DEC 2 3 2016

W9-CKJ-088

NAPA COUNTY LIBRARY
580 COOMBS STREET
NAPA, CA 94559

Headquarters USA

A Directory of Contact Information for Headquarters and Other Central Offices of Major Businesses & Organizations in the United States and in Canada

2017

39th EDITION

Volume 2:
Classification by Subject

Mailing Addresses, Telephone Numbers, Toll-Free Phone Numbers, Fax Numbers, and World Wide Web Addresses for:

- Associations, Foundations, and Similar Organizations
- Businesses, Industries, and Professions of All Types
- Colleges, Universities, Vocational & Technical Schools, and Other Educational Institutions
- Electronic Resources, including Internet Companies, Organizations, and Web Sites
- Embassies, Consulates, and UN Missions & Agencies
- Government Agencies & Offices at All Levels — City, County, State, Federal
- Libraries, Museums & Galleries, Zoos & Botanical Gardens, Performing Arts Organizations & Facilities, and Other Cultural Institutions
- Media Newspapers, Magazines, Newsletters; and Radio & Television Companies, Networks, Stations and Syndicators
- Research Centers & Organizations, including Scientific, Public Policy, and Market Research
- Professional Sports Teams, Other Sports Organizations, and Sports Facilities

and also including an Area/Zip Code Guide Covering more than 12,000 US Cities and Towns, as well as Area Code Tables in State & Numerical Order; and a detailed Index to Classified Headings under which listings are organized in the Directory's Classified Section.

Omnigraphics

Omnigraphics
A Part of Relevant Information

Pearline Jaikumar, *Editor*
Karthikeyan Ponnambalam, *Research Manager*

* * *

Keith Jones,
Managing Editor

Copyright © 2017 Omnigraphics Inc.

The editors of this publication have added value to the factual information contained in it through original selection, arrangement, and classification of that information. This work is fully protected by copyright and other laws. While every effort has been made to ensure the reliability of data contained in this directory, the publisher will not assume liability for damages caused by inaccuracies in the data and makes no warranty, express or implied, on the accuracy of the information contained herein.

No charge is made for listings in this publication. The inclusion of any company, organization, agency, inst-tution, or service does not imply endorsement by the editorial staff or the publisher.

ISBN 978-0-7808-1503-2

ISSN 1531-2909

Printed in the United States of America

Relevant Information
615 Griswold, Ste. 901, Detroit, MI 48226
Phone Orders: 800-234-1340 • Fax Orders: 800-875-1340
Mail Orders: P.O. Box 8002 • Aston, PA 19014-8002
www.omnigraphics.com

Table of Contents

Volume 1: Alphabetical by Organization Name

Volume 2: Classified by Subject

Classified Headings Table

Listed here are all of the headings under which listings are categorized in the Classified Section of this directory. The headings are numbered sequentially, and these numbers correspond to those printed in the "Class' column that accompanies listings in the Alphabetical Section. Just match the number in the "Class" column to the corresponding number printed in this table in order to identify the type of business or organization of any white pages listing. Use this table, too, to locate the page on which that subject category appears in the classified section.

For a more detailed list of classified headings, including "See" and "See also" references, please see the Index to Classified Headings at the back of this book.

A

B

C

Still can't find what you're looking for? *For a more detailed subject selection, see the Index to Classified Headings at the back of this directory.*

D

E

F

Still can't find what you're looking for? *For a more detailed subject selection, see the Index to Classified Headings at the back of this directory.*

G

H

I

Still can't find what you're looking for? *For a more detailed subject selection, see the Index to Classified Headings at the back of this directory.*

J

L

M

Still can't find what you're looking for? *For a more detailed subject selection, see the Index to Classified Headings at the back of this directory.*

Still can't find what you're looking for? *For a more detailed subject selection, see the Index to Classified Headings at the back of this directory.*

S

Still can't find what you're looking for? *For a more detailed subject selection, see the Index to Classified Headings at the back of this directory.*

T

Still can't find what you're looking for? *For a more detailed subject selection, see the Index to Classified Headings at the back of this directory.*

U

V

W

Z

Classified Section

Listings in the Classified Section are organized alphabetically (or, where noted, by city or state names) under subject headings denoting a business or organization type. Alphabetizing is on a word-by-word rather than letter-by-letter basis.

For a detailed explanation of the scope and arrangement of listings, please refer to ""How to Use This Directory' at the beginning of this book. Page elements and listing formats are illustrated on the sample pages with accompanying explanatory notes found just inside the back cover.

1 ABRASIVE PRODUCTS

Name / Address	City	State	ZIP	Phone	Fax
Abrasive Technology Inc 8400 Green Meadows Dr *Web:* www.abrasive-tech.com	Lewis Center	OH	43035	740-548-4100	
Acme Holding Co 24200 Marmon Ave *Web:* www.acmeabrasive.com	Warren	MI	48089	586-759-3332	759-3334
Agsco Corp 160 W Hintz Rd *Web:* www.agsco.com	Wheeling	IL	60090	847-520-4455	
Avery Abrasives Inc 2225 Reservoir Ave **Fax:* Cust Svc ■ *Web:* www.averyabrasives.com	Trumbull	CT	06611	203-372-3513	372-3714*
Basic Carbide Corp 900 Main St *TF:* 800-426-4291 ■ *Web:* www.basiccarbide.com	Lowber	PA	15660	724-446-1630	446-1656
Bullard Abrasives Inc 6 Carol Dr *TF:* 800-227-4469 ■ *Web:* www.bullardabrasives.com	Lincoln	RI	02865	401-333-3000	
Camel Grinding Wheels 7525 N Oak Pk Ave *Web:* www.cgwheels.com	Niles	IL	60714	847-647-5994	647-1861
Comco Inc 2151 N Lincoln St *TF:* 800-796-6626 ■ *Web:* www.comcoinc.com	Burbank	CA	91504	818-841-5500	955-8365
Composition Materials Company Inc 249 Pepes Farm Rd *TF:* 800-262-7763 ■ *Web:* compomat.com	Milford	CT	06460	203-874-6500	874-6505
Diagrind Inc 10491 164th Pl *Web:* www.diagrind.com	Orland Park	IL	60467	708-460-4333	460-8842
Eagle Grinding Wheel Corp 2519 W Fulton St *Web:* www.eaglegrindingwheel.com	Chicago	IL	60612	312-733-1770	733-5949
Emerald Creek Garnet Ltd 59652 Hwy 3 Rt 4 *Web:* www.emeraldcreekgarnet.com	Fernwood	ID	83830	208-245-2096	
Equipment Development Company Inc 100 Thomas Johnson Dr *Web:* www.edcoinc.com	Frederick	MD	21702	301-663-1600	
Ervin Industries Inc 3893 Research Pk Dr *TF:* 800-748-0055 ■ *Web:* www.ervinindustries.com	Ann Arbor	MI	48108	734-769-4600	663-0136
Formax Manufacturing Corp 168 Wealthy St SW *TF:* 800-242-2833 ■ *Web:* formaxmfg.com	Grand Rapids	MI	49503	616-456-5458	456-7507
Garfield Industries 62 Clinton Rd *Web:* garfieldbuff.com	Fairfield	NJ	07004	973-575-8800	575-6840
Gemtex Abrasives 234 Belfield Rd *TF:* 800-387-5100 ■ *Web:* www.gemtexabrasives.com	Toronto	ON	M9W1H3	416-245-5605	245-3723
Global Material Technologies 1540 E Dundee Rd Ste 210 *Web:* www.gmt-inc.com	Palatine	IL	60074	847-202-7000	215-4838
Hermes Abrasives Ltd PO Box 2389 *TF:* 800-464-8314 ■ *Web:* www.hermesabrasives.com	Virginia Beach	VA	23450	757-486-6623	
Kennametal Inc 2879 Aero Pk Dr *NYSE: KMT* ■ **Fax:* Sales ■ *TF:* 800-662-2131 ■ *Web:* www.kennametal.com	Traverse City	MI	49686	231-946-2100	946-3025*
Marvel Abrasive Products Inc 6230 S Oak Pk Ave *TF:* 800-621-0673 ■ *Web:* www.marvelabrasives.com	Chicago	IL	60638	800-621-0673	701-0187
Micro Surface Finishing Products Inc 1217 W Third St *TF:* 800-225-3006 ■ *Web:* www.micro-surface.com	Wilton	IA	52778	563-732-3240	
Modern Abrasive Corp PO Box 219 *Web:* www.modernabrasive.com	Spring Grove	IL	60081	815-675-2352	
Mosher Co 15 Exchange St *Web:* www.mocomfg.com	Chicopee	MA	01014	413-598-8341	
Moyco Technologies Inc 200 Commerce Dr	Montgomeryville	PA	18936	215-855-4300	362-3809
Norton Sandblasting Equipment 1006 Executive Blvd *TF:* 800-366-4341 ■ *Web:* www.nortonsandblasting.com	Chesapeake	VA	23320	757-548-4842	
Precision H2O Inc 6328 E Utah Ave *TF:* 800-425-2098 ■ *Web:* www.precisionh2o.com	Spokane	WA	99212	509-536-9214	536-9205
Premix-Marbletite Manufacturing Co 1259 NW 21st St *Web:* www.premixmarbletite.com	Pompano Beach	FL	33069	954-917-7665	
Radiac Abrasives Inc 1015 S College Ave **Fax:* Cust Svc ■ *TF:* 800-851-1095 ■ *Web:* www.radiac.com	Salem	IL	62881	618-548-4200	548-4207*
Raytech Industries 475 Smith St *TF Cust Svc:* 800-243-7163 ■ *Web:* www.raytech-ind.com	Middletown	CT	06457	860-632-2020	632-1699
Red Hill Grinding Wheel 335 Dotts St	Pennsburg	PA	18073	215-679-7964	
Sancap Abrasives 16123 Armour St NE *TF:* 800-433-6663	Alliance	OH	44601	330-821-3510	821-3516
Sandusky-Chicago Abrasive Wheel Co 532 W 4th St *Web:* www.sanduskychicago.com	Michigan City	IN	46360	219-879-6601	
Schaffner Mfg Company Inc 21 Herron Ave Schaffner Ctr *Web:* www.schaffnermfg.com	Pittsburgh	PA	15202	412-761-9902	761-8998
Shark Industries Ltd 6700 Bleck Dr *Web:* www.sharkind.com	Rockford	MN	55373	763-565-1900	
Superior Abrasives Inc 1620 Fieldstone Way *TF:* 800-235-9123 ■ *Web:* www.superiorabrasives.com	Vandalia	OH	45377	937-278-9123	
Trumbull Industries Inc 400 Dietz Rd NE *TF:* 800-477-1799 ■ *Web:* www.trumbull.com	Warren	OH	44482	330-393-6624	399-4421
Uneeda Enterprizes Inc 640 Chestnut Ridge Rd Spring Valley *Web:* www.sandpaper.com	New York	NY	10977	845-426-2800	
United Abrasives Inc 185 Boston Post Rd *Web:* www.unitedabrasives.com	North Windham	CT	06256	860-456-7131	456-8341
US Technology Corp 4200 Munson St NW *Web:* www.ustechnology.com	Canton	OH	44718	330-455-1181	
Virginia Materials & Supplies Inc 3306 Peterson St *Web:* www.sandblaster.com	Norfolk	VA	23509	757-855-0155	
VSM Abrasives 1012 E Wabash St *TF Cust Svc:* 800-737-0176 ■ *Web:* www.vsmabrasives.com	O'Fallon	MO	63366	636-272-7432	272-7434
Washington Mills Electro Minerals Co 20 N Main St *Web:* www.washingtonmills.com	North Grafton	MA	01536	508-839-6511	839-7675

2 ACCOUNTING FIRMS

Name / Address	City	State	ZIP	Phone	Fax
A D Singleton & Company CPA Inc 441 S Escondido Blvd *Web:* adscpa.com	Escondido	CA	92025	760-747-4605	
Aarons Grant & Habif LLC 3500 Piedmont Rd Ste 500 *Web:* www.aghllc.com	Atlanta	GA	30305	404-233-5486	
Abbott Company Ltd 345 E Flower St *Web:* acoabbott.com	Phoenix	AZ	85012	602-224-9092	
Abbott Stringham & Lynch 1550 Leigh Ave *Web:* www.aslcpa.com	San Jose	CA	95125	408-377-8700	
Abrams Foster Nole & Williams PA West Quadrangle 2 Hamill Rd Ste 241 *Web:* www.afnw.com	Baltimore	MD	21210	410-433-6830	
Accountants in Transition Inc 10509 Vista Sorrento Pkwy Ste 300 *Web:* calltsg.com	San Diego	CA	92121	858-404-9900	
Accounting Career Consultants 1001 Craig Rd Ste 391 *Web:* www.careeradvancers.com	Saint Louis	MO	63146	314-569-9898	
Accounts Payable Chexs Inc 1829 Ranchlands Blvd Nw *TF:* 888-437-0624 ■ *Web:* www.apchexs.com	Calgary	AB	T3G2A7	403-247-8913	
AccuPay Payroll Inc 50 S Penn St Ste A5 *Web:* www.accupay.net	Hatboro	PA	19040	267-803-1213	
Accurecord Inc 200 Broadhollow Rd Ste 308 *Web:* www.accurecord.com	Melville	NY	11747	631-243-6400	
Accutrack Medical Billing 15703 Freeman Ave	Lawndale	CA	90260	310-679-2141	
Ace Payroll Services Inc 1860 Walt Whitman Rd Ste 600 *Web:* www.acepayroll.com	Melville	NY	11747	516-420-9500	
Acsel Corp 2876 Guardian Ln *Web:* acsel.org	Virginia Beach	VA	23452	757-463-5240	
Active Captive Management 16485 Laguna Canyon Rd Ste 200 *TF:* 800-921-0155 ■ *Web:* www.activecaptive.com	Irvine	CA	92618	949-727-0155	
ACU Serve Corp 2020 Front St Ste 205 *TF:* 800-887-8965 ■ *Web:* acuservecorp.com	Cuyahoga Fls	OH	44221	330-923-5258	
Adserts Inc 14750 W Capitol D Ste 200 *Web:* adserts.com	Brookfield	WI	53005	262-794-9010	
Advanced Payroll Solutions LLC 201 W Passaic St Ste 202A *Web:* www.advpayrollsolutions.com	Rochelle Park	NJ	07662	201-587-0320	
Ahern Adcock Devlin LLP 1650 Iowa Ave Ste 200 *TF:* 888-226-9449 ■ *Web:* aadcpas.com	Riverside	CA	92507	951-683-0672	
Ahola Corp, The 6820 W Snowville Rd *TF:* 800-727-2849 ■ *Web:* www.ahola.com	Brecksville	OH	44141	440-717-7620	
Akin Doherty Klein & Feuge PC 8610 N New Braunfels Ste 101 *Web:* www.adkf.com	San Antonio	TX	78217	210-829-1300	
Albert R Maccani CPA 1537 S Delsea Dr	Vineland	NJ	08360	856-691-3279	
Albrecht- Viggiano- Zureck & Co 25 Suffolk Ct *Web:* www.avz.com	Hauppauge	NY	11788	631-434-9500	

Company / Address	City	State	ZIP	Phone	Fax
Aldagen Inc 2810 Meridian Pkwy Ste 148	Durham	NC	27713	919-484-2571	
Alex Alonzo Accountancy Corp 650 N First St	San Jose	CA	95112	408-295-3214	
Alexander X Kuhn & Co 123 W Front St Ste 200	Wheaton	IL	60187	630-681-8100	
Web: www.axk.com					
Alfred M Shiver Pa 260 E Court St	Marion	NC	28752	828-652-7319	
Web: shivercpa.com					
Alkon & Levine PC 29 Crafts St	Newton	MA	02458	617-969-6630	
Web: alkon-levine.com					
Allan S Feinberg An Acct Corp					
16311 Ventura Blvd Ste 610	Encino	CA	91436	818-325-2800	
Allen Gibbs & Houlik LC 301 N Main Ste 1700	Wichita	KS	67202	316-267-7231	
Allison Knapp & Siekmann Ltd					
2810 Frank Scott Pkwy W	Belleville	IL	62223	618-233-2641	
Almich & Assoc An Accountancy Corp					
26463 Rancho Pkwy S	Lake Forest	CA	92630	949-600-7550	
Web: almichcpa.com					
Almquist, Maltzahn, Galloway & Luth PC					
1203 W Second St	Grand Island	NE	68802	308-381-1810	
Web: www.gicpas.com					
Altera Payroll Inc 2400 Northside Crossing	Macon	GA	31210	478-477-6060	
TF: 877-474-6060 ■ *Web:* www.alterapayroll.com					
Amani Fahmy-Jensen CPA PC 763 N St	White Plains	NY	10605	914-948-1880	
Ambrico & Company PA					
425 W Colonial Dr Ste 305	Orlando	FL	32804	407-316-8900	
Anchin Block & Anchin LLP 1375 Broadway	New York	NY	10018	212-840-3456	840-7066
Web: www.anchin.com					
Andaloro, Smith & Krueger LLP					
N19W24400 Riverwood Dr Ste 200	Waukesha	WI	53188	262-544-2000	
Web: www.askcpas.com					
Anderson Satuloff Machado					
20700 Ventura Blvd Ste 205	Woodland Hills	CA	91364	818-710-0622	
Web: asmmcpa.com					
Andrews Hooper Pavlik Plc 5300 Gratiot Rd	Saginaw	MI	48638	989-497-5300	
TF: 888-754-8478 ■ *Web:* ahpplc.com					
Angell & Company Pllc					
3250 W Big Beaver Rd Ste 139	Troy	MI	48084	248-649-8720	
Web: angellcompany.com					
Angelo & O'Brien Pa 340 N Ave E	Cranford	NJ	07016	908-276-8300	
Anstiss & Company PC 1115 Westford St	Lowell	MA	01851	978-452-2500	
Web: anstisscpa.com					
Appleone Payroll & Tax Filing 990 Knox St	Torrance	CA	90502	310-516-1572	
Web: www.appleone.com					
AppleOne Services Ltd 50 Paxman Rd Ste 8	Etobicoke	ON	M9C1B7	416-622-0100	
Web: www.appleone.ca					
Arend Laukhuf & Stoller Inc 117 N Main St	Paulding	OH	45879	419-399-3686	
Web: www.brsw-cpa.com					
Arledge & Assoc Inc 309 N Bryant Ave	Edmond	OK	73034	405-348-0615	348-0931
Web: www.jmacpas.com					
Armanino LLP 12667 Alcosta Blvd Ste 500	San Ramon	CA	94583	925-790-2600	790-2601
Web: www.armaninollp.com					
Arnold Walker & Arnold & Company PC					
915 N Jefferson Ave	Mount Pleasant	TX	75455	903-572-6606	
Web: www.awacpa.com					
Aronson & Co 805 King Farm Blvd Ste 300	Rockville	MD	20850	301-231-6200	231-7630
Web: www.aronsonllc.com					
Arrone Appel CPA Professional 2425 Balsam Dr	Boulder	CO	80304	303-545-5755	
Web: appel-cpa.com					
Ascend Hr Solutions					
450 East 1000 North	North Salt Lake	UT	84054	801-299-6400	
Web: www.ascendhr.com					
Astra Group Corp 5913 Woodson Rd	Mission	KS	66202	913-378-1900	
Web: cobaltastra.com					
Athey & Company PA 1015 N Pearl St	Bridgeton	NJ	08302	856-451-8277	
Web: www.atheycocpa.com					
Audit Logistics LLC					
1172 W Century Dr Ste 245	Louisville	CO	80027	303-951-9000	
Web: www.auditlogistics.com					
Auerr Zajac & Assoc LLP 29 Dean Ave	Franklin	MA	02038	508-528-1305	
Web: auerr-zajaccpa.com					
Axley & Rode LLP 1307 S First St	Lufkin	TX	75901	936-634-6621	634-8183
Web: www.axleyrode.com					
Babush Neiman Komman Johnson LLP					
5909 Peachtree Dunwoody 800	Atlanta	GA	30328	770-261-1900	
Web: www.bnkj.com					
Baden Gage & Schroeder LLC					
6920 Pointe Inverness Way Ste 300	Fort Wayne	IN	46804	260-422-2551	422-7862
Web: badencpa.com					
Bain Freibaum & Company LLC					
3515 N Arnoult Rd	Metairie	LA	70002	504-568-0086	
Web: bfscpa.com					
Baker Tilly 8219 Leesburg Pk Ste 800	Vienna	VA	22182	703-923-8300	
Web: www.bakertilly.com					
Bansley & Kiener LLP					
8745 W Higgins Rd Ste 200	Chicago	IL	60631	312-263-2700	
Web: www.bk-cpa.com					
Barfield Murphy Shank & Smith PC					
1121 Riverchase Office Rd	Birmingham	AL	35244	205-982-5500	
Web: bmss.com					
Barrett & Company Pllc					
4910 NW Camas Meadows Dr	Camas	WA	98607	360-210-5100	
Barson Group Pa 60 E Main St PO Box 8018	Somerville	NJ	08876	908-203-9800	
Web: barsongroup.com					
Bart Morrill CPA PC 24 S 200 E PO Box 355	Roosevelt	UT	84066	435-725-1900	
Web: morrillcpa.com					
Bates Coughtry Reiss LLP 2601 Saturn St Ste 210	Brea	CA	92821	714-871-2422	
Web: bcrcpas.com					
Batson Acctg & Tax pa 20 Washington Pk	Greenville	SC	29601	864-235-6824	
Web: www.batsontax.net					
Battelle Rippe Kingston LLP					
2000 W Dorothy Ln	Cincinnati	OH	45202	937-298-0201	
Web: rsmus.com/who-we-are/welcome-battelle-rippe-kingston.html					
Bauman Associates Ltd PO Box 1225	Eau Claire	WI	54702	715-834-2001	
TF: 888-952-2866 ■ *Web:* baumancpa.com					
Beacon Acctg Group LLC					
10 Pidgeon Hill Dr Ste 110	Sterling	VA	20165	703-430-7666	
Web: beaconaccountinggroup.com					
Beasley Mitchell Co 509 S Main St Ste A	Las Cruces	NM	88004	575-528-6700	
Web: www.bmc-cpa.com					
Beason & Nalley Inc 101 Monroe St Ne	Huntsville	AL	35801	256-533-1720	
TF: 800-416-1946 ■ *Web:* www.beasonnalley.com					
Belfint Lyons & Shuman Pa					
1011 Centre Rd Ste 310	Wilmington	DE	19805	302-225-0600	
Web: belfint.com					
Bement & Company PC					
39 E Eagle Ridge Dr Ste 200	North Salt Lake	UT	84054	801-936-1900	
Web: bementcompany.com					
BendaGrace Stulz & Company PC					
38800 Van Dyke Ave	Sterling Heights	MI	48312	586-883-6240	
Web: bgscpas.com					
BenefitMall 3450 Lakeside Dr Ste 400	Miramar	FL	33027	954-874-4800	
TF: 877-729-6299 ■ *Web:* www.benefitmall.com					
Benham, Ichen & Knox LLP					
7600 County Line Rd Ste 6	Burr Ridge	IL	60527	847-362-4310	
Web: www.bikcpa.com					
Benjamin H Moore & Company Inc					
720 N Maitland Ave Ste 105	Maitland	FL	32751	407-644-3119	
Web: bhmcpapa.com					
Benko & Piane CPA'S 8301 Florence Ave Ste 316	Downey	CA	90240	562-923-9231	
Bennett & Middendorf Ltd 901 York	Quincy	IL	62301	217-222-1142	
Web: bennettandmiddendorf.com					
Bennett-Thrasher PC 3625 Cumberland Blvd	Atlanta	GA	30339	770-396-2200	
Web: btcpa.net					
Benson Piombo & Co 300 Tamal Plz Ste 180	Corte Madera	CA	94925	415-924-2292	
Web: bbensoncpa.com					
Berdon LLP 360 Madison Ave 8th Fl	New York	NY	10017	212-832-0400	371-1159
Web: www.berdonllp.com					
Berger & Company PA 95 Thames Blvd	Bergenfield	NJ	07621	201-384-6667	
Berger Assoc PC 1700 Bedford St Ste 101	Stamford	CT	06905	203-325-9727	
Web: bergerassociatespc.com					
Bergey & Co 616 Williams St	Berlin	MD	21811	410-641-1101	
Web: bergeycpa.com					
Berkowitz Dick Pollack & Brant LLP					
200 S Biscayne Blvd 6th Fl	Miami	FL	33131	305-379-7000	379-8200
TF: 800-999-1272 ■ *Web:* www.bpbcpa.com					
Bernard N Ackerman CPA PA					
596 Herrons Ferry Rd 5th fl	Rock Hill	SC	29730	803-366-8371	
Web: www.bnacpa.com					
Berry Dunn Mcneil & Parker					
100 Middle St 4th Fl	Portland	ME	04101	207-775-2387	774-2375
TF: 800-908-4490 ■ *Web:* www.berrydunn.com					
Bianchi Kasavan & Pope LLP					
243 Sixth St Ste 220	Hollister	CA	95023	831-638-2111	
Web: www.blhhcpa.com					
Bigelow & Co 500 N Commercial St	Manchester	NH	03101	603-627-7659	
Web: www.bigelowcpa.com					
BiggsKofford & Co					
630 Southpointe Ct Ste 200	Colorado Springs	CO	80906	719-579-9090	
Web: www.biggskofford.com					
Bill Pollard Jr CPA 79 E Eleventh St	Tracy	CA	95376	209-832-5110	
Web: billpollardcpa.com					
Binetti & Feerick CPAs PA					
381 Broadway Ste 45	Westwood	NJ	07675	201-664-9151	
Black & Soli PC CPA					
81 W Esperanza Blvd Ste E	Green Valley	AZ	85614	520-625-5988	
Web: blackandsoli.com					
Black Bashor & Porsch LLP 270 E Connelly Blvd	Sharon	PA	16146	724-981-7510	
Web: bbpcpa.com					
Blackman Kallick 10 S Riverside Plaza	Chicago	IL	60606	312-207-1040	207-1066
TF: 866-939-3921 ■ *Web:* www.plantemoran.com					
Blanski Peter Kronage & Zoch					
7500 Olson Memorial Hwy Ste 200	Minneapolis	MN	55427	763-546-6211	
Web: www.bpkz.com					
Blinn Farrell & Co 60 Bailey Blvd	Haverhill	MA	01830	978-372-8518	
Web: blinnfarrell.com					
Blue & Co 12800 N Meridian St Ste 400	Carmel	IN	46032	317-848-8920	573-2458
TF: 800-717-2583 ■ *Web:* www.blueandco.com					
Blum Shapiro 29 S Main St PO Box 272000	West Hartford	CT	06107	860-561-4000	521-9241
Bohr Dahm Greif & Assoc PC					
1845 51st St Ne	Cedar Rapids	IA	52402	319-366-8400	
Web: bdgcpas.com					
Bolden Lipkin PC					
3993 Huntingdon Pk	Huntingdon Valley	PA	19006	215-947-3750	
TF: 888-947-3750 ■ *Web:* blicpa.com					
Boldt Carlisle & Smith LLC					
1255 Lee St SE Ste 210	Salem	OR	97302	503-585-7751	
Web: www.bcsllc.com					
Bollus Lynch LLP 89 Shrewsbury St	Worcester	MA	01604	508-755-7107	
Web: bolluslynch.com					
Bolnick & Snow LLP 39 Old Doansburg Rd	Brewster	NY	10509	845-279-6300	
Web: bolnickandsnow.com					
Bolon Hart & Buehler Inc					
100 E Broad St Ste 2450	Columbus	OH	43215	614-228-2691	
Web: bhbcpa.com					
Bolton, Sullivan, Taylor & Weber LLP					
1023 N Mallard	Palestine	TX	75801	903-729-2229	
Web: bstwcpa.com					
Bonadio Group, The					
171 Sully's Trail Ste 201	Pittsford	NY	14534	585-381-1000	381-3131
TF: 877-917-3077 ■ *Web:* www.bonadio.com					
Bonanno, Savino & Davies PC					
105 Chestnut St Ste 32	Needham	MA	02492	781-449-3919	
Web: www.bsdcpa.com					
Bonari & Company CPAs 3724 Lakeside Dr Ste 201	Reno	NV	89509	775-322-5850	
Web: bonaricpas.com					
Bond Andiola & Company PC 600 Rt 206 S	Raritan	NJ	08869	908-722-5885	
Web: www.bac-cpa.com					

Name / Address	City	State	Zip	Phone	Fax
Boohaker Schillaci & Company PC 601 Vestavia Pkwy Ste 300 *Web:* www.bsccpa.com	Birmingham	AL	35216	205-824-1617	
Booker Arceneaux & Laskowski LLP 1100 NW Loop 410 Ste 207	San Antonio	TX	78213	210-341-2538	
Bookkeeping Express Enterprises LLC 671 N. Glebe Rd Ste 1610 *Web:* www.bookkeepingexpress.com	Arlington	VA	22203	703-766-5757	
Botz Deal & Company PC 2 Wbury Dr. *Web:* www.botzdeal.com	Saint Charles	MO	63301	636-946-2800	
Bowen & Bowen 16 W 445 S Frontage Rd *Web:* bowencpa.com	Burr Ridge	IL	60527	630-325-9800	
Bowman & Company LLP 601 White Horse Rd *Web:* www.bowmanllp.com	Voorhees	NJ	08043	856-435-6200	
Boyarsky Silbert & Silverman PA 6151 Executive Blvd	Rockville	MD	20852	301-231-0535	
Boyle & Stoll CPAs PC 3755 Brickway Blvd. *Web:* boyle-stoll.com	Santa Rosa	CA	95403	707-571-1951	
Brabo & Carlsen LLP 1111 E Tahquitz Canyon Way *Web:* brabo-carlsen.com	Palm Springs	CA	92262	760-320-0848	
Bradley J Mcdonough CPA 2645 Frederica St Ste 200	Owensboro	KY	42301	270-852-2733	
Bradshaw- Smith & Co 5851 W Charleston *Web:* www.bradshawsmith.com	Las Vegas	NV	89146	702-878-9788	
Brady Martz & Assoc PC 401 Demers Ave Ste 300 *Web:* bradymartz.com	Grand Forks	ND	58201	701-775-4685	795-7498
Branter Thibodeau & Associate 674 Mt Hope Ave Ste 1 *Web:* btacpa.com	Bangor	ME	04401	207-947-3325	
Brantley Janson Yost & Ellison CPA 1617 S 325th St *Web:* www.brantleyjanson.com	Federal Way	WA	98003	253-838-3484	
Briggs & Veselka Co 9 Greenway Plaza Ste 1700 *Web:* bvccpa.com	Houston	TX	77046	713-667-9147	626-7832
Brimmer Burek & Keelan LLP 5601 Mariner St Ste 200 *Web:* www.bbkm.com	Tampa	FL	33609	813-282-3400	
Brockman Coats Gedelian & Co 1735 Merriman Rd *TF:* 800-968-6661 ■ *Web:* bcgcompany.com	Akron	OH	44313	330-864-6661	
Broniec Assoc Inc 4855 Peachtree Industrial Blvd Ste 215 *TF:* 800-432-8348 ■ *Web:* www.broniec.com	Norcross	GA	30092	770-729-9664	
Brooks Mcginnis & Company LLC 5871 Glenridge Dr Ste 200 *Web:* brooksmcginnis.com	Atlanta	GA	30328	404-531-4940	
Brown Armstrong Accountancy Corp 4200 Truxtun Ave Ste 300 *Web:* www.bacpas.com	Bakersfield	CA	93309	661-324-4971	
Brown Graham & Company PC 7431 Continental Pkwy *Web:* www.bgc-cpa.com	Amarillo	TX	79114	806-355-8241	
Brown Ronald & Assoc pa 551 Ave K SE *Web:* ronaldbrowncpa.com	Winter Haven	FL	33880	863-299-1500	
Brown Schultz Sheridan & Fritz 210 Grandview Ave *Web:* bssf.com	Camp Hill	PA	17011	717-761-7171	
Bruce Hersh CPA Accountancy Corp 17547 Ventura Blvd	Encino	CA	91316	818-905-0533	
Bruno Skorheim 9665 Chesapeake Dr Ste 470 *Web:* www.brunoskorheim.com	San Diego	CA	92123	858-300-3141	
Bryant Katt & Assoc PC 6211 O St *Web:* bka-cpa.com	Lincoln	NE	68510	402-486-1040	
Buckeye Payroll Services 5749 Park Ctr Ct *Web:* www.buckeyepayroll.com	Toledo	OH	43615	419-472-7377	
Buckley Gent Macdonald & Cary PC 100 Great Oaks Blvd Ste 121	Albany	NY	12203	518-437-0430	
Buddy H Coffey CPA PC 201 N Thornton Ave	Dalton	GA	30720	706-226-7924	
Bunker Clark Winnell Nuorala PC 2301 Mitchell Park Dr. *Web:* bcwncpa.com	Petoskey	MI	49770	231-347-3963	
Burke & Schindler PLL 901 Adams Crossing *Web:* www.burkecpa.com	Cincinnati	OH	45202	513-455-8200	
Burr Pilger & Mayer LLP (BPMLLP) 600 California St Ste 1300 *Web:* www.bpmcpa.com	San Francisco	CA	94108	415-421-5757	288-6288
Business Strategy Inc 944 52nd St SE	Grand Rapids	MI	49508	616-261-2200	
C J Schlosser & Company LLC 233 E Ctr Dr PO Box 416 *Web:* www.cjsco.com	Alton	IL	62002	618-465-7717	465-7710
C&I Value Advisors LLC 4805 W Laurel St Ste 100 *Web:* clvalue.com	Tampa	FL	33607	813-286-7373	
Cachet Financial Services 750 E Green St Ste 315 *Web:* www.cachetbanq.com	Pasadena	CA	91101	626-578-9400	
Calegari & Morris 123 Mission St 18th Fl *Web:* calegariandmorris.com	San Francisco	CA	94105	415-981-8766	
Callero & Callero LLP 7800 N Milwaukee Ave *Web:* callero.com	Niles	IL	60714	847-966-2040	
Camp Moring & Cannon LLC 1418 Laurel St *Web:* cmccpas.net	Columbia	SC	29201	803-252-9375	
Campbell Rappold & Yurasits LLP 1033 S Cedar Crest Blvd *Web:* crycpas.com	Allentown	PA	18103	610-435-7489	
Candy & Schonwald Pllc 3116 Live Oak St. *Web:* cscpa.com	Dallas	TX	75204	214-826-6660	
Cannon Wright Blount Pllc 756 Ridge Lk Blvd Ste 100 *Web:* www.cannonwrightblount.com	Memphis	TN	38120	901-685-7500	
Cantor & Cantor CPA'S 31550 Northwestern Hwy Ste 110	Farmington Hills	MI	48334	248-851-0664	
Carbis Walker LLP 2599 Wilmington Rd *Web:* carbis.com	New Castle	PA	16105	724-658-1565	
Care Acctg Inc 110 Central Sq Dr.	Beaver Falls	PA	15010	724-843-1400	
Carmichael Brasher Tuvell & Co 1647 Mt Vernon Rd *Web:* www.cbtcpa.com	Atlanta	GA	30338	678-443-9200	
Carothers & Vlasman CPA'S PC 3555 Stanford Rd Ste 104	Fort Collins	CO	80525	970-223-7471	
Carr Riggs & Ingram LLC 1117 Boll Weevil Cir PO Box 311070 *Web:* www.cricpa.com	Enterprise	AL	36330	334-347-0088	347-7650
Carver Florek & James LLC 2246 University Park Blvd *Web:* cfjcpa.com	Layton	UT	84041	801-926-1177	
Case Sabatini & Co 470 Sts Run Rd Ste 1 *Web:* www.casesabatini.com	Pittsburgh	PA	15236	412-881-4411	
Casey Neilon & Assoc LLC 503 N Division St *Web:* caseyneilon.com	Carson City	NV	89703	775-283-5555	
Cast & Crew Entertainment Services LLC 2300 Empire Ave *Web:* www.castandcrew.com	Burbank	CA	91504	818-848-6022	
Catanese Group PC 307 State St *Web:* catanesegroup.com	Johnstown	PA	15905	814-255-8400	
Caufield & Flood 407 E Congress Pkwy Ste A *Web:* www.cfcpas.com	Crystal Lake	IL	60014	847-669-5950	
CBIZ Tofias PC 500 Boylston St. *TF:* 888-761-8835 ■ *Web:* www.cbiz.com	Boston	MA	02116	617-761-0600	761-0601
Cbm Chartered Accountants 152 Jackson St E Ste 200 *Web:* www.cbmca.com	Hamilton	ON	L8N1L3	905-572-7220	
Cerow & Company CPA'S PA 1801 Sarno Rd Ste 3	Melbourne	FL	32935	321-242-2511	
Certipay 199 Ave B NW Ste 270 *TF:* 800-422-3782 ■ *Web:* www.certipay.com	Winter Haven	FL	33881	863-299-2400	299-2131
CGA Canada 4200 N Fraser Way *Web:* www.cga-canada.org	Burnaby	BC	V5J5K7	604-669-3555	
Charles E Reed & AssocPC 3636 Professional Dr	Port Arthur	TX	77642	409-983-3277	
Cherry Bekaert & Holland LLP 200 S 10th St Ste 900 *Web:* www.cbh.com	Richmond	VA	23219	804-673-5700	673-4290
Chiampou Travis Besaw & Kershner LLP 45 Bryant Woods N *Web:* www.chiampou.com	Amherst	NY	14228	716-630-2400	
Cicinelli & Dippolito CPAs PC 1858 Commerce St *Web:* cdcpas.com	Yorktown Heights	NY	10598	914-302-2290	
CIS Group Ltd 55 rue Castonguay Ste 301 *Web:* www.cis-group.com	St-jerome	QC	J7Y2H9	450-432-1550	
Citrin Cooperman & Company LLP 529 Fifth Ave *Web:* www.citrincooperman.com	New York	NY	10017	212-697-1000	697-1004
CJBS LLC 2100 Sanders Rd Ste 200 *Web:* www.cjbs.com	Northbrook	IL	60062	847-945-2888	
Clark Nuber PS 10900 NE Fourth St Ste 1700 *TF General:* 800-504-8747 ■ *Web:* www.clarknuber.com	Bellevue	WA	98004	425-454-4919	454-4620
Clark Schaefer Hackett & Co 1 E Fourth St Ste 1200 *Web:* www.cshco.com	Cincinnati	OH	45202	513-241-3111	
Clausman & Assoc PC 1980 E 116th St.	Carmel	IN	46032	317-844-3110	
Clayton & Mckervey PC 2000 Town Ctr Ste 1800 *Web:* www.claytonmckervey.com	Southfield	MI	48075	248-208-8860	
CLC Inc 4170 Douglas Blvd. *Web:* www.clcincorporated.com	Granite Bay	CA	95746	916-789-7600	
CliftonLarsonAllen - CLA 301 SW Adams St Ste 1000 *TF:* 800-354-5849 ■ *Web:* www.claconnect.com	Peoria	IL	61602	309-671-4500	671-4508
Clinic Service Corp 3464 S Willow St *TF:* 800-929-5395 ■ *Web:* www.clinicservice.com	Denver	CO	80231	303-755-2900	
Cole & Reed PC 531 Couch Dr *Web:* rsmus.com/who-we-are/welcome-cole-reed.html	Oklahoma City	OK	73102	405-239-7961	
Collins Barrow Calgary LLP 1400 First Alberta Pl 777 - Eighth Ave SW *Web:* www.collinsbarrow.com	Calgary	AB	T2P3R5	403-298-1500	
Colusa Casino & Bingo 3770 Hwy 45 *Web:* www.colusacasino.com	Colusa	CA	95932	530-458-8844	
Community hospitals and Wellness centers 6050 Oak Tree Blvd S Ste 500 *NYSE: CBZ* ■ *Web:* www.cbizinc.com	Cleveland	OH	44131	216-447-9000	
Complete Business Consultants 1901 Jefferson Ave Ste 105	Tacoma	WA	98402	253-383-3700	
Complete Payroll Processing Inc 7488 SR- 39 Po Box 190 *TF:* 888-237-5800 ■ *Web:* www.completepayroll.com	Perry	NY	14530	585-237-5800	
Computer Business Applications Inc 507 N Mulberry St *Web:* www.cbatech.com	Elizabethtown	KY	42701	270-737-1888	
ComputerSearch Corp 331 Audubon Pkwy	Amherst	NY	14228	716-689-0511	
Comyns, Smith, McCleary & Deaver LLP 3470 Mount Diablo Blvd Ste A110 *Web:* csmllp.com	Lafayette	CA	94549	925-299-1040	
Condley & Co LLP 993 N 3rd St *Web:* www.condley.com	Abilene	TX	79601	325-677-6251	677-0006
Cone & Smith PC 3421 Rainbow Pkwy	Rainbow City	AL	35906	256-413-3057	
Conner Ash PC 12101 Woodcrest Exec Dr 300 *TF:* 877-366-1690 ■ *Web:* www.connerash.com	Saint Louis	MO	63141	314-205-2510	
Considine & Considine 1501 Fifth Ave Ste 400 *Web:* www.cccpa.com	San Diego	CA	92101	619-231-1977	

				Phone	Fax
Contingent Workforce Solutions Inc 2430 Meadowpine Blvd Ste 101 *TF:* 866-837-8630 ■ *Web:* cwsolutions.ca	Mississauga	ON	L5N6S2	866-837-8630	
Cooper, Travis & Company PLC 3008 Poston Ave *Web:* www.coopertravis.com	Nashville	TN	37203	615-329-4500	
Corbett Duncan & Hubly PC 100 E Pierce Rd Ste 100 *Web:* www.cdhcpa.com	Itasca	IL	60143	630-285-0215	
Corcoran Ender & Assoc 4010 S California Av *Web:* cpa-chicago.com	Chicago	IL	60632	773-247-7132	
Correll Assoc PC 26026 Telegraph Rd Ste 200 *Web:* correllcpa.com	Southfield	MI	48033	248-355-5151	
Coulter & Justus PC 9717 Cogdill Rd Ste 201 *Web:* cj-pc.com	Knoxville	TN	37932	865-637-4161	
Cowan Bolduc Doherty CPAs & Advisors 231 Sutton St *Web:* www.cbdcpa.com	North Andover	MA	01845	978-620-2000	
CPA Tax Solutions LLC 375 Mather St *Web:* cpataxsolutionsllc.com	Hamden	CT	06514	203-248-8600	
Crisell & Assoc 2199 E Willow St *Web:* crisellcpas.com	Signal Hill	CA	90755	562-595-0501	
Criticaledge Group Inc 2751 Dixwell Ave	Hamden	CT	06518	203-281-0006	
Crowe Horwath LLP 1 Mid America Plz Ste 700 *Web:* www.crowehorwath.com	Oak Brook	IL	60522	630-574-7878	
Cummings & Carroll PC 175 Great Neck Rd	Great Neck	NY	11021	516-482-3260	
Curtis Blakely & Company PC 2403 Judson Rd *Web:* cbandco.com	Longview	TX	75605	903-758-0734	
Cygan Hayes Ltd 20635 Abbey Woods Ct N *Web:* cyganhayes.com	Frankfort	IL	60423	815-534-5713	534-5523
D'Huyvetter & Swichkow PC 519 Johnson Ferry Rd Ste A-100 *Web:* www.dspccpa.com	Marietta	GA	30068	404-231-3500	
Dahl Hatton Muir & Reese Ltd 217 S Birch Ave PO Box 698 *Web:* dhmrcpa.com	Hallock	MN	56728	218-843-2645	
Dal Poggetto & Company LLP 149 Stony Cir	Santa Rosa	CA	95401	707-545-3311	
Dale M Long PC CPA'S 5945 Ward Rd Ste 200 *Web:* dalelongpc.com	Arvada	CO	80004	303-431-2666	
Dannible & McKee LLP 221 S Warren St *Web:* www.dmconsulting.com	Syracuse	NY	13202	315-472-9127	
Danser Balaam & Frank 5 Independence Way	Princeton	NJ	08540	609-987-0300	
Darmody, Merlino & Company LLP 75 Federal St 15th Fl *Web:* www.darmodymerlino.com	Boston	MA	02110	617-426-7300	
Davis Smith Accounting Associates pa 5582 Milford Harrington Hwy *Web:* www.davis-smithaccounting.com	Harrington	DE	19952	302-398-4020	
Dee J Wolfe CPA PC 818 NW 14th Ave *Web:* deejwolfe.com	Portland	OR	97209	503-295-0366	
Delap LLP 5885 Meadows Rd Ste 200 *Web:* delapcpa.com	Lake Oswego	OR	97035	503-697-4118	
Delisi & Assoc PC 217 S Pennsylvania Ave *Web:* delisiassociates.com	Greensburg	PA	15601	724-832-8585	
Deloitte & Touche USA LLP 1633 Broadway *Web:* www.deloitte.com	New York	NY	10019	212-489-1600	489-1687
Deloitte Touche Tohmatsu 1633 Broadway *Web:* www.deloitte.com	New York	NY	10019	212-489-1600	
Demello Mcauley Mcreynolds & Holland LLP 351 G St *Web:* dmmh-cpa.com	Eureka	CA	95501	707-445-0871	
Deming Malone Livesay & Ostroff 9300 Shelbyville Rd Ste 1100 *Web:* www.dmlo.com	Louisville	KY	40222	502-426-9660	
Denney & Company Chtd 1096 N Eastland Dr Ste 200 *Web:* denneycpa.com	Twin Falls	ID	83301	208-733-3223	
Dermody, Burke & Brown CPAs LLC 443 N Franklin St *Web:* www.dbbllc.com	Syracuse	NY	13204	315-471-9171	
Desmond & Ahern Ltd 10827 S Western Ave *Web:* www.desmondcpa.com	Chicago	IL	60643	773-779-4720	
DFrank Plater Jr Prof Corp 610 Colcord Dr	Oklahoma City	OK	73102	405-236-3739	
Diclaudio & Kramer LLC 50 Abele Rd Ste 1001	Bridgeville	PA	15017	412-220-7722	
Diebold & Assoc Ltd 1340 Remington Rd *Web:* dieboldcpa.com	Schaumburg	IL	60173	847-755-9000	
Dipietro & Thornton 9550 Prototype Ct Ste 101 *Web:* dipietro-thornton.com	Reno	NV	89521	775-825-1040	
Dix Barrett & Stiltner Pc 5670 Greenwood Plz Blvd Ste 505 *Web:* www.dbs-cpas.com	Greenwood Village	CO	80111	303-689-0844	
Dixon Hughes PLLC 6525 Morrison Blvd Ste 500 *Web:* www.dhgllp.com	Charlotte	NC	28211	704-367-7020	367-7760
Doeren Mayhew 305 West Big Beaver Rd Ste 200 *Web:* www.doeren.com	Troy	MI	48084	248-244-3000	244-3090
Doling Chang Ashmore CPA Inc 430 Sherman Ave *Web:* doling.com	Palo Alto	CA	94306	650-321-8744	
Don Farmer CPA Pa 508 Mulberry St PO Box 1858 *Web:* donfarmercpa.com	Lenoir	NC	28645	828-754-1613	
Donald E Graves CPA LLC 377 Main St Ste 400 *Web:* donaldegravescpa.com	Greenfield	MA	01301	413-774-6036	
Donald T Ostop & Company PC 790 Farmington Ave Bldg 2 *Web:* dtoco.com	Farmington	CT	06032	860-677-0779	
Douglas Daw CPA 1101 California Ave Ste 211	Corona	CA	92881	951-582-9023	
Draper & Mcginley Pa 365 W Patrick St 1st Fl *Web:* drapermcginleypa.com	Frederick	MD	21701	301-694-7411	694-0954
DS & B Ltd 222 S Ninth St *Web:* dsb-cpa.com	Minneapolis	MN	55402	612-359-9630	
Duggan Joiner & Company PA 334 NW Third Ave *Web:* djcocpa.com	Ocala	FL	34475	352-732-0171	
Dworken-Hillman-LaMorte & Sterczala 4 Corporate Dr Ste 488 *Web:* dhls.com	Shelton	CT	06484	203-929-3535	
Eadie & Payne LLP 1839 W Redlands Blvd *Web:* eadiepaynellp.com	Redlands	CA	92373	909-793-2406	
Easter & Stoney Ps 206 E First St	Aberdeen	WA	98520	360-533-7272	
Eckhoff Accountancy Corp 145 N Redwood Dr *Web:* www.eckhoff.com	San Rafael	CA	94903	415-499-9400	
ECS Financial Services Inc 3400 Dundee Rd *TF:* 800-826-7070 ■ *Web:* ecsfinancial.com	Northbrook	IL	60062	847-291-1333	
Edmond A Swad P C 38701 Seven Mile Rd *Web:* swadco.com	Livonia	MI	48152	734-462-9333	
Edward D Astrin CPA A P C 16633 Ventura Blvd Ste 1450	Encino	CA	91436	818-501-3022	
Ehrhardt Keefe Steiner & Hottman PC 7979 E Tufts Ave Ste 400 *Web:* www.eksh.com	Denver	CO	80237	303-740-9400	740-9009
Eichen & Di Meglio 1 Dupont St *Web:* eanddcpa.com	Plainview	NY	11803	516-576-3333	
Eide Bailly LLP 4310 17th Ave S *Web:* www.eidebailly.com	Fargo	ND	58103	701-239-8500	239-8600
Eisenberg Group AC CPAs, The 2260 Avenida De La Playa	La Jolla	CA	92037	858-551-5500	
Eisner & Maglione CPA'S LLC 66 Commack Rd Ste 201 *Web:* emcpallc.com	Commack	NY	11725	631-499-4039	
Eisner LLP 750 Third Ave *Web:* www.eisneramper.com	New York	NY	10017	212-949-8700	
Ekmanian Tax & Acctg A Professional Corp 404 East Branch St Ste 210 *Web:* ekmaniancpa.com	Pismo Beach	CA	93449	805-556-4512	
Elerick & Elerick PA 265 N Wymore Rd *Web:* elerickandelerick.com	Winter Park	FL	32789	407-629-9995	
Elliott Davis Decosimo LLC 629 Market St Ste 100 *TF:* 800-782-8382 ■ *Web:* www.elliottdavis.com	Chattanooga	TN	37402	423-756-7100	756-2939
Elliott Davis LLC 200 E Broad St PO Box 6286 *TF:* 800-503-4721 ■ *Web:* www.elliottdavis.com	Greenville	SC	29606	864-242-3370	
Elliott Lewis Leiber & Stumpf Inc Certif 1611 e Fourth st *Web:* www.ellscpas.com	Santa Ana	CA	92701	714-569-1000	
Engelson Assoc 3317 Mormon Coulee Rd *Web:* eacpas.net	La Crosse	WI	54601	608-788-2181	
Ennis Pellum & Assoc Cpas 5150 Belfort Rd S Bldg 600 *Web:* www.jaxcpa.com	Jacksonville	FL	32256	904-396-5965	399-4094
Ernst & Young Ernst & Young Tower 222 Bay St PO Box 251 *TF:* 800-291-3380 ■ *Web:* www.ey.com	Toronto	ON	M5K1J7	416-864-1234	864-1174
Ernst & Young 5 Times Sq **Fax:* Mail Rm ■ *Web:* www.ey.com	New York	NY	10036	212-773-3000	773-6350*
Ernst Swedean & Assoc PC 4125 Gordon Dr *Web:* esacpaonline.com	Sioux City	IA	51106	712-274-6617	
Erwin & Co 6311 Ranch Dr *Web:* erwinco.com	Little Rock	AR	72223	501-868-7486	
Estep-Doctor & Company PC 3737 W Bethel Ave *Web:* edcpa.com	Muncie	IN	47304	765-289-5366	
Fair Anderson & Langeman 3065 S Jones Blvd Ste 100 *Web:* www.falcpa.com	Las Vegas	NV	89146	702-870-7999	
Fairchild Lebel & Rice PC 5123 W St Joseph	Lansing	MI	48917	517-321-5990	
Farmers Insurance Group 6060 W Manchester Ave Ste 302 *TF:* 888-327-6335 ■ *Web:* farmers.com	Los Angeles	CA	90045	888-327-6335	
Faske Lay & Co 3508 Far W Blvd 300 *Web:* www.faskelay.com	Austin	TX	78731	512-346-9623	346-8109
Faust & Assoc 200 Third St *Web:* faustcpa.com	Mccomb	MS	39648	601-684-6382	
Federal Management Systems Inc 462 K St NW *TF:* 877-637-8277 ■ *Web:* www.fmshq.com	Washington	DC	20001	202-842-3003	829-4470
Feeley Bonaventura & Hyzy CPAsPc 5695 Main St *Web:* fbhcpa.com	Williamsville	NY	14221	716-632-0606	
Fenster & Fenster 1514 S D St *Web:* fensterandfenster.com	San Bernardino	CA	92408	909-889-0288	
Ferguson & Redelsperger PC 1026 Main St	Duncan	OK	73533	580-255-2190	
Ferrarabuckworth LLC 60 Pompton Ave	Verona	NJ	07044	973-857-8800	
Ferrell Wealth Management Inc 1400 W Fairbanks Ave *Web:* ferrellwm.com	Winter Park	FL	32789	407-629-7008	
Fiducial 1370 Ave of the Americas 31st Fl *TF:* 866-343-8242 ■ *Web:* www.fiducial.com	New York	NY	10019	212-207-4700	308-2613
Filomeno & Company PC 80 S Main St *Web:* www.filomeno.com	Hartford	CT	06107	860-561-0020	
Finkler & Company CPAs Inc 16600 Sprague Rd 285 *Web:* finklercpa.com	Middleburg Hts	OH	44130	440-826-1550	
Fischer Cunnane & Assoc Ltd 11 Turner Ln *Web:* www.fischercunnane.com	West Chester	PA	19380	610-431-1003	
Fitts Roberts & Co PC 5718 Westheimer Rd Ste 800 *Web:* www.fittsroberts.com	Houston	TX	77057	713-260-5230	
Flackman Goodman & Potter 106 Prospect St *Web:* www.fgpcpa.com	Ridgewood	NJ	07450	201-445-0500	
Flagel Huber Flagel and Co 3400 S Dixie Dr *Web:* fhf-cpa.com	Dayton	OH	45439	937-299-3400	

				Phone	Fax
Fletcher & Assoc PC 424 E Jackson St *Web:* fletchcpa.com	Thomasville	GA	31792	229-226-2241	
Flex Checks Inc PO Box 141215 *TF:* 866-791-7900 ■ *Web:* www.flexchecks.com	Grand Rapids	MI	49514	616-791-7900	
Flynn Walker Diggin CPA PC 50 Seward St *Web:* flynnwalkerdiggin.com	Saratoga Springs	NY	12866	518-583-1234	
Fontana CPAs Pa 2519 N Mcmullen Booth Rd Ste 5 *Web:* fontanacpas.com	Clearwater	FL	33761	727-799-9533	
Fox CPA Group Ltd 204 E Cherry St	Watseka	IL	60970	815-432-3126	
Frank J Larusso CPA PC 550 Mamaroneck Ave- Ste 509	Harrison	NY	10528	914-698-8303	
Frank Rimerman & Company LLP 1801 Page Mill Rd *Web:* www.frankrimerman.com	Palo Alto	CA	94304	650-845-8100	494-1975
Frank Seringer & Chaney Inc 197 N Leavitt Rd *Web:* fsc-cpa.com	Amherst	OH	44001	440-984-2441	
Frankie Friend & Assoc Inc 2305 E Arapahoe Rd Ste 132 *Web:* www.frankiefriend.com	Centennial	CO	80122	303-768-8577	
Franzen & Franzen LLP 125 E De La Guerra St Ste 201 *Web:* franzencpa.com	Santa Barbara	CA	93101	805-563-0821	
Frasier Dean & Howard PLLC 3310 W End Ave Ste 550 *Web:* www.fdhcpa.com	Nashville	TN	37203	615-383-6592	
Freed Maxick & Battaglia CPAs 800 Liberty Bldg *Web:* www.freedmaxick.com	Buffalo	NY	14202	716-847-2651	
Freedman & Goldberg CPA'S PC 31150 Northwestern Hwy Ste 200 *Web:* freedmangoldberg.com	Farmington Hills	MI	48334	248-626-2400	
Freyberg Hinkle Ashland Powers & Stowell Sc CPA 15420 W Capitol Dr *TF:* 800-413-8799 ■ *Web:* www.freyberg-hinkle.com	Brookfield	WI	53005	262-784-6210	
Friedberg Smith & Co PC 855 Main St *TF:* 800-772-1213 ■ *Web:* www.fscocpa.com	Bridgeport	CT	06604	203-366-5876	366-1924
Friedman & Huey Assoc LLP 1313 W 175th St *Web:* www.fhassoc.com	Homewood	IL	60430	708-799-6800	
Friedman LLP 1700 Broadway *TF:* 800-372-1033 ■ *Web:* www.friedmanllp.com	New York	NY	10019	212-842-7000	842-7001
Frohm Kelley Butler & Ryan PC 333 Ft St	Port Huron	MI	48060	810-987-2727	987-2734
Frost PLLC 425 W Capitol Ave Ste 3300 *Web:* www.frostpllc.com	Little Rock	AR	72201	501-376-9241	
Frost Ruttenberg & Rothblatt PC 111 S Pfingsten Rd Ste 300 *Web:* www.marcumllp.com	Deerfield	IL	60015	847-282-6300	
Fulbright & Fulbright 5410 NC 55 Greenwood Commons #AC Ste 104 *Web:* www.moneyful.com	Durham	NC	27713	919-544-0398	
Fuller Landau LLP 1010 De La Gauchetiere St W Pl du Canada Ste 200 *Web:* www.fullerlandau.com	Montreal	QC	H3B2S1	514-875-2865	
Furst & Jinks PA 170 Changebridge Rd *Web:* furstandjinks.com	Montville	NJ	07045	973-575-9191	
Fust Charles Chambers LLP 5786 Widewaters Pkwy *Web:* www.fcc-cpa.com	Syracuse	NY	13214	315-446-3600	446-3899
G. R. Rush & Co 5720 Skurlock Rd 6500 Bldg Osborne Office Pk *Web:* www.rushcpa.com	Chattanooga	TN	37411	423-899-5162	
Gable- Peritz- Miskin & Co 323 NORRISTOWN Rd *Web:* gpmllp.net	Spring House	PA	19477	215-628-0500	
Gail Rosen CPA PC 2032 Washington Vly Rd *Web:* gailrosencpa.com	Martinsville	NJ	08836	732-469-4202	
Galanti & Company Pc 1834 Independence Sq *Web:* www.galanticpa.com	Dunwoody	GA	30338	770-393-0399	
Gallagher Flynn & Company LLP 55 Community Dr *Web:* www.gfc.com	South Burlington	VT	05403	802-863-1331	651-7305
Gallina LLP 925 Highland Pointe Dr Ste 450 *TF:* 877-638-1188 ■ *Web:* www.gallina.com	Roseville	CA	95678	916-638-1188	638-1782
Gardenswartz & Dodds PC 600 17th St Ste 1800 N *Web:* gndpc.com	Denver	CO	80202	303-534-6770	
Gary A Halpert CPA 20335 Ventura Blvd Ste 400	Woodland Hills	CA	91364	818-715-9081	
Gary L Schutz PC 900 NW Joy Ave	Portland	OR	97229	503-520-1120	
Gatewood Hughey & Company CPA 2000 W First St Ste 411	Winston-Salem	NC	27104	336-724-4446	
GBQ Partners LLC 230 W St Ste 700 *Web:* www.gbq.com	Columbus	OH	43215	614-221-1120	
Gekakis & Co 901 Mariners Island Blvd Ste 610	San Mateo	CA	94404	650-349-5700	
Gelfand Rennert & Feldman LLP 1880 Century Park E Ste 1600 *Web:* www.grfllp.com	Los Angeles	CA	90067	310-553-1707	
Gentile Pismeny & Brengel LLP 159 Northern Blvd *Web:* www.gpb.net	Great Neck	NY	11021	516-487-4110	
George Bagley & Company LLC 1315 W 22nd St Ste 305 *Web:* bagleycpa.com	Oak Brook	IL	60523	630-990-0355	
Gerbel & Company PC 830 Pleasant St PO Box 44 *Web:* gerbel.com	St Joseph	MI	49085	269-983-0534	
Ghirardo CPA 7200 Redwood Blvd Ste 403 *Web:* www.ghirardocpa.com	Novato	CA	94945	415-897-5678	
Gibbons & Kawash 707 Virginia St Bank One Ctr Ste 500 *Web:* gandkcpas.com	Charleston	WV	25301	304-345-8400	
Gibgot Willenbacher & Co 310 E Shore Rd *Web:* gw-cpa.com	Great Neck	NY	11023	516-482-3660	
Gilbert & Calabrese LLC 181 Rt 206 *Web:* gcllc-cpa.com	Flanders	NJ	07863	973-448-1099	
Gilbert Associates Inc 2880 Gateway Oaks Dr Ste 100 *Web:* www.gilbertcpa.com	Sacramento	CA	95833	916-646-6464	
Gilbert Metzger & Madigan LLP 6029 Park Dr PO Box 677 *Web:* gmmcpa.com	Charleston	IL	61920	217-345-2128	
Gillispie & Ogilbee Pc 4400 N Meridian Ave *Web:* www.gocpas.com	Oklahoma City	OK	73112	405-947-3030	942-0017
Gilmore Jasion & Mahler Ltd 1715 Indianwood Cir Ste 100 *Web:* www.gjmltd.com	Maumee	OH	43537	419-794-2000	
Gitlin & Assoc LLP 55 S Main St	Liberty	NY	12754	845-292-7780	
Gitomer & Berenholz PC 445 Shady Ln *Web:* gbm-cpa.com	Huntingdon Valley	PA	19006	215-379-3500	
Glass & Company CPAs PC 515 Congress Ave Ste 1900 *Web:* glasscpa.com	Austin	TX	78701	512-480-8182	
Glass, Jacobson & Medallion Financial Services LLC 10711 Red Run Blvd Ste 101 *Web:* www.glassjacobson.com	Owings Mills	MD	21117	410-356-1000	
Glenn m Gelman & Assoc Certified Public Accountants 1940 E 17th St *Web:* www.gelmanllp.com	Santa Ana	CA	92705	714-667-2600	
Gold Meltzer Plasky & Wise PA 505 Pleasant Vly Ave *Web:* www.gmpw.com	Moorestown	NJ	08057	856-727-0100	
Goldberg Harder Adelstein & Co 132 Lincoln St	Boston	MA	02111	617-426-3350	
Gompers & Assoc PLLC 117 Edgington Ln *TF:* 844-805-9844 ■ *Web:* gomperscpa.com	Wheeling	WV	26003	304-242-9300	
Gordon Stockman & Waugh PC 8726 Industrial Rd *Web:* gswcpa.com	Peoria	IL	61615	309-692-4030	692-4159
Gorfine Schiller & Gardyn PA 10045 Red Run Blvd Ste 250	Owings Mills	MD	21117	410-356-5900	
Gorman & Assoc PC Certifi 1825 Franklin St Ste B *Web:* www.gaapc.com	Northampton	PA	18067	610-262-1280	
Gottlieb Flekier & Company PA 12721 Metcalf Ave Ste 201 *Web:* gfccpa.com	Overland Park	KS	66213	913-491-6655	
Grant Bennett Accountants 1375 Exposition Blvd Ste 230 *TF:* 888-763-7323 ■ *Web:* www.gbacpa.com	Sacramento	CA	95815	916-922-5109	
Grant J Milleret CPA 10777 W Twain Ave	Las Vegas	NV	89135	702-367-0341	
Grant Thornton (CCRLLP) 1400 Computer Dr *Web:* www.grantthornton.com	Westborough	MA	01581	508-926-2200	616-2972
Grant Thornton International Ltd 175 W Jackson Blvd 20th Fl *Web:* www.grantthornton.com	Chicago	IL	60604	312-856-0200	
Grant Thornton LLP 175 W Jackson Blvd 20th Fl *Web:* www.grantthornton.com	Chicago	IL	60604	312-856-0200	602-8099
Grantham Poole CPAs 1062 Highland Colony Pkwy Ste 201 *Web:* www.granthampoole.com	Ridgeland	MS	39157	601-499-2400	
Grassi & Co 488 Madison Ave *Web:* www.grassicpas.com	New York	NY	10022	212-661-6166	
Graves & Company PC 20550 Vernier Rd *Web:* gravescpa.com	Harper Woods	MI	48225	313-886-8892	
Gray Blodgett & Company Pllc 629 24th Ave SW *Web:* cpagray.com	Norman	OK	73069	405-360-5533	
Gray Callison & Company PA 3813 Forrestgate Dr *Web:* graycallison.com	Winston-Salem	NC	27103	336-760-3210	
Gray Hunter Stenn LLP 500 Maine St *Web:* www.gray-hunter-stenn.com	Quincy	IL	62301	217-222-0304	
Greenberg Ettlin & Assoc PA 109 Bridge St *Web:* ge-cpa.com	Elkton	MD	21921	410-398-1961	
Greenberg Rosenblatt Kull & Bitsoli PC The Day Bldg 306 Main St Ste 400 *Web:* www.grkb.com	Worcester	MA	01615	508-791-0901	
Greenstein Rogoff Olsen & Company LLP 39159 Paseo Padre Pkwy Ste 315 *Web:* www.groco.com	Fremont	CA	94538	510-797-8661	
Gregory & Assoc Pllc 14 E Tabb St *Web:* gregory-cpas.com	Petersburg	VA	23803	804-733-4511	
Gregory, Sharer & Stuart PA 100 Second Ave S Ste 600 *Web:* www.gsscpa.com	Saint Petersburg	FL	33701	727-821-6161	
Grimbleby Coleman CPA's Inc 200 W Roseburg Ave *Web:* www.grimbleby-coleman.com	Modesto	CA	95350	209-527-4220	
Gross Mendelsohn & Assoc pa 36 S Charles St 18th fl *TF:* 800-899-4623 ■ *Web:* www.gma-cpa.com	Baltimore	MD	21201	410-685-5512	
Grossman & Grossman LLP 4 Executive Park Dr	Albany	NY	12203	518-438-3509	
Guess CPA PC 4000 Eagle Point Corporate Dr	Birmingham	AL	35242	205-259-1905	
Gumbiner Savett Inc 1723 Cloverfield Blvd *TF:* 800-989-9798 ■ *Web:* www.gscpa.com	Santa Monica	CA	90404	310-828-9798	
Habenicht Novak & Birckbichler 287 Pittsburgh Rd *Web:* hnbcpa.net	Butler	PA	16002	724-283-8661	
Habif Arogeti & Wynne LLP 5 Concourse Pkwy NE Ste 1000 *Web:* www.hawcpa.com	Atlanta	GA	30328	404-892-9651	
Hacker Johnson & Smith PA 500 N Wshore Blvd Ste 1000 *TF:* 800-366-7126 ■ *Web:* www.hackerjohnson.com	Tampa	FL	33609	813-286-2424	

	City	State	ZIP	Phone	Fax
Haddox Reid Burkes & Calhoun PLLC					
PO Box 22507	Jackson	MS	39225	601-948-2924	
Web: www.haddoxreid.com					
Hagen Streiff Newton Oshiro PC					
15601 Dallas Pkwy Ste 1050	Addison	TX	75001	972-980-5060	
Web: www.hsno.com					
Hague Sahady & Company PC					
126 President Ave Ste 201	Fall River	MA	02720	508-675-7889	
Web: hague-sahady.com					
Hall Kistler & Company LLP					
220 Market Ave S Ste 700	Canton	OH	44702	330-453-7633	
Web: www.hallkistler.com					
Ham, Langston & Brezina LLP					
11550 Fuqua St Ste 475	Houston	TX	77034	281-481-1040	
Web: www.hlb-cpa.com					
Hanrahan Carey & Company PLC					
306 S Troy PO Box 1049	Royal Oak	MI	48068	248-544-1484	
Web: www.hccplc.com					
Hantzmon Wiebel LLP					
818 E Jefferson St	Charlottesville	VA	22902	434-296-2156	
Web: www.hantzmonwiebel.com					
Harding Shymanski & Company PSC					
21 SE Third St Ste 500	Evansville	IN	47708	812-464-9161	
Web: www.hsccpa.com					
Harper & Pearson Company PC					
1 Riverway Ste 1000	Houston	TX	77056	713-622-2310	
Web: harperpearson.com					
Harshad Kothari CPA Inc					
14752 Beach Blvd Ste 205	La Mirada	CA	90638	714-523-9802	
Hartman Blitch & Gartside					
4929 Atlantic Blvd	Jacksonville	FL	32207	904-396-9802	396-1528
Web: www.hbgcpa.com					
Haskell & White LLP 8001 Irvine Ctr Dr Ste 300	Irvine	CA	92618	949-450-6200	
Web: www.hwcpa.com					
Hein & Assoc LLP 1999 Broadway Ste 4000	Denver	CO	80202	303-298-9600	298-8118
Web: www.heincpa.com					
Heinfeld Meech & Company PC 10120 N Oracle Rd	Tucson	AZ	85704	520-742-2611	
Web: heinfeldmeech.com					
Hellam Varon & Company Inc PS					
1750 112th Ave Ne	Bellevue	WA	98004	425-453-9192	
Web: hellamvaron.com					
Henry & Peters PC 3310 S Broadway Ste 100	Tyler	TX	75701	903-597-6311	597-0343
Web: www.henrypeters.com					
Herbein & Company Inc 2763 Century Blvd	Reading	PA	19610	610-378-1175	
Web: herbein.com					
Hesley Hunt & Assoc Ltd					
2607 White Bear Ave N	Maplewood	MN	55109	651-770-8505	
Web: heshcpa.com					
Hicko CPA Group PC, The 310 E 90th Dr	Merrillville	IN	46410	219-738-2863	
Hilburn & Lein CPA'S 5520 S Ft Apache	Las Vegas	NV	89148	702-597-1945	
Web: hilburn-lein.com					
Hill Barth & King LLC 7680 Market St	Youngstown	OH	44512	330-758-8613	758-0357
TF: 800-733-8613 ■ *Web:* www.hbkcpa.com					
Hill Larson Walth & Benda Pa 326 N Main St	Austin	MN	55912	507-433-2264	
Web: hlwb-cpa.com					
Hill Schroderus & Company LLP 923 Spring St	Petoskey	MI	49770	231-347-4136	
Web: hs-co.com					
Hobe & Lucas					
1 Independence Pl 4807 Rockside Rd					
Ste 510	Independence	OH	44131	216-524-8900	
Web: www.hobe.com					
Hocking & Reid LLC 5757 S 34th St Ste 100	Lincoln	NE	68516	402-441-0140	
Holly A Carlin CPA 1912 Sidewinder Dr 211A	Park City	UT	84060	435-649-0909	
Web: carlincpa.com					
Holly C Roundtree 5001 Spring Vly Rd Ste 250E	Dallas	TX	75244	972-404-4434	
Web: hcroundtreecpa.com					
Holthouse Carlin & Van Trigt LLP					
11444 W Olympic Blvd Ste 300-S	Los Angeles	CA	90064	310-566-1900	566-1901
Web: www.hcvt.com					
Honegger Ringger & Company Inc					
1905 N Main St	Bluffton	IN	46714	260-824-4107	
TF: 888-853-5906 ■ *Web:* www.hrc-cpa.com					
Honkamp Krueger & Company PC					
2345 JFK Rd PO Box 699	Dubuque	IA	52004	563-556-0123	556-8762
TF: 888-556-0123 ■ *Web:* www.honkamp.com					
Horizon Business Solutions Inc					
1589 Brice Rd	Reynoldsburg	OH	43068	614-577-1700	
Web: horizonbiz.com					
Horne LLP 26 Security Dr	Jackson	TN	38305	731-668-7070	355-6521*
**Fax Area Code:* 601 ■ *Web:* hornellp.com					
House Park & Dobratz Pc					
605 W 47th St Ste 301	Kansas City	MO	64112	816-931-3393	931-9636
Web: www.hpdco.com					
Howard Cunningham Houchin & Turner LLP					
6901 Quaker Ave Ste 100	Lubbock	TX	79413	806-799-6699	
Web: hchtcpa.com					
Howson & Simon LLP					
101 Ygnacio Vly Rd Ste 310	Walnut Creek	CA	94596	925-977-9060	
Hoyman Dobson & Company PA 215 Baytree Dr	Melbourne	FL	32940	321-255-0088	
Web: www.hoyman.com					
HR&P Solutions Inc 14550 Torrey Chase Ste 100	Houston	TX	77014	281-880-6525	
Web: www.hrp.net					
Huckstep & Assoc LLC 3734 S Ave Ste E	Springfield	MO	65807	417-889-8991	
TF: 800-269-6466 ■ *Web:* www.huckstep.com					
Huggins & Company CPA Pa					
6148-D Brookshire Blvd	Charlotte	NC	28216	704-394-2364	
Hulsey Harwood & Sheridan LLC					
1900 Roselawn Ave	Monroe	LA	71201	318-325-6500	
Web: hhcpa.net					
Hulslander SUSAn d CPA PC					
24 First Ave E Ste D	Kalispell	MT	59901	406-755-3092	
Hutchinson & Bloodgood LLP					
579 Auto Ctr Dr	Watsonville	CA	95076	818-637-5000	
Web: www.hbllp.com					
Infonaut Inc 255 Consumers Rd Ste 500	Toronto	ON	M2J1R4	716-881-7578	
Web: www.infonaut.ca					
Internal Audit Services by John Capizzi					
6231 Pga Blvd Ste 104	Palm Bch Gdns	FL	33418	561-626-7746	
Web: internalauditservices.com					
Iprocess Online Inc 1050 Hull St Ste 100	Baltimore	MD	21230	410-547-3270	
Web: www.iprocessonline.com					
J Hall & Associates Inc: Hall Johnathan W CPA					
327 S Market St	Troy	OH	45373	937-339-8417	
James B Mcevoy CPA 280 N Bedford Rd	Mt Kisco	NY	10549	914-241-0460	
Web: jmcevoycpa.com					
James E Raftery CPA PC 606 N Stapley Dr	Mesa	AZ	85203	480-835-1040	
James R Swab 1707 Myrtle Rd	Silver Spring	MD	20902	301-681-7935	
Jankins & Jablonski SC 15400 W Capitol Dr	Brookfield	WI	53005	262-781-2121	
Jefferson Urian Doane & Sterner Inc					
651 N Bedford St Extn PO Box 830	Georgetown	DE	19947	302-856-3900	
Web: juds.com					
Jeffrey D Stewart & Company CPA'S					
6663 Western Row Rd	Mason	OH	45040	513-573-9600	
Jennifer A Jones CPA Ltd					
10615 Judicial Dr Ste 701	Fairfax	VA	22030	703-352-1587	
Web: jajonescpa.com					
Jobe Hastings & Assoc CPA's					
745 S Church St Ste 105	Murfreesboro	TN	37133	615-893-7777	
TF: 866-207-2384 ■ *Web:* jobehastings.com					
John A Culhane CPA 755 Main St Bldg Ste 1	Monroe	CT	06468	203-268-4431	
Web: culhanecpa.com					
John Gerlach & Co LLP 37 W Broad St Ste 530	Columbus	OH	43215	614-224-2164	224-1391
Web: www.johngerlach.com					
John Waddell & Company CPAs					
3416 American River Dr Ste A	Sacramento	CA	95864	916-488-2460	
Web: jwaddell.com					
Johnson & Mackowiak 70 E Main St	Fredonia	NY	14063	716-672-4770	679-1512
Web: jma-cpas.com					
Johnson & Shute PS 11130 NE 33rd Pl	Bellevue	WA	98004	425-827-5755	
Web: johnsonandshute.com					
Johnson Lambert & Company LLP					
700 Spring Forest Rd	Raleigh	NC	27609	919-719-6400	
Web: www.johnsonlambert.com					
Jones & Kolb 10 Piedmont Ctr Ste 100	Atlanta	GA	30305	404-262-7920	
Web: www.joneskolb.com					
Jones CPA Group 749 Boush St	Norfolk	VA	23510	757-627-7672	
Web: stricklandandjones.com					
Jones Ham & Cluff P C					
14475 SW Allen Blvd Ste A	Beaverton	OR	97005	503-643-6333	
Web: www.jonesandham.com					
Jones Henle & Schunck 135 Town & Country Dr	Danville	CA	94526	925-820-1821	
Web: www.jhs.com					
Jones Kohanski & Company LLP					
6 Brookhill Sq S	Sugarloaf	PA	18249	570-788-7000	
Web: jk-cpa.com					
Joseph Crnkovich Jr CPA					
1053 Mclaughlin Run Rd	Bridgeville	PA	15017	412-257-0844	
Joyce Swanson CPA 6715 Grover St	Omaha	NE	68106	402-390-2722	
JPMS Cox PLLC 11300 Cantrell Rd Ste 301	Little Rock	AR	72212	501-227-5800	227-5851
Web: www.jpmscox.com					
JST Enterprises 5120 Summerhill Rd	Texarkana	TX	75503	903-794-3743	
Web: www.jstent.com					
Julian J Rodriguez PA 95 Merrick Way	Coral Gables	FL	33134	305-445-0777	
Web: jjrpa.net					
Junkermier Clark Campanella Stevens PC					
501 Park Dr S Ste 100	Great Falls	MT	59403	406-761-2820	
Web: www.jccscpa.com					
Kahn Litwin Renza & Company Ltd					
951 N Main St	Providence	RI	02904	401-274-2001	
TF: 888-557-8557 ■ *Web:* www.kahnlitwin.com					
Kalfsbeek & Company Accountancy Corp					
4529 Quail Lakes Dr Ste C	Stockton	CA	95207	311-742-9189	
Kallman & Company LLP					
125 S Barrington Pl	Los Angeles	CA	90049	310-909-1900	
Kalmanowitz & Lee CPAs Pllc					
575 Eighth Ave Ste 1706	New York	NY	10018	212-687-2628	
Katz Abosch Windesheim Gershman & Freedman PA					
9690 Deereco Rd Ste 500	Lutherville Timonium	MD	21093	410-828-2727	
Web: www.katzabosch.com					
Katz Sapper & Miller					
800 E 96th St Ste 500	Indianapolis	IN	46240	317-580-2000	580-2117
Web: www.ksmcpa.com					
Kauffmann & Assoc Pllc					
4350 Brownsboro Rd Ste 170	Louisville	KY	40207	502-893-8067	
Web: kaacpas.com					
Kaufman & Kabani					
800 S Figueroa St Ste 900	Los Angeles	CA	90017	213-488-6180	
Web: kkcpa.com					
Kaufman Rossin & Co PA 2699 S Bayshore Dr	Miami	FL	33133	305-858-5600	856-3284
TF: 866-357-9634 ■ *Web:* www.kaufmanrossin.com					
Keefe McCullough & Co LLP Certified Public Accountants					
6550 N Federal Hwy Ste 410	Fort Lauderdale	FL	33308	954-771-0896	938-9353
Web: www.kmccpa.com					
Keith A Shibou CPA Accountancy Corp					
1900 E Tahquitz Canyon Way	Palm Springs	CA	92262	760-325-1214	
Kellogg & Andelson					
14724 Ventura Blvd 2nd Fl	Sherman Oaks	CA	91403	818-971-5100	
Web: www.k-a.com					
Kelly Dunn & Nestor 921 Bergen Ave	Jersey City	NJ	07306	201-795-1122	
Kenefick & Company CPA'S PA 2809 Cavan Ct	Charlotte	NC	28270	704-544-6757	
Web: kenefickandco.com					
Kennedy & Coe LLC 3030 Cortland Cir	Salina	KS	67401	785-825-1561	825-5371
Web: www.kcoe.com					
Kenneth Delarbre & Company PA					
1618 S Highland Ave	Clearwater	FL	33756	727-585-4708	
Kernutt Stokes LLP 1600 Executive Pkwy	Eugene	OR	97401	541-687-1170	
Web: kernuttstokes.com					

Phone Fax

Kesner, Godes & Morrissey LLC
15 Pacella Park Dr Ste 200 ... Randolph MA 02368 781-961-2900
Web: www.kesnermorrissey.com

Kessler Orlean Silver & Company PC
1101 Lk Cook Rd Ste C ... Deerfield IL 60015 847-580-4100
Web: koscpa.com

Kevin J Goering CPA Pa 2201 W 25th St ... Lawrence KS 66047 785-832-8300
Web: goeringcpa.com

Keystone Payroll
355 Colonnade Blvd Ste C ... State College PA 16803 814-234-2272
TF: 877-717-2272 ■ *Web:* www.keystonepayroll.com

KFMR Katz Ferraro McMurtry PC
300 Benedum-Trees Bldg 223 Fourth Ave ... Pittsburgh PA 15222 412-471-0200
Web: www.kfmr.com

Kieckhafer Dietzler & Hauser LLP
627 Elm St ... West Bend WI 53095 262-334-2341
Web: kdhcpa.com

Kingery & Crouse PA 2801 W Busch Blvd Ste 200 ... Tampa FL 33618 813-874-1280
Web: www.tampacpa.com

Kirkpatrick Phillips & Miller
1445 E Republic Rd ... Springfield MO 65804 417-882-4300 882-4343
Web: www.kpmcpa.com

Kiwi Partners Inc 30 Soundview Ln ... Port Washington NY 11050 516-767-6678
Web: www.kiwipartners.com

Klatzkin & Company Jr CPA's
1670 Whitehorse Hamilton Sq Rd Ste 7 ... Hamilton NJ 08690 609-890-9189
Web: www.klatzkin.com

Klingher Nadler LLP
580 Sylvan Ave Ste Ma ... Englewood Cliffs NJ 07632 201-731-3025
Web: klinghernadler.com

Knutte & Assoc PC 7900 S Cass Ave ... Darien IL 60561 630-960-3317
Web: www.knutte.com

Koch Group & Company LLP
333 Seventh Ave Rm 8 ... New York NY 10001 212-631-0700
Web: www.kgcpas.com

Koller & Company LLP 206 S Iowa Ave ... Washington IA 52353 319-653-6561
Web: kollerandcompany.com

Komisar Brady & Company LLP
135 S 84th St Ste 200 ... Milwaukee WI 53214 414-271-3966
Web: www.komisarbrady.com

Kositzka Wicks & Co
5500 Cherokee Ave Ste 400 ... Alexandria VA 22312 703-642-2700
Web: www.kwccpa.com

Kovash & Dasovick PC 148 W First St ... Dickinson ND 58601 701-483-1156

KPMG LLP US 3 Chestnut Ridge Rd ... Montvale NJ 07645 201-307-7000 307-7575
Web: www.kpmg.com

KraftCPAs Pllc 555 Great Cir Rd ... Nashville TN 37228 615-242-7351
Web: kraftcpas.com

Kramer Accountancy Corp
120 N Topanga Canyon Blvd Ste 111 ... Topanga CA 90290 310-455-9300
Web: kramercpa.com

Kramer Fiduciary Services
1500 Ardmore Blvd Ste 205 ... Pittsburgh PA 15221 412-351-2150
Web: kramerfiduciary.com

Kruggel Lawton & Company LLC
210 S Michigan St Ste 200 ... South Bend IN 46601 574-289-4011
Web: klcpas.com

Kuhn & Company CPAs 1730 Park St ... Naperville IL 60563 630-416-7700
Web: kuhnandcompany.com

Kurtz & Hornak PA 354 N Ave E ... Cranford NJ 07016 908-276-3380

Kutchins, Robbins, & Diamond Ltd
1101 Perimter Dr Ste 760 ... Schaumburg IL 60173 847-240-1040
Web: krdcpas.com

L f L Veritas LLC 1086 Teaneck Rd Ste 2C ... Teaneck NJ 07666 201-833-2266
Web: www.lflveritas.com

Labenz & Assoc LLC 4535 Normal Blvd Ste 195 ... Lincoln NE 68506 402-437-8383
Web: labenz.com

Lanaux & Felger CPAs Apc 5779 Hwy 311 ... Houma LA 70360 985-851-0883

Lance Soll & Lunghard LLP
203 N Brea Blvd Ste 203 ... Brea CA 92821 714-672-0022
Web: www.lslcpas.com

Lane Gorman Trubitt LLP 2626 Howell St Ste 700 ... Dallas TX 75204 214-871-7500 871-0011
Web: www.lgt-cpa.com

Langdon & Company LLP 223 Us 70 Hwy E Ste 100 ... Garner NC 27529 919-662-1001
Web: www.langdoncpa.com

Lanigan, Ryan, Malcolm & Doyle PC
555 Quince Orchard Rd Ste 600 ... Gaithersburg MD 20878 301-258-8900
Web: lrmd-cpa.com

Lanni Restifo LLC 21-00 Rt 208 S Ste 210 ... Fair Lawn NJ 07410 201-797-1600
Web: lannirestifo.com

Lapp, Fatch, Myers & Gallagher Accountants, A Professional Corp
2401 Professional Pkwy ... Santa Maria CA 93455 805-934-0015
Web: lfmgcpas.com

Larry Associates Inc
6136 170th St Ste M1 ... Fresh Meadows NY 11365 718-321-0384
Web: www.accountingbylarry.com

Latta Harris Hanon & Penningroth LLP
2730 Naples Ave SW Ste 101 ... Iowa City IA 52240 319-358-0520
Web: lattaharris.com

Lattimore Black Morgan & Cain PC
5250 Virginia Way ... Brentwood TN 37027 615-377-4600
Web: www.lbmc.com

Lavine Lofgren Morris & Engelberg CPAs
4180 La Jolla Village Dr Ste 300 ... La Jolla CA 92037 858-455-0898
Web: www.llme.com

Lazer Grant Inc 309 Mcdermot Ave ... Winnipeg MB R3A1T3 204-942-0300 957-5611
TF: 800-220-0005 ■ *Web:* www.lazergrant.ca

Leaf, Miele, Manganelli, Fortunato & Engel
310 Passaic Ave ... Fairfield NJ 07004 973-808-9500
Web: www.leafsaltzman.com

Leffler Accountancy Corp
16030 Ventura Blvd Ste 490 ... Encino CA 91436 818-501-1181

Phone Fax

Lefkowitz Garfinkel Champi & DeRienzo PC
10 Weybosset St ... Providence RI 02903 401-421-4800
TF: 800-927-5423 ■ *Web:* www.lgcd.com

Lenning & Company Inc
13924 Seal Beach Blvd Ste C ... Seal Beach CA 90740 562-594-9729
TF: 800-200-4829 ■ *Web:* lenning.com

Leone Mcdonnell & Roberts pa Cpa 5 Nelson St ... Dover NH 03820 603-749-2700
Web: www.lmrpa.com

Lerch Vinci & Higgins 17-17 State Rt 208 ... Fair Lawn NJ 07410 201-791-7100
Web: www.lvhcpa.com

Lester Halpern & Company PC 14 Bobala Rd ... Holyoke MA 01040 413-536-3970
Web: halperncpa.com

Levin, Swedler & Company Inc
3501 Embassy Pkwy Ste 200 ... Akron OH 44333 330-666-4199
Web: www.levinswedler.com

Lewellen Accountancy Corp
23521 Paseo De Valencia 205 ... Laguna Hills CA 92653 949-859-4644

Lewis & Company PC
3804 Poplar Hill Rd Ste B ... Chesapeake VA 23321 757-638-4566

Lewis & Knopf CPAs PC
5206 Gateway Centre Ste 100 ... Flint MI 48507 810-238-4617
TF: 877-244-1787 ■ *Web:* www.lewis-knopf.com

LH Frishkoff & Co 529 Fifth Ave Ste 901 ... New York NY 10017 212-808-0070
Web: www.lhfrishkoff.com

Libero & Kappel CPAs 57 Old Country Rd ... Westbury NY 11590 516-333-5511

Limsky Kypriotis & Co 220 Ridgedale Ave ... Florham Park NJ 07932 973-822-3400

Lindquist Von Husen & Joyce LLP
90 New Montgomery St 11th Fl ... San Francisco CA 94105 415-957-9999
Web: lvhj.com

Lindstrom Sorenson & Assoc LLP
3815 N Mulford Rd ... Rockford IL 61114 815-282-1288
Web: lsallp.com

Linger Peterson Shrum & Co
575 E Locust Ave Ste 308 ... Fresno CA 93720 559-438-8740

Link Murrel & Co 18831 Bardeen Ave Ste 200 ... Irvine CA 92612 949-261-1120
Web: www.link-murrel.com

Lipsey Youngren Means Ogren & Sandberg LLP
525 B St Ste 1400 ... San Diego CA 92101 619-234-0877 234-9319
Web: www.lymscpa.com

LMGW Certified Public Accountants LLP
20520 Prospect Rd Ste 200 ... Saratoga CA 95070 408-252-1800
Web: www.wheelerco.com

Lmo Reps LLC 21 Roulston Rd ... Windham NH 03087 603-893-4178
Web: lmoreps.com

Lodgen, Lacher, Golditch, Sardi, Saunders, & Howard LLP
16530 Ventura Blvd Ste 305 ... Encino CA 91436 818-783-0570
Web: www.lgshcpa.com

Loeb & Loeb LLP 345 Park Ave ... New York NY 10154 212-407-4000 407-4990
Web: www.loeb.com

Logan Simpson Design Inc 51 W Third St Ste 450 ... Tempe AZ 85281 480-967-1343
Web: www.logansimpson.com

Long Chilton LLP 3125 Central Blvd ... Brownsville TX 78520 956-546-1655
Web: www.longchilton.com

Loomis & Company CPA's LLP
267 E Campbell Ave Ste 200 ... Campbell CA 95008 408-385-3400
Web: www.loomiscpas.com

Lopata Flegel & Company LLP
600 Mason Ridge Ctr Dr Ste 100 ... Saint Louis MO 63141 314-514-8881
Web: www.lopataflegel.com

Lott (TE) & Co 221 N Seventh St ... Columbus MS 39701 662-328-5387
Web: www.telott.com

Louis Plung & Company LLP
420 Ft Duquesne Blvd Ste 1900 ... Pittsburgh PA 15222 412-281-8771
Web: www.louisplung.com

Love Scherle & Bauer PC
310 Grant St Ste 1020 ... Pittsburgh PA 15219 412-281-8270
Web: lovescherlebauer.com

Lucas Horsfall Murphy & Pindroh LLP
100 E Corson St Ste 200 ... Pasadena CA 91103 626-744-5100
Web: www.lhmp.com

Lutz & Carr 300 E 42nd St ... New York NY 10017 212-697-2299
Web: www.lutzandcarr.com

Lynn a Sylvester CPA PA 675 S Haywood St ... Waynesville NC 28786 828-456-6505
Web: www.lascpa-nc.com

M & K CPAs PLLC 4100 Nsam Houston Pkwy ... Houston TX 77086 832-242-9950
TF: 866-770-5931 ■ *Web:* mkacpas.com

Maglin Miskiv & Assoc CPA'S PA
299 Cherry Hill Rd Ste 100 ... Parsippany NJ 07054 973-263-3300

Mahoney Ulbrich Christiansen & Russ P A
30 E Plato Blvd ... Saint Paul MN 55107 651-227-6695
Web: www.mucr.com

Mallah Furman & Co
Brickell Bay Office Tower 1001 Brickell Bay Dr
Ste 1400 ... Miami FL 33131 305-371-6200
Web: www.mallahfurman.com

Maloney & Kennedy Pllc 15 Dartmouth Dr Ste 203 ... Auburn NH 03032 603-624-8819
Web: maloneyandkennedy.com

Mann Urrutia Nelson CPA's & Assoc LLP
2901 Douglas Blvd Ste 290 ... Roseville CA 95661 916-774-4208 774-4230
Web: www.muncpas.com

Manning Elliott LLP
1050 W Pender St 11th Fl ... Vancouver BC V6E3S7 604-714-3600
Web: www.manningelliott.com

Mantyla Mcreynolds LLC
178 S Rio Grande St Ste 200 ... Salt Lake City UT 84101 801-269-1818
Web: www.mmacpa.com

Manzi, Pino & Company PC
1895 Walt Whitman Rd - Ste 5 ... Melville NY 11747 631-420-5620
Web: manzipinocpa.com

Marc B Freedman CPA PC 215 W 95th St ... New York NY 10025 212-678-2418
Web: mbfcpa.com

Marcheschi Plankis & Pogore
9951 W 190th St Ste A ... Mokena IL 60448 708-479-7333
Web: mppcpa.com

Name / Address	City	State	Zip	Phone	Fax
Marcus Errico Emmer & Brooks PC 45 Braintree Hill Pk Ste 107	Braintree	MA	02184	781-843-5000	
Web: www.meeb.com					
Margolin Winer & Evens LLP 400 Garden City Plz 5th Fl	Garden City	NY	11530	516-747-2000	747-6707
Web: www.mwellp.com					
Mark Bailey & Co Ltd 1495 Ridgeview Dr Ste 200	Reno	NV	89519	775-332-4200	
Web: www.markbaileyco.com					
Marks Paneth & Shron LLP 622 Third Ave 7th Fl	New York	NY	10017	212-503-8800	503-8800
Web: www.markspaneth.com					
Martin & Martin CPA'S Ltd 1001 W. Hawthorn Dr Ste 360	Itasca	IL	60143	847-250-5074	
Web: mmcpasltd.com					
Martin & Orr LLC 127 Peachtree St Ste 500	Atlanta	GA	30303	404-525-3007	
Maruji & Raines PS 775 S Main St Ste A	Colville	WA	99114	509-684-5289	
Web: www.mrcpas.com					
Marvin & Company PC 11 British American Blvd	Latham	NY	12110	518-785-0134	
Web: marvincpa.com					
Massachusetts Society of Certified Public Accountants 105 Chauncy St 10th Fl	Boston	MA	02111	617-556-4000	
TF: 800-392-6145 ■ *Web:* www.mscpaonline.org					
Mather & Company CPAs LLC 9100 Shelbyville Rd	Louisville	KY	40222	502-429-0800	
Web: matherandcompany.com					
Matthews Carter & Boyce PC 12500 Fair Lakes Cir Ste 260	Fairfax	VA	22030	703-218-3600	
Web: www.mcb-cpa.com					
Mauldin & Jenkins Certified Public Accountants LLC 200 Galleria Pkwy SE	Atlanta	GA	30339	770-955-8600	446-3664*
**Fax Area Code:* 229 ■ *TF:* 800-277-0080 ■ *Web:* www.mjcpa.com					
Maxson & Assoc Accountancy Corp 6700 E Pacific Coast Hwy	Long Beach	CA	90803	562-594-4681	
Web: maxson-accounting.com					
May & Co 110 Monument Pl	Vicksburg	MS	39180	601-636-4762	
Web: www.maycpa.com					
May Cocagne & King Pc 1353 E Mound Rd Ste 300	Decatur	IL	62526	217-762-3136	
Web: www.mckcpa.com					
Mayer, Shanzer, & Mayer PC 918 Maple St	Conshohocken	PA	19428	610-828-0200	
Web: www.msmpc.com					
McConnell Jones Lanier & Murphy LLP The Lakes On Post Oak 3040 Post Oak Blvd Ste 1600	Houston	TX	77056	713-968-1600	
TF: 866-908-4650 ■ *Web:* www.mcconnelljones.com					
Mccormack Guyette & Assoc PC 66 Grove St	Rutland	VT	05701	802-775-3221	
Web: cpa-vermont.com					
Mcelrath Geyer Sandler & Fisher 1500 Quail St Ste 450	Newport Beach	CA	92660	949-252-0252	
McGowen Hurst Clark & Smith PC 1601 W Lakes Pkwy Ste 300	West Des Moines	IA	50266	515-288-3279	
Web: www.mhcscpa.com					
Mcgreal & Company PC 5740 W 95th St	Oak Lawn	IL	60453	708-422-8600	
Web: mcgreal.com					
McGregor & Company LLP 1190 Blvd Ne	Orangeburg	SC	29115	803-536-1015	
Web: mcgregorcpa.com					
Mcguire Peck & Co 630 Silver St	Agawam	MA	01001	413-789-2551	
Mckenna & Assoc PC 1515 S Washington St	Grand Forks	ND	58206	701-772-4819	
Web: mckennaandassociates.net					
McKonly & Asbury LLP 415 Fallowfield Rd	Camp Hill	PA	17011	717-761-7910	761-7944
Web: www.macpas.com					
McNair McLemore Middlebrooks & Company LLP 389 Mulberry St	Macon	GA	31202	478-746-6277	
Web: www.mmmcpa.com					
Mcruer & & Associates Cpas 1251 Nw Briarcliff Pkwy Ste 100	Kansas City	MO	64116	816-741-7882	
Web: kccpa.com					
Mcswain & Co PS 612 Woodland Sq Loop SE Ste 300	Lacey	WA	98503	360-357-9304	
TF: 800-282-1301 ■ *Web:* mcswaincpa.net					
McSweeney & Assoc A Professional Corp 350 Crown Point Cir Ste 200	Grass Valley	CA	95945	530-272-5555	
Web: mcsweeneyandassociates.com					
Medical Billing Concepts Inc 16001 Ventura Blvd Ste 135	Encino	CA	91436	818-817-9832	
Web: www.medbillconcepts.com					
Medical Billing Unlimited Inc 5959 Gateway Blvd W Ste 120	El Paso	TX	79925	915-779-1716	
Web: mbuinc.com					
Medical Management Specialists 4100 Embassy Dr SE Ste 200	Grand Rapids	MI	49546	616-975-1845	
TF: 888-707-2684 ■ *Web:* www.mms.med.pro					
Medwig & Co 401 Wood St	Pittsbugh	PA	15222	412-562-9061	
Melanson Heath & Company PC 102 Perimeter Rd	Nashua	NH	03063	603-882-1111	
Web: melansonheath.com					
Messina & Company LLC 1615 Pontiac Ave	Cranston	RI	02920	401-463-6800	
Michael Bossy Group 251 James St	Delhi	ON	N4B2B2	519-582-1260	
Web: www.bnggroup.ca					
Michael J Liccar & Co 231 s la salle st	Chicago	IL	60604	312-702-1861	
TF: 800-922-6604 ■ *Web:* www.liccar.com					
Michael R Rubenstein & Assoc 12527 New Brittany Blvd	Fort Myers	FL	33907	239-489-4443	
TF: 888-616-1222 ■ *Web:* mrubensteincpa.com					
Michael S Kaslik PC 1123 Vesper Rd	Ann Arbor	MI	48103	734-995-4455	
Michalik & Daniels LLC 934 Western Ave	Pittsburgh	PA	15233	412-322-2662	
Mickey Casanova & Sack 1735 - 28th St	Bakersfield	CA	93301	661-325-9451	
Millard, Rouse & Rosebrugh LLP 96 Nelson St	Brantford	ON	N3T5N3	519-863-3557	
Web: www.millards.com					
Miller & Company Plc 900 S Shackleford Rd Ste 100	Little Rock	AR	72211	501-221-3343	
Web: millercocpas.net					
Miller & Miller Accountancy Corp 1320 E Shaw Ave Ste 167	Fresno	CA	93710	559-225-6211	
Web: millermillerpc.com					
Miller Cooper & Company Ltd 1751 Lk Cook Rd Ste 400	Deerfield	IL	60015	847-205-5000	
Web: www.millercooper.com					
Miller Giangrande LLP 915 W Imperial Hwy	Brea	CA	92821	714-494-2200	
Web: mngcpa.com					
Miller Kaplan Arase & Company LLP 4123 Lankershim Blvd	Hollywood	CA	91602	818-769-2010	
Web: www.millerkaplan.com					
Milluzzo & Company PC 182 Kelsey St	Newington	CT	06111	860-667-9991	
MNP LLP 715 Fifth Ave SW 7th Fl	Calgary	AB	T2P2X6	403-444-0150	
Web: www.mnp.ca					
Mondorf & Fenwick Pllc 523 Columbia Dr	Johnson City	NY	13790	607-797-4339	
Web: mfcpas.com					
Monroe Shine & Company Inc 222 E Market St	New Albany	IN	47150	812-945-2311	
Web: www.monroeshine.com					
Mooney & Thomas PC 2111 Plum St Ste 150	Aurora	IL	60506	630-844-5272	
Web: mooneythomas.com					
Moore & Company PA 560 Riverside Dr Ste A-102	Salisbury	MD	21801	410-749-3211	
Web: moore-company.com					
Moore & Neidenthal Inc 3034 N Wooster Ave	Dover	OH	44622	330-364-7774	
TF: 866-364-7774 ■ *Web:* mnpinnacle.com					
Moore Reichl & Baker P C 11200 Wheimer Ste 410	Houston	TX	77042	281-558-9800	
Web: mrbcpas.com					
Moore Stephens Lovelace PA 1201 S Orlando Ave Ste 400	Winter Park	FL	32789	407-740-5400	740-0012
TF: 800-683-5401 ■ *Web:* www.mslcpa.com					
Morrison Brown Argiz & Farra LLP 1001 Brickell Bay Dr 9th Fl	Miami	FL	33131	305-373-5500	373-0056
TF: 800-239-3843 ■ *Web:* www.mbafcpa.com					
Morton Leben 270 N Ave	New Rochelle	NY	10801	914-636-1800	
Moss Adams LLP 999 Third Ave Ste 2800	Seattle	WA	98104	206-302-6500	622-9975
Web: www.mossadams.com					
Mowat Mackie & Anderson LLP 1999 Harrison St Ste 1500	Oakland	CA	94612	510-893-1120	
Web: www.mowat.com					
Mrasek & Assoc PC 6193 Miller Rd Ste A	Swartz Creek	MI	48473	810-635-2409	
Muckel Anderson CPAs 300 E Second St	Reno	NV	89501	775-686-3200	
Web: muckelanderson.com					
Nagy & Croniser CPA'S LLP 5564 Woodlawn Ave	Lowville	NY	13367	315-376-6518	
Nearman Maynard Vallez CPAs & Consultants pa 205 Brandywine Blvd Ste 200	Fayetteville	GA	30214	770-461-5706	
TF: 800-288-0293 ■ *Web:* nearman.com					
Nethaway & Clausen PC 6000 W St Joseph Ste 101	Lansing	MI	48917	517-321-0019	
Web: nethawayclausen.com					
Nichols Accounting Group PC, The 230 N Oregon St	Ontario	OR	97914	541-881-1433	
Web: www.nicholsaccounting.com					
Nicholson & Company PA 2 Southern Pointe Pkwy Ste 100	Hattiesburg	MS	39404	601-264-3519	
Web: www.nicholsoncpas.com					
Nietzke & Faupel PC 7274 Hartley St	Pigeon	MI	48755	989-453-3122	
TF: 855-999-3122 ■ *Web:* nfcpa.com					
Nightlinger Colavita & Volpa Pa 991 S Black Horse Pk	Williamstown	NJ	08094	856-629-3111	
Web: colavita.net					
Nimensky Gallinson & Buren PA CPAs 316 Eisenhower Pkwy	Livingston	NJ	07039	973-533-9200	
Web: ngbcpa.com					
Nisivoccia & Company LLP 200 Valley Rd Ste 300	Mt Arlington	NJ	07856	973-328-1825	
Web: www.nisivoccia.com					
Nolan O Luke CPA Pa 830 N Main	Wichita	KS	67203	316-265-0599	
Norman Jones Enlow & Co 226 N Fifth St Ste 500	Columbus	OH	43215	614-228-4000	
Norman W Marcoux CPA Inc 788 University Ave Ste 107	Sacramento	CA	95825	916-927-7772	
Web: marcouxcpa.com					
Novogradac & Company LLP 246 First St 5th Fl	San Francisco	CA	94105	415-356-8000	356-8001
Web: www.novoco.com					
Nperspective LLC 5971 Brick Ct Ste 100-B	Winter Park	FL	32792	407-679-7600	
Web: www.nperspective.net					
NSF-GFTC 88 McGilvray St	Guelph	ON	N1G2W1	519-821-1246	
TF: 800-673-6275 ■ *Web:* www.gftc.ca					
O'Connor & Drew PC 25 Braintree Hill Office Park Suit	Braintree	MA	02184	617-471-1120	
Web: ocd.com					
Olsen & Thompson Pa 970 Mt Kemble Ave	Morristown	NJ	07960	973-425-3212	
Web: otcpa.com					
Oprs 1615 Ellis St	Kewaunee	WI	54216	920-388-2788	
Opus 21 Management Solutions 680 Commerce Dr Ste 160	St Paul	MN	55125	651-905-0400	
Web: www.opus21ms.com					
Ostrow Reisin Berk & Abrams Ltd 455 N Cityfront Plz Dr	Chicago	IL	60611	312-670-7444	670-8301
Web: www.orba.com					
Packer Thomas 6601 Westford Pl Ste 101	Canfield	OH	44406	330-533-9777	
TF: 800-943-4278 ■ *Web:* www.packerthomas.com					
Padgett Business Services 160 Hawthorne Pk	Athens	GA	30606	800-723-4388	543-8537*
**Fax Area Code:* 706 ■ *TF:* 800-723-4388 ■ *Web:* www.padgettbusinessservices.com					
Paduano Di Tommaso & Golda 220 Monmouth Rd	Oakhurst	NJ	07755	732-531-4100	
Web: www.pdgcpa.com					
Pannell Kerr Forster Of Texas Pc 5847 San Felipe St	Houston	TX	77057	713-860-1400	355-3909
TF: 800-829-3676 ■ *Web:* www.pkftexas.com					
Parker Swearngin LLP 215 Se Douglas St	Lees Summit	MO	64063	816-434-6770	
Web: parkerswearngin.biz					
Patel & Assoc 266 17th St Ste 200	Oakland	CA	94612	510-452-5051	
Web: patelcpa.com					

Firm / Address	City	State	ZIP	Phone	Fax
Patrick & Buzarellos LLP 1900 Point W Way Ste 102	Sacramento	CA	95815	916-920-1604	
Web: pbpcpas.com					
Patrick J Kozlowski Accountancy 1127 11th St 225	Sacramento	CA	95814	916-448-5191	
Patrick Mcguire Certified Public Accountant 314 W 18th St.	Cheyenne	WY	82001	307-634-2151	
TF: 800-544-2151 ■ *Web:* www.mhpllp.com					
Patrick T Hsu CPA 7927 Garden Grove Blvd.	Garden Grove	CA	92841	714-895-6516	
Paulson Professional Corp 975 Willagillespie Rd Ste 202	Eugene	OR	97401	541-484-1881	
Paylogic 2843 Brownsboro Rd Ste 111	Louisville	KY	40206	502-894-0088	
Web: www.epaylogic.com					
Paylogix 1025 Old Country Rd Ste 310	Westbury	NY	11590	516-408-7800	
Web: paylogix.com					
Paymetric Inc 1225 Northmeadow Pkwy Ste 110	Roswell	GA	30076	678-242-5281	
TF: 888-445-4901 ■ *Web:* www.paymetric.com					
Payright Payroll Service Inc 468 Great Rd (2A)	Acton	MA	01720	978-263-5004	
Web: www.payrightpayroll.com					
Payroll 1 Inc 34100 Woodward Ave Ste 250	Birmingham	MI	48009	248-548-7020	
Web: www.payroll1.com					
Payroll Masters 855 Bordeaux Way	Napa	CA	94558	707-226-1428	
Web: www.payrollmasters.com					
PDR Certified Public Accountants Inc 29750 Us Hwy 19 N	Clearwater	FL	33761	727-785-4447	
Web: pdr-cpa.com					
Peachin Schwartz & Weingardt Pc 9449 Priority Way W Dr Ste 150	Indianapolis	IN	46240	317-574-4280	574-4286
Web: www.psw-cpa.com					
Pearce Bevill Leesburg & Moore Pc 110 Office Pk Dr	Birmingham	AL	35223	205-323-5440	328-8523
Web: www.pearcebevill.com					
Peck & Peck CPAs PC 312 S Pacific	Dillon	MT	59725	406-683-4254	
Pennock Acheson Nielsen Devaney Chartered Accountants 2201 Toronto Dominion Tower 102 Ave Ste 10088	Edmonton	AB	T5J2Z1	780-496-7774	
Web: www.pand.ca					
Pereira & Azevedo Cpa LLC 52-54 Rome St.	Newark	NJ	07105	973-466-1663	
Web: www.njcpas.com					
Perelson Weiner LLP 1 Dag Hammarskjold Plz 42nd Fl	New York	NY	10017	212-605-3100	
Web: www.pwcpa.com					
Perioperative Services LLC 111 Continental Dr Ste 412	Newark	DE	19713	302-733-0806	
Web: periopradonc.com					
Perkins Lund Collar & Assoc PLLC 2607 Oberlin Rd #200	Raleigh	NC	27608	919-781-1721	
Web: www.plccpa.com					
Peter Bell CPA 1735 Dilworth Rd E.	Charlotte	NC	28203	704-525-9999	
Web: peterbellpllc.com					
Peter J Bertuglia CPA PC 775 Park Ave	Huntington	NY	11743	631-385-7003	
Web: bertugliacpa.com					
Peters & Company PC 610 S W Alder St 910	Portland	OR	97205	503-241-8080	
Web: peterscopc.com					
Pfeffer Hanniford & Palka CPA's PC 225 E Grand River Ave Ste 104	Brighton	MI	48116	810-229-5550	
Web: phpcpa.com					
Phillips Gold & Company LLP 1430 Broadway Rm 1200	New York	NY	10018	212-730-1112	
TF: 800-772-1213 ■ *Web:* www.pgcebiz.com					
Pickens Snodgrass Koch & Company PC 3001 Medlin Dr Ste 100	Arlington	TX	76015	817-664-3000	
TF: 800-424-5790 ■ *Web:* www.pskcpa.com					
Piehl, Hanson, Beckman PA 700 S Grade Rd Sw.	Hutchinson	MN	55350	320-234-4430	
Web: www.phbcpa.com					
Piercy Bowler Taylor & Kern 6100 Elton Ave Ste 1000	Las Vegas	NV	89107	702-384-1120	
Web: pbtk.com					
Pilarski Sinkel & Hankes Ltd 5100 Eden Ave S Ste 304	Edina	MN	55436	952-929-2580	
Piltz Williams Larosa & Co 1077 Tommy Munro Dr	Biloxi	MS	39532	228-374-4141	
Web: pwlcpa.com					
Pinto Mucenski Hooper VanHouse & Company Certified Public Accountants PC 42 Market St.	Potsdam	NY	13676	315-265-6080	
Web: www.pmhvcpa.com					
PJ Schneiders & Company LLP 152 Himmelein Rd Village Greene E.	Medford	NJ	08055	609-654-8300	
Web: corrugatedcpa.com					
Plante & Moran PLLC 27400 NW Hwy.	Southfield	MI	48034	248-352-2500	352-0018
TF: 866-639-9991 ■ *Web:* www.plantemoran.com					
Playfair Planning Services 1640 E 94th St	Brooklyn	NY	11236	718-629-5898	
Web: www.playfairplanning.com					
PMB Helin Donovan LLP 5918 W Courtyard Dr.	Austin	TX	78730	512-258-9670	
Web: pmbhd.com					
Port & Company CPA'S 5730 Commons Park Dr.	East Syracuse	NY	13057	315-449-1200	
Port Kashdin & Mcsherry CPAs 111 W Rd	Cortland	NY	13045	607-756-5681	
Web: pkmcpa.com					
Porter & Company PC CPAs 241 Summit Ave Ste 100	Greensboro	NC	27401	336-370-1000	
Web: porterandco.com					
Porter & Porter PC 1370 Ramar Rd Ste B	Bullhead City	AZ	86442	928-758-4106	
Portnoy CPA 9283 San Jose Blvd	Jacksonville	FL	32257	904-731-8005	
Web: www.portnoycpa.com					
Pradip Patel & Company Ltd Certified Public Accountants 999 Plz Dr.	Schaumburg	IL	60173	847-413-0414	
Web: patel-cpa.com					
Presnell Gage Pllc 1216 Idaho St	Lewiston	ID	83501	208-746-8281	746-5174
Web: www.presnellgage.com					
PRG-Schultz International Inc 600 Galleria Pkwy Ste 100	Atlanta	GA	30339	770-779-3900	779-3133
TF: 800-752-5894 ■ *Web:* www.prgx.com					
Price Stagner & Company Pllc 501 Darby Creek Rd No 6	Lexington	KY	40509	859-263-1944	
Web: pricestagner.com					
PricewaterhouseCoopers LLP 300 Madison Ave.	New York	NY	10017	646-471-4000	286-6000*
**Fax Area Code:* 813 ■ *TF:* 800-993-9971 ■ *Web:* www.pwc.com					
Pritchard Bieler Gruver & Willison PC 590 Bethlehem Pk.	Colmar	PA	18915	215-997-6700	
Web: www.pbgw.com					
Pro HR Plus 724 Garland St	Little Rock	AR	72201	501-537-7747	
Pro Pay LLC 7450 W 130th St Ste 220	Overland Park	KS	66213	913-826-6300	
Quality Medical Reimbursement Services 6695 Highland Rd Ste 106	Waterford	MI	48327	248-666-4266	
Quast Janke & Co 1010 N Johnson St	Bay City	MI	48708	989-892-4549	
Web: qjc.com					
R J Williams 585 Rugh St	Greensburg	PA	15601	724-834-3403	
Radakovich Shaw & Blythe LLP 3220 S Higuera St Ste 201	San Luis Obispo	CA	93401	805-544-1557	
Web: radshaw.com					
Raffa PC 1899 L St NW Ste 900	Washington	DC	20036	202-822-5000	
Web: www.raffa.com					
Raimondo Pettit & Glassman 21515 Hawthorne Blvd Ste 1250	Torrance	CA	90503	310-540-5990	
Web: www.rpgcpa.com					
Ramberg & Assoc Pa 1080 SW Wanamaker Rd	Topeka	KS	66604	785-273-7276	
Web: rambergandassociates.com					
REA & Assoc Inc 419 W High Ave PO Box 1020	New Philadelphia	OH	44663	330-339-6651	308-9506
Web: www.reacpa.com					
Realty Consulting Services Inc 1628 Colonial Pkwy	Inverness	IL	60067	847-241-2900	
Reed & Brinkman Acctg Inc 208 Sherman St	Jackson	MN	56143	507-847-4222	
Rehmann Group 5800 Gratiot St Ste 201	Saginaw	MI	48638	989-799-9580	799-0227
TF: 866-799-9580 ■ *Web:* www.rehmann.com					
Reid Hurst Nagy 105-13900 Maycrest Way	Richmond	BC	V6V3E2	604-273-9338	
Web: www.rhncpa.com					
Reilly Penner & Benton LLP 1233 N Mayfair Rd	Milwaukee	WI	53226	414-271-7800	
Web: rpb.biz					
Repanich & Clevenger CPA'S 12715 Bel Red Rd Ste 200	Bellevue	WA	98005	425-451-4019	
Web: repanichclevenger.com					
Revens Revens & St Pierre 946 Centerville Rd	Warwick	RI	02886	401-822-2900	
Web: rrsplaw.com					
Reynolds Hix & Company PA 6729 Academy Rd Ne Ste D	Albuquerque	NM	87109	505-828-2900	
Web: rhcocpa.com					
Reznick Group PC 7501 Wisconsin Ave Ste 400 E	Bethesda	MD	20814	301-652-9100	
Web: cohnreznick.com					
RF Murray & Co CPAs PC 3741 Wilder Rd	Bay City	MI	48706	989-686-7740	686-7742
Web: rfmurraycpa.com					
Rich Gelwarg & Lampf LLP 4 Ethel Rd	Edison	NJ	08817	732-287-5565	
Web: www.rglcpa.com					
Richard L Brown & Company PA 1810 S Macdill Ave	Tampa	FL	33629	813-258-0338	
Richardson Pennington & Skinner Psc 513 S Second St	Louisville	KY	40202	502-583-9587	
TF: 800-654-3699 ■ *Web:* www.rps-cpa.com					
Richey May & Company PC 9605 S Kingston Ct Ste 200	Englewood	CO	80112	303-721-6131	
Web: www.richeymay.com					
Ringold Financial Management Services Inc 850 S Wabash Ave Ste 210	Chicago	IL	60605	312-566-9705	
Web: www.ringoldfinancial.com					
Ritz, Holman, Butala, Fine LLP 330 E Kilbourn Ave Two Plz E Ste 550	Milwaukee	WI	53202	414-271-1451	
Web: www.ritzholman.com					
Robert I Goldstein 6507 Wilkins Ave Ste 202	Pittsburgh	PA	15217	412-362-9040	
Robert K Taylor 2890 N Main St Ste 305	Walnut Creek	CA	94597	925-944-7660	
Robert M Grum Jr CPA 4540 Kearny Villa Rd Ste 108	San Diego	CA	92123	858-560-5449	
Roberts & Allan 2824 Park Ave Ste B	Merced	CA	95348	209-383-2442	
Robertson & Assoc CPA'S 1101 N Main St.	Lakeport	CA	95453	707-263-9012	
Web: robertsoncpa.com					
Robinson Hughes & Christopher Psc 459 W Martin Luther King Blvd	Danville	KY	40422	859-236-6628	
Web: rhccpas.com					
Rodefer Moss & Company PLLC 608 Mabry Hood Rd	Knoxville	TN	37932	865-583-0091	
Web: www.rodefermoss.com					
Roger D Perry PC 3050 Business Park Cir	Goodlettsville	TN	37072	615-851-6081	
Roger Sipe CPA Firm LLC 5742 Coventry Ln.	Fort Wayne	IN	46804	260-432-9996	
TF: 888-747-3272 ■ *Web:* sipecpa.com					
Rogers Huber & Assoc 973 Lycoming Mall Dr	Muncy	PA	17756	570-546-2238	
Web: rogershuber.com					
Ronald T Karpowich CPA 725 Front St	Freeland	PA	18224	570-636-2358	
Roscoe & Swanson Accountancy 3848 W Carson St Ste 215	Torrance	CA	90503	310-540-5300	
Web: rscpa.com					
Rosen Sapperstein & Friedlander Cht 300 Red Brook Blvd	Owings Mills	MD	21117	410-581-0800	
Web: rsfchart.com					
Rosen Seymour Shapss Martin & Company LLP 757 Third Ave 6th Fl	New York	NY	10017	212-303-1800	755-5600
Web: www.rssmcpa.com					
RosenbaumRollins & Olah PC 30230 Orchard Lk Rd Ste 200	Farmington Hills	MI	48334	248-855-6640	
Web: rra-cpas.com					

Name / Address	City	State	Zip	Phone	Fax
Rosenblum & Cohen CPAs					
100 Merrick Rd	Rockville Centre	NY	11570	516-763-1212	
Ross Buehler Falk & Company LLP (RBF)					
1500 Lititz Pk	Lancaster	PA	17601	717-393-2700	393-1743
Web: www.rbfco.com					
Rossmann Macdonald & Benetti Inc					
3838 Watt Ave Ste E500	Sacramento	CA	95821	916-488-8360	
Web: www.rmb-cpa.com					
Rotenberg Meril Solomon					
Park 80 W Plz 1 250 Pehle Ave Ste 101	Saddle Brook	NJ	07663	201-487-8383	
Web: www.rmsbg.com					
Roth & Company PC 666 Walnut Ste 1450	Des Moines	IA	50309	515-244-0266	
Web: www.rothcpa.com					
Roy & Assoc PC 433 Frye Farm Rd Ste 7	Greensburg	PA	15601	724-834-3900	
Web: royandassociates.wordpress.com					
Rozovics & Wojocicki Pc					
1580 N Northwest Hwy Ste 120	Park Ridge	IL	60068	847-699-7600	
RubinBrown LLP					
1 N Brentwood Blvd Ste 1100	Saint Louis	MO	63105	314-290-3300	290-3400
Web: www.rubinbrown.com					
Ruby Stein Wagner					
300 Rue Leo-pariseau Ste 1900	Montreal	QC	H2X4B5	514-842-3911	
TF: 866-842-3911 ■ *Web:* rsw.ca					
Ryan & Coscia PC 256 Essex St	Salem	MA	01970	978-744-1760	
Web: ryancoscia.com					
Ryansharkey LLP 12700 Sunrise Vly Dr	Reston	VA	20191	703-652-1124	
Web: ryansharkey.com					
S & p Tax Solutions Ltd 95 Revere Dr Ste A	Northbrook	IL	60062	847-480-4400	
Web: www.sandptax.com					
S R Snodgrass AC 2100 Corporate Dr	Wexford	PA	15090	724-934-0344	934-0345
TF: 800-580-7738 ■ *Web:* www.srsnodgrass.com					
Sackrider & Company Inc 1925 Wabash Ave	Terre Haute	IN	47807	812-232-9492	
Web: sackrider.com					
Sales Tax Resource Group					
16882 Bolsa Chica St Ste 206	Huntington Beach	CA	92649	714-377-2600	
Web: www.salestaxresource.com					
Sanford & Company PA 812 Dequeen	Mena	AR	71953	479-394-5414	
Web: sanford-cpa.com					
Sansiveri Kimball & Company LLP					
55 Dorrance St	Providence	RI	02903	401-331-0500	
Web: sansiveri.com					
Santa Monica Partners					
1865 Palmer Ave Ste 108	Larchmont	NY	10538	914-833-0958	
Web: www.smplp.com					
Santora CPA Group					
220 Continental Dr					
Ste 112 Christiana Executive Campus	Newark	DE	19713	302-737-6200	
TF: 800-347-0116 ■ *Web:* www.santoracpagroup.com					
Sara E Cooley CPA					
2240 Shelter Island Dr Ste 205	San Diego	CA	92106	619-758-9743	
Sarfino & Rhoades LLP					
11921 Rockville Pk Ste 501	North Bethesda	MD	20852	301-770-5500	
Web: www.sarfinoandrhoades.com					
Sattell Johnson Appel & Co Sc					
111 Heritage Reserve Ste 100	Menomonee Falls	WI	53051	414-273-0500	
Web: sattell.com					
SC&H Group LLC 910 Ridgebrook Rd	Sparks	MD	21152	410-403-1500	403-1570
TF: 800-832-3008 ■ *Web:* www.scandh.com					
Scafidi Cranston & Assoc LLC					
42 S Main St	Medford Lakes	NJ	08055	609-953-8699	
Web: scafidicranston.com					
Scheinkman & ScheinkmanPA					
18 NE Second Ave	Dania Beach	FL	33004	954-920-6173	
Schenck Business Solutions					
200 E Washington St	Appleton	WI	54911	920-731-8111	731-8037
TF: 800-236-2246 ■ *Web:* www.schenckc.com					
Schlenner Wenner & Co 630 Roosevelt Rd	Saint Cloud	MN	56301	320-251-0286	
TF: 877-616-0286 ■ *Web:* www.swcocpas.com					
Schmidt Assoc PC 2530 S Grand Ave	Carthage	MO	64836	417-358-6090	
Web: schmidt-cpapc.com					
Schmidt Westergard & Company PLLC					
77 W University Dr	Mesa	AZ	85201	480-834-6030	
Web: sw-cpa.com					
Schneider Downs & Company Inc					
1133 Penn Ave	Pittsburgh	PA	15222	412-261-3644	261-4876
Web: www.schneiderdowns.com					
Schroer & Assoc 300 W Broadway 41	Council Bluffs	IA	51503	712-322-8734	
Web: schroer-cpa.com					
Schulz & Urbanski PC 6 Forest Park Dr	Farmington	CT	06032	860-678-9042	
Schwartz & Nesbitt PC 281 Farmington Ave	Farmington	CT	06030	860-677-4585	
Schwartz Lasson Harris Ltd 2 Walnut Grove Dr	Horsham	PA	19044	215-956-9700	
Web: slhcpas.com					
Schwendiman Sutton & Simmons Pllc / Psp Inc					
39 Professional Plz	Rexburg	ID	83440	208-356-3452	
Web: ssscpa.net					
Scribner Cohen & Company SC					
400 E Mason St Ste 300	Milwaukee	WI	53202	414-271-1700	
TF: 888-730-0045 ■ *Web:* scribnercohen.com					
Seidel Schroeder & Co 304 E Blue Bell Rd	Brenham	TX	77833	979-846-8980	830-8131
Web: www.ssccpa.com					
Seiler LLP 3 Lagoon Dr Ste 400	Redwood City	CA	94065	650-365-4646	368-4055
Web: www.seiler.com					
Selden Fox Ltd 619 Enterprise Dr	Oak Brook	IL	60523	630-954-1400	
Web: www.seldenfox.com					
Self Maples & Copeland Pc 1601 Second Ave E	Oneonta	AL	35121	205-625-3472	
Web: cpasmc.com					
Seligman Friedman & Company PC					
235 St Charles Way Ste 250	York	PA	17402	717-741-0004	
Web: www.sfc-cpa.com					
Serna & Co PC 6031 W Ih-20 Ste 251	Arlington	TX	76017	817-483-3884	
Web: serna.com					
Seward & Monde 296 State St	North Haven	CT	06473	203-248-9341	
Web: sewardmonde.com					
Seybold John & Company Ltd					
800 Busse Hwy Ste 200	Park Ridge	IL	60068	847-696-1060	
Web: www.johnseybold.com					
Shajani LLP 5212 48 St	Red Deer	AB	T4N7C3	403-347-1384	
Web: shajani.ca					
Shannon & Assoc LLP 1851 Central Pl S Ste 225	Kent	WA	98030	253-852-8500	
Web: www.shannon-cpas.com					
Sharpe Kawam Carmosino & Company LLC					
1 Mars Ct Ste 1	Boonton	NJ	07005	973-335-1112	
Web: skcandco.com					
Sharrard McGee & Company PA 1321 Long St	High Point	NC	27262	336-884-0410	
Web: www.sharrardmcgee.com					
Shaw & Sullivan P C 1221 Cameron St	Alexandria	VA	22314	703-548-2776	
Web: shawcpa.com					
Sherman & Armbruster LLP 609 Treybourne Dr	Greenwood	IN	46142	317-881-6670	
Web: shermanandarmbruster.com					
Siegfried Group LLP, The 1201 Market St	Wilmington	DE	19801	302-984-1800	
Web: siegfriedgroup.com					
Siepert & Company LLP Cpa					
1920 W Hart Rd Side Side	Beloit	WI	53511	608-365-2266	
Web: www.siepert.com					
Sikich LLP 1415 W Diehl Rd Ste 400	Naperville	IL	60563	630-566-8400	566-8401
TF: 877-279-1900 ■ *Web:* www.sikich.com/sg					
Silberman Langner Assoc 6050 Santo Rd	San Diego	CA	92124	858-268-3330	
Web: silbermanlangner.com					
Simon Lever & Co 444 Murry Hill Cir	Lancaster	PA	17601	717-569-7081	
Web: www.simonlever.com					
Simons Bitzer & Assoc PC					
8350 S Emerson Ave Ste 100	Indianapolis	IN	46237	317-782-3070	
TF: 866-702-5090 ■ *Web:* www.simonsbitzer.com					
Singer Lewak Greenbaum & Goldstein LLP					
10960 Wilshire Blvd 7th Fl	Los Angeles	CA	90024	310-477-3924	478-6070
TF: 877-754-4557 ■ *Web:* www.singerlewak.com					
Sini & Reeves LLP CPA					
348 Main St Rt 25A	East Setauket	NY	11733	631-751-5225	
SJ Grillo 420 Jericho Tpke	Jericho	NY	11753	516-681-3433	
Slade Quilty & Assoc CPA'S LLP					
26619 Carmel Ctr Pl Ste 102	Carmel	CA	93923	831-625-8740	
Smith & Howard PC 271 17th St NW Ste 1600	Atlanta	GA	30363	404-874-6244	874-1658
Web: www.smith-howard.com					
Smith & Smith CPAs PC 2423 Us Hwy 2 E	Kalispell	MT	59901	406-755-4567	
Smith Anglin & Co 17738 Preston Rd	Dallas	TX	75252	972-267-1244	
Web: www.smithanglin.com					
Smith Brooks Bolshoun & CoLLP					
2680 18th St Ste 200	Denver	CO	80211	303-480-1200	
Web: sbbllp.com					
Smith Goolsby Artis & Reams Psc					
1330 Carter Ave	Ashland	KY	41101	606-329-1171	
Smith Koelling Dykstra & Ohm PC					
1605 N Convent	Bourbonnais	IL	60914	815-937-1997	
Web: skdocpa.com					
Smith Linden & Basso					
5120 Birch St Ste 200	Newport Beach	CA	92660	949-752-0660	
Web: www.slb-cpa.com					
Smith Schafer & Assoc Ltd					
220 S Broadway Ste 102	Rochester	MN	55904	507-288-3277	
Web: www.smithschafer.com					
Smoak Davis & Nixon LLP					
5011 Gate Pkwy Bldg 100 Ste 300	Jacksonville	FL	32256	904-396-5831	
Web: www.sdnllp.com					
Smoker Smith & Associates Pc					
339 W Governor Rd Ste 202	Hershey	PA	17033	717-533-5154	
TF: 888-277-1040 ■ *Web:* www.smokersmith.com					
Smolin, Lupin & Company PA					
165 Passaic Ave 4th Fl	Fairfield	NJ	07004	973-439-7200	
Web: www.smolin.com					
Smoll & Banning CPAs LLC 2410 Central Ave	Dodge City	KS	67801	620-225-6100	
TF: 800-499-8881 ■ *Web:* smollbanning.com					
Smythe Ratcliffe LLP 700 - 355 Burrard St	Vancouver	BC	V6C2G8	604-687-1231	
Web: www.smythecpa.com					
Sobel & Company LLC					
293 Eisenhower Pkwy Ste 290	Livingston	NJ	07039	973-994-9494	
TF: 800-471-2468 ■ *Web:* www.sobel-cpa.com					
Software Solutions Unlimited Inc					
9595 SW Gemini Dr	Beaverton	OR	97008	971-249-5400	
Web: www.ssui.com					
Sol Schwartz & Assoc					
7550 W Interstate 10 Ste 1200	San Antonio	TX	78229	210-384-8000	384-8011
Web: www.ssacpa.com					
Somerset CPAs PC					
3925 River Crossing Pkwy Ste 300	Indianapolis	IN	46240	317-472-2200	
Web: somersetcpas.com					
Sonnabend & Shu CPAS Inc 5832 Melvin Ave	Tarzana	CA	91356	818-776-0060	
Sorensen Vance & Company PC					
3115 East Lion Ln Ste 220	Salt Lake City	UT	84121	801-733-5055	
Web: sorensenvance.com					
Soukup Bush & Assoc CPAs PC					
2032 Caribou Dr Ste 200	Fort Collins	CO	80525	970-223-2727	
Web: soukupbush.com					
Spicer Jeffries & Company LLP					
5251 S Quebec St Ste 200	Greenwood Village	CO	80111	303-753-1959	
Web: spicerjeffries.com					
Spritzer Kaufman LLP 19 W 44th St Ste 1703	New York	NY	10036	212-593-1040	
Web: spritzerkaufman.com					
Sproles- Woodard- & Co					
777 Main St Ste 3250	Fort Worth	TX	76102	817-332-1328	
Web: www.sproles.com					
Squar Milner Peterson Miranda & Williamson LLP					
4100 Newport Pl Dr Ste 600	Newport Beach	CA	92660	949-222-2999	222-2989
Web: www.squarmilner.com					
Squire & Company PC 1329 South 800 East	Orem	UT	84097	801-225-6900	
Web: www.squire.com					
SS&G Financial Services Inc 32125 Solon Rd	Solon	OH	44139	440-248-8787	248-0841
Web: www.ssandg.com					

Firm	City	State	ZIP	Phone	Fax
Stanisky & Co 2550 Leechburg Rd *Web:* stanisky.com	Lower Burrell	PA	15068	724-339-7340	
Stanislawski & Harrison 301 N Lake Ave Ste 900 *Web:* www.snh-cpa.com	Pasadena	CA	91101	626-793-3600	
Stanley Benefit Services Inc 300 E Wendover Ave Ste 101 *Web:* www.stanleybenefits.com	Greensboro	NC	27401	336-271-4450	
Stanley R Hinckley CPA Inc 9292 Cincinnati-Columbus Rd	Cincinnati	OH	45241	513-777-4505	
Stealth Mktg Services 4424 Via De La Plz	Yorba Linda	CA	92886	714-693-3823	
Steinke Vertal Langdon & Drum Inc 3511 Center Rd PO Box 8 *Web:* svldcpa.com	Brunswick	OH	44212	330-225-3377	
Stephen A Kepniss & Assoc PC 211 Mountain Ave	Springfield	NJ	07081	973-921-1250	
Stephen M Meltz & Assoc CPA'S PC 6954 W Touhy Ave	Niles	IL	60714	847-647-6701	
Stephen Wojdowski CPA 8885 Rio San Diego Dr 3215	San Diego	CA	92108	619-296-0150	
Steven A Doyle Ltd 1565 82nd St W	Inver Grove Heights	MN	55077	651-688-8141	
Steven F Thurn CPA Psc 2134 Nicholasville Rd Ste 2 *Web:* thurncpa.com	Lexington	KY	40503	859-276-3782	
Stevenson Jones & Holmaas PC 5920 E Pima Ste 170	Tucson	AZ	85712	520-886-5495	
Stewart Archibald & Barney LLP 7881 W Charleston Blvd Ste 250 *Web:* www.sabcpa.com	Las Vegas	NV	89117	702-579-7000	
Stinnett & Assoc LLC 8801 S Yale Ave Ste 330 *Web:* www.stinnett-associates.com	Tulsa	OK	74137	918-728-3300	
Stockman Kast Ryan & Scruggs PC 102 N Cascade Ste 400 *Web:* www.skrco.com	Colorado Springs	CO	80903	719-630-1186	
Stockton Accountancy Corp 3355 Cerritos Ave	Los Alamitos	CA	90720	562-493-3591	
Stone & Company LLC 57 Bedford St *Web:* stonecpas.com	Lexington	MA	02420	781-863-6300	
Stone Parker & Company CPA 7512 Ridge Rd *Web:* stoneparkercpa.com	Port Richey	FL	34668	727-842-3180	
Strategic Account Management Assn 33 N La Salle St Ste 3700 *Web:* www.strategicaccounts.org	Chicago	IL	60602	312-251-3131	
Stratton & Assoc Pllc 398 S Ninth St Ste 290 *Web:* strattoncpa.com	Boise	ID	83702	208-336-4953	
Strothman & Company PSC 1600 Waterfront Plz *Web:* strothman.com	Louisville	KY	40202	502-585-1600	
Stuedle Spears & Company PSC 2821 S Hurstbourne Pkwy Ste 1	Louisville	KY	40220	502-491-5253	
Suby Von Haden & Assoc SC 1221 John Q Hammons Dr *TF:* 800-279-2616 ■ *Web:* www.sva.com	Madison	WI	53717	608-831-8181	
Sullivan & Menendez LLP 5510 Merrick Rd	Massapequa	NY	11758	516-795-2500	
Surgent Mccoy Cpe LLC 237 Lancaster Ave *Web:* cpenow.com	Devon	PA	19333	610-688-4477	
Susan Carlisle CPA A Professional 21243 Ventura Blvd Ste 138 *Web:* carlislecpa.com	Woodland Hills	CA	91364	818-888-3223	
Synter Resource Group LLC 5935 Rivers Ave Ste 102 *Web:* www.synterresource.com	Charleston	SC	29406	843-746-2200	
T James Williams & Company AC 7210 N Whitney Ave Ste 101 *Web:* tjwco.com	Fresno	CA	93720	559-322-9100	
Talbot Korvola & Warwick LLP 4800 Meadows Rd Ste 200 *Web:* tkw.com	Lake Oswego	OR	97035	503-274-2849	274-2853
Taycom Business Solutions Inc 719 Griswold Ave Ste 820 *TF:* 866-482-9266 ■ *Web:* www.taycomsolves.com	Detroit	MI	48226	866-482-9266	
Taylor Polson & Company PSC 101 Mckenna St	Glasgow	KY	42141	270-651-8877	
Teal Becker & Chiramonte (TBC) 7 Washington Sq *Web:* www.tbccpa.com	Albany	NY	12205	518-456-6663	456-3975
Team Jenn Corp 13323 W Washington Blvd Ste 205 *Web:* teamjenncorp.com	Los Angeles	CA	90066	310-822-8552	
Telniasoft Inc 1802 Brightseat Rd Ste 101 *Web:* telniasoft.com	Landover	MD	20785	301-918-4011	
Templeton & Company LLP 222 Lakeview Ave Ste 1200	West Palm Beach	FL	33401	561-798-9988	
Terry Jones & Assoc PC 5910 Grelot Rd *Web:* tjonescpa.com	Mobile	AL	36609	251-341-4593	
Theriot Charles C CPA 306 Grinage St *Web:* theriotaccountingfirm.com	Houma	LA	70360	985-872-9036	
Thomas A Lirot CPA PSC 551 State St *Web:* lirotcpa.com	Radcliff	KY	40160	270-351-1540	
Thomas C Jones CPA 105 S St *Web:* tomjonescpa.com	Elkton	MD	21921	410-398-9382	
Thomas E Holter PC 2730 E Broadway Blvd Ste 130	Tucson	AZ	85716	520-577-8818	
Thomas E Thevenin CPA PC 30 Wapping Rd	Kingston	MA	02364	781-582-1211	
Thomas Gammill & Company Ltd 5026 Old Greenwood St *Web:* gammillcpa.com	Fort Smith	AR	72903	479-648-1121	
Thomas W Daniels & Company PC 1310 Eagle Ridge Dr *Web:* thomaswdaniels.com	Schererville	IN	46375	219-864-7010	
Thombley & Simmons PC 78 Cole St Ste 200	Marietta	GA	30060	770-423-1234	
Thompson Greenspon & Company PC 4035 Ridgetop Rd Ste 700 *Web:* www.tgccpa.com	Fairfax	VA	22030	703-385-8888	
Tice Brunell & Baker Cpa Pc 14 Corporate Woods Blvd *Web:* www.tbbcpas.com	Albany	NY	12211	518-482-1887	
Tilton & Company CPA's PC 4015 S Mcclintock Dr Ste 105 *Web:* tiltonco.com	Tempe	AZ	85282	480-897-7708	
TimePlus Payroll Inc 695 Mansell Rd Ste 250 *Web:* www.timeplus.com	Roswell	GA	30076	770-998-5790	
Timmins Kroll & Jacobson LLP 10550 New York Ave Ste 200 *Web:* www.tkjcpa.com	Des Moines	IA	50322	515-270-8080	276-8329
Timpson Garcia 70 Washington St Ste 300 *Web:* www.timpsongarcia.com	Oakland	CA	94607	510-832-2325	
Tipton Marler Garner & Chastain 501 W 19th St *Web:* cpagroup.com	Panama City	FL	32405	850-769-9491	
TMG Company LLC 1718 Briarcrest Dr Ste 100 *TF:* 800-720-1563 ■ *Web:* www.tmgco.com	Bryan	TX	77802	979-774-4492	
Tobias Financial Advisors 1000 S Pine Island Rd Ste 250 *Web:* www.tobiasfinancial.com	Plantation	FL	33324	954-424-1660	
Todd Rivenbark Puryear Company Inc 2405 Robeson St *Web:* www.trpcpa.com	Fayetteville	NC	28305	910-323-3600	
Tollefson & Clancey CPA'S 151 Callan Ave Ste 310	San Leandro	CA	94577	510-483-0145	
Tomkiewicz Wright LLC 6111 P'Tree Dunwoody Rd Bld E 102 *Web:* twcpaga.com	Atlanta	GA	30328	770-351-0411	
Torosian & Walter Financial Services LLC 7225 N First St Ste 101 *Web:* www.twcpa.com	Fresno	CA	93720	559-256-5600	
Toukan & Co 575 Charring Cross Dr Ste 200 *Web:* toukan.com	Westerville	OH	43081	614-901-7100	
Tower Accounting 3435 Blue Mtn Dr *Web:* www.toweraccounting.com	San Jose	CA	95127	408-929-4576	
Trager Kevy & Trager 575 Hempstead Tpke Ste 1 *Web:* tktcpa.com	W Hempstead	NY	11552	516-292-9494	
Trout Ebersole & Groff 1705 Oregon Pk *Web:* www.troutcpa.com	Lancaster	PA	17601	717-569-2900	
Troutt, Beeman & Company PC 1212 Locust St *Web:* www.tbco.net	Harrisonville	MO	64701	816-380-5500	
Truitt Tingle & Paramore LLC 5346 Stadium Trace Pkwy Ste 202 *Web:* ttpcpa.com	Hoover	AL	35244	205-733-8265	
Turlington & Co 509 E Ctr St PO Box 1697 *Web:* www.turlingtonandcompany.com	Lexington	NC	27292	336-249-6856	
Turner Vedrenne & Howard PC 9330 Lbj Fwy Ste 875 *Web:* tvhcpas.com	Dallas	TX	75243	972-644-4131	
Turner Warren Hwang & Conrad 100 N First St Ste 202 *Web:* www.twhc.com	Burbank	CA	91502	818-955-9537	
TYS LLP 3150 Crow Canyon Pl Ste 170 *Web:* tysllp.com	San Ramon	CA	94583	925-498-6200	
UHY Advisors Inc 30 S Wacker Dr *Web:* www.uhyadvisors-us.com	Chicago	IL	60606	312-578-9600	346-6500
UHY Advisors NY Inc 66 S Pearl St *Web:* uhy-us.com	Albany	NY	12207	518-449-3171	449-5832
United Paramount Tax Group Inc 4025 Woodland Park Blvd Ste 310 *TF:* 888-829-8829 ■ *Web:* uptg.com	Arlington	TX	76013	817-983-0099	
Unity HR LLC 2400 Meridian St Bldg B *Web:* www.unityhr.com	Bellingham	WA	98225	360-671-0762	
Updegrove Combs Mcdaniel & Wilson Plc 10 Rock Pointe Ln Ste 3 *Web:* ucmcpas.com	Warrenton	VA	20186	540-347-5681	
Urish Popeck & Co 3 Gateway Ctr Ste 2400 *Web:* www.urishpopeck.com	Pittsburgh	PA	15222	412-391-1994	
Vanacore Debenedictus Digovanni Waddell LLP 11 Racquet Rd PO Box 10009 *Web:* www.vddw.com	Newburgh	NY	12552	845-567-9000	
Vavro & Company Inc 4725 Grayton Rd Ste 1040	Cleveland	OH	44135	440-886-0400	
Venturity Financial Partners 14131 Midway Rd Ste 112 *Web:* www.venturity.net	Addison	TX	75001	972-692-0380	
Verdolino & Lowey PC 124 Washington St Ste 101 *Web:* vlpc.com	Foxboro	MA	02035	508-543-1720	
Verlyn G Adamson CPA 708 S Second St *Web:* vacpa.cc	Mount Horeb	WI	53572	608-437-6322	
Vestal & Wiler Cpas 201 E Pine St Ste 801 *Web:* vestal-wiler.com	Orlando	FL	32801	407-843-4433	
Vicenti Lloyd & Stutzman LLP 2210 E Rt 66 *Web:* vlsllp.com	Glendora	CA	91740	626-857-7300	
Virginia Society of Certified Public Accountants 4309 Cox Rd *TF:* 800-733-8272 ■ *Web:* vscpa.com	Glen Allen	VA	23060	804-270-5344	
W Harold Talley Company Inc 4905 Radford Ave Ste 200	Richmond	VA	23230	804-359-5313	
Wakoff Andriulli & Company LLC 100 Craig Rd Ste 109 *Web:* njcpa.com	Manalapan	NJ	07726	732-866-8882	
Walker & Armstrong LLP 3838 N Central Ave *Web:* wa-cpas.com	Phoenix	AZ	85012	602-230-1040	
Walker & Massey CPAs 150 W Rialto Ave	Rialto	CA	92376	909-875-0244	
Wall, Einhorn & Chernitzer PC 555 E Main St Ste 1600 *Web:* www.wec-cpa.com	Norfolk	VA	23510	757-625-4700	

Name / Address	City	State	Zip	Phone	Fax
Walsh Kelliher & Sharp Apc					
1292 Sadler Way Ste 220	Fairbanks	AK	99701	907-456-2222	
Web: wkscpa.com					
Walter G Grady CPA 2843 Johnson Ave	Alameda	CA	94501	510-523-2310	
Walter L Weisman CPA 8911 La Mesa Blvd 201	La Mesa	CA	91942	619-697-7878	
Warady & Davis LLP 1717 Deerfield Rd	Deerfield	IL	60015	847-267-9600	
Web: waradydavis.com					
Warren Averett Kimbrough & Marino LLC					
2500 Acton Rd	Birmingham	AL	35243	205-979-4100	979-6313
Web: warrenaverett.com					
Watson Rice & Co 301 Rt 17 N	Rutherford	NJ	07070	201-460-4590	
TF: 800-945-5985 ■ *Web:* watsonrice.com					
Weber Obrien Ltd 5580 Monroe St	Sylvania	OH	43560	419-885-8338	
Web: www.weberobrien.com					
Weinstein & Anastasio PC					
2319 Whitney Ave Ste 2a	Hamden	CT	06518	203-397-2525	
Weiser LLP 135 W 50th St	New York	NY	10020	212-812-7000	375-6888
Web: weisermazars.com					
Weissberg & Speller CPA'S PC					
3601 Hempstead Tpke	Levittown	NY	11756	516-796-2727	
Web: weissbergandspeller.com					
Wells Coleman & Co 3800 Patterson Ave	Richmond	VA	23221	804-358-1150	
Web: www.wellscoleman.com					
West & Company CPAs PC 97 N Main St	Gloversville	NY	12078	518-725-7127	
Web: westcpapc.com					
Whiteman & Co PA					
111 2nd Avenue Northeast Ste 1600	St Petersburg	FL	33701	727-896-2727	
Whitley Penn 3411 Richmond Ave Ste 500	Houston	TX	77046	713-621-1515	621-1570
Web: www.whitleypenn.com					
Wiebe & Assoc 377 N Central Ave	Upland	CA	91786	909-985-5357	
Web: www.wiebecpas.com					
Wilcoxon Research Inc					
20511 Seneca Meadows Pkwy	Germantown	MD	20876	301-330-8811	
TF: 800-945-2696 ■ *Web:* www.wilcoxon.com					
Wilkin & Guttenplan PC 1200 Tices Ln	East Brunswick	NJ	08816	732-846-3000	
Web: wgcpas.com					
William Burton & Company Inc 99 Walnut St	Saugus	MA	01906	781-233-2204	
Web: cpaburton.com					
William G Koch & Assoc 2650 Wview Dr	Wyomissing	PA	19610	610-678-9700	
Web: wgkcpa.com					
Williams Benator & Libby LLP					
1040 Crown Pinte Pkwy NE Ste 400	Atlanta	GA	30338	770-512-0500	512-0200
Web: www.wblcpa.com					
Williamson Employment Services Inc					
213 Hilltop Rd	St. Joseph	MI	49085	269-983-0142	
Web: www.williamsonemployment.com					
Wilson Harris & Co 1602 W Franklin St	Boise	ID	83702	208-344-1355	
Web: wilsonharris.com					
Windham Brannon PC 3630 Peachtree Rd Ne	Atlanta	GA	30326	404-898-2000	
Web: windhambrannon.com					
Winer & Bevilacqua Inc 82 N Miller Rd	Fairlawn	OH	44333	330-867-3578	
Web: wb-cpa.com					
Winkler & Whittenberg Inc CPA'S					
15446 E Valley Blvd	City Of Industry	CA	91746	626-330-2224	961-0156
Web: whittenbergcpa.com					
Winther Stave & Company LLP					
1316 W 18th St PO Box 175	Spencer	IA	51301	712-262-3117	
Web: www.winther-stave.com					
Wipfli LLP 10000 Innovation Dr Ste 250	Milwaukee	WI	53226	414-431-9300	431-9303
Web: www.wipfli.com					
Wireless Watchdogs LLC					
5800 Hannum Ave Ste B	Culver City	CA	90230	866-522-0688	
TF: 866-522-0688 ■ *Web:* www.wirelesswatchdogs.com					
Wishnow Ross Warsavsky & Co					
16130 Ventura Blvd	Encino	CA	91436	818-981-2240	
WithumSmith+Brown 5 Vaughn Dr	Princeton	NJ	08540	609-520-1188	520-9882
TF: 866-455-7438 ■ *Web:* www.withum.com					
Wojteczko Snyder Group PC 5583 S Prince St	Littleton	CO	80120	303-730-7999	
Web: wsgrouppc.com					
Wolf Tesar & Company PC 1415 Valle Vista	Pekin	IL	61554	309-346-4106	
Wong & Knowles CPA PC 340 W Butterfield Rd	Elmhurst	IL	60126	630-993-2223	993-2229
TF: 866-966-4272 ■ *Web:* wongknowles.com					
Woodfield Fund Admin LLC					
3601 Algonquin Rd Ste 900	Rolling Meadows	IL	60008	847-255-3500	
Web: www.woodfieldllc.com					
Woronoff Hyman Levenson & Sweet PC					
30600 Northwestern Hwy Ste 302	Farmington Hills	MI	48334	248-487-2600	
Web: whls.com					
Wyatt & Company Inc 6846 S Trenton Ave	Tulsa	OK	74136	918-488-0311	
Web: www.wyattandcompany.com					
XPS Group Inc 888 Ft St 2nd Fl	Victoria	BC	V8W1H8	250-383-4135	
Web: www.xpsgroup.net					
Yeo & Yeo PC 3023 Davenport Ave	Saginaw	MI	48602	989-793-9830	
Web: yeoandyeo.com					
YFF & Scholma PC 688 Cascade W Pkwy SE	Grand Rapids	MI	49546	616-942-6530	
Web: yffandscholma.com					
Yodice & Co PC 1259 Rt # 46	Parsippany	NJ	07054	973-263-8228	
Web: yodiceco.com					
Young & Company CPAS					
11200 SW Allen Blvd Ste 100	Beaverton	OR	97005	503-646-4800	
Web: youngcocpas.com					
Yount Hyde & Barbour PC 50 S Cameron St	Winchester	VA	22601	540-662-3417	
Web: www.yhbcpa.com					
Zeisler, Zeisler, Rawson & Johnson LLP					
901 A St Ste C	San Rafael	CA	94901	415-451-1703	
Web: zzrjllp.com					
Zisook & Greenberg Ltd					
208 S Lasalle St Ste 1600	Chicago	IL	60604	312-641-1090	

3 ADHESIVES & SEALANTS

Name / Address	City	State	Zip	Phone	Fax
Adco Global Inc					
100 Tri State International Ste 135	Lincolnshire	IL	60069	847-282-3485	282-3481
Web: www.adcoglobal.com					
Adhesives Research Inc					
400 Seaks Run Rd PO Box 100	Glen Rock	PA	17327	717-235-7979	235-8320
TF: 800-445-6240 ■ *Web:* www.adhesivesresearch.com					
Arclin 1000 Holcomb Woods Pkwy Ste 342	Roswell	ON	L5R1B8	905-712-0900	
Web: www.dynea.com					
Arlon Graphics 2811 S Harbor Blvd	Santa Ana	CA	92704	714-540-2811	329-2756*
**Fax Area Code:* 800 ■ *TF:* 800-232-7161 ■ *Web:* www.arlon.com					
Atlas Minerals & Chemicals Inc					
1227 Valley Rd	Mertztown	PA	19539	610-682-7171	682-9200
TF Cust Svc: 800-523-8269 ■ *Web:* www.atlasmin.com					
Avery Dennison Corp 207 Goode Ave	Glendale	CA	91203	626-304-2000	
NYSE: AVY ■ *TF Cust Svc:* 888-567-4387 ■ *Web:* www.averydennison.com					
Axson North America Inc					
31200 Stephenson Hwy	Madison Heights	MI	48071	248-588-2270	663-0523*
**Fax Area Code:* 517 ■ *Web:* www.axson-technologies.com/us/index.html					
BASF Corp/Bldg Systems 889 Valley Pk Dr	Shakopee	MN	55379	952-496-6000	
TF Cust Svc: 800-433-9517 ■ *Web:* www.master-builders-solutions.basf.us/en-us					
Basic Adhesives Inc 60 Webro Rd	Clifton	NJ	07012	973-614-9000	
Web: www.elektromek.com					
Bemis Assoc Inc 1 Bemis Way	Shirley	MA	01464	978-425-6761	425-2278
Web: www.bemisworldwide.com					
Bestolife Corp 2777 Stemmons Fwy Ste 1800	Dallas	TX	75207	214-583-0271	631-3047
TF: 855-243-9164 ■ *Web:* www.bestolife.com					
Bonstone Materials Corp 707 Swan Dr	Mukwonago	WI	53149	262-363-9877	
TF: 800-425-2214 ■ *Web:* bonstone.com					
BR 111 Exotic Hardwood Flooring 1 NE 40th St	Miami	FL	33137	800-525-2711	
TF: 800-525-2711 ■ *Web:* www.br111.com					
Brady Coated Products 6555 W Good Hope Rd	Milwaukee	WI	53223	414-358-6600	541-1686*
**Fax Area Code:* 800 ■ *TF:* 800-662-1191 ■					
Web: www.bradyid.com/en-us/standards-and-compliance/custom-coating-services/overview					
CFC International Inc 500 State St	Chicago Heights	IL	60411	708-891-3456	758-5989
TF: 800-393-4505 ■ *Web:* www.cfcintl.com					
Chase Corp 26 Summer St	Bridgewater	MA	02324	781-332-0700	697-6419*
NYSE: CCF ■ **Fax Area Code:* 508 ■ *Web:* www.chasecorp.com					
Chemence Inc 185 Bluegrass Valley Pkwy	Alpharetta	GA	30005	770-664-6624	664-6620
Web: www.chemence.com					
Colloid Environmental Technologies Co (CETCO)					
2870 Forbs Ave	Hoffman Estates	IL	60192	847-851-1899	527-9948*
**Fax Area Code:* 800 ■ *TF:* 800-527-9948 ■ *Web:* www.cetco.com					
Concrete Sealants Inc 9325 SR- 201	Tipp City	OH	45371	937-845-8776	
Web: www.conseal.com					
Covalent Medical Inc					
4750 S State St Ste 301	Ann Arbor	MI	48108	734-429-2451	
Web: www.covamed.com					
Custom Bldg Products					
13001 Seal Beach Blvd	Seal Beach	CA	90740	562-598-8808	
TF: 800-272-8786 ■ *Web:* www.custombuildingproducts.com					
DAP Products Inc 2400 Boston St Ste 200	Baltimore	MD	21224	410-675-2100	558-1068*
**Fax:* Cust Svc ■ *TF Cust Svc:* 800-543-3840 ■ *Web:* www.dap.com					
Dehco Inc 58263 Charlotte Ave	Elkhart	IN	46517	574-294-2684	
Web: www.dehco.com					
Devcon Inc 30 Endicott St	Danvers	MA	01923	855-489-7262	774-0516*
**Fax Area Code:* 978 ■ *TF:* 800-626-7226 ■ *Web:* www.devcon.com					
Dymax Corp 318 Industrial Ln	Torrington	CT	06790	860-482-1010	496-0608
TF: 877-396-2963 ■ *Web:* www.dymax.com					
Eclectic Products Inc					
1075 Arrowsmith St PO Box 2280	Eugene	OR	97402	800-693-4667	746-1983*
**Fax Area Code:* 541 ■ *TF:* 800-693-4667 ■ *Web:* www.eclecticproducts.com					
EFTEC North America LLC 20219 Northline Rd	Taylor	MI	48180	248-585-2200	374-2050*
**Fax Area Code:* 734 ■ *Web:* www.eftec.ch					
Elmer's Products Inc 1 Easton Oval	Columbus	OH	43219	888-435-6377	
TF: 888-435-6377 ■ *Web:* www.elmers.com					
Euclid Chemical Co 19218 Redwood Rd	Cleveland	OH	44110	216-531-9222	531-9596
TF: 800-321-7628 ■ *Web:* www.euclidchemical.com					
Foster Construction Products Inc					
1105 S Frontenac St	Aurora	IL	60504	800-231-9541	942-6856
TF: 800-231-9541 ■ *Web:* www.fosterproducts.com					
Fox Industries Inc 3100 Falls Cliff Rd	Baltimore	MD	21211	410-243-8856	243-2701
TF: 888-760-0369 ■ *Web:* strongtie.com					
Franklin International 2020 Bruck St	Columbus	OH	43207	614-443-0241	445-1813
TF: 800-877-4583 ■ *Web:* www.franklininternational.com					
Geocel Corp PO Box 398	Elkhart	IN	46515	574-264-0645	348-7009*
**Fax Area Code:* 800 ■ *TF:* 800-348-7615 ■ *Web:* www.geocelusa.com					
H B Fuller Construction Products Inc					
1105 S Frontenac Rd	Aurora	IL	60504	800-832-9002	942-6856
TF: 800-832-9002 ■ *Web:* www.tecspecialty.com					
HB Fuller Co					
1200 Willow Lk Blvd PO Box 64683	Saint Paul	MN	55164	651-236-5900	236-5898
NYSE: FUL ■ *TF:* 888-423-8553 ■ *Web:* www.hbfuller.com					
Henkel Corp 1 Henkel Way	Rocky Hill	CT	06067	860-571-5100	571-5465
TF Cust Svc: 800-243-4874 ■ *Web:* www.henkel.com					
Hercules Chemical Company Inc 111 S St	Passaic	NJ	07055	973-778-5000	777-4115
TF: 800-221-9330 ■ *Web:* www.oatey.com					
Hexion Specialty Chemicals Inc					
180 E Broad St	Columbus	OH	43215	614-225-4000	
Web: www.momentive.com					
Houghton International Inc					
945 Madison Ave PO Box 930	Valley Forge	PA	19482	610-666-4000	666-0174
TF: 888-459-9844 ■ *Web:* www.houghtonintl.com					
IDQ Holdings Inc 2901 W Kingsley Rd	Garland	TX	75041	214-778-4600	
Web: www.idqusa.com					
Inovex Industries Inc					
45681 Oakbrook Ct Ste 102	Sterling	VA	20166	703-421-9778	421-1967
TF: 888-374-3366 ■ *Web:* www.ride-on.com					

Phone Fax

Integral Products Inc 24030 Frampton Ave.......... Harbor City CA 90710 310-326-8889
Web: www.integralproducts.com
IPS Corp 455 W Victoria St.......................... Compton CA 90220 310-898-3300 853-5008*
**Fax Area Code:* 901 ■ *TF:* 800-888-8312 ■ *Web:* www.ipscorp.com
ITW Polymers Sealants North America
111 S Nursery R.................................. Irving TX 75060 972-438-9111 231-8222*
**Fax Area Code:* 800 ■ *TF Hotline:* 888-751-0409 ■ *Web:* itwsealants.com
Key Polymer Corp 17 Shepherd St.................. Lawrence MA 01843 978-683-9411 686-7729
Web: www.keypolymer.com
L & L Products Inc 160 McLean Dr.................. Romeo MI 48065 586-336-1700 336-1699
Web: www.llproducts.com
LaPolla Industries Inc
15402 Vantage Pkwy E Ste 322..................... Houston TX 77032 281-219-4700 219-4102
OTC: LPAD ■ *Web:* lapolla.com/investor-relations
Laticrete International Inc 91 Amity Rd.............. Bethany CT 06524 203-393-0010 393-1684
TF: 800-243-4788 ■ *Web:* www.laticrete.com
Lord Corp 111 Lord Dr................................ Cary NC 27511 919-468-5979
TF: 877-275-5673 ■ *Web:* www.lord.com
Manus Products of Minnesota Inc
866 Industrial Blvd.............................. Waconia MN 55387 952-442-3323 442-3327
Web: www.manus.net
MAPEI Corp 1144 E Newport Ctr Dr.............. Deerfield Beach FL 33442 954-246-8888 246-8800
TF: 800-426-2734 ■ *Web:* www.mapei.com
Mask-Off Company Inc 345 W Maple Ave............ Monrovia CA 91016 626-359-3261 359-7160
Web: www.mask-off.com
Morgan Adhesives Co 4560 Darrow Rd.................. Stow OH 44224 330-688-1111 688-2540
TF: 866-262-2822 ■ *Web:* www.mactac.com
Multiseal Inc 4320 Hitch Peters Rd.................. Evansville IN 47711 812-428-3422 428-3432
Web: www.multiseal-usa.com
National Casein Co 601 W 80th St.................... Chicago IL 60620 773-846-7300 487-5709
Web: www.nationalcasein.com
Nylok Corp 15260 Hallmark Dr......................... Macomb MI 48042 586-786-0100 786-0598
TF: 800-826-5161 ■ *Web:* www.nylok.com
Pacific Polymers Inc 12271 Monarch St.......... Garden Grove CA 92841 714-898-0025
TF: 800-888-8340 ■ *Web:* www.pacpoly.com
Para-Chem Southern Inc
863 SE Main St PO Box 127..................... Simpsonville SC 29681 864-967-7691 963-1241
TF: 800-763-7272 ■ *Web:* www.parachem.com
Pecora Corp 165 Wambold Rd..................... Harleysville PA 19438 215-723-6051 799-2518
TF: 800-523-6688 ■ *Web:* www.pecora.com
Red Devil Inc 1437 S Boulder............................ Tulsa OK 74119 800-423-3845 585-8120*
**Fax Area Code:* 918 ■ *TF:* 800-423-3845 ■ *Web:* www.reddevil.com
Ritrama 800 Kasota Ave SE...................... Minneapolis MN 55414 612-378-2277 378-9327
TF: 800-328-5071 ■ *Web:* www.ritrama.com
Solar Compounds Corp 1201 W Blancke St.............. Linden NJ 07036 908-862-2813 862-8061
Web: www.solarcompounds.com
Southern Grouts & Mortars Inc
1502 SW Second Pl........................ Pompano Beach FL 33069 954-943-2288 943-2402
TF: 800-641-9247 ■ *Web:* www.sgm.cc
Super Glue Corp
9420 Santa Anita Ave.................... Rancho Cucamonga CA 91730 909-987-0550 987-0490
TF: 800-538-3091 ■ *Web:* www.supergluecorp.com
Super-Tek Products Inc 25-44 Borough Pl........... Woodside NY 11377 718-278-7900
Web: www.super-tek.com
Surteco USA Inc 7104 Cessna Dr.................. Greensboro NC 27409 336-668-9555 668-7795
Web: www.canplast.com
Tailored Chemical Products Inc
700 12th St Dr NW................................ Hickory NC 28601 828-322-6512 322-7688
TF: 800-627-1687 ■ *Web:* www.tailoredchemical.com
Tremco Inc Roofing Div 3735 Green Rd............ Beachwood OH 44122 216-292-5000
TF: 800-852-6013 ■ *Web:* www.tremcoroofing.com
Uniseal Inc 1800 W Maryland St..................... Evansville IN 47712 812-436-4840 429-1831
TF: 800-443-9081 ■ *Web:* www.uniseal.com
W.F. Taylor Company Inc 11545 Pacific Ave........... Fontana CA 92337 951-360-6677 360-1177
TF: 800-397-4583 ■ *Web:* www.wftaylor.com
Western American National Bank
1518 Taney St................................ Kansas City MO 64116 816-421-3000 421-3122
Worthen Industries Inc 3 E Spit Brook Rd.............. Nashua NH 03060 603-888-5443 888-7945
Web: www.worthenind.com
&Barr 600 E Washington St........................... Orlando FL 32801 407-849-0100
Web: andbarr.co

4 ADVERTISING AGENCIES

See Also Public Relations Firms p. 2994

Phone Fax

160 Over 90 510 Wallnut St 19th Fl................ Philadelphia PA 19106 215-732-3200
Web: www.160over90.com
22 Squared 1170 Peachtree St NE 14th Fl................ Atlanta GA 30309 404-347-8700
Web: www.22squared.com
2B Productions Inc 1674 Broadway Ste 902........... New York NY 10019 212-765-8202
Web: www.2binc.com
3marketeers Advertising Inc 785 The Almeda......... San Jose CA 95126 408-293-3233 293-2433
Web: www.3marketeers.com
5 Star Sports Calendar LLC
3340 N College Ave............................ Fayetteville AR 72703 479-444-8428
Web: www.fivestarsports.com
9summer LLC 7 Research Dr...................... Woodbridge CT 06525 203-397-0500
A Bright Idea LLC 210 Archer St........................ Bel Air MD 21014 410-836-7180
Web: www.abrightideaonline.com
A Web That Works 2733 Concession Rd 7.......... Bowmanville ON L1C3K6 905-263-2666 263-8989
TF: 800-579-9253 ■ *Web:* www.awebthatworks.com
Abelson-Taylor Inc 33 W Monroe St................. Chicago IL 60603 312-894-5500 894-5658
Web: abelsontaylor.com
Acento Adv Inc 2254 S Sepulveda Blvd............. Los Angeles CA 90064 310-943-8300
Web: www.acento.com
Ackerman McQueen Inc (AM)
1601 NW Expy Ste 1100...................... Oklahoma City OK 73118 405-843-7777 848-8034
Web: www.am.com
Ad Partners Inc
4631 Woodland Corporate Blvd Ste 109................. Tampa FL 33614 813-418-4645
Web: adpartnersagency.com

Phone Fax

Adams & Knight Inc 80 Avon Meadow Ln................ Avon CT 06001 860-676-2300
Web: www.adamsknight.com
Adasia Communications Inc
400 Sylvan Ave Ste 200..................... Englewood Cliffs NJ 07632 201-608-0388
Web: www.adasia-us.com
Addwater2 Inc 383 First St W......................... Sonoma CA 95476 707-938-1223
Web: addwater2.com
AdMasters 16901 Dallas Pkwy Ste 204................ Addison TX 75001 972-866-9300
Web: www.admasters.com
Adnet Adv Agency Inc 116 John St Fl 35............. New York NY 10038 212-587-3164
Web: www.adnet-nyc.com
Advertising Premium Sales Inc
11675 Lilburn Park Rd......................... Saint Louis MO 63146 314-872-7000
Web: apspromos.com
Agent 16 79 Fifth Ave.............................. New York NY 10003 212-367-3800 367-3884
Aj Ross Creative Media 1149 NY 17M............... Chester NY 10918 845-783-5770
TF: 800-723-4644 ■ *Web:* www.ajross.com
AKQA Inc 360 Third St 5th Fl.................... San Francisco CA 94107 415-645-9400 645-9420
Web: www.akqa.com
Alesco Data Group LLC
5276 Summerlin Commons Way................... Fort Myers FL 33907 239-275-5006
TF: 800-701-6531 ■ *Web:* www.alescodata.com
Alison Group Inc, The
2090 NE 163rd St........................ North Miami Beach FL 33162 305-893-6255
Web: www.alisongroup.com
All-Ways Adv Co 1442 Broad St.................... Bloomfield NJ 07003 973-338-0700 338-1410
TF: 800-255-9291 ■ *Web:* www.awadv.com
Allen & Gerritsen 2 Seaport Ln........................ Boston MA 02210 857-300-2000
Web: www.a-g.com
Alliance Communications Inc
15310 Amberly Dr Ste 215.......................... Tampa FL 33647 813-978-1992
American Telecast Corp
835 Springdale Dr Ste 206........................... Exton PA 19341 610-430-7800
Web: www.americantelecast.com
AMP Agency 77 N Washington St..................... Boston MA 02114 617-723-8929
Web: www.ampagency.com
Anderson Communications
1691 Phoenix Blvd Ste 390.......................... Atlanta GA 30349 404-766-8000 767-5264
Web: www.andercom.com
Anderson Partners Inc 6919 Dodge St................. Omaha NE 68132 402-341-4807
Web: www.andersonpartners.com
Animated Designs LLC
31336 Via Colinas Ste 103.................. Westlake Village CA 91362 818-889-2348
Web: www.anides.com
Apple Rock Adv & Promotion
7602 Business Park Dr.......................... Greensboro NC 27409 336-232-4800
Web: www.applerock.com
Archer/Malmo Adv Inc 65 Union Ave Ste 500.......... Memphis TN 38103 901-523-2000 523-7654
Web: www.archermalmo.com
Argus Communications Inc 280 Summer St Fl 4......... Boston MA 02210 617-261-7676
Arrowhead Agency 16155 N 83rd Ave Ste 205........... Peoria AZ 85382 623-979-3000
Web: arrowhead.agency
Arvizu Adv & Promotions Inc
3111 N Central Ave Ste 1240........................ Phoenix AZ 85012 602-279-4669
Web: www.arvizu.com
AskMencom Solutions Canada Inc
4200 St Laurent Ste 801.......................... Montreal QC H2W2R2 514-908-2552
Aspen Marketing Services 1240 N Ave.......... West Chicago IL 60185 630-293-9600 293-9600
TF: 800-848-0212 ■ *Web:* www.aspenms.com
ATD Austin PO Box 13324............................ Austin TX 78711 512-395-8101
Web: theredphonebook.com
Augie Leopold Adv Specialties Inc
3214 Roman St.................................... Metairie LA 70001 504-836-0525
Web: augieleopold.com
Automated Presort Inc
1400 Centre Cir Dr......................... Downers Grove IL 60515 630-620-7678
Avid Neo Geo 108 Lake Ave.......................... Orlando FL 32801 407-246-0092
Web: www.avidneogeo.com
Avrett Free Ginsberg (AFG)
885 Second Ave Dag Hammarskjold Plz.............. New York NY 10017 212-832-3800
Web: avrettfreeginsberg.com
Azul 7 Inc 800 Hennepin Ave Ste 700.............. Minneapolis MN 55403 612-767-4335
Web: azul7.com
Bader Rutter & Assoc Inc 13845 Bishops Dr......... Brookfield WI 53005 262-784-7200 938-5595
Web: www.baderrutter.com
Bailey Lauerman & Assoc Inc
1299 Farnam St Ste 1400........................... Lincoln NE 68102 402-514-9400
Web: www.baileylauerman.com
Bakersfield Californian Inc 1707 Eye St........... Bakersfield CA 93301 661-395-7500
Web: www.bakersfield.com
Balcom Agency, The 1500 Ballinger St............. Fort Worth TX 76102 817-877-9933
Web: www.balcomagency.com
Barkley 1740 Main St............................ Kansas City MO 64108 816-842-1500
Web: barkleyus.com
Barnhart 1641 California St.......................... Denver CO 80202 303-626-7200
Web: www.barnhartusa.com
Bbdo Atlanta Inc 3500 Lenox Rd Ne Ste 1900........... Atlanta GA 30326 404-231-1700
Web: bbdoatl.com
BBDO Worldwide Inc 1285 Ave of the Americas......... New York NY 10019 212-459-5000
Web: www.bbdo.com
Beehive Specialty Co 8701 Wall St Ste 900............ Austin TX 78754 512-912-7940 997-7944
TF: 866-898-8774 ■ *Web:* www.beehivespecialty.com
Bemis Balkind LLC 6135 Wilshire Blvd............ Los Angeles CA 90048 323-965-4800
Web: www.bemisbalkind.com
Bernstein-Rein 4600 Madison Ave Ste 1500......... Kansas City MO 64112 816-756-0640 399-6000
Web: www.b-r.com
Beyond Spots & Dots 1034 Fifth Ave................ Pittsburgh PA 15219 412-281-6215
Web: www.beyondspotsanddots.com
Binary Pulse Inc
3545 Harbor Gateway S Ste 102................... Costa Mesa CA 92626 714-429-0110
Web: www.binarypulse.com
Birdsong Gregory LLC
715 N Church St Ste 101.......................... Charlotte NC 28202 704-332-2299
Web: www.birdsonggregory.com

Name / Address	City	State	Zip	Phone	Fax
Blue Sky Agency 950 Joseph E Lowery Blvd Ste 30 *Web:* www.bluesky-agency.com	Atlanta	GA	30318	404-876-0202	
Bonnie Heneson Communications Inc 9199 Reisterstown Rd Ste 212C *Web:* www.bonnieheneson.com	Owings Mills	MD	21117	410-654-0000	
Borden Agency, The 1975 Pioneer Rd *Web:* aardvarkel.com	Huntingdon Valley	PA	19006	215-442-0590	
Boyden & Youngblutt Adv & Mktg Inc 120 W Superior St *Web:* b-y.net	Fort Wayne	IN	46802	260-422-4499	
Brand Pharm 79 Madison Ave	New York	NY	10016	212-684-0909	
Bromley Communications LLC 401 E Houston St *Web:* bromley.biz	San Antonio	TX	78205	210-244-2000	
Bros & Co 4860 S Lewis Ave *Web:* www.broco.com	Tulsa	OK	74105	918-743-8822	
Brown Parker & Demarinis Adv Inc 3333 S Congress Ave Ste 305b *Web:* bpdadvertising.com	Delray Beach	FL	33445	561-276-7701	
Bryan Mills Iradesso Inc 1129 Leslie St *Web:* www.bmir.com	Toronto	ON	M3C2K5	416-447-4740	
Buntin Group, The 1001 Hawkins St *Web:* www.buntingroup.com	Nashville	TN	37203	615-244-5720	244-6511
Burgess Adv & Assoc Inc 1290 Congress St *Web:* www.burgessadv.com	Portland	ME	04102	207-775-5227	
Burrell 233 N Michigan Ave Ste 2900 *Web:* www.burrell.com	Chicago	IL	60601	312-297-9600	297-9601
Cade & Assoc Adv Inc 1645 Metropolitan Blvd *TF:* 800-715-2233 ■ *Web:* www.cade1.com	Tallahassee	FL	32308	850-385-0300	
Cambridge BioMarketing Group LLC 245 First St 12th Fl *Web:* www.cambridgebmg.com	Cambridge	MA	02142	617-225-0001	
Cameron Christopher Thomas Adv Inc 1441 29th St *Web:* www.cctadvertising.com	Denver	CO	80205	303-531-7180	
Camnet Inc 3201 Fourth St NW *Web:* camnet.us	Albuquerque	NM	87107	505-761-4500	
Campbell-Ewald 2000 Brush St Ste 601 *Web:* www.c-e.com	Detroit	MI	48226	586-574-3400	
Carol H Williams Adv 555 12th St Ste 1700 *Web:* www.carolhwilliams.com	Oakland	CA	94607	510-763-5200	763-9266
Carton Donofrio Partners Inc 100 N Charles St *Web:* www.cartondonofrio.com	Baltimore	MD	21201	410-576-9000	
Celtic Inc 330 S Executive Dr Ste 206 *Web:* www.celticinc.com	Brookfield	WI	53005	262-789-7630	
Charles Tombras Adv Inc 630 Concord St *Web:* www.tombras.com	Knoxville	TN	37919	865-524-5376	
Ciceron Inc 126 N Third St Ste 200 *Web:* www.ciceron.com	Minneapolis	MN	55401	612-204-1919	
Clarity Coverdale Fury (CCF) 120 S Sixth St 1 Financial Plz Ste 1300 *Web:* www.claritycoverdalefury.com	Minneapolis	MN	55402	612-339-3902	
Clean Design Inc 6601 Six Forks Rd Ste 400 *Web:* www.cleandesign.com	Raleigh	NC	27615	919-544-2193	
Cline Davis & Mann Inc (CDM) 220 E 42nd St *Web:* www.clinedavis.com	New York	NY	10017	212-907-4300	687-5411
CMD 1631 NW Thurman St *Web:* www.cmdpdx.com	Portland	OR	97209	503-223-6794	223-2430
Cole & Weber United 221 Yale Ave N Ste 600 *Web:* www.coleweber.com	Seattle	WA	98109	206-447-9595	233-0178
Colle & McVoy Inc 400 First Ave N Ste 700 *Web:* www.collemcvoy.com	Minneapolis	MN	55401	612-305-6000	305-6500
Commercial Mailing Accessories Inc 28220 Playmor Beach Rd *TF:* 800-325-7303 ■ *Web:* www.dispensamatic.com	Rocky Mount	MO	65072	800-325-7303	
Communications Media Inc 2200 Renaissance Blvd *Web:* www.cmimedia.com	King Of Prussia	PA	19406	484-322-0880	
Compas Inc 4300 Haddonfield Rd Ste 200 *Web:* www.compasonline.com	Pennsauken	NJ	08109	856-667-8577	
Concept Group Inc 380 Cooper Rd *Web:* conceptgroup.com	Saint Paul	NJ	08091	651-221-9710	
Connelly Partners LLC 46 Waltham St 4th Fl *Web:* www.connellypartners.com	Boston	MA	02118	617-521-5400	
Cooper-smith Adv LLC 4444 Bennett Rd *TF:* 800-215-8812 ■ *Web:* cooper-smith.com	Toledo	OH	43612	419-470-5900	
Corbett Accel Healthcare Group 211 E Chicago Ave	Chicago	IL	60611	312-475-2500	649-7232
Cormark Securities Inc 200 Bay St Royal Bank Plz S Tower Ste 2800 *Web:* www.cormark.com	Toronto	ON	M5J2J2	416-362-7485	
Cotton & Co 633 SE Fifth St *TF:* 800-266-9076 ■ *Web:* www.thecottonsolution.com	Stuart	FL	34994	772-287-6612	
Cramer 425 University Ave *Web:* www.cramer.com	Norwood	MA	02062	781-278-2300	278-8464
Cramer-Krasselt 246 E Chicago St *Web:* www.c-k.com	Milwaukee	WI	53202	414-227-3500	
Cranford Johnson Robinson Woods 303 W Capitol Ave *Web:* www.cjrw.com	Little Rock	AR	72201	501-975-6251	975-4241
Crawford Strategy 200 E Camperdown Way *Web:* www.crawfordstrategy.com	Greenville	SC	29601	864-232-2302	
Create Adv Group LLC 6022 Washington Blvd *Web:* createadvertising.com	Culver City	CA	90232	310-280-2999	
Creative Alliance Inc 437 W Jefferson St *TF:* 800-525-0294 ■ *Web:* scoppechio.com	Louisville	KY	40202	502-584-8787	589-9900
Creative Broadcast Concepts 56 Industrial Park Rd *Web:* www.cbcads.com	Saco	ME	04072	207-283-9191	

Name / Address	City	State	Zip	Phone	Fax
Creative Fire 313 Ontario Ave *Web:* creative-fire.com	Saskatoon	SK	S7K3J7	306-934-3337	
Creative Marketing Alliance Inc 191 Clarksville Rd *Web:* www.cmasolutions.com	Princeton Junction	NJ	08550	609-799-6000	799-7032
Creative Producers Group Inc 1220 Olive St Ste 210 *Web:* www.creativeworks.com	Saint Louis	MO	63103	314-367-2255	
Customized Newspaper Advertising 319 E Fifth St Fl 2nd *Web:* www.cnaads.com	Des Moines	IA	50309	515-244-2145	
Dailey & Assoc 8687 Melrose Ave **Fax:* Acctg ■ *Web:* www.daileyideas.com	West Hollywood	CA	90069	310-360-3100	360-3100*
Dalton Agency Inc, The 140 W Monroe St Ste 200 *Web:* www.daltonagency.com	Jacksonville	FL	32202	904-398-5222	398-5220
Dana Communications Inc 2 E Broad St *Web:* www.danacommunications.com	Hopewell	NJ	08525	609-466-9187	
Dastmalchi Enterprises Inc 31 East Macarthur Crescent Ste 111 *TF:* 888-358-0331 ■ *Web:* dastmalchi.com	Santa Ana	CA	92707	888-358-0331	
Davis Elen Adv 865 S Figueroa St Ste 1200 *Web:* www.daviselen.com	Los Angeles	CA	90017	213-688-7000	
Daxon Mktg 679 Buttonwood Dr	Brea	CA	92821	714-529-1218	
DDB Worldwide 437 Madison Ave *Web:* www.ddb.com	New York	NY	10022	212-415-2000	415-3414
Dealer Impact Systems LLC 7733 Douglas Ave *Web:* flickfusion.com	Urbandale	IA	50322	515-334-9638	
Dentsu America Inc 32 Ave of the Americas *Web:* 360i.com	New York	NY	10013	212-397-3333	
Design 446 Inc 2411 Atlantic Ave *Web:* www.design446.com	Manasquan	NJ	08736	732-292-2400	
Detrow & Underwood Inc 12 W Main St *Web:* www.detrowunderwood.com	Ashland	OH	44805	419-289-0265	
Deutsch Inc 330 W 34th St *Web:* www.deutsch.com	New York	NY	10001	212-981-7600	981-7525
DGWB Inc 217 N Main St Ste 200 *Web:* www.dgwb.com	Santa Ana	CA	92701	714-881-2300	
Diablo Media LLC 2641 Walnut St *Web:* www.diablomedia.com	Denver	CO	80205	303-305-4052	
Dieste 1999 Bryan St Ste 2700 *Web:* www.dieste.com	Dallas	TX	75201	214-259-8000	
Dillon Works! Inc 11775 Harbour Reach Dr *Web:* www.dillonworks.com	Mukilteo	WA	98275	425-493-8309	
Doe Anderson Inc 620 W Main St *Web:* www.doeanderson.com	Louisville	KY	40202	502-589-1700	
Doner Adv 25900 NW Hwy **Fax:* PR ■ *Web:* doner.com	Southfield	MI	48075	248-354-9700	827-0880*
Doremus 200 Varick St *Web:* www.doremus.com	New York	NY	10014	212-366-3000	366-3060
Dudnyk 5 Walnut Grove Dr Ste 280 *TF:* 800-767-3263 ■ *Web:* www.dudnyk.com	Horsham	PA	19044	215-443-9406	443-0207
Dudnyk Exchange 5 Walnut Grove *Web:* dudnyk.com	Horsham	PA	19044	215-443-9406	
Duffy & Shanley Inc 10 Charles St *Web:* www.duffyshanley.com	Providence	RI	02904	401-274-0001	
DW Green Co 8100 S Priest Dr *TF:* 800-253-7146 ■ *Web:* www.dwgreen.com	Tempe	AZ	85284	480-491-8483	
Dynamic Digital Adv 1265 Industrial Blvd *Web:* www.zeroonezero.com	Southampton	PA	18966	215-355-6442	
E Morris Communications Inc 820 N Orleans *Web:* www.emorris.com	Chicago	IL	60610	312-943-2900	943-5856
Easterly & Co 1177 W Loop S Ste 950 *Web:* www.easterly.com	Houston	TX	77027	713-529-2949	
Educationdynamics LLC 5 Marine View Plaza Ste 212 *Web:* www.educationdynamics.com	Hoboken	NJ	07030	201-377-3000	377-3081
Edward Howard & Co 1100 Superior Ave Ste 1600 *Web:* www.edwardhoward.com	Cleveland	OH	44114	216-781-2400	781-8810
Elad National Properties LLC 1301 International Pkwy Ste 200 *Web:* www.eladnational.com	Sunrise	FL	33323	954-846-7800	
Elevate Group Holdings LLC 615 Regal Row *Web:* www.elevate-group.com	Dallas	TX	75247	214-951-9502	
Elevation B2B Marketing 1955 S Val Vista Dr Ste 101 *Web:* www.canyoncomm.com	Mesa	AZ	85204	480-775-8880	
Epoch Adv Agency Inc 888 E Brighton Ave *Web:* www.epoch-adv.com	Syracuse	NY	13205	315-492-3270	
Eric Mower & Assoc 211 W Jefferson St *Web:* www.mower.com	Syracuse	NY	13202	315-466-1000	
Ernst-Van Praag Inc 433 Plaza Real Ste 275 *Web:* www.evpconsulting.com	Boca Raton	FL	33432	561-447-0557	
Evans Hardy & Young Inc 829 De La Vina St *Web:* www.ehy.com	Santa Barbara	CA	93101	805-963-5841	
Exclaim Inc 220 N Smith St Ste 204 *Web:* www.exclaim-inc.com	Palatine	IL	60067	847-392-0008	
Explore Communications Inc 3213 Zuni St *Web:* www.explorehq.com	Denver	CO	80211	303-393-0567	
Fahlgren Inc 4030 Easton Station Ste 300 *TF:* 800-731-8927 ■ *Web:* www.fahlgrenmortine.com	Columbus	OH	43219	614-383-1500	383-1501
Fallon 901 Marquette Ave Ste 2400 *Web:* www.fallon.com	Minneapolis	MN	55402	612-758-2345	758-2346
Finelight Inc 30500 Whipple Rd	Union City	CA	94587	812-339-6700	
Fire & Rain LLC 40 N First Ave *Web:* www.firerain.com	Evansville	IN	47710	812-464-5244	
Fitzgerald & Co 3333 Piedmont Rd 11th Fl *Web:* www.fitzco.com	Atlanta	GA	30305	404-504-6900	
Fitzmartin Inc 2917 Central Ave Ste 211 *Web:* fitzmartin.com	Homewood	AL	35209	205-322-1010	

Company	City	State	ZIP	Phone	Fax
Fleming & Van Metre Adv 600 W Germantown Pk *Web:* thinkfvm.com	Plymouth Meeting	PA	19462	610-941-0395	
Flying Bridge Technologies 2709 Water Ridge Pkwy Ste 480 *Web:* www.flyingbridge.net	Charlotte	NC	28217	704-357-8011	
Frogdesign Inc 660 Third St 4th Fl *Web:* www.frogdesign.com	San Francisco	CA	94107	415-442-4804	442-4803
G S Design 6665 N Sidney Pl *Web:* www.gsdesign.com	Milwaukee	WI	53209	414-228-9666	
G2 USA 200 Fifth Ave *Web:* www.geometry.com	New York	NY	10010	212-546-2222	
Garza Communications Inc 414 Country View Ln *Web:* www.garzacommunications.com	Garland	TX	75043	214-720-3888	
Get a Clue Design 1026 14th Ave Dr NW	Hickory	NC	28601	828-324-4262	
Gigante Vaz Partners Inc 915 Bwy Ste 1408 *Web:* www.gigantevaz.com	New York	NY	10010	212-343-0004	
Gilmour Craves 455 Irwin St Ste 201 *Web:* gilmourcraves.com	San Francisco	CA	94107	415-431-9955	
Gish Sherwood & Friends Inc 209 10th Ave S Ste 222 *Web:* www.gsandf.com	Nashville	TN	37203	615-385-1100	
GKV 1500 Whetstone Way 4th Fl *Web:* www.gkv.com	Baltimore	MD	21230	410-539-5400	234-2441
Global Hue 4000 Town Ctr Ste 1600 **Fax Area Code:* 646 ■ *Web:* www.globalhue.com	Southfield	MI	48075	248-223-8900	871-6216*
GlobalWorks Group LLC 220 Fifth Ave *Web:* www.globalworks.com	New York	NY	10001	212-252-8800	
Glynndevins Adv & Mktg 11230 College Blvd *Web:* www.glynndevins.com	Overland Park	KS	66210	913-491-0600	
Godfrey Adv Inc 40 N Christian St *Web:* www.godfrey.com	Lancaster	PA	17602	717-393-3831	
Goodby Silverstein & Partners 720 California St *Web:* www.goodbysilverstein.com	San Francisco	CA	94108	415-392-0669	
Graham Group Inc, The 2014 W Pinhook Rd Ste 210 *Web:* www.graham-group.com	Lafayette	LA	70508	337-232-8214	235-3787
Graphica 4501 Lyons Rd *Web:* www.graphicadesign.com	Miamisburg	OH	45342	937-866-4013	
GREENCREST Marketing Inc 120 Northwoods Blvd *Web:* www.greencrest.com	Columbus	OH	43235	614-885-7921	
Grey Group 200 Fifth Ave *Web:* www.grey.com	New York	NY	10010	212-546-2000	546-1495
Grey Healthcare Group Inc 200 Fifth Ave *Web:* www.ghgroup.com	New York	NY	10010	212-886-3000	
GSD & M Idea City 828 W Sixth St *Web:* www.gsdm.com	Austin	TX	78703	512-242-4736	242-4700
GSW Worldwide 500 Old Worthington Rd *Web:* www.gsw-w.com	Westerville	OH	43082	614-848-4848	
Hal Lewis Group 1700 Market St 6th Fl *Web:* www.hlg.com	Philadelphia	PA	19103	215-563-4461	
Haley Miranda Group 8654 Washington Blvd *Web:* www.haleymiranda.com	Culver City	CA	90232	310-842-7369	
Hamilton Communications Group 20 N Wacker Dr *Web:* hamiltongrp.com	Chicago	IL	60606	312-321-5000	
Hammer Creative Inc 6311 Romaine St 3rd Fl *Web:* www.hammercreative.com	Hollywood	CA	90038	323-606-4700	
Hanson Directory Service Inc 1501 N 15th Ave E *Web:* www.hansondirectory.com	Newton	IA	50208	641-792-2855	
Hanson Watson Assoc 1411 15th St *Web:* www.hansonwatson.com	Moline	IL	61265	309-764-8315	
Harrison & Star 75 Varick St *Web:* www.harrisonandstar.com	New York	NY	10013	212-727-1330	
Hart Associates Inc 1915 Indian Wood Cir *Web:* www.hartinc.com	Maumee	OH	43537	419-893-9600	
Harvey & Company LLC 5000 Birch St Ste 9200 *Web:* www.harveyllc.com	Newport Beach	CA	92660	949-757-0400	
Healthcare Consultancy Group 711 Third Ave 17th Fl *Web:* www.hcgrp.com	New York	NY	10017	212-849-7935	
HealthSTAR Communications Inc 1000 Wyckoff Ave *Web:* www.healthstarcom.com	Mahwah	NJ	07430	201-560-5370	
HEILBrice Inc 9840 Irvine Ctr Dr *Web:* www.heilbrice.com	Irvine	CA	92618	949-336-8800	
High Velocity Communications LLC 1720 Dolphin Dr Ste D *Web:* www.highvelocityllc.com	Waukesha	WI	53186	262-544-6600	
Hudson Fusion 30 State St *Web:* www.hudsonfusion.com	Ossining	NY	10562	914-762-0900	
Hunter Hamersmith 725 NE 125th St *Web:* www.hhadvertising.net	North Miami	FL	33161	305-895-8430	
Hyphen 711 Third Ave 12th Fl *Web:* hyphendigital.com	New York	NY	10017	212-856-8700	
Ideal Adv & Printing 116 N Winnebago St *TF:* 800-208-0294 ■ *Web:* www.idealad.com	Rockford	IL	61101	815-965-1713	
Image Group 31 E Eighth St Ste 200 *Web:* www.imagegroup.com	Holland	MI	49423	616-393-9588	
Image Makers Adv LLC 514 Lincoln Ave PO Box 368	Wamego	KS	66547	386-236-1200	
Imaginasium Inc 110 S Washington St *Web:* www.imaginasium.biz	Green Bay	WI	54301	920-431-7872	
Impact - Proven Solutions 4600 Lyndale Ave N *Web:* www.impactconnects.com	Minneapolis	MN	55412	612-521-6245	
In Focus Adv Inc 29219 Canwood St Ste 101 *Web:* infocusadv.com	Agoura Hills	CA	91301	818-889-1342	
Innis Maggiore Group Inc 4715 Whipple Ave NW *TF:* 800-460-4111 ■ *Web:* www.innismaggiore.com	Canton	OH	44718	330-492-5500	492-5568
Innovage LLC 19511 Pauling *Web:* www.innovage.net	Foothill Ranch	CA	92610	949-587-9207	
Integrative Logic Inc 2397 Huntcrest Way Ste 200 *Web:* www.integrativelogic.com	Lawrenceville	GA	30043	678-638-2600	
Intermark Group Inc 101 25th St N *TF:* 800-624-9239 ■ *Web:* www.intermarkgroup.com	Birmingham	AL	35243	205-803-0000	870-3843
Internet Business Systems Inc 595 Millich Dr Ste 210 *Web:* www.ibsystems.com	Campbell	CA	95008	408-850-9202	
Interpublic Group 1114 Ave of the Americas *NYSE:* IPG ■ *Web:* www.interpublic.com	New York	NY	10036	212-704-1200	
Iris Group Inc, The 1675 Faraday Ave *TF:* 800-347-1103 ■ *Web:* www.irisgroup.com	Carlsbad	CA	92008	760-431-1103	
J Walter Thompson 466 Lexington Ave *Web:* www.jwt.com	New York	NY	10017	212-210-7000	
James Group Inc, The 33 W 17th St Ste 202 *Web:* www.thejamesgroup.com	New York	NY	10011	212-243-2022	
Jeff Scott & Assoc 2356 University Ave W Ste 400 *Web:* www.jeffscottandassociates.com	St. Paul	MN	55114	651-968-1457	
Jennings & Assoc 2121 Palomar Airport Rd Ste 220 *Web:* jandacommunications.com	Carlsbad	CA	92011	760-431-7466	
Johnson Group, The 436 Market St *Web:* www.johngroup.com	Chattanooga	TN	37402	423-756-2608	
Keiler & Co 304 Main St	Farmington	CT	06032	860-677-8821	676-8164
King Agency Inc, The 3 N Lombardy St *Web:* thekingagency.com	Richmond	VA	23220	804-249-7500	
Kirshenbaum Bond Senecal & Partners LLC 160 Varick St Fl 4 *Web:* www.kbsp.com	New York	NY	10013	212-633-0080	
Kleber & Assoc 1215 Hightower Trial Bldg C *Web:* www.kleberandassociates.com	Atlanta	GA	30350	770-518-1000	
Koopman Ostbo Inc 412 NW Eighth Ave *Web:* koopmanostbo.com	Portland	OR	97209	503-223-2168	
Korey Kay & Partners 130 Fifth Ave *Web:* www.koreykay.com	New York	NY	10011	212-620-4300	
Kovel/Fuller LLC 9925 Jefferson Blvd *Web:* www.kovelfuller.com	Culver City	CA	90232	310-841-4444	841-4599
KSC Adv & PR 40 Sarasota Ctr Blvd Ste 107 *Web:* kscadvpr.com	Sarasota	FL	34240	941-906-1555	
Kuno Creative Group LLC 36901 American Wy Ste 2A *TF:* 800-303-0806 ■ *Web:* www.kunocreative.com	Avon	OH	44011	800-303-0806	
Laird Partners LLC 475 Tenth Ave 7th Fl *Web:* www.lairdandpartners.com	New York	NY	10018	212-478-8181	478-8210
Laplaca Cohen Adv Inc 43 W 24th St Fl 10 *Web:* www.laplacacohen.com	New York	NY	10010	212-675-4106	
Latorra Paul & Mccann Inc 120 E Washington St University Bldg 10th Fl *Web:* www.lpm-adv.com/Home.aspx	Syracuse	NY	13202	315-476-1646	476-1611
Laughlin/Constable Inc 207 E Michigan St *TF:* 800-432-8747 ■ *Web:* www.laughlin.com	Milwaukee	WI	53202	414-272-2400	272-3056
Launch Agency LP 4100 Midway Rd Ste 2110 *TF:* 866-427-5013 ■ *Web:* launchagency.com	Carrollton	TX	75007	972-818-4100	
Launchpad Adv LLC 149 Fifth Ave 9th Fl *Web:* www.lpnyc.com	New York	NY	10010	212-303-7650	
Lawrence & Schiller Inc 3932 S Willow Ave *Web:* www.l-s.com	Sioux Falls	SD	57105	605-338-8000	338-8892
Leader Promotions Inc 790 E Johnstown Rd *Web:* www.leaderpromos.com	Columbus	OH	43230	614-416-6565	
Leo Burnett Company Inc 35 W Wacker Dr *Web:* www.leoburnett.com	Chicago	IL	60601	312-220-5959	220-3299
Lessing-Flynn Adv Co 3106 Ingersoll Ave *Web:* www.lessingflynn.com	Des Moines	IA	50312	515-274-9271	
Lewis Communications Inc 600 Meadow Brook Corp 2 *Web:* www.lewiscommunications.com	Birmingham	AL	35242	205-980-0774	
Lindsay Stone & Briggs Inc 1 South Pinckney St Ste 500 *Web:* www.lsb.com	Madison	WI	53703	608-251-7070	251-8989
Linnihan Foy Adv 615 First Ave Ne Ste 320 *Web:* www.linnihanfoy.com	Minneapolis	MN	55413	612-331-3586	
Liquid Adv Inc 499 Santa Clara Ave *Web:* www.liquidadvertising.com	Venice	CA	90291	310-450-2653	
Lopez Negrete Communications Inc 3336 Richmond Ave Ste 200 *Web:* www.lopeznegrete.com	Houston	TX	77098	713-877-8777	877-8796
Losasso Adv Inc 4853 N Ravenswood Ave *Web:* www.losasso.com	Chicago	IL	60640	773-271-2100	
Lost Planet Editorial 113 Spring St Fl 4 *Web:* www.quakebasket.com	New York	NY	10012	212-226-5678	
Love Adv Inc 770 S Post Oak Ln Ste 101 *Web:* www.loveadv.com	Houston	TX	77056	713-552-1055	552-9155
Lucid Fusion Inc 8935 Research Dr Ste 200 *Web:* www.lucidfusion.com	Irvine	CA	92618	949-502-7750	
Luckie & Co 600 Luckie Dr Ste 150 *Web:* www.luckie.com	Birmingham	AL	35223	205-879-2121	877-9713
Luquire George Andrews Inc 4201 Congress St Ste 400 *Web:* www.lgaadv.com	Charlotte	NC	28209	704-552-6565	552-1972
LyonHeart Communications Inc 220 E 42nd St 3rd Fl	New York	NY	10017	212-771-3000	771-3010
Mangan Holcomb Partners 2300 Cottondale Ln *Web:* www.manganholcomb.com	Little Rock	AR	72202	501-376-0321	
MARC USA 225 W Stn Sq Dr Ste 500 *Web:* www.marcusa.com	Pittsburgh	PA	15219	412-562-2000	562-2022
Marca Hispanic LLC 1320 S Dixie Hwy *Web:* marcamiami.com	Coral Gables	FL	33146	305-665-5410	

				Phone	Fax
Marcel Media LLC 445 W Erie St Ste 200 *Web:* www.marcelmedia.com	Chicago	IL	60654	312-255-8044	
Maricich Brand Communications 18201 McDurmott W Ste A *Web:* www.maricich.com	Irvine	CA	92614	949-223-6455	
Maris West & Baker Inc 18 Northtown Dr *Web:* www.mwb.com	Jackson	MS	39211	601-977-9200	
Marketing Directions 28005 Clemens Rd *Web:* ideaswithapoint.com	Westlake	OH	44145	440-835-5550	
Marketing Support Inc 200 E Randolph Dr Ste 5000 *Web:* agencymsi.com	Chicago	IL	60601	312-565-0044	946-6100
Mars Adv Company Inc 25200 Telegraph Rd *Web:* themarsagency.com	Southfield	MI	48034	248-936-2200	
Marshad Technology Group 99 Hudson St Fl 5 *Web:* www.marshad.com	New York	NY	10013	212-925-8656	292-8912
Marshall Adv & Design 2729 Bristol St	Costa Mesa	CA	92626	714-545-5757	
Martin Agency Inc 1 Shockoe Plz *Web:* www.martinagency.com	Richmond	VA	23219	804-698-8000	698-8001
Martin Thomas Inc 42 Riverside Dr **Fax Area Code:* 866 ■ *Web:* www.martinthomas.com	Barrington	RI	02806	401-245-8500	899-2710*
Martin-Williams Adv 150 S 5th st Ste 900 *TF:* 800-632-1388 ■ *Web:* www.martinwilliams.com	Minneapolis	MN	55402	612-340-0800	342-9700
Matlock Adv & Public Relations 107 Luckie St *Web:* www.matlock-adpr.com	Atlanta	GA	30303	404-872-3200	876-4929
Matthews Group Inc, The 400 Lake St *Web:* www.thematthewsgroup.com	Bryan	TX	77801	979-823-3600	
May Adv 718 Washington Ave N Ste 306 *Web:* www.mayads.com	Minneapolis	MN	55401	612-332-2450	
Mcdougall & Duval Adv Inc 24 Millyard Ste 8 *Web:* mcdougallduval.com	Amesbury	MA	01913	978-388-3100	
McKee Wallwork Cleveland LLC 1030 18th St NW *Web:* mckeewallwork.com	Albuquerque	NM	87104	505-821-2999	821-0006
McKinney 318 Blackwell St *Web:* www.mckinney.com	Durham	NC	27701	919-313-0802	313-0805
Media Buying Services Inc 4545 E Shea Blvd Ste 162 *TF:* 888-996-2232 ■ *Web:* www.mediabuyingservices.com	Phoenix	AZ	85028	602-996-2232	
Media Logic USA LLC 59 Wolf Rd *TF:* 866-353-3011 ■ *Web:* medialogic.com	Albany	NY	12205	518-456-3015	456-4279
Media Storm LLC 99 Washington St *Web:* www.mediastorm.biz	South Norwalk	CT	06854	203-852-8001	852-0746
Media Two Interactive LLC 111 E Hargett St Ste 200 *Web:* www.mediatwo.net	Raleigh	NC	27601	919-553-1246	
Media-Max Inc 12 N Washington St *Web:* www.mediamaxinc.net	Montoursville	PA	17754	570-368-7633	
MedPoint Digital Inc 909 Davis St Ste 500 *Web:* www.medpt.com	Evanston	IL	60201	847-869-4700	
Merkley & Partners 200 Varick St 12th Fl *Web:* www.merkleyandpartners.com	New York	NY	10014	212-805-7500	
MGH Adv Inc 100 Painters Mill Rd Ste 600 *Web:* www.mghus.com	Owings Mills	MD	21117	410-902-5000	902-8712
Miller Brooks Inc 11712 N Michigan Rd *Web:* millerbrooks.com	Zionsville	IN	46077	317-873-8100	
Mindgrub Technologies LLC 1215 E Ft Ave Ste 200 *TF:* 855-646-3472 ■ *Web:* www.mindgrub.com	Baltimore	MD	21230	410-988-2444	
MindShare 498 Seventh Ave *Web:* www.mindshareworld.com	New York	NY	10018	212-297-7000	297-7777
Mindstorm Communications Group Inc 10316 Feld Farm Ln Ste 200 *Web:* www.gomindstorm.com	Charlotte	NC	28210	704-331-0870	
Minnow Project a Creative Lab 815 O St Ste 3 *Web:* www.minnowproject.com	Lincoln	NE	68508	402-475-3322	
MKTG Inc 32 Ave of the Americas 20th Fl *OTC:* CMKG ■ *Web:* www.mktg.com	New York	NY	10013	212-366-3400	
MMG Worldwide 4601 Madison Ave *Web:* www.mmgyglobal.com	Kansas City	MO	64112	816-472-5988	
Mob Media Inc 27042 Towne Centre Dr Ste 260 *Web:* mobmedia.com	Foothill Ranch	CA	92610	949-222-0220	
Momentum Worldwide 250 Hudson St 2nd Fl *Web:* www.momentumww.com	New York	NY	10013	646-638-5400	638-5401
Moroch Partners 3625 N Hall St Ste 1100 *Web:* www.moroch.com	Dallas	TX	75219	214-520-9700	
Moses Anshell Inc 20 W Jackson St *Web:* mosesinc.com	Phoenix	AZ	85003	602-254-7312	
MRM//McCANN 622 Third Ave *Web:* mrm-mccann.com/en/index.html	New York	NY	10017	646-865-6230	
Mthink 55 New Montgomery St Ste 617 *Web:* www.mthink.com	San Francisco	CA	94105	415-371-8800	
Mullen 40 Broad St *Web:* us.mullenlowe.com	Boston	MA	02109	617-226-9000	226-9100
Muse Communications Inc 9543 Culver Blvd 2nd Fl *Web:* www.museusa.com	Culver City	CA	90232	310-945-4100	
Nap I Inc 2154 W Northwest Hwy *Web:* www.napiinc.com	Dallas	TX	75220	972-401-7488	
NAS Recruitment Communications 9700 Rockside Rd Ste 170 *TF:* 866-627-7327 ■ *Web:* www.nasrecruitment.com	Cleveland	OH	44125	866-627-7327	
Nasuti & Hinkle 7768 Woodmont Ave Ste 202 *Web:* nasuti.com	Bethesda	MD	20814	301-222-0010	
Neathawk Dubuque & Packett 1 E Cary St *Web:* ndp.agency	Richmond	VA	23219	804-783-8140	
Network Journal, The 39 Broadway Rm 2120 *TF:* 866-259-1465 ■ *Web:* www.tnj.com	New York	NY	10006	212-962-3791	
New Millenium Directories 1630 S Galena Ave *Web:* www.bigprintphonebook.com	Freeport	IL	61032	815-233-5797	
Newman Grace Inc 6133 Fallbrook Ave *Web:* www.newmangrace.com	Woodland Hills	CA	91367	818-713-1678	
Next Communications Inc 10249 Yellow Cir Dr Ste 100 *Web:* www.nextcom.com	Minnetonka	MN	55343	952-934-8220	
Norm Marshall & Assoc Inc 11059 Sherman Way *Web:* normmarshall.com	Sun Valley	CA	91352	818-982-3505	
North Charles Street Design Organization 222 W Saratoga St *Web:* www.ncsdo.com	Baltimore	MD	21201	410-539-4040	
Northlich 720 E Pete Rose Way *Web:* www.northlich.com	Cincinnati	OH	45202	513-421-8840	287-1858
Nowak Assoc Inc 6075 E Molloy Rd *Web:* www.nowakagency.com	Syracuse	NY	13211	518-452-4200	
Ocean Bridge Group 2032 Armacost Ave *Web:* www.oceanbridgemedia.com	Los Angeles	CA	90404	310-392-3200	
Off Madison Ave Inc 5555 E Van Buren St Ste 215 *Web:* www.offmadisonave.com	Phoenix	AZ	85008	480-505-4500	
Ogden Publications Inc 1503 SW 42nd St *Web:* www.ogdenpubs.com	Topeka	KS	66609	785-274-4300	
Ogilvy & Mather Worldwide 636 11th Ave *Web:* www.ogilvy.com	New York	NY	10036	212-237-4000	237-5123
Ogilvy One Worldwide 636 11th Ave *Web:* www.ogilvy.com	New York	NY	10036	212-237-6000	237-6757
Olson 420 N Fifth St *Web:* olson.com	Minneapolis	MN	55401	612-215-9800	
Orange Label Art & Advrtg 4000 MacArthur Blvd Ste 520 *Web:* www.orangelabeladvertising.com	Newport Beach	CA	92660	949-631-9900	
Orangeseed Design Inc 901 N Third St Ste 305 *Web:* www.orangeseed.com	Minneapolis	MN	55401	612-252-9757	
Osborn & Barr 914 Spruce St *Web:* osbornbarr.com	Saint Louis	MO	63102	314-726-5511	726-6350
Overlay TV Inc 80 Aberdeen St Ste 401 *Web:* www.overlay.tv	Ottawa	ON	K1S5R5	613-761-6152	
Pacific Communications 18581 Teller Ave Ste 900 *Web:* www.pacificcommunications.com	Irvine	CA	92612	714-427-1900	
Pacifico Inc 1190 Coleman Ave Ste 110 *Web:* www.pacifico.com	San Jose	CA	95110	408-327-8888	
Page 1 Solutions LLC 17301 W Colfax Ave Ste 275 *Web:* www.page1solutions.com	Golden	CO	80401	303-233-3886	
Paradise Adv & Mktg Inc 150 Second Ave N Ste 800 *Web:* www.paradiseadv.com	Saint Petersburg	FL	33701	727-821-5155	
Parkerwhite Inc 230 Birmingham Dr *Web:* www.parkerwhite.com	Cardiff By The Sea	CA	92007	760-783-2020	
Partners Riley 1375 Euclid Ave Ste 410 *Web:* www.partnersriley.com	Cleveland	OH	44115	216-241-2141	
Patient Recruiting Agency LLC, The 6207 Bee Cave Rd Ste 288 *Web:* tpra.com	Austin	TX	78746	512-345-7788	
Pavone Inc 1006 Market St *Web:* www.pavone.net	Harrisburg	PA	17101	717-234-8886	
Pedone 49 W 27th St *Web:* www.pedonepartners.com	New York	NY	10001	212-627-3300	627-3966
Penny Ohlmann Neiman Inc 1605 N Main St *Web:* ohlmanngroup.com	Dayton	OH	45405	937-278-0681	
Periscope Inc 921 Washington Ave S *Web:* www.periscope.com	Minneapolis	MN	55415	612-399-0500	399-0600
Peterson Milla Hooks 1315 Harmon Pl *Web:* www.pmhadv.com	Minneapolis	MN	55403	612-349-9116	
Petrol Adv Inc 443 N Varney St *Web:* petrolad.com	Burbank	CA	91502	323-644-3720	
Phelps Group, The 901 Wilshire Blvd *Web:* phelpsagency.com	Santa Monica	CA	90401	310-752-4400	752-4444
PJA Adv & Mktg 12 Arrow St *Web:* www.agencypja.com	Cambridge	MA	02138	617-492-5899	
PKA Marketing 1009 W Glen Oaks Ln Ste 107 *Web:* pkamar.publishpath.com	Mequon	WI	53092	262-241-9414	241-9454
Plan b 116 W Illinois St *Web:* www.thisisplanb.com	Chicago	IL	60654	312-222-0303	
Plowshare Group Inc 1 Dock St *Web:* www.plowsharegroup.com	Stamford	CT	06902	203-425-3949	
Pm Group Inc, The 7550 W Interstate 10 Ste 500 *Web:* thepmgrp.com	San Antonio	TX	78229	210-490-2554	490-5496
Point to Point Inc 23240 Chagrin Blvd Ste 200 *Web:* www.p2pcom.com	Cleveland	OH	44122	216-831-4421	
Posner Adv 30 Broad St *Web:* www.posnermiller.com	New York	NY	10004	212-867-3900	480-3440
Post No Bills Inc 801 Gervais St *Web:* www.postnobills.com	Columbia	SC	29201	803-254-4334	
Power Creative 11701 Commonwealth Dr *Web:* www.poweragency.com	Louisville	KY	40299	502-267-0772	
Prime Adv & Design Inc 7351 Kirkwood Ln N Ste 144 *TF:* 800-275-8777 ■ *Web:* www.primeadvertising.com	Maple Grove	MN	55369	763-424-9406	
Princeton Partners Inc 205 Rockingham Row *Web:* www.princetonpartners.com	Princeton	NJ	08540	609-452-8500	452-7212
Proact Marketing Group Inc 2604 Ne Industrial Dr Ste 230 *Web:* www.proactmarketing.com	Kansas City	MO	64117	816-472-9898	
Product Mktg Group Inc 978 Douglas Ave *Web:* eternalmessage.com	Altamonte Springs	FL	32714	407-774-6363	
ProEd Communications Inc 25101 Chagrin Blvd Ste 230 *Web:* www.proedcom.com	Beachwood	OH	44122	216-595-7919	
Publicis & Hal Riney 2001 Embarcadero *Web:* www.hrp.com	San Francisco	CA	94133	415-293-2001	

	City	State	Zip	Phone	Fax
Publicis Touchpoint Solutions Inc 1000 Floral Vale Blvd Ste 400 *Web:* www.touchpointsolutions.com	Yardley	PA	19067	215-525-9800	
Publicis USA 950 Sixth Ave *Web:* publicisna.com	New York	NY	10001	212-279-5550	
Purchase Planners Group Inc 801 S Grand Ave Ste 425 *Web:* www.ppg-la.com	Los Angeles	CA	90017	213-687-4206	
Purematter 350 W Julian St Bldg 3 *Web:* www.purematter.com	San Jose	CA	95110	408-297-7800	
R2c Group Inc 207 NW Pk Ave *Web:* www.r2cgroup.com	Portland	OR	97209	503-222-0025	276-4096
Rabinovici & Assoc Inc 800 Silks Run Ste 2320 *Web:* www.rabinovicionline.com	Hallandale	FL	33009	305-655-0021	
Rdw Group Inc 125 Holden St *Web:* www.rdwgroup.com	Providence	RI	02908	401-521-2700	521-0014
Re Group Inc 213 W Liberty St Ste 100 *Web:* www.regroup.us	Ann Arbor	MI	48104	734-213-0200	
ReachLocal Inc 21700 Oxnard St Ste 1600 *NASDAQ: RLOC* ■ *Web:* www.reachlocal.com	Woodland Hills	CA	91367	818-274-0260	
Red Tettemer Inc 1 S Broad St 24th Fl *Web:* rtop.com	Philadelphia	PA	19107	267-402-1410	
Redstone Communications Group Inc 10031 Maple St *Web:* www.redstoneweb.com	Omaha	NE	68134	402-393-5435	
Redux Media Inc 1100 Rene-Levesque W Fl 24 *Web:* www.reduxmedia.com	Montreal	QC	H3B4X9	514-866-4343	
Regan Group, The 4895 W 147th St *Web:* www.theregangroup.com	Hawthorne	CA	90250	310-935-0372	
Regency Outdoor Adv Inc 8820 Sunset Blvd *Web:* www.regencyoutdoor.com	West Hollywood	CA	90069	310-657-8883	
Regina Villa Associates Inc 51 Franklin St Ste 400 *Web:* www.reginavilla.com	Boston	MA	02110	617-357-5772	
Register Tapes Unlimited Inc 1445 Langham Creek *TF:* 800-247-4793 ■ *Web:* www.rtui.com	Houston	TX	77084	281-206-2500	
Reply Inc 12667 Alcosta Blvd Ste 200 *Web:* www.reply.eu/en	San Ramon	CA	94583	925-983-3400	
Research Horizons LLC 6423 Montgomery St Ste 12 *Web:* www.phoenixmi.com	Rhinebeck	NY	12572	845-876-8228	
Revolution Agency Inc 1210 E Windsor Ave *Web:* revolutionagency.com	Phoenix	AZ	85006	602-956-5465	
Rhea & Kaiser 400 E Diehl Rd *Web:* www.rkconnect.com	Naperville	IL	60563	630-505-1100	
RHR Adpro Adv LLC 105 Library Rd *Web:* adpro-ads.com	Dover	AR	72837	479-331-2526	
Richard Harrison Bailey Inc 121 S Niles Ave *TF:* 866-404-8333 ■ *Web:* www.rhb.com	South Bend	IN	46617	574-287-8333	
Richards Group 2801 N Central Expy Ste 100 *Web:* www.richards.com	Dallas	TX	75204	214-891-5700	891-5230
Richards/Carlberg 1900 W Loop S Ste 1100 *Web:* www.richardscarlberg.com	Houston	TX	77027	713-965-0764	
Riley Hayes Adv 333 S First St *Web:* www.rileyhayes.com	Minneapolis	MN	55401	612-338-7161	
Risdall Adv Agency 550 Main St *TF:* 888-747-3255 ■ *Web:* www.risdall.com	New Brighton	MN	55112	651-286-6700	631-2561
Ritta & Assoc 568 Grand Ave *Web:* www.ritta.com	Englewood	NJ	07631	201-567-4400	
RMD Adv 6116 Cleveland Ave *Web:* www.rmdadvertising.com	Columbus	OH	43231	614-794-2008	
Roberts Communications Inc 64 Commercial St *Web:* www.robertscomm.com	Rochester	NY	14614	585-325-6000	325-6001
Ron Foth Adv 8100 N High St *Web:* www.ronfoth.com	Columbus	OH	43235	614-888-7771	
Rubin Postaer & Assoc 2525 Colorado Ave *Web:* www.rpa.com	Santa Monica	CA	90404	310-394-4000	
Saatchi & Saatchi 375 Hudson St *Web:* www.saatchiny.com	New York	NY	10014	212-463-2000	463-9856
Sagon Phior 2107 Sawtelle Blvd *Web:* sagonphior.com	Los Angeles	CA	90025	310-575-4441	
Salva O'renick 1810 Cherry St	Kansas City	MO	64108	816-842-6996	
Sanders/Wingo Adv Inc 221 N Kansas Ste 900 *Web:* www.sanderswingo.com	El Paso	TX	79901	915-533-9583	533-3601
Sawtooth Group 141 W Front St *Web:* www.sawtoothgroup.com	Red Bank	NJ	07701	732-945-1004	
SBC Adv Ltd 333 W Nationwide Blvd *Web:* www.sbcadvertising.com	Columbus	OH	43215	614-255-2333	255-2600
Scott Howell & Company Inc 3900 Willow St Ste 200 *Web:* www.scotthowell.com	Dallas	TX	75226	214-951-9494	688-0555
Seiden Group 112 Madison Ave *Web:* www.seidenadvertising.com	New York	NY	10016	212-223-8700	
Serino Coyne Inc 1515 Broadway 36th Fl *Web:* www.serinocoyne.com	New York	NY	10036	212-626-2700	626-2799
Seven Dials Media 2449 Wendover Dr	Naperville	IL	60565	630-355-6199	
Shaker Recruitment Adv & Communications 1100 Lake St 3rd Fl *TF:* 800-323-5170 ■ *Web:* www.shaker.com	Oak Park	IL	60301	708-383-5320	
Sheehy & Assoc 2297 Lexington Rd *Web:* www.sheehy1.com	Louisville	KY	40206	502-456-9007	
Sherry Matthews Inc 200 S Congress Ave *TF:* 877-478-4397 ■ *Web:* www.sherrymatthews.com	Austin	TX	78704	512-478-4397	478-4978
Shumsky Enterprises Inc 811 E Fourth St *TF:* 800-223-2203 ■ *Web:* www.shumsky.com	Dayton	OH	45402	937-223-2203	223-2252
SIDES & Assoc Inc 222 Jefferson St Ste B PO Box 3267 *Web:* www.sides.com	Lafayette	LA	70501	337-233-6473	233-6485
Siegel & Gale 625 Ave of the Americas 4th Fl *Web:* siegelgale.com	New York	NY	10011	212-453-0400	453-0401
Sierra Select Distributors 4320 Roseville Rd *Web:* www.sierraselect.com	North Highlands	CA	95660	916-483-9295	
Simon Group Inc, The 1506 Old Bethlehem Pk *Web:* www.simongroup.com	Sellersville	PA	18960	215-453-8700	
Sky Adv Inc 14 E 33rd St APT 7s *Web:* www.skyad.com	New York	NY	10016	212-677-2500	
Slingshot LLC 208 N Market St Ste 500 *Web:* www.slingshot.com	Dallas	TX	75202	214-634-4411	634-5511
Source Communications Inc 433 Hackensack Ave *Web:* www.sourcead.com	Hackensack	NJ	07601	201-343-5222	343-5710
SPAR Group Inc 560 White Plains Rd *NASDAQ: SGRP* ■ *Web:* www.sparinc.com	Tarrytown	NY	10591	914-332-4100	332-0741
Spawn Ideas Inc 808 E St *Web:* spawnak.com	Anchorage	AK	99501	907-274-9553	
SPM Marketing & Communications 15 W Harris Ave Ste 300 *Web:* www.spmmarketing.com	La Grange	IL	60525	708-246-7700	
Springer Mktg & Adv 65 Wilkie Way *Web:* www.springermktadv.com	Fletcher	NC	28732	828-687-0334	
Stackpole & Partners Ltd 222 Merrimac St *Web:* www.stackpolepartners.com	Newburyport	MA	01950	978-463-6600	
Stephan & Brady Inc 1850 Hoffman St *Web:* www.stephanbrady.com	Madison	WI	53704	608-241-4141	241-4246
Stephenz Group Inc, The 75 E Santa Clara St Ste 900 *Web:* www.stephenz.com	San Jose	CA	95113	408-286-9899	
Sterling-Rice Group, The (SRG) 1801 13th St Ste 400 *Web:* www.srg.com	Boulder	CO	80302	303-381-6400	444-6637
Stern Adv Inc 950 Main Ave *Web:* www.sternadvertising.com	Cleveland	OH	44113	216-464-4850	464-4512
Stone & Ward Inc 225 E Markham St *Web:* www.stoneward.com	Little Rock	AR	72201	501-375-3003	375-8314
Streamworks LLC 3770 Dunlap St N *Web:* streamworksmn.com	Arden Hills	MN	55112	651-486-0252	
Sudler & Hennessey 230 Pk Ave S **Fax:* Hum Res ■ *Web:* www.sudler.com	New York	NY	10003	212-614-4100	598-6907*
Sullivan Higdon & Sink Inc 255 N Mead *Web:* www.wehatesheep.com	Wichita	KS	67202	316-263-0124	
Swanson Russell 1222 P St *Web:* www.swansonrussell.com	Lincoln	NE	68508	402-437-6400	
TBWA Chiat/Day Inc 488 Madison Ave *Web:* tbwachiatday.com	New York	NY	10022	212-804-1000	804-1200
TDG Communications Inc 93 Sherman St *Web:* www.tdgcommunications.com	Deadwood	SD	57732	605-722-7111	
Team One 13031 W Jefferson Blvd *Web:* www.teamone-usa.com	Los Angeles	CA	90094	310-437-2500	
Thayer Media Inc 9000 E Nichols Ave Ste 202 *Web:* www.thayermedia.com	Centennial	CO	80112	303-221-2221	
Thomasarts Inc 240 South 200 West *Web:* www.thomasarts.com	Farmington	UT	84025	801-451-5365	
Thompson Marketing 70 NE Loop 410 Ste 1050 *Web:* www.thompsonmarketinginc.com	San Antonio	TX	78216	239-772-5408	
Tinsley Adv 2000 S Dixie Hwy *TF:* 800-432-2242 ■ *Web:* www.tinsley.com	Miami	FL	33133	305-856-6060	858-3877
Topin & Associates Inc 205 N Michigan Ave Ste 2315 *Web:* www.topin.com	Chicago	IL	60601	312-645-0100	
Trahan Burden & Charles Inc (TBC) 900 S Wolfe St *Web:* www.tbc.us	Baltimore	MD	21231	410-347-7500	986-1299
Treasure Valley Reminder 1160 Sw Fourth St *Web:* www.argusobserver.com	Ontario	OR	97914	541-889-5387	
Tribal DDB Worldwide 437 Madison Ave 8th Fl *Web:* tribalworldwide.com	New York	NY	10022	212-515-8600	515-8660
Trolex Corp 55-57 Bushes Ln *Web:* www.trolexcorp.com	Elmwood Park	NJ	07407	201-794-8004	
Trone 1823 Eastchester Dr *Web:* www.tronebrandenergy.com	High Point	NC	27265	336-886-1622	886-4242
Unit 7 30 Irving Pl Fl 11	New York	NY	10003	212-209-1600	
UniWorld Group Inc 1 Metro Ctr N *Web:* uwg.is	Brooklyn	NY	11201	212-219-1600	219-6395
Verso Adv Inc 50 W 17th St Fl 5	New York	NY	10011	212-292-2990	
VIA Agency 619 Congress St *Web:* www.theviaagency.com	Portland	ME	04101	207-221-3000	761-9422
Vidal Partnership Inc, The 228 E 45th St Fl 14 *Web:* www.vidalpartnership.com	New York	NY	10017	212-867-5185	
Vistacomm 1401 N C Ave	Sioux Falls	SD	57104	605-977-2100	
VML Inc 250 NW RichaRds Rd *Web:* www.vml.com	Kansas City	MO	64116	816-283-0700	283-0954
Walker Brand Communication 1810 W Kennedy Blvd *Web:* www.walkerbrands.com	Tampa	FL	33606	813-875-3322	
Wasserman Media Group LLC 10960 Wilshire Blvd Ste 2200 *Web:* www.teamwass.com	Los Angeles	CA	90024	310-407-0200	407-0300
Weintraub Adv Inc 7745 Carondelet Ave Ste 308 *Web:* www.weintraubadv.com	Saint Louis	MO	63105	314-721-5050	721-6850
White & Partners Inc 13665 Dulles Tech Dr Ste 150 *Web:* white64.com	Herndon	VA	20171	703-793-3000	793-1495

Phone | Fax

Whitespace Creative Inc 24 N High St Ste 200 .... Akron OH 44308 330-762-9320
Web: www.whitespace-creative.com
Wieden & Kennedy 224 NW 13th Ave .... Portland OR 97209 503-937-7000 937-8000
Web: www.wk.com
Williams & Assoc Inc 247 S Wilmot Rd .... Tucson AZ 85711 520-745-8500
Web: www.wasoc.com
Williams Whittle Assoc Inc
711 Princess St .... Alexandria VA 22314 703-836-9222
Web: www.williamswhittle.com
Wingate Healthcare Inc 63 Kendrick St .... Needham MA 02494 781-707-9500
Web: www.wingate.com
WM Martin Adv Inc 6705 Levelland Rd Ste A .... Dallas TX 75252 972-732-8040
Web: www.wmmadv.com
World 50 Inc 3525 Piedmont Rd NE Bldg 7-600 .... Atlanta GA 30305 404-816-5559
Web: www.w50.com
WPP Group USA Inc 125 Pk Ave 4th Fl .... New York NY 10017 212-632-2200
Web: www.wpp.com
WYSE Adv 668 Euclid Ave .... Cleveland OH 44114 216-696-2424
Web: wyseadv.com
Zazoom 7600 E Doubletree Ranch Rd Ste 300 .... Scottsdale AZ 85258 480-998-3200
Zubi Adv Services Inc
2990 Ponce De Leon Blvd Ste 600 .... Coral Gables FL 33134 305-448-9824
Web: www.zubiad.com

ADVERTISING DISPLAYS

See Displays - Exhibit & Trade Show p. 2196; Displays - Point-of-Purchase p. 2197; Signs p. 3185

5 ADVERTISING SERVICES - DIRECT MAIL

Phone | Fax

29 Prime Inc 9701 Jeronimo Rd .... Irvine CA 92618 888-513-7746
TF: 888-513-7746 ■ *Web:* www.29prime.com
3D Internet
633 W Fifth St US Bank Twr Fl 28 .... Los Angeles CA 90071 800-442-5299
TF: 800-442-5299
3D2B Inc 80-02 Kew Gardens Rd Ste 903 .... Kew Gardens NY 11415 718-709-0900
Web: www.3d2b.com
3Q Digital Inc 1710 S Amphlett Blvd Ste 320 .... San Mateo CA 94002 650-539-4124
Web: 3qdigital.com
4Mads 834 Bush St Ste A .... San Francisco CA 94108 415-795-3686
Web: 4mads.com
614 Media Group Inc 458 E Main St .... Columbus OH 43215 614-488-4400
Web: www.614mediagroup.com
A M Solutions 100 Interstate Blvd .... Edgerton WI 53534 608-884-3452
Web: www.amsolutionswi.com
A Plus Letter Service Inc 200 Syracuse Ct .... Lakewood NJ 08701 732-830-1600
Web: www.aplusletter.com
Aa Temps Inc 7002 little river tpke .... Annandale VA 22003 703-642-9050
TF: 800-901-8367 ■ *Web:* www.ardelle.com
AAyuja Inc 35453B Dumbarton Ct .... Newark CA 94560 415-658-6070
Web: www.aayuja.com
ABR Services Inc 14849 Persistence Dr Ste .... Woodbridge VA 22191 703-490-5559
Web: www.abrservices.com
Access Direct Systems Inc
91 Executive Blvd .... Farmingdale NY 11735 631-420-0770 420-1647
Web: accessdirect.com
Access Worldwide Inc
5192 Southridge Pkwy Ste 112 .... Atlanta GA 30349 404-675-0633
TF: 877-564-8581 ■ *Web:* www.accessworldwide.net
Accurate Mailings Inc 215 O'Neill Ave .... Belmont CA 94002 650-508-8885
TF: 800-732-3290 ■ *Web:* www.accuratemailings.com
Accutrend Data Corp
7860 E Berry Pl .... Greenwood Village CO 80111 303-488-0011
Web: www.newbusinessreporter.com
Action Mailing Corp 3165 W Heartland Dr .... Liberty MO 64068 816-415-9000
TF: 866-990-9001 ■ *Web:* action-mailing.com
Acxiom Corp 601 E Third St .... Little Rock AR 72201 501-342-7799
NASDAQ: ACXM ■ *TF:* 888-337-7699 ■ *Web:* www.acxiom.com
Ad-mail Inc 905 Nw 17th Ave .... Portland OR 97209 503-223-1101
Web: www.admailinc.com
ad2 Inc 1990 E Grand Ave Ste 200 .... El Segundo CA 90245 310-356-7500
Web: www.ad2.com
Adinch Inc 2670 Leavenworth St Ste E .... San Francisco CA 94133 415-800-4475
Web: adinch.com
AdKarma LLC 3806 Buttonwood Dr Ste 101 .... Columbia MO 65201 573-446-7366
Web: adkarma.net
ADS Media Group Inc
15265 Capital Port Ste 100 .... San Antonio TX 78249 210-655-6613
Web: www.adsmediagroup.com
AdStaff Media LLC 4841 Summer Ave Ste 300 .... Memphis TN 38122 901-271-6700
Web: adstaffmedia.com
Adtegrity com Inc 5910 Tahoe Dr SE .... Grand Rapids MI 49546 616-285-5429
Web: www.adtegrity.com
Adtron Inc 1700 Morrissey Dr .... Bloomington IL 61704 309-662-1221 663-6691
Advance Design Inc
7100 E Vly Green Rd .... Fort Washington PA 19034 215-774-1000
Web: www.advancewebdesign.com
Advanced Distributor Products LLC
2175 W Park Pl Blvd .... Stone Mountain GA 30087 770-465-5560
Web: www.adpnow.com
Adventist Media Center Inc
101 W Cochran St .... Simi Valley CA 93065 805-955-7777
Web: www.adventistmediacenter.com
Advertical Media LLC
14 Palm Harbor Village Way .... Palm Coast FL 32137 386-986-1600
Web: www.adverticalmedia.com
Adviso Consulting Inc 909 Mont-Royal E .... Montreal QC H2J1X3 514-598-1881
Web: www.adviso.ca
Adwerx Inc 307 W Main St .... Durham NC 27701 888-746-5678
TF: 888-746-5678 ■ *Web:* www.adwerx.com

Phone | Fax

Adzzup LLC 8240 S Kyrene Rd Ste 101 .... Tempe AZ 85284 888-723-9987
TF: 888-723-9987 ■ *Web:* adzzup.com
Affnet Inc 1 City Blvd W Ste 840 .... Orange CA 92868 949-608-0839
Web: www.affnet.com
Agency Revolution 698 NW .... Bend OR 97701 800-606-0477
TF: 800-606-0477 ■ *Web:* www.agencyrevolution.com
agencyQ Inc 1100 13Th St. NW Ste 450 .... Washington DC 20005 202-776-9090
Web: www.agencyq.com
Aid Mailing & Fulfillment
1988 Leghorn St .... Mountain View CA 94043 650-919-1999
Web: aidmail.com
Airbrush Action Inc PO Box 438 .... Allenwood NJ 08720 732-223-7878
TF: 800-876-2472 ■ *Web:* www.airbrushaction.com
AKA Direct Inc 19217 SW 119th Ave .... Tualatin OR 97062 503-454-2200
Web: www.akadirect.com
AKT Enterprises 6424 Forest City Rd .... Orlando FL 32810 877-306-3651
TF: 877-306-3651 ■ *Web:* www.aktenterprises.com
Alaska Laser Printing & Mailing Services
165 E 56th Ave .... Anchorage AK 99518 907-561-8000
Web: www.alaskalaserprint.com
All Direct Mail Services Inc 15392 Cobalt St .... Sylmar CA 91342 818-833-7773
All Needs Computer & Mailing Services Inc
8100 S 13th St .... Lincoln NE 68512 402-421-1083
Web: www.ancms.com
Allstyle Coil Company LP 7037 Brittmore Dr .... Houston TX 77041 713-466-6333
Web: www.allstyle.com
Alltranmedia Ltd 1232 Harmony St Ste 670 .... New Orleans LA 70115 318-255-0524
Web: advercar.com
Allview Networks LLC
8303 Arlington Dr Ste 210 .... Fairfax VA 22031 888-982-8489
TF: 888-982-8489 ■ *Web:* www.allviewnetworks.com
Amazing Mail-print Center
2130 S 7th Ave Ste 170 .... Phoenix AZ 85007 888-681-1214
TF: 888-681-1214 ■ *Web:* amazingmail.com
Amazing Media Inc 133 Eglin Pkwy SE .... Ft Walton Beach FL 32563 850-833-2648
Web: amazingmediainc.com
American List Counsel Inc 4300 US Hwy 1 .... Princeton NJ 08543 609-580-2800 580-2888
Web: www.alc.com
American Mailers - Illinois Inc
820 Frontenac Rd .... Naperville IL 60563 630-579-8800
Web: anetorder.us
American Target Advertising Inc
9625 Surveyor Ct Ste 400 .... Manassas VA 20110 703-392-7676
Web: www.nonprofitprosperity.com
Americomm 804 Greenbrier Cir .... Chesapeake VA 23320 757-622-2724
TF: 800-527-6757 ■ *Web:* americommllc.com
Ameripack Inc 107 N Gold Dr .... Robbinsville NJ 08691 609-259-7004 259-8975
TF: 800-456-7963 ■ *Web:* www.ameripack.com
Ami 4407 Wheeler Ave .... Alexandria VA 22304 703-370-4606
Web: amidirect.com
Anderson DDB Health & Lifestyle
33 Bloor St E .... Toronto ON M4W3H1 416-960-3830
Web: www.andersonddb.com
Andrew Associates Inc 6 Pearson Way .... Enfield CT 06082 860-253-0000
Web: www.andrewmail.com
Ansira Inc 2300 Locust St .... Saint Louis MO 63103 314-783-2300
Web: www.thenationalsystem.com
AnswersMedia Inc 30 N Racine Ave Ste 300 .... Chicago IL 60607 312-421-0113
Web: www.answersmediainc.com
Argonaut Inc 576 Folsom St .... San Francisco CA 94105 415-633-8200
Web: www.argonautinc.com
Arista Information Systems Inc
1105 Fairchild Rd .... Winston-Salem NC 27105 336-776-1105
Web: www.aristainfo.com
Asico LLC 26 Plz Dr .... Westmont IL 60559 630-789-1291
Web: www.asico.com
Avenue Marketing & Communication
363 W Erie St #4E Chicago, ... Chicago IL 60654 312-787-8300
Web: www.avenue-inc.com
AXIAL360 3500 Marmenco Ct .... Baltimore MD 21230 410-789-5300
Web: www.axial360.com
Ballantine Corp, The 55 Lane Rd Ste 350 .... Fairfield NJ 07004 973-305-1500
Web: ballantine.com
Bancroft & Sons Transportation Inc
3390 High Prairie Rd .... Grand Prairie TX 75050 972-790-3777
Web: www.bancroftandsons.com
BandMerch LLC 3120 W Empire Ave .... Burbank CA 91504 818-736-4800
Web: www.bandmerch.com
BBDO Chicago Inc 410 N Michigan Ave .... Chicago IL 60611 312-337-7860
Web: www.energybbdo.com
Belo Interactive Media 900 Jackson St Ste 400 .... Dallas TX 75202 214-977-4000
Web: www.belointeractive.com
Berline Group Inc, The 70 E Long Lk .... Bloomfield Hills MI 48304 248-593-4744
Web: www.berline.com
Big m p G Inc 811 E Vienna Ave .... Milwaukee WI 53212 414-332-3900
Web: www.bigmpg.com
Bindery Associates Inc 2025 Horseshoe Rd .... Lancaster PA 17602 717-295-7443
Web: www.binderyassociates.com
Blow Me Away Media Corp 229 N Sherman Ave .... Corona CA 92882 951-299-6595
Web: www.blowmeawaymedia.tv
Blue Interactive Agency
608 SW Fourth Ave .... Fort Lauderdale FL 33315 954-779-2801
Web: www.blueinteractiveagency.com
BlueSpire Strategic Marketing
7650 Edinborough Way Ste 500 .... Minneapolis MN 55435 800-727-6397
TF: 800-727-6397 ■ *Web:* bluespiremarketing.com
Boostability Inc
2600 West Executive Pkwy Ste 200 .... Lehi UT 84043 800-261-1537
TF: 800-261-1537 ■ *Web:* www.boostability.com
Booth 4900 Nautilus Ct N Ste 220 .... Boulder CO 80301 323-805-0150
TF: 800-332-6684 ■ *Web:* www.thebooth.net/homeset.html
BPI Communications LLC
121 W Long Lk Rd Ste 100 .... Bloomfield Hills MI 48304 248-645-0001
Web: www.bpicommunications.com

Company	City	State	ZIP	Phone	Fax
Branding Farm, The 2112 Zeno Pl *Web:* branding.farm	Venice	CA	90291	310-822-6888	
Brandpoint 850 5Th St S *TF:* 877-374-5270 ■ *Web:* www.brandpoint.com	Hopkins	MN	55343	877-374-5270	
Bridg com 11390 W Olympic Blvd Ste 450 *Web:* bridg.com	Los Angeles	CA	90064	310-299-7939	
Brierley & Partners 5465 Legacy Dr Ste 300 *TF:* 800-899-8700 ■ *Web:* www.brierley.com	Plano	TX	75024	214-760-8700	743-5511
Bruen Productions International Inc 5235 Gulf Stream Court 2nd Fl *Web:* www.bruen.com	Loveland	CO	80538	970-593-6300	
BubbleLife Media LLC 4600 Greenville Ave Ste 240 *Web:* www.bubblelifemedia.com	Dallas	TX	75206	214-736-7090	
Buddy Group Inc, The 722 Lombard St Ste 202 *Web:* www.thebuddygroup.com	San Francisco	CA	94133	415-240-4160	
BuildCentral Inc 200 W Madison St Ste 1110 *Web:* www.buildcentral.com	Chicago	IL	60606	312-223-1600	
Bulldog Solutions LLC 7600 N Capital of Texas Hwy Bldg C Ste 250 *TF:* 877-402-9199 ■ *Web:* www.bulldogsolutions.com	Austin	TX	78731	877-402-9199	
Burdiss Lettershop Services Co 9765 Widmer Rd *Web:* www.burdiss.com	Lenexa	KS	66215	913-492-0545	
Burst Marketing LLC 122 Industrial Park Rd 2nd Fl *Web:* www.burstmarketing.net	Albany	NY	12206	518-907-0186	
Buy Owner Inc 1192 E Newport Ctr Dr Ste 200 *Web:* www.buyowner.com	Deerfield Beach	FL	33442	954-202-7777	
Buyer Group, The 805 E Hillsboro Blvd Ste 208 *Web:* www.thebuyergroup.com	Deerfield Beach	FL	33441	954-354-1411	
Cactus Mailing Co 16121 N 78th St Ste 103 *Web:* www.cactusmailing.com	Scottsdale	AZ	85260	480-443-1442	
Calmark Inc 1400 W 44th St	Chicago	IL	60609	773-247-7200	
Canyon International Marketing and Media P.O.Box 2223 *Web:* www.canyoninternational.com	Folsom	CA	95763	916-933-3026	
Cardagin Networks Inc 120 Buckingham Rd *Web:* www.cardagin.com	Charlottesville	NC	22903	703-963-7576	
Cardenas Marketing Network Inc 1459 W Hubbard St *Web:* www.cmnevents.com	Chicago	IL	60642	312-492-6424	
Cardlytics Inc 675 Ponce de Leon Ave NE Ste 6000 *TF:* 888-798-5802 ■ *Web:* www.cardlytics.com	Atlanta	GA	30308	888-798-5802	
Carl Bloom Assoc Inc 81 Main St Ste 126 *Web:* www.carlbloom.com	White Plains	NY	10601	914-761-2800	761-2744
Carousel30 500 Montgomery St Ste 650 *Web:* www.carousel30.com	Alexandria	VA	22314	703-260-1180	
Cass Data & Mailing Services Inc 26 Eglin Pkwy Se Ste 4 *Web:* cassdata.com	Fort Walton Beach	FL	32548	850-862-5110	
Catalina Marketing Corp 200 Carillon Pkwy *TF:* 888-322-3814 ■ *Web:* www.catalina.com	Saint Petersburg	FL	33716	727-579-5000	556-2700
Catawba Print & Mail Inc 1215 15th St Dr Ne *Web:* www.imagemarkonline.com/press-releases/imagemark-acquires-catawba-direct-marketing-solutions-to-expand-direct-mail-services	Hickory	NC	28601	828-324-2021	
Causemedia Group LLC 811 El Capitan Ste 130 *Web:* www.causemediagroup.com	San Luis Obispo	CA	93401	805-786-0150	
Cenoplex LLC 5121 Bee Cave Rd Ste 106 *Web:* www.cenoplex.com	Austin	TX	78746	512-843-0036	
Centron Data Services Inc 1175 Devin Dr **Fax Area Code:* 231 ■ *TF Cust Svc:* 800-732-8787 ■ *Web:* www.centrondata.com	Norton Shores	MI	49441	800-732-8787	799-0092*
Century Direct LLC 15 Enter Ln 3rd Fl **Fax Area Code:* 718 ■ *Web:* www.centurydirect.net	Islandia	NY	11749	212-763-0600	349-9528*
Cenveo Inc 201 Broad St 1 Canterberry Green *NYSE:* CVO ■ *Web:* www.cenveo.com	Stamford	CT	06901	203-595-3000	
Ces Mail Communications Inc 2319 Atlantic Ave *Web:* www.cesmail.com	Raleigh	NC	27604	919-833-5785	
Checkd-In Corp 4117 Hillsboro Pk Ste 103-135 *Web:* www.checkd.in	Nashville	TN	37215	615-390-4728	
Chicago Style SEO Inc 2020 N Lincoln Park W Ste 3 *Web:* www.chicagostyleseo.com	Chicago	IL	60614	773-809-5002	
Chillybears 6 Brook Rd *Web:* www.chillybears.com	Needham Heights	MA	24942	781-455-6321	
Ciplex 475 Washington Blvd Ste A *TF:* 866-406-8258 ■ *Web:* www.ciplex.com	Marina Del Rey	CA	90292	310-461-0330	
ClickGen LLC 1613 NW 136th Ave Ste 100 *Web:* www.clickgen.com	Sunrise	FL	33323	954-653-9200	
Clixo LLC 222 Milwaukee St Ste 307 *Web:* www.clixosearch.com	Denver	CO	80206	303-632-8722	
Club Marketing Services Inc 101 W Central *Web:* www.clubmarketing.com	Bentonville	AR	72712	479-696-3100	
Code and Theory Inc 575 Broadway 5th Fl *Web:* www.codeandtheory.com	New York	NY	10012	212-358-0717	
Cohen & Company Creative Inc 12002 Miramar Pkwy Ste C *Web:* www.cohenadv.com	Miramar	FL	33025	954-923-8133	
Colorado Data Mail Inc 2525 W Fourth Ave *Web:* www.coloradodatamail.com	Denver	CO	80219	303-629-6155	
Comark Direct 507 S Main St *TF:* 888-742-0405 ■ *Web:* comarkdirect.com	Ft. Worth	TX	76104	888-742-0405	
Command Partners LLC 2125 Southend Dr Ste 453 *Web:* commandpartners.com	Charlotte	NC	28203	704-910-5727	
Connexio Media 904 Fournie Ln *Web:* connexiomedia.com	Collinsville	IL	62234	309-635-2677	
Coresco Inc 1407 Airport Rd *Web:* www.coresco.com	Monroe	NC	28110	704-296-5600	
Create Digital Inc 100 Concourse Blvd Ste 150 *Web:* createdigital.com	Glen Allen	VA	23059	804-955-4400	
Crispin Porter & Bogusky LLC 3390 Mary St Ste 300 Coconut Grove *Web:* www.cpbgroup.com	Miami	FL	33133	305-859-2070	
Critical Mass Inc 1011 Ninth Ave SE Ste 300 *Web:* www.criticalmass.com	Calgary	AB	T2G0H7	403-262-3006	
Cruising Gide Publications Inc 1130 Pinehurst Rd Ste B *TF:* 800-330-9542 ■ *Web:* www.cruisingguides.com	Dunedin	FL	34698	727-733-5322	
Crusader Deals Enterprises LLC 1103 Marquina de Avila *Web:* www.crusaderdeals.com	Tampa	FL	33613	541-525-0124	
CSE, Inc. 5400 S Wridge Dr *Web:* www.csepromo.com	New Berlin	WI	53151	262-786-8400	
CSG Direct Inc 640 Maestro Dr Ste 100 *Web:* www.csgdirect.com	Reno	NV	89511	775-852-9777	
CTM Media Group Inc 11 Largo Dr S *Web:* www.ctmmediagroup.com	Stamford	CT	06907	203-323-5161	
CTRAC Computer Services Inc 16855 Foltz Pkwy *Web:* www.ctrac.com	Strongsville	OH	44149	440-572-1000	572-3330
Current360 1324 E Washington St *Web:* current360.com	Louisville	KY	40206	502-589-3567	
Custom Direct Inc 715 E Irving Park Rd *Web:* www.customdirect.com	Roselle	IL	60172	630-529-1936	
D&R Lathian LLC 40 Ave at the Commons Ste 105, *Web:* www.drlathian.com	Shrewsbury	NJ	07702	732-460-2500	
Darkside Productions Inc 248 3rd St Ste 644 *Web:* www.darksideproductions.net	Oakland	CA	94607	510-208-2100	
Data & Mailing Resources Inc 4929 Blalock Rd *Web:* www.dmr-inc.net	Houston	TX	77041	713-426-1550	
DataSphere Technologies Inc 3350 161st Ave SE *Web:* www.secondspace.com	Bellevue	WA	98008	425-644-7540	
David J Thompson Mailing Corp 21 Naus Way PO Box 150 *Web:* www.thompsonmailing.com	Bloomsburg	PA	17815	570-759-6690	
DB Studios Inc 17032 Murphy Ave *Web:* dbstudios.com	Irvine	CA	92614	949-833-0100	
DB5 202 N Ave 64 *Web:* www.dogsbollocks5.com	Los Angeles	CA	90042	646-884-3940	
Dealer Media Group Inc 2201 W Plano Pkwy Ste 100 *Web:* dealermediagroup.com	Plano	TX	75075	972-881-1106	
Deans Mailing & List Services Inc 3015 W Weldon Ave *Web:* www.deansmailing.com	Phoenix	AZ	85017	602-272-2100	
Delucchi Plus LLC 2101 L St NW Ste 650 *Web:* www.delucchiplus.com	Washington	DC	20037	202-349-4000	
Detroit Media Partnership L P 615 W Lafayette Blvd *Web:* www.detroitmedia.com	Detroit	MI	48226	313-222-2437	
Digital Operative 3990 Old Town Ave Ste C300 *Web:* www.digitaloperative.com	San Diego	CA	92110	619-795-0630	
DigitalSherpa 2 Sun Ct Ste 300 *Web:* www.digitalsherpa.com	Norcross	GA	30092	913-648-5757	
Diji Integrated Press 4920 W Cypress St Ste 100 *Web:* www.dijipress.com	Tampa	FL	33607	813-289-1660	
Direct Answer Inc 106 Paul Mellon Ct Ste 200 *Web:* directanswer.com	Waldorf	MD	20602	301-932-9801	
Direct Mail Processors Inc 1150 Conrad Ct *Web:* www.directmailprocessors.com	Hagerstown	MD	21740	301-714-4700	
Direct Resource Solutions LLC 6912 N 97th Cir *Web:* www.uaaclearinghouse.com	Omaha	NE	68122	402-991-2810	
DirectMailcom 201 Skipjack Rd *TF:* 866-284-5816 ■ *Web:* www.directmail.com	Prince Frederick	MD	20678	301-855-1700	
DL Blair Inc 400 Post Ave Ste 400 *Web:* www.dlblair.com	Westbury	NY	11590	516-746-3700	
Dme Global Marketing Fulfillment Distribution Inc 4915 Nw 159th St *Web:* www.dmeglobal.com	Miami	FL	33014	305-621-6245	
DMNmedia 508 Young St *Web:* dmnmedia.com	Dallas	TX	75202	214-842-6864	
Dms 100 S Keowee St *Web:* www.daytonmailing.com	Dayton	OH	45402	937-222-5056	
DMW Worldwide LLC 701 Lee Rd Ste 103 *Web:* www.dmwdirect.com	Chesterbrook	PA	19087	610-407-0407	407-0410
Do It Sports Inc 615 S Mansfield *Web:* www.doitsports.com	Ypsilanti	MI	48197	734-544-7700	
DogTime Media Inc 27 Maiden Ln Ste 700 *Web:* www.dogtime.com	San Francisco	CA	94108	415-830-9300	
DOMOREGOOD 125 Ottawa Ave NW Ste 205 *Web:* www.hanon-mckendry.com	Grand Rapids	MI	49503	616-776-1111	
Doochoo Inc 1 Daniel Burnham Ct Ste 308 *Web:* www.pick1.com	San Francisco	CA	94109	415-787-2466	
Dp Murphy Company Inc 945 Grand Blvd *TF:* 800-424-8724 ■ *Web:* dpmurphy.com	Deer Park	NY	11729	631-673-9400	
Dream Local Digital LTD 33 Roxbury St *Web:* www.dreamlocal.com	Thomaston	ME	04861	207-354-7073	
Droga5 LLC 400 Lafayette St 5th Fl *Web:* www.droga5.com	New York	NY	10003	917-237-8888	

Phone *Fax*

DropThought Inc 1900 Lafayette St Ste 230.......... Santa Clara CA 95050 408-306-2126
Web: www.dropthought.com
Dxo Communications Inc 1 Townline Cir............ Rochester NY 14623 716-685-4395
Web: dxocom.com
Dynamicard 332 S Juniper St Ste 101................ Escondido CA 92025 800-928-7670
TF: 800-928-7670 ■ *Web:* www.dynamicard.com
Early Advantage Llc 79 Sanford St.................. Fairfield CT 06824 203-259-6480
Web: www.early-advantage.com
Early Express Services Inc 1333 E 2nd St............. Dayton OH 45403 937-223-5801
Web: www.earlyexpress.com
EchoPoint Media 409 Massachusetts Ave........... Indianapolis IN 46204 317-264-8400
Web: echopointmedia.com
EdgeTheory LLC 800 Woodlands Pkwy Ste 210........ Ridgeland MS 39157 650-830-5752
Web: www.edgetheory.com
Edmunds & Associates Inc 301 Tilton Rd........... Northfield NJ 82251 609-645-7333
Web: www.edmundsassoc.com
EGC Group Inc, The
1175 Walt Whitman Rd Ste 200...................... Melville NY 11747 516-935-4944
Web: www.egcgroup.com
eLocal Listing LLC
28765 Single Oak Dr Ste 250...................... Temecula CA 92590 800-285-0484
TF: 800-285-0484 ■ *Web:* www.elocallisting.com
ELS Marketing Inc 3133 Orlando Dr............. Mississauga ON L4V1C5 905-612-1060
TF: 877-612-2673 ■ *Web:* www.corelogistics.net
Empyre Media 1150 N Carroll Ave.................. Southlake TX 76092 866-996-9893
TF: 866-996-9893 ■ *Web:* www.empyremedia.com
Encompass Media Inc 11-11 44th Dr 9th Fl......... Long Island NY 10016 212-993-9429
Web: emgmediainc.com
Encore Image Group Inc
1445 W Sepulveda Blvd........................... Torrance CA 90509 310-534-7500
Web: www.encoreimagegroup.com
Engageclick 430 Sherman Ave...................... Palo Alto CA 94306 650-328-2000
Web: engageclick.com
Enventys LLC 520 Elliot St Ste 200.................. Charlotte NC 28202 704-333-5335
Web: www.enventys.com
Envoy Inc 3317 N 107th St Ste 102..................... Omaha NE 68106 402-558-0637
Web: www.envoyinc.com
EQ Inc 1255 Bay St Ste 400.......................... Toronto ON M5R2A9 416-597-8889
Web: www.eqworks.com
eTagz Inc 108 1st Ave S Ste 450...................... Seattle WA 98104 800-831-0399
TF: 800-831-0399 ■ *Web:* www.etagz.com
EventPro Strategies LLC
7373 E Stetson Dr Ste B120...................... Scottsdale AZ 85251 480-449-4100 283-1190
Web: www.eventprostrategies.com
EventRebels com Inc 10013 Fox Den Rd........... Ellicott City MD 21042 877-883-1786
TF: 877-883-1786 ■ *Web:* www.eventrebels.com
eVision LLC 179 E Main St.......................... Branford CT 06405 203-481-8005
Web: www.evisionsem.com
evoke interaction One 13 S Broad St............. Philadelphia PA 19107 267-765-4992
Web: www.evokehealth.com
EWI Worldwide Inc 13211 Merriman Rd............... Livonia MI 48150 734-525-9010
Web: www.ewiworldwide.com
eWinery Solutions 1700 Soscol Ave Ste 3................ Napa CA 94559 707-253-7400
Web: www.vinsuite.com/home
Exopolis Inc 3000 E Cesar Chavez..................... Austin TX 78702 512-708-1113
Web: www.exopolis.com
eyeReturn Marketing
110 Eglinton Ave E Ste 705......................... Toronto ON M4P2Y1 416-929-4834
TF: 866-878-3335 ■ *Web:* www.eyereturnmarketing.com
Fanscape Inc 4721 Alla Rd...................... Marina Del Rey CA 90292 323-851-3267
Web: www.fanscape.com
Farmer, Lumpe & Mcclelland Advertising Agency Ltd
500 W Wilson Bridge Rd Ste 316................ Worthington OH 43085 614-601-5195
Web: www.wideopenthinking.com
FetchBack Inc 100 W University Ste 101................ Tempe AZ 85281 480-289-5555
Web: www.fetchback.com
FFF Enterprises Inc 41093 County Ctr Dr............. Temecula CA 92591 951-296-2500
TF: 800-843-7477 ■ *Web:* www.fffenterprises.com
Fisher Vista LLC 119 Marina Ave....................... Aptos CA 95003 831-685-9700
Web: www.fishervista.com
FlockTAG LLC 401 E Stadium Ste 106............... Ann Arbor MI 48104 734-707-1250
Web: deals.flocktag.com
FLS Group 405 Madison Ave Ste 1550.................. Toledo OH 43604 419-241-1244
Web: flsmarketing.com
Fmi Direct Mail 2100 Kubach Rd Rear............. Philadelphia PA 19116 215-464-0111
Web: fmidm.com
Focus Direct LLC 9707 Broadway.................. San Antonio TX 78217 210-805-9185 247-1691
TF: 800-555-1551 ■ *Web:* mysanantonio.com
Forthea 3355 W Alabama St Ste 1230................ Houston TX 77098 713-568-2763
TF: 800-882-5905 ■ *Web:* www.forthea.com
Frampton Mailing Systems 450 Horton St E........... London ON N6B1M3 519-680-6245
Web: fms.ca
Franklin Press Inc 1391 Highland Rd............. Baton Rouge LA 70802 225-387-0504
Web: gofranklingo.com
Freenters LLC 5555 S Ellis Ave...................... Chicago IL 60637 773-834-1414
Web: www.freenters.com
Friendemic Inc
307 West 200 South Ste 5200................. Salt Lake City UT 84101 801-415-9314
Web: friendemic.com
Frozen Fire Films Inc 420 S Cesar Chavez Blvd.......... Dallas TX 75201 214-745-3456
Web: frozenfire.com
FRWD Co 712 Ontario Ave W..................... Minneapolis MN 55403 612-235-5030
Web: frwdco.com
FUEL Digital Marketing & Branding
25 E Court St Ste 100........................... Greenville SC 29601 864-627-1676
Web: www.fuelingbrands.com
Full E-media Marketing Inc
2122 S El Camino Real Ste F.................. San Clemente CA 92672 949-940-0198
Funnel Science Internet Marketing LLC
1802 N Carson St.............................. Carson City NV 89701 877-301-0001
TF: 877-301-0001 ■ *Web:* www.funnelscience.com
Fusion Imaging inc 601 Boro St..................... Kaysville UT 84037 801-546-4567
Web: www.fusionimaging.com

Phone *Fax*

G2 USA 200 Fifth Ave............................... New York NY 10010 212-546-2222
Web: www.geometry.com
gamerDNA Media Inc 678 Broadway 5th Fl............ New York NY 10012 212-929-0900
Web: www.gamerdnamedia.com
Gannett Direct Marketing Services Inc
3400 Robards Ct.................................. Louisville KY 40218 502-454-6660 452-8518*
Gate6 Inc 23460 N 19th Ave Ste 110.................. Phoenix AZ 85027 623-572-7725
Web: www.gate6.com
Genesis Direct 8514 Sunstate St........................ Tampa FL 33634 813-855-4274
Web: www.genesisdirect.com
Gennesaret Media LLC 1990 Main St Ste 750.......... Sarasota FL 34236 941-621-2504
Web: www.gennesaretmedia.com
Get Found First LLC 160 W 2nd S.................... Rexburg ID 83440 208-991-3463
Web: www.getfoundfirst.com
GET IT Mobile Inc
2880 Stevens Creek Blvd Ste 350.................. San Jose CA 95128 408-694-3370
Web: www.corp.get.it
Glass McClure Inc 2700 J St..................... Sacramento CA 95816 916-448-6956
Web: glassagency.com
Go2 Communications Inc 8 Cedar St Ste 57........... Woburn MA 01810 781-376-2100
Web: www.go2communications.com
GoGo Cast Inc 161 Comstock Pkwy.................. Cranston RI 02921 401-646-2123
Web: www.gogocast.com
Graham Advertising
525 Communication Cir.................... Colorado Springs CO 80905 719-635-7335
Web: www.grahamoleson.com
Graphics & Mailing Service Inc
2026 Locust St................................. Montgomery AL 36107 334-263-3419
Web: www.graphicsandmailing.com
Greater Data & Mailing Inc 551 Acorn St............ Deer Park NY 11729 631-667-1450
Web: greaterdata.com
Green Canary Sustainability Consulting LLC
1717 W Sixth St Ste 400............................. Austin TX 78703 512-225-5853
Web: www.greencanary.net
Gregory Welteroth Advertising Inc
356 Laurens Rd............................ Montoursville PA 17754 570-433-3366
Web: www.gwa-inc.com
Griffin Tabor Communications
8445 camino santa fe............................ San Diego CA 92121 858-625-0070
TF: 800-795-4472 ■ *Web:* www.taborcommunications.com
Group 55 Marketing Inc
3011 W Grand Blvd 329 Fisher Bldg.................. Detroit MI 48202 313-875-1155
Web: www.group55.com
Grow (Norfolk, VA) 427 Granby St.................... Norfolk VA 23510 757-248-5274
Web: www.thisisgrow.com
Guest Communications Corp
15009 W 101st Ter.......................... Shawnee Mission KS 66215 913-888-1217
TF: 800-637-8525 ■ *Web:* www.gcckc.com
Guidemark Health Inc 6 Campus Dr............... Parsippany NJ 07054 201-740-6160
Web: www.guidemarkhealth.com
Guthrie & Associates Meeting & Event Management Inc
10889 La Alberca Ave........................... San Diego CA 92127 858-487-7759
Web: www.guthrie-meetings-events.com
Gyro Creative Group 400 Grand River Ave.............. Detroit MI 48226 313-964-0100
Web: www.gyrocreative.com
Haines & Company Inc 8050 Freedom Ave......... North Canton OH 44720 800-843-8452 494-3862*
**Fax Area Code:* 330 ■ *TF:* 800-843-8452 ■ *Web:* www.haines.com
Hands on Mailing & Fulfillment Inc
6840 Orangethorpe Ave Ste E..................... Buena Park CA 90620 714-522-3979
Web: handsonmailing.com
Hangout Industries Inc 110 Chauncy St............... Boston MA 02111 617-447-2160
Web: www.hangout.net
Harte-Hanks Inc
9601 McAllister Fwy Ste 610..................... San Antonio TX 78216 210-829-9000 829-9403
NYSE: HHS ■ *TF:* 800-456-9748 ■ *Web:* hartehanks.com
Hawkeye 2828 Routh St Ste 300......................... Dallas TX 75201 704-344-7900
Web: www.hawkeyeww.com
Haystak Digital Marketing LLC
1514 Broadway Ste 201.......................... Fort Myers FL 33901 866-292-0194
TF: 866-292-0194 ■ *Web:* www.haystak.com
Headrick Companies Inc, The 1 Freedom Sq........... Laurel MS 39440 601-649-1977
Web: www.headricks.com
Heartbeat Ideas 200 Hudson St 9th Fl............... New York NY 10013 212-812-2233
Web: www.heartbeatdigital.com
Heaven Group Inc 515 Broadway Ste 2AF............ New York NY 10012 508-654-5700
Web: www.heavengroup.com
Hecks Direct Mail & Printing Service Inc
202 W Florence Ave................................. Toledo OH 43605 419-661-6000 661-6036
Web: www.heckspринting.com
Heritage Co, The
2402 Wildwood Ave Ste 500.................. North Little Rock AR 72120 501-835-5000
TF: 800-643-8822 ■ *Web:* www.theheritagecompany.com
HERO Entertainment Marketing Inc
4590 Ish Dr Ste 140............................. Simi Valley CA 93063 805-527-2000
Web: www.heropp.com
HEROweb Marketing and Design Inc
4660 Main St Bldg D Ste 600-1................... Springfield OR 97478 541-746-6418
Web: www.hero-web.com
Hibbert Company Inc, The 400 Pennington Ave......... Trenton NJ 08650 609-394-7500
Web: www.hibbertgroup.com
Hkm Direct Market Communications Inc
5501 Cass Ave................................... Cleveland OH 44102 216-651-9500 961-6330
TF General: 800-860-4456 ■ *Web:* www.hkmdirectmarket.com
Hobart Group Holdings LLC 240 Main St.......... Gladstone NJ 07934 908-470-1780
Web: thehobartgroup.com
Honestly Now Inc 5 S Bedford Rd.............. Pound Ridge NY 10576 914-764-5615
Web: www.honestlynow.com
HouseLens Inc 720 Rundle Ave...................... Nashville TN 37210 615-209-9441
Web: houselens.com
Houston Production Guide Film 2054 W Main St....... Houston TX 77098 713-523-5387
Web: www.houstonproductionguide.com
Huntsinger & Jeffer Inc 809 Brook Hill Cir........... Richmond VA 23227 804-266-2499
Web: huntsinger-jeffer.com

Company	City	State	Zip	Phone	Fax
I Imagine Studio Inc 152 W Huron Ste 100 *TF:* 855-792-7263 ■ *Web:* www.iimaginestudio.com	Chicago	IL	60654	847-467-0308	
Icon Media Direct Inc 5910 Lemona Ave *Web:* www.iconmediadirect.com	Sherman Oaks	CA	91411	818-995-6400	
iConnected Marketing Corp 125 Tech Park Dr *Web:* www.iconnectedmarketing.com	Rochester	NY	14623	585-444-8500	
Ideal Media US Inc 526 7th Ave Fl 7 *Web:* idealmedia.com	New York	NY	10018	646-681-3356	
iDirect Marketing Inc 6789 Quail Hill Pkwy Ste 550 *Web:* www.idirectmarketing.com	Irvine	CA	92603	949-753-7300	269-0198
IGT Media Holdings Inc 21 SE First Ave *Web:* www.igtmh.com	Miami	FL	33131	305-573-2800	
Immediate Mailing Services Inc 245 Commerce Blvd *TF:* 800-466-4189 ■ *Web:* imsdirect.com	Liverpool	NY	13088	800-466-4189	
Impact Directories 1251 N Cole Rd *Web:* www.impactyp.com	Boise	ID	83704	208-375-2220	
Impact Mailing Services Inc 100 Forsyth Hall Dr Ste A1 *Web:* impactmailingservices.com	Charlotte	NC	28273	704-583-9490	
Indiemark LLC 120 Laurens St S.W. Second Fl *Web:* www.indiemark.com	Aiken	SC	29801	214-716-0268	
infoGroup Inc 1020 E First St *TF:* 866-414-7848 ■ *Web:* www.infousacity.com	Papillion	NE	68046	402-836-5290	
Innocean USA 180 Fifth St Ste 200 *Web:* www.innocean.com	Huntington Beach	CA	92648	714-861-5200	
Innovid Inc 30 Irving P Fl 12 *Web:* www.innovid.com	New York	NY	10003	212-966-7555	
Insegment Inc 313 Washington St Ste 401 *Web:* www.insegment.com	Newton	MA	02458	617-965-0800	
International Delivery Solutions LLC 7340 S Howell Ave *TF:* 877-437-8722 ■ *Web:* www.idstrac.com	Milwaukee	WI	53154	877-437-8722	
Interrupt Marketing 6622 Maplewood Ave *Web:* www.interruptdelivers.com	Sylvania	OH	43560	419-724-9900	
Intrigue Media Solutions Inc 151 Westmount Rd *Web:* www.intrigueme.ca	Guelph	ON	N1H5J3	519-265-4933	
Involve LLC 16 E Poplar Ave. *Web:* www.getinvolve.com	Columbus	OH	43215	614-545-3464	
Jack Nadel International Inc 8701 Bellanca Ave *Web:* www.nadel.com	Los Angeles	CA	90045	310-815-2600	
Jacobs & Clevenger Inc 515 N State St Ste 1700 *Web:* www.jacobsclevenger.com	Chicago	IL	60654	312-894-3000	894-3005
JLS Mailing Services Inc 672 Crescent St *TF:* 866-557-6245 ■ *Web:* www.jlsms.com	Brockton	MA	02302	508-313-1000	
Johnson & Quin Inc 7460 N Lehigh Ave. *Web:* www.j-quin.com	Niles	IL	60714	847-588-4800	647-6949
justClick media Inc 16782-B Red Hill Ave *Web:* www.justclickmedia.com	Irvine	CA	92606	949-863-0066	
Karcher Group Inc, The 14221-A Willard Rd Ste 1500 *Web:* karchergroup.com	Chantilly	VA	20151	703-631-6626	
Karner Blue Marketing LLC 2 Nott Ter *Web:* www.karnerbluemarketing.com	Schenectady	NY	12308	518-935-4101	
KDA Group Inc 7015 College Blvd Ste 700 *Web:* www.kda.com	Overland Park	KS	66211	913-344-1900	
Kepler Group LLC 6 E 32nd St 9th Fl. *Web:* www.keplergrp.com	New York	NY	10016	646-524-6896	
Kirk Integrated Marketing Services Ltd 11388 No 5 Rd Ste 110 *TF:* 888-275-5475 ■ *Web:* www.kirkmarketing.com	Richmond	BC	V7A4E7	604-279-8484	
KnowEm LLC 58 Phoenix Ave. *TF:* 800-691-5669 ■ *Web:* www.knowem.com	Morristown	NJ	07960	800-691-5669	
Kroll Direct Marketing Inc 3914 Netherlee Wy Ste 120 *Web:* www.krolldirect.com	Wellington	NJ	08536	609-275-2900	
KTC Media Group 9891 Hamilton Ave. *Web:* www.ktcmediagroup.com	Huntington Beach	CA	92646	714-378-1660	
Kyne Communications Inc 647 Franklin Ave Ste 200 *Web:* www.kynecommunications.com	Garden City	NY	11530	516-307-1409	
L & D Mail Masters Inc 110 Security Pkwy *Web:* www.ldmailmasters.com	New Albany	IN	47150	812-981-7161	
L & m Mail Service Inc 2452 Truax Blvd *Web:* www.lmmailservice.com	Eau Claire	WI	54703	715-836-0138	
Lake Group Media Inc 1 Byram Brook Pl. *Web:* www.lakegroupmedia.com	Armonk	NY	10504	914-925-2400	925-2499
Lake Michigan Mailers 3777 Sky King Blvd *Web:* www.lakemichiganmailers.com	Kalamazoo	MI	49009	269-383-9333	
Lawler Direct Mail 10300 Drummond Rd Ste 200 *Web:* www.lawlerdirect.com	Philadelphia	PA	19154	215-824-3290	
LeadDog Marketing Group 440 9th Ave 17th Fl *Web:* www.leaddogmarketing.com	New York	NY	10001	212-488-6530	
LeadingResponse LLC 263 Tresser Blvd *Web:* leadingresponse.com	Stamford	CT	06901	201-387-7272	
LeadMinders LLC 1643 VIVIAN ST *Web:* www.leadminders.com	Longmont	CO	80501	720-552-5650	
LeadRival 1207 S White Chapel Blvd Ste 250 *TF:* 800-332-8017 ■ *Web:* www.leadrival.com	Southlake	TX	76092	800-332-8017	
LEAP 2500 Technology Dr *Web:* www.leapagency.com	Louisville	KY	40299	502-212-1390	
Lemon Peak Marketing Services 500 W Putnam Ave Ste 400 *TF:* 888-253-7348 ■ *Web:* www.lemonpeak.com	Greenwich	CT	06831	888-253-7348	
Leon Henry Inc 200 N Central Ave Ste 220 *Web:* www.leonhenryinc.com	Hartsdale	NY	10530	914-285-3456	
Leonie Industries LLC 17383 Sunset Blvd Ste 420A *Web:* www.leoniegroup.com	Pacific Palisades	CA	90272	310-573-9505	

Company	City	State	Zip	Phone	Fax
LetterLogic Inc 1209 Fourth Ave S *Web:* www.letterlogic.com	Nashville	TN	37210	615-783-0070	
Level Interactive 241 Fourth Ave *TF:* 877-733-8625 ■ *Web:* level.agency	Pittsburgh	PA	15222	877-733-8625	
Lewis Direct Marketing 325 E Oliver St *TF:* 800-533-5394 ■ *Web:* www.lewisdirect.com	Baltimore	MD	21202	410-539-5100	685-5144
Lewis Media Partners LLC 500 Libbie Ave Ste 2-C *Web:* www.lewismediapartners.com	Richmond	VA	23226	804-741-7115	
Lexinet Corp, The 701 N Union St *TF:* 800-767-1577 ■ *Web:* www.lexinetcorporation.com	Council Grove	KS	66846	620-767-7000	
Licher Direct Mail Inc 980 Seco St *Web:* www.licherdm.com	Pasadena	CA	91103	626-795-3333	
List Services Corp 6 Trowbridge Dr *Web:* www.listservices.com	Bethel	CT	06810	203-743-2600	
Lodestone Social 1011 Westlake Dr *Web:* lodestonesocial.com	Austin	TX	78746	512-410-1204	
Loomis Group Inc 345 Spear St Ste 110 *Web:* www.loomisgroup.com	San Francisco	CA	94105	415-882-9494	
LOOP88 INC 1001 N 19th St Ste 930 *Web:* pinbooster.com	Arlington	VA	22209	202-595-9545	
Lorraine Gregory Corp 110 Schmitt Blvd *Web:* www.lorrainegregorycorp.com	Farmingdale	NY	11735	631-694-1500	
LOUD3R Inc 87 E Green St Ste 301 *Web:* www.loud3r.com	Pasadena	CA	91105	626-768-2023	
Loyalty 360 Inc 4120 Dumont St. *Web:* loyalty360.org	Cincinnati	OH	45226	513-800-0360	
Luntz Global LLC 9165 Key Commons Ct *Web:* www.luntzglobal.com	Manassas	VA	20110	571-299-2050	
Lynden Tribune 113 Sixth St. *Web:* lyndentribune.com	Lynden	WA	98264	360-354-4444	
M5 Marketing Communications Inc 42 O'Leary Ave *Web:* www.m5.ca	St. John's	NL	A1B4B7	709-753-5559	
Magnetic Media Online Inc 311 W 43rd St Ste 1406 *Web:* www.magnetic.com	New York	NY	10036	212-757-3189	
Mail America Communications Inc 1174 Elkton Farm Rd *Web:* www.mail-america.com	Forest	VA	24551	434-534-8000	
Mail Bag Inc 201 Commerce Dr *Web:* www.mailbaginc.com	Baltimore	MD	21230	301-249-7800	
Mail Right Inc 4470 Yankee Hill Rd *Web:* mailright.com	Rocklin	CA	95677	916-315-8235	
Mail Source Inc 111 Boardwalk *Web:* mailsourceinc.com	Fall Creek	WI	54742	715-877-3711	
Mail Unlimited Inc 4607 Metric Dr. *Web:* mailunlimited.com	Winter Park	FL	32792	407-657-9333	
Mail-Marketing Systems Inc 9420 Gerwig Ln *TF:* 800-878-9537 ■ *Web:* www.mail-marketing.com	Columbia	MD	21046	800-878-9537	
Mailer's Choice Inc 1504 Elm Hill Pk *Web:* www.mailerschoice.com	Nashville	TN	37210	615-883-0070	
Mailing Services of Pittsburgh Inc 155 Commerce Dr *Web:* msp-pgh.com	Freedom	PA	15042	724-774-3244	
Mailing Systems Inc 2431 Mercantile Dr Ste A *TF:* 877-577-2647 ■ *Web:* www.msimail.net	Rancho Cordova	CA	95742	916-674-2035	
Mailings Unlimited 116 Riverside Industrial Pkwy *TF:* 800-773-7417 ■ *Web:* www.growwithmail.com	Portland	ME	04103	207-347-5000	
Mailmark Enterprises LLC 8587 Canoga Ave *Web:* mailmark.com	Canoga Park	CA	91304	818-407-0660	
Mailrite Print & Mail Inc 834 Striker Ave Ste C *Web:* www.mailritemail.com	Sacramento	CA	95834	916-927-6245	
Mailroom Service Center Inc 3075 Shattuck Rd *Web:* www.mailroomservicecenter.com	Saginaw	MI	48603	989-790-2166	
Mailways Enterprises Inc 6105 Factory Rd Ste 1 *Web:* mailways.net	Crystal Lake	IL	60014	815-455-4850	
Major Fulfillment Inc 13707 S Figueroa St *Web:* www.majorfulfillment.com	Los Angeles	CA	90061	310-204-1874	
Manzama Inc 328 NW Bond St Ste 201 *Web:* www.manzama.com	Bend	OR	97701	541-701-2267	
Maple Direct Inc 2349 Haddonfield Rd *Web:* www.mapledirect.com	Pennsauken	NJ	08110	856-488-4700	
Market Data Retrieval 6 Armstrong Rd *TF:* 800-333-8802 ■ *Web:* www.schooldata.com	Shelton	CT	06484	203-926-4800	926-0784
Marketing Drive LLC 800 Connecticut Ave. *Web:* www.matchmg.com	Norwalk	CT	06854	203-857-6100	
Marketing Resource Group Inc (MRG) 225 S Washington Sq *Web:* mrgmi.com	Lansing	MI	48933	517-372-4400	372-4045
MarketLeverage LLC 701 International Pkwy Ste 200 *Web:* www.marketleverage.com	Lake Mary	FL	32746	407-268-7700	
Marketsmith Inc 2 Wing Dr *Web:* www.marketsmithinc.com	Cedar Knolls	NJ	07927	973-889-0006	
Martino & Binzer 29 W Main St Ste 3 *Web:* www.goodbait.com	Avon	CT	06001	860-678-4300	
Mason Inc 23 Amity Rd *Web:* www.mason-madison.com	Bethany	CT	06524	203-393-1101	
Masterworks 19265 Powder Hill Pl NE *Web:* www.masterworks.com	Poulsbo	WA	98370	360-394-4300	
Maxmedia Inc 2160 Hills Ave Ste A *Web:* www.maxmedia.com	Atlanta	GA	30318	404-564-0063	
McCann WorldGroup Inc 622 Third Ave *Web:* www.mccannworldgroup.com	New York	NY	10017	646-865-2000	487-9610
McGuffin Creative Group 566 W Adams St Ste 440 *Web:* mcguffincg.com	Chicago	IL	60661	312-715-9812	

Company / Address	City	State	ZIP	Phone	Fax
McMurry Inc 1010 E Missouri Ave McMurry Campus Center	Phoenix	AZ	85014	602-395-5850	
Web: www.mcmurry.com					
Medley Com Inc 220 Humboldt Ct.	Sunnyvale	CA	94089	408-745-5418	
Web: medley.com					
MedTera Solutions 40 W 37th St Ste 1203	New York	NY	10018	212-488-2130	
Web: www.medterasolutions.com					
Meridian Display & Merchandising Inc 162 York Ave E.	St Paul	MN	55117	651-227-3020	
TF: 800-786-2501 ■ *Web:* www.meridiandisplay.com					
Merrick Towle Associates Inc 5801-F Ammendale Rd.	Beltsville	MD	20705	301-974-6000	
Web: www.merricktowle.com					
MetaResponse Group Inc 700 W Hillsboro Blvd Ste 4-107	Deerfield Beach	FL	33441	954-360-0644	
Web: www.metaresponse.com					
Metro Mailing Service Inc 4251 Gateway Park Blvd	Sacramento	CA	95834	916-928-0801	
TF: 877-269-7055 ■ *Web:* www.mmsmail.com					
Mila Displays Inc 1315B Broadway Ste 108	Hewlett	NY	11557	516-791-2643	
TF: 800-295-6452 ■ *Web:* www.miladisplays.com					
Miller's Presort Inc 1147 Sweitzer Ave	Akron	OH	44301	330-434-9200	
Web: millerspresort.com					
MineAfrica Inc 769 Euclid Ave	Toronto	ON	M6G2V3	416-588-7749	
Web: www.mineafrica.com					
Mint Magazine Inc 6960 Bonneval Rd Ste 102	Jacksonville	FL	32216	904-281-8800	
Web: mintmag.com					
MLB Advertising 182 N Franklin St.	Wilkes-barre	PA	18702	570-824-1500	
Web: mlbadvertising.com					
Mobivity Inc 58 W Buffalo Ste 200	Chandler	AZ	85225	877-282-7660	
TF: 877-282-7660 ■ *Web:* mobivity.com					
Mohan Group, The 2345 Stanfield Rd Ste 200	Mississauga	ON	L4Y1R6	416-255-2500	
Web: www.mohangroup.com					
Momentus Media Inc 650 Alabama St	San Francisco	CA	94110	415-895-0571	
Web: momentusmedia.com					
Money Mailer LLC 12131 Western Ave.	Garden Grove	CA	92841	714-889-3800	265-7624*
**Fax Area Code:* 847 ■ *TF:* 800-468-5865 ■ *Web:* www.moneymailer.com					
Monigle Associates Inc 150 Adams St.	Denver	CO	80206	303-388-9358	
TF: 800-346-4710 ■ *Web:* www.monigle.com					
Motive Entertainment Inc 1303 Oakgrove Pl Ste 100	Westlake Village	CA	91362	805-778-1930	
Web: www.moviemarketing.biz					
Motor City Interactive Inc 49145 Wixom Tech Dr	Wixom	MI	48393	888-340-4638	
TF: 888-340-4638 ■ *Web:* www.motorcityinteractive.com					
Move Networks Inc 796 E Utah Vly Dr	American Fork	UT	84003	801-756-5805	
Moving Off Campus LLC 5257 Shaw Blvd Ste 102	St. Louis	MO	63110	314-367-2456	
Web: www.movingoffcampus.com					
Moxy Commerce Inc 965-A Detroit Ave	Concord	CA	94518	206-257-2121	
Web: www.moxy-commerce.com					
mphoria LLC 1245 Rosemont Dr	Indian Land	SC	29707	888-415-4933	
TF: 888-415-4933 ■ *Web:* www.sweetrelish.com					
Mpress Inc 4100 Howard Ave	New Orleans	LA	70125	504-524-8248	
Web: www.mpressnow.com					
MUNDO Media Inc 120 E Beaver Creek Rd Ste 200	Richmond Hill	ON	L4B4V1	416-342-5646	
Web: www.mundomedia.com					
Nationwide Biweekly Administration Inc 855 Lower Bellbrook Rd	Xenia	OH	45385	888-802-1296	
TF: 888-802-1296 ■ *Web:* www.nbabiweekly.com					
Neo Marketing LLC 4607 Woodland Ave NW	Canton	OH	44709	330-933-1843	
Web: www.neomarketingonline.com					
Neverblue Email 233 California St	El Segundo	CA	90245	310-706-6950	
Web: www.globalwidemedia.com					
New Channel Direct 2659 Center Rd	Hinckley	OH	44233	330-225-8950	
Web: www.newchanneldirect.com					
New Idea Engineering Inc 2784 Homestead Rd Ste 173	Santa Clara	CA	95051	408-446-3460	
TF: 866-433-2364 ■ *Web:* www.ideaeng.com					
NewClients Inc 3900 Gaskins Rd	Richmond	VA	23233	804-560-7000	
Web: www.newclients.com					
News America Marketing 1185 Ave of the Americas 27	New York	NY	10036	212-782-8000	575-5845
TF: 800-462-0852 ■ *Web:* www.newsamerica.com					
Next Day Flyers 18711 S Broadwick St	Rancho Dominguez	CA	90220	800-251-9948	
TF: 800-251-9948 ■ *Web:* www.nextdayflyers.com					
North Georgia Brick Company Inc 2405 Oak St W	Cumming	GA	30041	770-886-6555	
Web: www.northgeorgiabrick.com					
NowSpots Inc 210 W Hill St Ste 3	Chicago	IL	60610	269-861-5280	
Web: www.perfectaudience.com					
Numero Uno Web Solutions Inc 7000 Pine Valley Dr Ste 200	Vaughan	ON	L4L4Y8	905-856-2012	
Web: www.numerounoweb.com					
O'Halloran Adv Inc 270 Saugatuck Ave	Westport	CT	06880	203-341-9400	
TF: 877-466-6616 ■ *Web:* www.ohalloranagency.com					
Oboxmedia Inc 4200 St Laurent Blvd Ste 900	Montreal	QC	H2W2R2	514-282-5020	
Web: oboxmedia.com					
Odell Simms & Lynch Inc 7704 Leesburg Pk.	Falls Church	VA	22043	703-903-9797	903-8850
Web: www.odellsimms.com					
Ogilvy One Worldwide 636 11th Ave	New York	NY	10036	212-237-6000	237-6757
Web: www.ogilvy.com					
Olympia Media Group LLC 5201 W 86th St.	Indianapolis	IN	46268	888-272-2595	
TF: 888-272-2595 ■ *Web:* olympiamediagroup.com					
OneKreate Inc 3850 N 29th Terrace	Hollywood	FL	33020	954-322-7600	
Web: www.onekreate.com					
OnMedia Communications Company Inc 4400 College Blvd Ste 195	Overland Park	KS	66211	913-491-4030	
Web: www.onmediaadsales.com					
Onsite Management Group 4400 Bishop Ln Ste 214	Louisville	KY	40218	502-583-1664	
TF: 800-207-4807 ■ *Web:* omgservices.com					
Oohology LLC 1236 S Shelby St.	Louisville	KY	40203	502-749-2899	
Web: www.oohology.com					
Opposing Views Inc 11963 San Vicente Blvd Ste 901	Los Angeles	CA	90049	310-531-7400	
Web: www.opposingviews.com					
Orlandi Inc 131 Executive Blvd.	Farmingdale	NY	11735	631-756-0110	
Web: www.orlandi-usa.com					
Passkey Systems 4395 Polaris Ave	Las Vegas	NV	89103	702-798-7999	
Web: www.passkeysys.com					
Patton-Kiehl Group Inc 17026 Bull Church Rd	Woodford	VA	22580	888-388-0725	
TF: 888-388-0725 ■ *Web:* www.pattonkiehl.com					
Pc Mailing Services Inc 8120 Exchange Dr Ste 100	Austin	TX	78754	512-929-7785	
Web: pcmailingservices.com					
Perfekt Marketing Inc 3015 S 48th St	Tempe	AZ	85282	602-453-3333	
Web: www.perfektmarketing.com					
Phluant Inc 71 W 47th St Ste 203	New York	NY	10036	646-476-8740	
Web: www.phluant.com					
Pitch 8825 National Blvd.	Culver City	CA	90232	424-603-6000	
Web: www.thepitchagency.com					
PlayMyAd Inc 33 Hammond Ste 207	Irvine	CA	92618	949-600-9777	
Web: www.playmyad.com					
Podaddies Inc 1169 Howard St Ste 203	San Francisco	CA	94103	415-552-9000	
Web: www.podaddies.com					
PolyQuest Inc 1985 Eastwood Rd Ste 206	Wilmington	NC	28403	910-342-9554	
Web: www.polyquest.com					
POP Displays USA LLC 555 Tuckahoe Rd	Yonkers	NY	10710	914-771-4200	
Web: www.diam-int.com					
Position Marketing Group Inc 215 N DesPlaines St 1st Fl	Chicago	IL	60661	312-224-8755	
Web: positionmarketinggroup.com					
Post Haste Mailing Inc 2962 Cleveland Ave N	Roseville	MN	55113	651-639-8359	
Web: www.posthastemailing.com					
Post Masters 2101 Fillmore St	Fort Wayne	IN	46802	260-744-7400	
Web: postmastersaz.com					
Postal Presort Inc 820 W Second St N	Wichita	KS	67203	316-262-3333	
Web: www.postalpresort.com					
PowerChord Inc 100 Second Ave S Ste 200 S	Saint Petersburg	FL	33701	727-823-1530	
Web: www.powerchordsystem.com					
Precise Resource Group Inc 3016 Skyway Cir S	Irving	TX	75038	972-570-0121	
Web: preciseresourcegroup.com					
Presort America Ltd 4227 Williams Rd	Groveport	OH	43125	614-836-5120	
Web: www.presort.com					
PrimeNet Direct Mktg Solutions LLC 7320 Bryan Dairy Rd.	Largo	FL	33777	727-447-6245	
TF: 800-826-2869 ■ *Web:* www.primenet.com					
Promotional Media Management 528 Bridge St Nw Ste 7	Grand Rapids	MI	49504	616-456-5555	
Web: promedmgt.com					
Promotions Unlimited 7601 Durand Ave	Sturtevant	WI	53177	262-681-7000	681-7001
TF: 800-992-9307 ■ *Web:* www.promot.com					
Prompt Mailers Inc 66 Willow Ave.	Staten Island	NY	10305	718-447-6206	
Web: www.promptmailers.com					
Prospectr Marketing 3508 W 22nd St.	Minneapolis	MN	55416	800-908-3523	
TF: 800-908-3523 ■ *Web:* www.prospectrmarketing.com					
Purple Strategies LLC 815 Slaters Ln	Alexandria	VA	22314	703-548-7877	
Web: www.purplestrategies.com					
Pushtwentytwo 22 W Huron	Pontiac	MI	48342	248-335-9500	
Web: www.pushtwentytwo.com					
QuadW International Inc 333 N Wood Dale Rd Ste D.	Villa Park	IL	60181	630-694-4444	
Web: www.quadwinc.com					
QuantumDigital Inc 8702 Cross Park Dr Ste 200	Austin	TX	78754	512-837-2300	837-2777
Web: quantumdigital.com					
R O I Media Solutions LLC 11500 W Olympic Blvd Ste 400	Los Angeles	CA	90064	866-211-2580	
TF: 866-211-2580 ■ *Web:* www.roims.com					
R.W. Lynch Company Inc 2333 San Ramon Vly Blvd	San Ramon	CA	94583	925-837-3877	
TF: 800-594-8940 ■ *Web:* www.rwlynch.com					
Radius Advertising 10883 Pearl Rd Ste 100	Strongsville	OH	44136	440-638-3800	
Web: www.radiuscleveland.com					
RAJ Manufacturing Inc 2692 Dow Ave	Tustin	CA	92780	714-838-3110	
Web: rajswim.com					
Ratespecial LLC 35 N Arroyo Pkwy Ste 250	Pasadena	CA	91103	626-376-4702	
Web: www.ratespecial.com					
Rauxa Direct LLC 275 McCormick Ave A	Costa Mesa	CA	92626	714-427-1271	427-0661
Web: www.rauxa.com					
RDI Marketing Services 4350 Glendale Milford Rd Ste 250	Cincinnati	OH	45242	513-984-5927	984-9735
TF: 800-388-7636 ■ *Web:* www.rdimarketing.com					
ReadyPulse 1600 A El Camino Real	San Carlos	CA	94070	888-998-7412	
TF: 888-998-7412 ■ *Web:* www.readypulse.com					
RealTechNetwork Corp 75A Lk Rd Ste 150	Congers	NY	10920	877-279-4904	
TF: 877-279-4904 ■ *Web:* www.realtechnetwork.com					
Redfin 9890 S Maryland Pkwy Ste 200	Las Vegas	NV	89183	877-973-3346	313-9320*
**Fax Area Code:* 702 ■ *TF:* 800-561-5463 ■ *Web:* www.redfin.com/city/10201/nv/las-vegas					
Renkim Corp 13333 Allen Rd.	Southgate	MI	48195	734-374-8300	
Web: www.renkim.com					
Results:Digital LLC 91 Montvale Ave Ste 104	Stoneham	MA	02180	617-250-8580	
Web: resultsdigital.com					
Retail Benefits Inc 9403 Caserta St	Lake Worth	FL	33467	866-904-6044	
TF: 866-904-6044 ■ *Web:* retailbenefits.com					
RevenueAds Affiliate Network 2304 S Post Rd.	Midwest City	OK	73130	405-622-5046	
Web: www.leadvisionmedia.com					

Company / Address	City	State	Zip	Phone	Fax
Rewarder Inc 564 Market St Ste 705 *Web:* www.rewarder.com	San Francisco	CA	94104	415-217-8855	
Rich Ltd 3809 Ocean Ranch Blvd Ste 110 *Web:* www.richltd.com	Oceanside	CA	92056	760-722-2300	
Ripple6 Inc 520 Eighth Ave 17th Fl *Web:* www.ripple6.com	New York	NY	10018	646-254-6780	
RME360 4805 Independence Pkwy Ste 250 *TF:* 888-383-8770 ■ *Web:* www.rme360.com	Tampa	FL	33634	888-383-8770	
Rocket Direct Communications Inc 532 Central Dr *Web:* rocketdirectmail.com	Virginia Beach	VA	23454	757-463-9161	
RR Donnelley Logistics 1000 Windham Pkwy *TF:* 888-744-7773 ■ *Web:* www.rrdonnelley.com	Bolingbrook	IL	60490	630-226-6100	
RR Donnelley Response Marketing Services 4101 Winfield Rd *TF:* 800-722-9001 ■ *Web:* www.rrdonnelley.com	Warrenville	IL	60555	630-963-9494	
RSVP Publications 6730 W Linebaugh Ave Ste 201 *TF:* 800-360-7787 ■ *Web:* www.rsvppublications.com	Tampa	FL	33625	813-960-7787	549-3306
Rtc Direct Mailing Inc 56 Seip Ln *Web:* rtcdirect.net	Shoemakersville	PA	19555	610-562-5122	
RTC Relationship Marketing 1055 Thomas Jefferson St NW Ste 200 *Web:* www.rtcdirect.com	Washington	DC	20007	202-625-2111	424-7900
Russ Reid Company Inc 2 N Lake Ave Ste 600 *Web:* www.russreid.com	Pasadena	CA	91101	626-449-6100	449-6190
Russell Johns Associates LLC 5020 W Linebaugh Ave Ste 210 *Web:* russelljohns.com	Tampa	FL	33624	727-443-7667	
Sage Direct Inc 3400 Raleigh Dr Se *Web:* www.sagedirect.com	Grand Rapids	MI	49512	616-940-8311	
Sales Benchmark Index 1595 Peachtree Pkwy Ste 204-328 *TF:* 888-556-7338 ■ *Web:* www.salesbenchmarkindex.com	Cumming	GA	30041	888-556-7338	
San Jose Mailing & Printing 1445 Monterey Hwy *Web:* sanjosemailing.com	San Jose	CA	95110	408-971-1911	
Sanctuary Marketing Group Inc 219 E Maple St Ste 125 *Web:* www.sanctuarymg.com	North Canton	OH	44720	330-266-1188	
Savveo Inc 2108 S Blvd Ste 104 *Web:* savveo.com	Charlotte	NC	28203	704-295-0100	
ScreenPlay Inc 3411 Thorndyke Ave W *Web:* www.screenplayinc.com	Seattle	WA	98119	206-625-9901	
Seattle Mailing Bureau Inc 700 Sw 34th St *Web:* seattlemailing.com	Renton	WA	98057	206-431-5700	
Sebis Direct Inc 6516 W 74th St *Web:* www.sebis.com	Bedford	IL	60638	312-243-9300	
Secret Location Inc 777 Richmond St W Unit 102 *Web:* www.thesecretlocation.com	Toronto	ON	M6J0C2	416-545-0800	
Selectable Media Inc 168 Fifth Ave Ste 302 *Web:* selectablemedia.com	New York	NY	10010	212-796-6214	
Semcasting Inc 41 High St *Web:* semcasting.com	North Andover	MA	01845	978-684-7580	
Senior Alternatives For Living 26211 Central Park Blvd *TF:* 800-350-0770 ■ *Web:* www.alternativesforseniors.com	Southfield	MI	48076	800-350-0770	
Sherman & Assoc 333 Harmon Ave NW *Web:* www.shermanexperience.com	Warren	OH	44483	330-399-4500	399-6747
Sherpa Digital Media Inc 509 Seaport Ct *TF:* 877-989-7794 ■ *Web:* www.sherpadigitalmedia.com	Redwood City	CA	94063	877-989-7794	
ShiftCentral Inc 210 John St Ste 100 *TF:* 866-551-5533 ■ *Web:* www.shiftcentral.com	Moncton	NB	E1C0B8	866-551-5533	
Shikatani Lacroix Design Inc 387 Richmond E *Web:* www.sld.com	Toronto	ON	M5A1P6	416-367-1999	
Shoot The Hoop Inc 30911 1st Ave S *Web:* www.shootthehoop.com	Federal Way	WA	98003	253-835-5049	
SightWorks Inc 2505 SE 11th Ave Ste 250 *Web:* www.sightworks.com	Portland	OR	97202	503-223-4184	
Signs Now Corp 4900 Manatee Ave W Ste 201 *Web:* m.signsnow.com	Bradenton	FL	34209	941-747-7747	
Simage LLC 300 N Elizabeth St Ste 100C *TF:* 888-729-7796 ■ *Web:* www.simagenetwork.com	Chicago	IL	60607	888-729-7796	
Smart Transaction Systems Inc 1803 S Foothills Hwy Ste 205 *Web:* www.smart-transactions.com	Boulder	CO	80303	303-494-9760	
SmithGifford Inc 106 W Jefferson St *Web:* www.smithgifford.com	Falls Church	VA	22046	703-532-5992	
SMS Marketing Services Inc 777 Terrace Ave Ste 401 *Web:* www.sms-inc.com	Hasbrouck Heights	NJ	07604	201-865-5800	
Social Creature Media LLC 6031 Airport Way S *Web:* www.projectbionic.com	Seattle	WA	98108	206-501-7253	
SocialCode LLC 302 Fifth Ave 4th Fl *Web:* www.socialcode.com	New York	NY	10001	917-261-3045	
Soloflight Design 126 Sloan St *Web:* www.soloflightdesign.com	Roswell	GA	30075	770-925-1115	
Sonobi 444 W New England Ave Ste 215 *Web:* sonobi.com	Winter Park	FL	32789	386-320-5400	
Source One Distribution Services 1220 Morse Ave *TF:* 877-763-3976 ■ *Web:* www.sourceone-dist.com	Royal Oak	MI	48067	248-399-5060	
SourceLink Inc 500 Pk Blvd Ste 415 **Fax Area Code:* 847 ■ *TF:* 866-947-6872 ■ *Web:* www.sourcelink.com	Itasca	IL	60143	866-947-6872	350-0491*
Spectra Products LLC 520 Columbia Dr *Web:* www.spectraproducts.com	Johnson City	NY	13790	607-770-1985	
Speedy Automated Mailers Inc 2200 Queen St Ste 15 *Web:* speedy-inc.com	Bellingham	WA	98229	360-676-4775	
Spring Venture Group LLC 3500 W 75th St *Web:* www.springventuregroup.com	Prairie Village	KS	66208	913-653-8718	
SproutLoud Media Networks LLC 15431 SW 14th St *Web:* www.sproutloud.com	Sunrise	FL	33326	954-476-6211	
Spyder Trap Inc 1625 hennepin ave *Web:* www.spydertrap.com	Minneapolis	MN	55403	612-871-2270	
Square 2 Marketing Inc 555 N Ln Ste 5050 *Web:* www.square2marketing.com	Conshohocken	PA	18976	215-491-0100	
Stagnito Media LLC 570 Lk Cook Rd Ste 310	Deerfield	IL	60015	224-632-8200	
Starshot Ventures Inc 3555 Lakeshore Blvd W *Web:* www.starshot.com	Toronto	ON	M8W1P4	416-503-8362	
Statlistics Inc 69 Kenosia Ave *Web:* www.statlistics.com	Danbury	CT	06810	203-778-8700	
Steel House Inc 3644 Eastham Dr *TF:* 888-978-3354 ■ *Web:* www.steelhouse.com	Culver City	CA	90232	888-978-3354	
Step Saver Inc 213 Spring St *Web:* www.stepsaver.com	Southington	CT	06489	860-628-9645	621-1841
STIR LLC 330 E Kilbourn Ave Ste 222 *Web:* www.stirmarketing.com	Milwaukee	WI	53202	414-278-0040	
Stoltz Marketing Group LLC 913 W River St Ste 410 *Web:* www.stoltzgroup.com	Boise	ID	83702	208-388-0766	
Storeimage Programs Inc 250 rue Deveault *Web:* www.storeimage.com	Gatineau	QC	J8Z1S6	819-778-0114	
Straightforward Media LLC 8088 N 110th Dr *Web:* www.straightforwardmedia.com	Peoria	AZ	85345	623-266-3962	
StreamTrack Media Inc 345 Chapala St *Web:* streamtrack.com	Santa Barbara	CA	93101	805-308-9196	
Struck Axiom Inc 159 West Broadway Ste 200 *Web:* www.struck.com	Salt Lake City	UT	84101	801-531-0122	
Studio Center Worldwide Audio Inc 200 W 22nd St *Web:* www.studiocenter.com	Norfolk	VA	23517	757-622-2111	
StudioGood 1880 Santa Barbara St Ste 260 *Web:* www.studiogood.com	San Luis Obispo	CA	93401	805-786-0150	
Sub Rosa 353 W 12Th St *Web:* www.wearesubrosa.com	New York	NY	10014	212-414-8605	
Subway Franchisee Advertising Fund Trust 488 Wheelers Farms Rd Ste 2 *Web:* www.sfaft.org	Milford	CT	06461	203-878-0232	
SuperCoups 350 Revolutionary Dr *TF:* 800-626-2620 ■ *Web:* www.supercoups.com	East Taunton	MA	02718	508-977-2000	
Sussex Publishers LLC 115 E 23rd St 9th Fl	New York	NY	10010	212-260-7210	
TailCurrent Technologies Pvt Ltd Suite 4000, L40, 17 State St *Web:* www.tailcurrent.com	New York	NY	10004	312-224-1615	
Tandem Interactive Inc 2455 Hollywood Blvd Ste 204 *Web:* www.tandem-interactive.com	Hollywood	FL	33020	954-453-1140	
Target Direct Mailing Services 1206 Esi Dr *Web:* targetdirectmail.com	Springdale	AR	72764	479-750-4900	
TargetClick Powered by Mudd Advertising 8120 Jennings Dr Ste 13b *Web:* www.targetclickmarketing.com	Cedar Falls	IA	50613	319-575-0235	
TechPad Agency LLC 10824 SE Oak St Ste 205 *Web:* www.TechPadAgency.com	Milwaukie	OR	97222	619-749-8444	
Tel-e Technologies 7 Kodiak Crescent *TF:* 800-661-2340 ■ *Web:* www.tel-e-technologies.com	Toronto	ON	M3J3E5	416-631-1300	635-1711
Tension Envelope Corp 819 E 19th St **Fax Area Code:* 816 ■ *TF:* 800-388-5122 ■ *Web:* tensionenvelope.com	Kansas City	MO	64108	800-388-5122	283-1498*
Texas Mailhouse Inc 8606 Wall St Ste 1740 *Web:* texasmailhouse.com	Austin	TX	78754	512-837-2046	
Tgi Direct 5365 Hill 23 Dr *TF:* 800-337-2237 ■ *Web:* www.tgidirect.com	Flint	MI	48507	800-337-2237	
thelab LLC 637 W 27th St 8th Fl *Web:* www.thelabnyc.com	New York	NY	10001	212-209-1333	
Thorburn Group, The 811 Glenwood Ave Ste 920 *Web:* thethorburngroup.com	Minneapolis	MN	55405	612-226-3861	
TINK Profitabilite numerique Inc 87 Prince Ste 140 *Web:* www.tink.ca	Montreal	QC	H3C2M7	514-866-0995	
Tk Media Direct Inc 5062 Lankershim Blvd Ste 3033 *Web:* tkmediadirect.com	N. Hollywood	CA	91601	818-851-1483	
Tmr Mailing Services Inc 506 Manchester Expy Ste A1 *Web:* www.tmrmailing.com	Columbus	GA	31904	706-653-2090	
Total Outdoor Corp 414 Stewart St Ste 204 *Web:* www.totaloutdoor.com	Seattle	WA	98101	206-430-6080	
Totem Communications Group Inc 37 Front St E *Web:* totem.tc	Toronto	ON	M5E1B3	416-360-7339	
Towne AllPoints Communications Inc 3441 W MacArthur Blvd *Web:* www.towne.com	Santa Ana	CA	92704	714-540-3095	
Towne Mailer 2424 S Garfield St *Web:* www.townemailer.com	Missoula	MT	59801	406-541-6245	
Tractenberg & Co LLC 116 E 16th St 2nd Fl *Web:* www.tractenbergandco.com	New York	NY	10003	212-929-7979	
TriMax Direct 106 W Water St Ste 201 *Web:* www.trimaxdirect.com	St. Paul	MN	55107	651-292-0165	
Trinity Direct LLC 10 Park Pl *Web:* www.trinitydirect.net	Butler	NJ	07405	973-283-3600	
TripleLift Inc 134 Fifth Ave Fl 5 *Web:* triplelift.com	New York	NY	10011	502-354-3801	
True[X] Media Inc 11925 Wilshire Blvd, Ste 200 *Web:* www.socialvibe.com	Los Angeles	CA	90025	310-657-9900	
TrustWorkz 2449 Towne Lk Pkwy *Web:* trustworkz.com	Woodstock	GA	30189	770-615-3275	
Tutor Universe Inc 316 E Court Ste 7 *Web:* www.tutoruniverse.com	Iowa City	IA	52240	319-855-1595	

	City	State	Zip	Phone	Fax
Two West Inc 514 W 26th St	Kansas City	MO	64108	816-471-3255	
Web: www.twowest.com					
U S Monitor 86 Maple Ave	New City	NY	10956	845-634-1331	
TF: 800-767-7967 ■ *Web:* usmonitor.com					
Ubiquitous Media 27 Union Sq W Ste 204	New York City	NY	10003	212-386-7070	
Web: www.ubimedia.com					
Ultimate Lead Systems Inc 401 Frnt St	Berea	OH	44017	440-826-1908	
Web: ultimatelead.com					
Underdog Media 10 E Yanonali St Ste 2C	Santa Barbara	CA	93101	805-880-6910	
Web: www.underdogmedia.com					
Uniguest Inc 1035 Acorn Dr	Nashville	TN	37210	615-259-4500	
Web: www.ushospitality.com					
Unique Mailing Services Inc 325 Marmon Dr	Bolingbrook	IL	60440	630-739-4848	
United Letter Service Inc 1231 N Ellis St	Bensenville	IL	60106	312-427-3537	
Web: www.unitedgmg.com					
Universal Wilde 26 Dartmouth St	Westwood	MA	02090	781-251-2700	251-2613
TF: 866-825-5515 ■ *Web:* www.universalwilde.com					
UpClose Marketing & Printing 120 W White St	Champaign	IL	61820	217-359-3200	
Web: www.upcloseprinting.com					
Update Services Inc 7634 Washington Ave S	Eden Prairie	MN	55344	952-937-5447	
Web: www.updateservicesinc.com					
Valassis 1 Targeting Ctr	Windsor	CT	06095	860-285-6100	
Web: www.valassis.com					
Valassis Canada Inc 47 Jutland Rd Etobicoke	Toronto	ON	M8Z2G6	416-259-3600	
Web: www.valassis.ca					
Valpak Direct Marketing Systems Inc 8605 Largo Lakes Dr	Largo	FL	33773	800-237-6266	
TF: 800-237-6266 ■ *Web:* www.valpak.com					
Varvid Inc 705 Sunset Pond Lane Ste 2	Bellingham	WA	98226	360-738-7168	
TF: 855-827-8434 ■ *Web:* www.varvid.com					
Verso Group Enterprises LLC 148 Main St	Toledo	OH	43605	419-693-5302	
Vertical Vision Financial Marketing LLC 145 Towne Lk Pkwy	Woodstock	GA	30188	866-984-1585	
TF: 866-984-1585 ■ *Web:* www.v2fm.com					
Viamedia Inc 220 Lexington Green Cir Ste 300	Lexington	KY	40503	859-977-9000	
Web: www.viamediatv.com					
Voicetrak Inc 4500 E Speedway Blvd Ste 5	Tucson	AZ	85712	520-628-9221	
Web: www.voicetrak.com					
Voltage Ltd 901 Front St Ste 340	Louisville	CO	80027	303-664-1687	
Web: voltagead.com					
Wahl Media Inc 580 Packetts Landing	Fairport	NY	14450	585-377-8129	
Web: www.wahlmedia.com					
Walls+Forms Inc 204 Airline Dr Ste 200	Coppell	TX	75019	972-745-0800	
Web: www.wallsforms.com					
Walts Mailing Service Ltd 9610 E First Ave	Spokane Valley	WA	99206	509-924-5939	
TF: 888-549-2006 ■ *Web:* waltsmailing.com					
Wave Direct Inc 1616-102 W Cape Coral Pkwy Ste 243	Cape Coral	FL	33914	239-574-8181	
Web: www.wave-direct.com					
Weekleys Mailing Service Inc 1420 W Bagley Rd	Berea	OH	44017	440-234-4325	
Web: www.weekleysmailing.com					
Weinberg Capital Group 5005 Rockside Rd Ste 1140	Cleveland	OH	44131	216-503-8303	
Web: www.weinbergcap.com					
Welcome Wagon International Inc 5830 Coral Ridge Dr Ste 240	Coral Springs	FL	33076	516-333-9400	
Web: www.welcomewagon.com					
Welded Fixtures Inc 8155 Byron Rd	Whittier	CA	90606	562-907-7007	
Web: www.weldedfixtures.com					
Whitefield Group: Local Seo & Web Design LLC 6130 Plumas St Ste 200	Reno	NV	89519	775-230-7095	
Web: whitefieldgroup.net					
Whitespeed 1559 7th St	Santa Monica	CA	90401	310-899-9114	
Web: www.whitespeed.com					
WiderFunnel Marketing Inc 409 Granville St Ste 551	Vancouver	BC	V6C1T2	604-800-6450	
Web: www.widerfunnel.com					
Wilkins Media Co 8010 Roswell Rd Ste 120	Atlanta	GA	30350	770-804-1818	
Web: outofhomeamerica.com					
WireBuzz LLC 7762 E Gray Rd Ste 200	Scottsdale	AZ	85260	480-699-8053	
Web: www.wirebuzz.com					
Words, Data & Images LLC 3190 Rider Trl South	Earth City	MO	63045	314-743-5700	
Web: www.gabrielgroup.com					
World Marketing 7950 Joliet Rd	McCook	IL	60525	708-871-6006	
Yeck Bros Co 2222 Arbor Blvd	Dayton	OH	45439	937-294-4000	294-6985
TF: 800-417-2767 ■ *Web:* www.yeck.com					
Yiftee Inc 565 Middlefield Rd	Menlo Park	CA	94025	650-564-4438	
Web: yiftee.com					
Yovia LLC 2593 Mayport Rd Ste 101	Atlantic Beach	FL	32233	904-242-2669	
Web: yovia.com					
YP Intellectual Property LLC 611 N Brand Blvd Fifth Fl Ste 500	Glendale	CA	91203	818-937-5500	
Web: corporate.yp.com					
Zambezi 248 Westminster Ave	Venice	CA	90291	310-450-6800	
Web: www.zambezi-la.com					
Zemanta Inc 33 W 17th St 9th Fl	New York	NY	10010	216-536-1109	
Web: www.zemanta.com					
Zip Mail Services Inc 288 Hanley Industrial Ct	Saint Louis	MO	63144	314-645-5055	
Web: www.zipmailservices.com					
ZOG Digital Inc 11201 N Tatum Blvd Ste 200	Phoenix	AZ	85028	480-426-9952	
Web: www.zogdigital.com					

6 ADVERTISING SERVICES - MEDIA BUYERS

	City	State	Zip	Phone	Fax
Allan Hackel Organization Inc 1330 Ctr St	Newton Center	MA	02459	617-965-4400	527-6005
Web: www.hackelbarter.com					
Anvil Media Inc 310 NE Failing St	Portland	OR	97212	503-595-6050	
Web: www.anvilmediainc.com					
ARS Adv Inc 1001 Reads Lk Rd	Chattanooga	TN	37415	423-875-3743	
Web: aislerocket.com					
Backchannelmedia Inc 105 S St	Boston	MA	02111	617-210-8100	
Web: backchannelmedia.com					
Beachbody LLC 3301 Exposition Blvd	Santa Monica	CA	90404	310-883-9000	
Web: www.beachbody.com					
Billups Inc 340 Oswego Pointe Dr Ste 101	Lake Oswego	OR	97034	503-454-0714	
Web: billups.com					
Corinthian Media 500 Eigth Ave 5th Fl	New York	NY	10018	212-279-5700	
Web: www.mediabuying.com					
CRN International Inc 1 Circular Ave	Hamden	CT	06514	203-288-2002	
Web: www.skiwatchca.com					
EFX Media 2300 S Ninth St Ste 136	Arlington	VA	22204	703-486-2303	
Web: www.efxmedia.com					
Ektron Inc 542 Amherst St (Rt 101A)	Nashua	NH	03063	603-594-0249	594-0258
TF: 877-383-0885 ■ *Web:* www.ektron.com					
EMC Outdoor 5074 W Chester Pike 2nd Fl	Newtown Square	PA	19073	610-353-9300	
Web: www.emcoutdoor.com					
Envision Creative Group 3400 Northland Dr	Austin	TX	78731	512-292-1049	
Web: www.envisioncreativegroup.com					
Flip Publicity and Promotions 500 Bloor St W	Toronto	ON	M5S1Y3	416-533-7710	
Web: www.flip-publicity.com					
Harmelin Media 525 Righters Ferry Rd	Bala Cynwyd	PA	19004	610-668-7900	
Web: www.harmelin.com					
Haworth Marketing & Media Co 45 S Seventh St Plz 7 Bldg Ste 2400	Minneapolis	MN	55402	612-677-8900	
Web: www.haworthmedia.com					
JL Media Inc 1600 Rt 22 E Second Fl	Union	NJ	07083	908-687-8700	
Web: www.jlmedia.com					
MacDonald Media LLC 185 Madidon Ave 4th Fl	New York	NY	10016	212-578-8735	
Web: www.macdonaldmedia.com					
MAGNA Global USA 100 W 33rd St 9th Fl	New York	NY	10001	212-883-4751	
Web: www.magnaglobal.com					
Media Brokers International Inc 11720 Amberpark Dr Ste 600	Alpharetta	GA	30009	678-514-6200	
Web: www.media-brokers.com					
Media Space Solutions 904 MainSt	Hopkins	MN	55343	612-253-3900	454-2848
TF: 888-672-2100 ■ *Web:* www.mediaspacesolutions.com					
Media Works Ltd 1425 Clarkview Rd Ste 500	Baltimore	MD	21209	443-470-4400	
Web: www.medialtd.com					
Mediaedge:cia LLC 825 Seventh Ave	New York	NY	10019	212-474-0000	
Web: www.mecglobal.com					
Mediaspot Inc 1550 Bayside Dr	Corona Del Mar	CA	92625	949-721-0500	
Web: www.mediaspot.com					
Newton Media Associates Inc 824 Greenbrier Pkwy Ste 200	Chesapeake	VA	23320	757-547-5400	
Web: www.newtonmedia.com					
Oceanos Inc 892 Plain St	Marshfield	MA	02050	781-804-1010	
Web: www.oceanosinc.com					
Parr Media Group Inc, The 13120 Westlinks Ter Blvd Unit 4	Fort Myers	FL	33913	239-561-8090	
Web: www.parrmedia.com					
Petry Media Corp 200 Pk Ave Ste 1700	New York	NY	10166	212-230-5600	
PGR Media 34 Farnsworth St 2nd Fl	Boston	MA	02210	617-502-8400	
Web: www.pgrmedia.com					
TaigMarks Inc 223 S Main St Ste 100	Elkhart	IN	46516	574-294-8844	294-8855
Web: www.taigmarks.com					
Tangible Media Inc 417 Fifth Ave 11th Fl	New York	NY	10016	212-576-8500	
Web: www.tangiblemedia.com					
Telerep Inc 1 Dag Hammarskjold Plz	New York	NY	10017	212-759-8787	
Web: www.telerepinc.com					
Transvideo Studios 990 Villa St	Mountain View	CA	94041	650-965-4898	962-1753
Web: www.transvideo.com					
True Media 500 Business Loop 70 W Ste 201	Columbia	MO	65203	573-443-8783	
Web: www.truemediaservices.com					
Universal McCann 100 W 33rd St 8th Fl	New York	NY	10001	212-883-4700	
Web: www.umww.com					
Winstar Interactive Media (WIMS) 1675 Palm Beach Lakes Blvd Ste 1000	West Palm Beach	Fl	33401	561-227-0626	
Web: www.winstarinteractive.com					
Worldata 3000 N Military Trl	Boca Raton	FL	33431	561-393-8200	368-8345
TF: 800-331-8102 ■ *Web:* www.worldata.com					

7 ADVERTISING SERVICES - ONLINE

	City	State	Zip	Phone	Fax
1938 Media 1 Astor Pl Ph Ste J	New York	NY	10003	917-407-7600	
Web: 1938media.com					
2Advanced Studios LLC 32 Journey Ste 200	Aliso Viejo	CA	92656	949-521-7000	
Web: www.2advanced.com					
5 Metacom Inc 630 W Carmel Dr Ste 180	Carmel	IN	46032	317-580-7540	
Web: www.5metacom.com					
802 Creative Partners Inc 768 S Main St PO Box 54	Bethel	VT	05032	802-234-9755	
Web: www.802creative.com					
A-Team Advertising Advisors LLC 4 Park Ave Ste 15R	New York	NY	10016	646-530-8670	
Web: www.a-teamadvisors.com					
Absolute Media Inc 1150 Summer St	Stamford	CT	06905	203-327-9090	
Web: www.absolutemediainc.com					

Company / Address	City	State	ZIP	Phone	Fax
Access To Media 432 Front St *TF:* 866-612-0034 ■ *Web:* www.accesstomedia.com	Chicopee	MA	01013	866-612-0034	
Active Network 10182 Telesis Ct Ste 100 *TF:* 888-543-7223 ■ *Web:* www.activenetwork.com	San Diego	CA	92121	858-964-3800	551-7619
Ad Cetera Inc 15540 Spectrum Dr *Web:* www.adceterainc.com	Addison	TX	75001	972-387-5577	
Ad Results Inc 6110 Clarkson Ln *Web:* www.adresultsinc.com	Houston	TX	77055	713-783-1800	
Adams & Longino Advertising Inc 605 Lynndale Ct Ste F *Web:* www.adamsadv.com	Greenville	NC	27858	252-355-5566	
Adco Advertising Agency 1302 W Pioneer Pkwy Ste 100 *Web:* www.adcoagency.com	Peoria	IL	61615	309-692-7880	
ADFLOW Networks Inc 3170 Harvester Rd Ste 102 *Web:* adflownetworks.com	Burlington	ON	L7N3W8	905-333-0200	
Adler Display Studio Inc 7140 Windsor Blvd *Web:* www.adlerdisplay.com	Baltimore	MD	21244	410-281-1200	
Admerasia Inc 159 W 25th St 6th Fl *Web:* www.admerasia.com	New York	NY	10001	212-686-3333	
Adprint International Inc 6500 Greenbriar St *Web:* www.adprint.com	Houston	TX	77030	713-665-4578	
Adsport Inc 389 E Palm Ln *Web:* www.adsport.com	Phoenix	AZ	85004	602-262-0500	
Adstrategies Inc 101 Bay St Ste 201 *Web:* www.adstrategies.com	Easton	MD	21601	410-822-2450	
Advance Digital Inc 185 Hudson St *Web:* www.advancedigital.com	Jersey City	NJ	07302	201-459-2888	
Advance Notice Inc 24 Winter St *Web:* www.advancenotice.com	Peabody	MA	01960	978-531-6722	
Adwerks Inc 512 N Main Ave *Web:* www.adwerks.com	Sioux Falls	SD	57104	605-357-3690	
Adz Etc Inc N88w16749 Main St Ste 3 *Web:* www.adzetc.com	Menomonee Falls	WI	53051	262-502-0507	
Affinitive LLC 135 W 26th St 8th Fl	New York	NY	10001	212-684-9100	
Agency Mabu 1003 Gateway Ave *TF:* 800-568-9346 ■ *Web:* www.agencymabu.com	Bismarck	ND	58503	701-250-0728	
agencytwofifteen 215 Leidesdorff St *Web:* 215mccann.com	San Francisco	CA	94111	415-262-3500	
Alamo Tee's & Advertising 12814 Cogburn *TF:* 888-562-3800 ■ *Web:* alamotees.com	San Antonio	TX	78249	210-699-3800	
Alcone Marketing Group Inc 4 Studebaker *Web:* www.alconemarketing.com	Irvine	CA	92618	949-770-4400	
Allis Information Management Inc 204 W Wackerly St *Web:* www.allisinfo.com	Midland	MI	48640	989-835-5811	
Almighty LLC 300 Western Ave Fl 2 *Web:* www.bealmighty.com	Boston	MA	02134	617-782-1511	
Aloft Group Inc 26 Parker St *Web:* www.aloftgroup.com	Newburyport	MA	01950	978-462-0002	
Alt Studios LLC 506 3rd St Ste 200 *Web:* www.innovaideasandservices.com	Des Moines	IA	50309	515-697-7200	
Alterra Group PO Box 201355 *Web:* www.alterra-group.com	Cleveland	OH	44120	216-539-9710	
Altitude Digital Inc 1037 Broadway Unit B *Web:* www.altitudedigital.com	Denver	CO	80203	303-292-1414	
AMCI 4755 Alla Rd Ste 1000 *TF:* 855-486-5527 ■ *Web:* www.amciglobal.com	Marina Del Rey	CA	90292	855-486-5527	
Ammirati Ready Inc 19 Union Sq W 11th Fl *Web:* www.ammirati.com	New York	NY	10003	212-925-2111	
Anderson Marketing Group 7420 Blanco Rd Ste 200 *Web:* www.andadv.com	San Antonio	TX	78216	210-223-6233	
Annodyne Inc 920 Harvest Dr Ste 240 *Web:* www.annodyne.com	Blue Bell	PA	19422	215-540-9110	
Anson-Stoner Inc 111 E Fairbanks Ave *Web:* www.anson-stoner.com	Winter Park	FL	32789	407-629-9484	
Apex Advertising Inc 2959 Old Tree Dr *Web:* www.apexadv.com	Lancaster	PA	17603	717-396-7100	
Apple Printing & Advertising Specialties Inc 5055 Nw 10th Ter *Web:* appleprinting.com	Fort Lauderdale	FL	33309	954-776-5691	
Arc Worldwide 35 W Wacker Dr 15th Fl *Web:* www.arcww.com	Chicago	IL	60601	312-220-5959	220-6212
Archer Communications Inc 252 Alexander St *Web:* www.archercom.com	Rochester	NY	14607	585-461-1570	
Archer Group, The 233 N King St 1st Fl *Web:* www.archer-group.com	Wilmington	DE	19801	302-429-9120	
Archmill House Inc 1276 Osprey Dr *Web:* www.archmillhouse.com	Ancaster	ON	L9G4V5	905-648-7330	
Archrival Inc 720 O St *Web:* www.archrival.com	Lincoln	NE	68508	402-435-2525	
Atlas Advertising LLC 1128 Grant St *Web:* www.atlas-advertising.com	Denver	CO	80203	303-292-3300	
Atomic Direct LLC 1219 Se Lafayette St *Web:* atomicdirect.com	Portland	OR	97202	503-296-6131	
August Lang & Husak Inc 4630 Montgomery Ave Ste 400 *Web:* www.alhadv.com	Bethesda	MD	20814	301-657-2772	
Augustine & Associates 6620 Sierra College Blvd Ste 100 *Web:* www.augustineideas.com	Rocklin	CA	95677	916-774-9600	
Austin & Williams 125 Kennedy Dr Ste 100 *Web:* www.austin-williams.com	Hauppauge	NY	11788	631-231-6600	
Axis Creative Group 1713 Larchwood Dr Ste B *Web:* axis-creative.com	Troy	MI	48083	248-743-0501	
Ayzenberg Group Inc 49 E Walnut St *Web:* www.ayzenberg.com	Pasadena	CA	91103	626-584-4070	
Babcock & Jenkins Inc 1233 NW 12th Ave Ste 100 *Web:* www.bnj.com	Portland	OR	97209	503-382-8613	
Bagwell Marketting 13211 Deer Run Trl *Web:* www.oklahoma-advertising.com	Dallas	TX	75243	972-480-8192	
Banik Communications Inc 121 4th St N Ste 1b2 *Web:* banik.com	Great Falls	MT	59401	406-454-3422	
Banner Retail Marketing Group LLC 23305 E Knox Ave *Web:* www.bannerretail.com	Liberty Lake	WA	99019	509-922-7828	
Barber Martin & Associates 7400 beaufont springs Dr *Web:* www.barbermartin.com	Richmond	VA	23225	804-320-3232	
BARD Advertising Inc 4900 Lincoln Dr *Web:* www.bardadvertising.com	Edina	MN	55436	952-345-8000	
Barefoot Advertising Inc 700 W Pete Rose Way *Web:* www.thinkbarefoot.com	Cincinnati	OH	45203	513-861-3668	
Barnes Advertising Corp 1580 Fairview Rd *TF:* 800-458-1410 ■ *Web:* barnesadvertisingcorp.com	Zanesville	OH	43701	740-453-6836	
Barnett & Murphy Inc 1323 Brookhaven Dr *Web:* www.bmdm.com	Orlando	FL	32803	407-650-0264	
Barnett Cox & Associates 711 Tank Farm Rd Ste 210 *Web:* www.barnettcox.com	San Luis Obispo	CA	93401	805-545-8887	
Bazzirk Inc 1027 E Riverside Dr *Web:* www.bazzirk.com	Austin	TX	78704	512-418-8500	
Beber Silverstein Group 89 Ne 27th St Unit 119 *Web:* www.thinkbsg.com	Miami	FL	33137	305-856-9800	
Belmont Icehouse Llc 3116 Commerce St Ste D *Web:* www.belmonticehouse.com	Dallas	TX	75226	972-755-3200	
Benchworks Inc 860 High St *Web:* www.benchworks.com	Chestertown	MD	21620	410-810-8862	
Bensimon Byrne Inc 420 Wellington St W *Web:* bensimonbyrne.com	Toronto	ON	M5V1E3	416-922-2211	
Bfg Communications Hilton Head IS 6 Anolyn Ct *Web:* www.bfgcom.com	Bluffton	SC	29910	843-837-9115	
Big Frey Promotional Products 707 Lk Cook Rd Ste 300 *Web:* www.bigfrey.com	Deerfield	IL	60015	847-753-6611	
Big Think Studios 1426 18th St *Web:* www.bigthinkstudios.com	San Francisco	CA	94107	415-934-1111	
Biggs/Gilmore Communications 261 E Kalamazoo Ave	Kalamazoo	MI	49007	269-349-7711	349-3051
Bigmouth 244 Kearny St Fl 6 *Web:* www.bigmouth.com	San Francisco	CA	94108	415-394-6680	
Blade Creative Branding Inc 150 Laird Dr *Web:* www.bladecreativebranding.com	Toronto	ON	M4G3V7	416-467-4770	
Blaine Warren Advertising LLC 7120 Smoke Ranch Rd *Web:* www.blainewarren.com	Las Vegas	NV	89128	702-435-6947	
Blast Radius Inc 1146 Homer St *Web:* www.blastradius.com	Vancouver	BC	V6B2X6	604-647-6500	
Blf Marketing LLC 220 Athens Way Ste 110 *Web:* blfmarketing.com	Nashville	TN	37228	615-726-2360	
Blohm Creative Partners 1331 E Grand River Ave Ste 210 *Web:* www.blohmcreative.com	East Lansing	MI	48823	517-333-4900	
Blue C Communications 3421 Via Oporto # 200 *Web:* www.bluecusa.com	Newport Beach	CA	92663	949-723-9202	
Blue Cat Design Mastwoods Rd *TF:* 888-258-3228 ■ *Web:* www.bluecatdesign.com	Port Hope	ON	L1A3V5	905-753-1017	753-2777
Blue Iceberg LLC 146 W 29th St Studio 11W *Web:* www.blue-iceberg.com	New York	NY	10001	212-337-9920	
Blue State Digital LLC 406 Seventh St NW 3rd Fl *Web:* bluestatedigital.com	Washington	DC	20004	202-449-5600	
Blue Zebra Appointment Setting 25 PEQUOT AVE Ste A *TF:* 800-755-0094 ■ *Web:* www.bluezebrausa.com	Port Washington	NY	11050	800-755-0094	
boathouse group Inc 260 Charles St *Web:* www.boathouseinc.com	Waltham	MA	02453	781-663-6600	
Bob Wolfe Partners Tpg 202 San Vicente Blvd Apt 16 *Web:* www.bwp-tpg.com	Santa Monica	CA	90402	310-260-1340	
BOC Partners Inc 1030 South Ave W *Web:* bocpartners.com	Westfield	NJ	07090	908-232-2177	
Bock Communications Inc 3750 S Susan St Ste 100 *Web:* bockpr.com	South Coast Metro	CA	92704	714-540-1030	
Bolin Marketing & Advertising 2523 Wayzata Blvd Ste 300 *TF:* 800-876-6264 ■ *Web:* www.bolinmarketing.com	Minneapolis	MN	55405	612-374-1200	
Bon Advertising Inc 307 W Muhammad Ali Blvd *Web:* www.bch.com	Louisville	KY	40202	502-589-7711	
Bond Group The Inc 2419 N Ashland Ave *Web:* www.bondgrp.com	Chicago	IL	60614	773-549-2710	
BOONE|OAKLEY 101 W Worthington Ave Suit 200 *Web:* booneoakley.com	Charlotte	NC	28203	704-333-9797	
Boscobel Marketing Communications Inc 8606 Second ave *Web:* www.boscobel.com	Silver Spring	MD	20910	301-588-2900	
Bradshaw Advertising 811 Nw 19th Ave *Web:* bradshawads.com	Portland	OR	97209	503-221-5000	
Brand Innovation Group 8902 Airport Dr Pyramid Plza Ste A *Web:* www.gotobig.com	Fort Wayne	IN	46809	260-469-4060	
Brand Launcher Inc 4703 Falls Rd *Web:* www.brandlauncher.com	Baltimore	MD	21209	410-235-7070	
BrandingBusiness Inc One Wrigley *Web:* www.brandingbusiness.com	Irvine	CA	92618	949-273-6330	

Company / Address	City	State	Zip	Phone	Fax
Brandon Advertising 3023 Church St	Myrtle Beach	SC	29577	843-916-2000	
Web: www.thebrandonagency.com					
Brandspring Solutions LLC 14500 Martin Dr Ste 1000	Eden Prairie	MN	55344	952-345-7260	
Web: www.brandspringsolutions.com					
Brandt Ronat & Co 60 Mcleod St	Merritt Island	FL	32953	321-453-3101	
Web: brc60.com					
Brandtailers 17838 Fitch	Irvine	CA	92614	949-442-0500	
Web: www.brandtailers.com					
Bravado International Group Merchandising Services Inc 1755 Broadway 2nd Fl	New York	NY	10019	212-445-3400	
Web: www.bravadousa.com					
Brogan Tennyson Group Inc 2245 US Hwy 130 Ste 102	Dayton	NJ	08810	732-355-0700	
Web: www.brogantennyson.com					
BROOKSLACAYO Advertising Branding and Public Relations 7825 Baymeadows Way Ste 101-A	Jacksonville	FL	32256	904-636-5085	
Web: www.brookslacayo.com					
Brownstein Group Inc 215 S Broad St	Philadelphia	PA	19107	215-735-3470	
Web: m.brownsteingroup.com					
Brunet-Garcia Advertising Inc 1510 Hendricks Ave	Jacksonville	FL	32207	904-346-1977	
TF: 866-346-1977 ■ *Web:* www.brunetgarcia.com					
Brunner Inc 11 Stanwix St 5th Fl	Pittsburgh	PA	15222	412-995-9500	
Web: www.brunnerworks.com					
Brush Art Corp 343 W Us Hwy 24	Downs	KS	67437	785-454-3383	
Web: www.brushart.com					
Burdette Ketchum 1023 Kings Ave	Jacksonville	FL	32207	904-645-6200	
Web: www.burdetteketchum.com					
Burkhart Advertising Inc 1335 Mishawaka Ave	South Bend	IN	46615	574-233-2101	
Web: www.burkhartadv.com					
Business Direct Inc 5620 Old Bullard Rd Ste 128	Tyler	TX	75703	888-580-7799	
TF: 888-580-7799					
Butler Shine Stern & Partners 20 Liberty Ship Way	Sausalito	CA	94965	415-331-6049	331-3524
Web: bssp.com					
BVK Inc 250 W Coventry Ct Ste 300	Milwaukee	WI	53217	414-228-1990	
Web: www.bvk.com					
C L Graphics Inc 134 Virginia Rd Ste A	Crystal Lake	IL	60014	815-455-0900	
Web: www.clgraphics.com					
C2 Imaging LLC 274 Fillmore Ave E	Saint Paul	MN	55107	646-557-6300	
Web: www.c2imagingllc.com					
Cabello Associates 8340 Little Eagle Ct Ste 200	Indianapolis	IN	46234	317-209-9991	
Web: www.cabelloassociates.com					
Campus Media Group Inc 2 Appletree Sq 4th Fl	Bloomington	MN	55425	952-854-3100	
Web: www.campusmediagroup.com					
Cannonball Advertising & Promotion 8251 Maryland Ave Ste 200	Saint Louis	MO	63105	314-445-6400	
Web: www.cannonballagency.com					
Carrera & Partners Inc 388 SW 12th Ave	Deerfield Beach	FL	33442	954-360-9111	
Web: www.carreraadvertising.com					
Carson Group Advertising, The 1708 Hwy 6 S	Houston	TX	77077	281-496-2600	
Web: www.carsongroupadvertising.com					
Cartis Group 3011 N Lamar	Austin	TX	78705	512-476-2600	
Web: carterstrategy.com					
Casanova Pendrill Publicidad Inc 275-A McCormick Ave Ste 100	Costa Mesa	CA	92626	714-918-8200	
Web: casanova.com					
Catalpha Advertising & Design Inc 6801 Loch Raven Blvd	Towson	MD	21286	410-337-0066	
Web: www.catalpha.com					
Catalyst Direct Inc 110 Marina Dr	Rochester	NY	14626	585-453-8300	
Web: www.catalystinc.com					
Catral Doyle Creative Co 231 E Buffalo St Ste 301	Milwaukee	WI	53202	414-276-3075	
Web: www.cdcreative.com					
Central Address Systems Inc 10303 Crown Point Ave	Omaha	NE	68134	402-964-9998	
Web: www.cas-online.com					
ChemPetitive Group, The 657 W Lake St 5th Fl	Chicago	IL	60661	312-997-2436	
Web: chempetitive.com					
Cheryl Andrews Marketing Communications 331 Almeria Ave	Coral Gables	FL	33134	305-444-4033	
Web: www.cam-pr.com					
Cheshire Center Pediatric Comm 2500 N Church St	Greensboro	NC	27405	336-375-2240	
Web: www.cheshirecenter.net					
ChoiceStream Inc 25 Drydock Ave Fifth Fl	Boston	MA	02210	617-498-7800	
Web: www.choicestream.com					
Chrisad Inc 11 Professional Ctr Pkwy	San Rafael	CA	94903	415-924-8575	
TF: 800-505-4150 ■ *Web:* www.chrisad.com					
Chuck Thomas Creative Inc 214 W River Dr	Saint Charles	IL	60174	630-587-6000	
Web: ctcreative.com					
Chumney & Associates 660 US-1 Ste 2	North Palm Beach	FL	33408	561-882-0066	
Web: chumneyads.com					
Circle s Studio LLC 201 W Seventh St	Richmond	VA	23224	804-232-2908	
Web: www.circlesstudio.com					
City of Com, The 1559 S Brownlee Blvd	Corpus Christi	TX	78404	888-785-0500	
TF: 888-785-0500 ■ *Web:* cityof.com					
CKR Interactive Inc 399 NThird St	Campbell	CA	95008	408-517-1400	
Web: www.ckrinteractive.com					
Clear Agency, The 290 MLK St N Ste 203	St. Petersburg	FL	33705	727-289-7204	
Web: www.theclearagency.com					
ClickCulture Inc 9121 Anson Way Ste 200	Raleigh	NC	27615	919-420-7736	
Web: www.clickculture.com					
CMG Worldwide Inc 10500 Crosspoint Blvd	Indianapolis	IN	46256	317-570-5000	
Web: www.cmgworldwide.com					
Cmsa Inc 2142 Alt 19 Ste A	Palm Harbor	FL	34683	727-447-3396	
Web: www.cmsa.com					
Colangelo Synergy Marketing Inc 120 Tokeneke Rd	Darien	CT	06820	203-662-6600	
Web: www.colangelo-sm.com					
Cold Open Inc 1313 Innes Pl	Venice	CA	90291	310-399-3307	
Web: www.coldopen.com					
Colsky Media 2740 Van Ness Ave Ste 220	San Francisco	CA	94109	415-673-5400	
Web: www.colskymedia.com					
Commission Junction Inc 530 E Montecito St	Santa Barbara	CA	93103	805-730-8000	730-8001
TF: 800-761-1072 ■ *Web:* www.cj.com					
Compass Marketing Inc 222 Severn Ave Building 14 Ste 200	Annapolis	MD	21403	410-268-0030	
Web: www.compassmarketinginc.com					
Concerto Marketing Group Inc 128 Hastings St W	Vancouver	BC	V6B1G8	604-684-8933	
TF: 877-873-2738 ■ *Web:* www.concertomarketing.com					
Concussion LLP 707 W Vickery Blvd #103	Fort Worth	TX	76104	817-336-6824	
Web: www.pavlovagency.com					
Confluent Translations LLC 340 Mansfield Ave	Pittsburgh	PA	15220	412-539-1410	
TF: 888-539-9077 ■ *Web:* www.confluenttranslations.com					
Conroy Media Ltd 6713 Kingery Hwy	Willowbrook	IL	60527	630-920-7800	
Web: conroymedialtd.squarespace.com					
Conway Marketing Communications 6400 Baum Dr	Knoxville	TN	37919	865-588-5731	
TF: 800-882-7875 ■ *Web:* www.conwaymktg.com					
Copia Creative Inc 3122 Santa Monica Blvd Ste 203	Santa Monica	CA	90404	310-826-7422	
Web: www.copiacreative.com					
Core Twelve Inc 600 W Van Buren #1010	Chicago	IL	60607	312-274-1270	
Web: www.core12.com					
Creative Outdoor Advertising 2402 Stouffville Rd	Gormley	ON	L0H1G0	800-661-6088	
TF: 800-661-6088 ■ *Web:* www.creativeoutdoor.com					
Cronin & Company LLC 50 Nye Rd	Glastonbury	CT	06033	860-659-0514	
Web: www.cronin-co.com					
Crosby Marketing Communications Inc The Crosby Bldg 705 Melvin Ave Ste 200	Annapolis	MD	21401	410-626-0805	
Web: www.crosbymarketing.com					
Crosby-Wright 5907 N Rocking Rd	Scottsdale	AZ	85250	480-367-1112	
Web: www.crosby-wright.com					
Cross Agency, The 8133 Baymeadows Way	Jacksonville	FL	32256	904-642-8902	
Web: thecrossagency.com					
Crouch Group Inc, The 300 N Carroll Blvd Ste 103	Denton	TX	76201	940-383-1990	
TF: 888-211-0273 ■ *Web:* thecrouchgroup.com					
customedialabs 460 E Swedesford Rd Ste 2020	Wayne	PA	19087	610-225-0350	
Web: www.customedialabs.com					
Customer Magnetism Inc 2697 Intl Pkwy 1 Ste 201	Virginia Beach	VA	23452	757-689-2875	
Web: www.customermagnetism.com					
Cyphers Agency Inc, The 53 Old Solomons Is Rd Ste G	Annapolis	MD	21401	888-412-7469	
TF: 888-412-7469 ■ *Web:* thecyphersagency.com					
D M 2 Design Consultancy 100 Challenger Rd Ste 306	Ridgefield Park	NJ	07660	201-840-8910	
Web: thinkdm2.com					
D&S Creative Communications Inc 140 Park Ave E	Mansfield	OH	44902	419-524-4312	
Web: www.blackriverdisplay.com					
D2 Creative 28 World's Fair Dr	Somerset	NJ	08873	732-507-7300	
Web: www.d2creative.com					
Dailey Marketing Group Inc 29829 Santa Margarita Pkwy Ste 100	Rancho Santa Margarita	CA	92688	949-454-0751	
TF: 888-364-6584 ■ *Web:* www.daileymarketing.com					
Daniels & Roberts Inc 209 N Seacrest Blvd Ste 2	Boynton Beach	FL	33435	561-241-0066	
TF: 800-488-0066 ■ *Web:* www.danielsandroberts.com					
Datamine Internet Marketing Solutions Inc 330 S Lake St	Gary	IN	46403	219-939-9987	
TF: 877-328-2646 ■ *Web:* www.datamine.net					
Davco Advertising Inc 89 N Kinzer Rd PO Box 288	Kinzers	PA	17535	717-442-4155	
TF: 800-283-2826 ■ *Web:* davcoadvertising.com					
Davie Brown Entertainment Inc 2225 S Carmelina Ave	Los Angeles	CA	90064	310-979-1980	
Web: www.daviebrown.com					
Dayner Hall Marketing & Advertising 621 E Pine St	Orlando	FL	32801	407-428-5750	
Web: www.daynerhall.com					
DCG ONE 5501 Cass Ave	Cleveland	OH	44102	216-281-2866	
Web: www.directconnectgroup.com					
De La Cruz & Associates Metro Office Park, St 1 #9, Ste 201	Guyanabo	PR	00968	787-622-4141	
Web: www.delacruz.com					
Decker Advertising 99 Citizens Dr	Glastonbury	CT	06033	860-659-1311	
Web: www.deckerdoesit.com					
Definition 6 LLC 2115 Monroe Dr Ste 100	Atlanta	GA	30324	404-870-0323	
Web: www.definition6.com					
Denmark Group Inc, The 6285 Barfield Rd NE Ste 200	Atlanta	GA	30328	404-256-3681	
Web: www.denmarktheagency.com					
DeSantis Breindel Inc 30 W 21 St	New York	NY	10010	212-994-7680	
Web: www.desantisbreindel.com					
Designsensory Inc 1740 Commons Point Dr Centerpoint Commons Bldg 1	Knoxville	TN	37932	865-690-2249	
Web: www.designsensory.com					
Dexter Hospitality Inc 3493 Lamar Ave	Memphis	TN	38118	901-365-4742	
Web: dexterhospitality.com					
Dhx Advertising Inc 217 Ne Eighth Ave	Portland	OR	97232	503-872-9616	
Web: www.dhxadv.com					
Dicom Inc 1650 Des Peres Rd Ste 100	St. Louis	MO	63131	314-909-0900	
Web: dicominc.com					

				Phone	Fax
Digital Lightbridge LLC 11902 Little Rd . . . . New Port Richey *Web:* www.digitallightbridge.com	FL	34654		727-863-7806	
Digital Pulp Inc 220 E 23rd St Ste 900 . . . . New York *Web:* www.digitalpulp.com	NY	10010		212-679-0676	679-6217
Dinkel r a & Associates Inc 4641 Willoughby Rd . . . . Holt *Web:* ideasideas.com	MI	48842		517-699-7000	
Direct Choice 480 E Swedesford Rd Ste 210 . . . . Wayne *Web:* www.directchoiceinc.com	PA	19087		610-995-8201	
Direct Partners Inc 4755 Alla Rd . . . . Marina Del Rey *Web:* www.directpartners.com	CA	90292		310-482-4200	
Discover Mediaworks Inc 5236 Hwy 70 W . . . . Eagle River *Web:* discovermediaworks.com	WI	54521		715-477-1500	
Dky Inc 6009 Penn Ave S . . . . Minneapolis *Web:* dkyinc.com	MN	55419		612-798-4070	
Dogwood Productions Inc 757 Government St . . . . Mobile *TF:* 800-254-9903 ■ *Web:* www.dogwoodproductions.com	AL	36602		251-476-0858	
Donahue Purohit Miller 1 Speedwell Ave . . . . Morristown *Web:* cpeducate.com	NJ	07960		973-644-5055	
Donovan Advertising & Marketing Services 180 W Airport Rd, P.O. Box 5423 . . . . Lititz *Web:* www.donovanadv.com	PA	17543		717-560-1333	
DoublePositive Marketing Group Inc 1501 S Clinton St Ste 1520 . . . . Baltimore *Web:* www.doublepositive.com	MD	21224		410-332-0464	
Downtown Partners Chicago 200 E Randolph St Ste 3400 . . . . Chicago *Web:* www.downtownpartners.com	IL	60601		312-552-5800	
Dreamentia Inc 453 S Spring St Ste 1101 . . . . Los Angeles *Web:* www.dreamentia.com	CA	90013		213-347-6000	
E t Mktg. Solutions Ltd 207-3833 Henning Dr . . . . Burnaby *Web:* www.etmarketingsolutions.com	BC	V5C6N5		604-801-6168	
Eagle Direct LLC 635 Commerce Dr . . . . Upper Marlboro *Web:* www.eagledirects.com	MD	20774		301-390-3700	
eCreative Group Inc 2349 Jamestown Ave . . . . Independence *Web:* www.ecreativegroup.com	IA	50644		319-334-5115	
Eleven Inc 445 Bush St . . . . San Francisco *Web:* www.eleveninc.com	CA	94108		415-707-1111	
Elkins Retail Advertising Inc 6040 Hellyer Ave Ste 100 . . . . San Jose *Web:* elkinsadvertising.com	CA	95138		408-249-1411	
Ellison Advertising 3410 Se 20th Ave . . . . Portland *Web:* www.ellisonadvertising.com	OR	97202		503-236-8400	
Ellison Media Co 14804 N Cave Creek Rd . . . . Phoenix *Web:* www.ellisonmedia.com	AZ	85032		602-404-4000	
Emisare Inc 620 S Elm St Ste 332 . . . . Greensboro *Web:* www.emisare.com	NC	27406		336-378-0510	
Epicenter Network Inc 3500 188th St SW Ste 480 . . . . Lynnwood *Web:* www.epicenter.net	WA	98037		425-744-1474	
Ervin & Smith Advertising & Public Relations Inc 16934 Frances St . . . . Omaha *Web:* www.ervinandsmith.com	NE	68130		402-334-6969	
Esrock Recruitment Advertising 14550 S 94th Ave . . . . Orland Park *Web:* www.esrock.com	IL	60462		708-349-8400	
Everett Studios Inc 5 N Greenwich Rd . . . . Armonk *Web:* www.goeverett.com	NY	10504		914-997-2200	
Evins Communications Ltd 635 Madison Ave . . . . New York *Web:* www.evins.com	NY	10022		212-688-8200	
Evo Exhibits 399 Wegner Dr . . . . West Chicago *TF:* 888-404-4224 ■ *Web:* www.evoexhibits.com	IL	60185		630-520-0710	
Evok Advertising Inc 2500 Kunze Ave . . . . Orlando *Web:* www.evokad.com	FL	32806		407-302-4416	
Evolve Media Inc 175 N Indian Hill Blvd Ste B 200 . . . . Claremont *Web:* www.evolvemedia.tv	CA	91711		714-528-1133	
Exl Media Corp 803 Tahoe Blvd Ste 7 . . . . Incline Village *Web:* www.exlmedia.com	NV	89451		775-832-0202	
Expert Communications Inc 394 Pacific Ave . . . . San Francisco *Web:* www.eciww.com	CA	94111		415-981-9900	
ExpoPlus 1055 Research Ctr Atlanta Dr Sw . . . . Atlanta *Web:* www.expoplus.com	GA	30331		404-699-0650	
Extreme Communications Ltd 47 Fraser Ave N Entrance 2nd Fl . . . . Toronto *Web:* www.extremegroup.com	ON	M6K1Y7		416-607-6665	
Extreme Packing Solutions 5 Dodge St . . . . Beverly *Web:* extremepackingsolutions.com	MA	01915		978-232-9190	
Eyecon Marketing Group 6738 Jamestown Dr . . . . Alpharetta *Web:* www.eyeconmktg.com	GA	30005		770-752-0043	
F p i s Inc 220 Story Rd . . . . Ocoee *TF:* 800-346-5977 ■ *Web:* www.fpis.com	FL	34761		407-656-8818	
Faction Media LLP 1730 Blake St Ste 200 . . . . Denver *TF:* 866-788-5306 ■ *Web:* www.factionmedia.com	CO	80202		866-788-5306	
Factory Design Labs 1037 Broadway Ste B . . . . Denver *Web:* www.factorylabs.com	CO	80203		303-573-9100	
Fairly Painless Advertising Inc 44 E 8th St . . . . Holland *Web:* fairlypainless.com	MI	49423		616-394-5900	
Flourish Inc 1001 Huron Rd E Ste 102 . . . . Cleveland *Web:* www.freddiegeorges.com	OH	44115		216-696-9116	
Foster Marketing LLC 3909-F Ambassador Caffery . . . . Lafayette *Web:* www.fostermarketing.com	LA	70503		337-235-1848	
Foundry 9 LLC 44 W 28th St 6th Fl . . . . New York *Web:* www.foundry9.com	NY	10001		212-989-7999	
Freed Advertising LP 1650 Hwy 6 Ste 400 . . . . Sugar Land *Web:* www.freedad.com	TX	77478		281-240-4949	
Furman Roth Advertising 801 2nd Ave Rm 1400 . . . . New York *Web:* www.furmanroth.com	NY	10017		212-687-2300	
Fuse Inc 802 N First St . . . . St. Louis *Web:* www.fuseadvertising.com	MO	63102		314-421-4040	
FUSION b2b Inc 1548 Bond St Ste 114 . . . . Naperville *Web:* www.fusionb2b.com	IL	60563		630-579-8300	
Fusionary Media 220 Grandville SW . . . . Grand Rapids *Web:* www.fusionary.com	MI	49503		616-454-2357	
Fusionbox Inc 2031 Curtis St . . . . Denver *Web:* www.fusionbox.com	CO	80205		303-952-7490	
Gabriel deGrood Bendt LLC 608 Second Ave S Ste 129 . . . . Minneapolis *Web:* www.gdbagency.com	MN	55402		612-547-5000	
Garrigan Lyman Group Inc, The 1524 Fifth Ave Ste 400 . . . . Seattle *Web:* www.glg.com	WA	98101		206-223-5548	
Gary Stock Co 597 Rt 22 . . . . Brewster *Web:* www.gstockco.com	NY	10509		914-276-2700	
Gateway Design Inc 4299 San Felipe St Ste 100 . . . . Houston *Web:* www.gatewaydesign.com	TX	77027		713-572-9600	
Gauger & Associates 360 Post St Ste 901 . . . . San Francisco *Web:* www.gauger-associates.com	CA	94108		415-434-0303	
Gay Ad Network 1628 Ne 17th Way . . . . Ft Lauderdale *Web:* gayadnetwork.com	FL	33305		954-485-9910	
Gbsa Inc 2710 N ave . . . . Bridgeport *TF:* 800-544-0005 ■ *Web:* www.graystoneadv.com	CT	06604		203-549-0060	
Gift Card Partners Inc 47 pine plain rd . . . . Wellesley Hills *Web:* www.giftcardpartners.com	MA	02481		781-237-1742	
Giovatto Advertising & Consulting Inc 95 New Jersey 17 . . . . Paramus *Web:* www.giovatto.com	NJ	07652		201-226-9700	
Global TV Concepts Ltd 676 S Military Trl . . . . Deerfield Beach *Web:* www.globaltvconcepts.com	FL	33442		954-570-9999	
Global Village Marketing & Data Services Inc 2710 Thomes Ave . . . . Cheyenne *Web:* www.globalvillagemktg.com	WY	82001		307-222-4135	
Gorrie Marketing Services 2770 Matheson Blvd E . . . . Mississauga *Web:* www.gorrie.com	ON	L4W4M5		416-760-9100	
Grafik Marketing Communications Ltd 625 N Washington St Ste 302 . . . . Alexandria *Web:* www.grafik.com	VA	22314		703-299-4500	
Gragg Advertising Inc 450 E Fourth St Ste 100 . . . . Kansas City *Web:* www.graggadv.com	MO	64106		816-931-0050	
Graham Communications 40 Oval Rd . . . . Quincy *Web:* www.grahamcomm.com	MA	02170		617-328-0069	
Grapevine Communications International Inc 5201 Paylor Ln . . . . Sarasota *Web:* www.grapeinc.com	FL	34240		941-351-0024	
Grapevine Media & Marketing 1055 E Colorado Blvd Fl 5 . . . . Pasadena *Web:* www.gmmla.com	CA	91101		626-240-4667	
Gray & Associates Diversity Advertising & Public Relations Inc 2677 Tritt Springs Trce Ne . . . . Marietta *Web:* www.grayassoc.net	GA	30062		678-560-9272	
Greenhaus Inc 2660 First Ave . . . . San Diego *Web:* greenhaus.com	CA	92103		619-744-4024	
Grey Matter Group Inc 131 Division Ave S Ste 300 . . . . Grand Rapids *Web:* greymattergroup.com	MI	49503		616-458-8750	
Grip Ltd 179 John St 6th Fl . . . . Toronto *Web:* www.griplimited.com	ON	M5T1X4		416-340-7111	
Grupo Gallegos 401 E Ocean Blvd 6th Fl . . . . Long Beach *Web:* www.grupogallegos.com	CA	90802		562-256-3600	
Grupo Uno Intl 2199 Ponce De Leon Blvd Fl 5 . . . . Coral Gables *Web:* www.grupouno.com	FL	33134		305-448-6111	
Hacker Group Inc 1215 Fourth Ave Ste 2100 . . . . Seattle *Web:* hal2l.com	WA	98161		206-805-1500	805-1599
Hanser & Associates Public Relations 4401 Westown Pkwy Ste 212 . . . . West Des Moines *Web:* www.hanser.com	IA	50266		515-224-1086	
Harmonic International LLC 10 E Lee St Ste 2704 . . . . Baltimore *Web:* www.harmonicinternational.com	MD	21202		410-727-3554	
Harrison & Shriftman 141 W 36th St 12th Fl . . . . New York *Web:* www.hs-pr.com	NY	10018		917-351-8600	
Hart-Boillot LLC 134 Rumford Ave Ste 307 . . . . Newton *Web:* www.hbagency.com	MA	02466		781-893-0053	
Harvey & Daughters Inc 952 Ridgebrook Rd . . . . Sparks Glencoe *Web:* www.harveyagency.com	MD	21152		410-771-5566	
Helgeson Enterprises Inc 4461 White Bear Pkwy . . . . White Bear Lake	MN	55110		651-762-9700	
Hellman Associates Inc 1225 W Fourth St PO Box 627 . . . . Waterloo *Web:* www.hellman.com	IA	50704		319-234-7055	
HelloWorld 3000 Town center ste 2100 . . . . South Field *TF:* 877-837-7493 ■ *Web:* www.helloworld.com	MI	48075		877-837-7493	
Hightower Advertising Agency 1624 60th St . . . . Garrison *Web:* www.hightoweragency.com	IA	52229		319-477-6070	
Hitchcock Fleming & Associates Inc 500 Wolf Ledges Pkwy . . . . Akron *Web:* www.teamhfa.com	OH	44311		330-376-2111	
Hobbs Herder 2240 University Dr . . . . Newport Beach *Web:* www.hobbsherder.com	CA	92660		949-515-5000	
Hodges and Associates 2829 2nd Ave S Ste 300 . . . . Birmingham *Web:* hodgesusa.com	AL	35233		205-328-4357	
Hoffman G W Inc 757 Post Rd . . . . Darien *Web:* www.gwhoffman.com	CT	06820		203-655-8321	
HotLink Inc 2700 Oakmont Dr . . . . Round Rock *Web:* www.hotlink.com	TX	78665		512-491-7500	

Company / Address	City	State	Zip	Phone	Fax
Hub Strategy & Communication 39 Mesa St Ste 212 *Web:* hubsanfrancisco.com	San Francisco	CA	94129	415-561-4345	
Humongo 155 Main St 4th Fl *Web:* www.humongoagency.com	Danbury	CT	06810	203-730-6300	
Hunt Adkins Inc 15 S 5th St Ste 300 *Web:* www.huntadkins.com	Minneapolis	MN	55402	612-339-8003	
HY Connect 1000 N Water St Ste 1600 *Web:* www.hoffmanyork.com	Milwaukee	WI	53202	312-787-2330	
Hyperquake LLC 205 W Fourth St Ste 1010 *Web:* www.hyperquake.com	Cincinnati	OH	45202	513-563-6555	
IBIS Communications 1024 17th Ave South *Web:* www.ibiscommunications.com	Nashville	TN	37212	615-777-1900	
Ice Worldwide Llc 155 Fleet St *Web:* www.iceworldwide.com	Portsmouth	NH	03801	978-707-2000	
Idea Lab Marketing 7 E Main St Ste 100 *Web:* www.idealabmarketing.com	Moorestown	NJ	08057	856-642-0007	
Ideaology Advertising Inc 4223 Glencoe Ave Ste A127 *Web:* www.ideaology.biz	Marina Del Rey	CA	90292	310-306-6501	
Ideaworks 1110 N Palafox St *Web:* ideaworks.co	Pensacola	FL	32501	850-434-9095	
Identity Group, The 505 N Tustin Ave Ste 234 *Web:* theidgroup.com	Santa Ana	CA	92705	714-573-0010	
Ignited LLC 2221 Park Pl *Web:* ignitedusa.com	El Segundo	CA	90245	310-773-3100	
Images Usa 1320 Ellsworth Industrial Blvd *Web:* www.imagesusa.net	Atlanta	GA	30318	404-892-2931	
Imtek Inc 2075 High Hill Rd *Web:* www.imtek.com	Bridgeport	NJ	08014	856-467-0047	
inferno LLC 505 Tennessee St Ste 108 *Web:* www.creativeinferno.com	Memphis	TN	38103	901-278-3773	
Inside Ideas Inc 49 Broadway St Ste 203 *Web:* www.thegossagency.com	Asheville	NC	28801	828-225-6888	
Intech Direct 105 E Marquardt Dr *Web:* intechdirect.com	Wheeling	IL	60090	847-850-5999	
Integra Marketing Group 1000 5th Ave *Web:* www.integramarketinggroup.com	Beaver Falls	PA	15010	724-843-8844	
Interbrand Design Forum LLC 7575 Paragon Rd *Web:* www.interbranddesignforum.com	Dayton	OH	45459	937-439-4400	
Interlex Communications 4005 Broadway St *Web:* www.interlexusa.com	San Antonio	TX	78209	210-930-3339	
Interline Creative Group 553 North N Ct Ste 160 *Web:* www.interlinegroup.com	Palatine	IL	60067	847-358-4848	
Internet Matrix Inc 10179 Huennekens St *TF:* 800-462-8749 ■ *Web:* www.imatrix.com	San Diego	CA	92121	800-462-8749	
Introworks Inc 13911 Ridgedale Dr Ste 280 *Web:* introworks.net	Minnetonka	MN	55305	952-593-1800	
IOMEDIA Inc 91 Fifth Ave Fourth Fl *Web:* www.io-media.com	New York	NY	10003	212-352-1115	
Ion Design Inc 948 7th Ave W *Web:* www.iondesign.ca	Vancouver	BC	V5Z1C3	604-682-6787	
IZEA Inc 480 N Orlando Ave Ste 200 *Web:* www.izea.com	Winter Park	FL	32789	407-674-6911	
J & L Mail Services Inc 2100 Nelson Miller Pkwy *Web:* www.jandlmarketing.com	Louisville	KY	40223	502-261-9292	
J e b Advertising Inc 616 E Market St Ste 618 *Web:* www.jebadvertising.com	Louisville	KY	40202	502-625-1800	
J m Fox Associates Inc 616 Dekalb St *Web:* jmfox.com	Norristown	PA	19401	610-275-5957	
Jackson Marketing Group Inc 2 Task Industrial Ct *Web:* www.jacksonmg.com	Greenville	SC	29650	864-272-3000	
Jacobs Agency Inc 430 W Erie St Ste 403 *Web:* www.jacobsagency.com	Chicago	IL	60610	312-664-5000	
Jacobson Rost Inc 233 N Water St Ste 6	Milwaukee	WI	53202	414-220-4888	
Jajo Inc 131 N Rock Island *Web:* www.jajo.agency	Wichita	KS	67202	316-267-6700	
Jarrard Phillips Cate & Hancock Inc 219 Ward Cir *TF:* 888-844-6274 ■ *Web:* www.jarrardinc.com	Brentwood	TN	37027	312-419-0575	
Jay Advertising Inc 170 Linden Oaks *Web:* www.jayww.com	Rochester	NY	14625	585-264-3600	
Jayray Ads & Pr Inc 535 Dock St Ste 205 *Web:* www.jayray.com	Tacoma	WA	98402	253-627-9128	
Jdm & Associates Marketing Llc 3405 Park Pl *Web:* www.jdmandassociates.com	Evanston	IL	60201	847-570-9100	
Jeffrey Scott Agency Inc 670 P St *Web:* jsaweb.com	Fresno	CA	93721	559-268-9741	
Jibe Media Llc 774 South 300 West Unit B *Web:* jibemedia.com	Salt Lake City	UT	84101	801-433-5423	
Jobelephantcom Inc 5443 Fremontia Ln *TF:* 800-311-0563 ■ *Web:* www.jobelephant.com	San Diego	CA	92115	619-795-0837	
Johannes Leonardo LLC 95 Morton St 8th Fl *Web:* www.johannesleonardo.com	New York	NY	10014	212-462-8111	
John St 172 John St *Web:* www.johnst.com	Toronto	ON	M5T1X5	416-348-0048	
Jordan Associates Inc 3201 Quail Springs Pkwy Ste 100 *Web:* www.jordanet.com	Oklahoma City	OK	73134	405-840-3201	
JT Mega 4020 Minnetonka Blvd *TF:* 800-923-6342 ■ *Web:* www.jtmega.com	Minneapolis	MN	55416	952-929-1370	
Juice Studios 1648 10th St *Web:* www.juicestudios.tv	Santa Monica	CA	90404	310-460-7830	
Jumboshrimp Advertising Inc 544 Bryant St *Web:* www.jumboshrimp.com	San Francisco	CA	94107	415-369-0500	
Kastner & Partners 150 Pico Blvd *Web:* www.kastnernetwork.us	Santa Monica	CA	90405	310-458-2000	
Kathy Floam Pomerantz Agency 914 Bay Ridge Rd Ste 180 *Web:* www.pomagency.com	Annapolis	MD	21403	410-216-9447	
Kelley Advertising Co 818 Fulton St *Web:* kellyadvertising.com	Fort Wayne	OK	46802	260-426-1843	
Klondike Advertising Specialty House 1900 w benson blvd *Web:* www.klondikeadv.com	Anchorage	AK	99517	907-274-3535	
Knoodle Sales & Marketing Corp 4450 N 12th St Ste 120 *Web:* www.knoodleshop.com	Phoenix	AZ	85014	602-530-9900	
Knupp & Watson Inc 5201 Old Middleton Rd *Web:* knupp-watson.com	Madison	WI	53705	608-232-2300	
Koeppel Direct Inc 16200 Dallas Pkwy Ste 270 *Web:* koeppeldirect.com	Dallas	TX	75248	972-732-6110	
KPS3 Inc 50 W Liberty St Ste 640 *Web:* kps3.com	Reno	NV	89501	775-686-7439	
Kuhn & Wittenborn Advertising 2405 Grand Blvd *Web:* kuhnwitt.com	Kansas City	MO	64108	816-471-7888	
Kutoka Interactive Inc 225 Roy E Ste 100 *TF:* 877-858-8652 ■ *Web:* www.kutoka.com	Montreal	QC	H2W1M5	514-849-4800	
Labov & Beyond Inc 609 E Cook Rd *Web:* labov.com	Fort Wayne	IN	46825	260-497-0111	
LaneTerralever LLC 725 W McDowell rd *Web:* www.eblane.com	Phoenix	AZ	85007	602-258-5263	
Lapiz Hispanic Marketing 35 W Wacker Dr Fl Twelve *Web:* www.lapizusa.com	Chicago	IL	60601	312-220-5000	
Lattimer Communications Inc 934 glenwood ave se *Web:* www.lattimercommunications.com	Atlanta	GA	30316	404-526-9321	
Lavidge Co, The 2777 E Camelback Rd Ste 300 *Web:* www.lavidge.com	Phoenix	AZ	85016	480-998-2600	
Lazbro Inc 12840 Bonaparte Ave *Web:* www.lazbro.com	Los Angeles	CA	90066	310-989-6111	
Lead Pulse Media 3535 hayden ave *Web:* www.leadpulsemedia.com	Culver City	CA	90232	310-439-2334	
LeapFrog Solutions Inc 3201 Jermantown Rd Ste 350 *Web:* www.leapfrogit.com	Fairfax	VA	22030	703-273-7900	
Leone Advertising 2024 Santa Cruz Ave *Web:* leonead.com	Menlo Park	CA	94025	650-854-5895	
Leopold Ketel & Partners 112 SW First Ave *Web:* www.leoketel.com	Portland	OR	97204	503-295-1918	
LePoidevin Rickinger Group, The 245 S Executive Dr Ste 365 *Web:* www.thelrgroup.com	Brookfield	WI	53005	262-754-9550	
Les Howe Associates Inc 41 W High St *Web:* www.leshoweassociates.com	East Hampton	CT	06424	860-267-6651	
Lewis Advertising Inc 1050 Country Club Rd *Web:* www.lewisadvertising.com	Rocky Mount	NC	27802	252-443-5131	
LHWH Advertising & Public Relations 3005 Hwy 17 N Bypass *Web:* www.lhwh.com	Myrtle Beach	SC	29577	843-448-1123	
LiveWorld Inc 4340 Stevens Creek Blvd Ste 101 *Web:* www.liveworld.com	San Jose	CA	95129	408-871-5200	
Lkh & s 54 W Hubbard St Ste 100 *Web:* www.lkhs.com	Chicago	IL	60654	312-595-0200	
Lmi Advertising 24e E Roseville Rd *Web:* lmiadvertising.com	Lancaster	PA	17601	717-569-8826	
Lockard & Wechsler Inc 2 Bridge St Ste 200 *Web:* www.lwdirect.com	Irvington	NY	10533	914-591-6600	
Loomis Agency LLC, The 17120 Dallas Pkwy Ste 200 *Web:* www.theloomisagency.com	Dallas	TX	75248	972-331-7000	
Lopez Marketing Group Inc 11169 La Quinta Pl *Web:* www.lopezgroup.com	El Paso	TX	79936	915-772-8018	
Lyon Advertising 600 Escarpment Blvd 745 28 *Web:* www.lyonadvertising.com	Austin	TX	78749	512-480-5966	
M&C Saatchi LA Inc 2032 Broadway *Web:* mcsaatchi-la.com	Santa Monica	CA	90404	310-401-6070	
Mack Sign Advertising 893 Main St *Web:* www.battensign.com	Wakefield	MA	01880	617-387-1010	
MacKinnon Calderwood Advertising Inc 1555 Dundas St W *Web:* www.mackinnoncalderwood.com	Mississauga	ON	L5C1E3	905-281-6146	
Macquarium Intelligent Communications 1800 Peachtree St NW Ste 250 *Web:* www.macquarium.com	Atlanta	GA	30309	404-554-4000	554-4001
Macrovision Inc 301 S Main St Ste 3w *Web:* www.macrovis.com	Doylestown	PA	18901	215-348-1010	
Mad 4 Marketing Inc 5255 NW 33rd Ave *Web:* www.mad4marketing.com	Fort Lauderdale	FL	33309	954-485-5448	
Maddock Douglas Inc 111 Adell Pl *Web:* www.maddockdouglas.com	Elmhurst	IL	60126	630-279-3939	
MadeToOrder 1244-A Quarry Ln *Web:* www.madetoorder.com	Pleasanton	CA	94566	925-484-0600	
Madwire Media LLC 550 W Eisenhower Blvd *Web:* www.madwiremedia.com	Loveland	CO	80537	970-663-7635	
Magna Group Inc, The 17-17 Rt 208 N *Web:* www.themagnagroup.com	Fair Lawn	NJ	07410	201-652-8600	
Magner Sanborn 111 N Post Ste 400 *Web:* www.magnersanborn.com	Spokane	WA	99201	509-688-2200	
Mallof, Abruzino & Nash Marketing 765 Kimberly Dr *Web:* www.manmarketing.com	Carol Stream	IL	60188	630-929-5200	
Mambo Sprouts Marketing Corp 923 Haddonfield Rd Ste 300 *Web:* www.mambosprouts.com	Cherry Hill	NJ	08002	856-833-1933	

Company	City	State	Zip	Phone	Fax
Manahan Group, The 900 Lee St Ste 1710 *Web:* manahangroup.com	Charleston	WV	25301	304-343-2800	
Mandala Agency, The 2855 Nw Crossing Dr *Web:* mandala.agency	Bend	OR	97701	541-389-6344	
Mangos Graphics Inc 10 Great Vly Pkwy *Web:* mangos.agency	Malvern	PA	19355	610-296-2555	
Marchex Inc 520 Pike St Ste 2000 *NASDAQ: MCHX* ■ *TF:* 800-840-1012 ■ *Web:* www.marchex.com	Seattle	WA	98101	206-331-3300	331-3695
Marco Corp, The 470 Hardy Rd *Web:* www.themarcocorporation.biz/marcohome	Brantford	ON	N3V6T1	519-751-2227	
Marden-Kane Inc 36 Maple Pl. *Web:* www.mardenkane.com	Manhasset	NY	11030	516-365-3999	
Market Resource Partners LLC 1880 JFK Blvd Nineteenth Fl *Web:* www.marketresourcepartners.com	Philadelphia	PA	19103	215-587-8800	
MarketLauncher Inc 1800 Pembroke Dr Ste 300. *TF:* 800-901-3803 ■ *Web:* www.marketlauncher.com	Orlando	FL	32810	800-901-3803	
Marlin Network Inc 1200 E Woodhurst Bldg V *Web:* marlinco.com	Springfield	MO	65804	417-885-4500	
Marriner Marketing Communications Inc 6731 Columbia Gateway Dr Ste 250 *Web:* www.marriner.com	Columbia	MD	21046	410-715-1500	
Mary Pomerantz Advertising 300 Route 27 *Web:* www.marypomerantzadvertising.com	Highland Park	NJ	08904	732-214-9600	
MasonBaronet Inc 1801 N Lamar St Ste 250 *Web:* www.masonbaronet.com	Dallas	TX	75202	214-954-0316	
MatchCraft Inc 2701 Ocean Park Blvd Ste 220 *Web:* www.matchcraft.com	Santa Monica	CA	90405	310-314-3320	
MBI Direct Mail Inc 710 W New Hampshire Ave. *Web:* www.directmail-mbi.com	Deland	FL	32720	386-736-9998	
McClenahan Bruer Communications 1500 SW 12th Ave *Web:* www.mcbru.com	Portland	OR	97201	503-546-1000	
McGarrah Jessee LP 205 Brazos *Web:* www.mc-j.com	Austin	TX	78701	512-225-2000	
McGill Buckley Inc 2206 Anthony Ave. *Web:* www.mcgillbuckley.com	Ottawa	ON	K2B6V2	613-728-4199	
Mdi Imaging & Mail Llc 21955 Cascades Pkwy *Web:* mdimail.biz	Sterling	VA	20166	703-433-1200	
Media Fusion Inc 4951 Century St. *Web:* www.fusiononline.com	Huntsville	AL	35816	256-532-3874	
Mediabidscom Inc 448 Main St. *Web:* www.mediabids.com	Winsted	CT	06098	860-379-9602	
Mediassociates Inc One Ives St *Web:* www.mediassociates.com	Danbury	CT	06810	203-797-9500	
Mekanism Inc 640 Second St Fl 3. *Web:* www.mekanism.com	San Francisco	CA	94107	415-908-4000	
Mercury Communication Partners 13414 Watertown Plank Rd. *Web:* www.mercuryww.com	Elm Grove	WI	53122	262-782-4637	
MercuryCSC 22 S Grand Ave *Web:* www.mercurycsc.com	Bozeman	MT	59715	406-586-2280	
Meringcarson 1700 I St 2nd Fl *Web:* www.meringcarson.com	Sacramento	CA	95811	916-441-0571	
Merlot Marketing 4430 Duckhorn Dr. *Web:* www.merlotmarketing.com	Sacramento	CA	95834	916-285-9835	
Merz Group, The 1570 Mcdaniel Dr *Web:* www.themerzgroup.com	West Chester	PA	19380	610-429-3160	
MetaDesign North America 615 Battery St 6th Fl. *Web:* www.metadesign.com	San Francisco	CA	94111	415-627-0790	627-0795
Method Inc 585 Howard St Ground Fl *Web:* www.method.com	San Francisco	CA	94105	415-901-6300	
Meyocks Group Inc, The 6800 Lk Dr Ste 150. *Web:* www.meyocks.com	West Des Moines	IA	50266	515-225-1200	
Midwest Presort Mailing Services Corp Inc 2222 W 110th St. *Web:* www.mw-direct.com	Cleveland	OH	44102	216-251-2500	
Milici Valenti Ng Pack Inc First Hawaiian Ctr 999 Bishop St 24th Fl *Web:* www.mvnp.com	Honolulu	HI	96813	808-536-0881	
Mindpower Inc 337 Georgia Ave SE *Web:* www.mindpowerinc.com	Atlanta	GA	30312	404-581-1991	
Minimus LLC 914 tourmaline dr. *Web:* www.minimus.biz	Newbury Park	CA	91320	805-480-1415	
Mintz & Hoke Inc 40 Tower Ln *Web:* www.mintz-hoke.com	Avon	CT	06001	860-678-0473	
Mission Creative 140 E 9th St *Web:* www.missioncreative.biz	Dubuque	IA	52001	563-583-0853	
Mitchell & Resnikoff 8003 Old York Rd	Elkins Park	PA	19027	215-635-1000	
Mjs Advertising Marketing Consulting LLC 301 Yamato Rd Ste 4100 *Web:* www.mjsadvertising.com	Boca Raton	FL	33431	561-443-0440	
MMA Creative Inc 705 N Dixie Ave. *Web:* www.mmacreative.com	Cookeville	TN	38501	931-528-8852	
Modea Corp 902 Prices Fork Rd Ste 2100 *Web:* www.modea.com	Blacksburg	VA	24060	540-552-3210	
Modern Marketing Partners 1220 Iroquois Ave Ste 210 *Web:* www.modernmarketingpartners.com	Naperville	IL	60563	630-868-5060	
Monarch Creative 309 N Water St Ste 360. *Web:* monarchcreative.net	Milwaukee	WI	53202	414-277-0077	
Mondo Mannequins LLC 300 Karin Ln *Web:* www.mondomannequins.com	Hicksville	NY	11801	516-935-8983	
Moore & Scarry Advertising Inc 12601 Westlinks Dr Ste 7. *Web:* www.mooreandscarry.com	Fort Myers	FL	33913	239-689-4000	
Moore Communications Group Inc 2011 Delta Blvd *Web:* www.moorecommgroup.com	Tallahassee	FL	32303	850-224-0174	
More Media Group 1427 Goodman Ave *Web:* www.moremediagroup.com	Redondo Beach	CA	90278	310-991-9798	
Morrison and Abraham Inc 322 N Main St Ste 6 *Web:* www.morrisonandabraham.com	Randolph	MA	02368	781-986-2100	
MossWarner 33332 Valle Rd Ste 200 *Web:* mosswarner.com	Mission Viejo	CA	92765	949-429-2266	
Mr Youth LLC 11 W 19th St. *Web:* mry.com	New York	NY	10011	212-779-8700	
Munn Rabot Llc 33 W 17th St Fl 3 *Web:* www.munnrabot.com	New York	NY	10011	212-727-3900	
Murray Multi-media 2 Cahart Rd *Web:* www.murraymedia.com	Blairstown	NJ	07825	908-362-8174	
MZD Advertising 1800 N Meridian St # 200 *Web:* www.zmarketingpartners.com	Indianapolis	IN	46202	317-924-6271	
n-tara Inc 2214 E Fairview Ave. *Web:* www.ntara.com	Johnson City	TN	37601	423-926-8272	
Nail Communications Inc 63 Eddy St *Web:* nail.cc	Providence	RI	02903	401-331-6245	
Naylor LLC 5950 NW 1st Pl *Web:* www.naylor.com	Gainesville	FL	32607	352-332-1252	
Neal Advertising LLC 153 Andover St Ste 201 *Web:* nealadv.com	Danvers	MA	01923	978-774-4444	
Nelson & Gilmore 1604 Aviation Blvd. *Web:* www.nelsongilmore.com	Redondo Beach	CA	90278	310-376-0296	
Nelson Schmidt Inc 600 E Wisconsin Ave *Web:* nelsonschmidt.com	Milwaukee	WI	53202	414-224-0210	
NetGain Technology Inc 720 W St Germain St *Web:* www.netgainhosting.com	Saint Cloud	MN	56301	320-251-4700	251-5030
NeuroSource Inc 4501 N Winchester Ave Ste *Web:* neurosource.com	Chicago	IL	60640	773-250-0000	
New Day Marketing Ltd 923 Olive St. *Web:* www.newdaymarketing.com	Santa Barbara	CA	93101	805-965-7833	
NOBLE 2215 W Chesterfield Blvd. *Web:* www.noble.net	Springfield	MO	65807	417-875-5000	
non-linear creations Inc 987 Wellington St Ste 201 *TF:* 866-915-2997 ■ *Web:* www.nonlinearcreations.com	Ottawa	ON	K1Y2Y1	613-241-2067	241-3086
Nova Creative Group Inc 571 Congress Park Dr *Web:* www.novacreative.com	Dayton	OH	45459	937-434-9200	
Nuzoo Media Inc 606 W 18th St Apt 3 *Web:* www.nuzoo.com	Chicago	IL	60616	312-421-2129	
Obrien et Al Advertising Inc 3113 Pacific Ave. *Web:* www.obrienetal.com	Virginia Beach	VA	23451	757-422-3231	
Office Products Marketing & Advertising Inc 4211 Division Ave N. *Web:* opma.com	Comstock Park	MI	49321	616-785-6061	
Okeeffe & Company Marketing Inc 921 King St. *Web:* www.ikco.com	Alexandria	VA	22314	703-883-9000	
Open Road Entertainment LLC 9570 W Pico Blvd Ste 200 *Web:* www.openroadent.com	Los Angeles	CA	90035	310-248-3300	
Openjar Concepts Inc 27710 jefferson ave *TF:* 877-673-6527 ■ *Web:* www.openjar.com	Temecula	CA	92590	877-673-6527	
Optimization Group Inc 320 S. Main St. Ste D. *Web:* www.optimizationgroup.com	Ann Arbor	MI	48104	734-212-2044	
Organic Inc 600 California St 8th Fl. *Web:* www.organic.com	San Francisco	CA	94108	415-581-5300	
Ostler Group Inc, The 7430 S. Creek Rd Ste 204. *Web:* www.ostlergroup.com	Sandy	UT	84093	801-566-6081	
Out There Advertising Inc 22 E Second St *Web:* outthereadvertising.com	Duluth	MN	55802	218-720-6002	
Overit Media Inc 303 Hamilton St *Web:* overit.com	Albany	NY	12210	518-465-8829	
Owen Media Inc 3130 E Madison St Ste 206 *Web:* www.owenmedia.com	Seattle	WA	98112	206-322-1167	
Pace & Partners 1223 Turner St Ste 101 *Web:* www.gudmarketing.com	Lansing	MI	48906	517-267-9800	
Pacifico Inc 1190 Coleman Ave Ste 110 *Web:* www.pacifico.com	San Jose	CA	95110	408-327-8888	
Palio Communications LLC 260 Broadway *Web:* www.palio.com	Saratoga Springs	NY	12866	212-849-9455	
Palmer Advertising 466 Geary St Ste 301 *Web:* palmeradagency.com	San Francisco	CA	94102	415-771-2327	
Panthera Interactive LLC 2831 St Rose Pkwy Ste 232 *Web:* www.pantherainteractive.com	Henderson	NV	89052	702-202-4740	
PAPA Advertising Inc 1673 W Eighth St *Web:* www.papaadvertising.com	Erie	PA	16505	814-454-6236	
Pappas Macdonnell Inc 135 Rennell Dr *Web:* www.pappasmacdonnell.com	Southport	CT	06890	203-254-1944	
Partners Napier Inc 192 Mill St Ste 600 *Web:* www.partnersandnapier.com	Rochester	NY	14614	585-454-1010	
Patient Marketing Group Inc 155 Village Boulavard Ste 200 *Web:* www.patientmarketing.com	Princeton	NJ	08540	609-779-6200	
Patriot Advertising Inc 1801 E Ave *Web:* www.patriotadvertising.com	Katy	TX	77493	832-239-5775	
Payne, Ross & Associates Advertising Inc 206 E Jefferson St. *Web:* www.payneross.com	Charlottesville	VA	22902	434-977-7607	
Peter A. Mayer Advertising Inc 324 Camp St. *Web:* www.peteramayer.com	New Orleans	LA	70130	504-581-7191	
Phoenix Advertising & Graphics Inc 6101 Adamsville Rd *Web:* phoenix4banners.com	Gibsonton	FL	33534	813-672-1991	

				Phone	Fax
Pierce Promotions & Event Management Inc 1 Monument Sq., Ste. 400 Ste *Web:* www.ppem.com	Portland	ME	04101	207-523-1700	
Pierce-Cote Advertising 683 Main St. *Web:* www.pierce-cote.com	Osterville	MA	02655	508-420-5566	
Pinckney Hugo Group 760 W Genesee St *Web:* www.pinckneyhugo.com	Syracuse	NY	13204	315-478-6700	
Pinnacle Advertising and Marketing 1435 N Plum Grove Rd Ste C *Web:* www.pinnacle-advertising.com	Schaumburg	IL	60173	847-255-0000	
Pinnacle Exhibits Inc 22400 NW Westmark Dr *Web:* www.pinnacle-exhibits.com	Hillsboro	OR	97124	503-844-4848	
PL Communications 417 Victor St *Web:* plcommunications.com/	Scotch Plains	NJ	07076	908-889-8888	
Planet Propaganda 605 Williamson St *Web:* planetpropaganda.com	Madison	WI	53703	608-256-0000	
Play Advertising Inc 1455 Lakeshore Rd Ste 208 S. *Web:* playadvertising.com	Burlington	ON	L7S2J1	905-631-8299	
Pod1 Inc 628 - 630 Broadway Ste 403 *Web:* www.pod1.com	New York	NY	10012	212-625-8590	
Poretta & Orr Inc 450 East St *Web:* porettaorr.com	Doylestown	PA	18901	215-345-1515	
Powers Agency Inc 1 W Fourth St 5th Fl *Web:* www.powersagency.com	Cincinnati	OH	45202	513-721-5353	
Prairie Dog LLC 6155 Oak St. *Web:* www.pdog.com	Kansas City	MO	64113	816-822-3636	
Precise Mailing Inc 168 Beacon St *Web:* www.precisemailing.com	South San Francisco	CA	94080	650-589-4000	
PriceWeber Marketing Communications Inc 10701 Shelbyville Rd *Web:* www.priceweber.com	Louisville	KY	40243	502-499-9220	
Primacy 1577 New Britain Ave *Web:* www.theprimacy.com	Farmington	CT	06032	860-679-9332	679-9344
Primary Media Outdoor Advertising 2511 Boll St *Web:* primarymedia.com	Dallas	TX	75204	214-880-0440	
Priority Marketing 8200 College Pkwy Ste 201 *Web:* www.prioritymarketing.com	Fort Myers	FL	33919	239-267-2638	
ProMark Direct Inc 300 N Midland Ave Ste 2 *Web:* www.promarkdirect.com	Saddle Brook	NJ	07663	201-398-9000	
Proof Advertising LLC 114 W Seventh St Ste 500 *Web:* www.proof-advertising.com	Austin	TX	78701	512-345-6658	
Propaganda Inc 3115 S Grand Blvd Ste 500 *Web:* www.propaganda-inc.com	St. Louis	MO	63118	314-664-8516	
Prospects Influential Inc 3888 Sound Way *TF:* 888-982-0766 ■ *Web:* www.prospectsinfluential.com	Bellingham	WA	98227	888-982-0766	
Protagon Display Inc 719 Tapscott Rd. *Web:* www.protagon.com	Toronto	ON	M1X1A2	416-293-9500	
Publipage Inc 2055 Rue Peel *Web:* publipage.com	Montreal	QC	H3A1V4	514-286-1550	
Push Inc 101 Ernestine St. *Web:* www.pushhere.com	Orlando	FL	32801	407-841-2299	
Q Interactive Inc 1601 NW 136th Ave **Fax Area Code:* 312	Sunrise	FL	33323	954-653-9000	469-1744*
Quenzel Associates Inc 12801 University Dr *Web:* www.quenzel.com	Fort Myers	FL	33907	239-226-0040	
Quest Companies Inc 8011 N Point Blvd Ste 201 *TF:* 800-467-9409 ■ *Web:* www.questcompaniesinc.com	Winston-salem	NC	27106	800-467-9409	
Questus Inc 675 Davis St. *Web:* www.questus.com	San Francisco	CA	94111	415-677-5700	
Quiet Light Communications Inc 220 E State St *Web:* www.quietlightcom.com	Rockford	IL	61104	815-398-6860	
Quinlan & Company Inc 385 N French Rd Ste 106 *Web:* www.quinlanco.com	Amherst	NY	14228	716-691-6200	
Quirks Marketing Rsch Review 4662 Slater Rd *Web:* www.quirks.com	Saint Paul	MN	55122	651-379-6200	
R C Romine Advertising & Marketing 1250 Executive Pl Ste 601 *Web:* www.rcromine.com	Geneva	IL	60134	630-208-1020	
R/GA 350 W 39th St *Web:* www.rga.com	New York	NY	10018	212-946-4000	946-4010
Rainbow Advertising Lp 3904 W Vickery Blvd *TF:* 800-646-3477 ■ *Web:* www.rainbowadvertising.com	Fort Worth	TX	76107	817-738-3838	
Rakuten Marketing LLC 215 Pk Ave S 9th Fl *TF:* 888-880-8430 ■ *Web:* www.linkshareuk.com	New York	NY	10003	646-943-8200	943-8204
Rapp Advertising 30 Commerce St Ste 2 *Web:* www.rappadvertising.com	Springfield	NJ	07081	973-467-5570	
Rare Bird Inc 8555 Cedar Pl Dr Ste 114 *Web:* rarebirdinc.com	Indianapolis	IN	46240	317-251-6744	
Rc Productions Inc 1756 Lakeshore Dr *Web:* www.rcproductions.com	Muskegon	MI	49441	231-759-3160	
Real Integrated 40900 woodward ave. *Web:* www.realintegrated.com	Bloomfield Hills	MI	48304	248-540-0660	
Real World Inc 8098 N Via De Negocio *Web:* www.realworldinc.com	Scottsdale	AZ	85258	480-296-0160	
Rector Communications Inc 2300 Chestnut St Ste 340a *Web:* rector.com	Philadelphia	PA	19103	215-963-9661	
Red Door Interactive Inc 350 10th Ave Ste 1100 *Web:* www.reddoor.biz	San Diego	CA	92101	619-398-2670	
Red Square Agency Inc 54 Saint Emanuel St *Web:* redsquaregaming.com	Mobile	AL	36602	251-476-1283	
Red7e Inc 637 W Main St. *Web:* www.red7e.com	Louisville	KY	40202	502-585-3403	
RedPeg Marketing 727 N Washington St. *Web:* www.redpegmarketing.com	Alexandria	VA	22314	703-519-9000	
Reid & Odonahue & Associates Advertising Inc 419 S Perry St *Web:* reid-odonahue.com	Montgomery	AL	36104	334-263-7812	
Remer Inc 205 Marion St *Web:* www.remerinc.com	Seattle	WA	98104	206-624-1010	
Renegade LLC 437 Fifth Ave 4th Fl *Web:* www.renegade.com	New York	NY	10016	646-486-7702	
Rennies Advertising Ideas Inc 711 Twinridge Ln *Web:* www.renniesadv.com	Richmond	VA	23235	804-272-4442	
Republica LLC 2153 Coral Way The Republica Bldg *Web:* republica.net	Miami	FL	33145	786-347-4700	
Republik, The 211 Rigsbee Ave. *Web:* therepublik.net	Durham	NC	27701	919-956-9400	
RES Exhibit Services LLC 435 Smith St. *TF:* 800-482-4049 ■ *Web:* www.res-exhibits.com	Rochester	NY	14608	585-546-2040	
Return Path Inc 3 Park Ave 41st Fl *Web:* www.returnpath.com	New York	NY	10016	212-905-5500	905-5501
Riester Corp 3344 E Camelback Rd *Web:* www.riester.com	Phoenix	AZ	85018	602-462-2200	
Ripcord Llc 3455 Ringsby Ct Ste 103 *Web:* ripcordsolutions.com	Denver	CO	80216	303-221-2824	
Robert Michael Communications Inc 101 Laurel Rd *Web:* www.rmei.com	Voorhees	NJ	08043	856-547-4141	
Rodgers Townsend LLC 1000 Clark Ave *Web:* www.rodgerstownsend.com	Saint Louis	MO	63102	314-436-9960	
Roi Advertising & Communication 5001 Brentwood Stair Rd *Web:* www.roiac.com	Fort Worth	TX	76112	900-464-9564	
Room 214 Inc 3390 Valmont Rd Ste 214 *TF:* 866-624-1851 ■ *Web:* room214.com	Boulder	CO	80301	866-624-1851	
Rosenberg Advertising 12613 Detroit Ave. *Web:* rosenbergadv.com	Lakewood	OH	44107	216-529-7910	
Royal Industries Inc 225 25th St *Web:* www.royalindustries.com	Brooklyn	NY	11232	718-369-3046	
Russell Herder 100 S Fifth St Ste 2200 *Web:* www.russellherder.com	Minneapolis	MN	55402	612-455-2360	
RW Advertising Inc 313 Canal St *Web:* www.rwadv.com	Lemont	IL	60439	630-257-1179	
SCA Direct 11200 Waples Mill Rd Ste 150 *Web:* www.scadirect.com	Fairfax	VA	22030	703-293-6339	
Schnake Turnbo Frank Inc 20 E Fifth St Ste 1500 *Web:* www.schnake.com	Tulsa	OK	74103	918-582-9151	
School of Advertising Art Inc 1725 E David Rd *Web:* www.saa.edu	Dayton	OH	45440	937-294-0592	
Schubert Communications Inc 112 Schubert Dr *Web:* www.schubertb2b.com	Downingtown	PA	19335	610-269-2100	
Schupp Company Inc 401 Pine St. *Web:* www.schuppco.com	St. Louis	MO	63102	314-421-5200	
Scott Brown Media Group 645 Pressley Rd Ste D *Web:* sbmg.com	Charlotte	NC	28217	704-525-9775	
Scream Agency LLC 1501 Wazee St Ste 1b *Web:* www.screamagency.com	Denver	CO	80202	303-893-8608	
Screamer Design LLC 107 Leland St Ste 3 *Web:* screamerco.com	Austin	TX	78704	512-691-7894	
ScreenScape Networks Inc 133 Queen St 3rd Fl. *Web:* www.screenscape.com	Charlottetown	PE	C1A7K4	902-368-1975	
Secret Weapon Marketing 5870 W Jefferson Blvd *Web:* www.secretweapon.net	Los Angeles	CA	90016	310-656-5999	
Seismic Productions Llc 7010 Santa Monica Blvd. *Web:* www.seismicproductions.com	Los Angeles	CA	90038	323-957-3350	
SenaReider Inc 299 Cannery Row Ste E. *Web:* www.senareider.com	Monterey	CA	93940	831-372-4961	
SEO com LLC 14870 S Pony Express Rd Ste 100 *Web:* www.seo.com	Bluffdale	UT	84065	801-983-3271	
SEOP Inc 1720 E Garry St Ste 103 *TF:* 877-231-1557 ■ *Web:* www.seop.com	Santa Ana	CA	92705	877-231-1557	
SGW Integrated Marketing Communications Inc 219 Changebridge Rd. *Web:* www.sgw.com	Montville	NJ	07045	973-299-8000	
Shine Advertising 612 W Main St Ste 105 *Web:* shineunited.com	Madison	WI	53703	608-442-7373	
Siegel & Gale 625 Ave of the Americas 4th Fl *Web:* siegelgale.com	New York	NY	10011	212-453-0400	453-0401
Silver Creative Group Llc 50 N Main St *Web:* silvercreativegroup.com	Norwalk	CT	06854	203-855-7705	
Simantel Group 321 SW Water St *Web:* www.simantel.com	Peoria	IL	61602	309-674-7747	
Simmonsflint 33 S Third St Ste D *Web:* www.simmonsflint.com	Grand Forks	ND	58201	701-746-4573	
Siquis Ltd 1340 Smith Ave Ste 300 *Web:* www.siquis.com	Baltimore	MD	21209	410-323-4800	
Smartguys Advertising & Design Inc 4322 Scotia Dr *Web:* www.smartguys.biz	Fort Wayne	IN	46814	260-625-6427	
Smith, Kaplan, Allen & Reynolds Advertising Agency Inc 111 S 108th Ave *Web:* skar.com	Omaha	NE	68154	402-330-0110	
Sonnhalter 633 W Bagley Rd Ste 4 *Web:* www.sonnhalter.com	Berea	OH	44017	440-234-1812	
Source Marketing LLC 761 Main Ave *Web:* www.sourcecxm.com	Norwalk	CT	06851	203-291-4000	
Souza Agency Inc, The 2547 Housley Rd *Web:* www.souza.com	Annapolis	MD	21401	410-573-1300	

Company / Address	City	State	ZIP	Phone	Fax
Spear Marketing Group					
1630 N Main St Ste 200	Walnut Creek	CA	94596	925-891-9050	
Web: www.spearmarketing.com					
Springbox Ltd 708 Congress Ave Ste A	Austin	TX	78701	512-391-0065	
Web: www.springbox.com					
St. Gregory Group					
4000 Executive Park Dr Ste 200	Sharonville	OH	45241	513-769-8440	
Web: stgregory.com					
Star Marketing & Media Inc					
11991 Presilla Rd	Santa Rosa Valley	CA	93012	805-552-9900	
Web: www.starmarketingmedia.com					
Starboard Advertising Group					
211 Village Dr	Saint Simons Island	GA	31522	912-638-8885	
Web: starboardadgroup.com					
Stealth 1617 locust st	Saint Louis	MO	63103	314-480-3606	
Web: stlautos.com					
Stein + Partners Brand Activation (SPBA)					
432 Pk Ave S	New York	NY	10016	212-213-1112	779-7305
Web: www.steinias.com					
Steinreich Communications LLC					
2125 Center Ave	Fort Fee	NJ	07024	201-498-1600	
Web: www.scompr.com					
Stephens Advertising Inc 417 E Stroop Rd	Dayton	OH	45429	937-299-4993	
Web: www.stephensdirect.com					
Stevenson Advertising					
16524 13th Ave W Ste 2012	Lynnwood	WA	98037	425-787-9686	
Web: www.stevensonadvertising.com					
stMovement LLC, The 1010 E Union St Ste 120	Pasadena	CA	91106	626-689-4993	
Web: www.the1stmovement.com					
Stonearch Creative 710 S Second St Fl 7	Minneapolis	MN	55401	612-200-5000	
Web: www.stonearchcreative.com					
Straight North LLC 1001 W 31st St	Downers Grove	IL	60515	866-353-3953	
TF: 866-353-3953 ■ *Web:* www.straightnorth.com					
StratMar Retail Services Inc					
109 Willett Ave	Port Chester	NY	10573	914-937-7171	
Web: www.stratmar.com					
Stream Companies Inc 400 Lapp Rd	Malvern	PA	19355	610-644-8637	
Web: www.streamcompanies.com					
Streng Design & Advertising Inc					
244 W River Dr	Saint Charles	IL	60174	630-584-3887	
Web: www.strengdesign.com					
Sullivan Direct Marketing Inc					
5509 Fair Ln	Cincinnati	OH	45227	513-342-1139	
Web: www.sullivandirect.com					
Sundin Associates Inc 34 Main St Fl 3 Fl 3	Natick	MA	01760	508-650-3972	
Web: www.sundininc.com					
Supergroup Creative Omnimedia Inc, The					
154 Krog St Ne Ste 185	Atlanta	GA	30307	404-877-1711	
Web: www.thesupergroup.com					
Tactical Magic Llc 1460 Madison Ave	Memphis	TN	38104	901-722-3001	
Web: www.tacticalmagic.com					
Taglairino Advertising Group Ny Inc					
75 Sw 15th Rd	Miami	FL	33129	305-577-9988	
TF: 800-226-9988 ■ *Web:* www.tagad.com					
Tanen Directed Advertising					
12 S Main St	South Norwalk	CT	06854	203-855-5855	
Web: www.tanendirected.com					
Taxi Canada Inc 495 Wellington St W Ste 102	Toronto	ON	M5V1E9	416-342-8294	
Web: taxi.ca					
Team Velocity Marketing LLC					
13825 Sunrise Valley Dr	Herndon	VA	20171	877-832-6848	
TF: 877-832-6848 ■ *Web:* www.thevdrive.com					
Tel Edge 2616 Mesilla St Ne Ste 3	Albuquerque	NM	87110	505-292-9477	
Web: wrightedge.com					
Ten Adams Corp 1112 Se First St	Evansville	IN	47713	812-422-7440	
Web: www.tenadams.com					
Teplow Cucurullo Communications LLC					
68 Harvard St	Brookline	MA	02445	617-566-6710	
Web: tepcuc.com					
Terry Hines & Associates Inc					
2550 N Hollywood Way Ste 600	Burbank	CA	91505	323-877-2900	
Web: www.terryhines.com					
Texas Press Association 305 S Congress Ave	Austin	TX	78704	512-477-6755	
Web: www.texaspress.com					
Think! Creative Advertising Inc					
813 W Saint Germain St	Saint Cloud	MN	56301	320-259-9400	
Web: ithinkcreative.com					
Third Rail Creative 112 E Seventh St	Austin	TX	78701	512-358-9907	
Web: thirdrailcreative.com					
Thomas J Paul West Inc 1061 Rydal Rd Ste 100	Rydal	PA	19046	215-886-3220	
Web: www.thomasjpaul.com					
Thomas Puckett Advertising Marketing and Public Relations Inc					
4680 Polaris Ave	Las Vegas	NV	89103	702-798-5300	
Web: www.thomaspuckett.com					
Thunder Tech Inc					
3635 Perkins Ave Studio 5 SW	Cleveland	OH	44114	216-391-2255	
TF: 888-321-8422 ■ *Web:* www.thundertech.com					
Thynk Design Inc 1111 Pasquinelli Dr Ste 550	Westmont	IL	60559	630-323-1020	
Web: www.thynk.com					
Timmons & Company Inc 1753 Kendarbren Dr	Jamison	PA	18929	267-483-8220	
Web: www.timmonsandcompany.com					
Tiziani Whitmyre Inc 2 Commercial St	Sharon	MA	02067	781-793-9380	
Web: www.tizinc.com					
Tobe Direct 9700 Park Plz Ave Ste 210	Louisville	KY	40241	866-820-7313	
TF: 866-820-7313 ■ *Web:* www.tobedirect.com					
Top Floor Technologies LLC					
2725 S Moorland Rd Ste 300	New Berlin	WI	53151	262-364-0010	
Web: www.topfloortech.com					
Topica Inc 1 Post St Ste 875	San Francisco	CA	94104	415-344-0800	344-0900
TF: 888-728-2465 ■ *Web:* www.topica.com					
Total Promotions 1340 Old Skokie Rd	Highland Park	IL	60035	847-831-9500	
Web: www.totalpromote.com					
TPG Direct					
7 N Columbus Blvd The Piers at Penn's Landing	Philadelphia	PA	19106	215-592-8381	
Web: www.tpgdirect.com					
Traction Corp 1349 Larkin St	San Francisco	CA	94109	415-962-5800	
Web: www.tractionco.com					
Trademark Media Corp 2400 Webberville Rd	Austin	TX	78702	512-459-7000	
Web: www.trademarkmedia.com					
Transcontinental Inc					
1100 Rene-Levesque Blvd W 24th Fl	Montreal	QC	H3B4X9	514-392-9000	
TF: 800-361-5479 ■ *Web:* tctranscontinental.com					
Tri-Auto Enterprises LLC					
7225 Georgetown Rd	Indianapolis	IN	46268	317-644-5700	
Web: perq.com					
Tri-Media Integrated Marketing Technologies Inc					
517 Niagara St	Welland	ON	L3C1L7	905-732-6431	
TF: 800-367-0766 ■ *Web:* www.tri-media.com					
Triad Advertising Inc 1017 TurnPk St Ste 32a	Canton	MA	02021	781-828-9290	
Web: triadadvertising.com					
Triple Strength Graphics 232 W Main St Ste 2	Palmyra	PA	17078	717-838-9590	
Web: triplestrength.com					
Troika Design Group 6715 Melrose Ave	Hollywood	CA	90038	323-965-1650	
Web: www.troika.tv					
Truth & Advertising 454 N Broadway	Santa Ana	CA	92701	714-542-8778	
Web: www.truthandadvertising.com					
Tukaiz Communications LLC					
2917 N Latoria Ln	Franklin Park	IL	60131	847-455-1588	
TF: 800-543-2674 ■ *Web:* www.tukaiz.com					
Twist Image 407 rue McGill 2nd Fl	Montreal	QC	H2Y2G3	514-987-9992	
Web: www.twistimage.com					
Two by Four Ltd 10 N Dearborn St Ste 1000	Chicago	IL	60602	312-382-0100	
Web: twoxfour.com					
Union Square Media Group					
22647 Ventura Blvd No. 323	Woodland Hills	CA	91364	800-691-1741	
TF: 800-691-1741 ■ *Web:* unionsquaremedia.com					
United Landmark Associates Inc					
100 N Tampa St Ste 1925	Tampa	FL	33602	813-229-6566	
Web: www.unitedlandmark.com					
Unleaded Communications Inc 1701 Commerce St	Houston	TX	77002	713-874-8200	
Web: ulcomm.com					
Uri Inc 3542 Hayden Ave Ste 110	Torrance	CA	90501	310-360-1212	
Web: uriglobal.com					
US Digital Partners LLC 311 Elm St	Cincinnati	OH	45202	513-929-4603	
Web: www.usdigitalpartners.com					
US Media Consulting 1801 SW Third Ave 3rd Fl	Miami	FL	33129	305-722-5500	
Web: www.usmediaconsulting.com					
Uzzell Advertising					
2260 Wednesday St Ste 100	Tallahassee	FL	32308	850-513-1990	
Web: www.uzzelladv.com					
ValueClick Inc					
30699 Russell Ranch Rd Ste 250	Westlake Village	CA	91362	818-575-4500	575-4501
NASDAQ: VCLK ■ *TF:* 877-361-3316 ■ *Web:* conversantmedia.com/valueclick					
ValueClick Media 530 E Montecito St	Santa Barbara	CA	93103	805-879-1600	456-6611
TF: 877-361-3316 ■ *Web:* conversantmedia.com/valueclickmedia					
Verdi Group Inc, The 400 Andrews St Ste 300	Rochester	NY	14604	585-325-6304	
Web: www.theverdigroup.com					
Vermont Media Publishing Company Ltd					
Rt 100 PO Box 310	West Dover	VT	05356	802-464-3388	464-7255
Web: www.dvalnews.com					
Versant Inc 11000 W Park Pl Ste A	Milwaukee	WI	53224	414-410-0500	
Web: www.versantsolutions.com					
Vibrant Media Inc 565 Fifth Ave 15th Fl	New York	NY	10017	646-312-6100	
Web: www.vibrantmedia.com					
Victors & Spoils Inc 1904 Pearl St	Boulder	CO	80302	720-305-9822	
Web: www.victorsandspoils.com					
Viewpoint Creative 254 Second Ave	Needham	MA	02494	781-449-5858	
Web: www.viewpointcreative.com					
Villing & Company Inc 5909 Nimtz Pkwy	South Bend	IN	46628	574-277-0215	
Web: villing.com					
Vimarc Group Inc, The					
11840 Commonwealth Dr	Louisville	KY	40299	502-261-9100	
Web: www.vimarc.com					
Vision Creative Group Inc 16 Wing Dr	Cedar Knolls	NJ	07927	973-984-3454	
Web: www.visioncreativegroup.com					
VisionMAX Solutions Inc					
5580 Explorer Dr Ste 601	Mississauga	ON	L4W4YL	905-282-0503	
Web: www.visionmax.com					
Vital Media 508 W 5th St, Ste. 100 Ste	Charlotte	NC	28202	866-863-3426	
TF: 866-863-3426 ■ *Web:* www.vitalmedia.com					
Viva Partnership Inc 3227 NE 2nd Ave	Miami	FL	33137	305-576-6007	
Web: www.vivamia.com					
Walker Advertising Inc 1010 S Cabrillo Ave	San Pedro	CA	90731	310-519-4050	
Web: www.losdefensores.com					
Walsh & Sheppard Inc 111 W Ninth Ave	Anchorage	AK	99501	907-338-3857	
Web: www.walshsheppard.com					
Walter F. Cameron Advertising Inc					
350 Motor Pkwy Ste 410	Hauppauge	NY	11788	631-232-3033	
Web: www.cameronadv.com					
Wasserman & Partners Advertising Inc					
1020 Mainland St Ste 160	Vancouver	BC	V6B2T5	604-684-1111	
Web: wasserman-partners.com					
Weber Advertising & Marketing					
533 Janet Ave	Lancaster	PA	17601	717-299-1277	
Web: weberadvertising.com					
Weinrib & Connor 297 Knollwood Rd	White Plains	NY	10607	914-686-3900	
Web: www.weinconn.com					
Wexley School for Girls Llc 2218 5th Ave	Seattle	WA	98121	206-438-8900	
Web: www.wexley.com					
Williams & Helde Inc 711 Sixth Ave N Ste 200	Seattle	WA	98109	206-285-1940	
Web: www.williams-helde.com					
Wingman Advertising Inc					
4061 Glencoe Ave Ste A	Marina Del Rey	CA	90292	888-294-6462	
TF: 888-294-6462 ■ *Web:* www.wingmanmedia.com					

	City	State	Zip	Phone	Fax
Words at Work 403 W Ponce De Leon Ave Ste 113 *Web:* wordsatwork.com	Decatur	GA	30030	404-270-9200	
Wordsworth & Company Llc 723 Raymond Ave *Web:* www.wordsworthandco.com	Santa Monica	CA	90405	310-452-1022	
Working Media Group LLC 21 W 38th St 13th Fl *Web:* www.workingmediagroup.com	New York	NY	10018	212-679-2681	
Worldwide Partners Inc 100 Spruce St Ste 203 *Web:* www.worldwidepartners.com	Denver	CO	80230	303-577-9760	
Wowza Inc 2601 Second Ave S Studio One *Web:* wowzamade.com	Minneapolis	MN	55408	612-435-7100	
Wray Ward Marketing Communications 900 Baxter St *Web:* www.wrayward.com	Charlotte	NC	28204	704-332-9071	
Write on Target Inc 7941 Washington Woods Dr *Web:* www.writetarget.com	Dayton	OH	45459	937-436-4565	
WRL Advertising Inc 4470 Dressler Rd NW *Web:* www.wrladv.com	Canton	OH	44718	330-493-8866	
X-15 Creative Marketing LLC 300 S Madison Ave *Web:* x-15marketing.com	La Grange	IL	60525	708-579-1623	
Xaxis LLC 31 Penn Plz 132 W 31st St *Web:* www.xaxis.com	New York	NY	10001	646-259-4200	
Xperience Interactive 2601 Ocean Park Blvd Ste 116	Santa Monica	CA	90405	424-214-1471	
Yaffe & Co 26913 Northwestern Hwy Ste 500 *Web:* www.yaffe.com	Southfield	MI	48033	248-262-1700	
Yearick-Millea 100 First Ave Ste 525 *Web:* www.yearick-millea.com	Pittsburgh	PA	15222	412-323-9320	
Yellowhammer Media Group Inc 44 W 28th St *Web:* www.yhmg.com	New York	NY	10001	646-490-9841	
Yesmail 421 SW Sixth Ave Ste 400 *TF:* 877-937-6245 ■ *Web:* www.yesmail.com	Portland	OR	97204	503-241-4185	
YuMe Inc 1204 Middlefield Rd *Web:* www.yume.com	Redwood City	CA	94063	650-591-9400	
Zachry Associates Inc 500 Chestnut St Ste 2000 *Web:* www.zachryinc.com	Abilene	TX	79602	325-677-1342	

8 ADVERTISING SERVICES - OUTDOOR ADVERTISING

	City	State	Zip	Phone	Fax
A & A Safety Inc 1126 Ferris Rd *Web:* www.aasafetyinc.com	Amelia	OH	45102	513-943-6100	
Above All Advertising Inc 9080 Activity Rd Ste A *Web:* www.abovealladvertising.net	San Diego	CA	92126	858-549-2226	
Adams Outdoor Adv Co 911 SW Adams St *Web:* www.adamsoutdoor.com	Peoria	IL	61602	309-692-2482	692-8452
Advanced Sign Co 2024 Fifth St NW *Web:* www.advancedsignco.com	Albuquerque	NM	87102	505-246-8458	
Affiliate Traction 2125 Delaware Ave Ste E *Web:* www.affiliatetraction.com	Santa Cruz	CA	95060	831-464-1441	
Alpak Display Group 575 N Midland Ave *Web:* www.alpak.com	Saddle Brook	NJ	07663	201-797-1411	
Barrett Outdoor Communications Inc 381 Highland St *Web:* www.barrettoc.com	West Haven	CT	06516	203-932-4601	
Blue Hive Inc 7 Coppage Dr *Web:* www.blue-hive.com	Worcester	MA	01603	508-581-9560	
Bowlin Travel Centers Inc 150 Louisiana NE *OTC:* BWTL ■ *Web:* www.bowlintc.com	Albuquerque	NM	87108	505-266-5985	
BriteVision Media LLC 50 First St Ste 600 *TF:* 877-479-7777 ■ *Web:* www.britevision.com	San Francisco	CA	94105	877-479-7777	
Chicago Scenic Studios Inc 1315 N North Branch St *Web:* www.chicagoscenic.com	Chicago	IL	60642	312-274-9900	
Cineplex Digital Networks 369 York St Ste 2C *TF:* 866-353-8324 ■ *Web:* ek3.com	London	ON	N6B3R4	519-438-0111	
Clear Ch Outdoor Inc 2325 E Camelback Rd Ste 400 *Web:* www.clearchanneloutdoor.com	Phoenix	AZ	85016	602-381-5700	381-5782
Compass Collective 2150 Button Gwinnett Dr *TF:* 800-492-3402 ■ *Web:* www.compasscollective.com	Atlanta	GA	30340	404-875-6543	
Dirextion Inc 2025 Kentucky Ave Ste A *Web:* www.dirextion.com	Vestavia Hills	AL	35216	205-823-7265	
Display Works Inc 335 Gordons Corner Rd *Web:* www.displayworks.com	Manalapan	NJ	07726	732-536-0800	
Dodd Technologies Inc 7979 W Fall Creek Dr *Web:* doddtechnologies.com	Pendleton	IN	46064	317-485-4604	
Fairway Outdoor Advertising Inc 814 Duncan-Reidville Rd *Web:* fairwayoutdoor.com	Duncan	SC	29334	864-439-6371	
Grand Image Inc 560 Main St Ste 3 *Web:* www.grandimageinc.com	Hudson	MA	01749	978-567-9408	
Impac International 11445 Pacific Ave *Web:* www.impac-international.com	Fontana	CA	92337	951-685-9660	
Ion Art Inc 407 Radam Ln Ste A100 *Web:* ionart.com	Austin	TX	78745	512-326-9333	
Kc Sign Express Inc 5033 Mackey St *Web:* kcsignexpress.com	Shawnee	KS	66203	913-432-2500	
Kegerreis Outdoor Advertising LLC 1310 Lincoln Way E *Web:* www.kegerreis.com	Chambersburg	PA	17202	717-263-6700	
Kubin-Nicholson Corp 8440 N 87th St *TF:* 800-858-9557 ■ *Web:* www.kubin.com	Milwaukee	WI	53224	414-586-4300	586-6802
Lamar Adv Co 5321 Corporate Blvd *NASDAQ:* LAMR ■ *TF:* 800-235-2627 ■ *Web:* www.lamar.com	Baton Rouge	LA	70808	225-926-1000	923-0658
MediaChoice LLC 3701 Bee Caves Rd Ste 101 *Web:* www.mediachoice.com	Austin	TX	78746	512-693-9905	
Metro Bench Advertisers 3014 W Horatio St *Web:* www.metrobench.com	Tampa	FL	33609	813-872-8502	
Midway Displays Inc 6554 S Austin Ave *Web:* www.midwaydisplays.com	Bedford Park	IL	60638	708-563-2323	
NextMedia Group Inc 6312 S Fiddlers Green Cir Ste 205E	Greenwood Village	CO	80111	303-694-9118	694-4940
Norton Outdoor Advertising 5280 Kennedy Ave *Web:* www.norton-outdoor.com	Cincinnati	OH	45213	513-631-4864	
Origin LLC 119 E Graham Pl *Web:* www.originpop.com	Burbank	CA	91502	818-848-1648	
OUTFRONT Media Inc 405 Lexington Ave *TF:* 800-926-8834 ■ *Web:* www.cbsoutdoor.com	New York	NY	10174	212-297-6400	
Peachtree Packaging Inc 770 Marathon Pkwy *Web:* www.peachtreepackaging.com	Lawrenceville	GA	30046	770-822-1304	995-8447
PG Exhibits 3510 Himalaya Rd *Web:* www.pgexhibits.com	Aurora	CO	80011	303-722-6565	
R.O.A. General Inc 1775 N Warm Springs Rd *Web:* reaganoutdoor.com	Salt Lake City	UT	84116	801-521-1775	
RCS Enterprises Inc 7075 W Parkland Ct *TF:* 800-373-6873 ■ *Web:* www.rcsinnovations.com	Milwaukee	WI	53223	414-354-6900	
Redstar Media Group LLC 7685 Williamsport Pk	Falling Waters	WV	25419	304-274-6943	
Skyline Displays Bay Area Inc 44111 Fremont Blvd *Web:* www.skyline.com/san-jose-san-francisco-sacramento-ca-reno-nv	Fremont	CA	94538	510-490-9900	
Skyline New York 60 Plant Ave Ste 5 *Web:* www.skyline.com	Hauppauge	NY	11788	631-586-9400	
Spec Personnel LLC 25 Walls Dr *Web:* www.speconthejob.com	Fairfield	CT	06824	203-254-9935	
Steen Outdoor Advertising 3201 S 26th St *TF:* 866-537-8336 ■ *Web:* steen.com	Philadelphia	PA	19145	866-537-8336	
Stott Outdoor Advertising Po Box 7209 *Web:* stottoutdoor.com	Chico	CA	95927	530-342-3235	
Studio y Creations Inc 1-6204 29 St Se *TF:* 800-243-4024 ■ *Web:* www.studioycreations.com	Calgary	AB	T2C1W3	403-253-5447	
Suite 66 366 Adelaide St W Ste 600 *TF:* 866-779-3486 ■ *Web:* www.suite66.com	Toronto	ON	M5V1R9	416-628-5565	
Thomas Direct Sales Inc 33 Plymouth St *Web:* www.thomasdirect.com	Montclair	NJ	07042	973-777-6500	
Vestcom International Inc 7302 Kanis Rd *Web:* www.vestcom.com	Little Rock	AR	72204	501-663-0100	
Witt Sign Company Inc 306 McCowan Dr *Web:* wittsigns.com	Lebanon	TN	37087	615-444-3898	444-3980
Woodlands Academy Preparatory School, The 27440 Kuykendahl Rd *Web:* woodlandsprep.org	Tomball	TX	77375	281-516-0600	
WSOS Community Action Commission Inc 109 S Front St *TF:* 800-775-9767 ■ *Web:* www.wsos.org	Fremont	OH	43420	419-334-8911	

9 ADVERTISING SPECIALTIES

See Also Signs p. 3185; Smart Cards p. 3186; Trophies, Plaques, Awards p. 3269

	City	State	Zip	Phone	Fax
Adco Litho Line Inc 2700 W Roosevelt Rd	Broadview	IL	60155	708-345-8200	
ADG Promotional Products 2300 Main St *TF:* 800-852-5208 ■ *Web:* www.adgpromo.com	Hugo	MN	55038	800-852-5208	886-6790
AIA Corporation (AIA) 800 Winneconne Ave *Web:* www.aiagearedforgrowth.com	Neenah	WI	54956	920-886-3700	886-3733
Airmate Co Inc 16280 County Rd D *TF:* 800-544-3614 ■ *Web:* www.airmatecompany.com	Bryan	OH	43506	419-636-3184	636-4210
Alexander Mfg Co 12978 Tesson Ferry Rd *TF General:* 800-258-2743 ■ *Web:* www.alexandermc.com	Sappington	MO	63128	314-842-3344	
Allen Co 712 E Main St *TF:* 800-329-2491 ■ *Web:* www.allenmugs.com	Blanchester	OH	45107	937-783-2491	783-4831
Americanna Co 29 Aldrin Rd *TF Cust Svc:* 888-747-5550 ■ *Web:* www.americanna.com	Plymouth	MA	02360	508-747-5550	
Amsterdam Printing & Litho Corp 166 Wallins Corners Rd *TF Cust Svc:* 800-833-6231 ■ *Web:* www.amsterdamprinting.com	Amsterdam	NY	12010	518-842-6000	
Arthur Blank & Co Inc 225 Rivermoor St *TF:* 800-776-7333 ■ *Web:* www.abnote.com	Boston	MA	02132	617-325-9600	327-1235
Atlas Match LLC 1801 S Airport Cir *TF:* 800-628-2426 ■ *Web:* www.atlasmatch.com	Euless	TX	76040	817-267-1500	
Bastian Co 15 Eagle St *Web:* www.bastiancompany.com	Phelps	NY	14532	315-548-2300	
Belaire Products Inc 763 S Broadway St *TF:* 800-886-3224	Akron	OH	44311	330-253-3116	376-7790
Bergamot Inc 820 E Wisconsin St **Fax:* Sales ■ *TF Cust Svc:* 800-922-6733 ■ *Web:* www.bergamot.net	Delavan	WI	53115	262-728-5572	728-3750*
Brown & Bigelow Inc 345 Plato Blvd E *TF Cust Svc:* 800-628-1755 ■ *Web:* www.brownandbigelow.com	Saint Paul	MN	55107	651-293-7000	
Churchwell Co 814 S Edgewood Ave *TF:* 877-537-6166 ■ *Web:* www.churchwellcompany.com	Jacksonville	FL	32205	904-356-5721	
Crown Products LLC 3107 Halls Mill Rd *Web:* www.crownprod.com	Mobile	AL	36606	251-665-3600	
Dard Products Inc 912 Custer Ave *Web:* www.tagmaster.net	Evanston	IL	60202	847-328-5000	
Dunn Manufacturing Inc 1400 Goldmine Rd *TF:* 800-868-7111 ■ *Web:* facebook.com	Monroe	NC	28110	704-283-2147	289-6857
EBSCO Creative Concepts 3500 Blue Lake Dr Ste 150 *TF:* 800-756-7023 ■ *Web:* www.ebscocreativeconcepts.com	Birmingham	AL	35243	205-262-2696	262-2693
Ever-Lite Company Inc 1717 N Bayshore Dr *Web:* www.ever-lite.com	Miami	FL	33132	305-577-0819	

Phone Fax

Flair Communications Agency Inc
214 W Erie St . . . . Chicago IL 60654 312-943-5959 943-6049
Web: flairagency.com
Geiger 70 Mt Hope Ave . . . . Lewiston ME 04240 207-755-2000 755-2422
Web: www.geiger.com
Gold Bond Inc 5485 Hixson Pike . . . . Hixson TN 37343 423-842-5844 842-7934
Web: www.goldbondinc.com
Hit Promotional Products Inc
7150 Bryan Dairy Rd . . . . Largo FL 33777 727-541-5561 541-5130
TF: 800-237-6305 ■ *Web:* www.hitpromo.net
Imageworks Manufacturing Inc 49 S St . . . . Park Forest IL 60466 708-503-1122 503-1133
Web: www.imageworksmfg.com
Instant Imprints 5897 Oberlin Dr Ste 200 . . . . San Diego CA 92121 858-642-4848 453-6513
TF: 800-542-3437 ■ *Web:* www.instantimprints.com
Marco Promotional Products
2640 Commerce Dr . . . . Harrisburg PA 17110 877-545-9322 545-5672*
**Fax Area Code:* 866 ■ *TF:* 877-545-9322 ■ *Web:* www.marcopromotionalproducts.com
Marietta Hospitality 37 Huntington St . . . . Cortland NY 13045 607-753-6746 756-0658*
**Fax:* Cust Svc ■ *TF:* 800-950-7772 ■ *Web:* www.mariettahospitality.com
Maryland Match Corp 605 Alluvion St . . . . Baltimore MD 21230 410-752-8164 752-3441
TF: 800-423-0013 ■ *Web:* www.marylandmatch.com
Mid-America Merchandising Inc
204 W Third St . . . . Kansas City MO 64105 816-471-5600 842-0952
TF: 800-333-6737 ■ *Web:* www.mmipromo.com
MMG Works/Status Promotions
4601 Madison Ave . . . . Kansas City MO 64112 800-945-4044 472-7107*
**Fax Area Code:* 816 ■ *TF:* 800-945-4044 ■ *Web:* www.mmgworks.com
Myron Corp 205 Maywood Ave . . . . Maywood NJ 07607 877-803-3358
TF: 877-803-3358 ■ *Web:* www.myron.com
National Pen Corp (NPC)
12121 Scripps Summit Dr Ste 200 . . . . San Diego CA 92131 858-675-3000 675-0890
TF: 800-854-1000 ■ *Web:* www.pens.com
Nationwide Adv Specialty Co
2025 S Cooper St . . . . Arlington TX 76010 817-461-6161 274-4301
Neely Mfg 2178 Hwy 2 . . . . Corydon IA 50060 641-872-1100
Web: www.neelymfg.com
Newton Mfg Co 1123 First Ave E . . . . Newton IA 50208 641-792-4121
Web: www.newtonmfg.net
Norscot Group Inc
1000 W Donges Bay Rd PO Box 998 . . . . Mequon WI 53092 262-241-3313 241-4904
TF: 800-653-3313 ■ *Web:* www.norscot.com
Norwood Promotional Products Inc
14421 Myerlake Cir . . . . Clearwater IN 33760 727-538-3527 275-2570*
**Fax Area Code:* 317 ■ *TF:* 877-555-2223 ■ *Web:* www.norwood.com
Numo Manufacturing Co 1072 E Hwy 175 . . . . Kaufman TX 75142 972-962-5400
Web: www.numomfg.com
Pilgrim Plastic Products Co
1200 W Chestnut St . . . . Brockton MA 02301 508-583-9046
Web: www.pilgrimplastics.com
Prime Resources Corp 1100 Boston Ave . . . . Bridgeport CT 06610 203-331-9100 330-0123
TF: 800-621-5463 ■ *Web:* www.primeline.com
Quick Point Inc 1717 Fenpark Dr . . . . Fenton MO 63026 636-343-9400
Web: www.quickpoint.com
Quikey Manufacturing Co 1500 Industrial Pkwy . . . . Akron OH 44310 330-633-8106
Web: www.quikey.com
Slack & Company Inc
233 N Michigan Ave Ste 3050 . . . . Chicago IL 60601 312-970-5800 970-5850
Web: www.slackandcompany.com
Staples Promotional Products
7500 W 110th St . . . . Overland Park KS 66210 913-319-3100
TF: 800-369-4669 ■ *Web:* www.staplespromotionalproducts.com
Vanguard East 1172 Azalea Garden Rd . . . . Norfolk VA 23502 800-221-1264 857-0222*
**Fax Area Code:* 757 ■ *TF:* 800-221-1264 ■ *Web:* www.vanguardmil.com
VATEX America 2395 Hermitage Rd . . . . Richmond VA 23220 804-353-9010
Web: www.vatex.com
Western Plastic Products Inc 8441 Monroe Ave . . . . Stanton CA 90680 800-453-1881 495-2232*
**Fax Area Code:* 562 ■ *TF:* 800-453-1881 ■ *Web:* www.wbadges.com
Zebra Marketing
7125 Laurel Canyon Blvd Ste B . . . . North Hollywood CA 91605 818-765-6442
Web: www.zebramerchandise.blogspot.in

AGRICULTURAL CHEMICALS

AGRICULTURAL MACHINERY & EQUIPMENT

See Farm Machinery & Equipment - Mfr p. 2278; Farm Machinery & Equipment - Whol p. 2280

10 AGRICULTURAL PRODUCTS

See Also Fruit Growers p. 2332; Horse Breeders p. 2482; Horticultural Products Growers p. 2482; Seed Companies p. 3176

Phone Fax

Border Valley Trading Ltd 604 E Mead Rd . . . . Brawley CA 92227 760-344-6700 344-4305
Web: www.bordervalley.com
United Farmers Co-op (UFC)
705 E Fourth St PO Box 461 . . . . Winthrop MN 55396 507-647-6600 647-6620
TF: 866-998-3266 ■ *Web:* www.ufcmn.com

10-1 Cattle Ranches, Farms, Feedlots (Beef Cattle)

Phone Fax

A Duda & Sons Inc 1200 Duda Trail . . . . Oviedo FL 32765 407-365-2111 365-2147
Web: www.duda.com
Agri Beef Co 1555 Shoreline Dr Ste 320 . . . . Boise ID 83702 208-338-2500 338-2605
TF: 800-657-6305 ■ *Web:* www.agribeef.com
AzTx Cattle Co PO Box 390 . . . . Hereford TX 79045 806-364-8871 364-3842
TF: 800-999-5065 ■ *Web:* www.aztx.com
Bar G Feed Yard 275 FM 1057 Rd . . . . Summerfield TX 79085 806-357-2241
Web: bar-g.com
Barton County Feeders Inc 1164 SE 40th Rd . . . . Ellinwood KS 67526 620-564-2200
Web: bartoncountyfeeders.com
Beef Belt Feeders Inc 1350 E Rd 70 . . . . Scott City KS 67871 620-872-3059
Beef Northwest Feeders Inc 3455 Victorio Rd . . . . Nyssa OR 97913 541-372-2101 372-5661
Web: www.beefnw.com
Bledsoe Cattle Co 41726 US 385 . . . . Wray CO 80758 970-332-4955
Boise Valley Feeders LLC
1555 Shoreline Dr Ste 320 . . . . Boise ID 83702 208-338-2605 657-6305*
**Fax Area Code:* 800 ■ *TF:* 800-657-6305 ■ *Web:* www.agribeef.com
Buffalo Feeders LLC E US Hwy 64 PO Box 409 . . . . Buffalo OK 73834 580-735-2511
Web: www.buffalofeeders.com
Cactus Feeders Inc 2209 W Seventh Ave . . . . Amarillo TX 79106 806-373-2333 371-4767
TF: 877-698-7355 ■ *Web:* www.cactusfeeders.com
Coyote Lake Feedyard Inc 1287 FM 1731 . . . . Muleshoe TX 79347 806-946-3321
TF: 800-299-3321 ■ *Web:* www.coyotelakefeedyard.com
Darr Feedlot Inc 42826 Rd 759 . . . . Cozad NE 69130 308-324-2363 324-2365
Web: www.darrfeedlot.com
Dean Cluck Feedyard Inc 105 Dean Cluck Ave . . . . Gruver TX 79040 806-733-5021 733-2244
TF: 888-458-4787 ■ *Web:* deancluckfeedyard.com
Dinklage Feedyards PO Box 274 . . . . Sidney NE 69162 308-254-5940 254-6260
TF: 888-343-5940 ■ *Web:* www.dinklagefeedyards.com
Fall River Feedyard LLC
27962 Angostura Rd . . . . Hot Springs SD 57747 605-745-4109
Ford County Feed Yard Inc 12466 US Hwy 400 . . . . Ford KS 67842 620-369-2252
Friona Feedyard 2370 FM 3140 . . . . Friona TX 79035 806-265-3574
TF: 800-658-6014 ■ *Web:* www.frionaind.com
Friona Industries LP
500 S Taylor St Ste 601 . . . . Amarillo TX 79101 806-374-1811 374-1324
TF: 800-658-6014 ■ *Web:* www.frionaind.com
Garden City Feed Yard
1805 W Annie Scheer Rd . . . . Garden City KS 67846 620-275-4191
TF: 800-272-4191 ■ *Web:* www.aztx.com
Gottsch Feeding Corp
20507 Nicholas Cir Ste 100 . . . . Elkhorn NE 68022 402-463-6215
Web: gottschcattlecompany.com
Gray County Feed Yard Inc 23405 SR 23 . . . . Cimarron KS 67835 620-855-3486
Web: graycountyfeed.com
Great Bend Feeding Inc 2006 Broadway Ave . . . . Great Bend KS 67530 620-793-9200
Web: www.ilsbeef.com
Hansford County Feeders LP
13800 County Rd 19 . . . . Spearman TX 79081 806-477-1900 477-1910
Web: hcflp.com
Hays Feeders LLC 1174 Feedlot Rd . . . . Hays KS 67601 785-625-3415
Web: www.prattfeeders.com
Herd Company Cattle Co 83973 489th Ave . . . . Bartlett NE 68622 402-482-5931 482-5971
High Choice Feeders LLC 553 W Rd 40 . . . . Scott City KS 67871 620-872-7271
Web: highchoicefeeders.com
Ingalls Feed Yard 10505 US Hwy 50 . . . . Ingalls KS 67853 620-335-5174
Web: www.irsikanddoll.com
Irsik & Doll Co PO Box 847 . . . . Cimarron KS 67835 620-855-3111 855-3748
Web: www.irsikanddoll.com
JR Simplot Co 999 W Main St Ste 1300 . . . . Boise ID 83702 208-336-2110 389-7515
TF: 800-832-8893 ■ *Web:* www.simplot.com
King Ranch Inc 3 Riverway Ste 1600 . . . . Houston TX 77056 832-681-5700
Web: www.king-ranch.com
Knight Feedlot Inc 1768 Ave J . . . . Lyons KS 67554 620-257-5106 257-3347
Littlefield Feedyard Farm to Market 37 . . . . Littlefield TX 79339 806-385-5141
TF: 800-658-6014 ■ *Web:* www.frionaind.com
Midwest Feeders Inc 5013 13 Rd . . . . Ingalls KS 67853 620-335-5790
Web: www.midwest-feeders.com
Morrison Enterprises 3303 W 12th St . . . . Hastings NE 68901 402-463-3191 462-8542
North Platte Livestock Feeders Inc
3303 W 12th St . . . . Hastings NE 68901 402-463-6215
Web: www.gottschcattlecompany.com
PM Beef Group LLC 2850 Hwy 60 E . . . . Windom MN 56101 507-831-2761 831-6216
TF: 800-622-5213 ■ *Web:* www.pmbeef.com
Pratt Feeders LLC PO Box 945 . . . . Pratt KS 67124 620-672-6448
Web: www.prattfeeders.com
Premium Feeders Inc 705 US Hwy 36 . . . . Scandia KS 66966 785-335-2221
Web: www.premiumfeeders.com
Quality Beef Producers 5000 IH- 40 . . . . Wildorado TX 79098 806-426-3325 426-3582
Randall County Feedyard 15000 FM 2219 . . . . Amarillo TX 79119 806-499-3701
Web: www.frionaind.com
Red Rock Feeding Co 35415 E Sasco Cir . . . . Red Rock AZ 85245 520-682-3448
Royal Beef Feed Yard 11060 N Falcon Rd . . . . Scott City KS 67871 620-872-5371 872-3380
Web: www.irsikanddoll.com
Sparrowk Livestock 18780 E Hwy 88 . . . . Clements CA 95227 209-759-3530 759-3831
Web: www.sparrowk.com
Sublette Feeders 1535 Uu Rd . . . . Sublette KS 67877 620-668-5501
Swisher County Cattle Co Farm Market 214 Rd . . . . Tulia TX 79088 806-627-4231
TF: 800-658-6014 ■ *Web:* www.frionaind.com
Tejas Feeders Ltd E Highway 152 . . . . Pampa TX 79066 806-665-2030 669-0210
Tejon Ranch Co 4436 Lebec Rd PO Box 1000 . . . . Lebec CA 93243 661-248-3000 248-3100
NYSE: TRC ■ *Web:* www.tejonranch.com
Tri-State Feeders Inc 3 Mile S Hwy 83 . . . . Turpin OK 73950 580-778-3600
Weborg Feeding Co 1737 V Rd . . . . Pender NE 68047 402-385-3441 385-2441
Web: www.weborgfeeding.com
Western Feed Yard Inc 548 S Rd I . . . . Johnson KS 67855 620-492-6256 492-6239

10-2 Cotton Farms

Phone Fax

JG Boswell Co 101 W Walnut St . . . . Pasadena CA 91103 626-583-3000 583-3090
NYSE: BWEL
Wesson Farms Inc 25 Victoria Rd . . . . Osceola AR 72370 870-563-2674 563-6927
Westlake Farms Inc 23311 Newton Ave . . . . Stratford CA 93266 559-947-3348

10-3 Dairy Farms

Phone Fax

Astia Inc 833 Market St Ste 605 . . . . San Francisco CA 94103 415-421-5500
Web: www.astia.org

Phone Fax

Avid Identification Systems Inc
3185 Hamner Ave . . . Norco CA 92860 951-371-7505
Web: www.avidid.com

Berry Bros General Contractors Inc
1414 River Rd . . . Berwick LA 70342 985-384-8770

Big D Ranch 7590 S 10 Mile Rd . . . Meridian ID 83642 208-888-1710 888-0075
Web: www.bigdranch.com

Biomedical Research Models Inc
67 Millbrook St . . . Worcester MA 01606 508-459-7544
Web: brmcro.com

Brown Packing Company Inc
1 Dutch Vly Dr . . . South Holland IL 60473 708-849-7990

DNA LandMarks Inc
84 Richelieu St . . . Saint Jean-Sur-Richelieu QC J3B6X3 450-358-2621
Web: www.dnalandmarks.com

Fred Rau Dairy 10255 W Manning Ave . . . Fresno CA 93706 559-237-3393 237-3879

G & R Foods Inc PO Box 610 . . . Reedsburg WI 53959 608-524-3776 524-1752
Web: www.grfoodsinc.com

Hollandia Dairy Inc 622 E Mission Rd . . . San Marcos CA 92069 760-744-3222 744-2789
Web: www.hollandiadairy.com

Kreider Farms 1461 Lancaster Rd . . . Manheim PA 17545 717-665-4415 665-9614
TF: 888-665-4415 ■ *Web:* www.kreiderfarms.com

Marburger Farm Dairy Inc
1506 Mars Evans City Rd . . . Evans City PA 16033 724-538-4800 538-3250
TF: 800-331-1295 ■ *Web:* www.marburgerdairy.com

Maytag Dairy Farms Inc 2282 E Eighth St N . . . Newton IA 50208 641-792-1133
Web: iowabackroads.com

McClellan Park LLC 3140 Peacekeeper Way . . . Mcclellan CA 95652 916-965-7100
Web: www.mcclellanpark.com

Meadow Gold Dairy 55 S Wakea Ave . . . Kahului HI 96732 808-877-5541
Web: www.lanimoo.com

Provimi Foods Inc W2103 County Rd W . . . Seymour WI 54165 920-833-6861
Web: www.provimi-veal.com

Ronnybrook Farm Dairy Inc
310 Prospect Hill Rd . . . Ancramdale NY 12503 518-398-6455
Web: www.ronnybrook.com

Shamrock Farms Co 40034 W Clayton Rd . . . Stanfield AZ 85172 480-988-1452
Web: www.shamrockfarms.net

Tree Top Ranches LP PO Box 8126 . . . Boise ID 83707 208-377-0998

Virginia Poultry Growers Co-op Inc
6349 Rawley Pk . . . Hinton VA 22831 540-867-4000
Web: www.vapoultrygrowers.com

10-4 General Farms

Phone Fax

ABF Farm Services Inc 7761 W Undine Rd . . . Stockton CA 95206 209-462-0208 462-9429

Agrex Inc 10975 Grandview Dr St Ste 200 . . . Overland Park KS 66210 913-851-6300 851-6210
TF: 800-523-8181 ■ *Web:* www.agrexinc.com

Amana Colonies 622 46th Ave . . . Amana IA 52203 319-622-7622
TF: 800-579-2294 ■ *Web:* www.amanacolonies.com

Belk Farms 57300 Desert Cactus Dr . . . Thermal CA 92274 760-399-5951

Burford Ranch 1443 W Sample Ave . . . Fresno CA 93711 559-431-0902 431-1625

DM Camp & Sons 31798 Merced Ave . . . Bakersfield CA 93308 661-399-5511
Web: www.dmcampandsons.com

Farmers Win Coop (FFC) 110 N Jefferson . . . Fredericksburg IA 50630 563-237-5324
TF: 800-562-8389 ■ *Web:* www.fburgcoop.com

FarmTek 1440 Field of Dreams Way . . . Dyersville IA 52040 563-875-2288
TF: 800-327-6835 ■ *Web:* www.farmtek.com

Gold-Eagle Co-op PO Box 280 PO Box 280 . . . Goldfield IA 50542 800-825-3331
TF: 800-825-3331 ■ *Web:* www.goldeaglecoop.com

Great American Farms Inc
1255 W Atlantic Blvd Ste 218 . . . Pompano Beach FL 33069 954-785-9400 941-2977

Mercer Canyons Inc 46 Sonova Rd . . . Prosser WA 99350 509-894-4773 894-4965
Web: mercercanyons.com

Mid Valley Agricultural Services Inc
16401 E Hwy 26 PO Box 593 . . . Linden CA 95236 209-931-7600 931-0747
Web: www.midvalleyag.com

Morrison Enterprises 3303 W 12th St . . . Hastings NE 68901 402-463-3191 462-8542

Oji Bros Farms Inc 8547 Sawtelle Ave . . . Yuba City CA 95991 530-673-0845 673-8742

OPC Farms Inc 22300 Railroad Ave . . . San Joaquin CA 93660 559-693-2700

Plains Grain & Agronomy LLC 109 Third Ave . . . Enderlin ND 58027 701-437-2400
TF: 800-950-2219 ■ *Web:* www.plainsgrain.com

River Garden Farms Co
41758 County Rd 112 . . . Knights Landing CA 95645 530-735-6274 735-6734

Star of the West Milling Co
121 E Tuscola St . . . Frankenmuth MI 48734 989-652-9971 652-6358
TF: 888-281-4161 ■ *Web:* www.starofthewest.com

Sumner Peck Ranch Inc (SPR) 14860 N Hwy 41 . . . Madera CA 93636 559-822-3301
Web: www.sumnerpeckranch.com

Tosh Farms 1586 Atlantic Ave . . . Henry TN 38231 731-243-4861 243-4860
Web: www.toshfarms.net

10-5 Grain Farms

Phone Fax

AgriNorthwest 6716 W Rio Grande . . . Kennewick WA 99336 509-734-1195
Web: www.agrinorthwest.com

Alger Farms Inc 950 NW Eigth St . . . Homestead FL 33030 305-247-4334
Web: www.algerfarms.com

Big River Resources West Burlington LLC
15210 103rd St . . . West Burlington IA 52655 319-753-1100 753-1103
Web: www.bigriverresources.com

Busch Agricultural Resources Inc
2101 26th St S . . . Moorhead MN 56560 218-233-8531
Web: www.anheuser-busch.com

Colusa Elevator Co 2531 N County Rd . . . Colusa IL 62329 217-755-4221
Web: www.colusaelevator.com

Country Pride Co-op (CPC) 201 S Monroe PO Box 529 . . . Winner SD 57580 605-842-2711 842-2715
TF: 888-325-7743 ■ *Web:* www.countrypridecoop.com

Phone Fax

Erwin-Keith Inc 1529 Hwy 193 . . . Wynne AR 72396 870-238-2079 238-8621
TF: 888-535-7333 ■ *Web:* progenyag.com

Golden Grain Energy LLC 1822 43rd St SW . . . Mason City IA 50401 641-423-8525 421-8457
TF: 888-443-2676 ■ *Web:* www.ggecorn.com

Hoegemeyer Hybrids Inc 1755 Hoegemeyer Rd . . . Hooper NE 68031 402-654-3399
TF: 800-245-4631 ■ *Web:* www.therightseed.com

Illinois Foundation Seeds Inc (IFSI)
1083 County Rd 900 N . . . Tolono IL 61880 217-485-6260 485-3687
Web: www.ifsi.com

MFA Inc 201 Ray Young Dr . . . Columbia MO 65201 573-874-5111 876-5505
Web: www.mfaincorporated.com

Minn-Dak Growers Ltd 4034 40th Ave N . . . Grand Forks ND 58203 701-746-7453 780-9050
Web: www.minndak.com

Moews Seed Co Inc 9821 IL Hwy 89 . . . Granville IL 60640 815-339-2201
TF: 800-663-9795 ■ *Web:* www.moews.com

Morrow County Grain Growers Inc (MCGG)
350 N Main St . . . Lexington OR 97839 541-989-8221 989-8229
TF: 800-452-7396 ■ *Web:* www.mcgg.net

Pioneer Hi-Bred International Inc
PO Box 1000 . . . Johnston IA 50131 515-535-3200 535-4415
TF: 800-247-6803 ■ *Web:* www.pioneer.com

Remington Seeds 4746 W US Hwy 24 PO Box 9 . . . Remington IN 47977 219-261-3444 261-2220
Web: www.remingtonseeds.com

Richard Gumz Farms 8905 S Gumz Rd . . . North Judson IN 46366 574-896-5441

Stonington Co-op Grain
402 Walnut St PO Box 350 . . . Stonington IL 62567 217-325-3211

Wesson Farms Inc 25 Victoria Rd . . . Osceola AR 72370 870-563-2674 563-6927

Westlake Farms Inc 23311 Newton Ave . . . Stratford CA 93266 559-947-3348

William F Renk & Sons Inc
6809 Wilburn Rd . . . Sun Prairie WI 53590 800-289-7365 825-6143*
**Fax Area Code:* 608 ■ *TF:* 800-289-7365 ■ *Web:* www.renkseed.com

Wyffels Hybrids Inc 13344 US Hwy 6 . . . Geneseo IL 61254 309-944-8334 944-8338
TF: 800-369-7833 ■ *Web:* www.wyffels.com

10-6 Hog Farms

Phone Fax

Cargill Inc 15407 McGinty Rd W . . . Wayzata MN 55391 952-742-7575
TF: 800-227-4455 ■ *Web:* www.cargill.com

Christensen Farms 23971 County Rd 10 . . . Sleepy Eye MN 56085 507-794-5310 794-2471
Web: www.christensenfarms.com

Goschie Farms Inc 7365 Meridian Rd NE . . . Silverton OR 97381 503-873-5638
Web: goschiefarms.com

Hanor Co E 4614 Hwy 14-60 . . . Spring Green WI 53588 608-588-9170
Web: hanorcompany.com

Hastings Pork 301 S Burlington Avenue . . . Hastings NE 68901 402-461-8400
Web: www.hastingschamber.com

Hog Slat Inc PO Box 300 . . . Newton Grove NC 28366 910-594-0219 594-1392
TF: 800-949-4647 ■ *Web:* www.hogslat.com

Iowa Select Farms LP
811 S Oak St PO Box 400 . . . Iowa Falls IA 50126 641-648-4479 648-4251
Web: www.iowaselect.com

Jeckel Pork Farm Inc 600 N Sherman . . . Delavan IL 61734 309-244-7281

NG Purvis Farms Inc 2504 Spies Rd . . . Robbins NC 27325 910-673-3121 948-3213

PIC USA
100 Bluegrass Commons Blvd Ste 2200 . . . Hendersonville TN 37075 615-265-2700
TF: 800-325-3398 ■ *Web:* na.picgenus.com/home.aspx

Prestage Farms 4651 Taylors Bridge Hwy . . . Clinton NC 28329 910-596-5700 592-9552
Web: www.prestagefarms.com

Schwartz Farms Inc 32296 190th St . . . Sleepy Eye MN 56085 507-794-5779
Web: schwartzfarms.com

Seaboard Foods 9000 W 67th St Ste 200 . . . Shawnee Mission KS 66202 913-261-2600 261-2626
TF: 800-262-7907 ■ *Web:* www.seaboardfoods.com

Smithfield Foods Inc 200 Commerce St . . . Smithfield VA 23430 757-365-3000
NYSE: SFD ■ *Web:* www.smithfieldfoods.com

Swine Graphics Enterprises LP
1620 Superior St PO Box 668 . . . Webster City IA 50595 515-832-5481 832-2237
Web: sgepork.com

Texas Farm LLC 4200 S Main St . . . Perryton TX 79070 806-435-5935 435-3656
Web: texasfarmpork.com

Tyson Foods Inc
2210 W Oaklawn Dr PO Box 2020 . . . Springdale AR 72762 479-290-4000
NYSE: TSN ■ *TF:* 800-643-3410 ■ *Web:* www.tyson.com

Wakefield Pork Inc 410 Main Ave E . . . Gaylord MN 55334 507-237-5581 237-5584
Web: www.wakefieldpork.com

Whole Hog Health 88155 Hwy 57 . . . Hartington NE 68739 402-254-2444
Web: wholehogai.com

10-7 Mushroom Growers

Phone Fax

Monterey Mushrooms Inc 260 Westgate Dr . . . Watsonville CA 95076 831-763-5300 929-0271*
**Fax Area Code:* 610 ■ *TF:* 800-333-6874 ■ *Web:* www.montereymushrooms.com

Ostrom Mushroom Farms 8322 Steilacoom Rd SE . . . Olympia WA 98513 360-491-1410
Web: www.ostrommushrooms.com

Phillips Mushroom Farms Inc
1011 Kaolin Rd . . . Kennett Square PA 19348 610-925-0520 925-0527
TF: 800-722-8818 ■ *Web:* www.phillipsmushroomfarms.com

Sylvan Inc 90 Glade Dr . . . Kittanning PA 16201 724-543-3900 543-7583
TF: 866-352-7520 ■ *Web:* www.sylvaninc.com

10-8 Poultry & Eggs Production

Phone Fax

Allen's Hatchery Inc 126 N Shipley St . . . Seaford DE 19973 302-629-9163 629-0514
Web: allenharimllc.com/index.cfm

Amick Farms Inc 2079 Batesburg Hwy . . . Batesburg SC 29006 803-532-1400
TF: 800-926-4257 ■ *Web:* www.amickfarms.com

Company	City	State	Zip	Phone	Fax
Aviagen Group 5015 Bradford Dr.	Huntsville	AL	35805	256-890-3800	890-3919
TF: 800-826-9685 ■ *Web:* aviagen.com					
Cagle's Farms Inc 1385 Collier Rd NW	Atlanta	GA	30318	404-355-2820	350-9605
Cobb-Vantress Inc PO Box 1030	Siloam Springs	AR	72761	479-524-3166	524-3043
TF: 800-748-9719 ■ *Web:* www.cobb-vantress.com					
Cooper Farms 22348 County Rd 140 PO Box 547	Oakwood	OH	45873	419-594-3325	594-3372
TF: 800-423-2765 ■ *Web:* www.cooperfarms.com					
Creighton Bros LLC PO Box 220	Atwood	IN	46502	574-267-3101	
Web: www.creightonbrothersllc.com					
Culver Duck Farms Inc PO Box 910	Middlebury	IN	46540	574-825-9537	825-2613
TF: 800-825-9225 ■ *Web:* www.culverduck.com					
Demler Egg Ranch 1455 N Warren Rd	San Jacinto	CA	92582	951-654-8166	487-9766
Diestel Turkey Ranch 22200 Lyons Bald Mtn Rd	Sonora	CA	95370	209-532-4950	
Web: www.diestelturkey.com					
Dorothy Egg Farms LLC 271 Turkey Ln	Winthrop	ME	04364	207-377-9927	377-6106
Echo Lake Farm Produce Co PO Box 279	Burlington	WI	53105	800-888-3447	
TF: 800-888-3447 ■ *Web:* www.echolakefoods.com					
Esbenshade Farms 220 Eby Chiques Rd	Mount Joy	PA	17552	717-653-8061	653-6922
Web: esbenshadefarmmill.com					
Foster Farms Inc PO Box 306 PO Box 457	Livingston	CA	95334	800-255-7227	
TF: 800-255-7227 ■ *Web:* www.fosterfarms.com					
Glenwood Foods LLC 20850 Jackson Ln	Jetersville	VA	23083	804-561-3447	561-3228
Hubbard ISA 195 Main St.	Walpole	NH	03608	603-756-3311	756-9034
Web: www.hubbardbreeders.com					
Hy-Line International 1755 W Lakes Pkwy	West Des Moines	IA	50266	515-225-6030	225-6425
Web: www.hyline.com					
Maple Leaf Farms Inc PO Box 308	Milford	IN	46542	574-658-4121	658-2208
TF: 800-348-2812 ■ *Web:* www.mapleleaffarms.com					
Mar-Jac Poultry Inc 1020 Aviation Blvd PO Box 1017	Gainesville	GA	30501	770-531-5007	
Web: www.marjacpoultry.com					
Michael Foods Inc 301 Carlson Pkwy Ste 400	Minnetonka	MN	55305	952-258-4000	258-4911
TF: 800-328-5474 ■ *Web:* www.michaelfoods.com					
PECO Foods Inc 3701 Kauloosa Ave	Tuscaloosa	AL	35401	205-345-3955	343-2401
Web: www.pecofoods.com					
Perdue Farms Inc 31149 Old Ocean City Rd	Salisbury	MD	21804	410-543-3000	543-3532
TF: 800-473-7383 ■ *Web:* www.perdue.com					
Pilgrim's Corp 1770 Promontory Cir.	Greeley	CO	80634	800-321-1470	
NASDAQ: PPC ■ *TF:* 800-321-1470 ■ *Web:* www.pilgrimspride.com					
Plainville Farms Inc 304 S Water St PO Box 38	New Oxford	PA	17350	717-624-2191	
Web: www.plainvillefarms.com					
Puglisi Egg Farms Inc 75 Easy St	Howell	NJ	07731	732-938-2373	938-2232
Ritewood Inc 3643 S 4000 E PO Box 120	Franklin	ID	83237	208-646-2213	646-2217
Simpson's Eggs Inc 5015 Hwy 218 E.	Monroe	NC	28110	704-753-1478	753-4762
TF: 800-726-1330 ■ *Web:* www.simpsonseggs.com					
Tyson Foods Inc 2210 W Oaklawn Dr PO Box 2020	Springdale	AR	72762	479-290-4000	
NYSE: TSN ■ *TF:* 800-643-3410 ■ *Web:* www.tyson.com					
Wayne Farms LLC 4110 Continental Dr	Oakwood	GA	30566	800-392-0844	
TF: 800-392-0844 ■ *Web:* www.waynefarms.com					
Weiss Lake Egg Company Inc 9602 County Rd 59	Centre	AL	35960	256-927-5546	
Wilcox Farms Inc 40400 Harts Lake Valley Rd	Roy	WA	98580	360-458-7774	458-3995
Web: www.wilcoxfarms.com					
Willmar Poultry Co, The (WPC) 3735 County Rd 5 SW	Willmar	MN	56201	320-235-8850	
TF: 800-328-8849					
Zacky Farms Inc 2020 SE Ave	Fresno	CA	93721	562-641-2020	641-2040
TF: 800-888-0235 ■ *Web:* www.zacky.com					
Zephyr Egg Co Inc 4622 Gall Blvd	Zephyrhills	FL	33542	813-782-1521	
TF: 800-333-4415 ■ *Web:* refrigeratedtransporter.com					

10-9 Sugarcane & Sugarbeets Growers

Company	City	State	Zip	Phone	Fax
A Duda & Sons Inc 1200 Duda Trail	Oviedo	FL	32765	407-365-2111	365-2147
Web: www.duda.com					
Alico Inc (ALCO) 10070 Daniels Interstate Ct Ste 100	Fort Myers	FL	33913	863-675-2966	
NASDAQ: ALCO ■ *Web:* www.alicoinc.com					
Florida Crystals Corp 1 N Clematis St Ste 200	West Palm Beach	FL	33401	561-366-5100	366-5158
Web: www.floridacrystals.com					
Gay & Robinson Inc PO Box 156	Kaumakani	HI	96747	808-335-3133	335-6424
Sugar Cane Growers Co-op of Florida 1500 W Sugar House Rd	Belle Glade	FL	33430	561-996-5556	
Web: www.scgc.org					
US Sugar Corp 111 Ponce de Leon Ave	Clewiston	FL	33440	863-983-8121	
Web: www.ussugar.com					
Wedgworth Farms Inc 300 North Dixie Hwy Ste 471	West Palm Beach	FL	33401	561-832-4164	832-7965
Web: pbchistoryonline.org					

10-10 Tree Nuts Growers

Company	City	State	Zip	Phone	Fax
Agri-World Co-op 31545 Donald Ave	Madera	CA	93636	559-673-1306	673-1318
Blue Diamond Growers 1802 C St.	Sacramento	CA	95811	916-442-0771	446-8461
Web: www.bluediamond.com					
Braden Farms Inc 6940 Hughson Ave	Hughson	CA	95326	209-883-4061	
Columbia Empire Farms 31461 NE Bell Rd.	Sherwood	OR	97140	503-538-2156	
Web: www.columbiaempirefarms.com					
Cummings Violich Inc 1750 Dayton Rd	Chico	CA	95928	530-894-5494	891-4946
Farmland Management Services 301 E Main St.	Turlock	CA	95380	209-669-0742	243-1873*
**Fax Area Code:* 785					
Green Valley Pecan Co 1625 E Sahuarita Rd.	Sahuarita	AZ	85629	520-791-2852	791-2853
Web: greenvalleypecan.com					
Lassen Land Co 320 E S St	Orland	CA	95963	530-865-7676	865-8085
MacFarms of Hawaii LLC 89-406 Mamalahoa Hwy.	Captain Cook	HI	96704	415-399-1211	328-8081*
**Fax Area Code:* 808 ■ *Web:* www.macfarms.com					
Mauna Loa Macadamia Nut Corp 16-701 Macadamia Rd	Keaau	HI	96749	808-966-8618	966-8410*
**Fax:* Cust Svc ■ *TF Cust Svc:* 888-628-6256 ■ *Web:* www.maunaloa.com					
ML Macadamia Orchards LP 26-238 Hawaii Belt Rd	Hilo	HI	96720	808-969-8057	969-8123
NYSE: NNUT					
Spycher Bros Farms 14827 W HaRding Rd	Turlock	CA	95380	209-668-2471	668-4988
Web: www.spycherbros.com					
Sunnyland Farms Inc PO Box 8200	Albany	GA	31706	800-999-2488	
TF: 800-999-2488 ■ *Web:* www.sunnylandfarms.com					
Tejon Ranch Co 4436 Lebec Rd PO Box 1000	Lebec	CA	93243	661-248-3000	248-3100
NYSE: TRC ■ *Web:* www.tejonranch.com					

10-11 Vegetable Farms

Company	City	State	Zip	Phone	Fax
A Duda & Sons Inc 1200 Duda Trail	Oviedo	FL	32765	407-365-2111	365-2147
Web: www.duda.com					
Abe-El Produce 42143 Rd 120	Orosi	CA	93647	559-528-3030	528-6772
Agri-Empire Corp 630 W Seventh St.	San Jacinto	CA	92583	951-654-7311	
Web: www.agri-empire.com					
Amigo Farms Inc 4245 E Hwy 80	Yuma	AZ	85365	928-726-3738	726-3744
Web: www.amigofarms.com					
Anderson Farms Inc 4600 Second St.	Davis	CA	95618	530-753-5695	
Barkley Co PO Box 5540	Yuma	AZ	85365	928-782-2571	782-4656
Web: www.barkleycompany.com					
Barnes Farming Corp 7840 Old Bailey Hwy	Spring Hope	NC	27882	800-367-2799	459-9020*
**Fax Area Code:* 252 ■ *TF:* 800-367-2799 ■ *Web:* www.farmpak.com					
Bergin Fruit & Nut Company Inc 2000 Energy Park Dr.	St Paul	MN	55108	651-642-1234	
Web: berginfruit.com					
Black Gold 4320 18th Ave S Grand Forks	Grand Forks	ND	58201	701-792-3414	772-0749
Web: blackgoldfarms.com					
Bo-Jac Seed Co 245 County Rd 1500 E	Mount Pulaski	IL	62548	217-792-5001	792-5006
Bolthouse Farms 7200 E Brundage Ln	Bakersfield	CA	93307	800-467-4683	366-2834*
**Fax Area Code:* 661 ■ **Fax:* Sales ■ *TF:* 800-467-4683 ■ *Web:* www.bolthouse.com					
Bonipak 1850 W Stowell Rd	Santa Maria	CA	93458	805-925-2585	922-7982
Web: www.bonipak.com					
Borzynski Bros Distributing Inc 10508 Kraut Rd.	Franksville	WI	53126	630-668-3500	
Boskovich Farms Inc 711 Diaz Ave	Oxnard	CA	93030	805-487-2299	487-5189
Web: www.boskovichfarms.com					
Buurma Farms Inc 3909 Kok Rd	Willard	OH	44890	419-935-6411	935-1918
TF: 888-428-8762 ■ *Web:* www.buurmafarms.com					
Caruso Inc 3465 Hauck Rd.	Cincinnati	OH	45241	513-860-9200	
TF: 800-759-7659 ■ *Web:* carusologistics.com					
Charles H West Farms Inc 2953 Tub Mill Pond Rd	Milford	DE	19963	302-335-3936	335-0438
Christopher Ranch 305 Bloomfield Ave	Gilroy	CA	95020	408-847-1100	847-5488
TF: 800-779-1156 ■ *Web:* primuslabs.com					
Coast Produce Co 1791 Bay St.	Los Angeles	CA	90021	213-955-4900	955-4949
Web: www.coastproduce.com					
CROPP Co-op 1 Organic Way	LaFarge	WI	54639	888-444-6455	625-3025*
**Fax Area Code:* 608 ■ *TF:* 888-444-6455 ■ *Web:* www.organicvalley.coop					
D'Arrigo Bros Company of California Inc PO Box 850	Salinas	CA	93902	831-455-4500	455-4445
TF Cust Svc: 800-995-5939 ■ *Web:* www.andyboy.com					
Dean Kincaid Inc Wisconsin 106	Palmyra	WI	53156	262-495-3000	
Dresick Farms Inc PO Box 1260	Huron	CA	93234	559-945-2513	945-9627
Earthbound Farm 1721 San Juan Hwy	San Juan Bautista	CA	95045	831-623-7880	623-4988
TF: 800-690-3200 ■ *Web:* www.earthboundfarm.com					
Everkrisp Vegetables Inc 9202 W Harrison St.	Tolleson	AZ	85353	623-936-3321	
Web: everkrispvegetables.com					
Far Niente Winery Inc 1350 Acacia Dr.	Oakville	CA	94562	707-944-2861	
Web: www.farniente.com					
Frank Capurro & Son LLC 2250 Hwy 1 PO Box 410	Moss Landing	CA	95039	831-786-0731	
Fresh Express Inc 4757 The Grove Rd Ste 1212	Windermere	NC	34786	800-242-5472	
TF Cust Svc: 800-242-5472 ■ *Web:* www.freshexpress.com					
George Wood Farms Inc 113 N Carolina 343	Camden	NC	27921	252-335-4357	
Gilead Group LLC 12444 Powerscourt Dr Ste 375	St Louis	MO	63131	314-821-2500	
Web: www.gileadgroup.net					
Grant Family Farms 12155 NCR 15	Wellington	CO	80549	970-568-7654	
Web: www.grantfarms.com					
Greenheart Farms Inc 902 Zenon Way	Arroyo Grande	CA	93420	805-481-2234	481-7374
TF: 800-549-5531 ■ *Web:* www.greenheartfarms.com					
Griffin Ranches Inc 9490 W County 19th St	Somerton	AZ	85350	928-627-8809	
Grimmway Farms Inc PO Box 81498	Bakersfield	CA	93380	800-301-3101	
TF: 800-301-3101 ■ *Web:* www.grimmway.com					
Harris Farms Inc 27366 W Oakland Ave	Coalinga	CA	93210	559-884-2859	884-2855
TF: 800-311-6211 ■ *Web:* www.harrisfarms.com					
Hartung Bros Inc 708 Heartland Trl Ste 2000	Madison	WI	53717	608-829-6000	829-6001
TF: 800-362-2522 ■ *Web:* www.hartungbrothers.com					
HFM FoodService Inc 716 Umi St	Honolulu	HI	96819	808-843-3200	
Web: www.hfmfoodservice.com					
Hundley Farms Inc 28200 Florida 80	Belle Glade	FL	33430	561-996-6855	
Jack Bros Co 551 W Main St.	Brawley	CA	92227	760-344-3781	
Leach Farms Inc W1102 Buttercup Ct PO Box 192	Berlin	WI	54923	920-361-1880	361-4474
Web: www.leachfarms.com					
Long Farms Inc 2849 Lust Rd	Apopka	FL	32703	407-889-4141	889-5069
Major Farms Inc 1060 Growers St	Salinas	CA	93901	831-422-9616	
Martori Farms 7332 E Butherus Dr	Scottsdale	AZ	85260	480-998-1444	
Web: www.martorifarms.com					
McEntire Produce Inc 2040 American Italian Way	Columbia	SC	29209	803-799-3388	
TF: 800-845-2334 ■ *Web:* www.mcentireproduce.com					

Phone | Fax

Mount Dora Farms 16398 Jacinto Ft Blvd ... Houston TX 77015 713-821-7439
Web: www.mountdorafarms.com
Mountain King 6950 Neuhaus St ... Houston TX 77061 713-923-5807 921-3565
My-T Acres Inc 8127 Lewiston Rd ... Batavia NY 14020 585-343-1026 343-2051
Nash Produce Co 6160 S N Carolina 58 ... Nashville NC 27856 252-443-6011
TF: 800-334-3032 ■ *Web:* www.nashproduce.com
Navajo Agricultural Products Industry
PO Box 1318 ... Farmington NM 87499 505-566-2600 324-9458
Web: www.navajopride.com
Ocean Mist Farms
10855 Ocean Mist Pkwy Ste A ... Castroville CA 95012 831-633-2144
Web: www.oceanmist.com
Papen Farms Inc 847 Papen Ln ... Dover DE 19904 302-697-3291 697-2380
Peri & Sons Farms Inc PO Box 35 ... Yerington NV 89447 775-463-4444 463-4028
Web: www.periandsons.com
Petrocco Farms 14110 Brighton Rd ... Brighton CO 80601 303-659-6498 659-7645
TF: 888-876-2207 ■ *Web:* www.petroccofarms.com
Prime Time International
86-705 Ave 54 Ste A ... Coachella CA 92236 760-399-4278 399-4281
Web: www.primetimeproduce.com
RDO Equipment Co 700 Seventh St S ... Fargo ND 58103 877-444-7363 526-9717*
**Fax Area Code:* 701 ■ *TF:* 800-726-5391 ■ *Web:* www.rdoequipment.com
Roth Farms Inc 27502 CR 880 PO Box 1300 ... Belle Glade FL 33430 561-996-2991 996-8501
Web: www.rothfarms.com
Rousseau Farming Co 9601 W Harrison Ave ... Tolleson AZ 85353 623-936-7100 936-9045
Russo Farms Inc 1962 SE Ave ... Vineland NJ 08360 856-692-5942
Web: russofarms.com
Sackett Ranch Inc 2939 Neff Rd NE ... Stanton MI 48888 989-762-5049 762-5500
Sakata Farms Inc E Bromley Ln ... Brighton CO 80601 303-659-1559
Sam S Accursio Farms & Well
1225 NW Second St ... Homestead FL 33030 305-246-3455
San Miguel Produce Inc 4444 Naval Air Rd ... Oxnard CA 93033 805-488-0981 488-2103
Web: www.cutnclean.com
Sea Mist Farms 10855 Ocean Mist Pkwy ... Castroville CA 95012 831-633-2144 633-8163
Web: www.oceanmist.com
SMT Farms 8420 US 95 ... Yuma AZ 85365 928-341-9616
Sun World International Inc
16350 Drive Rd ... Bakersfield CA 93308 661-392-5000
Web: www.sun-world.com
Tanimura & Antle Inc PO Box 4070 ... Salinas CA 93912 800-772-4542
TF: 800-772-4542 ■ *Web:* www.taproduce.com
Taylor & Fulton Inc 932 Fifth Ave W ... Palmetto FL 34221 941-729-3883 723-2969
TF: 800-457-5577 ■ *Web:* www.taylorfulton.com
Teixeira Farms Inc
2600 Bonita Lateral Rd ... Santa Maria CA 93458 805-928-3801 928-9405
Web: www.teixeirafarms.com
Thomas Produce Co 9905 Clint Moore Rd ... Boca Raton FL 33496 561-482-1111 852-0018
Web: www.thomasproduce.com
Tom Bengard Ranch Inc 634 W Market ... Salinas CA 93901 831-758-5770
Web: bengardranch.com
Torrey Farms Inc Maltby Rd ... Elba NY 14058 585-757-9941
Web: www.torreyfarms.com
Tri-Campbell Farms 15111 Hwy 17 ... Grafton ND 58237 701-352-3116 352-2008
Web: www.tricampbellfarms.com
Turek Farms 8558 State Rt 90 ... King Ferry NY 13081 315-364-8735 364-5257
Web: www.turekfarms.com
Twin Garden Farms 23017 Illinois 173 ... Harvard IL 60033 815-943-7448
Web: www.twingardenfarms.com
Village Farms LP 7 Christopher Way ... Eatontown NJ 07724 732-676-3000 936-1187*
**Fax Area Code:* 407 ■ *Web:* www.villagefarms.com
Wada Farms Potatoes Inc 326 S 1400 W ... Pingree ID 83262 208-684-9801 684-4157
Web: www.wadafarms.com
Weber Farms 3559 Rd 'K' NW ... Quincy WA 98848 509-787-3620 787-4465
West Coast Distributing Inc
Commerce Pl 350 Main St ... Boston MA 02148 781-665-9393
TF: 800-235-3730 ■ *Web:* www.wcd-network.com
Wiers Farm Inc 4465 St Rt 103 S PO Box 385 ... Willard OH 44890 419-935-0131 933-2017
TF: 800-777-6243 ■ *Web:* wiersfarm.com
Wilson Farm Inc 10 Pleasant St ... Lexington MA 02421 781-862-3900 863-0469
Web: www.wilsonfarm.com
Wolfsen Inc 1269 W 'I' St ... Los Banos CA 93635 209-827-7700 827-7780
Web: wolfseninc.com
Worzella & Sons Inc 2801 Hoover Ave ... Plover WI 54467 715-344-4098
Web: worzellaandsons.com
Wysocki Produce Farm Inc 6320 Third Ave ... Plainfield WI 54966 715-366-7175

11 AGRICULTURAL SERVICES

11-1 Crop Preparation Services

Phone | Fax

AG Plus Inc 401 N Main PO Box 306 ... South Whitley IN 46787 260-723-5141
Web: www.agplusinc.com
Agricor Inc 1626 S Joaquin Dr ... Marion IN 46953 765-662-0606
Web: www.agricor.org
American Raisin Packers Inc
2335 Chandler St PO Box 30 ... Selma CA 93662 559-896-4760 896-8942
Web: americanraisinpacking.com
Andrews Distribution Co 13650 Copus Rd ... Bakersfield CA 93313 661-858-2266 858-2965
Web: www.andrewsagInc.com
Baird-Neece Packing Corp 60 SE St ... Porterville CA 93257 559-784-3393
Borg Produce Co
1601 E Olympic Blvd Bldg 100 ... Los Angeles CA 90021 213-688-9388 688-9381
Web: www.borgproduce.com
Cecelia Packing Corp 24780 E S Ave ... Orange Cove CA 93646 559-626-5000
Web: ceceliapack.com
Chooljian Bros Packing Company Inc
3192 S Indianola St ... Sanger CA 93657 559-875-5501 875-1582
Web: www.chooljianbrothers.com
Cummins Family Produce Inc
2570 Eldridge Ave ... Twin Falls ID 83301 208-733-5371

Deardorff-Jackson Company Inc PO Box 1188 ... Oxnard CA 93032 805-487-7801 483-1286
Web: www.deardorfffamilyfarms.com
Delta Packing Co 6021 E Kettleman Ln ... Lodi CA 95240 209-334-1023 334-0811
Web: www.deltapacking.com
Diamond Fruit Growers Inc 3515 Chevron Dr ... Hood River OR 97031 541-354-5300 354-5394
Web: www.diamondfruit.com
DiMare Bros/New England Farms Packing Co
84 New England Produce Ctr ... Chelsea MA 02150 617-889-3800
Web: dimarefresh.com
Dundee Citrus Growers Assn 111 First St N ... Dundee FL 33838 863-439-1574 439-1535
Web: www.dun-d.com
Emerald Packing 2823 N Orange Blossom Trl ... Orlando FL 32804 407-420-9534
Erwin-Keith Inc 1529 Hwy 193 ... Wynne AR 72396 870-238-2079 238-8621
TF: 888-535-7333 ■ *Web:* progenyag.com
Farmers Co-op Union, The
225 S Broadway PO Box 159 ... Sterling KS 67579 620-278-2141
TF: 800-238-1843 ■ *Web:* cpcoop.us
Fillmore-Piru Citrus Assn (FPCA)
357 N Main St PO Box 350 ... Piru CA 93040 805-521-1781 521-0990
Web: www.fillmorepirucitrus.com
Fresh Express Inc
4757 The Grove Rd Ste 1212 ... Windermere NC 34786 800-242-5472
TF Cust Svc: 800-242-5472 ■ *Web:* www.freshexpress.com
Golden Peanut Company LLC
100 N Pt Ctr E Ste 400 ... Alpharetta GA 30022 770-752-8160 752-8308
Web: www.goldenpeanut.com
Great Lakes Packers Inc
400 Great Lakes Pkwy ... Bellevue OH 44811 419-483-2956
Gruma Corp 1159 Cottonwood L Ste 200 ... Irving TX 75038 972-232-5000 232-5176
TF: 800-147-8629 ■ *Web:* www.gruma.com
GTC-GTC LLC 14574 Weld County Rd 64 ... Greeley CO 80631 970-351-6000 351-6003
Haines City Citrus Growers Assn (HCCGA)
8 Railroad Ave PO Box 337 ... Haines City FL 33844 863-422-1174 422-6544
TF Sales: 800-327-6676 ■ *Web:* www.hilltopcitrus.com
Harllee Packing Inc 2308 US 301 N ... Palmetto FL 34221 941-722-7747
Web: www.harlleepacking.com
Harris Woolf California Almonds
26060 Colusa Rd ... Coalinga CA 93210 559-884-2147 884-2746
Web: www.harriswoolfalmonds.com
Hazelnut Growers of Oregon 401 N 26th Ave ... Cornelius OR 97113 503-648-4176 648-9515
TF: 800-273-4676 ■ *Web:* www.westnut.com
Hunt Bros 2404 Hunt Bros Rd SE ... Lake Wales FL 33898 863-676-9471 676-8362
Index Fresh Inc 18184 Slover Ave ... Bloomington CA 92316 909-877-0999 877-0495
TF: 800-352-6931 ■ *Web:* www.indexfresh.com
Indian River Exchange Packers Inc
7355 Ninth St SW ... Vero Beach FL 32968 772-562-2252
Web: irexp.com
JLG Harvesting Inc 1450 S Atlantic Ave ... Yuma AZ 85365 928-329-7548 329-7551
Kingsburg Apple Packers Inc
10363 E Davis Ave PO Box 38 ... Kingsburg CA 93631 559-897-5132 897-4532
Web: www.kingsburgorchards.com
Kingston Cos 477 Shoup Ave ... Idaho Falls ID 83402 208-522-2365 522-7488
Web: kingstoncorp.com
Klink Citrus Assn 32921 Rd 159 PO Box 188 ... Ivanhoe CA 93235 559-798-1881 798-0182
LA Hearne Company Inc 512 Metz Rd ... King City CA 93930 831-385-5441 385-4377
Web: www.hearneco.com
Lake Region Packing Assn Inc
1293 S Duncan Dr ... Tavares FL 32778 352-343-3111 448-3441*
**Fax Area Code:* 952
Mann Packing Company Inc PO Box 690 ... Salinas CA 93902 831-422-7405
TF: 800-285-1002 ■ *Web:* www.veggiesmadeeasy.com
Mariani Nut Co 709 Dutton St ... Winters CA 95694 530-662-3311 949-4042
Web: www.marianinut.com
Mariani Packing Company Inc 500 Crocker Dr ... Vacaville CA 95688 707-452-2800 452-2973
TF: 800-231-1287 ■ *Web:* www.mariani.com
Mesa Citrus Growers Assn 254 W Broadway Rd ... Mesa AZ 85210 480-964-8615
Mooney Farms 1220 Fortress St ... Chico CA 95973 530-899-2661 899-7746
Web: www.mooneyfarms.com
Northern Fruit Co 220 2nd St NE ... East Wenatchee WA 98802 509-884-6651 884-1990
Web: www.northernfruit.com/home
Packers of Indian River Ltd
5700 W Midway Rd ... Fort Pierce FL 34981 772-464-6575
Phelan & Taylor Produce Co 1860 Front St ... Oceano CA 93445 805-489-2413
Pleasant Valley Potato Inc 275 E Elmore Ave ... Aberdeen ID 83210 208-397-4194 397-4841
Web: www.pleasantvalleypotato.com
River Ranch Fresh Foods 1156 Abbott St ... Salinas CA 93901 831-758-1390 755-8270
TF: 800-538-5868
Rivermaid Travelling Co PO Box 350 ... Lodi CA 95240 209-369-3586 369-5465
Web: www.rivermaid.com
RPAC LLC 21490 S Ortigalita Rd ... Los Banos CA 93635 209-826-0272 826-3882
Web: www.rpacalmonds.com
Tracy-Luckey Company Inc 110 N Hicks St ... Harlem GA 30814 706-556-6216 556-6210
TF: 800-476-4796
Veg-Pro Inc 11800 Gordon Ave ... Grant MI 49327 231-834-5634
Wilco Peanut Co 3391 US Hwy 281 N ... Pleasanton TX 78064 830-569-3808 569-2743

11-2 Livestock Improvement Services

Phone | Fax

ABS Global Inc 1525 River Rd PO Box 459 ... DeForest WI 53532 608-846-3721 846-6442
TF Cust Svc: 800-356-5331 ■ *Web:* www.absglobal.com
Accelerated Genetics E 10890 Penny Ln ... Baraboo WI 53913 608-356-8357 356-4387
TF: 800-451-9275 ■ *Web:* www.accelgen.com
Alta California N8350 High Rd ... Watertown WI 53094 920-261-5065 262-8022
TF: 800-932-2855 ■ *Web:* web.altagenetics.com
AMS Genetics Inc
7441 Sharpsburg Pk PO Box 12 ... Boonsboro MD 21713 240-329-0169 469-4231
Web: www.amsgenetics.com
Certified Semen Services
401 Bernadette Dr PO Box 1033 ... Columbia MO 65203 573-445-4406 446-2279
Web: www.naab-css.org

				Phone	Fax
COBA/Select Sires Inc 1224 Alton Darby Creek Rd *TF:* 800-837-2621 ■ *Web:* www.cobaselect.com	Columbus	OH	43228	614-878-5333	870-2622
Cobb-Vantress Inc PO Box 1030 *TF:* 800-748-9719 ■ *Web:* www.cobb-vantress.com	Siloam Springs	AR	72761	479-524-3166	524-3043
Dairy One 730 Warren Rd *TF:* 800-344-2697 ■ *Web:* www.dairyone.com	Ithaca	NY	14850	607-257-1272	257-6808
Flatness International Inc 104 Stony Mtn Rd *Web:* www.flatnessintl.com	Tunkhannock	PA	18657	570-836-3527	836-1549
Genex Co-op Inc/CRI 117 E Green Bay St *TF:* 888-333-1783 ■ *Web:* genex.crinet.com	Shawano	WI	54166	715-526-2141	526-4511
Hagyard-Davidson-McGee Assoc PSC 4250 Iron Works Pike *TF:* 888-323-7798 ■ *Web:* www.hagyard.com	Lexington	KY	40511	859-255-8741	253-0196
NA of Animal Breeders (NAAB) 401 Bernadette Dr *Web:* www.naab-css.org	Columbia	MO	65203	573-445-4406	446-2279
National Dairy Herd Improvement Assn Inc 421 S 9 Mound Rd PO Box 930399 *Web:* www.dhia.org	Verona	WI	53593	608-848-6455	848-7675
Newsham Choice Genetics LC 1415 28th St Ste 400 *Web:* choice-genetics.com	West Des Moines	IA	50265	515-225-9420	
Reproduction Enterprises Inc 908 N Prairie Rd *TF:* 866-734-2855 ■ *Web:* www.reproductionenterprises.com	Stillwater	OK	74075	405-377-8037	377-4541
SEK Genetics 9525 70th Rd **Fax Area Code:* 620 ■ *TF:* 800-443-6389 ■ *Web:* www.sekgenetics.com	Galesburg	KS	66740	800-443-6389	763-2231*
Select Sires Inc 11740 US Hwy 42 N *Web:* www.selectsires.com	Plain City	OH	43064	614-873-4683	873-5751
Simonsen Laboratories Inc 1180-C Day Rd *Web:* www.simlab.com	Gilroy	CA	95020	408-847-2002	847-4176

12 AIR CARGO CARRIERS

				Phone	Fax
ABX Air Inc 145 Hunter Dr *TF:* 800-736-3973 ■ *Web:* www.abxair.com	Wilmington	OH	45177	937-382-5591	
Aeronet Worldwide 42 Corporate Pk **Fax Area Code:* 800 ■ *TF:* 800-552-3869 ■ *Web:* www.aeronet.com	Irvine	CA	92606	949-474-3000	559-7090*
Agility Holdings Inc 240 Commerce *Web:* www.geo-logistics.com	Irvine	CA	92602	714-617-6300	
Air Creebec Inc 101 Fecteau St *TF:* 800-567-6567 ■ *Web:* www.aircreebec.ca	Val-d'or	QC	J9P0G4	819-825-8375	
Air North Charter & Training Ltd 150 Condor Rd *TF:* 800-661-0407 ■ *Web:* www.flyairnorth.com	Whitehorse	YT	Y1A6E6	867-668-2228	
Air-Sea Forwarders Inc PO Box 90637 *Web:* www.airseainc.com	Los Angeles	CA	90009	310-216-1616	216-2625
Alex Nichols Agency 3800 Hampton Rd *Web:* www.anaht.com	Oceanside	NY	11572	516-678-9100	678-1344
Alpine Air Express 1177 Alpine Air Way *Web:* www.alpine-air.com	Provo	UT	84601	801-373-1508	377-3781
Ameriflight Inc 4700 Empire Ave Hngr 1 **Fax:* Cust Svc ■ *TF:* 800-800-4538 ■ *Web:* www.ameriflight.com	Burbank	CA	91505	818-847-0000	847-0305*
Amerijet International Inc 2800 S Andrews Ave *TF:* 800-927-6059 ■ *Web:* www.amerijet.com	Fort Lauderdale	FL	33316	954-320-5300	
Atlas Air Worldwide Holdings Inc 2000 Westchester Ave *NASDAQ: AAWW* ■ *TF:* 866-434-1617 ■ *Web:* www.atlasair.com	Purchase	NY	10577	914-701-8000	701-8001
Cathay Pacific Cargo 6040 Avion Dr Ste 338 *TF:* 800-628-6960 ■ *Web:* www.cathaypacificcargo.com	Los Angeles	CA	90045	310-417-0052	348-9789
Cayman Airways Cargo Services 6103 NW 72nd Ave *TF:* 800-252-2746 ■ *Web:* www.caymanairways.com	Miami	FL	33166	305-526-3190	455-5616
Central Airlines Inc 411 NW Lou Holland Dr *Web:* www.centralairsouthwest.com	Kansas City	MO	64116	816-472-7711	472-1682
Centurion Cargo 4500 NW36th St *Web:* www.centurioncargo.com	Miami	FL	33166	305-871-0130	871-0118
China Airlines Cargo Sales & Service 11201 Aviation Blvd **Fax Area Code:* 907 ■ *TF:* 800-778-4838 ■ *Web:* www.china-airlines.com	Los Angeles	CA	90045	310-646-4293	248-4176*
Delta Air Cargo PO Box 20559 Dept 670 **Fax Area Code:* 404 ■ *TF:* 800-352-2737 ■ *Web:* deltacargo.com	Atlanta	GA	30320	800-352-2737	714-5022*
Empire Airlines Inc 11559 N Atlas Rd *Web:* www.empireairlines.com	Hayden	ID	83835	208-292-3850	292-3851
ICL Express 2307 Coney Island Ave *Web:* www.icl-express.com	Brooklyn	NY	11223	718-376-1023	376-1073
Kalitta Flying Service 818 Willow Run Airport *TF:* 800-521-1590 ■ *Web:* www.kalittaair.com	Ypsilanti	MI	48198	734-484-0088	484-3640
Lynden Air Cargo LLC 6441 S Airpark Pl *TF:* 888-243-7248 ■ *Web:* www.lynden.com	Anchorage	AK	99502	907-243-7248	257-5124
MartinAire Aviation LLC 4553 Glenn Curtiss Dr *TF:* 866-557-1861 ■ *Web:* www.martinaire.com	Addison	TX	75001	972-349-5700	349-5750
Polar Air Cargo 2000 Westchester Ave *Web:* www.polaraircargo.com	Purchase	NY	10577	914-701-8000	701-8001
Qantas Airways Cargo 6555 W Imperial Hwy *TF General:* 800-227-0290 ■ *Web:* www.qantas.com/travel/airlines/home/us/en	Los Angeles	CA	90045	310-665-2280	665-2201
Rhoades Aviation Inc 4770 Ray Boll Blvd *Web:* www.jlrventures.net/default.asp?sec_id=180007186	Columbus	IN	47203	812-372-1819	
Ryan International Airlines Inc 4949 Harrison Ave	Rockford	IL	61108	815-316-5420	398-0192
Service by Air Inc 222 Crossways Pk Dr **Fax Area Code:* 516 ■ *TF:* 800-243-5545 ■ *Web:* www.sbaglobal.com	Woodbury	NY	11797	800-243-5545	921-4304*
Southwest Airlines Air Cargo 2702 Love Field Dr *TF:* 800-533-1222 ■ *Web:* www.swacargo.com	Dallas	TX	75235	800-533-1222	
Tampa Airlines Cargo 1650 NW 66th Ave Bldg 708 *Web:* aviancacargo.com	Miami	FL	33122	305-526-6720	
Thai Airways International Cargo 6501 W Imperial Hwy *Web:* www.thaicargo.com	Los Angeles	CA	90045	310-670-8591	
United Airlines Cargo PO Box 66100 *TF:* 800-822-2746 ■ *Web:* www.unitedcargo.com	Chicago	IL	60666	800-822-2746	
Virgin Atlantic Cargo JFK International Airport Bldg 15 *TF:* 800-828-6822 ■ *Web:* www.virgin-atlantic.com	Jamaica	NY	11430	516-775-2600	354-3760

13 AIR CHARTER SERVICES

See Also Aviation - Fixed-Base Operations p. 1835; Helicopter Transport Services p. 2463

				Phone	Fax
Active Aero Group 2068 E St **Fax:* Hum Res ■ *TF Cust Svc:* 800-872-5387 ■ *Web:* www.activeaero.com	Belleville	MI	48111	734-547-7200	547-7222*
Aero Air LLC 2050 NE 25th Ave *TF:* 800-448-2376 ■ *Web:* www.aeroair.com	Hillsboro	OR	97124	503-640-3711	681-6514
Air Charter Team 4151 N Mulberry Dr Ste 250 *TF:* 800-205-6610 ■ *Web:* www.aircharterteam.com	Kansas City	MO	64116	816-283-3280	283-3185
Air Palm Springs 145 S Gene Autry Trl Ste 14 *TF:* 800-760-7774 ■ *Web:* www.airps.com	Palm Springs	CA	92262	760-322-1104	
Airbus Helicopters Canada 1100 Gilmore Rd PO Box 250 *TF:* 800-267-4999 ■ *Web:* www.airbushelicopters.ca	Fort Erie	ON	L2A5M9	905-871-7772	
AirFlite Inc 3250 AirFlite Way *TF:* 800-241-3548 ■ *Web:* www.airflight.com	Long Beach	CA	90807	562-490-6200	490-6290
Airship Ventures Inc NASA Research Park Bldg 156 *Web:* www.airshipventures.com	Moffett Field	CA	94035	650-969-8100	
Alpine Helicopters Ltd 1295 Industrial Rd *Web:* www.alpinehelicopter.com	Kelowna	BC	V1Z1G4	250-769-4111	
American Air Charter Inc 577 Bell Ave *TF:* 888-532-2710 ■ *Web:* www.americanaircharter.com	Chesterfield	MO	63005	636-532-2707	532-1486
Avstar Aviation Ltd 12 N Haven Ln *TF:* 800-575-2359 ■ *Web:* www.avstaraviation.com	East Northport	NY	11731	631-499-0048	
Berry Aviation Inc 1807 Airport Dr *TF:* 800-229-2379 ■ *Web:* www.berryaviation.com	San Marcos	TX	78666	512-353-2379	353-2593
Bighorn Airways Inc 912 W Brundage Ln *Web:* www.bighornairways.com	Sheridan	WY	82801	307-672-3421	
Bluffton Flying Service Co 1080 Navajo Dr *Web:* www.blufftonflyingservice.com	Bluffton	OH	45817	419-358-7045	
Charter Flight Inc 1928 S Blvd *TF:* 800-521-3148 ■ *Web:* www.charterflightinc.com	Charlotte	NC	28208	704-359-9124	
Charter Services Inc 8400 Airport Rd W *Web:* www.csijets.com	Mobile	AL	36608	251-633-6090	
Chrysler Aviation Inc (CAI) 7120 Hayvenhurst Ave Ste 309 *TF:* 800-995-0825 ■ *Web:* www.chrysleraviation.com	Van Nuys	CA	91406	818-989-7900	
Clay Lacy Aviation 7435 Valjean Ave *TF:* 800-423-2904 ■ *Web:* www.claylacy.com	Van Nuys	CA	91406	818-989-2900	904-3450
Clintondale Aviation Inc 652 Rt Highland Ste 201 *Web:* www.clintondale.com	New York	NY	12528	845-883-9657	883-5277
Corporate Flight Inc 6150 Highland Rd *Web:* corporateflight.com	Waterford	MI	48327	248-666-8800	
CSI Aviation Services Inc 3700 Rio Grand Blvd NW *TF:* 800-765-9464 ■ *Web:* csiaviation.com	Albuquerque	NM	87107	505-761-9000	
Custom Helicopters Ltd 401 Helicopter Dr *Web:* www.customheli.com	St. Andrews	MB	R1A3P7	204-338-7953	
Elite Aviation LLC 7501 Hayvenhurst Pl *Web:* www.eliteaviation.com	Van Nuys	CA	91406	818-988-5387	988-2111
Era Helicopters LLC 600 Airport Service Rd PO Box 6550 *TF:* 800-256-2372 ■ *Web:* www.erahelicopters.com	Lake Charles	LA	70606	337-478-6131	474-3918
Exec Air Montana Inc 2430 Airport Rd *TF:* 800-513-2190 ■ *Web:* www.execairmontana.com	Helena	MT	59601	406-442-2190	442-2199
Executive Jet 4556 Airport Rd *TF:* 877-356-5387 ■ *Web:* www.executivejetmanagement.com	Cincinnati	OH	45226	513-979-6600	979-6600
Fair Winds Air Charter Inc 2525 SE Witham Field Hngr 7 *TF:* 800-989-9665 ■ *Web:* www.fwjets.com	Stuart	FL	34996	772-288-4130	288-4230
Flightstar Corp 7 Airport Rd Willard Airport *TF:* 800-747-4777 ■ *Web:* www.flightstar.com	Savoy	IL	61874	217-351-7700	351-9843
Hop-A-Jet Inc 5525 NW 15th Ave Ste 150 *TF:* 800-556-6633 ■ *Web:* www.hopajetworldwide.com	Fort Lauderdale	FL	33309	954-771-5779	772-6981
International Jet Aviation Services 8511 Aviator Ln *TF:* 800-858-5891 ■ *Web:* www.internationaljet.com	Centennial	CO	80112	303-790-0414	790-4144
Jet Resource Inc 455 Wilmer Ave Lunken Airport Hngr 27 *TF:* 800-404-5387 ■ *Web:* www.jetresource.com	Cincinnati	OH	45226	513-871-1554	
JetSuite 18952 MacArthur Blvd *TF:* 866-779-7770 ■ *Web:* www.jetsuite.com	Irvine	CA	92612	866-779-7770	
KaiserAir Inc 8735 Earhart Rd PO Box 2626 *TF:* 800-538-2625 ■ *Web:* www.kaiserair.com	Oakland	CA	94621	510-569-9622	255-5017
Key Air LLC 3 Juliano Dr Ste 201 *TF:* 888-539-2471 ■ *Web:* www.keyair.com	Oxford	CT	06478	203-264-0605	264-0218
Key Lime Air Corp 13252 E Control Tower Rd *Web:* www.keylimeair.com	Englewood	CO	80112	303-768-9626	
Kucera International Inc 38133 Western Pkwy *Web:* www.kucerainternational.com	Willoughby	OH	44094	440-975-4230	
Life Flight Network LLC 22285 Yellow Gate Ln NE *TF:* 800-232-0911 ■ *Web:* www.lifeflight.org	Aurora	OR	97002	503-678-4364	

Company	City	State	Zip	Phone	Fax
LR Services 602 Hayden Cir. *TF:* 888-675-9650 ■ *Web:* www.lrservices.com	Allentown	PA	18109	610-266-2500	266-3100
Mayo Aviation Inc 7735 S Peoria St. *TF:* 800-525-0194 ■ *Web:* www.mayoaviation.com	Englewood	CO	80112	303-792-4020	790-4909
Miami Air International Inc 5000 NW 36 St Ste 307 *Web:* www.miamiair.com	Miami	FL	33122	305-876-3600	871-4222
Million Air Interlink Inc 8501 Telephone Rd. **Fax Area Code:* 866 ■ *TF:* 888-589-9059 ■ *Web:* www.millionair.com	Houston	TX	77061	713-640-4000	283-8274*
Nashville Jet 635 Hangar Ln *Web:* www.nashvillejetcharters.com	Nashville	TN	37217	615-933-7894	
New England Life Flight Inc 1727 Robins St Hangar *TF:* 800-233-8998 ■ *Web:* www.bostonmedflight.org	Bedford	MA	01730	781-863-2213	
New World Aviation Inc 987 Postal Rd *Web:* www.newworldaviation.com	Allentown	PA	18109	610-231-9555	
Ohio Medical Transportation Inc 2827 W Dblin Granville Rd *TF:* 877-633-3598 ■ *Web:* www.medflight.com	Columbus	OH	43235	614-734-8001	
Pacific Coast Jet Charter Inc 10600 White Rock Rd *TF:* 800-655-3599 ■ *Web:* www.pacificjet.com	Rancho Cordova	CA	95670	916-631-6507	631-6687
Panorama Helicopters Ltd 360 Airport Rd. *Web:* www.helicopterespanorama.com	Alma	QC	G8B5V2	418-668-3046	
Pentastar Aviation 7310 Highland Rd **Fax:* Mktg ■ *TF:* 800-662-9612 ■ *Web:* www.pentastaraviation.com	Waterford	MI	48327	248-666-3630	666-9657*
Planemasters Ltd 32 W 611 Tower Rd DuPage Airport *TF:* 800-994-6400 ■ *Web:* www.planemasters.com	West Chicago	IL	60185	630-513-2100	377-3283
Premier Jets 2140 NE 25th Ave. *TF:* 800-635-8583 ■ *Web:* www.premierjets.com	Hillsboro	OR	97124	503-640-2927	681-3064
Presidential Aviation 1725 NW 51st Pl Ft Lauderdale Executive Airport *Web:* presidential-aviation.com	Fort Lauderdale	FL	33309	954-772-8622	
Priester Aviation 1061 S Wolf Rd. *TF:* 888-323-7887 ■ *Web:* www.priesterav.com	Wheeling	IL	60090	847-537-1133	459-0778
Ryan International Airlines Inc 4949 Harrison Ave	Rockford	IL	61108	815-316-5420	398-0192
S Jet 1251 W Blee Rd *Web:* www.spectrajetinc.com	Springfield	OH	45502	937-323-5804	323-8168
San Juan Airlines Co 4000 Airport Rd Ste A *TF:* 800-874-4434 ■ *Web:* www.sanjuanairlines.com	Anacortes	WA	98221	360-293-4691	
Seneca Flight Operations 2262 Airport Dr *Web:* www.senecaflight.com	Penn Yan	NY	14527	315-536-4471	536-4558
Sentient Jet LLC 100 Grossman Dr Ste 400 *TF:* 866-602-0044 ■ *Web:* www.sentient.com	Braintree	MA	02184	781-763-0200	
Skyservice Airlines Inc 9785 Ryan Ave. *TF:* 888-985-1402 ■ *Web:* skyservice.com	Dorval	QC	H9P1A2	514-636-3300	636-4855
Tavaero Jet Charter 7930 Airport Blvd *TF:* 800-343-3771 ■ *Web:* www.tavaero.com	Houston	TX	77061	713-643-5387	643-5398
Thunder Airlines Ltd 310 Hector Dougall Way *TF:* 800-803-9943 ■ *Web:* www.thunderair.com	Thunder Bay	ON	P7E6M6	800-803-9943	
Trans-Exec Air Service Inc 7240 Hayvenhurst Pl Ste 200 *Web:* www.transexec.com	Van Nuys	CA	91406	818-904-6900	
Tulip City Air Service Inc 1581 S Washington Ave *TF:* 800-748-0515 ■ *Web:* www.tulipcityair.com	Holland	MI	49423	616-392-7831	392-1841
Twin Cities Air Service Inc 81 Airport Dr *TF:* 800-564-3882 ■ *Web:* www.twincitiesairservice.com	Auburn	ME	04210	800-564-3882	
West Coast Aviation Services 19711 Campus Dr Ste 150 *TF:* 800-352-6153 ■ *Web:* www.westcoastaviationservices.net	Santa Ana	CA	92707	949-852-8340	260-3999

AIR CONDITIONING EQUIPMENT - AUTOMOTIVE

AIR CONDITIONING EQUIPMENT - WHOL

See Plumbing, Heating, Air Conditioning Equipment & Supplies - Whol p. 2959

14 AIR CONDITIONING & HEATING EQUIPMENT - COMMERCIAL/INDUSTRIAL

See Also Air Conditioning & Heating Equipment - Residential p. 1722; Refrigeration Equipment - Mfr p. 3057

Company	City	State	Zip	Phone	Fax
AAON Inc 2425 S Yukon Ave. *NASDAQ: AAON* ■ *Web:* www.aaon.com	Tulsa	OK	74107	918-583-2266	583-6094
Absolut Aire Inc 5496 N Riverview Dr. *TF:* 800-804-4000 ■ *Web:* www.absolutaire.com	Kalamazoo	MI	49004	269-382-1875	382-5291
ACS Group 1100 E Woodfield Rd Ste 588 *TF:* 800-783-7835 ■ *Web:* www.acscorporate.com/aec	Schaumburg	IL	60173	847-273-7700	273-7804
ACS Group, The 2900 S 160th St *Web:* www.acscorporate.com	New Berlin	WI	53151	262-641-8600	
Advantage Engineering Inc 525 E S- 18 Rd. *TF:* 800-669-1282 ■ *Web:* www.advantageengineering.com	Greenwood	IN	46142	317-887-0729	881-1277
Afcon Products Inc Elec Equip 35 Sargent Dr. *Web:* www.afconproducts.com	Bethany	CT	06524	203-393-9301	
Airco Mechanical Inc 8210 Demetre Ave *Web:* www.aircomech.com	Sacramento	CA	95828	916-381-4523	386-0350
Aitken Products Inc 566 N Eagle St PO Box 151 *Web:* www.aitkenproducts.com	Geneva	OH	44041	440-466-5711	466-5716
American Coolair Corp 3604 Mayflower St *TF:* 877-250-2822 ■ *Web:* www.coolair.com	Jacksonville	FL	32205	904-389-3646	387-3449
Aqua Cal Inc 2737 24th St N *Web:* www.aquacal.com	Saint Petersburg	FL	33713	727-823-5642	
Arctic Industries Inc 9731 NW 114th Way *TF:* 800-325-0123 ■ *Web:* arcticwalkins.com	Miami	FL	33178	305-883-5581	883-4651
Armstrong International Inc 2081 SE Ocean Blvd 4th Fl *TF:* 866-738-5125 ■ *Web:* www.armstronginternational.com	Stuart	FL	34996	772-286-7175	286-1001
Auer Steel & Heating Supply Co 2935 W Silver Spring Dr. *TF:* 800-242-0406 ■ *Web:* www.auersteel.com	Milwaukee	WI	53209	414-463-1234	463-0303
Bally Refrigerated Boxes Inc 135 Little Nine Rd. *Web:* www.ballyrefboxes.com	Morehead City	NC	28557	252-240-2829	240-0384
Birk Manufacturing 14 Capitol Dr Colton Rd Industrial Park Exit 71 off I-95 *Web:* www.birkmfg.com	East Lyme	CT	06333	860-739-4170	
Blissfield Manufacturing Co 626 Depot St *TF Cust Svc:* 800-626-1772 ■ *Web:* www.blissfield.com	Blissfield	MI	49228	517-486-2121	486-2128
Brainerd Compressor Rebuilders Inc 3034 Sandbrook St. *TF:* 800-228-4138 ■ *Web:* www.brainerdcompressor.com	Memphis	TN	38116	800-228-4138	
Bristol Compressors Inc 15185 Industrial Pk Rd *TF:* 855-601-0894 ■ *Web:* www.bristolcompressors.com	Bristol	VA	24202	276-466-4121	645-7500
Brooks Automation Inc Polycold Systems 3800 Lakeville Hwy. *TF:* 800-698-6149 ■ *Web:* www.brooks.com	Petaluma	CA	94954	707-769-7000	769-1380
Bruner Corp 3637 Lacon Rd. *Web:* www.brunercorp.com	Hilliard	OH	43026	614-334-9000	334-9001
Bry-Air Inc 10793 SR 37 W *TF:* 877-427-9247 ■ *Web:* www.bry-air.com	Sunbury	OH	43074	740-965-2974	965-5470
Buckley Associates Inc 385 King St. *Web:* www.buckleyonline.com	Hanover	MA	02339	781-878-5000	
Carnes Co 448 S Main St *Web:* www.carnes.com	Verona	WI	53593	608-845-6411	845-6470
Carrier Corp 1 Carrier Pl **Fax:* Hum Res ■ *TF:* 800-227-7437 ■ *Web:* www.carrier.com	Farmington	CT	06034	860-674-3000	674-3139*
CEI Enterprises Inc 245 WoodwaRd Rd SE **Fax Area Code:* 505 ■ *TF:* 800-545-4034 ■ *Web:* www.ceienterprises.com	Albuquerque	NM	87102	800-545-4034	243-1422*
Cembell Industries Inc 740 CCC Rd (Hwy 628) *Web:* www.cembell.com	Montz	LA	70068	985-652-1188	
Central Products LLC 7750 Georgetown Rd. *Web:* www.centralrestaurant.com	Indianapolis	IN	46268	317-876-1010	
Champion Energy Corp 1 Radisson Plz Ste 801 *Web:* www.championenergy.com	New Rochelle	NY	10801	914-576-6190	576-6126
Chiller Solutions LLC 101 Alexander Ave *Web:* www.edwards-eng.com	Pompton Plains	NJ	07444	973-835-2800	
Chromalox Inc 103 Gamma Dr Ext. *Web:* www.chromalox.com	Pittsburgh	PA	15238	412-967-3800	
ClimaCool Corp 15 S Virginia *Web:* www.climacoolcorp.com	Oklahoma City	OK	73106	405-815-3000	
ClimateMaster Inc 7300 SW 44th St **Fax:* Cust Svc ■ *TF:* 800-299-9747 ■ *Web:* www.climatemaster.com	Oklahoma City	OK	73179	405-745-6000	745-2006*
Cold Shot Chillers 14020 InterDr W *TF:* 800-473-9178 ■ *Web:* www.waterchillers.com	Houston	TX	77032	281-227-8400	
Colmac Coil Manufacturing Inc 370 N Lincoln St PO Box 571 *TF:* 800-845-6778 ■ *Web:* www.colmaccoil.com	Colville	WA	99114	509-684-2595	684-8331
Colonial Commercial Corp 275 Wagaraw Rd *OTC: CCOM* ■ *Web:* www.colonialcomm.com	Hawthorne	NJ	07506	973-427-8224	427-6981
Cummins Northwest LLC 811 SW Grady Way *TF:* 800-274-0336 ■ *Web:* www.cumminsnorthwest.com	Renton	WA	98055	425-235-3400	
Dais Analytic Corp 11552 Prosperous Dr. *Web:* www.daisanalytic.com	Odessa	FL	33556	727-375-8484	
Data Aire Inc 230 W BlueRidge Ave *Web:* www.dataaire.com	Orange	CA	92865	714-921-6000	
Dehumidification Manufacturing Gp LLC 6609 Ave U *TF:* 866-736-8348 ■ *Web:* www.rentdh.com	Houston	TX	77011	713-939-1166	
Desert Aire Corp N120 W18485 Freistadt Rd *Web:* www.desert-aire.com	Germantown	WI	53022	262-946-7400	
DiversiTech Inc 6650 Sugarloaf Pkwy Ste 100 *TF:* 800-995-2222 ■ *Web:* www.diversitech.com	Duluth	GA	30097	678-542-3600	542-3700
Dometic Corp 2320 Industrial Pkwy. *TF:* 800-544-4881 ■ *Web:* www.dometic.com	Elkhart	IN	46516	574-294-2511	293-9686
Doucette Industries Inc (DII) 20 Leigh Dr *TF:* 800-445-7511 ■ *Web:* www.doucetteindustries.com	York	PA	17406	717-845-8746	845-2864
Drink More Water Store 7595-A Rickenbacker Dr. *TF:* 800-697-2070 ■ *Web:* www.drinkmorewater.com	Gaithersburg	MD	20879	800-697-2070	
DRISTEEM Corp 14949 Technology Dr *TF:* 800-328-4447 ■ *Web:* www.dristeem.com	Eden Prairie	MN	55344	952-949-2415	229-3200
DRS Sustainment Systems Inc 7375 Industrial Rd *TF:* 800-694-5005 ■ *Web:* www.drs.com	Florence	KY	41042	859-372-8204	795-1475
Duro Dyne Corp 81 Spence St *TF:* 800-899-3876 ■ *Web:* www.durodyne.com	Bay Shore	NY	11706	631-249-9000	249-9000
Electro Impulse Laboratory Inc 1805 Rte 33 PO Box 278 *Web:* www.electroimpulse.com	Neptune	NJ	07753	732-776-5800	776-6793
Elliott-Lewis Corp 2900 Black Lk Pl. *Web:* www.elliottlewis.com	Philadelphia	PA	19154	215-698-4400	698-4436
Ellis & Watts Inc 4400 Glen Willow Lake Ln *Web:* www.elliswatts.com	Batavia	OH	45103	513-752-9000	752-4983
Emerson Climate Technologies 1675 Campbell Rd *Web:* www.emersonclimate.com	Sidney	OH	45365	937-498-3011	498-3334
Energy Labs Inc 9651 Airway Rd Ste E *Web:* www.cafepatterson.com	San Diego	CA	92154	619-671-0100	
Environmental Air Systems Inc 521 Banner Ave *Web:* www.easinc.net	Greensboro	NC	27401	336-273-1975	273-1975
Evapco Inc 5151 Allendale Ln *Web:* www.evapco.com	Taneytown	MD	21787	410-756-2600	756-6450

Company / Address	City	State	ZIP	Phone	Fax
Fidelity Engineering Corp 25 Loveton Cir PO Box 2500 TF: 800-787-6000 ■ Web: www.fidelityengineering.com	Sparks	MD	21152	410-771-9400	771-9412
First Operations LP 8273 Moberly Ln Web: www.firstco.com	Dallas	TX	75227	214-388-5751	388-2255
Focal Point Energy Inc 1650 Las Plumas Ave Web: www.focalpointenergy.com	San Jose	CA	95133	408-923-1541	
Friedrich 10001 Reunion Pl Ste 500 TF: 800-541-6645 ■ Web: www.friedrich.com	San Antonio	TX	78216	210-546-0500	357-4480
Fulton Precision Industries 300 Success Dr Web: www.fultonprecision.com	McConnellsburg	PA	17233	717-485-5158	
GHC Mechanical Inc 990 Pauly Dr Web: www.ghcmech.com	Elk Grove Village	IL	60007	847-593-0123	
GlassPoint Solar Inc 46485 Landing Pkwy Web: www.glasspoint.com	Fremont	CA	94538	415-778-2800	
Governair Corp 4841 N Sewell Ave Web: governair.com	Oklahoma City	OK	73118	405-525-6546	
Great Lakes Plumbing & Heating Company Inc 4521 W Diversey Ave Web: www.glph.com	Chicago	IL	60639	773-489-0400	489-1492
Gusmer Enterprises Inc 1165 Globe Ave Web: www.gusmerenterprises.com	Mountainside	NJ	07092	908-301-1811	
Haakon Industries (Canada) Ltd 11851 Dyke Rd Web: www.haakon.com	Richmond	BC	V7A4X8	604-273-0161	273-8397
Halton Group Americas Inc 103 Industrial Drive Web: www.halton.com	Scottsville	KY	42164	270-393-7214	
Hankison International 1000 Philadelphia St Web: www.spx.com	Canonsburg	PA	15317	724-745-1555	745-6040
Haskris Co 100 Kelly St Web: www.haskris.com	Elk Grove Village	IL	60007	847-956-6420	
Hastings HVAC Inc 3606 Yost Ave PO Box 669 TF Cust Svc: 800-228-4243 ■ Web: www.hastingshvac.com	Hastings	NE	68902	402-463-9821	463-6273
Heat Controller Inc 1900 Wellworth Ave Web: www.heatcontroller.com	Jackson	MI	49203	517-787-2100	787-9341
Heat Pipe Technology Inc 4340 NE 49th Ave Web: www.heatpipe.com	Gainesville	FL	32609	352-367-0999	367-1688
Heateflex Corp 405 Santa Clara St Web: www.heateflex.com	Arcadia	CA	91006	626-599-8566	
Henry Technologies 701 S Main St TF: 800-964-3679 ■ Web: www.henrytech.com	Chatham	IL	62629	217-483-2406	483-2408
Howden Buffalo Inc 7909 Parklane Rd Ste 300 *Fax Area Code: 866 ■ TF: 866-757-0908 ■ Web: www.howden.com	Columbia	SC	29223	803-741-2700	757-0908*
Hunton Group, The 10555 Westpark Dr Web: www.huntongroup.com	Houston	TX	77042	713-266-3900	
International Environmental Corp (IEC) PO Box 2598 Web: www.iec-okc.com	Oklahoma City	OK	73101	405-605-5000	605-5001
ITT Corp 1133 Westchester Ave *Fax: Mktg ■ Web: www.bellgossett.com	White Plains	NY	10604	914-641-2000	696-2950*
ITW Vortec 10125 Carver Rd TF: 800-441-7475 ■ Web: www.itw-air.com	Cincinnati	OH	45242	513-891-7485	891-4092
Jensen USA Inc 99 Aberdeen Loop Web: www.jensen-group.com	Panama City	FL	32405	850-271-5959	
Kobelco Compressors (America) Inc 3000 Hammond Ave Web: www.kobelcocompressors.com	Elkhart	IN	46516	574-295-3145	293-1641
Kooltronic Inc 30 Pennington-Hopewell Rd Web: www.kooltronic.com	Pennington	NJ	08534	609-466-3400	466-1114
Krack Corp 1300 N Arlington Heights Rd Ste 130 Web: www.krack.com	Itasca	IL	60143	630-629-7500	250-3537
Lawler Manufacturing Corp 7 Kilmer Ct Web: www.lawlercorp.com	Edison	NJ	08817	732-777-2040	777-4828
Layton Manufacturing Corp 825 Remsen Ave TF: 800-545-8002 ■ Web: www.laytonmfg.com	Brooklyn	NY	11236	718-498-6000	
Lintern Corp 8685 Stn St TF: 800-321-3638 ■ Web: www.lintern.com	Mentor	OH	44060	440-255-9333	255-6427
Lomanco Inc 2101 W Main St TF: 800-643-5596 ■ Web: www.lomanco.com	Jacksonville	AR	72076	501-982-6511	982-1258
Mammoth Inc 13200 Pioneer Trl Ste 150 Web: www.mammoth-inc.com	Chaska	MN	55318	952-358-6600	358-6700
Maradyne Corp 4540 W 160th St TF: 800-537-7444 ■ Web: www.maradyne.com	Cleveland	OH	44135	216-362-0755	
Marvair Airxcel Inc 156 Seedling Dr Web: www.marvair.com	Cordele	GA	31015	912-273-3636	
Master-Bilt Products 908 Hwy 15 N TF: 800-647-1284 ■ Web: www.master-bilt.com	New Albany	MS	38652	662-534-9061	534-6049
Mee Industries Inc 16021 Adelante St Web: www.meefog.com	Irwindale	CA	91702	626-359-4550	
Mermaid Manufacturing 2651 Park Windsor Dr Ste 203 TF: 800-330-3553 ■ Web: www.mmair.com	Fort Myers	FL	33901	239-418-0535	
Mestek Inc 260 N Elm St Web: www.mestek.com	Westfield	MA	01085	413-568-9571	
Midwest Towers Inc 1156 Hwy 19 East TF: 800-900-2190 ■ Web: www.midwesttowers.com	Chickasha	OK	73018	405-224-4622	224-4625
Mobile Climate Control Corp 17103 State Rd 4 E TF: 800-450-2211 ■ Web: www.mcc-hvac.com	Goshen	IN	46528	574-534-1516	533-4452
Multistack LLC 1065 Maple Ave Web: www.multistack.com	Sparta	WI	54656	608-366-2400	
Munters Corp 210 Sixth St PO Box 6428 *Fax: Cust Svc ■ TF: 800-843-5360 ■ Web: www.munters.com	Fort Myers	FL	33907	239-936-1555	278-8790*
Munters Corp DHI 79 Monroe St TF Sales: 800-843-5360 ■ Web: www.munters.com	Amesbury	MA	01913	978-241-1100	241-1215
National Refrigeration & Air Conditioning Canada Corp 159 Roy Blvd Web: www.trentonrefrigeration.com	Brantford	ON	N3T5Y6	519-751-0444	
Niagara Blower Co Inc 673 Ontario St TF: 800-426-5169 ■ Web: www.niagarablower.com	Buffalo	NY	14207	716-875-2000	875-1077
Nordyne Inc 8000 Phoenix Pkwy *Fax: Sales ■ TF: 800-422-4328 ■ Web: www.nortekhvac.com	O'Fallon	MO	63368	636-561-7300	561-7323*
Nortek Air Solutions LLC 13200 Pioneer Trl Ste 150 Web: www.nortekair.com	Eden Prairie	MN	55347	952-358-6600	
North American Filter Corp 200 W Shore Blvd Web: www.nafcoinc.com	Newark	NY	14513	315-331-7000	
Novelaire Technologies LLC 10132 Mammoth Ave Web: www.novelaire.com	Baton Rouge	LA	70814	225-924-0427	
Pacific Rim Mechanical 7655 Convoy Ct TF: 800-891-4822 ■ Web: www.prmech.com	San Diego	CA	92111	858-974-6500	974-6501
Packless Metal Hose Inc PO Box 20668 TF: 800-347-4859 ■ Web: www.packless.com	Waco	TX	76702	254-666-7700	666-7893
Peerless of America Inc 1201 Wabash Ave Web: www.peerlessofamerica.com	Effingham	IL	62401	217-342-0400	342-0412
Perry Products Corp 25 Mount Laurel Rd Web: www.perryproducts.com	Hainesport	NJ	08036	609-267-1600	267-8724
PH Windsolutions Inc 7562 Chemin de la Cte de Liesse Web: www.phwindsolutions.com	Montreal	QC	H4T1E7	514-522-6329	
Phelps Fan LLC 10701 I-30 Web: www.phelpsfan.com	Little Rock	AR	72209	501-568-5550	568-3363
Phoenix Manufacturing Inc 3655 E Roeser Rd TF Cust Svc: 800-325-6952 ■ Web: www.evapcool.com	Phoenix	AZ	85040	602-437-1034	437-4833
Pittsburgh Plumbing Heating & Industrial (PPHI) 434 Melwood Ave TF: 800-445-4155 ■ Web: www.pphind.com	Pittsburgh	PA	15213	412-622-8100	622-8145
Polar King International Inc 4424 New Haven Ave Web: www.polarking.com	Fort Wayne	IN	46803	260-428-2530	
Precision Pump & Valve Service Inc 517 Old Goff Mtn Rd Web: www.ppvs.com	Cross Lanes	WV	25313	304-776-1710	
Proair LLC 28731 County Rd 6 TF: 800-338-8544 ■ Web: www.proairllc.com	Elkhart	IN	46514	574-264-5494	264-2194
RAE Corp Technical Systems Div 4492 Hunt St Web: rae-corp.com	Pryor	OK	74361	918-825-7222	825-0723
Rama Corp 600 W Esplanade Ave TF: 800-472-5670 ■ Web: ramacorporation.com	San Jacinto	CA	92583	951-654-7351	654-3748
Refrigeration Research Inc 525 N Fifth St Web: www.refresearch.com	Brighton	MI	48116	810-227-1151	227-3700
Refrigerator Manufacturers Inc 17018 Edwards Rd Web: www.rmi-econocold.com	Cerritos	CA	90703	562-926-2006	
Rheem Mfg Company Air Conditioning Div 5600 Old Greenwood Rd Web: www.rheem.com	Fort Smith	AR	72903	479-646-4311	
Rink Systems Inc 1103 Hershey St TF: 800-944-7930 ■ Web: www.rinksystems.com	Albert Lea	MN	56007	507-373-9175	377-1060
Ritchie Engineering Company Inc 10950 Hampshire Ave S Web: www.yellowjacket.com	Bloomington	MN	55438	952-943-1300	
Ruskin Rooftop Systems 1625 Diplomat Dr Web: www.rooftopsystems.com	Carrollton	TX	75006	972-247-7447	
Russell Food Equipment Ltd 1255 Venables St TF: 800-663-0707 ■ Web: www.russellfood.ca	Vancouver	BC	V6A3X6	604-253-6611	
San Jamar Inc 555 Koopman Ln TF: 800-248-9826 ■ Web: www.sanjamar.com	Elkhorn	WI	53121	262-723-6133	
Sealed Unit Parts Company Inc 2230 Landmark Pl TF: 800-333-9125 ■ Web: www.supco.com	Allenwood	NJ	08720	732-223-6644	223-1617
Seasons-4 Inc 4500 Industrial Access Rd TF: 800-888-9900 ■ Web: www.seasons4.net	Douglasville	GA	30134	770-489-0716	489-2938
Shield Air Solutions Inc 3708 Greenhouse Rd TF: 800-237-2095 ■ Web: shieldair.com	Houston	TX	77084	281-944-4300	
Skuttle Manufacturing Co 101 Margaret St TF: 800-848-9786 ■ Web: www.skuttle.com	Marietta	OH	45750	740-373-9169	373-9565
Slant Fin Corp 100 Forest Dr Web: www.slantfin.com	Greenvale	NY	11548	516-484-2600	484-2600
Snyder Capital Corp 5110 Pk Ln	Dallas	TX	75220	214-754-0500	
So Low Environmental Equipment Company Inc 10310 Spartan Dr Web: www.so-low.com	Cincinnati	OH	45215	513-772-9410	
T Rad North America Inc 750 Frank Yost Ln PO Box 2300 Web: www.copar.net	Hopkinsville	KY	42240	270-885-9116	
Tecumseh Power Co 900 N St Web: www.tecumsehpower.com	Grafton	WI	53024	262-377-2700	
Tecumseh Products Company PAris Div 2700 W Wood St Web: tecumseh.com	Paris	TN	38242	731-642-6394	
Tekgard Inc 3390 Farmtrail Rd Web: www.tekgard.com	York	PA	17406	717-854-0005	
Temp-Control Mechanical Corp (TCM) 4800 N Ch Ave TF: 877-826-3828 ■ Web: www.tcmcorp.com	Portland	OR	97217	503-285-9851	285-9978
Temtrol LLC 106 N Industrial Blvd Web: www.temtrol.com	Okarche	OK	73762	405-263-7286	263-4924
Texas Air Systems Inc 6029 W Campus Cir Dr Web: www.texasairsystems.com	Irving	TX	75063	972-570-4700	
Therma-Flite Inc 849 Jackson St Web: www.therma-flite.com	Benicia	CA	94510	707-747-5949	
Thermal Care Inc 7720 N Lehigh Ave TF: 888-828-7387 ■ Web: www.thermalcare.com	Niles	IL	60714	847-966-2260	966-9358
Thermo King Corp 314 W 90th St Web: www.thermoking.com	Minneapolis	MN	55420	952-887-2200	887-2615
ThermoElectric Cooling America Corp 4048 W Schubert Ave TF: 888-832-2872 ■ Web: www.thermoelectric.com	Chicago	IL	60639	773-342-4900	342-0191

Phone | Fax

Tom Barrow Co (TBC) 2800 Plant Atkinson Rd .... Atlanta GA 30339 404-351-1010 350-9121
TF: 800-229-8226 ■ *Web:* www.tombarrow.com

Tom Richards Inc 7010 Lindsay Dr .... Mentor OH 44060 440-974-1300
Web: www.process-technology.com

Transitair Inc 27 Bank St .... Hornell NY 14843 607-324-7860
Web: www.transitairusa.com

Traulsen & Company Inc 4401 Blue Mound Rd .... Fort Worth TX 76106 800-825-8220 624-4302*
**Fax Area Code:* 817 ■ **Fax:* Cust Svc ■ *TF:* 800-825-8220 ■ *Web:* www.traulsen.com

Tulsa Heaters Inc 1215 S Boulder Ste 1200 .... Tulsa OK 74119 918-582-9918 582-9916
Web: www.tulsaheaters.com

Tutco Inc 500 Gould Dr .... Cookeville TN 38506 931-432-4141 432-4140
TF: 877-262-4533 ■ *Web:* www.tutco.com

United CoolAir Corp 491 E Princess St .... York PA 17403 717-843-4311 854-4462
TF: 877-905-1111 ■ *Web:* www.unitedcoolair.com

United Electric Company LP
501 Galveston St .... Wichita Falls TX 76301 940-397-2100
Web: www.magicaire.com

Vinotheque Wine Cellars 1738 E Alpine Ave .... Stockton CA 95205 209-466-9463
Web: www.vinotheque.com

Watsco Inc 2665 S Bayshore Dr Ste 901 .... Miami FL 33133 305-714-4100 858-4492
NYSE: WSO ■ *Web:* www.watsco.com

Watts Radiant Inc 4500 E Progress Pl .... Springfield MO 65803 417-864-6108 864-8161
TF: 800-276-2419 ■ *Web:* www.wattsradiant.com

WEBCO Inc 3300 E Pythian St .... Springfield MO 65802 417-866-7231
Web: www.webco-inc.com

Whalen Co, The PO Box 1390 .... Easton MD 21601 410-822-9200 822-8926
Web: www.whalencompany.com

Williams Distributing Co
658 Richmond NW .... Grand Rapids MI 49504 616-456-1613
Web: www.wmsdist.com

Williams Furnace Co 250 W Laurel St .... Colton CA 92324 909-825-0993
Web: www.williamscomfortprod.com

WSA Engineered Systems 2018 S First St .... Milwaukee WI 53207 414-481-4120 481-4121
Web: www.wsaes.com

15 AIR CONDITIONING & HEATING EQUIPMENT - RESIDENTIAL

See Also Air Conditioning & Heating Equipment - Commercial/Industrial p. 1720

Phone | Fax

Airefco Inc 18755 SW Teton Ave PO Box 1349 .... Tualatin OR 97062 503-692-3210 691-2392
TF: 800-869-1349 ■ *Web:* www.airefco.com

Allied Air Enterprises
215 Metropolitan Dr .... West Columbia SC 29170 800-448-5872 738-4001*
**Fax Area Code:* 803 ■ *TF:* 800-448-5872 ■ *Web:* www.alliedair.com

Amana Appliances Inc 2800 220th Trl .... Amana IA 52204 319-622-5511 622-2180
TF Cust Svc: 800-843-0304 ■ *Web:* www.amana.com

Bard Mfg Co Inc 1914 Randolph Dr .... Bryan OH 43506 419-636-1194 636-2640
TF: 800-563-5660 ■ *Web:* www.bardhvac.com

Behr Climate Systems 5020 Augusta Dr .... Fort Worth TX 76106 817-624-7273 624-3328
Web: www.mahle.com

Bergstrom Manufacturing Co
2390 Blackhawk Rd .... Rockford IL 61125 815-874-7821 874-2144
Web: www.bergstrominc.com

CalsonicKansei North America Inc
1 Calsonic Way .... Shelbyville TN 37160 931-684-4490 684-2724
Web: www.calsonic.com

Delphi Harrison Thermal Systems
200 Upper Mtn Rd .... Lockport NY 14094 716-439-2011
Web: delphi.com

Evans Tempcon Inc 701 Ann St NW .... Grand Rapids MI 49504 616-361-2681 361-9646
Web: www.evanstempcon.com

Friedrich 10001 Reunion Pl Ste 500 .... San Antonio TX 78216 210-546-0500 357-4480
TF: 800-541-6645 ■ *Web:* www.friedrich.com

Goodman Mfg Company LP
5151 San Felipe St Ste 500 .... Houston TX 77056 713-861-2500
Web: www.goodmanmfg.com

HDT Global 30500 Aurora Rd Ste 100 .... Solon OH 44139 216-438-6111 248-1691*
**Fax Area Code:* 440 ■ *TF:* 800-969-8527 ■ *Web:* www.hdtglobal.com

International Comfort Products Corp (ICP)
650 Heil Quaker Ave .... Lewisburg TN 37091 931-359-3511
Web: www.icpusa.com

Johnson Controls Inc - YORK
5757 N Green Bay Ave .... Milwaukee WI 53201 414-524-1200
Web: www.johnsoncontrols.com

Kim Hotstart Manufacturing Co
5723 E Alki Ave .... Spokane WA 99212 509-536-8660
TF: 800-224-5550 ■ *Web:* www.hotstart.com

Lennox Industries Inc 2100 Lake Pk Blvd .... Richardson TX 75080 800-953-6669 572-4001
TF Cust Svc: 800-953-6669 ■ *Web:* www.lennox.com

Lennox International Inc
2140 Lake Pk Blvd .... Richardson TX 75080 972-497-5000 497-5292*
NYSE: LII ■ **Fax:* Mail Rm ■ *TF:* 800-953-6669 ■ *Web:* www.lennoxinternational.com

Modine Manufacturing Co 1500 De Koven Ave .... Racine WI 53403 262-636-1200 636-1424
NYSE: MOD ■ *TF:* 800-828-4328 ■ *Web:* www.modine.com

National System of Garage Ventilation Inc
714 N Church St PO Box 1186 .... Decatur IL 62525 217-423-7314 422-5387
TF: 800-728-8368 ■ *Web:* www.nsgv.com

Nortek Inc 50 Kennedy Plz .... Providence RI 02903 401-751-1600 751-4610
NASDAQ: NTK ■ *Web:* www.nortek.com

Simpson Mfg Company Inc
5956 W Las Positas Blvd .... Pleasanton CA 94588 925-560-9000
NYSE: SSD ■ *TF:* 800-925-5099 ■ *Web:* www.simpsonmfg.com

Takagi Industrial Company USA Inc 500 Wald .... Irvine CA 92618 949-770-7171 770-3171
TF: 888-882-5244 ■ *Web:* www.takagi.com

TPI Corp PO Box 4973 .... Johnson City TN 37602 800-682-3398
TF: 800-682-3398 ■ *Web:* www.tpicorp.com

Trane Company Unitary Products Group
6200 Troup Hwy .... Tyler TX 75707 903-730-4000
Web: www.trane.com

Van Natta Mechanical Corp 25 Whitney Rd .... Mahwah NJ 07430 201-391-3700 930-0295
Web: www.vannattamechanical.com

Ventamatic Ltd 100 Washington Rd .... Mineral Wells TX 76067 800-433-1626 325-9311*
**Fax Area Code:* 940 ■ *TF:* 800-433-1626 ■ *Web:* www.bvc.com

Phone | Fax

Whirlpool Corp 2000 N M-63 .... Benton Harbor MI 49022 269-923-5000
NYSE: WHR ■ *TF:* 800-253-1301 ■ *Web:* www.whirlpoolcorp.com

16 AIR FARE CONSOLIDATORS

Phone | Fax

Airline Tariff Publishing Co (ATPCO)
45005 Aviation Dr .... Dulles VA 20166 703-471-7510 471-6584
Web: www.atpco.net

Brazilian Travel Service (BTS)
16 W 46th St 2nd Fl .... New York NY 10036 212-764-6161 719-4142
TF: 800-342-5746 ■ *Web:* www.btstravelonline.com

C & H International
4751 Wilshire Blvd Ste 201 .... Los Angeles CA 90010 323-933-2288 939-2286
TF: 800-833-8888 ■ *Web:* www.cnhintl.com

Centrav Inc 511 E Travelers Trl .... Burnsville MN 55337 952-886-7650 886-7640
TF: 800-874-2033 ■ *Web:* www.centrav.com

GTT Global 600 Data Dr Ste 101 .... Plano TX 75075 972-239-5069
TF: 800-485-6828 ■ *Web:* www.gttglobal.com

International Travel Systems Inc
64 Madison Ave .... Wood-Ridge NJ 07075 201-727-0470
TF: 800-258-0135 ■ *Web:* international-travel-systems.com

Mill-Run Inc 424 Madison Ave 12th Fl .... New York NY 10017 212-486-9840 223-8129
Web: www5.millrun.com

Picasso Travel
300 N Continental Blvd Ste 310 .... El Segundo CA 90245 310-645-4400
Web: picassotravel.com

Sky Bird Travel & Tours Inc 24701 Swanson .... Southfield MI 48033 248-372-4800 372-4810
TF: 888-759-2473

Skylink Travel 980 Ave of the Americas .... New York NY 10018 212-573-8980 573-8878
TF: 800-247-6659 ■ *Web:* www.skylinkus.com

Solar Tours 1629 K St NW Ste 604 .... Washington DC 20006 202-861-5864 452-0905
TF: 800-388-7652 ■ *Web:* www.solartours.com

Trans Am Travel 4222 King St Ste 130 .... Alexandria VA 22302 703-998-7676 824-8190
TF: 800-822-7600 ■ *Web:* www.transamtravel.com

17 AIR PURIFICATION EQUIPMENT - HOUSEHOLD

See Also Appliances - Small - Mfr p. 1737

Phone | Fax

Air Quality Engineering Inc
7140 Northland Dr N .... Brooklyn Park MN 55428 763-531-9823 531-9900
TF: 888-883-3273 ■ *Web:* www.air-quality-eng.com

Airguard Industries Inc
100 River Ridge Cir .... Jeffersonville IN 47130 866-247-4827
TF: 800-999-3458 ■ *Web:* clcair.com/brands-products/airguard

Dayton Reliable Air Filter Inc
2294 N Moraine Dr .... Dayton OH 45439 800-699-0747 293-3975*
**Fax Area Code:* 937 ■ *TF Orders:* 800-699-0747 ■ *Web:* www.reliablefilter.com

Field Controls LLC 2630 Airport Rd .... Kinston NC 28504 252-522-3031 522-0214
Web: www.fieldcontrols.com

Gaylord Industries Inc 10900 SW Avery St .... Tualatin OR 97062 503-691-2010 692-6048
TF: 800-547-9696 ■ *Web:* gaylordventilation.com

General Filters Inc 43800 Grand River Ave .... Novi MI 48375 866-476-5101 349-2366*
**Fax Area Code:* 248 ■ *TF:* 866-476-5101 ■ *Web:* www.generalfilters.com

HEPA Corp 3071 E Coronado St .... Anaheim CA 92806 714-630-5700 630-2894
Web: www.hepa.com

Home Care Industries Inc ALFCO Div
1 Lisbon St .... Clifton NJ 07013 973-365-1600 365-1770
TF Cust Svc: 800-325-1908 ■ *Web:* www.homecareind.com

Indoor Purification Systems Inc
Surround Air Div 334 N Marshall Way Ste C .... Layton UT 84041 801-547-1162 991-4838
TF: 888-812-1516 ■ *Web:* surroundair.com

Kaz Home Environment 250 Tpke Rd .... Southborough MA 01772 508-490-7000
Web: www.kaz.com

Koch Filter Corp 625 W Hill St .... Louisville KY 40208 502-634-4796 637-2280
TF: 800-757-5624 ■ *Web:* www.kochfilter.com

Permatron Group 2020 Touhy Ave .... Elk Grove Village IL 60007 847-434-1421
TF: 800-882-8012 ■ *Web:* www.permatron.com

PuriTec 4705 S Durango Dr Ste 100-102 .... Las Vegas NV 89147 610-268-5420 759-8905*
**Fax Area Code:* 888 ■ *TF:* 888-491-4100 ■ *Web:* www.puriteam.com

Rena Ware International Inc
15885 NE 28th St .... Bellevue WA 98008 425-881-6171 882-7500
Web: www.renaware.com

Research Products Corp 1015 E Washington Ave .... Madison WI 53703 608-257-8801 257-4357
TF: 800-334-6011 ■ *Web:* www.aprilaire.com

RPS Products Inc 281 Keyes Ave .... Hampshire IL 60140 847-683-3400 683-3939
Web: www.rpsproducts.com

Spencer Turbine Co 600 Day Hill Rd .... Windsor CT 06095 860-688-8361 688-0098
TF: 800-232-4321 ■ *Web:* www.spencerturbine.com

Tjernlund Products Inc 1601 Ninth St .... White Bear Lake MN 55110 651-426-2993 426-9547
TF: 800-255-4208 ■ *Web:* www.tjernlund.com

Vornado Air Circulation Systems Inc
415 E 13th St .... Andover KS 67002 316-733-0035 733-1544
TF: 800-234-0604 ■ *Web:* www.vornado.com

18 AIR PURIFICATION EQUIPMENT - INDUSTRIAL

Phone | Fax

AAF International Corp
10300 Ormsby Pk Pl Ste 600 .... Louisville KY 40223 502-637-0011 223-6500*
**Fax Area Code:* 888 ■ *TF:* 888-223-2003 ■ *Web:* www.aafintl.com

Acme Engineering & Manufacturing Corp
PO Box 978 .... Muskogee OK 74402 918-682-7791 682-0134
TF: 800-382-2263 ■ *Web:* www.acmefan.com

Advantec MFS Inc 6723 Sierra Ct Ste A .... Dublin CA 94568 925-479-0625 479-0630
TF: 800-334-7132 ■ *Web:* www.advantecmfs.com

Aerovent Inc 5959 Trenton Ln .... Minneapolis MN 55442 763-551-7500 551-7501
Web: www.aerovent.com

Company	City	State	ZIP	Phone	Fax
Aget Manufacturing Co 1408 E Church St *TF:* 800-832-2438 ■ *Web:* www.agetmfg.com	Adrian	MI	49221	517-263-5781	263-7154
Air Quality Engineering Inc 7140 Northland Dr N *TF:* 888-883-3273 ■ *Web:* www.air-quality-eng.com	Brooklyn Park	MN	55428	763-531-9823	531-9900
Airflow Systems Inc 11221 Pagemill Rd *TF:* 800-818-6185 ■ *Web:* www.airflowsystems.com	Dallas	TX	75243	214-503-8008	503-9596
Airfoil Impellers Corp PO Box 9966 *Web:* www.airfoil.com	College Station	TX	77842	979-822-6418	775-5588
Airguard Industries Inc 100 River Ridge Cir *TF:* 800-999-3458 ■ *Web:* clcair.com/brands-products/airguard	Jeffersonville	IN	47130	866-247-4827	
Airmaster Fan Co 1300 Falahee Rd *Web:* www.airmasterfan.com	Jackson	MI	49203	517-764-2300	764-3838
Alanco Technologies Inc 15575 N 83rd Way Ste 3 *OTC: ALAN* ■ *Web:* www.alanco.com	Scottsdale	AZ	85260	480-607-1010	607-1515
American Fan Company Inc 2933 Symmes Rd *TF:* 866-771-6266 ■ *Web:* www.americanfan.com	Fairfield	OH	45014	513-874-2400	870-6249
AMETEK Rotron Mil-Aero Products Div 55 Hasbrouck Ln *Web:* www.ametekaerodefense.com	Woodstock	NY	12498	845-679-1371	679-1371
AMETEK Technical & Industrial Products 100 E Erie St *Web:* www.ametekdfs.com	Kent	OH	44240	330-673-3452	677-3306
Anguil Environmental Systems Inc 8855 N 55th St *TF:* 800-488-0230 ■ *Web:* www.anguil.com	Milwaukee	WI	53223	414-365-6400	365-6410
Arrow Pneumatics Inc 2111 W 21st St *Web:* www.arrowpneumatics.com	Broadview	IL	60155	708-343-9595	
Baghouse & Industrial Sheet Metal Services Inc 1731 Pomona Rd *TF:* 888-224-4687 ■ *Web:* www.1888baghouse.com	Corona	CA	92880	951-272-6610	272-1241
Beckett Air Inc 37850 Beckett Pkwy *TF:* 800-831-7839 ■ *Web:* www.beckettair.com	North Ridgeville	OH	44039	440-327-9999	327-3569
Bruning & Federle Mfg Co 2503 Northside Dr *Web:* www.bruning-federle.com	Statesville	NC	28625	704-873-7237	
Buffalo Air Handling Co 467 Zane Snead Dr *Web:* www.buffaloair.com	Amherst	VA	24521	434-946-7455	946-7941
Cincinnati Fan & Ventilator 7697 Snider Rd *Web:* www.cincinnatifan.com	Mason	OH	45040	513-573-0600	573-0640
Clarcor Inc 840 Crescent Ctr Dr Ste 600 *NYSE: CLC* ■ *TF:* 800-252-7267 ■ *Web:* www.clarcor.com	Franklin	TN	37067	615-771-3100	771-5616
Cleanroom Systems 7000 Performance Dr *TF:* 800-825-3268 ■ *Web:* www.cleanroomsystems.com	North Syracuse	NY	13212	315-452-7400	452-7420
Clements National Co 6650 S Narragansett Ave *TF:* 800-966-0016 ■ *Web:* www.cadillacproducts.com	Chicago	IL	60638	708-594-5890	594-2481
Columbus Industries Inc 2938 SR-752 *TF:* 800-766-2552 ■ *Web:* www.colind.com	Ashville	OH	43103	740-983-2552	983-4622
CSM Worldwide Inc 269 Sheffield St *Web:* www.csmworldwide.com	Mountainside	NJ	07092	908-233-2882	233-1064
CUNO Inc 400 Research Pkwy *TF:* 800-243-6894 ■ *Web:* www.3m.com	Meriden	CT	06450	203-237-5541	238-8701
Daw Technologies Inc 1600 West 2200 South Ste 201 *Web:* www.dawtech.com	Salt Lake City	UT	84119	801-977-3100	973-6640
Disa Systems Inc 150 Transit Ave *TF:* 800-845-8508 ■ *Web:* www.disagroup.com	Thomasville	NC	27360	336-889-9187	
Donaldson Company Inc 1400 W 94th St *NYSE: DCI* ■ *Web:* www.donaldson.com	Bloomington	MN	55431	952-887-3131	
Ducon Technologies Inc 19 Engineers Ln *Web:* www.ducon.com	Farmingdale	NY	11735	631-694-1700	420-4985
Dustex Corp 100 Chastain Ctr Blvd Ste 195 *Web:* www.dustex.com	Kennesaw	GA	30144	770-429-5575	429-5556
Dynamic Air Engineering Inc 620 E Dyer Rd *Web:* www.dynamic-air.com	Santa Ana	CA	92705	714-540-1000	545-9145
EBM Industries Inc *EBM-papst Inc* 100 & 110 Hyde Rd *Web:* www.ebmpapst.us	Farmington	CT	06034	860-674-1515	674-8536
Epcon Industrial Systems Inc 17777 IH- 45 S	Conroe	TX	77385	936-273-1774	273-4600
Filtertech Inc 113 Fairgrounds Dr PO Box 527 *Web:* www.filtertech.com	Manlius	NY	13104	315-682-8815	682-8825
Filtration Group Inc 912 E Washington St **Fax Area Code:* 800 ■ *TF:* 877-603-1003 ■ *Web:* www.filtrationgroup.com	Joliet	IL	60433	815-726-4600	518-1162*
Flanders Corp 531 Flanders Filters Rd *OTC: FLDR* ■ *TF:* 800-637-2803 ■ *Web:* www.flanderscorp.com	Washington	NC	27889	252-946-8081	946-3425
Fuel Tech Inc 27601 Bella Vista Pkwy *NASDAQ: FTEK* ■ *TF General:* 800-666-9688 ■ *Web:* www.ftek.com	Warrenville	IL	60555	630-845-4500	845-4502
Gaylord Industries Inc 10900 SW Avery St *TF:* 800-547-9696 ■ *Web:* gaylordventilation.com	Tualatin	OR	97062	503-691-2010	692-6048
General Filters Inc 43800 Grand River Ave **Fax Area Code:* 248 ■ *TF:* 866-476-5101 ■ *Web:* www.generalfilters.com	Novi	MI	48375	866-476-5101	349-2366*
Glasfloss Industries Inc PO Box 150469 **Fax Area Code:* 800 ■ *Web:* www.glasfloss.com	Dallas	TX	75315	214-741-7056	435-8377*
Great Lakes Filters 301 Arch Ave **Fax Area Code:* 517 ■ *TF:* 800-521-8565 ■ *Web:* www.greatlakesfilters.com	Hillsdale	MI	49242	800-521-8565	437-8942*
Greenheck Fan Corp 1100 Greenheck Dr PO Box 410 *TF:* 800-355-5354 ■ *Web:* www.greenheck.com	Schofield	WI	54476	715-359-6171	355-2399
Griffin Filters 106 Metropolitan Pk Dr *Web:* www.griffinfilters.com	Liverpool	NY	13088	315-451-5300	451-2338
Hardie-Tynes Company Inc 800 28th St N *Web:* www.hardie-tynes.com	Birmingham	AL	35203	205-252-5191	
Hartzell Fan Inc 910 S Downing St *TF:* 800-336-3267 ■ *Web:* www.hartzellairmovement.com	Piqua	OH	45356	937-773-7411	773-8994
HEPA Corp 3071 E Coronado St *Web:* www.hepa.com	Anaheim	CA	92806	714-630-5700	630-2894
Home Care Industries Inc ALFCO Div 1 Lisbon St *TF Cust Svc:* 800-325-1908 ■ *Web:* www.homecareind.com	Clifton	NJ	07013	973-365-1600	365-1770
Honeyville Metal Inc 4200 S 900 W *TF:* 800-593-8377 ■ *Web:* www.honeyvillemetal.com	Topeka	IN	46571	260-593-2266	593-2486
Houston Service Industries Inc 7901 Hansen Rd *TF:* 800-725-2291 ■ *Web:* www.hsiblowers.com	Houston	TX	77061	713-947-1623	947-6409
Howden Buffalo Inc 7909 Parklane Rd Ste 300 **Fax Area Code:* 866 ■ *TF:* 866-757-0908 ■ *Web:* www.howden.com	Columbia	SC	29223	803-741-2700	757-0908*
King Engineering Corp 3201 S State St *TF Cust Svc:* 800-242-8871 ■ *Web:* www.king-gage.com	Ann Arbor	MI	48106	734-662-5691	662-6652
Koch Filter Corp 625 W Hill St *TF:* 800-757-5624 ■ *Web:* www.kochfilter.com	Louisville	KY	40208	502-634-4796	637-2280
La Calhene Inc 1325 Field Ave S *Web:* getinge.com/nuclear	Rush City	MN	55069	320-358-4713	358-4713
Loren Cook Co 2015 E Dale St *Web:* www.lorencook.com	Springfield	MO	65803	417-869-6474	862-3820
Lydall Inc 1 Colonial Rd *NYSE: LDL* ■ *Web:* www.lydall.com	Manchester	CT	06042	860-646-1233	646-4917
Marsulex Environmental Technology 200 N Seventh St *Web:* www.met-apc.com	Lebanon	PA	17046	717-274-7000	274-7103
McIntire Co 745 Clark Ave *TF:* 800-437-9247 ■ *Web:* www.mcintireco.com	Bristol	CT	06010	860-585-0050	314-4500
Met-Pro Corp Duall Div 1550 Industrial Dr *Web:* www.dualldiv.com	Owosso	MI	48867	989-725-8184	725-8188
Midwesco Filter Resources Inc 385 Battaile Dr *TF:* 800-336-7300 ■ *Web:* www.midwesco-tdcfilter.com	Winchester	VA	22601	540-667-8500	504-8051
Midwest International Standard Products Inc 105 Stover Rd *Web:* www.midwestmagic.com	Charlevoix	MI	49720	231-547-4000	547-9453
NAO Inc 1284 E Sedgley Ave *TF Cust Svc:* 800-523-3495 ■ *Web:* www.nao.com	Philadelphia	PA	19134	215-743-5300	743-3018
National Filter Media Corp 691 North 400 West *TF:* 800-777-4248 ■ *Web:* www.nfm-filter.com	Salt Lake City	UT	84103	801-363-6736	531-1293
New York Blower Co 7660 Quincy St *Web:* www.nyb.com	Willowbrook	IL	60527	630-794-5700	794-5776
Parker Hannifin Corp Finite Filtratio & Separation Div 500 Glaspie St *TF:* 800-521-4357 ■ *Web:* www.parker.com	Oxford	MI	48371	248-628-6400	628-1850
Pneumech Systems Mfg LLC 201 Pneu Mech Dr *TF:* 800-358-7374 ■ *Web:* www.pneu-mech.com	Statesville	NC	28625	704-873-2475	871-2780
Precipitator Services Group Inc 1625 Broad St	Elizabethton	TN	37643	423-543-7331	543-8737
Process Equipment Inc 2770 Welborn St PO Box 1607 *TF:* 888-663-2028 ■ *Web:* www.processbarron.com	Pelham	AL	35124	205-663-5330	663-6037
Purafil Inc 2654 Weaver Way *TF:* 800-222-6367 ■ *Web:* www.purafil.com	Doraville	GA	30340	770-662-8545	263-6922
Revcor Inc 251 E Edwards Ave **Fax Area Code:* 847 ■ *TF:* 800-323-8261 ■ *Web:* www.revcor.com	Carpentersville	IL	60110	800-323-8261	426-4630*
Robinson Industries Inc 400 Robinson Dr *Web:* www.robinsonfans.com	Zelienople	PA	16063	724-452-6121	452-0388
RP Fedder Corp 740 Driving Pk Ave *Web:* www.rpfedder.com	Rochester	NY	14613	585-288-1600	288-2481
RPS Products Inc 281 Keyes Ave *Web:* www.rpsproducts.com	Hampshire	IL	60140	847-683-3400	683-3939
Sly Inc 8300 Dow Cir *TF:* 800-334-2957 ■ *Web:* www.slyinc.com	Strongsville	OH	44136	440-891-3200	891-3210
Sonic Air Systems Inc 1050 Beacon St *TF:* 800-827-6642 ■ *Web:* www.sonicairsystems.com	Brea	CA	92821	714-255-0124	255-8366
SPE Amerex 201 Houston St Ste 200 *Web:* amerextech.com	Batavia	IL	60510	630-406-7756	
Spencer Turbine Co 600 Day Hill Rd *TF:* 800-232-4321 ■ *Web:* www.spencerturbine.com	Windsor	CT	06095	860-688-8361	688-0098
Standard Filter Corp 5928 Balfour Ct *TF:* 800-634-5837 ■ *Web:* www.standardfilter.com	Carlsbad	CA	92008	760-929-8559	929-1901
Sterling Blower Co 135 Vista Ctr Dr *Web:* www.sterlingblower.com	Forest	VA	24551	434-316-5310	316-5910
Strobic Air Corp 160 Cassell Rd PO Box 144 *TF:* 800-722-3267 ■ *Web:* www.strobicair.com	Harleysville	PA	19438	215-723-4700	723-7401
Terra Universal Inc 800 S Ramon Ave *Web:* www.terrauni.com	Fullerton	CA	92831	714-578-6000	578-6020
Tjernlund Products Inc 1601 Ninth St *TF:* 800-255-4208 ■ *Web:* www.tjernlund.com	White Bear Lake	MN	55110	651-426-2993	426-9547
Tri-Dim Filter Corp 93 Industrial Dr *TF:* 800-458-9835 ■ *Web:* www.tridim.com	Louisa	VA	23093	540-967-2600	967-2835
Tri-Mer Corp 1400 Monroe St PO Box 730 *Web:* www.tri-mer.com	Owosso	MI	48867	989-723-7838	723-7844
Trion Inc 101 McNeill Rd *Web:* www.trioniaq.com	Sanford	NC	27330	919-775-2201	774-8771
Tuthill Vacuum & Blower Systems 4840 W Kearney St *TF:* 800-825-6937 ■ *Web:* www.tuthill.com	Springfield	MO	65803	417-865-8715	865-2950
Twin City Fan Cos Ltd 5959 Trenton Ln N *Web:* www.tcf.com	Minneapolis	MN	55442	763-551-7600	551-7601
Venturedyne Ltd 600 College Ave *Web:* www.venturedyne.com	Pewaukee	WI	53072	262-691-9900	691-9901
Waco 2546 Gen Armistead Ave *TF:* 800-928-7159 ■ *Web:* www.wacofilters.com	Norristown	PA	19403	610-630-4800	630-4904

19 AIR TRAFFIC CONTROL SERVICES

The Federal Aviation Administration (a US government agency) and NAV CANADA (a private, not-for-profit Canadian firm) provide air traffic services nationwide in the US and Canada, respectively. The types of services provided include aircraft routing, approach and departure instruction, and weather information.

Company	City	State	ZIP	Phone	Fax
Federal Aviation Administration (FAA) 800 Independence Ave SW *TF:* 866-835-5322 ■ *Web:* www.faa.gov	Washington	DC	20591	866-835-5322	

Phone Fax

Great Lakes Region 2300 E Devon Ave .... Des Plaines IL 60018 847-294-7272 294-7036
Web: www.faa.gov

Federal Aviation Administration Northwest Mountain Region
1601 Lind Ave SW .... Renton WA 98057 425-227-2001
TF: 800-220-5715 ■ *Web:* www.faa.gov

Federal Aviation Administration Regional Offices (FAA)
Alaskan Region 222 W Seventh Ave Ste 14 .... Anchorage AK 99513 907-271-5438 271-2851
Web: www.faa.gov
Central Region Federal Bldg 901 Locust St ...... Kansas City MO 64106 816-329-3050
Web: www.faa.gov
Eastern Region 159-30 Rockaway Blvd .... Jamaica NY 11434 718-553-3001
Web: www.faa.gov
New England Region
12 New England Executive Pk .... Burlington MA 01803 781-238-7020 238-7608
Web: www.faa.gov/airports/new_england
Western Pacific Region 15000 Aviation Blvd .... Lawndale CA 90261 310-725-7800 725-6811
Web: www.faa.gov/airports/western_pacific

Federal Aviation Administration Southern Region
1701 Columbia Ave .... College Park GA 30337 404-305-5000
Web: www.faa.gov

FlightAware 8 Greenway Plz Ste 1300................. Houston TX 77046 713-877-9010
Web: www.flightaware.com

mPower Software Services LLC
770 Newtown-Yardley Rd Ste 225 .... Newtown PA 18940 215-497-9730
Web: ww.mpowerss.com

NAV CANADA 77 Metcalfe St PO Box 3411 Stn D.......... Ottawa ON K1P5L6 613-563-5588 563-3426
TF: 800-876-4693 ■ *Web:* www.navcanada.ca

Veracity Engineering
600 Maryland Ave Sw Ste 600e .... Washington DC 20024 202-488-0975
Web: www.veracity-eng.com

20 AIRCRAFT

See Also Airships p. 1733

Phone Fax

ACR Aircraft Component Repair Inc
25058 Anza Dr .... Valencia CA 91355 661-295-6677 295-6679
Web: www.acr.aero

Aeronautical Accessories Inc
Tri-County Industrial Park 423 Century Ct
.... Piney Flats TN 37686 423-538-5151
Web: www.edwardsassociates.com

Aerospace Technologies Group Inc
620 NW 35th St .... Boca Raton FL 33431 561-244-7400
Web: www.atgshades.com

AeroVironment Inc
181 W Huntington Dr Ste 202...................... Monrovia CA 91016 626-357-9983 359-9628
NASDAQ: AVAV ■ *TF:* 888-833-2148 ■ *Web:* www.avinc.com

Air Tractor Inc 1524 Lelind Snow Way...................... Olney TX 76374 940-564-5616 564-5625
Web: www.airtractor.com

Airbus Helicopters Inc 2701 Forum Dr.............. Grand Prairie TX 75052 972-641-0000 641-3550
TF: 800-873-0001 ■ *Web:* airbushelicoptersinc.com

AvCraft Technical Services Inc
3301 Mustang St .... Myrtle Beach SC 29577 843-232-1338
Web: www.avcrafttechnical.com

Axiam Inc 58 Blackburn Ctr....................... Gloucester MA 01930 978-281-3550
Web: www.axiam.com

Ballistic Recovery Systems Inc
380 Airport Rd .... South St. Paul MN 55075 651-457-7491
Web: www.brsparachutes.com

Bell Helicopter Textron Inc
600 E Hurst Blvd (State Hwy 10)........................ Hurst TX 76053 817-280-2011 280-2321
TF: 888-874-5884 ■ *Web:* www.bellhelicopter.com

Boeing Co, The 100 N Riverside Plz.................. Chicago IL 60606 312-544-2000
NYSE: BA ■ *Web:* www.boeing.com

Boeing Company Commercial Airplane Group
PO Box 3707 .... Seattle WA 98124 206-655-2121
Web: www.boeing.com/commercial

Bombardier Aerospace 400 Cote-Vertu Rd W........... Dorval QC H4S1Y9 514-855-5000 855-7401
TF General: 866-855-5001 ■ *Web:* www.bombardier.com

Bombardier Aerospace Learjet 1 Learjet Way......... Wichita KS 67209 316-946-2000 946-2220
Web: businessaircraft.bombardier.com

Bombardier Inc 800 RenT-LTvesque Blvd W........... Montreal QC H3B1Y8 514-861-9481 861-7769
TSE: BBD/B ■ *Web:* www.bombardier.com

Cessna Aircraft Co 1 Cessna Blvd................... Wichita KS 67215 316-517-6000 517-7250
Web: cessna.txtav.com

Composite Resources Inc 485 Lakeshore Pkwy........ Rock Hill SC 29730 803-366-9700
Web: www.composite-resources.com

Conair Group Inc 1510 Tower St................... Abbotsford BC V2T6H5 604-855-1171 855-1185
Web: conair.ca

Concorde Battery Corp
2009 W San Bernardino Rd .... West Covina CA 91790 626-813-1234
Web: www.concordebattery.com

CPI Manufacturing LLC 108 Ledyard St .... Hartford CT 06114 860-296-7980
Web: www.cpimanufacturing.com

Dallas Airmotive Inc 900 Nolen Dr Ste 100........... Grapevine TX 76051 214-956-3001 956-2825*
**Fax Area Code:* 817 ■ *Web:* www.dallasairmotive.com

Dassault Falcon Jet Corp
PO Box 2000 .... South Hackensack NJ 07606 201-440-6700 322-7221*
**Fax Area Code:* 302 ■ **Fax:* Hum Res ■ *TF:* 800-527-2463 ■ *Web:* www.dassaultfalcon.com

Diamond Aircraft Industries Inc
1560 Crumlin Sideroad .... London ON N5V1S2 519-457-4000
TF: 888-359-3220 ■ *Web:* www.diamondaircraft.com

Embraer Aircraft Corp 276 SW 34th St.......... Fort Lauderdale FL 33315 954-359-3700 359-3701
Web: www.embraer.com.br

Enstrom Helicopter Corp USA 2209 22nd St .... Menominee MI 49858 906-863-1200 863-6244
Web: www.enstromhelicopter.com

Epic AIR LLC 22590 Nelson Rd .... Bend OR 97701 541-318-8849
TF: 888-359-3742 ■ *Web:* www.epicaircraft.com

Erickson Air-Crane Co
5550 SW Macadam Ave Ste 200..................... Portland OR 97239 503-505-5800
TF: 877-870-5176 ■ *Web:* www.ericksonaircrane.com

Phone Fax

First Wave Aviation LLC 5440 S 101st E Ave .... Tulsa OK 74146 918-622-0007
Web: www.firstwave.aero

Gulfstream Aerospace Corp 500 Gulfstream Rd........ Savannah GA 31408 912-965-3000 395-8222
Web: www.gulfstream.com

Heli-One American Support LLC
120 NE Frontage Rd .... Fort Collins CO 80524 970-492-1000
Web: www.heli-one.ca

Honda Aircraft Company Inc
6430 Ballinger RdGreensboro.................... Greensboro NC 27410 336-662-0246
Web: hondajet.honda.com

Kaman Aerospace Corp
Old Windsor Rd PO Box 2 .... Bloomfield CT 06002 860-242-4461 243-7514
Web: www.kaman.com

Kay & Associates Inc
165 N Arlington Heights Rd Ste 150.............. Buffalo Grove IL 60089 847-255-8444
Web: www.kayinc.com

Lockheed Martin Aeronautics Co
1 Lockheed Blvd.............................. Fort Worth TX 76108 817-777-2000 777-2115
Web: www.lockheedmartin.com

Lockheed Martin Corp 6801 Rockledge Dr........... Bethesda MD 20817 301-897-6000
NYSE: LMT ■ *TF:* 866-562-2363 ■ *Web:* www.lockheedmartin.com

M7 Aerospace 10823 NE Entrance Rd.............. San Antonio TX 78216 210-824-9421
Web: www.m7aerospace.com

Maule Air Inc 2099 GA Hwy 133 S .... Moultrie GA 31788 229-985-2045 890-2402
Web: www.mauleairinc.com

Moller International Inc 1222 Research Park Dr .... Davis CA 95618 530-756-5086
Web: www.moller.com

Mooney Aircraft Corp 165 Al Mooney Rd .... Kerrville TX 78028 800-456-3033
TF: 800-456-3033 ■ *Web:* www.mooney.com

New Piper Aircraft Inc 2926 Piper Dr .... Vero Beach FL 32960 772-567-4361
Web: www.piper.com

North American Aircraft Services Inc
11502 Jones Maltsberger .... San Antonio TX 78216 210-805-0049
Web: www.naasinc.com

Northrop Grumman Corp
2980 Fairview Park Dr .... Falls Church VA 22042 703-280-2900
NYSE: NOC ■ *Web:* www.northropgrumman.com

Northrop Grumman Corp Military Aircraft Systems Div
1 Hornet Way .... El Segundo CA 90245 310-332-1000
Web: northropgrumman.com

Piedmont Aviation Component Services LLC
1031 E Mtn St Bldg 320......................... Kernersville NC 27284 336-776-6300
Web: www.piedmontaviation.com

Quicksilver Manufacturing Inc
42214 Sarah Way .... Temecula CA 92590 951-506-0061
Web: www.quicksilveraircraft.com

Robinson Helicopter Co 2901 Airport Dr............. Torrance CA 90505 310-539-0508 539-5198
TF: 800-905-0655 ■ *Web:* www.robinsonheli.com

Rockland Aerospace Inc 2111 Baldwin Ave Ste 8 .... Crofton MD 21114 410-451-0969
Web: www.mhdrockland.com

Sabreliner Corp 1390 Hwy H....................... Perryville MO 63775 573-543-2212
Web: www.sabrelineraviation.com

Scaled Composites Inc 1624 Flight Line Rd .... Mojave CA 93501 661-824-4541 824-4174
Web: www.scaled.com

Sikorsky Aircraft Corp
6900 Main St PO Box 9729 .... Stratford CT 06615 203-386-4000
Web: www.sikorsky.com

Spirit AeroSystems Inc 3801 S Oliver St.............. Wichita KS 67210 316-526-9000
Web: www.spiritaero.com

TDG Aerospace Inc 545 Corporate Dr .... Escondido CA 92029 760-466-1040
Web: www.tdgaerospace.com

Teledyne Continental Motors Inc 2039 Broad St......... Mobile AL 36615 251-438-3411
TF: 800-718-3411 ■ *Web:* www.continentalmotors.aero

Texas Pneumatics Systems Inc
2404 Superior Dr .... Arlington TX 76013 817-794-0068
TF: 800-211-9690 ■ *Web:* www.txps.com

Thrush Aircraft Inc 300 Old Pretoria Rd................ Albany GA 31721 229-883-1440 439-9790
Web: www.thrushaircraft.com

Valair Aviation 7301 NW 50th St .... Oklahoma City OK 73132 405-789-5000
Web: www.valairaviation.com

Van Horn Aviation LLC
1000 E Vista Del Cerro Dr.......................... Tempe AZ 85281 480-483-4202
Web: www.vanhornaviation.com

Vantage Associates Inc
900 Civic Ctr Dr .... National City CA 91950 619-477-6940
Web: www.vantagemmc.com

21 AIRCRAFT ENGINES & ENGINE PARTS

Phone Fax

A & B Aerospace Inc 612 Ayon Ave..................... Azusa CA 91702 626-334-2976 334-6539
Web: abaerospace.com

AAR Corp 1100 N Wood Dale Rd 1 AAR Pl............ Wood Dale IL 60191 630-227-2000 227-2019
NYSE: AIR ■ *TF:* 800-422-2213 ■ *Web:* www.aarcorp.com

Aberdeen Regional Airport 123 S Lincoln St.......... Aberdeen SD 57402 605-626-7020
Web: www.aberdeen.sd.us

Abipa Canada Inc 2000, Blvd Dagenais ouest .... Laval QC H7L5W2 450-963-6888 963-8881
TF: 877-963-6888 ■ *Web:* www.abipa.com

Able Engineering & Component Services Inc
2920 E Chambers St............................. Phoenix AZ 85040 602-304-1227
Web: www.ableengineering.com

Acme Aerospace Inc 528 W 21st St .... Tempe AZ 85282 480-894-6864
Web: www.acme-aero.com

Action Aircraft Lp 10570 Olympic Dr................. Dallas TX 75220 214-351-1284
TF: 800-909-7616 ■ *Web:* www.actionaircraft.com

ADEPT Technologies LLC
2865 Wall Triana Hwy.......................... Huntsville AL 35824 256-851-2932
Web: www.adept-technologies.com

Aero manufacturing Corp 100 Sam Fonzo Dr.......... Beverly MA 01915 978-720-1000
Web: www.aeromanufacturing.com

Aerospace & Commercial Technologies Inc
970 Fm 2871 .... Fort Worth TX 76126 817-560-6600
Web: www.aero-com-tech.com

Name / Address	City	State	ZIP	Phone	Fax
Aerotec International Inc 3007 E Chambers St *Web:* www.aerotecinternational.com	Phoenix	AZ	85040	602-253-4540	
Aerotron AirPower Inc 456 Aerotron Pkwy *Web:* www.aerotron.com	Lagrange	GA	30240	706-812-1700	
Agilis Engineering Inc 3930 Rca Blvd Ste 3000 *Web:* www.agilis.com	Palm Beach Gardens	FL	33410	561-626-8900	
Agusta Aerospace Corp 3050 Red Lion Rd *Web:* www.agustawestland.com	Philadelphia	PA	19114	215-281-1400	
Aimpoint Inc 14103 Mariah Ct. *Web:* www.aimpoint.com	Chantilly	VA	20151	703-263-9795	
Air Georgian Ltd 2450 Derry Rd E Shell Aerocentre *Web:* www.airgeorgian.ca	Mississauga	ON	L5S1B2	905-676-1221	
Airbus Group Inc 2550 Wasser Ter Ste 9000 *Web:* northamerica.airbus-group.com	Herndon	VA	20171	703-466-5600	
Airista LLC 913 Ridgebrook Rd *Web:* www.airista.com	Sparks Glencoe	MD	21152	410-878-2700	
All Power Mfg Company Inc 13141 Molette St *Web:* www.allpowermfg.com	Santa Fe Springs	CA	90670	562-802-2640	
Alpha Q Inc 87 Upton Rd *Web:* alphaqinc.com	Colchester	CT	06415	860-537-4681	537-4332
American Dynamics Flight Systems Inc 8264 Preston Ct Ste A *Web:* www.adflightsystems.com	Jessup	MD	20794	301-358-0747	
Arnprior Aerospace Inc 107 Baskin Dr E. *Web:* www.arnprioraerospace.com	Arnprior	ON	K7S3M1	613-623-4267	
AV & R 269 Prince St *Web:* avr-aerospace.com	Montreal	QC	H3C2N4	514-788-1420	
Avalex Technologies Corp 2665 Gulf Breeze Pkwy *Web:* www.avalex.com	Gulf Breeze	FL	32563	850-470-8464	
Aventure International Aviation Services LLC 108 International Dr *Web:* aventureaviation.com	Peachtree City	GA	30269	770-632-7930	
Averitt Air Inc 625 Hngr Ln Hngr 4 Nashville International Airport *Web:* www.averittair.com	Nashville	TN	37217	615-399-8077	
Aviation Systems of Northwest Florida Inc 175 E Olive Rd *TF:* 800-759-0953 ■ *Web:* lsijax.com	Pensacola	FL	32514	800-759-0953	
Avior Integrated Products Inc 1001 Autoroute 440 Ouest *Web:* www.avior.ca	Laval	QC	H7L3W3	450-629-6200	
Avtron Aerospace Inc 7900 E Pleasant Vly Rd. *Web:* www.avtronaero.com	Cleveland	OH	44131	216-750-5152	
Azmark Aero Systems LLC 944 Guadalupe Rd *Web:* www.azmark.aero	Gilbert	AZ	85233	480-926-8969	926-8970
BAE Systems Aerospace & Defense Group Inc 7822 S 46th St *Web:* www.baesystems.com	Phoenix	AZ	85044	602-643-7233	
BAE Systems Electronics & Integrated Solutions 65 Spit Brook Rd *Web:* www.baesystems.com/en/our-company/our-businesses/electronic-systems	Nashua	NH	03060	603-885-4321	
BAE Systems Simula Inc 7822 S 46th St.	Phoenix	AZ	85044	602-643-7233	
Barnes Aerospace 169 Kennedy Rd *Web:* www.barnesaerospace.com	Windsor	CT	06095	860-298-7740	298-7738
Beacon Industries Inc 12300 Old Tesson Rd *TF:* 800-454-7159 ■ *Web:* www.beacontechnology.com	Saint Louis	MO	63128	314-487-7600	487-0100
BH Aircraft Company Inc 2230 Smithtown Ave. *Web:* www.bhaircraft.com	Ronkonkoma	NY	11779	631-981-4200	981-0221
Big Fly Inc 13940 Cedar Rd Ste 227 *Web:* www.bigflyaviation.com	Cleveland	OH	44118	323-875-2273	
Blackcomb Aviation LP Vancouver International Airport 4360 Agar Dr *Web:* www.blackcombhelicopters.com	Richmond	BC	V7B1A3	604-273-5311	
Brown Precision Inc 90 Shields Rd *Web:* www.brownprecisioninc.com	Huntsville	AL	35811	256-746-0533	
Budney Industries Inc PO Box 8316 *Web:* www.budney.com	Berlin	CT	06037	860-828-1950	828-7528
Cadence Aerospace LLC 610 Newport Ctr Dr Ste 950 *Web:* www.prvaerospace.com	Newport Beach	CA	92660	949-877-3630	
California Amforge Corp 750 N Vernon Ave *Web:* www.cal-amforge.com	Azusa	CA	91702	626-334-4931	
Cbol Corp 19850 Plummer St. *Web:* www.cbol.com	Chatsworth	CA	91311	818-704-8200	704-4336
CBS Manufacturing Co, The 35 Kripes Rd *Web:* www.cbsmfg.com	East Granby	CT	06026	860-653-8100	844-8150
Centra Industries Inc 24 Cherry Blossom Rd *Web:* www.centra-ind.com	Cambridge	ON	N3H4R7	519-650-2828	650-7474
Chromalloy Gas Turbine LLC 330 Blaisdell Rd *Web:* www.chromalloy.com	Orangeburg	NY	10962	845-359-4700	
Chromalloy Nevada 3636 Arrowhead Dr. *Web:* chromalloy.com	Carson City	NV	89706	775-687-8833	
Cobham Electronic Systems Inc 1001 Pawtucket Blvd	Lowell	MA	01854	978-442-4700	
Continental Motors Inc 2039 Broad St *TF:* 800-718-3411 ■ *Web:* www.tcmlink.com	Mobile	AL	36615	251-438-3411	432-7352
Corporate Eagle Management Services Inc 6320 Highland Rd. *Web:* corporateeagle.com	Waterford	MI	48327	248-461-9000	
Dakota Air Parts International Inc 1801 23rd Ave N Ste 119 *Web:* www.dakotaairparts.com	Fargo	ND	58102	701-297-9999	
Dart Aerospace Ltd 1270 Aberdeen St *TF:* 800-556-4166 ■ *Web:* www.dartaerospace.com	Hawkesbury	ON	K6A1K7	613-632-3336	
Data Link Solutions LLC 350 Collins Rd NE *Web:* www.datalinksolutions.net	Cedar Rapids	IA	52498	319-295-4357	
Davidson Technologies Inc 530 Discovery Drive Cummings Research Park *Web:* www.davidson-tech.com	Huntsville	AL	35806	256-922-0720	971-6861
Delta Industries 39 Bradley Pk Rd *Web:* mbaerospace.com	East Granby	CT	06026	860-653-5041	653-5792
DNE Systems Inc 50 Barnes Industrial Park N *Web:* www.dne.com	Wallingford	CT	06492	203-265-7151	
Doncasters Inc 36 Spring Ln *Web:* www.doncasters.com	Farmington	CT	06032	860-677-1376	
Eaton Aerospace LLC 9650 Jeronimo Rd Ste 1200 *Web:* www.aerospace.eaton.com	Irvine	CA	92618	949-452-9500	
EFW Inc 4700 Marine Creek Pkwy *Web:* www.efw.com	Fort Worth	TX	76136	817-234-6600	234-6768
Electro-Methods Inc 330 Governors Hwy *Web:* electro-methods.com	South Windsor	CT	06074	860-289-8661	
Electroimpact Inc 4413 Chennault Beach Rd. *Web:* www.electroimpact.com	Mukilteo	WA	98275	425-348-8090	
Engine Components Inc (ECI) 9503 Middlex *TF:* 800-324-2359 ■ *Web:* eci.aero	San Antonio	TX	78217	210-820-8101	820-8102
Essner Manufacturing LP 6651 Will Rogers Blvd *Web:* www.essner.com	Fort Worth	TX	76140	817-551-5511	
Esterline Defense Group 85901 Ave 53 *Web:* www.armtecdefense.com	Coachella	CA	92236	760-398-0143	
Ferco Tech Corp 291 Conover Dr *Web:* www.fercotech.com	Franklin	OH	45005	937-746-6696	
FIELD AVIATION COMPANY Inc 2450 Derry Rd E Hngr 2 *Web:* www.fieldav.com	Mississauga	ON	L5S1B2	905-676-1540	
Flight Dimensions International Inc 4835 Cordell Ave Ste 150 *TF:* 866-235-6870 ■ *Web:* www.flightexplorer.com	Bethesda	MD	20814	301-634-8201	
Flightsafety Services Corp 10770 E Briarwood Ave Ste 100 *Web:* www.flightsafety.com	Centennial	CO	80112	303-783-1023	
G2 Solutions LLC 11410 Ne 124Th St *Web:* g2globalsolutions.com	Kirkland	WA	98034	425-789-0200	
GA Telesis LLC 1850 NW 49th St *Web:* www.gatelesis.com	Fort Lauderdale	FL	33309	954-676-3111	676-9998
Gama Aviation Inc 2 Corporate Dr Ste 1050 *Web:* www.gamaaviationllc.com	Shelton	CT	06484	203-337-4600	
Garsite LLC 539 S Tenth St *TF:* 888-427-7483 ■ *Web:* www.garsite.com	Kansas City	KS	66105	913-342-5600	342-0638
GE Aircraft Engines 1 Neumann Way *Web:* www.geaviation.com	Cincinnati	OH	45215	513-243-2000	
GE Aviation 1 Neumann Way *Web:* www.geaviation.com	Cincinnati	OH	45215	513-243-2000	
General Dynamics Armament & Technical Products Inc 2118 Water Ridge Pkwy *Web:* www.gdatp.com	Charlotte	NC	28217	704-714-8000	
General Kinetics Engineering Corp 110 E Dr *Web:* www.generalkinetics.com	Brampton	ON	L6T1C1	905-458-0888	458-7566
Geospatial Systems Inc 150 Lucius Gordon Dr	West Henrietta	NY	14586	585-427-8310	
Graco Supply Co 1001 Miller Ave *Web:* www.gracosupply.com	Fort Worth	TX	76105	817-535-3200	
Gros-Ite Industries 1790 New Britain Ave *TF:* 877-777-4778 ■ *Web:* www.edactechnologies.com	Farmington	CT	06032	860-677-2603	
Haley Industries Ltd 634 Magnesium Rd.	Haley	ON	K0J1Y0	613-432-8841	
Hartzell Engine Technologies LLC 2900 Selma Hwy. *TF:* 877-359-5355 ■ *Web:* hartzell.aero	Montgomery	AL	36108	334-386-5400	
HEICO Corp 3000 Taft St. *NYSE: HEI* ■ *Web:* www.heico.com	Hollywood	FL	33021	954-987-4000	987-8228
Imagine Air Jet Services LLC 460 Briscoe Blvd Ste 210 *Web:* www.imagineair.com	Lawrenceville	GA	30046	678-226-2329	
Indal Technologies Inc 3570 Hawkestone Rd *Web:* www.indaltech.cwfc.com	Mississauga	ON	L5C2V8	905-275-5300	
Innotech-Execaire Aviation Group 10225 Ryan Ave Montreal International Airport *Web:* www.innotech-execaire.com	Dorval	QC	H9P1A2	514-636-8484	636-8573
Insight Technology Inc 9 Akira Way *TF:* 866-509-2040 ■ *Web:* www.insighttechnology.com	Londonderry	NH	03053	603-626-4800	
Institute For Natural Resources PO Box 5757 *TF:* 877-246-6336 ■ *Web:* www.inrseminars.com	Concord	CA	94524	925-609-2820	
International Enterprises Inc 108 Allen St *Web:* www.ieionline.com	Talladega	AL	35160	256-362-8562	
ION Corp 7500 Equitable Dr *Web:* www.ioncorp.com	Eden Prairie	MN	55344	952-936-9490	
Jet Source Inc 2056 Palomar Airport Rd. *Web:* www.jetsource.com	Carlsbad	CA	92011	760-438-0877	
Jetlease Inc 5718 Westheimer 17th Fl *Web:* www.jetleaseinc.com	Houston	TX	77057	713-952-5100	
Jupitor Corporation USA 55 Fairbanks *Web:* www.jupitor.co.jp	Irvine	CA	92718	949-588-0505	
Kalitta Charters LLC 843 Willow Run Airport *TF:* 800-525-4882 ■ *Web:* www.kalittacharters.com	Ypsilanti	MI	48198	734-544-3400	
Kalogridis International Ltd 4819 Maple Ave *Web:* www.kalogridis.com	Dallas	TX	75219	214-637-0519	
Keddeg Co 10700 Pflumm Rd *Web:* www.keddeg.com	Lenexa	KS	66215	913-492-1222	
Kelly Aerospace Turbine Rotables Inc 1919 E Northern St *Web:* www.turbinerotables.com	Wichita	KS	67216	316-943-6100	

				Phone	Fax
KING AEROSPACE Inc 4444 Westgrove ... Web: www.kingaerospaceinc.com	Addison	TX	75001	972-248-4886	
Kreisler Industrial Corp 180 Van Riper Ave ... Web: www.kreislermfg.com	Elmwood Park	NJ	07407	201-791-0700	791-8015
Kreisler Mfg Corp 180 Van Riper Ave ... TF: 888-750-5834 ■ Web: www.kreislermfg.com	Elmwood Park	NJ	07407	201-791-0700	791-8015
L-3 Fuzing & Ordnance Systems 3975 Mcmann Rd	Cincinnati	OH	45245	513-943-2000	
Lancair International Inc 250 SE Timber Ave ... Web: www.aerocraftparts.com	Redmond	OR	97756	541-923-2233	
Le Bas International Air Division Inc 3440 Empresa Dr ... Web: www.lebas.com	San Luis Obispo	CA	93401	805-593-0510	
Lear Romec Crane Corp 241 S Abbe Rd PO Box 4014 ... Web: www.craneae.com	Elyria	OH	44036	440-323-3211	322-3378
Leesta Industries Ltd 6 Plateau ... Web: www.leesta.com	Pointe-Claire	QC	H9R5W2	514-694-3930	
Lockheed Martin Aeronautics Co 86 S Cobb Dr ... Web: www.lmaeronautics.com	Marietta	GA	30063	770-494-4411	
McNally Group 5445 DTC Pkwy P4 ... Web: www.mcnally-group.com	Greenwood Village	CO	80111	303-846-3035	
Meco Inc 2121 S Main St ... *Fax Area Code: 281	Paris	IL	61944	217-465-7575	313-0643*
Mesotec Inc 3575 Industrial Blvd ... Web: www.mesotec.ca	Sherbrooke	QC	J1L1X7	819-822-2777	822-4117
Mint Turbines LLC 2915 N State Hwy 99 ... Web: www.mintturbines.com	Stroud	OK	74079	918-968-9561	
Mist Mobility Integrated Systems Technology Inc 3 Iber Rd ... Web: www.mmist.ca	Ottawa	ON	K2S1E6	613-723-0403	723-8925
Moeller Mfg Company Inc Aircraft Div 30100 Beck Rd ... Web: www.moelleraircraft.com	Wixom	MI	48393	248-960-3999	960-1593
MTU Aero Engines North America Inc 795 Brook St Bldg 5 ... Web: www.mtu.de	Rocky Hill	CT	06067	860-258-9700	258-9797
National Board for Certified Counselors Inc 3 Terrace Way Ste D ... Web: www.nbcc.org	Greensboro	NC	27403	336-547-0607	
Navhouse Corp 10 Loring Dr ... TF: 877-628-6667 ■ Web: www.navhouse.com	Bolton	ON	L7E1J9	905-857-8102	
Near Space Systems Inc 2375 Telstar Dr Ste 115 ... Web: www.globalnearspace.com	Colorado Springs	CO	80920	719-685-8108	
Neptec Design Group Ltd 302 Legget Dr Ste 202 ... Web: www.neptec.com	Kanata	ON	K2K1Y5	613-599-7602	
Nexcelle LLC 30 Merchant St Mail Drop W28 Princeton Hill ... Web: www.nexcelle.com	Cincinnati	OH	45246	513-552-6659	
Nextant Aerospace LLC 355 Richmond Rd ... Web: www.nextantaerospace.com	Cleveland	OH	44143	216-261-9000	
Niles Precision Co PO Box 548 ... Web: www.nilesprecision.com	Niles	MI	49120	269-683-0585	683-7762
Noel-Smyser Engineering Corp 4005 Industrial Blvd ... Web: www.noel-smyser.com	Indianapolis	IN	46254	317-293-2215	
Northstar Aerospace Inc 6006 W 73rd St ... TSE: NAS ■ Web: www.nsaero.com	Bedford Park	IL	60638	708-728-2000	728-2009
Northwest Uav Propulsion Systems 2717 Ne Bunn Rd ... Web: www.nwuav.com	Mcminnville	OR	97128	503-434-6845	
Novaria Group Inc 306 W Seventh St Ste 310 ... Web: www.novariagroup.com	Fort Worth	TX	76102	817-381-3810	
Ordnance Technologies (NA) Inc 7380 Sand Lk Rd Ste 360 ... Web: www.otnausa.com	Orlando	FL	32819	407-354-3827	
Pacific Scientific Energetic Materials Company Inc 7073 W Willis Dr ... Web: www.psemc.com	Chandler	AZ	85226	480-763-3000	
Pankl Aerospace Systems Inc 16615 Edwards Rd ... Web: www.pankl.com	Cerritos	CA	90703	562-207-6300	
Paradigm Precision Holdings LLC 3651 SE Commerce Ave ... Web: www.paradigmprecision.com	Stuart	FL	34997	772-287-7770	
Parker Gas Turbine Fuel Systems Div (GTFSD) 8940 Tyler Blvd ... Web: parker.com	Mentor	OH	44060	440-266-2300	266-2311
Parker Hannifin Corp Control System Div 14 Robbins Pond Rd ... Web: parker.com	Devens	MA	01434	978-784-1200	
Phoenix Aerospace Inc 61B Industrial Pkwy	Mound House	NV	89706	775-882-9700	
Powill Manufacturing & Engineering Inc 21039 N 27th Ave ... Web: powill.com	Phoenix	AZ	85027	623-780-4100	
Pratt & Whitney 400 Main St ... *Fax: Sales ■ Web: www.pratt-whitney.com	East Hartford	CT	06108	860-565-4321	565-6609*
Pratt & Whitney 17900 Bee Line Hwy ... Web: pw.utc.com	Jupiter	FL	33478	860-565-4321	
Pratt & Whitney Canada Inc 1000 Marie-Victorin Blvd ... TF: 800-268-8000 ■ Web: www.pwc.ca	Longueuil	QC	J4G1A1	450-677-9411	647-3620
Preece Inc 26845 Vista Ter ... Web: www.preeceinc.com	Lake Forest	CA	92630	949-770-9411	
Prime Industries Inc 406 Dividend Dr ... Web: www.primeindustriesusa.com	Peachtree City	GA	30269	770-632-1851	
QED Instruments Inc 2920 S Halladay St ... Web: www.qedinstruments.com	Santa Ana	CA	92705	714-546-6010	
Quality Honeycomb LP 624 107th St ... Web: www.qualityhoneycomb.com	Arlington	TX	76011	817-640-1190	
RedXDefense LLC 7642 Standish Pl ... Web: www.redxdefense.com	Rockville	MD	20855	301-279-7970	
Robertson Fuel Systems LLC 800 W Carver Rd Ste 101 ... Web: www.robertsonfuelsystems.com	Tempe	AZ	85284	480-337-7050	
Rogerson Kratos Corp 403 S Raymond ... Web: rogersonaircraft.com/markets-rogerson-kratos	Pasadena	CA	91109	626-449-3090	
Rolls-Royce North America 1875 Explorer St Ste 200 ... TF: 888-269-2377 ■ Web: www.rolls-royce.com/northamerica/na	Reston	VA	20190	703-834-1700	709-6086
Saab Barracuda LLC 608 E Mcneill St ... Web: www.saabgroup.com	Lillington	NC	27546	910-893-2094	
Sandel Avionics Inc 2401 Dogwood Way ... TF: 877-726-3357 ■ Web: www.sandel.com	Vista	CA	92081	760-727-4900	
Senior Aerospace Ketema Div 790 Greenfield Dr ... TF: 800-669-6820 ■ Web: www.sfketema.com	El Cajon	CA	92021	619-442-3451	440-1456
SGB Enterprises Inc 24844 Anza Dr Ste A ... Web: www.sgbent.com	Valencia	CA	91355	661-294-8306	
Sheffield Manufacturing Inc 9131 Glenoaks Blvd ... Web: www.sheffield-mfg.com	Sun Valley	CA	91352	818-767-4948	
Shur-Lok Corp 2541 White Rd ... Web: www.shur-lok.com	Irvine	CA	92614	949-474-6000	
Sifco Industries Inc 970 E 64th St ... NYSE: SIF ■ Web: www.sifco.com	Cleveland	OH	44103	216-881-8600	432-6281
Spatial & Spectral Research LLC 13 Beech St ... Web: www.ssrllc.us	Bedford	NH	03110	603-472-2575	
St. Aerospace San Antonio LP 9800 John Saunders Rd ... Web: www.stasaa.com	San Antonio	TX	78216	210-293-3200	293-3680
Tactical Support Equipment Inc 4039 Barefoot Rd ... Web: www.tserecon.com	Fayetteville	NC	28306	910-425-3360	
Trident Systems Inc 10201 Fairfax Blvd Ste 300 ... Web: www.tridsys.com	Fairfax	VA	22030	703-273-1012	
Tulmar Safety Systems Inc 1123 Cameron St ... Web: www.tulmar.com	Hawkesbury	ON	K6A2B8	613-632-1282	632-2030
Turbomeca USA Inc 2709 N Forum Dr ... TF: 800-662-6322 ■ Web: www.turbomeca.com	Grand Prairie	TX	75052	972-606-7600	
Universal Asset Management Inc 5350 Poplar Ave Ste 150 ... Web: www.uaminc.com	Memphis	TN	38119	901-682-4064	
Universal Avionics Systems Corp 3260 E Universal Way ... Web: www.uasc.com	Tucson	AZ	85756	520-295-2300	
Vector Aerospace Helicopter Services Inc 22378 Billie Blackmon Rd Ste 2100 ... TF: 888-729-2276 ■ Web: www.vectoraerospace.com	Andalusia	AL	36421	604-276-7600	276-7675
VerTechs Enterprises Inc 1071 Industrial Pl ... Web: vertechsusa.com	El Cajon	CA	92020	253-252-3914	
Visioneering Inc 31985 Groesbeck Hwy ... Web: www.vistool.com	Fraser	MI	48026	586-293-1000	
VT Systems Inc 99 Canal Ctr Plz Ste 220 ... Web: www.vt-systems.com	Alexandria	VA	22314	703-739-2610	
Wall Colmonoy Corp 101 W Girard Ave ... Web: www.wallcolmonoy.com	Madison Heights	MI	48071	248-585-6400	585-7960
Wesco Aircraft Hardware Corp 27727 Ave Scott ... Web: www.wescoair.com	Valencia	CA	91355	661-775-7200	
Whitcraft LLC 76 County Rd ... Web: www.whitcraft.com	Eastford	CT	06242	860-974-0786	
Williams International 2280 E W Maple Rd PO Box 200 ... Web: www.williams-int.com	Walled Lake	MI	48390	248-624-5200	624-5345
Woodward HRT Inc 25200 W Rye Canyon Rd ... Web: www.hrtextron.com	Santa Clarita	CA	91355	661-294-6000	
XOJET Inc 2000 Sierra Point Pkwy ... Web: www.xojet.com	Brisbane	CA	94005	650-676-4700	

22 AIRCRAFT PARTS & AUXILIARY EQUIPMENT

See Also Precision Machined Products p. 2968

				Phone	Fax
A G H Industries Inc 7420 Whitehall St ... Web: www.aghindustries.com	Richland Hills	TX	76118	817-284-1742	
AAR Cargo Systems 2870 Cargo Cir ... Web: www.aarcorp.com	Memphis	TN	38118	919-705-2400	705-2499
AAR Composites 14201 Myerlake Cir ... TF: 800-422-2213 ■ Web: aarcorp.com	Clearwater	FL	33760	727-539-8585	539-0316
AAR Corp 1100 N Wood Dale Rd 1 AAR Pl ... NYSE: AIR ■ TF: 800-422-2213 ■ Web: www.aarcorp.com	Wood Dale	IL	60191	630-227-2000	227-2019
Ace Clearwater Enterprises 19815 Magellan Dr ... Web: www.aceclearwater.com	Torrance	CA	90502	310-538-5380	323-2137
Acromil Corp 18421 Railroad St ... Web: www.acromil.com	City of Industry	CA	91748	626-964-2522	810-6100
Advanced Technology Co 2858 E Walnut St ... TF: 800-447-2442 ■ Web: www.at-co.com	Pasadena	CA	91107	626-449-2696	793-9442
Aereon Corp 20 Nassau St Ste 223 ... Web: www.aereon.com	Princeton	NJ	08542	609-921-2131	
Aero Controls Inc 1610 20th St NW ... Web: www.aerocontrols.com	Auburn	WA	98001	253-269-3000	
Aero Gear Inc 1050 Day Hill Rd ... Web: www.aerogear.com	Windsor	CT	06095	860-688-0888	285-8514
Aero Parts Mfg & Repair Inc 431 Rio Rancho Blvd NE ... Web: www.aeroparts.aero	Rio Rancho	NM	87124	505-891-6600	891-6650

Phone | Fax

Aero Seating Technologies LLC
5079 Walnut Grove Ave San Gabriel CA 91776 626-286-1130
Web: www.aeroseating.com
Aero-mach Laboratories Inc 7707 E Funston St Wichita KS 67207 316-682-7707
Web: www.aeromach.com
Aerofit Inc 1425 S Acacia Ave Fullerton CA 92831 714-521-5060
Web: www.aerofit.com
Aerosource Inc 390 Campus Dr Somerset NJ 08873 732-469-9300
Web: www.aerosourceinc.com
Aerospace Products International (API)
3778 Distriplex Dr N Memphis TN 38118 901-365-3470 950-1411*
**Fax Area Code:* 800 ■ *TF:* 888-274-2497 ■ *Web:* www.apiworldwide.com
Aircraft Belts Inc 1176 Telecom Dr Creedmoor NC 27522 919-956-4395
Web: www.aircraftbelts.com
Airline Hydraulics Corp 3557 Progress Dr Bensalem PA 19020 215-638-4700
Web: www.airlinehyd.com
Airtex Manufacturing Inc
259 Lower Morrisville Rd Fallsington PA 19054 215-295-4115
Web: www.airtexinteriors.com
Alken Industries Inc 2175 Fifth Ave. Ronkonkoma NY 11779 631-467-2000
Web: www.alkenind.com
Ametek Advanced Industries Inc
4550 Southeast Blvd. Wichita KS 67210 316-522-0424
Web: www.advancedindustries.com
Ametek HSA Inc 7841 NW 56th St Miami FL 33166 305-599-8855
Web: www.highstandardaviation.com
Apex Composites LLC 5322 John Lucas Dr Burlington ON L7L6A6 905-331-8042
Web: www.apexcomposites.com
Arden Engineering Inc 1878 N Main St. Orange CA 92865 714-998-6410 998-0956
Web: www.cadenceaerospace.com
Arkwin Industries Inc 686 Main St Westbury NY 11590 516-333-2640 334-6786*
**Fax:* Sales ■ *TF:* 800-284-2551 ■ *Web:* www.arkwin.com
Arrow Gear Company Inc 2301 Curtiss St. Downers Grove IL 60515 630-969-7640 969-0253
Web: www.arrowgear.com
Arrowhead Products Corp
4411 Katella Ave. Los Alamitos CA 90720 714-828-7770 995-3452
Web: www.arrowheadproducts.net
Arvan Inc 14083 S Normandie Ave. Gardena CA 90249 310-327-1818 324-6634
Web: www.arvaninc.com
Aurora Flight Sciences Corp 9950 Wakeman Dr Manassas VA 20110 703-369-3633 369-4514
Web: www.aurora.aero
Avcorp Industries Inc 10025 River Way Delta BC V4G1M7 604-582-6677 582-2620
TF: 866-781-3111 ■ *Web:* www.avcorp.com
Avidyne Corp 55 Old Bedford Rd Ste 101 Lincoln MA 01773 781-402-7400
Web: www.avidyne.com
Avox Systems Inc 225 Erie St. Lancaster NY 14086 716-683-5100 681-1089
Web: www.avoxsys.com
Bauer Howden Inc 175 Century Dr. Bristol CT 06010 860-583-9100
Web: www.bauerct.com
Blair-HSM Group of Cos 3671 Horseblock Rd. Medford NY 11763 631-924-6600
Web: www.blair-hsm.com
Boeing Company Commercial Airplane Group
PO Box 3707 Seattle WA 98124 206-655-2121
Web: www.boeing.com/commercial
Bowhead 4900 Seminary Rd Ste 1200 Alexandria VA 22311 703-413-4226
Web: www.bowheadsupport.com
Burnham Composite Structures Inc
6262 W 34th St S Wichita KS 67215 316-946-5900
Web: www.burnhamcs.com
C&D Zodiac 7330 Lincoln Way. Garden Grove CA 92841 714-891-1906
Web: www.cdzodiac.com
Capps Manufacturing Inc 2121 S Edwards Wichita KS 67213 316-942-9351
Web: www.cappsmfg.com
Carleton Life Support Systems Inc
2734 Hickory Grove Rd. Davenport IA 52804 563-383-6000 383-6430
Web: www.cobham.com
CEF Industries Inc 320 S Church St. Addison IL 60101 630-628-2299 628-1386
TF: 800-888-6419 ■ *Web:* www.cefindustries.com
Cfan Co 1000 Technology Way San Marcos TX 78666 512-353-2832 353-2838
Web: www.cfan.com
Champion Aerospace LLC 1230 Old Norris Rd Liberty SC 29657 864-843-1162
Web: www.championaerospace.com
Conrad Co, The 1304 Farmville Rd Memphis TN 38122 901-323-5926
Web: www.theconradcompany.com
Coronado Manufacturing Inc
8991 Glenoaks Boulvard. Sun Valley CA 91352 818-768-5010
Web: www.coronadomfg.com
Cox & Company Inc 1664 Old Country Rd Plainview NY 11803 212-366-0200
Web: www.coxandco.com
Craft Manufacturing & Tooling Inc
7152 Central Ave Hot Springs AR 71913 501-525-0268
Web: www.cmtair.com
CRS Jet Spares Inc 6701 NW 12th Ave Fort Lauderdale FL 33309 954-972-2807 972-2708
TF: 800-338-5387 ■ *Web:* www.crsjetspares.com
CTL Aerospace Inc 5616 Spellmire Dr. Cincinnati OH 45246 513-874-7900 874-2499
Web: www.ctlaerospace.com
Curtiss-Wright Corp
10 Waterview Blvd 2nd Fl. Parsippany NJ 07054 973-541-3700 541-3699
NYSE: CW ■ *TF:* 855-449-0995 ■ *Web:* www.curtisswright.com
Curtiss-Wright Flight Systems
201 Old Boiling Springs Rd Shelby NC 28152 704-481-1150
Web: www.curtisswright.com
Davis Aircraft Products Company Inc
1150 Walnut Ave Bohemia NY 11716 631-563-1500
Web: www.davisaircraftproducts.com
Disan Engineering Corp 101 Mohawk Dr Nowata OK 74048 918-273-1636
Web: www.disancorp.com
Ducommun AeroStructures Inc
268 E Gardena Blvd Gardena CA 90248 310-380-5390
Web: www.ducommunaero.com
Dukes Aerospace 9060 Winnetka Ave Northridge CA 91324 818-350-1900
Web: www.dukesaerospace.com

Phone | Fax

Electromech Technologies Inc 2600 S Custer Wichita KS 67217 316-941-0400
Web: www.electromech.com
Enflite Inc 105 Cooperative Way Georgetown TX 78626 512-868-3399 868-3320
Web: www.enflite.com
Enviro Systems Inc 12037 N Hwy 99 Seminole OK 74868 405-382-0731 382-0737
Web: www.enviro-ok.com
Esterline Interface Technologies
600 W Wilbur Ave. Coeur d'Alene ID 83815 208-765-8000 292-2275
TF: 800-444-5923 ■ *Web:* www.esterline.com
Exotic Metals Forming Company LLC
5411 S 226th St Kent WA 98032 253-395-3710 872-8033
Web: www.exoticmetals.com
Fairchild Controls Corp 540 Highland St Frederick MD 21701 301-228-3400 682-6885
TF: 800-695-5378 ■ *Web:* www.fairchildcontrols.com
FFC Inc 4010 Pilot Dr Ste 103 Memphis TN 38118 901-842-7110
Web: www.ffcfuelcells.com
Fiber Art Inc 124 Industrial Dr. Cibolo TX 78108 210-658-8866
Web: www.fiberartinc.com
First Call International Inc
6329 Airport Fwy Fort Worth TX 76117 817-831-2220
Web: www.firstcallintl.com
FletchAir Inc 103 Turkey Run Ln. Comfort TX 78013 830-995-5900 995-5903
TF: 800-329-4647 ■ *Web:* www.fletchair.com
GE Aviation Systems Div
3290 Patterson Ave SE Grand Rapids MI 49512 616-241-8274
Web: www.geaviation.com
General Aviation Industries Inc
415 Jones Rd Weatherford TX 76088 817-598-4848
Web: www.gaiinc.net
General Electrodynamics Corporation Inc
8000 Calendar Rd. Arlington TX 76001 817-572-0366
TF: 800-551-6038 ■ *Web:* www.gecscales.com
GKN Aerospace Bandy Machining Inc
3420 N San Fernando Blvd Burbank CA 91504 818-846-9020
Web: www.gkn.com
GKN Aerospace Chem-tronics Inc
1150 W Bradley Ave El Cajon CA 92020 619-448-2320 258-5270
Web: www.gkn.com
Global Ground Support LLC 540 Old Hwy 56 Olathe KS 66061 913-780-0300 780-0829
TF: 888-780-0303 ■ *Web:* www.globalgroundsupport.com
Globe Engineering Company Inc PO Box 12407 Wichita KS 67277 316-943-1266 943-3089
Web: www.globeeng.com
Goodrich Corp Aircraft Interior Products Div
3420 S Seventh St Phoenix AZ 85040 602-243-2200 243-2300
TF: 877-808-7575 ■ *Web:* utcaerospacesystems.com
Goodrich Corp Landing Gear Div
6225 Oak Tree Blvd Independence OH 44131 216-341-1700 429-4806
Web: utcaerospacesystems.com
Goodrich Landing Gear Div
1400 S Service Rd W Oakville ON L6L5Y7 905-827-7777
Web: customers.goodrich.com
Growth Industries Inc
12523 Third St PO Box 900 Grandview MO 64030 816-763-7676 765-4925
Web: www.growthind.com
GSE Dynamics Inc 25 Corporate Dr Hauppauge NY 11788 631-231-1044
Web: www.gsedynamics.com
Hansen Engineering Company Inc
24050 Frampton Ave Harbor City CA 90710 310-534-3870
Web: www.hansenengineering.com
Harlow Aerostructures LLC 1501 McLean Blvd S. Wichita KS 67213 316-265-5268
Web: www.harlowair.com
Harter Industries Inc 401 W Gemini Dr. Tempe AZ 85283 480-345-9595
Web: www.harter.aero
Hartwell Corp 900 Richfield Rd Placentia CA 92870 714-993-4200 579-4419
Web: www.hartwellcorp.com
Hartzell Propeller Inc 1 Propeller Pl Piqua OH 45356 937-778-4200 778-4321
TF: 800-942-7767 ■ *Web:* www.hartzellprop.com
Heizer Aerospace Inc
8750 Pevely Industrial Dr Pevely MO 63070 636-475-6300 464-4206
Web: www.haiusa.com
Hiller Inc 630 N Washington Wichita KS 67214 316-264-8022
Web: www.hillerinc.com
Honeywell Aerospace 3520 Westmoor St South Bend IN 46628 574-231-2000
TF: 800-707-4555 ■ *Web:* honeywell.com
Honeywell Aerospace 1944 E Sky Harbor Cir Phoenix AZ 85034 800-601-3099 365-3343*
**Fax Area Code:* 602 ■ *TF:* 800-601-3099 ■ *Web:* www.honeywell.com
Hydro-Aire Inc 3000 Winona Ave Burbank CA 91504 818-526-2600 842-6117
Web: www.craneae.com
Inair Aviation Services Co
8225 Country Club Pl. Indianapolis IN 46214 317-271-0195
Web: www.inairaviation.com
Jamco America Inc 1018 80th St SW Everett WA 98203 425-347-4735 353-2343
Web: www.jamcoamerica.com
Jarvis Airfoil Inc 528 Glastonbury Tpke Portland CT 06480 860-342-5000
Web: www.jarvisairfoil.com
Jeff Bonner R & D Inc 10525 Mopac Dr San Antonio TX 78217 210-590-3133 590-3155
Web: www.jbrnd.com
Kaman Aerospace Corp
Old Windsor Rd PO Box 2 Bloomfield CT 06002 860-242-4461 243-7514
Web: www.kaman.com
Keith Products Inc 4554 Claire Chennault. Addison TX 75001 972-407-1234
Web: www.keithproducts.com
L-3 Communications Integrated Systems
10001 Jack Finney Blvd Greenville TX 75402 903-455-3450 457-4413
TF: 877-282-1168 ■ *Web:* www.l-3com.com
LMI Aerospace Inc (LMIA)
411 Fountain Lakes Blvd Saint Charles MO 63301 636-946-6525 949-1576
NASDAQ: LMIA ■ *Web:* www.lmiaerospace.com
Magellan Aerospace 2320 Wedekind Dr Middletown OH 45042 513-422-2751
Web: www.aeroncainc.com
Magellan Aerospace Corp 3160 Derry Rd E Mississauga ON L4T1A9 905-677-1889 677-5658
TSE: MAL ■ *Web:* www.magellan.aero
Mayday Manufacturing Co 3100 Jim Christal Rd. Denton TX 76207 940-898-8301 898-8305
Web: www.maydaymfg.com

	City	State	Zip	Phone	Fax
MC Gill Corp 4056 Easy St *Web:* www.thegillcorp.com	El Monte	CA	91731	626-443-6094	350-5880
Mecaer America Inc 3205 Rue Delaunay *Web:* www.mecaer.com	Laval	QC	H7L5A4	450-682-7117	682-8152
Middle River Aircraft Systems (MRAS) 103 Chesapeake Pk Plaza *TF:* 877-432-3272 ■ *Web:* www.mras-usa.com	Baltimore	MD	21220	410-682-1500	682-1230
Mnemonics Inc 3900 Dow Rd *Web:* www.mnemonicsinc.com	Melbourne	FL	32934	321-254-7300	242-0862
MSA Aircraft Products Inc 10000 Iota Dr *Web:* www.msaaircraft.com	San Antonio	TX	78217	210-590-6100	
Nasco Aircraft Brake Inc 13300 Estrella Ave *Web:* www.nascoaircraft.com	Gardena	CA	90248	310-532-4430	532-6014
Neill Aircraft Co 1260 W 15th St *Web:* www.neillaircraft.com	Long Beach	CA	90813	562-432-7981	491-0483
NMG Aerospace 4880 Hudson Dr *Web:* www.nmgaerospace.com	Stow	OH	44224	330-688-6494	
NORDAM Group 6911 N Whirlpool Dr **Fax:* Sales ■ *Web:* www.nordam.com	Tulsa	OK	74117	918-878-4000	878-4808*
North American Aviation 7330 N Broadway St *Web:* www.naavinc.com	Wichita	KS	67219	316-744-6450	
Northrop Grumman Corp 2980 Fairview Park Dr *NYSE: NOC* ■ *Web:* www.northropgrumman.com	Falls Church	VA	22042	703-280-2900	
Oakridge Holdings Inc 1003 400 W ONTARIO St Ste 1003 *Web:* www.oakridgeholdingsinc.com	Chicago	IL	60654	312-505-9267	
Pacific Precision Products Manufacturing 9671 Irvine Ctr Dr Koll Ctr II Bldg 6 *Web:* www.ppp.aero	Irvine	CA	92618	949-727-3844	
Paramount Panels Inc 1531 E Cedar *Web:* www.paramountpanels.com	Ontario	CA	91761	909-947-8008	947-8012
Parker Aerospace Group 14300 Alton Pkwy *Web:* parker.com	Irvine	CA	92618	949-833-3000	
Precise Flight Inc 63354 Powell Butte Hwy *Web:* www.preciseflight.com	Bend	OR	97701	541-382-8684	
Precision Components International Inc 8801 Macon Rd *Web:* www.pciga.com	Midland	GA	31820	706-568-5900	
R&B Electronics Inc 1520 Industrial Park Dr Sault *Web:* www.randbelectronics.com	Marie	MI	49783	906-632-1542	
RECARO Aircraft Seating Americas Inc 2275 Eagle Pkwy *Web:* www.recaro-as.com	Fort Worth	TX	76177	817-490-9160	
Rogerson Aircraft Corp 2201 Alton Pkwy *Web:* www.rogerson.com	Irvine	CA	92606	949-660-0666	
Rotair Industries Inc 964 Crescent Ave *Web:* www.rotair.com	Bridgeport	CT	06607	203-576-6545	
Senior Aerospace Composites 2700 S Custer Ave *Web:* www.seniorcomposites.com	Wichita	KS	67217	316-942-3208	
Shimadzu Precision Instruments inc 3645 N Lakewood Blvd *Web:* www.shimadzu.com	Long Beach	CA	90808	310-517-9910	517-9180
Sigma Tek Inc 1001 Industrial Rd *Web:* www.sigmatek.com	Augusta	KS	67010	316-775-6373	
Soundair Inc 1826 Bickford Ave *Web:* www.soundair.com	Snohomish	WA	98290	360-453-2300	
Spectrum Aerospace Inc 609 W Knox Rd *Web:* www.spectrum-aero.com	Tempe	AZ	85284	480-966-0077	
SPP Canada Aircraft Inc 2025 Meadowvale Blvd Unit 1 *Web:* www.spp-ca.com	Mississauga	ON	L5N5N1	905-821-9339	
SPX Corp 300 Fenn Rd *Web:* pcxaero.com	Newington	CT	06111	860-666-2471	
Star Aviation Inc 2150 Michigan Ave Brookley Complex *Web:* www.staraviation.com	Mobile	AL	36615	251-650-0600	
STS Component Solutions LLC 2910 SW 42 Ave *TF:* 888-777-2960 ■ *Web:* www.stsaviationgroup.com	Palm City	FL	34990	888-777-2960	
Supracor Inc 2050 Corporate Ct *Web:* www.supracor.com	San Jose	CA	95131	408-432-1616	
Symbolic Displays Inc 1917 E St Andrew Pl *Web:* www.symbolicdisplays.com	Santa Ana	CA	92705	714-258-2811	258-2810
Transaero Inc 35 Melville Park Rd Ste 100 *Web:* www.transaeroinc.com	Melville	NY	11747	631-752-1240	
Triumph Fabrications 1923 Central Ave *Web:* www.triumphgroup.com	Hot Springs	AR	71901	501-321-9325	
Triumph Gear Systems Inc 6125 Silver Creek Dr	Park City	UT	84098	435-649-1900	
Triumph Structures-Long Island LLC 717 Main St *Web:* www.triumphgrp.com	Westbury	NY	11590	516-997-5757	
Triumph Thermal Systems Inc 200 Railroad St *Web:* www.triumphgroup.com	Forest	OH	45843	419-273-2511	273-3285
Tronair Inc 1740 Eber Rd *TF:* 800-426-6301 ■ *Web:* www.tronair.com	Holland	OH	43528	419-866-6301	867-0634
United Tool & Die Co 1 Carney Rd *TF:* 877-262-0336 ■ *Web:* www.utdco.com	West Hartford	CT	06110	860-246-6531	
UTC Aerospace Systems 14300 Judicial Rd *NYSE: GR*	Burnsville	MN	55306	952-892-4000	
Vibro-Meter Inc 144 Harvey Rd *TF:* 800-842-4291 ■ *Web:* www.vibro-meter.com	Londonderry	NH	03053	603-669-0940	669-0931
Vought Aircraft Div 300 Austin Blvd *Web:* www.triumphgroup.com/companies/triumph-aerostructures-vought-aircraft-division	Red Oak	TX	75154	972-946-2011	
WestWind Technologies Inc 2901 Wall Triana Hwy Ste 124 *Web:* www.westwindcorp.com	Huntsville	AL	35824	256-319-0137	
Wittenstein Inc 1249 Humbracht Cir *Web:* www.wittenstein-us.com	Bartlett	IL	60103	630-540-5300	
Zee Systems Inc 406 W Rhapsody Dr *Web:* www.zeeco-zeesys.com	San Antonio	TX	78216	210-342-9761	341-2609

23 AIRCRAFT RENTAL

See Also Aviation - Fixed-Base Operations p. 1835

	City	State	Zip	Phone	Fax
Adler Tank Rentals LLC 260 Mack Pl *Web:* m.adlertankrentals.com	South Plainfield	NJ	07080	908-462-9800	
Aerion Rental Services 1088 Hwy 65 n *Web:* aerionrentals.com	Greenbrier	AR	72058	501-335-7165	
AeroCentury Corp 1440 Chapin Ave Ste 310 *NYSE: ACY* ■ *Web:* www.aerocentury.com	Burlingame	CA	94010	650-340-1888	696-3929
AeroTurbine Inc 2323 NW 82nd Ave *Web:* www.aeroturbine.com	Miami	FL	33122	305-590-2600	
Aircastle Ltd 300 First Stamford Pl 5th Fl *NYSE: AYR* ■ *Web:* www.aircastle.com	Stamford	CT	06902	203-504-1020	504-1021
AmQuip Crane Rental LLC 1150 Northbrook Dr Ste 100 *Web:* www.amquip.com	Trevose	PA	19053	215-639-9200	
Apple Discount Drugs 404 N Fruitland Blvd *TF:* 800-424-8401 ■ *Web:* www.appledrugs.com	Salisbury	MD	21801	410-749-8401	
Argus Supply Co 46400 Continental Dr *Web:* argus-hazco.com	Chesterfield	MI	48047	586-840-3200	
Armour Transportation Systems Inc 689 Edinburgh Dr *TF:* 800-561-7987 ■ *Web:* www.armour.ca	Moncton	NB	E1E2L4	506-857-0205	
Atlas Aircraft Center 115 Flight Line Ave *Web:* www.planesense.com	Portsmouth	NH	03801	603-501-7700	
ATT Metrology Services Inc 30210 SE 79th St Ste 100 *Web:* www.attinc.com	Issaquah	WA	98027	425-867-5356	
Aviation Capital Group Corp 840 Newport Ctr Dr Ste 300 *Web:* www.aviationcapitalgroup.com	Newport Beach	CA	92660	949-219-4600	759-5675
Aviation Leasing Group 8080 Ward Pkwy Ste 407	Kansas City	MO	64114	816-931-7300	931-8200
Avsi Group 4464 w 12th st *Web:* www.avsigroup.com	Houston	TX	77055	713-290-8300	
Axis Jet 6133 Freeport Blvd *Web:* www.axisjet.com	Sacramento	CA	95822	916-391-5000	
Bar XH Air Inc 575 Palmer Rd NE (Esso Avitat) *Web:* www.barxh.com	Calgary	AB	T2E7G4	403-291-3227	
Bartha Visual 600 N Cassady Ave *Web:* bartha.com	Columbus	OH	43219	614-252-7455	
Bigrentz Inc 1063 Mcgaw Ave Ste 200 *TF:* 855-999-5438 ■ *Web:* www.bigrentz.com	Irvine	CA	92614	855-999-5438	
Blue Dot Energy Services LLC Route 76 E *Web:* www.bluedotinc.com	Bridgeport	WV	26330	304-842-3829	
Boucher Brothers Management Inc 1451 Ocean Dr Ste 205 *Web:* www.boucherbrothers.com	Miami Beach	FL	33139	305-535-8177	
BSM 2nd Street LLC 5405 Wilshire Blvd *Web:* www.blankspaces.com	Los Angeles	CA	90036	323-330-9505	
Compact Power Equipment Centers LLC 3326 Hwy 51 *Web:* www.compactpowercenter.com	Fort Mill	SC	29715	803-548-4348	
Eagle Helicopters Inc 4130 Heliport Dr *Web:* www.kachinaaviation.com	Nampa	ID	83687	208-318-0100	
eLease Funding Inc 2820 Firstst Ave N *Web:* elease.com	St. Petersburg	FL	33713	727-209-1200	
Equipment Corporation of America 1000 Sta St PO Box 306 *Web:* www.ecanet.com	Coraopolis	PA	15108	412-264-4480	
Excel Railcar Corp 28367 Davis Pkwy Cantera Lakes Office Campus Ste 300 *Web:* excelrailcar.com	Warrenville	IL	60555	630-657-1100	
FlexShopper Inc 2700 N Military Trl Ste 200 *TF:* 855-353-9289 ■ *Web:* www.flexshopper.com	Boca Raton	FL	33431	855-353-9289	
Frain Group Inc, The 9377 W Grand Ave *Web:* www.fraingroup.com	Franklin Park	IL	60131	630-629-9900	
G P Aviation Services 95 Round Hill Rd *Web:* gpaviation.com	Armonk	NY	10504	914-273-0123	
GE Aviation Services 901 Main Ave *Web:* www.gecas.com	Norwalk	CT	06851	203-842-5200	
Groupe Lou-Tec Inc 8500 Jules L,ger *Web:* www.loutec.com	Anjou	QC	H1J1A7	514-356-0047	
Host t Parker of Maryland Inc 2200 Broening Hwy Ste 102 *Web:* www.tparkerhost.com	Baltimore	MD	21224	410-633-4666	
International Lease Finance Corp (ILFC) 10250 Constellation Blvd Ste 3400 *Web:* www.ilfc.com	Los Angeles	CA	90067	310-788-1999	788-1990
J.A. Riggs Tractor Company Inc 9125 Interstate 30 *Web:* www.riggscat.com	Little Rock	AR	72209	501-570-3100	
Jean Cartier Packaging Inc 2325, Industriel Blvd *Web:* www.cartierpackaging.com	St-cesaire	QC	J0L1T0	450-469-3168	
John J Enoch Inc 2400 york rd *Web:* www.enochoffice.com	Lutherville timonium	MD	21093	410-561-7600	
Kropp Equipment Inc 1020 Kennedy Ave *Web:* www.kropp.us	Schereville	IN	46375	219-865-1111	
Lease Equity Appreciation Fund I LP 110 S Poplar St Ste 101 *TF:* 800-819-5556 ■ *Web:* LEAFFinancial.com	Wilmington	DE	19801	800-819-5556	
Moncton Flight College 1719 Champlain St *Web:* www.mfc.nb.ca	Dieppe	NB	E1A7P5	506-857-3080	
NCSG Crane & Heavy Haul Services Ltd 11466 Winterburn Rd *Web:* www.ncsg.com	Edmonton	AB	T5S2Y3	780-455-1075	

Phone | Fax

Nesco LLC
6714 Pointe Inverness Way Ste 220 Fort Wayne IN 46804 260-824-6340
Web: nescoelectric.com

Northern Jet Management 5500 44th St SE Grand Rapids MI 49512 616-336-4800
TF: 800-462-7709 ■ *Web:* www.northernjet.net

OK3 Air 1980 Airport Rd Hngr A Heber City UT 84032 435-654-3962
Web: www.ok3air.com

Peterson Power Systems Inc
2828 Teagarden St San Leandro CA 94577 510-895-8400
Web: www.petersonpower.com

Prive Jets LLC
1250 E Hallandale Beach Blvd Ste 505 Hallandale FL 33009 305-917-1600
Web: www.privejets.com

Procrane Inc
2440-76 Ave Station S PO Box 8610 Edmonton AB T6E6R2 780-440-4434
Web: www.sterlingcrane.ca

Raydon Rentals Ltd 9520 - 51 Ave Edmonton AB T6E5A6 780-989-1301
Web: www.catrents.ca

Red-D-Arc Inc 667 S Service Rd PO Box 40 Grimsby ON L3M4G1 905-643-4212
Web: www.red-d-arc.com

Rent Rite Inc 7601 N Federal Hwy Boca Raton FL 33487 561-995-8832
Web: www.rentriterentals.com

RobotWorx Inc 370 W Fairground St Marion OH 43302 740-251-4312
Web: www.robots.com

SenovvA Inc 731 Ceres Ave Los Angeles CA 90021 213-689-6900
Web: www.senovva.com

Simplex Equipment Rental
9740 Boul de l'Acadie Montreal QC H4N1L8 514-331-7777
Web: www.simplex.ca

Sonsray Machinery LLC 1475 Pioneer Way El Cajon CA 92020 619-873-0123
Web: www.sonsraymachinery.com

Sound Image 2415 W Vineyard Ave Escondido CA 92029 760-737-3900
Web: www.sound-image.com

Sunset Aviation 351 Airport Rd Ste E Novato CA 94945 415-897-2403
Web: sunsetaviation.com

Sunwest Aviation Ltd 230 Aviation Pl Ne Calgary AB T2E7G1 403-275-8121
TF: 888-291-4566 ■ *Web:* www.sunwestaviation.ca

Swiftlift Inc 820 Phillips Rd Victor NY 14564 585-742-2160
TF: 888-292-3101 ■ *Web:* www.swiftlift.com

Tankmaster Rentals L T D Poplar St Ste 117 Red Deer AB T4E1B4 403-342-1105
Web: www.tankmaster.ca

Titan Formwork Systems LLC
7855 S River Pkwy Ste 105 Tempe AZ 85284 480-456-5833
Web: www.titanformwork.com

Total Oilfield Rentals Partnership
6517 51 Ave Whitecourt AB T7S1N3 780-778-6222
Web: www.totaloilfield.ca

Trench Plate Rental Co 13217 Laureldale Ave Downey CA 90242 800-821-4478
TF: 800-821-4478 ■ *Web:* www.tprco.com

Tri-state Aero Inc 6101 Flight Line Dr Evansville IN 47725 812-426-1221
Web: www.tristateaero.com

Twin Otter International Ltd
2806 Perimeter Rd North Las Vegas NV 89032 702-646-8837
Web: www.twinotter.com

Us Adventure Rv 5120 n brady st Davenport IA 52806 877-768-4678
TF: 877-768-4678 ■ *Web:* www.usadventurerv.com

Valley Supply & Equipment Company Inc
1109 Middle River Rd Baltimore MD 21220 800-633-5077
TF: 800-633-5077 ■ *Web:* www.valleysupplyequipment.com

Warren Power & Machinery LP
4501 W Reno Ave Oklahoma City OK 73127 405-947-6771
Web: www.warrencat.com

Why Not Lease It 1750 Elm St Ste 1200 Manchester NH 03104 603-665-9000
Web: whynotleaseit.com

Wood's CRW Corp
795 Marshall Ave PO Box 1099 Williston VT 05495 802-658-1700
Web: www.woodscrw.com

Wright Air Service Inc
3842 University Ave S PO Box 60142 Fairbanks AK 99706 907-474-0502 474-0375
Web: www.wrightairservice.com

24 AIRCRAFT SERVICE & REPAIR

Phone | Fax

AAR Aircraft Component Services
747 Zeckendorf Blvd Garden City NY 11530 516-222-9000 222-0987
TF: 800-422-2213 ■ *Web:* www.aarcorp.com

AAR Aircraft Services
6611 S Meridian Ave Oklahoma City OK 73159 630-227-2000
Web: www.aarcorp.com

AAR Corp 1100 N Wood Dale Rd 1 AAR Pl Wood Dale IL 60191 630-227-2000 227-2019
NYSE: AIR ■ *TF:* 800-422-2213 ■ *Web:* www.aarcorp.com

AAR Landing Gear Services 9371 NW 100th St Miami FL 33178 305-887-4027 887-9437
TF: 800-422-2213 ■ *Web:* www.aarcorp.com

Aero Twin Inc 2403 Merrill Field Dr Anchorage AK 99501 907-274-6166 274-4285
Web: www.aerotwin.com

Alabama Aircraft Industries
1943 50th St N Birmingham AL 35212 205-592-0011 592-0195

American Avionics 7023 Perimeter Rd S Seattle WA 98108 206-763-8530
TF Sales: 800-518-5858 ■ *Web:* www.americanavionics.com

Barfield Inc 4101 NW 29th St Miami FL 33142 305-894-5300 894-5301
TF: 800-321-1039 ■ *Web:* www.barfieldinc.com

Basler Turbo Conversions LLC 255 W 35th St Oshkosh WI 54902 920-236-7820 235-0381
Web: www.baslerturbo.com

Bridgestone Aircraft Tire USA Inc
802 S Ayersville Rd Mayodan NC 27027 336-548-8100 548-7441
Web: bridgestone.com

Byerly Aviation 6100 EM Dirkson Pkwy Peoria IL 61607 309-697-6300
Web: www.byerlyaviation.com

Christiansen Aviation Inc 200 Lear Jet Ln Tulsa OK 74132 918-298-6650 298-6656
Web: www.christiansenaviation.com

Phone | Fax

Cutter Aviation 2802 E Old Tower Rd Phoenix AZ 85034 602-273-1237 275-4010
TF: 800-234-5382 ■ *Web:* cutteraviation.com

Duncan Aviation Inc 3701 Aviation Rd Lincoln NE 68524 402-475-2611 475-5541
TF: 800-228-4277 ■ *Web:* www.duncanaviation.aero

Elbit Systems of America
4700 Marine Creek Pkwy Fort Worth TX 76179 817-234-6600
Web: www.elbitsystems-us.com

Elliott Aviation Inc 6601 74th Ave PO Box 100 Milan IL 61264 309-799-3183 799-2014
TF: 800-447-6711 ■ *Web:* www.elliottaviation.com

Emteq Inc 5349 S Emmer Dr New Berlin WI 53151 262-679-6170 679-6175
TF: 888-679-6170 ■ *Web:* www.emteq.com

GKN Aerospace Chem-tronics Inc
1150 W Bradley Ave El Cajon CA 92020 619-448-2320 258-5270
Web: www.gkn.com

Hawker Pacific Aerospace
11240 Sherman Way Sun Valley CA 91352 818-765-6201 765-8073
Web: www.hawker.com

Helicomb International Inc 1402 S 69th E Ave Tulsa OK 74112 918-835-3999 834-4451
Web: www.syncaero.com

Honeywell Aerospace 3520 Westmoor St South Bend IN 46628 574-231-2000
TF: 800-707-4555 ■ *Web:* honeywell.com

Jet Aviation 112 Charles A Lindbergh Dr Teterboro NJ 07608 201-288-8400 462-4005
TF: 800-538-0832 ■ *Web:* www.jetaviation.com

Kfs Inc 1840 West Airfield Dr Dallas TX 75261 817-488-4115 488-4350
TF: 800-364-4115 ■ *Web:* www.kfsinc.com

L-3 Communications Flight International Aviation LLC
1 Lear Dr Newport News VA 23602 757-886-5500 874-7481
TF: 800-358-4685 ■ *Web:* www.l-3com.com/fi

Martin Aviation 19300 Ike Jones Rd Santa Ana CA 92707 714-210-2945 557-0637
Web: martin-aviation.com

McKinley Air Transport Inc
5430 Lauby Rd North Canton OH 44720 330-499-3316 499-0444
TF General: 800-225-6446

Mercury Air Group Inc 5456 McConnell Ave Los Angeles CA 90066 310-827-2737 827-8921
Web: www.mercuryairgroup.com

Million Air Interlink Inc 8501 Telephone Rd Houston TX 77061 713-640-4000 283-8274*
**Fax Area Code:* 866 ■ *TF:* 888-589-9059 ■ *Web:* www.millionair.com

NORDAM Group 6911 N Whirlpool Dr Tulsa OK 74117 918-878-4000 878-4808*
**Fax:* Sales ■ *Web:* www.nordam.com

Pemco World Air Services 4102 N Westshore Blvd Tampa FL 33614 813-322-9600
Web: www.pemcoair.com

Precision Airmotive LLC 14800 40th Ave NE Marysville WA 98271 360-651-8282 651-8080*
**Fax:* Sales ■ *Web:* www.precisionairmotive.com

Priester Aviation 1061 S Wolf Rd Wheeling IL 60090 847-537-1133 459-0778
TF: 888-323-7887 ■ *Web:* www.priesterav.com

Rolls-Royce Engine Services Inc
7200 Earhart Rd Oakland CA 94621 510-613-1000 635-3221
TF: 888-255-4766 ■ *Web:* www.rolls-royce.com

Serco Inc 1818 Library St Ste 1000 Reston VA 20190 703-939-6000 939-6000
TF: 866-628-6458 ■ *Web:* www.serco-na.com

Servisair 151 Northpoint Dr Houston TX 77060 281-260-3900 999-3740
Web: www.servisair.com

SGT Inc 7701 Greenbelt Rd Ste 400 Greenbelt MD 20770 301-614-8600 614-8601
Web: www.sgt-inc.com

Sierra Industries Ltd 122 Howard Langford Dr Uvalde TX 78801 830-278-4481 278-7649
TF: 888-835-9377 ■ *Web:* www.sijet.com

Sifco Industries Inc 970 E 64th St Cleveland OH 44103 216-881-8600 432-6281
NYSE: SIF ■ *Web:* www.sifco.com

Southern California Aviation Inc
18438 Readiness St Victorville CA 92394 760-530-2400 246-1186
Web: comav.com/services/technical-services

Summit Aviation Inc
4200 Summit Bridge Rd PO Box 258 Middletown DE 19709 302-834-5400 378-7035
TF: 800-441-9343 ■ *Web:* www.summit-aviation.com

Triumph Accessory Services 411 NW Rd Wellington KS 67152 620-326-2235 326-3761
Web: www.triumphgroup.com

Triumph Group Inc 1550 Liberty Ridge Dr Ste 100 Wayne PA 19087 610-251-1000 251-1555
NYSE: TGI ■ *Web:* www.triumphgroup.com

Tulsair Beechcraft Inc 3207 N Sheridan Rd Tulsa OK 74115 918-835-7651 835-7413
TF: 800-331-4071 ■ *Web:* www.tulsair.com

West Star Aviation Inc
796 Heritage Way Grand Junction CO 81506 970-243-7500 248-5243
TF: 800-255-4193 ■ *Web:* www.weststaraviation.com

Windsor Airmotive 68 Deming St Newington CT 06111 860-666-1777

25 AIRLINES - COMMERCIAL

See Also Air Cargo Carriers p. 1719; Air Charter Services p. 1719; Airlines - Frequent Flyer Programs p. 1730

Phone | Fax

Aeroflot Russian International Airlines
10 Rockefeller Plaza Ste 1015 New York NY 10020 212-944-2300
TF: 866-879-7647 ■ *Web:* www.aeroflot.com

Air India 570 Lexington Ave 15th Fl New York NY 10022 800-223-7776
TF: 800-223-7776 ■ *Web:* www.airindia.com

Air Sunshine Inc PO Box 22237 Fort Lauderdale FL 33335 954-434-8900
TF: 800-435-8900 ■ *Web:* www.airsunshine.com

Air Tahiti Nui 1990 E Grand Ave El Segundo CA 90245 310-662-1860 640-3683
TF Cust Svc: 877-824-4846 ■ *Web:* www.airtahitinui.com/us-en

Air Wisconsin Airlines Corp
W6390 Challenger Dr Ste 203 Appleton WI 54914 920-739-5123 749-7588
Web: www.airwis.com

All Nippon Airways Company Ltd
2050 W 190th St Ste 100 Torrance CA 90504 800-235-9262
TF: 800-235-9262 ■ *Web:* www.ana.co.jp

Allegiant Air 8360 S Durango Dr Las Vegas NV 89113 702-851-7300 851-7301
NASDAQ: ALGT ■ *Web:* www.allegiantair.com

American Airlines Inc
4333 Amon Carter Blvd Fort Worth TX 76155 817-963-1234 967-4162*
**Fax:* Cust Svc ■ *TF:* 800-433-7300 ■ *Web:* www.aa.com

Phone *Fax*

Atlanta Airlines Terminal Corp
Hartsfield-Jackson Atlanta International Airport
PO Box 45170 Atlanta GA 30320 404-530-2100
Web: www.aatc.org

Bearskin Airlines 1475 W Walsh St Thunder Bay ON P7E4X6 807-577-1141 474-2647
TF: 800-465-2327 ■ *Web:* www.bearskinairlines.com

Bering Air 1470 Sepalla Dr PO Box 1650 Nome AK 99762 907-443-5464 443-5919
TF: 800-478-5422 ■ *Web:* www.beringair.com

Bulloch & Bulloch Inc
309 Cash Memorial Blvd Forest Park GA 30297 404-762-5063
TF: 800-339-8177 ■ *Web:* www.jphallexpress.com

Cape Air 660 Barnstable Rd Hyannis MA 02601 508-771-6944 227-3247*
**Fax Area Code:* 800 ■ *TF:* 800-227-3247 ■ *Web:* www.capeair.com

Cayman Airways Ltd 91 Owen Roberts Dr Grand Cayman KY 10092 345-949-8200 949-7607
TF: 800-422-9626 ■ *Web:* www.caymanairways.com

Commutair Inc
24950 Country Club Blvd Ste 300 North Olmsted OH 44070 802-951-2500
Web: www.commutair.com

Czech Airlines 1 Penn Plaza Ste 1416 New York NY 10001 855-359-2932 279-6602*
**Fax Area Code:* 212 ■ *TF:* 855-359-2932 ■ *Web:* www.csa.cz

Delta Air Lines Inc 1030 Delta Blvd Atlanta GA 30354 404-715-2600 773-2108
NYSE: DAL ■ *TF:* 800-221-1212 ■ *Web:* www.delta.com

EgyptAir 19 W 44th St Ste 1701 New York NY 10036 212-581-5600
Web: egyptair.com

El Al Israel Airlines Inc 15 E 26th St New York NY 10010 212-852-0600 852-0797
TF: 800-223-6700 ■ *Web:* www.elal.com/en/usa/pages/default.aspx

EVA Airways 200 N Sepulveda Blvd Ste 1600 El Segundo CA 90245 310-362-6600 362-6660
TF: 800-695-1188 ■ *Web:* www.evaair.com

ExpressJet Airlines Inc 990 Toffie Terr Atlanta GA 30354 404-856-1000
Web: www.expressjet.com

Great Lakes Aviation Ltd 1022 Airport Pkwy Cheyenne WY 82001 307-432-7000
OTC: GLUX ■ *TF:* 800-554-5111 ■ *Web:* www.greatlakesav.com

Hawaiian Airlines Inc
3375 Koapaka St Ste G350 Honolulu HI 96819 808-835-3700 835-3690
TF: 800-367-5320 ■ *Web:* www.hawaiianairlines.com

Helicopter Tech Inc 452 Swedeland Rd King Of Prussia PA 19406 610-272-8090
Web: www.helicoptertechinc.com

Kenmore Air Harbor Inc 6321 NE 175th St Kenmore WA 98028 425-486-1257 485-4774
TF: 866-435-9524 ■ *Web:* www.kenmoreair.com

Korean Air 6101 W Imperial Hwy Los Angeles CA 90045 310-417-5200
TF: 800-438-5000 ■ *Web:* www.koreanair.com

Malaysia Airlines
100 N Sepulveda Blvd Ste 1710 El Segundo CA 90245 310-535-9288
TF Resv: 800-552-9264 ■ *Web:* www.malaysiaairlines.com

MD Helicopters Inc 4555 E Mcdowell Rd Mesa AZ 85215 480-346-6344
Web: www.mdhelicopters.com

New England Airlines Inc 56 Airport Rd Westerly RI 02891 800-243-2460 596-7366*
**Fax Area Code:* 401 ■ *TF:* 800-243-2460 ■ *Web:* www.block-island.com/nea

Olympic Airways 7000 Austin St Forest Hills NY 11375 718-269-2200
Web: patch.com/foresthills

Pacific Air Cargo 5761 W Imperial Hwy Los Angeles CA 90045 310-645-2178
Web: www.pacificaircargo.com

Pacific Wings 1 Keolani Pl Ste 30 Kahului HI 96732 808-873-0877 873-7920
TF: 888-575-4546

Pakistan International Airlines Corp (PIA)
1200 New Jersey Ave SE Washington DC 20590 800-578-6786
TF: 800-578-6786 ■ *Web:* www.piac.com.pk

Peninsula Airways Inc 6100 Boeing Ave Anchorage AK 99502 907-771-2500 771-2661
TF: 800-448-4226 ■ *Web:* www.penair.com

Phoenix Air Group Inc
100 Phoenix Air Dr SW Cartersville GA 30120 770-387-2000 387-4545
Web: www.phoenixair.com

Piedmont Airlines Inc
5443 Airport Terminal Rd Salisbury MD 21804 410-742-2996
Web: www.piedmont-airlines.com

Pinnacle Airlines Corp
40 S Main St 1 Commerce Sq Memphis TN 38103 901-348-4100 348-4130
OTC: PNCLQ ■ *Web:* www.flypinnacle.com

PSA Airlines Inc 3400 Terminal Dr Vandalia OH 45377 937-665-2876 264-3911
TF Resv: 800-235-0986 ■ *Web:* www.psaairlines.com

Qantas Airways Ltd 6080 Ctr Dr Ste 400 Los Angeles CA 90045 310-726-1400 726-1485
TF: 800-227-4500 ■ *Web:* www.qantas.com/travel/airlines/home/us/en

Scandinavian Airlines System (SAS)
301 Route 17 N Ste 500 Rutherford NJ 07070 800-437-5807 896-3735*
**Fax Area Code:* 201 ■ *TF:* 800-221-2350 ■ *Web:* www.flysas.com

Silver Airways Corp
1100 Lee Wagener Blvd Ste 201 Fort Lauderdale FL 33315 954-985-1500
TF: 844-674-5837 ■ *Web:* www.silverairways.com

Singapore Airlines Ltd
222 N Sepulveda Blvd Ste 1600 El Segundo CA 90245 310-647-1922
TF: 800-742-3333 ■ *Web:* www.singaporeair.com

Skyservice Airlines Inc 9785 Ryan Ave Dorval QC H9P1A2 514-636-3300 636-4855
TF: 888-985-1402 ■ *Web:* skyservice.com

SkyWest Airlines 444 S River Rd Saint George UT 84790 435-634-3000 634-3105
Web: www.skywest.com

South African Airways
1200 S Pine Island Rd Ste 650 Plantation FL 33324 954-769-5000 769-5079*
**Fax:* Sales ■ *TF:* 800-722-9675 ■ *Web:* www.flysaa.com

Southwest Airlines Co
2702 Love Field Dr PO Box 36611 Dallas TX 75235 214-792-4000
NYSE: LUV ■ *TF:* 800-435-9792 ■ *Web:* www.southwest.com

Spirit Airlines Inc 2800 Executive Way Miramar FL 33025 800-772-7117
NASDAQ: SAVE ■ *TF:* 800-772-7117 ■ *Web:* www.spirit.com

SriLankan Airlines 379 Thornall St 6th Fl Edison NJ 08837 732-205-0017 205-0299
TF: 877-915-2652 ■ *Web:* www.srilankanusa.com

Sun Country Airlines Inc
1300 Mendota Heights Rd Mendota Heights MN 55120 651-681-3900
TF: 800-359-6786 ■ *Web:* www.suncountry.com

Thai Airways International Ltd
222 N Sepulveda Blvd Ste 100 El Segundo CA 90245 310-640-0097
TF: 800-426-5204 ■ *Web:* www.thaiairwaysusa.com

USA 3000 Airlines
335 Bishop Hollow Rd Newtown Square PA 19073 610-325-1280
Web: usa3000.com

Virgin Atlantic Airways Ltd 747 Belden Ave Norwalk CT 06850 800-821-5438 750-6430*
**Fax Area Code:* 203 ■ **Fax:* Mktg ■ *TF:* 888-747-7474 ■ *Web:* www.virgin-atlantic.com

WestJet Airlines Ltd 22 Aerial Pl NE Calgary AB T2E3J1 403-444-2600 253-0131*
TSE: WJA ■ **Fax Area Code:* 844 ■ *TF:* 888-293-7853 ■ *Web:* www.westjet.com

26 AIRLINES - FREQUENT FLYER PROGRAMS

Phone *Fax*

Aer Lingus Airlines Gold Cir Club
300 Jericho Quad Ste 130 Jericho NY 11753 800-474-7424 622-4287*
**Fax Area Code:* 516 ■ *TF:* 800-474-7424 ■ *Web:* www.aerlingus.com

British Airways Executive Club PO Box 300743 Jamaica NY 11430 800-452-1201 251-6767*
**Fax Area Code:* 212 ■ *TF:* 800-452-1201 ■ *Web:* www.britishairways.com

Continental Airlines Inc 900 Grand Plz Dr Houston TX 77067 713-952-1630
TF: 800-621-7467 ■ *Web:* www.united.com

Czech Airlines OK Plus
147 W 35th St Ste 1505 New York NY 10001 855-359-2932 279-6602*
**Fax Area Code:* 212 ■ *TF:* 855-359-2932 ■ *Web:* www.csa.cz

Hawaiian Airlines HawaiianMiles
PO Box 30008 Honolulu HI 96820 877-426-4537 838-6777*
**Fax Area Code:* 808 ■ *TF:* 877-426-4537 ■ *Web:* www.hawaiianairlines.com

Icelandair North America 1900 Crown Colony Dr Quincy MA 02169 800-223-5500
TF: 800-223-5500 ■ *Web:* www.icelandair.com

Korean Air Skypass
1813 Wilshire Blvd Ste 300 Los Angeles CA 90057 213-484-1900
TF: 800-438-5000 ■ *Web:* www.koreanair.com

Kuwait Airways Oasis Club 400 Kelby St Fort Lee NJ 07024 201-582-9222
TF: 800-458-9248 ■ *Web:* www.kuwaitairways.com

Miles & More PO Box 946 Santa Clarita CA 91380 800-581-6400 244-4950*
**Fax Area Code:* 661 ■ *TF:* 800-581-6400 ■ *Web:* www.miles-and-more.com

REACH Air Medical Services
451 Aviation Blvd Santa Rosa CA 95403 707-324-2400 324-2478
Web: reachair.com

Singapore Airlines KrisFlyer
380 World Way Ste 336B Los Angeles CA 90045 310-646-6221
TF: 800-742-3333 ■ *Web:* www.singaporeair.com

Virgin Atlantic Flying Club 747 Belden Ave Norwalk CT 06850 800-365-9500
TF: 800-365-9500 ■ *Web:* virgin-atlantic.com/us/en/flying-club.html

27 AIRPORTS

See Also Ports & Port Authorities p. 2965

Listings for airports in the US and Canada are organized by states and provinces, and then by city names within those groupings.

Phone *Fax*

Birmingham International Airport
5900 Messer Airport Hwy Birmingham AL 35212 205-595-0533 599-0538
Web: flybirmingham.com

Huntsville International Airport
1000 Glenn Hearn Blvd Ste 20008 Huntsville AL 35824 256-772-9395
Web: www.flyhuntsville.com

Mobile Regional Airport 8400 Airport Blvd Mobile AL 36608 251-633-4510 639-7437
TF: 800-357-5373 ■ *Web:* www.mobairport.com

Montgomery Regional Airport
4445 Selma Hwy Montgomery AL 36108 334-281-5040 281-5041
Web: www.flymgm.com

Ted Stevens Anchorage International Airport
5000 W International Airport Rd Anchorage AK 99502 907-266-2526
Web: dot.state.ak.us

Fairbanks International Airport
6450 Airport Way Fairbanks AK 99709 907-474-2500 474-2513
Web: www.dot.state.ak.us/faiiap

Juneau International Airport
1873 Shell Simmons Dr Ste 200 Juneau AK 99801 907-789-7821 789-1227
TF: 800-478-4176 ■ *Web:* www.juneau.org/airport

Calgary International Airport
2000 Airport Rd NE Calgary AB T2E6W5 403-735-1200 735-1281
TF: 877-254-7427 ■ *Web:* www.yyc.com

Edmonton International Airport
8340 Sparrow Crescent Edmonton AB T9E8B7 780-800-0622
TF: 800-854-9517 ■ *Web:* ramada.com

Flagstaff Pulliam Airport
6200 S Pulliam Dr Flagstaff AZ 86001 928-556-1234 556-1288
TF: 800-463-1389 ■ *Web:* www.flagstaff.az.gov

Phoenix Sky Harbor International Airport
3400 E Sky Harbor Blvd Ste 3300 Phoenix AZ 85034 602-273-3300
Web: skyharbor.com

Tucson International Airport
7250 S Tucson Blvd Tucson AZ 85706 520-573-8100 573-8008
TF: 800-758-1874 ■ *Web:* www.flytucson.com

Northwest Arkansas Regional Airport
1 Airport Blvd Ste 100 Bentonville AR 72712 479-205-1000 205-1001
TF: 800-433-7300 ■ *Web:* www.flyxna.com

Fort Smith Regional Airport
6700 McKennon Blvd Ste 200 Fort Smith AR 72903 479-452-7000 452-7008
TF: 800-992-7433 ■ *Web:* www.fortsmithairport.com

Hot Springs Memorial Field
525 Airport Rd Hot Springs AR 71913 501-321-6750 321-6754
TF: 800-992-7433 ■ *Web:* cityhs.net/442/flight-information

Bill & Hillary Clinton National Airport
1 Airport Dr Little Rock AR 72202 501-372-3439 372-0612
Web: www.fly-lit.com

Vancouver International Airport
Airport Postal Outlet PO Box 23750 Richmond BC V7B1Y7 604-207-7077
Web: www.yvr.ca

Meadows Field Airport
3701 Wings Way Ste 300 Bakersfield CA 93308 661-391-1800 391-1801
Web: www.meadowsfield.com

Bob Hope Airport 2627 N Hollywood Way Burbank CA 91505 818-840-8840 848-1173
Web: www.bobhopeairport.com

	City	State	Zip	Phone	Fax
Fresno Yosemite International Airport 5175 E Clinton Way *TF:* 800-244-2359 ■ *Web:* www.fresno.gov	Fresno	CA	93727	559-621-4500	251-4825
Long Beach Airport LGB 4100 Donald Douglas Dr *TF:* 800-331-1212 ■ *Web:* www.lgb.org	Long Beach	CA	90808	562-570-2600	570-2601
Modesto City Airport 617 Airport Way *Web:* www.modestogov.com	Modesto	CA	95354	209-577-5319	576-1985
Monterey Peninsula Airport 200 Fred Kane Dr Ste 200 *Web:* www.montereyairport.com	Monterey	CA	93940	831-648-7000	373-2625
Ontario International Airport 1923 E Avion St *Web:* www.lawa.org/welcomeont.aspx	Ontario	CA	91761	909-937-2700	937-2743
Oxnard Airport 2889 W Fifth St *Web:* iflyoxnard.com	Oxnard	CA	93030	805-382-3022	
Palm Springs International Airport 3200 E Tahquitz Canyon Way *TF:* 800-847-4389 ■ *Web:* www.palmspringsca.gov	Palm Springs	CA	92262	760-318-3800	318-3815
Palo Alto Airport 1925 Embarcadero Rd *Web:* www.countyairports.org	Palo Alto	CA	94303	408-918-7700	
Sacramento International Airport 6900 Airport Blvd *Web:* www.sacairports.org	Sacramento	CA	95837	916-929-5411	
San Diego International Airport - Lindbergh Field 3225 N Harbor Dr San Diego County Regl Airport Authority 3rd Fl *Web:* www.san.org	San Diego	CA	92101	619-400-2404	
San Francisco International Airport PO Box 8097 *TF:* 800-435-9736 ■ *Web:* www.flysfo.com	San Francisco	CA	94128	650-821-8211	821-5005
Norman Y Mineta San Jose International Airport 1701 Airport Blvd Ste B-1130 *Web:* www.flysanjose.com	San Jose	CA	95110	408-501-7600	441-4591
John Wayne Airport 18601 Airport Way *Web:* www.ocair.com	Santa Ana	CA	92707	949-252-5200	
Colorado Springs Municipal Airport 7770 Milton E Proby Pkwy *Web:* www.springsgov.com	Colorado Springs	CO	80916	719-550-1900	550-1901
Denver International Airport 8500 Pena Blvd *TF:* 800-247-2336 ■ *Web:* www.flydenver.com	Denver	CO	80249	303-342-2000	342-2215
Fort Collins/Loveland Municipal Airport 4900 Earhart Rd *Web:* www.fortloveair.com	Loveland	CO	80538	970-962-2850	962-2855
Tweed New Haven Regional Airport 155 Burr St *Web:* www.flytweed.com	New Haven	CT	06512	203-466-8833	466-1199
Ronald Reagan Washington National Airport 1 Aviation Cir **Fax:* PR ■ *Web:* www.mwaa.com	Washington	DC	20001	703-417-8000	417-8371*
Washington Dulles International Airport Dulles Airport Access Rd *Web:* flydulles.com/iad/dulles-international-airport	Washington	DC	20041	703-572-2700	572-5718
Daytona Beach International Airport 700 Catalina Dr Ste 300 *Web:* www.flydaytonafirst.com	Daytona Beach	FL	32114	386-248-8030	
Fort Lauderdale Executive Airport 5101 NW 21st Ave *Web:* fortlauderdale.gov	Fort Lauderdale	FL	33309	954-828-4955	938-4974
Fort Lauderdale/Hollywood International Airport 100 Aviation Blvd *TF:* 866-682-2258 ■ *Web:* www.broward.org	Fort Lauderdale	FL	33315	954-359-1200	359-0027
Southwest Florida International Airport 11000 Terminal Access Rd Ste 8671 *TF:* 800-359-6786 ■ *Web:* www.flylcpa.com	Fort Myers	FL	33913	239-590-4800	590-4511
Jacksonville International Airport 2400 Yankee Clipper Dr *Web:* www.flyjacksonville.com	Jacksonville	FL	32218	904-741-4902	741-2224
Key West International Airport 3491 S Roosevelt Blvd *Web:* keywestinternationalairport.com	Key West	FL	33040	305-809-5200	
Miami International Airport 2261 NW 66th Ave Bldg 702 Ste 217 *TF:* 800-825-5642 ■ *Web:* www.miami-airport.com	Miami	FL	33122	305-876-7000	876-8077
Naples Municipal Airport 160 Aviation Dr N *Web:* www.flynaples.com	Naples	FL	34104	239-643-0733	643-4084
Orlando International Airport 1 Jeff Fuqua Blvd *Web:* www.orlandoairports.net	Orlando	FL	32827	407-825-2001	
Pensacola Gulf Coast Regional Airport 2430 Airport Blvd Ste 225 *TF:* 800-874-6580 ■ *Web:* www.flypensacola.com	Pensacola	FL	32504	850-436-5000	436-5006
Sarasota-Bradenton International Airport 6000 Airport Cir *TF:* 800-711-1712 ■ *Web:* www.srq-airport.com	Sarasota	FL	34243	941-359-5200	359-5054
Tallahassee Regional Airport 3300 Capital Cir SW *Web:* talgov.com	Tallahassee	FL	32310	850-891-7800	891-7837
Tampa International Airport 4100 George J Bean Pkwy PO Box 22287 *TF:* 866-289-9673 ■ *Web:* www.tampaairport.com	Tampa	FL	33607	813-870-8700	875-6670
Palm Beach International Airport 1000 Turnage Blvd *Web:* www.pbia.org	West Palm Beach	FL	33406	561-471-7420	471-7427
Hartsfield-Jackson Atlanta International Airport 6000 N Terminal Pkwy Ste 4000 *TF:* 800-897-1910 ■ *Web:* www.atlanta-airport.com	Atlanta	GA	30320	404-530-6600	530-6803
Augusta Regional Airport - Bush Field (AGS) 1501 Aviation Way *TF:* 866-289-9673 ■ *Web:* flyags.com	Augusta	GA	30906	706-798-3236	798-1551
Columbus Metropolitan Airport 3250 W Britt David Rd *Web:* flycolumbusga.com	Columbus	GA	31909	706-324-2449	

	City	State	Zip	Phone	Fax
Middle Georgia Regional Airport 1000 Airport Dr *Web:* iflymacon.com	Macon	GA	31216	478-788-3760	
Savannah/Hilton Head International Airport 400 Airways Ave *Web:* www.savannahairport.com	Savannah	GA	31408	912-964-0514	964-0877
Honolulu International Airport 300 Rodgers Blvd *Web:* www.honoluluairport.com	Honolulu	HI	96819	808-831-3600	
Kahului Airport 1 Kahului Airport Rd *TF:* 800-321-3712 ■ *Web:* www.hawaii.gov/ogg	Kahului	HI	96732	808-872-3830	872-3829
Kona International Airport 73-200 Kupipi St *TF:* 800-321-3712 ■ *Web:* www.hawaii.gov/koa	Kailua-Kona	HI	96740	808-327-9520	838-8067
Boise Airport 3201 Airport Way *Web:* www.cityofboise.org	Boise	ID	83705	208-383-3110	343-9667
Pocatello Regional Airport 1950 Airport Way PO Box 4169 *Web:* www.pocatello.us	Pocatello	ID	83205	208-234-6154	233-8418
Chicago Midway Airport 5700 S Cicero Ave *TF:* 800-832-6352 ■ *Web:* www.flychicago.com	Chicago	IL	60638	773-838-0600	838-0588
O'Hare International Airport *Dept of Aviation* PO Box 66142 *TF:* 800-832-6352 ■ *Web:* www.flychicago.com	Chicago	IL	60666	773-686-3700	
Prospect Airport Services Inc 2130 S Wolf Rd *Web:* www.prospectair.com	Des Plaines	IL	60018	847-299-3636	299-3638
Peoria Regional Airport 6100 W Everett McKinley Dirksen Pkwy *Web:* www.flypia.com	Peoria	IL	61607	309-697-8272	697-8132
Greater Rockford Airport 60 Airport Dr *TF:* 800-517-2000 ■ *Web:* www.flyrfd.com	Rockford	IL	61109	815-969-4000	969-4001
Abraham Lincoln Capital Airport 1200 Capital Airport Dr *Web:* www.flyspi.com	Springfield	IL	62707	217-788-1060	788-8056
Du Page Airport Authority 2700 International Dr Ste 200 *TF:* 800-208-5690 ■ *Web:* www.dupageairport.com	West Chicago	IL	60185	630-584-2211	584-3022
Evansville Regional Airport 7801 Bussing Dr *Web:* flyevv.com	Evansville	IN	47725	812-421-4401	421-4412
Fort Wayne International Airport 3801 W Ferguson Rd Ste 209 *Web:* www.fwairport.com	Fort Wayne	IN	46809	260-747-4146	747-1762
South Bend Regional Airport 4477 Progress Dr *Web:* www.flysbn.com	South Bend	IN	46628	574-282-4590	
Eastern Iowa Airport, The 2515 Arthur Collins PkwySW *Web:* www.eiairport.org	Cedar Rapids	IA	52404	319-362-8336	362-1670
Des Moines International Airport 5800 Fleur Dr *TF:* 877-686-0029 ■ *Web:* www.dsmairport.com	Des Moines	IA	50321	515-256-5050	256-5025
Dubuque Regional Airport 11000 Airport Rd *Web:* www.flydbq.com	Dubuque	IA	52003	563-589-4128	
Midcontinent Airport 2173 Air Cargo Rd *Web:* www.flywichita.com	Wichita	KS	67209	316-946-4700	946-4793
Blue Grass Airport 4000 Terminal Dr *TF:* 800-800-4000 ■ *Web:* www.bluegrassairport.com	Lexington	KY	40510	859-425-3100	233-1822
Louisville International Airport 700 Administration Dr PO Box 9129 *Web:* flylouisville.com	Louisville	KY	40209	502-368-6524	367-0199
Baton Rouge Metropolitan Airport 9430 Jackie Cochran Dr Ste 300 *TF:* 877-359-2538 ■ *Web:* www.flybtr.com	Baton Rouge	LA	70807	225-355-0333	355-2334
Lafayette Regional Airport 222 Tower Dr *Web:* www.lftairport.com	Lafayette	LA	70508	337-266-4400	
Shreveport Regional Airport 5103 Hollywood Ave *Web:* www.shreveportla.gov	Shreveport	LA	71109	318-673-5370	
Augusta State Airport 75 Airport Rd *TF:* 800-654-3131 ■ *Web:* www.augustamaine.gov	Augusta	ME	04330	207-626-2306	626-2309
Bangor International Airport 287 Godfrey Blvd *TF:* 866-359-2264 ■ *Web:* www.flybangor.com	Bangor	ME	04401	207-992-4600	945-3607
Portland International Jetport 1001 Westbrook St *Web:* www.portlandjetport.org	Portland	ME	04102	207-874-8877	774-7740
Hancock County-Bar Harbor Airport 115 Caruso Dr *Web:* www.bhbairport.com	Trenton	ME	04605	207-667-7329	667-0218
Winnipeg James Armstrong Richardson International Airport 2000 Wellington Ave Rm 249 Administration Bldg *TF:* 855-500-6589 ■ *Web:* www.waa.ca	Winnipeg	MB	R3H1C2	204-987-9400	987-9401
Baltimore/Washington International Thurgood Marshall Airport (BWI) PO Box 8766 *TF:* 800-435-9294 ■ *Web:* www.bwiairport.com	Baltimore	MD	21240	410-859-7111	768-9452
Salisbury Ocean City-Wicomico County Regional Airport 5485 Airport Terminal Rd *Web:* flysbyairport.com	Salisbury	MD	21804	410-548-4827	
Worcester Regional Airport 375 Airport Dr *Web:* www.worcesterma.gov	Worcester	MA	01602	508-799-1350	799-1866
Alpena County Regional Airport 1617 Airport Rd *Web:* www.alpenaairport.com	Alpena	MI	49707	989-354-2907	358-9988
Coleman A Young International Airport 11499 Conner *Web:* www.detroitmi.gov	Detroit	MI	48213	313-628-2146	372-2448
Detroit Metropolitan Airport Smith Terminal - Mezzanine Level *Web:* www.metroairport.com	Detroit	MI	48242	734-942-3550	
Bishop International Airport G-3425 W Bristol Rd *TF:* 800-433-7300 ■ *Web:* www.bishopairport.org	Flint	MI	48507	810-235-6560	233-3065

	City	State	Zip	Phone	Fax
Gerald R Ford International Airport 5500 44th St SE *TF:* 866-289-9673 ■ *Web:* www.grr.org	Grand Rapids	MI	49512	616-233-6000	233-6025
Capital Region International Airport 4100 Capital City Blvd *TF:* 866-841-4900 ■ *Web:* www.flylansing.com	Lansing	MI	48906	517-321-6121	321-6197
Duluth International Airport 4701 Grinden Dr *TF:* 855-787-2227 ■ *Web:* www.duluthairport.com	Duluth	MN	55811	218-727-2968	727-2960
Rochester International Airport (RST) 7600 Helgerson Dr SW *Web:* flyrst.com	Rochester	MN	55902	507-282-2328	
Gulfport/Biloxi International Airport 14035 - L Airport Rd *Web:* www.flygpt.com	Gulfport	MS	39503	228-863-5951	863-5953
Jackson International Airport 100 International Dr Ste 300 *TF:* 800-227-7368 ■ *Web:* www.jmaa.com	Jackson	MS	39208	601-939-5631	939-3713
Hattiesburg-Laurel Regional Airport 1002 Terminal Dr *TF:* 800-433-7300 ■ *Web:* www.flypib.com	Moselle	MS	39459	601-649-2444	545-3155
Tupelo Regional Airport 105 Lemons Dr *TF:* 877-777-4778 ■ *Web:* www.flytupelo.com	Tupelo	MS	38801	662-823-4359	823-8329
Columbia Regional Airport 11300 S Airport Dr *Web:* www.flycou.com	Columbia	MO	65201	573-874-7508	874-0105
Kansas City International Airport 601 Brasilia Ave PO Box 20047 *Web:* www.flykci.com	Kansas City	MO	64153	816-243-5237	243-3171
Lambert Saint Louis International Airport 10701 Lambert International Blvd PO Box 10212 *TF:* 855-787-2227 ■ *Web:* www.flystl.com	Saint Louis	MO	63145	314-426-8000	426-1221
Springfield-Branson National Airport 2300 N Airport Blvd *Web:* www.flyspringfield.com	Springfield	MO	65802	417-868-0500	
Billings Logan International Airport 1901 Terminal Cir *Web:* www.ci.billings.mt.us	Billings	MT	59105	406-657-8495	657-8438
Great Falls International Airport 2800 Terminal Dr *Web:* flygtf.com	Great Falls	MT	59404	406-727-3404	727-6929
Helena Regional Airport 2850 Skyway Dr *Web:* www.helenaairport.com	Helena	MT	59601	406-442-2821	449-2340
Lincoln Airport 2400 W Adams St *Web:* www.lincolnairport.com	Lincoln	NE	68524	402-458-2480	458-2490
Eppley Airfield 4501 Abbott Dr Ste 2300 *Web:* flyoma.com	Omaha	NE	68110	402-661-8000	661-8000
McCarran International Airport 5757 Wayne Newton Blvd PO Box 11005 *TF:* 888-261-4414 ■ *Web:* www.mccarran.com	Las Vegas	NV	89119	702-261-5211	597-9553
Reno-Tahoe International Airport 2001 E Plumb Ln *TF:* 877-736-6359 ■ *Web:* www.renoairport.com	Reno	NV	89502	775-328-6400	328-6510
Atlantic City International Airport (ACY) 101 Atlantic City International Airport Ste 106 *Web:* www.sjta.com	Egg Harbor Township	NJ	08234	609-645-7895	
Newark Liberty International Airport 1 Hotel Rd *TF:* 888-397-4636	Newark	NJ	07114	973-961-6007	
Albuquerque International Sunport 2200 Sunport Blvd *Web:* cabq.gov	Albuquerque	NM	87106	505-244-7700	842-4278
Las Cruces International Airport 8990 Zia Blvd *Web:* www.las-cruces.org	Las Cruces	NM	88007	575-541-2471	
Santa Fe Municipal Airport (SAF) 121 Aviation Dr PO Box 909 *TF:* 866-773-2587 ■ *Web:* santafenm.gov/airport	Santa Fe	NM	87504	505-955-2900	955-2905
Buffalo Niagara International Airport 4200 Genesee St *TF:* 877-359-2642 ■ *Web:* www.buffaloairport.com	Cheektowaga	NY	14225	716-630-6000	630-6070
John F Kennedy International Airport (JFK) 150 Greenwich St **Fax Area Code:* 718 ■ *Web:* www.panynj.gov/airports/jfk.html	New York	NY	10007	212-435-7000	244-3505*
Greater Rochester International Airport 1200 Brooks Ave *Web:* www.monroecounty.gov	Rochester	NY	14624	585-753-7020	753-7008
Long Island MacArthur Airport 100 Arrival Ave Ste 100 *TF:* 888-542-4776 ■ *Web:* www.macarthurairport.com	Ronkonkoma	NY	11779	631-467-3300	467-3348
Syracuse Hancock International Airport 1000 Colonel Eileen Collins Blvd *Web:* www.syrairport.org	Syracuse	NY	13212	315-454-4330	454-8757
Westchester County Airport 240 Airport Rd Ste 202 *Web:* www.co.westchester.ny.us/airport	White Plains	NY	10604	914-995-4860	995-3980
Asheville Regional Airport 61 Terminal Dr Ste 1 *TF:* 866-719-3910 ■ *Web:* www.flyavl.com	Fletcher	NC	28732	828-684-2226	684-3404
Piedmont Triad International Airport 1000 A Ted Johnson Pkwy *Web:* www.flyfrompti.com	Greensboro	NC	27409	336-665-5600	
Raleigh-Durham International Airport PO Box 80001 *TF:* 800-252-7522 ■ *Web:* www.rdu.com	Raleigh	NC	27623	919-840-2123	840-0175
Smith Reynolds Airport 3801 N Liberty St *Web:* www.smithreynolds.org	Winston-Salem	NC	27105	336-767-6361	767-8556
Bismarck Municipal Airport 2301 University Dr Bldg 17 PO Box 991 *Web:* www.bismarckairport.com	Bismarck	ND	58502	701-355-1800	221-6886
Hector International Airport 2801 32nd Ave NW *Web:* www.fargoairport.com	Fargo	ND	58102	701-241-1501	241-1538
Halifax Stanfield International Airport (HIAA) 1 Bell Blvd *Web:* www.hiaa.ca	Enfield	NS	B2T1K2	902-873-4422	873-4750
Cincinnati-Northern Kentucky International Airport PO Box 752000 *Web:* www.cvgairport.com	Cincinnati	OH	45275	859-767-3151	
Cleveland Hopkins International Airport 5300 Riverside Dr *Web:* www.clevelandairport.com	Cleveland	OH	44135	216-265-6000	265-6021
Port Columbus International Airport 4600 International Gateway *Web:* www.columbusairports.com	Columbus	OH	43219	614-239-4000	
Akron-Canton Airport 5400 Lauby Rd NW *TF:* 888-434-2359 ■ *Web:* www.akroncantonairport.com	North Canton	OH	44720	330-499-4221	499-5176
Toledo Express Airport 11013 Airport Hwy *Web:* www.toledoexpress.com	Swanton	OH	43558	419-865-2351	
Dayton International Airport 3600 Terminal Dr Ste 300 *TF:* 877-359-3291 ■ *Web:* www.flydayton.com	Vandalia	OH	45377	937-454-8200	454-8284
Youngstown-Warren Regional Airport 1453 Youngstown-Kingsville Rd NE *TF:* 800-444-1440 ■ *Web:* www.yngwrnair.com	Vienna	OH	44473	330-856-1537	609-5371
Will Rogers World Airport 7100 Terminal Dr PO Box 937 *Web:* www.flyokc.com	Oklahoma City	OK	73159	405-680-3200	
Tulsa International Airport 7777 E Apache PO Box 581838 *Web:* www.tulsaairports.com	Tulsa	OK	74115	918-838-5000	838-5199
Ottawa Macdonald-Cartier International Airport 1000 Airport PkwyPrivate Ste 2500 *TF:* 888-901-6222 ■ *Web:* yow.ca/en	Ottawa	ON	K1V9B4	613-248-2000	248-2012
Eugene Airport 28801 Douglas Dr *Web:* www.eugene-or.gov	Eugene	OR	97402	541-682-5430	682-6838
Portland International Airport 7000 NE Airport Way *TF:* 800-547-8411 ■ *Web:* www.portofportland.com	Portland	OR	97218	503-460-4234	
Lehigh Valley International Airport 3311 Airport Rd *TF:* 800-359-5842 ■ *Web:* www.flylvia.com	Allentown	PA	18109	610-266-6000	264-0115
Wilkes-Barre/Scranton International Airport 100 Terminal Dr Ste 1 *TF:* 877-235-9287 ■ *Web:* www.flyavp.com	Avoca	PA	18641	570-602-2000	602-2010
Erie International Airport 4411 W 12th St *Web:* www.erieairport.org	Erie	PA	16505	814-833-4258	833-0393
Harrisburg International Airport 1 Terminal Dr Ste 300 *TF:* 888-235-9442 ■ *Web:* www.flyhia.com	Middletown	PA	17057	717-948-3900	948-4636
Philadelphia International Airport 8000 Essington Ave *TF:* 800-514-0301 ■ *Web:* www.phl.org	Philadelphia	PA	19153	215-937-6937	937-6497
Pittsburgh International Airport Landside Terminal Fourth Fl Mezz PO Box 12370 *TF:* 888-429-5377 ■ *Web:* www.pitairport.com	Pittsburgh	PA	15231	412-472-3525	472-3636
Rhode Island Airport Corp 2000 Post Rd Warwick *TF:* 888-268-7222 ■ *Web:* www.pvdairport.com	Warwick	RI	02886	401-691-2000	
Charleston International Airport 5500 International Blvd Ste 101 *Web:* www.chs-airport.com	Charleston	SC	29418	843-767-7000	760-3020
Columbia Metropolitan Airport 3000 Aviation Way W *Web:* www.columbiaairport.com	Columbia	SC	29170	803-822-5010	
Greenville-Spartanburg Airport (GSP) 2000 GSP Dr Ste 1 *TF:* 800-331-1212 ■ *Web:* www.gspairport.com	Greer	SC	29651	864-877-7426	848-6225
Hilton Head Island Airport 120 Beach City Rd *Web:* bcgov.net	Hilton Head Island	SC	29926	843-255-2950	689-5411
Myrtle Beach International Airport 1100 Jetport Rd *Web:* www.flymyrtlebeach.com	Myrtle Beach	SC	29577	843-448-1589	626-9096
Pierre Regional Airport 3800 Airport Rd *Web:* cityofpierre.org/154/airport	Pierre	SD	57501	605-773-7447	
Rapid City Regional Airport 4550 Terminal Rd Ste 102 *TF:* 888-279-2135 ■ *Web:* www.rcgov.org/airport	Rapid City	SD	57703	605-393-9924	394-6190
Sioux Falls Regional Airport 2801 Jaycee Ln *Web:* www.sfairport.com	Sioux Falls	SD	57104	605-336-0762	367-7374
McGhee Tyson Airport 2055 Alcoa Hwy *Web:* www.tys.org	Alcoa	TN	37701	865-342-3000	342-3050
Tri-Cities Regional Airport 2525 Hwy 75 PO Box 1055 *Web:* triflight.com	Blountville	TN	37617	423-325-6000	325-6060
Chattanooga Metropolitan Airport 1001 Airport Rd Ste 14 *Web:* www.chattairport.com	Chattanooga	TN	37421	423-855-2202	855-2212
Memphis International Airport 2491 Winchester Rd Ste 113 *Web:* www.mscaa.com	Memphis	TN	38116	901-922-8000	922-8099
Metropolitan Nashville Airport Authority 1 Terminal Dr Ste 501 *Web:* www.flynashville.com	Nashville	TN	37214	615-275-1675	
Abilene Regional Airport 2933 Airport Blvd *Web:* www.abilenetx.com/airport	Abilene	TX	79602	325-676-6367	676-6317
Rick Husband Amarillo International Airport 10801 Airport Blvd *Web:* airport.amarillo.gov	Amarillo	TX	79111	806-335-1671	335-1672
Austin-Bergstrom International Airport (ABIA) 3600 Presidential Blvd *Web:* www.ci.austin.tx.us	Austin	TX	78719	512-530-2242	530-7686
Corpus Christi International Airport 1000 International Dr *Web:* www.corpuschristiairport.com	Corpus Christi	TX	78406	361-289-0171	289-0251

				Phone	Fax
Dallas Love Field 8008 Cedar Springs Rd LB 16	Dallas	TX	75235	214-670-5683	670-6051
TF: 877-359-8474 ■ *Web:* www.dallas-lovefield.com					
Dallas-Fort Worth International Airport (DFW) 3200 E Airfield Dr PO Box 619428	Dallas	TX	75261	972-973-8888	574-5509
TF: 800-252-7522 ■ *Web:* www.dfwairport.com					
El Paso International Airport 6701 Convair Rd	El Paso	TX	79925	915-780-4749	
Web: www.elpasointernationalairport.com					
Bush Intercontinental Airport 2800 N Terminal Rd	Houston	TX	77032	281-233-3000	
Web: www.fly2houston.com/iah					
William P Hobby Airport (HOU) 7800 Airport Blvd	Houston	TX	77061	713-640-3000	641-7703
Web: fly2houston.com/hobbyhome					
Lubbock Preston Smith International Airport 5401 N Martin Luther King Blvd	Lubbock	TX	79403	806-775-2044	
Web: www.mylubbock.us/departmental-websites/departments/lubbock-airport/home					
Midland International Airport 9506 Laforce Blvd PO Box 60305	Midland	TX	79711	432-560-2200	
Web: www.midlandinternational.com					
San Antonio International Airport (SAT) 9800 Airport Blvd Rm 2041	San Antonio	TX	78216	210-207-3411	207-3500*
**Fax:* PR ■ *TF:* 800-237-6639 ■ *Web:* www.sanantonio.gov/aviation					
Ogden-Hinckley Airport 3909 Airport Rd	Ogden	UT	84405	801-629-8251	627-8104
Web: www.ogdencity.com					
Salt Lake City International Airport 776 N Terminal Dr PO Box 145550	Salt Lake City	UT	84116	801-575-2400	575-2645
TF: 800-595-2442 ■ *Web:* www.slcairport.com					
Burlington International Airport 1200 Airport Dr	South Burlington	VT	05403	802-863-1889	863-7947
Newport News/Williamsburg International Airport 900 Bland Blvd Ste G	Newport News	VA	23602	757-877-0221	
Web: flyphf.com					
Norfolk International Airport 2200 Norview Ave	Norfolk	VA	23518	757-857-3351	857-3265
Web: www.norfolkairport.com					
Richmond International Airport 1 Richard E Byrd Terminal D Ste C	Richmond	VA	23250	804-226-3000	
Web: www.flyrichmond.com					
Roanoke Regional Airport 5202 Aviation Dr NW	Roanoke	VA	24012	540-362-1999	563-4838
Web: flyroa.com					
Seattle-Tacoma International Airport (SEA-TAC) 17801 International Blvd PO Box 68727	Seattle	WA	98158	206-787-5388	
Web: portseattle.org/sea-tac					
Spokane International Airport 9000 W Airport Dr	Spokane	WA	99224	509-455-6455	624-6633
TF: 800-776-5263 ■ *Web:* www.spokaneairports.net					
Yeager Airport 100 Airport Rd Ste 175	Charleston	WV	25311	304-344-8033	344-8034
Web: www.yeagerairport.com					
Morgantown Municipal Airport 100 Hartfield Rd	Morgantown	WV	26505	304-291-7461	
Web: morgantownairport.com					
Austin Straubel International Airport 2077 Airport Dr Ste 18	Green Bay	WI	54313	920-498-4800	498-8799
Web: www.co.brown.wi.us					
Dane County Regional Airport 4000 International Ln	Madison	WI	53704	608-246-3380	246-3385
Web: www.msnairport.com					
General Mitchell International Airport 5300 S Howell Ave	Milwaukee	WI	53207	414-747-5300	747-4525
Web: www.mitchellairport.com					
Natrona County International Airport 8500 Airport Pkwy	Casper	WY	82604	307-472-6688	472-1805
Web: www.iflycasper.com					
Cheyenne Regional Airport 4000 Airport Pkwy PO Box 2210	Cheyenne	WY	82001	307-634-7071	632-1206
Web: www.cheyenneairport.com					
Jackson Hole Airport 1250 E Airport Rd PO Box 159	Jackson	WY	83001	307-733-7682	733-9270
Web: www.jacksonholeairport.com					

28 AIRSHIPS

See Also Aircraft p. 1724

				Phone	Fax
Boland Balloon Post Mills Airport PO Box 51	Post Mills	VT	05058	802-333-9254	333-9254
Web: www.myairship.com					
Cameron Balloons US PO Box 3672	Ann Arbor	MI	48106	734-426-5525	426-5026
TF: 866-423-6178 ■ *Web:* www.cameronballoons.com					
FireFly Balloons 850 Meacham Rd	Statesville	NC	28677	704-878-9501	878-9505
Web: www.fireflyballoons.net					
ILC Dover Inc 1 Moonwalker Rd	Frederica	DE	19946	302-335-3911	335-0762
TF: 800-631-9567 ■ *Web:* www.ilcdover.com					
ISL Information Systems Labs 10070 Barnes Canyon Rd	San Diego	CA	92121	858-535-9680	535-9848
Web: www.islinc.com					
Lindstrand Balloons USA 11440 Dandar St	Galena	IL	61036	815-777-6006	777-6004
Web: www.lindstrand.com					
Millennium Airship Inc Bremerton National Airport PO Box 1972	Belfair	WA	98528	360-674-2488	674-2494
Web: www.millenniumairship.com					
TCOM LP 7115 Thomas Edison Dr	Columbia	MD	21046	410-312-2400	312-2455
Web: www.tcomlp.com					
Worldwide Aeros Corp 1734 Gage Rd	Montebello	CA	90640	818-344-3999	201-8383*
**Fax Area Code:* 323 ■ *Web:* aeroscraft.com					

29 ALL-TERRAIN VEHICLES

See Also Sporting Goods p. 3193

				Phone	Fax
American Honda Motor Company Inc 1919 Torrance Blvd	Torrance	CA	90501	310-783-3170	
TF: 800-999-1009 ■ *Web:* www.honda.com					
American Suzuki Motor Corp 3251 Imperial Hwy	Brea	CA	92821	714-996-7040	
Web: www.suzuki.com					
Cycle Country Access Corp 205 N Depot St PO Box 107	Fox Lake	WI	53933	800-841-2222	
TF Sales: 800-841-2222 ■ *Web:* www.cyclecountry.com					
Kawasaki Motors Corp USA PO Box 25252	Santa Ana	CA	92799	949-770-0400	460-5600
TF: 866-802-9381 ■ *Web:* www.kawasaki.com					
Ontario Drive & Gear Ltd (ODG) 220 Bergey Ct	New Hamburg	ON	N3A2J5	519-662-2840	
TF: 877-274-6288 ■ *Web:* www.argoatv.com					
Polaris Industries Inc 2100 Hwy 55	Medina	MN	55340	763-542-0500	542-0599
NYSE: PII ■ *Web:* www.polaris.com					
Recreatives Industries Inc 60 Depot St	Buffalo	NY	14206	716-855-2226	855-1094
TF: 800-255-2511 ■ *Web:* www.maxatvs.com					
Yamaha Motor Corp USA 6555 Katella Ave	Cypress	CA	90630	800-656-7695	
TF Cust Svc: 800-656-7695 ■ *Web:* www.yamaha-motor.com					

30 AMBULANCE SERVICES

				Phone	Fax
Abbott Ambulance Inc 2500 Abbott Pl	Saint Louis	MO	63143	314-768-1000	781-3595
TF: 888-974-7035 ■ *Web:* www.abbottems.org					
Acadian Ambulance Service Inc 300 Hopkins St	Lafayette	LA	70501	800-259-3333	291-2211*
**Fax Area Code:* 337 ■ *TF:* 800-259-3333 ■ *Web:* www.acadian.com					
Air Trek Inc 28000 A-5 Airport Rd	Punta Gorda	FL	33982	941-639-7855	
Web: www.medjets.com					
American Ambulance Service Inc 1 American Way	Norwich	CT	06360	860-886-1463	
Web: www.americanamb.com					
American Medical Response (AMR) 6200 S Syracuse Way Ste 200	Greenwood Village	CO	80111	303-495-1200	495-1811
TF: 877-244-4890 ■ *Web:* www.amr.net					
Area Metropolitan Ambulance Authority 551 E Berry St	Fort Worth	TX	76110	817-923-3700	
Web: www.medstar911.org					
Armstrong Ambulance Service Inc 87 Mystic St	Arlington	MA	02474	781-648-0612	
Web: armstrongambulance.com					
ATI Ambulance 8400 W 183rd Pl	Tinley Park	IL	60487	708-802-8101	
Web: www.traceambulance.com					
Bangs Ambulance Service Inc 205 W Green St	Ithaca	NY	14850	607-273-1161	
Web: www.bangsambulance.com					
CareFlite 3110 S Great Southwest Pkwy	Grand Prairie	TX	75052	972-339-4200	
Web: www.careflite.org					
Carrier Coach Inc 271 Buffalo St	Gowanda	NY	14070	716-532-2600	
Web: www.coach.com					
Cataldo Ambulance Service Inc 137 Washington St	Somerville	MA	02143	617-625-0126	
Web: www.cataldoambulance.com					
County Rescue Services 1765 Allouez Ave	Green Bay	WI	54311	920-469-9779	
Web: www.countyrescue.com					
Critical Care Services Inc 3010 Broadway St NE	Minneapolis	MN	55413	612-638-4900	
Web: www.lifelinkiii.com					
Danville Ambulance Service Office 12 A St	Danville	PA	17821	570-275-3031	
TF: 877-721-3671 ■ *Web:* www.danvilleambulance.com					
Emergency Ambulance Service International Inc 3200 E Birch St Ste A	Brea	CA	92821	714-990-1331	
TF: 800-400-0689 ■ *Web:* www.emergencyambulance.com					
Emergycare Inc 1701 Sassafras St	Erie	PA	16502	814-870-1010	
Web: www.emergycare.org					
Excellance Inc 453 Lanier Rd	Madison	AL	35758	256-772-9321	
Web: www.excellance.com					
Global Air Response 5919 Approach Rd	Sarasota	FL	34238	800-631-6565	926-7690*
**Fax Area Code:* 941 ■ *TF:* 800-631-6565 ■ *Web:* www.airresponse.net					
Hunters Ambulance Service Inc 47 N Plains Industrial Rd Ste A	Wallingford	CT	06492	203-269-6586	
Web: www.huntersamb.com					
Industrial Paramedic Services Ltd 630 Fourth Ave SW Ste 100	Calgary	AB	T2P0J9	403-264-6435	
Web: ipsems.com					
Kenora District Services Board 51d Hwy 105	Red Lake	ON	P0V2M0	807-223-2100	
Web: kdsb.on.ca					
Keystone Quality Transport Co 1260 E Woodland Ave	Springfield	PA	19064	610-604-1421	
Web: keystonequalitytransport.com					
Lake EMS 2761 W Old U.S. Hwy 441	Mount Dora	FL	32757	352-383-4554	
Web: www.lakeems.org					
Lifenet Inc 6225 St Michaels Dr	Texarkana	TX	75503	903-832-8531	
TF: 800-832-6395 ■ *Web:* www.lifenetems.org					
LifeStar Response Corp 3710 Commerce Dr Ste 1006	Halethorpe	MD	21227	410-247-1178	
Web: www.lifestarcompanies.com					
Medic Rescue for Your Convenience You May Dial 313 Bridge St	Beaver	PA	15009	724-728-3620	
Web: www.medicrescue.org					
MedjetAssist 3500 Colonnade Pkwy Ste 500 PO Box 43099	Birmingham	AL	35243	205-595-6626	595-6658
TF: 800-527-7478 ■ *Web:* www.medjetassist.com					
Mercy Flights Inc 2020 Milligan Way	Medford	OR	97504	541-858-2600	
TF: 800-903-9000 ■ *Web:* www.mercyflights.com					
Metro Aviation Inc 1214 Hawn Ave PO Box 7008	Shreveport	LA	71137	318-222-5529	222-0503
Web: www.metroaviation.com					
Metro West Ambulance Service Inc 5475 Ne Dawson Creek Dr	Hillsboro	OR	97124	503-648-6658	
Web: www.metrowest.fm					
Midwest Ambulance Service of Iowa 2535 106th St	Urbandale	IA	50322	515-222-2222	
Web: www.midwestambulance.com					

				Phone	Fax
Midwood Ambulance & Oxygen Service Inc 2593 W 13th St. *Web:* www.midwoodambulance.com	Brooklyn	NY	11223	718-645-1000	
Mission Ambulance 1055 E Third St *TF:* 800-899-9100 ■ *Web:* www.missionambulance.com	Corona	CA	92879	800-899-9100	
Mobile Life Support Services Inc 3188 Us Rt 9w *Web:* www.mobilelife.com	New Windsor	NY	12553	845-562-4368	
Monroe Medi-Trans Inc 1669 Lyell Ave *Web:* www.monroeambulance.com	Rochester	NY	14606	585-454-6910	
MTS Ambulance 2431 Greenup Ave *TF:* 800-598-3458 ■ *Web:* www.mtsambulance.com	Ashland	KY	41101	606-324-3286	
NES Healthcare Group Inc 39 Main St PO Box 156 *Web:* www.neshealth-care.com	Tiburon	CA	94920	631-265-7450	
On Time Transport Inc 135 E Highland Pkwy Ste A *Web:* www.ontimetransport.com	Roselle	NJ	07203	908-298-9500	
Paramedics Plus LLC 352 Glenwood *Web:* www.paramedicsplus.com	Tyler	TX	75702	903-535-5802	
Paratech Ambulance Service 9401 W Brown Deer Rd *Web:* www.paratechambulance.com	Milwaukee	WI	53224	414-358-1111	
Peach State Ambulance Inc 105 Peach State Ct *Web:* www.peachstateambulance.com	Tyrone	GA	30290	678-364-0003	
PL Custom Body & Equipment Company Inc 2201 Atlantic Ave *Web:* www.plcustom.com	Manasquan	NJ	08736	732-223-1411	
Professional Ambulance & Oxygen Service Inc 31 Smith Pl. *Web:* www.proems.com	Cambridge	MA	02138	617-492-2700	
PROMPT Ambulance Central Inc 9835 Express Dr *Web:* www.promptambulance.com	Highland	IN	46322	219-934-1010	
REVA Air Ambulance Inc 1745 NW 51 Pl Hngr 73 *Web:* www.flyreva.com	Fort Lauderdale	FL	33309	954-730-9300	
Rural/Metro Corp 9221 E Via de Ventura *TF:* 800-352-2309 ■ *Web:* www.ruralmetro.com	Scottsdale	AZ	85258	800-352-2309	
Schaefer Ambulance Service Inc 4627 Beverly Blvd. *Web:* www.schaeferamb.com	Los Angeles	CA	90004	323-468-1600	
Shock Trauma Air Rescue Society (STARS) 1441 Aviation Pk NE *Web:* www.stars.ca	Calgary	AB	T2E8M7	403-295-1811	275-4891
Skyservice Airlines Inc 9785 Ryan Ave. *TF:* 888-985-1402 ■ *Web:* skyservice.com	Dorval	QC	H9P1A2	514-636-3300	636-4855
Transcare Pennsylvania 400 Seco Rd *Web:* transcare.com	Monroeville	PA	15146	412-373-6300	373-8263
Westlog Aviation 311 Cove Rd. *Web:* www.cal-ore.com	Brookings	OR	97415	541-469-7911	

31 AMUSEMENT PARK COMPANIES

See Also Circus, Carnival, Festival Operators p. 1939

				Phone	Fax
AAF Rose Bowl Aquatics Center 360 N Arroyo Blvd *Web:* www.rosebowlaquatics.org	Pasadena	CA	91103	626-564-0330	
Ada Community Library 10664 W Victory Rd *Web:* www.adalib.org	Boise	ID	83709	208-362-0181	
All Star Adventures 1010 N Webb Rd *Web:* www.allstarwichita.com	Wichita	KS	67206	316-682-3700	
Austins Entertainment LLC 16231 N Ih-35 *Web:* www.austinspark.com	Pflugerville	TX	78660	512-670-9600	
Bay Tek Games Inc 1077 E Glenbrook Dr. *Web:* www.bay-tek.com	Pulaski	WI	54162	920-822-3951	
Belle Haven Country Club Inc 6023 Ft Hunt Rd *Web:* www.bellehavencc.com	Alexandria	VA	22307	703-329-1448	
Bend Metro Parks & Recreation District 200 NW Pacific Park Ln *Web:* bendparksandrec.org	Bend	OR	97701	541-389-7275	
BounceU 1166 S Gilbert Rd *Web:* www.bounceu.com	Gilbert	AZ	85296	480-632-9663	
Bowlmor Holdings LLC 222 W 44th St. *Web:* www.bowlmor.com	New York	NY	10036	212-777-2214	
Buffalo Grove Park District 530 Bernard Dr *TF:* 800-526-0844 ■ *Web:* bgparks.org	Buffalo Grove	IL	60089	847-850-2100	
California Exposition & State Fair 1600 Exposition Blvd *Web:* www.calexpo.com	Sacramento	CA	95815	916-263-4041	
CAMELBACK MOUNTAIN 301 Resort Dr *Web:* www.skicamelback.com	Tannersville	PA	18372	570-629-1661	629-2388
Casino Pauma 777 Pauma Reservation Rd PO Box 1067 *Web:* www.casinopauma.com	Pauma Valley	CA	92061	760-742-2177	
Castles n Coasters 9445 N Metro Pkwy E *Web:* www.castlesncoasters.com	Phoenix	AZ	85051	602-997-7575	
Cedar Fair LP 1 Cedar Pt Dr *NYSE:* FUN ■ *Web:* www.cedarfair.com	Sandusky	OH	44870	419-627-2233	627-2260
City of Dearborn 1300 S Telegraph Rd *Web:* www.cityofdearborn.org	Dearborn	MI	48124	313-563-4653	
Clementon Amusement Park & Splash World Waterpark 144 Berlin Rd *Web:* www.clementonpark.com	Clementon	NJ	08021	856-783-0263	
Cliff's Amusement Park Inc 4800 Osuna Rd NE *Web:* www.cliffsamusementpark.com	Albuquerque	NM	87109	505-881-9373	
Cordova Recreation & Park District 2197 Chase Dr *Web:* www.crpd.com	Rancho Cordova	CA	95670	916-362-1841	

				Phone	Fax
Des Plaines Park District 2222 Birch St. *Web:* dpparks.org	Des Plaines	IL	60018	847-391-5700	
Downers Grove Park District 2455 Warrenville Rd *Web:* www.dgparks.org	Downers Grove	IL	60516	630-960-7500	
Flagship Marinas Acquisitions LLC 950 E Paces Ferry Rd *Web:* www.flagshipmarinas.com	Atlanta	GA	30320	770-965-7605	
Freedom Station Family Fun Center 2992 N Park Ave Ste A *Web:* www.freedomstationfun.com	Prescott Valley	AZ	86314	928-775-4040	
Georgia Public Library 1800 Century Pl NE Ste 150 *TF:* 800-248-6701 ■ *Web:* www.georgialibraries.org	Atlanta	GA	30345	404-235-7200	
Going Bonkers Inc 229 N 48th St *Web:* www.goingbonkers.com	Quincy	IL	62305	217-223-6331	
Golfland Entertainment Centers Inc 155 W Hampton Ave. *Web:* www.golfland.com	Mesa	AZ	85210	480-834-8319	
Harris Goldman Productions Inc 8885 Rio San Diego Dr Ste 335 *Web:* www.harrisgoldman.com	San Diego	CA	92108	619-299-7951	
Hawaiian Falls Waterparks 4550 N Garland Ave *Web:* hfalls.com	Garland	TX	75040	972-675-8888	
Herschend Family Entertainment Corp (HFE) 5445 Triangle Pkwy Ste 200 *Web:* hfecorp.com	Peachtree Corners	GA	30092	770-441-1940	
Hershey Entertainment & Resorts Co 100 W Hersheypark Dr *TF:* 800-437-7439 ■ *Web:* www.hersheypa.com	Hershey	PA	17033	800-437-7439	
HITS Inc 319 Main St *Web:* www.hitsshows.com	Saugerties	NY	12477	845-246-8833	
iFly USA LLC 31310 Alvarado-Niles Rd *Web:* www.iflyworld.com/sfbay	Union City	CA	94587	510-489-4359	
International Training Inc 1045 Ne Industrial Blvd *TF:* 888-778-9073 ■ *Web:* www.tdisdi.com	Jensen Beach	FL	34957	207-729-4201	
Island Global Yachting Ltd 515 E Las Olas Blvd Ste 900 *Web:* www.igymarinas.com	Fort Lauderdale	FL	33301	954-302-6000	
Island Windjammers Inc 165 Shaw Dr *TF:* 877-772-4549 ■ *Web:* www.islandwindjammers.com	Acworth	GA	30102	877-772-4549	
Kids Play Today LLC 837 Route 6 Unit 5 *Web:* www.kidsplaytoday.com	Shohola	PA	18458	570-296-2313	
Lake Quassapaug Park 2132 Middlebury Rd *TF:* 800-367-7275 ■ *Web:* www.quassy.com	Middlebury	CT	06762	203-758-2913	
Laser Quest Inc 1605 N Academy Blvd *Web:* www.laserquest.com	Colorado Springs	CO	80909	719-570-1115	
Laserdome 2050 Auction Rd *Web:* laserdome.com	Manheim	PA	17545	717-492-0002	
Leesburg Animal Park 19270 James Monroe Hwy *Web:* www.leesburganimalpark.com	Leesburg	VA	20175	703-669-0010	
Lisle Park District 1825 Short St *Web:* www.lisleparkdistrict.org	Lisle	IL	60532	630-964-3410	
Magic Mountain Fun Centers 5890 Scarborough Blvd *Web:* www.magicmountainfuncenter.com	Columbus	OH	43232	614-840-9600	
Michigan's Adventure Inc 4750 Whitehall Rd *Web:* www.miadventure.com	Muskegon	MI	49445	231-766-3377	
Mundelein Park & Recreation District 1401 N Midlathian Rd. *Web:* mundeleinparks.org	Mundelein	IL	60060	847-566-0650	
New Lenox Community Park District 1 Manor Dr *Web:* www.newlenoxparks.org	New Lenox	IL	60451	815-485-3584	
New York Botanical Garden, The 2900 Southern Blvd *Web:* www.nybg.org	Bronx	NY	10458	718-817-8700	
Northbrook Park District 545 Academy Dr *Web:* www.nbparks.org	Northbrook	IL	60062	847-291-2960	
Oak Lawn Park District 9400 S Kenton Ave *Web:* www.olparks.com	Oaklawn	IL	60453	708-857-2222	
Oak Park Park District 218 Madison St *Web:* pdop.org	Oak Park	IL	60302	708-383-0002	
Ober Gatlinburg Inc 1001 Pkwy Ste 2 *Web:* obergatlinburg.com	Gatlinburg	TN	37738	865-436-5423	
Ocean Breeze Waterpark 849 General Booth Blvd *Web:* www.oceanbreezewaterpark.com	Virginia Beach	VA	23451	757-422-4444	
Odyssey Fun World 3440 Odyssey Ct. *Web:* www.odysseyfunworld.com	Naperville	IL	60563	630-416-2222	
Optical Discount Corp 10415 Slusher Dr Ste 1	Santa Fe Springs	CA	90670	562-946-3050	
Park Ridge Recreation & Park District 2701 Sibley Ave *Web:* prparks.org	Park Ridge	IL	60068	847-692-5127	
Paul Gauguin Cruises Inc 11100 Main St Ste 300 *Web:* www.pgcruises.com	Bellevue	WA	98004	425-440-6171	
Pennsylvania Renaissance Faire 2775 Lebanon Rd *Web:* www.parenfaire.com	Manheim	PA	17545	717-665-7021	
Q Center 1405 N Fifth Ave *TF:* 877-774-4627 ■ *Web:* www.qcenter.com	Saint Charles	IL	60174	630-377-3100	
Rentschler Field 615 Silver Ln. *Web:* www.rentschlerfield.com	East Hartford	CT	06118	860-610-4700	
Ripley Entertainment Inc 7576 Kingspointe Pkwy Ste 188 *Web:* www.ripleys.com	Orlando	FL	32819	407-345-8010	345-0801
Sage YMCA of Metro Chicago 701 Manor Rd *Web:* www.ymcachicago.org	Crystal Lake	IL	60014	815-459-4455	
Santa Cruz Seaside Co 400 Beach St. *Web:* www.beachboardwalk.com	Santa Cruz	CA	95060	831-423-5590	

Phone Fax

Schaumburg Park District 235 E Beech Dr. . . . . Schaumburg IL 60193 847-985-2115
Web: www.parkfun.com

Sea Research Foundation Inc 55 Coogan Blvd. . . . . Mystic CT 06355 860-572-5955
Web: www.searesearch.com

Ski Shawnee Inc 339 Hollow Rd. . . . . Shawnee On Delaware PA 18356 570-421-7231
TF: 800-233-4218 ■ *Web:* www.shawneemt.com

Splash Lagoon Water Pk Resort 8091 Peach St . . . . Erie PA 16509 814-217-1111
Web: www.splashlagoon.com

Taos Ski Valley Inc 116 Sutton Pl . . . . Taos Ski Valley NM 87525 575-776-2291
Web: www.skitaos.com

Tweetsie Railroad Inc
300 Tweetsie Railroad Ln . . . . Blowing Rock NC 28605 828-264-9061
Web: tweetsie.com

Universal City Development Partners Ltd
1000 Universal Studios Plz. . . . . Orlando FL 32819 407-363-8000
Web: www.universalorlando.com

Universal Parks & Resorts
100 Universal City Plz . . . . Universal City CA 91608 818-777-1000 866-3444

Ville De Riviere-Du-Loup
65 Rue De Lehetel-De-Ville . . . . Riviere-du-loup QC G5R1L4 418-867-6700
Web: www.ville.riviere-du-loup.qc.ca

West Point Thoroughbreds Inc
2 Smith Bridge Rd . . . . Saratoga Springs NY 12866 518-583-6638
Web: www.westpointtb.com

West Suburban Special Recreation Association
2915 Maple St . . . . Franklin Park IL 60131 847-455-2100
Web: www.wssra.net

Westchester Park District 10201 Bond St. . . . . Westchester IL 60154 708-865-8200
Web: www.wpdparks.org

Wet 'n' Wild Hawaii 400 Farrington Hwy. . . . . Kapolei HI 96707 808-674-9283
Web: wetnwildhawaii.com

Wheaton Park District 102 E Wesley St . . . . Wheaton IL 60187 630-665-4710
Web: www.wheatonparkdistrict.com

Wheeling Park District 333 W Dundee Rd . . . . Wheeling IL 60090 847-465-3333
Web: www.wheelingparkdistrict.com

Wild Adventures Valdosta LLC
3766 Old Clyattville Rd. . . . . Valdosta GA 31601 229-219-7080
Web: www.wildadventures.com

Wisconsin Center District 500 W Kilbourn . . . . Milwaukee WI 53203 414-908-6000
Web: www.wcd.org

Woodridge Park District 2600 Center Dr . . . . Woodridge IL 60517 630-353-3300
Web: www.woodridgeparks.org

World Poker Tour 5700 Wilshire Blvd . . . . Los Angeles CA 90036 323-330-9900
Web: www.wptmag.com

Wunderland Electric Castle's
10306 Ne Halsey St . . . . Portland OR 97220 503-255-7333
Web: wunderlandgames.com

YMCA of Pikes Peak Region Inc
207 N Nevada Ave . . . . Colorado Springs CO 80903 719-473-9622
Web: www.ppymca.org

YMCA of Triangle Area 801 Corporate Ctr Dr . . . . Raleigh NC 27607 919-719-9622
Web: www.ymcatriangle.org

32 AMUSEMENT PARKS

Phone Fax

Adventure Landing 3311 Capital Blvd . . . . Raleigh NC 27604 919-872-1688 872-3408
Web: www.adventurelanding.com

Adventuredome 2880 Las Vegas Blvd S . . . . Las Vegas NV 89109 702-691-5861 794-3906
TF: 866-456-8894 ■ *Web:* www.adventuredome.com

Adventureland Park 305 34th Ave NW. . . . . Altoona IA 50009 515-266-2121 266-9831
TF: 800-532-1286 ■ *Web:* www.adventurelandpark.com

Busch Gardens Williamsburg
1 Busch Gardens Blvd . . . . Williamsburg VA 23185 800-343-7946 253-3399*
**Fax Area Code:* 757 ■ **Fax:* Mktg ■ *TF:* 800-343-7946 ■ *Web:* www.buschgardens.com

California's Great America
4701 Great America Pkwy. . . . . Santa Clara CA 95054 408-988-1776 986-5855*
**Fax:* Sales ■ *Web:* www.cagreatamerica.com

Camelbeach Mountain Waterpark
309 Resort Dr PO Box 168 . . . . Tannersville PA 18372 570-629-1661
Web: www.camelbeach.com

Casino Pier & Water Works
800 Ocean Terr. . . . . Seaside Heights NJ 08751 732-793-6488 793-0461
Web: www.casinopiernj.com

Castle Park 3500 Polk St. . . . . Riverside CA 92505 951-785-3000
Web: www.castlepark.com

Cedar Fair Parks 14523 Carowinds Blvd . . . . Charlotte NC 28273 704-588-2600
TF: 800-888-4386 ■ *Web:* www.carowinds.com

Cedar Point Amusement Park 1 Cedar Pt Dr . . . . Sandusky OH 44870 419-626-0830 627-2200*
**Fax:* Mktg ■ *Web:* www.cedarpoint.com

Children's Fairyland Theme Park
699 Bellevue Ave . . . . Oakland CA 94610 510-452-2259 452-2261
Web: www.fairyland.org

Coney Island Park 6201 Kellogg Ave . . . . Cincinnati OH 45230 513-232-8230 231-1352
Web: www.coneyislandpark.com

Darien Lake Theme Park Resort
9993 Allegheny Rd PO Box 91 . . . . Darien Center NY 14040 585-599-4641 599-4053
TF: 866-640-0652 ■ *Web:* www.darienlake.com

Disney's Animal Kingdom
2901 Osceola Pkwy . . . . Lake Buena Vista FL 32830 407-938-3000 938-4799
Web: disneyworld.disney.go.com/parks/animal-kingdom

Disney's Blizzard Beach
1534 Blizzard Beach Dr. . . . . Lake Buena Vista FL 32830 407-560-3400
Web: www.disneyworld.disney.go.com

Disney's California Adventure
1313 S Disneyland Dr. . . . . Anaheim CA 92802 714-781-7290
TF: 800-225-2024 ■ *Web:* disneyland.disney.go.com

Disney's Hollywood Studios 3111 World Dr. . . . . Orlando FL 32836 407-824-4321
Web: disneyworld.disney.go.com/parks/hollywood-studios

Disney's Typhoon Lagoon
1145 E Buena Vista Blvd. . . . . Lake Buena Vista FL 32830 407-560-7223
Web: disneyworld.disney.go.com

Disneyland 1313 S Harbor Blvd . . . . Anaheim CA 92802 714-781-4636

Phone Fax

Dollywood 2700 Dollywood Parks Blvd. . . . . Pigeon Forge TN 37863 800-365-5996
TF: 800-365-5996 ■ *Web:* www.dollywood.com

Dorney Park & Wildwater Kingdom
3830 Dorney Pk Rd. . . . . Allentown PA 18104 610-395-3724
TF: 800-747-0561 ■ *Web:* dorneypark.com

Dutch Wonderland Family Amusement Park
2249 Lincoln Hwy E . . . . Lancaster PA 17602 717-291-1888 291-1595
TF: 866-386-2839 ■ *Web:* www.dutchwonderland.com

Elitch Gardens 2000 Elitch Cir . . . . Denver CO 80204 303-595-4386 629-0740
Web: www.elitchgardens.com

EPCOT 1200 Epcot Resort Blvd . . . . Lake Buena Vista FL 32830 407-824-4321
Web: disneyworld.disney.go.com

Family Kingdom Amusement Park & Oceanfront Water Park
300 S Ocean Blvd. . . . . Myrtle Beach SC 29577 843-626-3447
Web: www.familykingdomfun.com

Frontier City Theme Park 11501 NE Expy . . . . Oklahoma City OK 73131 405-478-2140 478-2118
Web: www.frontiercity.com

Fun Town Splash Town USA Inc
US Rt 1 774 Portland Rd. . . . . Saco ME 04072 207-284-5139 283-4716
TF: 800-843-5678 ■ *Web:* www.funtownsplashtownusa.com

Geauga Lake Wildwater Kingdom 1100 Squires Rd . . . . . . Aurora OH 44202 330-562-8303
Web: www.wildwaterfun.com

Grand Harbor Resort & Waterpark 350 Bell St . . . . Dubuque IA 52001 563-690-4000
TF: 866-690-4006 ■ *Web:* www.grandharborresort.com

Great Escape & Splashwater Kingdom
Po Box 511. . . . . Lake George NY 12845 518-792-3500 792-3404
Web: www.sixflags.com

Hersheypark 100 Hershey Pk Dr . . . . Hershey PA 17033 717-534-3900 534-3153
TF: 844-330-1813 ■ *Web:* www.hersheypark.com

Holiday World & Splashin' Safari
452 E Christmas Blvd. . . . . Santa Claus IN 47579 812-937-4401
TF: 877-463-2645 ■ *Web:* www.holidayworld.com

Idlewild & Soak Zone Rt 30 E PO Box C . . . . Ligonier PA 15658 724-238-3666 238-6544
Web: www.idlewild.com

Indiana Beach 5224 E Indiana Beach Rd. . . . . Monticello IN 47960 574-583-4141 583-4125
Web: www.indianabeach.com

Kennywood Park 4800 Kennywood Blvd. . . . . West Mifflin PA 15122 412-461-0500
Web: www.kennywood.com

Knight's Action Park & Caribbean Water Adventure
1700 Recreation Dr. . . . . Springfield IL 62711 217-546-8881
Web: www.knightsactionpark.com

Knoebels Amusement Resort 391 Knoebels Blvd . . . . . . Elysburg PA 17824 570-672-2572
TF: 800-487-4386 ■ *Web:* www.knoebels.com

Knott's Berry Farm 8039 Beach Blvd. . . . . Buena Park CA 90620 714-220-5220 220-5124
TF: 800-742-6427 ■ *Web:* www.knotts.com

Knott's Soak City San Diego
2052 Entertainment Cir. . . . . Chula Vista CA 91911 714-220-5200
Web: www.knotts.com

Lagoon & Pioneer Village 375 N Lagoon Dr. . . . . Farmington UT 84025 801-451-8000
TF: 800-748-5246 ■ *Web:* www.lagoonpark.com

Lake Compounce Family Theme Park
822 Lake Ave . . . . Bristol CT 06010 860-583-3300 589-7974
Web: www.lakecompounce.com

Lake Winnepesaukah Amusement Park
1730 Lakeview Dr . . . . Rossville GA 30741 706-866-5681
Web: www.lakewinnie.com

LEGOLAND California 1 Legoland Dr . . . . Carlsbad CA 92008 760-438-5346 918-5459
TF: 877-534-6526 ■ *Web:* www.legoland.com

Magic Kingdom Park 3111 World Dr. . . . . Lake Buena Vista FL 32836 407-824-4321
Web: disneyworld.disney.go.com/parks/magic-kingdom

Magic Springs Theme Park & Crystal Falls Water Park
1701 E Grand Ave. . . . . Hot Springs AR 71901 501-624-0100 318-5367
Web: www.magicsprings.com

Marineland 7657 Portage Rd. . . . . Niagara Falls ON L2E6X8 905-356-9565 374-6652
Web: www.marinelandcanada.com

Morey's Piers & Raging Waters Waterparks
3501 Boardwalk . . . . Wildwood NJ 08260 609-522-3900 522-0788
Web: www.moreyspiers.com

Myrtle Waves Water Park
3000 Tenth Ave N Ext . . . . Myrtle Beach SC 29577 843-913-9250
Web: www.myrtlewaves.com

NASCAR SpeedPark 1545 Pkwy . . . . Sevierville TN 37862 865-908-5500
Web: www.nascarspeedpark.com

Oaks Amusement Park 7805 SE Oaks PkWy. . . . . Portland OR 97202 503-233-5777 236-9143
Web: www.oakspark.com

Paramount Canada's Wonderland 9580 Jane St. . . . . . . Vaughan ON L6A1S6 905-832-8131
Web: www.canadaswonderland.com

Paramount's Kings Dominion 16000 Theme Pkwy. . . . . . . Doswell VA 23047 804-876-5000 876-5864
TF: 800-367-7623 ■ *Web:* www.kingsdominion.com

Raging Waters 2333 S White Rd. . . . . San Jose CA 95148 408-238-9900 270-2022
Web: www.rwsplash.com

Raging Waters Sacramento
1600 Exposition Blvd . . . . Sacramento CA 95815 916-924-3747 924-1314
Web: www.rwsac.com

Sandcastle Water Park 1000 Sandcastle Dr . . . . Pittsburgh PA 15120 412-462-6666 462-0827
Web: www.sandcastlewaterpark.com

Santa Cruz Beach Boardwalk 400 Beach St. . . . . Santa Cruz CA 95060 831-423-5590
Web: www.beachboardwalk.com

Schlitterbahn Beach Waterpark
33261 State Pk Rd Hwy 100 . . . . South Padre Island TX 78597 956-772-7873 761-3960
Web: www.schlitterbahn.com

Schlitterbahn Waterpark Resort
381 E Austin St. . . . . New Braunfels TX 78130 830-625-2351 625-3515
Web: www.schlitterbahn.com

SeaWorld Orlando 7007 Sea World Dr . . . . Orlando FL 32821 407-351-3600
TF: 800-327-2424 ■ *Web:* seaworldparks.com

SeaWorld San Diego 500 SeaWorld Dr . . . . San Diego CA 92109 619-226-3901
TF: 800-257-4268 ■ *Web:* www.seaworld.com

Sesame Place 100 Sesame Rd . . . . Langhorne PA 19047 215-752-7070 741-5307
Web: www.sesameplace.com

Seven Peaks Water Park 1330 East 300 North. . . . . Provo UT 84606 801-373-8777
Web: www.sevenpeaks.com

	City	State	Zip	Phone	Fax
Silver Springs State Park 5656 E Silver Springs Blvd *Web:* www.floridastateparks.org	Silver Springs	FL	34488	352-236-7148	
Six Flags America 13710 Central Ave *Web:* www.sixflags.com/parks/america	Mitchellville	MD	20721	301-249-1500	
Six Flags Discovery Kingdom 1001 Fairgrounds Dr *Web:* www.sixflags.com	Vallejo	CA	94589	707-644-4000	
Six Flags Fiesta Texas 17000 IH-10 W *TF:* 800-370-7488 ■ *Web:* www.sixflags.com	San Antonio	TX	78257	210-697-5000	
Six Flags Great Adventure 1 Six Flags Blvd *TF:* 800-772-2287 ■ *Web:* www.sixflags.com/parks/greatadventure	Jackson	NJ	08527	732-928-1821	
Six Flags Great America 542 N Rt 21 *Web:* www.sixflags.com	Gurnee	IL	60031	847-249-2133	
Six Flags Hurricane Harbor Dallas 1800 E Lamar Blvd *Web:* www.sixflags.com/parks/hurricaneharbordallas	Arlington	TX	76006	817-265-3356	
Six Flags Hurricane Harbor Los Angeles 26101 Magic Mtn Pkwy *Web:* www.sixflags.com/parks/hurricaneharborla	Valencia	CA	91355	661-255-4527	
Six Flags Magic Mountain 26101 Magic Mtn Pkwy *Web:* www.sixflags.com	Valencia	CA	91355	661-255-4100	
Six Flags New England 1623 Main St **Fax:* Mktg ■ *TF:* 800-370-7488 ■ *Web:* www.sixflags.com	Agawam	MA	01001	413-786-9300	821-2402*
Six Flags Over Georgia 275 Riverside PkwySW *Web:* www.sixflags.com	Austell	GA	30168	770-948-9290	
Six Flags Over Texas 2201 Rd to Six Flags *Web:* www.sixflags.com/parks/overtexas	Arlington	TX	76011	817-640-8900	607-6148
Six Flags Saint Louis 4900 Six Flags Rd PO Box 60 *Web:* www.sixflags.com/parks/stlouis	Eureka	MO	63025	636-938-5300	
Six Flags White Water Park 250 Cobb Pkwy N Ste 100 **Fax Area Code:* 636 ■ *Web:* www.sixflags.com	Marietta	GA	30062	770-948-9290	587-2753*
Six Flags Wild Safari 1 Six Flags Blvd *TF:* 800-772-2287 ■ *Web:* www.sixflags.com/parks/wildsafari	Jackson	NJ	08527	732-928-1821	
Splashtown Water Park 21300 IH-45 N *Web:* www.wetnwildsplashtown.com	Spring	TX	77373	281-355-3300	353-7946
Splish Splash 2549 Splish Splash Dr *Web:* www.splishsplash.com	Calverton	NY	11933	631-727-3600	
Universal Orlando 6000 Universal Blvd *TF:* 877-801-9720 ■ *Web:* universalorlando.com	Orlando	FL	32819	407-363-8000	
Universal's Islands of Adventure 6000 Universal Studios Plz *TF:* 877-801-9720 ■ *Web:* universalorlando.com	Orlando	FL	32819	407-363-8000	
Valleyfair 1 Valleyfair Dr *Web:* www.valleyfair.com	Shakopee	MN	55379	952-445-7600	445-1539
Village Vacances Valcartier 1860 Valcartier Blvd *TF:* 888-384-5524 ■ *Web:* www.valcartier.com	Valcartier	QC	G0A4S0	418-844-2200	844-1239
Water Country USA 176 Water Country Pkwy **Fax Area Code:* 757 ■ *TF:* 800-343-7946 ■ *Web:* www.watercountryusa.com	Williamsburg	VA	23185	800-343-7946	253-3216*
Waterworld California 1950 Waterworld Pkwy *Web:* www.waterworldcalifornia.com	Concord	CA	94520	925-609-1364	609-1360
Western Playland Amusement Park 1249 Futurity Dr *Web:* www.westernplayland.com	Sunland Park	NM	88063	575-589-3410	
Wet 'n Wild Emerald Pointe 3910 S Holden Rd *TF:* 800-555-5900 ■ *Web:* www.emeraldpointe.com	Greensboro	NC	27406	336-852-9721	852-2391
Wet 'n Wild Orlando 6200 International Dr *TF General:* 800-992-9453 ■ *Web:* www.wetnwildorlando.com	Orlando	FL	32819	407-351-1800	363-1147
White Water Bay 3908 W Reno Ave *Web:* www.whitewaterbay.com	Oklahoma City	OK	73107	405-943-9687	
Wild Waves/Enchanted Village 36201 Enchanted Pkwy S *Web:* wildwaves.com	Federal Way	WA	98003	253-661-8000	
Wonderland Amusement Park 2601 Dumas Dr *TF:* 800-383-4712 ■ *Web:* www.wonderlandpark.com	Amarillo	TX	79107	806-383-0832	383-8737
Worlds of Fun & Oceans of Fun 4545 NE Worlds of Fun Dr *Web:* www.worldsoffun.com	Kansas City	MO	64161	816-454-4545	454-4655

33 ANIMATION COMPANIES

See Also Motion Picture Production - Special Interest p. 2780; Motion Picture & Television Production p. 2780

	City	State	Zip	Phone	Fax
Acoustiguide Inc 102 W 38th St 3rd Fl *Web:* www.acoustiguide.com	New York	NY	10018	212-329-1227	
Advanced Animations PO Box 34 *Web:* www.advancedanimations.com	Stockbridge	VT	05772	802-746-8974	746-8971
Atomic Cartoons Inc 112 W Sixth Sve *Web:* www.atomiccartoons.com	Vancouver	BC	V5Y1K6	604-734-2866	
Bix Pix Entertainment Inc 11630 Tuxford St *Web:* www.bixpix.com	Sun Valley	CA	91352	818-252-7474	252-7410
Blue Sky Studios Inc 1 American Ln *Web:* www.blueskystudios.com	Greenwich	CT	06831	203-992-6000	992-6001
Blur Studio 3960 Ince Blvd *Web:* www.blur.com	Culver City	CA	90232	424-298-4800	298-4801
Brilliant Digital Entertainment Inc 14011 Ventura Blvd Ste 501 *Web:* www.globalfileregistry.com	Sherman Oaks	CA	91423	818-386-2179	
Cine-tal Systems Inc 8383 Craig St Ste 130 *Web:* www.cine-tal.com	Indianapolis	IN	46250	317-576-0091	
Digital Kitchen LLC 1114 E Pk St Third Fl *Web:* d-kitchen.com	Seattle	WA	98122	206-267-0400	
Digital Lagoon Inc 14685 W 105th *Web:* www.lagoon.com	Lenexa	KS	66215	913-888-3468	
DUCK 2205 Stoner Ave	Los Angeles	CA	90064	310-478-0771	478-0773
Film Roman Inc 21600 Oxnard St Ste 1700 *Web:* www.filmroman.com	Los Angeles	CA	91367	818-748-4000	
Grace & Wild Inc 23689 Industrial Park Dr *Web:* www.ringsidecreative.com	Farmington Hills	MI	48335	248-471-6010	
JibJab Media Inc 228 Main St Ste 4 *Web:* www.jibjab.com	Venice	CA	90291	323-400-6307	
Jim Henson's Creature Shop 1416 N LaBrea Ave *Web:* www.creatureshop.com	Hollywood	CA	90028	323-802-1557	
Keith Watson Productions Inc 2425 Nw 71st Pl *Web:* www.keithwatsonproductions.com	Gainesville	FL	32653	352-264-8812	
Klasky Csupo Inc 1238 N Highland Ave *Web:* www.klaskycsupo.com	Los Angeles	CA	90038	323-468-2600	468-3021
Laika 1400 NW 22nd Ave *Web:* www.laika.com	Portland	OR	97210	503-225-1130	226-3746
Mbox Communications LLC 1653 Wisconsin Ave Nw *Web:* www.mboxcommunications.com	Washington	DC	20007	202-536-4903	
Medcom Inc 6060 Phyllis Dr *TF:* 800-541-0253 ■ *Web:* www.medcominc.com	Cypress	CA	90630	800-541-0253	
NestFamily 1461 S Beltline Rd Ste 500 *TF:* 800-634-4298 ■ *Web:* www.nestlearning.com	Coppell	TX	75019	972-402-7100	
Pixar Animation Studios 1200 Pk Ave *Web:* www.pixar.com	Emeryville	CA	94608	510-922-3000	752-3151
Rhythm & Hues Inc 5890 W Jefferson Blvd Ste Q *Web:* www.rhythm.com	Los Angeles	CA	90016	310-448-7500	448-7600
Smashing Ideas Inc 1601 Second Ave Ste 900 *Web:* smashingideas.com	Seattle	WA	98101	206-378-0100	
Sony Pictures Animation 9050 W Washington Blvd *Web:* sonypicturesanimation.com	Culver City	CA	90232	310-840-8000	
Stupid Fun Club LLC 701 Channing Way *Web:* www.stupidfunclub.com	Berkeley	CA	94710	510-841-2600	
Summit Training Source Inc 4170 Embassy Dr SE *Web:* www.safetyontheweb.com	Grand Rapids	MI	49546	616-949-4343	
Topix 35 McCaul St Ste 200 *Web:* www.topix.com	Toronto	ON	M5T1V7	416-971-7711	
Winnercomm Inc 4500 S 129th E Ave Ste 201 *Web:* www.winnercomm.com	Tulsa	OK	74134	918-496-1900	

34 APPAREL FINDINGS

	City	State	Zip	Phone	Fax
Agron Inc 2440 S Sepulveda Blvd Ste 201 *Web:* www.agron.com	Los Angeles	CA	90064	310-473-7223	
Blind Center, The 1001 N Bruce St *Web:* www.blindcenter.org	Las Vegas	NV	89101	702-642-6000	
Cushman & Marden Inc 56 Pulaski St PO Box 3001 *Web:* www.cushmanandmarden.com	Peabody	MA	01960	978-532-1670	532-1670
Dallas Bias Fabrics Inc 1401 N Carroll Ave *Web:* www.dallasbias.com	Dallas	TX	75204	214-824-2036	824-2036
Javits Eric 433 5th Ave Fl 5 *Web:* www.ericjavits.com	New York	NY	10016	212-213-4949	
Metric Products Inc 4630 Leahy St *Web:* www.metric-products.com	Culver City	CA	90232	310-815-9000	
Modern Quilters Inc 62038 Minnesota Hwy 24 PO Box 66 *Web:* modernquilters.com	Litchfield	MN	55355	320-693-7987	
QST Industries Inc 550 W Adams St Ste 200 *Web:* www.qst.com	Chicago	IL	60661	312-930-9400	648-0312
TeamWorld Inc 498 Conklin Ave *Web:* www.teamworld.com	Binghamton	NY	13903	607-770-1005	
Wiggy's Inc 2482 Industrial Blvd *Web:* www.wiggys.com	Grand Junction	CO	81505	970-241-6465	

35 APPLIANCE & HOME ELECTRONICS STORES

See Also Computer Stores p. 2036; Department Stores p. 2191; Furniture Stores p. 2344; Home Improvement Centers p. 2479

	City	State	Zip	Phone	Fax
A & A Mechanical Inc 1111 Ulrich Ave *Web:* aamechanical.com	Louisville	KY	40219	502-968-0164	
Aaca Parts & Supplies 3227 Military Pkwy Ste 244 *Web:* www.aacapartsandsupplies.com	Mesquite	TX	75149	972-223-8484	
ABC Appliance Inc 1 Silverdome Industrial Pk **Fax:* Hum Res ■ *TF:* 800-981-3866 ■ *Web:* www.abcwarehouse.com	Pontiac	MI	48343	248-335-4222	335-2568*
ACS of Texas 16622 Sperry Gardens Dr *Web:* www.acsoftexas.com	Houston	TX	77095	832-593-9990	
Air Cleaning Technologies Inc 1300 W Detroit *TF:* 800-351-1858 ■ *Web:* www.aircleaningtech.com	Broken Arrow	OK	74012	918-251-8000	
Air Systems of Sacramento Inc 10381 Old Placerville Rd *Web:* www.airsystems1.com	Sacramento	CA	95827	916-368-0336	
American TV & Appliance of Madison Inc 2404 W Beltline Hwy *Web:* www.americantv.com	Madison	WI	53713	608-271-1000	
Arthur F Schultz Co 939 W 26th St *Web:* www.arthurfschultz.com	Erie	PA	16508	814-454-8171	454-3052
Audio Direct 2004 E Irvington Rd Ste 264 *TF Cust Svc:* 888-628-3467 ■ *Web:* www.audio-direct.com	Tucson	AZ	85714	888-628-3467	
Best Buy Company Inc 7601 Penn Ave S *NYSE:* BBY ■ **Fax:* Cust Svc ■ *TF:* 888-237-8289 ■ *Web:* www.bestbuy.com	Minneapolis	MN	55423	612-291-1000	292-2323*

Phone Fax

Blencowe Group Inc, The 915 Lady St Ste 444 Columbia SC 29201 803-779-5866
Web: blencowe.com

Blume Mechanical LLC 11300 43rd St N Clearwater FL 33762 727-544-5993
Web: www.blume-mechanical.com

BrandsMart USA Corp 3200 SW 42nd St Fort Lauderdale FL 33312 800-432-8579
TF: 800-432-8579 ■ *Web:* www.brandsmartusa.com

Carey Sales & Services Inc
3141-47 Frederick Ave Baltimore MD 21229 410-945-7878
Web: www.careysales.com

Clay Dunn Enterprises Inc 1606 E Carson St Carson CA 90745 310-549-1698
Web: www.airtecperforms.com

Coilmaster Corp 440 Industrial Dr Moscow TN 38057 901-877-3333
Web: coilmastercorp.com

Conn's Inc 3295 College St Beaumont TX 77701 409-832-1696
NASDAQ: CONN ■ *TF Cust Svc:* 800-511-5750 ■ *Web:* www.conns.com

EarthLinked Technologies Inc
4151 S Pipkin Rd Lakeland FL 33811 863-701-0096
Web: earthlinked.com

East Coast Appliance Sales, Service & Parts Inc
2053 Laskin Rd Virginia Beach VA 23454 757-425-2883
Web: www.eastcoastappliance.com

Eklund's Appliance & TV Co
1007 Central Ave W Great Falls MT 59404 406-761-3430
Web: www.eklundsappliance.com

Farley Appliance 814 W Main St League City TX 77573 281-332-8000
Web: farleyapplianc.wpengine.com

Fry's Electronics 600 E Brokaw Rd San Jose CA 95112 408-350-1484 487-4700*
**Fax:* PR ■ *Web:* www.frys.com

GeoMicro Inc 3200 El Camino Real Ste 140 Irvine CA 92602 714-505-8868
Web: www.geomicro.com

GNP Audio Video Inc
122-A Foothill Blvd Ste 326 Arcadia CA 91006 626-577-7767
Web: www.gnpaudiovideo.com

Gregg Appliances Inc 4151 E 96th St Indianapolis IN 46240 317-848-8710 848-8723
NYSE: HGG ■ *TF:* 800-284-7344 ■ *Web:* www.hhgregg.com

Guardian Technologies LLC
7700 Saint Clair Ave Mentor OH 44060 440-942-6995
Web: www.guardiantechnologies.com

Harco Company Ltd 5915 Coopers Ave Mississauga ON L4Z1R9 905-890-1220
TF: 800-387-9503 ■ *Web:* www.harcoco.com

Howard's Appliance & Big Screen Superstores
901 E Imperial Hwy La Habra CA 90631 714-871-2700 871-5840
Web: www.howards.com

Interbond Corp of America
3200 SW 42nd St Fort Lauderdale FL 33312 800-432-8579 797-4061*
**Fax Area Code:* 954 ■ **Fax:* Hum Res ■ *TF:* 800-432-8579 ■ *Web:* www.brandsmartusa.com

JCM Associates Inc
301C Prince Georges Blvd Upper Marlboro MD 20774 301-390-5500
Web: www.gojcm.com

Midland Radio Corp 5900 Parretta Dr Kansas City MO 64120 816-241-8500 241-5713
Web: midlandusa.com

Mintie Corp 1114 San Fernando Rd Los Angeles CA 90065 323-225-4111
TF: 800-964-6843 ■ *Web:* www.mintie.com

National Auto Sound Inc 11001 E Hwy 40 Independence MO 64055 816-356-8700
Web: www.nationalautosound.com

Niederauer Inc 1976 W San Carlos St San Jose CA 95128 408-297-2440
Web: westernappliance.com

PC Richard & Son Inc 150 Price Pkwy Farmingdale NY 11735 631-773-4900
TF: 800-696-2000 ■ *Web:* www.pcrichard.com

Pieratt's 110 Mt Tabor Rd Lexington KY 40517 859-268-6000 268-9065
TF: 855-743-7288 ■ *Web:* www.pieratts.com

Queen City TV & Appliance Company Inc
2430 Queen City Dr Charlotte NC 28208 704-391-6000 391-6038
TF All: 800-365-6665 ■ *Web:* www.queencityonline.com

QuestSoft Corp 23441 S Pointe Dr Ste 270 Laguna Hills CA 92653 949-837-9506
Web: www.questsoft.com

RadioShack Corp 300 RadioShack Cir Fort Worth TX 76102 817-882-9380
NYSE: RSH ■ *TF:* 800-843-7422 ■ *Web:* www.radioshack.com

Radon Control Systems Inc 160 US Route 1 Freeport ME 04032 207-865-9200
Web: awqinc.com

Sherman Mechanical Inc 1075 Alexander Ct Cary IL 60013 847-462-1020
Web: www.shermanmech.com

Simutek Inc 3136 E Ft Lowell Rd Tucson AZ 85716 520-321-9077
Web: www.simutek.com

Sparkle Solutions LP
2700 Steeles Ave W Unit 4 Concord ON L4K3C8 905-660-2282
TF: 866-660-2282 ■ *Web:* www.sparklesolutions.ca

Starsound Audio Inc 2679 Oddie Blvd Reno NV 89512 775-331-1010
Web: www.starsound.com

Synaptec Software Inc
4155 E Jewell Ave Ste 600 Denver CO 80222 303-320-4420
Web: www.lawbase.com

Valu Home Centers Inc 45 S Rossler Ave Buffalo NY 14206 716-825-7377
Web: valuhomecenters.com

Videoland Inc 6808 Hornwood Dr Houston TX 77074 800-877-2900 772-0500*
**Fax Area Code:* 713 ■ *TF:* 800-877-2900 ■ *Web:* www.hometheaterstore.com

Wireless Zone 34 Industrial Pk Pl Middletown CT 06457 860-632-9494 652-0520*
**Fax Area Code:* 989 ■ *TF:* 888-881-2622 ■ *Web:* www.wirelesszone.com

Yale Appliance 296 Freeport St Dorchester MA 02122 617-825-9253
TF: 800-565-6435 ■ *Web:* www.yaleappliance.com

36 APPLIANCES - MAJOR - MFR

See Also Air Conditioning & Heating Equipment - Residential p. 1722

Phone Fax

Anaheim Mfg Co 2680 Orbiter St PO Box 4146 Brea CA 92821 310-542-5259 996-7073*
**Fax Area Code:* 714 ■ *TF Cust Svc:* 800-854-3229 ■ *Web:* www.anaheimmfg.com

AO Smith Corp
11270 W Pk Pl Ste 170 PO Box 245008 Milwaukee WI 53224 414-359-4000 359-4180
NYSE: AOS ■ *TF:* 800-359-4065 ■ *Web:* www.aosmith.com

Phone Fax

AO Smith Water Products Co
500 Tennessee Waltz Pkwy Ashland City TN 37015 800-527-1953 792-2163*
**Fax Area Code:* 615 ■ *TF:* 800-527-1953 ■ *Web:* www.hotwater.com

ASKO Appliances Inc PO Box 44848 Madison WI 53744 800-898-1879
TF: 800-898-1879 ■ *Web:* askona.com

Atlanta Attachment Co Inc
362 Industrial Pk Dr Lawrenceville GA 30045 770-963-7369 963-7641
TF: 877-206-5116 ■ *Web:* www.atlatt.com

Bock Water Heaters Inc 110 S Dickinson St Madison WI 53703 608-257-2225
Web: www.bockwaterheaters.com

Bradford White Corp 725 Talamore Dr Ambler PA 19002 215-641-9400 641-1612
TF: 800-523-2931 ■ *Web:* www.bradfordwhite.com

Brown Stove Works Inc 1422 Carolina Ave Cleveland TN 37320 423-476-6544 476-6599
TF All: 800-251-7485 ■ *Web:* www.brownstoveworksinc.com

Cemline Corp PO Box 55 Cheswick PA 15024 724-274-5430 274-5448
TF: 800-245-6268 ■ *Web:* www.cemline.com

Char-Broil 1442 Belfast Ave Columbus GA 31902 706-324-0421 576-6355*
**Fax:* Cust Svc ■ *TF Cust Svc:* 866-239-6777 ■ *Web:* www.charbroil.com

CookTek LLC 156 N Jefferson St Ste 300 Chicago IL 60661 312-563-9600 432-6220
TF: 888-266-5835 ■ *Web:* www.cooktek.com

Dwyer Products Corp 1226 Michael Dr Ste F Wood Dale IL 60191 630-741-7900 741-7974
TF: 800-822-0092 ■ *Web:* www.dwyerproducts.com

Ecosmart US LLC 3315 NW 167th St Miami Gardens FL 33056 305-623-7900
Web: www.ecosmartus.com

Electric Heater Co 45 Seymour St Stratford CT 06615 203-378-2659 378-3593
TF: 800-647-3165 ■ *Web:* www.hubbellheaters.com

Electrolux PO Box 212237 Ste 250 Augusta GA 30907 216-898-1800
Web: www.electroluxappliances.com

Electrolux Appliances PO Box 212237 Augusta GA 30907 877-435-3287
TF: 877-435-3287 ■ *Web:* www.electroluxappliances.com

Fisher & Paykel Appliances Inc
5900 Skylab Rd Huntington Beach CA 92647 888-936-7872 547-1971*
**Fax Area Code:* 800 ■ *TF:* 888-936-7872 ■ *Web:* www.fisherpaykel.com

In-Sink-Erator 4700 21st St Racine WI 53406 262-554-5432
TF: 800-558-5712 ■ *Web:* www.insinkerator.com

LG Electronics USA Inc
1000 Sylvan Ave Englewood Cliffs NJ 07632 201-816-2000
TF Tech Supp: 800-243-0000 ■ *Web:* www.lg.com

Lochinvar Corp 300 Maddox Simpson Pkwy Lebanon TN 37090 615-889-8900 547-1000
TF: 800-722-2101 ■ *Web:* www.lochinvar.com

Maytag Appliances 403 W Fourth St N Newton IA 50208 800-344-1274
TF Cust Svc: 800-344-1274 ■ *Web:* www.maytag.com

Miele Inc 9 Independence Way Princeton NJ 08540 609-419-9898 419-4298
TF: 800-843-7231 ■ *Web:* www.miele.com

Multi-Pak Corp 180 Atlantic St Hackensack NJ 07601 201-342-7474 342-6525
Web: www.multipakcorp.com

Northland Corp 1260 E Van Deinse St Greenville MI 48838 800-223-3900 754-9690*
**Fax Area Code:* 616 ■ *TF:* 800-223-3900

Peerless Premier Appliance Co
119 S 14th St Belleville IL 62222 941-763-3915 235-1771*
**Fax Area Code:* 618 ■ *TF:* 800-858-5844 ■ *Web:* www.premierrange.com

Roper Corp 1507 Broomtown Rd La Fayette GA 30728 706-638-5100
Web: roperappliances.com

Sanyo Fisher Co 21605 Plummer St Chatsworth CA 91311 818-998-7322 717-2759

Sharp Electronics Corp 1 Sharp Plz Mahwah NJ 07430 201-529-8200 529-8413
TF: 800-237-4277 ■ *Web:* www.sharpusa.com

Vaughn Manufacturing Corp
26 Old Elm St PO Box 5431 Salisbury MA 01952 978-462-6683 462-6497
TF: 800-282-8446 ■ *Web:* www.vaughncorp.com

Weber-Stephen Products Co 200 E Daniels Rd Palatine IL 60067 800-446-1071
TF Cust Svc: 800-446-1071 ■ *Web:* www.weber.com

Whirlpool Corp 2000 N M-63 Benton Harbor MI 49022 269-923-5000
NYSE: WHR ■ *TF:* 800-253-1301 ■ *Web:* www.whirlpoolcorp.com

Whirlpool Corp North American Region
2000 N M-63 Benton Harbor MI 49022 269-923-5000 923-3525*
**Fax:* Hum Res ■ *TF:* 800-253-1301 ■ *Web:* www.whirlpoolcorp.com

Wisco Industries Inc 736 Janesville St Oregon WI 53575 608-835-3106 835-7399
TF: 800-999-4726 ■ *Web:* www.wiscoind.com

37 APPLIANCES - SMALL - MFR

See Also Air Purification Equipment - Household p. 1722; Vacuum Cleaners - Household p. 3284

Phone Fax

Abatement Technologies
605 Satellite Blvd Ste 300 Suwanee GA 30024 678-889-4200 358-2394*
**Fax Area Code:* 800 ■ *TF:* 800-634-9091 ■ *Web:* www.abatement.com

Adams Mfg Company Inc 9790 Midwest Ave Cleveland OH 44125 216-587-6801 587-6807
Web: www.adamsmanufacturing.com

Aerus L L C 5420 Lyndon B Johnson Fwy Ste 800 Dallas TX 75240 214-378-4000
Web: www.aerushome.com

Aisin Holdings of America Inc
1665 E Fourth St Seymour IN 47274 812-524-8144 524-8146
Web: www.aisinworld.com

Andis Co 1800 County Rd H Sturtevant WI 53177 262-884-2600 884-1100
TF: 800-558-9441 ■ *Web:* www.andis.com

Bernina of America Inc 3702 Prairie Lake Ct Aurora IL 60504 630-978-2500 978-8214
Web: www.bernina.com

Broan-NuTone LLC 926 W State St PO Box 140 Hartford WI 53027 262-673-4340 673-8709
TF Cust Svc: 800-558-1711 ■ *Web:* www.broan.com

Bunn-O-Matic Corp 1400 Stevenson Dr Springfield IL 62703 217-529-6601
TF: 800-637-8606 ■ *Web:* www.bunn.com

Cadet Mfg Company Inc
2500 W Fourth Plain Blvd Vancouver WA 98660 360-693-2505 694-6939
TF: 800-442-2338 ■ *Web:* cadetheat.com

Casablanca Fan Co 761 Corporate Ctr Dr Pomona CA 91768 909-689-1477 629-0958
TF: 888-227-2178 ■ *Web:* www.casablancafanco.com

City of Chula Vista 276 Fourth Ave Chula Vista CA 91910 619-691-5047
TF: 877-478-5478 ■ *Web:* chulavistaca.gov

Conair Corp 1 Cummings Pt Rd Stamford CT 06902 203-351-9000 351-9180
OTC: CNGA ■ *TF:* 800-326-6247 ■ *Web:* www.conair.com

				Phone	Fax
Craftmade International Inc 650 S Royal Ln *OTC:* CRFT ■ *TF:* 800-486-4892 ■ *Web:* www.craftmade.com	Coppell	TX	75019	972-393-3800	304-1728
Cuisinart 1 Cummings Pt Rd *TF:* 800-726-0190 ■ *Web:* www.cuisinart.com	Stamford	CT	06902	203-975-4609	975-4660
El Electronics LLC 1800 Shames Dr *TF:* 877-346-3837 ■ *Web:* www.electroind.com	Westbury	NY	11590	516-334-0870	338-4741
Electro Industries Inc 2150 W River St *Web:* www.electromn.com	Monticello	MN	55362	763-295-4138	
Electrolux PO Box 212237 Ste 250 *Web:* www.electroluxappliances.com	Augusta	GA	30907	216-898-1800	
Fan-Tastic Vent Corp 2083 S Almont Ave *TF:* 800-521-0298 ■ *Web:* www.fantasticvent.com	Imlay City	MI	48444	810-724-3818	
Hamilton Beach/Proctor-Silex Inc 4421 Waterfront Dr *TF Cust Svc:* 800-851-8900 ■ *Web:* www.hamiltonbeach.com	Glen Allen	VA	23060	804-273-9777	
Hotronic USA Inc 25 Omega Dr *Web:* www.hotronic.com	Williston	VT	05495	802-862-7403	863-6519
Hunter Fan Co 7130 Goodlett Farms Pkwy Ste 400 *TF:* 888-830-1326 ■ *Web:* www.hunterfan.com	Memphis	TN	38016	901-743-1360	
Jarden Consumer Solutions 2381 Executive Ctr Dr *TF:* 800-777-5452 ■ *Web:* www.jardencs.com	Boca Raton	FL	33431	561-912-4100	
Kaz Home Environment 250 Tpke Rd *Web:* www.kaz.com	Southborough	MA	01772	508-490-7000	
KAZ Inc 250 Tpke Rd *TF:* 800-477-0457 ■ *Web:* www.kaz.com	Southborough	MA	01772	800-477-0457	
King Electrical Manufacturing Co 9131 Tenth Ave S *TF:* 800-603-5464 ■ *Web:* www.king-electric.com	Seattle	WA	98108	206-762-0400	763-7738
Lasko Metal Products Inc 820 Lincoln Ave *TF:* 800-233-0268 ■ *Web:* www.laskoproducts.com	West Chester	PA	19380	610-692-7400	696-4648
LG Electronics USA Inc 1000 Sylvan Ave *TF Tech Supp:* 800-243-0000 ■ *Web:* www.lg.com	Englewood Cliffs	NJ	07632	201-816-2000	
Marley Engineered Products 470 Beauty Spot Rd E *TF:* 800-452-4179 ■ *Web:* www.marleymep.com	Bennettsville	SC	29512	843-479-4006	479-8912
National Presto Industries Inc 3925 N Hastings Way *NYSE:* NPK ■ *TF:* 800-877-0441 ■ *Web:* www.gopresto.com	Eau Claire	WI	54703	715-839-2121	
Nellcor Puritan Bennett LLC 6135 Gunbarrel Ave *Web:* www.nellcor.com	Boulder	CO	80301	303-305-2512	
Nesco/American Harvest 1700 Monroe St PO Box 237 *TF Cust Svc:* 800-288-4545 ■ *Web:* www.nesco.com	Two Rivers	WI	54241	920-793-1368	793-1086
Schawbel Corp 26 Crosby Dr *TF:* 866-753-3837 ■ *Web:* www.thermacell.com/mosquito-repellent	Bedford	MA	01730	781-541-6900	
Sharp Electronics Corp 1 Sharp Plz *TF:* 800-237-4277 ■ *Web:* www.sharpusa.com	Mahwah	NJ	07430	201-529-8200	529-8413
Singer Sewing Co 1224 Hill Quaker Blvd PO Box 7017 *TF:* 877-738-9869 ■ *Web:* www.singerco.com	La Vergne	TN	37086	615-213-0880	213-0994
Vita-Mix Corp 8615 Usher Rd *TF:* 800-848-2649 ■ *Web:* www.vitamix.com	Cleveland	OH	44138	440-235-4840	235-3726
West Bend Housewares LLC 2845 Wingate St PO Box 2780 **Fax Area Code:* 224 ■ *TF:* 866-290-1851 ■ *Web:* www.westbend.com	West Bend	WI	53095	866-290-1851	513-2498*
Whirlpool Corp KitchenAid Div 553 Benson Rd *TF:* 800-422-1230 ■ *Web:* www.kitchenaid.com	Benton Harbor	MI	49022	800-422-1230	
World Dryer Corp 5700 McDermott Dr *TF:* 800-323-0701 ■ *Web:* www.worlddryer.com	Berkeley	IL	60163	708-449-6950	449-6958

38 APPLIANCES - WHOL

				Phone	Fax
All Inc 185 Plato Blvd W *TF:* 800-829-2127 ■ *Web:* www.allinc.com	Saint Paul	MN	55107	651-227-6331	292-0541
Almo Corp 2709 Commerce Way **Fax:* Hum Res ■ *TF:* 800-345-2566 ■ *Web:* www.almo.com	Philadelphia	PA	19154	215-698-4000	698-4080*
Aves Audio Visual Systems Inc PO Box 500 *TF:* 800-365-2837 ■ *Web:* www.avesav.com	Sugar Land	TX	77487	281-295-1300	295-1310
Blodgett Supply Co Inc 100 Ave D PO Box 759 *TF:* 888-888-3424 ■ *Web:* www.blodgettsupply.com	Williston	VT	05495	802-864-9831	229-5105
Brady Marketing Co 1331N California Blvd Ste 320 *Web:* www.bradymarketing.com	Walnut Creek	CA	94596	925-676-1300	676-3082
Brooke Distributors Inc 16250 NW 52nd Ave *TF:* 800-275-8792 ■ *Web:* brookedist.com	Hialeah	FL	33014	305-624-9752	620-3988
Bursma Electronic Distributing Inc 2851 Buchanan Ave SW *TF:* 800-777-2604 ■ *Web:* www.bursma.com	Grand Rapids	MI	49548	616-831-0080	
C & L Supply Co PO Box 578 *TF:* 800-256-6411 ■ *Web:* www.clsupplyinc.com	Vinita	OK	74301	800-256-6411	
Carl Schaedel & Company Inc 4 Sperry Rd *Web:* www.carlschaedel.com	Fairfield	NJ	07004	973-244-1311	
Ceavco Audio-visual Co 6240 W 54th Ave *Web:* www.ceavco.com	Arvada	CO	80002	303-539-3500	
Cowboy Maloney's Electric City 1313 Harding St *Web:* cowboy-maloney.com	Jackson	MS	39202	601-948-5600	
Cunningham Distributing Inc 2015 Mills Ave	El Paso	TX	79901	915-533-6993	545-1320
DAS Inc 724 Lawn Rd **Fax Area Code:* 800 ■ *TF:* 866-622-7979 ■ *Web:* www.das-roadpro.com	Palmyra	PA	17078	717-964-3642	437-3659*
E&S International Enterprises Inc 7801 Hayvenhurst Ave *Web:* www.esintl.com	Van Nuys	CA	91406	818-887-0700	
Eagle Distributors LLC 2439 Albany St *Web:* www.eagledistributors.com	Kenner	LA	70062	504-464-5991	
Electrical Distributing Inc 4600 NW St Helens Rd *TF:* 800-877-4229 ■ *Web:* www.edinw.com	Portland	OR	97210	503-226-4044	226-4040
Erb Company Inc 1400 Seneca St *Web:* erbco.com	Buffalo	NY	14210	716-825-1400	
Factory Direct Appliance Inc 14105 Marshall Dr *Web:* www.kcfda.com	Lenexa	KS	66215	913-888-8028	888-7570
Felix Storch Inc 770 Garrison Ave *Web:* www.summitappliance.com	Bronx	NY	10474	718-893-3900	
Gamla Enterprises North America Inc 875 Ave of The Americas Ste 205 *TF:* 800-442-6526	New York	NY	10001	212-947-3790	947-3559
Gerhard's Appliances 290 N Keswick Ave *Web:* www.gerhardsappliance.com	Glenside	PA	19038	215-884-8650	884-0349
Gotham Sales Co 302 Main St *Web:* www.gothamsales.com	Millburn	NJ	07041	973-912-8412	
H Schultz & Sons Inc 777 Lehigh Ave *Web:* www.housewaresandthings.com	Union	NJ	07083	908-687-5400	687-1788
HB Communications Inc 60 Dodge Ave *TF:* 800-243-4414 ■ *Web:* www.hbcommunications.com	North Haven	CT	06473	203-234-9246	234-2013
Helen of Troy Ltd 1 Helen of Troy Plz *NASDAQ:* HELE ■ *Web:* www.hotus.com	El Paso	TX	79912	915-225-8000	225-8004
Home Entertainment Distribution Inc 120 Shawmut Rd **Fax Area Code:* 866 ■ *TF:* 800-343-9619 ■ *Web:* www.enservio.com	Canton	MA	02021	888-567-7557	200-3764*
John m Hartel & Company Inc 144 N Kinderkamack Rd *Web:* jmhartel.com	Montvale	NY	07645	845-735-3666	
Klaus Cos 8400 N Allen Rd *Web:* www.klausco.com	Peoria	IL	61615	309-691-4840	
M.d.m. Commercial Enterprises Inc 1102 A1a N Ste 205 **Fax Area Code:* 904 ■ *TF:* 800-359-6741 ■ *Web:* www.mdmcommercial.com	Ponte Vedra	FL	32082	800-359-6741	241-3133*
Midwest Sales & Service Inc 917 S Chapin St *TF:* 800-772-7262 ■ *Web:* midwestsales.org	South Bend	IN	46601	574-287-3365	
Molok North America Ltd 179 Norpark Ave *TF:* 877-558-5576 ■ *Web:* molokna.com	Mount Forest	ON	N0G2L0	519-323-9909	
Nelson & Small Inc 212 Canco Rd *TF:* 800-341-0780 ■ *Web:* www.nelsonsmall.com	Portland	ME	04103	207-775-5666	775-4303
Next Plumbing Supply 1839 Old Okeechobee Rd *Web:* nextps.com	West Palm Beach	FL	33409	561-689-9060	
O'Rourke Sales Co 3885 Elmore Ave Ste 100 *Web:* www.orourkesales.com	Davenport	IA	52807	563-823-1501	823-1534
Oregon Scientific Inc 19861 SW 95th Pl *Web:* global.oregonscientific.com	Tualatin	OR	97062	503-783-5100	691-6208
Peirce-Phelps Inc 2000 N 59th St *TF:* 800-222-2742 ■ *Web:* www.peirce.com	Philadelphia	PA	19131	215-879-7000	879-5141
Potter Distributing Inc 4037 Roger B Chaffee Blvd *TF:* 800-748-0568 ■ *Web:* www.potterdistributing.com	Grand Rapids	MI	49548	616-531-6860	531-9578
Power Plus Sound & Lighting Inc 2460 Grand Ave *Web:* www.powerpluscorp.com	Vista	CA	92081	760-727-1717	
Precision Trading Corp 15800 NW 48th Ave *Web:* www.precisiontrading.com	Miami Gardens	FL	33014	305-592-4500	593-6169
Prudential Builders Ctr 3304 E Ferry *Web:* mystore411.com	Spokane	WA	99202	509-535-2401	
R & B Wholesale Distributors Inc 2350 S Milliken Ave *TF:* 800-627-7539 ■ *Web:* www.rbdist.com	Ontario	CA	91761	909-230-5400	230-5405
Radio Distributing Company Inc 27015 Trolley Industrial Dr *Web:* www.radiodistributing.com	Taylor	MI	48180	313-295-4500	
Roth Distributing Co 11300 W 47th St *TF:* 800-363-3818 ■ *Web:* www.rothliving.com	Minnetonka	MN	55343	952-933-4428	
Servall Co 6761 E Ten Mile Rd *TF:* 800-856-9874 ■ *Web:* 1stsourceservall.com	Center Line	MI	48015	586-754-9985	
Siano Appliance Distributors Inc 5372 Pleasant View Rd *TF:* 800-742-6699 ■ *Web:* www.sianoappliance.com	Memphis	TN	38134	901-382-5833	372-3621
Speco Technologies 200 New Hwy *TF:* 800-645-5516 ■ *Web:* www.specotech.com	Amityville	NY	11701	631-957-8700	957-9142
Tacony Corp 1760 Gilsinn Ln *Web:* www.tacony.com	Fenton	MO	63026	636-349-3000	349-2333
Telerent Leasing Corp 4191 Fayetteville Rd *TF:* 800-626-0682 ■ *Web:* www.telerent.com	Raleigh	NC	27603	919-772-8604	
Tri-State Video Services Inc 1379 Pittsburgh Rd *TF:* 888-382-7768 ■ *Web:* www.tristatevideo.com	Valencia	PA	16059	724-898-1630	
WASH Multifamily Laundry Systems 100 N Sepulveda Blvd 12th Fl *TF General:* 800-421-6897 ■ *Web:* www.washlaundry.com	El Segundo	CA	90245	800-421-6897	
Westland Sales PO Box 427 *TF:* 800-356-0766 ■ *Web:* www.splendide.com	Clackamas	OR	97015	503-655-2563	656-8829
Whirlpool Canada 200-6750 Century Ave *TF:* 800-807-6777	Mississauga	ON	L5N0B7	905-821-6400	821-7871
Williams Kitchen & Bath 658 Richmond NW *Web:* www.williamskitchen.com	Grand Rapids	MI	49504	616-771-0505	
Woodson & Bozeman Inc 3870 New Getwell Rd *TF:* 800-876-4243 ■ *Web:* www.woodsonbozeman.com	Memphis	TN	38118	901-362-1500	362-1509

39 APPLICATION SERVICE PROVIDERS (ASPS)

Application Service Providers rent, deliver, license, manage, and/or host proprietary and/or third-party business software ("applications") and/or computer services to multiple users (customers). Included here are companies that host software applications as well as companies that provide the equipment necessary to do so.

				Phone	Fax
Access Data Corp 2 Chatham Ctr 2nd Fl *Web:* access-data.broadridge.com	Pittsburgh	PA	15219	412-201-6000	201-6060

Phone Fax

AllMeds Inc 151 Lafayette Dr Ste 401 Oak Ridge TN 37830 865-482-1999 481-0921
TF: 888-343-6337 ■ *Web:* www.allmeds.com

Amber Road Inc 1 Meadowlands Plz East Rutherford NJ 07073 201-935-8588 935-5187
Web: www.amberroad.com

Application Consulting Group
1639 NJ-10 Ste 107 Parsippany NJ 07054 973-898-0012 898-6647
Web: www.acgi.com

Ariba Inc 807 11th Ave Sunnyvale CA 94089 650-390-1000
NASDAQ: ARBA ■ *TF:* 866-772-7422 ■ *Web:* www.ariba.com

Avanade Inc 818 Stewart St Seattle WA 98101 206-239-5600 239-5605
TF: 844-282-6233 ■ *Web:* www.avanade.com

Avazpour Networking Services Inc
10895 Grandview Dr Ste 250 Overland Park KS 66210 913-498-8777

Baillio's Inc 5301 Menaul Blvd NE Albuquerque NM 87110 505-883-7511
TF: 800-540-7511 ■ *Web:* baillios.com

BizLand Inc 70 BlanchaRd Rd Burlington MA 01803 800-249-5263
TF: 800-249-5263 ■ *Web:* www.bizland.com

BroadVision Inc
1600 Seaport Blvd Ste 550 Redwood City CA 94063 650-295-0716
NASDAQ: BVSN ■ *Web:* www.broadvision.com

Cayenta Canada Corp 4200 N Fraser Way Ste 201 Burnaby BC V5J5K7 604-570-4300 291-0742
TF: 866-229-3682 ■ *Web:* www.cayenta.com

Centric Software Inc
655 Campbell Technology Pkwy Ste 200 Campbell CA 95008 408-574-7802 866-5869
Web: www.centricsoftware.com

Chemical Safety Corp
5901 Christie Ave Ste 502 Emeryville CA 94608 510-594-1000 594-1100
TF: 888-594-1100 ■ *Web:* www.chemicalsafety.com

Cision Inc 12051 Indian Creek Ct Beltsville MD 20705 301-459-2590 459-2827
NASDAQ: VOCS ■ *TF:* 866-639-5087 ■ *Web:* www.vocus.com

CliniComp International 9655 Towne Ctr Dr San Diego CA 92121 858-546-8202 546-1801
TF: 800-350-8202 ■ *Web:* www.clinicomp.com

Cogency Software Inc
500 Airport Blvd Ste 152 Burlingame CA 94010 650-685-2500 685-2515
Web: www.cogencysoftware.com

Computer Programs & Systems Inc (CPSI)
6600 Wall St Mobile AL 36695 251-639-8100 639-8214
NASDAQ: CPSI ■ *Web:* www.cpsi.com

Connectria Hosting
10845 Olive Blvd Ste 300 Saint Louis MO 63141 314-587-7000 587-7090
TF: 800-781-7820 ■ *Web:* www.connectria.com

Crexendo Inc 1615 S 52nd St Tempe AZ 85281 801-431-4695
OTC: CXDO ■ *TF:* 866-621-6111 ■ *Web:* crexendo.com

CyberData Inc 20 Max Ave Hicksville NY 11801 516-942-8000 942-0800
Web: cyberdata.com

Daptiv 1008 Western Ave Ste 700 Seattle WA 98101 206-341-9117 341-9123
TF: 888-621-8361 ■ *Web:* www.daptiv.com

Digital River Inc 10380 Bren Rd W Minnetonka MN 55343 800-598-7450 253-8497*
NASDAQ: DRIV ■ **Fax Area Code:* 952 ■ *TF:* 800-598-7450 ■ *Web:* www.digitalriver.com

DigitalWork Inc
14300 N Northsight Blvd Ste 206 Scottsdale AZ 85260 877-496-7571 272-6923*
**Fax Area Code:* 480 ■ *TF:* 877-496-7571 ■ *Web:* www.digitalwork.com

DocMan Technologies 31300 Bainbridge Rd Cleveland OH 44122 440-542-9660
Web: www.docmantech.com

E-Builder Inc 1800 NW 69 Ave Ste 201 Plantation FL 33313 954-556-6701
TF: 800-580-9322 ■ *Web:* www.e-builder.net

E-Markets Inc 807 Mountain Ave Ste 200 Berthoud CO 80513 877-674-7419
TF: 877-674-7419 ■ *Web:* www.e-markets.com

eGain Communications Corp
1252 Borregas Ave Mountain View CA 94043 408-636-4500 230-7600*
NASDAQ: EGAN ■ **Fax Area Code:* 650 ■ *TF:* 888-603-4246 ■ *Web:* www.egain.com

Electric Mail Company Inc
3999 Henning Dr Ste 300 Burnaby BC V5C6P9 604-482-1111 482-1110
TF: 866-950-5333 ■ *Web:* www.electricmail.com

Emdeon Business Services LLC
3055 Lebanon Pk Nashville TN 37214 615-932-3000
Web: www.emdeon.com

ePlus Inc 13595 Dulles Technology Dr Herndon VA 20171 703-984-8400 984-8600
NASDAQ: PLUS ■ *TF:* 888-482-1122 ■ *Web:* www.eplus.com

FinancialCAD Corp 13450 102nd Ave Ste 1750 Surrey BC V3T5X3 604-957-1200 957-1201
TF: 800-304-0702 ■ *Web:* www.fincad.com

Flying Aces Technology LLC
305 N Westgate Rd Ste 100 Mount Prospect IL 60056 847-299-7815
Web: www.flying-aces.com

HealthMEDX 5100 N Towne Ctr Dr Ozark MO 65721 417-582-1816 582-0296
TF: 877-875-1200 ■ *Web:* www.healthmedx.com

Horseman's Guarantee Corp of America
25 W Palatine Rd Palatine IL 60067 847-394-4210 358-7635
Web: www.hgcaonline.com

I-Business Network LLC
2617 Sandy Plains Rd Ste B Marietta GA 30066 678-627-0646 627-0688
Web: www.i-bn.net

Infogain Corp 485 Alberto Way Los Gatos CA 95032 408-355-6000 355-7000
Web: www.infogain.com

Intacct Corp 300 Park Ave Ste 1400 San Jose CA 95110 408-878-0900
TF: 877-437-7765

Internap Network Services Corp
250 Williams St Ste E-100 Atlanta GA 30303 404-302-9700 475-0520
NASDAQ: INAP ■ *TF:* 877-843-7627 ■ *Web:* www.internap.com

IntraLinks Inc 150 E 42nd St Ste 8 New York NY 10017 212-543-7700 543-7978
TF: 888-546-5383 ■ *Web:* www.intralinks.com

Jamcracker Inc
4677 Old Ironsides Dr Ste 450 Santa Clara CA 95054 408-496-5500 496-9944
Web: www.jamcracker.com

Journyx Inc 7600 Burnet Rd Ste. 300 Austin TX 78757 512-834-8888 834-8858
TF: 800-755-9878 ■ *Web:* www.journyx.com

Kleinschmidt Inc 450 Lake Cook Rd Deerfield IL 60015 847-945-1000 945-4619
TF: 800-824-2330 ■ *Web:* www.kleinschmidt.com

LivePerson Inc 462 Seventh Ave 3rd Fl New York NY 10018 212-609-4200 609-4201
NASDAQ: LPSN ■ *Web:* www.liveperson.com

MetraTech Corp 200 W St Waltham MA 02451 781-839-8300 839-8301
Web: www.metratech.com

Mobile Smith 5400 Trinity Rd Ste 320 Raleigh NC 27607 800-578-9000
TF: 800-578-9000 ■ *Web:* www.mobilesmith.com

Phone Fax

NeoMedia Technologies Inc
1515 Walnut St Ste 100 Boulder CO 80302 678-638-0460 648-9922*
**Fax Area Code:* 636 ■ *TF:* 800-413-4559 ■ *Web:* www.neom.com

NetBase Corp 7960 Donegan Dr Ste 225 Manassas VA 20109 703-396-7909
Web: netbasecorp.net

onProject Inc PO Box 104 Franklin Lakes NJ 07417 973-971-9970 971-9970
TF: 877-936-6776 ■ *Web:* www.onproject.com

OpenTable Inc 799 Market St 4th Fl San Francisco CA 94103 415-344-4200
Web: www.opentable.com

Oracle Corp 500 Oracle Pkwy Redwood Shores CA 94065 650-506-7000 506-7200
NYSE: ORCL ■ *TF Sales:* 800-392-2999 ■ *Web:* www.oracle.com

Outstart Inc 745 Atlantic Ave 4th Fl Boston MA 02111 617-897-6800 897-6801
TF: 877-971-9171 ■ *Web:* www.outstart.com

Paramount Technologies Inc
1374 EW Maple Rd Walled Lake MI 48390 248-960-0909 960-1919
TF: 800-725-4408 ■ *Web:* paramounttechnologies.com

PBM Corp 20600 Chagrin Blvd Ste 450 Cleveland OH 44122 216-283-7999 283-7931
TF: 800-341-5809 ■ *Web:* www.pbmcorp.com

Perfect Commerce Inc
1 Compass Way Ste 120 Newport News VA 23606 757-766-8211
TF Sales: 877-871-3788 ■ *Web:* perfect.com

PhDx Systems Inc
1001 University Blvd SE Ste 103 Albuquerque NM 87106 505-764-0174 764-0074
TF: 888-999-7439 ■ *Web:* www.phdx.com

PicoSearch LLC 10 Fawcett St Cambridge MA 02138 617-547-4020 576-7227

Pointivity 5355 Mira Sorrento Pl # 600 San Diego CA 92121 858-777-6900 777-6915
Web: www.pointivity.com

Premiere Global Services Inc (PGI)
3280 Peachtree Rd NE Ste 1000 Atlanta GA 30305 719-457-6901
NYSE: PGI ■ *TF:* 866-548-3203 ■ *Web:* www.pgi.com

Prodata Systems Inc 11007 Slater Ave NE Kirkland WA 98033 425-296-4168 822-3443
TF: 866-582-7485 ■ *Web:* www.prodata.com

Prosum technology services
2201 Park Pl Ste 102 El Segundo CA 90245 310-426-0600 426-0690
TF: 888-477-6786 ■ *Web:* www.prosum.com

PureWorks Inc 5000 Meridian Blvd Ste 600 Franklin TN 37067 615-367-4404 367-3887
TF: 888-202-3016 ■ *Web:* www.ulworkplace.com

Radware Inc 575 Corporate Dr Lobby 2 Mahwah NJ 07430 201-512-9771 512-9774
TF: 888-234-5763 ■ *Web:* www.radware.com

Resource Development Corp
280 Daines St Ste 200 Birmingham MI 48009 248-646-2300 646-0789
TF: 800-360-7222 ■ *Web:* www.resourcedev.com

Salesnet 6340 Sugarloaf Pkwy Ste 200 Duluth GA 30097 866-732-8632
TF: 866-732-8632 ■ *Web:* www.salesnet.com

Strategic Systems Consulting Inc
7742 Spalding Dr Ste 363 Norcross GA 30092 770-448-2100 601-7454*
**Fax Area Code:* 404 ■ *Web:* www.eapps.com

Streamline Health Solutions Inc
10200 Alliance Rd Ste 200 Cincinnati OH 45242 513-794-7100 794-9770
NASDAQ: STRM ■ *TF:* 800-878-5269 ■ *Web:* streamlinehealth.net

Syntrio 50 California St Ste 3260 San Francisco CA 94111 415-951-7913 951-7915
TF: 888-289-6670 ■ *Web:* www.syntrio.com

Talisma Corp 777 Yamato Rd Boca Raton FL 33431 561-923-2500
TF: 866-397-2537 ■ *Web:* www.talisma.com

TALX Corp 11432 Lackland Dr Saint Louis MO 63146 314-214-7000 214-7588
TF: 800-888-8277 ■ *Web:* www.talx.com

Thoughtworks Inc 200 E Randolph St 25th Fl Chicago IL 60601 312-373-1000 373-1001
Web: www.thoughtworks.com

Toolwire Inc 7031 Koll Ctr Pkwy Ste 220 Pleasanton CA 94566 925-227-8500 227-8501
TF: 866-935-8665 ■ *Web:* www.toolwire.com

UnicornHRO 25 Hanover Rd Ste B Florham Park NJ 07932 973-360-0688
TF: 800-368-8149 ■ *Web:* www.unicornhro.com

WebMD Health Holdings Inc
111 Eigth Ave 7th Fl New York NY 10011 212-624-3700
NASDAQ: WBMD ■ *Web:* www.webmd.com

Workscape Inc 123 Selton St Marlborough MA 01752 508-861-5500 573-9500
Web: www.workscape.com

40 AQUARIUMS - PUBLIC

See Also Botanical Gardens & Arboreta p. 1870; Zoos & Wildlife Parks p. 3316

Phone Fax

Adventure Aquarium 1 Riverside Dr Camden NJ 08103 856-365-3300 365-3311
TF: 800-616-5297 ■ *Web:* www.adventureaquarium.com

Aquarium of the Bay
The Embarcadero at Beach St Pier 39 San Francisco CA 94133 415-623-5300 623-5324
Web: www.aquariumofthebay.org

Aquarium of the Pacific 100 Aquarium Way Long Beach CA 90802 562-590-3100
Web: www.aquariumofpacific.org

Arborcrest Gardens Inc 205 Evergreen Ln Boone NC 28607 828-265-4873
Web: www.arborcrestgardens.org

Atlantic City Aquarium
800 N New Hampshire Ave Atlantic City NJ 08401 609-348-2880
Web: acaquarium.com

Birch Aquarium at Scripps
2300 Expedition Way La Jolla CA 92037 858-534-3474 534-7114
Web: www.aquarium.ucsd.edu

Cabrillo Marine Aquarium
3720 Stephen M White Dr San Pedro CA 90731 310-548-7562 548-2649
Web: www.cabrillomarineaquarium.org

Clearwater Marine Aquarium
249 Windward Passage Clearwater FL 33767 727-441-1790
Web: www.cmaquarium.org

Dallas World Aquarium 1801 N Griffin St Dallas TX 75202 214-720-2224
Web: www.dwazoo.com

Dauphin Island Sea Lab Estuarium
101 Bienville Blvd Dauphin Island AL 36528 251-861-2141 861-4646
Web: www.disl.org

Downtown Aquarium 410 Bagby St & Memorial Dr Houston TX 77002 713-223-3474
Web: www.aquariumrestaurants.com

Downtown Aquarium - Denver 700 Water St Denver CO 80211 303-561-4450
Web: www.aquariumrestaurants.com

Phone Fax

Florida Aquarium 701 Channelside Dr Tampa FL 33602 813-273-4000
TF: 800-353-4741 ■ *Web:* www.flaquarium.org

Georgia Aquarium 225 Baker St Atlanta GA 30313 404-581-4000
Web: www.georgiaaquarium.org

Great Lakes Aquarium 353 Harbor Dr Duluth MN 55802 218-740-3474 740-2020
Web: www.glaquarium.org

Gulf Coast Research Laboratory
703 E Beach Dr Ocean Springs MS 39564 228-872-4200

John G Shedd Aquarium 1200 S Lk Shore Dr Chicago IL 60605 312-939-2438
Web: www.sheddaquarium.org

Key West Aquarium 1 Whitehead St Key West FL 33040 305-296-2051
TF: 888-544-5927 ■ *Web:* www.keywestaquarium.com

Maria Mitchell Assn Aquarium 4 Vestal St Nantucket MA 02554 508-228-9198 228-1031
Web: mariamitchell.org

Marineland of Florida
9600 Ocean Shore Blvd Saint Augustine FL 32080 904-460-1275 471-1111
TF: 877-933-3402 ■ *Web:* www.marineland.net

Marinelife Ctr of Juno Beach
14200 US Hwy 1 Loggerhead Pk Juno Beach FL 33408 561-627-8280 627-8305
TF: 800-843-5451 ■ *Web:* www.marinelife.org

Maritime Aquarium at Norwalk 10 N Water St Norwalk CT 06854 203-852-0700 838-5416
Web: www.maritimeaquarium.org

Maui Ocean Ctr 192 Maalaea Rd Wailuku HI 96793 808-270-7000 270-7070
TF: 800-350-5634 ■ *Web:* www.mauioceancenter.com

Miami Seaquarium 4400 Rickenbacker Cswy Miami FL 33149 305-361-5705 361-6077
Web: www.miamiseaquarium.com

Monterey Bay Aquarium 886 Cannery Row Monterey CA 93940 831-648-4800
TF: 866-963-9645 ■ *Web:* www.montereybayaquarium.org

Mystic Aquarium & Institute for Exploration
55 Coogan Blvd Mystic CT 06355 860-572-5955 572-5969
Web: www.mysticaquarium.org

National Aquarium in Baltimore
501 E Pratt St Pier 3 Baltimore MD 21202 410-576-3800 576-8641
Web: www.aqua.org

National Park Aquarium 209 Central Ave Hot Springs AR 71901 501-624-3474
Web: nationalparkaquarium.org

New England Aquarium 1 Central Wharf Boston MA 02110 617-973-5200
Web: www.neaq.org

Newport Aquarium 1 Aquarium Way Newport KY 41071 859-261-7444 261-5888
TF: 800-406-3474 ■ *Web:* www.newportaquarium.com

North Carolina Aquarium at Fort Fisher
900 Loggerhead Rd Kure Beach NC 28449 910-458-8257 458-6812
TF: 800-832-3474 ■ *Web:* www.ncaquariums.com

North Carolina Aquarium on Roanoke Island
374 Airport Rd PO Box 967 Manteo NC 27954 252-475-2300 473-1980
TF: 800-832-3474 ■ *Web:* www.ncaquariums.com

Oklahoma Aquarium 300 S Aquarium Dr Jenks OK 74037 918-296-3474
Web: www.okaquarium.org

Oregon Coast Aquarium 2820 SE Ferry Slip Rd Newport OR 97365 541-867-3474 867-6846
TF: 800-452-7888 ■ *Web:* www.aquarium.org

Parc Aquarium du Quebec 1675 des Hotels Ave Quebec QC G1W4S3 418-659-5264 646-9238
TF: 866-659-5264 ■ *Web:* www.sepaq.com

Pittsburgh Zoo & PPG Aquarium 1 Wild Pl Pittsburgh PA 15206 412-665-3640 665-3661
TF: 800-732-0999 ■ *Web:* www.pittsburghzoo.org

Point Defiance Zoo & Aquarium 5400 N Pearl St Tacoma WA 98407 253-591-5337 591-5448
Web: www.pdza.org

Ripley's Aquarium 1110 Celebrity Cir Myrtle Beach SC 29577 843-916-0888
TF: 800-734-8888 ■ *Web:* www.ripleys.com

Sea Life Park 41-202 Kalanianaole Hwy Waimanalo HI 96795 808-259-2500 259-7373
Web: www.sealifeparkhawaii.com

Seattle Aquarium 1483 Alaskan Way Pier 59 Seattle WA 98101 206-386-4300 386-4328
Web: www.seattleaquarium.org

SeaWorld Orlando 7007 Sea World Dr Orlando FL 32821 407-351-3600
TF: 800-327-2424 ■ *Web:* seaworldparks.com

South Carolina Aquarium
100 Aquarium Wharf Charleston SC 29401 843-577-3474 210-1059*
**Fax Area Code:* 866 ■ *TF:* 800-722-6455 ■ *Web:* www.scaquarium.org

Steinhart Aquarium
California Academy of Sciences
55 Music Concourse Dr Golden Gate Park San Francisco CA 94118 415-379-8000
Web: www.calacademy.org/aquarium

Tennessee Aquarium 1 Broad St Chattanooga TN 37402 423-802-6768
TF: 800-262-0695 ■ *Web:* www.tennis.org

Texas State Aquarium
2710 N Shoreline Blvd Corpus Christi TX 78402 361-881-1200 881-1257
TF General: 800-477-4853 ■ *Web:* www.texasstateaquarium.org

University of Georgia Aquarium
30 Ocean Science Cir Savannah GA 31411 912-598-2496 598-2302
Web: www.marex.uga.edu/aquarium

Vancouver Aquarium Marine Science Ctr
845 Avison Way Vancouver BC V6G3E2 604-659-3474 659-3515
TF: 800-931-1186 ■ *Web:* www.vanaqua.org

Waikiki Aquarium 2777 Kalakaua Ave Honolulu HI 96815 808-923-9741 923-1771
Web: waikikiaquarium.org

41 ARBITRATION SERVICES - LEGAL

Phone Fax

Aaron Riechert Carpol & Riffle APC
900 Veterans Blvd Ste 600 Redwood City CA 94063 650-368-4662
Web: www.arcr.com

Acceleros 11900 Metric Blvd Ste J-163 Austin TX 78758 512-736-8385
Web: www.acceleros.com

Acme Press Inc 2312 Stanwell Dr Concord CA 94520 925-682-1111
Web: www.calitho.com

Advance Case Loans LLC
205 W Wacker Dr Ste 901 Chicago IL 60606 312-332-4100
Web: www.advancecaseloans.com

Advanced Medical Systems 820 Bear Tavern Rd Ewing NJ 08628 609-882-6889
Web: www.advmedsys.com

Advanced Practice Strategies Inc
470 Atlantic Ave 14th Fl Boston MA 02210 617-275-7300
Web: www.aps-web.com

AFL Network Services Inc 170 Ridgeview Ctr Dr Duncan SC 29334 615-591-0098
Web: www.AFLglobal.com

Alan Jones Auctioneers
2470 Nw Dallas St Grand Prairie TX 75050 972-641-7115
Web: antiqueauctioncenter.com

Albany Door Systems
975A Old Norcross Rd Ste A Lawrenceville GA 30046 770-338-5000
Web: www.assaabloyentrance.com/en/aaes/aaes

Alex Lyon & Son Sales Managers & Auctioneers Inc
7697 Route 31 Bridgeport NY 13030 315-633-2944
Web: www.lyonauction.com

Allerair Industries Inc
9600 Rte Transcanadienne Saint-laurent QC H4S1V9 888-852-8247
TF: 888-852-8247

Alliance Abroad Group LP
1221 S Mo Pac Expy Ste 250 Austin TX 78746 512-457-8062
TF: 866-622-7623 ■ *Web:* www.allianceabroad.com

Alliance Credit Counseling Inc
15720 Brixham Hill Ave Ste 575 Charlotte NC 28277 704-341-1010
TF: 888-995-7856 ■ *Web:* www.knowdebt.org

AmbioPharm Inc 1024 Dittman Ct North Augusta SC 29842 415-921-3593
Web: www.ambiopharm.com

Amerge Corp 1406 W Sixth St Ste 200 Cleveland OH 44113 216-928-6007
Web: www.acquisitions-mergers.com

Americall 1502 Tacoma Ave S Tacoma WA 98402 253-272-4111
TF: 800-964-3556 ■ *Web:* www.americall.com

American Arbitration Assn Inc (AAA)
1633 Broadway 10th Fl New York NY 10019 212-716-5800 716-5905
TF: 800-778-7879 ■ *Web:* www.adr.org

Amirsys Inc
2180 South 1300 East Ste 405 Salt Lake City UT 84106 801-485-6500
Web: www.amirsys.com

Anderson Brule Architects Inc
325 S First St Fl 4 San Jose CA 95113 408-298-1885
Web: www.aba-arch.com

Angelo Gordon & Co 245 Park Ave New York NY 10167 212-692-2000
Web: www.angelogordon.com

Annuvia Inc 1725 Clay St Ste 100 San Francisco CA 94109 866-364-7940
TF: 866-364-7940 ■ *Web:* www.annuvia.com

Anresco Inc 1375 Van Dyke Ave San Francisco CA 94124 415-822-1100
TF: 800-359-0920 ■ *Web:* anresco.com

ap Services LLC, The
562 Watertown Ave Ste 3 Waterbury CT 06708 866-843-7270
TF: 866-843-7270 ■ *Web:* www.therapservices.net

APEX Financial Services Inc
11800 Singletree Ln Ste 314 Eden Prairie MN 55344 952-238-1315
Web: www.apexfsi.com

Arbitration Forums Inc
3350 Buschwood Pk Dr Ste 295 Tampa FL 33618 813-931-4004 931-4618
TF Cust Svc: 800-967-8889 ■ *Web:* www.arbfile.org

Arcturus Advisors
1643 Plantation Oaks Ln Fernandina Beach FL 32034 866-593-2207
TF: 866-593-2207 ■ *Web:* www.arcturusadvisors.com

Ashton Metzler & Associates Inc 2391 Shop Rd Sanibel FL 33957 239-395-3152
Web: www.ashtonmetzler.com

Assemblies Unlimited Inc
143 Covington Dr Bloomingdale IL 60108 630-980-0200
Web: www.assemblies.com

Asset Appraisal Services Inc 344 N 115th St Omaha NE 68154 402-390-0505
Web: www.assetappraisalservices.com

Asset Sales Inc 301 Post Office Dr Ste C Indian Trail NC 28079 704-821-4315
Web: www.asset-sales.com

Asynchrony Solutions Inc
900 Spruce St Ste 700 St. Louis MO 63102 314-678-2200
Web: www.asynchrony.com

Atwood & Cherny PC 101 Huntington Ave 25th Fl Boston MA 02199 617-262-6400
Web: www.atwoodcherny.com

August Law Group PC 19200 Von Karman Ste 900 Irvine CA 92612 949-752-7772
Web: www.augustlawgroup.com

Avant Business Services
60 E 42nd St Lowr Level New York NY 10165 212-687-5145
Web: www.nymessenger.com

Balasa Dinverno Foltz LLC
500 Park Blvd Ste 1400 Itasca IL 60143 630-875-4900
TF: 800-840-4740 ■ *Web:* www.bdfllc.com

Bandit Lites Inc 2233 Sycamore Dr Knoxville TN 37921 865-971-3071
Web: www.banditlites.com

Bass & Associates PC
3936 E Ft Lowell Rd Ste 200 Tucson AZ 85712 520-577-1544
Web: www.bass-associates.com

Bass Doherty & Finks PC 40 Soldiers Field Pl Boston MA 02135 617-787-5551
Web: www.bassdoherty.com

Beacon Application Services Corp
959 Concord St Ste 250 Framingham MA 01701 508-663-4433
Web: www.beaconservices.com

Bexar Appraisal District 411 N Frio St San Antonio TX 78207 210-224-8511
Web: www.bcad.org

Bird Marella Boxer Wolpert Nessim Drooks & Lincenberg PC
1875 Century Park E 23rd Fl Los Angeles CA 90067 310-201-2100
Web: www.birdmarella.com

Bluewater Industries Inc
5300 Memorial Ste 550 Houston TX 77007 713-802-2060

Bluteau DeVenney & Company Inc
5670 Spring Garden Rd Ste 901A Halifax NS B3J1H6 902-425-0467
TF: 877-210-9800 ■ *Web:* www.bluteaudevenney.com

Borden Ladner Gervais LLP 40 King St W Toronto ON M5H3Y4 416-367-6000
Web: www.blg.com

Braverman & Co 331 Madison Ave New York NY 10017 212-682-2900
Web: www.braverlaw.net

Brightmix 5018 Leavenworth St Omaha NE 68106 402-991-6199
Web: www.brightmix.com

	City	State	Zip	Phone	Fax
Brock Capital Group LLC 521 Fifth Ave 39th Fl *Web:* www.brockcapital.com	New York	NY	10175	212-209-3000	
Brown & Streza LLP 40 Pacifica 15th Fl *Web:* www.brownandstreza.com	Irvine	CA	92618	949-453-2900	
Brunswick School Inc 100 Maher Ave *TF:* 800-546-9425 ■ *Web:* www.brunswickschool.org	Greenwich	CT	06830	203-625-5800	
Burr & Forman LLP 420 N 20th St Ste 3400 *Web:* www.burr.com	Birmingham	AL	35203	205-251-3000	
Butzel Long PC 150 W Jefferson Ste 900 *Web:* www.butzel.com	Detroit	MI	48226	313-225-7000	
Buy Rite Liquidators 1076 Park Rd *Web:* buyriteliquidators.com	Blandon	PA	19510	610-926-4444	
California District Attorneys Association 921 11th St *Web:* www.cdaa.org	Sacramento	CA	95814	916-443-2017	
Capital Valuation Group Inc 10 E Doty St Ste 1002 *Web:* www.capvalgroup.com	Madison	WI	53703	608-257-2757	
Career T E A M LLC 3580 Main St *Web:* www.careerteam.com	Hartford	CT	06120	860-522-6550	
CareerCurve LLC 5005 Rockside Rd Ste 600 *Web:* www.careercurve.com	Cleveland	OH	44131	216-406-5542	
Careerpros LLC 3392 Hillcrest Rd *TF:* 800-383-7641 ■ *Web:* www.careerpros.com	Dubuque	IA	52002	563-556-3040	
Carlson & Messer LLP 5959 W Century Blvd Ste 1214 *Web:* www.cmtlaw.com	Los Angeles	CA	90045	310-242-2200	
Cauldwell Wingate Company LLC 380 Lexington Ave 53rd Fl *Web:* www.cauldwellwingate.com	New York	NY	10168	212-983-7150	
Certified Business Brokers Ltd 10301 Northwest Fwy Ste 200 *Web:* www.certifiedbb.com	Houston	TX	77092	713-680-1200	
CFO Connection LLC, The 15 Oakland St *Web:* www.thecfoconnection.com	Newburyport	MA	01950	978-255-1236	
Chapman Associates 16 E Schaumburg Rd Ste 3 *Web:* www.chapman-usa.com	Schaumburg	IL	60194	847-884-0010	
CharacTell Ltd 34 Wessex Rd *Web:* www.charactell.com	Newton Center	MA	02459	617-965-1014	
CheckFreePay Corp 15 Sterling Dr P.O. Box 5044 Ste *Web:* www.apsnet.com	Wallingford	CT	06492	203-679-4400	
CIR Law Offices LLP 8665 Gibbs Dr Ste 150 *TF:* 800-496-8909 ■ *Web:* www.cirlaw.com	San Diego	CA	92123	800-496-8909	
CKM Staffing Inc 2351 Sunset Blvd Ste 170 PMB-329 *Web:* www.ckmstaffing.com	Rocklin	CA	95765	916-669-8593	
Clark Wilson LLP 900 885 W Georgia St *Web:* www.cwilson.com	Vancouver	BC	V6C3H1	604-687-5700	687-6314
Classic Die Services Inc 6926 Trafalgar Dr Ste D *Web:* www.classicdieservices.com	Fort Wayne	IN	46803	260-748-6907	
Clayton Levy & Little Architects 1001 E 8th St *Web:* www.claytonlevylittle.com	Austin	TX	78702	512-477-1727	
Clean Air Engineering Inc 500 W Wood St *Web:* www.cleanair.com	Palatine	IL	60067	847-991-3300	
Clearinghouse Community Development Financial Institution 23861 El Toro Rd Ste 401 *Web:* www.clearinghousecdfi.com	Lake Forest	CA	92630	949-859-3600	
CMC-KUHNKE 250 Falls Rd *Web:* www.cmc-kuhnke.com	Hudson	NY	12534	518-828-9345	
Coblentz Patch Duffy & Bass LLP 1 Ferry Bldg Ste 200 *Web:* www.coblentzlaw.com	San Francisco	CA	94111	415-391-4800	
Conestoga Energy Partners LLC 300 N Lincoln Ave	Liberal	KS	67901	620-624-2901	
Conference Technologies Inc 11653 Adie Rd *Web:* www.conferencetech.com	Maryland Heights	MO	63043	314-993-1400	
Consensus Advisors LLC 73 Newbury St *Web:* www.consensusadvisors.com	Boston	MA	02116	617-437-6500	
Cotchett Pitre & McCarthy LLP San Francisco Airport Office Ctr 840 Malcolm Rd Ste 200 *Web:* www.cpmlegal.com	Burlingame	CA	94010	650-697-6000	
Council of Better Business Bureaus Inc *Dispute Resolution Services & Mediation Training* 4200 Wilson Blvd Ste 800 *TF:* 855-748-4600 ■ *Web:* www.bbb.org	Arlington	VA	22203	703-276-0100	525-8277
Cox & Palmer LLP 1100-1959 Upper Water St Purdy's Wharf Tower I *Web:* www.coxandpalmerlaw.com	Halifax	NS	B3J3N2	902-421-6262	
CPR Institute for Dispute Resolution 575 Lexington Ave 21st Fl *TF:* 866-723-1781 ■ *Web:* www.cpradr.org	New York	NY	10022	212-949-6490	949-8859
Creative HR Solutions Inc 13220 - 22Nd St N *Web:* www.creative-hr-solutions.com	Stillwater	MN	55082	651-436-4645	
Crowley Barrett & Karaba 20 S Clark St Ste 2310 *Web:* cbklaw.com	Chicago	IL	60603	312-726-2468	
D W Hammer & Company Inc 17480 Dallas Pkwy Ste 100 *Web:* www.dwhammerco.com	Dallas	TX	75287	972-250-2547	
D&A Building Services Inc 321 Georgia Ave *Web:* www.dabuildingservices.com	Longwood	FL	32750	407-831-5388	
D'Arcangelo & Co 510 Haight Ave *Web:* www.darcangelo.com	Poughkeepsie	NY	12603	845-473-7774	
David A Noyes & Co 209 S LaSalle St *Web:* www.danoyes.com	Chicago	IL	60604	312-782-0400	
Davies Ward Phillips & Vineberg LLP 155 Wellington St W *Web:* www.dwpv.com	Toronto	ON	M5V3J7	416-863-0900	
DB Squared LLC 2928 N McKee Cir	Fayetteville	AR	72703	479-521-2976	
de gobierno PO Box 190759 *Web:* www.de.gobierno.pr	San Juan	PR	91900	787-759-8910	
Devicix LLC 7680 Executive Dr *Web:* www.devicix.com	Eden Prairie	MN	55344	952-368-0073	
E Tech Systems Inc 1900 E Golf Rd Ste 950 *Web:* www.etechsys.com	Schaumburg	IL	60173	847-352-4770	
EA Services Inc 13850 Gulf Fwy Ste 250 *Web:* www.easervices.com	Houston	TX	77034	281-922-4412	
EBG Consulting 419 Hudson Rd *Web:* www.ebgconsulting.com	Sudbury	MA	01776	978-261-5552	
Emerald Technology Valuations LLC 231 Sansome St 5th Fl *Web:* www.emerald-tech.com	San Francisco	CA	94104	415-773-6310	
EmpXtrack 150 Motor Parkway Ste 401 *TF:* 888-840-2682 ■ *Web:* www.empxtrack.com	Hauppauge	NY	11788	888-840-2682	
ENTrigue Surgical Inc 12672 Silicon Dr Ste 150 *Web:* www.entriguesurgical.com	San Antonio	TX	78249	210-298-6398	
Epixx 3915 Heritage Colony Dr *Web:* www.epixx.com	Missouri City	TX	77459	281-208-1989	
Estabrook Capital Management LLC 875 Third Ave 15th Fl *Web:* www.estabrookcap.com	New York	NY	10022	212-605-5595	
Eurofase Inc 33 W Beaver Creek Rd *Web:* www.eurofase.com	Richmond Hill	ON	L4B1L8	905-695-2055	
Eye-To-Eye Communications Inc 2624 W Canyon Ave *Web:* www.eyetoeyepr.com	San Diego	CA	92123	858-565-9800	
Family Credit Counseling Service 111 N Wabash Ste 1408 *TF:* 800-994-3328 ■ *Web:* www.familycredit.org	Chicago	IL	60602	800-994-3328	
Farallones Marine Sanctuary Association PO Box 29386 *Web:* www.farallones.org	San Francisco	CA	94129	415-561-6625	
Farris Vaughan Wills & Murphy 700 W Georgia St Pacific Centre S 25th Fl PO Box 10026 *TF:* 877-684-9151 ■ *Web:* www.farris.com	Vancouver	BC	V7Y1B3	604-684-9151	
Fasken Martineau DuMoulin LLP 333 Bay St Bay Adelaide Centre Ste 2400 PO Box 20 *TF:* 800-268-8424 ■ *Web:* www.fasken.com	Toronto	ON	M5H2T6	416-366-8381	364-7813
Federal Mediation & Conciliation Service 2100 K St NW *Web:* www.fmcs.gov	Washington	DC	20427	202-606-8100	606-4251
Fennebresque & Company LLC 550 S Caldwell St NASCAR Plz Ste 755 *Web:* www.fennebresque.com	Charlotte	NC	28202	704-295-8900	
Florida Council Against Sexual Violence Inc 1820 E Park Ave Ste 100 *TF:* 888-956-7273 ■ *Web:* www.fcasv.org	Tallahassee	FL	32301	850-297-2000	
Florida Surplus Lines Service Office 1441 Maclay Commerce Dr *TF:* 800-562-4496 ■ *Web:* www.fslso.com	Tallahassee	FL	32312	850-224-7676	
Folger Levin LLP 199 Fremont St 20th Fl *Web:* www.folgerlevin.com	San Francisco	CA	94105	415-625-1050	
Fossil Energy Research Corp 23342 S Pointe Dr Ste C *Web:* www.ferco.com	Laguna Hills	CA	92653	949-859-4466	
Fraser Yachts Florida Inc 1800 Southeast 10th Ave Ste 400 *Web:* www.fraseryachts.com	Fort Lauderdale	FL	33316	954-463-0600	
Freedom Cad Services Inc 20 Cotton Rd Ste 201 *Web:* www.freedomcad.com	Nashua	NH	03063	603-864-1300	
Garland Power & Light PO Box 469002 *Web:* www.garlandpower-light.org	Garland	TX	75046	972-205-2650	
Global Imaging Inc 2011 Cherry St Ste 116 *Web:* www.globalimaginginc.com	Louisville	CO	80027	303-673-9773	
Gokeyless 3646 Cargo Rd *TF:* 877-439-5377 ■ *Web:* www.gokeyless.com	Vandalia	OH	45377	937-890-2333	
Goldman Sloan Nash & Haber LLP 480 University Ave Ste 1600 *Web:* www.gsnh.com	Toronto	ON	M5G1V2	416-597-9922	
Goodmans LLP 333 Bay St Ste 3400 *Web:* www.goodmans.ca	Toronto	ON	M5H2S7	416-979-2211	
Goodmind LLC 41 E 11Th St 11Th Fl *Web:* www.goodmind.com	New York	NY	10003	212-660-0110	
Gordon & Rees LLP 275 Battery St Ste 2000 *Web:* www.gordonrees.com	San Francisco	CA	94111	415-986-5900	
Gould & Ratner 222 N LaSalle Ste 800 *Web:* www.gouldratner.com	Chicago	IL	60601	312-236-3003	
Gowling Lafleur Henderson LLP 100 King St W 1 First Canadian Pl Ste 1600 *Web:* www.gowlings.com	Toronto	ON	M5X1G5	416-862-7525	862-7661
Gray Rust St Amand Moffett & Brieske LLP 950 E Paces Ferry Rd Ne *Web:* www.grsmb.com	Atlanta	GA	30326	404-870-7373	
Guidesoft Inc 5875 Castle Creek Pkwy Ste 400 *TF:* 877-256-6948 ■ *Web:* www.knowledgeservices.com	Indianapolis	IN	46250	317-578-1700	
Gunderson Dettmer Stough Villeneuve Franklin & Hachigian LLP 1200 Seaport Blvd *Web:* www.gunder.com	Redwood City	CA	94063	650-321-2400	
GWAVA Inc 100 Alexis Nihon Rd Ste 500 *Web:* www.gwava.com	Montreal	QC	H4M2P1	514-639-4850	
Hammerman & Hultgren PC 3101 N Central Ave Ste 500 *Web:* www.hammerman-hultgren.com	Phoenix	AZ	85012	602-264-2566	
Haztek Inc 143 Medford - Mt. Holly Rd *Web:* www.haztekinc.com	Medford	NJ	08055	609-714-1003	

Company / Address	City	State	Zip	Phone	Fax
Herzog & Co 4640 Lankershim Blvd Ste 400 *Web:* www.herzogcompany.com	North Hollywood	CA	91602	818-762-4640	
Higgins, Marcus & Lovett Inc 800 S Figueroa St Ste 710 *Web:* www.hmlinc.com	Los Angeles	CA	90017	213-617-7775	
Holland & Knight LLP 2115 Harden Blvd *Web:* www.hklaw.com	Lakeland	FL	33803	863-682-1161	
Honigman Miller Schwartz & Cohn LLP 660 Woodward Ave Ste 2290 *Web:* www.honigman.com	Detroit	MI	48226	313-465-7000	
Hrv Conformance Verification Associates Inc 420 Rouser Rd Ste 400 *Web:* www.hrvinc.com	Moon Township	PA	15108	412-299-2000	
Hughes Design Associates 7160 Beneva Rd *Web:* www.hughesdes.com	Sarasota	FL	34238	941-922-4767	
Huntzinger Management Group Inc, The 72 Glenmaura National Blvd Ste 105 *Web:* huntzingergroup.com	Moosic	PA	18507	570-824-4721	
I-Safe America Inc 5900 Pasteur Court Ste 100 *Web:* www.isafe.org	Carlsbad	CA	92008	760-603-7911	
ICSNetwork LLC 17450 Long Meadow Trl *Web:* www.icsnetwork.com	Chagrin Falls	OH	44023	216-509-6000	
Infinity Direct Inc 13220 County Rd 6 Ste 200 *Web:* www.infinitydirect.com	Plymouth	MN	55441	763-559-1111	
Inland Valley Arbitration & Mediation Service (IVAMS) 8287 White Oak Ave *Web:* www.ivams.com	Rancho Cucamonga	CA	91730	909-466-1665	466-1796
Innovara Inc 21 Pray St *Web:* www.innovara.com	Amherst	MA	01002	413-549-5888	
J p King Auction Company Texas Ltd 108 Fountain Ave *Web:* www.jpking.com	Gadsden	AL	35901	256-546-5217	
JAMS/Endispute 500 N State College Blvd 14th Fl *TF:* 800-352-5267 ■ *Web:* www.jamsadr.com	Orange	CA	92868	714-939-1300	939-8710
JDC Group Inc 990 Hammond Dr Ste 750 *Web:* www.jdc-group.com	Atlanta	GA	30328	404-601-3310	
Jeffrey Byrne & Associates 4042 Central St *TF:* 800-222-9233 ■ *Web:* www.fundraisingjba.com	Kansas City	MO	64111	800-222-9233	
Jivaro Group Inc 5433 S Emporia Ct *Web:* www.jivarogroup.com	Englewood	CO	80111	303-740-0022	
Johanson & Yau Accountancy Corp 160 W Santa Clara St Ste 900 *Web:* www.jyac.com	San Jose	CA	95113	408-288-5111	
JS Paluch Company Inc 3708 River Rd Ste 400 *TF:* 800-621-5197 ■ *Web:* www.jspaluch.com	Franklin Park	IL	60131	847-678-9300	
Judge Organization Companies, The 201A Export St *Web:* www.judgeorg.com	Newark	NJ	07114	973-491-0600	
Judicate West 1851 E First St Ste 1600 *TF:* 800-488-8805 ■ *Web:* www.judicatewest.com	Santa Ana	CA	92705	714-834-1340	834-1344
July Business Services 215 Mary Ave Ste 302 *TF:* 888-333-5859 ■ *Web:* www.julyservices.com	Waco	TX	76701	888-333-5859	
JumpSport Inc 2055 S Seventh St Ste A *Web:* www.jumpsport.com	San Jose	CA	95112	408-213-2551	
Kaufman Company Inc 19 Walkhill Rd *TF:* 800-338-8023 ■ *Web:* www.kaufmanco.com	Norwood	MA	02062	781-255-1000	
Keais Records Service Inc 1010 Lamar 18th Fl *Web:* keais.com	Houston	TX	77002	713-224-6865	
Kelley Executive Partners 1275 E 10th St *Web:* www.kelley.iu.edu	Bloomington	IN	47405	812-855-0229	
Kiely and Associates 329 Leroi Rd *Web:* www.kielyandassociates.com	Pittsburgh	PA	15208	412-243-2019	
KLS Professional Advisors Group LLC 111 Fifth Ave 8th Fl *Web:* www.caravan-ny.com	New York	NY	10003	212-355-0346	
Knoxville Locomotive Works 300 W Quincy Ave *Web:* knoxvillelocomotiveworks.com	Knoxville	TN	37917	865-522-7078	
Kobelco Construction Machinery America LLC 501 Richardson Rd SE *Web:* www.kobelcoamerica.com	Calhoun	GA	30701	706-629-5572	
Koster Industries Inc 40 Daniel St Ste 2 *Web:* www.kosterindustries.com	Farmingdale	NY	11735	631-454-1766	
Kubisys 200 Wanaque Ave Ste 201 *Web:* www.kubisys.com	Pompton Lakes	NJ	07442	973-513-9350	
Kynikos Associates LP 20 W 55th St 8th Fl *Web:* www.kynikos.com	New York	NY	10019	212-649-0200	
Lake Court Medical Supplies Inc 27733 Groesbeck Hwy *Web:* www.lakecourt.com	Roseville	MI	48066	586-771-3100	
Land Information Access Association Land Information Access Association 324 Munson Ave *Web:* www.liaa.org	Traverse City	MI	49686	231-929-3696	
Lang Richert & Patch 5200 N Palm Ave Fig Garden Financial Ctr 4th Fl *Web:* www.lrp.org	Fresno	CA	93704	559-228-6700	
Larwin Co 16633 Ventura Blvd Ste 1300	Encino	CA	91436	818-986-8890	
Lasership Inc 1912 Woodford Rd *Web:* www.lasership.com	Vienna	VA	22182	703-761-9030	
Leader's Edge 2 Bala Plz Ste 300 *Web:* www.the-leaders-edge.com	Bala Cynwyd	PA	19004	610-660-6684	
LEADERS Magazine Inc 59 E 54Th St *Web:* www.leadersmag.com	New York	NY	10022	212-758-0740	
Living Color Enterprises Inc 6850 NW 12th Ave *TF:* 800-878-9511 ■ *Web:* www.livingcolor.com	Fort Lauderdale	FL	33309	954-970-9511	
Loeb Equipment & Appraisal Co 4131 S State St *TF:* 800-560-5632 ■ *Web:* www.loebequipment.com	Chicago	IL	60609	773-548-4131	
London Company Investment Counsel, The 1801 Bayberry Ct Ste 301 *Web:* www.tlcadvisory.com	Richmond	VA	23226	804-775-0317	
Luan Enterprises 5624 W 79th St *Web:* www.alltite.com	Burbank	IL	60459	708-423-4547	
Lush Group Inc 24 Southwest Ave *Web:* www.lgisoftware.com	Jamestown	RI	02835	401-423-9111	
Lynn Senior Services Greater 2 Rice St *Web:* glss.iapplicants.com	Saugus	MA	01906	781-231-5648	
Manomet Center for Conservation Sciences 81 Stage Point Rd *Web:* www.manomet.org	Manomet	MA	02345	508-224-6521	
Mark IV Capital Inc 100 Bayview Cir Ste 4500 *Web:* www.markiv.com	Newport Beach	CA	92660	949-509-1444	
Marks Nelson Vohland & Campbel 7701 College Blvd Ste 150 *Web:* www.marksnelsoncpa.com	Overland Park	KS	66210	913-498-9000	
Mater Dei Academy 3695 Elm St *Web:* www.materdeiacademy.org	Columbus	OH	43213	614-231-1984	
McDonald Carano Wilson LLP 100 W Liberty St 10th Fl *Web:* www.mcdonaldcarano.com	Reno	NV	89505	775-788-2000	
Mecham Co, The 4107 S Forest Meadows *Web:* www.mechamcompany.com	Spokane	WA	99206	509-922-0535	
Medicount Management Inc 10361 Spartan Dr *Web:* www.medicount.com	Cincinnati	OH	45215	513-772-4465	
Mega Group Inc 720-1st Ave N *Web:* www.megagroup.ca	Saskatoon	SK	S7K6R9	306-242-7366	
Merchant Law Group LLP 2401 Saskatchewan Dr Saskatchewan Dr Plz *TF:* 888-567-7777 ■ *Web:* www.merchantlaw.com	Regina	SK	S4P4H8	306-359-7777	
Meristem LLP 601 Carlson Pkwy Ste 800 *Web:* www.meristemfw.com	Minnetonka	MN	55305	952-835-2577	
Meriwether Capital LLC 30 Rockefeller Plz Rm 5600 *Web:* www.meriwethercapital.net	New York	NY	10112	212-649-5890	
Merlin Law Group PA 777 S Harbour Island Blvd *Web:* www.merlinlawgroup.com	Tampa	FL	33602	813-229-1000	
Michael Best & Friedrich LLP 100 E Wisconsin Ave Ste 3300 *Web:* www.michaelbest.com	Milwaukee	WI	53202	414-271-6560	
Middleton & Company Inc 600 Atlantic Ave 18th Fl *TF:* 800-357-5101 ■ *Web:* www.middletonco.com	Boston	MA	02210	617-357-5101	
Miller Thomson LLP Scotia Plz 40 King St W Ste 5800 *TF:* 888-762-5559 ■ *Web:* www.millerthomson.com	Toronto	ON	M5H3S1	416-595-8500	
Missouri Protection & Advocacy Services 925 S Country Club Dr Ste 3 *Web:* www.moadvocacy.org	Jefferson City	MO	65109	573-893-3333	
Mixtec Group 9829 Blue Larkspur Ln *Web:* www.mixtec.net	Monterey	CA	93940	831-373-7077	
MovieTickets.com Inc 2255 Glades Rd Ste 100E *Web:* www.movietickets.com	Boca Raton	FL	33431	561-322-3200	
mSnap Inc 101 Empty Saddle Trail *Web:* www.msnapinc.com	Hailey	ID	83333	415-981-0812	
Mueller Law Office, The 404 W Seventh St *Web:* www.muellerlaw.com	Austin	TX	78701	512-478-1236	
Nathan Sommers Jacobs PC 2800 Post Oak Blvd 61st Fl *Web:* www.nathansommers.com	Houston	TX	77056	713-960-0303	
National Arbitration & Mediation 990 Stewart Ave *TF:* 800-358-2550 ■ *Web:* www.namadr.com	Garden City	NY	11530	516-794-8950	794-8518
NBS Technologies Inc 703 Evans Ave Ste 402 *Web:* www.nbstech.com	Toronto	ON	M9C5E9	416-621-1911	
Ncs Subsea Inc 3928 Bluebonnet Dr *Web:* ncs-subsea.com	Stafford	TX	77477	281-491-3123	
Neat Oh International 790 W Frontage Rd Ste 303 *Web:* www.neat-oh.com	Northfield	IL	60093	847-441-4290	
Neovia 801 Garden St Ste 300 *Web:* www.neoviainsurance.com	Santa Barbara	CA	93101	805-961-3111	
New York Cruise Lines Inc Pier 83 W 42nd St at the Hudson River *Web:* www.circleline42.com	New York	NY	10036	212-630-8120	
Nexus World Services Inc 7114 W Jefferson Ste 110 *Web:* www.nexusworldservices.com	Denver	CO	80235	303-988-1243	
Nichols Jackson Dillard Hager & Smith LLP 500 N Akard St 1800 Ross Twr *Web:* www.njdhs.com	Dallas	TX	75201	214-965-9900	
Nines Hotel, The 525 SW Morrison *TF:* 877-229-9995 ■ *Web:* www.thenines.com	Portland	OR	97204	877-229-9995	
Notus Career Management 5 Centerpointe Dr Ste 400 *TF:* 800-431-1990 ■ *Web:* www.getnotus.com	Lake Oswego	OR	97035	800-431-1990	
O'connor Company Inc 16910 W. 116th St *Web:* www.oconnor-hvac.com	Lenexa	KS	66219	913-894-8788	
Object CTalk Inc 1013 W 9th Ave *Web:* www.octalk.com	King Of Prussia	PA	19406	610-265-1278	
OCTG LLP 9200 Sheldon Rd *Web:* www.octg.org	Houston	TX	77049	281-456-9057	
OnCell Systems Inc 1160D Pittsford-Victor Rd *Web:* oncell.com	Pittsford	NY	14534	585-419-9844	
OneTouch Direct LLC 4902 W Sligh Ave *TF:* 866-948-4005 ■ *Web:* www.onetouchdirect.com	Tampa	FL	33634	866-948-4005	

	City	State	ZIP	Phone	Fax
Optimal Outsource 7 Rancho Cir *Web:* optimaloutsource.com	Lake Forest	CA	92630	949-916-3700	
ORC ProTel Inc 17233 Continental Dr *Web:* www.orcprotel.com	Lansing	IL	60438	708-418-0600	
Origo Direct Marketing Communications 20-4480 Chesswood Dr *Web:* www.origo.ca	Toronto	ON	M3J2B9	416-398-7678	
Osler Hoskin & Harcourt LLP 100 King St W 1 First Canadian Pl Ste 6100 *Web:* www.osler.com	Toronto	ON	M5X1B8	416-362-2111	
OTS 3924 Clock Pointe Trl *TF:* 877-445-2058 ■ *Web:* www.ots.net	Stow	OH	44224	877-445-2058	
P.W. Gillibrand Company Inc 4537 Ish Dr *Web:* www.pwgillibrand.com	Simi Valley	CA	93063	805-526-2195	
PACCESS LLC 700 NE Multnomah St Ste 1600 *Web:* www.paccessglobal.com	Portland	OR	97232	503-230-4890	
Paging Network of Canada Inc 1-1685 Tech Ave *Web:* www.pagenet.ca	Mississauga	ON	L4W0A7	905-614-3100	
Pamlico Capital 150 N College St Ste 2400 *Web:* www.pamlicocapital.com	Charlotte	NC	28202	704-414-7150	
Parker Rose Design Inc 10075 Mesa Rim Rd Ste A *TF:* 800-403-2711 ■ *Web:* www.parker-rose.com	San Diego	CA	92121	800-403-2711	
Parnell & Crum PA 641 S Lawrence St *TF:* 866-629-0912 ■ *Web:* www.parnellcrum.com	Montgomery	AL	36104	334-832-4200	
Patpro Inc 2111 Eisenhower Ave Ste 404 *Web:* www.epatpro.com	Alexandria	VA	22314	703-299-8500	
PAVAD Medical Inc 40539 Encyclopedia Cir *Web:* www.pavad.com	Fremont	CA	94538	510-226-7300	
Peak Sales Recruiting Inc 64 Beaver St Ste 119 *Web:* www.peaksalesrecruiting.com	New York	NY	10004	646-291-8960	
Pearl Law Group 567 Sutter St 3rd Fl *Web:* www.immigrationlaw.com	San Francisco	CA	94102	415-771-7500	
Pennsylvania Employees Benefit Trust Fund 150 S 43rd St *Web:* www.pebtf.org	Harrisburg	PA	17111	717-561-4750	
Perkins Investment Management LLC 1 S Wacker Dr *Web:* pwmco.com	Chicago	IL	60606	312-341-9727	341-9737
Pine Tree Equity Management LP 777 Brickell Ave Ste 1070 *Web:* www.pinetreeequity.com	Miami	FL	33131	305-808-9820	
Pite Duncan LLP 4375 Jutland Dr Ste 200 *Web:* www.piteduncan.com	San Diego	CA	92117	858-750-7600	
PMA Canada Ltd 231 Oak Park Blvd Ste 400 *Web:* www.pmacanada.com	Oakville	ON	L6H7S8	905-257-2116	
Polaris Capital Management LLC 121 High St *Web:* www.polariscapital.com	Boston	MA	02110	617-951-1365	
Prime NDT Services Inc 4345 Independence Dr *Web:* www.primendt.com	Schnecksville	PA	18052	610-262-4954	
Print Resources Inc 1500 E Riverside Dr *Web:* www.printindy.com	Indianapolis	IN	46202	317-833-7000	
PrismOne Group Inc 37 N Boyd St *Web:* www.prismone.net	Winter Garden	FL	34787	321-293-1000	
Prodo Laboratories 27402 Aliso Viejo Pkwy *Web:* prodolabs.com	Aliso Viejo	CA	92656	949-727-1972	
Project Access Inc 3900 Birch St Ste 113 *Web:* www.project-access.org	Newport Beach	CA	92660	949-253-6200	
Promotion Fulfillment Center 311 21st St *Web:* www.pfcfulfills.com	Camanche	IA	52730	563-259-0105	
Quatred LLC 532 Fourth Range Rd *TF:* 888-395-8534 ■ *Web:* www.quatred.com	Pembroke	NH	03275	888-395-8534	
Quiktrak Inc 9700 SW Nimbus Ave *Web:* www.quiktrak.com	Beaverton	OR	97008	503-968-9800	
Rachman Group, The 33 Walt Whitman Rd Ste 232 *Web:* www.mrhuntington.com	Huntington Station	NY	11746	631-547-5464	
Randall S Miller & Associates PC 43252 Woodward Ave Ste 180 *TF:* 844-322-6558 ■ *Web:* www.millerlaw.biz	Bloomfield Hills	MI	48302	248-335-9200	
Realty Capital Partners LLC 8333 Douglas Ave *Web:* www.rcpinvestments.com	Dallas	TX	75225	469-533-4000	
Resolute Systems Inc 1550 N Prospect Ave *TF:* 800-776-6060 ■ *Web:* www.resolutesystems.com	Milwaukee	WI	53202	414-276-4774	270-0932
RESOLVE Partners LLC 2010 New Garden Rd *Web:* www.resolve-partners.com	Greensboro	NC	27410	336-346-3095	
Resume Solutions 1033 Bay St *TF:* 866-361-1290 ■ *Web:* www.resumesolutions.ca	Toronto	ON	M5S3A5	416-361-1290	
Reyes | Browne | Reilley 5950 Berkshire Ln Ste 410 *Web:* www.reyeslaw.com	Dallas	TX	75225	214-526-7900	
Richard Henry Group LLC PO Box 45422 *Web:* www.rhgsolutions.com	Westlake	OH	44145	440-724-2658	
Roda Group, The 918 Parker St *Web:* www.rodagroup.com	Berkeley	CA	94710	510-649-1900	
Ronald Mark Associates Inc 1227 Central Ave *Web:* www.ronaldmark.com	Hillside	NJ	07205	908-558-0011	
Rosenthal Appraisal Company Inc 6 W Railroad Ave *Web:* www.rosappraisal.com	Tenafly	NJ	07670	201-567-4300	
Russ Blakely & Associates 620 Lindsay St Ste 201 *Web:* russblakelyassoc.com	Chattanooga	TN	37403	423-266-8306	
Safer Healthcare 7600 E Arapahoe Rd Ste 204 *Web:* www.saferhealthcare.com	Centennial	CO	80112	303-298-8083	
Safety First Systems LLC 65 Route 4 E *Web:* nationwideagribusiness.safetyfirst.com	River Edge	NJ	07661	201-267-8900	
Safety Management Systems Inc 2916 N University Ave *Web:* www.safetyms.com	Lafayette	LA	70507	337-521-3400	
San Pasqual Fiduciary Trust Co 550 S Hope St Ste 550 *Web:* www.spftc.com	Los Angeles	CA	90071	213-452-8500	
SCF Partners 600 Travis Ste 6600 *Web:* www.scfpartners.com	Houston	TX	77002	713-227-7888	227-7850
Schiller Ducanto & Fleck 225 E Deerpath Ste 270 *Web:* www.sdflaw.com	Lake Forest	IL	60045	847-615-8300	
Sector3 Appraisals Inc 8802 69th Rd *Web:* www.sector3appraisals.com	Forest Hills	NY	11375	718-268-4376	
Secure Network Systems LLC 4282 WCR 11 *Web:* www.securenetworksystems.com	Erie	CO	80516	303-637-7617	
Sedona Staffing 7380 Clairemont Mesa Blvd Ste 209 *Web:* www.sedonastaffing.com	San Diego	CA	92111	858-268-9844	
Sensor Geophysical Ltd 736-6 Ave SW Ste 1300 *Web:* sensorgeo.com	Calgary	AB	T2P3T7	403-237-7711	
Singlewire Software LLC 2601 W Beltline Hwy Ste 510 *Web:* www.singlewire.com	Madison	WI	53713	608-661-1140	
Smith Gambrell & Russell LLP 1230 Peachtree St NE Promenade II Ste 3100 *Web:* www.sgrlaw.com	Atlanta	GA	30309	404-815-3500	
SOMA Medical Assessments Ltd 7368 Yonge St Ste 206 *Web:* www.somamedical.com	Thornhill	ON	L4J8H9	905-881-8855	
Sperry Rail Inc 46 Shelter Rock Rd *Web:* www.sperryrail.com	Danbury	CT	06810	203-791-4500	
Sports Management Network Inc 1668 S Telegraph Rd Ste 200 *Web:* www.sportsmanagementnetwork.com	Bloomfield Hills	MI	48302	248-335-3535	
Spotts Fain PC 411 E Franklin St Ste 600 *Web:* www.spottsfain.com	Richmond	VA	23219	804-697-2000	
Stacey Braun Associates Inc 377 Broadway *Web:* www.staceybraun.com	New York	NY	10013	212-226-7707	
StratiMind 268 Bishops Forest Dr *Web:* www.stratimind.com	Waltham	MA	02452	781-373-3750	
SuccessWorks Inc 1413 Sudden Valley *Web:* www.searchenginewriting.com	Bellingham	WA	98229	360-224-6260	
Summa Strategies Canada Inc 100 Sparks St Ste 1000 *Web:* www.summa.ca	Ottawa	ON	K1P5B7	613-235-1400	
Surveillance Specialties Ltd 600 Research Dr *TF:* 800-354-2616 ■ *Web:* www.securadyne.com	Wilmington	MA	01887	800-354-2616	
Tab Services Inc 2065 S Raritan St *Web:* tabservicescolorado.com	Denver	CO	80223	303-649-1213	
Tarter Krinsky & Drogin LLP 1350 Broadway *Web:* www.tarterkrinsky.com	New York	NY	10018	212-216-8000	
Tech Networks of Boston 574 Dorchester Ave *Web:* techboston.com	Boston	MA	02127	617-269-0299	
Technomics Inc 201 12th St S Ste 612 *Web:* www.technomics.net	Arlington	VA	22202	571-366-1400	
TERRAMAI 8400 Agate Rd *TF:* 800-220-9062 ■ *Web:* www.terramai.com	White City	OR	97503	800-220-9062	
Timber Products Inspection Inc 1641 Sigman Rd NW *Web:* www.tpinspection.com	Conyers	GA	30012	770-922-8000	
Torys LLP 79 Wellington St W TD Centre 30th Fl 30th Fl *Web:* www.torys.com	Toronto	ON	M5K1N2	416-865-0040	
Total Safety Consulting LLC 751 Broadway *Web:* www.totalsafety.org	Bayonne	NJ	07002	201-437-5150	
Tranzon LLC 7204 Glen Forest Dr Ste 105 *TF:* 866-503-1212 ■ *Web:* www.tranzon.com	Richmond	VA	23226	207-775-4300	
Tri-Starr Investigations Inc 3525 Hwy 138 SW *TF:* 800-849-9841 ■ *Web:* www.tristarr.com	Stockbridge	GA	30281	770-388-9841	
Tricor Employment Screening Ltd 110 Blaze Industrial Pkwy Ste C *Web:* www.tricorinfo.com	Berea	OH	44017	216-267-0431	
Triton Diving Services LLC 3421 N Causeway Blvd Ste 601 *Web:* www.tritondiving.net	Metairie	LA	70002	504-846-5056	
Tti Environmental Inc 1253 N Church St *Web:* www.ttienvinc.com	Moorestown	NJ	08057	856-840-8800	
Tulsa Inspection Resources LLC 4111 S Darlington Ave Ste 1000 *Web:* www.tulsainspection.com	Tulsa	OK	74135	918-274-1100	
Turbo Mechanical Inc 515 McPhee Rd SW *Web:* www.turbomechanical.com	Olympia	WA	98502	360-943-1888	
UbiCare 284 Amory St G-101 *Web:* www.ubicare.com	Boston	MA	02130	617-524-8861	
UMIAQ LLC 6700 Arctic Spur Rd *Web:* www.uicprofessionalservices.com	Anchorage	AK	99518	907-677-8220	
University Physicians Inc 13199 E Montview Blvd *Web:* www.upicolo.org	Aurora	CO	80045	303-493-7000	
Usherwood Office Technology Inc 1005 W Fayette St *Web:* www.usherwood.com	Syracuse	NY	13204	315-472-0050	
Valley Internet Inc 102 Maple St East **Fax Area Code:* 615 ■ *TF:* 888-433-1924 ■ *Web:* vallnet.com	Fayetteville	TN	37334	931-433-1921	221-0119*
Vanguard Dealer Services L.L.C 30 Two Bridges Rd Ste 350 *Web:* www.vanguarddealerservices.com	Fairfield	NJ	07004	973-575-7171	
Varnum LLP Bridgewater Pl PO Box 352 *Web:* www.varnumlaw.com	Grand Rapids	MI	49501	616-336-6000	
Vehtech Inc 2890 Hwy 212 Ste 347 A *Web:* www.vehtechnology.com	Conyers	GA	30094	770-788-2032	

Name	City	State	ZIP	Phone	Fax
Veritas Capital 9 W 57th St 29th Fl *Web:* www.veritascapital.com	New York	NY	10019	212-415-6700	
Viant Group LLC 500 Washington St Ste 325 *Web:* www.viantgroup.com	San Francisco	CA	94111	415-820-6100	
Webb; County Appraisal Distric 3302 Clark Blvd *Web:* www.webbcad.org	Laredo	TX	78043	956-718-4091	
WelcomeMat Services Inc 3348 Peachtree Rd 200 Tower Pl Ste 1095 *Web:* www.welcomematservices.com	Atlanta	GA	30326	404-841-2226	
Wetherby Asset Management 580 California St 8th Fl *Web:* www.wetherby.com	San Francisco	CA	94104	415-399-9159	
Whitham Curtis Christofferson & Cook PC 11491 Sunset Hills Rd Ste 340 *Web:* www.wcc-ip.com	Reston	VA	20190	703-787-9400	
Wikibon Project, The 5 Mount Royal Ave Ste 280 *Web:* www.wikibon.org	Marlborough	MA	01752	774-463-3400	
WLC 200 Pronghorn St *Web:* www.wlcwyo.com	Casper	WY	82601	307-266-2524	
Wolfe Industrial Auctions Inc 9801 Hansonville Rd *TF:* 800-443-9580 ■ *Web:* wolfeauctions.com	Frederick	MD	21702	301-898-0340	
Workforce Board, The 69 W Washington Ste 2860 *Web:* wtb.wa.gov	Chicago	WA	60602	360-709-4600	
Xerces Society, The 4828 Se Hawthorne Blvd *Web:* xerces.org	Portland	OR	97215	503-232-6639	
Yosemite Sierra Services 6771 N Palm Ave *Web:* www.yosemitepark.com	Fresno	CA	93704	559-454-2025	
Zarzaur & Cunningham PC 2209 Morris Ave PO Box 11366 *Web:* zsattorneys.stratuspayments.net	Birmingham	AL	35203	205-250-8437	

ARCHITECTS

See Engineering & Design p. 2252

ART - COMMERCIAL

See Graphic Design p. 2442

42 ART DEALERS & GALLERIES

Name	City	State	ZIP	Phone	Fax
Abbozzo Gallery 401 Richmond Stt W Ste 128 *TF:* 866-844-4481 ■ *Web:* www.abbozzogallery.com	Toronto	ON	M5V3A8	416-260-2220	
ACA Galleries 529 W 20th St 5th Fl *Web:* www.acagalleries.com	New York	NY	10011	212-206-8080	206-8498
Acquavella Galleries Inc 18 E 79th St *Web:* www.acquavellagalleries.com	New York	NY	10075	212-734-6300	794-9394
Airway Surgical Appliances Ltd 189 Colonnade Rd *Web:* www.airwaysurgical.ca	Nepean	ON	K2E7J4	613-723-4790	
Alexander & Bonin LLC 132 Tenth Ave *Web:* www.alexanderandbonin.com	New York	NY	10011	212-367-7474	367-7337
Allan Stone Projects 535 W 22nd St 3rd Fl **Fax Area Code:* 917 ■ *Web:* www.allanstoneprojects.com	New York	NY	10011	212-987-4997	421-9895*
Alpha Gallery 460 Harrison Ave *Web:* www.alphagallery.com	Boston	MA	02116	617-536-4465	536-5695
Angles Gallery 2754 S La Cienega Blvd *Web:* www.anglesgallery.com	Los Angeles	CA	90034	310-396-5019	202-6330
Anna Kustera Gallery 520 W 21st St *Web:* www.annakustera.com	New York	NY	10011	212-989-0082	
Army & Navy Club, The 901 17th St NW *Web:* www.armynavyclub.org	Washington	DC	20006	202-628-8400	
Art Emporium 2928 Granville St *Web:* www.theartemporium.ca	Vancouver	BC	V6H3J7	604-738-3510	
Art Placement Inc 228 Third Ave S Ste 228 *Web:* www.artplacement.com	Saskatoon	SK	S7K1L9	306-664-3385	933-2521
Aspen Hill Club 14501 Homecrest Rd *Web:* www.aspenhillclub.com	Silver Spring	MD	20906	301-598-5200	
Babcock Galleries 724 Fifth Ave 11th Fl *Web:* www.artnet.com	New York	NY	10019	212-767-1852	767-1857
Barbara Gladstone Gallery 515 W 24th St *Web:* www.gladstonegallery.com	New York	NY	10011	212-206-9300	206-9301
Barbara Krakow Gallery 10 Newbury St 5th Fl *Web:* www.barbarakrakowgallery.com	Boston	MA	02116	617-262-4490	262-8971
Barbara Mathes Gallery 22 E 80th St *Web:* barbaramathesgallery.com	New York	NY	10075	212-570-4190	570-4191
Bau-Xi Gallery 3045 Granville St *Web:* www.bau-xi.com	Vancouver	BC	V6H3J9	604-733-7011	
Beckett Fine Art Ltd 33 Hazelton Ave Ste 212 *Web:* www.beckettfineart.com	Toronto	ON	M5R2E3	416-922-5582	
Berry-Hill Galleries Inc 11 E 70th St *Web:* www.berry-hill.com	New York	NY	10021	212-744-2300	744-2838
Brooke Alexander Editions 59 Wooster St *Web:* www.baeditions.com	New York	NY	10012	212-925-4338	941-9565
Catriona Jeffries Gallery 274 E First Ave *Web:* www.catrionajeffries.com	Vancouver	BC	V5T1A6	604-736-1554	736-1054
Chamber Music Society of Lincoln Center 70 Lincoln Ctr Plz *Web:* www.chambermusicsociety.org	New York	NY	10023	212-875-5788	
Cheim & Read 547 W 25th St *Web:* www.cheimread.com	New York	NY	10001	212-242-7727	242-7737
Christopher Cutts Gallery 21 Morrow Ave *Web:* www.cuttsgallery.com	Toronto	ON	M6R2H9	416-532-5566	532-7272
Conner Rosenkranz LLC 19 E 74th St *Web:* www.crsculpture.com	New York	NY	10021	212-517-3710	
Corkin Shopland Gallery 55 Mill St Bldg 61 *Web:* www.corkingallery.com	Toronto	ON	M5A3C4	416-979-1980	979-7018
Courts Plus Fitness Center 3491 University Dr S *Web:* www.courtsplus.org	Fargo	ND	58104	701-237-4805	
CRG Gallery 195 Chrystie St *Web:* crggallery.com	New York	NY	10002	212-229-2766	229-2788
D'Amelio Terras 525 W 22nd St *Web:* www.damelioterras.com	New York	NY	10011	212-352-9460	
Danese 535 W 24th St 6th Fl *Web:* danesecorey.com	New York	NY	10011	212-223-2227	605-1016
David Findlay Jr Fine Art 724 Fifth Ave *Web:* www.davidfindlayjr.com	New York	NY	10019	212-486-7660	
David Nolan Gallery 527 W 29th St *Web:* www.davidnolangallery.com	New York	NY	10001	212-925-6190	334-9139
David Zwirner Gallery 525 W 19th St *Web:* www.davidzwirner.com	New York	NY	10011	212-727-2070	727-2072
Davis & Langdale Company Inc 231 E 60th St *Web:* davisandlangdale.com	New York	NY	10022	212-838-0333	752-7764
Dickinson Roundell Inc 19 E 66th St *Web:* www.simondickinson.com	New York	NY	10065	212-772-8083	772-8186
Didier Aaron Inc 32 E 67th St *Web:* www.didieraaron.com	New York	NY	10065	212-988-5248	
Douglas Udell Gallery 10332 124th St *Web:* www.douglasudellgallery.com	Edmonton	AB	T5N1R2	780-488-4445	488-8335
Drabinsky Gallery 114 Yorkville Ave	Toronto	ON	M5R1B9	416-324-5766	324-5770
Edward Day Gallery Inc 952 Queen St W *Web:* www.edwarddaygallery.com	Toronto	ON	M6J1G8	416-921-6540	
Edwynn Houk Gallery 745 Fifth Ave 4th Fl *Web:* www.houkgallery.com	New York	NY	10151	212-750-7070	688-4848
Elkon Gallery Inc 18 E 81st St Ste 2-A	New York	NY	10028	212-535-3940	737-8479
Equinox Gallery 2321 Granville St *Web:* www.equinoxgallery.com	Vancouver	BC	V6H3G4	604-736-2405	736-0464
Feheley Fine Arts 65 George St **Fax Area Code:* 647 ■ *TF:* 877-904-9114 ■ *Web:* www.feheleyfinearts.com	Toronto	ON	M5A4L8	416-323-1373	361-7667*
Fischbach Gallery 210 11th Ave *Web:* www.fischbachgallery.com	New York	NY	10001	212-759-2345	366-1783
Forum Gallery 730 Fifth Ave *Web:* www.forumgallery.com	New York	NY	10019	212-355-4545	355-4547
Fraenkel Gallery 49 Geary St *Web:* www.artnet.com	San Francisco	CA	94108	415-981-2661	981-4014
Galerie Lelong 528 W 26th St *Web:* www.galerie-lelong.com	New York	NY	10001	212-315-0470	
Galerie Saint Etienne 24 W 57th St *Web:* www.gseart.com	New York	NY	10019	212-245-6734	765-8493
Galerie Valentin 1490 Sherbrooke Quest Ste 200 *Web:* www.galerievalentin.com	Montreal	QC	H3G1L3	514-939-0500	939-0413
Gallery 78 Inc 796 Queen St *TF:* 888-883-8322 ■ *Web:* www.gallery78.com	Fredericton	NB	E3B1C6	506-454-5192	443-0199
Gallery Moos Ltd 622 Richmond St W *Web:* www.gallerymoos.com	Toronto	ON	M5V1Y9	416-504-5445	
Gallery One 121 Scollard St *Web:* www.artgalleryone.com	Toronto	ON	M5R1G4	416-929-3103	
Gallery Paule Anglim 14 Geary St *Web:* www.gallerypauleanglim.com	San Francisco	CA	94108	415-433-2710	433-1501
George Adams Gallery 525 W 26th St *Web:* www.artnet.com	New York	NY	10001	212-564-8480	564-8485
Gotham Growth Group 301 Tory Turn *Web:* www.gothamgrowth.com	Wayne	PA	19087	484-433-9806	
Granite Links Golf Club 100 Quarry Hills Dr *Web:* www.granitelinksgolfclub.com	Quincy	MA	02169	617-689-1900	
Hans P Kraus Jr Inc 962 Pk Ave *Web:* www.sunpictures.com	New York	NY	10028	212-794-2064	
Harlow's Casino 4280 Harlow Blvd *Web:* www.harlowscasino.com	Greenville	MS	38701	662-335-9797	
Heffel Gallery Ltd 2247 Granville St *TF:* 800-528-9608 ■ *Web:* www.heffel.com/gallery	Vancouver	BC	V6H3G1	604-732-6505	732-4245
Hirschl & Adler Galleries Inc 730 Fifth Ave *Web:* www.hirschlandadler.com	New York	NY	10019	212-535-8810	772-7237
Inuit Gallery of Vancouver Ltd 206 Cambie St Gastown *TF:* 888-615-8399 ■ *Web:* www.inuit.com	Vancouver	BC	V6B2M9	604-688-7323	
Jack Kilgore & Company Inc 154 E 71st St 3rd Fl	New York	NY	10021	212-650-1149	650-1389
Jack Tilton Gallery 8 E 76th St *Web:* www.jacktiltongallery.com	New York	NY	10021	212-737-2221	396-1725
James Goodman Gallery 41 E 57th St Ste 802 *Web:* www.jamesgoodmangallery.com	New York	NY	10022	212-593-3737	980-0195
James Graham & Sons Inc 32 E 67th St *Web:* www.graham1857.com	New York	NY	10065	212-535-5767	
Jason McCoy Inc 41 E 57th St 11th Fl *Web:* www.jasonmccoyinc.com	New York	NY	10022	212-319-1996	319-4799
Jill Newhouse Gallery 4 E 81st St *Web:* www.jillnewhouse.com	New York	NY	10028	212-249-9216	734-4098
John Berggruen Gallery 228 Grant Ave *Web:* www.berggruen.com	San Francisco	CA	94108	415-781-4629	781-0126
June Kelly Gallery 166 Mercer St # 3C *Web:* www.junekellygallery.com	New York	NY	10012	212-226-1660	
Kinsman Robinson Galleries 108 Cumberland St *Web:* www.kinsmanrobinson.com	Toronto	ON	M5R1A6	416-964-2374	964-9042
Kraushaar Galleries Inc 15 E 71 St Ste 2B *Web:* www.kraushaargalleries.com	New York	NY	10021	212-288-2558	
LA Louver Inc 45 N Venice Blvd *Web:* www.lalouver.com	Venice	CA	90291	310-822-4955	821-7529
Laurence Miller Gallery 20 W 57th St 3rd Fl *Web:* www.laurencemillergallery.com	New York	NY	10019	212-397-3930	397-3932
Lennon Weinberg Inc 514 W 25th St *Web:* www.lennonweinberg.com	New York	NY	10001	212-941-0012	929-3265
Leo Castelli Gallery 18 E 77th St *Web:* www.castelligallery.com	New York	NY	10075	212-249-4470	
Leonard Hutton Galleries 790 Madison Ave Ste 506 *Web:* www.leonardhuttongalleries.com	New York	NY	10065	212-751-7373	832-2261

	City	State	Zip	Phone	Fax
Leslie Tonkonow Artworks & Projects 535 W 22nd St 6th Fl *Web:* www.tonkonow.com	New York	NY	10011	212-255-8450	
Locks Gallery 600 Washington Sq S *Web:* www.locksgallery.com	Philadelphia	PA	19106	215-629-1000	629-3868
Luhring Augustine Gallery 531 W 24th St *Web:* www.luhringaugustine.com	New York	NY	10011	212-206-9100	206-9055
Manny Silverman Gallery 619 N Almont Dr *Web:* mannysilvermangallery.com	Los Angeles	CA	90069	310-659-8256	659-1001
Margo Leavin Gallery 812 N Robertson Blvd *Web:* www.margoleavingallery.com	West Hollywood	CA	90069	310-273-0603	273-9131
Marian Goodman Gallery 24 W 57th St *Web:* www.mariangoodman.com	New York	NY	10019	212-977-7160	581-5187
Mary Ryan Gallery 515 W 26th St *Web:* www.maryryangallery.com	New York	NY	10001	212-397-0669	
Mary-Anne Martin Fine Art 23 E 73rd St 4th Fl *Web:* www.mamfa.com	New York	NY	10021	212-288-2213	861-7656
Masters Gallery Ltd 2115 Fourth St SW *TF:* 866-245-0616 ■ *Web:* www.mastersgalleryltd.com	Calgary	AB	T2S1W8	403-245-2064	244-1636
Matthew Marks Gallery 523 W 24th St *Web:* www.matthewmarks.com	New York	NY	10011	212-243-0200	
Maxwell Davidson Gallery 724 Fifth Ave 4th Fl *Web:* www.davidsongallery.com	New York	NY	10001	212-759-7555	759-5824
Mayberry Fine Art Inc 212 Mcdermot Ave *TF:* 877-871-9261 ■ *Web:* www.mayberryfineart.com	Winnipeg	MB	R3B0S3	204-255-5690	
McKee Gallery 745 Fifth Ave 4th Fl *Web:* www.mckeegallery.com	New York	NY	10151	212-688-5951	752-5638
Meredith Long & Co 2323 San Felipe *Web:* www.meredithlonggallery.com	Houston	TX	77019	713-523-6671	523-2355
Metro Pictures Gallery 519 W 24th St *Web:* metropicturesgallery.com	New York	NY	10011	212-206-7100	337-0070
Meyer East Gallery 225 Canyon Rd *Web:* www.meyergalleries.com	Santa Fe	NM	87501	505-983-1434	
Michael Gibson Gallery 157 Carling St *TF:* 866-644-2766 ■ *Web:* www.gibsongallery.com	London	ON	N6A1H5	519-439-0451	
Michael Rosenfeld Gallery 100 Eleventh Ave *Web:* www.michaelrosenfeldart.com	New York	NY	10011	212-247-0082	247-0402
Michael Werner Gallery 4 E 77th St 2nd Fl *Web:* www.michaelwerner.com	New York	NY	10075	212-988-1623	988-1774
Mira Godard Gallery 22 Hazelton Ave *Web:* www.godardgallery.com	Toronto	ON	M5R2E2	416-964-8197	964-5912
Miriam Shiell Fine Art Ltd 16-A Hazelton Ave *Web:* www.miriamshiell.com	Toronto	ON	M5R2E2	416-925-2461	925-2471
Mitchell-Iness & Nash Gallery 1018 Madison Ave *Web:* www.miandn.com	New York	NY	10075	212-744-7400	744-7401
Modernism Inc 685 Market St Ste 290 *Web:* www.modernisminc.com	San Francisco	CA	94105	415-541-0461	541-0425
Moeller Fine Art Ltd 35 E 64th St *Web:* www.moellerfineart.com	New York	NY	10065	212-644-2133	644-2134
Montgomery Gallery 406 Jackson St *Web:* www.montgomerygallery.com	San Francisco	CA	94111	415-788-8300	788-5469
Nancy Hoffman Gallery 520 W 27th St *Web:* www.nancyhoffmangallery.com	New York	NY	10001	212-966-6676	334-5078
Newmarket Public Library 438 Park Ave *Web:* www.newmarketpl.ca	Newmarket	ON	L3Y1W1	905-953-5110	
Newzones Gallery of Contemporary Art 730 11th Ave SW *Web:* www.newzones.com	Calgary	AB	T2R0E4	403-266-1972	266-1987
Nouveau Gallery 2146 Albert St *Web:* www.nouveaugallery.com	Regina	SK	S4P2T9	306-569-9279	
O'Hara Gallery 595 Madison Ave *Web:* www.johg.com	New York	NY	10022	212-644-3533	
Odon Wagner Gallery 196 Davenport Rd *TF:* 800-551-2465 ■ *Web:* www.odonwagnergallery.com	Toronto	ON	M5R1J2	416-962-0438	962-1581
Olga Korper Gallery 17 Morrow Ave *Web:* www.olgakorpergallery.com	Toronto	ON	M6R2H9	416-538-8220	
Otto Naumann Ltd 22 E 80th St *Web:* www.ottonaumannltd.com	New York	NY	10075	212-734-4443	535-0617
Pace Gallery, The 32 E 57th St 2th Fl *Web:* www.pacegallery.com	New York	NY	10022	212-421-3292	421-0835
Pace Prints 32 E 57th St 3rd Fl *Web:* www.paceprints.com	New York	NY	10022	212-421-3237	832-5162
Paul Kuhn Gallery 724 11th Ave SW *Web:* www.paulkuhngallery.com	Calgary	AB	T2R0E4	403-263-1162	
Paula Cooper Gallery 534 W 21st St *Web:* www.paulacoopergallery.com	New York	NY	10011	212-255-1105	255-5156
Peter Findlay Gallery 16 E 79th St *Web:* www.findlay.com	New York	NY	10075	212-644-4433	644-1675
Phyllis Kind Gallery 236 W 26th St Ste 503 *Web:* www.phylliskindgallery.com	New York	NY	10001	212-925-1200	941-7841
ProTravelGear com 10809 Southern Loop Blvd Unit 1 *Web:* www.protravelgear.com	Pineville	NC	28134	704-583-1100	
Rhona Hoffman Gallery 118 N Peoria St *Web:* www.artnet.com	Chicago	IL	60607	312-455-1990	
Richard Gray Gallery 875 N Michigan Ave 38th Fl *Web:* www.richardgraygallery.com	Chicago	IL	60611	312-642-8877	642-8488
Richard L Feigen & Co 34 E 69th St *Web:* www.rlfeigen.com	New York	NY	10021	212-628-0700	249-4574
Riva Yares Gallery 3625 Bishop Ln *Web:* www.rivayaresgallery.com	Scottsdale	AZ	85251	480-947-3251	
Robert Miller Gallery 524 W 26th St *Web:* www.robertmillergallery.com	New York	NY	10001	212-366-4774	
Roberts Gallery Ltd 641 Yonge St *Web:* www.robertsgallery.net	Toronto	ON	M4Y1Z9	416-924-8731	
Ronald Feldman Fine Arts Inc 31 Mercer St *Web:* www.feldmangallery.com	New York	NY	10013	212-226-3232	941-1536
Schwarz Gallery 1806 Chestnut St *Web:* www.schwarzgallery.com	Philadelphia	PA	19103	215-563-4887	561-5621
Sikkema Jenkins & Co 530 W 22nd St *Web:* www.sikkemajenkinsco.com	New York	NY	10011	212-929-2262	929-2340
Sperone Westwater 257 Bowery *Web:* www.speronewestwater.com	New York	NY	10002	212-999-7337	999-7338
Stephen Bulger Gallery 1026 Queen St W *Web:* www.bulgergallery.com	Toronto	ON	M6J1H6	416-504-0575	504-8929
Stephen Mazoh & Company Inc 19 Pink Ln	Rhinebeck	NY	12572	845-876-2723	876-5838
Susan Hobbs Gallery Inc 137 Tecumseth St *Web:* www.susanhobbs.com	Toronto	ON	M6J2H2	416-504-3699	504-8064
Susan Sheehan Gallery 136 E 16th St *Web:* www.susansheehangallery.com	New York	NY	10003	212-489-3331	489-4009
Tasende Gallery 820 Prospect St *Web:* www.tasendegallery.com	La Jolla	CA	92037	858-454-3691	454-0589
Tatar Art Projects 300 King St E *Web:* tatarartprojects.ca	Toronto	ON	M5A1K4	416-360-3822	
Thielsen Gallery 1038 Adelaide St N *Web:* www.thielsengallery.com	London	ON	N5Y2M9	519-434-7681	
Tibor de Nagy Gallery 724 Fifth Ave 12th Fl *Web:* www.tibordenagy.com	New York	NY	10019	212-262-5050	262-1841
TrepanierBaer Gallery 999 Eigth St SW Ste 105 *Web:* www.trepanierbaer.com	Calgary	AB	T2R1J5	403-244-2066	244-2094
Ubu Gallery 416 E 59th St *Web:* www.ubugallery.com	New York	NY	10022	212-753-4444	753-4470
Uno Langmann Ltd 2117 Granville St *TF:* 800-730-8825 ■ *Web:* www.langmann.com	Vancouver	BC	V6H3E9	604-736-8825	
Valley House Gallery Inc 6616 Spring Vly Rd *Web:* www.valleyhouse.com	Dallas	TX	75254	972-239-2441	239-1462
Vivian Horan Fine Art 35 E 67th St 2nd Fl *Web:* vivianhoran.com	New York	NY	10065	212-517-9410	772-6107
Wallace Galleries Ltd 500 Fifth Ave SW *Web:* www.wallacegalleries.com	Calgary	AB	T2P3L5	403-262-8050	264-7112
West End Gallery Ltd 12308 Jasper Ave *TF:* 855-488-4892 ■ *Web:* www.westendgalleryltd.com	Edmonton	AB	T5N3K5	780-488-4892	
Winchester Galleries Ltd 2260 Oak Bay Ave *Web:* www.winchestergalleriesltd.com	Victoria	BC	V8R1G7	250-595-2777	595-2310
WM Brady & Company Inc 22 E 80th St 4th Fl	New York	NY	10075	212-249-7212	628-6587
Wynick Tuck Gallery 401 Richmond St W Studio S27 *Web:* www.wynicktuckgallery.ca	Toronto	ON	M5V3A8	416-504-8716	504-8699
Zabriskie Gallery 400 E 57th St 19B 4th Fl *Web:* www.zabriskiegallery.com	New York	NY	10022	212-752-1223	752-1224
Zolla Lieberman Gallery 325 W Huron St *Web:* www.zollaliebermangallery.com	Chicago	IL	60654	312-944-1990	944-8967
Zwickers Gallery 5415 Doyle St *Web:* www.zwickersgallery.ca	Halifax	NS	B3J1H9	902-423-7662	422-3870

43 ART MATERIALS & SUPPLIES - MFR

See Also Pens, Pencils, Parts p. 2911

	City	State	Zip	Phone	Fax
Adco Inc PO Box 815382 *TF:* 800-486-4583 ■ *Web:* www.gluestick.com	Dallas	TX	75381	972-484-6177	484-1726
Alvin & Company Inc 1335 Blue Hills Ave *Fax Area Code: 800 ■ *TF:* 800-444-2584 ■ *Web:* www.alvinco.com	Bloomfield	CT	06002	860-243-8991	777-2896*
American Art Clay Co (AMACO) 6060 Guion Rd *TF:* 800-374-1600 ■ *Web:* www.amaco.com	Indianapolis	IN	46254	317-244-6871	248-9300
American Metalcraft Inc 2074 George St *TF:* 800-333-9133 ■ *Web:* www.amnow.com	Melrose Park	IL	60160	708-345-1177	345-5758
Ampersand Art Supply 1235 S Loop 4 Ste 400 *TF:* 800-822-1939 ■ *Web:* www.ampersandart.com	Buda	TX	78610	512-322-0278	322-9928
ART Studio Clay Co 9320 Michigan Ave *TF:* 800-323-0212 ■ *Web:* www.artclay.com	Sturtevant	WI	53177	262-884-4278	884-4343
Artist Brand Canvas 2448 Loma Ave *Fax Area Code: 323 ■ *TF Orders:* 888-579-2704 ■ *Web:* www.artistbrandcanvas.com	South El Monte	CA	91733	626-579-2740	686-2658*
Badger Air Brush Co 9128 Belmont Ave *TF:* 800-247-2787 ■ *Web:* www.badgerairbrush.com	Franklin Park	IL	60131	847-678-3104	671-4352
Canson Inc 21 Industrial Dr *Web:* www.cansonstudio.com	South Hadley	MA	01075	413-538-9250	534-7692
Chartpak Inc 1 River Rd *TF:* 800-628-1910 ■ *Web:* www.chartpak.com	Leeds	MA	01053	413-584-5446	584-6781
Daler-Rowney USA Ltd 7 Corporate Dr *Web:* www.daler-rowney.com	Cranbury	NJ	08512	609-655-5252	655-5852
DecoArt Inc 49 Cotton Ave *TF:* 800-367-3047 ■ *Web:* www.decoart.com	Stanford	KY	40484	606-365-3193	365-2997
Duncan Enterprises 5673 E Shields Ave *TF:* 800-438-6226 ■ *Web:* www.ilovetocreate.com	Fresno	CA	93727	559-291-4444	291-4444
Gare Inc 165 Rosemont St *Fax Area Code: 800 ■ *TF:* 888-289-4273 ■ *Web:* www.gare.com	Haverhill	MA	01832	978-373-9131	292-0885*
General Pencil Co Inc 3160 Bay Rd *Web:* www.generalpencil.com	Redwood City	CA	94063	650-369-4889	369-7169
Georgie's Ceramic & Clay Company Inc 756 NE Lombard St *TF:* 800-999-2529 ■ *Web:* www.georgies.com	Portland	OR	97211	503-283-1353	283-1387
Golden Artists Colors Inc 188 Bell Rd *TF:* 800-959-6543 ■ *Web:* www.goldenpaints.com	New Berlin	NY	13411	607-847-6154	847-6767
Jack Richeson & Company Inc 557 Marcella Dr *TF:* 800-233-2404 ■ *Web:* www.richesonart.com	Kimberly	WI	54136	920-738-0744	738-9156
Martin/F Weber Co 2727 Southampton Rd *TF:* 800-876-8076 ■ *Web:* www.weberart.com	Philadelphia	PA	19154	215-677-5600	677-3336
National Artcraft Supply Co 300 Campus Dr *TF:* 888-937-2723 ■ *Web:* www.nationalartcraft.com	Aurora	OH	44202	330-562-3500	562-3507
Paasche Airbrush Co 4311 N Normandy *TF Sales:* 800-621-1907 ■ *Web:* www.paascheairbrush.com	Chicago	IL	60634	773-867-9191	867-9198
Plaid Enterprises Inc 3225 Westech Dr *Fax: Mktg ■ *TF:* 800-842-4197 ■ *Web:* www.plaidonline.com	Norcross	GA	30092	678-291-8100	291-8368*
Sargent Art Inc 100 E Diamond Ave *TF:* 800-424-3596 ■ *Web:* www.sargentart.com	Hazleton	PA	18201	570-454-3596	459-1752

	City	State	Zip	Phone	Fax
Sinopia Pigments 2349 Third St PO Box 884354 *Web:* www.sinopia.com	San Francisco	CA	94107	415-433-2724	
Smooth-On Inc 2000 St John St *TF:* 800-762-0744 ■ *Web:* www.smooth-on.com	Easton	PA	18042	610-252-5800	252-6200
Testor Corp 440 Blackhawk Pk Ave *TF:* 800-837-8677 ■ *Web:* www.testors.com	Rockford	IL	61104	815-962-6654	962-7401
Tri-Chem 681 Main St Bldg 24 *Web:* www.trichem.com	Belleville	NJ	07109	973-751-9200	450-1260
Utrecht Art Supplies PO Box 1769 **Fax Area Code:* 800 ■ *TF:* 888-336-3114 ■ *Web:* www.utrechtart.com	Galesburg	IL	61402	609-409-8001	382-1979*

44 ART MATERIALS & SUPPLIES - WHOL

	City	State	Zip	Phone	Fax
American Hobby Craft Distributors Inc 2040 W N Ln	Phoenix	AZ	85021	602-861-1239	944-7124
Creative Hobbies Inc 900 Creek Rd *TF:* 800-843-5456 ■ *Web:* creativehobbies.com	Bellmawr	NJ	08031	856-933-2540	
CWI Gifts & Crafts 77 Cypress St SW *TF:* 800-666-5858 ■ *Web:* www.shopcwi.com	Reynoldsburg	OH	43068	740-964-6210	964-6212
D&L Art Glass Supply 1440 W 52nd Ave *TF:* 800-525-0940 ■ *Web:* www.dlstainedglass.com	Denver	CO	80221	303-449-8737	442-3429
Darice Inc 13000 Darice Pkwy **Fax Area Code:* 440 ■ *TF:* 866-432-7423 ■ *Web:* www.darice.com	Strongsville	OH	44149	866-432-7423	238-1680*
Decorator & Craft Corp (DC & C) 428 S Zelta St *Web:* www.dcccrafts.com	Wichita	KS	67207	316-685-6265	685-7606
Dumouchelle Art Gallery 409 E Jefferson Ave *Web:* www.dumouchelles.com	Detroit	MI	48226	313-963-6255	963-8199
Howell's Craftand Imports 6030 NE 112th Ave **Fax Area Code:* 503 ■ *TF:* 800-547-0368 ■ *Web:* www.howells-craftland.com	Portland	OR	97220	800-547-0368	255-6878*
King Craft Co 142 N Main St *Web:* www.kingcraftco.com	Herkimer	NY	13350	315-866-5500	866-8062
Pioneer Wholesale Co 500 W Bagley Rd *TF:* 888-234-5400 ■ *Web:* www.pioneerwholesaleco.com	Berea	OH	44017	440-234-5400	234-5403
Sbar's Inc 14 Sbar Blvd *TF:* 800-989-7227 ■ *Web:* www.sbarsonline.com	Moorestown	NJ	08057	856-234-8220	234-9159
Sepp Leaf Products Inc 381 Pk Ave S Ste 1301 *TF:* 800-971-7377 ■ *Web:* www.seppleaf.com	New York	NY	10016	212-683-2840	725-0308
Shop Hobby Lobby 7717 SW 44th St *TF:* 800-888-0321 ■ *Web:* www.hobbylobby.com	Oklahoma City	OK	73179	405-745-1275	

45 ART SUPPLY STORES

	City	State	Zip	Phone	Fax
Aaron Bros Inc 8001 Ridgepoint Dr Ste 500 *Web:* www.aaronbrothers.com	Irving	TX	75063	214-492-6200	
Able Infosat Communications Inc 5906 Broadway St *Web:* www.able-usa.com	Pearland	TX	77581	281-485-8800	
AC Moore Arts & Crafts Inc 130 AC Moore Dr *NASDAQ: ACMR* ■ *TF:* 888-226-6673 ■ *Web:* www.acmoore.com	Berlin	NJ	08009	888-226-6673	
Accord Carton 6155 W 115th St *TF:* 800-648-6780 ■ *Web:* accordcarton.com	Alsip	IL	60803	800-648-6780	
Al Friedman Company Inc 44 W 18th St *TF:* 800-204-6352 ■ *Web:* www.aifriedman.com	New York	NY	10011	212-243-9000	929-7320
Alabama Art Supply Inc 1006 23rd St S *TF Cust Svc:* 800-749-4741 ■ *Web:* www.alabamaart.com	Birmingham	AL	35205	205-322-4741	254-3116
All Copy Products LLC 4141 Colorado Blvd *Web:* www.allcopyproducts.com	Denver	CO	80216	303-295-0741	
All in One Poster Co 8521 Whitaker St *TF:* 800-273-0307 ■ *Web:* www.allinoneposters.com	Buena Park	CA	90621	714-521-7720	
All Media Art Supply 417 E Main St *Web:* allmediaartsupply.com	Kent	OH	44240	330-678-8078	
All-Fab Building Components Inc 1755 Dugald Rd *TF:* 800-665-0335 ■ *Web:* www.all-fab.com	Winnipeg	MB	R2J0H3	204-661-8880	
Alpina Manufacturing LLC 3418 N Knox Ave *TF:* 800-915-2828 ■ *Web:* www.fastchangeframes.com	Chicago	IL	60641	773-202-8887	
AmeriWater Inc 1303 Stanley Ave *Web:* ameriwater.com	Dayton	OH	45404	937-461-8833	
Aquinas & More Catholic Goods Inc 4727 N Academy Blvd Ste A *Web:* www.aquinasandmore.com	Colorado Springs	CO	80918	719-495-7493	
Arch Framing & Design Inc 7844 Manchester Rd Ste *Web:* www.archframing.com	Saint Louis	MO	63143	314-645-6621	
Arizona Art Supply 4025 N 16th St *TF:* 877-264-9514 ■ *Web:* www.arizonaartsupply.com	Phoenix	AZ	85016	602-264-9514	
Armor Security Inc 2601 Stevens Ave South *Web:* www.armorsecurity.com	Minneapolis	MN	55408	612-870-4142	
Art Corner, The 264 Washington St *Web:* artcornersalem.com	Salem	MA	01970	978-745-9524	
Art Essentials 32 E Victoria St *Web:* www.sbartessentials.com	Santa Barbara	CA	93101	805-965-5456	
Art Hardware 119 E Costilla *Web:* arthardware.wordpress.com	Colorado Springs	CO	80903	719-635-2348	
Art Supply Warehouse 6672 Westminster Blvd *TF:* 800-854-6467 ■ *Web:* www.artsupplywarehouse.com	Westminster	CA	92683	714-891-3626	895-6701
Artmart 2355 S Hanley Rd *Web:* www.artmartstl.com	Saint Louis	MO	63144	314-781-9999	781-3121
ASC Global Technologies 4430 Laven Way *Web:* www.ascglobaltechnologies.com	Colorado Springs	CO	80920	719-321-4975	
Asel Art Supply 2701 Cedar Springs *TF:* 888-273-5278 ■ *Web:* www.aselart.com	Dallas	TX	75201	214-871-2425	871-0007
Autotether Inc 3 Inspiration Ln Unit B3 *Web:* www.autotether.com	Chester	CT	06412	860-526-1700	
Backblaze Inc 500 Ben Franklin Ct *Web:* www.backblaze.com	San Mateo	CA	94401	650-352-3738	
Best Banner Sign Graphics Inc 630 Canion St *Web:* www.bannersigngraphics.com	Austin	TX	78752	512-458-5348	
Bestronics Inc 2060 Ringwood Ave *Web:* www.bestronics.com	San Jose	CA	95131	408-432-3222	
Bettendorf Office Products Inc 3280 Middle Rd *Web:* www.bettoffice.com	Bettendorf	IA	52722	563-359-3487	359-8901
Blaine's Art Supply 1025 Photo Ave *TF:* 866-561-4278 ■ *Web:* www.blainesart.com	Anchorage	AK	99503	907-561-5344	562-5988
Bobcat Central Inc 3516 Newton Rd *Web:* www.bobcatcentral.com	Stockton	CA	95205	209-466-9631	
Business Systems & Consultants Inc 113 Little Vly Ct *Web:* bscsolutions.com	Birmingham	AL	35244	205-988-3300	
Cannagrow Holdings Inc 3440 E. Russell Rd,Suite 206 *Web:* cannagrowholdings.com	Las Vegas	NV	89120	702-214-4249	
Care Wise Medical Products Corp 16110 Caputo Dr *Web:* www.carewise.com	Morgan Hill	CA	95038	408-779-5531	
Cashman Equipment Co 3300 St Rose Pkwy *Web:* www.cashmanequipment.com	Henderson	NV	89052	702-649-8777	
Cazenovia Equipment Company Inc 2 Remington Park Dr *Web:* www.cazenoviaequipment.com	Cazenovia	NY	13035	315-655-8620	
Cen-Cal Fire Systems Inc P.O. Box 1284 *Web:* cen-calfire.com	Lodi	CA	94070	209-334-9119	
Cody Pools Inc 2300 W Parmer Ln *Web:* www.codypools.com	Austin	TX	78727	512-835-4966	
Condor Reliability Services Inc 3400 De La Cruz Blvd Unit R *Web:* www.crsigroup.com	Santa Clara	CA	95054	408-486-9600	
Congdon's Aids To Daily Living Ltd 100 A Ave Ste 15830 *Web:* congdons.ab.ca	Edmonton	AB	T5P0L8	780-483-1762	
Continental Art Supplies 7041 Reseda Blvd *Web:* www.continentalart.com	Reseda	CA	91335	818-345-1044	
Controls Corporation of America 1501 Harpers Rd *Web:* www.concoa.com	Virginia Beach	VA	23454	757-422-8330	
Crafts Frames & Things 108 Owen Dr *Web:* www.craftsframesandthings.com	Fayetteville	NC	28304	910-485-4833	
Crime Alert Alarm Co 690 Lenfest Rd *Web:* www.crimealert.com	San Jose	CA	95133	408-729-6200	
Custom Automated Controls Inc 2019 Jefferson Ter *Web:* www.custautocont.com	New Iberia	LA	70560	337-369-1523	
Dick Blick Co PO Box 1267 *TF Orders:* 800-447-8192 ■ *Web:* www.dickblick.com	Galesburg	IL	61402	309-343-6181	
Douglas & Sturgess Inc 1023 Factory St *Web:* www.artstuf.com	Richmond	CA	94801	510-235-8411	235-4211
Ellis & Associates Inc 508 Goldenmoss Loop *Web:* www.jellis.com	Ocoee	FL	34761	407-401-7136	
Entegrity Networks Inc 6220 Avanti Dr *Web:* entegritynetworks.com	Arlington	TX	76001	214-432-5418	
Esna Technologies Inc 30 W Beaver Creek Rd Ste 101 *Web:* www.esna.com	Richmond Hill	ON	L4B3K1	905-707-9700	
EverGlow NA Inc 1122 Industrial Dr *Web:* www.everglow.us	Matthews	NC	28105	704-841-2580	
Excelleris Technologies Inc 4445 Lougheed Hwy Ste 201 *TF:* 866-728-4777 ■ *Web:* www.excelleris.com	Burnaby	BC	V5C0E4	866-728-4777	
Fastframe USA Inc 1200 Lawrence Dr Ste 300 *Web:* www.fastframe.com	Newbury Park	CA	91320	805-498-4463	498-8983
Flax Art & Design 1699 Market St *TF:* 844-352-9278 ■ *Web:* www.flaxart.com	San Francisco	CA	94103	415-552-2355	
Franks International Services Inc 10260 Westheimer Rd Ste 700 *Web:* www.franksintl.com	Houston	TX	77042	281-966-7300	
G & H Art Co 4300 Hamilton Rd	Columbus	GA	31904	706-576-5551	
General Welding Supply Company and Propane Co 15 Lombard St *Web:* www.generalwelding.net	Martins Ferry	OH	43935	740-635-1324	
Georgie's Ceramic & Clay Company Inc 756 NE Lombard St *TF:* 800-999-2529 ■ *Web:* www.georgies.com	Portland	OR	97211	503-283-1353	283-1387
Haber Vision LLC 15710 W Colfax Ave Ste 204 *Web:* www.habervision.com	Golden	CO	80401	303-459-2220	
Herweck's Art & Drafting Supplies 300 Broadway St *TF:* 800-725-1349 ■ *Web:* www.herwecks.com	San Antonio	TX	78205	210-227-1349	
Hobby Lobby Creative Centers 7707 SW 44th St *TF:* 855-329-7060 ■ *Web:* www.hobbylobby.com	Oklahoma City	OK	73179	405-745-1100	745-1547
Hobbytown USA 1233 Libra Dr *Web:* www.hobbytown.com	Lincoln	NE	68512	402-434-5050	
Imaging Office Systems Inc 4505 E Park 30 Dr *Web:* www.imagingoffice.com	Columbia City	IN	46725	260-248-9696	
Insight Instruments Inc 2580 SE Willoughby Blvd *Web:* www.insightinstruments.com	Stuart	FL	34994	772-219-9393	
J. D. Young Company Inc 116 W Third St *Web:* www.jdyoung.com	Tulsa	OK	74103	918-582-9955	
Kanson Electronics Inc 245 Forrest Ave *Web:* www.issc-kanson.com	Hohenwald	TN	38462	931-796-3050	
Lantana Communications Corp 1700 Tech Centre Pkwy Ste 100 *TF:* 800-345-4211 ■ *Web:* www.lantanacom.com	Arlington	TX	76014	800-345-4211	

Company	City	State	ZIP	Phone	Fax
Lee's Art Shop Inc 220 W 57th St	New York	NY	10019	212-247-0110	581-7023
Web: www.leesartshop.com					
Legend Data Systems Inc 18024 72nd Ave South	Kent	WA	98032	425-251-1670	
Web: www.legendid.com					
Longwall Associates Inc 212 Kendall Ave	Chilhowie	VA	24319	276-646-2004	
Web: www.longwall.com					
M C Electronics Inc 1891 Airway Dr	Hollister	CA	95023	831-637-1651	
Web: www.mcelectronics.com					
MarketFrames Group LLC					
5331 SW Macadam Ave Ste 357	Portland	OR	97239	503-892-0160	
Web: www.marketframes.com					
Masterman's LLP 11 C St	Auburn	MA	01501	508-755-7861	
Web: www.mastermans.com					
Michaels Stores Inc 8000 Bent Branch Dr	Irving	TX	75063	972-409-1300	409-7570*
**Fax:* Hum Res ■ *TF Cust Svc:* 800-642-4235 ■ *Web:* www.michaels.com					
Micron Industries Corp 1211 22nd St Ste 200	Oak Brook	IL	60523	630-516-1222	
Web: micronpower.com					
Millers Artist Supplies Co					
33332 W 12 Mile Rd	Farmington Hills	MI	48334	248-489-8070	489-8643
Web: www.millersart.com					
Model Electronics Inc 615 E Crescent Ave	Ramsey	NJ	07446	201-961-9200	
Web: www.modelelectronics.com					
Modern Farm Equipment Co 2929 N Bluff St	Fulton	MO	65251	573-642-5777	
Web: www.modernfarmequip.com					
Motion Specialties Inc 2720 12 St NE	Calgary	AB	T2E7N4	403-247-2222	
Web: www.motionspecialties.com					
National Art Shop 509 S National Ave	Springfield	MO	65802	417-866-3743	866-3748
Web: nationalartshop.com					
Nelson White Systems Inc					
8725-A Loch Raven Blvd	Baltimore	MD	21286	410-668-9628	
Web: www.nelsonwhite.com					
New York Central Art Supply 62 Third Ave	New York	NY	10003	800-950-6111	475-2513*
**Fax Area Code:* 212 ■ *TF:* 800-950-6111 ■ *Web:* www.nycentralart.com					
NovaMed Corp 30 Nutmeg Dr	Trumbull	CT	06611	203-380-6682	
Web: www.novamedcorp.com					
Omnipure Filter Company Inc					
1904 Industrial Way	Caldwell	ID	83605	208-454-2597	
Web: www.omnipure.com					
Orbit Medical Enterprises Inc					
716 East 4500 South Ste 2500 S	Salt Lake City	UT	84107	801-713-2020	
TF: 800-430-0539 ■ *Web:* www.orbitmedical.com					
Orthotic Prosthetic Center Inc					
8330 Professional Hill Dr	Fairfax	VA	22031	703-698-5007	
Web: opc1.com					
Pantronix Corp 2710 Lakeview Ct	Fremont	CA	94538	510-656-5898	
Web: www.pantronix.com					
Pat Catan's Craft Centers					
21160 Drake Rd	Strongsville	OH	44149	440-238-7318	
Web: www.patcatans.com					
Patten Monument Co 3980 W River Dr NE	Comstock Park	MI	49321	616-785-4141	
Web: www.pattenmonument.com					
Petersen Industries Inc 4000 SR 60 W	Lake Wales	FL	33859	863-676-1493	
Web: www.petersenind.com					
Plaza Art 633 Middleton St	Nashville	TN	37203	615-254-3368	254-1814
TF: 866-668-6714 ■ *Web:* www.plazaart.com					
Plaza Artists Materials of the MidAtlantic Inc					
1990 K Str NW	Washington	DC	20006	202-331-7090	331-3004
TF: 866-668-6714 ■ *Web:* www.plazaart.com					
Premier Pyrotechnics Inc 25255 Hwy K	Richland	MO	65556	888-647-6863	
TF: 888-647-6863 ■ *Web:* www.premierpyro.com					
Presentation Concepts Corp					
7243 State Fair Blvd	Syracuse	NY	13209	315-635-6226	
Web: www.pccav.com					
Proline Supply Co 6711 Bingle Rd	Houston	TX	77092	713-939-9730	
Web: www.prolinesupplyco.com					
Provisio Group Ltd, The					
10910 W Sam Houston Pkwy N Ste 500	Houston	TX	77064	281-894-7700	
Web: www.provisiogroup.com					
Quality Filtration LLC					
5215 Linbar Dr Ste 204	Nashville	TN	37211	615-833-2400	
Web: www.qualityfiltration.com					
Quality Lease Service LLC					
480 County Rd 355 PO Box 1215	El Campo	TX	77437	979-543-4738	
Web: www.rocaceia-es.com					
Rabbit Air 9242 1/2 Hall Rd	Downey	CA	90241	562-861-4688	
TF: 888-866-8862 ■ *Web:* www.rabbitair.com					
Ready Set Go Po Box 856	Ukiah	CA	95482	707-468-0213	
Web: rdysetgo.com					
Regali Inc 518 N Interurban St	Richardson	TX	75081	972-726-8830	
Web: www.regaliinc.com					
Repeat Business Systems Inc 4 Fritz Blvd	Albany	NY	12205	518-869-8116	
Web: www.repeatbusinesssystems.com					
Restaurant Solutions Inc 1423 Austell Rd	Marietta	GA	30008	770-421-1999	
Web: www.restaurantsolutionsinc.com					
Rex Artist Supplies 3160 SW 22 St	Miami	FL	33145	305-445-1413	445-1412
TF: 800-739-2782 ■ *Web:* www.rexart.com					
RISD Store Art Supplies 30 N Main St	Providence	RI	02903	401-454-6464	454-6453
Web: risdstore.com					
Riverside Art Shop 1600 Grand Army Hwy	Somerset	MA	02726	508-672-6735	
Web: www.riversideart.com					
Santa Fe Partners LLC					
1512 Pacheco St Ste D202	Santa Fe	NM	87505	505-989-8180	
Savoir-Faire 40 Leveroni Ct	Novato	CA	94949	415-884-8090	
Web: www.savoirfaire.com					
Schulz Electric Co 30 Gando Dr	New Haven	CT	06513	203-562-5811	
Web: schulzelectric.com					
Short Order Lp 12521 Amherst Dr	Austin	TX	78727	512-610-3600	
Web: www.shortorder.com					
Smarterville Productions LLC					
1407 Fleet St Ste 150	Baltimore	MD	21231	443-320-2044	
Web: smarterville.com					
Spokane Art Supply Inc 1303 N Monroe St	Spokane	WA	99201	509-327-6622	327-6629
TF: 800-556-5568 ■ *Web:* www.spokaneartsupply.com					

Company	City	State	ZIP	Phone	Fax
Stagecraft Industries Inc 5051 N Lagoon Ave	Portland	OR	97217	503-286-1600	
Web: www.stagecraftindustries.com					
Starvin' Artist Supplies 802 S Oak Pk	Oak Park	IL	60304	708-358-3600	
TF: 800-427-8478 ■ *Web:* www.starvinartistsupply.com					
Stewart Business Systems LLC					
105 Connecticut Dr	Burlington	NJ	08016	609-589-4800	
Web: www.stewartxerox.com					
Suder's Art Store 1309 Vine St	Cincinnati	OH	45202	513-241-0800	
Web: sudersartstore.com					
SVTronics Inc 3465 Technology	Plano	TX	75074	214-440-1234	
Web: www.svtronics.com					
Symon's Fire Protection Inc					
1050 Pioneer Way Ste R	El Cajon	CA	92020	619-588-6364	
Web: www.symonsfp.com					
Technical Resource Group Inc					
7225 Bryan Dairy Rd	Largo	FL	33777	727-533-9440	
Web: www.picktrg.com					
Texas Art Supply 2001 Montrose Blvd	Houston	TX	77006	713-526-5221	526-4062
TF: 800-888-9278 ■ *Web:* www.texasart.com					
Texas Deer Association					
403 E Ramsey Rd Ste 204	San Antonio	TX	78216	210-767-8300	
Web: www.texasdeerassociation.com					
Thomsons Art Supply Inc					
184 Mamaroneck Ave	White Plains	NY	10601	914-949-4885	949-4978
Web: www.thomsonsart.com					
Top Notch Art Ctr 411 S Craig St	Pittsburgh	PA	15213	412-683-4444	
Web: tnartsupply.com					
Tournament Games Inc 107 W High St	Lebanon	TN	37087	615-547-1777	
Web: play.tournamentgames.com					
Trinity Ceramic Supply Inc 9016 Diplomacy Row	Dallas	TX	75247	214-631-0540	
Web: www.trinityceramic.com					
Tristar Electronics Corp					
3610 Willowbend Blvd Ste 1020	Houston	TX	77054	713-667-7200	
Web: www.tristareca.com					
Versalift East Inc 2706 Brodhead Rd	Bethlehem	PA	18020	610-866-1400	
Web: www.versalifteast.com					
Village Art Supply 715 Hahman Dr	Santa Rosa	CA	95405	707-575-4501	568-2112
VMI Inc 211 E Weddell Dr	Sunnyvale	CA	94089	408-745-1700	
Web: www.vmivideo.com					
Walden Equipment Ltd 2479 Riverside Dr	Timmins	ON	P4N2X7	705-682-2084	
Web: www.waldenequipment.ca					
Wasatch Container Inc					
645 North 400 West	North Salt Lake	UT	84054	801-295-8888	
Web: www.wasatchcontainer.com					
Wet Paint Inc 1684 W Grand Ave	Saint Paul	MN	55105	651-698-6431	698-8041
Web: www.wetpaintart.com					
Wire & Plastic Machinery Co 800 E Second St	Bonham	TX	75418	903-583-2183	
Web: www.wireandplastic.com					
Woodcraft Supply LLC 1177 Rosemar Rd	Parkersburg	WV	26105	800-535-4482	428-8271*
**Fax Area Code:* 304 ■ *TF:* 800-535-4482 ■ *Web:* www.woodcraft.com					
Zistos Corp 1736 Church St	Holbrook	NY	11741	631-434-1370	
Web: www.zistos.com					

46 ASPHALT PAVING & ROOFING MATERIALS

Company	City	State	ZIP	Phone	Fax
AE Stone Inc 1435 Doughty Rd	Egg Harbor Township	NJ	08234	609-641-2781	
Web: www.aestone.com					
American Asphalt Paving Co 500 Chase Rd	Shavertown	PA	18708	570-696-1181	696-3486
Web: www.amerasphalt.com					
Asphalt Materials Inc PO Box 5	West Jordan	UT	84084	801-561-4231	561-7795
Web: asphaltmaterials.net					
Atlas Roofing Corp 2322 Valley Rd	Meridian	MS	39307	601-483-7111	483-7344
TF Cust Svc: 800-478-0258 ■ *Web:* www.atlasroofing.com					
Baker Rock Resources					
21880 SW Farmington Rd	Beaverton	OR	97007	503-642-2531	642-2534
TF: 800-340-7625 ■ *Web:* www.baker-rock.com					
Brannan Sand & Gravel Co 2500 Brannan Way	Denver	CO	80229	303-534-1231	534-1231
Web: www.brannan1.com					
Brewer Co 1354 US Hwy 50	Milford	OH	45150	513-576-6300	576-1414
TF: 800-394-0017 ■ *Web:* www.brewercote.com					
Brox Industries Inc 1471 Methuen St	Dracut	MA	01826	978-454-9105	805-9720
Web: www.broxindustries.com					
Burkholder Paving 621 Martindale Rd	Ephrata	PA	17522	717-354-1340	428-7469*
**Fax Area Code:* 888 ■ *TF:* 866-839-3426 ■ *Web:* www.burkholderpaving.com					
Capitol Aggregates Ltd					
12625 Wetmore Rd Ste 301	San Antonio	TX	78247	210-871-6100	
TF: 800-292-5315 ■ *Web:* www.capitolaggregates.com					
CertainTeed Corp 750 E Swedesford Rd	Valley Forge	PA	19482	610-341-7000	341-7777
TF Prod Info: 800-782-8777 ■ *Web:* www.certainteed.com					
Coastal Bridge Company LLC					
4825 Jamestown Ave PO Box 14715	Baton Rouge	LA	70898	225-766-0244	766-0423
Web: www.coastalbridge.com					
Community Asphalt Corp 9675 NW 117 Ave Ste 108	Miami	FL	33178	305-884-9444	884-9448
Web: www.cacorp.net					
Consolidated Fiberglass Products Co					
3801 Standard St	Bakersfield	CA	93308	661-323-6026	324-2635
Web: www.conglas.com					
Coopers Creek Chemical Corp					
884 River Rd	West Conshohocken	PA	19428	610-828-0375	828-9720
Web: www.cooperscreekchemical.com					
Crafco Inc 420 N Roosevelt Ave	Chandler	AZ	85226	602-276-0406	961-0513*
**Fax Area Code:* 480 ■ *TF:* 800-528-8242 ■ *Web:* www.crafco.com					
Dalrymple Gravel & Contracting Company Inc					
2105 S Broadway	Pine City	NY	14871	607-737-6200	737-1056
Web: www.dalrymplecompanies.com					
Dalton Enterprises Inc 131 Willow St	Cheshire	CT	06410	203-272-3221	271-3396
TF: 800-851-5606 ■ *Web:* www.latexite.com					
Dewitt Products Co 5860 Plumer Ave	Detroit	MI	48209	313-554-0575	554-2171
TF Cust Svc: 800-962-8599 ■ *Web:* www.dewittproducts.com					
Fields Company LLC 2240 Taylor Way	Tacoma	WA	98421	800-627-4098	383-2181*
**Fax Area Code:* 253 ■ *TF:* 800-627-4098 ■ *Web:* www.fieldscorp.com					

Phone Fax

GAF Materials Corp 1361 Alps Rd .... Wayne NJ 07470 973-628-3000
TF: 800-365-7353 ■ *Web:* www.gaf.com

Gardner-Gibson PO Box 5449 .... Tampa FL 33675 813-248-2101 248-6768
TF: 800-237-1155 ■ *Web:* www.gardner-gibson.com

Garland Company Inc 3800 E 91st St .... Cleveland OH 44105 216-641-7500 641-0633
TF: 800-321-9336 ■ *Web:* www.garlandco.com

General Asphalt Co Inc 4850 NW 72nd Ave .... Miami FL 33166 305-592-3480 477-4675

Glenn O Hawbaker Inc
1952 Waddle Rd Ste 203 .... State College PA 16803 814-237-1444
TF: 800-221-1355 ■ *Web:* www.goh-inc.com

Granite Construction Inc 585 W Beach St .... Watsonville CA 95076 831-724-1011 722-9657
NYSE: GVA ■ *Web:* www.graniteconstruction.com

Heely-Brown Company Inc
1280 Chattahoochee Ave .... Atlanta GA 30318 404-352-0022 350-2693
TF: 800-241-4628 ■ *Web:* www.heelybrown.com

Hempt Bros Inc 205 Creek Rd .... Camp Hill PA 17011 717-737-3411 761-5019
Web: hemptbros.com

Henry Co 909 N Sepulveda Blvd Ste 650 .... El Segundo CA 90245 310-955-9200 223-1285*
**Fax Area Code:* 866 ■ **Fax:* Cust Svc ■ *TF:* 800-598-7663 ■ *Web:* www.henry.com

HRI Inc 1750 W College Ave .... State College PA 16801 814-238-5071 238-0131
TF: 877-474-9999 ■ *Web:* www.hrico.com

Innovative Metals Company Inc (IMETCO)
4648 S Old Peachtree Rd .... Norcross GA 30084 770-908-1030 908-2264
TF: 800-646-3826 ■ *Web:* www.imetco.com

Jax Asphalt Co 1800 Waterworks Rd .... Mount Vernon IL 62864 618-244-0500

Karnak Corp, The 330 Central Ave .... Clark NJ 07066 732-388-0300 388-9422
TF: 800-526-4236 ■ *Web:* www.karnakcorp.com

Koppers Inc 436 Seventh Ave .... Pittsburgh PA 15219 412-227-2001 227-2333
NYSE: KOP ■ *TF:* 800-385-4406 ■ *Web:* www.koppers.com

Lunday-Thagard Co 9302 Garfield Ave .... South Gate CA 90280 562-928-7000 806-4032
TF: 800-266-6551 ■ *Web:* lundaythagard.com

Malarkey Roofing Products PO Box 17217 .... Portland OR 97217 503-283-1191 289-7644
TF: 800-545-1191 ■ *Web:* www.malarkeyroofing.com

Marathon Petroleum LLC PO Box 1 .... Findlay OH 45839 419-422-2121
TF: 866-462-7284 ■ *Web:* www.marathonpetroleum.com

Martin Asphalt Co 3 Riverway Ste 400 .... South Houston TX 77056 713-350-6800 350-6801
TF: 800-662-0987 ■ *Web:* www.themartincompanies.com

Midland Asphalt Materials Inc 640 Young St .... Tonawanda NY 14150 716-692-0730 692-0613
Web: www.midlandasphalt.com

Neyra Industries 10700 Evendale Dr .... Cincinnati OH 45241 513-733-1000
TF: 800-543-7077 ■ *Web:* www.neyra.com

Oldcastle Materials Inc
900 Ashwood Pkwy Ste 700 .... Atlanta GA 30338 770-522-5600 522-5608
Web: www.apac.com

Pace Products Inc
4510 W 89th St Ste 110 .... Prairie Village KS 66207 888-389-8203 469-4067*
**Fax Area Code:* 913 ■ *TF:* 888-389-8203 ■ *Web:* www.paceproducts.com

Package Pavement Company Inc PO Box 408 .... Stormville NY 12582 845-221-2224 221-0433
TF: 800-724-8193 ■ *Web:* www.packagepavement.com

Palmer Asphalt Co 196 W Fifth St PO Box 58 .... Bayonne NJ 07002 201-339-0855 339-8320
TF: 800-352-9898 ■ *Web:* www.palmerasphalt.com

Peckham Industries Inc 20 Haarlem Ave .... White Plains NY 10603 914-949-2000 949-2075
Web: www.peckham.com

PetersenDean Roofing and Solar
39300 Civic Center Dr Ste 300 .... Fremont CA 94538 877-552-4418
TF: 877-552-4418 ■ *Web:* petersendean.com

Pike Industries Inc 3 Eastgate Pk Rd .... Belmont NH 03220 603-527-5100 527-5101
TF: 800-283-0803 ■ *Web:* pikeindustries.com

Rason Asphalt Inc 44 Morris Ave .... Glen Cove NY 11542 516-671-1500

Russell Standard Corp 285 Kappa Dr Ste 300 .... Pittsburgh PA 15238 800-323-3053
TF General: 800-323-3053 ■ *Web:* www.russellstandard.com

Seaboard Asphalt Products Co
3601 Fairfield Rd .... Baltimore MD 21226 410-355-0330 355-5864
TF: 800-536-0332 ■ *Web:* www.seaboardasphalt.com

Sika Sarnafil Inc 100 Dan Rd .... Canton MA 02021 781-828-5400 828-5365
TF: 800-451-2504 ■ *Web:* usa.sarnafil.sika.com

Simon Roofing & Sheet Metal Corp
70 Karago Ave .... Youngstown OH 44512 330-629-7663 629-7399
TF: 800-523-7714 ■ *Web:* www.simonroofing.com

South State Inc 202 Reeves Rd .... Bridgeton NJ 08302 856-451-5300 455-3461
Web: southstateinc.com

Stavola Contracting PO Box 482 .... Red Bank NJ 07701 732-542-2328 389-6083
Web: www.stavola.com

Suit-Kote Corp 1911 Lorings Crossing Rd .... Cortland NY 13045 607-753-1100 756-8611
Web: www.suit-kote.com

Tilcon Connecticut Inc PO Box 1357 .... New Britain CT 06050 860-224-6010 225-1865
TF: 888-845-2666 ■ *Web:* www.tilconct.com

Vance Bros Inc
5201 Brighton PO Box 300107 .... Kansas City MO 64130 816-923-4325 923-6472
TF: 800-821-8549 ■ *Web:* www.vancebrothers.com

Vulcan Materials Co
1200 Urban Ctr Dr PO Box 385014 .... Birmingham AL 35238 205-298-3000
NYSE: VMC ■ *TF:* 800-615-4331 ■ *Web:* www.vulcanmaterials.com

Weldon Materials 141 Central Ave .... Westfield NJ 07090 908-233-4444 233-4215
Web: www.weldonmat.com

47 ASSOCIATION MANAGEMENT COMPANIES

Phone Fax

ABEO Group, The 1300 Baxter St Ste 360 .... Charlotte NC 28204 704-365-3622
Web: www.associationoffices.com

Able Management Solutions Inc
5310 E Main St Ste 104 .... Columbus OH 43213 614-868-1144 868-1177
Web: www.ablemgt.com

Administrative Systems Inc
5204 Fairmount Ave .... Downers Grove IL 60515 630-655-0112 493-0798

Advanced Management Concepts 136 S Keowee St .... Dayton OH 45402 937-222-1024 222-5794
Web: www.advmgtconcepts.com

Allen Press Inc 810 E Tenth St PO Box 1897 .... Lawrence KS 66044 785-843-1235 843-1274
TF: 800-627-0932 ■ *Web:* allenpress.com

Alliance Management Group
1901 Pennsylvania Ave NW Ste 804 .... Washington DC 20006 202-293-7642 293-0495
Web: www.alliancemg.com

Amber Assn Partners LLC
801 N Fairfax St Ste 211 .... Alexandria VA 22314 703-299-0000 299-9233
Web: amberllc.com

AMR Management Services
201 E Main St Ste 1405 .... Lexington KY 40507 859-514-9150 514-9207
Web: www.amrms.com

Applied Measurement Professionals Inc (AMP)
18000 W 105th St .... Olathe KS 66061 913-895-4600 895-4650
Web: www.goamp.com

Association & Society Management International Inc
201 Pk Washington Ct .... Falls Church VA 22046 703-533-0251 241-5603
Web: www.asmii.com

Association Assoc Inc
Mercerville Rd Bldg B Ste 514 .... Trenton NJ 08619 609-890-9207 581-8244
Web: www.hq4u.com

Association Enterprise Inc (AE)
1601 N Bond St Ste 303 .... Naperville IL 60563 630-369-7786 369-3773
Web: incentivemarketing.org

Association Headquarters Inc
1120 Rt 73 Ste 200 .... Mount Laurel NJ 08054 856-439-0500 439-0525
Web: ahredchair.com

Association Management & Communications
349 Granada Rd .... West Palm Beach FL 33401 561-802-4310

Association Management Ctr
8735 W Higgins Rd Ste 300 .... Chicago IL 60631 847-375-4700
Web: www.connect2amc.com

Association Management Group Inc (AMG)
8400 Westpark Dr 2nd Fl .... McLean VA 22102 703-610-9000 610-9005
Web: www.amg-inc.com

Association Management Resources
2123 University Park Dr Ste 100 .... Okemos MI 48864 850-656-8848
Web: www.mgmtresources.org

Association Management Solutions LLC (AMSL)
48377 Freemont Blvd Ste 117 .... Fremont CA 94538 510-492-4000 492-4001
Web: www.amsl.com

Association Management Specialists
275 E Hillcrest Dr Ste 215 .... Thousand Oaks CA 91360 805-557-1111 557-1133
Web: www.assoc-mgmt.net

Association Management Systems Inc
214 N Hale St .... Wheaton IL 60187 630-510-4500 510-4501
Web: www.association-mgmt.com

Association Resource Ctr (ARC)
555 Capitol Mall Ste 755 PO Box 276567 .... Sacramento CA 95814 916-932-2200 932-2209
Web: www.4arc.com

Association Resources Inc
342 N Main St .... West Hartford CT 06117 860-586-7500 586-7550
Web: www.associationresources.com

Association Solutions Ltd
1111 Burlington Ave Ste 102 .... Lisle IL 60532 630-241-3100 241-0142

Bannister & Assoc Inc 34 N High St .... New Albany OH 43054 614-895-1355 895-3466
Web: www.bannister.com

BTF Enterprises Inc 3540 Soquel Ave Ste A .... Santa Cruz CA 95062 831-464-4880 464-4881
Web: www.btfenterprises.com

Calabrese Management 2207 Forest Hills Dr .... Harrisburg PA 17112 717-238-9989 238-9985
Web: www.calabresemgt.com

Center for Assn Growth
1926 Waukegan Rd Ste 1 .... Glenview IL 60025 847-657-6700 657-6819
TF: 800-492-6462 ■ *Web:* tcag.us

Center for Assn Resources Inc
1901 N Roselle Rd Ste 920 .... Schaumburg IL 60195 888-705-1434 885-8393*
**Fax Area Code:* 847 ■ *TF:* 888-705-1434 ■ *Web:* www.association-resources.com

Challenge Management Inc (CMI)
4230 LBJ Fwy Ste 414 .... Dallas TX 75244 972-755-2560 755-2561
Web: www.challenge-management.com

CM Services Inc
800 Roosevelt Rd Bldg C Ste 312 .... Glen Ellyn IL 60137 630-858-7337 790-3095
TF: 800-613-6672 ■ *Web:* www.cmservices.com

Crow-Segal Management Co
341 N Maitland Ave Ste 130 .... Maitland FL 32751 407-647-8839 629-2502
Web: www.crowsegal.com

Custom Management Group LLC
154 Hansen Rd .... Charlottesville VA 22911 434-971-4788 977-1856
Web: www.custommanagement.com

Degnon Assoc Inc 6728 Old McLean Village Dr .... McLean VA 22101 703-556-9222 556-8729
Web: degnon.org

DeSantis Management Group
1950 Old Tustin Ave .... Santa Ana CA 92705 714-550-9155
Web: www.desantisgroup.com

Diversified Management Services
6919 Vista Dr W .... Des Moines IA 50266 515-282-8192 282-9117
Web: www.assoc-mgmt.com

Drake & Co
16020 Swingley Ridge Rd Ste 300 .... Chesterfield MO 63017 636-449-5050 449-5051
Web: www.drakeco.com

Drohan Management Group (DMG)
12100 Sunset Hills Rd Ste 130 .... Reston VA 20190 703-437-4377 435-4390
Web: www.drohanmgmt.com

Ewald Consulting Group Inc
1000 Westgate Dr Ste 252 .... Saint Paul MN 55114 651-290-6260 290-2266
Web: www.ewald.com

Executive Administration Inc
85 W Algonquin Rd Ste 550 .... Arlington Heights IL 60005 847-427-9600 427-9656
Web: www.execadmin.com

Executive Director Inc
555 E Wells St Ste 1100 .... Milwaukee WI 53202 414-276-6445 276-3349
Web: www.execinc.com

Executive Management Assoc
210 N Glenoaks Blvd Ste C .... Burbank CA 91502 818-843-5660 843-7423
Web: www.emaoffice.com

Fanning Group Inc
1280 Main St Second Fl PO Box 479 .... Hanson MA 02341 781-293-4100 294-0808
Web: www.fanningnet.com

				Phone	Fax
Fernley & Fernley Inc 100 N 20th St 4th Fl — Web: www.fernley.com	Philadelphia	PA	19103	215-564-3484	564-2175
Giuffrida Assoc Inc 204 E St NE — Web: www.giuffrida.org	Washington	DC	20002	202-547-6340	547-6348
Grassley Group, The (FMCI) 409 Washington St Ste A — *Fax Area Code: 703 ■ TF: 866-619-5580 ■ Web: www.grassleygroup.com	Cedar Falls	IA	50613	866-619-5580	342-0411*
Guild Assoc Inc, The 389 Main St Ste 202 — Web: www.guildassoc.com	Malden	MA	02148	781-397-8870	
Harrington Co 4248 Pk Glen Rd — Web: www.harringtoncompany.com	Minneapolis	MN	55416	952-928-7477	929-1318
Hauck & Assoc Inc 1025 Thomas Jefferson St Ste 500 E — TF: 800-767-7777 ■ Web: www.hauck.com	Washington	DC	20007	202-452-8100	833-3636
IMI Assn Executives Inc 2501 Aerial Ctr Pkwy Ste 103 — Web: www.imiae.com	Morrisville	NC	27560	919-459-2070	459-2075
Interactive Management Inc 12011 Tejon St Ste 700 — Web: www.imigroup.org	Westminster	CO	80234	303-433-4446	458-0002
J Edgar Eubanks & Assoc 1 Windsor Cove Ste 305 — TF: 800-445-8629 ■ Web: www.jee.com	Columbia	SC	29223	803-252-5646	765-0860
Kellen Co National Press Bldg 529 14th St NW Ste 750 — Web: www.kellencompany.com	Washington	DC	20045	404-252-3663	252-0774
King Stringfellow Group 2105 Laurel Bush Rd Ste 200 — Web: stringfellowgroup.net	Bel Air	MD	21015	443-640-1030	640-1031
LoBue & Majdalany Management Group 572B Ruger St PO Box 29920 — TF: 800-820-4690 ■ Web: www.lm-mgmt.com	San Francisco	CA	94129	415-561-6110	561-6120
Madeleine Crouch & Company Inc 14070 Proton Rd Ste 100 — Web: www.madcrouch.com	Dallas	TX	75244	972-233-9107	490-4219
Management Solutions Plus Inc 9707 Key W Ave Ste 100 — Web: www.mgmtsol.com	Rockville	MD	20850	301-258-9210	990-9771
McBride & Assoc Inc 1633 Normandy Ct Ste A-200 — Web: www.mcbridemanagement.com	Lincoln	NE	68512	402-476-3852	476-6547
Multiservice Management Co 994 Old Eagle School Rd Ste 1019 — Web: www.mmco1.com	Wayne	PA	19087	610-971-4850	971-4859
NeuStar Inc 21575 Ridgetop Cir — TF: 855-638-2677 ■ Web: www.neustar.biz	Sterling	VA	20166	571-434-5400	
Offinger Management Co 1100-H Brandywine Blvd — Web: www.offinger.com	Zanesville	OH	43701	740-452-4541	
Organization Management Group 638 Independence Pkwy Ste 100 — Web: www.managegroup.com	Chesapeake	VA	23320	757-473-8701	473-9897
PAI Management Corp 5272 River Rd Ste 630 — Web: www.paimgmt.com	Bethesda	MD	20816	301-656-4224	656-0989
Pathfinder Group 6009 Quinpool Rd — Web: www.pathfinder-group.com	Halifax	NS	B3K5S3	902-425-2445	
Prime Management Services 3416 Primm Ln — TF: 866-609-1599 ■ Web: primemanagement.net	Birmingham	AL	35216	205-823-6106	823-2760
Professional Management Assoc LLC 390 Amwell Rd Ste 403 — Web: www.association-partners.com	Hillsborough	NJ	08844	908-359-1184	359-7619
Queen Communications LLC 1215 Anthony Ave — Web: www.queencommunicationsllc.com	Columbia	SC	29201	803-779-0340	
R W Armstrong 300 S Meridian St — Web: www.rwa.com	Indianapolis	IN	46225	317-786-0461	788-0957
Raybourn Group International 9100 PuRdue Rd Ste 200 — TF: 800-362-2546 ■ Web: www.raybourn.com	Indianapolis	IN	46268	317-328-4636	280-8527
REM Assn Services 2001 Jefferson Davis Hwy Ste 1004 — Web: www.remservices.biz	Arlington	VA	22202	703-416-0010	
Resource Ctr for Assns 10200 W 44th Ave Ste 304	Wheat Ridge	CO	80033	303-422-2615	422-8894
Robstan Group Inc 400 Admiral Blvd — Web: www.robstan.com	Kansas City	MO	64106	816-472-8870	472-7765
Ruggles Service Corp 2209 Dickens Rd — Web: www.societyhq.com	Richmond	VA	23230	804-282-0062	282-0090
S & S Management Services Inc 1 Regency Dr — Web: www.ssmgt.com	Bloomfield	CT	06002	860-243-3977	286-0787
Sanford Organization Inc, The (TSO) 1000 N Rand Rd Ste 214 — Web: www.tso.net	Wauconda	IL	60084	847-526-2010	526-3993
Solutions for Assns Inc 140 N Bloomingdale Rd — Web: www.sfainc.biz	Bloomingdale	IL	60108	630-351-8669	351-8490
STAT Assn Marketing & Management Inc 11240 Waples Mill Rd Ste 200 — Web: www.statmarketing.com	Fairfax	VA	22030	703-934-0160	359-7562
Talley Management Group Inc 19 Mantua Rd — Web: www.talley.com	Mount Royal	NJ	08061	856-423-7222	423-3420
Technical Enterprises Inc 7044 S 13th St — Web: www.techenterprises.net	Oak Creek	WI	53154	414-768-8000	768-8001
Thomas Assoc Inc 1300 Sumner Ave — Web: www.taol.com	Cleveland	OH	44115	216-241-7333	
Total Management Solutions Inc 55 Harristown Rd — TF: 866-544-0707 ■ Web: www.totmgtsol.com	Glen Rock	NJ	07452	201-447-0707	447-3831
Verto Solutions 1620 'I' St NW Ste 925 — Web: www.vertosolutions.net	Washington	DC	20006	202-293-5800	463-8998
Virtual Inc 401 Edgewater Pl Ste 600 — Web: www.virtualmgmt.com	Wakefield	MA	01880	781-246-0500	224-1239
Wanner Assoc Inc 908 N Second St — Web: www.wannerassoc.com	Harrisburg	PA	17102	717-236-2050	236-2046
Ward Management Group Inc 10293 N Meridian St Ste 175 — Web: www.wardmanage.com	Indianapolis	IN	46290	317-816-1619	816-1633
Wherry Assoc Inc 30200 Detroit Rd — Web: www.wherryassoc.com	Cleveland	OH	44145	440-899-0010	892-1404
Williams Management Resources Inc (WMR) 1717 N Naper Blvd Ste 102 — Web: www.wmrhq.com	Naperville	IL	60563	630-416-1166	416-9798
Willow Group 1485 Laperriere Ave — Web: www.thewillowgroup.com	Ottawa	ON	K1Z7S8	613-722-8796	729-6206

48 ASSOCIATIONS & ORGANIZATIONS - GENERAL

See Also Performing Arts Organizations p. 2919; Political Action Committees p. 2963; Political Parties (Major) p. 2964

48-1 Accreditation & Certification Organizations

				Phone	Fax
AACSB International - Assn to Advance Collegiate Schools of Business 777 S Harbour Island Blvd Ste 750 — Web: www.aacsb.edu	Tampa	FL	33602	813-769-6500	769-6559
ABET Inc 415 North Charles St Ste 1050 — Web: www.abet.org	Baltimore	MD	21201	410-347-7700	625-2238
Accreditation Assn for Ambulatory Health Care (AAAHC) 5250 Old OrchaRd Rd Ste 200 — Web: www.aaahc.org	Skokie	IL	60077	847-853-6060	853-9028
Accreditation Commission for Acupuncture & Oriental Medicine (ACAOM) 7501 Greenway Ctr Dr Ste 760 — TF: 800-735-2968 ■ Web: www.acaom.org	Greenbelt	MD	20770	301-313-0855	313-0912
Accreditation Council for Accountancy & Taxation (ACAT) 1010 N Fairfax St — TF: 888-289-7763 ■ Web: www.acatcredentials.org	Alexandria	VA	22314	703-549-2228	549-2984
Accreditation Council for Graduate Medical Education (ACGME) 515 N State St Ste 2000 — Web: www.acgme.org	Chicago	IL	60610	312-755-5000	755-7498
Accreditation Council for Pharmacy Education 20 N Clark St Ste 2500 — Web: www.acpe-accredit.org	Chicago	IL	60602	312-664-3575	664-4652
Accreditation Review Commission on Education for the Physician Assistant Inc (ARC-PA) 12000 Findley Rd Ste 240 — Web: www.arc-pa.org	Duluth	GA	30097	770-476-1224	476-1738
Accrediting Bureau of Health Education Schools (ABHES) 7777 Leesburg Pike Ste 314 N — TF: 800-228-9290 ■ Web: www.abhes.org	Falls Church	VA	22043	703-917-9503	917-4109
Accrediting Commission of Career Schools & Colleges of Technology (ACCSCT) 2101 Wilson Blvd Ste 302 — Web: www.accsc.org	Arlington	VA	22201	703-247-4212	247-4533
Accrediting Council for Continuing Education & Training (ACCET) 1722 N St NW — Web: www.accet.org	Washington	DC	20036	202-955-1113	955-1118
Accrediting Council for Independent Colleges & Schools (ACICS) 750 First St NE Ste 980 — TF: 800-258-3826 ■ Web: www.acics.org	Washington	DC	20002	202-336-6780	842-2593
Accrediting Council on Education in Journalism & Mass Communications (ACEJMC) *Univ of Kansas School of Journalism Stauffer-Flint Hall* 1435 Jayhawk Blvd — Web: www2.ku.edu	Lawrence	KS	66045	785-864-3973	864-5225
American Academy for Liberal Education (AALE) 1200 G St NW Ste 883 — Web: www.aale.org	Washington	DC	20005	202-452-8611	452-8620
American Assn for Accreditation of Ambulatory Surgery Facilities Inc (AAAASF) 5101 Washington St Ste 2F PO Box 9500 — TF: 888-545-5222 ■ Web: www.aaaasf.org	Gurnee	IL	60031	847-775-1985	775-1985
American Assn for Laboratory Accreditation (A2LA) 5301 Buckeystown Pike Ste 350 — Web: www.a2la.org	Frederick	MD	21704	301-644-3248	662-2974
American Board of Internal Medicine (ABIM) 510 Walnut St Ste 1700 — TF: 800-441-2246 ■ Web: www.abim.org	Philadelphia	PA	19106	215-446-3500	446-3590
American Board of Medical Specialties (ABMS) 353 N Clark St Ste 1400 — Web: www.abms.org	Chicago	IL	60654	312-436-2600	
American Council for Construction Education (ACCE) 1717 N Loop 1604 E Ste 320 — Web: www.acce-hq.org	San Antonio	TX	78232	210-495-6161	495-6168
American Culinary Federation Inc (ACF) 180 Ctr Pl Way — TF: 800-624-9458 ■ Web: www.acfchefs.org	Saint Augustine	FL	32095	904-824-4468	825-4758
American National Standards Institute (ANSI) 25 W 43rd St 4th fl — TF: 800-374-3818 ■ Web: www.ansi.org	New York	NY	10036	212-642-4900	398-0023
American Osteopathic Assn (AOA) 142 E Ontario St — TF: 800-621-1773 ■ Web: www.osteopathic.org	Chicago	IL	60611	312-202-8000	202-8200
Association for Assessment & Accreditation of Laboratory Animal Care International 5283 Corporate Dr Ste 203 — TF: 800-926-0066 ■ Web: www.aaalac.org	Frederick	MD	21703	301-696-9626	696-9627
Association for Biblical Higher Education (AABC) 5850 T G Lee Blvd Ste 130 — Web: www.abhe.org	Orlando	FL	32822	407-207-0808	
Association for Clinical Pastoral Education (ACPE) 1549 Clairmont Rd Ste 103 — Web: www.acpe.edu	Decatur	GA	30033	404-320-1472	320-0849
Association of Advanced Rabbinical & Talmudic Schools (AARTS) 11 Broadway	New York	NY	10004	212-363-1991	533-5335
Association of Collegiate Business Schools & Programs (ACBSP) 11520 W 119th St — Web: www.acbsp.org	Overland Park	KS	66213	913-339-9356	339-6226
Association of Specialized & Professional Accreditors (ASPA) 3304 N Broadway St Ste 214 — Web: www.aspa-usa.org	Chicago	IL	60657	773-857-7900	

Phone | Fax

Canadian Architectural Certification Board
1 Nicholas St Ste 710 ... Ottawa ON K1N7B7 613-241-8399 241-7991
Web: cacb.ca/en/home

Canadian Assn of Occupational Therapists (CAOT)
1125 Colonel By Dr ... Ottawa ON K1S5R1 613-523-2268 523-2552
TF: 800-434-2268 ■ *Web:* www.caot.ca

Canadian Forestry Accreditation Board
18 Pommel Crescent ... Kanata ON K2M1A2 613-599-7259 599-8107
Web: www.cfab.ca

Canadian Information Processing Society (CIPS)
5090 Explorer Dr Ste 801 ... Mississauga ON L4W4T9 905-602-1370 602-7884
TF: 877-275-2477 ■ *Web:* www.cips.ca

Certified Financial Planner Board of Standards Inc
1425 K St NW Ste 500 ... Washington DC 20005 202-379-2200 379-2299
TF: 800-487-1497 ■ *Web:* www.cfp.net

CoAEMSP 8301 Lakeview Pkwy Ste 111-312 ... Rowlett TX 75088 817-330-0080 330-0089
Web: www.coaemsp.org

COLA 9881 Broken Land Pkwy Ste 200 ... Columbia MD 21046 410-381-6581 381-8611*
**Fax:* Hum Res ■ *TF:* 800-981-9883 ■ *Web:* www.cola.org

Commission on Accreditation for Dietetics Education (CADE)
120 S Riverside Plz Ste 2000 ... Chicago IL 60606 312-899-0040
TF: 800-877-1600 ■ *Web:* www.eatright.org

Commission on Accreditation for Law Enforcement Agencies (CALEA)
13575 Heathcote Blvd Ste 320 ... Gainesville VA 20155 703-352-4225 890-3126
TF: 877-789-6904 ■ *Web:* www.calea.org

Commission on Accreditation in Physical Therapy Education (CAPTE)
1111 N Fairfax St ... Alexandria VA 22314 703-706-3245 838-8910
TF: 800-999-2782 ■ *Web:* www.capteonline.org/home.aspx

Commission on Accreditation of Allied Health Education Programs (CAAHEP)
1361 Pk St ... Clearwater FL 33756 727-210-2350 210-2354
TF: 800-228-2262 ■ *Web:* www.caahep.org

Commission on Accreditation of Healthcare Management Education
6110 Executive Blvd Ste 614 ... Rockville MD 20852 301-298-1820
Web: www.cahme.org

Commission on Accreditation of Rehabilitation Facilities International (CARF)
6951 E Southpoint Rd ... Tucson AZ 85756 520-325-1044 318-1129
TF: 888-281-6531 ■ *Web:* www.carf.org

Commission on Collegiate Nursing Education
1 Dupont Cir NW Ste 530 ... Washington DC 20036 202-887-6791 887-8476
TF: 800-441-1414 ■ *Web:* www.aacn.nche.edu

Commission on Dental Accreditation of Canada
1815 Alta Vista Dr ... Ottawa ON K1G3Y6 613-523-7114 523-7736
TF: 866-521-2322 ■ *Web:* www.cda-adc.ca

Commission on English Language Program Accreditation (CEA)
801 N Fairfax St Ste 402A ... Alexandria VA 22314 703-665-3400 519-2071
Web: www.cea-accredit.org

Commission on Massage Therapy Accreditation (COMTA)
5335 Wisconsin Ave NW Ste 440 ... Washington DC 20015 202-895-1518
Web: www.comta.org

Community Health Accreditation Program Inc (CHAP)
1275 K St NW Ste 800 ... Washington DC 20005 202-862-3413 862-3419
TF: 800-656-9656 ■ *Web:* www.chapinc.org

Continuing Care Accreditation Commission (CARF-CCAC)
1730 Rhode Island Ave NW Ste 209 ... Washington DC 20036 202-587-5001 587-5009
TF: 866-888-1122 ■ *Web:* www.carf.org

Council for Higher Education Accreditation (CHEA)
1 Dupont Cir NW Ste 510 ... Washington DC 20036 202-955-6126 955-6129
Web: www.chea.org

Council for Interior Design Accreditation (CIDA)
206 Grandville Ave Ste 350 ... Grand Rapids MI 49503 616-458-0400 458-0460
Web: www.accredit-id.org

Council of the Section of Legal Education & Admissions to the Bar
321 N Clark St 21st Fl ... Chicago IL 60654 312-988-6738 988-5681
TF: 800-238-2667 ■ *Web:* www.americanbar.org

Council on Academic Accreditation in Audiology & Speech-Language Pathology
2200 Research Blvd ... Rockville MD 20850 301-296-5700
TF: 800-498-2071 ■ *Web:* www.asha.org

Council on Accreditation (COA)
45 Broadway 29th Fl ... New York NY 10006 212-797-3000 797-1428
TF: 866-262-8088 ■ *Web:* www.coanet.org

Council on Accreditation of Nurse Anesthesia Educational Programs
222 S Prospect Ave ... Park Ridge IL 60068 847-692-7050 692-6968
TF: 855-526-2262 ■ *Web:* www.aana.com

Council on Aviation Accreditation (CAA)
Aviation Accreditation Board International
3410 Skyway Dr ... Auburn AL 36830 334-844-2431 844-2432
TF: 800-767-4767 ■ *Web:* www.aabi.aero

Council on Chiropractic Education Commission on Accreditation
8049 N 85th Way ... Scottsdale AZ 85258 480-443-8877 483-7333
TF: 888-443-3506 ■ *Web:* www.cce-usa.org

Council on Education for Public Health
1010 Wayne Ave Ste 220 ... Silver Spring MD 20910 202-789-1050 789-1895
Web: www.ceph.org

Council on Naturopathic Medical Education
342 Main St ... Great Barrington MA 01230 413-528-8877 528-8880
Web: www.cnme.org

Council on Occupational Education
7840 Roswell Rd Bldg 300 Ste 325 ... Atlanta GA 30350 770-396-3898 396-3790
TF: 800-917-2081 ■ *Web:* www.council.org

Council on Quality & Leadership, The (CQL)
100 W Rd Ste 300 ... Towson MD 21204 410-583-0060
Web: www.c-q-l.org

Distance Education & Training Council (DETC)
1601 18th St NW Ste 2 ... Washington DC 20009 202-234-5100 332-1386
Web: www.deac.org

Engineers Canada 180 Elgin St Ste 1100 ... Ottawa ON K2P2K3 613-232-2474 230-5759
TF: 877-408-9273 ■ *Web:* www.engineerscanada.ca

Joint Commission on Accreditation of Healthcare Organizations (JCAHO)
1 Renaissance Blvd ... Oakbrook Terrace IL 60181 630-792-5000 792-5005
Web: www.jointcommission.org

Joint Review Committee on Education in Radiologic Technology (JRCERT)
20 N Wacker Dr Ste 2850 ... Chicago IL 60606 312-704-5300 704-5304
Web: www.jrcert.org

Joint Review Committee on Educational Programs in Nuclear Medicine Technology (JRCNMT)
2000 W Danforth Rd Ste 130 203 ... Edmond OK 73003 405-285-0546 285-0579
Web: www.jrcnmt.org

Liaison Committee on Medical Education (LCME)
330 N Wabash Ave Ste 39300 ... Chicago IL 60611 312-464-4933
Web: www.lcme.org

Middle States Commission on Higher Education
3624 Market St ... Philadelphia PA 19104 267-284-5000 662-5501*
**Fax Area Code:* 215 ■ *Web:* www.msche.org

Montessori Accreditation Council for Teacher Education (MACTE)
420 Park St ... Charlottesville VA 22902 434-202-7793 525-8838*
**Fax Area Code:* 888 ■ *Web:* www.macte.org

National Accrediting Agency for Clinical Laboratory Sciences (NAACLS)
8410 W Bryn Mawr Ave Ste 670 ... Chicago IL 60631 773-714-8880 714-8886
Web: www.naacls.org

National Accrediting Commission of Cosmetology Arts & Sciences (NACCAS)
4401 Ford Ave Ste 1300 ... Alexandria VA 22302 703-600-7600 379-2200
TF: 877-212-5752 ■ *Web:* www.naccas.org

National Architectural Accrediting Board (NAAB)
1735 New York Ave NW ... Washington DC 20006 202-783-2007 783-2822
Web: www.naab.org

National Certification Commission for Acupuncture & Oriental Medicine (NCCAOM)
76 S Laura St Ste 1290 ... Jacksonville FL 32202 904-598-1005 598-5001
Web: www.nccaom.org

National Commission on Certification of Physician Assistants
12000 Findley Rd Ste 200 ... Duluth GA 30097 678-417-8100 417-8135
Web: www.nccpa.net

National Council for Accreditation of Teacher Education (NCATE)
2010 Massachusetts Ave NW Ste 500 ... Washington DC 20036 202-466-7496 296-6620
TF: 800-255-8664 ■ *Web:* www.ncate.org

National Recreation & Park Assn
22377 Belmont Ridge Rd ... Ashburn VA 20148 703-858-0784 858-0794
TF: 800-626-6772 ■ *Web:* www.nrpa.org

New England Assn of Schools & Colleges (NEASC)
209 Burlington Rd ... Bedford MA 01730 781-271-0022 541-5400
Web: www.neasc.org

North Central Assn Commission on Accreditation & School Improvement (NCA CASI)
9115 Westside Pkwy ... Alpharetta GA 30009 888-413-3669
TF: 888-413-3669 ■ *Web:* advanc-ed.org

North Central Assn Higher Learning Commission
230 S LaSalle St ... Chicago IL 60604 312-263-0456 263-7462
TF: 800-621-7440 ■ *Web:* www.hlcommission.org

Northwest Assn of Accredited Schools (NAAS)
1510 Robert St Ste 103 ... Boise ID 83705 208-493-5077
Web: advanc-ed.org

Northwest Commission on Colleges & Universities (NWCCU)
8060 165th Ave NE Ste 100 ... Redmond WA 98052 425-558-4224 376-0596
Web: www.nwccu.org

Office of Social Work Accreditation & Education Excellence
1725 Duke St Ste 500 ... Alexandria VA 22314 703-683-8080 683-8099
Web: www.cswe.org

Society of Accredited Marine Surveyors Inc (SAMS)
7855 Argyle Forest Blvd Ste 203 ... Jacksonville FL 32244 904-384-1494 388-3958
TF: 800-344-9077 ■ *Web:* www.marinesurvey.org

Society of American Foresters (SAF)
5400 Grosvenor Ln ... Bethesda MD 20814 301-897-8720 897-3690
TF: 866-897-8720 ■ *Web:* www.safnet.org

Southern Assn of Colleges & Schools
1866 Southern Ln ... Decatur GA 30033 404-679-4500 679-4558
TF: 888-413-3669 ■ *Web:* www.sacs.org

Speech-Language and Audiology Canada (CASLPA)
1 Nicholas St Ste 1000 ... Ottawa ON K1N7B7 613-567-9968 567-2859
TF: 800-259-8519 ■ *Web:* sac-conference.ca

Teacher Education Accreditation Council (TEAC)
1 Dupont Cir Ste 320 ... Washington DC 20036 202-466-7236
Web: www.teac.org

TransNational Assn of Christian Colleges & Schools (TRACS)
15935 Forest Rd PO Box 328 ... Forest VA 24551 434-525-9539 525-9538
TF: 800-669-4000 ■ *Web:* www.tracs.org

URAC 1220 L St NW Ste 400 ... Washington DC 20005 202-216-9010 216-9006
Web: www.urac.org

Western Assn of Schools & Colleges (WASC)
985 Atlantic Ave ... Alameda CA 94501 510-748-9001
Web: wascsenior.org

48-2 Agricultural Organizations

Phone | Fax

Agricultural Retailers Assn (ARA)
1156 15th St NW Ste 500 ... Washington DC 20005 202-457-0825 457-0864
TF: 800-535-6272 ■ *Web:* www.aradc.org

Agriculture Council of America (ACA)
11020 King St Ste 205 ... Overland Park KS 66210 913-491-1895 491-6502
Web: www.agday.org

American Agricultural Economics Assn (AAEA)
555 E Wells St Ste 1100 ... Milwaukee WI 53202 414-918-3190
Web: www.aaea.org

American Angus Assn (AAA)
3201 Frederick Ave ... Saint Joseph MO 64506 816-383-5100 233-9703
TF: 800-821-5478 ■ *Web:* www.angus.org

American Assn of Bovine Practitioners (AABP)
3320 Skyway Dr Ste 802 PO Box 3610 ... Auburn AL 36831 334-821-0442 821-9532
TF: 800-269-2227 ■ *Web:* www.aabp.org

American Dairy Goat Assn (ADGA)
209 W Main St PO Box 865 ... Spindale NC 28160 828-286-3801 287-0476
Web: www.adga.org

American Dairy Science Assn (ADSA)
1111 N Dunlap Ave ... Savoy IL 61874 217-356-5146 398-4119
TF: 888-670-2250 ■ *Web:* www.adsa.org

American Egg Board (AEB)
1460 Renaissance Dr Ste 301 ... Park Ridge IL 60068 847-296-7043 296-7007
TF: 888-549-2140 ■ *Web:* www.aeb.org

American Farm Bureau Federation
600 Maryland Ave SW Ste 1000-W ... Washington DC 20024 202-406-3600
Web: www.fb.org

American Farmland Trust (AFT) 1200 18th St ... Washington DC 20036 202-331-7300 659-8339
TF: 800-431-1499 ■ *Web:* www.farmland.org

Organization	City	State	ZIP	Phone	Fax
American Feed Industry Assn (AFIA) 2101 Wilson Blvd Ste 916 *Web:* www.afia.org	Arlington	VA	22201	703-524-0810	524-1921
American Fisheries Society (AFS) 5410 Grosvenor Ln Ste 110 *Web:* www.fisheries.org	Bethesda	MD	20814	301-897-8616	897-8096
American Forest & Paper Assn (AF&PA) 1111 19th St NW Ste 800 *TF:* 800-878-8878 ■ *Web:* www.afandpa.org	Washington	DC	20036	202-463-2700	463-2785
American Forest Foundation (AFF) 2000 M St NW Ste 550 *Web:* www.forestfoundation.org	Washington	DC	20036	202-463-2462	463-2461
American Gelbvieh Assn 10900 Dover St *TF:* 800-529-0900 ■ *Web:* www.gelbvieh.org	Westminster	CO	80021	303-465-2333	465-2339
American Hereford Assn 1501 Wyandotte St *Web:* www.hereford.org	Kansas City	MO	64108	816-842-3757	842-6931
American Jersey Cattle Assn 6486 E Main St *Web:* www.usjersey.com	Reynoldsburg	OH	43068	614-861-3636	861-8040
American Land Rights Assn (ALRA) 30218 NE 82nd Ave PO Box 400 *Web:* www.landrights.org	Battle Ground	WA	98604	360-687-3087	687-2973
American National CattleWomen Inc (ANCW) 200 NW 66th St *Web:* www.ancw.org	Oklahoma City	OK	73116	303-694-0313	694-2390
American Nursery & Landscape Assn (ANLA) 1000 Vermont Ave NW Ste 300 *Web:* americanhort.org	Washington	DC	20005	202-789-2900	789-1893
American Royal Assn 1701 American Royal Ct *TF:* 866-844-2295 ■ *Web:* www.americanroyal.com	Kansas City	MO	64102	816-221-9800	221-8189
American Seed Trade Assn (ASTA) 1701 Duke St Ste 275 *TF:* 888-890-7333 ■ *Web:* www.betterseed.org	Alexandria	VA	22304	703-837-8140	837-9365
American Sheep Industry Assn (ASI) 9785 Maroon Cir Ste 360 *Web:* www.sheepusa.org	Englewood	CO	80112	303-771-3500	771-8200
American Simmental Assn (ASA) 1 Simmental Way *Web:* www.simmental.org	Bozeman	MT	59715	406-587-4531	587-9301
American Society for Horticultural Science (ASHS) 1018 Duke St *TF:* 800-331-1600 ■ *Web:* www.ashs.org	Alexandria	VA	22314	703-836-4606	836-2024
American Society of Agricultural Consultants (ASAC) N78W14573 Appleton Ave *Web:* www.agconsultants.org	Menomonee Falls	WI	53051	262-253-6902	
American Society of Agronomy (ASA) 5585 Guilford Rd *TF:* 866-359-9161 ■ *Web:* www.agronomy.org	Madison	WI	53711	608-273-8080	273-2021
American Society of Animal Science (ASAS) 1111 N Dunlap Ave *Web:* www.asas.org	Savoy	IL	61874	217-356-9050	398-4119
American Society of Farm Managers & Rural Appraisers (ASFMRA) 950 S Cherry St Ste 508 *Web:* www.asfmra.org	Denver	CO	80246	303-758-3513	758-0190
American Society of Landscape Architects (ASLA) 636 'I' St NW *TF:* 888-999-2752 ■ *Web:* www.asla.org	Washington	DC	20001	202-898-2444	898-1185
American Soybean Assn (ASA) 12125 Woodcrest Executive Dr Ste 100 *TF:* 800-688-7692 ■ *Web:* www.soygrowers.com	Saint Louis	MO	63141	314-576-1770	576-2786
American-International Charolais Assn (AICA) 11700 NW Plaza Cir *TF:* 800-270-7711 ■ *Web:* www.charolaisusa.com	Kansas City	MO	64153	816-464-5977	464-5759
Association of Consulting Foresters of America (ACF) 312 Montgomery St Ste 208 *TF:* 888-540-8733 ■ *Web:* www.acf-foresters.org	Alexandria	VA	22314	703-548-0990	548-6395
Association of Farmworker Opportunity Programs (AFOP) 1120 20th St NW Ste 300 *TF:* 866-487-9243 ■ *Web:* afop.org	Washington	DC	20036	202-828-6006	828-6005
Association of Water Technologies (AWT) 9707 Key W Ave Ste 100 *TF:* 800-858-6683 ■ *Web:* www.awt.org	Rockville	MD	20850	301-740-1421	990-9771
Beattie Farmers Union Co-op Assn PO Box 79 *Web:* www.beattiecoop.com	Beattie	KS	66406	785-353-2237	
Beefmaster Breeders United (BBU) 6800 Pk Ten Blvd Ste 290-W *Web:* www.beefmasters.org	San Antonio	TX	78213	210-732-3132	732-7711
Beet Sugar Development Foundation 800 Grant St Ste 300 *Web:* www.bsdf-assbt.org	Denver	CO	80203	303-832-4460	832-4468
Breg Inc 2885 Loker Ave E **Fax Area Code:* 800 ■ *TF:* 800-897-2734 ■ *Web:* www.breg.com	Carlsbad	CA	92010	760-599-3000	329-2734*
Brown Swiss Cattle Breeders Assn of the USA 800 Pleasant St *Web:* www.brownswissusa.com	Beloit	WI	53511	608-365-4474	365-5577
Burley Tobacco Growers Co-op Assn 620 S Broadway *Web:* www.burleytobacco.com	Lexington	KY	40508	859-252-3561	
Corn Refiners Assn Inc (CRA) 1701 Pennsylvania Ave *Web:* www.corn.org	Washington	DC	20006	202-331-1634	331-2054
Cotton Council International 1521 New Hampshire Ave NW *Web:* www.cottonusa.org	Washington	DC	20036	202-745-7805	483-4040
Cotton Inc 6399 Weston Pkwy *TF:* 800-334-5868 ■ *Web:* www.cottoninc.com	Cary	NC	27513	919-678-2220	678-2230
Crop Science Society of America (CSSA) 677 S Segoe Rd *Web:* www.crops.org	Madison	WI	53711	608-273-8080	273-2021
CropLife America 1156 15th St NW Ste 400 *TF:* 800-266-9432 ■ *Web:* www.croplifeamerica.org	Washington	DC	20005	202-296-1585	463-0474
Dairy Management Inc (DMI) 10255 W Higgins Rd Ste 900 *TF:* 800-853-2479 ■ *Web:* www.dairy.org	Rosemont	IL	60018	800-853-2479	
Decatur Co-op Assn 305 S York Ave *TF:* 800-886-2293 ■ *Web:* www.decaturcoop.net	Oberlin	KS	67749	785-475-2234	475-3469
Farm Equipment Manufacturers Assn (FEMA) 1000 Executive Pkwy Ste 100 *Web:* www.farmequip.org	Saint Louis	MO	63141	314-878-2304	732-1480
Farmer's Co-op Assn 110 S Keokuk Wash Rd *TF:* 877-843-4893 ■ *Web:* www.keotafarmerscoop.com	Keota	IA	52248	641-636-3748	636-2460
Farmers Co-op PO Box 1640 *Web:* www.farmercoop.com	Van Buren	AR	72957	479-474-6622	474-4787
Farmers Co-op Society 317 Third St NW *Web:* www.farmerscoopsociety.com	Sioux Center	IA	51250	712-722-2671	722-2674
Farmers Educational & Co-op Union of America 20 F St NW Ste 300 *Web:* www.nfu.org	Washington	DC	20001	202-554-1600	554-1654
Fertilizer Institute, The (TFI) 425 Third St SW Ste 950 *Web:* www.tfi.org	Washington	DC	20024	202-962-0490	962-0577
Forest Products Society 2801 Marshall Ct *Web:* www.forestprod.org	Madison	WI	53705	608-231-1361	231-2152
Golf Course Superintendents Assn of America (GCSAA) 1421 Research Pk Dr *TF:* 800-472-7878 ■ *Web:* www.gcsaa.org	Lawrence	KS	66049	785-841-2240	832-4455
Herb Growing & Marketing Network (HGMN) PO Box 245 *Web:* www.herbworld.com	Silver Spring	PA	17575	717-393-3295	393-9261
Hohman Assoc Inc (HAI) 6951 W Little York *TF:* 800-324-0978 ■ *Web:* www.hohmanassociates.com	Houston	TX	77040	713-896-0978	896-9419
Holstein Assn USA Inc 1 Holstein Pl PO Box 808 *TF Orders:* 800-952-5200 ■ *Web:* www.holsteinusa.com	Brattleboro	VT	05302	802-254-4551	254-8251
Humane Farming Assn (HFA) PO Box 3577 *Web:* www.hfa.org	San Rafael	CA	94912	415-485-1495	485-0106
International Brangus Breeders Assn (IBBA) 5750 Epsilon Dr *Web:* www.gobrangus.com	San Antonio	TX	78249	210-696-8231	696-8718
International Order-Hoo-Hoo 207 E Main St	Gurdon	AR	71743	870-353-4997	
International Plant Nutrition Institute (IPNI) 3500 PkwyLn Ste 550 *TF:* 800-521-3044 ■ *Web:* www.ipni.net	Norcross	GA	30092	770-447-0335	448-0439
International Society of Arboriculture (ISA) PO Box 3129 *TF:* 888-472-8733 ■ *Web:* www.isa-arbor.com	Champaign	IL	61826	217-355-9411	355-9516
Irrigation Assn (IA) 6540 Arlington Blvd *Web:* www.irrigation.org	Falls Church	VA	22042	703-536-7080	536-7019
Livestock Marketing Assn (LMA) 10510 N Ambassador Dr *TF:* 800-821-2048 ■ *Web:* www.lmaweb.com	Kansas City	MO	64153	816-891-0502	891-7108
Mid-Kansas Co-op Assn (MKC) PO Box D *TF:* 800-864-4428 ■ *Web:* mkcoop.com	Moundridge	KS	67107	620-345-6361	
Milk Industry Foundation (MIF) 1250 H St NW Ste 900 *TF:* 866-225-4821 ■ *Web:* www.idfa.org	Washington	DC	20005	202-737-4332	331-7820
Mohair Council of America 233 W Twohig Rd *TF:* 800-583-3161 ■ *Web:* www.mohairusa.com	San Angelo	TX	76903	325-655-3161	
National Agri-Marketing Assn (NAMA) 11020 King St Ste 205 *TF:* 800-530-5646 ■ *Web:* www.nama.org	Overland Park	KS	66210	913-491-6500	491-6502
National Agricultural Aviation Assn (NAAA) 1005 E St SE *Web:* www.agaviation.org	Washington	DC	20003	202-546-5722	546-5726
National Association of Landscape Professionals Inc (PLANET) 950 Herndon Pkwy Ste 450 *TF:* 800-395-2522 ■ *Web:* www.landscapeprofessionals.org	Herndon	VA	20170	703-736-9666	736-9668
National Cattlemen's Beef Assn (NCBA) 9110 E Nichols Ave Ste 300 *TF:* 866-233-3872 ■ *Web:* www.beefusa.org	Centennial	CO	80112	303-694-0305	694-2851
National Chicken Council 1015 15th St NW Ste 930 *Web:* www.eatchicken.com	Washington	DC	20005	202-296-2622	293-4005
National Christmas Tree Assn (NCTA) 16020 Swingley Ridge Rd Ste 300 *Web:* www.realchristmastrees.org	Chesterfield	MO	63017	636-449-5070	449-5051
National Corn Growers Assn (NCGA) 632 Cepi Dr *Web:* www.ncga.com	Chesterfield	MO	63005	636-733-9004	733-9005
National Cotton Council of America 7193 Goodlett Farms Pkwy *TF:* 888-232-1738 ■ *Web:* www.cotton.org	Memphis	TN	38016	901-274-9030	725-0510
National Council of Farmer Co-ops (NCFC) 50 F St NW Ste 900 *Web:* www.ncfc.org	Washington	DC	20001	202-626-8700	626-8722
National Crop Insurance Services (NCIS) 8900 Indian Creek Pkwy Ste 600 *TF:* 800-951-6247 ■ *Web:* www.ag-risk.org	Overland Park	KS	66210	913-685-2767	685-3080
National Dairy Council (NDC) 10255 W Higgins Rd Ste 900 *Web:* www.nationaldairycouncil.org	Rosemont	IL	60018	847-627-3790	
National Endangered Species Act Reform Coalition (NESARC) 1050 Thomas Jefferson St NW 6th Fl *Web:* www.nesarc.org	Washington	DC	20007	202-333-7481	338-2416
National Family Farm Coalition (NFFC) 110 Maryland Ave NE Ste 307 *Web:* www.nffc.net	Washington	DC	20002	202-543-5675	543-0978
National Farmers Organization (NFO) 528 Billy Sunday Rd Ste 100 PO Box 2508 *TF:* 800-247-2110 ■ *Web:* www.nfo.org	Ames	IA	50010	515-292-2000	292-7106
National FFA Organization 6060 FFA Dr *TF:* 800-772-0939 ■ *Web:* www.ffa.org	Indianapolis	IN	46268	317-802-6060	802-6061
National Fisheries Institute Inc 7918 Jones Branch Dr Ste 700 *Web:* www.aboutseafood.com	McLean	VA	22102	703-752-8880	
National Grain & Feed Assn (NGFA) 1250 'I' St NW Ste 1003 *Web:* www.ngfa.org	Washington	DC	20005	202-289-0873	289-5388

				Phone	Fax
National Grange 1616 H St NW	Washington	DC	20006	202-628-3507	347-1091
TF: 888-447-2643 ■ *Web:* www.nationalgrange.org					
National Oilseed Processors Assn					
1300 L St NW Ste 1020	Washington	DC	20005	202-842-0463	842-9126
Web: www.nopa.org					
National Onion Assn (NOA) 822 Seventh St Ste 510	Greeley	CO	80631	970-353-5895	353-5897
Web: www.onions-usa.org					
National Renderers Assn (NRA)					
801 N Fairfax St Ste 205	Alexandria	VA	22314	703-683-0155	683-2626
Web: www.nationalrenderers.org					
National Turkey Federation (NTF)					
1225 New York Ave NW Ste 400	Washington	DC	20005	202-898-0100	898-0203
TF: 866-536-7593 ■ *Web:* www.eatturkey.com					
National Woodland Owners Assn (NWOA)					
374 Maple Ave E Ste 310	Vienna	VA	22180	703-255-2700	
TF: 800-476-8733 ■ *Web:* www.woodlandowners.org					
North American Blueberry Council (NABC)					
80 Iron Pt Cir Dr	Folsom	CA	95630	916-983-0111	983-9370
Web: www.blueberry.org					
North American Limousin Foundation (NALF)					
7383 S Alton Way Ste 100	Englewood	CO	80112	303-220-1693	220-1884
TF: 888-320-8747 ■ *Web:* www.nalf.org					
Red Angus Assn of America 4201 N IH- 35	Denton	TX	76207	940-387-3502	829-6069*
**Fax Area Code:* 888 ■ *Web:* www.redangus.org					
River Country Co-op					
9072 Cahill Ave	Inver Grove Heights	MN	55076	651-451-1151	451-8582
Web: www.rivercountry.coop					
Rural Coalition					
1029 Vermont Ave NW Ste 601	Washington	DC	20005	202-628-7160	393-1816
Web: www.ruralco.org					
Santa Gertrudis Breeders International					
PO Box 1257	Kingsville	TX	78364	361-592-9357	592-8572
Web: www.santagertrudis.com					
Shelburne Farms 1611 Harbor Rd	Shelburne	VT	05482	802-985-8686	985-8123
TF: 800-286-6022 ■ *Web:* www.shelburnefarms.org					
Skagit Farmers Supply					
1833 Pk Ln PO Box 266	Burlington	WA	98233	360-757-6053	757-4143
Web: www.skagitfarmers.com					
Society of American Foresters (SAF)					
5400 Grosvenor Ln	Bethesda	MD	20814	301-897-8720	897-3690
TF: 866-897-8720 ■ *Web:* www.safnet.org					
Soil Science Society of America (SSSA)					
677 S Segoe Rd	Madison	WI	53711	608-273-8080	273-2021
Web: www.soils.org					
Southern Forest Products Assn (SFPA)					
6660 Riverside Dr Ste 212	Metairie	LA	70065	504-443-4464	443-6612
TF: 866-574-4155 ■ *Web:* www.sfpa.org					
Sugar Assn 1300 L St NW Ste 1001	Washington	DC	20005	202-785-1122	785-5019
Web: www.sugar.org					
Supima 4141 E Broadway Rd	Phoenix	AZ	85040	602-792-6002	792-6004
Web: www.supima.com					
Texas Longhorn Breeders Assn of America (TLBAA)					
2315 N Main St Ste 402	Fort Worth	TX	76164	817-625-6241	625-1388
Web: www.tlbaa.org					
Tobacco Assoc Inc 1306 Annapolis Dr Ste 102	Raleigh	NC	27608	919-821-7670	821-7674
Web: www.tobaccoassociatesinc.org					
Tobacco Merchants Assn (TMA) PO Box 8019	Princeton	NJ	08543	609-275-4900	275-8379
TF: 888-672-4991 ■ *Web:* www.tma.org					
United Fresh Produce Assn					
1901 Pennsylvania Ave NW Ste 1100	Washington	DC	20006	202-303-3400	303-3433
Web: www.unitedfresh.org					
United Producers Inc 8351 N High St Ste 250	Columbus	OH	43235	800-456-3276	
TF: 800-456-3276 ■ *Web:* www.uproducers.com					
United Soybean Board (USB)					
16305 Swingley Ridge Rd Ste 150	Chesterfield	MO	63017	636-530-1777	530-1560
TF: 800-989-8721 ■ *Web:* www.unitedsoybean.org					
US Apple Assn 8233 Old Courthouse Rd Ste 200	Vienna	VA	22182	703-442-8850	790-0845
TF: 800-781-4443 ■ *Web:* www.usapple.org					
US Grains Council 1400 K St NW Ste 1200	Washington	DC	20005	202-789-0789	898-0522
Web: www.grains.org					
US Potato Board (USPB) 4949 S Syracuse St Ste 400	Denver	CO	80237	303-369-7783	369-7718
Web: www.uspotatoes.com					
US Poultry & Egg Assn 1530 Cooledge Rd	Tucker	GA	30084	770-493-9401	493-9257
Web: www.uspoultry.org					
US Wheat Assoc (USW) 3103 Tenth St N Ste 300	Arlington	VA	22201	202-463-0999	524-4399*
**Fax Area Code:* 703 ■ *Web:* www.uswheat.org					
Western Wood Products Assn (WWPA)					
522 SW Fifth Ave Ste 500	Portland	OR	97204	503-224-3930	224-3934
Web: www2.wwpa.org					
Wheat Quality Council 1814 Abbey Rd	Pierre	SD	57501	605-224-5187	224-0517
Web: www.wheatqualitycouncil.org					
Wild Blueberry Assn of North America (WBANA)					
PO Box 100	Old Town	ME	04468	207-570-3535	581-3499
TF: 800-341-1758 ■ *Web:* www.wildblueberries.com					

48-3 Animals & Animal Welfare Organizations

				Phone	Fax
African Wildlife Foundation (AWF)					
1400 16th St NW Ste 120	Washington	DC	20036	202-939-3333	939-3332
TF: 888-494-5354 ■ *Web:* www.awf.org					
Alaska Wildlife Alliance 308 G St Ste 308	Anchorage	AK	99501	907-277-0897	
Web: www.akwildlife.org					
American Animal Hospital Assn (AAHA)					
12575 W Bayaud Ave	Lakewood	CO	80228	303-986-2800	986-1700
TF: 800-252-2242 ■ *Web:* www.aaha.org/default.aspx					
American Assn of Equine Practitioners (AAEP)					
4075 Iron Works Pkwy	Lexington	KY	40511	859-233-0147	233-1968
TF: 800-443-0177 ■ *Web:* www.aaep.org					
American Buckskin Registry Assn Inc (ABRA)					
1141 Hartnell Ave	Redding	CA	96002	530-223-1420	
Web: www.americanbuckskin.org					
American Cetacean Society (ACS)					
745 W Paseo Del Mar	San Pedro	CA	90731	310-548-6279	548-6950
Web: www.acsonline.org					
American Donkey & Mule Society (ADMS)					
1346 Morningside Ave	Lewisville	TX	75057	972-219-0781	420-9980
TF: 877-752-4068 ■ *Web:* www.lovelongears.com					
American Horse Council (AHC)					
1616 H St NW 7th Fl	Washington	DC	20006	202-296-4031	296-1970
Web: www.horsecouncil.org					
American Humane Assn (AHA) 63 Inverness Dr E	Englewood	CO	80112	303-792-9900	792-5333
TF: 800-227-4645 ■ *Web:* www.americanhumane.org					
American Miniature Horse Assn (AMHA)					
5601 S IH- 35 W	Alvarado	TX	76009	817-783-5600	783-6403
Web: www.amha.org					
American Morgan Horse Assn (AMHA)					
4066 Shelburne Rd Ste 5	Shelburne	VT	05482	802-985-4944	985-8897
TF: 888-436-3700 ■ *Web:* www.morganhorse.com					
American Paint Horse Assn (APHA)					
2800 Meacham Blvd	Fort Worth	TX	76137	817-834-2742	834-3152
Web: www.apha.com					
American Quarter Horse Assn (AQHA)					
1600 Quarter Horse Dr	Amarillo	TX	79104	806-376-4811	349-6411
TF: 800-291-7323 ■ *Web:* www.aqha.com					
American Rabbit Breeders Assn (ARBA)					
PO BOX 5667	Bloomington	IL	61702	309-664-7500	664-0941
Web: www.arba.net					
American Saddlebred Horse Assn (ASHA)					
4083 Iron Works Pkwy	Lexington	KY	40511	859-259-2742	259-1628
Web: www.asha.net					
American Shetland Pony Club (ASPC)					
81B E Queenwood Rd Ste 2	Morton	IL	61550	309-263-4044	263-5113
Web: shetlandminiature.com					
American Shorthorn Assn 8288 Hascall St	Omaha	NE	68124	402-393-7200	393-7203
TF: 877-272-0686 ■ *Web:* www.shorthorn.org					
American Society for the Prevention of Cruelty to Animals (ASPCA)					
424 E 92nd St	New York	NY	10128	212-876-7700	
Web: www.aspca.org					
American Warmblood Registry (AWR)					
PO Box 1332	DeLeon Springs	FL	32130	406-734-5499	667-0516*
**Fax Area Code:* 775 ■ *Web:* www.americanwarmblood.com					
Animal Alliance of Canada 221 Broadview Ave	Toronto	ON	M4M2G3	416-462-9541	462-9647
Web: www.animalalliance.ca					
Animal Health Institute (AHI)					
1325 G St NW Ste 700	Washington	DC	20005	202-637-2440	
Web: www.ahi.org					
Appaloosa Horse Club (ApHC) 2720 W Pullman Rd	Moscow	ID	83843	208-882-5578	882-8150
TF: 888-304-7768 ■ *Web:* www.appaloosa.com					
Arabian Horse Assn (AHA) 10805 E Bethany Dr	Aurora	CO	80014	303-696-4500	696-4599
Web: www.arabianhorses.org					
ASPCA Animal Poison Control Ctr					
424 E 92nd St	New York	NY	10128	212-876-7700	
TF: 888-426-4435 ■ *Web:* www.aspca.org					
Association of Zoos & Aquariums (AZA)					
8403 Colesville Rd Ste 710	Silver Spring	MD	20910	301-562-0777	562-0888
TF: 800-323-6593 ■ *Web:* www.aza.org					
Atlantic Salmon Federation (ASF)					
PO Box 5200	Saint Andrews	NB	E5B3S8	506-529-1033	529-4438
TF: 800-565-5666 ■ *Web:* www.asf.ca					
Bat Conservation International (BCI)					
500 N Capital of Texas Hwy	Austin	TX	78746	512-327-9721	327-9724
TF: 800-538-2287 ■ *Web:* batcon.org					
Belgian Draft Horse Corp of America					
125 Southwood Dr	Wabash	IN	46992	260-563-3205	
Web: www.belgiancorp.com					
Bird Studies Canada					
115 Front St PO Box 160	Port Rowan	ON	N0E1M0	519-586-3531	586-3532
TF: 888-448-2473 ■ *Web:* www.bsc-eoc.org					
Born Free USA United with Animal Protection Institute					
1122 S St	Sacramento	CA	95814	916-447-3085	
TF: 800-348-7387 ■ *Web:* bornfreeusa.org					
Canadian Federation of Humane Societies (CFHS)					
30 Concourse Gate Ste 102	Ottawa	ON	K2E7V7	613-224-8072	723-0252
TF: 888-678-2347 ■ *Web:* cfhs.ca					
Canadian Kennel Club (CKC)					
200 Ronson Dr Ste 400	Etobicoke	ON	M9W5Z9	416-675-5511	675-6506
TF: 800-250-8040 ■ *Web:* www.ckc.ca					
Canadian Peregrine Foundation					
1450 O'Connor Dr Bldg B Ste 214	Toronto	ON	M4B2T8	416-481-1233	481-7158
TF: 888-709-3944 ■ *Web:* www.peregrine-foundation.ca					
Certified Horsemanship Assn (CHA)					
1795 Alysheba Way Ste 7102	Lexington	KY	40509	859-259-3399	255-0726
TF: 800-399-0138 ■ *Web:* www.cha-ahse.org					
Defenders of Wildlife 1130 17th St NW	Washington	DC	20036	202-682-9400	682-1331
TF: 800-385-9712 ■ *Web:* www.defenders.org					
Delta Waterfowl Foundation PO Box 3128	Bismarck	ND	58502	701-222-8857	
TF: 888-987-3695 ■ *Web:* www.deltawaterfowl.org					
Dian Fossey Gorilla Fund International					
800 Cherokee Ave SE	Atlanta	GA	30315	404-624-5881	624-5867
TF: 800-851-0203 ■ *Web:* www.gorillafund.org					
Friends of Animals Inc (FOA) 777 Post Rd Ste 205	Darien	CT	06820	203-656-1522	656-0267
TF: 800-321-7387 ■ *Web:* www.friendsofanimals.org					
Fund for Animals, The 200 W 57th St	New York	NY	10019	212-246-2096	
Web: www.fundforanimals.org					
Greyhound Friends Inc 167 Saddle Hill Rd	Hopkinton	MA	01748	508-435-5969	435-0547
Web: www.greyhoundfds.org/?cfid=194333870&cftoken=69301682&jsessionid=843092a60e45e47f-4418366c2321391a436b					
Hawk Mountain Sanctuary (HMS) 1700 Hawk Mtn Rd	Kempton	PA	19529	610-756-6961	756-4468
Web: www.hawkmountain.org					
Humane Farming Assn (HFA) PO Box 3577	San Rafael	CA	94912	415-485-1495	485-0106
Web: www.hfa.org					
Humane Society of the US (HSUS) 2100 L St NW	Washington	DC	20037	202-452-1100	778-6132
Web: www.humanesociety.org					
In Defense of Animals (IDA) 3010 Kerner Blvd	San Rafael	CA	94901	415-448-0048	454-1031
TF: 800-705-0425 ■ *Web:* www.idausa.org					

Organization	City	State	Zip	Phone	Fax
International Fund for Animal Welfare (IFAW) 290 Summer St *TF:* 800-932-4329 ■ *Web:* www.ifaw.org	Yarmouth Port	MA	02675	508-744-2000	744-2009
International Primate Protection League (IPPL) 120 Primate Ln *Web:* www.ippl.org	Summerville	SC	29483	843-871-2280	871-7988
International Society for Animal Rights (ISAR) PO Box F *TF:* 888-589-6397 ■ *Web:* www.isaronline.org	Clarks Summit	PA	18411	570-586-2200	586-9580
International Veterinary Acupuncture Society (IVAS) 1730 S College Ave Ste 301 *Web:* www.ivas.org	Fort Collins	CO	80525	970-266-0666	266-0777
Jane Goodall Institute for Wildlife Research Education & Conservation (JGI) 1595 Spring Hill Rd Ste 550 *TF:* 800-592-5263 ■ *Web:* www.janegoodall.org	Vienna	VA	22182	703-682-9220	682-9312
Missouri Fox Trotting Horse Breed Assn Inc PO Box 1027 *TF:* 877-663-4203 ■ *Web:* www.mfthba.com	Ava	MO	65608	417-683-2468	683-6144
Mountain Lion Foundation PO Box 1896 *TF:* 800-319-7621 ■ *Web:* www.mountainlion.org	Sacramento	CA	95812	916-442-2666	442-2871
NA of Animal Breeders (NAAB) 401 Bernadette Dr *Web:* www.naab-css.org	Columbia	MO	65203	573-445-4406	446-2279
National Animal Control Assn 101 N Church St Ste C *Web:* www.nacanet.org	Olathe	KS	66061	913-768-1319	768-1378
National Anti-Vivisection Society (NAVS) 53 W Jackson Blvd Ste 1552 *TF:* 800-888-6287 ■ *Web:* www.navs.org	Chicago	IL	60604	312-427-6065	427-6524
National Cutting Horse Assn (NCHA) 260 Bailey Ave *Web:* www.nchacutting.com	Fort Worth	TX	76107	817-244-6188	244-2015
National Disaster Search Dog Foundation 501 E Ojai Ave *TF:* 888-459-4376 ■ *Web:* www.searchdogfoundation.org	Ojai	CA	93023	805-646-1015	640-1848
National Reining Horse Assn (NRHA) 3000 NW Tenth St *Web:* nrha1.com	Oklahoma City	OK	73107	405-946-7400	946-8425
National Wild Turkey Federation (NWTF) 770 Augusta Rd PO Box 530 *TF Cust Svc:* 800-843-6983 ■ *Web:* www.nwtf.org	Edgefield	SC	29824	803-637-3106	637-0034
National Wildlife Federation (NWF) 11100 Wildlife Ctr Dr *TF:* 800-822-9919 ■ *Web:* www.nwf.org	Reston	VA	20190	703-438-6000	438-3570
Paso Fino Horse Assn 4047 Iron Works Pkwy Ste 1 *Web:* www.pfha.org	Lexington	KY	40511	859-825-6000	258-2125
People for the Ethical Treatment of Animals (PETA) 501 Front St *TF:* 800-566-9768 ■ *Web:* www.peta.org	Norfolk	VA	23510	757-622-7382	622-0457
Performing Animal Welfare Society (PAWS) 11435 Simmerhorn Rd *TF:* 800-513-6560 ■ *Web:* www.pawsweb.org	Galt	CA	95632	209-745-2606	745-1809
Pet Sitters International (PSI) 201 E King St *TF:* 800-576-4229 ■ *Web:* www.petsit.com	King	NC	27021	336-983-9222	983-5266
Pinto Horse Assn of America 7330 NW 23rd St *Web:* www.pinto.org	Bethany	OK	73008	405-491-0111	
Racking Horse Breeders Assn of America (RHBAA) 67 Horse Ctr Rd *Web:* www.rackinghorse.com	Decatur	AL	35603	256-353-7225	
Ruffed Grouse Society (RGS) 451 McCormick Rd *TF:* 888-564-6747 ■ *Web:* www.ruffedgrousesociety.org	Coraopolis	PA	15108	412-262-4044	262-9207
Save the Manatee Club (SMC) 500 N Maitland Ave Ste 210 *TF:* 800-432-5646 ■ *Web:* www.savethemanatee.org	Maitland	FL	32751	407-539-0990	539-0871
Tennessee Walking Horse Breeders' & Exhibitors' Assn (TWHBEA) 250 N Ellington Pkwy PO Box 286 *Web:* www.twhbea.com	Lewisburg	TN	37091	931-359-1574	359-7530
Thoroughbred Owners & Breeders Assn (TOBA) PO Box 910668 *TF:* 888-606-8622 ■ *Web:* www.toba.org	Lexington	KY	40591	859-276-2291	276-2462
Trout Unlimited (TU) 1300 N 17th St Ste 500 *TF:* 800-834-2419 ■ *Web:* www.tu.org	Arlington	VA	22209	703-522-0200	284-9400
Wildlife Conservation Society (WCS) 2300 Southern Blvd *Web:* www.wcs.org	Bronx	NY	10460	718-220-5100	
Wildlife Forever 2700 Fwy Blvd Ste 1000 *Web:* www.wildlifeforever.org	Brooklyn Center	MN	55430	763-253-0222	560-9961
Wildlife Management Institute (WMI) 1440 Upper Bermudian Rd **Fax Area Code:* 802 ■ *Web:* www.wildlifemanagementinstitute.org	Gardners	PA	17324	717-677-4480	563-2157*
World Animal Protection (WSPA) 450 Seventh Avenue 31st Floor **Fax Area Code:* 212 ■ *Web:* www.wspa-usa.org	New York	NY	10123	646-783-2200	564-4250*
World Wildlife Fund (WWF) 1250 24th St NW PO Box 97180 *TF:* 800-225-5993 ■ *Web:* www.worldwildlife.org	Washington	DC	20090	202-293-4800	293-9211
World Wildlife Fund Canada (WWF) 245 Eglinton Ave E Ste 410 *TF:* 800-267-2632 ■ *Web:* www.wwf.ca	Toronto	ON	M4P3J1	416-489-8800	489-3611
Zoocheck Canada 788 1/2 O'Connor Dr *TF:* 888-801-3222 ■ *Web:* www.zoocheck.com	Toronto	ON	M4B2S6	416-285-1744	285-4670

48-4 Arts & Artists Organizations

Organization	City	State	Zip	Phone	Fax
Academy of Motion Picture Arts & Sciences 8949 Wilshire Blvd *Web:* www.oscars.org	Beverly Hills	CA	90211	310-247-3000	859-9619
Actors' Equity Assn 1560 Broadway *Web:* www.actorsequity.org	New York	NY	10036	212-869-8530	719-9815
Alliance of Motion Picture & Television Producers (AMPTP) 15301 Ventura Blvd Bldg E *Web:* www.amptp.org	Sherman Oaks	CA	91403	818-995-3600	
American Academy of Arts & Letters 633 W 155th St *Web:* www.artsandletters.org	New York	NY	10032	212-368-5900	
American Academy of Arts & Sciences 136 Irving St *TF:* 800-666-2211 ■ *Web:* www.amacad.org	Cambridge	MA	02138	617-576-5000	576-5050
American Antiquarian Society (AAS) 185 Salisbury St *Web:* www.americanantiquarian.org	Worcester	MA	01609	508-755-5221	753-3311
American Arts Alliance *Performing Arts Alliance* 1211 Connecticut Ave NW Ste 200 *Web:* www.theperformingartsalliance.org	Washington	DC	20036	202-207-3850	833-1543
American Assn for State & Local History (AASLH) 1717 Church St *Web:* www.aaslh.org	Nashville	TN	37203	615-320-3203	327-9013
American Assn of Museums (AAM) 1575 Eye St NW Ste 400 *TF:* 866-226-2150 ■ *Web:* www.aam-us.org	Washington	DC	20005	202-289-1818	289-6578
American Ceramic Society (ACerS) 600 N Cleveland Ave # 210 *TF:* 866-721-3322 ■ *Web:* www.ceramics.org	Westerville	OH	43082	614-890-4700	899-6109
American Choral Directors Assn (ACDA) 545 Couch Dr *Web:* www.acda.org	Oklahoma City	OK	73102	405-232-8161	232-8162
American College of Musicians 808 Rio Grande St *Web:* www.pianoguild.com	Austin	TX	78701	512-478-5775	
American Composers Alliance Inc (ACA) 802 W 190th St Ste 1B *Web:* www.composers.com	New York	NY	10040	212-925-0458	
American Craft Council 72 Spring St 6th Fl *TF:* 800-836-3470 ■ *Web:* www.craftcouncil.org	New York	NY	10012	212-274-0630	
American Design Drafting Assn (ADDA) 105 E Main St *Web:* www.adda.org	Newbern	TN	38059	731-627-0802	627-9321
American Federation of Arts (AFA) 305 E 47th St 10th Fl *Web:* www.afaweb.org	New York	NY	10017	212-988-7700	861-2487
American Federation of Musicians of the US & Canada (AFM) 1501 Broadway Ste 600 *TF:* 800-762-3444 ■ *Web:* www.afm.org	New York	NY	10036	212-869-1330	764-6134
American Film Institute (AFI) 2021 N Western Ave *TF:* 866-234-3378 ■ *Web:* www.afi.com	Los Angeles	CA	90027	323-856-7600	467-4578
American Guild of Musical Artists (AGMA) 1430 Broadway 14th Fl *TF:* 800-543-2462 ■ *Web:* www.musicalartists.org	New York	NY	10018	212-265-3687	262-9088
American Guild of Organists (AGO) 475 Riverside Dr Ste 1260 *TF:* 855-631-0759 ■ *Web:* www.agohq.org	New York	NY	10115	212-870-2310	870-2163
American Guild of Variety Artists (AGVA) 363 Seventh Ave 17th Fl *TF:* 800-331-0890 ■ *Web:* agvausa.com	New York	NY	10001	212-675-1003	633-0097
American Institute for Conservation of Historic & Artistic Works (AIC) 1156 15th St NW Ste 320 *Web:* www.conservation-us.org	Washington	DC	20005	202-452-9545	452-9328
American Institute of Architects (AIA) 1735 New York Ave NW *TF Orders:* 800-242-3837 ■ *Web:* www.aia.org	Washington	DC	20006	202-626-7300	626-7547
American Institute of Graphic Arts (AIGA) 164 Fifth Ave *TF:* 800-548-1634 ■ *Web:* www.aiga.org	New York	NY	10010	212-807-1990	807-1799
American Musicological Society (AMS) 6010 College Stn *TF:* 888-421-1442 ■ *Web:* www.ams-net.org	Brunswick	ME	04011	207-798-4243	798-4254
American Society of Artists PO Box 1326 *Web:* www.americansocietyofartists.info	Palatine	IL	60078	312-751-2500	
American Society of Cinematographers (ASC) 1782 N Orange Dr *TF:* 800-448-0145 ■ *Web:* www.theasc.com	Hollywood	CA	90028	323-969-4333	882-6391
American Society of Interior Designers (ASID) 608 Massachusetts Ave *Web:* www.asid.org	Washington	DC	20002	202-546-3480	546-3240
Americans for the Arts 1000 Vermont Ave NW 6th Fl *TF:* 866-471-2787 ■ *Web:* americansforthearts.org	Washington	DC	20005	202-371-2830	371-0424
Archives of American Art 750 Ninth St NW Ste 2200 *Web:* www.aaa.si.edu	Washington	DC	20001	202-633-7940	633-7994
Art Dealers Assn of America (ADAA) 205 Lexington Ave Ste 901 **Fax Area Code:* 646 ■ *Web:* www.artdealers.org	New York	NY	10016	212-488-5550	688-6809*
Art Directors Guild (ADG) 11969 Ventura Blvd Ste 200 *Web:* www.adg.org	Studio City	CA	91604	818-762-9995	762-9997
Arts & Business Council of Americans for the Arts 1 E 53rd St 2nd Fl *Web:* americansforthearts.org	New York	NY	10022	212-223-2787	980-4857
Association for Information Media & Equipment (AIME) PO Box 9844 *Web:* www.aime.org	Cedar Rapids	IA	52409	319-654-0608	654-0609
Association for Recorded Sound Collections (ARSC) PO Box 543 *Web:* www.arsc-audio.org	Annapolis	MD	21404	410-757-0488	
Association of Children's Museums (ACM) 2711 Jefferson Davis Hwy Ste 600 **Fax Area Code:* 202 ■ *Web:* www.childrensmuseums.org	Arlington	VA	22202	703-224-3100	898-1086*
Association of Film Commissioners International (AFCI) 109 E 17th St **Fax Area Code:* 413 ■ *TF:* 888-765-5777 ■ *Web:* www.afci.org	Cheyenne	WY	82001	307-637-4422	375-2903*
Association of Performing Arts Presenters 1211 Connecticut Ave NW Ste 200 *TF:* 888-820-2787 ■ *Web:* www.apap365.org	Washington	DC	20036	202-833-2787	833-1543

Phone Fax

Association of Talent Agents
9255 Sunset Blvd Ste 930 ... Los Angeles CA 90069 310-274-0628 274-5063
Web: www.agentsassociation.com

Ballet Theatre Foundation
American Ballet Theatre
890 Broadway Third Fl ... New York NY 10003 212-477-3030 254-5938
Web: www.abt.org

Bix Beiderbecke Memorial Society
PO Box 3688 ... Davenport IA 52808 563-324-7170 326-1732
TF: 888-249-5487 ■ *Web:* www.bixsociety.org

Broadcast Music Inc (BMI)
250 Greenwich St 7 World Trade Ctr ... New York NY 10007 212-220-3000 220-4474
Web: www.bmi.com

Broadway League, The 729 Seventh Ave 5th Fl ... New York NY 10019 212-764-1122 944-2136
TF: 866-442-9878 ■ *Web:* www.broadwayleague.com

Chamber Music America (CMA)
305 Seventh Ave 5th Fl ... New York NY 10001 212-242-2022 242-7955
TF: 888-221-9836 ■ *Web:* www.chamber-music.org

Choristers Guild 2834 W Kingsley Rd ... Garland TX 75041 972-271-1521
TF: 800-246-7478 ■ *Web:* www.choristersguild.org

Chorus America 1156 15th St NW Ste 310 ... Washington DC 20005 202-331-7577 331-7599
Web: www.chorusamerica.org

Clowns of America International (COAI)
PO Box 122 ... Eustis FL 32727 352-357-1676
TF: 877-816-6941 ■ *Web:* www.coai.org

Conductors Guild 719 Twinridge Ln ... Richmond VA 23235 804-553-1378 553-1876
Web: www.conductorsguild.org

Country Music Assn Inc (CMA) 1 Music Cir S ... Nashville TN 37203 615-244-2840 726-0314
TF: 800-788-3045 ■ *Web:* cmaworld.com

Dance/USA 1111 16 St NW Ste 300 ... Washington DC 20036 202-833-1717 833-2686
Web: www.danceusa.org

Design Management Institute (DMI)
38 Chauncy St Ste 800 ... Boston MA 02111 617-338-6380 338-6570
Web: www.dmi.org

Dramatists Guild of America Inc
1501 Broadway Ste 701 ... New York NY 10036 212-398-9366 944-0420
TF: 800-289-9366 ■ *Web:* www.dramatistsguild.com

Drum Corps International (DCI) PO Box 3129 ... Indianapolis IN 46206 317-275-1212 713-0690
TF Orders: 800-495-7469 ■ *Web:* www.dci.org

Earshot Jazz 3429 Fremont Pl Ste 309 ... Seattle WA 98103 206-547-6763 547-6286
Web: www.earshot.org

Educational Theatre Assn 2343 Auburn Ave ... Cincinnati OH 45219 513-421-3900 421-7077
Web: www.schooltheatre.org

Folk Alliance International
509 Delaware St Ste 101 ... Kansas City MO 64105 816-221-3655
Web: www.folk.org

Glass Art Society (GAS) 6512 23rd Ave NW Ste 329 ... Seattle WA 98121 206-382-1305 382-2630
TF: 800-636-2377 ■ *Web:* www.glassart.org

Gold Coast Jazz Society
1350 E Sunrise Blvd ... Fort Lauderdale FL 33304 954-524-0805 525-7880
Web: www.goldcoastjazz.org

Gospel Music Assn (GMA) 741 Cool Springs Blvd ... Franklin TN 37067 615-242-0303 254-9755
Web: www.gospelmusic.org

Graphic Artists Guild Inc
32 Broadway Ste 1114 ... New York NY 10004 212-791-3400 791-0333
Web: www.graphicartistsguild.org

Guild of American Luthiers 8222 S Pk Ave ... Tacoma WA 98408 253-472-7853
Web: www.luth.org

Hollywood Foreign Press Assn (HFPA)
646 N Robertson Blvd ... West Hollywood CA 90069 310-657-1731
Web: www.goldenglobes.com/hfpa

Independent Film & Television Alliance (IFTA)
10850 Wilshire Blvd 9th Fl ... Los Angeles CA 90024 310-446-1047 446-1600
Web: www.ifta-online.org

Indian Arts & Crafts Assn (IACA)
4010 Carlisle Blvd NE Ste C ... Albuquerque NM 87107 505-265-9149 265-8251
Web: www.iaca.com

International Ctr of Medieval Art (ICMA)
The Cloisters Fort Tryon Pk ... New York NY 10040 212-928-1146 928-9946
Web: www.medievalart.org

International Interior Design Assn (IIDA)
222 Merchandise Mart Plz Ste 567 ... Chicago IL 60654 312-467-1950 467-0779
TF: 888-799-4432 ■ *Web:* www.iida.org

International Society of Bassists (ISB)
14070 Proton Rd Ste 100 ... Dallas TX 75244 972-233-9107 490-4219
Web: www.isbworldoffice.com

International Ticketing Assn (INTIX)
5868 E 71st St Ste E367 ... Indianapolis IN 46220 212-629-4036 629-4036
Web: www.intix.org

Kansas City Jazz Ambassadors (KCJA)
PO Box 36181 ... Kansas City MO 64171 913-967-6767
Web: www.kcjazzambassadors.com

League of American Orchestras
33 W 60th St 5th Fl ... New York NY 10023 212-262-5161 262-5198
Web: www.americanorchestras.org

League of Resident Theatres (LORT)
1501 Broadway Ste 1801 ... New York NY 10036 212-944-1501 768-0785
Web: www.lort.org

Motion Picture & Television Fund
23388 Mulholland Dr ... Woodland Hills CA 91364 855-760-6783
TF: 855-760-6783 ■ *Web:* www.mptf.com

Motion Picture Assn (MPA)
15301 Ventura Blvd Bldg E Sherman Oaks ... Sherman Oaks CA 91403 818-995-6600
Web: www.mpaa.org

Motion Picture Assn of America
1600 Eye St NW ... Washington DC 20006 202-293-1966 296-7410
Web: www.mpaa.org

Mystery Writers of America Inc (MWA)
1140 Bdwy Ste 1507 ... New York NY 10001 212-888-8171 888-8107
Web: www.mysterywriters.org

National Academy of Recording Arts & Sciences
3030 Olympic Blvd ... Santa Monica CA 90404 310-392-3777 392-2306
TF: 800-423-2017 ■ *Web:* www.grammy.com

National Academy of Television Arts & Sciences
111 W 57th St Ste 600 ... New York NY 10019 212-586-8424 246-8129
Web: www.emmyonline.org

National Association of Theatre Owners. (NATO)
1705 N St NW Ste 1130 ... Washington DC 20036 202-962-0054 962-0370
TF General: 800-365-5701 ■ *Web:* www.natoonline.org

National Council for the Traditional Arts (NCTA)
1320 Fenwick Ln Ste 200 ... Silver Spring MD 20910 301-565-0654 565-0472
Web: ncta-usa.org

National Guild of Piano Teachers PO Box 1807 ... Austin TX 78767 512-478-5775
Web: pianoguild.com

National Humanities Alliance (NHA)
21 Dupont Cir NW Ste 800 ... Washington DC 20036 202-296-4994 872-0884
Web: www.nhalliance.org

National League of American Pen Women Inc
1300 17th St NW ... Washington DC 20036 202-785-1997 452-6868
Web: www.nlapw.org

National Music Publishers' Assn (NMPA)
975 F St NW Ste 375 ... Washington DC 20004 202-393-6672
Web: www.nmpa.org

National Speakers Assn (NSA) 1500 S Priest Dr ... Tempe AZ 85281 480-968-2552 968-0911
Web: www.nsaspeaker.org

Percussive Arts Society (PAS)
110 W Washington St ... Indianapolis IN 46204 317-974-4488 974-4499
TF: 888-990-6663 ■ *Web:* www.pas.org

PLASA North America 630 Ninth Ave Ste 609 ... New York NY 10036 212-244-1505 244-1502
Web: www.plasa.org

Professional Photographers of America Inc (PPA)
229 Peachtree St NE Ste 2200 ... Atlanta GA 30303 404-522-8600 614-6400
TF: 800-786-6277 ■ *Web:* www.ppa.com

Professional Picture Framers Assn (PPFA)
2282 Springport Rd Ste F ... Jackson MI 49202 517-788-8100 788-8371
TF: 800-762-9287 ■ *Web:* www.pmai.org/ppfa

Recording Industry Assn of America Inc (RIAA)
1025 F St NW 10th Fl ... Washington DC 20004 202-775-0101 775-7253
Web: www.riaa.com

Screen Actors Guild (SAG)
5757 Wilshire Blvd ... Los Angeles CA 90036 323-954-1600 549-6775
TF: 800-724-0767 ■ *Web:* www.sagaftra.org

SESAC Inc 55 Music Sq E ... Nashville TN 37203 615-320-0055 963-3527
TF: 800-826-9996 ■ *Web:* www.sesac.com

SITE Santa Fe 1606 Paseo de Peralta ... Santa Fe NM 87501 505-989-1199 989-1188
Web: www.sitesantafe.org

Society for Ethnomusicology (SEM)
Indiana University
1165 E 3rd St Morrison Hall 005 ... Bloomington IN 47405 812-855-6672 855-6673
TF: 800-933-9330 ■ *Web:* www.ethnomusicology.org

Society of American Archivists (SAA)
17 N State St Ste 1425 ... Chicago IL 60602 312-606-0722 606-0728
TF: 866-722-7858 ■ *Web:* www2.archivists.org

Society of Animal Artists Inc
5451 Sedona Hills Dr ... Berthoud CO 80513 970-532-3127 532-2537
Web: www.societyofanimalartists.com

Society of Glass & Ceramic Decorators (SGCD)
PO Box 2489 ... Zanesville OH 43702 740-588-9882 588-0245
Web: www.sgcd.org

Society of Motion Picture & Television Engineers (SMPTE)
3 Barker Ave ... White Plains NY 10601 914-761-1100 761-3115
Web: www.smpte.org

Songwriters Guild of America
5120 Virginia Way C22 Ste 321 ... Brentwood TN 37027 615-742-9945
Web: Www.sgacap.com

Stuntwomen's Association of Motion Pictures, Inc.
3760 Cahuenga Blvd Ste 104 ... Studio City CA 91604 818-762-0907
Web: www.stuntwomen.com

Tucson Jazz Society (TJS) PO Box 41071 Ste 206 ... Tucson AZ 85717 520-903-1265
Web: www.tucsonjazz.org

Women in Film (WIF)
6100 Wilshire Blvd Ste 710 ... Los Angeles CA 90048 323-935-2211
Web: www.wif.org

World Monuments Fund (WMF)
350 Fifth Ave Ste 2412 ... New York NY 10118 646-424-9594 424-9593
Web: www.wmf.org

Young Audiences Inc 171 Madison Ave Ste 200 ... New York NY 10016 212-831-8110
Web: www.youngaudiences.org

48-5 Charitable & Humanitarian Organizations

Phone Fax

ACDI/VOCA 50 F St NW Ste 1075 ... Washington DC 20001 202-638-4661 783-7204
TF: 800-929-8622 ■ *Web:* www.acdivoca.org

Action Against Hunger 247 W 37th St 10th Fl ... New York NY 10018 212-967-7800 967-5480
TF: 877-777-1420 ■ *Web:* www.actionagainsthunger.org

Adventist Community Services
12501 Old Columbia Pk ... Silver Spring MD 20904 301-680-6438 680-6125
TF: 877-227-2702 ■ *Web:* www.communityservices.org

Adventist Development & Relief Agency International (ADRA)
12501 Old Columbia Pk ... Silver Spring MD 20904 301-680-6380
TF: 800-424-2372 ■ *Web:* www.adra.org

Africare Inc 440 R St NW ... Washington DC 20001 202-462-3614 387-1034
Web: www.africare.org

Aga Khan Foundation USA (AKF)
1825 K St NW Ste 901 ... Washington DC 20006 202-293-2537 423-4216*
**Fax Area Code:* 416 ■ *TF:* 800-267-2532

Air Serv International
410 Rosedale Ct Ste 190 ... Warrenton VA 20186 540-428-2323 428-2326
Web: www.airserv.org

Alan Guttmacher Institute (AGI)
125 Maiden Ln 7th Fl ... New York NY 10038 212-248-1111 248-1951
TF: 800-355-0244 ■ *Web:* www.guttmacher.org

America's Second Harvest
35 E Wacker Dr Ste 2000 ... Chicago IL 60601 312-263-2303 263-5626
TF: 800-771-2303 ■ *Web:* www.feedingamerica.org

Organization / Address	City	State	Zip	Phone	Fax
American Anti-Slavery Group, The 198 Tremont St *Fax Area Code: 270 ■ TF: 800-884-0719 ■ Web: www.iabolish.org	Boston	MA	02116	617-426-8161	964-2716*
American Council for Voluntary International Action 1400 16th St NW Ste 210 Web: www.interaction.org	Washington	DC	20036	202-667-8227	667-8236
American Friends Service Committee (AFSC) 1501 Cherry St Web: www.afsc.org	Philadelphia	PA	19102	215-241-7000	
American Institute of Philanthropy (AIP) 3450 N Lk Shore Dr Web: www.charitywatch.org	Chicago	IL	60657	773-529-2300	529-0024
American Jewish Joint Distribution Committee (JDC) 711 Third Ave 10th Fl Web: www.jdc.org	New York	NY	10017	212-687-6200	370-5467
American Jewish World Service (AJWS) 45 W 36th St TF: 800-889-7146 ■ Web: www.ajws.org	New York	NY	10018	212-792-2900	792-2930
American Lebanese Syrian Associated Charities (ALSAC) 262 Danny Thomas Pl TF: 800-822-6344 ■ Web: www.stjude.org	Memphis	TN	38105	901-578-2000	578-2805
American Near East Refugee Aid (ANERA) 1111 14th St NW Ste 400 Web: www.anera.org	Washington	DC	20005	202-266-9700	266-9701
American Red Cross 2025 E St NW TF: 800-257-7575 ■ Web: www.redcross.org	Washington	DC	20006	202-303-4498	303-0044
American Refugee Committee (ARC) 430 Oak Grove St Ste 204 TF: 800-875-7060 ■ Web: www.arcrelief.org	Minneapolis	MN	55403	612-872-7060	607-6499
AmeriCares Foundation 88 Hamilton Ave TF: 800-486-4357 ■ Web: www.americares.org	Stamford	CT	06902	203-658-9500	327-5200
Amigos de las Americas 1800 West Loop S Ste 1325 TF: 800-231-7796 ■ Web: www.amigoslink.org	Houston	TX	77027	713-782-5290	
Amnesty International USA (AIUSA) 5 Penn Plaza 16th Fl TF: 866-273-4466 ■ Web: www.amnestyusa.org	New York	NY	10001	212-807-8400	627-1451
Arms Control Assn 1313 L St NW Ste 130 Web: www.armscontrol.org	Washington	DC	20005	202-463-8270	463-8273
Association of Fundraising Professionals (AFP) 4300 Wilson Blvd Ste 300 TF: 800-666-3863 ■ Web: www.afpnet.org	Arlington	VA	22203	703-684-0410	684-0540
Bread for the World 425 Third St SW Ste 1200 TF Cust Svc: 800-822-7323 ■ Web: www.bread.org	Washington	DC	20024	202-639-9400	639-9401
Brother's Brother Foundation (BBF) 1200 Galveston Ave Web: www.brothersbrother.org	Pittsburgh	PA	15233	412-321-3160	321-3325
Canadian Council for International Cooperation (CCIC) 450 Rideau St Ste 200 Web: www.ccic.ca	Ottawa	ON	K1N5Z4	613-241-7007	241-5302
CARE USA 151 Ellis St NE *Fax: Hum Res ■ TF: 800-521-2273 ■ Web: www.care.org	Atlanta	GA	30303	404-681-2552	577-5977*
Catholic Charities USA 2050 Ballenger Ave Ste 400 Web: www.catholiccharitiesusa.org	Alexandria	VA	22314	703-549-1390	549-1656
Catholic Medical Mission Board (CMMB) 10 W 17th St TF: 800-678-5659 ■ Web: www.cmmb.org	New York	NY	10011	212-242-7757	
Catholic Relief Services (CRS) 228 W Lexington St TF: 800-235-2772 ■ Web: www.crs.org	Baltimore	MD	21201	410-625-2220	685-1635
Center for Community Change (CCC) 1536 U St NW Web: www.communitychange.org	Washington	DC	20009	202-339-9300	387-4891
Center for Human Services 7200 Wisconsin Ave Ste 600 Web: www.chs-urc.org	Bethesda	MD	20814	301-654-8338	941-8427
Child Health Foundation 110 E Ridgely Rd Web: www.childhealthfoundation.org	Timonium	MD	21093	410-992-5512	992-5641
Children International 2000 E Red Bridge Rd TF: 800-888-3089 ■ Web: www.children.org	Kansas City	MO	64131	816-942-2000	942-3714
Children's Miracle Network 4220 Steeles Ave W Ste C18 Web: www.childrensmiraclenetwork.ca	Woodbridge	ON	L4L3S8	905-265-9750	265-9749
Christian Appalachian Project 6550 S KY Rt 321 PO Box 459 TF: 800-755-5322 ■ Web: www.christianapp.org	Hagerhill	KY	41222	800-755-5322	
Christian Blind Mission (CBM) 450 E Pk Ave TF: 800-937-2264 ■ Web: www.cbmus.org	Greenville	SC	29601	864-239-0065	239-0069
Christian Disaster Response International PO Box 3339 Web: www.cdresponse.org	Winter Haven	FL	33885	863-967-4357	
Christian Reformed World Relief Committee (CRWRC) 2850 Kalamazoo Ave SE TF: 800-552-7972 ■ Web: www.worldrenew.net	Grand Rapids	MI	49560	616-241-1691	224-0806
Church World Service 28606 Phillips St PO Box 968 TF: 800-297-1516 ■ Web: www.cwsglobal.org	Elkhart	IN	46515	574-264-3102	262-0966
Church World Service Emergency Response Program 475 Riverside Dr Ste 700 TF: 888-297-2767 ■ Web: www.cwserp.org	New York	NY	10115	212-870-2061	870-2236
Citizens Network for Foreign Affairs (CNFA) 1828 L St NW Ste 710 Web: www.cnfa.org	Washington	DC	20036	202-296-3920	
Coalition on Human Needs (CHN) 1120 Connecticut Ave NW TF: 800-822-7323 ■ Web: www.chn.org	Washington	DC	20036	202-223-2532	223-2538
Community Action Partnership 1140 Connecticut Ave NW Ste 1210 Web: www.communityactionpartnership.com	Washington	DC	20036	202-265-7546	265-5048
Community Food Bank of New Jersey Inc 31 Evans Terminal TF: 866-527-1087 ■ Web: www.cfbnj.org	Hillside	NJ	07205	908-355-3663	355-0270
Community Health Charities 200 N Glebe Rd Ste 801 TF: 800-654-0845 ■ Web: www.healthcharities.org	Arlington	VA	22203	703-528-1007	528-1365
Community Renewal Team Inc 555 Windsor St Web: www.crtct.org	Hartford	CT	06120	860-560-5600	
Compassion International 12290 Voyager Pkwy *Fax: Hum Res ■ TF: 800-336-7676 ■ Web: www.compassion.com	Colorado Springs	CO	80921	719-487-7000	481-1893*
Concern America 2015 N Broadway TF: 800-266-2376 ■ Web: www.concernamerica.org	Santa Ana	CA	92706	714-953-8575	953-1242
Council on Foundations 2121 Crystal Dr Ste 700 TF: 800-673-9036 ■ Web: www.cof.org	Arlington	VA	22202	703-879-0600	879-0800
CRISTA Ministries 19303 Fremont Ave N TF Cust Svc: 800-346-9140 ■ Web: www.crista.org	Seattle	WA	98133	206-546-7200	546-7458
Direct Relief International 27 S La Patera Ln TF: 800-676-1638 ■ Web: www.directrelief.org	Goleta	CA	93117	805-964-4767	681-4838
Doctors Without Borders USA Inc 333 Seventh Ave 2nd Fl TF: 888-392-0392 ■ Web: www.doctorswithoutborders.org	New York	NY	10001	212-679-6800	679-7016
Dress for Success Worldwide 32 E 31st St 7th Fl Web: www.dressforsuccess.org	New York	NY	10016	212-532-1922	
Enterprise Community Partners Inc 10227 Wincopin Cir TF: 800-624-4298 ■ Web: www.enterprisecommunity.com	Columbia	MD	21044	410-964-1230	964-1918
EnterpriseWorks/VITA 1100 H StNW Ste 1200 Web: www.enterpriseworks.org	Washington	DC	20005	202-639-8660	639-8664
Episcopal Migration Ministries (EMM) 815 Second Ave TF: 800-334-7626 ■ Web: episcopalchurch.org/page/episcopal-migration-ministries	New York	NY	10017	212-716-6258	
Episcopal Relief & Development 815 Second Ave *Fax Area Code: 212 ■ TF: 800-334-7626 ■ Web: www.episcopalrelief.org	New York	NY	10017	855-312-4325	687-5302*
Ethiopian Community Development Council Inc (ECDC) 901 S Highland St Web: www.ecdcus.org	Arlington	VA	22204	703-685-0510	685-0529
Evangelical Council for Financial Accountability (ECFA) 440 W Jubal Early Dr Ste 130 TF: 800-323-9473 ■ Web: www.ecfa.org	Winchester	VA	22601	540-535-0103	535-0533
Fair Labor Assn (FLA) 1111 19th St NW Ste 401 Web: www.fairlabor.org	Washington	DC	20036	202-898-1000	898-9050
Feed the Children (FTC) PO Box 36 TF: 800-627-4556 ■ Web: www.feedthechildren.org	Oklahoma City	OK	73101	405-942-0228	945-4177
First Book 1319 F St NW Ste 1000 Web: www.firstbook.org	Washington	DC	20004	202-393-1222	628-1258
Food for the Poor Inc (FFP) 6401 Lyons Rd TF: 800-427-9104 ■ Web: www.foodforthepoor.org	Coconut Creek	FL	33073	954-427-2222	
Foundation for International Community Assistance (FINCA) 1201 15th St NW 8th fl TF: 855-903-4622 ■ Web: www.finca.org	Washington	DC	20005	202-682-1510	682-1535
Freedom from Hunger 1460 Drew Ave Ste 300 TF: 800-708-2555 ■ Web: www.freedomfromhunger.org	Davis	CA	95618	530-758-6200	758-6241
Fund for Peace, The 1101 14th St Ste 1020 Web: global.fundforpeace.org	Washington	DC	20006	202-223-7940	223-7947
Giving Institute 303 W Madison St Ste 2650 Web: givinginstitute.org	Chicago	IL	60606	312-981-6794	
Global Children's Organization 3580 Wilshire Blvd # 1800 Web: www.globalchild.org	Los Angeles	CA	90010	213-368-8385	
Goodwill Industries International Inc 15810 Indianola Dr TF: 800-741-0197 ■ Web: www.goodwill.org	Rockville	MD	20855	301-530-6500	530-1516
Grantmakers in Health (GIH) 1100 Connecticut Ave NW Ste 1200 Web: www.gih.org	Washington	DC	20036	202-452-8331	452-8340
Habitat for Humanity International Inc 121 Habitat St TF: 800-422-4828 ■ Web: www.habitat.org	Americus	GA	31709	229-924-6935	924-6541
Healing the Children (HTC) 2624 W Beacon Ave TF: 888-233-9527 ■ Web: www.healingthechildren.org	Spokane	WA	99208	509-327-4281	327-4284
Healthrite International 80 Maiden Ln Web: www.healthright.org	New York	NY	10038	212-226-9890	226-7026
Heart to Heart International 401 S Clairborne Rd Ste 302 Web: www.hearttoheart.org	Olathe	KS	66062	913-764-5200	764-0809
Hebrew Immigrant Aid Society (HIAS) 333 Seventh Ave 16th Fl TF: 800-442-7714 ■ Web: www.hias.org	New York	NY	10001	212-967-4100	967-4483
Heifer International 1 World Ave TF: 800-422-0474 ■ Web: www.heifer.org	Little Rock	AR	72202	501-907-2600	907-2902
Helen Keller International 352 Pk Ave S Ste 1200 TF: 877-535-5374 ■ Web: www.hki.org	New York	NY	10010	212-532-0544	532-6014
HELP USA 5 Hanover Sq TF: 800-311-7999 ■ Web: www.helpusa.org	New York	NY	10004	212-400-7000	400-7005
Hole in the Wall Gang Camps Inc 265 Church St Ste 503 Web: www.seriousfunnetwork.org	New Haven	CT	06510	203-562-1203	562-1207
HOPE Worldwide 1285 Drummers Ln Ste 330 Web: www.hopeww.org	San Diego	CA	92117	610-254-8800	254-8989
Housing Assistance Council (HAC) 1025 Vermont Ave NW Ste 606 TF: 866-234-2689 ■ Web: www.ruralhome.org	Washington	DC	20005	202-842-8600	347-3441
Hunger Project, The 5 Union Sq W TF: 800-228-6691 ■ Web: www.thp.org	New York	NY	10003	212-251-9100	532-9785
I Have a Dream Foundation (IHAD) 330 Seventh Ave 20th Fl Web: www.ihaveadreamfoundation.org	New York	NY	10001	212-293-5480	293-5478
Independent Charities of America (ICA) 1100 Larkspur Landing Cir Ste 340 TF: 800-477-0733 ■ Web: www.independentcharities.org	Larkspur	CA	94939	415-925-2600	925-2650

Organization / Address	City	State	Zip	Phone	Fax
Independent Order of Foresters (IOF) 789 Don Mills Rd *TF:* 800-828-1540 ■ *Web:* www.foresters.com	Toronto	ON	M3C1T9	416-429-3000	429-3896
Independent Sector 1602 L St NW Ste 900 *TF:* 888-737-9477 ■ *Web:* www.independentsector.org	Washington	DC	20036	202-467-6100	467-6101
INMED Partnerships for Children 20110 Ashbrook Pl Ste 260 *Web:* www.inmed.org	Ashburn	VA	20147	703-729-4951	858-7253
Interchurch Medical Assistance Inc (IMA) 500 Main St PO Box 429 *TF:* 877-241-7952 ■ *Web:* www.imaworldhealth.org	New Windsor	MD	21776	410-635-8720	635-8726
International Aid Inc 17011 W Hickory St *TF:* 800-968-7490 ■ *Web:* www.internationalaid.org	Spring Lake	MI	49456	616-846-7490	846-3842
International Eye Foundation (IEF) 10801 Connecticut Ave *Web:* www.iefusa.org	Kensington	MD	20895	240-290-0263	290-0269
International Institute of Rural Reconstruction (IIRR) 601 W 26th St Ste 325-1 *Web:* www.iirr.org	New York	NY	10001	212-880-9147	
International Medical Corps (IMC) 1919 Santa Monica Blvd Ste 400 *TF:* 800-481-4462 ■ *Web:* www.internationalmedicalcorps.org	Santa Monica	CA	90404	310-826-7800	442-6622
International Orthodox Christian Charities (IOCC) 110 W Rd Ste 360 *TF:* 877-803-4622 ■ *Web:* www.iocc.org	Towson	MD	21204	410-243-9820	243-9824
International Planned Parenthood Federation - Western Hemisphere Region (IPPF/WHR) 125 Maiden Ln 9th Fl *TF:* 866-477-3947 ■ *Web:* www.ippfwhr.org	New York	NY	10005	212-248-6400	248-4221
International Rescue Committee (IRC) 122 E 42nd St 12th Fl *TF:* 800-435-7352 ■ *Web:* www.rescue.org	New York	NY	10168	212-551-3000	551-3179
Jesuit Refugee Service North America (JRS) 1016 16th St NW Ste 500	Washington	DC	20036	202-462-0400	
Lutheran Disaster Response 8765 W Higgins Rd **Fax Area Code:* 773 ■ *TF:* 800-638-3522 ■ *Web:* www.elca.org	Chicago	IL	60631	800-638-3522	380-2707*
Lutheran Immigration & Refugee Service (LIRS) 700 Light St *Web:* www.lirs.org	Baltimore	MD	21230	410-230-2700	230-2890
Make-A-Wish Foundation of America 4742 N 24th St Ste 400 *TF:* 800-722-9474 ■ *Web:* www.wish.org	Phoenix	AZ	85016	602-279-9474	279-0855
MAP International 4700 Glynco Pkwy *TF:* 800-225-8550 ■ *Web:* www.map.org	Brunswick	GA	31525	912-265-6010	265-6170
Marine Toys for Tots Foundation 18251 Quantico Gateway Dr *Web:* www.toysfortots.org	Triangle	VA	22172	703-640-9433	649-2054
Medical Care Development International (MCDI) 8401 Colesville Rd Ste 425 *Web:* www.mcd.org	Silver Spring	MD	20910	301-562-1920	562-1921
Medical Teams International (MTI) PO Box 10 *TF:* 800-959-4325 ■ *Web:* www.medicalteams.org	Portland	OR	97207	503-624-1000	624-1001
Mennonite Central Committee (MCC) 21 S 12th St PO Box 500 *TF:* 888-563-4676 ■ *Web:* www.mcc.org	Akron	PA	17501	717-859-1151	859-2171
Mennonite Disaster Service (MDS) 583 Airport Rd *TF:* 800-241-8111 ■ *Web:* www.mds.mennonite.net	Lititz	PA	17543	717-735-3536	859-4910
MENTOR/National Mentoring Partnership 201 South St Ste 615 *TF:* 877-333-2464 ■ *Web:* www.mentoring.org	Boston	MA	02111	703-224-2200	226-2581
Mercy-USA for Aid & Development Inc (M-USA) 44450 Pinetree Dr Ste 201 *TF:* 800-556-3729 ■ *Web:* www.mercyusa.org	Plymouth	MI	48170	734-454-0011	454-0303
Michigan Municipal League 1675 Green Rd PO Box 1487 *TF:* 800-653-2483 ■ *Web:* www.mml.org	Ann Arbor	MI	48105	734-662-3246	662-8083
Migration & Refugee Services US Conference of Catholic Bishops 3211 Fourth St NE	Washington	DC	20017	202-541-3000	722-8755
NA for the Exchange of Industrial Resources (NAEIR) 560 McClure St *TF:* 800-562-0955 ■ *Web:* www.naeir.org	Galesburg	IL	61401	309-343-0704	
National Alliance to End Homelessness 1518 K St NW Ste 410 *TF:* 800-657-3769 ■ *Web:* www.endhomelessness.org	Washington	DC	20005	202-638-1526	638-4664
National AMBUCS Inc (AMBUCS) 4285 Regency Ct PO Box 5127 *TF:* 800-838-1845 ■ *Web:* www.ambucs.org	High Point	NC	27265	336-852-0052	852-6830
National Benevolent Assn (NBA) 733 Union Blvd Ste 300 *Web:* www.nbacares.org	St. Louis	MO	63108	314-993-9000	
National Children's Advocacy Ctr (NCAC) 210 Pratt Ave *Web:* www.nationalcac.org	Huntsville	AL	35801	256-533-5437	534-6883
National Coalition for the Homeless (NCH) 2201 P St NW *TF:* 877-243-1576 ■ *Web:* www.nationalhomeless.org	Washington	DC	20037	202-462-4822	462-4823
National Committee for Responsive Philanthropy (NCRP) 2001 S St NW Ste 620 *Web:* www.ncrp.org	Washington	DC	20009	202-387-9177	332-5084
National Peace Corps Assn (NPCA) 1900 L St NW Ste 610 *TF:* 800-424-8580 ■ *Web:* peacecorpsconnect.org	Washington	DC	20036	202-293-7728	293-7554
National Student Campaign Against Hunger & Homelessness (NSCAHH) 294 Washington St Ste 500 *Web:* www.studentsagainsthunger.org	Boston	MA	02108	312-544-4436	
Near East Foundation 230 Euclid Ave 900 S Crouse Ave *Web:* www.neareast.org	Syracuse	NY	13210	315-428-8670	
Neighborhood Service Organization Inc 882 Oakman Blvd Ste 1200 *Web:* www.nso-mi.org	Detroit	MI	48238	313-961-4890	961-5120
North American Mission Board SBC 4200 N Pt Pkwy *TF:* 800-634-2462 ■ *Web:* namb.net	Alpharetta	GA	30022	770-410-6000	
Nuclear Age Peace Foundation (NAPF) 1187 Coast Village Rd Ste 1 PO Box 121 *Web:* www.wagingpeace.org	Santa Barbara	CA	93108	805-965-3443	568-0466
OIC International 1875 Connecticut Ave NW Fl 10 *Web:* www.oici.org	Washington	DC	20009	215-842-0220	842-2276
Operation USA 3617 Hayden Ave Ste A *TF:* 800-678-7255 ■ *Web:* www.opusa.org	Culver City	CA	90232	310-838-3455	838-3477
ORBIS International Inc 520 Eigth Ave 11th Fl *TF:* 800-672-4787 ■ *Web:* www.orbis.org	New York	NY	10018	646-674-5500	674-5599
Oregon Food Bank Inc 7900 NE 33rd Dr *TF:* 888-398-8702 ■ *Web:* www.oregonfoodbank.org	Portland	OR	97211	503-282-0555	282-0922
ORT American Inc 75 Maiden Ln 10th Fl *TF:* 800-519-2678 ■ *Web:* www.ortamerica.org	New York	NY	10038	212-505-7700	674-3057
Outreach International 129 W Lexington PO Box 210 *TF:* 888-833-1235 ■ *Web:* www.outreach-international.org	Independence	MO	64050	816-833-0883	833-0103
Oxfam America 226 Cswy St 5th Fl *TF:* 800-776-9326 ■ *Web:* www.oxfamamerica.org	Boston	MA	02114	617-482-1211	728-2594
Pan American Development Foundation (PADF) 1889 F St NW 2nd Fl *TF:* 877-572-4484 ■ *Web:* www.padf.org	Washington	DC	20006	202-458-3969	458-6316
Partners of the Americas 1424 K St NW Ste 700 *Web:* www.partners.net	Washington	DC	20005	202-628-3300	628-3306
Partnership for Philanthropic Planning (NCPG) 233 McCrea St Ste 400 *Web:* www.pppnet.org	Indianapolis	IN	46225	317-269-6274	269-6276
Pathfinder International 9 Galen St Ste 217 *Web:* www.pathfind.org	Watertown	MA	02472	617-924-7200	924-3833
Peace Action 8630 Fenton St *Web:* www.peace-action.org	Silver Spring	MD	20910	301-565-4050	565-0850
People-to-People Health Foundation 255 Carter Hall Ln *TF:* 800-544-4673 ■ *Web:* www.projecthope.org	Millwood	VA	22646	540-837-2100	837-1813
Physicians for Human Rights (PHR) 185 Devonshire St Ste M102 *Web:* physiciansforhumanrights.org	Boston	MA	02110	617-301-4200	301-4250
Physicians for Social Responsibility (PSR) 1875 Connecticut Ave NW Ste 1012 *TF:* 800-459-1887 ■ *Web:* www.psr.org	Washington	DC	20009	202-667-4260	667-4201
Points of Light Foundation & Volunteer Ctr National Network 1400 'I' St NW Ste 800 *TF:* 866-269-0510 ■ *Web:* www.pointsoflight.org	Washington	DC	20005	202-729-8000	729-8100
Population Action International (PAI) 1300 19th St NW Ste 200 *Web:* pai.org	Washington	DC	20036	202-557-3400	728-4177
Population Communication 1250 E Walnut St Ste 220 *Web:* populationcommunication.com	Pasadena	CA	91106	626-793-4750	793-4791
Population Connection 2120 L St NW Ste 500 *TF:* 800-767-1956 ■ *Web:* www.populationconnection.org	Washington	DC	20037	202-332-2200	332-2302
Population Resource Ctr (PRC) 1725 K St NW *Web:* prcdc.org	Washington	DC	20006	202-467-5030	
Presbyterian Disaster Assistance (PDA) 100 Witherspoon St **Fax Area Code:* 502 ■ *TF:* 800-728-7228 ■ *Web:* www.presbyterianmission.org	Louisville	KY	40202	800-728-7228	569-8039*
Project Concern International (PCI) 5151 Murphy Canyon Rd Ste 320 *TF:* 877-724-4673 ■ *Web:* www.pciglobal.org	San Diego	CA	92123	858-279-9690	694-0294
ProLiteracy Worldwide 1320 Jamesville Ave *TF:* 800-448-8878 ■ *Web:* www.proliteracy.org	Syracuse	NY	13210	315-422-9121	422-6369
Rainbow/PUSH Coalition Inc 930 E 50th St *Web:* www.rainbowpush.org	Chicago	IL	60615	773-373-3366	373-3571
Rebuilding Together Inc 1899 L St NW Ste 1000 **Fax Area Code:* 202 ■ *TF:* 800-473-4229 ■ *Web:* togetherwetransform.org	Washington	DC	20036	800-473-4229	483-9081*
Refugees International (RI) 2001 S St NW Ste 700-K *TF:* 800-733-8433 ■ *Web:* www.refugeesinternational.org	Washington	DC	20009	202-828-0110	828-0819
Research!America 1101 King St Ste 520 *TF:* 800-366-2873 ■ *Web:* www.researchamerica.org	Alexandria	VA	22314	703-739-2577	739-2372
Resource Foundation, The 237 W 35th St Ste 1203 *Web:* www.resourcefnd.org	New York	NY	10001	212-675-6170	268-5325
Resource Inc 1900 Chicago Ave S *Web:* www.resource-mn.org	Minneapolis	MN	55404	612-752-8000	752-8001
RESULTS 750 First St NE Ste 1040 *Web:* www.results.org	Washington	DC	20002	202-783-7100	783-2818
Ronald McDonald House Charities (RMHC) 1 Kroc Dr *TF:* 855-670-4787 ■ *Web:* www.rmhc.org	Oak Brook	IL	60523	630-623-7048	623-7488
Rotary Foundation, The 1560 Sherman Ave *TF:* 800-435-7352 ■ *Web:* www.rotary.org	Evanston	IL	60201	847-866-3000	328-8554
Second Harvest Food Bank of Central Florida 411 Mercy Dr	Orlando	FL	32805	407-295-1066	292-4758
Sertoma International 1912 E Meyer Blvd *TF:* 800-593-5646 ■ *Web:* www.sertoma.org	Kansas City	MO	64132	816-333-8300	333-4320
SHARE El Salvador 2425 College Ave *Web:* www.share-elsalvador.org	Berkeley	CA	94704	510-848-8487	
Share Our Strength 1730 M St NW Ste 700 *TF:* 800-969-4767 ■ *Web:* www.nokidhungry.org	Washington	DC	20036	202-393-2925	347-5868
Smile Train Inc 41 Madison Ave Ste 28 *TF:* 877-543-7645 ■ *Web:* www.smiletrain.org	New York	NY	10010	212-689-9199	689-9299
Society of Saint Andrew (SoSA) 3383 Sweet Hollow Rd *TF:* 800-333-4597 ■ *Web:* www.endhunger.org	Big Island	VA	24526	434-299-5956	299-5949
Soroptimist International of the Americas 1709 Spruce St *Web:* www.soroptimist.org	Philadelphia	PA	19103	215-893-9000	893-5200
Southeast Asia Resource Action Ctr (SEARAC) 1628 16th St NW 3rd Fl *TF:* 888-907-1485 ■ *Web:* www.searac.org	Washington	DC	20009	202-667-4690	667-6449

Phone Fax

Special Wish Foundation Inc
1250 Memory Ln N ... Columbus OH 43209 614-258-3186
Web: www.spwish.org

TechnoServe 1 Mechanic St ... Norwalk CT 06854 203-852-0377 838-6717
TF: 800-999-6757 ■ *Web:* www.technoserve.org

Trickle Up Program Inc 104 W 27th St 12th Fl ... New York NY 10001 212-255-9980 255-9974
TF: 866-246-9980 ■ *Web:* www.trickleup.org

Turning Point Community Programs
3440 Viking Dr Ste 114 ... Sacramento CA 95827 916-364-8395
Web: www.tpcp.org

Unitarian Universalist Service Committee (UUSC)
689 Massachusetts Ave ... Cambridge MA 02139 617-868-6600 868-7102
TF: 800-388-3920 ■ *Web:* www.uusc.org

United Nations Children's Fund (UNICEF)
3 United Nations Plz ... New York NY 10017 212-326-7000 888-7465
Web: www.unicef.org

United Nations Foundation (UNF)
1800 Massachusetts Ave NW Ste 400 ... Washington DC 20036 202-887-9040 887-9021
Web: www.unfoundation.org

United Way of America 701 N Fairfax St ... Alexandria VA 22314 703-836-7100 683-7840
TF: 800-892-2757 ■ *Web:* www.unitedway.org

US Committee for Refugees & Immigrants (USCRI)
2231 Crystal Dr Ste 350 ... Arlington VA 22202 703-310-1130 769-4241
Web: www.refugees.org

US Fund for UNICEF 125 Maiden Ln ... New York NY 10038 800-367-5437 779-1679*
**Fax Area Code:* 212 ■ *TF:* 800-367-5437 ■ *Web:* www.unicefusa.org

USA for UNHCR 1775 K St NW Ste 580 ... Washington DC 20006 202-296-1115
TF: 800-770-1100 ■ *Web:* www.unrefugees.org

Veterans for Peace Inc (VFP)
216 S Meramec Ave ... Saint Louis MO 63105 314-725-6005 725-7103
TF: 877-429-0678 ■ *Web:* www.veteransforpeace.org

Voices of September 11th 161 Cherry St ... New Canaan CT 06840 203-966-3911 966-5701
TF: 866-505-3911 ■ *Web:* www.voicesofseptember11.org

Volunteers of America 1660 Duke St ... Alexandria VA 22314 703-341-5000 341-7000
TF: 800-899-0089 ■ *Web:* www.voa.org

War Resisters League 339 Lafayette St ... New York NY 10012 212-228-0450 228-6193
TF: 800-975-9688 ■ *Web:* www.warresisters.org

Women's Action for New Directions (WAND)
691 Massachusetts Ave ... Arlington MA 02476 781-643-6740 643-6744
Web: www.wand.org

World Concern 19303 Fremont Ave N ... Seattle WA 98133 206-546-7201 546-7269
TF: 800-755-5022 ■ *Web:* www.worldconcern.org

World Education Inc 44 Farnsworth St ... Boston MA 02210 617-482-9485 482-0617
Web: www.worlded.org

World Food Program USA (WFP)
1725 Eye St NW Ste 510 ... Washington DC 20036 202-530-1694 530-1698
TF: 888-454-0555 ■ *Web:* wfpusa.org

World Hunger Year Inc (WHY)
505 Eigth Ave Ste 2100 ... New York NY 10018 212-629-8850 465-9274
TF: 800-548-6479 ■ *Web:* www.whyhunger.org

World Learning 1 Kipling Rd PO Box 676 ... Brattleboro VT 05302 802-257-7751 258-3248
TF: 800-257-7751 ■ *Web:* www.worldlearning.org

World Neighbors Inc (WN) 4127 NW 122nd St ... Oklahoma City OK 73120 405-752-9700
TF: 800-242-6387 ■ *Web:* www.wn.org

World Peace Prayer Society 26 Benton Rd ... Wassaic NY 12592 845-877-6093 877-6862
Web: www.worldpeace.org

World Relief 7 E Baltimore St ... Baltimore MD 21202 443-451-1900
TF: 800-535-5433 ■ *Web:* www.worldrelief.org

World Vision Inc
34834 Weyerhaeuser Way S PO Box 9716 ... Federal Way WA 98001 253-815-1000
TF: 888-511-6548 ■ *Web:* www.worldvision.org

48-6 Children & Family Advocacy Organizations

Phone Fax

AARP 601 E St NW ... Washington DC 20049 202-434-2277 434-7597
TF: 888-687-2277 ■ *Web:* www.aarp.org

AARP Grandparent Information Ctr
601 E St NW ... Washington DC 20049 202-434-3525 434-6474
TF: 888-687-2277 ■ *Web:* aarp.org/relationships/grandparenting

Adoption ARC Inc 4701 Pine St Ste J-7 ... Philadelphia PA 19143 215-748-1441 842-9881
TF: 800-884-4004 ■ *Web:* www.adoptionarc.com

Alliance for Aging Research (AAR)
750 17th St NW Ste 1100 ... Washington DC 20006 202-293-2856 234-5030*
**Fax Area Code:* 770 ■ *TF:* 866-840-6283 ■ *Web:* www.agingresearch.org

Alliance for Children & Families Inc
11700 W Lk Pk Dr ... Milwaukee WI 53224 414-359-1040 359-1074
TF: 800-221-3726 ■ *Web:* www.alliance1.org

Alliance for Retired Americans
815 16th St NW 4th Fl ... Washington DC 20006 202-637-5399 637-5398
TF: 888-373-6497 ■ *Web:* www.retiredamericans.org

America's Promise - the Alliance for Youth
909 N Washington St Ste 400 ... Alexandria VA 22314 703-684-4500
Web: www.americaspromise.org

American Academy of Pediatrics (AAP)
141 NW Pt Blvd ... Elk Grove Village IL 60007 847-434-4000 434-8000
TF: 800-433-9016 ■ *Web:* www.aap.org

American Adoption Congress (AAC)
PO Box 42730 ... Washington DC 20015 202-483-3399
Web: www.americanadoptioncongress.org

American Assn for Marriage & Family Therapy (AAMFT)
112 S Alfred St ... Alexandria VA 22314 703-838-9808 838-9805
Web: www.aamft.org

American Coalition for Fathers & Children (ACFC)
1718 M St NW Ste 1187 ... Washington DC 20036 800-978-3237
TF: 800-978-3237 ■ *Web:* www.acfc.org

American Humane Assn (AHA) 63 Inverness Dr E ... Englewood CO 80112 303-792-9900 792-5333
TF: 800-227-4645 ■ *Web:* www.americanhumane.org

American Seniors Housing Assn (ASHA)
5225 Wisconsin Ave NW # 502 ... Washington DC 20015 202-237-0900 237-1616
Web: www.seniorshousing.org

American SIDS Institute 528 Raven Way ... Naples FL 34110 239-431-5425 431-5536
Web: www.sids.org

Phone Fax

American Society on Aging (ASA)
575 Market St Ste 2100 ... San Francisco CA 94105 415-974-9600 974-0300
TF: 800-537-9728 ■ *Web:* www.asaging.org

Association for Couples in Marriage Enrichment (ACME)
PO Box 21374 ... Winston-Salem NC 27120 336-724-1526
TF: 800-634-8325 ■ *Web:* www.bettermarriages.org

Athletes & Entertainers for Kids (AEFK)
14340 Bolsa Chica Rd Unit C ... Westminster CA 92683 562-438-5905

Believe In Tomorrow National Children's Foundation
6601 Frederick Rd ... Baltimore MD 21228 410-744-1032 744-1984
TF: 800-933-5470 ■ *Web:* www.believeintomorrow.org

Blue Grass Regional Mental Health-Mental Retardation Board Inc
1351 Newtown Pike Bldg 1 ... Lexington KY 40511 859-253-1686 255-4866
TF: 800-928-8000 ■ *Web:* www.bluegrass.org

Boys Town 14100 Crawford St ... Boys Town NE 68010 402-498-1300
TF: 800-448-3000 ■ *Web:* www.boystown.org

Buckner International
600 N Pearl St Ste 2000 20th Fl ... Dallas TX 75201 214-758-8000
TF: 800-442-4800 ■ *Web:* www.buckner.org

Cal Farley's Boys Ranch
600 W 11th St PO Box 1890 ... Amarillo TX 79174 806-372-2341 372-6638
TF: 800-687-3722 ■ *Web:* www.calfarley.org

Camelot Community Care Inc
4910 D Creekside Dr ... Clearwater FL 33760 727-593-0003 595-0735
TF: 800-435-7352 ■ *Web:* www.camelotcommunitycare.org

Child Find Canada 212-2211 McPhillips St ... Winnipeg MB R2V3M5 204-339-5584 339-5587
TF: 800-387-7962 ■ *Web:* www.childfind.ca

Child Lures Prevention 5166 Shelburne Rd ... Shelburne VT 05482 802-985-8458 985-8418
TF: 800-552-2197 ■ *Web:* www.childluresprevention.com

Child Trends
4301 Connecticut Ave NW Ste 350 ... Washington DC 20008 240-223-9200 200-1238
Web: www.childtrends.org

Child Welfare League of America (CWLA)
2345 Crystal Dr Ste 250 ... Arlington VA 22202 202-688-4200 412-2401*
**Fax Area Code:* 703 ■ *Web:* www.cwla.org

Childhelp USA 4350 E Camelback Rd Bldg F250 ... Phoenix AZ 85018 480-922-8212 922-7061
TF: 800-422-4453 ■ *Web:* www.childhelp.org

Children Awaiting Parents Inc (CAP)
595 Blossom Rd Ste 306 ... Rochester NY 14610 585-232-5110 232-2634
TF: 888-835-8802 ■ *Web:* www.capbook.org

Children Inc 4205 Dover Rd ... Richmond VA 23221 804-359-4562
TF: 800-538-5381 ■ *Web:* childrenincorporated.org

Children of Deaf Adults Inc (CODA)
3131 Calle Mariposa ... Santa Barbara CA 93105 805-682-0997
Web: coda-international.wildapricot.org

Children of the Night 14530 Sylvan St ... Van Nuys CA 91411 818-908-4474 908-1468
TF: 800-551-1300 ■ *Web:* www.childrenofthenight.org

Children's Defense Fund (CDF) 25 E St NW ... Washington DC 20001 202-628-8787 662-3510
TF: 800-233-1200 ■ *Web:* www.childrensdefense.org

Christian Foundation for Children & Aging (CFCA)
1 Elmwood Ave ... Kansas City KS 66103 913-384-6500 384-2211
TF: 800-875-6564 ■ *Web:* unbound.org

CityKids Foundation 601 W 26th St Ste 325 ... New York NY 10001 212-925-3320
Web: www.citykids.com

Community Options Inc 16 Farber Rd ... Princeton NJ 08540 609-951-9900 951-9112
Web: www.comop.org

Connecting Generations
100 W Tenth St Ste 1115 ... Wilmington DE 19801 302-656-2122 656-2123
TF: 877-202-9050 ■ *Web:* www.connecting-generations.org

Consortium for Citizens with Disabilities (CCD)
1660 L St NW Ste 701 ... Washington DC 20036 202-783-2229 783-8250
Web: www.c-c-d.org

Corps Network, The 1275 K St NW Ste 1050 ... Washington DC 20005 202-737-6272 737-6277
TF: 800-245-5627 ■ *Web:* www.corpsnetwork.org

Council for Equal Rights in Adoption
444 E 76th St ... New York NY 10021 212-988-0110 988-0291
Web: www.adoptionhealing.com

Covenant House 5 Penn Plz Ste 2 ... New York NY 10001 212-727-4000
TF: 800-999-9999 ■ *Web:* www.covenanthouse.org

Crossroads For Youth 930 E Drahner PO Box 9 ... Oxford MI 48371 248-628-2561 628-3080
Web: www.crossroadsforyouth.org

DePelchin Children's Ctr 4950 Memorial Dr ... Houston TX 77007 713-730-2335 802-3801
TF: 888-730-2335 ■ *Web:* www.depelchin.org

Envision Inc 610 N Main St ... Wichita KS 67203 316-440-1500 440-1540
TF: 888-425-7072 ■ *Web:* www.envisionus.com

Evan B Donaldson Adoption Institute
120 E 38th St ... New York NY 10016 212-925-4089 796-6592*
**Fax Area Code:* 775 ■ *TF:* 800-837-2655 ■ *Web:* www.adoptioninstitute.org

Experience Works Inc
4401 Wilson Blvd Ste 1100 ... Arlington VA 22203 703-522-7272 522-0141
TF: 866-397-9757 ■ *Web:* www.experienceworks.org

Family Research Council (FRC) 801 G St NW ... Washington DC 20001 202-393-2100 393-2134
TF: 800-225-4008 ■ *Web:* www.frc.org

Federation of Families for Children's Mental Health (FFCMH)
9605 Medical Ctr Dr Ste 280 ... Rockville MD 20850 240-403-1901 403-1909
Web: www.ffcmh.org

Find the Children 2656 29th St Ste 203 ... Santa Monica CA 90405 310-314-3213
TF: 888-477-6721 ■ *Web:* www.findthechildren.com

First Candle 1314 Bedford Ave Ste 210 ... Baltimore MD 21208 410-653-8226 653-8709
TF: 800-221-7437 ■ *Web:* www.firstcandle.org

Focus on the Family
8605 Explorer Dr ... Colorado Springs CO 80920 719-531-3400 531-3424
TF Sales: 800-232-6459 ■ *Web:* www.focusonthefamily.com

Food Research & Action Ctr (FRAC)
1875 Connecticut Ave NW Ste 540 ... Washington DC 20009 202-986-2200 986-2525
Web: www.frac.org

Generations United (GU)
1333 H St NW Ste 500-W ... Washington DC 20005 202-289-3979 289-3952
TF: 800-677-1116 ■ *Web:* www.gu.org

Girls Inc 120 Wall St 3rd Fl ... New York NY 10005 212-509-2000 509-8708
TF: 800-374-4475 ■ *Web:* www.girlsinc.org

Grandparents Rights Organization (GRO)
1760 S Telegraph Rd Ste 250 ... Bloomfield Hills MI 48304 248-646-7177
Web: www.grandparentsrights.org

Organization	City	State	Zip	Phone	Fax
Healthy Teen Network 1501 St Paul St Ste 124 *Web:* www.healthyteennetwork.org	Baltimore	MD	21202	410-685-0410	685-0481
Human Life International (HLI) 4 Family Life Ln *TF Orders:* 800-549-5433 ■ *Web:* www.hli.org	Front Royal	VA	22630	540-635-7884	622-6247
Ignitus Worldwide 1199 Haywood Dr Ste 417 *Web:* www.ignitusworldwide.org	College Station	TX	77845	305-670-2409	
International Soundex Reunion Registry 901 E Second St *Web:* www.isrr.net	Carson City	NV	89701	775-882-7755	
Jewish Assn for Services for the Aged (JASA) 247 W 37th St *Web:* www.jasa.org	New York	NY	10018	212-273-5272	
Jewish Board of Family & Children Services (JBFCS) 120 W 57th St *TF:* 888-523-2769 ■ *Web:* jewishboard.org	New York	NY	10019	212-582-9100	956-5676
Justice in Aging (NSCLC) 1444 'I' St Ste 1100 *Web:* nsclc.org	Washington	DC	20005	202-289-6976	289-7224
Kansas Children's Service League (KCSL) 3545 SW 5th *TF:* 877-530-5275 ■ *Web:* www.kcsl.org	Topeka	KS	66606	785-274-3100	
Kempe Children's Ctr 13123 E 16th Ave *Web:* www.kempe.org	Aurora	CO	80045	303-864-5300	864-5302
KlaasKids Foundation PO Box 925 *Web:* www.klaaskids.org	Sausalito	CA	94966	415-331-6867	
Leading Age 2519 Connecticut Ave NW *TF:* 866-702-3278 ■ *Web:* www.leadingage.org	Washington	DC	20008	202-783-2242	783-2255
Little Flower Children & Family Services of New York 2450 N Wading River Rd *Web:* www.littleflowerny.org	Wading River	NY	11792	631-929-6200	
Margaret Sanger Ctr International (MSCI) 26 Bleecker St *Web:* www.plannedparenthood.org	New York	NY	10012	212-965-7000	274-7299
May Institute Inc 41 Pacella Pk Dr *TF:* 800-778-7601 ■ *Web:* www.mayinstitute.org	Randolph	MA	02368	781-440-0400	
Men Against Destruction Defending Against Drugs & Social Disorder Inc (MAD DADS) 3026 4th Ave S *Web:* www.maddads.com	Minneapolis	MN	55408	612-822-0802	253-0663
MENTOR/National Mentoring Partnership 201 South St Ste 615 *TF:* 877-333-2464 ■ *Web:* www.mentoring.org	Boston	MA	02111	703-224-2200	226-2581
Mentoring USA 5 Hanover Sq *Web:* www.helpusa.org	New York	NY	10004	212-400-8294	
MOPS International 2370 S Trenton Way *TF General:* 888-910-6677 ■ *Web:* www.mops.org	Denver	CO	80231	303-733-5353	733-5770
Mothers Against Drunk Driving (MADD) 511 E John Carpenter Fwy Ste 700 *TF:* 877-275-6233 ■ *Web:* www.madd.org	Irving	TX	75062	214-744-6233	
NA for Home Care & Hospice (NAHC) 228 Seventh St SE *Web:* www.nahc.org	Washington	DC	20003	202-547-7424	547-3540
National Adoption Ctr 1500 Walnut St Ste 701 *Web:* www.adopt.org	Philadelphia	PA	19102	215-735-9988	735-9410
National Alliance for Caregiving 4720 Montgomery Ln Ste 205 *Web:* caregiving.org	Bethesda	MD	20814	301-718-8444	652-7711
National Caregiving Foundation 801 N Pitt St *TF:* 800-930-1357 ■ *Web:* www.caregivingfoundation.org	Alexandria	VA	22314	703-299-9300	
National Caucus & Ctr on Black Aged Inc (NCBA) 1220 L St NW Ste 800 *Web:* www.ncba-aged.org	Washington	DC	20005	202-637-8400	347-0895
National Child Care Assn (NCCA) 1325 G St NW Ste 500 *TF:* 866-536-1945 ■ *Web:* www.nccanet.org	Washington	DC	20005	866-536-1945	
National Child Support Enforcement Assn (NCSEA) 1760 Old Meadow Rd Ste 500 *Web:* www.ncsea.org	McLean	VA	22102	703-506-2880	506-3266
National Coalition Against Domestic Violence (NCADV) 1 Broadway Ste B210 *TF:* 800-799-7233 ■ *Web:* www.ncadv.org	Denver	CO	80203	303-839-1852	831-9251
National Coalition for the Protection of Children & Families (NCPCF) 800 Compton Rd Ste 9224 *Web:* www.eos.net	Cincinnati	OH	45231	513-521-6227	
National Council for Adoption (NCFA) 225 N Washington St *Web:* www.adoptioncouncil.org	Alexandria	VA	22314	703-299-6633	299-6004
National Council on Family Relations (NCFR) 1201 W River Pkwy Ste 200 *TF:* 888-781-9331 ■ *Web:* www.ncfr.org	Minneapolis	MN	55454	888-781-9331	
National Council on the Aging (NCOA) 1901 L St NW 4th Fl *TF:* 800-677-1116 ■ *Web:* www.ncoa.org	Washington	DC	20036	202-479-1200	479-0735
National Court Appointed Special Advocate Assn (CASA) 100 W Harrison St N Twr Ste 500 *TF:* 800-628-3233 ■ *Web:* www.casaforchildren.org	Seattle	WA	98119	206-270-0072	270-0078
National Ctr for Children in Poverty (NCCP) 215 W 125th St 3rd Fl *Web:* www.nccp.org	New York	NY	10027	646-284-9600	284-9623
National Ctr for Family Literacy (NCFL) 325 W Main St Ste 300 *TF:* 855-937-5668 ■ *Web:* familieslearning.org	Louisville	KY	40202	502-584-1133	584-0172
National Ctr for Missing & Exploited Children (NCMEC) 699 Prince St *TF:* 800-843-5678 ■ *Web:* www.missingkids.com	Alexandria	VA	22314	703-274-3900	274-2200
National Domestic Violence Hotline (NDVH) PO Box 161810 *TF:* 800-799-7233 ■ *Web:* www.thehotline.org	Austin	TX	78716	512-794-1133	
National Family Caregivers Assn (NFCA) 10400 Connecticut Ave Ste 500 *TF:* 800-896-3650 ■ *Web:* caregiveraction.org	Kensington	MD	20895	301-942-6430	
National Healthy Mothers Healthy Babies Coalition (HMHB) 4401 Ford Ave Ste 300 *Web:* www.hmhb.org	Alexandria	VA	22302	703-837-4792	
National Hispanic Council on Aging (NHCOA) 734 15th St NW Ste 1050 *TF:* 800-633-4227 ■ *Web:* www.nhcoa.org	Washington	DC	20005	202-347-9733	347-9735
National Interfaith Coalition on Aging (NICA) 1901 L St NW 4th Fl *Web:* www.ncoa.org	Washington	DC	20036	202-479-1200	479-0735
National Network for Youth, The 741 Eigth St SE *Web:* www.nn4youth.org	Washington	DC	20003	202-783-7949	783-7955
National Organization of Mothers of Twins Clubs Inc (NOMOTC) PO Box 700860 *Web:* www.multiplesofamerica.org	Plymouth	MI	48170	248-231-4480	
National Resource Ctr on Domestic Violence (NRCDV) 6400 Flank Dr Ste 1300 **Fax Area Code:* 717 ■ *TF:* 800-799-7233 ■ *Web:* www.nrcdv.org	Harrisburg	PA	17112	800-799-7233	545-9456*
National Resource Ctr on Native American Aging (NRCNAA) 501 N Columbia Rd Rm 4535 *TF:* 800-896-7628 ■ *Web:* ruralhealth.und.edu	Grand Forks	ND	58202	701-777-6780	777-6779
National Resource Ctr on Nutrition Physical Activity & Aging Florida International Univ 11200 SW Eighth St Bldg OE200 *Web:* nutritionandaging.fiu.edu	Miami	FL	33199	305-348-1517	348-1518
National Runaway Switchboard (NRS) 3141 N Lincoln Ave *TF:* 800-786-2929 ■ *Web:* www.1800runaway.org	Chicago	IL	60657	773-880-9860	929-5150
National SAFE KIDS Campaign 1301 Pennsylvania Ave NW Ste 1000 *Web:* www.safekids.org	Washington	DC	20004	202-662-0600	393-2072
National Urban Technology Ctr 80 Maiden Ln Ste 606 *TF:* 800-998-3212 ■ *Web:* www.urbantech.org	New York	NY	10038	212-528-7350	528-7355
National WIC Assn (NWA) 2001 S St NW Ste 580 *TF:* 866-782-6246 ■ *Web:* www.nwica.org	Washington	DC	20009	202-232-5492	387-5281
North American Council on Adoptable Children (NACAC) 970 Raymond Ave Ste 106 *TF:* 877-823-2237 ■ *Web:* www.nacac.org	Saint Paul	MN	55114	651-644-3036	644-9848
Orphan Foundation of America (OFA) 21351 Gentry Dr Ste 130 *TF:* 800-950-4673 ■ *Web:* www.fc2success.org	Sterling	VA	20166	571-203-0270	203-0273
Parents Helping Parents (PHP) 1400 Parkmoor Ave Ste 100 *TF:* 855-727-5775 ■ *Web:* www.php.com	San jose	CA	95126	408-727-5775	286-1116
Parents of Murdered Children (POMC) 4960 Ridge Ave Ste 2 *TF:* 888-818-7662 ■ *Web:* www.pomc.com	Cincinnati	OH	45209	513-721-5683	345-4489
Parsons Child & Family Ctr 60 Academy Rd *TF:* 800-342-3009 ■ *Web:* www.parsonscenter.org	Albany	NY	12208	518-426-2600	447-5234
Pension Rights Ctr 1350 Connecticut Ave NW Ste 206 *TF:* 866-735-7737 ■ *Web:* www.pensionrights.org	Washington	DC	20036	202-296-3776	833-2472
Plan USA 155 Plan Way *TF:* 800-556-7918 ■ *Web:* www.planusa.org	Warwick	RI	02886	401-738-5600	738-5608
Planned Parenthood Federation of America 434 W 33rd St *TF:* 800-230-7526 ■ *Web:* www.plannedparenthood.org	New York	NY	10001	212-541-7800	245-1845
Pressley Ridge 5500 Corporate Dr Ste 400 *TF:* 800-718-0356 ■ *Web:* www.pressleyridge.org	Pittsburgh	PA	15237	412-872-9400	872-9478
Promise Keepers (PK) PO Box 11798 **Fax Area Code:* 303 ■ *TF:* 866-776-6473 ■ *Web:* promisekeepers.org	Denver	CO	80211	866-776-6473	433-1036*
Rainbows 1007 Church St Ste 408 *Web:* www.rainbows.org	Evanston	IL	60201	847-952-1770	952-1774
Rape Abuse & Incest National Network (RAINN) 2000 L St NW Ste 406 *TF:* 800-656-4673 ■ *Web:* www.rainn.org	Washington	DC	20036	202-544-1034	544-3556
Safer Foundation 571 W Jackson Blvd *Web:* www.saferfoundation.org	Chicago	IL	60661	312-922-2200	922-0839
SOS Children's Villages-USA 1001 Connecticut Ave NW Ste 1250 *TF General:* 888-767-4543 ■ *Web:* www.sos-usa.org	Washington	DC	20036	202-347-7920	
Spaulding for Children 16250 Northland Dr Ste 120 *Web:* www.spaulding.org	Southfield	MI	48075	248-443-7080	
Stepfamily Foundation 310 W 85th St *Web:* www.stepfamily.org	New York	NY	10024	212-877-3244	
Students Against Destructive Decisions (SADD) 255 Main St *TF:* 877-723-3462 ■ *Web:* www.sadd.org	Marlborough	MA	01752	508-481-3568	481-5759
United Way of Greater Cincinnati 2400 Reading Rd *Web:* www.uwgc.org	Cincinnati	OH	45202	513-762-7100	762-7146
Voices for America's Children 1000 Vermont Ave NW Ste 700 *Web:* www.voicesforamericaschildren.org	Washington	DC	20005	202-289-0777	
Well Spouse Assn 63 W Main St Ste H *TF:* 800-838-0879 ■ *Web:* www.wellspouse.org	Freehold	NJ	07728	732-577-8899	577-8644
YMCA of the USA (YMCA) 101 N Wacker Dr *TF:* 800-872-9622 ■ *Web:* www.ymca.net	Chicago	IL	60606	312-977-0031	977-9063
YWCA USA (YWCA) 2025 M St NW Ste 550 *TF:* 888-872-9259 ■ *Web:* www.ywca.org	Washington	DC	20036	202-467-0801	467-0802

48-7 Civic & Political Organizations

Organization	City	State	Zip	Phone	Fax
Advocates for Self-Government 1010 N Tennessee St Ste 215 *TF:* 800-932-1776 ■ *Web:* theadvocates.org	Cartersville	GA	30120	770-386-8372	
AIDS United 1424 K St NW Ste 200 *Web:* www.aidsunited.org	Washington	DC	20005	202-408-4848	408-1818

Phone Fax

Alliance for Justice (AFJ)
11 Dupont Cir NW 2nd Fl........................Washington DC 20036 202-822-6070 822-6068
Web: www.afj.org
Alliance of Nonprofit Mailers (ANM)
1211 Connecticut Ave NW Ste 610................Washington DC 20036 202-462-5132 462-0423
Web: www.nonprofitmailers.org
American Assn of Political Consultants (AAPC)
8400 W pk Dr 2nd Fl..............................McLean VA 22102 703-245-8020
Web: www.theaapc.org
American Cause, The 501 Church St Ste 315............Vienna VA 22180 703-255-2632 255-2219
Web: www.theamericancause.org
American Conservative Union, The (ACU)
1331 H St NW Ste 500..........................Washington DC 20005 202-347-9388
Web: www.conservative.org
American Council for an Energy-Efficient Economy (ACEEE)
529 14th St NW Ste 600.........................Washington DC 20045 202-507-4000 429-2248
Web: www.aceee.org
American Israel Public Affairs Committee (AIPAC)
251 H St..Washington DC 20001 202-639-5200
Web: aipac.org
American Jewish Congress
260 Madison Ave 2nd Fl..........................New York NY 10016 212-879-4500 758-1633
Web: www.ajcongress.org
American Legislative Exchange Council (ALEC)
1101 Vermont Ave NW 11th Fl....................Washington DC 20005 202-466-3800 466-3801
Web: www.alec.org
Americans for Democratic Action (ADA)
1625 K St NW Ste 210..........................Washington DC 20006 202-785-5980 785-5969
TF: 855-712-8441 ■ *Web:* www.adaction.org
Americans for Fair Taxation PO Box 4929..........Clearwater FL 33758 713-963-9023
Web: www.fairtax.org
Americans for Peace Now (APN)
1101 14th St NW 6th Fl........................Washington DC 20005 202-728-1893 728-1895
TF: 877-429-0678 ■ *Web:* www.peacenow.org
Americans United for Separation of Church & State
518 C St NE......................................Washington DC 20002 202-466-3234 466-2587
TF: 800-875-3707 ■ *Web:* www.au.org
Brady Campaign to Prevent Gun Violence
1225 'I' St NW Ste 1100.........................Washington DC 20005 202-898-0792 371-9615
TF: 800-732-0999 ■ *Web:* www.bradycampaign.org
Cair National (CAIR) 453 New Jersey Ave SE.........Washington DC 20003 202-488-8787 488-0833
Web: www.cair.com
Campaign Legal Ctr
Media Policy Program Campaign Legal Ctr..........Washington DC 20036 202-736-2200 736-2222
TF: 877-855-5007 ■ *Web:* www.campaignlegalcenter.org
CapitolWatch PO Box 650911...................Potomac Falls VA 20165 202-544-2600
Web: www.capitolwatch.org
Center for Democracy & Technology (CDT)
1634 'I' St NW 11th Fl..........................Washington DC 20006 202-637-9800 637-0968
TF: 800-869-4499 ■ *Web:* www.cdt.org
Christian Coalition of America
PO Box 37030....................................Washington DC 20013 202-479-6900 586-0006*
**Fax Area Code:* 808 ■ *TF:* 888-999-6778 ■ *Web:* www.cc.org
Citizens Against Government Waste (CAGW)
1301 Pennsylvania Ave NW Ste 1075..............Washington DC 20004 202-467-5300 467-4253
TF: 800-435-7352 ■ *Web:* www.cagw.org
Citizens Committee for the Right to Keep & Bear Arms (CCRKBA)
12500 NE Tenth Pl...............................Bellevue WA 98005 425-454-4911 451-3959
TF: 800-426-4302 ■ *Web:* www.ccrkba.org
Citizens for Tax Justice (CTJ)
1616 P St NW Ste 200-B........................Washington DC 20036 202-299-1066 299-1065
TF: 888-626-2622 ■ *Web:* www.ctj.org
Close Up Foundation
1330 Braddock Pl Ste 400........................Alexandria VA 22314 703-706-3300
TF: 800-256-7387 ■ *Web:* www.closeup.org
Coalition to Stop Gun Violence
805 15th St NW Ste 700..........................Washington DC 20005 202-408-0061
Web: www.csgv.org
Common Cause 1133 19th St NW 9th Fl.............Washington DC 20036 202-833-1200 659-3716
Web: www.commoncause.org
Community Assns Institute (CAI)
6402 Arlington Blvd Ste 500.....................Falls Church VA 22042 703-970-9220 970-9558
TF: 888-224-4321 ■ *Web:* www.caionline.org
Concord Coalition
1011 Arlington Blvd Ste 300.......................Arlington VA 22209 703-894-6222 894-6231
TF: 888-333-4248 ■ *Web:* www.concordcoalition.org
Congress Watch 215 Pennsylvania Ave SE..........Washington DC 20003 202-546-4996 547-7392
TF: 800-289-3787 ■ *Web:* www.citizen.org/congress
Constitutional Rights Foundation
601 S Kingsley Dr...............................Los Angeles CA 90005 213-487-5590 386-0459
TF: 800-488-4273 ■ *Web:* www.crf-usa.org
Council of Canadians 170 Laurier Ave W Ste 700.........Ottawa ON K1P5V5 613-233-2773 233-6776
TF: 800-387-7177 ■ *Web:* www.canadians.org
Council of the Americas 680 Pk Ave...............New York NY 10065 212-628-3200 249-5868
Web: as-coa.org
Democracy 21 1825 I St NW.......................Washington DC 20006 202-429-2008
Web: www.democracy21.org
Democratic Congressional Campaign Committee (DCCC)
430 S Capitol St SE.............................Washington DC 20003 202-863-1500
Web: www.dccc.org
Democratic Governors Assn (DGA)
1401 K St NW Ste 200............................Washington DC 20005 202-772-5600 772-5602
Web: www.democraticgovernors.org
Democratic Senatorial Campaign Committee (DSCC)
120 Maryland Ave NE.............................Washington DC 20002 202-224-2447 969-0354
Web: www.dscc.org
EMILY's List 1800 M St NW Ste 375N...............Washington DC 20036 202-326-1400 326-1415
TF: 800-683-6459 ■ *Web:* www.emilyslist.org
Evangelicals for Social Action (ESA) PO Box 367.......Wayne PA 19087 484-384-2990
TF: 800-650-6600 ■ *Web:* www.evangelicalsforsocialaction.org
Families USA 1201 New York Ave NW Ste 1100.......Washington DC 20005 202-628-3030 347-2417
TF: 888-392-5132 ■ *Web:* www.familiesusa.org
Federation for American Immigration Reform (FAIR)
25 Massachusetts Ave NW Ste 330.................Washington DC 20009 202-328-7004 387-3447
TF: 877-627-3247 ■ *Web:* www.fairus.org

Phone Fax

Foreign Policy Assn (FPA) 470 Pk Ave S.............New York NY 10016 212-481-8100 481-9275
TF: 800-628-5754 ■ *Web:* www.fpa.org
Foundation for Moral Law PO Box 4086..........Montgomery AL 36103 334-262-1245 262-1708
Web: www.morallaw.org
Freedom Forum 555 Pennsylvania Ave NW...........Washington DC 20001 202-639-0537
Web: www.newseuminstitute.org
FreedomWorks 400 N Capitol St NW Ste 765.........Washington DC 20001 202-783-3870 942-7649
TF: 888-564-6273 ■ *Web:* www.freedomworks.org
Girls Nation
American Legion Auxiliary
8945 N Meridian St..........................Indianapolis IN 46260 317-569-4500 569-4502
Web: www.alaforveterans.org
Global Exchange 2017 Mission St Ste 303.........San Francisco CA 94110 415-255-7296 255-7498
TF: 800-497-1994 ■ *Web:* www.globalexchange.org
Interfaith Alliance
1212 New York Ave NW Ste 1250..................Washington DC 20005 202-238-3300 238-3301
TF: 800-510-0969 ■ *Web:* www.interfaithalliance.org
International Society of Political Psychology (ISPP)
126 Ward St Ste 1213 PO Box 1213.................Columbus NC 28722 828-894-5422 894-5422
Web: www.ispp.org
Interreligious Foundation for Community Organization (IFCO)
418 W 145th St...................................New York NY 10031 212-926-5757 926-5842
Web: www.ifconews.org
Judicial Watch Inc 425 Third St SW Ste 800.........Washington DC 20024 202-646-5172 646-5199
TF: 888-593-8442 ■ *Web:* www.judicialwatch.org
Junior Chamber International (JCI)
15645 Olive Blvd..............................Chesterfield MO 63017 636-449-3100 449-3107
TF: 800-905-5499 ■ *Web:* www.jci.cc
Keep America Beautiful Inc
1010 Washington Blvd............................Stamford CT 06901 203-659-3000
Web: www.kab.org
Landmark Volunteers 800 N Main St.................Sheffield MA 01257 413-229-0255 229-2050
League of Conservation Voters
1920 L St NW Ste 800...........................Washington DC 20036 202-785-8683 835-0491
Web: www.lcv.org
League of Women Voters (LWV)
1730 M St NW Ste 1000..........................Washington DC 20036 202-429-1965 429-0854
Web: www.lwv.org
NA of Town Watch (NATW)
308 E Lancaster Ave Ste 115.....................Wynnewood PA 19096 800-648-3688 649-5456*
**Fax Area Code:* 610 ■ *TF:* 800-648-3688 ■ *Web:* www.nationaltownwatch.org
National Civic League (NCL) 1889 York St.............Denver CO 80206 303-571-4343 314-6053*
**Fax Area Code:* 888 ■ *Web:* www.nationalcivicleague.org
National Coalition on Black Civic Participation Inc (NCBCP)
1050 Connecticut Ave NW Ste 700.................Washington DC 20036 202-659-4929 659-5025
Web: ncbcp.org
National Committee to Preserve Social Security & Medicare (NCPSSM)
10 G St NE Ste 600..............................Washington DC 20002 202-216-0420 216-0451
TF: 800-966-1935 ■ *Web:* www.ncpssm.org
National Community Action Foundation (NCAF)
PO Box 78214....................................Washington DC 20013 202-842-2092 842-2095
Web: ncaf.org
National Council of Women of the US Inc (NCWO)
777 UN Plz.......................................New York NY 10017 212-697-1278
Web: ncwus.org
National Council on Public History (NCPH)
425 University Blvd 327 Cavanaugh Hall...........Indianapolis IN 46202 317-274-2716 278-5230
TF: 800-554-5542 ■ *Web:* www.ncph.org
National Ctr for Neighborhood Enterprise (NCNE)
1625 K St Ste 1200..............................Washington DC 20006 202-518-6500 588-0314
TF: 866-518-1263 ■ *Web:* www.cneonline.org
National Endowment for Democracy (NED)
1025 F St NW Ste 800............................Washington DC 20004 202-378-9700
Web: www.ned.org
National Federation of Democratic Women (NFDW)
7211 E Lincoln...................................Wichita KS 67207 316-612-9709
Web: www.nfdw.com
National Federation of Republican Women (NFRW)
124 N Alfred St..................................Alexandria VA 22314 703-548-9688 548-9836
TF: 800-373-9688 ■ *Web:* www.nfrw.org
National Taxpayers Union (NTU)
108 N Alfred St..................................Alexandria VA 22314 703-683-5700 683-5722
TF: 800-680-7289 ■ *Web:* www.ntu.org
National Women's Political Caucus (NWPC)
PO Box 50476....................................Washington DC 20091 202-785-1100
Web: www.nwpc.org
Native American Community Board (NACB)
PO Box 572......................................Lake Andes SD 57356 605-487-7072 487-7964
Web: www.nativeshop.org
OMB Watch 1742 Connecticut Ave NW................Washington DC 20009 202-234-8494 234-8584
TF: 866-544-7573 ■ *Web:* www.foreffectivegov.org
Organization of American States (OAS)
1889 F St NW.....................................Washington DC 20006 202-458-3000 458-3967
TF: 888-442-4887 ■ *Web:* www.oas.org
People for the American Way (PFAW)
2000 M St NW Ste 400............................Washington DC 20036 202-467-4999 293-2672
TF: 800-326-7329 ■ *Web:* www.pfaw.org
Population Reference Bureau (PRB)
1875 Connecticut Ave NW Ste 520.................Washington DC 20009 202-483-1100 328-3937
TF: 800-877-9881 ■ *Web:* www.prb.org
Population-Environment Balance Inc
2000 P St NW Ste 600............................Washington DC 20036 202-955-5700 955-6161
TF: 800-866-6269 ■ *Web:* www.balance.org
Preservation Action
1307 New Hampshire Ave NW 3rd Fl................Washington DC 20036 202-637-7873
Web: www.preservationaction.org
Project Vote 1350 I St NW Ste 1250.................Washington DC 20005 202-546-4173
TF: 888-546-4173 ■ *Web:* www.projectvote.org
Public Affairs Council (PAC)
2033 K St NW Ste 700............................Washington DC 20006 202-872-1790
Web: www.pac.org
Public Citizen 1600 20th St NW.....................Washington DC 20009 202-588-1000 588-7796
Web: www.citizen.org
Public Forum Institute
2300 M St NW Ste 900............................Washington DC 20037 202-467-2774

Organization	City	State	ZIP	Phone	Fax
Public Service Research Foundation 320-D Maple Ave E *Web:* www.psrf.org	Vienna	VA	22180	703-242-3575	
Republican Governors Assn (RGA) 1747 Pennsylvania Ave NW Ste 250 *Web:* www.rga.org	Washington	DC	20006	202-662-4140	
Ripon Society 1300 L St NW Ste 900 *Web:* www.riponsociety.org	Washington	DC	20005	202-216-1008	
Rock the Vote (RTV) 1001 Connecticut Ave NW Ste 640 *Web:* www.rockthevote.com	Washington	DC	20036	202-719-9910	
Secure America's Future Economy (SAFE) 214 N Spring Vly Rd *Web:* www.s-a-f-e.org	Wilmington	DE	19807	302-478-0676	
Sister Cities International (SCI) 1301 Pennsylvania Ave NW Ste 850 *Web:* www.sister-cities.org	Washington	DC	20004	202-347-8630	393-6524
US Junior Chamber of Commerce 7447 S Lewis Ave *TF:* 800-905-5499 ■ *Web:* www.jci.cc	Tulsa	OK	74136	636-681-1857	681-1401
US Term Limits (USTL) 1250 Connecticut Ave NW Ste 200 *Web:* www.termlimits.org	Washington	DC	20036	202-261-3532	
Violence Policy Ctr (VPC) 1730 Rhode Island Ave NW Ste 1014 *Web:* www.vpc.org	Washington	DC	20036	202-822-8200	
WISH List 333 N Fairfax St Ste 302 *Web:* www.thewishlist.org	Alexandria	VA	22314	703-778-5550	778-5554
Women's Campaign Fund (WCF) 1900 L St NW Ste 500 *Web:* www.wcfonline.org	Washington	DC	20036	202-393-8164	393-0649
Young America's Foundation 110 Elden St **Fax Area Code: 703* ■ *TF:* 800-292-9231 ■ *Web:* www.yaf.org	Herndon	VA	20170	800-872-1776	318-9122*
Young Democrats of America (YDA) PO Box 77496 *Web:* www.yda.org	Washington	DC	20013	202-639-8585	318-3221

48-8 Civil & Human Rights Organizations

Organization	City	State	ZIP	Phone	Fax
ACT UP 12 Wooster St *Web:* www.actupny.org	New York	NY	10013	212-966-4873	
American Civil Liberties Union (ACLU) 125 Broad St 18th Fl *TF:* 877-867-1025 ■ *Web:* www.aclu.org	New York	NY	10004	212-549-2500	549-2580
American Jewish Committee (AJC) 165 E 56th St *Web:* www.ajc.org	New York	NY	10022	212-751-4000	750-0326
American Society of Access Professionals (ASAP) 1444 'I' St NW Ste 700 *Web:* www.accesspro.org	Washington	DC	20005	202-712-9054	216-9646
American-Arab Anti Discrimination Committee (ADC) 1990 M St NW Ste 610 *Web:* www.adc.org	Washington	DC	20036	202-244-2990	244-3196
Americans for Effective Law Enforcement (AELE) 841 W Touhy Ave *TF:* 800-763-2802 ■ *Web:* www.aele.org	Park Ridge	IL	60068	847-685-0700	685-9700
Americans for Tax Reform (ATR) 722 12th St NW Ste 4 *Web:* www.atr.org	Washington	DC	20005	202-785-0266	785-0261
Anti-Defamation League (ADL) 605 Third Ave *TF:* 866-386-3235 ■ *Web:* www.adl.org	New York	NY	10158	212-885-7700	867-0779
Arab American Institute (AAI) 1600 K St NW Ste 601 *Web:* www.aaiusa.org	Washington	DC	20006	202-429-9210	429-9214
Asian American Legal Defense & Education Fund (AALDEF) 99 Hudson St 12th Fl *TF:* 800-966-5946 ■ *Web:* www.aaldef.org	New York	NY	10013	212-966-5932	966-4303
Association for Women's Rights in Development (AWID) 215 Spadina Ave Ste 150 *Web:* www.awid.org	Toronto	ON	M5T2C7	416-594-3773	594-0330
Becket Fund for Religious Liberty 1350 Connecticut Ave NW Ste 605 *Web:* www.becketfund.org	Washington	DC	20036	202-955-0095	955-0090
Center for Individual Rights (CIR) 1233 20th St NW Ste 300 *TF:* 877-426-2665 ■ *Web:* www.cir-usa.org	Washington	DC	20036	202-833-8400	833-8410
Center for Reproductive Rights 120 Wall St 14th Fl *Web:* www.reproductiverights.org	New York	NY	10005	917-637-3600	637-3666
Congress of Racial Equality (CORE) PO Box 264 3rd Fl *Web:* www.congressofracialequality.org	New York	NY	10276	212-598-4000	
Corporate Accountability International 10 Milk St Ste 610 *TF:* 800-688-8797 ■ *Web:* www.stopcorporateabuse.org	Boston	MA	02108	617-695-2525	695-2626
Cultural Survival Inc 215 Prospect St *Web:* www.culturalsurvival.org	Cambridge	MA	02139	617-441-5400	441-5417
Disability Rights Ctr Inc 18 Low Ave *TF:* 800-834-1721 ■ *Web:* www.drcnh.org	Concord	NH	03301	603-228-0432	225-2077
Drug Policy Alliance 70 W 36th St 16th Fl *Web:* www.drugpolicy.org	New York	NY	10018	212-613-8020	613-8021
Ethics Resource Ctr 2345 Crystal Dr Ste 201 *Web:* www.ethics.org	Arlington	VA	22202	703-647-2185	647-2180
Families Against Mandatory Minimums (FAMM) 1612 K St NW Ste 700 *TF:* 800-435-7352 ■ *Web:* www.famm.org	Washington	DC	20006	202-822-6700	822-6704
Grandparents Rights Organization (GRO) 1760 S Telegraph Rd Ste 250 *Web:* www.grandparentsrights.org	Bloomfield Hills	MI	48304	248-646-7177	
Human Rights Campaign 1640 Rhode Island Ave NW *TF:* 800-777-4723 ■ *Web:* www.hrc.org	Washington	DC	20036	202-628-4160	347-5323
Human Rights Watch 350 Fifth Ave 34th Fl *Web:* www.hrw.org	New York	NY	10118	212-290-4700	736-1300
Institute for Health Freedom 1825 I St NW *Web:* www.forhealthfreedom.org	Washington	DC	20006	202-429-6610	861-1973
International Organization for Migration 1752 N St NW Ste 700 *Web:* www.iom.int	Washington	DC	20036	202-862-1826	862-1879
King Ctr, The 449 Auburn Ave NE *Web:* www.thekingcenter.org	Atlanta	GA	30312	404-526-8900	
La Causa Inc PO Box 4188 *Web:* www.lacausa.org	Milwaukee	WI	53204	414-647-8750	647-8797
Lambda Legal Defense & Education Fund 120 Wall St Ste 1500 *TF:* 866-542-8336 ■ *Web:* www.lambdalegal.org	New York	NY	10005	212-809-8585	809-0055
Leadership Conference on Civil Rights (LCCR) 1629 K St NW Ste 1000 *TF:* 888-460-0813 ■ *Web:* www.civilrights.org	Washington	DC	20006	202-466-3311	466-3435
Legal Counsel for the Elderly 601 E St NW Bldg A 4th Fl *Web:* www.aarp.org	Washington	DC	20049	202-434-2170	434-6464
Media Watch PO Box 618 *TF:* 800-631-6355 ■ *Web:* www.mediawatch.com	Santa Cruz	CA	95061	831-423-6355	
Medicare Rights Ctr (MRC) 520 Eigth Ave N Wing 3rd Fl *TF Hotline:* 800-333-4114 ■ *Web:* www.medicarerights.org	New York	NY	10018	212-869-3850	869-3532
Migrant Legal Action Program (MLAP) 1001 Connecticut Ave NW Ste 915 *Web:* www.mlap.org	Washington	DC	20036	202-775-7780	775-7784
NA for the Advancement of Colored People (NAACP) 4805 Mt Hope Dr *TF:* 877-622-2798 ■ *Web:* www.naacp.org	Baltimore	MD	21215	410-580-5777	486-9255
NARAL Pro-Choice America 1156 15th St NW Ste 700 *Web:* www.naral.org	Washington	DC	20005	202-973-3000	973-3096
National Abortion Federation (NAF) 1755 Massachusetts Ave NW *TF:* 800-772-9100 ■ *Web:* www.prochoice.org	Washington	DC	20036	202-667-5881	667-5890
National Coalition Against Censorship (NCAC) 275 Seventh Ave 9th Fl *Web:* www.ncac.org	New York	NY	10001	212-807-6222	807-6245
National Coalition Against Domestic Violence (NCADV) 1 Broadway Ste B210 *TF:* 800-799-7233 ■ *Web:* www.ncadv.org	Denver	CO	80203	303-839-1852	831-9251
National Coalition to Abolish the Death Penalty (NCADP) 1620 L St Ste 250 *Web:* www.ncadp.org	Washington	DC	20036	202-331-4090	
National Conference on Citizenship (NCOC) 1875 K St NW 5th Fl *TF:* 800-745-7275 ■ *Web:* www.ncoc.net	Washington	DC	20006	202-729-8038	449-8276
National Consumer Law Ctr (NCLC) 7 Winthrop Sq *Web:* www.nclc.org	Boston	MA	02110	617-542-8010	542-8028
National Council on Crime & Delinquency (NCCD) 1970 Broadway Ste 500 *TF:* 800-306-6223 ■ *Web:* www.nccdglobal.org	Oakland	CA	94612	510-208-0500	208-0511
National Crime Prevention Council (NCPC) 2345 Crystal Dr Ste 500 *Web:* www.ncpc.org	Arlington	VA	22202	202-466-6272	296-1356
National Ctr for Juvenile Justice (NCJJ) 3700 S Water St Ste 200 *Web:* ncjj.org	Pittsburgh	PA	15203	412-227-6950	227-6955
National Ctr for Victims of Crime, The 2000 M St NW Ste 480 *TF:* 800-394-2255 ■ *Web:* www.victimsofcrime.org	Washington	DC	20036	202-467-8700	467-8701
National Freedom of Information Coalition Univ of Missouri *TF:* 866-682-6663 ■ *Web:* www.nfoic.org	Columbia	MO	65211	573-882-4856	884-6204
National Gay & Lesbian Task Force (NGLTF) 1325 Massachusetts Ave NW Ste 600 *Web:* www.thetaskforce.org	Washington	DC	20005	202-393-5177	393-2241
National Immigration Forum 50 F St NW Ste 300 *Web:* www.immigrationforum.org	Washington	DC	20001	202-347-0040	347-0058
National Organization for the Reform of Marijuana Laws (NORML) 1600 K St NW Ste 501 *TF:* 888-676-6765 ■ *Web:* www.norml.org	Washington	DC	20006	202-483-5500	483-0057
National Organization for Victim Assistance (NOVA) 510 King St Ste 424 *TF:* 800-879-6682 ■ *Web:* trynova.org	Alexandria	VA	22314	703-535-6682	535-5500
National Right to Life Committee Inc (NRLC) 512 Tenth St NW *Web:* www.nrlc.org	Washington	DC	20004	202-626-8800	737-9189
National Urban League Inc 120 Wall St 8th Fl *Web:* nul.iamempowered.com	New York	NY	10005	212-558-5300	558-5332
No Peace Without Justice (NPWJ) 866 UN Plz Ste 408 *Web:* www.npwj.org	New York	NY	10017	212-980-2558	980-1072
Nuclear Information & Resource Service (NIRS) 6930 Carroll Ave Ste 340 *Web:* www.nirs.org	Takoma Park	MD	20912	301-270-6477	270-4291
Osborne Assn 809 Westchester Ave *Web:* www.osborneny.org	Bronx	NY	10455	718-707-2600	
Parents Families & Friends of Lesbians & Gays (PFLAG) 1828 L St NW Ste 660 *Web:* community.pflag.org/page.aspx?pid=194&srcid=-2	Washington	DC	20036	202-467-8180	349-0788
Patients Rights Council (PRC) PO Box 760 *TF:* 800-958-5678 ■ *Web:* www.patientsrightscouncil.org	Steubenville	OH	43952	740-282-3810	
PEN American Ctr 588 Broadway *Web:* www.pen.org	New York	NY	10012	212-334-1660	334-2181
Pro-Life Action League 6160 N Cicero Ave Ste 600 *Web:* www.prolifeaction.org	Chicago	IL	60646	773-777-2900	777-3061
Rutherford Institute PO Box 7482 *TF:* 800-225-1791 ■ *Web:* www.rutherford.org	Charlottesville	VA	22906	434-978-3888	978-1789
Second Amendment Foundation 12500 NE Tenth Pl *TF:* 800-426-4302 ■ *Web:* www.saf.org	Bellevue	WA	98005	425-454-7012	451-3959

Phone Fax

Sentencing Project
1705 DeSales St NW 8th Fl .... Washington DC 20036 202-628-0871 628-1091
Web: sentencingproject.org
Simon Wiesenthal Ctr
1399 Roxbury Dr Ste 100 .... Los Angeles CA 90035 310-553-9036
TF: 800-900-9036 ■ *Web:* www.wiesenthal.com
Southern Poverty Law Ctr (SPLC)
400 Washington Ave. .... Montgomery AL 36104 334-956-8200
TF: 888-414-7752 ■ *Web:* www.splcenter.org
Thomas Jefferson Ctr for the Protection of Free Expression
400 Worrell Dr .... Charlottesville VA 22911 434-295-4784 296-3621
Web: www.tjcenter.org
Urban Land Institute (ULI)
1025 Thomas Jefferson St NW Ste 500W .... Washington DC 20007 202-624-7000 624-7140
TF Orders: 800-321-5011 ■ *Web:* www.uli.org
WeTip Inc PO Box 1296 .... Rancho Cucamonga CA 91729 909-987-5005 987-2477
TF: 800-782-7463 ■ *Web:* www.wetip.com

48-9 Computer & Internet Organizations

Phone Fax

1394 Trade Assn 23117 39th Ave SE .... Bothell WA 98021 425-870-6574 320-3897
Web: www.1394ta.org
American Registry for Internet Numbers (ARIN)
3635 Concorde Pkwy Ste 200 .... Chantilly VA 20151 703-227-9840 997-6200
Web: www.arin.net
Apache Software Foundation (ASF)
1901 Munsey Dr .... Forest Hill MD 21050 410-420-0140 803-2258
Web: www.apache.org
Association for Computing Machinery (ACM)
2 Penn Plz Ste 701 .... New York NY 10121 212-626-0500 944-1318
TF: 800-342-6626 ■ *Web:* www.acm.org
Association For Data Ctr Management Professionals (AFCOM)
742 E Chapman Ave .... Orange CA 92866 714-997-7966 997-9743
Web: www.afcom.com
Association for the Advancement of Artificial Intelligence (AAAI)
445 Burgess Dr Ste 100 .... Menlo Park CA 94025 650-328-3123 321-4457
Web: www.aaai.org
Association of Service & Computer Dealers International (ASCDI)
131 NW First Ave .... Delray Beach FL 33444 561-266-9016 431-6302
Web: www.ascdi.com
Association of Shareware Professionals (ASP)
PO Box 1522 .... Martinsville IN 46151 765-349-4740 301-3756*
**Fax Area Code:* 815 ■ *Web:* www.asp-software.org
Association of Support Professionals, The
38954 Proctor Blvd Ste 396 .... Sandy OR 02472 503-668-9004
Web: www.asponline.com
Broadband Forum 48377 Fremont Blvd Ste 117 .... Fremont CA 94538 510-492-4020
Web: www.broadband-forum.org
CANARIE 45 O'Connor St Ste 500 .... Ottawa ON K1P1A4 613-943-5454 943-5443
Web: www.canarie.ca
Coalition for Networked Information
21 Dupont Cir NW Euram Bldg Ste 800 .... Washington DC 20036 202-296-5098 872-0884
Web: www.cni.org
CommerceNet 169 University Ave .... Palo Alto CA 94301 650-289-4040
Web: commerce.net
Computer Assisted Language Instruction Consortium (CALICO)
214 Centennial Hall .... San Marcos TX 78666 512-245-1417
Web: www.calico.org
Computer Measurement Group (CMG)
3501 Rt 42 Ste 130 #121 .... Turnersville NJ 08012 856-401-1700 401-1708
Computing Research Assn 1828 L St NW .... Washington DC 20036 202-234-2111 667-1066
Web: www.cra.org
Computing Technology Industry Assn (CompTIA)
3500 Lacey Rd Ste 100 .... Downers Grove IL 60515 630-678-8300 678-8384
Web: www.comptia.org
Consortium for School Networking (CoSN)
1025 Vermont Ave NW Ste 1010 .... Washington DC 20005 202-861-2676 393-2011
TF: 866-267-8747 ■ *Web:* www.cosn.org
Data Interchange Standards Assn (DISA)
7600 Leesburg Pike Ste 430 .... Falls Church VA 22043 703-970-4480 970-4488
EDUCAUSE 1150 18th St NW Ste 1010 .... Washington DC 20036 202-872-4200 872-4318
Web: www.educause.edu
Electronic Frontier Foundation Inc (EFF)
454 Shotwell St .... San Francisco CA 94110 415-436-9333 436-9993
Web: www.eff.org
Electronic Privacy Information Ctr (EPIC)
1718 Connecticut Ave NW Ste 200 .... Washington DC 20009 202-483-1140 483-1248
Web: www.epic.org
Entertainment Software Assn (ESA)
575 Seventh St NW Ste 300 .... Washington DC 20004 202-223-2400 223-2401
Web: www.theesa.com
Information Systems Audit & Control Assn (ISACA)
3701 Algonquin Rd Ste 1010 .... Rolling Meadows IL 60008 847-253-1545 253-1443
TF: 888-491-8833 ■ *Web:* www.isaca.org
Information Technology Industry Council (ITI)
1101 K St NW Ste 610 .... Washington DC 20005 202-737-8888 638-4922
Web: www.itic.org
Institute for Certification of Computing Professionals (ICCP)
2400 E Devon Ave Ste 281 .... Des Plaines IL 60018 847-299-4227
TF: 800-843-8227 ■ *Web:* www.iccp.org
Institute for Women & Technology (IWT)
1501 Page Mill Rd MS 1105 .... Palo Alto CA 94304 650-236-4756 852-8172
International Webmasters Assn (IWA)
119 E Union St Ste A .... Pasadena CA 91103 626-449-3709
Web: www.iwanet.org
Internet Corp for Assigned Names & Numbers (ICANN)
4676 Admiralty Way Ste 330 .... Marina del Rey CA 90292 310-823-9358 823-8649
Web: www.icann.org
Internet Society (ISOC) 1775 Wiehle Ave Ste 102 .... Reston VA 20190 703-439-2120 326-9881
Web: www.internetsociety.org
Internet2 1000 Oakbrook Dr Ste 300 .... Ann Arbor MI 48108 734-913-4250 913-4255
Web: www.internet2.edu

Phone Fax

ITechLaw Assn 401 Edgewater Pl Ste 600 .... Wakefield MA 01880 703-506-2895 224-1239*
**Fax Area Code:* 781 ■ *Web:* itechlaw.wpengine.com
National Urban Technology Ctr
80 Maiden Ln Ste 606 .... New York NY 10038 212-528-7350 528-7355
TF: 800-998-3212 ■ *Web:* www.urbantech.org
Object Management Group (OMG)
140 Kendrick St Ste 300 .... Needham MA 02494 781-444-0404 444-0320
Web: www.omg.org
Open Group 44 Montgomery St Ste 960 .... San Francisco CA 94104 415-374-8280 374-8293
TF: 800-433-6611 ■ *Web:* www.opengroup.org
Portable Computer & Communications Assn (PCCA)
PO Box 680 .... Hood River OR 97031 541-490-5140 410-8447*
**Fax Area Code:* 413 ■ *Web:* www.pcca.org
Print Services & Distribution Assn (PSDA)
330 N. Wabash Ave Ste 2000 .... Chicago IL 60611 800-230-0175
TF: 800-336-4641 ■ *Web:* www.psda.org
Society for Information Display (SID)
1475 S Bascom Ave Ste 114 .... Campbell CA 95008 408-879-3901 879-3833
Web: www.sid.org
Society for Information Management (SIM)
15000 Commerce Pkwy Ste C .... Mount Laurel NJ 08054 312-527-6734
TF: 800-387-9746 ■ *Web:* www.simnet.org
Society for Modeling & Simulation International (SCS)
4838 Ronson Ct Ste L PO Box 17900 .... San Diego CA 92111 858-277-3888 277-3930
Web: www.scs.org
Software & Information Industry Assn (SIIA)
1090 Vermont Ave NW 6th Fl .... Washington DC 20005 202-289-7442 289-7097
Web: www.siia.net
TechNet 805 15th St NW Ste 708 .... Washington DC 20005 202-650-5100
Web: www.technet.org
TechServe Alliance 1420 King St Ste 610 .... Alexandria VA 22314 703-838-2050 838-3610
TF: 888-421-1442 ■ *Web:* www.techservealliance.org
Transaction Processing Performance Council (TPC)
572 Ruger St. .... San Francisco CA 94129 415-561-6272 561-6120
Web: www.tpc.org
USENIX Assn 2560 Ninth St Ste 215 .... Berkeley CA 94710 510-528-8649 548-5738
Web: www.usenix.org
World Wide Web Consortium (W3C)
32 Vassar St Rm 32-G515 .... Cambridge MA 02139 617-253-2613 258-5999
Web: www.w3.org

48-10 Consumer Interest Organizations

Phone Fax

Accuracy in Media Inc (AIM) 4350 EW Hwy Ste 555 .... Bethesda MD 20814 202-364-4401 364-4098
TF: 800-787-4567 ■ *Web:* www.aim.org
Advocates for Highway & Auto Safety
750 First St NE Ste 901 .... Washington DC 20002 202-408-1711 408-1699
TF: 877-366-0711 ■ *Web:* www.saferoads.org
American Council on Science & Health (ACSH)
110 E 42nd St Ste 1300 .... New York NY 10017 212-362-7044 362-4919
TF: 866-905-2694 ■ *Web:* www.acsh.org
Call for Action 11820 Parklawn Dr Ste 340 .... Rockville MD 20852 240-747-0225
Web: www.callforaction.org
Carpet & Rug Institute (CRI)
100 S Hamilton St PO Box 2048 .... Dalton GA 30720 706-278-3176 278-8835
Web: www.carpet-rug.org
Center for Auto Safety (CAS)
1825 Connecticut Ave NW Ste 330 .... Washington DC 20009 202-328-7700
Web: www.autosafety.org
Center for Science in the Public Interest (CSPI)
1875 Connecticut Ave NW Ste 300 .... Washington DC 20009 202-332-9110 265-4954
Web: www.cspinet.org
Consumer Federation of America (CFA)
1620 I St NW Ste 200 .... Washington DC 20006 202-387-6121 265-7989
TF: 877-382-4357 ■ *Web:* www.consumerfed.org
Consumers' Research Council of America (CRCA)
2020 Pennsylvania Ave NW Ste 300-A .... Washington DC 20006 202-835-9698 835-9739
TF: 877-774-6337 ■ *Web:* www.consumersresearchcncl.org
Council of Better Business Bureaus Inc Wise Giving Alliance
4200 Wilson Blvd Ste 800 .... Arlington VA 22203 703-276-0100 525-8277
Web: www.bbb.org
Funeral Consumers Alliance
33 Patchen Rd .... South Burlington VT 05403 802-865-8300 865-2626
TF: 800-765-0107 ■ *Web:* www.funerals.org
Green Seal 1001 Connecticut Ave NW Ste 827 .... Washington DC 20036 202-872-6400 872-4324
Web: www.greenseal.org
Insurance Information Institute Inc (III)
110 William St .... New York NY 10038 212-346-5500 732-1916
TF: 877-263-7995 ■ *Web:* www.iii.org
National Committee for Quality Assurance (NCQA)
1100 13th St. .... Washington DC 20005 202-955-3500 955-3599
TF: 888-275-7585 ■ *Web:* www.ncqa.org
National Consumers League (NCL)
1701 K St NW Ste 1200 .... Washington DC 20006 202-835-3323 835-0747
TF: 800-388-2227 ■ *Web:* www.natlconsumersleague.org
National Ctr for Employee Ownership (NCEO)
1736 Franklin St 8th Fl .... Oakland CA 94612 510-208-1300 272-9510
Web: www.nceo.org
National Endowment for Financial Education (NEFE)
1331 17th St Ste 1200 .... Denver CO 80202 303-741-6333 220-0838
Web: www.nefe.org
National Fireworks Assn (NFA)
8224 NW Bradford Ct .... Kansas City MO 64151 816-741-1826 741-1348
Web: www.nationalfireworks.org
National Fraud Information Ctr (NFIC)
1701 K St NW Ste 1200 .... Washington DC 20006 202-835-3323
TF: 800-333-4636 ■ *Web:* www.fraud.org
NeighborWorks America
999 N Capitol St NE Ste 900 .... Washington DC 20002 202-760-4000 376-2600
Web: www.neighborworks.org
Privacy Rights Clearinghouse
3100 Fifth Ave Ste B .... San Diego CA 92103 619-298-3396 298-5681
Web: www.privacyrights.org

				Phone	Fax
Private Citizen Inc PO Box 233	Naperville	IL	60566	630-393-1555	

TF: 888-382-1222 ■ *Web:* www.privatecitizen.com

Public Citizen 1600 20th St NW ..... Washington DC 20009 202-588-1000 588-7796
Web: www.citizen.org

Public Citizen Health Research Group
1600 20th St NW ..... Washington DC 20009 202-588-1000 588-7796
Web: www.citizen.org/hrg

SOCAP International
625 N Washington St Ste 304 ..... Alexandria VA 22314 703-519-3700 549-4886
Web: www.socap.org

US Metric Assn Inc (USMA) 10245 Andasol Ave ..... Northridge CA 91325 310-832-3763

48-11 Educational Associations & Organizations

Phone Fax

A Better Chance Inc 253 W 35th St 6th Fl ..... New York NY 10001 646-346-1310
TF: 800-562-7865 ■ *Web:* www.abetterchance.org

AACSB International - Assn to Advance Collegiate Schools of Business
777 S Harbour Island Blvd Ste 750 ..... Tampa FL 33602 813-769-6500 769-6559
Web: www.aacsb.edu

Academy for Educational Development (AED)
1825 Connecticut Ave NW Ste 800 ..... Washington DC 20009 202-884-8000 884-8400
Web: www.fhi360.org

Academy of Political Science
475 Riverside Dr Ste 1274 ..... New York NY 10115 212-870-2500 870-2202
Web: www.psqonline.org

AFS International Inc 71 W 23rd St 6th Fl ..... New York NY 10010 212-807-8686
Web: www.afs.org

Alliance for Excellent Education
1201 Connecticut Ave Ste 901 ..... Washington DC 20036 202-828-0828 828-0821
Web: www.all4ed.org

Alliance for International Educational & Cultural Exchange
1776 Massachusetts Ave NW Ste 620 ..... Washington DC 20036 202-293-6141 293-6144
TF: 888-304-9023 ■ *Web:* www.alliance-exchange.org

American Council of the Blind (ACB)
2200 Wilson Blvd Ste 650 ..... Arlington VA 22201 202-467-5081 465-5085*
**Fax Area Code:* 703 ■ *TF:* 800-424-8666 ■ *Web:* www.acb.org

American Indian College Fund
8333 Greenwood Blvd ..... Denver CO 80221 303-426-8900 426-1200
TF: 800-776-3863 ■ *Web:* www.collegefund.org

American Montessori Society (AMS)
281 Pk Ave S 6th Fl ..... New York NY 10010 212-358-1250 358-1256
Web: www.amshq.org

American Philosophical Society (APS)
104 S Fifth St ..... Philadelphia PA 19106 215-440-3400 440-3436
Web: www.amphilsoc.org

Americas Society 680 Pk Ave 68th St ..... New York NY 10065 212-628-3200 628-3200
Web: www.as-coa.org

Archaeological Institute of America (AIA)
656 Beacon St 4th Fl ..... Boston MA 02215 617-353-9361 353-6550
TF: 877-524-6300 ■ *Web:* www.archaeological.org

Associated Collegiate Press (ACP)
2221 University Ave SE Ste 121 ..... Minneapolis MN 55414 612-625-8335 626-0720
Web: www.studentpress.org

Association for Asian Studies (AAS)
825 Victors Way Ste 310 ..... Ann Arbor MI 48108 734-665-2490 665-3801
Web: www.asian-studies.org

Association of Jesuit Colleges & Universities (AJCU)
1 Dupont Cir NW Ste 405 ..... Washington DC 20036 202-862-9893 862-8523
Web: www.ajcunet.edu

Association of Writers & Writing Programs (AWP)
George Mason Univ MS 1E3 ..... Fairfax VA 22030 703-993-4301 993-4302
Web: awpwriter.org

Astronomical Society of the Pacific
390 Ashton Ave ..... San Francisco CA 94112 415-337-1100 337-5205
TF: 800-335-2624 ■ *Web:* www.astrosociety.org

Braille Institute of America Inc
741 N Vermont Ave ..... Los Angeles CA 90029 323-663-1111 663-0867
TF: 800-272-4553 ■ *Web:* www.brailleinstitute.org

Breakthrough Collaborative
545 Sansome St Ste 700 ..... San Francisco CA 94111 415-442-0600 442-0609
Web: www.breakthroughcollaborative.org

Bryan City School District
1350 Fountain Grove Dr ..... Bryan OH 43506 419-636-6973 633-6280
Web: www.bryan.k12.oh.us

Challenger Ctr for Space Science Education
422 First St SE 3rd Fl ..... Washington DC 20003 202-827-1580 969-5747*
**Fax Area Code:* 800 ■ *TF General:* 800-969-5747 ■ *Web:* www.challenger.org

Chickasaw Nation, The
520 Arlington St PO Box 1548 ..... Ada OK 74821 580-436-2603 436-7297
TF: 866-466-1481 ■ *Web:* www.chickasaw.net

College Board 45 Columbus Ave ..... New York NY 10023 212-713-8000 713-8282*
**Fax:* PR ■ *TF:* 800-927-4302 ■ *Web:* www.collegeboard.org

College Parents of America (CPA)
2200 Wilson Blvd Ste 102-396 ..... Arlington VA 22201 888-761-6702
TF: 888-761-6702 ■ *Web:* www.collegeparents.org

Columbia Scholastic Press Assn (CSPA)
Columbia University 90 Morningside Dr
Ste B01 ..... New York NY 10027 212-854-9400 854-9401
Web: cspa.columbia.edu

Committee for Education Funding (CEF)
1800 M St NW Ste 500 ..... Washington DC 20036 202-383-0083
Web: www.cef.org

Comstar Enterprises Inc PO Box 6698 ..... Springdale AR 72766 479-361-2111 361-1069
TF: 800-533-2343 ■ *Web:* comstar-inc.com

Council For Economic Opportunities In Greater Cleveland
1228 Euclid Ave Ste 700 ..... Cleveland OH 44115 216-696-9077 696-0770
Web: www.ceogc.org

Council for Opportunity in Education
1025 Vermont Ave NW Ste 900 ..... Washington DC 20005 202-347-7430 347-0786
Web: www.coenet.us

Education Development Ctr Inc (EDC) 55 Chapel St ..... Newton MA 02458 617-969-7100 969-5979
TF: 800-225-4276 ■ *Web:* www.edc.org

Education Trust 1250 H St NW Ste 700 ..... Washington DC 20005 202-293-1217 293-2605
Web: www.edtrust.org

Facing History & Ourselves 16 HuRd Rd ..... Brookline MA 02445 617-232-1595 232-0281
TF: 800-856-9039 ■ *Web:* www.facinghistory.org

Family Career & Community Leaders of America (FCCLA)
1910 Assn Dr ..... Reston VA 20191 703-476-4900 860-2713
TF: 800-234-4425 ■ *Web:* www.fcclainc.org

FIRST 200 Bedford St ..... Manchester NH 03101 603-666-3906 666-3907
TF: 800-871-8326 ■ *Web:* www.firstinspires.org

Foundation Ctr 79 Fifth Ave 2nd Fl ..... New York NY 10003 212-620-4230 807-3691
TF: 800-424-9836 ■ *Web:* www.foundationcenter.org

Future Business Leaders of America-Phi Beta Lambda Inc (FBLA-PBL)
1912 Assn Dr ..... Reston VA 20191 800-325-2946 500-5610*
**Fax Area Code:* 866 ■ *TF:* 800-325-2946 ■ *Web:* www.fbla-pbl.org

German Academic Exchange Service (DAAD)
871 United Nations Plz ..... New York NY 10017 212-758-3223 755-5780
Web: www.daad.org

Graduate Management Admission Council (GMAC)
11921 Freedom Dr Ste 300 ..... Reston VA 20190 703-668-9600 668-9601
TF: 866-505-6559 ■ *Web:* www.gmac.com

Great Books Foundation 35 E Wacker Dr Ste 400 ..... Chicago IL 60601 312-332-5870
TF: 800-222-5870 ■ *Web:* www.greatbooks.org

Institute for Education & the Arts
1156 15th St NW Ste 600 ..... Washington DC 20005 202-223-9721
Web: www.edartsinstitute.org

Institute of Consumer Financial Education
PO Box 34070 ..... San Diego CA 92163 619-239-1401 923-3284
Web: www.financial-education-icfe.org

Institute of General Semantics (IGS)
72-11 Austin St ..... Forest Hills NY 11375 212-729-7973 793-2527*
**Fax Area Code:* 718 ■ *TF:* 800-346-1359 ■ *Web:* www.generalsemantics.org

Institute of International Education (IIE)
809 United Nations Plaza # 1 ..... New York NY 10017 212-883-8200 984-5358
Web: www.iie.org

Intercollegiate Studies Institute (ISI)
3901 Centerville Rd ..... Wilmington DE 19807 302-652-4600 652-1760
TF: 800-526-7022 ■ *Web:* home.isi.org

Intercultural Development Research Assn (IDRA)
5815 Callaghan Rd Ste 101 ..... San Antonio TX 78228 210-444-1710 444-1714
Web: www.idra.org

International Montessori Council & The Montessori Foundation
19600 Florida 64 PO Box 130 ..... Bradenton FL 34212 941-729-9565 729-9594
TF: 800-655-5843 ■ *Web:* www.montessori.org

International Studies Assn (ISA)
324 Social Sciences University of Arizona ..... Tucson AZ 85721 860-486-5850
Web: www.isanet.org

Junior Achievement of Canada (JACAN)
1 Eva Rd Ste 218 ..... Toronto ON M9C4Z5 416-622-4602 622-6861
TF: 800-265-0699 ■ *Web:* jacanada.org

Junior State of America (JSA)
400 S El Camino Real Ste 300 ..... San Mateo CA 94402 650-347-1600 347-7200
TF: 800-334-5353 ■ *Web:* www.jsa.org

League for Innovation in the Community College
4505 E Chandler Blvd Ste 250 ..... Phoenix AZ 85048 480-705-8200 705-8201
Web: www.league.org

Linguistic Society of America (LSA)
1325 18th St NW Ste 211 ..... Washington DC 20036 202-835-1714 835-1717
Web: www.linguisticsociety.org

Medieval Academy of America, The
17 Dunster St Ste 202 ..... Cambridge MA 02138 617-491-1622 492-3303
Web: www.medievalacademy.org

Music for All 39 W Jackson Pl Ste 150 ..... Indianapolis IN 46225 317-636-2263 524-6200
TF: 800-848-2263 ■ *Web:* www.musicforall.org

National Ctr for Family Literacy (NCFL)
325 W Main St Ste 300 ..... Louisville KY 40202 502-584-1133 584-0172
TF: 855-937-5668 ■ *Web:* familieslearning.org

National Head Start Assn (NHSA)
1651 Prince St ..... Alexandria VA 22314 703-739-0875 739-0878
TF: 866-677-8724 ■ *Web:* www.nhsa.org

National Honor Society (NHS) 1904 Assn Dr ..... Reston VA 20191 703-860-0200 476-5432
TF: 800-253-7746 ■ *Web:* www.nhs.us

National Research Council (NRC)
500 Fifth St NW ..... Washington DC 20001 202-334-2000
Web: www.nationalacademies.org/nrc

National Scholastic Press Assn (NSPA)
2221 University Ave SE Ste 121 ..... Minneapolis MN 55414 612-625-8335 626-0720
Web: www.studentpress.org/nspa

National Speech and Debate Association's (NFL)
125 Watson St PO Box 38 ..... Ripon WI 54971 920-748-6206 748-9478
Web: www.speechanddebate.org

North-American Interfraternity Conference (NIC)
3901 W 86th St Ste 390 ..... Indianapolis IN 46268 317-872-1112 872-1134
Web: www.nicindy.org

Northwestern Illinois Assn
245 W Exchange St Ste 4 ..... Sycamore IL 60178 815-895-9227 895-2971
Web: www.thenia.org

Panhandle-Plains Higher Education Authority Inc (PPHEA)
1403 23rd St ..... Canyon TX 79015 806-324-4100 655-3669

Public Education Network (PEN)
601 13th St NW Ste 710-S ..... Washington DC 20005 212-620-4230
Web: www.publiceducation.org

Reading Is Fundamental Inc (RIF)
1825 Connecticut Ave NW Ste 400 ..... Washington DC 20009 202-536-3400
TF: 877-743-7323 ■ *Web:* www.rif.org

Rolling Readers USA
2515 Camino del Rio S Ste 330 ..... San Diego CA 92108 619-516-4095
Web: www.rollingreaders.org

Scholarship America
1 Scholarship Way PO Box 297 ..... Saint Peter MN 56082 507-931-1682 931-9168
TF: 800-537-4180 ■ *Web:* www.scholarshipamerica.org

SkillsUSA 14001 James Monroe Hwy ..... Leesburg VA 20176 703-777-8810 777-8999
TF: 800-321-8422 ■ *Web:* www.skillsusa.org

University of Minnesota
200 SE Oak St Ste 300 ..... Minneapolis MN 55455 612-625-1440 625-5673
TF: 800-922-1663 ■ *Web:* give.umn.edu

Organization	City	State	ZIP	Phone	Fax
White House Historical Assn 740 Jackson Pl NW *Web:* www.whitehousehistory.org	Washington	DC	20006	202-737-8292	789-0440
Woodrow Wilson National Fellowship Foundation 5 Vaughn Dr # 300 *Web:* www.woodrow.org	Princeton	NJ	08540	609-452-7007	452-0066
World Learning International Development Programs 1015 15th St NW Ste 750 *TF:* 800-345-2929 ■ *Web:* www.worldlearning.org	Washington	DC	20005	202-408-5420	408-5397
Young Astronaut Council 5200 27th St NW *Web:* youngastronauts.org	Washington	DC	20015	301-617-0923	
Youth For Understanding USA 6400 Goldsboro Rd Ste 100 *TF:* 800-424-3691 ■ *Web:* www.yfuusa.org	Bethesda	MD	20817	240-235-2100	235-2104

48-12 Energy & Natural Resources Organizations

Organization	City	State	ZIP	Phone	Fax
Air & Waste Management Assn (A&WMA) 420 Fort Duquesne Blvd 1 Gateway Ctr 3rd Fl *TF:* 800-270-3444 ■ *Web:* www.awma.org	Pittsburgh	PA	15222	412-232-3444	232-3450
Alliance to Save Energy (ASE) 1850 M St NW Ste 600 *TF:* 800-862-2086 ■ *Web:* www.ase.org	Washington	DC	20036	202-857-0666	331-9588
American Academy of Environmental Engineers 130 Holiday Ct Ste 100	Annapolis	MD	21401	410-266-3311	266-7653
American Assn of Petroleum Geologists (AAPG) 1444 S Boulder Ave PO Box 979 *TF:* 800-364-2274 ■ *Web:* www.aapg.org	Tulsa	OK	74119	918-584-2555	560-2665
American Assn of Professional Landmen (AAPL) 4100 Fossil Creek Blvd. *TF:* 888-566-2275 ■ *Web:* www.landman.org	Fort Worth	TX	76137	817-847-7700	847-7704
American Coal Ash Assn (ACAA) 15200 E Girard Ave Ste 3050 *Web:* www.acaa-usa.org	Aurora	CO	80014	720-870-7897	870-7889
American Coalition for Clean Coal Electricity (ACCCE) 1152 15th St NW Ste 400 *Web:* americaspower.org	Washington	DC	20005	202-459-4800	
American Coke & Coal Chemicals Institute (ACCCI) 25 Massachusetts AveNW Ste 800 *Web:* www.accci.org	Washington	DC	20001	202-452-7198	463-6573
American Gas Assn (AGA) 400 N Capitol St NW 4th Fl	Washington	DC	20001	202-824-7000	
American Hydrogen Assn (AHA) 2350 W Shangri La *Web:* www.clean-air.org	Phoenix	AZ	85029	602-328-4238	
American Institute of Mining Metallurgical & Petroleum Engineers (AIME) 12999 E Adam Aircraft Cir **Fax Area Code:* 888 ■ *TF:* 888-702-0049 ■ *Web:* www.aimehq.org	Englewood	CO	80112	303-325-5185	702-0049*
American Oil Chemists Society (AOCS) 2710 S Boulder PO Box 17190 *TF:* 866-535-2730 ■ *Web:* www.aocs.org	Urbana	IL	61802	217-359-2344	351-8091
American Petroleum Institute (API) 1220 L St NW *Web:* www.api.org	Washington	DC	20005	202-682-8000	
American Public Gas Assn (APGA) 201 Massachusetts Ave NE Ste C-4 *TF:* 800-927-4204 ■ *Web:* www.apga.org	Washington	DC	20002	202-464-2742	464-0246
American Public Power Assn (APPA) 1875 Connecticut Ave Ste 1200 *TF:* 800-369-6220 ■ *Web:* www.publicpower.org	Washington	DC	20009	202-467-2900	467-2910
American Solar Energy Society (ASES) 2525 Arapahoe Ave Ste E4 253 *Web:* www.ases.org	Boulder	CO	80302	303-443-3130	
American Water Works Assn (AWWA) 6666 W Quincy Ave *TF:* 800-926-7337 ■ *Web:* www.awwa.org	Denver	CO	80235	303-794-7711	347-0804
American Wind Energy Assn (AWEA) 1501 M St NW Ste 1000 *Web:* www.awea.org	Washington	DC	20005	202-383-2500	383-2505
Association of Energy Engineers (AEE) 4025 Pleasantdale Rd Ste 420 *TF:* 877-407-0784 ■ *Web:* www.aeecenter.org	Atlanta	GA	30340	770-447-5083	446-3969
Association of Energy Service Cos (AESC) 14531 Fm 529 Ste 250 *TF:* 800-692-0771 ■ *Web:* www.aesc.net	Houston	TX	77095	713-781-0758	781-7542
Cooling Technology Institute (CTI) 2611 FM 1960 Rd W Ste A-101 *Web:* www.cti.org	Houston	TX	77068	281-583-4087	537-1721
Edison Electric Institute (EEI) 701 Pennsylvania Ave NW *TF:* 800-649-1202 ■ *Web:* www.eei.org	Washington	DC	20004	202-508-5000	508-5051
Electric Power Supply Assn (EPSA) 1401 New York Ave NW 11th Fl *Web:* www.epsa.org	Washington	DC	20005	202-628-8200	628-8260
Electricity Consumers Resource Council (ELCON) 1333 H St NW W Twr 8th Fl *Web:* www.elcon.org	Washington	DC	20005	202-682-1390	289-6370
Energy Recovery Council (IWSA) 1730 Rhode Island Ave NW Ste 700 *Web:* energyrecoverycouncil.org	Washington	DC	20036	202-467-6240	
Environmental Industry Assn 4301 Connecticut Ave NW Ste 300 *TF:* 800-424-2869 ■ *Web:* www.environmentalistseveryday.org	Washington	DC	20008	202-244-4700	966-4824
Environmental Technology Council (ETC) 1112 16th St Ste 420 *Web:* www.etc.org	Washington	DC	20036	202-783-0870	
Gas Processors Assn (GPA) 6526 E 60th St *Web:* www.gpaglobal.org	Tulsa	OK	74145	918-493-3872	493-3875
Gas Processors Suppliers Assn (GPSA) 6526 E 60th St *Web:* www.gpaglobal.org	Tulsa	OK	74145	918-493-3872	
Independent Petroleum Assn of America (IPAA) 1201 15th St NW Ste 300 *TF:* 800-433-2851 ■ *Web:* www.ipaa.org	Washington	DC	20005	202-857-4722	857-4799
Institute of Clean Air Cos (ICAC) 1730 M St NW Ste 206 *TF:* 800-631-9505 ■ *Web:* www.icac.com	Washington	DC	20036	202-457-0911	367-2114
Institute of Hazardous Materials Management (IHMM) 11900 Parklawn Dr Ste 450 *TF:* 800-437-0137 ■ *Web:* www.ihmm.org	Rockville	MD	20852	301-984-8969	984-1516
Institute of Nuclear Power Operations 700 Galleria Pkwy SE Ste 100 *Web:* www.inpo.info	Atlanta	GA	30339	770-644-8000	644-8549
Institute of Scrap Recycling Industries Inc (ISRI) 1615 L St NW Ste 600 *Web:* www.isri.org	Washington	DC	20036	202-662-8500	626-0900
Interstate Oil & Gas Compact Commission (IOGCC) 900 NE 23rd St PO Box 53127 *Web:* iogcc.publishpath.com	Oklahoma City	OK	73152	405-525-3556	525-3592
Methanol Institute (MI) 4100 Fairfax Dr Ste 740 *Web:* www.methanol.org	Arlington	VA	22203	703-248-3636	248-3997
National Ground Water Assn (NGWA) 601 Dempsey Rd *TF:* 800-551-7379 ■ *Web:* www.ngwa.org	Westerville	OH	43081	614-898-7791	898-7786
National Mining Assn (NMA) 101 Constitution Ave NW Ste 500-E *Web:* www.nma.org	Washington	DC	20001	202-463-2600	463-2666
National Ocean Industries Assn (NOIA) 1120 G St NW Ste 900 *TF:* 800-558-9994 ■ *Web:* www.noia.org	Washington	DC	20005	202-347-6900	347-8650
National Petrochemical & Refiners Assn (NPRA) 1667 K St NW Ste 700 *Web:* www.afpm.org	Washington	DC	20006	202-457-0480	457-0486
National Propane Gas Assn (NPGA) 1899 L St NW Ste 350 *Web:* www.npga.org	Washington	DC	20036	202-466-7200	466-7205
National Rural Electric Co-op Assn (NRECA) 4301 Wilson Blvd *TF:* 866-759-2619 ■ *Web:* www.nreca.coop	Arlington	VA	22203	703-907-5939	907-6885
National Rural Water Assn (NRWA) 2915 S 13th St *Web:* www.nrwa.org	Duncan	OK	73533	580-252-0629	255-4476
National Water Resources Assn (NWRA) 3800 Fairfax Dr # 4 **Fax Area Code:* 928 ■ *TF:* 800-468-3533 ■ *Web:* www.nwra.org	Arlington	VA	22203	703-524-1544	343-9483*
Natural Gas Supply Assn (NGSA) 805 15th St NW Ste 510 *Web:* www.ngsa.org	Washington	DC	20005	202-326-9300	326-9330
North American Electric Reliability Council (NERC) 1325 G St NW Ste 600 *Web:* www.nerc.com	Washington	DC	20005	609-452-8060	452-9550
Nuclear Energy Institute (NEI) 1776 'I' St NW Ste 400 *Web:* www.nei.org	Washington	DC	20006	202-739-8000	785-4019
Renewable Fuels Assn (RFA) 425 Third St SW *Web:* www.ethanolrfa.org	Washington	DC	20024	202-289-3835	289-7519
Society of Exploration Geophysicists (SEG) 8801 S Yale Ave Ste 500 PO Box 702740 *Web:* www.seg.org	Tulsa	OK	74137	918-497-5500	497-5557
Society of Petroleum Engineers (SPE) 222 Palisades Creek Dr *TF:* 800-456-6863 ■ *Web:* www.spe.org	Richardson	TX	75080	972-952-9393	952-9435
Society of Petrophysicists & Well Log Analysts (SPWLA) 8866 Gulf Fwy Ste 320 *Web:* www.spwla.org	Houston	TX	77017	713-947-8727	947-7181
Solar Energy Industries Assn (SEIA) 505 Ninth St NW Ste 800 *Web:* www.seia.org	Washington	DC	20004	202-682-0556	682-0559
U.S. Lumber Coalition 1750 K St NW *Web:* www.uslumbercoalition.org	Washington	DC	20006	202-582-0021	
US Energy Assn (USEA) 1300 Pennsylvania Ave NW Ste 550 *Web:* www.usea.org	Washington	DC	20004	202-312-1230	
Water Quality Assn (WQA) 4151 Naperville Rd *Web:* www.wqa.org	Lisle	IL	60532	630-505-0160	505-9637
Western Forestry & Conservation Assn 4033 SW Canyon Rd *TF:* 888-722-9416 ■ *Web:* www.westernforestry.org	Portland	OR	97221	503-226-4562	226-2515

48-13 Environmental Organizations

Organization	City	State	ZIP	Phone	Fax
Adirondack Council 103 Hand Ave Ste 3 Ste 3 *TF:* 877-873-2240 ■ *Web:* www.adirondackcouncil.org	Elizabethtown	NY	12932	518-873-2240	873-6675
Alaska Wilderness League 122 C St NW Ste 240 *Web:* www.alaskawild.org	Washington	DC	20001	202-544-5205	544-5197
Alliance for Responsible Atmospheric Policy 2111 Wilson Blvd 8th Fl *Web:* www.alliancepolicy.org	Arlington	VA	22201	703-243-0344	243-2874
American Cave Conservation Assn 119 E Main St *Web:* www.hiddenrivercave.com	Horse Cave	KY	42749	270-786-1466	
American Farmland Trust (AFT) 1200 18th St *TF:* 800-431-1499 ■ *Web:* www.farmland.org	Washington	DC	20036	202-331-7300	659-8339
American Forests 1220 L St NW Ste 750 *TF:* 800-368-5748 ■ *Web:* www.americanforests.org	Washington	DC	20005	202-737-1944	
American Lands Alliance 726 Seventh St SE *Web:* www.americanlands.org	Washington	DC	20003	202-547-9400	
American Littoral Society (ALS) 18 Hartshorne Dr Ste 1 *TF:* 800-424-8802 ■ *Web:* www.littoralsociety.org	Highlands	NJ	07732	732-291-0055	291-3551
American Rivers 1101 14th St NW Ste 1400 *TF:* 877-347-7550 ■ *Web:* www.americanrivers.org	Washington	DC	20005	202-347-7550	347-9240

Organization	City	State	Zip	Phone	Fax
American Shore & Beach Preservation Assn (ASBPA) 5460 Beaujolais Ln. *TF:* 800-331-1600 ■ *Web:* www.asbpa.org	Fort Myers	FL	33919	239-489-2616	489-9917
Appalachian Mountain Club (AMC) 5 Joy St *TF Orders:* 800-262-4455 ■ *Web:* www.outdoors.org	Boston	MA	02108	617-523-0655	523-0722
APVA Preservation Virginia 204 W Franklin St. *Web:* apva.org	Richmond	VA	23220	804-648-1889	775-0802
Audubon Naturalist Society 8940 Jones Mill Rd *TF:* 888-744-4723 ■ *Web:* www.audubonnaturalist.org	Chevy Chase	MD	20815	301-652-9188	951-7179
Beyond Pesticides 701 E St SE Ste 200. *TF:* 866-260-6653 ■ *Web:* www.beyondpesticides.org	Washington	DC	20003	202-543-5450	543-4791
Big Bend Natural History Assn PO Box 196 *Web:* www.bigbendbookstore.org	Big Bend National Park	TX	79834	432-477-2236	477-2234
Canadian Parks & Wilderness Society (CPAWS) 250 City Ctr Ave Ste 506 *TF:* 800-333-9453 ■ *Web:* www.cpaws.org	Ottawa	ON	K1R6K7	613-569-7226	569-7098
Canadian Water Resources Assn (CWRA) 9 Corvus Ct *Web:* www.cwra.org	Ottawa	ON	K2E7Z4	613-237-9363	594-5190
Canadian Wildlife Federation (CWF) 350 Michael Cowpland Dr *TF:* 800-563-9453 ■ *Web:* www.cwf-fcf.org	Kanata	ON	K2M2W1	613-599-9594	599-4428
Charles A & Anne Morrow Lindbergh Foundation 2150 Third Ave N Ste 310. *Web:* www.lindberghfoundation.org	Anoka	MN	55303	763-576-1596	
Citizens Network for Sustainable Development (CitNet) PO Box 7458 *Web:* www.citnet.org	Silver Spring	MD	20907	301-588-5550	
Civil War Preservation Trust (CWPT) 1331 H St NW Ste 1001 *TF:* 888-606-1400 ■ *Web:* www.civilwar.org	Washington	DC	20005	202-367-1861	367-1865
Clean Water Action 4455 Connecticut Ave NW *TF:* 800-657-3864 ■ *Web:* www.cleanwateraction.org	Washington	DC	20008	202-895-0420	895-0438
Co-op America 1612 K St NW Ste 600 *TF:* 800-584-7336 ■ *Web:* www.greenamerica.org	Washington	DC	20006	202-872-5307	331-8166
Coalition for Responsible Waste Incineration (CRWI) 1615 L St NW Ste 1350 *Web:* www.crwi.org	Washington	DC	20036	202-452-1241	887-8044
Coastal Conservation Assn (CCA) 6919 Portwest Dr Ste 100. *TF:* 800-201-3474 ■ *Web:* www.joincca.org	Houston	TX	77024	713-626-4234	626-5852
Conservation Fund 1655 N Fort Myer Dr Ste 1300 *TF:* 877-347-7550 ■ *Web:* www.conservationfund.org	Arlington	VA	22209	703-525-6300	525-4610
Conservation International (CI) 2011 Crystal Dr Ste 500 *TF:* 800-406-2306 ■ *Web:* www.conservation.org	Arlington	VA	22202	703-341-2400	553-0654
Conservation Treaty Fund (CTSF) 3705 CaRdiff Rd	Chevy Chase	MD	20815	301-652-6390	
Earth Day Network (EDN) 1616 P St NW Ste 340 *Web:* www.earthday.org	Washington	DC	20036	202-518-0044	518-8794
Earth Island Institute 2150 Allston Wy Ste 460 *Web:* www.earthisland.org	Berkeley	CA	94704	415-788-3666	788-7324
Earth Share 7735 Old Georgetown Rd Ste 900 *TF:* 800-875-3863 ■ *Web:* www.earthshare.org	Bethesda	MD	20814	240-333-0300	333-0301
EarthRights International 1612 K St NW Ste 401 *TF:* 888-224-9043 ■ *Web:* www.earthrights.org	Washington	DC	20006	202-466-5188	466-5189
Earthwatch Institute 114 Western Ave *TF:* 800-776-0188 ■ *Web:* www.earthwatch.org	Boston	MA	02134	978-461-0081	461-2332
Ecojustice Canada 131 Water St Ste 214. *TF:* 800-926-7744 ■ *Web:* www.ecojustice.ca	Vancouver	BC	V6B4M3	604-685-5618	685-7813
Educational Communications Inc PO Box 351419 *Web:* www.ecoprojects.org	Los Angeles	CA	90035	310-559-9160	559-9160
Environmental Defense 257 Pk Ave S. *TF:* 800-505-0703 ■ *Web:* www.edf.org	New York	NY	10010	212-505-2100	505-2100
Environmental Information Assn (EIA) 6935 Wisconsin Ave Ste 306 *TF:* 888-343-4342 ■ *Web:* www.eia-usa.org	Chevy Chase	MD	20815	301-961-4999	961-3094
Environmental Law Institute (ELI) 2000 L St NW Ste 620 *TF:* 800-433-5120 ■ *Web:* www.eli.org	Washington	DC	20036	202-939-3800	939-3868
Environmental Protection Information Ctr (EPIC) 145 G St Ste A *Web:* www.wildcalifornia.org	Arcata	CA	95521	707-822-7711	822-7712
Forest Guild 80 E San Francisco PO Box 519 *Web:* forestguild.org	Santa Fe	NM	87504	505-983-8992	986-0798
Forest History Society 701 William Vickers Ave. *Web:* www.foresthistory.org	Durham	NC	27701	919-682-9319	682-2349
Forest Landowners Assn (FLA) 900 Cir 75 Pkwy Ste 205 *TF:* 800-325-2954 ■ *Web:* www.forestlandowners.com	Atlanta	GA	30339	404-325-2954	325-2955
Freshwater Society 2500 Shadywood Rd *TF:* 888-471-9773 ■ *Web:* www.freshwater.org	Excelsior	MN	55331	952-471-9773	471-7685
Friends of the Earth 1717 Massachusetts Ave NW Ste 600 *TF:* 877-843-8687 ■ *Web:* www.foe.org	Washington	DC	20036	202-783-7400	783-0444
Friends of the Everglades 11767 S Dixie Hwy Ste 232 *Web:* www.everglades.org	Miami	FL	33156	305-669-0858	
Friends of the River 1418 20th St Ste 100. *TF:* 888-464-2477 ■ *Web:* www.friendsoftheriver.org	Sacramento	CA	95811	916-442-3155	442-3396
Grand Canyon Trust 2601 N Fort Valley Rd *Web:* www.grandcanyontrust.org	Flagstaff	AZ	86001	928-774-7488	774-7570
Greater Yellowstone Coalition (GYC) 215 S Wallace Ave Ste 2. *TF:* 800-775-1834 ■ *Web:* www.greateryellowstone.org	Bozeman	MT	59715	406-586-1593	556-2839
Greenpeace Canada 33 Cecil St *TF:* 800-320-7183 ■ *Web:* www.greenpeace.org	Toronto	ON	M5T1N1	416-597-8408	597-8422
Greenpeace USA 702 H St NW Ste 300 *TF:* 800-326-0959 ■ *Web:* www.greenpeace.org	Washington	DC	20001	202-462-1177	462-4507
Ground Water Protection Council (GWPC) 13308 N MacArthur Blvd *Web:* www.gwpc.org	Oklahoma City	OK	73142	405-516-4972	516-4973
Hells Canyon Preservation Council 105 Fir St Ste 327 PO Box 2768. *Web:* www.hellscanyon.org	La Grande	OR	97850	541-963-3950	
Heritage Canada Foundation 5 Blackburn Ave *TF:* 866-964-1066 ■ *Web:* www.nationaltrustcanada.ca	Ottawa	ON	K1N8A2	613-237-1066	237-5987
Historic New England 141 Cambridge St. *TF:* 800-722-2256 ■ *Web:* www.historicnewengland.org	Boston	MA	02114	617-227-3956	227-9204
International Assn of Wildland Fire (IAWF) 3416 Primm Ln. *Web:* www.iawfonline.org	Birmingham	AL	35216	205-824-7614	
International Society of Tropical Foresters (ISTF) 5400 Grosvenor Ln. **Fax Area Code:* 877 ■ *TF:* 866-897-8720 ■ *Web:* www.istf-bethesda.org	Bethesda	MD	20814	301-530-4514	665-6473*
Island Nature Trust PO Box 265 *Web:* www.islandnaturetrust.ca	Charlottetown	PE	C1A7K4	902-566-9150	628-6331
Izaak Walton League of America (IWLA) 707 Conservation Ln *TF:* 800-453-5463 ■ *Web:* www.iwla.org	Gaithersburg	MD	20878	301-548-0150	548-0146
Land Trust Alliance (LTA) 1660 L St NW Ste 1100 *Web:* www.landtrustalliance.org	Washington	DC	20036	202-638-4725	638-4730
League to Save Lake Tahoe 2608 Lake Tahoe Blvd *TF:* 888-844-9904 ■ *Web:* www.keeptahoeblue.org	South Lake Tahoe	CA	96150	530-541-5388	541-5454
Montana Wilderness Assn (MWA) 80 South Warren St. *Web:* www.wildmontana.org	Helena	MT	59601	406-443-7350	443-0750
Mount Rushmore Society 711 N Creek Dr *Web:* www.mountrushmoresociety.com	Rapid City	SD	57703	605-341-8883	341-0433
National Alliance of Preservation Commissions 1242 1/2 S Lumpkin St University of Georgia. *Web:* www.uga.edu/sed/pso/programs/napc/napc.htm	Athens	GA	30602	706-542-8924	
National Arbor Day Foundation 100 Arbor Ave. *TF:* 888-448-7337 ■ *Web:* www.arborday.org	Nebraska City	NE	68410	402-474-5655	474-0820
National Audubon Society (NAS) 225 Varick St. *TF:* 800-274-4201 ■ *Web:* www.audubon.org	New York	NY	10014	212-979-3000	979-3188
National Council for Air & Stream Improvement Inc (NCASI) PO Box 13318 *TF:* 888-448-2473 ■ *Web:* www.ncasi.org	Research Triangle Park	NC	27709	919-941-6400	941-6401
National Fish & Wildlife Foundation 1133 15th St NW Ste 1100. *Web:* www.nfwf.org	Washington	DC	20005	202-857-0166	857-0162
National Forest Foundation 27 Ft Missoula Rd Bldg 27 Ste 3 *Web:* www.nationalforests.org	Missoula	MT	59804	406-542-2805	542-2810
National Marine Sanctuary Foundation 8601 Georgia Ave Ste 501 *Web:* www.marinesanctuary.org	Silver Spring	MD	20910	301-608-3040	608-3044
National Park Foundation (NPF) 1201 Eye St NW Ste 550-B. *Web:* www.nationalparks.org	Washington	DC	20005	202-354-6460	371-2066
National Park Trust (NPT) 401 E Jefferson St Ste 102 *Web:* www.parktrust.org	Rockville	MD	20850	301-279-7275	279-7211
National Parks Conservation Assn (NPCA) 1300 19th St NW Ste 300. *TF:* 800-628-7275 ■ *Web:* www.npca.org	Washington	DC	20036	202-223-6722	
National Trust for Historic Preservation 1785 Massachusetts Ave NW *TF:* 800-944-6847 ■ *Web:* www.preservationnation.org	Washington	DC	20036	202-588-6000	588-6038
National Wildlife Refuge Assn (NWRA) 1250 Connecticut Ave NW Ste 600. *Web:* www.refugeassociation.org	Washington	DC	20036	202-292-2402	
Natural Areas Assn (NAA) PO Box 1504 *Web:* www.naturalareas.org	Bend	OR	97709	541-317-0199	317-0140
Natural Resources Defense Council (NRDC) 40 W 20th St. *Web:* www.nrdc.org	New York	NY	10011	212-727-2700	727-1773
Nature Conservancy 4245 N Fairfax Dr Ste 100 *TF Cust Svc:* 800-628-6860 ■ *Web:* www.nature.org	Arlington	VA	22203	703-841-5300	841-1283
Nature Conservancy of Canada 36 Eglinton Ave W Ste 400. *TF:* 800-465-8005 ■ *Web:* www.natureconservancy.ca	Toronto	ON	M4R1A1	416-932-3202	932-3208
Negative Population Growth (NPG) 2861 Duke St Ste 36. *Web:* www.npg.org	Alexandria	VA	22314	703-370-9510	370-9514
New England Wild Flower Society 180 Hemenway Rd *TF:* 888-636-0033 ■ *Web:* www.newfs.org	Framingham	MA	01701	508-877-7630	877-3658
Ocean Conservancy 1300 19th St NW 8th Fl. *TF:* 800-519-1541 ■ *Web:* www.oceanconservancy.org	Washington	DC	20036	202-429-5609	872-0619
Ocean Futures Society 325 Chapala St. *TF:* 800-477-7500 ■ *Web:* www.oceanfutures.org	Santa Barbara	CA	93101	805-899-8899	899-8898
Open Space Institute (OSI) 1350 Broadway Ste 201 *Web:* www.osiny.org	New York	NY	10018	212-290-8200	244-3441
Pacific Rivers Council (PRC) 1326 SW 16th Ave. *Web:* www.pacificrivers.org	Portland	OR	97201	503-228-3555	228-3556
Pew Charitable Trust 901 E St NW *Web:* www.pewtrusts.org	Washington	DC	20004	202-887-8800	
Pollution Probe 150 Ferrand Dr Ste 208. *TF:* 877-926-1907 ■ *Web:* www.pollutionprobe.org	Toronto	ON	M3C3E5	416-926-1907	926-1601
Project for Public Spaces 700 Broadway 4th Fl. *Web:* www.pps.org	New York	NY	10003	212-620-5660	620-3821
Public Lands Foundation (PLF) PO Box 7226 *TF:* 866-985-9636 ■ *Web:* www.publicland.org	Arlington	VA	22207	703-790-1988	821-3490

Organization / Address	City	State	Zip	Phone	Fax
Rails-to-Trails Conservancy (RTC) 2121 Ward Ct NW 5th Fl. *Web:* www.railstotrails.org	Washington	DC	20037	202-331-9696	223-9257
Rainforest Action Network (RAN) 221 Pine St 5th Fl. *TF:* 800-368-1819 ■ *Web:* www.ran.org	San Francisco	CA	94104	415-398-4404	398-2732
Renewable Natural Resources Foundation (RNRF) 5430 Grosvenor Ln. *Web:* www.rnrf.org	Bethesda	MD	20814	301-493-9101	493-6148
Royal Oak Foundation, The 35 W 35th St Ste 1200 *TF:* 800-913-6565 ■ *Web:* www.royal-oak.org	New York	NY	10001	212-480-2889	785-7234
Save America's Forests 4 Library Ct SE *TF:* 800-729-1363 ■ *Web:* www.saveamericasforests.org	Washington	DC	20003	202-544-9219	544-7462
Sea Grant Assn (SGA) 5784 York Complex University of Maine *Web:* www.sga.seagrant.org	Orono	ME	04469	207-581-1435	581-1426
Shelburne Farms 1611 Harbor Rd. *TF:* 800-286-6022 ■ *Web:* www.shelburnefarms.org	Shelburne	VT	05482	802-985-8686	985-8123
Sierra Club 85 Second St 2nd Fl *Web:* www.sierraclub.org	San Francisco	CA	94105	415-977-5500	977-5799
Sierra Club Canada 412-1 Nicholas St. *TF:* 888-810-4204 ■ *Web:* www.sierraclub.ca	Ottawa	ON	K1N7B7	613-241-4611	241-2292
Society for Ecological Restoration International (SERI) 1017 O St NW. **Fax Area Code:* 270 ■ *TF:* 866-895-4735 ■ *Web:* ser.org	Washington	DC	20001	202-299-9518	626-5485*
Society of Architectural Historians (SAH) 1365 N Astor St *Web:* www.sah.org	Chicago	IL	60610	312-573-1365	573-1141
Soil & Water Conservation Society (SWCS) 945 SW Ankeny Rd. *TF:* 800-843-7645 ■ *Web:* www.swcs.org	Ankeny	IA	50023	515-289-2331	289-1227
Southern Utah Wilderness Alliance (SUWA) 425 East 100 South *Web:* www.suwa.org	Salt Lake City	UT	84111	801-486-3161	
Student Conservation Assn (SCA) 689 River Rd PO Box 550 *TF:* 888-722-9675 ■ *Web:* www.thesca.org	Charlestown	NH	03603	603-543-1700	543-1828
Tall Timbers 13093 Henry Beadel Dr. *Web:* www.talltimbers.org	Tallahassee	FL	32312	850-893-4153	893-6470
Thornton W Burgess Society 6 Discovery Hill Rd. *TF:* 800-844-4542 ■ *Web:* www.thorntonburgess.org	East Sandwich	MA	02537	508-888-6870	888-1919
Tongass Conservation Society (TCS) PO Box 23377 *Web:* www.tongassconservation.org	Ketchikan	AK	99901	907-225-3275	
Tree Care Industry Assn (TCIA) 136 Harvey Rd Ste 101 *TF:* 800-733-2622 ■ *Web:* tcia.org	Londonderry	NH	03053	603-314-5380	314-5386
Trust for Public Land (TPL) 116 New Montgomery St 4th Fl *TF:* 800-714-5263 ■ *Web:* www.tpl.org	San Francisco	CA	94105	415-495-4014	495-4103
Union of Concerned Scientists (UCS) 2 Brattle Sq 6th Fl. *TF:* 800-666-8276 ■ *Web:* www.ucsusa.org	Cambridge	MA	02238	617-547-5552	864-9405
Upper Mississippi River Conservation Committee (UMRCC) 555 Lester Ave *Web:* www.umrcc.org	Onalaska	WI	54650	608-783-8432	783-8450
Walden Woods Project, The 44 Baker Farm Rd *TF:* 800-554-3569 ■ *Web:* www.walden.org	Lincoln	MA	01773	781-259-4700	259-4710
Water Environment Federation (WEF) 601 Wythe St *TF:* 800-666-0206 ■ *Web:* www.wef.org	Alexandria	VA	22314	703-684-2400	684-2492
Western Canada Wilderness Committee (WCWC) 227 Abbott St *TF:* 800-661-9453 ■ *Web:* www.wildernesscommittee.org	Vancouver	BC	V6B2K7	604-683-8220	683-8229
Wilderness Society 1615 M St NW *TF:* 800-843-9453 ■ *Web:* www.wilderness.org	Washington	DC	20036	202-833-2300	
Wildlife Habitat Council (WHC) 8737 Colesville Rd Ste 800 *Web:* www.wildlifehc.org	Silver Spring	MD	20910	301-588-8994	
World Forestry Ctr 4033 SW Canyon Rd *Web:* www.worldforestry.org	Portland	OR	97221	503-228-1367	228-4608
World Resources Institute (WRI) 10 G St NE Ste 800 *Web:* www.wri.org	Washington	DC	20002	202-729-7600	729-7610
Yosemite Assn *Yosemite Conservancy* 5020 El Portal Rd PO Box 230 *TF:* 800-469-7275 ■ *Web:* www.yosemiteconservancy.org	El Portal	CA	95318	209-379-2317	379-2486

48-14 Ethnic & Nationality Organizations

Organization / Address	City	State	Zip	Phone	Fax
Africa-America Institute (AAI) 420 Lexington Ave Ste 1706 *Web:* www.aaionline.org	New York	NY	10170	212-949-5666	682-6174
American Folklore Society (AFS) 1501 Neil Ave 1501 Neil Ave *TF:* 866-311-1200 ■ *Web:* www.afsnet.org	Columbus	OH	43201	614-292-4715	292-2407
American Hellenic Educational Progressive Assn (AHEPA) 1909 Q St NW Ste 500 *TF:* 855-473-3512 ■ *Web:* www.ahepa.org	Washington	DC	20009	202-232-6300	232-2140
American Historical Society of Germans from Russia 631 D St *Web:* www.ahsgr.org	Lincoln	NE	68502	402-474-3363	474-7229
American Latvian Assn Inc 400 Hurley Ave *Web:* www.alausa.org	Rockville	MD	20850	301-340-1914	340-8732
Arab American Institute (AAI) 1600 K St NW Ste 601 *Web:* www.aaiusa.org	Washington	DC	20006	202-429-9210	429-9214
Armenian Assembly of America 734 15th St NW Ste 500 *Web:* www.aaainc.org	Washington	DC	20005	202-393-3434	638-4904
Armenian General Benevolent Union (AGBU) 55 E 59th St 7th Fl *Web:* www.agbu.org	New York	NY	10022	212-319-6383	319-6507
ASPIRA Assn Inc 1444 'I' St NW Ste 800 *Web:* www.aspira.org	Washington	DC	20005	202-835-3600	835-3613
Assembly of Turkish American Assn (ATAA) 1526 18th St NW *TF:* 800-627-7692 ■ *Web:* www.ataa.org	Washington	DC	20036	202-483-9090	483-9092
Center for Cuban Studies 231 W 29th St Ste 401 *Web:* centerforcubanstudies.org	New York	NY	10001	212-242-0559	242-1937
China Institute in America 125 E 65th St. *Web:* www.chinainstitute.org	New York	NY	10065	212-744-8181	628-4159
Congress of Russian-Americans 2460 Sutter St. *Web:* www.russian-americans.org	San Francisco	CA	94115	415-928-5841	
Croatian Fraternal Union of America (CFU) 100 Delaney Dr. *Web:* www.croatianfraternalunion.org	Pittsburgh	PA	15235	412-843-0380	823-1594
Cuban American National Council 1223 SW Fourth St *Web:* www.cnc.org	Miami	FL	33135	305-642-3484	642-9122
First Nations Development Institute 2217 Princess Anne St Ste 111-1 **Fax Area Code:* 888 ■ *TF:* 888-371-3686 ■ *Web:* www.firstnations.org	Fredericksburg	VA	22401	540-371-5615	371-3686*
Foundation for Jewish Culture 330 Seventh Ave 21st Fl PO Box 489	New York	NY	10001	212-629-0500	629-0508
French Institute Alliance Francaise (FIAF) 22 E 60th St *Web:* www.fiaf.org	New York	NY	10022	212-355-6100	935-4119
German-American National Congress (DANK) 4740 N Western Ave Ste 206 *TF:* 888-872-3265 ■ *Web:* www.dank.org	Chicago	IL	60625	773-275-1100	275-4010
Hispanic Society of America 613 W 155th St *Web:* www.hispanicsociety.org	New York	NY	10032	212-926-2234	
Ibero-American Action League Inc 817 E Main St. *Web:* www.iaal.org	Rochester	NY	14605	585-256-8900	256-0120
Japan Society 333 E 47th St *Web:* www.japansociety.org	New York	NY	10017	212-832-1155	755-6752
Japanese American Citizens League (JACL) 1765 Sutter St. *Web:* www.jacl.org	San Francisco	CA	94115	415-921-5225	931-4671
Korean American Coalition (KAC) 3727 W Sixth St Ste 305 *Web:* www.kacla.org	Los Angeles	CA	90020	213-365-5999	380-7990
Mexican American Legal Defense & Educational Fund (MALDEF) 634 S Spring St *Web:* www.maldef.org	Los Angeles	CA	90014	213-629-2512	629-0266
Mexican-American Opportunity Foundation (MAOF) 401 N Garfield Ave *Web:* www.maof.org	Montebello	CA	90640	323-890-9600	890-9637
National Congress of American Indians (NCAI) 1516 P St NW *Web:* www.ncai.org	Washington	DC	20005	202-466-7767	466-7797
National Council of La Raza (NCLR) 1126 16th St NW 6th Fl *Web:* www.nclr.org	Washington	DC	20036	202-785-1670	776-1792
National Hispanic Institute (NHI) 472 FM 1966 Rd.	Maxwell	TX	78656	512-357-6137	357-2206
National Slovak Society of the USA (NSS) 351 Vly Brook Rd *TF:* 800-488-1890 ■ *Web:* www.nsslife.org	McMurray	PA	15317	724-731-0094	731-0145
Order Sons of Italy in America (OSIA) 219 E St NE *TF:* 800-552-6742 ■ *Web:* www.osia.org	Washington	DC	20002	202-547-2900	546-8168
Organization of Chinese Americans (OCA) 1322 18th St NW *Web:* www.ocanational.org	Washington	DC	20036	202-223-5500	296-0540
Polish American Congress 5711 N Milwaukee Ave *Web:* www.pac1944.org	Chicago	IL	60646	773-763-9944	
Scottish Heritage USA 315 Page Rd Ste 10 *Web:* www.scottishheritageusa.org	Pinehurst	NC	28374	910-295-4448	295-3147
Sons of Norway 1455 W Lake St 2nd Fl *TF:* 800-945-8851 ■ *Web:* www.sofn.com	Minneapolis	MN	55408	612-827-3611	827-0658
Swedish Council of America 3030 W River Pkwy *Web:* www.swedishcouncil.org	Minneapolis	MN	55406	612-871-0593	
Tolstoy Foundation Inc 104 Lake Rd PO Box 578 *Web:* www.tolstoyfoundation.org	Valley Cottage	NY	10989	845-268-6722	268-6937
Ukrainian NA Inc (UNA) 2200 Rt 10 **Fax Area Code:* 973 ■ *TF:* 800-253-9862 ■ *Web:* www.ukrainiannationalassociation.org	Parsippany	NJ	07054	800-253-9862	292-0900*
US Pan Asian American Chamber of Commerce (US PAACC) 1329 18th St NW *TF:* 800-696-7818 ■ *Web:* www.uspaacc.com	Washington	DC	20036	202-296-5221	296-5225
Venezuelan-American Assn of the US 641 Lexington Ave Ste 1430 *Web:* www.venezuelanamerican.org	New York	NY	10022	212-233-7776	233-7779

48-15 Fraternal & Social Organizations

Organization / Address	City	State	Zip	Phone	Fax
American Mensa Ltd 1229 Corporate Dr W *TF:* 800-666-3672 ■ *Web:* www.us.mensa.org	Arlington	TX	76006	817-607-0060	649-5232
Association of Junior Leagues International Inc (AJLI) 80 Maiden Ln Ste 305 *TF:* 800-955-3248 ■ *Web:* www.ajli.org	New York	NY	10038	212-951-8300	481-7196
Astor Home For Children, The 6339 Mill St PO Box 5005 *Web:* www.astorservices.org	Rhinebeck	NY	12572	845-871-1000	
Athletes in Action 651 Taylor Dr *Web:* www.athletesinaction.org	Xenia	OH	45385	937-352-1000	

Organization / Address	City	State	Zip	Phone	Fax
Benevolent & Protective Order of Elks of the USA 2750 N Lakeview Ave *Web:* www.elks.org	Chicago	IL	60614	773-755-4700	755-4790
Boy Scouts of America (BSA) 1325 W Walnut Hill Ln PO Box 152079 *Web:* www.scouting.org	Irving	TX	75015	972-580-2000	
Boys & Girls Clubs of America 1275 Peachtree St NE *TF:* 800-995-3579 ■ *Web:* www.bgca.org	Atlanta	GA	30309	404-487-5700	487-5757
Citizens For Citizens Inc 264 Griffin St *Web:* www.cfcinc.org	Fall River	MA	02724	508-679-0041	324-7503
Civitan International PO Box 130744 *TF:* 800-248-4826 ■ *Web:* www.civitan.org	Birmingham	AL	35213	205-591-8910	591-8910
Community Counseling & Correctional Service (CCCS) 471 E Mercury St *Web:* www.cccscorp.com	Butte	MT	59701	406-782-0417	782-6964
Cosmopolitan International 7341 W 80th St PO Box 4588 *TF:* 800-648-4331 ■ *Web:* www.cosmopolitan.org	Lancaster	PA	17604	913-648-4330	648-4330
DeMolay International 10200 NW Ambassador Dr *TF Orders:* 800-336-6529 ■ *Web:* www.demolay.org	Kansas City	MO	64153	816-891-8333	891-9062
English-Speaking Union of the US 144 E 39th St *Web:* www.esuus.org	New York	NY	10016	212-818-1200	818-1200
Fraternal Order of Police (FOP) 701 Marriott Dr *TF:* 800-451-2711 ■ *Web:* www.fop.net	Nashville	TN	37214	615-399-0900	399-0400
Friars Club 57 E 55th St *Web:* www.friarsclub.com	New York	NY	10022	212-751-7272	
General Grand Chapter Order of the Eastern Star 1618 New Hampshire Ave NW *Web:* www.easternstar.org	Washington	DC	20009	202-667-4737	462-5162
Girl Scouts of the USA 420 Fifth Ave *TF:* 800-478-7248 ■ *Web:* www.girlscouts.org	New York	NY	10018	212-852-8000	852-6517
Goodwill Industries of Central Texas 1015 Norwood Pk Blvd *TF:* 800-735-2989 ■ *Web:* www.goodwillcentraltexas.org	Austin	TX	78753	512-637-7106	637-7400
Grand Aerie Fraternal Order of Eagles 1623 Gateway Cir S *TF:* 877-829-5500 ■ *Web:* www.foe.com	Grove City	OH	43123	614-883-2200	883-2201
House of, The Good Shepherd, The 1550 Champlin Ave *Web:* www.hgs-utica.com	Utica	NY	13502	315-235-7600	
Independent Order of Odd Fellows 422 N Trade St *TF:* 800-235-8358 ■ *Web:* www.ioof.org	Winston-Salem	NC	27101	336-725-5955	722-7317
International Assn of Lions Clubs 300 W 22nd St *TF:* 800-710-7822 ■ *Web:* www.lionsclubs.org	Oak Brook	IL	60523	630-571-5466	571-8890
KenCrest Services Inc 502 W Germantown Pk Ste 200 *Web:* www.kencrest.org	Plymouth Meeting	PA	19462	610-825-9360	
Key Club International 3636 Woodview Trace *TF:* 800-549-2647 ■ *Web:* www.keyclub.org	Indianapolis	IN	46268	317-875-8755	879-0204
Klingberg Family Centers Inc 370 Linwood St *TF:* 877-696-6775 ■ *Web:* www.klingberg.org	New Britain	CT	06052	860-224-9113	832-8221
Knights of Columbus 1 Columbus Plz *TF Cust Svc:* 800-380-9995 ■ *Web:* www.kofc.org	New Haven	CT	06510	203-752-4000	
Life Inc 2609 Royall Ave *Web:* www.lifeincorporated.com	Goldsboro	NC	27534	919-778-1900	778-1911
Life's WORC 1501 Franklin Ave PO Box 8165 *Web:* www.lifesworc.org	Garden City	NY	11530	516-741-9000	741-5560
Lifestream Inc PO Box 50487 *Web:* www.lifestreaminc.com	New Bedford	MA	02745	508-993-1991	991-5228
Louisiana Baptist Children's Home Inc (LBCH) 7200 DeSiard St *TF:* 877-345-7411 ■ *Web:* www.lbch.org	Monroe	LA	71203	318-343-2244	
Lutheran Homes Society Inc 2021 N McCord Rd *TF:* 877-646-4050 ■ *Web:* www.lutheranhomessociety.org	Toledo	OH	43615	419-861-4990	861-4949
Lutheran Social Services of Illinois 1001 E Touhy Ave Ste 50 *TF:* 888-671-0300 ■ *Web:* www.lssi.org	Des Plaines	IL	60018	847-635-4600	
Masonic Service Assn of North America (MSANA) 8120 Fenton St Ste 203 *TF:* 855-476-4010 ■ *Web:* www.msana.com	Silver Spring	MD	20910	301-588-4010	608-3457
Mennonite Home 1520 Harrisburg Pk *Web:* www.mennonitehome.org	Lancaster	PA	17601	717-393-1301	393-1389
Mile High United Way Inc 2505 18th St *Web:* www.unitedwaydenver.org	Denver	CO	80211	303-433-8383	455-6462
Moose International Inc 155 S International Dr *Web:* www.mooseintl.org	Mooseheart	IL	60539	630-859-2000	
National Exchange Club 3050 W Central Ave *TF:* 800-924-2643 ■ *Web:* www.nationalexchangeclub.org	Toledo	OH	43606	419-535-3232	535-1989
Neighbor To Family Inc 220 S Ridgewood Ave Ste 260 *Web:* www.neighbortofamily.org	Daytona Beach	FL	32114	386-523-1440	
Optimist International 4494 Lindell Blvd *TF:* 800-500-8130 ■ *Web:* www.optimist.org	Saint Louis	MO	63108	314-371-6000	371-6006
Oswego County Opportunities Inc 239 Oneida St *TF:* 877-342-7618 ■ *Web:* www.oco.org	Fulton	NY	13069	315-598-4717	592-7533
Partnerships In Community Living Inc 480 Main St E PO Box 129 *TF:* 800-222-1222 ■ *Web:* www.pclpartnership.org	Monmouth	OR	97361	503-838-2403	838-5815
Presbyterian Homes Inc, The 2109 Sandy Ridge Rd *TF:* 800-225-9573 ■ *Web:* www.presbyhomesinc.org	Colfax	NC	27235	336-886-6553	886-4102
Professional Bull Riders Inc (PBR) 101 W Riverwalk *TF:* 800-366-8538 ■ *Web:* www.pbr.com	Pueblo	CO	81003	719-242-2800	242-2855
Quota International 1420 21st St NW *Web:* quota.org	Washington	DC	20036	202-331-9694	331-4395
Rotary International 1560 Sherman Ave 1 Rotary Ctr *Web:* www.rotary.org	Evanston	IL	60201	847-866-3000	328-8554
Ruritan National 5451 Lyons Rd PO Box 487 *TF:* 877-787-8727 ■ *Web:* www.ruritan.org	Dublin	VA	24084	540-674-5431	674-2304
Skill Creations Inc 2101 Royall Ave PO Box 10628 *Web:* www.skillcreations.com	Goldsboro	NC	27532	919-734-7398	735-5064
Spectrum Health Systems Inc 10 Mechanic St Ste 302 *TF:* 800-464-9555 ■ *Web:* www.spectrumhealthsystems.org	Worcester	MA	01608	508-792-5400	
Starr Commonwealth 13725 Starr Commonwealth Rd *TF:* 800-837-5591 ■ *Web:* www.starr.org	Albion	MI	49224	517-629-5591	630-2400
Sunnyvale Lumber Inc 870 W Evelyn Ave *Web:* www.sunnyvalelumber.com	Sunnyvale	CA	94086	408-736-5411	736-6738
TelecomPioneers 1801 California St Ste 225 *TF:* 800-872-5995 ■ *Web:* www.telecompioneers.org	Denver	CO	80202	303-571-1200	572-0520
TERI Inc 251 Airport Rd *Web:* www.teriinc.org	Oceanside	CA	92058	760-721-1706	
Toastmasters International 23182 Arroyo Vista *Web:* www.toastmasters.org	Rancho Santa Margarita	CA	92688	949-858-8255	858-1207
Uhlich Children's Advantage Network (UCAN) 3737 N Mozart St *Web:* ucanchicago.org	Chicago	IL	60618	773-588-0180	588-7762
Up With People 6830 Broadway *TF:* 877-264-8856 ■ *Web:* www.upwithpeople.org	Denver	CO	80221	303-460-7100	225-4649
Wabash Ctr Inc 2000 Greenbush St *Web:* www.wabashcenter.com	Lafayette	IN	47904	765-423-5531	
Way Station Inc 230 W Patrick St PO Box 3826 *TF:* 888-549-0629 ■ *Web:* www.waystationinc.org	Frederick	MD	21705	301-662-0099	694-9932

48-16 Greek Letter Societies

Organization / Address	City	State	Zip	Phone	Fax
Alpha Beta Gamma International Business Honor Society 75 Grasslands Rd *Web:* www.abg.org	Valhalla	NY	10595	914-606-6877	
Alpha Chi National College Honor Scholarship Society 915 E Market Ave *Web:* www.harding.edu	Searcy	AR	72143	501-279-4443	279-5438
Alpha Chi Omega 5939 Castle Creek Pkwy N Dr *TF:* 800-328-0522 ■ *Web:* www.alphachiomega.org	Indianapolis	IN	46250	317-579-5050	579-5051
Alpha Chi Rho Fraternity Inc 109 Oxford Way *Web:* www.alphachirho.org	Neptune	NJ	07753	732-869-1895	988-5357
Alpha Chi Sigma 2141 N Franklin Rd *TF:* 800-252-4369 ■ *Web:* www.alphachisigma.org	Indianapolis	IN	46219	317-357-5944	351-9702
Alpha Delta Phi International Fraternity 21 Byron Place *Web:* www.alphadeltaphi.org	New Haven	CT	06515	847-965-1832	965-1871
Alpha Delta Pi 1386 Ponce de Leon Ave NE *Web:* www.alphadeltapi.org	Atlanta	GA	30306	404-378-3164	373-0084
Alpha Epsilon Delta (AED) Texas Christian University PO Box BOX 298810 *Web:* aednational.tcu.edu	Fort Worth	TX	76129	817-257-4550	257-0201
Alpha Epsilon Phi Sorority (AEPhi) 11 Lake Ave Ext Ste 1-A *TF:* 888-668-4293 ■ *Web:* www.aephi.org	Danbury	CT	06811	203-748-0029	748-0039
Alpha Epsilon Pi Fraternity Inc 8815 Wesleyan Rd *TF:* 800-684-3608 ■ *Web:* www.aepi.org	Indianapolis	IN	46268	317-876-1913	876-1057
Alpha Gamma Delta 8701 Founders Rd *Web:* www.alphagammadelta.org	Indianapolis	IN	46268	317-872-2655	
Alpha Gamma Rho 10101 NW Ambassador Dr *TF:* 888-241-4546 ■ *Web:* www.alphagammarho.org	Kansas City	MO	64153	816-891-9200	891-9401
Alpha Kappa Alpha Sorority Inc 5656 S Stony Island Ave *Web:* www.aka1908.com	Chicago	IL	60637	773-684-1282	
Alpha Kappa Psi (AKPsi) 7801 E 88th St *Web:* www.akpsi.com	Indianapolis	IN	46256	317-872-1553	872-1567
Alpha Omega International Dental Fraternity 50 W Edmonston Dr *TF:* 877-368-6326 ■ *Web:* www.ao.org	Rockville	MD	20852	301-738-6400	738-6403
Alpha Omicron Pi International 5390 Virginia Way *TF:* 855-230-1183 ■ *Web:* www.alphaomicronpi.org	Brentwood	TN	37027	615-370-0920	371-9736
Alpha Phi Alpha Fraternity Inc 2313 St Paul St *Web:* www.apa1906.net	Baltimore	MD	21218	410-554-0040	554-0054
Alpha Phi Delta Fraternity Inc 257E Camden-Wyoming Ave Ste A *Web:* www.apd.org	Camden	DE	19934	302-538-6145	
Alpha Phi International Fraternity 1930 Sherman Ave *Web:* www.alphaphi.org	Evanston	IL	60201	847-475-0663	475-6820
Alpha Phi Omega (APO) 14901 E 42nd St *Web:* www.apo.org	Independence	MO	64055	816-373-8667	373-5975
Alpha Sigma Alpha (ASA) 9002 Vincennes Cir *Web:* www.alphasigmaalpha.org	Indianapolis	IN	46268	317-871-2920	871-2924
Alpha Sigma Phi National Fraternity 710 Adams St *TF:* 866-515-4747 ■ *Web:* www.alphasigmaphi.org	Carmel	IN	46032	317-843-1911	843-2966
Alpha Tau Omega Fraternity (ATO) 1 N Pennsylvania St 12th Fl *TF:* 800-798-9286 ■ *Web:* www.ato.org	Indianapolis	IN	46204	317-684-1865	684-1862
Alpha Xi Delta Women's Fraternity 8702 Founders Rd *Web:* www.alphaxidelta.org	Indianapolis	IN	46268	317-872-3500	872-2947

Organization	City	State	ZIP	Phone	Fax
Beta Alpha Psi 220 Leigh Farm Rd *Web:* www.bap.org	Durham	NC	27707	919-402-4044	402-4040
Beta Beta Beta National Biological Honor Society Univ of N Alabama PO Box 5079 *Web:* www.tri-beta.org	Florence	AL	35632	256-765-6220	765-6221
Beta Gamma Sigma Inc (BGS) 125 Weldon Pkwy *TF:* 800-337-4677 ■ *Web:* www.betagammasigma.org	Maryland Heights	MO	63043	314-432-5650	432-7083
Beta Phi Mu *Florida State Univ College of Information* 3141 Chestnut St *Web:* beta-phi-mu.org	Philadelphia	PA	19104	215-895-2492	895-2494
Beta Theta Pi 5134 Bonham Rd **Fax Area Code:* 513 ■ *TF:* 800-800-2382	Oxford	OH	45056	800-800-2382	523-2381*
Chi Alpha Campus Ministries USA 1445 Booneville Ave *TF:* 855-700-2457 ■ *Web:* www.chialpha.com	Springfield	MO	65802	417-862-2781	865-9947
Chi Omega Fraternity 3395 Players Club Pkwy *Web:* www.chiomega.com	Memphis	TN	38125	901-748-8600	748-8686
Chi Phi Fraternity 1160 Satellite Blvd *TF:* 800-849-1824 ■ *Web:* www.chiphi.org	Suwanee	GA	30024	404-231-1824	
Chi Psi Fraternity 45 Rutledge St *Web:* www.chipsi.org	Nashville	TN	37210	615-736-2520	736-2366
Delta Chi Fraternity Inc 314 Church St	Iowa City	IA	52245	319-337-4811	
Delta Delta Delta Fraternity 2331 Brookhollow Plz Dr *TF:* 877-746-7333 ■ *Web:* www.tridelta.org	Arlington	TX	76006	817-633-8001	652-0212
Delta Gamma 3250 Riverside Dr PO Box 21397 *Web:* www.deltagamma.org	Columbus	OH	43221	614-481-8169	
Delta Kappa Epsilon Fraternity (DKE) 611 1/2 E William St *Web:* www.dke.org	Ann Arbor	MI	48104	734-302-4210	
Delta Phi Epsilon International Sorority 251 S Camac St *Web:* www.dphie.org	Philadelphia	PA	19107	215-732-5901	732-5906
Delta Pi Epsilon (DPE) 1914 Association Dr *Web:* www.dpe.org	Reston	VA	20191	501-219-1866	
Delta Sigma Phi Fraternity 1331 N Delaware St *Web:* www.deltasig.org	Indianapolis	IN	46202	317-634-1899	634-1410
Delta Sigma Pi 330 S Campus Ave *Web:* www.deltasigmapi.org	Oxford	OH	45056	513-523-1907	523-7292
Delta Sigma Theta Sorority Inc 1707 New Hampshire Ave NW *TF:* 866-615-6464 ■ *Web:* www.deltasigmatheta.org	Washington	DC	20009	202-986-2400	986-2513
Delta Tau Delta Fraternity 10000 Allisonville Rd *TF:* 800-335-8795 ■ *Web:* www.delts.org	Fishers	IN	46038	317-284-0203	284-0214
Delta Theta Phi 225 Hillsborough St Ste 432 *TF:* 800-783-2600 ■ *Web:* www.deltathetaphi.org	Raleigh	NC	27603	800-783-2600	
Delta Upsilon International Fraternity 8705 Founders Rd PO Box 68942 *Web:* www.deltau.org	Indianapolis	IN	46268	317-875-8900	876-1629
Delta Zeta Sorority 202 E Church St *Web:* www.deltazeta.org	Oxford	OH	45056	513-523-7597	523-1921
Epsilon Sigma Phi Inc 450 Falls Ave Ste 106 *Web:* www.espnational.org	Twin Falls	ID	83301	208-736-4495	736-6081
Eta Sigma Gamma 2000 University Ave *TF:* 800-715-2559 ■ *Web:* www.etasigmagamma.org	Muncie	IN	47306	765-285-2258	285-3210
Fraternity of Alpha Kappa Lambda 354 Gradle Dr *Web:* www.akl.org	Carmel	IN	46032	317-564-8003	
Gamma Beta Phi Society 78 Mitchell Rd Ste A *TF:* 800-628-9920 ■ *Web:* www.gammabetaphi.org	Oak Ridge	TN	37830	865-483-6212	
Gamma Phi Beta International Sorority (GPB) 12737 E Euclid Dr *Web:* www.gammaphibeta.org	Centennial	CO	80111	303-799-1874	799-1876
International Fraternity of Phi Gamma Delta 1201 Red Mile Rd PO Box 4599 *TF:* 888-668-4293 ■ *Web:* www.phigam.org	Lexington	KY	40544	859-255-1848	253-0779
Kappa Alpha Order 115 Liberty Hall Rd *TF:* 888-922-6335 ■ *Web:* www.kappaalphaorder.org	Lexington	VA	24450	540-463-1865	463-2140
Kappa Alpha Psi Fraternity Inc 2322-24 N Broad St *Web:* www.kappaalphapsi1911.com	Philadelphia	PA	19132	215-228-7184	228-7181
Kappa Alpha Theta Fraternity 8740 Founders Rd *TF:* 800-526-1870 ■ *Web:* www.kappaalphatheta.org	Indianapolis	IN	46268	317-876-1870	876-1925
Kappa Delta Pi 3707 Woodview Trace *TF:* 800-284-3167 ■ *Web:* www.kdp.org	Indianapolis	IN	46268	317-871-4900	704-2323
Kappa Delta Sorority 3205 Players Ln *TF:* 800-536-1897 ■ *Web:* www.kappadelta.org	Memphis	TN	38125	901-748-1897	748-0949
Kappa Kappa Gamma PO Box 38 *TF:* 866-554-1870 ■ *Web:* www.kappakappagamma.org	Columbus	OH	43216	614-228-6515	228-7809
Kappa Sigma Fraternity 1610 Scottsville Rd *Web:* www.kappasigma.org	Charlottesville	VA	22902	434-295-3193	296-9557
Lambda Chi Alpha International Fraternity 8741 Founders Rd *Web:* www.lambdachi.org	Indianapolis	IN	46268	317-872-8000	
Mu Phi Epsilon International Music Fraternity PO Box 1369 *TF:* 888-259-1471 ■ *Web:* www.muphiepsilon.org	Fort Collins	CO	80522	888-259-1471	
National Alpha Lambda Delta 328 Orange St *TF:* 800-925-7421 ■ *Web:* www.nationalald.org	Macon	GA	31201	478-744-9595	744-9924
National Fraternity of Kappa Delta Rho (KDR) 331 S Main St *TF:* 800-536-5371 ■ *Web:* www.kdr.com	Greensburg	PA	15601	724-838-7100	838-7101
National Kappa Kappa Iota Inc 1875 E 15th St *TF:* 800-678-0389 ■ *Web:* www.nationalkappakappaiota.org	Tulsa	OK	74104	918-744-0389	744-0578
Omega Psi Phi Fraternity Inc 3951 Snapfinger Pkwy *Web:* www.oppf.org	Decatur	GA	30035	404-284-5533	284-0333
Phi Alpha Theta *National History Honor Society* 4202 E Fowler Ave SOC 107 **Fax Area Code:* 813 ■ *TF:* 800-394-8195 ■ *Web:* www.phialphatheta.org	Tampa	FL	33620	800-394-8195	974-8215*
Phi Beta Kappa Society 1606 New Hampshire Ave NW *Web:* www.pbk.org/home	Washington	DC	20009	202-265-3808	986-1601
Phi Beta Sigma Fraternity Inc 145 Kennedy St NW *Web:* www.phibetasigma1914.org	Washington	DC	20011	202-726-5434	882-1681
Phi Chi Theta 1508 E Beltline Rd Ste 104 *Web:* www.phichitheta.org	Carrollton	TX	75006	972-245-7202	
Phi Delta Kappa International (PDK) 408 N Union St *TF:* 800-766-1156 ■ *Web:* www.pdkintl.org	Bloomington	IN	47407	812-339-1156	339-0018
Phi Delta Phi International Legal Fraternity 1426 21st St NW *TF:* 800-368-5606 ■ *Web:* www.phideltaphi.org	Washington	DC	20036	202-223-6801	223-6808
Phi Delta Theta 2 S Campus Ave *TF:* 888-373-9855 ■ *Web:* www.phideltatheta.org	Oxford	OH	45056	513-523-6345	523-9200
Phi Eta Sigma National Honor Society 1906 College H8s Boulevard Ste 11062 *Web:* www.phietasigma.org	Bowling Green	KY	42101	270-745-6540	745-3893
Phi Kappa Psi 5395 Emerson Way *TF:* 800-486-1852 ■ *Web:* www.phikappapsi.com	Indianapolis	IN	46226	317-632-1852	
Phi Kappa Sigma International Fraternity Inc 2 Timber Dr *Web:* www.pks.org	Chester Springs	PA	19425	610-469-3282	469-3286
Phi Kappa Tau 5221 Morning Sun Rd *TF:* 800-758-1906 ■ *Web:* www.phikappatau.org	Oxford	OH	45056	513-523-4193	523-9325
Phi Kappa Theta National Fraternity 3901 W 86th St Ste 360 *Web:* www.phikaps.org	Indianapolis	IN	46268	317-872-9934	879-1889
Phi Mu Alpha Sinfonia Fraternity of America Inc 10600 Old State Rd *TF:* 800-473-2649 ■ *Web:* www.sinfonia.org	Evansville	IN	47711	812-867-2433	867-0633
Phi Mu Fraternity 400 Westpark Dr *TF:* 888-744-6824 ■ *Web:* www.phimu.org	Peachtree City	GA	30269	770-632-2090	632-2136
Phi Sigma Kappa International 2925 E 96th St *TF:* 888-846-6851 ■ *Web:* www.phisigmakappa.org	Indianapolis	IN	46240	317-573-5420	573-5430
Phi Sigma Pi National Honor Fraternity Inc 2119 Ambassador Cir *TF:* 800-366-1916 ■ *Web:* www.phisigmapi.org	Lancaster	PA	17603	717-299-4710	390-3054
Phi Sigma Sigma Fraternity Inc 8178 Lark Brown Rd Ste 202 *Web:* www.phisigmasigma.org	Elkridge	MD	21075	410-799-1224	799-9186
Phi Theta Kappa International Honor Society 1625 Eastover Dr *TF:* 800-946-9995 ■ *Web:* www.ptk.org	Jackson	MS	39211	601-984-3504	984-3550
Pi Beta Phi Fraternity for Women 1154 Town & Country Commons Dr *Web:* www.pibetaphi.org	Town and Country	MO	63017	636-256-0680	256-8095
Pi Kappa Alpha Fraternity 8347 W Range Cove *Web:* pikes.org	Memphis	TN	38125	901-748-1868	748-3100
Pi Kappa Phi Fraternity 2015 Ayrsley Town Blvd Ste 200 *Web:* www.pikapp.org	Charlotte	NC	28273	704-504-0888	504-0880
Pi Lambda Phi Fraternity Inc 60 Newtown Rd Ste 118 *Web:* www.pilambdaphi.org	Danbury	CT	06810	203-740-1044	740-1644
Pi Sigma Alpha 1527 New Hampshire Ave NW *Web:* office2248.wix.com/pi-sigma-alpha	Washington	DC	20036	202-349-9285	483-2657
Pi Sigma Epsilon (PSE) 3747 S Howell Ave *TF:* 800-761-9350 ■ *Web:* www.pse.org	Milwaukee	WI	53207	414-328-1952	328-1953
Psi Chi National Honor Society in Psychology 825 Vine St *Web:* www.psichi.org	Chattanooga	TN	37403	423-756-2044	
PSI Upsilon Fraternity 3003 E 96th St *TF:* 800-394-1833 ■ *Web:* www.psiu.org	Indianapolis	IN	46240	317-571-1833	844-5170
Sigma Alpha Epsilon Fraternity (SAE) 1856 Sheridan Rd *TF:* 800-233-1856 ■ *Web:* www.sae.net	Evanston	IL	60201	847-475-1856	475-2250
Sigma Alpha Iota (SAI) 1 Tunnel Rd *Web:* www.sai-national.org	Asheville	NC	28805	828-251-0606	251-0644
Sigma Chi Fraternity 1714 Hinman Ave *TF:* 877-829-5500 ■ *Web:* www.sigmachi.org	Evanston	IL	60201	847-869-3655	869-4906
Sigma Delta Tau 714 Adams St *Web:* sigmadeltatau.org	Carmel	IN	46032	317-846-7747	575-5562
Sigma Gamma Rho Sorority Inc 1000 Southhill Dr Ste 200 *Web:* www.sgrho1922.org	Cary	NC	27513	919-678-9720	678-9721
Sigma Kappa Sorority 8733 Founders Rd *Web:* www.sigmakappa.org	Indianapolis	IN	46268	317-872-3275	872-0716
Sigma Nu Fraternity Inc 9 N Lewis St PO Box 1869 *Web:* www.sigmanu.org	Lexington	VA	24450	540-463-1869	463-1669
Sigma Phi Epsilon Fraternity 310 S Blvd *TF:* 800-767-1901 ■ *Web:* www.sigep.org	Richmond	VA	23220	804-353-1901	359-8160
Sigma Pi Fraternity 106 N Castle Heights Ave *TF:* 800-332-1897 ■ *Web:* www.sigmapi.org	Lebanon	TN	37087	615-373-5728	373-8949
Sigma Tau Gamma 101 Ming St PO Box 54 *Web:* websites.omegafi.com/omegaws/sigmataugamma/	Warrensburg	MO	64093	660-747-2222	
Sigma Theta Tau International 550 W N St *TF:* 888-634-7575 ■ *Web:* www.nursingsociety.org	Indianapolis	IN	46202	317-634-8171	634-8188
Sigma Xi Scientific Research Society 3106 E NC Hwy 54 PO Box 13975 *TF:* 800-243-6534 ■ *Web:* www.sigmaxi.org	Research Triangle Park	NC	27709	919-549-4691	549-0090
Tau Alpha Chi 82 Thompson St	Alpharetta	GA	30009	770-475-4253	475-4408
Tau Beta Pi Assn 1512 Middle Dr *TF:* 877-829-5500 ■ *Web:* www.tbp.org	Knoxville	TN	37996	865-546-4578	546-4579

Organization	City	State	Zip	Phone	Fax
Tau Beta Sigma National Honorary Band Sorority PO Box 849 *TF Cust Svc:* 800-543-6505 ■ *Web:* www.tbsigma.org	Stillwater	OK	74076	405-372-2333	372-2363
Tau Kappa Epsilon (TKE) 7439 Woodland Dr Ste 100 *Web:* www.tke.org	Indianapolis	IN	46278	317-872-6533	875-8353
Theta Delta Chi Inc 214 Lewis Wharf *TF:* 800-999-1847 ■ *Web:* www.thetadeltachi.net	Boston	MA	02110	617-742-8886	
Theta Phi Alpha Fraternity Inc 27025 Knickerbocker Rd *Web:* www.thetaphialpha.org	Bay Village	OH	44140	440-899-9282	899-9293
Theta Tau Professional Engineering Fraternity 1011 San Jacinto Ste 205 *TF:* 800-264-1904 ■ *Web:* www.thetatau.org	Austin	TX	78701	512-472-1904	472-4820
Zeta Beta Tau Fraternity Inc (ZBT) 3905 Vincennes Rd Ste 100 *Web:* www.zbt.org	Indianapolis	IN	46268	317-334-1898	334-1899
Zeta Phi Beta Sorority Inc 1734 New Hampshire Ave NW *TF:* 800-393-2503 ■ *Web:* zphib1920.org	Washington	DC	20009	202-387-3103	
Zeta Psi Fraternity of North America 15 S Henry St *TF:* 800-477-1847 ■ *Web:* www.zetapsi.org	Pearl River	NY	10965	845-735-1847	735-1989
Zeta Tau Alpha Fraternity (ZTA) 3450 Founders Rd *Web:* www.zetataualpha.org	Indianapolis	IN	46268	317-872-0540	876-3948

48-17 Health & Health-Related Organizations

Organization	City	State	Zip	Phone	Fax
Acoustic Neuroma Assn (ANA) 600 Peachtree Pkwy Ste 108 *TF:* 877-200-8211 ■ *Web:* www.anausa.org	Cumming	GA	30041	770-205-8211	205-0239
Alliance for Aging Research (AAR) 750 17th St NW Ste 1100 **Fax Area Code:* 770 ■ *TF:* 866-840-6283 ■ *Web:* www.agingresearch.org	Washington	DC	20006	202-293-2856	234-5030*
Alliance for Lupus Research (ALR) 28 W 44th St Ste 501 *TF:* 800-867-1743 ■ *Web:* www.lupusresearch.org	New York	NY	10036	212-218-2840	218-2848
Alzheimer's Assn 225 N Michigan Ave Fl 17 **Fax Area Code:* 866 ■ *TF:* 800-272-3900 ■ *Web:* www.alz.org	Chicago	IL	60601	312-335-8700	699-1246*
American Academy for Cerebral Palsy & Developmental Medicine (AACPDM) 555 E Wells St Ste 1100 *Web:* www.aacpdm.org	Milwaukee	WI	53202	414-918-3014	276-2146
American Academy of Medical Acupuncture (AAMA) 1970 E Grand Ave Ste 330 *Web:* www.medicalacupuncture.org	El Segundo	CA	90245	310-364-0193	
American Academy of Sleep Medicine (AASM) 2510 N Frontage Rd Ste 920 *Web:* www.aasmnet.org	Darien	IL	60561	708-492-0930	492-0943
American Assn of Acupunture & Oriental Medicine (AAAOM) PO Box 162340 *TF:* 866-455-7999 ■ *Web:* www.aaaomonline.org	Sacramento	CA	95816	916-443-4770	443-4766
American Assn of Drugless Practitioners (AADP) 2200 Market St Ste 803 *TF:* 888-764-2237 ■ *Web:* www.aadp.net	Galveston	TX	77550	409-621-2600	
American Assn of Naturopathic Physicians (AANP) 818 18th St Ste 250 *TF:* 866-538-2267 ■ *Web:* www.naturopathic.org	Washington	DC	20006	202-237-8150	237-8152
American Assn of Suicidology (AAS) 5221 Wisconsin Ave NW 2nd Fl *Web:* www.suicidology.org	Washington	DC	20015	202-237-2280	237-2282
American Assn on Intellectual & Developmental Disabilities (AAIDD) 444 N Capitol St NW Ste 846 *TF:* 800-424-3688 ■ *Web:* www.aaidd.org	Washington	DC	20001	202-387-1968	387-2193
American Autoimmune Related Disease Assn (AARDA) 22100 Gratiot Ave *TF:* 800-598-4668 ■ *Web:* www.aarda.org	Eastpointe	MI	48021	586-776-3900	776-3903
American Botanical Council 6200 Manor Rd PO Box 144345 *TF:* 800-373-7105 ■ *Web:* www.abc.herbalgram.org	Austin	TX	78723	512-926-4900	926-2345
American Brain Tumor Assn (ABTA) 2720 River Rd *TF:* 800-886-2282 ■ *Web:* www.abta.org	Des Plaines	IL	60018	847-827-9910	827-9918
American Cancer Society (ACS) 250 William St NW *TF:* 800-227-2345 ■ *Web:* www.cancer.org	Atlanta	GA	30303	404-320-3333	
American Chronic Pain Assn (ACPA) PO Box 850 *TF:* 800-533-3231 ■ *Web:* www.theacpa.org	Rocklin	CA	95677	916-632-0922	632-3208
American Council for Headache Education (ACHE) 19 Mantua Rd *Web:* www.achenet.org	Mount Royal	NJ	08061	856-423-0043	423-0082
American Council of the Blind (ACB) 1155 15th St NW Ste 1004 *TF:* 800-424-8666 ■ *Web:* www.acb.org	Washington	DC	20005	202-467-5081	467-5085
American Council on Alcoholism (ACA) 1000 E Indian School Rd *TF:* 800-527-5344	Phoenix	AZ	85014	800-527-5344	
American Council on Exercise (ACE) 4851 Paramount Dr *TF:* 800-825-3636 ■ *Web:* www.acefitness.org	San Diego	CA	92123	858-576-6500	576-6564
American Diabetes Assn (ADA) 1701 N Beauregard St *TF:* 800-232-3472 ■ *Web:* www.diabetes.org	Alexandria	VA	22311	703-549-1500	
American Epilepsy Society (AES) 342 N Main St *TF:* 888-233-2334 ■ *Web:* www.aesnet.org	West Hartford	CT	06117	860-586-7505	586-7550
American Foundation for AIDS Research (AmFAR) 120 Wall St 13th Fl *Web:* www.amfar.org	New York	NY	10005	212-806-1600	806-1601
American Foundation for Suicide Prevention (AFSP) 120 Wall St 22nd Fl *TF:* 888-333-2377 ■ *Web:* www.afsp.org	New York	NY	10005	212-363-3500	363-6237
American Foundation for the Blind (AFB) 2 Penn Plaza *TF:* 800-232-5463 ■ *Web:* www.afb.org	New York	NY	10001	212-502-7600	502-7777
American Hearing Research Foundation 275 N York St Ste 401 *Web:* www.american-hearing.org	Elmhurst	IL	60126	312-726-9670	
American Heart Assn (AHA) 7272 Greenville Ave *TF:* 800-242-8721 ■ *Web:* www.heart.org	Dallas	TX	75231	214-373-6300	706-1191
American Holistic Health Assn (AHHA) PO Box 17400 *Web:* www.ahha.org	Anaheim	CA	92817	714-779-6152	
American Holistic Nurses' Assn (AHNA) 323 N San Francisco St Ste 201 *TF:* 800-278-2462 ■ *Web:* www.ahna.org	Flagstaff	AZ	86001	928-526-2196	526-2752
American Institute of Stress, The (AIS) 124 Pk Ave *Web:* www.stress.org	Yonkers	NY	10703	914-963-1200	
American Kidney Fund (AKF) 6110 Executive Blvd Ste 1010 **Fax Area Code:* 301 ■ *TF:* 800-638-8299 ■ *Web:* www.akfinc.org	Rockville	MD	20852	800-638-8299	881-0898*
American Liver Foundation (ALF) 39 Broadway *TF:* 800-465-4837 ■ *Web:* www.liverfoundation.org	New York	NY	10006	212-668-1000	483-8179
American Lung Assn (ALA) 14 Wall St *TF:* 800-586-4872 ■ *Web:* www.lung.org	New York	NY	10005	212-315-8700	
American Massage Therapy Assn (AMTA) 500 Davis St Ste 900 *TF:* 877-905-2700 ■ *Web:* www.amtamassage.org	Evanston	IL	60201	847-864-0123	864-1178
American Music Therapy Assn Inc (AMTA) 8455 Colesville Rd Ste 1000 *Web:* www.musictherapy.org	Silver Spring	MD	20910	301-589-3300	589-5175
American Naturopathic Medical Assn (ANMA) PO Box 96273 *Web:* www.anma.org	Las Vegas	NV	89193	702-450-3477	
American Organization for Bodywork Therapies of Asia (AOBTA) 1010 Haddonfield-Berlin Rd Ste 408 *Web:* www.aobta.org	Voorhees	NJ	08043	856-782-1616	782-1653
American Orthotic & Prosthetic Assn (AOPA) 330 John Carlyle St Ste 200 *Web:* www.aopanet.org	Alexandria	VA	22314	571-431-0876	431-0899
American Pain Society (APS) 4700 W Lake Ave *TF:* 877-752-4754 ■ *Web:* www.americanpainsociety.org	Glenview	IL	60025	847-375-4715	375-6479
American Parkinson Disease Assn (APDA) 135 Parkinson Ave *TF:* 800-223-2732 ■ *Web:* www.apdaparkinson.org	Staten Island	NY	10305	718-981-8001	981-4399
American Polarity Therapy Assn (APTA) 122 N Elm St Ste 512 *Web:* www.polaritytherapy.org	Greensboro	NC	27401	336-574-1121	574-1151
American SIDS Institute 528 Raven Way *Web:* www.sids.org	Naples	FL	34110	239-431-5425	431-5536
American Sleep Apnea Assn (ASAA) 6856 Eastern Ave NW #203 *TF:* 888-293-3650 ■ *Web:* www.sleepapnea.org	Washington	DC	20012	202-293-3650	293-3656
American Social Health Assn (ASHA) PO Box 13827 *TF:* 800-552-4375 ■ *Web:* www.ashastd.org	Research Triangle Park	NC	27709	919-361-8400	361-8425
American Therapeutic Recreation Assn (ATRA) 629 N Main St *TF:* 800-433-5255 ■ *Web:* www.atra-online.com	Hattiesburg	MS	39401	601-450-2872	582-3354
American Tinnitus Assn (ATA) 522 SW Fifth Ave Ste 825 *TF:* 800-634-8978 ■ *Web:* www.ata.org	Portland	OR	97204	503-248-9985	248-0024
Americans for Nonsmokers' Rights (ANR) 2530 San Pablo Ave Ste J *Web:* www.no-smoke.org	Berkeley	CA	94702	510-841-3032	841-3071
Anxiety Disorders Assn of America (ADAA) 8730 Georgia Ave Ste 600 *TF:* 800-922-8947 ■ *Web:* www.adaa.org	Silver Spring	MD	20910	240-485-1001	485-1035
Arc of the US 1010 Wayne Ave Ste 650 *TF:* 800-433-5255 ■ *Web:* www.thearc.org	Silver Spring	MD	20910	301-565-3842	565-3843
Arthritis Foundation 1330 W Peachtree St Ste 100 *TF:* 800-283-7800 ■ *Web:* www.arthritis.org	Atlanta	GA	30309	404-872-7100	872-0457
Associated Bodywork & Massage Professionals (ABMP) 25188 Genesee Trl Rd Ste 200 **Fax Area Code:* 800 ■ *TF:* 800-458-2267 ■ *Web:* www.abmp.com	Golden	CO	80401	303-674-8478	667-8260*
Association for Applied & Therapeutic Humor (AATH) 65 Enterprise **Fax Area Code:* 949 ■ *TF:* 888-747-2284 ■ *Web:* www.aath.org	Aliso Viejo	CA	92656	815-708-6587	715-6931*
Association for Children with Down Syndrome Inc (ACDS) 4 Fern Pl *Web:* www.acds.org	Plainview	NY	11803	516-933-4700	933-9524
Association for Macular Diseases Inc 210 E 64th St 8th Fl *Web:* www.macula.org	New York	NY	10065	212-605-3719	
Association for Research & Enlightenment (ARE) 215 67th St *TF:* 800-333-4499 ■ *Web:* www.edgarcayce.org	Virginia Beach	VA	23451	757-428-3588	422-6921
Association for the Advancement of the Blind & Retarded (AABR) 1508 College Pt Blvd *Web:* www.aabr.org	College Point	NY	11356	718-321-3800	
Asthma & Allergy Foundation of America (AAFA) 8201 Corporate Dr Ste 1000 *TF:* 800-727-8462 ■ *Web:* www.aafa.org	Landover	MD	20785	202-466-7643	466-8940
Autism Research Institute (ARI) 4182 Adams Ave *TF:* 866-366-3361 ■ *Web:* www.autism.com	San Diego	CA	92116	619-281-7165	563-6840
Autism Society of America (ASA) 4340 EW Hwy Ste 350 *TF:* 800-328-8476 ■ *Web:* www.autism-society.org	Bethesda	MD	20814	301-657-0881	657-0869
BACCHUS Network, The 111 K St NE 10th fl *Web:* www.naspa.org	Washington	DC	20002	303-871-0901	
BEGINNINGS 156 Wind Chime Ct Ste A *TF:* 800-541-4327 ■ *Web:* www.ncbegin.org	Raleigh	NC	27605	919-715-4092	715-4093

Organization	City	State	Zip	Phone	Fax
Better Hearing Institute (BHI) 1444 I St NW Ste 700 *TF:* 800-639-3884 ■ *Web:* www.betterhearing.org	Washington	DC	20005	202-449-1100	
Better Sleep Council 501 Wythe St *Web:* www.bettersleep.org	Alexandria	VA	22314	703-683-8371	683-4503
Better Vision Institute, The (BVI) *Vision Council, The* 225 Reinekers Ln Ste 700 *TF:* 800-372-3937	Alexandria	VA	22314	703-548-4560	
Brain Injury Assn of America 1608 Spring Hill Rd Ste 110 *TF:* 800-444-6443 ■ *Web:* www.biausa.org	Vienna	VA	22182	703-761-0750	761-0755
Campaign for Tobacco-Free Kids 1400 'I' St NW Ste 1200 *Web:* www.tobaccofreekids.org	Washington	DC	20005	202-296-5469	296-5427
Cancer Care Inc 275 Seventh Ave 22nd Fl *TF:* 800-813-4673 ■ *Web:* www.cancercare.org	New York	NY	10001	212-712-8400	712-8495
Candlelighters Childhood Cancer Foundation 10920 Connecticut Ave Suiute A PO Box 498 *TF:* 800-366-2223 ■ *Web:* www.acco.org	Kensington	MD	20895	301-962-3520	962-3521
Canine Companions for Independence Inc (CCI) 2965 Dutton Ave PO Box 446 *TF:* 800-572-2275 ■ *Web:* www.cci.org	Santa Rosa	CA	95402	707-577-1700	
Carcinoid Cancer Foundation Inc 333 Mamaroneck Ave Ste 492 *TF:* 888-722-3132 ■ *Web:* www.carcinoid.org	White Plains	NY	10605	212-722-3132	
Center for Practical Bioethics 1111 Main St Ste 500 *TF:* 800-344-3829 ■ *Web:* www.practicalbioethics.org	Kansas City	MO	64105	816-221-1100	221-2002
Center on Human Policy 805 S Crouse Ave *Web:* www.thechp.syr.edu	Syracuse	NY	13244	315-443-3851	
CFIDS Assn of America Inc 6827 Fairview Rd PO Box 220398 *Web:* solvecfs.org	Charlotte	NC	28222	704-365-2343	
Children & Adults with Attention-Deficit/Hyperactivity Disorder (CHADD) 8181 Professional Pl Ste 150 *TF:* 800-233-4050 ■ *Web:* www.chadd.org	Landover	MD	20785	301-306-7070	306-7090
Children's Eye Foundation 1631 Lancaster Dr Ste 200 *Web:* www.childrenseyefoundation.org	Grapevine	TX	76051	817-310-2641	
Children's Leukemia Research Assn 585 Stewart Ave Ste 18 *Web:* www.childrensleukemia.org	Garden City	NY	11530	516-222-1944	222-0457
Children's Organ Transplant Assn (COTA) 2501 W Cota Dr *TF:* 800-366-2682 ■ *Web:* www.cota.org	Bloomington	IN	47403	812-336-8872	336-8885
Children's Tumor Foundation 95 Pine St 16th Fl *TF:* 800-323-7938 ■ *Web:* www.ctf.org	New York	NY	10005	212-344-6633	747-0004
Children's Wish Foundation International 8615 Roswell Rd *TF:* 800-323-9474 ■ *Web:* www.childrenswish.org	Atlanta	GA	30350	770-393-9474	393-0683
Christopher Reeve Foundation 636 Morris Tpke Ste 3A *TF:* 800-225-0292 ■ *Web:* www.christopherreeve.org	Short Hills	NJ	07078	973-379-2690	
CJE SeniorLife 3003 W Touhy Ave *Web:* www.cje.net	Chicago	IL	60645	773-508-1000	508-1028
Cleft Palate Foundation (CPF) 1504 E Franklin St Ste 102 *TF:* 800-242-5338 ■ *Web:* www.cleftline.org	Chapel Hill	NC	27514	919-933-9044	933-9604
Compassion & Choices PO Box 101810 **Fax Area Code: 866* ■ *TF:* 800-247-7421 ■ *Web:* www.compassionandchoices.org	Denver	CO	80250	303-639-1202	312-2690*
Cornelia de Lange Syndrome Foundation Inc (CdLS) 302 W Main St Ste 100 *TF:* 800-753-2357 ■ *Web:* www.cdlsusa.org	Avon	CT	06001	860-676-8166	676-8337
Council for Affordable Health Insurance (CAHI) 127 S Peyton St Ste 210	Alexandria	VA	22314	703-836-6200	836-6550
Council on Size & Weight Discrimination (CSWD) PO Box 305 *Web:* www.cswd.org	Mount Marion	NY	12456	845-679-1209	679-1206
Creutzfeldt-Jakob Disease Foundation Inc 341 W 38th St Ste 501 *TF:* 800-659-1991 ■ *Web:* www.cjdfoundation.org	New York	NY	10018	212-719-5900	256-0359
Crohn's & Colitis Foundation of America (CCFA) 386 Pk Ave S 17th Fl *TF:* 800-932-2423 ■ *Web:* www.ccfa.org	New York	NY	10016	212-685-3440	779-4098
Cystic Fibrosis Foundation 6931 Arlington Rd Ste 200 *TF:* 800-344-4823 ■ *Web:* www.cff.org	Bethesda	MD	20814	301-951-4422	951-6378
Deafness Research Foundation (DRF) 641 Lexington Ave 15th Fl *Web:* hearinghealthfoundation.org	New York	NY	10022	212-328-9480	
Delta Society 875 124th Ave NE Ste 101 *Web:* www.petpartners.org	Bellevue	WA	98005	425-679-5500	
Dental Lifeline Network 1800 15th St Ste 100 *TF:* 888-471-6334 ■ *Web:* dentallifeline.org	Denver	CO	80202	303-534-5360	534-5290
Depression & Bipolar Support Alliance (DBSA) 730 N Franklin St Ste 501 *TF:* 800-826-3632 ■ *Web:* www.dbsalliance.org	Chicago	IL	60610	312-642-0049	642-7243
Disability Rights Ctr Inc 18 Low Ave *TF:* 800-834-1721 ■ *Web:* www.drcnh.org	Concord	NH	03301	603-228-0432	225-2077
Disabled & Alone/Life Services for the Handicapped 1440 Broadway 23rd Floor *TF:* 800-995-0066 ■ *Web:* www.disabledandalone.org	New York	NY	10018	212-532-6740	532-6740
Dystonia Medical Research Foundation 1 E Wacker Dr Ste 2810 *TF General:* 800-377-3978 ■ *Web:* www.dystonia-foundation.org	Chicago	IL	60601	312-755-0198	803-0138
Easter Seals 230 W Monroe St Ste 1800 *TF:* 800-221-6827 ■ *Web:* www.easterseals.com	Chicago	IL	60606	312-726-6200	726-1494
ECRI Institute 5200 Butler Pike *TF:* 866-247-3004 ■ *Web:* www.ecri.org	Plymouth Meeting	PA	19462	610-825-6000	834-1275
El Paso First Health Plans Inc 1145 Westmoreland Dr *TF:* 877-532-3778 ■ *Web:* www.epfirst.com	El Paso	TX	79925	915-532-3778	532-2877
Elizabeth Glaser Pediatric AIDS Foundation 1140 Connecticut Ave NW Ste 200 *TF:* 888-499-4673 ■ *Web:* www.pedaids.org	Washington	DC	20036	202-296-9165	296-9185
Endometriosis Assn 8585 N 76th Pl *TF:* 800-992-3636 ■ *Web:* www.endometriosisassn.org	Milwaukee	WI	53223	414-355-2200	355-6065
EngenderHealth 440 Ninth Ave 13th Fl *TF:* 800-564-2872 ■ *Web:* www.engenderhealth.org	New York	NY	10001	212-561-8000	561-8067
Epilepsy Foundation 8301 Professional Pl E *TF:* 800-332-1000 ■ *Web:* epilepsy.com	Landover	MD	20785	301-459-3700	577-2684
Euthanasia Research & Guidance Organization (ERGO) 24829 Norris Ln *Web:* www.finalexit.org	Junction City	OR	97448	541-998-1873	
FaithTrust Institute 2400 N 45th St Ste 101 *TF:* 877-860-2255 ■ *Web:* www.faithtrustinstitute.org	Seattle	WA	98103	206-634-1903	634-0115
Family Caregiver Alliance (FCA) 180 Montgomery St Ste 900 *TF:* 800-445-8106 ■ *Web:* www.caregiver.org	San Francisco	CA	94104	415-434-3388	434-3508
Family of the Americas Foundation PO Box 1170 *TF:* 800-443-3395 ■ *Web:* www.familyplanning.net	Dunkirk	MD	20754	301-627-3346	627-0847
Feingold Assn of the US 37 Shell Rd 2nd Fl *TF:* 800-321-3287 ■ *Web:* www.feingold.org	Rocky Point	NY	11778	631-369-9340	369-2988
First Candle 1314 Bedford Ave Ste 210 *TF:* 800-221-7437 ■ *Web:* www.firstcandle.org	Baltimore	MD	21208	410-653-8226	653-8709
Food Allergy & Anaphylaxis Network (FAAN) 11781 Lee Jackson Hwy Ste 160 *TF:* 800-929-4040 ■ *Web:* www.foodallergy.org	Fairfax	VA	22033	703-691-3179	691-2713
Foundation Fighting Blindness 11435 Cron Hill Dr *TF:* 800-683-5555 ■ *Web:* www.blindness.org	Owings Mills	MD	21117	410-568-0150	
Freedom From Fear (FFF) 308 Seaview Ave *Web:* www.freedomfromfear.org	Staten Island	NY	10305	718-351-1717	
Gay Men's Health Crisis (GMHC) 119 W 24th St *TF:* 800-243-7692 ■ *Web:* www.gmhc.org	New York	NY	10011	212-367-1000	
Genetic Alliance Inc 4301 Connecticut Ave NW Ste 404 *Web:* www.geneticalliance.org	Washington	DC	20008	202-966-5557	966-8553
Gift of Life Bone Marrow Foundation 800 Yamato Rd Ste 101 *TF:* 800-962-7769 ■ *Web:* www.giftoflife.org	Boca Raton	FL	33431	561-982-2900	
Glaucoma Foundation (TGF) 80 Maiden Ln Ste 700 *Web:* www.glaucomafoundation.org	New York	NY	10038	212-285-0080	651-1888
Glaucoma Research Foundation 251 Post St Ste 600 *TF:* 800-826-6693 ■ *Web:* www.glaucoma.org	San Francisco	CA	94108	415-986-3162	986-3763
Gluten Intolerance Group (GIG) 31214 124th Ave SE *Web:* www.gluten.org	Auburn	WA	98092	253-833-6655	833-6675
Guide Dog Foundation for the Blind Inc 371 E Jericho Tkpe *TF:* 800-548-4337 ■ *Web:* www.guidedog.org	Smithtown	NY	11787	800-548-4337	
Guide Dogs for the Blind 350 Los Ranchitos Rd *TF:* 800-295-4050 ■ *Web:* www.guidedogs.com	San Rafael	CA	94903	415-499-4000	499-4035
Guide Dogs of America 13445 Glenoaks Blvd *TF:* 800-459-4843 ■ *Web:* www.guidedogsofamerica.org	Sylmar	CA	91342	818-362-5834	362-6870
Head Injury Hotline 212 Pioneer Bldg *Web:* www.headinjury.com	Seattle	WA	98104	206-621-8558	
Health Physics Society 1313 Dolley Madison Blvd Ste 402 *TF:* 888-624-8373 ■ *Web:* www.hps.org	McLean	VA	22101	703-790-1745	790-2672
Healthcare Leadership Council (HLC) 750 Ninth St NW Ste 500 *Web:* hlc.org	Washington	DC	20001	202-452-8700	296-9561
Hearing Loss Assn of America 7910 Woodmont Ave Ste 1200 *TF:* 800-221-6827 ■ *Web:* www.hearingloss.org	Bethesda	MD	20814	301-657-2248	913-9413
Hepatitis Foundation International (HFI) 504 Blick Dr *TF:* 800-891-0707 ■ *Web:* www.hepfi.org	Silver Spring	MD	20904	301-622-4200	
Herb Research Foundation (HRF) 4140 15th St *TF:* 800-748-2617 ■ *Web:* www.herbs.org	Boulder	CO	80304	303-449-2265	449-7849
Hereditary Disease Foundation (HDF) 3960 Broadway 6th Fl *Web:* www.hdfoundation.org	New York	NY	10032	212-928-2121	928-2172
Herpes Resource Center, The (HRC) PO Box 13827 *TF:* 877-478-5868	Research Triangle Park	NC	27709	919-361-8400	361-8425
Hospice Education Institute 3 Unity Sq PO Box 98 *TF:* 800-331-1620 ■ *Web:* www.hospiceworld.org	Machiasport	ME	04655	207-255-8800	255-8008
Human Factors & Ergonomics Society (HFES) 1124 Montana Ave Ste B PO Box 1369 *TF:* 800-233-1234 ■ *Web:* www.hfes.org	Santa Monica	CA	90406	310-394-1811	394-2410
Human Growth Foundation 997 Glen Cove Ave Ste 5 *TF:* 800-451-6434 ■ *Web:* www.hgfound.org	Glen Head	NY	11545	516-671-4041	671-4055
Huntington's Disease Society of America (HDSA) 505 Eigth Ave Ste 902 *TF:* 800-345-4372 ■ *Web:* www.hdsa.org	New York	NY	10018	212-242-1968	239-3430
Hysterectomy Educational Resources & Services Foundation (HERS) 422 Bryn Mawr Ave *TF:* 888-750-4377 ■ *Web:* www.hersfoundation.com	Bala Cynwyd	PA	19004	610-667-7757	667-8096
Icahn School of Medicine at Mount Sinai 1 Gustave L Levy Pl *Web:* icahn.mssm.edu/research/programs/jewish-genetics-disease-center	New York	NY	10029	212-241-6500	
Immune Deficiency Foundation (IDF) 40 W Chesapeake Ave Ste 308 *TF:* 800-296-4433 ■ *Web:* www.primaryimmune.org	Towson	MD	21204	410-321-6647	321-9165
International Assn for the Study of Pain (IASP) 111 Queen Anne Ave N Ste 501 *TF:* 866-574-2654 ■ *Web:* www.iasp-pain.org	Seattle	WA	98109	206-283-0311	283-9403

Phone | Fax

International Ctr for the Disabled (ICD)
340 E 24th St ..... New York NY 10010 212-585-6020
Web: www.icdnyc.org

International Dyslexia Assn, The (IDA)
40 York Rd 4th Fl ..... Towson MD 21204 410-296-0232 321-5069
TF: 800-222-3123 ■ Web: eida.org

International Hearing Society (IHS)
16880 Middlebelt Rd Ste 4 ..... Livonia MI 48154 734-522-7200 522-0200
TF: 800-521-5247 ■ Web: www.ihsinfo.org

International OCD Foundation (OCF) PO Box 961029 ..... Boston MA 02196 617-973-5801 973-5803
Web: iocdf.org

Jannus Inc (MSG) 1607 W Jefferson St ..... Boise ID 83702 208-336-5533 336-0880
Web: www.jannus.org

Juvenile Diabetes Research Foundation International (JDRF)
120 Wall St ..... New York NY 10005 212-785-9500 785-9595
TF: 800-533-2873 ■ Web: www.jdrf.org

Kristin Brooks Hope Ctr (KBHC)
1250 24th St NW ..... Washington DC 20037 202-536-3200
TF: 800-784-2433 ■ Web: www.hopeline.com

La Leche League International Inc (LLLI)
957 N Plum Grove Rd ..... Schaumburg IL 60173 847-519-7730 969-0460
TF: 800-525-3243 ■ Web: www.lalecheleague.org

Lamaze International 2025 M St NW Ste 800 ..... Washington DC 20036 202-367-1128 367-2128
TF: 800-368-4404 ■ Web: www.lamaze.org

Laurent Clerc National Deaf Education Ctr
800 Florida Ave NE ..... Washington DC 20002 202-651-5050 651-5708
TF: 866-637-0102 ■ Web: www.gallaudet.edu

Learning Disabilities Assn of America (LDA)
4156 Library Rd ..... Pittsburgh PA 15234 412-341-1515 344-0224
TF: 888-300-6710 ■ Web: ldaamerica.org

Lifespire 350 Fifth Ave Ste 301 ..... New York NY 10118 212-741-0100 242-0696
TF: 800-221-5594 ■ Web: www.lifespire.org

Light for Life Foundation International
PO Box 644 ..... Westminster CO 80036 303-429-3530 426-4496
TF: 800-273-8255 ■ Web: www.yellowribbon.org

Living Bank PO Box 6725 ..... Houston TX 77027 713-961-9431 961-0979
TF: 800-528-2971 ■ Web: www.livingbank.org

Lupus Foundation of America Inc (LFA)
2000 L St NW Ste 410 ..... Washington DC 20036 202-349-1155 349-1156
TF: 800-558-0121 ■ Web: www.lupus.org

Lymphoma Research Foundation (LRF)
115 Broadway Ste 1301 ..... New York NY 10006 212-349-2910 349-2886
TF: 800-500-9976 ■ Web: www.lymphoma.org

Macula Foundation Inc 210 E 64th St ..... New York NY 10065 212-605-3777
TF: 800-622-8524 ■ Web: www.maculafoundation.org

Male Survivor 4768 BRdway Ste 527 ..... New York NY 10034 800-738-4181
TF: 800-738-4181 ■ Web: www.malesurvivor.org

March of Dimes Foundation
1275 Mamaroneck Ave ..... White Plains NY 10605 914-428-7100
Web: www.marchofdimes.org

MCS Referral & Resources Inc
6101 Gentry Ln ..... Baltimore MD 21210 410-889-6666 889-4944
Web: www.mcsrr.org

MedicAlert Foundation International
2323 Colorado Ave ..... Turlock CA 95382 209-668-3333 669-2495
TF Cust Svc: 800-432-5378 ■ Web: www.medicalert.org

Medicare Rights Ctr (MRC)
520 Eigth Ave N Wing 3rd Fl ..... New York NY 10018 212-869-3850 869-3532
TF Hotline: 800-333-4114 ■ Web: www.medicarerights.org

Mended Hearts Inc, The
8150 N Central Expy M2075 ..... Dallas TX 75206 214-296-9252 295-9552
TF: 888-432-7899 ■ Web: www.mendedhearts.org

Mental Health America (MHA)
2000 N Beauregard St 6th Fl ..... Alexandria VA 22311 703-684-7722 684-5968
TF Help Line: 800-969-6642 ■ Web: mentalhealthamerica.net

Mothers Supporting Daughters with Breast Cancer (MSDBC)
25235 Fox Chase Dr ..... Chestertown MD 21620 410-778-1982 778-1411
Web: www.mothersdaughters.org

Multiple Sclerosis Foundation (MSF)
6520 N Andrews Ave ..... Fort Lauderdale FL 33309 954-776-6805
TF: 800-225-6495 ■ Web: www.msfocus.org

Muscular Dystrophy Assn (MDA) 3300 E Sunrise Dr ..... Tucson AZ 85718 520-529-2000
TF: 800-572-1717 ■ Web: www.mda.org

NA of People with AIDS (NAPWA)
8401 Colesville Rd Ste 505 ..... Silver Spring MD 20910 240-247-0880
TF: 866-846-9366

Narcolepsy Network Inc
46 Union Dr Ste A212 ..... North Kingstown RI 02852 401-667-2523 633-6567
TF: 888-292-6522 ■ Web: www.narcolepsynetwork.org

National Adrenal Diseases Foundation (NADF)
505 Northern Blvd ..... Great Neck NY 11021 516-487-4992
Web: www.nadf.us

National Allergy Bureau (NAB)
555 E Wells St 11th Fl ..... Milwaukee WI 53202 414-272-6071 272-6070
Web: aaaai.org/global/nab-pollen-counts.aspx

National Alliance for Hispanic Health
1501 16th St NW ..... Washington DC 20036 202-387-5000 797-4353
Web: www.hispanichealth.org

National Alliance on Mental Illness (NAMI)
3803 N Fairfax Dr Ste 100 ..... Arlington VA 22203 703-524-7600 524-9094
TF: 800-950-6264 ■ Web: www.nami.org

National Alopecia Areata Foundation (NAAF)
14 Mitchell Blvd ..... San Rafael CA 94903 415-472-3780 472-5343
Web: www.naaf.org

National Amputation Foundation 40 Church St ..... Malverne NY 11565 516-887-3600
Web: www.nationalamputation.org

National Breast Cancer Coalition (NBCC)
1101 17th St NW Ste 1300 ..... Washington DC 20036 202-296-7477 265-6854
TF: 800-622-2838 ■ Web: www.breastcancerdeadline2020.org

National Cancer Registrars Assn (NCRA)
1340 Braddock Pl Ste 203 ..... Alexandria VA 22314 703-299-6640 299-6620
TF: 800-621-4111 ■ Web: www.ncra-usa.org

Phone | Fax

National Citizens' Coalition for Nursing Home Reform (NCCNHR)
National Consumer Voice for Quality Long-Term Care, The
1828 L St NW Ste 801 ..... Washington DC 20036 202-332-2275 332-2949
TF: 866-992-3668 ■ Web: www.theconsumervoice.org

National Coalition for Cancer Survivorship (NCCS)
1010 Wayne Ave Ste 315 ..... Silver Spring MD 20910 877-622-7937
TF: 877-622-7937 ■ Web: www.canceradvocacy.org

National Coalition on Health Care
1120 G St NW Ste 810 ..... Washington DC 20005 202-638-7151
Web: www.nchc.org

National Committee for Quality Assurance (NCQA)
1100 13th St ..... Washington DC 20005 202-955-3500 955-3599
TF: 888-275-7585 ■ Web: www.ncqa.org

National Council on Alcoholism & Drug Dependence Inc (NCADD)
217 Broadway Ste 712 ..... New York NY 10007 212-269-7797 269-7510
TF: 800-622-2255 ■ Web: www.ncadd.org

National Ctr for Homeopathy (NCH)
101 S Whiting St Ste 16 ..... Alexandria VA 22304 703-548-7790 548-7792
TF: 877-624-0613

National Down Syndrome Congress (NDSC)
1370 Ctr Dr Ste 102 ..... Atlanta GA 30338 770-604-9500 604-9898
TF: 800-232-6372 ■ Web: www.ndsccenter.org

National Down Syndrome Society (NDSS)
666 Broadway 8th Fl ..... New York NY 10012 800-221-4602 979-2873*
*Fax Area Code: 212 ■ TF: 800-221-4602 ■ Web: www.ndss.org

National Eating Disorders Assn
603 Stewart St Ste 803 ..... Seattle WA 98101 800-931-2237 829-8501*
*Fax Area Code: 206 ■ TF: 800-931-2237 ■ Web: www.nationaleatingdisorders.org

National Federation of the Blind (NFB)
1800 Johnson St ..... Baltimore MD 21230 410-659-9314 685-5653
TF: 800-392-5671 ■ Web: www.nfb.org

National Fibromyalgia Partnership Inc (NFP)
140 Zinn Way ..... Linden VA 22642 866-725-4404
TF: 866-725-4404 ■ Web: www.fmpartnership.org

National Fire Protection Assn (NFPA)
1 Batterymarch Pk ..... Quincy MA 02169 617-770-3000 770-0700
TF: 800-344-3555 ■ Web: www.nfpa.org

National Gaucher Foundation (NGF)
5410 Edson Ln Ste 220 ..... Rockville MD 30084 770-934-2910 934-2911
TF: 800-504-3189 ■ Web: www.gaucherdisease.org

National Headache Foundation (NHF)
820 N Orleans St Ste 217 ..... Chicago IL 60610 888-643-5552 640-9049*
*Fax Area Code: 312 ■ TF: 888-643-5552 ■ Web: www.headaches.org

National Health Council (NHC)
1730 M St NW Ste 500 ..... Washington DC 20036 202-785-3910 785-5923
Web: www.nationalhealthcouncil.org

National Healthy Mothers Healthy Babies Coalition (HMHB)
4401 Ford Ave Ste 300 ..... Alexandria VA 22302 703-837-4792
Web: www.hmhb.org

National Hearing Conservation Assn (NHCA)
3030 W 81st Ave ..... Westminster CO 80031 303-224-9022 458-0002
TF: 877-766-6629 ■ Web: www.hearingconservation.org

National Hemophilia Foundation (NHF)
116 W 32nd St 11th Fl ..... New York NY 10001 212-328-3700 328-3777
TF: 800-424-2634 ■ Web: www.hemophilia.org

National HPV & Cervical Cancer Prevention Resource Ctr
PO Box 13827 ..... Research Triangle Park NC 27709 919-361-8400 361-8425
Web: www.ashastd.org

National Industries for the Blind (NIB)
1310 Braddock Pl ..... Alexandria VA 22314 703-310-0500
TF Cust Svc: 800-433-2304 ■ Web: www.nib.org

National Inhalant Prevention Coalition (NIPC)
318 Lindsay St ..... Chattanooga TN 37405 423-265-4662 265-4889
TF: 800-269-4237 ■ Web: www.inhalants.org

National Kidney Foundation (NKF)
30 E 33rd St 8th Fl ..... New York NY 10016 212-889-2210 779-8056
TF: 800-622-9010 ■ Web: www.kidney.org

National Marfan Foundation (NMF)
22 Manhasset Ave ..... Port Washington NY 11050 516-883-8712 883-8040
TF: 800-862-7326 ■ Web: www.marfan.org

National Marrow Donor Program (NMDP)
3001 Broadway St NE Ste 100 ..... Minneapolis MN 55413 612-627-5800
TF: 800-526-7809 ■ Web: bethematch.org

National Multiple Sclerosis Society
733 Third Ave 3rd Fl ..... New York NY 10017 212-986-3240 986-7981
TF: 800-344-4867 ■ Web: www.nationalmssociety.org

National Niemann-Pick Disease Foundation Inc (NNPDF)
401 Madison Ave Ste B PO Box 49 ..... Fort Atkinson WI 53538 920-563-0930 563-0931
TF: 877-287-3672 ■ Web: www.nnpdf.org

National Odd Shoe Exchange PO Box 1120 ..... Chandler AZ 85244 480-892-3484
Web: www.oddshoe.org

National Oral Health Information Clearinghouse (NIDCR)
1 NOHIC Way ..... Bethesda MD 20892 301-496-4261 480-4098
TF: 866-232-4528 ■ Web: www.nidcr.nih.gov

National Organization for Albinism & Hypopigmentation (NOAH)
PO Box 959 ..... East Hampstead NH 03826 603-887-2310
TF: 800-648-2310 ■ Web: www.albinism.org

National Organization for Rare Disorders (NORD)
55 Kenosia Ave PO Box 1968 ..... Danbury CT 06813 203-744-0100 798-2291
TF: 800-999-6673 ■ Web: www.rarediseases.org

National Organization of Circumcision Information Resource Centers (NOCIRC)
PO Box 2512 ..... San Anselmo CA 94979 415-488-9883 488-9660
TF: 800-727-8622 ■ Web: www.nocirc.org

National Organization of Restoring Men (NORM)
3205 Northwood Dr Ste 209 ..... Concord CA 94520 925-827-4077 827-4119
Web: www.norm.org

National Organization on Disability (NOD)
910 16th St NW Ste 410 ..... Washington DC 20006 646-505-1191
Web: www.nod.org

National Osteoporosis Foundation (NOF)
251 18th St S Ste 630 ..... Arlington VA 22202 202-223-2226 223-2237
TF: 800-231-4222 ■ Web: www.nof.org

National Ovarian Cancer Coalition (NOCC)
2501 Oak Lawn Ave Ste 435 ..... Dallas TX 75219 888-682-7426 273-4201*
*Fax Area Code: 214 ■ TF: 888-682-7426 ■ Web: www.ovarian.org

Organization	City	State	Zip	Phone	Fax
National Pesticide Information Ctr (NPIC) 333 Weniger Hall **Fax Area Code:* 541 ■ *TF:* 800-858-7378 ■ *Web:* www.npic.orst.edu	Corvallis	OR	97331	800-858-7378	737-0761*
National Psoriasis Foundation (NPF) 6600 SW 92nd Ave Ste 300 *TF:* 800-723-9166 ■ *Web:* www.psoriasis.org	Portland	OR	97223	503-244-7404	245-0626
National Rehabilitation Assn (NRA) 633 S Washington St *TF:* 888-258-4295 ■ *Web:* www.nationalrehab.org	Alexandria	VA	22314	703-836-0850	836-0848
National Rehabilitation Information Ctr (NARIC) 8400 Corporate Dr Ste 500 *TF:* 800-346-2742 ■ *Web:* www.naric.com	Landover	MD	20785	301-459-5900	459-4263
National Reye's Syndrome Foundation (NRSF) 426 N Lewis St *TF:* 800-233-7393 ■ *Web:* www.reyessyndrome.org	Bryan	OH	43506	419-924-9000	924-9999
National Rosacea Society 800 S NW Hwy Ste 200 *TF:* 888-662-5874 ■ *Web:* www.rosacea.org	Barrington	IL	60010	847-382-8971	382-5567
National SAFE KIDS Campaign 1301 Pennsylvania Ave NW Ste 1000 *Web:* www.safekids.org	Washington	DC	20004	202-662-0600	393-2072
National Safety Council (NSC) 1121 Spring Lk Dr *TF:* 800-621-7615 ■ *Web:* www.nsc.org	Itasca	IL	60143	630-285-1121	285-1315
National Sleep Foundation (NSF) 1522 K St NW Ste 500 *Web:* www.sleepfoundation.org	Washington	DC	20005	202-347-3471	347-3472
National Society of Genetic Counselors (NSGC) 330 N Wabash Ave Ste 2000 *Web:* www.nsgc.org	Chicago	IL	60611	312-321-6834	673-6972
National Spinal Cord Injury Assn (NSCIA) 75-20 Astoria Blvd Ste 120 *TF:* 800-962-9629 ■ *Web:* www.spinalcord.org	East Elmhurst	NY	11370	718-512-0010	
National Stroke Assn (NSA) 9707 E Easter Ln **Fax Area Code:* 303 ■ *TF Cust Svc:* 800-787-6537 ■ *Web:* www.stroke.org	Centennial	CO	80112	800-787-6537	649-1328*
National Stuttering Assn (NSA) 119 W 40th St 14th Fl *TF:* 800-937-8888 ■ *Web:* www.westutter.org	New York	NY	10018	212-944-4050	944-8244
National Tay-Sachs & Allied Diseases Assn (NTSAD) 2001 Beacon St Ste 204 *TF:* 800-906-8723 ■ *Web:* www.ntsad.org	Brighton	MA	02135	617-277-4463	277-0134
National Vaccine Information Ctr (NVIC) 407 Church St Ste H *Web:* www.nvic.org	Vienna	VA	22180	703-938-0342	938-5768
National Wellness Institute (NWI) 1300 College Ct PO Box 827 *TF:* 877-800-2729 ■ *Web:* www.nationalwellness.org	Stevens Point	WI	54481	715-342-2969	342-2979
New West Health Services 130 Neill Ave *TF:* 888-500-3355 ■ *Web:* www.newwestmedicare.com	Helena	MT	59601	406-457-2200	457-2299
NISH 8401 Old Courthouse Rd *Web:* www.sourceamerica.org	Vienna	VA	22182	703-560-6800	
North American Menopause Society, The (NAMS) 5900 Landerbrook Dr Ste 390 *Web:* www.menopause.org	Mayfield Heights	OH	44124	440-442-7550	442-2660
North Shore Elder Services, Inc 300 Rosewood Dr Ste 200 *Web:* www.pacenorthshore.org	Danvers	MA	01923	781-715-6608	
Oley Foundation 214 Hun Memorial MC-28 Albany Medical Ctr *TF:* 800-776-6539 ■ *Web:* www.oley.org	Albany	NY	12208	518-262-5079	262-5528
Oral Health America 410 N Michigan Ave Ste 352 *TF:* 800-523-3438 ■ *Web:* www.oralhealthamerica.org	Chicago	IL	60611	312-836-9900	836-9986
Parkinson's Disease Foundation (PDF) 1359 Broadway *TF:* 800-457-6676 ■ *Web:* www.pdf.org	New York	NY	10018	212-923-4700	923-4778
Partnership for a Drug-Free America 405 Lexington Ave Ste 1601 *TF:* 855-378-4373 ■ *Web:* www.drugfree.org	New York	NY	10174	212-922-1560	922-1570
Pedorthic Footwear Assn (PFA) 2025 M St NW Ste 800 *TF:* 800-673-8447 ■ *Web:* www.pedorthics.org	Washington	DC	20036	202-367-1145	367-2145
Phoenix Society for Burn Survivors Inc 1835 RW Berends Dr SW *TF:* 800-888-2876 ■ *Web:* www.phoenix-society.org	Grand Rapids	MI	49519	616-458-2773	458-2831
Population Services International (PSI) 1120 19th St NW Ste 600 *Web:* www.psi.org	Washington	DC	20036	202-785-0072	785-0120
Postpartum Support International 2200 Pacific Coast Hwy Ste 304A *TF:* 800-944-4773 ■ *Web:* www.postpartum.net	Hermosa Beach	CA	90254	800-944-4773	
Prader-Willi Syndrome Assn (USA) 8588 Potter Pk Dr Ste 500 *TF:* 800-926-4797 ■ *Web:* www.pwsausa.org	Sarasota	FL	34238	941-312-0400	312-0142
Prevent Blindness America 211 W Wacker Dr Ste 1700 *TF:* 800-331-2020 ■ *Web:* www.preventblindness.org	Chicago	IL	60606	800-331-2020	
Prevent Cancer Foundation (PCF) 1600 Duke St Ste 500 *TF:* 800-227-2732 ■ *Web:* preventcancer.org	Alexandria	VA	22314	703-836-4412	836-4413
Program for Appropriate Technology in Health (PATH) 1455 NW Leary Way *Web:* www.path.org	Seattle	WA	98107	206-285-3500	285-6619
Project Inform 273 Ninth St *TF:* 877-435-7443 ■ *Web:* www.projectinform.org	San Francisco	CA	94103	415-558-8669	558-0684
Public Health Institute 555 12th St 10th Fl *TF:* 866-632-9992 ■ *Web:* www.phi.org	Oakland	CA	94607	510-285-5500	285-5501
Recording for the Blind & Dyslexic (RFB&D) 20 Roszel Rd **Fax Area Code:* 609 ■ *TF:* 800-221-4792 ■ *Web:* www.rfbd.org	Princeton	NJ	08540	800-221-4792	987-8116*
Registry of Interpreters for the Deaf Inc (RID) 333 Commerce St *Web:* www.rid.org	Alexandria	VA	22314	703-838-0030	838-0454
Rehabilitation Engineering & Assistive Technology Society of North America (RESNA) 1700 N Moore St Ste 1540 *Web:* www.resna.org	Arlington	VA	22209	703-524-6686	524-6630
Research to Prevent Blindness Inc (RPB) 645 Madison Ave 21st Fl *TF:* 800-621-0026 ■ *Web:* www.rpbusa.org	New York	NY	10022	212-752-4333	688-6231
RESOLVE: National Infertility Assn 1760 Old Meadow Rd Ste 500 *TF:* 888-592-4449 ■ *Web:* www.resolve.org	McLean	VA	22102	703-556-7172	506-3266
Restless Legs Syndrome Foundation Inc 1610 14th St NW Ste 300 *TF:* 877-463-6757 ■ *Web:* www.rls.org	Rochester	MN	55901	507-287-6465	287-6312
Rolf Institute of Structural Integration 5055 Chaparral Ct Ste 103 *TF:* 800-530-8875 ■ *Web:* www.rolf.org	Boulder	CO	80301	303-449-5903	449-5978
RP International PO Box 900 *TF:* 877-999-8322 ■ *Web:* www.rpinternational.org	Woodland Hills	CA	91365	818-992-0500	992-3265
Scleroderma Foundation 300 Rosewood Dr Ste 105 *TF:* 800-722-4673 ■ *Web:* www.scleroderma.org	Danvers	MA	01923	978-463-5843	463-5809
Scoliosis Assn Inc 2500 N Military Trail	Boca Raton	FL	33431	561-994-4435	
Sickle Cell Disease Assn of America (SCDAA) 3700 Koppers St Ste 570 *TF:* 800-421-8453 ■ *Web:* www.sicklecelldisease.org	Baltimore	MD	21202	410-528-1555	528-1495
Simon Foundation for Incontinence PO Box 815 *Web:* www.simonfoundation.org	Wilmette	IL	60091	847-864-3913	864-9758
Skin Cancer Foundation 149 Madison Ave Ste 901 *Web:* www.skincancer.org	New York	NY	10016	212-725-5176	725-5751
Society for Women's Health Research 1025 Connecticut Ave NW Ste 601 *Web:* www.womenshealthresearch.org	Washington	DC	20036	202-223-8224	
Spina Bifida Assn (SBAA) 4590 MacArthur Blvd NW Ste 250 *TF:* 877-686-6444 ■ *Web:* www.spinabifidaassociation.org	Washington	DC	20007	202-944-3285	
Stuttering Foundation of America 3100 Walnut Grove Rd Ste 603 *TF:* 800-992-9392 ■ *Web:* www.stutteringhelp.org	Memphis	TN	38111	901-452-7343	452-3931
Support Dogs Inc 11645 Lilburn Pk Rd *Web:* www.supportdogs.org	Saint Louis	MO	63146	314-997-2325	997-7202
Susan G Komen for the Cure 5005 LBJ Fwy Ste 250 *TF:* 800-227-2345 ■ *Web:* ww5.komen.org	Dallas	TX	75244	972-855-1600	
TASH 1001 Connecticut Ave NW Ste 235 *Web:* www.tash.org	Washington	DC	20006	202-540-9020	540-9019
TOPS Club Inc 4575 S Fifth St *TF:* 800-932-8677 ■ *Web:* www.tops.org	Milwaukee	WI	53207	414-482-4620	482-1655
Tourette Syndrome Assn Inc 42-40 Bell Blvd Ste 205 *TF:* 888-486-8738 ■ *Web:* www.tourette.org	Bayside	NY	11361	718-224-2999	279-9596
Trichotillomania Learning Ctr Inc (TLC) 207 McPherson St Ste H	Santa Cruz	CA	95060	831-457-1004	426-4383
UCare Minnesota 500 Stinson Blvd NE PO Box 52 *TF:* 866-457-7144 ■ *Web:* www.ucare.org	Minneapolis	MN	55413	612-676-6500	676-6501
Undersea & Hyperbaric Medical Society (UHMS) 21 W Colony Pl Ste 280 *TF:* 877-533-8467 ■ *Web:* www.uhms.org	Durham	NC	27705	919-490-5140	490-5140
United Network for Organ Sharing (UNOS) 700 N Fourth St *TF:* 888-894-6361 ■ *Web:* www.unos.org	Richmond	VA	23219	804-782-4800	782-4817
Vegan Action PO Box 7313 *Web:* vegan.org	Richmond	VA	23221	804-577-8341	
Vegetarian Resource Group, The (VRG) PO Box 1463 *Web:* www.vrg.org	Baltimore	MD	21203	410-366-8343	366-8804
Virginia Hospital & Healthcare Assn (VHHA) 4200 Innslake Dr *Web:* www.vhha.com	Glen Allen	VA	23060	804-965-1227	
Washington Business Group on Health (WBGH) 20 F St NW Ste 200 *Web:* www.businessgrouphealth.org	Washington	DC	20001	202-628-9320	628-9244
Well Spouse Assn 63 W Main St Ste H *TF:* 800-838-0879 ■ *Web:* www.wellspouse.org	Freehold	NJ	07728	732-577-8899	577-8644
Women Alive 1566 Burnside Ave *TF:* 800-472-2321 ■ *Web:* www.women-alive.org	Los Angeles	CA	90019	800-472-2321	

48-18 Hobby Organizations

Organization	City	State	Zip	Phone	Fax
Academy of Model Aeronautics (AMA) 5161 E Memorial Dr *TF:* 800-435-9262 ■ *Web:* www.modelaircraft.org	Muncie	IN	47302	765-287-1256	289-4248
American Bonanza Society (ABS) 1922 Midfield Rd *Web:* www.bonanza.org	Wichita	KS	67206	316-945-1700	945-1710
American Contract Bridge League (ACBL) 6575 Windchase Blvd *TF Sales:* 800-264-2743 ■ *Web:* www.acbl.org	Horn Lake	MS	38637	662-253-3100	253-3187
American Craft Council 72 Spring St 6th Fl *TF:* 800-836-3470 ■ *Web:* www.craftcouncil.org	New York	NY	10012	212-274-0630	
American Federation of Astrologers (AFA) 6535 S Rural Rd *TF:* 888-301-7630 ■ *Web:* www.astrologers.com	Tempe	AZ	85283	480-838-1751	838-8293
American Horticultural Society (AHS) 7931 E Blvd Dr *TF:* 800-777-7931 ■ *Web:* www.ahs.org	Alexandria	VA	22308	703-768-5700	768-8700
American Kennel Club (AKC) 260 Madison Ave *Web:* www.akc.org	New York	NY	10016	212-696-8200	696-8299
American Philatelic Society (APS) 100 Match Factory Pl *Web:* www.stamps.org	Bellefonte	PA	16823	814-933-3803	933-6128
American Radio Relay League (ARRL) 225 Main St *TF:* 888-277-5289 ■ *Web:* www.arrl.org	Newington	CT	06111	860-594-0200	594-0259

	City	State	Zip	Phone	Fax
American Rose Society (ARS) 8877 Jefferson Paige Rd TF: 800-637-6534 ■ Web: rose.org	Shreveport	LA	71119	318-938-5402	938-5405
Antique Automobile Club of America (AACA) 501 W Governor Rd PO Box 417 Web: www.aaca.org	Hershey	PA	17033	717-534-1910	534-9101
Art & Creative Materials Institute Inc (ACMI) 1280 Main St PO Box 479 Web: www.acminet.org	Hanson	MA	02341	781-293-4100	294-0808
Barbershop Harmony Society 110 Seventh Ave N TF: 800-876-7464 ■ Web: www.barbershop.org	Nashville	TN	37203	615-823-3993	313-7619
BMW Motorcycle Owners of America PO Box 3982 Web: www.bmwmoa.org	Ballwin	MO	63022	636-394-7277	391-1811
Craft & Hobby Assn (CHA) 319 E 54th St TF: 800-822-0494 ■ Web: www.craftandhobby.org	Elmwood Park	NJ	07407	201-835-1200	797-0657
Embroiderers Guild of America (EGA) 426 W Jefferson St Web: www.egausa.org	Louisville	KY	40202	502-589-6956	584-7900
Experimental Aircraft Assn (EAA) 3000 Poberezny Rd TF: 800-236-4800 ■ Web: www.eaa.org	Oshkosh	WI	54902	920-426-4800	426-4828
Handweavers Guild of America (HGA) 1255 Hwy 23 NW Ste 211 Web: www.weavespindye.org	Suwanee	GA	30024	678-730-0010	730-0836
Knitting Guild of America, The (TKGA) 1100-H Brandywine Blvd Web: www.tkga.com	Zanesville	OH	43701	740-452-4541	452-2552
National Garden Clubs Inc (NGC) 4401 Magnolia Ave TF: 800-550-6007 ■ Web: www.gardenclub.org	Saint Louis	MO	63110	314-776-7574	776-5108
National Gardening Assn (NGA) 1100 Dorset St TF: 800-538-7476 ■ Web: www.garden.org	South Burlington	VT	05403	802-863-5251	864-6889
National Genealogical Society (NGS) 3108 Columbia Pk Ste 300 TF: 800-473-0060 ■ Web: www.ngsgenealogy.org	Arlington	VA	22204	703-525-0050	525-0052
National Model Railroad Assn (NMRA) 4121 Cromwell Rd TF: 800-654-2256 ■ Web: www.nmra.org	Chattanooga	TN	37421	423-892-2846	899-4869
National NeedleArts Assn, The (TNNA) 1100-H Brandywine Blvd TF: 800-889-8662 ■ Web: www.tnna.org	Zanesville	OH	43701	740-455-6773	452-2552
National Scrabble Assn 403 Front St PO Box 700	Greenport	NY	11944	416-876-7675	
National Wood Carvers Assn (NWCA) 7424 Miami Ave Web: chipchats.org	Cincinnati	OH	45243	513-561-9051	
Philatelic Foundation 341 W 38th St 5th Fl Web: www.philatelicfoundation.org	New York	NY	10018	212-221-6555	221-6208
Society of Decorative Painters 393 N McLean Blvd Web: www.decorativepainters.org	Wichita	KS	67203	316-269-9300	269-9191
Sports Car Club of America (SCCA) 6700 SW Topeka Blvd Ste 300 TF: 800-770-2055 ■ Web: www.scca.com	Topeka	KS	66619	785-357-7222	232-7228
Sweet Adelines International 9110 S Toledo Ave TF: 800-992-7464 ■ Web: sweetadelines.com	Tulsa	OK	74137	918-622-1444	665-0894
US Chess Federation (USCF) PO Box 3967 TF: 800-903-8723 ■ Web: www.uschess.org	Crossville	TN	38557	931-787-1234	787-1200

48-19 Military, Veterans, Patriotic Organizations

	City	State	Zip	Phone	Fax
Air Force Assn (AFA) 1501 Lee Hwy 4th Fl TF: 800-727-3337 ■ Web: www.afa.org	Arlington	VA	22209	703-247-5800	247-5853
American Legion Auxiliary 8945 N Meridian St 2nd Fl Web: www.alaforveterans.org	Indianapolis	IN	46260	317-569-4500	569-4502
American Legion, The 700 N Pennsylvania St TF Cust Svc: 800-433-3318 ■ Web: www.legion.org	Indianapolis	IN	46204	317-630-1200	630-1223
American Logistics Assn (ALA) 1133 15th St NW Ste 640 TF: 800-791-7146 ■ Web: www.ala-national.org	Washington	DC	20005	202-466-2520	296-4419
American Society of Military Comptrollers (ASMC) 415 N Alfred St TF: 800-462-5637 ■ Web: www.asmconline.org	Alexandria	VA	22314	703-549-0360	549-3181
AMVETS 4647 Forbes Blvd TF: 877-726-8387 ■ Web: www.amvets.org	Lanham	MD	20706	301-459-9600	459-7924
Armed Forces Communications & Electronics Assn (AFCEA) 4400 Fair Lakes Ct TF: 800-336-4583 ■ Web: www.afcea.org	Fairfax	VA	22033	703-631-6100	631-4693
Armed Services Mutual Benefit Assn (ASMBA) PO Box 160384 TF: 800-251-8434 ■ Web: www.asmba.com	Nashville	TN	37216	615-851-0800	851-9484
Army Aviation Assn of America (AAAA) 593 Main St Web: www.quad-a.org	Monroe	CT	06468	203-268-2450	268-5870
Army Distaff Foundation 6200 Oregon Ave NW TF: 800-541-4255 ■ Web: www.armydistaff.org	Washington	DC	20015	202-541-0149	
Association of Civilian Technicians (ACT) 12620 Lk Ridge Dr Web: www.actnat.com	Woodbridge	VA	22192	703-494-4845	494-0961
Association of Old Crows (AOC) 1000 N Payne St Ste 300 TF: 800-247-5626 ■ Web: www.crows.org	Alexandria	VA	22314	703-549-1600	549-2589
Association of the US Army (AUSA) 2425 Wilson Blvd TF: 800-336-4570 ■ Web: www.ausa.org	Arlington	VA	22201	703-841-4300	525-9039
Disabled American Veterans (DAV) 3725 Alexandria Pike TF: 877-426-2838 ■ Web: www.dav.org	Cold Spring	KY	41076	859-441-7300	441-1416
Enlisted Assn of the National Guard of the US (EANGUS) 3133 Mt Vernon Ave TF: 800-234-3264 ■ Web: www.memberconnections.com	Alexandria	VA	22305	703-519-3846	519-3849
Fleet Reserve Assn (FRA) 125 NW St TF: 800-372-1924 ■ Web: www.fra.org	Alexandria	VA	22314	703-683-1400	549-6610
Marine Corps Assn (MCA) PO Box 1775 TF: 800-336-0291 ■ Web: www.mca-marines.org	Quantico	VA	22134	703-640-6161	640-0823
Military Benefit Assn (MBA) 14605 Avion Pkwy PO Box 221110 TF: 800-336-0100 ■ Web: www.militarybenefit.org	Chantilly	VA	20153	703-968-6200	968-6423
Military Officers Assn of America (MOAA) 201 N Washington St TF: 800-234-6622 ■ Web: www.moaa.org	Alexandria	VA	22314	703-549-2311	
NA for Uniformed Services (NAUS) 5535 Hempstead Way TF: 800-842-3451 ■ Web: www.naus.org	Springfield	VA	22151	703-750-1342	354-4380
National Committee for Employer Support of the Guard & Reserve (ESGR) 1555 Wilson Blvd Ste 319 TF: 800-336-4590 ■ Web: www.esgr.mil	Arlington	VA	22209	703-696-1386	
National Defense Industrial Assn (NDIA) 2111 Wilson Blvd Ste 400 Web: www.ndia.org	Arlington	VA	22201	703-522-1820	522-1885
National Fallen Firefighters Foundation PO Box 498 TF: 888-744-6513 ■ Web: www.firehero.org	Emmitsburg	MD	21727	301-447-1365	447-1645
National Guard Assn of the US (NGAUS) 1 Massachusetts Ave NW Ste 200 TF: 888-226-4287 ■ Web: www.ngaus.org	Washington	DC	20001	202-789-0031	682-9358
National League of Families of American Prisoners & Missing in Southeast Asia 5673 Columbia Pk Ste 100 Web: www.pow-miafamilies.org	Falls Church	VA	22041	703-465-7432	
National Society Daughters of the American Revolution (DAR) 1776 D St NW Web: www.dar.org	Washington	DC	20006	202-628-1776	879-3252
National Society of the Sons of the American Revolution (NSSAR) 1000 S Fourth St Web: www.sar.org	Louisville	KY	40203	502-589-1776	589-1671
Naval Enlisted Reserve Assn (NERA) 6703 Farragut Ave TF: 800-776-9020 ■ Web: www.nera.org	Falls Church	VA	22042	703-534-1329	
Naval Reserve Assn (NRA) 1619 King St *Fax Area Code: 866 ■ TF: 877-628-9411 ■ Web: ausn.org	Alexandria	VA	22314	703-548-5800	683-3647*
Navy League of the US 2300 Wilson Blvd TF: 800-356-5760 ■ Web: www.navyleague.org	Arlington	VA	22201	703-528-1775	528-2333
Navy-Marine Corps Relief Society (NMCRS) 875 N Randolph St Ste 225 TF: 800-654-8364 ■ Web: www.nmcrs.org	Arlington	VA	22203	703-696-4904	696-0144
Non Commissioned Officers Assn (NCOA) 9330 Corporate Dr Ste 701 TF: 800-662-2620 ■ Web: www.ncoausa.org	Selma	TX	78154	210-653-6161	637-3337
Reserve Officers Assn of the US (ROA) 1 Constitution Ave NE TF: 800-809-9448 ■ Web: www.roa.org	Washington	DC	20002	202-479-2200	547-1641
Retired Enlisted Assn (TREA) 15821 E Centre Tech Cir Web: www.trea.org	Aurora	CO	80011	303-340-3939	340-4516
Society of American Military Engineers (SAME) 607 Prince St Web: www.same.org	Alexandria	VA	22314	703-549-3800	684-0231
Tailhook Assn 9696 Businesspark Ave TF: 800-322-4665 ■ Web: www.tailhook.net	San Diego	CA	92131	858-689-9223	578-8839
United Service Organizations (USO) 2111 Wilson Blvd Ste 1200 Web: www.uso.org	Arlington	VA	22201	703-908-6400	
US Coast Guard Chief Petty Officers Assn 5520-G Hempstead Way Web: www.uscgcpoa.org	Springfield	VA	22151	703-941-0395	941-0397
US Naval Institute 291 Wood Rd TF: 800-233-8764 ■ Web: www.usni.org	Annapolis	MD	21402	410-268-6110	295-1084
Veterans for Peace Inc (VFP) 216 S Meramec Ave TF: 877-429-0678 ■ Web: www.veteransforpeace.org	Saint Louis	MO	63105	314-725-6005	725-7103
Veterans of Foreign Wars of the US (VFW) 406 W 34th St TF: 800-963-3180 ■ Web: www.vfw.org	Kansas City	MO	64111	816-756-3390	968-1149
Women in Military Service for America Memorial Foundation Inc Dept 560 TF: 800-222-2294 ■ Web: www.womensmemorial.org	Washington	DC	20042	703-533-1155	931-4208

48-20 Religious Organizations

	City	State	Zip	Phone	Fax
92nd St Young Men's & Young Women's Hebrew Assn 1395 Lexington Ave Web: www.92y.org	New York	NY	10128	212-415-5500	415-5788
Aberdeen Alliance Church of The Christian & Missionary Alliance, The 1106 S Roosevelt St	Aberdeen	SD	57401	605-225-9724	
Abiding Faith Free Lutheran Church 433 Crestview Ave Web: aflc.org	Ortonville	MN	56278	320-839-3949	
Abundant Life Tabernacle Upci 591 Broadway	Kingston	NY	12401	845-338-9883	
Abundant Love Church Inc 2615 New Haven Ave Web: abundantlove.faithweb.com	Fort Wayne	IN	46803	260-420-5683	
Adrian Dominican Sisters 1257 E Siena Heights Dr	Adrian	MI	49221	517-266-3400	
Aldersgate United Methodist Church 460 W Aldersgate Dr Web: aldersgatechurch.com	Nixa	MO	65714	417-725-4949	
Allegheny West Conference of Seventh Day Adventists 1339 E Broad St Web: www.awconf.org	Columbus	OH	43205	614-252-5271	

Organization	City	State	Zip	Phone	Fax
American Academy of Religion (AAR) 825 Houston Mill Rd NE Ste 300 *TF:* 800-282-6632 ■ *Web:* www.aarweb.org	Atlanta	GA	30329	404-727-3049	727-7959
American Baptist Assn (ABA) 4605 N State Line Ave *TF:* 800-264-2482 ■ *Web:* www.abaptist.org	Texarkana	TX	75503	903-792-2783	792-8128
American Baptist Churches USA PO Box 851 *TF:* 800-222-3872 ■ *Web:* www.abc-usa.org	Valley Forge	PA	19482	610-768-2000	768-2275
American Theological Library Assn (ATLA) 300 S Wacker Dr Ste 2100 *TF:* 888-665-2852 ■ *Web:* www.atla.com	Chicago	IL	60606	312-454-5100	454-5505
Answers in Genesis Ky Inc 2800 Bullittsburg Church Rd *Web:* www.answersingenesis.org	Petersburg	KY	41080	859-727-2222	
Antiochian Orthodox Christian Archdiocese of North America 358 Mountain Rd *TF:* 888-421-1442 ■ *Web:* www.antiochian.org	Englewood	NJ	07631	201-871-1355	871-7954
Apostolic Assembly of The Faith In Christ Jesus 10807 Laurel St *Web:* www.apostolicassembly.org	Rancho Cucamonga	CA	91730	909-987-3013	481-5691
Archdiocese of Louisville 212 E College St *Web:* www.archlou.org	Louisville	KY	40203	502-585-3291	
Archdiocese of Newark 171 Clifton Ave *Web:* www.rcan.org	Newark	NJ	07104	973-497-4126	
Archdiocese of Philadelphia 222 N 17th St *Web:* archphila.org	Philadelphia	PA	19103	215-965-4636	
Archdiocese of Portland in Oregon 2838 E Burnside St *Web:* www.archdpdx.org	Portland	OR	97214	503-234-5334	
Archdiocese of Saint Paul & Minneapolis 226 Summit Ave *TF:* 877-290-1605 ■ *Web:* www.archspm.org	Saint Paul	MN	55102	651-291-4411	
Archdiocese of San Francisco 1 Peter Yorke Way *Web:* www.sfarchdiocese.org	San Francisco	CA	94109	415-614-5500	
Arkansas Baptist Foundation 10 Remington Dr *TF:* 800-838-2272 ■ *Web:* abf.org	Little Rock	AR	72204	501-376-0732	
Armenian Church of America 630 Second Ave *Web:* www.armenianchurch.org	New York	NY	10016	212-686-0710	779-3558
Artman Lutheran Home 250 N Bethlehem Pk *Web:* www.libertylutheran.org	Ambler	PA	19002	215-643-6335	
Assemblies of God (A/G) 1445 N Boonville Ave *TF:* 800-641-4310 ■ *Web:* www.ag.org	Springfield	MO	65802	417-862-2781	862-8558
Association of Professional Chaplains (APC) 1701 E Woodfield Rd Ste 400 *Web:* www.professionalchaplains.org	Schaumburg	IL	60173	847-240-1014	240-1015
Association of Vineyard Churches 5115 Grove W Blvd *Web:* www.vineyardusa.org	Stafford	TX	77477	281-313-8463	
Automated Assembly Corp 20777 Kensington Blvd *Web:* www.autoassembly.com	Lakeville	MN	55044	952-469-6556	
Avant Ministries 10000 N Oak Trafficway *TF:* 800-468-1892 ■ *Web:* www.avantministries.org	Kansas City	MO	64155	816-734-8500	
B'nai B'rith International 2020 K St NW 7th Fl *TF:* 888-388-4224 ■ *Web:* www.bnaibrith.org	Washington	DC	20006	202-857-6600	857-6609
B'nai B'rith Youth Organization (BBYO) 2020 K St NW *Web:* www.bbyo.org	Washington	DC	20006	202-857-6633	857-6568
Bannockburn Baptist Church 7100 Brodie Ln *Web:* bbcfamily.com	Austin	TX	78745	512-892-2703	
Bapitst Campus Ministry Unc Charlotte 1328 John Kirk Dr *Web:* bcmcharlotte.org	Charlotte	NC	28262	704-547-7472	
Baptist Bible Fellowship International (BBFI) 720 E Kearney St *Web:* www.bbfi.org	Springfield	MO	65803	417-862-5001	865-0794
Baptist General Convention of Texas 333 N Washington Ave *Web:* texasbaptists.org	Dallas	TX	75246	214-828-5100	
Baptist Mid-Missions 7749 Webster Rd *Web:* www.bmm.org	Cleveland	OH	44130	440-826-3930	826-4457
Baptist Missionary Assn of America (BMA) 611 Locust Ave *Web:* bmamissions.org	Conway	AR	72034	501-455-4977	
Baptist Village of Hugo 1200 W Finley St *Web:* baptistvillage.org	Hugo	OK	74743	580-326-8383	
Baptist World Alliance 405 N Washington St *TF:* 844-862-2739 ■ *Web:* www.bwanet.org	Falls Church	VA	22046	703-790-8980	790-5719
Bell Shoals Baptist Church of Brandon Inc 2102 Bell Shoals Rd *Web:* bellshoals.com	Brandon	FL	33511	813-689-4229	
Benny Hinn Ministries PO Box 162000 *TF:* 800-433-1900 ■ *Web:* www.bennyhinn.org	Irving	TX	75016	817-722-2000	
Berean Baptist Church Unaffiliated Inc 517 Glensford Dr *Web:* bereanbaptistchurch.org	Fayetteville	NC	28314	910-868-5156	
Beth Medrash Govoha of America Inc 617 Sixth St	Lakewood	NJ	08701	732-367-1060	
Bethel Baptist Church 1196 N Academy St *Web:* www.mybethel.com	Galesburg	IL	61401	309-342-3166	
Bethel World Outreach Ministries International Inc 8252 Georgia Ave *Web:* cityofhope.bwomi.org	Silver Spring	MD	20910	301-588-8099	
Bethesda Ministries 2200 Peacock Rd *Web:* mybwc.org	Richmond	IN	47374	765-939-2975	
Bible League 3801 Eagle Nest Dr *TF:* 866-825-4636 ■ *Web:* www.bibleleague.org	Crete	IL	60417	817-595-1664	

Organization	City	State	Zip	Phone	Fax
Bible Way Fellowship Baptist Church 10120 Hartsook St *Web:* www.bibleway1.org	Houston	TX	77034	713-943-2215	
Billy Graham Evangelistic Assn 1 Billy Graham Pkwy *TF:* 877-247-2426 ■ *Web:* www.billygraham.org	Charlotte	NC	28201	704-401-2432	
Brainerd Baptist Church 212 Brookfield Ave *Web:* brainerdbaptist.org	Chattanooga	TN	37411	423-629-4202	
Brandywine Valley Baptist Church 7 Mt Lebanon Rd *Web:* brandywineonline.org	Wilmington	DE	19803	302-478-4255	
Breakthrough Urban Ministries 3330 W Carroll Ave *Web:* breakthrough.org	Chicago	IL	60624	773-722-1144	
Brooklyn Tabernacle 17 Smith St *Web:* www.brooklyntabernacle.org	Brooklyn	NY	11201	718-290-2000	
Buddhist Churches of America (BCA) 1710 Octavia St *Web:* buddhistchurchesofamerica.org	San Francisco	CA	94109	415-776-5600	771-6293
California Southern Baptist Convention 678 E Shaw Ave *Web:* www.csbc.com	Fresno	CA	93710	559-229-9533	229-2824
Calvary Baptist Christian Academy 543 Randolph St *Web:* calvarymeadville.com	Meadville	PA	16335	814-724-8099	
Calvary Chapel 13500 Philmont Ave *Web:* www.ccphilly.org	Philadelphia	PA	19116	215-969-1520	
Calvary Chapel of Costa Mesa Inc 3800 S Fairview St *Web:* www.calvarychapelcostamesa.com	Santa Ana	CA	92704	714-979-4422	
Camp Hill Presbyterian Church 101 N 23rd St *Web:* www.thechpc.org	Camp Hill	PA	17011	717-737-0488	
Campus Crusade for Christ International 100 Lk Hart Dr *TF:* 888-278-7233 ■ *Web:* www.cru.org	Orlando	FL	32832	407-826-2500	
Campus Outreach 2200 Briarwood Way *Web:* campusoutreach.org	Birmingham	AL	35243	205-776-5500	
Canon Law Society of America (CLSA) 3025 Fourth St NE Ste 111 *Web:* www.clsa.org	Washington	DC	20017	202-832-2350	832-2331
Canyon Ridge Christian Church 6200 W Lone Mtn Rd *Web:* www.canyonridge.org	Las Vegas	NV	89130	702-658-2722	
Capital Christian Center 9470 Micron Ave *Web:* capitalonline.cc	Sacramento	CA	95827	916-856-5683	
Cathedral School for Boys 1275 Sacramento St *Web:* www.cathedralschool.net	San Francisco	CA	94108	415-771-6600	
Catholic Biblical Assn of America 433 Caldwell Hall *Web:* www.catholicbiblical.org	Washington	DC	20064	202-319-5519	319-4799
Catholic Church Extension Society of the USA 150 S Wacker Dr 20th Fl **Fax Area Code:* 312 ■ *TF:* 800-842-7804 ■ *Web:* www.catholicextension.org	Chicago	IL	60606	800-842-7804	236-5276*
Catholic Social Services 8815 99 St *Web:* www.catholicsocialservices.ab.ca	Edmonton	AB	T6E3V3	780-432-1137	
Catholic Supply of st Louis Inc 6759 Chippewa St *TF:* 800-325-9026 ■ *Web:* www.catholicsupply.com	Saint Louis	MO	63109	314-644-0643	
Catholic Transcript Inc, The 467 Bloomfield Ave *TF:* 800-726-2381 ■ *Web:* www.catholictranscript.org	Bloomfield	CT	06002	860-286-2828	
CE National Inc 1003 Presidential Dr *Web:* cenational.org	Winona Lake	IN	46590	574-267-6622	
Center for Action & Contempla 1823 Five Points Rd SW *Web:* www.cac.org	Albuquerque	NM	87105	505-242-9588	
Central Baptist Village 4747 N Canfield Ave *Web:* www.cbvillage.org	Norridge	IL	60706	708-583-8500	
Central Conference of American Rabbis (CCAR) 355 Lexington Ave *Web:* www.ccarnet.org	New York	NY	10017	212-972-3636	
Centre Street United Methodist Church 217 N Centre St *Web:* centrestreetumc.com	Cumberland	MD	21502	301-722-5370	
Child Evangelism Fellowship Inc 17482 Hwy M *TF:* 800-748-7710 ■ *Web:* www.cefonline.com	Warrenton	MO	63383	636-456-4321	456-2078
Childrens Hopechest PO Box 63842 *Web:* www.hopechest.org	Colorado Springs	CO	80962	719-487-7800	
Christ & Grace Episcopal Church 1545 S Sycamore St *Web:* christandgrace.org	Petersburg	VA	23805	804-733-7202	
Christ Church of Universal Love, The 11699 130th Ave	Largo	FL	33778	727-585-5088	
Christ Church Xp 8800 Vaughn Rd *Web:* christchurchxp.net	Montgomery	AL	36117	334-387-0566	
Christ in Youth Inc PO Box B *TF:* 855-999-7238 ■ *Web:* ciy.com	Joplin	MO	64801	417-781-2273	781-5958
Christ Universal Temple 11901 S Ashland Ave Apt S *Web:* www.cutemple.org	Chicago	IL	60643	773-568-2282	
Christian & Missionary Alliance 8595 Explorer Dr *TF:* 800-700-2651 ■ *Web:* www.cmalliance.org	Colorado Springs	CO	80920	719-599-5999	
Christian Aid Ministries PO Box 360 *Web:* christianaidministries.org	Berlin	OH	44610	330-893-2428	893-2305
Christian Church (Disciples of Christ) 130 E Washington St *Web:* www.disciples.org	Indianapolis	IN	46204	317-635-3100	635-3700
Christian Fellowship Church Foundation 21673 Beaumeade Cir *Web:* www.cfellowshipc.org	Ashburn	VA	20147	703-729-3900	

Phone Fax

Christian Reformed Church in North America (CRC)
2850 Kalamazoo Ave SE Grand Rapids MI 49560 616-241-1691 224-0834
TF: 800-272-5125 ■ *Web:* www.crcna.org

Christophers, The 5 Hanover Sq 11th Fl New York NY 10004 212-759-4050 838-5073
TF: 888-298-4050 ■ *Web:* www.christophers.org

Christus Victor Lutheran Church Inc of Knox County Tennessee
4110 Central Ave Pike Knoxville TN 37912 865-687-6622
Web: christusvictorknoxville.org

Church of God in Christ Inc 930 Mason St. Memphis TN 38126 901-947-9300
TF: 877-746-8578 ■ *Web:* www.cogic.org

Church of God Ministries 1201 E Fifth St. Anderson IN 46012 765-642-0256 642-5652
TF: 800-848-2464 ■ *Web:* jesusisthesubject.org

Church of God World Missions (COGWM)
2490 Keith St PO Box 8016 Cleveland TN 37320 423-478-7190
TF: 800-345-7492 ■ *Web:* www.cogwm.org

Church of Jesus Christ of Latter-Day Saints
50 E N Temple St Salt Lake City UT 84150 801-240-1000
Web: www.lds.org

Church of Our Lady of Lourdes
901 Atwells Ave Providence RI 02909 401-272-8127
Web: parishesonline.com

Church of Scientology Flag Service Organization
503 Cleveland St Clearwater FL 33755 727-445-4387
Web: scientology-fso.org

Church of the Brethren 1451 Dundee Ave. Elgin IL 60120 847-742-5100 742-1407
TF: 800-323-8039 ■ *Web:* www.brethren.org

Church of The Holy Communion
218 Ashley Ave. Charleston SC 29403 843-722-2024
Web: www.holycomm.org

Church of the Nazarene
17001 Prairie Star Pkwy Lenexa KS 66220 913-577-0500
Web: www.nazarene.org

Church Women United (CWU)
475 Riverside Dr Ste 243 New York NY 10115 212-870-2347 870-2338
TF: 800-298-5551 ■ *Web:* www.churchwomen.org

City of Truth or Consequences
685 Marie St. Truth Or Consequences NM 87901 575-894-2603
Web: www.torcnm.org

City Union Mission Inc 1100 E 11th St Kansas City MO 64106 816-474-9380
Web: cityunionmission.org

Colonial Hills Baptist Church
5375 W Mt Morris Rd. Mount Morris MI 48458 810-687-1570

Columbia Lutheran Home 4700 Phinney Ave N Seattle WA 98103 206-632-7400
Web: www.columbialutheranhome.com

Commons at Orlando Lutheran Towers, The
300 E Church St Orlando FL 32801 407-872-7088
TF: 800-859-1033 ■ *Web:* orlandoseniorhealth.org

Community of Christ 1001 W Walnut St Independence MO 64050 816-833-1000 521-3085*
**Fax:* Hum Res ■ *TF:* 800-825-2806 ■ *Web:* www.cofchrist.org

Compassion Canada 985 Adelaide St S London ON N6E4A3 519-668-0224
TF: 800-563-5437 ■ *Web:* compassion.ca

Congregation Rodeph Sholom 7 W 83rd St New York NY 10024 212-362-8800
Web: www.rodephsholom.org

Connecting Businessmen to Christ (CBMC)
5746 Marlin Rd Ste 602 Osborne Ctr Chattanooga TN 37411 423-698-4444 629-4434
TF: 800-566-2262 ■ *Web:* www.cbmc.com

Connection Pointe Christian Church of Brownsburg
1800 N Green St Brownsburg IN 46112 317-852-2221
Web: www.connectionpointe.org

Coral Ridge Presbyterian Church Inc
5555 N Federal Hwy Fort Lauderdale FL 33308 954-771-8840
Web: www.crpc.org

Cornerstone United Methodist Church Inc
8200 Immokalee Rd Naples FL 34119 239-354-9160
Web: cornerstonenaples.org

Coupland-Moran Engineers Inc
6001 Indian School Rd Ne Ste 200 Albuquerque NM 87110 505-314-7500
Web: www.cmenm.com

Covenant United Methodist Church
6824 Tuckaseegee Rd Charlotte NC 28214 704-392-3925
Web: www.gbgm-umc.org

Crestview Baptist Church Georgetown Texas
2300 Williams Dr Georgetown TX 78628 512-863-6576
Web: crestviewbaptist.church

Crossgates Baptist Church Inc
8 Crosswoods Rd Brandon MS 39042 601-825-2562
Web: crossgates.org

Crossings Community Church
14600 N Portland Ave. Oklahoma City OK 73134 405-755-2227
Web: crossings.church

Crossway Community Church 13905 75th St. Bristol WI 53104 262-857-4488
Web: cwc.church

Crossworld 306 Bala Ave Bala Cynwyd PA 19004 888-785-0087
TF: 888-785-0087 ■ *Web:* www.crossworld.org

Crowes Mortuary & Chapel
118 Us Hwy 74A. Rutherfordton NC 28139 828-286-2304
Web: crowemortuary.com

Crux, The 2216 E S St Anaheim CA 92806 714-563-2024

Dane Street Congregational Church 10 Dane St Beverly MA 01915 978-922-4325
Web: www.danestchurch.org

Dare 2 Share Ministries International
PO Box 745323 Arvada CO 80006 303-425-1606
TF: 800-462-8355 ■ *Web:* dare2share.org

Destination America Inc
2255 Kuhio Ave Ste 1002 Honolulu HI 96815 808-971-0500

Diocese of Davenport 2706 N Gaines St Davenport IA 52804 563-324-1911
Web: www.davenportdiocese.org

Diocese of Greensburg 723 E Pittsburgh St Greensburg PA 15601 724-837-0901 837-0857
TF: 866-409-6455 ■ *Web:* www.dioceseofgreensburg.org

Diocese of Harrisburg
4800 Union Deposit Rd Harrisburg PA 17111 717-657-4804
Web: hbgdiocese.org

Diocese of La Crosse 3710 E Ave S. La Crosse WI 54601 608-788-7700
Web: diolc.org

Diocese of Metuchen PO Box 191 Metuchen NJ 08840 732-562-1990
Web: www.diometuchen.org

Diocese of Nashville 2400 21st Ave S. Nashville TN 37212 615-383-6393
Web: www.dioceseofnashville.com

Diocese of Phoenix 400 E Monroe St Phoenix AZ 85004 602-257-0030
Web: dphx.org

Diocese of Rochester 1150 Buffalo Rd Roch NY 14624 585-328-3210
TF: 800-388-7177 ■ *Web:* www.dor.org

Diocese of San Bernardino Education & Welfare Corp
1201 E Highland Ave San Bernardino CA 92404 909-475-5300
Web: sbdiocese.org

Diocese of St. Augustine Inc
11625 Old St Augustine Jacksonville FL 32258 904-262-3200
TF: 800-775-4659 ■ *Web:* www.dosafl.com

Divine Redeemer United Presbyterian Church
407 N Calaveras San Antonio TX 78207 210-433-9551
Web: divineredeemersa.org

Door Creek Church 6602 Dominion Dr. Madison WI 53718 608-222-8586
Web: www.doorcreekchurch.org

E3 Partners Ministry
16787 Bernardo Ctr Dr Ste 7 San Diego CA 92128 858-485-9904
Web: e3partners.org

Eagle Rock Baptist Church
1499 Colorado Blvd Los Angeles CA 90041 323-255-4611
Web: www.erockchurch.com

Eastern Star Church 5750 E 30th St Indianapolis IN 46218 317-591-5050
Web: www.easternstarchurch.org

Emmanuel Gospel Center Inc 2 San Juan St Boston MA 02118 617-262-4567
Web: egc.org

Episcopal Church USA 815 Second Ave New York NY 10017 212-716-6000 867-0395
TF: 800-334-7626 ■ *Web:* www.episcopalchurch.org

Episcopal Diocese of West Texas
111 Torcido Dr San Antonio TX 78209 210-824-5387
TF: 888-824-5387 ■ *Web:* dwtx.org

Evangelical Church Alliance (ECA)
205 W Broadway St PO Box 9. Bradley IL 60915 815-937-0720 937-0720
TF: 888-855-6060 ■ *Web:* www.ecainternational.org

Evangelical Fellowship of Canada (EFC)
600 Alden Rd Ste 300 Markham Industrial Pk Markham ON L3R0E7 905-479-5885 479-4742
TF: 866-302-3362 ■ *Web:* www.evangelicalfellowship.ca

Evangelical Free Church of America, The
901 E 78th St Minneapolis MN 55420 952-854-1300
TF: 800-745-2202 ■ *Web:* www.efca.org

Evangelical Lutheran Church in America (ELCA)
8765 W Higgins Rd Chicago IL 60631 773-380-2700 380-1465
TF: 800-638-3522 ■ *Web:* www.elca.org

Evangelical Presbyterian Church of Plant City
1107 Charlie Griffin Rd Plant City FL 33566 813-759-9383
Web: www.gracepointpc.org

Evangelical Training Assn (ETA) PO Box 327 Wheaton IL 60187 800-369-8291
TF General: 800-369-8291 ■ *Web:* www.etaworld.org

Faith Tabernacle Pentecostal Church of Montgomery County Mo
121 W Fourth St Montgomery City MO 63361 573-564-3700

Faithbridge United Methodist Church
18000 Stuebner Airline Rd Spring TX 77379 281-320-7588
Web: faithbridge.org

Family Life Worship Center Worldwide Ministries Inc
1517 Joyner Pond Rd Aiken SC 29803 803-641-0218

Felician Sisters Cssf 1600 W Oklahoma Ave. Milwaukee WI 53215 414-645-5329

Fellowship Community 3000 Fellowship Dr Whitehall PA 18052 610-799-3000
Web: www.fellowshipcommunity.com

Fellowship Village Dining Service Dept
8000 Fellowship Rd Basking Ridge NJ 07920 908-580-3806
Web: fellowshipseniorliving.org

Fifth Baptist Church of The City of st Louis Mo
3736 Natural Bridge Ave. Saint Louis MO 63107 314-531-2602

First Assembly of God 1701 N E Ave. Panama City FL 32405 850-769-3558
Web: firstassemblypc.org

First Baptist Church Dallas
1707 San Jacinto St Dallas TX 75201 214-969-0111
Web: www.firstdallas.org

First Baptist Church of Orlando Inc, The
3000 S John Young Pkwy. Orlando FL 32805 407-425-2555 425-2954
Web: www.firstorlando.com

First Christian Church 531 Fifth St Columbus IN 47201 812-379-4491
Web: www.fccoc.org

First Church of Christ Scientist
210 Massachusetts Ave P05-10 Boston MA 02115 617-450-2000
TF: 800-288-7155 ■ *Web:* www.christianscience.com

First Evangelical Free Church of st Louis County
1375 Carman Rd. Manchester MO 63021 636-227-0125
Web: efree.org

Focus 603 Park Point Dr Ste 200 Genesee CO 80401 303-962-5750
Web: www.focus.org

Fourth Presbyterian Church
3016 Preston Hwy Louisville KY 40217 502-634-8021
Web: fourthpc.org

Franciscan Sisters of Chicago Inc
11500 Theresa Dr Lemont IL 60439 800-524-6126
TF: 800-524-6126 ■ *Web:* www.franciscanministries.org

Friends General Conference
1216 Arch St Ste 2B Philadelphia PA 19107 215-561-1700
TF: 800-966-4556 ■ *Web:* www.fgcquaker.org

General Assn of Regular Baptist Churches (GARBC)
1300 N Meacham Rd Schaumburg IL 60173 847-585-0816
TF: 888-588-1600 ■ *Web:* www.garbcinternational.org

Glad Tidings Assembly of God Church
1110 Snyder Rd Reading PA 19609 610-678-0266
Web: www.gladtidingsonline.com

Glori Energy Inc 4315 S Dr. Houston TX 77053 713-237-8880
Web: www.glorienergy.com

God Owns This Company Inc 777 Hill Ave Muskegon MI 49442 231-727-3333
Web: godownsthiscompany.com

	City	State	Zip	Phone	Fax
Good Hope Lutheran Church					
3359 New Zoarville Rd Ne	Zoarville	OH	44656	330-859-2480	
Web: www.nclutheran.org					
Grace Church 802 Broadway	New York	NY	10003	212-254-2000	
Web: www.gracechurchnyc.org					
Grace Episcopal Church 33 Church St	White Plains	NY	10601	914-949-3098	
Web: www.gracecommunitycenter.org					
Grace Place Lutheran Retreats					
8460 Watson Rd Ste 136	Saint Louis	MO	63119	314-842-3077	
Web: graceplacewellness.org					
Graceworks Church Inc 16131 Hwy 44	Prairieville	LA	70769	225-622-7805	
Greater Atlanta Christian					
1575 Indian Trl Lilburn Rd	Norcross	GA	30093	770-243-2000	
TF: 800-450-1327 ■ *Web:* www.greateratlantachristian.org					
Green Acres Baptist Church					
16163 N Peninsula Rd	Whitehouse	TX	75791	903-566-2515	
Web: www.gabc.org					
Guild Shop of The Church of st John The Divine, The					
2009 Dunlavy St	Houston	TX	77006	713-528-5095	
Web: theguildshop.org					
Harvest Christian Fellowship					
6115 Arlington Ave	Riverside	CA	92504	951-687-6902	
Web: harvest.org					
Harvest Word of Life Ministries International Inc					
2260 Lake Ave	Fort Wayne	IN	46805	260-422-5750	
Heathwood Hall Episcopal School					
3000 S Beltline Blvd	Columbia	SC	29201	803-765-2309	
Web: www.heathwood.org					
Hella Corporate Center USA Inc					
43811 Plymouth Oaks Blvd	Plymouth	MI	48170	734-414-0900	
Web: www.hella.com					
Henderson Hills Baptist Church					
1200 E I 35 Frontage Rd	Edmond	OK	73034	405-341-4639	
TF: 877-901-4639 ■ *Web:* www.hhbc.com					
Highline United Methodist Church					
13015 First Ave S	Burien	WA	98168	206-241-5520	
Web: highlineunitedmethodistchurch.org					
Hillcrest Church of Christ 307 Oak St	Tunnel Hill	GA	30755	706-673-2234	
Hilldale Church of Christ Inc 501 Hwy 76	Clarksville	TN	37043	931-647-5264	
Web: hilldalecc.org					
Hillel: The Foundation for Jewish Campus Life					
800 Eighth St NW	Washington	DC	20001	202-449-6500	
Web: www.hillel.org					
Holy Cross Family Ministries					
518 Washington St	North Easton	MA	02356	508-238-4095	
TF: 800-299-7729 ■ *Web:* www.hcfm.org					
Holy Spirit Catholic School					
540 N Seventh Ave	Pocatello	ID	83201	208-232-5763	
Web: www.hscssa.org					
Horizon Christian Fellowship PO Box 17480	San Diego	CA	92177	858-277-4991	
Web: www.horizonchristianfellowship.org					
Hunter Memorial Presbyterian Church Inc					
109 Rosemont Gdn	Lexington	KY	40503	859-277-5126	
Web: hunterlex.org					
IFCA International 3520 Fairlane Ave SW	Grandville	MI	49418	616-531-1840	531-1814
TF: 800-347-1840 ■ *Web:* www.ifca.org					
Iglesia Adventista Del Septimo Dia					
9735 N Houston Rosslyn Rd	Houston	TX	77040	713-937-1200	
Iglesia Ni Cristo Church of Christ					
505 E 36th St	Long Beach	CA	90807	562-490-9757	
Web: incmedia.org					
Immanuel Lutheran Church 2120 Lakewood Ave	Lima	OH	45805	419-222-2541	
Web: www.wcoil.com					
Immanuel Lutheran Communities					
185 Crestline Ave	Kalispell	MT	59901	406-752-9622	
Web: ilcorp.org					
Incarnation Lutheran Church					
4880 Hodgson Rd	Saint Paul	MN	55126	651-766-0723	
Web: www.incarnationmn.org					
Interfaith Action of Greater Saint Paul					
1671 Summit Ave	Saint Paul	MN	55105	651-646-8805	
Web: interfaithaction.org					
Interfaith Ministries for Greater Houston					
3217 Montrose Blvd	Houston	TX	77006	713-533-4900	
TF: 800-511-0999 ■ *Web:* www.imgh.org					
International Bible Society (IBS)					
Biblica 1820 Jet Stream Dr	Colorado Springs	CO	80921	719-488-9200	867-2870
TF Cust Svc: 800-524-1588 ■ *Web:* www.biblica.com					
International Centers for Spiritual Living					
2825 E 33rd Ave	Spokane	WA	99223	509-534-1011	
Web: www.cslspokane.org					
International Church of the Foursquare Gospel (ICFG)					
1910 W Sunset Blvd PO Box 26902	Los Angeles	CA	90026	213-989-4234	989-4590
TF: 888-635-4234 ■ *Web:* www.foursquare.org					
International Pentecostal Holiness Church (IPHC)					
PO Box 12609	Oklahoma City	OK	73157	405-787-7110	789-3957
TF: 888-474-2966 ■ *Web:* www.iphc.org					
Interserve USA PO Box 418	Upper Darby	PA	19082	610-352-0581	
TF: 800-809-4440 ■ *Web:* www.interserveusa.org					
InterVarsity Christian Fellowship/USA					
6400 Schroeder Rd	Madison	WI	53711	608-274-9001	274-7882
TF: 866-734-4823 ■ *Web:* www.intervarsity.org					
Jericho Road Ministries Inc					
1090 Mondon Hill Rd	Brooksville	FL	34601	352-799-2912	
Web: www.jericho-road.net					
Jesse Duplantis Ministries					
1973 Ormond Blvd	Destrehan	LA	70047	985-764-2000	
Jewish Community Centers Assn of North America					
520 Eigth Ave	New York	NY	10018	212-532-4949	481-4174
Web: www.jcca.org					
Jewish National Fund (JNF) 42 E 69th St	New York	NY	10021	212-879-9300	
TF: 800-542-8733 ■ *Web:* www.jnf.org					
Jewish Reconstructionist Federation (JRF)					
101 Greenwood Ave	Jenkintown	PA	19046	215-885-5601	885-5603
TF: 877-226-7573 ■ *Web:* archive.jewishrecon.org					

	City	State	Zip	Phone	Fax
Jewish United Fund/Jewish Federation of Metropolitan Chicago (JUF)					
30 S Wells St	Chicago	IL	60606	312-346-6700	444-2086
TF: 855-275-5237 ■ *Web:* www.juf.org					
Jews for Jesus 60 Haight St	San Francisco	CA	94102	415-864-2600	552-8325
TF: 800-366-5521 ■ *Web:* jewsforjesus.org					
Jimmy Swaggart Ministries (JSM)					
8919 World Ministry Blvd PO Box 262550	Baton Rouge	LA	70810	225-768-8300	
TF Orders: 800-288-8350 ■ *Web:* www.jsm.org					
Kalamazoo Community Foundation					
151 S Rose St Ste 332	Kalamazoo	MI	49007	269-381-4416	
Web: www.kalfound.org					
Kalamazoo Gospel Mission 448 N Burdick St	Kalamazoo	MI	49007	269-345-2974	
Web: kzoogospel.org					
Kensington Community Church 1825 E Sq Lake Rd	Troy	MI	48085	248-786-0600	
Web: kensingtonchurch.org					
Kingsway Charities 1119 Commonwealth Ave	Bristol	VA	24201	276-466-3014	466-0955
TF: 800-321-9234 ■ *Web:* www.kingswaycharities.org					
Lake Junaluska Assembly					
Lake Junaluska Conference					
Retreat Ctr 689 N Lakeshore Dr	Lake Junaluska	NC	28745	828-452-2881	
TF: 800-482-1442 ■ *Web:* www.lakejunaluska.com					
Lakewood United Methodist Church of North Little Rock					
1922 Topf Rd	North Little Rock	AR	72116	501-753-6186	
Web: www.expandingthelight.org					
Life Baptist Church Mission Cottage					
158 Sandy Acres Way	Saint Stephen	SC	29479	843-567-4775	
Life of Learning Foundation 459 Galice Rd	Merlin	OR	97532	541-476-1200	
Web: guyfinley.org					
Life Outreach International					
1801 W Euless Blvd	Euless	TX	76040	817-267-4211	
Web: www.lifetoday.org					
Lifechurch-tv 4600 E Second St	Edmond	OK	73034	405-478-5433	
Web: www.life.church					
Lincoln Lutheran of Racine Inc 2132 Center St	Racine	WI	53403	262-634-1426	
Little Promise Keepers					
12320 Cypress N Houston Rd	Cypress	TX	77429	281-807-0009	807-0009
Living Faith Christian Church					
19503 Business Ctr Dr	Northridge	CA	91324	818-709-8532	
Web: living.org					
Lone Oak First Baptist Church Inc					
3601 Lone Oak Rd	Paducah	KY	42003	270-554-1441	
Web: loneoakfbc.org					
Lord of Life Lutheran Church Lcms					
3601 W 15th St	Plano	TX	75075	972-867-5588	
Web: planolutheran.com					
Lutheran Church Missouri Synod (LCMS)					
1333 S Kirkwood Rd	Saint Louis	MO	63122	314-965-9000	
TF: 888-843-5267 ■ *Web:* www.lcms.org					
Lutheran Church of Hope					
925 Jordan Creek Pkwy	West Des Moines	IA	50266	515-222-1520	
Web: www.hopewdm.org					
Lutheran Home at Hollidaysburg, The					
916 Hickory St	Hollidaysburg	PA	16648	814-696-4527	
TF: 800-400-2285 ■ *Web:* www.alsm.org					
Lutheran Home of The Cannon Valley Inc					
900 Cannon Vly Dr	Northfield	MN	55057	507-645-9511	
Web: www.northfieldretirement.org					
Lutheran Metropolitan Ministry Admin					
1468 W 25th St	Cleveland	OH	44113	216-696-5507	
Web: www.lutheranmetro.org					
Mandarin Presbyterian Church Inc, The					
11844 Mandarin Rd	Jacksonville	FL	32223	904-680-9944	
Mel Trotter Ministries 363 E State St	Belding	MI	48809	616-794-9844	
Web: meltrotter.org					
Messiah Lutheran Church					
303 Rt- 101 PO Box 488	Amherst	NH	03031	603-673-2011	
Web: www.messiahnh.org					
Messiah Village 100 Mt Allen Dr Ofc	Mechanicsburg	PA	17055	717-790-8232	
Web: messiahlifeways.org/residential-communities/messiah-village					
Mission Aviation Fellowship (MAF)					
112 N Pilatus Ln	Nampa	ID	83687	208-498-0800	498-0801
TF: 800-359-7623 ■ *Web:* www.maf.org					
Mission Springs Community Church of Fremont Inc					
48989 Milmont Dr	Fremont	CA	94538	510-490-0446	
Web: msccfremont.org					
Missouri Slope Lutheran Care Center Foundation					
2425 Hillview Ave	Bismarck	ND	58501	701-223-9407	
Web: www.mslcc.com					
Morningside Ministries 700 Babcock Rd	San Antonio	TX	78201	210-734-1000	
Web: mmliving.org					
Morris Cerullo World Evangelism					
3545 Aero Ct Frnt	San Diego	CA	92123	858-277-2200	
Web: www.mcwe.com					
Muslim Community Assn 2301 Plymouth Rd	Ann Arbor	MI	48105	734-665-6772	
Web: www.mca-aa.org					
NA of Congregational Christian Churches (NACCC)					
8473 S Howell Ave	Oak Creek	WI	53154	414-764-1620	764-0319
TF: 800-262-1620 ■ *Web:* www.naccc.org					
NA of Free Will Baptists (NAFWB)					
5233 Mt View Rd	Antioch	TN	37013	615-731-6812	731-0771
TF: 877-767-7659 ■ *Web:* www.nafwb.org					
Nashville Rescue Mission 639 Lafayette St	Nashville	TN	37203	615-255-2475	
Web: www.nashvillerescuemission.org					
Nation of Islam 7351 S Stony Island	Chicago	IL	60649	773-324-6000	
Web: www.noi.org					
National Baptist Convention of America Inc					
777 SRL Thornton Fwy	Dallas	TX	75203	214-942-3311	942-4696
Web: www.nbcainc.com					
National Baptist Convention USA Inc					
1700 Baptist World Ctr Dr	Nashville	TN	37207	615-228-6292	262-3917
TF: 866-531-3054 ■ *Web:* www.nationalbaptist.com					
National Spiritual Assembly of the Baha'is of the US					
1233 Central St	Evanston	IL	60201	847-733-3400	
Web: www.bahai.us					

Organization	City	State	Zip	Phone	Fax
Navigators of Canada 11 St John'S Dr *TF:* 866-202-6287 ■ *Web:* www.navigators.ca	Arva	ON	N0M1C0	519-660-8300	
Navigators, The 3820 N 30th St PO Box 6000 *TF:* 866-568-7827 ■ *Web:* www.navigators.org	Colorado Springs	CO	80934	719-598-1212	260-0479
Nebraska Synod Evangelical Lutheran Church in America 4980 S 118th St Ste D *TF:* 877-366-7242 ■ *Web:* nebraskasynod.org	Omaha	NE	68137	402-896-5311	
New Covenant Fellowship Church 18901 Waring Stn Rd *Web:* www.fellowshipusa.com	Germantown	MD	20874	301-444-3100	
New Hampshire Catholic Charities Inc 215 Myrtle St *TF:* 800-562-5249 ■ *Web:* www.cc-nh.org	Manchester	NH	03104	603-669-3030	626-1252
New Hope Housing Inc 8407-E Richmond Hwy *Web:* www.newhopehousing.org	Alexandria	VA	22309	703-799-2293	
New Tribes Mission (NTM) 1000 E First St *TF:* 800-321-5375 ■ *Web:* ntm.org	Sanford	FL	32771	407-323-3430	
Oak Cliff Bible Fellowship 1808 W Camp Wisdom Rd *Web:* www.ocbfchurch.org	Dallas	TX	75232	972-228-1281	
Oklahoma Methodist Manor Inc 4134 E 31st St *Web:* www.ommtulsa.org	Tulsa	OK	74135	918-743-2565	
Open Door Mission 5803 Harrisburg Blvd *Web:* www.opendoorhouston.org	Houston	TX	77011	713-923-8743	921-4206
Orgill Singer 8360 W Sahara Ave Ste 110 *TF:* 800-745-3065 ■ *Web:* www.orgillsinger.com	Las Vegas	NV	89117	702-796-9100	
Orlando Union Rescue Mission 1525 W Washington St *Web:* www.ourm.org	Orlando	FL	32805	407-423-2131	
Orthodox Union (OU) 11 Broadway *TF:* 855-505-7500 ■ *Web:* www.ou.org	New York	NY	10004	212-563-4000	564-9058
Oshkosh Convention & Visitors Bureau 2401 W Waukau Ave *TF:* 877-303-9200 ■ *Web:* www.visitoshkosh.com	Oshkosh	WI	54904	920-303-9200	
Palma Ceia United Methodist Church Day School & Day Care 3723 W Bay To Bay Blvd *Web:* palmaceiaumc.org	Tampa	FL	33629	813-837-1541	837-3600
Pathway to Peace Christian Church 5808 Lynn Rd	Tampa	FL	33624	813-908-0893	
Pentecostal Assemblies 3214 S Service Rd *TF:* 800-295-6368 ■ *Web:* www.paoc.org	Burlington	ON	L7N3J2	905-637-7558	
Perimeter Church 9500 Medlock Bridge Rd *Web:* www.perimeter.org	Johns Creek	CO	30097	678-405-2000	405-2009
Pioneers 10123 William Carey Dr *TF:* 800-359-9297 ■ *Web:* www.pioneers.org	Orlando	FL	32832	407-382-6000	382-1008
Potomac Conference Corp of Seventh Day Adventists 606 Greenville Ave *TF:* 800-732-1844 ■ *Web:* www.pcsda.org	Staunton	VA	24401	540-886-0771	886-5734
Presby's Inspired Life 2000 Joshua Rd *TF:* 877-977-3729 ■ *Web:* www.presbysinspiredlife.org	Lafayette Hill	PA	19444	610-834-1001	
Presbyterian Childrens Services Inc 1220 N Lindbergh Blvd *TF:* 800-383-8147 ■ *Web:* missouri.pchas.org	St. Louis	MO	63132	314-989-9727	427-2682
Presbyterian Church in America (PCA) 1700 N Brown Rd Ste 105 *Web:* pcanet.org	Lawrenceville	GA	30043	678-825-1000	825-1001
Presbyterian Church (USA) 100 Witherspoon St *TF:* 888-728-7228 ■ *Web:* www.pcusa.org	Louisville	KY	40202	502-569-5000	
Prince of Peace United Methodist Church of Elk Grove Village 1400 S Arlington Heights Rd *Web:* princeofpeaceumc.org	Elk Grove Village	IL	60007	847-439-0668	439-0715
Progressive National Baptist Convention Inc (PNBC) 601 50th St NE *TF:* 800-876-7622 ■ *Web:* www.pnbc.org	Washington	DC	20019	202-396-0558	398-4998
Promise Keepers (PK) PO Box 11798 *Fax Area Code: 303 ■ *TF:* 866-776-6473 ■ *Web:* promisekeepers.org	Denver	CO	80211	866-776-6473	433-1036*
Rabbinical Assembly 3080 Broadway *Web:* www.rabbinicalassembly.org	New York	NY	10027	212-280-6000	
Reconstructionist Rabbinical Assn (RRA) 1299 Church Rd *Web:* www.therra.org	Wyncote	PA	19095	215-576-5210	576-8051
Redeemer Lutheran Church of Waverly Bremer County Iowa 2001 W Bremer Ave *Web:* redeemerwaverly.org	Waverly	IA	50677	319-352-1325	
Redemptorist, The 1 Liguori Dr *TF:* 800-325-9521 ■ *Web:* www.liguori.org	Liguori	MO	63057	636-464-2500	
Reformed Church in America 475 Riverside Dr 18th Fl *TF:* 800-722-9977 ■ *Web:* www.rca.org	New York	NY	10115	212-870-3071	870-2499
Reid Temple African Methodist Episcopal Church 11400 Glenn Dale Blvd *Web:* reidtemple.org	Glenn Dale	MD	20769	301-352-0320	
Revival Slavic Christian Center of The Assemblies of God 5601 Hemlock St *Web:* revivalscc.com	Sacramento	CA	95841	916-332-2897	
Rio Grande Bible Institute & Language School 4300 S Us Hwy 281 *Web:* www.riogrande.edu	Edinburg	TX	78539	956-380-8100	
Rock Family Worship Center, The 2300 Memorial Pkwy SW *Web:* www.therockfwc.org	Huntsville	AL	35801	256-533-9292	
Saint Luke Baptist Church 476 Glen Iris Dr Ne	Atlanta	GA	30308	404-688-0528	
Seat of the Soul Foundation PO Box 3310 *TF:* 877-733-4279 ■ *Web:* www.seatofthesoul.com	Ashland	OR	97520	541-482-1515	482-9417
Seventh-day Adventist World Church 12501 Old Columbia Pike *TF:* 800-226-1119 ■ *Web:* www.adventist.org	Silver Spring	MD	20904	301-680-6000	680-6090
Shandon Baptist Church 5250 Forest Dr *Web:* www.shandon.org	Columbia	SC	29206	803-782-1300	
Sim USA Inc PO Box 7900 *TF:* 800-521-6449 ■ *Web:* www.simusa.org	Charlotte	NC	28241	800-521-6449	
Sisters of Mercy of The Americas Northeast Community Inc 55 E Cedar St	Newington	CT	06111	860-594-8619	
Sisters of Saint Francis 1545 S Layton Blvd *Web:* www.lbwn.org	Milwaukee	WI	53215	414-383-9038	
Sisters of st Francis of Assisi of 3221 S Lake Dr *Web:* lakeosfs.org	Saint Francis	WI	53235	414-744-1160	
Sisters of The Presentation 281 Masonic Ave *Web:* www.presentationsisterssf.org	San Francisco	CA	94118	415-422-5001	
Sixth & i Historic Synagogue 600 I St NW *Web:* sixthandi.org	Washington	DC	20001	202-408-3100	
Smith Chapel Free Will Baptist Church 519 Boundary Ln	Fayetteville	NC	28301	910-483-4437	
Society of Biblical Literature (SBL) The Luce Ctr 825 Houston Mill Rd *TF:* 866-727-9955 ■ *Web:* www.sbl-site.org	Atlanta	GA	30329	404-727-3100	727-3101
Southern Baptist Convention (SBC) 901 Commerce St *TF:* 866-722-5433 ■ *Web:* www.sbc.net	Nashville	TN	37203	615-244-2355	
St. Athanasius Rectory 2050 E Walnut Ln *Web:* stathanasiuschurch.us	Philadelphia	PA	19138	215-548-2700	
St. Barnabas Episcopal Church in The City of Lafayette 400 Camellia Blvd *Web:* saintbarnabas.us	Lafayette	LA	70503	337-984-3848	
St. Benedict's Monastery 104 Chapel Ln *Web:* sbm.osb.org	St Joseph	MN	56374	320-363-7116	
St. Brendans Church 333 E 206th St *Web:* saintbrendanchurch.org	Bronx	NY	10467	718-547-6655	
St. David's Episcopal Church & School 1300 Wiltshire Ave *Web:* saintdavids.net	San Antonio	TX	78209	210-824-2481	
St. George Greek Orthodox Church 1200 Klockner Rd *Web:* stgeorgetrenton.nj.goarch.org	Trenton	NJ	08619	609-586-4448	
St. John Lutheran Church 1140 W River Rd N *Web:* stjohnlutheran-elyria.org	Elyria	OH	44035	440-324-4070	
St. Johns Ev Lutheran Church & School 20801 W Forest View Dr	Lannon	WI	53046	262-251-2910	
St. Marks Evangelical Lutheran Church of North st Paul Minnesota Paul Minn 2499 Helen St N *Web:* stmarks-nsp.org	Saint Paul	MN	55109	651-777-7451	
St. Mary Missionary Baptist Church of Plant City 1840 E State Rd 60	Plant City	FL	33567	813-737-3668	
St. Mary's Catholic Church 120 E Miller St	Alpena	MI	49707	989-354-2322	
St. Matthews Parish School 1031 Bienveneda Ave *Web:* www.stmatthewsschool.com	Pacific Palisades	CA	90272	310-454-1350	
St. Peter The Apostle Church 19851 Anita St	Harper Woods	MI	48225	313-885-0975	
St. Stephens Episcopal Church 351 Main St *Web:* www.ststephens-ridgefield.org	Ridgefield	CT	06877	203-438-3789	
St. Thomas Aquinas Catholic Newman Center at Unlv 4765 Brussels St	Las Vegas	NV	89119	702-736-0887	
Summit Publications Inc 63 Summit Way *Web:* www.summitlighthouse.org	Gardiner	MT	59030	406-848-9200	
Sun Valley Community Church 456 E Ray Rd *Web:* www.sunvalleycc.com	Gilbert	AZ	85296	480-632-8920	
Sunrise Community Evangelical Free Church Inc 298 Aquatic Dr *Web:* sccjax.org	Atlantic Beach	FL	32233	904-249-3030	
TD Jakes Ministries 3635 Dan Morton Dr *Web:* tdjakes.org	Dallas	TX	75236	225-407-2291	
Tennessee Baptist Convention 5001 Maryland Way *TF:* 800-558-2090 ■ *Web:* www.tnbaptist.org	Brentwood	TN	37027	615-371-2029	
Texas Presbyterian Foundation 6100 Colwell Blvd Ste 250 *TF:* 800-955-3155 ■ *Web:* www.tpf.org	Irving	TX	75039	214-522-3155	522-3157
Thankful Baptist Church 1608 W Allegheny Ave	Philadelphia	PA	19132	215-229-5024	
Third Millennium Ministries 316 Live Oaks Blvd *TF:* 877-443-6455 ■ *Web:* www.thirdmill.org	Casselberry	FL	32707	407-830-0222	
Traditional Values Coalition (TVC) 139 C St SE *Web:* www.traditionalvalues.org	Washington	DC	20003	202-547-8570	546-6403
Union for Reformed Judaism 633 Third Ave *Web:* www.urj.org	New York	NY	10017	212-650-4000	
Unitarian Universalist Assn (UUA) 25 Beacon St *Web:* www.uua.org	Boston	MA	02108	617-742-2100	367-3237
United Church of Christ (UCC) 700 Prospect Ave *TF:* 866-822-8224 ■ *Web:* www.ucc.org	Cleveland	OH	44115	216-736-2100	736-2103
United Church of God an International Assocation 555 Techne Ctr Dr *Web:* www.ucg.org	Milford	OH	45150	513-576-9796	
United Methodist Retirement & Health Care Center Inc, The 2316 W Modelle Ave *Web:* umhcc-clinton.com	Clinton	OK	73601	580-323-0912	
United Pentecostal Church International (UPCI) 8855 Dunn Rd *Web:* www.upci.org	Hazelwood	MO	63042	314-837-7300	
United Synagogue of Conservative Judaism (USCJ) 820 Second Ave *Web:* www.uscj.org	New York	NY	10017	212-533-7800	353-9439
Urban Alternative PO Box 4000 *TF:* 800-800-3222 ■ *Web:* www.tonyevans.org	Dallas	TX	75208	214-943-3868	
US Conference of Catholic Bishops (USCCB) 3211 Fourth St NE *TF:* 866-582-0943 ■ *Web:* www.usccb.org	Washington	DC	20017	202-541-3000	541-3322
US National Committee to the International Dairy Federation PO Box 930398 *Web:* www.usnac.org	Verona	WI	53593	608-219-4115	262-1278

Phone | Fax

Vanguard Communications of Falls Church Inc
2121 K St NW Ste 650 — Washington DC 20037 — 202-331-4323
Web: www.vancomm.com

Voice of God Recordings Inc, The
5911 Charlestown Pk — Jeffersonville IN 47130 — 812-256-1177
Web: www.branham.org

Watchtower Bible & Tract Society Inc
25 Columbia Heights — Brooklyn NY 11201 — 718-560-5000
Web: www.jw.org

Welborn Baptist Foundation Inc
21 SE 3rd St Ste 610 — Evansville IN 47708 — 812-437-8260 — 437-8269
Web: welbornfdn.org

Wesbury United Methodist Community
31 N Park Ave — Meadville PA 16335 — 814-332-9000
TF: 877-937-2879 ■ *Web:* www.wesbury.com

Westside Baptist Church Inc of Haines City
1416 Polk City Rd — Haines City FL 33844 — 863-422-4720

Westwood Baptist Church 41 State Farm Rd — Alexandria AL 36250 — 256-820-2211
Web: www.westwoodbaptist.net

Westwood Community Church 401 Wwood Dr — Winnipeg MB R3K1G4 — 204-888-1771
Web: westwood.mb.ca

Wheat Ridge Ministries 1 Pierce Pl Ste 250E — Itasca IL 60143 — 630-766-9066 — 766-9622
TF: 800-762-6748 ■ *Web:* www.wheatridge.org

White Chapel Church of God Inc
1730 S Ridgewood Ave — South Daytona FL 32119 — 386-760-6834
Web: www.wcaeagles.org

Wider Church Ministries 700 Prospect Ave — Cleveland OH 44115 — 216-736-3200 — 736-3203
TF: 866-822-8224 ■ *Web:* www.ucc.org

Wisconsin Evangelical Lutheran Synod (WELS)
2929 N Mayfair Rd — Milwaukee WI 53222 — 414-256-3888 — 256-3899
Web: www.wels.net

Woman's Missionary Union (WMU)
100 Missionary Ridge — Birmingham AL 35242 — 205-991-8100
TF: 800-968-7301 ■ *Web:* www.wmu.com

Women in Touch Ministries Wit Inc
1044 W 37th St — Indianapolis IN 46208 — 317-925-4177

Word of Faith Family Worship Cathedral
212 Riverside Pkwy — Austell GA 30168 — 770-874-8400
Web: woffamily.org

Word of Life Fellowship Church Inc, The
3650 Greenbush St — Lafayette IN 47905 — 765-449-4008

World Gospel Mission (WGM)
3783 E State Rd 18 PO Box 948 — Marion IN 46952 — 765-664-7331 — 671-7230
TF: 800-426-0846 ■ *Web:* www.wgm.org

World Literature CrUSAde
640 Chapel Hills Dr — Colorado Springs CO 80920 — 719-260-8888
TF: 800-423-5054 ■ *Web:* ehc.org

World Methodist Council PO Box 518 — Lake Junaluska NC 28745 — 828-456-9432
Web: www.worldmethodistcouncil.org

WorldVenture 1501 W Mineral Ave — Littleton CO 80120 — 720-283-2000 — 283-9383
Web: www.worldventure.com

Worship Center Christian Church, The
9553 Pkwy E — Birmingham AL 35215 — 205-451-1750
Web: www.theworshipcentercc.org

Wycliffe Bible Translators
11221 John Wycliffe Blvd — Orlando FL 32832 — 407-852-3600 — 852-3601
TF: 800-992-5433 ■ *Web:* www.wycliffe.org

Yogi Divine Society 2437 Yeoman St — Waukegan IL 60087 — 847-336-6451

Young Israel of New Rochelle 1149 N Ave — New Rochelle NY 10804 — 914-636-2215
TF: 888-942-3638 ■ *Web:* www.youngisrael.org

Young Life 420 N Cascade Ave — Colorado Springs CO 80903 — 719-381-1800
Web: www.younglife.org

Youth for Christ/USA 7670 S Vaughn Ct — Englewood CO 80112 — 303-843-9000 — 843-9002
Web: yfc.givingfuel.com/30913

48-21 Self-Help Organizations

Phone | Fax

Adult Children of Alcoholics World Service Organization Inc (ACAWSO)
PO Box 3216 — Torrance CA 90510 — 562-595-7831
Web: www.adultchildren.org

Al-Anon Family Group Inc
1600 Corporate Landing Pkwy — Virginia Beach VA 23454 — 757-563-1600 — 563-1655
TF: 888-425-2666 ■ *Web:* www.al-anon.org

Alcoholics Anonymous (AA)
475 Riverside Dr 11th Fl — New York NY 10115 — 212-870-3400 — 870-3003
Web: www.aa.org

ARTS Anonymous PO Box 230175 — New York NY 10023 — 718-251-3828
Web: www.artsanonymous.org

Bereaved Parents of the USA PO Box 95 — Park Forest IL 60466 — 708-748-7866
Web: www.bereavedparentsusa.org

Calix Society, The 3881 Highland Ave Ste 201 — St Paul MN 55110 — 651-773-3117
TF: 800-398-0524 ■ *Web:* www.calixsociety.org

Candlelighters Childhood Cancer Foundation
10920 Connecticut Ave Suuite A PO Box 498 — Kensington MD 20895 — 301-962-3520 — 962-3521
TF: 800-366-2223 ■ *Web:* www.acco.org

Chemically Dependent Anonymous (CDA)
PO Box 423 — Severna Park MD 21146 — 888-232-4673
TF: 888-232-4673 ■ *Web:* cdawebsitedev.com

Children of Lesbians & Gays Everywhere (COLAGE)
3815 S Othello St Ste 100 — Seattle WA 98118 — 415-861-5437
TF: 800-657-3717 ■ *Web:* www.colage.org

Co-Anon Family Groups PO Box 12722 — Tucson AZ 85732 — 520-513-5028
TF: 800-898-9985 ■ *Web:* www.co-anon.org

Co-Dependents Anonymous Inc (CODA) PO Box 33577 — Phoenix AZ 85067 — 602-277-7991
TF: 888-444-2359 ■ *Web:* www.codependents.org

Cocaine Anonymous World Services Inc (CA)
PO Box 492000 — Los Angeles CA 90049 — 310-559-5833 — 559-2554
TF: 800-347-8998 ■ *Web:* www.ca.org

Community Teamwork Inc 155 Merrimack St — Lowell MA 01852 — 978-459-0551
Web: www.commteam.org

Compassionate Friends PO Box 3696 — Oak Brook IL 60522 — 630-990-0010 — 990-0246
TF: 877-969-0010 ■ *Web:* www.compassionatefriends.org

Compulsive Eaters Anonymous - HOW (CEA-HOW)
5500 E Atherton St Ste 227B — Long Beach CA 90815 — 562-342-9344
Web: www.ceahow.org

Concerned United Birthparents Inc (CUB)
PO Box 503475 — San Diego CA 92150 — 800-822-2777 — 712-3317*
**Fax Area Code:* 858 ■ *TF:* 800-822-2777 ■ *Web:* www.cubirthparents.org

Concerns of Police Survivors Inc (COPS)
846 Old S 5 PO Box 3199 — Camdenton MO 65020 — 573-346-4911 — 346-1414
TF: 800-784-2677 ■ *Web:* www.nationalcops.org

Crystal Meth Anonymous General Service Organization (CMA)
4470 W Sunset Blvd Ste 107 PO Box 555 — Los Angeles CA 90027 — 877-262-6691
TF: 877-262-6691 ■ *Web:* www.crystalmeth.org

Debtors Anonymous (DA) PO Box 920888 — Needham MA 02492 — 781-453-2743 — 453-2745
TF: 800-421-2383 ■ *Web:* www.debtorsanonymous.org

Depressed Anonymous PO Box 17414 — Louisville KY 40217 — 502-569-1989
Web: www.depressedanon.com

DignityUSA Inc PO Box 376 — Medford MA 02155 — 202-861-0017 — 397-0584*
**Fax Area Code:* 781 ■ *TF:* 800-877-8797 ■ *Web:* www.dignityusa.org

Food Addicts In Recovery Anonymous (FA)
400 W Cummings Pk Ste 1700 — Woburn MA 01801 — 781-932-6300 — 932-6322
Web: www.foodaddicts.org

Gam-Anon International Service Office Inc
PO Box 157 — Whitestone NY 11357 — 718-352-1671 — 746-2571
Web: www.gam-anon.org

Gamblers Anonymous (GA) PO Box 17173 — Los Angeles CA 90017 — 626-960-3500 — 960-3501
Web: www.gamblersanonymous.org

GROW Inc 2403 W Springfield Ave PO Box 3667 — Champaign IL 61826 — 217-352-6989 — 352-8530
Web: www.growinamerica.org

HEARTBEAT/Survivors After Suicide Inc
2015 Devon St — Colorado Springs CO 80909 — 719-596-2575
Web: www.heartbeatsurvivorsaftersuicide.org

Incest Survivors Anonymous (ISA)
PO Box 17245 — Long Beach CA 90807 — 562-428-5599
Web: www.lafn.org/medical/isa

International Lawyers in Alcoholics Anonymous (ILAA)
415-1080 Mainland St — Vancouver BC V6B2T4 — 604-685-2171
TF: 888-685-2171 ■ *Web:* www.ilaa.org

Jewish Alcoholics Chemically Dependent Persons & Significant Others
135 W 50th St 6th Fl — New York NY 10020 — 212-632-4600 — 399-3525
Web: jewishboard.org/listing/jewish-alcoholics-chemically-dependent-persons-and-significant-others-jacs

LifeRing Secular Recovery
1440 Broadway Ste 312 — Oakland CA 94612 — 510-763-0779 — 763-1513
TF: 800-811-4142 ■ *Web:* www.lifering.org

Lightning Strike & Electric Shock Survivors International Inc (LSESSI)
PO Box 1156 — Jacksonville NC 28541 — 910-346-4708
Web: www.lightning-strike.org

Marijuana Anonymous World Services (MAWS)
PO Box 7807 — Torrance CA 90504 — 800-766-6779
TF: 800-766-6779 ■ *Web:* www.marijuana-anonymous.org

MISS Foundation PO Box 5333 — Peoria AZ 85385 — 623-979-1000 — 979-1001
TF: 888-455-6477 ■ *Web:* www.missfoundation.org

Moderation Management Network Inc (MM)
22 W 27th St — New York NY 10001 — 212-871-0974
Web: www.moderation.org

Native American Indian General Service Office of Alcoholics Anonymous (NAIGSO-AA)
PO Box 1253 — Lakeside CA 92040 — 951-927-2626
Web: www.naigso-aa.org

Overcomers in Christ PO Box 34460 — Omaha NE 68134 — 402-573-0966
TF: 866-573-0966 ■ *Web:* www.overcomersinchrist.org

Overcomers Outreach PO Box 922950 — Sylmar CA 91392 — 818-833-1803 — 833-1546
TF: 800-310-3001 ■ *Web:* www.overcomersoutreach.org

Overeaters Anonymous Inc (OA) PO Box 44020 — Rio Rancho NM 87174 — 505-891-2664 — 891-4320
TF: 866-505-4966 ■ *Web:* www.oa.org

Rest Ministries Inc PO Box 502928 — San Diego CA 92150 — 858-486-4685
Web: www.restministries.com

S-Anon International Family Groups Inc
PO Box 111242 — Nashville TN 37222 — 615-833-3152
TF: 800-210-8141 ■ *Web:* www.sanon.org

Secular Organizations for Sobriety (SOS)
4773 Hollywood Blvd — Hollywood CA 90027 — 323-666-4295 — 666-4271
Web: www.cfiwest.org/sos

Sex & Love Addicts Anonymous (SLAA)
1550 NE Loop 410 Ste 118 — San Antonio TX 78209 — 210-828-7900 — 828-7922
Web: www.slaafws.org

Sex Addicts Anonymous (SAA) PO Box 70949 — Houston TX 77270 — 713-869-4902 — 692-0105
TF: 800-477-8191 ■ *Web:* www.saa-recovery.org

Sexaholics Anonymous (SA) PO Box 3565 — Brentwood TN 37024 — 615-370-6062 — 370-0882
TF: 866-424-8777 ■ *Web:* www.sa.org

SHARE Pregnancy & Infant Loss Support Inc
402 Jackson St — Saint Charles MO 63301 — 636-947-6164 — 947-7486
TF: 800-821-6819 ■ *Web:* www.nationalshare.org

Single Mothers by Choice Inc (SMC) PO Box 1642 — New York NY 10028 — 212-988-0993
Web: www.singlemothersbychoice.org

Sisters Network Inc 2922 Rosedale St — Houston TX 77004 — 713-781-0255 — 780-8998
TF: 866-781-1808 ■ *Web:* www.sistersnetworkinc.org

SMART Recovery 7304 Mentor Ave Ste F — Mentor OH 44060 — 440-951-5357 — 951-5358
TF: 866-951-5357 ■ *Web:* www.smartrecovery.org

Straight Spouse Network (SSN) PO Box 4985 — Chicago IL 60080 — 773-413-8213
Web: www.straightspouse.org

Survivors Network of Those Abused by Priests (SNAP)
PO Box 6416 — Chicago IL 60680 — 312-455-1499
TF: 877-762-7432 ■ *Web:* www.snapnetwork.org

Survivors of Incest Anonymous (SIA) PO Box 190 — Benson MD 21018 — 410-893-3322
Web: www.siawso.org

TOPS Club Inc 4575 S Fifth St — Milwaukee WI 53207 — 414-482-4620 — 482-1655
TF: 800-932-8677 ■ *Web:* www.tops.org

Twinless Twins Support Group International (TTSG)
PO Box 980481 — Ypsilanti MI 48198 — 888-205-8962
TF: 888-205-8962 ■ *Web:* www.twinlesstwins.org

Valley of the Sun United Way
1515 E Osborn Rd — Phoenix AZ 85014 — 602-631-4800 — 631-4809
TF: 877-322-8228 ■ *Web:* www.vsuw.org

Organization	City	State	ZIP	Phone	Fax
White Bison Inc 5585 Erindale Dr Ste 203 *TF:* 877-871-1495 ■ *Web:* www.whitebison.org	Colorado Springs	CO	80918	719-548-1000	548-9407
Wings Foundation (WINGS) 7550 W Yale Ave Ste B 201 *TF:* 800-373-8671 ■ *Web:* www.wingsfound.org	Denver	CO	80227	303-238-8660	238-4739
Women for Sobriety Inc (WFS) PO Box 618 *Web:* www.womenforsobriety.org	Quakertown	PA	18951	215-536-8026	538-9026
Workaholics Anonymous World Service Organization PO Box 289 *Web:* www.workaholics-anonymous.org	Menlo Park	CA	94026	510-273-9253	

48-22 Sports Organizations

Organization	City	State	ZIP	Phone	Fax
Adventure Cycling Assn 150 E Pine St PO Box 8308 *TF:* 800-755-2453 ■ *Web:* www.adventurecycling.org	Missoula	MT	59807	406-721-1776	721-8754
Aerobics & Fitness Assn of America (AFAA) 15250 Ventura Blvd Ste 200 *TF:* 877-968-7263 ■ *Web:* www.afaa.com	Sherman Oaks	CA	91403	818-905-0040	990-5468
Amateur Athletic Union of the US (AAU) 1910 Hotel Plaza Blvd *TF:* 800-228-4872 ■ *Web:* www.aausports.org	Lake Buena Vista	FL	32830	407-934-7200	934-7242
Amateur Trapshooting Assn (ATA) 601 W National Rd *TF:* 800-671-8042 ■ *Web:* www.shootata.com	Vandalia	OH	45377	937-898-4638	898-5472
American Alliance for Health Physical Education Recreation & Dance (AAH-PERD) 1900 Assn Dr *TF:* 800-213-7193 ■ *Web:* shapeamerica.org	Reston	VA	20191	703-476-3400	476-9527
American Amateur Baseball Congress (AABC) 100 W Broadway *Web:* www.aabc.us	Farmington	NM	87401	505-327-3120	
American Baseball Coaches Assn (ABCA) 108 S University Ave Ste 3 *Web:* www.abca.org	Mount Pleasant	MI	48858	989-775-3300	
American Bicycle Assn (ABA) 1645 W Sunrise Blvd *TF:* 866-650-4867 ■ *Web:* www.usabmx.com	Gilbert	AZ	85233	480-961-1903	961-1842
American Canoe Assn (ACA) 503 Sophia St Ste 100 **Fax Area Code:* 888 ■ *TF:* 888-229-3792 ■ *Web:* www.americancanoe.org	Fredericksburg	VA	22401	540-907-4460	229-3792*
American Council on Exercise (ACE) 4851 Paramount Dr *TF:* 800-825-3636 ■ *Web:* www.acefitness.org	San Diego	CA	92123	858-576-6500	576-6564
American Football Coaches Assn (AFCA) 100 Legends Ln *TF:* 877-557-5338 ■ *Web:* www.afca.com	Waco	TX	76706	254-754-9900	754-7373
American Motorcyclist Assn (AMA) 13515 Yarmouth Dr *TF:* 800-262-5646 ■ *Web:* www.americanmotorcyclist.com	Pickerington	OH	43147	614-856-1900	856-1920
American Poolplayers Assn Inc (APA) 1000 Lk St Louis Blvd Ste 325 *Web:* www.poolplayers.com	Lake Saint Louis	MO	63367	636-625-8611	625-2975
American Running Assn 4405 E W Hwy Ste 405 *TF:* 800-776-2732 ■ *Web:* www.americanrunning.org	Bethesda	MD	20814	301-913-9517	913-9520
American Society of Golf Course Architects (ASGCA) 125 N Executive Dr Ste 106 *Web:* www.asgca.org	Brookfield	WI	53005	262-786-5960	786-5919
American Sportfishing Assn (ASA) 1001 N Fairfax St Ste 501 *Web:* www.asafishing.org	Alexandria	VA	22314	703-519-9691	519-1872
American Sports Institute (ASI) 116 E Blithedale Ave	Mill Valley	CA	94941	415-383-5750	
American Volkssport Assn (AVA) 1001 Pat Booker Rd Ste 101 *TF:* 855-999-5200 ■ *Web:* www.ava.org	Universal City	TX	78148	210-659-2112	659-1212
American Youth Soccer Organization (AYSO) 19750 S Vermont Ave Ste 200 **Fax Area Code:* 310 ■ *TF:* 800-872-2976 ■ *Web:* ayso.org	Torrance	CA	90502	800-872-2976	525-1155*
AMOA-National Dart Assn (NDA) 9100 PuRdue Rd Ste 200 *TF:* 800-808-9884 ■ *Web:* www.ndadarts.com	Indianapolis	IN	46268	317-387-1299	387-0999
Association of Professional Ball Players of America 101 S Kraemer Ave Ste 112 *Web:* www.apbpa.org	Placentia	CA	92870	714-528-2012	528-2037
ATP Tour Inc 201 ATP Tour Blvd *Web:* www.atpworldtour.com	Ponte Vedra Beach	FL	32082	904-285-8000	285-5966
Babe Ruth League Inc 1770 Brunswick Pk PO Box 5000 *TF:* 800-880-3142 ■ *Web:* www.baberuthleague.org	Trenton	NJ	08638	609-695-1434	695-2505
Billiard Congress of America 12303 Airport Way Ste 140 *Web:* bca-pool.com/?	Broomfield	CO	80021	303-243-5070	243-5075
Boat Owners Assn of the US 880 S Pickett St *TF:* 800-395-2628 ■ *Web:* www.boatus.com	Alexandria	VA	22304	703-823-9550	
Cross Country Ski Areas Assn (CCSAA) 259 Bolton Rd *TF:* 877-779-2754 ■ *Web:* www.xcski.org	Winchester	NH	03470	603-239-4341	239-6387
Disabled Sports USA (DS/USA) 451 Hungerford Dr Ste 100 *TF:* 800-543-2754 ■ *Web:* www.disabledsportsusa.org	Rockville	MD	20850	301-217-0960	217-0968
Fellowship of Christian Athletes (FCA) 8701 Leeds Rd *TF:* 800-289-0909 ■ *Web:* www.fca.org	Kansas City	MO	64129	816-921-0909	921-8755
Hockey North America (HNA) 45570 Shepard Dr *TF:* 800-446-2539 ■ *Web:* www.hna.com	Sterling	VA	20164	703-430-8100	421-9205
Ice Skating Institute (ISI) 6000 Custer Rd Bldg 9 *Web:* www.skateisi.com	Plano	TX	75023	972-735-8800	735-8815
IDEA Inc 10455 Pacific Ctr Ct *TF:* 800-999-4332 ■ *Web:* www.ideafit.com	San Diego	CA	92121	858-535-8979	535-8234
International Assn of Approved Basketball Officials (IAABO) PO Box 355 *TF:* 800-526-1379 ■ *Web:* www.iaabo.org	Carlisle	PA	17013	717-713-8129	718-6164
International Collegiate Licensing Assn (ICLA) 24651 Detroit Rd *TF:* 877-887-2261 ■ *Web:* www.nacda.com/icla/nacda-icla.html	Westlake	OH	44145	440-892-4000	892-4007
International Health Racquet & Sportsclub Assn (IHRSA) 70 Fargo St *TF:* 800-228-4772 ■ *Web:* www.ihrsa.org	Boston	MA	02210	617-951-0055	951-0056
International Professional Rodeo Assn (IPRA) 1412 South Agnew *Web:* www.ipra-rodeo.com	Oklahoma City	OK	73108	405-235-6540	
Jockey Club 40 E 52nd St 15th Fl *Web:* www.jockeyclub.com	New York	NY	10022	212-371-5970	371-6123
Jockeys' Guild Inc 103 Wind Haven Dr Ste 200 *TF:* 866-465-6257 ■ *Web:* www.jockeysguild.com	Nicholasville	KY	40356	859-305-0606	219-9892
Ladies Professional Golf Assn (LPGA) 100 International Golf Dr *Web:* www.lpga.com	Daytona Beach	FL	32124	386-274-6200	274-1099
League of American Bicyclists 1612 K St NW Ste 800 *Web:* www.bikeleague.org	Washington	DC	20006	202-822-1333	822-1334
Little League Baseball Inc 539 US Rt 15 Hwy PO Box 3485 *Web:* www.littleleague.org	Williamsport	PA	17701	570-326-1921	326-1074
Maccabi USA/Sports for Israel 1926 Arch St Ste 4R *Web:* www.maccabiusa.com	Philadelphia	PA	19103	215-561-6900	561-5470
Major League Baseball Players Assn 12 E 49th St 24th Fl *Web:* mlbplayers.mlb.com/nasapp/mlb/pa	New York	NY	10017	212-826-0808	752-4378
Minor League Baseball 9550 16th St N *Web:* www.milb.com	Saint Petersburg	FL	33716	727-822-6937	821-5819
NA for Stock Car Auto Racing (NASCAR) 1801 W International Speedway Blvd **Fax Area Code:* 386 ■ **Fax:* Mktg ■ *Web:* www.nascar.com	Daytona Beach	FL	32114	704-348-7131	252-8804*
NA of Collegiate Directors of Athletics (NACDA) 24651 Detroit Rd *TF:* 877-887-2261 ■ *Web:* www.nacda.com	Westlake	OH	44145	440-892-4000	892-4007
NA of Intercollegiate Athletics (NAIA) 1200 Grand Blvd *Web:* www.naia.org	Kansas City	MO	64106	816-595-8000	595-8200
National Aeronautic Assn Hanger 7 1 S Smith Blvd Ste 202 *TF:* 800-644-9777 ■ *Web:* naa.aero	Washington	DC	20001	703-416-4888	
National Alliance for Youth Sports 2050 Vista Pkwy *TF:* 800-729-2057 ■ *Web:* www.nays.org	West Palm Beach	FL	33411	561-684-1141	684-2546
National Athletic Trainers Assn (NATA) 2952 N Stemmons Fwy Ste 200 *TF:* 800-879-6282 ■ *Web:* www.nata.org	Dallas	TX	75247	214-637-6282	637-2206
National Basketball Players Assn (NBPA) 310 Malcolm X Blvd *Web:* www.nbpa.com	New York	NY	10027	212-655-0880	655-0881
National Collegiate Athletic Assn (NCAA) 700 W Washington St PO Box 6222 *Web:* www.ncaa.org	Indianapolis	IN	46206	317-917-6222	917-6888
National Ctr for Bicycling & Walking (NCBW) 8120 Woodmont Ave Ste 520 **Fax Area Code:* 301 ■ *Web:* www.bikewalk.org	Bethesda	MD	20814	202-223-3621	656-4225*
National Federation of State High School Assn (NFHS) PO Box 690 *TF Cust Svc:* 800-776-3462 ■ *Web:* www.nfhs.org	Indianapolis	IN	46206	317-972-6900	822-5700
National Football League Players (NFLPA) 1133 20th St NW *Web:* www.nflpa.com	Washington	DC	20036	202-463-2200	
National Golf Foundation (NGF) 1150 S US Hwy 1 Ste 401 *TF:* 800-733-6006 ■ *Web:* www.ngf.org	Jupiter	FL	33477	561-744-6006	744-6107
National Greyhound Assn (NGA) 729 Old US 40 *Web:* www.ngagreyhounds.com	Abilene	KS	67410	785-263-4660	263-4689
National Hockey League Players Assn (NHLPA) 20 Bay St Ste 1700 *Web:* www.nhlpa.com	Toronto	ON	M5J2N8	416-907-9801	313-2301
National Intramural-Recreational Sports Assn (NIRSA) 4185 SW Research Way *Web:* www.nirsa.org	Corvallis	OR	97333	541-766-8211	766-8284
National Junior College Athletic Assn (NJCAA) 1755 Telstar Dr Ste 103 *Web:* www.njcaa.org	Colorado Springs	CO	80920	719-590-9788	590-7324
National Little Britches Rodeo Assn (NLBRA) 5050 Edison Ave Ste 105 *TF:* 800-763-3694 ■ *Web:* www.nlbra.org	Colorado Springs	CO	80915	719-389-0333	578-1367
National Senior Golf Assn (NSGA) 200 Perrine Rd Ste 201 **Fax Area Code:* 732 ■ *TF:* 800-282-6772 ■ *Web:* www.nationalseniorgolf.com	Old Bridge	NJ	08857	800-282-6772	525-9590*
National Shooting Sports Foundation (NSSF) 11 Mile Hill Rd *Web:* www.nssf.org	Newtown	CT	06470	203-426-1320	426-1087
National Soccer Coaches Assn of America (NSCAA) 800 Ann Ave *TF:* 800-458-0678 ■ *Web:* www.nscaa.com	Kansas City	KS	66101	913-362-1747	362-3439
National Strength & Conditioning Assn (NSCA) 1885 Bob Johnson Dr *TF:* 800-815-6826 ■ *Web:* www.nsca.com	Colorado Springs	CO	80906	719-632-6722	632-6367
National Thoroughbred Racing Assn (NTRA) 2525 Harrodsburg Rd Ste 510 *TF:* 800-792-6872 ■ *Web:* www.ntra.com	Lexington	KY	40504	800-792-6872	
National Tractor Pullers Assn (NTPA) 6155-B Huntley Rd *Web:* www.ntpapull.com	Columbus	OH	43229	614-436-1761	436-0964
National Youth Sports Coaches Assn (NYSCA) 2050 Vista Pkwy *TF:* 800-729-2057 ■ *Web:* www.nays.org	West Palm Beach	FL	33411	561-684-1141	684-2546
New York Arm Wrestling Assn (NYAWA) PO Box 670952 *Web:* www.nycarms.com	Flushing	NY	11367	718-544-4592	261-8111

	Phone	Fax

PGA of America
100 Ave of the Champions .... Palm Beach Gardens FL 33418 561-624-8400 624-8439
TF: 800-477-6465 ■ *Web:* www.pga.com

PGA Tour Inc 112 PGA Tour Blvd .... Ponte Vedra Beach FL 32082 904-285-3700
Web: www.pgatour.com

PONY Baseball/Softball Inc
1951 Pony Pl PO Box 225 .... Washington PA 15301 724-225-1060 225-9852
TF: 800-853-2414 ■ *Web:* www.pony.org

Pop Warner Little Scholars Inc
586 Middletown Blvd Ste C-100..................... Langhorne PA 19047 215-752-2691 752-2879
TF: 800-257-4268 ■ *Web:* www.popwarner.com

Professional Assn of Diving Instructors International (PADI)
30151 Tomas St...................... Rancho Santa Margarita CA 92688 949-858-7234 267-1267
TF Sales: 800-729-7234 ■ *Web:* www.padi.com

Professional Bowlers Assn (PBA)
719 Second Ave Ste 701.............................. Seattle WA 98104 206-332-9688 654-6030
TF: 877-910-2695 ■ *Web:* www.pba.com

Professional Rodeo Cowboys Assn (PRCA)
101 Pro Rodeo Dr......................... Colorado Springs CO 80919 719-593-8840
Web: www.prorodeo.com

Professional Tennis Registry
PO Box 4739 .... Hilton Head Island SC 29938 843-785-7244 686-2033
TF: 800-421-6289 ■ *Web:* www.ptrtennis.org

Roller Skating Assn International (RSAI)
6905 Corporate Dr .... Indianapolis IN 46278 317-347-2626 347-2636
Web: rollerskating.com

Senior Softball USA 2701 K St Ste 101A .... Sacramento CA 95816 916-326-5303 326-5304
TF: 888-244-9499 ■ *Web:* www.seniorsoftball.com

Special Olympics Inc
1133 19th St NW 11th Fl .... Washington DC 20036 202-628-3630 824-0200
TF: 800-700-8585 ■ *Web:* www.specialolympics.org

Sports Turf Managers Assn (STMA)
805 New Hampshire Ste E .... Lawrence KS 66044 785-843-2549 843-2977
TF: 800-323-3875 ■ *Web:* www.stma.org

Thoroughbred Racing Assn (TRA)
420 Fair Hill Dr Ste 1 .... Elkton MD 21921 410-392-9200 398-1366
Web: www.tra-online.com

United States Olympic Committee
1 Olympic Plaza .... Colorado Springs CO 80909 719-866-4567 632-0979
Web: www.teamusa.org

US Biathlon Assn
49 Pineland Dr Ste 301-A.................... New Gloucester ME 04260 207-688-6500 688-6505
TF General: 800-242-8456 ■ *Web:* www.teamusa.org

US Bobsled & Skeleton Federation (USBSF)
196 Old Military Rd .... Lake Placid NY 12946 518-523-1842 523-9491
TF: 888-431-3598 ■ *Web:* www.teamusa.org

US Curling Assn (USCA) 5525 Clem's Way......... Stevens Point WI 54482 715-344-1199 344-2279
TF: 888-287-5377 ■ *Web:* teamusa.org/usa-curling

US Equestrian Federation Inc
4047 Iron Works Pkwy .... Lexington KY 40511 859-258-2472 231-6662
Web: www.usef.org

US Equestrian Team Foundation Inc (USET)
1040 Pottersville Rd PO Box 355 .... Gladstone NJ 07934 908-234-1251 234-0670
Web: www.uset.org

US Fencing Assn (USFA) 1 Olympic Plaza ...... Colorado Springs CO 80909 719-866-4511 632-5737
TF: 888-431-3598 ■ *Web:* www.usfencing.org

US Figure Skating Assn (USFSA)
20 First St.............................. Colorado Springs CO 80906 719-635-5200 635-9548
Web: www.usfsa.org

US Golf Assn (USGA) 77 Liberty Corner Rd............. Far Hills NJ 07931 908-234-2300 234-9687
TF Orders: 800-336-4446 ■ *Web:* www.usga.org

US Luge Assn 57 Church St.......................... Lake Placid NY 12946 518-523-2071 523-4106
Web: www.teamusa.org/usa-luge

US Olympic Committee (USOC)
1 Olympic Plz............................ Colorado Springs CO 80909 719-632-5551
Web: www.teamusa.org

US Parachute Assn (USPA)
5401 Southpoint Ctr Blvd..................... Fredericksburg VA 22407 540-604-9740 604-9741
Web: www.uspa.org

US Professional Tennis Assn (USPTA)
3535 Briarpark Dr Ste 1 .... Houston TX 77042 713-978-7782 978-7780
TF: 800-877-8248 ■ *Web:* uspta.com

US Racquetball Assn (USRA)
2812 W Colorado Ave Ste 220 .... Colorado Springs CO 80904 719-635-5396 635-0685
Web: www.teamusa.org

US Rowing Assn 2 Wall St.......................... Princeton NJ 08540 609-924-1578 924-1578
TF: 800-314-4769 ■ *Web:* www.usrowing.org

US Sailing Assn 15 Maritime Dr PO Box 1260 .... Portsmouth RI 02871 401-683-0800 683-0840
TF: 800-877-2451 ■ *Web:* ussailing.org

US Soccer Federation 1801 S Prairie Ave............. Chicago IL 60616 312-808-1300 808-1301
TF: 800-745-3000 ■ *Web:* www.ussoccer.com

US Synchronized Swimming
1 Olympic Plaza .... Colorado Springs CO 80909 317-237-5700 237-5705
TF: 800-775-8762 ■ *Web:* www.teamusa.org

US Taekwondo Union
1 Olympic Plz Ste 104C .... Colorado Springs CO 80909 719-866-4632 866-4642
Web: www.teamusa.org

US Trotting Assn (USTA) 750 Michigan Ave .... Columbus OH 43215 614-224-2291 224-4575
TF: 877-800-8782 ■ *Web:* www.ustrotting.com

USA Archery (NAA) 1 Olympic Plz............. Colorado Springs CO 80909 719-866-4576 632-4733
Web: www.teamusa.org

USA Baseball 403 Blackwell St .... Durham NC 27701 919-474-8721 474-8822
Web: usabaseball.com

USA Basketball
5465 Mark Dabling Boulevard .... Colorado Springs CO 80918 719-590-4800 590-4811
TF: 888-284-5383 ■ *Web:* www.usab.com

USA Boxing Inc 1 Olympic Plz.............. Colorado Springs CO 80909 719-228-6800 866-2132
Web: www.teamusa.org/USA-Boxing

USA Canoe/Kayak (USACK)
725 S Lincoln Blvd............................ Oklahoma City OK 73129 405-552-4040
Web: www.teamusa.org

USA Cycling Inc 1 Olympic Plz .... Colorado Springs CO 80909 719-866-4581
Web: www.usacycling.org

	Phone	Fax

USA Diving Inc
132 E Washington St Ste 850..................... Indianapolis IN 46204 317-237-5252 237-5257
Web: www.teamusa.org/usa-diving

USA Gymnastics 201 S Capitol Ave Ste 300.......... Indianapolis IN 46225 317-237-5050 237-5069
TF: 800-345-4719 ■ *Web:* usagym.org

USA Hockey 1775 Bob Johnson Dr .... Colorado Springs CO 80906 719-576-8724 538-1160
TF: 800-566-3288 ■ *Web:* www.usahockey.com

USA Judo Inc 1 Olympic Plaza Ste 505 .... Colorado Springs CO 80909 719-866-4730 866-4733
TF: 800-775-8762 ■ *Web:* www.teamusa.org

USA Roller Sports 4730 S St.......................... Lincoln NE 68506 402-483-7551 483-1465
Web: www.teamusa.org

USA Swimming 1 Olympic Plaza .... Colorado Springs CO 80909 719-866-4578 866-4669
TF: 800-333-3333 ■ *Web:* www.usaswimming.org

USA Table Tennis 1 Olympic Plaza............ Colorado Springs CO 80909 719-866-4583 632-6071
TF: 800-775-8762 ■ *Web:* www.teamusa.org

USA Track & Field (USATF)
132 E Washington St Ste 800..................... Indianapolis IN 46204 317-261-0500 261-0481
TF: 800-222-8733 ■ *Web:* www.usatf.org

USA Triathlon 5825 Delmonico Dr............ Colorado Springs CO 80919 719-597-9090 597-2121
Web: www.teamusa.org/usa-triathlon

USA Water Polo 2124 Main St Ste 210......... Huntington Beach CA 92648 714-500-5445 960-2431
TF: 888-712-2166 ■ *Web:* usawaterpolo.org

USA Water Ski 1251 Holy Cow Rd............................ Polk City FL 33868 863-324-4341 325-8259
TF: 800-533-2972 ■ *Web:* www.usawaterski.org

USA Weightlifting (USAW)
1 Olympic Plaza .... Colorado Springs CO 80909 719-866-4508 866-4741
TF: 800-775-8762 ■ *Web:* www.teamusa.org

USA Wrestling 6155 Lehman Dr .... Colorado Springs CO 80918 719-598-8181 598-9440
TF: 888-431-3598 ■ *Web:* teamusa.org/usa-wrestling

USAC Racing (USAC) 4910 W 16th St.............. Speedway IN 46224 317-247-5151
Web: www.usacracing.com

Wheelchair & Ambulatory Sports USA
PO Box 5266 .... Kendall Park NJ 08824 732-266-2634 355-6500
Web: www.wasusa.org

Women's Sports Foundation
1899 Hempstead Tpke
Ste 400 Eisenhower Pk........................ East Meadow NY 11554 516-542-4700 542-4716
TF: 800-227-3988 ■ *Web:* www.womenssportsfoundation.org

WTA Tour Inc 1 Progress Plz Ste 1500 .... Saint Petersburg FL 33701 727-895-5000 894-1982
Web: www.wtatennis.com

48-23 Travel & Recreation Organizations

	Phone	Fax

Adirondack Mountain Club 814 Goggins Rd .... Lake George NY 12845 518-668-4447 668-3746
TF Orders: 800-395-8080 ■ *Web:* www.adk.org

Alberta Hotel & Lodging Assn (AHLA)
2707 Ellwood Dr....................................... Edmonton AB T6X0P7 780-436-6112 436-5404
TF: 888-436-6112 ■ *Web:* www.ahla.ca

America Outdoors 5816 Kingston Pk .... Knoxville TN 37919 865-558-3595 558-3598
TF: 800-524-4814 ■ *Web:* www.americaoutdoors.org

American Amusement Machine Assn (AAMA)
450 E Higgins Rd Ste 201.................... Elk Grove Village IL 60007 847-290-9088 290-9121
TF: 866-372-5190 ■ *Web:* www.coin-op.org

American Assn for Physical Activity & Recreation (AAPAR)
1900 Assn Dr .... Reston VA 20191 703-476-3400 476-9527
TF: 800-213-7193 ■ *Web:* shapeamerica.org/aapar

American Automobile Assn Inc (AAA) 1000 AAA Dr ... Heathrow FL 32746 407-444-4240 444-4247
Web: www.aaa.com

American Camp Assn (ACA)
5000 State Rd 67 N............................... Martinsville IN 46151 765-342-8456 342-2065
TF: 800-428-2267 ■ *Web:* www.acacamps.org

American Gaming Assn (AGA)
1299 Pennsylvania Ave NW Ste 1175............... Washington DC 20004 202-552-2675 552-2676
Web: www.americangaming.org

American Hiking Society (AHS)
1422 Fenwick Ln .... Silver Spring MD 20910 301-565-6704 565-6714
TF: 800-972-8608 ■ *Web:* www.americanhiking.org

American Hotel & Lodging Assn (AH&LA)
1201 New York Ave NW Ste 600.................. Washington DC 20005 202-289-3100 289-3185
Web: www.ahla.com

American Park & Recreation Society (APRS)
22377 Belmont Ridge Rd .... Ashburn VA 20148 703-858-0784 858-0794
TF: 800-765-3110 ■ *Web:* www.arcat.com

American Recreation Coalition (ARC)
1225 New York Ave NW Ste 450.................. Washington DC 20005 202-682-9530 682-9529
Web: www.funoutdoors.com

American Society of Travel Agents (ASTA)
1101 King St Ste 200 .... Alexandria VA 22314 703-739-2782 684-8319
TF: 800-275-2782 ■ *Web:* www.asta.org

American Trails PO Box 491797........................ Redding CA 96049 530-547-2060 547-2035
TF: 866-363-7226 ■ *Web:* www.americantrails.org

American Whitewater (AW) PO Box 1540 .... Cullowhee NC 28723 828-586-1930 586-2840
TF: 866-262-8429 ■ *Web:* americanwhitewater.org

Amusement & Music Operators Assn (AMOA)
600 Spring Hill Ring Rd Ste 111................. West Dundee IL 60118 847-428-7699 428-7719
TF: 800-937-2662 ■ *Web:* amoa.memberclicks.net

Appalachian Mountain Club (AMC) 5 Joy St .... Boston MA 02108 617-523-0655 523-0722
TF Orders: 800-262-4455 ■ *Web:* www.outdoors.org

Appalachian Trail Conservancy (ATC)
799 Washington St PO Box 807 .... Harpers Ferry WV 25425 304-535-6331 535-2667
TF Sales: 888-287-8673 ■ *Web:* appalachiantrail.org

Association of Corporate Travel Executives (ACTE)
515 King St Ste 440 .... Alexandria VA 22314 703-683-5322 683-2720
Web: www.acte.org

Association of Destination Management Executives (ADME)
11 W Monument Ave .... Dayton OH 45402 937-586-3727 586-3699
Web: www.adme.org

Back Country Horsemen of America (BCHA)
PO Box 1367 .... Graham WA 98338 360-832-2461 832-2471
TF: 888-893-5161 ■ *Web:* www.bcha.org

Phone | Fax

Bowling Proprietors' Assn of America (BPAA)
621 Six Flags Dr PO Box 5802 ..... Arlington TX 76011 817-649-5105 633-2940
TF: 800-343-1329 ■ *Web:* www.bpaa.com

Canadian Automobile Assn (CAA) 2151 Thurston Dr ..... Ottawa ON K1G6C9 613-820-1890 247-0118
TF: 800-267-8713 ■ *Web:* www.caa.ca

Canadian Parks & Recreation Assn (CPRA)
1180 Walkley Rd PO Box 83069 ..... Ottawa ON K1V2M5 613-523-5315 523-1182
Web: www.cpra.ca

Colorado Dude & Guest Ranch Assn (CDGRA)
PO Box D ..... Shawnee CO 80475 866-942-3472
TF: 866-942-3472 ■ *Web:* www.coloradoranch.com

Continental Divide Trail Society (CDT)
3704 N Charles St Ste 601 ..... Baltimore MD 21218 410-235-9610
Web: www.cdtsociety.org

Cruise Lines International Assn (CLIA)
1201 F St NW Ste 250 ..... Washington DC 20004 754-224-2200
TF: 855-444-2542 ■ *Web:* www.cruising.org

Dude Ranchers' Assn 1122 12th St PO Box 2307 ..... Cody WY 82414 307-587-2339 587-2776
TF: 866-399-2339 ■ *Web:* www.duderanch.org

Elderhostel Inc 11 Ave de Lafayette ..... Boston MA 02111 800-454-5768 426-2166*
**Fax Area Code:* 877 ■ *TF:* 800-454-5768 ■ *Web:* www.roadscholar.org

Environmental Traveling Companions (ETC)
2 Marina Blvd Bldg C ..... San Francisco CA 94123 415-474-7662 474-3919
Web: www.etctrips.org

Escapees RV Club 100 Rainbow Dr ..... Livingston TX 77399 936-327-8873 327-4388
TF: 800-231-9896 ■ *Web:* www.escapees.com

Family Campers & RVers (FCRV)
4804 Transit Rd Bldg 2 ..... Depew NY 14043 716-668-6242
TF: 800-245-9755 ■ *Web:* www.fcrv.org

Family Motor Coach Assn (FMCA)
8291 Clough Pk ..... Cincinnati OH 45244 513-474-3622 474-2332
TF: 800-543-3622 ■ *Web:* www.fmca.com

Global Business Travel Assn, The (GBTA)
123 N Pitt St ..... Alexandria VA 22314 703-684-0836 684-0263
TF: 888-574-6447 ■ *Web:* www.gbta.org

Good Sam Club PO Box 6888 ..... Englewood CO 80155 800-234-3450
TF: 800-234-3450 ■ *Web:* www.goodsamclub.com

Hostelling International USA - American Youth Hostels (HI-AYH)
8401 Colesville Rd Ste 600 ..... Silver Spring MD 20910 301-495-1240 495-6697
TF: 800-725-2331 ■ *Web:* www.hiusa.org

International Airline Passengers Assn (IAPA)
PO Box 700188 ..... Dallas TX 75370 972-404-9980 233-5348
TF: 800-821-4272 ■ *Web:* www.iapa.com

International Assn for Medical Assistance to Travellers (IAMAT)
2162 Gordon St ..... Guelph ON N1L1G6 519-836-0102
Web: www.iamat.org

International Assn of Amusement Parks & Attractions (IAAPA)
1448 Duke St ..... Alexandria VA 22314 703-836-4800 836-6742
Web: www.iaapa.org

International Assn of Fairs & Expositions, The (IAFE)
3043 E Cairo ..... Springfield MO 65802 417-862-5771
TF: 800-516-0313 ■ *Web:* www.fairsandexpos.com

International Festivals & Events Assn (IFEA)
2603 W Eastover Terr ..... Boise ID 83706 208-433-0950 433-9812
Web: www.ifea.com

International Gay & Lesbian Travel Assn (IGLTA)
1201 NE 26th St Ste 103 ..... Fort Lauderdale FL 33305 954-630-1637 630-1652
TF: 888-789-3090 ■ *Web:* www.iglta.org

International Mountain Bicycling Assn (IMBA)
4888 Pearl E Cir Ste 200E ..... Boulder CO 80301 303-545-9011 545-9026
TF: 888-442-4622 ■ *Web:* www.imba.com

Leave No Trace Ctr for Outdoor Ethics Inc
1830 17th St ..... Boulder CO 80302 303-442-8222 442-8217
TF: 800-332-4100 ■ *Web:* www.lnt.org

Lewis & Clark Trail Heritage Foundation
4201 Giant Springs Rd ..... Great Falls MT 59405 406-454-1234 771-9237
TF: 888-701-3434 ■ *Web:* www.lewisandclark.org

Lincoln Highway Assn 136 N Elm St ..... Franklin Grove IL 61031 815-456-3030
Web: www.lincolnhighwayassoc.org

Loners on Wheels (LOW) 1795 O'Kelley Rd SE ..... Deming NM 88030 575-544-7303
Web: www.lonersonwheels.com

Mountaineers, The 7700 Sand Pt Way NE ..... Seattle WA 98115 206-521-6000 523-6763
TF: 800-573-8484 ■ *Web:* www.mountaineers.org

National Club Assn (NCA)
1201 15th St NW Ste 450 ..... Washington DC 20005 202-822-9822 822-9808
TF: 800-625-6221 ■ *Web:* nationalclub.org

National Forest Recreation Assn (NFRA)
PO Box 488 ..... Woodlake CA 93286 559-564-2365 564-2048
TF: 800-282-2444 ■ *Web:* www.nfra.org

National Golf Course Owners Assn (NGCOA)
291 Seven Farms Dr 2nd Fl ..... Charleston SC 29492 843-881-9956 881-9958
TF: 800-933-4262 ■ *Web:* www.ngcoa.org

National Indian Gaming Assn (NIGA)
224 Second St SE ..... Washington DC 20003 202-546-7711 546-1755
Web: www.indiangaming.org

National Recreation and Park Association (NSPR)
22377 Belmont Ridge Rd
22377 Belmont Ridge Rd ..... Ashburn VA 20148 703-858-0784 858-0794
TF: 800-626-6772 ■ *Web:* www.nrpa.org

National Ski Areas Assn (NSAA)
133 S Van Gordon St Ste 300 ..... Lakewood CO 80228 303-987-1111 986-2345
Web: www.nsaa.org

National Tour Assn (NTA) 546 E Main St ..... Lexington KY 40508 859-226-4444 226-4404
TF: 800-682-8886 ■ *Web:* www.ntaonline.com

North Country Trail Assn 229 E Main St ..... Lowell MI 49331 616-897-5987 897-6605
TF: 866-445-3628 ■ *Web:* www.northcountrytrail.org

Oregon-California Trails Assn
524 S Osage St PO Box 1019 ..... Independence MO 64051 816-252-2276 836-0989
TF: 888-811-6282 ■ *Web:* www.octa-trails.org

Pacific Crest Trail Assn (PCTA)
1331 Garden Hwy ..... Sacramento CA 95833 916-285-1846 285-1865
TF: 888-728-7245 ■ *Web:* www.pcta.org

Pennsylvania AAA Federation
600 N Third St ..... Harrisburg PA 17101 717-238-7192 238-6574
Web: www.aaapa.org

Phone | Fax

Relais & Chateaux Assn 10 E 53rd St ..... New York NY 10022 212-319-4880
TF: 800-735-2478 ■ *Web:* relaischateaux.com

RVing Women (RVW)
879 N Plaza Dr Ste B103 ..... Apache Junction AZ 85120 480-671-6226 671-6230
TF: 888-557-8464 ■ *Web:* rvingwomen.org

Society of Incentive & Travel Executives (SITE)
401 N Michigan Ave ..... Chicago IL 60611 312-321-5148
Web: www.siteglobal.com

Special Military Active Retired Travel Club (SMART)
600 University Office Blvd Ste 1A ..... Pensacola FL 32504 850-478-1986
TF: 800-354-7681

Statue of Liberty-Ellis Island Foundation Inc, The
17 Battery Pl Ste 210 ..... New York NY 10004 212-561-4500 779-1990
Web: libertyellisfoundation.org

Travel Institute 945 Concord St Ste 305 ..... Framingham MA 01701 781-237-0280 237-3860
TF: 800-542-4282 ■ *Web:* www.thetravelinstitute.com

Washington Trails Assn (WTA)
705 Second Ave Ste 300 ..... Seattle WA 98121 206-625-1367 625-9249
Web: www.wta.org

Western National Parks Assn (WNPA)
12880 N Vistoso Village Dr ..... Tucson AZ 85755 520-622-1999 623-9519
Web: www.wnpa.org

Wilderness Inquiry (WI) 808 14th Ave SE ..... Minneapolis MN 55414 612-676-9400 676-9401
TF: 800-728-0719 ■ *Web:* www.wildernessinquiry.org

48-24 Women's Organizations

Phone | Fax

Association for Women's Rights in Development (AWID)
215 Spadina Ave Ste 150 ..... Toronto ON M5T2C7 416-594-3773 594-0330
Web: www.awid.org

Center for Women Policy Studies
1776 Masachusetts Ave NW Ste 450 ..... Washington DC 20036 202-872-1770 296-8962
Web: www.centerwomenpolicy.org

Coalition of Labor Union Women (CLUW)
815 16th St NW 2nd Fl ..... Washington DC 20006 202-508-6969 508-6968
Web: www.cluw.org

Equal Rights Advocates (ERA)
1170 Market St Ste 700 ..... San Francisco CA 94102 415-621-0672 621-6744
TF: 800-839-4372 ■ *Web:* www.equalrights.org

Feminist Majority Foundation-East Coast (FMF)
1600 Wilson Blvd Ste 801 ..... Arlington VA 22209 703-522-2214 522-2219
Web: www.feminist.org

General Federation of Women's Clubs (GFWC)
1734 N St NW ..... Washington DC 20036 202-347-3168 835-0246
TF: 800-443-4392 ■ *Web:* www.gfwc.org

Girls Inc 120 Wall St 3rd Fl ..... New York NY 10005 212-509-2000 509-8708
TF: 800-374-4475 ■ *Web:* www.girlsinc.org

Inter-American Commission of Women (CIM)
1889 F St NW ..... Washington DC 20006 202-458-6084 458-6094
Web: www.oas.org/cim

International Alliance for Women (TIAW)
1101 Pennsylvania Ave NW Fl 6 ..... Washington DC 20004 888-712-5200
TF: 888-712-5200 ■ *Web:* www.tiaw.org

International Ctr for Research on Women (ICRW)
1120 20th St NW Ste 500-N ..... Washington DC 20036 202-797-0007 797-0020
Web: www.icrw.org

MS Foundation for Women
12 MetroTech Ctr 26th Fl ..... Brooklyn NY 11201 212-742-2300 742-1653
Web: forwomen.org

National Congress of Neighborhood Women
249 Manhattan Ave ..... Brooklyn NY 11211 718-388-8915
Web: neighborhoodwomen.org

National Council of Jewish Women (NCJW)
475 Riverside Dr Ste 1901 ..... New York NY 10115 212-645-4048 645-7466
TF: 800-829-6259 ■ *Web:* www.ncjw.org

National Council of Negro Women Inc (NCNW)
633 Pennsylvania Ave NW ..... Washington DC 20004 202-737-0120 737-0476
TF: 800-462-6420 ■ *Web:* www.ncnw.org

National Organization for Women (NOW)
1100 H St NW 3rd Fl ..... Washington DC 20005 202-628-8669 785-8576
TF: 855-212-0212 ■ *Web:* www.now.org

National Partnership for Women & Families
1875 Connecticut Ave NW Ste 650 ..... Washington DC 20009 202-986-2600 986-2539
Web: www.nationalpartnership.org

National Woman's Party
144 Constitution Ave NE ..... Washington DC 20002 202-546-1210 546-3997
Web: www.sewallbelmont.org

National Women's Law Ctr (NWLC)
11 Dupont Cir NW Ste 800 ..... Washington DC 20036 202-588-5180 588-5185
Web: www.nwlc.org

New Ways to Work Inc 103 Morris St Ste A ..... Sebastopol CA 95472 707-824-4000 824-4410
Web: www.newwaystowork.org

Ninety-Nines Inc
4300 Amelia Earhart Rd ..... Oklahoma City OK 73159 405-685-7969 685-7985
TF: 800-994-1929 ■ *Web:* www.ninety-nines.org

Wider Opportunities for Women (WOW)
1001 Connecticut Ave NW Ste 930 ..... Washington DC 20036 202-464-1596 464-1660
Web: www.wowonline.org

Women Employed 65 E Wacker Pl ..... Chicago IL 60601 312-782-3902 782-5249
Web: www.womenemployed.org

Women's Economic Agenda Project (WEAP)
160 Franklin St Ste 208 ..... Oakland CA 94607 510-986-8620 986-8628
Web: www.weap.org

Women's Sports Foundation
1899 Hempstead Tpke
Ste 400 Eisenhower Pk ..... East Meadow NY 11554 516-542-4700 542-4716
TF: 800-227-3988 ■ *Web:* www.womenssportsfoundation.org

Zonta International 1211 W 22nd St Ste 900 ..... Oak Brook IL 60523 630-928-1400 928-1559
Web: www.zonta.org

49 ASSOCIATIONS & ORGANIZATIONS - PROFESSIONAL & TRADE

See Also Bar Associations - State p. 1849; Dental Associations - State p. 2190; Labor Unions p. 2618; Library Associations - State & Province p. 2671; Medical Associations - State p. 2736; Nurses Associations - State p. 2842; Pharmacy Associations - State p. 2937; Realtor Associations - State p. 3054; Veterinary Medical Associations - State p. 3295

49-1 Accountants Associations

Organization / Address	City	State	Zip	Phone	Fax
AACE International - Assn for the Advancement of Cost Engineering 209 Prairie Ave Ste 100 *TF:* 800-858-2678 ■ *Web:* www.aacei.org	Morgantown	WV	26501	304-296-8444	291-5728
AGN International-North America 2851 S Parker Rd Ste 850 *TF:* 800-782-2272 ■ *Web:* www.agn.org/namain	Aurora	CO	80014	303-743-7880	743-7660
American Acctg Assn 5717 Bessie Dr *Web:* www.aaahq.org	Sarasota	FL	34233	941-921-7747	923-4093
American Institute of Certified Public Accountants (AICPA) 1211 Ave of the Americas *TF:* 888-777-7077 ■ *Web:* www.aicpa.org	New York	NY	10036	212-596-6200	596-6213
American Institute of Professional Bookkeepers (AIPB) 6001 Montrose Rd Ste 500 *TF:* 800-622-0121 ■ *Web:* www.aipb.org	Rockville	MD	20852	800-622-0121	541-0066
American Woman's Society of Certified Public Accountants (AWSCPA) 1430 Yale St *Web:* www.awscpa.org	Houston	OH	77008	937-222-1872	222-5794
Association of Certified Fraud Examiners (ACFE) 716 W Ave *TF:* 800-245-3321 ■ *Web:* www.acfe.com	Austin	TX	78701	512-478-9000	478-9297
Association of Government Accountants (AGA) 2208 Mt Vernon Ave *TF:* 800-242-7211 ■ *Web:* www.agacgfm.org	Alexandria	VA	22301	703-684-6931	548-9367
Association of Healthcare Internal Auditors (AHIA) 10200 W 44th Ave Ste 304 *TF:* 888-275-2442 ■ *Web:* www.ahia.org	Wheat Ridge	CO	80033	303-327-7546	422-8894
BKR International 19 Fulton St Ste 401 *TF:* 800-257-4685 ■ *Web:* www.bkr.com	New York	NY	10038	212-964-2115	964-2133
Construction Financial Management Assn (CFMA) 100 Village Blvd Ste 200A *TF:* 877-462-7827 ■ *Web:* www.cfma.org	Princeton	NJ	08540	609-452-8000	452-0474
CPA Assoc International Inc 301 Rt 17 N *Web:* www.cpaai.com	Rutherford	NJ	07070	201-804-8686	804-9222
CPA Auto Dealer Consultants Assn (CADCA) 1801 W End Ave Ste 800 *TF:* 800-231-2524 ■ *Web:* autodealercpas.com	Nashville	TN	37203	615-373-9880	377-7092
CPAmerica International 11801 Research Dr *TF:* 800-992-2324 ■ *Web:* www.cpamerica.org	Alachua	FL	32615	386-418-4001	418-4002
Financial Acctg Foundation (FAF) 401 Merritt 7 PO Box 5116 *Web:* fasb.org	Norwalk	CT	06856	203-847-0700	849-9714
Financial Acctg Standards Board (FASB) 401 Merritt 7 PO Box 5116 *TF:* 800-748-0659 ■ *Web:* www.fasb.org	Norwalk	CT	06856	203-847-0700	849-9714
Hospitality Financial & Technology Professionals (HFTP) 11709 Boulder Ln Ste 110 *TF:* 800-646-4387 ■ *Web:* www.hftp.org	Austin	TX	78726	512-249-5333	249-1533
IGAF Worldwide 3235 Satellite Blvd NW	Duluth	GA	30097	678-417-7730	417-6977
Institute of Internal Auditors (IIA) 247 Maitland Ave *Web:* na.theiia.org	Altamonte Springs	FL	32701	407-937-1100	937-1101
Institute of Management Accountants Inc (IMA) 10 Paragon Dr Ste 1 *TF:* 800-638-4427 ■ *Web:* www.imanet.org	Montvale	NJ	07645	201-573-9000	474-1600
International Federation of Accountants 545 Fifth Ave 14th Fl *TF:* 888-272-2001 ■ *Web:* www.ifac.org	New York	NY	10017	212-286-9344	286-9570
National Acctg & Finance Council (NAFC) American Trucking Assn 950 N Glebe Rd *Web:* www.trucking.org	Arlington	VA	22203	703-838-1700	
National Association of Nonprofit Accountants & Consultants (NSA) 624 Grassmere Park Dr Ste 15 *TF:* 800-231-2524 ■ *Web:* www.nonprofitcpas.com	Nashville	TN	37211	615-373-9880	377-7092
National CPA Health Care Advisors Assn (HCAA) 1801 W End Ave Ste 800 *TF:* 800-231-2524 ■ *Web:* www.hcaa.com	Nashville	TN	37203	615-373-9880	377-7092
National Society of Accountants (NSA) 1010 N Fairfax St *TF:* 800-966-6679 ■ *Web:* www.nsacct.org	Alexandria	VA	22314	703-549-6400	549-2984
New York State Society of Certified Public Accountant (FAE) 14 Wall St 19th Fl *TF General:* 800-537-3635 ■ *Web:* www.nysscpa.org/page/continuing-education/fae-conferences	New York	NY	10005	212-719-8300	719-3365
Tax Executives Institute (TEI) 1200 G St NW Ste 300 *TF:* 877-244-7711 ■ *Web:* www.tei.org	Washington	DC	20005	202-638-5601	638-5607

49-2 Banking & Finance Professionals Associations

Organization / Address	City	State	Zip	Phone	Fax
ABA Marketing Network 1120 Connecticut Ave NW *TF:* 800-226-5377 ■ *Web:* www.aba.com/marketingnetwork	Washington	DC	20036	202-663-5000	828-5053
ACA International - Assn of Credit & Collection Professionals 4040 W 70th St PO Box 390106 *TF:* 800-844-5654 ■ *Web:* www.acainternational.org	Minneapolis	MN	55439	952-926-6547	926-1624
Accuplan Benefits Services 515 East 4500 South Ste G200 **Fax Area Code:* 877 ■ *TF:* 800-454-2649 ■ *Web:* www.accuplan.net	Salt Lake City	UT	84107	801-266-9900	890-0929*
America's Community Bankers (ACB) 1120 Connecticut Ave NW *TF:* 800-226-5377 ■ *Web:* www.aba.com	Washington	DC	20036	800-226-5377	
American Assn of Daily Money Managers (AADMM) 174 Crestview Dr **Fax Area Code:* 814 ■ *TF:* 877-326-5991 ■ *Web:* www.aadmm.com	Bellefonte	PA	16823	877-326-5991	355-2452*
American Assn of Individual Investors (AAII) 625 N Michigan Ave Ste 1900 *TF:* 800-428-2244 ■ *Web:* www.aaii.com	Chicago	IL	60611	312-280-0170	280-9883
American Bankers Assn (ABA) 1120 Connecticut Ave NW *TF Cust Svc:* 800-226-5377 ■ *Web:* www.aba.com	Washington	DC	20036	202-663-5000	
American Benefits Council 1501 M St NW Ste 600 *TF:* 877-829-5500 ■ *Web:* www.americanbenefitscouncil.org	Washington	DC	20005	202-289-6700	289-4582
American Council for Capital Formation (ACCF) 1001 Connecticut Ave NW Ste 620 *Web:* www.accf.org	Washington	DC	20036	202-293-5811	785-8165
American Economic Assn (AEA) 2014 Broadway Ste 305 *Web:* www.aeaweb.org	Nashville	TN	37203	615-322-2595	343-7590
American Finance Assn (AFA) 350 Main St *TF:* 800-835-6770 ■ *Web:* www.afajof.org	Malden	MA	02148	781-388-8599	
American Institute of Certified Planners (AICP) 1776 Massachusetts Ave NW Ste 400 *Web:* www.planning.org/aicp	Washington	DC	20036	202-872-0611	872-0643
Association for Financial Professionals (AFP) 4520 E W Hwy Ste 750 *Web:* www.afponline.org	Bethesda	MD	20814	301-907-2862	907-2864
Bank Administration Institute (BAI) 115 S LaSalle St Ste 3300 **Fax:* Cust Svc ■ *TF Cust Svc:* 800-224-9889 ■ *Web:* www.bai.org	Chicago	IL	60603	312-683-2464	683-2373*
Better Investing PO Box 220 *TF:* 877-275-6242 ■ *Web:* www.betterinvesting.org	Royal Oak	MI	48068	248-583-6242	583-4880
Certified Financial Planner Board of Standards Inc 1425 K St NW Ste 500 *TF:* 800-487-1497 ■ *Web:* www.cfp.net	Washington	DC	20005	202-379-2200	379-2299
CFA Institute 915 E High St PO Box 3668 *TF:* 800-247-8132 ■ *Web:* www.cfainstitute.org	Charlottesville	VA	22903	434-951-5499	951-5262
Community Banking Advisory Network (CBAN) 1801 W End Ave Ste 800 *TF:* 800-231-2524 ■ *Web:* www.bankingcpas.com	Nashville	TN	37203	615-373-9880	377-7092
Consumer Data Industry Assn (CDIA) 1090 Vermont Ave NW Ste 200 *Web:* www.cdiaonline.org	Washington	DC	20005	202-371-0910	371-0134
Council of Institutional Investors 888 17th St NW Ste 500 *Web:* www.cii.org	Washington	DC	20006	202-822-0800	
Credit Professionals International PO Box 220714 *Web:* www.creditprofessionals.org	Saint Louis	MO	63122	314-821-9393	821-7171
Credit Research Foundation (CRF) 8840 Columbia 100 Pkwy *TF:* 866-265-3298 ■ *Web:* www.crfonline.org	Columbia	MD	21045	410-740-5499	740-4620
Credit Union Executives Society (CUES) 5510 Research Pk Dr *TF:* 800-252-2664 ■ *Web:* www.cues.org	Madison	WI	53711	608-271-2664	271-2303
Electronic Funds Transfer Assn (EFTA) 11350 Random Hills Rd Ste 800 *Web:* www.efta.org	Fairfax	VA	22030	703-934-6052	934-6058
Emerging Markets Traders Assn (EMTA) 360 Madison Ave 18th Fl *Web:* www.emta.org	New York	NY	10017	212-313-1100	313-1016
Farm Credit Council 50 F St NW Ste 900 *TF:* 866-632-9992 ■ *Web:* www.fccouncil.com	Washington	DC	20001	202-626-8710	626-8718
Financial Executives International (FEI) 200 Campus Dr PO Box 674 *Web:* www.financialexecutives.org	Florham Park	NJ	07932	973-765-1000	765-1018
Financial Industry Regulatory Authority (FINRA) 9509 Key W Ave *Web:* www.finra.org	Rockville	MD	20850	301-590-6500	
Financial Management Assn International (FMA) 4202 E Fowler Ave *Web:* www.fma.org	Tampa	FL	33620	813-974-2084	
Financial Managers Society (FMS) 100 W Monroe St Ste 810 *TF Cust Svc:* 800-275-4367 ■ *Web:* www.fmsinc.org	Chicago	IL	60603	312-578-1300	578-1308
Financial Planning Assn (FPA) 7535 E Hampden Ave Ste 600 *TF:* 800-322-4237 ■ *Web:* www.plannersearch.org	Denver	CO	80231	303-759-4900	759-0749
Financial Service Centers of America Inc (FiSCA) 21 Main St 1st Fl *Web:* www.fisca.org	Hackensack	NJ	07602	201-487-0412	487-3954
Financial Services Roundtable 1001 Pennsylvania Ave NW Ste 500 *Web:* fsroundtable.org/bits	Washington	DC	20005	202-289-4322	628-2507
FINRA 1735 K St NW *TF:* 800-289-9999 ■ *Web:* www.finra.org	Washington	DC	20006	202-728-8000	
Futures Industry Assn (FIA) 2001 Pennsylvania Ave NW Ste 600 *Web:* fia.org	Washington	DC	20006	202-466-5460	296-3184
Independent Community Bankers of America (ICBA) 1615 L St NW Ste 900 *TF:* 800-422-8439 ■ *Web:* www.icba.org	Washington	DC	20036	202-659-8111	
Industry Council for Tangible Assets (ICTA) 1510 Circle Dr *Web:* www.ictaonline.org	Annapolis	MD	21409	410-626-7005	
Institute of International Bankers (IIB) 299 Pk Ave 17th Fl *Web:* www.iib.org	New York	NY	10171	212-421-1611	421-1119

Phone Fax

Institute of International Finance (IIF)
1333 H St NW Ste 800-E .... Washington DC 20005 202-857-3600 775-1430
Web: www.iif.com

International Swaps & Derivatives Assn (ISDA)
360 Madison Ave 16th Fl .... New York NY 10017 212-901-6000 901-6001
Web: www2.isda.org

Investment Company Institute (ICI)
1401 H St NW Ste 1200 .... Washington DC 20005 202-326-5800 326-5841
Web: www.ici.org

Investment Management Consultants Assn (IMCA)
5619 DTC Pkwy Ste 500 .... Greenwood Village CO 80111 303-770-3377 770-1812
TF: 800-250-9083 ■ *Web:* www.imca.org

Investor Protection Trust
919 18th St NW Ste 300 .... Washington DC 20006 202-775-2111
Web: www.investorprotection.org

Mortgage Bankers Assn (MBA)
1919 M St NW 5th Fl .... Washington DC 20036 202-557-2700 721-0245*
**Fax:* Cust Svc ■ *TF:* 800-793-6222

Municipal Securities Rulemaking Board (MSRB)
1900 Duke St Ste 600 .... Alexandria VA 22314 703-797-6600 797-6700
TF: 888-475-8376 ■ *Web:* www.msrb.org

NA of Credit Management (NACM)
8840 Columbia 100 Pkwy .... Columbia MD 21045 410-740-5560 740-5574
TF: 800-955-8815 ■ *Web:* www.nacm.org

NA of Federal Credit Unions (NAFCU)
3138 Tenth St N .... Arlington VA 22201 703-522-4770 524-1082
TF: 800-336-4644 ■ *Web:* www.nafcu.org

NA of Government Guaranteed Lenders (NAGGL)
215 E Ninth Ave .... Stillwater OK 74074 405-377-4022 377-3931
Web: www.naggl.org

NACHA - Electronic Payments Assn
13665 Dulles Technology Dr Ste 300 .... Herndon VA 20171 703-561-1100 787-0996
TF: 800-487-9180 ■ *Web:* www.nacha.org

National Federation of Community Development Credit Unions (NFCDCU)
39 Broadway Ste 2140 .... New York NY 10006 212-809-1850 809-3274
TF: 800-437-8711 ■ *Web:* www.cdcu.coop

National Futures Assn (NFA)
300 S Riverside Plz Ste 1800 .... Chicago IL 60606 312-781-1300 781-1467
TF: 800-621-3570 ■ *Web:* www.nfa.futures.org

National Investment Co Service Assn (NICSA)
8400 Westpark Dr 2nd Fl .... McLean VA 22102 508-485-1500 485-1560
TF: 800-426-1122 ■ *Web:* www.nicsa.org

National Investor Relations Institute (NIRI)
8020 Towers Crescent Dr Ste 250 .... Vienna VA 22182 703-506-3570 506-3571
Web: www.niri.org

North American Securities Administrators Assn (NASAA)
750 First St NE Ste 1140 .... Washington DC 20002 202-737-0900 783-3571
TF: 800-222-1253 ■ *Web:* www.nasaa.org

Pension Real Estate Assn (PREA)
100 Pearl St 13th Fl .... Hartford CT 06103 860-692-6341 692-6351
Web: www.prea.org

Risk Management Assn (RMA)
1801 Market St Ste 300 .... Philadelphia PA 19103 215-446-4000 446-4101
TF Cust Svc: 800-677-7621 ■ *Web:* www.rmahq.org

Securities Industry & Financial Markets Assn (SIFMAA)
120 Broadway 35th Fl .... New York NY 10271 212-313-1200 313-1301
TF: 888-367-7966 ■ *Web:* www.sifma.org

Security Traders Assn 1115 Broadway .... New York NY 10010 212-837-7765 659-5249*
**Fax Area Code:* 202 ■ *Web:* www.securitytraders.org

Smart Card Alliance Inc
191 Clarkville Rd .... Princeton Junction NJ 08550 609-799-5654 799-7032
TF: 800-556-6828 ■ *Web:* www.smartcardalliance.org

Western Economic Assn International (WEAI)
18837 Brookhurst St Ste 304 .... Fountain Valley CA 92708 714-965-8800 965-8829
Web: www.weai.org

Winter Kloman Moter & Repp SC (WKMR)
235 N Executive Dr Ste 160 .... Brookfield WI 53005 262-797-9050 797-8251
Web: www.wkmr.com

World Council of Credit Unions Inc (WOCCU)
5710 Mineral Pt Rd .... Madison WI 53705 608-395-2000 395-2001
Web: www.woccu.org

49-3 Construction Industry Associations

Phone Fax

Air Conditioning Contractors of America (ACCA)
2800 S Shirlington Rd Ste 300 .... Arlington VA 22206 703-575-4477 575-8107
Web: www.acca.org

Air Movement & Control Assn International Inc (AMCA)
30 W University Dr .... Arlington Heights IL 60004 847-394-0150 253-0088
Web: www.amca.org

American Architectural Manufacturers Assn (AAMA)
1827 Walden Office Sq Ste 550 .... Schaumburg IL 60173 847-303-5664 303-5774
Web: www.aamanet.org

American Concrete Institute International (ACI)
38800 Country Club Dr PO Box 9094 .... Farmington Hills MI 48331 248-848-3700 848-3701
Web: www.concrete.org

American Concrete Pavement Assn (ACPA)
5420 Old OrchaRd Rd Ste A-100 .... Skokie IL 60077 847-966-2272 966-9970
Web: www.acpa.org

American Concrete Pipe Assn
8445 Freeport Pkwy Ste 350 .... Irving TX 75063 972-506-7216 506-7682
Web: www.concretepipe.org

American Fence Assn (AFA)
800 Roosevelt Rd Bldg C-312 .... Glen Ellyn IL 60137 630-942-6598 790-3095
TF: 800-822-4342 ■ *Web:* www.americanfenceassociation.com

American Fire Sprinkler Assn (AFSA)
12750 Merit Dr Ste 350 .... Dallas TX 75251 214-349-5965 343-8898
Web: www.firesprinkler.org

American Institute of Constructors (AIC)
700 N Fairfax St Ste 510 .... Alexandria VA 22314 703-683-4999 527-3105*
**Fax Area Code:* 571 ■ *Web:* www.professionalconstructor.org

Phone Fax

American Institute of Steel Construction (AISC)
1 E Wacker Dr Ste 3100 .... Chicago IL 60601 312-670-2400 670-5403
Web: www.aisc.org

American Institute of Timber Construction (AITC)
7012 S Revere Pkwy Ste 140 .... Centennial CO 80112 303-792-9559 792-0669
Web: www.aitc-glulam.org

American Road & Transportation Builders Assn (ARTBA)
1219 28th St NW .... Washington DC 20007 202-289-4434 289-4435
TF: 800-636-2377 ■ *Web:* www.artba.org

American Society of Heating Refrigerating & Air-Conditioning Engineers Inc (ASHRAE)
1791 Tullie Cir NE .... Atlanta GA 30329 404-636-8400 321-5478
TF Cust Svc: 800-527-4723 ■ *Web:* www.ashrae.org

American Society of Home Inspectors (ASHI)
932 Lee St Ste 101 .... Des Plaines IL 60016 847-759-2820 759-1620
TF: 800-743-2744 ■ *Web:* www.homeinspector.org

American Society of Professional Estimators (ASPE)
2525 Perimeter Pl Dr Ste 103 .... Nashville TN 37214 615-316-9200 316-9800
TF: 888-378-6283 ■ *Web:* www.aspenational.org

American Subcontractors Assn Inc (ASA)
1004 Duke St .... Alexandria VA 22314 703-684-3450 836-3482
TF: 866-378-8866 ■ *Web:* www.asaonline.com

American Welding Society (AWS) 550 NW 42nd Ave ..... Miami FL 33126 305-443-9353 443-7559
TF: 800-443-9353 ■ *Web:* www.aws.org

APA - Engineered Wood Assn 7011 S 19th St .... Tacoma WA 98466 253-565-6600 565-7265
Web: www.apawood.org

Architectural Precast Assn (APA)
6710 Winkler Rd Ste 8 .... Fort Myers FL 33919 239-454-6989 454-6787
Web: www.archprecast.org

Architectural Woodwork Institute (AWI)
46179 Westlake Dr Ste 120 .... Potomac Falls VA 20165 571-323-3636 323-3630
TF: 866-877-6933 ■ *Web:* www.awinet.org

Asphalt Institute 2696 Research Pk Dr. .... Lexington KY 40511 859-288-4960 288-4999
Web: www.asphaltinstitute.org

Asphalt Roofing Manufacturers Assn (ARMA)
529 14th St NW Ste 750 .... Washington DC 20045 202-207-0917 223-9741
TF: 800-247-6637 ■ *Web:* www.asphaltroofing.org

Associated Builders & Contractors Inc (ABC)
4250 Fairfax Dr. .... Arlington VA 22203 703-812-2000 812-8235
TF: 877-889-5627 ■ *Web:* www.abc.org

Associated General Contractors of America (AGC)
2300 Wilson Blvd Ste 400 .... Arlington VA 22201 703-548-3118 548-3119
TF: 800-242-1766 ■ *Web:* www.agc.org

Associated Locksmiths of America (ALOA)
3500 Easy St. .... Dallas TX 75247 214-819-9733 819-9736
TF: 800-532-2562 ■ *Web:* www.aloa.org

Association for Retail Environment (ARE)
4651 Sheridan St Ste 470 .... Hollywood FL 33021 954-893-7300 893-7500
TF: 800-421-3483 ■ *Web:* www.retailenvironments.org

Association of the Wall & Ceiling Industries International (AWCI)
513 W Broad St Ste 210 .... Falls Church VA 22046 703-538-1600 534-8307
Web: www.awci.org

Brick Industry Assn (BIA)
1850 Centennial Pk Dr Ste 301 .... Reston VA 20191 703-620-0010 620-3928
TF: 866-644-1293 ■ *Web:* www.gobrick.com

Building & Construction Trades Dept AFL-CIO
815 16th St NW Ste 600 .... Washington DC 20006 202-347-1461 628-0724
Web: www.bctd.org

Building Material Dealers Assn (BMDA)
1006 SE Grand Ave Ste 301 .... Portland OR 97214 503-208-3763 620-1016
TF: 888-960-6329 ■ *Web:* www.bmda.com

Cedar Shake & Shingle Bureau
7101 Horne St Ste 2 .... Mission BC V2V7A2 604-820-7700 820-0266
Web: www.cedarbureau.org

Ceilings & Interior Systems Construction Assn (CISCA)
1010 Jorie Blvd Ste 30 .... Oak Brook IL 60523 630-584-1919 560-8537*
**Fax Area Code:* 866 ■ *TF:* 866-560-8537 ■ *Web:* cisca.org

Cement Assn of Canada (CAC) 502-350 Sparks St .... Ottawa ON K1R7S8 613-236-9471 563-4498
Web: www.cement.ca

Central Station Alarm Assn (CSAA)
8150 Leesburg Pk Ste 700 .... Vienna VA 22180 703-242-4670 242-4675
Web: www.csaaintl.org

Composite Panel Assn
19465 Deerfield Ave Ste 306 .... Leesburg VA 20176 703-724-1128
TF: 866-426-6767 ■ *Web:* compositepanel.org

Concrete Reinforcing Steel Institute (CRSI)
933 N Plum Grove Rd .... Schaumburg IL 60173 847-517-1200 517-1206
Web: www.crsi.org

Construction Financial Management Assn (CFMA)
100 Village Blvd Ste 200A .... Princeton NJ 08540 609-452-8000 452-0474
TF: 877-462-7827 ■ *Web:* www.cfma.org

Distribution Contractors Assn (DCA)
101 W Renner Rd Ste 460 .... Richardson TX 75082 972-680-0261 680-0461
Web: www.dca-online.org

Door & Hardware Institute (DHI)
14150 Newbrook Dr Ste 200 .... Chantilly VA 20151 703-222-2010 222-2410
Web: www.dhi.org

Electronic Security Assn Inc (ESA)
2300 Vly View Ln Ste 230 .... Irving TX 75062 214-260-5970 260-5979
TF: 888-447-1689 ■ *Web:* www.esaweb.org

Forest Resources Assn Inc
600 Jefferson Plz Ste 350 .... Rockville MD 20852 301-838-9385
Web: www.forestresources.org

Hardwood Plywood & Veneer Assn (HPVA)
1825 Michael Faraday Dr .... Reston VA 20190 703-435-2900 435-2537
Web: www.hpva.org

Interlocking Concrete Pavement Institute (ICPI)
14801 Murdock St Ste 2300 .... Chantilly VA 20151 202-712-9036 408-0285
TF: 800-241-3652 ■ *Web:* www.icpi.org

International Assn of Drilling Contractors (IADC)
10370 Richmond Ave Ste 760 .... Houston TX 77042 713-292-1945 292-1946
Web: www.iadc.org

International Assn of Electrical Inspectors (IAEI)
901 Waterfall Way Ste 602 .... Richardson TX 75080 972-235-1455 235-6858
TF: 800-786-4234 ■ *Web:* www.iaei.org

	Phone	Fax
International Code Council (ICC) 500 New Jersey Ave NW 6th Fl....Washington DC 20001 *TF:* 888-422-7233 ■ *Web:* www.iccsafe.org	202-370-1800	783-2348
International Council of Shopping Centers (ICSC) 1221 Ave of the Americas 41st Fl....New York NY 10020 **Fax Area Code:* 212 ■ *Web:* www.icsc.org	646-728-3800	589-5555*
International District Energy Assn (IDEA) 24 Lyman St Ste 230....Westborough MA 01581 *Web:* www.districtenergy.org	508-366-9339	366-0019
International Institute of Ammonia Refrigeration 1001 N Fairfax St Ste 503....Alexandria VA 22314 *TF:* 800-937-8461 ■ *Web:* www.iiar.org	703-312-4200	312-0065
International Masonry Institute (IMI) 17101 Science Dr....Bowie MD 20715 **Fax Area Code:* 301 ■ *TF:* 800-803-0295 ■ *Web:* www.imiweb.org	800-803-0295	261-2855*
International Road Federation (IRF) 500 Mongomery St 5th Fl....Alexandria VA 22314 *Web:* www.irfnews.org	703-535-1001	535-1007
International Union of Elevator Constructors (IUEC) 7154 Columbia Gateway Dr....Columbia MD 21046 *Web:* www.iuec.org	410-953-6150	
International Wood Products Assn (IWPA) 4214 King St....Alexandria VA 22302 *TF:* 855-435-0005 ■ *Web:* www.iwpawood.org	703-820-6696	820-8550
Manufactured Housing Institute (MHI) 2101 Wilson Blvd Ste 610....Arlington VA 22201 *TF:* 800-505-5500 ■ *Web:* www.manufacturedhousing.org	703-558-0400	558-0401
Marble Institute of America (MIA) 28901 Clemens Rd Ste 100....Westlake OH 44145 *TF:* 800-433-4903 ■ *Web:* www.marble-institute.com	440-250-9222	250-9223
Mason Contractors Assn of America (MCAA) 1481 Merchant Dr....Algonquin IL 60193 *TF:* 800-536-2225 ■ *Web:* www.masoncontractors.org	224-678-9709	678-9714
Mechanical Contractors Assn of America (MCAA) 1385 Piccard Dr....Rockville MD 20850 *TF:* 800-556-3653 ■ *Web:* www.mcaa.org	301-869-5800	990-9690
Monument Builders of North America (MBNA) 136 S Keowee St....Dayton OH 45402 **Fax Area Code:* 937 ■ *TF:* 800-233-4472 ■ *Web:* www.monumentbuilders.org	800-233-4472	222-5794*
NA of Women in Construction (NAWIC) 327 S Adams St....Fort Worth TX 76104 *TF:* 800-552-3506 ■ *Web:* www.nawic.org	817-877-5551	877-0324
National Association of Tower Erectors (NATE) 8 Second St SE....Watertown SD 57201 *TF:* 888-882-5865 ■ *Web:* natehome.com	605-882-5865	886-5184
National Community Renaissance of California 9421 Haven Ave....Rancho Cucamonga CA 91730 *Web:* www.nationalcore.org	909-483-2444	483-2448
National Concrete Masonry Assn 13750 Sunrise Vly Dr....Herndon VA 20171 *TF:* 877-343-6268 ■ *Web:* www.ncma.org	703-713-1900	713-1910
National Corrugated Steel Pipe Assn (NCSPA) 14070 Proton Rd Ste 100....Dallas TX 75244 *Web:* www.ncspa.org	972-850-1907	490-4219
National Council of Examiners for Engineering & Surveying (NCEES) 280 Seneca Creek Rd....Seneca SC 29678 *TF:* 800-250-3196 ■ *Web:* www.ncees.org	864-654-6824	654-6033
National Electrical Contractors Assn (NECA) 3 Bethesda Metro Ctr Ste 1100....Bethesda MD 20814 *TF:* 800-214-0585 ■ *Web:* www.necanet.org	301-657-3110	215-4500
National Elevator Industry Inc 1677 County Rd 64 PO Box 838....Salem NY 12865 *Web:* www.neii.org	518-854-3100	854-3257
National Fire Sprinkler Assn (NFSA) 40 Jon Barrett Rd....Patterson NY 12563 *Web:* www.nfsa.org	845-878-4200	878-4215
National Frame Builders Assn (NFBA) 8735 W Higgins Rd Ste 300....Chicago IL 60631 **Fax Area Code:* 847 ■ *TF:* 800-557-6957 ■ *Web:* www.nfba.org	800-557-6957	375-6495*
National Hardwood Lumber Assn (NHLA) 6830 Raleigh-LaGrange Rd....Memphis TN 38134 *TF:* 800-933-0318 ■ *Web:* www.nhla.com	901-377-1818	382-6419
National Housing Conference (NHC) 1801 K St NW Ste M-100....Washington DC 20006 *Web:* www.nhc.org	202-466-2121	466-2122
National Institute of Bldg Sciences (NIBS) 1090 Vermont Ave NW Ste 700....Washington DC 20005 *Web:* www.nibs.org	202-289-7800	289-1092
National Insulation Assn (NIA) 99 Canal Ctr Plz Ste 222....Alexandria VA 22314 *TF:* 877-968-7642 ■ *Web:* www.insulation.org	703-683-6422	549-4838
National Kitchen & Bath Assn (NKBA) 687 Willow Grove St....Hackettstown NJ 07840 **Fax Area Code:* 908 ■ *TF:* 800-843-6522 ■ *Web:* www.nkba.org	800-843-6522	852-1695*
National Parking Assn (NPA) 1112 16th St NW Ste 840....Washington DC 20036 *TF:* 800-647-7275	202-296-4336	296-3102
National Precast Concrete Assn (NPCA) 10333 N Meridian St Ste 272....Indianapolis IN 46290 *TF:* 800-366-7731 ■ *Web:* www.precast.org	317-571-9500	571-0041
National Ready Mixed Concrete Assn (NRMCA) 900 Spring St....Silver Spring MD 20910 *TF:* 888-846-7622 ■ *Web:* www.nrmca.org	301-587-1400	585-4219
National Roofing Contractors Assn (NRCA) 10255 W Higgins Rd Ste 600....Rosemont IL 60018 *TF Cust Svc:* 800-323-9545 ■ *Web:* www.nrca.net	847-299-9070	299-1183
National Stone Sand & Gravel Assn (NSSGA) 1605 King St....Alexandria VA 22314 *TF:* 800-342-1415 ■ *Web:* www.nssga.org	703-525-8788	525-7782
National Wood Flooring Assn (NWFA) 111 Chesterfield Industrial Blvd....Chesterfield MO 63005 *TF:* 800-422-4556 ■ *Web:* www.woodfloors.org	636-519-9663	
North American Bldg Material Distribution Assn (NBMDA) 330 N Wabash Ave Ste 2000....Chicago IL 60611 *TF:* 888-747-7862 ■ *Web:* www.nbmda.org	312-321-6845	644-0310
North American Insulation Manufacturers Assn (NAIMA) 44 Canal Ctr Plz Ste 310....Alexandria VA 22314 *Web:* insulationinstitute.org	703-684-0084	684-0427
Operative Plasterers' & Cement Masons' International Assn of the US & Canada (OPCMIA) 11720 Beltsville Dr Ste 700....Beltsville MD 20705 *TF:* 888-379-1558 ■ *Web:* www.opcmia.org	301-623-1000	623-1032
Painting & Decorating Contractors of America (PDCA) 2316 Millpark Dr....Maryland Heights MO 63043 *TF Cust Svc:* 800-332-7322 ■ *Web:* www.pdca.org	314-514-7322	514-9417
Plumbing Manufacturers International (PMI) 1921 Rohlwing Rd Unit G....Rolling Meadows IL 60008 *Web:* www.safeplumbing.org	847-481-5500	481-5501
Plumbing-Heating-Cooling Contractors NA (PHCC) 180 S Washington St....Falls Church VA 22040 *TF:* 800-533-7694 ■ *Web:* www.phccweb.org	703-237-8100	237-7442
Portland Cement Assn (PCA) 5420 Old OrchaRd Rd....Skokie IL 60077 *Web:* www.cement.org	847-966-6200	966-9781
Precast/Prestressed Concrete Institute (PCI) 200 W Adams St Ste 2100....Chicago IL 60606 *Web:* www.pci.org	312-786-0300	786-0353
Precision Metalforming Assn (PMA) 6363 Oak Tree Blvd....Independence OH 44131 *Web:* www.pma.org/home	216-901-8800	901-9190
Refrigeration Service Engineers Society (RSES) 1666 Rand Rd....Des Plaines IL 60016 *TF:* 800-297-5660 ■ *Web:* www.rses.org	847-297-6464	297-5038
Sheet Metal & Air Conditioning Contractors' NA (SMACNA) 4201 Lafayette Ctr Dr....Chantilly VA 20151 *Web:* www.smacna.org	703-803-2980	803-3732
Sheet Metal Workers International Assn (SMWIA) 1750 New York Ave NW 6th Fl....Washington DC 20006 *TF:* 800-251-7045 ■ *Web:* www.smwia.org	202-783-5880	662-0894
Steel Framing Alliance 25 Massachusetts Ave NW Ste 800....Washington DC 20001 *Web:* www.steelframingalliance.com	202-785-2022	452-1039
Tile Council of America Inc (TCA) 100 Clemson Research Blvd....Anderson SC 29625 *Web:* www.tcnatile.com	864-646-8453	646-2821
Tilt-up Concrete Assn (TCA) 113 First St NW....Mount Vernon IA 52314 **Fax Area Code:* 320 ■ *Web:* www.tilt-up.org	319-895-6911	213-5555*
US Society on Dams (USSD) 1616 17th St Ste 483....Denver CO 80202 *Web:* www.ussdams.org	303-628-5430	628-5431
Window & Door Manufacturers Assn (WDMA) 330 N Wabash Ave Ste 2000....Chicago IL 60611 **Fax Area Code:* 651 ■ *TF:* 800-223-2301 ■ *Web:* www.wdma.com	847-299-5200	264-5150*
Wood Moulding & Millwork Producers Assn (WMMPA) 507 First St....Woodland CA 95695 *TF:* 800-550-7889 ■ *Web:* www.wmmpa.com	530-661-9591	661-9586
Wood Products Manufacturers Assn (WPMA) PO Box 761....Westminster MA 01473 *Web:* www.wpma.org	978-874-5445	874-9946
Wood Truss Council of America (WTCA) 6300 Enterprise Ln....Madison WI 53719 *Web:* www.sbcindustry.com	608-274-4849	274-3329
World Millwork Alliance (AMD) 10047 Robert Trent Jones Pkwy....New Port Richey FL 34655 *Web:* worldmillworkalliance.com	727-372-3665	372-2879

49-4 Consumer Sales & Service Professionals Associations

	Phone	Fax
Advanced Medical Technology Assn 701 Pennsylvania Ave NW Ste 800....Washington DC 20004 *Web:* www.advamed.org	202-783-8700	783-8750
AHRI - Air-Conditioning Heating & Refrigeration Institute 4100 N Fairfax Dr Ste 200....Arlington VA 22203 *Web:* www.ahrinet.org	703-524-8800	528-3816
American Apparel & Footwear Assn (AAFA) 1601 N Kent St Ste 1200....Arlington VA 22209 *TF:* 800-520-2262 ■ *Web:* www.wewear.org	703-524-1864	522-6741
American Boat & Yacht Council Inc (ABYC) 613 Third St Ste 10....Annapolis MD 21403 *Web:* www.abycinc.org	410-990-4460	990-4466
American Gem Society (AGS) 8881 W Sahara Ave....Las Vegas NV 89117 *TF:* 866-805-6500 ■ *Web:* www.americangemsociety.org	702-255-6500	255-7420
American Gem Trade Assn (AGTA) 3030 LBJ Fwy Ste 840....Dallas TX 75234 *TF:* 800-972-1162 ■ *Web:* www.agta.org	214-742-4367	742-7334
American Hardware Manufacturers Assn (AHMA) 801 N Plz Dr....Schaumburg IL 60173 *Web:* www.ahma.org	847-605-1025	605-1030
American Institute of Floral Designers (AIFD) 720 Light St....Baltimore MD 21230 *TF:* 877-865-5320 ■ *Web:* www.aifd.org	410-752-3318	752-8295
American Lighting Assn (ALA) 2050 Stemmons Fwy Ste 10046....Dallas TX 75207 *TF:* 800-605-4448 ■ *Web:* www.americanlightingassoc.com	214-698-9898	698-9899
American Pet Products Manufacturers Assn (APPMA) 255 Glenville Rd....Greenwich CT 06831 *TF:* 800-452-1225 ■ *Web:* www.americanpetproducts.org	203-532-0000	532-0551
American Rental Assn (ARA) 1900 19th St....Moline IL 61265 *TF:* 800-334-2177 ■ *Web:* www.ararental.org	309-764-2475	764-1533
American Sportfishing Assn (ASA) 1001 N Fairfax St Ste 501....Alexandria VA 22314 *Web:* www.asafishing.org	703-519-9691	519-1872
American Watchmakers-Clockmakers Institute (AWI) 701 Enterprise Dr....Harrison OH 45030 *TF:* 866-367-2924 ■ *Web:* awci.com	513-367-9800	367-1414
Association for Linen Management 2161 Lexington Rd Ste 2....Richmond KY 40475 *TF:* 800-669-0863 ■ *Web:* www.almnet.org	859-624-0177	624-3580

Phone | Fax

Association of Home Appliance Manufacturers (AHAM)
1111 19th St NW Ste 402 Washington DC 20036 202-872-5955 872-9354
TF: 888-258-3247 ■ *Web:* www.aham.org

Association of Pool & Spa Professionals (APSP)
2111 Eisenhower Ave Ste 500 Alexandria VA 22314 703-838-0083 549-0493
TF: 800-323-3996 ■ *Web:* www.apsp.org

Automotive Recyclers Assn (ARA)
3975 Fair Ridge Dr Ste 20N Fairfax VA 22033 703-385-1001 385-1494
TF: 888-385-1005 ■ *Web:* www.a-r-a.org

Awards and Personalization Association (ARA)
8735 W Higgins Rd Ste 300 Chicago IL 60631 847-375-4800 375-6480
TF: 800-344-2148 ■ *Web:* awardspersonalization.org/default.aspx

Carpet & Rug Institute (CRI)
100 S Hamilton St PO Box 2048 Dalton GA 30720 706-278-3176 278-8835
Web: www.carpet-rug.org

Coin Laundry Assn (CLA)
1s660 Midwest Rd Ste 205 Oakbrook Terrace IL 60181 630-953-7920
TF: 800-570-5629 ■ *Web:* www.coinlaundry.org

Consumer Healthcare Products Assn (CHPA)
1150 Connecticut Ave NW # 700 Washington DC 20036 202-429-9260 223-6835
Web: www.chpa.org

Contact Lens Manufacturers Assn PO Box 29398 Lincoln NE 68529 402-465-4122 465-4187
TF: 800-344-9060 ■ *Web:* www.clma.net

Cremation Assn of North America (CANA)
499 Northgate Pkwy Wheeling IL 60090 312-245-1077 321-4098
Web: www.cremationassociation.org

Dental Trade Alliance (DTA)
4350 N Fairfax Dr Ste 220 Arlington VA 22203 703-379-7755 931-9429
Web: www.dentaltradealliance.org

Diamond Council of America (DCA)
3212 W End Ave Ste 202 Nashville TN 37203 615-385-5301 385-4955
TF: 877-283-5669 ■ *Web:* www.diamondcouncil.org

Diving Equipment & Marketing Assn (DEMA)
3750 Convoy St Ste 310 San Diego CA 92111 858-616-6408 616-6495
TF: 800-862-3483 ■ *Web:* www.dema.org

Drycleaning & Laundry Institute
14700 Sweitzer Ln Laurel MD 20707 301-622-1900 295-0685*
**Fax Area Code:* 240 ■ *TF:* 800-638-2627 ■ *Web:* www.dlionline.org

Envelope Manufacturers Assn (EMA)
500 Montgomery St Ste 550 Alexandria VA 22314 703-739-2200 739-2209
Web: www.envelope.org

Fashion Group International Inc (FGI)
8 W 40th St 7th Fl New York NY 10018 212-302-5511 302-5533
Web: www.fgi.org

Footwear Distributors & Retailers of America (FDRA)
1319 F St NW Ste 700 Washington DC 20004 202-737-5660
Web: www.fdra.org

Fragrance Foundation 621 2nd Ave 2nd Fl New York NY 10016 212-725-2755 786-3260*
**Fax Area Code:* 646 ■ *Web:* fragrance.org

Gemological Institute of America (GIA)
5345 Armada Dr Carlsbad CA 92008 760-603-4000 603-4003
TF: 800-421-7250 ■ *Web:* www.gia.edu

Hearth Patio & Barbecue Assn (HPBA)
1901 N Moore St Ste 600 Arlington VA 22209 703-522-0086 522-0548
Web: www.hpba.org

Home Furnishings Independents Assn (HFIA)
2050 Stemmons World Fwy Ste 292 Dallas TX 75207 800-422-3778
TF: 800-422-3778 ■ *Web:* myhfa.org

Independent Jewelers Organization (IJO)
136 Old Post Rd Southport CT 06890 800-624-9252 254-7429*
**Fax Area Code:* 203 ■ *TF:* 800-624-9252 ■ *Web:* www.ijo.com

Independent Office Products & Furniture Dealers Assn (IOPFDA)
3601 E Joppa Rd Baltimore MD 21234 410-931-8100 931-8111
Web: www.nopanet.org

Institute of Inspection Cleaning & Restoration Certification (IICRC)
4043 S E Ave Las Vegas NV 89119 360-693-5675
Web: www.iicrc.org

International Card Manufacturers Assn (ICMA)
191 Clarksville Rd Princeton Junction NJ 08550 609-799-4900 799-7032
Web: www.icma.com

International Cemetery Cremation & Funeral Assn (ICCFA)
107 Carpenter Dr Ste 100 Sterling VA 20164 703-391-8400 391-8416
TF: 800-645-7700 ■ *Web:* www.iccfa.com

International Engraved Graphics Assn
305 Plus Pk Blvd Nashville TN 37217 800-821-3138
TF: 800-821-3138 ■ *Web:* www.iega.org

International Executive Housekeepers Assn (IEHA)
1001 Eastwind Dr Ste 301 Westerville OH 43081 614-895-7166 895-1248
TF: 800-200-6342 ■ *Web:* www.ieha.org

International Furniture Rental Assn (IFRA)
950 F St NW 10th Fl Washington DC 20004 202-239-3818 654-4818
Web: www.ifra.org

International Housewares Assn (IHA)
6400 Shafer Ct Ste 650 Rosemont IL 60018 847-292-4200 292-4211
TF: 800-752-1052 ■ *Web:* www.housewares.org

International Order of the Golden Rule (OGR)
3520 Executive Ctr Dr Ste 300 Austin TX 78731 512-334-5504 334-5514
TF: 800-637-8030 ■ *Web:* www.ogr.org

International Precious Metals Institute (IPMI)
5101 N 12th Ave Ste C Pensacola FL 32504 850-476-1156 476-1548
Web: www.ipmi.org

International Sign Assn (ISA)
1001 N Fairfax St Ste 301 Alexandria VA 22314 703-836-4012 836-8353
TF: 866-949-7446 ■ *Web:* www.signs.org

International Sleep Products Assn (ISPA)
501 Wythe St Alexandria VA 22314 703-683-8371 683-4503
Web: www.sleepproducts.org

Jewelers Board of Trade (JBT) 95 Jefferson Blvd Warwick RI 02888 401-467-0055 467-6070
Web: www.jewelersboard.com

Jewelers of America (JA)
52 Vanderbilt Ave 19th Fl New York NY 10017 646-658-0246 658-0256
TF: 800-223-0673 ■ *Web:* www.jewelers.org

Leather Industries of America (LIA)
3050 K St NW Ste 400 Washington DC 20007 202-342-8497 342-8583
TF: 800-635-0617 ■ *Web:* www.leatherusa.com

Manufacturing Jewelers & Suppliers of America Inc (MJSA)
57 John L Dietsch Sq Attleboro MA 02763 401-274-3840 274-0265
TF: 800-444-6572 ■ *Web:* www.mjsa.org

National Beauty Culturists' League Inc (NBCL)
25 Logan Cir NW Washington DC 20005 202-332-2695
Web: www.nbcl.org

National Bicycle Dealers Assn (NBDA)
777 W 19th St Ste O Costa Mesa CA 92627 949-722-6909 722-1747
Web: www.nbda.com

National Cleaners Assn 252 W 29th St 2nd Fl New York NY 10001 212-967-3002 967-2240
TF General: 800-888-1622 ■ *Web:* www.nca-i.com

National Funeral Directors & Morticians Assn (NFDMA)
6290 Shannon Pkwy Union City GA 30291 770-969-0064 286-6573*
**Fax Area Code:* 404 ■ *TF:* 800-434-0958 ■ *Web:* www.nfdma.com

National Funeral Directors Assn (NFDA)
13625 Bishop's Dr Brookfield WI 53005 262-789-1880 789-6977
TF: 800-228-6332 ■ *Web:* nfda.org

National Home Furnishings Assn (NHFA)
500 Giuseppe Ct Ste 6 Roseville CA 95678 336-886-6100 801-6102
TF: 800-422-3778 ■ *Web:* myhfa.org

National Pest Management Assn Inc (NPMA)
10460 N St Fairfax VA 22030 703-352-6762 352-3031
Web: www.pestworld.org

National Shoe Retailers Assn (NSRA)
7386 N La Cholla Blvd Tucson AZ 85741 520-209-1710
TF: 800-673-8446 ■ *Web:* www.nsra.org

National Sporting Goods Assn (NSGA)
1601 Feehanville Dr Ste 300 Mount Prospect IL 60056 847-296-6742 391-9827
TF: 800-815-5422 ■ *Web:* www.nsga.org

National Volunteer Fire Council (NVFC)
7852 Walker Dr Ste 450 Greenbelt MD 20770 202-887-5700 887-5291
TF: 888-275-6832 ■ *Web:* www.nvfc.org

Outdoor Industry Assn (OIA)
4909 Pearl E Cir Ste 200 Boulder CO 80301 303-444-3353 444-3284
Web: www.outdoorindustry.org

Outdoor Power Equipment Institute Inc (OPEI)
341 S Patrick St Alexandria VA 22314 703-549-7600 549-7604
Web: www.opei.org

Pet Food Institute (PFI) 2025 M St NW Ste 800 Washington DC 20036 202-367-1120 367-2120
Web: www.petfoodinstitute.org

Pet Industry Joint Advisory Council (PIJAC)
1220 19th St NW Ste 400 Washington DC 20036 202-452-1525 293-4377
TF: 800-553-7387 ■ *Web:* www.pijac.org

Piano Technicians Guild 4444 Forest Ave Kansas City KS 66106 913-432-9975 432-9986
Web: www.ptg.org

Professional Assn of Innkeepers International (PAII)
108 S Cleveland St Merrill WI 54452 856-310-1102 895-0432
TF: 800-468-7244 ■ *Web:* www.paii.com

Recreation Vehicle Industry Assn (RVIA)
1896 Preston White Dr Reston VA 20191 703-620-6003 620-5071
TF: 800-336-0154 ■ *Web:* www.rvia.org

Security Industry Assn (SIA)
8405 Colesville Rd Ste 500 Silver Spring MD 20910 703-683-2075 683-2469
TF: 866-817-8888 ■ *Web:* www.siaonline.org

Selected Independent Funeral Homes
500 Lake Cook Rd Ste 205 Deerfield IL 60015 847-236-9401 236-9968
TF: 800-323-4219 ■ *Web:* www.selectedfuneralhomes.org

Shoe Service Institute of America (SSIA)
18 School St North Brookfield MA 01535 508-867-7731 569-8333*
**Fax Area Code:* 410 ■ *Web:* www.ssia.info

Silver Institute 888 16th St NW Ste 303 Washington DC 20006 202-835-0185 835-0155
Web: www.silverinstitute.org

SnowSports Industries America (SIA)
8377 Greensboro Dr # B McLean VA 22102 703-556-9020 821-8276
Web: www.snowsports.org

Society of American Florists (SAF)
1601 Duke St Alexandria VA 22314 703-836-8700 836-8705
TF: 800-336-4743 ■ *Web:* www.safnow.org

Specialty Sleep Assn (SSA) 46639 Jones Ranch Rd Friant CA 93626 559-868-4187
Web: www.sleepinformation.org

Sports & Fitness Industry Association, The
1150 17th St NW Ste 850 Washington DC 20036 202-775-1762 296-7462
Web: www.sfia.org

Textile Rental Services Assn (TRSA)
1800 Diagonal Rd Ste 200 Alexandria VA 22314 703-519-0029 519-0026
TF: 877-770-9274 ■ *Web:* www.trsa.org

Tire Industry Assn (TIA)
1532 Pointer Ridge Pl Ste G Bowie MD 20716 301-430-7280 430-7283
TF: 800-876-8372 ■ *Web:* www.tireindustry.org

Toy Industry Assn 1115 Broadway Ste 400 New York NY 10010 212-675-1141 633-1429
TF: 800-541-1345 ■ *Web:* www.toyassociation.org

Uniform & Textile Service Assn (UTSA)
1300 N 17th St Ste 750 Arlington VA 22209 703-247-2600
TF: 800-996-3426 ■ *Web:* www.glrppr.org

Vision Council, The
225 Reinekers Ln Ste 700 Alexandria VA 22314 703-548-4560 548-4580
TF: 866-826-0290 ■ *Web:* www.thevisioncouncil.org

Wallcoverings Assn
401 N Michigan Ave Ste 2200 Chicago IL 60611 312-644-6610 527-6705
TF: 800-575-8016 ■ *Web:* www.wallcoverings.org

World Floor Covering Assn (WFCA)
2211 Howell Ave Anaheim CA 92806 714-978-6440 978-6066
TF: 800-624-6880 ■ *Web:* www.wfca.org

World Gold Council 685 Third Ave Fl 27 New York NY 10017 212-317-3800 688-0410
Web: www.gold.org

49-5 Education Professionals Associations

Phone | Fax

American Anthropological Assn (AAA)
2200 Wilson Blvd Ste 600 Arlington VA 22201 703-528-1902 528-3546
Web: www.americananthro.org

Phone | Fax

American Assn for Adult & Continuing Education (AAACE)
1827 Powers Ferry Rd Bldg 14 Ste 100 Atlanta GA 30339 301-459-6261
Web: www.aaace.org

American Assn of Colleges for Teacher Education (AACTE)
1307 New York Ave NW Ste 300 Washington DC 20005 202-293-2450 457-8095
Web: www.aacte.org

American Assn of Colleges of Nursing (AACN)
1 Dupont Cir NW Ste 530 Washington DC 20036 202-463-6930 785-8320
Web: www.aacn.nche.edu

American Assn of Collegiate Registrars & Admissions Officers (AACRAO)
1 Dupont Cir NW Ste 520 Washington DC 20036 202-293-9161 872-8857
TF: 800-222-4922 ■ *Web:* www.aacrao.org

American Assn of Community Colleges (AACC)
1 Dupont Cir NW Ste 410 Washington DC 20036 202-728-0200 833-2467
Web: www.aacc.nche.edu

American Assn of Family & Consumer Sciences (AAFCS)
400 N Columbus St Ste 202 Alexandria VA 22314 703-706-4600 706-4663
TF: 800-424-8080 ■ *Web:* www.aafcs.org

American Assn of Physics Teachers (AAPT)
1 Physics Ellipse College Park MD 20740 301-209-3311 209-0845
Web: www.aapt.org

American Assn of School Administrators (AASA)
801 N Quincy St Ste 700 Arlington VA 22203 703-528-0700 841-1543
TF: 800-771-1162 ■ *Web:* www.aasa.org

American Assn of State Colleges & Universities (AASCU)
1307 New York Ave NW 5th Fl Washington DC 20005 202-293-7070 296-5819
TF: 800-558-3417 ■ *Web:* www.aascu.org

American Assn of Teachers of French (AATF)
302 N Granite St Marion IL 62959 618-453-5731 453-5733
Web: www.frenchteachers.org

American Assn of Teachers of German (AATG)
112 Haddontowne Ct Ste 104 Cherry Hill NJ 08034 856-795-5553 795-9398
TF: 800-835-6770 ■ *Web:* www.aatg.org

American Assn of Teachers of Spanish & Portuguese (AATSP)
900 Ladd Rd Walled Lake MI 48390 248-960-2180 960-9570
TF: 877-832-2457 ■ *Web:* www.aatsp.org

American Assn of University Professors (AAUP)
1133 Nineteenth St Ste 200 Washington DC 20036 202-737-5900 737-5526
TF: 800-424-2973 ■ *Web:* www.aaup.org

American Assn of University Women (AAUW)
1111 16th St NW Washington DC 20036 202-785-7700 872-1425
TF: 800-326-2289 ■ *Web:* www.aauw.org

American College Personnel Assn (ACPA)
1 Dupont Cir NW Ste 300 Washington DC 20036 202-835-2272 296-3286
Web: www.myacpa.org

American Council on Education (ACE)
1 Dupont Cir NW Ste 800 Washington DC 20036 202-939-9300 833-4760
Web: www.acenet.edu

American Council on the Teaching of Foreign Languages (ACTFL)
1001 N Fairfax St Ste 200 Alexandria VA 22314 703-894-2900 894-2905
TF: 844-685-4373 ■ *Web:* www.actfl.org

American Councils for International Education
1776 Massachusetts Ave NW Ste 700 Washington DC 20036 202-833-7522 833-7523
Web: www.americancouncils.org

American Dental Education Assn (ADEA)
1400 K St NW Ste 1100 Washington DC 20005 202-289-7201 289-7204
TF: 800-353-2237 ■ *Web:* www.adea.org

American Educational Research Assn (AERA)
1430 K St NW Ste 1200 Washington DC 20005 202-238-3200 238-3250
TF: 800-893-7950 ■ *Web:* www.aera.net

American Federation of School Administrators (AFSA)
1101 17th St NW Ste 408 Washington DC 20036 202-986-4209 986-4211

American Historical Assn (AHA) 400 A St SE Washington DC 20003 202-544-2422 544-8307
TF: 888-444-6664 ■ *Web:* www.historians.org

American Library Assn (ALA) 50 E Huron St Chicago IL 60611 312-944-6780 944-2641
TF: 800-545-2433 ■ *Web:* www.ala.org

American Medical Student Assn (AMSA)
1902 Assn Dr Reston VA 20191 703-620-6600 620-5873
TF: 800-767-2266 ■ *Web:* www.amsa.org

American Political Science Assn (APSA)
1527 New Hampshire Ave NW Washington DC 20036 202-483-2512 483-2657
Web: www.apsanet.org

American School Counselor Assn (ASCA)
1101 King St Ste 625 Alexandria VA 22314 703-683-2722 683-1619
TF: 800-306-4722 ■ *Web:* www.schoolcounselor.org

American School Health Assn (ASHA)
7263 State Rt 43 PO Box 708 Kent OH 44240 703-506-7675 506-3266
Web: netforum.avectra.com/eweb/startpage.aspx?site=asha1&webcode=homepage

American Society for Engineering Education (ASEE)
1818 N St NW Ste 600 Washington DC 20036 202-331-3500 265-8504
Web: www.asee.org

American Sociological Assn (ASA)
1307 New York Ave Washington DC 20005 202-383-9005 638-0882
TF: 800-524-9400 ■ *Web:* www.asanet.org

American String Teachers Assn (ASTA)
4155 Chain Bridge Rd Fairfax VA 22030 703-279-2113 279-2114
TF: 800-821-7303 ■ *Web:* www.astaweb.com

American Studies Assn (ASA)
1120 19th St NW Ste 301 Washington DC 20036 202-467-4783 467-4786
TF: 800-468-3571 ■ *Web:* www.theasa.net

American Translators Assn (ATA)
225 Reinekers Ln Ste 590 Alexandria VA 22314 703-683-6100 683-6122
TF: 800-253-2252 ■ *Web:* www.atanet.org

Association for Advanced Training in the Behavioral Sciences (AATBS)
5126 Ralston St Ventura CA 93003 805-676-3030 676-3033
TF: 800-472-1931 ■ *Web:* aatbs.com

Association for Career & Technical Education (ACTE)
1410 King St Alexandria VA 22314 703-683-3111 683-7424
TF: 800-826-9972 ■ *Web:* www.acteonline.org

Association for Childhood Education International (ACEI)
1101 16th St NW Ste 300 Washington DC 20036 202-372-9986 570-2212*
**Fax Area Code:* 301 ■ *TF:* 800-423-3563 ■ *Web:* www.acei.org

Association for Communications Technology Professionals in Higher Education (ACUTA)
152 W Zandale Dr Ste 200 Lexington KY 40503 859-278-3338 278-3268
Web: www.acuta.org

Association for Continuing Higher Education (ACHE)
1700 Asp Ave Norman OK 73072 800-807-2243
TF: 800-807-2243 ■ *Web:* www.acheinc.org

Association for Gerontology in Higher Education (AGHE)
1220 L St NW Ste 901 Washington DC 20005 202-289-9806 289-9824
Web: www.aghe.org

Association for Practical & Professional Ethics
618 E Third St Bloomington IN 47405 812-855-4848
Web: www.indiana.edu

Association for Supervision & Curriculum Development (ASCD)
1703 N Beauregard St Alexandria VA 22311 703-578-9600 575-5400
TF: 800-933-2723 ■ *Web:* www.ascd.org

Association for the Advancement of Computing in Education (AACE)
PO Box 1545 Chesapeake VA 23327 757-366-5606 997-8760*
**Fax Area Code:* 703 ■ *TF:* 800-352-5397 ■ *Web:* www.aace.org

Association of Advanced Rabbinical & Talmudic Schools (AARTS)
11 Broadway New York NY 10004 212-363-1991 533-5335

Association of American Colleges & Universities (AAC&U)
1818 R St NW Washington DC 20009 202-387-3760 265-9532
Web: www.aacu.org

Association of American Law Schools (AALS)
1201 Connecticut Ave NW Ste 800 Washington DC 20036 202-296-8851 296-8869
Web: www.aals.org

Association of American Medical Colleges (AAMC)
2450 N St NW Washington DC 20037 202-828-0400 828-1125
TF: 800-273-8255 ■ *Web:* www.aamc.org

Association of American Universities (AAU)
1200 New York Ave NW Ste 550 Washington DC 20005 202-408-7500 408-8184
Web: www.aau.edu

Association of Christian Schools International (ACSI)
731 Chapel Hills Dr Colorado Springs CO 80920 719-528-6906
TF Cust Svc: 800-367-0798 ■ *Web:* www.acsi.org

Association of College & University Housing Officers International (ACUHO-I)
941 Chatham Ln Ste 318 Columbus OH 43221 614-292-0099 292-3205
Web: www.acuho-i.org

Association of College Unions International (ACUI)
120 W Seventh St 1 City Ctr Ste 200 Bloomington IN 47404 812-245-2284 245-6710
Web: www.acui.org

Association of Collegiate Schools of Architecture (ACSA)
1735 New York Ave NW 3rd Fl Washington DC 20006 202-785-2324 628-0448
TF: 877-426-6323 ■ *Web:* www.acsa-arch.org

Association of Community College Trustees (ACCT)
1101 17th St NW Ste 300 Washington DC 20036 202-775-4667 223-1297
TF: 866-895-2228 ■ *Web:* www.acct.org

Association of Governing Boards of Universities & Colleges (AGB)
1133 20th St NW Ste 300 Washington DC 20036 202-296-8400 223-7053
TF: 800-356-6317 ■ *Web:* www.agb.org

Association of Higher Education Facilities Officers (APPA)
1643 Prince St Alexandria VA 22314 703-684-1446 549-2772
Web: www.appa.org

Association of Public & Land-grant Universities (APLU)
1307 New York Ave NW Ste 400 Washington DC 20005 202-478-6040 478-6046
Web: www.aplu.org

Association of Research Libraries (ARL)
21 Dupont Cir NW Ste 800 Washington DC 20036 202-296-2296 872-0884
Web: www.arl.org

Association of School Business Officials International (ASBO)
11401 N Shore Dr Reston VA 20190 866-682-2729 478-0205*
**Fax Area Code:* 703 ■ *TF:* 866-682-2729 ■ *Web:* asbointl.org

Association of Schools of Public Health (ASPH)
1900 M St NW Ste 710 Washington DC 20036 202-296-1099 296-1252
Web: www.aspph.org

Association of Test Publishers
601 Pennsylvania Ave NW Ste 900 Washington DC 20004 866-240-7909
TF: 866-240-7909 ■ *Web:* www.testpublishers.org

Association of Theological Schools in the US & Canada (ATS)
10 Summit Pk Dr Pittsburgh PA 15275 412-788-6505 788-6510
Web: www.ats.edu

Association of Universities for Research in Astronomy (AURA)
1200 New York Ave NW Ste 350 Washington DC 20005 202-483-2101 483-2106
TF: 888-624-8373 ■ *Web:* www.aura-astronomy.org

Association of University Centers on Disabilities (AUCD)
1100 Wayne Avenue Ste 1000 Silver Spring MD 20910 301-588-8252 588-2842
TF: 888-572-2249 ■ *Web:* www.aucd.org

Broadcast Education Assn (BEA) 1771 N St NW Washington DC 20036 202-429-3935
TF: 888-326-1415 ■ *Web:* www.beaweb.org

Business Professionals of America
5454 Cleveland Ave Columbus OH 43231 614-895-7277 895-1165
TF: 800-334-2007 ■ *Web:* www.bpa.org

Business-Higher Education Forum
2025 M St NW Ste 800 Washington DC 20036 202-367-1189 367-2269
Web: www.bhef.com

Career College Assn (CCA)
1101 Connecticut Ave NW Ste 900 Washington DC 20036 202-336-6700 336-6828
Web: www.career.org

Christian Schools International (CSI)
3350 E Paris Ave SE Grand Rapids MI 49512 616-957-1070 957-5022
TF: 800-635-8288 ■ *Web:* www.csionline.org

College & University Professional Assn for Hum Res (CUPA-HR)
1811 Commons Pt Dr Knoxville TN 37932 865-637-7673 637-7674
TF: 877-287-2474 ■ *Web:* www.cupahr.org

College Music Society (CMS) 312 E Pine St Missoula MT 59802 406-721-9616 721-9419
TF: 800-729-0235 ■ *Web:* www.music.org

Conference on College Composition & Communication (CCCC)
1111 W Kenyon Rd Urbana IL 61801 217-328-3870
TF: 877-369-6283 ■ *Web:* www.ncte.org/cccc

Council for Advancement & Support of Education (CASE)
1307 New York Ave NW Ste 1000 Washington DC 20005 202-328-5900 387-4973
TF Orders: 800-554-8536 ■ *Web:* www.case.org

Council for Christian Colleges & Universities (CCCU)
321 Eigth St NE Washington DC 20002 202-546-8713 546-8913
Web: www.cccu.org

Council for International Exchange of Scholars (CIES)
1400 K St NW Ste 700 Washington DC 20005 202-686-4000 362-3442
Web: www.cies.org

Phone Fax

Council for Professional Recognition
2460 16th St NW . . . Washington DC 20009 202-265-9090 265-9161
TF: 800-424-4310 ■ *Web:* www.cdacouncil.org

Council of Administrators of Special Education (CASE)
Osigian Office Centre 101 Katelyn Cir
Ste E . . . Warner Robins GA 31088 478-333-6892 333-2453
TF: 800-585-1753 ■ *Web:* www.casecec.org

Council of Chief State School Officers (CCSSO)
1 Massachusetts Ave NW Ste 700 . . . Washington DC 20001 202-336-7000 408-8072
Web: www.ccsso.org

Council of Graduate Schools (CGS)
1 Dupont Cir NW Ste 230 . . . Washington DC 20036 202-223-3791 331-7157
Web: www.cgsnet.org

Council of the Great City Schools
1301 Pennsylvania Ave NW Ste 702 . . . Washington DC 20004 202-393-2427 393-2400
TF: 888-280-7903 ■ *Web:* www.cgcs.org

Council on International Educational Exchange (CIEE)
300 Fore St 2nd Fl . . . Portland ME 04101 207-553-4000 553-5272
TF Cust Svc: 888-268-6245 ■ *Web:* www.ciee.org

Council on Social Work Education (CSWE)
1701 Duke St . . . Alexandria VA 22314 703-683-8080 683-8099
TF: 866-573-4235 ■ *Web:* www.cswe.org

Distance Education & Training Council (DETC)
1601 18th St NW Ste 2 . . . Washington DC 20009 202-234-5100 332-1386
Web: www.deac.org

Distributive Education Clubs of America (DECA)
1908 Assn Dr . . . Reston VA 20191 703-860-5000 860-4013
Web: www.deca.org

Econometric Society
New York Univ Dept of Economics
19 W Fourth St Sixth Fl . . . New York NY 10012 212-998-3820 995-4487
Web: www.econometricsociety.org

Education Commission of the States (ECS)
700 Broadway Ste 810 . . . Denver CO 80203 303-299-3600 296-8332
Web: www.ecs.org

Educational Housing Services Inc
55 Clark St . . . Brooklyn NY 11201 212-977-7622
TF: 800-385-1689 ■ *Web:* www.studenthousing.org

Hispanic Assn of Colleges & Universities (HACU)
8415 Datapoint Dr Ste 400 . . . San Antonio TX 78229 210-692-3805 692-0823
TF: 800-780-4228 ■ *Web:* www.hacu.net

Independent Educational Consultants Assn (IECA)
3251 Old Lee Hwy Ste 510 . . . Fairfax VA 22030 703-591-4850 591-4860
Web: iecaonline.com

International Council on Hotel Restaurant & Institutional Education (CHRIE)
2810 N Parham Rd Ste 230 . . . Richmond VA 23294 804-346-4800 346-5009
Web: www.chrie.org

International Society for Technology in Education (ISTE)
1530 Wilson Blvd Ste 730 . . . Arlington VA 22209 202-861-7777
TF General: 800-336-5191 ■ *Web:* www.iste.org

International Technology Education Assn (ITEA)
1914 Assn Dr Ste 201 . . . Reston VA 20191 703-860-2100 860-0353
Web: www.iteaconnect.org

Languages Canada 5886 169 A St . . . Surrey BC V3S6Z8 604-574-1532 277-0522*
**Fax Area Code:* 888 ■ *Web:* www.languagescanada.ca

MENC: NA for Music Education
1806 Robert Fulton Dr . . . Reston VA 20191 703-860-4000 860-1531
TF: 800-336-3768 ■ *Web:* nafme.org

Middle States Commission on Higher Education
3624 Market St . . . Philadelphia PA 19104 267-284-5000 662-5501*
**Fax Area Code:* 215 ■ *Web:* www.msche.org

Modern Language Assn (MLA) 26 Broadway 3rd Fl . . . New York NY 10004 646-576-5000 458-0030
TF: 800-323-4900 ■ *Web:* mla.org

Music Teachers NA (MTNA) 441 Vine St Ste 3100 . . . Cincinnati OH 45202 513-421-1420 421-2503
TF: 888-512-5278 ■ *Web:* www.mtna.org

NA of College Auxiliary Services (NACAS)
3 Boar's Head Ln Ste B . . . Charlottesville VA 22903 434-245-8425 245-8453
Web: www.nacas.org

NA of Colleges & Employers (NACE)
62 Highland Ave . . . Bethlehem PA 18017 610-868-1421 868-1421
TF: 800-544-5272 ■ *Web:* www.naceweb.org

NA of Elementary School Principals (NAESP)
1615 Duke St . . . Alexandria VA 22314 703-684-3345 548-6021
TF: 800-386-2377 ■ *Web:* www.naesp.org

NA of Independent Colleges & Universities (NAICU)
1025 Connecticut Ave NW Ste 700 . . . Washington DC 20036 202-785-8866 835-0003
Web: www.naicu.edu

NA of State Boards of Education (NASBE)
333 John Carlyle St Ste 530 . . . Alexandria VA 22314 703-684-4000
Web: www.nasbe.org

NAFSA: Assn of International Educators
1307 New York Ave NW 8th Fl . . . Washington DC 20005 202-737-3699 737-3657
Web: www.nafsa.org

National Academy of Education
500 Fifth St NW Ste 333 . . . Washington DC 20001 202-334-2341 334-2350
Web: www.naeducation.org

National Art Education Assn (NAEA)
1806 Robert Fulton Dr . . . Reston VA 20191 703-860-8000 860-2960
TF: 800-299-8321 ■ *Web:* www.arteducators.org

National Assn of Student Financial Aid Administrators (NASFAA)
1101 Connecticut Ave Ste 1100 . . . Washington DC 20036 202-785-0453 785-1487
TF: 800-877-8339 ■ *Web:* www.nasfaa.org

National Business Education Assn (NBEA)
1914 Assn Dr . . . Reston VA 20191 703-860-8300 620-4483
Web: www.nbea.org

National Catholic Educational Assn (NCEA)
1077 30th St NW Ste 100 . . . Washington DC 20007 202-337-6232 333-6706
TF: 800-711-6232 ■ *Web:* www.ncea.org

National Coalition of Girls' Schools (NCGS)
50 Leonard St Ste 2C . . . Belmont MA 02478 617-489-0013 489-0024
Web: www.ncgs.org

National Communication Assn (NCA)
1765 N St NW . . . Washington DC 20036 202-464-4622 464-4600
Web: www.natcom.org

National Council for the Social Studies (NCSS)
8555 16th St Ste 500 . . . Silver Spring MD 20910 301-588-1800 588-2049
TF Orders: 800-683-0812 ■ *Web:* socialstudies.org

National Council of Supervisors of Mathematics (NCSM)
6000 E Evans Ave Ste 3-205 . . . Denver CO 80222 303-758-9611 758-9616
Web: www.mathedleadership.org

National Council of Teachers of English (NCTE)
1111 W Kenyon Rd . . . Urbana IL 61801 217-328-3870 328-0977
TF: 877-369-6283 ■ *Web:* www.ncte.org

National Council of Teachers of Mathematics (NCTM)
1906 Assn Dr . . . Reston VA 20191 703-620-9840 476-2970
TF Orders: 800-235-7566 ■ *Web:* www.nctm.org

National Council on Economic Education (NCEE)
122 E 42nd St Ste 2600 . . . New York NY 10168 212-730-7007 730-1793
TF: 800-338-1192 ■ *Web:* www.councilforeconed.org

National Education Assn (NEA)
1201 16th St NW . . . Washington DC 20036 202-833-4000 822-7974
TF: 888-552-0624 ■ *Web:* www.nea.org

National Environmental Safety & Health Training Assn (NESHTA)
584 Main St . . . South Portland ME 04106 207-771-9020
Web: www.neshta.org

National Guild of Community Schools of the Arts
520 Eigth Ave Ste 302 . . . New York NY 10018 212-268-3337 268-3995
Web: www.nationalguild.org

National Middle School Assn (NMSA)
4151 Executive Pkwy Ste 300 . . . Westerville OH 43081 614-895-4730 895-4750
TF: 800-528-6672 ■ *Web:* www.amle.org

National School Boards Assn (NSBA)
1680 Duke St . . . Alexandria VA 22314 703-838-6722 683-7590
Web: www.nsba.org

National School Public Relations Assn (NSPRA)
15948 Derwood Rd . . . Rockville MD 20855 301-519-0496 519-0494
Web: www.nspra.org

National Science Teachers Assn (NSTA)
1840 Wilson Blvd . . . Arlington VA 22201 703-243-7100 243-7177
TF Sales: 800-722-6782 ■ *Web:* www.nsta.org

National Staff Development Council (NSDC)
504 S Locust St . . . Oxford OH 45056 513-523-6029 523-0638
TF: 800-727-7288 ■ *Web:* www.learningforward.org

North Central Assn Higher Learning Commission
230 S LaSalle St . . . Chicago IL 60604 312-263-0456 263-7462
TF: 800-621-7440 ■ *Web:* www.hlcommission.org

Oak Ridge Associated Universities (ORAU)
130 Badger Ave PO Box 117 . . . Oak Ridge TN 37831 865-576-3000 576-3643
Web: www.orau.org

Organization for Tropical Studies (OTS)
410 Swift Ave . . . Durham NC 27705 919-684-5774 684-5661
TF: 877-572-4484 ■ *Web:* www.ots.ac.cr

Organization of American Historians (OAH)
112 N Bryan Ave . . . Bloomington IN 47408 812-855-7311 855-0696
TF: 888-737-7006 ■ *Web:* www.oah.org

Registry of Interpreters for the Deaf Inc (RID)
333 Commerce St . . . Alexandria VA 22314 703-838-0030 838-0454
Web: www.rid.org

Society for American Archaeology (SAA)
900 Second St NE Ste 12 . . . Washington DC 20002 202-789-8200 789-0284
TF: 800-759-5219 ■ *Web:* www.saa.org

Society for College & University Planning (SCUP)
339 E Liberty St Ste 300 . . . Ann Arbor MI 48104 734-669-3270 998-6532
Web: www.scup.org

Society for Research in Child Development (SRCD)
2950 S State St Ste 401 . . . Ann Arbor MI 48104 734-926-0600 926-0601
Web: www.srcd.org

Southern Assn of Colleges & Schools
1866 Southern Ln . . . Decatur GA 30033 404-679-4500 679-4558
TF: 888-413-3669 ■ *Web:* www.sacs.org

Teach For America 315 W 36th St 7th Fl . . . New York NY 10018 212-279-2080
TF: 800-832-1230 ■ *Web:* www.teachforamerica.org

Teachers of English to Speakers of Other Languages (TESOL)
700 S Washington St Ste 200 . . . Alexandria VA 22314 703-836-0774 836-7864
TF: 888-547-3369 ■ *Web:* www.tesol.org

Teaching & Mentoring Communities (TMC)
PO Box 2579 . . . Laredo TX 78044 956-722-5174 725-0907
TF: 888-836-5151 ■ *Web:* www.tmccentral.org

Torah Umesorah-National Society for Hebrew Day Schools
620 Foster Ave . . . Brooklyn NY 11230 212-227-1000
Web: torah-umesorah.com

Trees for Tomorrow (TFT)
519 Sheridan St E PO Box 609 . . . Eagle River WI 54521 715-479-6456 479-2318
TF: 800-838-9472 ■ *Web:* www.treesfortomorrow.com

Washington Education Assn Inc
32032 Weyerhaeuser Way S PO Box 9100 . . . Federal Way WA 98001 253-941-6700
TF: 800-622-3393 ■ *Web:* www.washingtonea.org

Western Assn of Schools & Colleges (WASC)
985 Atlantic Ave . . . Alameda CA 94501 510-748-9001
Web: wascsenior.org

Women's College Coalition (WCC) PO Box 3983 . . . Decatur GA 30031 404-234-8715
Web: www.womenscolleges.org

49-6 Food & Beverage Industries Professional Associations

Phone Fax

American Assn of Cereal Chemists Inc (AACC)
3340 Pilot Knob Rd . . . Saint Paul MN 55121 651-454-7250 454-0766
TF: 800-328-7560 ■ *Web:* www.aaccnet.org/default.aspx

American Beverage Assn 1101 16th St NW . . . Washington DC 20036 202-463-6732 659-5349
Web: www.ameribev.org

American Beverage Licensees (ABL)
5101 River Rd Ste 108 . . . Bethesda MD 20816 301-656-1494 656-7539
TF: 800-656-3241 ■ *Web:* www.ablusa.org

American Culinary Federation Inc (ACF)
180 Ctr Pl Way . . . Saint Augustine FL 32095 904-824-4468 825-4758
TF: 800-624-9458 ■ *Web:* www.acfchefs.org

Organization	City	State	ZIP	Phone	Fax
American Dairy Products Institute (ADPI) 116 N York St Ste 200 *Web:* www.adpi.org	Elmhurst	IL	60126	630-530-8700	530-8707
American Institute of Food Distribution 10 Mountainview Rd Ste S125 *Web:* www.foodinstitute.com	Upper Saddle River	NJ	07458	201-791-5570	791-5222
American Malting Barley Assn (AMBA) 740 N Plankinton Ave Ste 830 *Web:* www.ambainc.org	Milwaukee	WI	53203	414-272-4640	
American Peanut Shellers Assn 2336 Lk Pk Dr *Web:* www.peanut-shellers.org	Albany	GA	31707	229-888-2508	888-5150
American Society for Nutrition (ASNS) 9211 Corporate Blvd Ste 300 *TF:* 800-627-8723 ■ *Web:* www.nutrition.org	Rockville	MD	20850	301-634-7050	634-7894
American Spice Trade Assn (ASTA) 1101 17th St NW Ste 700 *Web:* www.astaspice.org	Washington	DC	20036	202-331-2460	463-8998
Association of Food Industries Inc (AFI) 3301 Rt 66 Bldg C Ste 205 *Web:* afius.org	Neptune	NJ	07753	732-922-3008	922-3590
At-sea Processors Assn (APA) 4039 21st Ave W Ste 400 *Web:* www.atsea.org	Seattle	WA	98199	206-285-5139	285-1841
Beer Institute 440 First St NW Ste 350 *TF:* 800-379-2739 ■ *Web:* www.beerinstitute.org	Washington	DC	20001	202-737-2337	737-7004
Biscuit & Cracker Manufacturers Assn (B&CMA) 6325 Woodside Ct Ste 125 **Fax Area Code:* 410 ■ *TF:* 877-701-8111 ■ *Web:* www.thebcma.org	Columbia	MD	21046	443-545-1645	290-8585*
Confrerie de la Chaine des Rotisseurs 285 Madison Ave *Web:* www.chaineus.org	Madison	NJ	07940	973-360-9200	360-9330
Council for Responsible Nutrition (CRN) 1828 L St NW Ste 900 *Web:* www.crnusa.org	Washington	DC	20036	202-776-7929	204-7980
Distilled Spirits Council of the US Inc 1250 'I' St NW Ste 400 *Web:* www.discus.org	Washington	DC	20005	202-628-3544	682-8888
Flavor & Extract Manufacturers Assn of the US (FEMA) 1101 17th St NW Ste 700 *Web:* www.femaflavor.org	Washington	DC	20036	202-293-5800	463-8998
Food Marketing Institute (FMI) 2345 Crystal Dr Ste 800 *TF:* 800-732-2639 ■ *Web:* www.fmi.org	Arlington	VA	22202	202-220-0600	429-4519
Institute of Food Technologists (IFT) 525 W Van Buren St Ste 1000 *TF:* 800-438-3663 ■ *Web:* www.ift.org	Chicago	IL	60607	312-782-8424	782-8348
International Assn for Food Protection (IAFP) 6200 Aurora Ave Ste 200W *TF General:* 800-369-6337 ■ *Web:* www.foodprotection.org	Des Moines	IA	50322	515-276-3344	276-8655
International Assn of Culinary Professionals (IACP) 1221 Ave of the Americas 42nd fl *TF:* 800-928-4227 ■ *Web:* www.iacp.com	New York	NY	10020	866-358-2524	358-2524
International Bottled Water Assn (IBWA) 1700 Diagonal Rd Ste 650 *TF:* 800-928-3711 ■ *Web:* www.bottledwater.org	Alexandria	VA	22314	703-683-5213	683-4074
International Dairy Foods Assn (IDFA) 1250 H St NW Ste 900 *Web:* www.idfa.org	Washington	DC	20005	202-737-4332	331-7820
International Dairy-Deli-Bakery Assn (IDDBA) 636 Science Dr *TF:* 877-399-4925 ■ *Web:* www.iddba.org	Madison	WI	53705	608-238-7908	238-6330
International Food Information Council Foundation (IFIC) 1100 Connecticut Ave NW Ste 430 *TF:* 888-723-3366 ■ *Web:* www.foodinsight.org	Washington	DC	20036	202-296-6540	296-6547
International Foodservice Distributors Assn (IFDA) 1410 Spring Hill Rd Ste 210 *Web:* www.ifdaonline.org	McLean	VA	22102	703-532-9400	538-4673
International Foodservice Manufacturers Assn (IFMA) 180 N Stetson Ave 2 Prudential Plz Ste 4400 *Web:* www.ifmaworld.com	Chicago	IL	60601	312-540-4400	540-4401
International Ice Cream Assn 1250 H St NW Ste 900 *Web:* www.idfa.org	Washington	DC	20005	202-737-4332	331-7820
Master Brewers Assn of the Americas (MBAA) 3340 Pilot Knob Rd *TF:* 800-328-7560 ■ *Web:* www.mbaa.com	Saint Paul	MN	55121	651-454-7250	
NA of Catering And Events (NACE) 9891 Broken Land Pkwy Ste 301 *Web:* www.nace.net	Columbia	MD	21046	410-290-5410	290-5460
National Beer Wholesalers Assn (NBWA) 1101 King St Ste 600 *TF:* 800-300-6417 ■ *Web:* www.nbwa.org	Alexandria	VA	22314	703-683-4300	683-8965
National Coffee Assn of USA Inc (NCA) 45 Broadway Ste 1140 *Web:* www.ncausa.org	New York	NY	10006	212-766-4007	766-5815
National Confectioners Assn (NCA) 1101 30th St NW Ste 200 *TF:* 800-433-1200 ■ *Web:* www.candyusa.com	Washington	DC	20007	202-534-1440	337-0637
National Frozen & Refrigerated Foods Assn (NFRA) 4755 Linglestown Rd Ste 300 PO Box 6069 *Web:* www.nfraweb.org	Harrisburg	PA	17112	717-657-8601	657-9862
National Grocers Assn (NGA) 1005 N Glebe Rd Ste 250 *Web:* www.nationalgrocers.org	Arlington	VA	22201	703-516-0700	516-0115
National Meat Assn (NMA) 1970 Broadway Ste 825 *Web:* meatassociation.com	Oakland	CA	94612	510-763-1533	
National Milk Producers Federation (NMPF) 2101 Wilson Blvd Ste 400 *Web:* www.nmpf.org	Arlington	VA	22201	703-243-6111	841-9328
National Pork Producers Council (NPPC) 122 C St NW Ste 875 *Web:* www.nppc.org	Washington	DC	20001	202-347-3600	347-5265
National Restaurant Assn (NRA) 2055 L St NW Ste 700 *TF:* 800-424-5156 ■ *Web:* www.restaurant.org	Washington	DC	20036	202-331-5900	331-2429
North American Meat Processors Assn (NAMP) 1910 Assn Dr *Web:* meatassociation.com	Reston	VA	20191	703-758-1900	
North American Millers Assn (NAMA) 600 Maryland Ave SW Ste 825-W *Web:* www.namamillers.org	Washington	DC	20024	202-484-2200	488-7416
Popcorn Board 401 N Michigan Ave *Web:* www.popcorn.org	Chicago	IL	60611	312-644-6610	
Produce Marketing Assn (PMA) 1500 Casho Mill Rd *TF:* 800-660-4287 ■ *Web:* www.pma.com	Newark	DE	19711	302-738-7100	731-2409
Retail Confectioners International (RCI) 2053 S Waverly Ste C *TF:* 800-545-5381 ■ *Web:* www.retailconfectioners.org	Springfield	MO	65804	417-883-2775	883-1108
Salt Institute 700 N Fairfax St Ste 600 *Web:* www.saltinstitute.org	Alexandria	VA	22314	703-549-4648	548-2194
School Nutrition Assn (SNA) 700 S Washington St Ste 300 *TF:* 800-877-8822 ■ *Web:* www.schoolnutrition.org	Alexandria	VA	22314	703-739-3900	739-3915
Snack Food Assn 1600 Wilson Blvd Ste 650 *TF:* 800-628-1334 ■ *Web:* www.sfa.org	Arlington	VA	22209	703-836-4500	
Specialty Coffee Assn of America (SCAA) 117 W 4th St Ste 300 *TF:* 800-995-9019 ■ *Web:* www.scaa.org	Santa Ana	CA	92701	562-624-4100	624-4101
Tea Assn of the USA Inc 362 Fifth Ave Ste 801 *Web:* www.teausa.com	New York	NY	10001	212-986-9415	697-8658
Tea Council of the USA Inc 362 Fifth Ave Ste 801 *TF:* 877-212-5752 ■ *Web:* www.teausa.com	New York	NY	10001	212-986-9415	697-8658
US Dairy Export Council 2101 Wilson Blvd Ste 400 *Web:* www.usdec.org	Arlington	VA	22201	703-528-3049	528-3705
US Meat Export Federation Inc (USMEF) 1050 17th St Ste 2200 *Web:* www.usmef.org	Denver	CO	80265	303-623-6328	623-0297
USA Poultry & Egg Export Council (USAPEEC) 2300 W Pk Pl Blvd Ste 100 *Web:* www.usapeec.org	Stone Mountain	GA	30087	770-413-0006	413-0007
Wheat Foods Council 51 Red Fox Ln Unit D *Web:* www.wheatfoods.org	Ridgway	CO	81432	303-840-8787	840-6877
Wine & Spirits Shippers Assn Inc (WSSA) 11800 Sunrise Vly Dr *TF General:* 800-368-3167 ■ *Web:* www.wssa.com	Reston	VA	20191	703-860-2300	860-2422
Wine & Spirits Wholesalers of America Inc (WSWA) 805 15th St NW Ste 430 *Web:* www.wswa.org	Washington	DC	20005	202-371-9792	789-2405
Wine Institute 425 Market St Ste 1000 *Web:* www.wineinstitute.org	San Francisco	CA	94105	415-512-0151	442-0742
WineAmerica 818 Connecticut Ave Ste 1006 *TF:* 800-824-5419 ■ *Web:* www.wineamerica.org	Washington	DC	20006	202-783-2756	
World Cocoa Foundation (WCF) 1411 K St NW Ste 1300 *Web:* www.worldcocoafoundation.org	Washington	DC	20005	202-737-7870	737-7832

49-7 Government & Public Administration Professional Associations

Organization	City	State	ZIP	Phone	Fax
American Assn of Motor Vehicle Administrators (AAMVA) 4301 Wilson Blvd Ste 400 *Web:* www.aamva.org	Arlington	VA	22203	703-522-4200	522-1553
American Assn of State Highway & Transportation Officials (AASHTO) 444 N Capitol St NW Ste 249 *TF:* 800-880-4117 ■ *Web:* www.transportation.org	Washington	DC	20001	202-624-5800	624-5806
American Conference of Governmental Industrial Hygienists (ACGIH) 1330 Kemper Meadows Dr *Web:* www.acgih.org	Cincinnati	OH	45240	513-742-2020	742-3355
American Correctional Assn (ACA) 206 N Washington St Ste 200 *TF:* 800-222-5646 ■ *Web:* www.aca.org	Alexandria	VA	22314	703-224-0000	
American Federation of Police & Concerned Citizens 6350 Horizon Dr *TF:* 800-435-7352 ■ *Web:* www.afp-cc.org	Titusville	FL	32780	321-264-0911	264-0033
American Foreign Service Assn (AFSA) 2101 E St NW *TF:* 800-704-2372 ■ *Web:* www.afsa.org	Washington	DC	20037	202-338-4045	338-6820
American Foreign Service Protective Assn 1620 L St *Web:* www.afspa.org	Washington	DC	20036	202-833-4910	
American Jail Assn (AJA) 1135 Professional Ct *Web:* www.americanjail.org	Hagerstown	MD	21740	301-790-3930	790-2941
American Public Human Services Assn (APHSA) 1133 19th St NW Ste 400 *Web:* www.aphsa.org	Washington	DC	20036	202-682-0100	289-6555
American Public Works Assn (APWA) 2345 Grand Blvd Ste 700 *TF:* 800-848-2792 ■ *Web:* www.apwa.net	Kansas City	MO	64108	816-472-6100	472-1610
American Society for Public Administration (ASPA) 1301 Pennsylvania Ave NW Ste 840 *Web:* www.aspanet.org	Washington	DC	20004	202-393-7878	638-4952
Association of Maternal & Child Health Programs (AMCHP) 2030 M St NW Ste 350 *Web:* www.amchp.org	Washington	DC	20036	202-775-0436	
Association of Public Health Laboratories (APHL) 8515 Georgia Ave Ste 700 *TF:* 800-899-2278 ■ *Web:* www.aphl.org	Silver Spring	MD	20910	240-485-2745	485-2700
Association of Public-Safety Communications Officials International Inc 351 N Williamson Blvd *TF:* 888-272-6911 ■ *Web:* www.apcointl.org	Daytona Beach	FL	32114	386-322-2500	322-2501
Association of Racing Commissioners International (ARCI) 1510 Newtown Pike # 210 *Web:* www.arci.com	Lexington	KY	40511	859-224-7070	

				Phone	Fax
Association of Social Work Boards (ASWB)					
400 S Ridge Pkwy Ste B	Culpeper	VA	22701	540-829-6880	829-0142
TF: 800-225-6880 ■ *Web:* www.aswb.org					
Association of State & Interstate Water Pollution Control Administrators (ASIWPCA)					
1221 Connecticut Ave NW 2nd Fl	Washington	DC	20036	202-756-0600	
Web: www.acwa-us.org					
Association of State & Territorial Health Officials (ASTHO)					
2231 Crystal Dr Ste 450	Arlington	VA	22202	202-371-9090	527-3189*
**Fax Area Code:* 571 ■ *Web:* www.astho.org					
Association of State & Territorial Solid Waste Management Officials (ASTSWMO)					
444 N Capitol St NW Ste 315	Washington	DC	20001	202-624-5828	624-7875
Web: www.astswmo.org					
Association of State Wetland Managers					
32 Tandberg Trail Ste 2A	Windham	ME	04062	207-892-3399	892-3089
TF: 800-451-6027 ■ *Web:* www.aswm.org					
Commission on Accreditation for Law Enforcement Agencies (CALEA)					
13575 Heathcote Blvd Ste 320	Gainesville	VA	20155	703-352-4225	890-3126
TF: 877-789-6904 ■ *Web:* www.calea.org					
Conference of Radiation Control Program Directors (CRCPD)					
1030 Burlington Ln # 4B	Frankfort	KY	40601	502-227-4543	227-7862
Web: www.crcpd.org					
Conference of State Bank Supervisors (CSBS)					
1129 20th St NW 5th Fl	Washington	DC	20036	202-296-2840	296-1928
TF: 800-886-2727 ■ *Web:* www.csbs.org					
Council of State & Territorial Epidemiologists (CSTE)					
2872 Woodcock Blvd Ste 303	Atlanta	GA	30341	770-458-3811	458-8516
TF: 866-577-9956 ■ *Web:* www.cste.org					
Council of State Governments (CSG)					
2760 Research Pk Dr	Lexington	KY	40511	859-244-8000	244-8001
TF Sales: 800-800-1910 ■ *Web:* www.csg.org					
Council on Licensure Enforcement & Regulation (CLEAR)					
403 Marquis Ave	Lexington	KY	40502	859-269-1289	
Web: www.clearhq.org					
Federal Bureau of Investigation Agents Assn (FBIAA)					
PO Box 12650	Arlington	VA	22219	703-247-2173	247-2175
Federal Law Enforcement Officers Assn (FLEOA)					
1100 Connecticut Ave NW Ste 900	Washington	DC	20036	202-293-1550	
Web: www.fleoa.org					
Federal Managers Assn (FMA) 1641 Prince St	Alexandria	VA	22314	703-683-8700	683-8707
Web: www.fedmanagers.org					
Federally Employed Women (FEW)					
455 Massachusetts Ave NW Ste 306	Washington	DC	20001	202-898-0994	
Web: www.few.org					
Federation of State Medical Boards of the US Inc (FSMB)					
400 Fuller Wiser Rd Ste 300	Euless	TX	76039	817-868-4000	868-4098
TF: 800-793-7939 ■ *Web:* www.fsmb.org					
Federation of Tax Administrators (FTA)					
444 N Capitol St NW Ste 348	Washington	DC	20001	202-624-5890	624-7888
Web: www.taxadmin.org					
Forest Service Employees for Environmental Ethics (FSEEE)					
PO Box 11615	Eugene	OR	97440	541-484-2692	484-3004
TF: 800-270-7504 ■ *Web:* www.fseee.org					
Government Finance Officers Assn (GFOA)					
203 N LaSalle St Ste 2700	Chicago	IL	60601	312-977-9700	977-4806
Web: www.gfoa.org					
International Assn of Arson Investigators (IAAI)					
2111 Baldwin Ave # 203	Crofton	MD	21114	410-451-3473	451-9049
TF: 800-468-4224 ■ *Web:* www.firearson.com					
International Assn of Assessing Officers (IAAO)					
314 W Tenth St	Kansas City	MO	64105	816-701-8100	701-8149
TF: 800-616-4226 ■ *Web:* www.iaao.org					
International Assn of Auto Theft Investigators (IAATI)					
PO Box 223	Clinton	NY	13323	315-853-1913	793-0048
Web: www.iaati.org					
International Assn of Chiefs of Police (IACP)					
44 Canal Ctr Plz Ste 200	Alexandria	VA	22314	703-836-6767	836-4543
TF: 800-843-4227 ■ *Web:* www.theiacp.org					
International Assn of Fire Chiefs (IAFC)					
4025 Fair Ridge Dr Ste 300	Fairfax	VA	22033	703-273-0911	273-9363
TF: 866-385-9110 ■ *Web:* www.iafc.org					
International Assn of Fish & Wildlife Agencies (IAFWA)					
444 N Capitol St NW Ste 725	Washington	DC	20001	202-624-7890	624-7891
Web: www.fishwildlife.org					
International Assn of Plumbing & Mechanical Officials (IAPMO)					
4755 E Philadelphia St	Ontario	CA	91761	909-472-4100	472-4150
TF: 877-427-6601 ■ *Web:* www.iapmo.org					
International Bridge Tunnel & Turnpike Assn (IBTTA)					
1146 19th St NW Ste 600	Washington	DC	20036	202-659-4620	659-0500
Web: www.ibtta.org					
International City/County Management Assn (ICMA)					
777 N Capitol St NE Ste 500	Washington	DC	20002	202-289-4262	962-3500
TF: 800-745-8780 ■ *Web:* www.icma.org					
International Conference of Funeral Service Examining Boards Inc					
1885 Shelby Ln	Fayetteville	AR	72704	479-442-7076	442-7090
TF: 800-709-0180 ■ *Web:* www.theconferenceonline.org					
International Institute of Municipal Clerks (IIMC)					
8331 Utica Ave Ste 200	Rancho Cucamonga	CA	91730	909-944-4162	944-8545
TF: 800-251-1639 ■ *Web:* www.iimc.com					
International Municipal Signal Assn (IMSA)					
165 E Union St PO Box 539	Newark	NY	14513	315-331-2182	331-8205
TF: 800-723-4672 ■ *Web:* www.imsasafety.org					
International Society of Fire Service Instructors (ISFSI)					
14001C St Germain Dr	Centreville	VA	20121	800-435-0005	435-0005
TF: 800-435-0005 ■ *Web:* www.isfsi.org					
Kansas Assn of Counties (KAC)					
300 SW Eigth St 3rd Fl	Topeka	KS	66603	785-272-2585	272-3585
Web: www.kansascounties.org					
Maryland Assn of Counties (MACo)					
169 Conduit St	Annapolis	MD	21401	410-269-0043	268-1775
Web: www.mdcounties.org					
NA of Clean Water Agencies (NACWA)					
1816 Jefferson Pl NW	Washington	DC	20036	202-833-2672	833-4657
TF: 888-267-9505 ■ *Web:* www.nacwa.org					
NA of Conservation Districts (NACD)					
509 Capitol Ct NE	Washington	DC	20002	202-547-6223	547-6450
TF: 888-695-2433 ■ *Web:* www.nacdnet.org					
NA of Housing & Redevelopment Officials (NAHRO)					
630 'I' St NW	Washington	DC	20001	202-289-3500	289-8181
TF: 877-866-2476 ■ *Web:* www.nahro.org					
NA of Postmasters of the US (NAPUS)					
8 Herbert St	Alexandria	VA	22305	703-683-9027	683-6820
Web: www.napus.org					
NA of State Mental Health Program Directors (NASMHPD)					
66 Canal Ctr Plz Ste 302	Alexandria	VA	22314	703-739-9333	548-9517
Web: www.nasmhpd.org					
National Academy of Public Administration					
1600 K St Ste 400	Washington	DC	20006	202-347-3190	393-0993
TF: 800-883-3190 ■ *Web:* www.napawash.org					
National Alcohol Beverage Control Assn (NABCA)					
4401 Ford Ave Ste 700	Alexandria	VA	22302	703-578-4200	820-3551
Web: www.nabca.org					
National American Indian Housing Council (NAIHC)					
122 C S NW Ste 350	Washington	DC	20001	202-789-1754	789-1758
TF: 800-284-9165 ■ *Web:* www.naihc.net					
National Assembly of State Arts Agencies (NASAA)					
1029 Vermont Ave NW 2nd Fl	Washington	DC	20005	202-347-6352	737-0526
Web: www.nasaa-arts.org					
National Assn on Aging					
1201 15th St NW Ste 350	Washington	DC	20005	202-898-2578	
Web: www.nasuad.org					
National Board of Boiler & Pressure Vessel Inspectors					
1055 Crupper Ave	Columbus	OH	43229	614-888-8320	847-1147*
**Fax:* Cust Svc ■ *TF:* 877-682-8772 ■ *Web:* www.nationalboard.org					
National Conference of State Historic Preservation Officers					
444 N Capitol St NW Ste 342	Washington	DC	20001	202-624-5465	624-5419
Web: www.ncshpo.org					
National Conference of State Legislatures					
7700 E First Pl	Denver	CO	80230	303-364-7700	364-7800
TF: 866-229-2386 ■ *Web:* www.ncsl.org					
National Council of Architectural Registration Boards (NCARB)					
1801 K St NW Ste 700-K	Washington	DC	20006	202-783-6500	783-0290
Web: www.ncarb.org					
National Council of State Housing Agencies (NCSHA)					
444 N Capitol St NW Ste 438	Washington	DC	20001	202-624-7710	624-5899
Web: www.ncsha.org					
National Ctr for State Courts (NCSC)					
300 Newport Ave	Williamsburg	VA	23185	757-259-1525	220-0449
TF: 800-616-6164 ■ *Web:* www.ncsc.org					
National District Attorneys Assn (NDAA)					
99 Canal Ctr Plaza Ste 510	Alexandria	VA	22314	703-549-9222	836-3195
TF: 888-325-9943 ■ *Web:* www.ndaa.org					
National Emergency Management Assn (NEMA)					
PO Box 11910	Lexington	KY	40578	859-244-8000	244-8239
Web: www.nemaweb.org					
National Environmental Health Assn (NEHA)					
720 S Colorado Blvd Ste 1000-N	Denver	CO	80246	303-756-9090	691-9490
TF: 866-956-2258 ■ *Web:* www.neha.org					
National Fire Protection Assn (NFPA)					
1 Batterymarch Pk	Quincy	MA	02169	617-770-3000	770-0700
TF: 800-344-3555 ■ *Web:* www.nfpa.org					
National Forum for Black Public Administrators (NFBPA)					
777 N Capitol St NE Ste 807	Washington	DC	20002	202-408-9300	408-8558
Web: www.nfbpa.org					
National Governors Assn (NGA)					
444 N Capitol St NW Ste 267	Washington	DC	20001	202-624-5300	624-5313
Web: www.nga.org					
National Institute of Governmental Purchasing Inc (NIGP)					
151 Spring St	Herndon	VA	20170	703-736-8900	736-2818
TF: 800-367-6447 ■ *Web:* www.nigp.org					
National League of Cities (NLC)					
1301 Pennsylvania Ave NW Ste 550	Washington	DC	20004	202-626-3000	626-3043
Web: www.nlc.org					
National Organization of Black Law Enforcement Executives (NOBLE)					
4609 Pinecrest Office Pk Dr Ste F	Alexandria	VA	22312	703-658-1529	658-9479
Web: www.noblenatl.org					
National Sheriffs' Assn (NSA) 1450 Duke St	Alexandria	VA	22314	703-836-7827	683-6541
TF: 800-424-7827 ■ *Web:* www.sheriffs.org					
National Ski Patrol System Inc (NSP)					
133 S Van Gordon St Ste 100	Lakewood	CO	80228	303-988-1111	
Web: www.nsp.org					
National Volunteer Fire Council (NVFC)					
7852 Walker Dr Ste 450	Greenbelt	MD	20770	202-887-5700	887-5291
TF: 888-275-6832 ■ *Web:* www.nvfc.org					
Opportunity Finance Network					
620 Chestnut St Ste 572	Philadelphia	PA	19106	215-923-4754	923-4755
Web: ofn.org					
Police Executive Research Forum (PERF)					
1120 Connecticut Ave NW Ste 930	Washington	DC	20036	202-466-7820	466-7826
Web: www.policeforum.org					
Public Employees Roundtable (PER)					
PO Box 75248	Washington	DC	20013	202-927-4926	927-4920
Web: www.keyinsurancequotes.com					
Public Risk Management Assn (PRIMA)					
700 S Washington St Ste 218	Alexandria	VA	22314	703-528-7701	739-0200
Web: www.primacentral.org					
Public Technology Inc					
1420 Prince St Ste 200	Alexandria	VA	22314	202-626-2400	
TF: 866-664-6368 ■ *Web:* www.pti.org					
United Federations of Security					
540 N State Rd	Briarcliff Manor	NY	10510	914-941-4103	941-4472
TF: 800-227-4291 ■ *Web:* www.policefederation.com					
US Conference of Mayors					
1620 'I' St NW Ste 400	Washington	DC	20006	202-293-7330	293-2352
Web: www.usmayors.org					
US Travel Assn					
1100 New York Ave NW Ste 450	Washington	DC	20005	202-408-8422	408-1255
TF: 877-212-5752 ■ *Web:* www.ustravel.org					
West Virginia Assn of Counties (WVACO)					
2211 Washington St	Charleston	WV	25311	304-346-0591	346-0592
Web: www.wvaco.org					

49-8 Health & Medical Professionals Associations

	City	State	ZIP	Phone	Fax
Academy of General Dentistry (AGD) 211 E Chicago Ave Ste 900 *TF:* 888-243-3368 ■ *Web:* www.agd.org	Chicago	IL	60611	312-440-4300	440-0559
Academy of Managed Care Pharmacy (AMCP) 100 N Pitt St Ste 400 *TF:* 800-827-2627 ■ *Web:* www.amcp.org	Alexandria	VA	22314	703-683-8416	683-8417
Academy of Osseointegration 85 W Algonquin Rd Ste 550 *TF:* 800-656-7736 ■ *Web:* www.osseo.org	Arlington Heights	IL	60005	847-439-1919	439-1569
Academy of Pharmacy Practice & Management American Pharmacists Assn 1100 15th St NW Ste 400 *TF:* 800-237-2742 ■ *Web:* www.pharmacist.com	Washington	DC	20005	202-628-4410	783-2351
Academy of Students of Pharmacy American Pharmacists Assn 1100 15th St NW Ste 400 *TF:* 800-237-2742 ■ *Web:* www.pharmacist.com	Washington	DC	20005	202-628-4410	783-2351
AcademyHealth 1801 K St NW Ste 701 *Web:* www.academyhealth.org	Washington	DC	20006	202-292-6700	292-6800
Aerospace Medical Assn (AMA) 320 S Henry St *Web:* www.asma.org	Alexandria	VA	22314	703-739-2240	739-9652
Aging Life Care Association (GCM) 3275 W Ina Rd Ste 130 *Web:* www.aginglifecare.org	Tucson	AZ	85741	520-881-8008	325-7925
America's Blood Centers (ABC) 725 15th St NW Ste 700 *TF:* 888-872-5663 ■ *Web:* www.americasblood.org	Washington	DC	20005	202-393-5725	393-1282
America's Essential Hospitals (NAPH) 1301 Pennsylvania Ave NW Ste 950 *Web:* essentialhospitals.org	Washington	DC	20004	202-585-0100	585-0101
American Academy of Allergy Asthma & Immunology (AAAAI) 555 E Wells St Ste 1100 *TF:* 800-654-2452 ■ *Web:* www.aaaai.org	Milwaukee	WI	53202	414-272-6071	272-6070
American Academy of Audiology (AAA) 11730 Plz America Dr Ste 300 *TF:* 800-222-2336 ■ *Web:* www.audiology.org	Reston	VA	20190	703-790-8466	790-8631
American Academy of Cosmetic Dentistry (AACD) 402 W Wilson St. *TF:* 800-543-9220 ■ *Web:* www.aacd.com	Madison	WI	53703	608-222-8583	222-9540
American Academy of Cosmetic Surgery (AACS) 225 W Wacker Dr Ste 650 *Web:* www.cosmeticsurgery.org	Chicago	IL	60606	312-981-6760	981-6787
American Academy of Dental Group Practice (AADGP) 2525 E Arizona Biltmore Cir Ste 127 *Web:* www.aadgp.org	Phoenix	AZ	85016	602-381-1185	381-1093
American Academy of Dermatology (AAD) 930 E Woodfield Rd *TF:* 800-868-2472 ■ *Web:* www.aad.org	Schaumburg	IL	60173	847-330-0230	330-0050
American Academy of Disability Evaluating Physicians (AADEP) 223 W Jackson Blvd Ste 1104 *TF:* 800-456-6095 ■ *Web:* www.iaime.org	Chicago	IL	60606	312-663-1171	663-1175
American Academy of Facial Plastic & Reconstructive Surgery (AAFPRS) 310 S Henry St *Web:* aafprs.org	Alexandria	VA	22314	703-299-9291	299-8898
American Academy of Family Physicians (AAFP) 11400 Tomahawk Creek Pkwy *TF:* 800-274-2237 ■ *Web:* www.aafp.org	Leawood	KS	66211	913-906-6000	906-6075
American Academy of Home Care Physicians (AAHCP) PO Box 1037 *Web:* aahcm.org	Edgewood	MD	21040	410-676-7966	676-7980
American Academy of Hospice & Palliative Medicine (AAHPM) 4700 W Lk Ave **Fax Area Code: 877* ■ *Web:* www.aahpm.org	Glenview	IL	60025	847-375-4712	734-8671*
American Academy of Neurology (AAN) 1080 Montreal Ave *TF:* 800-879-1960 ■ *Web:* www.aan.com	Saint Paul	MN	55116	651-695-1940	695-2791
American Academy of Nurse Practitioners (AANP) PO Box 12846 *Web:* www.aanp.org	Austin	TX	78711	512-442-4262	442-6469
American Academy of Ophthalmology 655 Beach St *TF:* 866-561-8558 ■ *Web:* www.aao.org	San Francisco	CA	94109	415-561-8500	561-8575
American Academy of Optometry (AAO) 6110 Executive Blvd Ste 506 *TF:* 800-368-6263 ■ *Web:* www.aaopt.org	Rockville	MD	20852	301-984-1441	984-4737
American Academy of Orthopaedic Surgeons (AAOS) 6300 N River Rd *TF:* 800-346-2267 ■ *Web:* www.aaos.org	Rosemont	IL	60018	847-823-7186	823-8125
American Academy of Orthotists & Prosthetists (AAOP) 526 King St Ste 201 *TF:* 800-669-6024 ■ *Web:* www.oandp.org	Alexandria	VA	22314	703-836-0788	836-0737
American Academy of Otolaryngology-Head & Neck Surgery (AAO-HNS) 1650 Diagonal Rd *TF:* 877-722-6467 ■ *Web:* www.entnet.org	Alexandria	VA	22314	703-836-4444	683-5100
American Academy of Pain Management (AAPM) 13947 Mono Way Ste A *TF:* 888-519-9901 ■ *Web:* www.aapainmanage.org	Sonora	CA	95370	209-533-9744	533-9750
American Academy of Pediatric Dentistry (AAPD) 211 E Chicago Ave Ste 1600 *TF:* 800-974-3084 ■ *Web:* www.aapd.org	Chicago	IL	60611	312-337-2169	337-6329
American Academy of Pediatrics (AAP) 141 NW Pt Blvd *TF:* 800-433-9016 ■ *Web:* www.aap.org	Elk Grove Village	IL	60007	847-434-4000	434-8000
American Academy of Periodontology (AAP) 737 N Michigan Ave Ste 800 *TF:* 800-282-4867 ■ *Web:* www.perio.org	Chicago	IL	60611	312-787-5518	787-3670
American Academy of Physical Medicine & Rehabilitation (AAPM&R) 9700 W Bryn Mawr Ave Ste 200 *Web:* www.aapmr.org	Rosemont	IL	60018	847-737-6000	737-6001
American Academy of Physician Assistants (AAPA) 950 N Washington St *Web:* www.aapa.org	Alexandria	VA	22314	703-836-2272	684-1924
American Assn for Cancer Research (AACR) 615 Chestnut St 17th Fl *TF:* 866-423-3965 ■ *Web:* www.aacr.org	Philadelphia	PA	19106	215-440-9300	440-7228
American Assn for Homecare 2011 Crystal Dr Ste 725 *Web:* www.aahomecare.org	Arlington	VA	22202	703-836-6263	836-6730
American Assn for Respiratory Care (AARC) 9425 N MacArthur Blvd Ste 100 *Web:* www.aarc.org	Irving	TX	75063	972-243-2272	484-2720
American Assn for the Study of Liver Diseases (AASLD) 1001 N Fairfax St Ste 400 *Web:* www.aasld.org	Alexandria	VA	22314	703-299-9766	299-9622
American Assn for Thoracic Surgery (AATS) 900 Cummings Ctr Ste 221-U *TF:* 800-424-5249 ■ *Web:* www.aats.org	Beverly	MA	01915	978-927-8330	524-8890
American Assn of Bioanalysts (AAB) 906 Olive St Ste 1200 *TF:* 800-457-3332 ■ *Web:* www.aab.org	Saint Louis	MO	63101	314-241-1445	241-1449
American Assn of Clinical Endocrinologists (AACE) 245 Riverside Ave Ste 2000 *TF:* 800-435-7352 ■ *Web:* www.aace.com	Jacksonville	FL	32202	904-353-7878	353-8185
American Assn of Colleges of Osteopathic Medicine (AACOM) 5550 Friendship Blvd Ste 310 *TF:* 800-356-7836 ■ *Web:* www.aacom.org	Chevy Chase	MD	20815	301-968-4100	968-4101
American Assn of Colleges of Podiatric Medicine (AACPM) 15850 Crabbs Branch Way Ste 320 *Web:* www.aacpm.org	Rockville	MD	20855	301-948-9760	948-1928
American Assn of Critical-Care Nurses (AACN) 101 Columbia *TF:* 800-809-2273 ■ *Web:* www.aacn.org	Aliso Viejo	CA	92656	949-362-2000	362-2020
American Assn of Endodontists (AAE) 211 E Chicago Ave Ste 1100 *TF:* 800-872-3636 ■ *Web:* www.aae.org	Chicago	IL	60611	312-266-7255	266-9867
American Assn of Gynecological Laparoscopists (AAGL) 6757 Katella Ave *TF:* 800-554-2245 ■ *Web:* www.aagl.org	Cypress	CA	90630	714-503-6200	503-6201
American Assn of Immunologists (AAI) 9650 Rockville Pike *TF:* 888-503-1050 ■ *Web:* www.aai.org	Bethesda	MD	20814	301-634-7178	634-7887
American Assn of Integrated Healthcare Delivery Systems Inc (AAIHDS) 4435 Waterfront Dr Ste 101 *TF:* 888-491-8833 ■ *Web:* www.aaihds.org	Glen Allen	VA	23060	804-747-5823	747-5316
American Assn of Medical Assistants (AAMA) 20 N Wacker Dr Ste 1575 *TF:* 800-228-2262 ■ *Web:* www.aama-ntl.org	Chicago	IL	60606	312-899-1500	899-1259
American Assn of Medical Review Officers (AAMRO) PO Box 12873 *TF:* 800-489-1839 ■ *Web:* www.aamro.com	Research Triangle Park	NC	27709	919-489-5407	490-1010
American Assn of Medical Society Executives (AAMSE) 1000 Westgate Dr Ste 252 *Web:* www.aamse.org	St. Paul	MN	55114	414-221-9275	276-3349
American Assn of Neurological Surgeons (AANS) 5550 Meadowbrook Dr *TF:* 888-566-2267 ■ *Web:* www.aans.org	Rolling Meadows	IL	60008	847-378-0500	378-0600
American Assn of Neuromuscular & Electrodiagnostic Medicine (AANEM) 2621 Superior Dr NW *TF:* 844-347-3277 ■ *Web:* www.aanem.org	Rochester	MN	55901	507-288-0100	288-1225
American Assn of Neuroscience Nurses (AANN) 4700 W Lk Ave *TF:* 888-557-2266 ■ *Web:* www.aann.org	Glenview	IL	60025	847-375-4733	375-6430
American Assn of Nurse Anesthetists (AANA) 222 S Prospect Ave *TF:* 855-526-2262 ■ *Web:* www.aana.com	Park Ridge	IL	60068	847-692-7050	692-6968
American Assn of Oral & Maxillofacial Surgeons (AAOMS) 9700 W Bryn Mawr Ave *TF:* 800-822-6637 ■ *Web:* www.aaoms.org	Rosemont	IL	60018	847-678-6200	678-6286
American Assn of Orthodontists (AAO) 401 N Lindbergh Blvd. *Web:* www.mylifemysmile.org	Saint Louis	MO	63141	314-993-1700	
American Assn of Physician Specialists Inc (AAPS) 5550 W Executive Dr Ste 400 *Web:* www.aapsus.org	Tampa	FL	33609	813-433-2277	830-6599
American Assn of Poison Control Centers (AAPCC) 3201 New Mexico Ave Ste 310 *TF:* 800-222-1222 ■ *Web:* www.aapcc.org	Washington	DC	20016	800-222-1222	
American Assn of Preferred Provider Organizations (AAPPO) 974 Breckenridge Ln Ste 162 *Web:* nasho.org	Louisville	KY	40202	502-403-1122	403-1129
American Assn of Tissue Banks (AATB) 8200 Greensboro Dr Ste 320 *Web:* www.aatb.org	McLean	VA	22101	703-827-9582	356-2198
American Autoimmune Related Disease Assn (AARDA) 22100 Gratiot Ave *TF:* 800-598-4668 ■ *Web:* www.aarda.org	Eastpointe	MI	48021	586-776-3900	776-3903
American Burn Assn (ABA) 625 N Michigan Ave Ste 2550 *Web:* www.ameriburn.org	Chicago	IL	60611	312-642-9260	642-9130
American Cancer Society (ACS) 250 William St NW *TF:* 800-227-2345 ■ *Web:* www.cancer.org	Atlanta	GA	30303	404-320-3333	
American Chiropractic Assn (ACA) 1701 Clarendon Blvd 2nd Fl *TF:* 800-986-4636 ■ *Web:* www.acatoday.org	Arlington	VA	22209	703-276-8800	243-2593
American Cleft Palate-Craniofacial Assn 1504 E Franklin St Ste 102 *Web:* www.acpa-cpf.org	Chapel Hill	NC	27514	919-933-9044	933-9604
American College Health Assn (ACHA) 1362 Mellon Rd Ste 180 *Web:* www.acha.org	Hanover	MD	21076	410-859-1500	859-1510
American College of Allergy Asthma & Immunology (ACAAI) 85 W Algonquin Rd Ste 550 *TF:* 800-466-3649 ■ *Web:* www.acaai.org	Arlington Heights	IL	60005	847-427-1200	427-1294

Phone | Fax

American College of Cardiology (ACC)
2400 N St NW . . . Washington DC 20037 202-375-6000 375-7000
TF Cust Svc: 800-253-4636 ■ *Web:* www.acc.org

American College of Chest Physicians (ACCP)
3300 Dundee Rd . . . Northbrook IL 60062 847-498-1400 498-5460
TF: 800-343-2227 ■ *Web:* www.chestnet.org

American College of Clinical Pharmacy (ACCP)
13000 W 87th St Pkwy . . . Lenexa KS 66215 913-492-3311 492-0088
Web: www.accp.com

American College of Dentists (ACD)
839J Quince Orchard Blvd Ste J . . . Gaithersburg MD 20878 301-977-3223 977-3330
Web: www.acd.org

American College of Emergency Physicians (ACEP)
1125 Executive Cir PO Box 619911 . . . Dallas TX 75261 972-550-0911 580-2816
TF: 800-798-1822 ■ *Web:* www.acep.org

American College of Eye Surgeons/American Board of Eye Surgery (ACES)
334 E Lake Rd Ste 135 . . . Palm Harbor FL 34685 727-366-1487 836-9783
Web: www.aces-abes.org

American College of Foot & Ankle Surgeons (ACFAS)
8725 W Higgins Rd Ste 555 . . . Chicago IL 60631 773-693-9300 693-9304
TF: 800-421-2237 ■ *Web:* www.acfas.org

American College of Forensic Examiners International (ACFEI)
2750 E Sunshine St . . . Springfield MO 65804 417-881-3818 881-4702
TF: 800-423-9737 ■ *Web:* www.acfei.com

American College of Gastroenterology (ACG)
6400 Goldsboro Rd Ste 450 . . . Bethesda MD 20817 301-263-9000 263-9025
Web: gi.org

American College of Healthcare Executives (ACHE)
1 N Franklin St Ste 1700 . . . Chicago IL 60606 312-424-2800 424-0023
Web: www.ache.org

American College of Managed Care Medicine (ACMCM)
4435 Waterfront Dr Ste 101 . . . Glen Allen VA 23060 804-527-1905 747-5316
TF: 888-491-8833 ■ *Web:* www.acmcm.org

American College of Nurse-Midwives (ACNM)
8403 Colesville Rd Ste 1550 . . . Silver Spring MD 20910 240-485-1800 485-1818
Web: www.midwife.org

American College of Nutrition
300 S Duncan Ave Ste 225 . . . Clearwater FL 33755 727-446-6086 446-6202
Web: americancollegeofnutrition.org

American College of Obstetricians & Gynecologists (ACOG)
409 12th St SW PO Box 96920 . . . Washington DC 20090 202-863-1648
Web: acog.org

American College of Occupational & Environmental Medicine (ACOEM)
25 NW Pt Blvd Ste 700 . . . Elk Grove Village IL 60007 847-818-1800 818-9266
Web: www.acoem.org

American College of Osteopathic Family Physicians (ACOFP)
330 E Algonquin Rd Ste 1 . . . Arlington Heights IL 60005 847-952-5100 228-9755
TF: 800-323-0794 ■ *Web:* www.acofp.org

American College of Physician Executives (ACPE)
400 N Ashley Dr Ste 400 . . . Tampa FL 33602 813-287-2000 287-8993
TF: 800-562-8088 ■ *Web:* www.physicianleaders.org

American College of Physicians (ACP)
190 N Independence Mall W . . . Philadelphia PA 19106 215-351-2400 351-2594
TF: 800-523-1546 ■ *Web:* www.acponline.org

American College of Preventive Medicine (ACPM)
455 Massachusetts Ave NW . . . Washington DC 20001 202-466-2044 466-2662
Web: www.acpm.org

American College of Radiology (ACR)
1892 Preston White Dr . . . Reston VA 20191 703-648-8900
TF: 800-227-5463 ■ *Web:* www.acr.org

American College of Rheumatology (ACR)
2200 Lake Blvd NE . . . Atlanta GA 30319 404-633-3777 633-1870
Web: www.rheumatology.org

American College of Sports Medicine (ACSM)
401 W Michigan St PO Box 1440 . . . Indianapolis IN 46202 317-637-9200 634-7817
Web: www.acsm.org

American College of Surgeons (ACS)
633 N St Clair St . . . Chicago IL 60611 312-202-5000 202-5001
TF: 800-621-4111 ■ *Web:* www.facs.org

American Dental Assistants Assn (ADAA)
140 N Bloomingdale Rd . . . Bloomingdale IL 60108 312-541-1550 541-1496
TF: 877-874-3785 ■ *Web:* www.adaausa.org

American Dental Assn (ADA) 211 E Chicago Ave . . . Chicago IL 60611 312-440-2500
Web: www.ada.org

American Dental Hygienists' Assn (ADHA)
444 N Michigan Ave Ste 3400 . . . Chicago IL 60611 312-440-8900 467-1806
TF: 800-243-2342 ■ *Web:* www.adha.org

American Diabetes Assn (ADA)
1701 N Beauregard St . . . Alexandria VA 22311 703-549-1500
TF: 800-232-3472 ■ *Web:* www.diabetes.org

American Embryo Transfer Assn (AETA)
1111 N Dunlap Ave . . . Savoy IL 61874 217-356-3182 398-4119
Web: secure.fass.org

American Endodontic Society 265 N Main St . . . Glen Ellyn IL 60137 773-519-4879 858-0525*
**Fax Area Code:* 630 ■ *Web:* www.aesoc.com

American Epilepsy Society (AES)
342 N Main St . . . West Hartford CT 06117 860-586-7505 586-7550
TF: 888-233-2334 ■ *Web:* www.aesnet.org

American Federation for Aging Research (AFAR)
55 W 39th St 16th Fl . . . New York NY 10018 212-703-9977 997-0330
TF: 888-582-2327 ■ *Web:* www.afar.org

American Federation for Medical Research (AFMR)
900 Cummings Ctr Ste 221-U . . . Beverly MA 01915 978-927-8330 524-8890
TF: 888-737-9477 ■ *Web:* www.afmr.org

American Gastroenterological Assn (AGA)
4930 Del Ray Ave . . . Bethesda MD 20814 301-654-2055 654-5920
TF: 800-227-7888 ■ *Web:* www.gastro.org

American Headache Society (AHS)
19 Mantua Rd . . . Mount Royal NJ 08061 856-423-0043 423-0082
Web: www.americanheadachesociety.org

American Health Care Assn (AHCA)
1201 L St NW . . . Washington DC 20005 202-842-4444 842-3860
TF: 800-321-0343 ■ *Web:* www.ahcancal.org

American Health Information Management Assn (AHIMA)
233 N Michigan Ave Ste 2100 . . . Chicago IL 60601 312-233-1100 233-1090
TF: 800-335-5535 ■ *Web:* www.ahima.org

American Health Quality Assn (AHQA)
1155 21st St NW Ste 300 . . . Washington DC 20006 202-331-5790
Web: www.ahqa.org

American Healthcare Radiology Administrators (AHRA)
490-B Boston Post Rd Ste 200 . . . Sudbury MA 01776 978-443-7591 443-8046
TF: 800-334-2472 ■ *Web:* www.ahraonline.org

American Herbal Products Assn (AHPA)
8630 Fenton St Ste 918 . . . Silver Spring MD 20910 301-588-1171 588-1174
Web: www.ahpa.org

American Hospital Assn (AHA) 155 N Wacker Dr . . . Chicago IL 60606 312-422-3000 422-4796
TF: 800-424-4301 ■ *Web:* www.aha.org

American Institute of Ultrasound in Medicine (AIUM)
14750 Sweitzer Ln Ste 100 . . . Laurel MD 20707 301-498-4100 498-4450
TF: 800-638-5352 ■ *Web:* www.aium.org

American Lung Assn (ALA) 14 Wall St . . . New York NY 10005 212-315-8700
TF: 800-586-4872 ■ *Web:* www.lung.org

American Medical Assn (AMA) 515 N State St . . . Chicago IL 60610 312-464-5000 464-4184
TF: 800-621-8335 ■ *Web:* www.ama-assn.org

American Medical Directors Assn (AMDA)
11000 Broken Land Pkwy Ste 400 . . . Columbia MD 21044 410-740-9743 740-4572
TF: 800-876-2632 ■ *Web:* www.paltc.org

American Medical Group Assn (AMGA)
1422 Duke St . . . Alexandria VA 22314 703-838-0033 548-1890
Web: www.amga.org

American Medical Informatics Assn (AMIA)
4720 Montgomery Ln Ste 500 . . . Bethesda MD 20814 301-657-1291 657-1296
Web: www.amia.org

American Medical Rehabilitation Providers Assn (AMRPA)
1710 N St NW . . . Washington DC 20036 202-223-1920 223-1925
TF: 888-346-4624 ■ *Web:* www.amrpa.org

American Medical Technologists (AMT)
10700 W Higgins Rd Ste 150 . . . Rosemont IL 60018 847-823-5169 823-0458
TF: 800-275-1268 ■ *Web:* www.americanmedtech.org

American Nephrology Nurses Assn (ANNA)
200 E Holly Ave . . . Sewell NJ 08080 856-256-2320 589-7463
TF: 888-600-2662 ■ *Web:* www.annanurse.org

American Neurological Assn (ANA)
1120 Rte 73 Ste 200 . . . Mount Laurel NJ 08054 856-380-6892 545-6073*
**Fax Area Code:* 952 ■ *Web:* myana.org

American Nurses Assn (ANA)
8515 Georgia Ave Ste 400 . . . Silver Spring MD 20910 301-628-5000 628-5001
TF: 800-274-4262 ■ *Web:* nursingworld.org

American Occupational Therapy Assn Inc (AOTA)
4720 Montgomery Ln PO Box 31220 . . . Bethesda MD 20824 301-652-2682 652-7711
TF: 800-877-1383 ■ *Web:* www.aota.org

American Organization of Nurse Executives (AONE)
155 N Wacker Dr Ste 400 . . . Chicago IL 60606 312-422-2800 422-4503
Web: www.aone.org

American Orthopaedic Society for Sports Medicine (AOSSM)
6300 N River Rd Ste 500 . . . Rosemont IL 60018 847-292-4900 292-4905
TF: 877-321-3500 ■ *Web:* www.sportsmed.org

American Osteopathic Assn (AOA)
142 E Ontario St . . . Chicago IL 60611 312-202-8000 202-8200
TF: 800-621-1773 ■ *Web:* www.osteopathic.org

American Pain Society (APS) 4700 W Lake Ave . . . Glenview IL 60025 847-375-4715 375-6479
TF: 877-752-4754 ■ *Web:* www.americanpainsociety.org

American Physical Therapy Assn (APTA)
1111 N Fairfax St . . . Alexandria VA 22314 703-684-2782 706-8536
TF: 800-999-2782 ■ *Web:* www.apta.org

American Physiological Society (APS)
9650 Rockville Pk . . . Bethesda MD 20814 301-634-7164 634-7241
Web: www.the-aps.org

American Podiatric Medical Assn (APMA)
9312 Old Georgetown Rd . . . Bethesda MD 20814 301-581-9200 530-2752
TF: 800-275-2762 ■ *Web:* www.apma.org

American Psychiatric Nurses Assn (APNA)
1555 Wilson Blvd Ste 530 . . . Arlington VA 22209 703-243-2443 243-3390
TF: 866-243-2443 ■ *Web:* www.apna.org

American Public Health Assn (APHA)
800 'I' St NW . . . Washington DC 20001 202-777-2742 777-2533
Web: www.apha.org

American Registry of Diagnostic Medical Sonographers (ARDMS)
1401 Rockville Pike Ste 600 . . . Rockville MD 20852 301-738-8401 738-0312
TF: 800-541-9754 ■ *Web:* www.ardms.org

American Roentgen Ray Society (ARRS)
44211 Slatestone Ct . . . Leesburg VA 20176 703-729-3353 729-4839
TF: 800-438-2777 ■ *Web:* www.arrs.org

American Society for Aesthetic Plastic Surgery, The (ASAPS)
11262 Monarch St . . . Garden Grove CA 92841 562-799-2356 799-1098
TF: 800-364-2147 ■ *Web:* www.surgery.org

American Society for Bone & Mineral Research (ASBMR)
2025 M St NW Ste 800 . . . Washington DC 20036 202-367-1161 367-2161
Web: www.asbmr.org

American Society for Clinical Pathology (ASCP)
33 W Monroe St Ste 1600 . . . Chicago IL 60603 312-541-4999 541-4998
TF Cust Svc: 800-621-4142 ■ *Web:* www.ascp.org

American Society for Colposcopy & Cervical Pathology (ASCCP)
152 W Washington St . . . Hagerstown MD 21740 301-733-3640
TF: 800-787-7227 ■ *Web:* www.asccp.org

American Society for Dermatologic Surgery (ASDS)
5550 Meadowbrook Dr Ste 120 . . . Rolling Meadows IL 60008 847-956-0900 956-0999
Web: www.asds.net

American Society for Gastrointestinal Endoscopy (ASGE)
1520 Kensington Rd Ste 202 . . . Oak Brook IL 60523 630-573-0600 573-0691
TF: 866-353-2743 ■ *Web:* www.asge.org

American Society for Histocompatibility & Immunogenetics (ASHI)
15000 Commerce Pkwy Ste C . . . Mount Laurel NJ 08054 856-638-0428 439-0525
Web: www.ashi-hla.org

American Society for Laser Medicine & Surgery Inc (ASLMS)
2100 Stewart Ave Ste 240 . . . Wausau WI 54401 715-845-9283 848-2493
TF: 877-258-6028 ■ *Web:* www.aslms.org

American Society for Microbiology (ASM)
1752 N St NW . . . Washington DC 20036 202-737-3600
Web: www.asm.org

Phone | Fax

American Society for Parenteral & Enteral Nutrition (ASPEN)
8630 Fenton St Ste 412 Silver Spring MD 20910 301-587-6315 587-2365
TF: 800-727-4567 ■ *Web:* www.nutritioncare.org

American Society for Pharmacology & Experimental Therapeutics (ASPET)
9650 Rockville Pk Bethesda MD 20814 301-634-7060 634-7061
Web: www.aspet.org

American Society for Reproductive Medicine (ASRM)
1209 Montgomery Hwy Birmingham AL 35216 205-978-5000 978-5005
Web: www.asrm.org

American Society for Surgery of the Hand (ASSH)
822 W. Washington Blvd Chicago IL 60607 312-880-1900 384-1435*
**Fax Area Code:* 847 ■ *Web:* www.assh.org

American Society for Therapeutic Radiology & Oncology (ASTRO)
8280 Willow Oaks Corporate Dr Ste 500 Fairfax VA 22031 703-502-1550 502-7852
TF: 800-962-7876 ■ *Web:* www.astro.org

American Society of Abdominal Surgeons (ASAS)
824 Main St Second Fl Ste 1 Melrose MA 02176 781-665-6102 665-4127
Web: www.abdominalsurg.org

American Society of Addiction Medicine (ASAM)
4601 N Pk Ave Upper Arcade Ste 101 Chevy Chase MD 20815 301-656-3920 656-3815
Web: www.asam.org

American Society of Andrology (ASA)
1100 E Woodfield St Ste 350 Schaumburg IL 60173 847-517-1050 517-7229
Web: www.andrologysociety.org

American Society of Anesthesiologists (ASA)
520 N NW Hwy Park Ridge IL 60068 847-825-5586 825-1692
TF: 800-331-1600 ■ *Web:* www.asahq.org

American Society of Cataract & Refractive Surgery (ASCRS)
4000 Legato Rd Ste 700 Fairfax VA 22033 703-591-2220 591-0614
TF: 877-996-4464 ■ *Web:* www.ascrs.org

American Society of Clinical Hypnosis (ASCH)
140 N Bloomingdale Rd Bloomingdale IL 60108 630-980-4740 351-8490
Web: www.asch.net

American Society of Clinical Oncology (ASCO)
2318 Mill Rd Ste 800 Alexandria VA 22314 571-483-1300 299-0255*
**Fax Area Code:* 703 ■ *TF:* 888-282-2552 ■ *Web:* www.asco.org

American Society of Consultant Pharmacists (ASCP)
1321 Duke St Alexandria VA 22314 703-739-1300 739-1321
TF: 800-355-2727 ■ *Web:* www.ascp.com

American Society of Dermatopathology, The
111 Deer Lake Rd Ste 100 Deerfield IL 60015 847-686-2231 480-9282
TF: 800-445-8667 ■ *Web:* www.asdp.org

American Society of Echocardiography (ASE)
2100 Gateway Centre Blvd Ste 310 Morrisville NC 27560 919-861-5574 882-9900
Web: www.asecho.org

American Society of Health-System Pharmacists (ASHP)
7272 Wisconsin Ave Bethesda MD 20814 301-664-8700 664-8877
TF: 866-279-0681 ■ *Web:* www.ashp.org

American Society of Hematology (ASH)
1900 M St NW Ste 200 Washington DC 20036 202-776-0544 776-0545
Web: www.hematology.org

American Society of Hypertension (ASH)
148 Madison Ave 5th Fl New York NY 10016 212-696-9099 696-0711
Web: www.ash-us.org

American Society of Neuroradiology (ASNR)
2210 Midwest Rd Ste 207 Oak Brook IL 60523 630-574-0220 574-0661
Web: www.asnr.org

American Society of Nuclear Cardiology (ASNC)
4550 Montgomery Ave Ste 780-N Bethesda MD 20814 301-215-7575 215-7113
Web: www.asnc.org

American Society of PeriAnesthesia Nurses (ASPAN)
90 Frontage Rd Cherry Hill NJ 08034 856-616-9600 616-9601
TF: 877-737-9696 ■ *Web:* www.aspan.org

American Society of Plastic Surgeons (ASPS)
444 E Algonquin Rd Arlington Heights IL 60005 847-228-9900 228-9131
TF: 888-475-2784 ■ *Web:* www.plasticsurgery.org

American Society of Radiologic Technologists (ASRT)
15000 Central Ave SE Albuquerque NM 87123 505-298-4500 298-5063
TF: 800-444-2778 ■ *Web:* www.asrt.org

American Society of Regional Anesthesia & Pain Medicine (ASRA)
239 Fourth Ave Ste 1714 Pittsburgh PA 15222 412-471-2718 471-7503
TF: 855-795-2772 ■ *Web:* www.asra.com

American Society of Tropical Medicine & Hygiene
111 Deer Lk Rd Ste 100 Deerfield IL 60015 847-480-9592 480-9282
Web: www.astmh.org

American Speech-Language-Hearing Assn (ASHA)
2200 Research Blvd Rockville MD 20850 301-296-5700 296-8580
TF: 800-498-2071 ■ *Web:* www.asha.org

American Thoracic Society (ATS)
61 Broadway 4th Fl New York NY 10006 212-315-8600 315-6498
TF: 866-316-2673 ■ *Web:* www.thoracic.org

American Urological Assn (AUA)
1000 Corporate Blvd Linthicum MD 21090 410-689-3700 689-3800
TF: 866-746-4282 ■ *Web:* www.auanet.org

American Veterinary Medical Assn (AVMA)
1931 N Meacham Rd Ste 100 Schaumburg IL 60173 847-925-8070 925-1329
TF: 800-248-2862 ■ *Web:* www.avma.org

AORN Inc 2170 S Parker Rd Ste 300 Denver CO 80231 303-755-6300 750-3212*
**Fax:* Cust Svc ■ *TF:* 800-755-2676 ■ *Web:* www.aorn.org

Arthroscopy Assn of North America (AANA)
9400 W Higgins Rd Ste 200 Rosemont IL 60018 847-292-2262 292-2268
TF: 877-924-0305 ■ *Web:* www.aana.org

Assisted Living Federation of America (ALFA)
1650 King St Ste 602 Alexandria VA 22314 703-894-1805 894-1831
Web: www.alfa.org

Association for Applied Psychophysiology & Biofeedback (AAPB)
10200 W 44th Ave Ste 304 Wheat Ridge CO 80033 303-422-8436 422-8894
TF: 800-477-8892 ■ *Web:* www.aapb.org

Association for Death Education & Counseling (ADEC)
111 Deer Lk Rd Ste 100 Deerfield IL 60015 847-509-0403 480-9282
Web: www.adec.org

Association for Healthcare Documentation Integrity (AHDI)
4230 Kiernan Ave Ste 130 Modesto CA 95356 209-527-9620 527-9633
TF: 800-982-2182 ■ *Web:* www.ahdionline.org

Association for Healthcare Philanthropy (AHP)
313 Pk Ave Ste 400 Falls Church VA 22046 703-532-6243 532-7170
Web: www.ahp.org

Association for Professionals in Infection Control & Epidemiology Inc (APIC)
1275 K St NW Ste 1000 Washington DC 20005 202-789-1890 789-1899
TF: 800-650-9883 ■ *Web:* www.apic.org

Association for Research in Vision & Ophthalmology (ARVO)
12300 Twinbrook Pkwy Ste 250 Rockville MD 20852 240-221-2900 221-0370
TF: 888-503-1050 ■ *Web:* www.arvo.org

Association for the Advancement of Medical Instrumentation (AAMI)
4301 N Fairfax Dr Ste 301 Arlington VA 22203 703-525-4890 276-0793
TF: 800-332-2264 ■ *Web:* www.aami.org

Association for Vascular Access (AVA)
5526 West 13400 South Ste 229 Herriman UT 84096 801-792-9079 601-8012
TF: 888-576-2826 ■ *Web:* www.avainfo.org

Association of Academic Health Centers (AHC)
1400 16th St NW Ste 720 Washington DC 20036 202-265-9600 265-7514
Web: www.aahcdc.org

Association of American Indian Physicians (AAIP)
1225 Sovereign Row Ste 103 Oklahoma City OK 73108 405-946-7072 946-7651
Web: www.aaip.org

Association of Clinical Research Professionals (ACRP)
500 Montgomery St Ste 800 Alexandria VA 22314 703-254-8100 254-8101
TF: 888-508-5731 ■ *Web:* www.acrpnet.org

Association of Community Cancer Centers (ACCC)
11600 Nebel St Ste 201 Rockville MD 20852 301-984-9496 770-1949
Web: www.accc-cancer.org

Association of Emergency Physicians (AEP)
911 Whitewater Dr Mars PA 16046 724-772-1818 422-7794*
**Fax Area Code:* 866

Association of Military Surgeons of the United States (AMSUS)
9320 Old Georgetown Rd Bethesda MD 20814 301-897-8800 530-5446
TF: 800-761-9320 ■ *Web:* www.amsus.org

Association of Nurses in AIDS Care (ANAC)
3538 Ridgewood Rd Akron OH 44333 330-670-0101 670-0109
TF: 800-260-6780 ■ *Web:* www.nursesinaidscare.org

Association of Osteopathic Directors & Medical Educators (AODME)
142 E Ontario St Chicago IL 60611 312-202-8211 202-8224
TF: 800-621-1773 ■ *Web:* www.aodme.org

Association of Rehabilitation Nurses (ARN)
4700 W Lk Ave Glenview IL 60025 847-375-4710 375-6481
TF: 800-229-7530 ■ *Web:* www.rehabnurse.org

Association of Reproductive Health Professionals (ARHP)
1901 L St NW Ste 300 Washington DC 20036 202-466-3825 466-3826
TF: 877-311-8972 ■ *Web:* www.arhp.org

Association of Schools & Colleges of Optometry (ASCO)
6110 Executive Blvd Ste 420 Rockville MD 20852 301-231-5944 770-1828
TF: 800-397-2424 ■ *Web:* www.opted.org

Association of Schools of Allied Health Professions (ASAHP)
4400 Jenifer St NW Ste 333 Washington DC 20015 202-237-6481 237-6485
Web: www.asahp.org

Association of Staff Physician Recruiters (ASPR)
1000 Westgate Dr Ste 252 Saint Paul MN 55114 800-830-2777
TF: 800-830-2777 ■ *Web:* www.aspr.org

Association of Surgical Technologists (AST)
6 W Dry Creek Cir Ste 200 Littleton CO 80120 303-694-9130 694-9169
TF: 800-637-7433 ■ *Web:* www.ast.org

Association of University Programs in Health Administration (AUPHA)
2000 N 14th St Ste 780 Arlington VA 22201 703-894-0941 894-0941
TF: 877-275-6462 ■ *Web:* www.aupha.org

Association of Women's Health Obstetric & Neonatal Nurses (AWHONN)
2000 L St NW Ste 740 Washington DC 20036 202-261-2400 728-0575
TF: 800-673-8499 ■ *Web:* www.awhonn.org

Asthma & Allergy Foundation of America (AAFA)
8201 Corporate Dr Ste 1000 Landover MD 20785 202-466-7643 466-8940
TF: 800-727-8462 ■ *Web:* www.aafa.org

Canadian Academy of Sport Medicine (CASM)
180 Elgin St Ste 1400 Ottawa ON K2P2K3 613-748-5851 912-0128
TF: 877-585-2394 ■ *Web:* casem-acmse.org

Canadian Assn of Emergency Physicians (CAEP)
1785 Alta Vista Dr Ste 104 Ottawa ON K1G3Y6 613-523-3343 523-0190
TF: 800-463-1158 ■ *Web:* www.caep.ca

Canadian Medical Assn (CMA) 1867 Alta Vista Dr Ottawa ON K1G5W8 613-731-9331
TF: 800-663-7336 ■ *Web:* www.cma.ca

Canadian Veterinary Medical Assn (CVMA)
339 Booth St Ottawa ON K1R7K1 613-236-1162 236-9681
TF: 800-567-2862 ■ *Web:* canadianveterinarians.net

Case Management Society of America (CMSA)
6301 Ranch Dr Little Rock AR 72223 501-225-2229 221-9068
TF: 800-216-2672 ■ *Web:* www.cmsa.org

Catholic Health Assn of the US (CHA)
4455 Woodson Rd Saint Louis MO 63134 314-427-2500 427-0029
Web: www.chausa.org

Children's Hospice International (CHI)
500 Montgomery St Ste 400 Alexandria VA 22314 703-684-0330
Web: www.chionline.org

Christian Medical & Dental Assn (CMDA)
2604 Hwy 421 PO Box 7500 Bristol TN 37620 423-844-1000 844-1005
TF: 888-231-2637 ■ *Web:* www.cmda.org

Clinical & Laboratory Standards Institute (CLSI)
940 W Valley Rd Ste 1400 Wayne PA 19087 610-688-0100 688-0700

Clinical Immunology Society (CIS)
555 E Wells St Ste 1100 Milwaukee WI 53202 414-224-8095 272-6070
Web: www.clinimmsoc.org

COLA 9881 Broken Land Pkwy Ste 200 Columbia MD 21046 410-381-6581 381-8611*
**Fax:* Hum Res ■ *TF:* 800-981-9883 ■ *Web:* www.cola.org

College of American Pathologists (CAP)
325 Waukegan Rd Northfield IL 60093 847-832-7000 832-8168
TF: 800-323-4040 ■ *Web:* www.cap.org

Emergency Nurses Assn (ENA) 915 Lee St Des Plaines IL 60016 847-460-4000 460-4001
TF: 800-900-9659 ■ *Web:* www.ena.org

Endocrine Society
8401 Connecticut Ave Ste 900 Chevy Chase MD 20815 301-941-0200 941-0259
TF: 888-363-6274 ■ *Web:* www.endocrine.org

				Phone	Fax
Eye Bank Assn of America (EBAA) 1015 18th St NW Ste 1010	Washington	DC	20036	202-775-4999	429-6036
TF: 888-491-8833 ■ *Web:* www.restoresight.org					
Federation of American Hospitals 750 Ninth St NW Ste 600	Washington	DC	20004	202-624-1500	624-1500
Web: www.fah.org					
Federation of State Medical Boards of the US Inc (FSMB) 400 Fuller Wiser Rd Ste 300	Euless	TX	76039	817-868-4000	868-4098
TF: 800-793-7939 ■ *Web:* www.fsmb.org					
Gerontological Society of America, The 1220 L St NW Ste 901	Washington	DC	20005	202-842-1275	842-1150
TF: 800-677-1116 ■ *Web:* www.geron.org					
Gynecologic Oncology Group (GOG) 1600 JFK Blvd Ste 1020	Philadelphia	PA	19103	215-854-0770	854-0716
TF: 800-225-3053 ■ *Web:* www.gog.org					
Health Industry Business Communications Council (HIBCC) 2525 E Arizona Biltmore Cir Ste 127	Phoenix	AZ	85016	602-381-1091	381-1093
TF: 800-755-5505 ■ *Web:* www.hibcc.org					
Healthcare Financial Management Assn (HFMA) 2 Westbrook Corporate Ctr Ste 700	Westchester	IL	60154	708-531-9600	531-0032
TF: 800-252-4362 ■ *Web:* www.hfma.org					
Healthcare Information & Management Systems Society (HIMSS) 230 E Ohio St Ste 500	Chicago	IL	60611	312-664-4467	664-6143
Web: www.himss.org					
Heart Rhythm Society 1400 K St NW Ste 500	Washington	DC	20005	202-464-3400	464-3401
Web: www.hrsonline.org					
Hospice Foundation of America (HFA) 1710 Rhode Island Ave NW Ste 400	Washington	DC	20036	202-457-5811	457-5815
TF: 800-854-3402 ■ *Web:* www.hospicefoundation.org					
Infectious Diseases Society of America (IDSA) 1300 Wilson Blvd Ste 300	Arlington	VA	22209	703-299-0200	299-0204
TF: 888-844-4372 ■ *Web:* www.idsociety.org					
Infusion Nurses Society (INS) 315 Norwood Pk S	Norwood	MA	02062	781-440-9408	440-9409
TF: 800-694-0298 ■ *Web:* www.ins1.org					
Institute for Healthcare Improvement (IHI) 20 University Rd 7th Fl	Cambridge	MA	02138	617-301-4800	301-4848
TF: 866-787-0831 ■ *Web:* www.ihi.org					
Institute for the Advancement of Human Behavior (IAHB) PO BOX 5527	Santa Rosa	CA	95402	650-851-8411	755-3133*
**Fax Area Code:* 707 ■ *TF:* 800-258-8411 ■ *Web:* www.iahb.org					
Institute of Medicine 500 Fifth St NW	Washington	DC	20001	202-334-2352	334-1412
Web: www.nationalacademies.org/hmd					
Interamerican College of Physicians & Surgeons 233 Broadway	New York	NY	10279	212-777-3642	
Web: icps.org					
International Academy of Compounding Pharmacists (IACP) 4638 Riverstone Blvd	Missouri City	TX	77459	281-933-8400	495-0602
TF: 800-927-4227 ■ *Web:* www.iacprx.org					
International Assn for Dental Research (IADR) 1619 Duke St	Alexandria	VA	22314	703-548-0066	548-1883
Web: www.iadr.com					
International Chiropractors Assn (ICA) 6400 Arlington Blvd Ste 800	Falls Church	VA	22042	703-528-5000	528-5023
TF: 800-423-4690 ■ *Web:* www.chiropractic.org					
International College of Dentists (ICD) 51 Monroe St Ste 1400	Rockville	MD	20850	301-251-8861	738-9143
TF: 800-533-6825 ■ *Web:* www.icd.org					
International College of Surgeons (ICS) 1516 N Lk Shore Dr	Chicago	IL	60610	312-642-3555	
Web: www.icsglobal.org					
International Congress of Oral Implantologists (ICOI) 248 Lorraine Ave 3rd Fl	Upper Montclair	NJ	07043	973-783-6300	295-8509*
**Fax Area Code:* 267 ■ *TF:* 800-442-0525 ■ *Web:* www.icoi.org					
International Society for Heart & Lung Transplantation (ISHLT) 14673 Midway Rd Ste 200	Addison	TX	75001	972-490-9495	490-9499
TF: 888-722-2220 ■ *Web:* www.ishlt.org					
International Society for Magnetic Resonance in Medicine (ISMRM) 2030 Addison St Ste 700	Berkeley	CA	94704	510-841-1899	841-2340
TF: 800-445-8667 ■ *Web:* www.ismrm.org					
International Society for Peritoneal Dialysis (ISPD) 66 Martin St	Milton	ON	L9T2R2	905-875-2456	875-2864
TF: 888-834-1001 ■ *Web:* www.ispd.org					
International Society for Pharmacoeconomics & Outcomes Research (ISPOR) 3100 Princeton Pk Bldg 3 Ste E	Lawrenceville	NJ	08648	609-219-0773	219-0774
TF: 800-992-0643 ■ *Web:* www.ispor.org					
International Society for Pharmacoepidemiology (ISPE) 5272 River Rd Ste 630	Bethesda	MD	20816	301-718-6500	656-0989
TF: 888-887-7955 ■ *Web:* www.pharmacoepi.org					
International Society of Refractive Surgery (ISRS) 655 Beach St PO Box 7424	San Francisco	CA	94109	415-561-8581	561-8575
TF: 866-561-8558 ■ *Web:* www.aao.org					
International Society of Travel Medicine (ISTM) 315 W Ponce de Leon Ave Ste 245	Decatur	GA	30030	404-373-8282	373-8283
Web: www.istm.org					
International Transplant Nurses Society (ITNS) 1739 E Carson St PO Box 351	Pittsburgh	PA	15203	412-343-4867	343-3959
TF: 800-776-8636 ■ *Web:* www.itns.org					
Islamic Medical Assn of North America (IMANA) 101 W 22nd St Ste 106	Lombard	IL	60148	630-932-0000	932-0005
Web: www.imana.org					
Journal of Clinical Investigation (JCI) 15 Research Dr	Ann Arbor	MI	48103	734-222-6050	222-6058
Web: www.jci.org					
Lamaze International 2025 M St NW Ste 800	Washington	DC	20036	202-367-1128	367-2128
TF: 800-368-4404 ■ *Web:* www.lamaze.org					
Medical Group Management Assn (MGMA) 104 Inverness Terr E	Englewood	CO	80112	303-799-1111	784-6105
TF: 877-275-6462 ■ *Web:* www.mgma.com					
NA for Home Care & Hospice (NAHC) 228 Seventh St SE	Washington	DC	20003	202-547-7424	547-3540
Web: www.nahc.org					
NA of Neonatal Nurses (NANN) 4700 W Lk Ave	Glenview	IL	60025	847-375-3660	375-6491
TF: 800-451-3795 ■ *Web:* www.nann.org					
NA of Nurse Practitioners in Women's Health 505 C St NE	Washington	DC	20002	202-543-9693	543-9858
Web: www.npwh.org					
National Abortion Federation (NAF) 1755 Massachusetts Ave NW	Washington	DC	20036	202-667-5881	667-5890
TF: 800-772-9100 ■ *Web:* www.prochoice.org					
National Board of Medical Examiners (NBME) 3750 Market St	Philadelphia	PA	19104	215-590-9500	
Web: www.nbme.org					
National Community Pharmacists Assn (NCPA) 100 Daingerfield Rd	Alexandria	VA	22314	703-683-8200	683-3619
TF: 800-544-7447 ■ *Web:* www.ncpanet.org					
National Council of State Boards of Nursing (NCSBN) 111 E Wacker Dr Ste 2900	Chicago	IL	60601	312-525-3600	279-1032
TF: 866-293-9600 ■ *Web:* www.ncsbn.org					
National Council on Problem Gambling Inc 730 11th St NW Ste 601	Washington	DC	20001	202-547-9204	547-9206
TF: 800-522-4700 ■ *Web:* www.ncpgambling.org					
National Foundation for Infectious Diseases (NFID) 4733 Bethesda Ave Ste 750	Bethesda	MD	20814	301-656-0003	907-0878
Web: www.nfid.org					
National Home Infusion Assn (NHIA) 100 Daingerfield Rd	Alexandria	VA	22314	703-549-3740	683-1484
Web: www.nhia.org					
National Hospice & Palliative Care Organization (NHPCO) 1700 Diagonal Rd Ste 625	Alexandria	VA	22314	703-837-1500	837-1233
TF Help Line: 800-658-8898 ■ *Web:* www.nhpco.org					
National League for Nursing (NLN) 61 Broadway 33rd Fl	New York	NY	10006	212-363-5555	812-0391
TF: 800-669-1656 ■ *Web:* www.nln.org					
National Medical Assn (NMA) 8403 Colesville Rd Ste 920	Silver Spring	MD	20910	202-347-1895	347-0722
TF: 800-662-0554 ■ *Web:* www.nmanet.org					
National Nursing Staff Development Organization (NNSDO) 330 N Wabash Ave Ste 2000	Chicago	IL	60611	312-321-5135	673-6835
TF: 800-489-1995 ■ *Web:* www.anpd.org					
National Organization for Rare Disorders (NORD) 55 Kenosia Ave PO Box 1968	Danbury	CT	06813	203-744-0100	798-2291
TF: 800-999-6673 ■ *Web:* www.rarediseases.org					
National Pharmaceutical Council (NPC) 1894 Preston White Dr	Reston	VA	20191	703-620-6390	476-0904
Web: www.npcnow.org					
National Renal Administrators Assn (NRAA) 100 N 20th St	Philadelphia	PA	19103	215-320-4655	564-2175
Web: www.nraa.org					
National Student Nurses Assn (NSNA) 45 Main St Ste 606	Brooklyn	NY	11201	718-210-0705	210-0710
Web: www.nsna.org					
North American Menopause Society, The (NAMS) 5900 Landerbrook Dr Ste 390	Mayfield Heights	OH	44124	440-442-7550	442-2660
Web: www.menopause.org					
North American Spine Society (NASS) 7075 Veterans Blvd.	Burr Ridge	IL	60527	630-230-3600	
TF: 877-774-6337 ■ *Web:* www.spine.org					
Oncology Nursing Society (ONS) 125 Enterprise Dr	Pittsburgh	PA	15275	412-859-6100	369-5497*
**Fax Area Code:* 877 ■ *TF:* 866-257-4667 ■ *Web:* www.ons.org					
Optical Society of America (OSA) 2010 Massachusetts Ave NW	Washington	DC	20036	202-223-8130	223-1096
TF: 800-766-4672 ■ *Web:* www.osa.org					
Opticians Assn of America (OAA) 3740 Canada Rd.	Lakeland	TN	38002	901-388-2423	388-2348
Web: www.oaa.org					
Parental Drug Assn (PDA) 4350 East-West Hwy	Bethesda	MD	20814	301-656-5900	986-1093
Web: www.pda.org					
Pharmaceutical Care Management Assn (PCMA) 601 Pennsylvania Ave NW	Washington	DC	20004	202-756-7210	
Web: www.pcmanet.org					
Pharmaceutical Research & Manufacturers of America (PhRMA) 950 F St NW Ste 300	Washington	DC	20004	202-835-3400	835-3414
Web: www.phrma.org					
Physicians Committee for Responsible Medicine (PCRM) 5100 Wisconsin Ave NW Ste 400	Washington	DC	20016	202-686-2210	686-2216
TF: 866-416-7276 ■ *Web:* www.pcrm.org					
Physicians for Social Responsibility (PSR) 1875 Connecticut Ave NW Ste 1012	Washington	DC	20009	202-667-4260	667-4201
TF: 800-459-1887 ■ *Web:* www.psr.org					
Plasma Protein Therapeutics Assn (PPTA) 147 Old Solomon's Island Rd Ste 100	Annapolis	MD	21401	202-789-3100	
Web: usplaces.com					
Radiological Society of North America (RSNA) 820 Jorie Blvd	Oak Brook	IL	60523	630-571-2670	571-7837
TF: 800-381-6660 ■ *Web:* www.rsna.org					
Radiology Business Management Assn (RBMA) 10300 Eaton Pl Ste 460	Fairfax	VA	22030	703-621-3355	621-3356
TF: 888-224-7262 ■ *Web:* www.rbma.org					
Regulatory Affairs Professionals Society (RAPS) 5635 Fishers Ln Ste 550	Rockville	MD	20852	301-770-2920	770-2924
Web: www.raps.org					
Renal Physicians Assn (RPA) 1700 Rockville Pk Ste 220	Rockville	MD	20852	301-468-3515	468-3511
Web: www.renalmd.org					
Society for Academic Emergency Medicine (SAEM) 2340 S River Rd Ste 200	Des Plaines	IL	60018	847-813-9823	813-5450
Web: www.saem.org					
Society for Healthcare Epidemiology of America 1300 Wilson Blvd Ste 300	Arlington	VA	22209	703-684-1006	684-1009
Web: www.shea-online.org					
Society for Healthcare Strategy & Market Development (SHSMD) 155 N Wacker Dr Ste 400	Chicago	IL	60606	312-422-3888	278-0883
TF: 800-242-2626 ■ *Web:* www.shsmd.org					
Society for Investigative Dermatology Inc (SID) 526 Superior Ave E Ste 540	Cleveland	OH	44114	216-579-9300	579-9333
Web: www.sidnet.org					
Society for Medical Decision Making 390 Amwell Rd Ste 402	Hillsborough	NJ	08844	908-359-1184	450-1119
Web: www.smdm.org					

Phone *Fax*

Society for Neuroscience (SFN)
1121 14th St NW Ste 1010........................Washington DC 20005 202-962-4000 962-4941
Web: sfn.org

Society for Surgery of the Alimentary Tract (SSAT)
900 Cummings Ctr Ste 221-U .... Beverly MA 01915 978-927-8330 524-8890
TF: 866-849-5866 ■ *Web:* www.ssat.com

Society for Vascular Surgery (SVS)
633 N St Clair St 22nd Fl..........................Chicago IL 60611 312-334-2300 334-2320
TF: 800-258-7188 ■ *Web:* vascular.org

Society of American Gastrointestinal & Endoscopic Surgeons (SAGES)
11300 W Olympic Blvd Ste 600 ....Los Angeles CA 90064 310-437-0544 437-0585
Web: www.sages.org

Society of Cardiovascular Anesthesiologists (SCA)
2209 Dickens Rd .... Richmond VA 23230 804-282-0084 282-0090
Web: www.scahq.org

Society of Critical Care Medicine (SCCM)
500 Midway Dr Ste 200 ....Mount Prospect IL 60056 847-827-6869 827-6886
Web: www.sccm.org

Society of Diagnostic Medical Sonography (SDMS)
2745 Dallas Pkwy.......................................Plano TX 75093 214-473-8057 473-8563
TF: 800-229-9506 ■ *Web:* www.sdms.org

Society of Gastroenterology Nurses & Assoc Inc (SGNA)
401 N Michigan Ave................................Chicago IL 60611 312-321-5165 673-6694
TF: 800-245-7462 ■ *Web:* www.sgna.org

Society of Interventional Radiology (SIR)
3975 Fair Rdige Dr Ste 400 N..........................Fairfax VA 22033 703-691-1805 691-1855
TF: 800-488-7284 ■ *Web:* www.sirweb.org

Society of Laparoendoscopic Surgeons (SLS)
7330 SW 62nd Pl Ste 410 ....MIAMI FL 33143 305-665-9959 667-4123
Web: www.sls.org

Society of Nuclear Medicine (SNM)
1850 Samuel Morse Dr..............................Reston VA 20190 703-708-9000 708-9015
TF: 888-633-5343 ■ *Web:* snmmi.org

Society of Teachers of Family Medicine (STFM)
11400 Tomahawk Creek Pkwy Ste 540................Leawood KS 66211 913-906-6000 906-6096
TF: 800-274-7928 ■ *Web:* www.stfm.org

Society of Thoracic Surgeons (STS)
633 N St Clair St Ste 2320..........................Chicago IL 60611 312-202-5800 202-5801
TF: 877-865-5321 ■ *Web:* www.sts.org

Society of Toxicology (SOT)
1821 Michael Faraday Dr Ste 300......................Reston VA 20190 703-438-3115 438-3113
TF: 800-826-6762 ■ *Web:* www.toxicology.org

Southern Medical Assn (SMA)
35 W Lakeshore Dr.............................Birmingham AL 35209 205-945-1840 945-1548
TF: 800-423-4992

Special Care Dentistry Assn 330 N Wabash Ave ....Chicago IL 60611 312-527-6764 673-6805
Web: www.scdaonline.org

Sports Cardiovascular & Wellness Nutritionists (SCAN)
1450 Western Ave Ste 101...........................Albany NY 12203 518-254-6730
TF General: 800-249-2875 ■ *Web:* www.scandpg.org

Therapeutic Communities of America (TCA)
1601 Connecticut Ave NW Rm 574..................Washington DC 20006 202-296-3503
Web: www.treatmentcommunitiesofamerica.org

US Pharmacopeia (USP) 12601 Twinbrook Pkwy .... Rockville MD 20852 301-881-0666
TF: 800-227-8772 ■ *Web:* www.usp.org

Visiting Nurse Assns of America (VNAA)
900 19th St NW Ste 200..........................Washington DC 20006 202-384-1420 384-1444
TF: 888-866-8773 ■ *Web:* www.vnaa.org

World Allergy Organization (WAO)
555 E Wells St Ste 1100..........................Milwaukee WI 53202 414-276-1791 276-3349
Web: www.worldallergy.org

Wound Ostomy & Continence Nurses Society (WOCN)
1120 Rt 73 Ste 200............................Mount Laurel NJ 08054 888-224-9626
TF: 888-224-9626 ■ *Web:* www.wocn.org

49-9 Insurance Industry Associations

Phone *Fax*

America's Health Insurance Plans (AHIP)
601 Pennsylvania Ave NW Ste 500.................Washington DC 20004 202-778-3200 331-7487
Web: www.ahip.org

American Academy of Actuaries
1100 17th St NW 7th Fl ....Washington DC 20036 202-223-8196 872-1948
TF: 888-888-1778 ■ *Web:* www.actuary.org

American Assn of Crop Insurers (AACI)
1 Massachusetts Ave NW Ste 800 ....Washington DC 20001 202-789-4100 408-7763
Web: www.cropinsurers.com

American Assn of Insurance Services (AAIS)
1745 S Naperville Rd .... Wheaton IL 60189 630-681-8347 681-8356
TF: 800-564-2247 ■ *Web:* www.aaisonline.com

American Assn of Managing General Agents (AAMGA)
610 Freedom Business Ctr Ste 110 ....King of Prussia PA 19406 610-225-1999 225-1996
TF: 800-467-8725 ■ *Web:* www.aamga.org

American Council of Life Insurers (ACLI)
101 Constitution Ave NW Ste 700 W ....Washington DC 20001 202-624-2000 624-2319
Web: www.acli.com

American Institute for CPCU & Insurance Institute of America (AICPCU/IIA)
720 Providence Rd Ste 100 ....Malvern PA 19355 610-644-2100 640-9576
TF: 800-644-2101 ■ *Web:* www.theinstitutes.org

American Institute of Marine Underwriters (AIMU)
14 Wall St Ste 820 ....New York NY 10005 212-233-0550 227-5102
Web: www.aimu.org

American Insurance Assn (AIA) 2101 L St..........Washington DC 20037 202-828-7100 293-1219
Web: www.aiadc.org

American Nuclear Insurers (ANI)
95 Glastonbury Blvd Ste 300 ....Glastonbury CT 06033 860-682-1301 659-0002
Web: www.amnucins.com

Associated Risk Managers (ARM) 2 Pierce Pl ....Itasca IL 60143 630-285-4324 285-3590
TF: 800-735-5441 ■ *Web:* www.armiweb.com

Association for Advanced Life Underwriting (AALU)
11921 Freedom Dr Ste 1100..........................Reston VA 20190 703-641-9400 641-9885
TF: 888-275-0092 ■ *Web:* www.aalu.org

Phone *Fax*

Association for Co-op Operations Research & Development (ACORD)
1 Blue Hill Plz PO Box 1529.......................Pearl River NY 10965 845-620-1700 620-3600
TF: 800-444-3341 ■ *Web:* www.acord.org

Blue Cross & Blue Shield Assn
225 N Michigan Ave...................................Chicago IL 60601 312-297-6000
TF: 888-630-2583 ■ *Web:* www.bcbs.com

Casualty Actuarial Society (CAS)
4350 Fairfax Dr # 250............................Arlington VA 22203 703-276-3100 276-3108
Web: www.casact.org

Coalition Against Insurance Fraud
1012 14th St NW Ste 200........................Washington DC 20005 202-393-7330 318-9189
TF: 800-835-6422 ■ *Web:* www.insurancefraud.org

Consumer Credit Industry Assn (CCIA)
6300 Powers Ferry Rd Ste 600-286 ....Atlanta GA 30339 678-858-4001
Web: www.cciaonline.com

Council for Affordable Health Insurance (CAHI)
127 S Peyton St Ste 210..........................Alexandria VA 22314 703-836-6200 836-6550

Council of Insurance Agents & Brokers
701 Pennsylvania Ave NW Ste 750.................Washington DC 20004 202-783-4400 783-4410
TF: 877-267-9855 ■ *Web:* www.ciab.com

CPCU Society 720 Providence Rd ....Malvern PA 19355 800-932-2728 251-2780*
**Fax Area Code:* 610 ■ *TF:* 800-932-2728 ■ *Web:* www.cpcusociety.org

GAMA International 2901 Telestar Ct............. Falls Church VA 22042 800-345-2687
TF Cust Svc: 800-345-2687 ■ *Web:* gamaweb.com

Independent Insurance Agents & Brokers of America Inc (IIABA)
127 S Peyton St ....Alexandria VA 22314 703-683-4422 683-7556
TF: 800-221-7917 ■ *Web:* www.independentagent.com

Institute for Business & Home Safety (IBHS)
4775 E Fowler Ave ....Tampa FL 33617 813-286-3400 286-9960
TF: 866-657-4247 ■ *Web:* www.disastersafety.org

Insurance Information Institute Inc (III)
110 William St ....New York NY 10038 212-346-5500 732-1916
TF: 877-263-7995 ■ *Web:* www.iii.org

Insurance Institute for Highway Safety
1005 N Glebe Rd Ste 800.........................Arlington VA 22201 703-247-1500 247-1588
TF: 888-327-4236 ■ *Web:* www.iihs.org

Insurance Marketing Communications Assn (IMCA)
4248 Park Glen Rd .... Minneapolis MN 55416 952-928-4644 929-1318
Web: www.imcanet.com

Insurance Research Council (IRC)
718 Providence Rd.................................Malvern PA 19355 610-644-2212
TF: 800-644-2101 ■ *Web:* www.insurance-research.org

LIMRA International Inc 300 Day Hill Rd ....Windsor CT 06095 860-688-3358 298-9555
TF: 800-235-4672 ■ *Web:* www.limra.com

LOMA 2300 Windy Ridge Pkwy Ste 600...................Atlanta GA 30339 770-951-1770 984-0441
TF: 800-275-5662 ■ *Web:* www.loma.org

Million Dollar Round Table (MDRT)
325 W Touhy Ave...............................Park Ridge IL 60068 847-692-6378 518-8921
TF General: 877-883-4865 ■ *Web:* www.mdrt.org

Mortgage Insurance Cos of America (MICA)
1425 K St NW Ste 210...........................Washington DC 20005 202-682-2683
Web: usmi.org

NA of Dental Plans (NADP) 12700 Pk Central Dr .... Dallas TX 75251 972-458-6998 458-2258
Web: www.nadp.org

NA of Insurance & Financial Advisors (NAIFA)
2901 Telestar Ct............................. Falls Church VA 22042 703-770-8100
TF Sales: 877-866-2432 ■ *Web:* www.naifa.org

NA of Surety Bond Producers (NASBP)
1140 19th St NW Ste 800........................Washington DC 20036 202-686-3700 686-3656
Web: www.nasbp.org

National Council for Prescription Drug Programs (NCPDP)
9240 E Raintree Dr ....Scottsdale AZ 85260 480-477-1000 767-1042
TF: 888-665-2600 ■ *Web:* www.ncpdp.org

National Crop Insurance Services (NCIS)
8900 Indian Creek Pkwy Ste 600 .... Overland Park KS 66210 913-685-2767 685-3080
TF: 800-951-6247 ■ *Web:* www.ag-risk.org

National Insurance Crime Bureau (NICB)
1111 E Touhy Ave Ste 400 ....Des Plaines IL 60018 847-544-7002
TF: 800-447-6282 ■ *Web:* www.nicb.org

National Organization of Life & Health Insurance Guaranty Assn (NOLHGA)
13873 Pk Ctr Rd Ste 329 .... Herndon VA 20171 703-481-5206 481-5209
Web: www.nolhga.com

Physician Insurers Assn of America (PIAA)
2275 Research Blvd Ste 250........................ Rockville MD 20850 301-947-9000 947-9090
Web: www.piaa.us

Professional Insurance Marketing Assn (PIMA)
35 E Wacker Dr Ste 850 ....Chicago IL 60601 817-569-7462
Web: www.pima-assn.org

Professional Liability Underwriting Society
5353 Wayzata Blvd Ste 600 .... Minneapolis MN 55416 952-746-2580 746-2599
TF: 800-845-0778 ■ *Web:* www.plusweb.org

Property Casualty Insurers Assn of America
8700 W Bryn Mawr Ave ....Des Plaines IL 60018 847-297-7800 297-5064
Web: www.pciaa.net

Property Loss Research Bureau (PLRB)
3025 Highland Pkwy Ste 800 .... Downers Grove IL 60515 630-724-2200 724-2260
TF: 888-711-7572 ■ *Web:* www.plrb.org

Risk & Insurance Management Society Inc (RIMS)
1065 Ave of the Americas 13th Fl...................New York NY 10018 212-286-9292 986-9716
Web: www.rims.org

Society of Actuaries (SOA)
475 N Martingale Rd Ste 600.................... Schaumburg IL 60173 847-706-3500 706-3599
Web: www.soa.org

Society of Financial Service Professionals (SFSP)
19 Campus Blvd Ste 100 ....Newtown Square PA 19073 610-526-2500 527-4010
TF: 800-392-6900 ■ *Web:* www.financialpro.org

Surety & Fidelity Assn of America (SFAA)
1101 Connecticut Ave NW Ste 800.................Washington DC 20036 202-463-0600 463-0606
Web: www.surety.org

Workmen's Circle/Arbeter Ring Inc
247 W 37th St 5th Fl..............................New York NY 10018 212-889-6800 532-7518
TF: 800-922-2558 ■ *Web:* www.circle.org

49-10 Legal Professionals Associations

Phone | Fax

ABA Commission on Domestic Violence
321 N Clark St 9th Fl....Chicago IL 60654 312-988-5000 662-1594*
Fax Area Code: 202 ■ *TF:* 800-799-7233 ■
Web: www.americanbar.org/groups/domestic_violence.html

ABA Commission on Law & Aging (COLA)
1050 Connecticut Ave NW Ste 400....Washington DC 20036 202-662-1000 662-8698
Web: www.americanbar.org/groups/law_aging.html

American Academy of Psychiatry & the Law (AAPL)
1 Regency Dr PO Box 30....Bloomfield CT 06002 860-242-5450 286-0787
TF: 800-331-1389 ■ *Web:* www.aapl.org

American Arbitration Assn Inc (AAA)
1633 Broadway 10th Fl....New York NY 10019 212-716-5800 716-5905
TF: 800-778-7879 ■ *Web:* www.adr.org

American Assn for Justice (AAJ)
777 Sixth St NW Ste 200....Washington DC 20001 202-965-3500
TF: 800-424-2725 ■ *Web:* www.justice.org

American Bankruptcy Institute (ABI)
66 Canal Ctr Plz Ste 600....Alexandria VA 22314 703-739-0800 739-1060
Web: www.abi.org

American Bar Assn (ABA) 321 N Clark St....Chicago IL 60610 312-988-5000
TF: 800-285-2221 ■ *Web:* www.americanbar.org

American College of Trust & Estate Counsel (ACTEC)
901 15th St NW Ste 525....Washington DC 20005 202-684-8460 684-8459
Web: www.actec.org

American Health Lawyers Assn (AHLA)
1620 Eye St NW....Washington DC 20006 202-833-1100 833-1105
Web: www.healthlawyers.org

American Immigration Lawyers Assn (AILA)
918 F St NW....Washington DC 20004 202-216-2400 783-7853
Web: www.aila.org

American Intellectual Property Law Assn (AIPLA)
241 18th St S Ste 700....Arlington VA 22202 703-415-0780 415-0786
Web: www.aipla.org

American Judicature Society (AJS)
2700 University Ave....Des Moines IA 50311 515-271-2281 279-3090
TF: 800-626-4089

American Land Title Assn (ALTA)
1828 L St NW Ste 705....Washington DC 20036 202-296-3671 223-5843
TF: 800-787-2582 ■ *Web:* www.alta.org

American Law Institute (ALI)
4025 Chestnut St....Philadelphia PA 19104 215-243-1600 243-1636
TF: 800-253-6397 ■ *Web:* www.ali.org

American Society of International Law, The (ASIL)
2223 Massachusetts Ave NW....Washington DC 20008 202-939-6000 797-7133
Web: www.asil.org

American Tort Reform Assn (ATRA)
1101 Connecticut Ave NW Ste 400....Washington DC 20036 202-682-1163 682-1022
TF: 877-333-2227 ■ *Web:* www.atra.org

Association for Conflict Resolution (ACR)
12100 Sunset Hills Rd Ste 130....Reston VA 20190 703-234-4141 435-4390
TF: 800-880-7303 ■ *Web:* imis100us2.com/acr/acr/default.aspx

Association of American Law Schools (AALS)
1201 Connecticut Ave NW Ste 800....Washington DC 20036 202-296-8851 296-8869
Web: www.aals.org

Association of Corporate Counsel (ACC)
1025 Connecticut Ave NW Ste 200....Washington DC 20036 202-293-4103 293-4701
TF: 877-647-3411 ■ *Web:* www.acc.com

Association of Legal Administrators (ALA)
75 Tri-State International Ste 222....Lincolnshire IL 60069 847-267-1252 267-1329
TF: 877-675-5571 ■ *Web:* www.alanet.org

Battered Women's Justice Project
1801 Nicollet Ave S Ste 102....Minneapolis MN 55403 612-824-8768 824-8965
TF: 800-903-0111 ■ *Web:* www.bwjp.org

Christian Legal Society (CLS)
8001 Braddock Rd Ste 300....Springfield VA 22151 703-642-1070 642-1075
Web: www.clsnet.org

Commercial Law League of America (CLLA)
70 E Lake St Ste 630....Chicago IL 60601 312-781-2000 781-2010
TF: 800-978-2552 ■ *Web:* www.clla.org

Defense Research Institute (DRI)
55 W Monroe St Ste 20....Chicago IL 60603 312-795-1101 795-0749
TF: 866-525-6466 ■ *Web:* www.dri.org

Environmental Law Institute (ELI)
2000 L St NW Ste 620....Washington DC 20036 202-939-3800 939-3868
TF: 800-433-5120 ■ *Web:* www.eli.org

Federalist Society for Law & Public Policy Studies
1015 18th St NW Ste 425....Washington DC 20036 202-822-8138 296-8061
Web: www.fed-soc.org

Food & Drug Law Institute (FDLI)
1155 15th St NW Ste 800....Washington DC 20005 202-371-1420 371-0649
TF: 800-956-6293 ■ *Web:* www.fdli.org

Institute for Professionals in Taxation (IPT)
600 Northpark Town Ctr
1200 Abernathy Rd Ste L-2....Atlanta GA 30328 404-240-2300 240-2315
Web: www.ipt.org

International Assn of Defense Counsel (IADC)
303 W Madison St Ste 925....Chicago IL 60606 312-368-1494 368-1854
Web: www.iadclaw.org

International Law Institute (ILI)
1055 Thomas Jefferson St NW Ste M-100....Washington DC 20007 202-247-6006 247-6010
Web: www.ili.org

International Municipal Lawyers Assn (IMLA)
7910 Woodmont Ave Ste 1440....Bethesda MD 20814 202-466-5424 785-0152
TF: 800-942-7732 ■ *Web:* www.imla.org

Justice in Aging (NSCLC) 1444 'I' St Ste 1100....Washington DC 20005 202-289-6976 289-7224
Web: nsclc.org

Justice Research & Statistics Assn (JRSA)
777 N Capitol St NE Ste 801....Washington DC 20002 202-842-9330 842-9329
Web: www.jrsainfo.org

Lawyers for Civil Justice (LCJ)
1140 Connecticut Ave NW Ste 503....Washington DC 20036 202-429-0045 429-6982
Web: www.lfcj.com

Lawyers' Committee for Civil Rights Under Law
1401 New York Ave NW Ste 400....Washington DC 20005 202-662-8600 783-0857
TF: 888-299-5227 ■ *Web:* www.lawyerscommittee.org

Media Law Resource Ctr (MLRC)
266 W 37th St Ste 20....New York NY 10018 212-337-0200
Web: www.medialaw.org

NALS - Assn for Legal Professionals
8159 E 41st St....Tulsa OK 74145 918-582-5188 582-5907
Web: www.nals.org

National Bar Assn (NBA) 1225 11th St NW....Washington DC 20001 202-842-3900 289-6170
Web: www.nationalbar.org

National Council of Juvenile & Family Court Judges (NCJFCJ)
Univ of Nevada PO Box 8970....Reno NV 89507 775-784-6012 784-6628
TF: 800-527-3223 ■ *Web:* www.ncjfcj.org

National Court Reporters Assn (NCRA)
8224 Old Courthouse Rd....Vienna VA 22182 703-556-6272 556-6291
TF: 800-272-6272 ■ *Web:* www.ncra.org

National Employment Lawyers Assn (NELA)
417 Montgomery St 4th Fl....San Francisco CA 94104 415-296-7629 677-9445
Web: www.nela.org

National Federation of Paralegal Assn (NFPA)
23607 Hwy 99 Ste 2-C....Edmonds WA 98020 425-967-0045 771-9588

National Legal Aid & Defender Assn (NLADA)
1140 Connecticut Ave NW Ste 900....Washington DC 20036 202-452-0620 872-1031
TF: 800-725-4513 ■ *Web:* www.nlada.org

National Partnership for Women & Families
1875 Connecticut Ave NW Ste 650....Washington DC 20009 202-986-2600 986-2539
Web: www.nationalpartnership.org

Native American Rights Fund (NARF)
1506 Broadway....Boulder CO 80302 303-447-8760 443-7776
TF: 888-280-0726 ■ *Web:* www.narf.org

Pension Rights Ctr
1350 Connecticut Ave NW Ste 206....Washington DC 20036 202-296-3776 833-2472
TF: 866-735-7737 ■ *Web:* www.pensionrights.org

Practising Law Institute (PLI)
810 Seventh Ave 26th Fl....New York NY 10019 212-824-5700
TF: 800-260-4754 ■ *Web:* www.pli.edu

Taxpayers Against Fraud Education Fund (TAF)
1220 19th St NW Ste 501....Washington DC 20036 202-296-4826 296-4838
TF General: 800-873-2573 ■ *Web:* www.taf.org

Vera Institute of Justice
233 Broadway 12th Fl....New York NY 10279 212-334-1300 941-9407
Web: www.vera.org

World Jurist Assn (WJA)
7910 Woodmont Ave Ste 1440....Bethesda MD 20814 202-466-5428 452-8540
Web: www.worldjurist.org

49-11 Library & Information Science Associations

Phone | Fax

American Assn of Law Libraries (AALL)
53 W Jackson Blvd Ste 940....Chicago IL 60604 312-939-4764 431-1097
Web: www.aallnet.org

American Assn of School Librarians (AASL)
50 E Huron St....Chicago IL 60611 312-280-4386 664-7459
TF: 800-545-2433 ■ *Web:* www.ala.org/aasl

American Library Assn (ALA) 50 E Huron St....Chicago IL 60611 312-944-6780 944-2641
TF: 800-545-2433 ■ *Web:* www.ala.org

American Theological Library Assn (ATLA)
300 S Wacker Dr Ste 2100....Chicago IL 60606 312-454-5100 454-5505
TF: 888-665-2852 ■ *Web:* www.atla.com

Association for Library & Information Science Education (ALISE)
2150 N 107th St Ste 205....Seattle WA 98133 206-209-5267 367-8777
TF: 877-275-7547 ■ *Web:* www.alise.org

Association for Library Collections & Technical Services (ALCTS)
50 E Huron St....Chicago IL 60611 312-280-5038 280-5033
TF: 800-545-2433 ■ *Web:* www.ala.org/alcts

Association for Library Service to Children (ALSC)
50 E Huron St....Chicago IL 60611 312-280-2163 944-7671
TF: 800-545-2433 ■ *Web:* www.ala.org/alsc

Association for Library Trustees, Advocates, Friends & Foundations (ALTAFF)
50 E Huron St....Chicago IL 60611 800-545-2433
TF: 800-545-2433 ■ *Web:* ala.org

Association of College & Research Libraries (ACRL)
50 E Huron St....Chicago IL 60611 312-280-2519 280-2520
TF: 800-545-2433 ■ *Web:* www.ala.org/acrl/aboutacrl

Association of Jewish Libraries PO Box 1118....Teaneck NJ 07666 201-371-3255
Web: www.jewishlibraries.org

Association of Specialized & Co-op Library Agencies (ASCLA)
50 E Huron St....Chicago IL 60611 312-280-4395 944-8085
TF: 800-545-2433 ■ *Web:* www.ala.org/ascla

Cal Poly Pomona Foundation Inc
3801 W Temple Ave Bldg 55....Pomona CA 91768 909-869-2950 869-3716
Web: www.foundation.csupomona.edu

Canadian Assn of Special Libraries & Information Services (CASLIS)
1150 Morrison Dr Ste 400....Ottawa ON K2H8S9 613-232-9625 563-9895

Canadian Health Libraries Assn (CHLA)
39 River St....Toronto ON M5A3P1 416-646-1600 646-9460
Web: www.chla-absc.ca

Canadian Library Assn (CLA) 328 Frank St....Ottawa ON K2P0X8 613-232-9625 563-9895
Web: www.cla.ca

Library & Information Technology Assn (LITA)
50 E Huron St....Chicago IL 60611 312-280-4270 280-3257
TF: 800-545-2433 ■ *Web:* www.ala.org

Library Leadership & Management Assn (LLAMA)
50 E Huron St....Chicago IL 60611 800-545-2433
TF: 800-545-2433 ■ *Web:* www.ala.org/llama

Medical Library Assn (MLA)
65 E Wacker Pl Ste 1900....Chicago IL 60601 312-419-9094 419-8950
TF: 800-523-1850 ■ *Web:* www.mlanet.org

Phone Fax

Music Library Assn (MLA)
8551 Research Way Ste 180 ... Middleton WI 53562 608-836-5825 831-8200
Web: www.musiclibraryassoc.org

Online Computer Library Ctr Inc (OCLC)
6565 Kilgour Pl ... Dublin OH 43017 800-848-5878 764-6096*
**Fax Area Code:* 614 ■ *TF:* 800-848-5878 ■ *Web:* www.oclc.org

Public Library Assn (PLA) 50 E Huron St ... Chicago IL 60611 312-280-5752 280-5029
TF: 800-545-2433 ■ *Web:* www.ala.org

Reference & User Services Assn (RUSA)
50 E Huron St ... Chicago IL 60611 312-280-4398 944-8085
TF: 800-545-2433 ■ *Web:* www.ala.org/rusa

Special Libraries Assn (SLA)
331 S Patrick St ... Alexandria VA 22314 703-647-4900 647-4901
TF: 866-446-6069 ■ *Web:* www.sla.org

Urban Libraries Council (ULC)
125 S Wacker Dr Ste 1050 ... Chicago IL 60606 847-866-9999
Web: www.urbanlibraries.org

Young Adult Library Services Assn (YALSA)
50 E Huron St ... Chicago IL 60611 312-280-4390 664-7459
TF: 800-545-2433 ■ *Web:* www.ala.org/yalsa

49-12 Management & Business Professional Associations

Phone Fax

Academy of Management (AOM)
235 Elm Rd PO Box 3020 ... Briarcliff Manor NY 10510 914-923-2607 923-2615
TF: 800-633-4931 ■ *Web:* aom.org

AMC Institute 700 N Fairfax St Ste 510 ... Alexandria VA 22314 215-564-3484 963-9785
Web: amcinstitute.org

American Business Conference (ABC)
1828 L St NW Ste 908 ... Washington DC 20036 202-822-9300 467-4070
Web: www.americanbusinessconference.org

American Business Women's Assn (ABWA)
11050 Roe Ave Ste 200 ... Overland Park KS 66211 800-228-0007 660-0101*
**Fax Area Code:* 913 ■ *TF:* 800-228-0007 ■ *Web:* www.abwa.org

American Chamber of Commerce Executives (ACCE)
4875 Eisenhower Ave Ste 250 ... Alexandria VA 22304 703-998-0072 212-9512
TF: 800-394-2223 ■ *Web:* www.acce.org

American Payroll Assn (APA)
660 N Main Ave Ste 100 ... San Antonio TX 78205 210-226-4600 226-4027
Web: americanpayroll.org

American Seminar Leaders Assn (ASLA)
2405 E Washington Blvd ... Pasadena CA 91104 626-791-1211 791-0701
TF: 800-801-1886 ■ *Web:* www.asla.com

American Society of Assn Executives (ASAE)
1575 'I' St NW ... Washington DC 20005 202-626-2723
TF: 888-950-2723 ■ *Web:* www.asaecenter.org

American Society of Notaries (ASN)
PO Box 5707 ... Tallahassee FL 32314 850-671-5164 671-5165
Web: www.notaries.org

American Society of Pension Professionals & Actuaries (ASPPA)
4245 N Fairfax Dr Ste 750 ... Arlington VA 22203 703-516-9300 516-9308
Web: www.asppa.org

American Staffing Assn (ASA)
277 S Washington St Ste 200 ... Alexandria VA 22314 703-253-2020 253-2053
TF: 800-456-4324 ■ *Web:* www.americanstaffing.net

Appraisers Assn of America (AAA)
386 Pk Ave S Ste 2000 ... New York NY 10016 212-889-5404 889-5503
Web: appraisersassociation.org

APQC 123 N Post Oak Ln Ste 300 ... Houston TX 77024 713-681-4020 681-8578
TF: 800-776-9676 ■ *Web:* www.apqc.org

ARMA International
11880 College Blvd Ste 450 ... Overland Park KS 66210 913-341-3808 341-3742
TF: 800-422-2762 ■ *Web:* www.arma.org

ASIS International 1625 Prince St ... Alexandria VA 22314 703-519-6200 519-6299
Web: www.asisonline.org

Association for Business Communication
181 Turner St NW ... Blacksburg VA 24061 540-231-1939
Web: www.businesscommunication.org

Association for Corporate Growth (ACG)
125 S. Wacker Dr Ste 3100 ... Chicago IL 60606 312-957-4260
TF: 877-358-2220 ■ *Web:* www.acg.org

Association for Mfg Excellence (AME)
3701 W Algonquin Rd Ste 225 ... Rolling Meadows IL 60008 224-232-5980 232-5981
Web: www.ame.org

Association for Mfg Technology (AMT)
7901 Westpark Dr ... McLean VA 22102 703-893-2900 893-1151
TF: 800-524-0475 ■ *Web:* www.amtonline.org

Association of Fundraising Professionals (AFP)
4300 Wilson Blvd Ste 300 ... Arlington VA 22203 703-684-0410 684-0540
TF: 800-666-3863 ■ *Web:* www.afpnet.org

Association of Proposal Management Professionals (APMP)
PO Box 668 ... Dana Point CA 92629 949-493-9398
Web: www.apmp.org

Business Council for International Understanding (BCIU)
1212 Ave of the Americas 10th Fl ... New York NY 10036 212-490-0460 697-8526
Web: www.bciu.org

Business Executives for National Security (BENS)
1030 15th St NW Ste 200 ... Washington DC 20005 202-296-2125 296-2490
Web: www.bens.org

Business Forms Management Assn (BFMA)
3800 Old Cheney Rd Ste 101-285 ... Lincoln NE 68516 402-216-0479 204-5979*
**Fax Area Code:* 877 ■ *TF:* 888-367-3078 ■ *Web:* www.bfma.org

Business Roundtable (BR)
300 New Jersey Ave NW Ste 800 ... Washington DC 20001 202-872-1260 466-3509
Web: businessroundtable.org

Chief Executives Organization
7920 Norfolk Ave Ste 400 ... Bethesda MD 20814 301-656-9220
Web: www.ceo.org

Christian Leadership Alliance (CLA)
635 Camino De Los Mares Ste 216 ... San Clemente CA 92673 949-487-0900 487-0927
TF: 800-263-6317 ■ *Web:* www.christianleadershipalliance.org

Phone Fax

Club Managers Assn of America (CMAA)
1733 King St ... Alexandria VA 22314 703-739-9500 739-0124
TF: 800-409-7755 ■ *Web:* www.cmaa.org

Conference Board Inc 845 Third Ave ... New York NY 10022 212-759-0900 980-7014
Web: www.conference-board.org

Council for Community & Economic Research (C2ER)
1700 N Moore St Ste 2225 PO Box 100127 ... Arlington VA 22209 703-522-4980 393-5098*
**Fax Area Code:* 480 ■ *Web:* www.c2er.org

Council on State Taxation (COST)
122 C St NW Ste 330 ... Washington DC 20001 202-484-5222 484-5229
Web: www.cost.org

Employee Assistance Professionals Assn Inc (EAPA)
4350 N Fairfax Dr Ste 740 ... Arlington VA 22203 703-387-1000 522-4585
Web: www.eapassn.org

Employee Involvement Assn 11 W Monument Ave ... Dayton OH 45402 937-586-3724

Employers Council on Flexible Compensation (ECFC)
927 15th St NW Ste 700 ... Washington DC 20005 202-659-4300 216-9646
Web: www.ecfc.org

ESOP Assn 1726 M St NW Ste 501 ... Washington DC 20036 202-293-2971 293-7568
TF: 866-366-3832 ■ *Web:* www.esopassociation.org

Executive Women International (EWI)
3860 S 2300 E ... Salt Lake City UT 84109 801-355-2800 355-2852
TF: 877-439-4669 ■ *Web:* ewiconnect.com

Family Firm Institute (FFI)
200 Lincoln St Ste 201 ... Boston MA 02111 617-482-3045 482-3049
Web: www.ffi.org

Foundation on Economic Trends
4520 E W Hwy Ste 600 ... Bethesda MD 20814 301-656-6272 654-0208
Web: www.foet.org

HR People & Strategy (HRPS)
401 N Michigan Ave Ste 2200 ... Chicago IL 60611 312-321-6805 673-6944
TF: 800-337-9517 ■ *Web:* www.hrps.org

Institute for a Drug-Free Workplace (IDFW)
10701 Parkridge Blvd Ste 300 ... Reston VA 20191 703-391-7222 391-7223
TF: 877-696-6775 ■ *Web:* www.drugfreeworkplace.org

Institute for Alternative Futures (IAF)
100 N Pitt St Ste 307 ... Alexandria VA 22314 703-684-5880
Web: www.altfutures.com

Institute for Supply Management (ISM)
2055 Centennial Cir ... Tempe AZ 85284 480-752-6276 752-7890
TF Cust Svc: 800-888-6276 ■ *Web:* www.instituteforsupplymanagement.org

Institute of Business Appraisers (IBA)
1111 BrickyaRd Rd Ste 200 ... Salt Lake City UT 84106 800-299-4130 353-5406*
**Fax Area Code:* 866 ■ *TF:* 800-299-4130 ■ *Web:* www.go-iba.org

Institute of Certified Professional Managers (ICPM)
James Madison University MSC 5504 ... Harrisonburg VA 22807 540-568-3247
TF: 800-460-8013 ■ *Web:* www.icpm.biz

Institute of Management Consultants USA Inc (IMC USA)
2025 M St NW Ste 800 ... Washington DC 20036 202-367-1134 367-2134
TF: 800-221-2557 ■ *Web:* www.imcusa.org

International Assn for Human Resource Information Management Inc (IHRIM)
PO Box 1086 ... Burlington MA 01803 800-804-3983 998-8011*
**Fax Area Code:* 781 ■ *TF:* 800-804-3983 ■ *Web:* www.ihrim.org

International Assn for Impact Assessment (IAIA)
1330 23rd St S Ste C ... Fargo ND 58103 701-297-7908 297-7917
Web: www.iaia.org

International Assn of Administrative Professionals (IAAP)
10502 NW Ambassador Dr PO Box 20404 ... Kansas City MO 64153 816-891-6600 891-9118
Web: www.iaap-hq.org

International Assn of Business Communicators (IABC)
155 Montgomery St Ste 1210 ... San Francisco CA 94104 415-544-4700 544-4747
TF: 800-766-4222 ■ *Web:* www.iabc.com

International Assn of Conference Centers (IACC)
35 East Wacker Dr Ste 850 ... Chicago IL 60601 312-224-2580 644-8557
Web: www.iacconline.org

International Assn of Venue Managers Inc (IAVM)
635 Fritz Dr Ste 100 ... Coppell TX 75019 972-906-7441 906-7418
TF: 800-935-4226 ■ *Web:* www.iavm.org

International Assn of Workforce Professionals (IAPES)
1801 Louisville Rd ... Frankfort KY 40601 502-223-4459 223-4127
TF: 888-898-9960 ■ *Web:* www.iawponline.org

International Council of Shopping Centers (ICSC)
1221 Ave of the Americas 41st Fl ... New York NY 10020 646-728-3800 589-5555*
**Fax Area Code:* 212 ■ *Web:* www.icsc.org

International Economic Development Council (IEDC)
734 15th St NW Ste 900 ... Washington DC 20005 202-223-7800 223-4745
Web: www.iedconline.org

International Facility Management Assn (IFMA)
800 Gessner Rd Ste 900 ... Houston TX 77024 713-623-4362 623-6124
Web: www.ifma.org

International Graphoanalysis Society (IGAS)
842 Fifth Ave ... New Kensington PA 15068 724-472-9701 271-1149*
**Fax Area Code:* 509 ■ *Web:* www.igas.com

International Public Management Assn for Hum Res (IPMA-HR)
1617 Duke St ... Alexandria VA 22314 703-549-7100 684-0948
TF: 800-381-8378 ■ *Web:* www.ipma-hr.org

International Society for Performance Improvement (ISPI)
PO Box 13035 ... Silver Spring MD 20910 301-587-8570 587-8573
TF: 800-825-7550 ■ *Web:* www.ispi.org

International Society of Certified Employee Benefit Specialists (ISCEBS)
18700 W Bluemond Rd PO Box 209 ... Brookfield WI 53008 262-786-8771 786-8650
TF: 888-334-3327 ■ *Web:* www.iscebs.org

International Trademark Assn (INTA)
655 Third Ave 10th Fl ... New York NY 10017 212-768-9887 768-7796
TF: 800-995-3579 ■ *Web:* www.inta.org

Latin Business Assn (LBA)
120 S San Pedro St Ste 530 ... Los Angeles CA 90012 213-628-8510 628-8519
TF: 866-924-9757 ■ *Web:* lbausa.com

Manufacturers Alliance/MAPI Inc
1600 Wilson Blvd Ste 1100 ... Arlington VA 22209 703-841-9000 841-9514
Web: www.mapi.net

Meeting Professionals International (MPI)
3030 LBJ Fwy Ste 1700 ... Dallas TX 75234 972-702-3000 702-3070
TF: 866-748-9561 ■ *Web:* www.mpiweb.org

NA of Parliamentarians (NAP) 213 S Main St ... Independence MO 64050 816-833-3892 833-3893
TF: 888-627-2929 ■ *Web:* www.parliamentarians.org

Phone *Fax*

NA of Professional Employer Organizations (NAPEO)
707 N St Asaph St .... Alexandria VA 22314 703-836-0466 836-0976
Web: www.napeo.org

National Black MBA Assn (NBMBAA)
180 N Michigan Ave Ste 1400 .... Chicago IL 60601 312-236-2622 236-0390
Web: www.nbmbaa.org

National Business Assn (NBA)
5151 Beltline Rd Ste 1150 .... Dallas TX 75254 972-458-0900 960-9149
TF: 800-456-0440 ■ *Web:* www.nationalbusiness.org

National Business Coalition on Health (NBCH)
1015 18th St NW Ste 730 .... Washington DC 20036 202-775-9300 775-1569
TF: 800-223-4139 ■ *Web:* www.nbch.org

National Business Incubation Assn (NBIA)
12703 Research Pkwy Ste 100 .... Orlando FL 32826 740-593-4331
Web: www.nbia.org

National Co-op Business Assn (NCBA)
1401 New York Ave NW Ste 1100 .... Washington DC 20005 202-638-6222 638-1374
TF: 800-356-9655 ■ *Web:* www.ncba.coop

National Coalition of Black Meeting Planners (NCBMP)
700 N. Fairfax St Ste 510 .... Alexandria VA 22314 571-527-3110 588-0011*
**Fax Area Code:* 301 ■ *TF:* 800-551-9369 ■ *Web:* www.ncbmp.com

National Contract Management Assn (NCMA)
21740 Beaumeade Cir Ste 125 .... Ashburn VA 20147 571-382-0082 448-0939*
**Fax Area Code:* 703 ■ *TF:* 800-344-8096 ■ *Web:* www.ncmahq.org

National Council for Advanced Mfg (NACFAM)
2025 M St NW Ste 800 .... Washington DC 20036 202-429-2220 429-2422
Web: www.nacfam.org

National Institute for Work & Learning (NIWL)
1825 Connecticut Ave NW 7th Fl .... Washington DC 20009 202-884-8186 884-8422

National Management Assn (NMA) 2210 Arbor Blvd .... Dayton OH 45439 937-294-0421 294-2374
Web: www.nma1.org

National Notary Assn (NNA) 9350 DeSoto Ave .... Chatsworth CA 91313 818-739-4000
TF: 800-876-6827 ■ *Web:* www.nationalnotary.org

National Right to Work Committee (NRTWC)
8001 Braddock Rd Ste 500 .... Springfield VA 22160 703-321-8510 321-9319
TF: 800-325-7892 ■ *Web:* nrtw.org

National Small Business Assn (NSBA)
1156 15th St NW Ste 1100 .... Washington DC 20005 202-293-8830 872-8543
TF: 800-345-6728 ■ *Web:* www.nsba.biz

National Society of Compliance Professionals (NSCP)
22 Kent Rd .... Cornwall Bridge CT 06754 860-672-0843 672-3005
Web: www.nscp.org

New York Celebrity Assistants (NYCA)
459 Columbus Ave Ste 216 .... New York NY 10024 212-803-5444
Web: www.nycelebrityassistants.com

Organization for International Investment (OFII)
1225 19th St NW Ste 501 .... Washington DC 20036 202-659-1903 659-2293
Web: www.ofii.org

Product Development & Management Assn (PDMA)
330 N Wabash Ave Ste 2000 .... Chicago IL 60611 312-321-5145
TF: 800-232-5241 ■ *Web:* www.pdma.org

Professional Convention Management Assn (PCMA)
35 E Wacker Dr Ste 500 .... Chicago IL 60601 312-423-7262 423-7222
TF: 877-827-7262 ■ *Web:* www.pcma.org

Professional Services Council (PSC)
4401 Wilson Blvd Ste 1110 .... Arlington VA 22203 703-875-8059 875-8922
TF: 800-353-9118 ■ *Web:* www.pscouncil.org

Profit Sharing/401(k) Council of America (PSCA)
20 N Wacker Dr Ste 3700 .... Chicago IL 60606 312-419-1863 419-1864
TF: 866-614-8407 ■ *Web:* www.psca.org

Project Management Institute (PMI)
14 Campus Blvd .... Newtown Square PA 19073 610-356-4600 356-4647
TF: 866-276-4764 ■ *Web:* www.pmi.org

Religious Conference Management Assn Inc (RCMA)
7702 Woodland Dr Ste 120 .... Indianapolis IN 46278 317-632-1888 632-7909
TF: 800-221-8235 ■ *Web:* www.rcmaweb.org

SCORE Assn 1175 Herndon Pkwy Ste 900 .... Herndon VA 20170 800-634-0245 487-3066*
**Fax Area Code:* 703 ■ *TF:* 800-634-0245 ■ *Web:* www.score.org

Service Industry Assn (SIA)
2164 Histroic Decatur Rd Villa 19 .... San Diego CA 92106 619-221-9200
Web: www.servicenetwork.org

Small Business & Entrepreneurship Council
301 Maple Ave W Ste 690 .... Vienna VA 22180 703-242-5840 242-5841
Web: www.sbecouncil.org

Small Business Legislative Council (SBLC)
1010 Mass Ave NW Ste 400 .... Washington DC 20001 202-639-8500
Web: www.sblc.org

Society for Human Resource Management (SHRM)
1800 Duke St .... Alexandria VA 22314 703-548-3440 836-0367
TF: 800-283-7476 ■ *Web:* www.shrm.org

Society of Corporate Secretaries & Governance Professionals Inc
240 W 35th St Ste 400 .... New York NY 10001 212-681-2000 681-2005
Web: main.governanceprofessionals.org

Society of Professional Benefit Administrators (SPBA)
2 Wisconsin Cir Ste 670 .... Chevy Chase MD 20815 301-718-7722 718-9440
Web: www.spbatpa.org

Strategic and Competitive Intelligence Professionals (SCIP)
7550 IH 10 W Ste 400 .... San Antonio TX 78229 703-739-0696 739-2524
Web: www.scip.org

US Council for International Business (USCIB)
1212 Ave of the Americas 18th Fl .... New York NY 10036 212-354-4480 575-0327
Web: www.uscib.org

US-ASEAN Business Council
1101 17th St NW Ste 411 .... Washington DC 20036 202-289-1911 289-0519
Web: usasean.org

US-China Business Council, The
1818 N St NW Ste 200 .... Washington DC 20036 202-429-0340 775-2476
Web: www.uschina.org

US-Japan Business Council 1615 H St NW .... Washington DC 20062 202-463-5772
Web: www.usjbc.org

US-Russia Business Council
1110 Vermont Ave NW Ste 350 .... Washington DC 20005 202-739-9180 659-5920
Web: www.usrbc.org

World Trade Centers Assn (WTCA)
120 Broadway Ste 3350 .... New York NY 10271 212-432-2626 418-4801*
**Fax Area Code:* 479

WorldatWork 14040 N Northsight Blvd .... Scottsdale AZ 85260 202-315-5500 315-5550
TF: 877-951-9191 ■ *Web:* www.worldatwork.org

Worldwide Employee Benefits Network Inc (WEB)
11520 N Central Expressway Ste 201 .... Dallas TX 75243 202-349-2049 318-8778
Web: www.webnetwork.org

Young Presidents' Organization (YPO)
600 E Las Colinas Blvd Ste 1000 .... Irving TX 75039 972-587-1500 587-1611
TF: 800-773-7976 ■ *Web:* www.ypo.org

YPO-WPO 600 E Las Colinas Blvd Ste 1100 .... Irving TX 75039 972-587-1500 587-1600
TF: 800-773-7976 ■ *Web:* www.wpo.org

49-13 Manufacturing Industry Professional & Trade Associations

Phone *Fax*

Adhesive & Sealant Council Inc (ASC)
7101 Wisconsin Ave # 990 .... Bethesda MD 20814 301-986-9700 986-9795
Web: www.ascouncil.org

Aluminum Assn Inc 1525 Wilson Blvd Ste 600 .... Arlington VA 22209 703-358-2960 358-2961
Web: www.aluminum.org

Aluminum Extruders Council (AEC)
1000 N Rand Rd Ste 214 .... Wauconda IL 60084 847-526-2010 526-3993
Web: www.aec.org

American Assn of Textile Chemists & Colorists (AATCC)
1 Davis Dr PO Box 12215 .... Research Triangle Park NC 27709 919-549-8141 549-8933
Web: www.aatcc.org

American Boiler Manufacturers Assn (ABMA)
8221 Old Courthouse Rd Ste 207 .... Vienna VA 22182 703-356-7172 356-4543
TF: 800-227-1966 ■ *Web:* www.abma.com

American Composites Manufacturers Assn (ACMA)
3033 Wilson Blvd Ste 420 .... Arlington VA 22201 703-525-0743 525-0743
Web: www.acmanet.org

American Fiber Manufacturers Assn Inc (AFMA)
1530 Wilson Blvd Ste 690 .... Arlington VA 22209 703-875-0432 875-0907
Web: www.afma.org

American Foundry Society (AFS)
1695 N Penny Ln .... Schaumburg IL 60173 847-824-0181 824-2174
TF: 800-537-4237 ■ *Web:* www.afsinc.org

American Galvanizers Assn (AGA)
6881 S Holly Cir Ste 108 .... Centennial CO 80112 720-554-0900 554-0909
TF: 800-468-7732 ■ *Web:* www.galvanizeit.org

American Gear Manufacturers Assn (AGMA)
500 Montgomery St Ste 350 .... Alexandria VA 22314 703-684-0211 684-0242
Web: www.agma.org

American Industrial Hygiene Assn (AIHA)
2700 Prosperity Ave Ste 250 .... Fairfax VA 22031 703-849-8888 207-3561
Web: www.aiha.org

American Iron & Steel Institute (AISI)
1101 17th St NW .... Washington DC 20036 202-452-7100 463-6573
Web: www.steel.org

American Society for Quality (ASQ)
600 N Plankinton Ave .... Milwaukee WI 53203 414-272-8575 272-1734
TF: 800-248-1946 ■ *Web:* www.asq.org

American Textile Machinery Assn (ATMA)
201 Pk Washington Ct .... Falls Church VA 22046 703-538-1789
Web: www.atmanet.org

American Wire Producers Assn (AWPA)
801 N Fairfax St Ste 211 .... Alexandria VA 22314 703-299-4434 299-9233
Web: www.awpa.org

Asia America MultiTechnology Assn (AAMA)
1270 Oakmead Pkwy .... Sunnyvale CA 94085 408-736-2554
Web: www.aamasv.com

ASM International 9639 Kinsman Rd .... Materials Park OH 44073 440-338-5151 338-4634
TF: 800-336-5152 ■ *Web:* www.asminternational.org

Association for Facilities Engineering (AFE)
8200 Greensboro Dr Ste 400 .... McLean VA 22102 571-203-7171 766-2142
Web: www.afe.org

Association for Iron & Steel Technology (AIST)
186 Thorn Hill Rd .... Warrendale PA 15086 724-814-3000 814-3001
Web: www.aist.org

Association of Equipment Manufacturers (AEM)
6737 W Washington St Ste 2400 .... Milwaukee WI 53214 414-272-0943 272-1170
TF: 866-236-0442 ■ *Web:* www.aem.org

Association of Industrial Metallizers Coaters & Laminators (AIMCAL)
201 Springs St .... Fort Mill SC 29715 803-802-7820 802-7821
Web: www.aimcal.org

Association of Rotational Molders International (ARM)
800 Roosevelt Rd Ste C-312 .... Glen Ellyn IL 60137 630-942-6589 790-3095
Web: www.rotomolding.org

Association of Vacuum Equipment Manufacturers (AVEM)
201 Pk Washington Ct .... Falls Church VA 22046 703-538-3543 241-5603
Web: www.avem.org

Building Service Contractors Assn International (BSCAI)
401 N Michigan Ave Ste 2200 .... Chicago IL 60611 312-321-5167 673-6735
TF: 800-368-3414 ■ *Web:* www.bscai.org

Business & Institutional Furniture Manufacturers Assn (BIFMA)
678 Front Ave NW Ste 150 .... Grand Rapids MI 49504 616-285-3963 285-3765

Can Manufacturers Institute (CMI)
1730 Rhode Island Ave NW Ste 1000 .... Washington DC 20036 202-232-4677 232-5756
Web: www.cancentral.com

Chlorine Institute Inc 1300 Wilson Blvd .... Arlington VA 22209 703-894-4140 894-4130
Web: www.chlorineinstitute.org

Color Pigments Manufacturers Assn Inc
300 N Washington St Ste 105 .... Alexandria VA 22314 703-684-4044 684-1795
Web: www.pigments.org

Composite Can & Tube Institute (CCTI)
50 S Pickett St .... Alexandria VA 22304 703-823-7234 823-7237
Web: www.cctiwdc.org

Compressed Gas Assn (CGA)
4221 Walney Rd 5th Fl .... Chantilly VA 20151 703-788-2700 961-1831
Web: www.cganet.com

Phone / Fax

Consortium for Advanced Mfg International (CAM-I)
6836 Bee Cave Ste 256 .... Austin TX 78746 512-296-6872 347-1672
Web: www.cam-i.org

Copper Development Assn Inc
260 Madison Ave 16th Fl .... New York NY 10016 212-251-7200 251-7234
TF: 800-232-3282 ■ *Web:* www.copper.org

Cordage Institute
994 Old Eagle School Rd Ste 1019 .... Wayne PA 19087 610-971-4854 971-4859
Web: www.ropecord.com

Council of Industrial Boiler Owners (CIBO)
6801 Kennedy Rd Ste 102 .... Warrenton VA 20187 540-349-9043
Web: www.cibo.org

Crane Manufacturers Assn of America (CMAA)
8720 Red Oak Blvd Ste 201 .... Charlotte NC 28217 704-676-1190 676-1199
TF: 800-345-1815 ■ *Web:* www.mhi.org

Edison Welding Institute (EWI)
1250 Arthur E Adams Dr .... Columbus OH 43221 614-688-5000 688-5001
Web: www.ewi.org

Engine Manufacturers Assn (EMA)
333 W Wacker Dr Ste 810 .... Chicago IL 60606 312-929-1970 929-1975
Web: www.truckandenginemanufacturers.org

Equipment & Tool Institute (ETI)
134 W University Dr Ste 205 .... Rochester MI 48307 248-656-5080 971-2375*
**Fax Area Code:* 603 ■ *Web:* etools.org

Fabricators & Manufacturers Assn International (FMA)
833 Featherstone Rd .... Rockford IL 61107 815-399-8700 484-7700
TF: 888-394-4362 ■ *Web:* www.fmanet.org

Fibre Box Assn (FBA)
25 NW Pt Blvd Ste 510 .... Elk Grove Village IL 60007 847-364-9600 364-9639
Web: www.fibrebox.org

Flexible Packaging Assn (FPA)
971 Corporate Blvd Ste 403 .... Linthicum MD 21090 410-694-0800 694-0900
Web: www.flexpack.org

Fluid Controls Institute (FCI)
1300 Sumner Ave .... Cleveland OH 44115 216-241-7333 241-0105
Web: www.fluidcontrolsinstitute.org

Fluid Power Distributors Assn (FPDA)
PO Box 1420 .... Cherry Hill NJ 08034 856-424-8998 424-9248
Web: www.fpda.org

Food Processing Suppliers Assn (FPSA)
1451 Dolley Madison Blvd Ste 101 .... McLean VA 22101 703-761-2600 761-4334
TF: 855-670-4787 ■ *Web:* www.fpsa.org

Foodservice & Packaging Institute (FPI)
7700 Leesburg Pk .... Falls Church VA 22046 703-538-3551 241-5603
Web: www.fpi.org

Forging Industry Assn (FIA)
1111 Superior Ave Ste 615 .... Cleveland OH 44114 216-781-6260 781-0102
Web: www.forging.org

Glass Assn of North America (GANA)
800 SW Jackson St Ste 1500 .... Topeka KS 66612 785-271-0208 271-0166
TF: 877-275-2421 ■ *Web:* www.glasswebsite.com

Glass Packaging Institute (GPI)
700 N Fairfax St Ste 510 .... Alexandria VA 22314 703-684-6359 299-1543
Web: www.gpi.org

Gypsum Assn 6525 Belcrest Rd Ste 480 .... Hyattsville MD 20782 301-277-8686 277-8747
Web: www.gypsum.org

Illuminating Engineering Society of North America (IESNA)
120 Wall St 17th Fl .... New York NY 10005 212-248-5000 248-5017
Web: www.ies.org

INDA: Assn of the Nonwoven Fabrics Industry
1100 Crescent Green Ste 115 .... Cary NC 27518 919-233-1210 233-1282
Web: www.inda.org

Independent Lubricant Manufacturers Assn (ILMA)
400 N Columbus St Ste 201 .... Alexandria VA 22314 703-684-5574 836-8503
Web: www.ilma.org

Industrial Designers Society of America (IDSA)
45195 Business Ct Ste 250 .... Dulles VA 20166 703-707-6000 787-8501
Web: www.idsa.org

Industrial Diamond Assn of America (IDA)
6081 Central Pk Dr .... Columbus OH 43231 614-797-2265
Web: www.superabrasives.org

Industrial Fabrics Assn International (IFAI)
1801 County Rd 'B' W .... Roseville MN 55113 651-222-2508 631-9334
TF: 800-225-4324 ■ *Web:* www.ifai.com

Institute of Caster & Wheel Manufacturers (ICWM)
8720 Red Oak Blvd Ste 201 .... Charlotte NC 28217 704-676-1190 676-1199
TF: 877-522-5431 ■ *Web:* www.mhi.org

Institute of Industrial Engineers (IIE)
3577 PkwyLn Ste 200 .... Norcross GA 30092 770-449-0460 441-3295
TF Cust Svc: 800-494-0460 ■ *Web:* www.iienet2.org

Institute of Makers of Explosives (IME)
1120 19th St NW Ste 310 .... Washington DC 20036 202-429-9280 293-2420
TF: 800-461-8841 ■ *Web:* www.ime.org

Institute of Packaging Professionals (IoPP)
1833 Centre Point Cir Ste 123 .... Naperville IL 60563 630-544-5050 544-5055
TF: 800-432-4085 ■ *Web:* www.iopp.org

International AntiCounterfeiting Coalition (IACC)
1730 M St NW .... Washington DC 20036 202-223-6667
Web: www.iacc.org

International Copper Assn
260 Madison Ave 16th Fl .... New York NY 10016 212-251-7240 251-7245
Web: copperalliance.org

International Ground Source Heat Pump Assn (IGSHPA)
Oklahoma State University 374 Cordell S .... Stillwater OK 74078 405-744-5175 744-5283
TF: 800-626-4747 ■ *Web:* www.igshpa.okstate.edu

International Institute of Synthetic Rubber Producers Inc (IISRP)
3535 Briarpark Dr Ste 250 .... Houston TX 77042 713-783-7511 783-7253
Web: www.iisrp.com

International Magnesium Assn (IMA)
1000 N Rand Rd Ste 214 .... Wauconda IL 60084 847-526-2010 526-3993
Web: www.intlmag.org

Investment Casting Institute (ICI)
136 Summit Ave .... Montvale NJ 07645 201-573-9770 573-9771
Web: www.investmentcasting.org

Phone / Fax

Material Handling Equipment Distributors Assn (MHEDA)
201 US Hwy 45 .... Vernon Hills IL 60061 847-680-3500 362-6989
Web: www.mheda.org

Material Handling Industry of America (MHIA)
8720 Red Oak Blvd Ste 201 .... Charlotte NC 28217 704-676-1190 676-1199
TF: 800-345-1815 ■ *Web:* www.mhi.org

Metal Powder Industries Federation (MPIF)
105 College Rd E .... Princeton NJ 08540 609-452-7700 987-8523
Web: www.mpif.org

Metals Service Ctr Institute (MSCI)
4201 Euclid Ave .... Rolling Meadows IL 60008 847-485-3000 485-3001
Web: www.msci.org

Minerals Metals & Materials Society (TMS)
184 Thorn Hill Rd .... Warrendale PA 15086 724-776-9000 776-3770
TF: 800-759-4867 ■ *Web:* www.tms.org

NACE International: Corrosion Society
1440 S Creek Dr .... Houston TX 77084 281-228-6200 228-6300
TF: 800-797-6223 ■ *Web:* www.nace.org

National Coil Coating Assn (NCCA)
1300 Sumner Ave .... Cleveland OH 44115 216-241-7333 241-0105
TF: 800-532-0500 ■ *Web:* www.coilcoating.org

National Council of Textile Organizations (NCTO)
910 17th St NW .... Washington DC 20006 202-822-8028 822-8029
TF: 800-238-7192 ■ *Web:* www.ncto.org

National Electrical Manufacturers Assn (NEMA)
1300 N 17th St Ste 1752 .... Rosslyn VA 22209 703-841-3200 841-5900
TF: 800-699-9277 ■ *Web:* www.nema.org

National Fluid Power Assn (NFPA)
3333 N Mayfair Rd Ste 211 .... Milwaukee WI 53222 414-778-3344 778-3361
Web: www.nfpa.com

National Glass Assn (NGA)
8200 Greensboro Dr Ste 302 .... McLean VA 22102 703-442-4890 442-0630
TF: 866-342-5642 ■ *Web:* www.glass.org

National Marine Electronics Assn (NMEA)
7 Riggs Ave .... Severna Park MD 21146 410-975-9425 975-9450
TF: 800-808-6632 ■ *Web:* www.nmea.org

National Paint & Coatings Assn (NPCA)
1500 Rhode Island Ave NW .... Washington DC 20005 202-462-6272 462-8549
TF: 800-647-5527 ■ *Web:* www.paint.org

National Textile Assn (NTA) 6 Beacon St Ste 1125 .... Boston MA 02108 617-542-8220
Web: www.nationaltextile.org

National Tooling & Machining Assn (NTMA)
6363 Oak Tree Blvd .... Independence OH 44131 800-248-6862 248-7104*
**Fax Area Code:* 301 ■ *TF:* 800-248-6862 ■ *Web:* www.ntma.org

National Wooden Pallet & Container Assn (NWPCA)
1421 Prince St Ste 340 .... Alexandria VA 22314 703-519-6104 519-4720
Web: www.palletcentral.com

North American Assn of Food Equipment Manufacturers (NAFEM)
161 N Clark St Ste 2020 .... Chicago IL 60601 312-821-0201 821-0202
TF: 888-493-5961 ■ *Web:* www.nafem.org

North American Die Casting Assn (NADCA)
3250 N. Arlington Hts Rd Ste 101 .... Arlington Heights IL 60004 847-279-0001 279-0002
Web: www.diecasting.org

Open Applications Group Inc (OAGI) PO Box 4897 .... Marietta GA 30061 404-402-1962 740-0100*
**Fax Area Code:* 801 ■ *TF:* 800-236-4600 ■ *Web:* www.oagi.org

Packaging Machinery Manufacturers Institute (PMMI)
4350 N Fairfax Dr Ste 600 .... Arlington VA 22203 703-243-8555 243-8556
TF: 888-275-7664 ■ *Web:* www.pmmi.org

Polyurethane Manufacturers Assn (PMA)
6737 W Washington St Ste 1420 .... Milwaukee WI 53214 414-431-3094
Web: www.pmahome.org

Portable Rechargeable Battery Assn (PRBA)
1776 K St 4th Fl .... Washington DC 20006 202-719-4978
Web: www.prba.org

Precision Machined Products Assn (PMPA)
6700 W Snowville Rd .... Brecksville OH 44141 440-526-0300 526-5803
TF: 800-233-1234 ■ *Web:* www.pmpa.org

Recycled Paperboard Technical Assn PO Box 5774 .... Elgin IL 60121 847-622-2544
Web: www.rpta.org

Rubber Manufacturers Assn (RMA)
1400 K St NW Ste 900 .... Washington DC 20005 202-682-4800 682-4854
TF: 800-220-7622 ■ *Web:* www.rma.org

Sewn Products Equipment Suppliers Assn (SPESA)
9650 Strickland Rd Ste 103-324 .... Raleigh NC 27615 919-872-8909 872-1915
Web: www.spesa.org

Society for Mining Metallurgy & Exploration Inc (SME)
8307 Shaffer Pkwy .... Littleton CO 80127 303-973-9550 973-3845
TF: 800-763-3132 ■ *Web:* www.smenet.org

Society for Protective Coatings (SSPC)
40 24th St 6th Fl .... Pittsburgh PA 15222 412-281-2331 281-9995
TF: 877-281-7772 ■ *Web:* www.sspc.org

Society of Mfg Engineers (SME) 1 SME Dr .... Dearborn MI 48128 313-425-3000 425-3400
TF Cust Svc: 800-733-4763 ■ *Web:* www.sme.org

Society of Plastics Engineers (SPE)
13 Church Hill Rd .... Newtown CT 06470 203-775-0471 775-8490
Web: www.4spe.org

Society of Tribologists & Lubrication Engineers (STLE)
840 Busse Hwy .... Park Ridge IL 60068 847-825-5536 825-1456
Web: www.stle.org

Society of Vacuum Coaters (SVC)
71 Pinon Hill Pl NE .... Albuquerque NM 87122 505-856-7188 856-6716
TF: 800-443-8817 ■ *Web:* www.svc.org

Spring Manufacturers Institute (SMI)
2001 Midwest Rd Ste 106 .... Oak Brook IL 60523 630-495-8588 495-8595
TF: 866-482-5569 ■ *Web:* www.smihq.org

Steel Founders' Society of America (SFSA)
780 McArdle Dr Ste G .... Crystal Lake IL 60014 815-455-8240 455-8241
Web: www.sfsa.org

Steel Manufacturers Assn (SMA)
1150 Connecticut Ave NW Ste 715 .... Washington DC 20036 202-296-1515 296-2506
Web: www.steelnet.org

Steel Plate Fabricators Assn (SPFA)
944 Donata Ct .... Lake Zurich IL 60047 847-438-8265 438-8766
Web: www.steeltank.com

Organization	City	State	Zip	Phone	Fax
Steel Tank Institute (STI) 944 Donata Ct *Web:* www.steeltank.com	Lake Zurich	IL	60047	847-438-8265	438-8766
Sulphur Institute (TSI) 1140 Connecticut Ave NW Ste 612 *Web:* www.sulphurinstitute.org	Washington	DC	20036	202-331-9660	293-2940
Technical Assn of the Pulp & Paper Industry (TAPPI) 15 Technology Pkwy S *TF Sales:* 800-332-8686 ■ *Web:* www.tappi.org	Norcross	GA	30092	770-446-1400	446-6947
TRI/Princeton 601 Prospect Ave *Web:* www.triprinceton.org	Princeton	NJ	08540	609-430-4820	
Valve Manufacturers Assn of America (VMA) 1050 17th St NW Ste 280 *TF:* 800-468-3571 ■ *Web:* www.vma.org	Washington	DC	20036	202-331-8105	296-0378
Vinyl Siding Institute (VSI) 1201 15th St NW Ste 220 *Web:* www.vinylsiding.org	Washington	DC	20005	202-587-5100	
Wire Assn International Inc (WAI) 1570 Boston Post Rd PO Box 578 *Web:* www.wirenet.org	Guilford	CT	06437	203-453-2777	453-8384
Wiring Harness Manufacturers Assn (WHMA) 15490 101st Ave N Ste 100 *Web:* www.whma.org	Maple Grove	MN	55369	763-235-6461	
Wood Machinery Manufacturers of America (WMMA) 2105 Laurel Bush Rd Ste 201 **Fax Area Code:* 323 ■ *Web:* www.wmma.org	Bel Air	MD	21015	443-640-1052	215-0331*

49-14 Media Professionals Associations

Organization	City	State	Zip	Phone	Fax
Academy of Television Arts & Sciences 5220 Lankershim Blvd *Web:* emmys.com	North Hollywood	CA	91601	818-754-2800	
Accuracy in Media Inc (AIM) 4350 EW Hwy Ste 555 *TF:* 800-787-4567 ■ *Web:* www.aim.org	Bethesda	MD	20814	202-364-4401	364-4098
American Medical Writers Assn (AMWA) 30 W Gude Dr Ste 525 *Web:* www.amwa.org	Rockville	MD	20850	301-294-5303	294-9006
American Radio Relay League (ARRL) 225 Main St *TF:* 888-277-5289 ■ *Web:* www.arrl.org	Newington	CT	06111	860-594-0200	594-0259
American Society of Media Photographers (ASMP) 150 N Second St *Web:* www.asmp.org	Philadelphia	PA	19106	215-451-2767	451-0880
American Society of News Editors (ASNE) 11690-B Sunrise Vly Dr *Web:* www.asne.org	Reston	VA	20191	703-453-1122	453-1133
Association for Maximum Service Television (MSTV) 1776 Massachusetts Ave NW *Web:* www.mstv.org	Washington	DC	20016	202-966-1956	
Association for Women in Communications (AWC) 1717 E Republic Rd Ste A *Web:* www.womcom.org	Springfield	MO	65804	417-886-8606	
Association of Alternative Newsweeklies (AAN) 115615th St NW *TF:* 866-415-0704 ■ *Web:* www.altweeklies.com	Washington	DC	20005	202-289-8484	289-2004
Association of Independents in Radio (AIR) 42 Charles St 2nd Fl *Web:* www.airmedia.org	Dorchester	MA	02122	617-825-4400	
Association of Public Television Stations (APTS) 2100 Crystal Dr Ste 700 *Web:* www.apts.org	Arlington	VA	22202	202-654-4200	654-4236
Cable Television Laboratories Inc 858 Coal Creek Cir *Web:* www.cablelabs.com	Louisville	CO	80027	303-661-9100	661-9199
Catholic Press Assn (CPA) 205 W Monroe St Ste 470 *TF:* 800-777-7432 ■ *Web:* www.catholicpress.org	Chicago	IL	60606	312-380-6789	361-0256
Center for Media Literacy 23852 Pacific Coast Hwy Ste 472 *Web:* www.medialit.org	Malibu	CA	90265	310-456-1225	
Country Radio Broadcasters Inc (CRB) 819 18th Ave S *Web:* countryradioseminar.com	Nashville	TN	37203	615-327-4487	329-4492
Foundation for American Communications (FACS) 85 S Grand Ave	Pasadena	CA	91105	626-584-0010	
Inter American Press Assn (IAPA) 1801 SW Third Ave 8th Fl *Web:* sipiapa.org/index.php	Miami	FL	33129	305-634-2465	635-2272
International Communication Assn (ICA) 1500 21st St NW *Web:* www.icahdq.org	Washington	DC	20036	202-955-1444	955-1448
International Radio & Television Society Foundation Inc (IRTS) 1697 Broadway 10th Fl *Web:* www.irtsfoundation.org	New York	NY	10019	212-867-6650	
Media Coalition Inc 275 Seventh Ave Ste 1504	New York	NY	10001	212-587-4025	587-2436
Media Financial Management Assn (MFM) 550 W Frontage Rd Ste 3600 *Web:* www.bcfm.com	Northfield	IL	60093	847-716-7000	716-7004
NA of Broadcasters (NAB) 1771 N St NW *Web:* www.nab.org	Washington	DC	20036	202-429-5300	
NA of Television Program Executives (NATPE) 5757 Wilshire Blvd PH-10 *Web:* www.natpe.com	Los Angeles	CA	90036	310-453-4440	453-5258
National Cable & Telecommunications Assn (NCTA) 25 Massachusetts Ave NW Ste 100 *Web:* www.ncta.com	Washington	DC	20001	202-222-2300	
National Cable Television Co-op Inc (NCTC) 11200 Corporate Ave **Fax Area Code:* 202 ■ *TF:* 800-720-5850 ■ *Web:* www.ncta.com	Lenexa	KS	66219	913-599-5900	222-2311*
National Federation of Community Broadcasters (NFCB) 1970 Broadway Ste 1000 *Web:* www.nfcb.org	Oakland	CA	94612	510-451-8200	451-8208
National Newspaper Assn (NNA) PO Box 7540 *TF:* 800-829-4662 ■ *Web:* nnaweb.org	Columbia	MO	65205	573-777-4980	777-4985
National Press Club (NPC) 529 14th St NW *Web:* www.press.org	Washington	DC	20045	202-662-7500	662-7569
National Press Photographers Assn (NPPA) 3200 Croasdaile Dr Ste 306 *Web:* www.nppa.org	Durham	NC	27705	919-383-7246	383-7261
National Religious Broadcasters (NRB) 9510 Technology Dr *Web:* www.nrb.org	Manassas	VA	20110	703-330-7000	330-7100
Newspaper Assn of America (NAA) 4401 Wilson Blvd Ste 900 *Web:* www.naa.org	Arlington	VA	22203	571-366-1000	366-1195
Overseas Press Club of America (OPC) 40 W 45th St *Web:* www.opcofamerica.org	New York	NY	10036	212-626-9220	626-9210
Parents Television Council (PTC) 707 Wilshire Blvd Ste 2075 *Web:* w2.parentstv.org	Los Angeles	CA	90017	213-629-9255	629-9254
Radio-Television News Directors Assn (RTNDA) 1600 K St NW Ste 700 *TF:* 800-807-8632 ■ *Web:* www.rtdna.org	Washington	DC	20006	202-659-6510	223-4007
Satellite Broadcasting & Communications Assn (SBCA) 1730 M St NW Ste 600 *TF:* 800-541-5981 ■ *Web:* www.sbca.com	Washington	DC	20036	202-349-3620	349-3621
Society for News Design (SND) 424 E Central Blvd Ste 406 *Web:* www.snd.org	Orlando	FL	32801	407-420-7748	420-7697
Society for Technical Communication (STC) 9401 Lee Hwy Ste 300 *Web:* www.stc.org	Fairfax	VA	22031	703-522-4114	522-2075
Society of Broadcast Engineers Inc (SBE) 9102 N Meridian St Ste 150 *TF:* 800-237-1776 ■ *Web:* www.sbe.org	Indianapolis	IN	46260	317-846-9000	846-9120
Society of Environmental Journalists (SEJ) 115 W Ave *TF:* 866-208-3372 ■ *Web:* www.sej.org	Jenkintown	PA	19046	215-884-8174	884-8175
Society of Professional Journalists (SPJ) 3909 N Meridian St *TF:* 800-331-1212 ■ *Web:* www.spj.org	Indianapolis	IN	46208	317-927-8000	920-4789
Specialized Information Publishers Assn (SIPA) 8229 Boone Blvd Ste 260 *TF:* 800-356-9302 ■ *Web:* www.siia.net	Vienna	VA	22182	703-992-9339	992-7512
Women in Cable Telecommunications (WICT) 2000 K St Ste 350 *Web:* www.wict.org	Washington	DC	20006	202-827-4794	450-5596

49-15 Mental Health Professionals Associations

Organization	City	State	Zip	Phone	Fax
American Academy of Addiction Psychiatry (AAAP) 400 Massasoit Ave 2nd Fl Ste 307 *Web:* www.aaap.org	East Providence	RI	02914	401-524-3076	272-0922
American Academy of Child & Adolescent Psychiatry (AACAP) 3615 Wisconsin Ave NW *TF:* 800-333-7636 ■ *Web:* www.aacap.org	Washington	DC	20016	202-966-7300	966-2891
American Academy of Psychiatry & the Law (AAPL) 1 Regency Dr PO Box 30 *TF:* 800-331-1389 ■ *Web:* www.aapl.org	Bloomfield	CT	06002	860-242-5450	286-0787
American Assn for Geriatric Psychiatry (AAGP) 7910 Woodmont Ave Ste 1050 *Web:* www.aagponline.org	Bethesda	MD	20814	301-654-7850	654-4137
American College of Psychiatrists 122 S Michigan Ave # 1360 *Web:* www.acpsych.org	Chicago	IL	60603	312-662-1020	662-1025
American Council of Hypnotist Examiners 700 S Central Ave **Fax Area Code:* 818 ■ *Web:* www.hypnotistexaminers.org	Glendale	CA	91204	619-280-7200	247-9379*
American Counseling Assn (ACA) 5999 Stevenson Ave *TF:* 800-347-6647 ■ *Web:* www.counseling.org	Alexandria	VA	22304	703-823-9800	823-0252
American Group Psychotherapy Assn (AGPA) 25 E 21st St 6th Fl *TF:* 877-668-2472 ■ *Web:* www.agpa.org	New York	NY	10010	212-477-2677	979-6627
American Mental Health Counselors Assn (AMHCA) 801 N Fairfax St Ste 304 *TF:* 800-326-2642 ■ *Web:* www.amhca.org	Alexandria	VA	22314	703-548-6002	548-4775
American Psychiatric Assn (APA) 1000 Wilson Blvd Ste 1825 *TF:* 888-357-7924 ■ *Web:* www.psychiatry.org	Arlington	VA	22209	703-907-7300	907-1085
American Psychiatric Nurses Assn (APNA) 1555 Wilson Blvd Ste 530 *TF:* 866-243-2443 ■ *Web:* www.apna.org	Arlington	VA	22209	703-243-2443	243-3390
American Psychoanalytic Assn (APsaA) 309 E 49th St *Web:* www.apsa.org	New York	NY	10017	212-752-0450	593-0571
American Psychological Assn (APA) 750 First St NE *TF:* 800-374-2721 ■ *Web:* www.apa.org	Washington	DC	20002	202-336-5500	336-5962
American Society for Adolescent Psychiatry (ASAP) 1737 Omar Dr *Web:* adolescent-psychiatry.org	Mesquite	TX	75150	972-613-0985	613-5532
Arc Baltimore, The 7215 York Rd *Web:* www.thearcbaltimore.org	Baltimore	MD	21212	410-296-2272	296-2394
Arc of Stanly County, The 350 Pee Dee Ave Ste A *TF:* 800-230-7525 ■ *Web:* www.monarchnc.org	Albemarle	NC	28001	704-986-1500	
Association for Behavioral & Cognitive Therapies (ABCT) 305 Seventh Ave 16th Fl *TF:* 800-685-2228 ■ *Web:* www.abct.org/home	New York	NY	10001	212-647-1890	647-1865
Association for Play Therapy (APT) 3198 Willow Ave Ste 110 *Web:* www.a4pt.org	Clovis	CA	93612	559-294-2128	294-2129
Association for Psychological Type International (APTI) 1450 Western Ave Ste 101 *Web:* www.aptinternational.org	Albany	NY	12203	518-320-7416	

Organization	City	State	Zip	Phone	Fax
Catholic Charities of Buffalo New York Inc 741 Delaware Ave *Web:* www.ccwny.org	Buffalo	NY	14209	716-218-1400	856-2005
Depression & Related Affective Disorders Assn (DRADA) 8201 Greensboro Dr Ste 300 *Web:* www.drada.org	McLean	VA	22102	703-610-9026	
Edinburg Ctr Inc, The 1040 Waltham St *Web:* www.edinburgcenter.org	Lexington	MA	02421	781-862-3600	863-5903
Federation of Families for Children's Mental Health (FFCMH) 9605 Medical Ctr Dr Ste 280 *Web:* www.ffcmh.org	Rockville	MD	20850	240-403-1901	403-1909
International Assn of Marriage & Family Counselors (IAMFC) 5999 Stevenson Ave *TF:* 800-347-6647 ■ *Web:* www.counseling.org	Alexandria	VA	22304	800-347-6647	473-2329
International Neuropsychological Society (INS) 700 Ackerman Rd Ste 625 *Web:* www.the-ins.org	Columbus	OH	43202	614-263-4200	263-4366
International Society for Traumatic Stress Studies (ISTSS) 111 Deer Lk Rd Ste 100 *TF:* 877-469-7873 ■ *Web:* www.istss.org	Deerfield	IL	60015	847-480-9028	480-9282
Lifespring Inc 460 Spring St *TF:* 800-456-2117 ■ *Web:* lifespringhealthsystems.org	Jeffersonville	IN	47130	812-280-2080	
National Council for Therapeutic Recreation Certification Inc (NCTRC) 7 Elmwood Dr *Web:* www.nctrc.org	New City	NY	10956	845-639-1439	639-1471
National Psychological Assn for Psychoanalysis (NPAP) 40 W 13th St Ste 1 *TF:* 800-365-7006 ■ *Web:* www.npap.org	New York	NY	10011	212-924-7440	989-7543
New Ctr Community Mental Health Services 2051 W Grand Blvd *Web:* www.newcentercmhs.org	Detroit	MI	48208	313-961-3200	
Northern Arizona Regional Behavioral Health Authority Inc (NARBHA) 1300 S Yale St *TF:* 877-923-1400 ■ *Web:* www.narbha.org	Flagstaff	AZ	86001	928-774-7128	774-5665
Northwestern Counseling & Support Services Inc 107 Fisher Pond Rd *TF:* 800-834-7793 ■ *Web:* www.ncssinc.org	Saint Albans	VT	05478	802-524-6554	527-7801
SAVE - Suicide Awareness Voices of Education 8120 Penn Ave S Ste 470 *TF:* 888-511-7283 ■ *Web:* www.save.org	Bloomington	MN	55431	952-946-7998	829-0841
Scranton Counseling Ctr Inc 326 Adams Ave *Web:* www.scrantonscc.org	Scranton	PA	18503	570-348-6100	
Society for Social Work Leadership in Health Care 100 N 20th St 4th Fl *TF:* 866-237-9542 ■ *Web:* www.sswlhc.org	Philadelphia	PA	19103	215-599-6134	564-2175
Society of Behavioral Medicine (SBM) 555 E Wells St Ste 1100 *TF:* 800-784-8669 ■ *Web:* www.sbm.org	Milwaukee	WI	53202	414-918-3156	276-3349
Suncoast Ctr Inc PO Box 10970 *Web:* www.suncoastcenter.com	Saint Petersburg	FL	33733	727-327-7656	323-8978
Valeo Behavioral Health Care Inc 5401 SW Seventh St *Web:* www.valeotopeka.org	Topeka	KS	66606	785-233-1730	
West Oakland Health Council Inc (WOHC) 700 Adeline St *Web:* www.wohc.org	Oakland	CA	94607	510-835-9610	
Yakima Neighborhood Health Services (YNHS) 12 S Eigth St PO Box 2605 *Web:* www.ynhs.org	Yakima	WA	98907	509-454-4143	454-3651

49-16 Publishing & Printing Professional Associations

Organization	City	State	Zip	Phone	Fax
American Society of Business Publication Editors (ASBPE) 214 N Hale St *Web:* www.asbpe.org	Wheaton	IL	60187	630-510-4588	510-4501
American Society of Indexers (ASI) 1628 E Southern Ave Ste 9-223 *Web:* www.asindexing.org	Tempe	AZ	85282	480-245-6750	
Associated Church Press The (ACP) 924 Woodcrest Way *Web:* www.theacp.org	Oviedo	FL	32765	407-341-6615	386-3236
Association of American Publishers Inc (AAP) 71 Fifth Ave *TF:* 866-271-4968 ■ *Web:* www.publishers.org	New York	NY	10003	212-255-0200	255-7007
Association of American University Presses 28 W 36th St Ste 602 *Web:* www.aaupnet.org	New York	NY	10018	212-989-1010	989-0975
Association of Directory Publishers (ADP) PO Box 209 *TF:* 800-267-9002 ■ *Web:* www.adp.org	Traverse City	MI	49685	231-486-2182	486-2182
Book Industry Study Group Inc (BISG) 370 Lexington Ave Ste 900 *Web:* www.bisg.org	New York	NY	10017	646-336-7141	336-6214
Book Manufacturers Institute Inc (BMI) 2 Armand Beach Dr Ste 1-B *Web:* www.bmibook.org	Palm Coast	FL	32137	386-986-4552	986-4553
Canadian Newspaper Assn 890 Yonge St Ste 200 *TF:* 877-305-2262 ■ *Web:* www.newspaperscanada.ca	Toronto	ON	M4W3P4	416-923-3567	923-7206
Children's Book Council (CBC) 54 W 39th St 14th Fl *Web:* www.cbcbooks.org	New York	NY	10018	212-966-1990	
Copyright Clearance Ctr Inc (CCC) 222 Rosewood Dr *TF:* 855-239-3415 ■ *Web:* www.copyright.com	Danvers	MA	01923	978-750-8400	646-8600
Copyright Society of the USA 1 E 53rd St *Web:* www.csusa.org	New York	NY	10022	212-354-6401	354-2847
Editorial Freelancers Assn (EFA) 71 W 23rd St 4th Fl *TF:* 866-929-5400 ■ *Web:* www.the-efa.org	New York	NY	10010	212-929-5400	929-5439
Evangelical Christian Publishers Assn (ECPA) 9633 S 48th St Ste 140 *Web:* www.ecpa.org	Phoenix	AZ	85044	480-966-3998	966-1944
Flexographic Technical Assn (FTA) 3920 Veterans Memorial Hwy Ste 9 *Web:* www.flexography.org	Bohemia	NY	11716	631-737-6020	737-6813
Greeting Card Assn (GCA) 1133 Westchester Ave Ste N136 *Web:* www.greetingcard.org	White Plains	NY	10604	914-421-3331	948-1484
Idealliance 1600 Duke St Ste 420 *TF:* 800-255-8141 ■ *Web:* idealliance.org	Alexandria	VA	22314	952-896-1908	
Independent Book Publishers Assn, The (IBPA) 1020 Manhattan Beach Blvd Ste 204 *Web:* www.ibpa-online.org	Manhattan Beach	CA	90266	310-546-1818	546-3939
International Digital Enterprise Alliance 1421 Prince St Ste 230 *Web:* www.idealliance.org	Alexandria	VA	22314	703-837-1070	837-1072
International Reprographic Assn (IRgA) 401 N Michigan Ave Ste 2200 *TF:* 800-833-4742 ■ *Web:* www.irga.com	Chicago	IL	60611	312-245-1026	673-6724
Magazine Publishers of America (MPA) 810 Seventh Ave 24th Fl *TF:* 800-234-3368 ■ *Web:* www.magazine.org	New York	NY	10019	212-872-3700	888-4217
National Information Standards Organization (NISO) 3600 Clipper Mill Rd Ste 302 **Fax Area Code:* 410 ■ *TF:* 877-375-2160 ■ *Web:* www.niso.org	Baltimore	MD	21211	301-654-2512	685-5278*
National Press Foundation (NPF) 1211 Connecticut Ave NW Ste 310 *Web:* www.nationalpress.org	Washington	DC	20036	202-663-7280	
NPES: Assn for Suppliers of Printing Publishing & Converting Technologies 1899 Preston White Dr *TF:* 866-381-9839 ■ *Web:* www.npes.org	Reston	VA	20191	703-264-7200	620-0994
Printing Industries of America/Graphic Arts Technical Foundation (PIA/GATF) 200 Deer Run Rd *TF:* 800-910-4283 ■ *Web:* www.printing.org	Sewickley	PA	15143	412-741-6860	741-2311
Society for Imaging Science & Technology (IS&T) 7003 Kilworth Ln *Web:* www.imaging.org	Springfield	VA	22151	703-642-9090	642-9094
Society for Scholarly Publishing (SSP) 10200 W 44th Ave Ste 304 *Web:* www.sspnet.org	Wheat Ridge	CO	80033	303-422-3914	422-8894
Specialty Graphic Imaging Assn (SGIA) 10015 Main St *TF:* 888-385-3588 ■ *Web:* www.sgia.org	Fairfax	VA	22031	703-385-1335	273-0456

49-17 Real Estate Professionals Associations

Organization	City	State	Zip	Phone	Fax
American Homeowners Foundation (AHF) 6776 Little Falls Rd *Web:* www.americanhomeowners.org	Arlington	VA	22213	703-536-7776	
American Planning Assn (APA) 1030 15th St NW *Web:* www.planning.org	Washington	DC	20005	202-872-0611	872-0643
American Resort Development Assn (ARDA) 1201 15th St NW Ste 400 *Web:* www.arda.org	Washington	DC	20005	202-371-6700	289-8544
American Society of Appraisers (ASA) 555 Herndon Pkwy Ste 125 *TF:* 800-272-8258 ■ *Web:* www.appraisers.org	Herndon	VA	20170	703-478-2228	742-8471
Appraisal Institute 550 W Van Buren St Ste 1000 *TF:* 888-756-4624 ■ *Web:* www.appraisalinstitute.org	Chicago	IL	60607	312-335-4100	335-4400
Building Owners & Managers Assn International (BOMA) 1101 15th St NW Ste 800 *TF:* 800-426-6292 ■ *Web:* www.boma.org	Washington	DC	20005	202-408-2662	326-6377
CCIM Institute 430 N Michigan Ave Ste 800 *TF:* 800-621-7027 ■ *Web:* www.ccim.com	Chicago	IL	60611	312-321-4460	321-4530
CoreNet Global Inc 260 Peachtree St NW Ste 1500 *TF:* 800-726-8111 ■ *Web:* www.corenetglobal.org	Atlanta	GA	30303	404-589-3200	589-3201
Council of Real Estate Brokerage Managers (CRB) 430 N Michigan Ave **Fax Area Code:* 312 ■ *TF:* 800-621-8738 ■ *Web:* www.crb.com	Chicago	IL	60611	800-621-8738	329-8882*
Council of Residential Specialists 430 N Michigan Ave Ste 300 *TF:* 800-462-8841 ■ *Web:* www.crs.com	Chicago	IL	60611	312-321-4400	329-8882
Counselors of Real Estate (CRE) 430 N Michigan Ave 2nd Fl *Web:* www.cre.org	Chicago	IL	60611	312-329-8427	329-8881
Institute of Business Appraisers (IBA) 1111 BrickyaRd Rd Ste 200 **Fax Area Code:* 866 ■ *TF:* 800-299-4130 ■ *Web:* www.go-iba.org	Salt Lake City	UT	84106	800-299-4130	353-5406*
Institute of Real Estate Management (IREM) 430 N Michigan Ave **Fax Area Code:* 800 ■ *TF:* 800-837-0706 ■ *Web:* www.irem.org	Chicago	IL	60611	312-329-6000	338-4736*
International Downtown Assn (IDA) 1025 Thomas Jefferson St NW Ste 500 W *Web:* www.ida-downtown.org/eweb	Washington	DC	20007	202-393-6801	393-6869
NA of Master 303 W Cypress St *Web:* faqs.org	San Antonio	TX	78212	210-271-0781	
NA of REALTORS 430 N Michigan Ave **Fax:* Mktg ■ *TF:* 800-874-6500 ■ *Web:* www.realtor.org	Chicago	IL	60611	312-329-8200	329-8390*
National Apartment Assn (NAA) 4300 Wilson Blvd Ste 400 *TF:* 800-632-3007 ■ *Web:* www.naahq.org	Arlington	VA	22203	703-518-6141	248-9440
National Housing & Rehabilitation Assn (NH&RA) 1400 16th St NW Ste 420 *Web:* www.housingonline.com	Washington	DC	20036	202-939-1750	265-4435
National Multi Housing Council (NMHC) 1850 M St NW Ste 540 *Web:* www.nmhc.org	Washington	DC	20036	202-974-2300	775-0112
New Venture Communications 218 Commercial Ave SE PO Box 157 *TF:* 800-932-0637 ■ *Web:* www.igreenbuild.com	Highmore	SD	57345	650-343-2735	343-8492
Real Estate Buyer's Agent Council (REBAC) 430 N Michigan Ave **Fax Area Code:* 312 ■ *TF:* 800-648-6224 ■ *Web:* www.rebac.net	Chicago	IL	60611	800-648-6224	329-8632*

				Phone	Fax
Real Estate Roundtable 801 Pennsylvania Ave NW Ste 720 *Web:* www.rer.org	Washington	DC	20004	202-639-8400	639-8442
Society of Industrial & Office Realtors (SIOR) 1201 New York Ave NW Ste 350 *Web:* www.sior.com	Washington	DC	20005	202-449-8200	216-9325
Vacation Rental Managers Assn (VRMA) 9100 PuRdue Rd Ste 200 *Web:* www.vrma.com	Indianapolis	IN	46268	317-454-8315	
Women's Council of REALTORS (WCR) 430 N Michigan Ave **Fax Area Code:* 312 ■ *TF:* 800-245-8512 ■ *Web:* www.wcr.org	Chicago	IL	60611	800-245-8512	329-3290*

49-18 Sales & Marketing Professional Associations

				Phone	Fax
Advertising Council Inc 815 Second Ave 9th Fl *TF:* 888-200-4005 ■ *Web:* www.adcouncil.org	New York	NY	10016	212-922-1500	922-1676
Advertising Research Foundation (ARF) 432 Pk Ave S 6th Fl *Web:* thearf.org	New York	NY	10016	212-751-5656	319-5265
American Adv Federation (AAF) 1101 Vermont Ave NW Ste 500 *TF:* 800-999-2231 ■ *Web:* www.aaf.org	Washington	DC	20005	202-898-0089	898-0159
American Assn of Adv Agencies (AAAA) 1065 Ave of the Americas 16th Fl *Web:* www.aaaa.org	New York	NY	10018	212-682-2500	682-8391
American Assn of Exporters & Importers (AAEI) 1050 17th St NW Ste 810 *Web:* www.aaei.org	Washington	DC	20036	202-857-8009	857-7843
American Assn of Franchisees & Dealers (AAFD) PO Box 10158 **Fax Area Code:* 866 ■ *TF:* 800-733-9858 ■ *Web:* www.aafd.org	Palm Desert	CA	92255	619-209-3775	855-1988*
American Booksellers Assn (ABA) 200 White Plains Rd Ste 600 *TF:* 800-637-0037 ■ *Web:* www.bookweb.org	Tarrytown	NY	10591	914-591-2665	591-2720
American Hardwood Export Council (AHEC) 1825 Michael Faraday Dr *Web:* www.ahec.org	Reston	VA	20190	202-463-2720	
American International Automobile Dealers Assn (AIADA) 500 Montgomery St Ste 800 *TF:* 800-462-4232 ■ *Web:* www.aiada.org	Alexandria	VA	22314	703-519-7800	519-7810
American Machine Tool Distributors' Assn (AMTDA) 1445 Research Blvd Ste 450 *Web:* www.amtonline.org	Rockville	MD	20850	301-738-1200	
American Marketing Assn (AMA) 311 S Wacker Dr Ste 5800 *TF:* 800-262-1150 ■ *Web:* www.ama.org	Chicago	IL	60606	312-542-9000	542-9001
Associated Equipment Distributors (AED) 650 E Algonquin Rd Ste 305 *TF:* 800-388-0650 ■ *Web:* www.aednet.org	Schaumburg	IL	60173	630-574-0650	574-0132
Association for Postal Commerce 1901 Ft Myer Dr *Web:* www.postcom.org	Arlington	VA	22209	703-524-0096	524-1871
Association of National Advertisers (ANA) 708 Third Ave 33rd Fl *Web:* www.ana.net	New York	NY	10017	212-697-5950	687-7310
Association of Progressive Rental Organizations (APRO) 1504 Robin Hood Trl *TF:* 800-204-2776 ■ *Web:* www.rtohq.org	Austin	TX	78703	512-794-0095	794-0097
Audit Bureau of Circulations (ABC) 48 W Seegers Rd **Fax Area Code:* 847 ■ *TF:* 800-759-6397 ■ *Web:* www.auditedmedia.com	Arlington Heights	IL	60005	224-366-6939	605-0483*
Automotive Distribution Network 3085 Fountainside Dr Ste 210 *TF:* 800-727-8112 ■ *Web:* www.networkhq.org	Germantown	TN	38138	901-682-9090	
BPA Worldwide 100 BeaRd Sawmill Rd 6th Fl *Web:* www.bpaww.com	Shelton	CT	06484	203-447-2800	447-2900
Brick Industry Assn (BIA) 1850 Centennial Pk Dr Ste 301 *TF:* 866-644-1293 ■ *Web:* www.gobrick.com	Reston	VA	20191	703-620-0010	620-3928
Business Marketing Assn (BMA) 708 Third Ave 33rd Fl *Web:* www.marketing.org	New York	NY	10017	212-697-5950	687-7310
Business Technology Assn (BTA) 12411 Wornall Rd Ste 200 *TF:* 800-325-7219 ■ *Web:* www.bta.org	Kansas City	MO	64145	816-941-3100	941-2829
Center for Exhibition Industry Research (CEIR) 12700 Park Central Dr Ste 308 *Web:* www.ceir.org	Dallas	TX	75251	972-687-9242	692-6020
Chain Drug Marketing Assn (CDMA) 43157 W Nine-Mile Rd PO Box 995 *TF:* 800-935-2362 ■ *Web:* www.chaindrug.com	Novi	MI	48376	248-449-9300	449-9396
Clio Awards Inc 770 Broadway 6th Fl *Web:* www.clioawards.com	New York	NY	10003	212-683-4300	683-4796
Coalition for Employment Through Exports (CEE) 1625 K St NW Ste 200 *Web:* www.usaexport.org	Washington	DC	20006	202-296-6107	296-9709
Coalition for Government Procurement 1990 M St NW Ste 450 *Web:* thecgp.org	Washington	DC	20036	202-331-0975	822-9788
Color Marketing Group (CMG) 1908 Mount Vernon Ave *Web:* www.colormarketing.org	Alexandria	VA	22301	703-329-8500	535-3190
Council of Supply Chain Management Professionals 333 E Butterfield Rd Ste 140 *Web:* www.cscmp.org	Lombard	IL	60148	630-574-0985	574-0989
Dairyamerica Inc 7815 N Palm Ave Ste 250 *TF:* 800-722-3110 ■ *Web:* www.dairyamerica.com	Fresno	CA	93711	559-251-0992	251-1078
Direct Marketing Assn Inc (DMA) 1120 Ave of the Americas *TF:* 855-422-0749 ■ *Web:* thedma.org	New York	NY	10036	212-768-7277	302-6714
Direct Selling Assn (DSA) 1667 K St NW Ste 1100 *Web:* www.dsa.org	Washington	DC	20006	202-452-8866	452-9010
Electronics Representatives Assn (ERA) 111 N Canal St Ste 885 *Web:* www.era.org	Chicago	IL	60606	312-419-1432	
Entertainment Merchants Assn 16530 Ventura Blvd Ste 400 *Web:* www.entmerch.org	Encino	CA	91436	818-385-1500	933-0910
Equipment Dealers Assn (NAEDA) 165 N Meramec Ave Ste 430 *Web:* www.equipmentdealer.org	St. Louis	MO	63105	636-349-5000	349-5443
Equipment Leasing & Finance Assn (ELFA) 1825 K St NW Ste 900 *Web:* www.elfaonline.org	Washington	DC	20006	202-238-3400	238-3401
Exhibit Designers & Producers Assn (EDPA) 19 Compo Rd S *Web:* www.edpa.com	Westport	CT	06880	203-557-6321	
Food Marketing Institute (FMI) 2345 Crystal Dr Ste 800 *TF:* 800-732-2639 ■ *Web:* www.fmi.org	Arlington	VA	22202	202-220-0600	429-4519
Global Market Development Ctr (GMDC) 1275 Lk Plz Dr *Web:* www.gmdc.org	Colorado Springs	CO	80906	719-576-4260	576-2661
Global Offset & Countertrade Assn (GOCA) 818 Connecticut Ave NW 12th Fl *Web:* www.globaloffset.org	Washington	DC	20006	202-887-9011	872-8324
HARDI Hydronic Heating & Cooling Council 3455 Mill Run Dr Ste 820 *TF:* 888-253-2128 ■ *Web:* www.hardinet.org	Hilliard	OH	43026	614-345-4328	
Health Industry Distributors Assn (HIDA) 310 Montgomery St *TF:* 800-549-4432 ■ *Web:* www.hida.org	Alexandria	VA	22314	703-549-4432	549-6495
Healthcare Convention & Exhibitors Assn (HCEA) 7918 Jones Branch Dr Ste 300 *Web:* www.hcea.org	Atlanta	GA	30342	703-935-1961	506-3266
Healthcare Distribution Management Assn (HDMA) 901 N Glebe Rd Ste 1000 *Web:* www.healthcaredistribution.org	Arlington	VA	22203	703-787-0000	935-3200
Hospitality Sales & Marketing Assn International (HSMAI) 1760 Old Meadow Rd Ste 500 *Web:* www.hsmai.org	McLean	VA	22102	703-506-3280	610-9005
International Assn of Exhibitions & Events (IAEE) 12700 Park Central Dr Ste 308 *TF:* 866-266-3378 ■ *Web:* www.iaee.com	Dallas	TX	75251	972-458-8002	458-8119
International Assn of Plastics Distribution (IAPD) 6734 W 121 St *Web:* www.iapd.org	Overland Park	KS	66209	913-345-1005	345-1006
International Federation of Pharmaceutical Wholesalers (IFPW) 10569 Crestwood Dr *Web:* www.ifpw.com	Manassas	VA	20109	703-331-3714	331-3715
International Foodservice Distributors Assn (IFDA) 1410 Spring Hill Rd Ste 210 *Web:* www.ifdaonline.org	McLean	VA	22102	703-532-9400	538-4673
International Franchise Assn (IFA) 1501 K St NW Ste 350 *TF:* 800-543-1038 ■ *Web:* www.franchise.org	Washington	DC	20005	202-628-8000	628-0812
International Home Furnishings Representatives Assn (IHFRA) 209 S Main St PO Box 670 *Web:* www.ihfra.org	High Point	NC	27261	336-889-3920	
International Sanitary Supply Assn (ISSA) 3300 Dundee Rd *TF:* 800-225-4772 ■ *Web:* global.issa.com	Northbrook	IL	60062	847-982-0800	982-1012
Licensing Executives Society (LES) 1800 Diagonal Rd Ste 280 *Web:* www.lesi.org	Alexandria	VA	22314	703-836-3106	836-3107
Machinery Dealers NA (MDNA) 315 S Patrick St *TF:* 800-872-7807 ■ *Web:* www.mdna.org	Alexandria	VA	22314	703-836-9300	836-9303
Marketing Research Assn Inc (MRA) 110 National Dr **Fax Area Code:* 888 ■ *Web:* www.marketingresearch.org	Glastonbury	CT	06033	860-682-1000	512-1050*
Metals Service Ctr Institute (MSCI) 4201 Euclid Ave *Web:* www.msci.org	Rolling Meadows	IL	60008	847-485-3000	485-3001
Multi-Level Marketing International Assn (MLMIA) 119 Stanford Ct *Web:* www.mlmia.com	Irvine	CA	92612	949-854-0484	
NA of Chain Drug Stores (NACDS) 413 N Lee St *TF:* 800-678-6223 ■ *Web:* www.nacds.org	Alexandria	VA	22314	703-549-3001	836-4869
NA of College Stores (NACS) 500 E Lorain St *TF:* 800-622-7498 ■ *Web:* www.nacs.org	Oberlin	OH	44074	440-775-7777	775-4769
NA of Convenience Stores (NACS) 1600 Duke St *TF Cust Svc:* 800-966-6227 ■ *Web:* www.nacsonline.com	Alexandria	VA	22314	703-684-3600	836-4564
NA of Electrical Distributors Inc (NAED) 1181 Corporate Lk Dr *TF:* 888-791-2512 ■ *Web:* www.naed.org	Saint Louis	MO	63132	314-991-9000	991-3060
NA of Wholesaler-Distributors (NAWD) 1325 G St NW Ste 1000 *Web:* www.naw.org	Washington	DC	20005	202-872-0885	785-0586
NAMM - International Music Products Assn 5790 Armada Dr *TF:* 800-767-6266 ■ *Web:* www.namm.org	Carlsbad	CA	92008	760-438-8001	438-7327
National Agri-Marketing Assn (NAMA) 11020 King St Ste 205 *TF:* 800-530-5646 ■ *Web:* www.nama.org	Overland Park	KS	66210	913-491-6500	491-6502
National Art Materials Trade Assn 20200 Zion Ave *TF:* 800-349-1039 ■ *Web:* www.namta.org	Cornelius	NC	28031	704-892-6244	892-6247
National Auctioneers Assn (NAA) 8880 Ballentine St *TF:* 877-657-1990 ■ *Web:* www.auctioneers.org	Overland Park	KS	66214	913-541-8084	894-5281
National Auto Auction Assn (NAAA) 5320 Spectrum Dr Ste D *TF:* 800-232-5411 ■ *Web:* www.naaa.com	Frederick	MD	21703	301-696-0400	631-1359

				Phone	Fax
National Automatic Merchandising Assn (NAMA) 20 N Wacker Dr Ste 3500 *Web:* www.vending.org	Chicago	IL	60606	312-346-0370	704-4140
National Automobile Dealers Assn (NADA) 8400 Westpark Dr *TF:* 800-252-6232 ■ *Web:* www.nada.org	McLean	VA	22102	703-821-7000	821-7075
National Cotton Council of America 7193 Goodlett Farms Pkwy *TF:* 888-232-1738 ■ *Web:* www.cotton.org	Memphis	TN	38016	901-274-9030	725-0510
National Electrical Manufacturers Representatives Assn (NEMRA) 28 Deer St Ste 302 **Fax Area Code:* 603 ■ *TF:* 800-446-3672 ■ *Web:* www.nemra.org	Portsmouth	NH	03801	914-524-8650	319-1667*
National Electronic Distributors Assn (NEDA) 1111 Alderman Dr Ste 400 *Web:* www.eciaonline.org	Alpharetta	GA	30005	678-393-9990	393-9998
National Electronics Service Dealers Assn (NESDA) 3608 Pershing Ave *TF:* 800-946-0201 ■ *Web:* www.nesda.com	Fort Worth	TX	76107	817-921-9061	921-3741
National Foreign Trade Council (NFTC) 1625 K St NW Ste 200 *Web:* www.nftc.org	Washington	DC	20006	202-887-0278	452-8160
National Independent Automobile Dealers Assn (NIADA) 2521 Brown Blvd *TF:* 800-682-3837 ■ *Web:* www.niada.com	Arlington	TX	76006	817-640-3838	649-5866
National Independent Flag Dealers Assn (NIFDA) 7984 S Chicago Ave *Web:* www.nifda.net	Chicago	IL	60617	773-768-8076	768-3138
National Luggage Dealers Assn (NLDA) 1817 Elmdale Ave *Web:* www.nlda.com	Glenview	IL	60026	847-998-6869	998-6884
National Lumber & Bldg Material Dealers Assn (NLBMDA) 2025 M St NW *Web:* www.dealer.org	Washington	DC	20036	202-367-1169	367-2169
National Mail Order Assn LLC (NMOA) 2807 Polk St NE *TF:* 800-992-1377 ■ *Web:* www.nmoa.org	Minneapolis	MN	55418	612-788-1673	788-1147
National Marine Representatives Assn (NMRA) PO Box 360 *TF:* 800-890-3819 ■ *Web:* www.nmraonline.org	Gurnee	IL	60031	847-662-3167	336-7126
National Minority Supplier Development Council (NMSDC) 1359 Broadway 10th Fl *Web:* www.nmsdc.org	New York	NY	10018	212-944-2430	719-9611
National Retail Federation (NRF) 1101 New York Ave NW *TF:* 800-673-4692 ■ *Web:* www.nrf.com	Washington	DC	20005	202-783-7971	737-2849
National Retail Hardware Assn (NRHA) 5822 W 74th St *TF Cust Svc:* 800-772-4424 ■ *Web:* www.nrha.org	Indianapolis	IN	46278	317-290-0338	328-4354
National School Supply & Equipment Assn (NSSEA) 8380 Colesville Rd Ste 250 *TF:* 800-395-5550 ■ *Web:* edmarket.org	Silver Spring	MD	20910	301-495-0240	495-3330
National Shoe Retailers Assn (NSRA) 7386 N La Cholla Blvd *TF:* 800-673-8446 ■ *Web:* www.nsra.org	Tucson	AZ	85741	520-209-1710	
North American Bldg Material Distribution Assn (NBMDA) 330 N Wabash Ave Ste 2000 *TF:* 888-747-7862 ■ *Web:* www.nbmda.org	Chicago	IL	60611	312-321-6845	644-0310
NPTA Alliance 330 N Wabash Ave Ste 2000 *TF:* 800-355-6782 ■ *Web:* www.gonpta.com	Chicago	IL	60611	312-321-4092	
Paint & Decorating Retailers Assn (PDRA) 1401 Triad Ctr Dr *TF:* 800-737-0107 ■ *Web:* www.pdra.org	Saint Peters	MO	63376	636-326-2636	
Pet Industry Distributors Assn (PIDA) 2105 Laurel Bush Rd Ste 200 *Web:* www.pida.org	Bel Air	MD	21015	443-640-1060	640-1031
Petroleum Marketers Assn of America (PMAA) 1901 N Ft Myer Dr Ste 500 *Web:* www.pmaa.org	Arlington	VA	22209	703-351-8000	351-9160
Photo Marketing Assn International (PMA) 3000 Picture Pl *TF:* 800-762-9287 ■ *Web:* www.pmai.org	Jackson	MI	49201	517-788-8100	788-8371
Power Transmission Distributors Assn (PTDA) 230 W Monroe St Ste 1410 *Web:* www.ptda.org	Chicago	IL	60606	312-516-2100	516-2101
Private Label Manufacturers Assn (PLMA) 630 Third Ave 4th Fl *Web:* plma.com	New York	NY	10017	212-972-3131	
Professional Beauty Assn (PBA) 15825 N 71st St Ste 100 *TF:* 800-468-2274 ■ *Web:* www.probeauty.org	Scottsdale	AZ	85254	480-281-0424	905-0708
Promotional Products Assn International (PPAI) 3125 Skyway Cir N *TF:* 888-426-7724 ■ *Web:* www.ppai.org	Irving	TX	75038	972-252-0404	258-3004
Public Relations Society of America (PRSA) 33 Maiden Ln 11th Fl *TF:* 800-350-0111 ■ *Web:* www.prsa.org	New York	NY	10038	212-460-1400	995-0757
Radio Adv Bureau (RAB) 125 W 55th St 21st Fl *TF:* 800-232-3131 ■ *Web:* www.rab.com	New York	NY	10019	212-681-7200	
Recreation Vehicle Dealers Assn (RVDA) 3930 University Dr 3rd Fl *TF:* 800-336-0355 ■ *Web:* www.rvda.org	Fairfax	VA	22030	703-591-7130	591-0734
Retail Industry Leaders Assn (RILA) 1700 N Moore St Ste 2250 *Web:* www.rila.org	Arlington	VA	22209	703-841-2300	841-1184
Retail Solutions Providers Assn (RSPA) 10130 Perimeter Pkwy Ste 420 *TF:* 800-782-2693 ■ *Web:* www.gorspa.org	Charlotte	NC	28216	704-357-3124	357-3127
Society for Marketing Professional Services (SMPS) 99 Canal Ctr Plz *TF:* 800-292-7677 ■ *Web:* www.smps.org	Alexandria	VA	22314	703-549-6117	549-2498
Society of Independent Gasoline Marketers of America (SIGMA) 3930 Pender Dr Ste 340 *Web:* www.sigma.org	Fairfax	VA	22030	703-709-7000	709-7007
Specialty Tools & Fasteners Distributors Assn (STAFDA) 500 Elm Grove Rd Ste 210 PO Box 44 *TF:* 800-352-2981 ■ *Web:* www.stafda.org	Elm Grove	WI	53122	262-784-4774	784-5059
Television Bureau of Adv (TVB) 3 E 54th St 10th Fl *Web:* www.tvb.org	New York	NY	10022	212-486-1111	935-5631
Traffic Audit Bureau for Media Measurement (TAB) 271 Madison Ave Ste 1504 *Web:* www.tabonline.com	New York	NY	10016	212-972-8075	
Video Advertising Bureau (CAB) 830 Third Ave 2nd Fl *Web:* www.thevab.com	New York	NY	10022	212-508-1200	832-3268

49-19 Technology, Science, Engineering Professionals Associations

				Phone	Fax
ABET Inc 415 North Charles St Ste 1050 *Web:* www.abet.org	Baltimore	MD	21201	410-347-7700	625-2238
Acoustical Society of America (ASA) 1305 Walt Whitman Rd Ste 300 *Web:* www.acousticalsociety.org	Melville	NY	11747	516-576-2360	576-2377
AES Electrophoresis Society 1202 Ann St *TF:* 800-242-4363 ■ *Web:* www.aesociety.org	Madison	WI	53713	608-258-1565	258-1569
AIM Global - Assn for Automatic Identification & Mobility 20399 Rte 19 Ste 203 *Web:* www.aimglobal.org	Cranberry Township	PA	16066	724-934-4470	934-4495
American Assn for Clinical Chemistry Inc (AACC) 1850 K St NW Ste 625 *TF Cust Svc:* 800-892-1400 ■ *Web:* www.aacc.org	Washington	DC	20006	202-857-0717	887-5093
American Assn for Laboratory Accreditation (A2LA) 5301 Buckeystown Pike Ste 350 *Web:* www.a2la.org	Frederick	MD	21704	301-644-3248	662-2974
American Assn for Laboratory Animal Science (AALAS) 9190 Crestwyn Hills Dr *Web:* www.aalas.org	Memphis	TN	38125	901-754-8620	753-0046
American Assn for the Advancement of Science (AAAS) 1200 New York Ave NW *Web:* www.aaas.org	Washington	DC	20005	202-326-6400	682-0816
American Assn of Engineering Societies (AAES) 1620 'I' St NW Ste 210 *TF Orders:* 888-400-2237 ■ *Web:* www.aaes.org	Washington	DC	20006	202-296-2237	296-1151
American Assn of Pharmaceutical Scientists (AAPS) 2107 Wilson Blvd Ste 700 *TF:* 877-998-2277 ■ *Web:* www.aaps.org	Arlington	VA	22201	703-243-2800	243-9650
American Assn of Variable Star Observers (AAVSO) 49 Bay State Rd *TF:* 888-802-7827 ■ *Web:* www.aavso.org	Cambridge	MA	02138	617-354-0484	354-0665
American Astronomical Society (AAS) 2000 Florida Ave NW Ste 400 *Web:* www.aas.org	Washington	DC	20009	202-328-2010	234-2560
American Chemical Society (ACS) 1155 16th St NW *TF:* 800-227-5558 ■ *Web:* www.acs.org	Washington	DC	20036	202-872-4600	872-4615
American Council of Engineering Cos (ACEC) 1015 15th St NW 8th Fl *Web:* www.acec.org	Washington	DC	20005	202-347-7474	898-0068
American Council of Independent Laboratories (ACIL) 1875 I St NW Ste 500 *TF:* 800-368-1131 ■ *Web:* www.acil.org	Washington	DC	20006	202-887-5872	887-0021
American Council on Science & Health (ACSH) 110 E 42nd St Ste 1300 *TF:* 866-905-2694 ■ *Web:* www.acsh.org	New York	NY	10017	212-362-7044	362-4919
American Geological Institute (AGI) 4220 King St *TF:* 800-334-2564 ■ *Web:* www.agiweb.org	Alexandria	VA	22302	703-379-2480	379-7563
American Geophysical Union (AGU) 2000 Florida Ave NW *TF:* 800-966-2481 ■ *Web:* www.agu.org	Washington	DC	20009	202-462-6900	328-0566
American Indian Science & Engineering Society (AISES) 2305 Renard SE Ste 200 *TF:* 800-759-5219 ■ *Web:* www.aises.org	Albuquerque	NM	87106	505-765-1052	765-5608
American Institute of Aeronautics & Astronautics Inc (AIAA) 1801 Alexander Bell Dr Ste 500 *TF:* 800-639-2422 ■ *Web:* www.aiaa.org	Reston	VA	20191	703-264-7500	264-7551
American Institute of Biological Sciences (AIBS) 1444 'I' St NW Ste 200 *TF:* 800-992-2427 ■ *Web:* www.aibs.org	Washington	DC	20005	202-628-1500	628-1509
American Institute of Chemical Engineers (AIChE) 120 Wall St Fl 23 *TF Cust Svc:* 800-242-4363 ■ *Web:* www.aiche.org	New York	NY	10005	203-702-7660	775-5177
American Institute of Chemists (AIC) 315 Chestnut St *TF:* 800-829-0115 ■ *Web:* www.theaic.org	Philadelphia	PA	19106	215-873-8224	925-1954
American Institute of Physics 1 Physics Ellipse *Web:* www.aip.org	College Park	MD	20740	301-209-3100	209-0843
American Institute of Professional Geologists (AIPG) 1400 W 122nd Ave Ste 250 *Web:* www.aipg.org	Westminster	CO	80234	303-412-6205	253-9220
American Mathematical Society (AMS) 201 Charles St *TF Cust Svc:* 800-321-4267 ■ *Web:* www.ams.org	Providence	RI	02904	401-455-4000	331-3842
American Meteorological Society (AMS) 45 Beacon St *TF:* 800-824-0405 ■ *Web:* www.ametsoc.org	Boston	MA	02108	617-227-2425	742-8718
American Nuclear Society (ANS) 555 N Kensington Ave *TF:* 800-323-3044 ■ *Web:* www.ans.org	La Grange Park	IL	60526	708-352-6611	352-0499
American Physical Society (APS) 1 Physics Ellipse *TF:* 866-918-1164 ■ *Web:* www.aps.org	College Park	MD	20740	301-209-3200	209-0865
American Phytopathological Society, The (APS) 3340 Pilot Knob Rd *TF:* 800-328-7560 ■ *Web:* www.apsnet.org/pages/default.aspx	Saint Paul	MN	55121	651-454-7250	454-0766

Phone | Fax

American Rock Mechanics Assn (ARMA)
600 Woodland Terr .... Alexandria VA 22302 703-683-1808 683-1815
Web: www.armarocks.org

American Society for Biochemistry & Molecular Biology (ASBMB)
9650 Rockville Pk .... Bethesda MD 20814 301-634-7145 634-7126
Web: www.asbmb.org

American Society for Cell Biology (ASCB)
8120 Woodmont Ave Ste 750 .... Bethesda MD 20814 301-347-9300 347-9310
Web: www.ascb.org

American Society for Engineering Education (ASEE)
1818 N St NW Ste 600 .... Washington DC 20036 202-331-3500 265-8504
Web: www.asee.org

American Society for Nondestructive Testing Inc (ASNT)
1711 Arlingate Ln PO Box 28518 .... Columbus OH 43228 614-274-6003 274-6899
TF Orders: 800-222-2768 ■ *Web:* www.asnt.org

American Society for Photobiology (ASP)
PO Box 1897 .... Lawrence KS 66044 785-843-1234 843-1274
Web: www.photobiology.org

American Society for Photogrammetry & Remote Sensing, The (ASPRS)
5410 Grosvenor Ln Ste 210 .... Bethesda MD 20814 301-493-0290 493-0208
Web: www.asprs.org

American Society of Human Genetics (ASHG)
9650 Rockville Pike .... Bethesda MD 20814 301-634-7300 634-7079
TF: 800-720-4363 ■ *Web:* www.ashg.org

American Society of Ichthyologists & Herpetologists
PO Box 1897 .... Lawrence KS 66044 305-348-1235
Web: www.asih.org

American Society of Limnology & Oceanography (ASLO)
5400 Bosque Blvd Ste 680 .... Waco TX 76710 254-399-9635 776-3767
TF: 800-929-2756 ■ *Web:* www.aslo.org

American Society of Plant Biologists (ASPB)
15501 Monona Dr .... Rockville MD 20855 301-251-0560 279-2996
Web: my.aspb.org

American Society of Safety Engineers (ASSE)
1800 E Oakton St .... Des Plaines IL 60018 847-699-2929 768-3434
Web: www.asse.org

American Statistical Assn (ASA)
732 N Washington St .... Alexandria VA 22314 703-684-1221 684-2037
TF: 888-231-3473 ■ *Web:* www.amstat.org

AOAC International
481 N Frederick Ave Ste 500 .... Gaithersburg MD 20877 301-924-7077 924-7089
TF: 800-379-2622 ■ *Web:* www.aoac.org

ASME International Gas Turbine Institute (IGTI)
6525 the Corners Pkwy .... Norcross GA 30092 404-847-0072 847-0151
Web: www.asme.org

Association for Women in Science Inc (AWIS)
1321 Duke St Ste 210 .... Alexandria VA 22314 703-894-4490 894-4489
TF: 866-736-7343 ■ *Web:* www.awis.org

Association of American Geographers (AAG)
1710 16th St NW .... Washington DC 20009 202-234-1450 234-2744
TF: 800-696-7353 ■ *Web:* www.aag.org

Association of Consulting Chemists & Chemical Engineers (ACC&CE)
514 Corrigan Way .... Cary NJ 27519 973-729-6671
Web: www.chemconsult.org

Association of Science-Technology Centers Inc (ASTC)
1025 Vermont Ave NW Ste 500 .... Washington DC 20005 202-783-7200 783-7207
Web: www.astc.org

Association of University Technology Managers (AUTM)
111 Deer Lk Rd Ste 100 .... Deerfield IL 60015 847-559-0846 480-9282
Web: www.autm.net

ASTM International
100 Barr Harbor Dr PO Box C700 .... West Conshohocken PA 19428 610-832-9500 832-9555
TF: 800-814-1017 ■ *Web:* www.astm.org

Audio Engineering Society
60 E 42nd St Rm 2520 .... New York NY 10165 212-661-8528 682-0477
TF: 800-541-7299 ■ *Web:* www.aes.org

AVS Science & Technology Society
120 Wall St 32nd Fl .... New York NY 10005 212-248-0200 248-0245
Web: www.avs.org

Biophysical Society (BPS) 9650 Rockville Pk .... Bethesda MD 20814 301-634-7114 634-7133
Web: www.biophysics.org

Biotechnology Industry Organization
1201 Maryland Ave SW Ste 900 .... Washington DC 20024 202-962-9200 488-6301
TF: 866-356-5155 ■ *Web:* www.bio.org

Center for Chemical Process Safety (CCPS)
120 Wall St .... New York NY 10005 646-495-1371 495-1504
TF: 800-242-4363 ■ *Web:* www.aiche.org/CCPS

Center for Science in the Public Interest (CSPI)
1875 Connecticut Ave NW Ste 300 .... Washington DC 20009 202-332-9110 265-4954
Web: www.cspinet.org

Clinical Laboratory Management Assn (CLMA)
401 N Michigan Ave Ste 2000 .... Chicago IL 60611 312-321-5111 673-6927
Web: www.clma.org

Commission on Professionals in Science & Technology (CPST)
1200 New York Ave NW Ste 113 .... Washington DC 20005 202-326-7080

Coordinating Research Council Inc (CRC)
3650 Mansell Rd Ste 140 .... Alpharetta GA 30022 678-795-0506 795-0509
TF: 800-445-8667 ■ *Web:* www.crcao.com

Council for Chemical Research Inc (CCR)
1730 Rhode Island Ave NW Ste 302 .... Washington DC 20036 202-429-3971 429-3976
Web: www.ccrhq.org

Council for Responsible Genetics (CRG)
5 Upland Rd Ste 3 .... Cambridge MA 02140 617-868-0870 491-5344
TF: 888-591-3911 ■ *Web:* www.councilforresponsiblegenetics.org

Cryogenic Society of America Inc (CSA)
218 Lake St .... Oak Park IL 60302 708-383-6220 383-9337
Web: www.cryogenicsociety.org

Custom Electronic Design & Installation Assn (CEDIA)
7150 Winton Dr Ste 300 .... Indianapolis IN 46268 317-328-4336 735-4012
TF: 800-669-5329 ■ *Web:* www.cedia.net

Drug Chemical & Associated Technologies Assn (DCAT)
1 Washington Blvd Ste 7 .... Robbinsville NJ 08691 609-448-1000
TF: 800-640-3228 ■ *Web:* www.dcat.org

Earthquake Engineering Research Institute (EERI)
499 14th St Ste 320 .... Oakland CA 94612 510-451-0905 451-5411
Web: www.eeri.org

Phone | Fax

Ecological Society of America (ESA)
1990 M St Ste 700 .... Washington DC 20036 202-833-8773 833-8775
Web: www.esa.org

Electrical Apparatus Service Assn (EASA)
1331 Baur Blvd .... Saint Louis MO 63132 314-993-2220 993-1269
Web: www.easa.com

Electrochemical Society
65 S Main St Bldg D .... Pennington NJ 08534 609-737-1902 737-2743
Web: www.electrochem.org

Electronics Technicians Assn International (ETA)
5 Depot St .... Greencastle IN 46135 765-653-8262 653-4287
TF: 800-288-3824 ■ *Web:* www.eta-i.org

Engineering Contractors' Assn (ECA)
2190 S Towne Centre Pl .... Anaheim CA 92806 714-937-5000 937-5030
Web: www.ecaonline.net

Entomological Society of America
10001 Derekwood Ln Ste 100 .... Lanham MD 20706 301-731-4535 731-4538
TF: 800-523-8635 ■ *Web:* www.entsoc.org

Federation of American Scientists (FAS)
1725 DeSales St NW 6th Fl .... Washington DC 20036 202-546-3300 315-5847
Web: www.fas.org

Federation of American Societies for Experimental Biology (FASEB)
9650 Rockville Pk .... Bethesda MD 20814 301-634-7000 634-7001
TF: 800-433-2732 ■ *Web:* www.faseb.org

Foundation for Advanced Education in the Sciences (FAES)
1 Cloister Ct .... Bethesda MD 20814 301-496-7976 402-0174
Web: www.faes.org

Generic Pharmaceutical Assn (GPhA)
2300 Clarendon Blvd Ste 400 .... Arlington VA 22201 703-647-2480 647-2481
TF: 800-859-8003 ■ *Web:* www.gphaonline.org

Genetics Society of America (GSA)
9650 Rockville Pk .... Bethesda MD 20814 301-634-7300 634-7079
TF: 866-486-4363 ■ *Web:* www.genetics-gsa.org

Geological Society of America, The (GSA)
3300 Penrose Pl PO Box 9140 .... Boulder CO 80301 303-357-1000 357-1070
TF: 800-472-1988 ■ *Web:* www.geosociety.org

Geoprofessional Business Association
8811 Colesville Rd Ste G106 .... Silver Spring MD 20910 301-565-2733 589-2017
Web: www.geoprofessional.org

Geospatial Information & Technology Assn (GITA)
14456 E Evans Ave .... Aurora CO 80014 303-337-0513
Web: www.gita.org

IEEE Broadcast Technology Society (BTS)
445 Hoes Ln .... Piscataway NJ 08854 732-562-5407 981-1769
TF: 800-678-4333 ■ *Web:* bts.ieee.org

IEEE Computational Intelligence Society (CIS)
IEEE CIS / IEEE PELS 445 Hoes Ln .... Piscataway NJ 08855 732-465-5892 455-1560*
**Fax Area Code: 858* ■ *Web:* cis.ieee.org

IEEE Computer Society 2001 L St NW Ste 700 .... Washington DC 20036 202-371-0101 728-9614
TF: 800-272-6657 ■ *Web:* www.computer.org

IEEE Consumer Electronics Society (CES)
445 Hoes Ln .... Piscataway NJ 08854 732-981-0060 562-6380
TF: 800-678-4333 ■ *Web:* cesoc.ieee.org

IEEE Education Society (ES)
IEEE Operations Ctr 445 Hoes Ln .... Piscataway NJ 08854 732-981-0060 562-6380
TF: 800-678-4333 ■ *Web:* www.ewh.ieee.org/soc/es

IEEE Electromagnetic Compatibility Society (EMC)
IEEE Operations Ctr 445 Hoes Ln .... Piscataway NJ 08854 732-981-0060 562-6380
TF: 800-678-4333 ■ *Web:* www.ewh.ieee.org/soc/emcs

IEEE Electron Devices Society (EDS)
IEEE Operations Ctr 445 Hoes Ln .... Piscataway NJ 08854 732-981-0060 562-6380
TF: 800-678-4333 ■ *Web:* eds.ieee.org

IEEE Engineering Management Society (EMS)
IEEE Operations Ctr 445 Hoes Ln .... Piscataway NJ 08854 732-981-0060 562-6380
TF: 800-678-4333 ■ *Web:* www.ewh.ieee.org/soc/ems

IEEE Geoscience & Remote Sensing Society (GRSS)
IEEE Operations Ctr 445 Hoes Ln .... Piscataway NJ 08854 732-562-5550
TF: 800-678-4333 ■ *Web:* www.ewh.ieee.org

IEEE Industrial Electronics Society (IES)
IEEE Operations Ctr 445 Hoes Ln .... Piscataway NJ 08854 732-981-0060 562-6380
TF: 800-678-4333 ■ *Web:* www.ewh.ieee.org/soc/ies

IEEE Industry Applications Society
445 Hoes Ln .... Piscataway NJ 08854 732-465-5804
Web: ias.ieee.org

IEEE Instrumentation & Measurement Society (IM)
445 Hoes Ln .... Piscataway NJ 08854 732-562-3844 981-9019
TF: 800-327-6677 ■ *Web:* www.ieee-ims.org

IEEE Magnetics Society
445 Hoes Ln PO Box 459 .... Piscataway NJ 08855 908-981-0060 981-0225
TF: 800-678-4333 ■ *Web:* www.ieeemagnetics.org

IEEE Microwave Theory & Techniques Society (MTT-S)
5829 Bellanca Dr .... Elkridge MD 21075 410-796-5866
TF: 800-678-4333 ■ *Web:* www.mtt.org

IEEE Nuclear & Plasma Sciences Society (NPSS)
445 Hoes Ln .... Piscataway NJ 08854 732-562-5501 562-6380
TF: 800-678-4333 ■ *Web:* ieee-npss.org

IEEE Power Engineering Society (PES)
IEEE Operations Ctr 445 Hoes Ln .... Piscataway NJ 08854 732-562-3883 562-3881
TF: 800-678-4333 ■ *Web:* www.ieee-pes.org

IEEE Product Safety Engineering Society
IEEE Operations Ctr 445 Hoes Ln .... Piscataway NJ 08854 732-981-0060 562-6380
TF: 800-678-4333 ■ *Web:* www.ewh.ieee.org/soc/pses

IEEE Reliability Society (RS)
IEEE Operations Ctr 445 Hoes Ln .... Piscataway NJ 08854 732-981-0060 562-6380
TF: 800-678-4333 ■ *Web:* ieee.org

IEEE Signal Processing Society
IEEE Operations Ctr 445 Hoes Ln .... Piscataway NJ 08854 732-981-0060
TF: 800-678-4333 ■ *Web:* www.signalprocessingsociety.org

IEEE Society on Social Implications of Technology (SSIT)
IEEE Operations Ctr 445 Hoes Ln .... Piscataway NJ 08854 732-981-0060 562-6380
TF: 800-678-4333 ■ *Web:* standards.ieee.org

IEEE Solid State Circuits Society (SSCS)
445 Hoes Ln .... Piscataway NJ 08854 732-981-3400
TF: 800-678-4333 ■ *Web:* sscs.ieee.org

Phone | Fax

IEEE Ultrasonics Ferroelectrics & Frequency Control Society
IEEE Operations Ctr 445 Hoes Ln . . . . Piscataway NJ 08854 732-981-0060
TF: 800-678-4333 ■ *Web:* www.ieee-uffc.org

Industrial Research Institute Inc (IRI)
2200 Clarendon Blvd Ste 1102. . . . . Arlington VA 22201 703-647-2580 647-2581
Web: www.iriweb.org

Institute for Operations Research & the Management Sciences (INFORMS)
7240 Pkwy Dr Ste 300 . . . . Hanover MD 21076 443-757-3500 757-3515
TF: 800-446-3676 ■ *Web:* www.informs.org

Institute of Environmental Sciences & Technology (IEST)
2340 S Arlington Heights Rd
Ste 100. . . . . Arlington Heights IL 60005 847-981-0100 981-4130
Web: www.iest.org

International Biometric Society (IBS)
1444 'I' St NW Ste 700. . . . . Washington DC 20005 202-712-9049 216-9646
TF: 800-262-1171 ■ *Web:* www.biometricsociety.org

International Ctr for Technology Assessment (ICTA)
660 Pennsylvania Ave SE Ste 302 . . . . Washington DC 20003 415-826-2770
Web: www.icta.org

International Microelectronics & Packaging Society (IMAPS)
PO Box 110127 . . . . Research Triangle Park NC 27709 202-548-4001 548-6115
Web: www.imaps.org

International Society for Pharmaceutical Engineering (ISPE)
3109 W Dr ML King Jr Blvd Ste 250. . . . . Tampa FL 33607 813-960-2105 264-2816
Web: www.ispe.org

International Society of Automation, The
67 Alexander Dr PO Box 12277 . . . . Research Triangle Park NC 27709 919-549-8411 549-8288
Web: www.isa.org

International Society of Certified Electronics Technicians (ISCET)
3608 Pershing Ave. . . . . Fort Worth TX 76107 817-921-9101 921-3741
TF: 800-946-0201 ■ *Web:* www.iscet.org

International Titanium Assn (ITA)
2655 W Midway Blvd Ste 300. . . . . Broomfield CO 80020 303-404-2221 404-9111
Web: www.titanium.org

Laser Institute of America (LIA)
13501 Ingenuity Dr Ste 128 . . . . Orlando FL 32826 407-380-1553 380-5588
TF: 800-345-2737 ■ *Web:* www.lia.org

Materials Properties Council (MPC)
PO Box 201547 . . . . Shaker Heights OH 44122 216-658-3847 658-3854
Web: www.forengineers.org/mpc

Materials Research Society (MRS)
506 Keystone Dr. . . . . Warrendale PA 15086 724-779-3003 779-8313
Web: www.mrs.org

Mathematical Assn of America (MAA)
1529 18th St NW . . . . Washington DC 20036 202-387-5200 265-2384
TF: 800-331-1622 ■ *Web:* www.maa.org

MTM Assn for Standards & Research
1111 E Touhy Ave Ste 280. . . . . Des Plaines IL 60018 847-299-1111 299-3509
Web: www.mtm.org

National Academies 500 Fifth St NW. . . . . Washington DC 20001 202-334-2138 334-2158
TF: 800-624-6242 ■ *Web:* www.nas.edu

National Academy of Engineering
500 Fifth Ave . . . . Washington DC 20001 202-334-2431 334-2290
Web: www.nae.edu

National Council on Radiation Protection & Measurements (NCRP)
7910 Woodmont Ave Ste 400. . . . . Bethesda MD 20814 301-657-2652 907-8768
TF: 800-462-3683 ■ *Web:* www.ncrponline.org

National Environmental Balancing Bureau (NEBB)
8575 Grovemont Cir. . . . . Gaithersburg MD 20877 301-977-3698 977-9589
TF: 866-497-4447 ■ *Web:* www.nebb.org

National Geographic Society
1145 17th St NW . . . . Washington DC 20036 202-857-7000
TF: 800-647-5463 ■ *Web:* www.nationalgeographic.com

National Institute for Women in Trades Technology & Science (IWITTS)
1150 Ballena Blvd Ste 102. . . . . Alameda CA 94501 510-749-0200 749-0500
Web: www.iwitts.org

National Society of Black Physicists (NSBP)
1100 N Glebe Rd Ste 1010. . . . . Arlington VA 22201 703-536-4207
Web: www.nsbp.org

National Society of Professional Engineers (NSPE)
1420 King St. . . . . Alexandria VA 22314 703-684-2800 836-4875
TF: 888-285-6773 ■ *Web:* www.nspe.org

New York Academy of Medicine (NYAM)
1216 Fifth Ave . . . . New York NY 10029 212-822-7200
Web: www.nyam.org

New York Academy of Sciences
250 Greenwich St 40th Fl. . . . . New York NY 10007 212-298-8600 298-3650
TF: 800-843-6927 ■ *Web:* www.nyas.org

Plasma Protein Therapeutics Assn (PPTA)
147 Old Solomon's Island Rd Ste 100 . . . . Annapolis MD 21401 202-789-3100
Web: usplaces.com

Robotic Industries Assn (RIA)
900 Victors Way Ste 140 . . . . Ann Arbor MI 48108 734-994-6088 994-3338
Web: www.robotics.org

Scientific Equipment & Furniture Assn (SEFA)
65 Hilton Avenue . . . . Garden City NY 11530 516-294-5424 294-2758
TF: 877-294-5424 ■ *Web:* www.sefalabs.com

Semiconductor Environmental Safety & Health Assn (SESHA)
1313 Dolley Madison Blvd Ste 402 . . . . McLean VA 22101 703-790-1745 790-2672
Web: www.seshaonline.org

Semiconductor Equipment & Materials International
3081 Zenker Rd . . . . San Jose CA 95134 408-943-6900 428-9600
TF: 877-746-7788 ■ *Web:* www.semi.org

Silver Research Consortium (SRC)
2525 Meridian Pkwy Ste 100 . . . . Durham NC 27713 919-361-4647 361-1957
Web: www.ilzro.org

Society for Biomaterials
1120 Rte 73 Ste 200. . . . . Mount Laurel NJ 08054 856-439-0826 439-0525
TF: 800-337-9255 ■ *Web:* www.biomaterials.org

Society for Experimental Mechanics Inc (SEM)
7 School St. . . . . Bethel CT 06801 203-790-6373 790-4472
TF: 800-627-8258 ■ *Web:* www.sem.org

Society for Industrial & Applied Mathematics (SIAM)
3600 Market St 6th Fl. . . . . Philadelphia PA 19104 215-382-9800 386-7999
TF: 800-447-7426 ■ *Web:* www.siam.org

Phone | Fax

Society for Integrative & Comparative Biology (SICB)
1313 Dolley Madison Blvd Ste 402 . . . . McLean VA 22101 703-790-1745 790-2672
TF: 800-955-1236 ■ *Web:* www.sicb.org

Society for Risk Analysis (SRA)
1313 Dolley Madison Blvd Ste 402 . . . . McLean VA 22101 703-790-1745 790-2672
TF: 800-364-5800 ■ *Web:* www.sra.org

Society for Sedimentary Geology (SEPM)
4111 S Darlington Ste 100. . . . . Tulsa OK 74135 918-610-3361 621-1685
TF: 800-865-9765 ■ *Web:* www.sepm.org

Society for the Advancement of Material & Process Engineering (SAMPE)
1161 Pk View Dr Ste 200. . . . . Covina CA 91724 626-331-0616 262-1431*
**Fax Area Code:* 801 ■ *TF:* 800-562-7360 ■ *Web:* www.sampe.org

Society of Cable Telecommunications Engineers (SCTE)
140 Philips Rd . . . . Exton PA 19341 610-363-6888 363-5898
TF: 800-542-5040 ■ *Web:* www.scte.org

Society of Cosmetic Chemists (SCC)
120 Wall St Ste 2400 . . . . New York NY 10005 212-668-1500 668-1504
Web: www.scconline.org

Society of Environmental Toxicology & Chemistry (SETAC)
1010 N 12th Ave. . . . . Pensacola FL 32501 850-469-1500 469-9778
Web: www.setac.org

Society of Women Engineers (SWE)
120 S La Salle St Ste 1515. . . . . Chicago IL 60603 312-596-5223 596-5252
TF: 877-793-4636 ■ *Web:* societyofwomenengineers.swe.org

SPIE - International Society for Optical Engineering
1000 20th St. . . . . Bellingham WA 98225 360-676-3290 647-1445
Web: www.spie.org

Synthetic Organic Chemical Manufacturers Assn (SOCMA)
1850 M St NW Ste 700. . . . . Washington DC 20036 202-721-4100 296-8120
Web: www.socma.com

Universities Research Assn Inc (URA)
1140 19th St NW Ste 900. . . . . Washington DC 20036 202-293-1382 293-5012
Web: www.ura-hq.org

Universities Space Research Assn (USRA)
10211 Wincopin Cir Ste 500 . . . . Columbia MD 21044 410-730-2656 730-3496
Web: www.usra.edu

Vibration Institute
6262 Kingery Hwy # 212 . . . . Willowbrook IL 60527 630-654-2254 654-2271
Web: www.vi-institute.org

Women in Technology International (WITI)
11500 Olympic Blvd Ste 400 . . . . Los Angeles CA 90064 818-788-9484 788-9410
TF: 800-334-9484 ■ *Web:* www.witi.com

World Future Society
7910 Woodmont Ave Ste 450. . . . . Bethesda MD 20814 301-656-8274 951-0394
TF: 800-989-8274 ■ *Web:* www.wfs.org

49-20 Telecommunications Professionals Associations

Phone | Fax

Alliance for Telecommunications Industry Solutions (ATIS)
1200 G St NW Ste 500 . . . . Washington DC 20005 202-628-6380 393-5453
TF: 800-649-1202 ■ *Web:* www.atis.org

American Public Communications Council Inc (APCC)
625 Slaters Ln Ste 104 . . . . Alexandria VA 22314 703-739-1322 739-1324
TF: 800-868-2722 ■ *Web:* www.apcc.net

Communications Supply Service Assn (CSSA)
5700 Murray St. . . . . Little Rock AR 72209 501-562-7666 562-7616
TF: 800-252-2772 ■ *Web:* www.cssa.net

Computer & Communications Industry Assn (CCIA)
666 11th St NW . . . . Washington DC 20001 202-783-0070 783-0534
Web: www.ccianet.org

Enterprise Wireless Alliance (EWA)
8484 Westpark Dr Ste 630 . . . . McLean VA 22102 703-528-5115 524-1074
TF: 800-482-8282 ■ *Web:* www.enterprisewireless.org

Forest Industries Telecommunications (FIT)
1565 Oak St . . . . Eugene OR 97401 541-485-8441 485-7556
Web: www.landmobile.com

International Communications Industries Assn (ICIA)
11242 Waples Mill Rd Ste 200. . . . . Fairfax VA 22030 703-273-7200 278-8082
TF: 800-659-7469 ■ *Web:* www.infocomm.org

National Telecommunications Co-op Assn (NTCA)
4121 Wilson Blvd 10th Fl. . . . . Arlington VA 22203 703-351-2000 351-2001
Web: www.ntca.org

Society of Telecommunications Consultants (STC)
13275 California 89 . . . . Old Station CA 96071 530-335-7313 335-7360
TF: 800-782-7670 ■ *Web:* sctcconsultants.org/?

Telecommunications Industry Assn (TIA)
2500 Wilson Blvd Ste 300 . . . . Arlington VA 22201 703-907-7700 907-7727
Web: www.tiaonline.org

US Telecom Assn (USTA) 607-14th St NW Ste 400. . . . Washington DC 20005 202-326-7300 315-3603
TF: 877-869-6903 ■ *Web:* ustelecom.org

Utilities Telecom Council (UTC)
1129 20th St NW Ste 350. . . . . Washington DC 20036 202-872-0030 872-1331
Web: www.utc.org

Wireless Communications Assn International (WCA)
1333 H St NW Ste 700W . . . . Washington DC 20005 202-452-7823
Web: wcai.com

49-21 Transportation Industry Associations

Phone | Fax

Aerospace Industries Assn of America (AIA)
1000 Wilson Blvd Ste 1700 . . . . Arlington VA 22209 703-358-1000 358-1011
TF: 877-229-7555 ■ *Web:* www.aia-aerospace.org

Air Traffic Control Assn (ATCA)
1101 King St Ste 300. . . . . Alexandria VA 22314 703-299-2430 299-2437
TF: 866-953-2189 ■ *Web:* www.atca.org

Aircraft Owners & Pilots Assn (AOPA)
421 Aviation Way. . . . . Frederick MD 21701 301-695-2000 695-2375
TF: 800-872-2672 ■ *Web:* www.aopa.org

Airlines for America (ATA)
1301 Pennsylvania Ave NW Ste 1100. . . . . Washington DC 20004 202-626-4000
Web: airlines.org

	City	State	Zip	Phone	Fax
Airports Council International of North America (ACI-NA) 1775 K St NW Ste 500 *Web:* www.aci-na.org	Washington	DC	20006	202-293-8500	331-1362
American Ambulance Assn (AAA) 8400 Wpark Dr Fl 2 *TF:* 800-523-4447 ■ *Web:* www.the-aaa.org	McLean	VA	22102	703-610-9018	
American Assn of Airport Executives (AAAE) 601 Madison St Ste 400 *TF:* 800-609-7374 ■ *Web:* www.aaae.org	Alexandria	VA	22314	703-824-0500	820-1395
American Assn of Port Authorities (AAPA) 1010 Duke St *Web:* www.aapa-ports.org	Alexandria	VA	22314	703-684-5700	684-6321
American Assn of State Highway & Transportation Officials (AASHTO) 444 N Capitol St NW Ste 249 *TF:* 800-880-4117 ■ *Web:* www.transportation.org	Washington	DC	20001	202-624-5800	624-5806
American Boat & Yacht Council Inc (ABYC) 613 Third St Ste 10 *Web:* www.abycinc.org	Annapolis	MD	21403	410-990-4460	990-4466
American Bureau of Shipping (ABS) 16855 Northchase Dr *Web:* www.eagle.org	Houston	TX	77060	281-877-5800	877-5803
American Helicopter Society International (AHS) 217 N Washington St *TF:* 855-247-4685 ■ *Web:* www.vtol.org	Alexandria	VA	22314	703-684-6777	739-9279
American Highway Users Alliance 1920 L St NW Ste 525 *Web:* www.highways.org	Washington	DC	20036	202-857-1200	857-1220
American International Automobile Dealers Assn (AIADA) 500 Montgomery St Ste 800 *TF:* 800-462-4232 ■ *Web:* www.aiada.org	Alexandria	VA	22314	703-519-7800	519-7810
American Moving & Storage Assn (AMSA) 1611 Duke St *TF:* 888-849-2672 ■ *Web:* www.promover.org	Alexandria	VA	22314	703-683-7410	683-7527
American Pilots' Assn 499 S Capitol St SW Ste 409 *Web:* www.americanpilots.org	Washington	DC	20003	202-484-0700	484-9320
American Public Transportation Assn (APTA) 1666 K St NW Ste 1100 *Web:* www.apta.com	Washington	DC	20006	202-496-4800	496-4321
American Railway Engineering & Maintenance-of-Way Assn (AREMA) 4501 Forbes Blvd Ste 130	Lanham	MD	20706	301-459-3200	459-8077
American Short Line & Regional Railroad Assn (ASLRRA) 50 F St NW Ste 7020 *Web:* www.aslrra.org	Washington	DC	20001	202-628-4500	628-6430
American Society of Naval Engineers (ASNE) 1452 Duke St *Web:* www.navalengineers.org	Alexandria	VA	22314	703-836-6727	836-7491
American Traffic Safety Services Assn (ATSSA) 15 Riverside Pkwy Ste 100 *TF:* 800-272-8772 ■ *Web:* www.atssa.com	Fredericksburg	VA	22406	540-368-1701	368-1717
American Trucking Assn (ATA) 950 N Glebe Rd Ste 210 *TF:* 800-282-5463 ■ *Web:* www.trucking.org	Arlington	VA	22203	703-838-1700	
American Waterways Operators (AWO) 801 N Quincy St Ste 200 *Web:* www.americanwaterways.com	Arlington	VA	22203	703-841-9300	841-0389
Association of American Railroads (AAR) 425 Third St SW *Web:* www.aar.org	Washington	DC	20024	202-639-2100	639-2286
Automatic Transmission Rebuilders Assn (ATRA) 2400 Latigo Ave *TF:* 866-464-2872 ■ *Web:* www.atra.com	Oxnard	CA	93030	805-604-2000	604-2003
Automotive Aftermarket Industry Assn (AAIA) 7101 Wisconsin Ave *TF:* 800-936-8906 ■ *Web:* autocare.org	Bethesda	MD	20814	301-654-6664	654-3299
Automotive Engine Rebuilders Assn (AERA) 500 Coventry Ln Ste 180 *TF:* 888-326-2372 ■ *Web:* www.aera.org	Crystal Lake	IL	60014	847-541-6550	541-5808
Automotive Industry Action Group (AIAG) 26200 Lahser Rd Ste 200 *TF:* 877-275-2424 ■ *Web:* www.aiag.org	Southfield	MI	48033	248-358-3570	358-3253
Automotive Oil Change Assn (AOCA) 330 N. Wabash Ave Ste 2000 *TF:* 800-230-0702 ■ *Web:* www.aoca.org	Chicago	IL	60611	312-321-5132	673-6832
Automotive Parts Remanufacturers Assn (APRA) 4215 Lafayette Ctr Dr Ste 3 *TF:* 877-734-4827 ■ *Web:* www.apra.org	Chantilly	VA	20151	703-968-2772	968-2878
Automotive Recyclers Assn (ARA) 3975 Fair Ridge Dr Ste 20N *TF:* 888-385-1005 ■ *Web:* www.a-r-a.org	Fairfax	VA	22033	703-385-1001	385-1494
Automotive Service Assn (ASA) 1901 Airport Fwy **Fax Area Code:* 817 ■ *TF Cust Svc:* 800-272-7467 ■ *Web:* www.asashop.org	Bedford	TX	76021	800-272-7467	685-0225*
Brotherhood of Railroad Signalmen 917 Shenandoah Shores Rd *Web:* www.brs.org	Front Royal	VA	22630	540-622-6522	622-6532
Car Care Council 7101 Wisconsin Ave **Fax Area Code:* 301 ■ *Web:* www.carcare.org	Bethesda	MD	20814	240-333-1088	654-3299*
Cargo Airline Assn 1620 L St NW Ste 610 *Web:* cargoair.org	Washington	DC	20036	202-293-1030	
Center for Auto Safety (CAS) 1825 Connecticut Ave NW Ste 330 *Web:* www.autosafety.org	Washington	DC	20009	202-328-7700	
Coalition Against Bigger Trucks (CABT) 1001 N Fairfax St Ste 515 *Web:* www.cabt.org	Alexandria	VA	22314	703-535-3131	
Coalition for Auto Repair Equality (CARE) 105 Oronoco St Ste 115 *TF:* 800-229-5380 ■ *Web:* www.careauto.org	Alexandria	VA	22314	703-519-7555	519-7747
Community Transportation Assn of America (CTAA) 1341 G St NW 10th Fl *TF:* 800-891-0590 ■ *Web:* www.ctaa.org	Washington	DC	20005	202-628-1480	737-9197
Dangerous Goods Advisory Council (DGAC) 7501 Greenway Ctr Dr Ste 760 *Web:* www.dgac.org	Greenbelt	MD	20770	202-289-4550	289-4074
Flight Safety Foundation 801 N Fairfax St Ste 400 *Web:* www.flightsafety.org	Alexandria	VA	22314	703-739-6700	739-6708
General Aviation Manufacturers Assn (GAMA) 1400 K St NW Ste 801 *TF:* 866-427-3287 ■ *Web:* www.gama.aero	Washington	DC	20005	202-393-1500	842-4063
Helicopter Assn International (HAI) 1635 Prince St *TF:* 800-435-4976 ■ *Web:* www.rotor.org	Alexandria	VA	22314	703-683-4646	683-4745
Independent Liquid Terminals Assn (ILTA) 1444 'I' St NW Ste 400 *Web:* www.ilta.org	Washington	DC	20005	202-842-9200	326-8660
Institute of International Container Lessors (IICL) 1990 M St NW Ste 650 *Web:* www.iicl.org	Washington	DC	20036	202-223-9800	223-9810
Institute of Navigation Inc (ION) 8551 Rixlew Ln Ste 360 *TF:* 800-696-7353 ■ *Web:* www.ion.org	Manassas	VA	20109	703-366-2723	366-2724
Institute of Transportation Engineers (ITE) 1099 14th St NW Ste 300W *Web:* www.ite.org	Washington	DC	20005	202-289-0222	289-7722
Insurance Institute for Highway Safety 1005 N Glebe Rd Ste 800 *TF:* 888-327-4236 ■ *Web:* www.iihs.org	Arlington	VA	22201	703-247-1500	247-1588
Intelligent Transportation Society of America (ITS) 1100 17th St NW Ste 1200 *TF:* 800-374-8472 ■ *Web:* www.itsa.org	Washington	DC	20036	202-484-4847	484-3483
Intermodal Assn of North America (IANA) 11785 Beltsville Dr Ste 1100 *TF:* 877-438-8442 ■ *Web:* www.intermodal.org	Calverton	MD	20705	301-982-3400	982-4815
International Air Cargo Assn (TIACA) 5600 NW 36th St Ste 620 *Web:* www.tiaca.org	Miami	FL	33266	786-265-7011	265-7012
International Air Transport Assn 800 Pl Victoria PO Box 113 *TF:* 800-716-6326 ■ *Web:* www.iata.org	Montreal	QC	H4Z1M1	514-874-0202	874-9632
International Carwash Assn 230 E Ohio St **Fax Area Code:* 312 ■ *TF:* 888-422-8422 ■ *Web:* www.carwash.org	Chicago	IL	60611	888-422-8422	245-1085*
International Motor Coach Group Inc (IMG) 8695 College Blvd Ste 260 *TF:* 888-447-3466 ■ *Web:* www.imgcoach.com	Overland Park	KS	66210	913-906-0111	906-0115
International Parking Institute (IPI) 701 Kenmore Ave Ste 350 *Web:* www.parking.org	Alexandria	VA	22314	571-699-3011	
International Safe Transit Assn (ISTA) 1400 Abbott Rd Ste 160 *TF:* 888-299-2208 ■ *Web:* www.ista.org	East Lansing	MI	48823	517-333-3437	333-3813
International Warehouse Logistics Assn (IWLA) 2800 S River Rd Ste 260 *Web:* www.iwla.com	Des Plaines	IL	60018	847-813-4699	813-0115
Interstate Natural Gas Assn of America (INGAA) 10 G St NE Ste 700 *Web:* www.ingaa.org	Washington	DC	20002	202-216-5900	216-0870
Japan Automobile Manufacturers Assn (JAMA) 1050 17th St NW Ste 410 *Web:* www.jama.org	Washington	DC	20036	202-296-8537	872-1212
Jewelers Shipping Assn (JSA) 125 Carlsbad St *TF:* 800-688-4572 ■ *Web:* www.jewelersshipping.com	Cranston	RI	02920	401-943-6020	
Mid-West Truckers Assn Inc 2727 N Dirksen Pkwy *Web:* mid-westtruckers.com	Springfield	IL	62702	217-525-0310	525-0342
Mobile Air Conditioning Society Worldwide (MACS) 225 S Broad St *TF:* 800-641-1133 ■ *Web:* www.macsw.org	Lansdale	PA	19446	215-631-7020	631-7017
Motor & Equipment Manufacturers Assn (MEMA) 10 Laboratory Dr	Research Triangle Park	NC	27709	919-549-4800	406-1465
Motorcycle Industry Council (MIC) 2 Jenner St Ste 150 *Web:* www.mic.org	Irvine	CA	92618	949-727-4211	727-3313
National Air Carrier Assn (NACA) 1000 Wilson Blvd Ste 1700 *Web:* www.naca.cc	Arlington	VA	22209	703-358-8060	358-8070
National Air Transportation Assn (NATA) 4226 King St *TF:* 800-808-6282 ■ *Web:* www.nata.aero	Alexandria	VA	22302	703-845-9000	845-8176
National Automobile Dealers Assn (NADA) 8400 Westpark Dr *TF:* 800-252-6232 ■ *Web:* www.nada.org	McLean	VA	22102	703-821-7000	821-7075
National Automotive Radiator Service Assn (NARSA) 3000 Village Run Rd Ste 103 221 *Web:* www.narsa.org	Wexford	PA	15090	724-799-8415	799-8416
National Business Aviation Assn (NBAA) 1200 18th St NW Ste 400 *TF:* 800-394-6222 ■ *Web:* www.nbaa.org	Washington	DC	20036	202-783-9000	331-8364
National Cargo Bureau Inc (NCB) 17 Battery Pl Ste 1232 *Web:* www.natcargo.org	New York	NY	10004	212-785-8300	785-8333
National Customs Brokers & Forwarders Assn of America Inc (NCBFAA) 1200 18th St NW Ste 901 *Web:* www.ncbfaa.org	Washington	DC	20036	202-466-0222	466-0226
National Industrial Transportation League (NITL) 1700 N Moore St Ste 1900 *Web:* www.nitl.org	Arlington	VA	22209	703-524-5011	524-5017
National Marine Manufacturers Assn (NMMA) 200 E Randolph Dr Ste 5100 *Web:* www.nmma.org	Chicago	IL	60601	312-946-6200	946-0388
National Motor Freight Traffic Assn (NMFTA) 1001 N Fairfax St Ste 600 *TF:* 866-411-6632 ■ *Web:* www.nmfta.org	Alexandria	VA	22314	703-838-1810	683-6296
National Motorists Assn (NMA) 402 W Second St *TF:* 800-882-2785 ■ *Web:* www.motorists.org	Waunakee	WI	53597	608-849-6000	849-8697
National Private Truck Council (NPTC) 950 N Glebe Rd Ste 2300 *Web:* www.nptc.org	Arlington	VA	22203	703-683-1300	683-1217
National Tank Truck Carriers Inc 950 N Glebe Rd Ste 520 *Web:* www.tanktruck.org	Arlington	VA	22203	703-838-1960	

				Phone	Fax
National Truck Equipment Assn (NTEA) 37400 Hills Tech Dr *TF:* 800-441-6832 ■ *Web:* www.ntea.com	Farmington Hills	MI	48331	248-489-7090	489-8590
National Waterways Conference Inc (NWC) 4650 Washington Blvd Ste 608 *TF:* 866-371-1390 ■ *Web:* www.waterways.org	Arlington	VA	22201	703-243-4090	243-4155
NATSO Inc 1737 King St Ste 200 *TF:* 800-956-9160 ■ *Web:* www.natso.com	Alexandria	VA	22314	703-549-2100	684-4525
nternational Propeller Club of the United States 3927 Old Lee Hwy Ste 101-A *Web:* www.propellerclub.us/home	Fairfax	VA	22030	703-691-2777	691-4173
Owner-Operator Independent Drivers Assn Inc (OOIDA) 1 NW OOIDA Dr *TF:* 800-444-5791 ■ *Web:* www.ooida.com	Grain Valley	MO	64029	816-229-5791	229-0518
Passenger Vessel Assn (PVA) 103 Oronoco St Ste 200 *TF:* 800-807-8360 ■ *Web:* www.passengervessel.com	Alexandria	VA	22314	703-518-5005	518-5151
Railway Supply Institute Inc (RSI) 425 Third St Ste 920 *Web:* www.rsiweb.org	Washington	DC	20024	202-347-4664	347-0047
Recreation Vehicle Dealers Assn (RVDA) 3930 University Dr 3rd Fl *TF:* 800-336-0355 ■ *Web:* www.rvda.org	Fairfax	VA	22030	703-591-7130	591-0734
Recreation Vehicle Industry Assn (RVIA) 1896 Preston White Dr *TF:* 800-336-0154 ■ *Web:* www.rvia.org	Reston	VA	20191	703-620-6003	620-5071
Regional Airline Assn (RAA) 2025 M St NW Ste 800 *Web:* www.raa.org	Washington	DC	20036	202-367-1170	367-2170
Self Storage Assn (SSA) 1900 N Beauregard St Ste 450 *TF:* 888-735-3784 ■ *Web:* www.selfstorage.org	Alexandria	VA	22311	703-575-8000	575-8901
Shipbuilders Council of America (SCA) 20 F St, NW Ste 500 *Web:* www.shipbuilders.org	Washington	DC	20001	202-347-5462	
Shipowners Claims Bureau (SCB) 1 Battery Pk Plaza 31st Fl *TF:* 800-774-8724 ■ *Web:* www.american-club.com	New York	NY	10004	212-847-4500	847-4599
Society of Automotive Engineers Inc (SAE) 400 Commonwealth Dr *TF:* 877-606-7323 ■ *Web:* www.sae.org	Warrendale	PA	15096	724-776-4841	776-0790
Society of Naval Architects & Marine Engineers (SNAME) 601 Pavonia Ave Ste 400 *TF:* 800-798-2188 ■ *Web:* www.sname.org	Jersey City	NJ	07306	201-798-4800	798-4975
Specialized Carriers & Rigging Assn (SC&RA) 5870 Trinity Pkwy Ste 200 *Web:* www.scranet.org	Centreville	VA	20120	703-698-0291	698-0297
Specialty Equipment Market Assn (SEMA) 1575 S Vly Vista Dr *Web:* www.sema.org	Diamond Bar	CA	91765	909-396-0289	860-0184
Specialty Vehicle Institute of America (SVIA) 2 Jenner St Ste 150 *TF:* 800-887-2887 ■ *Web:* www.atvsafety.org	Irvine	CA	92618	949-727-3727	727-4216
Technology & Maintenance Council (TMC) American Trucking Assn 950 N Glebe Rd Ste 210 *Web:* www.trucking.org	Arlington	VA	22203	703-838-1763	
Transport Workers Union of America 501 Third St NW 9th Fl *TF:* 888-565-6898 ■ *Web:* www.twu.org	Washington	DC	20001	202-719-3900	347-0454
Transportation Institute 5201 Auth Way *Web:* transportationinstitute.org	Camp Springs	MD	20746	301-423-3335	423-0634
Transportation Intermediaries Assn (TIA) 1625 Prince St Ste 200 *TF:* 888-910-4747 ■ *Web:* www.tianet.org	Alexandria	VA	22314	703-299-5700	836-0123
Transportation Research Board (TRB) 500 Fifth St NW *TF:* 866-233-4642 ■ *Web:* www.trb.org	Washington	DC	20001	202-334-2934	334-2519
Truck Renting & Leasing Assn (TRALA) 675 N Washington St Ste 410 *Web:* www.trala.org	Alexandria	VA	22314	703-299-9120	299-9115
Truckload Carriers Assn (TCA) 555 E Braddock Rd *TF:* 800-666-2770 ■ *Web:* www.truckload.org	Alexandria	VA	22314	703-838-1950	836-6610
United Motorcoach Assn (UMA) 113 SW St 4th Fl *TF:* 800-424-8262 ■ *Web:* www.uma.org	Alexandria	VA	22314	703-838-2929	838-2950
Warehousing Education & Research Council (WERC) 1100 Jorie Blvd Ste 170 *Web:* www.werc.org	Oak Brook	IL	60523	630-990-0001	990-0256

50 ATTRACTIONS

See Also Amusement Parks p. 1735; Aquariums - Public p. 1739; Art Dealers & Galleries p. 1744; Botanical Gardens & Arboreta p. 1870; Cemeteries - National p. 1897; Presidential Libraries p. 2648; Special Collections Libraries p. 2665; Museums p. 2790; Museums - Children's p. 2812; Museums & Halls of Fame - Sports p. 2814; Parks - National - Canada p. 2871; Parks - National - US p. 2871; Parks - State p. 2878; Performing Arts Facilities p. 2912; Planetariums p. 2943; Zoos & Wildlife Parks p. 3316

50-1 Churches, Cathedrals, Synagogues, Temples

				Phone	Fax
Antioch Baptist Church 1057 Texas Ave	Shreveport	LA	71101	318-222-7090	222-5738
Arch Street Meeting House 320 Arch St *Web:* www.archstreetfriends.org	Philadelphia	PA	19106	215-627-2667	
Basilica of Saint Mary of the Immaculate Conception, The 232 Chapel St *Web:* www.basilicaofsaintmary.org	Norfolk	VA	23504	757-622-4487	625-7969
Basilica of the Assumption 409 Cathedral St *Web:* americasfirstcathedral.org	Baltimore	MD	21201	410-727-3565	539-0407
Black Madonna Shrine 100 St Joseph Hill Rd PO Box 181 *Web:* www.franciscancaring.org/blackmadonnashri.html	Pacific	MO	63069	636-938-5361	
Boardman Park 375 BoaRdman-Poland Rd *Web:* www.boardmanpark.com	Boardman	OH	44512	330-726-8107	726-4562
Carmel Mission 3080 Rio Rd *Web:* www.carmelmission.org	Carmel	CA	93923	831-624-1271	624-8050
Cathedral Basilica of Saint Joseph 80 S Market St *Web:* www.stjosephcathedral.org	San Jose	CA	95113	408-283-8100	
Cathedral Basilica of Saint Louis (New Cathedral) 4431 Lindell Blvd *Web:* www.cathedralstl.org	Saint Louis	MO	63108	314-373-8200	373-8290
Cathedral Basilica of the Sacred Heart 89 Ridge St *Web:* www.cathedralbasilica.org	Newark	NJ	07104	973-484-4600	483-8253
Cathedral Church of All Saints Martello St & University Ave *Web:* www.cathedralchurchofallsaints.com	Halifax	NS	B3H4Z1	902-423-6002	423-1437
Cathedral Church of Saint John the Divine 1047 Amsterdam Ave *Web:* www.stjohndivine.org	New York	NY	10025	212-316-7490	932-7347
Cathedral Church of Saint Mark 231 East 100 South	Salt Lake City	UT	84111	801-322-3400	322-3410
Cathedral of Christ the King 299 Colony Blvd *Web:* cathedralctk.org	Lexington	KY	40502	859-268-2861	268-8061
Cathedral of Our Lady of the Angels 555 W Temple St *TF:* 800-838-1356 ■ *Web:* www.olacathedral.org	Los Angeles	CA	90012	213-680-5200	620-1982
Cathedral of Saint Paul 239 Selby Ave *Web:* www.cathedralsaintpaul.org	Saint Paul	MN	55102	651-228-1766	
Cathedral of Saints Peter & Paul 30 Fenner St	Providence	RI	02903	401-331-2434	273-0687
Cathedral of the Blessed Sacrament 1017 11th St *Web:* www.blessedsaccathedral.org	Sacramento	CA	95814	916-444-3071	
Cathedral of the Immaculate Conception 2 S Claiborne St *Web:* www.mobilecathedral.org	Mobile	AL	36602	251-434-1565	434-1588
Cathedral of the Immaculate Conception 125 Eagle St *Web:* www.cathedralic.com	Albany	NY	12202	518-463-4447	436-5177
Cathedral of the Madeleine 331 E S Temple St *Web:* www.utcotm.org	Salt Lake City	UT	84111	801-328-8941	364-6504
Catholic Diocese of Peoria, The 607 NE Madison Ave *Web:* www.cdop.org	Peoria	IL	61603	309-682-5823	
Center Church 60 Gold St *Web:* www.centerchurchhartford.org	Hartford	CT	06103	860-249-5631	246-3915
Christ Church Cathedral 125 Monument Cir *Web:* www.cccindy.org	Indianapolis	IN	46204	317-636-4577	
Christ Church Cathedral 45 Church St *Web:* www.cccathedral.org	Hartford	CT	06103	860-527-7231	527-5313
Christ Church Cathedral 1210 Locust St *Web:* www.christchurchcathedral.us	Saint Louis	MO	63103	314-231-3454	231-3142
Christ Church Cathedral 690 Burrard St *Web:* thecathedral.ca	Vancouver	BC	V6C2L1	604-682-3848	682-8377
Christ Church in Philadelphia 20 N American St *Web:* www.christchurchphila.org	Philadelphia	PA	19106	215-922-1695	922-3578
Christ Episcopal Church 10 N Church St *Web:* www.ccgsc.org	Greenville	SC	29601	864-271-8773	242-0879
Christ Episcopal Church State & Water Streets PO Box 1374 *Web:* www.christchurchdover.org	Dover	DE	19903	302-734-5731	
Church of the Transfiguration 1 E 29th St *Web:* www.littlechurch.org	New York	NY	10016	212-684-6770	
Circular Congregational Church 150 Meeting St *Web:* www.circularchurch.org	Charleston	SC	29401	843-577-6400	958-0594
Congregation Beth Elohim 90 Hasell St *Web:* www.kkbe.org	Charleston	SC	29401	843-723-1090	723-0537
Congregation Mikveh Israel 44 N Fourth St *Web:* www.mikvehisrael.org	Philadelphia	PA	19106	215-922-5446	922-1550
Crystal Cathedral 12921 S Lewis St *Web:* www.crystalcathedral.org	Garden Grove	CA	92840	714-971-4000	
Dagom Gaden Tensung-Ling Monastery 2150 E Dolan Rd *Web:* www.ganden.org	Bloomington	IN	47404	812-334-3456	
Dexter Avenue King Memorial Baptist Church 454 Dexter Ave *Web:* www.dexterkingmemorial.org	Montgomery	AL	36104	334-263-3970	
Duke Memorial United Methodist Church 504 W Chapel Hill St *Web:* www.dukememorial.org	Durham	NC	27701	919-683-3467	682-3349
Ebenezer Baptist Church 407 Auburn Ave NE *Web:* www.historicebenezer.org	Atlanta	GA	30312	404-688-7300	521-1129
Emanuel African Methodist Episcopal Church 110 Calhoun St *Web:* www.emanuelamechurch.org	Charleston	SC	29401	843-722-2561	722-1869
First Congregational Church 62 Centre St *Web:* nantucketfcc.org	Nantucket	MA	02554	508-228-0950	
First Unitarian Church of Philadelphia 2125 Chestnut St *Web:* www.philauu.org	Philadelphia	PA	19103	215-563-3980	563-4209
Franciscan Monastery of the Holly Land 1400 Quincy St NE *Web:* www.myfranciscan.org	Washington	DC	20017	202-526-6800	

Name / Address	City	State	ZIP	Phone	Fax
Historic Trinity Lutheran Church 1345 Gratiot Ave	Detroit	MI	48207	313-567-3100	567-3209
TF: 800-268-3058 ■ *Web:* www.historictrinity.org					
Holy Trinity Catholic Church 315 Marshall St	Shreveport	LA	71101	318-221-5990	
Web: www.holytrinity-shreveport.com					
King's Chapel 58 Tremont St	Boston	MA	02108	617-227-2155	227-4101
Web: kings-chapel.org					
Landmark on the Park 160 Central Pk W	New York	NY	10023	212-595-1658	
Web: www.landmarkonthepark.org					
Ling Shen Ching Tze Temple 17012 NE 40th Ct	Redmond	WA	98052	425-882-0916	
Web: tbsseattle.org					
Martha's Vineyard Preservation Trust 99 Main St PO Box 5277	Edgartown	MA	02539	508-627-4440	627-8088
Web: www.mvpreservation.org					
Mesa Arizona Temple 101 S LeSueur	Mesa	AZ	85204	480-833-1211	827-2828
TF: 855-537-4357 ■ *Web:* www.lds.org/church/temples					
Mission Dolores 3321 16th St	San Francisco	CA	94114	415-621-8203	621-2294
Web: www.missiondolores.org					
Mission of Nombre de Dios & Shrine of Our Lady of La Leche 27 Ocean Ave	Saint Augustine	FL	32084	904-824-2809	
TF: 800-342-6529 ■ *Web:* www.missionandshrine.org					
Mission San Fernando Rey De Espana 15151 San Fernando Mission Blvd	Mission Hills	CA	91345	818-361-0186	
Web: missiontour.org					
Mission San Jose 701 E Pyron Ave	San Antonio	TX	78214	210-922-0543	
Web: www.nps.gov					
Mission San Luis Rey de Francia 4050 Mission Ave	Oceanside	CA	92057	760-757-3651	757-4613
Web: www.sanluisrey.org					
Mother Bethel AME Church 419 S Sixth St	Philadelphia	PA	19147	215-925-0616	925-1402
Web: www.motherbethel.org					
National Shrine of Our Lady of Lebanon, The 2759 N Lipkey Rd	North Jackson	OH	44451	330-538-3351	538-0455
Web: www.ourladyoflebanonshrine.com					
National Shrine of Our Lady of the Snows 442 S De Mazenod Dr	Belleville	IL	62223	618-397-6700	398-6549
TF: 800-682-2879 ■ *Web:* www.snows.org					
New England Peace Pagoda, The 100 Cave Hill Rd	Leverett	MA	01054	413-367-2202	
Web: newenglandpeacepagoda.org					
Oakland Mormon Temple 4770 Lincoln Ave	Oakland	CA	94602	510-531-3200	531-2646
Web: www.ldschurchtemples.com					
Old First Reformed Church of Christ 151 N Fourth St	Philadelphia	PA	19106	215-922-4566	
Web: www.oldfirstucc.org					
Old Mission San Jose 43148 Mission Blvd	Fremont	CA	94539	510-657-1797	
Web: www.saintjosephmsj.org					
Old North Church 193 Salem St	Boston	MA	02113	617-523-6676	725-0559
Web: www.oldnorth.com					
Old Pine Street Presbyterian Church 412 Pine St	Philadelphia	PA	19106	215-925-8051	
Web: www.oldpine.org					
Old Saint Ferdinand's Shrine 1 Rue St Francois	Florissant	MO	63031	314-837-2110	
TF: 800-366-2427 ■ *Web:* oldstferdinandshrine.com					
Old Saint Joseph's Church 321 Willings Alley	Philadelphia	PA	19106	215-923-1733	574-8529
Web: www.oldstjoseph.org					
Old Saint Mary's Church 123 E 13th St	Cincinnati	OH	45202	513-721-2988	
Web: www.oldstmarys.org					
Old Saint Patrick's Church 700 W Adams St	Chicago	IL	60661	312-648-1021	
Web: www.oldstpats.org					
Our Lady Queen of the Most Holy Rosary Cathedral 2535 Collingwood Blvd	Toledo	OH	43610	419-244-9575	
Web: www.rosarycathedral.org					
Queen of Angels Monastery 840 S Main St	Mount Angel	OR	97362	503-845-6141	845-6585
Web: www.benedictine-srs.com					
Saint George's Anglican Church 1101 Stanley St	Montreal	QC	H3B2S6	514-866-7113	866-6096
Web: www.st-georges.org					
Saint George's Church 2222 Brunswick St	Halifax	NS	B3K2Z3	902-423-1059	423-0897
Web: www.roundchurch.ca					
Saint Joseph Cathedral 521 N Duluth Ave	Sioux Falls	SD	57104	605-336-7390	
Web: stjosephcathedral.net					
Saint Louis Cathedral 615 Pere Antoine Alley	New Orleans	LA	70116	504-525-9585	525-9583
Web: www.stlouiscathedral.org					
Saint Mary's Cathedral 203 E Tenth St	Austin	TX	78701	512-476-6182	476-8799
Web: www.smcaustin.org					
Saint Mary's Catholic Church 155 Market St	Memphis	TN	38105	901-522-9420	522-8314
Saint Paul's Episcopal Church 1430 J St	Sacramento	CA	95814	916-446-2620	
Web: www.stpaulssacramento.org					
Saint Photios Greek Orthodox National Shrine 41 St George St	Saint Augustine	FL	32085	904-829-8205	829-8707
Web: www.stphotios.org					
Salt Lake Temple 50 W N Temple St	Salt Lake City	UT	84150	801-240-2640	240-1550
TF: 800-453-3860 ■ *Web:* www.lds.org					
San Gabriel Mission 428 S Mission Dr	San Gabriel	CA	91776	626-457-3035	282-5308
Web: www.sangabrielmissionchurch.org					
San Miguel Mission 401 Old Santa Fe Trl	Santa Fe	NM	87501	505-983-3974	
San Xavier Del Bac Mission 1950 W San Xavier Rd	Tucson	AZ	85746	520-294-2624	
Web: www.sanxaviermission.org					
Scottish Rite Cathedral 160 S Scott Ave	Tucson	AZ	85701	520-622-8364	
Web: tucsonscottishrite.org					
Shrine of Saint John Neumann 1019 N Fifth St	Philadelphia	PA	19123	215-627-3080	627-3296
Web: www.stjohnneumann.org					
Sixteenth Street Baptist Church 1530 Sixth Ave N	Birmingham	AL	35203	205-251-9402	251-9811
Southern Union Conference Assn of The Seventh Day Adventist Church 302 Research Dr NW	Norcross	GA	30092	404-299-1832	
Web: www.southernunion.com					
Touro Synagogue National Historic Site 85 Touro St	Newport	RI	02840	401-847-4794	
Web: www.tourosynagogue.org					
Trinity Cathedral 2230 Euclid Ave	Cleveland	OH	44115	216-771-3630	771-3657
Web: www.trinitycleveland.org					
Union Chapel 55 Narragansett Ave	Edgartown	MA	02539	508-627-4440	
Web: www.mvpreservation.org					
Union Church of Pocantico Hills 555 Bedford Rd	Sleepy Hollow	NY	10591	914-631-8200	631-0089
TF: 877-325-4822 ■ *Web:* www.hudsonvalley.org					
Wayfarers Chapel 5755 Palos Verdes Dr	Rancho Palos Verdes	CA	90275	310-377-1650	
Web: www.wayfarerschapel.org					
White Church Christian Church 2200 N 85th St	Kansas City	KS	66109	913-299-4056	
Ysleta Mission 131 S Zaragosa Rd	El Paso	TX	79907	915-859-9848	860-9340
Web: www.ysletamission.org					

50-2 Cultural & Arts Centers

Arizona

Name / Address	City	State	ZIP	Phone	Fax
Deer Valley Rock Art Ctr 3711 W Deer Vly Rd	Glendale	AZ	85308	623-582-8007	582-8831
Web: www.asu.edu					
Mesa Arts Ctr 1 E Main St PO Box 1466	Mesa	AZ	85201	480-644-6501	644-6503
Web: www.mesaartscenter.com					

Arkansas

Name / Address	City	State	ZIP	Phone	Fax
Arkansas Arts Ctr 501 E Ninth St	Little Rock	AR	72202	501-372-4000	375-8053
TF: 800-264-2787 ■ *Web:* www.arkarts.com					
Center for Art & Education 104 N 13th St	Van Buren	AR	72956	479-474-7767	474-4411
Web: www.art-ed.org					

California

Name / Address	City	State	ZIP	Phone	Fax
Aerie Art Garden 71-225 Aerie Rd	Palm Desert	CA	92260	760-568-6366	
Web: www.aerieartgarden.com					
African American Art & Culture Complex 762 Fulton St Ste 300	San Francisco	CA	94102	415-922-2049	922-5130
Web: www.aaacc.org					
Huntington Beach Arts Ctr 538 Main St	Huntington Beach	CA	92648	714-374-1650	
Web: huntingtonbeachartcenter.org					
Jurupa Mountains Discovery Ctr 7621 Granite Hill Dr	Riverside	CA	92509	951-685-5818	685-1240
Web: www.jmdc.org					
Mission Cultural Ctr for Latino Arts 2868 Mission St	San Francisco	CA	94110	415-821-1155	648-0933
Web: www.missionculturalcenter.org					
Oakland Asian Cultural Ctr 388 Ninth St Ste 290	Oakland	CA	94607	510-637-0455	637-0459
Web: www.oacc.cc					
Roy & Edna Disney/CALARTS Theater (REDCAT) (REDCAT) 631 W Second St	Los Angeles	CA	90012	213-237-2800	237-2811
Web: www.redcat.org					
Skirball Cultural Ctr 2701 N Sepulveda Blvd	Los Angeles	CA	90049	310-440-4500	440-4595
Web: www.skirball.org					

Colorado

Name / Address	City	State	ZIP	Phone	Fax
Anasazi Heritage Ctr 27501 Hwy 184	Dolores	CO	81323	970-882-5600	882-7035
Web: www.blm.gov					
Anderson Ranch Arts Ctr 5263 Owl Creek Rd PO Box 5598	Snowmass Village	CO	81615	970-923-3181	923-3871
TF: 800-525-6363 ■ *Web:* www.andersonranch.org					
Dairy Ctr for the Arts 2590 Walnut St	Boulder	CO	80302	303-440-7826	440-7104
Web: www.thedairy.org					
Durango Arts Ctr 802 E Second Ave	Durango	CO	81301	970-259-2606	259-6571
TF: 800-838-3006 ■ *Web:* durangoarts.org					
Southern Ute Cultural Ctr & Museum PO Box 737	Ignacio	CO	81137	970-563-9583	563-4641
Web: www.southernute-nsn.gov/southern-ute-museum-and-cultural-center					

Connecticut

Name / Address	City	State	ZIP	Phone	Fax
Charter Oak Cultural Ctr 21 Charter Oak Ave	Hartford	CT	06106	860-310-2580	
Web: www.charteroakcenter.org					
Rowayton Arts Ctr 145 Rowayton Ave	Rowayton	CT	06853	203-866-2744	866-1123
Web: www.rowaytonartscenter.org					
Silvermine Arts Ctr 1037 Silvermine Rd	New Canaan	CT	06840	203-966-9700	966-2763
Web: www.silvermineart.org					
Westport Arts Ctr 51 Riverside Ave	Westport	CT	06880	203-222-7070	222-7999
Web: www.westportartscenter.org					

Delaware

Name / Address	City	State	ZIP	Phone	Fax
Delaware Ctr for the Contemporary Arts 200 S Madison St	Wilmington	DE	19801	302-656-6466	656-6944
Web: www.thedcca.org					

Florida

	City	State	ZIP	Phone	Fax
African-American Research Library & Cultural Ctr 2650 Sistrunk Blvd	Fort Lauderdale	FL	33311	954-357-6282	
Armory Art Ctr 1700 Parker Ave *Web:* www.armoryart.org	West Palm Beach	FL	33401	561-832-1776	832-0191
ArtSouth 5825 SW 68th St Ste 2 Office 202 *Web:* www.artsouthhomestead.org	South Miami	FL	33143	305-247-9406	247-7308
Lighthouse Ctr for the Arts 373 Tequesta Dr Gallery Sq N *Web:* www.lighthousearts.org	Tequesta	FL	33469	561-746-3101	
Maitland Art Ctr 231 W Packwood Ave **Fax Area Code:* 888 ■ *TF:* 800-435-7352 ■ *Web:* www.artandhistory.org	Maitland	FL	32751	407-539-2181	316-5729*

Georgia

	City	State	ZIP	Phone	Fax
Atlanta Contemporary Art Ctr 535 Means St NW *Web:* atlantacontemporary.org	Atlanta	GA	30318	404-688-1970	577-5856
Callanwolde Fine Arts Ctr 980 Briarcliff Rd NE *Web:* www.callanwolde.org	Atlanta	GA	30306	404-872-5338	872-5175
Center for Puppetry Arts 1404 Spring St NW *TF:* 800-642-3629 ■ *Web:* www.puppet.org	Atlanta	GA	30309	404-873-3089	873-9907
City Market Art Ctr 219 W Bryan St Ste 207 *Web:* www.savannahcitymarket.com/art.html	Savannah	GA	31401	912-232-4903	

Idaho

	City	State	ZIP	Phone	Fax
Pocatello Art Ctr (PAC) 444 N Main St *Web:* www.pocatelloartctr.org	Pocatello	ID	83204	208-232-0970	

Illinois

	City	State	ZIP	Phone	Fax
City of Chicago 121 N LaSalle St *Web:* www.cityofchicago.org	Chicago	IL	60602	312-744-5000	
Irish American Heritage Ctr 4626 N Knox Ave *Web:* www.irish-american.org	Chicago	IL	60630	773-282-7035	
South Shore Cultural Ctr 7059 S Shore Dr *Web:* www.chicagoparkdistrict.com	Chicago	IL	60649	773-256-0149	

Indiana

	City	State	ZIP	Phone	Fax
Indianapolis Art Ctr 820 E 67th St *Web:* indplsartcenter.org	Indianapolis	IN	46220	317-255-2464	

Kentucky

	City	State	ZIP	Phone	Fax
Capital Gallery of Contemporary Art 314 Lewis St *Web:* ellenglasgow.com	Frankfort	KY	40601	502-223-2649	
Kentucky Ctr for African American Heritage 1701 W Muhammad Ali Blvd *Web:* www.kcaah.org	Louisville	KY	40203	502-583-4100	
Kentucky Museum of Art & Craft 715 W Main St *Web:* www.kmacmuseum.org	Louisville	KY	40202	502-589-0102	589-0154

Louisiana

	City	State	ZIP	Phone	Fax
Acadiana Ctr for the Arts 101 W Vermilion St *Web:* www.acadianacenterforthearts.org	Lafayette	LA	70501	337-233-7060	233-7062
Barnwell Garden & Art Ctr 601 Clyde Fant Pkwy	Shreveport	LA	71101	318-673-7703	

Maine

	City	State	ZIP	Phone	Fax
Maine Folklife Ctr 5773 S Stevens Hall University of Maine *Web:* www.umaine.edu/folklife	Orono	ME	04469	207-581-1891	581-1823

Manitoba

	City	State	ZIP	Phone	Fax
Jewish Heritage Ctr of Western Canada C116-123 Doncaster St *Web:* www.jhcwc.org	Winnipeg	MB	R3N2B2	204-477-7460	477-7465
Saint Norbert Arts & Cultural Centre (SNAC) 100 Rue des Ruines du Monastere *Web:* www.snac.mb.ca	Winnipeg	MB	R3V1B9	204-269-0564	261-1927

Maryland

	City	State	ZIP	Phone	Fax
Elizabeth Myers Mitchell Art Gallery 60 College Ave	Annapolis	MD	21401	410-626-2556	
Maryland Art Place (MAP) 218 W Saratoga St *Web:* www.mdartplace.org	Baltimore	MD	21201	410-962-8565	
Maryland Federation of Art Cir Gallery (MFA) 18 State Cir *Web:* www.mdfedart.com	Annapolis	MD	21401	410-268-4566	268-4570

Massachusetts

	City	State	ZIP	Phone	Fax
Worcester Ctr for Crafts 25 Sagamore Rd *Web:* www.worcester.edu	Worcester	MA	01605	508-753-8183	797-5626

Michigan

	City	State	ZIP	Phone	Fax
Ann Arbor Art Ctr 117 W Liberty St *Web:* www.annarborartcenter.org	Ann Arbor	MI	48104	734-994-8004	994-3610
Detroit Gallery-Contemporary 104 Fisher Rd Ste 104	Grosse Pointe Shores	MI	48230	313-873-7888	
Flint Cultural Ctr Corp 1310 E Kearsley St *TF:* 800-214-7275 ■ *Web:* www.flintculturalcenter.com	Flint	MI	48503	810-237-7333	
Lansing Art Gallery 119 N Washington Sq *Web:* www.lansingartgallery.org	Lansing	MI	48933	517-374-6400	
Nokomis Learning Ctr 5153 Marsh Rd *Web:* www.nokomis.org	Okemos	MI	48864	517-349-5777	
Oakland University Art Gallery Oakland University 208 Wilson Hall *Web:* www.ouartgallery.org	Rochester	MI	48309	248-370-3005	370-4208

Minnesota

	City	State	ZIP	Phone	Fax
Rochester Art Ctr 40 Civic Ctr Dr SE *Web:* www.rochesterartcenter.org	Rochester	MN	55904	507-282-8629	

Mississippi

	City	State	ZIP	Phone	Fax
Mississippi Arts Ctr 201 E Pascagoula St Ste 102 *Web:* www.arts.state.ms.us	Jackson	MS	39201	601-359-6030	960-1352
Municipal Art Gallery 839 N State St	Jackson	MS	39202	601-960-1582	960-2066

Missouri

	City	State	ZIP	Phone	Fax
Center of Contemporary Arts 524 Trinity Ave *Web:* www.cocastl.org	Saint Louis	MO	63130	314-725-6555	725-6222
Portfolio Gallery & Educational Ctr 3514 Delmar Blvd *Web:* www.portfoliogallerystl.org	Saint Louis	MO	63103	314-533-3323	

Nebraska

	City	State	ZIP	Phone	Fax
Bemis Ctr for Contemporary Arts 724 S 12th St *Web:* www.bemiscenter.org	Omaha	NE	68102	402-341-7130	341-9791
Gerald R Ford Conservation Ctr 1326 S 32nd St *TF:* 800-634-6932 ■ *Web:* www.nebraskahistory.org	Omaha	NE	68105	402-595-1180	595-1178

New Jersey

	City	State	ZIP	Phone	Fax
Great Falls Historic District Cultural Ctr 65 McBride Ave Ext *Web:* www.patersonnj.gov	Paterson	NJ	07501	973-279-9587	279-0587

New Mexico

	City	State	ZIP	Phone	Fax
Branigan Cultural Ctr 501 N Main St PO Box 20000 *Web:* www.las-cruces.org	Las Cruces	NM	88004	575-541-2154	541-2152
National Hispanic Cultural Ctr 1701 Fourth St SW *Web:* www.nhccnm.org	Albuquerque	NM	87102	505-246-2261	246-2613
South Broadway Cultural Ctr 1025 Broadway Blvd SE *TF:* 866-441-6075 ■ *Web:* cabq.gov	Albuquerque	NM	87102	505-848-1320	848-1329

New York

	City	State	ZIP	Phone	Fax
African American Cultural Ctr of Buffalo Inc 350 Masten Ave *Web:* aaccbuffalo.org	Buffalo	NY	14209	716-884-2013	
Burchfield-Penney Art Ctr *Buffalo State College* 1300 Elmwood Ave *Web:* www.burchfieldpenney.org	Buffalo	NY	14222	716-878-6011	878-6003
Hallwalls Contemporary Arts Ctr 341 Delaware Ave *Web:* www.hallwalls.org	Buffalo	NY	14202	716-854-1694	854-1696
Rochester Contemporary Art Ctr 137 E Ave *Web:* www.rochestercontemporary.org	Rochester	NY	14604	585-461-2222	461-2223

North Carolina

	City	State	ZIP	Phone	Fax
Afro-American Cultural Ctr 551 S Tryon St *Web:* www.ganttcenter.org	Charlotte	NC	28202	704-547-3700	
Center for Visual Arts - Greensboro 200 N Davie St PO Box 13 *Web:* www.greensboroart.org	Greensboro	NC	27401	336-333-7475	333-7477

	City	State	Zip	Phone	Fax
Delta Fine Arts Inc 2611 New Walkertown Rd *Web:* deltaartscenter.org	Winston-Salem	NC	27101	336-722-2625	
Pack Place 2 S Pack Sq. *Web:* www.packplace.org	Asheville	NC	28801	828-257-4500	
Page-Walker Arts & History Ctr 119 Ambassador Loop *Web:* www.townofcary.org	Cary	NC	27513	919-460-4963	388-1141
Southeastern Ctr for Contemporary Art 750 Marguerite Dr *Web:* www.secca.org	Winston-Salem	NC	27106	336-725-1904	722-6059

Ohio

	City	State	Zip	Phone	Fax
City of Dayton 40 S Edwin C Moses Blvd *Web:* www.daytonohio.gov/departments/rys/pages/default.aspx	Dayton	OH	45402	937-333-2489	
Contemporary Arts Ctr 44 E Sixth St *Web:* www.contemporaryartscenter.org	Cincinnati	OH	45202	513-345-8400	
Dayton Visual Arts Ctr 118 N Jefferson St *Web:* www.daytonvisualarts.org	Dayton	OH	45402	937-224-3822	
King Arts Complex, The 867 Mt Vernon Ave *Web:* kingartscomplex.com	Columbus	OH	43203	614-645-5464	645-0672

Oklahoma

	City	State	Zip	Phone	Fax
Greenwood Cultural Ctr 322 N Greenwood Ave *Web:* www.greenwoodculturalcenter.com	Tulsa	OK	74120	918-596-1020	

Oregon

	City	State	Zip	Phone	Fax
Bush Barn Art Ctr 600 Mission St SE *Web:* www.salemart.org	Salem	OR	97302	503-581-2228	371-3342
Maude Kerns Art Ctr 1910 E 15th Ave *Web:* www.mkartcenter.org	Eugene	OR	97403	541-345-1571	345-6248
Portland Institute for Contemporary Art 415 SW 10th Ave Ste 300 *Web:* www.pica.org	Portland	OR	97205	503-242-1419	243-1167

Pennsylvania

	City	State	Zip	Phone	Fax
Painted Bride Art Ctr 230 Vine St *Web:* www.paintedbride.org	Philadelphia	PA	19106	215-925-9914	925-7402
Pittsburgh Ctr for the Arts (PCA) 6300 Fifth Ave *Web:* center.pfpca.org	Pittsburgh	PA	15232	412-361-0873	361-8338
Silver Eye Ctr for Photography 1015 E Carson St *Web:* www.silvereye.org	Pittsburgh	PA	15203	412-431-1810	431-5777

South Dakota

	City	State	Zip	Phone	Fax
Dahl Arts Ctr 713 Seventh St *Web:* www.thedahl.org	Rapid City	SD	57701	605-394-4101	394-6121
Multi-Cultural Ctr of Sioux Falls 515 N Main Ave *Web:* www.sfmcc.org	Sioux Falls	SD	57104	605-367-7401	367-7404

Tennessee

	City	State	Zip	Phone	Fax
Beck Cultural Exchange Ctr Inc 1927 Dandridge Ave *Web:* beckcenter.net	Knoxville	TN	37915	865-524-8461	524-8462

Texas

	City	State	Zip	Phone	Fax
Art Ctr of Corpus Christi 100 N Shoreline Blvd *Web:* www.artcentercc.org	Corpus Christi	TX	78401	361-884-6406	
ArtCentre of Plano, The 901 18th St *Web:* www.artcentreofplano.org	Plano	TX	75074	972-423-7809	424-0745
Bath House Cultural Ctr (BHCC) 521 E Lawther Dr *Web:* www.dallasculture.org/bathhouseculturecenter	Dallas	TX	75218	214-670-8749	670-8751
Blue Star Contemporary Arts Ctr 116 Blue Star Rd *Web:* www.bluestarart.org	San Antonio	TX	78204	210-227-6960	229-9412
Carver Community Cultural Ctr 226 N Hackberry St *Web:* www.thecarver.org	San Antonio	TX	78202	210-207-7211	
Center for Contemporary Arts, The 220 Cypress St *Web:* www.center-arts.com	Abilene	TX	79601	325-677-8389	677-1171
Dallas Ctr for Contemporary Art 161 Glass St *Web:* www.thecontemporary.net	Dallas	TX	75207	214-821-2522	821-9103
Dougherty Arts Ctr, The (DAC) 1110 Barton Springs Rd *TF:* 855-787-2227	Austin	TX	78704	512-974-4000	974-1226
Guadalupe Cultural Arts Ctr 1300 Guadalupe St *Web:* www.guadalupeculturalarts.org	San Antonio	TX	78207	210-271-3151	
Ice House Cultural Ctr 1925 Elm St Ste 500 *Web:* www.dallasculture.org	Dallas	TX	75201	214-670-3687	
La Villita Historic Arts Village 418 Villita St	San Antonio	TX	78205	210-207-8614	207-4390
Latino Cultural Ctr 2600 Live Oak St *Web:* www.dallasculture.org	Dallas	TX	75204	214-671-0045	670-0633
Louise Hopkins Underwood Ctr for the Arts (LHUCA) 511 Ave K *Web:* www.lhuca.org	Lubbock	TX	79401	806-762-8606	
McKinney Avenue Contemporary (The MAC) 3120 McKinney Ave *Web:* www.the-mac.org	Dallas	TX	75204	214-953-1212	
Nasher Sculpture Ctr 2001 Flora St *Web:* www.nashersculpturecenter.org	Dallas	TX	75201	214-242-5100	242-5155

Utah

	City	State	Zip	Phone	Fax
Eccles Community Art Ctr 2580 Jefferson Ave *Web:* www.ogden4arts.org	Ogden	UT	84401	801-392-6935	392-5295

Virginia

	City	State	Zip	Phone	Fax
Arlington Arts Ctr (AAC) 3550 Wilson Blvd *Web:* www.arlingtonartscenter.org	Arlington	VA	22201	703-248-6800	248-6849
Contemporary Art Ctr of Virginia (CAC) 2200 Parks Ave *Web:* www.cacv.org	Virginia Beach	VA	23451	757-425-0000	
Ellipse Arts Ctr 3700 S Four Mile Run Dr *Web:* www.arlingtonarts.org	Arlington	VA	22206	703-228-7710	
Peninsula Fine Arts Ctr 101 Museum Dr *Web:* www.pfac-va.org	Newport News	VA	23606	757-596-8175	

Washington

	City	State	Zip	Phone	Fax
City of Spokane 507 W Seventh Ave *Web:* my.spokanecity.org/parksrec	Spokane	WA	99204	509-625-6677	
Daybreak Star Ctr 3801 W Government Way PO Box 99100 *TF:* 800-321-4321 ■ *Web:* www.unitedindians.org	Seattle	WA	98199	206-285-4425	282-3640

West Virginia

	City	State	Zip	Phone	Fax
Artworks Around Town Gallery & Art Ctr 2200 Market St *Web:* www.artworksaroundtown.org	Wheeling	WV	26003	304-233-7540	
Monongalia Arts Ctr (MAC) 107 High St PO Box 239 *Web:* www.monartscenter.com	Morgantown	WV	26507	304-292-3325	292-3326
Oglebay Institute's Stifel Fine Arts Ctr 1330 National Rd *TF:* 800-624-6988 ■ *Web:* www.oionline.com	Wheeling	WV	26003	304-242-7700	

Wisconsin

	City	State	Zip	Phone	Fax
Irish Cultural & Heritage Ctr of Wisconsin 2133 W Wisconsin Ave *Web:* www.ichc.net	Milwaukee	WI	53233	414-345-8800	

50-3 Historic Homes & Buildings

Alabama

	City	State	Zip	Phone	Fax
Battle-Friedman House & Gardens 1010 Greensboro Ave *Web:* www.historictuscaloosa.org	Tuscaloosa	AL	35401	205-758-6138	
Conde-Charlotte Museum House 104 Theatre St	Mobile	AL	36602	251-432-4722	
Fort Gaines Historic Site 51 Bienville Blvd *Web:* www.dauphinisland.org/fort.htm	Dauphin Island	AL	36528	251-861-6992	
Old Alabama Town 301 Columbus St *TF:* 888-240-1850 ■ *Web:* www.oldalabamatown.com	Montgomery	AL	36104	334-240-4500	
Tannehill Ironworks Historical State Park 12632 Confederate Pkwy *Web:* www.tannehill.org	McCalla	AL	35111	205-477-5711	477-9400

Arizona

	City	State	Zip	Phone	Fax
Cosanti Originals Inc 6433 Doubletree Ranch Rd *TF:* 800-752-3187 ■ *Web:* www.cosanti.com	Paradise Valley	AZ	85253	480-948-6145	998-4312
Goldfield Ghost Town & Mine 4650 N Mammouth Rd *Web:* www.goldfieldghosttown.com	Goldfield	AZ	85119	480-983-0333	
Historic Heritage Square 115 N Sixth St *Web:* www.phoenix.gov	Phoenix	AZ	85004	602-261-8063	
OK Corral 326 E Allen St *Web:* www.ok-corral.com	Tombstone	AZ	85638	520-457-3456	
Wrigley Mansion 2501 E Telawa Trl *Web:* www.wrigleymansion.com	Phoenix	AZ	85016	602-955-4079	956-8439

Arkansas

	City	State	Zip	Phone	Fax
Belle Grove Historic District 623 Garrison Ave Rm 331 *Web:* www.fortsmithar.gov	Fort Smith	AR	72902	479-784-2266	784-2462
Quapaw Quarter Curran Hall 615 E Capitol Ave *Web:* www.quapaw.com	Little Rock	AR	72202	501-371-0075	

California

Phone | Fax

Camron-Stanford House 1418 Lakeside Dr .... Oakland CA 94612 510-874-7802 874-7803
Web: www.cshouse.org

Casa del Herrero 1387 E Valley Rd .... Santa Barbara CA 93108 805-565-5653 969-2371
Web: www.casadelherrero.com

Dunsmuir Hellman Historic Estate
2960 Peralta Oaks Ct .... Oakland CA 94605 510-615-5555 562-8294
Web: dunsmuir-hellman.com

Kimberly Crest House & Gardens
1325 Prospect Dr .... Redlands CA 92373 909-792-2111 798-1716
Web: www.kimberlycrest.org

Marston House Museum & Gardens
3525 Seventh Ave .... San Diego CA 92103 619-297-9327
Web: www.sohosandiego.org

Old Sacramento Business Assn Inc
980 9th St Ste 400 .... Sacramento CA 95814 916-442-8575 442-2053
Web: www.oldsacramento.com

Old Sacramento Schoolhouse 1200 Front St .... Sacramento CA 95814 916-483-8818
Web: www.scoe.net/oldsacschoolhouse

Robinson Jeffers Tor House Foundation
26304 Ocean View Ave .... Carmel CA 93923 831-624-1813 624-3696
Web: www.torhouse.org

Village Green Heritage Ctr
221 S Palm Canyon Dr .... Palm Springs CA 92262 760-323-8297 320-2561
Web: www.pshistoricalsociety.org

WebHost4Life 1440 29th Ave .... Oakland CA 94601 510-536-1703
Web: www.cohenbrayhouse.info

Winchester Mystery House
525 S Winchester Blvd .... San Jose CA 95128 408-247-2000 247-2090
Web: www.winchestermysteryhouse.com

Connecticut

Phone | Fax

Bates-Scofield Homestead 45 Old King's Hwy N .... Darien CT 06820 203-655-9233 656-3892
Web: darienhistorical.org

Bush-Holley House 39 Strickland Rd .... Cos Cob CT 06807 203-869-6899 861-9720
Web: www.hstg.org

Hoyt-Barnum House, The 713 Bedford St .... Stamford CT 06903 203-329-1183 322-1607
Web: www.stamfordhistory.org/hbh.htm

Isham-Terry House 59 S Prospect St .... Hartford CT 06106 860-247-8996
Web: www.ctlandmarks.org

Mill Hill Historic Park & Museum
2 East Wall St .... Norwalk CT 06851 203-846-0525
Web: www.norwalkhistoricalsociety.org

Ogden House & Gardens 1520 Bronson Rd .... Fairfield CT 06824 203-259-1598 255-2716
Web: www.fairfieldhistoricalsociety.org

Old State House 800 Main St .... Hartford CT 06103 860-522-6766 522-2812
Web: www.cga.ct.gov/osh

Pardee-Morris House 325 Lighthouse Rd .... New Haven CT 06512 203-562-4183 562-2002
Web: newhavenmuseum.org

Delaware

Phone | Fax

Amstel House 30 Market St .... New Castle DE 19720 302-322-2794 322-8923
Web: www.newcastlehistory.org

Greenbank Mill 500 Greenbank Rd .... Wilmington DE 19808 302-999-9001
Web: www.greenbankmill.org

John Dickinson Plantation 340 Kitts Hummock Rd .... Dover DE 19901 302-739-3277
Web: history.delaware.gov

Preservation Delaware Inc
1405 Greenhill Ave .... Wilmington DE 19806 302-651-9617 651-9603
Web: www.preservationde.org

Read House & Gardens 42 The Strand .... New Castle DE 19720 302-322-8411
Web: www.hsd.org/read.htm

District of Columbia

Phone | Fax

Dumbarton House 2715 Q St NW .... Washington DC 20007 202-337-2288 337-0348
Web: www.dumbartonhouse.org

Old Stone House 3051 M St NW .... Washington DC 20007 202-426-6851
Web: www.nps.gov

Tudor Place Historic House & Garden
1644 31st St NW .... Washington DC 20007 202-965-0400 965-0164
Web: www.tudorplace.org

Florida

Phone | Fax

Ann Norton Sculpture Gardens
253 Barcelona Rd .... West Palm Beach FL 33401 561-832-5328 835-9305
Web: www.ansg.org

Ernest Hemingway Home & Museum
907 Whitehead St .... Key West FL 33040 305-294-1136 294-2755
Web: www.hemingwayhome.com

Historic Pensacola Village
120 Church St PO Box 12866 .... Pensacola FL 32502 850-595-5985 595-5989
Web: www.historicpensacola.org

Merrick House 907 Coral Way .... Coral Gables FL 33134 305-460-5361
Web: coralgables.com

Mission San Luis Apalachee
2100 W Tennessee St .... Tallahassee FL 32304 850-245-6406 488-6186
Web: www.missionsanluis.org

Pablo Historical Park
381 Beach Blvd .... Jacksonville Beach FL 32250 904-241-5657
Web: www.beachesmuseum.org

Phone | Fax

Ponce de Leon's Fountain of Youth
11 Magnolia Ave .... Saint Augustine FL 32084 904-829-3168
TF: 800-356-8222 ■ *Web:* www.fountainofyouthflorida.com

Sugar Mill Ruins 600 Mission Rd .... New Smyrna Beach FL 32168 386-427-2284
Web: www.volusia.org

Georgia

Phone | Fax

1797 Ezekiel Harris House 560 Reynolds St .... Augusta GA 30904 706-722-8454
Web: www.augustamuseum.org/harrishouse.php

Andrew Low House, The 329 Abercorn St .... Savannah GA 31401 912-233-6854
Web: www.andrewlowhouse.com

Boyhood Home of President Woodrow Wilson
419 Seventh St .... Augusta GA 30901 706-722-9828
Web: www.wilsonboyhoodhome.org

Georgia Trust, The 1516 Peachtree St NW .... Atlanta GA 30309 404-881-9980 875-2205
Web: www.georgiatrust.org

Gordon-Lee Mansion 217 Cove Rd .... Chickamauga GA 30707 706-375-4728
Web: leeandgordonsmills.com

Hammonds House 503 Peeples St SW .... Atlanta GA 30310 404-612-0500 752-8733
Web: www.hammondshouse.org

Historic Roswell District 617 Atlanta St .... Roswell GA 30075 800-776-7935
TF: 800-776-7935 ■ *Web:* www.visitroswellga.com

Juliette Gordon Low Girl Scout National Ctr
10 E Oglethorpe Ave .... Savannah GA 31401 912-233-4501 233-4659
Web: www.juliettegordonlowbirthplace.org

Margaret Mitchell House 990 Peachtree St NE .... Atlanta GA 30309 404-249-7015
Web: atlantahistorycenter.com/mmh

Pebble Hill Plantation Hwy 319 .... Thomasville GA 31792 229-226-2344
Web: pebblehill.com

Sidney Lanier Cottage 935 High St .... Macon GA 31201 478-743-3851
Web: historicmacon.org

Smith Plantation Home 935 Alpharetta St .... Roswell GA 30075 770-641-3978 641-3974
Web: www.roswellgov.com/discover-us/southern-trilogy-historic-house-museums/smith-plantation

Stately Oaks Plantation 100 Carriage Ln .... Jonesboro GA 30236 770-473-0197 473-9855
Web: historicaljonesboro.org

Swan House
Atlanta History Ctr 130 W Paces Ferry Rd .... Atlanta GA 30305 404-814-4000
Web: www.atlantahistorycenter.com

Wheeler House 510 Gilmer Ferry Rd .... Ball Ground GA 30107 770-402-1686
Web: www.thewheelerhouse.net

Hawaii

Phone | Fax

Queen Emma Summer Palace 2913 Pali Hwy .... Honolulu HI 96817 808-595-3167 595-4395
Web: daughtersofhawaii.org

Idaho

Phone | Fax

Old Idaho Penitentiary State Historic Site
2445 Old Penitentiary Rd .... Boise ID 83712 208-334-2844 334-3225
TF: 877-653-4367 ■ *Web:* history.idaho.gov

Illinois

Phone | Fax

Dana-Thomas House (DTH) 301 E Lawrence Ave .... Springfield IL 62703 217-782-6776
Web: www.dana-thomas.org

Jane Addams Hull-House Museum
800 S Halsted St .... Chicago IL 60607 312-413-5353 413-2092
TF: 800-625-2013 ■ *Web:* www.uic.edu

John C Flanagan House 942 NE Glen Oak Ave .... Peoria IL 61603 309-674-1921

Lewis & Clark State Historic Site
1 Lewis & Clark Trl .... Hartford IL 62048 618-251-5811
Web: www.campdubois.com

Lincoln-Herndon Law Offices State Historic Site
6th & Adams .... Springfield IL 62701 217-785-7289
Web: illinois.gov/ihpa

Sears Tower 233 S Wacker Dr .... Chicago IL 60606 312-875-9447 906-8193
TF: 877-759-3325 ■ *Web:* www.theskydeck.com

Stephen Mack Home & Whitman Trading Post
2221 Freeport Rd .... Rockton IL 61072 815-624-4200
Web: www.macktownlivinghistory.com

Indiana

Phone | Fax

Morris-Butler House Museum
1204 N Pk Ave .... Indianapolis IN 46202 317-636-5409
Web: indianalandmarks.org

President Benjamin Harrison Home
1230 N Delaware St .... Indianapolis IN 46202 317-631-1888 632-5488
Web: www.presidentbenjaminharrison.org

Swinney Homestead 1424 W Jefferson Blvd .... Fort Wayne IN 46802 260-424-7212
Web: www.settlersinc.org

Iowa

Phone | Fax

Brucemore 2160 Linden Dr SE .... Cedar Rapids IA 52403 319-362-7375
Web: www.brucemore.org

Mathias Ham House Historic Site
2241 Lincoln Ave .... Dubuque IA 52001 563-557-9545
TF: 800-226-3369 ■
Web: www.mississippirivermuseum.com/features_historicsites_ham.cfm

Seminole Valley Farm
1400 Seminole Vly Rd NE .... Cedar Rapids IA 52411 319-378-9240
Web: seminolevalleyfarmmuseum.net

	City	State	ZIP	Phone	Fax
Sherman Hill National Historic District 1620 Pleasant Ste 204 *Web:* www.historicshermanhill.com	Des Moines	IA	50314	515-284-5717	
Wallace House 756 16th St. *Web:* www.wallace.org	Des Moines	IA	50314	515-243-7063	243-8927

Kentucky

	City	State	ZIP	Phone	Fax
Ashland-The Henry Clay Estate 120 Sycamore Rd *TF:* 800-735-5251 ■ *Web:* www.henryclay.org	Lexington	KY	40502	859-266-8581	
Berry Hill Mansion 700 Louisville Rd.	Frankfort	KY	40601	502-564-3000	564-6505
Brennan House Historic Home 631 S Fifth St *Web:* www.thebrennanhouse.org	Louisville	KY	40202	502-540-5145	540-5165
Hunt-Morgan House (BGT) 201 N Mill St *Web:* www.bluegrasstrust.org/huntmorgantours.html	Lexington	KY	40507	859-253-0362	259-9210
Liberty Hall Historic Site 202 Wilkinson St *Web:* www.libertyhall.org	Frankfort	KY	40601	502-227-2560	
Locust Grove Historic Home 561 Blankenbaker Ln *Web:* www.locustgrove.org	Louisville	KY	40207	502-897-9845	897-0103
Loudoun House 209 Castlewood Dr. **Fax Area Code: 209* ■ *TF:* 866-945-7920 ■ *Web:* nps.gov	Lexington	KY	40505	859-254-7024	372-0739*
Mary Todd Lincoln House 578 W Main St. *Web:* www.mtlhouse.org	Lexington	KY	40507	859-233-9999	
Old Louisville Historic Preservation District 1340 S Fourth St *Web:* www.oldlouisville.com	Louisville	KY	40208	502-635-5244	635-5245
Riverside Farnsley-Moremen Landing 7410 Moorman Rd *Web:* riverside-landing.org	Louisville	KY	40272	502-935-6809	935-6821

Louisiana

	City	State	ZIP	Phone	Fax
Beauregard-Keyes House 1113 Chartres St *Web:* bkhouse.org	New Orleans	LA	70116	504-523-7257	523-7257
Destrehan Plantation 13034 River Rd. *Web:* www.destrehanplantation.org	Destrehan	LA	70047	985-764-9315	725-1929
Elms Mansion & Gardens 3029 St Charles Ave *Web:* www.elmsmansion.com	New Orleans	LA	70115	504-895-9200	
Greenwood Plantation 6838 Highland Rd. *TF:* 800-259-4475 ■ *Web:* www.greenwoodplantation.com	Saint Francisville	LA	70775	225-655-4475	655-3292
Houmas House Plantation & Gardens 40136 Hwy 942 *TF:* 800-979-3370 ■ *Web:* www.houmashouse.com	Darrow	LA	70725	225-473-7841	473-7891
Rosedown Plantation State Historic Site 12501 Hwy 10 *TF:* 888-376-1867 ■ *Web:* crt.state.la.us	Saint Francisville	LA	70775	225-635-3332	784-1382

Maine

	City	State	ZIP	Phone	Fax
Isaac Farrar Mansion 17 Second St *Web:* bangory.org	Bangor	ME	04401	207-941-2808	941-2812
Portland Head Light 1000 Shore Rd *Web:* www.portlandheadlight.com	Cape Elizabeth	ME	04107	207-799-2661	799-2800
Victoria Mansion 109 Danforth St *Web:* www.victoriamansion.org	Portland	ME	04101	207-772-4841	772-6290
Wadsworth-Longfellow House 489 Congress St *Web:* www.mainehistory.org/house_overview.shtml	Portland	ME	04101	207-774-1822	775-4301

Maryland

	City	State	ZIP	Phone	Fax
Barracks, The 43 Pinkney St. *Web:* www.annapolis.org	Annapolis	MD	21401	410-267-7619	
Chase-Lloyd House 22 Maryland Ave.	Annapolis	MD	21401	410-263-2723	
Historic Annapolis Foundation 18 Pinkney St *Web:* www.annapolis.org	Annapolis	MD	21401	410-267-7619	
Waterfront Warehouse 4 Pinkney St. *Web:* www.annapolis.org	Annapolis	MD	21401	410-267-7619	

Massachusetts

	City	State	ZIP	Phone	Fax
Captain Bangs Hallett House 11 Strawberry Ln PO Box 11 *Web:* www.hsoy.org	Yarmouth Port	MA	02675	508-362-3021	
Freedom Trail 99 Chauncy St Ste 401 *Web:* www.thefreedomtrail.org	Boston	MA	02111	617-357-8300	357-8303
Grange Hall 1067 State Rd *Web:* www.mvpreservation.org	Vineyard Haven	MA	02568	508-627-4440	627-8088
Hadwen House 96 Main St *Web:* www.nha.org	Nantucket	MA	02554	508-228-1894	228-5618
House of the Seven Gables 115 Derby St. *Web:* www.7gables.org	Salem	MA	01970	978-744-0991	741-4350
Hoxie House 18 Water St	Sandwich	MA	02563	508-888-1173	
Salisbury Mansion 40 Highland St. *Web:* www.worcesterhistory.org	Worcester	MA	01609	508-753-8278	753-9070
Wistariahurst Museum 238 Cabot St *Web:* www.wistariahurst.org	Holyoke	MA	01040	413-322-5660	534-2344

Michigan

	City	State	ZIP	Phone	Fax
Applewood the CS Mott Estate 1400 E Kearsley St *Web:* www.ruthmottfoundation.org	Flint	MI	48503	810-233-0170	233-7022
Edsel & Eleanor Ford House 1100 Lk Shore Rd. *Web:* www.fordhouse.org	Grosse Pointe Shores	MI	48236	313-884-4222	884-5977
Heritage Hill Historic District 126 College Ave SE *Web:* www.heritagehillweb.org	Grand Rapids	MI	49503	616-459-8950	459-2409
Meyer May House 450 Madison Ave SE. *Web:* meyermayhouse.steelcase.com	Grand Rapids	MI	49503	616-246-4821	
Turner-Dodge House & Heritage Ctr 100 E N St.	Lansing	MI	48906	517-483-4220	483-6081

Minnesota

	City	State	ZIP	Phone	Fax
Alexander Ramsey House (ARH) 265 S Exchange St *Web:* mnhs.org/visit	Saint Paul	MN	55102	651-296-8760	
Comstock Historic House 506 Eigth St S *Web:* mnhs.org/visit	Moorhead	MN	56560	218-291-4211	
Glensheen Mansion 3300 London Rd *TF:* 888-454-4536 ■ *Web:* www.d.umn.edu	Duluth	MN	55804	218-726-8910	726-8911
Historic Fort Snelling 200 Tower Ave Ft Snelling History Ctr *Web:* mnhs.org/visit	Saint Paul	MN	55111	612-726-1171	
History Ctr of Olmsted County 1195 W Cir Dr SW *Web:* olmstedhistory.com	Rochester	MN	55902	507-282-9447	289-5481
James J Hill House 240 Summit Ave *TF:* 888-727-8386 ■ *Web:* www.mnhs.org	Saint Paul	MN	55102	651-297-2555	
Plummer House 1091 SW Plummer Ln. *Web:* rochestermn.com	Rochester	MN	55902	507-328-2525	

Missouri

	City	State	ZIP	Phone	Fax
1859 Jail Marshal's Home & Museum 217 N Main St *Web:* www.jchs.org/jail/museum.html	Independence	MO	64050	816-252-1892	
Frank Lloyd Wright House in Ebbsworth Park 120 N Ballas Rd *Web:* www.ebsworthpark.org	Kirkwood	MO	63122	314-822-8359	
General Daniel Bissell House 10225 Bellefontaine Rd. *Web:* stlouisco.com	Saint Louis	MO	63137	314-544-5714	
Hanley House 7600 Westmoreland St *Web:* hanleyhouse.blogspot.com	Clayton	MO	63105	314-862-1247	290-8517
Harris-Kearney House 4000 Baltimore St *Web:* www.westporthistorical.com	Kansas City	MO	64111	816-561-1821	
Hawken House, The 1155 S Rock Hill Rd *Web:* thehotelnexus.com	Saint Louis	MO	63119	314-968-1857	
Historic Samuel Cupples House 3673 W Pine Mall *Web:* www.slu.edu	Saint Louis	MO	63108	314-977-3575	
Oakland House 7801 Genesta St *Web:* www.afftonoaklandhouse.com	Saint Louis	MO	63123	314-352-5654	
Vaile Mansion 1500 N Liberty St. *Web:* www.vailemansion.org	Independence	MO	64050	816-325-7430	

Montana

	City	State	ZIP	Phone	Fax
Moss Mansion 914 Div St *Web:* www.mossmansion.com	Billings	MT	59101	406-256-5100	

Nebraska

	City	State	ZIP	Phone	Fax
General Crook House Museum 5730 N 30th St Ste 11B	Omaha	NE	68111	402-455-9990	453-9448
Joslyn Castle 3902 Davenport St. *Web:* www.joslyncastle.com	Omaha	NE	68131	402-595-2199	
Thomas P Kennard House PO Box 82554 *Web:* www.nebraskahistory.org	Lincoln	NE	68501	402-471-4764	

New Hampshire

	City	State	ZIP	Phone	Fax
Kimball-Jenkins Estate 266 N Main St. *Web:* www.kimballjenkins.com	Concord	NH	03301	603-225-3932	225-9288

New Jersey

	City	State	ZIP	Phone	Fax
Absecon Lighthouse 31 S Rhode Island Ave *Web:* www.abseconlighthouse.org	Atlantic City	NJ	08401	609-449-1360	449-1919
Ballantine House 49 Washington St. *Web:* www.newarkmuseum.org	Newark	NJ	07102	973-596-6550	642-0459
Batsto Historic Village 31 Batsto Rd. *Web:* www.batstovillage.org	Hammonton	NJ	08037	609-561-0024	567-8116
Dey Mansion 199 Totowa Rd	Wayne	NJ	07470	973-696-1776	696-1365
Durand Hedden House & Garden Assn 523 Ridgewood Rd *Web:* durandhedden.org	Maplewood	NJ	07040	973-763-7712	

				Phone	Fax
Wayne Van Riper Hopper Museum 533 Berdan Ave	Wayne	NJ	07470	973-694-7192	
Web: waynetownship.com					
William Trent House 15 Market St	Trenton	NJ	08611	609-989-3027	
Web: www.williamtrenthouse.org					

New Mexico

				Phone	Fax
Coronado State Monument 485 Kuaua Rd	Bernalillo	NM	87004	505-867-5351	867-1733
Web: www.nmmonuments.org					
Taos Pueblo PO Box 1846	Taos	NM	87571	575-758-1028	758-4604*
**Fax Area Code: 505* ■ *Web:* www.taospueblo.com					

New York

				Phone	Fax
Camillus Octagon House 5420 W Genesee St	Camillus	NY	13031	315-488-7800	
Web: octagonhouseofcamillus.org					
Frank Lloyd Wright's Martin House Complex 125 Jewett Pkwy	Buffalo	NY	14214	716-856-3858	856-4009
TF: 877-377-3858 ■ *Web:* www.darwinmartinhouse.org					
Friend's of Pruyn House 207 Old Niskayuna Rd PO Box 1254	Latham	NY	12110	518-783-1435	783-1437
Web: www.pruynhouse.org					
George Eastman House & Gardens 900 E Ave	Rochester	NY	14607	585-271-3361	271-3970
Web: www.eastman.org					
Glenview Mansion 511 Warburton Ave Hudson River Museum	Yonkers	NY	10701	914-963-4550	
Web: www.hrm.org					
Gracie Mansion 88th St & E End Ave	New York	NY	10128	212-570-4751	
Web: www.nyc.gov/html/om/html/gracie.html					
High Falls Museum 60 Browns Race	Rochester	NY	14614	585-325-2030	
Web: www.cityofrochester.gov/highfallsmuseum					
Lyndhurst 635 S Broadway	Tarrytown	NY	10591	914-631-4481	
Web: www.lyndhurst.org					
Sleepy Hollow Cemetery 540 N Broadway	Sleepy Hollow	NY	10591	914-631-0081	
Web: www.sleepyhollowcemetery.org					
Washington Irving's Sunnyside W Sunnyside Ln	Tarrytown	NY	10591	914-591-8763	
Web: www.hudsonvalley.org					
Washington's Heaquarters/Miller House 140 Virginia Rd	White Plains	NY	10603	914-949-1236	
Web: westchestergov.com					

North Carolina

				Phone	Fax
Cashier's House 1940 Hwy 107 S	Cashiers	NC	28717	828-743-7710	454-6890*
**Fax Area Code: 814*					
Castle McCulloch 3925 Kivett Dr	Jamestown	NC	27282	336-887-5413	
Web: www.castlemcculloch.com					
Haywood Hall House & Gardens 211 New Bern Pl	Raleigh	NC	27601	919-832-8357	
Web: haywoodhall.org					
Historic Latta Plantation 5225 Sample Rd	Huntersville	NC	28078	704-875-2312	875-1724
Web: www.lattaplantation.org					
James K Polk Memorial State Historic Site 12031 Lancaster Hwy PO Box 475	Pineville	NC	28134	704-889-7145	889-3057
Web: www.nchistoricsites.org					
Mendenhall Plantation 603 W Main St PO Box 512	Jamestown	NC	27282	336-454-3819	
Web: www.mendenhallhomeplace.com					
Mordecai Historic Park 1 Mimosa St	Raleigh	NC	27604	919-857-4364	
Web: www.raleighnc.gov/mordecai					
Reed Gold Mine State Historic Site 9621 Reed Mine Rd	Midland	NC	28107	704-721-4653	721-4657
TF: 877-628-6386 ■ *Web:* www.nchistoricsites.org					
Tannenbaum Historic Park 2200 New Garden Rd	Greensboro	NC	27410	336-545-5315	
Web: www.greensboro-nc.gov					
Thomas Wolfe Memorial 52 N Market St	Asheville	NC	28801	828-253-8304	
Web: www.wolfememorial.com					
Vance Birthplace State Historic Site 911 Reems Creek Rd	Weaverville	NC	28787	828-645-6706	645-0936
TF: 800-767-1560 ■ *Web:* www.nchistoricsites.org/vance/vance.htm					

Ohio

				Phone	Fax
Fort Meigs State Memorial 29100 W River Rd	Perrysburg	OH	43551	419-874-4121	874-9446
TF: 800-283-8916 ■ *Web:* www.fortmeigs.org					
German Village 588 S Third St	Columbus	OH	43215	614-221-8888	222-4747
Web: germanvillage.com					
Loghurst Western Reserve 3967 BoaRdman-Canfield Rd	Canfield	OH	44406	330-533-4330	
Paul Laurence Dunbar House 219 N Paul Laurence Dunbar St	Dayton	OH	45402	937-224-7061	
TF: 800-860-0148 ■ *Web:* ohiohistory.org					
Perkins Stone Mansion 550 Copley Rd	Akron	OH	44320	330-535-1120	535-0250
Web: summithistory.org					
SunWatch Indian Village/Archaeological Park 2301 W River Rd	Dayton	OH	45417	937-268-8199	
Web: www.sunwatch.org					

Oregon

				Phone	Fax
Brunk House 5705 Salem-Dallas Hwy NW	Salem	OR	97304	503-371-8586	
Deepwood Museum & Gardens 1116 Mission St SE	Salem	OR	97302	503-363-1825	
Web: oregonlink.com/sorry_notfound.html					
Mission Mill Museum 1313 Mill St SE	Salem	OR	97301	503-585-7012	
Web: willametteheritage.org					
Shelton-McMurphey-Johnson House 303 Willamette St	Eugene	OR	97401	541-484-0808	
Web: www.smjhouse.org					

Pennsylvania

				Phone	Fax
Besty Ross House 239 Arch St	Philadelphia	PA	19106	215-686-1252	
Web: historicphiladelphia.org					
Carpenters' Hall 320 Chestnut St	Philadelphia	PA	19106	215-925-0167	
Web: www.ushistory.org/carpentershall					
Declaration House 599 S 7th St	Philadelphia	PA	19106	215-965-7676	
Web: www.nps.gov					
Eastern State Penitentiary Historic Site 22nd St & Fairmount Ave	Philadelphia	PA	19130	215-236-3300	236-5289
Web: www.easternstate.org					
Fallingwater 1491 Mill Run Rd	Mill Run	PA	15464	724-329-8501	329-0553
Web: waterlandlife.org					
Fort Hunter Mansion & Park 5300 N Front St	Harrisburg	PA	17110	717-599-5751	599-5838
Web: www.forthunter.org					
Glen Foerd on the Delaware 5001 Grant Ave	Philadelphia	PA	19114	215-632-5330	
Web: www.glenfoerd.org					
Hans Herr House & Museum 1849 Hans Herr Dr	Willow Street	PA	17584	717-464-4438	
Web: www.hansherr.org					
Hartwood Mansion 200 Hartwood Acres	Pittsburgh	PA	15238	412-767-9200	
Web: alleghenycounty.us					
Historic Rock Ford Plantation 881 Rockford Rd	Lancaster	PA	17602	717-392-7223	
TF: 800-732-0999 ■ *Web:* www.rockfordplantation.org					
Independence Hall & Congress Hall Chestnut St-between Fifth & Sixth Sts	Philadelphia	PA	19106	215-597-8787	597-8976
Web: www.nps.gov/inde					
John Chadds House 1736 N Creek Rd PO Box 27	Chadds Ford	PA	19317	610-388-7376	388-7480
Web: www.chaddsfordhistory.org					
John Harris-Simon Cameron Mansion, The 219 S Front St	Harrisburg	PA	17104	717-233-3462	233-6059
Web: www.dauphincountyhistory.org					
Lancaster County's Historical Society & President James Buchanan's Wheatland 230 N President Ave	Lancaster	PA	17603	717-392-4633	293-2739
Web: www.lancasterhistory.org					
Physick House 321 S Fourth St	Philadelphia	PA	19106	215-925-2251	
Web: www.philalandmarks.org					
Powel House 244 S Third St	Philadelphia	PA	19106	215-627-0364	
TF: 877-426-8056 ■ *Web:* www.philalandmarks.org					

Rhode Island

				Phone	Fax
Belcourt Castle 657 Bellevue Ave	Newport	RI	02840	401-846-0669	846-5345
Web: www.belcourtcastle.com					
Chateau-Sur-Mer 474 Bellevue Ave	Newport	RI	02840	401-847-1000	847-1361
Web: www.newportmansions.org					
Edward King House 35 King St	Newport	RI	02840	401-846-7426	846-8310
Web: www.edwardkinghouse.org					
Hunter House 54 Washington St	Newport	RI	02840	401-847-1000	847-1361
Web: www.newportmansions.org					
John Brown House Museum 52 Power St	Providence	RI	02906	401-273-7507	
Web: www.rihs.org					
Marble House 596 Bellevue Ave	Newport	RI	02840	401-847-1000	847-1361
Web: www.newportmansions.org					
Rose Island Lighthouse Foundation 365 Thames St Second Fl PO Box 1419	Newport	RI	02840	401-847-4242	847-7262
Web: www.roseislandlighthouse.org					
Samuel Whitehorne House 416 Thames St	Newport	RI	02840	401-849-7300	
Web: www.newportrestoration.org					

South Carolina

				Phone	Fax
Aiken-Rhett House 48 Elizabeth St	Charleston	SC	29401	843-723-1159	
Web: www.historiccharleston.org					
Boone Hall Plantation & Gardens 1235 Long Pt Rd	Mount Pleasant	SC	29464	843-884-4371	884-0475
Web: boonehallplantation.com					
Fort Hill The John C Calhoun House Clemson University Ft Hill St	Clemson	SC	29634	864-656-2475	
Web: clemson.edu					
Gassaway Mansion 106 Dupont Dr	Greenville	SC	29607	864-271-0188	242-9935
TF: 888-912-7469 ■ *Web:* www.gassawaymansion.com					
Hampton-Preston Mansion & Garden 1615 Blanding St	Columbia	SC	29201	803-252-1770	929-7695
Web: www.historiccolumbia.org					
Heyward-Washington House 87 Church St	Charleston	SC	29403	843-722-0354	
Web: charlestonmuseum.org					
Kilgore-Lewis House, The 560 N Academy St	Greenville	SC	29601	864-232-3020	
Web: www.kilgore-lewis.org					
Mann Simons Cottage 1403 Richland St	Columbia	SC	29201	803-252-7742	929-7695
Web: www.historiccolumbia.org					
Nathaniel Russell House 51 Meeting St	Charleston	SC	29401	843-724-8481	
Web: www.historiccharleston.org					
Old Exchange & Provost Dungeon 122 E Bay St	Charleston	SC	29401	843-727-2165	
TF: 888-763-0448 ■ *Web:* oldexchange.org					
Robert Mills House & Gardens 1616 Blanding St	Columbia	SC	29201	803-252-7742	929-7695
Web: www.historiccolumbia.org					

				Phone	Fax
Seibels House & Garden 1616 Blanding St *Web:* www.historiccolumbia.org	Columbia	SC	29201	803-252-1770	929-7695
Woodrow Wilson Family Home 1705 Hampton St *Web:* www.historiccolumbia.org	Columbia	SC	29201	803-252-7742	

South Dakota

				Phone	Fax
Corn Palace 604 N Main St *TF:* 800-289-7469 ■ *Web:* www.cornpalace.org	Mitchell	SD	57301	605-995-8430	

Tennessee

				Phone	Fax
Belmont Mansion 1900 Belmont Blvd *Web:* www.belmontmansion.com	Nashville	TN	37212	615-460-5459	460-5688
Blount Mansion 200 W Hill Ave *Web:* www.blountmansion.org	Knoxville	TN	37901	865-525-2375	546-5315
Confederate Memorial Hall 3148 Kingston Pk *Web:* www.knoxvillecmh.org	Knoxville	TN	37919	865-522-2371	
Davies Manor House 9336 Davies Plantation Rd *Web:* www.daviesmanorplantation.org	Memphis	TN	38133	901-386-0715	388-4677
Ramsey House 2614 Thorngrove Pk *Web:* www.ramseyhouse.org	Knoxville	TN	37914	865-546-0745	546-1851
Tipton-Haynes State Historic Site 2620 S Roan St *Web:* www.tipton-haynes.org	Johnson City	TN	37601	423-926-3631	
Travellers Rest Plantation & Museum 636 Farrell Pkwy *Web:* www.travellersrestplantation.org	Nashville	TN	37220	615-832-8197	832-8169
Woodruff-Fontaine House 680 Adams Ave *Web:* www.woodruff-fontaine.org	Memphis	TN	38105	901-526-1469	755-6075

Texas

				Phone	Fax
Guenther House 205 E Guenther St *TF:* 800-235-8186 ■ *Web:* www.guentherhouse.com	San Antonio	TX	78204	210-227-1061	
King William Historic District 122 Madison St *Web:* kwfair.org	San Antonio	TX	78204	210-271-3247	
Neill-Cochran House Museum 2310 San Gabriel St *Web:* www.nchmuseum.org	Austin	TX	78705	512-478-2335	
Sidbury House 1609 N Chaparral St	Corpus Christi	TX	78401	361-883-9352	

Utah

				Phone	Fax
This is the Place Heritage Park 2601 E Sunnyside Ave *Web:* www.thisistheplace.org	Salt Lake City	UT	84108	801-582-1847	583-1869

Vermont

				Phone	Fax
Ethan Allen Homestead 1 Ethan Allen Homestead *Web:* www.ethanallenhomestead.org	Burlington	VT	05408	802-865-4556	

Virginia

				Phone	Fax
Adam Thoroughgood House 1636 Parish Rd	Virginia Beach	VA	23455	757-385-5100	460-7644
Athenaeum, The 201 Prince St *Web:* www.nvfaa.org	Alexandria	VA	22314	703-548-0035	
Francis Land House 3131 Virginia Beach Blvd *Web:* museumsvb.org	Virginia Beach	VA	23452	757-385-5100	
Frank Lloyd Wright's Pope-Leighey House 9000 Richmond Hwy *Web:* www.woodlawnpopeleighey.org	Alexandria	VA	22309	703-780-4000	
George Washington's Mount Vernon Estate & Gardens George Washington Memorial Pkwy PO Box 110 *Web:* www.mountvernon.org	Mount Vernon	VA	22121	703-780-2000	
James Madison's Montpelier 11407 Constitution Hwy *Web:* www.montpelier.org	Montpelier Station	VA	22957	540-672-2728	672-0411
John Marshall House, The 818 E Marshall St *Web:* preservationvirginia.org	Richmond	VA	23219	804-648-7998	648-5880
Lynnhaven House 2040 Potters Rd *Web:* www.virginiabeachhistory.org	Virginia Beach	VA	23454	757-491-3490	
Monticello 931 Thomas Jefferson Pkwy PO Box 316 *TF:* 800-243-1743 ■ *Web:* www.monticello.org	Charlottesville	VA	22902	434-984-9822	977-7757
Old Cape Henry Lighthouse 583 Atlantic Ave	Fort Story	VA	23459	757-422-9421	
Pope-Leighey House 9000 Richmond Hwy *Web:* www.popeleighey1940.org	Alexandria	VA	22309	703-780-4000	
Shirley Plantation 501 Shirley Plantation Rd *Web:* www.shirleyplantation.com	Charles City	VA	23030	804-829-5121	
Sully Historic Site 3650 Historic Sully Way *Web:* www.fairfaxcounty.gov/parks/sully	Chantilly	VA	20151	703-437-1794	787-3314
Virginia House 4301 Sulgrave Rd *Web:* www.vahistorical.org	Richmond	VA	23221	804-353-4251	355-2399
Willoughby-Baylor House 601 E Freemason St *Web:* www.chrysler.org/about-the-museum/historic-houses/willoughby-baylor-house	Norfolk	VA	23510	757-333-1087	

Washington

				Phone	Fax
Covington House 4201 Main St *Web:* www.clark.wa.gov/community-planning/covington-house	Vancouver	WA	98663	360-695-6750	

West Virginia

				Phone	Fax
Pearl S Buck Birthplace US 219 PO Box 126 *Web:* www.pearlsbuckbirthplace.com	Hillsboro	WV	24946	304-653-4430	
TH Eckhart House 810 Main St *Web:* www.eckharthouse.com	Wheeling	WV	26003	304-232-5439	

Wisconsin

				Phone	Fax
Pabst Mansion 2000 W Wisconsin Ave *Web:* www.pabstmansion.com	Milwaukee	WI	53233	414-931-0808	
Taliesin 5607 County Hwy C *TF:* 877-588-7900 ■ *Web:* www.taliesinpreservation.org	Spring Green	WI	53588	608-588-7090	588-7514

50-4 Monuments, Memorials, Landmarks

				Phone	Fax
African-American Civil War Memorial & Museum 1200 U St NW *Web:* www.afroamcivilwar.org	Washington	DC	20001	202-667-2667	667-6771
Arkansas Post National Memorial 1741 Old Post Rd *Web:* www.nps.gov	Gillett	AR	72055	870-548-2207	548-2431
Buffalo & Erie County Naval & Military Park 1 Naval Pk Cove *Web:* www.buffalonavalpark.org	Buffalo	NY	14202	716-847-1773	
Bunker Hill Monument Monument Sq *Web:* www.nps.gov	Charlestown	MA	02129	617-242-5641	242-6006
Chamizal National Memorial 800 S San Marcial St *TF:* 877-642-4743 ■ *Web:* www.nps.gov	El Paso	TX	79905	915-532-7273	532-7240
Crazy Horse Memorial Ave of the Chiefs *Web:* www.crazyhorsememorial.org	Crazy Horse	SD	57730	605-673-4681	673-2185
De Soto National Memorial 8300 Desoto Memorial Hwy *TF:* 888-831-7526 ■ *Web:* www.nps.gov	Bradenton	FL	34209	941-792-0458	792-5094
Empire State Bldg 350 Fifth Ave Ste 100 *TF:* 877-692-8439 ■ *Web:* www.esbnyc.com	New York	NY	10118	212-736-3100	
First Church of Christ in New Haven, The *Center Church on-the-Green* 311 Temple St *Web:* www.newhavencenterchurch.org	New Haven	CT	06511	203-787-0121	787-2187
Flight 93 National Memorial *National Park Service* PO Box 911 *Web:* www.nps.gov/flni/index.htm	Shanksville	PA	15560	814-893-6322	443-2180
Fort Caroline National Memorial 12713 Ft Caroline Rd *Web:* www.nps.gov/foca	Jacksonville	FL	32225	904-641-7155	641-3798
Franklin Delano Roosevelt Memorial 900 Ohio Dr SW *Web:* www.nps.gov/fdrm	Washington	DC	20024	202-426-6841	
Gateway Arch 50 S Leonor K Sullivan Blvd *TF:* 877-982-1410 ■ *Web:* www.gatewayarch.com	Saint Louis	MO	63102	877-982-1410	
General Grant National Memorial Riverside Dr & W 122nd St *Web:* www.nps.gov/gegr	New York	NY	10027	212-666-1640	932-9631
George Washington Masonic National Memorial 101 Callahan Dr *TF:* 800-435-7352 ■ *Web:* www.gwmemorial.org	Alexandria	VA	22301	703-683-2007	519-9270
Golden Gate Bridge Golden Gate Bridge Toll Plz Presidio Stn PO Box 9000 *TF:* 877-229-8655 ■ *Web:* www.goldengate.org	San Francisco	CA	94129	415-921-5858	956-1663
Holocaust Memorial of the Greater Miami Jewish Federation 1933-1945 Meridian Ave *Web:* www.holocaustmmb.org	Miami Beach	FL	33139	305-538-1663	
Idaho Human Rights Education Ctr 777 S Eigth St *Web:* www.wassmuthcenter.org	Boise	ID	83702	208-345-0304	
Illinois Vietnam Veterans Memorial Oak Ridge Cemetery *Web:* www.illinois.gov	Springfield	IL	62702	217-782-2717	
Jefferson Memorial 701 E Basin Dr SW **Fax Area Code:* 912 ■ *Web:* www.nps.gov/thje	Washington	DC	20242	202-426-6841	673-7747*
Kansas City Kansas Convention & Visitors Bureau 755 Minnesota Ave *Web:* visitkansascityks.com	Kansas City	KS	66101	913-321-5800	
Korean War Veterans Memorial c/o National Capital Parks - Central 900 Ohio Dr SW *Web:* www.nps.gov/kowa	Washington	DC	20004	202-426-6841	
Liberty Bell Ctr 6th & Market Sts *Web:* www.nps.gov	Philadelphia	PA	19106	215-965-2305	861-4950
Lincoln Boyhood National Memorial 2916 E S St PO Box 1816 *Web:* www.nps.gov/libo	Lincoln City	IN	47552	812-937-4541	937-9929
Lincoln Memorial Shrine 125 W Vine St *Web:* www.lincolnshrine.org	Redlands	CA	92373	909-798-7632	
Lincoln Tomb Oak Ridge Cemetery 1500 Monument Ave *Web:* illinois.gov/ihpa	Springfield	IL	62702	217-782-2717	
Littleton Coin Company LLC 1309 Mt Eustis Rd *TF:* 800-645-3122 ■ *Web:* www.littletoncoin.com	Littleton	NH	03561	603-444-5386	444-0121

				Phone	Fax
Lyndon Baines Johnson Memorial Grove on the Potomac Turkey Run Pk George Washington Memorial Pkwy *Web:* www.nps.gov/lyba	McLean	VA	22101	703-289-2500	289-2598
Mason-Dixon Historical Park 79 Buckeye Rd	Core	WV	26541	304-879-4101	
Mormon Battalion Visitors Ctr 2510 Juan St *Web:* lds.org	San Diego	CA	92110	619-298-3317	
Mormon Trail Ctr at Historic Winter Quarter 3215 State St *Web:* lds.org	Omaha	NE	68112	402-453-9372	
New Mexico Veterans Memorial 1100 Louisiana Blvd SE *Web:* nmvetsmemorial.org	Albuquerque	NM	87108	505-256-2042	
Perry's Victory & International Peace Memorial 93 Delaware Ave PO Box 549 *Web:* www.nps.gov/pevi	Put-in-Bay	OH	43456	419-285-2184	285-2516
Philadelphia Vietnam Veterans Memorial 4720 Mercer St *Web:* pvvms646.org	Philadelphia	PA	19137	215-535-0643	
Pilgrim Monument & Provincetown Museum 1 High Pole Hill Rd *Web:* www.pilgrim-monument.org	Provincetown	MA	02657	508-487-1310	
Potomac Assn, The 540 Water St Jack London Sq *Web:* www.usspotomac.org	Oakland	CA	94607	510-627-1215	839-4729
Roger Williams National Memorial 282 N Main St *Web:* www.nps.gov/rowi	Providence	RI	02903	401-521-7266	521-7239
Rosedale Memorial Arch 1403 Southwest Blvd	Kansas City	KS	66103	913-677-5097	
Space Needle LLC 203 Sixth Ave N *TF:* 800-937-9582 ■ *Web:* www.spaceneedle.com	Seattle	WA	98109	206-905-2200	
Statue of Liberty National Monument & Ellis Island Liberty Island *Web:* www.nps.gov/stli	New York	NY	10004	212-363-3200	
Texas State Cemetery 909 Navasota St *TF:* 877-673-6839 ■ *Web:* www.cemetery.state.tx.us	Austin	TX	78702	512-463-0605	463-8811
Theodore Roosevelt Island Park c/o Turkey Run Pk George Washington Memorial Pkwy *Web:* www.nps.gov/this	McLean	VA	22101	703-289-2500	289-2598
Trenton Battle Monument 348 N Warren St *Web:* www.njparksandforests.org	Trenton	NJ	08625	609-737-0623	
US Navy Memorial & Naval Heritage Ctr 701 Pennsylvania Ave NW Ste 123 *Web:* www.navylog.org	Washington	DC	20004	202-737-2300	
USS Alabama Battleship Memorial Park 2703 Battleship Pkwy PO Box 65 *TF:* 888-414-4448 ■ *Web:* www.ussalabama.com	Mobile	AL	36602	251-433-2703	
USS Arizona Memorial 1 Arizona Memorial Pl *Web:* www.nps.gov/usar	Honolulu	HI	96818	808-422-0561	483-8608
USS Kidd Veterans Memorial & Museum 305 S River Rd *TF:* 800-638-0594 ■ *Web:* www.usskidd.com	Baton Rouge	LA	70802	225-342-1942	342-2039
USS Missouri Memorial Assn Inc 63 Cowpens St *TF:* 877-644-4896 ■ *Web:* ussmissouri.org	Honolulu	HI	96818	808-455-1600	455-1598
Vietnam Veterans of America 3027 Walnut St *Web:* vva.org	Kansas City	MO	64108	816-561-8387	
Vietnam Women's Memorial Foundation Inc 1735 Connecticut Ave NW 3rd Fl *TF:* 866-822-8963 ■ *Web:* www.vietnamwomensmemorial.org	Washington	DC	20009	866-822-8963	

50-5 Nature Centers, Parks, Other Natural Areas

				Phone	Fax
Anita Purves Nature Ctr 1505 N Broadway *Web:* www.urbanaparks.org	Urbana	IL	61801	217-384-4062	384-1052
Anne Kolb Nature Ctr 751 Sheridan St *Web:* www.floridanaturepictures.com/dadebrow/annkolb/ann.htm	Hollywood	FL	33019	954-357-5161	
Ansonia Nature & Recreation Ctr 10 Deerfield Ln *Web:* www.ansonianaturecenter.org	Ansonia	CT	06401	203-736-1053	
Aurora Reservoir 5800 S Powhaton Rd *Web:* www.auroragov.org	Aurora	CO	80016	303-690-1286	
Balboa Park 1549 El Prado Ste 1 *Web:* www.balboapark.org	San Diego	CA	92101	619-239-0512	
Bear Creek Nature Ctr 245 Bear Creek Rd *Web:* adm.elpasoco.com/parks	Colorado Springs	CO	80906	719-520-6387	636-8968
Beaver Lake Nature Ctr 8477 E Mud Lk Rd *Web:* www.onondagacountyparks.com	Baldwinsville	NY	13027	315-638-2519	638-7488
Biscayne Nature Ctr 6767 Crandon Blvd *Web:* www.biscaynenaturecenter.org	Key Biscayne	FL	33149	305-361-6767	365-8434
Black Hills Caverns 2600 Cavern Rd *TF:* 800-837-9358 ■ *Web:* www.blackhillscaverns.com	Rapid City	SD	57702	605-343-0542	
Blandford Nature Ctr 1715 Hillburn Ave NW *Web:* blandfordnaturecenter.org	Grand Rapids	MI	49504	616-735-6240	
Boulder Reservoir 5565 N 51st St *Web:* www.bouldercolorado.gov	Boulder	CO	80301	303-441-3461	441-1807
Boyden Caverns 5350 Moaning Cave Rd *TF:* 866-762-2837 ■ *Web:* www.caverntours.com	Vallecito	CA	95251	209-736-2708	736-0330
Butterfly House 11455 Obee Rd *Web:* www.wheelerfarms.com	Whitehouse	OH	43571	419-877-2733	
Butterfly House - Faust Park, The 15193 Olive Blvd *TF:* 800-642-8842 ■ *Web:* www.missouribotanicalgarden.org	Chesterfield	MO	63017	636-530-0076	530-1516
Butterfly World 3600 W Sample Rd Tradewinds Pk S *Web:* www.butterflyworld.com	Coconut Creek	FL	33073	954-977-4400	977-4501
Capen Hill Nature Sanctuary 56 Capen Rd PO Box 218 *Web:* www.capenhill.org	Charlton City	MA	01508	508-248-5516	248-5516
Carson Hot Springs 1500 Hot Springs Rd *TF:* 888-917-3711 ■ *Web:* www.carsonhotspringsresort.com	Carson City	NV	89706	775-885-8844	
Cascade Caverns Park 226 Cascade Caverns Rd *Web:* www.cascadecaverns.com	Boerne	TX	78006	830-755-8080	
Cave of the Mounds 2975 CAve of the Mounds Rd PO Box 148 *Web:* www.caveofthemounds.com	Blue Mounds	WI	53517	608-437-3038	437-4181
Cave of the Winds 100 Cave of the Winds Rd *Web:* www.caveofthewinds.com	Manitou Springs	CO	80829	719-685-5444	685-1712
Centennial Olympic Park 265 Pk Ave W NW *Web:* www.centennialpark.com	Atlanta	GA	30313	404-223-4412	223-4499
Central Park 830 Fifth Ave *Web:* www.centralparknyc.org	New York	NY	10065	212-360-1461	
Chattahoochee Nature Ctr 9135 Willeo Rd *Web:* chattnaturecenter.org	Roswell	GA	30075	770-992-2055	552-0926
Connecticut Audubon Society Nature Ctr 2325 Burr St *Web:* www.ctaudubon.org	Fairfield	CT	06824	203-259-6305	254-7365
Cypress Gardens 3030 Cypress Gardens Rd *Web:* www.cypressgardens.info	Moncks Corner	SC	29461	843-553-0515	569-0644
Darien Nature Ctr Inc 120 Brookside Rd *Web:* www.dariennaturecenter.org	Darien	CT	06820	203-655-7459	
DeGraaf Nature Ctr 600 Graafschap Rd *TF:* 888-535-5792 ■ *Web:* cityofholland.com	Holland	MI	49423	616-355-1057	355-1069
Devil's Den Preserve 33 Pent Rd *Web:* www.nature.org	Weston	CT	06883	203-226-4991	226-4807
Dodge Nature Ctr 365 Marie Ave W *Web:* www.dodgenaturecenter.org	West Saint Paul	MN	55118	651-455-4531	455-2575
Domaine Maizerets 2000 Montmorency Blvd *Web:* domainemaizerets.com	Quebec	QC	G1J5E7	418-641-6335	660-6295
Eagle River Nature Ctr 32750 Eagle River Rd *Web:* ernc.org	Eagle River	AK	99577	907-694-2108	694-2119
Earthplace 10 Woodside Ln *Web:* www.earthplace.org	Westport	CT	06880	203-227-7253	227-8909
El Dorado Nature Ctr 7550 E Spring St *TF:* 800-662-8887 ■ *Web:* longbeach.gov	Long Beach	CA	90815	562-570-1745	570-8530
Everglades Holiday Park 21940 Griffin Rd *Web:* www.evergladesholidaypark.com	Fort Lauderdale	FL	33332	954-434-8111	
Falls Park on the Reedy 601 S Main St *Web:* www.fallspark.com	Greenville	SC	29601	864-467-4350	
Fern Forest Nature Ctr 201 Lyons Rd S *Web:* www.broward.org/parks	Coconut Creek	FL	33063	954-970-0150	
Forest Park Nature Ctr 5809 Forest Pk Dr *Web:* peoriaparks.org	Peoria Heights	IL	61616	309-686-3360	
Genesee County Parks & Recreation 5045 Stanley Rd *TF:* 800-648-7275 ■ *Web:* www.geneseecountyparks.org	Flint	MI	48506	810-736-7100	736-7220
Golden Gate Park 970 47th Ave *Web:* goldengateparkgolf.com	San Francisco	CA	94121	415-751-8987	
Great Plains Nature Ctr 6232 E 29th St N *TF:* 800-222-1222 ■ *Web:* www.gpnc.org	Wichita	KS	67220	316-683-5499	688-9555
Gulf Branch Nature Ctr & Park Grounds 3608 N Military Rd *Web:* arlingtonva.us	Arlington	VA	22207	703-228-3403	
Gumbo Limbo Nature Ctr 1801 N Ocean Blvd *Web:* www.gumbolimbo.org	Boca Raton	FL	33432	561-544-8605	338-1483
Hanauma Bay Nature Preserve 100 Hanauma Bay Rd *TF:* 800-690-6200 ■ *Web:* www.honolulu.gov	Honolulu	HI	96825	808-396-4229	395-0468
Hemlock Bluffs Nature Preserve 2616 Kildaire Farm Rd *Web:* townofcary.org	Cary	NC	27518	919-387-5980	
Houston Arboretum & Nature Ctr 4501 Woodway Dr *TF:* 866-510-7219 ■ *Web:* www.houstonarboretum.org	Houston	TX	77024	713-681-8433	
Ijams Nature Ctr 2915 Island Home Ave *Web:* www.ijams.org	Knoxville	TN	37920	865-577-4717	577-1683
Indian Creek Nature Ctr 6665 Otis Rd SE *Web:* www.indiancreeknaturecenter.org	Cedar Rapids	IA	52403	319-362-0664	362-2876
Jefferson Barracks County Park 345 N Dr *TF:* 800-735-2966	Saint Louis	MO	63125	314-615-8800	615-4567
Katharine Ordway Preserve 4245 N Fairfax Dr Ste 100 *TF:* 800-628-6860 ■ *Web:* www.nature.org	Arlington	VA	22203	203-226-4991	226-4807
Lava Hot Springs State Foundation 430 E Main St PO Box 669 *TF:* 800-423-8597 ■ *Web:* www.lavahotsprings.com	Lava Hot Springs	ID	83246	208-776-5221	
Lewis & Clark National Historic Trail Interpretive Ctr 4201 Giant Springs Rd *Web:* www.fs.usda.gov/lcnf	Great Falls	MT	59405	406-727-8733	453-6157
Lincoln Memorial Garden & Nature Ctr 2301 E Lake Dr *Web:* www.lincolnmemorialgarden.org	Springfield	IL	62712	217-529-1111	529-0134
Linville Caverns Inc 19929 US 221 N **Fax Area Code:* 828 ■ *TF:* 800-419-0540 ■ *Web:* www.linvillecaverns.com	Marion	NC	28752	800-419-0540	756-4171*
Long Branch Nature Ctr 625 S Carlin Springs Rd *Web:* arlingtonva.us	Arlington	VA	22204	703-228-6535	
Lost River Caverns 726 Durham St PO Box M *TF:* 888-529-1907 ■ *Web:* www.lostcave.com	Hellertown	PA	18055	610-838-8767	838-2961
Martin Park Nature Ctr 5000 W Memorial Rd *Web:* okc.gov/parks/martin%5fpark	Oklahoma City	OK	73142	405-297-3882	
Mississippi Petrified Forest 124 Forest Pk Rd *Web:* www.mspetrifiedforest.com	Flora	MS	39071	601-879-8189	

	City	State	ZIP	Phone	Fax
Morikami Museum & Japanese Gardens 4000 Morikami Pk Rd	Delray Beach	FL	33446	561-495-0233	
Web: www.morikami.org					
Morrison-Knudsen Nature Ctr 600 S Walnut St	Boise	ID	83712	208-334-2225	287-2905
Mount Saint Helens National Volcanic Monument 42218 NE Yale Bridge Rd	Amboy	WA	98601	360-449-7800	449-7801
Web: www.fs.fed.us					
Natural Bridge Caverns 26495 Natural Bridge Caverns Rd	Natural Bridge Caverns	TX	78266	210-651-6101	651-6144
Web: www.naturalbridgecaverns.com					
New Canaan Nature Ctr 144 Oenoke Ridge	New Canaan	CT	06840	203-966-9577	966-6536
Web: www.newcanaannature.org					
New York State Office of Parks Recreation & Historic Preservation Empire State Plaza Agency Bldg 1	Albany	NY	12238	716-354-9101	486-1899*
**Fax Area Code: 518* ■ *TF:* 800-456-2267 ■ *Web:* nysparks.com					
Nisqually Reach Nature Ctr (NRNC) 4949 D'Milluhr Rd NE	Olympia	WA	98516	360-459-0387	
Web: www.nisquallyestuary.org					
Ogden Nature Ctr 966 W 12th St	Ogden	UT	84404	801-621-7595	621-1867
Web: www.ogdennaturecenter.org					
Olentangy Indian Caverns 1779 Home Rd	Delaware	OH	43015	740-548-7917	
Web: www.olentangyindiancaverns.com					
Oxbow Meadows Environmental Learning Ctr 3535 S Lumpkin Rd	Columbus	GA	31903	706-507-8550	507-8549
TF: 866-264-2035 ■ *Web:* oxbow.columbusstate.edu					
Parkersville Landing Historical Park 24 S A St	Washougal	WA	98671	360-835-2196	835-2197
Web: portcw.com					
Pike National Forest 601 S Weber St	Colorado Springs	CO	80903	719-636-1602	477-4233
Web: www.fs.fed.us					
Pine Jog Environmental Education Ctr 6301 Summit Blvd	West Palm Beach	FL	33415	561-686-6600	687-4968
Web: www.pinejog.fau.edu					
Plains Conservation Ctr 21901 E Hampden Ave	Aurora	CO	80013	303-693-3621	
Web: www.plainscenter.org					
Powder Valley Conservation Nature Ctr 11715 Cragwold Rd	Saint Louis	MO	63122	314-301-1500	301-1501
Web: mdc.mo.gov					
Prairie Wetlands Learning Ctr 602 State Hwy 210 E	Fergus Falls	MN	56537	218-998-4480	
Web: www.fws.gov					
Quarry Hill Nature Ctr 701 Silver Creek Rd NE	Rochester	MN	55906	507-328-3950	287-1345
Web: www.qhnc.org					
Raccoon Mountain Caverns 319 W Hills Dr	Chattanooga	TN	37419	423-821-9403	825-1289
TF: 800-823-2267 ■ *Web:* www.raccoonmountain.com					
Randall Davey Audubon Ctr 1800 Upper Canyon Rd PO Box 9314	Santa Fe	NM	87504	505-983-4609	983-2355
Web: www.audubon.org/chapter/nm/nm/rdac					
Red Rock Canyon National Conservation Area 4701 N Torrey Pines Dr	Las Vegas	NV	89130	702-515-5350	363-6779
Web: www.blm.gov					
Riveredge Nature Ctr 4458 W Hawthorne Dr PO Box 26	Newburg	WI	53060	262-375-2715	
TF: 800-287-8098 ■ *Web:* www.riveredgenaturecenter.org					
Rock City Gardens 1400 Patten Rd	Lookout Mountain	GA	30750	706-820-2531	
TF: 800-854-0675 ■ *Web:* www.seerockcity.com					
Ruby Falls 1720 S Scenic Hwy	Chattanooga	TN	37409	423-821-2544	821-6705
TF: 800-755-7105 ■ *Web:* www.rubyfalls.com					
Runge Conservation Nature Ctr 2901 W Truman Blvd	Jefferson City	MO	65109	573-751-4115	751-4467
TF: 800-392-1111 ■ *Web:* www.mdc.mo.gov					
Rushmore Cave 13622 Hwy 40	Keystone	SD	57751	605-255-4384	
Web: www.rushmorecave.com					
Santa Catalina Ranger District 5700 N Sabino Canyon Rd	Tucson	AZ	85750	520-749-8700	749-7723
Web: www.fs.fed.us					
Saw Mill River Audubon Inc 275 Millwood Rd	Chappaqua	NY	10514	914-666-6503	666-7430
Web: www.sawmillriveraudubon.org/pruyn.html					
Schilling Wildlife Management Area 17614 Schilling Refuge Rd	Plattsmouth	NE	68048	402-296-0041	
Web: calendar.outdoornebraska.gov					
Schlitz Audubon Nature Ctr 1111 E Brown Deer Rd	Bayside	WI	53217	414-352-2880	352-6091
Web: www.schlitzaudubon.org					
Sea Lion Caves 91560 Hwy 101	Florence	OR	97439	541-547-3111	547-3545
Web: www.sealioncaves.com					
Seven Falls Co 2850 S Cheyenne Canyon Rd	Colorado Springs	CO	80906	855-923-7272	632-0781*
**Fax Area Code: 719* ■ *TF:* 855-923-7272 ■ *Web:* www.sevenfalls.com					
Severson Dells Nature Ctr 8786 Montague Rd	Rockford	IL	61102	815-335-2915	335-2471
Web: www.seversondells.com					
Sitting Bull Crystal Caverns 13745 S Hwy 16	Rapid City	SD	57702	605-342-2777	
Snake River Birds of Prey National Conservation Area PO Box 84	Kuna	ID	83634	208-861-9131	
Web: www.snakeriverbirdsofpreyfestival.com					
Springfield Conservation Nature Ctr 4600 S Chrisman Ave	Springfield	MO	65804	417-888-4237	888-4241
TF: 800-392-1111 ■ *Web:* www.mdc.mo.gov					
T.O. Fuller State Park 1500 W Mitchell Rd	Memphis	TN	38109	901-543-7581	785-8485
Web: www.tennessee.gov					
Tacoma Nature Ctr 1919 S Tyler St	Tacoma	WA	98405	253-591-6439	593-4152
Web: metroparkstacoma.org					
Tree Hill Nature Ctr 7152 Lone Star Rd	Jacksonville	FL	32211	904-724-4646	724-9132
Web: www.treehill.org					
Vista House 40700 E Historic Columbia River Hwy	Corbett	OR	97019	503-695-2230	695-2250
Web: www.vistahouse.com					
Weedon Island Preserve Cultural & Natural History Ctr 1800 Weedon Dr NE	Saint Petersburg	FL	33702	727-453-6500	
Web: www.weedonislandcenter.org					
Wehr Nature Ctr 9701 W College Ave	Franklin	WI	53132	414-425-8550	425-6992
Web: county.milwaukee.gov					
Western North Carolina Nature Ctr 75 Gashes Creek Rd	Asheville	NC	28805	828-298-5600	298-2644
Web: www.wildwnc.org					
Westwood Hills Nature Ctr 8300 W Franklin Ave	Saint Louis Park	MN	55426	952-924-2544	797-9691
Web: stlouispark.org					
Woldumar Nature Ctr 5739 Old Lansing Rd	Lansing	MI	48917	517-322-0030	322-9394
Web: www.woldumar.org					
Woodcock Nature Ctr 54 Deer Run Rd	Wilton	CT	06897	203-762-7280	834-0062
Web: www.woodcocknaturecenter.org					
World Bird Sanctuary 125 Bald Eagle Ridge Rd	Valley Park	MO	63088	636-861-3225	861-3240
Web: www.worldbirdsanctuary.org					

50-6 Shopping/Dining/Entertainment Districts

	City	State	ZIP	Phone	Fax
Bannister's Wharf 1 Bannister's Wharf	Newport	RI	02840	401-846-4500	849-8750
TF: 800-395-1343 ■ *Web:* www.bannistersnewport.com					
Barefoot Landing 4898 Hwy 17 S	North Myrtle Beach	SC	29582	843-272-8349	272-1052
Web: www.bflanding.com					
Bayside Marketplace 401 Biscayne Blvd	Miami	FL	33132	305-577-3344	
Web: www.baysidemarketplace.com					
Bazaar del Mundo 4133 Taylor St	San Diego	CA	92110	619-296-3161	
Web: www.bazaardelmundo.com					
Beale Street Historic District 203 Beale St Ste 300	Memphis	TN	38103	901-526-0115	526-0125
Web: www.bealestreet.com					
Belmar 464 S Teller St	Lakewood	CO	80226	303-742-1520	987-7693
Web: www.belmarcolorado.com					
BOB the (Big Old Bldg) 20 Monroe Ave NW	Grand Rapids	MI	49503	616-356-2000	493-2011
Web: www.thebob.com					
Bricktown 2 S Mickey Mantle Dr	Oklahoma City	OK	73104	405-236-8666	
Web: welcometobricktown.com					
Brightleaf Square Gregson & Main Sts Ste 24	Durham	NC	27701	919-682-9229	688-1953
Web: www.historicbrightleaf.com					
Broadway at the Beach 1325 Celebrity Cir	Myrtle Beach	SC	29577	843-444-3200	
Web: www.broadwayatthebeach.com					
Cannery at Del Monte Square 2801 Leavenworth St Mezzanine Level	San Francisco	CA	94133	415-771-3112	
Web: www.delmontesquare.com					
Celebration Town Hall 851 Celebration Ave	Kissimmee	FL	34747	407-566-1200	
Web: www.celebration.fl.us					
Center in the Square 1 Market Sq SE 5th Fl	Roanoke	VA	24011	540-342-5700	
Web: www.centerinthesquare.org					
Centro Ybor 1600 E Eigth Ave	Tampa	FL	33605	813-242-4660	
Web: www.centroybor.com					
City Market 219 W Bryan St Ste 207	Savannah	GA	31401	912-232-4903	
Web: www.savannahcitymarket.com					
CityPlace 700 S Rosemary Ave	West Palm Beach	FL	33401	561-366-1000	366-1001
Web: www.cityplace.com					
CocoWalk 3015 Grand Ave	Coconut Grove	FL	33133	305-444-0777	441-8936
Web: www.cocowalk.net					
Cooper Young Business Assn 2120 Young Ave	Memphis	TN	38104	901-276-7222	
Web: lamplighter.cooperyoung.org					
Crocker Park 189 Crocker Pk Blvd	Westlake	OH	44145	440-871-6880	871-6889
Web: www.crockerpark.com					
Desert Ridge Marketplace 21001 N Tatum Blvd	Phoenix	AZ	85050	480-513-7586	563-1829
Web: www.shopdesertridge.com					
District, The 11 S Tenth St	Columbia	MO	65201	573-442-6816	
Web: www.discoverthedistrict.com					
Downtown at the Gardens 11701 Lk Victoria Gardens Ave Ste 2203	Palm Beach Gardens	FL	33410	561-340-1600	
Web: downtownatthegardens.com					
Downtown Disney S Disneyland Dr	Anaheim	CA	92802	714-781-4565	
Web: disneyland.disney.go.com					
East Town 770 N Jefferson St	Milwaukee	WI	53202	414-271-1416	271-6401
Web: www.easttown.com					
Faneuil Hall Marketplace 4 S Market Bldg 5th Fl	Boston	MA	02109	617-523-1300	523-1779
Web: www.faneuilhallmarketplace.com					
Fifth Street Public Market 296 E Fifth Ave	Eugene	OR	97401	541-484-0383	686-1220
Web: www.5stmarket.com					
Findlay Market PO Box 14727	Cincinnati	OH	45250	513-665-4839	665-3480
Web: www.findlaymarket.org					
FlatIron Crossing 1 W FlatIron Crossing Dr	Broomfield	CO	80021	720-887-0888	
Web: www.flatironcrossing.com					
Fort Worth Stockyards National Historic District PO Box 64203	Fort Worth	TX	76164	817-626-7921	740-8635
Web: www.fortworthstockyards.org					
Fourth Avenue 434 E Ninth St	Tucson	AZ	85705	520-624-5004	
Web: www.fourthavenue.org					
Gaslamp Quarter Assn 614 Fifth Ave Ste E	San Diego	CA	92101	619-233-5227	233-4693
Web: www.gaslamp.org					
Gateway, The 18 N Rio Grande St	Salt Lake City	UT	84101	801-456-0000	456-0005
Web: www.shopthegateway.com					
Ghirardelli Square 900 N Pt St Ste E-100	San Francisco	CA	94109	415-775-5500	775-0912
Web: www.ghirardellisq.com					
Great Lakes Crossing Outlets 4000 Baldwin Rd	Auburn Hills	MI	48326	248-454-5000	
TF: 877-746-7452 ■ *Web:* www.greatlakescrossingoutlets.com					
Harborplace & the Gallery 201 E Pratt St	Baltimore	MD	21202	410-332-4191	547-7317
TF: 800-722-8614 ■ *Web:* www.harborplace.com					
Hillcrest Historic District Markham & Kavanaugh	Little Rock	AR	72216	501-371-0075	374-8142
TF: 877-637-0037 ■ *Web:* www.arkansas.com					
Hollywood & Highland 6801 Hollywood Blvd	Hollywood	CA	90028	323-817-0200	460-6003
Web: www.hollywoodandhighland.com					

	City	State	Zip	Phone	Fax
Hyde Park Village 744 S Village Cir *Web:* www.hydeparkvillage.com	Tampa	FL	33606	813-251-3500	
International Plaza & Bay Street 2223 NW Shore Blvd *Web:* www.shopinternationalplaza.com	Tampa	FL	33607	813-342-3790	342-3788
John's Pass Village & Boardwalk 150 John's Pass Boardwalk Pl *Web:* www.johnspass.com	Madeira Beach	FL	33708	727-398-6577	
Laclede's Landing 710 N Second St *Web:* lacledeslanding.com	Saint Louis	MO	63102	314-241-5875	
Larimer Square 1430 Larimer St Ste 200 *Web:* www.larimersquare.com	Denver	CO	80202	303-534-2367	
Mellwood Arts & Entertainment Ctr 1860 Mellwood Ave *Web:* www.mellwoodartcenter.com	Louisville	KY	40206	502-895-3650	
Metreon 865 Market St *Web:* www.westfield.com	San Francisco	CA	94103	415-495-5656	
Miracle Mile Shops at Planet Hollywood 3663 Las Vegas Blvd S *TF:* 888-800-8284 ■ *Web:* www.miraclemileshopslv.com	Las Vegas	NV	89109	702-866-0703	
New Roc City 19 LeCount Pl *Web:* www.funfuzionline.com	New Rochelle	NY	10801	914-637-7575	
Newport on the Levee 1 Levee Way Ste 1113 *Web:* www.newportonthelevee.com	Newport	KY	41071	859-291-0550	291-7020
Ocean Walk Shoppes at the Village 250 N Atlantic Ave Ste 201 *Web:* www.oceanwalkshoppes.com	Daytona Beach	FL	32118	386-258-9544	238-3864
Peabody Place 100 Peabody Pl Ste 1400 *Web:* www.belz.com	Memphis	TN	38103	901-260-7348	
Penn's Landing 301 S Columbus Blvd *Web:* www.delawareriverwaterfront.com	Philadelphia	PA	19106	215-922-2386	923-2801
Pike Outlets, The 95 S Pine Ave *Web:* www.facebook.com/thepikeoutlets	Long Beach	CA	90802	562-432-8325	
Pike Place Market (PPM PDN) 85 Pike St Rm 500 *Web:* www.pikeplacemarket.org	Seattle	WA	98101	206-682-7453	625-0646
Pioneer Square 310 First Ave S *Web:* www.pioneersquare.org	Seattle	WA	98104	206-667-0687	
Ports O'Call Village Berth 75-79 *Web:* www.sanpedro.com/sp_point/portcall.htm	San Pedro	CA	90731	310-548-8076	
Power Plant Live! 34 Market St *Web:* www.powerplantlive.com	Baltimore	MD	21202	410-727-5483	
Renaissance Ctr Detroit River *Web:* marriott.com/hotels/propertypage/dtwdt	Detroit	MI	48243	313-568-8000	
River Walk 110 Broadway Ste 500 *TF:* 800-417-4139 ■ *Web:* www.thesanantonioriverwalk.com	San Antonio	TX	78204	210-227-4262	212-7602
Santana Row 3055 Olin Ave Ste 2100 *TF:* 888-509-7303 ■ *Web:* www.santanarow.com	San Jose	CA	95128	408-551-4611	
Seaport Village 849 W Harbor Dr Ste D *Web:* www.seaportvillage.com	San Diego	CA	92101	619-235-4014	696-0025
Shops at Columbus Circle, The 10 Columbus Cir *Web:* www.shopsatcolumbuscircle.com	New York	NY	10019	212-823-6300	
Shoreline Village 429 Shoreline Village Dr # 100 *Web:* www.shorelinevillage.com	Long Beach	CA	90802	562-435-2668	
South Street Seaport 19 Fulton St Pier 17 *Web:* www.southstreetseaport.com	New York	NY	10038	212-732-8257	964-8056
Stockyards Station 130 E Exchange Ave *Web:* www.stockyardsstation.com	Fort Worth	TX	76164	817-625-9715	
Streets at Southpoint & Main Street 6910 Fayetteville Rd *Web:* www.streetsatsouthpoint.com	Durham	NC	27713	919-572-8800	
Sundance Square 201 Main St Ste 700 *Web:* www.sundancesquare.com	Fort Worth	TX	76102	817-255-5700	
Underground Atlanta 50 Central Ave SW Ste 007 *Web:* www.underground-atlanta.com	Atlanta	GA	30303	404-523-2311	
Union Station 50 Massachusetts Ave *Web:* www.unionstationdc.com	Washington	DC	20002	202-289-1908	
Universal Studios CityWalk Hollywood Universal City Plz *Web:* www.citywalkhollywood.com	Los Angeles	CA	91608	818-622-4455	
Water Tower Place 835 N Michigan Ave *Web:* www.shopwatertower.com	Chicago	IL	60611	312-440-3166	440-1259
Waterside Festival Marketplace 333 Waterside Dr *Web:* www.watersidemarketplace.com	Norfolk	VA	23510	757-627-3300	
West Port Plaza 111 W Port Plz Ste 550 *Web:* www.westportstl.com	Saint Louis	MO	63146	314-576-7100	
Westport Historical Society 4000 Baltimore St *Web:* www.westporthistorical.com	Kansas City	MO	64111	816-561-1821	

50-7 Wineries

The wineries listed in this category feature wine-tasting as an attraction.

	City	State	Zip	Phone	Fax
A Nonini Winery Inc 2640 N Dickenson *Web:* www.noniniwinery.com	Fresno	CA	93723	559-275-1936	
Adams County Winery 251 Peach Tree Rd *TF:* 877-601-7936 ■ *Web:* www.adamscountywinery.com	Orrtanna	PA	17353	717-334-4631	334-4026
Alaska Denali Winery 1301 E Dowling Rd Ste 107 *Web:* denaliwinery.info	Anchorage	AK	99518	907-563-9434	563-9501
Arbor Crest Wine Cellars 4705 N Fruithill Rd *Web:* www.arborcrest.com	Spokane	WA	99217	509-927-9463	927-0574
Bogle Vineyards & Winery 37783 County Rd 144 *Web:* www.boglewinery.com	Clarksburg	CA	95612	916-744-1139	744-1187
Butler Winery 1022 N College Ave *Web:* www.butlerwinery.com	Bloomington	IN	47404	812-339-7233	
Cap*Rock Winery 408 E Woodrow Rd *Web:* www.caprockwinery.com	Lubbock	TX	79423	806-686-4452	
Casa Rondena Winery 733 Chavez Rd NW *Web:* www.casarondena.com	Albuquerque	NM	87107	505-344-5911	343-1823
Chaddsford Winery 632 Baltimore Pk *Web:* www.chaddsford.com	Chadds Ford	PA	19317	610-388-6221	
Chateau Elan Winery 100 Tour de France *TF:* 800-233-9463 ■ *Web:* www.chateauelan.com	Braselton	GA	30517	678-425-0900	425-6000
Chateau Julien Wine Estate 8940 Carmel Valley Rd *Web:* www.greatamericanwinegroup.com	Carmel	CA	93923	831-920-4736	624-6138
Chateau Morrisette Winery 287 Winery Rd SW *TF:* 866-695-2001 ■ *Web:* thedogs.com	Floyd	VA	24091	540-593-2865	593-2868
Chateau Saint Jean 8555 Sonoma Hwy *Web:* www.chateaustjean.com	Kenwood	CA	95452	707-833-4134	
Chateau Ste Michelle Winery 14111 NE 145th St *TF:* 800-267-6793 ■ *Web:* www.ste-michelle.com	Woodinville	WA	98072	425-415-3300	
Cherry Hill Winery 7867 Crowley Rd PO Box 66 *Web:* www.cherryhillwinery.com	Rickreall	OR	97371	503-623-7867	623-7878
Columbia Winery 14030 NE 145th St PO Box 1248 *TF:* 800-488-2347 ■ *Web:* www.columbiawinery.com	Woodinville	WA	98072	425-488-2776	
Countryside Vineyards Winery 658 Henry Harr Rd *Web:* cvwineryandsupply.com	Blountville	TN	37617	423-323-1660	
Easley Winery 205 N College Ave *Web:* www.easleywinery.com	Indianapolis	IN	46202	317-636-4516	974-0128
Eola Hills Wine Cellars 501 S Pacific Hwy 99 W *TF:* 800-291-6730 ■ *Web:* www.eolahillswinery.com	Rickreall	OR	97371	503-623-2405	623-0350
Forks of Cheat Winery 2811 Stewart Town Rd *TF:* 877-989-4637 ■ *Web:* www.wvwines.com	Morgantown	WV	26508	304-598-2019	
Georgia Winery, The 6469 Battlefield Pkwy *Web:* www.georgiawines.com	Ringgold	GA	30736	706-937-9463	937-9860
Gruet Winery 8400 Pan American Fwy NE *Web:* www.gruetwinery.com	Albuquerque	NM	87113	505-821-0055	857-0066
Honeywood Winery 1350 Hines St SE *TF:* 800-726-4101 ■ *Web:* www.honeywoodwinery.com	Salem	OR	97302	503-362-4111	
Huber's Orchard & Winery 19816 Huber Rd *TF:* 800-345-9463 ■ *Web:* huberwinery.com	Borden	IN	47106	812-923-9463	923-3013
J Lohr Vineyards & Wines 1000 Lenzen Ave *Web:* www.jlohr.com	San Jose	CA	95126	408-288-5057	993-2276
James Arthur Vineyards & Winery 2001 W Raymond Rd *Web:* www.jamesarthurvineyards.com	Raymond	NE	68428	402-783-5255	
King Estate Winery 80854 Territorial Rd *TF:* 800-884-4441 ■ *Web:* www.kingestate.com	Eugene	OR	97405	541-942-9874	942-9867
La Vina Winery 4201 S Hwy 28 *Web:* lavina.wolfep.com	La Union	NM	88021	575-882-7632	
Latah Creek Winery 13030 E Indiana Ave *TF:* 800-528-2427 ■ *Web:* www.latahcreek.com	Spokane	WA	99216	509-926-0164	
LaVelle Vineyards 89697 Sheffler Rd *Web:* www.lavellevineyards.com	Elmira	OR	97437	541-935-9406	
Llano Estacado Winery 3426 E FM 1585 *TF:* 800-634-3854 ■ *Web:* www.llanowine.com	Lubbock	TX	79404	806-745-2258	
Mazza Vineyards 11815 E Lake Rd *TF:* 800-796-9463 ■ *Web:* enjoymazza.com/mazza-vineyards	North East	PA	16428	814-725-8695	725-3948
Michael-David Winery 4580 W Hwy 12 *TF:* 888-707-9463 ■ *Web:* www.michaeldavidwinery.com	Lodi	CA	95242	209-368-7384	368-5801
Mountain Dome Winery 16315 E Temple Rd *Web:* www.mountaindome.com	Spokane	WA	99217	509-928-2788	
Nassau Valley Vineyards 32165 Winery Way *TF:* 800-425-2355 ■ *Web:* www.nassauvalley.com	Lewes	DE	19958	302-645-9463	645-6666
Oak Ridge Winery 6100 E Victor Rd *Web:* www.oakridgewinery.com	Lodi	CA	95240	209-369-4758	
Oliver Winery 8024 N SR-37 *TF:* 800-258-2783 ■ *Web:* www.oliverwinery.com	Bloomington	IN	47404	812-876-5800	
Orfila Vineyards & Winery 13455 San Pasqual Rd *Web:* www.orfila.com	Escondido	CA	92025	760-738-6500	
Penn Shore Vineyards & Winery 10225 Lake Rd *Web:* www.pennshore.com	North East	PA	16428	814-725-8688	725-8689
Redhawk Vineyard & Winery 2995 Michigan City Ave NW *Web:* www.redhawkwine.com	Salem	OR	97304	503-362-1596	
Saint Innocent Winery 5657 Zena Rd NW *Web:* www.stinnocentwine.com	Salem	OR	97304	503-378-1526	
Sakonnet Vineyards 162 W Main Rd *Web:* www.sakonnetwine.com	Little Compton	RI	02837	401-635-8486	
San Sebastian Winery 157 King St *TF:* 888-352-9463 ■ *Web:* www.sansebastianwinery.com	Saint Augustine	FL	32084	904-826-1594	826-1595
Silvan Ridge/Hinman Vineyards 27012 Briggs Hill Rd *Web:* www.silvanridge.com	Eugene	OR	97405	541-345-1945	
Talon Winery & Vineyards 7086 Tates Creek Rd *Web:* www.talonwine.com	Lexington	KY	40515	859-971-3214	971-8787
Westbend Vineyards 5394 Williams Rd *TF:* 866-901-5032 ■ *Web:* www.westbendvineyards.com	Lewisville	NC	27023	336-945-5032	
Williamsburg Winery Ltd 5800 Wessex Hundred *Web:* www.williamsburgwinery.com	Williamsburg	VA	23185	757-229-0999	229-0911
Winery at Wolf Creek 2637 Cleveland Massillon Rd *TF:* 800-436-0426 ■ *Web:* www.wineryatwolfcreek.com	Norton	OH	44203	330-666-9285	665-1445

51 AUCTIONS

Company	City	State	Zip	Phone	Fax
Abidon Leasing 5301 E State St Ste 215	Rockford	IL	61108	815-226-8700	226-8769
ADESA Inc 13085 Hamilton Crossing Blvd TF: 800-923-3725 ■ Web: www.adesa.com	Carmel	IN	46032	317-815-1100	249-4600
Akron Auto Auction Inc 2471 Ley Dr TF: 800-773-0033 ■ Web: www.akronautoauction.com	Akron	OH	44319	330-773-8245	773-1641
American Auction Co 951 W Watkins TF: 800-801-8880	Phoenix	AZ	85007	800-801-8880	
Bonhams & Butterfields 220 San Bruno Ave TF: 800-223-2854 ■ Web: www.bonhams.com	San Francisco	CA	94103	415-861-7500	861-8951
Collectors Universe Inc PO Box 6280 NASDAQ: CLCT ■ TF: 800-325-1121 ■ Web: www.collectors.com	Newport Beach	CA	92658	949-567-1234	833-7955
Doyle New York 175 E 87th St Web: doyle.com	New York	NY	10128	212-427-2730	369-0892
Earl's Auction Co 5199 Lafayette Rd Web: www.earlsauction.com	Indianapolis	IN	46254	317-291-5843	291-5844
eBay Inc 2065 Hamilton Ave NASDAQ: EBAY ■ TF: 800-322-9266 ■ Web: www.ebay.com	San Jose	CA	95125	408-376-7400	376-7401
Fasig-Tipton Co Inc 2400 Newtown Pike TF: 877-945-2020 ■ Web: www.fasigtipton.com	Lexington	KY	40511	859-255-1555	254-0794
Freeman/Fine Arts of Philadelphia 1808 Chestnut St Web: www.freemansauction.com	Philadelphia	PA	19103	215-563-9275	563-8236
Gallery of History Inc 3601 W Sahara Ave TF: 800-425-5379 ■ Web: www.galleryofhistory.com	Las Vegas	NV	89102	702-364-1000	364-1285
Greater Rockford Auto Auction Inc (GRAA) 5937 Sandy Hollow Rd TF: 800-830-4722 ■ Web: www.graa.net	Rockford	IL	61109	815-874-7800	874-1325
Harry Davis & Co 1725 Blvd of Allies TF: 800-775-2289 ■ Web: www.harrydavis.com	Pittsburgh	PA	15219	412-765-1170	765-1170
Henderson Auctions 13340 Florida Blvd PO Box 336 TF: 800-334-7443 ■ Web: www.hendersonauctions.com	Livingston	LA	70754	225-686-2252	686-0647
Heritage Place Inc 2829 S MacArthur TF: 888-343-9831 ■ Web: www.heritageplace.com	Oklahoma City	OK	73128	405-682-4551	686-1267
iCollector Technologies Inc 1750 Coast Meridian Rd Ste 114 TF: 866-313-0123 ■ Web: www.icollector.com	Port Coquitlam	BC	V3C6R8	604-941-2221	
Insurance Auto Auctions Inc 2 Westbrook Corporate Ctr Ste 500 TF: 800-872-1501 ■ Web: www.iaai.com	Westchester	IL	60154	708-492-7000	
Ironplanet Inc 3825 Hopyard Rd Ste 250 *Fax: Cust Svc ■ TF Cust Svc: 888-433-5426 ■ Web: www.ironplanet.com.au	Pleasanton	CA	94588	925-225-8600	225-8610*
Kennedy-Wilson Inc 9701 Wilshire Blvd Ste 700 TF: 800-522-6664 ■ Web: kennedywilson.com	Beverly Hills	CA	90212	310-887-6400	887-6414
Liquidity Services Inc 1920 L St NW 6th Fl NASDAQ: LQDT ■ TF: 800-310-4604 ■ Web: www.liquidityservices.com	Washington	DC	20036	202-467-6868	467-5475
NexTag.com Inc 555 Twin Dolphin Dr Ste 370 Web: www.nextag.com	Redwood City	CA	94065	650-645-4700	341-3779
Priceline.com LLC 800 Connecticut Ave NASDAQ: PCLN ■ TF: 800-774-2354 ■ Web: www.priceline.com	Norwalk	CT	06854	800-774-2354	
Rene Bates Auctioneers Inc 4660 County Rd 1006 Web: www.renebates.com	McKinney	TX	75071	972-548-9636	542-5495
Sotheby's Inc 1334 York Ave Web: www.sothebys.com	New York	NY	10021	212-606-7000	894-1141
Swann Galleries Inc 104 E 25th St Web: www.swanngalleries.com	New York	NY	10010	212-254-4710	979-1017
Theriault's PO Box 151 TF: 800-966-3655 ■ Web: www.theriaults.com	Annapolis	MD	21404	410-224-3655	224-2515
uBid Inc 740 Hilltop Dr TF: 866-946-8243	Itasca	IL	60143	866-946-8243	
Yahoo! Auctions 701 First Ave Web: about.yahoo.com	Sunnyvale	CA	94089	408-349-3300	616-3702

52 AUDIO & VIDEO EQUIPMENT

Company	City	State	Zip	Phone	Fax
Alfred Williams & Co 410 S Salisbury St Web: alfredwilliams.com	Raleigh	NC	27601	919-832-9570	
Alpine Electronics of America 19145 Gramercy Pl *Fax: Hum Res ■ TF: 800-257-4631 ■ Web: www.alpine-usa.com	Torrance	CA	90501	310-326-8000	320-5089*
Amplifier Technologies Inc 1749 Chapin Rd Web: www.bgw.com	Montebello	CA	90640	323-278-0001	278-0083
AmpliVox Sound Systems LLC 3995 Commercial Ave TF: 800-267-5486 ■ Web: www.ampli.com	Northbrook	IL	60062	847-498-9000	498-6691
Amx LLC 3000 Reseach Dr Web: amx.com	Richardson	TX	75082	469-624-8000	
Applied Research & Technology 215 Tremont St TF: 800-775-2427 ■ Web: artproaudio.com	Rochester	NY	14608	585-436-2720	436-3942
Atlas Sound 1601 Jack McKay Blvd *Fax Area Code: 800 ■ TF: 800-876-3333 ■ Web: www.atlasied.com	Ennis	TX	75119	972-875-8413	765-3435*
Audio America Inc 15132 Park Of Commerce Blvd Ste 100 Web: www.audioamerica.com	Jupiter	FL	33478	561-863-7704	
Audio Command Systems 694 Main St TF: 800-382-2939 ■ Web: www.audiocommand.com	Westbury	NY	11590	516-997-5800	997-2195
Audio Research Corp 3900 Annapolis Ln N Web: www.audioresearch.com	Plymouth	MN	55447	763-577-9700	577-0323
Audio-Video Corp 213 Broadway Web: www.audiovideocorp.com	Albany	NY	12204	518-449-7213	449-1205
Audiosears Corp 2 S St TF: 800-533-7863 ■ Web: www.audiosears.com	Stamford	NY	12167	607-652-7305	652-3653
Audiovox Corp 180 Marcus Blvd NASDAQ: VOXX ■ TF: 800-645-4994 ■ Web: www.voxxintl.com	Hauppauge	NY	11788	631-231-7750	
Automated Voice Systems Inc (AVSI) 17059 El Cajon Ave	Yorba Linda	CA	92886	714-524-4488	996-1127
Avidex Industries LLC 13555 Bel-Red Rd Ste 226 Web: www.avidex.com	Bellevue	WA	98005	425-643-0330	
Biamp Systems Inc 9300 SW Gemini Dr *Fax Area Code: 503 ■ TF: 800-826-1457 ■ Web: www.biamp.com	Beaverton	OR	97008	800-826-1457	626-0281*
Bogen Communications International Inc 50 Spring St OTC: BOGN ■ TF: 800-999-2809 ■ Web: www.bogen.com	Ramsey	NJ	07446	201-934-8500	934-6532
Bose Corp The Mountain TF Sales: 800-379-2073 ■ Web: global.bose.com	Framingham	MA	01701	508-766-1099	820-3465
Car Toys Inc 20 W Galer St TF: 800-997-3644 ■ Web: www.cartoys.com	Seattle	WA	98119	206-443-0980	443-2525
Cerwin-Vega Inc 3000 SW 42nd St Web: www.cerwinvega.com	Hollywood	FL	33312	954-316-1501	316-1590
Chemguard Inc 204 S Sixth Ave Web: www.chemguard.com	Mansfield	TX	76063	817-473-9964	
City of Chula Vista 276 Fourth Ave TF: 877-478-5478 ■ Web: chulavistaca.gov	Chula Vista	CA	91910	619-691-5047	
Clarion Corp of America 6200 Gateway Dr TF: 800-347-8667 ■ Web: www.clarion.com	Cypress	CA	90630	310-327-9100	327-1999
Community Professional Loudspeakers 333 E Fifth St TF: 800-523-4934 ■ Web: www.communitypro.com	Chester	PA	19013	610-876-3400	874-0190
Cornet Technology Inc 6800 Versar Ctr Ste 216 Web: www.cornet.com	Springfield	VA	22151	703-658-3400	658-3440
Creative Labs Inc 1901 McCarthy Blvd TF Cust Svc: 800-998-1000 ■ Web: www.us.creative.com	Milpitas	CA	95035	408-428-6600	428-6611
Crescendo Designs 641 County Rd 39A Web: crescendodesigns.com	Southampton	NY	11968	631-283-2133	
Crest Electronics Inc 3706 Alliance Dr TF: 888-502-7378 ■ Web: www.crestelectronics.com	Greensboro	NC	27407	336-855-6422	855-6676
Crown Audio Inc 1718 W Mishawaka Rd Web: www.crownaudio.com	Elkhart	IN	46517	574-294-8000	294-8301
Dana Innovations 212 Avenida Fabricante TF: 800-582-7777 ■ Web: www.sonance.com	San Clemente	CA	92672	949-492-7777	
Dangerous Music Inc 231 Stevens Rd Web: www.dangerousmusic.com	Edmeston	NY	13335	607-965-8011	
DEI Holdings Inc 1 Viper Way OTC: DEIX ■ TF: 800-876-0800 ■ Web: deiholdings.com	Vista	CA	92081	760-598-6200	598-6400
Digital Innovations 3436 N Kennicott Ste 200 Web: digitalinnovations.com	Arlington Heights	IL	60004	847-463-9000	463-9001
Digital Video Systems Inc (DVS) 357 Castro St Ste 5 Web: www.dvsystems.com	Mountain View	CA	94041	650-938-8815	938-8829
Dolby Laboratories Inc 100 Potrero Ave NYSE: DLB ■ Web: www.dolby.com/in/en/index.html	San Francisco	CA	94103	415-558-0200	645-4000
Dreamgear LLC 20001 S Western Ave Web: www.dreamgear.com	Torrance	CA	90501	310-222-5522	222-5577
DTS Inc 5220 Las Virgenes Rd NASDAQ: DTSI ■ Web: www.dts.com	Calabasas	CA	91302	818-436-1000	
Dynamic Instruments Inc 3860 Calle Fortunada TF: 800-793-3358 ■ Web: www.dynamicinst.com	San Diego	CA	92123	858-278-4900	278-6700
Echo Digital Audio Corp 6450 Via Real Ste 1 Web: www.echoaudio.com	Carpinteria	CA	93013	805-684-4593	
Educational Technology Inc 300 Bedford Ave Ste 202 Web: www.educationaltechnology.com	Bellmore	NY	11710	516-221-8440	
Eminence Speaker LLC 838 Mulberry Pike PO Box 360 TF: 800-897-8373 ■ Web: www.eminence.com	Eminence	KY	40019	502-845-5622	845-5622
Encore Productions Inc 5150 S Decatur Blvd Web: encore-us.com	Las Vegas	NV	89118	702-739-8803	739-8831
Extron Electronics 1230 S Lewis St TF Tech Supp: 800-633-9876 ■ Web: www.extron.com	Anaheim	CA	92805	714-491-1500	491-1517
FlexHead Industries Inc 56 Lowland St TF: 800-829-6975 ■ Web: www.flexhead.com	Holliston	MA	01746	508-893-9596	
Ford Audio-Video Systems Inc 4800 W I- 40 TF: 800-654-6744 ■ Web: www.fordav.com	Oklahoma City	OK	73128	405-946-9966	946-9991
Foster Electric America 1000 E State Pkwy Ste G Web: www.fosterelectric.com	Schaumburg	IL	60173	847-310-8200	310-8212
Fujitsu Ten Corp of America 19600 S Vermont Ave TF: 800-233-2216 ■ Web: www.eclipse-web.com	Torrance	CA	90502	310-327-2151	
Funai Corp 201 Rt 17 N Ste 903 Web: www.funai.us	Rutherford	NJ	07070	201-727-4560	288-8019
Furman Sound LLC 1690 Corporate Cir TF: 877-486-4738 ■ Web: www.furmansound.com	Petaluma	CA	94954	707-763-1010	763-1310
GlobalMedia Group LLC 15020 N 74th St Web: www.globalmed.com	Scottsdale	AZ	85260	480-922-0044	922-1090
Grass Valley Inc 3499 Douglas-B.-Floreani Web: www.grassvalley.com	Montreal	QC	H4S2C6	514-333-1772	333-9828
Harman International Industries Inc 400 Atlantic St 15th Fl NYSE: HAR ■ TF: 800-473-0602 ■ Web: www.harman.com	Stamford	CT	06901	203-328-3500	328-3964
Harman Kardon Inc 250 Crossways Pk Dr Web: www.harmankardon.com	Woodbury	NY	11797	516-496-3400	682-3520
Harman Music Group 8760 S Sandy Pkwy Web: www.dbxpro.com	Sandy	UT	84070	801-566-8800	566-7005
Harman/Becker Automotive Systems 39001 W 12 Mile Rd Web: www.harman.com	Farmington Hills	MI	48331	248-994-2100	994-2900

Phone | Fax

Interactive Digital Solutions Inc
14701 Cumberland Rd Ste 400 .... Noblesville IN 46060 317-770-3521
TF: 877-880-0022 ■ *Web:* www.e-idsolutions.com

JBL Professional 8500 Balboa Blvd .... Northridge CA 91329 818-894-8850 830-1220
TF: 800-852-5776 ■ *Web:* www.jblpro.com

Jeopardy Productions Inc
10202 Washington Blvd .... Culver City CA 90232 310-244-8855
Web: www.jeopardy.com

JVC Professional Products Co 1700 Valley Rd .... Wayne NJ 07470 973-317-5000 317-5030
TF: 800-252-5722 ■ *Web:* www.pro.jvc.com/prof

Kaleidescape 440 Potrero Ave .... Sunnyvale CA 94085 650-625-6100
Web: kaleidescape.com

Kenwood USA Corp 2201 E Dominguez St .... Long Beach CA 90810 310-639-9000
TF: 800-536-9663 ■ *Web:* www.kenwoodusa.com

KK Audio Inc 12620 Raymer St .... North Hollywood CA 91605 818-765-2921

KLH Audio Systems 11131 Dora St .... Sun Valley CA 91352 818-767-2843
Web: www.klhaudio.com

Klipsch LLC 137 Hempstead 278 .... Hope AR 71801 888-250-8561 777-6753*
**Fax Area Code:* 870 ■ *TF:* 888-250-8561 ■ *Web:* www.klipsch.com

Koss Corp 4129 N Port Washington Ave .... Milwaukee WI 53212 414-964-5000 964-8615
NASDAQ: KOSS ■ *TF:* 800-872-5677 ■ *Web:* www.koss.com

Krell Industries Inc 45 Connair Rd .... Orange CT 06477 203-799-9954 799-9796
Web: www.krellonline.com

KSC Industries Inc 881 Kuhn Dr Ste 200 .... Chula Vista CA 91914 619-671-0110 671-0330
Web: www.kscind.com

Law Enforcement Assoc Corp (LEA)
120 Penmarc Dr Ste 125 .... Raleigh NC 27616 919-872-6210 872-6431
OTC: LAWEQ ■ *TF:* 800-354-9669 ■ *Web:* www.leacorp.com

Lectrosonics Inc PO Box 15900 .... Rio Rancho NM 87174 505-892-4501 892-6243
TF: 800-821-1121 ■ *Web:* www.lectrosonics.com

LifeSize Communications Inc
1601 S Mopac Expwy Ste 100 .... Austin TX 78746 512-347-9300 347-9301
TF: 877-543-3749 ■ *Web:* www.lifesize.com

Line 6 26580 Agoura Rd .... Calabasas CA 91302 818-575-3600 575-3601
Web: www.line6.com

LKG Industries Inc 3660 Publisher's Dr .... Rockford IL 61109 815-874-2301
Web: www.crankinpower.com

Logitech Inc 6505 Kaiser Dr .... Fremont CA 94555 510-795-8500 792-8901
TF Sales: 800-231-7717 ■ *Web:* www.logitech.com

LOUD Technologies Inc
16220 Wood Red Rd NE .... Woodinville WA 98072 425-892-6500
OTC: LTEC ■ *TF:* 866-858-5832 ■ *Web:* www.loudtechinc.com

Loudspeaker Components Corp
7596 US Hwy 61 S .... Lancaster WI 53813 608-723-2127 723-7775
Web: loudspeakercomponents.com

Lowell Manufacturing Co 100 Integram Dr .... Pacific MO 63069 636-257-3400 257-6606
TF: 800-325-9660 ■ *Web:* www.lowellmfg.com

Marantz America Inc 100 Corporate Dr .... Mahwah NJ 07430 201-762-6500 762-6670
Web: www.marantz.com

MartinLogan Ltd 2101 Delaware St .... Lawrence KS 66046 785-749-0133 749-5320
Web: www.martinlogan.com

McIntosh Laboratory Inc 2 Chambers St .... Binghamton NY 13903 607-723-3512 724-0549
TF: 800-538-6576 ■ *Web:* mcintoshlabs.com

Metra Electronics Corp 460 Walker St .... Holly Hill FL 32117 386-257-1186 255-3965
TF Sales: 800-221-0932 ■ *Web:* www.metraonline.com

Meyer Sound Laboratories Inc
2832 San Pablo Ave .... Berkeley CA 94702 510-486-1166 486-8356
Web: www.meyersound.com

Microsearch 3903 Stoney Brook Dr .... Houston TX 77063 713-988-2818
Web: www.microsearch.com

Mitsubishi Digital Electronics America Inc
9351 Jeronimo Rd .... Irvine CA 92618 949-465-6000
TF: 800-332-2119 ■ *Web:* www.mitsubishi-tv.com

Monster Cable Products Inc 455 Valley Dr .... Brisbane CA 94005 415-840-2000
TF: 877-800-8989 ■ *Web:* www.monsterproducts.com

Nady Systems Inc 6701 Shellmound St .... Emeryville CA 94608 510-652-2411 652-5075
Web: www.nady.com

Norcon Communications Inc 510 Burnside Ave .... Inwood NY 11096 516-239-0300
Web: norconcomm.com

Omnitronics LLC 6573 Cochran Rd .... Solon OH 44139 440-349-4900 349-4900
TF: 800-762-9266 ■ *Web:* www.cadaudio.com

OSRAM Sylvania Inc 100 Endicott St .... Danvers MA 01923 978-777-1900 750-2152
Web: www.sylvania.com

Panasonic 3 Panasonic Way .... Secaucus NJ 07094 201-348-7000 553-0723*
**Fax Area Code:* 888 ■ *Web:* panasonic.com

Panasonic Avionics Corp
26200 Enterprise Way .... Lake Forest CA 92630 949-672-2000 462-7100
TF: 877-627-2300 ■ *Web:* panasonic.aero

Panasonic Consumer Electronics Co
1 Panasonic Way .... Secaucus NJ 07094 888-762-2097 392-6168*
NYSE: PC ■ **Fax Area Code:* 201 ■ *TF:* 800-103-1333 ■ *Web:* www.panasonic.com

Panasonic Corp of North America
1 Panasonic Way .... Secaucus NJ 07094 888-762-2097 348-7016*
**Fax Area Code:* 201 ■ **Fax:* Hum Res ■ *TF Cust Svc:* 800-211-7262 ■ *Web:* www.panasonic.com

Peavey Electronics Corp
5022 Hartley Peavey Dr .... Meridian MS 39305 601-483-5365 486-1278
TF: 877-732-8391 ■ *Web:* www.peavey.com

Phase Technology 6400 Youngerman Cir .... Jacksonville FL 32244 904-777-0700
TF: 888-742-7385 ■ *Web:* phasetech.mseaudio.com

Pioneer Electronics (USA) Inc
1925 E Dominguez St .... Long Beach CA 90810 310-952-2000 952-2402
TF: 800-421-1404 ■ *Web:* www.pioneerelectronics.com

Polk Audio Inc 5601 Metro Dr .... Baltimore MD 21215 410-358-3600 764-5266
TF: 800-377-7655 ■ *Web:* www.polkaudio.com

Precision Econowind Inc
8940 N Fork Dr .... North Fort Myers FL 33903 239-997-3860
Web: www.precisioneconowind.com

Primo Microphones Inc 1805 Couch Dr .... McKinney TX 75069 972-548-9807 548-1351
TF: 800-767-7466 ■ *Web:* www.primomic.com

QSC Audio Products LLC
1675 MacArthur Blvd .... Costa Mesa CA 92626 714-754-6175 754-6174*
**Fax:* Mktg ■ *TF:* 800-854-4079 ■ *Web:* www.qsc.com

Quam-Nichols Company Inc 234 E Marquette Rd .... Chicago IL 60637 773-488-5800 488-6944
TF: 800-633-3669 ■ *Web:* www.quamspeakers.com

Rane Corp 10802 47th Ave W .... Mukilteo WA 98275 425-355-6000 347-7757
TF: 877-764-0093 ■ *Web:* www.rane.com

Record Play Tek Inc 110 E Vistula St .... Bristol IN 46507 574-848-5233 848-5333
TF: 800-809-5233 ■ *Web:* www.recordplaytek.com

Remote Technologies Inc
5775 12th Ave E Ste 180 .... Shakopee MN 55379 952-253-3100
Web: www.rticorp.com

Renkus-heinz Inc 19201 Cook St .... Foothill Ranch CA 92610 949-588-9997 588-9514
TF: 855-411-2364 ■ *Web:* www.renkus-heinz.com

ReQuest Inc
100 Saratoga Village Blvd Ste 45 .... Ballston Spa NY 12020 518-899-1254 899-1251*
**Fax:* Sales ■ *TF Sales:* 800-236-2812 ■ *Web:* www.request.com

Roanwell Corp 2564 Pk Ave .... Bronx NY 10451 718-401-0288 401-0663
Web: www.roanwell.com

Robert Bosch LLC
38000 Hills Tech Dr .... Farmington Hills MI 48331 248-876-1000
TF Sales: 800-893-6342 ■ *Web:* www.bosch.us

Rockford Corp 600 S Rockford Dr .... Tempe AZ 85281 480-967-3565 966-3983
OTC: ROFO ■ *TF:* 800-903-2897 ■ *Web:* www.rockfordcorp.com

Sanyo Fisher Co 21605 Plummer St .... Chatsworth CA 91311 818-998-7322 717-2759

SDI Technologies Inc 1299 Main St .... Rahway NJ 07065 800-333-3092
TF: 800-333-3092 ■ *Web:* www.sditechnologies.com

Sharp Electronics Corp 1 Sharp Plz .... Mahwah NJ 07430 201-529-8200 529-8413
TF: 800-237-4277 ■ *Web:* www.sharpusa.com

Sherwood America
6120 Valley View Buena Pk .... Buena Park CA 90620 714-739-2000 739-2009
Web: www.sherwoodamerica.com

Shure Inc 5800 W Touhy Ave .... Niles IL 60714 847-866-2200 600-1212
TF: 800-257-4873 ■ *Web:* www.shure.com

Sima Products Corp 120 Pennsylvania Ave .... Oakmont PA 15139 412-828-3700 828-3775
TF: 800-345-7462 ■ *Web:* simaproducts.com

Skymicro Inc
2060 E Avenida De Los Arboles Ste D344 .... Thousand Oaks CA 91362 805-491-8995
Web: www.skymicro.com

Snell Acoustics 300 Jubilee Dr .... Peabody MA 01960 978-538-6262
Web: www.snellacoustics.com

Sony Corp of America 550 Madison Ave .... New York NY 10022 212-833-6800
TF: 800-282-2848 ■ *Web:* www.sony.com

Sony Electronics Inc 1 Sony Dr .... Park Ridge NJ 07656 201-930-1000
TF Cust Svc: 800-222-7669 ■ *Web:* www.sony.com

Sony of Canada Ltd 115 Gordon Baker Rd .... Toronto ON M2H3R6 416-499-1414 497-1774
Web: www.sony.com/all-electronics

Sound Com Corp 227 Depot St .... Berea OH 44017 440-234-2604 234-2614
TF: 800-628-8739 ■ *Web:* www.soundcom.net

Southern Audio Services
14763 Florida Blvd .... Baton Rouge LA 70819 225-272-7135 272-9844
TF Cust Svc: 800-843-8823 ■ *Web:* www.bazooka.com

Stancil Corp 2644 S Croddy Way .... Santa Ana CA 92704 714-546-2002 546-2092
Web: www.stancilcorp.com

Sunfire Corp 1969 Kellogg Ave .... Carlsbad CA 92008 760-710-0993
Web: www.sunfire.com

TDK USA Corp 525 RXR Plaza .... Uniondale NY 11556 516-535-2600 294-8318*
**Fax:* Sales ■ *Web:* www.tdk.com

TEAC America Inc 7733 Telegraph Rd .... Montebello CA 90640 323-726-0303 727-7656
Web: www.teac.com

Telex Communications Inc
12000 Portland Ave S .... Burnsville MN 55337 952-884-4051 884-0043
TF: 877-863-4169 ■ *Web:* www.telex.com

Toshiba America Inc
1251 Ave of the Americas Ste 4100 .... New York NY 10020 212-596-0600 593-3875
TF: 800-457-7777 ■ *Web:* www.toshiba.com

Universal Audio Inc
1700 Green Hills Rd .... Scotts Valley CA 95066 831-440-1176 461-1550
TF: 877-698-2834 ■ *Web:* www.uaudio.com

Universal Electronics Inc
201 E. Sandpointe Ave 8th Fl .... Santa Ana CA 92707 714-918-9500 918-4100
NASDAQ: UEIC ■ *Web:* www.uei.com

Verrex Corp 1130 Rt 22 W .... Mountainside NJ 07092 908-232-7000 232-7991
Web: www.verrex.com

Vialta Inc 48461 Fremont Blvd .... Fremont CA 94538 510-870-3088
Web: www.vialta.com

Washington Professional Systems (WPS)
109GaitherDr Ste 301 .... Mount Laurel NJ 08054 856-273-8688 273-8558
Web: www.wpsworld.com

Wisdom Audio Corp
1572 College Pkwy Ste 164 .... Carson City NV 89706 775-887-8850 887-8820
Web: www.wisdomaudio.com

Xantech Corp 1969 Kellogg Ave .... Carlsbad CA 92008 818-362-0353 492-6832*
**Fax Area Code:* 800 ■ *TF Sales:* 800-843-5465 ■ *Web:* www.xantech.com

Yamaha Electronics Corp
6660 Orangethorpe Ave .... Buena Park CA 90620 714-522-9888 634-0355*
**Fax Area Code:* 800 ■ *TF:* 800-292-2982 ■ *Web:* usa.yamaha.com

Z Systems 3724 Oregon Ave S .... Minneapolis MN 55426 952-974-3140
Web: www.zsyst.com

Zenith Electronics Corp
2000 Millbrook Dr .... Lincolnshire IL 60069 847-941-8000
Web: www.zenith.com

53 AUTO CLUBS

Phone | Fax

AAA Akron 111 W Ctr St .... Akron OH 44308 330-762-0631 762-5965
Web: www.aaa.com

AAA Allied Group Inc 15 W Central Pkwy .... Cincinnati OH 45202 513-762-3100 762-3282
TF: 800-543-2345 ■ *Web:* ohiovalley.aaa.com

AAA Carolinas 6600 AAA Dr .... Charlotte NC 28212 704-569-3600 285-6176
TF: 800-477-4222 ■
Web: locator.carolinas.aaa.com/nc/charlotte/1032?utm_source=google&utm_medium=distrib&utm_campaign=google-distrib

AAA Chicago Motor Club 975 Meridian Lake Dr .... Aurora IL 60504 866-968-7222 499-8200*
**Fax Area Code:* 630 ■ *TF:* 866-968-7222 ■ *Web:* www.aaa.com

Phone Fax

AAA Colorado 4100 E Arkansas Ave .... Denver CO 80222 303-753-8800 300-7710
TF: 866-625-3601 ■ Web: www.colorado.aaa.com

AAA East Central 5900 Baum Blvd.................. Pittsburgh PA 15206 412-363-5100 362-8943
Web: www.aaa.com

AAA East Penn 1020 W Hamilton St................. Allentown PA 18101 800-222-4357
TF: 800-222-4357 ■ Web: www.aaa.com

AAA Hawaii 1130 N Nimitz Hwy Ste A-170 .... Honolulu HI 96817 808-593-2221 591-9359
TF: 800-736-2886 ■ Web: hawaii.aaa.com/home.html

AAA Hoosier Motor Club 3750 Guion Rd............ Indianapolis IN 46222 317-923-1500 923-5991*
*Fax: Cust Svc ■ Web: www.aaa.com

AAA Hudson Valley 618 Delaware Ave .... Albany NY 12209 518-426-1000 426-1595
Web: www.aaa.com

AAA Massillon Auto Club 1972 Wales Rd NE......... Massillon OH 44646 330-833-1084
TF: 800-222-4357 ■ Web: www.aaa.com

AAA Merrimack Valley
49 OrchaRd Hill Rd.......................... North Andover MA 01845 978-681-9200
Web: www.aaa.com

AAA Michigan 1 Auto Club Dr....................... Dearborn MI 48126 800-222-6424
TF: 800-222-6424 ■ Web: www.aaa.com

AAA Minneapolis 5400 Auto Club Way............. Minneapolis MN 55416 952-927-2600 927-2559
Web: www.aaa.com

AAA Minnesota/Iowa 600 W Travelers Trl .... Burnsville MN 55337 952-707-4500
TF: 800-222-1333 ■ Web: www.aaa.com/ppinternational/international.html

AAA Missouri 12901 N Forty Dr................... Saint Louis MO 63141 314-523-7350
TF: 800-222-4357 ■ Web: aaa.com

AAA MountainWest 2100 11th Ave .... Helena MT 59601 406-447-8100 442-5671
TF: 800-332-6119 ■ Web: www.aaa.com

AAA Nebraska 910 N 96th St.......................... Omaha NE 68114 402-390-1000
TF: 800-222-6327 ■ Web: www.aaa.com/ppinternational/international.html

AAA North Penn 1035 N Washington Ave.............. Scranton PA 18509 570-348-2511 348-2563
TF: 800-222-4357 ■ Web: www.aaa.com

AAA Northampton County 3914 Hecktown Rd............ Easton PA 18045 610-258-2371 258-5256
Web: www.aaa.com

AAA Northern New England 68 Marginal Way .... Portland ME 04104 207-780-6800 780-6986
TF: 800-222-4357 ■ Web: www.northernnewengland.aaa.com

AAA Northway 112 Railroad St .... Schenectady NY 12305 518-374-4696 374-3140
TF: 866-222-7283 ■ Web: aaa.com

AAA Northwest Ohio 7150 W Central Ave .... Toledo OH 43617 419-843-1200 843-1249
TF: 800-428-0060 ■ Web: www.nwohio.aaa.com

AAA Ohio Auto Club 90 E Wilson Bridge Rd......... Worthington OH 43085 614-431-7901 431-7918
TF: 888-222-6446 ■ Web: ohio.aaa.com

AAA Oklahoma 2121 E 15th St .... Tulsa OK 74104 918-748-1000 748-1111
TF: 800-222-2582 ■ Web: www.ok.aaa.com

AAA Reading-Berks 920 Van Reed Rd .... Wyomissing PA 19610 610-374-4531 374-1325
Web: www.aaa.com

AAA Schuylkill County 340 S Centre St............... Pottsville PA 17901 570-622-4991 622-8179
Web: www.aaa.com

AAA Shelby County 920 Wapakoneta Ave................. Sidney OH 45365 937-492-3167 492-7297
Web: www.aaa.com

AAA South Jersey 700 Laurel Oak Rd................. Voorhees NJ 08043 856-783-4222
Web: www.aaa.com

AAA Southern New England
110 Royal Little Dr .... Providence RI 02904 401-868-2000 868-2085
TF: 800-222-7448 ■ Web: www.aaa.com

AAA Southern Pennsylvania 2840 Eastern Blvd............ York PA 17402 717-600-8700
TF: 800-222-1469 ■ Web: www.aaa.com

AAA Susquehanna Valley 1001 Market St.............. Sunbury PA 17801 570-286-4507
Web: www.aaa.com

AAA Tidewater Virginia
5366 Virginia Beach Blvd...................... Virginia Beach VA 23462 757-233-3800 233-3896
Web: www.aaa.com

AAA Utica & Central New York 409 Ct St .... Utica NY 13502 315-797-5000
Web: www.aaa.com

AAA Washington-Inland 1745 114th Ave SE............ Bellevue WA 98004 425-646-2058 467-7729
TF: 800-222-4357 ■ Web: newsroom.aaa.com

AAA Western & Central New York
100 International Dr .... Williamsville NY 14221 716-633-9860 633-4439
TF: 800-836-2582 ■ Web: westerncentralny.aaa.com

AAA Wisconsin 8401 Excelsior Dr.................... Madison WI 53717 608-828-2495
TF: 800-236-1300 ■ Web: newsroom.aaa.com

AARP Motoring Plan 601 E St NW................. Washington DC 20049 800-555-1121
TF: 888-687-2277 ■
Web: www.aarproadside.com/aarp/forwardto.do?pagename=contact_us

American Automobile Association, Inc.
321 Whittington Pkwy............................. Louisville KY 40222 502-582-3311 584-1455
TF: 800-727-2552 ■ Web: www.aaa.com

Auto Club Ltd PO Box 162526......................... Austin TX 78716 866-247-3728
TF: 866-247-3728 ■ Web: www.paragonmotorclub.com

Auto Club of America Corp (ACA)
9411 N Georgia St .... Oklahoma City OK 73120 405-751-4430 751-4462
TF: 800-411-2007 ■ Web: www.autoclubofamerica.com

Auto Club of New York Inc 1415 Kellum Pl .... Garden City NY 11530 516-746-7730 873-2320
Web: www.aaa.com/PPInternational/Benefits_Intl_to_US.html

Automobile Club of Southern California
2601 S Figueroa St............................. Los Angeles CA 90007 213-741-3686 741-4890
TF: 800-400-4222 ■ Web: www.aaa.com

BP MotorClub PO Box 4441 .... Carol Stream IL 60197 800-334-3300
TF: 800-334-3300 ■ Web: www.bpmotorclub.com

Brickell Financial Services Motor Club Inc
7300 Corporate Ctr Dr Ste 601....................... Miami FL 33126 305-392-4300 392-4301
TF: 800-262-7262 ■ Web: www.road-america.com

British Columbia Automobile Assn (BCAA)
4567 Canada Way................................. Burnaby BC V5G4T1 604-268-5000 268-5569
TF: 800-222-4357 ■ Web: www.bcaa.com

CAA Central Ontario 60 Commerce Vly Dr E .... Thornhill ON L3T7P9 905-771-3000 771-3101
TF: 800-268-3750 ■ Web: www.caasco.com

CAA Manitoba 870 Empress St....................... Winnipeg MB R3C2Z3 204-262-6166
TF: 800-222-4357 ■ Web: www.caamanitoba.com

CAA Maritimes Ltd 378 Westmorland Rd............. Saint John NB E2J2G4 506-634-1400 653-9500
TF: 800-471-1611 ■ Web: ww2.aaa.com

CAA North & East Ontario PO Box 8350................ Ottawa ON K1G3T2 613-820-1890 820-4646
TF: 800-267-8713 ■ Web: caaneo.ca

CAA Quebec 444 Bouvier St.......................... Quebec QC G2J1E3 418-624-8222
TF: 800-222-4357 ■ Web: www.caaquebec.com

CAA Stoney Creek 163 Centennial Pkwy N............. Hamilton ON L8E1H8 905-664-8000 664-8080
TF: 800-992-8143 ■ Web: www.caasco.com

California State Automobile Assn
150 Van Ness Ave.......................... San Francisco CA 94102 800-922-8228
TF Cust Svc: 800-922-8228 ■ Web: calstate.aaa.com

Canadian Automobile Assn (CAA) 2151 Thurston Dr ..... Ottawa ON K1G6C9 613-820-1890 247-0118
TF: 800-267-8713 ■ Web: www.caa.ca

Cross Country Automotive Services (CCAS)
1 Cabot Rd .... Medford MA 02155 781-393-9300 395-6706
Web: www.agero.com

Findlay Automobile Club 1550 Tiffin Ave .... Findlay OH 45840 419-422-4961 422-5620
TF: 800-222-4357 ■ Web: www.aaa.com

National Automobile Club (NAC)
373 Vintage Park Dr Ste E......................... Foster City CA 94404 650-294-7000 294-7040
Web: www.nacroadservice.com

National Motor Club of America Inc (NMC)
130 E John Carpenter Fwy .... Irving TX 75062 972-999-1099
TF: 800-523-4582 ■ Web: www.nmc.com

Pennsylvania AAA Federation
600 N Third St .... Harrisburg PA 17101 717-238-7192 238-6574
Web: www.aaapa.org

Pinnacle Motor Club 510 N Topeka St.................. Wichita KS 67214 800-446-1289
TF: 800-446-1289 ■ Web: www.pinnaclemotorclub.com

Travelers Motor Club 720 NW 50th St........... Oklahoma City OK 73154 405-848-1711
TF: 800-654-9208 ■ Web: www.travelersmotorclub.com

Zipcar Inc 35 Thomson Pl .... Boston MA 02210 877-353-9227 995-4300*
NASDAQ: ZIP ■ *Fax Area Code: 617 ■ TF: 877-353-9227 ■ Web: www.zipcar.com

54 AUTO SUPPLY STORES

Phone Fax

A 1 Auto Recyclers 7804 S Hwy 79 .... Rapid City SD 57701 605-348-8442
TF: 800-456-0715 ■ Web: www.a1autorecyclers.com

Advance Auto Parts Inc 5008 Airport Rd .... Roanoke VA 24012 877-238-2623
NYSE: AAP ■ TF: 877-238-2623 ■ Web: advanceautoparts.com

Aeromotive Inc 7805 Barton St........................ Lenexa KS 66214 913-647-7300
Web: www.aeromotiveinc.com

Air Lift Co 2727 Snow Rd............................ Lansing MI 48917 517-322-2144
TF: 800-248-0892 ■ Web: www.airliftcompany.com

Air Specialists Inc 27 Hollenberg Ct .... Bridgeton MO 63044 636-326-5900
Web: airspec.com

American Crane & Tractor Parts Inc
2200 State Line Rd .... Kansas City KS 66103 913-371-8585
Web: www.actparts.com

American Glass Distributors 3901 Airline Dr.......... Houston TX 77022 713-692-8522
TF: 800-570-3303 ■ Web: www.allamericanglass.com

Amex World Trade Corp 18765 Sw 78th Ct........... Cutler Bay FL 33157 305-238-3010
Web: www.amexworldtrade.com

Anatech Ltd 771 Crosspoint Dr....................... Denver NC 28037 704-489-1488
Web: www.anatechltd.com

Anthony Liftgates Inc 1037 W Howard St.............. Pontiac IL 61764 815-842-3383
Web: www.anthonyliftgates.com

Atlanta Commercial Tire Inc
146 Forest Pkwy............................... Forest Park GA 30297 404-675-9998
Web: www.actire.com

Ats All Tire Supply Co
6600 Long Point Rd Ste 101........................ Houston TX 77055 888-339-6665
TF: 888-339-6665 ■ Web: www.alltiresupply.com

Auto Barn 13 Harbor Pk Dr.................... Port Washington NY 11050 516-484-9500 484-4341
Web: www.autobarn.net

AutoZone Inc 123 S Front St....................... Memphis TN 38103 901-495-6500 495-8300
NYSE: AZO ■ TF: 800-288-6966 ■ Web: www.autozone.com

B & b Selectcom Inc 1109 S Fremont Ave.............. Tucson AZ 85719 520-882-0911
Web: bbselectcom.com

Bap Geon LLC
3310 Austin Bluffs Pkwy.................... Colorado Springs CO 80918 713-227-1544
Web: www.bap-geon.com

Bavarian Autosport Inc
275 Constitution Ave .... Portsmouth NH 03801 603-427-2002
Web: www.bavauto.com

Bennett Auto Supply Inc
3141 SW Tenth St.............................. Pompano Beach FL 33069 954-335-8700 924-0003*
*Fax Area Code: 899 ■ *Fax: Hum Res ■ Web: www.bennettauto.com

Benny's Inc 340 Waterman Ave..................... Smithfield RI 02917 401-231-1000 231-1080
Web: www.hellobennys.com

Bill Smith Auto Parts 400 Ash St..................... Danville IL 61832 217-442-0156
Web: www.billsmithauto.com

Black's Tire Service Inc 30 Bitmore Rd .... Whiteville NC 28472 910-642-4123
Web: www.blackstire.com

Blue Star Automobile Stores Inc
2001 S State St.................................. Chicago IL 60616 312-225-7174

BMW of Manhattan Inc 555 W 57th St............... New York NY 10019 212-586-2269
TF: 877-855-4607 ■ Web: www.bmwnyc.com

Bond Auto Parts 45 Summer St .... Barre VT 05641 802-476-3108
TF: 800-639-1982 ■ Web: www.bondauto.com

Bowditch Ford Inc 11291 Jefferson Ave........... Newport News VA 23601 757-595-2211
TF: 866-399-2616 ■ Web: bowditchford.com

Bridgestone Retail Operations LLC
535 Marriott Dr Ste 300 .... Nashville TN 60108 630-259-9000
Web: www.bsro.com

Briggs Auto Group Inc 2312 Stagg Hill Rd........... Manhattan KS 66502 785-537-8330
Web: www.briggsauto.com

Burien Toyota Collision Center
15025 First Ave S................................... Burien WA 98148 206-243-0700
Web: www.burientoyota.com

C & R Racing Inc 6950 Guion Rd .... Indianapolis IN 46268 317-293-4100
Web: www.crracing.com

Cape Electronics 19 Dupont Ave .... South Yarmouth MA 02664 508-394-2405
Web: capeelectronics.com

Company / Address	City	State	Zip	Phone	Fax
Carquest Corp 2635 E Millbrook Rd	Raleigh	NC	27604	919-573-3000	
TF: 800-876-1291 ■ *Web:* www.carquest.com					
CEC Industries Ltd 599 Bond St	Lincolnshire	IL	60069	847-821-1199	
TF: 800-572-4168 ■ *Web:* cecindustries.com					
Chet Nichols Inc 315 E Main St	Benton Harbor	MI	49022	269-925-2136	
Web: www.chetnichols.com					
Chris Alston Chassisworks Inc 8661 Younger Creek Dr	Sacramento	CA	95828	916-388-0288	
TF: 800-722-2269 ■ *Web:* www.cachassisworks.com					
Clark Brothers Instrument Company Inc 56680 Mound Rd	Shelby Township	MI	48316	586-781-7000	
Web: www.clarkbrothers.net					
Coan Engineering LLC 1602 E Havens St	Kokomo	IN	46901	765-456-3957	
Web: www.coanracing.com					
Coastal Automotive Service Garage 2006 Cottonwood Ave	Bay City	TX	77414	979-245-8361	
Web: www.awesomenet.net					
CRP 4X4 Truck OutFitters 2102 Ninth St Ste A	Greeley	CO	80631	970-351-8603	
Web: crptruck.com					
Cumberland Truck Parts 15 Sylmar Rd	Nottingham	PA	19362	610-932-1152	
TF: 800-364-6995 ■ *Web:* www.cumberlandtruck.com					
Custom Truck Accessories Inc 13408 Hwy 65 Ne	Ham Lake	MN	55304	763-757-5326	757-5994
TF: 800-333-1282 ■ *Web:* www.customtruckaccess.com					
Day Motor Sports LLC 6100 Hwy 69 N	Tyler	TX	75706	903-593-9815	
Web: www.daymotorsports.com					
Delco Diesel Services Inc 1100 S Agnew Ave	Oklahoma City	OK	73108	405-232-3595	
TF: 800-256-0395 ■ *Web:* www.delcodiesel.com					
Delta World Tire Co 203 Guilbeau Rd	Lafayette	LA	70506	337-984-3098	
Web: www.deltaworldtire.com					
Des-Case Corp 675 N Main St	Goodlettsville	TN	37072	615-672-8800	
Web: descase.com					
Doug Richert Pontiac Cadillac 1900 Sw Topeka Blvd	Topeka	KS	66612	785-233-1361	
Web: www.dougrichert.com					
Fabrication Technologies Industries Inc 2200 Haffley Ave	National City	CA	91950	619-477-4141	
Web: www.ftisd.com					
Fluke Electronics Canada LP 400 Britannia Rd E Unit 1	Mississauga	ON	L4Z1X9	905-890-7600	
Web: www.fluke.com/fluke/caen/home/default.htm					
Frank Millman Distributors Inc 8 Progress St	Edison	NJ	08820	908-561-7300	
Web: www.millmans.com					
Gallo Equipment Company Inc 11835 S Ave O	Chicago	IL	60617	773-374-5515	
Web: www.galloequipment.com					
Go Industries Inc 420 N Grove Rd	Richardson	TX	75081	972-783-7444	437-3425
Web: goindustries.com					
Green Oak Tire Inc 7480 Kensington Rd	Brighton	MI	48116	248-437-1753	
Web: www.greenoaktire.com					
Hedahls Inc 100 East Broadway	Bismarck	ND	58502	701-223-8393	221-4251
TF: 800-433-2457 ■ *Web:* www.hedahls.com					
Index Engines Inc 960 Holmdel Rd Bldg One 1st Fl	Holmdel	NJ	07733	732-817-1060	
Web: www.indexengines.com					
Inflexxion Inc 320 Needham St Ste 100	Newton	MA	02464	617-332-6028	
Web: www.inflexxion.com					
Jack's Tire & Oil Management Company Inc 1795 N Main St	North Logan	UT	84341	435-752-7811	
Web: www.jackstireandoil.com					
JE Adams Industries Ltd 1025 63rd Ave Sw	Cedar Rapids	IA	52404	319-363-0237	
TF: 800-553-8861 ■ *Web:* www.jeadams.com					
JohnDow Industries Inc 151 Snyder Ave	Barberton	OH	44203	330-753-6895	
Web: johndow.com					
Johnson Power Ltd 2530 Braga Dr	Broadview	IL	60155	708-345-4300	
Web: www.johnsonpower.com					
Knecht's Auto Parts 3400 Main St	Springfield	OR	97478	541-746-4446	746-0884
Web: www.knechts.com					
KOI Warehouse Inc 2701 Spring Grove Ave	Cincinnati	OH	45225	513-357-2400	723-9204
TF: 800-354-0408 ■ *Web:* www.koiautoparts.com					
Kuhn Honda 2522 N Dale Mabry Hwy	Tampa	FL	33607	813-872-4816	
Web: www.kuhnhonda.com					
Mar-K Quality Parts LLC 6625 W Wilshire Blvd	Oklahoma City	OK	73132	405-721-7945	
Web: mar-k.com					
Matsuo Industries USA Inc 408 Municipal Dr	Jefferson City	TN	37760	865-475-9085	
Web: www.matsuousa.com					
Max Auto Supply Co 1101 Monroe St	Toledo	OH	43604	419-243-7281	243-1626
Meridian Auto Parts 10211 Pacific Mesa Blvd Ste 404	San Diego	CA	92121	800-874-1974	
TF: 800-874-1974 ■ *Web:* www.meridianautoparts.com					
Merle's Automotive Supply Inc 33 W University Blvd	Tucson	AZ	85705	520-622-3526	
TF: 800-546-6040 ■ *Web:* www.merlesauto.com					
Midway Auto Supply Inc 1101 S Hampton Rd	Dallas	TX	75208	214-943-4341	
Web: www.midwayautosupply.com					
Midwest Automotive Inc 1065 Lee St	Des Plaines	IL	60016	847-827-8400	
Web: midwestautomotiveinc.com					
Mike Gatto Inc 15 W Hibiscus Blvd	Melbourne	FL	32901	321-676-2710	
Web: www.gattos.com					
Millennium Line X & Truck Accessories 905 N Raceway Rd	Indianapolis	IN	46234	317-209-8000	
Web: www.millenniumlinings.com					
Minor Tire & Wheel Company Inc 3512 Sixth Ave Se	Decatur	AL	35603	256-353-4957	
Web: www.visionwheel.com					
Momo Automotive Accessories Inc 20512 Crescent Bay Ste 104	Lake Forest	CA	92630	949-380-7556	
TF: 800-749-6666 ■ *Web:* www.momo.com					
Motor State Distributing 8300 Lane Dr	Watervliet	MI	49098	269-463-4113	
TF: 800-772-2678 ■ *Web:* www.motorstate.com					

Company / Address	City	State	Zip	Phone	Fax
Motorad of America 6292 Walmore Rd	Niagara Falls	NY	14304	716-731-6442	
Web: www.motoradusa.com					
Myers Brothers of Kansas City Inc 1210 W 28th St	Kansas City	MO	64108	816-931-5501	
TF: 800-264-2404 ■ *Web:* www.myersbrotherskc.com					
Nitto Denko Automotive Ohio Inc 1620 S Main St	Piqua	OH	45356	937-773-4820	
Web: www.piquatechnologies.com					
NORD Drivesystems 800 Nord Dr	Waunakee	WI	53597	888-314-6673	
TF: 888-314-6673 ■ *Web:* www.nord.com					
Northland Auto & Truck Accessories 1106 S 29th St W	Billings	MT	59102	406-245-0595	
TF: 800-736-5302 ■ *Web:* www.northlandautomotive.com					
Nu-Star Inc 1425 Stagecoach Rd	Shakopee	MN	55379	952-445-8295	
Web: www.nustarinc.com					
O'Reilly Automotive Inc 233 S Patterson	Springfield	MO	65802	417-862-6708	
NASDAQ: ORLY ■ *TF:* 888-327-7153 ■ *Web:* www.oreillyauto.com					
OC Seacrets Inc 117 49th St	Ocean City	MD	21842	410-524-4900	
Web: www.seacrets.com					
Original Parts Group Inc (OPGI) 1770 Saturn Way	Seal Beach	CA	90740	562-594-1000	594-1050
TF: 800-243-8355 ■ *Web:* www.opgi.com					
Palm Beach Motoring Accessories Inc 7744 Sw Jack James Dr	Stuart	FL	34997	772-286-2701	
Web: www.autogeek.net					
Parkhouse Tire Service Inc 5960 Shull St	Bell Gardens	CA	90201	562-928-0421	
Web: www.parkhousetire.com					
Parks Auto Parts Professionals 2320 Savannah Hwy	Charleston	SC	29414	843-556-4703	
Web: parksautoparts.com					
PDQ of The Rockies Inc 8214 Park Meadows Dr	Lone Tree	CO	80124	303-662-9100	
Peerless Tire Co 5000 Kingston St	Denver	CO	80239	303-371-4300	
TF: 800-999-7810 ■ *Web:* www.peerlesstyreco.com					
Phoenix USA Inc 51 E Borden St	Cookeville	TN	38501	931-526-6128	
Web: www.phoenixusa.com					
Pick Your Part Auto Wrecking Inc 1235 S Beach Blvd	Anaheim	CA	92804	714-385-1301	
Web: www.lkqpickyourpart.com					
PJS Used Cars & Auto Parts Inc 2708 Caledonia Leroy Rd	Caledonia	NY	14423	585-538-2391	
Web: www.pjs4lkq.com					
Power Station Inc 7360 Reseda Blvd	Reseda	CA	91335	818-344-8148	
Web: www.mauriss.com					
Precision Engine Controls Corp 11661 Sorrento Vly Rd	San Diego	CA	92121	858-792-3217	
Web: www.precisioneng.com					
R Cushman & Associates Inc 32840 W 8 Mile Rd	Farmington	MI	48336	248-477-9900	
Web: www.rcushman.com					
Rent A Tire Inc 2466 Jacksboro Hwy	Fort Worth	TX	76114	817-626-4294	
Web: www.rentatire.com					
Rent A Wheel 2500 Firestone Blvd Ste G	South Gate	CA	90280	818-786-7906	
Web: mobile.rentawheel.com					
Roadster Factory, The 328 Killen Rd	Armagh	PA	15920	814-446-4444	
Web: www.the-roadster-factory.com					
Robertson Tire Company Inc PO Box 472287	Tulsa	OK	74147	918-664-2211	622-7221
Web: www.robertson-tire.com					
Runway Tire Service Inc 4115 19th Ave	Astoria	NY	11105	718-545-5200	
Web: www.runwaytireservice.com					
S & S Tire & Auto Service Center 1475 Jingle Bell Ln	Lexington	KY	40509	800-685-6794	
TF: 800-685-6794 ■ *Web:* www.sstire.com					
S&R Truck Tire Center Inc 1402 Truckers Blvd	Jeffersonville	IN	47130	812-282-4799	
TF: 800-488-2670 ■ *Web:* www.srtrucktire.com					
Sales Automation Support Inc 17025 W Rogers Dr	New Berlin	WI	53151	262-754-8712	
Web: www.salesautomationsupport.com					
SAP USA Truck & Auto Parts Inc 5301 NW 74 Ave Ste 200	Miami	FL	33166	305-594-2844	
Web: www.sapcorp.net					
Spal-Usa Inc 1731 SE Oralabor Rd	Ankeny	IA	50021	515-289-7000	
Web: www.spalusa.com					
Specmo Auto Sound & Speed 1200 E Avis Dr	Madison Heights	MI	48529	800-545-7910	
TF: 800-545-7910 ■ *Web:* www.specmo.com					
Standard Auto Parts Corp 2020 Hollins Ferry Rd	Baltimore	MD	21230	410-659-5400	
Web: www.standardautoparts.com					
Suburban Wheel Cover Co 1420 Landmeier Rd	Elk Grove Village	IL	60007	847-758-0388	
Web: www.suburbanwheelcover.com					
Terry-haggerty Tire Company Inc 980 Broadway	Menands	NY	12204	518-449-5185	
Web: www.terry-haggerty.com					
Thieman Tailgates Inc 600 E Wayne St	Celina	OH	45822	419-586-7727	
Web: www.thieman.com					
Tire Warehouse 200 Holleder Pkwy	Rochester	NY	14615	800-876-6676	
TF: 800-876-6676 ■ *Web:* www.tirewarehouse.net					
Tireman Auto Service Centers Ltd PO Box 3456	Toledo	OH	43607	419-724-8473	
Web: www.thetireman.com					
TNT Parts Inc 3000 S Corporate Pkwy Ste 400	Forest Park	GA	30297	678-244-8532	
Web: www.tntpartsinc.com					
Total Quality Inc 229 Washington Ave	Grand Haven	MI	49417	616-846-4529	
Web: www.shiptqi.com					
Town Fair Tire Company Inc 460 Coe Ave	East Haven	CT	06512	800-972-2245	
TF: 800-972-2245 ■ *Web:* www.townfairtire.com					
Tradesman Truck Accessories LLC 305 N Frisco St	Winters	TX	79567	325-754-4561	
Transdiesel 1310 George Jenkins Blvd	Lakeland	FL	33815	863-688-5881	
Web: www.heavydutytransmissions.com					
Trew Industrial Wheels Inc 310 Wilhagan Rd	Nashville	TN	37217	615-360-9100	
TF: 888-977-8739 ■ *Web:* www.trew-wheels.com					

Phone | Fax

Turbo Parts LLC 767 Pierce Rd Ste 2 ... Clifton Park NY 12065 518-885-3199
Web: www.mdaturbines.com
United Auto Supply 625 Third St ... La Crosse WI 54601 608-784-9198
Web: www.uasparts.com
US Axle Inc 275 Shoemaker Rd ... Pottstown PA 19464 610-323-3800
Web: www.usaxle.com
Utilimaster Holding Co 603 Earthway Blvd ... Bristol IN 46507 800-237-7806
TF: 800-237-7806 ■ *Web:* www.utilimaster.com
Vanguard Trucks Centers 700 Ruskin Dr ... Forest Park GA 30297 866-216-7925 363-4659*
**Fax Area Code:* 404 ■ *TF:* 866-216-7925 ■ *Web:* www.vanguardtrucks.com
Weathers Auto Supply Inc 23308 Airpark Dr ... Petersburg VA 23803 804-861-1076
TF: 888-572-2886 ■ *Web:* www.weathers.com
Wellers Utility Trailers 16889 N Main St ... Bridgeville DE 19933 302-337-8228
Web: www.pacetrailers.com
West Coast Differentials
2429 Mercantile Dr Ste A ... Rancho Cordova CA 95742 916-635-0950
TF: 800-510-0950 ■ *Web:* www.differentials.com
Westbay Auto Parts Inc
2610 SE Mile Hill Dr ... Port Orchard WA 98366 360-876-8008 876-7999
Web: www.westbayautoparts.com
XKS Unlimited Inc 850 Fiero Ln ... San Luis Obispo CA 93401 805-544-7864
TF: 800-444-5247 ■ *Web:* www.xks.com

55 AUTOMATIC MERCHANDISING EQUIPMENT & SYSTEMS

See Also Food Service *p. 2315*

Phone | Fax

Affiliated Control Equipment Inc
640 Wheat Ln ... Wood Dale IL 60191 630-595-4680 595-6151
TF: 800-942-8753 ■ *Web:* www.affiliatedcontrol.com
AIR-serv Group LLC
1370 Mendota Heights Rd ... Mendota Heights MN 55120 651-454-0465 454-9542
TF: 800-247-8363 ■ *Web:* www.air-serv.com
American Coin Merchandising Inc
325 Interlocken Pkwy ... Broomfield CO 80021 303-444-2559 247-1728
American Vending Sales Inc
750 Morse Ave ... Elk Grove Village IL 60007 847-439-9400 439-9405
TF: 800-441-0009 ■ *Web:* www.americanvending.com
Automatic Products International Ltd
165 Bridgepoint Dr ... Saint Paul MN 55075 800-523-8363
TF: 800-523-8363 ■ *Web:* www.automaticproducts.com
Bastian Material Handling LLC (BMH)
10585 N Meridian St 3rd Fl ... Indianapolis IN 46290 317-575-9992 575-8596
TF: 800-772-0464 ■ *Web:* www.bastiansolutions.com
Betson Enterprises Inc
303 Patterson Plank Rd ... Carlstadt NJ 07072 201-438-1300 438-4837
TF: 800-524-2343 ■ *Web:* www.betson.com
Birmingham Vending Co 540 Second Ave N ... Birmingham AL 35204 205-324-7526 322-6639
TF: 800-288-7635 ■ *Web:* www.bhmvending.com
Coin Acceptors Inc 300 Hunter Ave ... Saint Louis MO 63124 314-725-0100 725-2896
TF: 800-325-2646 ■ *Web:* www.coinco.com
Coinstar Inc 1800 114th Ave SE ... Bellevue WA 98004 425-943-8000
TF: 800-928-2274 ■ *Web:* www.coinstar.com
Dixie-Narco Inc 3330 Dixie-Narco Blvd ... Williston SC 29853 803-266-5000 266-5000
TF: 800-688-9090 ■ *Web:* www.dixie-narco.com
Glacier Water Services Inc 1385 Pk Ctr Dr ... Vista CA 92081 760-560-1111
OTC: GWSV ■ *TF:* 800-452-2437 ■ *Web:* www.glacierwater.com
Harcourt Outlines Inc 7765 S 175 W PO Box 128 ... Milroy IN 46156 800-428-6584 278-5165
TF: 800-428-6584 ■ *Web:* www.harcourtoutlinesstore.com
Melo-Tone Vending Inc 130 Broadway ... Somerville MA 02145 617-666-4900 666-4906
Web: melo-tone-vending-inc.placestars.com
Northwestern Corp PO Box 490 ... Morris IL 60450 815-942-1300 942-4417
TF: 800-942-1316 ■ *Web:* www.nwcorp.com

56 AUTOMATIC TELLER MACHINES (ATMS)

Phone | Fax

Accu-time Systems Inc 420 Somers Rd ... Ellington CT 06029 860-870-5000 872-1511
TF: 800-355-4648 ■ *Web:* www.accu-time.com
Diebold Inc 5995 Mayfair Rd ... North Canton OH 44720 330-490-4000
NYSE: DBD ■ *TF:* 800-999-3600 ■ *Web:* www.diebold.com
Electronic Cash Systems Inc (ECS)
30352 Esperanza ... Rancho Santa Margarita CA 92688 949-888-8580 888-8024
TF: 888-327-2860 ■ *Web:* www.ecspayments.com
Everi Holdings Inc (GCA)
7250 S Tenaya Way Ste 100 ... Las Vegas NV 89113 702-855-3000
NYSE: EVRI ■ *TF:* 800-833-7110 ■ *Web:* www.everi.com
Tidel Engineering Inc
2025 W Belt Line Rd Ste 114 ... Carrollton TX 75006 972-484-3358 484-1014
TF: 800-678-7577 ■ *Web:* www.tidel.com

57 AUTOMOBILE DEALERS & GROUPS

See Also Automobile Sales & Related Services - Online *p. 1829*

Phone | Fax

#1 Cochran of Monroeville
4520 William Penn Hwy ... Monroeville PA 15146 412-373-3333
Web: cochran.com
15625 Ft Bend Ltd 15625 SW Fwy ... Sugar Land TX 77478 281-207-1500
32 Ford Mercury Inc 610 W Main St ... Batavia OH 45103 513-732-2124
A & T Chevrolet Inc 801 Bethlehem Pk ... Sellersville PA 18960 215-257-8022
A C Nelson Rv World 11818 L St ... Omaha NE 68137 402-333-1122 333-1054
TF: 888-655-2332 ■ *Web:* www.acnrv.com
AAA Aircraft Supply LLC 68 Shaker Rd ... Enfield CT 06082 860-749-5192
Web: aaa-aircraft.com
Aberdeen Chrysler Center Inc
901 Auto Plz Dr ... Aberdeen SD 57401 605-225-1656
Web: www.aberdeenchrysler.com
ACK Controls Inc 2600 Happy Vly Rd ... Glasgow KY 42141 270-678-6200

Phone | Fax

Action Tire 2405 Weaver Way ... Doraville GA 30340 770-263-9695 448-3888
Web: www.actiontireco.com
Acura Medical Systems Inc
8990 Cotter St ... Lewis Center OH 43035 614-781-0600
Web: acuramed.com
Acura Neon 1801 N Willow Ave ... Broken Arrow OK 74012 918-252-2258
Web: www.anisigns.com
Acura of Bellevue 13424 NE 20th St ... Bellevue WA 98005 425-644-3000
Web: www.acuraofbellevue.com
Adams Auto Corp 501 NE Colbern Rd ... Lees Summit MO 64086 816-358-7600
Adamson Motors Inc 4800 Hwy 52 N ... Rochester MN 55901 507-289-4004
Web: adamsonmotors.com
Advanced Auto Service & Tire Centers
1947 N Higley Rd ... Mesa AZ 85205 480-985-5400
Web: advancedauto.com
Aeroman 139 SW 51st Ter ... Cape Coral FL 33914 239-540-0040
Alberic Colon Auto Sales Inc
Ave John F Kennedy Carr Ste 2 KM 3.4 ... San Juan PR 00920 877-292-4610
TF: 877-292-4610 ■ *Web:* albericgm.com
Alden Buick Gmc Truck Inc 6 Whalers Way ... Fairhaven MA 02719 508-999-3300
Web: aldengmc.com
Alford Motors Inc Hwy 171 ... Leesville LA 71461 337-397-4144
Web: www.alfordmotors.com
All American Ford Inc 520 River St ... Hackensack NJ 07601 201-487-6700
Web: www.allamericanfordofhackensack.com
Allen Turner Hyundai Inc
6000 Pensacola Blvd ... Pensacola FL 32505 850-479-9667
Web: www.allenturnerhyundai.com
Allgeier Auto Parts Inc 7650 Harrison Ave ... Cincinnati OH 45247 513-353-3377
Web: allgeierautoparts.com
Allied Toyotalift 1640 Island Home Ave ... Knoxville TN 37920 865-573-0995
TF: 866-538-0667 ■ *Web:* www.alliedtoyotalift.com
America's Car-Mart Inc
802 SE Plz Ave Ste 200 ... Bentonville AR 72712 479-464-9944 273-7556
NASDAQ: CRMT ■ *Web:* www.car-mart.com
American Augers Inc 135 US Rt 42 ... West Salem OH 44287 419-869-7107 869-7727
TF: 800-324-4930 ■ *Web:* www.americanaugers.com
Anchor Subaru LLC
949 Eddie Dowling Hwy ... North Smithfield RI 02896 401-769-1199
Web: anchorsubaru.com
Ancira Winton Chevrolet 6111 Bandera Rd ... San Antonio TX 78238 210-762-4545
TF General: 800-299-5286 ■ *Web:* chevroletancira.com
Anthony Underwood Inc 4006 Bessemer Hwy ... Bessemer AL 35020 205-424-4033
Web: anthonyunderwood.com
Apple Tree Enterprises Inc 195 Underwood Rd ... Fletcher NC 28732 828-684-4400
Web: www.appletreeautos.com
Arizona Bus Sales Corp 3615 S 28th St ... Phoenix AZ 85040 602-437-2255
Web: www.arizonabussales.com
Arlington Toyota Inc
10939 Atlantic Blvd ... Jacksonville FL 32225 904-721-3000
Web: www.arlingtontoyota.com
Arrow Truck Sales Inc
3200 Manchester Trfy ... Kansas City MO 64129 816-923-5000 923-4005
TF: 800-311-7144 ■ *Web:* www.arrowtruck.com
Art Morrison Enterprises Inc 5301 Eighth St E ... Fife WA 98424 253-922-7188
TF: 888-640-0516 ■ *Web:* www.artmorrison.com
Asbury Automotive Group Inc
2905 Premiere Pkwy Ste 300 ... Duluth GA 30097 770-418-8200
NYSE: ABG ■ *Web:* www.asburyauto.com
Asheville Chevrolet Inc 205 Smokey Pk Hwy ... Asheville NC 28806 828-665-4444
TF: 866-921-1073 ■ *Web:* www.ashevillechevrolet.com
Associated Aircraft Mfg & Sales Inc
2735 NW 63rd Ct ... Fort Lauderdale FL 33309 954-772-6606
Web: www.aamsi.com
Astoria Ford 710 W Marine Dr ... Astoria OR 97103 503-325-6411
TF: 888-760-9303 ■ *Web:* www.astoriaford.net
Astron Wireless Technologies Inc
22560 Glenn Dr Ste 114 ... Sterling VA 20164 703-450-5517
Web: www.astronwireless.com
Atlanta Toyota Inc 2345 Pleasant Hill Rd ... Duluth GA 30096 770-476-8282
Web: www.atlantatoyota.com
Atlantic Automotive Corp 23 Walker Ave ... Baltimore MD 21208 410-602-6177
Web: www.mileonecorporate.com
Atlantic British Ltd
Halfmoon Light Industrial Pk 6 Enterprise Ave
... Clifton Park NY 12065 518-664-6169
TF: 800-533-2210 ■ *Web:* www.roverparts.com
Atlantic Tire & Supply Company Inc
1430 Saint Georges Ave ... Avenel NJ 07001 732-381-0100
Web: www.emcar.com
Atlantic Tractor LLC 31415 John Deere Dr ... Salisbury MD 21804 410-860-0676
Web: atlantictractor.net
Auto Credit Express Inc
3271 Five Points Dr Ste 200 ... Auburn Hills MI 48326 248-370-6600
Web: www.autocreditexpress.net
Auto Lenders Liquidation Center 104 Rt 73 ... Voorhees NJ 08043 888-305-5968
TF: 888-305-5968 ■ *Web:* www.autolenders.com
Auto Mall, The 800 Pytney Rd ... Brattleboro VT 05301 802-275-4510
Web: www.brattautomall.com
Auto Quotes
8800 Baymeadows Way W Ste 500 ... Jacksonville FL 32256 904-384-2279
Web: aqnet.com
Auto Supply Company Inc 1032 Winston St ... Greensboro NC 27405 336-275-6193
Web: www.ascodc.com
Auto Toy Store, The
727 N Federal Hwy ... Fort Lauderdale FL 33304 754-551-7900
Web: www.thenewautotoystore.com
AutoFair Automotive Group 200 Keller St ... Manchester NH 03103 603-634-1000
Web: www.autofair.com
Autoland 170 Rt 22 E ... Springfield NJ 07081 973-467-2900
TF Sales: 877-813-7239 ■ *Web:* www.1800autoland.com
Automann Inc 850 Randolph Rd ... Somerset NJ 08873 201-529-4996
Web: www.automann.com

				Phone	Fax

Automobile Racing Club of America
8117 Lewis Ave ... Temperance MI 48182 734-847-6726
TF: 800-385-2503 ■ *Web:* www.arcaracing.com

AutoNation Inc
200 SW First Ave Ste 1600 ... Fort Lauderdale FL 33301 954-769-7000 769-6537*
NYSE: AN ■ **Fax:* PR ■ *Web:* www.autonation.com/pages/homepage.aspx

Autorama Inc 5389 Poplar Ave ... Memphis TN 38119 901-345-6211
TF: 888-356-7636 ■ *Web:* www.mbofmemphis.com

AutoRevo LTD 7920 Belt Line Rd Ste 450 ... Dallas TX 75254 972-715-8600
TF: 888-311-7386 ■ *Web:* www.autorevo.com

Aviation Devices & Electronic Components LLC
1810 Mony St ... Fort Worth TX 76102 817-738-9161
Web: www.avdec.com

Aviation Ground Equipment Corp 53 Hanse Ave ... Freeport NY 11520 516-546-0003
TF: 800-758-0044 ■ *Web:* www.aviationgroundequip.com

B & b Automotive Inc 301 W Market St ... Aberdeen WA 98520 360-533-4113
Web: www.bbauto.org

Badger Truck Ctr Inc 2326 W St Paul Ave ... Milwaukee WI 53233 414-344-9500 344-4323
Web: www.badgertruck.com

Badger Utility Inc 4334 Daentl Rd ... Deforest WI 53532 608-249-5301
Web: www.badger-utility.com

Bain & Holden Tire Company Inc
100 N Amhurst Pl ... Englewood TN 37329 423-887-7932

Baker & Sons Equipment Co 45381 SR- 145 ... Lewisville OH 43754 740-567-3317
Web: www.bakerandsons.com

Baker Motor Company Inc 1511 Savannah Hwy ... Charleston SC 29407 843-852-4000
Web: www.bakermotorcompany.com

Bale Chevrolet Co 13101 Chenal Pkwy ... Little Rock AR 72211 501-221-9191 221-9484
Web: balechevrolet.com

Ball Automotive Group
1935 National City Blvd ... National City CA 91950 619-474-6431
TF: 888-318-6492 ■ *Web:* www.ballauto.com

Banner Equipment Company Inc 1370 Bungalow Rd ... Morris IL 60450 815-941-9600
Web: www.bannerbeer.com

Barry Bunker Chevrolet Inc 1307 N Wabash Ave ... Marion IN 46952 765-664-1275
TF Sales: 866-603-8625 ■ *Web:* barrybunker.com

Bartow Ford Co 2800 Us Hwy 98 N ... Bartow FL 33830 863-533-0425
Web: bartowford.com

Baskin Auto Truck & Tractor Inc
1844 Hwy 51 S ... Covington TN 38019 901-476-2626 476-2658
TF: 877-476-2626 ■ *Web:* www.baskintrandtr.com

Bates Ford 1673 W Main St ... Lebanon TN 37087 888-834-4671
TF: 888-834-4671 ■ *Web:* tonybatesfordsales.com

Baxter Chrysler Jeep Inc 17950 Burt St ... Omaha NE 68118 402-493-7800
Web: baxterchryslerjeepdodge.net

Bayway Lincoln-mercury Inc 12333 Gulf Fwy ... Houston TX 77034 888-262-9275
TF: 888-262-9275 ■ *Web:* clickmotive.com

Beach Ford Inc
2717 Virginia Beach Blvd ... Virginia Beach VA 23452 757-486-2717
Web: beachfordvirginiabeach.com

Becker Avionics Inc 10376 Usa Today Way ... Miramar FL 33025 954-450-3137
Web: www.becker-avionics.com

Bed Wood & Parts LLC
8345 Madisonville Rd ... Hopkinsville KY 42240 270-424-3000
TF: 877-205-9663 ■ *Web:* bedwoodandparts.com

Bell Aviation Inc 2404 Edmund Hwy ... West Columbia SC 29170 803-822-4114 822-8970
Web: www.bellaviation.com

Bell Ford Inc 2401 W Bell Rd ... Phoenix AZ 85023 602-866-1776
TF: 800-688-1776 ■ *Web:* www.bellford.com

Bellamy Automotive Group Inc
145 Industrial Blvd ... Mcdonough GA 30253 770-954-3000
Web: bellamystrickland.com

Ben Davis Chevrolet 931 W Seventh St ... Auburn IN 46706 260-570-4327
Web: bendavischevrolet.net

Berge Ford 460 E Auto Ctr Dr ... Mesa AZ 85204 480-497-1111
Web: www.bergefordfleet.com

Bergstrom Automotive 1 Neenah Ctr ... Neenah WI 54956 920-725-4444
Web: www.bergstromauto.com

Bergstrom of Kaukauna 2929 Lawe St ... Kaukauna WI 54130 866-939-0130
TF: 866-939-0130 ■ *Web:* www.bergstromchryslerjeep.com/contact-form.htm

Best Chevrolet Inc 128 Derby St ... Hingham MA 02043 866-208-7873 749-8153*
**Fax Area Code:* 781 ■ *TF:* 866-208-7873 ■ *Web:* www.thebestchevy.com

Big Country Autoland 4004 Spur Business 84 ... Snyder TX 79549 325-573-5456
Web: bigcountryautoland.com

Biggers Chevrolet 1385 E Chicago St ... Elgin IL 60120 847-742-9000 742-0061
TF: 866-431-1555 ■ *Web:* www.biggerschevy.com

Bill Abbott Inc 500 W Ctr ... Monticello IL 61856 217-762-2576
Web: billabbottinc.com

Bill Black Chevrolet Cadillac Inc
601 E Bessemer Ave ... Greensboro NC 27405 336-275-9641
Web: billblackauto.com

Bill Collins 4220 BaRdstown Rd ... Louisville KY 40218 502-459-9550
TF: 888-327-9095 ■ *Web:* billcollinsford.net

Bill Currie Ford Inc 5815 N Dale Mabry Hwy ... Tampa FL 33614 813-872-5555
Web: billcurrieford.com

Bill Penney Toyota 4808 University Dr NW ... Huntsville AL 35816 256-837-1111
Web: www.billpenneytoyota.com

Bill Snethkamp Lansing Dodge Inc
6131 S Pennsylvania Ave ... Lansing MI 48911 517-394-1200
TF: 800-863-6343 ■ *Web:* www.billsnethkamp.com

Bill Stasek Chevrolet Inc 700 W Dundee Rd ... Wheeling IL 60090 847-537-7000
Web: www.stasekchevrolet.com

Billings Nissan 2100 King Ave W ... Billings MT 59102 406-655-1111
Web: billingsnissan.com

Birchwood automative group
35D-3965 Portage Ave ... Winnipeg MB R3K2H7 204-832-1676
Web: birchwood.ca

Blaise Alexander Chevrolet Inc
933 Broad St ... Montoursville PA 17754 570-368-8677
Web: blaisealexander.com

Blossom Chevrolet Inc
1850 N Shadeland Ave ... Indianapolis IN 46219 317-357-1121
Web: www.blossomchevrolet.com

BMW of Darien 140 Ledge Rd ... Darien CT 06820 203-656-1804
TF: 855-349-6240 ■ *Web:* www.bmwdarien.com

BMW Toronto 11 Sunlight Park Rd ... Toronto ON M4M1B5 416-623-4269
Web: bmwtoronto.ca

Bob Allen Ford 9239 Metcalf Ave ... Overland Park KS 66212 913-381-3000
TF: 888-573-6364 ■ *Web:* www.boballenford.com

Bob Brown Chevrolet Inc 3600 111th St ... Urbandale IA 50322 515-278-7800
Web: bobbrownchevy.com

Bob Davidson Ford Lincoln 1845 E Joppa Rd ... Baltimore MD 21234 410-661-6400 668-4306
TF: 877-885-7890 ■ *Web:* www.bobdavidsonford.com

Bob Fisher Chevrolet Inc
4111 Pottsville Pike ... Reading PA 19605 610-370-6683
Web: www.bobfisherchev.com

Bob Montgomery Chevrolet Honda Inc
5340 Dixie Hwy ... Louisville KY 40216 502-448-2820
Web: www.bobmontgomery.com

Bob Sight Ford Inc 610 NW Blue Pkwy ... Lees Summit MO 64063 816-524-6550
Web: bobsightford.com

Bob Stall Chevrolet 7601 Alvarado Rd ... La Mesa CA 91942 619-460-1311
TF: 800-295-2695 ■ *Web:* www.bobstall.com

Bobby Murray Chevrolet Inc 1820 Capital Blvd ... Raleigh NC 27604 919-834-6441

Bohnert Equipment Company Inc
1010 S Ninth St ... Louisville KY 40203 502-584-3391
Web: www.bohnert.com

Bommarito Automotive Group
15736 Manchester Rd ... Ellisville MO 63011 636-391-7200 394-3241
TF: 800-367-2289 ■ *Web:* www.bommarito.com

Bonner Chevrolet Company Inc
694 Wyoming Ave ... Kingston PA 18704 570-763-4799 288-0853
Web: www.bonnerchevrolet.com

Bosserman Aviation Equipment Inc 2327 SR- 568 ... Carey OH 43316 419-396-6256
Web: www.bossermanaviationequip.com

Boucher Group Inc 4141 S 108th St ... Greenfield WI 53228 414-427-4141 427-4140
Web: www.boucher.com

Bozard Ford Co 540 Outlet Mall Blvd ... St Augustine FL 32084 904-824-1641
Web: bozardford.com

Brasher Motor Company of Weimar Inc
1700 I- 10 ... Weimar TX 78962 979-725-8515 725-8118
TF: 800-783-1746 ■ *Web:* www.brashermotors.com

Braxton Automotive Group Inc
1604 Howell Mill Rd NW ... Atlanta GA 30318 404-367-4767
Web: www.braxtonautogroup.com

Brickner Motors Inc 16450 County Rd A ... Marathon WI 54448 715-842-5611
Web: bricknermotors.net

Brighton Chrysler Plymouth Dodge Inc
9827 E Grand River ... Brighton MI 48116 810-355-4161

Brighton Ford Inc 8240 W Grand River ... Brighton MI 48114 810-227-1171
TF: 888-644-9991 ■ *Web:* brightonford.com

Brogan Cadillac Co 112 Rt 46 E ... Totowa NJ 07512 973-785-4300
Web: brogancadillac.com

Brown & Miller Racing Solutions LLC
4005 Dearborn Pl NW ... Concord NC 28027 704-793-4319
Web: www.bmrs.net

Brown Automotive Group LP 4300 S Georgia ... Amarillo TX 79110 806-353-7211
TF: 888-388-6728 ■ *Web:* smallerprofit.com

BTECH Inc 10 Astro Pl ... Rockaway NJ 07866 973-983-1120
Web: www.btechinc.com

Buchanan Automotive Group
50 Central Ave Ste 900 ... Sarasota FL 34236 941-364-9500
TF: 888-292-4883 ■ *Web:* www.buchananautogroup.com

Buckeye Nissan Inc 3820 Pkwy Ln ... Hilliard OH 43026 614-771-2345
TF: 800-686-4391 ■ *Web:* buckeyenissan.com

Bud Weiser Motors Inc 2676 Milwaukee Rd ... Beloit WI 53511 608-466-4172
Web: budweisermotors.com

Burr Truck & Trailer Sales Inc 2901 Vestal Rd ... Vestal NY 13850 607-729-2211 729-4375
Web: www.burrtruck.com

Bus Andrews Truck Equipment Inc
2828 N E Ave ... Springfield MO 65803 417-869-1541 869-1656
TF: 800-273-0733 ■ *Web:* busandrews.com

Bush Inc 2581 Hickory Blvd SE ... Lenoir NC 28645 828-728-4224
Web: www.roosterbush.com

Butler County Ford 400 S Main St ... Butler PA 16001 724-287-2766
Web: www.butlercountyford.net

Byerly Ford 4041 Dixie Hwy ... Louisville KY 40216 502-448-1661
TF: 888-436-0819 ■ *Web:* www.byerlyford.com

Cable-Dahmer Chevrolet Inc
1834 S Noland Rd ... Independence MO 64055 816-521-7508 521-7542
TF: 888-738-5260 ■ *Web:* www.cabledahmer.com

Cadillac Jack Inc 2450 Satellite Blvd ... Duluth GA 30096 770-908-2094
Web: cadillacjack.com

Cal Tech Precision Inc 1830 N Lemon St ... Anaheim CA 92801 714-992-4130
Web: www.caltechprecision.com

Callaway Cars Inc 3 High St ... Old Lyme CT 06371 860-434-9002
TF: 866-927-9400 ■ *Web:* www.callawaycars.com

Camar Aircraft Parts Co 743 Flynn Rd ... Camarillo CA 93012 805-389-8944
Web: www.camarac.com

Canfield Equipment Service 21533 Mound Rd ... Warren MI 48091 586-757-2020
TF: 800-637-3956 ■ *Web:* www.canfieldequipment.com

Capital Automobile Co 2210 Cobb Pkwy SE ... Smyrna GA 30080 770-952-2277 989-8439
Web: www.capitalcadillac.com

Capital Ford Inc 4900 Capital Blvd ... Raleigh NC 27616 919-790-4600 871-6900
TF: 877-659-2496 ■ *Web:* www.capitalford.com

Capitol Chevrolet Montgomery
711 Eastern Blvd ... Montgomery AL 36117 334-272-8700
TF Sales: 800-410-1137 ■ *Web:* www.capitolchevrolet.com

Car City Motor Company Inc
3100 S US Hwy 169 ... Saint Joseph MO 64503 816-233-9149
TF: 800-525-7008 ■ *Web:* www.carcitymotors.com

Cardinal Honda 531 Rt 12 ... Groton CT 06340 860-449-0411
Web: www.cardinalhonda.com

CarMax Inc 12800 Tuckahoe Creek Pkwy ... Richmond VA 23238 804-747-0422 217-6819
NYSE: KMX ■ *TF:* 888-722-7629 ■ *Web:* www.carmax.com

Name / Address	City	State	Zip	Phone	Fax
Carolina International Trucks Inc 1619 Bluff Rd *TF:* 800-868-4923 ■ *Web:* www.carolinainternational.com	Columbia	SC	29201	803-799-4923	
Carr Auto Group 11635 SW Canyon Rd *Web:* www.carrauto.com	Beaverton	OR	97005	503-644-2161	
Cars & Trucks r Us 7676 Happy Vly Rd *Web:* ucarsandtrucks.com	Cave City	KY	42127	270-773-2886	
Carter Motor Co 400 S Railroad St *Web:* www.cartermotor.com	Warren	IL	61087	815-745-2100	
Cascade Autocenter 148 Easy St *Web:* www.cascadeautocenter.com	Wenatchee	WA	98801	509-663-0011	
Cavender Cadillac Co 7625 N Loop 1604 E *Web:* www.cavendercadillac.com	San Antonio	TX	78233	210-226-7221	
Centric Parts Inc 14528 Bonelli St *Web:* centricparts.com	City Of Industry	CA	91746	626-961-5775	
CFI Tire Service 1520 E S Omaha Bridge Rd *Web:* cfitirecb.com	Council Bluffs	IA	51503	712-388-9744	
Champion Chevrolet Cadillac of Johnson City LLC 3606 Bristol Hwy *Web:* www.championjc.com	Johnson City	TN	37601	423-282-2121	
Champion Preferred Automotive 2020 Lexington Rd *Web:* www.championautos.com	Nicholasville	KY	40356	859-269-4141	
Chaplins Bellevue Subaru-volkswagen 15000 SE Eastgate Way *Web:* www.chaplins.com	Bellevue	WA	98007	425-641-2002	
Charles Gabus Ford Inc 4545 Merle Hay Rd *TF Sales:* 800-934-2287 ■ *Web:* charlesgabusford.com	Des Moines	IA	50310	515-270-0707	270-2162
Checkered Flag Motor Car Corp 5225 Virginia Beach Blvd *TF:* 866-414-7820 ■ *Web:* www.checkeredflag.com	Virginia Beach	VA	23462	757-687-3486	
Chenoweth Ford Inc Rt 50 E	Clarksburg	WV	26301	304-623-6501	
Cherry Creek Dodge 2727 S Havana St *TF Sales:* 888-891-7522 ■ *Web:* www.cherrycreekdodge.com	Denver	CO	80014	303-751-1104	
Chino Hills Ford 4480 Chino Hills Pkwy *Web:* chinohillsford.com	Chino	CA	91710	909-342-7466	
Chuck Patterson Inc 200 E Ave *Web:* www.chuckpattersontoyota.net	Chico	CA	95926	530-895-1771	
Circle Buick Gmc Inc 2440 45th St *Web:* circleautomotive.com	Highland	IN	46322	219-865-4400	
City Auto Sales 4932 Elmore Rd *Web:* www.cityauto.com	Memphis	TN	38128	901-377-9502	
City Motors of Cartersville 352 N Tennessee St	Cartersville	GA	30120	770-382-5780	
Cityside Subaru 790 Pleasant St *Web:* citysidesubaru.com	Belmont	MA	02478	617-826-5000	
Cliff Findlay Auto Ctr Inc 3730 Stockton Hill Rd	Kingman	AZ	86409	928-757-4041	757-9701
Clinton Family Ford Lincoln Mercury of Rock Hill Inc 1884 Canterbury Glen Ln *Web:* clintonfamilyford.com	Rock Hill	SC	29730	803-366-3181	
Coastal Tractor Inc 10 Harris Pl *Web:* www.coastaltractor.com	Salinas	CA	93901	831-757-4101	
Coastline Equipment 1930 Lockwood St *Web:* www.coastlineequipment.com	Oxnard	CA	93036	805-485-2106	
Cobalt Truck Equipment 4620 E Trent Ave *Web:* www.critzer.com	Spokane	WA	99212	509-534-0446	
Coffman Truck Sales 1149 W Lake St Rt 31 *TF:* 800-255-7641 ■ *Web:* www.coffmantrucks.com	Aurora	IL	60506	630-892-7093	892-1080
College Station Ford 1351 Earl Rudder Fwy S *TF:* 888-508-0241 ■ *Web:* www.collegestationford.com	College Station	TX	77845	979-694-2022	
Colussy Chevrolet 3073 Washington Pike *Web:* colussy.com	Bridgeville	PA	15017	412-564-4132	
Component Repair Technologies Inc 8507 Tyler Blvd *Web:* componentrepair.com	Mentor	OH	44060	440-255-1793	
Composite Solutions Corp 1820 W Vly Hwy N *Web:* www.compositesolutions.com	Auburn	WA	98001	253-833-1878	
Conant Auto Retail Group 18900 Studebaker Rd *TF:* 888-318-5001 ■ *Web:* www.thecargroup.com	Cerritos	CA	90703	888-318-5001	
Concord Road Equipment Manufacturing Inc 348 Chester St *TF:* 800-942-7623 ■ *Web:* www.concordroadequipment.com	Painesville	OH	44077	440-357-5344	
Concours Motors Inc 1400 W Silver Spring Dr *Web:* concoursmotors.com	Milwaukee	WI	53209	414-290-1400	
Consumer Safety Technology Inc 10520 Hickman Rd Ste F *Web:* www.intoxalock.com	Des Moines	IA	50325	515-331-7643	
Control Logistics Inc 1213 Pope Ln *Web:* www.aerowindows.com	Lake Worth	FL	33460	561-641-2031	
Cook Gm Super Store 1193 W Saginaw Rd *Web:* cookgm.com	Vassar	MI	48768	989-882-4074	
Cook Truck Equipment & Tools 3701 Harlee Ave *TF:* 800-241-4210 ■ *Web:* www.cooktruck.com	Charlotte	NC	28208	704-392-4138	
Cooley Motors Corp 401 N Greenbush Rd *TF:* 888-518-0245 ■ *Web:* www.cooleyvw.com	Rensselaer	NY	12144	518-283-2902	
Cooper Motors Inc 985 York St *TF:* 866-414-2809 ■ *Web:* coopermotors.com	Hanover	PA	17331	866-414-2809	
Coral Springs Auto Mall 9400 W Atlantic Blvd *TF:* 800-353-8660 ■ *Web:* www.coralspringsautomall.com	Coral Springs	FL	33071	954-369-1016	
Corning Ford Inc 2280 Short Dr *Web:* www.corningford.com	Corning	CA	96021	530-824-5434	
Costa Mesa Nissan 2850 Harbor Blvd *Web:* www.costamesanissan.com	Costa Mesa	CA	92626	714-444-4220	
Coulter Cadillac Inc 1188 E Camelback Rd *Web:* coulteroncamelback.com	Phoenix	AZ	85014	602-714-3112	
Country Club Nissan 55 Oneida St *Web:* www.countryclubnissan.com	Oneonta	NY	13820	607-432-2800	
Court Street Ford Inc 558 William Latham Dr *Web:* courtstreetford.com	Bourbonnais	IL	60914	815-939-9600	
Courtesy Chevrolet 1233 E Camelback Rd *TF:* 877-295-4648 ■ *Web:* www.houseofcourtesy.com	Phoenix	AZ	85014	602-235-0255	
Courtesy Chrysler Jeep Dodge 9207 Adamo Dr E *TF:* 866-343-9730 ■ *Web:* www.courtesychryslerjeepdodge.com	Tampa	FL	33619	813-620-4300	
Courtney Honda 767 Bridgeport Ave *Web:* courtneyhonda.com	Milford	CT	06460	203-877-2888	
Crescent Ford Truck Sales 6121 Jefferson Hwy *Web:* crescenttrucks.com	Harahan	LA	70123	504-818-1818	
Criswell Automotive 503 Quince Orchard Rd *Web:* www.criswellauto.com	Gaithersburg	MD	20878	301-948-0880	
Crivelli Chevrolet Buick Inc 600 N Church St	Mt Pleasant	PA	15666	724-547-2200	
Crivelli Ford Inc 2085 Brodhead Rd *Web:* crivelliford.com	Aliquippa	PA	15001	724-857-0400	
Crown Auto Dealerships Inc 5237 34th St N *Web:* crowncars.com	St Petersburg	FL	33714	727-527-7151	
Crown Motors Ltd 196 Regent Blvd *TF:* 800-466-7000 ■ *Web:* www.crownmotors.com	Holland	MI	49423	616-396-5268	
Cumberland Chrysler Ctr 1550 Interstate Dr *TF:* 888-277-4902 ■ *Web:* www.cumberlandchryslercenter.com	Cookeville	TN	38501	888-277-4902	
D-Patrick Motoplex Inc 200 N Green River Rd *TF:* 800-831-6870 ■ *Web:* www.dpat.com	Evansville	IN	47715	812-473-6500	
Daewoo Motor America Inc 159 W Orangethorpe Ave Ste A	Placentia	CA	90870	562-313-1020	
Dale Willey Automotive 2840 Iowa St *Web:* dalewilleyauto.com	Lawrence	KS	66046	785-727-1124	843-4903
Dan Wolf Chevrolet of Naperville 1515 W Ogden Ave *TF:* 800-243-8872 ■ *Web:* www.chevroletofnaperville.com	Naperville	IL	60540	630-596-1189	
DarCars Ltd 12210 Cherry Hill Rd *Web:* www.darcars.com	Silver Spring	MD	20904	301-622-0300	622-4915
Dave Sinclair Ford Inc 7466 S Lindbergh Blvd *Web:* www.davesinclairford.com	Saint Louis	MO	63125	314-892-2600	
Dave Walter 447 W Exchange St *Web:* www.davewaltervw.com	Akron	OH	44302	330-434-8989	
Dave White Chevrolet Inc 5880 Monroe St *TF:* 800-893-5217 ■ *Web:* www.davewhitechevy.com	Sylvania	OH	43560	419-517-6111	
David Taylor Cadillac Company Inc 10422 SW Fwy Bldg B *Web:* www.davidtaylor.com	Houston	TX	77074	713-777-7151	
Davis Automotive Group Inc 6135 Kruse Dr *Web:* www.davisautomotive.com	Solon	OH	44139	440-542-0600	542-0700
Day Automotive Group 1600 Golden Mile Hwy *Web:* dayauto.com	Monroeville	PA	15146	724-327-0900	
DCH Honda of Nanuet 10 Rt 304 *TF:* 888-495-8660 ■ *Web:* www.hondaofnanuet.com	Nanuet	NY	10954	845-623-1200	
Dean Team Automotive Group Inc 15121 Manchester Rd *TF:* 888-699-0663 ■ *Web:* www.deanteam.com	Ballwin	MO	63011	636-227-0100	
Dearth Motors Inc 520 Eigth St *TF:* 877-495-5321 ■ *Web:* www.dearthmotorsinc.com	Monroe	WI	53566	608-325-3181	
Delaney Automotive Group 626 Water St *Web:* www.delaneyauto.com	Indiana	PA	15701	724-349-3000	
Dellenbach Motors 3111 S College Ave *Fax Area Code: 970 ■ *TF:* 866-963-5689 ■ *Web:* www.dellenbach.com	Fort Collins	CO	80525	866-963-5689	226-0233*
DeMontrond 888 I- 45 S *TF Sales:* 888-843-6583 ■ *Web:* www.demontrond.com	Conroe	TX	77304	281-443-2500	
Dempewolf Ford Inc 2530 Us 41 N *Web:* dempewolfford.com	Henderson	KY	42420	270-827-3566	
Denooyer Chevrolet Inc 127 Wolf Rd *Web:* denooyerchevrolet.com	Albany	NY	12205	518-458-7700	
Desert Sun Motors Inc 2600 N White Sands Blvd *Web:* www.desertsunmotors.com	Alamogordo	NM	88310	575-437-7530	
Designer Auto Sales 1304 10th Dr SE	Austin	MN	55912	507-434-0123	
Diamond Motors/Mazda 10968 Airline Hwy *Web:* diamondmazda.com	Baton Rouge	LA	70816	225-295-3900	
Diamond Truck Body Manufacturing Inc 1908 E Fremont St *Web:* www.diamondtruckbody.com	Stockton	CA	95205	209-943-1655	
Dick Brantmeier Ford Inc 3624 Kohler Memorial Dr *TF:* 800-498-6111 ■ *Web:* dickbrantmeier.com	Sheboygan	WI	53082	920-458-6111	
Dick Masheter Ford Inc 1090 S Hamilton Rd *Web:* masheterford.net	Columbus	OH	43227	614-861-7150	
Diehl Automotive Group Inc 258 Pittsburgh Rd *Web:* www.diehlauto.com	Butler	PA	16002	724-282-8898	
Dillon Dennis Auto Park & Truck Ctr Inc 2777 S Orchard St *Web:* www.dennisdillon.com	Boise	ID	83705	208-336-6000	
Direct Tire & Auto Service 126 Galen St *Web:* directtire.com	Watertown	MA	02472	617-923-1800	
Don Beyer Motors Inc 1231 W Broad St *Web:* www.donbeyervolvo.com	Falls Church	VA	22046	703-237-5000	
Don Chalmers Ford Inc 2500 Rio Rancho Blvd *Web:* www.donchalmersford.com	Rio Rancho	NM	87124	505-897-2500	
Don Herring Enterprises Ltd 4225 W Plano Pkwy *Web:* www.donherring.com	Plano	TX	75093	972-387-8600	
Don Hewlett Chevrolet Buick Inc 7601 S Interstate 35 *Web:* www.donhewlett.com	Georgetown	TX	78626	512-681-3000	
Don McGill Toyota Inc 11800 Katy Fwy *TF:* 877-259-6888 ■ *Web:* www.donmcgilltoyota.com	Houston	TX	77079	281-496-2000	977-3097

				Phone	Fax
Don Rasmussen Co 720 NE Grand Ave *Web:* www.landroverportland.com	Portland	OR	97232	503-230-7700	
Dossett Big 4 Buick Pontiac Cadillac Gmc Inc 628 S Gloster St *Web:* dossettbig4.com	Tupelo	MS	38801	662-842-4162	
Dothan Chrysler-Dodge Inc 4074 Ross Clark Cir NW *TF:* 877-674-9574 ■ *Web:* www.dothanchryslerdodge.net	Dothan	AL	36303	877-674-9574	
Drivers Village 5885 E Cir Dr *Web:* burdickdodgechryslerjeep.com	Cicero	NY	13039	315-699-3846	
DriveTime Corp 4020 E Indian School Rd *TF:* 888-418-1212 ■ *Web:* www.drivetime.com	Phoenix	AZ	85018	888-418-1212	
Dueck Auto Group 12100 Featherstone Way *TF:* 877-993-8325 ■ *Web:* www.dueckgm.com	Richmond	BC	V6W1K9	604-273-1311	
Dunning Motors Inc 3745 Jackson Rd *Web:* www.dunningtoyota.com	Ann Arbor	MI	48103	734-997-7600	
Durand Chevrolet Inc 223 Washington St *Web:* durandchevrolet.com	Hudson	MA	01749	978-562-7915	
Durocher Auto Sales Inc 4651 Rt 9 *TF:* 877-215-8954 ■ *Web:* www.durocherauto.com	Plattsburgh	NY	12901	888-635-4599	
Dyna-Empire Inc 1075 Stewart Ave *Web:* www.dyna-empire.com	Garden City	NY	11530	516-222-2700	
Earnhardt Auto Centers 7300 W Orchid Ln *TF:* 888-378-7711 ■ *Web:* www.earnhardt.com	Chandler	AZ	85226	480-926-4000	
East Bay Ford Truck Sales Inc 70 Hegenberger Loop *TF:* 888-219-8551 ■ *Web:* www.eastbaytruckcenter.com	Oakland	CA	94621	510-272-4400	746-4486
Eastern Carolina Nissan 3315 Hwy 70 E *TF:* 888-944-7822 ■ *Web:* ecnissan.com	New Bern	NC	28564	252-636-1000	
Eau Claire Ford Lincoln Mercury 2909 Lorch Ave *Web:* www.eauclaireford.com	Eau Claire	WI	54701	715-852-1000	
Eckenrod Ford Lincoln Mercury of Cullman Inc 5255 Alabama Hwy 157 *TF:* 888-470-7346 ■ *Web:* eckenrodford.com	Cullman	AL	35058	256-734-3361	
Ed Bozarth Chevrolet Inc 2001 S Havana St *TF:* 877-626-9358 ■ *Web:* www.denver-chevy.com	Aurora	CO	80014	877-626-9358	
Ed Martin Inc 3800 E 96th St *TF:* 800-211-5410 ■ *Web:* edmartinacura.com	Indianapolis	IN	46240	317-846-3800	
Ed Schmidt Automotive Group Inc 26875 Dixie Hwy *Web:* edschmidt.com	Perrysburg	OH	43551	419-874-4331	
El Cajon Motors D/B/A El Cajon Ford 1595 E Main St *TF:* 877-375-1408 ■ *Web:* elcajonford.com	El Cajon	CA	92021	619-579-8888	
El Camino Store, The 420 Athena Dr *TF:* 888-685-5987 ■ *Web:* www.elcaminostore.com	Athens	GA	30601	706-546-9217	
ELCO Chevrolet Cadillac 15110 Manchester Rd *Web:* www.elcochevrolet.com	Ballwin	MO	63011	636-227-5333	
Electro Enterprises Inc 3601 N I-35 Service Rd *TF:* 800-324-6591 ■ *Web:* www.electroenterprises.com	Oklahoma City	OK	73111	405-427-6591	
Elk Grove Toyota 9640 W Stockton Blvd *Web:* www.elkgrovetoyota.com	Elk Grove	CA	95757	916-405-8000	
Elm Chevrolet Co Inc 301 E Church St *TF:* 877-265-6708 ■ *Web:* elmchevrolet.com	Elmira	NY	14901	607-734-4141	734-7649
Erhard Bmw Of Bloomfield Hills 4065 W Maple Rd *TF:* 888-481-4058 ■ *Web:* erhardbmw.com	Bloomfield Hills	MI	48301	248-642-6565	
Ernie Von Schledorn Country Inc N88 W14167 Main St *Web:* evsauto.com	Menomonee Falls	WI	53051	262-255-6000	
Ernst Auto Ctr Inc 615 E 23rd St *Web:* www.ernstauto.com	Columbus	NE	68601	402-835-4221	
F C Kerbeck & Sons 100 Rt 73 N *TF General:* 855-846-1500 ■ *Web:* www.fckerbeck.com	Palmyra	NJ	08065	856-829-8200	829-7036
Fair Oaks Ford Inc 2055 Wodgen Ave *Web:* fairoaksford.com	Naperville	IL	60540	630-355-8140	
Fairway Lincoln-Mercury Inc 10101 Abercorn St *Web:* www.fairwaylincolnmercury.com	Savannah	GA	31419	912-927-1000	
Feduke Ford 2200 Vestal Pkwy E *Web:* fedukeford.com	Vestal	NY	13850	607-754-5533	
Ferguson Buick Gmc 1015 N I- Dr *Web:* fergusonchallenge.com	Norman	OK	73069	405-253-0918	360-8854
Ferman Automotive Group 1306 W Kennedy Blvd *Web:* www.fermanauto.com	Tampa	FL	33606	813-251-2765	254-4798
Ferrotherm Corp 4758 Warner Rd *Web:* www.ferrotherm.com	Cleveland	OH	44125	216-883-9350	
Feussner'S Ford Inc 470 S St *Web:* feussnersford.com	Freeland	PA	18224	570-636-3920	
Finchey Corp of California Dba Pacific Bmw 800 S Brand Blvd	Glendale	CA	91204	818-246-5600	
Findlay Automotive Group 310 N Gibson Rd *Web:* www.findlayauto.com	Henderson	NV	89014	702-558-8888	
Finish Line Ford Inc 2211 W Pioneer Pkwy *TF:* 888-841-4002 ■ *Web:* www.greenfordstore.com	Peoria	IL	61615	309-693-2525	
First Truck Centre Inc 11313 170 St *TF:* 888-882-8530 ■ *Web:* www.firsttruck.ca	Edmonton	AB	T5M3P5	780-413-8800	
Fitzgerald Auto Mall 10915 Georgia Ave *TF:* 855-776-0552 ■ *Web:* www.fitzmall.com	Wheaton	MD	20902	855-776-0552	
Fitzgerald Auto Mall Inc 114 Baughmans Ln *Web:* www.fitzmall.com	Frederick	MD	21702	301-696-9200	
Five Star Dodge 3068 Riverside Dr *TF:* 877-748-9845 ■ *Web:* www.fivestaronline.com	Macon	GA	31210	478-474-3700	
Five Star International LLC 6100 Wattsburg Rd *Web:* fivestarinternational.com	Erie	PA	16509	814-825-6150	
Fletch's Inc 825 Charlevoix Ave PO Box 265 *TF:* 877-238-0816 ■ *Web:* www.fletchs.com	Petoskey	MI	49770	231-347-9651	
Fletcher Jones Imports 7300 W Sahara Ave *TF:* 888-927-3675 ■ *Web:* www.fjimports.com	Las Vegas	NV	89117	702-364-2700	
Folsom Buick Gmc 12640 Auto Mall Cir *Web:* folsombuickgmc.com	Folsom	CA	95630	916-358-8963	
Folsom Lake Ford 12755 Folsom Blvd *TF:* 800-730-0457 ■ *Web:* www.folsomlakeford.com	Folsom	CA	95630	916-353-2000	
Ford 504 N Main St	Frankenmuth	MI	48734	989-652-6157	
Ford of Montebello Inc 2747 Via Campo *TF:* 888-313-2305 ■ *Web:* www.fordofmontebello.com	Montebello	CA	90640	323-838-6920	
FordDirect 1740 Us Hwy 60 PO Box 700 *TF:* 888-865-2576 ■ *Web:* www.republicford.com	Republic	MO	65738	417-732-2626	
Fordham Auto Sales Inc 236 W Fordham Rd *TF:* 800-407-1153 ■ *Web:* www.fordhamtoyota.com	Bronx	NY	10468	800-407-1153	
Formula Ford Inc 265 River St *TF:* 888-872-9439 ■ *Web:* formulatruckland.com	Montpelier	VT	05602	802-223-5201	
Fowler Holding Company Inc 2721 NW 36th Ave *Web:* fowlerholding.com	Norman	OK	73072	405-573-9909	
Francis Coppola Winery LLC 620 Airpark Rd *Web:* www.francisfordcoppolawinery.com	Napa	CA	94558	707-251-3200	
Frank Kent Cadillac Inc 3800 W Loop 820 S *Web:* www.frankkentcadillac.com	Fort Worth	TX	76116	817-763-5000	
Frank W Diver Inc 2101 Pennsylvania Ave *Web:* www.diverchev.com	Wilmington	DE	19806	302-575-0161	658-4599
Franklin Truck Parts Inc 6925 Bandini Blvd *Web:* www.franklintruckparts.com	Commerce	CA	90040	323-726-1034	
Frederick Motor Co, The 1 Waverley Dr *TF:* 800-734-9118	Frederick	MD	21702	800-734-9118	
FreeFlight Systems Inc 8150 Springwood Dr Ste 100 *Web:* www.freeflightsystems.com	Irving	TX	75063	254-662-0000	
Freightliner of Hartford Inc 222 Roberts St *TF:* 800-453-6967 ■ *Web:* freightlinerofhartford.com	East Hartford	CT	06108	860-289-0201	610-6242
Friendship Automotive Inc 1855 Volunteer Pkwy *Web:* friendshipford.com	Bristol	TN	37620	423-652-6200	
Frontier Ford 3701 Stevens Creek Blvd *Web:* frontierford.com	Santa Clara	CA	95051	408-241-1800	
Gabrielli Truck Sales Ltd 153-20 S Conduit Ave *Web:* www.gabriellitruck.com	Jamaica	NY	11434	718-977-7348	
Galpin Motors Inc 15505 Roscoe Blvd **Fax:* Acctg ■ *TF:* 800-256-7137 ■ *Web:* www.galpin.com	North Hills	CA	91343	818-787-3800	778-2210*
Gateway Industrial Power Inc 921 Fournie Ln *TF:* 888-865-8675 ■ *Web:* gipower.com	Collinsville	IL	62234	618-345-0123	
Gatorland Toyota-scion 2985 N Main St *Web:* gatorlandtoyota.com	Gainesville	FL	32609	352-376-3262	
Gene Langley Ford Inc 3500 E End Dr *Web:* genelangleyford.com	Humboldt	TN	38343	731-784-9311	
Germain Motor Co *Stevegermain* 4300 Morse Crossing *Web:* www.germain.com	Columbus	OH	43219	614-759-3033	
Gettel Automotive Group 3500 Bee Ridge Rd *Web:* www.gettel.com	Sarasota	FL	34239	941-921-2655	
Gillman Cos 10595 W Sam Houston Pkwy S *TF:* 888-532-8956 ■ *Web:* www.gillmanauto.com	Houston	TX	77099	713-776-7000	
Gilroy Chevrolet Cadillac Inc 6720 Bear Cat Ct *TF:* 800-201-7241 ■ *Web:* gilroychevy.com	Gilroy	CA	95020	408-842-9301	846-0649
GKN Armstrong Wheels Inc 801 E Skinner St	Wichita	KS	67211	316-943-3571	
Gladstone Dodge 5610 N Oak Trafficway *TF:* 866-695-2043 ■ *Web:* www.gladstonedodgekansascity.com	Gladstone	MO	64118	866-695-2043	
Glendale Infiniti 812 S Brand Blvd	Glendale	CA	91204	818-543-5000	
Global Filtration Inc 9207 Emmott St *TF:* 888-717-0888 ■ *Web:* www.globalfiltration.com	Houston	TX	77040	713-856-9800	
GlobalPartsaero 901 Industrial Rd *Web:* www.globalparts.aero	Augusta	KS	67010	316-733-9240	
Globe Motor Car Co 1230 Bloomfield Ave *Web:* www.mbofcaldwell.com	Fairfield	NJ	07004	973-227-3600	575-7835
Globe Motors Inc 2275 Stanley Ave *TF:* 800-433-5700 ■ *Web:* www.globe-motors.com	Dayton	OH	45404	937-228-3171	
Godfrey Chevrolet-Buick Inc 1701 N Mitchell St *Web:* www.godfreychevroletbuick.com	Cadillac	MI	49601	231-775-4661	
Gore Design Completions Ltd 2060 Eagle Pkwy *Web:* www.gdctechnics.com	Fort Worth	TX	76177	210-496-5614	
Gorges Motor Company Inc 2660 S Oliver St	Wichita	KS	67210	316-265-6400	
Graff Truck Centers Inc 1401 S Saginaw St *TF:* 888-870-4203 ■ *Web:* www.grafftruckcenter.com	Flint	MI	48503	810-239-8300	239-8561
Gray Chevrolet Cadillac 1245 N Ninth St *Web:* graychevrolet.com	Stroudsburg	PA	18360	570-517-5500	
Gregory Logistics Inc 2844 Fair St *Web:* www.gregorylogistics.com	Poplar Bluff	MO	63901	573-785-1088	
Gregs Japanese Auto Parts & Service 1506 S 348th St *Web:* www.gregs.com	Federal Way	WA	98003	253-815-1500	
Gridley Country Ford-mercury 1709 State Hwy 99 *Web:* www.gridleycountryford.com	Gridley	CA	95948	530-846-4724	
Grossinger Motorcorp Inc 6900 N McCormick Blvd *Web:* grossinger.com	Lincolnwood	IL	60712	847-674-9000	
Grossinger Motors 1430 Fort Jesse Rd *TF:* 888-719-0095 ■ *Web:* www.sudsmotorcars.com	Normal	IL	61761	888-719-0095	
Group 1 Automotive Inc 800 Gessner Ste 500 *NYSE:* GPI ■ *TF:* 888-707-4094 ■ *Web:* www.group1auto.com	Houston	TX	77024	713-647-5700	
Grubbs Infiniti Ltd 1661 Airport Fwy *TF:* 800-685-1111 ■ *Web:* infiniti.grubbs.com	Euless	TX	76040	817-318-1200	359-4100
Gryphon Mobile Electronics LLC 489 Yorbita Rd *Web:* gryphonmobile.com	La Puente	CA	91744	626-810-7770	
Guardian Jet LLC 102 BRd St *Web:* www.guardianjet.com	Guilford	CT	06437	203-453-0800	
Gulf Coast Autoplex Inc 407 Shankland Ave *Web:* gulfcoastautoplex.net	Jennings	LA	70546	337-824-4486	

Phone | Fax

Gunn Automotive Group 227 Broadway San Antonio TX 78205 210-988-9598
Web: www.gunnauto.com

Gurley Leep Automotive Group 5302 Grape Rd Mishawaka IN 46545 574-272-0990 256-5427
Web: www.gurleyleep.com

Gurley Motor Co 701 W Coal Gallup NM 87301 505-722-6621
Web: gurleymotor.com

Gustman Chevrolet Sales Inc
1450 Delanglade St Kaukauna WI 54130 920-766-3581 766-0520
Web: www.gustman.com

H & H Chevrolet LLC 4645 S 84 St Omaha NE 68127 402-339-2222
Web: hhchevy.com

H&R Construction Parts & Equipment Inc
20 Milburn St Buffalo NY 14212 716-891-4311
TF: 800-333-0650 ■ *Web:* www.hrparts.com

Hainen Ford Inc 800 Hwy 5 S Tipton MO 65081 888-526-6979
TF: 888-526-6979 ■ *Web:* hainenford.com

Hall Automotive LLC 441 Viking Dr Virginia Beach VA 23452 757-431-9944
Web: www.hallauto.com

Hamilton Chevrolet 5800 E 14 Mile Rd Warren MI 48092 586-264-1400 276-1531
TF: 888-466-7827 ■ *Web:* hamiltonchevy.com

Harte Nissan Inc 165 W Service Rd Hartford CT 06120 860-549-2800
TF: 866-687-8971 ■ *Web:* www.hartenissan.com

Harvey Cadillac Co 2600 28th St SE Grand Rapids MI 49512 616-949-1140 954-1201
TF Sales: 877-845-1557 ■ *Web:* harveycadillac.com

Hastings Automotive Inc 3625 Vermillion St Hastings MN 55033 651-437-4030
Web: hastingsautos.com

Headquarter Toyota 5895 NW 167th St Miami FL 33015 305-364-9800
TF: 800-549-0947 ■ *Web:* www.headquartertoyota.com

Hendrick Automotive Group
6000 Monroe Rd Ste 100 Charlotte NC 28212 704-568-5550 566-3295
Web: www.hendrickauto.com

Hendrick Buick GMC Cadillac
1151 W 104th St Kansas City MO 64114 877-584-7140
TF: 888-255-9362 ■ *Web:* www.hendrickcadillackansascity.com

Henna Chevrolet Inc 8805 N Ih 35 Austin TX 78753 512-832-1888
Web: www.hennachevyaustin.com

Hennessy River View Ford 2200 US Hwy 30 Oswego IL 60543 630-897-8900
Web: www.riverviewford.com

Herb Chambers 259 McGrath Hwy Somerville MA 02145 617-666-8333 666-8448
Web: www.herbchambers.com

Herb Chambers I 95 Inc 107 Andover St Danvers MA 01923 877-907-1965
TF: 877-907-1965 ■ *Web:* www.herbchamberschevrolet.com

Herb Easley Motors Inc
1125 Central Fwy Wichita Falls TX 76306 940-723-6631 767-3655
Web: www.herbeasley.com

Herb Gordon Nissan
3131 Automobile Blvd Silver Spring MD 20904 866-399-7502
TF: 844-249-4077 ■ *Web:* www.herbgordonnissan.com

Heritage Ford Inc 2100 Sisk Rd Modesto CA 95350 209-529-5110
TF: 888-323-9990 ■ *Web:* www.heritagefordmodesto.com

Herson's Inc 15525 Frederick Rd Rockville MD 20855 888-203-8318
TF: 888-203-8318 ■ *Web:* www.hersonsauto.com

Hertrich Family of Automobile Dealerships
26905 Sussex Hwy Seaford DE 19973 302-629-4553
Web: www.hertrichs.com

Hesser Toyota Scion 1811 Humes Rd Janesville WI 53545 608-754-7754
Web: www.hessertoyota.com

High Country Performance 4x4 Inc
1695 W Hamilton Pl Englewood CO 80110 303-761-7379
Web: hcp4x4.com

Hiland Toyota 5500 45th Ave Dr Moline IL 61265 309-764-2481
Web: www.hilandtoyota.com

Hines Park Lincoln Inc 40601 Ann Arbor Rd Plymouth MI 48170 866-979-3919 453-8333*
**Fax Area Code: 734* ■ *TF:* 866-979-3919 ■ *Web:* www.hinesparklincoln.com

Hinshaws Acura/Honda 5955 20th St E Fife WA 98424 253-922-8830
TF: 800-752-2872 ■ *Web:* hinshawsacura.com

Holler Automotive Group 1011 N Wymore Rd Winter Park FL 32789 407-645-4969
Web: www.hollerclassic.com

Holman Cadillac Co 1200 Rt 73 S Mount Laurel NJ 08054 856-778-1000
TF: 866-865-6973 ■ *Web:* holmancadillac.com

Holz Motors Inc 5961 S 108th Pl Hales Corners WI 53130 414-425-2400
Web: www.holzmotors.com

HomeRunAutoSales 301 Green Ave N Stevens Point WI 54481 715-341-2440 341-5424
Web: homerunautogroup.com

Honda Carland 11085 Alpharetta Hwy Roswell GA 30076 770-993-2805
Web: hondacarland.com

Honda of Santa Monica
1726 Santa Monica Blvd Santa Monica CA 90404 310-264-4900
TF: 800-269-2031 ■ *Web:* www.hondaofsantamonica.com

Honda World 10645 Studebaker Rd Downey CA 90241 562-929-7000
TF: 888-458-9404 ■ *Web:* www.lahondaworld.com

Honolulu Ford Lincoln & Mercury
1370 N King St Honolulu HI 96817 808-532-1700
Web: www.honoluluford.com

Hoover Toyota 2686 Hwy 150 Hoover AL 35244 205-978-2600
TF: 866-980-8082 ■ *Web:* www.hoovertoyota.com

Horwith Trucks Inc PO Box 7 NorthHampton PA 18067 610-261-2220 261-2916
TF: 800-220-8807 ■ *Web:* www.horwithfreightliner.com

Hoselton Chevrolet Inc
909 Fairport Rd East Rochester NY 14445 585-586-7373
Web: hoselton.com

House Chevrolet Co 410 Main St S Stewartville MN 55976 507-533-4255
Web: housechevrolet.com

Hunt Ford Inc 6825 Crain Hwy La Plata MD 20646 301-934-8186
Web: huntfordinc.com

Ididit Inc 610 S Maumee St Tecumseh MI 49286 517-424-0577
Web: www.ididitinc.com

Igarashi Motor Sales USA LLC
710 Colomba Ct Saint Charles IL 60174 630-587-1177
Web: www.igusa.com

Imlay City Ford Inc 1788 S Cedar St Imlay City MI 48444 810-724-5900
Web: imlaycityford.com

Import Auto World 21571 Mission Blvd Hayward CA 94541 510-581-1200 581-1228
Web: importautoworldinc.com

Indy Honda 8455 US 31 S Indianapolis IN 46227 317-887-0800
Web: www.indyhonda.com

Injen Technology Company Ltd 244 Pioneer Pl Pomona CA 91768 909-839-0706
Web: www.injen.com

Island Lincoln-Mercury Inc
1850 E Merritt Island Cswy Merritt Island FL 32952 321-452-9220
TF: 800-392-3673

Jack Giambalvo Motor Co 1390 Eden Rd York PA 17402 717-781-2154 854-5509
Web: jackgiambalvo.com

Jack Powell Ford-Mercury Inc
1418 Se 1 St Mineral Wells TX 76067 940-325-1331
Web: jackpowellford.net

James Wood Motors Inc 2111 Us Hwy 287 S Decatur TX 76234 940-627-2177 627-8542
TF: 888-833-7230 ■ *Web:* www.jameswood.com

Jay Wolfe Automotive Group
1011 W 103rd St Kansas City MO 64114 816-943-6060
Web: www.jaywolfe.com

Jedco Inc 1615 Broadway NW Grand Rapids MI 49504 616-459-5161
Web: jedco.us

Jenkins & Wynne Inc 328 College St Clarksville TN 37040 931-647-3353
Web: www.jenkinsandwynne.com

Jerry Haag Motors Inc 1475 N High St Hillsboro OH 45133 937-402-2090
Web: www.jerryhaagmotors.com

Jet X Aerospace 400 N York Rd Bensenville IL 60106 847-750-8888
Web: www.jetxaerospace.com

Jim Ellis Auto Dealerships
5901 Peachtree Industrial Blvd S Atlanta GA 30341 770-458-6811
Web: www.jimellis.com

Jim McKay Chevrolet Inc 3509 University Dr Fairfax VA 22030 703-591-4800 591-8021
Web: jimmckaychevrolet.com

JM Family Enterprises Inc
100 Jim Moran Blvd Deerfield Beach FL 33442 954-429-2000 429-2244
Web: www.jmfamily.com

Joe Holland Chevrolet Inc
210 Maccorkle Ave SW South Charleston WV 25303 304-744-1561
TF: 855-468-9491 ■ *Web:* www.joeholland.com

Joe Van Horn Chevrolet Inc PO Box 238 Plymouth WI 53073 920-893-6361
TF: 800-236-1415 ■ *Web:* www.vanhornchev.com

John Hine Mazda Inc 1545 Camino Del Rio S San Diego CA 92108 619-297-4251
Web: www.johnhine.com

John Lance Ford Inc 23775 Ctr Ridge Rd Westlake OH 44145 440-871-8600
Web: autonationfordwestlake.com

John Mcclaren Chevrolet Inc
1015 E Mcgregor Dr Mcgregor TX 76657 254-840-3261
Web: johnmcclarenchevrolet.com

John Watson Chevrolet 3535 Wall Ave Ogden UT 84401 801-394-2611
TF: 866-647-9930 ■ *Web:* www.johnwatsonchevrolet.com

Johnny Londoff Chevrolet Inc 1375 Dunn Rd Florissant MO 63031 314-595-6586 837-0105

Johnson Lexus of Raleigh 5839 Capital Blvd Raleigh NC 27616 919-877-1800
Web: johnsonlexusraleigh.com

Johnson Motors Inc 1891 Blinker Pkwy Du Bois PA 15801 814-371-4444
TF: 800-537-1768 ■ *Web:* www.johnsonauto.com

Jon Lancaster Inc 3501 Lancaster Dr Madison WI 53718 608-243-5500
Web: eastmadisontoyota.com

Joyce Motors Corp 3166 SR- 10 Denville NJ 07834 973-361-3000
TF: 844-332-5955 ■ *Web:* www.joycehonda.com

Karl Tyler Chevrolet Inc 3663 N Reserve Missoula MT 59808 406-721-2438
Web: gmofmontana.com

Keeler Motor Car Co 1111 Troy Schenectady Rd Latham NY 12110 518-785-4197
TF: 800-474-4197 ■ *Web:* www.keeler.com

Ken Fowler Motors 1265 Airport Pk Blvd Ukiah CA 95482 707-468-0101 462-2475
TF: 800-287-0107 ■ *Web:* www.fowlerautocenter.com

Ken Garff Automotive Group
405 S Main St Salt Lake City UT 84111 801-257-3400
TF: 888-630-6838 ■ *Web:* www.kengarff.com

Ken Grody Ford 6211 Beach Blvd Buena Park CA 90621 714-521-3110
Web: www.kengrody.com

Ken Wilson Ford Inc 769 Champion Dr Canton NC 28716 828-648-2313
Web: www.kenwilsonford.net

Kendall Imports LLC 10943 S Dixie Hwy Miami FL 33156 305-665-6581
Web: www.kendalltoyota.com

Kenworth Northwest Inc
20220 International Blvd S SeaTac WA 98198 206-433-5911 878-7676
TF: 800-562-0060 ■ *Web:* www.kenworthnorthwest.com

Kenworth of Indianapolis Inc
2929 S Holt Rd Indianapolis IN 46241 317-247-8421 241-5742
TF: 800-827-8421 ■ *Web:* www.palmertrucks.com

Key Cadillac Inc 6825 York Ave S Edina MN 55435 952-920-4300 920-4821
Web: keycadillac.com

Keyes Toyota 5855 Van Nuys Blvd Van Nuys CA 91401 818-782-0122 907-4128
Web: www.keyestoyota.com

Keyser & Miller Ford Inc 8 E Main St Collegeville PA 19426 610-489-9366
Web: www.keysermillerford.com

Keyser Bros Cadillac Inc
4130 Sheridan Dr Williamsville NY 14221 716-568-7045 634-4326

Kightlinger Motors Inc 358 Rt 6 W Coudersport PA 16915 814-274-9660
Web: kightlingermotor.com

King-o'rourke Cadillac Inc
756 Smithtown Byp Smithtown NY 11787 631-724-4700 724-4784
Web: kingorourkeautogroup.com

Klick-lewis Inc 720 E Main St Palmyra PA 17078 717-838-1353
Web: www.klicklewiscars.com

Knippelmier Chevrolet Inc 1811 E Hwy 62 E Blanchard OK 73010 877-644-7255
TF: 877-644-7255 ■ *Web:* knippelmier.com

Koerner Ford of Syracuse Inc
805 W Genesee St Syracuse NY 13204 315-474-4275
Web: www.koernerford.net

Kolosso Toyota 3000 W Wisconsin Ave Appleton WI 54914 920-738-3666
TF: 877-756-2297 ■ *Web:* www.kolossotoyota.com

Koons Ford of Annapolis Inc 2540 Riva Rd Annapolis MD 21401 410-224-2100
TF: 888-313-5524 ■ *Web:* www.koonsford.com

	City	State	Zip	Phone	Fax
Kuni Automotive Group 17800 SE Mill Plain Blvd Ste 190 *Web:* www.kuniauto.com	Vancouver	WA	98683	360-553-7650	
L & S Truck Ctr of Appleton Inc 330 N Bluemound Dr *TF:* 888-617-3140 ■ *Web:* www.lstruck.com	Appleton	WI	54914	920-749-1700	749-0818
La Beau Bros Inc 295 N Harrison Ave *TF:* 800-747-9519 ■ *Web:* www.labeautrucks.com	Kankakee	IL	60901	815-933-5519	933-4366
La Belle Dodge Chrysler Jeep Inc 501 S Main St *TF:* 800-226-1193 ■ *Web:* www.labelledodgechryslerjeep.com	Labelle	FL	33935	863-675-2701	
La Mesa Rv Ctr Inc 7430 Copley Pk Pl *TF Sales:* 888-509-4199 ■ *Web:* www.lamesarv.com	San Diego	CA	92111	858-874-8000	874-8021
Lafferty Chevrolet 829 W St Rd *Web:* www.laffertychevy.com	Warminster	PA	18974	215-259-5817	672-3594
Lafontaine Honda 2245 S Telegraph Rd *TF:* 866-567-5088 ■ *Web:* lafontainehonda.com	Dearborn	MI	48124	866-567-5088	
Lakeside International LLC 11000 W Silver Spring Rd *TF:* 800-236-0444 ■ *Web:* www.lakesidetrucks.com	Milwaukee	WI	53225	414-353-4800	353-2743
Lakeside Toyota 3701 N Cswy Blvd *TF Sales:* 877-512-8274 ■ *Web:* www.lakesidetoyota.com	Metairie	LA	70002	504-833-3311	
Lambert Buick Pontiac-Gmc Truck Inc 2409 Front St *Web:* lambertgm.com	Cuyahoga Falls	OH	44221	330-923-9771	
Lancaster Toyota Inc 5270 Manheim Pk *TF:* 888-424-1295 ■ *Web:* www.lancastertoyota.com	East Petersburg	PA	17520	888-424-1295	
Land Rover of Calgary 175 Glendeer Cir SE *Web:* landrovercalgary.com	Calgary	AB	T2H2S8	403-255-1994	
Landers Ford Inc 2082 W Poplar Ave *TF:* 888-281-5266 ■ *Web:* www.landersfordmemphis.com	Collierville	TN	38017	888-281-5266	
Landmark Lincoln-Mercury Inc 5000 S Broadway *TF:* 888-318-9692 ■ *Web:* landmarklincoln.com	Englewood	CO	80113	303-761-1560	
Lankota Inc 270 Wpark Ave *TF:* 866-526-5682 ■ *Web:* www.lankota.com	Huron	SD	57350	605-352-4550	
Larry Green Chevrolet Oldsmobile & Geo Inc 2050 Rodeo Dr *Web:* larrygreenchevrolet.com	Cottonwood	AZ	86326	928-634-2227	
Larry Hopkins Honda 1048 W El Camino Real *Web:* www.larryhopkinshonda.com	Sunnyvale	CA	94087	408-720-1888	
Larry Roesch Chrysler-jeep-dodge LLC 200 W Grand Ave *Web:* www.larryroesch.com	Elmhurst	IL	60126	630-834-8000	
Lavery Chevrolet-Buick Inc 1096 W State St *Web:* laveryauto.com	Alliance	OH	44601	330-823-1100	
Lawrence Hall Chevrolet Inc 1385 S Danville Dr *TF:* 800-568-7158 ■ *Web:* www.lawrencehall.com	Abilene	TX	79605	325-695-8800	692-1657
Leach Enterprises 4304 Il Rt 176 *Web:* www.leach-ent.com	Crystal Lake	IL	60014	815-459-6917	
Lee Air Company Inc 7545 Wheatland Ave *Web:* www.leeairinc.com	Sun Valley	CA	91352	818-767-0777	
LEKTRO Inc 1190 SE Flightline Dr *TF:* 800-535-8767 ■ *Web:* www.lektro.com	Warrenton	OR	97146	503-861-2288	
Lemay Auto Group 8220-75th St *Web:* www.lemayautogroupwi.com	Kenosha	WI	53142	262-694-2000	
Les Stanford Chevrolet Inc 21730 Michigan Ave *TF:* 800-836-0972 ■ *Web:* lesstanfordchevrolet.com	Dearborn	MI	48124	313-457-0364	
Levin Tire Center 5713 Broadway *Web:* www.levintirecenter.com	Merrillville	IN	46410	219-887-0531	
Lewis Ford Sales Inc 3373 N College Ave PO Box 8430 *Web:* lewiscars.com	Fayetteville	AR	72703	479-442-5301	
Lexus of Memphis Inc 2600 Ridgeway Rd *TF Sales:* 877-876-9996 ■ *Web:* lexusofmemphis.com	Memphis	TN	38119	901-362-8833	
Lia Auto Group, The 1258 Central Ave PO Box 5789 *TF:* 855-212-7985 ■ *Web:* www.liacars.com	Albany	NY	12205	518-489-2111	489-2112
Liccardi Ford Inc 1615 Rt 22 W *Web:* liccardi.com	Watchung	NJ	07069	908-561-7500	
Lindsay Cadillac Co 1525 Kenwood Ave *Web:* lindsaycars.com	Alexandria	VA	22302	703-998-6600	
Lithia Motors Inc 360 E Jackson St *NYSE:* LAD ■ *TF:* 866-318-9660 ■ *Web:* www.lithia.com	Medford	OR	97501	866-318-9660	
Lockhart Cadillac Inc 9265 E 126th St *Web:* www.lockhartcadillac.com	Fishers	IN	46038	317-644-2817	
Loeber Motors Inc 4255 W Touhy Ave *TF:* 888-211-4485 ■ *Web:* www.loebermotors.com	Lincolnwood	IL	60712	847-675-1000	
Lordco Parts Ltd 22866 Dewdney Trunk Rd *TF:* 877-591-1581 ■ *Web:* www.lordco.com	Maple Ridge	BC	V2X3K6	604-467-1581	463-7557
Lou Bachrodt Auto Group 7070 Cherryvale N Blvd *TF:* 866-635-2349 ■ *Web:* www.bachrodt.com	Rockford	IL	61112	815-332-3000	
Lupient Automotive Group (LAG) 750 Pennsylvania Ave S *Web:* www.lupient.com	Minneapolis	MN	55426	763-544-6666	
Lynch Ford - Mt Vernon Inc 410 Hwy 30 SW *Web:* www.lynchfordchevrolet.com	Mount Vernon	IA	52314	319-895-8500	895-8100
Lynch Management Co 2165 River Blvd	Jacksonville	FL	32204	904-387-1537	
Lynn Layton Chevrolet Inc 2416 Hwy 31 S *Web:* www.lynnlaytonchevrolet.com	Decatur	AL	35601	256-274-4665	
Mac Haik Auto Group 11711 Katy Fwy *TF:* 866-721-8619 ■ *Web:* www.machaik.com	Houston	TX	77079	866-721-8619	
Mac Haik Ford Inc 10333 Katy Fwy *Web:* www.machaikford.com	Houston	TX	77024	713-932-5000	
Maclean Assoc LLC Dba Land Rover Guilford 1700 Boston Post Rd	Guilford	CT	06437	203-453-7060	
Magnussen Dealership Group 401 Burgess Dr Ste A	Menlo Park	CA	94025	650-327-4100	
Main Line Tire & Service 102 Robbins Rd *Web:* unitedtire.com	Downingtown	PA	19335	610-514-3600	
Maple Hill Auto Group 5622 W Main St *Web:* www.maplehillauto.com	Kalamazoo	MI	49009	269-342-6600	
Mark Chevrolet Inc 33200 Michigan Ave *Web:* www.markchevrolet.com	Wayne	MI	48184	734-629-4964	
Mark Thomas Motors Inc 2315 Santiam Hwy *Web:* www.markthomasmotors.com	Albany	OR	97321	541-967-9105	
Markley Motors 3325 S College Ave *TF:* 888-480-5167 ■ *Web:* www.markleymotors.com	Fort Collins	CO	80525	970-226-2214	
Marquette Public Service Garage 919 W Baraga Ave *Web:* www.publicservicegarage.com	Marquette	MI	49855	906-662-4395	
Marshal Mize Ford Inc 5348 Hwy 153 *TF:* 888-633-5038 ■ *Web:* marshalmizeford.net	Chattanooga	TN	37343	888-633-5038	
Martin Automotive Group 12101 W Olympic Blvd *Web:* martinautogroup.com	Los Angeles	CA	90064	310-622-9334	622-9334
Martin Automotive Group Inc 1065 Ashley St Ste 100 *Web:* www.martingp.com	Bowling Green	KY	42103	270-783-8080	781-4792
Marty Franich Ford Lincoln 550 Auto Ctr Dr	Watsonville	CA	95076	831-722-4181	724-6897
Marvin K. Brown Auto Ctr Inc 1441 Camino Del Rio S *Web:* www.mkb.com	San Diego	CA	92108	619-291-2040	
Massive Audio 2261 S Atlantic Blvd *Web:* www.massiveaudio.com	Commerce	CA	90040	323-262-2262	
Matt Blatt Inc 501 Delsea Dr N *TF:* 877-462-5288 ■ *Web:* www.mattblatt.com	Glassboro	NJ	08028	856-881-0444	
Matthews Currie Ford Company Inc 130 N Tamiami Trl *TF:* 855-491-3131 ■ *Web:* www.matthewscurrie.com	Nokomis	FL	34275	941-488-6787	
Mazda Knoxville 8814 Kingston Pk *Web:* www.mazdaknoxville.com	Knoxville	TN	37923	865-690-9395	
Mazda of Roswell 11185 Alpharetta Hwy *Web:* mazdaofroswell.com	Roswell	GA	30076	770-993-6999	
McCloskey Motors Inc 6710 N Academy Blvd *TF:* 877-389-6671 ■ *Web:* www.bigjoeauto.com	Colorado Springs	CO	80918	719-594-9400	
McDevitt Trucks Inc 1 Mack Ave PO Box 4640 *TF:* 800-370-6225 ■ *Web:* www.mctrucks.com	Manchester	NH	03108	603-668-1700	668-1865
McGrath Auto Group 4610 Ctr Pt Rd NE *TF:* 888-902-8414 ■ *Web:* www.mcgrathauto.com	Cedar Rapids	IA	52402	888-902-8414	
Mclean Implement Inc 793 Illinois Rte 130 *TF:* 888-720-4440 ■ *Web:* www.mcleanimp.com	Albion	IL	62806	618-445-3676	445-2846
Meade Auto Group 45001 Northpointe Blvd *Web:* meadelexus.com/v2	Utica	MI	48315	586-726-7900	
Medved Autoplex 11001 W I-70 Frontage Rd N *Web:* www.medved.com	Wheat Ridge	CO	80033	303-421-0100	
Medved Chevrolet Inc 11001 W I-70 Frontage Rd N *Web:* medved.com	Wheat Ridge	CO	80033	303-421-0100	
Meiji Corp 660 Fargo Ave *Web:* www.meijicorp.com	Elk Grove Village	IL	60007	847-364-9333	
Melloy Nissan 7707 Lomas Blvd NE *Web:* www.melloynissan.com	Albuquerque	NM	87110	505-265-8721	
Memering Motorplex Inc 1949 Hart St *Web:* www.memeringmotorplex.com	Vincennes	IN	47591	812-882-5367	
Mercedes-Benz Canada Inc 98 Vanderhoof Ave *Web:* www.mercedes-benz.ca	Toronto	ON	M4G4C9	416-425-3550	
Mercedes-Benz of San Francisco 500 Eigth St *TF:* 877-554-6016 ■ *Web:* www.sfbenz.com	San Francisco	CA	94103	415-673-2000	673-6100
Mercedes-Benz USA LLC 4500 Stevens Creek Blvd *Web:* mbofstevenscreek.com	San Jose	CA	95129	408-641-4610	615-4335
Merchants Automotive Group Inc 1278 Hooksett Rd *Web:* www.merchantsauto.com	Hooksett	NH	03106	603-669-4100	
Merollis Chevrolet Sales & Service Inc 21800 Gratiot Ave *Web:* www.merollischevy.com	Eastpointe	MI	48021	586-775-8300	
Metro Ford Inc 9000 NW Seventh Ave *TF:* 877-811-9402 ■ *Web:* www.metroford.com	Miami	FL	33150	877-811-9402	
Michael Roberts Auto Sales 9051 SR- 2830	Maceo	KY	42355	270-264-7100	
Mid-City Motor World 4800 N Hwy 101 *Web:* midcitymotorworld.com	Eureka	CA	95503	707-443-4871	
Mike Calvert Toyota Inc 2333 S Loop W *Web:* mikecalverttoyota.com	Houston	TX	77054	713-558-8100	
Mike Reed Chevrolet 1559 E Oglethorpe *TF:* 877-228-3943 ■ *Web:* mikereedchevy.com	Hinesville	GA	31313	877-228-3943	
Mike Savoie Chevrolet Inc PO Box 520 *Web:* www.mikesavoie.com	Troy	MI	48084	248-643-8000	649-3007
Miller Motorcars Inc 342 W Putnam Ave *Web:* www.millermotorcars.com	Greenwich	CT	06830	203-629-3890	
Milton Martin Toyota 2350 Browns Bridge Rd *Web:* www.miltonmartintoyota.com	Gainesville	GA	30504	770-532-4355	536-1385
Minato Auto LLC Dba Toyota of Portsmouth 150 Greenleaf Ave	Portsmouth	NH	03801	603-431-6100	
Mission Golf Cars 18865 Redland Rd *TF:* 800-324-7868 ■ *Web:* www.missiongolfcars.com	San Antonio	TX	78259	210-545-7868	
Mission Valley Ford Truck Sales Inc 780 E Brokaw Rd *TF:* 888-284-7471 ■ *Web:* missionvalleykubota.com	San Jose	CA	95112	408-933-2300	436-0313
Modern Chevrolet of Winston-Salem 5955 University Pkwy *TF General:* 888-306-0825 ■ *Web:* www.modernchevy.com	Winston-Salem	NC	27105	336-722-4191	785-8455
Molle Toyota Inc 601 W 103rd St *TF:* 888-510-7705 ■ *Web:* www.molletoyota.com	Kansas City	MO	64114	816-942-5200	
Montesi Motors Inc 444 State St *TF:* 844-282-1115 ■ *Web:* www.montesivolkswagen.com	North Haven	CT	06473	844-282-1115	
Morganton Honda 1600 Burkemont Ave *Web:* morgantonhonda.com	Morganton	NC	28655	828-437-3181	

Phone | Fax

Morrison Industrial Equipment Co
1825 Monroe NW....Grand Rapids MI 49505 616-447-3800 361-0885
Web: www.morrison-ind.com

Mossy Motors Inc 1331 S Broad St....New Orleans LA 70125 504-822-2050 826-5614
Web: www.mossymotors.com

Motor Inn of Knoxville LLC
114 S Sixth St....Estherville IA 51334 712-362-5834
Web: motorinnautogroup.com

Motorcars International 3015 E Cairo St....Springfield MO 65802 417-831-9999 831-9995
TF: 866-970-6800 ■ *Web:* www.motorcars-intl.com

Motors Management Inc D/B/Atroy Honda
1835 Maplelawn....Troy MI 48084 248-649-0202

Murray Motor Imports Co 4300 E Kentucky Ave....Glendale CO 80246 303-759-3400
Web: murraymotors.com

Muzi Motors Inc 557 Highland Ave....Needham Heights MA 02494 781-444-5300
Web: www.muzimotors.com

Nalley Lexus Smyrna 2750 Cobb Pkwy SE....Smyrna GA 30080 877-454-4206
TF: 877-454-4206 ■ *Web:* www.nalleylexussmyrna.com

National Auto Stores Inc
2512 Quakertown Rd....Pennsburg PA 18073 215-679-2300
Web: www.nationalautostores.com

National Car Mart Inc 9255 Brookpark Rd....Cleveland OH 44129 216-505-1750
Web: www.nationalcarmart.com

National Standard Parts Assoc Inc
4400 Mobile Hwy....Pensacola FL 32506 850-456-5771
TF: 800-874-6813 ■ *Web:* www.nspa.com

National Tire & Wheel 5 Garden Ct....Wheeling WV 26003 800-847-3287
TF: 800-847-3287 ■ *Web:* www.ntwonline.com

National Tool Warehouse
221 W Fourth St Ste 4....Carthage MO 64836 417-358-1919
Web: nationaltoolwarehouse.com

Nationwide Lift Trucks Inc
3900 N 28th Terr....Hollywood FL 33020 954-922-4645 922-8770
TF: 800-327-4431 ■ *Web:* www.toyotanlt.com

Nevada Auto Mall Inc 2501 E Austin Blvd....Nevada MO 64772 417-667-3385
Web: nevadaautomall.net

New Country Motor Car Group
358 Broadway Ste 403....Saratoga Springs NY 12866 518-584-7700 584-8611
Web: www.newcountry.com

New Country Volkswagen of Greenwich
200 W Putnam Ave....Greenwich CT 06830 866-584-6747
TF: 866-584-6747 ■ *Web:* newcountry.com

Newins Bay Shore Ford Inc 219 W Main St....Bay Shore NY 11706 631-665-1300
Web: www.newinsbayshoreford.com

Nextran Corp 1986 W Beaver St....Jacksonville FL 32209 904-354-3721
TF: 800-347-6225 ■ *Web:* www.nextrancorp.com

NFI Inc Dba Harrisonburg Honda Mitsubishi Hyundai
2885 S Main St....Harrisonburg VA 22801 540-433-1467

Nick Alexander Imports Inc
6333 S Alameda St....Los Angeles CA 90001 323-583-1901
Web: alexanderbmw.com

Nick Crivelli Chevrolet Inc 294 State Ave....Beaver PA 15009 724-987-5000
Web: nickcrivelli.com

Nielsen Dodge Chrysler Jeep Ram
175 Rt 10 E....East Hanover NJ 07936 973-884-2100
Web: nielsendodgechryslerjeepram

Nissan of Atlantic City
6021 Black Horse Pike....Egg Harbor Township NJ 08234 609-383-6100 646-0730
Web: www.admiralnissan.com

Nitrous Express Inc 5411 Seymour Hwy....Wichita Falls TX 76310 940-767-7694 767-7697
TF: 888-463-2781 ■ *Web:* www.nitrousexpress.com

Noarus Auto Group 6701 Ctr Dr W Ste 925....Los Angeles CA 90045 310-258-0920
Web: www.noarus.com

Norauto Inc 1161 Hwy 111 E....Amos QC J9T1N2 819-732-5352
Web: www.norautonissan.com

Norduyn Inc 6200 Henri-Bourassa W....Montreal QC H4R1C3 514-334-3210 334-2989
TF: 877-332-3210 ■ *Web:* www.norduyn.com

Norman Frede Chevrolet Co
16801 Feather Craft Ln....Houston TX 77058 281-486-2200
TF: 888-307-1703 ■ *Web:* www.fredechevrolet.com

Norris Ford 901 Merritt Blvd....Baltimore MD 21222 410-285-0200
TF Sales: 866-460-5275 ■ *Web:* www.norrisford.com

North Bay Nissan Inc 1250 Auto Ctr Dr....Petaluma CA 94952 707-769-7700
TF: 877-818-6866 ■ *Web:* www.northbaynissan.com

North Park Lincoln 9207 San Pedro St....San Antonio TX 78216 210-341-8841
TF: 888-696-5480 ■ *Web:* nplincoln.com

Northtown Automotive Cos Inc
1135 Millersport Hwy....Amherst NY 14226 716-614-7000
Web: www.northtownauto.com

Northway Toyota 727 New Loudon Rd....Latham NY 12110 877-800-5098 785-4957*
**Fax Area Code:* 518 ■ *TF:* 877-525-3488 ■ *Web:* www.northwaytoyota.com

O Neill's Chevrolet & Buick Inc 5 W Main St....Avon CT 06001 860-269-3279
Web: www.oneillschevybuick.com

O'Gara Coach Company LLC
8833 W Olympic Blvd....Beverly Hills CA 90211 888-291-5533 652-9656*
**Fax Area Code:* 310 ■ *TF:* 888-291-5533 ■ *Web:* www.ogaracoach.com

O'rielly Chevrolet Inc 6100 E Broadway Blvd....Tucson AZ 85711 520-829-4400
Web: www.orielly.com

Orange Coast Chrysler Jeep Dodge
2929 Harbor Blvd....Costa Mesa CA 92626 714-549-8023
Web: www.ocauto.com

Orange Motors Company Inc 799 Central Ave....Albany NY 12206 518-489-5414
TF: 888-912-5958 ■ *Web:* www.orangemotors.com

Orlando Dodge Chrysler Jeep
4101 W Colonial Dr....Orlando FL 32808 407-299-1120
Web: orlandododge.com

Otics USA Inc 5555 Interstate View Dr....Morristown TN 37813 423-581-9933
Web: oticsusa.com

Otto Instrument Service Inc 1441 Valencia Pl....Ontario CA 91761 909-930-5800
Web: www.ottoinstrument.com

Outten Chevrolet Inc 1701 W Tilghman St....Allentown PA 18104 610-628-3600 820-5774
Web: outtenchevyallentown.com

Paddock Chevrolet Inc 3232 Delaware Ave....Kenmore NY 14217 716-876-0945 876-4016
Web: www.paddockchevrolet.com

Palm Automotive Group 1801 Tamiami Trail....Punta Gorda FL 33950 941-639-1155
TF General: 800-643-2112 ■ *Web:* www.palmautomall.com

Palm Beach Motor Cars Ltd Inc
915 S Dixie Hwy....West Palm Beach FL 33401 561-659-6206
Web: www.jaguarpalmbeach.com

Palmetto Chevrolet Company Inc
1122 Fourth Ave....Conway SC 29526 843-248-4283
Web: palmettochevy.com

Papastavros Assoc Medical Imaging Inc
1701 Augustine Cut Off Bldg 4....Wilmington DE 19803 302-652-3016 652-2534
Web: www.papastavros.com

Paradise Chevrolet 6350 Leland St....Ventura CA 93003 805-642-0111
Web: www.paradisechevrolet.com

Park Place Volvo 3515 Inwood Rd....Dallas TX 75209 214-956-5500
Web: parkplace.com

Parsons Buick Co, The 151 E St....Plainville CT 06062 860-747-1693 747-5734
TF: 877-274-2613 ■ *Web:* www.parsonsbuick.com

Pat Milliken Ford Inc 9600 Telegraph Rd....Redford MI 48239 313-255-3100
Web: www.patmillikenford.com

Paul Heuring Motors Inc 720 N Hobart Rd....Hobart IN 46342 219-942-3673
TF: 888-851-9702 ■ *Web:* www.paulheuring.com

Paul Moak Automotive Inc 740 Larson St....Jackson MS 39202 601-352-2700
Web: www.paulmoak.com

PDQ Auto Supply of Manville Inc
240 N First Ave....Manville NJ 08835 908-526-0888

Pearman Motor Company Ltd 240 N Marcus....Alto TX 75925 936-858-4188
Web: pearmanmotor.com

Pepe Motors group/Mercedes-Benz of White Plains
50 Bank St....White Plains NY 10606 914-949-4000
Web: www.mbwhiteplains.com

Perth Amboy Spring Works 185 Sheridan St....Perth Amboy NJ 08861 732-442-4420

Pertronix Inc 440 E Arrow Hwy....San Dimas CA 91773 909-599-5955
Web: www.pertronix.com

Pete Baur Buick GMC Inc 14000 Pearl Rd....Cleveland OH 44136 440-580-4256
Web: petebaur.com

Peters of Nashua 300 Amherst St....Nashua NH 03063 603-889-1166
Web: www.petersauto.com

Phil Long Dealerships
1212 Motor City Dr....Colorado Springs CO 80905 866-644-1378
TF: 866-644-1378 ■ *Web:* phillong.com

Phil Smart Inc 600 E Pike St....Seattle WA 98122 206-324-5959
TF: 877-241-4528 ■ *Web:* www.mbseattle.com

Phil Smith Automotive Group
4250 N Federal Hwy....Lighthouse Point FL 33064 954-867-1234
Web: www.philsmithauto.com

Phillips Automotive Inc
4949 Virginia Beach Blvd....Virginia Beach VA 23462 757-499-3771
Web: mercedesbenzofvirginiabeach.com

Phillips Buick-Pontiac-Gmc Truck Inc
2160 US Hwy 441....Fruitland Park FL 34731 352-728-1212 728-1444
TF: 888-664-7454 ■ *Web:* www.phillips-buick.com

Piercey Automotive Group 16901 Millikan Ave....Irvine CA 92606 949-396-6000
Web: www.pierceyautogroup.com

Pignataro Volkswagon 10633 Evergreen Way....Everett WA 98204 425-348-3141
Web: www.pignatarovw.com

Pitts Toyota Inc 210 N Jeffreson St....Dublin GA 31021 478-272-3244 272-1524
TF: 888-561-8030 ■ *Web:* www.pittstoyota.com

Planet Honda 2285 Us Hwy 22 W....Union NJ 07083 908-964-1600
Web: www.planethondanj.com

Pollard Friendly Ford Co 3301 S Loop 289....Lubbock TX 79423 806-797-3441
Web: pollardfriendlyford.com

Porsche of Maplewood 2780 Maplewood Dr....Maplewood MN 55109 888-679-1698
TF: 888-852-8937 ■ *Web:* www.porscheofstpaul.com

Potamkin Automotive Group Inc
6200 NW 167th Ste B....Miami Lakes FL 33014 855-799-9965
TF: 855-799-9965

Potter-Webster Co 41 NE Walker St....Portland OR 97211 503-283-4792
Web: www.potterwebster.com

Premier Subaru LLC 150 N Main St....Branford CT 06405 203-481-0687 481-1861
TF: 888-690-6710 ■ *Web:* www.premiersubaru.com

Premier Truck Parts Inc 5800 W Canal Rd....Cleveland OH 44125 216-642-5000
Web: www.premiertruckparts.com

Prestige Chrysler Dodge Inc 200 Alpine St....Longmont CO 80501 303-651-3000
TF: 866-439-1926 ■ *Web:* www.prestigechryslerdodge.com

Price Ford of Turlock
5200 N Golden State Blvd....Turlock CA 95382 209-669-5200
Web: www.pricefordofturlock.com

Priority Chevrolet of Chesapeake
1495 S Military Hwy....Chesapeake VA 23320 757-424-1811
TF: 855-315-0212 ■ *Web:* www.priorityauto.com

Pro-system Inc 121 Oakpark Dr....Mooresville NC 28115 704-799-8100
Web: www.prosystems.com

Production Automation Co 6200 Bury Dr....Eden Prairie MN 55346 952-903-0333
Web: www.gotopac.com

Prostrollo Motor Sales Inc 500 Fourth St NE....Huron SD 57350 866-466-4515 352-9286*
**Fax Area Code:* 605 ■ *TF:* 866-466-4515 ■ *Web:* www.prostrollo.com

Puklich Chevrolet Inc 3701 State St....Bismarck ND 58502 701-223-5800
Web: puklichchevrolet.com

Purvis Ford Inc
3660 Jefferson Davis Hwy Ste 1 Ste 1....Fredericksburg VA 22408 540-898-3000
Web: purvisford.net

Putnam Lexus 390 Convention Way....Redwood City CA 94063 650-363-8500
TF: 888-231-8005 ■ *Web:* www.putnamlexus.com

Quality Tower Erectors & Service Inc
2280 10th St SE....Largo FL 33771 727-585-6176
Web: www.qualitytower.com

RAPCO Inc 445 Cardinal Ln....Hartland WI 53029 262-367-2292
Web: rapcoinc.com

Ray Catena Motor Car Corp 910 US Hiwy Rt 1....Edison NJ 08817 732-549-6600 549-6983
Web: www.raycatena.com

Ray Seraphin Ford Inc
100 Windsor Ave....Vernon Rockville CT 06066 860-875-3369
Web: rayseraphinfordinc.com

Phone Fax

RC Olsen Cadillac Inc 201 Cambridge Rd..............Woburn MA 01801 781-336-4814
Web: olsencadillac.com

Real Don Johnson Brownsville, The
2101 Central Blvd..............................Brownsville TX 78520 956-546-2288
Web: www.realdonjohnson.com

Reed Motors Inc 3776 W Colonial Dr..................Orlando FL 32808 407-297-7333
Web: www.reednissan.com

Reichard Buick GMC 161 Salem Ave..................Dayton OH 45406 937-401-2034 220-6746
Web: www.reichardbuick.com

Reliable Chevrolet Inc 800 N Central Expy..........Richardson TX 75080 972-330-4326 897-6000*
**Fax Area Code:* 505 ■ *Web:* www.reliablechev.com

Renntech Inc 1369 N Killian Dr......................Lake Park FL 33403 561-845-7888
Web: www.renntechmercedes.com

RF Inc T/A Frankel Acura 10400 York Rd.........Cockeysville MD 21030 410-666-5300

Rhoden Auto Ctr Inc 3400 S Expy St.............Council Bluffs IA 51501 712-309-4000 309-4001
TF: 866-562-6248

Ricart Automotive Group 4255 S Hamilton Rd........Columbus OH 43125 614-836-5321
TF: 888-225-6783 ■ *Web:* www.ricart.com

Rickenbaugh Cadillac Co 777 Broadway..............Denver CO 80203 303-573-7773
Web: rickenbaughvolvo.com

Rippy Cadillac LLC 4951 New Centre Dr...........Wilmington NC 28403 910-799-2421

River States Truck & Trailer
3959 N Kinney Coulee Rd.........................La Crosse WI 54601 608-784-1149
Web: www.riverstates.com

Riverside Ford 2625 Ludington St..................Escanaba MI 49829 906-786-1130
TF: 877-774-3171 ■ *Web:* www.riversidefordescanaba.com

Riverside Ford Inc 2089 Riverside Dr..................Macon GA 31204 478-464-2900 752-7850
TF Sales: 800-395-6210 ■ *Web:* www.riversideford.net

Rnr Custom Wheels & Tires
8030 Florida Blvd...........................Baton Rouge LA 70806 225-926-7466
Web: rnrwheels.com

RnR RV Ctr 23203 E Knox Ave....................Liberty Lake WA 99019 866-386-4875
TF: 866-386-4875 ■ *Web:* www.rnrrv.com

Robberson Ford Lincoln Mercury Mazda
2289 NE Third St...............................Prineville OR 97754 541-447-6820
Web: www.robberson.com

Roberson Motors Inc 3100 Ryan Dr SE.................Salem OR 97301 503-363-4117
TF: 888-281-6220 ■ *Web:* www.robersonmotorschryslerjeep.com

Roger Dean Chevrolet Inc
2235 Okeechobee Blvd.....................West Palm Beach FL 33409 561-683-8100 683-7332
TF: 877-827-4705 ■ *Web:* www.rogerdeanchevrolet.com

Roland D Kelly Infiniti Inc
155 Andover St Rt 114...........................Danvers MA 01923 978-774-1000
Web: www.kellyauto.com

Romero Mazda 1307 Kettering Dr....................Ontario CA 91761 909-390-8484 390-4595
TF: 888-317-2233 ■ *Web:* www.mazdaofontario.com

Ron Carter Automotive Group 3205 FM 528.............Alvin TX 77511 281-331-3111
Web: www.roncarter.com

Ron Tonkin Dealerships 122 NE 122nd Ave...........Portland OR 97230 503-255-4100
TF: 855-890-1823 ■ *Web:* tonkinchevrolet.com

Rosen Aviation LLC 1020 Owen Loop S...............Eugene OR 97402 541-342-3802
Web: www.rosenaviation.com

Rosenthal Automotive Organization
1902 Association Dr..............................Reston VA 20191 703-553-4300
Web: www.rosenthalauto.com

Rosewell Toyota 2211 W Second St..................Roswell NM 88201 575-622-5860
Web: www.roswelltoyota.com

Rosner Auto Group
3507 Jefferson Davis Hwy....................Fredericksburg VA 22408 540-907-4900
TF Sales: 855-270-6270 ■ *Web:* www.rosnerauto.com

Rowleys Tires & Automotive Services
3596 Wilder Rd..................................Bay City MI 48706 989-686-1144
Web: www.rowleystires.com

Roy Nichols Motors Ltd 2728 Courtice Rd............Courtice ON L1E2M7 905-436-2222
Web: roynicholsmotors.com

Ruggeri-Jensen-Azar & Assoc
4690 Chabot Dr................................Pleasanton CA 94588 925-227-9100
Web: rja-gps.com

Rush Truck Center - Whittier 2450 Kella Ave..........Whittier CA 90601 562-551-5000
TF: 877-605-7623 ■ *Web:* rushtruckcenters.com

Russ Darrow Group Inc
W133 N8569 Executive Pkwy................Menomonee Falls WI 53051 262-250-9600
Web: russdarrow.com

Russell Karting Specialties Inc PO Box 1220.........Raymore MO 64083 816-322-3330 322-2860
TF: 800-821-3359 ■ *Web:* russellkarting.com

Russo & Steele LLC 5230 S 39th St..................Phoenix AZ 85040 602-252-2697
Web: russoandsteele.com

RV World Inc of Nokomis 2110 Tamiami Trl N.........Nokomis FL 34275 941-966-2182
TF: 800-262-2182 ■ *Web:* www.rvworldinc.com

Ryan Automotive LLC 200 Carter Dr..................Edison NJ 08817 732-650-1550

Rye Ford Inc 1151 Boston Post Rd........................Rye NY 10580 914-967-6300
Web: ryeford.com

Saccucci Honda 1350 W Main Rd................Middletown RI 02842 401-847-4737
Web: www.saccuccihonda.com

Salisbury Motor Company Inc 700 W Innes St.........Salisbury NC 28144 704-636-1341
Web: www.salisburymotorcompany.com

Sam Swope Auto Group LLC
I-64 Hurstbourne Pkwy Ste I........................Louisville KY 40201 502-499-5020
Web: www.samswope.com

Sandy Sansing Chevrolet
6200 N Pensacola Blvd..........................Pensacola FL 32505 850-476-2480
TF Sales: 888-885-1844 ■ *Web:* www.sandysansingchevrolet.com

Santa Maria Ford Lincoln
1035 E Battles Rd...............................Santa Maria CA 93454 805-925-2445
Web: santamariaford.com

Santa Maria Tire Inc 249 Montgomery Ave.............Oxnard CA 93036 805-642-0174
Web: www.smtire.com

Saratoga Honda 3402 Rt 9..................Saratoga Springs NY 12866 888-658-2303
TF: 888-658-2303 ■ *Web:* www.saratogahonda.com

Scap Auto Group 421 Tunxis Hill Rd..................Fairfield CT 06825 203-384-9300
Web: www.scapauto.com

Phone Fax

Scat Enterprises Inc
1400 Kingsdale Ave.........................Redondo Beach CA 90278 310-370-5501
Web: www.procarbyscat.com

Schukei Chevrolet Inc 721 S Monroe.............Mason City IA 50401 641-423-5402
TF: 866-918-6497 ■ *Web:* www.schukeichevy.com

Schumacher European Ltd
18530 N Scottsdale Rd............................Phoenix AZ 85054 480-991-1155
Web: mbofnorthscottsdale.com

Scott Family of Dealerships 3333 Lehigh St.........Allentown PA 18103 800-274-1039 966-3742*
**Fax Area Code:* 610 ■ *TF:* 800-274-1039 ■ *Web:* www.scottcars.com

Scott-Mc Rae Advertising
701 Riverside Pk Pl.............................Jacksonville FL 32204 904-354-4000
Web: scottmcraejobs.com

Scranton Motors Inc 777 Talcottville Rd...............Vernon CT 06066 860-872-9145
Web: scrantonmotors.com

Sears Imported Autos Inc
13500 Wayzata Blvd............................Minnetonka MN 55305 952-546-5301 546-2899
TF Sales: 800-493-1720 ■ *Web:* sears.mercedesdealer.com

Seekins Ford Lincoln Inc
1625 Seekins Ford Dr............................Fairbanks AK 99701 907-459-4000
Web: seekins.com

Seneca Tank Inc 5585 NE 16th St................Des Moines IA 50313 515-262-5900
TF: 800-362-2910 ■ *Web:* www.senecatank.com

Serra Automotive 3118 E Hill Rd.................Grand Blanc MI 48439 810-694-1720
Web: serrausa.com

Servco Pacific Inc 2850 Pukoloa Ste 300............Honolulu HI 96819 808-564-1300 523-3937
Web: www.servco.com

Shamaley Buick GMC 955 Crockett Way..............El Paso TX 79922 915-317-5958 581-9203
Web: www.shamaleybuickgmc.com

Sheehy Auto Stores 12701 Fair Lakes Cir..............Fairfax VA 22033 703-802-3480
Web: www.sheehy.com

Shelly Automotive Group
Irvine BMW 9881 Research Dr.......................Irvine CA 92618 888-853-7429
TF: 888-853-7429 ■ *Web:* www.shellygroup.com

Sheppard Motors 2300 W Seventh Ave................Eugene OR 97402 541-343-8811
TF Sales: 877-362-1865 ■ *Web:* www.sheppardmotors.com

Shock Tech Inc 360 Rt 59..........................Airmont NY 10952 845-368-8600
Web: www.shocktech.com

Showcase Honda 1333 E Camelback Rd...............Phoenix AZ 85014 602-464-7145
Web: www.showcasehonda.com

Shults Management Group Inc
181 E Fairmount Ave............................Lakewood NY 14750 716-763-1551

Sierra Volkswagen Inc 510 E Norris Dr...............Ottawa IL 61350 866-374-5828
TF: 877-854-2771 ■ *Web:* www.sierravw.com

Silver Star Automotive Group
Lotus of Thousand Oaks
3601 Auto Mall Dr.......................Thousand Oaks CA 91362 800-472-5450
TF: 800-472-5450 ■ *Web:* www.silverstarcadillac.com

Simmons-rockwell Inc 784 County Rd 64..............Elmira NY 14903 607-796-5555
TF: 888-520-2213 ■ *Web:* www.simmons-rockwell.com

Simplex Manufacturing Co
13340 NE Whitaker Way...........................Portland OR 97230 503-257-3511
Web: simplex.aero

Simpsons on The Spot Auto Detailing
2953 Pleasant Grove Rd...........................Lansing MI 48910 517-393-7910

Sisbarro Dealerships 425 W Boutz Rd............Las Cruces NM 88005 575-524-7707
TF: 800-215-8021 ■ *Web:* www.sisbarro-buickgmc.com

Sitton Buick GMC 2640 Laurens Rd................Greenville SC 29607 864-990-3600
TF: 888-484-8009 ■ *Web:* www.sittongm.com

Sky Mart Sales Corp
9475 NW 13th St PO Box 522007.....................Miami FL 33172 305-592-0263 592-8359
Web: www.skymartsales.com

Skybooks Inc 1310 Tradeport Dr.................Jacksonville FL 32218 904-741-8700
TF: 866-929-8700 ■ *Web:* www.skybooks.com

Skycom Avionics Inc 2441 Aviation Rd.............Waukesha WI 53188 262-521-8180
TF: 800-443-4490 ■ *Web:* www.skycomavionics.com

Smith Motors Inc of Hammond
6405 Indianapolis Blvd.........................Hammond IN 46320 219-845-4000
TF: 877-392-2689 ■ *Web:* www.smithchevyusa.com

Smoky Mountain Truck Ctr LLC
841 Eastern Star Rd.............................Kingsport TN 37663 800-451-1508 349-0431*
**Fax Area Code:* 423 ■ *TF:* 800-451-1508 ■ *Web:* www.smtruckcenter.com

Smythe Volvo Inc 40 River Rd.......................Summit NJ 07901 908-273-4200
Web: smythevolvo.com

Snell MotorsInc 1900 Madison Ave..................Mankato MN 56001 507-345-4626
Web: snellmotors.com

Snowfire 100 Us Rt 2.............................Waterbury VT 05676 802-244-5606
TF: 800-287-5606 ■ *Web:* snowfireauto.com

Snyder Chevrolet 524 N Perry St...................Napoleon OH 43545 567-341-4132
TF: 800-569-3957 ■ *Web:* www.snyderchevrolet.com

Sommer's Automotive 7211 W Meq...................Mequon WI 53092 262-242-0100
TF: 888-494-4193 ■ *Web:* www.sommerscars.com

Sonic Automotive Inc 4401 Colwick Rd..............Charlotte NC 28211 704-566-2400
NYSE: SAH ■ *Web:* www.sonicautomotive.com

South Charlotte Nissan 9215 S Blvd.................Charlotte NC 28273 704-552-9191
TF: 888-411-1423 ■ *Web:* www.scottclarknissan.com

South Motors Infiniti 16915 S Dixie Hwy..............Miami FL 33157 305-256-2000
Web: www.southinfiniti.com

South Tacoma Honda 7802 S Tacoma Way............Tacoma WA 98409 253-472-2300
TF: 888-497-2416 ■ *Web:* www.southtacomahonda.com

Southfield Dodge Chrysler Jeep Ram
28100 Telegraph Rd............................Southfield MI 48034 248-354-2950 352-3776
TF Sales: 888-388-0451 ■ *Web:* www.southfieldchryslerdodgejeepram.com

Southwick Inc 2400 Shattuck Ave...................Berkeley CA 94704 510-845-2530
TF: 888-686-0046 ■ *Web:* www.toyotaofberkeley.com

Sparta Chevrolet 8955 Sparta Ave NW..................Sparta MI 49345 616-887-1791
Web: spartachevy.com

Specialty Hearse & Ambulance Sale Corp
60 Engineers Ln E..........................Farmingdale NY 11735 516-349-7700 349-0482
TF General: 800-349-6102 ■ *Web:* www.specialtyhearse.com

Sport Chevrolet 3101 Automobile Blvd............Silver Spring MD 20904 301-890-6000
Web: sportautomotive.com

Phone | Fax

St. Charles Nissan Inc
5625 Veterans Memorial Pkwy . . . . Saint Peters MO 63376 636-441-4481
Web: stcharlesauto.com

Stadium International Trucks Inc
105 Seventh N St . . . . Liverpool NY 13088 315-475-8471
Web: www.stadiumtrucks.com

Stadium Toyota 5088 N Dale Mabry Hwy . . . . Tampa FL 33614 813-872-4881
Web: www.stadiumtoyota.com

Staluppi Auto Group 133 US Hwy 1 . . . . Palm Beach FL 33408 561-844-7148

Standard Auto Parts 2930 Texas Ave. . . . . Texas City TX 77590 409-945-3333

Standard Motors Ltd 44 Second Ave NW. . . . . Swift Current SK S9H3V6 866-334-8985
TF: 866-334-8985 ■ *Web:* www.standardmotors.ca

Steele Truck Ctr Inc 2150 Rockfill Rd . . . . Fort Myers FL 33916 239-334-7300 334-4676
TF: 888-806-4839 ■ *Web:* www.steeletruck.com

Steve Barry Buick Inc 16000 Detroit Ave. . . . . Lakewood OH 44107 216-920-0866 221-7001
TF: 866-327-5818 ■ *Web:* www.stevebarrybuick.com

Steve Millen Sportparts Inc
3176 Airway Ave. . . . . Costa Mesa CA 92626 714-540-5566
TF: 866-250-5542 ■ *Web:* www.stillen.com

Stevens Creek Mitsubishi
3209 Stevens Creek Blvd . . . . San Jose CA 95117 408-264-9999
TF: 888-479-0842 ■ *Web:* www.stevenscreekmitsubishi.com

Stew Hansen Dodge Ram Chrysler Jeep
12103 Hickman Rd . . . . Urbandale IA 50323 515-331-2900
Web: www.stewhansens.com

Stillwater Motor Co
5900 Stillwater Blvd N . . . . Stillwater MN 55082 651-323-2245
Web: www.stillwatermotors.com

Stokes Automotive Inc
8650 Rivers Ave . . . . North Charleston SC 29406 843-572-4700
Web: www.stokeshondanorth.com

Stoops Freightliner- Quality Trailer Inc
1851 W Thompson Rd . . . . Indianapolis IN 46217 317-788-1533
Web: truckcountry.com

Suburban Collection 1810 Maplelawn Dr . . . . Troy MI 48084 877-471-7100
TF: 877-471-7100 ■ *Web:* www.suburbancollection.com

Sullivan Automotive Group 2406 N Section St. . . . . Sullivan IN 47882 812-268-4321 268-4323
Web: www.shopsullivanauto.com

Sulphur Springs Ford Lincoln Inc
1040 Gilmer St . . . . Sulphur Springs TX 75482 903-885-0502
Web: www.toliverford.com

Sunland Tire Co of Upland Inc
461 E Foothill Blvd . . . . Upland CA 91750 909-982-1396
Web: sunlandtire.com

Sunnyside Motor Co Inc 944 Main St . . . . Holden MA 01520 508-829-4333 829-5362
Web: www.sunnysideford.com

Sunset Logistics Inc 710 Fm 1620 . . . . Seguin TX 78155 830-560-1032
Web: sunsetlogistics.com

Superior Hyundai 110 S Quintard Ave. . . . . Anniston AL 36201 256-403-4991
Web: www.superiorhyundaial.com

Surf City Garage Inc
5872 Engineer Dr . . . . Huntington Beach CA 92649 714-894-1707
Web: www.surfcitygarage.com

Surrey Honda 15291 Fraser Hwy . . . . Surrey BC V3R3P3 604-583-7421
Web: surreyhonda.com

Susan Schein Automotive 3171 Pelham Pkwy . . . . Pelham AL 35124 205-664-1491
TF: 800-845-1578 ■ *Web:* www.susanschein.com

Sutton Ford Inc 21315 S Central Ave . . . . Matteson IL 60443 708-720-8115
TF: 866-232-2966 ■ *Web:* www.suttonford.com

Szott Ford 8800 E Holly Rd . . . . Holly MI 48442 248-634-4411
Web: szottford.com

T G H Aviation 2389 Rickenbacker Way . . . . Auburn CA 95602 530-823-6204
TF: 800-843-4976 ■ *Web:* www.tghaviation.com

Tallman Truck Centre Ltd 750 Dalton Ave . . . . Kingston ON K7M8N8 613-546-3336
Web: tallmangroup.ca

Taylor Ford Inc 13500 Telegraph . . . . Taylor MI 48180 313-291-0300
Web: shoptaylorford.com

Taylor's Auto Max 4100 10th Ave S . . . . Great Falls MT 59405 406-727-0380
Web: www.taylorsautomax.com

Team Volkswagen of Hayward Corp
25115 Mission Blvd . . . . Hayward CA 94544 866-308-2825
TF: 866-308-2825 ■ *Web:* www.vwhayward.com

Tennessee Tractor LLC 15 S Bells St Ste . . . . Alamo TN 38001 731-696-5598 696-4458
Web: www.tennesseetractor.com

Terry Thompson Chevrolet Olds 1402 Us Hwy 98 . . . . Daphne AL 36526 251-626-0631
TF: 800-287-9309 ■ *Web:* terry-thompson.com

Terrys Ford Lincoln 363 N Harlem Ave . . . . Peotone IL 60468 708-258-9200
Web: terrysfordofpeotone.com

Texas Direct Auto 12053 SW Fwy (Hwy 59). . . . . Stafford TX 77477 281-499-8200
Web: www.texasdirectauto.com

Thompson Lexus 50 W Swamp Rd . . . . Doylestown PA 18901 215-345-1110
Web: www.1800thompson.com

Thoroughbred Ford Inc
I-29 At Barry Rd 8501 N Boardwalk Ave . . . . Kansas City MO 64154 816-505-1818
Web: www.thoroughbredford.com

Tidewater Fleet Supply LLC
1324 Lindale Dr . . . . Chesapeake VA 23320 757-436-7679
Web: www.tidewaterfleetsupply.com

Tipotex Chevrolet Inc 1600 N Expy # 77 . . . . Brownsville TX 78521 956-541-3131
Web: www.tipotexchevrolet.com

Titus Will Ford 3606 S Sprague . . . . Tacoma WA 98409 253-475-4151
Web: tituswillford.com

Tom Bensen Chevrolet Co Inc
9400 San Pedro . . . . San Antonio TX 78216 210-341-3311
TF: 866-635-6971

Tom Gibbs Chevrolet Inc 5850 E Hwy 100 . . . . Palm Coast FL 32164 386-437-3314
Web: tomgibbschevy.com

Tom Hesser Chevrolet Inc
1001 N Washington Ave . . . . Scranton PA 18509 570-343-1221
Web: tomhesserbmw.com

Tom Holzer Ford Inc
39300 W Ten Mile . . . . Farmington Hills MI 48335 248-474-1234
Web: tholzerford.com

Tom Naquin Chevrolet Inc
2500 W Lexington Ave . . . . Elkhart IN 46514 574-293-8621
Web: www.tomnaquin.com

Toms Truck Ctr Inc
1008 E Fourth St PO Box 88 . . . . Santa Ana CA 92701 714-338-6060 836-6039
TF: 800-638-1015 ■ *Web:* www.ttruck.com

Toyota of Greenwich 75 E Putnam Ave . . . . Cos Cob CT 06807 203-661-5055
Web: www.toyotaofgreenwich.com

Toyota of Watertown Inc 149 Arsenal St . . . . Watertown MA 02472 617-926-5200
Web: toyotaofwatertown.com

Toyota Sunnyvale 898 W El Camino Real . . . . Sunnyvale CA 94087 408-245-6640
TF: 888-210-0091 ■ *Web:* toyotasunnyvale.com

Transource Inc 8700 Triad Dr . . . . Colfax NC 27235 336-996-6060
Web: www.transourcetrucks.com

Transwest 20770 I-76 Frontage Rd . . . . Brighton CO 80603 303-289-3161 288-2310
TF: 800-289-3161 ■ *Web:* www.transwest.com

Trebol Motors Corp PO Box 11204 . . . . San Juan PR 00910 787-793-2828
Web: www.trebolmotors.com

Trend Motors Ltd 221 Us Hwy 46 . . . . Rockaway NJ 07866 973-625-0100
Web: www.trendmotors.com

Tri County Ford Mercury Inc
4032 Commerce Pkwy PO Box 425 . . . . Buckner KY 40010 502-241-7333
TF: 800-945-2520 ■ *Web:* www.tricountyford.com

Tri-State Motors 298 S Main St . . . . Cedar City UT 84720 435-238-4342
Web: www.tristateofcedarcity.com

Triad Automation Group Inc
4994 Indiana Ave, Ste F PO Box 1065 . . . . Winston-Salem NC 27106 336-767-1379

Trident Auto Sales 550 Hollis Rd . . . . Hollis Center ME 04042 207-929-5858

Tropical Ford 9900 S Orange Blossom Trial . . . . Orlando FL 32837 407-851-3800 240-6116
TF Sales: 800-790-7137 ■ *Web:* www.tropicalford.com

Truck Enterprises Inc 3440 S Main St . . . . Harrisonburg VA 22801 540-564-6900
Web: www.truckenterprises.com

Truck Sales & Service Inc PO Box 262 . . . . Midvale OH 44653 740-922-3412 922-7239
TF: 800-282-6100 ■ *Web:* www.trksls.com

Truck Tire Sales Inc 426 W Pershing Rd . . . . Chicago IL 60609 773-285-3000
Web: trucktiresalesil.com

Truck Works Inc 1815 S 39th Ave . . . . Phoenix AZ 85009 602-233-3713
TF: 877-894-8757

Truckwell of Alaska Inc 5801 Silverado Way . . . . Anchorage AK 99518 907-349-8845
Web: www.truckwell.info

Tuffy Security Products Inc 25733 Rd H . . . . Cortez CO 81321 970-564-1762
TF: 800-348-8339 ■ *Web:* www.tuffyproducts.com

Tustin Nissan 30 Auto Ctr Dr . . . . Tustin CA 92782 714-669-8282
Web: www.tustinnissan.com

Ultimate Linings Ltd 6630 Roxburgh Dr Ste 175 . . . . Houston TX 77041 713-466-0302 937-0052
Web: www.ultimatelinings.com

Usem Inc 703 17th Ave NW . . . . Austin MN 55912 507-396-4083
Web: useminc.com

Utility Trailor Manufacturing Co
2921 Hwy 49 N . . . . Paragould AR 72450 870-236-9195
Web: www.utm.com

Utility/Keystone Trailer Sales Inc
1976 Auction Rd . . . . Manheim PA 17545 717-653-9444 653-9443
TF: 888-327-4236 ■ *Web:* www.utilitykeystone.com

V&H Inc 1505 S Central Ave . . . . Marshfield WI 54449 715-486-8800
TF: 800-826-2308 ■ *Web:* www.vhtrucks.com

Valley Freightliner Inc 277 Stewart Rd SW . . . . Pacific WA 98047 800-523-8014 863-6473*
**Fax Area Code:* 253 ■ *TF:* 800-523-8014 ■ *Web:* www.valleyfreightliner.com

Van Bortel Subaru 6327 SR- 96 . . . . Victor NY 14564 585-924-5230
TF: 888-902-7961 ■ *Web:* www.vanbortelsubaru.net

Van Boxtel Rv & Auto LLC 1956 Bond St . . . . Green Bay WI 54303 920-497-3072
TF: 888-831-5267 ■ *Web:* vanboxtelrv.com

Vendetti Motors Inc 411 W Central St . . . . Franklin MA 02038 508-528-3450
Web: vendettimotors.com

Vic Canever Chevrolet Inc 3000 Owen Rd . . . . Fenton MI 48430 810-519-5634 750-1307
Web: www.viccaneverchevy.com

Village Motors Inc 75 N Beacon St . . . . Boston MA 02134 617-560-1710
Web: www.villageautomotive.com

Vin Devers Inc 5570 Monroe St . . . . Sylvania OH 43560 419-885-5111 824-2595
TF: 888-847-9535 ■ *Web:* www.vindevers.com

Vip Auto Group 2006 Hwy 161 . . . . North Little Rock AR 72117 501-955-5556

VIP Motor Cars Ltd
4095 E Palm Canyon Dr . . . . Palm Springs CA 92264 760-328-6525

Virginia Truck Center Inc 3243 Lee Hwy . . . . Weyers Cave VA 24486 540-234-0999
Web: www.exceltruckgroup.com

Vision Ford Lincoln Hyundai
1500 S White Sands Blvd . . . . Alamogordo NM 88310 866-932-2441
TF: 866-932-2441 ■ *Web:* www.visionfordlm.com

Visionaire Inc 1502 109th St . . . . Grand Prairie TX 75050 972-647-1056
TF: 866-838-2810 ■ *Web:* www.visionaire-inc.com

Vista Auto 21501 Ventura Blvd . . . . Woodland Hills CA 91364 888-313-4252
TF: 888-887-6530 ■ *Web:* www.vistaford.com

Vogler Motor Co Inc 1170 E Main . . . . Carbondale IL 62901 618-457-8135
Web: voglermotorcompany.com

Volvo of Tucson 831 W Wetmore Rd . . . . Tucson AZ 85705 520-792-1070
Web: www.volvooftucson.com

Walker Ford Company Inc 17556 Us Hwy 19 N . . . . Clearwater FL 33764 727-535-3673
Web: walkerford.com

Walker Honda 1616 Macarthur Dr . . . . Alexandria LA 71301 318-445-6421
Web: www.walkerhonda.com

Wallingford Buick GMC
1122 Old N Colony Rd . . . . Wallingford CT 06492 866-582-4487
TF Cust Svc: 866-582-4487 ■ *Web:* www.wallingfordbuickgmc.com

Wareham Ford Inc 2628 Cranberry Hwy . . . . Wareham MA 02571 508-295-3643
Web: warehamford.com

Watson Quality Ford 6130 I-55 N . . . . Jackson MS 39211 601-956-7000
Web: watsonquality.com

Watson'S Manistee Chrysler Inc
208 Parkdale Ave . . . . Manistee MI 49660 231-723-6528
Web: watsonsmanisteechrysler.com

Wellesley Volkswagen Buick Inc
231 Linden St . . . . Wellesley MA 02482 781-237-3553
Web: buywellesleyvw.com

Phone | Fax

West-Herr Automotive Group Inc
3448 McKinley Pkwy ... Blasdell NY 14219 716-649-5640
TF: 800-643-2112 ■ *Web:* www.westherr.com

Westchester Toyota Service
75 Vredenburgh Ave ... Yonkers NY 10704 914-968-6500
TF: 866-232-7662 ■ *Web:* www.westchestertoyota.com

Western Automation Inc
23011 Moulton Pkwy Ste F1 ... Laguna Hills CA 92653 949-859-6988
Web: www.waisales.com

Western Bus Sales Inc 30355 SE Hwy 212 ... Boring OR 97009 503-905-0002 905-0003
TF: 800-258-2473 ■ *Web:* www.westernbus.com

Western Slope Auto Co 2264 Hwy 6 & 50 ... Grand Junction CO 81505 970-243-0843
TF: 888-461-3493 ■ *Web:* www.westernslopeauto.com

Westland Ford 3450 Wall Ave ... Ogden UT 84401 801-394-8803
Web: westlandford.com

Westman Freightliner Inc
2200 Fourth Ave Mankato PO Box 699 ... Mankato MN 56001 507-625-4118 625-4127
TF: 866-576-6914 ■ *Web:* www.westmanfreightliner.com

Westside Lexus 12000 Katy Fwy ... Houston TX 77079 281-558-3030 558-7859
Web: www.westsidelexus.com

Westway Ford 801 W Airport Fwy ... Irving TX 75062 844-877-9037
TF: 844-877-9037 ■ *Web:* westwayford.com

Whatever It Takes Transmission Parts Inc
4282 E Blue Lick Rd ... Louisville KY 40229 502-955-6035
Web: www.wittrans.com

Whitaker Buick Co 131 19th St SW ... Forest Lake MN 55025 651-674-3931
TF: 877-324-8885 ■ *Web:* whitakerauto.com

White Allen Chevrolet Inc 442 N Main St ... Dayton OH 45405 937-222-3701
Web: www.whiteallen.com

White Plains Honda 344 Central Ave ... White Plains NY 10606 914-948-3305
TF: 877-553-9292 ■ *Web:* www.whiteplainshonda.com

Whited Ford 207 Perry Rd ... Bangor ME 04401 207-947-3673
Web: www.whitedford.com

Wiers International Trucks Inc
2111 Jim Neu Dr ... Plymouth IN 46563 574-936-4076
TF: 888-889-4377 ■ *Web:* wiers.com

Wilcor Autos Inc Dba Toyota Vallejo
201 Auto Mall Pkwy ... Vallejo CA 94591 707-552-4545

Wilde Automotive Management of Wisc Onsin Inc
1710 A Hwy 164 ... Waukesha WI 53186 262-513-2770
TF: 888-379-5817 ■ *Web:* wildeauto.com

Wilkie Lexus 568 W Lancaster Ave ... Haverford PA 19041 610-525-0900
Web: wilkielexus.com

Willey Honda 2215 S 500 W ... Bountiful UT 84010 888-431-4490
TF Sales: 888-431-4490 ■ *Web:* performancehondautah.com

Williams Nationalease Ltd 400 W Northtown Rd ... Normal IL 61761 309-452-1110
TF: 800-779-8785 ■ *Web:* wnlgroup.com

Wilson Automotive Group 1400 N Tustin St ... Orange CA 92867 714-516-3111 997-9200
Web: www.davidwilsonautogroup.com

Winner Chevrolet Inc PO Box 1867 ... Colfax CA 95713 530-349-4151
Web: www.winnerchevy.com

Winslow BMW 730 N Cir Dr ... Colorado Springs CO 80909 719-473-1373
TF: 877-367-7357 ■ *Web:* www.winslowbmw.com

Wisconsin Kenworth 5100 E Pk Ave ... Madison WI 53718 608-241-5616
Web: www.csmtruck.com/companies/wisconsin-kenworth

Witt Lincoln 588 Camino Del Rio N ... San Diego CA 92108 619-358-5000 358-5008
TF: 877-937-3301 ■ *Web:* wittlincoln.com

WMK Inc 810 Moe Dr ... Akron OH 44310 330-633-1118
TF: 877-275-4912 ■ *Web:* www.mobilityworks.com

Woodbine Chrysler Ltd 8280 Woodbine Ave ... Markham ON L3R2N8 905-415-2260
Web: www.woodbinechrysler.ca

World Auto Group 3057 New Jersey ... Denville NJ 07834 973-442-0500
Web: www.denvillenissan.com

World Class Automotive Group 4730 Wistar Rd ... Richmond VA 23228 804-308-1877
Web: www.worldclassag.com

Wray Ford Inc 2851 Benton Rd ... Bossier City LA 71111 318-686-7300
Web: wrayford.net

Yonkers Motors Corp 2000 Central Pk Ave ... Yonkers NY 10710 914-961-8180
Web: www.yonkershonda.com

York Ford Inc 1481 Bwy ... Saugus MA 01906 781-231-1945
TF: 888-705-6229 ■ *Web:* www.yorkford.com

Zeigler Chevrolet Inc 13153 Dunnings Hwy ... Claysburg PA 16625 814-239-2125
Web: zeiglerchevy.com

Ziems Ford Corners Inc 5700 E Main St ... Farmington NM 87402 505-325-1961
Web: ziemsfordcorners.com

Zimmerman Auto Center 4001 First Ave ... Cedar Rapids IA 52402 319-313-5086
TF: 855-877-4223 ■ *Web:* www.gozimmerman.com

Zimmerman Ford Inc 2525 E Main St ... Saint Charles IL 60174 630-584-1800
Web: www.zimmermanford.com

AUTOMOBILE LEASING

See Credit & Financing - Commercial p. 2171; Credit & Financing - Consumer p. 2172; Fleet Leasing & Management p. 2287

58 AUTOMOBILE SALES & RELATED SERVICES - ONLINE

See Also Automobile Dealers & Groups p. 1820

Phone | Fax

Autobytel Inc 18872 MacArthur Blvd ... Irvine CA 92612 949-225-4500 225-4541
NASDAQ: ABTL ■ *TF:* 888-422-8999 ■ *Web:* www.autobytel.com

Autofusion Corp 6215 Ferris Sq Ste 200 ... San Diego CA 92121 858-270-9444 270-6116
TF: 800-410-7354 ■ *Web:* www.autofusion.com

Automobile Consumer Services Inc
6249 Stewart Rd ... Cincinnati OH 45227 513-527-7700 527-7705
TF: 800-223-4882 ■ *Web:* www.acscorp.com

Automotive Information Ctr
18872 MacArthur Blvd ... Irvine CA 92612 888-422-8999
TF: 888-422-8999 ■ *Web:* www.autobytel.com

AutoVIN Inc 50 Mansell Ct ... Roswell GA 30076 678-585-8000
Web: www.autovin.com

Cars.com 175 W Jackson Blvd Ste 800 ... Chicago IL 60604 312-601-5000 601-5755
TF: 888-246-6298 ■ *Web:* www.cars.com

CarsDirect.com Inc
909 N Sepulveda Blvd 11th Fl ... El Segundo CA 90245 888-227-7347
TF Cust Svc: 888-227-7347 ■ *Web:* www.carsdirect.com

CarSmart 18872 MacArthur Blvd Ste 200 ... Irvine CA 92612 949-225-4500
Web: www.autobytel.com

Kelley Blue Book Company Inc
195 Technology Dr ... Irvine CA 92623 949-770-7704 837-1904
TF: 800-258-3266 ■ *Web:* www.kbb.com

Williamson Cadillac Co 7815 SW 104th St ... Miami FL 33156 305-670-7100
TF: 877-228-6093 ■ *Web:* williamsonautomotivegroup.com

59 AUTOMOBILES - MFR

See Also All-Terrain Vehicles p. 1733; Motor Vehicles - Commercial & Special Purpose p. 2785; Motorcycles & Motorcycle Parts & Accessories p. 2787; Snowmobiles p. 3187

Phone | Fax

4 Guys Inc 230 Industrial Pk Rd ... Meyersdale PA 15552 814-634-8373 634-0076
Web: www.4guysfire.com

AM General LLC 105 N Niles Ave PO Box 7025 ... South Bend IN 46617 574-237-6222
Web: www.amgeneral.com

American Honda Motor Company Inc
1919 Torrance Blvd ... Torrance CA 90501 310-783-3170
TF: 800-999-1009 ■ *Web:* www.honda.com

American Suzuki Motor Corp 3251 Imperial Hwy ... Brea CA 92821 714-996-7040
Web: www.suzuki.com

Audi of America 3800 Hamlin Rd ... Auburn Hills MI 48326 888-237-2834
TF: 888-237-2834 ■ *Web:* www.audiusa.com

Bentley Motors Inc 2200 Ferdinand Porsche Dr ... Herndon VA 20171 703-364-7990
Web: www.bentleymotors.com

BMW Manufacturing Co 1400 Hwy 101 S ... Greer SC 29651 864-989-6000
Web: www.bmwusfactory.com

BMW of North America LLC
300 Chestnut Ridge Rd ... Woodcliff Lake NJ 07677 201-307-4000 307-4095
TF: 800-831-1117 ■ *Web:* www.bmwusa.com

Braun Industries Inc 1170 Production Dr ... Van Wert OH 45891 877-344-9990
TF: 877-344-9990 ■ *Web:* www.braunambulances.com

Chrysler Canada Inc 1 Riverside Dr W ... Windsor ON N9A5K3 519-973-2000
Web: www.fcacanada.ca/en

Chrysler Group LLC 1000 Chrysler Dr ... Auburn Hills MI 48326 800-423-6343
TF Cust Svc: 800-423-6343 ■ *Web:* www.dodge.com

Collins Bus Corp PO Box 2946 ... Hutchinson KS 67504 620-662-9000 662-3838
TF: 800-533-1850 ■ *Web:* www.collinsbuscorp.com

DaimlerChrysler Corp Jeep Div
PO Box 21-8004 ... Auburn Hills MI 48321 800-992-1997
TF Cust Svc: 800-992-1997 ■ *Web:* www.jeep.com

Eldorado National Inc 1655 Wall St ... Salina KS 67401 909-591-9557 823-9471*
**Fax Area Code: 785* ■ *TF:* 800-850-1287 ■ *Web:* www.enconline.com

Ferrara Fire Apparatus Inc PO Box 249 ... Holden LA 70744 225-567-7100 567-5260
TF: 800-443-9006 ■ *Web:* www.ferrarafire.com

Ferrari North America Inc
250 Sylvan Ave ... Englewood Cliffs NJ 07632 201-816-2600 816-2626
Web: www.ferrari.com

Ford Motor Co PO Box 6248 ... Dearborn MI 48126 313-845-8540
NYSE: F ■ *TF:* 800-392-3673 ■ *Web:* www.ford.com

Freightliner Specialty Vehicles Inc
2300 S 13th St ... Clinton OK 73601 580-323-4100 323-4111
TF: 800-358-7624 ■ *Web:* www.sportchassis.com

General Motors Corp (GMC) 100 Renaissance Ctr ... Detroit MI 48265 313-556-5000
NYSE: GM ■ *Web:* www.gm.com

General Motors Corp Buick Motor Div
300 Renaissance Ctr PO Box 33136 ... Detroit MI 48265 800-521-7300
TF Cust Svc: 800-521-7300 ■ *Web:* www.buick.com

Glaval Bus 914 County Rd 1 ... Elkhart IN 46514 574-262-2212 264-9036
TF: 800-445-2825 ■ *Web:* www.glavalbus.com

Honda Mfg of Alabama LLC 1800 Honda Dr ... Lincoln AL 35096 205-355-5000
Web: www.hondaalabama.com

Horton Emergency Vehicles
3800 McDowell Rd ... Grove City OH 43123 614-539-8181 539-8165
TF: 800-282-5113 ■ *Web:* www.hortonambulance.com

Hyundai Motor America
10550 Talbert Ave ... Fountain Valley CA 92708 714-965-3000
TF Cust Svc: 800-633-5151 ■ *Web:* www.hyundaiusa.com

International Armoring Corp 80 N 1400 W ... Centerville UT 84014 801-393-1075 298-0858
Web: www.armormax.com

Jefferson Industries Corp
6670 Ohio 29 ... West Jefferson OH 43162 614-879-5300 879-6806

Land Rover North America Inc
555 MacArthur Blvd ... Mahwah NJ 07430 800-637-6837
TF: 800-637-6837 ■ *Web:* www.landrover.com

Lincoln-Mercury Co PO Box 6128 ... Dearborn MI 48121 800-521-4140
TF: 800-521-4140 ■ *Web:* www.mercuryvehicles.com

Lotus Cars USA Inc
2402 Tech Ctr Pkwy NE ... Lawrenceville GA 30043 770-476-6540
TF Cust Svc: 800-245-6887 ■ *Web:* www.lotuscars.com

Mazda North American Operations
7755 Irvine Ctr Dr PO Box 19734 ... Irvine CA 92618 949-727-1990
TF Cust Svc: 800-222-5500 ■ *Web:* www.mazdausa.com

Medix Specialty Vehicles Inc 3008 Mobile Dr ... Elkhart IN 46514 574-266-0911
Web: www.medixambulance.com

Mercedes-Benz U.S. International Inc
1 Mercedes Dr ... Vance AL 35490 205-507-2252
TF: 888-286-8762 ■ *Web:* www.mbusi.com

Mercedes-Benz USA LLC 1 Mercedes Dr ... Montvale NJ 07645 201-573-0600
TF Cust Svc: 800-367-6372 ■ *Web:* www.mbusa.com

Mitsubishi Canada Ltd
2800-200 Granville St Ste 2800 ... Vancouver BC V6C1G6 604-654-8000 654-8222
Web: www.mitsubishicorp.com

Phone Fax

Mobile Concepts by Scotty Inc
480 Bessemer Rd .... Mount Pleasant PA 15666 724-542-7640
Web: www.mobileconcepts.com

Nissan Canada Inc (NCI) 5290 Orbitor Dr .... Mississauga ON L4W4Z5 800-387-0122 629-6553*
**Fax Area Code:* 905 ■ *TF:* 800-387-0122 ■ *Web:* www.nissan.ca

Nissan Motor Corp USA Infiniti Div
1 Nissan Way PO Box 685003 .... Franklin TN 37067 800-662-6200
TF: 800-662-6200 ■ *Web:* www.infinitiusa.com

Nissan North America Inc 25 Vantage way .... Nashville TN 37228 800-647-7261 629-9742*
**Fax Area Code:* 905 ■ *TF:* 800-647-7261 ■ *Web:* www.nissanusa.com

Peugeot Motors of America Inc
150 Clove Rd Ste 3 .... Little Falls NJ 07424 973-812-4444
Web: www.peugeot.com

Porsche Cars North America Inc
980 Hammond Dr Ste 1000 .... Atlanta GA 30328 770-290-3500 290-3708
TF: 800-505-1041 ■ *Web:* www.porsche.com

Saleen Automotive Inc 2735 Wardlow Rd .... Corona CA 92882 800-888-8945
TF: 800-888-8945 ■ *Web:* www.saleen.com

Subaru of America Inc
2235 Marlton Pike W .... Cherry Hill NJ 08002 856-488-8500 488-0485
TF: 800-782-2783 ■ *Web:* www.subaru.com

T3 Motion Inc 2990 Airway Ave Ste A .... Costa Mesa CA 92626 714-619-3600
Web: www.t3motion.com

Terrafugia Inc 23 Rainin Rd .... Woburn MA 01801 781-491-0812
Web: www.terrafugia.com

Tesla Motors Inc 3500 Deer Creek Rd .... Palo Alto CA 94304 650-681-5000
TF: 888-518-3752 ■ *Web:* www.teslamotors.com

Toyota Canada Inc 1 Toyota Pl .... Scarborough ON M1H1H9 416-438-6320
TF Cust Svc: 888-869-6828 ■ *Web:* www.toyota.ca

Toyota Motor Manufacturing Kentucky Inc
1001 Cherry Blossom Way .... Georgetown KY 40324 502-868-2000
Web: www.toyotageorgetown.com

Toyota Motor Sales USA Inc
19001 S Western Ave .... Torrance CA 90501 310-468-4000 468-7814
TF Cust Svc: 800-331-4331 ■ *Web:* www.toyota.com

Toyota Motor Sales USA Inc Lexus Div
19001 S Western Ave .... Torrance CA 90501 800-255-3987 468-7800*
**Fax Area Code:* 310 ■ *TF Cust Svc:* 800-255-3987 ■ *Web:* www.lexus.com

Trikon Design Inc 2295 N Opdyke Rd Ste F .... Auburn Hills MI 48326 248-340-0460
Web: www.trikoncorp.com

Verspeeten Cartage Ltd 274129 Wallace Line .... Ingersoll ON N5C3J7 519-425-7881
Web: www.verspeeten.com

Volkswagen Canada Inc 777 Bayly St W .... Ajax ON L1S7G7 905-428-6700 428-5898
TF: 800-822-8987 ■ *Web:* www.vw.ca

Volkswagen Group of America Inc
2200 Ferdinand Porsche Dr .... Herndon VA 20171 248-754-5000
Web: www.volkswagengroupamerica.com

Volkswagen of America Inc
3800 Hamlin Rd .... Auburn Hills MI 48326 800-822-8987
TF: 800-822-8987 ■ *Web:* www.vw.com

Volvo Cars of North America 1 Volvo Dr .... Rockleigh NJ 07647 201-768-7300
TF Cust Svc: 800-458-1552 ■ *Web:* www.volvocars.com

60 AUTOMOTIVE PARTS & SUPPLIES - MFR

See Also Carburetors, Pistons, Piston Rings, Valves p. 1892; Electrical Equipment for Internal Combustion Engines p. 2222; Engines & Turbines p. 2273; Gaskets, Packing, Sealing Devices p. 2351; Hose & Belting - Rubber or Plastics p. 2483; Motors (Electric) & Generators p. 2787

Phone Fax

Acadia Polymers Inc 5251 Concourse Dr .... Roanoke VA 24019 540-265-2700

Accuride Corp 7140 Office Cir .... Evansville IN 47715 812-962-5000
NYSE: ACW ■ *TF Cust Svc:* 800-823-8332 ■ *Web:* www.accuridecorp.com

Aer Mfg Inc PO Box 979 .... Carrollton TX 75011 972-417-2582
TF: 800-753-5237 ■ *Web:* www.aermanufacturing.com

Airtex Products 407 W Main St .... Fairfield IL 62837 618-842-2111
TF: 800-880-3056 ■ *Web:* www.airtexproducts.com

Aisin Holdings of America Inc
1665 E Fourth St .... Seymour IN 47274 812-524-8144 524-8146
Web: www.aisinworld.com

Aisin USA Mfg Inc 1700 E Fourth St .... Seymour IN 47274 812-523-1969 523-1984
Web: www.aisinusa.com

Alma Products Co 2000 Michigan Ave .... Alma MI 48801 989-463-1151 457-2719*
**Fax Area Code:* 800 ■ *TF:* 877-427-2624 ■ *Web:* almaproducts.sharepoint.com

AMBAC International Inc 910 Spears Creek Ct .... Elgin SC 29045 803-735-1400 735-2163
TF: 800-628-6894 ■ *Web:* ambacdiesel.com

American Auto Accessories Inc
35-06 Leavitt St Unit C .... Flushing NY 11354 718-886-6600 625-8600*
**Fax Area Code:* 347

AMSTED Industries Inc
180 N Stetson St Ste 1800 .... Chicago IL 60601 312-645-1700
Web: www.amsted.com

Angstrom Precision Metals Inc 8229 Tyler Blvd .... Mentor OH 44060 440-255-6700 255-4263

AP Exhaust Technologies Inc
300 Dixie Trial .... Goldsboro NC 27530 919-580-2000
TF: 800-277-2787 ■ *Web:* www.apexhaust.com

ARC Automotive Inc 1729 Midpark Rd Ste D .... Knoxville TN 37921 865-583-7800
Web: www.arcautomotive.com

ArvinMeritor Inc 2135 W Maple Rd .... Troy MI 48084 248-435-1000 435-1393
NYSE: MTOR ■ *Web:* www.meritor.com

Atwood Mobile Products 1120 N Main St .... Elkhart IN 46514 574-264-2131 262-2194
TF: 800-546-8759 ■ *Web:* www.atwoodmobile.com

Autocam Corp 4070 E Paris Ave .... Kentwood MI 49512 616-698-0707 698-6876
TF: 800-747-6978 ■ *Web:* www.autocam.com

Avis Industrial Corp 1909 S Main St .... Upland IN 46989 765-998-8100 998-8111
Web: www.avisindustrial.com

Aw Transmission Engineering USA Inc
14920 Keel St .... Plymouth MI 48170 734-454-1710 454-1091
Web: www.awtec.com

Baldwin Filters 4400 Hwy 30 .... Kearney NE 68847 800-822-5394 828-4453
TF: 800-822-5394 ■ *Web:* www.baldwinfilter.com

Phone Fax

Beach Manufacturing Co PO Box 129 .... Donnelsville OH 45319 937-882-6372 882-6153
TF: 800-543-5942 ■ *Web:* www.beachmfgco.com

Black River Manufacturing Inc
2625 20th St .... Port Huron MI 48060 810-982-9812 982-2074
Web: www.blackrivermfg.biz

Bode North America Inc 660 John Dodd Rd .... Spartanburg SC 29303 864-578-9683
Web: www.bodecorpusa.com

BorgWarner Automatic Transmission Systems
3800 Automation Ave .... Auburn Hills MI 48326 248-754-9600
Web: www.borgwarner.com

BorgWarner Inc 3850 Hamlin Rd .... Auburn Hills MI 48326 248-754-9200
NYSE: BWA ■ *Web:* www.borgwarner.com

BorgWarner Morse TEC 800 Warren Rd .... Ithaca NY 14850 607-257-6700
Web: www.borgwarner.com

BorgWarner TorqTransfer Systems
3800 Automation Ave .... Auburn Hills MI 48326 248-754-9600 754-9356
Web: www.borgwarner.com

Borla Performance Industries Inc
500 Borla Dr .... Johnson City TN 37604 423-979-4000 979-4099
TF: 877-462-6752 ■ *Web:* www.borla.com

Bushwacker Inc 6710 N Catlin Ave .... Portland OR 97203 503-283-4335 283-3007
TF: 800-234-8920 ■ *Web:* www.bushwacker.com

Car Parts Warehouse Inc 5200 W 130th St .... Akron OH 44311 216-676-5100 676-5516
Web: www.carpartswarehouse.net

Cardone Industries Inc
5501 Whitaker Ave .... Philadelphia PA 19124 215-912-3000 912-3700
TF Cust Svc: 800-777-4780 ■ *Web:* www.cardone.com

Carlisle Cos Inc
13925 Ballantyne Corporate Pl Ste 400 .... Charlotte NC 28277 704-501-1100 501-1190
NYSE: CSL ■ *TF:* 800-248-5995 ■ *Web:* www.carlisle.com

Carlisle Cos Inc
11605 N Community House Rd Ste 600 .... Charlotte NC 28277 704-501-1100 501-1190
NYSE: CSL ■ *Web:* www.carlisle.com

Carlisle Industrial Brake
1031 E Hillside Dr .... Bloomington IN 47401 812-336-3811 334-8775
TF: 800-873-6361 ■ *Web:* www.carlislebrake.com

Champion Laboratories Inc 200 S Fourth St .... Albion IL 62806 618-445-6011 445-4040
Web: www.champlabs.com

Clarcor Inc 840 Crescent Ctr Dr Ste 600 .... Franklin TN 37067 615-771-3100 771-5616
NYSE: CLC ■ *TF:* 800-252-7267 ■ *Web:* www.clarcor.com

Commercial Vehicle Group Inc
7800 Walton Pkwy .... New Albany OH 43054 614-289-5360 289-5361
NASDAQ: CVGI ■ *Web:* www.cvgrp.com

Competition Cams Inc 3406 Democrat Rd .... Memphis TN 38118 901-795-2400 366-1807
TF: 800-999-0853 ■ *Web:* www.compcams.com

Consolidated Metco Inc
13940 N Rivergate Blvd .... Portland OR 97203 800-547-9473 240-5488*
**Fax Area Code:* 503 ■ **Fax:* Sales ■ *TF Sales:* 800-547-9473 ■ *Web:* www.conmet.com

Cooper-Standard Automotive Fluid Systems Div
2110 Executive Hills Ct .... Auburn Hills MI 48326 248-836-9400 836-9116
Web: www.cooperstandard.com

Cooper-Standard Automotive Inc
39550 Orchard Hill Pl Dr .... Novi MI 48375 248-596-5900
Web: www.cooperstandard.com

Crower Cams & Equipment
6180 Business Ctr Ct .... San Diego CA 92154 619-661-6477 661-6466
Web: www.crower.com

Cummins Filtration 2931 Elm Hill Pike .... Nashville TN 37214 615-367-0040 999-8664*
**Fax Area Code:* 800 ■ *TF:* 800-777-7064 ■ *Web:* www.cumminsfiltration.com

Cummins Inc 500 Jackson St PO Box 3005 .... Columbus IN 47201 812-377-5000 377-3334
NYSE: CMI ■ *TF:* 800-343-7357 ■ *Web:* www.cummins.com

CWC Textron 1085 W Sherman Blvd .... Muskegon MI 49441 231-733-1331
TF: 800-999-0853 ■ *Web:* www.cwctextron.com

DACCO Transmission Parts
741 Dacco Dr PO Box 2789 .... Cookeville TN 38502 931-528-7581
TF Cust Svc: 866-645-1452 ■ *Web:* www.daccoinc.com

Danaher Corp
2200 Pennsylvania Ave NW Ste 800 .... Washington DC 20037 202-828-0850 828-0860
NYSE: DHR ■ *TF:* 800-833-9200 ■ *Web:* www.danaher.com

Davco Technology LLC
1600 Woodland Dr PO Box 487 .... Saline MI 48176 734-429-5665 429-0741
TF: 800-328-2611 ■ *Web:* www.davcotec.com

Dayton Parts LLC
3500 Industrial Rd PO Box 5795 .... Harrisburg PA 17110 717-255-8500 255-8500
TF Cust Svc: 800-225-2159 ■ *Web:* daytonparts.com

Decoma International Inc
Magna Exteriors & Interiors 50 Casmir Ct .... Concord ON L4K4J5 905-669-2888 528-6450*
**Fax Area Code:* 248 ■ *TF:* 888-348-2398 ■ *Web:* www.magna.com

Delphi Corp 5725 Delphi Dr .... Troy MI 48098 248-813-2334
Web: www.delphi.com

Delphi Energy & Chassis Systems 5725 Delphi Dr .... Troy MI 48098 248-813-2334
Web: www.delphi.com

Denso International America Inc
24777 Denso Dr .... Southfield MI 48033 248-350-7500 213-2337
Web: www.densocorp-na.com

Dexter Axle 2900 Industrial Pkwy .... Elkhart IN 46516 574-295-7888 295-8666
TF: 800-522-7291 ■ *Web:* www.dexteraxle.com

Dorman Products Inc 3400 E Walnut St .... Colmar PA 18915 215-997-1800
NASDAQ: DORM ■ *TF:* 800-523-2492 ■ *Web:* www.rbinc.com

Douglas Autotech Corp 300 Albers Rd .... Bronson MI 49028 517-369-2315 369-7217
Web: www.douglasautotech.com

Dreison International Inc 4540 W 160th St .... Cleveland OH 44135 216-265-8006 265-0130
Web: www.dreison.com

DST Industries Inc 34364 Goddard Rd .... Romulus MI 48174 734-941-0300
Web: www.dstindustries.com

Dura Automotive Systems Inc
1780 Pond Run .... Auburn Hills MI 48326 248-299-7500 211-7544*
**Fax Area Code:* 442 ■ *Web:* www.duraauto.com

Eagle Wings Industries Inc (EWI)
400 Shellhouse Dr .... Rantoul IL 61866 217-892-4322
Web: www.ewiusa.com

East Penn Mfg Co Inc PO Box 147 .... Lyon Station PA 19536 610-682-6361 682-6361
Web: eastpennmanufacturing.com

Company	City	State	ZIP	Phone	Fax
Eaton Corp 1111 Superior Ave Eaton Ctr *Web:* www.eaton.com	Cleveland	OH	44114	216-523-5000	
Edelbrock Corp 2700 California St *TF:* 800-739-3737 ■ *Web:* www.edelbrock.com	Torrance	CA	90503	310-781-2222	320-1187
Engine Power Components Inc 1333 Fulton St *Web:* www.engpwr.com	Grand Haven	MI	49417	616-846-0110	847-0500
EnPro Industries Inc 5605 Carnegie Blvd Ste 500 *NYSE: NPO*	Charlotte	NC	28209	704-731-1500	
Evercoat 6600 Cornell Rd *TF:* 800-729-7600 ■ *Web:* www.evercoat.com	Cincinnati	OH	45242	513-489-7600	489-9229
Faurecia Exhaust Systems Inc 543 Matzinger Rd *Web:* www.faurecia.com	Toledo	OH	43612	419-727-5000	727-5025
Federal-Mogul Corp 27300 W 11 Mile Rd *NASDAQ: FDML* ■ *TF Cust Svc:* 800-325-8886 ■ *Web:* www.federalmogul.com	Southfield	MI	48034	248-354-7700	354-7700
Firestone Industrial Products Co 250 W 96th St *TF:* 800-888-0650 ■ *Web:* www.firestoneip.com	Indianapolis	IN	46260	317-818-8600	818-8645
Flex-N-Gate Corp 1306 E University Ave *TF:* 800-398-1496 ■ *Web:* www.flex-n-gate.com	Urbana	IL	61802	217-278-2600	278-2616
Fontaine Fifth Wheel 7574 Commerce Cir *TF:* 800-874-9780 ■ *Web:* www.fifthwheel.com	Trussville	AL	35173	205-661-4900	655-9982
Fontaine Truck Equipment Co 7574 Commerce Cir *TF:* 800-874-9780 ■ *Web:* www.fontaine.com	Trussville	AL	35173	205-661-4900	655-9982
Franklin Precision Industry Inc (FPI) 3220 Bowling Green Rd *Web:* www.fpik.com	Franklin	KY	42134	270-598-4300	586-0180
Freudenberg-NOK General Partnership 47690 E Anchor Ct *Web:* www.fst.com	Plymouth	MI	48170	734-451-0020	451-0043
Griffin Thermal Products 100 Hurricane Creek Rd *TF:* 800-722-3723 ■ *Web:* www.griffinrad.com	Piedmont	SC	29673	864-845-5000	845-5001
Grote Industries Inc 2600 Lanier Dr *TF:* 800-628-0809 ■ *Web:* www.grote.com	Madison	IN	47250	812-273-2121	265-8440
Gunite Corp 302 Peoples Ave *TF:* 800-677-3786 ■ *Web:* www.accuridewheelendsolutions.com	Rockford	IL	61104	815-964-3301	964-0775
Hastings Manufacturing Co 325 N Hanover St *TF:* 800-776-1088 ■ *Web:* www.hastingspistonrings.com	Hastings	MI	49058	269-945-2491	945-4667
Hayden Automotive 1801 Waters Ridge Dr *TF:* 888-505-4567 ■ *Web:* www.haydenauto.com	Lewisville	TX	75057	888-505-4567	
Heckethorn Manfacturing Cos Inc 2005 Forrest St *Web:* www.hecomfg.com	Dyersburg	TN	38024	731-285-3310	286-2739
Hendrickson International 800 S Frontage Rd *TF:* 855-743-3733 ■ *Web:* www.hendrickson-intl.com	Woodridge	IL	60517	630-910-2800	910-2899
Hennessy Industries Inc 1601 JP Hennesey Dr **Fax Area Code:* 615 ■ **Fax:* Mktg ■ *TF:* 800-688-6359 ■ *Web:* www.hennessyind.com	La Vergne	TN	37086	855-876-3864	641-6069*
Holley Performance Products Inc 1801 Russellville Rd **Fax:* Cust Svc ■ *TF Sales:* 800-638-0032 ■ *Web:* www.holley.com	Bowling Green	KY	42101	270-782-2900	781-9940*
Hopkins Manufacturing Corp 428 Peyton St *TF:* 800-524-1458 ■ *Web:* www.hopkinsmfg.com	Emporia	KS	66801	620-342-7320	340-8590
Hutchens Industries Inc 215 N Patterson Ave **Fax:* Cust Svc ■ *TF:* 800-654-8824 ■ *Web:* hutchensindustries.com	Springfield	MO	65802	417-862-5012	862-2317*
HWH Corp 2096 Moscow Rd *TF:* 800-321-3494 ■ *Web:* www.hwhcorp.com	Moscow	IA	52760	563-724-3396	724-3408
Ilmor Engineering Inc 43939 Plymouth Oaks Blvd *Web:* www.ilmor.com	Plymouth	MI	48170	734-456-3600	
Indian Head Industries Inc 8530 Cliff Cameron Dr *TF:* 800-527-1534 ■ *Web:* mgmbrakes.com	Charlotte	NC	28269	704-547-7411	547-9367
Injex Industries Inc 30559 San Antonio St *Web:* injexindustries.com	Hayward	CA	94544	510-487-4960	487-8886
Insight USA Inc 23330 Cottonwood Pkwy Ste 333 *Web:* www.mds-inc.com	California	MD	20619	301-866-1990	
Interparts International Inc 190 Express St *Web:* www.interparts.com	Plainview	NY	11803	516-576-2000	
Irvin Automotive Products Inc 2600 Centerpoint Pkwy *Web:* www.irvinautomotive.com	Pontiac	MI	48341	248-451-4100	451-4101
J B Poindexter & Company Inc 600 Travis St Ste 200 *Web:* www.jbpoindexter.com	Houston	TX	77002	713-655-9800	951-9038
Jacobs Vehicle Systems Inc 22 E Dudley Town Rd *Web:* www.jacobsvehiclesystems.com	Bloomfield	CT	06002	860-243-1441	243-7632
Jason Inc 411 E Wisconsin Ave Ste 2120 *Web:* www.jasoninc.com	Milwaukee	WI	53202	414-277-9300	
JASPER Engines & Transmissions 815 Wernsing Rd PO Box 650 *TF:* 800-827-7455 ■ *Web:* www.jasperengines.com	Jasper	IN	47547	812-482-1041	634-1820
John Bean Co 309 Exchange Ave *TF:* 800-225-5786 ■ *Web:* www.johnbean.com	Conway	AR	72032	501-450-1500	
Johnson Controls Inc Automotive Systems Group 49200 Halyard Dr *Web:* www.johnsoncontrols.com	Plymouth	MI	48170	734-254-5000	
JSJ Corp 700 Robbins Rd *Web:* www.jsjcorp.com	Grand Haven	MI	49417	616-842-6350	847-3112
KONI North America 1961-A International Way *Web:* www.koni-na.com	Hebron	KY	41048	859-586-4100	334-3340
Linamar Corp 287 Speedvale Ave W *TSE: LNR* ■ *Web:* www.linamar.com	Guelph	ON	N1H1C5	519-836-7550	824-8479
Lorain County Automotive Systems Inc 7470 Industrial Pkwy Dr *Web:* www.camacollc.com	Lorain	OH	44053	440-960-7470	960-1878
LuK USA LLC 3401 Old Airport Rd *Web:* www.schaeffler.us	Wooster	OH	44691	330-264-4383	264-4333
Lund International Holdings Inc 4325 Hamilton Mill Rd Ste 400 *TF:* 800-241-7219 ■ *Web:* www.lundinternational.com	Buford	GA	30518	678-804-3912	
Luverne Truck Equipment Inc 1200 Birch St *Web:* www.luvernetruck.com	Brandon	SD	57005	605-582-7200	582-3486
MacLean-Fogg Co 1000 Allanson Rd *TF:* 800-323-4536 ■ *Web:* www.macleanfogg.com	Mundelein	IL	60060	847-566-0010	949-0285
Magna International Inc 337 Magna Dr *TSE: MG* ■ *Web:* www.magna.com	Aurora	ON	L4G7K1	905-726-2462	726-7164
Magna International of America 750 Tower Dr *Web:* www.magna.com	Troy	MI	48098	248-631-1100	
Magneti Marelli Powertrain USA Inc 2101 Nash St **Fax:* Mktg ■ *Web:* www.magnetimarelli.com	Sanford	NC	27330	919-776-4111	775-6337*
MAHLE Industries Inc 2020 Sanford St *TF:* 888-255-1942 ■ *Web:* www.us.mahle.com	Muskegon	MI	49444	231-722-1300	724-1941
Manley Performance Engineering 1960 Swarthmore Ave *Web:* manleyperformance.com	Lakewood	NJ	08701	732-905-3366	
Marmon-Herrington Co 13001 Magisterial Dr *TF:* 800-227-0727 ■ *Web:* marmon-herrington.com	Louisville	KY	40223	502-253-0277	253-0317
Mayco International LLC 42400 Merrill Rd *Web:* maycointernational.com	Sterling Heights	MI	48314	586-803-6000	
Melling Tool Co 2620 Saradan St PO Box 1188 *Web:* www.melling.com	Jackson	MI	49204	517-787-8172	787-5304
Metaldyne Corp 47603 Halyard Dr *Web:* www.metaldyne.com	Plymouth	MI	48170	734-207-6200	207-6500
Mikuni American Corp 8910 Mikuni Ave *Web:* www.mikuni.com	Northridge	CA	91324	818-885-1242	993-6877
Mitsuba Bardstown Inc 901 Withrow Ct *Web:* www.americanmitsuba.com	Bardstown	KY	40004	502-348-3100	
Neapco Inc 6735 Haggerty Rd PO Box 399 *TF:* 800-821-2374 ■ *Web:* www.neapco.com	Belleville	MI	48111	734-447-1380	
Omni Gear 7502 Mesa Rd *Web:* www.omnigear.com	Houston	TX	77028	713-635-6331	635-6360
P. T. M. Corp 6560 Bethuy Rd *TF:* 800-486-2212 ■ *Web:* www.ptmcorporation.com	Fair Haven	MI	48023	586-725-2211	725-6753
Penda Corp PO Box 449 *TF:* 800-356-7704 ■ *Web:* pendaform.com/markets_automotive.php	Portage	WI	53901	800-356-7704	
Penntecq Inc 106 Kuder Dr *Web:* www.penntecq.com	Greenville	PA	16125	724-646-4250	646-4261
Perfection Clutch Co 100 Perfection Way *TF:* 800-258-8312 ■ *Web:* www.perfectionclutch.com	Timmonsville	SC	29161	843-326-5544	
Phillips & Temro Industries 9700 W 74th St *TF:* 800-328-6108 ■ *Web:* www.phillipsandtemro.com	Eden Prairie	MN	55344	952-941-9700	941-2285
Powers & Sons LLC 1613 Magda Dr *Web:* www.powersandsonsllc.com	Montpelier	OH	43543	419-485-3151	485-5490
Prime Wheel Corp 17705 S Main St *Web:* www.primewheel.com	Gardena	CA	90248	310-516-9126	516-9676
Raybestos Powertrain LLC 711 Tech Dr *TF:* 800-729-7763 ■ *Web:* www.raybestospowertrain.com	Crawfordsville	IN	47933	800-729-7763	
Remy International Inc 600 Corp Dr *NYSE: REMY* ■ *TF:* 800-372-3555 ■ *Web:* www.remyinc.com	Pendleton	IN	46064	765-778-6499	
Ridewell Corp PO Box 4586 *TF:* 877-434-8088 ■ *Web:* www.ridewellcorp.com	Springfield	MO	65808	417-833-4565	
Rieter Automotive North America Inc 38555 Hills Tech Dr *Web:* www.rieter.com	Farmington Hills	MI	48331	248-848-0100	848-0130
Robert Bosch LLC 2800 S 25th Ave *Web:* www.bosch.us	Broadview	IL	60155	708-865-5200	
Roush Manufacturing Inc 12068 Market St *TF:* 800-215-9658 ■ *Web:* www.roush.com	Livonia	MI	48150	734-779-7006	
Ryobi Die Casting Inc 800 W Mausoleum Rd *Web:* www.ryobidiecasting.com	Shelbyville	IN	46176	317-398-3398	421-3725
SAF-Holland USA 1950 Industrial Blvd *Web:* corporate.safholland.com	Muskegon	MI	49442	231-773-3271	
Sealco Commercial Vehicle Products Inc 215 E Watkins St **Fax Area Code:* 800 ■ *Web:* www.sealcocvp.com	Phoenix	AZ	85004	602-253-1007	222-2334*
Simpson Performance Products Inc 328 FM 306 *Web:* www.simpsonraceproducts.com	New Braunfels	TX	78130	830-625-1774	
SmarTire Systems Inc 6900 Graybar Rd Ste 2110 *TF:* 800-247-2725 ■ *Web:* www.smartire.com	Richmond	BC	V3W0A5	604-276-9884	
Soucy Holding Inc 5450 Saint-Roch St *Web:* www.soucy-group.com	Drummondville	QC	J2B6W3	819-474-9008	
Spalding Automotive Inc 4529 Adams Cir **Fax Area Code:* 267 ■ *Web:* www.spaldingautomotive.com	Bensalem	PA	19020	215-826-4000	550-9035*
Stanadyne Corp 92 Deerfield Rd *TF:* 888-336-3473 ■ *Web:* www.stanadyne.com	Windsor	CT	06095	860-525-0821	687-4235
Standard Motor Products Inc 37-18 Northern Blvd *NYSE: SMP* ■ *Web:* www.smpcorp.com	Long Island	NY	11101	718-392-0200	729-4549
Stemco LP 300 Industrial Blvd PO Box 1989 **Fax:* Sales ■ *TF:* 800-527-8492 ■ *Web:* www.stemco.com	Longview	TX	75606	903-758-9981	232-3508*
Stoneridge Inc 9400 E Market St *NYSE: SRI* ■ *Web:* www.stoneridge.com	Warren	OH	44484	330-856-2443	856-3618
Strattec Security Corp 3333 W Good Hope Rd *NASDAQ: STRT* ■ *Web:* www.strattec.com	Milwaukee	WI	53209	414-247-3333	247-3329
Summit Polymers Inc 6717 S Sprinkle Rd *Web:* www.summitpolymers.com	Portage	MI	49002	269-324-9330	324-9311
Superior Industries International Inc 7800 Woodley Ave *NYSE: SUP* ■ *TF:* 800-322-2885 ■ *Web:* www.supind.com	Van Nuys	CA	91406	818-781-4973	780-3500
Systrand Manufacturing Corp 19050 Allen Rd *Web:* www.systrand.com	Brownstown	MI	48183	734-479-8100	479-8107

Phone | Fax

TAG Holdings LLC 2075 W Big Beaver Rd Ste 500 .... Troy MI 48084 248-822-8056 822-8012
Web: www.taghold.com

Taylor Devices Inc
90 Taylor Dr PO Box 748 .... North Tonawanda NY 14120 716-694-0800 695-6015
NASDAQ: TAYD ■ *Web:* www.taylordevices.com

TBDN Tennessee Co 1410 Hwy 70 Bypass.............. Jackson TN 38301 731-421-4800 421-4879
Web: www.tbdn.com

Teleflex Medical
2917 Weck Dr PO Box 12600............ Research Triangle Park NC 27709 919-544-8000 361-3914
TF: 866-246-6990 ■ *Web:* www.teleflex.com

TeleflexGFI Control Systems LP
100 Hollinger Crescent............................ Kitchener ON N2K2Z3 519-576-4270 576-7045
TF: 800-667-4275 ■ *Web:* www.gficontrolsystems.com

Tenneco Inc 500 N Field Dr.......................... Lake Forest IL 60045 847-482-5000 482-5940
NYSE: TEN ■ *TF:* 866-839-3259 ■ *Web:* www.tenneco.com

Thermacore Inc 780 Eden Rd .... Lancaster PA 17601 717-569-6551
Web: www.thermacore.com

Titan International Inc 2701 Spruce St................. Quincy IL 62301 217-228-6011 228-9331*
NYSE: TWI ■ **Fax:* Cust Svc ■ *TF:* 800-872-2327 ■ *Web:* www.titan-intl.com

Titan Wheel Corp 2701 Spruce St .... Quincy IL 62301 217-228-6011 228-9331*
**Fax:* Cust Svc ■ *TF:* 800-872-2327 ■ *Web:* www.titan-intl.com

Transform Automotive LLC
7026 Sterling Ponds Ct .... Sterling Heights MI 48312 586-826-8500 826-3656
Web: www.transformauto.com

Trelleborg Automotive Americas
400 Aylworth Ave .... South Haven MI 49090 269-637-2116 394-5005*
**Fax Area Code:* 828 ■ *TF:* 800-635-9331 ■ *Web:* www.trelleborg.com

Triangle Suspension Systems Inc
47 E Maloney Rd .... Du Bois PA 15801 814-375-7211 237-2396*
**Fax Area Code:* 800 ■ *TF:* 800-458-6077 ■ *Web:* www.triangleusa.com

Trico Products Corp 3255 W Hamlin Rd .... Rochester Hills MI 48309 248-371-1700 371-8300
Web: www.tricoproducts.com

TRW Automotive 12025 Tech Ctr Dr.................... Livonia MI 48150 734-855-2600
Web: www.trwauto.com

TS Trim Industries Inc 59 Gender Rd.......... Canal Winchester OH 43110 614-837-4114
Web: www.tstrim.com

Universal Manufacturing Co
405 Diagonal St PO Box 190 .... Algona IA 50511 515-295-3557 295-5537
OTC: UFMG ■ *TF:* 800-651-7445 ■ *Web:* www.universalmanf.com

US Chemical & Plastics 600 Nova Dr SE .... Massillon OH 44646 330-830-6000 830-6005
TF: 800-321-0672 ■ *Web:* www.uschem.com

US Manufacturing Corp 28201 Van Dyke Ave............ Warren MI 48093 586-467-1600 467-1630
Web: www.usmfg.com

Velvac Inc 2405 S Calhoun Rd .... New Berlin WI 53151 262-786-0700 786-7323
TF: 800-783-8871 ■ *Web:* www.velvac.com

Visteon Corp 1 Village Ctr Dr............... Van Buren Township MI 48111 734-710-5000
NYSE: VC ■ *Web:* www.visteon.com

Voith Turbo Inc 25 Winship Rd.................................. York PA 17406 717-767-3200 767-3210
Web: redirect.voith.com/index2.php?r=d939d1f104c0b

Webasto Roof Systems Inc
1757 Northfield Dr .... Rochester Hills MI 48309 248-997-5100 997-5581
Web: www.webasto.com

Webb Automotive Group Inc 3911 E Main St........ Farmington NM 87402 505-325-1911 325-1911
Web: webbauto.com

Webb Wheel Products Inc
2310 Industrial Dr SW .... Cullman AL 35055 256-739-6660 739-6246*
**Fax:* Sales ■ *TF:* 800-633-3256 ■ *Web:* www.webbwheel.com

Wescast Industries Inc
150 Savannah Oaks Dr............................ Brantford ON N3T5V7 519-750-0000 427-9895*
TSE: WCS.A ■ **Fax Area Code:* 570 ■ *Web:* www.wecast.com

Westport Innovations Inc
1750 W 75th Ave Ste 101......................... Vancouver BC V6P6G2 604-718-2000 718-2001
TSE: WPT ■ *Web:* www.westport.com

Wix Filtration Products
1 Wix Way PO Box 1967.......................... Gastonia NC 28053 704-864-6711 864-9277*
**Fax:* Cust Svc ■ *Web:* www.wixfilters.com

61 AUTOMOTIVE PARTS & SUPPLIES - WHOL

Phone | Fax

AA Wheel & Truck Supply Inc
717 E 16th Ave.............................. Kansas City MO 64116 816-221-9556 221-9558
TF: 800-486-4335 ■ *Web:* www.aawheel.com

Aapco Automotive Warehouse
2997 E La Palma Ave .... Anaheim CA 92806 714-630-5600 666-2913

ABM Equipment & Supply LLC 333 Second St NE......... Hopkins MN 55343 952-938-5451 938-0159
Web: www.abm-highway.com

Ace Tool Co 7337 Bryan Dairy Rd .... Largo FL 33777 727-544-4331 544-6211
TF: 800-777-5910 ■ *Web:* www.acetoolco.com

Acterra Group Inc
Corporate Centre 200 200 35th St .... Marion IA 52302 319-377-6357
Web: www.acterragroup.com

Advantage Truck Accessories Inc
6535 Jacson Rd .... Ann Arbor MI 48103 800-773-3110 227-8899*
**Fax Area Code:* 877 ■ *TF:* 800-773-3110 ■ *Web:* www.advantagetruckaccessories.com

Advantech International Inc PO Box 6739 .... Somerset NJ 08875 800-322-6150 805-0122*
**Fax Area Code:* 732 ■ *TF:* 800-322-6150 ■ *Web:* www.advantechinternational.com

AFX Industries LLC 522 Michigan St Ste B............ Port Huron MI 48060 810-966-4650 966-9522
Web: www.afxindustries.com

All Products Automotive Inc
4701 W Cortland St .... Chicago IL 60639 773-889-4500
Web: locations.autovalue.com

Allomatic Products Co
102 Jericho Tpke Ste 104 Floral Pk .... Floral Park NY 11001 516-775-0330
TF: 800-568-0330 ■ *Web:* www.allomatic.com

Alto Products Corp 1 Alto Way........................ Atmore AL 36502 251-368-7777
Web: www.altousa.com

Arnold Motor Supply & The Merrill Co
601 First Ave S W................................ Spencer IA 51301 712-262-1141
Web: www.arnoldmotorsupply.com

Atsco ReMfg Inc 4525 N 43rd Ave..................... Phoenix AZ 85031 623-842-4047 842-0485
Web: www.atscoreman.com

Phone | Fax

Auto Parts Warehouse Inc 1073 E Artesia Blvd .... Carson CA 90746 310-884-5000 604-5088
Web: www.apwks.com

Automotive Distributors Company Inc
2981 Morse Rd.................................. Columbus OH 43231 800-421-5556 476-9469*
**Fax Area Code:* 614 ■ *TF:* 800-421-5556 ■ *Web:* www.adw1.com

Automotive Mfg & Supply Co
90 Plant Ave Ste 1 .... Hauppauge NY 11788 631-435-1400
Web: www.amscovf.com

Automotive Parts Headquarters
2959 Clearwater Rd .... Saint Cloud MN 56301 320-252-5411 252-4256
TF: 800-247-0339 ■ *Web:* www.autopartshq.com

Balkamp Inc 2601 S Holt Rd .... Indianapolis IN 46241 317-244-7241 227-1100
Web: www.balkamp.com

Barron Motor Inc 1850 McCloud Pl NE .... Cedar Rapids IA 52402 319-393-6220

Battery Systems Inc 12322 Monarch St .... Garden Grove CA 92841 310-667-9320
Web: www.batterysystems.net

Bell Industries Inc Recreational Products Group
580 Yankee Doodle Rd .... Eagan MN 55121 651-203-2300
TF: 800-866-5017

Bendix Commercial Vehicle Systems LLC
901 Cleveland St .... Elyria OH 44035 440-329-9000 329-9557
TF: 800-247-2725 ■ *Web:* www.bendix.com

Brake & Wheel Parts Industries Inc (BWP)
2415 W 21st St PO Box 08375........................ Chicago IL 60608 773-847-7000 847-5149

Bucyrus 1232 Whetstone St .... Bucyrus OH 44820 419-562-7987 562-8577

CAM International LLC 503 Space Park S .... Nashville TN 37211 615-331-1550
Web: www.caminternational.com

Carolina Rim & Wheel Co
1308 Upper Asbury Ave .... Charlotte NC 28206 704-334-7276 334-7270
TF: 800-247-4337 ■ *Web:* www.truckpro.com

Carolinas Auto Supply House Inc
2135 Tipton Dr .... Charlotte NC 28206 704-334-4646 377-7016*
**Fax Area Code:* 800 ■ *TF:* 800-438-4070 ■ *Web:* www.autosupplyhouse.com

Carquest Corp 2635 E Millbrook Rd .... Raleigh NC 27604 919-573-3000
TF: 800-876-1291 ■ *Web:* www.carquest.com

Celltron Inc 1110 W Seventh St........................ Galena KS 66739 620-783-1333
Web: www.celltron.com

Chalmers Group 6400 Northam Dr .... Mississauga ON L4V1J1 905-362-6400
Web: www.chalmersgroup.com

Champion Power Equipment Inc
10006 Santa Fe Springs Rd .... Santa Fe Springs CA 90670 562-236-9422
TF: 877-338-0999 ■ *Web:* www.championpowerequipment.com

Coast Distribution System
350 Woodview Ave............................ Morgan Hill CA 95037 408-782-6686 782-7790
NYSE: CRV ■ *TF:* 800-495-5858 ■ *Web:* www.coastdistribution.com

Cold Air Distributors Warehouse of Florida Inc
3053 Industrial 31st St.......................... Fort Pierce FL 34946 772-466-3036
Web: www.coldairdistributors.com

Colonial Garage & Distributors Ltd
59 Majors Path .... St John'S NL A1A4Z9 709-579-4015
Web: www.colonialautoparts.ca

Crw Parts Inc 1211 68th St .... Baltimore MD 21237 410-866-3300
Web: www.crwparts.com

Custom Chrome Inc 155 E Main Ave Ste 150......... Morgan Hill CA 95037 408-778-0500
TF: 800-729-3332 ■ *Web:* www.customchrome.com

DAA Draexlmaier Automotive of America LLC
1751 E Main St.................................... Duncan SC 29334 864-433-8910

Delcoline Inc 4919 Lawrence St .... Hyattsville MD 20781 301-864-4455
Web: www.delcoline.com

Dero Bike Racks Inc
504 Malcolm Ave SE Ste 100 .... Minneapolis MN 55414 612-359-0689
TF: 888-337-6729 ■ *Web:* www.dero.com

Distributors Warehouse Inc 1900 Tenth St .... Paducah KY 42001 270-442-8201 442-4914
Web: btbauto.com

Dorian Drake International Inc
2 Westchester Park Dr .... White Plains NY 10604 914-697-9800 697-9683
Web: www.doriandrake.com

Dreyco Inc 263 Veterans Blvd .... Carlstadt NJ 07072 201-896-9000
Web: www.dreycoinc.com

Drive Products Income Fund
1665 Shawson Dr.............................. Mississauga ON L4W1T7 905-564-5800
Web: www.driveproducts.com

Drive Train Industries Inc 5555 Joliet St .... Denver CO 80239 303-292-5176 297-0473
TF: 800-525-6177 ■ *Web:* www.drivetrainindustries.com

Eagle Parts & Products Inc
1411 Marvin Griffin Rd............................ Augusta GA 30906 706-790-6687 790-6066
TF: 888-972-9911 ■ *Web:* www.eagleproducts.us

Enginetech Inc 1205 W Crosby Rd................. Carrollton TX 75006 972-245-0110 245-2093
TF: 800-869-8711 ■ *Web:* www.enginetech.com

Fast Undercar Inc 4277 Transport St................. Ventura CA 93003 805-676-3410
Web: www.fastundercar.com

Fisher Auto Parts
512 Greenville Ave PO Box 2248 .... Staunton VA 24401 540-885-8901
Web: www.fisherautoparts.com

Fleet Brake Parts & Service Ltd
7707 54 St SE.................................... Calgary AB T2C4R7 403-279-8661
Web: www.fleetbrake.com

Fleet Products LLC 6510 Golden Groves Ln .... Tampa FL 33610 813-621-1734
Web: www.fleetproductsfl.com

Fleetilla LLC 1745 Fritz Dr........................... Trenton MI 48183 734-676-5100
Web: www.fleetilla.com

Flowers Auto Parts Co 935 Hwy 70 SE................ Hickory NC 28602 828-322-5414 322-9070
TF Cust Svc: 800-538-6272 ■ *Web:* www.napaonline.com

Frank Edwards Co 3626 Pkwy Blvd .... West Valley City UT 84120 801-736-8000 736-8051
Web: feco.net

General Truck Parts & Equipment Co
3835 W 42nd St .... Chicago IL 60632 773-247-6900 247-2632
TF: 800-621-3914 ■ *Web:* www.generaltruckparts.com

Genuine Parts Co 2999 Cir 75 Pkwy.................... Atlanta GA 30339 770-953-1700
NYSE: GPC ■ *Web:* www.genpt.com

GK Industries Ltd 50 Precidio Ct .... Brampton ON L6S6E3 905-799-1972 799-0852
TF: 800-463-8889 ■ *Web:* www.gkindustries.com

Company	City	State	Zip	Phone	Fax
Global Parts Distributors LLC 3279 Avondale Mill Rd *Web:* www.globalpartsdist.com	Macon	GA	31216	478-781-9854	
Greddy Performance Products Inc Mnmt 9 Vanderbilt *Web:* www.greddy.com	Irvine	CA	92618	949-588-8300	588-6318
Grinstead Group Inc 13289 O'Bannon Stn Way	Louisville	KY	40223	502-966-9020	
Grupo Antolin Kentucky Inc 208 Commerce Ct. *Web:* www.grupoantolin.com	Hopkinsville	KY	42240	270-885-2703	
Hahn Automotive Warehouse Inc 415 W Main St *Web:* www.hahnauto.com	Rochester	NY	14608	585-235-1595	
Hanson Distributing Company Inc 10802 Rush St	South El Monte	CA	91733	626-448-4683	
Harada Industry of America Inc 22925 Venture Dr *Web:* www.harada.com	Novi	MI	48375	248-374-9000	374-9100
Harmonic Drive LLC 247 Lynnfield St. *TF:* 800-921-3332 ■ *Web:* www.harmonicdrive.net	Peabody	MA	01960	978-532-1800	
Hedahls Inc 100 East Broadway *TF:* 800-433-2457 ■ *Web:* www.hedahls.com	Bismarck	ND	58502	701-223-8393	221-4251
Henderson Wheel & Warehouse Supply 1825 South 300 West *TF:* 800-748-5111 ■ *Web:* www.hendersonwheel.com	Salt Lake City	UT	84115	801-486-2073	486-0353
Hilite International Inc 250 Kay Industrial Dr *Web:* www.hilite.com	Orion	MI	48359	248-475-4580	475-4581
IEA Inc 9625 55th St *Web:* www.iearad.com	Kenosha	WI	53144	262-942-1414	
IGD Industries Inc 4150 C St SW *Web:* www.igdindustries.com	Cedar Rapids	IA	52404	319-396-2222	
Indiana Heat Transfer Corp 500 W Harrison St *Web:* www.ihtc.net	Plymouth	IN	46563	574-936-3171	
Instrument Sales & Service Inc 16427 NE Airport Way **Fax Area Code:* 800 ■ *TF:* 800-333-7976 ■ *Web:* www.instrumentsales.com	Portland	OR	97230	503-239-0754	333-4678*
InterAmerican Motor Corp (IMC) 8901 Canoga Ave **Fax:* Sales ■ *TF:* 800-874-8925 ■ *Web:* www.imcparts.net	Canoga Park	CA	91304	818-678-1200	775-5152*
Interstate Batteries 12770 Merit Dr Ste 400 *TF:* 800-541-8419 ■ *Web:* www.interstatebatteries.com	Dallas	TX	75251	972-991-1444	
Intraco Corp 530 Stephenson Hwy *Web:* www.intracousa.com	Troy	MI	48083	248-585-6900	585-6920
Jead Auto Supply Corp 1810 E Tremont Ave *Web:* www.jeadauto.com	Bronx	NY	10460	718-792-7113	
JEGS Performance Auto Parts 101 Jeg'S Pl *TF:* 800-345-4545 ■ *Web:* www.jegs.com	Delaware	OH	43015	614-294-5050	
Jobbers Automotive Warehouse Inc 801 E Zimmerly St *Web:* www.jawinc.com	Wichita	KS	67211	316-267-4393	
Johnson Industries 5944 Peachtree Corners E. *TF Orders:* 800-922-8111 ■ *Web:* www.teamji.com	Norcross	GA	30071	770-441-1128	248-2896
Kansas City Peterbilt Inc 8915 Woodend Rd *TF:* 800-489-1122 ■ *Web:* www.kcpete.com	Kansas City	KS	66111	913-441-2888	422-5029
Kenmar Corp 17515 W 9 Mile Rd Ste 1200 *Web:* www.ekenmar.com	Southfield	MI	48075	248-424-8200	
Keystone Automotive Operations Inc 44 Tunkhannock Ave *TF:* 800-521-9999 ■ *Web:* www.keystoneautomotive.com	Exeter	PA	18643	570-655-4514	603-2003
Knopf Automotive 93 Shrewsbury Ave *Web:* www.mmknopf.com	Red Bank	NJ	07701	732-212-0444	212-0443
KYB America LLC 140 N Mitchell Ct *Web:* www.kyb.com	Addison	IL	60101	630-620-5555	
L & M Radiator Inc 1414 E 37th St. *TF:* 800-346-3500 ■ *Web:* www.mesabi.com	Hibbing	MN	55746	218-263-8993	
Lakeshirts Inc 750 Randolph Rd *TF:* 800-627-2780 ■ *Web:* www.lakeshirts.com	Detroit Lakes	MN	56501	218-847-2171	
LKQ Corp 500 W Madison St Ste 2800 *NASDAQ: LKQX* ■ *TF:* 877-557-2677 ■ *Web:* www.lkqcorp.com	Chicago	IL	60661	312-621-1950	621-1969
London Machinery Inc 15790 Robin's Hill Rd *TF:* 800-265-1098 ■ *Web:* www.lmi.ca	London	ON	N5V0A4	519-963-2500	
Lumbee Enterprises Inc 356 W Phillips Rd *Web:* www.lumbeena.com	Greer	SC	29650	864-989-0149	
Lynco Flange & Fitting Inc 5114 Steadmont Dr **Fax Area Code:* 903 ■ *Web:* www.lyncoflange.com	Houston	TX	77040	713-690-0040	690-5095*
Maxzone Vehicle Lighting Corp 15889 Slover Ave Ste A *Web:* www.maxzone.com	Fontana	CA	92337	909-822-3288	822-3399
McGard LLC 3875 California Rd *TF:* 800-444-5847 ■ *Web:* www.mcgard.com	Orchard Park	NY	14127	716-662-8980	662-8985
Mico Industries Inc 1425 Burlingame Ave SW *Web:* www.micoindustries.com	Grand Rapids	MI	49509	616-245-6426	
Mid America Motorworks 17082 N Us Hwy 45 PO Box 1368 *TF:* 866-350-4543 ■ *Web:* www.mamotorworks.com	Effingham	IL	62401	217-540-4200	540-4800
Midwest Action Cycle Inc 251 Host Dr *Web:* www.midwestactioncycle.com	Lake Geneva	WI	53147	262-249-0600	249-0608
Midwest Truck & Auto Parts Inc 1001 W Exchange *TF:* 800-934-2727 ■ *Web:* www.midwesttruck.com	Chicago	IL	60609	773-247-3400	579-3788
Mighty Distributing System of America Inc 650 Engineering Dr. *TF:* 800-829-3900 ■ *Web:* www.mightyautoparts.com	Norcross	GA	30092	770-448-3900	446-8627
Mile Marker International Inc 2121 BLOUNT Rd *TF:* 800-886-8647 ■ *Web:* milemarker.com	Pompano Beach	FL	33069	800-886-8647	
Milliron Industries Inc 2384 St Rt 39 *Web:* millironautoparts.com	Mansfield	OH	44903	419-747-6565	
Minnpar LLC 5273 Program Ave *Web:* www.minnpar.com	Mounds View	MN	55112	612-379-0606	
Mutual Wheel Co Inc 2345 Fourth Ave *TF:* 800-798-6926 ■ *Web:* www.mutualwheel.com	Moline	IL	61265	309-757-1200	757-1241
N.b.c. Truck Equipment Inc 28130 Groesbeck Hwy *TF:* 800-778-8207 ■ *Web:* www.nbctruckequip.com	Roseville	MI	48066	586-774-4900	772-1280
National Automotive Parts Assn (NAPA) 2999 Circle 75 Pkwy *TF:* 800-538-6272 ■ *Web:* genpt.com	Atlanta	GA	30339	770-953-1700	
Newstream Enterprises LLC 1925 E Chestnut Expy *Web:* www.newstreaming.com	Springfield	MO	65802	417-831-3112	
Northeast Battery & Alternator Inc 240 Washington St *TF:* 800-441-8824 ■ *Web:* www.northeastbattery.com	Auburn	MA	01501	508-832-2700	832-2706
Northern Factory Sales Inc PO Box 660 *TF:* 800-328-8900 ■ *Web:* www.northernfactory.com	Willmar	MN	56201	320-235-2288	235-2297
NTP Distribution Inc 27150 SW Kinsman Rd. *TF:* 800-242-6987 ■ *Web:* www.ntpdistribution.com	Wilsonville	OR	97070	503-570-0171	
O.E.M. Systems LLC PO Box 473 *TF:* 800-810-7252 ■ *Web:* www.oemsystems.net	Okarche	OK	73762	405-263-7488	
PACCAR Parts 750 Houser Way N. *Web:* www.paccar.com	Renton	WA	98057	425-254-4400	
Parts Authority Inc 495 Merrick Rd *Web:* www.partsauthority.com	Rockville Centre	NY	11570	516-678-3900	
Parts Central Inc 3243 Whitfield St *TF:* 800-226-9396 ■ *Web:* www.partscentral.net	Macon	GA	31204	478-745-0878	746-1177
PBE Warehouse Inc 12171 Pangborn Ave *Web:* www.pbewarehouse.com	Downey	CA	90241	562-803-4691	
Pioneer Inc 5184 Pioneer Rd *Web:* www.pioneerautoind.com	Meridian	MS	39301	601-482-6068	
Plaza Fleet Parts Inc 1520 S Broadway *TF:* 800-325-7618 ■ *Web:* plazafleetparts.com	Saint Louis	MO	63104	314-231-5047	231-5109
Pneumercator Inc 120 Finn Ct. *Web:* www.pneumercator.com	Farmingdale	NY	11735	631-293-8450	
Racer Parts Wholesale 411 Dorman *Web:* www.racerpartswholesale.com	Indianapolis	IN	46202	317-639-0725	
Rebuilders Automotive Supply Company Inc 1650 Flat River Rd *Web:* www.coresupply.com	Coventry	RI	02816	401-822-3030	
Regional International Corp 1007 Lehigh Stn Rd *TF:* 800-836-0409 ■ *Web:* www.regionalinternational.com	Henrietta	NY	14467	585-359-2011	359-2418
Rep Works Marketing LLC 7411 W Beverly Blvd *Web:* www.repworksmktg.com	Los Angeles	CA	90036	323-933-8211	
Service Champ Inc 180 New Britain Blvd *Web:* www.servicechamp.com	Chalfont	PA	18914	215-822-8500	
Six Robblees' Inc 11010 Tukwila International Blvd *TF:* 800-275-7499 ■ *Web:* www.sixrobblees.com	Tukwila	WA	98168	206-767-7970	763-7416
Six States Distributors Inc 247 West 1700 South *TF Cust Svc:* 800-453-5703 ■ *Web:* www.sixstates.com	Salt Lake City	UT	84115	801-488-4666	488-4676
Space Electronics LLC 81 Fuller Way *Web:* space-electronics.com	Berlin	CT	06037	860-829-0001	
Stewart Title Insurance Co 300 E 42nd St 10th Fl. *TF:* 800-913-4170 ■ *Web:* www.stewart.com/en.html	New York	NY	10017	713-625-8100	
TCG International Inc 8658 Commerce Ct. *Web:* www.tcgi.com	Burnaby	BC	V5A4N6	604-438-1000	
Trade Union International Inc 4651 State St *Web:* tradeunion.com	Montclair	CA	91763	909-628-7500	
Tri-City Glass & Door Inc 100 W Northland Ave *Web:* www.tricityglass-door.com	Appleton	WI	54911	920-731-8176	
Tucker Rocky Distributing Inc 4900 Alliance Gateway Fwy *Web:* www.tuckerrocky.com	Fort Worth	TX	76177	817-258-9000	
Twinco Romax 4635 Willow Dr *Web:* www.twincoromax.com	Medina	MN	55340	763-478-2360	478-3411
U S Auto Parts Network Inc 16941 Keegan Ave *NASDAQ: PRTS* ■ *Web:* www.usautoparts.net	Carson	CA	90746	310-735-0085	
UAP Inc 7025 Rue Ontario E *Web:* www.napacanada.com	Montreal	QC	H1N2B3	514-256-5031	256-8469
Uriman Inc 650 N Puente St *Web:* www.uriman.com	Brea	CA	92821	714-257-2080	
Vander Haag's Inc 3809 Fourth Ave W. *TF:* 888-940-5030 ■ *Web:* www.vanderhaags.com	Spencer	IA	51301	712-262-7000	262-7421
W. W. Tire Service Inc 204 Main St PO Box 22 *Web:* www.wwtireservice.com	Bryant	SD	57221	605-628-2501	628-2018
WAIglobal 411 Eagleview Blvd Ste 100 **Fax Area Code:* 800 ■ *TF:* 800-877-3340 ■ *Web:* waiglobal.com	Exton	PA	19341	484-875-6600	948-6121*
Warn Industries Inc 12900 SE Capps Rd *Web:* www.warn.com	Clackamas	OR	97015	503-722-1200	
Weddle Industries 7200 Hollister Ave Ste C *Web:* www.weddleindustries.com	Goleta	CA	93117	805-562-8600	
Western Truck Parts & Equip Co 3707 Airport Way S *TF:* 800-255-7383 ■ *Web:* westernpeterbilt.com/western-peterbilt-seattle-wa	Seattle	WA	98134	206-624-7383	
Westin Automotive Products Inc 5200 N Irwindale Ave Ste 220 *TF:* 800-345-8476 ■ *Web:* www.westinautomotive.com	Irwindale	CA	91706	626-960-6762	
WM Automotive Inc 208 Penland St *Web:* www.wmautomotive.com	Fort Worth	TX	76111	817-834-5559	
WORLDPAC Inc 37137 Hickory St *TF:* 800-888-9982 ■ *Web:* www.worldpac.com	Newark	CA	94560	510-742-8900	
Wurth USA Inc 93 Grant St *TF:* 800-987-8487 ■ *Web:* www.wurthusa.com	Ramsey	NJ	07446	201-825-2710	825-3706

62 AUTOMOTIVE SERVICES

See Also Gas Stations p. 2349

Company	City	State	Zip	Phone	Fax
7 Stars Test Only 7905 Balboa Ave Ste D *Web:* 7starstestonly.com	San Diego	CA	92111	858-278-8737	
Adaptive Driving Access Inc 3430 E Sam Houston Pkwy S *Web:* www.adaptivedriving.com	Pasadena	TX	77505	281-487-1969	
Boyd Group Inc, The 3570 Portage Ave *TF:* 800-385-5451 ■ *Web:* www.boydgroup.com	Winnipeg	MB	R3K0Z8	204-895-1244	
Canopies Party Rental 7234 N 60th St *Web:* canopiesevents.com	Milwaukee	WI	53223	414-760-0770	
Charles Agapiou Ltd 9017 Santa Monica Blvd *Web:* www.rollsandbentley.com	West Hollywood	CA	90069	310-274-6201	
Jeeps Unlimited 4245 County Rd 6 *Web:* jeepsunlimited.net	Erie	CO	80516	303-828-9020	
Kele Inc PO Box 34817 *Web:* www.kele.com	Memphis	TN	38184	901-382-4300	
Magoo's Automotive Consultants Inc 4580 Market St *Web:* magoos.net	Ventura	CA	93003	805-676-3440	
Speedemissions Inc 220 1015 Tyrone Rd Ste 710 *Web:* www.speedemissions.com	Tyrone	GA	30290	770-306-7667	

62-1 Appearance Care - Automotive

Company	City	State	Zip	Phone	Fax
Autobell Car Wash Inc 1521 E Third St *TF:* 800-582-8096 ■ *Web:* www.autobell.com	Charlotte	NC	28204	704-527-9274	333-0526
Blue Beacon International Inc 500 Graves Blvd *Web:* www.bluebeacon.com	Salina	KS	67401	785-825-2221	825-0801
Color-Glo International 7111 Ohms Ln *TF:* 800-333-8523 ■ *Web:* colorglo.com	Minneapolis	MN	55439	952-835-1338	
Creative Colors International Inc 19015 S Jodi Rd Ste E *TF:* 800-933-2656 ■ *Web:* www.wecanfixthat.com	Mokena	IL	60448	708-478-1437	478-1636
Dr Vinyl & Assoc Ltd 1350 SE Hamblen Rd *TF General:* 800-531-6600 ■ *Web:* www.drvinyl.com	Lees Summit	MO	64081	816-525-6060	
Flagstop Corp 11031 Ironbridge Rd *Web:* www.flagstopcarwash.com	Chester	VA	23831	804-768-0090	
Fleetwash Inc PO Box 1577 **Fax Area Code:* 973 ■ *TF:* 800-847-3735 ■ *Web:* www.fleetwash.com	West Caldwell	NJ	07007	800-847-3735	882-0585*
Hoffman Car Wash 1757 Central Ave *Web:* www.hoffmancarwash.com	Albany	NY	12205	518-869-3218	869-3574
Kaady Car Washes 7400 SW Barbur Blvd *Web:* www.kaady.com	Portland	OR	97219	503-246-7735	
Mister Car Wash 3101 E Speedway Blvd *TF Cust Svc:* 866-254-3229 ■ *Web:* www.mistercarwash.com	Tucson	AZ	85718	520-615-4000	
Mr.Clean Car Wash 2567 EW Conn SW *Web:* www.mrcleancarwash.com	Austell	GA	30106	770-222-5811	
Oasis Carwash LLC 3425 E Flamingo Rd *Web:* oasishandcarwash.com	Las Vegas	NV	89121	702-433-3680	
Precision Auto Care Inc 748 Miller Dr SE *OTC:* PACI ■ **Fax Area Code:* 703 ■ *TF:* 866-944-8863 ■ *Web:* www.precisiontune.com	Leesburg	VA	20175	866-944-8863	771-7108*
ScrubaDub Auto Wash Centers Inc 172 Worcester Rd *Web:* www.scrubadub.com	Natick	MA	01760	508-650-1155	655-9261
Simoniz Car Wash 435 Eastern Ave *Web:* www.washdepot.com	Malden	MA	02148	781-321-1900	
Vizza Wash Services LLC 2208 NW Loop 410 *TF Cust Svc:* 866-493-8822 ■ *Web:* washtub.com	San Antonio	TX	78230	210-493-8822	
Wash Depot Holdings Inc 14 Summer St *Web:* www.washdepot.com	Malden	MA	02148	781-324-2000	321-5483
Ziebart International Corp 1290 E Maple Rd **Fax:* Orders ■ *TF:* 800-877-1312 ■ *Web:* www.ziebart.com	Troy	MI	48083	248-588-4100	588-0431*

62-2 Glass Replacement - Automotive

Company	City	State	Zip	Phone	Fax
All Star Glass Co Inc 1845 Morena Blvd *TF:* 800-225-4184 ■ *Web:* www.allstarglass.net	San Diego	CA	92110	619-275-3343	275-6367
City Auto Glass Inc 116 S Concord Exchange **Fax Area Code:* 612 ■ *TF:* 888-552-4272 ■ *Web:* www.cityautoglass.com	South Saint Paul	MN	55075	651-552-1000	552-1080*
Martin Glass Co 25 Ctr Plz *TF:* 800-325-1946 ■ *Web:* www.martinglass.net	Belleville	IL	62220	618-277-1946	
Safelite Group Inc 2400 Farmers Dr *TF:* 877-664-8931 ■ *Web:* www.safelite.com	Columbus	OH	43235	877-664-8931	
Speedy Auto & Glass Inc 2422 Arctic Blvd	Anchorage	AK	99503	907-272-1435	
SuperGlass Windshield Repair Inc 6101 Chancellor Dr Ste 200 *TF:* 866-557-7497 ■ *Web:* www.superglass.com	Orlando	FL	32809	407-240-1920	240-3266

62-3 Mufflers & Exhaust Systems Repair - Automotive

Company	City	State	Zip	Phone	Fax
Car-X Assoc Corp 1375 E Woodfield Rd Ste 500 *Web:* www.carx.com	Schaumburg	IL	60173	847-273-8920	619-3310
Midas International Corp 1300 Arlington Heights Rd *TF:* 800-621-8545 ■ *Web:* www.midas.com	Itasca	IL	60143	630-438-3000	438-3700
Monro Muffler Brake Inc 200 Holleder Pkwy *NASDAQ:* MNRO ■ *TF:* 800-876-6676 ■ *Web:* www.monro.com	Rochester	NY	14615	585-647-6400	647-0945

62-4 Paint & Body Work - Automotive

Company	City	State	Zip	Phone	Fax
CARSTAR Quality Collision Service 8400 W 110th St Ste 200 *TF Cust Svc:* 800-227-7827 ■ *Web:* www.carstar.com	Overland Park	KS	66210	913-451-1294	
CK Technologies LLC 1701 Magda Dr *Web:* www.cktech.biz	Montpelier	OH	43543	419-485-1110	485-1405
Colors on Parade 125 Daytona St PO Box 50940 *TF Cust Svc:* 866-756-4207 ■ *Web:* www.colorsonparade.com	Conway	SC	29526	843-347-8818	
Dent Clinic 711 48th Ave SE *TF:* 888-722-3368 ■ *Web:* www.dentclinic.com	Calgary	AB	T2G2A7	403-255-3111	
Dent Wizard International 4710 Earth City Expway *TF:* 800-267-9369 ■ *Web:* www.dentwizard.com	Bridgeton	MO	63044	314-592-1800	592-1951
Gerber Auto Collision & Glass Centers Inc 8250 Skokie Blvd *TF:* 877-743-7237 ■ *Web:* www.gerbercollision.com	Skokie	IL	60077	847-679-0510	679-0549
Gerber Collision & Glass 44700 Enterprise Dr *TF General:* 877-743-7237 ■ *Web:* www.gerbercollision.com	Clinton Township	MI	48038	586-954-3850	954-0912
Holmes Body Shop Inc 1095 E Colorado Blvd	Pasadena	CA	91106	626-795-6447	795-9653
Maaco LLC 440 S Church St Ste 700 **Fax Area Code:* 866 ■ *TF:* 800-523-1180 ■ *Web:* www.maaco.com	Charlotte	NC	28202	704-377-8855	702-4602*
Mike Rose's Auto Body Inc 2260 Via de Marcardos *TF:* 855-340-1739 ■ *Web:* mikesautobody.com	Concord	CA	94520	925-689-1739	689-0991
Service King Collision Repair Centers 808 S Central Expy *TF:* 866-730-5464 ■ *Web:* www.serviceking.com	Richardson	TX	75080	972-960-7595	980-4266

62-5 Repair Service (General) - Automotive

Company	City	State	Zip	Phone	Fax
All Tune & Lube Brakes & More Inc 8334 Veteran's Hwy *TF:* 877-978-1758 ■ *Web:* www.alltuneandlube.com	Millersville	MD	21108	410-987-1011	
All Tune & Lube International Inc *ATL International Inc* 8334 Veterans Hwy *TF Cust Svc:* 877-978-1758 ■ *Web:* www.alltuneandlube.com	Millersville	MD	21108	410-987-1011	
Basin Tire & Auto Inc 2700 E Main St **Fax Area Code:* 970 ■ *TF:* 800-832-9832 ■ *Web:* directoryplus.com	Farmington	NM	87402	505-326-2231	385-2460*
Belle Tire Inc 1000 Enterprise Dr *TF:* 888-462-3553 ■ *Web:* www.belletire.com	Allen Park	MI	48101	313-271-9400	271-6793
Bergey's Inc 462 Harleysville Pike *TF:* 800-237-4397 ■ *Web:* www.bergeys.com	Souderton	PA	18964	215-723-6071	721-3479
Bridgestone Americas Holding Inc 535 Marriott Dr *TF Cust Svc:* 877-201-2373 ■ *Web:* www.bridgestoneamericas.com/en/index	Nashville	TN	37214	615-937-1000	937-3621
Clark Tire & Auto Supply Co Inc 220 S Ctr St *Web:* www.clarktire.com	Hickory	NC	28602	828-322-2303	324-2906
Cross-Midwest Tire Co 401 S 42nd St *Web:* www.crossmidwest.com	Kansas City	KS	66106	913-321-3003	
Evans Tire & Service Centers Inc 510 N Broadway *TF:* 877-338-2678 ■ *Web:* www.evanstire.com	Escondido	CA	92025	877-338-2678	
Express Oil Change 1880 S Pk Dr *TF:* 888-945-1771 ■ *Web:* www.expressoil.com	Hoover	AL	35244	205-945-1771	413-8732
Express Tire 1148 Industrial Ave *Web:* www.expresstire.com	Escondido	CA	92029	760-741-4044	741-5942
Fyda Freightliner Youngstown Inc 5260 76th Dr *TF:* 800-837-3932 ■ *Web:* www.fydafreightliner.com	Youngstown	OH	44515	330-797-0224	797-0230
Grease Monkey International 7450 E Progress Pl *TF:* 800-822-7706 ■ *Web:* www.greasemonkeyintl.com	Greenwood Village	CO	80111	303-308-1660	308-5908
Hunter Engineering Co 11250 Hunter Dr *TF:* 800-448-6848 ■ *Web:* www.hunter.com	Bridgeton	MO	63044	314-731-3020	731-1776
Jack Williams Tire Co Inc PO Box 3655 *TF:* 800-833-5051 ■ *Web:* www.jackwilliams.com	Scranton	PA	18505	800-833-5051	
Jensen Tire & Auto 10609 I St *Web:* www.jensentireandauto.com	Omaha	NE	68127	402-339-2917	
Jiffy Lube PO Box 4427 *TF:* 800-344-6933 ■ *Web:* www.jiffylube.com	Houston	TX	77210	800-344-6933	
Jubitz Corp 33 NE Middlefield Rd *TF:* 800-523-0600 ■ *Web:* www.jubitz.com	Portland	OR	97211	503-283-1111	240-5834
Kansas City Peterbilt Inc 8915 Woodend Rd *TF:* 800-489-1122 ■ *Web:* www.kcpete.com	Kansas City	KS	66111	913-441-2888	422-5029
Kolstad Company Inc 8501 Naples St NE *Web:* www.kolstadco.com	Blaine	MN	55449	763-792-1033	
Lamb's Tire & Automotive 2100 Kramer Ln *Web:* www.lambstire.com	Austin	TX	78758	512-257-2350	
Lucor Inc 790 Pershing Rd	Raleigh	NC	27608	919-828-9511	828-4847
Merlin Corp 3815 E Main St *TF:* 800-652-9910 ■ *Web:* www.merlins.com	Saint Charles	IL	60174	630-513-8200	513-1388
Mr Tire Auto Service Centers Inc 200 Holleder Pkwy *TF:* 800-876-6676 ■ *Web:* www.mrtire.com	Rochester	NY	14615	800-876-6676	
NDI Group Inc 310 Simmons Rd Ste B *Web:* ndigroup.com	Knoxville	TN	37922	865-777-1250	
Oil Butler International Corp 1599 US 22	Union	NJ	07083	908-687-3453	687-7617
Parrish Tire Company Inc 5130 Indiana Ave *TF:* 800-849-8473 ■ *Web:* www.parrishtire.com	Winston-Salem	NC	27106	336-767-0202	744-2716
Payne Trucking Co 10411 Hall Industrial Dr *Web:* www.paynetrucking.com	Fredericksburg	VA	22408	540-898-1346	
Perry Bros Tire Service Inc 610 Wicker St *Web:* www.perrybros.com	Sanford	NC	27330	919-775-7225	

Phone *Fax*

Plaza Tire Service
2075 Corporate Cr PO Box 2048 .... Cape Girardeau MO 63702 877-787-1691 334-0322*
**Fax Area Code:* 573 ■ *TF:* 877-787-1691 ■ *Web:* plazatireservice.com

Precision Auto Care Inc 748 Miller Dr SE.... Leesburg VA 20175 866-944-8863 771-7108*
OTC: PACI ■ **Fax Area Code:* 703 ■ *TF:* 866-944-8863 ■ *Web:* www.precisiontune.com

Raben Tire Company Inc
2100 N New York Ave.... Evansville IN 47711 812-465-5565
Web: www.rabentire.com

Schmidt's Auto Inc 1621 Beld St.... Madison WI 53715 608-257-0505
Web: www.schmidtsauto.com

Sullivan Tire Co Inc PO Box 370.... Rockland MA 02370 781-871-2299 871-7212
TF: 877-855-4826 ■ *Web:* www.sullivantire.com

Sun Devil Auto Inc 1824 E Elliot Rd.... Tempe AZ 85284 480-831-2831 491-4204
Web: www.sunautoservice.com

Techni-Car Inc 450 Commerce Blvd.... Oldsmar FL 34677 813-855-0022 855-2101
TF: 800-886-0022 ■ *Web:* www.techni-car.com

Tire-Rama Inc 1429 Grand Ave.... Billings MT 59102 406-245-4006
TF: 800-828-1642 ■ *Web:* www.tirerama.com

Tires Plus Total Car Care
2021 Sunnydale Blvd.... Clearwater FL 33765 727-441-3727 443-2401
TF: 800-440-4167 ■ *Web:* www.tiresplus.com

Tom Stinnett Rv's 520 Marriott Dr.... Clarksville IN 47129 812-282-7718
TF: 800-583-5685 ■ *Web:* www.stinnettrv.com

Tri-State Trailer Sales Inc
3111 Grand Ave.... Pittsburgh PA 15225 412-747-7777 777-4010
Web: www.tristatetrailer.com

Tuffy Assoc Corp 7150 Granite Cir.... Toledo OH 43617 419-865-6900 865-7343
TF: 800-228-8339 ■ *Web:* www.tuffy.com

VIP Tires & Service 12 Lexington St.... Lewiston ME 04240 207-784-5423 784-9178
Web: www.vipauto.com

Warren Tire Service Ctr Inc
4 Highland Ave.... Queensbury NY 12804 518-792-0316
Web: www.warrentiresvc.com

Wingfoot Commercial Tire Systems LLC
1000 S 21st St.... Fort Smith AR 72901 479-788-6400 788-6486
TF: 800-643-7330 ■ *Web:* goodyearctsc.com

62-6 Transmission Repair - Automotive

Phone *Fax*

Certified Transmission Rebuilders Inc
1801 S 54th St.... Omaha NE 68106 402-558-2117
Web: www.certifiedtransmission.com

Lee Myles Auto Group 914 Fern Ave.... Reading PA 19607 800-533-6953
TF: 800-533-6953 ■ *Web:* www.leemyles.com

Mr Transmission 9675 Yonge St 2nd Fl.... Richmond Hill ON L4C1V7 905-884-1511 884-4727
TF: 800-373-8432 ■ *Web:* www.mistertransmission.com

62-7 Van Conversions

Phone *Fax*

Clock Mobility 6700 Clay Ave.... Grand Rapids MI 49548 616-698-9400 698-9495
TF: 800-732-5625 ■ *Web:* www.clockmobility.com

Foley Inc 855 Centennial Ave.... Piscataway NJ 08854 732-885-5555 885-6612
TF: 888-417-6464 ■ *Web:* www.foleyinc.com

Land Rover Carolinas 1450 Laurens Rd.... Greenville SC 29607 864-232-7493
Web: www.landrovercarolinas.com

Marathon Coach 91333 Coburg Industrial Way.... Coburg OR 97408 541-343-9991 343-2401
TF: 800-234-9991 ■ *Web:* www.marathoncoach.com

Monaco Coach Corp 1031 US 224 E.... Decatur IN 46733 877-466-6226 724-5238*
**Fax Area Code:* 260 ■ **Fax:* Hum Res ■ *TF:* 877-466-6226 ■ *Web:* monacocoach.com

Rollx Vans 6591 Hwy 13 W.... Savage MN 55378 952-890-7851 890-1903
TF: 800-956-6668 ■ *Web:* www.rollxvans.com

Sherrod Vans Inc 3151 Industrial Blvd.... Waycross GA 31503 800-824-6333
TF: 800-824-6333 ■ *Web:* www.sherrodvans.com

Sidewinder Conversions 44658 Yale Rd W.... Chilliwack BC V2R0G5 604-792-2082 792-8920
TF: 888-266-2299 ■ *Web:* www.sidewinder-conversions.com

Unique Conversions Inc 1502 Hwy 157 N Ste D.... Mansfield TX 76063 817-477-5251
Web: laredoconversions.com

Vantage Mobility International (VMI)
5202 S 28th Pl.... Phoenix AZ 85040 602-243-2700 304-3290
TF: 800-348-8267 ■ *Web:* www.vantagemobility.com

Waldoch Crafts Inc 13821 Lake Dr NE.... Forest Lake MN 55025 651-464-3215 464-1117
TF: 800-328-9259 ■ *Web:* www.waldoch.com

63 AVIATION - FIXED-BASE OPERATIONS

See Also Air Cargo Carriers p. 1719; Air Charter Services p. 1719; Aircraft Rental p. 1728; Aircraft Service & Repair p. 1729

Phone *Fax*

A & M Aviation Inc
130 S Clow International Pkwy Ste B.... Bolingbrook IL 60490 630-759-1555
Web: www.aandmaviation.com

A&D Environmental Services Inc
2718 Uwharrie Rd.... Archdale NC 27261 336-434-7750
Web: www.adenviro.com

Abilene Aero 2850 Airport Blvd.... Abilene TX 79602 325-677-2601 671-8018
Web: www.abileneaero.com

Aero Industries Inc
5745 Huntsman Rd
Richmond International Airport.... Richmond VA 23250 804-226-7200 236-1670
TF: 800-845-1308 ■ *Web:* www.aeroind.com

Aerodynamics Inc
25700 Science Park Dr Ste 210.... Beachwood OH 30152 404-410-7612

Aerosmith Aviation 321 Corporate Rd.... Longview TX 75603 903-643-0898
Web: www.aerosmithaviation.com

Phone *Fax*

Aircraft Specialists Inc
6005 Propeller Ln.... Sellersburg IN 47172 812-246-4696 246-4365
Web: www.800projets.com

Airline Services International Inc
5160 Explorer Dr Ste 4.... Mississauga ON L4W4T7 905-629-4522
Web: www.airlineservices.com

American Aviation 2495 Broad St.... Brooksville FL 34604 352-796-5173 799-4681
Web: www.americanaviation.com

Atlantic Aviation 17725 John F Kennedy Blvd.... Houston TX 77032 281-443-3434
Web: www.atlanticaviation.com

Atlantic Aviation Services
19711 Campus Dr Ste 100 John Wayne Airport.... Santa Ana CA 92707 949-851-5061
Web: www.atlanticaviation.com

Aurora Aviation 22785 Airport Rd NE.... Aurora OR 97002 503-678-1217 678-1219
Web: www.auroraaviation.com

Banyan Air Service 5360 NW 20th Terr.... Fort Lauderdale FL 33309 954-491-3170 771-0281
TF: 800-200-2031 ■ *Web:* www.banyanair.com

Basler Flight Service
Wittman Regional Airport PO Box 2464.... Oshkosh WI 54903 920-236-7827 236-7833
Web: www.baslerflightservice.com

Bayview Environmental Services Inc
6925 San Leandro St.... Oakland CA 94621 510-562-6181
Web: www.bayviewenvironmental.com

Belshire Environmental Services Inc
25971 Towne Centre Dr.... Foothill Ranch CA 92610 949-460-5200
TF: 800-995-8220 ■ *Web:* www.belshire.com

BMG Aviation Inc 984 S Kirby Rd.... Bloomington IN 47403 812-825-7979 825-7978
TF: 888-457-3787 ■ *Web:* www.bmgaviation.com

Central Flying Service Inc 1501 Bond St.... Little Rock AR 72202 501-375-3245 375-7355
TF: 800-888-5387 ■ *Web:* www.flycfs.com

Channel Islands Aviation
305 Durley Ave Camarillo Airport.... Camarillo CA 93010 805-987-1301 987-8301
Web: www.flycia.com

Chicago Executive Airport 1020 Plant Rd.... Wheeling IL 60090 847-537-2580
Web: chiexec.com

Co-Mar Aviation 1020 Woodhurst St.... Bowling Green KY 42103 270-781-9797 793-0525
Web: www.comaraviation.com

Colonial Air 1605 Airport Rd.... New Bedford MA 02746 508-997-0620 990-2582
Web: www.colonial-air.com

Columbia Air Services
175 Tower Ave Groton-New London Airport.... Groton CT 06340 860-449-1400 405-7269
TF: 800-787-5001 ■ *Web:* columbiaaironline.com

Cook Aviation Inc 970 S Kirby Rd.... Bloomington IN 47403 812-825-2392 825-3701
TF: 800-880-3499 ■ *Web:* www.cookaviation.com

Corporate Air LLC
15 Allegheny County Airport.... West Mifflin PA 15122 412-469-6800
TF: 888-429-5377 ■ *Web:* www.travelredefined.com

Crow Executive Air Inc
28331 Lemoyne Rd Toledo Metcalf Airport.... Millbury OH 43447 419-838-6921 838-6911
TF: 800-972-2769 ■ *Web:* www.crowair.com

DB Aviation Inc 3550 N McAree Rd.... Waukegan IL 60087 847-244-8504
TF: 888-362-6738 ■ *Web:* www.landmarkaviation.com

Deer Horn Aviation Ltd Co PO Box 60248.... Midland TX 79711 432-563-2033

Dodgen Aircraft 740 Grand St.... Allegan MI 49010 269-673-4157
Web: www.dodgenaircraft.com

Dolphin Aviation Inc 8191 N Tamiami Tr.... Sarasota FL 34243 941-355-2902
Web: dolphinaviation.com

Dulles Aviation Inc
10501 Observation Rd Manassas Regl Airport.... Manassas VA 20110 703-361-2171
TF: 888-835-9324 ■ *Web:* www.dullesaviation.com

Dunkirk Aviation Sales & Service Inc
3389 Middle Rd.... Dunkirk NY 14048 716-366-6938 366-6986
Web: www.dkk.com

Dyersburg Avionics of Caruthersville
2204 Airport Dr.... Caruthersville MO 63830 573-333-4296

Eaa Environmental Abatement Associates Inc
239 Schuyler Ave Ste 125B.... Kingston PA 18704 570-283-0500
Web: environmental-abatement.com

Eagle Aviation
2861 Aviation Way
Columbia Metropolitan Airport.... West Columbia SC 29170 803-822-5555 822-5529
TF: 800-849-3245 ■ *Web:* www.eagle-aviation.com

Edmonton Regional Airports Authority
1000 Airport Rd Edmonton International Airport
.... Edmonton AB T9E0V3 780-890-8900
Web: www.flyeia.com

Edwards Jet Ctr 1691 Aviation Pl.... Billings MT 59105 406-252-0508 245-9491
TF: 866-353-8245 ■ *Web:* www.edwardsjetcenter.com

Epps Aviation Inc
1 Aviation Way DeKalb Peachtree Airport.... Atlanta GA 30341 770-458-9851 458-0320
TF: 800-241-6807 ■ *Web:* www.eppsaviation.com

Executive Air
2131 Airport Dr
Austin Straubel International Airport.... Green Bay WI 54313 920-498-4880 498-4890
Web: www.executiveair.com

Fargo Jet Center Inc 3802 20th St N.... Fargo ND 58102 701-235-3600
Web: www.fargojet.com

Felts Field Aviation Inc 6205 E Rutter Ave.... Spokane WA 99212 509-535-9011 535-9014
TF: 800-676-5538 ■ *Web:* www.feltsfield.com

Flight Light Inc 2708 47th Ave.... Sacramento CA 95822 916-394-2800
TF: 800-806-3548 ■ *Web:* www.flightlight.com

Flightline Group Inc 3256 Capital Cir SW.... Tallahassee FL 32310 850-574-4444 576-4210
Web: www.flightlinegroup.com

Galvin Flying Services 7001 Perimeter Rd.... Seattle WA 98108 206-763-9706
Web: www.galvinflying.com

Gibbs Flying Service Inc
3717 John J Montgomery Dr.... San Diego CA 92123 858-277-0310 277-0678
Web: gibbsflyingservice.com

Grand Aire Express Inc
11777 W Airport Service Rd.... Swanton OH 43558 800-704-7263 865-2965*
**Fax Area Code:* 419 ■ *TF:* 800-704-7263 ■ *Web:* www.grandaire.com

Grand Strand Airport
2800 Terminal St.... North Myrtle Beach SC 29582 843-848-7400

	City	State	ZIP	Phone	Fax
Greater Toronto Airports Authority					
Toronto Pearson International Airport 3111 Convair Dr					
PO Box 6031	Toronto	ON	L5P1B2	416-776-3000	
Web: www.torontopearson.com					
Holman Aviation Co 1940 Airport Ct	Great Falls	MT	59404	406-453-7613	
Web: www.holmanaviation.com					
Hunt Pan Am Aviation Inc					
505 Amelia Earhart Dr	Brownsville	TX	78521	956-542-9111	542-9133
TF: 800-888-7524 ■ *Web:* www.huntpanam.com					
Inter-State Aviation					
4800 Airport Complex N Airport Rd	Pullman	WA	99163	509-332-6596	334-1751
Web: inter-stateaviation.com					
Interstate Aviation 62 Johnson Ave	Plainville	CT	06062	860-747-5519	589-1853
TF: 800-573-5519 ■ *Web:* www.interstateaviation.com					
Jet Harbor Inc 2860 NW 59th St	Fort Lauderdale	FL	33309	954-772-2863	772-6510
Web: www.jetharbor.com					
Kansas City Aviation Ctr Inc					
15325 S Pflumm Rd	Olathe	KS	66062	913-782-0530	782-9462
TF: 800-720-5222 ■ *Web:* www.kcac.com					
Keystone Aviation Services Inc					
288 Christian St	Oxford	CT	06478	203-264-6525	264-0295
TF: 866-436-2177 ■ *Web:* keystoneav.com					
Landmark Aviation 3501 Aviation Ave	Sioux Falls	SD	57104	408-286-3832	
TF General: 800-888-1646 ■ *Web:* www.landmarkaviation.com					
Landmark Aviation 4360 Agar Dr	Richmond	BC	V7B1A3	604-279-9922	279-9942
TF: 888-298-7326 ■ *Web:* www.landmarkaviation.com					
Landmark Aviation 1500 CityWest Blvd Ste 600	Houston	TX	77042	713-895-9243	690-9553
Web: www.landmarkaviation.com					
Landmark Aviation Trenton Mercer Airport	Trenton	NJ	08628	609-882-1601	
Web: www.landmarkaviation.com					
Lane Aviation Corp					
4389 International Gateway	Columbus	OH	43219	614-237-3747	231-4741*
**Fax:* Cust Svc ■ *TF:* 800-848-6263 ■ *Web:* www.laneaviation.com					
LogiCore Corp 1015 Henderson Rd NW	Huntsville	AL	35816	256-533-5789	
Web: www.logicorehsv.com					
Loyd's Aviation Services Inc					
1601 Skyway Dr Ste 100 PO Box 80958	Bakersfield	CA	93308	661-393-1334	393-0824
TF: 800-284-1334 ■ *Web:* www.bakersfieldjetcenter.com					
Maine Instrument Flight Inc 215 Winthrop St	Augusta	ME	04330	207-622-1211	622-7858
TF: 888-643-3597 ■ *Web:* www.maineinstrumentflight.com					
Malloy Air East Inc Avenue B	WestHampton Beach	NY	11978	631-288-2917	
McCall Aviation 300 Deinhard Ln	McCall	ID	83638	208-634-7137	634-3917
TF: 800-992-6559 ■ *Web:* www.mccallaviation.com					
Mid-Ohio Aviation 6250 N Honeytown Rd	Smithville	OH	44677	330-669-2671	
TF: 800-669-4243 ■ *Web:* www.midohioaviation.com					
Midwest Corporate Aviation 3512 N Webb Rd	Wichita	KS	67226	316-636-9700	636-9747
TF: 800-435-9622 ■ *Web:* www.midwestaviation.com					
Millenium Aviation					
2365 Bernville Rd Reading Regional Airport	Reading	PA	19605	610-372-4728	374-7580
Web: www.majets.com					
Miller Environmental Services Inc					
401 Navigation Blvd	Corpus Christi	TX	78408	361-289-9800	
Web: www.millerenviro.com					
Million Air 4300 Westgrove Dr	Addison	TX	75001	972-248-1600	733-5803
TF: 800-248-1602 ■ *Web:* www.millionair.com					
Minuteman Aviation Inc (MAI)					
5225 HWY 10 W PO Box 16	Missoula	MT	59808	406-728-9363	
Web: www.minutemanaviation.com					
Monterey Jet Center LLC 300 Skypark Dr	Monterey	CA	93940	831-373-0100	
TF: 800-679-2992 ■ *Web:* www.montereyjetcenter.com					
Montgomery Aviation Corp 4525 Selma Hwy	Montgomery	AL	36108	334-288-7334	288-7337
TF: 800-392-8044 ■ *Web:* www.montgomeryaviation.com					
National Jets 3495 SW Ninth Ave	Fort Lauderdale	FL	33315	954-359-9900	359-0064
TF: 800-327-3710 ■ *Web:* www.nationaljets.com/natjet/jet					
Neuber Environmental Services Inc					
42 Ridge Rd	Phoenixville	PA	19460	610-933-4332	
Web: www.neuberenv.com					
North Coast Air 4645 W 12th St	Erie	PA	16505	814-836-9220	836-9901
Web: www.ncair.com					
Northeast Airmotive Inc 1011 Westbrook St	Portland	ME	04102	207-774-6318	874-4714
TF: 877-354-7881 ■ *Web:* www.northeastair.com					
Ocean Aire PO Box 1245	Toms River	NJ	08754	732-797-1077	797-1076
Web: www.oceanaire.net					
Pelican Aviation 1314 Hangar Dr	New Iberia	LA	70560	337-367-1401	
Perfect Sweep Inc 1202 S Expressway Dr	Toledo	OH	43608	419-726-1801	
Web: www.perfectsweep.com					
Premier Jet Ctr 3301 NE Cornell Rd Ste A	Hillsboro	OR	97124	503-693-1096	930-0124*
**Fax Area Code:* 760					
Prior Aviation Service Inc 50 N Airport Dr	Buffalo	NY	14225	716-633-1000	633-1432
Web: www.prioraviation.com					
Pro-Tec Fire Services Ltd 2129 S Oneida St	Green Bay	WI	54304	920-494-8851	
Web: www.protecfire.com					
PS Air Inc 3411 Beech Way SW	Cedar Rapids	IA	52404	319-846-3600	
Web: www.psair.com					
Regional Jet Ctr 12344 Tower Dr	Bentonville	AR	72712	479-205-1100	205-1101
Web: www.regionaljetcenter.com					
Richmor Aviation Inc					
1142 Rt 9 H Columbia County Airport	Hudson	NY	12534	518-828-9461	828-1303
TF: 800-331-6101 ■ *Web:* www.richmor.com					
Robinson Aviation 50 Thompson Ave	East Haven	CT	06512	203-467-9555	467-6346
Web: www.robinsonaviation.com					
Rose Aircraft Interiors Inc 132 Flight Ln	Mena	AR	71953	479-394-2551	
Web: www.roseaircraft.com					
Safegate Airport Systems					
7101 Northland Cir N Ste 110	Minneapolis	MN	55428	763-535-9299	
Web: www.safegate.com					
Saker Aviation Services Inc					
20 South St Pier 6 E River	New York	NY	10004	212-776-4046	
Web: www.sakeraviation.com					
Sanford Aircraft Services Inc					
701 Rod Sullivan Rd	Sanford	NC	27330	919-708-5549	
Web: www.sanford-aircraft.com					
Santa Fe Air Ctr Inc					
121 Aviation Dr Bldg 3005	Santa Fe	NM	87507	505-471-2525	
Web: www.santafejet.biz					
Shannon Airport					
3380 Shannon Airport Cir	Fredericksburg	VA	22408	540-373-4431	373-0035
SheltAir Aviation Services Fort Lauderdale					
4860 NE 12th Ave	Fort Lauderdale	FL	33334	954-771-2210	771-3745
TF: 800-700-2210 ■ *Web:* www.sheltairaviation.com					
Showalter Flying Service 600 Herndon Ave	Orlando	FL	32803	407-326-6062	
Web: www.showalter.com					
Signature Flight Support					
201 S Orange Ave Ste 1100-S	Orlando	FL	32801	407-648-7200	206-8428*
**Fax:* Hum Res ■ *Web:* www.signatureflight.com					
Silverhawk Aviation Inc 1751 W Kearney Ave	Lincoln	NE	68524	402-475-8600	
Web: www.silverhawkaviation.com					
Sky Bright 65 Aviation Dr	Gilford	NH	03249	603-528-6818	
TF: 800-639-6012 ■ *Web:* www.skybright.com					
Skyservice Airlines Inc 9785 Ryan Ave	Dorval	QC	H9P1A2	514-636-3300	636-4855
TF: 888-985-1402 ■ *Web:* skyservice.com					
SkyTech Inc 550 Airport Rd	Rock Hill	SC	29732	803-366-5108	366-1519
TF: 888-386-3596 ■ *Web:* www.skytechinc.com					
Smyrna Air Ctr 300 Doug Warpoole Rd	Smyrna	TN	37167	888-863-9996	
TF: 888-863-9996 ■ *Web:* www.smyrnaaircenter.com					
Snohomish Flying Service Inc					
9900 Airport Way	Snohomish	WA	98296	360-568-1541	568-6034
TF: 800-827-1000 ■ *Web:* www.snohomishflying.com					
Southwest Airport Services Inc					
11811 N Brantly Ave Ste 500	Houston	TX	77034	281-484-6551	996-8826*
**Fax Area Code:* 713 ■ *TF:* 888-362-6738					
Space Coast Jet Ctr 7003 Challenger Ave	Titusville	FL	32780	321-267-8355	267-0129
TF: 800-559-5473 ■ *Web:* www.spacecoastjetcenter.com					
Spanaflight 16705 103rd Ave Ct E	Puyallup	WA	98374	253-848-2020	840-5843
Web: www.spanaflight.com					
St. Paul Flight Ctr 270 Airport Rd Ste 5	Saint Paul	MN	55107	651-227-8108	227-6195
TF: 800-368-0107 ■ *Web:* www.stpaulflight.com					
Statesville Flying Service					
238 Airport Rd	Statesville	NC	28677	704-873-1111	
Web: statesvilleregion.com					
Stevens Aviation Inc 600 Delaware St	Greenville	SC	29605	864-678-6000	879-6215
TF: 800-359-7838 ■ *Web:* www.stevensaviation.com					
Stuart Jet Ctr LLC 2501 Aviation Way	Stuart	FL	34996	772-288-6700	288-3782
TF: 877-735-9538 ■ *Web:* www.stuartjet.com					
Sundance Aviation Inc					
Sundance Airpark NW 122nd & Sara Rd	Oklahoma City	OK	73099	405-373-3886	373-3893
Web: sundanceairport.com					
Swift Aviation 2710 E Old Tower Rd	Phoenix	AZ	85034	602-273-3770	273-3773
Web: www.swiftaviation.com					
Texas Jet Management LLC					
200 Texas Way Hngr 23n	Fort Worth	TX	76106	817-624-8438	
Web: www.texasjet.com					
Top Gun Aviation Inc 405 Industrial Pk Rd	Hammond	LA	70401	985-542-0719	542-2077
Web: www.airnav.com/airport/KHDC/TOP_GUN					
Truman Arnold Cos 701 S Robison Rd	Texarkana	TX	75501	903-794-3835	335-2612*
**Fax Area Code:* 806 ■ *Web:* www.tacair.com					
Unipak Aviation 2049 Ninth Ave	Ronkonkoma	NY	11779	631-471-9801	
Web: www.unipakaviation.net					
United States Aviation 4141 N Memorial Dr	Tulsa	OK	74115	918-836-7345	
TF: 800-897-5387 ■ *Web:* www.unitedstatesaviation.com					
Vail Valley Jet Center LLC					
871 Cooley Mesa Rd Eagle County Regional Airport					
	Gypsum	CO	81637	970-524-7700	
Web: vvjc.com					
Valley International Airport					
3002 Heritage Way	Harlingen	TX	78550	956-430-8605	
Web: www.flythevalley.com					
Vantage Airport Group Ltd					
West 73rd Ave Ste 1410 - 1200	Vancouver	BC	V6P6G5	604-269-0080	
Web: www.vantageairportgroup.com					
Vee Neal Aviation Inc 148 Aviation Ln Ste 109	Latrobe	PA	15650	724-539-4533	539-5501
TF: 800-278-2710 ■ *Web:* www.veeneal.com					
West Valley Flying Club					
1901 Embarcadero Rd	Palo Alto	CA	94303	650-856-2030	
Web: www.wvfc.org					
Western Aircraft Inc 4300 S Kennedy St	Boise	ID	83705	208-338-1800	338-1887
TF: 800-333-3442 ■ *Web:* www.westair.com					
Western Cardinal Inc 205 Durley Ave	Camarillo	CA	93010	805-482-2586	484-2713
TF: 800-882-3018 ■ *Web:* www.westerncardinal.com					
Wilson Air Ctr					
2930 Winchester Rd					
Memphis International Airport	Memphis	TN	38118	901-345-2992	
TF: 800-464-2992 ■ *Web:* www.wilsonair.com					
Wings Air Charter					
236 Airport Hanger Dr	Wisconsin Rapids	WI	54494	715-424-3737	424-3737
Web: www.wingsaircharter.com					
Wisconsin Aviation Inc 1741 River Dr	Watertown	WI	53094	920-261-4567	206-6386
TF: 800-657-0761 ■ *Web:* www.wisconsinaviation.com					
Woodland Aviation Inc 25170 Aviation Ave	Davis	CA	95616	530-759-6037	
TF: 800-442-1333 ■ *Web:* www.woodlandaviation.com					

64 BABY PRODUCTS

See Also Children's & Infants' Clothing p. 1942; Household Furniture p. 2341; Paper Products - Sanitary p. 2869; Toys, Games, Hobbies p. 3256

	City	State	ZIP	Phone	Fax
Baby Jogger Co 8575 Magellan Pkwy Ste 1000	Richmond	VA	23227	800-241-1848	262-6277*
**Fax Area Code:* 804 ■ *TF:* 800-241-1848 ■ *Web:* www.babyjogger.com					
Baby Trend Inc 1567 S Campus Ave	Ontario	CA	91761	800-328-7363	773-0108*
**Fax Area Code:* 909 ■ *TF Cust Svc:* 800-328-7363 ■ *Web:* www.babytrend.com					
Baby's Dream Furniture Inc					
411 Industrial Blvd	Buena Vista	GA	31803	229-649-4404	649-2007
TF: 800-835-2742 ■ *Web:* www.babysdream.com					

Phone Fax

Ball Bounce & Sport Inc/Hedstrom Plastics
1 Hedstrom Dr .... Ashland OH 44805 419-289-9310 281-3371
TF: 800-765-9665 ■ *Web:* www.hedstrom.com

Britax Child Safety Inc 4140 Pleasant Rd .... Fort Mill NC 29708 704-409-1700 409-1665*
**Fax:* Cust Svc ■ *TF:* 888-427-4829 ■ *Web:* us.britax.com

Cardinal Gates 79 Amlajack Way .... Newnan GA 30265 770-252-4200 252-4122
TF: 800-318-3380 ■ *Web:* www.cardinalgates.com

Central Specialties Ltd 220 Exchange Dr .... Crystal Lake IL 60014 815-459-6000 459-6562
TF: 800-873-4370 ■ *Web:* www.csltd.com

Crown Crafts Infant Products Inc
711 W Walnut St .... Compton CA 90220 310-763-8100 295-1954*
**Fax Area Code:* 562 ■ **Fax:* Cust Svc ■ *Web:* www.ccipinc.com

Delta Enterprises 114 W 26th St 8th Fl .... New York NY 10001 212-736-7000
TF: 800-377-3777 ■ *Web:* www.deltachildren.com

Dolly Packaging 320 N Fourth St .... Tipp City OH 45371 937-667-5414

Dorel Juvenile Group USA 2525 State St .... Columbus IN 47201 812-372-0141 372-0911
TF: 800-544-1108 ■ *Web:* na.doreljuvenile.com

Evenflo Company Inc 1801 Commerce Dr .... Piqua OH 45356 800-233-5921
TF: 800-233-5921 ■ *Web:* www.evenflo.com

Fisher-Price Inc 636 Girard Ave .... East Aurora NY 14052 716-687-3000 687-3476
TF: 800-432-5437 ■ *Web:* www.fisher-price.com

Gerber Products Co 445 State St .... Fremont MI 49412 800-284-9488
TF: 800-284-9488 ■ *Web:* www.gerber.com

Infantino LLC
4920 Carroll Canyon Rd Ste 200 .... San Diego CA 92121 800-840-4916 457-0181*
**Fax Area Code:* 858 ■ *TF:* 800-840-4916 ■ *Web:* www.infantino.com

Kelty 6235 Lookout Rd .... Boulder CO 80301 800-535-3589 504-2745
TF: 800-423-2320 ■ *Web:* www.kelty.com

KidCo Inc 1013 Technology Way .... Libertyville IL 60048 847-549-8600 549-8660
TF: 800-553-5529 ■ *Web:* www.kidco.com

Kids II 555 N Pt Ctr E Ste 600 .... Alpharetta GA 30022 770-751-0442 751-0543
TF: 800-230-8190 ■ *Web:* www.kidsii.com

Kolcraft Enterprises Inc 10832 NC Hwy 211 E .... Aberdeen NC 28315 910-944-9345
TF Cust Svc: 800-453-7673 ■ *Web:* www.kolcraft.com

Little Tikes Co, The 2180 Barlow Rd .... Hudson OH 44236 800-321-0183
TF Cust Svc: 800-321-0183 ■ *Web:* www.littletikes.com

Manhattan Toy 300 First Ave N Ste 200 .... Minneapolis MN 55401 800-541-1345
TF: 800-541-1345 ■ *Web:* www.manhattantoy.com

Peg-Perego USA Inc 3625 Independence Dr .... Fort Wayne IN 46808 260-482-8191 484-2940
TF Cust Svc: 800-671-1701 ■ *Web:* en.pegperego.com

Prince Lionheart Inc 2421 Westgate Rd .... Santa Maria CA 93455 805-922-2250 922-9442
TF: 800-544-1132 ■ *Web:* www.princelionheart.com

REI 1700 45th St E .... Sumner WA 98352 253-891-2500 891-2523
TF: 800-426-4840 ■ *Web:* www.rei.com

Sassy Inc 2305 Breton Industrial Pk Dr .... Kentwood MI 49508 616-243-0767 243-1042
TF: 800-323-6336 ■ *Web:* www.sassybaby.com

Step2 Co 10010 Aurora-Hudson Rd .... Streetsboro OH 44241 330-656-0440 655-9685
TF Cust Svc: 800-347-8372 ■ *Web:* www.step2.com

Tough Traveler Ltd 1012 State St .... Schenectady NY 12307 518-377-8526 377-5434
TF Cust Svc: 800-468-6844 ■ *Web:* www.toughtraveler.com

Triboro Quilt Mfg Inc 172 S Broadway .... White Plains NY 10605 914-428-7551 428-0130
Web: www.cuddletime.com

Triple Play Products LLC 904 Main St Ste 330 .... Hopkins MN 55343 952-938-0531 935-4835
TF: 800-829-1625 ■ *Web:* www.lillygold.com

65 BAGS - PAPER

Phone Fax

AJM Packaging Corp
E-4111 Andover Rd .... Bloomfield Hills MI 48302 248-901-0040 901-0061
Web: www.ajmpack.com

Bancroft Bag Inc 425 Bancroft Blvd .... West Monroe LA 71292 318-387-2550
TF: 800-551-4950 ■ *Web:* www.bancroftbag.com

Bemis Company Inc
1 Neenah Ctr Fourth Fl PO Box 669 .... Neenah WI 54957 920-727-4100
NYSE: BMS ■ *Web:* www.bemis.com

Bemis Company Inc Paper Packaging Div
2445 Deer Pk Blvd .... Omaha NE 68105 800-541-4303
TF: 800-541-4303 ■ *Web:* www.bemispaper.com

Bonita Pioneer Packaging Products Inc
7333 SW Bonita Rd .... Portland OR 97224 800-677-7725 323-6027
TF: 800-677-7725 ■ *Web:* www.bonitapioneer.com

Colonial Bag Co 1 Ocean Pond Ave PO Box 929 .... Lake Park GA 31636 229-559-8484 559-0085
TF: 800-392-4875 ■ *Web:* colonial-bag.com

Hood Packaging Corp 25 Woodgreen Pl .... Madison MS 39110 601-853-7260 853-7299
TF: 800-321-8115 ■ *Web:* www.hoodpkg.com

KapStone Paper and Packaging Corp
300 Fibre Way PO Box 639 .... Longview WA 98632 360-425-1550
Web: www.kapstonepaper.com

KYD Inc 2949 Koapaka St .... Honolulu HI 96819 808-836-3221 833-8995
Web: www.kydinc.com

Master Design Co 789 State Rt 94 E .... Fulton KY 42041 270-838-7060 838-7060
Web: www.masterdesign.org

Pacific Bag Inc
15300 Woodinville Redmond Rd NE Ste A .... Woodinville WA 98072 425-455-1128 990-8582
TF: 800-562-2247 ■ *Web:* www.pacificbag.com

Roses Southwest Papers Inc
1701 Second St SW .... Albuquerque NM 87102 505-842-0134 242-0342
Web: www.rosessouthwestpapers.com

Ross & Wallace Paper Products Inc
204 Old Covington Hwy .... Hammond LA 70403 800-854-2300 345-1370*
**Fax Area Code:* 985 ■ *TF:* 800-854-2300 ■ *Web:* www.rossandwallace.com

Stewart Sutherland Inc 5411 E 'V' Ave .... Vicksburg MI 49097 269-649-0530 649-3961
TF: 800-253-1034 ■ *Web:* www.ssbags.com

Werthan Packaging Inc 605 HWY 76 .... White House TN 37188 615-672-3336 242-2801
Web: www.werthan.com

Weyerhaeuser Co 33663 Weyerhaeuser Way S .... Federal Way WA 98003 253-924-2345
NYSE: WY ■ *TF:* 800-525-5440 ■ *Web:* www.weyerhaeuser.com

Zenith Specialty Bag Company Inc
17625 E Railroad St PO Box 8445 .... City of Industry CA 91748 626-912-2481 284-8493*
**Fax Area Code:* 800 ■ *TF:* 800-962-2247 ■ *Web:* zbags.com

66 BAGS - PLASTICS

Phone Fax

Aabaco Plastics Inc
9520 Midwest Ave .... Garfield Heights OH 44125 216-663-9494 663-9475*
**Fax:* Sales ■ *Web:* www.aabacoplastics.com

Admiral Packaging Inc 10 Admiral St .... Providence RI 02908 401-274-7000 331-1910
TF: 800-556-6454 ■ *Web:* www.admiralpkg.com

Ampac Packaging LLC 12025 Tricon Rd .... Cincinnati OH 45246 513-671-1777 671-2920*
**Fax:* Cust Svc ■ *TF:* 800-543-7030 ■ *Web:* www.ampaconline.com

Apco Extruders Inc 180 National Rd .... Edison NJ 08817 732-287-3000 287-1421
TF Orders: 800-942-8725

Armand Manufacturing Inc
2399 Silver Wolf Dr .... Henderson NV 89011 702-565-7500 565-3838
TF: 800-669-9811 ■ *Web:* www.armandmfg.com

Associated Bag Co 400 W Boden St .... Milwaukee WI 53207 800-926-6100 926-4610
TF: 800-926-6100 ■ *Web:* www.associatedbag.com

Bag Makers Inc 6606 S Union Rd .... Union IL 60180 800-458-9031 458-9023
TF: 800-458-9031 ■ *Web:* www.bagmakersinc.com

Bema Inc 744 N Oaklawn Ave .... Elmhurst IL 60126 630-279-7800 279-0284
Web: bemaprint.com

Bemis Company Inc
1 Neenah Ctr Fourth Fl PO Box 669 .... Neenah WI 54957 920-727-4100
NYSE: BMS ■ *Web:* www.bemis.com

Buckeye Boxes Inc 601 N Hague Ave .... Columbus OH 43204 614-274-8484 274-7381
Web: www.buckeyeboxes.com

Clear View Bag Co 5 Burdick Dr .... Albany NY 12205 518-458-7153 458-1401
TF: 800-458-7153 ■ *Web:* www.clearviewbag.com

Clorox Co 1221 Broadway .... Oakland CA 94612 510-271-7000 832-1463
NYSE: CLX ■ *TF Cust Svc:* 800-424-9300 ■ *Web:* www.thecloroxcompany.com

Colonial Bag Corp 205 E Fullerton Ave .... Carol Stream IL 60188 630-690-3999 690-1571
TF: 800-445-7496 ■ *Web:* www.colonialbag.com

Crown Poly Inc 5700 Bickett St .... Huntington Park CA 90255 323-585-5522
Web: www.crownpoly.com

Enviro-Tote Inc 4 Cote Ln .... Bedford NH 03110 603-647-7171 647-0116
TF: 800-868-3224 ■ *Web:* www.enviro-tote.com

Heritage Bags 1648 Diplomat Dr .... Carrollton TX 75006 800-527-2247
TF: 800-527-2247 ■ *Web:* www.heritage-bag.com

International Poly Bag Inc
990 Pk Ctr Dr Ste F & G .... Vista CA 92081 760-598-2468 598-2469
TF: 800-976-5922 ■ *Web:* www.intlpolybag.com

KYD Inc 2949 Koapaka St .... Honolulu HI 96819 808-836-3221 833-8995
Web: www.kydinc.com

Mexico Plastics Company (Inc) 2000 W Blvd .... Mexico MO 65265 800-325-0216
TF: 800-325-0216 ■ *Web:* www.continentalproducts.com

Pacific Bag Inc
15300 Woodinville Redmond Rd NE Ste A .... Woodinville WA 98072 425-455-1128 990-8582
TF: 800-562-2247 ■ *Web:* www.pacificbag.com

Pactiv Corp 1900 W Field Ct .... Lake Forest IL 60045 847-482-2000 482-4738
TF: 888-828-2850 ■ *Web:* www.pactiv.com

Pitt Plastics Inc 1400 Atkinson Ave .... Pittsburg KS 66762 800-835-0366 314-8449
TF: 800-835-0366 ■ *Web:* www.pittplastics.com

Plastic Packaging Inc 1246 Main Ave SE .... Hickory NC 28602 828-328-2466 322-1830*
**Fax:* Sales ■ *Web:* www.ppi-hky.com

Poly-America Inc 2000 W Marshall Dr .... Grand Prairie TX 75051 972-337-7100 647-8061
TF: 800-527-3322 ■ *Web:* www.poly-america.com

Poly-Pak Industries Inc 125 Spagnoli Rd .... Melville NY 11747 800-969-1993 454-6366*
**Fax Area Code:* 631 ■ *TF:* 800-969-1993 ■ *Web:* www.poly-pak.com

Presto Products Co
670 N Perkins St PO Box 2399 .... Appleton WI 54912 920-739-9471 738-1432
TF: 800-558-3525 ■ *Web:* www.prestoproducts.com

Ronpak Inc 4301 New Brunswick Ave .... South Plainfield NJ 07080 732-968-8000
Web: www.ronpak.com

Roplast Industries Inc 3155 S Fifth Ave .... Oroville CA 95965 530-532-9500 532-9576
TF: 800-767-5278 ■ *Web:* www.roplast.com

Shields Bag & Printing Co 1009 Rock Ave .... Yakima WA 98902 509-248-7500 248-6304
TF: 800-541-8630 ■ *Web:* shieldsbag.com

Star Packaging Corp 453 85th Cir .... Atlanta GA 30349 404-763-2800 763-1914
Web: www.interflexgroup.com

Superbag Corp 9291 Baythrone Dr .... Houston TX 77041 713-462-1173 462-8145
TF: 888-842-1177 ■ *Web:* www.superbag.com

Tara Plastics Corp 175 Lk Mirror Rd .... Forest Park GA 30297 404-366-4464 366-3816
Web: www.taraplastics.com

Waverly Plastics Company Inc PO Box 801 .... Waverly IA 50677 319-352-3333
TF: 800-454-6377 ■ *Web:* www.waverlyplastics.com

Webster Industries Inc
95 Chestnut Ridge Rd, ... Montvale NJ 07645 800-999-2374 474-9578*
**Fax Area Code:* 570 ■ *TF:* 800-955-2374 ■ *Web:* www.aepinc.com

Western Summit Manufacturing Corp
13290 Daum Dr .... City of Industry CA 91746 626-333-3333 961-2247

Wisconsin Film & Bag Inc 3100 E Richmond St .... Shawano WI 54166 715-524-2565 524-3527
TF: 800-765-9224 ■ *Web:* www.wifb.com

67 BAGS - TEXTILE

See Also Handbags, Totes, Backpacks p. 2449; Luggage, Bags, Cases p. 2688

Phone Fax

A Rifkin Co 1400 Sans Souci Pkwy .... Wilkes-Barre PA 18706 570-825-9551 825-5282
TF Cust Svc: 800-458-7300 ■ *Web:* www.arifkin.com

Bearse Manufacturing Co 3815 W Cortland St .... Chicago IL 60647 773-235-8710 235-8716
Web: www.bearseusa.com

Bulk Lift International Inc (BLI)
1013 Tamarac Dr .... Carpentersville IL 60110 847-428-6059 428-7180
TF: 800-879-2247 ■ *Web:* www.bulklift.com

Corman Bag Co 32 Arlington St .... Chelsea MA 02150 617-884-7600 437-7917
Web: www.cormanbag.com

Fox Packaging Co 2200 Fox Dr .... McAllen TX 78504 956-682-6176 682-5768
Web: www.foxbag.com

	City	State	Zip	Phone	Fax
Fulton-Denver Co 3500 Wynkoop St *Web:* fultonpacific.com	Denver	CO	80216	303-294-9292	
GEM Group 9 International Way *TF:* 800-800-3200 ■ *Web:* gemline.com	Lawrence	MA	01843	978-691-2000	691-2085
Halsted Corp 51 Commerce Dr Ste 3 *TF:* 800-843-5184 ■ *Web:* www.halstedbag.com	Cranbury	NJ	08512	201-433-3323	
HBD Inc 3901 Riverdale Rd *TF:* 800-403-2247 ■ *Web:* www.hbdinc.com	Greensboro	NC	27406	336-275-4800	
Indian Valley Industries Inc PO Box 810 *TF:* 800-659-5111 ■ *Web:* www.iviindustries.com	Johnson City	NY	13790	607-729-5111	729-5158
J & M Industries Inc 300 Ponchatoula Pkwy *TF:* 800-989-1002 ■ *Web:* www.jm-ind.com	Ponchatoula	LA	70454	985-386-6000	
Langston Cos Inc 1760 S Third St *Web:* langstonbag.com	Memphis	TN	38109	901-774-4440	
LBU Inc 217 Brook Ave *Web:* www.lbuinc.com	Passaic	NJ	07055	973-773-4800	773-6005
Menardi 1 Maxwell Dr *TF:* 800-321-3218 ■ *Web:* menardifilters.com	Trenton	SC	29847	803-663-6551	663-4029
NYP Corp 805 E Grand St *TF:* 800-524-1052 ■ *Web:* www.nyp-corp.com	Elizabeth	NJ	07201	908-351-6550	351-0108
Sacramento Bag Manufacturing Co 440 N Pioneer Ave Ste 300 *TF:* 800-287-2247 ■ *Web:* www.sacbag.com	Woodland	CA	95776	530-662-6130	662-6381

68 BAKERIES

	City	State	Zip	Phone	Fax
Ace Endico Corp 80 International Blvd *Web:* www.aceendico.com	Brewster	NY	10509	845-940-1501	940-1516
Alvarado Street Bakery 2225 S Mcdowell Blvd Ext *Web:* www.alvaradostreetbakery.com	Petaluma	CA	94954	707-283-0300	
American Harvest Baking Company Inc 823 Est Gate Dr Ste 3 *Web:* www.ahbfoods.com	Mt Laurel	NJ	08054	856-642-9955	
Andre-Boudin Bakeries 221 Main St Ste 1230 *Web:* www.boudinbakery.com	San Francisco	CA	94105	415-882-1849	
Atlanta Bread Co 1200 Wilson Way Ste 100 **Fax Area Code:* 678 ■ *Web:* www.atlantabread.com	Smyrna	GA	30082	770-432-0933	366-3361*
Au Bon Pain 19 Fid Kennedy Ave *Web:* www.aubonpain.com	Boston	MA	02210	617-423-2100	423-7879
Awrey Bakeries Inc 12301 Farmington Rd *TF:* 800-950-2253 ■ *Web:* www.awrey.com	Livonia	MI	48150	734-522-1100	
Benson's Bakery Inc 134 Elder St *Web:* www.bensonsbakery.com	Bogart	GA	30622	770-725-5711	
Big Apple Bagels 500 Lk Cook Rd Ste 475 *TF:* 800-251-6101 ■ *Web:* www.babcorp.com	Deerfield	IL	60015	847-948-7520	405-8140
Bimbo Bakery USA 5662 Eastgate Dr *Web:* bimbobakeriesusa.com	San Diego	CA	92121	858-457-9860	
Bruegger's Enterprises 159 Bank St *Web:* www.brueggers.com	Burlington	VT	05401	802-660-4020	
Busken Bakery Inc 2675 Madison Rd *Web:* www.busken.com	Cincinnati	OH	45208	513-871-5330	871-2662
Butterkrust Bakery Inc 3355 W Memorial Blvd *Web:* flowersfoods.com	Lakeland	FL	33815	863-682-1155	
Certified Oil Corp 949 King Ave *Web:* certifiedoil.com	Columbus	OH	43212	614-421-7500	
Cheryl & Co 646 McCorkle Blvd **Fax Area Code:* 614 ■ *TF:* 800-443-8124 ■ *Web:* www.cheryls.com	Westerville	OH	43082	800-443-8124	891-8699*
Coles Quality Foods Inc 25 Ottawa SW 4th Fl *Web:* www.coles.com	Grand Rapids	MI	49503	616-975-0081	
Collin Street Bakery Inc 401 W Seventh Ave **Fax Area Code:* 903 ■ *TF Sales:* 800-267-4657 ■ *Web:* www.collinstreet.com	Corsicana	TX	75151	800-267-4657	872-6879*
Cookies By Design Inc 1865 Summit Ave Ste 605 *TF:* 800-945-2665 ■ *Web:* www.cookiesbydesign.com	Plano	TX	75074	972-398-9536	398-9542
Cookies From Home Inc 1605 W University Dr Ste 106 *Web:* www.cookiesfromhome.com	Tempe	AZ	85281	480-894-1944	
Cookies in Bloom Inc 7208 La Casa Rd *Web:* www.cookiesinbloom.com	Dallas	TX	75248	425-688-7777	
Corner Bakery Cafe 12700 Pk Central Dr Ste 1300 *TF General:* 800-309-4642 ■ *Web:* www.cornerbakerycafe.com	Dallas	TX	75251	972-619-4100	
Crest Foods Inc 101 W Renner Rd Ste 240 *Web:* www.nestlecafe.com	Richardson	TX	75082	214-495-9533	853-5347
Damascus Bakery Inc 56 Gold St **Fax Area Code:* 718 ■ *TF:* 800-367-7482 ■ *Web:* www.damascusbakery.com	Brooklyn	NY	11201	800-367-7482	403-0948*
Dancing Deer Baking Company Inc 65 Sprague St W A *Web:* www.dancingdeer.com	Boston	MA	02136	617-442-7300	
Dare Foods Ltd 2481 Kingsway Dr *Web:* www.darefoods.com	Kitchener	ON	N2C1A6	519-893-5500	
Daylight Donut Flour Company LLC 11707 E 11th St *TF:* 800-331-2245 ■ *Web:* www.daylightdonuts.com	Tulsa	OK	74128	918-438-0800	438-0804
Dunkin' Donuts 130 Royall St *TF Cust Svc:* 800-859-5339 ■ *Web:* www.dunkindonuts.com	Canton	MA	02021	781-737-3000	737-4000
East Balt Inc 1801 W 31st Pl *TF:* 800-621-8555 ■ *Web:* www.eastbalt.com	Chicago	IL	60608	773-376-4444	376-8137
Eleni's 75 Ninth Ave *TF:* 888-435-3647 ■ *Web:* www.elenis.com	New York	NY	10011	888-435-3647	
Fiera Foods Co 50 Marmora St *Web:* www.fierafoods.com	Toronto	ON	M9M2X5	416-746-1010	
Freed's Bakery LLC 299 Pepsi Rd *Web:* www.freedsbakery.org	Manchester	NH	03109	603-627-7746	
Galasso's Inc 10820 San Sevaine Way *TF:* 800-339-7494 ■ *Web:* www.galassos.com	Mira Loma	CA	91752	951-360-1211	
Gold Medal Bakery Inc 1397 Bay St *TF:* 800-642-7568 ■ *Web:* www.goldmedalbakery.com	Fall River	MA	02724	508-674-5766	674-6090
Gonnella Baking Co 1001 W Chicago Ave *TF:* 800-262-3442 ■ *Web:* www.gonnella.com	Chicago	IL	60642	312-733-2020	733-7056
Great American Cookie Company Inc 3300 Chambers Rd Ste 170 *TF:* 877-639-2361 ■ *Web:* www.greatamericancookies.com	Horseheads	NY	14845	877-639-2361	
Great Harvest Bread Co 28 S Montana St *TF:* 800-442-0424 ■ *Web:* www.greatharvest.com	Dillon	MT	59725	406-683-6842	683-5537
Harbar LLC 320 Turnpike St *Web:* www.harber.com	Canton	MA	02021	781-828-0848	
Hill & Valley Inc 3915 9th St *TF:* 800-480-0055 ■ *Web:* www.hillandvalley.net	Rock Island	IL	61201	309-793-0161	
Holsum Bakery Inc 2322 W Lincoln St *TF:* 800-755-8167 ■ *Web:* www.holsumaz.com	Phoenix	AZ	85009	602-252-2351	
Honey Dew Assoc Inc 2 Taunton St *TF:* 800-946-6393 ■ *Web:* www.honeydewdonuts.com	Plainville	MA	02762	508-699-3900	699-3949
Horizon Snack Foods Inc 7066 Las Positas Rd Ste G	Livermore	CA	94551	925-373-7700	
Hot Stuff Pizza 2930 W Maple St *TF:* 800-336-1320 ■ *Web:* www.hotstuffpizza.com	Sioux Falls	SD	57107	605-336-6961	336-0141
Interbake Foods LLC 3951 Werre Pkwy *Web:* www.interbake.com	Richmond	VA	23233	804-755-7107	
Jessie Lord Bakery LLC 21100 S Western Ave *Web:* www.jessielordpies.com	Torrance	CA	90501	310-533-6010	328-2608
Joseph Campione Garlic Bread 2201 W S Branch Blvd *Web:* www.josephcampione.com	Oak Creek	WI	53154	414-761-8944	761-2005
Just Desserts Inc 351 California St Ste 600 *Web:* www.justdesserts.com	San Francisco	CA	94104	510-567-2900	
King Arthur Flour Co Inc, The 135 Rt 5 S *Web:* www.kingarthurflour.com	Norwich	VT	05055	802-649-3881	649-3365
Krispy Kreme Doughnuts Corp 370 Knollwood St Ste 500 *NYSE: KKD* ■ *TF:* 800-457-4779 ■ *Web:* www.krispykreme.com	Winston-Salem	NC	27103	336-725-2981	733-3796
Le Boulanger Inc 305 N Mathilda *Web:* www.leboulanger.com	Sunnyvale	CA	94085	408-774-9000	
Manhattan Bagel Co Inc 555 Zang St Ste 300 *TF:* 800-224-3563 ■ *Web:* www.manhattanbagel.com	Lakewood	CO	80228	303-568-8000	
Maple Donuts Inc 3455 E Market St *TF:* 800-627-5348 ■ *Web:* www.mapledonuts.com	York	PA	17402	717-757-7826	755-8725
New Horizons Baking Co Inc 211 Woodlawn Ave *Web:* www.genesisbaking.com	Norwalk	OH	44857	419-663-6432	
Olde Tyme Pastries 2225 Geer Rd *Web:* www.otpastries.com	Turlock	CA	95382	209-668-0928	
Orange Bakery Inc 17751 Cowan Ave *Web:* www.orangebakery.com	Irvine	CA	92614	949-863-1377	
Panera Bread Co 3630 S Geyer Rd *NASDAQ: PNRA* ■ *TF:* 800-301-5566 ■ *Web:* www.panerabread.com	Saint Louis	MO	63127	314-984-1000	909-3300
PARTNERS A Tasteful Choice Co 20232 72nd Ave *TF:* 800-632-7477 ■ *Web:* www.partnerscrackers.com	South Kent	WA	98032	253-867-1580	
Pioneer Frozen Foods Inc 627 Big Stone Gap *Web:* www.chguenther.com	Duncanville	TX	75137	972-298-4281	
Puritan Bakery Inc 1624 E Carson St *Web:* www.puritanbakery.com	Carson	CA	90745	310-830-5451	
Quality Naturally Foods 18830 E San Jose Ave *Web:* www.qnfoods.com	City of Industry	CA	91748	626-854-6363	965-0978
Rotella's Italian Bakery Inc 6949 S 108th St *Web:* www.rotellasbakery.com	La Vista	NE	68128	402-592-6600	592-2989
Schulze & Burch Biscuit Co 1133 W 35th St *Web:* schulzeburch.com/brands/pastries.asp	Chicago	IL	60609	773-927-6622	
Southern Maid Donut Flour Co 3615 Cavalier Dr *Web:* www.southernmaiddonuts.com	Garland	TX	75042	972-272-6425	276-3549
Sprinkles Cupcakes Inc 9635 S Santa Monica Blvd *Web:* www.sprinkles.com	Beverly Hills	CA	90210	310-274-8765	
Sterling Foods LLC 1075 Arion Pkwy *Web:* www.sterlingfoodsusa.com	San Antonio	TX	78216	210-490-1669	490-7964
Sunrise Bakery Inc 4564 Second Ave 47th St	Brooklyn	NY	11232	718-788-7884	
SuperMom's LLC 625 Second St	Saint Paul Park	MN	55071	651-459-2253	
Sweet Street Desserts Inc 722 Hiesters Ln *Web:* www.sweetstreet.com	Reading	PA	19605	610-921-8113	
Treats International Franchise Corp 238 Queen St S 2nd Fl *TF:* 800-461-4003 ■ *Web:* www.treats.com	Mississauga	ON	L5M1L5	613-563-4073	563-1982
Van's Natural Foods 3285 E Vernon Ave *Web:* www.vansfoods.com	Vernon	CA	90058	323-585-5581	
Vie de France Yamazaki Inc 2070 Chain Bridge Rd Ste 500 *TF General:* 800-446-4404 ■ *Web:* www.vdfy.com	Vienna	VA	22182	703-442-9205	821-2695
Wetzel's Pretzels LLC 35 Hugus Alley Ste 300 *Web:* www.wetzels.com	Pasadena	CA	91103	626-432-6900	432-6904
Wicks Pies Inc 217 Greenville Ave *Web:* www.wickspies.com	Winchester	IN	47394	765-584-8401	

69 BANKING-RELATED SERVICES

	City	State	Zip	Phone	Fax
Atm Merchant Systems 1667 Helm Dr *TF:* 888-878-8166 ■ *Web:* www.atmms.com	Las Vegas	NV	89119	702-837-8787	
Austin Trust Co 336 S Congress Ave Ste 100 *Web:* www.austintrust.com	Austin	TX	78704	512-478-2121	478-2616
Automatic Funds Transfer Services 151 S Landers St Ste C *TF:* 800-275-2033 ■ *Web:* www.afts.com	Seattle	WA	98134	206-254-0975	254-0968
Blackhawk Bank PO Box 719 *TF:* 888-769-2600 ■ *Web:* www.blackhawkbank.com	Beloit	WI	53511	608-364-4534	364-8946

	City	State	ZIP	Phone	Fax
Bremer Financial Corp 2100 Bremer Tower 445 Minnesota St *TF:* 800-908-2265 ■ *Web:* www.bremer.com	Saint Paul	MN	55101	651-227-7621	312-3675
Capital Farm Credit Aca 7000 Woodway Dr *TF:* 877-944-5500 ■ *Web:* www.capitalfarmcredit.com	Waco	TX	76712	254-776-7506	776-8112
Citizens Federal Savings & Loan Assn 110 N Main St PO Box 9 *TF:* 800-436-5177 ■ *Web:* www.citizensfederalsl.com	Bellefontaine	OH	43311	937-593-0015	593-6577
Civista Bank 100 E Water St *TF:* 888-645-4121 ■ *Web:* www.civistabank.com	Sandusky	OH	44870	419-625-4121	627-3359
Comdata Corp 5301 Maryland Way *TF:* 800-266-3282 ■ *Web:* www.comdata.com	Brentwood	TN	37027	615-370-7000	
Community Bank 505 E Colorado Blvd *TF:* 800-788-9999 ■ *Web:* www.cbank.com	Pasadena	CA	91101	800-788-9999	
Directcash Payments Inc 1420 28 St NE Bay 6 *Web:* www.directcash.net	Calgary	AB	T2A7W6	403-387-2103	
eCivis Inc 418 N Fair Oaks Ave Ste 301 *TF:* 877-232-4847 ■ *Web:* www.ecivis.com	Pasadena	CA	91103	877-232-4847	
Emida Corp 27442 Portola Pkwy Ste 150 *Web:* www.emida.net	Foothill Ranch	CA	92610	949-699-1401	699-1420
Emprise Financial Corp 257 N Broadway St PO Box 2970 *TF Cust Svc:* 800-201-7118 ■ *Web:* www.emprisebank.com	Wichita	KS	67202	316-383-4301	
Eureka Homestead 1922 Veterans Memorial Blvd *TF:* 855-858-5179 ■ *Web:* www.eurekahomestead.com	Metairie	LA	70005	504-834-0242	
Fiserv Inc 255 Fiserv Dr PO Box 979 *NASDAQ: FISV* ■ *TF Sales:* 800-872-7882 ■ *Web:* www.fiserv.com	Brookfield	WI	53008	262-879-5000	
Hawaii National Bank 45 N King St *TF:* 800-528-2273 ■ *Web:* www.hawaiinational.com	Honolulu	HI	96817	808-528-7711	
HomEquity Bank 1881 Yonge St Ste 300 *TF:* 866-522-2447 ■ *Web:* www.homequitybank.ca	Toronto	ON	M4S3C4	416-925-4757	
Lockwood Advisors Inc 760 Moore Rd *TF:* 800-200-3033	King Of Prussia	PA	19406	800-200-3033	
Mba Surety Agency Inc 207 E Capitol Ave *Web:* www.mobankers.com	Jefferson City	MO	65101	573-636-2142	
Minority Alliance Capital LLC 6960 Orchard Lk Rd Ste 306 *Web:* www.mac-leasing.com	West Bloomfield	MI	48322	248-855-8660	
Moelis & Co LLC 399 Pk Ave 5th Fl *Web:* www.moelis.com	New York	NY	10022	212-883-3800	880-4260
MoneyGram International Inc 2828 N Harwood Fl 15 *NASDAQ: MGI* ■ *TF:* 800-666-3947 ■ *Web:* www.moneygram.com	Dallas	TX	75201	800-666-3947	
Moneytree Inc 6720 Ft Dent Way *TF:* 877-613-6669 ■ *Web:* www.moneytreeinc.com	Seattle	WA	98188	206-246-3500	248-3400
NYCE Corp 400 Plaza Dr **Fax Area Code:* 201 ■ *TF:* 888-323-0310 ■ *Web:* www.nyce.net	Secaucus	NJ	07094	904-438-6000	330-3374*
Oak Ridge Financial 701 Xenia Ave S Ste 100 *TF:* 800-231-8364 ■ *Web:* www.oakridgefinancial.com	Minneapolis	MN	55416	763-923-2200	923-2283
OANDA Corp 140 Broadway 46th Fl *TF:* 800-826-8164 ■ *Web:* www.oanda.com	New York	NY	10005	416-593-9436	
Orchard First Source (OFS) 10 S Wacker Dr Ste 2500 *Web:* www.ofscapital.com	Chicago	IL	60606	847-734-2000	
Philadelphia Trust Co, The 1760 Market St 2nd Fl *Web:* philadelphiatrust.com	Philadelphia	PA	19103	215-979-3434	
PULSE 1301 McKinney St Ste 2500 *TF:* 800-420-2122 ■ *Web:* www.pulsenetwork.com	Houston	TX	77010	713-223-1400	223-1204
Rock Springs National Bank 200 Second St PO Box 880 *TF:* 800-469-8801 ■ *Web:* www.rsnb.com	Rock Springs	WY	82902	307-362-8801	362-9432
Sherman Financial Group LLC 335 Madison Ave *Web:* sfg.com	New York	NY	10017	212-922-1616	
Travelex Worldwide Money 122 E 42nd St Ste 2800 *TF:* 800-228-9792 ■ *Web:* www.travelex.com	New York	NY	10168	212-363-6206	
United Bank & Trust 935 Main St PO Box E **Fax Area Code:* 517	Sabetha	KS	66534	785-284-2187	423-5041*
Universal Money Centers Inc 6800 Squibb Rd *Web:* www.universalmoney.com	Shawnee Mission	KS	66202	913-831-2055	
Western Union Holdings Inc 12500 E Belford Ave *NYSE: WU* ■ *TF Cust Svc:* 800-325-6000 ■ *Web:* westernunion.com	Englewood	CO	80112	720-332-1000	332-4753
Your Community Bank 2323 Ring Rd *TF:* 800-314-2265 ■ *Web:* www.yourcommunitybank.com	Elizabethtown	KY	42701	270-765-2131	765-2135

70 BANKS - COMMERCIAL & SAVINGS

See Also Credit & Financing - Commercial p. 2171; Credit & Financing - Consumer p. 2172; Credit Unions p. 2174; Bank Holding Companies p. 2464

	City	State	ZIP	Phone	Fax
1st Bank 120 Second St NW	Sidney	MT	59270	406-433-3212	
1st Bank & Trust of Broken Bow 710 S Park Dr *Web:* 1stbankandtrust.com	Broken Bow	OK	74728	580-584-9123	
1st Colonial Bancorp Inc 1040 Haddon Ave *OTC: FCOB* ■ *TF:* 800-500-1044 ■ *Web:* www.1stcolonial.com	Collingswood	NJ	08108	856-858-1100	858-9255
1st Source Bank 100 N Michigan St **Fax:* Mktg ■ *TF:* 800-513-2360 ■ *Web:* www.1stsource.com	South Bend	IN	46601	574-235-2254	235-2948*
1st Summit Bancorp 125 Donald Ln *Web:* 1stsummit.com	Johnstown	PA	15904	814-262-4000	
3rd Federal Bank 3 Penns Trail *TF:* 800-822-3321 ■ *Web:* www.3rdfedbank.com	Newtown	PA	18940	215-579-4600	579-2381
Albany Bank & Trust Company NA 3400 W Lawrence Ave *Web:* www.albanybank.com	Chicago	IL	60625	773-267-7300	267-7337
Alderwood Capital LLC 505 Montgomery St 11th Fl *Web:* www.alderwoodcapital.com	San Francisco	CA	94111	415-874-3388	
Alerus Financial 2300 S Columbia Rd	Grand Forks	ND	58201	701-795-3200	
Allegiance Capital Corp 16400 Dallas Pkwy Ste 300 *Web:* www.allcapcorp.com	Dallas	TX	75248	214-217-7750	
Allied Irish Banks 1166 Ave of the Americas *Web:* www.aib.ie	New York	NY	10036	212-339-8080	
Alma Exchange Bank 501 W 12th St PO Box 1988 *Web:* www.aebalma.com	Alma	GA	31510	912-632-8631	
Alostar Bank 3680 Grandview Pkwy Ste 200 **Fax Area Code:* 866 ■ *TF:* 877-738-6391 ■ *Web:* www.alostarbank.com	Birmingham	AL	35243	205-298-6391	715-6601*
Alpine Capital Bank 680 Fifth Ave *Web:* www.alpinecapitalbank.com	New York	NY	10019	212-328-2555	
AltaCorp Capital Inc 1100 888-3rd St SW *Web:* www.altacorpcapital.com	Calgary	AB	T2P5C5	403-539-8600	
Amalgamated Bank of Chicago 30 N LaSalle *Web:* www.aboc.com	Chicago	IL	60603	312-822-3000	267-8767
Amalgamated Bank of New York 275 Seventh Ave *TF:* 800-662-0860 ■ *Web:* www.amalgamatedbank.com	New York	NY	10001	800-662-0860	
Amarillo National Bank 410 S Taylor St Plaza 1 **Fax:* Cust Svc ■ *TF:* 800-253-1031 ■ *Web:* www.anb.com	Amarillo	TX	79101	806-378-8000	378-8066*
Amboy National Bank 3590 US Hwy 9 S *TF:* 800-942-6269 ■ *Web:* www.amboybank.com	Old Bridge	NJ	08857	732-591-8700	591-0705
Amegy Bank of Texas 4400 Post Oak Pkwy *TF:* 800-287-0301 ■ *Web:* www.amegybank.com	Houston	TX	77027	713-235-8800	
American Bank 4029 W Tilghman St *Web:* ambk.com	Allentown	PA	18104	610-366-1800	
American Bank of Commerce 610 W Fifth St *Web:* www.theabcbank.com	Austin	TX	78701	512-391-5500	391-5599
American Bank of Texas NA 200 N Austin St *TF:* 800-567-1817 ■ *Web:* www.abtexas.com	Seguin	TX	78155	830-379-5236	
American Exchange Bank (AEB) 510 W Main St PO Box 818 *TF:* 888-652-3321 ■ *Web:* www.aebbank.net	Henryetta	OK	74437	918-652-3321	652-7057
American Express Centurion Bank 4315 South 2700 West *Web:* www.americanexpress.com	Salt Lake City	UT	84184	801-945-3000	
American First National Bank 9999 Bellaire Blvd *Web:* www.afnb.com	Houston	TX	77036	713-596-2888	596-2555
American Heritage Bank 2 S Main PO Box 1408 *Web:* www.ahb-ok.com	Sapulpa	OK	74067	918-224-3210	224-7689
American Metro Bank 4878 N Broadway *Web:* www.americanmetrobank.com	Chicago	IL	60640	773-769-6868	769-6288
American National Bank PO Box 2139 *TF Cust Svc:* 800-279-0007 ■ *Web:* www.anbank.com	Omaha	NE	68103	402-399-5000	
American Savings Bank FSB 1001 Bishop St PO Box 2300 *TF:* 800-272-2566 ■ *Web:* www.asbhawaii.com	Honolulu	HI	96813	808-627-6900	
AmericanWest Bank 2237 NW 57th St *Web:* www.bannerbank.com	Seattle	WA	98107	206-784-2200	784-6650
Ameriserv Financial 216 Franklin St PO Box 520 *NASDAQ: ASRV* ■ *TF:* 800-837-2265 ■ *Web:* www.ameriserv.com	Johnstown	PA	15907	814-533-5300	
Amfirst Bank NA Mccook 602 W B St *Web:* amfirstbank.com	Mccook	NE	69001	308-345-1555	
AmTrust Bank 1801 E Ninth St *TF:* 888-696-4444 ■ *Web:* www.mynycb.com	Cleveland	OH	44114	216-736-3480	987-8732
Anadarko Bank & Trust Co 110 W Oklahoma Ave *Web:* www.bocokonline.com	Anadarko	OK	73005	405-247-3311	
Anchor Bank 1055 Wayzata Blvd E *TF:* 800-425-5150 ■ *Web:* www.anchorlink.com	Wayzata	MN	55391	952-473-4606	476-5219
Anchor Commercial Bank 13951 Us Hwy One *Web:* www.anchorcommercialbank.com	Juno Beach	FL	33408	561-383-3150	
AnchorBank 25 W Main St PO Box 7933 *TF:* 800-252-6246 ■ *Web:* www.anchorbank.com	Madison	WI	53703	608-252-8827	252-8783
ANZ Securities Inc 1177 Ave of the Americas 6th Fl *Web:* www.anz.com	New York	NY	10036	212-801-9800	801-9163
Apple Bank for Savings 122 E 42nd St 9th Fl *TF:* 800-824-0710 ■ *Web:* www.applebank.com	New York	NY	10168	914-902-2775	
Apple Creek Banc Corp 3 W Main St PO Box 237 *TF:* 888-327-7533 ■ *Web:* www.applecreekbank.com	Apple Creek	OH	44606	330-698-2631	
Arthur State Bank 100 E Main St PO Box 769 *TF:* 877-226-5246 ■ *Web:* www.arthurstatebank.com	Union	SC	29379	864-427-1213	429-8537
Artisan's Bank 2961 Centerville Rd *TF:* 800-282-8255 ■ *Web:* www.artisansbank.com	Wilmington	DE	19808	302-658-6881	654-0559
Arundel FSB 333 E Patapsco Ave *Web:* arundelfederal.com	Baltimore	MD	21225	410-355-9300	355-0335
Asheville Savings Bank S S B PO Box 652 *TF:* 800-222-3230 ■ *Web:* www.ashevillesavings.com	Asheville	NC	28802	828-254-7411	252-1512
Ashir Capital Inc 40 Wall St 59th Fl	New York	NY	10005	212-269-2300	
Asia Bank NA 135-34 Roosevelt Ave	Flushing	NY	11354	718-961-9700	
Associated Bank 2870 Holmgren Way *TF:* 800-728-3501 ■ *Web:* www.associatedbank.com	Green Bay	WI	54304	262-879-0133	
Associated Bank Green Bay NA 200 N Adams St *TF:* 800-728-3501 ■ *Web:* www.associatedbank.com	Green Bay	WI	54301	920-433-3200	433-3028
Associated Bank Illinois NA 612 N Main St *TF:* 800-236-8866 ■ *Web:* www.associatedbank.com	Rockford	IL	61103	815-987-3500	
Associated Bank Milwaukee 401 E Kilbourn Ave *TF:* 800-236-8866 ■ *Web:* www.associatedbank.com	Milwaukee	WI	53202	414-271-1786	

	City	State	Zip	Phone	Fax
Associated Bank North 303 S First Ave *TF:* 800-236-8866 ■ *Web:* www.associatedbank.com	Wausau	WI	54401	715-848-4793	
Athens State Bank 6530 N State Rt 29 *TF:* 800-367-7576 ■ *Web:* athensstatebank.com	Springfield	IL	62707	217-487-7766	487-7733
Baldwin & Clarke Corporate Finance Inc Coldstream Park 116B S River Rd *Web:* baldwinclarke.com	Bedford	NH	03110	603-668-4353	
Banc Statements Inc 4700 Birmingham St *Web:* www.bsisite.com	Birmingham	AL	35217	205-956-5004	
Bancorp Bank 409 Silverside Rd Ste 105 *NASDAQ:* TBBK ■ *TF Cust Svc:* 866-255-9831 ■ *Web:* thebancorp.com	Wilmington	DE	19809	302-385-5000	385-5099
Bangor Savings Bank 99 Franklin St *TF:* 877-226-4671 ■ *Web:* www.bangor.com	Bangor	ME	04401	207-942-5211	
Bank Financial 6415 W 95th St *TF:* 800-894-6900 ■ *Web:* www.bankfinancial.com	Chicago Ridge	IL	60415	800-894-6900	
Bank First National PO Box 10 *Web:* www.bankfirstnational.com	Manitowoc	WI	54221	920-684-6611	
Bank Leumi USA 579 Fifth Ave *TF:* 800-892-5430 ■ *Web:* www.leumiusa.com	New York	NY	10017	917-542-2343	542-2254
Bank Midwest NA 1111 Main St *Web:* www.bankmw.com	Kansas City	MO	64105	816-471-9800	
Bank of Albuquerque NA 201 3rd St NW Ste 1400 *TF:* 800-583-0709 ■ *Web:* www.bankofalbuquerque.com	Albuquerque	NM	87102	505-855-0855	222-8481
Bank of Bartlett Inc 6281 Stage Rd *Web:* bankofbartlett.com	Bartlett	TN	38134	901-382-6600	
Bank of Bennington (Bennington NE) 12212 N 156th St *Web:* www.bankbenn.com	Bennington	NE	68007	402-238-2245	
Bank of Bennington, The 155 N St *Web:* www.thebankofbennington.com	Bennington	VT	05201	802-442-8121	
Bank of Blue Valley PO Box 26128 *Web:* www.bankbv.com	Overland Park	KS	66225	913-338-1000	
Bank of Cashton 723 Main St *Web:* bankofcashton.com	Cashton	WI	54619	608-654-5121	
Bank of Delmar Inc 2245 Northwood Dr *Web:* www.bankofdelmarvahb.com	Salisbury	MD	21801	410-548-1100	
Bank of Denver 810 E 17th Ave *Web:* thebankofdenver.com	Denver	CO	80218	303-572-3600	
Bank of Erath 105 W Edwards *Web:* bankoferath.com	Erath	LA	70533	337-937-5816	
Bank of Gleason 203 Main St PO Box 231 *Web:* www.gleasononline.com	Gleason	TN	38229	731-648-5506	648-5090
Bank of Glen Burnie, The 101 Crain Hwy SE *Web:* www.thebankofglenburnie.com	Glen Burnie	MD	21061	410-766-3300	
Bank of Gravett 211 Se Main St *Web:* bankofgravett.net	Gravette	AR	72736	479-787-5251	
Bank of Hazlehurst PO Box 628 *Web:* www.bankofhazlehurst.com	Hazlehurst	GA	31539	912-375-4228	
Bank of Herrin, The 101 S Park Ave	Herrin	IL	62948	618-942-6666	942-3618
Bank of Holly Springs PO Box 250 *Web:* www.bankofhollysprings.com	Holly Springs	MS	38635	662-252-2511	252-1816
Bank of Kirksville 214 S Franklin *Web:* bankofkirksville.com	Kirksville	MO	63501	660-665-7766	
Bank of Landisburg, The 100 N Carlisle St PO Box 179 *Web:* www.bankoflandisburg.com	Landisburg	PA	17040	717-789-3213	
Bank of Louisiana 300 St Charles Ave *TF:* 866-392-9952 ■ *Web:* www.bankoflouisiana.com	New Orleans	LA	70130	504-592-0600	592-0606
Bank of Marin 504 Tamalpais Dr *NASDAQ:* BMRC ■ *TF:* 800-654-5111 ■ *Web:* www.bankofmarin.com	Corte Madera	CA	94925	415-927-2265	927-8920
Bank of Mauston, The 503 State Rd 82 E PO Box 226 *Web:* www.bankofmauston.com	Mauston	WI	53948	608-847-6200	847-5372
Bank of McKenney 20718 First St *OTC:* BOMK ■ *TF:* 800-528-2273 ■ *Web:* www.bankofmckenney.com	McKenney	VA	23872	804-478-4434	478-4704
Bank of Montreal (BMO) 100 King St W 1 First Canadian Pl 19th Fl *NYSE:* BMO ■ *Web:* www.bmo.com	Toronto	ON	M5X1A1	416-867-6785	867-6793
Bank of Montreal 3 Times Sq *TF:* 877-225-5266 ■ *Web:* www.bmocm.com	New York	NY	10036	877-225-5266	
Bank of Morton 366 S Fourth St PO Box 229 *Web:* www.bankofmorton.com	Morton	MS	39117	601-732-8944	732-8599
Bank of Napa Na 2007 Redwood Rd Ste 101 *Web:* www.thebankofnapa.com	Napa	CA	94558	707-257-7777	
Bank of Nevada 2700 W Sahara Ave *TF:* 877-750-0010	Las Vegas	NV	89102	702-248-4200	248-8661
Bank of New Glarus 501 First St *Web:* www.thebankofnewglarus.bank	New Glarus	WI	53574	608-527-5205	
Bank of North Dakota 1200 Memorial Hwy *TF:* 800-472-2166 ■ *Web:* bnd.nd.gov	Bismarck	ND	58504	701-328-5600	328-5632
Bank of Nova Scotia 1 Liberty Plaza 26th Fl *TSE:* BNS ■ *TF:* 800-472-6842 ■ *Web:* www.scotiabank.com	New York	NY	10006	212-225-5000	
Bank of Oak Ridge 2211 Oak Ridge Rd *OTC:* BKOR ■ *Web:* www.bankofoakridge.com	Oak Ridge	NC	27310	336-644-9944	644-6644
Bank of Oklahoma NA PO Box 2300 *TF:* 800-234-6181 ■ *Web:* www.bankofoklahoma.com	Tulsa	OK	74192	918-588-6010	
Bank of Springfield 2600 Adlai Stevenson Dr *TF:* 877-698-3278 ■ *Web:* www.bankwithbos.com	Springfield	IL	62703	217-529-5555	529-5080
Bank of Stanly PO Box 338 *TF:* 800-438-6864 ■ *Web:* www.uwharrie.com	Albemarle	NC	28002	704-983-6181	983-5548
Bank of Stockton PO Box 1110 *TF:* 800-941-1494 ■ *Web:* www.bankofstockton.com	Stockton	CA	95201	209-929-1600	929-1434
Bank of Sunset & Trust Co 863 Napoleon Ave *TF:* 800-264-5578 ■ *Web:* www.bankofsunset.com	Sunset	LA	70584	337-662-5222	662-5705
Bank of Tampa, The 601 Bayshore Blvd *Web:* bankoftampa.com	Tampa	FL	33606	813-872-1216	
Bank of Tescott, The 600 S Santa Fe	Salina	KS	67401	785-825-1621	
Bank of the Carolinas 135 Boxwood Village Dr *OTC:* BCAR ■ *TF:* 877-751-5755 ■ *Web:* www.bankofthecarolinas.com	Mocksville	NC	27028	336-751-5755	
Bank of the Cascades 121 N Ninth St *Web:* botc.com	Boise	ID	83702	208-343-7848	
Bank of the Ozarks 4328 Old Spanish Trail *TF:* 800-274-4482 ■ *Web:* www.omnibank.com	Houston	TX	77021	713-747-9000	
Bank of the Sierra PO Box 1930 *TF Cust Svc:* 888-454-2265 ■ *Web:* www.bankofthesierra.com	Porterville	CA	93258	559-782-4900	
Bank of Tokyo-Mitsubishi Ltd 1251 Ave of the Americas **Fax:* Hum Res ■ *Web:* www.bk.mufg.jp	New York	NY	10020	212-782-4000	782-6570*
Bank of Tuscaloosa 2200 Jack Warner Pkwy *Web:* bankoftuscaloosa.synovus.com	Tuscaloosa	AL	35401	205-345-6200	
Bank Of Utica 222 Genesee St *OTC:* BKUT ■ *TF:* 800-442-1028 ■ *Web:* www.bankofutica.com	Utica	NY	13502	315-797-2700	797-2707
Bank of Virginia 11730 Hull St Rd *NASDAQ:* BOVA ■ *TF:* 800-500-1044 ■ *Web:* bankofva.com	Midlothian	VA	23112	804-744-7576	744-2306
Bank of Walterboro 1100 N Jeffries Blvd *Web:* bankofwalterboro.com	Walterboro	SC	29488	843-549-2265	
Bank Street Group LLC, The 4 Landmark Sq 3rd Fl *Web:* www.bankstreet.com	Stamford	CT	06901	203-252-2800	
Bank2 909 S Meridian *Web:* bank2online.com	Oklahoma City	OK	73108	405-946-2265	
BankAtlantic 200 W Second St *TF:* 800-226-5228 ■ *Web:* www.bbt.com	Winston-Salem	NC	27101	888-628-3926	
Bankeast 502 E Lamar Alexander Pkwy PO Box 24 *Web:* usbank.com	Maryville	TN	37804	865-984-0003	
Bankers' Bank 7700 Mineral Point Rd *TF:* 800-388-5550 ■ *Web:* www.bankersbankusa.com	Madison	WI	53717	608-833-5550	829-5590
Bankwest Corporation 2050 N California Blvd *TF:* 888-389-8668 ■ *Web:* www.bankofthewest.com	Walnut Creek	CA	94596	925-933-7810	
Bankwest Inc 420 S Pierre St PO Box 998 *TF:* 800-253-0362 ■ *Web:* www.bankwest-sd.com	Pierre	SD	57501	605-224-7391	224-7393
Banner Bank 10 S First Ave PO Box 907 **Fax:* Hum Res ■ *TF:* 800-272-9933 ■ *Web:* www.bannerbank.com	Walla Walla	WA	99362	509-527-3636	526-8898*
Banterra Corp 1404 US Rt 45 S *TF:* 877-541-2265 ■ *Web:* www.banterrabank.com	Eldorado	IL	62930	618-273-9346	
Baraboo BanCorp Inc, The 101 Third Ave	Baraboo	WI	53913	608-356-7703	
Barrington Bank & Trust Company Na 201 S Hough St *Web:* www.barringtonbank.com	Barrington	IL	60010	847-842-4500	304-6697
Bay Banks of Virginia Inc 100 S Main St PO Box 1869 *OTC:* BAYK ■ *Web:* www.bankoflancaster.com	Kilmarnock	VA	22482	804-435-1171	
Bay Business Credit 1460 Maria Ln Ste 300 *Web:* baybizcr.com	Walnut Creek	CA	94596	925-256-9003	
Baybank Corp 104 S 10th St *Web:* baybank.us	Gladstone	MI	49837	906-428-4040	
BB & T Corp 200 W Second St *NYSE:* BBT ■ *TF:* 800-226-5228 ■ *Web:* bbt.investorroom.com/corporate-information	Winston-Salem	NC	27101	336-733-1470	
BDO Capital Advisors LLC 1888 Century Park E *Web:* www.bdocap.com	Los Angeles	CA	90067	310-557-0300	
Beal Bank SSB 6000 Legacy Dr **Fax Area Code:* 972 ■ *Web:* www.bealbank.com	Plano	TX	75024	469-467-5000	309-3800*
Bear State Bank 600 Hwy 71 S *Web:* www.bearstatebank.com/home/home	Mena	AR	71953	479-394-3838	
Beneficial Mutual Savings Bank 530 Walnut St *TF:* 800-784-8490 ■ *Web:* www.thebeneficial.com	Philadelphia	PA	19106	215-864-6000	
Berkshire Bank PO Box 1308 *TF:* 800-773-5601 ■ *Web:* www.berkshirebank.com	Pittsfield	MA	01202	413-443-5601	443-3587
Better Banks 10225 N Knoxville Ave *Web:* betterbanks.com	Peoria	IL	61615	309-243-1000	
Blackbridge Partners LLC 800 W Cummings Pk Ste 2000 *Web:* www.blackbridgepartners.com	Woburn	MA	01801	617-273-2404	
Blue Ridge Bank & Trust Co 4240 Blue Ridge Blvd Ste 100 *TF:* 800-569-4287 ■ *Web:* www.blueridgebank.com	Kansas City	MO	64133	816-358-5000	252-2630
Blueharbor Bank 106 Corporate Park Dr *TF:* 877-322-8228 ■ *Web:* www.blueharborbank.com	Mooresville	NC	28117	704-662-7700	
BMO Harris Bank 111 W Monroe St *TF:* 888-340-2265 ■ *Web:* www.bmoharris.com	Chicago	IL	60603	847-238-2265	
BNA Bank 133 E Bankhead *Web:* bnabank.com	New Albany	MS	38652	662-534-8171	
BNC National Bank 322 E Main Ave *TF:* 800-262-2265 ■ *Web:* www.bncbank.com	Bismarck	ND	58501	701-250-3000	250-3028
Boiling Springs Savings Bank (BSSB) 25 Orient Way *TF:* 888-388-7459 ■ *Web:* www.bssbank.com	Rutherford	NJ	07070	201-939-5000	939-3957
Borel Private Bank & Trust Co 160 Bovet Rd *Web:* www.bostonprivate.com	San Mateo	CA	94402	650-378-3700	378-3774
Bowen Advisors Inc 25 Recreation Park Dr Ste 210 *Web:* www.bowenadvisors.com	Hingham	MA	02043	617-245-1660	
Branch Banking & Trust Company of South Carolina 301 College St *TF:* 800-226-5228 ■ *Web:* www.bbt.com	Greenville	SC	29601	800-226-5228	
BroadSpan Capital 1450 Brickell Ave Ste 2620 *Web:* www.brocap.com	Miami	FL	33131	305-424-3400	
Broadway Bank 1177 NE Loop 410 *Web:* www.broadwaybank.com	San Antonio	TX	78209	210-283-6500	
Brotherhood Bank & Trust 756 Minnesota Ave *TF:* 855-522-6722 ■ *Web:* www.brotherhoodbank.com	Kansas City	MO	66101	913-321-4242	
Brown Bros Harriman & Co 140 Broadway *Web:* www.bbh.com	New York	NY	10005	212-483-1818	
Burke & Herbert Bank & Trust Co 100 S Fairfax St *TF:* 877-440-0800 ■ *Web:* www.burkeandherbertbank.com	Alexandria	VA	22314	703-751-7701	

	City	State	Zip	Phone	Fax
Byline Bank 3639 N Broadway St.	Chicago	IL	60613	773-244-7000	
TF: 866-957-7700 ■ *Web:* www.northcommunitybank.com					
Byline Bank 3639 N Bdwy	Chicago	IL	60613	773-244-7000	
Web: www.bylinebank.com					
C1 Bank 2025 Lakewood Ranch Blvd	Lakewood Ranch	FL	34211	941-750-0700	
Web: www.c1bank.com					
Cabrillo Advisors LLC					
4330 La Jolla Village Dr Ste 270	San Diego	CA	92122	858-452-9500	
Web: www.cabrilloadvisors.com					
California Bank & Trust					
11622 El Camino Real Ste 200	San Diego	CA	92130	858-793-7400	793-7438
TF: 800-400-6080 ■ *Web:* www.calbanktrust.com					
Cambridge Savings Bank					
1374 Massachusetts Ave	Cambridge	MA	02138	617-441-4155	520-5306*
**Fax:* Cust Svc ■ *TF:* 888-418-5626 ■ *Web:* cambridgesavings.com					
Cambridge Trust Co 1336 Massachusetts Ave	Cambridge	MA	02138	617-876-5500	
Web: cambridgetrust.com					
Canadian Imperial Bank of Commerce (CIBC)					
199 Bay St Commerce Ct W	Toronto	ON	M5L1A2	800-465-2422	
NYSE: CM ■ *TF:* 800-465-2422 ■ *Web:* www.cibc.com					
Canadian Western Bank					
10303 Jasper Ave Ste 3000	Edmonton	AB	T5J3X6	780-423-8888	
TSE: CWB ■ *TF:* 866-317-0356 ■ *Web:* www.cwbank.com					
Canandaigua National Corp 72 S Main St	Canandaigua	NY	14424	585-394-4260	394-4001
OTC: CNND ■ *Web:* www.cnbank.com					
Cape Bank 225 N Main St	Cape May Court House	NJ	08210	609-465-5600	
Web: www.capebanknj.com					
Cape Cod Five Cents Savings Bank					
19 W Rd PO Box 20	Orleans	MA	02653	508-240-0555	
TF: 800-678-1855 ■ *Web:* www.capecodfive.com					
Capital Alliance Corp					
2777 N Stemmons Fwy Ste 1220	Dallas	TX	75207	214-638-8280	638-8009
Web: www.cadallas.com					
Capital City Bank					
2111 N Monroe St PO Box 900	Tallahassee	FL	32302	850-402-7500	
TF: 888-671-0400 ■ *Web:* www.ccbg.com					
Capital One Auto Finance Inc					
PO Box 60511	City of Industry	CA	91716	800-946-0332	
TF: 800-946-0332 ■ *Web:* www.capitalone.com					
Capital One FSB					
Capital One Bank 15000 Capital One Dr	Richmond	VA	23238	804-273-1144	
Web: www.capitalone.com					
Capitol FSB 700 S Kansas Ave	Topeka	KS	66603	785-235-1341	
TF: 888-822-7333 ■ *Web:* www.capfed.com					
Carolina Premier Bank					
13024 Ballantyne Corporate Pl Ste 100	Charlotte	NC	28277	704-752-9292	
Web: www.carolinapremierbank.com					
Carolina Trust Bank 901 E Main St	Lincolnton	NC	28092	704-735-1104	735-1104
NASDAQ: CART ■ *TF:* 877-983-5537 ■ *Web:* www.carolinatrust.com					
Carter Bank & Trust 1300 Kings Mtn Rd	Martinsville	VA	24112	276-656-1776	
Web: carterbankandtrust.com					
Carver FSB 75 W 125th St	New York	NY	10027	718-230-2900	
Web: www.carverbank.com					
Cascade Credit Services Inc					
1635 Se Malden St Ste D	Portland	OR	97202	503-722-2009	
Web: cascadecredit.com					
Casey State Bank 305-307 N Central Ave	Casey	IL	62420	217-932-2136	932-4370
TF: 866-666-2754 ■ *Web:* www.caseystatebank.com					
CBC National Bank 1891 S 14th St	Fernandina Beach	FL	32034	904-321-0400	277-0167
Web: cbcnationalbank.com					
CCB Community Bank 225 E Three Notch St	Andalusia	AL	36420	334-222-2561	
Web: bankccb.com					
CCC Investment Banking 150 King St W Ste 2020	Toronto	ON	M5H1J9	416-599-4206	
Web: www.cccinvestmentbanking.com					
CedarStone Bank 900 W Main St	Lebanon	TN	37087	615-443-1411	
Web: www.cedarstonebank.com					
Centerstate Banks Inc 42725 Us Hwy 27	Davenport	FL	33837	855-863-2265	
TF: 855-863-2265 ■ *Web:* centerstatebank.com					
Central BanCo 238 Madison St	Jefferson City	MO	65101	573-634-1155	
TF: 877-554-5535 ■ *Web:* www.centralbancompany.com					
Central Bank of Kansas City					
2301 Independence Ave	Kansas City	MO	64124	816-483-1210	483-2586
Web: www.centralbankkc.com					
Central National Bank 800 Se Quincy St	Topeka	KS	66612	785-234-2265	234-9660
Web: centralnational.com					
Centreville Savings Bank 1218 Main St	West Warwick	RI	02893	401-821-9100	
Web: www.centrevillebank.com					
Century National Bank 14 S Fifth St	Zanesville	OH	43701	740-454-2521	455-7201
TF Cust Svc: 800-548-3557 ■ *Web:* www.centurynationalbank.com					
CFG Community Bank 1422 Clarkview Rd	Baltimore	MD	21209	410-823-0500	823-6685
TF: 866-619-1417 ■ *Web:* www.cfgcommunitybank.com					
CharterBank 1233 OG Skinner Dr	West Point	GA	31833	706-645-1391	645-1370
TF: 800-763-4444 ■ *Web:* www.charterbk.com					
Chase Bank 1 Chase Manhattan Plz	New York	NY	10005	800-935-9935	
TF: 800-935-9935 ■ *Web:* www.chase.com					
Chesapeake Bank of Maryland					
2001 E Joppa Rd	Baltimore	MD	21234	410-661-1141	665-8604
Web: chesapeakebank.com					
Chiba Bank Ltd					
1133 Ave of the Americas 15th Fl	New York	NY	10036	212-354-7777	354-8575
Web: www.chibabank.co.jp/english/corporate/profile					
Chinatrust Bank USA					
801 S Figueroa St Ste 2300	Los Angeles	CA	90017	310-791-2828	
TF: 888-839-9000 ■ *Web:* www.chinatrustusa.com					
Choice Financial Group 645 Hill Ave	Grafton	ND	58237	701-352-0242	
Web: choicefinancialgroup.com					
Citibank (Delaware)					
4500 New Linden Hill Rd	Wilmington	DE	19808	302-323-3600	
TF: 800-374-9700					
Citibank NA 399 Pk Ave	New York	NY	10022	800-627-3999	
TF: 800-627-3999 ■ *Web:* citigroup.com					
Citibank (South Dakota) NA					
701 E 60th St N	Sioux Falls	SD	57104	605-331-2626	331-7518
TF: 800-627-3999 ■ *Web:* online.citi.com/us/welcome.c					
Citizen National Bank Of Bluffton, The					
102 S Main St PO Box 88	Bluffton	OH	45817	419-358-8040	
TF: 800-262-4663 ■ *Web:* www.cnbohio.com					
Citizens Bank of Clovis 420 Wheeler	Texico	NM	88135	575-482-3381	762-7259
TF: 844-657-3553 ■ *Web:* www.citizensbankofclovis.com					
Citizens Bank of Las Cruces 505 S Main St	Las Cruces	NM	88004	575-647-4100	
Web: www.citizenslc.com					
Citizens Bank of Massachusetts 28 State St	Boston	MA	02109	800-610-7300	
TF: 800-610-7300 ■ *Web:* www.citizensbank.com					
Citizens Bank of Mukwonago					
301 N Rochester St PO Box 223	Mukwonago	WI	53149	262-363-6500	363-6515
TF: 877-546-5868 ■ *Web:* www.citizenbank.com					
Citizens Bank of Rhode Island					
1 Citizens Plz	Providence	RI	02903	401-456-7000	455-5715
TF Cust Svc: 800-922-9999 ■ *Web:* www.citizensbank.com					
Citizens Business Bank (CBB) 701 N Haven Ave	Ontario	CA	91764	909-980-4030	481-2130
TF Cust Svc: 888-222-5432 ■ *Web:* www.cbbank.com					
Citizens Financial Services 707 Ridge Rd	Munster	IN	46321	219-836-5500	770-7572*
**Fax Area Code:* 317 ■ *TF:* 866-622-1370 ■ *Web:* www.firstmerchants.com					
Citizens State Bank					
1300 W Hildebrand Ave PO Box 5970	San Antonio	TX	78201	210-785-2300	785-2301
Web: Www.csbsa.com					
Citizens Trust Bank 1700 3rd Ave N	Birmingham	AL	35203	205-328-2041	
TF: 888-214-3099 ■ *Web:* www.ctbconnect.com					
City National Bank 400 N Roxbury Dr	Beverly Hills	CA	90210	310-888-6000	
TF Cust Svc: 800-773-7100 ■ *Web:* www.cnb.com					
City National Bank of Florida					
450 E Las Olas Blvd	Fort Lauderdale	FL	33301	954-467-6667	
TF: 800-762-2489 ■ *Web:* www.citynationalcm.com					
City National Bank of New Jersey (CNB)					
900 Broad St	Newark	NJ	07102	973-624-0865	624-5754
TF: 877-350-3524 ■ *Web:* www.citynatbank.com					
City National Bank of Sulphur Springs, The					
201 Connally	Sulphur Springs	TX	75482	903-885-7523	
City National Bank of West Virginia					
3601 McCorckle Ave	Charleston	WV	25304	304-926-3324	925-8073
TF: 888-816-8064 ■ *Web:* www.bankatcity.com					
City Savings Bank & Trust 301 N Pine St	Deridder	LA	70634	337-463-8661	
TF: 800-920-8661 ■ *Web:* citysavingsbank.com					
Clay County Savings Bank					
1178 W Kansas St PO Box 277	Liberty	MO	64069	816-781-4500	781-1668
Web: www.claycountysavings.com					
Clearfield Bank & Trust Co					
11 N Second St PO Box 171	Clearfield	PA	16830	814-765-7551	765-2943
TF: 888-765-7551 ■ *Web:* www.cbtfinancial.com					
Coast Capital Savings 645 Tyee Rd Ste 400	Victoria	BC	V9A6X5	250-483-7000	
TF: 888-517-7000 ■ *Web:* www.coastcapitalsavings.com					
College Savings Bank PO Box 3769	Princeton	NJ	08543	800-888-2723	987-3760*
**Fax Area Code:* 609 ■ *TF:* 800-888-2723 ■ *Web:* www.collegesavings.com					
Colorado East Bank & Trust Inc 100 W Pearl St	Lamar	CO	81052	719-336-5200	336-5944
Web: www.coloeast.com					
Colorado Fsb					
8400 E Prentice Ave Ste 545	Greenwood Village	CO	80111	303-793-3555	793-3560
TF: 877-484-2372 ■ *Web:* www.coloradofederalbank.com					
Colorado State Bank & Trust NA PO Box 2300	Tulsa	OK	74192	303-861-2111	
Web: www.csbt.com					
Columbia Bank, The 7168 Columbia Gateway Dr	Columbia	MD	21046	888-822-2265	
TF: 888-822-2265 ■ *Web:* www.thecolumbiabank.com					
Columbia Savings Bank 19-01 Rt 208	Fair Lawn	NJ	07410	800-522-4167	
TF Cust Svc: 800-747-4428 ■ *Web:* www.columbiabankonline.com					
Columbia State Bank PO Box 2156	Tacoma	WA	98401	253-305-1900	
TF: 800-305-1905 ■ *Web:* www.columbiabank.com					
Columbus Bank & Trust Co 1148 Broadway	Columbus	GA	31901	706-649-4900	
TF: 800-334-9007 ■ *Web:* columbusbankandtrust.synovus.com					
Comerica Bank 411 W Lafayette	Detroit	MI	48226	313-222-3344	
TF: 800-643-4418 ■ *Web:* www.comerica.com					
Comerica Bank-California					
333 W Santa Clara St	San Jose	CA	95113	408-556-5300	
TF: 800-522-2265 ■ *Web:* www.comerica.com					
Comerica Bank-Texas 1717 Main St	Dallas	TX	75201	800-925-2160	
TF: 800-925-2160 ■ *Web:* www.comerica.com					
Commerce Bank & Trust Co 386 Main St	Worcester	MA	01608	508-797-6842	797-6836
TF: 800-698-2265 ■ *Web:* www.bankatcommerce.com					
Commercewest Bank NA 2111 Business Ctr Dr	Irvine	CA	92612	949-251-6959	
OTC: CWBK ■ *Web:* www.cwbk.com					
Commercial Bank 301 N State St PO Box 638	Alma	MI	48801	989-463-2185	463-5996
OTC: CEFC ■ *TF:* 800-547-8531 ■ *Web:* www.commercial-bank.com					
Commerzbank AG 2 World Financial Ctr	New York	NY	10281	212-266-7200	266-7235
Web: www.corporates.commerzbank.com					
Commonwealth Bank of Australia					
599 Lexington Ave 17th Fl	New York	NY	10022	212-848-9200	
Web: www.commbank.com.au					
Commonwealth National Bank					
2214 St Stephens Rd	Mobile	AL	36617	251-476-5938	476-5946
Web: ecommonwealthbank.com					
Community Bank of Midwest					
2220 Broadway Ave	Great Bend	KS	67530	620-792-5111	
Web: www.communitybankmidwest.com					
Community Bank of Raymore PO Box 200	Raymore	MO	64083	816-322-2100	322-5915
TF: 800-322-6772 ■ *Web:* www.cbronline.net					
Community First Bank 925 Wisconsin Ave	Boscobel	WI	53805	608-375-4117	375-4119
Web: www.cfbank.com					
Community National Bank PO Box 259	Derby	VT	05829	802-334-7915	
Web: www.communitynationalbank.com					
Community State Bank					
1414 W 11th St PO Box 219	Coffeyville	KS	67337	620-251-1313	
Community Trust Bank NA					
346 N Mayo Trl PO Box 2947	Pikeville	KY	41501	606-432-1414	
TF: 800-422-1090 ■ *Web:* www.ctbi.com					
Confluence Advisors LLC 200 Wallace Rd	Wexford	PA	15090	724-940-1900	
Web: www.confluenceadvisorsllc.com					
Conneaut Savings Bank 305 Main St PO Box 740	Conneaut	OH	44030	440-599-8121	593-6446
TF: 888-453-2311 ■ *Web:* www.conneautsavings.com					

	City	State	Zip	Phone	Fax
Cornhusker Bank 1101 Cornhusker Hwy TF: 877-837-4481 ■ Web: www.cornhuskerbank.com	Lincoln	NE	68521	402-434-2265	434-2262
CorTrust Bank 1801 S Marion Rd Web: www.cortrustbank.com	Sioux Falls	SD	57106	605-361-8356	
Country Bank for Savings 75 Main St TF: 800-322-8233 ■ Web: www.countrybank.com	Ware	MA	01082	413-967-6221	967-3289
Creative Health Capital LLC 351 Hubbard St Ste 312 Web: www.chcapital.com	Chicago	IL	60654	312-574-3740	
Credit Union of Denver 9305 W Alameda Ave TF: 800-951-9014 ■ Web: www.cudenver.com	Lakewood	CO	80226	303-234-1700	239-1108
Crescent Bank & Trust 1100 Poydras St Ste 100 Web: cbtno.com	New Orleans	LA	70163	504-556-5950	552-4458
CRT Investment Banking LLC 262 Harbor Dr 3rd Fl Web: www.mmdillon.com	Stamford	CT	06902	203-569-6800	
CSB Bancshares Inc 203 N Douglas Web: csbanc.com	Ellsworth	KS	67439	785-472-3141	
CTS Capital Advisors LLC 7315 Wisconsin Ave Ste 500 E Web: www.ctsca.com	Bethesda	MD	20814	240-482-3240	
D L Evans Bank 397 N Overland PO Box 1188 TF: 888-873-9777 ■ Web: www.dlevans.com	Burley	ID	83318	208-678-9076	678-9093
Dakota Community Bank & Trust 1727 State St Web: dakotacommunitybank.com	Bismarck	ND	58501	701-255-9000	
Daroth Capital Advisors LLC 130 E 59th St 12th Fl Web: www.daroth.com	New York	NY	10022	212-687-2500	
Davis Capital Corp 200 S Wacker Dr 31st Fl Web: www.daviscapital.com	Chicago	IL	60606	312-623-4500	
DBS Bank Ltd 725 S Figueroa St TF: 800-209-4555 ■ Web: www.dbs.com	Los Angeles	CA	90017	213-627-0222	
Dedham Institution For Savings 55 Elm St PO Box 9107 TF: 888-289-0342 ■ Web: www.dedhamsavings.com	Dedham	MA	02026	781-329-6700	326-9893
Delta National Bank 2711 Mchenry Ave Web: www.deltabank.com	Modesto	CA	95350	209-527-3700	
Deutsche Bank Canada (DB) 199 Bay St Ste 4700 Commerce Ct W Web: www.db.com	Toronto	ON	M5L1E9	416-682-8000	682-8383
Devon Bank 6445 N Western Ave *Fax Area Code: 773 ■ TF: 866-683-3866 ■ Web: www.devonbank.com	Chicago	IL	60645	866-683-3866	973-5647*
Dexia Bank 445 Pk Ave 7th Fl Web: www.dexia.com	New York	NY	10022	212-515-7000	
Dime Bank, The 820 Church St PO Box 509 TF: 888-469-3463 ■ Web: www.thedimebank.com	Honesdale	PA	18431	570-253-1902	253-5845
Discover Bank PO Box 30416 TF: 800-347-7000 ■ Web: www.discover.com	Salt Lake City	UT	84130	302-323-7810	
Dollar Bank FSB 225 Forbes Ave TF: 800-828-5527 ■ Web: www.dollar.bank/personal	Pittsburgh	PA	15222	800-828-5527	
Durant Bancorp / First United Bank 1400 W Main TF: 800-924-4427 ■ Web: firstunitedbank.com	Durant	OK	74701	580-924-2211	
E*Trade Bank 671 N Glebe Rd *Fax Area Code: 678 ■ TF: 800-387-2331 ■ Web: us.etrade.com	Arlington	VA	22203	877-800-1208	624-8502*
East Boston Savings Bank 10 Meridian St TF: 800-657-3272 ■ Web: www.ebsb.com	Boston	MA	02128	617-567-1500	
Eastern Bank 1 Eastern Pl TF: 800-327-8376 ■ Web: www.easternbank.com	Lynn	MA	01901	781-599-2100	598-7697
El Dorado Savings Bank 4040 El Dorado Rd TF: 800-874-9779 ■ Web: www.eldoradosavingsbank.com	Placerville	CA	95667	530-622-1492	621-1659
Elmira Savings Bank 333 E Water St NASDAQ: ESBK ■ TF: 888-372-9299 ■ Web: www.elmirasavingsbank.com	Elmira	NY	14901	607-734-3374	
Empire State Bank 68 N Plank Rd Web: esbna.com	Newburgh	NY	12550	845-561-0003	
Encore Bank 3003 Tamiami Trail N Ste 100 TF: 800-472-3272 ■ Web: www.encorebank.com	Naples	FL	34103	239-919-5888	261-0578
Energy Capital Solutions LP 2651 N Harwood Ste 410 Web: www.nrgcap.com	Dallas	TX	75201	214-219-8200	
Ennis State Bank 815 W Ennis Ave Web: ennisstatebank.com	Ennis	TX	75119	972-875-9676	875-1574
Enterprise Bank of SC 13497 Broxton Bridge Rd PO Box 8 TF: 800-554-8969 ■ Web: www.ebanksc.com	Ehrhardt	SC	29081	803-267-3191	267-2316
Envoy Advisors 268 Summer St Web: www.envoyadvisors.com	Boston	MA	02210	617-292-7676	
Equitable Bank 113 N Locust St TF: 800-641-5046 ■ Web: equitableonline.com	Grand Island	NE	68802	308-382-3136	
Essex Savings Bank PO Box 950 TF: 877-377-3922 ■ Web: www.essexsavings.com	Essex	CT	06426	860-767-4414	767-4411
Euro Pacific Capital Inc 88 Post Rd W 2nd Fl TF: 800-727-7922 ■ Web: www.europac.com	Westport	CT	06880	203-662-9700	
Evangeline Bank & Trust Co, The 497 W Main St Web: www.therealbank.com	Ville Platte	LA	70586	337-363-5541	363-0678
Exchange State Bank 3992 Chandler St PO Box 68 TF: 888-488-9300 ■ Web: www.exchangestatebank.com	Carsonville	MI	48419	810-657-9333	
F&M Bank PO Box 1130 TF: 800-645-4199 ■ Web: www.myfmbank.com	Clarksville	TN	37041	931-645-2400	
Farm Bureau Bank 2165 Green Vista Dr Ste 204 *Fax Area Code: 866 ■ TF: 800-492-3276 ■ Web: farmbureaubank.com	Sparks	NV	89431	775-673-4566	913-5087*
Farmers Bank & Savings Company Inc 211 W Second St Web: www.fbsc.com	Pomeroy	OH	45769	740-992-2136	667-3162
Farmers Bank, The 9 E Clinton St PO Box 129 TF: 800-932-7368 ■ Web: www.thefarmersbank.com	Frankfort	IN	46041	765-654-8731	654-8738
Farmers Building & Savings Bank 290 W Park St	Rochester	PA	15074	724-774-4970	
Farmers Merchants Bank & Trust Co 100 S Main St PO Box 910 Web: www.fmbanking.com	Breaux Bridge	LA	70517	337-332-2115	332-5089
Farmers National Bank of Buhl 914 Main St PO Box 392 Web: www.farmersbankidaho.com	Buhl	ID	83316	208-543-4351	543-8323
Farmers National Bank of Prophetstown, The 114 W Third St Web: www.farmersnationalbank.com	Prophetstown	IL	61277	815-772-3700	
Farmers State Bancshares Inc 100 W Main St PO Box 9 Web: www.fsbankmctn.com	Mountain City	TN	37683	423-727-8121	727-5382
Farmers State Bank & Trust Co, The 200 W State St Web: www.fsbtco.com	Jacksonville	IL	62650	217-479-4000	
Fauquier Bank, The (TFB) 10 Courthouse Sq PO Box 561 TF: 800-638-3798 ■ Web: www.tfb.bank	Warrenton	VA	20186	540-347-2700	
Fidelity Bancshares Nc Inc PO Box 8 TF: 800-816-9608 ■ Web: www.fidelitybanknc.com	Fuquay Varina	NC	27526	919-552-2242	
Fidelity Bank 100 E English St *Fax Area Code: 316 ■ TF: 800-658-1637 ■ Web: www.fidelitybank.com	Wichita	KS	67201	800-658-1637	268-7383*
Fidelity Bank & Trust 9400 Old Hammond Hwy *Fax Area Code: 242	Baton Rouge	LA	70809	225-923-0232	326-3000*
Fidelity State Bank & Trust Co 600 S Kansas Ave Web: www.fidelitytopeka.com	Topeka	KS	66603	785-295-2100	233-7571
Fifth Third Bank Central Ohio 21 E State St TF: 866-671-5353 ■ Web: www.53.com	Columbus	OH	43215	800-972-3030	
First Alliance Bank 51 Germantown Ct Ste 100 Web: fabtn.com	Cordova	TN	38018	901-753-8339	
First American Bank 261 S Western Ave Web: www.firstambank.com	Carpentersville	IL	60110	847-426-6300	426-6300
First American Bank & Trust 2785 Hwy 20 W PO Box 550 TF: 800-738-2265 ■ Web: www.fabt.com	Vacherie	LA	70090	225-265-2265	265-7339
First Arkansas Bank & Trust 600 W Main St Web: www.fabandt.com	Jacksonville	AR	72076	501-982-4511	
First Bank Financial Centre (FBFC) 155 W Wisconsin Ave PO Box 1004 TF: 888-569-9909 ■ Web: www.fbfcwi.com	Oconomowoc	WI	53066	262-569-9900	
First Bank Muleshoe 202 S 1st PO Box 565 TF: 888-653-9558 ■ Web: fbmuleshoe.com	Muleshoe	TX	79347	806-272-4515	272-4436
First Bankers Trust Company NA 1201 Broadway PO Box 3566 Web: www.firstbankers.com	Quincy	IL	62305	217-228-8000	228-8091
First Bethany Bank & Trust 6500 NW 39th Expy Web: firstbethany.com	Bethany	OK	73008	405-789-1110	
First Business Financial Services Inc 401 Charmany Dr NASDAQ: FBIZ ■ TF: 888-455-2263 ■ Web: www.firstbusiness.com	Madison	WI	53719	608-238-8008	232-5994
First Calgary Savings 510 16th Ave NE *Fax Area Code: 403 ■ TF: 866-923-4778 ■ Web: www.firstcalgary.com	Calgary	AB	T2E1K4	866-923-4778	276-5299*
First Century Bank NA 500 Federal St TF: 877-214-9426 ■ Web: www.firstcentury.com	Bluefield	WV	24701	304-325-8181	325-3727
First Citizens Bank & Trust Co Inc 1230 Main St *Fax Area Code: 803 ■ TF: 888-612-4444 ■ Web: www.firstcitizens.com	Columbia	SC	29201	919-716-4588	733-2031*
First City Bank 1885 Northwest Blvd Web: bankcolumbusoh.com	Columbus	OH	43212	614-487-1010	
First Clover Leaf Bank 6814 Goshen Rd PO Box 540 Web: www.firstcloverleafbank.com	Edwardsville	IL	62025	618-656-6122	656-1712
First County Bank Inc, The 117 Prospect St Web: www.firstcountybank.com	Stamford	CT	06901	203-462-4407	
First Federal Bank Fsb 6900 N Executive Dr TF: 888-651-4759 ■ Web: www.ffbkc.com	Kansas City	MO	64120	816-241-7800	245-4348
First Federal Bank Of Ohio 1660 W Market St Ste A Web: www.firstfederalbankofohio.com	Tiffin	OH	44883	419-468-1518	468-2973
First Federal Lakewood 14806 Detroit Ave TF: 800-966-7300 ■ Web: www.ffl.net	Lakewood	OH	44107	216-529-2700	226-0622
First Financial Bank 1 First Financial Plz TF: 800-511-0045 ■ Web: www.first-online.com	Terre Haute	IN	47807	812-238-6000	238-6000
First Financial Bank 300 High St *Fax: Cust Svc ■ TF Cust Svc: 877-322-9530 ■ Web: www.bankatfirst.com	Hamilton	OH	45011	513-867-4744	867-3111*
First Financial Bank 301 W Beauregard Web: www.ffin.com	San Angelo	TX	76903	325-659-5900	
First Financial Bankshares 400 Pine St PO Box 701 NASDAQ: FFIN ■ Web: www.ffin.com	Abilene	TX	79601	806-363-8200	363-8295
First Foundation Bank 18101 Von Karman Ave Ste 750 TF: 800-224-7931 ■ Web: www.ff-inc.com	Irvine	CA	92612	949-202-4100	
First General Bank 1744 S Nogales St Web: www.fgbusa.com	Rowland Heights	CA	91748	626-820-1234	
First Hawaiian Bank 999 Bishop St TF: 888-844-4444 ■ Web: www.fhb.com	Honolulu	HI	96813	808-525-6340	
First Intercontinental Bank, The 5593 Buford Hwy Web: firsticbank.com	Doraville	GA	30340	770-451-7200	
First Interstate Bank 401 N 31st St TF: 888-752-3341 ■ Web: www.firstinterstatebank.com	Billings	MT	59101	406-255-5000	
First Jackson Bank 43243 Us Hwy 72 TF: 888-950-2265 ■ Web: firstjacksonbank.com	Stevenson	AL	35772	256-437-2107	
First Mercantile Trust Co 57 Germantown Ct 4th Fl TF: 800-753-3682 ■ Web: www.firstmerc.com	Cordova	TN	38018	901-753-9080	
First Metro Bank 406 Avalon Ave Web: www.firstmetro.com	Muscle Shoals	AL	35661	256-386-0600	386-0651

Name / Address	City	State	Zip	Phone	Fax
First Mid-Illinois Bank & Trust 1515 Charleston Ave *OTC: FMBH* ■ *Web:* www.firstmid.com	Mattoon	IL	61938	217-258-0653	258-0426
First National Bank PO Box 578 *TF:* 800-883-8773 ■ *Web:* www.1stnationalbank.com	Fort Collins	CO	80521	970-495-9450	
First National Bank 316 E Bremer Ave PO Box 837 *Web:* www.myfnbbank.com	Waverly	IA	50677	319-352-1340	352-6323
First National Bank Alaska 101 W 36 Ave PO Box 100720 *OTC: FBAK* ■ *TF:* 800-856-4362 ■ *Web:* www.fnbalaska.com	Anchorage	AK	99510	907-777-4362	
First National Bank Creston PO Box 445 *TF:* 877-782-2195 ■ *Web:* www.fnbcreston.com	Creston	IA	50801	641-782-2195	
First National Bank In Alamogordo 414 Tenth St PO Box 9 *Web:* fnbalamo.com	Alamogordo	NM	88311	575-437-4880	437-1631
First National Bank In Tremont 134 S Sampson St PO Box 23 *Web:* www.tremontbank.com	Tremont	IL	61568	309-925-2121	925-5448
First National Bank of Illinois Inc 3256 Ridge Rd *Web:* www.fnbiweb.com	Lansing	IL	60438	708-474-1300	
First National Bank Of Jasper 200 W 18th St *Web:* firstbankofjasper.synovus.com	Jasper	AL	35501	205-221-3121	
First National Bank of Muscatine 300 E Second St *Web:* www.fnbmusc.com	Muscatine	IA	52761	563-263-4221	262-4213
First National Bank of Omaha 1620 Dodge St *TF:* 800-462-5266 ■ *Web:* www.fnbomaha.com	Omaha	NE	68197	402-341-0500	342-4332
First National Bank of Oneida, The 18418 Alberta St PO Box 4699 *TF:* 866-546-8273 ■ *Web:* www.fnboneida.com	Oneida	TN	37841	423-569-8586	569-9826
First National Bank of Paragould 200 W Ct St *Web:* www.fnbank.net	Paragould	AR	72450	870-239-8521	
First National Bank of Santa Fe PO Box 609 *TF:* 888-912-2265 ■ *Web:* www.firstnationalsantafe.com	Santa Fe	NM	87504	505-992-2000	
First National Bank of South Miami 5750 Sunset Dr. *Web:* fnbsm.com	Miami	FL	33143	305-667-5511	662-5440
First National Bankers Bankshares Inc (FNBB) 7813 Office Pk Blvd *TF:* 800-421-6182 ■ *Web:* www.bankers-bank.com	Baton Rouge	LA	70809	225-924-8015	952-0899
First NBC (CPB) 29092 Kretel Rd *TF:* 800-423-7503 ■ *Web:* www.firstnbcbank.com	Lacombe	LA	70445	985-819-1200	
First Newton National Bank 100 N Second Ave W *Web:* firstnnb.com	Newton	IA	50208	641-792-3010	
First Niagara Financial Group 726 Exchange St Ste 618 *TF:* 800-421-0004 ■ *Web:* www.firstniagara.com	Buffalo	NY	14210	716-625-7500	
First Palmetto Savings Bank Fsb PO Box 430 *TF:* 800-922-7411 ■ *Web:* www.firstpalmetto.com	Camden	SC	29021	803-432-2265	
First Personal Bank 14701 Ravinia Ave *Web:* firstpersonalbank.net	Orland Park	IL	60462	708-226-2727	
First Pryority Bank 310 E Graham *Web:* www.firstpryoritybank.com	Pryor	OK	74361	918-825-2121	
First Reliance Bank 2170 W Palmetto St *Web:* firstreliance.com	Florence	SC	29501	843-656-5000	
First Republic Bank 111 Pine St *NYSE: FRC* ■ *TF:* 800-392-1400 ■ *Web:* www.firstrepublic.com	San Francisco	CA	94111	415-392-1400	392-1413
First Savings Bank 2804 N Telshor Blvd *TF:* 800-555-6895 ■ *Web:* www.firstsavingsbanks.com	Las Cruces	NM	88011	575-521-7931	
First Security Bank of Missoula 1704 Dearborn PO Box 4506 *TF:* 888-782-3115 ■ *Web:* www.fsbmsla.com	Missoula	MT	59801	406-728-3115	
First Security Bank of Sleepy Eye 100 E Main PO Box 469 *Web:* www.firstsecuritybanks.com	Sleepy	MN	56085	507-794-3911	794-5140
First Sentinel Bank 315 Railroad Ave *Web:* firstsentinelbank.com	Richlands	VA	24641	276-963-0836	
First State Bank 708 Azalea Dr PO Box 506 **Fax Area Code:* 601 ■ *TF:* 866-408-3582 ■ *Web:* www.firststatebnk.com	Waynesboro	MS	39367	866-408-3582	735-0231*
First State Bank & Trust Co 1005 E 23rd St *TF:* 888-674-4344 ■ *Web:* www.firststatebankandtrust.com	Fremont	NE	68025	402-721-2500	727-0208
First State Bank of Kansas City 650 Kansas Ave *TF:* 800-883-1242 ■ *Web:* www.cfbkc.com	Kansas City	KS	66105	913-371-1242	371-7516
First Tennessee Bank 165 Madison Ave **Fax:* Mktg ■ *TF:* 800-382-5465 ■ *Web:* www.firsttennessee.com	Memphis	TN	38103	901-523-4883	523-4145*
First Texas Bank 501 E Third St *TF:* 866-220-1598 ■ *Web:* www.firstexbank.com	Lampasas	TX	76550	512-556-3691	556-6104
First Utah BanCorp 3826 South 2300 East *Web:* firstutahbank.com	Salt Lake City	UT	84109	801-272-9454	
First Western Bank & Trust PO Box 1090 *TF:* 800-688-2584 ■ *Web:* bankfirstwestern.com	Minot	ND	58702	701-852-3711	857-7195
First Whitney Bank & Trust 223 Chestnut St PO Box 271 *Web:* firstwhitneybank.com	Atlantic	IA	50022	712-243-3195	
First-Knox National Bank 1 S Main St *TF:* 800-837-5266 ■ *Web:* www.firstknox.com	Mount Vernon	OH	43050	740-399-5500	
FirsTier Bank (Kimball NE) 115 S Walnut *Web:* www.firstierbanks.com	Kimball	NE	69145	308-235-4633	
Firstrust Savings Bank 15 E Ridge Pike 4th Fl *TF:* 800-220-2265 ■ *Web:* www.firstrust.com	Conshohocken	PA	19428	610-941-9898	941-5544
Flagstar Bank FSB 5151 Corporate Dr *TF:* 800-945-7700 ■ *Web:* www.flagstar.com	Troy	MI	48098	248-312-2000	
Florence Savings Bank 85 Main St PO Box 60700 *Web:* www.florencebank.com	Florence	MA	01062	413-586-1300	582-9947
Floridian Financial Group 175 Timacuan Blvd *Web:* floridianfinancialgroup.com	Lake Mary	FL	32746	407-321-3233	
Flushing Savings Bank FSB 144-51 Northern Blvd *Web:* www.flushingbank.com	Flushing	NY	11354	718-512-2929	
Foresight Financial Group Inc 3106 N Rockton Ave *Web:* foresightfg.com	Rockford	IL	61103	815-847-7500	
Foster Bank 5225 N Kedzie Ave *Web:* fosterbank.com	Chicago	IL	60625	773-588-7700	
Founders Community Bank 237 Higuera St *Web:* founderscommunitybank.com	San Luis Obispo	CA	93401	805-543-6500	
Four Oaks Bank & Trust Co PO Box 309 *TF:* 877-963-6257 ■ *Web:* www.fouroaksbank.com	Four Oaks	NC	27524	919-963-2177	963-2768
Fowler State Bank 300 E Fifth St PO Box 511 *TF:* 800-439-3951 ■ *Web:* www.fowlerstatebank.com	Fowler	IN	47944	765-884-1200	
Fox Chase Bank 4390 Davisville Rd *Web:* foxchasebank.com	Hatboro	PA	19040	215-682-7400	
Franchise Capital Advisors Inc 9903 E Bell Rd Ste 130 *Web:* www.franchisecapitaladvisors.com	Scottsdale	AZ	85260	480-355-4390	
Fremont Bank PO Box 5101 *TF:* 800-359-2265 ■ *Web:* www.fremontbank.com	Fremont	CA	94538	510-792-2300	
Frontenac Bank 3330 Rider Trl S *TF:* 877-205-5777 ■ *Web:* www.frontenacbank.com	Earth City	MO	63045	314-298-8200	
Galway Group LP 3009 Post Oak Blvd Ste 950 *Web:* www.galwaylp.com	Houston	TX	77056	713-952-0186	
Garden State Community Bank (GSCB) 36 Ferry St *NYSE: NYB* ■ *TF:* 877-786-6560	Newark	NJ	07105	973-589-8616	589-1141
Garnett State Savings Bank 106 E Fifth St PO Box 329 *Web:* www.gssb.us.com	Garnett	KS	66032	785-448-3111	448-6613
Gebsco Inc 245 S Eau Claire St	Mondovi	WI	54755	715-926-4234	
Genesis Capital LLC 3414 Peachtree Rd Ne Ste 700 *TF:* 800-998-8479 ■ *Web:* www.genesis-capital.com	Atlanta	GA	30326	404-816-7540	
Giantbank.com 6300 NE First Ave *TF:* 877-446-4200 ■ *Web:* www.giantbank.com	Fort Lauderdale	FL	33334	954-958-0001	958-0190
Gibraltar Savings Bank 1039 S Orange Ave *Web:* gibraltarbanknj.com	Newark	NJ	07106	973-372-1221	
Glenview State Bank 800 Waukegan Rd *Web:* gsb.com	Glenview	IL	60025	847-729-1900	
Glenwood State Bank 5 E Minnesota Ave PO Box 197 *TF:* 800-207-7333 ■ *Web:* www.glenwoodstate.com	Glenwood	MN	56334	320-634-5111	634-5114
Golden Valley Bank Community Foundation 190 Cohasset Rd Ste 170 *TF:* 800-808-2070 ■ *Web:* www.goldenvalleybank.com	Chico	CA	95926	530-894-1000	
Gorham Savings Bank 64 Main St *Web:* www.gorhamsavingsbank.com	Gorham	ME	04038	207-839-4450	839-4790
Grants State Bank 824 W Santa Fe Ave PO Box 1088 *TF:* 877-285-6611 ■ *Web:* www.grantsbank.com	Grants	NM	87020	505-285-6611	287-2260
Grayson National Bank (GNB) 113 W Main St *Web:* www.graysonnationalbank.com	Independence	VA	24348	276-773-2811	
Great Western Bank 6015 NW Radial Hwy **Fax Area Code:* 515 ■ *TF:* 800-952-2043 ■ *Web:* www.greatwesternbank.com	Omaha	NE	68104	402-952-6000	223-6057*
Greenfield Savings Bank 400 Main St PO Box 1537 *TF:* 888-324-3191 ■ *Web:* www.greenfieldsavings.com	Greenfield	MA	01302	413-774-3191	
Greensburg State Bank 240 S Main St *Web:* bestbank.us	Greensburg	KS	67054	620-723-2131	
GreensLedge Group LLC, The 520 Madison Ave 37th Fl *Web:* www.greensledge.com	New York	NY	10022	212-792-5270	
Greenville First Bank 100 Verdae Blvd Ste 100 *TF:* 877-679-9646 ■ *Web:* www.southernfirst.com	Greenville	SC	29072	864-679-9000	679-9099
Guaranty Bank 4000 W Brown Deer Rd *TF:* 800-235-4636 ■ *Web:* www.guarantybank.com	Brown Deer	WI	53209	414-362-4000	290-6433
Guaranty Bank & Trust Co PO Box 1807 *TF:* 800-362-2119 ■ *Web:* www.guaranty-bank.com	Cedar Rapids	IA	52406	319-286-6200	362-7894
Guaranty State Bank & Trust Company Beloit Kansas, The 201 S Mill St *TF:* 888-738-8000 ■ *Web:* guarantystate.com	Beloit	KS	67420	785-738-3501	
Guilford Savings Bank (GSB) PO Box 369 *TF:* 866-878-1480 ■ *Web:* www.gsb-yourbank.com	Guilford	CT	06437	203-453-2015	458-3927
Gulf Coast Bank 4310 Johnston St *TF:* 800-722-5363 ■ *Web:* www.gcbank.com	Lafayette	LA	70503	337-989-1133	
Habib American Bank 99 Madison Ave *Web:* www.habbank.com	New York	NY	10016	212-532-4444	532-7136
Hamler State Bank 210 Randolph St PO Box 358 *TF:* 888-508-3955 ■ *Web:* www.hamlerstatebank.com	Hamler	OH	43524	419-274-3955	
Hampton Roads Bankshares Inc 999 Waterside Dr *NASDAQ: HMPR* ■ *Web:* www.bankofhamptonroads.com	Norfolk	VA	23510	757-217-1000	
Hardin County Bank, The (HCB) 235 Wayne Rd PO Box 940 *Web:* www.hardincountybank.com	Savannah	TN	38372	731-925-9001	925-8106
Harvard Savings Bank 58 N Ayer St *Web:* harvardsavingsbank.com	Harvard	IL	60033	815-943-5261	
Hastings City Bank 150 W Court St *Web:* hastingscitybank.com	Hastings	MI	49058	269-945-2401	
Hatboro Federal Savings 221 S York Rd *Web:* www.hatborofed.com	Hatboro	PA	19040	215-675-4000	672-6684
Havana National Bank, The 112 S Orange St	Havana	IL	62644	309-543-3361	
Hebron Savings Bank (HSB) 101 N Main St PO Box 59 *Web:* www.hebronsavingsbank.com	Hebron	MD	21830	410-749-1185	543-0703
Hemet Bancorp 3715 Sunnyside Dr	Riverside	CA	92506	951-784-5771	
Heritage Group Inc 1101 12th St *TF:* 888-463-6611 ■ *Web:* www.bankonheritage.com	Aurora	NE	68818	402-694-3136	
Hibernia Bancorp Inc 325 Carondelet St *Web:* hibbank.com	New Orleans	LA	70130	504-522-3203	

Name / Address	City	State	ZIP	Phone	Fax
Hickory Point Bank & Trust FSB PO Box 2548 *TF Cust Svc:* 800-872-0081 ■ *Web:* www.hickorypointbank.com	Decatur	IL	62525	217-875-3131	
Highland Community Bank 307 Thacker Ave PO Box 1059 *Web:* www.highlandscommunitybank.com	Covington	VA	24426	540-962-2265	962-1203
Hills Bank & Trust Co 131 Main St PO Box 70 *TF:* 800-445-5725 ■ *Web:* www.hillsbank.com	Hills	IA	52235	319-679-2291	679-2180
Hingham Institution for Savings 55 Main St. *NASDAQ: HIFS* ■ *Web:* www.hinghamsavings.com	Hingham	MA	02043	781-749-2200	740-4889
Hocking Valley Bank 7 W Stimson Ave *TF:* 888-482-5854 ■ *Web:* www.hvbonline.com	Athens	OH	45701	740-592-4441	594-3147
Home Federal Bank 225 S Main Ave *TF:* 800-244-2149 ■ *Web:* www.homefederal.com	Sioux Falls	SD	57104	605-336-2470	333-7591
Home Savings & Loan Company of Youngstown 275 W Federal St *TF:* 888-822-4751 ■ *Web:* www.homesavings.com	Youngstown	OH	44503	330-742-0500	742-0615
HomeStreet Bank 601 Union St 2 Union Sq Ste 2000 *TF:* 800-654-1075 ■ *Web:* homestreet.com	Seattle	WA	98101	206-623-3050	389-4458
Hometown Bank 245 N Peters Ave *TF:* 877-261-2220 ■ *Web:* www.hometownbancorp.com	Fond du Lac	WI	54935	920-907-2220	
Hometrust Bank, The PO Box 10 *TF:* 800-627-1632 ■ *Web:* www.hometrustbanking.com	Asheville	NC	28802	828-259-3939	
Homewood FSB 3228-30 Eastern Ave *TF:* 800-554-8969 ■ *Web:* www.homewoodfsb.com	Baltimore	MD	21224	410-327-5220	558-1719
Hopkins Financial Corp 100 E Havens *Web:* cortrustbank.com	Mitchell	SD	57301	605-996-7775	
Houlihan Valuation Advisors Inc 28662 W Northwest Hwy Ste 3 *Web:* www.houlihan-hva.com	Lake Barrington	IL	60010	847-381-3616	
Hudson City Savings Bank W 80 Century Rd *TF:* 800-222-0194	Paramus	NJ	07652	201-967-1900	
Hudson Valley Bank 21 Scarsdale Rd *Web:* www.hudsonvalleybank.com	Yonkers	NY	10707	914-961-6100	
Huntington National Bank 41 S High St Huntington Ctr *TF:* 800-480-2265 ■ *Web:* www.huntington.com	Columbus	OH	43287	614-480-8300	480-4973
Huron Community Bank 301 Newman St *Web:* bankhcb.com	East Tawas	MI	48730	989-362-6700	
Hyden Citizens Bank 22023 Main St PO Box 948 *Web:* www.hydencitizensbank.com	Hyden	KY	41749	606-672-2344	672-3627
Iberville Bank 23405 Eden St *Web:* ibervillebank.com	Plaquemine	LA	70764	225-687-2091	687-0539
Illinois National Bank 322 E Capitol *TF:* 877-771-2316 ■ *Web:* www.illinoisnationalbank.com	Springfield	IL	62701	217-747-5500	747-5530
Illinois Service Federal S & L 4619 S King Dr *Web:* www.isfbank.com	Chicago	IL	60653	773-624-2000	624-5340
Independence FSB 1301 Ninth St NW *Web:* www.ifsb.com	Washington	DC	20001	202-628-5500	
Indiana Bankers Assn 6925 Parkdale Pl *Web:* www.indianabankers.org	Indianapolis	IN	46254	317-387-9380	
Industrial Bank NA 4812 Georgia Ave NW **Fax Area Code:* 800 ■ *Web:* www.industrial-bank.com	Washington	DC	20011	202-722-2000	461-5056*
Inova Federal Credit Union 358 S Elkhart Ave *Web:* inovafcu.org	Elkhart	IN	46516	574-294-6553	
InsurBanc 10 Executive Dr *TF:* 866-467-2262 ■ *Web:* www.insurbanc.com	Farmington	CT	06032	860-677-9701	677-9793
Integra Technologies LLC 3450 N Rock Rd Bldg 100 Ste 111 *Web:* integra-tech.com	Wichita	KS	67226	316-630-6800	
Inter-County Bakers Inc 1095 Long Island Ave *TF:* 800-696-1350 ■ *Web:* www.icbakers.com	Deer Park	NY	11729	631-957-1350	957-1013
InterBank 4921 N May Ave *Web:* www.interbank.com	Oklahoma City	OK	73112	405-782-4200	
Investors Savings Bank 101 Wood Ave S *NASDAQ: ISBC* ■ *TF:* 855-422-6548 ■ *Web:* www.myinvestorsbank.com	Iselin	NJ	08830	973-924-5100	376-5357
Inwood National Bank 7621 Inwood Rd *Web:* www.inwoodbank.com	Dallas	TX	75209	214-358-5281	351-7381
Iowa State Savings Bank 401 W Adams St *TF:* 888-508-0142 ■ *Web:* issbbank.com	Creston	IA	50801	641-782-1000	
Ireland Bank 33 Bannock St *Web:* ireland-bank.com	Malad City	ID	83252	208-766-2254	
Israel Discount Bank of New York (IDBB) 511 Fifth Ave *Web:* www.idbny.com	New York	NY	10017	212-551-8500	551-8540
Jeff Davis Bancshares Inc 507 N Main St PO Box 730 *OTC: JDVB* ■ *TF:* 800-789-5159 ■ *Web:* www.jdbank.com	Jennings	LA	70546	337-824-3424	824-7283
Jersey Shore State Bank 300 Market St PO Box 967 *TF:* 888-412-5772 ■ *Web:* www.jssb.com	Williamsport	PA	17701	570-322-1111	
Jersey State Bank 1000 S State St *Web:* jerseystatebank.com	Jerseyville	IL	62052	618-498-6466	
Johnson Bank 4001 N Main St *Web:* johnsonbank.com	Racine	WI	53402	262-639-6010	
JP Morgan Chase & Co 270 Pk Ave *Web:* www.jpmorganchase.com	New York	NY	10017	212-270-6000	
JumpStart Partners Inc 3616 Far W Blvd Ste 117-294 *Web:* www.jumpstartpartners.com	Austin	TX	78731	512-576-9000	
Kearny FSB 120 Passaic Ave **Fax Area Code:* 201 ■ *TF:* 800-273-3406 ■ *Web:* www.kearnybank.com	Fairfield	NJ	07004	973-244-4500	991-6713*
Kennebec Savings Bank 150 State St PO Box 50 *TF:* 888-303-7788 ■ *Web:* www.kennebecsavings.com	Augusta	ME	04332	207-622-5801	626-2858
Kentucky Bank PO Box 157 *TF:* 877-322-8228 ■ *Web:* www.kybank.com	Paris	KY	40362	859-987-1795	
Key Bank 65 Dutch Hill Rd *TF Cust Svc:* 800-539-2968 ■ *Web:* www.key.com	Orangeburg	NY	10962	800-539-2968	
Kingston National Bank 2 N Main St PO Box 613 *TF:* 866-642-2191 ■ *Web:* www.kingstonnationalbank.com	Kingston	OH	45644	740-642-2191	
Kirkwood Bank & Trust Co 2911 N 14th St *TF:* 800-492-4955 ■ *Web:* kirkwoodbank.com	Bismarck	ND	58503	701-258-6550	
Kish Bancorp Inc 4255 E Main St PO Box 917 *OTC: KISB* ■ *TF:* 888-554-4748 ■ *Web:* www.kishbank.com	Belleville	PA	17004	717-935-2191	935-5511
Klein Financial Inc 1550 Audubon Rd *Web:* kleinbank.com	Chaska	MN	55318	952-448-2484	
KPMG Corporate Finance LLC 345 Park Ave *Web:* corporatefinance.kpmg.us	New York	NY	10154	212-758-9700	
Labette Bank 4th & Huston PO Box 497 *TF:* 800-711-5311 ■ *Web:* www.labettebank.com	Altamont	KS	67330	620-784-5311	784-5323
Lake Bank Shares Inc 437 Bridge Ave	Albert Lea	MN	56007	507-373-1481	
Lakeside Bank 55 W Wacker Dr *TF:* 866-892-1572 ■ *Web:* www.lakesidebank.com	Chicago	IL	60601	312-435-5100	
Lamesa National Bank, The 602 S First St	Lamesa	TX	79331	806-872-5457	
Landmark Bank 801 E Broadway *Web:* landmarkbank.com	Columbia	MO	65201	573-499-7333	
LaPorte Savings Bank, The 710 Indiana Ave *TF:* 866-362-7511 ■ *Web:* www.laportesavingsbank.com	LaPorte	IN	46350	219-362-7511	324-2269
Laurentian Bank of Canada 1981 McGill College Ave *TSE: LB* ■ *TF:* 800-252-1846 ■ *Web:* www.laurentianbank.ca	Montreal	QC	H3A3K3	514-284-4500	284-3988
LCNB National Bank 3209 W Galbraith Rd *TF:* 800-344-2265 ■ *Web:* www.lcnb.com	Cincinnati	OH	45239	513-932-1414	741-0019
Leaders Bank, The 2001 York Rd Ste 150 *Web:* leadersbank.com	Oak Brook	IL	60523	630-572-5323	
Ledyard National Bank 320 Main St *Web:* www.ledyardbank.com	Norwich	VT	05055	802-649-2050	649-2060
Legacy Bank 1580 E Cheyenne Mtn Blvd *TF:* 866-627-0800 ■ *Web:* www.elegacybank.com	Colorado Springs	CO	80906	719-579-9150	226-6694
Liberty Bank 315 Main St *TF:* 800-622-6732 ■ *Web:* www.liberty-bank.com	Middletown	CT	06457	800-354-8950	
Liberty Bank & Trust Co PO Box 60131 *TF:* 800-883-3943 ■ *Web:* www.libertybank.net	New Orleans	LA	70160	504-240-5100	
Liberty Savings Bank FSB 2251 Rombach Ave *TF:* 800-436-6300 ■ *Web:* www.libertysavingsbank.com	Wilmington	OH	45177	800-436-6300	
Libertyville Bank & Trust Co 507 N Milwaukee Ave **Fax Area Code:* 866 ■ *Web:* www.libertyvillebank.com	Libertyville	IL	60048	847-367-6800	468-0952*
Litchfield National Bank 316 N State St *Web:* www.litchfieldnationalbank.com	Litchfield	IL	62056	217-324-6161	
Little Bank Inc, The 804 Carey Rd *OTC: LTLB* ■ *TF:* 855-449-0975 ■ *Web:* www.thelittlebank.com	Kinston	NC	28501	252-939-9990	317-2837
Llano National Bank 1001 Ford St *Web:* www.llanonationalbank.com	Llano	TX	78643	325-247-5701	247-3765
Lone Star National Bank Shares Neveda 520 E Nolana Ave Ste 110 *Web:* www.lonestarnationalbank.com	Mcallen	TX	78504	956-682-1722	
Lowell Five Cent Savings Bank, The 1 Merrimack Plz *Web:* www.lowellfive.com	Lowell	MA	01852	978-452-1300	
Lubbock National Bank 4811 50th St PO Box 6100 *Web:* lubbocknational.com	Lubbock	TX	79493	806-792-1000	792-0976
Luther Burbank Savings 804 Fourth St *TF:* 888-205-6005 ■ *Web:* www.lutherburbanksavings.com	Santa Rosa	CA	95404	707-578-9216	526-7844
M & I Bank Northeast 310 W Walnut St *Web:* www.bmoharris.com	Green Bay	WI	54303	920-436-1800	
M&T Bank 1 M & T Plz 13th Fl *NYSE: MTB* ■ *TF:* 800-724-2440 ■ *Web:* www.mtb.com	Buffalo	NY	14203	716-842-4470	
Machias Savings Bank 4 Ctr St PO Box 318 *TF:* 800-982-7179 ■ *Web:* www.machiassavings.com	Machias	ME	04654	207-255-3347	255-3170
Mackinac Savings Bank FSB 2901-A N Military Trl *Web:* www.mackbank.com	West Palm Beach	FL	33409	561-686-2352	638-2616
Macquarie Infrastructure Company Inc 125 W 55th St *NYSE: MIC* ■ *Web:* www.macquarie.com	New York	NY	10019	212-231-1000	231-1010
Magyar Bancorp Inc 400 Somerset St *NASDAQ: MGYR* ■ *Web:* www.magbank.com/home/home	New Brunswick	NJ	08901	732-342-7600	
Magyar Bank 400 Somerset St *TF:* 800-472-3272 ■ *Web:* www.magbank.com	New Brunswick	NJ	08901	732-342-7600	
Main Banc Inc 2424 Louisiana Blvd Ne *Web:* mainbank.com	Albuquerque	NM	87110	505-880-1700	
Main Source Bank 201 N Broadway **Fax Area Code:* 812 ■ *TF:* 800-713-6083 ■ *Web:* www.mainsourcebank.com	Greensburg	IN	47240	800-713-6083	663-4904*
Malvern FSB Inc 42 E Lancaster Ave *Web:* www.malvernfederal.com	Paoli	PA	19301	610-644-9400	
Maren Group LLC 11th Fl 400 Madison Ave	New York	NY	10017	212-584-2340	
Marine Bank of Champaign-Urbana 2434 Village Green Pl *Web:* www.ibankmarine.com	Champaign	IL	61822	217-239-0100	
Marquette Bank 10000 W 151st St *TF:* 888-254-9500 ■ *Web:* www.emarquettebank.com	Orland Park	IL	60462	708-226-8026	
Marquette Savings Bank 920 Peach St *TF:* 866-672-3743 ■ *Web:* www.marquettesavings.com	Erie	PA	16501	814-455-4481	453-5345
Maspeth Federal Savings 56-18 69th St *TF:* 888-558-1300 ■ *Web:* www.maspethfederal.com	Maspeth	NY	11378	718-335-1300	446-3671
Max Credit Union 400 Eastdale Cir *TF:* 800-776-6776 ■ *Web:* www.mymax.com	Montgomery	AL	36117	334-260-2600	
Mayville Savings Bank 200 S Main St *Web:* mayvillesavings.com	Mayville	WI	53050	920-387-2310	
Mc Kenzie Banking Co (MBC) 676 N Main St *Web:* www.foundationbank.org	McKenzie	TN	38201	731-352-2262	352-7778
McHenry Savings Bank 353 Bank Dr *Web:* www.mchenrysavings.com	McHenry	IL	60050	815-385-3000	385-4433
MCNB Bank & Trust Co PO Box 549 *TF:* 800-532-9553 ■ *Web:* www.mcnbbanks.com	Welch	WV	24801	304-436-4112	
MEA Advisors LLC Graybar Bldg Ste 300 420 Lexington Ave *Web:* www.meaadvisorsllc.com	New York	NY	10170	212-249-2239	

	City	State	Zip	Phone	Fax
Mechanics Savings Bank 100 Minot Ave PO Box 400	Auburn	ME	04210	207-786-5700	786-5709
TF: 877-886-1020 ■ *Web:* www.mechanicssavings.com/home/home					
Members Trust Co 14025 Riveredge Dr Ste 280	Tampa	FL	33637	813-631-9191	
TF: 888-727-9191 ■ *Web:* www.memberstrust.com					
Meramec Valley Bank 199 Clarkson Rd	Ellisville	MO	63011	636-230-3500	230-3191
Web: www.meramecvalleybank.com					
Mercana Growth Partners 390 Bay St Ste 1706	Toronto	ON	M5H2Y2	416-947-1300	
Web: www.mercanagrowth.com					
Merchants National Bank of Bangor Inc 25 Broadway PO Box 227	Bangor	PA	18013	610-588-0981	588-6886
TF: 877-678-6622 ■ *Web:* www.merchantsbangor.com					
Meredith Village Savings Bank (MVSB) 24 State Rt 25 PO Box 177	Meredith	NH	03253	603-279-7986	279-5710
TF: 800-922-6872 ■ *Web:* www.mvsb.com					
Mesa 85 Fifth Ave 6th Fl	New York	NY	10003	212-792-3950	
Web: www.mesaglobal.com					
Metairie Bank & Trust Co 3344 Metairie Rd	Metairie	LA	70001	504-834-6330	
Web: www.metairiebank.com					
Metropolitan National Bank 501 Main St	Pine Bluff	AR	71601	870-541-1000	
Web: simmonsfirst.com					
Midamerica National Bancshares 100 W Elm St	Canton	IL	61520	309-647-5000	647-8551
TF: 877-647-5050 ■ *Web:* www.midnatbank.com					
Middlebury National Corp PO Box 189	Middlebury	VT	05753	802-388-4982	
OTC: MDVT ■ *Web:* nbmvt.com					
Middlesex Savings Bank 120 Flanders Rd	Westborough	MA	01581	508-653-0300	
TF: 877-463-6287 ■ *Web:* www.middlesexbank.com					
MidFirst Bank PO Box 76149	Oklahoma City	OK	73147	405-943-8002	840-0862*
**Fax:* Cust Svc ■ *TF:* 888-643-3477 ■ *Web:* www.midfirst.com					
Midland National Bank 527 N Main	Newton	KS	67114	316-283-1700	283-3813
TF: 800-810-9457 ■ *Web:* www.midlandnb.com					
Midstate Financial Corp 1 E Main St PO Box 230	Brownsburg	IN	46112	317-852-2268	
Midwest Bank 105 E Soo St PO Box 40	Parkers Prairie	MN	56361	218-338-6054	338-5070
TF: 877-365-5155 ■ *Web:* www.midwestbank.net					
Midwest Federal Savings & Loan Assn of St Joseph 1901 Frederick Ave	St Joseph	MO	64501	816-233-5148	
Mifflinburg Bank & Trust Co (MBTC) 250 E Chestnut St PO Box 186	Mifflinburg	PA	17844	570-966-1041	966-7432
TF: 888-966-3131 ■ *Web:* www.mbtc.com					
Milford Bank 33 Broad St	Milford	CT	06460	203-783-5700	
TF: 800-340-4862 ■ *Web:* www.milfordbank.com					
Milford National Bank & Trust Co, The 300 E Main St	Milford	MA	01757	508-634-4100	634-4107
Web: www.milfordnational.com					
Minier Financial Inc 101 S Main PO Box 800	Minier	IL	61759	309-392-2623	
Web: firstfarmers.com					
Minster Bank 95 W Fourth St	Minster	OH	45865	419-628-2351	
Web: www.minsterbank.com					
Missouri Bank & Trust Co 1044 Main St	Kansas City	MO	64105	816-881-8200	
Web: www.mobank.com					
Mitchell Bank 1039 W Mitchell St	Milwaukee	WI	53204	414-645-0600	645-4020
Web: www.mitchellbank.com					
Monroe Bank & Trust 102 E Front St	Monroe	MI	48161	734-241-3431	384-8101*
**Fax:* Hum Res ■ *TF:* 800-321-0032 ■ *Web:* www.mbandt.com					
Montecito Bank & Trust 1000 State St	Santa Barbara	CA	93101	805-963-7511	
Web: montecito.bank					
Montgomery Bank 1 Montgomery Bank Plaza PO Box 948	Sikeston	MO	63801	573-471-2275	472-5595
TF: 800-455-2275 ■ *Web:* www.montgomerybank.com					
Morton Community Bank 721 W Jackson St	Morton	IL	61550	309-266-5337	
Web: hometownbanks.com					
Mountain Valley Bank 317 DAVIS Ave	Elkins	WV	26241	304-637-2265	637-2270
TF: 800-555-3503 ■ *Web:* www.mountainvalleybank.com					
MSB Financial Corp (MSBF) 1902 Long Hill Rd	Millington	NJ	07946	908-647-4000	647-6196
NASDAQ: MSBF ■ *TF:* 844-265-9680					
MT Mckinley Bank 500 Fourth Ave	Fairbanks	AK	99701	907-452-1751	
Web: mtmckinleybank.com					
Murray Bank, The 405 S 12th St	Murray	KY	42071	270-753-5626	
TF: 877-965-1122 ■ *Web:* www.themurraybank.com					
Mutual Bank 570 Washington St	Whitman	MA	02382	781-447-4488	
Web: www.mymutualbank.com					
Mutual of Omaha Bank 3333 Farnam St	Omaha	NE	68131	877-471-7896	
TF: 866-351-5646 ■ *Web:* www.mutualofomahabank.com					
Nantucket Bank 104 Pleasant St	Nantucket	MA	02554	508-228-0580	
TF: 800-533-9313 ■ *Web:* www.nantucketbank.com					
National Australia Bank Americas 245 Pk Ave 28th Fl	New York	NY	10167	212-916-9500	
TF: 866-706-0509 ■ *Web:* www.nab.com.au					
National Bank & Trust Company of Sycamore, The 230 W State St	Sycamore	IL	60178	815-895-2125	895-2592
National Bank of Arizona 335 N Wilmot Rd Ste 100	Tucson	AZ	85711	520-571-1500	513-0134
TF: 800-497-8168 ■ *Web:* www.nbarizona.com					
National Bank of Blacksburg PO Box 90002	Blacksburg	VA	24062	540-552-2011	951-6337
TF: 800-552-4123 ■ *Web:* www.nbbank.com					
National Bank of Gatesville PO Box 779	Gatesville	TX	76528	254-865-2211	865-8916
TF: 877-628-2265 ■ *Web:* www.natlbank.com					
National Bank, The 852 Middle Rd	Bettendorf	IA	52722	563-344-3935	823-3350
TF: 877-321-4347 ■ *Web:* www.bankwithtriumph.com					
National Exchange Bank & Trust 130 S Main St PO Box 988	Fond Du Lac	WI	54936	920-921-7700	923-7021
Web: www.nebat.com					
NBT Bank NA PO Box 351	Norwich	NY	13815	607-337-2265	
TF: 800-628-2265 ■ *Web:* www.nbtbank.com					
Neffs Bancorp Inc 5629 Rt 873 PO Box 10	Neffs	PA	18065	610-767-3875	767-1890
OTC: NEFB ■ *Web:* www.neffsnatl.com					
Neighborhood National Bank 3511 National Ave	San Diego	CA	92113	619-239-3360	
Web: mynnb.com					
Nevada State Bank PO Box 990	Las Vegas	NV	89125	702-383-0009	
TF: 800-727-4743 ■ *Web:* www.nsbank.com					
New Century Bank 700 W Cumberland St	Dunn	NC	28334	910-892-7080	
Web: www.selectbank.com					
New Omni Bank NA 1235 S Garfield Ave	Alhambra	CA	91801	626-284-5555	
Web: newomnibank.com					
New Washington State Bank 402 E Main St PO Box 10	New Washington	IN	47162	812-293-3321	293-3072
TF: 800-883-0131 ■ *Web:* www.newwashbank.com					
New West Banks of Colorado Inc 55 S Elm Ave	Eaton	CO	80615	970-454-1800	454-1802
Web: bankofcolorado.com					
New York Community Bank 615 Merrick Ave	Westbury	NY	11590	877-786-6560	
TF: 877-786-6560 ■ *Web:* www.mynycb.com					
New York Private Bank & Trust FSB 200 Bellevue Pkwy Ste 150	Wilmington	DE	19809	302-798-2160	
Web: www.nypbt.com					
NewBridge Bancorp 1501 Highwoods Blvd Ste 400	Greensboro	NC	27410	336-369-0900	509-0406*
NASDAQ: NBBC ■ **Fax Area Code:* 910 ■ *Web:* www.newbridgebank.com					
Newburyport Five Cents Savings Bank Inc, The 63 State St PO Box 350	Newburyport	MA	01950	978-462-3136	462-9672
TF: 877-462-3136 ■ *Web:* www.newburyportbank.com					
Newfield National Bank 18 SW Blvd	Newfield	NJ	08344	856-692-3440	697-3114
Web: www.newfieldbank.com					
Newtown Savings Bank Foundation Inc 39 Main St PO Box 497	Newtown	CT	06470	203-426-2563	
TF: 800-461-0672 ■ *Web:* www.nsbonline.com					
Noble Bank & Trust NA 1509 Quintard Ave	Anniston	AL	36202	256-741-1800	
Web: noblebank.com					
North American Development Bank 203 S St Mary'S Ste 300	San Antonio	TX	78205	210-231-8000	
TF: 800-499-6232 ■ *Web:* www.nadb.org					
North American Savings Bank (NASB) 12520 S 71 Hwy	Grandview	MO	64030	816-765-2200	
TF: 800-677-6272 ■ *Web:* www.nasb.com					
North Middlesex Savings Bank Inc 7 Main St PO Box 469	Ayer	MA	01432	978-772-3306	772-9131
TF: 800-762-3306 ■ *Web:* www.nmsb.com					
North Milwaukee State Bank (NMS) 5630 W Fond Du Lac Ave	Milwaukee	WI	53216	414-466-2344	466-6248
TF: 800-799-5630 ■ *Web:* www.nmsbank.com					
North Shore Bank FSB 15700 W Bluemound Rd	Brookfield	WI	53005	262-797-3858	797-3376*
**Fax:* Cust Svc ■ *TF:* 800-236-4672 ■ *Web:* www.northshorebank.com					
North Shore Trust & Savings 700 S Lewis Ave	Waukegan	IL	60085	847-336-4430	336-4438
Web: www.northshoretrust.com					
North Side Bank & Trust Co, The 4125 Hamilton Ave	Cincinnati	OH	45223	513-542-7800	541-6941
Web: nsbt.net					
Northeast Bank 77 Broadway St Ne	Minneapolis	MN	55413	612-379-8811	362-3262
Web: www.northeastbank-mn.com					
Northern Trust Co 50 S LaSalle St	Chicago	IL	60603	312-630-6000	
NASDAQ: NTRS ■ *TF:* 888-289-6542 ■ *Web:* www.northerntrust.com					
Northfield Savings Bank (NSB) PO Box 347	Northfield	VT	05663	802-485-5871	981-1572*
**Fax Area Code:* 718 ■ *TF:* 800-672-2274 ■ *Web:* www.nsbvt.com					
Northrim BanCorp Inc 3111 C St	Anchorage	AK	99503	907-562-0062	261-3594*
NASDAQ: NRIM ■ **Fax:* Mktg ■ *TF:* 800-478-3311 ■ *Web:* www.northrim.com					
Northstar Bank of Texas 400 N Carroll Blvd	Denton	TX	76201	940-591-1200	384-1947
Web: www.nstarbank.com					
Northstar Global Partners LLC The Prudential Tower 800 Boylston St	Boston	MA	02199	617-375-5800	
Northwest Community Bank 86 Main St PO Box 1019	Winsted	CT	06098	860-379-7561	
TF: 800-455-6668 ■ *Web:* www.nwcommunitybank.com					
Northwest Savings Bank 100 Liberty St PO Box 128	Warren	PA	16365	814-726-2140	728-7716*
**Fax:* Mktg ■ *TF:* 800-822-2009 ■ *Web:* www.northwestsavingsbank.com					
Northwestern Bank 202 N Bridge St PO Box 49	Chippewa Falls	WI	54729	715-723-4461	723-0586
Web: www.northwesternbank.com					
Norway Savings Bank 261 Main St	Norway	ME	04268	207-743-7986	
Web: norwaysavingsbank.com					
NovaFund Advisors 140 Rowayton Ave	Norwalk	CT	06853	203-831-0111	
Web: www.novafundadvisors.com					
Oak Bank 1000 N Rush St Ste 1	Chicago	IL	60611	312-440-4000	
OBA Financial Services Inc 20300 Seneca Meadows Pkwy	Germantown	MD	20876	301-916-0742	
NASDAQ: OBAF					
Ocean Bank 780 NW 42nd Ave	Miami	FL	33126	305-442-2660	
TF: 877-688-2265 ■ *Web:* www.oceanbank.com					
Ocean City Home Savings & Loan Inc 1001 Asbury Ave	Ocean City	NJ	08226	609-927-7722	399-3614
Web: www.ochome.com					
OceanFirst Bank 975 Hooper Ave PO Box 2009	Toms River	NJ	08753	732-240-4500	349-5070
TF: 888-623-2633 ■ *Web:* www.oceanfirstonline.com					
Ocwen Federal Bank FSB 1661 Worthington Rd Ste 100	West Palm Beach	FL	33409	561-682-8000	
TF: 800-746-2936 ■ *Web:* www.ocwen.com					
Old Line Bank 1525 Pointer Ridge Pl	Bowie	MD	20716	301-430-2500	430-8723
NASDAQ: WSB ■ *TF:* 800-416-6373 ■ *Web:* Www.oldlinebank.com					
Old National Bancorp 1 Main St	Evansville	IN	47708	812-464-1294	522-9561
Web: www.oldnational.com					
Old National Bank 1 Main St PO Box 718	Evansville	IN	47705	800-731-2265	464-1551*
**Fax Area Code:* 812 ■ **Fax:* Cust Svc ■ *TF:* 800-731-2265 ■ *Web:* www.oldnational.com					
Onebanc 300 W Capitol Ave	Little Rock	AR	72201	501-370-4400	370-4505
Web: www.onebanc.com					
OneUnited Bank 3683 Crenshaw Blvd	Los Angeles	CA	90016	323-290-4848	389-0548
TF: 877-663-8648 ■ *Web:* www.oneunited.com					
Oostburg State Bank 905 Center Ave	Oostburg	WI	53070	920-564-2336	
Web: oostburgbank.com					
Oritani Financial Corp 370 Pascack Rd PO Box 1329	Washington Township	NJ	07676	201-664-5400	497-1223
NASDAQ: ORIT ■ *TF:* 888-674-8264 ■ *Web:* www.oritani.com					
Ossian State Bank 102 N Jefferson St	Ossian	IN	46777	260-622-4141	
Web: ossianstatebank.com					

Phone Fax

Oversea-Chinese Banking Corp Ltd
1700 Broadway 18th Fl. New York NY 10019 212-586-6222 586-0636
Web: www.ocbc.com

Oxford Bank PO Box 129 Addison IL 60101 630-629-5000 628-1575
TF: 800-236-2442 ■ *Web:* www.oxford-bank.com

Pacific City Financial Corp
3701 Wilshire Blvd Ste 402 Los Angeles CA 90010 213-210-2000 210-2032
OTC: PFCF ■ *Web:* www.paccity.net

Pacific Continental Corp
111 W Seventh Ave PO Box 10727 Eugene OR 97440 541-686-8685 344-2807
NASDAQ: PCBK ■ *TF:* 877-231-2265 ■ *Web:* www.therightbank.com

Palmetto State Bank 601 First St W Hampton SC 29924 803-943-2671 943-5634
Web: www.palmettostatebank.com

Paragon Advising Group LP
3200 SW Fwy Ste 2350 Houston TX 77027 713-599-0111

Paragon National Bank 5400 Poplar Ave Ste 350 Memphis TN 38119 901-273-2900
Web: bankparagon.com

Paris National Bank 118 N Main St Paris MO 65275 660-327-4181
Web: parisnational.com

Parkway Bancorp Inc
4800 N Harlem Ave Harwood Heights IL 60706 708-867-6600 867-1119
Web: www.parkwaybank.com

Pasadera Capital LLC 115 W El Prado Ste 1 San Antonio TX 78212 210-804-4240
Web: www.pasaderacapital.com

Pathway Bank 306 S High St Cairo NE 68824 308-485-4232
Web: pathwaybank.com

PBK Bank Inc 120 Frontier Blvd Stanford KY 40484 606-365-7098
TF: 877-230-3711 ■ *Web:* pbkbank.com

Penn Liberty Bank 724 W Lancaster Ave Ste 210 Wayne PA 19087 610-535-4500
Web: www.pennlibertybank.com

Penseco Financial Services Corp
150 N Washington Ave Scranton PA 18503 570-346-7741
NASDAQ: PFIS ■ *Web:* psbt.com/index.php

Pentucket Bank 1 Merrimack St Haverhill MA 01830 978-372-7731 372-4499
Web: www.pentucketbank.com

People Bank 201 N Bardstown Rd Mount Washington KY 40047 502-538-7301 538-6606
Web: www.peoplesbankmtw.com

People's United Bank
850 Main St Bridgeport Ctr Bridgeport CT 06604 203-338-7171 338-2310
TF: 800-772-1090 ■ *Web:* www.peoples.com

Peoples Bank of Bullitt County
1612 Hwy 44 E Shepherdsville KY 40165 502-543-2226 543-3517
Web: www.pbofbc.com

Peoples Financial Services Corp
82 Franklin Ave Hallstead PA 18822 570-879-2175
NASDAQ: PFIS ■ *TF:* 888-868-3858 ■ *Web:* psbt.com/index.php

Peoples National Bank
5175 N Academy Blvd Colorado Springs CO 80918 719-528-4000 260-2256
TF: 800-862-6696 ■ *Web:* www.epeoples.com

Peoples Savings Bank (PSB)
414 N Adams PO Box 248 Wellsburg IA 50680 641-869-3721 869-3855
TF: 877-493-3799 ■ *Web:* www.bankpsb.com

Peoples State Bank 445 S Lewis Ave Tulsa OK 74104 918-583-9800 587-9307
Web: peoplesbanktulsa.com

Periculum Capital Company LLC
4 Ctr Green Ste 200 Carmel IN 46032 317-636-1800
Web: www.periculumcapital.com

Perrin Holden & Davenport Capital Corp
5 Hanover Sq New York NY 10004 212-269-3500

Petsky Prunier LLC 60 Broad St 38th Fl New York NY 10004 212-842-6020
Web: www.petskyprunier.com

Piedmont FSB (PFSB) 201 S Stratford Rd Winston-Salem NC 27103 336-770-1000 770-1055
Web: www.piedmontfederal.com

Pilgrim BanCorp 2401 S Jefferson Ave Mount Pleasant TX 75455 903-575-2150 575-1550
TF: 877-303-3111 ■ *Web:* pilgrimbank.com

Pine Country Bank 412 N Hwy 10 PO Box 25 Royalton MN 56373 320-584-5522 584-8385
Web: www.pinecountrybank.com

Pineries Bank, The 3601 Main St Stevens Point WI 54481 715-341-5600
Web: pineries.com

Pinnacle Trust Partners LLC
540 Hopmeadow St Simsbury CT 06070 860-264-1595
Web: www.pinnacletrustpartners.com

Pintoresco Advisors LLC
466 Foothill Blvd Ste 333 La Canada Flintridge CA 91011 213-223-2070
TF: 866-217-1140 ■ *Web:* www.pintorescoadvisors.com

Piqua State Bank 1356 Xylan Rd Piqua KS 66761 620-468-2555
Web: piquastatebank.com

Platte Valley Bank of Missouri
2400 Prairie View Rd PO Box 1250 Platte City MO 64079 816-858-5400
Web: www.plattevalleybank.com

Plaza Bank 7460 W Irving Pk Rd Norridge IL 60706 708-456-3440 452-2214*
**Fax Area Code: 760* ■ *TF General:* 877-714-9599

Plums Bank 35 S Lindan Ave Quincy CA 95971 530-283-7305 283-3557
NASDAQ: PLBC ■ *Web:* www.plumasbank.com

PNC Bank 1 PNC Plaza 249 Fifth Ave Pittsburgh PA 15222 412-762-2000 762-7829
TF: 888-762-2265 ■ *Web:* www.pnc.com

PNC Bank 600 Grant St Pittsburgh PA 15219 888-762-2265
NYSE: PNC-L ■ *TF:* 888-762-2265 ■ *Web:* www.pnc.com

PNC Bank Delaware 300 Delaware Ave Wilmington DE 19899 302-429-1361
TF: 888-762-2265 ■ *Web:* www.pnc.com

PNC Bank NA 249 Fifth Ave 1 PNC Plaza Pittsburgh PA 15222 412-762-2000
TF: 888-762-2265 ■ *Web:* www.pnc.com

Potter State Bank of Potter, The
301 Chestnut St Potter NE 69156 308-879-4451
Web: potterstatebank.com

Prairie State Bank & Trust
1361 Toronto Rd Springfield IL 62712 217-786-2509
Web: www.psbank.net

Preferred Bank Los Angeles
601 S Figueroa St 29th Fl Los Angeles CA 90017 213-891-1188 622-0369
NASDAQ: PFBC ■ *TF:* 888-673-1808 ■ *Web:* www.preferredbank.com

Premier Bank & Trust 600 S Main St North Canton OH 44720 330-499-1900
TF: 855-728-6010 ■ *Web:* www.mypremierbankandtrust.com

Premier Valley Bank 255 E River Pk Cir Ste 180 Fresno CA 93720 559-438-2002 432-0572
TF: 877-438-2002 ■ *Web:* www.premiervalleybank.com

Presidential Online Bank 4520 East-West Hwy Bethesda MD 20814 301-652-0700 951-3582
TF: 800-383-6266 ■ *Web:* www.presidential.com

Primebank 37 First Ave NW PO Box 1408 Le Mars IA 51031 712-546-4175
Web: primebank.com

Profile Bank 45 Wakefield St PO Box 1808 Rochester NH 03866 603-332-2610 332-2519
TF: 800-554-8969 ■ *Web:* www.profilebank.com

Progressive Bank NA 1090 E Bethlehem Blvd Wheeling WV 26003 304-238-0040
TF: 866-235-1923 ■ *Web:* www.progbank.com

Provident Bank 239 Washington St Jersey City NJ 07302 732-590-9200
Web: www.snl.com

Provident Savings Bank FSB
3756 Central Ave Riverside CA 92506 951-686-6060 786-4725
TF: 800-442-5201 ■ *Web:* www.myprovident.com

Prudential Savings Bank
1834 W Oregon Ave Philadelphia PA 19145 215-755-1500 336-7122
TF: 800-554-8969 ■ *Web:* www.prudentialsavingsbank.com

Pueblo Bank & Trust Co 301 W Fifth St Pueblo CO 81003 719-545-1834
Web: www.pbandt.com

Putnam Bank 40 Main St PO Box 151 Putnam CT 06260 860-928-6501
TF: 877-275-3342 ■ *Web:* www.putnambank.com

Pyramax Bank Fsb 7001 W Edgerton Ave Greenfield WI 53220 414-421-8200

QNB Corp 15 N Third St PO Box 9005 Quakertown PA 18951 215-538-5600 538-5765
OTC: QNBC ■ *TF:* 800-491-9070 ■ *Web:* qnbbank.com/2690/mirror/redirect.htm

Quarton Partners LLC 300 Park St Ste 480 Birmingham MI 48009 248-594-0400
Web: www.quartoninternational.com

Queens County Savings Bank
13665 Roosevelt Ave Flushing NY 11354 718-460-4800
Web: www.mynycb.com

Queenstown Bank of Maryland
7101 Main St PO Box 120 Queenstown MD 21658 410-827-8881 827-8190
TF: 888-827-4300 ■ *Web:* www.queenstown-bank.com

Rabo Bank 1026 E Grand Ave Arroyo Grande CA 93420 805-473-7710
TF: 800-942-6222 ■ *Web:* www.rabobankamerica.com

Randolph Savings Bank 129 N Main St Randolph MA 02368 781-963-2100 961-7916
TF: 877-963-2100 ■ *Web:* www.randolphsavings.com

RBC Royal Bank 1127 Blvd D,carie Montreal QC H4L3M8 800-769-2599 874-3055*
**Fax Area Code:* 514 ■ *TF:* 800-769-2599 ■ *Web:* www.rbcroyalbank.com

RBC Trust Company (Delaware) Ltd
4550 New Linden Hill Rd Ste 200 Wilmington DE 19808 302-892-6976
TF: 800-441-7698 ■ *Web:* www.rbctrust.com

Reelfoot Bank 1491 S First St Union City TN 38261 731-885-1010
Web: reelfootbank.com

Regents Bank NA PO Box 9137 La Jolla CA 92038 858-729-7700 454-9052
Web: www.regentsbank.com

Regions Bank 1900 Fifth Ave N Birmingham AL 35203 800-734-4667
TF: 800-734-4667 ■ *Web:* www.regions.com

Reliance Bancshares Inc 10401 Clayton Rd St. Louis MO 63131 314-569-7200
OTC: RLBS ■ *Web:* www.reliancebankstl.com

Ridgewood Savings Bank 71-02 Forest Ave Ridgewood NY 11385 718-240-4800
TF: 800-250-4832 ■ *Web:* www.ridgewoodbank.com

Rio Bank 1655 N 23rd Mcallen TX 78501 956-631-7890 972-1574
Web: riobk.com

River City Bank PO Box 15247 Sacramento CA 95851 916-567-2899
OTC: RCBC ■ *TF Cust Svc:* 800-564-7144 ■ *Web:* www.rivercitybank.com

Rockland Trust 435 Market St Boston MA 02135 617-254-0813
NASDAQ: PEOP ■ *Web:* www.rocklandtrust.com

Rockport National Bank 16 Main St Rockport MA 01966 978-546-3411
Web: www.institutionforsavings.com

Roselle Savings Bank Inc
235 Chestnut St PO Box 349 Roselle NJ 07203 908-245-1885
Web: www.rosellesavings.com

Royal Bank America 732 Montgomery Ave Narberth PA 19072 610-668-4700 668-3670
Web: www.royalbankamerica.com

Royal Bank of Canada 200 Bay St 9th Fl S Twr Toronto ON M5J2J5 416-955-7806 974-3535
TSE: RY ■ *TF:* 800-769-2599 ■ *Web:* www.rbc.com

Royal Savings Bank 9226 S Commercial Ave Chicago IL 60617 773-768-4800
Web: www.royalbankweb.com

S&T Bank 800 Philadelphia St PO Box 190 Indiana PA 15701 724-349-1800 465-6874
TF Cust Svc: 800-325-2265 ■ *Web:* www.stbank.com

Safra National Bank of New York
546 Fifth Ave New York NY 10036 212-704-5500 704-9397
Web: www.safra.com

Salem Five & Savings Bank 210 Essex St Salem MA 01970 978-745-5555 745-1073
TF Cust Svc: 800-850-5000 ■ *Web:* www.salemfive.com

Sandhills Bank 300 King St E Bethune SC 29009 843-334-2265
Web: www.sandhillsbank.com

SCB Bancorp Inc 1501 E Eldorado St Decatur IL 62521 217-428-7781
TF: 888-769-2265 ■ *Web:* www.soybank.com

Scottdale Bank & Trust 125 S Arch St Connellsville PA 15425 724-628-3200
Web: sbtbank.com

Seamen's Bank
221 Commercial St PO Box 659 Provincetown MA 02657 508-487-0035 487-8421
TF: 855-227-5347 ■ *Web:* www.seamensbank.com

Seaway Bank & Trust Co 645 E 87th St Chicago IL 60619 773-487-4800 487-0452
Web: www.seawaybank.us

Security Bank of Pulaski County
110 Lynn St PO Box S Waynesville MO 65583 573-774-6417 774-6465
Web: www.sbpc.com

Security National Bank 40 S Limestone St Springfield OH 45502 937-324-6800 324-6861
Web: www.securitynationalbank.com

Security National Bank of Enid 201 W Maine Ave Enid OK 73701 580-234-5151 249-9199
Web: www.snbenid.com

Security National Bank of Omaha (Inc)
1120 S 101st St PO Box 31400 Omaha NE 68124 402-344-7300
Web: www.snbconnect.com

Security National Bank of Sioux City Iowa
PO Box 147 Sioux City IA 51101 712-277-6666
Web: www.snbonline.com

Security State Bank & Trust (Inc)
201 W Main St PO Box 471 Fredericksburg TX 78624 830-997-7575 997-7994
Web: www.ssbtexas.com

				Phone	Fax
Severn Bancorp Inc 200 Westgate Cir Ste 200	Annapolis	MD	21401	410-260-2000	841-6296
NASDAQ: SVBI ■ *TF:* 800-752-5854 ■ *Web:* www.severnbank.com					
Shelby State Bank 242 N Michigan Ave	Shelby	MI	49455	231-861-2123	
Web: shelbybank.com					
Signature Bank 565 Fifth Ave 12th Fl	New York	NY	10017	646-822-1500	
NASDAQ: SBNY ■ *TF:* 866-744-5463 ■ *Web:* www.signatureny.com					
Silicon Valley Bank (SVB) 3003 Tasman Dr	Santa Clara	CA	95054	408-654-7400	
Web: www.svb.com					
Silvergate Bank 4275 Executive Sq Ste 800	La Jolla	CA	92037	858-362-6300	362-6333
TF: 800-595-5856 ■ *Web:* www.silvergatebank.com					
Societe Generale USA 245 Park Ave	New York	NY	10167	212-278-6000	278-6789
Web: cib.societegenerale.com/en					
Solvay Bank 1537 Milton Ave	Solvay	NY	13209	315-468-1661	
Web: www.solvaybank.com					
Somerset Trust Co 151 W Main St PO Box 777	Somerset	PA	15501	814-443-9200	
TF: 800-972-1651 ■ *Web:* www.somersettrust.com					
Sooner Southwest Bankshares Inc 1751 E 71st St	Tulsa	OK	74136	918-496-4242	
South Louisiana Bank (SLB)					
1362 W Tunnel Blvd PO Box 1718	Houma	LA	70361	985-851-3434	879-3095
TF: 877-275-3342 ■ *Web:* ayeee.com					
Southbridge Savings Bank Inc					
253-257 Main St PO Box 370	Southbridge	MA	01550	508-765-9103	765-1187
TF: 800-939-9103 ■ *Web:* www.southbridgesavingsbank.com					
Southern Michigan Bank & Trust					
51 W Pearl St PO Box 309	Coldwater	MI	49036	517-279-5500	278-7358
TF: 800-379-7628 ■ *Web:* www.smb-t.com					
SouthWest Capital Bank 622 Douglas Ave	Las Vegas	NM	87701	505-425-7565	425-8501
TF: 800-748-2406 ■ *Web:* www.southwestcapital.com					
Southwest Missouri Bank 2417 S Grand Ave	Carthage	MO	64836	417-358-1770	358-4081
TF: 800-943-8488 ■ *Web:* www.smbonline.com					
Sovereign Bank FSB PO Box 12646	Reading	PA	19612	877-768-2265	
TF Cust Svc: 877-768-2265 ■ *Web:* www.santanderbank.com					
Spencer Savings Bank PO Box 912	Spencer	MA	01562	508-885-5313	
TF: 800-547-2885 ■ *Web:* www.spencerbankonline.com					
Spencer Savings Bank SLA 611 River Dr	Elmwood Park	NJ	07407	973-772-6700	
TF: 800-363-8115 ■ *Web:* www.spencersavings.com					
St. Martin Bank & Trust Co					
301 S Main St	Saint Martinville	LA	70582	337-394-7800	394-7831
Web: www.stmartinbank.com					
Standard Bank & Trust Co					
7800 W 95th St	Hickory Hills	IL	60457	708-598-7400	
TF: 866-499-2265 ■ *Web:* www.standardbanks.com					
Standard Chartered Bank 1 Madison Ave	New York	NY	10010	212-667-0700	667-0380
Web: www.sc.com					
Star Bank 201 Second Ave NW PO Box 188	Bertha	MN	56437	218-924-4055	924-2265
Web: www.starbank.net					
STAR Financial Group Inc PO Box 11409	Fort Wayne	IN	46858	260-467-5507	
OTC: SFIGA ■ *Web:* www.starfinancial.com					
State Bank 175 N Leroy St	Fenton	MI	48430	810-629-2263	629-3892
TF: 800-535-0517 ■ *Web:* www.thestatebank.com					
State Bank & Trust 3100 13th Ave S	Fargo	ND	58103	701-298-1500	
Web: www.bellbanks.com					
State Bank & Trust Co 1025 Sixth St PO Box 327	Nevada	IA	50201	515-382-2191	382-3826
Web: www.banksbt.com					
State Bank of Countryside Inc (SBC)					
6734 Joliet Rd	Countryside	IL	60525	708-485-3100	485-3106
Web: www.bankcountryside.com					
State Bank of Cross Plains					
1205 Main St PO Box 218	Cross Plains	WI	53528	608-798-3961	798-3591
Web: www.crossplainsbank.com					
State Bank of Toledo 100 E High St PO Box 309	Toledo	IA	52342	641-484-2980	
Web: www.banktoledo.com					
State Bank of Waterloo PO Box 148	Waterloo	IL	62298	618-939-7194	939-4140
TF: 800-367-7576 ■ *Web:* www.sbw.bank					
State Farm Financial Services FSB					
PO Box 2316	Bloomington	IL	61702	877-734-2265	
TF: 877-734-2265 ■ *Web:* www.statefarm.com/bank/bank.htm					
State National Bank & Trust Co					
122 Main St PO Box 130	Wayne	NE	68787	402-375-1130	
Web: www.state-national-bank.com					
State Street Corp 1 Lincoln St	Boston	MA	02111	617-786-3000	664-6316*
NYSE: STT ■ **Fax:* Mktg ■ *Web:* www.statestreet.com					
Stephenson National Bank & Trust, The					
1820 Hall Ave PO Box 137	Marinette	WI	54143	715-732-1732	732-5478
Web: www.snbt.com					
Sterling Bank & Trust FSB					
1 Town Sq Ste 1900	Southfield	MI	48076	248-351-3442	359-6660
TF: 877-438-4338 ■ *Web:* www.sterlingbank.com					
Sterling Savings Bank 105 W Simpson Ave	Mccleary	WA	98557	800-650-7141	
TF: 800-650-7141 ■ *Web:* www.umpquabank.com					
Steuben Trust Co 1 Steuben Sq	Hornell	NY	14843	607-324-5010	
TF: 866-783-8236 ■ *Web:* steubentrust.com					
Stillman Banccorp NA PO Box 150	Stillman Valle	IL	61084	815-645-2000	645-2341
TF: 866-546-8273 ■ *Web:* www.stillmanbank.com					
Stock Exchange Bank 103 S Main PO Box 273	Caldwell	KS	67022	620-845-6431	
Web: stockxbank.com					
Stockmans Bank 100 Kennedy	Gould	OK	73544	580-676-3921	
Web: stockmansbankok.com					
Stonegate Bank 1430 N Federal Hwy	Fort Lauderdale	FL	33304	954-315-5500	
Web: stonegatebank.com					
Stoneham Savings Bank					
359 Main St PO Box 80071	Stoneham	MA	02180	781-438-9400	
Sturgis Bank & Trust Co					
113-125 E Chicago Rd PO Box 600	Sturgis	MI	49091	269-651-9345	651-5512*
OTC: STBI ■ **Fax Area Code:* 616 ■ *Web:* www.sturgisbank.com					
Sumitomo Mitsui Banking Corp (SMBC) 277 Pk Ave	New York	NY	10172	212-224-4000	593-9522
Web: www.smbcgroup.com					
Sumitomo Mitsui Trust Bank (USA) (SMTBUSA)					
111 River St	Hoboken	NJ	07030	201-420-9470	983-3730*
**Fax Area Code:* 718 ■ *Web:* logon.sumitomotrustusa.com					
Summit Bank 2969 Broadway	Oakland	CA	94611	510-839-8800	839-8853
TF: 800-380-9333 ■ *Web:* www.summitbanking.com					

				Phone	Fax
Sun National Bank					
350 Fellowship Rd Ste. 101	Mount Laurel	NJ	08054	800-786-9066	
TF: 800-786-9066 ■ *Web:* www.sunnationalbank.com					
Suntrust Bank PO Box 4418	Atlanta	GA	30302	800-786-8787	
NYSE: STI ■ *TF:* 800-786-8787 ■ *Web:* www.suntrust.com					
Svenska Handelsbanken 875 Third Ave 4th Fl	New York	NY	10022	212-326-5100	
Web: www.handelsbanken.se					
Swedbank 1 Penn Plz 15th Fl	New York	NY	10119	646-674-0789	486-3220*
**Fax Area Code:* 212 ■ *Web:* www.swedbank.com					
Swineford National Bank					
1255 N Susquehanna Trial PO Box 241	Hummels Wharf	PA	17831	570-743-7786	743-8562
TF: 866-762-1903 ■ *Web:* www.swineford.com					
Tallahassee State Bank					
2720 W Tennessee St	Tallahassee	FL	32304	850-576-1182	893-7192
Web: talstatebank.synovus.com					
Talmer Bancorp Inc 2301 W Big Beaver Rd Ste 525	Troy	MI	48084	248-649-2301	
Web: talmerbank.com					
TAP Advisors LLC 152 W 57th St 34th Fl	New York	NY	10019	212-909-9010	
Web: www.tapadvisors.com					
TCF National Bank 801 Marquette Ave	Minneapolis	MN	55402	612-823-2265	
Web: www.tcfbank.com					
TD Bank NA 1701 Rt 70 E	Cherry Hill	NJ	08034	856-751-2739	761-8536*
**Fax Area Code:* 207 ■ *TF:* 888-751-9000 ■ *Web:* www.tdbank.com					
TD Banknorth Massachusetts 295 Pk Ave	Worcester	MA	01609	508-752-2584	
TF Cust Svc: 800-747-7000 ■ *Web:* www.tdbank.com					
Tempo Bank 28 W Broadway	Trenton	IL	62293	618-224-9228	
Web: tempobank.com					
Tennessee Commerce Bank					
381 Mallory Stn Rd Ste 207	Franklin	TN	37067	877-275-3342	
TF: 877-275-3342 ■ *Web:* fdic.gov					
Texas Bank & Trust Co					
300 E Whaley PO Box 3188	Longview	TX	75606	903-237-5500	237-1890
Web: www.texasbankandtrust.com					
Texas Capital Bank 2000 McKinney Ave Ste 700	Dallas	TX	75201	214-932-6600	932-6604
TF: 877-839-2265 ■ *Web:* www.texascapitalbank.com					
Texas Star Bank					
177 E Jefferson PO Box 608	Van Alstyne	TX	75495	903-482-5234	482-5239
TF: 866-546-8273 ■ *Web:* www.texasstarbank.com					
Third Federal Savings & Loan Assn of Cleveland					
7007 Broadway Ave	Cleveland	OH	44105	216-429-5228	
TF: 888-844-7333 ■ *Web:* www.thirdfederal.com					
Thomas Capital Group Inc					
4221 Harborview Dr Ste 200	Gig Harbor	WA	98332	253-777-4477	
Web: www.thomascapital.com					
Thomaston Savings Bank					
203 Main St PO Box 907	Thomaston	CT	06787	860-283-1874	283-6621
TF General: 855-344-1874 ■ *Web:* www.thomastonsavingsbank.com					
Thumb National Bank & Trust Co					
7254 Michigan Ave	Pigeon	MI	48755	989-453-3113	
Web: thumbnational.com					
Tompkins Trust Co PO Box 460	Ithaca	NY	14851	607-273-3210	
NYSE: TMP ■ *TF:* 888-273-3210 ■ *Web:* www.tompkinstrust.com					
Town Bank 850 W N Shore Dr	Hartland	WI	53029	262-367-1900	
TF: 800-433-3076 ■ *Web:* www.townbank.us					
TowneBank 4501 Cox Rd PO Box 5310	Glen Allen	VA	23060	804-967-7026	
Web: www.franklinfederal.com					
Traditional Bank					
49 W Main St PO Box 326	Mount Sterling	KY	40353	859-498-0414	498-0643
TF: 800-498-0414 ■ *Web:* www.traditionalbank.com					
Transportation Alliance Bank Inc					
4185 Harrison Blvd Ste 200	Ogden	UT	84403	801-624-4800	
Web: www.tabbank.com					
Tri City Bankshares Corp 6400 S 27th St	Oak Creek	WI	53154	414-761-1610	761-2019
OTC: TRCY ■ *Web:* www.tcnb.com					
Tri-State Bank & Trust 4321 Youree Dr	Shreveport	LA	71105	318-861-6184	861-9046
Tristar Bank 719 E College St	Dickson	TN	37055	615-446-7100	
Web: tristarbank.com					
Triumph Savings Bank SSB					
5220 Spring Valley Rd Ste 160	Dallas	TX	75254	214-237-3170	
Web: www.triumphbancorp.com/savings-bank					
Trust Bank 600 E Main St PO Box 158	Olney	IL	62450	618-395-4311	395-4312
TF: 800-766-3451 ■ *Web:* www.trustbank.net					
Trust Company of Virginia, The					
9030 Stony Point Pkwy Ste 300	Richmond	VA	23235	804-272-9044	
TSG Partners					
The Promenade Ii 1230 Peachtree St 24th Fl	Atlanta	GA	30309	630-818-7302	
Web: www.tsg-partners.com					
Twin River National Bank 1507 G St	Lewiston	ID	83501	208-746-4848	746-4949
TF: 877-743-4948 ■ *Web:* www.twinriverbank.com					
UBS AG 1285 Ave of the Americas	New York	NY	10019	212-713-2000	
TF: 877-827-8001 ■ *Web:* www.ubs.com					
Ulster Savings Bank					
180 Schwenk Dr PO Box 3337	Kingston	NY	12401	845-338-6322	
Web: www.ulstersavings.com/home/home					
UMB Bank NA 1010 Grand Blvd	Kansas City	MO	64106	816-860-7000	860-4642
TF: 800-821-2171 ■ *Web:* www.umb.com					
Umpqua Bank PO Box 1820	Roseburg	OR	97470	503-973-5945	973-5943
TF: 866-486-7782 ■ *Web:* www.umpquabank.com					
Unibank For Savings 49 Church St	Whitinsville	MA	01588	508-234-8112	234-4648
TF: 800-578-4270 ■ *Web:* www.unibank.com					
Union Bank & Trust Inc					
312 Central Ave SE	Minneapolis	MN	55414	612-379-3222	379-8837
Web: www.ubtmn.com					
Union Bank of California NA					
400 California St 1st Fl	San Francisco	CA	94104	415-765-3434	
TF: 800-238-4486 ■ *Web:* www.unionbank.com					
Union FSB 1565 Mineral Spring Ave	North Providence	RI	02904	401-353-8900	353-8938
TF: 888-226-0819					
Union Savings Bank					
223 W Stephenson St PO Box 540	Freeport	IL	61032	815-235-0800	
Web: www.unionsavingsbank.com					
Union SQUARE Advisors LLC					
2 Embarcadero Ctr Ste 1330	San Francisco	CA	94111	415-501-8000	
Web: www.usadvisors.com					

Phone Fax

Union State Bank 127 S Summit St .... Arkansas City KS 67005 620-442-5200 442-8081
Web: www.myunionstate.com

United American Bank 101 S Ellsworth Ave .... San Mateo CA 94401 650-579-1500 579-1501
OTC: UABK ■ *TF:* 877-822-4822 ■ *Web:* www.unitedamericanbank.com

United Americas Bank NA 3789 Roswell Rd.............. Atlanta GA 30342 404-240-0101 240-0101

United Bank 11185 Fairfax Blvd......................... Fairfax VA 22030 703-219-4850 352-8730
TF: 800-327-9862 ■ *Web:* www.bankwithunited.com

United Bank of Philadelphia
30 S 15th St Ste 1200.......................... Philadelphia PA 19102 215-351-4600
Web: www.ubphila.com

United Financial Bancorp Inc
95 Elm St PO Box 9020 .... West Springfield MA 01090 413-787-1700
NASDAQ: UBNK ■ *TF:* 866-959-2265 ■ *Web:* www.bankatunited.com

United Overseas Bank Ltd (UOB)
592 Fifth Ave 10th Fl 48th St .... New York NY 10036 212-382-0088 382-1881
Web: www.uob.com.sg

United Security Bancshares 2126 Inyo St.............. Fresno CA 93721 559-248-4943
NASDAQ: UBFO ■ *TF:* 888-683-6030 ■ *Web:* www.unitedsecuritybank.com

UPS Capital Business Credit
35 Glenlake Pkwy NE .... Atlanta GA 30328 877-263-8772
TF: 877-263-8772 ■ *Web:* www.upscapital.com

US Bank NA 1900 N University Dr .... Fargo ND 58102 701-280-3547
Web: www.usbank.com

US Bank NA 800 Nicollet Mall .... Minneapolis MN 55402 651-466-3000
TF: 800-872-2657 ■ *Web:* www.usbank.com

USAA FSB (USAAFSB) 10750 McDermott Fwy .... San Antonio TX 78288 800-531-8722 531-5717
TF: 800-531-8722 ■ *Web:* www.usaa.com

Vakifbank 399 Park Ave.............................. New York NY 10022 212-319-4630

Valley National Bank 615 Main Ave .... Passaic NJ 07055 973-777-6768
TF: 800-522-4100 ■ *Web:* valleynationalbank.com

Valley Republic Bank
5000 California Ave Ste 110...................... Bakersfield CA 93309 661-371-2000
Web: valleyrepublicbank.com

Vectra Bank Colorado NA
2000 S Colorado Blvd Ste 2-1200 .... Denver CO 80222 720-947-7700 947-7760
TF: 800-232-8948 ■ *Web:* www.vectrabank.com

Velocity Credit Union 610 E 11th St .... Austin TX 78701 512-469-7000 469-7024
Web: www.velocitycu.com

Village Bank & Trust 234 W NW Hwy .... Arlington Heights IL 60004 847-670-1000 670-7744
Web: www.bankatvillage.com

VirtualBank
3801 PGA Blvd Ste 700
PO Box 109638 .... Palm Beach Gardens FL 33410 877-998-2265 776-6378*
**Fax Area Code:* 561 ■ *TF:* 877-998-2265 ■ *Web:* www.virtualbank.com

Wachovia Bank 3800 Wilshire Blvd Ste 110e......... Los Angeles CA 90025 310-477-8004
TF: 800-225-5935 ■ *Web:* www.wellsfargo.com

Wachovia Bank NA 301 S College St................. Charlotte NC 28202 704-335-5878
Web: www.wellsfargo.com

Wallace H Coulter Foundation, The
790 NW 107th Ave .... Miami FL 33172 305-559-2991
Web: www.whcf.org

Wallkill Valley Federal Savings & Loan Assn
23 Wallkill Ave .... Wallkill NY 12589 845-895-2051
Web: www.wallkill.com

Walpole Co-op Bank Inc 982 Main St.................... Walpole MA 02081 508-668-1080 660-2690
TF: 877-322-8228 ■ *Web:* www.walpolecoop.com

Waterman State Bank
248 W Lincoln Hwy PO Box 209..................... Waterman IL 60556 815-264-3201
Web: watermanbank.com

Waterstone Bank 7500 W State St .... Wauwatosa WI 53213 414-258-5880
Web: www.wsbonline.com

Waukesha State Bank
151 E St Paul Ave PO Box 648 .... Waukesha WI 53187 262-549-8500 549-8593
Web: www.waukeshabank.com

Weatherbank Inc 1015 Waterwood Pkwy Ste J .... Edmond OK 73034 405-359-0773 341-0115
TF: 800-687-3562 ■ *Web:* www.weatherbank.com

Wellesley Bank 40 Central St......................... Wellesley MA 02482 781-235-2550
Web: wellesleybank.com

Wells Fargo Bank 5622 Third St............................. Katy TX 77493 281-391-2101
TF: 800-869-3557 ■ *Web:* www.wellsfargo.com

Wells Fargo Bank Indiana NA
111 E Wayne St .... Fort Wayne IN 46802 260-461-6430
TF: 800-869-3557 ■ *Web:* www.wellsfargo.com

Wells Fargo Bank Iowa NA
666 Walnut St PO Box 837...................... Des Moines IA 50309 800-869-3557
TF: 800-869-3557 ■ *Web:* www.wellsfargo.com

Wells Fargo Bank Minnesota South NA
21 First St SW .... Rochester MN 55902 507-285-2800
Web: www.wellsfargo.com

Wells Fargo Bank Montana NA 175 N 27th St........... Billings MT 59101 406-657-1903
Web: www.wellsfargo.com

Wells Fargo Bank NA 420 Montgomery St.......... San Francisco CA 94104 415-222-4292
TF: 800-869-3557 ■ *Web:* www.wellsfargo.com

Wells Fargo Bank Nebraska NA 1919 Douglas St......... Omaha NE 68102 402-536-2022
Web: www.wellsfargo.com

Wells Fargo Bank South Dakota NA
101 N Phillips Ave .... Sioux Falls SD 57104 605-575-6900
Web: www.wellsfargo.com

Wells Fargo Bank Texas NA
707 Castroville Rd .... San Antonio TX 78237 210-856-6224
TF: 800-869-3557 ■ *Web:* www.wellsfargo.com

WesBanco Inc 1 Bank Plz .... Wheeling WV 26003 304-234-9000
NASDAQ: WSBC ■ *TF:* 800-328-3369 ■ *Web:* www.wesbanco.com

West Alabama Bank & Trust
509 First Ave W PO Box 310 .... Reform AL 35481 205-375-6261 375-2289
Web: www.wabt.com

West Coast Bank 506 SW Coast Hwy.................. Newport OR 97365 877-272-3678
TF Cust Svc: 800-895-3345 ■ *Web:* www.columbiabank.com

West Milton State Bank 940 High St .... West Milton PA 17886 570-568-6851
Web: westmiltonstatebank.com

West Suburban Bank 711 Westmore Meyers Rd .... Lombard IL 60148 630-652-2000 629-0278
TF: 800-258-4009 ■ *Web:* www.westsuburbanbank.com

Westamerica Bancorp 1108 Fifth Ave............... San Rafael CA 94901 415-257-8000
NASDAQ: WABC ■ *Web:* www.westamerica.com

Phone Fax

Western Commerce Bank
1910 Wyoming Blvd Ne .... Albuquerque NM 87112 505-271-9964 271-9879
Web: www.wcb.net

Western Security Bank 2812 First Ave N .... Billings MT 59101 406-371-8200
TF: 800-983-5537 ■ *Web:* www.westernsecuritybank.com

Western State Bank 110 Fourth St S............... Devils Lake ND 58301 701-662-4936
Web: www.westernbanks.com

Westfield Bank 140 Portage Trail .... Cuyahoga Falls OH 44221 330-923-0454
Web: www.westfield-bank.com

Westpac Banking Corp Americas Div
575 Fifth Ave 39th Fl .... New York NY 10017 212-551-1800 551-1999
TF: 888-269-2377 ■ *Web:* www.westpac.com.au

White Sands Federal Credit Union
2190 E Lohman Ave .... Las Cruces NM 88001 575-647-4500 647-4540
TF: 800-658-9933 ■ *Web:* www.wsfcu.org

Whitney National Bank 228 St Charles Ave .... New Orleans LA 70130 504-586-7456
TF: 800-844-4450 ■ *Web:* www.whitneybank.com

Wilcox | Swartzwelder & Company LLC
102 Decker Crt Ste 204.............................. Irving TX 75062 972-831-1300
Web: www.ws-ibank.com

Wilmington Trust Co 1100 N Market St............ Wilmington DE 19890 302-651-1000 651-8937*
**Fax:* Hum Res ■ *TF:* 800-441-7120 ■ *Web:* www.wilmingtontrust.com

Wilshire State Bank
3200 Wilshire Blvd Ste 1400 .... Los Angeles CA 90010 213-368-7700 427-6562*
**Fax:* Cust Svc ■ *TF:* 866-886-2265 ■ *Web:* www.wilshirebank.com

Wilson Bank Holding Co 623 W Main St.............. Lebanon TN 37087 615-444-2265 443-7117
OTC: WBHC ■ *Web:* www.wilsonbank.com

Winnsboro State Bank & Trust Co
3875 Front St .... Winnsboro LA 71295 318-435-7535
TF: 866-205-4026 ■ *Web:* winnsborobank.com

Winter Hill Bank 342 Broadway .... Somerville MA 02145 617-666-8600 629-3327
TF: 800-444-4300 ■ *Web:* www.winterhillbank.com/Default.asp

Woodforest Financial Group Inc PO Box 7889.......... Spring TX 77387 832-375-2000
TF: 877-968-7962 ■ *Web:* www.woodforest.com

Woodsville Guaranty Savings Bank
10 Pleasant St PO Box 266...................... Woodsville NH 03785 603-747-2735 747-3267
TF: 800-564-2735 ■ *Web:* www.theguarantybank.com

WoodTrust Financial Corp
181 Second St S......................... Wisconsin Rapids WI 54494 715-423-7600 422-0300
TF: 800-716-3742 ■ *Web:* www.woodtrust.com

Yadkin Bank 1318 N Bridge St .... Elkin NC 28621 336-526-6371
NASDAQ: YDKN ■ *TF:* 866-867-9979 ■ *Web:* www.yadkinbank.com

Yakima Federal Savings & Loan Assn
118 E Yakima Ave.................................... Yakima WA 98901 509-248-2634
TF: 800-331-3225 ■ *Web:* www.yakimafed.com

Ynb 401 Elm St PO Box 851700 .... Yukon OK 73099 405-354-5281
Web: ynbok.com

Yoakum National Bank 301 W Grand Ave............. Yoakum TX 77995 361-293-5225 293-7322
Web: yoakumnationalbank.com

York State Bank & Trust Co 700 N Lincoln AvE............ York NE 68467 402-362-4411 362-4192
TF: 888-295-5540 ■ *Web:* www.yorkstatebank.com

Zions First National Bank 1 S Main St............ Salt Lake City UT 84111 801-974-8800
TF: 800-974-8800 ■ *Web:* www.zionsbank.com

71 BANKS - FEDERAL RESERVE

Phone Fax

Federal Reserve Bank of Atlanta
1000 Peachtree St NE................................ Atlanta GA 30309 404-498-8353
TF: 888-500-7390 ■ *Web:* www.frbatlanta.org
Birmingham Branch 524 Liberty Pkwy............ Birmingham AL 35242 205-968-6700
TF: 800-257-7013 ■ *Web:* www.frbatlanta.org
Jacksonville Branch 800 Water St .... Jacksonville FL 32204 904-632-1000
Web: federalreserve.gov
Miami Branch 9100 NW 36th St .... Miami FL 33178 305-591-2065
Web: frbatlanta.org
Nashville Branch 301 Rosa L Parks................ Nashville TN 37203 615-251-7100
Web: www.frbatlanta.org
New Orleans Branch 525 St Charles Ave .... New Orleans LA 70130 504-593-3200
TF: 877-638-7003 ■ *Web:* www.frbatlanta.org

Federal Reserve Bank of Boston
600 Atlantic Ave.. Boston MA 02210 617-973-3000 619-8501
Web: www.bostonfed.org

Federal Reserve Bank of Chicago
230 S LaSalle St....................................... Chicago IL 60604 312-322-5322 322-5515
Web: www.chicagofed.org
Detroit Branch 1600 E Warren Ave..................... Detroit MI 48207 313-961-6880
Web: chicagofed.org

Federal Reserve Bank of Cleveland
1455 E Sixth St PO Box 6387 .... Cleveland OH 44101 216-579-2000
Web: www.clevelandfed.org
Cincinnati Branch 150 E Fourth St............... Cincinnati OH 45202 513-721-4787
TF: 877-372-2457 ■ *Web:* www.clevelandfed.org

Federal Reserve Bank of Dallas
2200 N Pearl St PO Box 655906.......................... Dallas TX 75201 214-922-6000 922-5268
TF: 800-333-4460 ■ *Web:* www.dallasfed.org
El Paso Branch 301 E Main St......................... El Paso TX 79901 915-521-5200
TF: 800-333-4460 ■ *Web:* www.dallasfed.org
Houston Branch 1801 Allen Pkwy .... Houston TX 77019 713-483-3000
Web: www.dallasfed.org
San Antonio Branch 402 Dwyer Ave........... San Antonio TX 78204 210-978-1200
TF: 800-333-4460 ■ *Web:* www.dallasfed.org

Federal Reserve Bank of Kansas City
1 Memorial Dr PO Box 1200.................... Kansas City MO 64198 816-881-2000 881-2704
TF: 800-333-1010 ■ *Web:* www.kansascityfed.org
Denver Branch 1 Memorial Dr .... Kansas City MO 64198 888-851-1920 881-2704*
**Fax Area Code:* 816 ■ *TF:* 888-851-1920 ■ *Web:* kansascityfed.org
Oklahoma City Branch
226 Dean A McGee Ave.......................... Oklahoma City OK 73102 405-270-8400 270-8676
TF: 800-333-1030 ■ *Web:* www.kansascityfed.org
Omaha Branch 2201 Farnam St........................ Omaha NE 68102 402-221-5500
TF: 800-333-1040 ■ *Web:* www.kansascityfed.org

				Phone	Fax
Federal Reserve Bank of Minneapolis					
90 Hennepin Ave	Minneapolis	MN	55401	612-204-5000	204-5905
TF: 800-553-9656 ■ *Web:* www.minneapolisfed.org					
Helena Branch 100 Neill Ave	Helena	MT	59601	406-447-3800	
Web: federalreserve.gov					
Federal Reserve Bank of Philadelphia					
10 Independence Mall	Philadelphia	PA	19106	215-574-6000	
TF: 877-574-1776 ■ *Web:* www.phil.frb.org					
Federal Reserve Bank of Richmond					
701 E Byrd St	Richmond	VA	23219	804-697-8000	
Web: www.richmondfed.org					
Baltimore Branch 502 S Sharp St	Baltimore	MD	21201	410-576-3300	
Web: www.richmondfed.org					
Federal Reserve Bank of Saint Louis					
701 Convention Plaza	Saint Louis	MO	63101	314-444-8444	
TF: 800-333-0810 ■ *Web:* www.stlouisfed.org					
Little Rock Branch					
111 Ctr St Ste 1000 Stephens Bldg	Little Rock	AR	72201	501-324-8300	
TF: 877-372-2457 ■ *Web:* frbservices.org					
Louisville Branch 101 S Fifth St Ste 1920	Louisville	KY	40202	502-568-9200	
Web: frbservices.org					
Federal Reserve Bank of San Francisco (FRBSF)					
101 Market St	San Francisco	CA	94105	415-974-2000	974-2855
TF: 800-227-4133 ■ *Web:* www.frbsf.org					
Los Angeles Branch 950 S Grand Ave	Los Angeles	CA	90015	213-683-2300	
Web: www.frbsf.org					
Portland Branch 1500 SW First Ave Ste 100	Portland	OR	97201	503-276-3000	
TF: 800-227-4133 ■ *Web:* www.frbsf.org					
Salt Lake City Branch 101 Market St	San Francisco	CA	94105	415-974-2000	974-2168
TF: 800-227-4133 ■ *Web:* www.frbsf.org					
First Federal of Northern Michigan					
100 S Second Ave	Alpena	MI	49707	989-356-9041	354-8671
NASDAQ: FFNM ■ *TF:* 800-916-8800 ■ *Web:* www.first-federal.com					
First FSB 633 La Salle St	Ottawa	IL	61350	815-434-3500	
TF: 800-443-8780 ■ *Web:* www.ffsbweb.com					
First Shore Federal					
106-108 S Div St PO Box 4248	Salisbury	MD	21803	410-546-1101	546-9590
TF: 800-634-6309 ■ *Web:* www.firstshorefederal.com					
Frandsen Bank & Trust 501 Chestnut St W	Virginia	MN	55792	507-744-2361	
Web: www.frandsenbank.com					
Home Federal Bank 221 S Locust St	Grand Island	NE	68801	308-382-4000	382-9235
Web: www.homefederalne.com					
Lake Shore Bancorp Inc 128 E Fourth St	Dunkirk	NY	14048	716-366-4070	366-2965
NASDAQ: LSBK ■ *Web:* www.lakeshoresavings.com					
Lincoln FSB 1101 N St 68508	Lincoln	NE	68501	402-474-1400	474-1585
TF: 800-333-2158 ■ *Web:* www.lincolnfed.com					
Martha's Vineyard Savings Bank					
78 Main St PO Box 1069	Edgartown	MA	02539	508-627-4266	627-7588
Web: mvbank.com					
Milford Federal Savings & Loan Assn					
PO Box 210	Milford	MA	01757	508-634-2500	634-2500
TF: 800-478-6990 ■ *Web:* www.milfordfederal.com					
Naugatuck Savings Bank 87 Church St	Naugatuck	CT	06770	203-729-5291	
TF: 877-729-4442 ■ *Web:* www.naugatucksavingsbank.com					
Pioneer Bank 21 Second St PO Box 1048	Troy	NY	12181	518-274-4800	
TF: 866-873-9573 ■ *Web:* www.pioneerbanking.com					
Ponce De Leon Fsb 2244 Westchester Ave	Bronx	NY	10462	718-931-9000	542-9733
Web: www.poncedeleonbank.com					
Putnam County Savings Bank (PCSB)					
2477 Rt 6 PO Box 417	Brewster	NY	10509	845-279-7101	279-9321
Web: www.pcsb.com					
Security Federal Bank (SFB) 238 Richland Ave W	Aiken	SC	29801	803-641-3000	
TF: 866-851-3000 ■ *Web:* www.securityfederalbank.com					
Sterling Federal Bank					
110 E Fourth St PO Box 617	Sterling	IL	61081	815-626-0614	626-6921
Web: www.sterlingfederal.com					
Summit State Bank					
500 Bicentennial Way PO Box 6188	Santa Rosa	CA	95406	707-568-6000	568-7090
NASDAQ: SSBI ■ *TF:* 800-428-5008 ■ *Web:* www.summitstatebank.com					
Thomas County Federal Savings & Loan Assn Inc					
131 S Dawson St PO Box 1197	Thomasville	GA	31799	229-226-3221	226-3459
Web: www.tcfederal.com					
Webster First Federal Credit Union					
271 Greenwood St	Worcester	MA	01607	508-671-5000	
TF: 800-962-4452 ■ *Web:* www.websterfirst.com					

72 BAR ASSOCIATIONS - STATE

See Also Legal Professionals Associations p. 1794

				Phone	Fax
Alabama State Bar 415 Dexter Ave	Montgomery	AL	36104	334-269-1515	261-6310
TF: 800-392-5660 ■ *Web:* www.alabar.org					
Alaska Bar Assn					
550 W Seventh Ave Ste 1900 PO Box 100279	Anchorage	AK	99501	907-272-7469	272-2932
TF: 800-478-4372 ■ *Web:* www.alaskabar.org					
Arkansas Bar Assn 2224 Cottondale Ln	Little Rock	AR	72202	501-375-4606	375-4901
Web: arkbar.com					
Colorado Bar Assn 1900 Grant St Ste 900	Denver	CO	80203	303-860-1115	894-0821
Web: www.cobar.org					
Connecticut Bar Assn					
30 Bank St PO Box 350	New Britain	CT	06050	860-223-4400	223-4400
Web: www.ctbar.org					
Delaware State Bar Assn 405 N King St	Wilmington	DE	19801	302-658-5279	
TF: 855-872-5911					
District of Columbia Bar, The					
1101 K St NW Ste 200	Washington	DC	20005	202-737-4700	626-3453
TF: 877-333-2227 ■ *Web:* www.dcbar.org					
Florida Bar 651 E Jefferson St	Tallahassee	FL	32399	850-561-5600	561-1141
TF: 800-342-8060 ■ *Web:* www.floridabar.org					
Hawaii State Bar Assn (HSBA)					
1100 Alakea St Ste 1000	Honolulu	HI	96813	808-537-1868	521-7936
Web: www.hsba.org					
Idaho State Bar 525 W Jefferson St	Boise	ID	83702	208-334-4500	334-4515
TF: 800-221-3295 ■ *Web:* www.isb.idaho.gov					
Illinois State Bar Assn 424 S Second St	Springfield	IL	62701	217-525-1760	525-0712
TF: 800-252-8908 ■ *Web:* www.isba.org					
Indiana State Bar Assn					
1 Indiana Sq Ste 530	Indianapolis	IN	46204	317-639-5465	266-2588
TF: 800-266-2581 ■ *Web:* www.inbar.org					
Iowa State Bar Assn 625 E Ct Ave	Des Moines	IA	50309	515-243-3179	243-2511
Web: www.iowabar.org					
Kansas Bar Assn 1200 SW Harrison St	Topeka	KS	66612	785-234-5696	234-3813
TF: 800-928-3111 ■ *Web:* www.ksbar.org					
Kentucky Bar Assn 514 W Main St	Frankfort	KY	40601	502-564-3795	564-3225
Web: www.kybar.org					
Louisiana State Bar Assn (LSBA)					
601 St Charles Ave	New Orleans	LA	70130	504-566-1600	566-0930
TF: 800-421-5722 ■ *Web:* www.lsba.org					
Maine State Bar Assn 124 State St	Augusta	ME	04330	207-622-7523	623-0083
TF: 800-475-7523 ■ *Web:* www.mainebar.org					
Maryland State Bar Assn Inc					
520 W Fayette St	Baltimore	MD	21201	410-685-7878	685-1016
TF: 800-492-1964 ■ *Web:* www.msba.org					
Massachusetts Bar Assn 20 W St	Boston	MA	02111	617-338-0500	
Web: mass.gov					
Minnesota State Bar Assn					
600 Nicollet Mall Ste 380	Minneapolis	MN	55402	612-333-1183	333-4927
TF: 800-882-6722 ■ *Web:* www.mnbar.org					
Mississippi Bar 643 N State St	Jackson	MS	39202	601-948-4471	355-8635
Web: www.msbar.org					
Missouri Bar, The					
326 Monroe St PO Box 119	Jefferson City	MO	65102	573-635-4128	635-2811
TF: 888-253-6013 ■ *Web:* www.mobar.org					
Nebraska State Bar Assn 635 S 14th St Ste 200	Lincoln	NE	68501	402-475-7091	475-7098
TF: 800-927-0117 ■ *Web:* www.nebar.com					
New Hampshire Bar Assn 2 Pillsbury St Ste 300	Concord	NH	03301	603-224-6942	224-2910
Web: www.nhbar.org					
New Jersey State Bar Assn					
1 Constitution Sq New Jersey Law Ctr	New Brunswick	NJ	08901	732-249-5000	249-2815
Web: www.njsba.com					
New York State Bar Assn 1 Elk St	Albany	NY	12207	518-463-3200	487-5517
TF: 800-342-3661 ■ *Web:* www.nysba.org					
North Carolina State Bar					
217 E Edenton St PO Box 25996	Raleigh	NC	27601	919-828-4620	821-9168
TF: 800-662-7407 ■ *Web:* ncbar.gov					
Ohio State Bar Assn (OSBA) 1700 Lk Shore Dr	Columbus	OH	43204	614-487-2050	487-1008
TF: 800-282-6556 ■ *Web:* www.ohiobar.org					
Oklahoma Bar Assn					
1901 N Lincoln Blvd PO Box 53036	Oklahoma City	OK	73105	405-416-7000	416-7001
TF: 800-522-8065 ■ *Web:* www.okbar.org					
Oregon State Bar Assn					
16037 SW Upper Boones Ferry Rd	Tigard	OR	97224	503-620-0222	684-1366
TF: 800-452-8260 ■ *Web:* www.osbar.org					
Pennsylvania Bar Assn 100 S St	Harrisburg	PA	17101	717-238-6715	238-1204
TF: 800-932-0311 ■ *Web:* www.pabar.org					
Rhode Island Bar Assn 115 Cedar St	Providence	RI	02903	401-421-5740	421-2703
TF: 877-659-0801 ■ *Web:* www.ribar.com					
South Carolina Bar 950 Taylor St	Columbia	SC	29201	803-799-6653	799-4118
TF: 877-797-2227 ■ *Web:* www.scbar.org					
State Bar Assn of North Dakota					
504 N Washington St PO Box 2136	Bismarck	ND	58502	701-255-1404	224-1621
TF: 800-472-2685 ■ *Web:* www.sband.org					
State Bar of Arizona 4201 N 24th St Ste 200	Phoenix	AZ	85016	602-252-4804	271-4930
TF: 866-482-9227 ■ *Web:* www.azbar.org					
State Bar of California 180 Howard St	San Francisco	CA	94105	415-538-2000	538-2304
Web: www.calbar.ca.gov					
State Bar of Georgia					
104 Marietta St NW Ste 100	Atlanta	GA	30303	404-527-8700	527-8717
TF: 800-334-6865 ■ *Web:* www.gabar.org					
State Bar of Michigan 306 Townsend St	Lansing	MI	48933	517-346-6300	482-6248
TF: 800-968-1442 ■ *Web:* www.michbar.org					
State Bar of Montana PO Box 577	Helena	MT	59624	406-442-7660	442-7763
Web: www.montanabar.org					
State Bar of Nevada 600 E Charleston Blvd	Las Vegas	NV	89104	702-382-2200	385-2878
TF: 800-254-2797 ■ *Web:* www.nvbar.org					
State Bar of New Mexico					
5121 Masthead St NE PO Box 92860	Albuquerque	NM	87109	505-797-6000	828-3765
TF: 800-876-6227 ■ *Web:* www.nmbar.org					
State Bar of South Dakota					
222 E Capitol Ave Ste 3	Pierre	SD	57501	605-224-7554	224-0282
Web: statebarofsouthdakota.com					
State Bar of Texas 1414 Colorado St	Austin	TX	78701	512-427-1463	427-4100
TF: 800-204-2222 ■ *Web:* www.texasbar.com					
State Bar of Wisconsin 5302 Eastpark Blvd	Madison	WI	53718	608-257-3838	
Web: www.wisbar.org					
Tennessee Bar Assn 221 Fourth Ave N Ste 400	Nashville	TN	37219	615-383-7421	297-8058
TF: 800-899-6993 ■ *Web:* tba.org					
Utah State Bar 645 S 200 E	Salt Lake City	UT	84111	801-531-9077	531-0660
TF: 877-752-2611 ■ *Web:* www.utahbar.org					
Vermont Bar Assn (VBA) 35-37 Ct St PO Box 100	Montpelier	VT	05601	802-223-2020	223-1573
TF: 800-639-7036 ■ *Web:* www.vtbar.org					
Virginia State Bar 707 E Main St Ste 1500	Richmond	VA	23219	804-775-0500	775-0544
TF: 800-552-7977 ■ *Web:* www.vsb.org					
Washington State Bar Assn					
1325 Fourth Ave Ste 600	Seattle	WA	98101	206-727-8200	727-8320
TF: 800-945-9722 ■ *Web:* www.wsba.org					
West Virginia State Bar					
2000 Deitrick Blvd	Charleston	WV	25311	304-553-7220	558-2467
TF: 866-989-8227 ■ *Web:* www.wvbar.org					
Wyoming State Bar 4124 Laramie St	Cheyenne	WY	82001	307-632-9061	632-3737
TF: 855-445-8058 ■ *Web:* www.wyomingbar.org					

73 BASKETS, CAGES, RACKS, ETC - WIRE

See Also Pet Products p. 2928

Company	City	State	Zip	Phone	Fax
Adrian Fabricators Inc 545 Industrial Dr. *Web:* adrian.cylex-usa.com	Adrian	MI	49221	517-266-5700	
Apco Products Inc PO Box 236 *Web:* www.apco-products.com	Essex	CT	06426	860-767-2108	767-7259
Archer Wire International Corp 7300 S Narragansett Ave *Web:* www.archerwire.com	Bedford Park	IL	60638	708-563-1700	563-1740
Bright Co-op Inc 803 W Seale St *TF:* 800-562-0730 ■ *Web:* www.brightcoop.com	Nacogdoches	TX	75964	936-564-8378	564-3281
Equipment Fabricating Corp 729 45th Ave *Web:* www.equipmentfabricating.com	Oakland	CA	94601	510-261-0343	261-0715
Glamos Wire Products Company Inc 5561 N 152nd St *TF:* 800-328-5062 ■ *Web:* www.glamoswire.com	Hugo	MN	55038	651-429-5386	429-7733
InterMetro Industries Corp 651 N Washington St **Fax:* Hum Res ■ *TF Cust Svc:* 800-992-1776 ■ *Web:* www.metro.com	Wilkes-Barre	PA	18705	570-825-2741	823-2852*
Kewanna Metal Specialties Inc (KMS) 419 W Main St *Web:* www.kmswire.com	Kewanna	IN	46939	574-653-2554	653-2556
Lab Products Inc 742 Sussex Ave PO Box 639 *TF:* 800-526-0469 ■ *Web:* www.labproductsinc.com	Seaford	DE	19973	302-628-4300	628-4309
Marlboro Wire 2403 N 24th St *Web:* www.marlborowire.com	Quincy	IL	62305	217-224-7989	224-7990
Midwest Wire Products Inc 800 Woodward Heights *TF:* 800-989-9881 ■ *Web:* www.midwestwire.com	Ferndale	MI	48220	248-399-5100	542-7104
Nashville Wire Products Manufacturing Co 199 Polk Ave *TF:* 800-448-2125 ■ *Web:* www.nashvillewire.com	Nashville	TN	37210	615-743-2500	242-4225
Progress Wire Products Inc 3535 W 140th St *Web:* www.progresswire.com	Cleveland	OH	44111	216-251-2181	251-2699
Riverdale Mills Corp 130 Riverdale St *TF:* 800-762-6374 ■ *Web:* www.riverdale.com	Northbridge	MA	01534	508-234-8715	234-9593
Stevens Wire Products Inc 351 NW 'F' St *Web:* www.stevenswire.com	Richmond	IN	47374	765-966-5534	962-3586
Technibilt Ltd 700 E P St PO Box 310 **Fax Area Code:* 800 ■ *Web:* www.technibilt.com	Newton	NC	28658	828-464-7388	968-8934*
Wirefab Inc 75 Blackstone River Rd *Web:* www.wirefab.com	Worcester	MA	01607	508-754-5359	797-3620

74 BATTERIES

Company	City	State	Zip	Phone	Fax
A123 Systems Inc 200 W St *TF:* 800-224-7654 ■ *Web:* www.a123systems.com	Waltham	MA	02451	617-778-5700	924-8910
Applied Energy Solutions LLC 1 Technology Pl **Fax:* Sales ■ *TF:* 800-836-2132 ■ *Web:* www.appliedenergysol.com	Caledonia	NY	14423	585-538-4421	538-6345*
Atlantic Battery Company Inc 309 Main St *Web:* www.atlanticbatterycompany.com	Watertown	MA	02472	617-924-2868	
Battery Handling Systems Inc 1488 Page Industrial Ct *Web:* www.bhs1.com	Saint Louis	MO	63132	314-423-7091	
Bren-Tronics Inc 10 Brayton Ct *Web:* www.bren-tronics.com	Commack	NY	11725	631-499-5155	499-5504
C & D Technologies Inc 1400 Union Meeting Rd PO Box 3053 *TF:* 800-543-8630 ■ *Web:* www.cdtechno.com	Blue Bell	PA	19422	215-619-2700	619-7899
Cell-con Inc 305 Commerce Dr Ste 300 *TF:* 800-771-7139 ■ *Web:* www.cell-con.com	Exton	PA	19341	610-280-7630	280-7685
Continental Battery Corp 4919 Woodall St *TF:* 800-442-0081 ■ *Web:* www.continentalbattery.com	Dallas	TX	75247	214-631-5701	634-7846
Crown Battery Manufacturing Co 1445 Majestic Dr *TF:* 800-487-2879 ■ *Web:* www.crownbattery.com	Fremont	OH	43420	419-334-7181	334-7416
Douglas Battery Manufacturing Co 500 Battery Dr *TF:* 800-368-4527 ■ *Web:* www.douglasbattery.com	Winston-Salem	NC	27107	800-368-4527	
Duracell 14 Research Dr **Fax Area Code:* 866 ■ *TF:* 800-551-2355 ■ *Web:* www.duracell.com	Bethel	CT	06801	800-544-5454	889-7911*
EaglePicher Technologies LLC C & Porter St *Web:* www.eaglepicher.com	Joplin	MO	64801	417-623-8000	
Ener1 Inc 3023 Distribution Wy *Web:* www.ener1.com	Greenfield	IN	46140	317-703-1800	
EnerSys 2366 Bernville Rd *NYSE:* ENS ■ *TF:* 800-538-3627 ■ *Web:* enersys.com	Reading	PA	19605	610-208-1991	372-8457
EnerSys Inc 617 N Ridgeview Dr *Web:* www.enersys.com/globallanding.aspx	Warrensburg	MO	64093	660-429-2165	429-1758
Exide Technologies 13000 Deerfield Pkwy Bldg 200 *NASDAQ:* XIDE ■ *TF:* 888-563-6300 ■ *Web:* www.exideworld.com	Milton	GA	30004	678-566-9000	566-9188
Hawker Powersource Inc 9404 Ooltewah Industrial Dr PO Box 808 *TF:* 800-238-8658 ■ *Web:* www.hawkerpowersource.com	Ooltewah	TN	37363	423-238-5700	238-6060
Industrial Battery & Charger Inc 5831 Orr Rd *TF:* 800-833-8412 ■ *Web:* www.ibcipower.com	Charlotte	NC	28213	704-597-7330	597-0855
MarathonNorco Aerospace Inc 8301 Imperial Dr *Web:* www.mnaerospace.com	Waco	TX	76712	254-776-0650	776-6558
Mathews Assoc Inc 220 Power Ct *TF:* 800-871-5262 ■ *Web:* www.maifl.com	Sanford	FL	32771	407-323-3390	323-3115
Power Battery Co Inc 25 McLean Blvd *Web:* powerbatteryco.com	Paterson	NJ	07514	973-523-8630	523-3023
PulseTech Products Corp 1100 S Kimball Ave *Web:* www.pulsetech.net	Southlake	TX	76092	817-329-6099	
R & D Batteries Inc 3300 Corporate Ctr Dr PO Box 5007 *TF:* 800-950-1945 ■ *Web:* www.rdbatteries.com	Burnsville	MN	55306	952-890-0629	890-7912
Staab Battery Manufacturing Co 931 S 11th St *Web:* www.staabbattery.com	Springfield	IL	62703	217-528-0421	
Surefire LLC 18300 Mt Baldy Cir *TF:* 800-828-8809 ■ *Web:* www.surefire.com	Fountain Valley	CA	92708	714-545-9444	545-9537
Tadiran Batteries 2001 Marcus Ave Ste 125E *TF:* 800-537-1368 ■ *Web:* www.tadiranbat.com	New Hyde Park	NY	11042	516-621-4980	621-4517
TNR Technical Inc 301 Central Pk Dr *OTC:* TNRK ■ *TF:* 800-346-0601 ■ *Web:* www.batterystore.com	Sanford	FL	32771	407-321-3011	321-3208
Trojan Battery Co 12380 Clark St *TF Cust Svc:* 800-423-6569 ■ *Web:* www.trojanbattery.com	Santa Fe Springs	CA	90670	562-236-3000	236-3282
Ultralife Batteries Inc 2000 Technology Pkwy *NASDAQ:* ULBI ■ *TF:* 800-332-5000 ■ *Web:* www.ultralifecorporation.com	Newark	NY	14513	315-332-7100	331-7800
Valence Technology Inc 12303 Technology Blvd Ste 950 *TF:* 888-825-3623 ■ *Web:* www.valence.com	Austin	TX	78727	512-527-2900	527-2910
Yardney Technical Products Inc 82 Mechanic St *Web:* www.yardney.com	Pawcatuck	CT	06379	860-599-1100	599-3903

75 BEARINGS - BALL & ROLLER

Company	City	State	Zip	Phone	Fax
Accurate Bushing Company Inc 443 N Ave *TF Sales:* 800-932-0076 ■ *Web:* www.smithbearing.com	Garwood	NJ	07027	908-789-1121	789-9429
ACL Distribution Inc 4722 Danvers Dr *Web:* www.aclperformance.com.au	Grand Rapids	MI	49512	616-956-1300	
Advanced Green Components LLC 4005 Corporate Dr *Web:* www.advgreen.com	Winchester	KY	40391	859-737-6000	
Aetna Bearing Co 1081 Sesame St *Web:* www.aetnabearing.com	Franklin Park	IL	60131	630-694-0024	
Alinabal Inc 28 Woodmont Rd *Web:* www.alinabal.com	Milford	CT	06460	203-877-3241	874-5063
American Roller Bearing Co 400 Second Ave NW *Web:* www.amroll.com	Hickory	NC	28601	828-624-1460	
AST Bearings 115 Main Rd *TF:* 800-526-1250 ■ *Web:* www.astbearings.com	Montville	NJ	07045	973-335-2230	335-6987
Aurora Bearing Co 901 Aucutt Rd *Web:* www.aurorabearing.com	Montgomery	IL	60538	630-859-2030	
Avon Bearings Inc 1500 Nagle Rd *Web:* www.kaydonbearings.com	Avon	OH	44011	440-871-2500	
Bearing Inspection Inc 4500 Mount Pleasant NW *TF Cust Svc:* 800-416-8881 ■ *Web:* www.timken.com	North Canton	OH	44720	234-262-3000	
Bearing Service Co of Pennsylvania 630 Alpha Dr RIDC Park *TF:* 800-783-2327 ■ *Web:* www.bearing-service.com	Pittsburgh	PA	15238	412-963-7710	963-8005
Berliss Bearing Co 644 Rt 10 Po Box 45 *Web:* www.berliss.com	Livingston	NJ	07039	973-992-4242	992-6669
C & S Engineering Corp 956 Old Colony Rd *Web:* www.cscos.com	Meriden	CT	06451	203-235-5727	
Cooper Split Roller Bearing Corp, The 5365 Robin Hood Rd Ste B *Web:* www.cooperbearings.com	Norfolk	VA	23513	757-460-0925	
Del-tron Precision Inc 5 Trowbridge Dr *Web:* deltron.com	Bethel	CT	06801	203-778-2727	
EDT Corp 1006-J NE 146th St *Web:* www.edtcorp.com	Vancouver	WA	98685	360-574-7294	
Flexible Concepts 1620 Middlebury St *Web:* www.flexibleconcepts.com	Elkhart	IN	46516	574-296-0941	
Freeway Corp 9301 Allen Dr **Fax:* Sales ■ *Web:* www.freewaycorp.com	Cleveland	OH	44125	216-524-9700	524-7396*
General Bearing Corp 44 High St *TF Sales:* 800-431-1766 ■ *Web:* www.generalbearing.com	West Nyack	NY	10994	845-358-6000	358-6277
Hartford Technologies 1022 Elm St *Web:* www.hartfordtechnologies.com	Rocky Hill	CT	06067	860-571-3602	571-3604
JTEKT Corporation 29570 Clemens Rd *TF Cust Svc:* 800-263-5163 ■ *Web:* www.jtekt-na.com	Westlake	OH	44145	440-835-1000	835-9347
LSB Industries Inc 16 S Pennsylvania Ave *NYSE:* LXU ■ *Web:* www.lsbindustries.com	Oklahoma City	OK	73107	405-235-4546	235-5067
Lutco Bearings Inc 130 Higgins St *Web:* www.lutco.com	Worcester	MA	01606	508-853-2114	
Lutco Inc 677 Cambridge St *Web:* www.lutco.com	Worcester	MA	01610	508-756-6296	799-6848
Mechatronics Inc 8152 304th Ave SE PO Box 5012 *Web:* www.mechatronicsinc.com	Preston	WA	98050	425-222-5900	
Nachi America Inc 715 Pushville Rd *TF:* 888-340-2747 ■ *Web:* www.nachiamerica.com	Greenwood	IN	46143	317-530-1001	530-1011
National Bearing Co 1596 Manheim Pk *Web:* www.nationalbearings.com	Lancaster	PA	17604	717-569-0485	569-1605
New Hampshire Ball Bearings Inc 175 Jaffrey Rd **Fax:* Cust Svc ■ *Web:* www.nhbb.com	Peterborough	NH	03458	603-924-3311	924-4419*
NSK-AKS Precision Ball Co 1100A N First St *Web:* www.aksball-us.com	Clarinda	IA	51632	712-542-6515	
Ntn Bower 2086 Military St S *Web:* ntnbower.com	Hamilton	AL	35570	205-952-9355	
Peer Bearing Co 2200 Norman Dr S **Fax:* Orders ■ *TF:* 800-433-7337 ■ *Web:* www.peerbearing.com	Waukegan	IL	60085	847-578-1000	578-1200*
Professional Instruments Co 7800 Powell Rd *Web:* www.airbearings.com	Hopkins	MN	55343	952-933-1222	933-3315
Roller Bearing Company of America 400 Sullivan Way *TF:* 800-390-3300 ■ *Web:* www.rbcbearings.com	West Trenton	NJ	08628	609-882-5050	882-5533

Phone Fax

Rotek Inc 1400 S Chillicothe Rd PO Box 312 ....Aurora OH 44202 330-562-4000 562-4620*
Fax: Sales ■ *TF:* 800-221-8043 ■ *Web:* www.rotek-inc.com
S/n Precision Enterprises Inc 145 Jordan Rd ....Troy NY 12180 518-283-8002 283-8032
Web: www.pacamor.com
Schaeffler Group USA Inc
308 Springhill Farm Rd ....Fort Mill SC 29715 803-548-8500 548-8599
TF: 800-361-5841 ■ *Web:* www.schaeffler.us
Schatz Bearing Corp 10 Fairview Ave ....Poughkeepsie NY 12601 845-452-6000 452-1660
TF: 800-554-1406 ■ *Web:* www.schatzbearing.com
SKF USA Inc Roller Bearing Div
20 Industrial Dr.............Hanover PA 17331 717-637-8981
Web: skf.com
Timken Co 1835 Dueber Ave SW.............Canton OH 44706 330-438-3000 458-6006
NYSE: TKR ■ *TF:* 800-223-1954 ■ *Web:* www.timken.com
Universal Bearings Inc 431 N Birkey St ....Bremen IN 46506 574-546-2261 546-5085
Web: www.univbrg.com
Virginia Industries Inc 1022 Elm St ....Rocky Hill CT 06067 860-571-3600 571-3604
Web: www.virginia.gov
Wecsys LLC 8825 Xylon Ave N.............Minneapolis MN 55445 763-504-1069
TF: 888-493-2797 ■ *Web:* www.wecsysllc.com
Wieland Metals Inc 567 Northgate Pkwy.............Wheeling IL 60090 847-537-3990 537-4085
Web: www.wielandus.com
Winsted Precision Ball Corp
159 Colebrook River Rd ....Winsted CT 06098 860-379-2788 379-9650
TF: 800-462-3075 ■ *Web:* www.winball.com

76 BEAUTY SALON EQUIPMENT & SUPPLIES

Phone Fax

Arbonne International 9400 Jeronimo Rd.............Irvine CA 92618 949-770-2610
Web: arbonne.com
Beaute Craft Supply Co 600 W Maple Rd.............Troy MI 48084 248-362-0400 362-7996*
Belvedere USA Corp 1 Belvedere Blvd.............Belvidere IL 61008 815-544-3131 626-9750*
**Fax Area Code:* 800 ■ *TF:* 800-435-5491 ■ *Web:* www.belvedere.com
Betty Dain Creations Inc 9701 NW 112 Ave Ste 10 ....Miami FL 33178 305-769-3451
TF General: 800-327-5256 ■ *Web:* www.bettydain.com
Brad-Pak Enterprises Inc 124 S Ave ....Garwood NJ 07027 908-233-1234
Web: brad-pak.com
Burmax Co 28 Barretts Ave.............Holtsville NY 11742 800-645-5118 289-7590*
**Fax Area Code:* 631 ■ *TF:* 800-645-5118 ■ *Web:* www.burmax.com
Cedar Bay Inc 1224 Whitestone Dr.............Murphy TX 75094 972-384-0410
Collins Manufacturing Co 2000 Bowser Rd.............Cookeville TN 38506 931-528-5151 528-5472
TF: 800-292-6450 ■ *Web:* www.collinsmfgco.com
Dr Kern USA Inc 221 S Franklin Rd.............Indianapolis IN 46219 317-472-0873 472-0873
TF: 800-908-9885 ■ *Web:* www.drkern.com
European Touch Ltd II 8301 W Parkland Ct.............Milwaukee WI 53223 414-357-7016
IdeaVillage Products Corp 155 Rt 46 W 4th Fl.............Wayne NJ 07470 973-826-8418
Web: www.ideavillage.com
Jerdon Style LLC
1820 N Glenville Dr Ste 124.............Richardson TX 75081 972-690-4286
Web: www.jerdonstyle.com
Jeunesse Global LLC
650 Douglas Ave ....Altamonte Springs FL 32714 407-215-7414
TF: 800-400-2676 ■ *Web:* www.jeunesseglobal.com
Living Earth Crafts 3210 Executive Ridge Dr.............Vista CA 92081 760-597-2155
TF: 800-358-8292 ■ *Web:* www.livingearthcrafts.com
Middlebridge Mktg Inc
1525 Old Louisquisset Pk.............Lincoln RI 02865 401-728-0040
National Salon Resources Inc
3109 Louisiana Ave N.............Minneapolis MN 55427 763-541-1000 577-2512*
**Fax Area Code:* 800 ■ *TF:* 800-622-0003 ■ *Web:* www.nationalsalon.com
Pibbs Industries 133-15 32nd Ave.............Flushing NY 11354 718-445-8046 461-3910
TF: 800-551-5020 ■ *Web:* www.pibbs.com
Sally Beauty Company Inc 3001 Colorado Blvd.............Denton TX 76210 940-898-7500
TF: 800-777-5706 ■ *Web:* www.sallybeauty.com
T3 Micro Inc 228 Main St Ste 12.............Venice CA 90291 310-452-2888
Takara Belmont USA Inc 101 Belmont Dr.............Somerset NJ 08873 877-283-1289 283-1687*
**Fax Area Code:* 732 ■ *TF:* 877-283-1289 ■ *Web:* www.takarabelmont.com
TouchAmerica 1403 S Third St Ext.............Hillsborough NC 27278 919-732-6968 732-1173
TF: 800-678-6824 ■ *Web:* www.touchamerica.com
Valley Barber & Beauty Supply
413 W Harrison St ....Harlingen TX 78550 956-423-0727 423-0757
William Marvy Company Inc
1540 St Clair Ave ....Saint Paul MN 55105 651-698-0726 698-4048
TF: 800-874-2651 ■ *Web:* www.wmmarvyco.com

77 BEAUTY SALONS

Phone Fax

A b Salon Interiors Inc
14220 66th St N Ste E ....Clearwater FL 33764 727-531-5405
Web: www.absalonequipment.com
A-tech Security Inc
10001 Wilshire Ave Ne.............Albuquerque NM 87122 505-821-5777
Web: www.atechsecurity.com
Adam Broderick Salon & Spa 89 Danbury Rd ....Ridgefield CT 06877 203-431-3994
TF: 800-438-3834 ■ *Web:* www.adambroderick.com
Aedes De Venustas Inc
9 Christopher St Frnt B.............New York NY 10014 212-206-8674
Web: aedes.com
Alejandra Hair Salon
14208 Palm Dr.............Desert Hot Springs CA 92240 954-447-9561
Web: www.alejandrahair.com
Alexandre de Paris Inc
12751 Federal Systems Park Dr.............Fairfax VA 22033 703-222-7661
Web: www.alexandredeparis.com
Aloe Up Suncare 9700 W 76th St Ste 112.............Eden Prairie MN 55344 952-933-7724
Web: www.aloeup.com
Amber Waves Inc 11 S Ave W ....Richardton ND 58652 701-974-4230
Web: www.amberwavesinc.com

Phone Fax

Ambiance Day Spa & Salon
1777 Monte Vista Ave.............Claremont CA 91711 909-625-5535
Web: www.claremontclub.com
Aromaland Inc 1326 Rufina Cir.............Santa Fe NM 87507 505-438-0402
TF: 800-933-5267 ■ *Web:* www.aromaland.com
Ascent Biomedical Ventures
142 W 57th St Ste 4A.............New York NY 10019 212-303-1680
Web: www.ankarcapital.com
Balance Day Spa LLC 2138 Lawndale Dr.............Greensboro NC 27408 336-574-2556
Web: www.balancedayspa.com
Ball Beauty Supplies 416 N Fairfax Ave.............Los Angeles CA 90036 323-655-2330
TF: 800-588-0244 ■ *Web:* www.ballbeauty.com
Beauty Bar LLC 2919 W Central Ave.............Toledo OH 43606 419-537-5400
Web: www.beauty-bar.com
Beauty Brands Inc 4600 Madison St Ste 400.............Kansas City MO 64112 816-531-2266
TF: 877-640-2248 ■ *Web:* www.beautybrands.com
Beauty Collection Inc 7862 Burnet Ave.............Van Nuys CA 91405 818-785-7447
Web: beautycollection.com
Beauty Craft Supply & Equipment Co
11110 Bren Rd W.............Minnetonka MN 55343 952-935-4420
TF: 800-328-5010 ■ *Web:* www.beautycraft.com
Beauty Management Inc 270 Beavercreek Rd.............Oregon City OR 97045 503-723-3200
Web: www.perfectlooksalons.com
Beauty Schools of America
1176 Southwest 67 Ave ....Miami FL 33144 305-824-2070
Web: www.bsa.edu
Belpointe Capital 125 Greenwich Ave ....Greenwich CT 06830 203-629-3300
Web: www.belpointe.com
Beyer Barber Co 1136 Hamilton St Ste 103 ....Allentown PA 18101 610-435-9577
Web: www.beyerbarber.com
Borealis Compounds LLC 176 Thomas Rd ....Port Murray NJ 07865 908-850-6200
Web: www.borealisgroup.com
Boyd Brothers Inc 425 E 15th St ....Panama City FL 32405 850-763-1741
Web: www.boyd-printing.com
Bullhead City Bee 1905 Lakeside Dr ....Bullhead City AZ 86442 928-763-9339
Web: www.bullheadcitybee.com
Buy Me Beauty 4221 NE 12th Terrace.............Oakland Park FL 33334 954-568-7150
Web: www.buymebeauty.com
Cain's Barber College Inc 365 E 51st St.............Chicago IL 60615 773-536-4441
Web: www.cbcon51st.org
Cartoon Cuts LP 927 N University Dr ....Coral Springs FL 33071 954-341-4221
Web: www.cartooncuts.com
Celadon Spa 1180 F St Nw Frnt 1 ....Washington DC 20004 202-347-3333
Web: www.celadonspa.com
Changes Salon & Day Spa Inc
1475 N Broadway ....Walnut Creek CA 94596 925-947-1814
Web: changessalon.com
Charles Penzone Inc 1480 Manning Pkwy.............Powell OH 43065 614-898-1200
Web: www.charlespenzone.com
Chella Professional Skin Care
507 Calle San Pablo.............Camarillo CA 93012 805-383-7711
TF: 877-424-3552 ■ *Web:* www.chella.com
Cinta Salon 23 Grant Ave.............San Francisco CA 94108 415-989-1000
Web: cinta.com
Colourbox Hairdressing 305 Cordova St W.............Vancouver BC V6B1E5 604-669-6354
Web: colourboxhair.com
Daired's Salon & Spa Pangea
2400 W Interstate 20.............Arlington TX 76017 817-465-9797
Web: daireds.com
Denver Dermatology Consultants Pc
1551 Milky Way ....Thornton CO 80260 303-426-4525
Web: www.denverderm.com
Dermatology Associates of Tyler
1367 Dominion Plz.............Tyler TX 75703 903-534-6200
Web: www.easttexasderm.com
Desiccare Inc 3400 Pomona Blvd.............Pomona CA 91768 909-444-8272
Web: www.desiccare.com
Dipietro Todd Salon 177 Post St Fl 2.............San Francisco CA 94108 415-397-0177
Web: www.dipietrotodd.com
Dosha Salon & Spa 3490 Se Hawthorne Blvd.............Portland OR 97214 503-231-4993
Web: www.dosha.org
Dunwoody Village 3500 W Chester Pk.............Newtown Square PA 19073 610-359-4400
Web: www.dunwoody.org
Durham Christian Homes Hair Styling
200 Glen Hill Dr.............Whitby ON L1N7J7 905-668-3840
Web: durhamchristianhomes.salonpages.ca
EG Capital Group LLC 39 W 54th St.............New York NY 10019 212-956-2600
Web: www.egcapitalgroup.com
Evelinecharles Salons-spas
100 Anderson Rd Se Ste 5 ....Calgary AB T2J3V1 403-571-5666
Web: www.evelinecharles.com
Fantastic Sams Inc 500 Cummings Ctr Ste 1100 ....Beverly MA 01915 651-770-1449
Web: www.fantasticsams.com
Farmington Center Salem an Oregon LP
960 Boone Rd SE ....Salem OR 97306 503-715-0727
Web: www.farmingtonsquare-salem.com
Fintronx LLC 5995 Chapel Hill Rd Ste 119.............Raleigh NC 27607 919-324-3960
Web: www.fintronx.com
Floral Plant Growers LLC North 781 Curran Rd ....Denmark WI 54208 920-863-2107
Web: www.naturalbeautygrowers.com
Fountain, The 1100 State Rt 17.............Ramsey NJ 07446 201-327-5155
Web: www.fountain.com
Fuga 3853 N Southport Ave.............Chicago IL 60613 773-880-1280
Web: www.salonfuga.com
Gadabout Inc
6393 E Grant Near Grant and Tanque Verde Near Costco
.............Tucson AZ 85715 520-885-0000
Web: www.gadabout.com
Genesis Biosystems Inc
1500 Eagle Ct # 75057.............Lewisville TX 75057 972-315-7888
TF: 888-577-7335 ■ *Web:* www.genesisbiosystems.com
Geralds of Northville Inc
41012 Five Mile Rd ....Plymouth MI 48170 734-420-0111
Web: www.geraldssalon.com

				Phone	Fax
Ginger Bay Salon Group Ltd 437 S kirkwood Rd *Web:* www.gingerbay.com	kirkwood	MO	63122	314-966-0655	
Gino Morena Enterprises LLC 111 Starlite St *TF:* 800-227-6905 ■ *Web:* www.ginomorena.com	South San Francisco	CA	94080	800-227-6905	
Gould's Styling Salons 2760 N Germantown Pkwy Ste 197 *Web:* gouldsalonspa.com	Memphis	TN	38133	901-386-5101	
Great Clips Inc 7700 France Ave S Ste 425 *TF:* 800-999-5959 ■ *Web:* www.greatclips.com	Minneapolis	MN	55435	952-893-9088	844-3444
Green Tangerine Spa & Salon 238 Patriot Pl *Web:* www.greentangerinespa.com	Foxborough	MA	02035	508-203-9414	
Hair Club for Men LTD Inc 1515 S Federal Hwy Ste 401 *Web:* www.hairclub.com	Boca Raton	FL	33432	561-361-7600	
Hair It Is 977 Perry Hwy Ste 4 *Web:* www.hairitis.biz	Pittsburgh	PA	15237	412-366-5511	
Hairart International Inc 400 W 157th St *Web:* hairartinc.com	Gardena	CA	90248	818-905-7730	
HK Enterprises Inc 3190-B Coronado Dr	Santa Clara	CA	95054	408-988-5880	
Holiday Hair 7201 Metro Blvd *TF:* 800-345-7811 ■ *Web:* www.signaturestyle.com/brands/holiday-hair.html	Minneapolis	MN	55439	800-345-7811	
Holtzman Enterprises Inc 8501 Turnpike Dr Ste 103 *Web:* greatclips.com	Westminster	CO	80031	303-428-3364	
Ideal Image Development Inc 1 Urban Ctr 4830 W Kennedy Blvd Ste 440 *Web:* www.idealimage.com	Tampa	FL	33609	813-286-8100	
Imperial Salon & Spa Inc 3 Suntree Pl *Web:* www.imperialsalonandspa.com	Melbourne	FL	32940	321-254-4432	
In Stock Retail 128 Holiday Ct Ste 105 *Web:* instockrs.com	Franklin	TN	37067	615-790-2934	
Instyle Hair Designs Inc 175 Littleton Rd *Web:* www.instylehd.com	Westford	MA	01886	978-692-7851	
J D Beauty 5 Adams Ave *Web:* www.jdbeauty.com	Hauppauge	NY	11788	631-273-2800	
Jai Transforme Salon 12730 Olive Blvd *Web:* www.jaitransformesalon.com	Saint Louis	MO	63141	314-439-5542	
John Masters Organic Hair Care Inc 77 Sullivan St *Web:* www.johnmasters.com	New York	NY	10012	212-343-9590	
Just Hair 1845 Eastwest Pkwy *Web:* www.justhair.mobi	Fleming Island	FL	32003	904-215-2995	
Kenneth Shuler School of Cosmetology & Hair Design Inc 449 Saint Andrews Rd *Web:* www.kennethshuler.com	Columbia	SC	29210	803-772-6042	
L Salon & Color Group 223 S San Mateo Dr	San Mateo	CA	94401	650-342-6668	
La Camarilla Racquet Fitness & Swim Club 5320 E Shea Blvd *Web:* www.lacamarilla.com	Scottsdale	AZ	85254	480-998-3388	
Las Olas Beauty 1503 E Las Olas Blvd *Web:* www.lasolasbeauty.com	Fort Lauderdale	FL	33301	954-779-2616	
Los Angeles School of Make-up Inc 129 S San Fernando Blvd *Web:* www.makeupschool.com	Burbank	CA	91502	818-729-9420	
Maka Beauty Systems 3959 E Speedway Blvd Ste 308 *Web:* www.maka.com	Tucson	AZ	85712	520-322-6252	
Mane Street Manor Hair Salon & Day Spa 1108 S Main St *Web:* manestreetmanorspa.com	Hampstead	MD	21074	410-239-1425	
Mango Hair Salon 123 Libbie Ave *Web:* mangosalon.com	Richmond	VA	23226	804-285-2800	
Mark Anthony Inc 300 W Hubbard St Ste 301 *Web:* www.mitchellspas.com	Chicago	IL	60654	919-467-9641	
Meriwether Godsey Inc 4944 Old Boonsboro Rd *Web:* www.merig.com	Lynchburg	VA	24503	434-384-3663	
Mi Pueblito Beauty Salon 4534 E Tropicana Ave	Las Vegas	NV	89121	702-433-6435	
Miracell Botanicals 921 North 1430 West *Web:* www.miracell.com	Orem	UT	84057	801-434-8165	
Mitchells Salon & Day Spa 5901 E Galbraith Rd *Web:* www.mitchellssalon.com	Cincinnati	OH	45236	513-793-0900	
Mohegan Tribal Gaming Authority 1 Mohegan Sun Blvd *TF:* 888-226-7711 ■ *Web:* www.mtga.com	Uncasville	CT	06382	888-226-7711	
Moxie Hair Salon 2649 Lyndale Ave S *Web:* moxiesalon.com	Minneapolis	MN	55408	612-813-0330	
Naimies Beauty Center Inc 12640 Riverside Dr *Web:* www.naimies.com	Valley Village	CA	91607	818-655-9933	
Navii Salon Spa 316 E Us Hwy 30 *Web:* www.navii.com	Schererville	IN	46375	219-865-6515	
Noelle Spa-beauty & Wellness 1100 High Ridge Rd *Web:* www.noelle.com	Stamford	CT	06905	203-322-3445	
OC Jones & Sons Inc 1520 Fourth St *Web:* www.ocjones.com	Berkeley	CA	94710	510-526-3424	
One Step Logic 17615 Mayall St *Web:* www.onesteplogic.com	Northridge	CA	91325	818-700-7837	
Ovation Hair Design 18 Davenport St *Web:* ovationhairdesign.com	Somerville	NJ	08876	908-526-5110	
Over The Rainbow Children & Adult Hair Styling Salon 8300 Tampa Ave Ste C *Web:* www.overtherainbowchildrenssalon.com	Northridge	CA	91324	818-886-9325	
Panzer Dermatology Association 537 Stanton Christiana Rd Ste 107 *Web:* www.premierdermde.com	Newark	DE	19713	302-633-7550	
Paragon Salons Inc 6775 Harrison Ave *Web:* paragonsalon.com	Cincinnati	OH	45247	513-574-7610	
Perry Anthony Design Group 5331 Limestone Rd *Web:* www.perryanthony.com	Wilmington	DE	19808	302-239-6161	
Pino's Salon & Spa 70 Victoria St N *Web:* www.pinosalon.com	Kitchener	ON	N2H5C2	519-578-8898	
Pizzazz Hair Design at Abacoa Inc 771 Village Blvd Ste 208 *Web:* www.wellingtoncomputer.com	West Palm Beach	FL	33409	561-689-1177	
Planet 21 8040 Providence Rd Ste 300 *Web:* www.planet21salon.com	Charlotte	NC	28277	704-543-1083	
Planet Beauty Inc 3199 Red Hill Ave Ste A *Web:* www.planet-beauty.com	Costa Mesa	CA	92626	949-752-1885	
Preston Wynne Spa Inc 14567 Big Basin Way *Web:* www.prestonwynne.com	Saratoga	CA	95070	408-741-5525	
Pro-Link Inc 510 Chapman St *Web:* www.prolinkhq.com	Canton	MA	02021	781-828-9550	
Quinn Medical Day Spa 6920 W 121st St Ste 102 *Web:* www.quinnplasticsurgery.com	Leawood	KS	66209	913-663-5483	
Rasmussen John 730 Sand Lk Rd *Web:* www.rasmussen-usa.com	Orlando	FL	32809	407-859-5255	
Ratner co 1577 Spring Hill Rd Ste 500 *Web:* www.ratnerco.com	Vienna	VA	22182	703-269-5400	
Redex Industries Inc 1176 Salem Pkwy *Web:* www.uddercream.com	Salem	OH	44460	330-332-9800	
Regis Corp 7201 Metro Blvd *NYSE: RGS* ■ *TF:* 888-888-7778 ■ *Web:* www.regiscorp.com	Minneapolis	MN	55439	952-947-7777	
Regis Corp MasterCuts Div 7201 Metro Blvd *TF:* 877-857-2070 ■ *Web:* www.regiscorp.com	Minneapolis	MN	55439	952-947-7777	947-7801
Regis Corp Pro-Cuts Div 7201 Metro Blvd *TF:* 877-857-2070 ■ *Web:* www.procuts.com	Minneapolis	MN	55439	952-947-7777	
Regis Corp Regis Hairstylists Div 7201 Metro Blvd *TF:* 877-857-2070 ■ *Web:* www.regissalons.com	Minneapolis	MN	55439	952-947-7777	
Regis Corp SmartStyle Div 7201 Metro Blvd *TF:* 877-857-2070 ■ *Web:* www.smartstyle.com	Minneapolis	MN	55439	952-947-7777	
Regis Group Inc, The 102 N King St PO Box 3323 *Web:* www.regisgroup.com	Leesburg	VA	20176	703-777-2233	
Retreat Spa & Salon LLC 4246 Washington Rd *Web:* retreatspaandsalon.com	Evans	GA	30809	706-364-8292	
Rick Engineering Co 5620 Friars Rd *Web:* www.rickengineering.com	San Diego	CA	92110	619-291-0707	
Rios Golden Cut Inc 121 N Pk Blvd	San Antonio	TX	78204	210-227-4996	
Rip Curl Inc 3030 Airway Ave *Web:* www.ripcurl.com	Costa Mesa	CA	92626	714-422-3642	
Rita Hazan Salon 720 Fifth Ave Fl 11 *Web:* www.ritahazan.com	New York	NY	10019	212-586-4343	
River City Engineering 1011 W County Line Rd *Web:* www.rcetx.com	New Braunfels	TX	78130	830-626-3588	626-3601
Robert Jeffrey Hair Studio 3434 N Halsted St *Web:* robertjeffrey.com	Chicago	IL	60657	773-525-8800	
Rocco Altobelli Inc 14301 Burnsville Pkwy W *Web:* roccoaltobellisalons.com	Burnsville	MN	55306	952-707-1900	
RZ & Company Inc 6602 Odana Rd *Web:* rzco.com	Madison	WI	53719	608-827-7979	
Sagittarius Hair Designs Ltd 1136 Conrad Ct *Web:* www.sagittariussalon.com	Hagerstown	MD	21740	301-797-8008	
Salon Service Group Inc 1859 W Arbor Ct *TF:* 800-933-5733 ■ *Web:* www.salonservicegroup.com	Springfield	MO	65807	800-933-5733	
Salon Services & Supplies Inc 740 SW 34th St *Web:* www.salonservicesnw.com	Renton	WA	98057	425-251-8840	
Scentisphere LLC 97 Old Rt 6 *Web:* www.oscom.net	Carmel	NY	10512	845-225-3600	
Shelter Mortgage Company LLC 4000 W Brown Deer Rd *Web:* www.sheltermortgage.com	Milwaukee	WI	53209	414-716-2800	
Sport Clips Inc 110 Briarwood Dr *TF:* 800-872-4247 ■ *Web:* www.sportclips.com	Georgetown	TX	78628	512-869-1201	
Steiner Leisure Ltd 770 S Dixie Hwy Ste 200 *NASDAQ: STNR* ■ *Web:* www.steinerleisure.com	Coral Gables	FL	33146	305-358-9002	
Stewart School of Cosmetology 604 NW Ave *TF:* 800-537-2625 ■ *Web:* www.stewartschool.com	Sioux Falls	SD	57104	605-336-2775	
Studio Booth LLC 6343 Penn Ave *Web:* studio-booth.com	Pittsburgh	PA	15206	412-362-6684	
Sue Kolve'S Salon & Day Spa 230 Main St *Web:* suekolves.com	Onalaska	WI	54650	608-784-2363	
Sugar House Day Spa & Salon 111 N Alfred St *Web:* sugarhousedayspa.com	Alexandria	VA	22314	703-549-9940	
Supercuts 7201 Metro Blvd **Fax Area Code:* 952 ■ *TF:* 877-857-2070 ■ *Web:* www.supercuts.com	Minneapolis	MN	55439	877-857-2070	947-7300*
Theraderm and Therapon Skin Health Inc 2081 Dime Dr *Web:* theraderm.net	Springdale	AR	72764	479-751-7345	
Toni & Guy USA Inc 2311 Midway Rd **Fax Area Code:* 972 ■ *TF:* 800-256-9391 ■ *Web:* www.toniguy.com	Carrollton	TX	75006	800-256-9391	931-1999*
Total Beauty Media Inc 3420 Ocean Park Blvd Ste 3050 *Web:* www.totalbeautymedia.com	Santa Monica	CA	90405	310-399-7400	
Tutta Bella Hair Salon 17400 Monterey St *Web:* tuttabellasalon.com	Morgan Hill	CA	95037	408-778-6949	
Twizzle Hair Studio 2670 Fourth Ave W *Web:* twizzle.ca	Vancouver	BC	V6K1P7	604-738-1733	
Ultraderm Medspa 3311 Mission Dr *Web:* ultraderm.com	Santa Cruz	CA	95065	831-475-4315	

Phone Fax

Universal Companies Inc 18260 Oak Park Dr ... Abingdon VA 24210 276-466-9110
Web: www.universalcompanies.com

Victoria & Albert Hair Studio
10715 Charter Dr Ste 160 ... Columbia MD 21044 410-992-3000
Web: www.victoriaandalberthair.com

Vidal Sassoon Salons 399 Boylston St ... Boston MA 02116 617-536-5496
Web: www.sassoon.com

Visage Solutions LLC
8601 Six Forks Rd Ste 400 ... Raleigh NC 27615 919-882-2056
Web: www.visagesolutions.com

Visible Changes Inc 1303 Campbell Rd ... Houston TX 77055 713-984-8800
Web: www.visiblechanges.com

Windflower Spa Hyatt Hill Country Resort
9800 Hyatt Resort Dr ... San Antonio TX 78251 210-767-5577
Web: www.hillcountry.hyatt.com

Wood River Technologies Inc
191 Sun Valley Rd Ste 202 ... Ketchum ID 83340 888-661-4094
TF: 888-661-4094 ■ *Web:* www.fedmarket.com

Xanadu Salon & Spa 3351 W Sheridan St ... Hollywood FL 33021 954-983-0100
Web: xanadusalonspa.com

Xpres Spa 3 East 54th St 9th Fl ... New York NY 10022 212-750-9595
Web: www.xpresspa.com

Z Salon & Spa Inc 9407 Shelbyville Rd ... Louisville KY 40222 502-426-2226
Web: www.zsalon.com

Ziba Beauty Center Inc 17832 Pioneer Blvd ... Artesia CA 90701 562-402-5131
Web: zibabeauty.com

78 BETTER BUSINESS BUREAUS - CANADA

Phone Fax

Council of Better Business Bureaus
3033 Wilson Blvd Ste 600 ... Arlington VA 22201 416-644-4936 644-4945
Web: www.bbb.org

AAA of Minnesota & Iowa
600 W Travelers Trail ... Burnsville MN 55337 952-707-4200
Web: mn-ia.aaa.com

Aboriginal Human Resource Council
708 2nd Ave N ... Saskatoon SK S7K2E1 306-956-5360
Web: aboriginalhr.ca

Arelia James Island 10880 angelfish way ... Jacksonville FL 32256 904-641-0500
Web: areliajamesisland.com

Arizona Technology Council
2800 N Central Ave Ste 1920 ... Phoenix AZ 85004 602-343-8324
Web: www.aztechcouncil.org

Atheer Inc 155 Ave b ... New York NY 10009 212-228-5974
Web: atheerlabs.com

Better Business Bureau of Eastern Ontario & the Outaouais Inc
700 Industrial Ave Unit 505 ... Ottawa ON K1G0Y9 613-237-4856 237-4878

Better Business Bureau of Quebec
1565 Boul de l'Avenir Ste 206 ... Laval QC H7S2N5 514-905-3893 663-6316*
**Fax Area Code:* 450 ■ *Web:* www.occq-qcco.com

Better Business Bureau of Saskatchewan
980 Albert St Ste 201 ... Regina SK S4R2P7 306-352-7601 565-6236
TF: 888-352-7601 ■ *Web:* bbb.org/saskatchewan

Better Business Bureau of Southern Alberta
1709 8 Ave NE Ste 5 ... Calgary AB T2E0S9 403-531-8784 640-2514
Web: www.bbb.org/calgary

Better Business Bureau of the Maritime Provinces
1888 Brunswick St Ste 805 ... Halifax NS B3J3J8 902-422-6581 429-6457
Web: bbb.org/atlantic-provinces

Better Business Bureau of Vancouver Island
220-1175 Cook St Ste 220 ... Victoria BC V8V4A1 250-386-6348 386-2367
TF: 877-826-4222 ■ *Web:* bbb.org/vancouver-island

Better Business Bureau Serving Central & Northern Alberta
16102 100 Ave NW ... Edmonton AB T5P0L3 780-482-2341 482-1150
Web: www.bbb.org/edmonton

Better Business Bureau Serving Mainland British Columbia
788 Beatty St Ste 404 ... Vancouver BC V6B2M1 604-682-2711 681-1544
TF: 888-803-1222 ■ *Web:* www.bbb.org/mbc

Better Business Bureau Serving Western Ontario
190 Wortley Rd Ste 206 ... London ON N6C4Y7 519-673-3222 673-5966
TF: 877-283-9222 ■ *Web:* bbb.org/western-ontario

Better Business Bureau Serving Windsor & Southwestern Ontario
880 Ouellette Ave Ste 302 ... Windsor ON N9A1C7 519-258-7222
Web: www.bbb.org/western-ontario

Better Business Bureau Serving Winnipeg & Manitoba
1030B Empress St ... Winnipeg MB R3G3H4 204-989-9010 989-9016
TF: 800-385-3074 ■ *Web:* www.bbb.org/manitoba

Builders Association of The Twin Cities
2960 Centre Pointe Dr ... Saint Paul MN 55113 651-697-1954
Web: www.batconline.org

Building Performance Contractors Association of New York State, The
P.O. Box 1113 ... Bridgehampton NY 11932 631-324-2861
Web: www.home-performance.org

Canadian Association of Petroleum Producers
350 - 7th Ave S W Ste 2100 ... Calgary AB T2P3N9 403-267-1100
Web: www.capp.ca

Canadian Business for Social Responsibility
205 - 535 Thurlow St ... Vancouver BC V6E3L2 604-323-2715
Web: www.cbsr.ca

Canadian Sport Centre Atlantic
26 Thomas Raddall Dr ... Halifax NS B3S0E2 902-425-0942
Web: cscatlantic.ca

Canadian Wood Council 99 Bank St Ste 400 ... Ottawa ON K1P6B9 613-747-5544
Web: cwc.ca

Cree Nation of Eastmain
78 Nouchimi PO Box 90 ... Eastmain QC J0M1W0 819-977-0211
Web: eastmain.ca

Fcis Llc 206 mapeat ln ... New Castle PA 16101 724-652-0528
Web: www.fcisllc.com

Florida Academy of Family Physicians
6720 Atlantic Blvd ... Jacksonville FL 32211 800-223-3237
TF: 800-223-3237 ■ *Web:* www.fafp.org

Phone Fax

Florida Regional Minority Business Council Inc
9499 Ne 2nd Ave Ste 201 ... Miami Shores FL 33138 305-762-6151
Web: www.sfmsdc.org

Fondation Rues Principales
870 De Salaberry Ave Ste 204 ... Quebec QC G1R2T9 418-694-9944
Web: www.fondationruesprincipales.com

Going Global Inc 258 college ln ... Mobile AL 36608 251-342-9811
Web: www.goinglobal.com

Hampton Roads Shipping Association, The
236 E Plume St ... Norfolk VA 23510 757-622-2639
Web: hrsa.portofhamptonroads.com

Hospital Association of Southern California
515 S Figueroa St Ste 1300 ... Los Angeles CA 90071 213-538-0700
Web: www.hasc.org

Indiana Rural Health Association
1024 s 6th st ... Terre haute IN 47807 812-478-3919
Web: www.indianaruralhealth.org

Intracon Na Inc 1175 e iron eagle dr ... Eagle ID 83616 208-672-0888
Web: www.intracon.com

Kansas Bankers Association
610 SW Corporate View ... Topeka KS 66615 785-272-7836
Web: www.ksbankers.com

Kentucky Association School
152 Consumer Ln Ste 154 ... Frankfort KY 40601 502-875-3411
Web: server.kasa.org

Latinos In Information Sciences & Technology Association
5935 s norcross tucker rd ... Norcross GA 30093 678-620-3173
Web: www.a-lista.org

Lets Talk Business Network
54 W 39th At Av Of The Americas ... New York NY 10018 212-742-1553
Web: ltbn.com

Maine International Trade Center
511 Congress St Ste 100 ... Portland ME 04101 207-541-7400
Web: www.mitc.com

Metacred Inc 6324 georgetown Pk ... Mc Lean VA 22101 703-327-2733
Web: metacred.com

Metalscope Building Systems Inc
3930 fm 1960 rd e ... Humble TX 77338 832-644-1706
Web: www.metalscopebuildings.com

Midwest Energy Association
7825 Telegraph Rd ... Bloomington MN 55438 651-289-9600
Web: www.midwestenergy.org

MRN Inc 5353 South 960 East Ste 200 ... Salt Lake City UT 84117 888-674-6741
TF: 888-674-6741 ■ *Web:* www.mrn.com

Multicultural Foodservice & Hospitality Alliance
1144 Narragansett Blvd ... Providence RI 02905 401-461-6342
Web: www.mfha.net

Nciv 427 N. Shaw Ln Rm 300F ... East Lansing MI 48824 202-842-1414
Web: cvip.isp.msu.edu

North Delta Planning & Development District
130 Leflore Ave ... Clarksdale MS 38614 662-627-3401
Web: www.ndpdd.com

Oates 415 Pablo Ave ... Jacksonville Beach FL 32250 904-242-0075
Web: www.oatesenergy.com

Ontario Hockey Federation
1185 Eglinton Ave E ... North York ON M3C3C6 226-533-9070
Web: www.ohf.on.ca

Ontario Medical Association
150 Bloor St W Ste 900 ... Toronto ON M5S3C1 416-599-2580
Web: www.oma.org

Ordre Des Ingenieurs Du Quebec
2020 Rue University ... Montreal QC H3A2A5 514-845-6141
Web: www.oiq.qc.ca

Oregon Business Council
1100 Sw 6th Ave Ste 1608 ... Portland OR 97204 503-220-0691
Web: orbusinesscouncil.org

Peccole Ranch Community Association
9501 Red Hills Rd ... Las Vegas NV 89117 702-255-3351
Web: peccoleran.com

Reemployability Inc 3212 parkside Ctr cir ... Tampa FL 33619 813-663-9880
Web: www.reemployability.com

Retail Merchants Association of Tidewater Virginia Inc
500 Plume St E Ste 500 ... Norfolk VA 23510 757-466-1600
Web: www.retail-alliance.com

SACA Technologies LLC
5101 E La Palma Ave Ste 200 ... Anaheim Hills CA 92807 714-777-3222
Web: www.sacatech.com

Sales Lead Management Association
17853 Santiago Blvd., Ste #107-339 ... Villa Park CA 92861 714-637-6989
Web: www.salesleadmgmtassn.com

Seattle Marathon Association
1500 Westlake Ave. N Ste #008 ... Seattle WA 98109 206-729-3660
Web: www.seattlemarathon.org

Skotdal Enterprises Inc
2910 Colby Ave Ste 200 ... Everett WA 98201 425-252-5400
Web: www.skotdal.com

Society Of Hospital Medicine
190 N Independence Mall W ... Philadelphia PA 19106 215-351-2585
Web: www.hospitalmedicine.org

Tennis Canada 285 Rue Gary-carter ... Montreal QC H2R2W1 514-273-1515
Web: www.tenniscanada.com

Texas Association of School Business Officials
6611 Boeing Dr ... El Paso TX 79925 512-462-1711
Web: www.tasbo.org

Utah League of Cities and Towns, The
50 South 600 East Ste 150 ... Salt Lake City UT 84102 801-328-1601
Web: ulct.org

Xplor International 24238 Hawthorne Blvd ... Torrance CA 90505 310-373-3633
Web: xplor.org

79 BETTER BUSINESS BUREAUS - US

See Also Consumer Interest Organizations p. 1761

Phone | Fax

Better Business Bureau Online
Council of Better Business Bureaus, The
4200 Wilson Blvd Ste 800 — Arlington VA 22203 — 703-276-0100 525-8277
TF: 800-459-8875 ■ *Web:* www.bbb.org

Better Business Bureau Heartland 11811 P St. — Omaha NE 68137 — 402-391-7612 391-7535
TF: 800-649-6814 ■ *Web:* bbb.org/nebraska

Better Business Bureau In Alaska Oregon & Western Washington
341 W Tudor Rd Ste 209 — Anchorage AK 99503 — 907-562-0704
Web: bbb.org/alaskaoregonwesternwashington

Better Business Bureau Inc
1000 Broadway Ste 625 — Oakland CA 94607 — 510-844-2000 844-2100
TF: 866-411-2221 ■ *Web:* bbb.org/greater-san-francisco

Better Business Bureau of Acadiana
4007 W Congress St Ste B — Lafayette LA 70506 — 337-981-3497 981-7559
Web: bbb.org/acadiana

Better Business Bureau of Alaska Oregon & Western Washington
1000 Stn Dr Ste 222 — Dupont WA 98327 — 206-431-2222 431-2200
Web: bbb.org/alaskaoregonwesternwashington

Better Business Bureau of Ark-La-Tex
401 Edwards St Ste 135 — Shreveport LA 71101 — 318-222-7575
TF: 800-372-4222 ■ *Web:* bbb.org/shreveport

Better Business Bureau of Arkansas
12521 Kanis Rd — Little Rock AR 72211 — 501-664-7274 664-0024
Web: bbb.org

Better Business Bureau of Asheville/Western North Carolina
112 Executive Pk — Asheville NC 28801 — 828-253-2392 252-5039
TF: 800-452-2882 ■ *Web:* bbb.org/asheville

Better Business Bureau of Brazos Valley & Deep East Texas
418 Tarrow — College Station TX 77840 — 979-260-2222 846-0276
Web: bbb.org/bryan

Better Business Bureau of Canton Region/West Virginia
1434 Cleveland Ave NW — Canton OH 44703 — 330-454-9401 456-8957
TF: 800-362-0494 ■ *Web:* bbb.org/canton

Better Business Bureau of Central & Eastern Kentucky
1460 Newtown Pk — Lexington KY 40511 — 859-259-1008 259-1639
TF: 800-866-6668 ■ *Web:* bbb.org/lexington

Better Business Bureau of Central & South Central Texas
1005 La Posada Dr — Austin TX 78752 — 512-445-2096 445-2096
Web: bbb.org/central-texas

Better Business Bureau of Central Alabama & the Wiregrass Area
4750 Woodmere Blvd Ste D — Montgomery AL 36106 — 334-273-5530
Web: bbb.org/csal

Better Business Bureau of Central Alabama & the Wiregrass Area Dothan Branch
1971 S Brannon Stand Rd — Dothan AL 36305 — 334-794-0492 794-0659
Web: bbb.org/csal

Better Business Bureau of Central East Texas
3600 Old BullaRd Rd Bldg 1 — Tyler TX 75701 — 903-581-5704 534-8644
TF: 800-443-0131 ■ *Web:* bbb.org/east-texas

Better Business Bureau of Central East Texas Longview Branch
102 Commander Ste 7 — Longview TX 75605 — 903-758-3222 534-8644
TF: 800-443-0131 ■ *Web:* bbb.org/east-texas

Better Business Bureau of Central Florida
1600 S Grant St — Longwood FL 32750 — 407-621-3300 786-2625
Web: bbb.org/central-florida

Better Business Bureau of Central Georgia
277 ML King Jr Blvd Ste 102 — Macon GA 31201 — 478-742-7999 742-8191
Web: bbb.org/central-georgia

Better Business Bureau of Central Illinois
112 Harrison St — Peoria IL 61602 — 309-688-3741 681-7290
TF: 800-763-4222 ■ *Web:* bbb.org/central-illinois

Better Business Bureau of Central Indiana
151 N Delaware St — Indianapolis IN 46204 — 317-488-2222 488-2224
TF: 866-463-9222 ■ *Web:* bbb.org/indy

Better Business Bureau of Central Louisiana & Ark-La-Tex
5220-C Rue Verdun — Alexandria LA 71303 — 318-473-4494 473-8906
TF General: 800-372-4222 ■ *Web:* bbb.org/shreveport

Better Business Bureau of Central New England & Northeast Connecticut
340 Main St Ste 802 — Worcester MA 01608 — 508-755-3340 754-4158

Better Business Bureau of Central North Carolina
3608 W Friendly Ave — Greensboro NC 27410 — 336-852-4240 852-7540
Web: bbb.org/greensboro

Better Business Bureau of Central Northeast Northwest & Southwest Arizona
4428 N 12th St — Phoenix AZ 85014 — 602-264-1721 263-0997
TF: 877-291-6222 ■ *Web:* bbb.org/phoenix

Better Business Bureau of Central Ohio
1169 Dublin Rd — Columbus OH 43215 — 614-486-6336 486-6631
TF: 800-759-2400 ■ *Web:* bbb.org/centralohio

Better Business Bureau of Central Oklahoma
17 S Dewey Ave — Oklahoma City OK 73102 — 405-239-6081 235-5891
Web: bbb.org/oklahoma-city

Better Business Bureau of Central Texas
445 Central TX Expy Ste 1 — Harker Heights TX 76548 — 512-445-2911 445-2096
Web: bbb.org/central-texas

Better Business Bureau of Central Virginia
720 Moorefield Pk Dr Ste 300 — Richmond VA 23236 — 804-648-0016 320-0248
Web: bbb.org/richmond

Better Business Bureau of Chicago & Northern Illinois
330 N Wabash Ave Ste 2006 — Chicago IL 60611 — 312-832-0500 832-9985
Web: bbb.org/chicago

Better Business Bureau of Cincinnati
7 W Seventh St Ste 1600 — Cincinnati OH 45202 — 513-421-3015 621-0907
Web: bbb.org/cincinnati

Better Business Bureau of Coastal North & South Carolina
314 Laurel St Ste 203 — Conway SC 29526 — 843-488-0238 488-0998
Web: bbb.org/myrtle-beach

Better Business Bureau of Connecticut
94 S Tpke Rd — Wallingford CT 06492 — 203-269-2700 294-3694
Web: bbb.org/connecticut

Better Business Bureau of Dayton/Miami Valley
15 W Fourth St Ste 300 — Dayton OH 45402 — 937-222-5825 222-3338
Web: bbb.org/dayton

Better Business Bureau of Delaware
60 Reads Way — New Castle DE 19720 — 302-221-5255 221-5265
Web: bbb.org/delaware

Better Business Bureau of Detroit & Eastern Michigan
26777 Central Pk Blvd Ste 100 — Southfield MI 48076 — 248-223-9400 356-5135
Web: bbb.org/detroit

Better Business Bureau of Eastern Massachusetts Maine Rhode Island & Vermont
290 Donald Lynch Blvd Ste 102 — Marlborough MA 01752 — 508-652-4800 652-4820
TF: 800-422-2811 ■ *Web:* bbb.org/boston

Better Business Bureau of Eastern Missouri & Southern Illinois
211 N Broadway Ste 2060 — Saint Louis MO 63102 — 314-645-3300 645-2666
Web: bbb.org/stlouis

Better Business Bureau of Eastern North Carolina
5540 Munford Rd Ste 130 — Raleigh NC 27612 — 919-277-4222 277-4221
Web: bbb.org/raleigh-durham

Better Business Bureau of Eastern Oklahoma
1722 S Carson Ave Ste 3200 — Tulsa OK 74119 — 918-492-1266 492-1276
Web: bbb.org/tulsa

Better Business Bureau of Eastern Pennsylvania
1880 JFK Blvd Ste 1330 — Philadelphia PA 19103 — 215-985-9313 563-4907
Web: bbb.org/washington-dc-eastern-pa

Better Business Bureau of El Paso
720 Arizona Ave — El Paso TX 79902 — 915-577-0191 577-0209
Web: bbb.org/elpaso

Better Business Bureau of Four Corners & Grand Junction Colorado
308 N Locke Ave — Farmington NM 87401 — 505-326-6501

Better Business Bureau of Greater East Tennessee
255 N Peters Rd Ste A PO Box 31377 — Knoxville TN 37923 — 865-692-1600 692-1590
Web: bbb.org/knoxville

Better Business Bureau of Greater Iowa Quad Cities & Sioux Land Region
505 Fifth Ave Ste 950 — Des Moines IA 50309 — 515-243-8137 243-2227
Web: www.bbb.org/iowa

Better Business Bureau of Greater Kansas City
8080 Ward Pkwy Ste 401 — Kansas City MO 64114 — 816-421-7800 472-5442
TF: 877-606-0695 ■ *Web:* bbb.org/kansas-city

Better Business Bureau of Greater Maryland
502 S Sharp St Ste 1200 — Baltimore MD 21201 — 410-347-3990 347-3936
Web: bbb.org/greater-maryland

Better Business Bureau of Greater New Orleans
710 Baronne St Ste C — New Orleans LA 70113 — 504-581-6222 524-9110
Web: bbb.org/new-orleans

Better Business Bureau of Hampton Roads
586 Virginian Dr — Norfolk VA 23505 — 757-531-1300 531-1388
Web: bbb.org/norfolk

Better Business Bureau of Hawaii
1132 Bishop St Ste 615 — Honolulu HI 96813 — 808-536-6956 628-3970
TF: 877-222-6551 ■ *Web:* bbb.org/hawaii

Better Business Bureau of Kansas Inc
345 N Riverview St Ste 720 — Wichita KS 67203 — 316-263-3146 263-3063
TF: 800-856-2417 ■ *Web:* bbb.org/nebraska

Better Business Bureau of Louisville Southern Indiana & Western Kentucky
844 S Fourth St — Louisville KY 40203 — 502-583-6546 589-9940
TF: 800-388-2222 ■ *Web:* bbb.org/louisville

Better Business Bureau of Maine
290 Donald Lynch Blvd Ste 102 — Marlborough MA 01752 — 508-652-4800 652-4820
TF: 800-422-2811 ■ *Web:* www.bbb.org/boston

Better Business Bureau of Metro Washington DC & Eastern Pennsylvania
1411 K St NW Ste 1000 — Washington DC 20005 — 202-393-8000 393-1198
Web: bbb.org/washington-dc-eastern-pa

Better Business Bureau of Metropolitan Atlanta
503 Oak Pl Ste 590 — Atlanta GA 30349 — 404-766-0875 768-1085
Web: bbb.org/atlanta

Better Business Bureau of Metropolitan Dallas & Northeast Texas
1601 Elm St Ste 3838 — Dallas TX 75201 — 214-220-2000 740-0321
Web: bbb.org/dallas

Better Business Bureau of Metropolitan Houston
1333 W Loop S Ste 1200 — Houston TX 77027 — 713-868-9500 867-4947
Web: bbb.org/houston

Better Business Bureau of Metropolitan New York
257 Pk Ave S — New York NY 10010 — 212-533-6200 477-4912
TF: 800-684-3322 ■ *Web:* bbb.org/new-york-city

Better Business Bureau of Middle Tennessee Inc
201 Fourth Ave N Ste 100 — Nashville TN 37219 — 615-242-4222 250-4245
Web: bbb.org/nashville

Better Business Bureau of Minnesota & North Dakota
220 River Ridge Cir S — Burnsville MN 55337 — 651-699-1111 695-2488
Web: bbb.org/minnesota

Better Business Bureau of New Jersey
1700 Whitehorse-Hamilton Sq Rd Ste D-5 — Trenton NJ 08690 — 609-588-0808 588-0546
TF: 888-494-4009 ■ *Web:* bbb.org/new-jersey

Better Business Bureau of North Central Texas
4245 Kemp Blvd Ste 900 — Wichita Falls TX 76308 — 940-691-1172 691-1175
Web: bbb.org/wichita-falls

Better Business Bureau of Northeast California
3075 Beacon Blvd. — West Sacramento CA 95691 — 916-443-6843 443-0376
TF: 866-334-6272 ■ *Web:* bbb.org/northeast-california

Better Business Bureau of Northeast Florida & The Southeast Atlantic
4417 Beach Blvd Ste 202 — Jacksonville FL 32207 — 904-721-2288
TF: 800-713-6661 ■ *Web:* bbb.org/north-east-florida

Better Business Bureau of Northeast Kansas
345 N. Riverview St Ste 720 — Wichita KS 67203 — 316-263-3146

Better Business Bureau of Northeast Louisiana
1900 N 18th St Ste 411 — Monroe LA 71201 — 318-387-4600
Web: bbb.org/north-east-louisiana

Better Business Bureau of Northeast Ohio
2800 Euclid Ave 4th Fl — Cleveland OH 44115 — 216-241-7678 861-6365
TF: 800-233-0361 ■ *Web:* bbb.org/cleveland

Better Business Bureau of Northeastern & Central Pennsylvania
1054 Oak St — Scranton PA 18508 — 570-342-5100 342-1282
Web: bbb.org/washington-dc-eastern-pa

Better Business Bureau of Northern Alabama
107 Lincoln St — Huntsville AL 35804 — 256-533-1640 533-1177
Web: bbb.org/northern-alabama

Phone | Fax

Better Business Bureau of Northern Colorado & East Central Wyoming
8020 S County Rd 5 Ste 100 ... Fort Collins CO 80528 970-484-1348 221-1239
TF: 800-564-0371 ■ *Web:* bbb.org/wyoming-and-northern-colorado

Better Business Bureau of Northern Indiana
4011 Parnell Ave ... Fort Wayne IN 46805 260-423-4433 423-3301
TF: 800-552-4631 ■ *Web:* bbb.org/northernindiana

Better Business Bureau of Northern Nevada
4834 Sparks Blvd Ste 102 ... Sparks NV 89436 775-322-0657 322-8163
Web: bbb.org/reno

Better Business Bureau of Northwest Florida
912 E Gadsden St ... Pensacola FL 32501 850-429-0002 429-0006
Web: bbb.org/northwest-florida

Better Business Bureau of Northwest Indiana
7863 Broadway Ste 124 ... Merrillville IN 46410 260-423-4433 884-2123*
**Fax Area Code:* 219 ■ *Web:* bbb.org/northernindiana

Better Business Bureau of Northwest North Carolina
500 W Fifth St Ste 202 ... Winston-Salem NC 27101 336-725-8348 777-3727
TF: 800-777-8348 ■ *Web:* bbb.org/northwestern-north-carolina

Better Business Bureau of Northwest Ohio & Southeast Michigan
7668 King's Pt Rd ... Toledo OH 43617 419-531-3116 578-6001
TF: 800-743-4222 ■ *Web:* bbb.org/toledo

Better Business Bureau of Rockford
330 North Wabash Ave Ste 3120 ... Chicago IL 60611 312-832-0500 832-9985
TF: 800-955-5100 ■ *Web:* www.bbb.org/chicago

Better Business Bureau of San Diego & Imperial Counties
5050 Murphy Canyon Rd Ste 110 ... San Diego CA 92123 858-637-6199 496-2141
Web: bbb.org/sdoc

Better Business Bureau of South Central Louisiana
748 Main St ... Baton Rouge LA 70802 225-346-5222 346-1029
Web: bbb.org/baton-rouge

Better Business Bureau of South Texas
1333 W Loop S Ste 1200 ... Houston TX 77027 713-868-9500 867-4947
Web: bbb.org/houston

Better Business Bureau of Southeast Florida & the Caribbean
4411 Beacon Cir Ste 4 ... West Palm Beach FL 33407 561-842-1918 845-7234
TF: 866-966-7226 ■ *Web:* bbb.org/south-east-florida

Better Business Bureau of Southeast Tennessee & Northwest Georgia
508 N Market St ... Chattanooga TN 37405 423-266-6144 267-1924
TF: 800-548-4456 ■ *Web:* bbb.org/chattanooga

Better Business Bureau of Southeast Texas
550 Fannin St Ste 100 ... Beaumont TX 77701 409-835-5348 838-6858
TF: 800-685-7650 ■ *Web:* bbb.org/southeast-texas

Better Business Bureau of Southern Arizona
434 S Williams Blvd Ste 102 ... Tucson AZ 85711 520-888-5353 888-6262
Web: bbb.org/tucson

Better Business Bureau of Southern Colorado
25 N Wahsatch Ave ... Colorado Springs CO 80903 719-636-1155 636-5078
Web: bbb.org/southern-colorado

Better Business Bureau of Southern Nebraska
3 Wilson Blvd Ste 1 ... Omaha NE 68137 402-436-2345 476-8221
Web: bbb.org/nebraska

Better Business Bureau of Southern Nevada
6040 S Jones Blvd ... Las Vegas NV 89118 702-320-4500 320-4560
Web: bbb.org/southern-nevada

Better Business Bureau of Southern Piedmont Carolinas
13860 Ballantyne Corporate Pl Ste 225 ... Charlotte NC 28277 704-927-8611 927-8615
Web: bbb.org/charlotte

Better Business Bureau of Southwest Georgia
PO Box 2587 ... Columbus GA 31902 706-324-0712 324-2181
TF: 800-768-4222 ■ *Web:* bbb.org/columbus-georgia

Better Business Bureau of Southwest Idaho & Eastern Oregon
1200 N Curtis Rd PO Box 9817 ... Boise ID 83706 208-342-4649 342-5116
TF: 800-218-1001 ■ *Web:* bbb.org/snakeriver

Better Business Bureau of Southwest Louisiana Inc
2309 E Prien Lk Rd ... Lake Charles LA 70601 337-478-6253 474-8981
TF: 800-542-7085 ■ *Web:* bbb.org/lakecharles

Better Business Bureau of Southwest Missouri
430 S Glenstone Ave ... Springfield MO 65802 417-862-4222 869-5544
Web: bbb.org/southwestern-missouri

Better Business Bureau of the Abilene Area
3300 S 14th St Ste 307 ... Abilene TX 79605 325-691-1533 691-0309
Web: bbb.org/abilene

Better Business Bureau of the Akron Inc
222 W Market St ... Akron OH 44303 330-253-4590 253-6249
TF: 800-825-8887 ■ *Web:* bbb.org/akron

Better Business Bureau of the Bakersfield Area
1601 H St Ste 101 ... Bakersfield CA 93301 661-322-2074 322-8318
TF: 800-675-8118 ■ *Web:* bbb.org/central-california-inland-empire

Better Business Bureau of the Denver-Boulder Metro Area
1020 Cherokee St ... Denver CO 80204 303-758-2100 758-8321
TF: 800-356-6333 ■ *Web:* bbb.org/denver

Better Business Bureau of the Mid-Hudson
150 White Plains Rd Ste 107 ... Tarrytown NY 10591 914-333-0550 333-7519
Web: bbb.org/new-york-city

Better Business Bureau of the Mid-South
3693 Tyndale Dr ... Memphis TN 38125 901-759-1300 757-2997
TF: 800-222-8754 ■ *Web:* bbb.org/memphis

Better Business Bureau of the Permian Basin Area of West Texas
1005 La Posada Dr ... Austin TX 78752 432-563-1880 445-2096*
**Fax Area Code:* 512 ■ *Web:* www.bbb.org

Better Business Bureau of the San Angelo Area
3134 Executive Dr ... San Angelo TX 76904 325-949-2989 949-3514
Web: bbb.org/san-angelo

Better Business Bureau of the Santa Clara Valley San Benito Santa Cruz & Monterey Inc
1112 S Bascom Ave ... San Jose CA 95128 408-278-7400 278-7444
Web: bbb.org/losangelessiliconvalley

Better Business Bureau of the South Central Area
1800 NE Loop 410 Ste 400 ... San Antonio TX 78217 210-828-9441 828-3101
Web: bbb.org/central-texas

Better Business Bureau of the South Plains of Texas
3333 66th St ... Lubbock TX 79413 806-763-0459 744-9748
Web: bbb.org/south-plains-texas

Better Business Bureau of the Southeast Atlantic
6555 Abercorn St Ste 120 ... Savannah GA 31405 912-354-7521 354-5068
Web: bbb.org/north-east-florida

Better Business Bureau of the Southland Inc
315 N La Cadena Dr ... Colton CA 92324 909-825-7280 503-1890

Better Business Bureau of the Southwest
2625 Pennsylvania St NE Ste 2050 ... Albuquerque NM 87110 505-326-6501 346-0696
Web: bbb.org/new-mexico-southwest-colorado

Better Business Bureau of the Texas Panhandle
600 S Tyler Ste 1300 ... Amarillo TX 79101 806-379-6222 379-8206
Web: bbb.org/amarillo

Better Business Bureau of the Tri-Counties
PO Box 129 ... Santa Barbara CA 93102 805-963-8657 962-8557
Web: bbb.org/santa-barbara

Better Business Bureau of the Tri-Parish Area
801 Barrow St Ste 400 ... Houma LA 70360 985-868-3456
Web: bbb.org/new-orleans

Better Business Bureau of Upstate New York
100 Bryant Woods S ... Amherst NY 14228 716-881-5222 883-5349
TF: 800-828-5000 ■ *Web:* bbb.org/upstate-new-york

Better Business Bureau of Utah
5673 S Redwood Rd ... Salt Lake City UT 84123 801-892-6009 892-6002
TF: 800-456-3907 ■ *Web:* bbb.org/utah

Better Business Bureau of West Central Ohio
219 N McDonel St ... Lima OH 45801 419-223-7010
Web: www.bbb.org/phoenix/businessreviews/betterbusinessbureaus/thebbbservingwestcentralohioinli-maoh97003194

Better Business Bureau of West Florida
2655 McCormick Dr ... Clearwater FL 33759 727-535-5522 539-6301
TF: 800-525-1447 ■ *Web:* bbb.org/west-florida

Better Business Bureau of West Georgia & East Alabama
PO Box 2587 ... Columbus GA 31902 706-324-0712 324-2181
TF: 800-768-4222 ■ *Web:* bbb.org/columbus-georgia

Better Business Bureau of Western Massachusetts
35 Ctr St Ste 203 ... Chicopee MA 01013 866-566-9222
TF: 866-566-9222 ■ *Web:* bbb.org/central-western-massachusetts

Better Business Bureau of Western Michigan
40 Pearl St NW Ste 354 ... Grand Rapids MI 49503 616-774-8236 774-2014
Web: bbb.org/western-michigan

Better Business Bureau of Western Pennsylvania
400 Holiday Dr Ste 220 ... Pittsburgh PA 15220 412-456-2700 922-8656
Web: bbb.org/pittsburgh

Better Business Bureau of Wisconsin
10101 W Greenfield Ave Ste 125 ... Milwaukee WI 53214 414-847-6000 302-0355
Web: bbb.org/wisconsin

Better Business Bureau Serving Central California
4201 W Shaw Ave Ste 107 ... Fresno CA 93722 559-222-8111 228-6518
TF: 800-675-8118 ■ *Web:* bbb.org/central-california-inland-empire

Better Business Bureau Serving Eastern Washington North Idaho & Montana Inc
152 S Jefferson St Ste 200 ... Spokane WA 99201 509-455-4200 838-1079
Web: www.bbb.org

Better Business Bureau Upstate South Carolina
408 N Church St Ste C ... Greenville SC 29601 864-242-5052
Web: bbb.org/upstatesc

Tri-State Better Business Bureau
5401 Vogel Rd Ste 410 ... Evansville IN 47715 812-473-0202 473-3080
TF: 800-359-0979 ■ *Web:* bbb.org/evansville

80 BEVERAGES - MFR

See Also Breweries p. 1876; Water - Bottled p. 3305

80-1 Liquor - Mfr

Phone | Fax

A. Smith Bowman Distillery
1 Bowman Dr ... Fredericksburg VA 22408 540-373-4555 371-2236
Web: www.asmithbowman.com

Anheuser-Busch Cos Inc 1 Busch Pl ... Saint Louis MO 63118 314-577-2000 525-0810
TF: 800-342-5283 ■ *Web:* www.anheuser-busch.com

Bacardi USA Inc 2701 S Le Jeune Rd ... Coral Gables FL 33134 305-573-8511 573-7507*
**Fax:* Hum Res ■ *Web:* www.bacardi.com

Beam Inc 510 Lk Cook Rd ... Deerfield IL 60015 847-948-8888
Web: www.jimbeam.com

Black Prince Distillery Inc 691 Clifton Ave ... Clifton NJ 07011 973-365-2050 365-0746
Web: www.blackprincedistillery.com

City Brewing Company LLC 925 S Third St ... La Crosse WI 54601 608-785-4200 785-4300
Web: www.citybrewery.com

Diageo North America 801 Main Ave ... Norwalk CT 06851 203-229-2100
Web: www.diageo.com

Dickel George A Co 1950 Cascade Hollow Rd ... Tullahoma TN 37388 931-857-4110
Web: www.dickel.com

Four Roses Distillery LLC
1224 Bonds Mill Rd ... Lawrenceburg KY 40342 502-839-3436 839-8338
Web: www.fourrosesbourbon.com

Gekkeikan Sake USA Inc 1136 Sibley St ... Folsom CA 95630 916-985-3111 985-2221
Web: www.gekkeikan-sake.com

Heavenhill Distilleries Inc
1064 Loretto Rd ... Bardstown KY 40004 502-348-3921
Web: heavenhill.com

Jack Daniel Distillery 182 Lynchburg Hwy ... Lynchburg TN 37352 931-759-6357
Web: www.jackdaniels.com

Jacquin Charles et Cie Inc
2633 Trenton Ave ... Philadelphia PA 19125 215-425-9300 425-9438

Laird & Co 1 LaiRd Rd ... Scobeyville NJ 07724 732-542-0312 542-2244
TF: 877-438-5247 ■ *Web:* www.lairdandcompany.com

Maker's Mark Distillery Inc
3350 Burke Spring Rd ... Loretto KY 40037 270-865-2881 865-2196
Web: www.makersmark.com

McCormick Distilling Co Inc 1 McCormick Ln ... Weston MO 64098 816-640-2276 640-3082
Web: www.mccormickdistilling.com

Montebello Brands Inc
1919 Willow Spring Rd ... Baltimore MD 21222 410-282-8800 282-8809

Pernod Ricard USA 100 Manhattanville Rd ... Purchase NY 10577 914-848-4800
Web: www.pernod-ricard-usa.com

Phone | Fax

Sunrich LLC 3824 SW 93rd St PO Box 128 .... Hope MN 56046 507-451-6030 451-8201
TF: 800-297-5997 ■ *Web:* www.sunrich.com

Takara Sake USA Inc 708 Addison St .... Berkeley CA 94710 510-540-8250 486-8758
Web: takarasake.com

Walker MS Inc 20 Third Ave .... Somerville MA 02143 617-776-6700 776-5808
TF: 800-528-2787 ■ *Web:* www.mswalker.com

80-2 Soft Drinks - Mfr

Phone | Fax

Adirondack Beverages Inc 701 Corporations Pk .... Scotia NY 12302 518-370-3621 370-3762
Web: www.adirondackbeverages.com

American Beverage Corp 1 Daily Way .... Verona PA 15147 412-828-9020 828-3462
Web: www.ambev.com

Classic Distributing & Beverage Group Inc
120 N Puente Ave........................... City Of Industry CA 91746 626-934-3700
Web: www.cdbginc.com

Coca-Cola Co 1 Coca-Cola Plz PO Box 1734 .... Atlanta GA 30313 404-676-2121 676-6792
NYSE: KO ■ *TF:* 800-438-2653 ■ *Web:* us.coca-cola.com

Cosco International Inc
1633 Sands Pl SE Cumberland Business Pk .... Marietta GA 30067 770-303-0797 303-0795
Web: www.coscous.com

Cott Corp 6525 Viscount Rd...................... Mississauga ON L4V1H6 905-672-1900 881-1926*
NYSE: COT ■ **Fax Area Code:* 813 ■ *TF:* 866-732-8683 ■ *Web:* www.cott.com

Crystal Rock Holdings Inc
1050 Buckingham St .... Watertown CT 06795 860-945-0661
NYSE: AMEX ■ *TF:* 800-525-0070 ■ *Web:* www.crystalrock.com

Davis Beverage Group 1530-A Bobali Dr............ Harrisburg PA 17104 717-914-1295

Double Cola Company USA
537 Market St Ste 100 .... Chattanooga TN 37402 423-267-5691
Web: double-cola.com

Dr Pepper/Seven-Up Inc 5301 Legacy Dr .... Plano TX 75024 972-673-7000 673-7000*
**Fax:* Hum Res ■ *TF:* 800-696-5891 ■ *Web:* www.drpeppersnapplegroup.com

Faygo Beverages Inc 3579 Gratiot Ave .... Detroit MI 48207 313-925-1600
Web: www.faygo.com

Fiji Water Company LLC
11444 W Olympic Blvd 2nd Fl .... Los Angeles CA 90064 310-312-2850 312-2828
TF: 888-426-3454 ■ *Web:* www.fijiwater.com

Great Plains Coca-Cola Bottling Company Inc
600 N May Ave.............................. Oklahoma City OK 73107 405-280-2000 946-5739
TF: 800-753-2653 ■ *Web:* www.greatplainscocacola.com

Jones Soda Co 66 S Hanford St Ste 150 .... Seattle WA 98134 206-624-3357 624-6857
OTC: JSDA ■ *TF:* 800-690-6903 ■ *Web:* www.jonessoda.com

Middlesboro Coca-Cola Bottling Works Inc
1324 Cumberland Ave .... Middlesboro KY 40965 877-692-4679
TF: 800-442-0102 ■ *Web:* www.mccbw.com

Monarch Beverage Co
1123 Zonolite Rd NE Ste 10 .... Atlanta GA 30306 404-262-4040 612-3389*
**Fax Area Code:* 317

Oneta Co 1401 S Padre Island Dr................. Corpus Christi TX 78416 361-853-0123 853-5327
Web: www.onetacc.com

Pepsi-Cola Bottling Company of Yuba City Inc
750 Sutter St................................... Yuba City CA 95991 530-673-9205
Web: pepsico.com

Polar Beverages Inc 1001 Southbridge St............ Worcester MA 01610 508-753-4300 793-0813
TF Cust Svc: 800-734-9800 ■ *Web:* www.polarbev.com

Primal Essence Inc 1351 Maulhardt Ave.................. Oxnard CA 93030 805-981-2409
Web: www.primalessence.com

Procesadora Campo Fresco Inc PO Box 755 .... Santa Isabel PR 00757 787-845-4747 845-3490
Web: www.campofresco.com

Shasta Beverages Inc 26901 Industrial Blvd........... Hayward CA 94545 510-783-3200 783-8681*
**Fax:* Sales ■ *TF:* 800-834-9980 ■ *Web:* www.shastapop.com

Wallingford Coffee Mills Inc
11401 Rockfield Ct............................ Cincinnati OH 45241 513-771-4570 771-3138
TF: 800-533-3690 ■ *Web:* www.wallingfordcoffee.com

White Rock Products Corp
141-07 20th Ave Ste 403 .... Whitestone NY 11357 718-746-3400 767-0413
TF: 800-969-7625 ■ *Web:* www.whiterockbeverages.com

80-3 Wines - Mfr

Phone | Fax

A Bommarito Wines Inc
2827 S Brentwood Blvd .... Saint Louis MO 63144 314-961-8996
Web: www.abommaritowines.com

Ambiente Wine Importing Company Inc
2314 Rutland Dr Ste 205 .... Austin TX 78758 512-835-2299
Web: www.ambientewine.com

Barton Brescome Inc 69 Defco Park Rd........... North Haven CT 06473 203-239-4901
TF: 800-922-4840 ■ *Web:* www.brescomebarton.com

Beaulieu Vineyard 1960 St Helena Hwy.............. Rutherford CA 94573 707-967-5233
TF: 800-373-5896 ■ *Web:* www.bvwines.com

Benziger Family Winery
1883 London Ranch Rd .... Glen Ellen CA 95442 707-935-3000 935-3016
Web: www.benziger.com

Bronco Wine Co 6342 Bystrum Rd .... Ceres CA 95307 209-538-3131 538-2178
TF: 855-874-2394 ■ *Web:* classicwinesofcalifornia.com

Brotherhood Winery
100 Brotherhood Plz Dr PO Box 190 .... Washingtonville NY 10992 845-496-3661
Web: www.brotherhood-winery.com

Bully Hill Vineyards
8843 Greyton H Taylor Memorial Dr............ Hammondsport NY 14840 607-868-3610 868-3205
Web: www.bullyhillvineyards.com

Canandaigua Wine Company Inc
235 N Bloomfield Rd .... Canandaigua NY 14424 585-396-7600
TF: 888-659-7900 ■ *Web:* www.cbrands.com

Chateau Montelena Winery 1429 Tubbs Ln........... Calistoga CA 94515 707-942-5105 942-4221
Web: www.montelena.com

Chatham Imports Inc 245 Fifth Ave.................... New York NY 10016 212-473-1100
Web: www.chathamimports.com

Phone | Fax

Classic Wines LLC 6489 E 39th Ave.................... Denver CO 80207 303-825-1360
Web: www.classicwines.net

Clos du Bois 19410 Geyserville Ave.................. Geyserville CA 95441 707-857-1651
TF Sales: 800-222-3189 ■ *Web:* www.closdubois.com

Columbia Crest Winery
178810 State Rt 221 PO Box 231 .... Paterson WA 99345 509-875-4227 415-3657*
**Fax Area Code:* 425 ■ *TF:* 888-309-9463 ■ *Web:* www.columbiacrest.com

Crossroad Vintners 6429 Guion Rd .... Indianapolis IN 46268 317-471-1038
Web: crossroadvintners.com

Diageo Chateau & Estate Wines Co
240 Gateway Rd W .... Napa CA 94558 707-299-2600 299-2777
Web: www.diageowines.com

Dolce Winery Inc PO Box 327 .... Oakville CA 94562 707-944-8868 944-2312
Web: www.dolcewine.com

Domaine Chandon Inc 1 California Dr .... Yountville CA 94599 888-242-6366 944-1123*
**Fax Area Code:* 707 ■ *TF:* 888-242-6366 ■ *Web:* www.chandon.com

Domaine Select Wine Estates LLC
105 Madison Ave Ste 2302.......................... New York NY 10016 212-279-0799
Web: www.domaineselect.com

Dreyfus Ashby & Co 630 Third Ave 15th Fl............ New York NY 10017 212-818-0770
Web: www.dreyfusashby.com

F Korbel & Bros Inc 13250 River Rd .... Guerneville CA 95446 707-824-7000 869-2506
Web: www.korbel.com

Franciscan Estates 1178 Galleron Rd............. Saint Helena CA 94574 707-967-3830 396-7831*
**Fax Area Code:* 585 ■ *Web:* www.franciscan.com

Freixenet USA 967 Broadway .... Sonoma CA 95476 707-996-4981 996-0720
Web: www.freixenetusa.com

Garvey Wholesale Beverage Inc
2542 San Gabriel Blvd .... Rosemead CA 91770 626-280-5244
TF: 800-287-2075 ■ *Web:* garveywholesalebeverage.com

Hogue Cellars 2800 Lee Rd.......................... Prosser WA 99350 800-565-9779 786-4580*
**Fax Area Code:* 509 ■ *TF:* 800-565-9779 ■ *Web:* www.hoguecellars.com

i2c Inc 1300 Island Dr Ste 105.................. Redwood City CA 94065 650-593-5400
Web: www.i2cinc.com

Imperial Brands Inc
11505 Fairchild Gardens Ave
Ste 204.................................. Palm Beach Gardens FL 33410 561-624-5662
Web: www.ibrandsinc.com

Jarboe Sales Co 6833 E Reading Pl .... Tulsa OK 74115 918-836-2511
Web: www.jarboesales.com

Jefferson Vineyards LP
1353 Thmas Jefferson Pkwy .... Charlottesville VA 22902 434-977-3042
Web: www.jeffersonvineyards.com

Jwsieg Wines
1180 Seminole Trl Ste 290..................... Charlottesville VA 22901 434-244-5300

Kendall-Jackson Wine Estates Ltd
425 Aviation Blvd .... Santa Rosa CA 95403 707-544-4000
TF: 800-769-3649 ■ *Web:* www.kj.com

Kysela Pere Et Fils Ltd 331 Victory Rd .... Winchester VA 22602 540-722-9228
TF: 877-492-7917 ■ *Web:* www.kysela.com

Laetitia Vineyards & Winery Inc
453 Laetitia Vineyard Dr .... Arroyo Grande CA 93420 805-481-1772 481-6920
TF: 888-809-8463 ■ *Web:* www.laetitiawine.com

Louis M Martini Winery
254 S St Helena Hwy .... Saint Helena CA 94574 866-549-2582 963-8750*
**Fax Area Code:* 707 ■ *TF:* 866-549-2582 ■ *Web:* www.louismartini.com

Magnotta Winery Corp 271 Chrislea Rd .... Vaughan ON L4L8N6 905-738-9463 738-5551
TF: 800-461-9463 ■ *Web:* www.magnotta.com

Major Brands Inc 6701 SW Ave .... St Louis MO 63143 314-645-1843
Web: www.majorbrands.com

Meier's Wine Cellars Inc
6955 Plainfield Rd .... Cincinnati OH 45236 513-891-2900 891-6370
Web: www.meierswinecellars.com

Mendocino Wine Co 501 PaRducci Rd................... Ukiah CA 95482 707-463-5350 462-7260
TF: 800-362-9463 ■ *Web:* www.mendocinowineco.com

MHW Ltd 1129 Northern Blvd Ste 312 .... Manhasset NY 11030 516-869-9170
Web: www.mhwltd.com

Michel-Schlumberger Partners LP
4155 Wine Creek Rd............................ Healdsburg CA 95448 707-433-7427 433-0444
TF: 800-447-3060 ■ *Web:* www.michelschlumberger.com

Monsieur Touton Selections of Massachusetts Ltd
230 Lowell St Ste 2i .... Wilmington MA 01887 978-657-0405
Web: www.mtouton.com

Newlands Systems Inc 602-30731 Simpson Rd .... Abbotsford BC V2T6Y7 604-855-4890 855-8826
TF: 877-855-4890 ■ *Web:* nsibrew.com

Noble Wines Ltd 9860 40th Ave S......................... Seattle WA 98118 206-326-5274
Web: www.noblewinesltd.com

Old Mill Winery 403 S Broadway....................... Geneva OH 44041 800-227-6972 466-4417*
**Fax Area Code:* 440 ■ *TF:* 800-227-6972 ■ *Web:* www.ohiowines.org

Opici Import Co 25 Deboer Dr...................... Glen Rock NJ 07452 201-689-1200
Web: www.opici.com

Ozeki Sake (USA) Inc 249 Hillcrest Rd.................. Hollister CA 95023 831-637-9217
Web: www.ozekisake.com

Pine Ridge Winery LLC 5901 Silverado Trail.............. Napa CA 94558 800-575-9777
TF: 800-575-9777 ■ *Web:* www.pineridgevineyards.com

Ravenswood Winery Inc 18701 Gehricke Rd............... Sonoma CA 95476 888-669-4679
TF: 888-669-4679 ■ *Web:* www.ravenswoodwinery.com

Raymond Vineyard 849 Zinfandel Ln .... Saint Helena CA 94574 707-963-6941
TF: 800-525-2659 ■ *Web:* www.raymondvineyards.com

Renault Winery Resort
72 N Bremen Ave .... Egg Harbor City NJ 08215 609-965-2111
Web: www.renaultwinery.com

Roanoke Valley Wine Co 1250 Intervale.................. Salem VA 24153 540-444-4440
TF: 877-478-9463 ■ *Web:* rvwc.com

Robert Mondavi Co 7801 St Helena Hwy .... Oakville CA 94562 707-226-1395
TF: 888-766-6328 ■ *Web:* www.robertmondaviwinery.com

Rodney Strong Vineyards
11455 Old Redwood Hwy .... Healdsburg CA 95448 707-431-1533
TF: 800-678-4763 ■ *Web:* www.rodneystrong.com

Royal Wine Corp 63 Le Fante Ln..................... Bayonne NJ 07002 201-437-9131 388-8444*
**Fax Area Code:* 718 ■ *Web:* www.royalwine.com

Sebastiani Vineyards Inc 389 Fourth St E .... Sonoma CA 95476 707-933-3230 933-3370
TF: 855-232-2338 ■ *Web:* www.sebastiani.com

Company / Address	City	State	Zip	Phone	Fax
Trefethen Vineyards Winery Inc 1160 Oak Knoll Ave — *TF:* 866-895-7696 ■ *Web:* www.trefethen.com	Napa	CA	94558	707-255-7700	
Tryon Distributing Company LLC 4701 Stockholm Ct — *Web:* www.tryondist.com	Charlotte	NC	28273	704-334-0849	
Vie-Del Co 11903 S Chestnut	Fresno	CA	93725	559-834-2525	834-1348
Warner Vineyards Inc 706 S Kalamazoo St — *TF:* 800-756-5357 ■ *Web:* warnerwines.com	Paw Paw	MI	49079	269-657-3165	
Weatherford Laboratories Inc 8845 Fallbrook Dr — *Web:* labs.weatherford.com	Houston	TX	77064	832-237-4000	
Weibel Vineyards 1 Winemaster Way — *TF:* 800-932-9463 ■ *Web:* www.weibel.com	Lodi	CA	95240	209-365-9463	365-9469
Willamette Valley Vineyards Inc 8800 Enchanted Way SE — *NASDAQ: WVVI* ■ *TF Sales:* 800-344-9463 ■ *Web:* www.wvv.com	Turner	OR	97392	503-588-9463	588-8894
Wilson Daniels Ltd 1201 Dowdell Ln — *Web:* www.wilsondaniels.com	St Helena	CA	94574	707-963-9661	
WineCommune LLC 7305 Edgewater Dr Ste D — *Web:* www.winecommune.com	Oakland	CA	94621	510-632-5300	

81 BEVERAGES - WHOL

81-1 Beer & Ale - Whol

Company / Address	City	State	Zip	Phone	Fax
All State Beverage Co 130 Sixth St — *Web:* www.allstatebeverage.com	Montgomery	AL	36104	334-265-0507	
Allentown Beverage Company Inc 1249 N Quebec St — *Web:* allentownbeverage.com	Allentown	PA	18109	610-432-4581	
Anheuser-Busch, Inc., 900 John St — *Web:* www.lakebeverage.com	West Henrietta	NY	14586	585-427-0090	
Arkansas Distributing Company LLC 800 E Barton Ave — *TF:* 877-735-3506	West Memphis	AR	72301	870-735-3506	735-0052
Associated Distributors LLC 401 Woodlake Dr — *TF:* 800-308-2600	Chesapeake	VA	23320	757-424-6300	424-4616
Atlas Distributing Corp 44 Southbridge St — *TF:* 800-649-6221 ■ *Web:* www.atlasdistributing.com	Auburn	MA	01501	508-791-6221	791-0812
Banko Beverage Co 5001 Crackersport Rd — *TF General:* 800-322-9295	Allentown	PA	18104	610-434-0147	
Beauchamp Distributing Co 1911 S Santa Fe Ave — *Web:* www.beauchampdist.com	Compton	CA	90221	310-639-5320	537-8641
Bergseth Bros Co 1211 47th St N — *Web:* bergsethbeer.com	Fargo	ND	58102	701-232-8818	
Birmingham Beverage Company Inc 211 Citation Ct — *Web:* alabev.com	Birmingham	AL	35209	205-942-9403	
Blach Distributing Co 131 W Main St — *TF:* 800-310-5099 ■ *Web:* www.abwholesaler.com	Elko	NV	89801	775-738-7111	
Blue Ridge Beverage Company Inc 44-46 Barley Dr — *Web:* www.blueridgebeverage.com	Salem	VA	24153	540-380-2000	
Bonanza Beverage Co 6333 Ensworth St — *Web:* www.bonanzabev.com	Las Vegas	NV	89119	702-361-4166	361-6408
Buck Distributing Company Inc 15827 Commerce Ct — *TF Cust Svc:* 800-750-2825 ■ *Web:* www.buckdistributing.com	Upper Marlboro	MD	20774	301-952-0400	
Burke Beverages Inc 4900 S Vernon Ave — *Web:* www.burkebev.com	McCook	IL	60525	708-688-2000	688-2050
Carenbauer Distributing Corp 1900 Jacob St — *Web:* www.abwholesaler.com	Wheeling	WV	26003	304-232-3000	232-3630
Central Distributors Inc 15 Foss Rd — *Web:* www.centraldistributors.com	Lewiston	ME	04240	207-784-4026	784-7869
Central European Distribution Corp (CEDC) 3000 Atrium Way Ste 265 — *NASDAQ: CEDC* ■ *Web:* www.cedc.com	Mount Laurel	NJ	08054	822-456-6000	
Cherokee Distributing Company Inc 200 Miller Main Cir — *Web:* cherokeedistributing.com	Knoxville	TN	37919	865-588-7641	558-8941
Chicago Beverage Systems LLC 4239 W Ferdinand St — *Web:* reyesholdings.com	Chicago	IL	60624	773-826-4100	
City Beverages of Orlando 10928 Florida Crown Dr — *Web:* www.abwholesaler.com	Orlando	FL	32824	407-251-4049	851-7100
Clare Rose Inc 100 Rose Executive Blvd — *Web:* www.clarerose.com/agecheck.aspx	East Yaphank	NY	11967	631-475-1840	650-4331
Classic City Beverages LLC 530 Calhoun Dr — *Web:* jandlventuresllc.com	Athens	GA	30601	706-353-1650	353-1655
Coastal Beverage Co Inc 301 Harley Rd — *Web:* www.coastalbev.com	Wilmington	NC	28405	910-799-3011	392-3674
Columbia Distributing Co 6840 N Cutter Cir — *TF:* 888-417-5001 ■ *Web:* www.columbia-dist.com	Portland	OR	97217	503-289-9600	
Commercial Distributing Co Inc 46 S Broad St — *Web:* commercialdist.com	Westfield	MA	01085	413-562-9691	562-7302
Consolidated Beverages Inc 12 St Mark St — *Web:* consolidatedbeverages.com	Auburn	MA	01501	508-832-5311	
Coors Distributing Co (CBC) 5400 N Pecos St — *Web:* www.coors.com	Denver	CO	80221	303-433-6541	964-5577
Couch Distributing Company Inc 104 Lee Rd — *Web:* www.couchdistributing.com	Watsonville	CA	95076	831-724-0649	724-4293
Crescent Crown Distributing 5900 Almonaster Ave — *Web:* crescentcrown.com	New Orleans	LA	70126	504-240-5900	
Crest Beverage Co 8870 Liquid Ct — *Web:* www.crestbeverage.com	San Diego	CA	92121	858-452-2300	
D Canale Beverages Inc 45 W EH Crump Blvd — *Web:* www.abwholesaler.com/dcanalebeverages	Memphis	TN	38106	901-948-4543	
DBI Beverage 245 S Spruce Ave Ste 900 — *Web:* www.dbibeverage.com	San Francisco	CA	94080	415-643-9900	
DET Distributing Co 301 Great Cir Rd — **Fax Area Code:* 617 ■ *Web:* www.detdist.com	Nashville	TN	37228	615-244-4113	255-0122*
Dutchess Beer Distributors Inc 5 Laurel St — *Web:* dutchessbeer.com	Poughkeepsie	NY	12601	845-452-0940	452-0958
Eagle Distributing Co Inc 1100 S Bud Blvd — **Fax Area Code:* 865	Fremont	NE	68025	402-721-0620	525-9530*
Eagle Distributing Company Inc 310 Radford Pl — *Web:* eagledistributing.com	Knoxville	TN	37917	865-637-3311	525-9530
Eastown Distributors Co 14400 Oakland Ave — *Web:* www.eastown.com	Highland Park	MI	48203	313-867-6900	
Fahr Beverage Inc PO Box 358 — *Web:* www.fahrbeverage.com	Waterloo	IA	50704	319-234-2605	234-5644
Five Star Distributing Inc 4055 E Parl 30 Dr — *Web:* www.fivestardistributing.net	Columbia City	IN	46725	260-244-3775	
Frank B Fuhrer Wholesale Co 3100 E Carson St — *TF:* 800-837-2212 ■ *Web:* www.fuhrerwholesale.com	Pittsburgh	PA	15203	412-488-8844	488-0195
Gambrinus Co, The 14800 San Pedro Ave 3rd Fl — *TF:* 800-596-6486 ■ *Web:* www.gambrinusco.com	San Antonio	TX	78232	210-490-9128	490-9984
General Distributing Co 5350 Amelia Earhart Dr — *Web:* generaldistributing.weebly.com	Salt Lake City	UT	84116	801-531-7895	363-4924
Georgia Crown Distributing Co 100 Georgia Crown Dr — *TF:* 800-342-2350 ■ *Web:* www.georgiacrown.com	McDonough	GA	30253	770-302-3000	302-3080
Girardi Distributors LLC 5 Railroad Pl — *Web:* businessfinder.masslive.com	Athol	MA	01331	978-249-3581	
Golden Eagle Distributors Inc 705 E Ajo Way — *Web:* www.gedaz.com	Tucson	AZ	85713	520-884-5999	884-1804
Golden Eagle of Arkansas Inc 1900 E 15th St	Little Rock	AR	72202	501-372-2800	376-2404
Grantham Distributing Co Inc 2685 Hansrob Rd	Orlando	FL	32804	407-299-6446	295-7104
Great Bay Distributors Inc 2310 Starkey Rd — *Web:* www.greatbaybud.com	Largo	FL	33771	727-584-8626	
Gretz Beer Co 710 E Main St — *TF General:* 800-310-5099	Norristown	PA	19401	610-275-0285	
Guiffre Distributing Co 6839 Industrial Rd — *Web:* guiffredistributing.com	Springfield	VA	22151	703-642-1700	642-2855
Gusto Brands Inc 707 Douglas St — *Web:* gustobrands.com	LaGrange	GA	30240	706-882-2573	882-2412
Heineken USA 360 Hamilton Ave Ste 1103 — *Web:* www.heineken.com	White Plains	NY	10601	914-681-4100	681-1900
Henry A Fox Sales Co 4494 36th St SE — *Web:* henryfoxsales.com	Grand Rapids	MI	49512	616-949-1210	
Hensley & Co 4201 N 45th Ave — **Fax Area Code:* 623 ■ *Web:* www.abwholesaler.com	Phoenix	AZ	85031	602-264-1635	247-7094*
High Grade Beverage Inc 891 Georges Rd — *Web:* www.highgradebeverage.com	Monmouth Junction	NJ	08852	732-821-7600	821-2898
Hill Distributing Co 2555 Harrison Rd	Columbus	OH	43204	614-276-6533	276-8888
House of Schwan Inc 3636 Comotara St — *Web:* wichitabeer.com	Wichita	KS	67226	316-636-9100	
Hubert Distributors Inc 1200 Auburn Rd — *Web:* www.abwholesaler.com	Pontiac	MI	48342	248-858-2340	858-7777
Iron City Distributing Co 2670 Commercial Ave — *TF Cust Svc:* 800-759-2671 ■ *Web:* www.ironcitydist.com	Mingo Junction	OH	43938	740-598-4171	598-4677
JJ Taylor Cos Inc 655 N AIA — *Web:* www.jjtaylor.com	Jupiter	FL	33477	561-354-2900	
Koerner Distributors Inc 1305 W Wabash St PO Box 67 — *Web:* www.koernerdistributor.com	Effingham	IL	62401	217-347-7113	347-8736
Labatt Breweries of Canada 207 Queen's Quay W Ste 299 — *TF Cust Svc:* 800-268-2337 ■ *Web:* www.labatt.com	Toronto	ON	M5J1A7	416-361-5050	
Leon Farmer & Co 100 Rail Ridge Rd — *Web:* www.leonfarmer.com	Athens	GA	30607	706-353-1166	
Lion Brewery Inc 700 N Pennsylvania Ave — *Web:* www.lionbrewery.com	Wilkes-Barre	PA	18705	570-823-8801	823-6686
Louis Glunz Beer Inc 7100 N Capitol Dr — *Web:* www.glunzbeers.com	Lincolnwood	IL	60712	847-676-9500	675-5678
Maple City Ice Co Inc 371 Cleveland Rd — *TF Cust Svc:* 877-762-9119 ■ *Web:* norwalkreflector.com	Norwalk	OH	44857	419-668-2531	
Markstein Beverage Co 505 S Pacific St — *Web:* abwholesaler.com/group08/markstein	San Marcos	CA	92078	760-744-9100	
Mautino Distributing Co 500 N Richards St — *TF Cust Svc:* 800-851-2756	Spring Valley	IL	61362	815-664-4311	664-2224
McLaughlin & Moran Inc 40 Slater Rd — *TF:* 800-423-0156	Cranston	RI	02920	401-463-5454	
Merrimack Valley Distributing Co 50 Prince St — *Web:* mvdc.com	Danvers	MA	01923	978-777-2213	774-7487
Metz Beverage Company Inc 302 N Custer St	Sheridan	WY	82801	307-674-4818	
Mission Beverage Co 550 S Mission Rd	Los Angeles	CA	90033	323-266-6238	266-6559
Moon Distributors Inc 2800 Vance St — *Web:* moondist.com	Little Rock	AR	72206	501-375-8291	
Muller Inc 2800 Grant Ave — *Web:* mullerbev.com	Philadelphia	PA	19114	215-676-7575	698-0414
New Hampshire Distributors Inc 65 Regional Dr — *Web:* nhdist.com	Concord	NH	03301	603-224-9991	224-0415

Phone Fax

NKS Distributors Inc 399 Churchmans Rd........... New Castle DE 19720 302-322-1811 324-4024
TF: 800-310-5099 ■ *Web:* www.abwholesaler.com

Pacific Beverage Co 5305 Ekwill St............. Santa Barbara CA 93111 805-964-3574
Web: www.pacificbeveragecompany.com

Paradise Beverages Inc 94-1450 Moaniani St......... Waipahu HI 96797 808-678-4000 677-8280*
**Fax:* Sales ■ *Web:* www.paradisebeverages.com

Pepin Distributing Co 4121 N 50th St.................. Tampa FL 33610 813-626-6176 626-5800
Web: www.pepindistributing.com

Pike Distributors Inc
401 E John St PO Box 465........................Newberry MI 49868 906-293-8611
Web: pikedistributors.com

Pine State Trading Co 8 Ellis Ave.................... Augusta ME 04330 207-622-3741
TF: 800-873-3825 ■ *Web:* www.pinestatetrading.com

Powers Distributing Company Inc
3700 Giddings Rd.................................Orion MI 48359 248-393-3700
Web: powersdistributing.com

Premium Distributors
3500 Fort Lincoln Dr NE.........................Washington DC 20018 202-526-3900
Web: reyesholdings.com

Premium Distributors of Maryland LLC
530 Monocacy Blvd .... Frederick MD 21701 301-662-0372
Web: www.reyesholdings.com

Premium Distributors of VA LLC
15001 Northridge Dr............................. Chantilly VA 20151 703-227-1200 227-1202
Web: reyesholdings.com

Quality Beverage Inc 525 Miles Standish Blvd.......... Taunton MA 02780 508-822-6200 823-9092

Richland Beverage Assoc
2415 Midway Rd Ste 115......................... Carrollton TX 75006 214-357-0248 357-9581

Saccani Distributing Co
2600 Fifth St PO Box 1764......................Sacramento CA 95818 916-441-0213 441-0806
Web: www.saccanidist.com

Saratoga Eagle Sales & Service Inc
45 Duplainville Rd ....Saratoga Springs NY 12866 518-581-7377 581-7777
TF: 800-310-5099 ■ *Web:* www.abwholesaler.com

Savannah Distributing Co Inc
2425 W Gwinnett St ....Savannah GA 31415 912-233-1167 233-1557
TF General: 800-551-0777 ■ *Web:* www.savdist.com

Silver Eagle Distributors LP
7777 Washington Ave..............................Houston TX 77007 713-869-4361 867-8112
TF: 855-332-2110 ■ *Web:* silvereagle.com

Skokie Valley Beverage Co 199 Shepard Ave ....Wheeling IL 60090 847-541-1500 541-2059
Web: www.svbco.com

Southern Wine & Spirits of Colorado
5270 Fox St PO Box 5603 ....Denver CO 80216 303-292-1711 297-9967
TF: 800-776-0180 ■ *Web:* www.southernwine.com

Standard Beverage Corp 2416 E 37th St N............. Wichita KS 67219 316-838-7707 838-1396
TF: 800-999-8797 ■ *Web:* www.standardbeverage.com

Standard Sales Co Inc 4800 E 42nd St Ste 400.......... Odessa TX 79762 432-367-7662 367-9526
Web: standardsalescompanylp.com

Star Distributors Inc 460 Frontage Rd............. West Haven CT 06516 203-932-3636 932-5977
TF: 877-922-3501

Stoudt Co 1618 Judson Rd..........................Longview TX 75601 903-753-7239

Three Lakes Distributing Co
111 Overton St ....Hot Springs AR 71901 501-623-8201 624-4499

Town & Country Distributors Inc
1050 W Ardmore Ave ....Itasca IL 60143 630-250-0590
Web: tcbeer.com

Treu House of Munch Inc 8000 Arbor Dr ....Northwood OH 43619 419-666-7770 666-5712
Web: www.treuhouse.com

Tri-County Beverage Co 2651 E 10 Mile Rd ....Warren MI 48091 586-757-4900
Web: www.tricountybeverage.com

United Distributors Inc 5500 United Dr SE............. Smyrna GA 30082 678-305-2080
Web: udiga.com

Watson Kunda & Sons Inc
349 S Henderson Rd........................ King of Prussia PA 19406 610-265-3113
Web: www.kundabev.com

Western Beverages Inc 4545 E 51st Ave ....Denver CO 80216 303-388-5755 336-3336
Web: western-beverage-distributing-company.placestars.com

Western Wyoming Beverages Inc
100 Reliance Rd..............................Rock Springs WY 82901 307-362-6332
Web: www.westernwyomingbeverages.com

Williams Distributing Corp 880 Burnett Rd ....Chicopee MA 01020 413-594-4900
Web: williamsdistributing.com

Wright Wisner Distributing Corp
3165 Brighton-Henrietta Town Line Rd.............. Rochester NY 14623 585-427-2880 272-1216*
**Fax Area Code:* 716 ■ *Web:* wrightbev.com

81-2 Soft Drinks - Whol

Phone Fax

Admiral Beverage Corp
721 Pulliam Ave PO Box 58..........................Worland WY 82401 307-347-4201
Web: www.admiralbeverage.com

All State Beverage Co 130 Sixth St.............. Montgomery AL 36104 334-265-0507
Web: www.allstatebeverage.com

Atlas Distributing Corp 44 Southbridge St .... Auburn MA 01501 508-791-6221 791-0812
TF: 800-649-6221 ■ *Web:* www.atlasdistributing.com

Buffalo Rock Co 111 Oxmoor Rd ....Birmingham AL 35209 205-942-3435 942-2601
TF: 800-822-9799 ■ *Web:* www.buffalorock.com

Carolina Canners Inc PO Box 1628.................... Cheraw SC 29520 843-537-5281 537-6743
Web: carolinacanners.com

Coca-Cola Bottling Co 725 E Erie Ave............. Philadelphia PA 19134 215-427-4500 423-5557

Coca-Cola Bottling Co Consolidated
4100 Coca-Cola Plaza ....Charlotte NC 28211 704-557-4000
NASDAQ: COKE ■ *TF:* 800-777-2653 ■ *Web:* www.cokeconsolidated.com

Coca-Cola Enterprises Inc
2500 Windy Ridge Pkwy.............................Atlanta GA 30339 770-989-3000
NYSE: CCE ■ *Web:* www.cokecce.com

Gusto Brands Inc 707 Douglas St.....................LaGrange GA 30240 706-882-2573 882-2412
Web: gustobrands.com

Made-Rite Co PO Box 3283..........................Longview TX 75606 903-753-8604 236-9743
Web: www.themade-ritecompany.com

Malolo Beverages & Supplies Ltd
120 Sand Island Access Rd ....Honolulu HI 96819 808-845-4830 845-4835
Web: malolobeverages.com

Markstein Beverage Co 505 S Pacific St ....San Marcos CA 92078 760-744-9100
Web: abwholesaler.com/group08/markstein

Metz Beverage Company Inc 302 N Custer St......... Sheridan WY 82801 307-674-4818

Nor-Cal Beverage Company Inc
2286 Stone Blvd...........................West Sacramento CA 95691 916-372-0600
Web: www.ncbev.com

Swire Coca-Cola USA 12634 S 265 W.................. Draper UT 84020 801-816-5300 816-5423
TF: 800-497-2653 ■ *Web:* swirecc.com

Temple Bottling Company Ltd 3510 Pkwy Dr .... Temple TX 76504 254-773-3376 778-5414
Web: www.templebot.com

Vital Pharmaceuticals Inc 1600 N Pk Dr.............. Weston FL 33326 954-641-0570 641-4960
Web: www.vpxsports.com

Western Wyoming Beverages Inc
100 Reliance Rd..............................Rock Springs WY 82901 307-362-6332
Web: www.westernwyomingbeverages.com

Wis-Pak Inc 860 W St PO Box 496 .... Watertown WI 53094 920-262-6300 262-9273
Web: wis-pak.com

81-3 Wine & Liquor - Whol

Phone Fax

Alabama Crown Distributing
421 Industrial Ln ....Birmingham AL 35211 205-941-1155
TF: 800-548-1869 ■ *Web:* georgiacrown.com

Bacardi Bottling Corp 12200 N Main St ....Jacksonville FL 32218 904-757-1290 751-1397

Badger Liquor Company Inc
850 S Morris St .... Fond du Lac WI 54936 920-923-8160 923-8169
TF: 800-242-9708 ■ *Web:* www.badgerliquor.com

Badger West Wine & Spirits LLC
5400 Old Town Hall Rd........................... Eau Claire WI 54701 715-836-8600 836-8609
TF: 800-472-6674 ■ *Web:* www.badgerliquor.com

Ben Arnold Beverage Company LP
101 Beverage Blvd ....Ridgeway SC 29130 803-337-3500 337-5310*
**Fax:* Cust Svc ■ *TF Acctg:* 888-262-9787 ■ *Web:* www.charmer-sunbelt.com

Beverage Distributors Co 14200 E Moncrieff Pl.......... Aurora CO 80011 303-371-3421 270-5983*
**Fax Area Code:* 334 ■ *TF General:* 888-262-9787 ■
Web: www.charmer-sunbelt.com/beveragedistr/Pages/Welcome.aspx

Blue Ridge Beverage Company Inc
44-46 Barley Dr .... Salem VA 24153 540-380-2000
Web: www.blueridgebeverage.com

Capitol-Husting Company Inc
12001 W Carmen Ave............................Milwaukee WI 53225 414-353-1000 353-0768
Web: www.capitol-husting.com

Cardinal Distributing Company LLC
269 Jackrabbit Ln.................................Bozeman MT 59718 406-586-0241 587-1156
Web: www.cardinaldistributing.com

Castle Brands Inc 122 E 42nd St Ste 4700.............New York NY 10168 646-356-0200 356-0222
NYSE: ROX ■ *TF:* 800-882-8140 ■ *Web:* www.castlebrandsinc.com

Central Distributors Inc 15 Foss Rd................. Lewiston ME 04240 207-784-4026 784-7869
Web: www.centraldistributors.com

Charmer Sunbelt Group, The
60 E 42nd St Ste 1915 ....New York NY 10165 212-699-7000 699-7099
TF: 888-262-9787 ■ *Web:* www.charmer-sunbelt.com

Columbia Distributing Co 6840 N Cutter Cir............Portland OR 97217 503-289-9600
TF: 888-417-5001 ■ *Web:* www.columbia-dist.com

Constellation Brands Inc
207 High Pt Dr Bldg 100 ....Victor NY 14564 888-724-2169
NYSE: STZ ■ *TF:* 888-724-2169 ■ *Web:* www.cbrands.com

Diageo Chateau & Estate Wines Co
240 Gateway Rd W .... Napa CA 94558 707-299-2600 299-2777
Web: www.diageowines.com

Dichello Distributors Inc 55 Marsh Hill Rd.............Orange CT 06477 203-891-2100
Web: www.dichello.com

Fedway Assoc Inc 505 Westgate Dr..............Basking Ridge NJ 07920 973-624-6444
Web: www.fedway.com

Frederick Wildman & Sons Ltd 307 E 53rd St.........New York NY 10022 212-355-0700 355-4719
TF General: 800-733-9463 ■ *Web:* www.frederickwildman.com

General Beer Distributors 6169 McKee Rd............Fitchburg WI 53719 608-271-1237
Web: visitmadison.com

General Wine & Liquor Co
373 Victor Ave ....Highland Park MI 48203 313-867-0521 867-4039
Web: www.gwlc.com

Georgia Crown Distributing Co
100 Georgia Crown Dr .... McDonough GA 30253 770-302-3000 302-3080
TF: 800-342-2350 ■ *Web:* www.georgiacrown.com

Glazer's Wholesale Drug Company Inc
14911 Quorum Dr Ste 400.............................. Dallas TX 75254 972-392-8200 702-8508
TF: 800-275-2854 ■ *Web:* www.glazers.com

Goldring Gulf Distributing Co
8245 Opportunity Dr.................................Milton FL 32583 850-432-9883 432-5509
Web: www.goldringgulf.com

Grantham Distributing Co Inc 2685 Hansrob Rd........ Orlando FL 32804 407-299-6446 295-7104

Hammer Company Inc 9450 Rosemont Dr........... Streetsboro OH 44241 330-422-1471

Henry A Fox Sales Co 4494 36th St SE ....Grand Rapids MI 49512 616-949-1210
Web: henryfoxsales.com

Horizon Wine & Spirits Nashville
3851 Industrial Pkwy ....Nashville TN 37218 615-320-7292 321-4173
Web: www.hwas.com

Johnson Bros Wholesale Liquor Co
1999 ShepaRd Rd.................................. Saint Paul MN 55116 651-649-5800 649-5894
Web: www.johnsonbrothers.com

Kings Liquor Inc 2810 W Berry St.................. Fort Worth TX 76109 817-923-3737
Web: www.kingsliquor.com

Luxco 5050 Kemper Ave .... Saint Louis MO 63139 314-772-2626 772-6021
Web: www.luxco.com

Maisons Marques & Domaines USA Inc
383 Fourth St Ste 400.............................Oakland CA 94607 510-286-2000 286-2010
Web: www.mmdusa.net

	City	State	Zip	Phone	Fax
Merrimack Valley Distributing Co 50 Prince St *Web:* mvdc.com	Danvers	MA	01923	978-777-2213	774-7487
Moet Hennessy USA 85 Tenth Ave *Web:* www.mhusa.com	New York	NY	10011	212-251-8200	251-8388
Moon Distributors Inc 2800 Vance St *Web:* moondist.com	Little Rock	AR	72206	501-375-8291	
National Wine & Spirits Inc PO Box 2187 *Web:* www.nwscorp.com	Indianapolis	IN	46206	317-602-6644	602-6720
NKS Distributors Inc 399 Churchmans Rd *TF:* 800-310-5099 ■ *Web:* www.abwholesaler.com	New Castle	DE	19720	302-322-1811	324-4024
Paradise Beverages Inc 94-1450 Moaniani St **Fax:* Sales ■ *Web:* www.paradisebeverages.com	Waipahu	HI	96797	808-678-4000	677-8280*
Pernod Ricard USA 100 Manhattanville Rd *Web:* www.pernod-ricard-usa.com	Purchase	NY	10577	914-848-4800	
Phillips Distributing Corp 3010 Nob Hill Rd *TF:* 800-236-7269 ■ *Web:* www.phillipsdistributing.com	Madison	WI	53713	608-222-9177	222-0558
Premier Beverage Company of Florida 9801 Premier Pkwy *Web:* www.charmer-sunbelt.com	Miramar	FL	33025	954-436-9200	436-9039
Quality Beverage Inc 525 Miles Standish Blvd	Taunton	MA	02780	508-822-6200	823-9092
R & R Marketing LLC 10 Patton Dr *Web:* www.charmer-sunbelt.com	West Caldwell	NJ	07006	973-228-5100	403-8679
Remy Cointreau USA Inc 1290 Ave of the Americas *Web:* www.remy-cointreau.com	New York	NY	10104	212-399-4200	424-2259
Republic National Distributing Co (RNDC) 6511 Tri County Pkwy *Web:* www.rndc-usa.com	Schertz	TX	78154	210-224-7531	
Savannah Distributing Co Inc 2425 W Gwinnett St *TF General:* 800-551-0777 ■ *Web:* www.savdist.com	Savannah	GA	31415	912-233-1167	233-1557
Southern Wine & Spirits of America Inc 1600 NW 163rd St *TF:* 800-776-0180 ■ *Web:* www.southernwine.com	Miami	FL	33169	305-625-4171	
Southern Wine & Spirits of Colorado 5270 Fox St PO Box 5603 *TF:* 800-776-0180 ■ *Web:* www.southernwine.com	Denver	CO	80216	303-292-1711	297-9967
Southern Wine & Spirits of Illinois 300 E Crossroads Pkwy Bolingbrook Corp Ctr *TF:* 800-776-0180 ■ *Web:* www.southernwine.com	Bolingbrook	IL	60440	630-685-3000	685-3700
Southern Wine & Spirits of New York 313 Underhill Blvd PO Box 9034 *Web:* www.southernwine.com	Syosset	NY	11791	516-921-9005	
Standard Beverage Corp 2416 E 37th St N *TF:* 800-999-8797 ■ *Web:* www.standardbeverage.com	Wichita	KS	67219	316-838-7707	838-1396
Sterling Distributing Co 4433 S 96th St	Omaha	NE	68127	402-339-2300	339-3772
Terlato Wine Group, The (TWG) 900 Armour Dr *TF:* 800-950-7676 ■ *Web:* terlatowines.com	Lake Bluff	IL	60044	847-604-8900	
William Grant & Sons Inc 130 Fieldcrest Ave *Web:* www.grantusa.com	Edison	NJ	08837	732-225-9000	
Winebow Inc 75 Chestnut Ridge Rd *TF:* 800-859-0689 ■ *Web:* www.thewinebowgroup.com	Montvale	NJ	07645	201-445-0620	
Wisconsin Distributors Inc 900 Progress Way *Web:* www.wisconsindistributors.com	Sun Prairie	WI	53590	608-834-2337	834-2300
Young's Market Company LLC 500 S Central Ave **Fax:* Hum Res ■ *TF:* 800-627-2777 ■ *Web:* www.youngsmarket.com	Los Angeles	CA	90013	213-612-1248	612-1238*

82 BICYCLES & BICYCLE PARTS & ACCESSORIES

See Also Sporting Goods p. 3193; Toys, Games, Hobbies p. 3256

	City	State	Zip	Phone	Fax
Cane Creek Cycling Components 355 Cane Creek Rd *TF:* 800-234-2725 ■ *Web:* www.canecreek.com	Fletcher	NC	28732	828-684-3551	684-1057
Giant Bicycle USA 3587 Old Conejo Rd **Fax Area Code:* 800 ■ *Web:* www.giant-bicycles.com	Newbury Park	CA	91320	805-267-4600	637-9704*
Haro Bicycles 1230 Avenida Chelsea *Web:* www.harobikes.com	Vista	CA	92081	760-599-0544	599-1237
Huffy Bicycle Co 6551 Centerville Business Pkwy *TF:* 800-872-2453 ■ *Web:* www.huffybikes.com	Centerville	OH	45459	937-865-2800	865-5470
K2 Bike 1600 Calebs Path Ext Ste 203 *Web:* www.eccyclesupply.com	Hauppauge	NY	11788	631-780-5360	780-5358
Quality Bicycle Products Inc 6400 W 105th St *Web:* peopleforbikes.org	Bloomington	MN	55438	952-941-9391	
Raleigh America Inc 6004 S 190th St Ste 101 **Fax Area Code:* 253 ■ *TF:* 800-222-5527 ■ *Web:* www.diamondback.com	Kent	WA	98032	800-222-5527	872-0257*
Raleigh USA 6004 S 190th St Ste 101 *TF:* 800-222-5527 ■ *Web:* www.raleighusa.com	Kent	WA	98032	253-395-1100	872-0257
Shimano American Corp 1 Holland Dr *Web:* www.shimano.com	Irvine	CA	92618	949-951-5003	768-0920
SMITH Mfg Company Inc 1610 S Dixie Hwy *TF:* 800-653-9311 ■ *Web:* www.smithmfg.com	Pompano Beach	FL	33060	954-941-9744	545-0348
Specialized Bicycle Components 15130 Concord Cir *TF:* 877-808-8154 ■ *Web:* www.specialized.com	Morgan Hill	CA	95037	408-779-6229	779-1631
SRAM Corp 1333 N Kingsbury St 4th Fl *TF:* 800-346-2928 ■ *Web:* www.sram.com	Chicago	IL	60622	312-664-8800	664-8826
Terry Precision Bicycles for Women Inc 47 Maple St **Fax Area Code:* 802 ■ *TF:* 800-289-8379 ■ *Web:* www.terrybicycles.com	Burlington	VT	05401	800-289-8379	861-2956*
Trek Bicycle Corp 801 W Madison St *Web:* www.trekbikes.com	Waterloo	WI	53594	920-478-2191	478-2774
Wald LLC 800 E Fifth St **Fax:* Sales ■ *Web:* www.waldllc.com	Maysville	KY	41056	606-564-4077	564-5248*
Worksman Trading Corp 94-15 100th St *TF:* 800-962-2453 ■ *Web:* www.worksman.com	Ozone Park	NY	11416	718-322-2000	529-4803

83 BIO-RECOVERY SERVICES

Companies listed here provide services for managing and eliminating biohazard dangers that may be present after a death or injury. These services include cleaning, disinfecting, and deodorizing biohazard scenes resulting from accidents, homicides, suicides, natural deaths, and similar events.

	City	State	Zip	Phone	Fax
Advanced Ozone Engineering Inc 6038 Oakwood Ave	Cincinnati	OH	45224	513-681-3871	681-3991
Allied Services 3001 1/2 Gill St Ste E	Bloomington	IL	61704	309-662-0008	
Bio-Recovery Corp 1863 Pond Rd Ste 4 *TF:* 800-556-0621 ■ *Web:* www.biorecovery.com	Ronkonkoma	NY	11779	631-676-2600	
Bio-Scene Recovery 13191 Meadow St NE *TF:* 877-380-5500 ■ *Web:* www.bioscene.com	Alliance	OH	44601	330-823-5500	
Biocare Inc 122 Clair Dr	Piedmont	SC	29673	864-295-9000	
Grangeville Environmental Services (GES) *GES Property Pros LLC* 585 McAllister St *TF:* 866-437-5151 ■ *Web:* www.gespropertypros.com	Hanover	PA	17331	717-637-6152	630-2713
JP Maguire Assoc Inc 266 Brookside Rd *TF:* 877-576-2484 ■ *Web:* www.fixmydamage.com	Waterbury	CT	06708	203-755-2297	573-8547
Peerless Cleaners Inc 519 N Monroe St *TF:* 800-879-7056 ■ *Web:* www.peerlessrestoration.com	Decatur	IL	62522	217-423-7703	
Richey Restoration Inc 9574 Lebanon Rd *Web:* www.richeyrestoration.com	Mount Juliet	TN	37122	615-533-3760	
RMRC Services Inc 5870 S Walden Ct *Web:* www.rockymountainmold.com	Centennial	CO	80015	303-667-0400	

84 BIOMETRIC IDENTIFICATION EQUIPMENT & SOFTWARE

	City	State	Zip	Phone	Fax
AcSys Biometrics Corp 1100 Burloak Dr Ste 703 *Web:* www.acsysbiometrics.com	Burlington	ON	L7L6B2	905-331-7337	634-1101
Aspect Business Solutions 7550 IH-10 W 14th Fl	San Antonio	TX	78229	210-298-5000	298-5001
AuthenTec Inc 100 Rialto Pl # 100	Melbourne	FL	32901	321-308-1300	308-1430
Bio Medic Data Systems Inc 1 Silas Rd *TF:* 800-526-2637 ■ *Web:* www.bmds.com	Seaford	DE	19973	302-628-4100	628-4110
BIO-key International Inc 300 Nickerson Rd *Web:* www.bio-key.com	Marlborough	MA	01752	508-460-4000	
Communication Intelligence Corp (CIC) 275 Shoreline Dr Ste 500 *OTC: CICI* ■ *Web:* www.cic.com	Redwood Shores	CA	94065	650-802-7888	
Count Me In LLC 1530 E Dundee Ste 150 **Fax Area Code:* 702 ■ *TF:* 866-514-5888 ■ *Web:* www.countmeinllc.com	Palatine	IL	60074	866-514-5888	515-7473*
Cross Match Technologies 3950 RCA Blvd Ste 5001 *Web:* www.crossmatch.com	Palm Beach Gardens	FL	33410	561-622-1650	622-9938
Crossmatch 720 Bay Rd Ste 100 *TF:* 866-463-7792 ■ *Web:* www.crossmatch.com	Redwood City	CA	94063	650-474-4000	298-8313
Honeywell Aerospace 1944 E Sky Harbor Cir **Fax Area Code:* 602 ■ *TF:* 800-601-3099 ■ *Web:* www.honeywell.com	Phoenix	AZ	85034	800-601-3099	365-3343*
International Biometric Group LLC 1 Battery Pk Plz Ste 2901 *Web:* www.ibgweb.com	New York	NY	10004	212-809-9491	809-6197
Lightning Powder Company Inc 13386 International Pkwy	Jacksonville	FL	32218	904-485-1836	741-5407
MorphoTrak Inc 113 S Columbus St 4th Fl *TF:* 800-601-6790 ■ *Web:* www.morphotrak.com	Alexandria	VA	22314	703-797-2600	706-9549
NEC Corp of America 10850 Gold Ctr Dr Ste 200 *TF:* 800-632-4636 ■ *Web:* www.necam.com	Rancho Cordova	CA	95670	916-463-7000	
SecuGen Corp 2065 Martin Ave Ste 108 *Web:* www.secugen.com	Santa Clara	CA	95050	408-727-7787	834-7762
Security First Corp 29811 Santa Margarita Pkwy Ste 600 *TF:* 888-884-7152 ■ *Web:* securityfirstcorp.com	Rancho Santa Margarita	CA	92688	949-858-7525	858-7092
SIRCHIE Finger Print Laboratories Inc 100 Hunter Pl *TF:* 800-356-7311 ■ *Web:* www.sirchie.com	Youngsville	NC	27596	919-554-2244	554-2266

85 BIOTECHNOLOGY COMPANIES

See Also Diagnostic Products p. 2192; Medicinal Chemicals & Botanical Products p. 2748; Pharmaceutical Companies p. 2934; Pharmaceutical Companies - Generic Drugs p. 2936

	City	State	Zip	Phone	Fax
ACADIA Pharmaceuticals Inc 3911 Sorrento Vly Blvd *NASDAQ: ACAD* ■ *Web:* www.acadia-pharm.com	San Diego	CA	92121	858-558-2871	558-2872
Acorda Therapeutics Inc 420 Saw Mill River RD *NASDAQ: ACOR* ■ *Web:* www.acorda.com	Ardsley	NY	10502	914-347-4300	347-4560
Acusphere Inc 99 Hayden Ave Ste 385 *OTC: ACUS* ■ **Fax Area Code:* 978 ■ *Web:* www.acusphere.com	Lexington	MA	02421	617-648-8800	863-9993*
Aeolus Pharmaceuticals Inc 26361 Crown Vly Pkwy Ste 150 *Web:* www.aeoluspharma.com	Mission Viejo	CA	92691	949-481-9825	
AEterna Zentaris Inc 1405 Parc Technologique Blvd *TSE: AEZ* ■ *Web:* www.aezsinc.com/en/index.php	Quebec	QC	G1P4P5	418-652-8525	652-0881
Affymax Inc 19200 Stevens Creek Blvd Ste 240 *OTC: AFFY* ■ *Web:* www.affymax.com	Cupertino	CA	95014	650-812-8700	

Company	City	State	ZIP	Phone	Fax
Alexion Pharmaceuticals Inc 352 Knotter Dr *NASDAQ: ALXN* ■ *Web:* alexion.com	Cheshire	CT	06410	203-272-2596	271-8198
Alexza Pharmaceuticals Inc 2091 Stierlin Ct *NASDAQ: ALXA* ■ *Web:* www.alexza.com	Mountain View	CA	94043	650-944-7000	944-7999
Alkermes Inc 852 Winter St *NASDAQ: ALKS* ■ *TF:* 800-848-4876 ■ *Web:* www.alkermes.com	Waltham	MA	02451	781-609-6000	
Allos Therapeutics Inc 11080 Cir Pt Rd Ste 200 *NASDAQ: ALTH*	Westminster	CO	80020	303-426-6262	426-4731
Alnylam Pharmaceuticals Inc 300 Third St 3rd Fl *NASDAQ: ALNY* ■ *TF:* 866-330-0326 ■ *Web:* www.alnylam.com	Cambridge	MA	02142	617-551-8200	551-8101
Amarillo Biosciences Inc 4134 Business Pk Dr *Web:* www.amarbio.com	Amarillo	TX	79110	806-376-1741	376-9301
American Bio Medica Corp (ABMC) 122 Smith Rd *OTC: ABMC* ■ *TF General:* 800-227-1243 ■ *Web:* www.abmc.com	Kinderhook	NY	12106	518-758-8158	758-8172
Amgen Canada Inc 6775 Financial Dr Ste 100 *TF:* 800-665-4273 ■ *Web:* www.amgen.ca	Mississauga	ON	L5N0A4	905-285-3000	285-3100
Amgen Inc 1 Amgen Ctr Dr *TF:* 800-563-9798 ■ *Web:* www.amgen.com	Thousand Oaks	CA	91320	805-447-1000	
AmpliPhi Biosciences Corp 3579 Valley Centre Dr Ste 100 *OTC: APHB* ■ *TF:* 877-795-3647 ■ *Web:* www.ampliphibio.com	San Diego	CA	92130	804-205-5069	
Antibodies Inc PO Box 1560 **Fax Area Code: 530* ■ *TF:* 800-824-8540 ■ *Web:* www.antibodiesinc.com	Davis	CA	95617	800-824-8540	758-6307*
Applied Molecular Evolution Inc (AME) 10300 Campus Pt Dr Ste 200	San Diego	CA	92121	858-597-4990	597-4950
Apricus Biosciences 11975 El Camino Real Ste 300 *NASDAQ: APRI* ■ *Web:* www.apricusbio.com	San Diego	CA	92130	858-222-8041	866-0482
Arboretum, The 1800 S Lincoln Ave *Web:* arboretum.illinois.edu	Urbana	IL	61802	217-333-7579	
Ardea Biosciences Inc 4939 Directors Pl *Web:* ardeabio.com	San Diego	CA	92121	858-652-6500	625-0760
Arena Pharmaceuticals Inc 6166 Nancy Ridge Dr *NASDAQ: ARNA* ■ *Web:* www.arenapharm.com	San Diego	CA	92121	858-453-7200	453-7210
ARIAD Pharmaceuticals Inc 26 Landsdowne St *NASDAQ: ARIA* ■ *Web:* www.ariad.com	Cambridge	MA	02139	617-494-0400	494-8144
Aridis Pharmaceuticals LLC 5941 Optical Ct *Web:* www.aridispharma.com	San Jose	CA	95138	408-385-1742	
ArQule Inc 19 Presidential Way *NASDAQ: ARQL* ■ *TF:* 800-373-7827 ■ *Web:* www.arqule.com	Woburn	MA	01801	781-994-0300	376-6019
Array BioPharma Inc 3200 Walnut St *NASDAQ: ARRY* ■ *TF:* 877-633-2436 ■ *Web:* www.arraybiopharma.com	Boulder	CO	80301	303-381-6600	449-5376
Astellas Pharma US Inc 1 Astellas Way **Fax Area Code: 877* ■ *TF:* 800-695-4321 ■ *Web:* www.astellas.us	Northbrook	IL	60062	800-695-4321	829-7942*
Astex Pharmaceuticals 4140 Dublin Blvd Ste 200 *Web:* astx.com	Dublin	CA	94568	925-560-0100	560-0101
AtriCure Inc 6217 Centre Pk Dr *NASDAQ: ATRC* ■ *TF:* 888-347-6403 ■ *Web:* www.atricure.com	West Chester	OH	45069	513-755-4100	755-4567
Autoimmune Technologies LLC 1010 Common St Ste 1705 *Web:* www.autoimmune.com	New Orleans	LA	70112	504-529-9944	529-8982
AVANIR Pharmaceuticals 30 Enterprise Ste 400 *NASDAQ: AVNR* ■ *Web:* www.avanir.com	Aliso Viejo	CA	92656	949-389-6700	643-6800
AVAX Technologies Inc 2000 Hamilton St Ste 204 *Web:* avax-tech.com	Philadelphia	PA	19130	215-241-9760	241-9684
Bayer CropScience 2 TW Alexander Dr *Web:* www.cropscience.bayer.us	Research Triangle Park	NC	27709	919-549-2000	
BD Biosciences PharMingen 10975 Torreyana Rd **Fax Area Code: 619* ■ *TF:* 800-848-6227 ■ *Web:* www.bdbiosciences.com	San Diego	CA	92121	858-812-8800	812-8888*
Bellus Health Inc 275 Armand Frappier Blvd *TSE: BLU* ■ *TF:* 877-680-4500 ■ *Web:* www.bellushealth.com	Laval	QC	H7V4A7	450-680-4500	680-4501
BioCryst Pharmaceuticals Inc 2190 Pkwy Lk Dr *NASDAQ: BCRX* ■ *Web:* www.biocryst.com	Birmingham	AL	35244	205-444-4600	444-4640
BioDelivery Sciences International Inc (BDSI) 801 Corporate Ctr Dr Ste 210 *NASDAQ: BDSI* ■ *Web:* www.bdsi.com	Raleigh	NC	27607	919-582-9050	582-9051
BioLife Solutions Inc 3303 Monte Villa Pkwy Ste 310 *Web:* biolifesolutions.com	Bothell	WA	98021	425-402-1400	
BioMarin Pharmaceutical Inc 105 Digital Dr *NASDAQ: BMRN* ■ *Web:* www.biomarin.com	Novato	CA	94949	415-506-6700	382-7889
BioNumerik Pharmaceuticals Inc 8023 Vantage Dr Ste Lobby 1 *Web:* www.bionumerik.com	San Antonio	TX	78229	210-614-1701	615-8030
Bioo Scientific Corp 3913 Todd Ln Ste 312 *Web:* www.biooscientific.com	Austin	TX	78744	512-707-8993	
Bioqual Corp 4 Research Ct *Web:* www.bioqual.com	Rockville	MD	20850	301-251-2801	251-1260
BioReliance Corp 14920 Broschart Rd *TF:* 800-553-5372 ■ *Web:* www.bioreliance.com	Rockville	MD	20850	301-738-1000	610-2590
BioTechLogic Inc 717 Indian Rd *Web:* www.biotechlogic.com	Glenview	IL	60025	847-730-3475	
BioTime Inc 101 Atlantic Ave Ste 102 *Web:* www.biotimeinc.com	Alameda	CA	94501	510-521-3390	521-3389
Callisto Pharmaceuticals Inc 420 Lexington Ave Ste 2012 *AMEX: KAL* ■ *Web:* www.synergypharma.com	New York	NY	10170	212-297-0010	297-0019
Cangene Corp 155 Innovation Dr *TSE: CNJ* ■ *Web:* www.cangene.com	Winnipeg	MB	R3T5Y3	204-275-4200	
Cardiome Pharma Corp 6190 Agronomy Rd 6th Fl *NASDAQ: CRME* ■ *TF:* 800-330-9928 ■ *Web:* www.cardiome.com	Vancouver	BC	V6T1Z3	604-677-6905	677-6915
CEL-SCI Corp 8229 Boone Blvd Ste 802 *NYSE: CVM* ■ *TF:* 800-422-6237 ■ *Web:* www.cel-sci.com	Vienna	VA	22182	703-506-9460	506-9471
Celera Genomics Group 1401 Harbor Bay Pkwy *Web:* www.celera.com	Alameda	CA	94502	510-749-4200	
Celgene Corp 86 Morris Ave *NASDAQ: CELG* ■ *TF:* 888-771-0141 ■ *Web:* www.celgene.com	Summit	NJ	07901	908-673-9000	673-9001
Cell Therapeutics Inc (CTI) 501 Elliott Ave W Ste 400 *NASDAQ: CTIC* ■ *TF:* 800-215-2355	Seattle	WA	98119	206-282-7100	284-6206
Cerus Corp 2550 Stanwell Dr *NASDAQ: CERS* ■ *TF:* 800-401-1957 ■ *Web:* www.cerus.com	Concord	CA	94520	925-288-6000	288-6001
Cima Labs Inc 7325 Aspen Ln *Web:* www.cimalabs.com	Brooklyn Park	MN	55428	763-488-4700	488-4800
CMC Biologics 22021 20th Ave SE *Web:* www.cmcbio.com	Bothell	WA	98021	425-485-1900	486-0300
Colorado Serum Co 4950 York St PO Box 16428 *TF Orders:* 800-525-2065 ■ *Web:* www.colorado-serum.com	Denver	CO	80216	303-295-7527	295-1923
CombiMatrix Corp 300 Goddard Ste 100 *NASDAQ: CBMX* ■ *TF:* 800-710-0624 ■ *Web:* www.combimatrix.com	Irvine	CA	92618	949-753-0624	753-1504
Cook Biotech Inc 1425 Innovation Pl *TF:* 888-299-4224 ■ *Web:* www.cookbiotech.com	West Lafayette	IN	47906	765-497-3355	497-2361
Corcept Therapeutics Inc 149 Commonwealth Dr *NASDAQ: CORT* ■ *Web:* www.corcept.com	Menlo Park	CA	94025	650-327-3270	327-3218
Covance Inc 210 Carnegie Ctr *NYSE: CVD* ■ *TF:* 888-268-2623 ■ *Web:* www.covance.com	Princeton	NJ	08540	609-419-2240	
Cryolife Inc 1655 Roberts Blvd NW *NYSE: CRY* ■ *TF:* 800-438-8285 ■ *Web:* www.cryolife.com	Kennesaw	GA	30144	770-419-3355	
Curis Inc 4 Maguire Rd *NASDAQ: CRIS* ■ *Web:* www.curis.com	Lexington	MA	02421	617-503-6500	503-6501
Cytokinetics Inc 280 E Grand Ave *NASDAQ: CYTK* ■ *Web:* www.cytokinetics.com	South San Francisco	CA	94080	650-624-3000	624-3010
Cytori Therapeutics Inc 3020 Callan Rd *NASDAQ: CYTX* ■ *Web:* www.cytori.com	San Diego	CA	92121	858-458-0900	
CytRx Corp 11726 San Vicente Blvd Ste 650 *NASDAQ: CYTR* ■ *Web:* www.cytrx.com	Los Angeles	CA	90049	310-826-5648	826-6139
Danisco US Inc Genencor Div 925 Page Mill Rd *Web:* biosciences.dupont.com	Palo Alto	CA	94304	650-846-7500	845-6500
Dendreon Corp 301 2nd Ave *OTC: DNDNQ* ■ *TF:* 877-256-4545 ■ *Web:* www.dendreon.com	Seattle	WA	98101	206-256-4545	256-0571
DepoMed Inc 7999 Gateway Blvd Ste 300 *NASDAQ: DEPO* ■ *Web:* depomed.com	Newark	CA	94560	510-744-8000	
DexCom Inc 6340 Sequence Dr *NASDAQ: DXCM* ■ *TF:* 888-738-3646 ■ *Web:* www.dexcom.com	San Diego	CA	92121	858-200-0200	
diaDexus Inc 349 Oyster Pt Blvd *OTC: DDXS* ■ *Web:* www.diadexus.com	South San Francisco	CA	94080	650-246-6400	246-6499
Discovery Laboratories Inc 2600 Kelly Rd Ste 100 *NASDAQ: DSCO* ■ *Web:* www.discoverylabs.com	Warrington	PA	18976	215-488-9300	
Dow AgroSciences LLC 9330 Zionsville Rd **Fax Area Code: 800* ■ *TF:* 800-331-6451 ■ *Web:* www.dowagro.com	Indianapolis	IN	46268	317-337-3000	905-7326*
DURECT Corp 2 Results Way *NASDAQ: DRRX* ■ *Web:* www.durect.com	Cupertino	CA	95014	408-777-1417	777-3577
DUSA Pharmaceuticals Inc 25 Upton Dr *NASDAQ: DUSA* ■ *TF:* 877-533-3872 ■ *Web:* www.dusapharma.com	Wilmington	MA	01887	978-657-7500	657-9193
Dyadic International Inc 140 Intracoastal Pointe Dr Ste 404 *OTC: DYAI* ■ *Web:* www.dyadic.com	Jupiter	FL	33477	561-743-8333	743-8343
Elite Pharmaceuticals Inc 165 Ludlow Ave *OTC: ELTP* ■ *Web:* www.elitepharma.com	Northvale	NJ	07647	201-750-2646	750-2755
Elusys Therapeutics Inc 25 Riverside Dr *Web:* www.elusys.com	Pine Brook	NJ	07058	973-808-0222	
EMD Serono Inc 1 Technology Pl *TF:* 800-283-8088 ■ *Web:* www.emdserono.com	Rockland	MA	02370	781-982-9000	871-6754
Emergent Biosolutions Inc 2273 Research Blvd Ste 400 *Web:* www.emergentbiosolutions.com	Rockville	MD	20850	301-795-1800	795-1899
Emisphere Technologies Inc 240 Cedar Knolls Rd Ste 200 *Web:* www.emisphere.com	Cedar Knolls	NJ	07927	973-532-8000	532-8115
Encore Medical Corp 9800 Metric Blvd *TF:* 800-456-8696 ■ *Web:* www.djoglobal.com	Austin	TX	78758	512-832-9500	834-6300
Enzo Biochem Inc 527 Madison Ave *NYSE: ENZ* ■ *TF:* 800-522-5052 ■ *Web:* www.enzo.com	New York	NY	10022	212-583-0100	583-0150
Enzon Pharmaceuticals Inc 20 Kingsbridge Rd *NASDAQ: ENZN* ■ *Web:* www.enzon.com	Piscataway	NJ	08854	732-980-4500	
Exelixis Inc 210 E Grand Ave *NASDAQ: EXEL* ■ *Web:* www.exelixis.com	South San Francisco	CA	94080	650-837-7000	837-8300
Fate Therapeutics Inc 3535 General Atomics Ct Ste 200 *Web:* www.fatetherapeutics.com	San Diego	CA	92121	858-875-1800	
Galectin Therapeutics 4960 Peachtree Industrial Blvd Ste 240 *TF:* 888-286-8010 ■ *Web:* www.galectintherapeutics.com	Norcross	GA	02459	617-559-0033	928-3450
Genaera Corp 5110 Campus Dr *TF:* 800-299-9156 ■ *Web:* www.genaera.com	Plymouth Meeting	PA	19462	610-941-4020	
Generex Biotechnology Corp 555 Richmond St W Ste 202 *OTC: GNBT* ■ *TF:* 800-391-6755 ■ *Web:* www.generex.com	Toronto	ON	M5J2G2	416-364-2551	364-9363
GeneThera Inc 7577 W 103rd Ave Ste 212 *Web:* www.genethera.net	Westminster	CO	80021	303-439-2085	
Genomic Health Inc 101 Galveston Dr *NASDAQ: GHDX* ■ *TF:* 866-662-6897 ■ *Web:* www.genomichealth.com	Redwood City	CA	94063	650-556-9300	556-1132
GenVec Inc 65 W Watkins Mill Rd *NASDAQ: GNVC* ■ *Web:* www.genvec.com	Gaithersburg	MD	20878	240-632-0740	632-0735
Genzyme Corp 500 Kendall St *TF:* 800-745-4447 ■ *Web:* www.genzyme.com	Cambridge	MA	02142	617-252-7500	
Geron Corp 149 Commonwealth Dr *NASDAQ: GERN* ■ *Web:* www.geron.com	Menlo Park	CA	94025	650-473-7700	473-7750
Gilead 5045 Orbitor Dr *TSE: GILD* ■ *Web:* www.gilead.com	Mississauga	ON	L4W4Y4	905-629-9761	

Company	City	State	ZIP	Phone	Fax
Gilead Sciences Inc 333 Lakeside Dr *NASDAQ: GILD* ■ *TF:* 800-445-3235 ■ *Web:* www.gilead.com	Foster City	CA	94404	650-574-3000	578-9264
Grifols USA LLC 2410 Lillyvale Ave *TF:* 888-474-3657 ■ *Web:* www.grifolsusa.com	Los Angeles	CA	90032	888-474-3657	
GTC Biotherapeutics Inc 175 Crossing Blvd *Web:* revobiologics.com	Framingham	MA	01702	508-620-9700	370-3797
GTx Inc 175 Toyota Plz 7th Fl *NASDAQ: GTXI* ■ *Web:* www.gtxinc.com	Memphis	TN	38103	901-523-9700	844-8075
Helix Biopharma Corp 305 Industrial Pkwy S Unit 3 *TSE: HBP* ■ *Web:* www.helixbiopharma.com	Aurora	ON	L4G6X7	905-841-2300	841-2244
Hemispherx Biopharma Inc 1617 JFK Blvd Ste 500 *NYSE: HEB* ■ *Web:* www.hemispherx.net	Philadelphia	PA	19103	215-988-0080	988-1730
Idenix Pharmaceuticals Inc 320 Bent St 4th fl *NYSE: MRK* ■ **Fax Area Code:* 215 ■ *TF:* 800-770-4674 ■ *Web:* www.merck.com/contact/home.html	Cambridge	MA	02141	908-423-1000	631-5996*
Idera Pharmaceuticals Inc 167 Sidney St *NASDAQ: IDRA* ■ *Web:* www.iderapharma.com	Cambridge	MA	02139	617-679-5500	679-5592
Illumina Inc 9885 Towne Centre Dr *NASDAQ: ILMN* ■ *TF:* 800-809-4566 ■ *Web:* www.illumina.com	San Diego	CA	92121	858-202-4500	202-4545
ImmunoGen Inc 830 Winter St *NASDAQ: IMGN* ■ *Web:* www.immunogen.com	Waltham	MA	02451	781-895-0600	895-0611
Immunomedics Inc 300 American Rd *NASDAQ: IMMU* ■ *TF:* 800-327-7211 ■ *Web:* www.immunomedics.com	Morris Plains	NJ	07950	973-605-8200	605-8282
Incyte Corp 1801 Augustine Cut-Off *NASDAQ: INCY* ■ *Web:* www.incyte.com	Wilmington	DE	19803	302-498-6700	
Innovus Pharmaceuticals, Inc. 1981 Murray Holladay R *Web:* innovuspharma.com	Salt Lake City	UT	84117	801-272-9294	
INSMED Inc 4851 Lk Brook Dr Ste 200 *NASDAQ: INSM* ■ *Web:* www.insmed.com	Glen Allen	VA	23060	804-565-3000	
Intarcia Therapeutics Inc 24650 Industrial Blvd *Web:* www.intarcia.com	Hayward	CA	94545	510-782-7800	782-7801
Integra LifeSciences Holdings Corp 311 Enterprise Dr *NASDAQ: IART* ■ *TF:* 800-654-2873 ■ *Web:* www.integra-ls.com	Plainsboro	NJ	08536	609-275-0500	799-3297
ioGenetics LLC 3591 Anderson St Ste 218 *Web:* www.iogenetics.com	Madison	WI	53704	608-310-9540	
Irvine Scientific 2511 Daimler St *TF:* 800-577-6097 ■ *Web:* www.irvinesci.com	Santa Ana	CA	92705	949-261-7800	261-6522
Ivers-Lee Inc 31 Hansen S *TF:* 800-265-1009 ■ *Web:* jonespackaging.com	Brampton	ON	L6W3H7	905-451-5535	
La Jolla Pharmaceutical Co 10182 Telesis Ct 6th Fl *Web:* lajollapharmaceutical.com	San Diego	CA	92121	858-207-4264	
Leo Pharma Inc 123 Commerce Vly Dr E Ste 400 *Web:* www.leo-pharma.com	Thornhill	ON	L3T7W8	905-886-9822	886-6622
Lescarden Inc 420 Lexington Ave Ste 212 *Web:* www.lescarden.com	New York	NY	10170	212-687-1050	
Lexicon Pharmaceuticals Inc 8800 Technology Forest Pl *NASDAQ: LXRX* ■ *TF:* 855-828-4651 ■ *Web:* www.lexicon-genetics.com	The Woodlands	TX	77381	281-863-3000	863-8088
LifeCore Biomedical LLC 3515 Lyman Blvd *TF Cust Svc:* 800-348-4368 ■ *Web:* www.lifecore.com	Chaska	MN	55318	952-368-4300	368-3411
LiphaTech Inc 3600 W Elm St **Fax Area Code:* 414 ■ *TF:* 888-331-7900 ■ *Web:* www.liphatech.com	Milwaukee	WI	53209	888-331-7900	247-8166*
Lundbeck Canada Inc 1000 de la GauchetiFre W Ste 500 *Web:* www.lundbeck.com	Montreal	QC	H3B4W5	514-844-8515	844-5495
MannKind Corp 28903 N Ave Paine *NASDAQ: MNKD* ■ *Web:* www.mannkindcorp.com	Valencia	CA	91355	661-775-5300	775-2081
Martek Biosciences Corp 6480 Dobbin Rd *Web:* www.lifesdha.com	Columbia	MD	21045	410-740-0081	740-2985
Medicines Co 8 Sylvan Way *NASDAQ: MDCO* ■ *TF:* 800-388-1183 ■ *Web:* www.themedicinescompany.com	Parsippany	NJ	07054	973-290-6000	656-9898
MediGene Inc 10650 Scripps Ranch Blvd Ste 206 *Web:* www.medigene.com	San Diego	CA	92131	858-586-2240	
Mera Pharmaceuticals Inc 73-4460 Queen Kaahumanu Hwy Ste 110 *TF:* 800-480-6515 ■ *Web:* www.merapharma.com	Kailua-Kona	HI	96740	808-326-9301	326-9401
Millennium Pharmaceuticals Inc 40 Lansdowne St *Web:* www.millennium.com	Cambridge	MA	02139	617-679-7000	
Momenta Pharmaceuticals Inc 675 W Kendall St *NASDAQ: MNTA* ■ *Web:* www.momentapharma.com	Cambridge	MA	02142	617-491-9700	621-0431
Myriad Genetics Inc 320 Wakara Way *NASDAQ: MYGN* ■ *TF:* 800-469-7423 ■ *Web:* www.myriad.com	Salt Lake City	UT	84108	801-584-3600	584-3640
N.E.T. Inc 5651 Palmer Way Ste C *TF:* 800-888-4638 ■ *Web:* www.netmindbody.com	Carlsbad	CA	92010	760-929-5980	929-5981
Natural Industries Inc 12320 Cutten Rd	Houston	TX	77066	281-580-1643	
Nektar Therapeutics 455 Mission Bay Blvd S *NASDAQ: NKTR* ■ *Web:* www.nektar.com	San Francisco	CA	94158	415-482-5300	
Neuralstem Inc 9700 Great Seneca Hwy *Web:* investor.neuralstem.com	Rockville	MD	20850	301-366-4841	
Neurocrine Biosciences Inc 12790 El Camino Rl *NASDAQ: NBIX* ■ *Web:* www.neurocrine.com	San Diego	CA	92130	858-617-7600	617-7602
Nordion 447 March Rd *NYSE: NDZ* ■ *TF:* 800-465-3666 ■ *Web:* www.nordion.com	Ottawa	ON	K2K1X8	613-592-2790	592-6937
Novartis Vaccines & Diagnostics 350 Massachusetts Ave *NYSE: NVS* ■ *Web:* www.novartis-vaccines.com	Cambridge	MA	02139	862-778-8300	
Novavax Inc 9920 Belward Campus Dr *NASDAQ: NVAX* ■ *TF:* 800-642-1687 ■ *Web:* www.novavax.com	Rockville	MD	20850	240-268-2000	268-2100
Nucro-Technics 2000 Ellesmere Rd Unit 16 *Web:* www.nucro-technics.com	Scarborough	ON	M1H2W4	416-438-6727	438-3463
Nuo Therapeutics Inc 207A Perry Pkwy Ste 1 *OTC: NUOT* ■ *TF:* 866-298-6633 ■ *Web:* www.nuot.com	Gaithersburg	MD	20877	866-298-6633	
Oakwood Laboratories LLC 7670 First Pl Ste A *Web:* www.oakwoodlabs.com	Oakwood Village	OH	44146	440-359-0000	359-0001
Oncolytics Biotech Inc 1167 Kensington Crescent NW Ste 210 *TSE: ONC* ■ *TF:* 800-731-5319 ■ *Web:* www.oncolyticsbiotech.com	Calgary	AB	T2N1X7	403-670-7377	283-0858
Oncothyreon Inc 2601 Fourth Ave Ste 500 *Web:* www.oncothyreon.com	Seattle	WA	98121	206-801-2100	801-2101
Organogenesis Inc 150 Dan Rd *Web:* www.organogenesis.com	Canton	MA	02021	781-575-0775	
Osiris Therapeutics Inc 7015 Albert Einstein Dr *NASDAQ: OSIR* ■ *Web:* www.osiristx.com	Columbia	MD	21046	443-545-1800	545-1701
Osteotech Inc 710 Medtronic Pkwy *TF:* 800-633-8766 ■ *Web:* www.medtronic.com	Minneapolis	MN	55432	763-514-4000	
OXiGENE Inc 701 Gateway Blvd Ste 210 *NASDAQ: OXGN* ■ *Web:* www.oxigene.com	South San Francisco	CA	94080	650-635-7000	635-7001
Oxis International Inc 468 N Camden Dr 2nd Fl *OTC: OXIS* ■ *Web:* www.oxis.com	Beverly Hills	CA	90210	310-860-5184	
Pacira Inc 10450 Science Ctr Dr *Web:* www.pacira.com	San Diego	CA	92121	858-625-2424	625-2439
Paladin Labs Inc 100 Blvd Alexis Nihon Ste 600 *TSE: PLB* ■ *TF:* 888-376-7830 ■ *Web:* www.paladin-labs.com	St-Laurent	QC	H4M2P2	514-340-1112	
Palatin Technologies Inc 4 B Cedar Brook Dr Cedar Brook Corporate Ctr *NYSE: PTN* ■ *Web:* www.palatin.com	Cranbury	NJ	08512	609-495-2200	
Paratek Pharmaceuticals Inc 75 Kneeland St *Web:* paratekpharma.com	Boston	MA	02111	617-275-0040	275-0039
Peregrine Pharmaceuticals Inc 14282 Franklin Ave Ste 100 *NASDAQ: PPHM* ■ *TF:* 800-987-8256 ■ *Web:* www.peregrineinc.com	Tustin	CA	92780	714-508-6000	838-5817
Pharmacyclics Inc 995 E Arques Ave *NASDAQ: PCYC* ■ *TF:* 855-859-2056 ■ *Web:* www.pharmacyclics.com	Sunnyvale	CA	94085	408-774-0330	
Poniard Pharmaceuticals Inc 750B Attery St Ste 330 *OTC: PARD*	South San Francisco	CA	94111	650-583-3774	
Pozen Inc 1414 Raleigh Rd Ste 400 *NASDAQ: POZN* ■ *Web:* www.pozen.com	Chapel Hill	NC	27517	919-913-1030	913-1039
PRA International *PRA* 4130 Parklake Ave Ste 400 *Web:* prahs.com	Raleigh	NC	27612	919-786-8200	786-8201
Pressure BioSciences Inc 14 Norfolk Ave *OTC: PBIO* ■ *Web:* pressurebiosciences.com	South Easton	MA	02375	508-230-1828	230-1829
Primorigen Biosciences Inc 510 Charmany Dr *TF:* 866-372-7442 ■ *Web:* www.primorigen.com	Madison	WI	53719	608-441-8332	
Progenics Pharmaceuticals Inc 777 Old Saw Mill River Rd *NASDAQ: PGNX* ■ *TF:* 866-644-7188 ■ *Web:* www.progenics.com	Tarrytown	NY	10591	914-789-2800	789-2817
Protein Sciences Corp 1000 Research Pkwy *TF:* 800-488-7099 ■ *Web:* www.proteinsciences.com	Meriden	CT	06450	203-686-0800	686-0268
pSivida Inc 400 Pleasant St *NASDAQ: PSDV* ■ *Web:* www.psivida.com	Watertown	MA	02472	617-926-5000	926-5050
Psychemedics Corp 125 Nagog Pk Ste 200 *NASDAQ: PMD* ■ *TF:* 800-628-8073 ■ *Web:* www.psychemedics.com	Acton	MA	01720	978-206-8220	264-9236
QLT Inc 887 Great Northern Way Ste 101 *NASDAQ: QLT* ■ *TF:* 800-663-5486 ■ *Web:* www.qltinc.com	Vancouver	BC	V5T4T5	604-707-7000	707-7001
Regeneron Pharmaceuticals Inc 777 Old Saw Mill River Rd *NASDAQ: REGN* ■ *Web:* www.regeneron.com	Tarrytown	NY	10591	914-847-7000	
Repligen Corp 41 Seyon St *NASDAQ: RGEN* ■ *TF Sales:* 800-622-2259 ■ *Web:* www.repligen.com	Waltham	MA	02453	781-250-0111	250-0115
Repros Therapeutics Inc 2408 Timberloch Pl Ste B-7 *NASDAQ: RPRX* ■ *Web:* www.reprosrx.com	The Woodlands	TX	77380	281-719-3400	719-3446
Research Triangle Park Laboratories 7201 Acc Blvd # 104 *Web:* www.rtp-labs.com	Raleigh	NC	27617	919-510-0228	510-0141
Revivicor Inc 1700 Kraft Dr Ste 2400 *Web:* www.revivicor.com	Blacksburg	VA	24060	540-961-5559	961-7958
Rigel Pharmaceuticals Inc 1180 Veterans Blvd *NASDAQ: RIGL* ■ *Web:* www.rigel.com	South San Francisco	CA	94080	650-624-1100	624-1101
Roche Palo Alto LLC 4300 Hacienda Dr *TF:* 888-545-2443 ■ *Web:* www.roche.com	Pleasanton	CA	94588	925-730-8000	730-8388
Royalty Pharma 110 E 59th St 33rd Fl *Web:* www.royaltypharma.com	New York	NY	10022	212-883-0200	883-2260
RTI Biologics Inc 11621 Research Cir *NASDAQ: RTIX* ■ *TF:* 877-343-6832 ■ *Web:* www.rtix.com	Alachua	FL	32615	386-418-8888	418-0342
Samaritan Pharmaceuticals Inc 101 Convention Ctr Dr Ste 310 *OTC: SPHC*	Las Vegas	NV	89109	702-735-7001	737-7016
Sangamo BioSciences Inc 501 Canal Blvd Ste A100 *NASDAQ: SGMO* ■ *Web:* www.sangamo.com	Richmond	CA	94804	510-970-6000	236-8951
Sanofi Pasteur Inc Discovery Dr **Fax:* Hum Res ■ *TF Orders:* 800-822-2463 ■ *Web:* www.sanofipasteur.us	Swiftwater	PA	18370	570-839-7187	839-7187*
Sanofi-Aventis Canada 2150 St Elzear Blvd W *TF:* 800-363-6364 ■ *Web:* sanofi-aventis.ca/index.html	Laval	QC	H7L4A8	514-331-9220	
Seattle Genetics Inc 21823 30th Dr SE *NASDAQ: SGEN* ■ *Web:* www.seattlegenetics.com	Bothell	WA	98021	425-527-4000	527-4001
Selexys Pharmaceuticals Corp 840 Research Pkwy Ste 516 *Web:* www.selexys.com	Oklahoma City	OK	73104	405-319-8195	
Sequenom Inc 3595 John Hopkins Ct *NASDAQ: SQNM* ■ *TF:* 877-821-7266 ■ *Web:* www.sequenom.com	San Diego	CA	92121	858-202-9000	202-9001
Soligenix Inc 29 Emmons Dr Ste C-10 *OTC: SNGX* ■ *Web:* soligenix.com	Princeton	NJ	08540	609-538-8200	452-6467

	City	State	Zip	Phone	Fax
Spectrum Pharmaceuticals Inc 11500 S Eastern Ave Ste 240 *NASDAQ: SPPI* ■ *TF:* 800-332-1088 ■ *Web:* www.sppirx.com	Henderson	NV	89052	702-835-6300	260-7405
SRP Environmental LLC 348 Aero Dr. *Web:* www.srpenvironmental.com	Shreveport	LA	71107	318-222-2364	
Supernus Pharmaceuticals Inc 1550 E Gude Dr *NASDAQ: SUPN* ■ *Web:* www.supernus.com	Rockville	MD	20850	301-838-2500	
Takeda Canada Inc 435 N Service Rd W Ste 101 *TF:* 888-367-3331 ■ *Web:* www.takedacanada.com	Oakville	ON	L6M4X8	905-469-9333	469-4883
Tamir Biotechnology Inc 12625 High Bluff Dr Ste 113 *OTC: ACEL* ■ *Web:* www.alfacell.com	San Diego	CA	92130	732-823-1003	652-4575
Telesta Therapeutics Inc 275 Labrosse Ave *TSE: TST* ■ *TF:* 800-387-0825 ■ *Web:* www.telestatherapeutics.com	Pointe-Claire	QC	H9R1A3	514-697-6636	697-7966
Theratechnologies Inc 2015 Peel St 5th Fl *TSE: TH* ■ *Web:* www.theratech.com	Montreal	QC	H3A1T8	514-336-7800	336-7242
Theravance Inc 901 Gateway Blvd *NASDAQ: THRX* ■ *Web:* www.theravance.com	South San Francisco	CA	94080	650-808-6000	
Threshold Pharmaceuticals Inc 170 Harbor Way Ste 300 *NASDAQ: THLD* ■ *TF:* 866-276-9886 ■ *Web:* www.thresholdpharm.com	South San Francisco	CA	94080	650-474-8200	474-2529
Titan Pharmaceuticals Inc 400 Oyster Pt Blvd Ste 505 *OTC: TTNP* ■ *TF:* 888-417-8516 ■ *Web:* www.titanpharm.com	South San Francisco	CA	94080	650-244-4990	244-4956
Unigene Laboratories Inc 81 Fulton St *Web:* www.unigene.com	Boonton	NJ	07005	973-265-1100	
United Biomedical Inc 25 Davids Dr *Web:* www.unitedbiomedical.com	Hauppauge	NY	11788	631-273-2828	273-1717
Urigen Pharmaceuticals Inc 501 Silverside Rd PO Box 95 *Web:* www.urigen.com	Wilmington	DE	19809	925-280-2861	280-2861
Verdezyne Inc 2715 Loker Ave W *Web:* www.verdezyne.com	Carlsbad	CA	92010	760-707-5200	
Vericel Corp 24 Frank Lloyd Wright Dr Domino's Farms Lobby K *NASDAQ: ASTM* ■ *Web:* vcel.com	Ann Arbor	MI	48105	734-418-4400	665-0485
Vical Inc 10390 Pacific Ctr Ct *NASDAQ: VICL* ■ *Web:* www.vical.com	San Diego	CA	92121	858-646-1100	646-1150
Viventia Biotechnologies Inc 147 Hamelin St **Fax Area Code:* 905 ■ *Web:* www.viventia.com	Winnipeg	MB	R3T3Z1	204-478-1023	362-2973*
XenoPort Inc 3410 Central Expy *NASDAQ: XNPT* ■ *Web:* www.xenoport.com	Santa Clara	CA	95051	408-616-7200	616-7210
XOMA (US) LLC 2910 Seventh St *NASDAQ: XOMA* ■ *TF:* 800-468-9716 ■ *Web:* www.xoma.com	Berkeley	CA	94710	510-204-7200	644-2011
ZymoGenetics Inc 1201 Eastlake Ave E *TF:* 800-332-2056 ■ *Web:* www.bms.com	Seattle	WA	98102	206-442-6600	442-6608

86 BLANKBOOKS & BINDERS

See Also Checks - Personal & Business p. 1932

	City	State	Zip	Phone	Fax
Abco Inc 1621 Wall St *TF:* 800-969-2226 ■ *Web:* abcodigital.com	Dallas	TX	75215	214-565-1191	428-8996
Acme Sample Books Inc 2410 Schirra Pl *Web:* www.acmesample.com	High Point	NC	27263	336-883-4187	883-4565
Advanced Looseleaf Technologies Inc 1424 Somerset Ave *TF:* 800-339-6354 ■ *Web:* www.binder.com	Dighton	MA	02715	508-669-6354	669-6143
Allison Payment Systems LLC 2200 Production Dr **Fax Area Code:* 317 ■ *TF:* 800-755-2440 ■ *Web:* www.apsllc.com	Indianapolis	IN	46241	800-755-2440	808-2477*
American Thermoplastic Co (ATC) 106 Gamma Dr *TF:* 800-245-6600 ■ *Web:* www.binders.com	Pittsburgh	PA	15238	800-245-6600	
Avery Dennison Corp 207 Goode Ave *NYSE: AVY* ■ *TF Cust Svc:* 888-567-4387 ■ *Web:* www.averydennison.com	Glendale	CA	91203	626-304-2000	
Blackbourn 200 Fourth Ave N **Fax Area Code:* 507 ■ *TF:* 800-842-7550 ■ *Web:* www.blackbourn.com	Edgerton	MN	56128	800-842-7550	442-4313*
Blair Packaging Inc 1515 Independence St *TF:* 800-624-3150	Cape Girardeau	MO	63703	573-334-2146	
Colad Group 801 Exchange St *TF:* 800-950-1755 ■ *Web:* www.colad.com	Buffalo	NY	14210	716-961-1776	961-1753
Colwell Industries Inc 123 N Third St *Web:* www.colwellindustries.com	Minneapolis	MN	55401	612-340-0365	
Continental Binder & Specialty Corp 407 W Compton Blvd *TF:* 800-872-2897 ■ *Web:* www.continentalbinder.com	Gardena	CA	90248	310-324-8227	715-6740
Continental Loose Leaf Inc 1122 16th Ave *TF:* 888-719-5013 ■ *Web:* www.continentallooseleaf.com	Minneapolis	MN	55414	612-378-4800	378-7680
Daret Inc 287 Margaret King Ave *Web:* daret.com	Ringwood	NJ	07456	973-962-6001	
Data Management Inc 537 New Britain Ave **Fax Area Code:* 800 ■ *TF Orders:* 800-243-1969 ■ *Web:* www.datamanage.com	Farmington	CT	06034	860-677-8586	428-1951*
Dilley Manufacturing Co 215 E Third St *TF:* 800-247-5087 ■ *Web:* www.dilleymfg.com	Des Moines	IA	50309	515-288-7289	288-4210
EBSCO Industries Inc Vulcan Information Packaging Div PO Box 29 *TF:* 800-633-4526 ■ *Web:* www.binders.com	Vincent	AL	35178	800-633-4526	344-8939
Eckhart & Company Inc 4011 W 54th St *TF:* 800-443-3791 ■ *Web:* www.eckhartandco.com	Indianapolis	IN	46254	317-347-2665	347-2666
Federal Business Products Inc 95 Main Ave *TF:* 800-927-5123 ■ *Web:* www.feddirect.com	Clifton	NJ	07014	973-667-9800	
Fey Industries Inc 200 Fourth Ave N *TF:* 800-533-5340 ■ *Web:* fey-line.com	Edgerton	MN	56128	507-442-4311	442-3686
Formflex Inc PO Box 218 *TF:* 800-255-7659 ■ *Web:* www.formflexproducts.com	Bloomingdale	IN	47832	800-255-7659	
General Loose Leaf Bindery Co 3811 Hawthorn Ct *TF:* 800-621-0493 ■ *Web:* www.looseleaf.com	Waukegan	IL	60087	847-244-9700	244-9741
General Products 4045 N Rockwell St	Chicago	IL	60618	773-463-2424	463-3028
HALO Branded Solutions Inc 1980 Industrial Dr *Web:* www.halo.com	Sterling	IL	61081	815-625-0980	632-6900
HC Miller Co 3030 Lowell Dr *Web:* hcmillerpress.com	Green Bay	WI	54311	920-465-3030	465-3035
Holum & Sons Company Inc 740 Burr Oak Dr *TF:* 800-447-4479 ■ *Web:* www.holumandsons.com	Westmont	IL	60559	630-654-8222	654-2929
Kurtz Bros Company Inc 400 Reed St PO Box 392 *TF:* 800-252-3811 ■ *Web:* www.kurtzbros.com	Clearfield	PA	16830	814-765-6561	765-8690
Leed Selling Tools Corp 9700 Hwy 57 *TF:* 855-687-5333 ■ *Web:* leedsamples.com	Evansville	IN	47725	812-867-4340	
Michael Lewis Co 8900 W 50th St *Web:* www.mlco.com	McCook	IL	60525	708-688-2200	688-2880
NAPCO Inc 120 Trojan Ave *TF:* 800-854-8621 ■ *Web:* www.napcousa.com	Sparta	NC	28675	336-372-5228	372-8602
Northeast Data Services 1316 College Ave	Elmira	NY	14901	607-733-5541	
Pioneer Photo Albums Inc 9801 Deering Ave *Web:* www.pioneerphotoalbums.com	Chatsworth	CA	91311	818-882-2161	882-6239
Roaring Spring Blank Book Co 740 Spang St *TF:* 800-441-1653 ■ *Web:* www.rspaperproducts.com	Roaring Spring	PA	16673	814-224-5141	224-5429
Samsill Corp 5740 Hartman Rd *TF:* 800-255-1100 ■ *Web:* www.samsill.com	Fort Worth	TX	76119	817-536-1906	535-6900
Southwest Plastic Binding Co 109 Millwell Ct *TF:* 800-325-3628 ■ *Web:* www.swplastic.com	Maryland Heights	MO	63043	314-739-4400	
Spiral Binding Company Inc 1 Maltese Dr **Fax:* Cust Svc ■ *TF:* 800-631-3572 ■ *Web:* www.spiralbinding.com	Totowa	NJ	07511	973-256-0666	256-5981*
Superior Press Inc 11930 Hamden Pl *TF Cust Svc:* 888-590-7998 ■ *Web:* www.superiorpress.com	Santa Fe Springs	CA	90670	562-948-1866	948-4966
Trendex Inc 240 E Maryland Ave *TF:* 800-328-9200 ■ *Web:* www.trendex.com	Saint Paul	MN	55117	651-489-4655	489-4423
Unified Packaging Inc 1187 E 68th Ave *Web:* www.unifiedbinders.com	Denver	CO	80229	303-733-1000	733-6789
Union Group 649 Alden St *TF:* 800-289-3523 ■ *Web:* www.theuniongroup.com	Fall River	MA	02722	508-675-4545	677-0130
US Ring Binder 6800 Arsenal St *TF:* 800-888-8772 ■ *Web:* www.usring.com	Saint Louis	MO	63139	314-645-7880	645-7239
ViaTech Publishing Solutions 1440 Fifth Ave *TF:* 800-645-8558 ■ *Web:* www.viatechpub.com	Bay Shore	NY	11706	631-968-8500	968-0830
West Coast Samples Inc 14450 Central Ave	Chino	CA	91710	909-464-1616	465-9982

87 BLINDS & SHADES

	City	State	Zip	Phone	Fax
Aeroshade Inc 433 Oakland Ave *TF:* 800-331-7179	Waukesha	WI	53186	262-547-2101	547-0546
Beauti-Vue Products Inc 8555 194th Ave **Fax Area Code:* 800 ■ *TF:* 800-558-9431 ■ *Web:* www.beautivue.com	Bristol	WI	53104	262-857-2306	329-9431*
Budget Blinds Inc 1927 N Glassell St *TF:* 800-800-9250 ■ *Web:* www.budgetblinds.com	Orange	CA	92865	714-637-2100	637-1400
Carnegie Fabrics Inc 110 N Centre Ave *Web:* www.carnegiefabrics.com	Rockville Centre	NY	11570	516-678-6770	678-6875
Comfortex Window Fashions Inc 21 Elm St **Fax Area Code:* 800 ■ *TF Cust Svc:* 800-843-4151 ■ *Web:* www.comfortex.com	Maplewood	NY	12189	518-273-3333	336-4580*
Delaine James Inc 10508C Boyer Blvd **Fax Area Code:* 800 ■ *TF Claims:* 800-999-5333	Austin	TX	78758	512-835-5333	999-5555*
Dixon Blind & Awning Service 1800 Sunset Ave	Rocky Mount	NC	27804	252-442-2145	
Hunter Douglas Inc 1 Hunter Douglas Dr **Fax Area Code:* 800 ■ *TF:* 800-365-3399 ■ *Web:* my.hunterdouglas.com/dc	Cumberland	MD	21502	301-722-7700	950-3399*
Kenney Mfg Co 1000 Jefferson Blvd *TF Cust Svc:* 800-753-6639 ■ *Web:* www.kenney.com	Warwick	RI	02886	401-739-2200	736-1822
Lafayette Venetian Blind Inc 3000 Klondike Rd. PO Box 2838 **Fax Area Code:* 765 ■ *TF:* 800-342-5523 ■ *Web:* www.lafvb.com	West Lafayette	IN	47996	800-342-5523	423-2402*
Levolor Kirsch Window Fashions 4110 Premier Dr *TF:* 800-752-9677 ■ *Web:* www.levolor.com	High Point	NC	27265	336-812-8181	
Mill Supply Div 266 Morse St *TF General:* 888-585-9354 ■ *Web:* www.millsupplydiv.com	Hamden	CT	06517	203-777-7668	
Ralph Friedland & Bros 17 Industrial Dr *TF:* 800-631-2162 ■ *Web:* friedlandshades.com	Keyport	NJ	07735	732-290-9800	
Sun Control Products Window Shades 1908 Second St SW *TF:* 800-533-0010 ■ *Web:* suncontrolwindowshades.com	Rochester	MN	55902	507-282-2620	
Superior Shade & Blind Company Inc 1571 N Powerline Rd *Web:* www.superiorshade.com	Pompano Beach	FL	33069	954-975-8122	975-2938
Warm Co 5529 186th Pl SW *TF:* 800-234-9276 ■ *Web:* www.warmcompany.com	Lynnwood	WA	98037	425-248-2424	248-2422

88 BLISTER PACKAGING

	City	State	Zip	Phone	Fax
A-1 Creative Packaging Corp 400 Industrial Blvd *Web:* creativeplastics.com	Palmyra	WI	53156	262-495-2151	
Aaron Thomas Company Inc 7421 Chapman Ave *Web:* www.packaging.com	Garden Grove	CA	92841	714-894-4468	
Accu-Tec Inc 1735 W Burnett St *Web:* www.accu-tec.com	Louisville	KY	40210	502-339-7511	
Adec Industries 2700 Industrial Pkwy *TF:* 866-730-3111 ■ *Web:* www.adecinc.com	Elkhart	IN	46516	574-295-3167	
Aero Fulfillment Services Corp 3900 Aero Dr *Web:* www.aerofulfillment.com	Mason	OH	45040	513-459-3900	

Phone Fax

Andex Industries Inc 1911 Fourth Ave N Escanaba MI 49829 800-338-9882 786-3133*
*Fax Area Code: 906 ■ *TF:* 800-338-9882 ■ *Web:* www.andex.net
Andpak Inc 400 Jarvis Dr. Morgan Hill CA 95037 408-782-2500
Web: www.andpak.com
AQL Decorating Company Inc 215 Bergen Blvd Fairview NJ 07022 201-941-1610
Web: www.aqldecorating.com
Axiom Label 1360 W Walnut Pkwy. Compton CA 90220 310-603-8910
Web: www.axiomlabel.com
Bms Management Inc 1200 W Commerce Way. Lincoln NE 68521 402-474-4014
Web: www.bmslogisticsinc.com
Brisar Industries Inc 150 E Seventh St Paterson NJ 07524 973-278-2500
Web: www.brisar.com
Card Pak Inc 29601 Solon Rd Solon OH 44139 440-542-3100 542-3399
TF: 800-824-3342 ■ *Web:* www.cardpak.com
Chrysalis Packaging & Assembly Corp
130 W Edgerton Ave Ste 130 Milwaukee WI 53207 414-744-8550
Web: www.chryspac.com
CS Packaging Inc 1620 Fullerton Ct. Glendale Heights IL 60139 630-534-4500
Display Pack 1340 Monroe Ave NW Grand Rapids MI 49505 616-451-3061 451-8907
Web: www.displaypack.com
DIY Group Inc 2401 W 26th Muncie IN 47302 765-284-9000
Web: www.diygroup.com
EPC Industries Ltd 12 Tupper Blvd. Amherst NS B4H4S7 902-667-7241
Web: www.polycello.com
Genesee Packaging Inc 2010 Dort Hwy Flint MI 48506 810-235-6120
Web: www.genpackaging.com
Genie Manufacturing Corp
999 Rush Henrietta Townli Rush NY 14543 585-359-4100
Web: www.geniemfg.com
GSC Packaging Inc 575 Wharton Dr. Atlanta GA 30336 404-505-9925
Web: www.gscpackaging.com
Guernsey Industries 60772 Southgate Rd Byesville OH 43723 740-439-5017
Web: guernseycountydd.org
Guy Chemical Company Inc 150 Dominion Dr Somerset PA 15501 814-443-9455
Web: www.guychemical.com
Helm Inc 47911 Halyard Dr. Plymouth MI 48170 313-865-5000
Web: www.helm.com
Hmc Products Inc 5196 27th Ave. Rockford IL 61109 815-397-9145
Web: www.hmcproducts.com
Hy-Test Packaging Corp 515 E 41st St. Paterson NJ 07504 973-754-7000
Web: www.hy-testpackaging.com
Imperial Dax Company Inc 120 New Dutch Ln Fairfield NJ 07004 973-227-6105
Web: www.daxhaircare.com
Innovated Packaging Company Inc
38505 Cherry St Newark CA 94560 510-745-8180
Web: www.innovpak.com
James Alexander Corp 845 Route 94 Blairstown NJ 07825 908-362-9266
Web: www.james-alexander.com
Jay Packaging Group (JPG)
100 Warwick Industrial Dr Warwick RI 02886 401-739-7200 738-0137*
*Fax: Cust Svc ■ *Web:* www.jaypack.com
Jenco Productions Inc 401 South J St San Bernardino CA 92410 909-381-9453
Web: www.jencoproductions.com
Kent Sussex Industries Inc
301 N Rehoboth Blvd Milford DE 19963 302-422-4014
Web: www.ksiinc.org
Metro Label Group Inc 999 Progress Ave Toronto ON M1B6J1 416-292-6600
TF: 800-668-4405 ■ *Web:* www.metrolabel.com
Nelson Packaging Company Inc 1801 Reservoir Rd Lima OH 45804 419-229-3471
TF: 888-229-3471 ■ *Web:* www.nelsonpackagingco.com
Nk Parts Industry Inc Main Facility
777 S Kuther Rd Sidney OH 45365 937-498-4651
Web: www.nkparts.com
Nurol Corp 1531 Marietta Blvd Nw Atlanta GA 30318 404-352-3587
Web: www.nurol.com
Package Right Corp 811 Development Dr Tipton IN 46072 765-675-2323
Web: www.packageright.com
PackageX Inc 17100 Ventura Blvd Ste 223 Encino CA 91316 818-789-6910
Web: www.packagex.com
Pak-Rite Ltd 2395 S Burrell St. Milwaukee WI 53207 414-489-0450
Web: www.pak-rite.com
Placon Corp 6096 McKee Rd Madison WI 53719 608-271-5634 271-3162
TF: 800-541-1535 ■ *Web:* www.placon.com
Pozzetta Products Inc
3219 S Platte River Dr Englewood CO 80110 303-783-3172
Web: www.pozzetta.com
Pri-Pak Inc 2000 Schenley Pl Greendale IN 47025 812-537-7300
Web: www.pripak.com
Primary Packaging Inc
10810 Industrial Pkwy NW Bolivar OH 44612 330-874-3131 874-3811
TF: 800-774-2247 ■ *Web:* www.primarypackaging.com
Pro-Tech Design & Manufacturing Inc
14561 Marquardt Ave Santa Fe Springs CA 90670 562-207-1680
Web: www.protechdesign.com/sitepages/protech.aspx
Quetico LLC 5521 Schaefer Ave. Chino CA 91710 909-628-6200
Web: www.queticollc.com
Remar Inc 6200 E Division St. Lebanon TN 37090 615-449-0231
Web: www.remarinc.com
Sealed Air Corp 200 Riverfront Blvd Elmwood Park NJ 07407 201-791-7600
NYSE: SEE ■ *Web:* www.sealedair.com
Software Partners Inc
447 Old Boston Rd Rt 1 Topsfield MA 01983 978-887-6409
Web: www.softwarepartners.com
Sourcentra Inc 150 Speen St Framingham MA 01701 508-405-2605
Web: www.sourcentra.com
Sun Packing Inc 10077 Wallisville Rd Houston TX 77013 713-673-4600
Web: www.sunpacking.com
Tailored Label Products Inc
W165 N5731 Ridgewood Dr Menomonee Falls WI 53051 262-703-5000
Web: www.tailoredlabel.com
Tpgtex Label Solutions Inc 5830 Ludington Dr Houston TX 77035 713-726-9636
Web: www.tpgtex.com

Phone Fax

Unified Solutions Inc 9801 80th Ave Pleasant Prairie WI 53158 262-942-5200
Web: usipackaging.com
Valley Packaging Industries Inc
110 N Kensington Dr Appleton WI 54915 920-749-5840
Web: www.vpind.com
Virtual Images 1177 Idaho St Ste 100 Redlands CA 92374 408-649-2240
Web: www.vuclip.com
Visual Pak Co 1909 Waukegan Rd Waukegan IL 60085 847-689-1000
Web: www.visualpak.com
Vulsay Industries Ltd 35 Regan Rd Brampton ON L7A1B2 905-846-2200
Web: www.vulsay.com
WePackItAll Inc 2745 Huntington Dr Duarte CA 91010 626-301-9214
Web: www.wepackitall.com
Westpak Inc 10326 Roselle St Ste 101 San Diego CA 92121 858-623-8100
Web: www.westpak.com
Wynalda Packaging 8221 Graphic Dr NE. Belmont MI 49306 616-866-1561 866-4316
Web: www.wynalda.com
Xela Pack Inc 8300 Boettner Rd Saline MI 48176 734-944-1300
Web: www.xelapack.com
Zouire L L C 7226 W Frntage Rd Merriam KS 66203 913-384-6888
Web: www.zouire.com

89 BLOOD CENTERS

See Also Laboratories - Drug-Testing p. 2622; Laboratories - Genetic Testing p. 2622; Laboratories - Medical p. 2622

The centers listed here are members of America's Blood Centers (ABC), the national network of non-profit, independent community blood centers. ABC members are licensed and regulated by the US Food & Drug Administration.

Phone Fax

Belle Bonfils Memorial Blood Ctr
717 Yosemite St Denver CO 80230 303-341-4000 363-2239
TF: 800-365-0006 ■ *Web:* www.bonfils.org
Blood & Tissue Ctr of Central Texas
4300 N Lamar Blvd. Austin TX 78756 512-206-1266
Web: www.bloodandtissue.org
Blood Assurance Inc 705 E Fourth St Chattanooga TN 37403 423-756-0966
TF: 800-962-0628 ■ *Web:* www.bloodassurance.org
Blood Bank of Alaska 4000 Laurel St Anchorage AK 99508 907-222-5600 563-1371
Web: www.bloodbankofalaska.org
Blood Bank of Delmarva 100 Hygeia Dr Newark DE 19713 302-737-8405 737-8233
TF: 800-548-4009 ■ *Web:* www.delmarvablood.org
Blood Bank of Hawaii 2043 Dillingham Blvd. Honolulu HI 96819 808-845-9966
TF: 800-372-9966 ■ *Web:* www.bbh.org
Blood Bank of the Redwoods
2324 Bethards Dr Santa Rosa CA 95405 707-545-1222
TF: 888-393-4483 ■ *Web:* www.bloodcenters.org
Blood Centers of the Pacific
250 Bush St Ste 136 San Francisco CA 94104 415-567-6400
TF: 888-393-4483 ■ *Web:* www.bloodcenters.org
Blood Ctr of Northcentral Wisconsin
211 Forest St Wausau WI 54403 715-842-0761 845-6429
Blood Ctr, The 2609 Canal St New Orleans LA 70112 504-524-1322 592-1580
TF: 800-862-5663 ■ *Web:* www.thebloodcenter.org
BloodCenter of Wisconsin 638 N 18th St. Milwaukee WI 53233 414-933-5000
TF: 877-232-4376 ■ *Web:* www.bcw.edu
BloodSource 1608 Q St Sacramento CA 95811 916-456-1500
TF: 800-995-4420 ■ *Web:* www.bloodsource.org
Carter BloodCare 2205 Hwy 121 Bedford TX 76021 817-412-5000 412-5992
TF: 800-366-2834 ■ *Web:* www.carterbloodcare.org
Cascade Regional Blood Services 220 S 'I' St Tacoma WA 98405 253-383-2553
TF: 877-242-5663 ■ *Web:* www.crbs.net
Central California Blood Ctr
4343 W Herndon Ave Fresno CA 93722 559-389-5433 225-1602
Web: donateblood.org
Central Illinois Community Blood Ctr
1134 S Seventh St Springfield IL 62703 217-753-1530 753-8116
TF Help Line: 800-448-3253 ■ *Web:* bloodcenter.org/home.aspx?region=104&sap=1
Central Jersey Blood Ctr 494 Sycamore Ave Shrewsbury NJ 07702 732-842-5750
TF: 888-712-5663 ■ *Web:* www.cjbcblood.org
Central Kentucky Blood Ctr
3121 Beaumont Centre Cir Lexington KY 40513 859-276-2534 233-4166
TF: 800-775-2522 ■ *Web:* www.ckbc.org
Central Pennsylvania Blood Bank
8167 Adams Dr. Hummelstown PA 17036 717-566-6161
TF: 800-771-0059 ■ *Web:* www.cpbb.org
Coastal Bend Blood Ctr
209 N Padre Island Dr Corpus Christi TX 78406 361-855-4943 855-2641
TF: 800-299-4943 ■ *Web:* www.coastalbendbloodcenter.org
Coffee Memorial Blood Ctr 7500 Wallace Dr Amarillo TX 79124 806-358-4563
Web: www.thegiftoflife.org
Community Blood Bank of Northwest Pennsylvania
2646 Peach St Erie PA 16508 814-456-4206 452-3966
TF: 877-842-0631 ■ *Web:* www.fourhearts.org
Community Blood Ctr 349 S Main St. Dayton OH 45402 937-461-3450 461-9217
TF: 800-388-4483 ■ *Web:* www.cbccts.org
Blue Springs Ctr 4040 Main St Kansas City MO 64111 816-753-4040 968-4047
TF: 888-647-4040 ■ *Web:* www.savealifenow.org
Gladstone Ctr 7265 N Oak Trafficway. Gladstone MO 64118 816-468-9813
TF: 877-468-6844 ■ *Web:* www.savealifenow.org
Community Blood Ctr Inc 4406 W Spencer St. Appleton WI 54914 920-738-3131 738-3139
TF: 800-280-4102 ■ *Web:* www.communityblood.org
Community Blood Ctr of the Ozarks
220 W Plainview Rd Springfield MO 65810 417-227-5000
TF: 800-280-5337 ■ *Web:* www.cbco.org
Community Blood Services
970 Linwood Ave W PO Box 39 Paramus NJ 07653 201-444-3900 670-6174
TF: 866-228-1500 ■ *Web:* www.communitybloodservices.org
Community Blood Services of Illinois
1408 W University Ave Urbana IL 61801 217-367-2202
TF: 800-217-4483 ■ *Web:* bloodcenter.org/home.aspx?region=134&sap=2

	City	State	ZIP	Phone	Fax
Delta Blood Bank 65 N Commerce St	Stockton	CA	95202	209-943-3830	462-0221
TF: 888-942-5663 ■ *Web:* www.deltabloodbank.org					
Gulf Coast Regional Blood Ctr					
1400 La Concha Ln	Houston	TX	77054	713-790-1200	
TF: 888-482-5663 ■ *Web:* www.giveblood.org					
Heartland Blood Centers 1200 N Highland Ave	Aurora	IL	60506	630-892-7055	892-4590
TF: 800-786-4483 ■ *Web:* www.heartlandbc.org					
Hemacare Corp 15350 Sherman Way Ste 350	Van Nuys	CA	91406	818-226-1968	251-5300
TF: 877-310-0717 ■ *Web:* www.hemacare.com					
Houchin Community Blood Bank					
5901 Truxtun Ave	Bakersfield	CA	93309	661-327-8541	
Web: www.hcbb.com					
Hoxworth Blood Ctr University of Cincinnati Medical Ctr					
3130 Highland Ave ML0055	Cincinnati	OH	45267	513-558-1200	558-1209
TF: 800-265-1515 ■ *Web:* www.hoxworth.org					
Inland Northwest Blood Ctr 210 W Cataldo Ave	Spokane	WA	99201	509-624-0151	232-4523
TF: 800-423-0151 ■ *Web:* www.inbcsaves.org					
Lane Memorial Blood Bank 2211 Willamette St	Eugene	OR	97405	541-484-9111	484-6976
Web: lanebloodcenter.org					
Lifeblood Mid-South Regional Blood Ctr					
1040 Madison Ave	Memphis	TN	38104	901-522-8585	523-8671
TF: 888-543-3256 ■ *Web:* www.lifeblood.org					
DeSoto Ctr 1040 Madison Ave	Memphis	TN	38104	901-271-1260	349-2427*
**Fax Area Code:* 662 ■ *Web:* www.lifeblood.org					
LifeServe Blood Ctr 431 E Locust St	Des Moines	IA	50309	800-287-4903	288-0833*
**Fax Area Code:* 515 ■ *TF:* 800-287-4903 ■ *Web:* www.lifeservebloodcenter.org					
LifeShare Blood Centers 8910 Linwood Ave	Shreveport	LA	71106	318-222-7770	222-8886
TF: 800-256-4483 ■ *Web:* www.lifeshare.org					
LifeShare Community Blood Services					
105 Cleveland St	Elyria	OH	44035	440-322-5700	322-6240
TF: 800-317-5412 ■ *Web:* www.lifeshare.cc					
LifeSource Blood Services 2764 Aurora Ave	Naperville	IL	60540	877-543-3768	
TF: 877-543-3768 ■ *Web:* lifesource.org					
LifeSouth Community Blood Centers					
4039 Newberry Rd	Gainesville	FL	32607	888-795-2707	224-1650*
**Fax Area Code:* 352 ■ *TF:* 888-795-2707 ■ *Web:* www.lifesouth.org					
LifeSouth Community Blood Centers Atlanta					
4891 Ashford Dunwoody Rd	Atlanta	GA	30338	404-329-1994	
TF: 888-795-2707 ■ *Web:* lifesouth.org					
Memorial Blood Centers (MBC) 737 Pelham Blvd	Saint Paul	MN	55114	651-332-7000	332-7001
TF Cust Svc: 888-448-3253 ■ *Web:* www.mbc.org					
Michigan Community Blood Centers					
1036 Fuller Ave NE	Grand Rapids	MI	49503	616-774-2300	
TF: 866-642-5663 ■ *Web:* www.miblood.org					
Michigan Community Blood Centers					
4005 Orchard Dr	Midland	MI	48670	989-839-3490	
TF: 866-642-5663 ■ *Web:* www.miblood.org					
Michigan Community Blood Centers Northwest					
2575 Aero Pk Dr	Traverse City	MI	49686	231-935-3030	
TF General: 866-642-5663 ■ *Web:* www.miblood.org					
Miller-Keystone Blood Ctr					
1465 Vly Ctr Pkwy	Bethlehem	PA	18017	610-691-5850	
Web: www.hcsc.org					
Mississippi Blood Services 115 Tree St	Flowood	MS	39232	601-981-3232	
TF: 888-902-5663 ■ *Web:* www.msblood.com					
Mississippi Valley Regional Blood Ctr					
5500 Lakeview Pkwy	Davenport	IA	52807	563-359-5401	359-8603
TF: 800-747-5401 ■ *Web:* www.bloodcenter.org					
MVRBC 5500 Lakeview Pkwy	Davenport	IA	52501	641-682-8149	
TF: 800-747-5401 ■ *Web:* bloodcenter.org					
Nebraska Community Blood Bank 100 N 84th St	Lincoln	NE	68505	402-486-9414	486-9429
TF: 877-486-9414 ■ *Web:* www.ncbb.org					
New York Blood Ctr 310 E 67th St	New York	NY	10065	646-456-4281	
Web: www.nybloodcenter.org					
Northern California Community Blood Bank					
2524 Harrison Ave	Eureka	CA	95501	707-443-8004	443-8007
Web: www.nccbb.org					
Northwest Florida Blood Ctr					
2209 N Ninth Ave	Pensacola	FL	32503	850-434-2535	432-8941
Web: www.oneblood.org					
Oklahoma Blood Institute (OBI)					
1001 N Lincoln Blvd	Oklahoma City	OK	73104	405-278-3100	477-0446*
**Fax Area Code:* 918 ■ *TF:* 866-708-4995 ■ *Web:* www.obi.org					
Puget Sound Blood Ctr 921 Terry Ave	Seattle	WA	98104	206-292-6500	292-8030
TF: 800-366-2831 ■ *Web:* www.psbc.org					
Rhode Island Blood Ctr 405 Promenade St	Providence	RI	02908	401-453-8360	453-8557
TF: 800-283-8385 ■ *Web:* www.ribc.org					
Rock River Valley Blood Ctr					
3065 N Perryville Rd Ste 105	Rockford	IL	61114	815-965-8751	965-8756
TF General: 877-778-2299 ■ *Web:* www.rrvbc.org					
SeraCare Life Sciences Inc 37 Birch St	Milford	MA	01757	508-244-6400	634-3394
NASDAQ: SRLS ■ *TF:* 800-676-1881 ■ *Web:* www.seracare.com					
Shepeard Community Blood Ctr					
1533 Wrightsboro Rd	Augusta	GA	30904	706-737-4551	
Web: www.shepeardblood.org					
South Texas Blood & Tissue Ctr					
6211 IH-10 W	San Antonio	TX	78201	210-731-5555	731-5501
TF: 800-292-5534 ■ *Web:* southtexasblood.org					
Suncoast Communities Blood Bank					
1760 Mound St	Sarasota	FL	34236	941-954-1600	951-2629
TF: 866-972-5663 ■ *Web:* www.scbb.org					
Texoma Regional Blood Ctr 3911 N Texoma Pkwy	Sherman	TX	75090	903-893-4314	893-8628
Web: texomablood.org					
United Blood Services					
6210 E Oak St PO Box 1867	Scottsdale	AZ	85252	480-946-4201	
TF: 800-288-2199 ■ *Web:* www.unitedbloodservices.org					
united blood services 4119 Broad St	San luis obispo	CA	93401	805-543-4290	
Web: www.unitedbloodservices.org					
United Blood Services of Arizona					
Chandler 6220 E Oak St	Scottsdale	AZ	85252	877-827-4376	
TF: 877-827-4376 ■ *Web:* www.unitedbloodservices.org					
San Luis Obispo 4119 Broad St Ste 100	San Luis Obispo	CA	93401	805-543-4290	543-4926
TF: 877-827-4376 ■ *Web:* www.unitedbloodservices.org					
United Blood Services of Colorado					
146 Sawyer Dr	Durango	CO	81303	970-385-4601	
TF: 800-288-2199 ■ *Web:* www.unitedbloodservices.org					
United Blood Services of Louisiana					
Baton Rouge 8234 1 Calais Ave	Baton Rouge	LA	70809	225-769-7233	
Web: www.unitedbloodservices.org/louisiana					
Lafayette 1503 Bertrand Dr	Lafayette	LA	70506	337-235-5433	
Web: www.unitedbloodservices.org					
United Blood Services of Mississippi					
Hattiesburg 805 S 28th Ave	Hattiesburg	MS	39402	601-264-0743	
Web: www.unitedbloodservices.org					
Meridian 1115 25th Ave	Meridian	MS	39301	601-482-2482	483-4204
TF: 877-827-4376 ■ *Web:* www.unitedbloodservices.org					
Tupelo 4326 S Eason Blvd	Tupelo	MS	38801	662-842-8871	
TF: 800-844-8870 ■ *Web:* www.unitedbloodservices.org/nt					
United Blood Services of Montana					
Billings 1444 Grand Ave	Billings	MT	59102	406-248-9168	248-1025
TF: 800-365-4450 ■ *Web:* www.unitedbloodservices.org					
Butte 3745 Harrison Ave	Butte	MT	59701	406-723-3264	
Web: www.unitedbloodservices.org					
United Blood Services of Nevada					
Carson City 256 E Winnie Ln	Carson City	NV	89706	775-887-9111	
Web: www.unitedbloodservices.org					
Las Vegas 6930 W Charleston Blvd	Las Vegas	NV	89117	702-228-4483	
Web: www.unitedbloodservices.org					
Las Vegas 4950 W Craig Rd	Las Vegas	NV	89130	702-228-4483	
Web: www.unitedbloodservices.org					
United Blood Services of New Mexico					
1515 University Blvd NE	Albuquerque	NM	87102	800-333-8037	
TF: 800-333-8037 ■ *Web:* www.unitedbloodservices.org					
Albuquerque 1515 University Blvd NE	Albuquerque	NM	87102	800-333-8037	
TF: 800-333-8037 ■ *Web:* www.unitedbloodservices.org/nm					
Farmington 475 E 20th St	Farmington	NM	87401	888-804-9913	
TF: 877-827-4376 ■ *Web:* www.unitedbloodservices.org					
Las Cruces 1515 University Blvd NE	Albuquerque	NM	87102	575-527-1322	
TF General: 877-827-4376 ■ *Web:* www.unitedbloodservices.org					
United Blood Services of North Dakota					
Bismarck 3231 S 11th St	Fargo	ND	58104	800-456-6159	
TF: 800-456-6159 ■ *Web:* www.unitedbloodservices.org/nd					
Fargo 3231 S 11th St	Fargo	ND	58104	701-293-9453	
TF General: 800-288-2199 ■ *Web:* www.unitedbloodservices.org/nd					
United Blood Services of South Dakota					
Rapid City 2209 W Omaha St	Rapid City	SD	57702	605-342-8585	
Web: www.unitedbloodservices.org					
United Blood Services of Texas					
El Paso 424 S Mesa Hills	El Paso	TX	79912	915-544-5422	
TF: 877-827-4376 ■ *Web:* www.unitedbloodservices.org					
Lubbock 2523 48th St	Lubbock	TX	79413	806-797-6804	
TF: 800-333-6920 ■ *Web:* www.unitedbloodservices.org					
McAllen 1400 S Sixth St	McAllen	TX	78501	956-213-7500	
TF General: 888-827-4376 ■ *Web:* www.unitedbloodservices.org/RG					
San Angelo 2020 W Beauregard Ave	San Angelo	TX	76901	325-223-7500	
TF General: 800-756-0024 ■ *Web:* www.unitedbloodservices.org					
United Blood Services of Wyoming					
Casper 112 E. 8th Ave Ste 102	Cheyenne	WY	82001	307-638-3326	
Web: www.unitedbloodservices.org					
Cheyenne 112 E Eigth Ave	Cheyenne	WY	82001	307-638-3326	
TF: 800-955-7057 ■ *Web:* www.unitedbloodservices.org					

90 BOATS - RECREATIONAL

	City	State	ZIP	Phone	Fax
Action Craft Inc 830 NE 24th Ln	Cape Coral	FL	33909	239-574-7800	574-7805
Web: www.actioncraft.com					
Albemarle Sportfishing Boats Inc					
140 Midway Dr	Edenton	NC	27932	252-482-7600	482-8289
Web: www.albemarleboats.com					
Albin Marine Inc 143 River Rd PO Box 228	Cos Cob	CT	06807	203-661-4341	661-6040
Web: www.albinmarine.com					
Albury Bros Boats 1401 Broadway	Riviera Beach	FL	33404	561-863-7006	863-7746
Web: www.alburybrothers.com					
Alpin Haus Ski Shop 4850 State Hwy 30	Amsterdam	NY	12010	518-843-4400	
Web: www.alpinhaus.com					
Alumacraft Boat Co 315 St Julien St	Saint Peter	MN	56082	507-931-1050	931-9056
Web: www.alumacraft.com					
Alumaweld Boats Inc 1601 Ave F	White City	OR	97503	541-826-7171	830-6907
TF: 800-401-2628 ■ *Web:* www.alumaweldboats.com					
Arima Boats 7510 Bree Dr	Bremerton	WA	98312	360-813-3600	813-3513
Web: www.arimaboats.com					
Avalon Pontoon Boats 903 Michigan Ave	Alma	MI	48801	989-463-2112	
Web: boatersbook.com					
B & B Boats Inc 3568 Old Winter Garden Rd	Orlando	FL	32805	407-299-2190	
Baja Marine Corp 1653 Whichards Beach Rd	Washington	NC	27889	252-975-2000	975-6793
Web: www.bajamarine.com					
Bay Craft Inc 1785 Langley Ave	DeLand	FL	32724	386-943-8877	943-8617
Web: www.baycraftinc.com					
Beneteau America Inc 1313 Hwy 76 W	Marion	SC	29571	843-629-5320	
Web: www.beneteau.com/us					
Bertram Yacht Inc 3663 NW 21st St	Miami	FL	33142	305-633-8011	633-2868
Boston Whaler Inc 100 Whaler Way	Edgewater	FL	32141	877-294-5645	423-8589*
**Fax Area Code:* 386 ■ *TF:* 877-294-5645 ■ *Web:* www.bostonwhaler.com					
Briggs Boat Works Inc 370 Harbor Rd	Wanchese	NC	27981	252-473-2393	473-2392
Web: www.briggsboatworks.com					
Brunswick Boat Group 800 S Gay St 17th Fl	Knoxville	TN	37929	865-582-2200	582-2301
Web: brunswick.com					
Brunswick Corp 1 N Field Ct	Lake Forest	IL	60045	847-735-4700	735-4765
NYSE: BC ■ *Web:* www.brunswick.com					
Brunswick Corp Sea Ray Group					
2600 Sea Ray Blvd	Knoxville	TN	37914	865-522-4181	
Web: global.searay.com					

Company / Address	City	State	ZIP	Phone	Fax
Cape Cod Shipbuilding Co					
7 Narrows Rd PO Box 152	Wareham	MA	02571	508-295-3550	295-3551
Web: www.capecodshipbuilding.com					
Carolina Classic Boats Inc					
109 Anchors Way Dr	Edenton	NC	27932	252-482-3699	
Web: www.carolinaclassicboats.com					
Carolina Skiff Inc 3231 Fulford Rd	Waycross	GA	31503	912-287-0547	287-0533
TF: 800-422-7282 ■ *Web:* www.carolinaskiff.com					
Carver Boat Corp LLC					
790 Markham Dr PO Box 1010	Pulaski	WI	54162	920-822-3214	
Web: www.carveryachts.com					
Catalina Yachts Inc					
21200 Victory Blvd	Woodland Hills	CA	91367	818-884-7700	884-3810
Web: www.catalinayachts.com					
Chaparral Boats Inc					
300 Industrial park Blvd	Nashville	GA	31639	229-686-7481	686-3660
Web: www.chaparralboats.com					
Chris-Craft Boats 8161 15th St E	Sarasota	FL	34243	941-351-4900	358-3717
TF: 800-845-5255 ■ *Web:* chriscraft.com					
Cigarette Racing Team LLC 4355 NW 128th St	Opa Locka	FL	33054	305-931-4564	769-4355
Web: www.cigaretteracing.com					
Cobalt Boats LLC 1715 N Eigth St	Neodesha	KS	66757	620-325-2653	325-2361
TF: 800-468-5764 ■ *Web:* www.cobaltboats.com					
Concept Boats Corp 2410 NW 147th St	Opa Locka	FL	33054	305-635-8712	635-9543
TF: 888-635-8712 ■ *Web:* www.conceptboats.com					
Correct Craft Inc 14700 Aerospace Pkwy	Orlando	FL	32809	407-855-4141	855-4141
TF: 800-346-2092 ■ *Web:* www.nautique.com					
Crestliner Inc 9040 Quaday Ave NE	Ostego	MN	55330	866-301-8544	256-4676*
**Fax Area Code:* 320 ■ *TF:* 866-301-8544 ■ *Web:* www.crestliner.com					
Crownline Boats Inc					
11884 Country Club Rd	West Frankfort	IL	62896	618-937-6426	
Web: www.crownline.com					
Defiant Marine Inc 228 Redbud Ln	Bostic	NC	28018	828-245-2059	245-2079
Web: defiantmarine.net					
Donzi Marine 1653 WhichaRds Beach Rd	Washington	NC	27889	800-624-3304	
TF: 800-624-3304 ■ *Web:* www.donzimarine.com					
Ebbtide Corp 2545 Jones Creek Rd	White Bluff	TN	37187	615-797-3193	797-4889
TF: 866-467-4010 ■ *Web:* www.ebbtideboats.com					
EdgeWater Power Boats 211 Dale St	Edgewater	FL	32132	386-426-5457	427-9783
Web: www.ewboats.com					
Egg Harbor Yachts Inc					
801 Philadelphia Ave PO Box 702	Egg Harbor City	NJ	08215	609-965-2300	965-3517
Web: www.eggharboryachts.com					
Everglades Boats 544 Air Pk Rd	Edgewater	FL	32132	386-409-2202	409-7939
TF: 800-368-5647 ■ *Web:* www.evergladesboats.com					
Fishing Holdings, LLC PO Box 179	Flippin	AR	72634	870-453-2222	
Web: www.rangerboats.com					
Flats Cat Boats 1565 Patton Rd	Rosenberg	TX	77471	281-342-3940	
Web: www.flatscat.com					
Four Winns Inc 925 Frisbie St	Cadillac	MI	49601	231-775-1343	779-2345
Web: www.fourwinns.com					
Garlington Landeweer Marine Inc					
3370 SE Slater St	Stuart	FL	34997	772-283-7124	220-1049
Web: www.garlingtonyachts.com					
Glastron Boats 710 Co Rd 75	St Joseph	MN	56374	320-433-2141	
Web: www.glastron.com					
Grady-White Boats Inc					
5121 Martin Luther King Jr Hwy	Greenville	NC	27834	252-752-2111	752-4217
Web: www.gradywhite.com					
Grand Banks Yachts Ltd					
2288 W Commodore Way Ste 200	Seattle	WA	98199	206-352-0116	352-1711
Web: www.grandbanks.com					
Hatteras Yachts Inc 110 N Glenburnie Rd	New Bern	NC	28560	252-633-3101	634-4813
Web: www.hatterasyachts.com					
Hinckley Co, The 1 Little Harbor Landing	Portsmouth	RI	02871	401-683-7005	
TF: 866-446-2553 ■ *Web:* www.hinckleyyachts.com					
Hobie Cat Co 4925 Oceanside Blvd	Oceanside	CA	92056	760-758-9100	758-1841
TF: 800-462-4349 ■ *Web:* www.hobiecat.com					
Intrepid Powerboats 11700 S Belcher Rd	Largo	FL	33773	727-548-1260	544-1796
Web: www.intrepidboats.com					
Jersey Cape Yachts Inc 2143 River Rd	Lower Bank	NJ	08215	609-965-8650	965-7480
Web: www.jerseycapeyachts.com					
Johnson Outdoors Inc 555 Main St	Racine	WI	53403	262-631-6600	631-6601
NASDAQ: JOUT ■ *TF:* 800-468-9716 ■ *Web:* www.johnsonoutdoors.com					
KenCraft Manufacturing Inc 4155 Dixie Inn Rd	Wilson	NC	27893	252-291-0271	
Web: www.kencraftboats.com					
Key West Boats Inc					
593 Ridgeville Rd PO Box 399	Ridgeville	SC	29472	843-873-0112	821-6334
Web: www.keywestboatsinc.com					
Klamath Boat Co 5199 Fulton Dr Ste I	Fairfield	CA	94534	707-643-0447	643-0483
Web: www.klamathboats.com					
Knight & Carver Yachtcenter Inc					
1313 Bay Marina Dr	National City	CA	91950	619-336-4141	336-4050
KYS 700 E Market St	Jeffersonville	IN	47130	812-282-2660	
Web: www.kys-marlago.com					
L & H Boats Inc 3350 SE Slater St	Stuart	FL	34997	772-288-2291	
Web: www.lhboats.com					
Larson Boats					
700 Paul Larson Memorial Dr	Little Falls	MN	56345	320-632-5481	
Web: www.larsonboats.com					
Lowe Boats 2900 Industrial Dr	Lebanon	MO	65536	417-532-9101	532-8991
TF: 800-641-4372 ■ *Web:* www.loweboats.com					
Mainship Corp 255 Diesel Rd	St Augustine	FL	32084	904-827-2007	
TF: 800-771-5556 ■ *Web:* www.mainship.com					
Marine Safety Corp PO Box 465	Farmingdale	NJ	07727	732-938-5668	938-4839
Web: marinesafetycorporation.com					
MasterCraft Boat Co 100 Cherokee Cove Dr	Vonore	TN	37885	423-884-2221	884-2295
TF: 800-443-8774 ■ *Web:* mastercraft.com					
Maverick Boat Company Inc					
3207 Industrial 29th St	Fort Pierce	FL	34946	772-465-0631	489-2168
Web: www.maverickboats.com					
Melges Boatworks Inc PO Box 1	Zenda	WI	53195	262-275-1110	275-8012
Web: www.melges.com					
Merritt's Boat & Engine Works Inc					
2931 NE 16th St	Pompano Beach	FL	33062	954-943-6250	
Web: www.merrittboat.com					
Monterey Boats 1579 SW 18th St	Williston	FL	32696	352-528-2628	529-2628
Web: www.montereyboats.com					
Pacific Seacraft PO Box 189	Washington	NC	27889	252-948-1421	948-1422
Web: www.pacificseacraft.com					
Parker Boats 2570 N Carolina 101	Beaufort	NC	28516	252-728-5621	728-2770
Web: www.parkerboats.net					
Port Harbor Marine Inc 1 Spring Pt Dr	South Portland	ME	04106	207-767-3254	767-5940
Web: www.portharbormarine.com					
Porta-Bote International					
1074 Independence Ave	Mountain View	CA	94043	650-961-5334	961-3800
TF: 800-227-8882 ■ *Web:* www.porta-bote.com					
Porter Inc 2200 W Monroe St	Decatur	IN	46733	260-724-9111	
TF: 800-736-7685 ■ *Web:* www.formulaboats.com					
Pursuit Boats 3901 St Lucie Blvd	Fort Pierce	FL	34946	772-465-6006	465-6177
TF: 800-947-8778 ■ *Web:* www.pursuitboats.com					
Regal Marine Industries Inc 2300 Jetport Dr	Orlando	FL	32809	407-851-4360	857-1256*
**Fax:* Sales ■ *TF:* 800-877-3425 ■ *Web:* www.regalboats.com					
Riverside Marine Inc 600 Riverside Dr	Essex	MD	21221	410-335-1500	
TF: 800-448-6872 ■ *Web:* www.riversideboats.com					
Rybovich Spencer Group					
4200 N Flagler Dr	West Palm Beach	FL	33407	561-844-1800	
Web: www.rybovich.com					
Sabre Corp PO Box 134	South Casco	ME	04077	207-655-3831	655-5050
Web: www.sabreyachts.com					
Scout Boats Inc 2531 US 78	Summerville	SC	29483	843-821-0068	821-4786
Web: www.scoutboats.com					
Sea Cat Boats Inc 1005 Marina Rd	Titusville	FL	32796	321-268-2628	269-8483
Web: www.seacatboats.com					
Sea Fox Boat Company Inc 2550 Hwy 52	Moncks Corner	SC	29461	843-761-6090	761-6139
Web: www.seafoxboats.com					
Seminole Marine 2501 Milestone Industrial Pk	Cairo	GA	39828	229-377-2125	377-1855
Web: www.sailfishboats.com					
Silverton Marine Corp 301 Riverside Dr	Millville	NJ	08332	609-965-2300	825-2064*
**Fax Area Code:* 856 ■ **Fax:* Mktg ■ *Web:* www.eggharborgroup.com					
Skeeter Products Inc 1 Skeeter Rd	Kilgore	TX	75662	903-984-0541	
Web: www.skeeterboats.com					
Skier's Choice Inc 1717 Henry G Ln St	Maryville	TN	37801	865-856-3035	
TF: 800-970-3744 ■ *Web:* www.supraboats.com					
Smoker Craft PO Box 65	New Paris	IN	46553	866-719-7873	
TF: 866-719-7873 ■ *Web:* www.smokercraft.com					
Sonic power boats 309 Angle Rd	Fort Pierce	FL	34947	772-429-8888	
Web: www.sonicboats.net					
Stamas Yacht Inc 300 Pampas Ave	Tarpon Springs	FL	34689	727-937-4118	
Web: www.stamas.com					
Starcraft Marine LLC					
68143 Clunette St PO Box 65	New Paris	IN	46553	574-831-2103	
TF: 888-327-4236 ■ *Web:* www.starcraftmarine.com					
Stevens Marine Inc 9180 SW Burnham St	Tigard	OR	97223	503-620-7023	
TF: 800-225-7023 ■ *Web:* www.stevensmarine.com					
Stoltzfus RV's & Marine					
1335 Wilmington Pike	West Chester	PA	19382	866-755-8858	
TF: 866-755-8858 ■ *Web:* stoltzfus-rec.com					
Sundance Boats Inc 6131 Sundance Rd	Blackshear	GA	31516	912-449-0033	
Web: www.sundanceboats.com					
Tartan Yachts					
1920 Fairport Nursery Rd	Fairport Harbor	OH	44077	440-332-0578	
Web: www.tartanyachts.com					
Tiara Yachts Inc 725 E 40th St	Holland	MI	49423	616-392-7163	394-7466
Web: www.tiarayachts.com					
Tracker Marine Group LLC					
2500 E Kearney St	Springfield	MO	65803	417-873-5900	873-5068*
**Fax:* Mktg ■ *Web:* www.trackermarine.com					
Valiant Yachts Inc 500 Harbour View Rd	Gordonville	TX	76245	903-523-4899	523-4077
Web: www.valiantsailboats.com					
Viking Yacht Company Inc PO Box 308	New Gretna	NJ	08224	609-296-6000	296-3956
Web: www.vikingyachts.com					
Willard Marine Inc 1250 N Grove St	Anaheim	CA	92806	714-666-2150	632-8136
Web: www.willardmarine.com					
Wooldridge Boats Inc 1303 S 96th St	Seattle	WA	98108	206-722-8998	
Web: www.wooldridgeboats.com					
World Cat 1090 W St James St	Tarboro	NC	27886	252-641-8000	
TF: 866-485-8899 ■ *Web:* www.worldcat.com					
Xpress Boats 199 Extrusion Pl	Hot Springs	AR	71901	501-262-5300	262-5053
Web: www.xpressboats.com					
Zodiac of North America Inc					
540 Thompson Creek Rd	Stevensville	MD	21666	410-643-8123	643-4491
Web: www.zodiacmilpro.com					

91 BOILER SHOPS

Company / Address	City	State	ZIP	Phone	Fax
A & A Industries Inc 320 Jubilee Dr	Peabody	MA	01960	978-977-9660	
Web: www.aandaindustries.com					
Adamson Global Technology Corp					
13101 N Eron Church Rd	Chester	VA	23836	800-525-7703	796-2037*
**Fax Area Code:* 804 ■ *TF:* 800-525-7703 ■ *Web:* www.adamsontank.com					
Aerofin Corp 4621 Murray Pl PO Box 10819	Lynchburg	VA	24506	434-845-7081	528-6242*
**Fax:* Sales ■ *TF:* 800-237-6346 ■ *Web:* www.aerofin.com					
Aesys Technologies LLC 693 N Hills Rd	York	PA	17402	717-755-1081	755-0020
Web: www.aesystech.com					
AlfaLaval Inc 5400 International Trade Dr	Richmond	VA	23231	804-222-5300	236-3276
Web: www.alfalaval.com					
American Welding & Tank Co					
4718 Old Gettysburg Rd Ste 300	Mechanicsburg	PA	17055	717-763-5080	763-5081
TF: 800-345-2495 ■ *Web:* www.propanetank.com					
Amtrol Inc 1400 Div Rd	West Warwick	RI	02893	401-884-6300	885-2567
Web: www.amtrol.com					
API Heat Transfer Inc 2777 Walden Ave	Buffalo	NY	14225	716-684-6700	684-2129
TF: 877-274-4328 ■ *Web:* www.apiheattransfer.com					

Company	City	State	ZIP	Phone	Fax
Armstrong Engineering Assoc Inc PO Box 566 *Web:* www.rmarmstrong.com	West Chester	PA	19381	610-436-6080	436-0374
Arrow Tank & Engineering Co 650 N Emerson St *TF:* 888-892-7769 ■ *Web:* www.arrowtank.com	Cambridge	MN	55008	763-689-3360	689-1263
AustinMohawk & Company Inc 2175 Beechgrove Pl *TF:* 800-765-3110 ■ *Web:* www.austinmohawk.com	Utica	NY	13501	315-793-3000	793-9370
Babcock & Wilcox Co 20 S Van Buren Ave *TF:* 800-222-2625 ■ *Web:* www.babcock.com	Barberton	OH	44203	330-753-4511	860-1886
Babcock Power Inc 6 Kimball Ln Ste 210 *TF:* 800-523-0480 ■ *Web:* www.babcockpower.com	Lynnfield	MA	01940	978-646-3300	646-3301
Benicia Fabrication & Machine Inc 101 E Ch Rd *Web:* www.beniciafab.com	Benicia	CA	94510	707-745-8111	745-8102
Bristol Metals LP 390 Bristol Metals Rd *Web:* www.brismet.com	Bristol	TN	37620	423-989-4700	
Bryan Steam LLC 783 Chili Ave *Web:* www.bryanboilers.com	Peru	IN	46970	765-473-6651	473-3074
C Burgett & Assoc Inc 1462 N FM 2199 Rd	Scottsville	TX	75688	903-938-6638	938-6638
Caldwell Tanks Inc 4000 Tower Rd *Web:* www.caldwelltanks.com	Louisville	KY	40219	502-964-3361	966-8732
Chart Industries Inc 1 Infinity Corporate Centre Dr Ste 300 *Web:* www.chartindustries.com	Garfield Heights	OH	44125	440-753-1490	753-1491
Chicago Boiler Co 1300 NW Ave *TF Cust Svc:* 800-522-7343 ■ *Web:* cbmills.com	Gurnee	IL	60031	847-662-4000	662-4003
Clawson Tank Co 4701 White Lake Rd *TF:* 800-272-1367 ■ *Web:* www.clawsontank.com	Clarkston	MI	48346	248-625-8700	625-3066
Cleaver Brooks 11950 W Lk Pk Dr *Web:* cleaver-brooks.com	Milwaukee	WI	53224	414-359-0600	
Cleaver Brooks Thomasville 221 Law St *TF:* 800-250-5883 ■ *Web:* www.cleaver-brooks.com	Thomasville	GA	31792	229-226-3024	226-3027
Coen Co Inc 11920 East Apache St *Web:* www.coen.com	Tulsa	CA	74116	918-234-1800	
Columbia Boiler Co 390 Old Reading Pk PO Box 1070 *Web:* www.columbiaboiler.com	Pottstown	PA	19464	610-323-2700	323-7292
Columbian Tectank 2101 S 21st St *Web:* www.cstindustries.com	Parsons	KS	67357	620-421-0200	421-9122
Connell LP 1 International Pl 31st Fl *Web:* www.connell-lp.com	Boston	MA	02110	617-391-5577	737-1617
CP Industries Inc (CPI) 2214 Walnut St **Fax:* Sales ■ *Web:* www.cp-industries.com	McKeesport	PA	15132	412-664-6604	664-6653*
CP Industries Inc 12767 Industrial Dr PO Box 690 *Web:* www.cpind.com	Granger	IN	46530	574-273-3000	273-4000
DCI Inc 600 N 54th Ave *Web:* www.dciinc.com	Saint Cloud	MN	56303	320-252-8200	252-0866
Delta Industries 39 Bradley Pk Rd *Web:* mbaerospace.com	East Granby	CT	06026	860-653-5041	653-5792
Dynasteel Corp 4334 Old Millington Rd *Web:* www.dynasteel.net	Memphis	TN	38127	901-358-6231	
Eaton Metal Products Co 4803 York St *TF:* 800-208-2657 ■ *Web:* www.eatonsalesservice.com	Denver	CO	80216	303-296-4800	296-4800
Ecodyne MRM 8203 Market St *Web:* www.ecodynehx.com	Houston	TX	77029	713-675-3511	675-7922
Enerfab Inc 4955 Spring Grove Ave *TF:* 800-772-5066 ■ *Web:* www.enerfab.com	Cincinnati	OH	45232	513-641-0500	242-6833
Energy Exchanger Co 1844 N Garnett Rd *Web:* www.energyexchanger.com	Tulsa	OK	74116	918-437-3000	437-7144
Engineered Storage Products Co 345 Harvestore Dr *TF:* 800-880-3663 ■ *Web:* www.cstindustries.com	DeKalb	IL	60115	815-756-1551	756-7821
Essick Air Products Inc 5800 Murray St *TF:* 800-643-8341 ■ *Web:* www.essickair.com	Little Rock	AR	72209	501-562-1094	562-9485
Exothermics Inc 5040 Enterprise Blvd *Web:* www.eclipsenet.com	Toledo	OH	43612	419-729-9726	729-9705
Fafco Inc 435 Otterson Dr *TF:* 800-994-7652 ■ *Web:* www.fafco.com	Chico	CA	95928	530-332-2100	332-2109
Fisher Tank Co 3131 W Fourth St *Web:* www.fishertank.com	Chester	PA	19013	610-494-7200	485-0157
Geiger & Peters Inc 761 S Sherman Dr PO Box 33807 *Web:* www.gpsteel.com	Indianapolis	IN	46203	317-359-9521	359-9525
General Welding Works Inc 2060 N Loop W Ste 200 PO Box 925749 *Web:* www.generalwelding.com	Houston	TX	77018	713-869-6401	869-5405
Goodhart Sons Inc 2515 Horseshoe Rd *Web:* www.goodhartsons.com	Lancaster	PA	17605	717-656-2404	656-3301
Hammersmith Mfg & Sales Inc 401 Central Ave *TF:* 800-375-8245 ■ *Web:* www.vailproducts.com	Horton	KS	66439	785-486-2121	486-2454
Harsco Industrial Air-X-Changers 5215 Arkansas Rd *TF:* 800-404-3904 ■ *Web:* www.harscoaxc.com	Catoosa	OK	74015	918-619-8000	384-5000
HB Smith Company Inc 47 Westfield Industrial Pk Rd *Web:* hbsmith.com	Westfield	MA	01085	413-568-3148	
Highland Tank & Manufacturing Co 1 Highland Rd *Web:* www.highlandtank.com	Stoystown	PA	15563	814-893-5701	893-6126
Hughes-Anderson Heat Exchangers Inc 1001 N Fulton Ave *Web:* www.hughesanderson.com	Tulsa	OK	74115	918-836-1681	836-5967
Hurst Boiler & Welding Company Inc 100 Boilermaker Ln *TF:* 877-994-8778 ■ *Web:* www.hurstboiler.com	Coolidge	GA	31738	229-346-3545	346-3874
Indeck Energy Services Inc 600 N Buffalo Grove Rd Ste 300 *Web:* indeckenergy.com	Buffalo Grove	IL	60089	847-520-3212	520-9883
ITT Standard 175 Standard Pkwy **Fax Area Code:* 716 ■ *TF:* 800-447-7700 ■ *Web:* www.ittstandard.com	Cheektowaga	NY	14227	800-281-4111	897-1777*
Joseph Oat Corp 2500 Broadway *Web:* www.josephoat.com	Camden	NJ	08104	856-541-2900	541-0864
Koch Heat Transfer Company LP 12602 FM 529 *Web:* www.kochheattransfer.com	Houston	TX	77041	713-466-3535	466-3701
Krueger Engineering & Manufacturing Co 12001 Hirsch Rd PO Box 11308 *Web:* www.kemco.net	Houston	TX	77293	281-442-2537	442-6668
Metalforms Manufacturing Inc 7218 Garth St *Web:* www.metalformsltd.com	Beaumont	TX	77705	409-842-1626	842-1503
Mgs Inc 178 Muddy Creek Church Rd *TF:* 800-952-4228 ■ *Web:* www.mgsincorporated.com	Denver	PA	17517	717-336-7528	336-0514
Mississippi Tank & Manufacturing Co 3000 W Seventh St *Web:* www.mstank.com	Hattiesburg	MS	39403	601-264-1800	264-0769
MiTek Industries Inc 14515 N Outer 40 Rd Ste 300 *TF:* 800-325-8075 ■ *Web:* mii.com	Chesterfield	MO	63017	314-434-1200	434-5343
Mitternight Boiler Works Inc 5301 Hwy 43 N PO Box 489 *Web:* www.mitternight.com	Satsuma	AL	36572	251-675-2550	675-2671
Modern Welding Company Inc 2880 New Hartford Rd *TF:* 800-922-1932 ■ *Web:* www.modweldco.com	Owensboro	KY	42303	270-685-4400	684-6972
Ohmstede 895 N Main St *TF:* 800-568-2328 ■ *Web:* www.ohmstede.com	Beaumont	TX	77704	409-833-6375	839-4948
Ottenweller Company Inc 3011 Congressional Pkwy *Web:* www.ottenweller.com	Fort Wayne	IN	46808	260-484-3166	484-9798
Pasadena Tank Corp 15915 Jacintoport Blvd *Web:* www.ptctanks.com	Houston	TX	77015	281-457-3996	
Pentair Residential Filtration LLC 20580 Enterprise Ave *TF:* 888-784-9065 ■ *Web:* waterpurification.pentair.com/en-us	Brookfield	WI	53008	262-784-4490	785-6535
Plant Maintenance Service Corp 3000 Fite Rd *Web:* www.pmscmphs.com	Memphis	TN	38127	901-353-9880	353-0882
Precision Custom Components 500 Lincoln St **Fax:* Mktg ■ *Web:* www.pcc-york.com	York	PA	17401	717-848-1126	843-5733*
PVI Industries LLC 3209 Galvez Ave PO Box 7124 *TF:* 800-784-8326 ■ *Web:* www.pvi.com	Fort Worth	TX	76111	817-335-9531	332-6742
R. W. Fernstrum & Co 1716 11th Ave PO Box 97 *Web:* www.fernstrum.com	Menominee	MI	49858	906-863-5553	863-5634
Reco Constructors Inc 710 Hospital St *Web:* www.recoconstructors.com	Richmond	VA	23219	804-644-2611	643-3561
Redman Equipment & Mfg Co 19800 Normandie Ave *TF:* 888-733-2602 ■ *Web:* www.redmaneq.com	Torrance	CA	90502	310-329-1134	324-5656
Rocky Mountain Fabrication Inc PO Box 16409 *TF:* 888-763-5307 ■ *Web:* www.rmf-slc.com	Salt Lake City	UT	84116	801-596-2400	322-2702
Ross Technology Corp 104 N Maple Ave *TF:* 800-345-8170 ■ *Web:* www.rosstechnology.com	Leola	PA	17540	717-656-2200	656-3281
Roy E Hanson Jr Mfg 1600 E Washington Blvd *TF:* 800-421-9395 ■ *Web:* www.hansontank.com	Los Angeles	CA	90021	213-747-7514	747-7724
Sen-Dure Products Inc 6785 NW 17th Ave *TF:* 800-394-5112 ■ *Web:* www.sen-dure.com	Fort Lauderdale	FL	33309	954-973-1260	968-7213
Sivalls Inc 2200 E Second St *Web:* www.sivalls.com	Odessa	TX	79761	432-337-3571	337-2624
Smithco Engineering Inc 6312 S 39th W Ave *Web:* www.smithco-eng.com	Tulsa	OK	74132	918-446-4406	445-2857
Snap-Tite Autoclave Engineers Div 8325 Hessinger Dr *TF:* 800-458-0409 ■ *Web:* snap-tite.com	Erie	PA	16509	814-838-5700	
SPX Cooling Technologies 7401 W 129th St *TF:* 800-462-7539 ■ *Web:* www.spxcooling.com	Overland Park	KS	66213	913-664-7400	664-7439
Super Steel Products Corp 7900 W Tower Ave *Web:* www.supersteel.com	Milwaukee	WI	53223	414-355-4800	355-0372
Superior Boiler Works Inc 3524 E Fourth St PO Box 1527 *TF:* 800-444-6693 ■ *Web:* www.superiorboiler.com	Hutchinson	KS	67504	620-662-6693	662-7586
Superior Die Set Corp 900 W Drexel Ave **Fax Area Code:* 800 ■ *TF:* 800-558-6040 ■ *Web:* www.supdie.com	Oak Creek	WI	53154	414-764-4900	657-0855*
Sussman Automatic Corp 43-20 34th St *TF:* 800-727-8326 ■ *Web:* www.mrsteam.com	Long Island	NY	11101	718-937-4500	
Tampa Tank Inc 2710 E Fifth Ave *Web:* www.tampatank.com	Tampa	FL	33605	813-623-2675	
Taylor Forge Engineered Systems Inc 208 N Iron St *Web:* www.tfes.com	Paola	KS	66071	913-294-5331	294-5337
Taylor-Wharton 4718 Gettysburg Rd Ste 300 *Web:* www.taylorwharton.com	Mechanicsburg	PA	17055	717-763-5060	731-7988
Thermal Engineering International Inc 10375 Slusher Dr *Web:* www.babcockpower.com	Santa Fe Springs	CA	90670	323-726-0641	726-9592
Thermal Transfer Corp 50 N Linden St *Web:* www.hamonusa.com	Duquesne	PA	15110	412-460-4004	466-2899
ThermaSys Corp 2776 Gunter Pk Dr E Ste RS *Web:* www.thermasys.com	Montgomery	AL	36109	334-244-9240	244-9248
Thermodynetics Inc 651 Day Hill Rd *OTC:* TDYT ■ *TF:* 800-394-1633 ■ *Web:* www.thermodynetics.com	Windsor	CT	06095	860-683-2005	285-0139
Titanium Fabrication Corp 110 Lehigh Dr *Web:* www.tifab.com	Fairfield	NJ	07004	973-227-5300	227-6541
Tranter Inc 1900 Old Burk Hwy *TF:* 800-414-6908 ■ *Web:* www.tranter.com	Wichita Falls	TX	76306	940-723-7125	723-5131
Ultraflote Corp 3640 W 12th St *Web:* www.ultraflote.com	Houston	TX	77008	713-461-2100	461-2213
Weil-McLain Co 500 Blaine St *Web:* www.weil-mclain.com	Michigan City	IN	46360	219-879-6561	879-4025

Phone Fax

Winbco Tank Co 1200 E Main St PO Box 618 .... Ottumwa IA 52501 800-822-1855 683-8265*
Fax Area Code: 641 ■ *TF:* 800-822-1855 ■ *Web:* www.winbco.com

Worthington Industries
200 Old E Wilson Bridge Rd .... Columbus OH 43085 614-438-3013 438-3083
TF: 866-928-2657 ■ *Web:* worthingtonindustries.com/home

Zak Inc 1 Tibbits Ave .... Green Island NY 12183 518-273-3912
Web: www.zakinc.com

92 BOOK BINDING & RELATED WORK

See Also Printing Companies - Book Printers p. 2976

Phone Fax

360 Imaging Inc 120 Fredette St .... Gardner MA 01440 978-632-7100
Web: www.360imaging.com

Area Trade Bindery Co 157 W Providencia Ave .... Burbank CA 91502 818-846-6041

Bindagraphics Inc 2701 Wilmarco Ave .... Baltimore MD 21223 410-362-7200 362-7233
TF: 800-326-0300 ■ *Web:* www.bindagraphics.com

Bindtech Inc 1232 Antioch Pk .... Nashville TN 37211 615-834-0404
Web: www.bindtechinc.com

Bison Bookbinding and Letterpress
1420 N State St .... Bellingham WA 98225 360-734-0481
Web: bisonbookbinding.com

Blooming Color Inc 230 Eisenhower Ln N .... Lombard IL 60148 630-705-9200
Web: www.bloomingcolor.com

Booksource Inc 1230 Macklind Ave .... Saint Louis MO 63110 314-647-0600 647-1923*
Fax Area Code: 800 ■ *TF:* 800-444-0435 ■ *Web:* www.booksource.com

Bound to Stay Bound Books Inc (BTSB)
1880 W Morton Ave .... Jacksonville IL 62650 217-245-5191 747-2872*
Fax Area Code: 800 ■ *TF:* 800-637-6586 ■ *Web:* www.btsb.com

Capital Spectrum Inc 6800 Burleson Rd Ste 180 .... Austin TX 78744 512-443-0088
Web: www.capspec.com

Color Optics Inc 216 Midland Ave .... Saddle Brook NJ 07663 973-772-1007
Web: www.coloroptics.com

Composition Systems Inc
205 W Jefferson St .... Falls Church VA 22046 703-205-0000
Web: csi2.com

Continental Bindery Corp
700 Fargo Ave .... Elk Grove Village IL 60007 847-439-6811 439-6847

Contract Converting LLC PO Box 247 .... Greenville WI 54942 920-757-4000
Web: www.contractconverting.com

David Dobbs Enterprises Inc
4600 US Hwy 1 N .... Saint Augustine FL 32095 904-824-6171
Web: www.menudesigns.com

Dekker Bookbinding 2941 Clydon Ave SW .... Grand Rapids MI 49519 616-538-5160 538-0720
Web: www.dekkerbook.com

Document Centre, The
470 Mission St Unit 5 .... Carol Stream IL 60188 630-588-1900
Web: www.thedocumentcentre.com

Finishing Plus Inc 4546 W 47th St .... Chicago IL 60632 773-523-5510
Web: finishingplus.com

Form House, The 4640 S Kolmar .... Chicago IL 60632 773-577-8500 523-9155
Web: theformhouse.com

HF Group, The 8844 Mayfield Rd .... Chesterland OH 44026 440-729-2445
Web: hfgroup.com/index.php

John C Otto Company Inc, The
341 Shaker Rd .... East Longmeadow MA 01028 413-525-4131
Web: www.jco.com

Kater-Crafts Bookbinders Inc
4860 Gregg Rd .... Pico Rivera CA 90660 562-692-0665 692-7920
Web: www.katercrafts.com

Lake Book Manufacturing Inc
2085 N Cornell Ave .... Melrose Park IL 60160 708-345-7000 345-1544
Web: www.lakebook.com

Lazer Inc 1150 University Ave Ste 20 .... Rochester NY 14607 585-247-6600
Web: www.lazerinc.com

Library Binding Service (LBS)
1801 Thompson Ave .... Des Moines IA 50316 515-262-3191 262-4091*
Fax Area Code: 800 ■ *TF:* 800-247-5323 ■ *Web:* www.lbsbind.com

Marshall & Bruce Printing Co
689 Davidson St .... Nashville TN 37213 615-256-3661 256-6803
Web: www.marbruco.com

National Library Bindery Co
100 Hembree Pk Dr .... Roswell GA 30076 770-442-5490 442-0183

Parker Powis Inc 775 Heinz Ave .... Berkeley CA 94710 510-848-2463 848-2462
TF: 800-321-2463 ■ *Web:* www.powis.com

Perma-Bound 617 E Vandalia Rd .... Jacksonville IL 62650 217-243-5451 551-1169*
Fax Area Code: 800 ■ *TF:* 800-637-6581 ■ *Web:* www.perma-bound.com

Reindl Bindery Company Inc
W194 N11381 McCormick Dr .... Germantown WI 53022 262-293-1444 293-1445
TF: 800-878-1121 ■ *Web:* www.reindlbindery.com

Rickard Circular Folding Co
325 N Ashland Ave .... Chicago IL 60607 312-243-6300 243-6323
TF: 800-747-1389 ■ *Web:* www.rickardbindery.com

Riverside Group 655 Driving Pk Ave .... Rochester NY 14613 585-458-2090 458-2123
TF: 800-777-2463 ■ *Web:* www.riversidegroup.com

Roswell Bookbinding Co 2614 N 29th Ave .... Phoenix AZ 85009 602-272-9338 272-9786
TF: 888-803-8883 ■ *Web:* www.roswellbookbinding.com

Talas Inc 330 Morgan Ave .... Brooklyn NY 11211 212-219-0770 219-0735
Web: www.talas-nyc.com

United Bindery Service Inc
1845 W Carroll Ave .... Chicago IL 60612 312-243-0240 243-3080

Wert Bookbinding Inc 9975 Allentown Blvd .... Grantville PA 17028 717-469-0629 469-0629
TF Cust Svc: 800-344-9378 ■ *Web:* www.wertbookbinding.com

93 BOOK, MUSIC, VIDEO CLUBS

Phone Fax

Booksfree.com 8453 Tyco Rd # P .... Vienna VA 22182 703-748-2390
Web: www.booksfree.com

Crossings Book Club PO Box 916400 .... Rantoul IL 61866 717-918-2665
Web: www.crossings.com

Phone Fax

Direct Brands Inc 1225 S Market St .... Mechanicsburg PA 17055 717-697-0311

eMusic.com Inc 511 Avenue of the Americas .... New York NY 10011 212-201-9240
Web: www.emusic.com

GameFly Inc 3000 Ocean Pk Blvd .... Santa Monica CA 90405 310-664-6400
Web: www.gamefly.com

NetFlix Inc 100 Winchester Cir .... Los Gatos CA 95032 408-540-3700
NASDAQ: NFLX ■ *TF:* 800-290-8191 ■ *Web:* netflix.com

Science Fiction Book Club PO Box 916400 .... Rantoul IL 61866 717-918-2665
Web: www.sfbc.com

Writer's Digest Book Club
4700 E Galbraith Rd .... Cincinnati OH 45236 513-531-2690 445-4087*
Fax Area Code: 715 ■ *TF Cust Svc:* 800-759-0963 ■ *Web:* www.writersdigestshop.com

94 BOOK PRODUCERS

Book producers, or book packagers, work with authors, editors, printers, publishers, and others to provide all publication services except sales and order fulfillment. These publication services include editing of manuscripts, formatting of computer disks, producing books as a finished product, and helping the book publisher to develop marketing plans. Book producers listed here are members of the American Book Producers Association.

Phone Fax

Agincourt Press 25 Main St .... Chatham NY 12037 518-392-2898

AGS BookWorks PO Box 460313 .... San Francisco CA 94146 415-285-8799
Web: www.agsbookworks.com

Ardent Media Inc 522 E 82nd St .... New York NY 10028 212-861-1501 861-0998

Attic Technologies Inc
1199 Amboy Ave Tano Professional Bldg .... Edison NJ 08837 732-767-0660
Web: www.attictechnologies.com

Becker & Mayer! Ltd 11120 NE 33rd Pl # 101 .... Bellevue WA 98004 425-827-7120 828-9659
Web: www.beckermayer.com

Current Medical Directions Inc 230 Pk Ave S .... New York NY 10003 212-614-6218 598-6909
Web: www.cmdny.com

Emprise Publishing Inc 1104 Murrayhill Rd .... Vestal NY 13850 607-772-0559

Evanston Publishing Inc
4824 Brownsboro Ctr .... Louisville KY 40207 502-899-1919
Web: www.evanstonpublishing.com

Focus Strategic Communications Inc
2474 Waterford St .... Oakville ON L6L5E6 905-825-8757
TF: 866-263-6287 ■ *Web:* www.focussc.com

GGP Publishing Inc 105 Calvert St Ste 201 .... Harrison NY 10528 914-834-8896 834-7566
Web: ggppublishing.com

Gonzalez Defino 7 E 14th St Ste 20s .... New York NY 10003 212-414-1058
Web: www.gonzalezdefino.com

Guru Labs
1148 W Legacy Crossing Blvd Ste 200 .... Centerville UT 84010 801-298-5227
Web: www.gurulabs.com

Innovative USA Inc 50 Washington St .... Norwalk CT 06854 203-838-6400 855-5582
Web: www.innovativekids.com

Learning Source Ltd 644 Tenth St .... Brooklyn NY 11215 718-768-0231 369-3467
Web: www.learningsourceltd.com

MetriTech Inc 4106 Fieldstone Rd .... Champaign IL 61826 217-398-4868
Web: www.metritech.com

Mountain Lion Inc 9 Voorhees Ct .... Hopewell NJ 08525 609-730-1665
Web: www.mtlioninc.com

MTM Publishing Inc 435 W 23rd St Ste 8C .... New York NY 10011 212-242-6930 242-6906
Web: www.mtmpublishing.com

Palace Printing & Design 100 N Maple Ave .... Greensburg PA 15601 415-526-1370
TF: 800-247-0108 ■ *Web:* www.palaceprinter.com

Philip Lief Group Inc (PLG) 130 Wall St .... Princeton NJ 08540 609-430-1000 430-0300
Web: www.philipliefgroup.com

Rosa + Wesley Inc 400 S Knoll St Ste B .... Wheaton IL 60187 630-588-9801 588-9804
Web: www.rosawesley.com

Schlager Group Inc 325 N Saint Paul Ste 3425 .... Dallas TX 75201 888-416-5727 347-9469*
Fax Area Code: 214 ■ *TF:* 888-416-5727 ■ *Web:* www.schlagergroup.com

Shackleton Group Inc 1410 Vance St Ste 205 .... Lakewood CO 80214 303-482-2370
Web: shkgrp.com

Shoreline Publishing Group
125 Santa Rosa Pl .... Santa Barbara CA 93109 805-564-1004 840-6713*
Fax Area Code: 800 ■ *Web:* www.shorelinepublishing.com

Sideshow Media 611 Broadway Ste 734 .... New York NY 10012 212-674-5335
Web: www.sideshowbooks.com

Smallwood & Stewart Inc 5 E 20th St .... New York NY 10003 212-505-3268
Web: www.smallwoodandstewart.com

Stonesong Press LLC 270 W 39th St Ste 201 .... New York NY 10018 212-929-4600
Web: www.stonesong.com

Training to Inc 2200 N Central Ave Ste 400 .... Phoenix AZ 85004 602-266-1500
Web: www.trainingtoyou.com

Victory Productions Inc 55 Linden St .... Worcester MA 01609 508-755-0051
Web: victoryprd.com

Welcome Enterprises Inc 6 W 18th St Ste 4B .... New York NY 10011 212-989-3200 989-3205
Web: www.welcomebooks.com

95 BOOK STORES

Phone Fax

710 Book Store 819 S Illinois Ave .... Carbondale IL 62901 618-549-7304
Web: www.seventen.com

Alibris Inc 1250 45th St Ste 100 .... Emeryville CA 94608 510-594-4500 550-6052
Web: www.alibris.com

Amazon.com Inc 1200 12th Ave S Ste 1200 .... Seattle WA 98144 206-266-1000
NASDAQ: AMZN ■ *TF Cust Svc:* 800-201-7575 ■ *Web:* www.amazon.com

Antigone Books 411 N Fourth Ave .... Tucson AZ 85705 520-792-3715 882-8802
Web: www.antigonebooks.com

Artisan Books & Bindery
509 Pendleton Point Rd .... Islesboro ME 04848 207-734-6852
Web: www.artisanbooksandbindery.com

Associated Students Ucla
308 Westwood Plz .... Los Angeles CA 90095 310-825-7711
Web: www.asucla.ucla.edu

Phone | Fax

Bakersfield Magazine Inc
1601 New Stine Rd Ste 200 ... Bakersfield CA 93309 661-834-4126
Web: www.bakersfieldmagazine.net

Barbour Publishing Inc
1810 Barbour Dr PO Box 719 ... Uhrichsville OH 44683 740-922-6045
Web: www.barbourbooks.com

Barnes & Noble College Bookstores Inc
120 Mtn View Blvd ... Basking Ridge NJ 07920 908-991-2665
Web: www.bncollege.com

Barnes & Noble Inc 122 Fifth Ave ... New York NY 10011 212-633-3300 727-4827*
NYSE: BKS ■ **Fax:* Cust Svc ■ *Web:* www.barnesandnoble.com

barnesandnoble.com Inc 122 Fifth Ave ... New York NY 10011 212-414-6000
TF: 800-843-2665 ■ *Web:* www.barnesandnoble.com

BarristerBooks Inc 615 Florida St ... Lawrence KS 66044 785-856-2772
Web: www.barristerbooks.com

Bauman Rare Books 535 Madison Ave Frnt 1 ... New York NY 10022 212-751-0011
Web: www.baumanrarebooks.com

Bear Pond Books 77 Main St ... Montpelier VT 05602 802-229-0774
Web: www.bearpondbooks.com

Becks Bookstores Inc 4520 N Broadway ... Chicago IL 60640 773-784-7963 784-0066
Web: www.becksbooks.com

Better World Books Inc 55740 Currant Rd ... Mishawaka IN 46545 574-252-5303
Web: www.betterworldbooks.com

Bon Venture Services Inc 34 Ironia Rd ... Flanders NJ 07836 973-584-5699
Web: www.bonventure.net

Book Exchange Inc 152 Willey St ... Morgantown WV 26505 304-292-7354
TF: 800-339-7691 ■ *Web:* www.bookexchangewv.com

Book House Inc, The 208 W Chicago St ... Jonesville MI 49250 800-248-1146
TF: 800-248-1146

Book Loft 631 S Third St ... Columbus OH 43206 614-464-1774
Web: www.bookloft.com

Book Passage 51 Tamal Vista Blvd ... Corte Madera CA 94925 415-927-0960
TF: 800-999-7909 ■ *Web:* www.bookpassage.com

Book Revue 313 New York Ave ... Huntington NY 11743 631-271-1442 271-5890
Web: www.bookrevue.com

Book Soup 8818 Sunset Blvd ... West Hollywood CA 90069 310-659-3110 659-3410
Web: www.booksoup.com

BookBuyers 317 Castro St ... Mountain View CA 94041 650-968-7323
Web: www.bookbuyers.com

Bookmans Entertainment Exchange
8034 N 19th Ave ... Phoenix AZ 85021 602-433-0255
Web: www.bookmans.com

BookPal LLC 18101 Von Karman Ave Ste 1240 ... Irvine CA 92612 866-522-6657
TF: 866-522-6657 ■ *Web:* book-pal.com

BookPeople 603 N Lamar ... Austin TX 78703 512-472-5050 482-8495
TF: 800-853-9757 ■ *Web:* www.bookpeople.com

Books & Books 265 Aragon Ave ... Coral Gables FL 33134 305-442-4408 444-9751
Web: www.booksandbooks.com

Books Inc 2251 Chestnut St ... San Francisco CA 94123 415-931-3633
Web: www.booksinc.net

Books of Discovery 2539 Spruce St ... Boulder CO 80302 303-443-1794
Web: www.booksofdiscovery.com

Books on the Square 471 Angell St ... Providence RI 02906 401-331-9097
TF: 888-669-9660 ■ *Web:* www.booksq.com

Books-A-Million Inc 402 Industrial Ln ... Birmingham AL 35211 205-942-3737
NASDAQ: BAMM ■ *TF:* 800-201-3550 ■ *Web:* www.booksamillion.com

Boston Consumers Checkbook 185 Franklin St ... Boston MA 02110 888-382-1222
TF: 888-382-1222 ■ *Web:* www.checkbook.org

Boulder Book Store 1107 Pearl St ... Boulder CO 80302 303-447-2074 447-3946
TF: 800-244-4651 ■ *Web:* www.boulderbookstore.com

BPDI Corp 1000 S Lynndale Dr Apt O ... Appleton WI 54914 920-830-7897
Web: www.bookworldstores.com

Brazos Bookstore 2421 Bissonnet ... Houston TX 77005 713-523-0701
Web: www.brazosbookstore.com

Brookline Booksmith 279 Harvard St ... Brookline MA 02446 617-566-6660 734-9125
Web: www.brooklinebooksmith.com

Changing Hands Bookstore 6428 S McClintock Dr ... Tempe AZ 85283 480-730-0205 730-1196
Web: www.changinghands.com

Chaucer's Books 3321 State St ... Santa Barbara CA 93105 805-682-6787
Web: www.chaucersbooks.com

Chicago Architecture Foundation
224 S Michigan Ave ... Chicago IL 60604 312-922-3432
Web: www.architecture.org

Childrens Plus Inc 1387 Dutch American Way ... Beecher IL 60401 800-230-1279
TF: 800-230-1279 ■ *Web:* www.childrensplusinc.com

Chinati Foundation PO Box 1135 ... Marfa TX 79843 432-729-4362 729-4597
Web: www.chinati.org

City Lights Booksellers
261 Columbus Ave ... San Francisco CA 94133 415-362-8193 362-4921
Web: www.citylights.com

Collector Books 5801 Kentucky Dam Rd ... Paducah KY 42003 270-898-6211
Web: www.collectorbooks.com

Comic Strip Live 1568 Second Ave Frnt ... New York NY 10028 212-861-9386
Web: www.comicstriplive.com

Curious George Goes to WordsWorth
1 John F Kennedy St ... Cambridge MA 02138 617-547-4500
Web: thecuriousgeorgestore.com

Curtis Circulation Company LLC
730 River Rd ... New Milford NJ 07646 201-634-7400
Web: www.curtiscirc.com

Daedalus Books Inc 9645 Gerwig Ln ... Columbia MD 21046 410-309-2706
TF: 800-395-2665 ■ *Web:* www.daedalusbooks.com

Dallas Bar Association 2101 Ross Ave ... Dallas TX 75201 214-220-7400
Web: www.dallasbar.org

Deseret Book Co 57 W S Temple ... Salt Lake City UT 84111 801-534-1515
TF: 800-453-4532 ■ *Web:* www.deseretbook.com

Dickens Books Ltd 219 N Milwaukee St ... Milwaukee WI 53202 800-236-7323 274-8690*
**Fax Area Code:* 414 ■ *TF:* 800-236-7323 ■ *Web:* 800ceoread.com

Digital Manga Inc 1487 W 178th St Ste 300 ... Gardena CA 90248 310-817-8010
Web: www.digitalmanga.com

Dillard University 2601 Gentilly Blvd ... New Orleans LA 70122 504-283-8822
Web: www.dillard.edu

Doodles Campus Store 935 Main St ... Montevallo AL 35115 205-665-1719
Web: www.doodlesbooks.com

Drama Book Shop Inc 250 E 40th St Frnt 2 ... New York NY 10018 212-944-0595 730-8739
TF: 800-322-0595 ■ *Web:* www.dramabookshop.com

Dunn & Company Inc 75 Green St ... Clinton MA 01510 978-368-8505
Web: booktrauma.com

East West Bookshop of Palo Alto
324 Castro St ... Mountain View CA 94041 650-988-9800
Web: www.eastwest.com

Eastern National
470 Maryland Dr Ste 1 ... Fort Washington PA 19034 215-283-6900
Web: www.easternnational.org

EC Council University Inc
6330 Riverside Plz Ln Nw Ste 210 ... Albuquerque NM 87120 505-341-3228
Web: www.eccouncil.org

Elliott Bay Book Co 101 S Main St ... Seattle WA 98104 206-624-6600 903-1601
TF: 800-962-5311 ■ *Web:* www.elliottbaybook.com

Elmendorf Strategies LLC
900 Seventh St Nw Ste 750 ... Washington DC 20001 202-737-1010
Web: www.elmendorfryan.com

Emmanuel Books 702 Delaware St PO Box 321 ... New Castle DE 19720 302-325-9515
Web: www.emmanuelbooks.com

EOIR Technologies Inc
10300 Spotsylvania Ave Ste 420 ... Fredericksburg VA 22408 540-834-4888
Web: www.eoir.com

Evangel Cathedral 13901 Central Ave ... Upper Marlboro MD 20774 301-249-9400
Web: www.evangelcathedral.net

Family Christian Stores Inc
5300 Patterson Ave ... Grand Rapids MI 49530 616-554-8700 554-8608
Web: www.familychristian.com

Fanfare Sports & Entertainment
4415 S Westnedge Ave ... Kalamazoo MI 49008 269-349-8866
Web: www.fanfare-se.com

FJH Music Company Inc, The
2525 Davie Rd Ste 360 ... Davie FL 33317 954-382-6061
Web: www.fjhmusic.com

Florida Instructional Materials Center
5002 N Lois Ave ... Tampa FL 33614 813-872-5281
Web: www.fimcvi.org

Follett Corp
3 Westbrook Corporate Center Ste 200 ... Westchester IL 60154 708-884-0000
TF: 800-365-5388 ■ *Web:* www.follett.com

Follett Higher Education Group
3 Westbrook Corporate Ctr Ste 200 ... Westchester IL 60154 800-323-4506 279-2569*
**Fax Area Code:* 630 ■ *TF:* 800-323-4506 ■ *Web:* www.follett.com/higher-ed

Full Cir Bookstore 1900 NW Expy ... Oklahoma City OK 73118 405-842-2900 842-2894
Web: www.fullcirclebooks.com

Half Price Books Records & Magazines Inc
5803 E Northwest Hwy ... Dallas TX 75231 214-360-0833 379-8010
Web: www.hpb.com

Harvard Book Store Inc
1256 Massachusetts Ave ... Cambridge MA 02138 617-661-1515
TF: 800-542-7323 ■ *Web:* harvard.com

Harvard Square Co-op Society
1400 Massachusetts Ave ... Cambridge MA 02238 617-499-2000
Web: www.harvardsquare.com

Hastings Entertainment Inc 3601 Plains Blvd ... Amarillo TX 79102 877-427-8464
NASDAQ: HAST ■ *TF Cust Svc:* 877-427-8464 ■ *Web:* www.gohastings.com

Horizon Books 243 E Front St ... Traverse City MI 49684 231-946-7290
TF: 800-587-2147 ■ *Web:* www.horizonbooks.com

Hosanna 2421 Aztec Rd Ne ... Albuquerque NM 87107 505-881-3321
TF: 800-545-6552 ■ *Web:* www.faithcomesbyhearing.com

I See Me! Inc 4305 Chimo E St ... Wayzata MN 55391 952-473-3939
Web: www.myveryownname.com

In The Line of Duty
10727 Indian Head Industrial Blvd ... Saint Louis MO 63132 314-890-8733
Web: www.lineofduty.com

Indigo Books & Music Inc
468 King St W Ste 500 ... Toronto ON M5V1L8 416-364-4499 364-0355
NYSE: IDG ■ *TF Cust Svc:* 800-832-7569 ■ *Web:* www.chapters.indigo.ca

Jessica's Biscuit Mobile Book Fair
82 Needham St ... Newton MA 02461 617-965-0530

Jimmy Bs Audiobooks 324 Ave I ... Redondo Beach CA 90277 310-375-3134
Web: www.audiobooks.com

Kalkomey Enterprises Inc 14086 Proton Rd ... Dallas TX 75244 214-351-0461
Web: www.kalkomey.com

Karrass Seminars
8370 Wilshire Blvd Fl 3 ... Beverly Hills CA 90211 323-951-7500
Web: www.karrass.com

Keyano College 8115 Franklin Ave ... Fort Mcmurray AB T9H2H7 780-791-4800
TF: 800-251-1408 ■ *Web:* www.keyano.ca

Kinetic Books Company Inc
2003 Western Ave Ste 100 ... Seattle WA 98121 206-448-1141
Web: www.kineticbooks.com

Kinokuniya Book Stores of America Company Ltd
1581 Webster St ... San Francisco CA 94115 415-673-7431
Web: www.kinokuniya.com

Kinokuniya Bookstores
1073 Ave of the Americas ... New York NY 10018 212-869-1700 869-1703
Web: www.kinokuniya.co.jp

Lee & Low Books Inc 95 Madison Ave Ste 1205 ... New York NY 10016 212-779-4400
Web: www.leeandlow.com

Left Bank Books 399 N Euclid Ave ... Saint Louis MO 63108 314-367-6731 367-3256
Web: www.left-bank.com

LibertyTree 100 Swan Way ... Oakland CA 94621 510-632-1366 568-6040
TF: 800-927-8733 ■ *Web:* www.independent.org

Mastermind LP 2134 Queen St E ... Toronto ON M4E1E3 416-699-3797
Web: www.mastermindtoys.com

Matthews Book Co
11559 Rock Island Ct ... Maryland Heights MO 63043 314-432-1400 432-7044
TF: 800-633-2665 ■ *Web:* www.matthewsbooks.com

MCE Technologies LLC 30 Hughes Ste 203 ... Irvine CA 92618 949-458-0800
Web: www.mcetech.com

Phone | Fax

McNally Robinson Booksellers Inc
1120 Grant Ave Winnipeg MB R3M2A6 204-475-0483
TF: 800-561-1833 ■ *Web:* www.mcnallyrobinson.com

Merchant One Payment Systems Inc
524 Arthur Godfrey Rd 3rd Fl Miami Beach FL 33140 800-610-4189
TF: 800-610-4189 ■ *Web:* www.merchantone.com

Millman Search Group Inc
11419 Cronridge Dr Ste 17 Owings Mills MD 21117 410-902-6600
Web: www.millmansearch.com

Moe's Books 2476 Telegraph Ave Berkeley CA 94704 510-849-2087 849-9938
Web: www.moesbooks.com

Mountaineers Books
1001 Sw Klickitat Way Ste 201 Seattle WA 98134 206-223-6303
TF: 800-553-4453 ■ *Web:* www.mountaineersbooks.org

Mrs Nelsons Library Service
1650 W Orange Grove Ave Pomona CA 91768 909-397-7820
TF: 800-875-9911 ■ *Web:* www.mrsnelsons.com

National Book Network Inc
4501 Forbes Blvd Ste 200 Lanham MD 20706 301-459-3366
Web: www.nbnbooks.com

Newbury Comics Inc 5 Guest St Brighton MA 02135 617-254-1666 254-1085
Web: www.newbury.com

Newslink Group LLC 6910 NW 12th St Miami FL 33126 305-594-5754
Web: newslinkgroup.net

Northshire Information Inc
4869 Main St Manchester Center VT 05255 802-362-2200 362-1233
TF: 800-437-3700 ■ *Web:* www.northshire.com

On Demand Books 584 Broadway Rm 1100 New York NY 10012 212-966-2222
Web: www.ondemandbooks.com

Page One Bookstore
?5850 Eubank Blvd Ste B-41 Albuquerque NM 87111 505-294-2026 294-5576
Web: www.page1book.com

Parable Christian Stores
3563 Empleo St San Luis Obispo CA 93401 805-248-7395 201-9026
Web: www.parable.com

Paragraph Book Store Inc
2220 McGill College Ave Montreal QC H3A3P9 514-845-5811
Web: www.paragraphbooks.com

Park Place Mobile Homes
731 E Arrow Hwy Ste A Glendora CA 91740 626-914-2992
Web: www.reasons.org

Pentecostals of Alexandria, The
2817 Rapides Ave Alexandria LA 71301 318-487-8976
Web: www.thepentecostals.org

Poetry Pals Inc 295 SW Brushy Mound Rd Burleson TX 76028 817-295-6680
Web: www.poetrypals.com

Poisoned Pen Bookstore
4014 N Goldwater Blvd Scottsdale AZ 85251 480-947-2974 945-1023
TF: 888-560-9919 ■ *Web:* www.poisonedpen.com

Politics & Prose Bookstore
5015 Connecticut Ave NW Washington DC 20008 202-364-1919 966-7532
TF: 800-722-0790 ■ *Web:* www.politics-prose.com

Powell's Books Inc 7 NW Ninth Ave Portland OR 97209 503-228-0540 228-1142
TF: 800-878-7323 ■ *Web:* www.powells.com

Powell's City of Books 1005 W Burnside St Portland OR 97209 503-228-4651
TF: 800-878-7323 ■ *Web:* www.powells.com

Prairie Lights Bookstore 15 S Dubuque St Iowa City IA 52240 319-337-2681
TF: 800-295-2665 ■ *Web:* www.prairielights.com

Printed Matter Inc 231 11th Ave New York NY 10001 212-925-0325
Web: www.printedmatter.org

R J Julia Booksellers LLC 768 Boston Post Rd Madison CT 06443 203-245-3959
Web: booksasgifts.com

Regulator Bookshop 720 Ninth St Durham NC 27705 919-286-2700
Web: regulatorbookshop.com

Remuda Ranch Co 1 E Apache St Wickenburg AZ 85390 928-684-3913
Web: www.remudaranch.com

Safari Books Online LLC
1003 Gravenstein Hwy N Sebastopol CA 95472 707-827-4100
Web: my.safaribooksonline.com

Samuel French Inc 45 W 25th St New York NY 10010 212-206-8990
Web: www.samuelfrench.com

Schuler Books & Music Inc
2660 28th St SE Grand Rapids MI 49512 616-942-2561
Web: www.schulerbooks.com

SciTech Publishing Inc
911 Paverstone Dr Ste B Raleigh NC 27615 919-847-2434
Web: www.theiet.org/resources/books/scitech

Seagull Book & Tape Inc
1720 S Redwood Rd Salt Lake City UT 84104 800-999-6257
TF: 800-999-6257 ■ *Web:* www.seagullbook.com

Seminary Co-op Bookstore
5757 S University Ave Chicago IL 60637 773-752-4381 752-8507
Web: www.semcoop.com

Skylight Books 1818 N Vermont Ave Los Angeles CA 90027 323-660-1175 660-0232
Web: www.skylightbooks.com

Social Studies School Service
10200 Jefferson Blvd PO Box 802 Culver City CA 90232 310-839-2436 944-5432*
**Fax Area Code:* 800 ■ *TF:* 800-421-4246 ■ *Web:* www.socialstudies.com

Square Books 160 Courthouse Sq Oxford MS 38655 662-236-2262
TF: 800-648-4001 ■ *Web:* www.squarebooks.com

Strand Book Store Inc 828 Broadway New York NY 10003 212-473-1452
Web: www.strandbooks.com

Student Book Store
421 E Grand River Ave East Lansing MI 48823 517-351-4210
TF: 800-968-1111 ■ *Web:* www.sbsmsu.com

Sunshine Books Inc 49 River St Ste 3 Waltham MA 02453 781-398-0754
TF: 800-472-5425 ■ *Web:* www.clickertraining.com

Tatnuck Bookseller 18 Lyman St Westborough MA 01581 508-366-4959 366-7929
Web: www.tatnuck.com

Tattered Cover Book Store Inc 1628 16th St Denver CO 80202 303-436-1070 629-1704
TF: 800-833-9327 ■ *Web:* www.tatteredcover.com

Textbook Brokers Inc 911 Rochester Rd Ste Sparta MO 65753 417-485-3440
Web: www.k12textbookbrokers.com

That Bookstore in Blytheville
316 W Main St Blytheville AR 72315 870-763-3333 763-1125
Web: thatbookstoreinblytheville.com

Title Wave Inc 1360 W Northern Lights Blvd Anchorage AK 99503 907-278-9283
Web: www.wavebooks.com

Travis Avenue Baptist Church
800 E Berry St Fort Worth TX 76110 817-924-4266 921-9620
Web: www.travis.org

University Book Store, The 711 State St Madison WI 53703 608-257-3784
Web: www.uwbookstore.com

University of Oregon Bookstore Inc
895 E 13th Ave Eugene OR 97401 541-346-4331
TF: 800-352-1733 ■ *Web:* www.uoduckstore.com

University Press Books (UPB) 2430 Bancroft Way Berkeley CA 94704 510-548-0585 849-9214
TF: 800-676-8722 ■ *Web:* www.universitypressbooks.com

Valley Books PO Box 2127 Amherst MA 01004 413-256-1508
Web: www.valleybooks.com

Viewpoint Books 548 Washington St Columbus IN 47201 812-376-0778
Web: www.viewpointbooks.com

Vroman's Bookstore 695 E Colorado Blvd Pasadena CA 91101 626-449-5320
Web: www.vromansbookstore.com

Western Continental Book Co
6425 Washington St Denver CO 80229 303-289-1761
TF: 800-364-0350 ■ *Web:* www.continentalbook.com

Wild Onion Books 3441 N Ashland Ave Chicago IL 60657 773-281-1818
TF: 800-621-1008 ■ *Web:* www.loyolapress.com

Word Among Us Inc 9639 Doctor Perry Rd Ijamsville MD 21754 301-874-1700
TF: 800-775-9673 ■ *Web:* wau.org

96 BOOKS, PERIODICALS, NEWSPAPERS - WHOL

Phone | Fax

21st Century Christian Inc PO Box 40526 Nashville TN 37204 615-383-3842
TF: 800-251-2477 ■ *Web:* www.21stcc.com

Advantage Mktg Inc 14 W Main St Ashland OH 44805 419-281-4762
TF: 800-670-7479 ■ *Web:* www.advantagemkt.com

Alexander City Outlook
548 Cherokee Rd Alexander City AL 35010 256-234-4281
Web: www.alexcityoutlook.com

Alliance Paper & Food Service Inc
11058 W Addison St Franklin Park IL 60131 847-349-1500
Web: www.allpfs.com

American Book Co
11130 Kingston Pk Ste 1-183 Knoxville TN 37934 865-966-7454 675-0557
Web: www.americanbookco.com

American Overseas Book Company Inc
550 Walnut St Norwood NJ 07648 201-767-7600
Web: www.aobc.com

ATA Retail Services Inc 30773 Wiegman Rd Hayward CA 94544 510-401-5300
Web: www.ataretail.com

Auto Export Shipping Inc
187 Mill Ln Ste 103 Mountainside NJ 07092 908-436-2150
TF: 800-829-4933 ■ *Web:* aesshipping.com

Baker & Taylor Inc 2550 W Tyvola Rd Ste 300 Charlotte NC 28217 800-775-1800 998-3316*
**Fax Area Code:* 704 ■ *TF:* 800-775-1800 ■ *Web:* www.btol.com

BMI Educational Services PO Box 800 Dayton NJ 08810 732-329-6991 986-9393*
**Fax Area Code:* 800 ■ *TF:* 800-222-8100 ■ *Web:* www.bmionline.com

Book Depot Inc 67 Front St N Thorold ON L2V1X3 905-680-7230
TF: 888-402-7323 ■ *Web:* www.bookdepot.com

Bookazine Company Inc 75 Hook Rd Bayonne NJ 07002 201-339-7777 339-7778
TF: 800-221-8112 ■ *Web:* www.bookazine.com

Booksource Inc 1230 Macklind Ave Saint Louis MO 63110 314-647-0600 647-1923*
**Fax Area Code:* 800 ■ *TF:* 800-444-0435 ■ *Web:* www.booksource.com

C2F Inc 6600 SW 111th Ave Beaverton OR 97008 503-643-9050
TF: 800-544-8825 ■ *Web:* www.c2f.com

Campus Text Inc 107 Forrest Ave Narberth PA 19072 610-664-6900
Web: campustext.com

Canadian Industrial Distributors Inc
175 Sun Pac Blvd Brampton ON L6S5Z6 905-595-0411

Capitol Fiber Inc 6610 Electronics Dr Springfield VA 22151 703-658-0200 658-0212
Web: capitolfiber.com

Choice Books LLC 2387 Grace Chapel Rd Harrisonburg VA 22801 540-434-1827 434-9894
TF: 800-224-5006 ■ *Web:* www.choicebooks.org

Comag Marketing Group LLC
155 Village Blvd 3rd Fl Princeton NJ 08540 609-524-1800 524-1629
TF: 866-790-9353 ■ *Web:* www.i-cmg.com

Comint Apparel Group LLC
463 Seventh Ave 11th Fl New York NY 10018 212-947-7474
Web: www.comintapparel.com

Command Spanish Inc PO Box 1091 Petal MS 39465 601-582-8378 582-5177
TF: 800-250-8637 ■ *Web:* www.commandspanish.com

Consortium Book Sales & Distribution Inc
The Keg House 34 Thirteenth Ave NE
Ste 101 Minneapolis MN 55413 612-746-2600
Web: www.cbsd.com

Coppel Corp 503 Scaroni Rd Calexico CA 92231 760-357-3707
Web: www.coppel.com

Cousin Corp of America 12333 Enterprise Blvd Largo FL 33773 727-536-3568
Web: www.cousin.com

Csubs 155 Chestnut Ridge Rd Montvale NJ 07645 201-307-9900
Web: www.csubs.com

Davidson Titles Inc 2345 Dr F E Wright Dr Jackson TN 38305 731-988-5333
Web: www.davidsontitles.com

Direct Holdings Americas Inc
8280 Willow Oaks Corporate Dr Fairfax VA 22031 800-950-7887
TF: 800-950-7887 ■ *Web:* www.timelife.com

Directory Distributing Assoc (DDA)
1602 Pk 370 Ct Hazelwood MO 63042 314-592-8600 592-8790
TF General: 800-325-1964

EBSCO Subscription Services
110 Olmsted St Ste 100 Birmingham AL 35242 205-995-1596 995-1518
TF: 800-653-2726 ■ *Web:* www.ebsco.com/home/about/ess.asp

Phone *Fax*

Educational Development Corp 10302 E 55th Pl Tulsa OK 74146 918-622-4522 665-7919
NASDAQ: EDUC ■ *TF:* 800-475-4522 ■ *Web:* www.edcpub.com

Emery-Pratt Co 1966 W M 21 Owosso MI 48867 989-723-5291
Web: www.emery-pratt.com

ePromos Promotional Products Inc
120 Broadway Ste 1360 New York NY 10271 212-286-8008
TF: 877-377-6667 ■ *Web:* www.epromos.com

Fall River News Co 25 Westwood Ave New London CT 06320 860-442-4394

Flexpak Inc 1894 West 2425 South Woods Cross UT 84087 801-956-0696
Web: www.flexpak.net

Follett Corp
3 Westbrook Corporate Center Ste 200 Westchester IL 60154 708-884-0000
TF: 800-365-5388 ■ *Web:* www.follett.com

Follett Educational Services
1433 International Pkwy Woodridge IL 60517 630-972-5600 638-4424*
**Fax Area Code:* 800 ■ *TF:* 800-621-4272 ■ *Web:* www.fes.follett.com

General Pet Supply Inc 7711 N 81st St Milwaukee WI 53223 414-365-3400
TF: 800-433-9786 ■ *Web:* www.generalpet.com

Independent Publishers Group
814 N Franklin St Chicago IL 60610 312-337-0747 337-5985
TF Orders: 800-888-4741 ■ *Web:* www.ipgbook.com

InfraRed Imaging Systems Inc
22718 Holycross Epps Rd Marysville OH 43040 888-987-5768
TF: 888-987-5768 ■ *Web:* www.irimagesys.com

Ingram Book Group 1 Ingram Blvd La Vergne TN 37086 615-793-5000 213-5710
TF: 800-937-8000 ■ *Web:* www.ingrambookgroup.com

Kable News Company Inc 14 Wall St Ste 4C New York NY 10005 513-671-2800 705-4666*
**Fax Area Code:* 212 ■ *Web:* www.kablefulfillment.com

Kirk Co 201 St Helens Ave Tacoma WA 98402 253-627-2133
Web: www.kirktrees.com

MacKellar Assoc Inc
1729 Northfield Dr Rochester Hills MI 48309 248-335-4440
Web: www.mackellar.com

MBS Textbook Exchange Inc 2711 W Ash St Columbia MO 65203 573-445-2243 446-5254
TF Cust Svc: 800-325-0530 ■ *Web:* www.mbsbooks.com

Midwest Library Service Inc
11443 St Charles Rock Rd Bridgeton MO 63044 314-739-3100 739-1326
TF: 800-325-8833 ■ *Web:* www.midwestls.com

Milligan News Co Inc 150 N Autumn St San Jose CA 95110 408-286-7604
Web: www.milligannews.com

Nebraska Book Co 4700 S 19th St Lincoln NE 68512 402-421-7300 421-0001
TF: 800-869-0366 ■ *Web:* www.nebook.com

Network Paper & Packaging Ltd
1391 Kebet Way Port Coquitlam BC V3C6G1 604-941-2999
Web: www.netpak.net

Neway Packaging Corp
1973 E Via Arado Rancho Dominguez CA 90220 310-898-3400
TF: 800-456-3929 ■ *Web:* www.newaypackaging.com

Newsways Distributors Inc
1324 Cypress Ave Los Angeles CA 90065 323-258-6000 256-9999
Web: www.newsways.com

Packaging Progressions Inc
102 G P Clement Dr Collegeville PA 19426 610-489-8601
Web: www.pacproinc.com

Product Development Corp
20 Ragsdale Dr Ste 100 Monterey CA 93940 831-333-1100 333-0110
TF: 800-819-6910 ■ *Web:* teampdc.com

Publishers Group West (PGW) 1700 Fourth St Berkeley CA 94710 510-809-3700 809-3777
Web: www.pgw.com

Publishers' Warehouse 2700 Crestwood Blvd Irondale AL 35210 205-956-2078
TF: 800-653-2726 ■ *Web:* ebscoind.com

Quality Books Inc 1003 W Pines Rd Oregon IL 61061 815-732-4450 732-4499
TF Cust Svc: 800-323-4241 ■ *Web:* www.quality-books.com

Readerlink Distribution Services LLC
1420 Kensington Rd Ste 300 Oak Brook IL 60523 708-547-4400
TF: 800-549-5389 ■ *Web:* www.levybooks.com

Rittenhouse Book Distributors Inc
511 Feheley Dr King of Prussia PA 19406 800-345-6425 223-7488*
**Fax:* Orders ■ *TF Cust Svc:* 800-345-6425 ■ *Web:* www.rittenhouse.com

Saddleback Educational Publishing Inc
3 Watson Costa Mesa CA 92626 949-860-2500
Web: www.sdlback.com

SCB Distributors 15608 New Century Dr Gardena CA 90248 310-532-9400
TF: 800-729-6423 ■ *Web:* scbdistributors.com

Scholastic Book Fairs Inc
1080 Greenwood Blvd Lake Mary FL 32746 573-632-1687
TF: 800-874-4809 ■ *Web:* www.scholastic.com/bookfairs

Seda France Inc 8301 Springdale Rd Ste 800 Austin TX 78724 512-206-0105
TF: 800-474-0854 ■ *Web:* www.sedafrance.com

Selamat Designs 231 S Maple Ave South San Francisco CA 94080 650-243-4840
Web: www.selamatdesigns.com

Send The Light Distribution LLC
100 Biblica Way Elizabethton TN 37643 423-547-5100

Service Paper Co 4501 W Vly Hwy E Ste A Sumner WA 98390 253-321-3300
Web: bunzldistribution.com

Smith Mountain Industries Inc 1000 Dillard Dr Forest VA 24551 434-385-1305

Snack Factory LLC 11 Tamarack Cir Skillman NJ 08558 609-683-5400
Web: www.snackfactory.com

Source Interlink Cos Inc
27500 Riverview Ctr Blvd Bonita Springs FL 34134 239-949-4450 949-7623

Southwestern/Great American
2451 Atrium Way Nashville TN 37214 888-602-7867
TF Cust Svc: 888-602-7867 ■ *Web:* www.southwestern.com

Spring Arbor Distributors 1 Ingram Blvd La Vergne TN 37086 615-793-5000
TF: 800-395-4340 ■ *Web:* www.ingramcontent.com

Tarps & Tie-Downs Inc 24967 Huntwood Ave Hayward CA 94544 510-782-8772
Web: tarpstiedowns.com

Texas Book Co 8501 Technology Cir Greenville TX 75402 903-455-6937 454-2442
Web: www.texasbook.com

Vulcan Service 5724 Hwy 280 E Birmingham AL 35242 800-841-9600 980-3891*
**Fax Area Code:* 205 ■ *TF:* 800-841-9600 ■ *Web:* www.vulcanservice.com

YBP Library Services 999 Maple St Contoocook NH 03229 603-746-3102 746-5628
TF: 800-258-3774 ■ *Web:* www.ybp.com

97 BOTANICAL GARDENS & ARBORETA

See Also Zoos & Wildlife Parks *p. 3316*

Phone *Fax*

Adkins Arboretum 12610 Eveland Rd PO Box 100 Ridgely MD 21660 410-634-2847 634-2878
Web: www.adkinsarboretum.org

Airlie Gardens 300 Airlie Rd Wilmington NC 28403 910-798-7700 256-5083
Web: airliegardens.org

Alaska Botanical Garden
4601 Campbell Airstrip Rd Anchorage AK 99507 907-770-3692 770-0555
Web: www.alaskabg.org

Aldridge Botanical Gardens 3530 Lorna Rd Hoover AL 35216 205-682-8019
Web: www.aldridgegardens.com

Alexandra Botanic Gardens
Wellesley College 106 Central St Wellesley MA 02481 781-283-1000
Web: www.wellesley.edu

Alfred B Maclay State Gardens
3540 Thomasville Rd Tallahassee FL 32309 850-487-4556 487-8808
Web: www.floridastateparks.org/maclaygardens

Alta Vista Gardens 1270 Vale Ter Dr Vista CA 92084 760-945-3954
Web: www.altavistagardens.org

Amarillo Botanical Gardens 1400 Streit Dr Amarillo TX 79106 806-352-6513 352-6227
Web: www.amarillobotanicalgardens.org

Anderson Japanese Gardens
318 Spring Creek Rd Rockford IL 61107 815-229-9390
Web: andersongardens.org

Annmarie Garden 13480 Dowell Rd PO Box 99 Dowell MD 20629 410-326-4640 326-4887
Web: www.annmariegarden.org

Applewood the CS Mott Estate
1400 E Kearsley St Flint MI 48503 810-233-0170 233-7022
Web: www.ruthmottfoundation.org

Arboretum at California State University Fresno
2351 E Barstow Ave Fresno CA 93740 559-278-7422 278-7698
Web: www.fresnostate.edu

Arboretum at Flagstaff 4001 S Woody Mtn Rd Flagstaff AZ 86001 928-774-1442 774-1441
Web: www.thearb.org

Arboretum at Penn State
336 Forest Resources Bldg University Park PA 16802 814-865-9118 865-3725
Web: www.arboretum.psu.edu

Arboretum at Penn State Behrend
4701 College Dr Glenhill Farmhouse Erie PA 16563 814-898-6160 898-6461
Web: www.psbehrend.psu.edu

Arboretum at the University of California Santa Cruz
1156 High St Santa Cruz CA 95064 831-427-2998 427-1524
Web: arboretum.ucsc.edu

Arboretum of the Barnes Foundation
300 N Latch's Ln Merion PA 19066 610-667-0290 664-4026
Web: www.barnesfoundation.org

Arboretum, The
Arboretum Rd University of Guelph Guelph ON N1G2W1 519-824-4120 763-9598
TF: 877-674-1610 ■ *Web:* www.uoguelph.ca/arboretum

Arnold Arboretum of Harvard University
125 Arborway Jamaica Plain MA 02130 617-524-1718 524-1418
Web: arboretum.harvard.edu

Atlanta Botanical Garden
1345 Piedmont Ave NE Atlanta GA 30309 404-876-5859 876-7472
Web: atlantabg.org

Awbury Arboretum & Historic Estate
1 Awbury Rd Francis Cope House Philadelphia PA 19138 215-849-2855 849-0213
Web: www.awbury.org

Bartlett Arboretum & Gardens
151 Brookdale Rd Stamford CT 06903 203-322-6971 595-9168
Web: www.bartlettarboretum.org

Bartram's Garden
54th St & Lindbergh Blvd Philadelphia PA 19143 215-729-5281 729-1047
Web: www.bartramsgarden.org

Beardsley Zoo 1875 Noble Ave Bridgeport CT 06610 203-394-6565
Web: www.beardsleyzoo.org

Bellevue Botanical Garden 12001 Main St Bellevue WA 98005 425-452-2750 452-2748
Web: www.bellevuebotanical.org

Bellingrath Gardens & Home
12401 Bellingrath Garden Rd Theodore AL 36582 251-973-2217 973-0540
TF: 800-247-8420 ■ *Web:* bellingrath.org

Berkshire Botanical Garden
5 W Stockbridge Rd PO Box 826 Stockbridge MA 01262 413-298-3926 298-4897
Web: www.berkshirebotanical.org

Bernheim Arboretum & Research Forest
2499 Clermont Rd PO Box 130 Clermont KY 40110 502-955-8512 955-4039
Web: bernheim.org

Betty Ford Alpine Gardens 183 Gore Creek Dr Vail CO 81657 970-476-0103 476-1685
Web: bettyfordalpinegardens.org

Bicentennial Gardens 1105 Hobbs Rd Greensboro NC 27410 336-297-4162
Web: greensborobeautiful.org

Bickelhaupt Arboretum 340 S 14th St Clinton IA 52732 563-242-4771
Web: bick-arb.org

Birmingham Botanical Gardens
2612 Ln Pk Rd Birmingham AL 35223 205-414-3900
Web: www.bbgardens.org

Blithewold Mansion Gardens & Arboretum
101 Ferry Rd Rt 114 Bristol RI 02809 401-253-2707 253-0412
Web: www.blithewold.org

Bloedel Reserve, The
7571 NE Dolphin Dr Bainbridge Island WA 98110 206-842-7631 842-3295
Web: bloedelreserve.org

Boerner Botanical Gardens
9400 Boerner Dr Hales Corners WI 53130 414-525-5601
Web: www.boernerbotanicalgardens.org

Botanic Garden of Smith College
Smith College NorthHampton MA 01063 413-585-2740 585-2744
Web: www.smith.edu/garden

	City	State	ZIP	Phone	Fax
Botanica the Wichita Gardens 701 N Amidon Ave *Web:* www.botanica.org	Wichita	KS	67203	316-264-0448	264-0587
Botanical Garden of the Ozarks 4703 N Crossover Rd PO Box 10407 *Web:* www.bgozarks.org	Fayetteville	AR	72764	479-750-2620	756-1920
Botanical Gardens at Asheville 151 WT Weaver Blvd *TF:* 888-823-4622 ■ *Web:* www.ashevillebotanicalgardens.org	Asheville	NC	28804	828-252-5190	252-1211
Botanical Research Institute of Texas 1700 University Dr *Web:* www.brit.org	Fort Worth	TX	76102	817-332-4441	332-4112
Bowman's Hill Wildflower Preserve 1635 River Rd PO Box 685 *Web:* www.bhwp.org	New Hope	PA	18938	215-862-2924	862-1846
Boxerwood Nature Ctr & Woodland Garden 963 Ross Rd *Web:* www.boxerwood.org	Lexington	VA	24450	540-463-2697	
Boyce Thompson Arboretum 37615 US Hwy 60 *TF:* 877-763-5315 ■ *Web:* cals.arizona.edu	Superior	AZ	85273	520-689-2723	689-5858
Brenton Arboretum 25141 260th St *Web:* www.thebrentonarboretum.org	Dallas Center	IA	50063	515-992-4211	992-3303
Brookgreen Gardens 1931 Brookgreen Dr *TF:* 800-849-1931 ■ *Web:* www.brookgreen.org	Murrells Inlet	SC	29576	843-235-6000	235-6039
Brooklyn Botanic Garden 1000 Washington Ave *Web:* www.bbg.org	Brooklyn	NY	11225	718-623-7200	
Brookside Gardens 1800 Glenallan Ave *TF:* 800-366-2012 ■ *Web:* www.montgomeryparks.org	Wheaton	MD	20902	301-962-1400	962-7878
Buffalo & Erie County Botanical Gardens 2655 S Pk Ave *Web:* www.buffalogardens.com	Buffalo	NY	14218	716-827-1584	
Butchart Gardens, The 800 Benvenuto Ave *TF:* 866-652-4422 ■ *Web:* www.butchartgardens.com	Brentwood Bay	BC	V8M1J8	250-652-4422	652-7751
Calgary Zoo Botanical Garden & Prehistoric Park 1300 Zoo Rd NE *TF:* 800-588-9993 ■ *Web:* www.calgaryzoo.com	Calgary	AB	T2E7V6	403-232-9300	237-7582
Callaway Gardens 17800 Hwy 27 *TF:* 800-225-5292 ■ *Web:* www.callawaygardens.com	Pine Mountain	GA	31822	706-663-2281	663-5122
Camden Children's Garden 3 Riverside Dr *Web:* www.camdenchildrensgarden.org	Camden	NJ	08103	856-365-8733	365-8733
Cape Fear Botanical Garden 536 N Eastern Blvd PO Box 53485 *Web:* capefearbg.org	Fayetteville	NC	28301	910-486-0221	486-4209
Carleen Bright Arboretum 9001 Bosque Blvd *Web:* www.woodway-texas.com	Woodway	TX	76712	254-399-9204	
Casa del Herrero 1387 E Valley Rd *Web:* www.casadelherrero.com	Santa Barbara	CA	93108	805-565-5653	969-2371
Cave Hill Cemetery & Arboretum 701 Baxter Ave *Web:* www.cavehillcemetery.com	Louisville	KY	40204	502-451-5630	451-5655
Cedar Crest College 100 College Dr *Fax: Admissions ■ *TF Admissions:* 800-360-1222 ■ *Web:* www.cedarcrest.edu	Allentown	PA	18104	610-437-4471	606-4647*
Cedar Valley Arboretum & Botanic Gardens 1927 E Orange Rd *Web:* www.cedarvalleyarboretum.org	Waterloo	IA	50701	319-226-4966	226-4966
Chanticleer Garden 786 Church Rd *Web:* www.chanticleergarden.org	Wayne	PA	19087	610-687-4163	293-0149
Cheekwood Museum of Art & Botanical Garden 1200 Forrest Pk Dr *TF:* 877-356-8150 ■ *Web:* www.cheekwood.org	Nashville	TN	37205	615-356-8000	353-0919
Chesapeake Arboretum 624 Oak Grove Rd *Web:* chesarbor.org	Chesapeake	VA	23328	757-382-7060	
Cheyenne Botanic Gardens 710 S Lions Pk Dr *Web:* www.botanic.org	Cheyenne	WY	82001	307-637-6458	
Chicago Botanic Garden 1000 Lake Cook Rd *TF:* 877-829-5500 ■ *Web:* www.chicagobotanic.org	Glencoe	IL	60022	847-835-5440	835-4484
Chihuahuan Desert Research Institute (CDRI) 43869 State Hwy 118 PO Box 905 *Web:* cdri.org	Fort Davis	TX	79734	432-364-2499	364-2686
Chimney Rock Park 431 Main St *TF:* 800-277-9611 ■ *Web:* www.chimneyrockpark.com	Chimney Rock	NC	28720	828-625-9611	625-9610
Cincinnati Zoo & Botanical Garden 3400 Vine St *TF:* 800-944-4776 ■ *Web:* www.cincinnatizoo.org	Cincinnati	OH	45220	513-281-4700	559-7790
Clark County Museum 1830 S Boulder Hwy *Web:* clarkcountynv.gov	Henderson	NV	89002	702-455-7955	455-7948
Cleveland Botanical Garden 11030 E Blvd *Web:* www.cbgarden.org	Cleveland	OH	44106	216-721-1600	721-2056
Cleveland Metroparks Zoo 3900 Wildlife Way *Web:* clevelandmetroparks.com/zoo/zoo.aspx	Cleveland	OH	44109	216-661-6500	
Clovis Botanical Garden 945 N Clovis Ave *Web:* clovisbotanicalgarden.org	Clovis	CA	93611	559-298-3091	
Coastal Maine Botanical Gardens PO Box 234 *Web:* www.mainegardens.org	Boothbay	ME	04537	207-633-4333	633-2366
Como Zoo & Conservatory 1225 Estabrook Dr *Web:* comozooconservatory.org	Saint Paul	MN	55103	651-487-8200	
Connecticut College Arboretum 270 Mohegan Ave PO Box 5201 *Web:* www.conncoll.edu	New London	CT	06320	860-439-5020	439-5482
Conservatory Garden 14 E 60th St Central Pk *Web:* www.centralparknyc.org	New York	NY	10022	212-310-6600	
Conservatory of Flowers San Francisco Recreation & Pk Dept 100 John F Kennedy Dr *Web:* www.conservatoryofflowers.org	San Francisco	CA	94118	415-846-0538	
Cornell Plantations 1 Plantations Rd *TF:* 800-269-8368 ■ *Web:* www.cornellplantations.org	Ithaca	NY	14850	607-255-2400	255-2404
Cox Arboretum MetroPark 6733 Springboro Pike *TF:* 800-865-6543 ■ *Web:* www.metroparks.org/Parks/CoxArboretum	Dayton	OH	45449	937-434-9005	
Crosby Arboretum 370 Ridge Rd *Web:* www.msstate.edu	Picayune	MS	39466	601-799-2311	799-2372
CW Post Community Arboretum *Long Island University* 720 Northern Blvd *Web:* www.liu.edu	Brookville	NY	11548	516-299-2000	299-3223
Dallas Arboretum & Botanical Garden 8525 Garland Rd *Web:* www.dallasarboretum.org	Dallas	TX	75218	214-515-6500	515-6522
Daniel Stowe Botanical Garden 6500 S New Hope Rd *Web:* www.dsbg.org	Belmont	NC	28012	704-825-4490	829-1240
Dawes Arboretum 7770 Jacksontown Rd SE *TF:* 800-443-2937 ■ *Web:* www.dawesarb.org	Newark	OH	43056	740-323-2355	
Delaware Ctr for Horticulture 1810 N DuPont St *Web:* www.thedch.org	Wilmington	DE	19806	302-658-6262	658-6267
Denver Botanic Gardens 1005 York St *Web:* www.botanicgardens.org	Denver	CO	80206	720-865-3500	
Des Moines Botanical Ctr 909 Robert D Ray Dr *Web:* www.dmbotanicalgarden.com	Des Moines	IA	50316	515-323-6290	
Descanso Gardens 1418 Descanso Dr *Web:* www.descansogardens.org	La Canada	CA	91011	818-949-4200	
Desert Botanical Garden 1201 N Galvin Pkwy *TF:* 888-314-9480 ■ *Web:* www.dbg.org	Phoenix	AZ	85008	480-941-1225	481-8124
Devonian Botanic Garden University of Alberta *Web:* www.ales.ualberta.ca	Edmonton	AB	T6G2M7	780-987-3054	987-4141
Dixon Gallery & Gardens 4339 Pk Ave *Web:* www.dixon.org	Memphis	TN	38117	901-761-5250	682-0943
Dothan Area Botanical Gardens 5130 Headland Ave *Web:* www.dabg.com	Dothan	AL	36303	334-793-3224	793-5275
Dow Gardens 1809 Eastman Ave *Web:* www.dowgardens.org	Midland	MI	48640	989-631-2677	
Dr Sun Yat-Sen Classical Chinese Garden 578 Carrall St *Web:* www.vancouverchinesegarden.com	Vancouver	BC	V6B5K2	604-662-3207	682-4008
Dubuque Arboretum & Botanical Gardens 3800 Arboretum Dr *Web:* www.dubuquearboretum.com	Dubuque	IA	52001	563-556-2100	556-2443
Duke Farms 80 Rt 206 S *Web:* www.dukefarms.org	Hillsborough	NJ	08844	908-722-3700	
Dyck Arboretum of the Plains 177 W Hickory St *Web:* www.dyckarboretum.org	Hesston	KS	67062	620-327-8127	
Earl Burns Miller Japanese Garden 1250 Bellflower Blvd *TF:* 800-985-8880 ■ *Web:* www.csulb.edu/~jgarden	Long Beach	CA	90840	562-985-8885	985-5362
East Texas Arboretum (ETABS) 1601 Patterson Rd PO Box 2231 *Web:* www.eastexasarboretum.org	Athens	TX	75751	903-675-5630	
Edith J Carrier Arboretum & Botanical Gardens at James Madison University 780 University Blvd MSC 3705 *TF:* 888-568-2586 ■ *Web:* www.jmu.edu	Harrisonburg	VA	22807	540-568-3194	568-5115
Elizabeth Gamble Garden 1431 Waverley St *Web:* www.gamblegarden.org	Palo Alto	CA	94301	650-329-1356	329-1688
Elizabeth Park Rose Gardens 1561 Asylum Ave	West Hartford	CT	06117	860-231-9443	
Elizabethan Gardens 1411 National Pk Dr *Web:* www.elizabethangardens.org	Manteo	NC	27954	252-473-3234	473-3244
Enid A Haupt Glass Garden 400 E 34th St NYU Medical Ctr Rusk Inst of Rehabilitative Medicine *Web:* www.med.nyu.edu	New York	NY	10016	212-263-6058	263-2091
Erie Zoo 423 W 38th St *TF:* 877-371-5422 ■ *Web:* www.eriezoo.org	Erie	PA	16508	814-864-4091	864-1140
Fairchild Tropical Botanic Garden 10901 Old Cutler Rd *Web:* www.fairchildgarden.org	Coral Gables	FL	33156	305-667-1651	661-8953
Fernwood Botanical Gardens & Nature Preserve 13988 Range Line Rd *Web:* www.fernwoodbotanical.org	Niles	MI	49120	269-695-6491	
Filoli 86 Canada Rd *TF:* 866-691-9080 ■ *Web:* www.filoli.org	Woodside	CA	94062	650-364-8300	366-7836
Flamingo Gardens 3750 S Flamingo Rd *TF:* 800-435-7352 ■ *Web:* www.flamingogardens.org	Davie	FL	33330	954-473-2955	473-1738
Florida Botanical Gardens 12520 Ulmerton Rd *Web:* www.flbg.org	Largo	FL	33774	727-582-2100	
Foellinger-Freimann Botanical Conservatory 1100 S Calhoun St *TF:* 866-220-8842 ■ *Web:* www.botanicalconservatory.org	Fort Wayne	IN	46802	260-427-6440	427-6450
For-Mar Nature Preserve & Arboretum 2142 N Genesee Rd *Web:* www.geneseecountyparks.org	Burton	MI	48509	810-789-8567	
Forestiere Underground Gardens 5021 W Shaw Ave *Web:* www.undergroundgardens.com	Fresno	CA	93722	559-271-0734	
Fort Worth Botanic Garden 3220 Botanic Garden Blvd *Web:* www.fwbg.org	Fort Worth	TX	76107	817-392-5510	
Foster Botanical Garden 50 N Vineyard Blvd *Web:* www.honolulu.gov/parks/hbg/fbg.htm	Honolulu	HI	96817	808-522-7066	522-7050
Founders Memorial Garden 2450 Milledge Ave *Web:* gardenclub.uga.edu	Athens	GA	30602	706-227-5369	227-5370
Franklin Park Conservatory & Botanical Gardens 1777 E Broad St *Web:* www.fpconservatory.org	Columbus	OH	43203	614-715-8000	715-8199
Frederik Meijer Gardens & Sculpture Park 1000 E Beltline Ave NE *TF:* 877-975-3171 ■ *Web:* www.meijergardens.org	Grand Rapids	MI	49525	616-957-1580	957-5792
Friends of the Topiary Park 480 E Town St *Web:* www.topiarygarden.org	Columbus	OH	43215	614-645-0197	
Fruit & Spice Park 24801 SW 187th Ave *Web:* www.floridaplants.com/fruit&spice	Homestead	FL	33031	305-247-5727	245-3369
Fullerton Arboretum 1900 Associated Rd *Web:* www.fullertonarboretum.org	Fullerton	CA	92831	657-278-3407	278-7066

				Phone	Fax
Ganna Walska Lotusland 695 Ashley Rd *Web:* www.lotusland.org	Santa Barbara	CA	93108	805-969-3767	969-4423
Garden of the Coastal Plain at Georgia Southern University 1505 Bland Ave PO Box 8039 *Web:* academics.georgiasouthern.edu	Statesboro	GA	30460	912-871-1149	871-1777
Gardens of the American Rose Ctr 8877 Jefferson-Paige Rd *TF:* 800-637-6534 ■ *Web:* rose.org/arc/gardens.htm	Shreveport	LA	71119	318-938-5402	938-5402
Gardens on Spring Creek 2145 Centre Ave *Web:* www.fcgov.com	Fort Collins	CO	80526	970-416-2486	416-2280
Garfield Park Conservatory 300 N Central Pk Ave **Fax Area Code: 773* ■ *Web:* www.garfield-conservatory.org	Chicago	IL	60624	312-746-5100	638-1777*
Gari Melchers Home and Studio 224 Washington St *Web:* garimelchers.umw.edu	Fredericksburg	VA	22405	540-654-1015	654-1785
Garvan Woodland Gardens 550 Arkridge Rd PO Box 22240 *TF:* 800-366-4664 ■ *Web:* www.garvangardens.org	Hot Springs	AR	71903	501-262-9300	262-9301
George Eastman House & Gardens 900 E Ave *Web:* www.eastman.org	Rochester	NY	14607	585-271-3361	271-3970
George L Luthy Memorial Botanical Gardens 2520 N Prospect *Web:* www.peoriaparks.org	Peoria	IL	61603	309-686-3362	
Gifford Arboretum 1301 Memorial Dr University of Miami *Web:* www.bio.miami.edu/arboretum	Coral Gables	FL	33146	305-284-5364	284-3039
Gilroy Gardens Family Theme Park 3050 Hecker Pass Hwy *Web:* www.gilroygardens.org	Gilroy	CA	95020	408-840-7100	
Glacier Gardens Rainforest Adventure 7600 Old Glacier Hwy *Web:* www.glaciergardens.com	Juneau	AK	99801	907-790-3377	790-3907
Goodstay Gardens 26002800 Pennsylvania Ave *Web:* www.udel.edu	Wilmington	DE	19806	302-573-4450	
Goodwood Museum & Gardens 1600 Miccosukee Rd *Web:* www.goodwoodmuseum.org	Tallahassee	FL	32308	850-877-4202	877-3090
Green Bay Botanical Garden 2600 Larsen Rd *TF:* 877-355-4224 ■ *Web:* www.gbbg.org	Green Bay	WI	54303	920-490-9457	490-9461
Green Spring Gardens Park 4603 Green Spring Rd *Web:* www.fairfaxcounty.gov/parks/gsgp	Alexandria	VA	22312	703-642-5173	642-8095
Grotto, The 8840 NE Skidmore St *Web:* www.thegrotto.org	Portland	OR	97220	503-254-7371	254-7948
Guadalupe River Park & Gardens 438 Coleman Ave *Web:* www.grpg.org	San Jose	CA	95110	408-298-7657	288-9048
Harry P Leu Gardens 1920 N Forest Ave *Web:* www.leugardens.org	Orlando	FL	32803	407-246-2620	246-2849
Hawaii Tropical Botanical Garden 27-717 Old Mamalahoa Hwy PO Box 80 *Web:* www.hawaiigarden.com	Papaikou	HI	96781	808-964-5233	964-1338
Heathcote Botanical Gardens 210 Savannah Rd *Web:* www.heathcotebotanicalgardens.org	Fort Pierce	FL	34982	772-464-4672	
Hendricks Park & Gardens 2198 Summit Ave *Web:* www.eugene-or.gov	Eugene	OR	97403	541-682-4812	
Henry Schmieder Arboretum *Delaware Valley College* 700 E Butler Ave *Web:* www.delval.edu	Doylestown	PA	18901	215-489-2283	489-2404
Hershey Gardens 170 Hotel Rd *Web:* www.hersheygardens.org	Hershey	PA	17033	717-534-3492	533-5095
Hidden Lake Gardens 6214 Monroe Rd *Web:* www.hiddenlakegardens.msu.edu	Tipton	MI	49287	517-431-2060	431-9148
Highline SeaTac Botanical Gardens 13735 24th Ave S PO Box 69384 *Web:* www.highlinegarden.org	SeaTac	WA	98168	206-391-4003	
Highstead Arboretum 127 Lonetown Rd PO Box 1097 *Web:* highstead.net	Redding	CT	06875	203-938-8809	938-0343
Hilltop Arboretum 11855 Highland Rd *Web:* sites01.lsu.edu/wp/hilltop	Baton Rouge	LA	70810	225-767-6916	768-7740
Hilltop Garden & Nature Ctr *Indiana University Campus* 2367 E Tenth St	Bloomington	IN	47408	812-855-8808	
Hillwood Estate Museum & Gardens 4155 Linnean Ave NW *Web:* www.hillwoodmuseum.org	Washington	DC	20008	202-686-5807	966-7846
Holden Arboretum 9500 Sperry Rd *Web:* www.holdenarb.org	Kirtland	OH	44094	440-946-4400	602-3857
Honolulu Botanical Gardens 50 N Vineyard Blvd *Web:* www.honolulu.gov/parks/hbg	Honolulu	HI	96817	808-768-3003	768-3053
Hoyt Arboretum 4000 SW Fairview Blvd *Web:* www.hoytarboretum.org	Portland	OR	97221	503-865-8733	
Hudson Gardens & Event Ctr 6115 S Santa Fe Dr *Web:* www.hudsongardens.org	Littleton	CO	80120	303-797-8565	797-8647
Humber Arboretum 205 Humber College Blvd *Web:* www.humberarboretum.on.ca	Toronto	ON	M9W5L7	416-675-6622	675-2755
Humboldt Botanical Gardens 402 E St PO Box 6117 *Web:* www.hbgf.org	Eureka	CA	95501	707-442-5139	442-6634
Huntington Library Art Collections & Botanical Gardens, The 1151 Oxford Rd *Web:* www.huntington.org	San Marino	CA	91108	626-405-2100	
Huntington Museum of Art Inc 2033 McCoy Rd *Web:* www.hmoa.org	Huntington	WV	25701	304-529-2701	529-7447
Huntsville Botanical Garden 4747 Bob Wallace Ave *TF:* 800-300-4916 ■ *Web:* www.hsvbg.org	Huntsville	AL	35805	256-830-4447	830-5314
Idaho Botanical Garden 2355 N Penitentiary Rd *TF:* 877-527-8233 ■ *Web:* www.idahobotanicalgarden.org	Boise	ID	83712	208-343-8649	343-3601
Inniswood Metro Gardens 940 S Hempstead Rd *Web:* www.inniswood.org	Westerville	OH	43081	614-895-6216	895-6352
Iowa Arboretum 1875 Peach Ave *Web:* www.iowaarboretum.org	Madrid	IA	50156	515-795-3216	
J Paul Getty Museum 1200 Getty Ctr Dr **Fax:* Hum Res ■ *Web:* www.getty.edu	Los Angeles	CA	90049	310-440-7300	440-7720*
James Madison's Montpelier 11407 Constitution Hwy *Web:* www.montpelier.org	Montpelier Station	VA	22957	540-672-2728	672-0411
Japanese Garden 611 SW Kingston Ave *Web:* www.japanesegarden.com	Portland	OR	97205	503-223-1321	223-8303
JC Raulston Arboretum North Carolina State University PO Box 7522 *TF:* 888-842-2442 ■ *Web:* www.ncsu.edu/jcraulstonarboretum	Raleigh	NC	27695	919-513-7457	515-5361
Jenkins Arboretum (JA) 631 Berwyn Baptist Rd *Web:* www.jenkinsarboretum.org	Devon	PA	19333	610-647-8870	647-6664
JJ Neilson Arboretum Ridgetown College University of Guelph 120 Main St E *Web:* www.ridgetownc.uoguelph.ca/aboutus/arboretum.cfm	Ridgetown	ON	N0P2C0	519-674-1500	674-1515
Journey Museum 222 New York St *TF:* 877-343-8220 ■ *Web:* www.journeymuseum.org	Rapid City	SD	57701	605-394-6923	394-6940
Jungle Gardens Hwy 329 *Web:* www.junglegardens.org	Avery Island	LA	70513	337-369-6243	369-6254
Jungle Island 1111 Parrot Jungle Trl *Web:* www.jungleisland.com	Miami	FL	33132	305-400-7000	400-7290
Kalmia Gardens of Coker College 1624 W Carolina Ave *Web:* www.coker.edu	Hartsville	SC	29550	843-383-8145	
Kenilworth Aquatic Gardens 1550 Anacostia Ave NE *TF:* 877-642-4743 ■ *Web:* www.nps.gov/keaq	Washington	DC	20019	202-426-6905	426-5991
Key West Botanical Garden 5210 College Rd *Web:* www.keywestbotanicalgarden.org	Key West	FL	33040	305-296-1504	296-2242
Kingwood Ctr 900 Pk Ave W *Web:* www.kingwoodcenter.org	Mansfield	OH	44906	419-522-0211	
Klehm Arboretum & Botanic Garden 2715 S Main St *Web:* www.klehm.org	Rockford	IL	61102	815-965-8146	965-5914
Kruckeberg Botanic Garden 20312 15th Ave NW *Web:* www.kruckeberg.org	Shoreline	WA	98177	206-546-1281	
Ladew Topiary Gardens 3535 Jarettsville Pk *Web:* www.ladewgardens.com	Monkton	MD	21111	410-557-9466	557-7763
Lady Bird Johnson Wildflower Ctr 4801 LaCrosse Ave *TF:* 877-945-3357 ■ *Web:* www.wildflower.org	Austin	TX	78739	512-292-4200	232-0156
Lake Wilderness Arboretum 22520 SE 248th St PO Box 72 *Web:* www.lakewildernessarboretum.org	Maple Valley	WA	98038	425-413-2572	
Lakewold Gardens 12317 Gravelly Lk Dr SW *TF:* 888-858-4106 ■ *Web:* lakewoldgardens.org	Lakewood	WA	98499	253-584-4106	584-3021
Landis Arboretum 174 Lape Rd PO Box 186 *Web:* www.landisarboretum.org	Esperance	NY	12066	518-875-6935	
Lauritzen Gardens Omaha's Botanical Ctr 100 Bancroft St *Web:* www.lauritzengardens.org	Omaha	NE	68108	402-346-4002	346-8948
Leach Botanical Garden 6704 SE 122 Ave PO Box 90667 *Web:* www.leachgarden.org	Portland	OR	97236	503-823-9503	823-9504
Leila Arboretum Society 928 W Michigan Ave *Web:* www.leilaarboretumsociety.org	Battle Creek	MI	49037	269-969-0270	969-0616
Lewis Ginter Botanical Garden 1800 Lakeside Ave *Web:* www.lewisginter.org	Richmond	VA	23228	804-262-9887	262-6329
Lincoln Botanical Garden & Arboretum (BGA) University of Nebraska 1309 N 17th St *TF:* 800-742-8800 ■ *Web:* www.unl.edu/bga	Lincoln	NE	68588	402-472-2679	472-9615
Living Desert Zoo & Gardens 47900 Portola Ave *Web:* www.livingdesert.org	Palm Desert	CA	92260	760-346-5694	568-9685
Lockerly Arboretum 1534 Irwinton Rd *Web:* www.lockerly.org	Milledgeville	GA	31061	478-452-2112	452-1020
Long House Reserve 133 Hands Creek Rd *Web:* longhouse.org	East Hampton	NY	11937	631-329-3568	329-4299
Longue Vue House & Gardens 7 Bamboo Rd *Web:* www.longuevue.com	New Orleans	LA	70124	504-488-5488	486-7015
Longwood Gardens PO Box 501 *TF:* 800-737-5500 ■ *Web:* longwoodgardens.org	Kennett Square	PA	19348	610-388-1000	388-5488
Los Angeles County Arboretum & Botanic Garden 301 N Baldwin Ave *Web:* www.arboretum.org	Arcadia	CA	91007	626-821-3222	445-1217
Los Angeles Zoo & Botanical Gardens 5333 Zoo Dr *Web:* www.lazoo.org	Los Angeles	CA	90027	323-644-4200	662-9786
Lubbock Memorial Arboretum 4111 University Ave *Web:* www.lubbockarboretum.org	Lubbock	TX	79413	806-797-4520	
Luther Burbank Home & Gardens 204 Santa Rosa Ave *Web:* www.lutherburbank.org	Santa Rosa	CA	95404	707-524-5445	524-5827
Magnolia Plantation & Gardens 3550 Ashley River Rd *TF:* 800-367-3517 ■ *Web:* www.magnoliaplantation.com	Charleston	SC	29414	843-571-1266	
Marie Selby Botanical Gardens 811 S Palm Ave *Web:* www.selby.org	Sarasota	FL	34236	941-366-5731	366-9807
Marjorie McNeely Conservatory at Como Park 1225 Estabrook Dr *Web:* www.comozooconservatory.org	Saint Paul	MN	55103	651-487-8201	

Name / Address	City	State	Zip	Phone	Fax
Markham Regional Arboretum 1202 La Vista Ave *Web:* www.markhamarboretum.org	Concord	CA	94521	925-681-2968	
Marywood University Arboretum 2300 Adams Ave. *TF:* 866-279-9663 ■ *Web:* www.marywood.edu	Scranton	PA	18509	570-348-6218	
Matthaei Botanical Gardens 1800 N Dixboro Rd *TF:* 800-666-8693 ■ *Web:* www.lsa.umich.edu/mbg	Ann Arbor	MI	48105	734-647-7600	998-6205
McKee Botanical Garden 350 US 1 *Web:* www.mckeegarden.org	Vero Beach	FL	32962	772-794-0601	794-0602
Meadowlark Botanical Gardens 9750 Meadowlark Gardens Ct. *Web:* www.novaparks.com/parks/meadowlark-botanical-gardens	Vienna	VA	22182	703-255-3631	255-2392
Memphis Botanic Garden 750 Cherry Rd *TF:* 877-829-5500 ■ *Web:* www.memphisbotanicgarden.com	Memphis	TN	38117	901-576-4100	682-1561
Mendocino Coast Botanical Gardens 18220 N Hwy 1 *Web:* www.gardenbythesea.org	Fort Bragg	CA	95437	707-964-4352	964-3114
Mepkin Abbey Botanical Garden 1098 Mepkin Abbey Rd *Web:* www.mepkinabbey.org	Moncks Corner	SC	29461	843-761-8509	761-6719
Mercer Arboretum & Botanic Gardens 22306 Aldine Westfield Rd *TF:* 877-321-2652 ■ *Web:* www.hcp4.net/mercer	Humble	TX	77338	281-443-8731	209-9767
Miami Beach Botanical Garden 2000 Convention Ctr Dr *Web:* www.mbgarden.org	Miami Beach	FL	33139	305-673-7256	
Minnesota Landscape Arboretum 3675 Arboretum Dr *Web:* www.arboretum.umn.edu	Chaska	MN	55318	952-443-1400	443-2521
Missouri Botanical Garden 4344 Shaw Blvd *TF:* 800-642-8842 ■ *Web:* www.missouribotanicalgarden.org	Saint Louis	MO	63110	314-577-5100	
Mobile Botanical Gardens 5151 Museum Dr *Web:* www.mobilebotanicalgardens.org	Mobile	AL	36608	251-342-0555	
Montgomery Botanical Ctr 11901 Old Cutler Rd *TF:* 800-435-7352 ■ *Web:* www.montgomerybotanical.org	Miami	FL	33156	305-667-3800	661-5984
Monticello 931 Thomas Jefferson Pkwy PO Box 316 *TF:* 800-243-1743 ■ *Web:* www.monticello.org	Charlottesville	VA	22902	434-984-9822	977-7757
Montreal Botanical Garden 4101 Sherbrooke St E *Web:* ville.montreal.qc.ca	Montreal	QC	H1X2B2	514-872-1400	872-1455
Morris Arboretum of the University of Pennsylvania 100 E NW Ave. *Web:* www.business-services.upenn.edu/arboretum	Philadelphia	PA	19118	215-247-5777	247-7862
Morton Arboretum 4100 Illinois Rt 53 *Web:* www.mortonarb.org	Lisle	IL	60532	630-968-0074	
Morven Museum & Gardens 55 Stockton St. *Web:* morven.org	Princeton	NJ	08540	609-924-8144	
Mount Pisgah Arboretum 34901 Frank Parrish Rd *Web:* mountpisgaharboretum.org	Eugene	OR	97405	541-747-1504	741-4904
Mountain Top Arboretum Rt 23C Maude Adams Rd PO Box 379 *Web:* www.mtarboretum.org	Tannersville	NY	12485	518-589-3903	
Mounts Botanical Garden 531 N Military Trl *Web:* www.mounts.org	West Palm Beach	FL	33415	561-233-1757	
Muttart Conservatory 9626 96A St *Web:* www.edmonton.ca	Edmonton	AB	T6C4L8	780-496-8755	496-8747
Mynelle Gardens 4736 Clinton Blvd *TF:* 800-354-7695 ■ *Web:* www.jacksonms.gov	Jackson	MS	39209	601-960-1894	960-1576
Myriad Botanical Gardens/Crystal Bridge Tropical Conservatory 301 W Reno Ave *Web:* oklahomacitybotanicalgardens.com	Oklahoma City	OK	73102	405-445-7080	297-3620
Naples Botanical Garden 4820 Bayshore Dr. *TF:* 877-433-1874 ■ *Web:* www.naplesgarden.org	Naples	FL	34112	239-643-7275	649-7306
National Garden 100 Maryland Ave *Web:* www.usbg.gov	Washington	DC	20001	202-225-8333	
Native Plant Ctr at Westchester Community College 75 Grasslands Rd *Web:* www.sunywcc.edu	Valhalla	NY	10595	914-606-7870	606-6143
Nebraska Statewide Arboretum UNL Keim Hall 102 PO Box 830964 *Web:* www.arboretum.unl.edu	Lincoln	NE	68583	402-472-2971	472-8095
New England Tropical Conservatory (NETC) 413 US Rt 7S PO Box 4715 *Web:* oneworldconservationcenter.org	Bennington	VT	05201	802-447-7419	
New England Wild Flower Society 180 Hemenway Rd *TF:* 888-636-0033 ■ *Web:* www.newfs.org	Framingham	MA	01701	508-877-7630	877-3658
Niagara Parks Botanical Gardens 2565 Niagara Pkwy N PO Box 150 *TF:* 877-642-7275 ■ *Web:* niagaraparks.com/garden-trail/botanical-gardens.html	Niagara Falls	ON	L2E6T2	905-356-8554	356-5488
Nichols Aboretum *University of Michigan* 1600 Washington Heights *Web:* www.lsa.umich.edu	Ann Arbor	MI	48104	734-647-7600	
Nikka Yuko Japanese Garden PO Box 751 *Web:* www.nikkayuko.com	Lethbridge	AB	T1J3Z6	403-328-3511	328-0511
Norfolk Botanical Garden 6700 Azalea Garden Rd *Web:* norfolkbotanicalgarden.org	Norfolk	VA	23518	757-441-5830	
North Carolina Arboretum 100 Frederick Law Olmsted Way *Web:* www.ncarboretum.org	Asheville	NC	28806	828-665-2492	665-2371
North Carolina Botanical Garden *University of North Carolina, The* CB 3375 Totten Ctr PO Box 3375 *Web:* www.ncbg.unc.edu	Chapel Hill	NC	27599	919-962-0522	962-3531
Oklahoma Botanical Garden & Arboretum Oklahoma State University Dept of Horticulture 358 Ag Hall *Web:* botanicgarden.okstate.edu	Stillwater	OK	74078	405-744-4531	744-9709
Olbrich Botanical Gardens 3330 Atwood Ave. *Web:* www.olbrich.org	Madison	WI	53704	608-246-4550	246-4719
Old City Cemetery Museums & Arboretum 401 Taylor St *Web:* www.gravegarden.org	Lynchburg	VA	24501	434-847-1465	856-2004
Oldfields - Lilly House & Gardens 4000 Michigan Rd *Web:* www.imamuseum.org	Indianapolis	IN	46208	317-923-1331	931-1978
Oregon Garden, The 879 W Main St PO Box 155 *TF:* 877-674-2733 ■ *Web:* www.oregongarden.org	Silverton	OR	97381	503-874-8100	339-2996
Overfelt Gardens 368 Educational Pk Dr. *Web:* www.sanjoseca.gov	San Jose	CA	95133	408-251-3323	
Philbrook Museum of Art & Gardens 2727 S Rockford Rd *Web:* www.philbrook.org	Tulsa	OK	74114	918-749-7941	
Phipps Conservatory & Botanical Gardens 1 Schenley Pk. *Web:* www.phipps.conservatory.org	Pittsburgh	PA	15213	412-622-6914	622-7363
Pine Tree State Arboretum 153 Hospital St *Web:* www.vilesarboretum.org	Augusta	ME	04330	207-626-7989	
Pinecrest Gardens 11000 Red Rd *Web:* www.pinecrest-fl.gov	Pinecrest	FL	33156	305-669-6990	669-6944
Polly Hill Arboretum 809 State Rd PO Box 561 *Web:* www.pollyhillarboretum.org	West Tisbury	MA	02575	508-693-9426	
Polynesian Cultural Ctr 55-370 Kamehameha Hwy *TF:* 800-367-7060 ■ *Web:* www.polynesia.com	Laie	HI	96762	808-293-3005	293-3027
Powell Gardens 1609 NW US Hwy 50. *Web:* www.powellgardens.org	Kingsville	MO	64061	816-697-2600	697-2619
Preservation Delaware Inc 1405 Greenhill Ave *Web:* www.preservationde.org	Wilmington	DE	19806	302-651-9617	651-9603
Quad City Botanical Ctr 2525 Fourth Ave *Web:* www.qcgardens.com	Rock Island	IL	61201	309-794-0991	
Quarryhill Botanical Garden 12841 Sonoma Hwy PO Box 232 *Web:* www.quarryhillbg.org	Glen Ellen	CA	95442	707-996-3166	996-3198
Queens Botanical Garden 43-50 Main St. *Web:* www.queensbotanical.org	Flushing	NY	11355	718-886-3800	463-0263
Rancho Santa Ana Botanic Garden 1500 N College Ave *Web:* www.rsabg.org	Claremont	CA	91711	909-625-8767	626-7670
Red Butte Garden & Arboretum 300 Wakara Way University of Utah *Web:* www.redbuttegarden.org	Salt Lake City	UT	84108	801-581-4747	
Reeves-Reed Arboretum 165 Hobart Ave *Web:* www.reeves-reedarboretum.org	Summit	NJ	07901	908-273-8787	273-6869
Reflection Riding Arboretum & Botanical Garden 400 Garden Rd *Web:* www.reflectionriding.org	Chattanooga	TN	37419	423-821-1160	
Reiman Gardens *Iowa State University* 1407 University Blvd *Web:* www.reimangardens.com	Ames	IA	50011	515-294-2710	
Reynolda Gardens of Wake Forest University 100 Reynolda Village *Web:* www.reynoldagardens.org	Winston-Salem	NC	27106	336-758-5593	
Rhododendron Species Botanical Garden 2525 S 336th St PO Box 3798 *TF:* 877-242-2528 ■ *Web:* www.rhodygarden.org	Federal Way	WA	98063	253-838-4646	838-4686
Riverbanks Zoo & Botanical Garden 500 Wildlife Pkwy *Web:* www.riverbanks.org	Columbia	SC	29210	803-779-8717	253-6381
Robert Allerton Park & Conference Ctr 515 Old Timber Rd *Web:* www.allerton.illinois.edu	Monticello	IL	61856	217-333-3287	762-3742
Rotary Botanical Gardens 1455 Palmer Dr. *Web:* rotarybotanicalgardens.org	Janesville	WI	53545	608-752-3885	752-3853
Royal Botanical Gardens (RBG) 680 Plains Rd W *TF:* 800-694-4769 ■ *Web:* www.rbg.ca	Burlington	ON	L7T4H4	905-527-1158	577-0375
Rutgers Gardens 112 Ryders Ln Cook College/Rutgers University *Web:* www.rutgersgardens.rutgers.edu	New Brunswick	NJ	08901	732-932-8451	932-7060
Ruth Bancroft Garden 1552 Bancroft Rd *Web:* www.ruthbancroftgarden.org	Walnut Creek	CA	94598	925-210-9663	256-1889
San Antonio Botanical Garden & Lucile Halsell Conservatory 555 Funston Pl *Web:* www.sabot.org	San Antonio	TX	78209	210-207-3250	207-3274
San Diego Botanic Garden 230 Quail Gardens Dr PO Box 230005 *Web:* www.sdbgarden.org	Encinitas	CA	92023	760-436-3036	632-0917
San Francisco Botanical Garden 9th Ave & Lincoln Way *Web:* www.sfbotanicalgarden.org	San Francisco	CA	94122	415-661-1316	331-1316
San Jose Heritage Rose Garden (SJHRG) 438 Coleman Ave *Web:* www.grpg.org	San Jose	CA	95110	408-298-7657	
San Luis Obispo Botanical Garden 3450 Dairy Creek Rd. *Web:* www.slobg.org	San Luis Obispo	CA	93405	805-541-1400	541-1466
Sandhills Horticultural Gardens 3395 Airport Rd *Web:* sandhillshorticulturalgardens.com	Pinehurst	NC	28374	910-695-3882	
Santa Barbara Botanic Garden 1212 Mission Canyon Rd *Web:* www.sbbg.org	Santa Barbara	CA	93105	805-682-4726	563-0352
Sarah P Duke Gardens 420 Anderson St *Web:* gardens.duke.edu	Durham	NC	27708	919-684-3698	668-3610
Sawtooth Botanical Garden (SBG) 11 Gimlet Rd PO Box 928 *Web:* www.sbgarden.org	Ketchum	ID	83340	208-726-9358	
Schedel Arboretum & Gardens 19255 W Portage River S Rd *Web:* www.schedel-gardens.org	Elmore	OH	43416	419-862-3182	

Phone | Fax

Schoepfle Garden 12882 Diagonal Rd . . . La Grange OH 44050 440-458-5121 458-8924
TF: 800-526-7275 ■
Web: www.metroparks.cc/reservation-schoepfle-garden.php

Schreiner's Iris Gardens 3625 Quinaby Rd NE . . . Salem OR 97303 503-393-3232 393-5590
TF: 800-525-2367 ■ *Web:* www.schreinersgardens.com

Scott Arboretum of Swarthmore College
500 College Ave . . . Swarthmore PA 19081 610-328-8025
Web: www.scottarboretum.org

Secrest Arboretum 1680 Madison Ave. . . . Wooster OH 44691 330-464-2148 263-3886
Web: secrest.osu.edu

Shambhala Mountain Ctr
151 Shambhala Wy. . . . Red Feather Lakes CO 80545 970-881-2184 881-2909
TF: 888-788-7221 ■ *Web:* www.shambhalamountain.org

Shangri La Botanical Gardens & Nature Ctr
2111 W Pk Ave. . . . Orange TX 77630 409-670-9113 670-9341
Web: starkculturalvenues.org

Sherman Library & Gardens
2647 E Coast Hwy . . . Corona del Mar CA 92625 949-673-2261 675-5458
Web: www.slgardens.org

Sherwood Fox Arboretum
University of Western Ontario
1151 Richmond St. . . . London ON N6A5B7 519-850-2542 661-3935
Web: uwo.ca//biology/research/biology_facilities/arboretum.html

Skylands PO Box 302 . . . Ringwood NJ 07456 973-962-9534 962-1553
Web: www.njbg.org

Slayton Arboretum of Hilsdale College
33 E College St. . . . Hillsdale MI 49242 517-607-2241
Web: hillsdale.edu/home

Sonnenberg Gardens 151 Charlotte St. . . . Canandaigua NY 14424 585-394-4922 394-2192
Web: www.sonnenberg.org

South Carolina Botanical Garden
150 Discovery Ln Clemson University . . . Clemson SC 29634 864-656-3405 656-6230
Web: www.clemson.edu/public/scbg

South Coast Botanic Garden
26300 Crenshaw Blvd. . . . Palos Verdes Peninsula CA 90274 310-544-6815
Web: www.southcoastbotanicgarden.org

South Texas Botanical Gardens & Nature Ctr
8545 S Staples St. . . . Corpus Christi TX 78413 361-852-2100 852-7875
Web: www.stxbot.org

Stan Hywet Hall & Gardens 714 N Portage Path. . . . Akron OH 44303 330-836-5533
TF: 888-836-5533 ■ *Web:* www.stanhywet.org

State Arboretum of Virginia 400 Blandy Farm Ln . . . Boyce VA 22620 540-837-1758 837-1523
Web: www.virginia.edu

State Botanical Garden of Georgia
2450 S Milledge Ave . . . Athens GA 30605 706-542-1244 542-3091
Web: botgarden.uga.edu

Stonecrop Gardens 81 Stonecrop Ln . . . Cold Spring NY 10516 845-265-2000
Web: www.stonecrop.org

Stranahan Arboretum 4131 Tantara Dr . . . Toledo OH 43623 419-841-1007 530-4421
Web: www.utoledo.edu

Texas Discovery Gardens
3601 Martin Luther King Junior Blvd . . . Dallas TX 75210 214-428-7476 428-5338
Web: www.texasdiscoverygardens.org

Tofino Botanical Gardens Foundation
1084 Pacific Rim Hwy. . . . Tofino BC V0R2Z0 250-725-1220
Web: www.tbgf.org

Tohono Chul Park 7366 N Paseo del Norte. . . . Tucson AZ 85704 520-742-6455 797-1213
Web: www.tohonochulpark.org

Toledo Botanical Garden 5403 Elmer Dr . . . Toledo OH 43615 419-536-5566 536-5574
Web: www.toledogarden.org

Tower Hill Botanic Garden
11 French Dr PO Box 598. . . . Boylston MA 01505 508-869-6111 869-0314
Web: www.towerhillbg.org

Tucson Botanical Gardens 2150 N Alvernon Way . . . Tucson AZ 85712 520-326-9686
Web: www.tucsonbotanical.org

Tulsa Garden Ctr 2435 S Peoria Ave. . . . Tulsa OK 74114 918-746-5125 746-5128
Web: www.tulsagardencenter.com

Tyler Arboretum 515 Painter Rd . . . Media PA 19063 610-566-9134 891-1490
Web: www.tylerarboretum.org

UC Davis Arboretum
University of California La Ru Rd . . . Davis CA 95616 530-752-4880 752-5796
Web: arboretum.ucdavis.edu

University of Alabama Arboretum
PO Box 870344 . . . Tuscaloosa AL 35487 205-553-3278 553-3728
Web: www.arboretum.ua.edu

University of British Columbia Botanical Garden & Centre for Plant Research
6804 SW Marine Dr . . . Vancouver BC V6T1Z4 604-822-4208 822-2016
Web: www.botanicalgarden.ubc.ca

University of California Botanical Garden at Berkeley
200 Centennial Dr. . . . Berkeley CA 94720 510-643-2755 642-5045
Web: www.botanicalgarden.berkeley.edu

University of California Riverside Botanic Gardens
900 University Ave . . . Riverside CA 92521 951-784-6962 784-6962
Web: gardens.ucr.edu

University of Chicago Botanic Garden
5555 S Ellis Ave. . . . Chicago IL 60637 773-702-1700 702-5814
Web: www.uchicago.edu

University of Delaware Botanic Garden
University of Delaware
Plant & Soil Science Dept 152 Townsend Hall . . . Newark DE 19716 302-831-0153 831-0605
Web: www.ag.udel.edu/udbg

University of Idaho Arboretum & Botanical Garden
875 Perimeter Dr PO Box 442281. . . . Moscow ID 83844 208-885-5978 885-5748
Web: www.uidaho.edu/arboretum

University of Kentucky Lexington-Fayette Urban County Government Arboretum
500 Alumni Dr . . . Lexington KY 40503 859-257-6955
Web: www.ca.uky.edu/arboretum

University of Missouri Botanic Garden
General Services Bldg. . . . Columbia MO 65211 573-882-4240 884-3032
TF: 800-856-2181 ■ *Web:* gardens.missouri.edu/about/index.php

University of Rochester Arboretum
612 Wilson Blvd. . . . Rochester NY 14627 585-275-3340 461-3055
Web: www.facilities.rochester.edu/arboretum

Phone | Fax

University of South Florida Botanical Gardens
4202 E Fowler Ave . . . Tampa FL 33620 813-974-2329 974-4808
Web: gardens.usf.edu

University of Southern Maine Arboretum
PO Box 9300 . . . Portland ME 04104 800-800-4876 780-5143*
**Fax Area Code:* 207 ■ *TF:* 800-800-4876 ■ *Web:* www.usm.maine.edu/arboretum

University of Tennessee Arboretum
901 S Illinois Ave . . . Oak Ridge TN 37830 865-483-3571 483-3572
Web: forestry.tennessee.edu

University of Tennessee Gardens
2431 Joe Johnson Dr . . . Knoxville TN 37996 865-974-7324 974-1947
Web: utgardens.tennessee.edu

University of Wisconsin-Madison Arboretum
1207 Seminole Hwy . . . Madison WI 53711 608-263-7888 262-5209
Web: arboretum.wisc.edu

US Botanic Garden 100 Maryland Ave . . . Washington DC 20001 202-225-8333
Web: www.aoc.gov

US National Arboretum
3501 New York Ave NE. . . . Washington DC 20002 202-245-2726 245-4575
Web: www.usna.usda.gov

Utah Botanical Ctr
920 South 50 West PO Box 265 . . . Kaysville UT 84037 801-593-8969
Web: usubotanicalcenter.org

Van Vleck House & Gardens 21 Van Vleck St . . . Montclair NJ 07042 973-744-4752 746-1082
Web: www.vanvleck.org

Vander Veer Botanical Park
215 W Central Pk Ave. . . . Davenport IA 52803 563-326-7818
Web: www.cityofdavenportiowa.com

Vanderbilt University 2201 W End Ave . . . Nashville TN 37240 615-322-7311 343-7765
TF: 800-288-0432 ■ *Web:* www.vanderbilt.edu

Vermont Garden Park 1100 Dorset St. . . . South Burlington VT 05403 802-863-5251 864-6889
TF: 800-538-7476 ■ *Web:* www.garden.org

Virginia Tech Horticulture Garden (VTHG)
Virginia Tech 301 Saunders Hall . . . Blacksburg VA 24061 540-231-5451
Web: www.hort.vt.edu/vthg

Waddell Barnes Botanical Gardens
100 College Stn Dr Macon State College . . . Macon GA 31206 478-471-2780
Web: www.mga.edu

Washington Park Arboretum
2300 Arboretum Dr E . . . Seattle WA 98112 206-543-8800 616-2871
Web: www.depts.washington.edu

Washington Park Botanical Garden
1740 W Fayette Ave . . . Springfield IL 62704 217-753-6228 546-0257
Web: www.springfieldparks.org

Wave Hill W 249th St & Independence Ave . . . Bronx NY 10471 718-549-3200 884-8952
Web: www.wavehill.org

Wegerzyn Gardens MetroPark
1301 E Siebenthaler Ave. . . . Dayton OH 45414 937-275-7275
Web: www.metroparks.org

Welkinweir 1368 Prizer Rd . . . Pottstown PA 19465 610-469-7543
Web: www.welkinweir.org

West Virginia Botanic Garden
714 Venture Dr . . . Morgantown WV 26508 304-376-2717
Web: www.wvbg.org

White River Gardens
1200 W Washington St PO Box 22309. . . . Indianapolis IN 46222 317-630-2001 630-5153
Web: www.indianapoliszoo.com

Wing Haven Gardens & Bird Sanctuary
248 Ridgewood Ave . . . Charlotte NC 28209 704-331-0664 331-9368
Web: www.winghavengardens.com

Winterthur Museum & Country Estate
5105 Kennett Pk . . . Winterthur DE 19735 302-888-4600
TF: 800-448-3883 ■ *Web:* www.winterthur.org

WJ Beal Botanical Garden
Michigan State University 412 Olds Hall . . . East Lansing MI 48824 517-355-9582 432-1090
Web: www.cpa.msu.edu

Woodland Cemetery & Arboretum Foundation
118 Woodland Ave . . . Dayton OH 45409 937-228-3221 222-7259
Web: www.woodlandcemetery.org

Wrigley Memorial & Botanical Garden
125 Claressa Ave . . . Avalon CA 90704 310-510-2897 510-2325
Web: www.catalinaconservancy.org/index.php?s=portal

WW Seymour Botanical Conservatory
316 S 'G' St. . . . Tacoma WA 98405 253-591-5330
Web: metroparkstacoma.org

Yale University Marsh Botanical Gardens
Yale University
Corner of Prospect & Hillside St. . . . New Haven CT 06511 203-432-6320
Web: marshbotanicalgarden.yale.edu

Yew Dell Gardens
6220 Old LaGrange Rd PO Box 1334 . . . Crestwood KY 40014 502-241-4788
Web: www.yewdellgardens.org

Zilker Botanical Garden
2220 Barton Springs Rd . . . Austin TX 78746 512-477-8672 481-8254
Web: www.zilkergarden.org

ZooMontana & Botanical Gardens
2100 S Shiloh Rd . . . Billings MT 59106 406-652-8100
Web: www.zoomontana.org

BOTTLES - GLASS

See Glass Jars & Bottles p. 2353

98 BOTTLES - PLASTICS

Phone | Fax

Alpha Packaging
1555 Page Industrial Blvd. . . . Saint Louis MO 63132 314-427-4300 427-5445
TF: 800-421-4772 ■ *Web:* www.alphap.com

Amcor Packaging 935 Technology Dr Ste 100. . . . Ann Arbor MI 48108 734-428-9741 562-6059*
**Fax Area Code:* 714 ■ *Web:* www.amcor.com/petpackaging

CCW Products Inc 5861 Tennyson St. . . . Arvada CO 80003 303-427-9663
Web: www.ccwproducts.com

Company	City	State	Zip	Phone	Fax
Colt's Plastics Co 969 N Main St PO Box 429 *TF:* 800-222-2658 ■ *Web:* www.coltsplastics.com	Dayville	CT	06241	860-774-2301	774-2301
Comar LLC 141 N Fifth St *TF:* 800-962-6627 ■ *Web:* www.comar.com	Saddle Brook	NJ	07663	201-909-3400	
Cortland Plastics International LLC 211 Main St *Web:* www.cortlandplastics.com	Cortland	NY	13045	607-662-0120	
Drug Plastics & Glass Company Inc 1 Bottle Dr *Web:* www.drugplastics.com	Boyertown	PA	19512	610-367-5000	367-9800
Graham Packaging Company Inc 2401 Pleasant Vly Rd *Web:* www.grahampackaging.com	York	PA	17402	717-849-8500	854-4269
In Zone Brands 2859 Paces Ferry Rd SE Ste 2100	Atlanta	GA	30339	678-718-2000	718-2031
Midland Mfg Company Inc 101 E County Line Rd PO Box 899 *Web:* www.midlandmfgco.com	Monroe	IA	50170	641-259-2625	259-3216
NEW Plastics Corp 112 Fourth St *TF:* 800-666-5207 ■ *Web:* www.newplasticscorp.com	Luxemburg	WI	54217	920-845-2326	845-2439
Nutrifaster Inc 209 S Bennett St *TF:* 800-800-2641 ■ *Web:* www.nutrifaster.com	Seattle	WA	98108	206-767-5054	762-2209
Ozarks Coca-Cola Dr Pepper Bottling Co 1777 N Packer Rd *TF:* 866-223-4498 ■ *Web:* www.cocacolaozarks.com	Springfield	MO	65803	417-865-9900	865-7967
Plastipak Packaging Inc 41605 Ann Arbor Rd *Web:* www.plastipak.com	Plymouth	MI	48170	734-455-3600	354-7391
Pluto Corp PO Box 391 *Web:* www.plutocorp.com	French Lick	IN	47432	812-936-9988	936-2828
Poly-Tainer Inc 450 W Los Angeles Ave *Web:* www.polytainer.com	Simi Valley	CA	93065	805-526-3424	526-3430
Progressive Plastics Inc 14801 Emery Ave *TF:* 800-252-0053 ■ *Web:* www.progressive-plastics.com	Cleveland	OH	44135	216-252-5595	252-6327
Quality Containers of New England 247 Portland St *TF:* 800-639-1550 ■ *Web:* www.qualitycontainersne.com	Yarmouth	ME	04096	207-846-5420	
Redi Bag USA 135 Fulton Ave *TF:* 800-517-2247 ■ *Web:* www.redibagusa.com	New Hyde Park	NY	11040	516-746-0600	
RN Fink Mfg Company Inc 1530 Noble Rd PO Box 245 *Web:* www.rnfink.com	Williamston	MI	48895	517-655-4351	655-5119
Silgan Plastics Corp 14515 N Outer Forty Ste 210 *Fax Area Code: 314 ■ *TF:* 800-274-5426 ■ *Web:* www.silganplastics.com	Chesterfield	MO	63017	800-274-5426	469-5387*
Weber International Packing Company LLC 318 Cornelia St *Web:* www.weberintl.com	Plattsburgh	NY	12901	518-561-8282	561-4509
Western Container Corp 1600 First Ave *Web:* westerncontainercoke.com	Big Spring	TX	79720	432-263-8361	263-8075

99 BOWLING CENTERS

Company	City	State	Zip	Phone	Fax
Allen's Crosley Lanes 2400 E Evergreen Blvd *Web:* www.crosleylanes.com	Vancouver	WA	98661	360-693-4789	
AMF Bowling Worldwide Inc 7313 Bell Creek Rd *TF:* 800-342-5263 ■ *Web:* www.amf.com	Mechanicsville	VA	23111	800-342-5263	
Bowl America Inc 6446 Edsall Rd *NYSE: BWL.A* ■ *Web:* www.bowl-america.com	Alexandria	VA	22312	703-941-6300	
Bowl-A-Roll Lanes 1560 Jefferson Rd *Web:* www.bowl-a-roll.com	Rochester	NY	14623	585-427-7250	
Collins Bowling Centers Inc 750 E New Cir Rd *TF:* 866-252-2695 ■ *Web:* www.collinsbowling.com	Lexington	KY	40505	859-252-3429	
Fourth Street Bowl 1441 N Fourth St *Web:* www.4thstreetbowl.com	San Jose	CA	95112	408-453-5555	
Freeway Lanes Bowling Group 7300 Palisades Pkwy *Web:* freewaylanes.com	Mentor	OH	44060	440-946-5131	
George Pappas' Liberty Lanes 2501 S York Rd *Web:* www.georgepappaslibertylanes.com	Gastonia	NC	28052	704-868-2695	
Holiday Lanes 3316 Old Minden Rd *Web:* www.bowlholidaylanes.com	Bossier City	LA	71112	318-746-7331	
Lucky Strike Lanes Orange 20 City Blvd W Ste G2 *Web:* www.bowlluckystrike.com	Orange	CA	92868	714-937-5263	
Oakwood Lanes Inc 234 State Route 31 N *Web:* www.oakwoodlanes.com	Washington	NJ	07882	908-689-0310	
Olympic Lanes 110 Mason St *Web:* bizwi.rr.com	Greeneville	TN	37745	423-639-5166	
Plano Super Bowl Inc 2521 K Ave *Web:* planosuperbowl.com	Plano	TX	75074	972-881-0242	
Rowlett Bowl-A-Rama 5021 Lakeview Pkwy *Web:* www.rowlettbowlarama.com	Rowlett	TX	75088	972-475-7080	
Southern Bowl 1010 Us Hwy 31 S *Web:* www.royalpin.com	Greenwood	IN	46143	317-881-8686	

100 BOXES - CORRUGATED & SOLID FIBER

Company	City	State	Zip	Phone	Fax
Accurate Box Company Inc 86 Fifth Ave *Web:* www.accuratebox.com	Paterson	NJ	07524	973-345-2000	
Action Box Co Inc 6207 N Houston Rosslyn Rd *Web:* www.actionboxinc.com	Houston	TX	77091	713-869-7701	869-2086
Action Packaging 6995 Southbelt Dr Se *Web:* www.actionpackaging.com	Caledonia	MI	49316	616-871-5200	
Advance Packaging Corp 4459 40th St SE PO Box 888311 *Web:* www.advancepkg.com	Grand Rapids	MI	49588	616-949-6610	954-7373
Advanced Design 5090 McDougall Dr SW *Web:* www.stronghaven.com	Atlanta	GA	30336	404-699-1952	
Age Industries Ltd 3601 County Rd 316c *Web:* www.ageindustries.com	Cleburne	TX	76031	817-641-8178	641-2509
Akers Packaging Service Inc 2820 Lefferson Rd *Web:* www.akers-pkg.com	Middletown	OH	45044	513-422-6312	422-2829
Alma Container Corp 1000 Charles Ave *Web:* www.almacontainer.com	Alma	MI	48801	989-463-2106	
American Corrugated Products Inc 4700 Alkire Rd *TF:* 800-248-6840 ■ *Web:* www.americancorrugated.com	Columbus	OH	43228	614-870-2000	
American Environmental Container Corp 2302 Lasso Ln *TF:* 800-535-7946 ■ *Web:* www.sanjuanpools.com	Lakeland	FL	33801	863-666-3020	
Anchor Bay Packaging Corp 30905 23 Mile Rd *Web:* www.anchorbaypackaging.com	New Baltimore	MI	48047	586-949-4040	949-9998
Arrowhead Containers Inc 4330 Clary Blvd *TF:* 888-861-9225 ■ *Web:* www.smcpackaging.com	Kansas City	MO	64130	816-861-8050	
Artistic Carton Co 1975 Big Timber Rd *TF:* 800-735-7225 ■ *Web:* www.artisticcarton.com	Elgin	IL	60123	847-741-0247	741-8529
Arvco Container Corp 845 Gibson St *TF:* 800-968-9127 ■ *Web:* www.arvco.com	Kalamazoo	MI	49001	269-381-0900	381-2919
Atlas Container Corp 8140 Telegraph Rd *TF:* 800-394-4894 ■ *Web:* www.atlascontainer.com	Severn	MD	21144	410-551-6300	551-2703
Bates Container 6433 Davis Blvd *TF:* 888-541-0192 ■ *Web:* www.batescontainer.com	North Richland Hills	TX	76182	817-498-3200	581-8802
Bay Corrugated Container Inc 1655 W Seventh St *Web:* www.baycorr.com	Monroe	MI	48161	734-243-5400	
Beacon Container Corp 700 W First St *TF:* 800-422-8383 ■ *Web:* www.beaconcontainer.com	Birdsboro	PA	19508	610-582-2222	582-3992
Bell Container Corp 615 Ferry St *Web:* www.bellcontainer.com	Newark	NJ	07105	973-344-4400	344-0817
Boxes of St Louis Inc 1833 Knox Ave *Web:* www.boxesinc.com	Saint Louis	MO	63139	314-781-2600	
Brandt Box & Paper Company Inc 6 W Crisman Rd *Web:* www.brandtboxnj.com	Columbia	NJ	07832	908-496-4500	
Buckeye Container Inc 3350 Long Rd *TF:* 800-968-6894	Wooster	OH	44691	330-264-6336	264-0127
Buckeye Corrugated Inc 275 Springside Dr *Web:* www.bcipkg.com	Akron	OH	44333	330-576-0590	576-0600
Bulk-pack Inc 1025 N Ninth St *TF:* 800-498-4215 ■ *Web:* www.bulk-pack.com	Monroe	LA	71201	318-387-3260	387-6362
Cano Container Corp 3920 Enterprise Ct *Web:* www.canocontainer.com	Aurora	IL	60504	630-585-7500	
Capitol City Container Corp 8240 Zionsville Rd *TF:* 800-233-5145 ■ *Web:* www.capcitycont.com	Indianapolis	IN	46268	317-875-0290	
Carolina Container Co 909 Prospect St *TF:* 800-627-0825 ■ *Web:* www.carolinacontainer.com	High Point	NC	27260	336-883-7146	883-7576
Central Florida Box Corp 2950 Lk Emma Rd *Web:* www.centralfloridabox.com	Lake Mary	FL	32746	407-936-1277	
Central Graphics & Container Group Ltd 5526 Timberlea Blvd *Web:* www.centralgraphics.ca	Mississauga	ON	L4W2T7	905-238-8400	238-8127
Colorado Container Corp 4221 Monaco St *Web:* www.packagingcorp.com	Denver	CO	80216	303-331-0400	331-9455
Columbus Container Inc 3460 Commerce Dr *Web:* www.columbuscontainer.com	Columbus	IN	47201	812-376-9301	
Cornell Paper & Box Co 162 Van Dyke St *Web:* cornellpaper.com	Brooklyn	NY	11231	718-875-3202	875-3281
Corrugated Container Corp 6405 Commonwealth Dr SW *Web:* www.cccbox.com	Roanoke	VA	24018	540-774-0500	
DanHil Containers II Ltd 3715 Lucius McCelvey Dr *Web:* www.danhilcontainers.com	Temple	TX	76503	254-773-0704	
DeLine Box & Display 3700 Lima St *Web:* www.delinebox.com	Denver	CO	80239	303-373-1430	373-2325
Delta Corrugated Paper Products Corp W Ruby Ave *Web:* www.deltacorrugated.com	Palisades Park	NJ	07650	201-941-1910	941-9399
EMT International Inc 780 Centerline Dr *Web:* www.emtinternational.com	Hobart	WI	54155	920-468-5475	
Ferguson Supply & Box Manufacturing Co 10820 Quality Dr *TF:* 800-821-1023 ■ *Web:* www.fergusonbox.com	Charlotte	NC	28278	704-597-0310	597-5623
Flutes Inc 8252 Zionsville Rd *Web:* www.flutesllc.com	Indianapolis	IN	46268	317-870-6010	
Great Lakes Packaging Corp W 190 N 11393 Carnegie Dr *TF:* 800-261-4572 ■ *Web:* www.glpc.com	Germantown	WI	53022	262-255-2100	255-7290
Great Northern Corp 395 Stroebe Rd *TF:* 800-236-3671 ■ *Web:* www.greatnortherncorp.com	Appleton	WI	54914	920-739-3671	739-7096
Green Bay Packaging Inc 1700 Webster Ct *TF:* 800-236-8400 ■ *Web:* www.gbp.com	Green Bay	WI	54302	920-433-5111	
Island Container Group 44 Island Container Plz *Web:* www.islandcontainer.com	Wyandanch	NY	11798	631-253-4400	
KapStone Paper and Packaging Corp 300 Fibre Way PO Box 639 *Web:* www.kapstonepaper.com	Longview	WA	98632	360-425-1550	
Kearny Steel Container Corp 401 S St *Web:* www.kearnysteel.com	Newark	NJ	07105	973-589-2070	
Kelly Box & Packaging Corp 2801 Covington Rd *Web:* www.kellybox.com	Fort Wayne	IN	46802	260-432-4570	
Key Container Corp 21 Campbell St *TF:* 800-343-8811 ■ *Web:* www.keycontainercorp.com	Pawtucket	RI	02861	401-723-2000	725-5980
Lakeway Container Inc 5715 Superior Dr *Web:* www.lakewaycontainer.com	Morristown	TN	37814	423-581-2164	

				Phone	Fax
Landaal Packaging Systems Inc 3256 B Iron St *Web:* www.landaal.com	Burton	MI	48529	810-742-2730	
Lawrence Paper Co 2801 Lakeview Rd *TF:* 800-535-4553 ■ *Web:* www.lpco.net	Lawrence	KS	66049	785-843-8111	749-3904
Lone Star Container Corp 700 N Wildwood Dr **Fax Area Code:* 972 ■ *TF:* 800-552-6937 ■ *Web:* www.lonestarcontainer.com	Irving	TX	75061	800-552-6937	554-6081*
Menasha Corp 1645 Bergstrom Rd *TF:* 800-558-5073 ■ *Web:* www.menasha.com	Neenah	WI	54956	920-751-1000	751-1236
Menasha Packaging Co 1645 Bergstrom Rd *TF:* 800-558-5073 ■ *Web:* www.menasha.com	Neenah	WI	54956	920-751-1000	751-1075
Midland Packaging & Display Inc 3545 Nicholson Rd *Web:* midlandpkg.com	Franksville	WI	53126	262-886-8851	
Miller Container Corp 3402 78th Ave W *Web:* www.millercontainer.com	Rock Island	IL	61201	309-787-6161	
Montebello Container Corp 13220 Molette St *Web:* www.montcc.com	Santa Fe Springs	CA	90670	562-404-6221	
New England Wooden Ware Corp 205 School St Ste 201 *TF:* 800-252-9214 ■ *Web:* www.newoodenware.com	Gardner	MA	01440	978-632-3600	630-1513
North American Container Corp 1811 W Oak Pkwy Ste D *TF:* 800-929-0610 ■ *Web:* www.nacontainer.com	Marietta	GA	30062	770-431-4858	431-6957
Packaging Corp of America 1955 W Field Ct *NYSE: PKG* ■ *TF:* 800-456-4725 ■ *Web:* www.packagingcorp.com	Lake Forest	IL	60045	800-456-4725	
Packaging Services Inc of Tennessee 120 T Elmer Cox Rd *Web:* www.psipack.com	Greeneville	TN	37743	423-787-7711	
Pactiv Corp 1900 W Field Ct *TF:* 888-828-2850 ■ *Web:* www.pactiv.com	Lake Forest	IL	60045	847-482-2000	482-4738
Paragon Packaging Products Inc 625 Beaver Rd *Web:* www.parapack.com	Girard	PA	16417	814-774-9621	
Planet Paper Box Inc 2841 Langstaff Rd *Web:* www.planetpaper.com	Concord	ON	L4K4W7	416-798-7641	
President Container Inc 200 W Commercial Ave *Web:* www.presidentcontainergroup.com	Moonachie	NJ	07074	201-933-7500	
Progress Container Corp 635 Patrick Mill Rd SW *Web:* www.progresscontainer.com	Winder	GA	30680	678-425-2000	
R & R Corrugated Container Inc 360 Minor Rd *Web:* www.randrcorrugated.com	Bristol	CT	06010	860-584-1194	
R D A Container Corp 70 Cherry Rd *Web:* www.rdacontainer.com	Gates	NY	14624	585-247-2323	
Reliable Container Corp 9206 Santa Fe Springs Rd *Web:* www.reliablecontainer.com	Santa Fe Springs	CA	90670	562-861-6226	
Romanow Inc 346 University Ave *Web:* www.romanowcontainer.com	Westwood	MA	02090	781-320-9200	
Royal Group 1301 S 47th Ave *Web:* royalbox.com	Cicero	IL	60804	708-656-2020	
Sacramento Container Corp 4841 Urbani Ave *Web:* www.saccontainer.biz	Mcclellan	CA	95652	916-614-0580	
Sharpsville Container Corp 600 Main St *Web:* sharpsvillecontainer.com	Sharpsville	PA	16150	724-962-1100	
Shoreline Container Inc 4450 N 136th Ave PO Box 1993 *TF:* 800-968-2088 ■ *Web:* www.shorelinecontainer.com	Holland	MI	49422	616-399-2088	399-7240
Southern Container Ltd 10410 Papalote St Ste 130 *Web:* www.southerncontainer.com	Houston	TX	77041	713-466-5661	466-4223
Specialty Container Corp 1608 Plantation Rd *Web:* www.specialtycontainer.com	Dallas	TX	75235	214-637-0160	
Stephen Gould Corp 35 S Jefferson Rd *Web:* www.stephengould.com	Whippany	NJ	07981	973-428-1500	428-5274
Strathcona Paper LP 77 County Rd 16 RR #7 *Web:* www.strathconapaper.com	Napanee	ON	K7R3L2	613-378-6672	
Stronghaven Inc 5090 McDougall Dr SW *TF:* 800-331-7835 ■ *Web:* www.stronghaven.com	Atlanta	GA	30336	404-699-1952	699-1825
Technology Container Corp 207 Greenwood St *Web:* www.techcontainer.com	Worcester	MA	01607	508-752-8000	
TimBar Packaging & Display 148 N Penn St *TF:* 800-572-6061 ■ *Web:* www.timbar.com	Hanover	PA	17331	717-632-4727	632-1243
Tri-Lakes Container 533 S First St *Web:* www.tri-lakes.com	Pierceton	IN	46562	574-594-2217	
Valiant Enterprise LLC 2300 Mcdermott Rd	Plano	TX	75025	972-390-7410	447-9156
Victory Packaging LP 3555 Timmons Ln Ste 1440 *Web:* www.victorypackaging.com	Houston	TX	77027	713-961-3299	
Welch Packaging Group 1020 Herman St *TF:* 800-246-2475 ■ *Web:* www.welchpkg.com	Elkhart	IN	46516	574-295-2460	295-1527
York Container 138 Mt Scion Rd PO Box 3008 *Web:* www.yorkcontainer.com	York	PA	17402	717-757-7611	755-8090

101 BOXES - PAPERBOARD

Products made by these companies include setup, folding, and nonfolding boxes.

				Phone	Fax
Advance Paper Box Co 6100 S Gramercy Pl *Web:* www.advancepaperbox.com	Los Angeles	CA	90047	323-750-2550	752-8133
Apex Paper Box Co 5601 Walworth Ave *TF Cust Svc:* 800-438-2269 ■ *Web:* boxit.com	Cleveland	OH	44102	216-416-9475	
Arkay Packaging Corp 350 E Pk Dr *Web:* www.arkay.com	Roanoke	VA	24019	540-977-3031	977-2503
Astronics Corp 130 Commerce Way *NASDAQ: ATRO* ■ *Web:* www.astronics.com	East Aurora	NY	14052	716-805-1599	655-0309
Boelter Industries Inc 202 Galewski Dr *Web:* www.wspackaging.com	Winona	MN	55987	507-452-2315	452-2649
Boutwell Owens & Co Inc 251 Authority Dr *Web:* www.boutwellowens.com	Fitchburg	MA	01420	978-343-3067	343-9132
Burd & Fletcher 3000 W Geospace Dr *TF:* 800-821-2776 ■ *Web:* www.burdfletcher.com	Independence	MO	64056	816-257-0291	
Calpine Containers Inc 9499 N Ford Wahington Rd Ste 103 *Web:* www.calpinecontainers.com	Fresno	CA	93730	559-519-7199	
Caraustar Industries Inc 5000 Austell-Powder Springs Rd Ste 300 *TF:* 800-858-1438 ■ *Web:* www.caraustar.com	Austell	GA	30106	770-948-3100	
Carton Service Inc First Quality Dr PO Box 702 *TF General:* 800-533-7744 ■ *Web:* www.cartonservice.com	Shelby	OH	44875	419-342-5010	342-4804
Climax Packaging Inc 4515 Easton Rd *TF:* 800-225-4629	Saint Joseph	MO	64503	816-233-3181	233-2475
Colbert Packaging Corp 28355 N Bradley Rd *Web:* www.colbertpkg.com	Lake Forest	IL	60045	847-367-5990	367-4403
Complemar Partners 500 Lee Rd Ste 200 *TF:* 800-388-7254 ■ *Web:* www.complemar.com	Rochester	NY	14606	585-647-5800	647-5800
Cornell Paper & Box Co 162 Van Dyke St *Web:* cornellpaper.com	Brooklyn	NY	11231	718-875-3202	875-3281
Curtis Packaging Corp 44 Berkshire Rd *Web:* www.curtispackaging.com	Sandy Hook	CT	06482	203-426-5861	426-2684
Dee Paper Box Company Inc 100 Broomall St *TF:* 800-359-0041 ■ *Web:* deepaperbox.com	Chester	PA	19013	610-876-9285	876-7040
Diamond Packaging Company Inc 111 Commerce Dr PO Box 23620 *TF:* 800-333-4079 ■ *Web:* www.diamondpackaging.com	Rochester	NY	14692	585-334-8030	334-9141
Fuller Box Co 150 Chestnut St *Web:* www.fullerbox.com	North Attleboro	MA	02760	508-695-2525	695-2187
Graphic Packaging International 1500 Riveredge Parkway NW Ste 100 *NYSE: GPK* ■ *TF:* 888-548-8395 ■ *Web:* www.graphicpkg.com	Atlanta	GA	30328	770-240-7200	
House of Packaging Inc 2225 Via Cerro Ste B *Web:* www.hopbox.com	Riverside	CA	92509	626-369-3371	
Hub Folding Box Co Inc 774 Norfolk St *TF:* 800-334-1113 ■ *Web:* www.hubfoldingbox.com	Mansfield	MA	02048	508-339-0005	339-0102
Knight Paper Box Company Inc 4651 W 72nd St *Web:* knightpack.com	Chicago	IL	60629	773-585-2035	585-3824
Mafcote Industries Inc 108 Main St *Web:* www.mafcote.com	Norwalk	CT	06851	203-847-8500	849-9177
Malnove Inc 13434 F St *TF:* 800-228-9877 ■ *Web:* www.malnove.com	Omaha	NE	68137	402-330-1100	330-2941
Menasha Corp 1645 Bergstrom Rd *TF:* 800-558-5073 ■ *Web:* www.menasha.com	Neenah	WI	54956	920-751-1000	751-1236
MOD-PAC Corp 1801 Elmwood Ave *NASDAQ: MPAC* ■ *TF Cust Svc:* 866-216-6193 ■ *Web:* www.modpac.com	Buffalo	NY	14207	716-873-0640	873-6008
Pactiv Corp 1900 W Field Ct *TF:* 888-828-2850 ■ *Web:* www.pactiv.com	Lake Forest	IL	60045	847-482-2000	482-4738
Panoramic Inc 1500 N Parker Dr *TF:* 800-333-1394 ■ *Web:* www.panoramicinc.com	Janesville	WI	53545	608-754-8850	754-5703
Paragon Packaging Inc 7700 Centerville Rd *TF:* 888-615-0065 ■ *Web:* www.paragonpackaging.com	Ferndale	CA	95536	707-786-4004	
Rice Packaging Inc 356 Somers Rd *TF:* 800-367-6725 ■ *Web:* www.ricepackaging.com	Ellington	CT	06029	860-872-8341	
Royal Paper Box Company of California Inc PO Box 458 *Web:* www.royalpaperbox.com	Montebello	CA	90640	323-728-7041	722-2646
RTS Packaging LLC 504 Thrasher St **Fax Area Code:* 770 ■ *TF:* 800-558-6984 ■ *Web:* www.rtspackaging.com	Norcross	GA	30071	800-558-6984	449-0261*
Rusken Packaging Inc PO Box 2100 *TF:* 800-232-8108 ■ *Web:* www.rusken.com	Cullman	AL	35056	256-734-0092	734-3008
Seaboard Folding Box Co Inc 35 Daniels St *TF:* 800-225-6313 ■ *Web:* www.seaboardbox.com	Fitchburg	MA	01420	978-342-8921	342-1105
Sheboygan Paper Box Co 716 Clara Ave PO Box 326 *Web:* www.spbox.com	Sheboygan	WI	53082	920-458-8373	458-2901
Southern Standard Cartons Inc 2415 Plantside Dr *Web:* thestandardgroup.com	Louisville	KY	40299	502-491-2760	491-2767
Stephen Gould Corp 35 S Jefferson Rd *Web:* www.stephengould.com	Whippany	NJ	07981	973-428-1500	428-5274
Sterling Paper Co 2155 E Castor Ave *Web:* fieldnotesphilly.wordpress.com	Philadelphia	PA	19134	215-546-1146	546-1180
Tetra Pak Inc 753 Geneva Pkwy N *Web:* www.tetrapak.com	Lake Geneva	WI	53147	262-249-7400	
Thoro-Packaging Inc 1467 Davril Cir *Web:* www.thoropackaging.com	Corona	CA	92880	951-278-2100	
Triumph Packaging Group 515 W Crossroads Pkwy	Bolingbrook	IL	60440	630-771-0900	
Utah Paper Box Company Inc 920 South 700 West *Web:* www.upbslc.com	Salt Lake City	UT	84104	801-363-0093	

102 BREWERIES

See Also Malting Products p. 2710

				Phone	Fax
Abita Brewing Co 21084 Hwy 36 *TF:* 800-737-2311 ■ *Web:* www.abita.com	Covington	LA	70433	985-893-3143	898-3546
Alaskan Brewing Co 5429 Shaune Dr *Web:* www.alaskanbeer.com	Juneau	AK	99801	907-780-5866	780-4514
Anchor Brewing Co 1705 Mariposa St *Web:* www.anchorbrewing.com	San Francisco	CA	94107	415-863-8350	552-7094
Anheuser-Busch InBev 250 Pk Ave *Web:* www.ab-inbev.com	New York	NY	10177	212-573-8800	
Asahi Beer USA Inc 3625 Del Amo Blvd Ste 250 *Web:* www.asahibeerusa.com	Torrance	CA	90503	310-214-9051	542-5108
Boston Beer Co 1 Design Ctr Pl Ste 850 *NYSE: SAM* ■ *TF:* 888-661-2337 ■ *Web:* www.bostonbeer.com	Boston	MA	02210	617-368-5000	368-5500
Boulder Beer Co 2880 Wilderness Pl *Web:* www.boulderbeer.com	Boulder	CO	80301	303-444-8448	
Boulevard Brewing Co 2501 SW Blvd *Web:* www.boulevard.com	Kansas City	MO	64108	816-474-7095	474-1722

Company	City	State	Zip	Phone	Fax
BridgePort Brewing Co 1318 NW Northrup St. TF: 888-834-7546 ■ Web: www.bridgeportbrew.com	Portland	OR	97209	503-241-7179	
Brooklyn Brewery, The 79 N 11th St. Web: www.brooklynbrewery.com	Brooklyn	NY	11211	718-486-7422	486-7440
Capital Brewery 7734 Terr Ave. Web: www.capital-brewery.com	Middleton	WI	53562	608-836-7100	
Cold Spring Brewing Co 219 Red River Ave N PO Box 476 Web: www.coldspringbrewery.com	Cold Spring	MN	56320	320-685-8686	685-8318
Craft Brew Alliance 929 N Russell St NASDAQ: BREW ■ Web: craftbrew.com	Portland	OR	97227	503-331-7270	
DG Yuengling & Son Inc 5th & Mahantongo St Web: www.yuengling.com	Pottsville	PA	17901	570-622-4141	622-4011
DL Geary Brewing Company Inc 38 Evergreen Dr Web: www.gearybrewing.com	Portland	ME	04103	207-878-2337	878-2388
Flying Dog Brewery LLC 4607 Wedgewood Blvd. Web: www.flyingdogales.com	Frederick	MD	21703	301-694-7899	694-2971
Fresh Ale Pubs LLC 1317 W Northern Lights Blvd Web: freshalepubs.com	Anchorage	AK	99503	907-222-1560	
Harpoon Brewery 306 Northern Ave Web: www.harpoonbrewery.com	Boston	MA	02210	617-574-9551	
Heineken USA 360 Hamilton Ave Ste 1103 Web: www.heineken.com	White Plains	NY	10601	914-681-4100	681-1900
Humboldt Brews 856 Tenth St. Web: www.humbrews.com	Arcata	CA	95521	707-826-2739	
Jacob Leinenkugel Brewing Co 124 E Elm St. TF General: 888-534-6437 ■ Web: www.leinie.com	Chippewa Falls	WI	54729	715-723-5558	723-7158
Keurig Inc 53 S Ave TF: 866-901-2739 ■ Web: www.keurig.com	Burlington	MA	01867	866-901-2739	
Labatt Breweries of Canada 207 Queen's Quay W Ste 299 TF Cust Svc: 800-268-2337 ■ Web: www.labatt.com	Toronto	ON	M5J1A7	416-361-5050	
Latrobe Brewing Co 119 Jefferson St. Web: www.rollingrock.com	Latrobe	PA	15650	724-537-5545	
Lion Brewery Inc 700 N Pennsylvania Ave Web: www.lionbrewery.com	Wilkes-Barre	PA	18705	570-823-8801	823-6686
Long Trail Brewing Co 5520 Rt 4 Web: www.longtrail.com	Bridgewater Corners	VT	05035	802-672-5011	672-5012
Malt Products Corp 88 Market St. TF: 800-526-0180 ■ Web: www.maltproducts.com	Saddle Brook	NJ	07663	201-845-4420	845-0028
Matt Brewing Co 811 Edward St. Web: www.saranac.com	Utica	NY	13502	315-624-2400	624-2452
McMenamins 430 N Killingsworth TF: 800-669-8610 ■ Web: www.mcmenamins.com	Portland	OR	97217	503-223-0109	294-0837
Mendocino Brewing Co 455 Kunzler Ranch Rd. Web: www.mendobrew.com	Ukiah	CA	95482	707-462-1697	462-1699
Minhas Craft Brewery 1208 14th Ave Web: www.minhasbrewery.com	Monroe	WI	53566	608-325-3191	325-3198
Molson Coors Brewing Co 1225 17th St Ste 3200 NYSE: TAP ■ TF: 800-645-5376 ■ Web: www.molsoncoors.com	Denver	CO	80202	303-927-2337	
New Belgium Brewing Co 500 Linden St. Web: www.newbelgium.com	Fort Collins	CO	80524	970-221-0524	221-0535
North Coast Brewing Company Inc 455 N Main St Web: www.northcoastbrewing.com	Fort Bragg	CA	95437	707-964-2739	964-8768
Odell Brewing Co 800 E Lincoln Ave Web: www.odellbrewing.com	Fort Collins	CO	80524	970-498-9070	498-0706
Pabst Brewing Co, The 10635 Santa Monica Blvd Ste 350 TF: 800-947-2278 ■ Web: www.pabstbrewingco.com	Los Angeles	CA	90025	800-947-2278	
Pittsburgh Brewing Co 3340 Liberty Ave. Web: www.pittsburghbrewing.com	Pittsburgh	PA	15201	412-682-7400	
Pyramid Brewing Co 91 S Royal Brougham Way Web: www.pyramidbrew.com	Seattle	WA	98134	206-682-8322	682-8420
Rogue Ales Co 2320 OSU Dr. Web: www.rogue.com	Newport	OR	97365	541-867-3660	867-3260
Sierra Nevada Brewing Co 1075 E 20th St Web: www.sierranevada.com	Chico	CA	95928	530-893-3520	893-1275
Summit Brewing Co 910 Montreal Cir Web: www.summitbrewing.com	Saint Paul	MN	55102	651-265-7800	265-7801
Widmer Bros Brewing Co 929 N Russell St. Web: www.widmerbrothers.com	Portland	OR	97227	503-281-2437	281-1496

BROKERS

See Commodity Contracts Brokers & Dealers p. 1996; Electronic Communications Networks (ECNs) p. 2226; Insurance Agents, Brokers, Services p. 2570; Mortgage Lenders & Loan Brokers p. 2778; Real Estate Agents & Brokers p. 3041; Securities Brokers & Dealers p. 3163

103 BRUSHES & BROOMS

See Also Art Materials & Supplies - Mfr p. 1745

Company	City	State	Zip	Phone	Fax
A & B Brush Manufacturing Corp 1150 Three Ranch Rd Web: abbrush.com	Duarte	CA	91010	626-303-8856	303-1207
Abco Cleaning Products 6800 NW 36th Ave. TF: 888-694-2226 ■ Web: www.abcoproducts.com	Miami	FL	33147	305-694-2226	694-0451
American Brush Company Inc 300 Industrial Blvd Web: www.americanbrush.com	Claremont	NH	03743	603-542-9951	
Brush Research Mfg Company Inc 4642 Floral Dr Web: www.brushresearch.com	Los Angeles	CA	90022	323-261-2193	268-6587
Brushes Corp 5400 Smith Rd. Web: www.brushescorp.com	Cleveland	OH	44142	216-267-8084	267-9077
Brushtech Inc 4 Matt Ave Web: brushtechbrushes.com	Plattsburgh	NY	12901	518-563-8420	563-0581
Carlisle Sanitary Maintenance Products 402 S Black River St *Fax Area Code: 800 ■ TF: 800-654-8210 ■ Web: www.carlislefsp.com	Sparta	WI	54656	608-269-2151	872-4701*
Corona Brushes Inc 5065 Savarese Cir TF: 800-458-3483 ■ Web: www.coronabrushes.com	Tampa	FL	33634	813-885-2525	882-9810
Crystal Lake Manufacturing Inc 2225 Alabama 14 PO Box 159 TF: 800-633-8720 ■ Web: www.crystallakemfg.com	Autaugaville	AL	36003	334-365-3342	365-3332
Detroit Quality Brush Mfg 32165 Schoolcraft Rd. TF: 800-722-3037 ■ Web: dqb.com	Livonia	MI	48150	734-525-5660	525-0437
Felton Brush Inc 7 Burton Dr TF: 800-258-9702 ■ Web: www.feltoninc.com	Londonderry	NH	03053	603-425-0200	425-0200
Fuller Brush Co, The PO Box 729 1 Fuller Way TF Cust Svc: 800-522-0499 ■ Web: www.fuller.com	Great Bend	KS	67530	620-792-1711	
Gordon Brush Mfg Company Inc 6247 Randolph St. TF: 800-950-7950 ■ Web: www.gordonbrush.com	Commerce	CA	90040	323-724-7777	724-1111
Greenwood Mop & Broom Inc 312 Palmer St. TF: 800-635-6849 ■ Web: www.greenwoodmopandbroom.com	Greenwood	SC	29646	864-227-8411	227-3200
Harper Brush Works Inc 400 N Second St. TF: 800-223-7894 ■ Web: www.harperbrush.com	Fairfield	IA	52556	641-472-5186	472-3187
Industrial Brush Company Inc 105 Clinton Rd TF: 800-241-9860 ■ Web: www.indbrush.com	Fairfield	NJ	07004	973-575-0455	575-6169
Industries for the Blind 445 S Curtis Rd. TF: 800-642-8778 ■ Web: www.ibmilwaukee.com	West Allis	WI	53214	414-778-3040	778-3041
Industries of the Blind Inc 920 W Lee St Web: www.industriesoftheblind.com	Greensboro	NC	27403	336-274-1591	
Kline Hawkes & Co 11726 San Vicente Blvd Ste 300	Los Angeles	CA	90049	310-442-4700	826-2299
Laitner Brush Co 1561 Laitner Dr TF Cust Svc: 800-423-6805	Traverse City	MI	49686	231-929-3300	929-7219
Libman Co 220 N Sheldon St *Fax Area Code: 217 ■ TF: 877-818-3380 ■ Web: www.libman.com	Arcola	IL	61910	877-818-3380	268-4168*
Linzer Products Corp 248 Wyandanch Ave Web: www.linzerproducts.com	West Babylon	NY	11704	631-253-3333	253-9750
Magnolia Brush Mfg Ltd 1000 N Cedar PO Box 932 *Fax Area Code: 800 ■ TF: 800-248-2261 ■ Web: www.magnoliabrush.com	Clarksville	TX	75426	903-427-2261	427-5231*
Mill-Rose Co 7995 Tyler Blvd TF: 800-321-3533 ■ Web: www.millrose.com	Mentor	OH	44060	440-255-9171	255-5039
Osborn International 5401 Hamilton Ave. TF Cust Svc: 800-720-3358 ■ Web: www.osborn.com	Cleveland	OH	44114	216-361-1900	361-1913
Padco Inc 2220 Elm St SE TF: 800-328-5513 ■ Web: www.padco.com	Minneapolis	MN	55414	612-378-7270	378-9388
PFERD Milwaukee Brush Company Inc 30 Jytek Dr TF: 800-342-9015 ■ Web: www.pferdusa.com	Leominster	MA	01453	978-840-6420	840-6421
Rubberset Co 101 W Prospect Ave TF: 800-345-4939 ■ Web: www.rubberset.com	Cleveland	OH	44115	800-345-4939	
Sanderson-MacLeod Inc 1199 S Main St PO Box 50 TF: 866-522-3481 ■ Web: www.sandersonmacleod.com	Palmer	MA	01069	413-283-3481	289-1919
SM Arnold Inc 7901 Michigan Ave TF Cust Svc: 800-325-7865 ■ Web: www.smarnold.com	Saint Louis	MO	63111	314-544-4103	544-3159
Super Brush Co 800 Worcester St Web: www.superbrush.com	Springfield	MA	01151	413-543-1442	543-1523
Sweepster Inc 2800 N Zeeb Rd. TF: 800-456-7100 ■ Web: www.paladinlightconstructiongroup.com	Dexter	MI	48130	734-996-9116	996-9014
Universal Brush Manufacturing Co 16200 Dixie Hwy TF: 800-323-3474 ■ Web: www.universalbrush.com	Markham	IL	60428	708-331-1700	331-4923
Weiler Corp 1 Wildwood Dr. TF Cust Svc: 800-835-9999 ■ Web: www.weilercorp.com	Cresco	PA	18326	570-595-7495	595-2002
Wooster Brush Co 604 Madison Ave TF: 800-392-7246 ■ Web: www.woosterbrush.com	Wooster	OH	44691	330-264-4440	263-0495
Zephyr Mfg Company Inc 200 Mitchell Rd TF: 800-821-7197 ■ Web: www.zephyrmfg.com	Sedalia	MO	65301	660-827-0352	827-0713

104 BUILDING MAINTENANCE SERVICES

See Also Cleaning Services p. 1940

Company	City	State	Zip	Phone	Fax
Ability Janitorial Services Ltd 884 Churchill Ave S	Ottawa	ON	K1Z5H2	613-722-3566	
Able Service Contractors Inc 13505 Dulles Technology Dr Ste 2 Web: www.ableservice.com	Herndon	VA	20171	571-323-2990	
Action Maintenance Systems Inc 251 251 E Empire St St. Web: actionmaintenance.net	San Jose	CA	95112	408-287-8000	
Advance Building Maintenance 9601 Wilshire Blvd Ste Gl25 Web: www.advancemaintenance.com	Beverly Hills	CA	90210	310-247-0077	
AHI Facility Services Inc 625 Yuma Ct. Web: www.ahifs.com	Dallas	TX	75208	214-741-3714	
Aid Maintenance Co 300 Roosevelt Ave TF: 800-886-6627 ■ Web: www.aidmaintenance.com	Pawtucket	RI	02860	401-722-6627	723-6860
Allied Building Service Company of Detroit Inc 1801 Howard St Web: www.teamallied.com	Detroit	MI	48216	313-230-0800	
AM Facility Services 8481 Bash St Ste 1700 Web: www.amincorporated.com	Indianapolis	IN	46250	317-578-2290	
Ambius Inc 485 E Half Day Rd Ste 450 Web: www.ambius.com	Buffalo Grove	IL	60089	847-634-4258	
AME Services Inc 23 Barreca St.	Norco	LA	70079	504-712-3220	

Company / Address	City	State	ZIP	Phone	Fax
Anka Behavioral Health Inc 1850 Gateway Blvd Ste 900 *Web:* www.ankabhi.org	Concord	CA	94520	925-825-4700	
Associated Building Maintenance Company Inc 2140 Priest Bridge Ct *Web:* www.abmcoinc.com	Crofton	MD	21114	410-721-1818	
Aztec Landscaping Inc 7980 Lemon Grove Way *Web:* www.azteclandscaping.com	Lemon Grove	CA	91945	619-464-3303	
Broadway Services Inc 3709 E Monument St *Web:* www.broadwayservices.com	Baltimore	MD	21205	410-563-6900	563-6960
Building Maintenance Services LLC 1541 S Beretania St Ste 204 *Web:* www.bmsnationwide.com	Honolulu	HI	96826	808-983-1250	
Building Restoration Inc 2423 Ravine Rd *Web:* www.gobri.com	Kalamazoo	MI	49004	269-345-0567	
Burns Janitor Service 1631 W Hill St *Web:* www.burnsjanitor.com	Louisville	KY	40210	502-585-4548	
Busy Bee Cleaning Company Inc 18 Wilson Ave *Web:* busybeecleaningcompany.com	West Chester	PA	19382	610-430-6888	
Calico Building Services Inc 15550-C Rockfield Blvd *TF:* 800-576-7313 ■ *Web:* www.calicoweb.com	Irvine	CA	92618	800-576-7313	
Castle Keepers of Charleston Inc 2030 Harley St *Web:* www.castle-keepers.com	North Charleston	SC	29406	843-572-4757	
CBM Systems Inc 13515 Sw Millikan Way	Beaverton	OR	97005	503-520-1660	
CCS of South Carolina Inc 2325 Prosperity Way Ste 8 *Web:* www.cleanworldusa.com	Florence	SC	29501	843-669-2273	
Coastal Building Maintenance 15405 Nw Seventh Ave *Web:* www.cbmflorida.com	Miami	FL	33169	305-681-6100	
Courtesy Building Services Inc 2154 W Northwest Hwy Ste 214 *TF:* 800-479-3853 ■ *Web:* www.courtesybldgservices.com	Dallas	TX	75220	972-831-1444	
Cristi Cleaning Service Corp 77 Trinity Pl *Web:* www.cristicleaning.com	Hackensack	NJ	07601	201-883-1717	
Cummins Facility Services 5202 Marion Waldo Rd *TF:* 800-451-5629 ■ *Web:* www.cumminsfs.com	Prospect	OH	43342	740-726-9800	
Customized Performance Inc 1342 Ridder Park Dr *Web:* www.custgroup.com	San Jose	CA	95131	408-437-1720	
D & d Elevator Maintenance Inc 38 Hayes St *Web:* ddelevator.com	Elmsford	NY	10523	914-347-4344	
Data Clean Corp 1033 Graceland Ave *Web:* www.dataclean.com	Des Plaines	IL	60016	847-296-3100	
Davis Professional Services Inc 820 Greenbrier Cir Ste 18 *Web:* www.davisproserv.com	Chesapeake	VA	23320	757-431-1344	
Defender Services Inc 9031 Garners Ferry Rd *Web:* www.defenderservices.com	Hopkins	SC	29061	803-776-4220	
DMS Facility Services Inc 417 East Huntington Dr *TF:* 800-443-8677 ■ *Web:* www.dmsfacilityservices.com	Monrovia	CA	91016	626-305-8500	
Dominion Due Diligence Group 4121 Cox Rd Ste 200 *Web:* d3g.com	Glen Allen	VA	23060	804-358-2020	
Drayton Group 2295 N Opdyke Rd Ste D *TF:* 888-655-4442 ■ *Web:* www.draytongroupinc.com	Auburn Hills	MI	48326	888-655-4442	
E- Konomy Pool Service Inc 3821 W Costco Dr Ste 115 *Web:* www.e-konomy.com	Tucson	AZ	85711	520-325-6427	
Eagle Cleaning Service Inc 525 Belview St *TF:* 877-864-5696 ■ *Web:* www.eaglecleaningservice.com	Bessemer	AL	35020	205-424-5252	
Ecolo Odor Control Technologies Inc 59 Penn Dr *TF:* 800-667-6355 ■ *Web:* www.ecolo.com	Toronto	ON	M9L2A6	416-740-3900	740-3800
Empire Maintenance Co Inc 624 S Palm Ave *Web:* www.empiremaintenance.com	Alhambra	CA	91803	626-289-8755	
Epic Industries Inc 1007 Jersey Ave *Web:* www.epicindustries.com	New Brunswick	NJ	08901	732-249-6867	
FBG Service Corp 407 S 27th Ave *TF:* 800-777-8326 ■ *Web:* www.fbgservices.com	Omaha	NE	68131	402-346-4422	595-5044
Flagship Facility Services Inc 1050 N Fifth St *Web:* www.flagshipinc.com	San Jose	CA	95112	408-977-0155	
Fresh Start Janitorial & Property Services Inc 806 E Ninth St *Web:* www.freshstartjanitorial.com	South Sioux City	NE	68776	402-494-9980	
Gerrus Maintenance Inc 95 Northfield Ave *Web:* www.gerrus.com	Edison	NJ	08837	732-225-0662	
GFS Building Maintenance Inc 20 Blaine St *Web:* www.gfsservices.com	Manchester	NH	03102	603-668-6612	
Goodwill Ind of Fort Worth PO Box 15520 *Web:* www.goodwillfortworth.org	Fort Worth	TX	76119	817-332-7866	
Griesbach Diamond Water N1022 Quality Dr *TF:* 800-236-8931 ■ *Web:* www.diamondh2o.com	Greenville	WI	54942	920-757-5440	
Hastings Water Works Inc 10331 Brecksville Rd *Web:* hastingswaterworks.com	Brecksville	OH	44141	440-832-7700	
HB Management Group Inc 7100 Broadway Ste 6L *Web:* www.hbmgmt.com	Denver	CO	80221	303-428-1873	
Home Tester, The 10555 Sw Tigard St Apt 57 *Web:* www.thehometester.com	Tigard	OR	97223	503-515-1833	
Horizon Services Co 250 Governor St *TF:* 800-949-5323 ■ *Web:* www.horizonsvcs.com	East Hartford	CT	06108	800-949-5323	
Interstate Contract Cleaning Services Inc 509 Blairhill Rd *Web:* www.interstateccs.com	Charlotte	NC	28217	704-522-7773	
ISS Facilities Services Inc 1019 Central Pkwy N Ste 100 *Web:* www.us.issworld.com	San Antonio	TX	78232	210-495-6021	
James City Service Authority Water Treatment 101 Mounts Bay Rd *Web:* www.james-city.va.us	Williamsburg	VA	23185	757-229-1611	
James L Maher Center 120 Hillside Ave *Web:* www.mahercenter.org	Newport	RI	02840	401-846-0340	
Janitronics Bldg Services 29 Sawyer Rd *Web:* www.janitronics.com	Waltham	MA	02453	781-647-5570	893-5878
Kleen Air Research Inc 4510 Helton Dr *Web:* www.filterpro.com	Florence	AL	35630	256-767-5122	
Landmark Building Maintenance Inc 1725 W 17th St *Web:* www.landmarkcleaning.com	Tempe	AZ	85281	480-303-0244	
M&I Professional Services Inc 7667 N Ave *Web:* www.mlproclean.com	Lemon Grove	CA	91945	619-469-1604	
Man-maid Cleaning Services Inc 29 Fox Creek Dr *Web:* www.manmaidcleaning.com	Rehoboth Beach	DE	19971	631-281-5308	
Master Klean Janitorial Inc 2149 S Clermont St *Web:* www.masterklean.com	Denver	CO	80222	303-753-6084	
Master-Lee Energy Services Corp 5631 Route 981 *TF:* 800-662-4493 ■ *Web:* www.masterlee.com	Latrobe	PA	15650	724-539-8060	
Metroclean Commercial Building Services Inc 9000 Southwest Fwy Ste 412 *Web:* www.metrocleanonline.com	Houston	TX	77074	713-255-0100	
Meyer Brothers Building Company Inc 800 E 101st Ter Ste 120 *Web:* www.meyerbro.com	Kansas City	MO	64131	816-246-4800	
Midwest Janitorial Service 2831 Falls Ave *Web:* midwestjanitorialservice.com	Waterloo	IA	50701	319-233-6787	
Mister Kleen Maintenance Company Inc 7302 Beulah St *Web:* www.misterkleen.com	Alexandria	VA	22315	703-719-6900	
My Cleaning Service Inc 2701 Cresmont Ave *Web:* www.mycleaningservice.com	Baltimore	MD	21211	410-889-0505	
Pacific Building Maintenance Inc 2646 Palma Dr Ste 320 *Web:* www.pacificbuildingmaintenance.com	Ventura	CA	93003	805-642-0214	
Peerless Maintenance Service 1100 S Euclid St *Web:* www.peerlesssvc.com	Fullerton	CA	92832	714-871-3380	
Peninsula Cleaning Service Inc 12610 Patrick Henry Dr Ste A *Web:* www.peninsulacleaning.com	Newport News	VA	23602	757-833-1603	
Power Vac Services 50 Goebel Ave *Web:* www.powervac.ca	Cambridge	ON	N3C1Z1	519-658-4140	
Powerlink Facilities Management Services 3031 W Grand Blvd Ste 640 *Web:* www.powerlinkonline.com	Detroit	MI	48202	313-309-2020	
Powerplant Maintenance Specialists Inc (PMSI) 2900 Bristol St Ste H202 *Web:* www.pmsipower.com	Costa Mesa	CA	92626	714-427-6900	427-6906
Professional Maintenance Care 4912 Naples St *Web:* www.pmsjanitorial.com	San Diego	CA	92110	619-276-1150	
PureChoice Inc 11481 Rupp Dr *Web:* www.purechoice.com	Burnsville	MN	55112	952-985-0500	
Rembrandt Commercial Cleaning 20900 Swenson Dr Ste 250 *Web:* www.rembrandtcleaning.com	Waukesha	WI	53186	262-798-1038	
Roof to deck Decoration Inc 365 Webster St Ste 6 *Web:* www.rooftodeckdecoration.com	Saint Paul	MN	55102	651-699-3504	
Sealco Data Center Services Ltd 1761 International Pkwy Ste 127 *Web:* www.sealco.net	Richardson	TX	75081	972-234-5567	
Shamrock Acquisition Corp 10901 Danka Cir N Ste B *Web:* www.shamrockclean.com	Saint Petersburg	FL	33716	727-585-6007	
Shannon Diversified Inc 1190 N Del Rio Pl *TF:* 800-794-2345 ■ *Web:* www.shannoncompany.com	Ontario	CA	91764	800-794-2345	
Sonitec-Vortisand Inc 1400 Tees St *Web:* www.sonitec.com	St-laurent	QC	H4R2B6	514-335-2200	
Style Crest Inc 2450 Enterprise St *TF:* 800-925-4440 ■ *Web:* www.stylecrestinc.com	Fremont	OH	43420	419-332-7369	332-8763
Temco Service Industries Inc 417 Fifth Ave 9th Fl *Web:* temcoservices.com	New York	NY	10016	212-889-6353	213-9854
Toledo Building Services 2121 Adams St *Web:* www.toledobuildingservices.com	Toledo	OH	43604	419-241-3101	
Treco Service Inc 904 N Zarzamora St *Web:* www.trecoservices.com	San Antonio	TX	78207	210-432-4100	
Unichem Inc 8 N Kings Rd *Web:* www.unichem.com	Greenville	SC	29605	864-422-0191	
United Building Maintenance Inc 165 Easy St *Web:* www.ubm-usa.com	Carol Stream	IL	60188	630-653-4848	
UV Pure Technologies Inc 60 Venture Dr Unit 19 *TF:* 888-407-9997 ■ *Web:* www.uvpure.com	Toronto	ON	M1B3S4	416-208-9884	
Vanguard Resources Inc 17300 Henderson Pass Ste 200 *Web:* www.vanguardresources.com	San Antonio	TX	78232	210-495-1950	
Whitehall Associates Inc 416 Southview Ave	Silver Spring	MD	20905	301-879-1421	
Xpicor Inc 4411 W Market St Ste 100 *Web:* www.xpicor.com	Greensboro	NC	27407	336-510-0333	
Zazula Process Equipment Ltd 4609 Manitoba Rd Se *Web:* www.zazula.com	Calgary	AB	T2G4B9	403-244-0751	

105 BUILDINGS - PREFABRICATED - METAL

Company	City	State	Zip	Phone	Fax
American Buildings Co 1150 State Docks Rd *TF:* 888-307-4338 ■ *Web:* www.americanbuildings.com	Eufaula	AL	36027	334-687-2032	688-2261
American Modular Technologies (AMT) 6306 Old 421 Rd PO Box 1069 *Web:* www.americanmodulartechnologies.com	Liberty	NC	27298	336-622-6200	622-6473
Behlen Manufacturing Co 4025 E 23rd St *Web:* www.behlenmfg.com	Columbus	NE	68601	402-564-3111	563-7405
Butler Manufacturing Co 1540 Genessee St **Fax:* Hum Res ■ *Web:* www.butlermfg.com	Kansas City	MO	64102	816-968-3000	968-6506*
Canatal Industries Inc 2885 Boul Frontenac E *Web:* www.canatal.com	Thetford Mines	QC	G6G6P6	418-338-6044	338-6829
Ceco Bldg Systems 2400 Hwy 45 N *Web:* www.cecobuildings.com	Columbus	MS	39705	662-328-6722	
CEMCO 263 N Covina Ln **Fax Area Code:* 626 ■ *TF:* 800-775-2362 ■ *Web:* www.cemcosteel.com	City Of Industry	CA	91744	800-775-2362	330-7598*
Clearspan Components Inc 6110 Old Hwy 80 W *Web:* merchantcircle.com	Meridian	MS	39307	601-483-3941	483-3941
Dean Steel Buildings Inc 2929 Industrial Ave *Web:* www.deanintl.com	Fort Myers	FL	33901	239-334-1051	334-2432
DeRaffele Mfg Company Inc 2525 Palmer Ave	New Rochelle	NY	10801	914-636-6850	636-6596
Dura-Bilt Products Inc PO Box 188 *Web:* www.durabilt.com	Wellsburg	NY	14894	570-596-2000	
Empire Iron Works Ltd 21104 - 107 Ave *Web:* www.empireiron.com	Edmonton	AB	T5S1X2	780-447-4650	447-4005
Erect-A-Tube Inc 701 W Pk St PO Box 100 *TF:* 800-624-9219 ■ *Web:* www.erect-a-tube.com	Harvard	IL	60033	815-943-4091	943-4095
Four Seasons Solar Products LLC 5005 Veterans Memorial Hwy *TF:* 800-368-7732 ■ *Web:* www.fourseasonssunrooms.com	Holbrook	NY	11741	631-563-4000	563-4010
Garco Bldg Systems 2714 S Garfield Rd *TF:* 800-941-2291 ■ *Web:* www.garcobuildings.com	Airway Heights	WA	99001	509-244-5611	244-2850
Gichner Systems Group Inc 490 E Locust St *Web:* www.gichner.us	Dallastown	PA	17313	717-244-7611	246-5496
Gulf States Manufacturers 101 Airport Rd PO Box 1128 *Web:* gsmnucor.com	Starkville	MS	39760	662-323-8021	324-2984
Imperial Industries Inc 505 Industrial Pk Ave *TF:* 800-558-2945 ■ *Web:* www.imperialind.com	Rothschild	WI	54474	715-359-0200	355-5349
Kirby Bldg Systems Inc 124 Kirby Dr *TF:* 800-348-7799 ■ *Web:* www.kirbybuildingsystems.com	Portland	TN	37148	615-325-4165	
Lark Builders Inc 409 Dixon St *Web:* www.larkbuilders.com	Vidalia	GA	30474	912-538-1888	
Ludwig Buildings Inc 521 Timesaver Ave *Web:* ludwigbuildings.com	Harahan	LA	70123	504-733-6260	733-7458
Madison Industries Inc of Georgia 1035 Iris Dr *Web:* www.madisonind.com	Conyers	GA	30094	770-483-4401	785-7967
Mesco Bldg Solutions 5244 Bear Creek Ct *TF:* 800-556-3726 ■ *Web:* www.mescobuildingsolutions.com	Irving	TX	75061	214-687-9999	687-9736
Metl-Span LLC 1720 Lakepointe Dr Ste 101 *TF:* 877-585-9969 ■ *Web:* www.metlspan.com	Lewisville	TX	75057	972-221-6656	420-9382
Mid-West Steel Bldg Co 7301 Fairview *TF:* 800-777-9378 ■ *Web:* www.mid-weststeel.com	Houston	TX	77041	713-466-7788	466-3194
Morton Buildings Inc 252 W Adams St PO Box 399 *TF:* 800-447-7436 ■ *Web:* www.mortonbuildings.com	Morton	IL	61550	309-263-7474	266-5123
Mueller Inc 1913 Hutchins Ave *TF:* 877-268-3553 ■ *Web:* www.muellerinc.com	Ballinger	TX	76821	325-365-3555	365-8181
NCI Bldg Systems Inc 10943 N Sam Houston PkwyWest *NYSE:* NCS ■ *TF:* 888-624-8677 ■ *Web:* www.ncibuildingsystems.com	Houston	TX	77064	281-897-7788	477-9674
Pacific Building Systems (PBS) 2100 N Pacific Hwy *TF General:* 800-727-7844 ■ *Web:* www.pbsbuildings.com	Woodburn	OR	97071	503-981-9581	981-9584
Package Industries Inc 15 Harback Rd *TF:* 800-225-7242 ■ *Web:* www.packagesteel.com	Sutton	MA	01590	508-865-5871	865-9130
Parkline Inc PO Box 65 *TF:* 800-786-4855 ■ *Web:* www.parkline.com	Winfield	WV	25213	304-586-2113	586-3842
Porta-Fab Corp 18080 Chesterfield Airport Rd *TF:* 800-325-3781 ■ *Web:* www.portafab.com	Chesterfield	MO	63005	636-537-5555	537-2955
PorterCorp 4240 136th Ave *TF:* 800-354-7721 ■ *Web:* www.portercorp.com	Holland	MI	49424	616-399-1963	399-9123
Protect Controls Inc (PCI) 3212 Old Hwy 105 E *Web:* www.protectcontrols.com	Conroe	TX	77301	713-691-5183	691-0159
Red Dot Corp 1209 W Corsicana St *TF Cust Svc:* 800-657-2234 ■ *Web:* www.reddotbuildings.com	Athens	TX	75751	800-657-2234	
Ruffin Bldg Systems Inc 6914 Louisiana 2 *TF:* 800-421-4232 ■ *Web:* www.ruffinbuildingsystems.com	Oak Grove	LA	71263	318-428-2305	428-2231
ShelterLogic Corp 150 Callendar Rd *TF:* 800-932-9344 ■ *Web:* www.shelterlogic.com	Watertown	CT	06795	860-945-6442	
Star Bldg Systems 8600 S I-35 **Fax Area Code:* 405 ■ *TF:* 800-879-7827 ■ *Web:* www.starbuildings.com	Oklahoma City	OK	73149	800-879-7827	636-2419*
Tampa Tank Inc 2710 E Fifth Ave *Web:* www.tampatank.com	Tampa	FL	33605	813-623-2675	
Temo Sunrooms Inc 20400 Hall Rd *TF:* 800-344-8366 ■ *Web:* www.temosunrooms.com	Clinton Township	MI	48038	800-344-8366	
Trachte Bldg Systems Inc 314 Wilburn Rd *TF:* 800-356-5824 ■ *Web:* www.trachte.com	Sun Prairie	WI	53590	800-356-5824	981-9014
Tyler Bldg Systems LP 3535 Shiloh Rd	Tyler	TX	75701	903-561-3000	
United Structures of America Inc 1912 Buschong *Web:* www.usabldg.com	Houston	TX	77039	281-442-8247	442-2125
Varco Pruden Buildings 3200 Players Club Cir *Web:* www.vp.com	Memphis	TN	38125	901-748-8000	748-9323
Whirlwind Steel 8234 Hansen Rd **Fax Area Code:* 832 ■ *TF:* 800-324-9992 ■ *Web:* www.whirlwindsteel.com	Houston	TX	77075	713-946-7140	553-4992*
Winandy Greenhouse Co 2211 Peacock Rd *Web:* winandygreenhouse.com	Richmond	IN	47374	765-935-2111	
Worldwide Steel Buildings PO Box 588 *TF:* 800-825-0316 ■ *Web:* www.worldwidesteelbuildings.com	Peculiar	MO	64078	800-825-0316	
XS Smith Inc 932 Page Rd *TF:* 800-631-2226 ■ *Web:* www.xssmith.com	Washington	NC	27889	252-940-5060	946-0724

106 BUILDINGS - PREFABRICATED - WOOD

Company	City	State	Zip	Phone	Fax
A & S Building Systems LP 1880 Hwy 116 *Web:* www.a-s.com	Caryville	TN	37714	865-426-2141	
Acorn Deck House Co 852 Main St *TF:* 800-727-3325 ■ *Web:* www.deckhouse.com	Acton	MA	01720	978-263-6800	263-4159
Alenco Inc 16201 W 110th St *Web:* www.alenconline.com	Lenexa	KS	66219	913-438-1902	
Alfresco Grills Inc 7039 E Slauson Ave *Web:* www.alfrescogrills.com	Commerce	CA	90040	323-722-7900	
Algeco Scotsman Inc 901 S Bond St Ste 600 *Web:* www.algecoscotsman.com	Baltimore	MD	21231	410-931-6000	
Barden & Robeson Corp 103 Kelly Ave *TF:* 800-724-0141 ■ *Web:* www.bardenhomes.com	Middleport	NY	14105	716-735-3732	735-3752
Bebco Industries Inc 4725 Lawndale *Web:* www.okbebco.com	La Marque	TX	77568	409-935-5743	
Bellcomb Inc 5001 Boone Ave N	Minneapolis	MN	55428	763-746-0000	
Blazer Industries Inc PO Box 489 *TF:* 877-211-3437 ■ *Web:* www.blazerind.com	Aumsville	OR	97325	503-749-1900	749-3969
BOXX Modular Inc 555 Jubilee Ln Ste 750 *Web:* www.boxxmodularus.com	Denver	CO	80202	972-492-4040	
Cardinal Homes Inc 525 Barnesville Hwy *Web:* www.cardinalhomes.com	Wylliesburg	VA	23976	434-735-8111	735-8824
Cedarstore.com 5410 Rt 8 *TF:* 888-885-3806 ■ *Web:* www.cedarstore.com	Gibsonia	PA	15044	724-444-5300	
Dacro Industries Inc 9325-51 Ave *Web:* www.dacro.com	Edmonton	AB	T6E4W8	780-434-8900	433-3138
Deluxe Bldg Systems Inc 499 W Third St *TF:* 800-843-7372 ■ *Web:* deluxecrm.com/crm	Berwick	PA	18603	570-752-5914	752-1525
Design Homes Inc 600 N Marquette Rd *TF:* 800-627-9443 ■ *Web:* www.designhomes.com	Prairie du Chien	WI	53821	608-326-6041	326-4233
Dickinson Homes Inc 404 N Stephenson Ave Hwy US-2 PO Box 2245 *TF:* 800-438-4687 ■ *Web:* www.dickinsonhomes.com	Iron Mountain	MI	49801	906-774-2186	774-5207
Dynamic Homes LLC 525 Roosevelt Ave **Fax:* Orders ■ *TF:* 800-492-4833 ■ *Web:* www.dynamichomes.com	Detroit Lakes	MN	56501	218-847-2611	847-2617*
Fleetwood Homes of California Inc 7007 Jurupa Ave *Web:* www.fleetwoodhomes.com	Riverside	CA	92504	951-351-2494	
Flexospan Steel Buildings Inc 253 Railroad St *TF:* 800-245-0396 ■ *Web:* www.flexospan.com	Sandy Lake	PA	16145	724-376-7221	
Foremost Industries Inc 2375 Buchanan Trl W *TF:* 877-284-5334 ■ *Web:* www.foremosthomes.com	Greencastle	PA	17225	717-597-7166	597-5579
Gary Doupnik Manufacturing Inc 3237 Rippey Rd	Loomis	CA	95650	916-652-9291	652-9021
General Shelters of Texas Ltd 1639 State Hwy 87 N *Web:* www.generalshelters.com	Center	TX	75935	936-598-3389	598-1432
Global Precast Inc 2101 Teston Rd *Web:* www.globalprecast.com	Maple	ON	L6A1R3	905-832-4307	832-4388
Gold Capital LLC 3566 Olivet Church Rd *Web:* www.goldcapitalky.com	Paducah	KY	42001	270-408-4653	
Harbor Technologies LLC 681 Riverside Dr *Web:* www.harbortech.us	Augusta	ME	04330	207-725-4878	
Haven Homes Inc 554 Eagle Vly Rd *Web:* lockhaven.com	Beech Creek	PA	16822	570-962-2111	
Heckaman Homes Inc 2676 E Market St *Web:* www.heckamanhomes.com	Nappanee	IN	46550	574-773-4167	
Heritage Log Homes Inc 119 W Dumplin Vly Rd *Web:* thegreatsmokeymountainsparkway.com	Kodak	TN	37764	865-932-0202	
Homes by Keystone Inc 13338 Midvale Rd PO Box 69 *TF:* 800-890-7926 ■ *Web:* www.homesbykeystone.com	Waynesboro	PA	17268	800-890-7926	
Imperial Manufacturing Inc 2271 NE 194th *Web:* www.imperialmfg.com	Portland	OR	97230	503-665-5539	
Indaco Metal 3 American Way *TF:* 877-750-5614 ■ *Web:* www.indacometals.com	Shawnee	OK	74804	877-300-7334	
Industries Bonneville Ltee 601 rue de l'Industrie *Web:* www.maisonsbonneville.com	Beloeil	QC	J3G4S5	450-464-1001	
International Homes of Cedar Inc (IHC) PO Box 886 *TF:* 800-767-7674 ■ *Web:* www.ihoc.com	Woodinville	WA	98072	360-668-8511	668-5562
Keiser Homes 56 Mechanic Falls Rd Rte 121 **Fax Area Code:* 207 ■ *TF:* 888-333-1748 ■ *Web:* www.keisermaine.com	Oxford	ME	04270	888-333-1748	539-0944*
Kerkstra Precast Inc 3373 Busch Dr *Web:* www.kerkstra.com	Grandville	MI	49418	616-224-6176	
KIT HomeBuilders West LLC 1124 Garber St *TF:* 800-859-0347 ■ *Web:* www.kitwest.com	Caldwell	ID	83605	208-454-5000	455-2995
Kontek Industries Inc 1200 Dawson Rd *Web:* www.kontekindustries.com	New Madrid	MO	63869	573-748-5561	
Lester Bldg Systems LLC 1111 Second Ave S *TF:* 800-826-4439 ■ *Web:* www.lesterbuildings.com	Lester Prairie	MN	55354	320-395-2531	395-5393
Lindal Cedar Homes Inc 4300 S 104th Pl *TF Prod Info:* 800-426-0536 ■ *Web:* www.lindal.com	Seattle	WA	98178	206-725-0900	725-1615
Log Cabin Homes Ltd 410 N Pearl St *Web:* www.logcabinhomes.com	Rocky Mount	NC	27804	252-454-1500	

	City	State	Zip	Phone	Fax
Manufactured Structures Corp (MSC) 3089 E Fort Wayne Rd PO Box 350	Rochester	IN	46975	574-223-4794	
Web: www.mscoffice.com					
Modtech Holdings Inc 1660 Chicago Ave Ste M-21	Riverside	CA	92507	951-686-3633	
Web: www.modtech.com					
Montana Idaho Log & Timber 1069 Us Hwy 93 N	Victor	MT	59875	406-961-3092	
TF: 800-600-8604 ■ *Web:* www.mtidlog.com					
Morgan Bldg Systems Inc 2800 McCree Rd	Garland	TX	75041	972-864-7300	
TF: 800-935-0321 ■ *Web:* www.morganusa.com					
Nassal Co, The 415 W Kaley St	Orlando	FL	32806	407-648-0400	648-0841
Web: www.nassal.com					
National Barn Co 818 N Broadway	Portland	TN	37148	615-325-2700	
Web: www.nationalbarn.com					
Nationwide Custom Homes 1100 Rives Rd	Martinsville	VA	24115	800-216-7001	632-1181*
**Fax Area Code:* 276 ■ *TF:* 800-216-7001 ■ *Web:* www.nationwide-homes.com					
Natural Structures 2005 Tenth St	Baker City	OR	97814	541-523-0224	
Web: www.naturalstructures.com					
New Acton Mobile Industries LLC 809 Gleneagles Ct	Baltimore	MD	21286	800-251-1600	
TF: 800-251-1600 ■ *Web:* www.actonmobile.com					
New England Homes 270 Ocean Rd	Greenland	NH	03840	603-436-8830	431-8540
TF: 800-800-8831 ■ *Web:* www.newenglandhomes.net					
Nexus Corp 10983 Leroy Dr	Northglenn	CO	80233	303-457-9199	
TF: 800-228-9639 ■ *Web:* www.nexuscorp.com					
Northeastern Log Homes Inc 10 Ames Rd	Kenduskeag	ME	04450	207-884-7000	884-3000
TF: 800-624-2797 ■ *Web:* www.northeasternlog.com					
Original Lincoln Logs Ltd 5 Riverside Dr PO Box 135	Chestertown	NY	12817	800-833-2461	494-3008*
**Fax Area Code:* 518 ■ *TF:* 800-833-2461 ■ *Web:* www.lincolnlogs.com					
Pacific Modern Homes Inc (PMHI) 9723 Railroad St	Elk Grove	CA	95624	916-685-9514	
TF: 800-395-1011 ■ *Web:* www.pmhi.com					
Pan Abode Cedar Homes Inc 1100 Maple Ave SW	Renton	WA	98057	425-255-8260	255-8630
TF: 800-782-2633 ■ *Web:* www.panabodehomes.com					
Pittsville Homes Inc 5094 Second Ave	Pittsville	WI	54466	715-884-2511	884-2136
Rocky Mountain Log Homes 1883 Hwy 93 S	Hamilton	MT	59840	406-363-5680	363-2109
Web: www.rockymountainloghomes.com					
Sand Creek Post & Beam 116 W First St	Wayne	NE	68787	402-833-5600	
Web: www.sandcreekpostandbeam.com					
Satellite Shelters Inc 2530 Xenium Ln N	Plymouth	MN	55441	763-553-1900	
Web: www.satelliteco.com					
Schulte Building Systems Inc 17600 Badtke Rd	Hockley	TX	77447	281-304-6111	
TF: 877-257-2534 ■ *Web:* www.sbslp.com					
Simplex Homes 1 Simplex Dr	Scranton	PA	18504	570-346-5113	346-3732
Web: www.simplexind.com					
Southern Bleacher Company Inc 801 Fifth St	Graham	TX	76450	940-549-0733	
Web: www.southernbleacher.com					
Starrco Company Inc 11700 Fairgrove Industrial Blvd	Maryland Heights	MO	63043	314-567-5533	
Web: www.starrco.com					
Sterling Bldg Systems PO Box 8005	Wausau	WI	54402	800-455-0545	
TF: 800-455-0545 ■ *Web:* sterlingbldg.com/contact-us					
Stratford Homes LP 402 S Weber Ave	Stratford	WI	54484	715-687-3133	687-3453
TF: 800-448-1524 ■ *Web:* www.stratfordhomes.com					
Suntec Concrete Inc 2221 W Shangri-La Rd	Phoenix	AZ	85029	602-997-0937	
Web: www.suntecconcrete.com					
Timberland Homes Inc 1201 37th St NW	Auburn	WA	98001	253-735-3435	939-8803
TF: 800-488-5036 ■ *Web:* www.timberland-homes.com					
Trading Post Homes 490 Sparrow Dre	Shepherdsville	KY	40165	502-955-5622	
Web: www.tphomes.com					
Unibilt Industries Inc 8005 Johnson Stn Rd PO Box 373	Vandalia	OH	45377	800-777-9942	890-8303*
**Fax Area Code:* 937 ■ *TF:* 800-777-9942 ■ *Web:* www.unibiltcustomhomes.com					
Ward Cedar Log Homes 37 Bangor St PO Box 72	Houlton	ME	04730	800-341-1566	532-7806*
**Fax Area Code:* 207 ■ *TF Cust Svc:* 800-341-1566 ■ *Web:* www.wardcedarloghomes.com					
Wausau Homes Inc PO Box 8005	Wausau	WI	54402	715-359-7272	
Web: www.wausauhomes.com					
Weatherhaven Global Resources Ltd 2120 Hartley Ave	Coquitlam	BC	V3K6W5	604-451-8900	
Web: www.weatherhaven.com					
Westchester Modular Homes Inc 30 Reagans Mill Rd	Wingdale	NY	12594	845-832-9400	
Web: www.westchestermodular.com					
Whitley Manufacturing Inc 201 W First St PO Box 496	South Whitley	IN	46787	260-723-5131	723-6949
Web: www.whitleyman.com					
Wisconsin Homes Inc 425 W McMillan St	Marshfield	WI	54449	715-384-2161	387-3627
Web: www.wisconsinhomesinc.com					
Yankee Barn Homes 131 Yankee Barn Rd	Grantham	NH	03753	800-258-9786	
TF: 800-258-9786 ■ *Web:* www.yankeebarnhomes.com					

107 BUS SERVICES - CHARTER

	City	State	Zip	Phone	Fax
A Yankee Line 370 W First St	Boston	MA	02127	617-268-8890	268-6960
TF: 800-942-8890 ■ *Web:* www.yankeeline.us					
Agape Tours & Charter 3306 Cumberland Ave	Wichita Falls	TX	76301	940-767-4935	
Web: agapetourstx.com					
All West Coach Lines 7701 Wilbur Way	Sacramento	CA	95828	916-423-4000	
TF: 800-843-2121 ■ *Web:* coachusa.com					
Anderson Coach & Travel 1 Anderson Plz	Greenville	PA	16125	724-588-8310	588-0257
TF: 800-345-3435 ■ *Web:* www.goanderson.com					
Arrow Stage Lines 720 E Norfolk Ave	Norfolk	NE	68701	402-371-3850	
TF: 800-672-8302 ■ *Web:* www.arrowstagelines.com					
B & C Transportation Inc 427 Continental Dr	Maryville	TN	37804	865-983-4653	
TF: 877-812-2287 ■ *Web:* bctransportation.net					
Badger Bus 5501 Femrite Dr	Madison	WI	53718	608-255-1511	
TF: 800-442-8259 ■ *Web:* www.badgerbus.com					
Blue Lakes Charters & Tours 12154 N Saginaw Rd	Clio	MI	48420	810-686-4287	686-9772
TF: 800-282-4287 ■ *Web:* www.bluelakes.com					
Boise-Winnemucca Stage Lines Inc 1105 S La Pt St	Boise	ID	83706	208-336-3300	336-3303
TF: 800-448-5692 ■ *Web:* www.boise-winnemuccastages.com					
Brown Coach Inc 50 Venner Rd	Amsterdam	NY	12010	518-843-4700	843-3600
TF: 800-424-4700 ■ *Web:* www.browntours.com					
Butler Motor Transit Company Inc 210 S Monroe St PO Box 1602	Butler	PA	16003	724-282-1000	
TF: 800-222-8750 ■ *Web:* www.coachusa.com/butler					
C & H Bus Lines Inc 448 Pine St	Macon	GA	31201	478-746-6441	743-5597
Carl R Bieber Tourways Inc 320 Fair St PO Box 180	Kutztown	PA	19530	610-683-7333	
TF: 800-243-2374 ■ *Web:* www.biebertourways.com					
Central States Coach Repairs 3426 Gilbert Rd	Grand Prairie	TX	75050	972-399-1059	986-7262
TF: 800-533-1939 ■ *Web:* www.bus-charter.com					
Chippewa Trucking 510 E S Ave	Chippewa Falls	WI	54729	715-726-2457	726-2455
TF: 866-777-1399					
Citizen Auto Stage Co 3594 E Lincoln St	Tucson	AZ	85714	520-622-8811	
TF: 800-276-1528 ■ *Web:* graylinearizona.com					
Coach Tours Ltd 475 Federal Rd	Brookfield	CT	06804	203-740-1118	
TF: 800-822-6224 ■ *Web:* www.coachtour.com					
Colorado Charter Lines 4960 Locust St	Commerce	CO	80022	303-287-0239	287-2819
TF: 800-821-7491 ■ *Web:* www.bus-charter.com/coloradocharter.htm					
Conestoga Tours Inc 1619 Manheim Pike Ste A	Lancaster	PA	17601	717-569-1111	
Web: www.conestogatours.com					
Covered Wagon Tours LLC 158 Thacher St	Hornell	NY	14843	607-324-3900	
Web: www.coveredwagontours.net					
Cowtown Bus Charters Inc 5504 Forest Hill Dr	Fort Worth	TX	76119	817-531-3287	
TF: 877-287-4897 ■ *Web:* www.cowtowncharters.com					
Croswell Bus Lines Inc 975 W Main St	Williamsburg	OH	45176	513-724-2206	724-3261
TF: 800-782-8747 ■ *Web:* gocroswell.com					
CYR Bus Lines 153 Gilman Falls Ave	Old Town	ME	04468	207-827-2335	827-6763
TF: 800-244-2335 ■ *Web:* johntcyrandsons.com					
DATTCO Inc 583 S St	New Britain	CT	06051	860-229-4878	826-1115
TF: 800-229-4879 ■ *Web:* dattco.com					
Delta Bus Lines Inc 3107 Hwy 82E	Greenville	MS	38701	662-335-2633	335-2634
Web: deltabuslines.net					
Discovery Care Centre Corp 601 N Tenth St	Hamilton	MT	59840	406-363-2273	
Web: www.discoverycare.com					
Easton Coach Co 1200 Conroy Pl	Easton	PA	18040	610-253-4055	
Web: eastoncoach.com					
Elite Coach 1685 W Main St	Ephrata	PA	17522	717-733-7710	733-7133
TF: 800-722-6206 ■ *Web:* www.elitecoach.com					
Escot Bus Lines Inc 6890 142nd Ave	Largo	FL	33771	727-545-2088	
Web: www.escotbuslines.com					
Eyre Bus Service Inc 13600 Triadelphia Rd PO Box 239	Glenelg	MD	21737	410-442-1330	442-0010
TF: 800-321-3973 ■ *Web:* www.eyre.com					
Gold Coast Tours 105 Gemini Ave	Brea	CA	92821	714-449-6888	
TF: 800-638-6427 ■ *Web:* www.goldcoasttours.com					
Good Time Tours 455 Corday St	Pensacola	FL	32503	850-476-0046	476-7637
TF: 800-446-0886 ■ *Web:* www.goodtimetours.com					
Gray Line Worldwide 1835 Gaylord St	Denver	CO	80206	303-394-6920	394-6950
TF: 800-472-9546 ■ *Web:* www.grayline.com					
Great Southern Coaches 900 Burke Ave	Jonesboro	AR	72401	870-935-5569	
Web: yellowpagesgoesgreen.org					
Greyhound Canada Transportation Corp 1111 International Blvd Ste 700	Burlington	ON	L7L6W1	800-661-8747	
TF: 800-661-8747 ■ *Web:* www.greyhound.ca					
Hampton Jitney Inc (HJ) 395 County Rd 39A Ste 6	SouthHampton	NY	11968	631-283-4600	287-4759
Web: www.hamptonjitney.com					
Harms Charters 532 S Vly View Rd	Sioux Falls	SD	57106	605-336-3339	
TF: 800-678-6543 ■ *Web:* www.foremanchartersandtours.com					
Hawkeye Stages Inc 703 Dudley St	Decorah	IA	52101	563-382-3639	
TF: 877-464-2954 ■ *Web:* www.hawkeyestages.com					
Indian Trails Inc 109 E Comstock St	Owosso	MI	48867	989-725-5105	
TF: 800-292-3831 ■ *Web:* www.indiantrails.com					
Kerrville Bus Co 1 S Main St	Del Rio	TX	78840	830-775-7515	
TF: 800-474-3352 ■ *Web:* www.iridekbc.com					
Lamers Bus Lines Inc 2407 S Pt Rd	Green Bay	WI	54313	920-496-3600	496-3611
TF: 800-236-1240 ■ *Web:* www.golamers.com					
Marin Charter & Tours 8 Lovell Ave	San Rafael	CA	94901	415-256-8830	256-8839
Web: www.marinairporter.com					
Martz First Class Coach Company Inc 4783 37th St N	Saint Petersburg	FL	33714	727-526-9086	522-5548
TF: 800-282-8020 ■ *Web:* www.martzfirstclass.com					
Mid-America Charter Lines 2513 E Higgins Rd	Elk Grove Village	IL	60007	847-437-3779	437-4978
TF: 800-323-0312 ■ *Web:* bus-charter.com					
MV Transportation Inc 5910 N Central Expy Ste 1145	Dallas	TX	75206	972-391-4600	863-8944*
**Fax Area Code:* 707 ■ *Web:* www.mvtransit.com					
Northfield Lines Inc 32611 Northfield Blvd	Northfield	MN	55057	507-645-5267	645-5635
TF: 888-670-8068 ■ *Web:* www.northfieldlines.com					
Onondaga Coach Corp PO Box 277	Auburn	NY	13021	315-255-2216	255-0925
TF: 800-451-1570 ■ *Web:* www.onondagacoach.com					
Pacific Western Transportation Ltd 6999 ordan Dr	Mississauga	ON	L5T1K6	905-564-3232	564-5959
TF: 800-387-6787 ■ *Web:* www.pacificwesterntoronto.com					
Peter Pan Bus Lines PO Box 1776	Springfield	MA	01102	800-343-9999	
TF: 800-343-9999 ■ *Web:* www.peterpanbus.com					
Peter Pan Bus Lines Inc 1776 Main St	Springfield	MA	01103	800-343-9999	747-7626*
**Fax Area Code:* 413 ■ *TF:* 800-343-9999 ■ *Web:* www.peterpanbus.com					
Premier Coach Company Inc 946 Rte 7 S	Milton	VT	05468	802-655-4456	655-4213
TF: 800-532-1811 ■ *Web:* www.premiercoach.net					
Punchbowl Inc 50 Speen St Ste 202	Framingham	MA	01701	508-589-4486	
TF: 877-570-4340 ■ *Web:* punchbowl.com					

	City	State	Zip	Phone	Fax
Red Carpet Charters 4820 SW 20th *TF:* 888-878-5100 ■ *Web:* www.redcarpetcharters.com	Oklahoma City	OK	73128	405-672-5100	
Riteway Bus Service Inc Motorcoach Div W201 N13900 Fond du Lac Ave *TF:* 800-776-7026 ■ *Web:* goriteway.com	Richfield	WI	53076	262-677-3282	677-3121
Rockland Coaches Inc 180 Old Hook Rd *Web:* www.coachusa.com/rockland	Westwood	NJ	07675	201-263-1254	
Salter Bus Lines Inc 212 Hudson Ave *TF:* 800-223-8056 ■ *Web:* www.salter.us	Jonesboro	LA	71251	318-259-2522	259-2522
SBS Transit Inc 3747 Colorado Ave *Web:* loraincounty.com	Sheffield Village	OH	44054	440-949-8121	
Shafer's Tour & Charter 500 N St *TF:* 800-287-8986 ■ *Web:* www.shaferbus.com	Endicott	NY	13760	607-797-2006	
Sharp Bus Lines Ltd 567 Oak Park Rd *Web:* www.sharpbus.com	Brantford	ON	N3T5L8	519-426-0050	
Silver Fox Tours & Motorcoaches 3 Silver Fox Dr *TF:* 800-342-5998 ■ *Web:* www.silverfoxcoach.com	Millbury	MA	01527	508-865-6000	865-4660
Southeastern Stages Inc 260 University Ave SW *Web:* www.southeasternstages.com	Atlanta	GA	30315	404-591-2780	591-2745
Starr Bus Charter & Tours 2531 E State St *TF:* 800-782-7703 ■ *Web:* www.starrtours.com	Trenton	NJ	08619	609-587-0626	587-3052
Storer Coachways 3519 McDonald Ave *TF:* 800-621-3383 ■ *Web:* www.storercoachways.com	Modesto	CA	95358	209-521-8250	578-4888
Swarthout Coaches Inc 115 Graham Rd *TF:* 800-772-7267 ■ *Web:* www.goswarthout.com	Ithaca	NY	14850	607-257-2277	257-0218
Trailways Transportation System Inc 3554 Chain Bridge Rd Ste 202 *TF:* 877-467-3346 ■ *Web:* www.trailways.com	Fairfax	VA	22030	703-691-3052	691-9047
Triple J Tours Inc 4455 S Cameron St *Web:* www.lasvegasbus.com	Las Vegas	NV	89103	702-261-0131	736-5103
Van Galder Bus Co 715 S Pearl St *TF:* 800-747-0994 ■ *Web:* www.coachusa.com	Janesville	WI	53548	608-752-5407	
VIP Tour & Charter Bus Co 129-137 Fox St *TF General:* 800-231-2222 ■ *Web:* www.vipchartercoaches.com	Portland	ME	04101	207-772-4457	772-7020
Voyageur Transportation Services 573 Admiral Ct *TF:* 855-263-7163 ■ *Web:* www.voyageurtransportation.ca	London	ON	N5V4L3	519-455-4580	
White Hat Management LLC 159 S Main St Ste 600 *Web:* www.whitehatmgmt.com	Akron	OH	44308	330-535-6868	
Wilson Bus Lines Inc 203 Patriots Rd PO Box 415 *TF:* 800-253-5235 ■ *Web:* www.wilsonbus.com	East Templeton	MA	01438	978-632-3894	632-9005
Winn Transportation 1831 Westwood Ave *TF:* 800-296-9466 ■ *Web:* www.winnbus.com	Richmond	VA	23227	804-358-9466	353-2606
Wisconsin Coach Lines Inc 1520 Arcadian Ave *TF:* 877-324-7767 ■ *Web:* www.coachusa.com	Waukesha	WI	53186	262-542-8861	542-2036
Young Transportation & Tours 843 Riverside Dr *TF:* 800-622-5444 ■ *Web:* www.youngtransportation.com	Asheville	NC	28804	828-258-0084	252-3342

108 BUS SERVICES - INTERCITY & RURAL

See Also Bus Services - School p. 1881; Mass Transportation (Local & Suburban) p. 2731

	City	State	Zip	Phone	Fax
A. J. Edmond Co 1530 W 16th St *Web:* ajedmondco.com	Long Beach	CA	90813	562-437-1802	
Adirondack Trailways 499 Hurley Ave *TF:* 800-858-8555 ■ *Web:* www.trailwaysny.com	Hurley	NY	12443	845-339-4230	
Autobus Girardin Inc 4000 Girardin St *Web:* www.girardinbluebird.com	Drummondville	QC	J2E0A1	819-477-3222	
C & L Bus Company Inc 12200 W Broward Blvd *Web:* www.ahschool.com	Plantation	FL	33325	954-472-7800	
Calgary Handi-bus Assn 231 37 Ave Ne *Web:* www.calgaryhandibus.com	Calgary	AB	T2E8J2	403-276-8028	
Colorado Valley Transit Inc 108 Cardinal Ln PO Box 940 *TF:* 800-548-1068 ■ *Web:* www.gotransit.org	Columbus	TX	78934	979-732-6281	732-6283
Elgie Bus Lines Ltd 5137 Cobble Hills Rd *Web:* www.elgiebuslines.com	Thamesford	ON	N0M2M0	519-461-1227	
Everything Parking Inc 1415 S Church St Ste T *TF:* 877-751-6683 ■ *Web:* www.parkinc.com	Charlotte	NC	28203	704-377-1755	
Gary Public Transportation Corp 2101 W 35th Ave *Web:* www.gptcbus.com	Gary	IN	46408	219-884-6100	
GATRA 2 Oak St *TF:* 800-483-2500 ■ *Web:* www.gatra.org	Taunton	MA	02780	508-823-8828	
Geauga County Transit 12555 Merritt Rd *TF Cust Svc:* 888-287-7190 ■ *Web:* www.geaugatransit.org	Chardon	OH	44024	440-279-2150	285-9476
Girardin Minibus Inc 3000 rue Girardin *Web:* www.girardin.com	Drummondville	QC	J2E0A1	819-477-2012	
Greyhound Canada Transportation Corp 1111 International Blvd Ste 700 *TF:* 800-661-8747 ■ *Web:* www.greyhound.ca	Burlington	ON	L7L6W1	800-661-8747	
Indianapolis Public Transportation Corporation 1501 W Washington St *Web:* www.indygo.net	Indianapolis	IN	46204	317-635-3344	
Jefferson Partners LP 2100 E 26th St *TF Cust Svc:* 800-767-5333 ■ *Web:* www.jeffersonlines.com	Minneapolis	MN	55404	612-359-3400	359-3437
Long Beach Transit 1963 E Anaheim St *Web:* www.lbtransit.com	Long Beach	CA	90813	562-591-2301	
M & L Transit Systems Inc 60 Olympia Ave Ste 1 *Web:* www.mltsi.com	Woburn	MA	01801	781-938-8646	
Martha's Vineyard Regional Transit Authority 11 A St MV Business Pk *Web:* www.vineyardtransit.com	Edgartown	MA	02539	508-693-9440	693-9953
Martz Trailways 239 Old River Rd *Web:* www.martztrailways.com	Wilkes-Barre	PA	18702	570-821-3838	821-3835
Merced Transportation Co 300 Grogan Ave	Merced	CA	95341	209-384-2575	
Mid-City Transit Corp 518 State Rt 17M *Web:* www.midcitytransit.com	Middletown	NY	10940	845-343-4702	
Ozark Regional Transit 2423 E Robinson Ave *TF:* 800-865-5901 ■ *Web:* www.ozark.org	Springdale	AR	72764	479-756-5901	
Pacific Transit System 216 N Second St *TF:* 800-833-6388 ■ *Web:* www.pacifictransit.org	Raymond	WA	98577	360-875-9418	942-3193
Pelivan Transit 333 S Oak St PO Box B *TF:* 800-482-4594 ■ *Web:* okladot.state.ok.us	Big Cabin	OK	74332	918-783-5793	
Peter Pan Bus Lines Inc 1776 Main St *Fax Area Code: 413 ■ *TF:* 800-343-9999 ■ *Web:* www.peterpanbus.com	Springfield	MA	01103	800-343-9999	747-7626*
Pima County Dept of Transportation Transportation Systems Div 201 N Stone Ave 4th Fl *Web:* www.dot.pima.gov	Tucson	AZ	85701	520-740-6410	740-6341
Powder River Transportation 1700 U S 14 *TF:* 888-970-7233 ■ *Web:* www.coachusa.com	Gillette	WY	82716	307-682-0960	
Rail Transit Consultants Inc 901 S Railroad St *Web:* www.railtransit.com	Penn	PA	15675	724-527-2386	
RailCrew Xpress LLC 15729 College Blvd *Web:* www.railcrewxpress.com	Lenexa	KS	66219	913-928-5000	
Ramblin Express Transportation 3465 Astrozon Pl *Web:* www.ramblinexpress.com	Colorado Springs	CO	80910	719-590-8687	
Rural Community Transportation Inc (RCT) 1161 Portland St *Web:* sites.google.com/a/rctvt.org/riderct	Saint Johnsbury	VT	05819	802-748-8170	748-5275
Rural Transit Enterprises Coordinated Inc (RTEC) 100 E Main St *TF:* 800-321-7832 ■ *Web:* www.4rtec.com	Mount Vernon	KY	40456	606-256-9835	
Southeastern Stages Inc 260 University Ave SW *Web:* www.southeasternstages.com	Atlanta	GA	30315	404-591-2780	591-2745
Spokane Transit Authority Route & Schedule Information 328 Ride 701 W Riverside Ave *Web:* www.spokanetransit.com	Spokane	WA	99201	509-456-7277	
Star Shuttle & Charter 1343 Hallmark Dr *Web:* www.starshuttle.com	San Antonio	TX	78216	210-341-6000	
Suburban Transit Corp 750 Somerset St *TF:* 800-222-0492 ■ *Web:* www.coachusa.com	New Brunswick	NJ	08901	732-249-1100	
Thunderbird Rural Public Transportation System 2801 W Loop 306 Ste A PO Box 60050 *TF:* 877-947-8729 ■ *Web:* www.cvcog.org/cvcog/trans_rural.html	San Angelo	TX	76904	325-944-9666	947-8286
Tornado Bus Company Inc 535 E Jefferson Blvd *Web:* www.tornadobus.com	Dallas	TX	75203	214-941-7399	
Training Advantage, The PO Box 800 *TF:* 800-659-2656 ■ *Web:* www.sucap.org	Ignacio	CO	81137	970-563-4517	
Trans-Bridge Lines Inc 2012 Industrial Dr *Web:* www.transbridgelines.com	Bethlehem	PA	18017	610-868-6001	868-9057
Veolia Transport Quebec Inc 720 rue Trotter	Saint-jean-sur-richelieu	QC	J3B8T2	514-787-1998	
Viking Trailways 201 Glendale Rd *TF:* 800-400-2779 ■ *Web:* trailways.com	Joplin	MO	64804	417-781-2779	

109 BUS SERVICES - SCHOOL

	City	State	Zip	Phone	Fax
Birnie Bus Service Inc 248 Otis St *TF:* 800-734-3950 ■ *Web:* birniebus.com	Rome	NY	13441	315-336-3950	339-5957
Brown Bus Co 2111 E Sherman Ave *TF:* 800-574-1580 ■ *Web:* www.brownbuscompany.com	Nampa	ID	83686	208-466-4181	466-2861
Cook-Illinois Corp 2100 Clearwater Dr Ste 300 *Web:* cookillinois.com	Oak Brook	IL	60523	708-560-9840	560-0661
Davidsmeyer Bus Service Inc 2513 E Higgins Rd *TF:* 800-323-0312 ■ *Web:* www.bus-charter.com/aboutus-dsm.htm	Elk Grove Village	IL	60007	847-437-3767	437-4978
Dean Transportation Inc 4812 Aurelius Rd *TF:* 800-282-3326 ■ *Web:* deantransportation.com	Lansing	MI	48910	517-319-8300	319-8384
First Student Inc 600 Vine St *Web:* www.firststudentinc.com	Cincinnati	OH	45202	513-241-2200	
Hastings Bus Co 425 31st St E *TF:* 800-210-6362 ■ *Web:* www.minnesotacoaches.com	Hastings	MN	55033	651-437-1888	438-3319
Independent Coach Corp 25 Wanser Ave *Web:* independentcoach.com	Inwood	NY	11096	516-239-1100	
John T Cyr & Sons Inc 153 Gilman Falls Ave *TF:* 800-244-2335 ■ *Web:* johntcyrandsons.com	Old Town	ME	04468	207-827-2335	827-6763
Johnson School Bus Services Inc 2151 W Washington St PO Box 285 *Web:* www.johnsonschoolbus.com	West Bend	WI	53095	262-334-3146	334-8019
Kobussen Buses Ltd W914 County Rd CE *TF:* 800-447-0116 ■ *Web:* www.kobussen.com	Kaukauna	WI	54130	920-766-0606	766-0797
Krise Bus Service Inc 119 Bus Ln	Punxsutawney	PA	15767	814-938-5250	
Michael's Transportation Service Inc 140 Yolano Dr *TF Cust Svc:* 800-295-2448 ■ *Web:* bustransportation.com	Vallejo	CA	94589	707-643-2099	643-1906
Mid-Columbia Bus Co PO box 1108 *Web:* www.midcobus.com	Pendleton	OR	97801	541-278-1444	
Monroe School Transportation 970 Emerson St *Web:* monroeschooltrans.com	Rochester	NY	14606	585-458-3230	458-9159
Pioneer Transportation Corp 2890 Arthur Kill Rd *Web:* pioneerbus.com	Staten Island	NY	10309	718-984-8077	984-6588
Riteway Bus Service Inc Motorcoach Div W201 N13900 Fond du Lac Ave *TF:* 800-776-7026 ■ *Web:* goriteway.com	Richfield	WI	53076	262-677-3282	677-3121
Rocky Mountain Transportation Inc 1410 E Edgewood *Web:* www.rockymountaintrans.com	Whitefish	MT	59937	406-863-1200	863-1213
Royal Coach Lines Inc 924 Broadway *Web:* royalcoachlines.com	Thornwood	NY	10594	914-747-9494	747-9497
Safe-Way Bus Co 6030 Carmen Ave	Inver Grove Heights	MN	55076	651-451-1375	451-3525

				Phone	Fax
Stock Transportation Ltd 128 Wellington St W Ste 201 *TF:* 888-952-0878 ■ *Web:* www.stocktransportation.com	Barrie	ON	L4N1K9	888-952-0878	
Student Transportation of America Inc (STA) 3349 Hwy 138 Bldg B Ste D *TF:* 888-942-2250 ■ *Web:* www.ridestbus.com	Wall	NJ	07719	732-280-4200	280-4214
Suffolk Transportation Service Inc 10 Moffitt Blvd *Web:* www.suffolkbus.com	Bay Shore	NY	11706	631-665-3245	665-3186
WE Transport Inc 75 Commercial St. *Web:* www.wetransport.com	Plainview	NY	11803	516-349-8200	349-8275
Williams Bus Lines Inc PO Box 1272 *Web:* www.williamsbus.com	Springfield	VA	22151	703-560-5355	560-7851

110 BUSINESS FORMS

See Also Printing Companies - Commercial Printers p. 2976

				Phone	Fax
Ace Forms of Kansas Inc 2900 N Rotary Terr **Fax Area Code:* 620 ■ *TF:* 800-223-9287 ■ *Web:* www.aceforms.com	Pittsburg	KS	66762	800-223-9287	232-1111*
Allison Payment Systems LLC 2200 Production Dr **Fax Area Code:* 317 ■ *TF:* 800-755-2440 ■ *Web:* www.apsllc.com	Indianapolis	IN	46241	800-755-2440	808-2477*
Amsterdam Printing & Litho Corp 166 Wallins Corners Rd *TF Cust Svc:* 800-833-6231 ■ *Web:* www.amsterdamprinting.com	Amsterdam	NY	12010	518-842-6000	
Apex Color 200 N Lee St *TF:* 800-367-6790 ■ *Web:* www.apexcolor.net	Jacksonville	FL	32204	800-367-6790	
Bestforms Inc 1135 Avenida Acaso *TF:* 800-350-0618 ■ *Web:* www.bestforms.com	Camarillo	CA	93012	805-383-6993	987-5280
Central States Business Forms Inc 2500 Industrial Pkwy **Fax Area Code:* 918 ■ *TF:* 800-331-0920 ■ *Web:* www.centralstates.net	Dewey	OK	74029	800-331-0920	534-3470*
Champion Industries Inc PO Box 2968 PO Box 2968 *OTC:* CHMP ■ *TF:* 800-624-3431 ■ *Web:* champion-industries.com	Huntington	WV	25728	304-528-2791	528-2746
Curtis 1000 Inc 1725 Breckinridge Pkwy Ste 500 **Fax Area Code:* 800 ■ *TF:* 877-287-8715 ■ *Web:* www.curtis1000.com	Duluth	GA	30096	678-380-9095	944-8817*
Custom Business Forms Inc 210 Edge Pl *TF General:* 800-234-1221 ■ *Web:* www.cbfnet.com	Minneapolis	MN	55418	612-789-0002	789-6321
DATA Group (DBF) 9195 Torbram Rd *Web:* www.datacm.com	Brampton	ON	L6S6H2	905-791-3151	791-3277
Data Papers Inc 468 Industrial Pk Rd **Fax Area Code:* 888 ■ *TF:* 800-233-3032 ■ *Web:* www.datapapers.com	Muncy	PA	17756	800-233-3032	546-2366*
Data Source Inc 1400 Universal Ave *TF:* 877-846-9120 ■ *Web:* www.data-source.com	Kansas City	MO	64120	816-483-3282	483-3284
Datatel Resources Corp 1729 Pennsylvania Ave *TF:* 800-245-2688 ■ *Web:* www.datatelcorp.com	Monaca	PA	15061	724-775-5300	775-0688
DFS Group 500 Main St *TF General:* 800-225-9528 ■ *Web:* www.dfsonline.com/dfsecat/loginservlet	Groton	MA	01471	800-225-9528	876-6337
Dupli-Systems Inc 8260 Dow Cir *TF:* 800-321-1610 ■ *Web:* www.dupli-systems.com	Strongsville	OH	44136	440-234-9415	234-2350
Eagle Graphics Inc 150 N Moyer St *Web:* www.eaglegraphic.com	Annville	PA	17003	717-867-5576	867-5579
Eastern Business Forms Inc PO Box 10 *TF:* 800-387-2648 ■ *Web:* www.ebf-inc.com	Mauldin	SC	29662	800-387-2648	
Federal Business Products Inc 95 Main Ave *TF:* 800-927-5123 ■ *Web:* www.feddirect.com	Clifton	NJ	07014	973-667-9800	
FedEx 450 W First Ave *TF:* 800-463-3339 ■ *Web:* www.fedex.com/us/office/commercialpress	Roselle	NJ	07203	406-252-6265	
Flesh Co 2118 59th St **Fax:* Sales ■ *TF:* 800-869-3330 ■ *Web:* www.fleshco.com	Saint Louis	MO	63110	314-781-4400	781-5546*
Forms Manufacturers Inc 312 E Forest Ave *TF:* 800-835-0614 ■ *Web:* www.ennis.com/our-network/forms-manufacturers	Girard	KS	66743	620-724-8225	724-8188
Freedom Graphic Systems Inc (FGS) 1101 S Janesville St *TF:* 800-334-3540 ■ *Web:* fgs.com	Milton	WI	53563	800-334-3540	
General Credit Forms Inc (GCF) 3595 Rider Trl S *TF:* 888-423-6397 ■ *Web:* www.gcfinc.com	Earth City	MO	63045	314-216-8600	216-8570
Genoa Business Forms Inc 445 Pk Ave **Fax Area Code:* 815 ■ *TF:* 800-383-2801 ■ *Web:* www.genoabusforms.com	Sycamore	IL	60178	800-383-2801	895-8206*
Gulf Business Forms Inc 2460 S IH-35 PO Box 1073 *TF:* 800-433-4853 ■ *Web:* www.gulfforms.com	San Marcos	TX	78667	512-353-8313	353-8866
Highland Computer Forms Inc 1025 W Main St **Fax Area Code:* 800 ■ **Fax:* Sales ■ *TF:* 800-669-5213 ■ *Web:* www.hcf.com	Hillsboro	OH	45133	937-393-4215	842-6485*
Hospital Forms & Systems Corp 8900 Ambassador Row *TF:* 800-527-5081 ■ *Web:* www.hforms.com	Dallas	TX	75247	214-634-8900	
IBS Direct 431 Yerkes Rd *TF:* 800-220-1255 ■ *Web:* www.ibsdm.com	King of Prussia	PA	19406	610-265-8210	265-7997
Imperial Graphics Inc 3100 Walkent Dr NW **Fax Area Code:* 616 ■ *TF:* 800-777-2591 ■ *Web:* www.imperialcrs.com	Grand Rapids	MI	49544	800-777-2591	784-8256*
Integrated Print & Graphics (IPG) 645 Stevenson Rd *Web:* www.ipandginc.com	South Elgin	IL	60177	847-695-6777	
Kaye-Smith 4101 Oakesdale Ave SW *TF:* 800-822-9987 ■ *Web:* www.kayesmith.com	Renton	WA	98057	425-228-8600	
Liberty-Pittsburgh Systems Inc 3498 Grand Ave **Fax Area Code:* 877	Pittsburgh	PA	15225	412-771-9900	577-3456*
NCP Solutions 5200 E Lake Blvd *Web:* www.ncpsolutions.com	Birmingham	AL	35217	205-849-5200	421-7387
New Jersey Business Forms Manufacturing Co 55 W Sheffield Ave *TF:* 800-466-6523 ■ *Web:* www.njbf.com	Englewood	NJ	07631	201-569-4500	
Paris Business Products 800 Highland Dr *TF Cust Svc:* 800-523-6454 ■ *Web:* www.pariscorp.com	Westampton	NJ	08060	609-265-9200	261-4853
Patterson Office Supplies 3310 N Duncan Rd *TF:* 800-637-1140 ■ *Web:* www.pattersonofficesupplies.com	Champaign	IL	61822	317-733-4900	
Performance Office Papers 21565 Hamburg Ave *TF:* 800-458-7189 ■ *Web:* www.perfpapers.com	Lakeville	MN	55044	800-458-7189	488-5058
PrintEdd Products of North America 2641 N Forum Dr *TF:* 800-367-6728 ■ *Web:* www.printedd.com	Grand Prairie	TX	75052	972-660-3800	641-2564
Quality Forms 4317 W US Rt 36 **Fax Area Code:* 888 ■ *TF:* 866-773-4595 ■ *Web:* www.qualforms.com	Piqua	OH	45356	937-773-4595	550-3937*
Rotary Forms Press Inc 835 S High St *TF:* 800-654-2876 ■ *Web:* www.rotaryfp.com	Hillsboro	OH	45133	937-393-3426	393-8473
Royal Business Forms Inc 3301 Ave E E *TF:* 800-255-9303 ■ *Web:* royalbf.com	Arlington	TX	76011	817-640-5248	633-2164
Source4 3944 S Morgan *Web:* www.source4.com	Chicago	IL	60609	773-247-4141	247-1313
Specialized Printed Forms Inc 352 Ctr St *TF:* 800-688-2381 ■ *Web:* www.spforms.com	Caledonia	NY	14423	585-538-2381	538-4922
Sterling Business Forms PO Box 2486 *TF Cust Svc:* 800-759-3676 ■ *Web:* www.sbfnet.com	White City	OR	97503	800-759-3676	234-2409
Stry-Lenkoff Co Inc 1100 W Broadway *TF:* 800-626-8247 ■ *Web:* www.strylenkoff.com	Louisville	KY	40232	502-587-6804	587-6822
United Business Forms Inc 8482 W Allens Bridge Rd *Web:* greenevillesun.com	Greeneville	TN	37743	423-639-5551	
Victor Printing Inc 1 Victor Way *TF:* 800-443-2845 ■ *Web:* www.victorptg.com	Sharon	PA	16146	724-342-2106	342-6147
Ward-Kraft Inc 2401 Cooper St *TF:* 800-821-4021 ■ *Web:* www.wardkraft.com	Fort Scott	KS	66701	620-223-5500	223-6953
Wilmer Service Line 515 W Sycamore St *TF:* 800-494-5637 ■ *Web:* www.4wilmer.com	Coldwater	OH	45828	800-494-5637	553-4849
Wise Business Forms Inc 555 McFarland 400 Dr *TF:* 888-815-9473 ■ *Web:* www.wbf.com	Alpharetta	GA	30004	770-442-1060	442-9849
Witt Printing Company Inc 301 Oak St *TF:* 800-641-4342 ■ *Web:* www.wittprinting.com	El Dorado Springs	MO	64744	417-876-4721	876-4794
Wright Business Forms Inc 645 Stevenson Rd	South Elgin	IL	60177	708-865-7600	
Wright Business Graphics (WBG) 18440 NE San Rafael St *TF:* 800-547-8397 ■ *Web:* www.wrightbg.com	Portland	OR	97230	800-547-8397	

111 BUSINESS MACHINES - MFR

See Also Business Machines - Whol p. 1884; Calculators - Electronic p. 1889; Computer Equipment p. 1998; Photocopying Equipment & Supplies p. 2939

				Phone	Fax
Aaxon Laundry Systems 6100 N Powerline Rd *Web:* www.aaxon.com	Ft. Lauderdale	FL	33309	954-772-7100	
Abbott Vascular 26531 Ynez Rd *TF:* 800-227-9902 ■ *Web:* www.abbottvascular.com	Temecula	CA	92591	800-227-9902	
ACR Supply Company Inc 4040 S Alston Ave *Web:* www.acrsupply.com	Durham	NC	27713	919-765-8081	
Action Industrial Group LLC 1623 Cedar Line Dr *Web:* www.actionindgroup.com	Rock Hill	SC	29730	803-324-2658	
Agissar Corp 526 Benton St *TF:* 800-627-8256 ■ *Web:* www.agissar.com	Stratford	CT	06615	203-375-8662	
Amano Cincinnati Inc 140 Harrison Ave *TF:* 800-526-2559 ■ *Web:* www.amano.com	Roseland	NJ	07068	973-403-1900	364-1086
Americ Machinery Corp 1001 3rd Ave S *Web:* www.americmachinery.com	Kent	WA	98032	253-236-8555	
Atlantic Zeiser Inc 15 Patton Dr *Web:* www.atlanticzeiser.com	West Caldwell	NJ	07006	973-228-0800	228-9064
Atlas Companies, The 5101 Commerce Crossing Dr *Web:* www.atlas-co.com	Louisville	KY	40229	502-779-2100	
Aurora Instruments Ltd 1001 E Pender St *Web:* www.aurorabiomed.com/	Vancouver	BC	V6A1W2	604-215-8700	
Autometrix Precision Cutting Systems Inc 12098 Charles Dr *Web:* www.autometrix.com	Grass Valley	CA	95945	530-477-5065	
Better Packages Inc 255 Canal St PO Box 711 *TF:* 800-237-9151 ■ *Web:* www.betterpackages.com	Shelton	CT	06484	203-926-3722	926-3706
Bidwell Industrial Group Inc 2055 S Main St *Web:* www.bidwellinc.com	Middletown	CT	06457	860-346-9283	347-8775
Biosafe Engineering LLC 485 Southpoint Cir Ste 200 *Web:* biosafeeng.com	Brownsburg	IN	46112	317-858-8099	
Borin Manufacturing Inc 5741 Buckingham Pkwy Unit B *Web:* borin.com	Culver City	CA	90230	310-822-1000	
Brandt Tractor Ltd Hwy 1 E PO Box 3856 *TF:* 888-227-2638 ■ *Web:* www.brandt.ca	Regina	SK	S4P3R8	306-791-7777	
Brother International Corp 100 Somerset Corporate Blvd *TF Cust Svc:* 877-552-6255 ■ *Web:* www.brother-usa.com	Bridgewater	NJ	08807	908-704-1700	704-8235
Broudy Precision Equipment Co 9 Union Hill Rd *Web:* www.broudyprecision.com	West Conshohocken	PA	19428	610-825-7200	
CCTF Corp 5407 - 53 Ave NW *TF:* 800-661-3633 ■ *Web:* www.cctf.com	Edmonton	AB	T6B3G2	780-463-8700	
CCX Corp 1399 Horizon Ave *Web:* www.ccxcorp.com	Lafayette	CO	80026	303-666-5206	
Checker Industrial Ltd 3345 Wyandotte St *Web:* www.checkerindustrial.com	East Windsor	ON	N8Y4S2	519-258-2022	
CMD Corp 2901-3005 E Pershing St PO Box 1279 *Web:* www.cmd-corp.com	Appleton	WI	54912	920-730-6888	

Company	City	State	ZIP	Phone	Fax
CNC Industries Inc 3810 Fourier Dr *Web:* www.cncind.com	Fort Wayne	IN	46818	260-490-5700	
Col-Met Spray Booths Inc 1635 Innovation Dr *Web:* www.colmetsb.com	Rockwall	TX	75032	972-772-1919	
Con-tek Machine Inc 3575 Hoffman Rd E *Web:* www.con-tek.com	Saint Paul	MN	55110	651-779-6058	
Coop Purdel LA 155 Rue Saint-Jean-Baptiste *Web:* www.purdel.qc.ca	Le Bic	QC	G0L1B0	418-736-4363	
Corma Inc 10 McCleary Court Concord *Web:* www.corma.com	Toronto	ON	L4K2Z3	905-669-9397	
CP Bourg Inc 50 Samuel Barnet Blvd *Web:* www.cpbourg.com	New Bedford	MA	02745	508-998-2171	
CRANE Merchandising Systems 2043 Woodland Pkwy Ste 102 *Web:* www.cranems.com	St. Louis	MO	63146	314-298-3500	
Crown Lift Trucks LLC 10685 Medallion Dr *Web:* www.okisys.com	Cincinnati	OH	45241	513-874-2600	
Cubeit Portable Storage Canada Inc 100 Canadian Rd *TF:* 888-428-2348 ■ *Web:* www.cubeit.ca	Scarborough	ON	M1R4Z5	888-428-2348	
Cummins-Allison Corp 852 Feehanville Dr *TF:* 800-786-5528 ■ *Web:* www.cumminsallison.com	Mount Prospect	IL	60056	847-299-9550	299-9550
Data Cable Technologies Inc 1306 Enterprise Dr *Web:* www.datacabletech.com	Romeoville	IL	60446	630-226-5600	
Dedoes Industries Inc 1060 W West Maple Rd *Web:* www.dedoes.com	Walled Lake	MI	48390	248-624-7710	
Dillin Engineered Systems Corp 8030 Broadstone Rd *Web:* www.dillinautomation.com	Perrysburg	OH	43551	419-666-6789	
Distek Inc 121 N Ctr Dr *Web:* www.distekinc.com	North Brunswick	NJ	08902	732-422-7585	
Dynetics Engineering Corp 515 Bond St *TF:* 800-888-8110 ■ *Web:* www.dyneticsengineering.com	Lincolnshire	IL	60069	847-541-7300	541-7488
Ecco Business Systems Inc 60 W 38th St 4th Fl *TF:* 800-558-6777 ■ *Web:* www.eccobusiness.com	New York	NY	10018	212-921-4545	921-2198
ECRM Inc 554 Clark Rd *TF:* 800-537-3276 ■ *Web:* www.ecrm.com	Tewksbury	MA	01876	978-851-0207	851-7016
Edgewater Automation LLC 481 Renaissance Dr *Web:* www.edgewaterautomation.com	St. Joseph	MI	49085	269-983-1300	
Elliot Equipment Corp 1131 Country Club Rd *Web:* www.elliottequipment.com	Indianapolis	IN	46234	317-271-3065	
Engrenage Provincial Inc 165, boulevard des CŠdres *Web:* www.engrenageprovincial.com	Quebec	QC	G1L1M8	418-683-2745	
Epygi Technologies Ltd 6900 Dallas Pkwy Ste 850 *Web:* www.epygi.com	Plano	TX	75024	972-692-1166	
Ernest Green & Son Ltd 2395 Skymark Ave *TF:* 800-387-7577 ■ *Web:* www.ernestgreen.com	Mississauga	ON	L4W4Y6	905-629-8999	
Essex Electro Engineering Inc 2015 Mitchell Blvd *Web:* www.essexelectro.com	Schaumburg	IL	60193	847-891-4444	
Exocor Inc 271 Ridley Rd *TF:* 888-317-2209 ■ *Web:* exocor.com	St. Catharines	ON	L2R6P7	905-704-0603	
Fabgroups Technologies Inc 1100 Saint Amour *Web:* www.fabgroups.com	Saint-laurent	QC	H4S1J2	514-331-3712	
Fargo Automation Inc 969 34th St N *Web:* www.fargoautomation.com	Fargo	ND	58102	701-232-1780	
FCA LLC 7601 John Deere Pkwy PO Box 758 *Web:* www.fcapackaging.com	Moline	IL	61266	309-792-3444	
Felins USA Inc 8306 W Parkland Ct *Web:* www.felins.com	Milwaukee	WI	53223	414-355-7747	
Fellowes Inc 1789 Norwood Ave **Fax:* Cust Svc ■ *TF:* 800-945-4545 ■ *Web:* www.fellowes.com	Itasca	IL	60143	630-893-1600	893-1600*
Fireside Hearth & Home 7571 215th St W *TF:* 800-669-4328 ■ *Web:* www.fireside.com	Lakeville	MN	55044	651-452-3399	
Fogg Filler Co 3455 John F Donnelly Dr *Web:* www.foggfiller.com	Holland	MI	49424	616-786-3644	
Foremost Machine Builders Inc 23 Spielman Rd *Web:* foremostmachine.com	Fairfield	NJ	07004	973-227-0700	
Fountain Industries Co 922 E 14th St *TF:* 800-328-3594 ■ *Web:* www.fountainindustries.com	Albert Lea	MN	56007	507-373-2351	
G & O Thermal Supply Co 5435 N Northwest Hwy *TF:* 800-621-4997 ■ *Web:* www.gothermal.com	Chicago	IL	60630	773-763-1300	
GalFab Inc 612 W 11th St PO Box 39 *Web:* www.galfab.com	Winamac	IN	46996	574-946-7767	
GenServe Inc 80 Sweeneydale Ave *TF:* 800-247-7215 ■ *Web:* www.genserveinc.com	Bay Shore	NY	11706	631-435-0437	
Global Payment Technologies Inc 170 Wilbur Pl *OTC: GPTX*	Bohemia	NY	11716	631-563-2500	563-2630
Gradco USA Inc 871 Coronado Ctr Dr Ste 200 *Web:* www.gradco.com	Henderson	NV	89052	949-595-4374	
Groves Industrial Supply Inc 7301 Pinemont Dr *Web:* www.grovesindustrial.com	Houston	TX	77040	713-675-4747	
Hewitt Material Handling Inc 425 Millway Ave *Web:* www.hewittmaterialhandling.ca	Concord	ON	L4K3V8	905-669-6590	
HILLS Inc 7785 Ellis Rd *Web:* www.hillsinc.net	West Melbourne	FL	32904	321-724-2370	
HTS Engineering Ltd 115 Norfinch Dr *Web:* www.htseng.com	Toronto	ON	M3N1W8	416-661-3400	
Imaging Business Machines LLC 2750 Crestwood Blvd *TF:* 877-627-8325 ■ *Web:* www.ibml.com	Birmingham	AL	35210	205-439-7100	956-5309
Industrial Shredders 12037 S Ave PO Box 218 *Web:* www.industrialshredders.com	North Lima	OH	44452	330-549-9960	549-9961
International Business Machines Corp (IBM) 1 New OrchaRd Rd *NYSE: IBM* ■ *TF:* 800-426-4968 ■ *Web:* www.ibm.com	Armonk	NY	10504	914-499-1900	
J C Foodservice Inc 415 S Atlantic Blvd *Web:* www.actionsales.com	Monterey Park	CA	91754	626-308-1988	
Korsch America Inc 18 Bristol Dr *Web:* www.korschamerica.com	South Easton	MA	02375	508-238-9080	
Lakeside Process Controls Ltd 2475 Hogan Dr *TF:* 800-265-1005 ■ *Web:* www.lakesidecontrols.ca	Mississauga	ON	L5N0E9	905-629-9340	
Lathem Time Corp 200 Selig Dr SW **Fax Area Code:* 800 ■ *TF:* 800-241-4990 ■ *Web:* www.lathem.com	Atlanta	GA	30336	404-691-0400	252-2208*
Leeson Canada Inc 320 Superior Blvd *TF:* 800-563-0949 ■ *Web:* www.leeson.ca	Mississauga	ON	L5T2N7	905-670-4770	
Lynde-Ordway Company Inc 3308 W Warner Ave *TF:* 800-762-7057 ■ *Web:* www.lynde-ordway.com	Santa Ana	CA	92704	714-957-1311	433-2166
MAAC Machinery Corp 590 Tower Blvd *TF:* 800-588-6222 ■ *Web:* maacmachinery.com	Carol Stream	IL	60188	630-665-1700	
Magnatech International Inc 17 E Meadow Ave *TF:* 800-523-8193 ■ *Web:* magnatech-int.com	Robesonia	PA	19551	610-693-8866	
Manitex Liftking ULC 7135 Islington Ave *Web:* www.manitexliftking.com	Woodbridge	ON	L4L1V9	905-851-3988	
Maple Farm Equipment Partnership Hwy 10 E *Web:* www.maplefarm.ca	Yorkton	SK	S3N2V7	306-783-9459	
Martin Yale Industries Inc 251 Wedcor Ave *TF:* 800-225-5644 ■ *Web:* www.martinyale.com	Wabash	IN	46992	260-563-0641	563-4575
MBM Corp (MBM) 3134 Industry Dr *TF Cust Svc:* 800-223-2508 ■ *Web:* www.mbmcorp.com	North Charleston	SC	29418	843-552-2700	552-2974
Morehouse-COWLES 13930 Magnolia Ave *Web:* www.morehousecowles.com	Chino	CA	91710	909-627-7222	
National Lift Truck Inc 3333 Mount Prospect Rd *Web:* www.nlt.com	Franklin Park	IL	60131	630-782-1000	
Neopost Inc Canada 150 Steelcase Rd W *TF:* 800-636-7678 ■ *Web:* www.neopost.ca	Markham	ON	L3R3J9	905-475-3722	475-7699
Newbold Corp 450 Weaver St *TF:* 800-552-3282 ■ *Web:* www.newboldcorp.com/addressograph	Rocky Mount	VA	24151	540-489-4400	489-4417
Nissei America Inc 1480 N Hancock St *Web:* www.nisseiamerica.com	Anaheim	CA	92807	714-693-3000	
Noble Trade Inc 7171 Jane St *TF:* 800-529-9805 ■ *Web:* www.noble.ca	Concord	ON	L4K1A7	416-754-5533	
Norchem Corp 5649 Alhambra Ave *Web:* norchemcorp.com	Los Angeles	CA	90032	323-221-0221	
Nordon Inc 1 Cabot Blvd E *Web:* www.nordoninc.com	Langhorne	PA	19047	215-504-4700	
Norsask Farm Equipment Ltd Box 49 *TF:* 888-446-8128 ■ *Web:* www.norsaskfarmequipmentltd.com	North Battleford	SK	S9A2X6	306-445-8128	
Norwesco Industries (1983) Ltd 6908L - Sixth St SE *Web:* www.norwesco.ab.ca	Calgary	AB	T2H2K4	403-258-3883	
Ossur 27412 Aliso Viejo Pkwy *TF:* 800-233-6263 ■ *Web:* www.ossur.com	Aliso Viejo	CA	92656	800-233-6263	
Outotec (Canada) Ltd 1551 Corporate Dr *Web:* www.outotec.com	Burlington	ON	L7L6M3	905-335-0002	
Paymaster Technologies Inc 61 Garlisch Dr *Web:* www.paymastertech.com	Elk Grove Village	IL	60007	847-758-1234	
Peerless Inc 79 Perry St *Web:* www.peerless-inc.com	Buffalo	NY	14203	716-852-4784	
Pitney Bowes Inc 1 Elmcroft Rd *NYSE: PBI* ■ *TF:* 800-672-6937 ■ *Web:* pitneybowes.com/us	Stamford	CT	06926	203-356-5000	
PLC Diagnostics Inc 5743 Corsa Ave Ste 119 *Web:* www.plcds.com	Westlake Village	CA	91362	805-405-4620	
Preston Phipps Inc 6400 Vanden Abeele *Web:* prestonphipps.com	Montreal	QC	H4S1R9	514-333-5340	
Process Control Corp 6875 Mimms Dr *Web:* www.process-control.com	Atlanta	GA	30340	770-449-8810	
Proco Machinery 1111 Brevik Pl *Web:* procomachinery.com	Mississauga	ON	L4W3R7	905-602-6066	
Proline Concrete Tools Inc 2560 Jason Ct *Web:* www.prolinestamps.com	Oceanside	CA	92056	760-758-7240	
Pubco Corp 3830 Kelley Ave *TF:* 800-878-3399 ■ *Web:* fundinguniverse.com	Cleveland	OH	44114	216-881-5300	881-8380
Puregas LLC 226 Commerce St *TF:* 800-521-5351 ■ *Web:* puregas.com	Broomfield	CO	80020	303-427-3700	
Rapid Line Industries Inc 455 N Ottawa St *TF:* 877-444-9955 ■ *Web:* rapidline.com	Joliet	IL	60432	815-727-4362	
Red Streak Corp 1627 Main St Ste 901	Kansas City	MO	64108	816-471-6979	471-1143
Reed Machinery Inc 10A New Bond St *Web:* www.reed-machinery.com	Worcester	MA	01606	508-595-9090	
Refron Inc 38-18 33rd St *Web:* www.refron.com	Long Island City	NY	11101	718-392-8002	
Rimex Supply Ltd 9726 186th St *TF:* 800-663-9883 ■ *Web:* www.rimex.com	Surrey	BC	V4N3N7	604-888-0025	
Royal Consumer Information Products Inc 379 Campus Dr 2nd Fl **Fax Area Code:* 800 ■ *TF Sales:* 888-261-4555 ■ *Web:* www.royalsupplies.com	Somerset	NJ	08873	732-627-9977	232-9769*
Russell Forest Products Inc 719 Railroad St SW *Web:* www.russellforest.com	Hartselle	AL	35640	256-773-1607	
Schaumburg Specialties Co 550 Albion Ave Unit 30 *TF:* 800-834-8125 ■ *Web:* www.shopcraftracks.com	Schaumburg	IL	60193	800-834-8125	
Schold Machine Corp 7201 W 64th Pl *Web:* www.schold.com	Chicago	IL	60638	708-458-3788	

Company	City	State	ZIP	Phone	Fax
Schuneman Equipment Co 15058 SD Hwy 15 PO Box 229	Milbank	SD	57252	605-432-5523	
Web: www.schunemanequipment.com					
Seamless Technologies Inc 35 Airport Rd	Morristown	NJ	07960	973-326-8900	
Web: www.seamlessti.com					
Security Check LLC 2612 Jackson Ave W	Oxford	MS	38655	662-234-0440	281-8400
Security Engineered Machinery Company Inc 5 Walkup Dr PO Box 1045	Westborough	MA	01581	508-366-1488	836-4154
TF Sales: 800-225-9293 ■ *Web:* www.semshred.com					
Shalon Ventures 155 Island Dr	Palo Alto	CA	94301	650-566-8200	
Web: www.shalon.com					
Sharp Electronics Corp 1 Sharp Plz	Mahwah	NJ	07430	201-529-8200	529-8413
TF: 800-237-4277 ■ *Web:* www.sharpusa.com					
Skyjack Inc 55 Campbell Rd	Guelph	ON	N1H1B9	519-837-0888	
Web: www.skyjack.com					
Sonar Products Inc 609 Industrial Rd	Carlstadt	NJ	07072	201-729-1116	
Web: sonarproductsinc.com					
Spartan Controls Ltd 305 - 27 St SE	Calgary	AB	T2A7V2	403-207-0700	
Web: www.spartancontrols.com					
Staplex Co 777 Fifth Ave	Brooklyn	NY	11232	718-768-3333	965-0750
TF Cust Svc: 800-221-0822 ■ *Web:* www.staplex.com					
Stemmerich Inc 4728 Gravois Ave	Saint Louis	MO	63116	314-832-7726	
Web: www.stemmerich.com					
STT Enviro Corp 8485 Parkhill Dr	Milton	ON	L9T5E9	905-693-9301	
Web: www.sttsemcan.com					
Sturtevant Inc 348 Circuit St	Hanover	MA	02339	781-829-6501	
Web: www.sturtevantinc.com					
Supfina Machine Company Inc 181 Circuit Dr	North Kingstown	RI	02852	401-294-6600	
Web: www.supfina.com					
Swintec Corp 320 W Commercial Ave	Moonachie	NJ	07074	201-935-0115	933-9745
TF: 800-225-0867 ■ *Web:* www.swintec.com					
TeraDiode Inc 30 Upton Dr	Wilmington	MA	01887	978-988-1040	
Web: www.teradiode.com					
Tundra Process Solutions Ltd 7523 Flint Rd SE	Calgary	AB	T2H1G3	403-255-5222	
TF: 800-265-1166 ■ *Web:* www.tundrasolutions.ca					
Updike Supply Inc 8241 Expansion Way	Huber Heights	OH	45424	937-482-4000	
Web: www.updikesupply.com					
Vincent Corp 2810 E Fifth Ave	Tampa	FL	33605	813-248-2650	
Web: www.vincentcorp.com					
Westward Parts Services Ltd 6517 - 67 St	Red Deer	AB	T4P1A3	403-347-2200	
TF: 888-937-7278 ■ *Web:* www.westwardparts.com					
William F. White International Inc 800 Islington Ave	Toronto	ON	M8Z6A1	416-239-5050	
Web: www.whites.com					
Wolseley Canada Inc 880 Laurentian Dr	Burlington	ON	L7N3V6	905-335-7373	
Web: www.wolseleyinc.ca					
Wright Implement Company LLC 3225 Carter Rd	Owensboro	KY	42301	270-683-3606	
Web: wrightimp.com					

112 BUSINESS MACHINES - WHOL

See Also Business Machines - Mfr p. 1882; Computer Equipment & Software - Whol p. 2002; Photocopying Equipment & Supplies p. 2939

Company	City	State	ZIP	Phone	Fax
ABC Electric Corp 2425 46th St	Astoria	NY	11103	718-956-0000	
Web: www.abcelectriccorp.com					
Adams Remco Inc PO Box 3968	South Bend	IN	46619	574-288-2113	
TF: 800-627-2113 ■ *Web:* www.adamsremco.com					
Airdyne Ltd 14910 Henry Rd	Houston	TX	77060	281-820-0000	
Web: www.airdyne.net					
Arkansas Power Steering & Hydraulics Inc 900 Fiber Optic Dr	North Little Rock	AR	72117	501-372-4828	
Web: apshyd.com					
Black Equipment Co Inc 1050 N Congress Ave	Evansville	IN	47716	812-477-6481	
Web: www.blackequipment.com					
Blue Technologies 5885 Grant Ave	Cleveland	OH	44105	216-271-4800	271-0084*
**Fax:* Sales ■ *Web:* www.bluetechnologiesinc.com					
Brahma Compression Ltd 43rd Ave SE Ste 1310	Calgary	AB	T2G2A2	403-287-6990	
Web: www.brahmacompression.com					
C J Nolte Co, The 649 Central Ave Ste 19	Westfield	NJ	07090	908-789-0377	
Web: cjnolte.com					
Canon Business Solutions-Central 425 N Martingale Rd Ste 100	Schaumburg	IL	60173	847-706-3400	706-3419*
**Fax:* Hum Res ■ *TF:* 800-706-3303 ■ *Web:* csa.canon.com/online/portal/csa/csa/home/!ut/p/a1/04_sj9cpykssy0xplmnmz0vmafgjzoi9lvwcdt1mdl-wtzeondbz9q0l9demcdq0stiakioekdhaarwnc-gtyqxubjfroha!!/dl5/d5/l2dbisevz0fbis9nqseh					
Carr Business Systems Inc 130 Spagnoli Rd	Melville	NY	11747	631-249-9880	
TF: 800-720-2277 ■ *Web:* www.carr-global.com					
Collicutt Energy Services Ltd 8133 Edgar Industrial Close	Red Deer	AB	T4P3R4	403-309-9250	
Web: collicutt.com					
Copiers Northwest Inc 601 Dexter Ave N	Seattle	WA	98109	206-282-1200	282-2010
TF: 866-692-0700 ■ *Web:* www.copiersnw.com					
CRS Inc 4851 White Bear Pkwy	Saint Paul	MN	55110	651-294-2700	294-2900
TF: 800-333-4949 ■ *Web:* www.crs-usa.com					
Daisy IT Supplies Sales & Service 8575 Red Oak Ave	Rancho Cucamonga	CA	91730	909-989-5585	989-5585
TF: 800-266-5585 ■ *Web:* daisyit.com					
Datamax Office Systems Inc 6717 Waldemar Ave	Saint Louis	MO	63139	314-633-1400	633-1402
TF: 800-325-9299 ■ *Web:* www.datamaxstl.com					
Dieterich-Post Co 616 Monterey Pass Rd	Monterey Park	CA	91754	626-289-5021	688-3729*
**Fax Area Code:* 800 ■ *TF:* 800-955-3729 ■ *Web:* www.dieterich-post.com					
Don-Nan Pump & Supply Co 3427 E Garden City Hwy	Midland	TX	79706	432-682-7742	
Web: www.don-nan.com					
DTI LLC 1196 FM 529	Houston	TX	77041	713-856-8735	
Web: dtillc.com					
EcoPower Hybrid Systems Inc 9995 Ave de Catania Ste G	Brossard	QC	J4Z3V7	450-676-7755	
Web: ecopowerhs.com					
El Dorado Trading Group Inc 760 San Antonio Rd	Palo Alto	CA	94303	800-227-8292	494-1995*
**Fax Area Code:* 650 ■ *TF:* 800-227-8292 ■ *Web:* www.edtg.com					
FP Mailing Solutions 140 N Mitchell Ct	Addison	IL	60101	630-827-5500	
TF: 800-341-6052 ■ *Web:* www.fp-usa.com					
G C Peterson Machinery Co Inc 2300 Myrtle Ave Ste 100	St. Paul	MN	55114	651-789-5360	
Web: www.gcpeterson.com					
Global Imaging Systems Inc 3820 Northdale Blvd Ste 200A	Tampa	FL	33624	813-960-5508	264-7877
TF: 888-628-7834 ■ *Web:* www.global-imaging.com					
GS Precision Inc 101 John Seitz Dr 1 Industrial Pk	Brattleboro	VT	05301	802-257-5200	257-7937
Web: www.gsprecision.com					
Hewitt Equipment Limited 5001, Trans-Canada Hwy	Pointe-Claire	QC	H9R1B8	514-630-3100	
Web: www.hewitt.ca					
Huston-Patterson Corp 123 W N St Fl 4	Decatur	IL	62522	217-429-5161	
Web: www.hustonpatterson.com					
Illinois Wholesale Cash Register Inc 2790 Pinnacle Dr	Elgin	IL	60124	847-310-4200	310-8490
TF: 800-544-5493 ■ *Web:* www.illinoiswholesale.com					
Inspectech Ltd 450 Midwest Rd	Toronto	ON	M1P3A9	416-757-1179	
Web: www.inspectech.ca					
Konica Minolta Business Solutions USA Inc 100 Williams Dr	Ramsey	NJ	07446	201-825-4000	
Web: www.kmbs.konicaminolta.us					
Leyman Manufacturing Corp 10900 Kenwood Rd	Cincinnati	OH	45242	513-891-6210	
Web: www.leymanlift.com					
Mead O'brien Inc 1429 Atlantic Ave	North Kansas City	MO	64116	816-471-3993	
Web: www.meadobrien.com					
Merchants Solutions Co 19252 S Blackhawk Pkwy Unit 75	Mokena	IL	60448	708-449-6650	449-1432
TF: 800-486-3214					
Metro - Sales Inc 1640 E 78th St	Minneapolis	MN	55423	612-861-4000	866-8069
TF: 800-862-7414 ■ *Web:* www.metrosales.com					
Numeridex Inc 632 S Wheeling Rd	Wheeling	IL	60090	800-323-7737	541-8392*
**Fax Area Code:* 847 ■ *TF:* 800-323-7737 ■ *Web:* www.numeridex.com					
Pitney Bowes Inc 1 Elmcroft Rd	Stamford	CT	06926	203-356-5000	
NYSE: PBI ■ *TF:* 800-672-6937 ■ *Web:* pitneybowes.com/us					
Power Systems & Controls Inc 3206 Lanvale Ave	Richmond	VA	23230	804-355-2803	
Web: www.pscpower.com					
Ricoh Americas Corp 5 Dedrick Pl	West Caldwell	NJ	07006	973-882-2000	
TF: 800-727-1885 ■ *Web:* www.ricoh-usa.com					
Secap USA Inc 10 Clipper Rd	Conshohocken	PA	19428	610-825-6205	825-6205
TF: 800-523-0320 ■ *Web:* www.pitneybowes.com/us					
Shoppa's Material Handling Ltd 15217 Grand River Rd	Fort Worth	TX	76155	817-359-1100	
Web: www.shoppas.com					
Standard Duplicating Machines Corp 10 Connector Rd	Andover	MA	01810	978-470-1920	
TF: 800-526-4774 ■ *Web:* www.sdmc.com					
Stewart Engineering Supply Inc 3221 E Pioneer Pkwy	Arlington	TX	76010	817-640-1767	
TF: 800-533-1265 ■ *Web:* www.sesisupply.com					
Systel Business Equipment Company Inc 2604 Fort Bragg Rd	Fayetteville	NC	28303	910-321-7700	483-2846
TF: 800-849-5900 ■ *Web:* www.systeloa.com					
Tomra Pacific Inc 150 Klug Cir	Corona	CA	92880	951-520-1700	
Web: replanetusa.com					
Transco Business Technologies (TBT) 34 Leighton Rd	Augusta	ME	04330	207-622-6251	621-8620
TF: 800-322-0003 ■ *Web:* www.transcobusiness.com					
W C Weil Co Inc 3812 William Flynn Hwy Ste 2	Allison Park	PA	15101	412-487-7140	
Web: www.wcweil.com					
WellDynamics Inc 445 Woodline Dr	Spring	TX	77386	281-297-1200	
Web: www.welldynamics.com					
Winternitz Inc 235 Anthony Trail	Northbrook	IL	60062	847-272-0440	
Web: www.winternitz.com					
Zero Waste Energy Systems Inc 143 Old Humber Crescent	Kleinberg	ON	L0J1C0	905-266-0314	
Web: www.zwes.ca					

BUSINESS ORGANIZATIONS

See Chambers of Commerce - Canadian p. 1899; Chambers of Commerce - International p. 1900; Chambers of Commerce - US - Local p. 1903; Chambers of Commerce - US - State p. 1931; Management & Business Professional Associations p. 1795

113 BUSINESS SERVICE CENTERS

Company	City	State	ZIP	Phone	Fax
A & d Technical Supply Company Inc 4320 S 89th St	Omaha	NE	68127	402-592-4950	
Web: www.adtechsupply.com					
A e Graphics Inc 4075 N 124th St Ste A	Brookfield	WI	53005	262-241-5860	
Web: aegraphics.com					
Acclaim Print & Copy Centers Inc 6345 Scarlett Ct	Dublin	CA	94568	925-829-7750	
Web: www.acclaimprint.com					
Accurate Printing Inc 2380 Research Court Ste 100	Woodbridge	VA	22192	703-494-0707	
Web: www.accurateprinting.com					

	City	State	Zip	Phone	Fax
Allegra Graphic Design Group 3983 Linden Ave SE *Web:* allegragr.com	Grand Rapids	MI	49548	616-248-4110	
Allegra Network LLC 47585 Galleon Dr *TF General:* 800-726-9050 ■ *Web:* allegramarketingprint.com	Plymouth	MI	48170	248-596-8600	596-8601
Aloha Petroleum Ltd 1132 Bishop St Ste 1700 *TF:* 800-621-4654 ■ *Web:* www.alohagas.com	Honolulu	HI	96813	808-522-9700	522-9707
Alphanumeric Systems Inc 3801 Wake Forest Rd *TF:* 800-638-6556 ■ *Web:* www.alphanumeric.com	Raleigh	NC	27609	919-781-7575	872-1440
Aminian Business Services Inc 50 Tesla *TF:* 888-800-5207 ■ *Web:* www.aminian.com	Irvine	CA	92618	949-724-1155	
Annex Brands Inc 7580 Metropolitan Dr Ste 200 *TF:* 877-722-5236 ■ *Web:* www.gopackagingstore.com	San Diego	CA	92108	619-563-4800	563-9850
Ares Corp 1440 Chapin Ave Ste 390 *Web:* www.arescorporation.com	Burlingame	CA	94010	650-401-7100	401-7101
Asi System Integration Inc 48 W 37th St *Fax Area Code: 212 ■ *TF:* 866-308-3920 ■ *Web:* www.asisystem.com	New York	NY	10018	866-308-3920	629-3944*
Avalon Copy Centers of America Inc 901 N State St *Web:* www.teamavalon.com	Syracuse	NY	13208	315-471-3333	
B2B Workforce Inc 200 N Pt Ctr E Ste 150 *Fax Area Code: 404	Alpharetta	GA	30022	770-667-7200	479-2423*
Barrister Digital Solutions LLC 1700 K St Nw Ste B100	Washington	DC	20006	202-289-7279	
Belmark Inc 600 Heritage Rd PO Box 5310 *Web:* www.belmark.com	De Pere	WI	54115	920-336-2848	336-4577
Bright Trading LLC 4850 Harrison Dr *Web:* www.stocktrading.com	Las Vegas	NV	89121	702-739-1393	739-1398
Capitol Copy Service 116 W State St *Web:* capitol-copy.com	Trenton	NJ	08608	609-989-8776	
Client Solution Architects 52 Gettysburg Pk *Web:* www.csaassociates.com	Mechanicsburg	PA	17055	717-795-9104	
Cmbs Medical Business Services 223 N 1st Ave Ste 201 *Web:* cmbsllc.net	Arcadia	CA	91006	626-821-1411	
Coastal Reprographics Services 880 Via Esteban Ste B *Web:* gocrs.com	San Luis Obispo	CA	93401	805-543-5247	
Color Reflections 10795 Rockley Rd *Web:* www.colorreflections.com	Houston	TX	77099	713-626-4045	
Composites Horizons Inc 1471 Industrial Pk St *Web:* aipaerospace.com/composites-home	Covina	CA	91722	626-331-0861	339-3220
Concentrix Corp 3750 Monroe Ave *TF:* 800-747-0583 ■ *Web:* www.concentrix.com	Pittsford	NY	14534	585-218-5300	218-5301
Conlins Copy Center Inc 52 Lancaster Ave Ste *Web:* www.conlinscopy.com	Malvern	PA	19355	610-647-6100	
Copymat Digibranch 191 Battery St *Web:* www.copymat3.com	San Francisco	CA	94111	415-981-1300	
Core Bts Inc 201 W 103rd St Ste 240 *TF:* 855-267-3287 ■ *Web:* www.corebts.com	Indianapolis	IN	46290	855-267-3287	
Corporation Service Co 2711 Centerville Rd Ste 400 *TF:* 866-403-5272 ■ *Web:* www.cscglobal.com	Wilmington	DE	19808	302-636-5400	636-5454
Craters & Freighters 331 Corporate Cir Ste J *Fax Area Code: 303 ■ *TF:* 800-736-3335 ■ *Web:* www.cratersandfreighters.com	Golden	CO	80401	800-736-3335	399-9964*
Crush Creative 1919 Empire Ave *Web:* www.crushcreative.com	Burbank	CA	91504	818-842-1121	
Csbs Business Services Llc 200 Gary Rd *Web:* www.csbsllc.com	Carrboro	NC	27510	919-932-7109	
Davinci Institute Inc 9191 Sheridan Blvd Ste 300 *Web:* davinciinstitute.com	Westminster	CO	80031	303-666-4133	
Ditto Document Solutions 610 Smithfield St *Web:* www.dittodocument.com	Pittsburgh	PA	15222	412-434-6666	
Dollar Bill Copying 611 Church St Ste 4 *Web:* www.dollarbillcopying.com	Ann Arbor	MI	48104	734-665-9200	
Dragonfly Technologies 48 Wall St Ste 1100 *Web:* www.dragonflytech.com	New York	NY	10005	212-713-5250	
Duncan-Parnell Inc 900 S McDowell St *TF:* 800-849-7708 ■ *Web:* www.duncan-parnell.com	Charlotte	NC	28204	704-372-7766	333-3845
e4e Inc 10720 Gilroy Rd *Web:* www.e4e.com	Hunt Valley	MD	21031	410-568-3075	
Elbar Duplicator Corp 10526 Jamaica Ave *Web:* www.edcbizsolutions.com	Richmond Hill	NY	11418	718-441-1123	
Errand Solutions LLC 118 S Clinton St Ste 760 *Web:* www.errandsolutions.com	Chicago	IL	60661	312-475-3800	
Evolve Discovery Inc 611 Mission St 4th Fl *TF:* 866-488-1032 ■ *Web:* www.evolvediscovery.com	San Francisco	CA	94105	415-398-8600	
FedEx Kinko's Office & Print Services Inc 7900 Legacy Dr *Web:* fedex.com	Plano	TX	75024	214-550-7000	550-7001
Galaxie Coffee Services 110 Sea Ln *TF:* 800-564-9104 ■ *Web:* galaxiecoffee.com	Farmingdale	NY	11735	631-694-2688	
Group O Inc 4905 77th Ave *TF Cust Svc:* 800-752-0730 ■ *Web:* www.groupo.com	Milan	IL	61264	309-736-8300	736-8301
Hackworth Reprographics 1700 Liberty St *TF:* 800-676-2424 ■ *Web:* www.hackworth.co	Chesapeake	VA	23324	757-545-7675	
Himes Vending Inc 4654 Groves Rd *Web:* himesvending.com	Columbus	OH	43232	614-868-6931	
Inter Technologies Corp 7716 Middle Valley Dr *Web:* intertechav.com	Springfield	VA	22153	703-451-1083	
JAD Business Services Inc PO Box 953 *Web:* www.jadbsi.com	Shady Side	MD	20764	301-261-5538	
Java Dave's Executive Coffee Service 6239 E 15th St *TF:* 800-725-7315 ■ *Web:* www.javadavescoffee.com	Tulsa	OK	74112	918-836-5570	
Juran Institute Inc 160 Main St Ste 100 *TF:* 800-338-7726 ■ *Web:* www.juran.com	Southington	CT	06489	203-267-3445	
Kabel Business Services 1454 30th St Ste 202 *Web:* www.kabelbiz.com	Wdm	IA	50266	515-224-9400	
Kal-blue Reprographics Inc 914 E Vine St *Web:* www.kalblue.com	Kalamazoo	MI	49001	269-349-8681	
Kens Reproductions Llip 2220 Curtis St *Web:* www.kensrepro.com	Denver	CO	80205	303-297-9191	
Key Blue Prints Inc 195 E Livingston Ave *Web:* www.key-evidence.com	Columbus	OH	43215	614-225-7787	
Mej Personal Business Services Inc 245 E 116th St *Web:* www.mejpbs.com	New York	NY	10029	212-426-6017	
Mele Printing Company LLC 619 N Tyler St *Web:* www.meleprinting.com	Covington	LA	70433	985-893-9522	
Mid-West Fabricating Co 313 N Johns St *Web:* www.midwestfab.com	Amanda	OH	43102	740-969-4411	969-4433
Miller Systems Inc 175 Portland St 5th fl *Web:* www.millersystems.com	Boston	MA	02114	617-266-4200	
MRSCO Inc 801 N Capitol Ave *Web:* www.marbaugh.com	Indianapolis	IN	46204	317-631-1000	
Ms Dallas Reprographics Inc 2300 Reagan St *Web:* www.msdallas.com	Dallas	TX	75219	214-521-7000	
Navis Logistics Network 6551 S Revere Pkwy Ste 250 *Fax Area Code: 303 ■ *TF:* 800-344-3528 ■ *Web:* www.gonavis.com	Centennial	CO	80111	800-344-3528	741-6653*
Navis Pack & Ship Centers 6551 S Revere Pkwy Ste 250 *Fax Area Code: 303 ■ *TF:* 800-344-3528 ■ *Web:* www.gonavis.com	Centennial	CO	80111	800-344-3528	741-6653*
New Jersey Legal Copy Inc 501 King Ave *TF:* 800-426-7965 ■ *Web:* njlone.com	Cherry Hill	NJ	08002	856-910-0202	
Objectwin Technology Inc 14800 St Mary's Ln Ste 100 *Web:* www.objectwin.com	Houston	TX	77079	713-782-8200	782-8283
Office Depot Inc 2200 Old Germantown Rd *NASDAQ: ODP* ■ *TF:* 800-937-3600 ■ *Web:* www.officedepot.com	Delray Beach	FL	33445	561-438-4800	
Pacific Event Productions Inc 6989 Corte Santa Fe *Web:* www.pacificevents.com	San Diego	CA	92121	858-458-9908	458-1173
Pak Mail Centers of America Inc 7173 S Havana St Ste 600 *TF Cust Svc:* 800-778-6665 ■ *Web:* www.pakmail.com	Centennial	CO	80112	303-957-1000	957-1015
Parcel Plus Inc 13121 Louetta Rd *Web:* www.parcelpluscypress.com	Cypress	TX	77429	281-376-0054	376-0056
Parcel Pro Inc 1867 Western Way Ste *Web:* www.parcelpro.com	Torrance	CA	90501	310-328-8484	
Peachtree Planning Corp 5040 Roswell Rd NE *TF:* 800-366-0839 ■ *Web:* www.peachtreeplanning.com	Atlanta	GA	30342	404-260-1600	260-1700
Peniel Solutions LLC 4311 Communications Dr *Web:* www.penielsolutions.com	Norcross	GA	30093	770-982-8350	
Postal Connections of America 6136 Frisco Sq Blvd Ste 400 *TF:* 800-767-8257 ■ *Web:* www.postalconnections.com	Frisco	TX	75034	800-767-8257	
PostalAnnex+ Inc 7580 Metropolitan Dr Ste 200 *TF:* 800-456-1525 ■ *Web:* www.postalannex.com	San Diego	CA	92108	619-563-4800	563-9850
PostNet International Franchise Corp 1819 Wazee St *TF:* 800-841-7171 ■ *Web:* www.postnet.com	Denver	CO	80202	303-771-7100	771-7133
Property One Inc 4141 Veterans Memorial Blvd Ste 300 *Web:* www.property-one.com	Metairie	LA	70002	504-681-3400	681-3438
Rodney Babar Inc 3135 Millbranch Rd *Web:* www.baberweb.com	Memphis	TN	38116	901-794-4445	
Schoeneckers Inc 7630 Bush Lake Rd *Web:* www.biworldwide.com	Minneapolis	MN	55439	952-835-4800	844-4033
Sharp Decisions Inc 1040 Ave of the A *TF:* 800-742-7792 ■ *Web:* www.sharpdecisions.com	New York	NY	10018	212-481-5533	481-8751
Shawmut Mills 2770 Dove St *Web:* www.darlexx.com	Port Huron	MI	48060	810-987-2222	
Shee Atika Inc 315 Lincoln St Ste 300 *TF:* 800-478-3534 ■ *Web:* www.sheeatika.com	Sitka	AK	99835	907-747-3534	747-5727
Sir Speedy Inc 26722 Plaza Dr *TF:* 800-854-8297 ■ *Web:* www.sirspeedy.com	Mission Viejo	CA	92691	949-348-5000	348-5066
Speedway Printing & Copy Center Inc 2575 N Causeway Blvd *Web:* speedwayprinting.net	Mandeville	LA	70471	985-626-0032	
Stone Rudolph & Henry PLC 124 Ctr Pointe Dr *Web:* www.srhcpas.com	Clarksville	TN	37040	931-648-4786	647-5445
Sunrise Business Services Inc 35 W Main St Ste 3 *Web:* www.sunrisebusiness.com	Kings Park	NY	11787	631-366-0504	
Target Copy 635 W Tennessee St *Web:* targetprintmail.com	Tallahassee	FL	32304	850-224-3007	
Team National Inc 8210 W State Rd 84 *Web:* www.bign.com	Davie	FL	33324	954-584-2151	584-2747
Technical Training Inc (TTI) 3903 W. Hamlin Rd *Web:* www.tti-global.com	Rochester Hills	MI	48309	248-853-5550	853-2411
Total Energy Solutions LLC (TES) 100 International Dr Ste 260 *TF:* 877-436-9812 ■ *Web:* www.totalenergyllc.com	Portsmouth	NH	03801	877-436-9812	
Toth Financial Advisory Corp 608 S King St Ste 300 *TF:* 800-445-1880 ■ *Web:* www.tothfinancial.com	Leesburg	VA	20175	703-443-8684	
Ubics Inc 333 Technology Dr Ste 210 *OTC: UBIX* ■ *TF:* 800-441-0077 ■ *Web:* www.ubics.com	Canonsburg	PA	15317	724-746-6001	743-4115
Unique Copy Center of New York 252 Greene St *Web:* uniquecopycenter.com	New York	NY	10003	212-420-9198	
UPS Store, The 6060 Cornerstone Ct W *TF:* 800-789-4623 ■ *Web:* www.theupsstore.com	San Diego	CA	92121	858-455-8800	
Zoom Information Inc 307 Waverley Oaks Rd *TF:* 800-949-7040 ■ *Web:* www.zoominfo.com	Waltham	MA	02452	781-693-7500	693-7510

114 BUYER'S GUIDES - ONLINE

See Also Investment Guides - Online p. 2611

Company	City	State	Zip	Phone	Fax
Ace Mart - Downtown San Antonio 1220 S St Mary's *TF:* 888-898-8079 ■ *Web:* acemart.com	San Antonio	TX	78210	210-224-0082	224-1629
ePublicEye.com 1010 N Central Ave	Glendale	CA	91202	818-547-0222	
InsWeb Inc 11290 Pyrites Way *TF:* 866-697-9085	Gold River	CA	95670	916-853-3300	853-3325
Market America Inc 1302 Pleasant Ridge Rd *TF:* 866-420-1709 ■ *Web:* www.marketamerica.com	Greensboro	NC	27409	336-605-0040	605-0041
Parke-Bell Ltd Inc 709 W 12th St *TF:* 800-457-7456 ■ *Web:* www.touchofclass.com	Huntingburg	IN	47542	812-683-3707	683-5921
Shopping.com Inc 8000 Marina Blvd 5th Fl *Web:* www.shopping.com	Brisbane	CA	94005	650-616-6500	616-6510

115 CABINETS - WOOD

See Also Carpentry & Flooring Contractors p. 2081; Household Furniture p. 2341

Company	City	State	Zip	Phone	Fax
Allen Lumber Company Inc 502 N Main St *TF:* 800-696-2666 ■ *Web:* www.allenlumbercompany.com	Barre	VT	05641	802-476-4156	
American Woodmark Corp 3102 Shawnee Dr *NASDAQ: AMWD* ■ *Web:* www.americanwoodmark.com	Winchester	VA	22601	540-665-9100	665-9176
Ampco Products Inc 11400 NW 36th Ave **Fax Area Code:* 866 ■ *Web:* www.ampco.com	Miami	FL	33167	305-821-5700	642-5300*
Anton Cabinetry 2002 W Pioneer Pkwy *Web:* www.antoncabinetry.com	Pantego	TX	76013	817-460-8681	
Bertch Cabinet Manufacturing Inc 4747 Crestwood Dr *Web:* www.bertch.com	Waterloo	IA	50702	319-296-2987	296-2315
Bloch Industries 140 Commerce Dr *Web:* www.blochindustries.com	Rochester	NY	14623	585-334-9600	
Britten Woodworks 1954 N Betsie River Rd *Web:* www.brittenwoodworks.com	Interlochen	MI	49643	231-275-5457	
Cabinetry By Karman Inc 6000 Stratler St *TF:* 800-255-3581 ■ *Web:* www.cabinetrybykarman.com	Salt Lake City	UT	84107	801-281-6400	
Cabinets 2000 Inc 11100 Firestone Blvd *Web:* www.cabinets2000.com	Norwalk	CA	90650	562-868-0909	
California Kitchen Cabinet Door Corp 400 Cochrane Cir *Web:* www.caldoor.com	Morgan Hill	CA	95037	408-782-5700	782-9000
Cambria Inc 31496 Cambria Ave Ste 220 *Web:* www.cambriausa.com	Le Sueur	MN	56058	507-665-5003	
Candlelight Cabinetry Inc 24 Michigan St *Web:* www.candlelightcab.com	Lockport	NY	14094	716-434-6543	434-6748
Canyon Creek Cabinet Co 16726 Tye St SE *TF:* 800-228-1830 ■ *Web:* www.canyoncreek.com	Monroe	WA	98272	360-348-4973	348-4810
Capitol Granite & Marble 1700 Oak Lk Blvd *Web:* www.capitolgraniteandmarble.com	Midlothian	VA	23112	804-379-2641	
Cardell Cabinetry 3215 N Panam Expy *Web:* www.cardellcabinetry.com	San Antonio	TX	78219	210-225-0290	
Chandlers Plywood Products Inc 3716 Waverly Rd *Web:* www.chandlerkitchens.com	Huntington	WV	25704	304-429-1311	429-1331
Cole Kepro International LLC 4170-103 Distribution Cir *Web:* colekepro.com	North Las Vegas	NV	89030	702-633-4270	
Commercial Wood Products Co 10019 Yucca Rd *Web:* www.commercialwood.com	Adelanto	CA	92301	760-246-4530	
Conestoga Wood Specialties Inc 245 Reading Rd *TF:* 800-964-3667 ■ *Web:* www.conestogawood.com	East Earl	PA	17519	800-964-3667	
Continental Cabinet Inc 2841 Pierce St *Web:* www.continentalcabinet.com	Dallas	TX	75233	214-467-4444	
Crystal Cabinet Works Inc 1100 Crystal Dr *TF:* 800-347-5045 ■ *Web:* www.ccworks.com	Princeton	MN	55371	763-389-4187	389-5846
Cutting Edge Countertops Inc 1300 Flagship Dr *Web:* www.cectops.com	Perrysburg	OH	43551	419-873-9500	
Cygnus Inc 1701 Standish Ave *Web:* www.cygnusinc.net	Petoskey	MI	49770	231-347-5404	
Dalia Kitchen Design Inc 1 Design Ctr Pl Ste 643 *Web:* www.daliakitchendesign.com	Boston	MA	02210	617-482-2566	
Decore-ative Specialties Inc 2772 S Peck Rd *TF:* 800-729-7277 ■ *Web:* www.decore.com	Monrovia	CA	91016	626-254-9191	254-1515
Designers Choice Cabinetry Inc 100 TGK Cir *Web:* www.dccabinetry.com	Rockledge	FL	32955	321-632-0772	
Dewils Industries Inc 6307 NE 127th Ave *Web:* www.dewils.com	Vancouver	WA	98682	360-892-0300	
Doormark Inc 430 Goolsby Blvd *TF:* 888-969-0124 ■ *Web:* www.doormark.com	Deerfield Beach	FL	33442	954-418-4700	
Dura Supreme Inc 300 Dura Dr *Web:* www.durasupreme.com	Howard Lake	MN	55349	320-543-3872	543-3310
Dutch Made Custom Cabinetry 10415 Roth Rd *Web:* www.dutchmade.com	Grabill	IN	46741	260-657-3311	657-5778
EGR Inc 601 N Miller Blvd *Web:* egronline.com	Oklahoma City	OK	73107	405-943-0900	
Evans Cabinet Corp 1321 N Franklin St *Web:* www.evanscabinet.com	Dublin	GA	31021	478-272-2530	
Fashion Cabinet Mfg Inc 5440 Axel Pk Rd *Web:* www.fashioncabinet.com	West Jordan	UT	84081	801-280-0646	280-8934
Fixture Exchange Corp 3000 W Pafford St *Web:* fixturex.com	Fort Worth	TX	76110	817-429-2496	
Flo-Form Industries Ltd 125 Hamelin St *Web:* www.floform.com	Winnipeg	MB	R3T3Z1	204-474-2334	453-0639
Fortune Brands Home & Hardware Inc 520 Lk Cook Rd *Web:* www.fbhs.com	Deerfield	IL	60015	847-484-4400	
Grabill Cabinet Company Inc 13844 Sawmill Dr *TF:* 877-472-2782 ■ *Web:* www.grabillcabinets.com	Grabill	IN	46741	877-472-2782	
Grandview Products Co 1601 Superior Dr *TF:* 800-247-9105 ■ *Web:* www.grandviewcabinets.com	Parsons	KS	67357	620-421-6950	421-4211
Granite-Tops Inc 1480 Prairie Dr *Web:* www.granite-tops.com	Cold Spring	MN	56320	320-685-3005	
Haas Cabinet Company Inc 625 W Utica St *TF:* 800-457-6458 ■ *Web:* www.haascabinet.com	Sellersburg	IN	47172	812-246-4431	
Halabi Inc 2100 Huntington Dr *Web:* www.duracite.com	Fairfield	CA	94533	707-402-1600	
Helmut Guenschel Inc 10 Emala Ave *Web:* www.guenschel.com	Baltimore	MD	21220	410-686-5900	
Hoff Enterprises Inc 151 Freidhoff Ln *Web:* www.hoffent.com	Johnstown	PA	15902	814-535-8371	
HomeCrest Cabinetry 1002 Eisenhower Dr N *Web:* www.homecrestcabinetry.com	Goshen	IN	46526	574-535-9300	
Huntwood Industries 23800 E Apple Way *TF:* 800-873-7350 ■ *Web:* www.huntwood.com	Liberty Lake	WA	99019	509-924-5858	
Innovative Surfaces Inc 515 Spiral Blvd *Web:* www.innovativesurfaces.com	Hastings	MN	55033	651-437-1004	
Jim Bishop Cabinets Inc 5640 Bell Rd *TF:* 800-410-2444 ■ *Web:* www.bishopcabinets.com	Montgomery	AL	36116	800-410-2444	
Kabinart Corp 3650 Trousdale Dr	Nashville	TN	37204	615-833-1961	781-8026
Kitchen Craft Cabinetry 1180 Springfield Rd *Web:* www.kitchencraft.com	Winnipeg	MB	R2C2Z2	204-224-3211	222-7608
Kitchen Kompact Inc 911 E 11th St *Web:* www.kitchenkompact.com	Jeffersonville	IN	47130	812-282-6681	282-7880
Kraftmaid Cabinetry Inc 15535 S State Ave PO Box 1055 *TF:* 888-562-7744 ■ *Web:* www.kraftmaid.com	Middlefield	OH	44062	888-562-7744	
Legere Group Ltd PO Box 1527 *Web:* www.legeregroup.com	Avon	CT	06001	860-674-0392	674-0469
Marsh Furniture Co PO Box 870 *TF:* 800-696-2774 ■ *Web:* www.marshfurniture.com	High Point	NC	27261	336-884-7363	884-3553
Martin Cabinet Inc 336 S Washington St *Web:* martincabinet.com	Plainville	CT	06062	860-747-5769	747-9595
Masco Cabinetry LLC 5353 W US 223 *TF:* 866-850-8557 ■ *Web:* www.merillat.com	Adrian	MI	49221	517-263-0771	265-3325
Masco Corp 21001 Van Born Rd *NYSE: MAS* ■ *TF:* 888-627-6397 ■ *Web:* www.masco.com	Taylor	MI	48180	313-274-7400	792-4177
Mastercraft Industries Inc 777 S St *TF:* 800-835-7812 ■ *Web:* mastercraftusa.com	Newburgh	NY	12550	845-565-8850	565-9392
Medallion Cabinetry 2222 Camden Ct *TF:* 800-543-4074 ■ *Web:* www.medallioncabinetry.com	Oak Brook	IL	60523	952-442-5171	
Mesa Fully Formed Inc 1111 S Sirrine *Web:* www.mesa.org	Mesa	AZ	85210	480-834-9331	
Mid-America Cabinet Inc 20980 Marion Lee Rd *Web:* www.midamericacabinets.com	Gentry	AR	72734	479-736-2671	736-8086
Mouser Custom Cabinetry 2112 N Hwy 31 W *TF:* 800-345-7537 ■ *Web:* www.mousercc.com	Elizabethtown	KY	42701	270-737-7477	
Norcraft cabinetry 3020 Denmark Ave *TF:* 877-888-0002 ■ *Web:* www.norcraftcompanies.com	Eagan	MN	55121	651-234-3300	
Northern Contours Inc 1355 Mendota Heights Rd Ste 100 *TF:* 866-344-8132 ■ *Web:* www.northerncontours.com	Mendota Heights	MN	55120	651-695-1698	695-1714
Omega Cabinetry Ltd 1205 Peters Dr **Fax:* Cust Svc ■ *Web:* www.omegacabinetry.com	Waterloo	IA	50703	319-235-5700	235-5860*
Patella Industries Inc 721 Grand Bernier N	Saint-Jean-Sur-Richelieu	QC	J3B8H6	450-359-0040	
Patrick Industries Inc 107 W Franklin St PO Box 638 *NASDAQ: PATK* ■ *TF:* 800-331-2151 ■ *Web:* www.patrickind.com	Elkhart	IN	46515	574-294-7511	522-5213
Plato Woodwork Inc 200 Third St SW *TF:* 800-328-5924 ■ *Web:* www.platowoodwork.com	Plato	MN	55370	320-238-2193	
Precision Countertops Inc 26200 SW 95th Ave Ste 303 *Web:* www.precisioncountertops.com	Wilsonville	OR	97070	503-692-6660	
Republic Industries Inc 1400 Warren Dr *TF:* 866-284-0941 ■ *Web:* republicind.com	Marshall	TX	75672	903-935-3680	935-3697
Rosebud Mfg Co Inc 701 SE 12th St *TF:* 800-256-4561 ■ *Web:* www.rosebudmfg.com	Madison	SD	57042	605-256-4561	256-3842
Roy's Wood Products Inc 329 Thrush Ln *TF:* 800-727-1590 ■ *Web:* www.royswoodproducts.com	Lugoff	SC	29078	803-438-1590	
Royal Cabinets 1299 E Phillips Blvd *Web:* www.royalcabinets.com	Pomona	CA	91766	909-629-8565	629-7762
RSI Home Products Inc 400 E Orangethorpe Ave **Fax:* Cust Svc ■ *TF:* 888-774-8062 ■ *Web:* www.rsihomeproducts.com	Anaheim	CA	92801	714-449-2200	449-2222*
Rutt HandCrafted Cabinetry 215 Diller Ave *Web:* ruttcabinetry.com	New Holland	PA	17557	717-351-1700	
Rynone Mfg Corp PO Box 128 *TF:* 800-839-1654 ■ *Web:* www.rynone.com	Sayre	PA	18840	570-888-5272	888-1175
Shamrock Cabinet & Fixture Corp 10201 E 65th St *Web:* www.shamrockcabinet.com	Raytown	MO	64133	816-737-2300	356-7835
Showplace Wood Products Inc 1 Enterprise St *TF:* 877-512-2500 ■ *Web:* www.showplacewood.com	Harrisburg	SD	57032	605-743-2200	
Spectrum Cabinet Sales Inc 90 Crossways Park Dr W *Web:* www.spectrumkitchens.com	Woodbury	NY	11797	516-496-9888	
Starmark Cabinetry 600 E 48th St N *TF:* 800-755-7789 ■ *Web:* www.starmarkcabinetry.com	Sioux Falls	SD	57104	800-594-9444	
Thomasville Furniture Industries Inc 401 E Main St PO Box 339 *Web:* www.thomasville.com	Thomasville	NC	27361	336-472-4000	

Phone Fax

Tri-Star Cabinet & Top Co Inc 1000 S Cedar . . . New Lenox IL 60451 815-485-2564
Web: www.tristarcabinets.com
Ultracraft Co 6163 Old 421 Rd . . . Liberty NC 27298 800-262-4046
TF: 800-262-4046 ■ *Web:* www.ultracraft.com
Valley Cabinet Inc 845 Prosper Rd . . . De Pere WI 54115 920-336-3174 383-5580
Web: www.valleycabinetinc.com
WM Ohs-Kitchen Showroom 115 Madison St . . . Denver CO 80206 303-321-3232
Web: www.wmohs.com
Woodcase Fine Cabinetry Inc
8340 East Raintree Dr . . . Scottsdale AZ 85260 480-948-0756
Web: www.woodcaseinc.net
Woodcraft Industries Inc
525 Lincoln Ave SE . . . Saint Cloud MN 56304 320-252-1503 656-2199
Web: www.woodcraftind.com
WW Wood Products Inc 10182 Old Hwy 60 . . . Dudley MO 63936 573-624-7090
Web: wwwoodproducts.com

116 CABLE & OTHER PAY TELEVISION SERVICES

Phone Fax

Aboriginal People's Television Network Inc
339 Portage Ave . . . Winnipeg MB R3B2C3 204-947-9331
Web: www.aptn.ca
Access Cable Television Inc
302 Enterprise Dr . . . Somerset KY 42501 606-677-2444
Web: www.accesshsd.net
Access Communications Co-operative Ltd
2250 Park St . . . Regina SK S4N7K7 306-569-2225
TF: 866-211-6334 ■ *Web:* www.myaccess.ca
Aegis Film Group Inc
7510 Sunset Blvd Ste 275 . . . Los Angeles CA 90046 323-848-7977
Web: www.aegisfilmgroup.com
All West Communications Inc 50 West 100 North . . . Kamas UT 84036 435-783-4361
TF: 866-255-9378 ■ *Web:* www.allwest.net
Allen's TV Cable Service Inc
800 Victor II Blvd . . . Morgan City LA 70380 985-384-8335
Web: www.atvc.net
Almega Cable Inc 4001 W Airport Fwy Ste 530 . . . Bedford TX 76021 817-685-9588 685-6488
Alpine Communications LC 923 Humphrey St . . . Elkader IA 52043 563-245-4000
Web: www.alpinecom.net
American Cable Company Inc
231 E Luzerne St . . . Philadelphia PA 19124 215-456-0700
Web: www.americancableco.com
Antietam Cable Television Inc
1000 Willow Cir . . . Hagerstown MD 21740 301-797-5000
Web: www.antietamcable.com
Areacall Inc 7803 Stratford Rd . . . Bethesda MD 20814 301-657-2718
Web: www.areacall.com
Armstrong Group of Cos 1 Armstrong Pl . . . Butler PA 16001 724-283-0925 283-9655
Web: www.armstrongonewire.com
Astral Media Inc 1800 McGill College Ste 600 . . . Montreal QC H3A3J6 514-939-5000 939-1515
Web: www.bellmedia.ca
Azteca America Inc 1139 Grand Central Ave . . . Glendale CA 91201 818-241-5400
Web: www.aztecaamerica.com
Barre y Lane LLC 9318 Drawbridge Rd . . . Mechanicsville VA 23116 804-723-4035
Web: www.barreylane.com
Big Bend Telephone Company Inc 808 N Fifth St . . . Alpine TX 79830 432-364-1000
TF: 800-520-0092 ■ *Web:* www.bigbend.net
Black Rock Cable 1512 Fairview St . . . Bellingham WA 98229 360-738-3116
Broadband Solutions Inc 1886 Commerce Dr . . . De Pere WI 54115 920-339-8056
Web: www.broadband-solutions.com
Broadcast Equipment Corp 1035 44th Dr . . . Long Island NY 11101 718-784-5540
Web: www.becny.com
Broadnet Teleservices LLC
1805 Shea Ctr Dr Ste 160 . . . Highlands Ranch CO 80129 877-579-4929
TF: 877-579-4929 ■ *Web:* www.broadnet.com
Buckeye CableSystem 5566 Southwick Blvd . . . Toledo OH 43614 419-724-9802 724-7074
Web: www.buckeyecablesystem.com
Buford Media Group LLC (BMG) 6125 Paluxy Dr . . . Tyler TX 75703 903-561-4411 561-4031
Cable Center, The 2000 Buchtel Blvd . . . Denver CO 80210 720-502-7500
Web: www.cablecenter.org
Cable Com Inc 12115 Roxie Dr . . . Austin TX 78729 512-250-5901
Web: www.cablecominc.com
Cable Connection, The 52 Heppner Dr . . . Carson City NV 89706 775-885-1443 885-2734
TF: 800-851-2961 ■ *Web:* www.thecableconnection.com
Cable Coop 27 E College St . . . Oberlin OH 44074 440-775-4001
Web: www.oberlin.net
Cable Line Inc 239 Main St Ste 102 . . . East Greenville PA 18041 215-258-1380
Web: www.cable-line.com
Cable One Inc 210 E Earll Drive . . . Phoenix AZ 85012 602-364-6000 364-6010
TF: 877-692-2253 ■ *Web:* www.cableone.net
Cable Vision Services 1701 Cogswell Ave . . . Pell City AL 35125 501-223-7539
Cable-Comm Technologies Inc
800 Enterprise Ct . . . Naperville IL 60563 630-717-7179
Web: www.cable-comm.com
CableAmerica Corp 7822 E Gray Rd . . . Scottsdale AZ 85260 866-871-4492
TF: 866-871-4492 ■ *Web:* www.cableamerica.com
Cablecom LLC 3701 W Burnham St Ste C . . . Milwaukee WI 53215 414-226-2205
Web: cablecomllc.com
Cablevision Systems Corp 1111 Stewart Ave . . . Bethpage NY 11714 516-803-2300
NYSE: CVC ■ *Web:* www.cablevision.com
Campus Televideo Inc 100 First Stamford Pl . . . Stamford CT 06902 203-983-5400
TF: 866-615-8674 ■ *Web:* www.campustelevideo.com
Capital News 9 104 Watervliet Ave Ext . . . Albany NY 12206 518-459-9999
Web: www.twcnews.com/nys/rochester.html
Capitol Connection 4400 University Dr MS 1D2 . . . Fairfax VA 22030 703-993-3100
TF: 844-504-7161 ■ *Web:* capitolconnection.org
CaptionMax Inc 2438 27th Ave South . . . Minneapolis MN 55406 612-341-3566
Web: www.captionmax.com
Cass Cable Tv Inc 100 Redbud Rd . . . Virginia IL 62691 217-452-7725
TF: 800-252-1799 ■ *Web:* www.casscomm.com

Phone Fax

CDR Data Corp 1028 N Lake Ave Ste 105 . . . Pasadena CA 91104 626-791-9700
Web: www.cdrdata.com
Charter Communications Inc
12405 Powerscourt Dr Ste 100 . . . Saint Louis MO 63131 314-965-0555 965-9745
NASDAQ: CHTR ■ *TF:* 888-438-2427 ■ *Web:* www.charter.com
Chisholm Trail Broadcasting Co 316 E Willow Rd . . . Enid OK 73701 580-237-1390
Citizens Telephone Co 26 S Main St . . . Hammond NY 13646 315-324-5911
Web: www.cit-tele.com
Coast Communications Company Inc
349 Damon Rd . . . Ocean Shores WA 98569 360-289-2252
Web: www.coastaccess.com
Cogeco Cable Inc 5 Pl Ville-Marie Ste 915 . . . Montreal QC H3B4M7 514-874-2600 874-2625
TF: 800-855-0511 ■ *Web:* www.cogeco.ca
Comcast Cable Communications LLC
1701 John F Kennedy Blvd . . . Philadelphia PA 19103 215-665-1700 981-7790
Web: www.xfinity.com
Comcast SPORTSNET Bay Area LP
360 Third St 2nd Fl . . . San Francisco CA 94107 415-296-8900
Web: www.csnbayarea.com
Comcast Wholesale 1899 Wynkoop St Ste 550 . . . Denver CO 80202 720-504-9524
Web: www.comcastwholesale.com
ComSouth Telecommunications Inc
99 Broad St PO Box 1298 . . . Hawkinsville AK 31036 478-783-4001
Web: www.comsouth.net
Concierge Communications LLC
4801 S Lkshore Dr Ste 106 . . . Tempe AZ 85282 888-624-2643
TF: 888-624-2643 ■ *Web:* www.conciergecom.com
Connect802 Corp 111 Deerwood Rd Ste 200 . . . San Ramon CA 94583 925-552-0802
Web: www.connect802.com
Country Cablevision Inc
9449 State Hwy 197 S . . . Burnsville NC 28714 828-682-4074
TF: 800-722-4074 ■ *Web:* www.ccvn.com
Cox Communications Inc 1400 Lake Hearn Dr . . . Atlanta GA 30319 404-843-5000 843-5000
TF: 866-961-0027 ■ *Web:* cox.com
Curious Pictures Corp 440 Lafayette St . . . New York NY 10003 212-674-1400
Web: www.curiouspictures.com
Custom Cable Corp 242 Butler St . . . Westbury NY 11590 516-334-3600
TF: 800-832-3600 ■ *Web:* www.customwireandcable.com
Data Cell Systems Inc 250 Hwy 3201 . . . Winnsboro LA 71295 318-435-5800
Web: www.data-cell.com
Datacom Inc 2517 S Santa Fe Ave . . . Vista CA 92083 760-598-6000
Web: www.datacom.com
DC Connections 22650 Executive Dr Ste 125 . . . Sterling VA 20166 703-471-9757
Web: www.dcconnections.com
Decibels Inc 1551 Center St . . . Tacoma WA 98409 253-473-5855
Web: decibelsinc.com
Defender Security Company Inc
3750 Priority Way S Dr Ste 200 . . . Indianapolis IN 46240 317-810-4720
DIRECTV Inc 2230 E Imperial Hwy . . . El Segundo CA 90245 310-535-5000
TF Cust Svc: 800-531-5000 ■ *Web:* www.directv.com
DISH Network LLC 9601 S Meridian Blvd . . . Englewood CO 80112 800-823-4929
NASDAQ: DISH ■ *TF:* 800-823-4929 ■ *Web:* www.dish.com
E-Z Form Cable Corp 285 Welton St . . . Hamden CT 06517 203-785-8215
Web: www.ezform.com
Electric Cable Compounds Inc 108 Rado Dr . . . Naugatuck CT 06770 203-723-2590
Web: www.electriccablecompounds.com
Engineered Environments Inc
1620 Timocuan Way Ste 130 . . . Longwood FL 32750 407-831-6998
Web: www.eeigc.net
EOSPACE Inc 6222 185th AVE NE . . . Redmond WA 98052 425-869-8673
Web: www.eospace.com
Everest Production Corp 300 Franklin Sq Dr . . . Somerset NJ 08873 732-560-0800
Web: www.everestpro.com
Excell Communications Inc
6247 Amber Hills Rd . . . Trussville AL 35173 205-956-0198
Web: www.excellcommunications.com
Fandango Inc 12200 W Olympic Blvd Ste 400 . . . Los Angeles CA 90064 310-954-0278
Web: www.fandango.com
Favorite Office Automation
2011 W State St Ste B . . . New Castle PA 16101 724-658-8300
Web: www.favorite1.com
Fibercomm Lc 1605 Ninth St . . . Sioux City IA 51101 712-224-2020
TF: 800-836-2472 ■ *Web:* www.fibercomm.net
Fidelity Communications Company Inc
64 N Clark St . . . Sullivan MO 63080 573-468-8081
Web: www.fidelitycommunications.com
Florida Cable Inc 23505 State Rd 40 . . . Astor FL 32102 352-759-2788
Web: www.floridacable.com
Fluent Media Group LLC 5230 Alton Rd . . . Miami Beach FL 33140 305-424-1030
Web: www.fluentmediagroup.com
Giant Communications Inc 418 W Fifth St Ste C . . . Holton KS 66436 785-362-9331
Web: www.giantcomm.net
GM Cable Contractors Inc 9232 Joor Rd . . . Baton Rouge LA 70818 225-261-9800
Web: gmcable.com
Grace To You 28001 Harrison Pkwy . . . Valencia CA 91355 661-295-5777
Web: gty.org
Greater Media Detroit Wcsx Wmg
1 Radio Plz St . . . Ferndale MI 48220 248-591-6800
Web: www.greatermedia.biz/greatermediadetroit
Green Earth Cleaning 51 W 135th St . . . Kansas City MO 64145 816-926-0895
TF: 877-926-0895 ■ *Web:* www.greenearthcleaning.com
Haefele Tv Inc 24 E Tioga St . . . Spencer NY 14883 607-589-6235
Web: www.htva.net
Hamilton Telephone Co 1001 12th St . . . Aurora NE 68818 402-694-5101
TF: 800-821-1831 ■ *Web:* www.hamiltontelephone.com
Harlan Community Television Inc
124 S First St . . . Harlan KY 40831 606-573-2945
Web: www.harlanonline.net
Hawaii Pacific Teleport LP
91-340 Farrington Hwy . . . Kapolei HI 96707 808-674-9157
Web: www.hawaiiteleport.com
Heartland Video Systems Inc 1311 Pilgrim Rd . . . Plymouth WI 53073 920-893-4204
Web: hvs-inc.com

Phone *Fax*

High Power Technical Services Inc (HPTS)
2230 Ampere Dr .... Louisville KY 40299 866-310-5377
TF: 866-310-5377 ■ *Web:* inc.com

Home Town Cable TV LLC
10486 SW Village Ctr Dr .... Port Saint Lucie FL 34987 772-345-6000

Horvath Communications Inc
312 W Colfax Ave .... South Bend IN 46601 574-237-0464
Web: www.horvathcommunications.com

ImOn Communications LLC 625 First St SE .... Cedar Rapids IA 52401 319-298-6484
Web: www.imon.net

Inside Edition Inc 1700 Broadway 33rd Fl .... New York NY 10019 212-817-5423
Web: www.insideedition.com

Inter Mountain Cable Inc
20 Laynesville Rd PO Box 159 .... Harold KY 41635 606-478-9406
Web: www.imctv.com

Isotropic Networks Inc W2835 Krueger Rd .... Lake Geneva WI 53147 262-248-9600
Web: www.isosat.net

ITV Studios America Inc
15303 Ventura Blvd Bldg C Ste 800 .... Los Angeles CA 91403 818-455-4600
Web: www.itvstudios.com

J P Diamond Co 25 E James St .... Falconer NY 14733 716-665-4100
Web: www.jpdiamond.com

Kable Link Communications
15273 Flight Path Dr .... Brooksville FL 34604 352-796-7639
Web: www.kablelink.com

Keene Valley Video Inc 1948 nys Rt 73 .... Keene Valley NY 12943 518-576-4510
Web: www.kvvi.net

Kelly Cable Corp 9065 Quince St .... Henderson CO 80640 303-287-1112
Web: www.sitewise.net

KenCast Inc 290 Harbor Dr .... Stamford CT 06902 203-359-6984
Web: www.kencast.com

KFDM-TV Channel 6 2955 I-10 E .... Beaumont TX 77702 409-892-6622
Web: www.kfdm.com

Kincardine Cable TV Ltd 223 Bruce Ave .... Kincardine ON N2Z2P2 519-396-8880
TF: 800-265-3064 ■ *Web:* www.tnt21.com

Kmtelecom 18 Second Ave NW .... Kasson MN 55944 507-634-2511
TF: 888-232-3796 ■ *Web:* www.kmtel.com

Knight Enterprises Inc 6056 Ulmerton Rd .... Clearwater FL 33760 727-524-6235
Web: www.knight-enterprises.com

Ksbj 1722 Treble Dr .... Humble TX 77338 281-446-5725 540-2198
TF: 877-644-5725 ■ *Web:* www.ksbj.org

Ksby-Tv 1772 Calle Joaquin .... San Luis Obispo CA 93405 805-541-6666
TF: 800-583-4135 ■ *Web:* www.ksby.com

Kytx-Tv Cbs 19 2211 Ese Loop 323 .... Tyler TX 75701 903-581-2211
Web: www.cbs19.tv

Lanshack.com 155 Meadow Rd Ste 100 .... Clark NJ 07066 732-396-3600
Web: www.lanshack.com

Lincolnville Telephone Co
133 Back Meadow Rd .... Nobleboro ME 04555 207-763-9911
Web: www.lintelco.net

Link Electronics Inc 2137 Rust Ave .... Cape Girardeau MO 63703 573-334-4433
TF: 800-776-4411 ■ *Web:* www.linkelectronics.com

Live Wire Net 4577 Pecos St .... Denver CO 80211 303-458-5667
Web: www.livewirenet.com

Louisiana Radio Network Inc
10500 Coursey Blvd Ste 104 .... Baton Rouge LA 70816 225-291-2727
Web: louisianaradionetwork.com

Main Line Equipment Inc 20917 Higgins Ct .... Torrance CA 90501 310-357-4450

Manhattan Neighborhood Network
537 W 59th St .... New York NY 10019 212-757-2670
Web: www.mnn.org

Max Media LLC 900 Laskin Rd .... Virginia Beach VA 23451 757-437-9800
Web: www.maxmediallc.com

Mediacom Communications Corp
100 Crystal Run Rd .... Middletown NY 10941 845-695-2600
TF General: 800-479-2082 ■ *Web:* mediacomcable.com

MediaOne Services LLC
901 Battery St Ste 220 .... San Francisco CA 94111 415-262-4222
Web: www.linktv.org

Metrocast Cablevision of New Hampshire LLC
9 Apple Rd .... Belmont NH 03220 603-524-4425
Web: www.metrocast.com

Mid-Coast Cablevision LP 505 N Mechanic St .... El Campo TX 77437 979-543-6858
Web: www.warpspeed1.net

Midcontinent Communications PO Box 5010 .... Sioux Falls SD 57117 605-274-9810
TF: 800-888-1300 ■ *Web:* www.midco.com

Middleburgh Telephone Co, The
103 Cliff St .... Middleburgh NY 12122 518-827-5211
Web: www.midtel.net

Multicom Inc 1076 Florida Central Pkwy .... Longwood FL 32750 407-331-7779
Web: www.multicominc.com

National Cable Television Co-op Inc (NCTC)
11200 Corporate Ave .... Lenexa KS 66219 913-599-5900 222-2311*
**Fax Area Code:* 202 ■ *TF:* 800-720-5850 ■ *Web:* www.ncta.com

Newport Television LLC 460 Nichols Rd .... Kansas City MO 64112 816-751-0200

Nistica Inc 745 Rt 202-206 .... Bridgewater NJ 08807 908-707-9500
Web: www.nistica.com

No Good Entertainment Inc
9944 Santa Monica Blvd .... Beverly Hills CA 90212 310-556-8600
Web: www.ngtv.com

North Shore Communications Group Inc
85 Eastern Ave Ph Ste 107 .... Gloucester MA 01930 978-282-8222
Web: www.northshorecommunications.com

Northland Telecommunications Corp
101 Stewart St Ste 700 .... Seattle WA 98101 206-621-1351
Web: yournorthland.com

Npg of Oregon Inc 62990 O B Riley Rd .... Bend OR 97701 541-383-2121
Web: www.ktvz.com

Oceanic Time Warner Cable 200 Akamainui St .... Mililani HI 96789 808-643-2100
Web: www.oceanic.com

Oceanside Community Service Television Corp
3038 Industry St .... Oceanside CA 92054 760-722-4433
Web: www.koct.org

Phone *Fax*

Omega Communications Inc
41 E Washington Ste 110 .... Indianapolis IN 46204 317-264-4000 264-4020
Web: www.omegac.com

OrbitCom Inc 1701 N Louise Dr .... Sioux Falls SD 57107 605-977-6900
Web: www.orbitcom.biz

Otter Tail Telcom 230 W Lincoln Ave .... Fergus Falls MN 56537 218-826-6161
TF: 800-247-2706 ■ *Web:* www.prtel.com

Panora Cooperative Telephone Association Inc
114 E Main St .... Panora IA 50216 641-755-2424
Web: www.panoratelco.com

Paragould Light Water & Cable (PLWC)
1901 Jones Rd .... Paragould AR 72450 870-239-7700 239-7798
Web: www.paragould.com

Phoenix Cable Inc (PCI) 145 N Franklin Tpke .... Ramsey NJ 07446 201-825-9090

Phonoscope Ltd 6105 Wline Dr .... Houston TX 77036 713-272-4600
Web: www.phonoscope.com

Pine Telephone System Inc 104 Ctr St .... Halfway OR 97834 541-742-2201
Web: www.pinetel.com

Polar Communications 110 Fourth St E .... Park River ND 58270 701-284-7221
Web: www.polarcomm.com

Premier Communications 339 First Ave Ne .... Sioux Center IA 51250 712-722-3451
Web: www.mtcnet.net

Quality Cable & Electronics
1780 Nw 15th Ave Ste 400 .... Pompano Beach FL 33069 954-532-0165
Web: www.qualitycable.com

Quebecor Media Inc 612 Rue St Jacques .... Montreal QC H3C4M8 514-380-1999
Web: www.quebecor.com

Quick Cable Corp 3700 Quick Dr .... Franksville WI 53126 262-824-3100
Web: www.quickcable.com

Rainbow Network Communications
620 Hicksville Rd .... Bethpage NY 11714 516-803-0300
Web: www.rncnetwork.com

Real Hip-Hop Network Inc, The
1455 Pennsylvania Ave NW Ste 400 .... Washington DC 20004 202-379-3115
Web: rhn.tv

Richard A Foreman Assoc Inc 330 Emery Dr E .... Stamford CT 06902 203-327-2800
Web: www.rafamedia.com

Rifkin & Assoc Inc 360 S Monroe St .... Denver CO 80209 303-333-1215
Web: www.rifkinco.com

River Valley Telecommunications Coop & Cable Tv
1607 Rolling St .... Ruthven IA 51358 712-837-5522
Web: www.ruthventel.com

RLTV 5525 Research Park Dr .... Baltimore MD 21228 800-754-8464
TF: 800-754-8464 ■ *Web:* www.rl.tv/about-rltv

Romanoff Group, The 1288 Research Rd .... Gahanna OH 43230 614-755-4500
Web: www.romanoffgroup.cc

Rooftop Media Inc 188 Spear St Ste 250 .... San Francisco CA 94105 800-860-0293
TF: 800-860-0293 ■ *Web:* rooftopcomedy.com

RTM Productions Inc 130 SE Pkwy Ct .... Franklin TN 37064 615-503-9700
Web: www.horsepowertv.com

Satellite Receivers Ltd
1740 Cofrin Dr Ste 2 .... Green Bay WI 54302 920-432-5777
Web: www.cashdepotplus.com

Scio Cablevision 38770 N Main St PO Box 1100 .... Scio OR 97374 503-394-2995
Web: www.smt-net.com

See World Satellites Inc 1321 Wayne Ave .... Indiana PA 15701 724-463-3200
Web: www.seeworld.biz

Service Electric Cable TV & Communications
2260 Ave A .... Bethlehem PA 18017 610-865-9100 865-7888
TF: 800-232-9100 ■ *Web:* www.sectv.com

Shaw Communications Inc 630 Third Ave SW .... Calgary AB T2P4L4 403-750-4500 750-4501*
TSE: SJR/B ■ **Fax:* Mktg ■ *TF:* 888-472-2222 ■ *Web:* www.shaw.ca

Shen-Heights TV Assoc Inc 38 N Main St .... Shenandoah PA 17976 570-462-1911
Web: www.shenhgts.net

Silverado Cable Co 1840 W First Ave .... Mesa AZ 85202 480-655-8751
Web: www.silveradocable.com

Sky Radio Network Inc
5320 Laurel Canyon Blvd .... Valley Village CA 91607 818-762-6800

Soup2Nuts Inc 311 Arsenal St .... Watertown MA 02472 617-600-2222

Southern Cable Communications
2101 S Fraser St .... Georgetown SC 29440 843-546-2200
Web: www.sccc.tv

Southern Vermont Cable Co PO Box 166 .... Bondville VT 05340 800-544-5931
TF: 800-544-5931 ■ *Web:* www.svcable.net

Specialty Cable Corp 2 Tower Dr .... Wallingford CT 06492 203-265-7126
Web: www.specialtycable.com

Spencer Municipal Utilities 712 Grand Ave .... Spencer IA 51301 712-580-5800
Web: www.smunet.net

Suddenlink Communications 6151 Paluxy Dr .... Tyler TX 75703 877-694-9474
TF: 877-694-9474 ■ *Web:* www.suddenlink.com

Syringa Networks LLC 3795 S Development Ave .... Boise ID 83705 208-229-6100
Web: www.syringanetworks.net

TCI Tire Centers LLC 10 Mt Read Blvd Ste A .... Rochester NY 14611 585-436-1120

Techni Logic Communications
959 E Collins Blvd Ste 120 .... Richardson TX 75081 972-455-5500

Technical Cable Concepts Inc 350 Lear Ave .... Costa Mesa CA 92626 714-835-1081
Web: www.techcable.com

Tel Star Cablevison Inc 1295 Lourdes Rd .... Metamora IL 61548 309-383-2677
TF: 888-842-0258 ■ *Web:* www.telstar-online.net

Tel Tech Networks Inc 810 E Hammond Ln .... Phoenix AZ 85034 602-431-9399
Web: www.teltechnetworks.com

Tele-Media Corp
804 Jacksonville Rd PO Box 39 .... Bellefonte PA 16823 814-353-2025 353-2072
TF: 800-704-4254 ■ *Web:* www.tele-media.com

Telecommunication Support Services Inc
720 N Dr .... Melbourne FL 32934 321-242-0000
Web: www.tssincorp.com

Telepictures Production Inc
3500 W Olive St Ste 1000 .... Burbank CA 91505 818-972-0777
Web: www.telepicturestv.com

Terrasat Communications Inc
315 Digital Dr .... Morgan Hill CA 95037 408-782-5911
Web: www.terrasatinc.com

Company	City	State	Zip	Phone	Fax
Third Screen Media Inc 2 Oliver St 4th Fl *Web:* corp.aol.com	Boston	MA	02109	617-531-6400	
Titan Broadcast Management LLC 888 Third St NW Ste A *Web:* www.titanbroadcast.com	Atlanta	GA	30318	678-904-0555	
TiVo Inc 2160 Gold St *NASDAQ: TIVO* ■ *TF:* 877-367-8486 ■ *Web:* www.tivo.com	Alviso	CA	95002	408-519-9100	519-5330
Touch Base 620 Sixth St Fl 3 *TF:* 800-605-6920 ■ *Web:* touchbaseglobal.com	Denver	CO	80202	303-862-3300	
TowerComm LLC 6017 Triangle Dr *Web:* www.towercommonline.com	Raleigh	NC	27617	919-781-3496	
TV5 Quebec Canada 1755 Blvd Rene-Levesque E Bureau 101 *Web:* www.tv5.ca	Montreal	QC	H2K4P6	514-522-5322	
TVWorks LLC 2 Belvedere Pl Ste 200 *Web:* www.tvworks.com	Mill Valley	CA	94941	415-380-6200	
United Telephone Mutual Aid Corp 411 Seventh Ave *Web:* www.utma.com	Langdon	ND	58249	701-256-5156	
US Cable Corp 28 W Grand Ave Ste 10	Montvale	NJ	07645	201-930-9000	
USA Communications 124 Main St *Web:* www.usacomm.coop	Shellsburg	IA	52332	319-436-2224	
V-me Media Inc 450 W 33rd St 11th Fl *Web:* www.vmetv.com	New York	NY	10001	212-273-4800	
Vernon Telephone Company Inc 103 N Main St *Web:* www.vernontel.com	Westby	WI	54667	608-634-3136	
Vertical Structures Inc 309 Spangler Dr Ste E *Web:* verticalstructures.com	Richmond	KY	40475	859-624-8360	
Viodi LLC 5255 Stevens Creek Blvd Ste 127 *Web:* www.viodi.com	Santa Clara	CA	95051	408-551-0320	
VISTA Satellite Communications Inc 73-104 SW 12th Ave *Web:* vistaworldlink.com	Dania Beach	FL	33004	954-838-0900	
Voyport LLC 8200 Greensboro Dr *Web:* www.voyport.com	Mc Lean	VA	22102	703-462-5468	
W H Q r 913 Fm 254 N Front St Ste 300 *Web:* www.whqr.org	Wilmington	NC	28401	910-343-1640	
Wally World Satellite Local Direct Tv Dealer 524 Cemetery Rd	Park City	MT	59063	406-633-2811	
WBOY-TV Inc 904 W Pike St *Web:* www.wvalways.com	Clarksburg	WV	26301	304-623-3311	
Wbsd 400 Mc Canna Pkwy	Burlington	WI	53105	262-763-0195	
WDMP Radio 2163 State Rd 23-151 *Web:* d99point3.com	Dodgeville	WI	53533	608-935-2302	
Wehco Video Inc 115 E Capitol Ave *Web:* www.wehco.com	Little Rock	AR	72201	501-378-3529	376-8594
Westar Satellite Services LP 777 Westar Ln *Web:* www.westarsat.com	Cedar Hill	TX	75104	972-291-6000	
Wght Radio 1878 Lincoln Ave *Web:* www.ghtradio.com	Pompton Lakes	NJ	07442	973-839-1500	
White Mountain Cable Construction LLC 2113 Dover Rd *Web:* www.wmc1.com	Epsom	NH	03234	603-736-4766	
Wiat-tv 2075 Golden Crest Dr *Web:* wiat.com	Birmingham	AL	35209	205-322-4200	
Wirelesswerks USA Inc 7981 168th Ave Ne *Web:* www.wirelesswerks.com	Redmond	WA	98052	425-869-2356	
Wjac-Tv 49 Old Hickory Ln *Web:* www.wjactv.com	Johnstown	PA	15905	814-255-7600	
YKK AP America Inc 7680 The Bluffs Ste 100 *Web:* www.ykkap.com	Austell	GA	30168	678-838-6000	
Young Broadcasting of San Francisco Inc 599 Lexington Ave *Web:* kron4.com	New York	NY	10022	212-754-7070	
Zero Point Zero Production Inc 875 Ave of the Americas 19th Fl *Web:* www.zeropointzero.com	New York	NY	10001	212-620-2730	
Zito Media LP 102 S Main St *Web:* www.zitomedia.net	Coudersport	PA	16915	814-260-9570	

117 CABLE REELS

Company	City	State	Zip	Phone	Fax
American Reeling Devices Inc 15 Airpark Vista Blvd *TF Sales:* 800-354-7335 ■ *Web:* americanreeling.net	Dayton	NV	89403	800-354-7335	
Conductix 10102 F St *TF:* 800-521-4888 ■ *Web:* www.conductix.us	Omaha	NE	68127	402-339-9300	339-9627
Gleason Reel Corp 600 S Clark St *TF:* 888-504-5151 ■ *Web:* www.hubbell-gleason.com	Mayville	WI	53050	920-387-4120	387-4189
Hannay Reels Inc 553 SR 143 *TF:* 877-467-3357 ■ *Web:* www.hannay.com	Westerlo	NY	12193	518-797-3791	797-3259

118 CALCULATORS - ELECTRONIC

Company	City	State	Zip	Phone	Fax
Calculated Industries Inc 4840 Hytech Dr *TF:* 800-854-8075 ■ *Web:* www.calculated.com	Carson City	NV	89706	775-885-4900	885-4949
Sharp Electronics Corp 1 Sharp Plz *TF:* 800-237-4277 ■ *Web:* www.sharpusa.com	Mahwah	NJ	07430	201-529-8200	529-8413
Sweda Company LLC 17411 Vly Blvd *TF:* 800-848-8417 ■ *Web:* www.swedausa.com	City of Industry	CA	91744	626-357-9999	357-6080
Texas Instruments Inc 12500 TI Blvd *NASDAQ: TXN* ■ *TF Cust Svc:* 800-336-5236 ■ *Web:* www.ti.com	Dallas	TX	75243	972-995-3773	927-6377
Victor Technology LLC 175 E Crossroads Pkwy *TF:* 800-628-2420 ■ *Web:* www.victortech.com	Bolingbrook	IL	60440	630-754-4400	972-3902

119 CAMERAS & RELATED SUPPLIES - RETAIL

Company	City	State	Zip	Phone	Fax
Adorama Camera Inc 42 W 18th St *TF:* 800-223-2500 ■ *Web:* www.adorama.com	New York	NY	10011	212-741-0052	463-7223
B & H Photo-Video-Pro Audio Corp 420 Ninth Ave *TF:* 800-947-9954 ■ *Web:* www.bhphotovideo.com	New York	NY	10001	212-444-6615	239-7770
Beach Camera 203 Rt 22 E *TF:* 800-572-3224 ■ *Web:* www.beachcamera.com	Green Brook	NJ	08812	732-968-6400	968-7709
Black Photo Corp 200 Consilium Pl Ste 1600 *TF:* 800-668-3826 ■ *Web:* www.blacks.ca	Toronto	ON	M1H3J3	416-279-0007	
CambridgeWorld 34 Franklin Ave *TF:* 800-221-2253 ■ *Web:* www.cambridgeworld.com	Brooklyn	NY	11205	718-858-5002	858-5437
Camera Corner Inc PO Box 1899 *TF:* 800-868-2462 ■ *Web:* www.camcor.com	Burlington	NC	27216	336-228-0251	222-8011
Cress Photo PO Box 4262 *Web:* www.flashbulbs.com	Wayne	NJ	07474	973-694-1280	694-6965
Dodd Camera 2077 E 30th St *TF:* 800-507-1676 ■ *Web:* www.doddcamera.com	Cleveland	OH	44115	216-361-6800	361-6819
Dury's 701 Ewing Ave *TF:* 800-824-2379 ■ *Web:* www.durys.com	Nashville	TN	37203	615-255-3456	255-3506
F-11 Photographic Supplies 16 E Main St *TF:* 888-548-0203 ■ *Web:* www.f11photo.com	Bozeman	MT	59715	406-586-3281	
Focus Camera Inc 905 McDonald Ave *TF:* 800-221-0828 ■ *Web:* www.focuscamera.com	Brooklyn	NY	11218	718-437-8810	437-8895
Foto Source Canada Inc 2333 Wyecroft Rd *Web:* www.fotosource.com	Oakville	ON	L6L6L4	905-465-2759	465-0470
Kenmore Camera Inc 18031 67th Ave NE PO Box 82467 *TF:* 888-485-7447 ■ *Web:* www.kenmorecamera.com	Kenmore	WA	98028	425-485-7447	489-2843
Lawrence Photo & Video Inc 2550 S Campbell St *Web:* www.lawrencephotovideo.com	Springfield	MO	65807	417-883-8300	
Ritz Camera & Image 2 Bergen Turnpike *TF Cust Svc:* 855-622-7489 ■ *Web:* www.ritzcamera.com	Ridgefield Park	NJ	07660	855-622-7489	
Samy's Camera Inc 431 S Fairfax Ave *TF:* 800-321-4726 ■ *Web:* www.samys.com	Los Angeles	CA	90036	323-938-2420	692-0750

120 CAMPERS, TRAVEL TRAILERS, MOTOR HOMES

Company	City	State	Zip	Phone	Fax
A & N Trailer Parts 6028 S 118th E Ave *TF:* 800-272-1898 ■ *Web:* www.antrailerparts.com	Tulsa	OK	74146	918-461-8404	
Aerospace Engineering & Support Inc 1307 West 2550 South *Web:* aesut.com	Ogden	UT	84401	801-394-9565	
Airstream Inc 419 W Pike St *Web:* www.airstream.com	Jackson Center	OH	45334	937-596-6111	
Alaskan Campers Inc 801 NW Kerron Ave *Web:* www.alaskancamper.net	Winlock	WA	98596	360-748-6494	
Benlee Dunright 30383 Ecorse Rd *Web:* www.benlee.com	Romulus	MI	48174	734-722-8100	
Cam Superline Inc 4763 Zane A Miller Dr *Web:* www.camsuperline.com	Waynesboro	PA	17268	717-749-3369	
Coach House Inc 3480 Technology Dr *TF:* 800-235-0984 ■ *Web:* www.coachhouserv.com	Nokomis	FL	34275	941-485-0984	
Cool Amphibious Manufacturers International LLC 714 Okeetee Rd *Web:* www.camillc.com	Ridgeland	SC	29936	843-717-2444	717-2424
Cruise America 11 W Hampton Ave *TF:* 800-671-8042 ■ *Web:* www.cruiseamerica.com	Mesa	AZ	85210	480-464-7300	464-7321
Custom Fiberglass Mfg Corp *Snugtop* 1711 Harbor Ave PO Box 121 *TF:* 800-768-4867 ■ *Web:* www.snugtop.com	Long Beach	CA	90813	562-432-5454	435-2992
Davidson-Kennedy Co 800 Industrial Park Dr *TF:* 800-733-3434 ■ *Web:* www.equipmentinnovators.com	Marietta	GA	30062	770-427-9467	
Dexter Chassis Group 501 Miller Dr *Web:* dexterchassisgroup.com	White Pigeon	MI	49099	269-483-7681	
Doepker Industries Ltd 300 Doepker Ave *Web:* www.doepker.com	Annaheim	SK	S0K0G0	306-598-2171	
Dutchmen Mfg Inc 2164 Caragana Ct PO Box 2164 *TF:* 866-425-4369 ■ *Web:* www.dutchmen.com	Goshen	IN	46527	574-537-0600	
Exiss Aluminum Trailers Inc 900 East Trailer Blvd *TF:* 877-553-9477 ■ *Web:* www.exiss.com	El Reno	OK	73036	877-553-9477	
Forest River Inc 58277 SR 19 S *Web:* www.forestriverinc.com	Elkhart	IN	46517	574-296-7700	295-8749
Foretravel Motorcoach Inc 1221 NW Stallings Dr *TF:* 800-955-6226 ■ *Web:* www.foretravel.com	Nacogdoches	TX	75964	936-564-8367	564-0391
Four Wheel Campers 1460 Churchill Downs Ave *TF:* 800-242-1442 ■ *Web:* www.fourwh.com	Woodland	CA	95776	530-666-1442	666-1486
Gulf Stream Coach Inc 503 S Oakland Ave PO Box 1005 *TF:* 800-289-8787 ■ *Web:* www.gulfstreamcoach.com	Nappanee	IN	46550	574-773-7761	773-5761
Jayco Inc 903 S Main St *TF Cust Svc:* 800-283-8267 ■ *Web:* www.jayco.com	Middlebury	IN	46540	574-825-5861	825-7354
Keystone RV Co 2642 Hackberry Dr PO Box 2000 *TF:* 866-425-4369 ■ *Web:* www.keystonerv.com	Goshen	IN	46527	574-535-2100	535-2199
Lance Camper Mfg Corp 43120 Venture St *Web:* www.lancecampers.com	Lancaster	CA	93535	661-949-3322	949-1262
Monaco Coach Corp 1031 US 224 E **Fax Area Code:* 260 ■ **Fax:* Hum Res ■ *TF:* 877-466-6226 ■ *Web:* monacocoach.com	Decatur	IN	46733	877-466-6226	724-5238*
Myco Trailers LLC 2703 29th Ave E *Web:* www.mycotrailers.com	Bradenton	FL	34208	941-748-2397	
New Horizons RV Corp 2401 Lacy Dr *TF:* 800-235-3140 ■ *Web:* www.horizonsrv.com	Junction City	KS	66441	785-238-7575	238-4992

				Phone	Fax
Newell Coach Corp 3900 N Main St *TF:* 888-363-9355 ■ *Web:* www.newellcoach.com	Miami	OK	74354	918-542-3344	542-2028
Newmar Corp 355 Delaware St *TF:* 800-731-8300 ■ *Web:* www.newmarcorp.com	Nappanee	IN	46550	574-773-7791	773-2895
Nu-Wa Industries Inc 3701 Johnson Rd *TF:* 800-835-0676 ■ *Web:* www.nuwa.com	Chanute	KS	66720	620-431-2088	431-2513
Pace-Edwards 2400 Commercial Rd *TF:* 800-338-3697 ■ *Web:* www.pace-edwards.com	Centralia	WA	98531	360-736-9991	736-9992
Palomino RV 1200 New Jersey Ave *TF:* 888-327-4236 ■ *Web:* www.palominorv.com	Washington	MI	20590	269-432-3271	432-2516
Peterson Industries Inc 616 E Hwy 36 *Web:* www.petersonind.com	Smith Center	KS	66967	785-282-6825	282-3810
Renegade/Kibbi LLC 52216 State Rd 15 *TF:* 888-522-1126 ■ *Web:* www.renegaderv.com	Bristol	IN	46507	574-848-1126	848-1127
Rexhall Industries Inc 46147 Seventh St W *OTC: REXLQ* ■ *TF:* 800-765-7500 ■ *Web:* www.rexhall.com	Lancaster	CA	93534	661-726-0565	
Skyline Corp 2520 By-Pass Rd *NYSE: SKY* ■ *TF:* 800-348-7469 ■ *Web:* www.skylinecorp.com	Elkhart	IN	46514	574-294-6521	
Thor Industries Inc 419 W Pike St *NYSE: THO* ■ **Fax Area Code:* 877 ■ *Web:* thorindustries.com	Jackson Center	OH	45334	937-596-6111	596-6111*
Tiffin Motor Homes Inc (TMH) 105 Second St NW *Web:* www.tiffinmotorhomes.com	Red Bay	AL	35582	256-356-8661	356-8219
Vanguard National Trailer Corp 289 E Water Tower Dr *Web:* www.vanguardtrailer.com	Monon	IN	47959	219-253-2000	
Viking Recreational Vehicles LLC 580 W Burr Oak St PO Box 549 *Web:* coachmenrv.com	Centreville	MI	49032	269-467-6321	467-6021
Walt's Drive-A-Way Services Inc 321 N Kerth Ave *Web:* www.waltsonline.com	Evansville	IN	47711	812-424-8927	
Winnebago Industries Inc 605 W Crystal Lk Rd PO Box 152 *NYSE: WGO* ■ *TF:* 800-643-4892 ■ *Web:* www.winnebagoind.com	Forest City	IA	50436	641-585-3535	585-6966

121 CAMPGROUND OPERATORS

				Phone	Fax
Banner Day Camp 1225 Riverwoods Rd *Web:* www.bannerdaycamp.com	Lake Forest	IL	60045	847-295-4900	
Campfire 62 White St Ste 3E *Web:* www.campfirenyc.com	New York	NY	10013	212-612-9600	
CanaDream Corp 2510 27 St NE *Web:* www.canadream.com	Calgary	AB	T1Y7G1	403-291-1000	
Carson Valley Inn Inc 1627 US Hwy 395 N *TF:* 866-284-7766 ■ *Web:* www.cvinn.com	Minden	NV	89423	775-782-9711	
Champion Electric Inc 3950 Garner Rd *Web:* www.championelec.com	Riverside	CA	92501	951-276-9619	
Coan Construction Company Inc 1481 E Grand Ave *Web:* www.coanconstruction.com	Pomona	CA	91766	909-868-6812	
F Visions Services 500 Greenwich St Fl 3 *TF:* 888-245-8333 ■ *Web:* www.visionsvcb.org	New York	NY	10013	212-625-1616	
Glen Eden Corp 25999 Glen Eden Rd *TF:* 800-843-6833 ■ *Web:* www.gleneden.com	Corona	CA	92883	951-277-4650	
Hart Ranch Camping Resort Club 23756 Arena Dr *Web:* www.hartranchresort.com	Rapid City	SD	57702	605-399-2582	
Holiday Trails Resorts (Western) Inc 53730 Bridal Falls Rd *TF:* 800-663-2265 ■ *Web:* www.holidaytrailsresorts.com	Rosedale	BC	V0X1X1	604-794-7876	794-3756
Kampgrounds of America Inc (KOA) PO Box 30558 *TF:* 888-562-0000 ■ *Web:* www.koa.com	Billings	MT	59114	888-562-0000	
Lakeshore Golf and Rv Resort 100 Silver Creek Trl *Web:* www.golfatthelakes.com	Wentworth	SD	57075	605-483-3800	
Leisure Systems Inc 502 TechneCenter Dr Ste D *TF:* 866-928-9644 ■ *Web:* www.jellystonefranchise.com	Milford	OH	45150	513-831-2100	576-8670
Morgan RV Resorts LLC 63 Putnam St Ste 201 *Web:* www.morganrvresorts.com	Saratoga Springs	NY	12866	518-615-0552	
Pismo Coast Village Inc 165 S Dolliver St *Web:* www.pismocoastvillage.com	Pismo Beach	CA	93449	805-773-5649	
Red River Computer Company Inc 21 Water St Ste 500 *Web:* www.redriver.com	Claremont	NH	03743	603-448-8880	
Swan Lake Resort & Campground 17463 County Hwy 29 *TF:* 800-697-4626 ■ *Web:* swanlkresort.com	Fergus Falls	MN	56537	218-736-4626	
Touch of Nature Environmental Center 1206 Touch Of Nature Rd *Web:* www.pso.siu.edu	Makanda	IL	62958	618-453-1121	
Western Horizon Resorts (WHR) 103 W Tomichi Ave Ste 201A *TF:* 800-378-3709 ■ *Web:* www.westernhorizonresorts.net	Gunnison	CO	81230	970-641-5387	642-4591

122 CANDLES

See Also Gift Shops p. 2352

				Phone	Fax
Dadant & Sons Inc 51 S Second St *TF:* 888-922-1293 ■ *Web:* www.dadant.com	Hamilton	IL	62341	217-847-3324	847-3660
General Wax & Candle Co 6863 Beck Ave PO Box 9398 *TF:* 800-929-7867 ■ *Web:* www.generalwax.com	North Hollywood	CA	91605	818-765-5800	765-0555
Knorr Beeswax Products Inc 14906 Via De La Valle *TF:* 800-807-2337 ■ *Web:* www.knorrbeeswax.com	Del Mar	CA	92014	760-431-2007	431-8977
Original Cake Candle Co, The 102 Sundale Rd *TF:* 888-444-2253 ■ *Web:* cakecandle.com	Norwich	OH	43767	740-872-3248	
Reed Candle Co 1531 W Poplar St *Web:* reedcandlecompany.com	San Antonio	TX	78207	210-734-4243	734-2342
Root Candles Co 623 W Liberty St *TF:* 800-289-7668 ■ *Web:* www.rootcandles.com	Medina	OH	44256	330-725-6677	725-5624
Swans Candles 16524 Tilley Rd S *TF:* 888-848-7926 ■ *Web:* www.swanscandles.com	Tenino	WA	98589	888-848-7926	

123 CANDY STORES

				Phone	Fax
Adamson Associates Architects 401 Wellington St W 3rd Fl *Web:* www.adamson-associates.com	Toronto	ON	M5V1E7	416-967-1500	
Burdette Beckmann Inc 5851 Johnson St *Web:* www.bbiteam.com	Hollywood	FL	33021	954-983-4360	
Candy Bouquet International Inc 510 Mclean St *TF:* 877-226-3901 ■ *Web:* www.candybouquet.com	Little Rock	AR	72202	501-375-9990	375-9998
Candy Express 3320 Greencastle Rd *Web:* candyexpress.com	Burtonsville	MD	20866	301-384-5889	384-1788
Gardners Candies Inc 2600 Adams Ave PO Box E *TF:* 800-242-2639 ■ *Web:* www.gardnerscandies.com	Tyrone	PA	16686	814-684-3925	684-3928
Gertrude Hawk Chocolates Inc 9 Keystone Pk **Fax Area Code:* 570 ■ *TF:* 866-932-4295 ■ *Web:* www.gertrudehawkchocolates.com	Dunmore	PA	18512	800-822-2032	338-0947*
Gorant Candies 8301 Market St *Web:* gorant.com	Youngstown	OH	44512	330-726-8821	726-0325
JaCiva's Chocolate 4733 SE Hawthorne Ave *Web:* www.jacivas.com	Portland	OR	97215	503-234-8115	
Kilwins Quality Confections Inc (KQC) 1050 Bay View Rd *TF:* 888-454-5946 ■ *Web:* www.kilwins.com	Petoskey	MI	49770	888-454-5946	
Lammes Candies Since 1885 Inc PO Box 1885 *TF:* 800-252-1885 ■ *Web:* www.lammes.com	Austin	TX	78767	512-310-2223	238-2019
Provide Commerce Inc 4840 Eastgate Mall *TF Cust Svc:* 800-776-3569	San Diego	CA	92121	858-729-2800	909-4201
Rocky Mountain Chocolate Factory Inc (RMCF) 265 Turner Dr *NASDAQ: RMCF* ■ *TF Cust Svc:* 888-525-2462 ■ *Web:* www.rmcf.com	Durango	CO	81303	970-259-0554	382-7371
See's Candies Inc 210 El Camino Real *TF Cust Svc:* 800-877-7337 ■ *Web:* www.sees.com	South San Francisco	CA	94080	650-761-2490	

124 CANS - METAL

See Also Containers - Metal (Barrels, Drums, Kegs) p. 2141

				Phone	Fax
Allstate Can Corp 1 Wood Hollow Rd *Web:* www.allstatecan.com	Parsippany	NJ	07054	973-560-9030	560-9217
BWAY Corp 8607 Roberts Dr Ste 250 *TF:* 800-527-2267 ■ *Web:* www.bwaycorp.com	Atlanta	GA	30350	770-645-4800	645-4810
Can Corp of America Inc 326 June Ave *Web:* www.cancorpam.com	Blandon	PA	19510	610-926-3044	926-5041
Carolina Fabricators Inc 3831 Hwy 321 *Web:* www.carolinafab.net	West Columbia	SC	29169	803-794-4906	
CCL Container Corp 1 Llodio Dr *Web:* www.cclcontainer.com	Hermitage	PA	16148	724-981-4420	
Champion Container Corp 1455 N Michael Dr PO Box 90 *Web:* www.championcontainer.com	Wood Dale	IL	60191	732-636-6700	855-8663
Consolidated Fabricators Corp 14620 Arminta St *Web:* www.con-fab.com	Van Nuys	CA	91402	818-901-1005	
Container Supply Company Inc 12571 Western Ave *Web:* containersupplycompany.com	Garden Grove	CA	92841	714-892-8321	892-3824
Cork Supply USA Inc 531 Stone Rd *Web:* corksupply.com	Benicia	CA	94510	707-746-0353	
Crown Holdings Inc 1 Crown Way *NYSE: CCK* ■ *TF:* 800-523-3644 ■ *Web:* www.crowncork.com	Philadelphia	PA	19154	215-698-5100	
DS Containers Inc 1789 Hubbard Ave *Web:* www.dscontainers.com	Batavia	IL	60510	630-406-9600	
Eagle Mfg Company Inc 2400 Charles St *Web:* www.eagle-mfg.com	Wellsburg	WV	26070	304-737-3171	737-3171
Euclid Spiral Paper Tube Corp 339 Mill St *Web:* www.euclidspiral.com	Apple Creek	OH	44606	330-698-4711	
Exal Corp 1 Performance Pl *Web:* www.exal.com	Youngstown	OH	44502	330-744-2267	
G3 Enterprises Inc 502 E Whitmore Ave *Web:* www.g3enterprises.com	Modesto	CA	95358	209-341-4045	
Hupp & Assoc Inc 1690 Summit St *Web:* www.huppaerospace.com	New Haven	IN	46774	260-748-8282	
Independent Can Co 1300 Brass Mill Rd *Web:* www.independentcan.com	Belcamp	MD	21017	410-272-0090	273-7500
Intertape Polymer US Inc 3647 Cortez Rd W *Web:* www.itape.com	Bradenton	FL	34210	941-727-5788	
JL Clark Mfg Co 923 23rd Ave *TF:* 877-482-5275 ■ *Web:* www.jlclark.com	Rockford	IL	61104	815-962-8861	
JL Clark Mfg Co Lancaster Div 303 N Plum St *TF:* 877-482-5275 ■ *Web:* www.jlclark.com	Lancaster	PA	17602	717-392-4125	
KOR Water Inc 95 Enterprise Ste 310 *TF:* 877-708-7567 ■ *Web:* www.korwater.com	Aliso Viejo	CA	92656	714-708-7567	
Liberty Bottle Co 2900 Sutherland Dr *Web:* libertybottles.com	Union Gap	WA	98903	509-834-6500	494-0189
Peak International Inc 3432 Greystone Dr Ste 202 *Web:* www.peakf.com	Austin	TX	78731	512-339-4684	
Pochet of America Inc 415 Hamburg Tpke Ste D21	Wayne	NJ	07470	973-942-4923	
Polar Tech Industries Inc 415 E Railroad Ave *Web:* www.polar-tech.com	Genoa	IL	60135	815-784-9000	

				Phone	Fax
Protectoseal Co 225 W Foster Ave TF: 800-323-2268 ■ Web: www.protectoseal.com	Bensenville	IL	60106	630-595-0800	595-8059
Rexam Beverage Can Americas 8770 W Bryn Mawr Ave Web: rexam.com	Chicago	IL	60631	773-399-3000	399-8088
Ring Container Technology 1 Industrial Park Rd *Fax Area Code: 901 ■ TF: 800-280-6333 ■ Web: www.ringcontainer.com	Oakland	TN	38060	800-280-6333	465-1179*
Silgan Containers Corp 21800 Oxnard St Ste 600 Web: www.silgancontainers.com	Woodland Hills	CA	91367	818-348-3700	593-2255
Silgan Holdings Inc 4 Landmark Sq Ste 400 NASDAQ: SLGN ■ Web: www.silganholdings.com	Stamford	CT	06901	203-975-7110	975-7902

125 CANS, TUBES, DRUMS - PAPER (FIBER)

				Phone	Fax
Acme Spirally Wound Paper Products Inc 4810 W 139th St PO Box 35320 TF: 800-274-2797 ■ Web: www.acmespiral.com	Cleveland	OH	44135	216-267-2950	267-0239
Armbrust Paper Tubes Inc 6255 S Harlem Ave Web: www.tubesrus.com	Chicago	IL	60638	773-586-3232	
Callenor Company Inc N 60 W 15725 Kohler Ln TF: 800-813-7429 ■ Web: www.callenor.com	Menomonee Falls	WI	53051	262-252-3343	252-3873
Caraustar Industries Inc 5000 Austell-Powder Springs Rd Ste 300 TF: 800-858-1438 ■ Web: www.caraustar.com	Austell	GA	30106	770-948-3100	
Chicago Mailing Tube Co 400 N Leavitt St Web: www.mailing-tube.com	Chicago	IL	60612	312-243-6050	243-6545
Custom Paper Tubes Inc 15900 Industrial Pkwy TF: 800-343-8823 ■ Web: www.custompapertubes.com	Cleveland	OH	44135	216-362-2964	362-2980
Fibercorp Mills Inc 670 17th St NW Web: fibercorr.com	Massillon	OH	44646	330-837-5151	
Greif Inc 425 Winter Rd NYSE: GEF ■ TF: 877-781-9797 ■ Web: www.greif.com	Delaware	OH	43015	740-549-6000	657-6592
Industrial Paper Tube Inc 1335 E Bay Ave *Fax Area Code: 718 ■ TF: 800-345-0960 ■ Web: www.mailingtubes-ipt.com	Bronx	NY	10474	800-345-0960	378-0055*
LCH Paper Tube & Core Co 11930 Larc Industrial Blvd TF: 800-472-3477 ■ Web: www.lchpapertube.com	Burnsville	MN	55337	952-358-3587	224-0087
Master Package Corp 200 Madson St TF: 800-396-8425 ■ Web: www.masterpackage.com	Owen	WI	54460	715-229-2156	
New England Paper Tube Company Inc PO Box 186 Web: nepapertube.com	Pawtucket	RI	02862	401-725-2610	
NYSCO Products Inc 2350 Lafayette Ave Web: www.nysco.com	Bronx	NY	10473	718-792-9000	792-7732
Ohio Paper Tube Co 3422 Navarre Rd SW Web: www.ohiopapertube.com	Canton	OH	44706	330-478-5171	
OX Paper Tube & Core Inc 331 Maple Ave TF: 800-414-2476 ■ Web: oxpapertube.com	Hanover	PA	17331	800-414-2476	
Pacific Paper Tube Inc 1025 98th Ave TF: 888-377-8823 ■ Web: www.pacificpapertube.com	Oakland	CA	94603	510-562-8823	562-9002
Precision Paper Tube Company Inc 1033 S Noel Ave Web: www.pptube.com	Wheeling	IL	60090	847-537-4250	537-5777
Self-Seal Container Corp 401 E Fourth St TF: 800-334-1428 ■ Web: www.selfsealtubes.com	Bridgeport	PA	19405	610-275-2300	
TEKPAK Inc 1410 Washington St Web: www.tekpakinc.com	Marion	AL	36756	334-683-6121	
Trend-Pak of Canada 71 Railside Rd Web: www.trendpak.com	North York	ON	M3A1B2	416-510-3129	510-8371
Yankee Containers 110 Republic Dr Web: www.yankeecontainers.com	North Haven	CT	06473	203-288-3851	288-9936
Yazoo Mills Inc PO Box 369 TF Cust Svc: 800-242-5216 ■ Web: www.yazoomills.com	New Oxford	PA	17350	717-624-8993	624-4420

126 CAR RENTAL AGENCIES

See Also Fleet Leasing & Management p. 2287; Truck Rental & Leasing p. 3270

				Phone	Fax
A Betterway Rent-a-car Inc 1110 Northchase Pkwy SE TF: 800-527-0700 ■ Web: www.budgetatl.com	Marietta	GA	30067	770-240-3305	240-3340
ACE Rent A Car 4529 W 96th St TF: 888-261-7368 ■ Web: www.acerentacar.com	Indianapolis	IN	46268	317-248-5686	
Advantage Rent-A-Car 1288 Old Bayshore Hwy TF Cust Svc: 800-777-5500 ■ Web: www.advantage.com	Burlingame	CA	94010	800-777-5500	
Affiliated Car Rental 105 Hwy 36 *Fax Area Code: 732 ■ TF: 800-367-5159 ■ Web: www.affiliatedcarrental.com	Eatontown	NJ	07724	800-367-5159	380-0404*
Affordable Car Rental LC 105 Hwy 36 TF: 800-367-5159 ■ Web: www.affiliatedcarrental.com	Eatontown	NJ	07724	732-380-0888	380-0404
Aulick Leasing Corp 305 Ninth Ave PO Box 1369 Web: www.aulickleasing.com	Scottsbluff	NE	69361	308-220-4000	
Auto Europe 39 Commercial St TF: 800-223-5555 ■ Web: www.autoeurope.com	Portland	ME	04101	207-842-2000	842-2222
Avis Rent A Car System Inc 6 Sylvan Way *Fax: Sales ■ TF: 800-331-1212 ■ Web: www.avis.com	Parsippany	NJ	07054	973-496-3500	496-3444*
Budget Rent A Car System Inc 6 Sylvan Way TF: 800-527-0700 ■ Web: www.budget.com	Parsippany	NJ	07054	800-283-4382	
Car Rentals Inc 1570 S Washington Ave Web: www.avisnj.com	Piscataway	NJ	08854	732-752-6800	
Communauto Inc 335 rue St-Joseph Est Ste 310 Web: www.communauto.com	Quebec	QC	G1K3B4	418-523-1788	
Dewey Ford Inc 3055 SE Delaware Ave TF: 877-704-6793 ■ Web: www.deweyford.com	Ankeny	IA	50021	877-704-6793	
Discount Car & Truck Rentals Ltd 720 Arrow Rd *Fax Area Code: 416 ■ TF: 866-742-5968 ■ Web: www.discountcar.com	North York	ON	M9M2M1	866-742-5968	744-8340*
Dollar Rent A Car Inc 5330 E 31st St *Fax: Sales ■ TF: 800-800-4000 ■ Web: www.dollar.com	Tulsa	OK	74135	918-669-3000	669-3009*
Dollar Thrifty Automotive Group Inc 5330 E 31st St PO Box 35985 TF: 800-334-1705 ■ Web: www.thrifty.com	Tulsa	OK	74135	918-660-7700	
Driving Force Inc, The 60 King Rd Web: www.drivingforce.ca	Inuvik	NT	X0E0T0	867-777-2346	
Enterprise Rent-A-Car 600 Corporate Pk Dr TF: 844-377-0171 ■ Web: www.enterprise.com	Saint Louis	MO	63105	314-512-5000	
Europe by Car 40 Exchange Pl Ste 1720 TF: 800-223-1516 ■ Web: www.europebycarblog.com	New York	NY	10005	212-581-3040	246-1458
Foss National Leasing 7200 Yonge St TF: 800-461-3677 ■ Web: www.fossnational.com	Thornhill	ON	L4J1V8	905-886-4244	
Hale Trailer Brake & Wheel Inc Rt 73 & Cooper Rd TF: 800-232-6535 ■ Web: www.haletrailer.com	Voorhees	NJ	08043	856-768-1330	
Hertz Global Holdings Inc 225 Brae Blvd NYSE: HTZ ■ TF: 800-654-3131 ■ Web: www.hertz.com	Park Ridge	NJ	07656	201-307-2000	
Kemwel Inc 39 Commercial St TF: 800-678-0678 ■ Web: www.kemwel.com	Portland	ME	04112	207-842-2285	842-2147
Omaha Truck Center Inc 10710 I St PO Box 27379 TF: 800-866-2204 ■ Web: truckcentercompanies.com	Omaha	NE	68127	402-592-2440	
P V Rentals Ltd 5810 S Rice Ave TF: 800-275-7878 ■ Web: www.pvrentals.com	Houston	TX	77081	713-667-0665	
Steve Foley Cadillac 100 Skokie Blvd TF: 888-670-1429 ■ Web: www.foleycadillac.com	Northbrook	IL	60062	888-670-1429	
Thrifty Car Rental 5330 E 31st St TF: 888-400-8877 ■ Web: www.thrifty.com	Tulsa	OK	74135	918-660-7700	
Tnt Automotive Leasing Ltd 10124 W Broad St Ste G Web: tntauto.com	Glen Allen	VA	23060	804-270-2912	
Trailer Wizards Ltd 10387 Nordel Ct Web: www.trailerwizards.com	Delta	BC	V4G1J9	604-464-2220	
U-Save Auto Rental of America Inc 1052 Highland Colony Pkwy Ste 204 TF General: 800-438-2300 ■ Web: www.usave.com	Ridgeland	MS	39157	601-713-4333	

127 CARBON & GRAPHITE PRODUCTS

				Phone	Fax
Advance Carbon Products Inc 2036 National Ave TF: 800-283-1249 ■ Web: store.advancecarbon.com	Hayward	CA	94545	510-293-5930	293-5939
Carbonyx International USA Inc 1255 W 15th St Ste 320 Web: www.carbonyx.com	Plano	TX	75025	972-943-3355	
Fiber Materials Inc 5 Morin St Web: www.fibermaterialsinc.com	Biddeford	ME	04005	207-282-5911	282-7529
GrafTech International Holdings Inc 12900 Snow Rd NYSE: GTI ■ Web: www.graftech.com	Parma	OH	44130	216-676-2000	
Graphite Machining Inc 240 N Main St Web: www.graphitemachininginc.com	Topton	PA	19562	610-682-0080	
Graphite Systems Inc 1613 Danciger Dr	Fort Worth	TX	76112	817-457-1851	457-2664
Helwig Carbon Products Inc 8900 W Tower Ave TF: 800-365-3113 ■ Web: www.helwigcarbon.com	Milwaukee	WI	53224	414-354-2411	354-2421
Hyper-Therm HTC 18411 Gothard St Ste B Web: www.htcomposites.com	Huntington Beach	CA	92648	714-375-4085	
Mersen USA BN Corp 400 Myrtle Ave *Fax Area Code: 973 ■ TF General: 800-526-0877 ■ Web: www.mersen.com	Boonton	NJ	07005	800-526-0877	334-6394*
Micro Mech Inc 33 Tpke Rd	Ipswich	MA	01938	978-356-2966	
National Electrical Carbon 251 Forrester Dr *Fax Area Code: 408 ■ TF: 800-471-7842 ■ Web: ndt.org	Greenville	SC	29607	864-284-9728	280-7706*
Oxbow Carbon & Minerals Inc 1601 Forum Pl Ste 1400 Web: www.oxbow.com	West Palm Beach	FL	33401	561-697-4300	697-1876
Process Engineering Corp PO Box 279 Web: www.pecfrictionfighters.com	Crystal Lake	IL	60039	815-459-1734	459-3676
Pyrotek Inc 9503 E Montgomery Ave Web: www.pyrotek-inc.com	Spokane Valley	WA	99206	509-926-6212	927-2408
Saint Marys Carbon Co 259 Eberl St Web: www.stmaryscarbon.com	Saint Marys	PA	15857	814-781-7333	834-9201
Saturn Industries Inc 157 Union Tpke TF: 800-775-1651 ■ Web: www.saturnedm.com	Hudson	NY	12534	518-828-9956	828-9868
SCHUNKÿGmbHÿ&ÿCo.ÿKG 211 Kitty Hawk Dr Web: www.schunk.com	Morrisville	NC	27560	919-572-2705	
Scion Aviation LLC 3693 E County Rd 30 Web: www.scionaviation.com	Fort Collins	CO	80528	970-207-1721	
SGL Carbon LLC 307 Jamestown Rd TF: 800-828-6601 ■ Web: www.sglgroup.com	Morganton	NC	28655	828-437-3221	432-5885
SPARTA Inc 25531 Commercentre Dr Ste 120	Lake Forest	CA	92630	949-768-8161	
Superior Graphite 10 S Riverside Plaza Ste 1470 *Fax Area Code: 800 ■ TF Cust Svc: 800-325-0337 ■ Web: www.superiorgraphite.com	Chicago	IL	60606	312-559-2999	542-0200*
TEC Industries LLC 403 14th St SE Web: www.quatrocomposites.com	Orange City	IA	51041	712-707-9200	
US Graphite Inc 1620 E Holland Ave Web: www.usggledco.co.uk	Saginaw	MI	48601	989-755-0441	755-0445
Vector Composites Inc 3251 Mc Call St	Dayton	OH	45417	937-281-1444	
Zoltek Cos Inc 3101 McKelvey Rd NASDAQ: ZOLT ■ Web: www.zoltek.com	Bridgeton	MO	63044	314-291-5110	291-8536

128 CARBURETORS, PISTONS, PISTON RINGS, VALVES

See Also Aircraft Engines & Engine Parts p. 1724; Automotive Parts & Supplies - Mfr p. 1830

Phone / Fax

Compressor Products International
4410 Greenbriar Dr. Stafford TX 77477 281-207-4600 207-4612
TF: 800-675-6646 ■ *Web:* www.c-p-i.com

Dexter Automatic Products Co
2500 Bishop Cir E Dexter MI 48130 734-426-8900 426-2622
Web: www.dapcoind.com

Grant Piston Rings 1360 Jefferson St. Anaheim CA 92807 714-996-0050
Web: www.grantpistonrings.com

Grover Corp 2759 S 28th St Milwaukee WI 53234 414-384-9472 384-0201
TF: 800-776-3602 ■ *Web:* www.grovercorp.com

Hastings Manufacturing Co 325 N Hanover St Hastings MI 49058 269-945-2491 945-4667
TF: 800-776-1088 ■ *Web:* www.hastingspistonrings.com

Helio Precision Products Inc
601 N Skokie Hwy Lake Bluff IL 60044 847-473-1300 473-1306
Web: www.hnprecision.com

Holley Performance Products Inc
1801 Russellville Rd. Bowling Green KY 42101 270-782-2900 781-9940*
**Fax:* Cust Svc ■ *TF Sales:* 800-638-0032 ■ *Web:* www.holley.com

Hydreco 1500 County Naple Blvd Charlotte NC 28273 704-295-7575 295-7574
Web: www.hydreco.com

IMPCO Technologies Inc 3030 S Susan St. Santa Ana CA 92704 714-656-1200 656-1400*
**Fax:* Sales ■ *Web:* www.impcotechnologies.com

LE Jones Co 1200 34th Ave Menominee MI 49858 906-863-4411 863-4867
Web: www.lejones.com

MAHLE Industries Inc 2020 Sanford St Muskegon MI 49444 231-722-1300 724-1941
TF: 888-255-1942 ■ *Web:* www.us.mahle.com

Martin Wells Industries 5886 Compton Ave. Los Angeles CA 90001 323-581-6266 589-2334
TF: 800-421-6000

Pacific Piston Ring Co Inc
3620 Eastham Dr Culver City CA 90232 310-836-3322
Web: www.pacificpistonring.com

Safety Seal Piston Ring Co 4000 Airport Rd Marshall TX 75672 903-938-9241 938-9317*
**Fax:* Sales ■ *TF Sales:* 800-962-3631 ■ *Web:* www.sswesco.com

Total Seal Inc 22642 N 15th Ave. Phoenix AZ 85027 623-587-7400 587-7600
TF: 800-874-2753 ■ *Web:* www.totalseal.com

United Engine & Machine Company Inc
1040 Corbett St Carson City NV 89706 775-882-7790 882-7773
TF: 800-648-7970 ■ *Web:* www.uempistons.com

Wiseco Piston Inc 7201 Industrial Pk Blvd Mentor OH 44060 440-951-6600 951-6606
TF: 800-321-1364 ■ *Web:* www.wiseco.com

Zenith Fuel Systems Inc
14570 Industrial Pk Rd Bristol VA 24202 276-669-5555 645-8696
Web: www.zenithfuelsystems.com

129 CARD SHOPS

See Also Gift Shops p. 2352

Phone / Fax

Ad-venture Promotions LLC 2625 Regency Rd. Lexington KY 40503 859-263-4299
TF: 800-218-5488 ■ *Web:* www.ad-venturepromotions.com

Captiv 8 102 W 38th St 5th Fl. New York NY 10018 212-473-2440
Web: www.captiv8promos.com

Coral Productions Inc 100 Bickford St Rochester NY 14606 585-254-2580
Web: www.coralproductions.com

Design It Yourself Gift Baskets LLC
7999 Hansen Rd Ste 204 Houston TX 77061 713-944-3440
TF: 800-589-7553 ■ *Web:* www.designityourselfgiftbaskets.com

Enhanced Retail Solutions Inc
214 W 39th St Rm 1202a New York NY 10018 212-938-1991
Web: www.enhancedretailsolutions.com

Future of Flight Foundation
8415 Paine Field Blvd. Mukilteo WA 98275 425-438-8100
TF: 888-467-4777 ■ *Web:* www.futureofflight.org

Get Noticed Promotions Inc 152 Sonwil Dr. Buffalo NY 14225 716-688-8152
TF: 877-296-7179 ■ *Web:* getnoticedpromotions.com

Hallmark Cards Inc 2501 McGee St. Kansas City MO 64108 816-274-5111 274-5061*
**Fax:* Mail Rm ■ *TF:* 800-425-5627 ■ *Web:* www.hallmark.com

Howe Caverns Inc 255 Discovery Dr Howes Cave NY 12092 518-296-8900
Web: www.howecaverns.com

L a Party Rents Inc 13520 Saticoy St. Van Nuys CA 91402 818-989-4300
Web: lapartyrents.com

Papyrus Franchise Corp 500 Chadbourne Rd. Fairfield CA 94533 800-789-1649
TF: 800-789-1649 ■ *Web:* www.papyrusonline.com

Party Concepts
4691 S Butterfield Dr Palo Verde Tucson AZ 85714 520-750-0550
Web: party-concepts.com

Recycled Paper Greetings Inc
111 N Canal St Ste 700 Chicago IL 60606 800-777-3331
TF: 800-777-3331 ■ *Web:* www.prgreetings.com

130 CARDS - GREETING - MFR

Phone / Fax

123Greetingscom Inc 1674 Broadway Ste 403 New York NY 10019 212-246-0044
Web: www.123greetings.com

Amber Lotus Publishing PO Box 11329 Portland OR 97211 503-284-6400 284-6417
TF: 800-326-2375 ■ *Web:* www.amberlotus.com

American Artists Group Inc PO Box 49313 Athens GA 30604 706-227-0708 637-3105*
**Fax Area Code:* 270 ■ *Web:* www.americanartistsgroup.com

American Greetings Corp 1 American Rd. Cleveland OH 44144 216-252-7300 252-6778
NYSE: AM ■ *TF Sales:* 800-777-4891 ■ *Web:* www.corporate.americangreetings.com

AtticSalt Greetings Inc PO Box 5773 Topeka KS 66605 888-345-6005 333-0225*
**Fax Area Code:* 866 ■ *TF:* 888-345-6005 ■ *Web:* www.atticsaltgreetings.com

Avanti Press Inc 155 W Congress St Ste 200 Detroit MI 48226 313-961-0022 875-9690*
**Fax Area Code:* 800 ■ *TF:* 800-228-2684 ■ *Web:* www.avantipress.com

B Designs Letterpress 23 Noel St Ste 2 Amesbury MA 01913 978-388-1052
Web: www.bdesignsletterpress.com

Bayview Press 30 Knox St PO Box 153 Thomaston ME 04861 207-354-9919 354-9919
TF: 800-903-2346 ■ *Web:* www.bayviewpress.com

Birchcraft Studios Inc 10 Railroad St Abington MA 02351 781-878-5152 678-5151*
**Fax Area Code:* 800 ■ *TF:* 800-333-0405 ■ *Web:* www.birchcraft.com

Blue Mountain Arts Inc PO Box 4549 Boulder CO 80306 303-449-0536 417-6496*
**Fax:* Cust Svc ■ *TF Sales:* 800-545-8573 ■ *Web:* www.sps.com

Blue Turtle Studio 4884 Broiles Rd Christiana TN 37037 615-585-5757
Web: www.blueturtlestudio.com

Bonair Daydreams PO Box 1522 Wrightsville Beach NC 28480 910-617-3887 509-4108
TF: 888-226-6247 ■ *Web:* www.bonairdaydreams.com

Carole Joy Creations Inc
1087 Federal Rd Unit 8 Brookfield CT 06804 203-740-4490 740-4495
TF Sales: 800-223-6945

Checkerboard Ltd 216 W Boylston St West Boylston MA 01583 508-835-2475 835-4355
Web: checkernet.com

Colors By Design 7723 Densmore Ave Van Nuys CA 91406 800-832-8436 824-2530
TF: 800-832-8436 ■ *Web:* www.cbdcards.com

Curiosities Greeting Cards 21 Ashwood Ct Lancaster NY 14086 716-681-2801
Web: www.curiosities.com

DaySpring Cards Inc 21154 Hwy 16 E Siloam Springs AR 72761 479-524-9301
TF: 800-944-8000 ■ *Web:* www.dayspring.com

Design Design Inc 19 La Grave SE Grand Rapids MI 49503 616-774-2448 774-4020
TF: 800-334-3348 ■ *Web:* www.designdesign.us

Eclectik 1332 W Lake St Chicago IL 60607 312-676-2442 751-2075*
**Fax Area Code:* 773 ■ *TF:* 866-308-1231 ■ *Web:* www.eclectik.com

Fantus Paper Products P.S. Greetings Inc
5730 N Tripp Ave Chicago IL 60646 773-267-6069 267-6055
TF Sales: 800-621-8823 ■ *Web:* www.psg-fpp.com

Fotofolio Inc 33 W 34th St Ste 3 New York NY 10001 212-226-0923
Web: www.fotofolio.com

Freedom Greeting Card Company Inc
774 American Dr. Bensalem PA 19020 215-604-0300 604-0436
TF Sales: 800-359-3301 ■ *Web:* www.freedomgreetings.com

Galison Publishing LLC 28 W 44th St Ste 1411 New York NY 10036 212-354-8840
TF: 800-670-7441 ■ *Web:* www.galison.com

Gallant Greetings Corp
4300 United Pkwy. Schiller Park IL 60176 847-671-6500
TF: 800-621-4279 ■ *Web:* www.gallantgreetings.com

Gina B Designs Inc
12700 Industrial Pk Blvd Ste 40 Plymouth MN 55441 763-559-7595 559-3899
TF: 800-228-4856 ■ *Web:* www.ginabdesigns.com

Graphique De France 9 State St. Woburn MA 01801 781-935-3405 935-5145
TF Sales: 800-444-1464 ■ *Web:* www.graphiquedefrance.com

Great Arrow Graphics 2495 Main St Ste 457 Buffalo NY 14214 716-836-0408 836-0702
TF: 800-835-0490 ■ *Web:* www.greatarrow.com

Hallmark Cards Inc 2501 McGee St. Kansas City MO 64108 816-274-5111 274-5061*
**Fax:* Mail Rm ■ *TF:* 800-425-5627 ■ *Web:* www.hallmark.com

Hallmark International PO Box 419034 Kansas City MO 64141 816-274-5111
TF: 800-425-5627 ■ *Web:* www.hallmark.com

JewishCard 7360 Viewpoint Rd Aptos CA 95003 831-469-8883 662-2746
Web: www.jewishcard.com

Laughing Elephant 3645 Interlake Ave N Seattle WA 98103 800-354-0400
TF: 800-354-0400 ■ *Web:* www.laughingelephant.com

Laurel Ink 911 N 145th St Seattle WA 98133 800-850-0081
TF Cust Svc: 800-850-0081 ■ *Web:* www.laurelink.com

Leanin' Tree Inc 6055 Longbow Dr Boulder CO 80301 303-530-1442
Web: www.leanintree.com

Marian Heath Greeting Cards Inc
9 Kendrick Rd. Wareham MA 02571 508-291-0766 291-2976
TF Sales: 800-688-9998 ■ *Web:* www.marianheath.com

Meri Meri 63 Leonard St Belmont MA 02478 617-484-5571
TF: 800-638-2881 ■ *Web:* www.merimeri.com

Museum Facsimiles 117 Fourth St Pittsfield MA 01201 413-499-0020
TF: 877-499-0020 ■ *Web:* www.museumfacsimiles.com

NobleWorks Inc 500 Paterson Plank Rd Union City NJ 07087 201-420-0095
TF: 800-346-6253 ■ *Web:* www.nobleworkscards.com

Northern Exposure Greeting Cards
2301 Circadian Way Ste 300 Santa Rosa CA 95407 707-546-2153
TF: 800-237-3524 ■ *Web:* www.necards.com

Nouvelles Images Inc 68 Morgan Ave. Danbury CT 06810 203-730-1004
TF: 800-345-1383 ■ *Web:* www.nouvellesimages.com

Palm Press Inc 1442A Walnut St Ste 120 Berkeley CA 94709 510-486-0502
Web: www.palmpressinc.com

Paperdoll Co 4944 Encino Ave Encino CA 91316 818-906-8411 907-0225
TF: 866-223-1145 ■ *Web:* thepaperdollcompany.com

Peaceable Kingdom Press
950 Gilman St Ste 200 Berkeley CA 94710 877-444-5195
TF: 877-444-5195 ■ *Web:* www.peaceablekingdom.com

Penny Laine Papers
2211 Century Ctr Blvd Ste 110 Irving TX 75062 972-812-3000 812-3004
TF: 800-456-6484 ■ *Web:* pennylainepapers.com

Perma-Greetings Inc 2470 Schuetz Rd Maryland Heights MO 63043 314-567-4606
Web: permagraphics.net

Persimmon Press PO Box 297 Belmont CA 94002 650-802-8325 910-5095*
**Fax Area Code:* 800 ■ *TF:* 800-910-5080 ■ *Web:* www.persimmoncards.com

PostMark Press Inc 16 Spruce St Watertown MA 02472 617-924-3520
Web: www.postmarkpress.com

Posty Cards 1600 Olive St Kansas City MO 64127 816-231-2323 577-3800*
**Fax Area Code:* 888 ■ *TF:* 800-821-7968 ■ *Web:* www.postycards.com

Potluck Press 920 S Bayview St Seattle WA 98134 206-268-0458 328-4633
Web: www.potluckpress.com

Quotable Cards Inc 611 Broadway Rm 810 New York NY 10012 212-420-7552 420-7558
Web: www.quotablecards.com

Recycled Paper Greetings Inc
111 N Canal St Ste 700 Chicago IL 60606 800-777-3331
TF: 800-777-3331 ■ *Web:* www.prgreetings.com

Schurman Fine Papers 500 Chadbourne Rd Fairfield CA 94533 800-789-1649 428-0641*
**Fax Area Code:* 707 ■ *TF Sales:* 800-789-1649 ■ *Web:* www.papyrusonline.com

Sillies Greeting Card Co 14762 Oak Run Ln Burnsville MN 55306 952-892-5666

Phone Fax

StellArt 2012 Waltzer Rd.......................... Santa Rosa CA 95403 707-569-1378 569-1379
TF: 866-621-1987 ■ *Web:* www.stellart.com
Sunshine Business Class 150 Kingswood Dr.......... Mankato MN 56001 800-873-7681 842-9371
TF: 800-873-7681 ■ *Web:* www.sunshinebusinessclass.com
Sunshine Girl Creations Inc
11111 Excelsior Blvd.............................. Hopkins MN 55343 952-931-2464 931-2575
Web: www.sunshinegirlcreations.net
Up With Paper 6049 Hi-Tek Ct........................ Mason OH 45040 513-759-7473 293-8471*
**Fax Area Code:* 800 ■ *TF:* 800-852-7677 ■ *Web:* www.upwithpaper.com
US Allegiance Inc 63075 NE 18th St..................... Bend OR 97701 541-330-6282 622-8212*
**Fax Area Code:* 800
Victorian Trading Co 15600 W 99th St.................. Lenexa KS 66219 913-438-3995 724-7697*
**Fax Area Code:* 800 ■ *TF Cust Svc:* 800-700-2035 ■ *Web:* www.victoriantradingco.com
Viktorina Cards 89 Stonehurst Ave Ste 311.............. Ottawa ON K1Y4R6 613-422-6337
Web: www.amazzzingcards.com
Willow Creek Press Inc
9931 Hwy 70 W PO Box 147...................... Minocqua WI 54548 715-358-7010 358-2807
TF Cust Svc: 800-850-9453 ■ *Web:* www.willowcreekpress.com
ZPR International Inc
27900 Chagrin Blvd Ste 208...................... Beachwood OH 44122 216-464-2667

131 CARPETS & RUGS

See Also Flooring - Resilient p. 2288; Tile - Ceramic (Wall & Floor) p. 3247
The companies listed here include carpet finishers and makers of mats and padding.

Phone Fax

Americas Floor Source 3442 Millennium Ct.......... Columbus OH 43219 614-237-3181
Web: www.americasfloorsource.com
Architectural Floor Systems Inc
595 Supreme Dr.................................. Bensenville IL 60106 877-437-3567
TF: 877-437-3567 ■ *Web:* www.gerflorusa.com
Art of The Knot Inc 5893 Sunset Dr............... South Miami FL 33143 305-667-2000
Artisans Inc W4146 Second St PO Box 278.............. Glen Flora WI 54526 715-322-5285
TF: 800-311-8756 ■ *Web:* www.artisanscarpet.com
Atlas Carpet Mills Inc 2200 Saybrook Ave.......... Los Angeles CA 90040 323-724-9000 724-4526
TF: 800-272-8527 ■ *Web:* www.atlascarpetmills.com
Bacova Guild Ltd 1000 Commerce Ctr Dr............. Covington VA 24426 540-863-2600 863-2645
Web: www.bacova.com
Barrett Carpet Mills Inc 2216 Abutment Rd............. Dalton GA 30721 800-241-4064
TF: 800-241-4064 ■ *Web:* krausflooring.com/barrett
Beaulieu of America Inc
1502 Coronet Dr PO Box 1248........................ Dalton GA 30722 800-227-7211
TF: 800-227-7211 ■ *Web:* usa.beaulieuflooring.com
Bentley Prince Street
14641 E Don Julian Rd....................... City of Industry CA 91746 800-423-4709 741-7420
TF: 800-423-4709 ■ *Web:* www.bentleymills.com
Blackton Inc 1714 Alden Rd.......................... Orlando FL 32803 407-898-2661
Web: www.blacktoninc.com
Bloomsburg Carpet Industries Inc
4999 Columbia Blvd............................ Bloomsburg PA 17815 570-784-9188
TF: 800-233-8773 ■ *Web:* www.bloomsburgcarpet.com
Brintons USA
1000 Cobb Pl Blvd Bldg 200 Ste 200............... Kennesaw GA 30144 678-594-9300
Web: brintons.net
Camelot Carpet Mills Inc 17111 Red Hill Ave............ Irvine CA 92614 949-474-4000 553-8238
TF: 800-854-8331 ■ *Web:* www.camelotcarpetmills.com
Capel Inc 831 N Main St............................... Troy NC 27371 800-382-6574 572-7040*
**Fax Area Code:* 910 ■ *TF:* 800-334-3711 ■ *Web:* www.capelrugs.com
Carpet Cushions & Supplies Inc
1520 Pratt Blvd............................ Elk Grove Village IL 60007 847-364-6760 364-6785
Web: www.carpetcushions.com
Carpet Exchange 1133 S Platte River Dr................ Denver CO 80223 303-744-3300
Web: www.carpetexchangeonline.com
Carpets Plus by Design 330 Lockwood.............. Woodville WI 54028 715-698-2200
Web: carpetsplusbydesign.com
Challenger Industries Inc 743 Hill Rd................... Dalton GA 30721 706-278-7707
Web: www.challengerturf.com
CMH Space Flooring Products Inc
2732 Hwy 74 W................................. Wadesboro NC 28170 704-694-6213
Web: www.cmhspace.com
Compagnie Beaulieu Canada 335 Ch Roxton........ Acton Vale QC J0H1A0 450-546-5000
Consolidated Carpet Assoc LLC
45 W 25th St 8th Fl.............................. New York NY 10010 212-226-4600
Web: www.consolidatedcarpet.com
Continental Precision Corp
230 Saint Nicholas Ave...................... South Plainfield NJ 07080 908-754-7663
Web: www.montrosemolders.com
Culver Floor Covering Company Inc
2411 Ave X.................................... Brooklyn NY 11235 718-332-3434
Web: www.culverfloors.org
Delaware Valley Corp 500 Broadway................. Lawrence MA 01841 978-688-6995 688-5825
Web: www.dvc500.com
Dixie Group Inc 104 Nowlin Ln Ste 101............ Chattanooga TN 37421 423-510-7000
NASDAQ: DXYN ■ *TF:* 800-289-4811 ■ *Web:* www.thedixiegroup.com
Dorsett Industries Inc 1304 May St PO Box 805.......... Dalton GA 30721 706-278-1961 217-1775
TF: 800-241-4035 ■ *Web:* www.dorsettind.com
Durkan Patterned Carpet Inc 405 Virgil Dr.............. Dalton GA 30721 800-981-2009
TF: 800-981-2009 ■ *Web:* www.durkan.com
EMW Carpets & Furniture 2141 S Broadway............ Denver CO 80210 303-744-2754
Web: emwcarpets.com
Flex Foam 617 N 21st Ave........................... Phoenix AZ 85009 602-252-5819
TF: 800-266-3626 ■ *Web:* www.flexfoam.net
Floors Are Us Inc 2275 Seminole Ln............. Charlottesville VA 22901 434-978-4454
Web: www.floorsareusinc.com
Floors by Foutch 5555 Woodland Hills Dr............. Denton TX 76208 940-383-4499
Forbo Flooring Inc
8 Maplewood Dr Humboldt Industrial Pk
PO Box 667..................................... Hazleton PA 18202 570-459-0771
Web: www.forbo.com/flooring/en-us
Fortune Contract Inc 272 Kraft Dr..................... Dalton GA 30721 706-279-3669
Web: www.fortunecontract.com

Phone Fax

Garland Sales Inc PO Box 1870....................... Dalton GA 30720 706-278-7880
TF: 800-524-0361 ■ *Web:* www.garlandrug.com
H & s Floors & Furnishings Inc
210 Russell St................................. Darlington SC 29532 843-393-0456
Home Dynamix LLC 1 Carol Pl.................... Moonachie NJ 07074 201-807-0111
TF: 800-726-9290 ■ *Web:* www.homedynamix.com
Indian Summer Carpet Mills Inc
601 Callahan Rd PO Box 3577........................ Dalton GA 30719 706-277-6277 279-1884
TF: 800-824-4010 ■ *Web:* www.southwindcarpet.com
Interface Inc 2859 Paces Ferry Rd Ste 2000.............. Atlanta GA 30339 770-437-6800
NASDAQ: TILE ■ *Web:* www.interfaceglobal.com
J & J Industries Inc 818 J & J Dr PO Box 1287........... Dalton GA 30721 706-529-2100 275-4433
TF: 800-241-4586 ■ *Web:* www.jjflooringgroup.com
Jaipur Rugs Inc 2775 Pacific Dr................... Norcross GA 30071 404-351-2360
TF: 888-676-7330 ■ *Web:* www.jaipurliving.com
Johnson Wholesale Floors Inc
1874 Defoor Ave NW.............................. Atlanta GA 30318 404-352-2700
TF: 800-345-9318 ■ *Web:* johnsonwholesalefloors.com
Johnsonite Inc 16910 Munn Rd.................. Chagrin Falls OH 44023 440-543-8916
TF: 800-899-8916 ■ *Web:* www.johnsonite.com
KAS Oriental Rugs Inc 62 Veronica Ave.............. Somerset NJ 08873 732-545-1900
Web: www.kasrugs.com
Langhorne Carpet Co
201 W Lincoln Hwy PO Box 7175..................... Penndel PA 19047 215-757-5155 757-2212
Web: www.langhornecarpets.com
Lexmark Carpet Mills Inc 285 Kraft Dr............... Dalton GA 30721 800-871-3211
TF: 800-871-3211 ■ *Web:* www.lexmarkcarpet.com
Manufacturers Chemicals LLC
4325 Old Tasso Rd.............................. Cleveland TN 37320 423-476-6518
Web: synalloychemicals.com
Maples Industries Inc 2210 Moody Ridge Rd......... Scottsboro AL 35768 256-259-1327 259-2072
TF Hum Res: 800-537-5447
Marglen Industries Inc 1748 WaRd Mtn Rd.............. Rome GA 30161 706-295-5621
Web: www.marglen.us
Masland Carpets Inc 716 Bill Myles Dr................ Saraland AL 36571 800-633-0468
TF: 800-633-0468 ■ *Web:* www.maslandcarpets.com
Mats Inc 37 Shuman Ave.......................... Stoughton MA 02072 781-344-1536
Web: www.matsinc.com
Milliken & Co 920 Milliken Rd.................... Spartanburg SC 29303 864-503-2020 503-2100*
**Fax:* Hum Res ■ *Web:* www.milliken.com
Milliken & Co KEX Div PO Box 1926 MS 801.......... Spartanburg SC 29304 706-880-5511 880-5358*
**Fax:* Cust Svc ■ *TF:* 800-241-4826 ■ *Web:* www.millikencarpet.com
Mohawk Industries Inc 160 S Industrial Blvd........... Calhoun GA 30703 706-629-7721
NYSE: MHK ■ *TF:* 800-241-4494 ■ *Web:* www.mohawkind.com
Mohawk Industries Inc Karastan Div
508 E Morris St.................................. Dalton GA 30721 800-234-1120
TF: 800-234-1120 ■ *Web:* www.karastan.com
Mohawk Industries Inc Lees Carpets Div
160 S Industrial Blvd............................. Calhoun GA 30701 706-629-7721
TF: 800-241-4494 ■ *Web:* mohawkind.com/content.aspx?id=1785
Natco Products Corp 155 Brookside Ave........... West Warwick RI 02893 401-828-0300 823-7670
Netchannel Inc 8310 Rio Grande Blvd NW.......... Albuquerque NM 87114 505-843-8282
TF: 888-843-8282 ■ *Web:* www.netchannel.com
Oriental Weavers of America
3252 Lower Dug Gap Rd SW......................... Dalton GA 30720 706-277-9666 277-9639
Web: www.orientalweavers.com
Packerland Rent-a-mat Inc 12580 W Rohr Ave........... Butler WI 53007 262-781-5321
TF: 800-472-9339 ■ *Web:* www.packerland.net
Quality Mat Co 6550 Tram Rd...................... Beaumont TX 77713 409-722-4594
TF: 800-227-8159 ■ *Web:* www.qmat.com
Rieter Automotive North America - Carpet
480 W Fifth St.............................. Bloomsburg PA 17815 570-784-4100 848-0130*
**Fax Area Code:* 248
Rite Rug Co 3949 Business Park Dr.................. Columbus OH 43204 614-261-6060
Web: www.riterug.com
Royalty Carpet Mills Inc 17111 Red Hill Ave............ Irvine CA 92614 949-474-4000 553-8238
TF: 800-854-8331 ■ *Web:* www.royaltycarpetmills.com
RTY Installations Inc
13903 Ballantyne Meadows Dr...................... Charlotte NC 28277 704-544-0726
S & S Mills Inc 414 C N Pk Dr........................ Dalton GA 30720 706-277-3677
TF: 800-241-4013 ■ *Web:* www.ssmillsinc.com
Schmidt Custom Floors Inc
N8W22590 Johnson Dr.......................... Waukesha WI 53186 262-547-8763
Web: www.schmidtflooring.com
Scottdel Inc 400 Church St......................... Swanton OH 43558 419-825-2341 825-1523
TF: 800-446-2341 ■ *Web:* www.scottdel.com
Shaw Industries Inc 616 E Walnut Ave.................. Dalton GA 30722 800-441-7429
TF: 800-441-7429 ■ *Web:* www.shawfloors.com
Southwind Carpet Mills
601 Callahan Rd SE PO Box 3577..................... Dalton GA 30719 706-277-6277
Web: www.cherokeecarpet.com
Subaru of Indiana Automotive Inc
5500 State Rd 38 E.............................. Lafayette IN 47905 765-449-1111 449-6888
Web: www.subaru-sia.com
Syntec Industries LLC
438 Lavender Dr PO Box 1653........................ Rome GA 30162 706-235-1158 235-1768
Web: www.syntecind.com
Tandus Centiva
311 Smith Industrial Blvd PO Box 1447................ Dalton GA 30722 706-259-9711 259-9711*
**Fax:* Mktg ■ *TF:* 800-248-2878 ■ *Web:* tandus-centiva.com
Tri State Wholesale Flooring Inc
3900 W 34th St N............................ Sioux Falls SD 57107 605-336-3080
TF: 800-353-3080 ■ *Web:* tsf.com
Unique Carpets Ltd 7360 Jurupa Ave................. Riverside CA 92504 951-352-8125 352-8140
TF: 800-547-8266 ■ *Web:* www.uniquecarpetsltd.com
Universal Rugs & Oil Paintings Inc
325 N Brand Blvd................................ Glendale CA 91203 818-549-0095

132 CASINO COMPANIES

See Also Games & Gaming p. 2348

Phone Fax

7clans Paradise Casino 7500 Hwy 177.............. Red Rock OK 74651 580-723-4005
Web: www.okparadisecasino.com

				Phone	Fax
Affinity Gaming LLC 3440 W Russel Rd · *Web:* www.affinitygaming.com	Las Vegas	NV	89118	702-889-7695	
Ameristar Casinos Inc 3773 Howard Hughes Pkwy Ste 490-S · *NASDAQ: ASCA* ■ *TF:* 888-708-5699 ■ *Web:* www.ameristar.com	Las Vegas	NV	89169	702-567-7000	
Angel of The Winds Casino 3438 Stoluckquamish Ln · *Web:* www.angelofthewinds.com	Arlington	WA	98223	360-474-9740	
Baystar Hotel Group 500N Westshore Blvd Ste 740 · *Web:* baystarhotels.com	Largo	FL	33609	727-585-3333	
BeDynamic Inc 1725 Westlake Ave N Ste 150 · *Web:* bedynamic.com	Seattle	WA	98109	206-285-1407	
Boomtown Inc 2100 Garson Rd · *TF:* 800-648-3790 ■ *Web:* www.boomtownreno.com	Verdi	NV	89439	775-345-6000	
Boyd Gaming Corp 3883 Howard Hughes Pkwy 9th Fl · *NYSE: BYD* ■ *TF:* 800-522-4700 ■ *Web:* boydgaming.com	Las Vegas	NV	89169	702-792-7200	
Buffalo Run Casino 1000 Buffalo Run Blvd · *Web:* www.buffalorun.com	Miami	OK	74354	918-542-7140	
Casino One Corp 999 N 2nd St · *Web:* www.lumiereplace.com	St. Louis	MO	63102	341-881-7777	
Century Casinos Inc 2860 S Cir Dr Ste 350 · *NASDAQ: CNTY* ■ *TF:* 888-966-2257 ■ *Web:* www.cnty.com	Colorado Springs	CO	80906	719-527-8300	527-8301
Cherokee Nation Entertainment State Hwy 62 4 Miles S. · *Web:* www.cherokeecasino.com	Tahlequah	OK	74465	918-207-3600	
Colony Palms Hotel 572 N Indian Canyon Dr · *TF:* 800-557-2187 ■ *Web:* www.colonypalmshotel.com	Palm Springs	CA	92262	760-969-1800	
Elgin Riverboat Resort 250 S Grove Ave · *Web:* www.grandvictoria-elgin.com	Elgin	IL	60120	847-468-7000	
Empire Resorts Inc 204 Rt 17B · *NASDAQ: NYNY* ■ *Web:* www.empireresorts.com	Monticello	NY	12701	845-807-0001	
Fond du Lac Band of Lake Superior Chippewa 1720 Big Lake Rd · *TF:* 888-888-6007 ■ *Web:* fdlrez.com	Cloquet	MN	55720	218-879-4593	878-7169
Fort Mojave Tribal Council 500 Merriman Ave · *Web:* mojaveindiantribe.com	Needles	CA	92363	760-629-4591	
Fortune House All Suites Hotel 185 Se 14th Ter · *Web:* fortunehousehotel.com	Miami	FL	33131	305-349-5200	
Four Winds Casino Resort 11111 Wilson Rd · *TF:* 866-494-6371 ■ *Web:* www.fourwindscasino.com	New Buffalo	MI	49117	866-494-6371	
Full House Resorts Inc 4670 S Fort Apache Rd Ste 190 · *NASDAQ: FLL* ■ *Web:* www.fullhouseresorts.com	Las Vegas	NV	89147	702-221-7800	
Granite Gaming Group 115 N First St	Las Vegas	NV	89101	702-385-4250	385-4935
Gulph Creek Hotels Inc 150 Strafford Ave Ste 215 · *Web:* gulphcreekhotels.com	Wayne	PA	19087	610-687-9283	
Hilton Ponce Golf & Casino Resort 1150 Ave Caribe · *Web:* www3.hilton.com/en/hotels/puerto-rico/hilton-ponce-golf-and-casino-resort-pnchihh/index.html	Ponce	PR	00716	787-259-7676	
Hotel Fusion 140 Ellis St · *Web:* hotelfusionsf.com	San Francisco	CA	94102	415-568-2525	
Kerzner International Ltd 1000 S Pine Island Rd Ste 800 · *Web:* www.kerzner.com	Plantation	FL	33324	954-809-2000	809-2317
Kickapoo Traditional Tribe Of Texas 162 Chick Kazen Rd · *Web:* www.ktttribe.org	Eagle Pass	TX	78852	830-773-2105	
Lake Tahoe Horizon Casino Resort 50 Hwy 50 · *Web:* www.tropicanacasinos.com	Stateline	NV	89449	775-588-6211	
Los Gatos Lodge Inc 50 Los Gatos Saratoga Rd · *Web:* losgatoslodge.com	Los Gatos	CA	95032	408-354-3301	
Mille Lacs Band of Ojibwe 43408 Oodena Dr. · *TF:* 800-709-6445 ■ *Web:* www.millelacsband.com	Onamia	MN	56359	320-532-4181	532-7505
Mountain High Resort 24510 State Hwy 2 · *Web:* www.mthigh.com	Wrightwood	CA	92397	760-316-7889	
Mountaineer Park Inc Route 2 · *Web:* www.moreatmountaineer.com	Chester	WV	26034	304-387-8300	
Nevada Gold & Casinos Inc 133 E Warm Springs Rd Ste 102 · *NYSE: UWN* ■ **Fax Area Code:* 713 ■ *Web:* www.nevadagold.com	Las Vegas	NV	89119	702-685-1000	621-6919*
Nevada Property 1 LLC 3708 Las Vegas Blvd South · *Web:* www.cosmopolitanlasvegas.com	Las Vegas	NV	89109	702-698-7000	
New York Hotel Trades 707 Eighth Ave · *Web:* www.hotelworkers.org	New York	NY	10036	212-245-8100	
Northmere The Sro Hotel 4943 N Kenmore Ave	Chicago	IL	60640	773-561-4234	
Overton Hotel & Conference Center 2320 Mac Davis Ln · *Web:* www.overtonhotel.com	Lubbock	TX	79401	806-776-7000	
Palace Casino 158 Howard Ave · *TF:* 800-725-2239 ■ *Web:* www.palacecasinoresort.com	Biloxi	MS	39530	228-432-8888	
Park House Hotel Corp 1206 48th St · *Web:* www.parkhousehotelbrooklyn.com	Brooklyn	NY	11219	718-871-8100	
Pinnacle Entertainment Inc 3980 Howard Hughes Pkwy · *NYSE: PNK* ■ *TF:* 877-764-8750 ■ *Web:* www.pnkinc.com	Las Vegas	NV	89169	702-541-7777	
Proximity Hotel 704 Green Vly Rd · *TF:* 800-379-8200 ■ *Web:* www.proximityhotel.com	Greensboro	NC	27408	336-379-8200	
Red Lake Gaming Enterprises Inc PO Box 543 · *TF:* 888-679-2501 ■ *Web:* www.sevenclanscasino.com	Red Lake	MN	56671	218-679-2111	679-2191
Savannah Suites 3421 Wrightsboro Rd · *Web:* www.savannahsuites.com	Augusta	GA	30909	706-849-3100	
Shoalwater Bay Casino 4112 State Hwy 105 · *TF:* 866-992-3675 ■ *Web:* www.swbcasino.com	Tokeland	WA	98590	360-267-2048	
Silver Reef Casino 4876 Haxton Way · *TF:* 866-383-0777 ■ *Web:* silverreefcasino.com	Ferndale	WA	98248	360-383-0777	
Station Casinos Inc 1505 S Pavilion Ctr Dr · *TF Resv:* 800-634-3101 ■ *Web:* www.sclv.com	Las Vegas	NV	89135	702-495-3000	
Tachi Palace Hotel & Casino, The 17225 Jersey Ave · *Web:* tachipalace.com	Lemoore	CA	93245	559-924-7751	
Tivoli Hotel 936 Warren Ave · *Web:* tivolihotel.net	Downers Grove	IL	60515	630-968-6450	
Trump Plaza Associates LLC The Boardwalk at Mississippi Ave · *Web:* www.trumpplaza.com	Atlantic City	NJ	08401	609-441-6060	
Trump Taj Mahal 1000 Boardwalk at Virginia Ave · *Web:* www.trumptaj.com	Atlantic City	NJ	08401	609-449-1000	449-6586
Verdanza Hotel 8020 Calle Tartak · *Web:* www.verdanzahotel.com	Carolina	PR	00979	787-253-9000	
Zia Partners LLC 3901 West Millen Dr · *Web:* www.ziapartners.com	Hobbs	NM	88240	505-492-7000	

133 CASINOS

See Also Games & Gaming p. 2348

Listings for casinos are alphabetized by states.

				Phone	Fax
Birmingham Race Course 1000 John Rogers Dr · *TF:* 800-998-8238 ■ *Web:* www.birminghamracecourse.com	Birmingham	AL	35210	205-838-7500	838-7407
Baccarat Casino 10128 104th Ave · *Web:* www.gatewaycasinos.com	Edmonton	AB	T5J4Y8	780-413-3178	
Deerfoot Inn & Casino 1000 11500 35th St SE · *TF:* 877-236-5225 ■ *Web:* www.deerfootinn.com	Calgary	AB	T2Z3W4	403-236-7529	252-4767
Palace Casino 2710 8882-170th St W Edmonton Mall · *Web:* www.palacecasino.com	Northwest Edmonton	AB	T5T4J2	780-444-2112	444-1155
Pure Canadian Gaming Corp 7055 Argyll Rd · *Web:* www.purecanadiangaming.com	Edmonton	AB	T6C4A5	780-465-5377	
Apache Greyhound Park 3801 E Washington · *TF:* 800-772-0852 ■ *Web:* phoenixgreyhoundpark.com	Phoenix	AZ	85034	480-982-2371	
Casino Arizona at Salt River 524 N 92nd St · *TF General:* 866-877-9897 ■ *Web:* www.casinoarizona.com	Scottsdale	AZ	85256	480-850-7777	
Fort McDowell Casino 10424 N Ft McDowell Rd · *TF:* 800-843-3678 ■ *Web:* www.fortmcdowellcasino.com	Fort Mcdowell	AZ	85264	800-843-3678	
Tucson Greyhound Park 2601 S 3rd Ave. · *Web:* tucsongreyhound.com	Tucson	AZ	85713	520-884-7576	624-9389
River Rock Casino Resort 8811 River Rd · *TF:* 866-748-3718 ■ *Web:* www.riverrock.com	Richmond	BC	V6X3P8	604-247-8900	207-2641
Agua Caliente Casino Resort Spa 32-250 Bob Hope Dr · *TF:* 888-999-1995 ■ *Web:* www.hotwatercasino.com	Rancho Mirage	CA	92270	760-321-2000	
Augustine Casino 84-001 Ave 54 · *TF:* 888-752-9294 ■ *Web:* www.augustinecasino.com	Coachella	CA	92236	760-391-9500	
Barona Resort & Casino 1932 Wildcat Canyon Rd · *TF:* 888-722-7662 ■ *Web:* www.barona.com	Lakeside	CA	92040	619-443-2300	443-2856
Cache Creek Casino Resort 14455 Hwy 16 · *Web:* cachecreek.com	Brooks	CA	95606	530-796-3118	
Club One Casino 1033 Van Ness Ave · *Web:* www.clubonecasino.com	Fresno	CA	93721	559-497-3000	237-2582
Commerce Casino 6131 Telegraph Rd · *Web:* www.commercecasino.com	Commerce	CA	90040	323-721-2100	
Eagle Mountain Casino 681 S Tule Resv Rd · *TF:* 800-903-3353 ■ *Web:* www.eaglemtncasino.com	Porterville	CA	93257	559-788-6220	788-6223
Fantasy Springs Resort Casino 84-245 Indio Springs Pkwy · *TF Cust Svc:* 800-827-2946 ■ *Web:* www.fantasyspringsresort.com	Indio	CA	92203	760-342-5000	
Golden West Casino 1001 S Union Ave · *TF:* 800-267-3983 ■ *Web:* www.goldenwestcasino.net	Bakersfield	CA	93307	661-324-6936	324-6977
Hawaiian Gardens Casino 11871 Carson St · *Web:* www.thegardenscasino.com	Hawaiian Gardens	CA	90716	562-860-5887	
Pala Casino Resort & Spa 35008 Pala-Temecula Rd · *TF:* 877-946-7252 ■ *Web:* www.palacasino.com	Pala	CA	92059	760-510-5100	510-5191
Pechanga Resort & Casino 45000 Pechanga Pkwy · *TF:* 877-711-2946 ■ *Web:* www.pechanga.com	Temecula	CA	92592	951-693-1819	695-7410
San Manuel Indian Bingo & Casino 777 San Manuel Blvd · **Fax Area Code:* 909 ■ *TF:* 800-359-2464 ■ *Web:* www.sanmanuel.com	Highland	CA	92346	800-359-2464	425-3557*
Spa Resort Casino 401 E Amado Rd · *TF:* 888-999-1995 ■ *Web:* www.sparesortcasino.com	Palm Springs	CA	92262	888-999-1995	
Spotlight 29 Casino 46-200 Harrison Pl · *Web:* www.spotlight29.com	Coachella	CA	92236	760-775-5566	775-7677
Sycuan Casino & Resort 5469 Casino Way · *TF General:* 800-279-2826 ■ *Web:* www.sycuan.com	El Cajon	CA	92019	619-445-6002	445-1961
Table Mountain Casino 8184 Table Mountain Rd · *TF:* 800-541-3637 ■ *Web:* www.tmcasino.com	Friant	CA	93626	559-822-7777	822-2081
Thunder Valley Casino 1200 Athens Ave · *TF:* 877-468-8777 ■ *Web:* www.thundervalleyresort.com	Lincoln	CA	95648	916-408-7777	408-8370
Viejas Casino 5000 Willows Rd · *TF:* 800-847-6537 ■ *Web:* www.viejas.com	Alpine	CA	91901	619-445-5400	
Black Hawk Station Casino 141 Gregory St PO Box 417 · *Web:* blackhawkcolorado.com	Black Hawk	CO	80422	303-582-5582	582-5590
Bronco Billy's Casino 233 E Bennett Ave PO Box 590 · *TF:* 877-989-2142 ■ *Web:* www.broncobillyscasino.com	Cripple Creek	CO	80813	719-689-2142	
Canyon Casino 131 Main St · *Web:* www.canyoncasino.com	Black Hawk	CO	80422	303-777-1111	
Dostal Alley Casino 1 Dostal Alley · *TF:* 888-949-2757 ■ *Web:* www.centralcitycolorado.com	Central City	CO	80427	303-582-1610	582-0143
Double Eagle Hotel & Casino 442 E Bennett Ave · *TF:* 800-711-7234 ■ *Web:* decasino.com	Cripple Creek	CO	80813	719-689-5000	689-5096

	City	State	Zip	Phone	Fax
Famous Bonanza Casino 107 Main St.	Central City	CO	80427	303-582-5914	
Web: www.famousbonanza.com					
Gilpin Hotel Casino 111 Main St	Black Hawk	CO	80422	303-582-1133	
Web: thegilpincasino.com					
Golden Gates Casino 300 Main St	Black Hawk	CO	80422	303-582-5600	
Web: thegoldengatescasino.com					
Golden Mardi Gras 300 Main St.	Black Hawk	CO	80422	303-582-5600	
Web: thegoldengatescasino.com					
Grande Plateau Casino 131 Main St.	Black Hawk	CO	80422	303-777-1111	582-0311
Web: www.blackhawkcolorado.com					
Isle of Capri Casino 401 Main St.	Black Hawk	CO	80422	303-998-7777	582-9601
TF resv: 800-843-4753 ■ *Web:* www.isleofcapricasinos.com					
Lodge Casino 240 Main St PO Box 50.	Black Hawk	CO	80422	303-582-1771	582-6464
Web: www.thelodgecasino.com					
Midnight Rose Hotel & Casino					
256 E Bennett Ave.	Cripple Creek	CO	80813	719-689-2446	689-3413
TF: 800-635-5825 ■ *Web:* triplecrowncasinos.com					
Red Dolly Casino 530 Gregory St	Black Hawk	CO	80422	303-582-1100	582-1435
Web: reddollycasino.net					
Reserve Casino Hotel 321 Gregory St	Central City	CO	80427	303-582-0800	
TF: 800-924-6646 ■ *Web:* www.reservecasinohotel.com					
Sky Ute Casino 14324 US Hwy 172 N.	Ignacio	CO	81137	970-563-7777	
TF: 888-842-4180 ■ *Web:* www.skyutecasino.com					
Ute Mountain Casino 3 Weeminuche Dr	Towaoc	CO	81334	970-565-8800	565-6553
TF: 800-258-8007 ■ *Web:* www.utemountaincasino.com					
Wild Card Saloon & Casino 120 Main St	Black Hawk	CO	80422	303-639-1111	582-3508
Mohegan Sun Resort & Casino					
1 Mohegan Sun Blvd	Uncasville	CT	06382	860-862-8150	
TF: 888-226-7711 ■ *Web:* www.mohegansun.com					
Winners Sports Haven 600 Long Wharf Dr	New Haven	CT	06511	800-468-2260	
TF: 800-468-2260 ■ *Web:* www.mywinners.com					
Gulfstream Park 901 S Federal Hwy	Hallandale	FL	33009	954-454-7000	457-6510
Web: www.gulfstreampark.com					
Seminole Casino Hollywood					
4150 N State Rd 7	Hollywood	FL	33021	954-961-3220	
TF: 866-222-7466 ■ *Web:* www.seminolehollywoodcasino.com					
Seminole Casino Immokalee 506 S First St.	Immokalee	FL	34142	800-218-0007	
TF: 800-218-0007 ■ *Web:* www.seminoleimmokaleecasino.com					
Seminole Coconut Creek Casino					
5550 NW 40th St	Coconut Creek	FL	33073	954-977-6700	
Web: www.seminolecoconutcreekcasino.com					
Seminole Hard Rock Hotel & Casino Tampa (SHRH & C)					
5223 N Orient Rd	Tampa	FL	33610	813-627-7625	983-0242*
**Fax Area Code:* 954 ■ *TF General:* 866-388-4263 ■ *Web:* www.seminolehardrocktampa.com					
Argosy's Alton Belle Casino 1 Piasa St	Alton	IL	62002	800-711-4263	
TF: 800-711-4263 ■ *Web:* www.argosyalton.com					
Casino Queen 200 S Front St.	East Saint Louis	IL	62201	618-874-5000	874-5081
TF: 800-777-0777 ■ *Web:* www.casinoqueen.com					
Harrah's Joliet 151 N Joliet St	Joliet	IL	60432	815-740-7800	740-2223
TF: 800-522-4700 ■ *Web:* www.caesars.com/harrahs-joliet					
Hollywood Casino Joliet 777 Hollywood Blvd	Joliet	IL	60436	800-426-2537	
TF: 800-426-2537 ■ *Web:* www.hollywoodcasinojoliet.com					
Belterra Casino Resort 777 Belterra Dr.	Florence	IN	47020	812-427-7777	427-7823
TF: 888-235-8377 ■ *Web:* www.belterracasino.com					
Blue Chip Casino Inc 777 Blue Chip Dr.	Michigan City	IN	46360	219-879-7711	
TF: 888-879-7711 ■ *Web:* www.bluechipcasino.com					
Casino Aztar 421 NW Riverside Dr	Evansville	IN	47708	812-433-4000	
TF: 800-342-5386 ■ *Web:* www.tropevansville.com					
Horseshoe Casino 777 Casino Ctr Dr.	Hammond	IN	46320	219-473-7000	
TF: 800-522-4700 ■ *Web:* www.totalrewards.com					
Majestic Star Casino & Hotel					
1 Buffington Harbor Dr	Gary	IN	46406	219-977-7777	
TF: 800-522-4700 ■ *Web:* www.majesticstarcasino.com					
Rising Star Casino Resort					
777 Rising Star Dr	Rising Sun	IN	47040	812-438-1234	
TF: 800-472-6311 ■ *Web:* www.risingstarcasino.com					
Ameristar Casino Hotel Council Bluffs					
2200 River Rd.	Council Bluffs	IA	51501	712-328-8888	
TF: 866-667-3386 ■ *Web:* www.ameristar.com					
Harrah's Council Bluffs					
1 Harrahs Blvd	Council Bluffs	IA	51501	712-329-6000	329-6491
TF: 800-342-7724 ■ *Web:* www.caesars.com/harrahs-council-bluffs					
Horseshoe Council Bluffs					
2701 23rd Ave	Council Bluffs	IA	51501	712-323-2500	
Web: www.totalrewards.com					
Meskwaki Bingo Hotel Casino 1504 305th St.	Tama	IA	52339	800-728-4263	
TF: 800-728-4263 ■ *Web:* www.meskwaki.com					
Peninsula Gaming Corp 301 Bell St	Dubuque	IA	52001	563-690-4975	
Web: www.diamondjo.com					
Prairie Meadows Racetrack & Casino					
1 Prairie Meadows Dr PO Box 1000	Altoona	IA	50009	515-967-1000	967-1344
TF: 800-325-9015 ■ *Web:* www.prairiemeadows.com					
Rhythm City Casino 7077 Elmore Ave	Davenport	IA	52807	563-328-8000	
TF: 844-852-4386 ■ *Web:* rhythmcitycasino.co					
Prairie Band Casino & Resort 12305 150th Rd	Mayetta	KS	66509	785-966-7777	966-7799
TF: 888-727-4946 ■ *Web:* www.prairieband.com					
Sac & Fox Casino 1322 Us Hwy 75	Powhattan	KS	66527	785-467-8000	
Web: www.sacandfoxcasino.com					
Belle of Baton Rouge Casino					
103 France St	Baton Rouge	LA	70802	800-676-4847	
TF: 800-676-4847 ■ *Web:* www.belleofbatonrouge.com					
Boomtown Casino New Orleans 4132 Peters Rd	Harvey	LA	70058	504-366-7711	
Web: www.boomtownneworleans.com					
Boomtown Hotel Casino 300 Riverside Dr	Bossier City	LA	71111	318-746-0711	
Web: www.boomtownbossier.com					
Coushatta Casino Resort					
777 Coushatta Dr PO Box 1510	Kinder	LA	70648	800-584-7263	
TF: 800-584-7263 ■ *Web:* coushattacasinoresort.com					
DiamondJacks Casino Resort					
711 Diamond Jacks Blvd	Bossier City	LA	71111	318-678-7777	
TF: 866-552-9629 ■ *Web:* diamondjacks.com					
Eldorado Resort Casino Shreveport					
451 Clyde Fant Pkwy	Shreveport	LA	71101	318-220-0711	
TF: 877-602-0711 ■ *Web:* www.eldoradoshreveport.com					
Harrah's New Orleans 8 Canal St.	New Orleans	LA	70130	504-533-6000	
TF: 800-427-7247 ■ *Web:* www.caesars.com/harrahs-new-orleans					
Hollywood Casino Baton Rouge					
1717 River Rd N	Baton Rouge	LA	70802	225-709-7777	
TF: 800-447-6843 ■ *Web:* www.hollywoodbr.com					
Isle of Capri Casino Hotel Lake Charles					
100 W Lake Ave	Westlake	LA	70669	800-843-4753	
TF: 800-843-4753 ■ *Web:* www.lake-charles.isleofcapricasinos.com					
Paragon Casino Resort 711 Paragon Pl	Marksville	LA	71351	800-946-1946	
TF: 800-946-1946 ■ *Web:* www.paragoncasinoresort.com					
Sam's Town Hotel & Casino Shreveport					
315 Clyde Fant Pkwy	Shreveport	LA	71101	877-770-7867	
TF: 877-770-7867 ■ *Web:* www.samstownshreveport.com					
Treasure Chest Casino 5050 Williams Blvd	Kenner	LA	70065	504-443-8000	
TF: 800-298-0711 ■ *Web:* www.treasurechest.com					
Pimlico Race Course 5201 Park Heights Ave	Baltimore	MD	21215	410-542-9400	
TF: 800-638-1859 ■ *Web:* pimlico.com					
Rosecroft Raceway 6336 Rosecroft Dr	Fort Washington	MD	20744	301-567-4500	567-1053
Web: www.rosecroft.com					
Suffolk Downs 111 Waldemar Ave.	East Boston	MA	02128	617-567-3900	
TF: 800-225-3460 ■ *Web:* www.suffolkdowns.com					
Greektown Superholdings Inc 555 E Lafayette.	Detroit	MI	48226	313-223-2999	
Web: www.greektowncasino.com					
MGM Grand Detroit 1777 Third St	Detroit	MI	48226	313-465-1400	
TF: 877-888-2121 ■ *Web:* www.mgmgranddetroit.com					
MotorCity Casino Hotel 2901 Grand River Ave	Detroit	MI	48201	313-237-7711	
TF: 866-752-9622 ■ *Web:* www.motorcitycasino.com					
Rock Gaming LLC 1086 Woodward Ave	Detroit	MI	48226	313-373-3700	
Web: www.rock-gaming.com					
Soaring Eagle Casino & Resort					
6800 E Soaring Eagle Blvd	Mount Pleasant	MI	48858	888-732-4537	
TF: 888-732-4537 ■ *Web:* www.soaringeaglecasino.com					
Black Bear Casino Resort					
1785 Hwy 210 PO Box 777.	Carlton	MN	55718	218-878-2327	878-2414
TF: 888-771-0777 ■ *Web:* www.blackbearcasinohotel.com					
Grand Casino Hinckley 777 Lady Luck Dr	Hinckley	MN	55037	800-472-6321	
TF: 800-472-6321 ■ *Web:* www.grandcasinomn.com					
Grand Casino Mille Lacs					
777 Grand Ave PO Box 343	Onamia	MN	56359	800-626-5825	
TF: 800-626-5825 ■ *Web:* www.grandcasinomn.com					
Jackpot Junction Casino Hotel					
39375 County Hwy 24 PO Box 420	Morton	MN	56270	507-697-8000	
TF: 800-946-2274 ■ *Web:* www.jackpotjunction.com					
Mystic Lake Casino Hotel					
2400 Mystic Lk Blvd.	Prior Lake	MN	55372	952-445-9000	
TF: 800-262-7799 ■ *Web:* www.mysticlake.com					
Ameristar Casino Hotel Vicksburg					
4116 Washington St	Vicksburg	MS	39180	601-638-1000	
Web: www.ameristar.com					
Bally's Casino Tunica					
1450 Bally's Blvd	Robinsonville	MS	38664	866-422-5597	
TF: 866-422-5597 ■ *Web:* www.ballystunica.com					
Boomtown Casino Biloxi 676 Bayview Ave	Biloxi	MS	39530	228-435-7000	435-7964
TF: 800-627-0777 ■ *Web:* www.boomtownbiloxi.com					
Fitzgeralds Casino & Hotel Tunica					
711 Lucky Ln	Robinsonville	MS	38664	662-363-5825	
TF: 888-766-5825 ■ *Web:* www.fitzgeraldstunica.com					
Gold Strike Casino Resort					
1010 Casino Ctr Dr.	Tunica Resorts	MS	38664	662-357-1111	
TF Resv: 888-245-7829 ■ *Web:* www.goldstrikemississippi.com					
Golden Nugget Hotels & Casinos 151 Beach Blvd	Biloxi	MS	39530	228-435-5400	
TF: 800-777-7568 ■ *Web:* www.goldennugget.com					
Hard Rock Hotel & Casino Biloxi					
777 Beach Blvd.	Biloxi	MS	39530	228-374-7625	276-7655
TF: 877-877-6256 ■ *Web:* www.hrhcbiloxi.com					
Harrah's Tunica 1021 Casino Ctr Dr.	Robinsonville	MS	38664	800-303-7463	
TF: 800-946-4946 ■ *Web:* www.caesars.com/horseshoe-tunica					
Hollywood Casino Bay Saint Louis					
711 Hollywood Blvd	Bay Saint Louis	MS	39520	866-758-2591	
TF: 866-758-2591 ■ *Web:* hollywoodgulfcoast.com					
IP Casino Resort & Spa 850 Bayview Ave	Biloxi	MS	39530	228-436-3000	
TF Resv: 888-946-2847 ■ *Web:* www.ipbiloxi.com					
Island View Casino Resort					
3300 W Beach Blvd PO Box 1600.	Gulfport	MS	39502	228-314-2100	
TF General: 888-777-9696 ■ *Web:* www.islandviewcasino.com					
Isle of Capri Casino 1800 E Front St	Kansas City	MO	64120	816-855-7777	855-4247
TF: 800-843-4753 ■ *Web:* www.kansas-city.isleofcapricasinos.com					
St. Jo Frontier Casino 777 Winners Cir.	St Joseph	MO	64505	816-279-5514	
Web: www.stjocasino.com					
Horsemen's Park 6303 Q St	Omaha	NE	68117	402-731-2900	731-5122
Web: www.horsemenspark.com					
Aquarius Casino Resort 1900 S Casino Dr	Laughlin	NV	89029	702-298-5111	
TF: 888-662-5825 ■ *Web:* www.aquariuscasinoresort.com					
Arizona Charlie's Boulder Casino & Hotel					
4575 Boulder Hwy	Las Vegas	NV	89121	702-951-5800	
TF: 888-236-9066 ■ *Web:* www.arizonacharliesboulder.com					
Arizona Charlie's Decatur Casino & Hotel					
740 S Decatur Blvd.	Las Vegas	NV	89107	702-258-5200	258-5192
TF: 888-236-8645 ■ *Web:* www.arizonacharliesdecatur.com					
Atlantis Casino Resort 3800 S Virginia St	Reno	NV	89502	775-825-4700	
TF: 800-723-6500 ■ *Web:* www.atlantiscasino.com					
Bally's Las Vegas 3645 Las Vegas Blvd S	Las Vegas	NV	89109	702-967-4111	739-4379
TF Resv: 800-522-4700 ■ *Web:* www.caesars.com/ballys-las-vegas					
Binion's Gambling Hall & Hotel					
128 E Fremont St	Las Vegas	NV	89101	702-382-1600	
TF: 800-937-6537 ■ *Web:* www.binions.com					
Boomtown Casino & Hotel Reno 2100 Garson Rd.	Verdi	NV	89439	775-345-6000	
TF Resv: 800-648-3790 ■ *Web:* boomtownreno.com					
Boulder Station Hotel & Casino					
4111 Boulder Hwy	Las Vegas	NV	89121	702-432-7777	367-6138*
**Fax:* Circulation Desk ■ *TF:* 800-683-7777 ■ *Web:* boulderstation.sclv.com					
Buffalo Bill's Resort & Casino					
31900 Las Vegas Blvd S.	Primm	NV	89019	702-386-7867	
TF: 888-774-6668 ■ *Web:* primmvalleyresorts.com					

	City	State	Zip	Phone	Fax
Cactus Jack's Casino 420 N Carson St	Carson City	NV	89701	775-882-8770	
California Hotel & Casino 12 E Ogden Ave *TF:* 800-634-6505 ■ *Web:* www.thecal.com	Las Vegas	NV	89101	702-385-1222	388-2660
Carson City Nugget 507 N Carson St *TF:* 800-426-5239 ■ *Web:* www.ccnugget.com	Carson City	NV	89701	775-882-1626	883-1106
Casino Fandango 3800 S Carson St *Web:* www.casinofandango.com	Carson City	NV	89701	775-885-7000	
Casino Royale Hotel 3411 Las Vegas Blvd S *TF:* 800-854-7666 ■ *Web:* www.casinoroyalehotel.com	Las Vegas	NV	89109	702-737-3500	
Circus Circus Hotel & Casino Reno 500 N Sierra St *TF:* 800-648-5010 ■ *Web:* www.circusreno.com	Reno	NV	89503	775-329-0711	328-9652
Circus Circus Hotel Casino & Theme Park Las Vegas 2880 Las Vegas Blvd S *TF Resv:* 800-634-3450 ■ *Web:* www.circuscircus.com	Las Vegas	NV	89109	702-734-0410	
Colorado Belle Hotel & Casino 2100 S Casino Dr *TF Resv:* 877-460-0777 ■ *Web:* www.coloradobelle.com	Laughlin	NV	89029	702-298-4000	
Don Laughlin's Riverside Resort & Casino 1650 Casino Dr *TF:* 800-227-3849 ■ *Web:* www.riversideresort.com	Laughlin	NV	89029	702-298-2535	
Edgewater Hotel & Casino 2020 S Casino Dr **Fax:* Mktg ■ *TF Resv:* 866-352-3553 ■ *Web:* www.edgewater-casino.com	Laughlin	NV	89029	702-298-2453	298-5606*
El Cortez Hotel & Casino 600 E Fremont St *TF:* 800-634-6703 ■ *Web:* www.elcortezhotelcasino.com	Las Vegas	NV	89101	702-385-5200	
Eldorado Hotel Casino 345 N Virginia St *TF Resv:* 800-879-8879 ■ *Web:* www.eldoradoreno.com	Reno	NV	89501	775-786-5700	322-7124
Excalibur Hotel & Casino 3850 Las Vegas Blvd S *TF:* 877-750-5464 ■ *Web:* www.excalibur.com	Las Vegas	NV	89109	702-597-7777	597-7009
Fiesta Rancho Casino Hotel 2400 N Rancho Dr *TF Resv:* 800-731-7333 ■ *Web:* fiestarancho.sclv.com	Las Vegas	NV	89130	702-631-7000	638-3645
Fremont Hotel & Casino 200 Fremont St *TF:* 800-634-6460 ■ *Web:* www.fremontcasino.com	Las Vegas	NV	89101	702-385-3232	
Gold Coast Hotel & Casino 4000 W Flamingo Rd *TF:* 800-331-5334 ■ *Web:* www.goldcoastcasino.com	Las Vegas	NV	89103	702-367-7111	
Gold Dust West Carson City 2171 E William St *TF:* 877-519-5567 ■ *Web:* www.gdwcasino.com	Carson City	NV	89701	775-885-9000	888-8018
Gold Ranch Casino & RV Resort 350 Gold Ranch Rd *TF:* 877-914-6789 ■ *Web:* www.goldranchrvcasino.com	Verdi	NV	89439	775-345-6789	
Gold Spike Hotel & Casino 217 Las Vegas Blvd N *Web:* goldspike.com	Las Vegas	NV	89101	702-476-4923	
Gold Strike Hotel & Gambling Hall 1 Main St *TF:* 800-634-1359 ■ *Web:* goldstrikejean.com	Jean	NV	89019	702-477-5000	
Golden Nugget Laughlin 2300 S Casino Dr *TF:* 800-950-7700 ■ *Web:* www.goldennugget.com	Laughlin	NV	89029	702-298-7111	298-3023
Grand Sierra Resort & Casino 2500 E Second St *TF:* 800-501-2651 ■ *Web:* www.grandsierraresort.com	Reno	NV	89595	775-789-2000	789-2130
Green Valley Ranch Resort Casino & Spa 2300 Paseo Verde Pkwy *TF Resv:* 866-782-9487 ■ *Web:* greenvalleyranch.sclv.com	Henderson	NV	89052	702-617-7777	
Harrah's Laughlin 2900 S Casino Dr *TF:* 800-427-7247 ■ *Web:* www.totalrewards.com	Laughlin	NV	89029	702-298-4600	298-1234
Harveys Lake Tahoe Hwy 50 at Stateline Ave PO Box 128 *TF:* 800-522-4700 ■ *Web:* www.caesars.com/harveys-tahoe	Lake Tahoe	NV	89449	775-588-6611	
Hooters Casino Hotel 115 E Tropicana Ave *TF:* 866-584-6687 ■ *Web:* www.hooterscasinohotel.com	Las Vegas	NV	89109	702-739-9000	
Hyatt Regency Lake Tahoe Resort & Casino 111 Country Club Dr *TF:* 800-233-1234 ■ *Web:* laketahoe.regency.hyatt.com/en/hotel/home.html	Incline Village	NV	89451	775-832-1234	831-2171
Laughlin River Lodge. 2700 S Casino Dr	Laughlin	NV	89029	702-298-2242	
Luxor Hotel & Casino 3900 Las Vegas Blvd S *TF Resv:* 800-288-1000 ■ *Web:* www.luxor.com	Las Vegas	NV	89119	702-262-4000	262-4404
M Resort LLC, The 12300 Las Vegas Blvd S *Web:* www.themresort.com	Henderson	NV	89044	702-797-1000	
Mandalay Bay Resort & Casino 3950 Las Vegas Blvd S *TF:* 877-632-7800 ■ *Web:* www.mandalaybay.com	Las Vegas	NV	89119	702-632-7777	632-7234
MGM Grand Hotel & Casino 3799 Las Vegas Blvd S *TF:* 877-880-0880 ■ *Web:* www.mgmgrand.com	Las Vegas	NV	89109	702-891-1111	891-3036
Monte Carlo Resort & Casino 3770 Las Vegas Blvd S *TF:* 800-311-8999 ■ *Web:* www.montecarlo.com	Las Vegas	NV	89109	702-730-7777	730-7200
New York New York Hotel & Casino 3790 Las Vegas Blvd S *TF:* 800-689-1797 ■ *Web:* www.newyorknewyork.com	Las Vegas	NV	89109	702-740-6969	740-6700
Orleans Las Vegas Hotel & Casino 4500 W Tropicana Ave *TF:* 800-675-3267 ■ *Web:* www.orleanscasino.com	Las Vegas	NV	89103	702-365-7111	
Palace Station Hotel & Casino 2411 W Sahara Ave *TF Resv:* 800-634-3101 ■ *Web:* palacestation.sclv.com	Las Vegas	NV	89102	702-367-2411	
Palms Casino Resort 4321 W Flamingo Rd *TF:* 866-942-7777 ■ *Web:* palms.com	Las Vegas	NV	89103	702-942-7777	
Peppermill Hotel & Casino 2707 S Virginia St *TF:* 800-648-6992 ■ *Web:* www.peppermillreno.com	Reno	NV	89502	775-826-2121	689-7041
Railroad Pass Hotel & Casino 2800 S Boulder Hwy *TF:* 800-654-0877 ■ *Web:* www.railroadpass.com	Henderson	NV	89002	702-294-5000	294-0092
Red Rock Resort Spa & Casino 11011 W Charleston Blvd *TF:* 866-767-7773 ■ *Web:* redrock.sclv.com	Las Vegas	NV	89135	702-797-7777	797-7890
Sam's Town Hotel & Gambling Hall 5111 Boulder Hwy *TF:* 800-897-8696 ■ *Web:* www.samstownlv.com	Las Vegas	NV	89122	702-456-7777	
Santa Fe Station 4949 N Rancho Dr *TF Resv:* 888-786-7389 ■ *Web:* santafestation.sclv.com	Las Vegas	NV	89130	702-658-4900	
Silver Legacy Resort & Casino 407 N Virginia St *TF:* 800-687-8733 ■ *Web:* www.silverlegacyreno.com	Reno	NV	89501	775-325-7401	325-7474
Silverton Hotel & Casino 3333 Blue Diamond Rd *TF:* 866-722-4608 ■ *Web:* www.silvertoncasino.com	Las Vegas	NV	89139	702-263-7777	
South Point Hotel & Casino 9777 Las Vegas Blvd S *TF:* 866-796-7111 ■ *Web:* www.southpointcasino.com	Las Vegas	NV	89183	702-796-7111	
Stratosphere Tower Hotel & Casino 2000 S Las Vegas Blvd **Fax:* Sales ■ *TF:* 800-998-6937 ■ *Web:* www.stratospherehotel.com	Las Vegas	NV	89104	702-380-7777	383-4755*
Suncoast Hotel & Casino 9090 Alta Dr *TF:* 877-677-7111 ■ *Web:* www.suncoastcasino.com	Las Vegas	NV	89145	702-636-7111	
Sunset Station Hotel & Casino 1301 W Sunset Rd *TF:* 888-786-7389 ■ *Web:* sunsetstation.sclv.com	Henderson	NV	89014	702-547-7777	
Texas Station Gambling Hall & Hotel 2101 Texas Star Ln *TF Resv:* 800-654-8888 ■ *Web:* texasstation.sclv.com	North Las Vegas	NV	89032	702-631-1000	
Treasure Island Hotel & Casino 3300 Las Vegas Blvd S *TF:* 800-288-7206 ■ *Web:* www.treasureisland.com	Las Vegas	NV	89109	702-894-7111	894-7414
Tropicana Express 2121 S Casino Dr *TF:* 800-243-6846 ■ *Web:* troplaughlin.com	Laughlin	NV	89029	702-298-4200	298-4619
Tuscany Suites & Casino 255 E Flamingo Rd *TF Resv:* 877-887-2261 ■ *Web:* www.tuscanylv.com	Las Vegas	NV	89169	702-893-8933	947-5994
Western Village Inn & Casino 815 Nichols Blvd *TF:* 800-648-1170 ■ *Web:* www.westernvillagesparks.com	Sparks	NV	89434	800-648-1170	
Westin Casuarina Las Vegas Hotel Casino & Spa 160 E Flamingo Rd *Web:* www.starwoodhotels.com	Las Vegas	NV	89109	702-836-5900	836-9776
Wynn Las Vegas 3131 Las Vegas Blvd S *TF:* 877-321-9966 ■ *Web:* www.wynnlasvegas.com	Las Vegas	NV	89109	702-770-7000	
Casino New Brunswick LP 21 Casino Dr *TF:* 877-859-7775 ■ *Web:* www.casinonb.ca	Moncton	NB	E1G0R7	506-859-7770	
Harrah's Resort Atlantic City 777 Harrah's Blvd *TF:* 800-342-7724 ■ *Web:* www.caesars.com/harrahsac	Atlantic City	NJ	08401	609-441-5000	
Resorts Casino Hotel 1133 Boardwalk *TF:* 800-334-6378 ■ *Web:* www.resortsac.com	Atlantic City	NJ	08401	800-334-6378	
Tropicana Entertainment 2831 Boardwalk *OTC: TPCA* ■ *TF:* 800-843-8767 ■ *Web:* www.tropicana.net	Atlantic City	NJ	08401	800-843-8767	
Trump Taj Mahal Casino Resort 1000 Boardwalk & Virginia Ave *TF:* 800-426-2537 ■ *Web:* www.trumptaj.com	Atlantic City	NJ	08401	609-449-1000	
Camel Rock Casino 17486A Hwy 84/285 *TF:* 800-483-1040 ■ *Web:* www.camelrockcasino.com	Santa Fe	NM	87506	505-983-2667	982-2331
Cities of Gold Casino 10-B Cities of Gold Rd *TF:* 800-455-3313 ■ *Web:* www.citiesofgold.com	Santa Fe	NM	87506	505-455-3313	
Route 66 Casino Hotel 14500 Central Ave *TF:* 866-352-7866 ■ *Web:* www.rt66casino.com	Albuquerque	NM	87121	505-352-7866	
Sandia Resort & Casino 30 Rainbow Rd NE *TF:* 800-526-9366 ■ *Web:* www.sandiacasino.com	Albuquerque	NM	87113	505-796-7500	
Seneca Niagara Casino 310 Fourth St *TF:* 877-873-6322 ■ *Web:* www.senecaniagaracasino.com	Niagara Falls	NY	14303	716-299-1100	
Turning Stone Resort Casino LLC 5218 Patrick Rd *TF:* 800-771-7711 ■ *Web:* turningstone.com	Verona	NY	13478	315-361-7711	
Harrah's Cherokee Casino & Hotel 777 Casino Dr *TF General:* 877-811-0777 ■ *Web:* www.caesars.com/harrahs-cherokee	Cherokee	NC	28719	828-497-7777	497-5076
Prairie Knights Casino & Resort 7932 Hwy 24 *TF:* 800-425-8277 ■ *Web:* www.prairieknights.com	Fort Yates	ND	58538	701-854-7777	854-7786
Casino Nova Scotia 1983 Upper Water St *TF:* 888-642-6376 ■ *Web:* www.casinonovascotia.com	Halifax	NS	B3J3Y5	902-425-7777	425-7777
Caesars License Company LLC 377 Riverside Dr E *TF:* 800-991-7777 ■ *Web:* www.caesars.com/caesars-windsor	Windsor	ON	N9A7H7	519-258-7878	258-0020
Casino Niagara 5705 Falls Ave *TF:* 888-325-5788 ■ *Web:* www.casinoniagara.com	Niagara Falls	ON	L2E6T3	888-325-5788	
Fallsview Casino Resort 6380 Fallsview Blvd **Fax Area Code:* 905 ■ *TF:* 888-325-5788 ■ *Web:* www.fallsviewcasinoresort.com	Niagara Falls	ON	L2G7X5	888-325-5788	371-7952*
Bluberi Gaming & Technologies inc 2120 Rue Letendre *Web:* www.bluberi.com	Drummondville	QC	J2C7E9	819-475-5155	
Newport Grand Jai Alai 150 Admiral Kalbfus Rd *Web:* www.newportgrand.com	Newport	RI	02840	401-849-5000	846-0290
Saskatchewan Indian Gaming Authority 250 - 103 C Packham Ave *TF:* 800-306-6789 ■ *Web:* www.siga.sk.ca	Saskatoon	SK	S7N4K4	306-477-7777	
Speaking Rock Entertainment Centre 122 S Old Pueblo Rd *Web:* www.speakingrockentertainment.com	El Paso	TX	79907	915-860-7777	
Emerald Downs 2300 Emerald Downs Dr PO Box 617 *TF:* 888-931-8400 ■ *Web:* www.emeralddowns.com	Auburn	WA	98001	253-288-7000	
Emerald Queen Casino (EQC) 2024 E 29th St *TF:* 888-831-7655 ■ *Web:* www.emeraldqueen.com	Tacoma	WA	98404	253-594-7777	
Great American Casino 10117 S Tacoma Way *Web:* www.greatamericancasino.com	Lakewood	WA	98499	253-396-0500	
Lucky Eagle Casino 12888 188th Ave SW *TF:* 800-720-1788 ■ *Web:* www.luckyeagle.com	Rochester	WA	98579	360-273-2000	
Northern Quest Casino 100 N Hayford Rd *TF:* 877-871-6772 ■ *Web:* www.northernquest.com	Airway Heights	WA	99001	509-242-7000	
Red Wind Casino 12819 Yelm Hwy *TF:* 866-946-2444 ■ *Web:* www.redwindcasino.com	Olympia	WA	98513	360-412-5000	
Skagit Valley Casino Resort 5984 N Darrk Ln *TF:* 877-275-2448 ■ *Web:* www.theskagit.com	Bow	WA	98232	360-724-7777	

Phone Fax

Snoqualmie Entertainment Authority
37500 SE N Bend Way .... Snoqualmie WA 98065 425-888-1234
Web: www.snocasino.com

Wheeling Island Gaming Inc 1 S St1 St .... Wheeling WV 26003 304-232-5050
TF: 877-946-4373 ■ *Web:* www.wheelingisland.com

Dairyland Greyhound Park 5522 104th Ave .... Kenosha WI 53144 262-657-8200

Ho-Chunk Casino S 3214 County Rd BD .... Baraboo WI 53913 800-746-2486
TF: 800-746-2486 ■ *Web:* www.ho-chunk.com

Lake of the Torches Resort Casino
510 Old Abe Rd .... Lac du Flambeau WI 54538 715-588-7070
TF: 800-258-6724 ■ *Web:* www.lakeofthetorches.com

Potawatomi Bingo Casino 1721 W Canal St .... Milwaukee WI 53233 414-645-6888 847-7727
TF: 800-729-7244 ■ *Web:* www.paysbig.com

134 CASKETS & VAULTS

See Also Mortuary, Crematory, Cemetery Products & Services p. 2779

Phone Fax

American Wilbert Vault Corp
7525 W 99th Pl .... Bridgeview IL 60455 708-366-3210 366-3281
Web: www.americanwilbert.com

Batesville Casket Co 1 Batesville Blvd .... Batesville IN 47006 812-934-7500 934-7613
TF Cust Svc: 800-622-8373 ■ *Web:* www.batesville.com

Brown-Wilbert Inc 2280 Hamline Ave N .... Saint Paul MN 55113 651-631-1234
Web: www.wilbert.net

Clark Grave Vault Co, The 375 E Fifth Ave .... Columbus OH 43201 614-294-3761
Web: www.clarkvault.com

CSI Care Services Inc 432 First St PO Box 172 .... Eynon PA 18403 570-876-2642 876-5613
Web: www.casketshellsinc.com

Norwalk-Wilbert Vault Co 425 Harral Ave .... Bridgeport CT 06604 203-366-5678
Web: www.norwalkwilbert.com

Paul Casket Co 505 S Green St .... Cambridge City IN 47327 765-478-3991 962-0911
TF: 800-521-8202

Pettigrew & Sons Casket Co
6151 Power Inn Rd .... Sacramento CA 95824 916-383-0777 383-2445
Web: www.pettigrewcaskets.com

Providence Casket Co 1 Industrial Cir .... Lincoln RI 02865 401-726-1700 726-1700

Sound Casket Co 20350 71st Ave NE Ste G .... Arlington WA 98223 360-403-3132

York Group Inc 2 Northshore Ctr Ste 100 .... Pittsburgh PA 15212 412-995-1600 995-1690
Web: www.yorkgrp.com

Zane Casket Co 1201 Hall Ave .... Zanesville OH 43701 740-452-4680

135 CEMENT

Phone Fax

Adjustable Forms Inc 1 E Progress Rd .... Lombard IL 60148 630-953-8700
Web: www.adjustableforms.com

All Rite Ready Mix Inc 108 Williams Way .... Wilder KY 41076 859-572-9951
Web: www.allritereadymix.com

Ash Grove Cement Co
8900 Indian Creek Pkwy .... Overland Park KS 66210 913-451-8900
OTC: ASHG ■ *TF:* 800-545-1882 ■ *Web:* www.ashgrove.com

California Portland Cement Co
2025 E Financial Way .... Glendora CA 91741 626-852-6200
TF Cust Svc: 800-272-1891 ■ *Web:* www.calportland.com

Carriere Bernier Ltee
25 Petit Bernier CP 548 .... Saint-jean-sur-richelieu QC J3B6Z8 450-545-2000
Web: www.carrierebernier.com

Cemex USA 840 Gessner Ste 1400 .... Houston TX 77024 713-650-6200 317-6047*
NYSE: CX ■ **Fax Area Code:* 212 ■ *TF:* 888-292-0070 ■ *Web:* www.cemex.com

CGM Inc 1445 Ford Rd .... Bensalem PA 19020 215-638-4400 638-7949
TF: 800-523-6570 ■ *Web:* www.cgmbuildingproducts.com

Coastal Cement Corp 36 Drydock Ave .... Boston MA 02210 617-350-0183

Continental Cement Company LLC
14755 N Outer 40 Ste 514 .... Chesterfield MO 63017 636-532-7440 532-7445
TF: 800-625-1144 ■ *Web:* www.continentalcement.com

Daniel G Schuster LLC 3717 Crondall Ln .... Owings Mills MD 21117 410-363-3837
Web: www.schusterconcrete.com

Dragon Products Co 960 Ocean Ave .... Portland ME 04103 207-774-6355

E Z Grout Corp 405 Watertown Rd .... Waterford OH 45786 740-749-3512
TF: 888-344-7688 ■ *Web:* www.ezgrout.com

Eagle Materials Inc
3811 Turtle Creek Blvd Ste 1100 .... Dallas TX 75219 214-432-2000 432-2100
NYSE: EXP ■ *Web:* www.eaglematerials.com

ESSROC Materials Inc 3251 Bath Pike .... Nazareth PA 18064 610-837-6725 837-9614
TF: 800-437-7762 ■ *Web:* www.essroc.com

Faddis Concrete Products
2206 Horseshoe Pk .... Honey Brook PA 19344 610-269-4685
Web: www.faddis.com

Federal White Cement Ltd PO Box 1609 .... Woodstock ON N4S0A8 519-485-5410 485-5892
TF Sales: 800-265-1806 ■ *Web:* www.federalwhitecement.com

Folsom Ready Mix Inc
3401 Fitzgerald Rd .... Rancho Cordova CA 95742 916-851-8300
Web: www.folsomreadymix.com

GCC of America Inc 130 Rampart Way Ste 200 .... Denver CO 80230 303-739-5900
Web: www.gccusa.com

Grand Junction Concrete Pipe Co
2868 I-70 Business Loop .... Grand Junction CO 81501 970-243-4604
Web: www.gjpipe.com

Hawaiian Cement 99-1300 Halawa Vly St .... Aiea HI 96701 808-532-3400 532-3499
Web: www.hawaiiancement.com

Illinois Cement Co 1601 Rockwell Rd .... La Salle IL 61301 815-224-2112
Web: www.eaglematerials.com

Knife River Corp 1150 W Century Ave .... Bismarck ND 58506 701-530-1400 530-1451
Web: www.kniferiver.com

Lafarge North America Inc
8700 W Bryn Mawr Ave Ste 300 .... Chicago VA 60631 703-480-3600 480-3899
Web: www.lafarge-na.com

Lee's Ready-Mix & Trucking Inc
1100 W John F Kennedy Dr .... North Vernon IN 47265 812-346-9767

Phone Fax

Lehigh Inland Cement Ltd 12640 Inland Way .... Edmonton AB T5V1K2 780-420-2500 420-2550
TF Orders: 800-252-9304 ■ *Web:* www.lehighhansoncanada.com

Maxxon Corp 920 Hamel Rd .... Hamel MN 55340 763-478-9600
TF: 800-356-7887 ■ *Web:* www.maxxon.com

Monarch Cement Co 449 1200 St PO Box 1000 .... Humboldt KS 66748 620-473-2222 473-2447
OTC: MCEM ■ *Web:* www.monarchcement.com

Mountain Cement Co 5 Sand Creek Rd .... Laramie WY 82070 307-745-4879 742-4534
Web: www.mountaincement.com

Nashville Ready Mix Inc 605 Cowan St .... Nashville TN 37207 615-256-2071
Web: www.nashvillereadymix.net

Ozinga Ready Mix Concrete Inc 400 Blaine St .... Gary IN 46406 219-949-9800
Web: www.ozinga.com

Permatile Concrete Products Co 100 Beacon Rd .... Bristol VA 24203 276-669-5332
TF: 800-662-5332 ■ *Web:* www.permatile.com

Phoenix Cement Co
8800 E Chaparral Rd Ste 155 .... Scottsdale AZ 85250 480-850-5757 850-5758
Web: www.srmaterials.com

Prairie Group Inc 7601 W 79th St .... Bridgeview IL 60455 708-458-0400 458-7626
TF Sales: 800-649-3690

Prestressed Systems Inc
4955 Walker Rd Hwy 401 .... Windsor ON N9A6J3 519-737-1216
Web: www.theprecaster.com

RJS & Assoc Inc 1675 Sabre St .... Hayward CA 94545 510-670-9111

Titan America Inc 1151 Azalea Garden Rd .... Norfolk VA 23502 757-858-6500 855-7707
TF: 800-468-7622 ■ *Web:* www.titanamerica.com

136 CEMETERIES - NATIONAL

See Also Historic Homes & Buildings p. 1808;
Parks - National - US p. 2871

Phone Fax

Alexandria National Cemetery
209 E Shamrock St .... Pineville LA 71360 318-449-1793 449-9327
TF: 800-827-1000 ■ *Web:* www.cem.va.gov

Alton National Cemetery 600 Pearl St .... Alton IL 62003 314-845-8320
TF: 800-535-1117 ■ *Web:* www.cem.va.gov

Balls Bluff National Cemetery Rt 7 .... Leesburg VA 22075 540-825-0027 825-6684
Web: www.cem.va.gov

Baltimore National Cemetery
5501 Frederick Ave .... Baltimore MD 21228 410-644-9696 644-1563
TF: 800-535-1117 ■ *Web:* cem.va.gov

Barrancas National Cemetery
Naval Air Stn 80 Hovey Rd .... Pensacola FL 32508 850-453-4108 453-4635
Web: www.cem.va.gov

Bath National Cemetery VA Medical Ctr .... Bath NY 14810 607-664-4853 664-4761
Web: www.cem.va.gov

Battleground National Cemetery
6625 Georgia Ave NW .... Washington DC 20012 202-829-4650
Web: www.nps.gov

Bay Pines National Cemetery
10000 Bay Pines Blvd .... Saint Petersburg FL 33708 727-398-9426 398-9520
Web: www.cem.va.gov

Beaufort National Cemetery 1601 Boundary St .... Beaufort SC 29902 843-524-3925 524-8538
TF: 800-273-8255 ■ *Web:* www.cem.va.gov

Beverly National Cemetery 916 Bridgeboro Rd .... Beverly NJ 08010 215-504-5610 871-4691*
**Fax Area Code:* 609 ■ *Web:* www.cem.va.gov/cems/nchp/beverly.asp

Biloxi National Cemetery 400 Veterans Ave .... Biloxi MS 39531 228-388-6668 523-5784
Web: www.cem.va.gov

Black Hills National Cemetery
20901 Pleasant Vly Dr .... Sturgis SD 57785 605-347-3830 720-7298
Web: www.cem.va.gov

Calverton National Cemetery
210 Princeton Blvd .... Calverton NY 11933 631-727-5410 727-5815
TF: 800-829-1040 ■ *Web:* www.cem.va.gov

Camp Butler National Cemetery
5063 Camp Butler Rd .... Springfield IL 62707 217-492-4070 492-4072
TF: 877-907-8585 ■ *Web:* www.cem.va.gov/cems/nchp/campbutler.asp

Camp Nelson National Cemetery
6980 Danville Rd .... Nicholasville KY 40356 859-885-5727 887-4860
TF: 800-827-1000 ■ *Web:* www.cem.va.gov

Chattanooga National Cemetery
1200 Bailey Ave .... Chattanooga TN 37404 423-855-6590 855-6597
TF: 877-907-8585 ■ *Web:* www.cem.va.gov

City Point National Cemetery
10th Ave & Davis St .... Hopewell VA 23860 804-795-2031 795-1064
Web: www.cem.va.gov/cems/nchp/citypoint.asp

Corinth National Cemetery 1551 Horton St .... Corinth MS 38834 901-386-8311 382-0750
TF: 800-273-8255 ■ *Web:* www.cem.va.gov

Crown Hill National Cemetery
700 W 38th St .... Indianapolis IN 46208 765-674-0284
Web: www.cem.va.gov

Culpeper National Cemetery 305 US Ave .... Culpeper VA 22701 540-825-0027 825-6684
TF: 800-827-1000 ■ *Web:* www.cem.va.gov/cems/nchp/culpeper.asp

Cypress Hills National Cemetery
625 Jamaica Ave .... Brooklyn NY 11208 631-454-4949 694-5422
TF: 800-535-1117 ■ *Web:* www.cem.va.gov/cems/nchp/cypresshills.asp

Danville National Cemetery 721 Lee St .... Danville VA 24541 704-636-2661 636-1115
Web: www.cem.va.gov/cems/nchp/danvilleva.asp

Danville National Cemetery 1900 E Main St .... Danville IL 61832 217-554-4550 554-4803
TF: 800-827-1000 ■ *Web:* www.cem.va.gov

Dayton National Cemetery 4100 W Third St .... Dayton OH 45428 937-262-2115 262-2187
TF: 800-273-8255 ■ *Web:* www.cem.va.gov

Eagle Point National Cemetery
2763 Riley Rd .... Eagle Point OR 97524 541-826-2511 826-2888
TF: 800-535-1117 ■ *Web:* www.cem.va.gov

Fayetteville National Cemetery
700 S Government Ave .... Fayetteville AR 72701 479-444-5051 444-5094
Web: www.cem.va.gov

Finn's Point National Cemetery
454 Ft. Mott Rd .... Pennsville NJ 08070 215-504-5610 504-5611
TF: 800-827-1000 ■ *Web:* www.cem.va.gov/cems/nchp/finnspoint.asp

	City	State	Zip	Phone	Fax
Florence National Cemetery 803 E National Cemetery Rd *TF:* 877-907-8585 ■ *Web:* www.cem.va.gov	Florence	SC	29506	843-669-8783	662-8318
Florida National Cemetery 6502 SW 102nd Ave *TF:* 877-907-8585 ■ *Web:* www.cem.va.gov	Bushnell	FL	33513	352-793-7740	793-9560
Fort Bayard National Cemetery 200 Camino De Paz PO Box 44 *Web:* www.cem.va.gov/cems/nchp/ftbayard.asp	Fort Bayard	NM	88036	915-564-0201	564-3746
Fort Bliss National Cemetery PO Box 6342 *TF:* 800-273-8255 ■ *Web:* www.cem.va.gov	El Paso	TX	79906	915-564-0201	564-3746
Fort Custer National Cemetery 15501 Dickman Rd *TF:* 800-273-8255 ■ *Web:* www.cem.va.gov	Augusta	MI	49012	269-731-4164	731-2428
Fort Gibson National Cemetery 1423 Cemetery Rd *Web:* www.cem.va.gov	Fort Gibson	OK	74434	918-478-2334	478-2661
Fort Leavenworth National Cemetery 395 Biddle Blvd *Web:* www.cem.va.gov	Fort Leavenworth	KS	66027	913-758-4105	758-4136
Fort Logan National Cemetery 4400 W Kenyon Ave *Web:* www.cem.va.gov	Denver	CO	80236	303-761-0117	781-9378
Fort Lyon National Cemetery 15700 County Rd HH *Web:* www.cem.va.gov	Las Animas	CO	81054	303-761-0117	781-9378
Fort Mitchell National Cemetery 553 Hwy 165 *Web:* www.cem.va.gov	Fort Mitchell	AL	36856	334-855-4731	855-4740
Fort Richardson National Cemetery Bldg 58-512 Davis Hwy PO Box 5-498 *Web:* www.cem.va.gov/cems/nchp/ftrichardson.asp	Fort Richardson	AK	99505	907-384-7075	384-7111
Fort Rosecrans National Cemetery PO Box 6237 *Web:* www.cem.va.gov/cems/nchp/ftrosecrans.asp	San Diego	CA	92166	619-553-2084	553-6593
Fort Sam Houston National Cemetery 1520 Harry Wurzbach Rd *Web:* cem.va.gov	San Antonio	TX	78209	210-820-3891	820-3445
Fort Scott National Cemetery 900 E National Ave *Web:* www.cem.va.gov/cems	Fort Scott	KS	66701	620-223-2840	223-2505
Fort Smith National Cemetery 522 Garland Ave *TF:* 800-535-1117 ■ *Web:* www.cem.va.gov	Fort Smith	AR	72901	479-783-5345	785-4189
Fort Snelling National Cemetery 7601 34th Ave *Web:* www.cem.va.gov	Minneapolis	MN	55450	612-726-1127	726-9119
Golden Gate National Cemetery 1300 Sneath Ln *Web:* cem.va.gov	San Bruno	CA	94066	650-589-7737	873-6578
Grafton National Cemetery 431 Walnut St *TF:* 800-535-1117 ■ *Web:* www.cem.va.gov	Grafton	WV	26354	304-265-2044	265-4336
Hampton National Cemetery Cemetery Rd at Marshall Ave *Web:* www.cem.va.gov	Hampton	VA	23669	757-723-7104	728-3144
Houston National Cemetery 10410 Veterans Memorial Dr *Web:* www.cem.va.gov	Houston	TX	77038	281-447-8686	447-0580
Indiantown Gap National Cemetery RR 2 PO Box 484 *Web:* www.cem.va.gov/cems/nchp/indiantowngap.asp	Annville	PA	17003	717-865-5254	865-5256
Jefferson Barracks National Cemetery 2900 Sheridan Rd **Fax Area Code:* 703 ■ *TF:* 800-827-1000	Saint Louis	MO	63125	314-845-8320	221-2185*
Jefferson City National Cemetery 1024 E McCarty St *TF:* 877-907-8585 ■ *Web:* www.cem.va.gov/cems/nchp/jeffersoncity.asp	Jefferson City	MO	65101	314-845-8320	845-8355
Keokuk National Cemetery 1701 J St **Fax Area Code:* 319 ■ *TF:* 800-273-8255 ■ *Web:* www.cem.va.gov/cems/nchp/keokuk.asp	Keokuk	IA	52632	309-782-2094	524-8118*
Kerrville National Cemetery 3600 Memorial Blvd *TF:* 800-273-8255 ■ *Web:* www.cem.va.gov	Kerrville	TX	78028	210-820-3891	820-3445
Knoxville National Cemetery 939 Tyson St NW *Web:* www.cem.va.gov/cems/nchp/knoxville.asp	Knoxville	TN	37917	423-855-6590	855-6597
Leavenworth National Cemetery 150 Muncie Rd *Web:* www.cem.va.gov/cems	Leavenworth	KS	66048	913-758-4105	758-4136
Lebanon National Cemetery 20 Hwy 208 *Web:* www.cem.va.gov	Lebanon	KY	40033	270-692-3390	692-0018
Little Rock National Cemetery 2523 Confederate Blvd *Web:* www.cem.va.gov	Little Rock	AR	72206	501-324-6401	324-7182
Long Island National Cemetery 2040 Wellwood Ave *Web:* www.cem.va.gov/cems/nchp/longisland.asp	Farmingdale	NY	11735	631-454-4949	694-5422
Los Angeles National Cemetery 950 S Sepulveda Blvd *Web:* www.cem.va.gov	Los Angeles	CA	90049	310-268-4494	268-3257
Loudon Park National Cemetery 3445 Frederick Rd *Web:* www.cem.va.gov/cems/nchp/loudonpark.asp	Baltimore	MD	21228	410-644-9696	644-1563
Marietta National Cemetery 500 Washington Ave **Fax Area Code:* 770 ■ *TF:* 866-236-8159 ■ *Web:* www.cem.va.gov	Marietta	GA	30060	866-236-8159	479-9311*
Marion National Cemetery 1700 E 38th St *Web:* www.cem.va.gov	Marion	IN	46953	765-674-0284	674-4521
Massachusetts National Cemetery Conery Rd **Fax Area Code:* 703 ■ *TF:* 800-827-1000 ■ *Web:* www.cem.va.gov	Bourne	MA	02532	508-563-7113	221-2185*
Memphis National Cemetery 3568 Townes Ave *Web:* www.cem.va.gov	Memphis	TN	38122	901-386-8311	382-0750
Mill Springs National Cemetery 9044 W Hwy 80 *Web:* www.cem.va.gov/cems/nchp/millsprings.asp	Nancy	KY	42544	859-885-5727	887-4860
Mobile National Cemetery 1202 Virginia St *TF:* 800-827-1000 ■ *Web:* www.cem.va.gov	Mobile	AL	36604	850-453-4108	453-4635
Mound City National Cemetery Hwy 37 & 51 PO Box 128 *Web:* www.cem.va.gov/cems/nchp/moundcity.asp	Mound City	IL	62963	314-845-8320	845-8355
Mountain Home National Cemetery PO Box 8 *TF:* 800-827-1000 ■ *Web:* www.cem.va.gov/cems/nchp/mountainhome.asp	Mountain Home	TN	37684	423-979-3535	979-3521
Nashville National Cemetery 1420 Gallatin Rd S *Web:* www.cem.va.gov	Madison	TN	37115	615-860-0086	860-8691
Natchez National Cemetery 41 Cemetery Rd *Web:* www.cem.va.gov	Natchez	MS	39120	601-445-4981	445-8815
National Memorial Cemetery of Arizona 23029 N Cave Creek Rd *Web:* www.cem.va.gov	Phoenix	AZ	85024	480-513-3600	513-1412
New Albany National Cemetery 1943 Ekin Ave *Web:* www.cem.va.gov/cems/nchp/newalbany.asp	New Albany	IN	47150	502-893-3852	893-6612
New Bern National Cemetery 1711 National Ave *TF:* 800-827-1000 ■ *Web:* www.cem.va.gov	New Bern	NC	28560	252-637-2912	637-7145
Philadelphia National Cemetery Haines St & Limekiln Pike *Web:* www.cem.va.gov/cems/nchp/philadelphia.asp	Philadelphia	PA	19138	215-504-5610	504-5611
Port Hudson National Cemetery 20978 Port Hickey Rd *Web:* www.cem.va.gov	Zachary	LA	70791	225-654-3767	654-3728
Prescott National Cemetery 500 Hwy 89 N **Fax Area Code:* 703 ■ *TF:* 800-827-1000	Prescott	AZ	86301	928-717-7569	221-2185*
Quantico National Cemetery 18424 Joplin Rd *Web:* www.cem.va.gov	Triangle	VA	22172	703-221-2183	221-2185
Quincy National Cemetery 36th & Maine St *Web:* www.cem.va.gov/cems/nchp/quincy.asp	Quincy	IL	62301	309-782-2094	782-2097
Raleigh National Cemetery 501 Rock Quarry Rd *Web:* www.cem.va.gov/cems/nchp/raleigh.asp	Raleigh	NC	27610	252-637-2912	637-7145
Riverside National Cemetery 22495 Van Buren Blvd *Web:* www.cem.va.gov	Riverside	CA	92518	951-653-8417	653-5233
Rock Island National Cemetery Bldg 118 *Web:* www.cem.va.gov/cems/nchp/rockisland.asp	Rock Island	IL	61299	309-782-2094	782-2097
Roseburg National Cemetery 1770 Harvard Blvd *TF:* 800-535-1117 ■ *Web:* www.cem.va.gov/cems/nchp/roseburg.asp	Roseburg	OR	97470	541-826-2511	826-2111
Saint Augustine National Cemetery 104 Marine St *TF:* 800-273-8255 ■ *Web:* www.cem.va.gov/cems/nchp/staugustine.asp	Saint Augustine	FL	32084	352-793-7740	793-9560
Salisbury National Cemetery 501 Statesville Blvd *Web:* www.cem.va.gov/cems/nchp/salisbury.asp	Salisbury	NC	28144	704-636-2661	636-1115
San Antonio National Cemetery 1520 Harry Wurzback Rd *Web:* www.cem.va.gov	San Antonio	TX	78209	210-820-3891	820-3445
San Francisco National Cemetery Presidio of San Francisco 1 Lincoln Blvd *Web:* www.cem.va.gov/cems/nchp/sanfrancisco.asp	San Francisco	CA	94129	650-589-7737	873-6578
San Joaquin Valley National Cemetery 32053 W McCabe Rd *Web:* www.cem.va.gov/cems/nchp/sanjoaquinvalley.asp	Santa Nella	CA	95322	209-854-1040	854-3944
Santa Fe National Cemetery 501 N Guadalupe St *Web:* www.cem.va.gov	Santa Fe	NM	87501	505-988-6400	988-6497
Seven Pines National Cemetery 400 E Williamsburg Rd *TF:* 800-535-1117 ■ *Web:* www.cem.va.gov/cems/nchp/sevenpines.asp	Sandston	VA	23150	804-795-2031	795-1064
Sitka National Cemetery 803 Sawmill Creek Rd *TF:* 800-273-8255 ■ *Web:* www.cem.va.gov	Sitka	AK	99835	907-384-7075	384-7111
Springfield National Cemetery 1702 E Seminole St *Web:* www.cem.va.gov	Springfield	MO	65804	417-881-9499	881-7862
Staunton National Cemetery 901 Richmond Ave *TF:* 800-273-8255 ■ *Web:* www.cem.va.gov/cems/nchp/staunton.asp	Staunton	VA	24401	540-825-0027	825-6684
Tahoma National Cemetery 18600 SE 240th St *TF:* 800-827-1000 ■ *Web:* www.cem.va.gov	Kent	WA	98042	425-413-9614	413-9618
Togus National Cemetery VA Regional Office Ctr *TF:* 800-273-8255 ■ *Web:* www.cem.va.gov/cems/nchp/togus.asp	Togus	ME	04330	508-563-7113	564-9946
West Virginia National Cemetery 42 Veterans Memorial Lane *TF:* 800-273-8255 ■ *Web:* www.cem.va.gov/cems/nchp/westvirginia.asp	Grafton	WV	26354	304-265-2044	265-4336
Willamette National Cemetery 11800 SE Mt Scott Blvd *Web:* www.cem.va.gov	Portland	OR	97086	503-273-5250	273-5330
Wilmington National Cemetery 2011 Market St **Fax Area Code:* 252 ■ *TF:* 800-535-1117 ■ *Web:* www.cem.va.gov	Wilmington	NC	28403	910-815-4877	637-7145*
Winchester National Cemetery 401 National Ave *Web:* www.cem.va.gov/cems/nchp/winchester.asp	Winchester	VA	22601	540-825-0027	825-6684
Wood National Cemetery 5000 W National Ave Bldg 1301 *TF:* 888-878-3256 ■ *Web:* www.cem.va.gov	Milwaukee	WI	53295	414-382-5300	382-5321
Woodlawn National Cemetery 1825 Davis St *TF:* 877-907-8585 ■ *Web:* www.cem.va.gov	Elmira	NY	14901	607-732-5411	732-1769
Yorktown National Cemetery PO Box 210 *Web:* www.nps.gov/york/index.htm	Yorktown	VA	23690	757-898-2410	898-6346
Zachary Taylor National Cemetery 4701 Brownsboro Rd *Web:* www.cem.va.gov	Louisville	KY	40207	502-893-3852	893-6612

137 CHAMBERS OF COMMERCE - CANADIAN

Listings are organized by provinces and then are alphabetized within each province grouping according to the name of the city in which each chamber is located.

Chamber / Address	City	Prov	Postal Code	Phone	Fax
Brooks & District Chamber of Commerce 403-2 Ave W Suite 6 Ste 4 *Web:* www.brookschamber.ab.ca	Brooks	AB	T1R1B4	403-362-7641	362-6893
Calgary Chamber of Commerce 237 8th Ave SE *Web:* www.calgarychamber.com	Calgary	AB	T2G5C3	403-750-0400	266-3413
Alberta Chambers of Commerce 10025 - 102A Ave Edmonton Ctr Ste 1808 *TF:* 800-272-8854 ■ *Web:* www.abchamber.ca	Edmonton	AB	T5J2Z2	780-425-4180	429-1061
Edmonton Chamber of Commerce 9990 Jasper Ave Ste 600 *Web:* www.edmontonchamber.com	Edmonton	AB	T5J1P7	780-426-4620	424-7946
Fort McMurray Chamber of Commerce 9612 Franklin Ave Ste 304 *Web:* www.fortmcmurraychamber.ca	Fort McMurray	AB	T9H2J9	780-743-3100	790-9757
Grande Prairie & District Chamber of Commerce 11330 106th St Ste 127 *Web:* www.grandeprairiechamber.com	Grande Prairie	AB	T8V6T7	780-532-5340	532-2926
Lethbridge Chamber of Commerce 529 Sixth St S Ste 200 *Web:* lethbridgechamber.com	Lethbridge	AB	T1J2E1	403-327-1586	327-1001
Medicine Hat & District Chamber of Commerce 413 Sixth Ave SE *Web:* www.medicinehatchamber.com	Medicine Hat	AB	T1A2S7	403-527-5214	527-5182
Peace River Chamber of Commerce 9309-100 St PO Box 6599 *TF:* 888-525-4423 ■ *Web:* www.peaceriverchamber.com	Peace River	AB	T8S1S4	780-624-4166	624-4663
Red Deer Chamber of Commerce 3017 Gaetz Ave. *Web:* www.reddeerchamber.com	Red Deer	AB	T4N5Y6	403-347-4491	343-6188
Saint Albert Chamber of Commerce 71 St Albert Rd *TF:* 800-243-2378 ■ *Web:* www.stalbertchamber.com	Saint Albert	AB	T8N6L5	780-458-2833	458-6515
Abbotsford Chamber of Commerce 32900 S Fraser Way Ste 207 *Web:* www.abbotsfordchamber.com	Abbotsford	BC	V2S5A1	604-859-9651	850-6880
Burnaby Board of Trade 4555 Kings Way Ste 201 *Web:* www.bbot.ca	Burnaby	BC	V5H4T8	604-412-0100	412-0102
Campbell River & District Chamber of Commerce 900 Alder St PO Box 459 *Web:* www.campbellriverchamber.ca	Campbell River	BC	V9W2P6	250-287-4636	286-6490
Chilliwack Chamber of Commerce 46093 Yale Rd Ste 201 *Web:* www.chilliwackchamber.com	Chilliwack	BC	V2P2L8	604-793-4323	793-4303
Tri-Cities Chamber of Commerce 1209 Pinetree Way *Web:* www.tricitieschamber.com	Coquitlam	BC	V3B7Y3	604-464-2716	464-6796
Comox Valley Chamber of Commerce 2040 Cliffe Ave *TF:* 888-357-4471 ■ *Web:* www.comoxvalleychamber.com	Courtenay	BC	V9N2L3	250-334-3234	334-4908
Delta Chamber of Commerce 6201 60th Ave *Web:* www.deltachamber.ca	Delta	BC	V4K4E2	604-946-4232	946-5285
Duncan Cowichan Chamber of Commerce 2896 Drinkwater Rd *Web:* duncancc.bc.ca	Duncan	BC	V9L2C6	250-748-1111	746-8222
Fort Saint John & District Chamber of Commerce 9325 100th St. *Web:* www.fsjchamber.com	Fort Saint John	BC	V1J4N4	250-785-6037	785-6050
Kamloops Chamber of Commerce 615 Victoria St *Web:* www.kamloopschamber.ca	Kamloops	BC	V2C2B3	250-372-7722	828-9500
Kelowna Chamber of Commerce 544 Harvey Ave *Web:* www.kelownachamber.org	Kelowna	BC	V1Y6C9	250-861-3627	861-3624
Langley Chamber of Commerce 8047 199 St Ste 207 *Web:* www.langleychamber.com	Langley	BC	V2Y0E2	604-530-6656	530-7066
Mission Regional Chamber of Commerce 34033 Lougheed Hwy *Web:* www.missionchamber.bc.ca	Mission	BC	V2V5X8	604-826-6914	826-5916
Greater Nanaimo Chamber of Commerce 2133 Bowen Rd *Web:* www.nanaimochamber.bc.ca	Nanaimo	BC	V9S1H8	250-756-1191	756-1584
New Westminster Chamber of Commerce 601 Queens Ave *Web:* www.newwestchamber.com	New Westminster	BC	V3M1L1	604-521-7781	521-0057
Saanich Peninsula Chamber of Commerce 10382 Pat Bay Hwy. *Web:* www.peninsulachamber.ca	North Saanich	BC	V8L5S8	250-656-3616	656-7111
North Vancouver Chamber of Commerce 124 W First St Ste 102 *Web:* www.nvchamber.ca	North Vancouver	BC	V7M3N3	604-987-4488	987-8272
Parksville Chamber of Commerce (PDCC) PO Box 99 *Web:* parksvillechamber.com	Parksville	BC	V9P2G3	250-248-3613	248-5210
Penticton & Wine Country Chamber of Commerce 553 Railway St *TF:* 800-663-5052 ■ *Web:* www.penticton.org	Penticton	BC	V2A8S3	250-492-4103	492-6119
Alberni Valley Chamber of Commerce 2533 Port Alberni Hwy *Web:* www.albernichamber.ca	Port Alberni	BC	V9Y8P2	250-724-6535	724-6560
Prince George Chamber of Commerce 890 Vancouver St *Web:* www.pgchamber.bc.ca	Prince George	BC	V2L2P5	250-562-2454	562-6510
Richmond Chamber of Commerce 5811 Cooney Rd Ste 101 *Web:* www.richmondchamber.ca	Richmond	BC	V6X3M1	604-278-2822	278-2972
Surrey Board of Trade 14439 104th Ave Ste 101 *TF:* 866-848-7130 ■ *Web:* www.businessinsurrey.com	Surrey	BC	V3R1M1	604-581-7130	588-7549
British Columbia Chamber of Commerce 750 W Pender St Ste 1201 *TF:* 800-669-9655 ■ *Web:* www.bcchamber.org	Vancouver	BC	V6C2T8	604-683-0700	683-0416
Vancouver Board of Trade 400-999 Canada Pl Ste 400 *Web:* www.boardoftrade.com	Vancouver	BC	V6C3E1	604-681-2111	681-0437
Greater Vernon Chamber of Commerce 2901 32nd St Ste 102 *Web:* vernonchamber.ca	Vernon	BC	V1T5M2	250-545-0771	545-3114
Greater Victoria Chamber of Commerce 852 Ft St Ste 100 *Web:* www.victoriachamber.ca	Victoria	BC	V8W1H8	250-383-7191	385-3552
West Shore Chamber of Commerce 2830 Aldwynd Rd *TF:* 888-234-3566 ■ *Web:* www.westshore.bc.ca	Victoria	BC	V9B3S7	250-478-1130	478-1584
West Vancouver Chamber of Commerce 2235 Marine Dr *TF:* 888-471-9996 ■ *Web:* www.westvanchamber.com	West Vancouver	BC	V7V1K5	604-926-6614	925-7220
Westbank & District Chamber of Commerce 2372 Dobbin Rd *Web:* gwboardoftrade.com	Westbank	BC	V4T2H9	250-768-3378	768-3465
Brandon Chamber of Commerce 1043 Rosser Ave *Web:* www.brandonchamber.ca	Brandon	MB	R7A0L5	204-571-5340	571-5347
Portage & District Chamber of Commerce 56 Royal Rd N. *Web:* www.portagechamber.com	Portage la Prairie	MB	R1N1V1	204-857-7778	856-5001
Saint-Boniface Chamber of Commerce 383 boul Provencher PO Box 204 *Web:* www.ccfsb.mb.ca	Saint-Boniface	MB	R2H3B4	204-235-1406	377-8514
Selkirk & District Chamber of Commerce (SDCC) 200 Eaton Ave. *Web:* www.selkirkanddistrictchamber.ca	Selkirk	MB	R1A0W6	204-482-7176	482-5448
Manitoba Chambers of Commerce 227 Portage Ave *Web:* www.mbchamber.mb.ca	Winnipeg	MB	R3B2A6	204-948-0100	948-0110
Winnipeg Chamber of Commerce, The 259 Portage Ave Ste 100 *Web:* www.winnipeg-chamber.com	Winnipeg	MB	R3B2A9	204-944-8484	944-8492
Fredericton Chamber of Commerce 270 Rookwood Rd Ste 200 *Web:* www.frederictonchamber.ca	Fredericton	NB	E3B4Y9	506-458-8006	451-1119
Miramichi Chamber of Commerce 120 Newcastle Blvd Ste 2 PO Box 342 *Web:* www.miramichichamber.com	Miramichi	NB	E1N3A7	506-622-5522	622-5959
Greater Moncton Chamber of Commerce 1273 Main St Ste 200 *Web:* www.gmcc.nb.ca	Moncton	NB	E1C0P4	506-857-2883	857-9209
Saint John Board of Trade (SJBT) 40 King St PO Box 6037 *Web:* www.sjboardoftrade.com	Saint John	NB	E2L4R5	506-634-8111	632-2008
Greater Corner Brook Board of Trade 11 Confederation Dr PO Box 475 *Web:* www.gcbbt.com	Corner Brook	NL	A2H6E6	709-634-5831	639-9710
Gander & Area Chamber of Commerce 109 Trans Canada Hwy *Web:* www.ganderchamber.nf.ca	Gander	NL	A1V1P6	709-256-7110	256-4080
Northwest Territories Chamber of Commerce 4802 - 50th Ave Unit 13 *Web:* www.nwtchamber.com	Yellowknife	NT	X1A1C4	867-920-9505	873-4174
Bridgewater & Area Chamber of Commerce 373 King St *Web:* www.bridgewaterchamber.com	Bridgewater	NS	B4V1B1	902-543-4263	543-1156
Metropolitan Halifax Chamber of Commerce 656 Windmill Rd Ste 200 *Web:* www.halifaxchamber.com	Dartmouth	NS	B3B1B8	902-468-7111	468-7333
Pictou County Chamber of Commerce 980 E River Rd *Web:* www.pictouchamber.com	New Glasgow	NS	B2H3S8	902-755-3463	
Sydney & Area Chamber of Commerce 275 Charlotte St *Web:* www.sydneyareachamber.ca	Sydney	NS	B1P1C6	902-564-6453	539-7487
Truro & District Chamber of Commerce 605 Prince St	Truro	NS	B2N1G2	902-895-6328	897-6641
Aurora Chamber of Commerce 6-14845 Yonge St Ste 321 *Web:* www.aurorachamber.on.ca	Aurora	ON	L4G6H8	905-727-7262	841-6217
Greater Barrie Chamber of Commerce 97 Toronto St *Web:* www.barriechamber.com	Barrie	ON	L4N1V1	705-721-5000	726-0973
Belleville Chamber of Commerce 5 Moira St E *TF:* 888-852-9992 ■ *Web:* www.bellevillechamber.ca	Belleville	ON	K8P2S3	613-962-4597	962-3911
Caledon Chamber of Commerce 12598 Hwy Ste 50 S *Web:* www.caledonchamber.com	Bolton	ON	L7E1T6	905-857-7393	857-7405
Brampton Board of Trade 36 Queen St E Ste 101 *Web:* www.bramptonbot.com	Brampton	ON	L6V1A2	905-451-1122	450-0295
Brantford Brant Chamber of Commerce (BBCC) 77 Charlotte St *Web:* www.brantfordbrantchamber.com	Brantford	ON	N3T2W8	519-753-2617	753-0921
Burlington Chamber of Commerce 414 Locust St Ste 201 *TF:* 888-635-8687 ■ *Web:* www.burlingtonchamber.com	Burlington	ON	L7S1T7	905-639-0174	333-3956
Cambridge Chamber of Commerce 750 Hespeler Rd *TF General:* 800-749-7560 ■ *Web:* www.cambridgechamber.com	Cambridge	ON	N3H5L8	519-622-2221	622-0177
Chatham-Kent Chamber of Commerce 54 Fourth St *Web:* www.chatham-kentchamber.ca	Chatham	ON	N7M2G2	519-352-7540	352-8741
Cornwall & Area Chamber of Commerce 113 Second St E *Web:* www.chamber.cornwall.on.ca	Cornwall	ON	K6H1Y5	613-933-4004	933-8466
Dryden District Chamber of Commerce 284 Government St Hwy 17 *Web:* www.drydenchamber.ca	Dryden	ON	P8N2P3	807-223-2622	223-2626

Organization / Address	City	State	Postal Code	Phone	Fax
Flamborough Chamber of Commerce 7 Innovation Dr Ste 227 *Web:* www.flamboroughchamber.ca	Flamborough	ON	L9H7H9	905-689-7650	689-1313
Halton Hills Chamber of Commerce 328 Guelph St. *Web:* www.haltonhillschamber.on.ca	Georgetown	ON	L7G4B5	905-877-5117	877-5117
Guelph Chamber of Commerce 111 Farquhar St *Web:* www.guelphchamber.com	Guelph	ON	N1H3N4	519-822-8081	822-8451
Hamilton Chamber of Commerce 120 King St W Plz level *Web:* www.hamiltonchamber.ca	Hamilton	ON	L8P4V2	905-522-1151	522-1154
Greater Kingston Chamber of Commerce 67 Brock St. *Web:* kingstonchamber.ca	Kingston	ON	K7L1R8	613-548-4453	548-4743
Chamber of Commerce of Kitchener & Waterloo 80 Queen St N PO Box 2367 *Web:* www.greaterkwchamber.com	Kitchener	ON	N2H6L4	519-576-5000	742-4760
Leamington District Chamber of Commerce 318 Erie St S. *TF:* 800-393-3769 ■ *Web:* www.leamingtonchamber.com	Leamington	ON	N8H3C5	519-326-2721	326-3204
London Chamber of Commerce 244 Pall Mall St Ste 101 *Web:* www.londonchamber.com	London	ON	N6A5P6	519-432-7551	432-8063
Markham Board of Trade 80 F Centurian Dr Ste 206 *Web:* www.markhamboard.com	Markham	ON	L3R8C1	905-474-0730	474-0685
Southern Georgia Bay Chamber of Commerce 208 King St. *Web:* southerngeorgianbay.ca	Midland	ON	L4R3L9	705-526-7884	526-1744
Milton Chamber of Commerce 251 Main St E Ste 104 *Web:* miltonchamber.ca	Milton	ON	L9T1P1	905-878-0581	878-4972
Mississauga Board of Trade 77 City Centre Dr Ste 701 *Web:* www.mbot.com	Mississauga	ON	L5B1M5	905-273-6151	273-4937
Newmarket Chamber of Commerce 470 Davis Dr *Web:* www.newmarketchamber.com	Newmarket	ON	L3Y2P3	905-898-5900	
Niagara Falls Canada Chamber of Commerce 4056 Dorchester Rd *Web:* www.niagarafallschamber.com	Niagara Falls	ON	L2E6M9	905-374-3666	374-2972
North Bay & District Chamber of Commerce 1375 Seymour St *TF:* 888-249-8998 ■ *Web:* www.northbaychamber.com	North Bay	ON	P1B8J8	705-472-8480	472-8027
Oakville Chamber of Commerce 700 Kerr St Ste 200 *Web:* www.oakvillechamber.com	Oakville	ON	L6K3W5	905-845-6613	845-6475
Greater Oshawa Chamber of Commerce 44 Richmond St W Ste 100 *Web:* www.oshawachamber.com	Oshawa	ON	L1G1C7	905-728-1683	432-1259
Canadian Chamber of Commerce 360 Albert St Ste 420 *Web:* www.chamber.ca	Ottawa	ON	K1R7X7	613-238-4000	238-7643
Ottawa Chamber of Commerce 328 Somerset St W *Web:* www.ottawachamber.ca	Ottawa	ON	K2P0J9	613-236-3631	236-7498
Upper Ottawa Valley Chamber of Commerce 224 Pembroke St W *Web:* www.upperottawavalleychamber.com	Pembroke	ON	K8A5N2	613-732-1492	
Perth & District Chamber of Commerce 34 Herriott St *Web:* www.perthchamber.com	Perth	ON	K7H1T2	613-267-3200	267-6797
Greater Peterborough Chamber of Commerce 175 George St N *TF:* 877-640-4037 ■ *Web:* www.peterboroughchamber.ca	Peterborough	ON	K9J3G6	705-748-9771	743-2331
Port Colborne-Wainfleet Chamber of Commerce 76 Main St W *Web:* www.pcwchamber.com	Port Colborne	ON	L3K3V2	905-834-9765	834-1542
Richmond Hill Chamber of Commerce (RHCOC) 376 Church St S *Web:* www.rhcoc.com	Richmond Hill	ON	L4C9V8	905-884-1961	884-1962
Timmins Chamber of Commerce PO Box 985 *Web:* www.timminschamber.on.ca	Schumacher	ON	P4N7H6	705-360-1900	360-1193
Simcoe & District Chamber of Commerce 95 Queensway W *Web:* www.simcoechamber.on.ca	Simcoe	ON	N3Y2M8	519-426-5867	428-7718
Stratford & District Chamber of Commerce 55 Lorne Ave E *Web:* www.stratfordchamber.com	Stratford	ON	N5A6S4	519-273-5250	273-2229
Greater Sudbury Chamber of Commerce 40 Elm St Ste 1 *Web:* sudburychamber.ca	Sudbury	ON	P3C1S8	705-673-7133	673-1951
Thunder Bay Chamber of Commerce 200 Syndicated Ave S Ste 102 *Web:* www.tbchamber.ca	Thunder Bay	ON	P7E1C9	807-624-2626	622-7752
Canadian Chamber of Commerce Toronto Office 55 University Ave Ste 901 *Web:* www.chamber.ca	Toronto	ON	M5J2H7	416-868-6415	868-0189
Ontario Chamber of Commerce 180 Dundas St W Ste 505 *Web:* www.occ.ca	Toronto	ON	M5G1Z8	416-482-5222	482-5879
Vaughan Chamber of Commerce 25 Edilcan Dr Ste 2 *TF:* 888-943-8937 ■ *Web:* vaughanchamber.ca	Vaughan	ON	L4K3S4	905-761-1366	761-1918
Welland/Pelham Chamber of Commerce 32 E Main St.	Welland	ON	L3B3W3	905-732-7515	732-7175
Whitby Chamber of Commerce 128 Brock St S *Web:* www.whitbychamber.org	Whitby	ON	L1N4J8	905-668-4506	668-1894
Windsor-Essex Regional Chamber of Commerce 2575 Ouellette Pl *Web:* www.windsorchamber.org	Windsor	ON	N8X1L9	519-966-3696	966-0603
Woodstock District Chamber of Commerce 476 Peel St Ste 3 *Web:* woodstockchamber.ca	Woodstock	ON	N4S1K1	519-539-9411	456-1611
Greater Charlottetown Area Chamber of Commerce PO Box 67 *Web:* www.charlottetownchamber.com	Charlottetown	PE	C1A7K2	902-628-2000	368-3570
La Chambre de Commerce de Drummond 234 Rue St Marcel CP 188 *Web:* www.ccid.qc.ca	Drummondville	QC	J2B6V7	819-477-7822	477-2823
Chambre de Commerce Haute-Yamaska Region (CDCHY) 90 Rue Robinson S Ste 102 *Web:* cchyr.ca	Granby	QC	J2G7L4	450-372-6100	372-3161
Laval Chamber of Commerce 1555 boul Chomedey Ste 200 *Web:* www.ccilaval.qc.ca	Laval	QC	H7V3Z1	450-682-5255	682-5735
Mont-Laurier Chamber of Commerce 385 Rue Du Pont *Web:* www.ccmont-laurier.com	Mont-Laurier	QC	J9L2R5	819-623-3642	623-5220
Canadian Chamber of Commerce Montreal Office 1155 University St Ste 709 *Web:* www.chamber.ca	Montreal	QC	H3B3A7	514-866-4334	866-7296
Chambre de Commerce du Quebec 17 rue St-Louis *Web:* www.fccq.ca	Quebec	QC	G1R3Y8	418-692-3853	
Chambre de Commerce et d'Industrie du Quebec Metropolitain 17 St Louis St *Web:* www.cciquebec.ca	Quebec	QC	G1R3Y8	418-692-3853	694-2286
Sept-Iles Chamber of Commerce 700 boul Laure Bureau 237 *Web:* www.ccseptiles.com	Sept-Iles	QC	G4R1Y1	418-968-3488	968-3432
Chambre de Commerce de la Region Sherbrookoise 9 Rue Wellington S *Web:* www.ccsherbrooke.com	Sherbrooke	QC	J1H5C8	819-822-6151	822-6156
Moose Jaw & District Chamber of Commerce 88 Saskatchewan St E *Web:* www.mjchamber.com	Moose Jaw	SK	S6H0V4	306-692-6414	694-6463
Battlefords Chamber of Commerce PO Box 1000 Jcts of Hws 16 & 40 E *Web:* www.battlefordschamber.com	North Battleford	SK	S9A3E6	306-445-6226	445-6633
Prince Albert & District Chamber of Commerce 3700 Second Ave W *Web:* www.princealbertchamber.com	Prince Albert	SK	S6W1A2	306-764-6222	922-4727
Regina Chamber of Commerce 2145 Albert St *Web:* www.reginachamber.com	Regina	SK	S4P2V1	306-757-4658	757-4668
Greater Saskatoon Chamber of Commerce 104-202 Fourth Ave N *Web:* www.saskatoonchamber.com	Saskatoon	SK	S7K0K1	306-244-2151	244-8366
Whitehorse Chamber of Commerce 302 Steele St Ste 101 *Web:* www.whitehorsechamber.com	Whitehorse	YT	Y1A2C5	867-667-7545	667-4507

138 CHAMBERS OF COMMERCE - INTERNATIONAL

See Also Chambers of Commerce - Canadian p. 1899

Included here are organizations that work to promote business and trade relationships between the United States and other countries.

Organization / Address	City	State	Postal Code	Phone	Fax
262 With Donna 11762 marco beach dr *Web:* breastcancermarathon.com	Jacksonville	FL	32224	904-551-0732	
AAAA Benefits 11020 David Taylor Dr Ste 305 *Web:* www.aaaabenefits.com	Charlotte	NC	28262	704-594-6270	
Ace Charter High School 1929 N Stone Ave *Web:* www.acehs.org	Tucson	AZ	85705	520-628-8316	
Alaska Primary Care Association Inc 903 W Northern Lights Blvd Ste 200 *Web:* www.alaskapca.org	Anchorage	AK	99503	907-929-2722	
Alberta Association of Municipal Districts & Counties 2510 Sparrow Dr *Web:* www.aamdc.com	Nisku	AB	T9E8N5	780-955-3639	
Alberta Senior Citizens Housing Association 9711 47 Ave Nw *Web:* www.ascha.com	Edmonton	AB	T6E5M7	780-439-6473	
Alberta Soccer 9023 111 Ave Nw *TF:* 866-250-2200 ■ *Web:* www.albertasoccer.com	Edmonton	AB	T5B0C3	780-474-2200	
Alent Technologies LLC 8201 Bondage Dr *Web:* www.alent.net	Gaithersburg	MD	20882	301-520-3080	
America-Israel Chamber of Commerce - Chicago 247 S State St Ste 1325 *Web:* www.israeltrade.org	Chicago	IL	60604	312-641-2937	641-2941
American Egyptian Cooperation Foundation 1535 W Loop S.	Houston	TX	77027	713-624-7113	
American-Indonesian Chamber of Commerce 317 Madison Ave Ste 1619 *Web:* www.aiccusa.org	New York	NY	10017	212-687-4505	687-5844
American-Israel Chamber of Commerce & Industry of Minnesota 13100 Wayzata Blvd *Web:* www.aiccmn.org	Minnetonka	MN	55305	952-593-8666	
American-Israel Chamber of Commerce Southeast Region (AICC) 400 Northridge Rd Ste 260 *Web:* www.aiccse.org	Atlanta	GA	30350	404-843-9426	843-1416
American-Russian Chamber of Commerce & Industry 1101 Pennsylvania Ave NW 6th Fl *Web:* www.arcci.org	Washington	DC	20004	202-756-4943	362-4634
Aqtis 533 Rue Ontario E *Web:* www.aqtis.qc.ca	Montreal	QC	H2L1N8	514-844-2113	
Arizona Automobile Dealers Association 4701 N 24th St Ste B3 *TF:* 800-678-3875 ■ *Web:* www.aada.com	Phoenix	AZ	85016	602-468-0888	
Arizona Bankers Association 111 W Monroe St Ste 440 *Web:* www.azbankers.org	Phoenix	AZ	85003	602-258-1200	
Aski Financial Inc 419 Notre Dame Ave *TF:* 866-987-7180 ■ *Web:* www.askifinancial.ca	Winnipeg	MB	R3B1R3	204-987-7180	
Association of American Chambers of Commerce in Latin America 1615 H St NW 3rd Fl *TF:* 800-638-6582 ■ *Web:* www.aaccla.org	Washington	DC	20062	202-463-5485	463-3126
Australian American Chamber of Commerce of Houston 1300 McGowen St Ste 120 **Fax Area Code: 832* ■ *Web:* www.aacc-houston.org	Houston	TX	77004	713-527-9688	415-0545*

Phone Fax

Australian-American Chamber of Commerce - San Francisco
PO Box 471285 San Francisco CA 94147 415-485-6718
Web: sfaussies.com

Bc Maritime Employers Assn 349 Railway St. Vancouver BC V6A1A4 604-688-1155
Web: www.bcmea.com

Belgian-American Chamber of Commerce in the US (BACC)
1177 Ave of the Americas 8th Fl. New York NY 10036 212-541-0779
Web: www.belcham.org

BPI Information Systems
6055 W Snowville Rd Brecksville OH 44141 440-717-4112
Web: www.bpiohio.com

Brazilian-American Chamber of Commerce Inc
509 Madison Ave Ste 304 New York NY 10022 212-751-4691 751-7692
Web: www.brazilcham.com

Brazilian-American Chamber of Commerce of Florida
PO Box 310038 Miami FL 33231 305-579-9030 579-9756
Web: www.brazilchamber.org

British-American Business Council (BABC)
52 Vanderbilt Ave 20th Fl New York NY 10017 212-661-4060 661-4074
Web: www.babc.org

British-American Business Council of Los Angeles
15303 Ventura Blvd Ste 1040 Sherman Oaks CA 91403 310-312-1962 995-4124*
*Fax Area Code: 818 ■ *Web:* www.babcla.org

British-American Chamber of Commerce Great Lakes Region (BACC)
4700 Millenia Blvd Ste 175 Orlando FL 32839 216-621-0222
Web: www.baccohio.org

British-American Chamber of Commerce of Miami
501 Brickell Key Dr Ste 410 Miami FL 33131 305-377-0992

Buffalo Economic Renaissance Corp
920 City Hall Buffalo NY 14202 716-842-6923
Web: www.berc.org

Burns Bog Conservation Society 7953 120 St Delta BC V4C6P6 604-572-0373
TF: 888-850-6264 ■ *Web:* www.burnsbog.org

Canadian Advanced Technology Alliance
388 Albert St Ottawa ON K1R5B2 613-236-6550
Web: www.cata.ca

Canadian Bar Assn 845 Cambie St 10th Fl Vancouver BC V6B5T3 604-687-3404
Web: www.cba.org

Canadian Cancer Society 10 Alcorn Ave Ste 200 Toronto ON M4V3B1 416-961-7223
Web: www.cancer.ca

Canadian Electricity Association 66 Slater St Ottawa ON K1P5H1 613-230-9263
Web: www.electricity.ca

Canadian Finance & Leasing Association
15 Toronto St Toronto ON M5C2E3 416-860-1133
TF: 877-213-7373 ■ *Web:* www.cfla-acfl.ca

Canadian Manufacturers & Exporters
1 Nicholas St Ste 1500 Ottawa BC K1N7B7 613-238-8888
Web: www.cme-mec.ca

Canadian Mental Health Association
8 King St E Ste 810 Toronto ON M5C1B5 416-484-7750
Web: www.cmha.ca

Canadian Musical Reproduction Rights Agency Ltd The
56 Wellesley St W Ste 320 Toronto ON M5S2S3 416-926-1966
Web: www.cmrra.ca

Canadian Payroll Association 250 Bloor St E Toronto ON M4W1E6 416-487-3380
TF: 800-387-4693 ■ *Web:* www.payroll.ca

Canadian Seed Growers' Association
240 Catherine St Ottawa ON K2P2G8 613-236-0497
Web: www.seedgrowers.ca

Canadian Society of Customs Brokers
55 Murray St Ste 320 Ottawa ON K1N5M3 613-562-3543
Web: cscb.ca

Cape Jourimain Nature Centre Inc
5039 Route 16 Bayfield NB E4M3Z8 506-538-2220
Web: www.capejourimain.ca

Carefirst Seniors & Community Services Association
3601 Victoria Park Ave Scarborough ON M1W3Y3 416-502-2323
Web: www.carefirstseniors.com

Chicago Automobile Trade Association
18 W 200 Butterfield Rd Oakbrook Terrace IL 60181 630-495-2282
Web: cata.info

Chile-US Chamber of Commerce
8333 NW 53rd St Ste 450 Doral FL 33166 305-403-9760
Web: www.chileus.org

Chinese Chamber of Commerce of Hawaii
8 S King St Honolulu HI 96817 808-533-3181
TF: 877-533-2444 ■ *Web:* www.chinesechamber.com

Chinese Chamber of Commerce of Los Angeles
977 N Broadway Ground Fl Ste E Los Angeles CA 90012 213-617-0396 617-2128
TF: 800-400-7115 ■ *Web:* www.lachinesechamber.org

Chinese Chamber of Commerce of San Francisco
730 Sacramento St San Francisco CA 94108 415-982-3000 982-4720

Cic Plus Inc 7321 ridgeway ave Skokie IL 60076 847-677-9800
Web: www.cicplus.com

CIO Association of Canada
7270 Woodbine Ave Ste 204 Markham ON L3R4B9 905-752-1899
Web: www.ciocan.ca

Coach Canada's Health Informatics Association
250 Consumers Rd North York ON M2J4V6 416-494-9324
TF: 888-253-8554 ■ *Web:* www.coachorg.com

Colombian American Chamber of Commerce
2305 NW 107 Ave Ste 1m14 box 105 Miami FL 33172 305-446-2542 446-2038
Web: www.colombiachamber.com

Constructors Association of Western Pennsylvania
1201 Banksville Rd Pittsburgh PA 15216 412-343-8000
TF: 877-343-2297 ■ *Web:* www.cawp.org

Dairy Farmers of Ontario
6780 Campobello Rd Mississauga ON L5N2L8 905-821-8970
Web: www.milk.org

Danish-American Chamber of Commerce
885 Second Ave 18th Fl New York NY 10017 646-790-7169
Web: www.daccny.com

Deaf Inter-link 100 Saint Francois St Florissant MO 63031 314-837-7757
Web: www.deafinterlink.com

Phone Fax

Downtown Austin Alliance
211 E Seventh St Ste 818 Austin TX 78701 512-469-1766
Web: downtownaustin.com

Ecuadorian-American Chamber of Commerce of Greater Miami
1640 Town Center Cir Ste 210 Weston FL 33326 305-539-0010

Eden i & r Inc 570 B St Hayward CA 94541 510-537-2710
Web: www.edenir.org

Edmonton Folk Music Festival
10115 97a Ave Nw Edmonton AB T6E4T2 780-429-1899
Web: www.edmontonfolkfest.org

Electric Cooperatives of South Carolina Inc, The
808 Knox Abbott Dr Cayce SC 29033 803-796-6060
Web: www.ecsc.org

Electronic Transactions Association, The
1101 16th St NW Ste 402 Washington DC 20036 202-828-2635
TF: 800-695-5509 ■ *Web:* www.electran.org

Empire Building Services
1570 E Edinger Ave Santa Ana CA 92705 714-836-7700
TF: 888-296-2078 ■ *Web:* www.ebuildingservices.com

European-American Business Council
919 18th St NW Ste 220 Washington DC 20006 202-828-9104 828-9106
Web: transatlanticbusiness.org

Ex-Students' Association, The
2110 San Jacinto Blvd Austin TX 78712 512-471-8839
Web: www.texasexes.org

Federal Bar Council 123 Main St Ste L100 White Plains NY 10601 914-682-8800
Web: federalbarcouncil.org

Fine Arts Association, The
38660 Mentor Ave Willoughby OH 44094 440-951-7500
Web: www.fineartsassociation.org

Finnish American Chamber of Commerce Inc
866 United Nations Plz Ste 250 New York NY 10017 212-821-0225 750-4418
Web: www.facc-ny.com

Flagship Fire Inc 1500 15th Ave dr e Palmetto FL 34221 941-723-7230
TF: 866-242-3307 ■ *Web:* www.flagshipfire.com

Flashbanc LLC 185 nw spanish river blvd Boca Raton FL 33431 561-278-8888
Web: www.flashbanc.com

Florida Association of Counties
100 S Monroe St Tallahassee FL 32301 850-922-4300
Web: www.fl-counties.com

Florida Retail Federation Services Inc
227 S Adams St Tallahassee FL 32301 850-222-4082
Web: www.frf.org

Florida Venture Forum Inc, The 707 W Azeele St Tampa FL 33606 813-335-8116
TF: 888-375-7136 ■ *Web:* www.flventure.org

French-American Chamber of Commerce in New York
1350 Broadway Ste 2101 New York NY 10018 212-867-0123 867-9050
TF: 800-821-2241 ■ *Web:* www.faccnyc.org

French-American Chamber of Commerce of Atlanta
3399 Peachtree Rd NE Ste 500 Atlanta GA 30326 404-997-6800 997-6810
Web: www.facc-atlanta.com

French-American Chamber of Commerce of Chicago (FACC)
35 E Wacker Dr Ste 670 Chicago IL 60601 312-578-0444 578-0445
Web: www.facc-chicago.com

French-American Chamber of Commerce of Florida
100 N Biscayne Blvd Ste 1105 Miami FL 33131 305-374-5000 358-8203
Web: www.faccmiami.com

French-American Chamber of Commerce of Houston
777 Post Oak Blvd Ste 600 Houston TX 77056 713-985-3280

French-American Chamber of Commerce of Philadelphia (FACC)
1617 John F Kennedy Blvd Ste 555 Philadelphia PA 19103 215-545-0123
Web: www.faccphila.org

French-American Chamber of Commerce of San Francisco
26 O'Farrell St Ste 500 San Francisco CA 94108 415-442-4717 442-4621
Web: www.faccsf.com

French-American Chamber of Commerce of the Pacific Northwest (FACCPNW)
2200 Alaskan Way Ste 490 Seattle WA 98121 206-443-4703 448-4218
Web: www.faccpnw.org

FSNA 1052 St Laurent Blvd Ottawa ON K1K3B4 613-745-2559
TF: 855-304-4700 ■ *Web:* www.fsna.com

Georgia Poultry Improvement Assn
3235 Abit Massey Way Ganesville GA 30501 770-535-5996

Georgia Society of Cpa's
3353 Peachtree Rd NE Ste 400 Alpharetta GA 30326 404-231-8676
TF: 800-330-8889 ■ *Web:* www.gscpa.org

German-American Chamber of Commerce Inc
75 Broad St 21st Fl New York NY 10004 212-974-8830 974-8867
Web: www.gaccny.com

German-American Chamber of Commerce Inc - Philadelphia
1617 John F Kennedy Blvd Ste 340
1 Penn Ctr Philadelphia PA 19103 215-665-1585 665-0375
Web: www.gaccphiladelphia.com

German-American Chamber of Commerce of the Midwest Inc
321 N Clark St Ste 1425 Chicago IL 60654 312-644-2662 644-0738
Web: www.gaccmidwest.org

German-American Chamber of Commerce of the Southern US Inc
1170 Howell Mill Rd Ste 300 Atlanta GA 30318 404-586-6800 586-6820
Web: www.gaccsouth.com

Global Hope Network Po Box 560026 Orlando FL 32856 407-207-3256
Web: www.ghni.org

Grants Manager Network
1666 K St NW Ste 440 Washington DC 02006 504-834-9656
TF: 888-466-1996 ■ *Web:* gmnetwork.org

Graphic Arts Association
1210 Northbrook Dr Ste 200 Trevose PA 19053 215-396-2300
Web: www.graphicartsassociation.org

Hass Avocado Board 38 Discovery Ste 150 Irvine CA 92618 949-341-3250
Web: www.hassavocadoboard.com

Health Unit Brant County 194 Ter Hill St Brantford ON N3R1G7 519-753-4937
Web: www.bchu.org

Healthshare Inc Po Box 679010 Austin TX 78767 512-465-1000
Web: www.healthshare-tha.com

Heart of Virginia Council Inc Boy Scouts of America
4015 Fitzhugh Ave Richmond VA 23230 804-355-4306
Web: hovc.org

Phone Fax

Hellenic-American Chamber of Commerce (HACC)
370 Lexington Ave 27th Fl, New York NY 10017 212-629-6380 564-9281
Web: www.hellenicamerican.cc

Heritage Solar 5035 surfside dr, San diego CA 92154 619-200-9073

Hive Modern Design 820 nw glisan st, Portland OR 97209 503-242-1967
TF: 866-663-4483 ■ *Web:* hivemodern.com

Home Builders Association of Washtenaw County
179 Little Lk Dr, Ann Arbor MI 48103 734-996-0100
Web: bragannarbor.com

Honolulu-Japanese Chamber of Commerce
2454 S Beretania St Ste 201, Honolulu HI 96826 808-949-5531 949-3020
Web: hjcc.org

Houston Apartment Association Inc
4810 Westway Park Blvd, Houston TX 77041 713-595-0300
Web: www.haaonline.org

Houston Area Safety Council 1301 W 13th St, Deer Park TX 77536 281-476-9900
TF: 888-955-7233 ■ *Web:* hacsc.com

Iada Services Inc
1111 Office Park Rd, West Des Moines IA 50265 515-440-7621
Web: www.iada.com

Ibb Design Group 5798 Genesis Ct, Frisco TX 75034 214-618-6600
TF: 800-355-9195 ■ *Web:* www.ibbdesign.com

Icelandic-American Chamber of Commerce
800 Third Ave 36th Fl, New York NY 10022 212-593-2700 593-6269
Web: www.iceland.is

Illinois Soybean Assoc
1605 Commerce Pkwy, Bloomington IL 61704 309-662-3373
Web: www.ilsoy.org

Indiana Black Expo Inc
3145 N Meridian St, Indianapolis IN 46208 317-925-2702
Web: www.indianablackexpo.com

Info. Quality Healthcare
385b Highland Colony Pkwy Ste 504, Ridgeland MS 39157 601-957-1575
TF: 800-844-0500 ■ *Web:* www.iqh.org

Inland Press Association
701 Lee St Ste 925, Des Plaines IL 60016 847-795-0380
Web: inlandpress.org

Intensity Corp 12730 High Bluff Dr Ste 300, San Diego CA 92130 858-876-9101
Web: intensity.com

Iowa Soybean Association 4554 114th st, Urbandale IA 50322 515-251-8640
TF: 800-383-1423 ■ *Web:* www.iasoybeans.com

Ireland Chamber of Commerce in the US
556 Central Ave, New Providence NJ 07974 908-286-1300 286-1200
Web: www.iccusa.org

Italian American Chamber of Commerce of Chicago (IACC)
500 N Michigan Ave Ste 506, Chicago IL 60611 312-553-9137 553-9142
Web: www.iacc-chicago.com

Italy-America Chamber of Commerce Inc
730 Fifth Ave Ste 600, New York NY 10019 212-459-0044 459-0090
Web: www.italchamber.org

Italy-America Chamber of Commerce of Texas Inc
1800 W Loop S Ste 1120, Houston TX 77027 713-626-9303 626-9309
Web: www.iacctexas.com

Italy-America Chamber of Commerce Southeast Inc
2 S Biscayne Blvd Ste 1880, Miami FL 33131 305-577-9868 577-3956
TF: 800-428-3003 ■ *Web:* www.iacc-miami.com

Italy-America Chamber of Commerce West Inc
10537 Santa Monica Blvd Ste 210, Los Angeles CA 90025 310-557-3017 557-1217
Web: www.iaccw.net

Japanese Chamber of Commerce & Industry of Chicago
541 N Fairbanks Ct Ste 2050, Chicago IL 60611 312-245-8344 245-8355
Web: jccc-chi.org/ja/ai1ec_event/environmentallaw

Japanese Chamber of Commerce & Industry of Hawaii
714 Kanoelehua Ave, Hilo HI 96720 808-934-0177 934-0178
Web: jccih.org

Japanese Chamber of Commerce & Industry of New York Inc
145 W 57th St 6th Fl, New York NY 10019 212-246-8001 246-8002
Web: www.jcciny.org

Japanese Chamber of Commerce of Northern California
1875 S Grant St Ste 760, San Mateo CA 94402 650-522-8500 522-8300
Web: www.jccnc.org

JJ Kane 8008 US Hwy 130 Bldg One Ste 214, Delran NJ 08075 856-764-7163
Web: www.jjkane.com

Johnnie Appleseed Visitor Center
1000 Rte 2 Westbound, Lancaster MA 01523 978-534-2302
Web: www.appleseed.org

Kids Help Phone 300-439 University Ave, Toronto ON M5G1Y8 416-586-5437
TF: 800-268-3062 ■ *Web:* www.kidshelpphone.ca

Kieckhafer & Co 6201 Oak Canyon Dr, Irvine CA 92618 949-250-3900
Web: www.ksandco.com

Korean Chamber of Commerce
3435 Wilshire Blvd Ste 2450, Los Angeles CA 90010 213-480-1115

Korean Chamber of Commerce & Industry in the USA Inc
460 Pk Ave Ste 410, New York NY 10022 212-644-0140 644-9106
Web: www.kocham.org

Labor Law Center Inc 12534 Vly view st, Garden Grove CA 92845 800-745-9970
TF: 800-745-9970 ■ *Web:* www.laborlawcenter.com

Latin Chamber of Commerce of the US (CAMACOL)
1417 W Flagler St, Miami FL 33135 305-642-3870 642-0653
Web: www.camacol.org

Lernia Training Solutions
3603 winding way, Newtown Square PA 19073 610-356-1792
Web: www.lernia-ts.com

Lignite Energy Council 1016 E Owens Ave, Bismarck ND 58502 701-258-7117
TF: 800-932-7117 ■ *Web:* www.lignite.com

Maine Hospital Association 33 Fuller Rd, Augusta ME 04330 207-622-4794
Web: themha.org

MANTEC Inc 600 N Hartley St Ste 100, York PA 17404 717-843-5054
Web: www.mantec.org

Marine Corps Reserve Association
8626 Lee Hwy Ste 205, Fairfax VA 22031 703-207-0626
Web: www.nationalmcla.org

Mavro Imaging LLC 22 maple tree dr, Westampton NJ 08060 609-265-3803
Web: www.mavroimaging.com

Phone Fax

Meclabs LLC
1300 Marsh Landing Pkwy Ste 106, Jacksonville Beach FL 32250 800-517-5531
TF: 800-517-5531 ■ *Web:* www.meclabs.com

Mercer Engineering & Research
135 Osigian Blvd, Warner Robins GA 31088 478-953-6800
TF: 877-650-6372 ■ *Web:* www.merc-mercer.org

Merlino Foods po box 80069, Seattle WA 98108 206-723-4700
Web: www.merlino.com

Michigan Association of Insurance Agents
1141 Centennial Way, Lansing MI 48917 517-323-9473
Web: www.michagent.org

Michigan Bankers Association 507 S Grand Ave, Lansing MI 48933 517-485-3600
Web: www.mibankers.com

Michigan Manufacturers Association, The
620 S Capitol Ave, Lansing MI 48901 517-372-5900
Web: mimfg.org

Milyli Inc 415 n sangamon st, Chicago IL 60642 312-265-0136
Web: www.milyli.com

Minnesota Multi Housing Services Inc
1600 W 82nd St Ste 110, Bloomington MN 55431 952-854-8500
Web: www.mmha.com

Mobius Executive Leadership
177 worcester st, Wellesley Hills MA 02481 781-237-1362
Web: www.mobiusleadership.com

N.c. Center for Nonprofit Organizations Inc
1110 Navaho Dr Ste 200, Raleigh NC 27609 919-790-1555
Web: www.ncnonprofits.org

Nacm Chicago-midwest
3005 Tollview Dr, Rolling Meadows IL 60008 847-483-6400
Web: www.nacmchicago.org

Naffs 3301c State Rt 66 Ste 205, Neptune NJ 07753 732-922-3218
Web: naffs.org

Namgis First Nation 49 Atli St, Alert Bay BC V0N1A0 250-974-5556
Web: www.namgis.bc.ca

National Swine Registry
2639 Yeager Rd, West Lafayette IN 47906 765-463-3594
Web: www.nationalswine.com

National US-Arab Chamber of Commerce
1023 15th St NW Ste 400, Washington DC 20005 202-289-5920 289-5938
Web: www.nusacc.org

National US-Arab Chamber of Commerce
1101 17th St, NW Ste 1220, Washington DC 20036 713-963-4620 963-4609
Web: www.nusacc.org

Nazcare Inc 599 White Spar Rd, Prescott AZ 86303 928-442-9205
TF: 877-756-4090 ■ *Web:* www.nazcare.org

Nbcot 12 S Summit Ave Ste 100, Gaithersburg MD 20877 301-990-7979
Web: www.nbcot.org

Neal Systems Inc 122 Terry Dr, Newtown PA 18940 215-968-7577
Web: www.nealsystems.com

Nebraska Bankers Association Inc
233 S 13th St Ste 700, Lincoln NE 68508 402-474-1555
Web: www.nebankers.org

Nebraska Beef Council 1319 Central Ave, Kearney NE 68848 308-236-7551
TF: 800-421-5326 ■ *Web:* www.nebeef.org

Nebraska Farm Bureau Federation
5225 S 16th St, Lincoln NE 68512 402-421-4400
Web: www.nefb.org

NEDMA 396 Washington St Ste 387, Wellesley Hills MA 02481 781-237-1366
Web: www.nedma.com

Netherlands Chamber of Commerce
267 Fifth Ave, New York NY 10016 212-265-6460

New Tech Network 1250 Main St Ste 100, Napa CA 94559 707-253-6951
TF: 800-856-7038 ■ *Web:* www.newtechnetwork.org

New York Women in Film & Television
6 E 39th St Ste 1200, New York NY 10016 212-679-0870
Web: www.nywift.org

NJ Assn-Osteopathic
1 Distribution Way, Monmouth Junction NJ 08852 732-940-9000
Web: www.njosteo.com

Nofa-ny Certified Organic LLC
840 Upper Front St, Binghamton NY 13905 607-724-9851
Web: www.nofany.org

Norwegian-American Chamber of Commerce Inc, The
655 Third Ave Ste 1810, New York NY 10017 212-885-9737 885-9710
Web: www.naccusa.org

Norwegian-American Chamber of Commerce Southwest Chapter (NACC)
5219 Pine Arbor Dr, Houston TX 77066 281-537-6879 587-9284
Web: www.nacchouston.org

Ohio Contractors Association 1313 Dublin Rd, Columbus OH 43215 614-488-0724
TF: 800-229-1388 ■ *Web:* ohiocontractors.org

Ohio Health Care Association, The
55 Green Meadows Dr S PO Box 447, Lewis Center OH 43035 614-436-4154
Web: www.ohca.org

Ohio Manufacturers' Association
33 N High St, Columbus OH 43215 614-224-5111
TF: 800-662-4463 ■ *Web:* www.ohiomfg.com

Ohio Motorcycle Dealers Association
655 Metro Pl S Ste 270, Dublin OH 43017 614-766-9100
Web: oada.com

Oklahoma Alliance for Manufacturing Excellence Inc
525 S Main St Ste 210, Tulsa OK 74103 918-592-0722
Web: www.okalliance.com

Oklahoma Primary Care Association
4300 N Lincoln Blvd Ste 203, Oklahoma City OK 73105 405-424-2282
Web: okpca.publishpath.com/default.aspx

Ontario Association of Archietects
111 Moatfield Dr, North York ON M3B3L6 416-449-5756
Web: www.oaa.on.ca

Ontario Dental Nurses & Assistants Association
869 Dundas St, London ON N5W2Z8 519-679-2566
TF: 800-461-4348 ■ *Web:* odaa.org

Ontario Equestrian Federation
1 W Pearce St, Richmond Hill ON L4B3K3 905-709-6545
Web: horse.on.ca

Organization	City	State	Zip	Phone	Fax
Open Geospatial Consortium Inc 35 Main St Ste 5 *Web:* www.opengeospatial.org	Wayland	MA	01778	508-655-5858	
Oregon Bankers Association 777 13th St Se Ste 130 *Web:* oregonbankers.com	Salem	OR	97301	503-581-3522	
Oregon Primary Care Association 310 SW 4th Ave Ste 200 *Web:* www.orpca.org	Portland	OR	97204	503-228-8852	
Palm Beach Chamber of Commerce 400 Royal Palm Way *Web:* www.palmbeachchamber.com	Palm Beach	FL	33480	561-655-3282	
Pathways to Independence 25 Dundas St W *Web:* www.pathwaysind.com	Belleville	ON	K8P3M7	613-962-2541	
Pce Systems 28530 orchard Lk rd *Web:* www.pcesystems.com	Farmington hills	MI	48334	248-932-4888	
Pennag Industries Association 2215 Forest Hills Dr Ste 39 *Web:* pennag.com	Harrisburg	PA	17112	717-651-5920	
Portugal-US Chamber of Commerce 590 Fifth Ave 4th Fl *Web:* www.portugal-us.com	New York	NY	10036	212-354-4627	575-4737
Poteet Strawberry Festival Association 9199 N State Hwy 16 *TF:* 888-742-8144 ■ *Web:* www.strawberryfestival.com	Poteet	TX	78065	830-742-8144	
Project Lifesaver International Headquarters 815 Battlefield Blvd S *TF:* 877-580-5433 ■ *Web:* www.projectlifesaver.org	Chesapeake	VA	23322	757-546-5502	
PromaxBDA 1522 E Cloverfield Blvd *Web:* www.promaxbda.org	Santa Monica	CA	90404	310-788-7600	
Prores Group Inc 16526 W 78th St Ste 310 *Web:* proresgroup.com	Eden Prairie	MN	55346	952-449-1000	
Puerto Rican Chamber of Commerce of South Florida 3550 Biscayne Blvd Ste 306 *Web:* www.puertoricanchamber.com	Miami	FL	33137	305-571-8007	571-8007
Pump It Up Party 11411 W 183rd St *Web:* www.pumpitupparty.com	Orland Park	IL	60467	708-479-2220	
Quadis Technologies Inc 5925 s 56th st *Web:* www.summitgroupsoftware.com	Lincoln	NE	68516	402-423-4660	
Regional Plan Association Inc 4 Irving Place 7th Fl *Web:* www.rpa.org	New York	NY	10003	212-253-2727	
Representative of German Industry & Trade 1776 I St NW Ste 1000 *Web:* www.rgit-usa.com	Washington	DC	20006	202-659-4777	659-4779
RJ & Makay LLC 100 S Ridge St Ste 101 *Web:* www.rjandmakay.com	Breckenridge	CO	80424	970-306-0600	
Rlj Financial Services Inc 1788 Mitchell Rd Ste 102 *TF:* 800-240-1050 ■ *Web:* www.rljfinancial.com	Ceres	CA	95307	209-538-7758	
ROC USA LLC 7 Wall St *Web:* www.rocusa.org	Concord	NH	03301	603-224-6669	
Rosewood Care Center Holding Co 100 Rosewood Village Dr *Web:* www.rosewoodnursing.com	Swansea	IL	62226	618-236-1391	
Royal Canadian Yacht Club, The 141 St George St *Web:* rcyc.ca	Toronto	ON	M5R2L8	416-967-7245	
Safety Training Seminars 598 Vermont St *Web:* www.cprcpr.com	San Francisco	CA	94107	415-437-1600	
Santie Oil Co 126 Larcel Dr *TF:* 800-748-7788 ■ *Web:* www.santiemidwest.com	Sikeston	MO	63801	314-436-3569	
Scoliosis Research Society 555 E Wells St Ste 1100 *Web:* www.srs.org	Milwaukee	WI	53202	414-289-9107	
Sierra Club of Canada Bc Chapter 304-733 Johnson St *Web:* www.sierraclub.bc.ca	Victoria	BC	V8W3C7	250-386-5255	
SMC Business Councils 600 Cranberry Woods Dr Ste 190 *TF:* 800-553-3260 ■ *Web:* www.smc.org	Cranberry Township	PA	16066	412-371-1500	
SOCAN 41 Valleybrook Dr *TF:* 800-557-6226 ■ *Web:* www.socan.ca	Toronto	ON	M3B2S6	416-445-8700	
Spain-US Chamber of Commerce 80 Broad St Ste 2103 *Web:* www.spainuscc.org	New York	NY	10004	212-967-2170	564-1415
SPEECH Morphing SYSTEMS Inc 1320 White Oaks Rd *Web:* www.speechmorphing.com	Campbell	CA	95008	408-371-8014	
Speed Skating Canada 2781 Lancaster Rd *TF:* 877-572-4772 ■ *Web:* www.speedskating.ca	Ottawa	ON	K1B1A7	613-260-3660	
Sports Inc 333 Second Ave N *Web:* www.sportsinc.com	Lewistown	MT	59457	406-538-3496	
St. Louis Association of Realtors 12777 Olive Blvd *Web:* www.stlrealtors.com	St. Louis	MO	63141	314-576-0033	
Stanford Alumni Association 326 Galvez St *Web:* alumni137.stanford.edu/protocol_message.html?pem=8hftl3	Stanford	CA	94305	650-723-2021	
Suzuki Association of The Americas Inc 1900 Folsom St Ste 101 *TF:* 888-378-9854 ■ *Web:* www.suzukiassociation.org	Boulder	CO	80302	303-444-0948	
Swedish-American Chamber of Commerce Atlanta Inc (SACC) 4775 Peachtree Industrial Blvd Bldg 300 Ste 300 *Web:* www.sacc-georgia.org	Norcross	GA	30092	770-670-2480	
Swedish-American Chamber of Commerce Inc New York Chapter 570 Lexington Ave 20th Fl *Web:* www.saccny.org	New York	NY	10022	212-838-5530	755-7953
Swedish-American Chamber of Commerce San Diego 4475 Mission Blvd Ste 201 *Web:* www.sacc-sandiego.org	San Diego	CA	92109	858-598-4809	598-4809
Swedish-American Chamber of Commerce Washington DC Inc 2900 K St NW *Web:* sacc-usa.org/beta/dc	Washington	DC	20007	202-536-1570	
Swiss-American Chamber of Commerce *New York Chapter* 500 Fifth Ave Rm 1800 *Web:* www.amcham.ch	New York	NY	10110	212-246-7789	246-1366
Syncratec Solutions LLC 7 upton ln *Web:* www.syncratec.com	Yardley	PA	19067	267-266-5596	
Tahoe Keys Property Owners Association 356 Ala Wai Blvd *Web:* www.tahoekeyspoa.org	South Lake Tahoe	CA	96150	530-542-6444	
TerraLex Inc 2050 Coral Way Ste 601 *Web:* www.terralex.org	Miami	FL	33145	305-858-8825	
Texas Oil & Gas Association Inc 304 W 13th St *Web:* www.txoga.org	Austin	TX	78701	512-478-6631	
Theatre Historical Society of America 152 N York St 2nd Fl *Web:* www.historictheatres.org	Elmhurst	IL	60126	630-782-1800	
Toronto Construction Association 70 Leek Cres *Web:* www.tcaconnect.com/home.html	Richmond Hill	ON	L4B1H1	416-499-4000	
Toronto Law Office Management Association PO Box 1029 Toronto Dominion Ctr *Web:* www.tloma.com	Toronto	ON	M5K1P2	416-410-1979	
Tourism Industry Association of Pei 25 Queen St *Web:* www.tiapei.pe.ca	Charlottetown	PE	C1A4A2	902-566-5008	
Trackers Earth Inc 1424 se 76th ave *Web:* trackerspdx.com	Portland	OR	97202	503-345-3312	
TransferOnline 512 SE Salmon St *Web:* www.transferonline.com	Portland	OR	97214	503-227-2950	
Travel Goods Association 301 N Harrison St Ste 412 *TF:* 877-842-1938 ■ *Web:* www.travel-goods.org	Princeton	NJ	08540	877-842-1938	
Trusted Computing Group 3855 SW 153rd Dr *Web:* www.trustedcomputinggroup.org	Beaverton	OR	97006	503-619-0562	
Tsleil-Waututh Nation, The 3075 Takaya Dr *Web:* www.twnation.ca	North Vancouver	BC	V7H3A8	604-929-3454	
Turfgrass Producers International 1855-A Hicks Rd *Web:* www.turfgrasssod.org	Rolling Meadows	IL	60008	847-705-9898	
Uni-Bell PVC Pipe Association 2711 LBJ Fwy Ste 1000 *Web:* www.uni-bell.org	Dallas	TX	75234	972-243-3902	
US-Angola Chamber of Commerce 1100 17th St NW Ste 1000 *Web:* www.us-angola.org	Washington	DC	20036	202-857-0789	
US-Austrian Chamber of Commerce 1133 Ave of the Americas 16th Fl *Web:* usaustrianchamber.org	New York	NY	10036	212-819-0117	
US-Mexico Chamber of Commerce 1300 Pennsylvania Ave NW Ste 0003 *Web:* www.usmcoc.org	Washington	DC	20004	202-312-1520	312-1530
US-Mexico Chamber of Commerce California Pacific Chapter 2450 Colorado Ave Ste 400E *TF:* 800-997-9148 ■ *Web:* www.usmcocca.org	Santa Monica	CA	90404	310-586-7901	586-7800
Vietnamese-American Chamber of Commerce of Hawaii PO Box 240352 *Web:* www.vacch.org	Honolulu	HI	96824	808-545-1889	
Volunteer Calgary 1202 Centre St Se *Web:* www.volunteercalgary.ab.ca	Calgary	AB	T2G5A5	403-265-5633	
Wireless Network Group Warehouse 220 w Pkwy *Web:* www.wnginc.com	Pompton Plains	NJ	07444	973-831-4015	
Wisconsin Hospital Association Inc 5510 Research Park Dr *Web:* www.wha.org	Fitchburg	WI	53711	608-274-1820	
Women Lawyers Association of Los Angeles 634 S Spring St Ste 617 *Web:* www.wlala.org	Los Angeles	CA	90014	213-892-8982	
Wyoming Hospital Association 2005 Warren Ave *Web:* www.wyohospitals.com	Cheyenne	WY	82001	307-632-9344	
Ymca Canada 42 Charles St E *Web:* www.ymca.ca	Toronto	ON	M4Y1T4	416-967-9622	
Young Drivers of Canada Inc 1 James St S Ste 300 *Web:* www.yd.com	Hamilton	ON	L8P4R5	905-529-5501	

139 CHAMBERS OF COMMERCE - US - LOCAL

See Also Civic & Political Organizations p. 1758

Chambers listed here represent areas with a population of 25,000 or more. Listings are organized by states and then are alphabetized within each state grouping according to the name of the city in which each chamber is located.

Alabama

Organization	City	State	Zip	Phone	Fax
Alexander City Chamber of Commerce 120 Tallapoosa St *Web:* www.alexandercity.org	Alexander City	AL	35010	256-234-3461	234-0094
Calhoun County Chamber of Commerce 1330 Quintard Ave *Web:* www.calhounchamber.com	Anniston	AL	36201	256-237-3536	237-0126
Greater Limestone County Chamber of Commerce 101 S Beaty St *TF:* 866-953-6565 ■ *Web:* www.tourathens.com	Athens	AL	35611	256-232-2600	232-2609
Auburn Chamber of Commerce 714 E Glenn Ave PO Box 1370 *Web:* www.auburnchamber.com	Auburn	AL	36831	334-887-7011	821-5500
North Baldwin Chamber of Commerce 301 McMeans Ave *Web:* www.northbaldwinchamber.com	Bay Minette	AL	36507	251-937-5665	937-5670

Chamber	City	State	Zip	Phone	Fax
Bessemer Area Chamber of Commerce 321 N 18th St *TF:* 888-423-7736 ■ *Web:* www.bessemerchamber.com	Bessemer	AL	35020	205-425-3253	425-4979
Birmingham Business Alliance 505 N 20th St Ste 200 *Web:* birminghambusinessalliance.com	Birmingham	AL	35203	205-324-2100	324-2560
Cullman Area Chamber of Commerce 301 Second Ave SW *TF:* 800-313-5114 ■ *Web:* www.cullmanchamber.org	Cullman	AL	35055	256-734-0454	737-7443
Eastern Shore Chamber of Commerce 29750 Larry Dee Cawyer Dr PO Box 310 *Web:* www.eschamber.com	Daphne	AL	36526	251-621-8222	621-8001
Decatur-Morgan County Chamber of Commerce 515 Sixth Ave NE *Web:* www.dcc.org	Decatur	AL	35601	256-353-5312	353-2384
Dothan Area Chamber of Commerce 102 Jamestown Blvd *TF:* 800-221-1027 ■ *Web:* www.dothan.com	Dothan	AL	36301	334-792-5138	794-4796
Eufaula/Barbour County Chamber of Commerce 333 E Broad St *TF:* 800-524-7529 ■ *Web:* eufaulachamber.com	Eufaula	AL	36027	334-687-6664	
Shoals Chamber of Commerce 20 Hightower Pl PO Box 1331	Florence	AL	35630	256-764-4661	331-5386
South Baldwin Chamber of Commerce (SBCC) 112 W Laurel Ave PO Box 1117 *TF:* 877-461-3712 ■ *Web:* www.southbaldwinchamber.com	Foley	AL	36535	251-943-3291	943-6810
Gadsden & Etowah County Chamber 1 Commerce Sq *TF:* 800-659-2955 ■ *Web:* www.gadsdenchamber.com	Gadsden	AL	35901	256-543-3472	543-9887
Greenville Area Chamber of Commerce 1 Depot Sq *TF:* 800-959-0717 ■ *Web:* www.greenvillealchamber.com	Greenville	AL	36037	334-382-3251	
Hoover Chamber of Commerce PO Box 36005 *Web:* www.hooverchamber.org	Hoover	AL	35236	205-988-5672	988-8383
Chamber of Commerce of Huntsville/Madison County 225 Church St *Web:* www.huntsvillealabamausa.com	Huntsville	AL	35801	256-535-2000	535-2015
Walker County Chamber of Commerce 204 19th St E Ste 101 *TF General:* 800-384-4571 ■ *Web:* www.walkerchamber.us	Jasper	AL	35501	205-384-4571	
Greater Valley Area Chamber of Commerce 2102 S Broad Ave PO Box 205 *Web:* www.greatervalleyarea.com	Lanett	AL	36863	334-642-1411	642-1410
Mobile Area Chamber of Commerce 451 Government St *TF:* 800-422-6951 ■ *Web:* www.mobilechamber.com	Mobile	AL	36602	251-433-6951	432-1143
Monroeville Area Chamber of Commerce 86 Alabama 21 *Web:* www.monroecountyal.com	Monroeville	AL	36460	251-743-2879	743-2189
Montgomery Area Chamber of Commerce 41 Commerce St PO Box 79 *Web:* www.montgomerychamber.com	Montgomery	AL	36104	334-834-5200	265-4745
Blount County-Oneonta Chamber of Commerce 225 Second Ave E *Web:* bocc.publishpath.com	Oneonta	AL	35121	205-274-2153	274-2099
Ozark Area Chamber of Commerce 294 Painter Ave *TF:* 800-582-8497 ■ *Web:* www.ozarkalchamber.com	Ozark	AL	36360	334-774-9321	774-8736
Greater Shelby County Chamber of Commerce 1301 County Services Dr *Web:* www.shelbychamber.org	Pelham	AL	35124	205-663-4542	663-4524
Phenix City-Russell County Chamber of Commerce 1107 Broad St *TF:* 800-892-2248 ■ *Web:* www.pc-rcchamber.com	Phenix City	AL	36867	334-298-3639	
Franklin County Chamber of Commerce 103 N Jackson Ave *Web:* www.franklincountychamber.org	Russellville	AL	35653	256-332-1760	332-1740
Greater Jackson County Chamber of Commerce PO Box 973 *TF:* 800-259-5508 ■ *Web:* www.jacksoncountychamber.com	Scottsboro	AL	35768	256-259-5500	259-4447
Selma-Dallas County Chamber of Commerce 912 Selma Ave *TF:* 800-457-3562 ■ *Web:* www.selmaalabama.com	Selma	AL	36701	334-875-7241	875-7142
Greater Talladega Area Chamber of Commerce 210 E St S PO Box A *Web:* www.talladegachamber.com	Talladega	AL	35160	256-362-9075	362-9093
Chamber of Commerce of West Alabama 2200 University Blvd *Web:* www.tuscaloosachamber.com	Tuscaloosa	AL	35401	205-758-7588	391-0565

Alaska

Chamber	City	State	Zip	Phone	Fax
Anchorage Chamber of Commerce 1016 W Sixth Ave Ste 303 *Web:* www.anchoragechamber.org	Anchorage	AK	99501	907-272-2401	272-4117
Fairbanks Chamber of Commerce 100 Cushman St Ste 102 *Web:* www.fairbankschamber.org	Fairbanks	AK	99701	907-452-1105	456-6968
Juneau Chamber of Commerce 9301 Glacier Hwy Ste 110 *TF:* 888-581-2201 ■ *Web:* www.juneauchamber.com	Juneau	AK	99801	907-463-3488	463-3489

Arizona

Chamber	City	State	Zip	Phone	Fax
Apache Junction Chamber of Commerce 567 W Apache Trl *Web:* www.ajchamber.com	Apache Junction	AZ	85220	480-982-3141	982-3234
Bullhead Area Chamber of Commerce 1251 Hwy 95 *TF:* 800-987-7457 ■ *Web:* bullheadareachamber.com	Bullhead City	AZ	86429	928-754-4121	754-5514
Chandler Chamber of Commerce 25 S Arizona Pl Ste 201 *TF:* 800-963-4571 ■ *Web:* www.chandlerchamber.com	Chandler	AZ	85225	480-963-4571	963-0188
Cottonwood Chamber of Commerce 1010 S Main St *Web:* www.cottonwoodchamberaz.org	Cottonwood	AZ	86326	928-634-7593	634-7594
Flagstaff Chamber of Commerce 101 W Rt 66 *Web:* www.flagstaffchamber.com	Flagstaff	AZ	86001	928-774-4505	779-1209
Gilbert Chamber of Commerce 119 N Gilbert Rd Ste 101 PO Box 527 **Fax Area Code:* 602 ■ *Web:* www.gilbertaz.com	Gilbert	AZ	85299	480-892-0056	892-1980*
Southwest Valley Chamber of Commerce 289 N Litchfield Rd *Web:* www.southwestvalleychamber.org	Goodyear	AZ	85338	623-932-2260	932-9057
Kingman Area Chamber of Commerce 120 W Andy Devine Ave *Web:* www.kingmanchamber.com	Kingman	AZ	86401	928-753-6253	753-1049
Lake Havasu Area Chamber of Commerce 314 London Bridge Rd *TF:* 800-307-3610 ■ *Web:* www.havasuchamber.com	Lake Havasu City	AZ	86403	928-855-4115	680-0010
Mesa Chamber of Commerce 120 N Ctr St *Web:* www.mesachamber.org	Mesa	AZ	85201	480-969-1307	827-0727
Nogales Chamber of Commerce 123 W Kino Pk *Web:* thenogaleschamber.com	Nogales	AZ	85621	520-287-3685	
Rim Country Regional Chamber of Commerce 100 W Main St *TF:* 800-249-2678 ■ *Web:* www.rimcountrychamber.com	Payson	AZ	85547	928-474-4515	474-8812
Greater Phoenix Chamber of Commerce 201 N Central Ave Ste 2700 *Web:* www.phoenixchamber.com	Phoenix	AZ	85004	602-495-2195	495-8913
Prescott Chamber of Commerce 117 W Goodwin St *TF:* 800-266-7534 ■ *Web:* www.prescott.org	Prescott	AZ	86303	928-445-2000	445-0068
Prescott Valley Chamber of Commerce 3001 N Main St Ste 2A *TF:* 800-355-0843 ■ *Web:* www.pvchamber.org	Prescott Valley	AZ	86314	928-772-8857	772-4267
Graham County Chamber of Commerce 1111 Thatcher Blvd *TF:* 888-837-1841 ■ *Web:* www.graham-chamber.com	Safford	AZ	85546	928-428-2511	428-0744
Scottsdale Area Chamber of Commerce 7501 E McCormick Pkwy Ste 202-N *Web:* www.scottsdalechamber.com	Scottsdale	AZ	85258	480-355-2700	355-2710
Greater Sierra Vista Area Chamber of Commerce 21 E Wilcox Dr *TF:* 800-288-3861 ■ *Web:* www.sierravistachamber.org	Sierra Vista	AZ	85635	520-458-6940	452-0878
Tempe Chamber of Commerce 909 E Apache Blvd *Web:* www.tempechamber.org	Tempe	AZ	85281	480-967-7891	966-5365
Tucson Metropolitan Chamber of Commerce 465 W St Mary's Rd PO Box 991 *Web:* www.tucsonchamber.org	Tucson	AZ	85702	520-792-2250	882-5704
Yuma County Chamber of Commerce 180 W First St Ste A *TF:* 877-782-0438 ■ *Web:* www.yumachamber.org	Yuma	AZ	85364	928-782-2567	343-0038

Arkansas

Chamber	City	State	Zip	Phone	Fax
Bentonville/Bella Vista Chamber of Commerce (BBVCC) 200 E Central St PO Box 330 *Web:* www.bbvchamber.com	Bentonville	AR	72712	479-273-2841	273-2180
Berryville Chamber of Commerce 506 S Main PO Box 402 *Web:* www.berryvillear.com	Berryville	AR	72616	870-423-3704	
Conway Area Chamber of Commerce 900 Oak St *Web:* www.conwaychamber.org	Conway	AR	72032	501-327-7788	327-7790
Fayetteville Chamber of Commerce 21 W Mtn Ste 300 *Web:* www.fayettevillear.com	Fayetteville	AR	72701	479-521-1710	521-1791
Fort Smith Regional Chamber of Commerce 612 Garrison Ave *Web:* www.fortsmithchamber.org	Fort Smith	AR	72901	479-783-3111	783-6110
Phillips County Chamber of Commerce 111 Hickory Hill Dr PO Box 447 *Web:* www.phillipscountychamber.org	Helena	AR	72342	870-338-8327	
Greater Hot Springs Chamber of Commerce 659 Ouachita Ave *Web:* www.hotspringschamber.com	Hot Springs	AR	71901	501-321-1700	321-3551
Jacksonville Chamber of Commerce 200 Dupree Dr *TF:* 888-857-3019 ■ *Web:* www.jacksonville-arkansas.com	Jacksonville	AR	72076	501-982-1511	982-1464
Jonesboro Regional Chamber of Commerce PO Box 789 *Web:* jonesborochamber.com	Jonesboro	AR	72403	870-932-6691	933-5758
Little Rock Regional Chamber of Commerce 1 Chamber Plz *Web:* www.littlerockchamber.com	Little Rock	AR	72201	501-374-2001	374-6018
Magnolia-Columbia County Chamber of Commerce 211 W Main St PO Box 866 *Web:* www.magnoliachamber.com	Magnolia	AR	71753	870-234-4352	234-9291
Mountain Home Area Chamber of Commerce 1023 Hwy 62 *TF:* 800-822-3536 ■ *Web:* www.enjoymountainhome.com	Mountain Home	AR	72653	870-425-5111	425-4446
Paragould Regional Chamber of Commerce 300 W Ct St PO Box 124 *Web:* www.paragould.org	Paragould	AR	72451	870-236-7684	236-7142
Rogers-Lowell Area Chamber of Commerce 317 W Walnut St *TF:* 800-364-1240 ■ *Web:* www.rogerslowell.com	Rogers	AR	72756	479-636-1240	636-5485
Russellville Area Chamber of Commerce 708 W Main St *TF:* 855-678-2447 ■ *Web:* www.russellvillechamber.org	Russellville	AR	72801	479-968-2530	968-5894
Springdale Chamber of Commerce 202 W Emma **Fax Area Code:* 202 ■ *Web:* www.springdale.com	Springdale	AR	72765	479-872-2222	228-1371*
West Memphis Chamber of Commerce 108 W Broadway *Web:* www.wmcoc.com	West Memphis	AR	72301	870-735-1134	735-6283

California

Organization	City	State	ZIP	Phone	Fax
Alameda Chamber of Commerce 2210D S Shore Ctr	Alameda	CA	94501	510-522-0414	522-7677
Web: www.alamedachamber.com					
Alhambra Chamber of Commerce 104 S First St	Alhambra	CA	91801	626-282-8481	282-5596
Web: www.alhambrachamber.org					
Altadena Chamber of Commerce 730 E Altadena Dr	Altadena	CA	91001	626-794-3988	
Web: altadenachamber.org					
Anaheim Chamber of Commerce 2400 E Katella Ave Ste 725	Anaheim	CA	92806	714-758-0222	758-0468
Web: www.anaheimchamber.org					
Antioch Chamber of Commerce 101 H St #4	Antioch	CA	94509	925-757-1800	757-5286
Web: www.antiochchamber.com					
Apple Valley Chamber of Commerce 16010 Apple Vly Rd	Apple Valley	CA	92307	760-242-2753	242-0303
Web: avchamber.org					
Aptos Chamber of Commerce 7605-A Old Dominion Ct	Aptos	CA	95003	831-688-1467	688-6961
Web: www.aptoschamber.com					
Arcadia Chamber of Commerce 388 W Huntington Dr	Arcadia	CA	91007	626-447-2159	445-0273
Web: arcadiacachamber.org					
Atascadero Chamber of Commerce 6904 El Camino Real	Atascadero	CA	93422	805-466-2044	466-9218
TF: 877-204-9830 ■ *Web:* www.atascaderochamber.org					
Atwater Chamber of Commerce 1181 Third St	Atwater	CA	95301	209-358-4251	
TF: 844-269-9688 ■ *Web:* atwaterchamberofcommerce.com					
Auburn Area Chamber of Commerce 601 Lincoln Way	Auburn	CA	95603	530-885-5616	885-5854
TF: 800-310-2355 ■ *Web:* www.auburnchamber.net					
Azusa Chamber of Commerce 240 W Foothill Blvd	Azusa	CA	91702	626-334-1507	334-5217
Web: www.azusachamber.org					
Greater Bakersfield Chamber of Commerce 1725 Eye St	Bakersfield	CA	93301	661-327-4421	327-8751
Web: www.bakersfieldchamber.org					
Kern County Board of Trade 2101 Oak St	Bakersfield	CA	93301	661-868-5376	868-5376
TF General: 800-787-9920 ■ *Web:* www.visitkern.com					
Beaumont Chamber of Commerce 726 Beaumont Ave	Beaumont	CA	92223	951-845-9541	769-9080
Web: www.beaumontcachamber.com					
Bell Chamber of Commerce 4401 Gage Ave	Bell	CA	90201	323-560-8755	560-2060
Bell Gardens Chamber of Commerce 7535 Perry Rd	Bell Gardens	CA	90201	562-806-2355	
Web: www.bellgardenschamber.org					
Bellflower Chamber of Commerce 16730 Bellflower Blvd	Bellflower	CA	90706	562-867-1744	866-7545
Web: www.bellflowerchamber.com					
Belmont Chamber of Commerce 1059 Alameda De Las Pulgas	Belmont	CA	94002	650-595-8696	204-6232
Web: www.belmontchamber.org					
Benicia Chamber of Commerce 601 First St Ste 100	Benicia	CA	94510	707-745-2120	745-2275
Web: www.beniciachamber.com					
Berkeley Chamber of Commerce 1834 University Ave	Berkeley	CA	94703	510-549-7000	549-1789
TF: 800-847-4823 ■ *Web:* www.berkeleychamber.com					
Beverly Hills Chamber of Commerce Santa Monica Blvd 2nd Fl	Beverly Hills	CA	90210	310-248-1000	248-1020
Web: www.beverlyhillschamber.com					
Blythe Area Chamber of Commerce 207 E Hobsonway	Blythe	CA	92225	760-922-8166	922-4010
Web: www.blythechamberofcommerce.com					
Brea Chamber of Commerce 1 Civic Ctr Cir	Brea	CA	92821	714-529-4938	
Web: www.breachamber.com					
Burbank Chamber of Commerce 200 W Magnolia Blvd	Burbank	CA	91502	818-846-3111	846-0109
Web: www.burbankchamber.org					
Burlingame Chamber of Commerce 417 California Dr	Burlingame	CA	94010	650-344-1735	344-1763
Web: www.burlingamechamber.org					
Camarillo Chamber of Commerce 2400 Ventura Blvd	Camarillo	CA	93010	805-484-4383	484-1395
Web: camarillochamber.org					
Campbell Chamber of Commerce 1628 W Campbell Ave	Campbell	CA	95008	408-378-6252	378-0192
Web: campbellchamber.net					
Canoga Park/West Hills Chamber of Commerce 7248 Owensmouth Ave	Canoga Park	CA	91303	818-884-4222	
Web: www.cpwhchamber.org					
Carlsbad Chamber of Commerce 5934 Priestly Dr	Carlsbad	CA	92008	760-931-8400	931-9153
Web: www.carlsbad.org					
Carmichael Chamber of Commerce 6825 Fair Oaks Blvd Ste 100	Carmichael	CA	95608	916-481-1002	481-1003
Web: carmichaelchamber.com					
Carson Chamber of Commerce 530 E Del Amo Blvd	Carson	CA	90746	310-217-4590	217-4591
Web: www.carsonchamber.com					
Castro Valley Chamber of Commerce 3467 Castro Vly Blvd	Castro Valley	CA	94546	510-537-5300	537-5335
Web: www.edenareachamber.com					
Cathedral City Chamber of Commerce 68950 E Palm Canyon Dr	Cathedral City	CA	92234	760-328-1213	321-0659
Web: www.cathedralcitycc.com					
Ceres Chamber of Commerce 2491 Lawrence St	Ceres	CA	95307	209-537-2601	
Web: www.cereschamber.org					
Cerritos Chamber of Commerce 13259 S St	Cerritos	CA	90703	562-467-0800	467-0840
Web: www.cerritos.org					
Chatsworth Chamber of Commerce 10038 Old Depot Plz Rd	Chatsworth	CA	91311	818-341-2428	341-4930
Web: www.chatsworthchamber.com					

Organization	City	State	ZIP	Phone	Fax
Chico Chamber of Commerce 441 Main St	Chico	CA	95928	530-891-5556	891-3613
TF: 800-852-8570 ■ *Web:* www.chicochamber.com					
Chino Valley Chamber of Commerce 13150 Seventh St	Chino	CA	91710	909-627-6177	627-4180
Web: chinovalleychamberofcommerce.com					
Chula Vista Chamber of Commerce 233 Fourth Ave	Chula Vista	CA	91910	619-420-6603	420-1269
Web: www.chulavistachamber.org					
Citrus Heights Chamber of Commerce 7115 Greenback Ln # A	Citrus Heights	CA	95621	916-722-4545	722-4543
Web: www.chchamber.com					
Claremont Chamber of Commerce 205 Yale Ave	Claremont	CA	91711	909-624-1681	624-6629
Web: www.claremontchamber.org					
Clovis Chamber of Commerce 325 Pollasky Ave	Clovis	CA	93612	559-299-7363	299-2969
Web: www.clovischamber.com					
Colton Chamber of Commerce 655 N La Cadena Dr	Colton	CA	92324	909-825-2222	824-1650
Web: coltonchamber.org					
Greater Concord Chamber of Commerce 2280 Diamond Blvd Ste 200	Concord	CA	94520	925-685-1181	685-5623
TF: 800-427-8686 ■ *Web:* www.concordchamber.com					
Corona Chamber of Commerce 904 E Sixth St	Corona	CA	92879	951-737-3350	737-3531
Web: www.mychamber.org					
Coronado Chamber of Commerce 875 Orange Ave Ste 102	Coronado	CA	92118	619-435-9260	522-6577
Web: www.coronadochamber.com					
Costa Mesa Chamber of Commerce 1700 Adams Ave Ste 101	Costa Mesa	CA	92626	714-885-9092	885-9094
Web: www.costamesachamber.com					
Covina Chamber of Commerce 935 W Badillo St Ste 100	Covina	CA	91722	626-967-4191	966-9660
Web: www.covina.org					
Culver City Chamber of Commerce 6000 Sepulveda Blvd Ste 1260	Culver City	CA	90230	310-287-3850	
Web: www.culvercitychamber.com					
Cupertino Chamber of Commerce 20455 Silverado Ave	Cupertino	CA	95014	408-252-7054	
Web: cupertino-chamber.org					
Cypress Chamber of Commerce 5550 Cerritos Ave Ste D	Cypress	CA	90630	714-827-2430	
Web: www.cypresschamber.org					
Daly City-Colma Chamber of Commerce 355 Gellert Blvd Ste 138	Daly City	CA	94015	650-755-3900	755-5160
Web: www.dalycity-colmachamber.org					
Dana Point Chamber of Commerce 24681 La Plz Ste 115	Dana Point	CA	92629	949-496-1555	
Web: www.danapoint-chamber.com					
Davis Chamber of Commerce 604 3 St	Davis	CA	95616	530-756-5160	756-5190
Web: www.davischamber.com					
San Diego Coastal Chamber of Commerce 1104 Camino Del Mar Ste 1	Del Mar	CA	92014	858-755-4844	793-5293
Web: www.delmarchamber.org					
Downey Chamber of Commerce 11131 Brookshire Ave	Downey	CA	90241	562-923-2191	869-0461
TF: 888-201-0995 ■ *Web:* www.downeychamber.com					
Dublin Chamber of Commerce 7080 Donlon Way Ste 110	Dublin	CA	94568	925-828-6200	828-4247
Web: www.dublinchamberofcommerce.org					
San Diego East County Chamber of Commerce 201 S Magnolia Ave	El Cajon	CA	92020	619-440-6161	440-6164
Web: eastcountychamber.org					
El Centro Chamber of Commerce & Visitors Bureau 1095 S Fourth St	El Centro	CA	92243	760-352-3681	352-3246
Web: www.elcentrochamber.org					
El Monte/South El Monte Chamber of Commerce 10505 Valley Blvd Ste 312	El Monte	CA	91731	626-443-0180	
Web: www.emsem.com					
Encinitas Chamber of Commerce 527 Encinitas Blvd	Encinitas	CA	92024	760-753-6041	753-6270
TF: 800-953-6041 ■ *Web:* www.encinitaschamber.com					
Encino Chamber of Commerce 4933 Balboa Blvd	Encino	CA	91316	818-789-4711	789-2485
Web: encinochamber.org					
Escondido Chamber of Commerce 720 N Broadway	Escondido	CA	92025	760-745-2125	745-1183
Web: www.escondidochamber.org					
Greater Eureka Chamber of Commerce, The 2112 Broadway	Eureka	CA	95501	707-442-3738	442-0079
TF: 866-267-4255 ■ *Web:* www.eurekachamber.com					
Fairfield-Suisun Chamber of Commerce 1111 Webster St	Fairfield	CA	94533	707-425-4625	425-0826
Web: www.ffsc-chamber.com					
Fallbrook Chamber of Commerce 111 S Main Ave	Fallbrook	CA	92028	760-728-5845	728-4031
Web: www.fallbrookchamberofcommerce.org					
Folsom Chamber of Commerce 200 Wool St	Folsom	CA	95630	916-985-2698	985-4117
Web: www.folsomchamber.com					
Fontana Chamber of Commerce 8491 Sierra Ave	Fontana	CA	92335	909-822-4433	822-6238
Web: www.fontanachamber.org					
Mendocino Coast Chamber of Commerce 217 S Main St PO Box 1141	Fort Bragg	CA	95437	707-961-6300	964-2056
TF: 800-382-7244 ■ *Web:* www.mendocinocoast.com					
Foster City Chamber of Commerce 1031 E Hillsdale Blvd Ste F	Foster City	CA	94404	650-573-7600	573-5201
Web: www.fostercitychamber.com					
Fountain Valley Chamber of Commerce 10055 Slater Ave Ste 250	Fountain Valley	CA	92708	714-962-3822	
Web: www.fvchamber.com					
Fremont Chamber of Commerce 39488 Stevenson Pl Ste 100	Fremont	CA	94539	510-795-2244	795-2240
Web: www.fremontbusiness.com					
Fresno Chamber of Commerce 2331 Fresno St	Fresno	CA	93721	559-495-4800	495-4811
Web: www.fresnochamber.com					
Fullerton Chamber of Commerce 444 N Harbor Blvd Ste 200	Fullerton	CA	92832	714-871-3100	871-2871
Web: www.nocchamber.com					

Phone Fax

Garden Grove Chamber of Commerce
12866 Main St Ste 102 .... Garden Grove CA 92840 714-638-7950 636-6672
TF: 800-959-5560 ■ *Web:* gardengrovechamber.com

Gardena Valley Chamber of Commerce
1204 W Gardena Blvd Ste E .... Gardena CA 90247 310-532-9905 329-7307
Web: www.gardenachamber.com

Gilroy Chamber of Commerce 7471 Monterey St. .... Gilroy CA 95020 408-842-6437 842-6010
Web: www.gilroy.org

Glendale Chamber of Commerce
200 S Louise St .... Glendale CA 91205 818-240-7870 240-2872
Web: www.glendalechamber.com

Glendora Chamber of Commerce
131 E Foothill Blvd .... Glendora CA 91741 626-963-4128 914-4822
TF: 800-926-4478 ■ *Web:* www.glendora-chamber.org

Goleta Valley Chamber of Commerce
271 N Fairview Ave Ste 104 .... Goleta CA 93117 805-967-2500
TF: 800-646-5382 ■ *Web:* www.goletavalley.com

Granada Hills Chamber of Commerce
17723 Chatsworth St .... Granada Hills CA 91344 818-368-3235
Web: www.granadachamber.com

Hanford Chamber of Commerce 113 Ct St .... Hanford CA 93230 559-582-0483
Web: www.hanfordchamber.com

Hawthorne Chamber of Commerce
12519 Crenshaw Blvd .... Hawthorne CA 90250 310-676-1163 676-7661
TF: 800-977-4770 ■ *Web:* www.hawthorne-chamber.com

Hayward Chamber of Commerce 22561 Main St .... Hayward CA 94541 510-537-2424
Web: www.hayward.org

Hemet Jacinto Valley Chamber of Commerce
615 N San Jacinto St .... Hemet CA 92543 951-658-3211 766-5013
Web: hsjvc.com

Hesperia Chamber of Commerce
16816 Main St Ste D .... Hesperia CA 92345 760-244-2135 244-1333
TF: 855-574-7337 ■ *Web:* www.hesperiachamber.org

Highland Area Chamber of Commerce
27255 Messina St .... Highland CA 92346 909-864-4073 864-4583
Web: www.highlandchamber.org

Hollywood Chamber of Commerce
7018 Hollywood Blvd .... Hollywood CA 90028 323-469-8311
Web: walkoffame.com

Huntington Beach Chamber of Commerce
2134 Main St Ste 100 .... Huntington Beach CA 92648 714-536-8888 960-7654
Web: hbchamber.com

Greater Huntington Park Area Chamber of Commerce
6330 Pacific Blvd Ste 208 .... Huntington Park CA 90255 323-585-1155 585-2176
Web: www.hpchamber.org

Imperial Beach Chamber of Commerce & Visitors Bureau
702 Seacoast Dr .... Imperial Beach CA 91932 619-424-3151 424-3008
Web: www.ib-chamber.com

Indio Chamber of Commerce 82921 Indio Blvd .... Indio CA 92201 760-347-0676
Web: www.indiochamber.org

Inglewood Chamber of Commerce
330 E Queen St .... Inglewood CA 90301 310-677-1121 677-1001
Web: www.inglewoodchamber.com

Irvine Chamber of Commerce
2485 McCabe Way Ste 150 .... Irvine CA 92614 949-660-9112 660-0829
TF General: 800-321-2211 ■ *Web:* www.irvinechamber.com

Orange County Business Council
2 Pk Plz Ste 100 .... Irvine CA 92614 949-476-2242 476-9240
Web: www.ocbc.org

Amador County Chamber of Commerce
115 Main St PO Box 596 .... Jackson CA 95642 209-223-0350 223-4425
TF General: 800-822-9466 ■ *Web:* amadorchamber.com

Crescenta Valley Chamber of Commerce
3131 Foothill Blvd Ste D .... La Crescenta CA 91214 818-248-4957 248-9625
Web: www.crescentavalleychamber.org

La Habra Area Chamber of Commerce
321 E La Habra Blvd .... La Habra CA 90631 562-697-1704 697-8359
Web: www.lahabrachamber.com

La Jolla Town Council
1150 Silverado St Ste 2131 .... La Jolla CA 92037 858-454-1444
Web: lajollatowncouncil.org

La Verne Chamber of Commerce
2078 Bonita Ave .... La Verne CA 91750 909-593-5265 596-0579
Web: www.lavernechamber.org

Laguna Beach Chamber of Commerce
357 Glenneyre St .... Laguna Beach CA 92651 949-494-1018
Web: www.lagunabeachchamber.org

Laguna Niguel Chamber of Commerce
28062 Forbes Rd Ste C .... Laguna Niguel CA 92677 949-363-0136 363-9026
Web: www.lnchamber.com

Lake Elsinore Valley Chamber of Commerce
132 W Graham Ave .... Lake Elsinore CA 92530 951-245-8848 245-9127
Web: www.lakeelsinorechamber.com

Lakeport Regional Chamber of Commerce
875 Lakeport Blvd PO Box 295 .... Lakeport CA 95453 707-263-5092 263-5104
TF: 866-525-3767 ■ *Web:* www.lakecochamber.com

Lakeside Chamber of Commerce 9924 Vine St .... Lakeside CA 92040 619-561-1031 561-7951
Web: lakesidechamber.org

Lakewood Chamber of Commerce
24 Lakewood Ctr Mall .... Lakewood CA 90712 562-531-9733
Web: www.lakewoodchamber.com

Antelope Valley Chambers of Commerce
554 W Lancaster Blvd .... Lancaster CA 93534 661-948-4518 949-1212
Web: lancasterchamber.org

Livermore Chamber of Commerce
2157 First St .... Livermore CA 94550 925-447-1606 447-1641
Web: www.livermorechamber.org

Lodi District Chamber of Commerce
35 S School St .... Lodi CA 95240 209-367-7840 369-9344
Web: www.lodichamber.com

Lompoc Valley Chamber of Commerce & Visitors Bureau
PO Box 626 .... Lompoc CA 93438 805-736-4567 737-0453
TF: 800-240-0999 ■ *Web:* www.lompoc.com

Phone Fax

Long Beach Area Chamber of Commerce
1 World Trade Ctr Ste 206 .... Long Beach CA 90831 562-436-1251 436-7099
Web: www.lbchamber.com

Los Altos Chamber of Commerce
321 University Ave .... Los Altos CA 94022 650-948-1455 948-6238
Web: www.losaltoschamber.org

Century City Chamber of Commerce
2029 Century Pk E Concourse Level .... Los Angeles CA 90067 310-553-2222 553-4623
TF: 800-462-7899 ■ *Web:* www.centurycitycc.com

Eagle Rock Chamber of Commerce
PO Box 41354 .... Los Angeles CA 90041 323-257-2197 257-4245
Web: www.eaglerockchamberofcommerce.com

East Los Angeles Chamber of Commerce
4716 E Cesar Chavez Ave .... Los Angeles CA 90022 323-263-2005
Web: www.eastlachamber.com

LAX Coastal Area Chamber of Commerce
9100 S Sepulveda Blvd Ste 210 .... Los Angeles CA 90045 310-645-5151 645-0130
Web: laxcoastal.com

Lincoln Heights Chamber of Commerce
2716 N Broadway Ste 210 .... Los Angeles CA 90031 323-221-6571 221-1513

Los Angeles Area Chamber of Commerce
350 S Bixel St .... Los Angeles CA 90017 213-580-7500 580-7511
Web: www.lachamber.com

Los Gatos Chamber of Commerce
349 N Santa Cruz Ave .... Los Gatos CA 95030 408-354-9300 399-1594
Web: www.losgatoschamber.com

Madera District Chamber of Commerce 120 NE St .... Madera CA 93638 559-673-3563 673-5009*
**Fax:* Acctg ■ *TF:* 866-382-7822 ■ *Web:* www.maderachamber.com

Malibu Chamber of Commerce
23805 Stuart Ranch Rd Ste 210 .... Malibu CA 90265 310-456-9025 456-0195
TF: 800-442-4988 ■ *Web:* www.malibu.org

Manhattan Beach Chamber of Commerce
425 15th St .... Manhattan Beach CA 90266 310-545-5313
Web: manhattanbeachchamber.com

Manteca Chamber of Commerce 183 W N St Ste 6 .... Manteca CA 95336 209-823-6121 239-6131
Web: www.manteca.org

Marina Chamber of Commerce PO Box 425 .... Marina CA 93933 831-384-0155
Web: www.marinachamber.com

Martinez Area Chamber of Commerce
603 Marina Vista .... Martinez CA 94553 925-228-2345 228-2356
TF: 877-855-5506 ■ *Web:* www.martinezchamber.com

Menifee Valley Chamber of Commerce
29683 New Hub Dr Ste C .... Menifee CA 92586 951-672-1991 672-4022
Web: www.menifeevalleychamber.com

Menlo Park Chamber of Commerce
1100 Merrill St .... Menlo Park CA 94025 650-325-2818 325-0920
Web: www.menloparkchamber.com

Greater Merced Chamber of Commerce
1640 N St Ste 120 .... Merced CA 95340 209-384-7092 384-8472
TF: 800-877-2345 ■ *Web:* www.merced-chamber.com

Merced County Chamber of Commerce
860 W 18th St .... Merced CA 95340 209-722-3864
Web: www.mercedcountychamber.com

Modesto Chamber of Commerce 1114 J St .... Modesto CA 95354 209-577-5757 577-2673
Web: www.modchamber.org

Monrovia Chamber of Commerce
620 S Myrtle Ave .... Monrovia CA 91016 626-358-1159 357-6036
Web: www.monroviacc.com

Montclair Chamber of Commerce
5220 Benito St .... Montclair CA 91763 909-624-4569 625-2009
Web: www.montclairchamber.com

Montebello Chamber of Commerce
109 N 19th St .... Montebello CA 90640 323-721-1153 721-7946
Web: www.montebellochamber.org

Monterey Peninsula Chamber of Commerce
30 Ragsdale Dr #200 .... Monterey CA 93940 831-648-5360 649-3502
Web: www.montereychamber.com

Monterey Park Chamber of Commerce
700 El Mercado Ave .... Monterey Park CA 91754 626-570-9429
Web: montereyparkchamber.org

Moorpark Chamber of Commerce 18 E High St .... Moorpark CA 93021 805-529-0322 529-5304
Web: www.moorparkchamber.com

Moreno Valley Chamber of Commerce
12625 Frederick St .... Moreno Valley CA 92553 951-697-4404 697-0995
Web: www.movalchamber.org

Morgan Hill Chamber of Commerce
17485 Monterey St Ste 105 .... Morgan Hill CA 95037 408-779-9444 779-5405
Web: www.morganhill.org

Chamber of Commerce Mountain View
580 Castro St .... Mountain View CA 94041 650-968-8378 968-5668
Web: www.chambermv.org

Murrieta Chamber of Commerce
25125 Madison Ave Ste 108 .... Murrieta CA 92562 951-677-7916 677-9976
Web: www.murrietachamber.org

Napa Chamber of Commerce 1556 First St .... Napa CA 94559 707-226-7455 226-1171
TF: 877-807-2249 ■ *Web:* napachamber.com

National City Chamber of Commerce
901 National City Blvd .... National City CA 91950 619-477-9339 477-5018
Web: www.nationalcitychamber.org

Newark Chamber of Commerce 37101 Newark Blvd .... Newark CA 94560 510-744-1000
TF: 844-245-8925 ■ *Web:* www.newark-chamber.com

Newport Beach Chamber of Commerce
1470 Jamboree Rd .... Newport Beach CA 92660 949-729-4400 729-4417
Web: www.newportbeach.com

Universal City-North Hollywood Chamber of Commerce
6369 Bellingham Ave .... North Hollywood CA 91606 818-508-5155 508-5156
Web: www.noho.org

North Valley Regional Chamber of Commerce
9401 Reseda Blvd Ste 100 .... Northridge CA 91324 818-349-5676 349-4343
Web: northridgechamber.org

Norwalk Chamber of Commerce 12040 Foster Rd .... Norwalk CA 90650 562-864-7785 864-8539
TF: 800-427-2200 ■ *Web:* norwalkchamber.com

Novato Chamber of Commerce 807 DeLong Ave .... Novato CA 94945 415-897-1164 898-9097
TF: 800-897-1164 ■ *Web:* www.novatochamber.com

			Phone	Fax
Oakhurst Area Chamber of Commerce 49074 Civic Cir . . . . . Oakhurst *Web:* www.oakhurstchamber.com	CA	93644	559-683-7766	658-2942
Oakland Metropolitan Chamber of Commerce 475 14th St Ste 100 . . . . . Oakland *Web:* www.oaklandchamber.com	CA	94612	510-874-4800	839-8817
Oceanside Chamber of Commerce 928 N Coast Hwy . . . . . Oceanside *Web:* www.oceansidechamber.com	CA	92054	760-722-1534	722-8336
Ojai Valley Chamber of Commerce 201 S Signal St . . . . . Ojai *Web:* www.ojaichamber.org	CA	93023	805-646-8126	646-9762
Ontario Chamber of Commerce 3200 Inland Empire Blvd Ste 130 . . . . . Ontario *Web:* www.ontario.org	CA	91764	909-984-2458	
Orange Chamber of Commerce 1940 N Tustin St . . . . . Orange *TF:* 888-676-1040 ■ *Web:* www.orangechamber.com	CA	92865	714-538-3581	532-1675
Orangevale Chamber of Commerce 9267 Greenback Ln Ste B-91 . . . . . Orangevale *TF:* 800-962-1106 ■ *Web:* www.orangevalechamber.com	CA	95662	916-988-0175	988-1049
Oroville Area Chamber of Commerce 1789 Montgomery St . . . . . Oroville *TF:* 800-655-4653 ■ *Web:* www.orovillechamber.net	CA	95965	530-538-2542	538-2546
Oxnard Chamber of Commerce 400 E Esplanade Dr Ste 302 . . . . . Oxnard *Web:* www.oxnardchamber.org	CA	93036	805-983-6118	604-7331
Pacifica Chamber of Commerce 225 Rockaway Beach Ave Ste 1 . . . . . Pacifica *Web:* pacificachamber.com	CA	94044	650-355-4122	355-6949
Palm Desert Chamber of Commerce (PDCC) 72559 Hwy 111 . . . . . Palm Desert *Web:* www.pdcc.org	CA	92260	760-346-6111	346-3263
Palm Springs Chamber of Commerce 190 W Amado Rd . . . . . Palm Springs *Web:* www.pschamber.org	CA	92262	760-325-1577	
Antelope Valley Board of Trade 41319-12th St W Ste 104 . . . . . Palmdale *Web:* www.avbot.org	CA	93551	661-947-9033	
Palmdale Chamber of Commerce 817 E Ave Q-9 . . . . . Palmdale *Web:* www.palmdalechamber.org	CA	93550	661-273-3232	273-8508
Palo Alto Chamber of Commerce 355 Alma St . . . . . Palo Alto *Web:* www.paloaltochamber.com	CA	94301	650-324-3121	324-1215
Paradise Chamber of Commerce 5550 Sky Way Ste 1 . . . . . Paradise *TF:* 800-838-3006 ■ *Web:* www.paradisechamber.com	CA	95969	530-877-9356	877-1865
Paramount Chamber of Commerce 15357 Paramount Blvd . . . . . Paramount *Web:* paramountchamber.com	CA	90723	562-634-3980	634-0891
Pasadena Chamber of Commerce & Civic Assn 844 E Green St Ste 208 . . . . . Pasadena *Web:* www.pasadena-chamber.org	CA	91101	626-795-3355	795-5603
Petaluma Area Chamber of Commerce 6 Petaluma Blvd N Ste A-2 . . . . . Petaluma *Web:* www.petalumachamber.com	CA	94952	707-762-2785	762-4721
Pico Rivera Chamber of Commerce 5016 Passons Blvd . . . . . Pico Rivera *Web:* www.picoriverachamber.org	CA	90660	562-949-2473	
Pittsburg Chamber of Commerce 985 Railroad Ave . . . . . Pittsburg *Web:* pittsburgchamber.org	CA	94565	925-432-7301	427-5555
Placentia Chamber of Commerce 201 E Yorba Linda Blvd Ste C . . . . . Placentia *TF:* 844-730-0418 ■ *Web:* www.placentiachamber.com	CA	92870	714-528-1873	528-1879
El Dorado County Chamber of Commerce 542 Main St . . . . . Placerville *TF:* 800-457-6279 ■ *Web:* www.eldoradocounty.org	CA	95667	530-621-5885	642-1624
Pleasant Hill Chamber of Commerce 91 Gregory Ln Ste 11 . . . . . Pleasant Hill *Web:* www.pleasanthillchamber.com	CA	94523	925-687-0700	676-7422
Pleasanton Chamber of Commerce 777 Peters Ave . . . . . Pleasanton *TF:* 877-807-2249 ■ *Web:* www.pleasanton.org	CA	94566	925-846-5858	846-9697
Pomona Chamber of Commerce 101 W Mission Blvd Ste 223 . . . . . Pomona *Web:* www.pomonachamber.org	CA	91766	909-622-8484	620-5986
Porterville Chamber of Commerce 93 N Main St Ste A . . . . . Porterville *Web:* www.portervillechamber.org	CA	93257	559-784-7502	
Poway Chamber of Commerce 14005-B Midland Rd . . . . . Poway *Web:* www.poway.com	CA	92064	858-748-0016	748-1710
Ramona Chamber of Commerce 960 Main St . . . . . Ramona *TF:* 800-411-7343 ■ *Web:* www.ramonachamber.com	CA	92065	760-789-1311	789-1317
Rancho Cordova Chamber of Commerce 2729 Prospect Pk Dr Ste 117 . . . . . Rancho Cordova *Web:* www.ranchocordova.org	CA	95670	916-273-5688	
Rancho Cucamonga Chamber of Commerce 9047 Arrow Route Ste 180 . . . . . Rancho Cucamonga *TF:* 800-677-5434 ■ *Web:* www.ranchochamber.org	CA	91730	909-987-1012	987-5917
Greater Redding Chamber of Commerce 747 Auditorium Dr . . . . . Redding *Web:* www.reddingchamber.com	CA	96001	530-225-4433	225-4398
Redlands Chamber of Commerce 1 E Redlands Blvd . . . . . Redlands *TF:* 800-966-6428 ■ *Web:* www.redlandschamber.org	CA	92373	909-793-2546	335-6388
Redondo Beach Chamber of Commerce & Visitors Bureau 200 N Pacific Coast Hwy . . . . . Redondo Beach *Web:* www.redondochamber.org	CA	90277	310-376-6911	374-7373
Redwood City-San Mateo County Chamber of Commerce 1450 Veterans Blvd Ste 125 . . . . . Redwood City *Web:* www.redwoodcitychamber.com	CA	94063	650-364-1722	364-1729
Rialto Chamber of Commerce 120 N Riverside Ave . . . . . Rialto *TF:* 800-597-4955 ■ *Web:* www.rialtochamber.org	CA	92376	909-875-5364	875-6790
Richmond Chamber of Commerce 3925 Macdonald Ave . . . . . Richmond *TF:* 866-568-4642 ■ *Web:* www.rcoc.com	CA	94805	510-234-3512	234-3540

			Phone	Fax
Ridgecrest Chamber of Commerce 128-B E California Ave Ste B . . . . . Ridgecrest *Web:* www.ridgecrestchamber.com	CA	93555	760-375-8331	375-0365
Greater Riverside Chambers of Commerce 3985 University Ave . . . . . Riverside *Web:* www.riverside-chamber.com	CA	92501	951-683-7100	683-2670
Rocklin Area Chamber of Commerce 3700 Rocklin Rd . . . . . Rocklin *TF:* 800-228-3380 ■ *Web:* www.rocklinchamber.com	CA	95677	916-624-2548	624-5743
Rohnert Park Chamber of Commerce 101 Golf Course Dr Ste C-7 . . . . . Rohnert Park *TF:* 888-364-7379 ■ *Web:* www.rohnertparkchamber.org	CA	94928	707-584-1415	584-2945
Palos Verdes Peninsula Chamber of Commerce 707 Silver Spur Rd Ste 100 . . . . . Rolling Hills Estates *Web:* www.palosverdeschamber.com	CA	90274	310-377-8111	377-0614
Rosemead Chamber of Commerce 3953 Muscatel Ave . . . . . Rosemead *Web:* rosemeadchamber.org	CA	91770	626-288-0811	288-2514
Roseville Chamber of Commerce 650 Douglas Blvd . . . . . Roseville *Web:* www.rosevillechamber.com	CA	95678	916-783-8136	
Sacramento Metro Chamber of Commerce 1 Capital Mall Ste 300 . . . . . Sacramento *Web:* www.metrochamber.org	CA	95814	916-552-6800	443-2672
Salinas Valley Chamber of Commerce 119 E Alisal St . . . . . Salinas *TF:* 888-678-2871 ■ *Web:* www.salinaschamber.com	CA	93901	831-751-7725	424-8639
San Bernardino Area Chamber of Commerce PO Box 658 . . . . . San Bernardino *TF:* 800-928-5091 ■ *Web:* www.sbachamber.org	CA	92402	909-885-7515	384-9979
San Bruno Chamber of Commerce 618 San Mateo Ave . . . . . San Bruno *Web:* www.sanbrunochamber.com	CA	94066	650-588-0180	588-6473
San Carlos Chamber of Commerce 610 Elm St Ste 206 . . . . . San Carlos *Web:* www.sancarloschamber.org	CA	94070	650-593-1068	593-9108
San Clemente Chamber of Commerce 1100 N El Camino Real . . . . . San Clemente *TF:* 877-411-3662 ■ *Web:* www.scchamber.com	CA	92672	949-492-1131	492-3764
Peninsula Chamber of Commerce PO Box 6015 . . . . . San Diego *Web:* www.peninsulachamber.com	CA	92166	619-223-1629	225-1294
San Diego Regional Chamber of Commerce 402 W Broadway Ste 1000 . . . . . San Diego *Web:* www.sdchamber.org	CA	92101	619-544-1300	
San Dimas Chamber of Commerce 246 E Bonita Ave . . . . . San Dimas *Web:* www.sandimaschamber.com	CA	91773	909-592-3818	592-8178
San Francisco Chamber of Commerce 235 Montgomery St 12th Fl . . . . . San Francisco *TF:* 855-808-2387 ■ *Web:* www.sfchamber.com	CA	94104	415-392-4520	392-0485
San Gabriel Chamber of Commerce 620 W Santa Anita St . . . . . San Gabriel *Web:* sangabrielchamber.org	CA	91776	626-576-2525	289-2901
San Jose Silicon Valley Chamber of Commerce (SJSVCC) 101 W Santa Clara St . . . . . San Jose *Web:* www.sjchamber.com	CA	95113	408-291-5250	286-5019
San Juan Capistrano Chamber of Commerce 31421 La Matanza St . . . . . San Juan Capistrano *Web:* www.sanjuanchamber.com	CA	92675	949-493-4700	489-2695
San Leandro Chamber of Commerce 120 Estudillo Ave . . . . . San Leandro *Web:* www.sanleandrochamber.com	CA	94577	510-317-1400	317-1404
San Luis Obispo Chamber of Commerce 1039 Chorro St . . . . . San Luis Obispo *Web:* www.slochamber.org	CA	93401	805-781-2777	543-1255
San Marcos Chamber of Commerce 904 W San Marcos Blvd . . . . . San Marcos *TF:* 800-814-7241 ■ *Web:* www.sanmarcoschamber.com	CA	92078	760-744-1270	744-5230
San Mateo Area Chamber of Commerce 1700 S El Camino Real Ste 108 . . . . . San Mateo *Web:* www.sanmateoca.org	CA	94402	650-401-2440	
San Pablo Chamber of Commerce 13925 San Pablo Ave . . . . . San Pablo *Web:* ci.san-pablo.ca.us	CA	94806	510-234-2067	234-0604
San Pedro Peninsula Chamber of Commerce 390 W Seventh St . . . . . San Pedro *Web:* www.sanpedrochamber.com	CA	90731	310-832-7272	832-0685
San Rafael Chamber of Commerce 817 Mission Ave . . . . . San Rafael *TF:* 888-378-0777 ■ *Web:* srchamber.com	CA	94901	415-454-4163	454-7039
San Ramon Chamber of Commerce 2410 Camino Ramon #125 . . . . . San Ramon *Web:* www.sanramon.org	CA	94583	925-242-0600	242-0603
San Ysidro Chamber of Commerce 663 E San Ysidro Blvd . . . . . San Ysidro *Web:* www.sanysidrochamber.org	CA	92173	619-428-1281	
Santa Ana Chamber of Commerce 1631 W Sunflower Ave Ste C35 . . . . . Santa Ana *Web:* www.santaanachamber.com	CA	92704	714-541-5353	541-2238
Santa Barbara Region Chamber of Commerce 924 Anacapa St Ste 1 . . . . . Santa Barbara *Web:* www.sbchamber.org	CA	93101	805-965-3023	966-5954
Santa Clara Chamber of Commerce 1850 Warburton Ave . . . . . Santa Clara *Web:* www.santaclarachamber.com	CA	95050	408-244-8244	244-7830
Santa Clarita Valley Chamber of Commerce 27451 Tourney Rd Ste 160 . . . . . Santa Clarita *Web:* www.scvchamber.com	CA	91355	661-702-6977	702-6980
Santa Cruz Chamber of Commerce 611 Ocean St Ste 1 . . . . . Santa Cruz *TF:* 866-282-5900 ■ *Web:* www.santacruzchamber.org	CA	95060	831-457-3713	423-1847
Santa Maria Valley Chamber of Commerce 614 S Broadway . . . . . Santa Maria *TF:* 800-331-3779 ■ *Web:* www.santamaria.com	CA	93454	805-925-2403	925-0840

				Phone	Fax
Santa Monica Chamber of Commerce 1234 Sixth St Ste 100 *Web:* www.smchamber.com	Santa Monica	CA	90401	310-393-9825	394-1868
Santa Paula Chamber of Commerce 200 N Tenth St **Fax Area Code: 858* ■ *Web:* santapaulachamber.net	Santa Paula	CA	93060	805-525-5561	546-0770*
Santa Rosa Chamber of Commerce 637 First St *Web:* www.santarosachamber.com	Santa Rosa	CA	95404	707-545-1414	545-6914
Santee Chamber of Commerce 10315 Mission Gorge Rd *Web:* santeechamber.com	Santee	CA	92071	619-449-6572	562-7906
Saratoga Chamber of Commerce 14485 Big Basin Way *Web:* www.saratogachamber.org	Saratoga	CA	95070	408-867-0753	867-5213
Seal Beach Chamber & Business Assn 201 Eigth St Ste 120 *Web:* www.sealbeachchamber.org	Seal Beach	CA	90740	562-799-0179	795-5637
Sebastopol Area Chamber of Commerce 265 S Main St *Web:* www.sebastopol.org	Sebastopol	CA	95472	707-823-3032	823-8439
Greater Sherman Oaks Chamber of Commerce 14827 Ventura Blvd Ste 207 *Web:* www.shermanoakschamber.org	Sherman Oaks	CA	91403	818-906-1951	783-3100
Simi Valley Chamber of Commerce 40 W Cochran St Ste 100 *Web:* www.simivalleychamber.org	Simi Valley	CA	93065	805-526-3900	526-6234
Sonoma Valley Chamber of Commerce 651A Broadway *Web:* www.sonomachamber.org	Sonoma	CA	95476	707-996-1033	996-9402
Tuolumne County Chamber of Commerce 222 S Shepherd St *TF:* 877-532-4212 ■ *Web:* www.tcchamber.com	Sonora	CA	95370	209-532-4212	532-8068
South Gate Chamber of Commerce 3350 Tweedy Blvd *Web:* sgchamber.org	South Gate	CA	90280	323-567-1203	
South San Francisco Chamber of Commerce 213 Linden Ave *Web:* www.ssfchamber.com	South San Francisco	CA	94080	650-588-1911	588-2534
Spring Valley Chamber of Commerce 3322 Sweetwater Springs Blvd Ste 202 *Web:* www.springvalleychamber.org	Spring Valley	CA	91977	619-670-9902	670-9924
Stanton Chamber of Commerce 8381 Katella Ave Ste H *Web:* www.stantonchamber.org	Stanton	CA	90680	714-995-1485	
Greater Stockton Chamber of Commerce 445 W Weber Ave Ste 220 *Web:* www.stocktonchamber.org	Stockton	CA	95203	209-547-2770	
Studio City Chamber of Commerce 4024 Radford Ave Edit 2 Ste F *Web:* www.studiocitychamber.com	Studio City	CA	91604	818-655-5916	
Sun Valley Area Chamber of Commerce 11501 Strathern St PO Box 308 *TF:* 877-834-7064 ■ *Web:* www.svacc.com	Sun Valley	CA	91352	818-768-2014	
Sunland-Tujunga Chamber of Commerce 8250 Foothill Blvd Ste A *Web:* www.stchamber.com	Sunland	CA	91040	818-352-4433	353-7551
Sunnyvale Chamber of Commerce 260 S Sunnyvale Ave Ste 4 *Web:* www.svcoc.org	Sunnyvale	CA	94086	408-736-4971	736-1919
Lassen County Chamber of Commerce 75 N Weatherlow St *TF:* 877-686-7878 ■ *Web:* www.lassencountychamber.org	Susanville	CA	96130	530-257-4323	
Greater Tehachapi Chamber of Commerce 209 E Tehachapi Blvd PO Box 401 *Web:* www.tehachapi.com	Tehachapi	CA	93581	661-822-4180	822-9036
Temecula Valley Chamber of Commerce (TVCC) 26790 Ynez Ct Ste A *TF:* 866-676-5090 ■ *Web:* www.temecula.org	Temecula	CA	92591	951-676-5090	694-0201
Temple City Chamber of Commerce 9050 Las Tunas Dr *Web:* www.templecitychamber.org	Temple City	CA	91780	626-286-3101	
Harbor City-Harbor Gateway Chamber of Commerce 19401 S Vermont Ave Ste H-112 *Web:* www.hchgchamber.com	Torrance	CA	90502	310-534-3143	516-7734
Torrance Area Chamber of Commerce 3400 Torrance Blvd Ste 100 *Web:* www.torrancechamber.com	Torrance	CA	90503	310-540-5858	540-7662
Tracy Chamber of Commerce 223 E Tenth St *Web:* www.tracychamber.org	Tracy	CA	95376	209-835-2131	833-9526
Greater Tulare Chamber of Commerce 220 E Tulare Ave *Web:* www.tularechamber.org	Tulare	CA	93274	559-686-1547	686-4915
Turlock Chamber of Commerce 115 S Golden State Blvd *TF:* 800-834-0401 ■ *Web:* turlockchamber.com	Turlock	CA	95380	209-632-2221	632-5289
Tustin Chamber of Commerce 700 W First St Ste 7 *Web:* www.tustinchamber.org	Tustin	CA	92780	714-544-5341	544-2083
Twentynine Palms Chamber of Commerce 73484 Twentynine Palms Hwy *Web:* www.29chamber.org	Twentynine Palms	CA	92277	760-367-3445	
Ukiah Chamber of Commerce 200 S School St *Web:* www.ukiahchamber.com	Ukiah	CA	95482	707-462-4705	462-2088
Union City Chamber of Commerce 3939 Smith St *Web:* www.unioncitychamber.com	Union City	CA	94587	510-952-9637	952-9647
Upland Chamber of Commerce 215 N Second Ave Ste D *Web:* www.uplandchamber.org	Upland	CA	91786	909-204-4465	204-4464
Vacaville Chamber of Commerce 300 Main St *Web:* www.vacavillechamber.com	Vacaville	CA	95688	707-448-6424	448-0424
Vallejo Chamber of Commerce 427 York St *TF:* 877-397-7936 ■ *Web:* www.vallejochamber.com	Vallejo	CA	94590	707-644-5551	644-5590
Mid Valley Chamber of Commerce 7120 Hayvenhurst Ave Ste 114 *Web:* www.sanfernandovalleychamber.com	Van Nuys	CA	91406	818-989-0300	989-3836
Venice Chamber of Commerce 327 Washington Blvd PO Box 202 *Web:* www.venicechamber.net	Venice	CA	90294	310-822-5425	
Ventura Chamber of Commerce 505 Poli St 2nf Fl *Web:* venturachamber.com	Ventura	CA	93001	805-643-7222	653-8015
Victorville Chamber of Commerce 14174 Green Tree Blvd *Web:* vvchamber.com	Victorville	CA	92395	760-245-6506	245-6505
Visalia Chamber of Commerce 222 N Garden St Ste 300 *Web:* www.visaliachamber.org	Visalia	CA	93291	559-734-5876	734-7479
Regional Chamber of Commerce San Gabriel Valley 19720 E Walnut Dr Ste 100A *Web:* www.regionalchambersgv.com	Walnut	CA	91789	909-869-0701	
Walnut Creek Chamber of Commerce 1280 Civic Dr Ste 100 *Web:* www.walnut-creek.com	Walnut Creek	CA	94596	925-934-2007	934-2404
Pajaro Valley Chamber of Commerce 44 Brennan St PO Box 1748 *Web:* www.pajarovalleychamber.com	Watsonville	CA	95076	831-724-3900	724-5821
West Hollywood Chamber of Commerce 8272 Santa Monica Blvd *Web:* www.wehochamber.com	West Hollywood	CA	90046	323-650-2688	650-2689
West Sacramento Chamber of Commerce 1414 Merkley Ave Ste 1 *Web:* www.westsacramentochamber.com	West Sacramento	CA	95691	916-371-7042	371-7007
Westminster Chamber of Commerce 1025 Westminster Mall *TF:* 800-545-5585 ■ *Web:* www.westminsterchamber.org	Westminster	CA	92683	714-898-2559	373-1499
Whittier Area Chamber of Commerce 8158 Painter Ave *Web:* www.whittierchamber.com	Whittier	CA	90602	562-698-9554	693-2700
Willows Chamber of Commerce 118 W Sycamore *TF:* 855-233-6362 ■ *Web:* willowschamber.com	Willows	CA	95988	530-934-8150	
Wilmington Chamber of Commerce 544 N Avalon Blvd Ste 104 *Web:* www.wilmington-chamber.com	Wilmington	CA	90744	310-834-8586	834-8887
Woodland Chamber of Commerce 307 First St *TF:* 888-843-2636 ■ *Web:* www.woodlandchamber.org	Woodland	CA	95695	530-662-7327	662-4086
Woodland Hills Chamber of Commerce 20121 Ventura Blvd Ste 309 *TF:* 888-852-9961 ■ *Web:* www.woodlandhillscc.net	Woodland Hills	CA	91364	818-347-4737	347-3321
Yorba Linda Chamber of Commerce 17670 Yorba Linda Blvd *Web:* www.yorbalindachamber.org	Yorba Linda	CA	92886	714-993-9537	993-7764
Yucaipa Valley Chamber of Commerce 35139 Yucaipa Blvd *Web:* yucaipachamber.org	Yucaipa	CA	92399	909-790-1841	363-7373
Yucca Valley Chamber of Commerce 56711 29 Palms Hwy *TF:* 855-568-5348 ■ *Web:* www.yuccavalley.org	Yucca Valley	CA	92284	760-365-6323	365-0763

Colorado

				Phone	Fax
Arvada Chamber of Commerce 7305 Grandview Ave *Web:* www.arvadachamber.org	Arvada	CO	80002	303-424-0313	424-5370
Aspen Chamber Resort Assn 425 Rio Grande Pl *TF:* 800-670-0792 ■ *Web:* www.aspenchamber.org	Aspen	CO	81611	970-925-1940	920-1173
Aurora Chamber of Commerce 14305 E Alameda Ave Ste 300 *TF:* 877-770-4438 ■ *Web:* www.aurorachamber.org	Aurora	CO	80012	303-344-1500	344-1564
Vail Valley Chamber of Commerce 101 Fawcett Rd Ste 240 *Web:* www.visitvailvalley.com	Avon	CO	81620	970-476-1000	
Boulder Chamber of Commerce 2440 Pearl St *Web:* www.boulderchamber.com	Boulder	CO	80302	303-442-1044	938-8837
Canon City Chamber of Commerce 403 Royal Gorge Blvd *TF:* 800-876-7922 ■ *Web:* www.canoncity.com	Canon City	CO	81212	719-275-2331	275-2332
South Metro Denver Chamber of Commerce 6840 S University Blvd *Web:* www.bestchamber.com	Centennial	CO	80122	303-795-0142	795-7520
Colorado Springs Regional Business Alliance 102 S Tejon St Ste 430 *TF:* 866-804-8763 ■ *Web:* www.coloradospringsbusinessalliance.com	Colorado Springs	CO	80903	719-471-8183	
Delta Area Chamber of Commerce 301 Main St *Web:* www.deltacolorado.org	Delta	CO	81416	970-874-8616	874-8618
Broomfield Chamber of Commerce 350 Interlocken Blvd Ste 200 *Web:* www.broomfieldchamber.com	Denver	CO	80202	303-466-1775	466-4481
Denver Metro Chamber of Commerce 1445 Market St *Web:* www.denverchamber.org	Denver	CO	80202	303-534-8500	534-3200
Fort Collins Area Chamber of Commerce 225 S Meldrum St *TF:* 877-652-8607 ■ *Web:* www.fortcollinschamber.com	Fort Collins	CO	80521	970-482-3746	482-3774
Fort Morgan Area Chamber of Commerce 300 Main St *TF:* 800-354-8660 ■ *Web:* www.fortmorganchamber.org	Fort Morgan	CO	80701	970-867-6702	
Greater Golden Chamber of Commerce 1010 Washington Ave *Web:* goldenchamber.org	Golden	CO	80401	303-279-3113	279-0332
West Chamber of Commerce 1667 Cole Blvd Bldg 19 Ste 400 *Web:* www.westchamber.org	Golden	CO	80401	303-233-5555	237-7633
Grand Junction Area Chamber of Commerce 360 Grand Ave *TF:* 800-352-5286 ■ *Web:* www.gjchamber.org	Grand Junction	CO	81501	970-242-3214	242-3694

	City	State	ZIP	Phone	Fax
Greeley-Weld Chamber of Commerce 902 Seventh Ave *TF:* 800-449-3866 ■ *Web:* www.greeleychamber.com	Greeley	CO	80631	970-352-3566	352-3572
La Veta/Cuchara Chamber of Commerce 132 W Ryus Ave *TF:* 866-277-5550 ■ *Web:* www.lavetacucharachamber.com	La Veta	CO	81055	719-742-3676	
Longmont Area Chamber of Commerce 528 Main St *Web:* www.longmontchamber.org	Longmont	CO	80501	303-776-5295	776-5657
Loveland Chamber of Commerce 5400 Stone Creek Cir Ste 200 *TF:* 800-216-0680 ■ *Web:* www.loveland.org	Loveland	CO	80538	970-667-6311	667-5211
Montrose Chamber of Commerce 1519 E Main St *TF:* 800-923-5515 ■ *Web:* montrosechamber.com	Montrose	CO	81401	970-249-5000	249-2907
Parker Chamber of Commerce 19590 E Main St Ste 100 *Web:* www.parkerchamber.com	Parker	CO	80138	303-841-4268	841-8061
Greater Pueblo Chamber of Commerce 302 N Santa Fe Ave *TF:* 800-233-3446 ■ *Web:* www.pueblochamber.org	Pueblo	CO	81003	719-542-1704	542-1624
Metro North Chamber of Commerce 14583 Orchard Pkwy Ste 300 *TF:* 877-888-8811 ■ *Web:* www.metronorthchamber.com	Westminster	CO	80023	303-288-1000	227-1050

Connecticut

	City	State	ZIP	Phone	Fax
Shoreline Chamber Of Commerceÿ 764 E Main St *Web:* shorelinechamberct.com	Branford	CT	06405	203-488-5500	488-5046
Bridgeport Regional Business Council 10 Middle St Ste 1401 *Web:* www.brbc.org	Bridgeport	CT	06604	203-335-3800	
Greater Bristol Chamber of Commerce 200 Main St *TF:* 855-344-1874 ■ *Web:* www.centralctchambers.org	Bristol	CT	06010	860-584-4718	584-4722
Cheshire Chamber of Commerce 195 S Main St. *Web:* www.cheshirechamber.org	Cheshire	CT	06410	203-272-2345	271-3044
Greater Danbury Chamber of Commerce 39 W St *Web:* www.danburychamber.com	Danbury	CT	06810	203-743-5565	794-1439
Northeastern Connecticut Chamber of Commerce 3 Central St.	Danielson	CT	06239	860-774-8001	774-4299
East Haven Chamber of Commerce 200 Kimberly Ave PO Box 120055 *Web:* www.easthavenchamber.com	East Haven	CT	06512	203-467-4305	
Fairfield Chamber of Commerce 1597 Post Rd. *Web:* www.fairfieldctchamber.com	Fairfield	CT	06824	203-255-1011	256-9990
Glastonbury Chamber of Commerce 2400 Main St Ste 2 *Web:* www.glastonburychamber.net	Glastonbury	CT	06033	860-659-3587	659-0102
Greenwich Chamber of Commerce 45 E Putnam Ave Ste 121 *Web:* www.greenwichchamber.com	Greenwich	CT	06830	203-869-3500	869-3502
Hamden Chamber of Commerce 2969 Whitney Ave *Web:* hamdenregionalchamber.com	Hamden	CT	06518	203-288-6431	288-4499
MetroHartford Alliance 31 Pratt St 5th Fl. *Web:* www.metrohartford.com	Hartford	CT	06103	860-525-4451	293-2592
Greater Manchester Chamber of Commerce 20 Hartford Rd *Web:* www.manchesterchamber.com	Manchester	CT	06040	860-646-2223	646-5871
Greater Meriden Chamber of Commerce 3 Colony St Ste 301 *TF:* 877-283-8158 ■ *Web:* www.midstatechamber.com/default.asp	Meriden	CT	06451	203-235-7901	686-0172
Middlesex County Chamber of Commerce 393 Main St *Web:* www.middlesexchamber.com	Middletown	CT	06457	860-347-6924	346-1043
Milford Chamber of Commerce 5 Broad St *Web:* www.milfordct.com	Milford	CT	06460	203-878-0681	876-8517
Mystic Chamber of Commerce 12 Roosevelt Ave,2nd Fl PO Box 143 *TF:* 866-572-9578 ■ *Web:* www.mysticchamber.org	Mystic	CT	06355	860-572-9578	572-9273
Chamber of Commerce 195 Water St *Web:* www.waterburychamber.com	Naugatuck	CT	06770	203-729-4511	729-4512
Greater New Britain Chamber of Commerce 1 Ct St 4th Fl *Web:* www.newbritainchamber.com	New Britain	CT	06051	860-229-1665	223-8341
Greater New Haven Chamber of Commerce 900 Chapel St 10th Fl. *Web:* www.gnhcc.com	New Haven	CT	06510	203-787-6735	782-4329
Greater New Milford Chamber of Commerce 11 Railroad St. *Web:* www.newmilford-chamber.com	New Milford	CT	06776	860-354-6080	354-8526
Greater Norwalk Chamber of Commerce 101 E Ave *Web:* www.norwalkchamberofcommerce.com	Norwalk	CT	06851	203-866-2521	852-0583
Old Saybrook Chamber of Commerce 1 Main St *Web:* www.oldsaybrookchamber.com	Old Saybrook	CT	06475	860-388-3266	388-9433
Greater Valley Chamber of Commerce 900 Bridgeport Ave 2nd Fl *Web:* www.greatervalleychamber.com	Shelton	CT	06484	203-925-4981	925-4984
Greater Southington Chamber of Commerce 1 Factory Sq Ste 202 *Web:* www.southingtonchamber.com	Southington	CT	06489	860-628-8036	276-9696
Business Council of Fairfield County (SACIA) 1 Landmark Sq Ste 300 *Web:* www.businessfairfield.com	Stamford	CT	06901	203-359-3220	967-8294
Stamford Chamber of Commerce 733 Summer St Ste 104 *TF:* 866-262-4548 ■ *Web:* www.stamfordchamber.com	Stamford	CT	06901	203-359-4761	363-5069
Chamber of Commerce of Northwest Connecticut 333 Kennedy Dr Ste R101 PO Box 59 *Web:* www.nwctchamberofcommerce.org	Torrington	CT	06790	860-482-6586	489-8851
Tolland County Chamber of Commerce 30 Lafayette Sq *Web:* www.tollandcountychamber.org	Vernon	CT	06066	860-872-0587	872-0588
Quinnipiac Chamber of Commerce 50 N Main St *Web:* www.quinncham.com	Wallingford	CT	06492	203-269-9891	269-1358
Greater Waterbury Chamber of Commerce 83 Bank St *Web:* www.waterburychamber.com	Waterbury	CT	06702	203-757-0701	
Chamber of Commerce of Eastern Connecticut Inc 914 Hartford Tpke *Web:* www.chamberect.com	Waterford	CT	06385	860-464-7373	
West Hartford Chamber of Commerce 948 Farmington Ave *Web:* www.whchamber.com	West Hartford	CT	06107	860-521-2300	521-1996
West Haven Chamber of Commerce 355 Main St Ground Fl *Web:* www.westhavenchamber.com	West Haven	CT	06516	203-933-1500	931-1940
Windham Region Chamber of Commerce 1010 Main St *TF:* 800-683-4564 ■ *Web:* www.windhamchamber.com	Willimantic	CT	06226	860-423-6389	423-8235
Windsor Chamber of Commerce 261 Broad St *Web:* www.windsorcc.org	Windsor	CT	06095	860-688-5165	688-0809

Delaware

	City	State	ZIP	Phone	Fax
Rehoboth Beach-Dewey Beach Chamber of Commerce 501 Rehoboth Ave *TF:* 800-441-1329 ■ *Web:* www.beach-fun.com	Rehoboth Beach	DE	19971	302-227-2233	227-8351
Yazoo County Chamber of Commerce 1615 H St NW *TF:* 800-638-6582 ■ *Web:* uschamber.com	Washington	DC	20062	662-746-1273	

Florida

	City	State	ZIP	Phone	Fax
Apalachicola Bay Chamber of Commerce 122 Commerce St. *TF:* 866-269-3022 ■ *Web:* www.apalachicolabay.org	Apalachicola	FL	32320	850-653-9419	653-8219
SouthShore Chamber of Commerce 137 Harbor Village Ln. *Web:* www.southshorechamberofcommerce.org	Apollo Beach	FL	33570	813-645-1366	645-2099
DeSoto County Chamber of Commerce 16 S Volusia Ave *Web:* www.desotochamberfl.com	Arcadia	FL	34266	863-494-4033	494-3312
Belleview-South Marion Chamber of Commerce 5331 SE Abshier Blvd. *Web:* belleviewsouthmarionchamber.org	Belleview	FL	34420	352-245-2178	
Lower Keys Chamber of Commerce 31020 Overseas Hwy *TF:* 800-872-3722 ■ *Web:* www.lowerkeyschamber.com	Big Pine Key	FL	33043	305-872-2411	872-0752
Greater Boca Raton Chamber of Commerce 1800 N Dixie Hwy *TF:* 800-435-7352 ■ *Web:* www.bocaratonchamber.com	Boca Raton	FL	33432	561-395-4433	392-3780
Bonita Springs Area Chamber of Commerce 25071 Chamber of Commerce Dr *TF:* 800-226-2943 ■ *Web:* www.bonitaspringschamber.com	Bonita Springs	FL	34135	239-992-2943	992-5011
Greater Boynton Beach Chamber of Commerce 1880 N Congress Ave Ste 106 *Web:* www.boyntonbeach.org	Boynton Beach	FL	33426	561-732-9501	734-4304
Manatee Chamber of Commerce 222 Tenth St W *Web:* www.manateechamber.com	Bradenton	FL	34205	941-748-3411	745-1877
Greater Brandon Chamber of Commerce 330 Pauls Dr Ste 100 *Web:* www.brandonchamber.com	Brandon	FL	33511	813-689-1221	689-9440
Greater Hernando County Chamber of Commerce 15588 Aviation Loop Dr *Web:* www.hernandochamber.com	Brooksville	FL	34604	352-796-0697	796-3704
Clearwater Regional Chamber of Commerce 401 Cleveland St *TF:* 877-447-7356 ■ *Web:* www.clearwaterflorida.org	Clearwater	FL	33755	727-461-0011	449-2889
Coral Gables Chamber of Commerce 224 Catalonia *Web:* coralgableschamber.org	Coral Gables	FL	33134	305-446-1657	446-9900
Coral Springs Chamber of Commerce 11805 Heron Bay Blvd *Web:* www.cschamber.com	Coral Springs	FL	33076	954-752-4242	827-0543
Crestview Area Chamber of Commerce 1447 Commerce Dr *Web:* www.crestviewchamber.com	Crestview	FL	32539	850-682-3212	682-7413
Citrus County Chamber of Commerce 28 NW Us Hwy 19 *Web:* www.citruscountychamber.com	Crystal River	FL	34428	352-795-3149	
Davie-Cooper City Chamber of Commerce 4185 Davie Rd *Web:* www.davie-coopercity.org	Davie	FL	33314	954-581-0790	581-9684
Greater Deerfield Beach Chamber of Commerce 1601 E Hillsboro Blvd. *TF:* 866-551-9805 ■ *Web:* www.deerfieldchamber.com	Deerfield Beach	FL	33441	954-427-1050	427-1056
DeLand Area Chamber of Commerce 336 N Woodland Blvd. *TF:* 800-611-5207 ■ *Web:* www.delandchamber.org	DeLand	FL	32720	386-734-4331	734-4333
Greater Delray Beach Chamber of Commerce 140 NE 1st St *Web:* www.delraybeach.com	Delray Beach	FL	33444	561-278-0424	278-6012
Destin Area Chamber of Commerce 4484 Legendary Dr Ste A *Web:* www.destinchamber.com	Destin	FL	32541	850-837-6241	654-5612
Dunedin Chamber of Commerce 301 Main St *Web:* www.dunedin-fl.com	Dunedin	FL	34698	727-733-3197	734-8942
Dunnellon Area Chamber of Commerce 20500 E Pennsylvania Ave *Web:* www.dunnellonchamber.org	Dunnellon	FL	34432	352-489-2320	

Name / Address	City	State	Zip	Phone	Fax
Englewood-Cape Haze Area Chamber of Commerce 601 S Indiana Ave *TF:* 800-603-7198 ■ *Web:* www.englewoodchamber.com	Englewood	FL	34223	941-474-5511	475-9257
Amelia Island-Fernandina Beach-Yulee Chamber of Commerce 961687 Gateway Blvd Ste 101-G *Web:* www.islandchamber.com	Fernandina Beach	FL	32034	904-261-3248	261-6997
Broward County Chamber of Commerce 2425 E Commercial Blvd #103 *TF:* 877-653-4752 ■ *Web:* www.browardbiz.com	Fort Lauderdale	FL	33308	954-565-5750	
Greater Fort Lauderdale Chamber of Commerce 512 NE Third Ave *TF:* 800-683-8338 ■ *Web:* www.ftlchamber.com	Fort Lauderdale	FL	33301	954-462-6000	527-8766
Chamber of Southwest Florida 5237 Summerlin Commons Blvd Ste 114 *Web:* www.chamber-swflorida.com	Fort Myers	FL	33907	239-278-4001	275-2103
Greater Fort Myers Chamber of Commerce 2310 Edwards Dr *TF:* 800-366-3622 ■ *Web:* www.fortmyers.org	Fort Myers	FL	33901	239-332-3624	332-7276
Fort Myers Beach Chamber of Commerce 17200 San Carlos Blvd *TF:* 866-998-9250 ■ *Web:* www.fortmyersbeach.org	Fort Myers Beach	FL	33931	239-454-7500	454-7910
Greater Fort Walton Beach Chamber of Commerce 34 Miracle Strip Pkwy SE *Web:* www.fwbchamber.org	Fort Walton Beach	FL	32548	850-244-8191	244-1935
Gainesville Area Chamber of Commerce 300 E University Ave Ste 100 *TF:* 888-795-2707 ■ *Web:* www.gainesvillechamber.com	Gainesville	FL	32601	352-334-7100	334-7141
Goldenrod Area Chamber of Commerce 4755 Palmetto Ave PO Box 61 *Web:* www.goldenrodchamber.com	Goldenrod	FL	32733	407-677-5980	677-4928
Hallandale Beach Chamber of Commerce 400 S Federal Hwy Ste 192 *Web:* www.hallandalebeachchamber.com	Hallandale Beach	FL	33009	954-454-0541	454-0930
Hialeah Chamber of Commerce & Industries 240 E First Ave Ste 217	Hialeah	FL	33010	305-888-7780	888-7804
Greater Hollywood Chamber of Commerce 330 N Federal Hwy *Web:* www.hollywoodchamber.org	Hollywood	FL	33020	954-923-4000	
Citrus County Chamber of Commerce 401 Tompkins St *Web:* www.citruscountychamber.com	Inverness	FL	34450	352-726-2801	637-1921
Islamorada Chamber of Commerce PO Box 915 *TF:* 800-322-5397 ■ *Web:* www.islamoradachamber.com	Islamorada	FL	33036	305-664-4503	664-4289
Jacksonville Chamber of Commerce 3 Independent Dr *Web:* www.myjaxchamber.com	Jacksonville	FL	32202	904-366-6600	
Jacksonville Chamber of Commerce Beaches Div 3 Independent Dr *Web:* www.myjaxchamber.com	Jacksonville	FL	32202	904-366-6600	
North Palm Beach County Chamber of Commerce 800 N US Hwy 1 *Web:* www.npbchamber.com	Jupiter	FL	33477	561-746-7111	745-7519
Key Largo Chamber of Commerce 106000 Overseas Hwy *TF:* 800-680-9701 ■ *Web:* keylargochamber.org	Key Largo	FL	33037	305-451-1414	451-4726
Kissimmee/Osceola County Chamber of Commerce 1425 E Vine St *Web:* www.kissimmeechamber.com	Kissimmee	FL	34744	407-847-3174	870-8607
Lake City/Columbia County Chamber of Commerce 162 S Marion Ave *Web:* www.lakecitychamber.com	Lake City	FL	32025	386-752-3690	755-7744
Greater Lake Placid Chamber of Commerce 18 N Oak Ave *Web:* www.lpfla.com	Lake Placid	FL	33852	863-465-4331	465-2588
Lake Wales Area Chamber of Commerce 340 W Central Ave *Web:* www.lakewaleschamber.com	Lake Wales	FL	33859	863-676-3445	676-3446
Greater Lake Worth Chamber of Commerce 501 Lake Ave *Web:* www.cpbchamber.com	Lake Worth	FL	33460	561-582-4401	
Lakeland Area Chamber of Commerce 35 Lk Morton Dr *Web:* www.lakelandchamber.com	Lakeland	FL	33801	863-688-8551	683-7454
Central Pasco Chamber of Commerce 2810 Land O' Lakes Blvd *Web:* www.centralpascochamber.com	Land O Lakes	FL	34639	813-909-2722	909-0827
Central Pinellas Chamber of Commerce 151 Third St NW *Web:* www.centralchamber.biz	Largo	FL	33770	727-584-2321	586-3112
Lehigh Acres Chamber of Commerce 25 Homestead Rd N *Web:* www.lehighacreschamber.org	Lehigh Acres	FL	33936	239-369-3322	368-0500
Maitland Area Chamber of Commerce 110 N Maitland Ave *Web:* www.maitlandchamber.com	Maitland	FL	32751	407-644-0741	539-2529
Greater Marathon Chamber of Commerce 12222 Overseas Hwy *TF:* 800-262-7284 ■ *Web:* www.floridakeysmarathon.com	Marathon	FL	33050	305-743-5417	289-0183
Marco Island Chamber of Commerce 1102 N Collier Blvd *TF:* 800-788-6272 ■ *Web:* www.marcoislandchamber.org	Marco Island	FL	34145	239-394-7549	394-3061
Jackson County Chamber of Commerce 4318 Lafayette St *Web:* www.jacksoncounty.com	Marianna	FL	32446	850-482-8060	
Cocoa Beach Area Chamber of Commerce 400 Fortenberry Rd *Web:* www.cocoabeachchamber.com	Merritt Island	FL	32952	321-459-2200	459-2232
Greater Miami Chamber of Commerce 1601 Biscayne Blvd *TF:* 888-660-5955 ■ *Web:* www.miamichamber.com	Miami	FL	33132	305-350-7700	374-6902
Miami-Dade Chamber of Commerce 11380 NW 27th Ave Ste 1328 *Web:* www.m-dcc.org	Miami	FL	33167	305-751-8648	
North Dade Regional Chamber of Commerce 1300 NW 167th St Ste 2 *Web:* www.thechamber.cc	Miami	FL	33169	305-690-9123	
Miami Beach Chamber of Commerce 1920 Meridian Ave 3rd Fl *TF:* 800-501-0401 ■ *Web:* www.miamibeachchamber.com	Miami Beach	FL	33139	305-672-1270	538-4336
Santa Rosa County Chamber of Commerce 5247 Stewart St *TF:* 800-239-8732 ■ *Web:* www.srcchamber.com	Milton	FL	32570	850-623-2339	623-4413
Greater Naples Chamber of Commerce, The 2390 Tamiami Trl N Ste 210 *Web:* www.napleschamber.org	Naples	FL	34103	239-262-6376	262-8374
West Pasco Chamber of Commerce 5443 Main St *Web:* www.westpasco.com	New Port Richey	FL	34652	727-842-7651	848-0202
Southeast Volusia Chamber of Commerce 115 Canal St *Web:* www.sevchamber.com	New Smyrna Beach	FL	32168	386-428-2449	423-3512
Niceville-Valparaiso Chamber of Commerce 1055 E John Sims Pkwy *Web:* www.nicevillechamber.com	Niceville	FL	32578	850-678-2323	678-2602
North Fort Myers Chamber of Commerce 2787 N Tamiami Trl Unit 10 *Web:* nfmchamber.org	North Fort Myers	FL	33903	239-997-9111	997-4026
Greater North Miami Chamber of Commerce 13100 W Dixie Hwy *Web:* www.northmiamichamber.com	North Miami	FL	33161	305-891-7811	893-8522
North Miami Beach Chamber of Commerce 16901 NE 19th Ave *Web:* www.nmbchamber.com	North Miami Beach	FL	33162	305-944-8500	944-8191
Ocala-Marion County Chamber of Commerce 310 SE Third St *TF:* 800-466-5055 ■ *Web:* ocalacep.com	Ocala	FL	34471	352-629-8051	629-7651
Okeechobee Chamber of Commerce 55 S Parrott Ave *Web:* www.okeechobeebusiness.com	Okeechobee	FL	34972	863-467-6246	
Upper Tampa Bay Regional Chamber of Commerce 101 State St W *Web:* www.utbchamber.com	Oldsmar	FL	34677	813-855-4233	854-1237
Clay County Chamber of Commerce 1734 Kingsley Ave *TF:* 800-435-7352 ■ *Web:* www.claychamber.com	Orange Park	FL	32073	904-264-2651	264-0070
Orlando Regional Chamber of Commerce 75 S Ivanhoe Blvd *Web:* www.orlando.org	Orlando	FL	32804	407-425-1234	835-2500
Ormond Beach Chamber of Commerce 165 W Granada Blvd *Web:* www.ormondchamber.com	Ormond Beach	FL	32174	386-677-3454	677-4363
Putnam County Chamber of Commerce 1100 Reid St *Web:* www.putnamcountychamber.com	Palatka	FL	32177	386-328-1503	328-7076
Northern Palm Beach County Chamber of Commerce 5520 PGA Blvd Ste 200 *Web:* www.npbchamber.com	Palm Beach Gardens	FL	33418	561-746-7111	745-7519
Flagler County Chamber of Commerce 20 Airport Rd Ste C *Web:* www.flaglerchamber.org	Palm Coast	FL	32164	386-437-0106	437-5700
Greater Palm Harbor Area Chamber of Commerce 1151 Nebraska Ave *Web:* www.palmharborcc.org	Palm Harbor	FL	34683	727-784-4287	786-2336
Bay County Chamber of Commerce 235 W Fifth St *Web:* www.panamacity.org	Panama City	FL	32401	850-785-5206	763-6229
Panama City Beaches Chamber of Commerce 309 Richard Jackson Blvd *Web:* www.pcbeach.org	Panama City Beach	FL	32407	850-235-1159	235-2301
Miramar-Pembroke Pines Regional Chamber of Commerce 10100 Pines Blvd 4th Fl *Web:* www.miramarpembrokepines.org	Pembroke Pines	FL	33026	954-432-9808	432-9193
Pensacola Area Chamber of Commerce 117 W Garden St *Web:* www.pensacolachamber.com	Pensacola	FL	32502	850-438-4081	438-6369
Pinellas Park Mid-County Chamber of Commerce 5851 Pk Blvd *Web:* www.pinellasparkchamber.com	Pinellas Park	FL	33781	727-544-4777	209-0837
Greater Plant City Chamber of Commerce 106 N Evers St *TF:* 800-760-2315 ■ *Web:* www.plantcity.org	Plant City	FL	33563	813-754-3707	752-8793
Greater Plantation Chamber of Commerce 7401 NW Fourth St *Web:* www.plantationchamber.org	Plantation	FL	33317	954-587-1410	587-1886
Greater Pompano Beach Chamber of Commerce 2200 E Atlantic Blvd *Web:* www.pompanobeachchamber.com	Pompano Beach	FL	33062	954-941-2940	785-8358
Port Orange-South Daytona Chamber of Commerce 3431 S Ridgewood Ave *Web:* www.pschamber.com	Port Orange	FL	32129	386-761-1601	788-9165
Charlotte County Chamber of Commerce 311 W Retta Esplanade *Web:* www.charlottecountychamber.org	Punta Gorda	FL	33950	941-639-6330	639-6330
Gadsden County Chamber of Commerce 208 N Adams St *TF:* 800-627-9231 ■ *Web:* www.gadsdencc.com	Quincy	FL	32351	850-627-9231	875-3299
Greater Riverview Chamber of Commerce 10011 Water Works Ln *Web:* www.riverviewchamber.com	Riverview	FL	33578	813-234-5944	234-5945
Saint Johns County Chamber of Commerce 1 News Place *Web:* www.stjohnscountychamber.com	Saint Augustine	FL	32084	904-829-5681	829-6477
Saint Cloud/Greater Osceola Chamber of Commerce 1200 New York Ave *Web:* www.stcloudflchamber.com	Saint Cloud	FL	34769	407-892-3671	892-5289
Tampa Bay Beaches Chamber of Commerce 6990 Gulf Blvd *TF:* 866-450-9222 ■ *Web:* www.tampabaybeaches.com	Saint Pete Beach	FL	33706	727-360-6957	360-2233
Sanford Chamber of Commerce 400 E First St *Web:* www.sanfordchamber.com	Sanford	FL	32771	407-322-2212	322-8160

Phone Fax

Sanibel & Captiva Islands Chamber of Commerce
1159 Cswy Rd . . . Sanibel FL 33957 239-472-1080 472-1070
Web: www.sanibel-captiva.org

Walton Area Chamber of Commerce
63 S Centry Trl . . . Santa Rosa Beach FL 32459 850-267-0683 267-0603
TF: 800-435-7352 ■ *Web:* waltonareachamber.com

Greater Sarasota Chamber of Commerce
1945 Fruitville Rd . . . Sarasota FL 34236 941-955-8187 366-5621
Web: www.sarasotachamber.com

Sebastian River Area Chamber of Commerce
700 Main St . . . Sebastian FL 32958 772-589-5969 589-5993
Web: www.sebastianchamber.com

Greater Sebring Chamber of Commerce
227 US 27 N . . . Sebring FL 33870 863-385-8448 385-8810
Web: sebring.org

Greater Seminole Area Chamber of Commerce
7995 113th St N . . . Seminole FL 33772 727-392-3245 397-7753
Web: www.seminolechamber.net

Chamber South 6410 SW 80th St . . . South Miami FL 33143 305-661-1621 666-0508
TF: 800-206-3715 ■ *Web:* www.chambersouth.com

Stuart-Martin County Chamber of Commerce
1650 S Kanner Hwy . . . Stuart FL 34994 772-287-1088 220-3437
TF: 800-962-2873 ■ *Web:* www.stuartmartinchamber.org

Sumter County Chamber of Commerce
PO Box 100 . . . Sumterville FL 33535 352-793-3099 793-2120
Web: www.sumterchamber.org

Sunny Isles Beach Tourism & Marketing Council
18070 Collins Ave . . . Sunny Isles Beach FL 33160 305-792-1952
Web: www.sunnyislesbeachmiami.com

Sunrise Chamber of Commerce
6800 Sunset Strip Ste 318 . . . Sunrise FL 33313 954-835-2428 561-9685
Web: www.sunrisechamber.org

Greater Tallahassee Chamber of Commerce
115 N Calhoun St . . . Tallahassee FL 32301 850-224-8116 561-3860
Web: www.talchamber.com

Tamarac Chamber of Commerce
7525 NW 88th Ave # 103 . . . Tamarac FL 33321 954-722-1520 721-2725
Web: www.tamaracchamber.org

Greater Tampa Chamber of Commerce
201 N Franklin St Ste 201 . . . Tampa FL 33602 813-228-7777 223-7899
TF: 800-707-8846 ■ *Web:* www.tampachamber.com

North Tampa Chamber of Commerce PO Box 82043 . . . Tampa FL 33682 813-961-2420 961-2903
Web: northtampachamberofcommerce.wildapricot.org

Ybor City Chamber of Commerce 1800 E Ninth Ave . . . Tampa FL 33605 813-248-3712 247-1764
Web: www.ybor.org

Tarpon Springs Chamber of Commerce
111 E Tarpon Ave . . . Tarpon Springs FL 34689 727-937-6109 937-2879
Web: tarponspringschamber.com

Titusville Area Chamber of Commerce
2000 S Washington Ave . . . Titusville FL 32780 321-267-3036 264-0127
TF: 800-435-7352 ■ *Web:* www.titusville.org

Venice Area Chamber of Commerce
597 Tamiami Trl S . . . Venice FL 34285 941-488-2236 484-5903
Web: www.venicechamber.com

Indian River County Chamber of Commerce
1216 21st St . . . Vero Beach FL 32960 772-567-3491 778-3181
TF: 877-646-6889 ■ *Web:* www.indianriverchamber.com

Palms West Chamber of Commerce
12794 W Forest Hill Blvd Ste 19 . . . Wellington FL 33414 561-790-6200 791-2069
Web: www.cpbchamber.com

Chamber of Commerce of the Palm Beaches
401 N Flagler Dr . . . West Palm Beach FL 33401 561-833-3711 833-5582
Web: www.palmbeaches.org

West Orange Chamber of Commerce
12184 W Colonial Dr . . . Winter Garden FL 34787 407-656-1304 656-0221
TF: 877-999-9981 ■ *Web:* www.wochamber.com

Greater Winter Haven Area Chamber of Commerce
401 Ave 'B' NW . . . Winter Haven FL 33881 863-293-2138 297-5818
Web: winterhavenchamber.com

Winter Park Chamber of Commerce
151 W Lyman Ave . . . Winter Park FL 32789 407-644-8281 644-7826
TF Help Line: 877-972-4262 ■ *Web:* www.winterpark.org

Zephyrhills Chamber of Commerce
38550 Fifth Ave . . . Zephyrhills FL 33542 813-782-1913 783-6060
TF: 800-851-8754 ■ *Web:* www.zephyrhillschamber.org

Georgia

Phone Fax

Albany Area Chamber of Commerce
225 W Broad Ave . . . Albany GA 31701 229-434-8700 434-8716
TF: 800-475-8700 ■ *Web:* www.albanyga.com

Greater North Fulton Chamber of Commerce (GNFCC)
11605 Haynes Bridge Rd Ste 100 . . . Alpharetta GA 30009 770-993-8806 594-1059
TF: 866-840-5770 ■ *Web:* www.gnfcc.com

Americus-Sumter County Chamber of Commerce
409 Elm Ave PO Box 724 . . . Americus GA 31709 229-924-2646 924-8784
Web: www.sumtercountychamber.com

Athens Area Chamber of Commerce
246 W Hancock Ave . . . Athens GA 30601 706-549-6800 549-5636
Web: www.athensga.com

Cobb Chamber of Commerce 240 I- N Pkwy . . . Atlanta GA 30339 770-980-2000 980-9510
TF: 800-228-2545 ■ *Web:* www.cobbchamber.org

Metro Atlanta Chamber of Commerce
235 International Blvd NW . . . Atlanta GA 30303 404-880-9000
Web: www.metroatlantachamber.com

Augusta Metro Chamber of Commerce
1 10th St Ste 120 . . . Augusta GA 30901 706-821-1300 821-1330
TF: 888-639-8188 ■ *Web:* augustametrochamber.com

Bainbridge-Decatur County Chamber of Commerce
100 Earl May Boat Basin Cir . . . Bainbridge GA 39819 229-246-4774 243-7633
Web: www.bainbridgega.com

Brunswick-Golden Isles Chamber of Commerce
1505 Richmond St 2nd Fl . . . Brunswick GA 31520 912-265-0620 265-0629
TF: 888-453-5955 ■ *Web:* www.brunswickgoldenisleschamber.com

Phone Fax

Gordon County Chamber of Commerce
300 S Wall St . . . Calhoun GA 30701 706-625-3200 625-5062
TF: 800-887-3811 ■ *Web:* www.gordonchamber.org

Cherokee County Chamber of Commerce
3605 Marietta Hwy . . . Canton GA 30114 770-345-0400
Web: www.cherokee-chamber.com

Carroll County Chamber of Commerce
200 Northside Dr . . . Carrollton GA 30117 770-832-2446 832-1300
Web: www.carroll-ga.org

Cartersville-Bartow County Chamber of Commerce
122 W Main St PO Box 307 . . . Cartersville GA 30120 770-382-1466 382-2704
Web: www.cartersvillechamber.com

Chatsworth-Murray County Chamber of Commerce
PO Box 516 . . . Chatsworth GA 30705 706-695-2834 517-1623
TF: 800-969-9490 ■ *Web:* www.murraycountychamber.org

White County Chamber of Commerce
122 N Main St . . . Cleveland GA 30528 706-865-5356 865-0758
TF: 800-392-8279 ■ *Web:* www.whitecountychamber.org

Greater Columbus Chamber of Commerce
1200 Sixth Ave PO Box 1200 . . . Columbus GA 31902 706-327-1566 327-7512
TF: 800-360-8552 ■ *Web:* www.columbusgachamber.com

Conyers-Rockdale Chamber of Commerce
1186 Scott St . . . Conyers GA 30012 770-483-7049 922-8415
Web: www.conyers-rockdale.com

Habersham County Chamber of Commerce
668 Clarkesville St . . . Cornelia GA 30531 706-778-4654 776-1416
TF: 800-835-2559 ■ *Web:* www.habershamchamber.com

Newton County Chamber of Commerce
2101 Clark St . . . Covington GA 30014 770-786-7510 786-1294
Web: gocovington.com/chamber

Cumming-Forsyth County Chamber of Commerce
212 Kelly Mill Rd . . . Cumming GA 30040 770-887-6461 781-8800
Web: www.cummingforsythchamber.org

Paulding County Chamber of Commerce
455 Jimmy Campbell Pkwy . . . Dallas GA 30132 770-445-6016 445-3050
Web: www.pauldingchamber.org

Dalton-Whitfield Chamber of Commerce
890 College Dr . . . Dalton GA 30720 706-278-7373 226-8739
Web: www.daltonchamber.org

Douglas-Coffee County Chamber of Commerce
211 S Gaskin Ave . . . Douglas GA 31533 912-384-1873 383-6304
TF: 888-426-3334 ■ *Web:* www.douglasga.org

Douglas County Chamber of Commerce
6658 Church St . . . Douglasville GA 30134 770-942-5022 942-5876
Web: www.douglascountygeorgia.com

Dublin-Laurens County Chamber of Commerce
1200 Bellvue . . . Dublin GA 31021 478-272-5546 275-0811
TF: 800-829-4933 ■ *Web:* www.dublin-georgia.com

Gwinnett Chamber of Commerce
6500 Sugarloaf Pkwy . . . Duluth GA 30097 770-232-3000 232-8807
Web: www.gwinnettchamber.org

Fayette County Chamber of Commerce
600 W Lanier Ave Ste 250 . . . Fayetteville GA 30214 770-461-9983 461-9622
Web: www.fayettechamber.org

Greater Hall Chamber of Commerce
230 EE Butler Pkwy . . . Gainesville GA 30501 770-532-6206 535-8419
Web: www.ghcc.com

Griffin-Spalding Chamber of Commerce
143 N Hill St . . . Griffin GA 30223 770-228-8200 228-8031
Web: www.griffinchamber.com

Liberty County Chamber of Commerce
425 W Oglethorpe Hwy . . . Hinesville GA 31313 912-368-4445 368-4677
TF: 855-846-3940 ■ *Web:* www.libertycounty.org

Jackson County Area Chamber of Commerce
270 Athens St PO Box 629 . . . Jefferson GA 30549 706-387-0300 387-0304
TF: 800-243-6921 ■ *Web:* www.jacksoncountyga.com

Clayton County Chamber of Commerce
2270 Mt Zion Rd . . . Jonesboro GA 30236 678-610-4021 610-4025
TF: 877-790-1831 ■ *Web:* www.claytonchamber.org

LaGrange-Troup County Chamber of Commerce
111 Bull St . . . LaGrange GA 30240 706-884-8671 882-8012
Web: www.lagrangechamber.com

Greater Macon Chamber of Commerce
305 Coliseum Dr . . . Macon GA 31217 478-621-2000 621-2021
Web: www.maconchamber.com

Henry County Chamber of Commerce
1709 Hwy 20 W . . . McDonough GA 30253 770-957-5786 957-8030
Web: www.henrycounty.com

Milledgeville-Baldwin County Chamber of Commerce
130 S Jefferson St . . . Milledgeville GA 31061 478-453-9311
Web: milledgevillega.com

Walton County Chamber of Commerce
132 E Spring St . . . Monroe GA 30655 770-267-6594 267-0961
Web: www.waltonchamber.org

Moultrie-Colquitt County Chamber of Commerce
116 First Ave SE . . . Moultrie GA 31768 229-985-2131
TF: 888-408-4748 ■ *Web:* www.moultriechamber.com

Newnan-Coweta Chamber of Commerce
23 Bullsboro Dr . . . Newnan GA 30263 770-253-2270 253-2271
Web: www.newnancowetachamber.org

Catoosa County Area Chamber of Commerce
264 Catoosa Cir . . . Ringgold GA 30736 706-965-5201 965-8224
Web: www.catoosachamberofcommerce.com

Walker County Chamber of Commerce
10052 N Hwy 27 . . . Rock Spring GA 30739 706-375-7702 375-7797
TF: 800-321-8128 ■ *Web:* www.walkercochamber.com

Polk County Chamber of Commerce/Development Authority
133 S Marble St . . . Rockmart GA 30153 770-684-8760
Web: www.polkgeorgia.com

Greater Rome Chamber of Commerce
1 Riverside Pkwy . . . Rome GA 30161 706-291-7663 232-5755
Web: www.romega.com

Camden County Chamber of Commerce
2603 Osborne Rd Unit CC . . . Saint Marys GA 31558 912-729-5840 576-7924
TF: 888-331-8226 ■ *Web:* www.camdenchamber.com

Phone Fax

Effingham County Chamber of Commerce
520 W Third St PO Box 1078 .... Springfield GA 31329 912-754-3301 754-1236
TF: 800-241-3333 ■ *Web:* www.effinghamcounty.com

Statesboro-Bulloch Chamber of Commerce
102 S Main St. .... Statesboro GA 30458 912-764-6111
Web: www.statesboro-chamber.org

Thomaston-Upson Chamber of Commerce
110 W Main St .... Thomaston GA 30286 706-647-9686 647-1703
Web: www.thomastonchamber.com

Tifton-Tift County Chamber of Commerce
100 Central Ave .... Tifton GA 31794 229-382-6200 386-2232
TF: 800-550-8438 ■ *Web:* www.tiftonison.com

Toccoa-Stephens County Chamber of Commerce
160 N Alexander St. .... Toccoa GA 30577 706-886-2132 886-2133
Web: www.toccoagachamber.com

DeKalb Chamber of Commerce
125 Clairemont Ave Ste 235 .... Tucker GA 30084 404-378-8000 378-3397
TF: 800-428-7337 ■ *Web:* www.dekalbchamber.org

Valdosta-Lowndes County Chamber of Commerce
416 N Ashley St .... Valdosta GA 31601 229-247-8100 245-0071
Web: www.valdostachamber.com

Warner Robins Area Chamber of Commerce
1228 Watson Blvd .... Warner Robins GA 31093 478-922-8585 328-7745
Web: www.robinsregion.com

Waycross-Ware County Chamber of Commerce
315 Plant Ave Ste B .... Waycross GA 31501 912-283-3742 283-0121
Web: www.waycrosschamber.org

Barrow County Chamber of Commerce PO Box 456 ..... Winder GA 30680 770-867-9444 867-6366
Web: www.barrowchamber.com

Hawaii

Phone Fax

Hawaii Island Chamber of Commerce 117 Keawe St....... Hilo HI 96720 808-935-7178 961-4435
TF: 877-482-4411 ■ *Web:* hicc.biz

Kailua Chamber of Commerce
600 Kailua Rd Ste 107 .... Kailua HI 96734 808-261-2727
TF: 888-261-7997 ■ *Web:* kailuachamber.com

Kona-Kohala Chamber of Commerce
75-5737 Kuakini Hwy Ste 208 .... Kailua-Kona HI 96740 808-329-1758 329-8564
Web: www.kona-kohala.com

Kaua'i Chamber of Commerce 2970 Kele St # 112 .... Lihue HI 96766 808-245-7363 245-8815
Web: www.kauaichamber.org

Idaho

Phone Fax

Boise Metro Chamber of Commerce PO Box 2368 .... Boise ID 83701 208-472-5205 472-5201
Web: www.boisechamber.org

Caldwell Chamber of Commerce 704 Blaine St .... Caldwell ID 83605 208-459-7493 454-1284
TF: 877-375-7382 ■ *Web:* www.cityofcaldwell.com

Coeur d'Alene Area Chamber of Commerce
105 N First St Ste 100 .... Coeur d'Alene ID 83814 208-664-3194 667-9338
TF: 877-782-9232 ■ *Web:* www.cdachamber.com

Mini-Cassia Chamber of Commerce (MCC)
1177 Seventh St .... Heyburn ID 83336 208-679-4793 679-4794
Web: www.minicassiachamber.com

Sun Valley/Ketchum Chamber & Visitors Bureau
491 Sun Vly Rd. .... Ketchum ID 83340 208-726-3423 726-4533
TF: 800-634-3347 ■ *Web:* www.visitsunvalley.com

Meridian Chamber of Commerce
215 E Franklin Rd .... Meridian ID 83642 208-888-2817 888-2682
TF: 866-833-3330 ■ *Web:* www.meridianchamber.org

Moscow Chamber of Commerce 411 S Main St .... Moscow ID 83843 208-882-1800
TF: 866-770-2020 ■ *Web:* www.moscowchamber.com

Nampa Chamber of Commerce 315 11th Ave S.......... Nampa ID 83651 208-466-4641 466-4677
Web: www.nampa.com

Greater Pocatello Chamber of Commerce
324 S Main St. .... Pocatello ID 83204 208-233-1525 233-1527
Web: www.pocatelloidaho.com

Twin Falls Area Chamber of Commerce
2015 Neilsen Point Pl. .... Twin Falls ID 83301 208-733-3974 733-9216
TF: 866-734-3838 ■ *Web:* www.twinfallschamber.com

Illinois

Phone Fax

Addison Chamber of Commerce & Industry
777 W Army Trl Blvd Ste D. .... Addison IL 60101 630-543-4300 543-4355
Web: www.addisonchamber.org

Arlington Heights Chamber of Commerce
311 S Arlington Heights Rd Ste 20 .... Arlington Heights IL 60005 847-253-1703 253-9133

Aurora Chamber of Commerce 43 W Galena Blvd........ Aurora IL 60506 630-256-3180 256-3189
TF: 866-947-8081 ■ *Web:* www.aurorachamber.com

Barrington Area Chamber of Commerce
325 N Hough St .... Barrington IL 60010 847-381-2525 381-2540
Web: www.barringtonchamber.com

Bartlett Chamber of Commerce 138 S Oak Ave .... Bartlett IL 60103 630-830-0324 830-9724
Web: www.bartlettchamber.com

Belvidere Area Chamber of Commerce
130 S State St Ste 300 .... Belvidere IL 61008 815-544-4357 547-7654
Web: www.belviderechamber.com

Berwyn Development Corp
3322 S Oak Pk Ave 2nd Fl .... Berwyn IL 60402 708-788-8100 788-0966
Web: www.berwyn.net

McLean County Chamber of Commerce
2203 E Empire St .... Bloomington IL 61704 309-829-6344 827-3940
Web: www.mcleancochamber.org

Bolingbrook Area Chamber of Commerce & Industry
201 Canterbury Ln Unit B .... Bolingbrook IL 60440 630-226-8420 226-8426
Web: www.bolingbrookchamber.org

Phone Fax

Buffalo Grove Area Chamber of Commerce
50 1/2 Raupp Blvd PO Box 7124 .... Buffalo Grove IL 60089 847-541-7799 541-7819
Web: www.bgacc.org

Calumet City Chamber of Commerce
80 River Oaks Ctr PO Box 2406 .... Calumet City IL 60409 708-891-5888
Web: www.calumetcitychamber.com

Carbondale Chamber of Commerce
131 S Illinois Ave .... Carbondale IL 62901 618-549-2146 529-5063
Web: www.carbondalechamber.com

Northern Kane County Chamber of Commerce
20 S Grove St Ste 101 .... Carpentersville IL 60110 847-426-8565
Web: www.nkcchamber.com

Champaign County Chamber of Commerce
1817 S Neil St Ste 201 .... Champaign IL 61820 217-359-1791 359-1809
TF: 800-328-1627 ■ *Web:* champaigncounty.org

Charleston Area Chamber of Commerce
501 Jackson Ave. .... Charleston IL 61920 217-345-7041 345-7042
Web: www.charlestonchamber.com

Albany Park Chamber of Commerce
3403 W Lauren Ave Ste 201 .... Chicago IL 60625 773-478-0202 478-0282
Web: www.albanyparkchamber.org

Chicagoland Chamber of Commerce
410 N Michigan Ave Ste 900 .... Chicago IL 60611 312-494-6700 861-0660
Web: www.chicagolandchamber.org

Cosmopolitan Chamber of Commerce
30 E Adams St Ste 1050 .... Chicago IL 60603 312-499-0611
Web: www.cosmococ.org

East Side Chamber of Commerce
3501 E 106th St Ste 200 .... Chicago IL 60617 773-721-7948
Web: www.eastsidechamber.com

Hyde Park Chamber of Commerce
5501 S Everett Ave .... Chicago IL 60637 773-288-0124 288-0464
Web: www.hydeparkchamberchicago.org

Lincoln Park Chamber of Commerce
1925 N Clybourn Ave Ste 301 .... Chicago IL 60614 773-880-5200 880-0266
Web: www.lincolnparkchamber.com

Portage Park Chamber of Commerce
5829 W Irving Pk Rd. .... Chicago IL 60634 773-777-2020 777-0202

Collinsville Chamber of Commerce
221 W Main St .... Collinsville IL 62234 618-344-2884 344-7499
Web: www.discovercollinsville.com

Crete Area Chamber of Commerce
1182 Main St PO Box 263 .... Crete IL 60417 708-672-9216 672-7640
Web: www.cretechamber.com

Crystal Lake Chamber of Commerce
427 W Virginia St .... Crystal Lake IL 60014 815-459-1300 459-0243
TF: 800-946-2248 ■ *Web:* www.clchamber.com

Vermillion Advantage 28 W N St. .... Danville IL 61832 217-442-6201 442-6228
Web: www.vermilionadvantage.com

Greater Decatur Chamber of Commerce
101 S Main St Ste 102 .... Decatur IL 62523 217-422-2200 422-4576
Web: www.decaturchamber.com

Deerfield Bannockburn & Riverwoods Chamber of Commerce
601 Deerfield Rd Ste 200 .... Deerfield IL 60015 847-945-4660 940-0381
Web: www.dbrchamber.com

DeKalb Chamber of Commerce 164 E Lincoln Hwy .... DeKalb IL 60115 815-756-6306 756-5164
TF: 888-428-5237 ■ *Web:* www.dekalb.org

Des Plaines Chamber of Commerce & Industry
1401 E Oakton St .... Des Plaines IL 60018 847-824-4200 824-7932
Web: www.dpchamber.com

Elgin Area Chamber of Commerce 31 S Grove Ave .... Elgin IL 60120 847-741-5660 741-5677
TF: 800-621-3362 ■ *Web:* www.elginchamber.com

Greater O'Hare Assn of Industry & Commerce
PO Box 1516 .... Elk Grove Village IL 60009 630-773-2944
TF: 877-355-4768 ■ *Web:* thegoa.com

Elmhurst Chamber of Commerce & Industry
300 A W Lk St Ste 201 .... Elmhurst IL 60126 630-834-6060 834-6002
Web: www.elmhurstchamber.org

Mont Clare-Elmwood Park Chamber of Commerce
11 Conti Pkwy .... Elmwood Park IL 60707 708-456-8000 456-8680
Web: grandchamber.org

Evanston Chamber of Commerce 1840 Oak Ave....... Evanston IL 60201 847-328-1500 328-1510
Web: evchamber.com

Evergreen Park Chamber of Commerce
9449 S Kedzie Ave Ste 196 .... Evergreen Park IL 60805 708-423-1118
Web: www.evergreenparkchamber.org

Freeport Area Chamber of Commerce
27 W Stephenson St .... Freeport IL 61032 815-233-1350 235-4038
Web: www.freeportilchamber.com

Galesburg Area Chamber of Commerce
185 S Kellogg St. .... Galesburg IL 61401 309-343-1194
Web: www.galesburg.org

Glen Ellyn Chamber of Commerce
800 Roosevelt Rd Bldg D Ste 108 .... Glen Ellyn IL 60137 630-469-0907 469-0426
TF: 800-622-9000 ■ *Web:* www.glenellynchamber.com

Glenview Chamber of Commerce
2320 Glenview Rd. .... Glenview IL 60025 847-724-0900 724-0202
Web: www.glenviewchamber.com

Growth Assn of Southwestern Illinois
5800 Godfrey Rd Alden Hall .... Godfrey IL 62035 618-467-2280 466-8289
TF: 855-852-9460 ■ *Web:* www.growthassociation.com

Chamber of Commerce of Southwestern Madison County
3600 Nameoki Rd Ste 202 .... Granite City IL 62040 618-876-6400 876-6448
Web: www.chamberswmadisoncounty.com

Lake County Chamber of Commerce
5221 Grand Ave .... Gurnee IL 60031 847-249-3800
Web: www.lakecountychamber.com

Highland Park Chamber of Commerce
508 Central Ave Ste 206 .... Highland Park IL 60035 847-432-0284 432-2802
Web: www.chamberhp.com

West Suburban Chamber of Commerce
9440 Joliet Rd Ste B .... Hodgkins IL 60525 708-387-7550 387-7556
TF: 800-796-9696 ■ *Web:* www.wscci.org

Hoffman Estates Chamber of Commerce
2200 W Higgins Rd Ste 201 .... Hoffman Estates IL 60169 847-781-9100 781-9172
Web: www.hechamber.com

	City	State	Zip	Phone	Fax
Chicago Southland Chamber of Commerce 920 W 175th St *Web:* www.chicagosouthlandchamber.com	Homewood	IL	60430	708-957-6950	957-6968
Jacksonville Area Chamber of Commerce 310 E State St *TF:* 800-593-5678 ■ *Web:* www.jacksonvilleil.org	Jacksonville	IL	62650	217-243-5678	
Joliet Region Chamber of Commerce & Industry 63 N Chicago St *TF:* 877-499-9669 ■ *Web:* www.jolietchamber.com	Joliet	IL	60432	815-727-5371	727-5374
Algonquin/Lake in the Hills Chamber of Commerce 2114 W Algonquin Rd *Web:* www.alchamber.com	Lake In the Hills	IL	60156	847-658-5300	658-6546
Lake Zurich Area Chamber of Commerce 444 S Rand Rd Ste 308 *Web:* www.lzacc.com	Lake Zurich	IL	60047	847-438-5572	438-5574
Lansing Chamber of Commerce 3330 181st Pl Ste 103 *Web:* www.chamberoflansing.com	Lansing	IL	60438	708-474-4170	
GLMV Chamber of Commerce 1123 S Milwaukee Ave *Web:* www.glmvchamber.org	Libertyville	IL	60048	847-680-0750	680-0760
Lincoln/Logan County Chamber of Commerce 1555 Fifth St *Web:* www.lincolnillinois.com	Lincoln	IL	62656	217-735-2385	735-9205
Lombard Area Chamber of Commerce 10 Lilac Ln. *Web:* www.lombardchamber.com	Lombard	IL	60148	630-627-5040	627-5519
Parks Chamber of Commerce 100 Heart Blvd *Web:* www.parkschamber.com	Loves Park	IL	61111	815-633-3999	633-4057
Macomb Area Chamber of Commerce & Downtown Development Corp 214 N Lafayette St *Web:* www.macombareachamber.com	Macomb	IL	61455	309-837-4855	837-4857
Greater Marion Area Chamber of Commerce 2305 W Main St *Web:* www.marionillinois.com	Marion	IL	62959	618-997-6311	233-8765
McHenry Area Chamber of Commerce 1257 N Green St *Web:* www.mchenrychamber.com	McHenry	IL	60050	815-385-4300	385-9142
Illinois Quad City Chamber of Commerce 1601 River Dr Ste 310 *Web:* www.quadcitieschamber.com	Moline	IL	61265	309-757-5416	
Grundy County Chamber of Commerce & Industry 909 Liberty St *TF:* 800-892-1412 ■ *Web:* www.grundychamber.com	Morris	IL	60450	815-942-0113	942-0117
Mount Prospect Chamber of Commerce 662 E NW Hwy *TF:* 800-584-4452 ■ *Web:* www.mountprospectchamber.org	Mount Prospect	IL	60056	847-398-6616	398-6780
Jefferson County Chamber of Commerce 200 Potomac Blvd *Web:* www.southernillinois.com	Mount Vernon	IL	62864	618-242-5725	242-5130
Naperville Area Chamber of Commerce 55 S Main St Ste 351 *Web:* www.naperville.net	Naperville	IL	60540	630-355-4141	355-8335
Niles Chamber of Commerce 8060 Oakton St *Web:* www.nileschamber.com	Niles	IL	60714	847-268-8180	268-8186
Northbrook Chamber of Commerce & Industry 2002 Walters Ave *TF:* 855-354-3337 ■ *Web:* www.northbrookchamber.org	Northbrook	IL	60062	847-498-5555	498-5510
Oak Forest - Crestwood Area Chamber of Commerce 15440 S Central Ave *Web:* oc-chamber.org	Oak Forest	IL	60452	708-687-4600	
Oak Lawn Chamber of Commerce 5120 Museum Dr *Web:* www.oaklawnchamber.com	Oak Lawn	IL	60453	708-424-8300	
Oak Park-River Forest Chamber of Commerce PO Box 4554 *Web:* www.oprfchamber.org	Oak Park	IL	60304	708-613-0550	
Orland Park Area Chamber of Commerce 8799 W 151 St *Web:* www.orlandparkchamber.org	Orland Park	IL	60462	708-349-2972	349-7454
Palatine Area Chamber of Commerce 579 First Bank Dr #205 *Web:* www.palatinechamber.com	Palatine	IL	60067	847-359-7200	359-7246
Pekin Area Chamber of Commerce 402 Ct St *Web:* www.pekinchamber.com	Pekin	IL	61554	309-346-2106	346-2104
Peoria Area Chamber of Commerce 100 SW Water St *TF:* 888-681-6561 ■ *Web:* www.peoriachamber.org	Peoria	IL	61602	309-676-0755	676-7534
Illinois Valley Area Chamber of Commerce & Economic Development 1320 Peoria St *Web:* www.ivaced.org	Peru	IL	61354	815-223-0227	223-4827
Quincy Area Chamber of Commerce 300 Civic Ctr Plz Ste 245 *Web:* www.quincychamber.org	Quincy	IL	62301	217-222-7980	222-3033
Rockford Chamber of Commerce 308 W State St Ste 190 *TF:* 866-767-2629 ■ *Web:* www.rockfordchamber.com	Rockford	IL	61101	815-987-8100	987-8122
Rolling Meadows Chamber of Commerce 2775 Algonquin Rd Ste 310 *Web:* rmchamber.org	Rolling Meadows	IL	60008	847-398-3730	398-3745
Round Lake Area Chamber of Commerce & Industry 2007 Civic Ctr Way *TF:* 800-334-7661 ■ *Web:* www.rlchamber.org	Round Lake Beach	IL	60073	847-546-2002	546-2254
Skokie Chamber of Commerce 5002 Oakton St PO Box 106 *Web:* www.skokiechamber.org	Skokie	IL	60077	847-673-0240	673-0249
Greater Springfield Chamber of Commerce, The 1011 S Second St *Web:* www.gscc.org	Springfield	IL	62701	217-525-1173	525-8768
Illinois Assn of Chamber of Commerce Executives 215 E Adams St *Web:* www.iacce.org	Springfield	IL	62701	217-522-5512	522-5518
Streamwood Chamber of Commerce 22 W Streamwood Blvd PO Box 545 *Web:* www.streamwoodchamber.com	Streamwood	IL	60107	630-837-5200	837-5251
Streator Area Chamber of Commerce & Industry 320 E Main St PO Box 360 *Web:* www.streatorchamber.com	Streator	IL	61364	815-672-2921	672-1768
Tinley Park Chamber of Commerce 17316 Oak Pk Ave *Web:* www.tinleychamber.org	Tinley Park	IL	60477	708-532-5700	532-1475
Wheaton Chamber of Commerce 108 E Wesley St *Web:* www.wheatonchamber.com	Wheaton	IL	60187	630-668-6464	668-2744
Wheeling/Prospect Heights Area Chamber of Commerce & Industry 2 Community Blvd Ste 203 *Web:* www.wphchamber.com	Wheeling	IL	60090	847-541-0170	541-0296
Wilmette Chamber of Commerce (WCC) 351 Linden Ave *Web:* www.wilmettechamber.org	Wilmette	IL	60091	847-251-3800	251-6321
Woodridge Area Chamber of Commerce 6440 Main St Ste 330 *Web:* chamber630.com	Woodridge	IL	60517	630-960-7080	852-2316
Woodstock Chamber of Commerce & Industry 136 Cass St *Web:* www.woodstockilchamber.com	Woodstock	IL	60098	815-338-2436	338-2927

Indiana

	City	State	Zip	Phone	Fax
Greater Bloomington Chamber of Commerce 400 W Seventh St Ste 102 *Web:* www.chamberbloomington.org	Bloomington	IN	47404	812-336-6381	336-0651
Warrick County Chamber of Commerce 224 W Main St Ste 203 *Web:* warrickchamber.org	Boonville	IN	47601	812-897-2340	897-2360
Columbus Area Chamber of Commerce 500 Franklin St *Web:* www.columbusareachamber.com	Columbus	IN	47201	812-379-4457	
Connersville Chamber-Commerce 504 N Central Ave *Web:* connersvillechamber.com	Connersville	IN	47331	765-825-2561	825-4613
Chamber of Commerce of Harrison County 111 W Walnut St *Web:* www.harrisonchamber.org	Corydon	IN	47112	812-738-0120	738-0500
Crawfordsville-Montgomery County Chamber of Commerce 309 N Green St *Web:* www.crawfordsvillechamber.com	Crawfordsville	IN	47933	765-362-6800	362-6900
Greater Elkhart Chamber of Commerce 418 S Main St *Web:* www.elkhart.org	Elkhart	IN	46516	574-293-1531	294-1859
Chamber of Commerce of Southwest Indiana 318 Main St Ste 401 *Web:* swinchamber.com	Evansville	IN	47708	812-425-8147	421-5883
Greater Fort Wayne Chamber of Commerce 826 Ewing St *Web:* greaterfortwayneinc.com	Fort Wayne	IN	46802	260-424-1435	426-7232
Clinton County Chamber of Commerce 259 E Walnut St *Web:* www.ccinchamber.org	Frankfort	IN	46041	765-654-5507	654-9592
Gary Chamber of Commerce 839 Broadway Ste S103 *Web:* www.garychamber.com	Gary	IN	46402	219-885-7407	
Goshen Chamber of Commerce 232 S Main St *TF:* 800-307-4204 ■ *Web:* www.goshen.org	Goshen	IN	46526	574-533-2102	533-2103
Greencastle Chamber of Commerce 16 S Jackson St *Web:* www.gogreencastle.com	Greencastle	IN	46135	765-653-4517	
Greater Greenwood Chamber of Commerce 65 Airport Pkwy *TF:* 800-462-7585 ■ *Web:* www.greenwoodchamber.com	Greenwood	IN	46143	317-888-4856	865-2609
Lakeshore Chamber of Commerce 5246 Hohman Ave Ste 100 *TF:* 855-464-6368 ■ *Web:* www.lakeshorechamber.com	Hammond	IN	46320	219-931-1000	937-8778
Greater Indianapolis Chamber of Commerce 111 Monument Cir Ste 1950 *Web:* www.indychamber.com	Indianapolis	IN	46204	317-464-2200	464-2217
Greater Lawrence Township Chamber of Commerce 9120 Otis Ave Ste 100 *TF:* 800-473-2328 ■ *Web:* www.lawrencechamberofcommerce.org	Indianapolis	IN	46216	317-541-9876	541-9875
Kokomo/Howard County Chamber of Commerce 325 N Main St *Web:* greaterkokomo.com	Kokomo	IN	46901	765-457-5301	452-4564
Lafayette-West Lafayette Chamber of Commerce 337 Columbia St *Web:* www.lafayettechamber.com	Lafayette	IN	47902	765-742-4041	742-6276
LaGrange County Chamber of Commerce 901 S Detroit St Ste A *Web:* www.lagrangechamber.org	LaGrange	IN	46761	260-463-2443	463-2683
Dearborn County Chamber of Commerce 320 Walnut St *TF:* 800-322-8198 ■ *Web:* www.dearborncountychamber.org	Lawrenceburg	IN	47025	812-537-0814	537-0845
Boone County Chamber of Commerce 221 N Lebanon St *Web:* www.boonechamber.org	Lebanon	IN	46052	765-482-1320	482-3114
Logansport/Cass County Chamber of Commerce 300 E Broadway Ste 103 *Web:* www.logan-casschamber.com	Logansport	IN	46947	574-753-6388	735-0909
Madison Area Chamber of Commerce 301 E Main St *Web:* www.madisonindiana.com/chamber	Madison	IN	47250	812-265-3135	265-9784
Marion-Grant County Chamber of Commerce 215 S Adams St *Web:* www.marionchamber.org	Marion	IN	46952	765-664-5107	668-5443
Michigan City Area Chamber of Commerce 200 E Michigan Blvd *Web:* www.michigancitychamber.com	Michigan City	IN	46360	219-874-6221	873-1204
Greater Monticello Chamber of Commerce 116 N Main St *TF:* 800-541-7906 ■ *Web:* www.monticelloin.com	Monticello	IN	47960	574-583-7220	583-3399

Chamber	City	State	ZIP	Phone	Fax
Muncie-Delaware County Chamber of Commerce 401 S High St *TF:* 800-336-1373 ■ *Web:* www.muncie.com	Muncie	IN	47305	765-288-6681	751-9151
One Southern Indiana 4100 Charlestown Rd *TF:* 800-521-2232 ■ *Web:* www.1si.org	New Albany	IN	47150	812-945-0266	948-4664
Noblesville Chamber of Commerce 601 Conner St *Web:* www.noblesvillechamber.com	Noblesville	IN	46060	317-773-0086	773-1966
Jennings County Chamber of Commerce 203 N State St PO Box 340 *TF:* 866-382-4968 ■ *Web:* www.jenningscountychamber.com	North Vernon	IN	47265	812-346-2339	
Miami County Chamber of Commerce 13 E Main St *TF:* 800-521-9945 ■ *Web:* www.miamicochamber.com	Peru	IN	46970	765-472-1923	472-7099
Greater Portage Chamber of Commerce 2642 Eleanor St *Web:* www.portageinchamber.com	Portage	IN	46368	219-762-3300	763-2450
Wayne County Area Chamber of Commerce 33 S Seventh St Ste 2 *Web:* www.wcareachamber.org	Richmond	IN	47374	765-962-1511	966-0882
Schererville Chamber of Commerce 149 E Joliet St *Web:* www.46375.org	Schererville	IN	46375	219-322-5412	322-0598
Shelby County Chamber of Commerce 501 N Harrison St *TF:* 800-318-4083 ■ *Web:* www.shelbychamber.net	Shelbyville	IN	46176	317-398-6647	392-3901
Chamber of Commerce of Saint Joseph County 401 E Colfax Ave Ste 310 *Web:* www.sjchamber.org	South Bend	IN	46617	574-234-0051	289-0358
Winchester Area Chamber of Commerce 211 S Main St *Web:* www.winchesterareachamber.org	Winchester	IN	47394	765-584-3731	584-5544

Iowa

Chamber	City	State	ZIP	Phone	Fax
Ames Chamber of Commerce 1601 Golden Aspen Dr Ste 110 *TF:* 800-288-7470 ■ *Web:* www.ameschamber.com	Ames	IA	50010	515-232-2310	232-6716
Burlington/West Burlington Area Chamber of Commerce 610 N Fourth St Ste 200 *TF:* 800-827-4837 ■ *Web:* www.greaterburlington.com	Burlington	IA	52601	319-752-6365	752-6454
Greater Cedar Falls Chamber of Commerce 312 W 1st St *Web:* cedarvalleyalliance.com	Cedar Falls	IA	50613	319-266-3593	277-4325
Cedar Rapids Area Chamber of Commerce 424 First Ave NE *Web:* www.cedarrapids.org	Cedar Rapids	IA	52401	319-398-5317	398-5228
Clinton Area Chamber of Commerce 721 S Second St *Web:* www.clintonia.com	Clinton	IA	52732	563-242-5702	242-5803
Council Bluffs Area Chamber of Commerce 149 W Bdwy *TF:* 800-228-6878 ■ *Web:* www.councilbluffsiowa.com	Council Bluffs	IA	51503	712-325-1000	322-5698
Greater Des Moines Partnership 700 Locust St Ste 100 *TF:* 866-487-9243 ■ *Web:* www.desmoinesmetro.com	Des Moines	IA	50309	515-286-4950	286-4974
Dubuque Area Chamber of Commerce 300 Main St Ste 200 *TF:* 800-798-4748 ■ *Web:* www.dubuquechamber.com	Dubuque	IA	52001	563-557-9200	557-1591
Fort Dodge Chamber of Commerce 24 N 9th St Ste A *Web:* www.greaterfortdodge.com	Fort Dodge	IA	50501	515-955-5500	955-3245
Iowa City Area Chamber of Commerce 325 E Washington St Ste 100 *Web:* www.iowacityarea.com	Iowa City	IA	52240	319-337-9637	338-9958
Keokuk Area Chamber of Commerce 329 Main St *Web:* www.keokukchamber.wildapricot.org	Keokuk	IA	52632	319-524-5055	524-5016
Marion Chamber of Commerce 1225 Sixth Ave Ste 100 *Web:* www.cedarrapids.org	Marion	IA	52302	319-377-6316	
Marshalltown Area Chamber of Commerce 709 S Ctr St PO Box 1000 *TF:* 800-725-5301 ■ *Web:* www.marshalltown.org	Marshalltown	IA	50158	641-753-6645	752-8373
Mason City Area Chamber of Commerce 25 W State St *Web:* www.masoncityia.com	Mason City	IA	50401	641-423-5724	423-5725
Ottumwa Area Chamber of Commerce 217 E Main St *Web:* www.ottumwaiowa.com	Ottumwa	IA	52501	641-682-3465	682-3466
Siouxland Chamber of Commerce 101 Pierce St *TF:* 800-228-7903 ■ *Web:* www.siouxlandchamber.com	Sioux City	IA	51101	712-255-7903	258-7578
Urbandale Chamber of Commerce 3600 NW 86th St *Web:* uniquelyurbandale.com	Urbandale	IA	50322	515-331-6855	331-2987
Greater Cedar Valley Chamber of Commerce 10 W 4th St Ste 310 *TF:* 800-288-1047 ■ *Web:* cedarvalleyalliance.com	Waterloo	IA	50703	319-232-1156	233-4580
West Des Moines Chamber of Commerce 650 S Prairie View Dr Ste 110 *Web:* www.wdmchamber.org	West Des Moines	IA	50266	515-225-6009	

Kansas

Chamber	City	State	ZIP	Phone	Fax
Arkansas City Area Chamber of Commerce PO Box 795 *Web:* www.arkcity.org	Arkansas City	KS	67005	620-442-0230	
Dodge City Area Chamber of Commerce 311 W Spruce St *Web:* www.dodgechamber.com	Dodge City	KS	67801	620-227-3119	227-2957
Emporia Area Chamber of Commerce 719 Commercial St *TF:* 800-279-3730 ■ *Web:* www.emporiakschamber.org	Emporia	KS	66801	620-342-1600	342-3223
Garden City Area Chamber of Commerce 1511 E Fulton Terr *Web:* www.gardencity.net	Garden City	KS	67846	620-275-1900	
Hutchinson/Reno County Chamber of Commerce 117 N Walnut St *TF:* 800-691-4262 ■ *Web:* www.hutchchamber.com	Hutchinson	KS	67501	620-662-3391	662-2168
Junction City Area Chamber of Commerce 222 W Sixth St PO Box 26 *Web:* www.junctioncitychamber.org	Junction City	KS	66441	785-762-2632	
Kansas City Kansas Area Chamber of Commerce 727 Minnesota Ave *Web:* www.kckchamber.com	Kansas City	KS	66117	913-371-3070	371-3732
Women's Chamber of Commerce PO Box 171337 *Web:* www.womenschamberkck.org	Kansas City	KS	66117	913-371-3165	
Leavenworth-Lansing Area Chamber of Commerce 518 Shawnee St *Web:* www.llchamber.com	Leavenworth	KS	66048	913-682-4112	682-8170
Liberal Area Chamber of Commerce PO Box 676 *Web:* www.liberalkschamber.com	Liberal	KS	67905	620-624-3855	624-8851
Manhattan Area Chamber of Commerce 501 Poyntz Ave *TF:* 800-759-0134 ■ *Web:* www.manhattan.org	Manhattan	KS	66502	785-776-8829	776-0679
Olathe Chamber of Commerce 18001 W 106th St Ste 160 *Web:* www.olathe.org	Olathe	KS	66061	913-764-1050	782-4636
Overland Park Chamber of Commerce 9001 W 110th St Ste 150 *Web:* opchamber.org/	Overland Park	KS	66210	913-491-3600	491-0393
Pittsburg Area Chamber of Commerce 117 W Fourth St *TF:* 800-794-4780 ■ *Web:* www.pittsburgareachamber.com	Pittsburg	KS	66762	620-231-1000	231-3178
Salina Area Chamber of Commerce 120 W Ash St *TF:* 877-725-4625 ■ *Web:* www.salinakansas.org	Salina	KS	67401	785-827-9301	827-9758
Shawnee Chamber of Commerce 15100 W 67th St Ste 202 *Web:* www.shawneekschamber.com	Shawnee	KS	66217	913-631-6545	631-9628
Greater Topeka Chamber of Commerce 120 SE Sixth St Ste 110 *Web:* www.topekachamber.org	Topeka	KS	66603	785-234-2644	234-8656
Wichita Area Chamber of Commerce 350 W Douglas Ave *Web:* www.wichitachamber.org	Wichita	KS	67202	316-265-7771	265-7502

Kentucky

Chamber	City	State	ZIP	Phone	Fax
Ashland Alliance Chamber of Commerce 1733 Winchester Ave *TF:* 800-233-3826 ■ *Web:* www.ashlandalliance.com	Ashland	KY	41101	606-324-5111	325-4607
Marshall County Chamber of Commerce 17 US Hwy 68 W *Web:* www.marshallcounty.net	Benton	KY	42025	270-527-7665	527-9193
Bowling Green Area Chamber of Commerce 710 College St *TF:* 866-330-2422 ■ *Web:* www.bgchamber.com	Bowling Green	KY	42101	270-781-3200	843-0458
Danville-Boyle County Chamber of Commerce 105 East Walnut St *Web:* www.betterindanville.com	Danville	KY	40422	859-236-2805	
Elizabethtown-Hardin County Chamber of Commerce (HCCC) 111 W Dixie Ave *Web:* hardinchamber.com	Elizabethtown	KY	42701	270-765-4334	737-0690
Northern Kentucky Chamber of Commerce 300 Buttermilk Pk Ste 330 *Web:* www.nkychamber.com	Fort Mitchell	KY	41017	859-578-8800	578-8802
Frankfort Area Chamber of Commerce 100 Capitol Ave *Web:* www.frankfortky.info	Frankfort	KY	40601	502-223-8261	223-5942
Georgetown-Scott County Chamber of Commerce 160 E Main St *Web:* www.gtown.org	Georgetown	KY	40324	502-863-5424	863-5756
Glasgow-Barren County Chamber of Commerce 118 E Public Sq *TF:* 800-264-3161 ■ *Web:* www.glasgowbarrenchamber.com	Glasgow	KY	42141	270-651-3161	651-3122
Greenville-Muhlenberg Chamber of Commerce 100 E Main Cross *Web:* www.greatermuhlenberg.com	Greenville	KY	42345	270-338-5422	338-5440
Harlan County Chamber of Commerce PO Box 268 *Web:* www.harlancountychamber.com	Harlan	KY	40831	606-573-4717	
Hopkinsville-Christian County Chamber of Commerce 2800 Port Campbell Blvd *TF:* 800-842-9959 ■ *Web:* www.christiancountychamber.com	Hopkinsville	KY	42240	270-885-9096	881-9366
Jeffersontown Chamber of Commerce 10434 Watterson Tr *Web:* www.jtownchamber.com	Jeffersontown	KY	40299	502-267-1674	
Oldham County Chamber of Commerce 412 E Main St *Web:* www.oldhamcountychamber.com	LaGrange	KY	40031	502-222-1635	222-3159
Greater Lexington Chamber of Commerce Inc 330 E Main St Ste 100 *Web:* www.commercelexington.com	Lexington	KY	40507	859-254-4447	233-3304
Greater Louisville Inc 614 W Main St *Web:* www.greaterlouisville.com	Louisville	KY	40202	502-625-0000	625-0010
Madisonville-Hopkins County Chamber of Commerce 15 E Ctr St *Web:* www.hopkinschamber.com	Madisonville	KY	42431	270-821-3435	821-9190
Mayfield-Graves County Chamber of Commerce 201 E College St *Web:* www.mayfieldchamber.com	Mayfield	KY	42066	270-247-6101	
Bell County Chamber of Commerce PO Box 788 *Web:* www.bellcountychamber.net	Middlesboro	KY	40965	606-248-1075	248-8851
Chamber of Commerce - Murray-Calloway County, The 805 N 12th St *Web:* www.mymurray.com	Murray	KY	42071	270-753-5171	

				Phone	Fax
Greater Owensboro Chamber of Commerce 200 E Third St PO Box 825 *Web:* www.owensboro.com	Owensboro	KY	42302	270-926-1860	926-3364
Paducah Area Chamber of Commerce 300 S Third St *Web:* www.paducahchamber.org	Paducah	KY	42003	270-443-1746	442-9152
Pike County Chamber of Commerce 178 College St *Web:* www.sekchamber.com	Pikeville	KY	41501	606-432-5504	432-7295
Radcliff Hardin County Chamber of Commerce 306 N Wilson Rd *Web:* www.hardinchamber.com	Radcliff	KY	40160	270-351-4450	352-4449
Logan County Chamber of Commerce 116 S Main St *TF:* 800-811-8379 ■ *Web:* www.loganchamber.com	Russellville	KY	42276	270-726-2206	
Shelby County Chamber of Commerce 316 Main St *Web:* www.shelbycountykychamber.com	Shelbyville	KY	40065	502-633-1636	633-7501
Bullitt County Chamber of Commerce 295 N Buckman St PO Box 1656 *Web:* www.bullittchamber.org	Shepherdsville	KY	40165	502-955-9641	
Somerset-Pulaski County Chamber of Commerce 445 S Hwy 27 Ste 101 *TF:* 877-629-9722 ■ *Web:* somersetpulaskichamber.com	Somerset	KY	42501	606-679-7323	679-1744
Winchester-Clark County Chamber of Commerce 2 S Maple St *Web:* www.winchesterkychamber.com	Winchester	KY	40391	859-744-6420	744-9229

Louisiana

				Phone	Fax
Central Louisiana Chamber of Commerce 1118 Third St PO Box 992 *Web:* www.cenlachamber.org	Alexandria	LA	71309	318-442-6671	442-6734
Bastrop-Morehouse Parish Chamber of Commerce 110 N Franklin St *Web:* bastroplacoc.org	Bastrop	LA	71220	318-281-3794	
Greater Baton Rouge Chamber of Commerce 564 Laurel St *Web:* www.brac.org	Baton Rouge	LA	70801	225-381-7125	336-4306
Bossier Chamber of Commerce 710 Benton Rd *TF:* 800-659-2955 ■ *Web:* www.bossierchamber.com	Bossier City	LA	71111	318-746-0252	746-0357
Saint Tammany West Chamber of Commerce 610 Hollycrest Blvd *Web:* www.sttammanychamber.org	Covington	LA	70433	985-892-3216	893-4244
Livingston Parish Chamber of Commerce PO Box 591 *Web:* www.livingstonparishchamber.org	Denham Springs	LA	70726	225-665-8155	665-2411
Greater Beauregard Chamber of Commerce 111 N Washington St *Web:* www.beauchamber.org	DeRidder	LA	70634	337-463-5533	463-2244
Ascension Chamber of Commerce 1006 W Hwy 30 *Web:* www.ascensionchamber.com	Gonzales	LA	70737	225-647-7487	647-5124
Houma-Terrebonne Chamber of Commerce 6133 Louisiana 311 *Web:* www.houmachamber.com	Houma	LA	70360	985-876-5600	876-5611
One Acadiana 804 E St Mary Blvd *Web:* www.lafchamber.org	Lafayette	LA	70503	337-233-2705	234-8671
Chamber/Southwest Louisiana 120 W Pujo St *Web:* allianceswla.org	Lake Charles	LA	70601	337-433-3632	436-3727
Chamber of Lafourche & the Bayou Region 107 W 26th St *Web:* www.lafourchechamber.com	Larose	LA	70373	985-693-6700	693-6702
Greater Vernon Chamber of Commerce PO Box 1228 *Web:* www.chambervernonparish.com	Leesville	LA	71496	337-238-0349	238-0340
DeSoto Parish Chamber of Commerce 115 N Washington Ave *Web:* www.desotoparishchamber.net	Mansfield	LA	71052	318-872-1310	871-1875
Jefferson Chamber of Commerce 3421 N Cswy Blvd Ste 203 *Web:* jeffersonchamber.org	Metairie	LA	70002	504-835-3880	835-3828
Monroe Chamber of Commerce 212 Walnut St Ste 100 *TF:* 888-677-5200 ■ *Web:* www.monroe.org	Monroe	LA	71201	318-323-3461	322-7594
Natchitoches Area Chamber of Commerce 780 Front St Ste 101 *TF:* 877-646-6689 ■ *Web:* www.natchitocheschamber.com	Natchitoches	LA	71457	318-352-6894	352-5385
Greater Iberia Chamber of Commerce 111 W Main St *Web:* iberiachamber.org	New Iberia	LA	70560	337-364-1836	367-7405
New Orleans Chamber of Commerce 1515 Poydras St Ste 1010 *Web:* www.neworleanschamber.org	New Orleans	LA	70112	504-799-4260	799-4259
Iberville Parish Chamber of Commerce 23675 Church St *TF:* 800-266-2692 ■ *Web:* www.ibervillechamber.com	Plaquemine	LA	70764	225-687-3560	687-3575
Ruston/Lincoln Chamber of Commerce 2111 N Trenton St *TF:* 800-392-9032 ■ *Web:* www.rustonlincoln.org	Ruston	LA	71270	318-255-2031	255-3481
Greater Shreveport Chamber of Commerce 400 Edwards St *TF:* 800-448-5432 ■ *Web:* www.shreveportchamber.org	Shreveport	LA	71101	318-677-2500	677-2541
East St Tammany Chamber of Commerce 118 W Hall Ave *TF:* 800-870-3673 ■ *Web:* estchamber.com	Slidell	LA	70460	985-643-5678	649-2460
Thibodaux Chamber of Commerce 318 E Bayou Rd PO Box 467 *Web:* thibodauxchamber.com	Thibodaux	LA	70302	985-446-1187	446-1191

Maine

				Phone	Fax
Kennebec Valley Chamber of Commerce 21 University Dr *Web:* www.augustamaine.com	Augusta	ME	04330	207-623-4559	626-9342
Bangor Region Chamber of Commerce 208 Maine Ave *Web:* www.bangorregion.com	Bangor	ME	04401	207-947-0307	990-1427
Bar Harbor Chamber of Commerce 2 Cottage St *TF:* 888-540-9990 ■ *Web:* www.barharborinfo.com	Bar Harbor	ME	04609	207-288-5103	667-9080
Belfast Area Chamber of Commerce 14 Main St *TF:* 877-338-9015 ■ *Web:* www.belfastmaine.org	Belfast	ME	04915	207-338-5900	338-3808
Biddeford-Saco Chamber of Commerce & Industry 28 Water St Ste 101 *Web:* www.biddefordsacochamber.org	Biddeford	ME	04005	207-282-1567	
Saint Croix Valley Chamber of Commerce 39 Union St *Web:* www.visitcalais.com	Calais	ME	04619	207-454-2308	
Ellsworth Area Chamber of Commerce 163 High St *Web:* www.ellsworthchamber.org	Ellsworth	ME	04605	207-667-5584	667-2617
Greater Lincoln Lakes Region Chamber of Commerce 256 W Broadway *Web:* www.lincolnmechamber.org	Lincoln	ME	04457	207-794-8065	
Portland Regional Chamber 443 Congress St *Web:* www.portlandregion.com	Portland	ME	04101	207-772-2811	772-1179
Sanford-Springvale Chamber of Commerce & Economic Development 917 Main St Ste B *Web:* www.sanfordchamber.org	Sanford	ME	04073	207-324-4280	
Oxford Hills Chamber of Commerce 4 Western Ave *Web:* www.oxfordhillsmaine.com	South Paris	ME	04281	207-743-2281	743-0687
Southern Midcoast Maine Chamber 2 Main St Border Trust Business Ctr *TF:* 877-725-8797 ■ *Web:* www.midcoastmaine.com	Topsham	ME	04086	207-725-8797	725-9787
Mid-Maine Chamber of Commerce 50 Elm St *Web:* www.midmainechamber.com	Waterville	ME	04901	207-873-3315	877-0087

Maryland

				Phone	Fax
Annapolis & Anne Arundel County Chamber of Commerce 134 Holiday Ct Ste 316 *Web:* www.annearundelchamber.org	Annapolis	MD	21401	410-266-3960	266-8270
Harford County Chamber of Commerce 108 S Bond St *TF:* 800-682-8536 ■ *Web:* www.harfordchamber.org	Bel Air	MD	21014	410-838-2020	893-4715
Greater Bethesda-Chevy Chase Chamber of Commerce 7910 Woodmont Ave Ste 1204 *TF:* 800-333-6778 ■ *Web:* www.bccchamber.org	Bethesda	MD	20814	301-652-4900	657-1973
Greater Bowie Chamber of Commerce 1525 Pointer Ridge Pl Ste 117 *Web:* www.bowiechamber.org	Bowie	MD	20715	301-262-0920	262-0921
Dorchester Chamber of Commerce 528 Poplar St *Web:* www.dorchesterchamber.org	Cambridge	MD	21613	410-228-3575	228-6848
Queen Anne's County Chamber of Commerce 1561 Postal Rd *Web:* www.qacchamber.com	Chester	MD	21619	410-643-8530	643-8477
Howard County Chamber of Commerce 5560 Sterrett Pl Ste 105 *Web:* www.howardchamber.com	Columbia	MD	21044	410-730-4111	730-4584
Greater Crofton Chamber of Commerce PO Box 4146 **Fax Area Code:* 443 ■ *Web:* www.greatercroftonchamberofcommerce.wildapricot.org	Crofton	MD	21114	410-721-9131	274-6060*
Allegany County Chamber of Commerce 24 Frederick St *Web:* www.alleganycountychamber.com	Cumberland	MD	21502	301-722-2820	722-5995
Caroline County Chamber of Commerce 24820 Meeting House Rd Ste 1 *Web:* www.carolinechamber.org	Denton	MD	21629	410-479-4638	479-4862
Talbot County Chamber of Commerce 101 Marlboro Ave Ste 53 *Web:* www.talbotchamber.org	Easton	MD	21601	410-822-4606	822-7922
Cecil County Chamber of Commerce 106 E Main St Ste 101 *Web:* www.cecilchamber.com	Elkton	MD	21921	410-392-3833	
Frederick County Chamber of Commerce 8420 Gas House Pk Ste B *Web:* www.frederickchamber.org	Frederick	MD	21701	301-662-4164	846-4427
Gaithersburg-Germantown Chamber of Commerce 910 Clopper Rd Ste 205N *Web:* www.ggchamber.org	Gaithersburg	MD	20878	301-840-1400	963-3918
Hagerstown-Washington County Chamber of Commerce 28 W Washington St *Web:* www.hagerstown.org	Hagerstown	MD	21740	301-739-2015	739-1278
Charles County Chamber of Commerce 101 Centennial St Ste A *TF:* 800-992-3194 ■ *Web:* www.charlescountychamber.org	La Plata	MD	20646	301-932-6500	932-3945
Prince George's Chamber of Commerce 4640 Forbes Blvd Ste 130 *Web:* www.pgcoc.org	Lanham	MD	20706	301-731-5000	
Baltimore/Washington Corridor Chamber of Commerce 312 Marshall Ave Ste 104 *Web:* www.baltwashchamber.org	Laurel	MD	20707	301-725-4000	725-0776
Garrett County Chamber of Commerce 15 Visitors Ctr Dr *TF:* 888-387-5237 ■ *Web:* www.visitdeepcreek.com	McHenry	MD	21541	301-387-4386	387-2080
Essex-Middle River-White Marsh Chamber of Commerce 405 Williams Ct Ste 108 *Web:* www.chesapeakechamber.org	Middle River	MD	21220	443-317-8763	317-8772

Phone *Fax*

Greater Ocean City Chamber of Commerce
12320 Ocean Gateway ... Ocean City MD 21842 410-213-0144 213-7521
TF: 888-626-3386 ■ *Web:* www.oceancity.org

West Anne Arundel County Chamber of Commerce
8385 Piney Orchard Pkwy ... Odenton MD 21113 410-672-3422 672-3475
Web: www.westcountychamber.org

Olney Chamber of Commerce
3460 Olney-Laytonsville Rd Ste 211 ... Olney MD 20832 301-774-7117 774-4944
Web: www.olneymd.org

Pikesville Chamber of Commerce
7 Church Ln Ste 14 ... Pikesville MD 21208 410-484-2337 484-4151
Web: www.pikesvillechamber.org

Calvert County Chamber of Commerce
PO Box 9 ... Prince Frederick MD 20678 410-535-2577 295-7213*
**Fax Area Code:* 443 ■ *Web:* www.calvertchamber.org

Montgomery County Chamber of Commerce
51 Monroe St Ste 1800 ... Rockville MD 20850 301-738-0015 738-8792
Web: www.montgomerycountychamber.com

Rockville Chamber of Commerce
1 Research Ct # 450 ... Rockville MD 20850 301-424-9300 762-7599
Web: www.rockvillechamber.org

Salisbury Area Chamber of Commerce
144 E Main St ... Salisbury MD 21801 410-749-0144 860-9925
Web: www.salisburyarea.com

Snow Hill Chamber of Commerce
5485 Airport Terminal Rd ... Salisbury MD 21804 410-632-2080
Web: www.snowhillmd.com

Greater Severna Park Chamber of Commerce
1 Holly Ave ... Severna Park MD 21146 410-647-3900 647-3999
Web: www.severnaparkchamber.com

Greater Silver Spring Chamber of Commerce
8601 Georgia Ave Ste 203 ... Silver Spring MD 20910 301-565-3777 565-3377
Web: www.gsscc.org

Baltimore County Chamber of Commerce
102 W Pennsylvania Ave Ste 101 ... Towson MD 21204 410-825-6200 821-9901
Web: www.baltcountycc.com

Eastern Baltimore Area Chamber of Commerce
102 W Pennsylvania Ave Ste 101 ... Towson MD 21204 410-825-6200 821-9901
Web: www.baltcountycc.com

Carroll County Chamber of Commerce
700 Corporate Ctr Ct # L ... Westminster MD 21157 410-848-9050 876-1023
Web: www.carrollcountychamber.org

Wheaton-Kensington Chamber of Commerce
2401 Blueridge Ave Ste 101 ... Wheaton MD 20902 301-949-0080 949-0081
TF: 800-927-9061 ■ *Web:* www.wkchamber.org

Massachusetts

Phone *Fax*

Middlesex West Chamber of Commerce
179 Great Rd Ste 104B ... Acton MA 01720 978-263-0010 264-0303
TF: 800-439-0183 ■ *Web:* www.mwcoc.com

Amherst Area Chamber of Commerce 28 Amity St ... Amherst MA 01002 413-253-0700 256-0771
Web: www.amherstarea.com

Arlington Chamber of Commerce
611 Massachusetts Ave ... Arlington MA 02474 781-643-4600 646-5581
Web: www.arlcc.org

North Quabbin Chamber of Commerce
251 Exchange St ... Athol MA 01331 978-249-3849 249-7151
Web: www.northquabbinchamber.com

United Regional Chamber of Commerce
42 Union St ... Attleboro MA 02703 508-222-0801 222-1498
Web: www.unitedregionalchamber.org

Beverly Chamber of Commerce
100 Cummings Ctr Ste 107K ... Beverly MA 01915 978-232-9559 232-9372
TF: 800-924-8167 ■ *Web:* www.greaterbeverlychamber.com

Greater Boston Chamber of Commerce
265 Franklin St ... Boston MA 02110 617-227-4500 227-7505
TF: 800-476-3094 ■ *Web:* www.bostonchamber.com

Metro South Chamber of Commerce
60 School St ... Brockton MA 02301 508-586-0500 587-1340
TF: 877-777-4414 ■ *Web:* www.metrosouthchamber.com

Brookline Chamber of Commerce
251 Harvard St Ste 1 ... Brookline MA 02446 617-739-1330 739-1200
Web: www.brooklinechamber.com

Cape Cod Canal Regional Chamber of Commerce
70 Main St ... Buzzards Bay MA 02532 508-759-6000 759-6965
TF: 888-332-2732 ■ *Web:* www.capecodcanalchamber.org

Cambridge Chamber of Commerce
859 Massachusetts Ave ... Cambridge MA 02139 617-876-4100 354-9874
Web: www.cambridgechamber.org

Cape Cod Chamber of Commerce
5 Shoot Flying Hill Rd ... Centerville MA 02632 508-362-3225 362-3698
TF: 888-332-2732 ■ *Web:* www.capecodchamber.org

Chicopee Chamber of Commerce
264 Exchange St ... Chicopee MA 01013 413-594-2101 594-2103
Web: www.chicopeechamber.org

North Shore Chamber of Commerce
5 Cherry Hill Dr Ste 100 ... Danvers MA 01923 978-774-8565 774-3418
Web: www.northshorechamber.org

Nashoba Valley Chamber of Commerce
100 Sherman Ave ... Devens MA 01434 978-772-6976 772-3503
TF: 877-322-8228 ■ *Web:* www.nvcoc.com

Everett Chamber of Commerce 467 Broadway ... Everett MA 02149 617-387-9100 389-6655
Web: www.everettmachamber.com

Fall River Area Chamber of Commerce & Industry
200 Pocasset St ... Fall River MA 02721 508-676-8226 675-5932
TF: 800-647-2824 ■ *Web:* www.fallriverchamber.com

Falmouth Chamber of Commerce 20 Academy Ln ... Falmouth MA 02540 508-548-8500 548-8521
TF: 800-526-8532 ■ *Web:* www.falmouthchamber.com

North Central Massachusetts Chamber of Commerce
860 S St ... Fitchburg MA 01420 978-353-7600 353-4896
Web: www.northcentralmass.com

Phone *Fax*

Metro West Chamber of Commerce
1671 Worcester Rd Ste 201 ... Framingham MA 01701 508-879-5600 875-9325
TF: 866-709-9401 ■ *Web:* www.metrowest.org

Greater Gardner Chamber of Commerce
29 Parker St PO Box 1381 ... Gardner MA 01440 978-632-1780 630-1767
Web: www.gardnerma.com

Cape Ann Chamber of Commerce
33 Commercial St ... Gloucester MA 01930 978-283-1601 283-4740
Web: capeannchamber.com

Franklin County Chamber of Commerce
395 Main St ... Greenfield MA 01301 413-773-5463 773-7008
Web: franklincc.org

Greater Haverhill Chamber of Commerce
80 Merrimack St ... Haverhill MA 01830 978-373-5663 373-8060
Web: www.haverhillchamber.com

Greater Holyoke Chamber of Commerce
177 High St ... Holyoke MA 01040 413-534-3376
Web: www.holycham.com

Assabet Valley Chamber of Commerce
18 Church St PO Box 578 ... Hudson MA 01749 978-568-0360 562-4118
Web: www.assabetvalleychamber.org

Hyannis Area Chamber of Commerce 397 Main St ... Hyannis MA 02601 508-775-2201
Web: www.hyannis.com

Merrimack Valley Chamber of Commerce
264 Essex St ... Lawrence MA 01840 978-686-0900 794-9953
TF: 800-966-3375 ■ *Web:* www.merrimackvalleychamber.com

Lexington Chamber of Commerce
1875 Massachusetts Ave ... Lexington MA 02420 781-862-2480
Web: www.lexingtonchamber.org

Greater Lowell Chamber of Commerce
131 Merrimack St ... Lowell MA 01852 978-459-8154 452-4145
TF: 800-338-0221 ■ *Web:* greaterlowellcc.org

Lynn Area Chamber of Commerce
583 Chestnut St Unit 8 ... Lynn MA 01901 781-592-2900 592-2903
Web: www.lynnareachamber.com

Malden Chamber of Commerce
200 Pleasant St Ste 416 ... Malden MA 02148 781-322-4500 322-4866
Web: www.maldenchamber.org

Marlborough Regional Chamber of Commerce
11 Florence St ... Marlborough MA 01752 508-485-7746 481-1819
Web: www.marlboroughchamber.org

Medford Chamber of Commerce
1 Shipyard Way Ste 302 ... Medford MA 02155 781-396-1277 396-1278
Web: medfordchambermass.com

Melrose Chamber of Commerce 1 W Foster St ... Melrose MA 02176 781-665-3033
Web: www.melrosechamber.org

Cranberry Country Chamber of Commerce
40 N Main St ... Middleboro MA 02346 508-947-1499 947-1446
Web: www.cranberrycountry.org

Milford Area Chamber of Commerce
258 Main St PO Box 621 ... Milford MA 01757 508-473-6700 473-8467
Web: www.milfordchamber.org

New Bedford Area Chamber of Commerce
794 Purchase St ... New Bedford MA 02740 508-999-5231 999-5237
Web: www.newbedfordchamber.com

Newton-Needham Chamber of Commerce
281 Needham St ... Newton MA 02464 617-244-5300 244-5302
Web: www.nnchamber.com

Greater Northampton Chamber of Commerce
99 Pleasant St ... NorthHampton MA 01060 413-584-1900 584-1934
TF: 800-392-6090 ■ *Web:* www.explorenorthampton.com

Neposet Valley Chamber of Commerce
190 Vanderbilt Ave ... Norwood MA 02062 781-769-1126 769-0808
Web: www.nvcc.com

Quaboag Valley Chamber of Commerce
3 Converse St Ste 103 ... Palmer MA 01069 413-283-2418 289-1355

Peabody Chamber of Commerce (PACC)
24 Main St Ste 28 ... Peabody MA 01960 978-531-0384 532-7227
Web: www.peabodychamber.com

Berkshire Chamber of Commerce 66 Allen St ... Pittsfield MA 01201 413-499-4000 447-9641
Web: 1berkshire.com

Plymouth Area Chamber of Commerce
10 Cordage Pk Cir Ste 231 ... Plymouth MA 02360 508-830-1620 830-1621
Web: www.plymouthchamber.com

Reading-North Reading Chamber of Commerce
PO Box 771 ... Reading MA 01867 978-664-5060
Web: www.readingnreadingchamber.org

South Shore Chamber of Commerce
1050 Hingham St ... Rockland MA 02370 781-421-3900 479-9274*
**Fax Area Code:* 617 ■ *Web:* www.southshorechamber.org

Salem Chamber of Commerce 265 Essex St ... Salem MA 01970 978-744-0004 745-3855
Web: www.salem-chamber.org

Somerville Chamber of Commerce
2 Alpine St PO Box 44034 ... Somerville MA 02144 617-776-4100
Web: www.somervillechamber.org

Affiliated Chamber of Commerce of Greater Springfield
1441 Main St ... Springfield MA 01103 413-787-1555 731-8530
TF: 888-283-3757 ■ *Web:* www.myonlinechamber.com

West Springfield Chamber of Commerce
1441 Main St ... Springfield MA 01103 413-787-1555 731-8530
Web: www.myonlinechamber.com

Taunton Area Chamber of Commerce
12 Taunton Green Ste 201 ... Taunton MA 02780 508-824-4068 884-8222
Web: www.tauntonareachamber.org

Wakefield Chamber of Commerce 5 Common St ... Wakefield MA 01880 781-245-0741
Web: wakefieldchamber.org

Waltham/West Suburban Chamber of Commerce
84 S St ... Waltham MA 02453 781-894-4700
Web: www.walthamchamber.com

Watertown-Belmont Chamber of Commerce
182 Main St PO Box 45 ... Watertown MA 02471 617-926-1017 926-2322
Web: www.wbcc.org

Wellesley Chamber of Commerce
1 Hollis St Ste 232 ... Wellesley MA 02482 781-235-2446 235-7326
Web: www.wellesleychamber.org

Phone | Fax

Greater Westfield Chamber of Commerce
16 N Elm St — Westfield MA 01085 413-568-1618
Web: www.westfieldbiz.org/contact-us.html

Blackstone Valley Chamber of Commerce
110 Church St — Whitinsville MA 01588 508-234-9090 234-5152
TF: 800-841-0919 ■ *Web:* www.blackstonevalley.org

North Suburban Chamber of Commerce
76-R Winn St Ste 3D — Woburn MA 01801 781-933-3499 933-1071
Web: www.northsuburbanchamber.com

Worcester Regional Chamber of Commerce
446 Main St Ste 200 — Worcester MA 01608 508-753-2924 754-8560
Web: www.worcesterchamber.org

Michigan

Phone | Fax

Lenawee Economic Development Corp
5285 W US Hwy 223 — Adrian MI 49221 517-265-5141
Web: www.lenaweenow.org

Allen Park Chamber of Commerce
6543 Allen Rd — Allen Park MI 48101 313-382-7303 382-4409
Web: www.allenparkchamber.org

Gratiot Area Chamber of Commerce
110 W Superior St PO Box 516 — Alma MI 48801 989-463-5525 463-6588
Web: www.gratiot.org

Alpena Area Chamber of Commerce
235 W Chisholm St — Alpena MI 49707 989-354-4181 356-3999
TF: 800-425-7362 ■ *Web:* www.alpenachamber.com

Battle Creek Area Chamber of Commerce
1 Riverwalk Ctr ste 3A 34 W Jackson St — Battle Creek MI 49017 269-962-4076 962-6309
Web: www.battlecreek.org

Bay Area Chamber of Commerce 901 Saginaw St — Bay City MI 48708 989-893-4567 895-5594
Web: www.baycityarea.com

Belleville Area Chamber of Commerce
248 Main St — Belleville MI 48111 734-697-7151 697-1415
Web: www.bellevilleareachamber.org

Cornerstone Alliance Chamber Services
38 W Wall St — Benton Harbor MI 49022 269-925-6100 925-4471
Web: www.cstonealliance.org

Mecosta County Area Chamber of Commerce
246 N State St — Big Rapids MI 49307 231-796-7649 796-1625
Web: www.mecostacounty.com

Birmingham-Bloomfield Chamber of Commerce
725 S Adams Rd Ste 130 — Birmingham MI 48009 248-644-1700 644-0286
Web: www.bbcc.com

Greater Brighton Area Chamber of Commerce
218 E Grand Riv — Brighton MI 48116 810-227-5086 227-5940
Web: www.brightoncoc.org

Brooklyn-Irish Hills Chamber of Commerce
131 N Main St PO Box 805 — Brooklyn MI 49230 517-592-8907
Web: irishhills.com

Cadillac Area Chamber of Commerce
222 N Lake St — Cadillac MI 49601 231-775-9776 775-1440
Web: www.cadillac.org

Canton Chamber of Commerce 45525 Hanford Rd — Canton MI 48187 734-453-4040 453-4503
Web: www.cantonchamber.com

Clarkston Area Chamber of Commerce
5856 S Main St — Clarkston MI 48346 248-625-8055 625-8041
Web: www.clarkston.org

Cold Water Area Chamber of Commerce
20 Div St — Coldwater MI 49036 517-278-5985 278-8369
Web: coldwaterchamber.com

Dearborn Chamber of Commerce
22100 Michigan Ave — Dearborn MI 48124 313-584-6100 584-9818
TF: 800-844-5440 ■ *Web:* dearbornareachamber.org

Dearborn Heights Chamber of Commerce
22100 Michigan Ave Ste 2 — Dearborn Heights MI 48124 313-274-7480
Web: www.dearbornareachamber.org

Detroit Regional Chamber
1 Woodward Ave Ste 1900 — Detroit MI 48226 313-964-4000 964-0183
Web: detroitchamber.com

Delta County Area Chamber of Commerce
230 Ludington St — Escanaba MI 49829 906-786-2192 786-8830
TF: 800-221-2001 ■ *Web:* www.deltami.org

Ferndale Chamber of Commerce
407 E 9-Mile Rd — Ferndale MI 48220 248-542-2160 542-8979
Web: www.ferndaleareachamber.com

Genesee Regional Chamber of Commerce
519 S Saginaw St Ste 200 — Flint MI 48502 810-600-1404 600-1461
TF: 800-829-3676 ■ *Web:* www.flintandgenesee.org

Grand Blanc Chamber of Commerce
512 E Grand Blanc Rd — Grand Blanc MI 48439 810-695-4222 695-0053
Web: www.grandblancchamber.org

Chamber of Commerce - Grand Haven-Spring Lake-Ferrysburg
1 S Harbor Dr — Grand Haven MI 49417 616-842-4910 842-0379
Web: www.grandhavenchamber.org

Grand Rapids Area Chamber of Commerce
111 Pearl St NW — Grand Rapids MI 49503 616-771-0300 771-0318
Web: www.grandrapids.org

Holland Area Chamber of Commerce
272 E Eigth St — Holland MI 49423 616-392-2389 392-7379
Web: www.westcoastchamber.org

Howell Area Chamber of Commerce (HACC)
123 E Washington St — Howell MI 48843 517-546-3920 546-4115
Web: www.howell.org

Dickinson Area Partnership
600 S Stephenson Ave — Iron Mountain MI 49801 906-774-2002 774-2004
TF: 888-543-2139 ■ *Web:* www.dickinsonchamber.com

Greater Jackson Chamber of Commerce
141 S Jackson St — Jackson MI 49201 517-782-8221 780-3688
TF: 800-366-3699 ■ *Web:* www.jacksonchamber.org

Orion Area Chamber of Commerce
PO Box 484 Ste 112 — Lake Orion MI 48361 248-693-6300
Web: orionlibrary.org

Phone | Fax

Lansing Regional Chamber of Commerce
500 E Michigan Ave Ste 200 — Lansing MI 48912 517-487-6340 484-6910
Web: www.lansingchamber.org

Lapeer Area Chamber of Commerce 108 W Pk St — Lapeer MI 48446 810-664-6641 664-4349
Web: www.lapeerareachamber.org

Livonia Chamber of Commerce 33233 5 Mile Rd — Livonia MI 48154 734-427-2122 427-6055
Web: www.livonia.org

Madison Heights-Hazel Park Chamber of Commerce (MHP)
939 E 12 Mile Rd — Madison Heights MI 48071 248-542-5010 542-6821
Web: www.madisonheightschamber.com

Midland Area Chamber of Commerce
300 Rodd St Ste 101 — Midland MI 48640 989-839-9901 835-3701
TF: 800-715-0074 ■ *Web:* www.macc.org

Huron Valley Chamber of Commerce
317 Union St — Milford MI 48381 248-685-7129 685-9047
Web: www.huronvcc.com

Monroe County Chamber of Commerce
1645 N Dixie Hwy Ste 20 — Monroe MI 48162 734-384-3366 384-3367
TF: 855-386-1280 ■ *Web:* monroecountychamber.com

Macomb County Chamber 28 First St Ste B — Mount Clemens MI 48043 586-493-7600 493-7602
TF: 800-564-3136 ■ *Web:* macombcountychamber.com

Macomb County Chamber of Commerce
28 First St — Mount Clemens MI 48043 586-493-7600 493-7602
Web: macombcountychamber.com

Muskegon Area Chamber of Commerce
380 W Western Ste 202 — Muskegon MI 49440 231-722-3751 728-7251
TF: 800-659-2955 ■ *Web:* www.muskegon.org

Four Flags Area Chamber of Commerce
321 E Main St — Niles MI 49120 269-683-3720 683-3722
Web: www.nilesmi.com

Novi Chamber of Commerce, The
41875 W 11 Mile Rd Ste 201 — Novi MI 48375 248-349-3743 349-9719
TF: 888-440-7325 ■ *Web:* www.novichamber.com

Petoskey Regional Chamber of Commerce
401 E Mitchell St — Petoskey MI 49770 231-347-4150 348-1810
Web: www.petoskeychamber.com

Plymouth Community Chamber of Commerce
850 W Ann Arbor Trl — Plymouth MI 48170 734-453-1540
Web: www.plymouthchamber.org

Pontiac Regional Chamber of Commerce
402 N Telegraph Rd — Pontiac MI 48341 248-335-9600
Web: www.pontiacchamber.com

Blue Water Area Chamber of Commerce
512 McMorran Blvd — Port Huron MI 48060 810-985-7101 985-7311
TF: 800-361-0526 ■ *Web:* www.bluewaterchamber.com

Redford Township Chamber of Commerce
26050 5-Mile Rd — Redford MI 48239 313-535-0960 535-6356
Web: www.redfordchamber.com

Greater Rochester Chamber of Commerce
71 Walnut Blvd — Rochester MI 48307 248-651-6700

Rockford Area Chamber of Commerce
598 Byrne Industrial Dr — Rockford MI 49341 616-866-2000 866-2141
Web: www.rockfordmichamber.com

Romeo-Washington Chamber of Commerce
228 N Main St PO Box 175 — Romeo MI 48065 586-752-4436 752-2835
Web: www.rwchamber.com

Saginaw County Chamber of Commerce
515 N Washington Ave 2nd Fl — Saginaw MI 48607 989-752-7161 752-9055
TF: 866-657-9357 ■ *Web:* www.saginawchamber.org

Sault Area Chamber of Commerce
2581 I-75 Business Spur — Sault Sainte Marie MI 49783 906-632-3301 632-2331
Web: www.saultstemarie.org

South Lyon Area Chamber of Commerce
125 N Lafayette St — South Lyon MI 48178 248-760-6308 437-4116
Web: www.southlyonchamber.com

Southfield Chamber of Commerce
24300 Southfield Rd Ste 101 — Southfield MI 48075 248-557-6661 557-3931
Web: www.southfieldchamber.com

Sterling Heights Area Chamber of Commerce
12900 Hall Rd Ste 100 — Sterling Heights MI 48313 586-731-5400 731-3521
Web: www.shrcci.com

Southern Wayne County Chamber of Commerce
20904 Northline Rd — Taylor MI 48180 734-284-6000 284-0198
Web: swcrc.com

Traverse City Area Chamber of Commerce
202 E Grandview Pkwy — Traverse City MI 49684 231-947-5075 946-2565
TF: 844-900-0500 ■ *Web:* www.tcchamber.org

Troy Chamber of Commerce
4555 Investment Dr Ste 300 — Troy MI 48098 248-641-8151 641-0545
Web: www.troychamber.com

Lakes Area Chamber of Commerce
305 N Pontiac Trl Ste B — Walled Lake MI 48390 248-624-2826 624-2892
Web: www.lakesareachamber.com

West Bloomfield Chamber of Commerce
5745 W Maple Rd Ste 206 — West Bloomfield MI 48322 248-626-3636 626-4218
Web: www.westbloomfieldchamber.com

Westland Chamber of Commerce 36900 Ford Rd — Westland MI 48185 734-326-7222 326-6040
TF: 800-737-4859 ■ *Web:* www.westlandchamber.com

Wyoming-Kentwood Area Chamber of Commerce
4415 Byron Ctr Ave SW — Wyoming MI 49519 616-531-5990 531-0252
Web: www.southkent.org

Minnesota

Phone | Fax

Albert Lea-Freeborn County Chamber of Commerce
2580 Bridge Ave — Albert Lea MN 56007 507-373-3938 373-0344
Web: www.albertlea.org

Alexandria Lakes Area Chamber of Commerce
206 Broadway — Alexandria MN 56308 320-763-3161 763-6857
TF: 800-235-9441 ■ *Web:* www.alexandriamn.org

Anoka Area Chamber of Commerce 12 Bridge Sq — Anoka MN 55303 763-421-7130 421-0577
Web: www.anokaareachamber.com

Phone | Fax

Apple Valley Chamber of Commerce
14800 Galaxie Ave Ste 101 . . . Apple Valley MN 55124 952-432-8422 432-7964
TF: 800-301-9435 ■ *Web:* www.applevalleychamber.com

Bemidji Area Chamber of Commerce
300 Bemidji Ave . . . Bemidji MN 56601 218-444-3541 444-4276
TF: 800-458-2223 ■ *Web:* www.bemidji.org

Brainerd Lakes Area Chamber of Commerce
7393 State Hwy 371 PO Box 356 . . . Brainerd MN 56401 218-829-2838 829-8199
TF: 800-450-2838 ■ *Web:* www.explorebrainerdlakes.com

Burnsville Chamber of Commerce
350 W Burnsville Pkwy Ste 425 . . . Burnsville MN 55337 952-435-6000 435-6972
Web: www.burnsvillechamber.com

Cloquet Area Chamber of Commerce
225 Sunnyside Dr . . . Cloquet MN 55720 218-879-1551 878-0223
TF: 800-554-4350 ■ *Web:* www.cloquet.com

Cottage Grove Area Chamber of Commerce
7516 80th St S Ste 205 PO Box 16 . . . Cottage Grove MN 55016 651-458-8334 458-8383
Web: www.cottagegrovechamber.org

Detroit Lakes Regional Chamber of Commerce
700 Summit Ave . . . Detroit Lakes MN 56501 218-847-9202 847-9082
TF: 800-542-3992 ■ *Web:* www.visitdetroitlakes.com

Duluth Area Chamber of Commerce
5 W First St Ste 101 . . . Duluth MN 55802 218-722-5501 722-3223
TF: 800-385-8842 ■ *Web:* www.duluthchamber.com

Dakota County Regional Chamber of Commerce
1121 Town Ctr Dr Ste 102 . . . Eagan MN 55123 651-452-9872 452-8978
Web: www.dcrchamber.com

Eden Prairie Chamber of Commerce
11455 Viking Dr Ste 270 . . . Eden Prairie MN 55344 952-944-2830 944-0229
Web: www.epchamber.org

Forest Lake Area Chamber of Commerce
56 E Broadway Ave . . . Forest Lake MN 55025 651-464-3200 464-3201
Web: forestlakechamber.org

Grand Rapids Area Chamber of Commerce
1 NW Third St . . . Grand Rapids MN 55744 218-326-6619 326-4825
TF: 800-472-6366 ■ *Web:* www.grandmn.com

Hastings Area Chamber of Commerce & Tourism Bureau
111 E Third St . . . Hastings MN 55033 651-437-6775 437-2697
TF: 888-612-6122 ■ *Web:* www.hastingsmn.org

River Heights Chamber of Commerce
5782 Blackshire Path . . . Inver Grove Heights MN 55076 651-451-2266 451-0846
Web: www.riverheights.com

Lakeville Area Chamber of Commerce & Convention & Visitors Bureau
19950 Dodd Blvd Ste 101 . . . Lakeville MN 55044 952-469-2020 469-2028
TF: 888-525-3845 ■ *Web:* www.lakevillechamber.org

Minneapolis Regional Chamber of Commerce
81 S Ninth St Ste 200 . . . Minneapolis MN 55402 612-370-9100 370-9195
Web: www.minneapolischamber.org

Richfield Chamber of Commerce
6601 Lyndale Ave S Ste 106 . . . Minneapolis MN 55423 612-866-5100
Web: richfieldmnchamber.org

Chamber of Commerce of Fargo Moorhead
202 First Ave N . . . Moorhead MN 56560 218-233-1100 233-1200
Web: www.fmchamber.com

Twin Cities North Chamber of Commerce
525 Main St Ste 200 . . . New Brighton MN 55112 763-571-9781 572-7950
Web: www.twincitiesnorth.org

North Hennepin Chamber of Commerce
229 First Ave NE . . . Osseo MN 55369 763-424-6744 424-6927
Web: www.nhachamber.com

Owatonna Area Chamber of Commerce & Tourism
320 Hoffman Dr . . . Owatonna MN 55060 507-451-7970 451-7972
TF: 800-423-6466 ■ *Web:* www.owatonna.org

TwinWest Chamber of Commerce
10700 Old County Rd 15 . . . Plymouth MN 55441 763-450-2220 450-2221
Web: www.twinwest.com

Rochester Area Chamber of Commerce
220 S Broadway Ste 100 . . . Rochester MN 55904 507-288-1122 282-8960
Web: www.rochestermnchamber.com

Saint Paul Area Chamber of Commerce
401 N Robert St Ste 150 . . . Saint Paul MN 55101 651-223-5000 223-5119
Web: www.saintpaulchamber.com

Greater Stillwater Chamber of Commerce
200 Chestnut St E Ste 204 . . . Stillwater MN 55082 651-439-4001
Web: www.ilovestillwater.com

Leech Lake Area Chamber of Commerce
205 Minnesota Ave E . . . Walker MN 56484 218-547-1313 547-1338
TF: 800-833-1118 ■ *Web:* www.leech-lake.com

White Bear Lake Area Chamber of Commerce
4751 Hwy 61 . . . White Bear Lake MN 55110 651-429-8593 429-8592
Web: www.whitebearchamber.com

Willmar Lakes Area Chamber of Commerce
2104 Hwy 12 E . . . Willmar MN 56201 320-235-0300 231-1948
Web: www.willmarareachamber.com

Mississippi

Phone | Fax

Monroe County Chamber of Commerce
124 W Commerce St . . . Aberdeen MS 39730 662-369-6488 369-6489
Web: www.gomonroe.org

Panola Partnership Inc 150-A Public Sq . . . Batesville MS 38606 662-563-3126 563-0704
TF: 888-872-6652 ■ *Web:* www.panolacounty.com

Rankin County Chamber of Commerce
101 Service Dr . . . Brandon MS 39043 601-825-2268 825-1977
TF: 800-987-8280 ■ *Web:* www.rankinchamber.com

Brookhaven-Lincoln County Chamber of Commerce
230 S Whitworth Ave . . . Brookhaven MS 39601 601-833-1411 833-1412
TF: 800-613-4667 ■ *Web:* brookhavenchamber.org

Clarksdale-Coahoma County Chamber of Commerce & Industrial Foundation
1540 DeSoto Ave . . . Clarksdale MS 38614 662-627-7337 627-1313
TF: 800-626-3764 ■ *Web:* www.clarksdale.com

Cleveland-Bolivar County Chamber of Commerce
600 Third St . . . Cleveland MS 38732 662-843-2712 843-2718
Web: clevelandmschamber.com

Marion County Development Partnership (MCDP)
412 Courthouse Sq PO Box 272 . . . Columbia MS 39429 601-736-6385 736-6392
Web: www.mcdp.info

Alliance, The 810 Tate St . . . Corinth MS 38834 662-287-5269
TF: 877-347-0545 ■ *Web:* www.corinthalliance.com

Greenwood-Leflore County Chamber of Commerce
402 Hwy 82 . . . Greenwood MS 38930 662-453-4152 453-8003
TF: 800-844-7483 ■ *Web:* www.greenwoodms.com

Gulfport Chamber of Commerce
11975-E Seaway Rd . . . Gulfport MS 39503 228-604-0014 604-0105
Web: mscoastchamber.com

Mississippi Gulf Coast Chamber of Commerce
11975-E Seaway Rd . . . Gulfport MS 39503 228-604-0014 604-0105
Web: www.mscoastchamber.com

Area Development Partnership
1 Convention Ctr Plz . . . Hattiesburg MS 39401 601-296-7500 296-7505
TF: 800-238-4288 ■ *Web:* www.theadp.com

Greater Jackson Chamber Partnership
PO Box 22548 . . . Jackson MS 39225 601-948-7575 352-5539
Web: www.greaterjacksonpartnership.com

East Mississippi Business Development Corp
1901 Front St PO Box 790 . . . Meridian MS 39302 601-693-1306 693-5638
Web: www.embdc.org

Natchez-Adams County Chamber of Commerce
108 S Commerce St . . . Natchez MS 39120 601-445-4611 445-9361
Web: www.natchezchamber.com

Olive Branch Chamber of Commerce
9123 Pigeon Roost PO Box 608 . . . Olive Branch MS 38654 662-895-2600 895-2625
Web: www.olivebranchms.com

Oxford-Lafayette County Chamber of Commerce
299 W Jackson Ave . . . Oxford MS 38655 662-234-4651
TF: 800-880-6967 ■ *Web:* www.oxfordms.com

Jackson County Chamber of Commerce
720 Krebs Ave . . . Pascagoula MS 39567 228-762-3391 769-1726
Web: www.jcchamber.com

Community Development Partnership
256 W Beacon Str 256 W Beacon . . . Philadelphia MS 39350 601-656-1000 656-1066
TF: 877-752-2643 ■ *Web:* www.neshoba.org

Madison County Chamber of Commerce
618 Crescent Blvd Ste 101 . . . Ridgeland MS 39157 601-605-2554 605-2260
Web: www.madisoncountychamber.com

Southaven Chamber of Commerce
8700 NW Dr Ste 100 . . . Southaven MS 38671 662-342-6114 342-6365
Web: www.southavenchamber.com

Greater Starkville Development Partnership
200 E Main St . . . Starkville MS 39759 662-323-3322 323-5815
TF: 800-649-8687 ■ *Web:* www.starkville.org

Pike County Chamber of Commerce & Economic Development District
PO Box 5302 . . . Summit MS 39666 601-684-2291 684-4899
TF: 800-844-2653 ■ *Web:* www.pikeinfo.com

Vicksburg-Warren County Chamber of Commerce
2020 Mission 66 . . . Vicksburg MS 39180 601-636-1012 636-4422
Web: www.vicksburgchamber.org

Missouri

Phone | Fax

Affton Chamber of Commerce 9815 Mackenzie Rd . . . Affton MO 63123 314-631-3100
Web: www.afftonchamber.com

Blue Springs Chamber of Commerce
1000 W Main St . . . Blue Springs MO 64015 816-229-8558 229-1244
Web: bluespringschamber.com

Branson/Lakes Area Chamber of Commerce
PO Box 1897 . . . Branson MO 65615 417-334-4084 334-4139
TF: 800-214-3661 ■ *Web:* www.bransonchamber.com

Cape Girardeau Area Chamber of Commerce
1267 N Mt Auburn Rd . . . Cape Girardeau MO 63701 573-335-3312 335-4686
Web: www.capechamber.com

Cassville Area Chamber of Commerce
504 Main St . . . Cassville MO 65625 417-847-2814
Web: www.cassville.com

Chesterfield Chamber of Commerce
101 Chesterfield Business Pkwy . . . Chesterfield MO 63005 636-532-3399 532-7446
TF: 888-242-4262 ■ *Web:* www.chesterfieldmochamber.com

Columbia Chamber of Commerce
300 S Providence Rd . . . Columbia MO 65203 573-874-1132 443-3986
Web: www.columbiamochamber.com

West Saint Louis County Chamber of Commerce
15965 Manchester Rd Ste 102 . . . Ellisville MO 63011 636-230-9900 230-9912
Web: www.westcountychamber.com

Twin City Area Chamber of Commerce
114 Main St . . . Festus MO 63028 636-931-7697
Web: www.twincity.org

Greater North County Chamber of Commerce
420 W Washington St . . . Florissant MO 63031 314-831-3500 831-9682
Web: greaternorthcountychamber.com

Gladstone Area Chamber of Commerce
7001 N Oak Trfwy . . . Gladstone MO 64118 816-436-4523 436-4352
Web: gladstonechamber.com

Independence Chamber of Commerce
210 W Truman Rd . . . Independence MO 64050 816-252-4745 252-4917
Web: ichamber.biz

Jefferson City Area Chamber of Commerce
213 Adams St . . . Jefferson City MO 65101 573-634-3616 634-3805
TF: 866-223-6535 ■ *Web:* www.jcchamber.org

Joplin Area Chamber of Commerce
320 E Fourth St . . . Joplin MO 64801 417-624-4150 624-4303
Web: www.joplincc.com

Greater Kansas City Chamber of Commerce
911 Main St Ste 2600 . . . Kansas City MO 64105 816-221-2424 221-7440
Web: www.kcchamber.com

Northland Regional Chamber of Commerce
634 NW Englewood Rd . . . Kansas City MO 64118 816-455-9911
Web: www.northlandchamber.com

	City	State	Zip	Phone	Fax
South Kansas City Chamber of Commerce 406 E Bannister Rd Ste F *Web:* southkcchamber.com	Kansas City	MO	64131	816-761-7660	761-7340
Lebanon Area Chamber of Commerce 186 N Adams St *TF:* 888-588-5710 ■ *Web:* www.lebanonmissouri.com	Lebanon	MO	65536	417-588-3256	588-3251
Lee's Summit Chamber of Commerce 220 SE Main St *TF:* 888-816-5757 ■ *Web:* lschamber.com	Lees Summit	MO	64063	816-524-2424	524-5246
Kirkwood-Des Peres Area Chamber of Commerce 108 W Adams Ave *Web:* www.kirkwooddesperes.com	Louis	MO	63122	314-821-4161	821-5229
Neosho Area Chamber of Commerce 216 W Spring St *Web:* www.neoshocc.com	Neosho	MO	64850	417-451-1925	451-8097
O'Fallon Chamber of Commerce 2145 Bryan Vly Commercial Dr *TF:* 888-349-1897 ■ *Web:* www.ofallonchamber.org	O'Fallon	MO	63366	636-240-1818	
Park Hills Leadington Chamber of Commerce (PHLCOC) 12 Municipal Dr *Web:* www.phlcoc.net	Park Hills	MO	63601	573-431-1051	431-2327
Raytown Area Chamber of Commerce 5909 Raytown Trafficway *Web:* www.raytownchamber.com	Raytown	MO	64133	816-353-8500	353-8525
Rolla Area Chamber of Commerce 1311 KingsHwy *TF:* 888-809-3817 ■ *Web:* www.rollachamber.org	Rolla	MO	65401	573-364-3577	364-5222
Saint Charles Chamber of Commerce 2201 First Capitol Dr *Web:* www.gstccc.com	Saint Charles	MO	63301	636-946-0633	
Saint Joseph Area Chamber of Commerce 3003 Frederick Ave *TF:* 800-748-7856 ■ *Web:* www.saintjoseph.com	Saint Joseph	MO	64506	816-232-4461	364-4873
Maryland Heights Chamber of Commerce 547 W Port Plz *Web:* www.mhcc.com	Saint Louis	MO	63146	314-576-6603	576-6855
South County Chamber of Commerce 4179 Crescent Dr Ste A *Web:* southcountychamber.org	Saint Louis	MO	63129	314-894-6800	
Waynesville-Saint Robert Area Chamber of Commerce 137 St Robert Blvd Ste B *Web:* www.waynesville-strobertchamber.com	Saint Robert	MO	65584	573-336-5121	336-5472
Sedalia Area Chamber of Commerce 600 E Third St *Web:* www.sedaliachamber.com	Sedalia	MO	65301	660-826-2222	826-2223
Springfield Area Chamber of Commerce 202 S John Q Hammons Pkwy *Web:* www.springfieldchamber.com	Springfield	MO	65806	417-862-5567	862-1611
Northwest Chamber of Commerce 8944 St Charles Rock Rd Ste 300 *Web:* www.northwestchamber.com	St. Louis	MO	63114	314-291-2131	291-2153
Washington Area Chamber of Commerce 323 W Main St *Web:* www.washmo.org	Washington	MO	63090	636-239-2715	

Montana

	City	State	Zip	Phone	Fax
Billings Area Chamber of Commerce 815 S 27th St *TF:* 855-328-9116 ■ *Web:* www.billingschamber.com	Billings	MT	59101	406-245-4111	245-7333
Bozeman Area Chamber of Commerce 2000 Commerce Way *Web:* www.bozemanchamber.com	Bozeman	MT	59715	406-586-5421	586-8286
Butte-Silver Bow Chamber of Commerce 1000 George St *TF:* 800-735-6814 ■ *Web:* www.buttechambersite.org	Butte	MT	59701	406-723-3177	723-1215
Great Falls Area Chamber of Commerce 100 First Ave N *TF:* 800-735-8535	Great Falls	MT	59401	406-761-4434	761-6129
Bitterroot Valley Chamber of Commerce 105 E Main St *Web:* bitterrootchamber.com	Hamilton	MT	59840	406-363-2400	363-2402
Helena Area Chamber of Commerce 225 Cruse Ave *TF:* 800-743-5362 ■ *Web:* www.helenachamber.com	Helena	MT	59601	406-442-4120	447-1532
Kalispell Area Chamber of Commerce 15 Depot Pk *Web:* www.kalispellchamber.com	Kalispell	MT	59901	406-758-2800	758-2805
Missoula Area Chamber of Commerce 825 E Front St *TF:* 800-814-2342 ■ *Web:* www.missoulachamber.com	Missoula	MT	59802	406-543-6623	543-6625

Nebraska

	City	State	Zip	Phone	Fax
Bellevue Chamber of Commerce 1102 Galvin Rd S *Web:* www.bellevuenebraska.com	Bellevue	NE	68005	402-898-3000	291-8729
Grand Island Area Chamber of Commerce 309 W Second St *Web:* gichamber.com	Grand Island	NE	68802	308-382-9210	382-1154
Kearney Area Chamber of Commerce 1007 Second Ave PO Box 607 *TF:* 800-227-8340 ■ *Web:* www.kearneycoc.org	Kearney	NE	68848	308-237-3101	237-3103
Lincoln Chamber of Commerce 1135 M St PO Box 83006 *Web:* www.lcoc.com	Lincoln	NE	68508	402-436-2350	436-2360
North Platte Area Chamber & Development 502 S Dewey St *Web:* www.nparea.com	North Platte	NE	69101	308-532-4966	532-4827
Greater Omaha Chamber of Commerce 1301 Harney St *Web:* www.omahachamber.org	Omaha	NE	68102	402-346-5000	346-7050
Sarpy County Chamber of Commerce 7775 Olson Dr Ste 207 *Web:* www.sarpychamber.org	Papillion	NE	68046	402-339-3050	339-9968

Nevada

	City	State	Zip	Phone	Fax
Carson City Area Chamber of Commerce 1900 S Carson St Ste 200 *Web:* www.carsoncitychamber.com	Carson City	NV	89701	775-882-1565	882-4179
Elko Area Chamber of Commerce 1405 Idaho St *Web:* www.elkonevada.com	Elko	NV	89801	775-738-7135	738-7136
Fallon Chamber of Commerce 85 N Taylor St *Web:* www.fallonchamber.com	Fallon	NV	89406	775-423-2544	423-0540
Carson Valley Chamber of Commerce & Visitors Authority 1477 Hwy 395 N Ste A *TF:* 800-727-7677 ■ *Web:* www.carsonvalleynv.org	Gardnerville	NV	89410	775-782-8144	782-1025
Henderson Chamber of Commerce 590 S Boulder Hwy *Web:* www.hendersonchamber.com	Henderson	NV	89015	702-565-8951	565-3115
Las Vegas Chamber of Commerce 575 Symphony Park Ave Ste 100 *TF:* 888-635-7272 ■ *Web:* www.lvchamber.com	Las Vegas	NV	89105	702-641-5822	735-0406
Latin Chamber of Commerce 300 N 13th St *Web:* www.lvlcc.com	Las Vegas	NV	89101	702-385-7367	385-2614
North Las Vegas Chamber of Commerce 3365 W Craig Rd Ste 25 *Web:* www.nlvchamber.org	North Las Vegas	NV	89032	702-642-9595	
Lake Tahoe Chamber of Commerce 169 Hwy 50 *Web:* www.tahoechamber.org	Stateline	NV	89449	775-588-1728	588-1941
Tonopah Chamber of Commerce 301 Brougher Ave *Web:* www.tonopahnevada.com	Tonopah	NV	89049	775-482-3859	

New Hampshire

	City	State	Zip	Phone	Fax
Souhegan Valley Chamber of Commerce 69 New Hampshire 101A *Web:* www.souhegan.net	Amherst	NH	03031	603-673-4360	673-5018
Greater Concord Chamber of Commerce 49 S Main St *Web:* www.concordnhchamber.com	Concord	NH	03301	603-224-2508	224-8128
Greater Derry Chamber of Commerce 29 W Broadway *Web:* www.gdlchamber.org	Derry	NH	03038	603-432-8205	
Greater Dover Chamber of Commerce 550 Central Ave *Web:* www.dovernh.org	Dover	NH	03820	603-742-2218	749-6317
Hampton Area Chamber of Commerce 1 Layfayette Rd *Web:* www.hamptonchamber.com	Hampton	NH	03842	603-926-8718	926-9977
Hanover Area Chamber of Commerce 53 S Main St *Web:* www.hanoverchamber.org	Hanover	NH	03755	603-643-3115	643-5606
Greater Keene Chamber of Commerce 48 Central Sq *Web:* www.keenechamber.com	Keene	NH	03431	603-352-1303	358-5341
Lakes Region Chamber 383 S Main St *Web:* lakesregionchamber.org	Laconia	NH	03246	603-524-5531	
Greater Nashua Chamber of Commerce 142 Main St *Web:* www.nashuachamber.com	Nashua	NH	03060	603-881-8333	881-7323
Greater Portsmouth Chamber of Commerce 500 Market St PO Box 239 *Web:* www.portsmouthchamber.org	Portsmouth	NH	03802	603-610-5510	436-5118
Greater Rochester Chamber of Commerce 18 S Main St *Web:* www.rochesternh.org	Rochester	NH	03867	603-332-5080	332-5216
Greater Salem Chamber of Commerce 81 Main St *Web:* www.gschamber.com	Salem	NH	03079	603-893-3177	894-5158

New Jersey

	City	State	Zip	Phone	Fax
Asbury Park Chamber of Commerce 1201 Springwood Ave *Web:* www.asburyparkchamber.com	Asbury Park	NJ	07712	732-775-7676	775-7675
Greater Atlantic City Chamber 12 S Virginia Ave *TF:* 800-123-4567 ■ *Web:* acchamber.com	Atlantic City	NJ	08401	609-345-4524	345-1666
Bayonne Chamber of Commerce 621 Ave C *Web:* www.bayonnenj.org	Bayonne	NJ	07002	201-436-4333	
Brick Township Chamber of Commerce 270 Chambers Bridge Rd *TF:* 877-539-2020 ■ *Web:* brickchamber.com	Brick	NJ	08723	732-477-4949	477-5788
Bridgeton Area Chamber of Commerce 76 Magnolia Ave PO Box 1063 *Web:* www.baccnj.com	Bridgeton	NJ	08302	856-455-1312	453-9795
Somerset County Business Partnership 360 Grove St *Web:* www.scbp.org	Bridgewater	NJ	08807	908-218-4300	722-7823
Mount Olive Area Chamber of Commerce PO Box 192 *Web:* www.mtolivechambernj.com	Budd Lake	NJ	07828	973-691-0109	
Cape May County Chamber of Commerce 13 Crest Haven Rd PO Box 74 *Web:* www.capemaycountychamber.com	Cape May Court House	NJ	08210	609-465-7181	465-5017
Cherry Hill Regional Chamber of Commerce 1060 Kings Hwy N Ste 200	Cherry Hill	NJ	08034	856-667-1600	667-1464
North Jersey Regional Chamber of Commerce 205 Rt 46 W Ste A103 *Web:* northjerseychamber.org	Clifton	NJ	07013	973-470-9300	470-9245
Edison Chamber of Commerce 1028 Amboy Ave *Web:* www.edisonchamber.com	Edison	NJ	08837	732-738-9482	738-9485

Phone Fax

Gateway Regional Chamber of Commerce
135 Jefferson Ave PO Box 300 ..... Elizabeth NJ 07207 908-352-0900 352-0865
Web: www.gatewaychamber.com

Englewood Chamber of Commerce
2-10 N Van Brunt St ..... Englewood NJ 07631 201-567-2381
Web: www.englewood-chamber.com

Fair Lawn Chamber of Commerce
12-45 River Rd ..... Fair Lawn NJ 07410 201-796-7050 475-0619
Web: www.fairlawnchamber.org

Hunterdon County Chamber of Commerce
14 Mine St ..... Flemington NJ 08822 908-782-7115 782-7283
Web: www.hunterdon-chamber.org

Greater Fort Lee Chamber of Commerce (GFLCOC)
210 Whiteman St ..... Fort Lee NJ 07024 201-944-7575 944-5168
Web: www.fortleechamber.com

Greater Monmouth Chamber of Commerce
57 Schanck Rd Ste C-3 ..... Freehold NJ 07728 732-462-3030 462-2123
TF: 800-700-6400 ■ *Web:* www.greatermonmouthchamber.com

Greater Hackensack Chamber of Commerce
5 University Plz Dr ..... Hackensack NJ 07601 201-489-3700 489-1741
Web: www.hackensackchamber.org

MIDJersey Chamber of Commerce
1A Quakerbridge Plaza Dr Ste 2 ..... Hamilton NJ 08619 609-689-9960
Web: www.midjerseychamber.org

Greater Hammonton Chamber of Commerce
10 S Egg Harbor Rd ..... Hammonton NJ 08037 609-561-9080

Northern Monmouth Chamber of Commerce
1340 State Hwy 36 Ste 22 Ste 22 ..... Hazlet NJ 07730 732-203-0340 676-7778
Web: www.monmouthcountychamber.com

Howell Chamber of Commerce
103 W Second St PO Box 196 ..... Howell NJ 07731 732-363-4114 363-8747
Web: www.howellchamber.com

Hudson County Chamber of Commerce
857 Bergen Ave 3rd Fl ..... Jersey City NJ 07306 201-386-0699 386-8480
Web: www.hudsonchamber.org

Parsippany Area Chamber of Commerce
14 N Beverwyck Rd ..... Lake Hiawatha NJ 07034 973-402-6400
Web: www.parsippanychamber.org

Greater Long Branch Chamber of Commerce
228 Broadway PO Box 628 ..... Long Branch NJ 07740 732-222-0400 571-3385
Web: www.longbranchchamber.org

Matawan-Aberdeen Chamber of Commerce
201 Broad St PO Box 522 ..... Matawan NJ 07747 732-290-1125 290-1125
Web: macocnj.com

Millville Chamber of Commerce 4 City Pk Dr ..... Millville NJ 08332 856-825-2600 825-5333
Web: www.millville-nj.com

North Essex Chamber of Commerce
26 Park St Ste 2062 ..... Montclair NJ 07042 973-226-5500 783-4407
Web: www.northessexchamber.com

Morris County Chamber of Commerce
25 Lindsley Dr Ste 105 ..... Morristown NJ 07960 973-539-3882 539-3960
Web: www.morrischamber.org

Randolph Area Chamber of Commerce
PO Box 391 ..... Mount Freedom NJ 07970 973-361-3462
Web: www.randolphchamber.org

Burlington County Regional Chamber of Commerce
100 Technology Way Ste 110 ..... Mount Laurel NJ 08054 856-439-2520 439-2523
Web: www.bcls.lib.nj.us/burlington-county-chamber-commerce

Middlesex County Regional Chamber of Commerce
109 Church St ..... New Brunswick NJ 08901 732-745-8090 745-8098
Web: www.mcrcc.org

Newark Regional Business Partnership
744 Broad St 26th Fl ..... Newark NJ 07102 973-522-0099 824-6587
TF: 888-337-3339 ■ *Web:* www.newarkrbp.org

Sussex County Chamber of Commerce
120 Hampton House Rd ..... Newton NJ 07860 973-579-1811 579-3031
TF: 844-256-7328 ■ *Web:* www.sussexcountychamber.org

Nutley Chamber of Commerce 172 Chestnut St ..... Nutley NJ 07110 973-667-5300
Web: www.nutleychamber.com

Commerce & Industry Assn of New Jersey (CIANJ)
61 S Paramus Rd ..... Paramus NJ 07652 201-368-2100 368-3438
Web: www.cianj.org

Greater Paramus Chamber of Commerce
58 E Midland Ave ..... Paramus NJ 07652 201-261-3344 261-3346
Web: paramuschamber.org

Greater Paterson Chamber of Commerce
100 Hamilton Plaza Ste 1201 ..... Paterson NJ 07505 973-881-7300 881-8233
TF: 800-220-2892 ■ *Web:* www.greaterpatersoncc.org

Piscataway/Middlesex/South Plainfield Chamber of Commerce
275 Old New Brunswick Rd Ste 105 ..... Piscataway NJ 08854 732-394-0220 394-0223

Point Pleasant Beach Chamber of Commerce
517-A Arnold Ave ..... Point Pleasant Beach NJ 08742 732-899-2424 899-0103
Web: pointpleasantbeachchamber.com

Princeton Regional Chamber of Commerce
9 Vandeventer Ave ..... Princeton NJ 08542 609-924-1776 924-5776
Web: www.princetonchamber.org

Meadowlands Regional Chamber of Commerce
201 Rt 17 ..... Rutherford NJ 07070 201-939-0707 939-0522
Web: www.meadowlands.org

Southern Ocean County Chamber of Commerce
265 W Ninth St ..... Ship Bottom NJ 08008 609-494-7211 494-5807
TF: 800-292-6372 ■ *Web:* www.visitlbiregion.com

Franklin Township Chamber of Commerce
675 Franklin Blvd ..... Somerset NJ 08873 732-545-7044
Web: www.franklinchamber.com

Suburban Chambers of Commerce 71 Summit Ave ..... Summit NJ 07901 908-522-1700 522-9252
Web: www.suburbanchambers.org

Toms River-Ocean County Chamber of Commerce
1027 Hooper Ave Bldg 1, 2nd Fl Ste 5 ..... Toms River NJ 08753 732-349-0220 349-1252

Union Township Chamber of Commerce
355 Chestnut St 2nd Fl ..... Union NJ 07083 908-688-2777 688-0338
Web: www.unionchamber.com

Greater Vineland Chamber of Commerce
2115 S Delsea Dr ..... Vineland NJ 08360 856-691-7400 691-2113
TF: 800-922-1766 ■ *Web:* www.vinelandchamber.org

Chamber of Commerce of Southern New Jersey
4015 Main St ..... Voorhees NJ 08043 856-424-7776 424-8180
Web: www.chambersnj.com

Jersey Shore Chamber of Commerce
2510 Belmar Blvd Ste I-20 ..... Wall NJ 07719 732-280-8800 280-8505
Web: www.jerseyshorechambernj.com/kickoff.asp

Tri-County Chamber of Commerce PO Box 2420 ..... Wayne NJ 07474 973-831-7788
Web: www.tricounty.org

Westfield Area Chamber of Commerce (WACC)
173 Elm St 3rd Fl ..... Westfield NJ 07090 908-233-3021 654-8183
Web: www.gwaccnj.com

New Mexico

Phone Fax

Alamogordo Chamber of Commerce
1301 N White Sands Blvd ..... Alamogordo NM 88310 575-437-6120 437-6334
TF: 800-826-0294 ■ *Web:* www.alamogordo.com

Greater Albuquerque Chamber of Commerce
115 Gold Ave SW # 201 ..... Albuquerque NM 87102 505-764-3700 764-3714
Web: www.abqchamber.com

Carlsbad Chamber of Commerce 302 S Canal St ..... Carlsbad NM 88220 575-887-6516 885-1455
Web: www.carlsbadchamber.com

Clovis/Curry County Chamber of Commerce
105 E Third St ..... Clovis NM 88101 575-763-3435 763-7266
TF: 800-261-7656 ■ *Web:* www.clovisnm.org

Espanola Valley Chamber of Commerce
1 Calle de las Espanolas Ste F & G ..... Espanola NM 87532 505-753-2831 753-1252
Web: www.espanolanmchamber.com

Farmington Chamber of Commerce
100 W Broadway ..... Farmington NM 87401 505-325-0279 327-7556
Web: www.gofarmington.com

Grants/Cibola County Chamber of Commerce
100 N Iron Ave ..... Grants NM 87020 505-287-4802 287-8224
TF: 866-270-5110 ■ *Web:* www.grants.org

Hobbs Chamber of Commerce 400 N Marland Blvd ..... Hobbs NM 88240 575-397-3202 397-1689
TF: 800-658-6291 ■ *Web:* www.hobbschamber.org

Greater Las Cruces Chamber of Commerce
760 W Picacho Ave ..... Las Cruces NM 88005 575-524-1968 527-5546
Web: www.lascruces.org

Rio Rancho Chamber of Commerce
4001 Southern Blvd SE ..... Rio Rancho NM 87124 505-892-1533 892-6157
Web: www.rrchamber.org

Roswell Chamber of Commerce 131 W Second St ..... Roswell NM 88202 575-623-5695 624-6870
TF: 877-849-7679 ■ *Web:* www.roswellnm.org

Santa Fe Chamber of Commerce
1644 St Michael's Dr ..... Santa Fe NM 87507 505-988-3279 984-2205
Web: www.santafechamber.com

Silver City-Grant County Chamber of Commerce
201 N Hudson St ..... Silver City NM 88061 575-538-3785 538-3786
TF: 800-548-9378 ■ *Web:* www.silvercity.org

New York

Phone Fax

Albany-Colonie Regional Chamber of Commerce
5 Computer Dr S ..... Albany NY 12205 518-431-1400 431-1402
Web: capitalregionchamber.com

Orleans County Chamber of Commerce
102 N Main St Ste 1 ..... Albion NY 14411 585-589-7727 589-7326
Web: www.orleanschamber.com

Cayuga County Chamber of Commerce 2 State St ..... Auburn NY 13021 315-252-7291 255-3077
Web: www.cayugacountychamber.com

Genesee County Chamber of Commerce
210 E Main St ..... Batavia NY 14020 585-343-7440 343-7487
TF: 877-788-6846 ■ *Web:* www.geneseeny.com

Steuben County Chamber of Commerce
110 Liberty St PO Box 488 ..... Bath NY 14810 607-776-7122 776-7122
Web: www.centralsteubenchamber.com

Bay Shore Chamber of Commerce
77 E Main St PO Box 5110 ..... Bay Shore NY 11706 631-665-7003
Web: www.bayshorecommerce.com

Greater Binghamton Chamber of Commerce
49 Ct St ..... Binghamton NY 13901 607-772-8860 722-4513
Web: www.greaterbinghamtonchamber.com

Bronx Chamber of Commerce
1200 Waters Pl Ste 106 ..... Bronx NY 10461 718-828-3900
Web: www.bronxmall.com

Brooklyn Chamber of Commerce
335 Adams St Ste 2700 ..... Brooklyn NY 11201 718-875-1000 237-4274
Web: www.ibrooklyn.com

Buffalo Niagara Partnership
665 Main St Ste 200 ..... Buffalo NY 14203 716-852-7100 852-2761
TF: 844-308-9165 ■ *Web:* www.thepartnership.org

St. Lawrence County Chamber of Commerce
101 Main St ..... Canton NY 13617 315-386-4000 379-0134
TF: 877-228-7810 ■ *Web:* www.northcountryguide.com

Greene County Chamber of Commerce
327 Main St PO Box 248 ..... Catskill NY 12414 518-943-4222 943-1700
Web: greenecountychamber.com

Cheektowaga Chamber of Commerce
2875 Union Rd Ste 50 ..... Cheektowaga NY 14227 716-684-5838 684-5571
Web: www.cheektowaga.org

Chamber of Southern Saratoga County
58 Clifton Country Rd Ste 102 ..... Clifton Park NY 12065 518-371-7748 371-5025
Web: www.southernsaratoga.org

Corning Area Chamber of Commerce
1 W Market St Ste 302 ..... Corning NY 14830 607-936-4686 936-4685
TF: 866-463-6264 ■ *Web:* www.corningny.com

Bethlehem Chamber of Commerce
318 Delaware Ave Ste 11 ..... Delmar NY 12054 518-439-0512 475-0910
Web: www.bethlehemchamber.com

Phone Fax

Chautauqua County Chamber of Commerce
10785 Bennett Rd . . . Dunkirk NY 14048 716-366-6200 366-4276
Web: www.chautauquachamber.org
Greater East Aurora Chamber of Commerce
652 Main St . . . East Aurora NY 14052 716-652-8444 652-8384
TF: 800-441-2881 ■ *Web:* www.eanycc.com
Chemung County Chamber of Commerce
400 E Church St . . . Elmira NY 14901 607-734-5137 734-4490
TF General: 800-627-5892 ■ *Web:* www.chemungchamber.org
Livingston County Chamber of Commerce
4635 Millennium Dr . . . Geneseo NY 14454 585-243-2222 243-4824
TF: 800-538-7365 ■ *Web:* www.fingerlakeswest.com
Adirondack Regional Chambers of Commerce
136 Glen St Ste 3 . . . Glens Falls NY 12801 518-798-1761 792-4147
Web: www.adirondackchamber.org
Montgomery County Chamber of Commerce
2 N Main St PO Box 836 . . . Gloversville NY 12078 518-725-0641 725-0643
Web: fultonmontgomeryny.org
Guilderland Chamber of Commerce
2050 Western Ave Ste 109 . . . Guilderland NY 12084 518-456-6611 456-6690
Web: www.guilderlandchamber.com
Hicksville Chamber of Commerce
10 W Marie St . . . Hicksville NY 11801 516-931-7170 931-8546
Web: www.hicksvillechamber.com
Southern Ulster County Chamber of Commerce
3553 Rt 9W PO Box 320 . . . Highland NY 12528 845-691-6070
Web: www.southernulsterchamber.org
Schoharie County Chamber of Commerce
143 Caverns Rd . . . Howes Cave NY 12092 518-296-8820 296-8825
Web: www.schohariechamber.com
Columbia County Chamber of Commerce
507 Warren St . . . Hudson NY 12534 518-828-4417 822-9539
Web: columbiachamber-ny.com
Huntington Township Chamber of Commerce
164 Main St . . . Huntington NY 11743 631-423-6100 351-8276
TF: 888-962-9932 ■ *Web:* www.huntingtonchamber.com
Hyde Park Chamber of Commerce PO Box 17 . . . Hyde Park NY 12538 845-229-8612 229-8638
Web: www.hydeparkchamber.org
Tompkins County Chamber of Commerce
904 E Shore Dr . . . Ithaca NY 14850 607-273-7080 272-7617
TF: 888-568-9816 ■ *Web:* www.tompkinschamber.org
Queens Chamber of Commerce
75-20 Astoria Blvd Ste 140 . . . Jackson Heights NY 11370 718-898-8500 898-8599
TF: 800-931-2297 ■ *Web:* www.queenschamber.org
Jamaica Chamber of Commerce
15711 Rockaway Blvd . . . Jamaica NY 11434 718-877-7704
Web: jamaicachambernyc.com
Chautauqua County Chamber of Commerce
512 Falconer St . . . Jamestown NY 14701 716-484-1101 487-0785
Web: www.chautauquachamber.org
Kenmore-Town of Tonawanda Chamber of Commerce
3411 Delaware Ave . . . Kenmore NY 14217 716-874-1202 874-3151
TF: 888-710-6626 ■ *Web:* www.ken-ton.org
Chamber of Commerce of Ulster County
55 Albany Ave . . . Kingston NY 12401 845-338-5100 338-0968
Web: www.ulsterchamber.org
Greater Liverpool Chamber of Commerce
314 Second St . . . Liverpool NY 13088 315-457-3895 234-3226
Web: www.liverpoolchamber.com
Long Beach Chamber of Commerce
350 National Blvd . . . Long Beach NY 11561 516-432-6000 432-0273
Web: www.thelongbeachchamber.com
Lewis County Chamber of Commerce
7576 S State St . . . Lowville NY 13367 315-376-2213 376-0326
TF: 800-724-0242 ■ *Web:* www.lewiscountychamber.org
Greater Mahopacs-Carmel Chamber of Commerce
953 S Lake Blvd PO Box 160 . . . Mahopac NY 10541 845-628-5553 628-5962
Web: www.mahopaccarmelonline.com
Chamber of Commerce of the Massapequas Inc
674 Broadway . . . Massapequa NY 11758 516-541-1443 541-8625
Web: massapequachamber.org
Long Island Assn
300 Broadhollow Rd Ste 110-W . . . Melville NY 11747 631-493-3000 499-2194
Web: longislandassociation.org
Herkimer County Chamber of Commerce
28 W Main St . . . Mohawk NY 13407 315-866-7820 866-7833
TF: 877-984-4636 ■ *Web:* www.herkimercountychamber.com
Orange County Chamber of Commerce
30 Scott's Corners Dr . . . Montgomery NY 12549 845-457-9700 457-8799
Web: www.orangeny.com
Sullivan County Chamber of Commerce
196 Bridgeville Rd Ste 7 . . . Monticello NY 12701 845-791-4200 791-4220
Web: www.catskills.com
Mount Vernon Chamber of Commerce
65 Haven Ave . . . Mount Vernon NY 10553 914-775-8127 699-0139
Chamber of Commerce of New Rochelle
459 Main St . . . New Rochelle NY 10801 914-632-5700
Web: www.newrochellechamber.org
Greater New York Chamber of Commerce
20 W 44th St 4th Fl . . . New York NY 10036 212-686-7220 686-7232
Web: www.chamber.nyc/default.asp
Manhattan Chamber of Commerce
1375 Broadway 3rd F . . . New York NY 10018 212-479-7772 473-8074
Web: www.manhattancc.org
New York City Partnership & Chamber of Commerce Inc
1 Battery Pk Plz 5th Fl . . . New York NY 10004 212-493-7400 344-3344
Web: www.pfnyc.org
Chamber of Commerce of the Tonawandas
15 Webster St . . . North Tonawanda NY 14120 716-692-5120 692-1867
Web: www.the-tonawandas.com
Commerce Chenango 15 S Broad St . . . Norwich NY 13815 607-334-1400 336-6963
Web: www.chenangony.org
Oceanside Chamber of Commerce
2721 Harrison Ave . . . Oceanside NY 11572 516-763-9177

Phone Fax

Greater Olean Area Chamber of Commerce
120 N Union St . . . Olean NY 14760 716-372-4433 372-7912
Web: www.oleanny.com
Otsego County Chamber 189 Main St Ste 201 . . . Oneonta NY 13820 607-432-4500 432-4506
Web: otsegocc.com
Orchard Park Chamber of Commerce
4211 N Buffalo St Ste 14 . . . Orchard Park NY 14127 716-662-3366 662-5946
Web: orchardparkchamber.org
Greater Oswego-Fulton Chamber of Commerce (GOFCC)
44 E Bridge St . . . Oswego NY 13126 315-343-7681 342-0831
Web: www.oswegofultonchamber.com
Tioga County Chamber of Commerce 80 N Ave . . . Owego NY 13827 607-687-2020 687-9028
Web: www.tiogachamber.com
Hudson Valley Gateway Chamber of Commerce
1 S Div St . . . Peekskill NY 10566 914-737-3600 737-0541
Web: www.hvgatewaychamber.com
Plattsburgh North Country Chamber of Commerce
7061 Rt 9 . . . Plattsburgh NY 12901 518-563-1000 563-1028
Web: www.northcountrychamber.com
Tri-State Chamber of Commerce
5 S Broome St . . . Port Jervis NY 12771 845-856-6694 856-6695
Web: tristatechamber.org
Port Washington Chamber of Commerce
329 Main St . . . Port Washington NY 11050 516-883-6566 883-6591
Web: www.pwguide.com
Dutchess County Regional Chamber of Commerce
1 Civic Ctr Plaza Ste 400 . . . Poughkeepsie NY 12601 845-454-1700 454-1702
TF: 800-817-2918 ■ *Web:* www.dcrcoc.org
Rome Area Chamber of Commerce 139 W Dominick St . . . Rome NY 13440 315-337-1700 337-1715
Web: www.romechamber.com
Niagara USA Chamber of Commerce
6311 Inducon Corporate Dr Ste 2 . . . Sanborn NY 14132 716-285-9141 285-0941
Web: niagarachamber.org
Saratoga County Chamber of Commerce
28 Clinton St . . . Saratoga Springs NY 12866 518-584-3255 798-0163
TF: 855-765-7873 ■ *Web:* www.saratoga.org
Chamber of Schenectady County
306 State St . . . Schenectady NY 12305 518-372-5656
Web: www.schenectadychamber.org
Seneca County Chamber of Commerce
2020 Rt 5 & 20 W . . . Seneca Falls NY 13148 315-568-2906 568-1730
Web: fingerlakesgateway.com
Smithtown Chamber of Commerce
79 E Main St Ste E . . . Smithtown NY 11787 631-979-8069 979-2206
Web: www.smithtownchamber.org
Southampton Chamber of Commerce
76 Main St . . . SoutHampton NY 11968 631-283-0402 283-8707
Web: www.southamptonchamber.com
Staten Island Chamber of Commerce
130 Bay St . . . Staten Island NY 10301 718-727-1900 727-2295
Web: www.sichamber.com
Rensselaer County Regional Chamber of Commerce
255 River St . . . Troy NY 12180 518-274-7020 272-7729
Web: www.renscochamber.com
Mohawk Valley Chamber of Commerce
200 Genesee St . . . Utica NY 13502 315-724-3151 724-3177
Web: greateruticachamber.org
Warwick Valley Chamber of Commerce (WVCC)
PO Box 202 . . . Warwick NY 10990 845-986-2720 986-6982
Web: www.warwickcc.org
Greater Watertown-North Country Chamber of Commerce
1241 Coffeen St . . . Watertown NY 13601 315-788-4400 788-3369
TF: 800-924-5145 ■ *Web:* www.watertownny.com
Webster Chamber of Commerce
1110 Crosspointe Ln Ste C . . . Webster NY 14580 585-265-3960 265-3702
Web: www.websterchamber.com
Business Council of Westchester
108 Corporate Pk Dr Ste 101 . . . White Plains NY 10604 914-948-2110 948-0122
Web: thebcw.org
Amherst Chamber of Commerce
400 Essjay Rd Ste 150 . . . Williamsville NY 14221 716-632-6905 632-0548
Web: www.amherst.org
Yonkers Chamber of Commerce 55 Main St 2nd Fl . . . Yonkers NY 10701 914-963-0332 963-0455
Web: www.yonkerschamber.com

North Carolina

Phone Fax

Ahoskie Chamber of Commerce
310 Catherine Creek Rd . . . Ahoskie NC 27910 252-332-2042 332-8617
Web: ahoskiechamber.net
Stanly County Chamber of Commerce
116 E N St . . . Albemarle NC 28001 704-982-8116 983-5000
Web: www.stanlychamber.org
Archdale-Trinity Chamber of Commerce
213 Balfour Dr . . . Archdale NC 27263 336-434-2073 431-5845
Web: www.archdaletrinitychamber.com
Asheville Area Chamber of Commerce
36 Montford Ave . . . Asheville NC 28802 828-258-6101 251-0926
TF: 888-314-1041 ■ *Web:* www.ashevillechamber.org
Black Mountain-Swannanoa Chamber of Commerce
201 E State St . . . Black Mountain NC 28711 828-669-2300 669-1407
TF: 800-669-2301 ■ *Web:* www.blackmountain.org
Blowing Rock Chamber of Commerce
7738 Vly Blvd . . . Blowing Rock NC 28605 828-295-7851
TF: 800-295-7851 ■ *Web:* www.blowingrock.com
Brevard-Transylvania Chamber of Commerce
175 E Main St . . . Brevard NC 28712 828-883-3700 883-8550
TF: 800-648-4523 ■ *Web:* www.brevardncchamber.org
Alamance County Area Chamber of Commerce
610 S Lexington Ave . . . Burlington NC 27215 336-228-1338 228-1330
Web: www.alamancechamber.com
Cary Chamber of Commerce 307 N Academy St . . . Cary NC 27513 919-467-1016 469-2375
Web: www.carychamber.com

				Phone	Fax
Chapel Hill-Carrboro Chamber of Commerce 104 S Estes Dr *TF:* 800-694-9784 ■ *Web:* www.carolinachamber.org	Chapel Hill	NC	27515	919-967-7075	968-6874
Charlotte Chamber of Commerce 330 S Tryon St PO Box 32785 *Web:* www.charlottechamber.com	Charlotte	NC	28202	704-378-1300	374-1903
Lake Norman Chamber of Commerce 19900 W Catawba Ave Ste 101 *TF:* 800-305-2508 ■ *Web:* www.lakenormanchamber.org	Cornelius	NC	28031	704-892-1922	892-5313
Greater Durham Chamber of Commerce 300 W Morgan St Ste 1400 PO Box 3829 *Web:* www.durhamchamber.org	Durham	NC	27702	919-328-8700	688-8351
Elizabeth City Area Chamber of Commerce 502 E Ehringhaus St *Web:* www.elizabethcitychamber.org	Elizabeth City	NC	27909	252-335-4365	335-5732
Yadkin Valley Chamber of Commerce 116 E Market St PO Box 496 *Web:* www.yadkinvalley.org	Elkin	NC	28621	336-526-1111	526-1879
Cumberland County Business Council 1019 Hay St	Fayetteville	NC	28305	910-483-8133	483-0263
Fuquay-Varina Area Chamber of Commerce 121 N Main St *Web:* www.fuquay-varina.com	Fuquay Varina	NC	27526	919-552-4947	552-1029
Gaston Chamber of Commerce 601 W Franklin Blvd *TF:* 800-933-3909 ■ *Web:* www.gastonchamber.com	Gastonia	NC	28052	704-864-2621	854-8723
Wayne County Chamber of Commerce 308 N Williams St *Web:* www.waynecountychamber.com	Goldsboro	NC	27530	919-734-2241	734-2247
Greenville-Pitt County Chamber of Commerce 302 S Greene St *Web:* www.greenvillenc.org	Greenville	NC	27834	252-752-4101	752-5934
Henderson-Vance County Chamber of Commerce 414 S Garnett St *Web:* www.hendersonvance.org	Henderson	NC	27536	252-438-8414	
Hendersonville County Chamber of Commerce 204 Kanuga Rd *Web:* www.hendersoncountychamber.org	Hendersonville	NC	28739	828-692-1413	693-8802
Catawba County Chamber of Commerce 1055 Southgate Corporate Pk SW PO Box 1828 *Web:* www.catawbachamber.org	Hickory	NC	28603	828-328-6111	328-1175
High Point Chamber of Commerce 1634 N Main St *TF:* 844-704-3663 ■ *Web:* www.highpointchamber.org	High Point	NC	27262	336-882-5000	889-9499
Jacksonville/Onslow Chamber of Commerce 1099 Gum Branch Rd *TF:* 800-877-8339 ■ *Web:* www.jacksonvilleonline.org	Jacksonville	NC	28541	910-347-3141	347-4705
Cabarrus Regional Chamber of Commerce 3003 Dale Earnhardt Blvd *Web:* www.cabarrus.biz	Kannapolis	NC	28083	704-782-4000	782-4050
Outer Banks Chamber of Commerce 101 Town Hall Dr PO Box 1757 *Web:* www.outerbankschamber.com	Kill Devil Hills	NC	27948	252-441-8144	
Kinston-Lenoir County Chamber of Commerce 301 N Queen St *Web:* www.kinstonchamber.com	Kinston	NC	28501	252-527-1131	527-1914
Laurinburg/Scotland County Area Chamber of Commerce 606 Atkinson St *Web:* www.laurinburgchamber.com	Laurinburg	NC	28352	910-276-7420	277-8785
Caldwell County Chamber of Commerce 1909 Hickory Blvd SE *Web:* caldwellchambernc.com	Lenoir	NC	28645	828-726-0616	726-0385
Lincolnton-Lincoln County Chamber of Commerce 101 E Main St *Web:* www.lincolnchambernc.org	Lincolnton	NC	28092	704-735-3096	735-5449
Lumberton Area Chamber of Commerce 800 N Chestnut St *Web:* www.lumbertonchamber.com	Lumberton	NC	28358	910-739-4750	671-9722
Western Rockingham Chamber of Commerce 112 W Murphy St *Web:* www.westernrockinghamchamber.com	Madison	NC	27025	336-548-6248	548-4466
McDowell County Chamber of Commerce 1170 W Tate St *Web:* www.mcdowellchamber.com	Marion	NC	28752	828-652-4240	659-9620
Davie County Chamber of Commerce 135 S Salisbury St *Web:* www.daviechamber.com	Mocksville	NC	27028	336-751-3304	751-5697
Union County Chamber of Commerce 903 Skyway Dr PO Box 1789 *Web:* www.unioncountycoc.com	Monroe	NC	28110	704-289-4567	282-0122
Mooresville-South Iredell Chamber of Commerce 149 E Iredell Ave *Web:* www.mooresvillenc.org	Mooresville	NC	28115	704-664-3898	664-2549
Carteret County Chamber of Commerce 801 Arendell St Ste 1 *TF:* 800-622-6278 ■ *Web:* www.nccoastchamber.com	Morehead City	NC	28557	252-726-6350	726-3505
Burke County Chamber of Commerce 110 E Meeting St *Web:* burkecountychamber.org	Morganton	NC	28655	828-437-3021	437-1613
Greater Mount Airy Chamber of Commerce 200 N Main St *TF:* 800-948-0949 ■ *Web:* www.mtairyncchamber.org	Mount Airy	NC	27030	336-786-6116	786-1488
Mount Olive Area Chamber of Commerce 123 N Ctr St *Web:* www.moachamber.com	Mount Olive	NC	28365	919-658-3113	
Cherokee County Chamber of Commerce (CCCC) 805 W US 64 Hwy *Web:* www.cherokeecountychamber.com	Murphy	NC	28906	828-837-2242	837-6012
New Bern Area Chamber of Commerce 316 S Front St *TF:* 877-811-1776 ■ *Web:* www.newbernchamber.com	New Bern	NC	28560	252-637-3111	637-7541
Wilkes Chamber of Commerce 717 Main St *Web:* wilkeschamber.com	North Wilkesboro	NC	28659	336-838-8662	838-3728
Granville County Chamber of Commerce 124 Hillsboro St *Web:* www.granville-chamber.com	Oxford	NC	27565	919-693-6125	693-6126
Raeford-Hoke Chamber of Commerce 101 N Main St *Web:* www.raefordhokechamber.com	Raeford	NC	28376	910-875-5929	
Greater Raleigh Chamber of Commerce PO Box 2978 *TF:* 888-456-8535 ■ *Web:* www.raleighchamber.org	Raleigh	NC	27602	919-664-7000	664-7097
Roanoke Valley Chamber of Commerce 260 Premier Blvd *Web:* www.rvchamber.com	Roanoke Rapids	NC	27870	252-537-3513	535-5767
Richmond County Chamber of Commerce 101 W Broad Ave PO Box 86 *Web:* www.richmondcountychamber.com	Rockingham	NC	28380	910-895-9058	895-9056
Rocky Mount Area Chamber of Commerce 100 Coastline St Ste 200 *TF:* 800-682-6746 ■ *Web:* www.rockymountchamber.org	Rocky Mount	NC	27804	252-446-0323	446-5103
Roxboro Area Chamber of Commerce 211 N Main St *Web:* www.roxboronc.com	Roxboro	NC	27573	336-599-8333	599-8335
Rutherford County Chamber of Commerce 162 N Main St *TF:* 866-478-4646 ■ *Web:* www.rutherfordcoc.org	Rutherfordton	NC	28139	828-287-3090	287-0799
Rowan County Chamber of Commerce 204 E Innes St Ste 110 *Web:* www.rowanchamber.com	Salisbury	NC	28144	704-633-4221	639-1200
Sanford Area Chamber of Commerce 115 Chatham St Ste 4 PO Box 519 **Fax Area Code:* 855 ■ *Web:* growsanfordnc.com/chamber	Sanford	NC	27330	919-775-7341	884-2547*
Brunswick County Chamber of Commerce 4948 Main St *TF:* 800-426-6644 ■ *Web:* www.brunswickcountychamber.org	Shallotte	NC	28459	910-754-6644	754-6539
Cleveland County Chamber of Commerce 200 S Lafayette St *Web:* www.clevelandchamber.org	Shelby	NC	28150	704-487-8521	487-7458
Chatham Chamber of Commerce 531 E Third St *Web:* www.ccucc.net	Siler City	NC	27344	919-742-3333	742-1333
Greater Smithfield-Selma Area Chamber of Commerce 1115 Industrial Pk Dr *Web:* www.smithfieldselma.com	Smithfield	NC	27577	919-934-9166	934-1337
Moore County Chamber of Commerce 10677 Hwy 15-501 *Web:* www.moorecountychamber.com	Southern Pines	NC	28387	910-692-3926	692-0619
Jackson County Chamber of Commerce 773 W Main St *TF:* 800-962-1911 ■ *Web:* www.mountainlovers.com	Sylva	NC	28779	828-586-2155	586-4887
Tarboro Edgecombe Chamber of Commerce 509 Trade St *Web:* www.tarborochamber.com	Tarboro	NC	27886	252-823-7241	823-1499
Thomasville Area Chamber of Commerce PO Box 1400 *Web:* www.thomasvillechamber.net	Thomasville	NC	27361	336-475-6134	475-4802
Carolina Foothills Chamber of Commerce 2753 Lynn Rd Ste A *Web:* www.carolinafoothillschamber.com	Tryon	NC	28782	828-859-6236	
Greater Franklin County Chamber of Commerce 3124 Heritage Trade Dr Ste 104 *Web:* www.franklin-chamber.org	Wake Forest	NC	27287	919-496-3056	496-0422
Washington-Beaufort County Chamber of Commerce 102 Stewart Pkwy PO Box 665 *Web:* www.wbcchamber.com	Washington	NC	27889	252-946-9168	946-9169
Haywood County Chamber of Commerce 28 Walnut St *TF:* 877-456-3073 ■ *Web:* haywoodchamber.com	Waynesville	NC	28786	828-456-3021	452-7265
Martin County Chamber of Commerce 415 E Blvd *Web:* martincountync.com	Williamston	NC	27892	252-792-4131	792-1013
Greater Wilmington Chamber of Commerce 1 Estell Lee Pl *TF:* 800-829-4477 ■ *Web:* www.wilmingtonchamber.org	Wilmington	NC	28401	910-762-2611	762-9765
Wilson Chamber of Commerce 200 Nash St NE *TF:* 855-905-0604 ■ *Web:* www.wilsonncchamber.com	Wilson	NC	27893	252-237-0165	243-7931
Windsor-Bertie Area Chamber of Commerce 121 Granville St PO Box 572 *TF:* 800-334-5010 ■ *Web:* www.windsorbertiechamber.com	Windsor	NC	27983	252-794-4277	794-5070
Greater Winston-Salem Chamber of Commerce 411 W Fourth St Ste 211 *Web:* www.winstonsalem.com	Winston-Salem	NC	27101	336-728-9200	721-2209
Yadkin County Chamber of Commerce 205 S Jackson St PO Box 1840 *TF:* 877-492-3546 ■ *Web:* www.yadkinchamber.org	Yadkinville	NC	27055	336-679-2200	679-3034

North Dakota

				Phone	Fax
Bismarck Mandan Chamber of Commerce 1640 Burnt Boat Dr *Web:* www.bismarckmandan.com	Bismarck	ND	58502	701-223-5660	255-6125
Grand Forks Chamber of Commerce 202 N Third St *TF:* 855-233-6362 ■ *Web:* www.gochamber.org	Grand Forks	ND	58203	701-772-7271	772-9238
Jamestown Area Chamber of Commerce 120 Second St SE PO Box 1530 *Web:* www.jamestownchamber.com	Jamestown	ND	58402	701-252-4830	952-4837
Minot Area Chamber of Commerce 1020 20th Ave SW *Web:* www.minotchamber.org	Minot	ND	58701	701-852-6000	838-2488

Ohio

				Phone	Fax
Greater Akron Chamber 1 Cascade Plz 17th Fl *Web:* www.greaterakronchamber.org	Akron	OH	44308	330-376-5550	379-3164

				Phone	Fax
Alliance Area Chamber of Commerce 210 E Main St *Web:* www.allianceohiochamber.org	Alliance	OH	44601	330-823-6260	823-4434
Ashtabula Area Chamber of Commerce 4536 Main Ave *Web:* www.ashtabulachamber.net	Ashtabula	OH	44004	440-998-6998	992-8216
Athens Area Chamber of Commerce 449 E State St Ste 1 *TF:* 877-360-3608 ■ *Web:* www.athenschamber.com	Athens	OH	45701	740-594-2251	594-2252
Barberton South Summitt Chamber of Commerce 503 W Pk Ave *Web:* www.southsummitchamber.org	Barberton	OH	44203	330-745-3141	
Beavercreek Chamber of Commerce 3210 Beaver-Vu Dr *Web:* www.beavercreekchamber.org	Beavercreek	OH	45431	937-426-2202	426-2204
Logan County Chamber of Commerce 100 S Main St *TF:* 877-360-3608 ■ *Web:* www.logancountyohio.com	Bellefontaine	OH	43311	937-599-5121	599-2411
Muskingum Valley Area Chamber of Commerce PO Box 837 *Web:* www.mvacc.com	Beverly	OH	45715	740-984-8259	
Bowling Green Chamber of Commerce (BGCC) 130 S. Main St PO Box 31 *Web:* www.bgchamber.net	Bowling Green	OH	43402	419-353-7945	353-3693
Brunswick Area Chamber of Commerce 1324 Pearl Rd M2 *Web:* www.brunswickareachamber.org	Brunswick	OH	44212	330-225-8411	273-8172
Cambridge Area Chamber of Commerce 918 Wheeling Ave *Web:* www.cambridgeohiochamber.com	Cambridge	OH	43725	740-439-6688	439-6689
Canton Regional Chamber of Commerce 222 Market Ave N *TF:* 800-533-4302 ■ *Web:* www.cantonchamber.org	Canton	OH	44702	330-456-7253	452-7786
Carroll County Chamber of Commerce & Economic Development 61 N Lisbon St PO Box 277 *TF:* 800-956-4684 ■ *Web:* www.carrollohchamber.com	Carrollton	OH	44615	330-627-4811	627-3647
Celina-Mercer County Chamber of Commerce 226 N Main St *Web:* www.celinamercer.com	Celina	OH	45822	419-586-2219	586-8645
Chagrin Valley Chamber of Commerce 83 N Main St *Web:* www.cvcc.org	Chagrin Falls	OH	44022	440-247-6607	
Chillicothe-Ross Chamber of Commerce 45 E Main St *Web:* www.chillicotheohio.com	Chillicothe	OH	45601	740-702-2722	702-2727
Anderson Area Chamber of Commerce 7850 Five Mile Rd *Web:* www.andersonareachamber.org	Cincinnati	OH	45230	513-474-4802	474-4857
Cincinnati USA Regional Chamber 441 Vine St Ste 300 *Web:* www.cincinnatichamber.com	Cincinnati	OH	45202	513-579-3100	579-3102
Clermont Chamber of Commerce 4355 Ferguson Dr Ste 150 *Web:* www.clermontchamber.com	Cincinnati	OH	45245	513-576-5000	576-5001
Pickaway County Chamber of Commerce PO Box 841 *Web:* www.pickaway.com	Circleville	OH	43113	740-474-4923	
Greater Cleveland Partnership 1240 Huron Rd E Ste 300 *TF:* 888-304-4769 ■ *Web:* www.gcpartnership.com	Cleveland	OH	44115	216-621-3300	621-6013
Columbus Chamber of Commerce 150 S Front St Ste 200 *TF:* 877-771-5202 ■ *Web:* www.columbus.org	Columbus	OH	43215	614-221-1321	221-1408
Coshocton County Chamber of Commerce 401 Main St *Web:* www.coshoctoncounty.net	Coshocton	OH	43812	740-622-5411	622-9902
Cuyahoga Falls Chamber of Commerce (CFCC) 151 Portage Trl Ste 1 *Web:* cfchamber.com	Cuyahoga Falls	OH	44221	330-929-6756	929-4278
Dayton Area Chamber of Commerce 1 Chamber Plaza Ste 200 *TF:* 800-621-9131 ■ *Web:* www.daytonchamber.org	Dayton	OH	45402	937-226-1444	226-8254
South Metro Regional Chamber of Commerce 683 Miamisburg Centerville Rd Ste 210 *Web:* www.smrcoc.org	Dayton	OH	45459	937-433-2032	433-6881
Defiance Area Chamber of Commerce 325 Clinton St *Web:* www.defiancechamber.com	Defiance	OH	43512	419-782-7946	782-0111
Southern Columbiana County Regional Chamber of Commerce 529 Market St PO Box 94 *Web:* www.sccregionalchamber.org	East Liverpool	OH	43920	330-385-0845	385-0581
Eaton-Preble County Chamber of Commerce 122 W Decatur St PO Box 303 *Web:* www.preblecountyohio.com	Eaton	OH	45320	937-456-4949	456-4949
Lorain County Chamber of Commerce 226 Middle Ave *Web:* www.loraincountychamber.com	Elyria	OH	44035	440-328-2550	328-2557
Englewood-Northmont Chamber of Commerce PO Box 62 *Web:* www.northmontchamber.com	Englewood	OH	45322	937-836-2550	836-2485
Euclid Chamber of Commerce 22639 Euclid Ave PO Box 32611 *Web:* www.euclidchamber.com	Euclid	OH	44117	216-731-9322	865-4925
Fairborn Area Chamber of Commerce 12 N Central Ave *Web:* www.fairborn.com	Fairborn	OH	45324	937-878-3191	878-3197
Fairfield Chamber of Commerce 670 Wessel Dr	Fairfield	OH	45014	513-881-5500	881-5503
Findlay-Hancock County Chamber of Commerce 123 E Main Cross St *Web:* www.findlayhancockalliance.com	Findlay	OH	45840	419-422-3313	422-9508
Fostoria Area Chamber of Commerce (FACC) 121 N Main St *Web:* www.fostoriaohio.org	Fostoria	OH	44830	419-435-7789	435-0936
Chamber of Commerce of Sandusky County 215 Croghan St *Web:* www.scchamber.org	Fremont	OH	43420	419-332-1591	332-8666
Gahanna Area Chamber of Commerce 181 Granville St Ste 200 *Web:* www.gahannaareachamber.com	Gahanna	OH	43230	614-471-0451	471-5122
Gallia County Chamber of Commerce 16 State St PO Box 465 *Web:* galliacountychamber.org	Gallipolis	OH	45631	740-446-0596	446-7031
Garfield Heights Chamber of Commerce 5522 Turney Rd *Web:* www.garfieldchamber.com	Garfield Heights	OH	44125	216-475-7775	
Geneva Area Chamber of Commerce 866 E Main St *Web:* www.genevachamber.org	Geneva	OH	44041	440-466-8694	
Brown County Chamber of Commerce PO Box 21606 *Web:* www.browncountyohiochamber.com	Georgetown	OH	45121	937-378-4784	378-1634
Darke County Chamber of Commerce 622 S Broadway *Web:* www.darkecountyohio.com	Greenville	OH	45331	937-548-2102	
Greater Hamilton Chamber of Commerce 201 Dayton St *Web:* www.hamilton-ohio.com	Hamilton	OH	45011	513-844-1500	844-1999
Highland County Chamber of Commerce PO Box 183 *Web:* www.highlandcountychamber.com	Hillsboro	OH	45133	937-393-1111	
Huber Heights Chamber of Commerce 4707 Brandt Pk PO Box 24006 *Web:* huberheightschamber.com	Huber Heights	OH	45424	937-233-5700	
Jackson Area Chamber of Commerce 234 Broadway St *Web:* www.jacksonohio.org	Jackson	OH	45640	740-286-2722	286-8443
Jackson-Beldon Chamber of Commerce 5735 Wales Ave NW *Web:* www.jbcc.org	Jackson Township	OH	44646	330-833-4400	833-4456
Kent Area Chamber of Commerce 138 E Main St Ste 102 *Web:* www.kentbiz.com	Kent	OH	44240	330-673-9855	
Hardin County Chamber of Commerce (HCCBA) 225 S Detroit St *TF:* 888-642-7346 ■ *Web:* www.hardincountyoh.org	Kenton	OH	43326	419-673-4131	674-4876
Kettering-Moraine-Oakwood Area Chamber of Commerce 2977 Far Hills Ave *Web:* www.kmo-coc.org	Kettering	OH	45419	937-299-3852	299-3851
Lakewood Chamber of Commerce 16017 Detroit Ave *Web:* www.lakewoodchamber.org	Lakewood	OH	44107	216-226-2900	226-1340
Lancaster-Fairfield County Chamber of Commerce 109 N Broad St Ste 100 *Web:* www.lancoc.org	Lancaster	OH	43130	740-653-8251	653-7074
Lima/Allen County Chamber of Commerce 144 S Main St Ste 100 *Web:* www.limachamber.com	Lima	OH	45801	419-222-6045	229-0266
Logan-Hocking Chamber of Commerce 4 E Hunter St *Web:* www.hockinghillschamber.com	Logan	OH	43138	740-385-6836	385-7259
Madison-Perry Area Chamber of Commerce 5965 N Ridge Rd *Web:* www.easternlakecountychamber.org	Madison	OH	44057	440-428-3760	428-6668
Richland Area Chamber of Commerce 55 N Mulberry St *Web:* www.richlandareachamber.com	Mansfield	OH	44902	419-522-3211	526-6853
Marietta Area Chamber of Commerce 100 Front St Ste 200 *Web:* www.mariettachamber.com	Marietta	OH	45750	740-373-5176	373-7808
Marion Area Chamber of Commerce 267 W Ctr St Ste 100 *Web:* www.marionareachamber.org	Marion	OH	43302	740-382-2181	387-7722
Union County Chamber of Commerce 227 E Fifth St *TF:* 800-642-0087 ■ *Web:* www.unioncounty.org	Marysville	OH	43040	937-642-6279	644-0422
Massillon Area Chamber of Commerce 137 Lincoln Way E *Web:* www.massillonohchamber.com	Massillon	OH	44646	330-833-3146	833-8944
Mentor Chamber of Commerce 6972 Spinach Dr *TF:* 800-292-5707 ■ *Web:* www.mentorchamber.org	Mentor	OH	44060	440-255-1616	255-1717
Chamber of Commerce serving Middletown Monroe & Trenton 1500 Central Ave *TF:* 800-837-3200 ■ *Web:* thechamberofcommerce.org	Middletown	OH	45044	513-422-4551	422-6831
Milford-Miami Township Chamber of Commerce 983 Lila Ave *TF:* 877-723-0513 ■ *Web:* www.milfordmiamitownship.com	Milford	OH	45150	513-831-2411	831-3547
Holmes County Chamber of Commerce 35 N Monroe St *Web:* www.holmescountychamber.com	Millersburg	OH	44654	330-674-3975	674-3976
Morrow County Chamber of Commerce 17 1/2 W High St PO Box 174 *Web:* www.morrowchamber.org	Mount Gilead	OH	43338	419-946-2821	
Mount Vernon-Knox County Chamber of Commerce 400 S Gay St *Web:* www.knoxchamber.com	Mount Vernon	OH	43050	740-393-1111	393-1590
Napoleon/Henry County Chamber of Commerce 611 N Perry St *TF:* 800-322-6849 ■ *Web:* henrycountychamber.org	Napoleon	OH	43545	419-592-1786	592-4945
Tuscarawas County Chamber of Commerce 1323 Fourth St NW *Web:* www.tuschamber.com	New Philadelphia	OH	44663	330-343-4474	343-6526
Licking County Chamber of Commerce 50 W Locust St *Web:* www.lickingcountychamber.com	Newark	OH	43055	740-345-9757	345-5141
North Canton Area Chamber of Commerce 121 S Main St *Web:* www.northcantonchamber.org	North Canton	OH	44720	330-499-5100	499-7181
North Olmsted Chamber of Commerce 28938 Lorain Rd Ste 204 *Web:* www.nolmstedchamber.org	North Olmsted	OH	44070	440-777-3368	777-9361

Organization / Address	City	State	ZIP	Phone	Fax
North Royalton Chamber of Commerce 13737 State Rd *Web:* www.nroyaltonchamber.com	North Royalton	OH	44133	440-237-6180	237-6181
Eastern Maumee Bay Chamber of Commerce 2460 Navaree Ave *Web:* www.embchamber.org	Oregon	OH	43616	419-693-5580	693-9990
Parma Area Chamber of Commerce 7908 Day Dr *Web:* www.parmaareachamber.org	Parma	OH	44129	440-886-1700	886-1770
Perrysburg Area Chamber of Commerce 105 W Indiana Ave *Web:* www.perrysburgchamber.com	Perrysburg	OH	43551	419-874-9147	872-9347
Portsmouth Area Chamber of Commerce 342 Second St PO Box 509 *TF:* 800-648-2574 ■ *Web:* www.portsmouth.org	Portsmouth	OH	45662	740-353-7647	353-5824
Reynoldsburg Area Chamber of Commerce 1580 Brice Rd *Web:* www.reynoldsburgchamber.com	Reynoldsburg	OH	43068	614-866-4753	866-7313
Salem Area Chamber of Commerce 713 E State St *Web:* www.salemohiochamber.org	Salem	OH	44460	330-337-3473	337-3474
Erie County Chamber of Commerce 225 W Washington Row *Web:* eriecountychamber.com	Sandusky	OH	44870	419-625-6421	625-7914
Sidney-Shelby County Chamber of Commerce 101 S Ohio Ave 2nd Fl *Web:* www.sidneyshelbychamber.com	Sidney	OH	45365	937-492-9122	498-2472
Greater Lawrence County Area Chamber of Commerce 216 Collins Ave *TF:* 800-408-1334 ■ *Web:* www.lawrencecountyohio.org	South Point	OH	45680	740-377-4550	377-2091
Jefferson County Chamber of Commerce 630 Market St *Web:* www.jeffersoncountychamber.com	Steubenville	OH	43952	740-282-6226	
Stow-Munroe Falls Chamber of Commerce 4381 Hudson Dr Ste 2450 *Web:* www.smfcc.com	Stow	OH	44224	330-688-1579	688-6234
Strongsville Chamber of Commerce 18829 Royalton Rd *Web:* www.strongsvillechamber.com	Strongsville	OH	44136	440-238-3366	238-7010
Sylvania Area Chamber of Commerce 5632 Main St *Web:* www.sylvaniachamber.org	Sylvania	OH	43560	419-882-2135	885-7740
Tiffin Area Chamber of Commerce 62 S Washington St *Web:* www.tiffinchamber.com	Tiffin	OH	44883	419-447-4141	447-5141
Toledo Regional Chamber of Commerce 300 Madison Ave Ste 200 *Web:* www.toledochamber.com	Toledo	OH	43604	419-243-8191	241-8302
Trotwood Chamber of Commerce 5790 Denlinger Rd *Web:* www.trotwoodchamber.org	Trotwood	OH	45426	937-837-1484	837-1508
Champaign County Chamber of Commerce 113 Miami St *TF:* 877-873-5764 ■ *Web:* www.champaignohio.com	Urbana	OH	43078	937-653-5764	652-1599
Vandalia-Butler Chamber of Commerce 544 W National Rd *Web:* www.vandaliabutlerchamber.org	Vandalia	OH	45377	937-898-5351	898-5491
Fayette County Chamber of Commerce 101 E East St *Web:* www.fayettecountyohio.com	Washington Court House	OH	43160	740-335-0761	335-0762
West Chester Chamber Alliance 8922 Beckett Rd *Web:* www.thechamberalliance.com	West Chester	OH	45069	513-777-3600	777-0188
Adams County Travel & Visitors Bureau 509 E Main St *TF:* 877-232-6764 ■ *Web:* www.adamscountytravel.org	West Union	OH	45693	937-544-5639	
Westerville Area Chamber of Commerce 99 Commerce Pk Dr # A *Web:* www.westervillechamber.com	Westerville	OH	43082	614-882-8917	882-2085
West Shore Chamber of Commerce PO Box 45297 Ste204 *Web:* www.westshorechamber.org	Westlake Village	OH	44145	440-835-8787	835-8798
Willougby Area Chamber of Commerce 28 Public Sq *TF:* 877-229-4361 ■ *Web:* www.wwlcchamber.com	Willoughby	OH	44094	440-942-1632	942-0586
Wilmington Clinton County Chamber of Commerce (WCCC) 100 W Main St *Web:* www.wccchamber.com	Wilmington	OH	45177	937-382-2737	
Wooster Area Chamber of Commerce 377 W Liberty St *Web:* www.woosterchamber.com	Wooster	OH	44691	330-262-5735	262-5745
Worthington Area Chamber of Commerce 25 W New England Ave Ste 100 *Web:* www.worthingtonchamber.org	Worthington	OH	43085	614-888-3040	841-4842
Xenia Area Chamber of Commerce 334 W Market St *Web:* xacc.com	Xenia	OH	45385	937-372-3591	372-2192
Youngstown Warren Regional Chamber 11 Central Sq Ste 1600 *TF:* 877-807-2249 ■ *Web:* www.regionalchamber.com	Youngstown	OH	44503	330-744-2131	746-0330
Zanesville-Muskingum County Chamber of Commerce 205 N Fifth St *TF:* 800-743-2303 ■ *Web:* www.zmchamber.com	Zanesville	OH	43701	740-455-8282	454-2963

Oklahoma

Organization / Address	City	State	ZIP	Phone	Fax
Ada Area Chamber of Commerce 209 W Main St *Web:* www.adachamber.com	Ada	OK	74820	580-332-2506	
Bartlesville Area Chamber of Commerce 201 S Keeler Ave *Web:* www.bartlesville.com	Bartlesville	OK	74003	918-336-8708	337-0216
Broken Arrow Chamber of Commerce 210 N Main Ste C *Web:* www.brokenarrow.org	Broken Arrow	OK	74012	918-251-1518	
Del City Chamber of Commerce PO Box 15643 *Web:* www.delcitychamber.com	Del City	OK	73155	405-677-1910	
Durant Area Chamber of Commerce 215 N Fourth St *Web:* www.durantchamber.org	Durant	OK	74701	580-924-0848	924-0348
Edmond Area Chamber of Commerce 825 E Second St *Web:* www.edmondchamber.com	Edmond	OK	73034	405-341-2808	340-5512
Greater Enid Chamber of Commerce PO Box 907 *TF:* 877-334-2665 ■ *Web:* www.enidchamber.com	Enid	OK	73702	580-237-2494	237-2497
Midwest City Chamber of Commerce 5905 Trosper Rd *Web:* www.midwestcityok.com	Midwest City	OK	73110	405-733-3801	
Moore Chamber of Commerce 305 W Main St *Web:* www.moorechamber.com	Moore	OK	73160	405-794-3400	794-8555
Greater Muskogee Area Chamber of Commerce PO Box 797 *TF:* 866-381-6543 ■ *Web:* www.visitmuskogee.com	Muskogee	OK	74402	918-682-2401	682-2403
Greater Oklahoma City Chamber of Commerce 123 Pk Ave *Web:* www.okcchamber.com	Oklahoma City	OK	73102	405-297-8900	297-8916
South Oklahoma City Chamber of Commerce 701 SW 74 St *Web:* www.southokc.com	Oklahoma City	OK	73139	405-634-1436	634-1462
Owasso Chamber of Commerce 315 S Cedar St *Web:* www.owassochamber.com	Owasso	OK	74055	918-272-2141	272-8564
Ponca City Area Chamber of Commerce 420 E Grand Ave *TF:* 866-763-8092 ■ *Web:* www.poncacitychamber.com	Ponca City	OK	74601	580-765-4400	765-2798
Poteau Chamber of Commerce 201 S Broadway *Web:* poteauchamber.com	Poteau	OK	74953	918-647-9178	647-4099
Sallisaw Chamber of Commerce 301 E Cherokee Ave *Web:* sallisawchamber.com	Sallisaw	OK	74955	918-775-2558	775-4021
Greater Shawnee Area Chamber of Commerce 131 N Bell Ave *TF:* 800-762-7695 ■ *Web:* www.shawneechamber.com	Shawnee	OK	74801	405-273-6092	275-9851
Stillwater Chamber of Commerce 409 S Main St *TF:* 800-593-5573 ■ *Web:* www.stillwaterchamber.org	Stillwater	OK	74075	405-372-5573	372-4316
Tulsa Metro Chamber 1 West Third St Ste 100 *TF:* 888-424-9411 ■ *Web:* www.tulsachamber.com	Tulsa	OK	74103	918-585-1201	
Yukon Chamber of Commerce 510 Elm St *Web:* www.yukoncc.com	Yukon	OK	73099	405-354-3567	350-0724

Oregon

Organization / Address	City	State	ZIP	Phone	Fax
Albany Area Chamber of Commerce 435 W First Ave W *Web:* www.albanychamber.com	Albany	OR	97321	541-926-1517	926-7064
Beaverton Area Chamber of Commerce 12655 SW Ctr St Ste 140 *Web:* www.beaverton.org	Beaverton	OR	97005	503-644-0123	526-0349
Bend Chamber of Commerce 777 NW Wall St *TF:* 800-905-2363 ■ *Web:* www.bendchamber.org	Bend	OR	97701	541-382-3221	385-9929
Bay Area Chamber of Commerce 145 Central Ave *Web:* www.oregonsbayarea.org	Coos Bay	OR	97420	541-266-0868	267-6704
Corvallis Area Chamber of Commerce 420 NW Second St *Web:* www.corvallischamber.com	Corvallis	OR	97330	541-757-1505	
Eugene Chamber of Commerce 1401 Willamette St *Web:* www.eugenechamber.com	Eugene	OR	97401	541-484-1314	484-4942
Florence Area Chamber of Commerce 290 Hwy 101 *Web:* www.florencechamber.com	Florence	OR	97439	541-997-3128	997-4101
Grants Pass Chamber of Commerce 1995 NW Vine St PO Box 970 *TF:* 800-547-5927 ■ *Web:* www.grantspasschamber.org	Grants Pass	OR	97526	541-476-7717	476-9574
Gresham Area Chamber of Commerce 701 NE Hood Ave *Web:* www.greshamchamber.org	Gresham	OR	97030	503-665-1131	666-1041
Hermiston Chamber of Commerce 415 S Hwy 395 PO Box 185 *Web:* www.hermistonchamber.com	Hermiston	OR	97838	541-567-6151	564-9109
Hillsboro Chamber of Commerce 5193 NE Elam Young Pkwy Ste A *Web:* hillsborochamberor.com	Hillsboro	OR	97124	503-648-1102	
Keizer Chamber of Commerce 980 Chemawa Rd NE *Web:* www.keizerchamber.com	Keizer	OR	97303	503-393-9111	393-1003
Klamath County Chamber of Commerce 205 Riverside Dr *Web:* www.klamath.org	Klamath Falls	OR	97601	541-884-5193	884-5195
La Grande-Union County Chamber of Commerce 102 Elm St *TF:* 800-848-9969 ■ *Web:* www.unioncountychamber.org	La Grande	OR	97850	541-963-8588	963-3936
Lake Oswego Chamber of Commerce 242 B Ave *Web:* www.lake-oswego.com	Lake Oswego	OR	97034	503-636-3634	636-7427
Chamber of Medford/Jackson County 101 E Eigth St *Web:* www.medfordchamber.com	Medford	OR	97501	541-779-4847	776-4808
North Clackamas County Chamber of Commerce 7740 SE Harmony Rd *Web:* www.yourchamber.com	Milwaukie	OR	97222	503-654-7777	653-9515
Greater Newport Chamber of Commerce 555 SW Coast Hwy *TF:* 800-262-7844 ■ *Web:* www.newportchamber.org	Newport	OR	97365	541-265-8801	265-5589
Oregon City Chamber of Commerce 1201 Washington St *Web:* www.oregoncity.org	Oregon City	OR	97045	503-656-1619	656-2274
Portland Business Alliance 200 SW Market St Ste 150 *TF:* 800-224-1180 ■ *Web:* www.portlandalliance.com	Portland	OR	97201	503-224-8684	323-9186

				Phone	Fax
Salem Area Chamber of Commerce 1110 Commercial St NE *Web:* www.salemchamber.org	Salem	OR	97301	503-581-1466	581-0972
Springfield Chamber of Commerce 101 S 'A' St *Web:* www.springfield-chamber.org	Springfield	OR	97477	541-746-1651	726-4727
Tigard Area Chamber of Commerce (TACC) 12345 SW Main St *Web:* www.tigardareachamber.org	Tigard	OR	97223	503-639-1656	

Pennsylvania

				Phone	Fax
Greater Lehigh Valley Chamber of Commerce 840 Hamilton St Ste 205 *TF:* 800-845-7941 ■ *Web:* www.lehighvalleychamber.org	Allentown	PA	18101	610-841-5800	437-4907
Two Rivers Area Chamber of Commerce 840 Hamilton St Ste 205 *Web:* www.lehighvalleychamber.org	Allentown	PA	18101	610-841-5800	437-4907
Altoona-Blair County Chamber of Commerce 3900 Industrial Pk Dr Ste 12 *Web:* www.blairchamber.com	Altoona	PA	16602	814-943-8151	943-5239
Beaver County Chamber of Commerce 798 Turnpike St *Web:* beavercountychamber.com	Beaver	PA	15009	724-775-3944	728-9737
Bedford County Chamber of Commerce 137 E Pitt St *TF:* 800-732-0999 ■ *Web:* bedfordcountychamber.com	Bedford	PA	15522	814-623-2233	623-6089
Bellefonte Intervalley Chamber of Commerce 320 W High St *Web:* www.bellefonte.com	Bellefonte	PA	16823	814-355-2917	355-2761
Lehigh Valley Chamber of Commerce 1 E BRd St Ste 560 *Web:* www.lehighvalleychamber.org	Bethlehem	PA	18018	610-841-5862	758-9533
Bloomsburg Area Chamber of Commerce 238 Market St *Web:* www.bloomsburg.org	Bloomsburg	PA	17815	570-784-2522	784-2661
Columbia Montour chamber of Commerce, The 238 Market St *Web:* www.columbiamontourchamber.com	Bloomsburg	PA	17815	570-784-2522	784-2661
Butler County Chamber of Commerce 101 E Diamond St Ste 116 *Web:* www.butlercountychamber.com	Butler	PA	16001	724-283-2222	283-0224
West Shore Chamber of Commerce 4211 E Trindle Rd *Web:* www.wschamber.org	Camp Hill	PA	17011	717-761-0702	761-4315
Washington County Chamber of Commerce 375 Southpointe Blvd Ste 240 *TF:* 800-242-6422 ■ *Web:* www.washcochamber.com	Canonsburg	PA	15301	724-225-3010	228-7337
Greater Chambersburg Chamber of Commerce 100 Lincoln Way E Ste A *Web:* www.chambersburg.org	Chambersburg	PA	17201	717-264-7101	267-0399
Clarion Area Chamber of Business & Industry 21 N Sixth Ave *Web:* www.clarionpa.com	Clarion	PA	16214	814-226-9161	226-4903
Perkiomen Valley Chamber of Commerce 351 E Main St *Web:* perkiomenvalleychamber.org	Collegeville	PA	19426	610-489-6660	454-1270
Central Bucks Chamber of Commerce 252 W Swamp Rd Ste 23 *Web:* www.centralbuckschamber.com	Doylestown	PA	18901	215-348-3913	348-7154
Montgomery County Chamber of Commerce PO Box 200 *Web:* www.montgomerycountychamber.org	Eagleville	PA	19408	610-265-1776	265-0473
Erie Regional Chamber & Growth Partnership 208 E Bayfront Pkwy *TF:* 888-300-3743 ■ *Web:* www.eriepa.com	Erie	PA	16507	814-454-7191	459-0241
Exton Region Chamber of Commerce 185 Exton Square Mall *Web:* www.ercc.net	Exton	PA	19341	610-363-7746	
Lower Bucks County Chamber of Commerce 409 Hood Blvd *TF:* 800-786-2234 ■ *Web:* www.lbccc.org	Fairless Hills	PA	19030	215-943-7400	943-7404
Franklin Area Chamber of Commerce (FACC) 1259 Liberty St *TF:* 888-547-2377 ■ *Web:* www.franklinareachamber.org	Franklin	PA	16323	814-432-5823	437-2453
Gettysburg-Adams County Area Chamber of Commerce 18 Carlisle St Ste 203 *TF:* 800-699-1176 ■ *Web:* www.gettysburg-chamber.org	Gettysburg	PA	17325	717-334-8151	334-3368
Westmoreland Chamber of Commerce 241 Tollgate Hill Rd *TF:* 866-468-1231 ■ *Web:* www.westmorelandchamber.com	Greensburg	PA	15601	724-834-2900	837-7635
Hanover Area Chamber of Commerce 146 Carlisle St *Web:* www.hanoverchamber.com	Hanover	PA	17331	717-637-6130	637-9127
Harrisburg Regional Chamber 3211 N Front St Ste 201 *TF:* 877-883-8339 ■ *Web:* www.harrisburgregionalchamber.org	Harrisburg	PA	17110	717-232-4099	232-5184
Huntingdon County Business & Industry 9136 William Penn Hwy *Web:* www.hcbi.com	Huntingdon	PA	16652	814-506-8287	
Indiana County Chamber of Commerce 1019 Philadelphia St *Web:* www.indianapa.com	Indiana	PA	15701	724-465-2511	
Norwin Chamber of Commerce 321 Main St *TF:* 800-395-5665 ■ *Web:* www.norwinchamber.com	Irwin	PA	15642	724-863-0888	863-5133
Greater Johnstown/Cambria County Chamber of Commerce 245 Market St Ste 100 *TF:* 800-790-4522 ■ *Web:* www.johnstownchamber.com	Johnstown	PA	15901	814-536-5107	539-5800
Southern Chester County Chamber of Commerce 217 W State St *TF:* 800-343-6583 ■ *Web:* www.scccc.com	Kennett Square	PA	19348	610-444-0774	444-5105
Chamber of Commerce 101 Bill Smith Blvd *Web:* montgomerycountychamber.org	King of Prussia	PA	19406	610-265-1776	265-0473
Armstrong County Chamber of Commerce 124 Market St *Web:* allekiskistrong.com	Kittanning	PA	16201	724-543-1305	
Lancaster Chamber of Commerce & Industry PO Box 1558 *Web:* lancasterchamber.com	Lancaster	PA	17608	717-397-3531	293-3159
PennSuburban Chamber of Commerce 34 Susquehanna Ave *Web:* pennsuburban.org	Lansdale	PA	19446	215-362-9200	362-0393
Latrobe Area Chamber of Commerce PO Box 463 *Web:* www.latrobelaurelvalley.org	Latrobe	PA	15650	724-537-2671	537-2690
Lebanon Valley Chamber of Commerce 604 Cumberland St *Web:* www.lvchamber.org	Lebanon	PA	17042	717-273-3727	273-7940
Juniata Valley Area Chamber of Commerce 1 W Market St *TF:* 866-377-1234 ■ *Web:* www.juniatarivervalley.org	Lewistown	PA	17044	717-248-6713	248-6714
Clinton County Economic Partnership 212 N Jay St *TF:* 888-388-6991 ■ *Web:* www.clintoncountyinfo.com	Lock Haven	PA	17745	570-748-5782	893-0433
Meadville-Western Crawford County Chamber of Commerce 908 Diamond Pk *Web:* www.meadvillechamber.com	Meadville	PA	16335	814-337-8030	337-8022
Delaware County Chamber of Commerce 602 E Baltimore Pk *Web:* www.delcochamber.org	Media	PA	19063	610-565-3677	
Pike County Chamber of Commerce 209 E Hartford St *Web:* www.pikechamber.com	Milford	PA	18337	570-296-8700	296-3921
Monroeville Area Chamber of Commerce 4268 Northern Pike *TF:* 800-527-8941 ■ *Web:* www.monroevillechamber.com	Monroeville	PA	15146	412-856-0622	856-1030
Pittsburgh Airport Area Chamber of Commerce 850 Beaver Grade Rd *Web:* www.paacc.com	Moon Township	PA	15108	412-264-6270	264-1575
Laurel Highlands Chamber of Commerce 537 W Main St *Web:* www.westmorelandchamber.com	Mount Pleasant	PA	15666	724-547-7521	
Nazareth Area Chamber of Commerce 201 N Main St PO Box 173 *TF:* 866-776-8240 ■ *Web:* www.nazarethchamber.com	Nazareth	PA	18064	610-759-9188	759-5262
Lawrence County Chamber of Commerce 138 W Washington St *Web:* www.lawrencecountychamber.org	New Castle	PA	16101	724-654-5593	654-3330
Pennridge Chamber of Commerce 538 W Market St *Web:* www.pennridge.com	Perkasie	PA	18944	215-257-5390	257-6840
Greater Northeast Philadelphia Chamber of Commerce 8025 Roosevelt Blvd Ste 200 *Web:* www.nephilachamber.com	Philadelphia	PA	19152	215-332-3400	332-6050
Greater Philadelphia Chamber of Commerce 200 S Broad St Ste 700 *Web:* www.greaterphilachamber.com	Philadelphia	PA	19102	215-545-1234	790-3600
Moshannon Valley Economic Development Partnership 200 Shady Ln *Web:* www.mvedp.org	Philipsburg	PA	16866	814-342-2260	342-2878
Phoenixville Regional Chamber of Commerce 171 Bridge St *Web:* www.phoenixvillechamber.org	Phoenixville	PA	19460	610-933-3070	917-0503
East Liberty Quarter Chamber of Commerce 5907 Penn Ave Ste 305 *Web:* www.eastlibertychamber.org	Pittsburgh	PA	15206	412-661-9660	
Greater Pittsburgh Chamber of Commerce 425 Sixth Ave Ste 1100 *TF:* 877-392-1300 ■ *Web:* www.alleghenyconference.org	Pittsburgh	PA	15219	412-392-4500	392-1040
North Side Chamber of Commerce 809 Middle St *Web:* www.northsidechamberofcommerce.com	Pittsburgh	PA	15212	412-231-6500	321-6760
Penn Hills Chamber of Commerce 12013 Frankstown Rd *Web:* www.pennhillschamber.org	Pittsburgh	PA	15235	412-795-8741	795-7993
South Hills Chamber of Commerce 1910 Cochran Rd Ste 140 *Web:* www.shchamber.org	Pittsburgh	PA	15220	412-306-8090	306-8093
South Side Chamber of Commerce 1100 E Carson St *Web:* www.southsidechamber.org	Pittsburgh	PA	15203	412-431-3360	
Tri County Area Chamber of Commerce 152 E High St Ste 360 *TF:* 800-223-8477 ■ *Web:* www.tricountyareachamber.com	Pottstown	PA	19464	610-326-2900	970-9705
Schuylkill Chamber of Commerce 91 S Progress Ave *TF:* 800-755-1942 ■ *Web:* www.schuylkillchamber.com	Pottsville	PA	17901	570-622-1942	622-1638
Upper Bucks Chamber of Commerce 2170 Portzer Rd *TF:* 888-942-8257 ■ *Web:* www.ubcc.org	Quakertown	PA	18951	215-536-3211	536-7767
Greater Reading Chamber of Commerce & Industry 201 Penn St *Web:* www.greaterreadingchamber.org	Reading	PA	19601	610-376-6766	376-4135
Greater Scranton Chamber of Commerce 222 Mulberry St *Web:* www.scrantonchamber.com	Scranton	PA	18503	570-342-7711	347-6262
Greater Susquehanna Valley Chamber of Commerce 2859 N Susquehanna Trl PO Box 10 *TF:* 800-410-2880 ■ *Web:* www.gsvcc.org	Shamokin Dam	PA	17876	570-743-4100	743-1221
Shenango Valley Chamber of Commerce 41 Chestnut St *TF:* 800-732-0993 ■ *Web:* www.svchamber.com	Sharon	PA	16146	724-981-5880	981-5480
Shippensburg Area Chamber of Commerce 53 W King St *Web:* www.shippensburg.org	Shippensburg	PA	17257	717-532-5509	532-7501
Somerset County Chamber of Commerce 601 N Ctr Ave *Web:* www.somersetcountychamber.com	Somerset	PA	15501	814-445-6431	443-4313

Phone | Fax

Chamber of Business & Industry of Centre County
200 Innovation Blvd Ste 150 .... State College PA 16803 814-234-1829 234-5869
TF: 877-234-5050 ■ *Web:* www.cbicc.org

Indian Valley Chamber of Commerce
100 Penn Ave .... Telford PA 18969 215-723-9472 723-2490
Web: www.indianvalleychamber.com

Fayette Chamber of Commerce 65 W Main St .... Uniontown PA 15401 724-437-4571 438-3304
TF: 800-916-9365 ■ *Web:* www.fayettechamber.com

StrongLand Chamber of Commerce
1129 Industrial Pk Rd Ste 108 PO Box 10 .... Vandergrift PA 15690 724-845-5426
Web: allekiskistrong.com

Warren County Chamber of Commerce (WCCBI)
308 Market St .... Warren PA 16365 814-723-3050 723-6024
Web: www.wccbi.org

Main Line Chamber of Commerce
175 Strafford Ave Ste 130 .... Wayne PA 19087 610-687-6232 687-8085
Web: www.mlcc.org

Greater Waynesboro Chamber of Commerce
118 Walnut St Ste 111 .... Waynesboro PA 17268 717-762-7123 762-7124
Web: www.waynesboro.org

Greater West Chester Chamber of Commerce
119 N High St .... West Chester PA 19380 610-696-4046 696-9110
Web: www.greaterwestchester.com

Greater Wilkes-Barre Chamber of Business & Industry
2 Public Sq PO Box 5340 .... Wilkes-Barre PA 18710 570-823-2101 822-5951
TF: 800-701-8449 ■ *Web:* www.wilkes-barre.org

Williamsport/Lycoming Chamber of Commerce
100 W Third St .... Williamsport PA 17701 570-326-1971 321-1208
TF: 800-732-2258 ■ *Web:* www.williamsport.org

York County Chamber of Commerce
96 S George St Ste 300 .... York PA 17401 717-848-4000 843-6737
Web: www.ycea-pa.org

Rhode Island

Phone | Fax

East Providence Chamber of Commerce
1011 Waterman Ave .... East Providence RI 02914 401-438-1212 435-4581
Web: www.eastprovidenceareachamber.com

North Central Chamber of Commerce
255 Greenville Ave .... Johnston RI 02919 401-349-4674 349-4676
Web: www.nrichamber.com

Northern Rhode Island Chamber of Commerce
6 Blackstone Vly Pl Ste 402, 2nd Fl .... Lincoln RI 02865 401-334-1000 334-1009
Web: www.nrichamber.com

Newport County Chamber of Commerce
35 Valley Rd .... Middletown RI 02842 401-847-1600 849-5848
Web: www.newportchamber.com

North Kingstown Chamber of Commerce
8045 Post Rd .... North Kingstown RI 02852 401-295-5566 295-5582
Web: nkchamberri.com

Greater Providence Chamber of Commerce
30 Exchange Terr .... Providence RI 02903 401-521-5000 621-6109
Web: www.providencechamber.com

Southern Rhode Island Chamber of Commerce
230 Old Tower Hill Rd .... Wakefield RI 02879 401-783-2801 789-3120
Web: www.srichamber.com

East Bay Chamber of Commerce
16 Cutler St Ste 102 .... Warren RI 02885 401-245-0750 245-0110
TF: 877-797-9790 ■ *Web:* www.eastbaychamberri.org

Central Rhode Island Chamber of Commerce
3288 Post Rd .... Warwick RI 02886 401-732-1100 732-1107
Web: www.centralrichamber.com

South Carolina

Phone | Fax

Abbeville Chamber of Commerce 107 Ct Sq .... Abbeville SC 29620 864-366-4600
Web: www.visitabbevillesc.com

Greater Aiken Chamber of Commerce
121 Richland Ave E PO Box 892 .... Aiken SC 29802 803-641-1111 641-4174
Web: www.aikenchamber.net

Anderson Area Chamber of Commerce
907 N Main St Ste 200 .... Anderson SC 29621 864-226-3454 226-3300
TF: 800-922-1150 ■ *Web:* www.andersonscchamber.com

Kershaw County Chamber of Commerce
607 S Broad St .... Camden SC 29020 803-432-2525 432-4181
TF: 800-968-4037 ■ *Web:* www.kershawcountychamber.org

West Metro Chamber of Commerce 1006 12th St .... Cayce SC 29033 803-794-6504 794-6505
Web: wmvc.publishpath.com

Chester County Chamber of Commerce
109 Gadsden St .... Chester SC 29706 803-581-4142 581-2431
Web: www.chesterchamber.com

Laurens County Chamber of Commerce
291 Professional Pk Rd .... Clinton SC 29325 864-833-2716 833-6935
TF: 866-548-9674 ■ *Web:* www.laurenscounty.org

Greater Columbia Chamber of Commerce
930 Richland St .... Columbia SC 29201 803-733-1110 733-1149
Web: www.columbiachamber.com

Conway Area Chamber of Commerce 203 Main St .... Conway SC 29526 843-248-2273 248-0003
Web: www.conwayscchamber.com

Greater Darlington Chamber of Commerce
38 Public Sq .... Darlington SC 29532 843-393-2641 393-8059
Web: darlingtonchamber.wix.com/darlingtonchamber

Dillon County Chamber of Commerce
100 N MacArthur Ave .... Dillon SC 29536 843-774-8551 774-0114
Web: www.cityofdillonsc.us

Greater Easley Chamber of Commerce
2001 E Main St PO Box 241 .... Easley SC 29641 864-859-2693 859-1941
Web: www.easleychamber.net

Cherokee County Chamber of Commerce
225 S Limestone St .... Gaffney SC 29340 864-489-5721
Web: www.cherokeechamber.org

Georgetown County Chamber of Commerce
531 Front St .... Georgetown SC 29440 843-546-8436 520-4876
TF: 800-777-7705 ■ *Web:* www.visitgeorge.com

Greater Greenville Chamber of Commerce
24 Cleveland St .... Greenville SC 29601 864-242-1050 282-8509*
*Fax: PR ■ *TF:* 866-485-5262 ■ *Web:* www.greenvillechamber.org

Greenwood Chamber of Commerce
110 Phoenix St .... Greenwood SC 29646 864-223-8431 229-9785
Web: www.greenwoodscchamber.org

Greater Hartsville Chamber of Commerce
PO Box 578 .... Hartsville SC 29551 843-332-6401 332-8017
TF: 866-747-0060 ■ *Web:* www.hartsvillechamber.org

Hilton Head Island-Bluffton Chamber of Commerce
1 Chamber Dr .... Hilton Head Island SC 29928 843-785-3673 785-7110
TF: 800-523-3373 ■ *Web:* www.hiltonheadisland.org

Williamsburg Hometown Chamber of Commerce
136 N Academy St PO Box 696 .... Kingstree SC 29556 843-355-6431 355-3343
Web: www.williamsburgsc.org

Lancaster County Chamber of Commerce
PO Box 430 .... Lancaster SC 29721 803-283-4105 286-4360
Web: www.lancasterchambersc.org

Lexington Chamber of Commerce
311 W Main St .... Lexington SC 29072 803-359-6113 359-0634
Web: www.lexingtonsc.org

Berkeley County Chamber of Commerce
PO Box 968 .... Moncks Corner SC 29461 843-761-8238 899-6491
TF: 800-882-0337 ■ *Web:* www.berkeleysc.org

Myrtle Beach Area Chamber of Commerce
1200 N Oak St .... Myrtle Beach SC 29577 843-626-7444 626-0009
TF: 800-356-3016 ■ *Web:* www.visitmyrtlebeach.com

Newberry County Chamber of Commerce
1209 Caldwell St PO Box 396 .... Newberry SC 29108 803-276-4274 276-4373
Web: newberrycountychamber.com

North Augusta Chamber of Commerce
406 W Ave .... North Augusta SC 29841 803-279-2323 279-0003
Web: www.northaugustachamber.org

Charleston Metro Chamber of Commerce
4500 Leeds Ave Ste 100 .... North Charleston SC 29405 843-577-2510 723-4853
Web: www.charlestonchamber.net

Orangeburg County Chamber of Commerce
155 Riverside Dr SW PO Box 328 .... Orangeburg SC 29116 803-534-6821 531-9435
TF: 800-545-6153 ■ *Web:* www.orangeburgchamber.com

York County Regional Chamber of Commerce
116 E Main St .... Rock Hill SC 29731 803-324-7500 324-1889
Web: www.yorkcountychamber.com

Spartanburg Area Chamber of Commerce
105 N Pine St .... Spartanburg SC 29302 864-594-5000 594-5055
Web: www.spartanburgchamber.com

Greater Summerville-Dorchester County Chamber of Commerce
402 N Main St .... Summerville SC 29483 843-873-2931 875-4464
Web: greatersummerville.org

Greater Sumter Chamber of Commerce
32 E Calhoun St .... Sumter SC 29150 803-775-1231 775-0915
Web: www.sumterchamber.com

Union County Chamber of Commerce 135 W Main St .... Union SC 29379 864-427-9039 427-9030
TF: 877-202-8755 ■ *Web:* www.unionsc.info

Walterboro-Colleton Chamber of Commerce
109 Benson St .... Walterboro SC 29488 843-549-9595 549-5775
Web: walterboro.org

South Dakota

Phone | Fax

Aberdeen Area Chamber of Commerce
516 S Main St .... Aberdeen SD 57401 605-225-2860 225-2437
TF: 800-874-9038 ■ *Web:* www.aberdeen-chamber.com

Pierre Area Chamber of Commerce
800 W Dakota Ave .... Pierre SD 57501 605-224-7361 224-6485
TF: 800-962-2034 ■ *Web:* www.pierre.org

Rapid City Area Chamber of Commerce
444 Mt Rushmore Rd N .... Rapid City SD 57701 605-343-1744 343-6550
Web: www.rapidcitychamber.com

Sioux Falls Area Chamber of Commerce
200 N Phillips Ave Ste 102 .... Sioux Falls SD 57104 605-336-1620
Web: www.siouxfalls.com

Tennessee

Phone | Fax

Cheatham County Chamber of Commerce
108 N Main St PO Box 354 .... Ashland City TN 37015 615-792-6722 792-5001
Web: www.cheathamchamber.org

Bartlett Area Chamber of Commerce
2969 Elmore Pk Rd .... Bartlett TN 38134 901-372-9457 372-9488
Web: www.bartlettchamber.org

Bristol Chamber of Commerce
20 Volunteer Pkwy .... Bristol TN 37620 423-989-4850 989-4867
Web: www.bristolchamber.com

Chattanooga Area Chamber of Commerce
811 Broad St .... Chattanooga TN 37402 423-756-2121 267-7242
TF: 877-756-1684 ■ *Web:* www.chattanoogachamber.com

Clarksville Area Chamber of Commerce
25 Jefferson St Ste 300 .... Clarksville TN 37040 931-647-2331 645-1574
TF: 800-530-2487 ■ *Web:* www.clarksvillechamber.com

Cleveland/Bradley Chamber of Commerce
225 Keith St .... Cleveland TN 37311 423-472-6587 472-2019
TF: 800-533-9930 ■ *Web:* www.clevelandchamber.com

Anderson County Chamber of Commerce
245 N Main St Ste 200 .... Clinton TN 37716 865-457-2559 463-7480
Web: www.andersoncountychamber.org

Collierville Chamber of Commerce
485 Halle Pk Dr .... Collierville TN 38017 901-853-1949 853-2399
Web: www.colliervillechamber.com

Maury Alliance 106 W Sixth St .... Columbia TN 38401 931-388-2155 380-0335
Web: www.mauryalliance.com

Phone Fax

Cookeville Area-Putnam County Chamber of Commerce
1 W First St. Cookeville TN 38501 931-526-2211 526-4023
TF: 800-264-5541 ■ *Web:* www.cookevillechamber.com

Covington-Tipton County Chamber of Commerce
PO Box 683 Covington TN 38019 901-476-9727 476-0056
Web: www.covington-tiptoncochamber.com

Crossville Cumberland County Chamber of Commerce
34 S Main St. Crossville TN 38555 931-484-8444 484-7511
TF: 877-465-3861 ■ *Web:* www.crossville-chamber.com

Jefferson County Chamber of Commerce
532 Patriot Dr Dandridge TN 37725 865-397-9642 397-0164
TF: 877-237-3847 ■ *Web:* www.jefferson-tn-chamber.org

Dickson County Chamber of Commerce
119 Hwy 70 E Dickson TN 37055 615-446-2349 441-3112
TF: 877-718-4967 ■ *Web:* www.dicksoncountychamber.com

Weakley County Chamber of Commerce
114 W Maple St PO Box 67 Dresden TN 38225 731-364-3787 364-2099
Web: www.weakleycountychamber.com

Dyersburg/Dyer County Chamber of Commerce
2000 Commerce Ave Dyersburg TN 38024 731-285-3433 286-4926
Web: dyerchamber.com

Elizabethton/Carter County Chamber of Commerce
Hwy 19 E Elizabethton TN 37644 423-547-3850 547-3854
Web: www.elizabethtonchamber.com

Fayetteville-Lincoln County Chamber of Commerce
208 S Elk Ave Fayetteville TN 37334 931-433-1234 433-9087
TF: 888-433-1238 ■ *Web:* www.fayettevillelincolncountychamber.com

Williamson County-Franklin Chamber of Commerce
5005 Meridian Blvd Ste 150 Franklin TN 37067 615-771-1912 790-5337
TF: 877-811-0002 ■ *Web:* williamsonchamber.com

Germantown Area Chamber of Commerce
2195 S Germantown Rd Germantown TN 38138 901-755-1200 755-9168
Web: www.germantownchamber.com

Greene County Partnership & Chamber of Commerce
115 Academy St Greeneville TN 37743 423-638-4111 638-5345
Web: www.greenecountypartnership.com

Hendersonville Area Chamber of Commerce
100 Country Dr Ste 104 Hendersonville TN 37075 615-824-2818 250-3637
Web: www.hendersonvillechamber.com

Carroll County Chamber of Commerce
20740 Main St E Huntingdon TN 38344 731-986-4664 986-2029
Web: www.carrollcounty-tn-chamber.com

Jackson Area Chamber of Commerce
197 Auditorium St Jackson TN 38301 731-423-2200 424-4860
TF: 866-262-8867 ■ *Web:* www.jacksontn.com

Johnson City/Jonesborough/Washington County Chamber of Commerce
603 E Market St Johnson City TN 37601 423-461-8000 461-8047
Web: www.johnsoncitytnchamber.com

Kingsport Area Chamber of Commerce
151 E Main St. Kingsport TN 37660 423-392-8800
Web: www.kingsportchamber.org

Roane County Chamber of Commerce
1209 N Kentucky St Kingston TN 37763 865-376-5572 376-4978
Web: www.roanealliance.org

Knoxville Area Chamber Partnership
17 Market Sq Ste 201 Knoxville TN 37902 865-637-4550 523-2071
Web: www.knoxvillechamber.com

Lawrence County Tennessee Chamber of Commerce
25B Public Sqr PO Box 86 Lawrenceburg TN 38464 931-762-4911 762-3153
TF: 877-388-4911 ■ *Web:* www.selectlawrence.com

Lebanon-Wilson County Chamber of Commerce
149 Public Sq. Lebanon TN 37087 615-444-5503 443-0596
Web: www.lebanonwilsontnchamber.org

Loudon County Chamber of Commerce (LCCC)
318 Angel Row Loudon TN 37774 865-458-2067 458-1206
Web: www.loudoncountychamberofcommerce.com

Madison Rivergate Area Chamber of Commerce
301 Madison St Madison TN 37115 615-865-5400
Web: www.madisonrivergatechamber.com

Monroe County Chamber of Commerce
520 Cook St Ste A Madisonville TN 37354 423-442-4588 442-9016
TF: 800-245-5428 ■ *Web:* www.monroecountychamber.org

Blount County Chamber of Commerce
201 S Washington St Maryville TN 37804 865-983-2241 984-1386
TF: 855-257-3964 ■ *Web:* www.blountchamber.com

McMinnville-Warren County Chamber of Commerce
110 S Ct Sq McMinnville TN 37110 931-473-6611 473-4741
Web: www.warrentn.com

Memphis Regional Chamber of Commerce
22 N Front St Ste 200 Memphis TN 38103 901-543-3500 543-3510
TF: 800-829-1040 ■ *Web:* www.memphischamber.com

Morristown Area Chamber of Commerce
825 W First N St Morristown TN 37814 423-586-6382 586-6576
Web: www.morristownchamber.com

Mount Juliet Chamber of Commerce
46 W Caldwell St Mount Juliet TN 37122 615-758-3478 754-8595
Web: www.mjchamber.org

Rutherford County Chamber of Commerce
501 Memorial Blvd Murfreesboro TN 37129 615-893-6565 890-7600
TF: 800-716-7560 ■ *Web:* www.rutherfordchamber.org

Donelson-Hermitage Chamber of Commerce
125 Donelson Pike PO Box 140200 Nashville TN 37214 615-883-7896 391-4880
TF: 800-688-9889 ■ *Web:* www.d-hchamber.com

Nashville Chamber of Commerce
211 Commerce St Ste 100 Nashville TN 37201 615-743-3000 743-3004
Web: www.nashvillechamber.com

Newport/Cocke County Chamber of Commerce
433-B Prospect Ave Newport TN 37821 423-623-7201
Web: www.cockecounty.org

Oak Ridge Chamber of Commerce
1400 Oak Ridge Tpke Oak Ridge TN 37830 865-483-1321 483-1678
Web: www.oakridgechamber.org

Paris-Henry County Chamber of Commerce
2508 Eastwood St. Paris TN 38242 731-642-3431 642-3454
TF: 800-345-1103 ■ *Web:* www.paristnchamber.com

Phone Fax

Giles County Chamber of Commerce
110 N Second St. Pulaski TN 38478 931-363-3789 363-7279
Web: www.gilescountychamber.com

Rogersville/Hawkins County Chamber of Commerce
107 E Main St Ste 100 Rogersville TN 37857 423-272-2186 272-2186
Web: www.rogersvillechamber.us

Shelbyville-Bedford County Chamber of Commerce
100 N Cannon Blvd Shelbyville TN 37160 931-684-3482 684-3483
TF: 888-662-2525 ■ *Web:* www.shelbyvilletn.com

Robertson County Chamber ofCommerce
503 W Ct Sq Springfield TN 37172 615-384-3800 384-1260
Web: robertsonchamber.org

Claiborne County Chamber of Commerce
1732 Main St Ste 1 Tazewell TN 37879 423-626-4149 626-1611
TF: 800-332-8164

Greater Gibson County Area Chamber of Commerce
200 E Eaton St Trenton TN 38382 731-855-0973 855-0979
Web: www.gibsoncountytn.com

Franklin County Chamber of Commerce
44 Chamber Way PO Box 280 Winchester TN 37398 931-967-6788 967-9418
Web: www.franklincountychamber.com

Texas

Phone Fax

Abilene Chamber of Commerce
174 Cypress St Ste 200 Abilene TX 79601 325-677-7241
Web: www.abilenechamber.com

Alice Chamber of Commerce (ACC)
612 E Main St PO Box 1609 Alice TX 78333 361-664-3454 664-2291
Web: www.alicetxchamber.org

Allen Chamber of Commerce 210 W McDermott Dr Allen TX 75013 972-727-5585 727-9000
Web: www.allenfairviewchamber.com

Alvin-Manvel Area Chamber of Commerce
105 W Willis St. Alvin TX 77511 281-331-3944 585-8662
TF: 888-755-6864 ■ *Web:* alvinmanvelchamber.com

Amarillo Chamber of Commerce 1000 S Polk St. Amarillo TX 79101 806-373-7800 373-3909
Web: www.amarillo-chamber.org

Arlington Chamber of Commerce
505 E Border St Arlington TX 76010 817-275-2613 701-0893
Web: www.arlingtontx.com

Atlanta Area Chamber of Commerce 101 NE St. Atlanta TX 75551 903-796-3296
Web: www.atlantatexas.org

Greater Austin Chamber of Commerce
535 E 5th St Austin TX 78701 512-478-9383 478-9615
TF: 888-409-5380 ■ *Web:* www.austinchamber.com

Bastrop Chamber of Commerce 927 Main St Bastrop TX 78602 512-303-0558 303-0305
Web: www.bastropchamber.com

Baytown Chamber of Commerce
1300 Rolling Brook Ste 400 Baytown TX 77521 281-422-8359 428-1758
Web: www.baytownchamber.com

Beaumont Chamber of Commerce 1110 Pk St Beaumont TX 77701 409-838-6581 833-6718
Web: www.bmtcoc.org

Hurst-Euless-Bedford Chamber of Commerce
2109 Martin Dr Bedford TX 76021 817-283-1521 267-5111
Web: www.heb.org

Bee County Chamber of Commerce
1705 N St Mary Beeville TX 78102 361-358-3267
Web: www.beecountychamber.org

Bonham Area Chamber of Commerce 327 N. Main Bonham TX 75418 903-583-4811 583-7972
Web: www.fannincountytexas.com

Washington County Chamber of Commerce
314 S Austin St. Brenham TX 77833 979-836-3695 836-2540
TF: 888-273-6426 ■ *Web:* www.brenhamtexas.com

Brownsville Chamber of Commerce
1600 University Blvd Brownsville TX 78520 956-542-4341 504-3348
Web: www.brownsvillechamber.com

Brownwood Area Chamber of Commerce
600 E Depot St Brownwood TX 76801 325-646-9535 643-6686
Web: www.brownwoodchamber.org

Bryan-College Station Chamber of Commerce
4001 E 29th St Ste 175 Bryan TX 77802 979-260-5200 164-9791
Web: www.bcschamber.org

Burleson Area Chamber of Commerce
1044 SW Wilshire Blvd. Burleson TX 76028 817-295-6121 295-6192
Web: burlesonchamber.com

Canyon Chamber of Commerce 1518 Fifth Ave Canyon TX 79015 806-655-7815 655-4608
TF: 800-999-9481 ■ *Web:* www.canyonchamber.org

Panola County Chamber of Commerce
300 W Panola St. Carthage TX 75633 903-693-6634 693-8578
Web: www.carthagetexas.us

Cleburne Chamber of Commerce
1511 W Henderson St. Cleburne TX 76033 817-645-2455 641-3069
Web: www.cleburnechamber.com

Greater Conroe-Lake Conroe Area Chamber of Commerce
505 W Davis St. Conroe TX 77301 936-756-6644 756-6462
Web: www.conroe.org

Greater Conroe/Lake Conroe Area Chamber of Commerce
PO Box 2347 Conroe TX 77305 936-756-6644 756-6462
Web: www.conroe.org

Coppell Chamber of Commerce
509 W Bethel Rd Ste 200 Coppell TX 75019 972-393-2829 393-0659
Web: www.coppellchamber.org

Copperas Cove Chamber of Commerce
204 E Robertson Ave Copperas Cove TX 76522 254-547-7571 547-5015
Web: www.copperascove.com

Corsicana Area Chamber of Commerce
120 N 12th St Corsicana TX 75110 903-874-4731 874-4187
TF: 866-222-7100 ■ *Web:* www.corsicana.org

Cy-Fair Houston Chamber of Commerce
11734 Barker Cypress Ste 105 Cypress TX 77433 281-373-1390 373-1394
Web: www.cyfairchamber.com

Dallas Northeast Chamber of Commerce
9543 Losa Dr Ste 118 Dallas TX 75218 214-328-4100
Web: www.eastdallaschamber.com

Chamber / Address	City	State	ZIP	Phone	Fax
Greater Dallas Chamber of Commerce 700 N Pearl St Ste 1200 *Web:* www.dallaschamber.org	Dallas	TX	75201	214-746-6600	746-6799
Metrocrest Chamber of Commerce 5100 Belt Line Rd Ste 430 *Web:* www.metrocrestchamber.com	Dallas	TX	75254	469-587-0420	587-0428
North Dallas Chamber of Commerce 10707 Preston Rd *Web:* www.ndcc.org	Dallas	TX	75230	214-368-6485	691-5584
Oak Cliff Chamber of Commerce 400 S Zang Blvd Ste 110 *Web:* www.oakcliffchamber.org	Dallas	TX	75208	214-943-4567	943-4582
Southeast Dallas Chamber of Commerce 802 S Buckner Blvd *Web:* www.sedallaschamber.org	Dallas	TX	75217	214-398-9590	398-9591
Deer Park Chamber of Commerce 110 Ctr St *Web:* www.deerparkchamber.org	Deer Park	TX	77536	281-479-1559	476-4041
Del Rio Chamber of Commerce (DRCoC) 1915 Veterans Blvd *TF General:* 877-218-5117 ■ *Web:* www.drchamber.com	Del Rio	TX	78840	830-775-3551	774-1813
Denton Chamber of Commerce 414 W Pkwy St *TF:* 800-747-2316 ■ *Web:* www.denton-chamber.org	Denton	TX	76201	940-382-9693	382-0040
DeSoto Chamber of Commerce 2010 N Hampton Rd Ste 200 *Web:* www.desotochamber.org	DeSoto	TX	75115	972-224-3565	354-1022
North Galveston County Chamber of Commerce 218 FM 517 W *Web:* www.northgalvestoncountychamber.com	Dickinson	TX	77539	281-534-4380	534-4389
Duncanville Chamber of Commerce 300 E Wheatland Rd *Web:* www.duncanvillechamber.org	Duncanville	TX	75116	972-780-4990	298-9370
Eagle Pass Chamber of Commerce 400 E Garrison St *TF:* 888-355-3224 ■ *Web:* eaglepasstexas.com	Eagle Pass	TX	78852	830-773-3224	773-8844
Edinburg Chamber of Commerce 602 W University Dr *TF:* 800-800-7214 ■ *Web:* www.edinburg.com	Edinburg	TX	78540	956-383-4974	383-6942
Greater El Paso Chamber of Commerce 10 Civic Ctr Plz *Web:* www.elpaso.org	El Paso	TX	79901	915-534-0500	534-0510
Farmers Branch Chamber of Commerce 2815 Valley view Ln Ste 118 *Web:* farmersbranchchamber.org	Farmers Branch	TX	75234	972-243-8966	243-8968
Flower Mound Chamber of Commerce 700 Parker Sq Ste 100 *Web:* www.flowermoundchamber.com	Flower Mound	TX	75028	972-539-0500	539-4307
Fort Worth Chamber of Commerce 777 Taylor St Ste 900 *TF:* 800-433-5747 ■ *Web:* www.fortworthchamber.com	Fort Worth	TX	76102	817-336-2491	877-4034
Friendswood Chamber of Commerce 1100 S Friendswood Dr *Web:* www.friendswood-chamber.com	Friendswood	TX	77546	281-482-3329	
Garland Chamber of Commerce 520 N Glenbrook Dr *Web:* www.garlandchamber.com	Garland	TX	75040	972-272-7551	276-9261
Georgetown Chamber of Commerce 1 Chamber Wy *Web:* www.georgetownchamber.org	Georgetown	TX	78626	512-930-3535	930-3587
Gilmer Area Chamber of Commerce 106 Buffalo St *Web:* gilmerareachamber.wix.com/chamber	Gilmer	TX	75644	903-843-2413	843-3759
Lake Granbury Area Chamber of Commerce 3408 E Hwy 377 *Web:* www.granburychamber.com	Granbury	TX	76049	817-573-1622	573-0805
Grapevine Chamber of Commerce 200 Vine St *TF:* 866-322-8667 ■ *Web:* www.grapevinechamber.org	Grapevine	TX	76051	817-481-1522	424-5208
Northeast Tarrant Chamber of Commerce 5001 Denton Hwy *Web:* www.netarrant.org	Haltom City	TX	76117	817-281-9376	281-9379
Harlingen Area Chamber of Commerce 311 E Tyler St *Web:* www.harlingen.com	Harlingen	TX	78550	956-423-5440	425-3870
Henderson Area Chamber of Commerce 201 N Main St *Web:* www.hendersontx.com	Henderson	TX	75652	903-657-5528	657-9454
Clear Lake Area Chamber of Commerce 1201 NASA Pkwy *TF:* 800-877-8339 ■ *Web:* www.clearlakearea.com	Houston	TX	77058	281-488-7676	488-8981
Galleria Area Chamber of Commerce 10370 Richmond Ave Ste 125 *Web:* www.hwcoc.org	Houston	TX	77042	713-785-4922	785-4944
Greater Heights Area Chamber of Commerce 545 W 19th St 2nd Fl *Web:* www.heightschamber.com	Houston	TX	77008	713-861-6735	861-9310
Greater Houston Partnership 1200 Smith St Ste 700 *Web:* www.houston.org	Houston	TX	77002	713-844-3600	844-0200
Houston Intercontinental Chamber of Commerce 250 N Sam Houston Pkwy E Ste 200 *Web:* www.nhgcc.org	Houston	TX	77060	281-408-0866	
Houston Northwest Chamber of Commerce (HNW) 3920 Cypress Creek Pkwy *Web:* www.houstonnwchamber.org	Houston	TX	77068	281-440-4160	440-5302
Houston West Chamber of Commerce 10370 Richmond Ave Ste 125 *Web:* www.hwcoc.org	Houston	TX	77042	713-785-4922	785-4944
North Ch Area Chamber of Commerce 13301 E Fwy # 100 *Web:* www.northchannelarea.com	Houston	TX	77015	713-450-3600	450-0700
South Belt-Ellington Chamber of Commerce 10500 Scarsdale Blvd *Web:* www.southbeltchamber.com	Houston	TX	77089	281-481-5516	922-7045
Lake Houston Area Chamber of Commerce, The 110 W Main St *Web:* www.lakehouston.org	Humble	TX	77338	281-446-2128	446-7483
Huntsville-Walker County Chamber of Commerce 1327 11th St *TF:* 800-289-0389 ■ *Web:* www.chamber.huntsville.tx.us	Huntsville	TX	77340	936-295-8113	295-0571
Kerrville Area Chamber of Commerce 1700 Sidney Baker St Ste 100 *Web:* www.kerrvilletx.com	Kerrville	TX	78028	830-896-1155	896-1175
Greater Killeen Chamber of Commerce 1 Santa Fe Plz *TF:* 866-790-4769 ■ *Web:* www.killeenchamber.com	Killeen	TX	76540	254-526-9551	526-6090
Kingsville Chamber of Commerce 635 E King Ave # 124 *Web:* www.kingsville.org	Kingsville	TX	78363	361-592-6438	592-0866
La Porte-Bayshore Chamber of Commerce 712 W Fairmont Pkwy *Web:* www.laportechamber.org	La Porte	TX	77571	281-471-1123	471-1710
Brazosport Area Chamber of Commerce 300 Abner Jackson Pkwy *Web:* www.brazosport.org	Lake Jackson	TX	77566	979-285-2501	285-2505
Laredo-Webb County Chamber of Commerce 2310 San Bernardo Ave *TF:* 800-292-2122 ■ *Web:* www.laredochamber.com	Laredo	TX	78042	956-722-9895	791-4503
Lewisville Chamber of Commerce 551 N Valley Pkwy *Web:* www.lewisvillechamber.org	Lewisville	TX	75067	972-436-9571	436-5949
Liberty-Dayton Area Chamber of Commerce 1801 Trinity St *Web:* www.libertydaytonchamber.com	Liberty	TX	77575	936-336-5736	336-1159
Longview Partnership 410 N Ctr St *TF:* 800-338-7232 ■ *Web:* www.longviewchamber.com	Longview	TX	75601	903-237-4000	237-4049
Lubbock Chamber of Commerce 1500 Broadway Ste 101 *Web:* www.lubbockchamber.com	Lubbock	TX	79401	806-761-7000	761-7013
Lufkin/Angelina County Chamber of Commerce 1615 S Chestnut St *TF:* 800-409-5659 ■ *Web:* www.lufkintexas.org	Lufkin	TX	75901	936-634-6644	634-8726
Greater Cedar Creek Lake Area Chamber of Commerce 604 S Third St Ste E *TF:* 800-331-6844 ■ *Web:* www.cclake.net	Mabank	TX	75147	903-887-3152	887-3695
Greater Marshall Chamber of Commerce 213 W Austin St *Web:* www.marshall-chamber.com	Marshall	TX	75670	903-935-7868	
McAllen Chamber of Commerce 1200 Ash Ave *Web:* mcallen.org	McAllen	TX	78501	956-682-2871	687-2917
McKinney Chamber of Commerce 2150 S Central Expy # 150 *Web:* www.mckinneychamber.com	McKinney	TX	75070	972-542-0163	548-0876
Mesquite Chamber of Commerce 617 N Ebrite St *Web:* www.mesquitechamber.com	Mesquite	TX	75149	972-285-0211	285-3535
Midland Chamber of Commerce 109 N Main St *TF:* 800-624-6435 ■ *Web:* www.midlandtxchamber.com	Midland	TX	79701	432-683-3381	686-3556
Mineral Wells Area Chamber of Commerce 511 E Hubbard St *TF:* 800-252-6989 ■ *Web:* www.mineralwellstx.com	Mineral Wells	TX	76067	940-325-2557	328-0850
Mission Chamber of Commerce 202 W Tom Landry St *Web:* www.missionchamber.com	Mission	TX	78572	956-585-2727	585-3044
Mount Pleasant-Titus County Chamber of Commerce 1604 N Jefferson Ave *Web:* www.mtpleasanttx.com	Mount Pleasant	TX	75455	903-572-8567	572-0613
Nacogdoches County Chamber of Commerce 2516 N St *Web:* www.nacogdoches.org	Nacogdoches	TX	75965	936-560-5533	560-3920
New Braunfels Chamber of Commerce 390 S Seguin St *TF:* 800-572-2626 ■ *Web:* innewbraunfels.com	New Braunfels	TX	78130	830-625-2385	625-7918
Odessa Chamber of Commerce 700 N Grant St Ste 200 *TF:* 800-780-4678 ■ *Web:* www.odessachamber.com	Odessa	TX	79761	432-332-9111	333-7858
Greater Orange Area Chamber of Commerce 1012 Green Ave *Web:* www.orangetexaschamber.org	Orange	TX	77630	409-883-3536	886-3247
Lamar County Chamber of Commerce 1125 Bonham St *TF:* 800-727-4789 ■ *Web:* www.paristexas.com	Paris	TX	75460	903-784-2501	784-2503
Pasadena Chamber of Commerce 4334 Fairmont Pkwy *Web:* www.pasadenachamber.org	Pasadena	TX	77504	281-487-7871	487-5530
Pearland Area Chamber of Commerce 6117 Broadway St *TF:* 888-604-5888 ■ *Web:* www.pearlandtexaschamber.us	Pearland	TX	77581	281-485-3634	485-2420
Greater Pflugerville Chamber of Commerce 101 S Third St PO Box 483 *Web:* www.pfchamber.com	Pflugerville	TX	78691	512-251-7799	251-7802
Pharr Chamber of Commerce 308 W Pk St *Web:* www.pharrchamber.com	Pharr	TX	78577	956-787-1481	
Plainview Chamber of Commerce 1906 W Fifth St *Web:* www.plainviewtexaschamber.com	Plainview	TX	79072	806-296-7431	296-0819
Plano Chamber of Commerce 1200 E 15th St *Web:* www.planochamber.org	Plano	TX	75074	972-424-7547	422-5182
Greater Port Arthur Chamber of Commerce 4749 Twin City Hwy Ste 300 *Web:* www.portarthurtexas.com	Port Arthur	TX	77642	409-963-1107	962-1997
Richardson Chamber of Commerce 411 Belle Grove Dr *Web:* www.richardsonchamber.com	Richardson	TX	75080	972-792-2800	792-2825
Rockwall County Chamber of Commerce 697 E IH- 30 *Web:* www.rockwallchamber.org	Rockwall	TX	75087	972-771-5733	772-3642
Rosenberg-Richmond Area Chamber of Commerce 4120 Ave H *TF:* 877-382-7414 ■ *Web:* www.cfbca.org	Rosenberg	TX	77471	281-342-5464	342-2990

Phone *Fax*

Round Rock Chamber of Commerce
212 E Main St. . . . . Round Rock TX 78664 512-255-5805
Web: www.roundrockchamber.org

Rowlett Chamber of Commerce 3910 Main St . . . . . Rowlett TX 75088 972-475-3200 463-1699
Web: www.rowlettchamber.com

Greater San Antonio Chamber of Commerce
602 E Commerce St . . . . . San Antonio TX 78205 210-229-2100 229-1600
TF: 888-828-8680 ■ *Web:* www.sachamber.org

North San Antonio Chamber of Commerce
12930 Country Pkwy . . . . . San Antonio TX 78216 210-344-4848 525-8207
TF: 877-495-5888 ■ *Web:* www.northsachamber.com

South San Antonio Chamber of Commerce
7902 Challenger Dr . . . . . San Antonio TX 78235 210-533-1600 533-1611
Web: www.southsachamber.org

San Marcos Area Chamber of Commerce
202 N CM Allen Pkwy. . . . . San Marcos TX 78666 512-393-5900 393-5912
TF: 888-200-5620 ■ *Web:* www.sanmarcostexas.com

Seguin Area Chamber of Commerce 116 N Camp St. . . . . Seguin TX 78155 830-379-6382 379-6971
TF: 888-674-7224 ■ *Web:* www.seguinchamber.com

Springtown Chamber of Commerce
112 S Main St. . . . . Springtown TX 76082 817-220-7828
Web: www.springtowntexas.com

Fort Bend Chamber of Commerce
445 Commerce Green Blvd. . . . . Sugar Land TX 77478 281-491-0800 491-0112
Web: www.fortbendchamber.com

Hopkins County Chamber of Commerce
300 Connally St . . . . . Sulphur Springs TX 75482 903-885-6515 885-6516
Web: www.sulphursprings-tx.com

Temple Chamber of Commerce 2 N Fifth St . . . . . Temple TX 76501 254-773-2105 773-0661
Web: www.templetx.org

Texarkana Chamber of Commerce
819 N State Line Ave . . . . . Texarkana TX 75501 903-792-7191 793-4304
TF: 877-275-5289 ■ *Web:* www.texarkanachamber.com

Texas City-La Marque Chamber of Commerce
9702 Emmett F Lowry Expy . . . . . Texas City TX 77591 409-935-1408 316-0901
TF General: 877-986-8719 ■ *Web:* www.texascitychamber.com

South Montgomery County Woodlands Chamber of Commerce
1400 Woodloch Forest Dr Ste 300 . . . . . The Woodlands TX 77380 281-367-5777 292-1655
Web: www.woodlandschamber.org

Tyler Area Chamber of Commerce
315 N Broadway Ave. . . . . Tyler TX 75702 903-592-1661 593-2746
TF: 800-235-5712 ■ *Web:* www.tylertexas.com

Victoria Chamber of Commerce
3404 N Ben Wilson St . . . . . Victoria TX 77901 361-573-5277
Web: www.victoriachamber.org

Greater Waco Chamber of Commerce 101 S Third St . . . . . Waco TX 76701 254-752-6551 752-6618
Web: www.wacochamber.com

Weatherford Chamber of Commerce
401 Ft Worth St . . . . . Weatherford TX 76086 817-596-3801 613-9216
TF: 888-594-3801 ■ *Web:* www.weatherford-chamber.com

Rio Grande Valley Chamber of Commerce
322 S Missouri St. . . . . Weslaco TX 78596 956-968-3141 968-0210
TF: 800-628-5115 ■ *Web:* www.valleychamber.com

Weslaco Area Chamber of Commerce
301 W Railroad. . . . . Weslaco TX 78596 956-968-2102 968-6451
TF: 800-700-2443 ■ *Web:* www.weslaco.com

Lake Tawakoni Regional Chamber of Commerce
100 Hwy 276 W PO Box 1149 . . . . . West Tawakoni TX 75474 903-447-3020
Web: www.laketawakonichamber.org

Wichita Falls Board of Commerce & Industry
900 Eigth St Ste 218. . . . . Wichita Falls TX 76301 940-723-2741 723-8773
Web: wichitafallschamber.com

Utah

Phone *Fax*

Davis Chamber of Commerce
450 Simmons Way Ste 220 . . . . . Kaysville UT 84037 801-593-2200 593-2212
Web: www.davischamberofcommerce.com

Cache Chamber of Commerce 160 N Main St. . . . . Logan UT 84321 435-752-2161 753-5825
Web: www.cachechamber.com

Murray Area Chamber of Commerce (MACC)
5250 S Commerce Dr Ste 180 . . . . . Murray UT 84107 801-263-2632 263-8262
Web: www.murraychamber.org

Commission for Economic Development in Orem
56 N State St Rm 101 . . . . . Orem UT 84058 801-229-7172 226-2678
Web: econdev.orem.org

Provo/Orem Chamber of Commerce
111 S University Ave . . . . . Provo UT 84601 801-851-2555
Web: thechamber.org

St. George Area Chamber of Commerce
97 E St George Blvd . . . . . Saint George UT 84770 435-628-1658 673-1587
Web: www.stgeorgechamber.com

Salt Lake City Chamber of Commerce
175 East University Blvd 400 S
Ste 600. . . . . Salt Lake City UT 84111 801-364-3631 328-5098
Web: www.slchamber.com

Sandy Area Chamber of Commerce 35 East 9270 . . . . . Sandy UT 84070 801-566-0344 566-0346
Web: www.sandychamber.com

South Salt Lake Chamber of Commerce
220 E Morris Ave Ste 150. . . . . South Salt lake City UT 84115 801-466-3377
Web: www.sslchamber.com

Tooele County Chamber of Commerce 154 S Main. . . . . Tooele UT 84074 435-882-0690 833-0946
Web: www.tooelechamber.com

West Jordan Chamber of Commerce
8000 Redwood Rd . . . . . West Jordan UT 84088 801-569-5151 569-5153
Web: www.westjordanchamber.com

ChamberWest
1241 W Village Main Dr Ste B . . . . . West Valley City UT 84119 801-977-8755 977-8329
Web: chamberwest.com

Vermont

Phone *Fax*

Great Falls Region Chamber of Commerce
5 Westminster St . . . . . Bellows Falls VT 05101 802-463-4280
Web: www.gfrcc.org

Bennington Area Chamber of Commerce
100 Veterans Memorial Dr . . . . . Bennington VT 05201 802-447-3311 447-1163
TF: 800-229-0252 ■ *Web:* www.bennington.com

Central Vermont Chamber of Commerce
33 Stewart Rd. . . . . Berlin VT 05602 802-229-5711 229-5713
TF: 877-887-3678 ■ *Web:* www.central-vt.com

Brattleboro Area Chamber of Commerce
180 Main St . . . . . Brattleboro VT 05301 802-254-4565 254-5675
TF: 877-254-4565 ■ *Web:* www.brattleborochamber.org

Lake Champlain Regional Chamber of Commerce
60 Main St Ste 100. . . . . Burlington VT 05401 802-863-3489 863-1538
TF: 877-686-5253 ■ *Web:* www.vermont.org

Addison County Chamber of Commerce
93 Ct St . . . . . Middlebury VT 05753 802-388-7951 388-8066
Web: www.addisoncounty.com

Vermont's North Country Chamber of Commerce
246 Cswy St. . . . . Newport VT 05855 802-334-7782
TF: 800-266-2278 ■ *Web:* www.vtnorthcountry.org

Franklin County Regional Chamber of Commerce
2 N Main St Ste 101 . . . . . Saint Albans VT 05478 802-524-2444
Web: www.visitfranklincountyvt.com

Virginia

Phone *Fax*

Washington County Chamber of Commerce
1 Government Ctr Pl Ste D. . . . . Abingdon VA 24210 276-628-8141 628-3984
Web: www.washingtonvachamber.org

Alexandria Chamber of Commerce
801 N Fairfax St Ste 402. . . . . Alexandria VA 22314 703-549-1000 739-3805
Web: www.alexchamber.com

Mount Vernon-Lee Chamber of Commerce
6911 Richmond Hwy Ste 320. . . . . Alexandria VA 22306 703-360-6925 360-6928
Web: www.mtvernon-leechamber.org

Amherst County Chamber of Commerce
154 S Main St. . . . . Amherst VA 24521 434-946-0990 946-0879
Web: www.amherstvachamber.com

Annandale Chamber of Commerce
7263 Maple Pl Ste 207. . . . . Annandale VA 22003 703-256-7232 256-7233
Web: www.annandalechamber.com

Arlington Chamber of Commerce
2009 14th St N Ste 111 . . . . . Arlington VA 22201 703-525-2400
Web: www.arlingtonchamber.org

Bedford Area Chamber of Commerce
305 E Main St. . . . . Bedford VA 24523 540-586-9401
Web: www.bedfordareachamber.com

Danville Pittsylvania County Chamber of Commerce
8653 US Hwy 29 PO Box 99. . . . . Blairs VA 24527 434-836-6990 836-6955
Web: www.dpchamber.org

Charlottesville Regional Chamber of Commerce
209 Fifth St NE. . . . . Charlottesville VA 22902 434-295-3141 295-3144
Web: www.cvillechamber.com

Montgomery County Chamber of Commerce
1520 North Franklin St. . . . . Christiansburg VA 24073 540-382-3020 981-1970
Web: www.montgomerycc.org

Pulaski County Chamber of Commerce
4440 Cleburne Blvd Ste B. . . . . Dublin VA 24084 540-674-1991 674-4163
TF: 866-256-8864 ■ *Web:* www.pulaskichamber.info

Central Fairfax Chamber of Commerce
11166 Fairfax Blvd Ste 407. . . . . Fairfax VA 22030 703-591-2450 591-2820
Web: www.cfcc.org

Botetourt County Chamber of Commerce
13 W Main St . . . . . Fincastle VA 24090 540-473-8280 473-8365
Web: botetourtchamber.com

Greater Augusta Regional Chamber of Commerce
30 Ladd Rd PO Box 1107. . . . . Fishersville VA 22939 540-324-1133 324-1136
TF: 866-922-2514 ■ *Web:* augustava.com

Franklin-Southampton Area Chamber of Commerce
108 W Third Ave PO Box 531. . . . . Franklin VA 23851 757-562-4900 562-6138
Web: fsachamber.com

Fredericksburg Regional Chamber of Commerce
2300 Fall Hill Ave Ste 240 . . . . . Fredericksburg VA 22401 540-373-9400 373-9570
TF: 888-338-0252 ■ *Web:* www.fredericksburgchamber.org

Front Royal-Warren County Chamber of Commerce
106 Chester St . . . . . Front Royal VA 22630 540-635-3185 635-9758
Web: www.frontroyalchamber.com

Galax-Carroll-Grayson Chamber of Commerce
405 N Main St . . . . . Galax VA 24333 276-236-2184 236-1338
Web: twincountychamber.com

Virginia Peninsula Chamber of Commerce
21 Enterprise Pkwy Ste 100 . . . . . Hampton VA 23666 757-262-2000 262-2009
TF: 800-462-3204 ■ *Web:* www.virginiapeninsulachamber.com

Harrisonburg-Rockingham Chamber of Commerce
800 Country Club Rd. . . . . Harrisonburg VA 22802 540-434-3862 434-4508
Web: www.hrchamber.org

Hopewell-Prince George Chamber of Commerce
210 N Second Ave . . . . . Hopewell VA 23860 804-458-5536
Web: hpgchamber.org

Loudoun County Chamber of Commerce
19301 Winmeade Dr Ste 210 . . . . . Lansdowne VA 20176 703-777-2176 777-1392
Web: www.loudounchamber.org

Lexington-Rockbridge County Chamber of Commerce
100 E Washington St . . . . . Lexington VA 24450 540-463-5375 463-3567
Web: www.lexrockchamber.com

Lynchburg Regional Chamber of Commerce
2015 Memorial Ave . . . . . Lynchburg VA 24501 434-845-5966 522-9592
Web: www.lynchburgregion.org

Phone Fax

Prince William County-Greater Manassas Chamber of Commerce
9720 Capital Ct Ste 203 Manassas VA 20110 703-368-6600 368-4733
TF: 877-867-3853 ■ *Web:* www.pwchamber.org

Prince William Regional Chamber of Commerce
9720 Capital Ct Ste 203 Manassas VA 20110 703-368-6600 368-4733
TF: 877-867-3853 ■ *Web:* pwchamber.org

Chamber of Commerce of Smyth County
214 W Main St Marion VA 24354 276-783-3161
Web: www.smythchamber.org

Martinsville-Henry County Chamber of Commerce
115 Broad St Martinsville VA 24112 276-632-6401 632-5059
TF: 800-811-6302 ■ *Web:* www.martinsville.com

Eastern Shore of Virginia Chamber of Commerce
19056 Pkwy Rd Melfa VA 23410 757-787-2460 787-8687
Web: www.esvachamber.org

Hampton Roads Chamber of Commerce
500 E Main St Ste 700 Norfolk VA 23510 757-622-2312 622-5563
Web: www.hamptonroadschamber.com

Hampton Roads Chamber of Commerce-Suffolk
500 E Main St Ste 700 Norfolk VA 23510 757-622-2312 622-5563
Web: www.hamptonroadschamber.com

Wise County Chamber of Commerce
765 Pk Ave PO Box 226 Norton VA 24273 276-679-0961 679-2655
Web: www.wisecountychamber.org

Petersburg Chamber of Commerce
325 E Washington St Petersburg VA 23804 804-733-8131 733-9891
Web: www.petersburgvachamber.com

Greater Reston Chamber of Commerce
1763 Fountain Dr Reston VA 20190 703-707-9045 707-9049
TF: 888-274-2912 ■ *Web:* www.restonchamber.org

Greater Richmond Chamber of Commerce
600 E Main St 7th Fl Richmond VA 23219 804-648-1234 783-9366
Web: www.grcc.com

Roanoke Regional Chamber of Commerce
210 S Jefferson St Roanoke VA 24011 540-983-0700 983-0723
TF: 800-924-3543 ■ *Web:* www.roanokechamber.org

Salem/Roanoke County Chamber of Commerce
611 E Main St Salem VA 24153 540-387-0267 387-4110
Web: www.s-rcchamber.org

Halifax County Chamber of Commerce
PO Box 399 South Boston VA 24592 434-572-3085
TF: 800-283-0098 ■ *Web:* www.halifaxchamber.net

Greater Springfield Chamber of Commerce
6434 Brandon Ave Ste 208 Springfield VA 22150 703-866-3500 866-3501
Web: www.springfieldchamber.org

Tazewell Area Chamber of Commerce
Tazewell Mall PO Box 6 Tazewell VA 24651 276-988-5091
TF: 855-233-6362 ■ *Web:* www.tazewellchamber.com

Fairfax County Chamber of Commerce (FCCC)
8230 Old Courthouse Rd Ste 350 Vienna VA 22182 703-749-0400 749-9075
Web: www.novachamber.org

Vienna-Tysons Regional Chamber of Commerce
513 Maple Ave W 2nd Fl Vienna VA 22180 703-281-1333 242-1482
Web: www.tysonschamber.org

Fauquier County Chamber of Commerce
205-1 Keith St Warrenton VA 20186 540-347-4414 347-7510
Web: www.fauquierchamber.org

Williamsburg Area Chamber of Commerce
421 N Boundary St PO Box 3495 Williamsburg VA 23187 757-229-6511 253-1397
TF: 800-368-6511 ■ *Web:* www.williamsburgcc.com

Top of Virginia Regional Chamber
407 S Loudoun St Winchester VA 22601 540-662-4118
Web: www.regionalchamber.biz

Wytheville-Wythe-Bland Chamber of Commerce Inc
150 E Monroe St PO Box 563 Wytheville VA 24382 276-223-3365 223-3412
Web: www.wwbchamber.com

Washington

Phone Fax

Grays Harbor Chamber of Commerce
506 Duffy St Aberdeen WA 98520 360-532-1924 533-7945
TF: 800-321-1924 ■ *Web:* www.graysharbor.org

Auburn Area Chamber of Commerce 25 2nd St NW Auburn WA 98001 253-833-0700 735-4091
Web: www.auburnareawa.org

Bellevue Chamber of Commerce
330 112th Ave NE Ste 100 Bellevue WA 98004 425-454-2464 462-4660
Web: www.bellevuechamber.org

Bellingham/Whatcom Chamber of Commerce & Industry
119 N Commercial St Ste 110 Bellingham WA 98225 360-734-1330 734-1332
Web: bellingham.com

Bremerton Area Chamber of Commerce
286 Fourth St Bremerton WA 98337 360-479-3579 479-1033
Web: www.bremertonchamber.org

Camas-Washougal Chamber of Commerce
422 NE Fourth Ave Camas WA 98607 360-834-2472 834-9171
TF: 800-468-5865 ■ *Web:* www.cwchamber.com

Centralia-Chehalis Chamber of Commerce
500 NW Chamber of Commerce Way Chehalis WA 98532 360-748-8885 748-8763
TF: 800-525-3323 ■ *Web:* www.chamberway.com

Greater Edmonds Chamber of Commerce
121 Fifth Ave N Edmonds WA 98020 425-670-1496 712-1808
Web: www.edmondswa.com

Enumclaw Area Chamber of Commerce
1421 Cole St Enumclaw WA 98022 360-825-7666 825-8369
Web: www.enumclawchamber.com

Greater Federal Way Chamber of Commerce
31919 First Ave S Ste 202 Federal Way WA 98003 253-838-2605 661-9050
Web: www.federalwaychamber.com

Gig Harbor/Peninsula Area Chamber of Commerce
3125 Judson St Ste 101 Gig Harbor WA 98332 253-851-6865 851-6881
Web: www.gigharborchamber.net

Greater Issaquah Chamber of Commerce
155 NW Gilman Blvd Issaquah WA 98027 425-392-7024 392-8101
Web: www.issaquahchamber.com

Phone Fax

Tri-City Area Chamber of Commerce
7130 W Grandridge Blvd Kennewick WA 99336 509-736-0510 783-1733
Web: www.tricityregionalchamber.com

Kent Chamber of Commerce 524 W Meeker St Ste 1 Kent WA 98032 253-854-1770 854-8567
TF: 800-321-2808 ■ *Web:* www.kentchamber.com

Greater Kirkland Chamber of Commerce
440 Central Way Ste 102 Kirkland WA 98033 425-822-7066 827-4878
Web: www.kirklandchamber.org

Lacey-Thurston County Chamber of Commerce
8300 Quinault Dr NE # A Lacey WA 98516 360-491-4141 491-9403
Web: www.laceysschamber.com

Lakewood Chamber of Commerce
4650 Steilacoom Blvd SW Ste 109 Lakewood WA 98499 253-582-9400 581-5241
Web: lakewood-chamber.com

Kelso Longview Chamber of Commerce
1563 Olympia Way Longview WA 98632 360-423-8400 423-0432
Web: www.kelsolongviewchamber.org

Greater Maple Valley-Black Diamond Chamber of Commerce
23745 225th Way SE Ste 205 Maple Valley WA 98038 425-432-0222
Web: www.maplevalleychamber.org

Moses Lake Area Chamber of Commerce
324 S Pioneer Way Moses Lake WA 98837 509-765-7888
TF: 800-992-6234 ■ *Web:* www.moseslake.com

Greater Oak Harbor Chamber of Commerce
32630 SR 20 PO Box 883 Oak Harbor WA 98277 360-675-3755 679-1624
Web: www.oakharborchamber.com

Olympia/Thurston County Chamber of Commerce
809 Legion Way Olympia WA 98501 360-357-3362 357-3376
Web: www.thurstonchamber.com

Port Orchard Chamber of Commerce
1014 Bay St Ste 8 Port Orchard WA 98366 360-876-3505 895-1920
Web: www.portorchard.com

Pullman Chamber of Commerce 415 N Grand Ave Pullman WA 99163 509-334-3565 332-3232
TF: 800-365-6948 ■ *Web:* www.pullmanchamber.com

Eastern Pierce County Chamber of Commerce
323 N Meridian PO Box 1298 Puyallup WA 98371 253-845-6755
Web: www.puyallupsumnerchamber.com

Redmond Chamber of Commerce
8383 158th Ave NE Ste 225 Redmond WA 98052 425-885-4014
Web: www.oneredmond.org

Greater Renton Chamber of Commerce
625 S Fourth St Renton WA 98057 425-226-4560 226-4287
TF: 877-467-3686 ■ *Web:* www.gorenton.com

Ballard Chamber of Commerce
2208 NW Market St Ste 100 Seattle WA 98107 206-784-9705 783-8154
Web: www.ballardchamber.com

Greater Seattle Chamber of Commerce
1301 Fifth Ave Ste 1500 Seattle WA 98101 206-389-7200
TF: 866-978-2997 ■ *Web:* www.seattlechamber.com

Greater University Chamber of Commerce
4710 University Way NE Ste 114 Seattle WA 98105 206-547-4417
Web: udistrictpartnership.org

Lake City Chamber of Commerce
12345 30th Ave NE Ste FG Seattle WA 98125 206-363-3287
Web: www.lakecitychamber.org

Shelton-Mason County Chamber of Commerce
215 W Railroad Ave PO Box 2389 Shelton WA 98584 360-426-2021 426-8678
TF: 800-576-2021 ■ *Web:* www.sheltonchamber.org

Shoreline Chamber of Commerce
18560 First Ave NE Shoreline WA 98155 206-361-2260 361-2268

Greater Spokane Inc
801 W Riverside Ave Ste 100 Spokane WA 99201 509-624-1393 747-0077
TF: 800-776-5263 ■ *Web:* www.greaterspokane.org

Spokane Valley Chamber of Commerce
9507 E Sprague Ave Spokane Valley WA 99206 509-924-4994 924-4992
TF: 866-475-1436 ■ *Web:* www.spokanevalleychamber.org

Tacoma-Pierce County Chamber of Commerce
950 Pacific Ave Ste 300 Tacoma WA 98402 253-627-2175 597-7305
Web: www.tacomachamber.org

Southwest King County Chamber of Commerce
14220 Interurban Ave S Ste 134 Tukwila WA 98168 206-575-1633 575-2007
TF: 800-638-8613 ■ *Web:* www.sschamber.com

Greater Vancouver Chamber of Commerce
1101 Broadway Ste 100 Vancouver WA 98660 360-694-2588 693-8279
Web: www.vancouverusa.com

Walla Walla Valley Chamber of Commerce
29 E Sumach St Walla Walla WA 99362 509-525-0850 522-2038
TF: 866-826-9422 ■ *Web:* www.wwvchamber.com

Wenatchee Valley Chamber of Commerce
2 S Mission St Wenatchee WA 98801 509-662-2116 663-2022
TF: 800-572-7753 ■ *Web:* www.wenatchee.org

Greater Yakima Chamber of Commerce
10 N 9th St PO Box 1490 Yakima WA 98901 509-248-2021 248-0601
Web: www.yakima.org

West Virginia

Phone Fax

Beckley-Raleigh County Chamber of Commerce
245 N Kanawha St Beckley WV 25801 304-252-7328 252-7373
TF: 877-987-3847 ■ *Web:* www.brccc.com

Buckhannon-Upshur Chamber of Commerce
14 E Main St Buckhannon WV 26201 304-472-1722
Web: www.buchamber.com

Jefferson County Chamber of Commerce
201 E Washington St Charles Town WV 25414 304-725-2055
TF: 800-624-0577 ■ *Web:* www.jeffersoncountywvchamber.org

Charleston Regional Chamber of Commerce
1116 Smith St Charleston WV 25301 304-340-4253 340-4275
TF: 800-792-4326 ■ *Web:* www.charlestonareaalliance.org

Harrison County Chamber of Commerce
520 W Main St Clarksburg WV 26301 304-624-6331 624-5190
Web: www.harrisoncountychamber.com

Organization	City	State	Zip	Phone	Fax
Elkins-Randolph County Chamber of Commerce (ERCCC) 200 Executive Plz *Web:* www.erccc.com	Elkins	WV	26241	304-636-2717	636-8046
Marion County Chamber of Commerce 110 Adams St *Web:* www.marionchamber.com	Fairmont	WV	26554	304-363-0442	363-0480
Huntington Regional Chamber of Commerce 720 Fourth Ave *Web:* www.huntingtonchamber.org	Huntington	WV	25701	304-525-5131	525-5158
Mineral County Chamber of Commerce 40« Main St *Web:* www.mineralchamber.com	Keyser	WV	26726	304-788-2513	
Greater Greenbrier Chamber of Commerce 200 W Washington St Ste C *Web:* www.greenbrierwvchamber.org	Lewisburg	WV	24901	304-645-2818	497-3001
Logan County Chamber of Commerce 214 Stratton St *Web:* www.logancountychamberofcommerce.com	Logan	WV	25601	304-752-1324	
Martinsburg-Berkeley County Chamber of Commerce 198 Viking Way *TF:* 800-332-9007 ■ *Web:* www.berkeleycounty.org	Martinsburg	WV	25401	304-267-4841	263-4695
Morgantown Area Chamber of Commerce 1029 University Ave Ste 101 *TF General:* 800-618-2525 ■ *Web:* www.morgantownchamber.org	Morgantown	WV	26505	304-292-3311	296-6619
Marshall County Chamber of Commerce 609 Jefferson Ave *Web:* www.marshallcountychamber.com	Moundsville	WV	26041	304-845-2773	845-2773
Wetzel County Chamber of Commerce 201 Main St PO Box 271 *Web:* www.wetzelcountychamber.com	New Martinsville	WV	26155	304-455-3825	455-3637
Mason County Area Chamber of Commerce 305 Main St *Web:* www.masoncountychamber.org	Point Pleasant	WV	25550	304-675-1050	675-1601
Wheeling Area Chamber of Commerce 1310 Market St *Web:* www.wheelingchamber.com	Wheeling	WV	26003	304-233-2575	233-1320
Putnam County Chamber of Commerce 5664 State Re 34 *Web:* www.putnamchamber.org	Winfield	WV	25213	304-757-6510	757-6562

Wisconsin

Organization	City	State	Zip	Phone	Fax
Fox Cities Chamber of Commerce & Industry 125 N Superior St *TF:* 888-249-2587 ■ *Web:* www.foxcitieschamber.com	Appleton	WI	54911	920-734-7101	734-7161
Greater Beloit Chamber of Commerce 500 Public Ave *TF:* 866-981-5969 ■ *Web:* greaterbeloitchamber.org	Beloit	WI	53511	608-365-8835	365-6850
Greater Brookfield Chamber of Commerce 17100 W Bluemound Rd Ste 202 *Web:* www.brookfieldchamber.com	Brookfield	WI	53005	262-786-1886	786-1959
Chippewa Falls Area Chamber of Commerce 10 S Bridge St *TF:* 888-723-0024 ■ *Web:* www.chippewachamber.org	Chippewa Falls	WI	54729	715-723-0331	723-0332
Eau Claire Area Chamber of Commerce 101 N Farwell St Ste 101 *Web:* www.eauclairechamber.org	Eau Claire	WI	54703	715-834-1204	834-1956
Fond du Lac Area Assn of Commerce 207 N Main St *TF:* 800-279-8811 ■ *Web:* www.fdlac.com	Fond du Lac	WI	54935	920-921-9500	921-9559
Green Bay Area Chamber of Commerce PO Box 1660 *Web:* www.titletown.org	Green Bay	WI	54305	920-437-8704	
Greenfield Chamber of Commerce 4818 S 76th St Ste 129 *Web:* www.thegreenfieldchamber.com	Greenfield	WI	53220	414-327-8500	
Heart of the Valley Chamber of Commerce 101 E Wisconsin Ave *Web:* www.heartofthevalleychamber.com	Kaukauna	WI	54130	920-766-1616	766-5504
Kenosha Area Chamber of Commerce 600 52nd St Ste 130 *Web:* www.kenoshaareachamber.com	Kenosha	WI	53140	262-654-1234	654-4655
Greater Madison Chamber of Commerce PO Box 71 *Web:* www.greatermadisonchamber.com	Madison	WI	53701	608-256-8348	256-0333
Manitowoc-Two Rivers Area Chamber of Commerce 1515 Memorial Dr *TF:* 866-727-5575 ■ *Web:* chambermanitowoccounty.org	Manitowoc	WI	54220	920-684-5575	684-1915
Menomonee Falls Chamber of Commerce N 88 W 16621 Appleton Ave *Web:* www.fallschamber.com	Menomonee Falls	WI	53051	262-251-2430	
Greater Menomonie Area Chamber of Commerce 342 E Main St *TF:* 800-283-1862 ■ *Web:* www.menomoniechamber.org	Menomonie	WI	54751	715-235-9087	235-2824
Merrill Area Chamber of Commerce 705 N Ctr Ave *TF:* 877-907-2757 ■ *Web:* www.merrillchamber.org	Merrill	WI	54452	715-536-9474	539-2043
Metropolitan Milwaukee Assn of Commerce 756 N Milwaukee St *TF:* 800-362-9472 ■ *Web:* www.mmac.org	Milwaukee	WI	53202	414-287-4100	271-7753
Monroe Chamber of Commerce & Industry 1505 Ninth St *Web:* www.monroechamber.org	Monroe	WI	53566	608-325-7648	328-2241
Oconomowoc Area Chamber of Commerce 175 E Wisconsin Ave *Web:* www.oconomowoc.org	Oconomowoc	WI	53066	262-567-2666	567-3477
Oshkosh Chamber of Commerce 120 Jackson St *Web:* www.oshkoshchamber.com	Oshkosh	WI	54901	920-303-2266	303-2263
Racine Area Mfg & Commerce 300 Fifth St *Web:* www.racinechamber.com	Racine	WI	53403	262-634-1931	634-7422
Ripon Area Chamber of Commerce 114 Scott St PO Box 305 *Web:* www.ripon-wi.com	Ripon	WI	54971	920-748-6764	748-6784
Shawano Country Chamber of Commerce 1263 S Main St *TF:* 800-235-8528 ■ *Web:* www.shawanocountry.com	Shawano	WI	54166	715-524-2139	524-3127
Sheboygan County Chamber of Commerce 621 S Eigth St *TF:* 800-457-9497 ■ *Web:* www.sheboygan.org	Sheboygan	WI	53081	920-457-9491	457-6269
Portage County Business Council 5501 Vern Holmes Dr *TF:* 800-333-6668 ■ *Web:* www.portagecountybiz.com	Stevens Point	WI	54481	715-344-1940	344-4473
Superior-Douglas County Chamber of Commerce 205 Belknap St *TF:* 800-942-5313 ■ *Web:* www.superiorchamber.org	Superior	WI	54880	715-394-7716	394-3810
Waukesha County Chamber of Commerce 2717 N Grandview Blvd Ste 204 *TF:* 800-727-1344 ■ *Web:* www.waukesha.org	Waukesha	WI	53188	262-542-4249	542-8068
Wausau Area Chamber of Commerce 200 Washington St Ste 120 *Web:* www.wausauchamber.com	Wausau	WI	54403	715-845-6231	845-6235
Wauwatosa Chamber of Commerce 10437 Innovation Dr *Web:* tosachamber.org	Wauwatosa	WI	53226	414-453-2330	
West Allis-West Milwaukee Chamber of Commerce 6737 W Washington St Ste 2141 *TF:* 800-554-1448 ■ *Web:* www.wawmchamber.com	West Allis	WI	53214	414-302-9901	302-9918
West Bend Area Chamber of Commerce 304 S Main St *TF:* 888-338-8666 ■ *Web:* www.wbachamber.org	West Bend	WI	53095	262-338-2666	338-1771
Heart of Wisconsin Business & Economic Alliance 1120 Lincoln St *Web:* www.wisconsinrapidschamber.com	Wisconsin Rapids	WI	54494	715-423-1830	423-1865

Wyoming

Organization	City	State	Zip	Phone	Fax
Casper Area Chamber of Commerce 500 N Ctr St *TF:* 866-234-5311 ■ *Web:* www.casperwyoming.org	Casper	WY	82601	307-234-5311	265-2643
Greater Cheyenne Chamber of Commerce 121 W 15th St Ste 204 *Web:* www.cheyennechamber.org	Cheyenne	WY	82001	307-638-3388	778-1407
Campbell County Chamber of Commerce 314 S Gillette Ave *TF:* 800-448-7801 ■ *Web:* www.gillettechamber.com	Gillette	WY	82716	307-682-3673	682-0538
Jackson Hole Chamber of Commerce 112 Ctr St *Web:* www.jacksonholechamber.com	Jackson	WY	83001	307-733-3316	733-5585
Laramie Area Chamber of Commerce 800 S Third St *TF:* 866-876-1012 ■ *Web:* www.laramie.org	Laramie	WY	82070	307-745-7339	745-4624
Rock Springs Chamber of Commerce 1897 Dewar Dr *TF:* 800-463-8637 ■ *Web:* rockspringschamber.com	Rock Springs	WY	82901	307-362-3771	362-3838
Sheridan County Chamber of Commerce 1517 E Fifth St *TF:* 800-453-3650 ■ *Web:* www.sheridanwyomingchamber.org	Sheridan	WY	82801	307-672-2485	672-7321

140 CHAMBERS OF COMMERCE - US - STATE

Organization	City	State	Zip	Phone	Fax
US Chamber of Commerce 1615 H St NW *TF:* 800-638-6582 ■ *Web:* www.uschamber.com	Washington	DC	20062	202-659-6000	
Alaska State Chamber of Commerce 471 W 36th Ave *Web:* www.alaskachamber.com	Anchorage	AK	99503	907-278-2722	
Arizona Chamber of Commerce & Industry 3200 N Central Ave Ste 1125 *TF:* 866-275-5816 ■ *Web:* www.azchamber.com	Phoenix	AZ	85012	602-248-9172	265-1262
Arkansas State Chamber of Commerce 1200 W Capitol Ave PO Box 3645 *TF:* 800-482-1127 ■ *Web:* www.arkansasstatechamber.com	Little Rock	AR	72203	501-372-2222	372-2722
Association of Washington Business PO Box 658 *TF:* 800-521-9325 ■ *Web:* www.awb.org	Olympia	WA	98507	360-943-1600	943-5811
Business Council of Alabama 2 N Jackson St Ste 501 *TF:* 800-665-9647 ■ *Web:* www.bcatoday.org	Montgomery	AL	36101	334-834-6000	
Business Council of New York State Inc 152 Washington Ave *TF:* 800-358-1202 ■ *Web:* www.bcnys.org	Albany	NY	12210	518-465-7511	465-4389
California Chamber of Commerce 1215 K St Ste 1400 PO Box 1736 *Web:* www.calchamber.com	Sacramento	CA	95812	916-444-6670	325-1272
Colorado Assn of Commerce & Industry 1600 Broadway Ste 1000 *Web:* www.cochamber.com	Denver	CO	80202	303-831-7411	860-1439
Connecticut Business & Industry Assn 350 Church St *Web:* www.cbia.com	Hartford	CT	06103	860-244-1900	278-8562
Delaware State Chamber of Commerce 1201 N Orange St Ste 200 PO Box 671 *TF:* 800-292-9507 ■ *Web:* www.dscc.com	Wilmington	DE	19899	302-655-7221	654-0691
District of Columbia Chamber of Commerce 506 Ninth St NW *Web:* www.dcchamber.org	Washington	DC	20004	202-347-7201	
Florida Chamber of Commerce 136 S Bronough St PO Box 11309 *TF:* 877-521-1230 ■ *Web:* www.flchamber.com	Tallahassee	FL	32302	850-521-1200	
Georgia Chamber of Commerce 233 Peachtree St NE Ste 2000 *TF:* 800-241-2286 ■ *Web:* www.gachamber.com	Atlanta	GA	30303	404-223-2264	223-2290
Idaho Assn of Commerce & Industry 816 W Bannock St Ste 5B PO Box 389 *Web:* www.iaci.org	Boise	ID	83701	208-343-1849	
Illinois State Chamber of Commerce 300 S Wacker Dr Ste 1600 *Web:* www.ilchamber.org	Chicago	IL	60606	312-983-7100	983-7101

Phone *Fax*

Indiana State Chamber of Commerce
115 W Washington St Ste 850-S .... Indianapolis IN 46204 317-264-3110 264-6855
Web: www.indianachamber.com

Iowa Assn of Business & Industry
400 E Ct Ave Ste 100 .... Des Moines IA 50309 515-280-8000
TF: 800-383-4224 ■ *Web:* www.iowaabi.org

Kansas Chamber of Commerce & Industry
835 SW Topeka Blvd .... Topeka KS 66612 785-357-6321 357-4732
Web: www.kansaschamber.org

Kentucky Chamber of Commerce
464 Chenault Rd .... Frankfort KY 40601 502-695-4700
TF: 800-533-0127 ■ *Web:* www.kychamber.com

Louisiana Assn of Business & Industry
3113 Vly Creek Dr PO Box 80258 .... Baton Rouge LA 70898 225-928-5388 929-6054
TF: 888-816-5224 ■ *Web:* www.labi.org

Maine State Chamber of Commerce
125 Community Dr Ste 101 .... Augusta ME 04330 207-623-4568 622-7723
Web: www.mainechamber.org

Maryland Chamber of Commerce
60 W St Ste 100 .... Annapolis MD 21401 410-269-0642 269-5247
Web: www.mdchamber.org

Michigan Chamber of Commerce 600 S Walnut St ...... Lansing MI 48933 517-371-2100 371-7224
TF: 800-748-0266 ■ *Web:* www.michamber.com

Minnesota Chamber of Commerce
400 Robert St N Ste 1500 .... Saint Paul MN 55101 651-292-4650 292-4656
TF: 800-821-2230 ■ *Web:* www.mnchamber.com

Mississippi Economic Council PO Box 23276 .... Jackson MS 39225 601-969-0022 353-0247
TF: 800-748-7626 ■ *Web:* www.msmec.com

Missouri Chamber of Commerce
428 E Capitol Ave PO Box 149 .... Jefferson City MO 65102 573-634-3511 634-8855
Web: www.mochamber.com

Montana Chamber of Commerce
900 Gibbon St PO Box 1730 .... Helena MT 59624 406-442-2405 442-2409
TF: 888-442-6668 ■ *Web:* www.montanachamber.com

Nebraska Chamber of Commerce & Industry
1320 Lincoln Mall # 201A .... Lincoln NE 68508 402-474-4422 474-5681
Web: www.nechamber.net

New England Council Inc
98 N Washington St Ste 201 .... Boston MA 02114 617-723-4009 723-3943
Web: www.newenglandcouncil.com

New Jersey State Chamber of Commerce
216 W State St .... Trenton NJ 08608 609-989-7888 989-9696
Web: www.njchamber.com

New Mexico Assn of Commerce & Industry (ACI)
2201 Buena Vista Dr SE Ste 410
PO Box 9706 .... Albuquerque NM 87106 505-842-0644 842-0734
Web: www.nmaci.org

North Carolina Chamber
701 Corporate Ctr Dr Ste 400 .... Raleigh NC 27607 919-836-1400 836-1425
Web: www.ncchamber.net/mx/hm.asp?id=home

North Dakota Chamber of Commerce
2000 Schafer St PO Box 2639 .... Bismarck ND 58502 701-222-0929 222-1611
TF: 800-382-1405 ■ *Web:* www.ndchamber.com

Ohio Chamber of Commerce
230 E Town St PO Box 15159 .... Columbus OH 43215 614-228-4201 228-6403
TF: 800-533-2794 ■ *Web:* www.ohiochamber.com

Oklahoma State Chamber 330 NE Tenth St .... Oklahoma City OK 73104 405-235-3669 235-3670
Web: www.okstatechamber.com

Pennsylvania Chamber of Business & Industry
417 Walnut St .... Harrisburg PA 17101 717-255-3252 255-3298
TF: 800-225-7224 ■ *Web:* www.pachamber.org

Puerto Rico Chamber of Commerce
PO Box 9024033 .... San Juan PR 00902 787-721-6060 723-1891
Web: www.camarapr.org

South Carolina Chamber of Commerce
1201 Main St Ste1100 .... Columbia SC 29201 803-799-4601 779-6043
TF: 800-799-4601 ■ *Web:* www.scchamber.net

South Dakota Chamber of Commerce & Industry
108 N Euclid Ave .... Pierre SD 57501 605-224-6161 224-7198
TF: 800-742-8112 ■ *Web:* www.sdchamber.biz

Tennessee Chamber of Commerce & Industry
414 Union St Ste 107 .... Nashville TN 37219 615-256-5141
Web: www.tnchamber.org

Texas Assn of Business 1209 Nueces St .... Austin TX 78701 512-477-6721 477-0836
Web: www.txbiz.org

Vermont Chamber of Commerce PO Box 37 .... Montpelier VT 05601 802-223-3443 223-4257
TF: 800-451-4279 ■ *Web:* www.vtchamber.com

Virginia Chamber of Commerce 919 E Main St .... Richmond VA 23219 804-644-1607 783-6112
TF: 800-228-9290 ■ *Web:* www.vachamber.com

West Virginia Chamber of Commerce
1624 Kanawha Blvd E .... Charleston WV 25311 304-342-1115 342-1130
Web: www.wvchamber.com

Wisconsin Manufacturers & Commerce
PO Box 352 .... Madison WI 53701 608-258-3400 258-3413
TF: 800-236-5414 ■ *Web:* www.wmc.org

141 CHECK CASHING SERVICES

Phone *Fax*

ACE Cash Express 1231 Greenway Dr Ste 600 .... Irving TX 75038 972-550-5000 550-5150
TF: 800-817-5106 ■ *Web:* www.acecashexpress.com

Advance America Cash Advance Centers Inc
135 N Church St .... Spartanburg SC 29306 864-342-5600
NYSE: AEA ■ *TF:* 800-538-1579 ■ *Web:* www.advanceamerica.net

Cash Plus Inc 3002 Dow Ave Ste 120 .... Tustin CA 92780 714-731-2274 731-2099
Web: www.cashplusinc.com

Check Cashing Store (CCS)
6340 NW Fifth Way .... Fort Lauderdale FL 33309 800-361-1407
TF: 800-361-1407 ■ *Web:* www.thecheckcashingstore.com

Check Cashing USA Inc 899 NW 37th Ave .... Miami FL 33125 305-644-1840
Web: www.checkcashingusa.com

Dollar Financial Corp
1436 Lancaster Ave Ste 300 .... Berwyn PA 19312 610-296-3400 296-7844
Web: www.dfcglobalcorp.com

Phone *Fax*

Enviro-Pro-Tech Inc 3210 Barrancas Ave .... Pensacola FL 32507 850-587-5588

Extra Help Inc 3911 W Ernestine Dr .... Marion IL 62959 618-993-9675
Web: www.extrahelpinc.com

First Cash Financial Services Inc
690 E Lamar Blvd Ste 400 .... Arlington TX 76011 817-460-3947 461-7019
NASDAQ: FCFS ■ *TF:* 800-290-4598 ■ *Web:* ww2.firstcash.com

First Fidelity Funding & Mortgage Corp
6000 Lk Forrest Dr Ste 290 .... Atlanta GA 30328 404-943-1533
Web: firstfidelityfunding.com

Midland Credit Management Inc
8875 Aero Dr Ste 200 .... San Diego CA 92123 800-265-8825
TF: 800-265-8825 ■ *Web:* www.encorecapitalgroup.com

Mister Money Investment 2057 Vermont Dr .... Fort Collins CO 80525 800-290-4598 490-2099*
**Fax Area Code:* 970 ■ *TF:* 888-336-0403 ■ *Web:* ww2.firstcash.com

NIX Neighborhood Lending
1440 Rosecrans Ave .... Manhattan Beach CA 90266 310-603-5889
Web: nixlending.com

Pay-O-Matic Corp 160 Oak Dr .... Syosset NY 11791 516-496-4900
TF: 888-545-6311 ■ *Web:* www.payomatic.com

Policy Research Associates Inc
345 Delaware Ave .... Delmar NY 12054 518-439-7415
TF: 800-311-4246 ■ *Web:* www.prainc.com

QC Holdings Inc
9401 Indian Creek Pkwy Ste 1500 .... Overland Park KS 66210 866-660-2243
NASDAQ: QCCO ■ *TF:* 866-660-2243 ■ *Web:* www.qcholdings.com

Service General Corp 13 E Laurel St .... Georgetown DE 19947 302-856-3500
Web: www.servicegeneral.net

Stoneleigh Recovery Associates Llc
810 Springer Dr .... Lombard IL 60148 630-812-2820
Web: www.stoneleighrecoveryassociates.com

United Financial Services Group
325 Chestnut St Ste 3000 .... Philadelphia PA 19106 215-238-0300 238-9056
Web: www.unitedfsg.com

VERICO One Link Mortgage & Financial
200-1215 Henderson Hwy .... Winnipeg MB R2G1L8 204-954-7620
Web: onelinkmortgage.com

Waterfield Technologies Inc
1 W Third St Ste 1115 .... Tulsa OK 74103 918-858-6400
TF: 800-324-0936 ■ *Web:* www.waterfieldtechnologies.com

Widearea Systems Inc 201A Broadway St .... Frederick MD 21701 301-418-6180
Web: wideareasystems.com

142 CHECKS - PERSONAL & BUSINESS

Phone *Fax*

4checks.com 8245 N Union Blvd .... Colorado Springs CO 80920 800-995-9925
TF: 800-995-9925 ■ *Web:* www.4checks.com

Artistic Checks Inc
1809 Fashion Ct PO Box 1000 .... Conyers GA 30012 800-824-3255
TF: 800-243-2577 ■ *Web:* www.artisticchecks.com

Check Printers Inc 1530 Antioch Pike .... Antioch TN 37013 800-766-1217 324-3323*
**Fax Area Code:* 615 ■ *TF:* 800-766-1217 ■ *Web:* www.check-printers.com

Checks In The Mail Inc 2435 Goodwin Ln .... New Braunfels TX 78135 800-733-4443 609-6522*
**Fax Area Code:* 830 ■ *TF:* 800-733-4443 ■ *Web:* www.secure.checksinthemail.com

Checks Unlimited 8245 N Union Blvd .... Colorado Springs CO 80920 719-531-3900
TF: 800-210-0468 ■ *Web:* www.checksunlimited.com

Safeguard Business Systems Inc
8585 N Stemmons Fwy Ste 600 N .... Dallas TX 75247 800-523-2422 439-3423
TF: 800-523-2422 ■ *Web:* www.gosafeguard.com

CHEMICALS - AGRICULTURAL

See Fertilizers & Pesticides p. 2283

143 CHEMICALS - INDUSTRIAL (INORGANIC)

Phone *Fax*

Advance Research Chemicals Inc
1110 Keystone Ave .... Catoosa OK 74015 918-266-6789 266-6796
Web: www.fluoridearc.com

Air Liquide America LP
2700 Post Oak Blvd Ste 1800 .... Houston TX 77056 877-855-9533
TF: 877-855-9533 ■ *Web:* www.airliquide.com

Air Products & Chemicals Inc
7201 Hamilton Blvd .... Allentown PA 18195 610-481-4911
NYSE: APD ■ *TF Prod Info:* 800-345-3148 ■ *Web:* www.airproducts.com

AkzoNobel Surface Chemistry LLC
525 W Van Buren St .... Chicago IL 60607 312-544-7000 544-7410
TF Cust Svc: 800-937-5449 ■ *Web:* www.akzonobel.com

Almatis Inc 501 W Pk Rd .... Leetsdale PA 15056 412-630-2800 630-2900
TF: 800-643-8771 ■ *Web:* www.almatis.com

American Chemet Corp 740 Waukegan Rd .... Deerfield IL 60015 847-948-0800 948-0811
Web: www.chemet.com

Americhem Inc 2000 Americhem Way .... Cuyahoga Falls OH 44221 330-929-4213 929-4144
TF: 800-228-3476 ■ *Web:* www.americhem.com

Ampacet Corp 660 White Plains Rd .... Tarrytown NY 10591 914-631-6600 631-7197
TF Cust Svc: 800-888-4267 ■ *Web:* www.ampacet.com

Ashta Chemicals Inc 3509 Middle Rd .... Ashtabula OH 44004 440-997-5221 992-0151
TF Cust Svc: 800-492-5082 ■ *Web:* www.ashtachemicals.com

Baerlocher production USA LLC
5890 Highland Ridge Dr .... Cincinnati OH 45232 513-482-6300 242-9213
Web: www.baerlocher.com

BASF Canada 100 Milverton Dr 5th Fl .... Mississauga ON L5R4H1 289-360-1300 360-6000
TF Cust Svc: 866-485-2273 ■ *Web:* www2.basf.us/basf-canada

BASF Corp 100 Campus Dr .... Florham Park NJ 07932 973-245-6000 895-8002
TF: 800-526-1072 ■ *Web:* www.basf.com

Bio-Lab Inc
1725 N Brown Rd PO Box 30000 .... Lawrenceville GA 30043 678-502-4000
TF: 800-859-7946 ■ *Web:* www.biolabinc.com

BWX Technologies Inc
13024 Ballantyne Corporate Pl Ste 700 .... Charlotte NC 28277 704-625-4900
Web: www.babcock.com

	City	State	ZIP	Phone	Fax
Cabot Corp 2 Seaport Ln Ste 1300	Boston	MA	02210	617-345-0100	342-6103
NYSE: CBT ■ *TF:* 800-322-1236 ■ *Web:* www.cabotcorp.com					
Calgon Carbon Corp 3000 GSK Dr	Moon Township	PA	15108	412-787-6700	787-6676
NYSE: CCC ■ *TF Cust Svc:* 800-422-7266 ■ *Web:* www.calgoncarbon.com					
Carus Corp 315 Fifth St	Peru	IL	61354	815-223-1500	224-6697
TF: 800-435-6856 ■ *Web:* www.caruscorporation.com					
Centrus Energy Corp 6903 Rockledge Dr Ste 800	Bethesda	MD	20817	301-564-3200	564-3201
NYSE: USU ■ *TF:* 800-273-7754 ■ *Web:* www.centrusenergy.com					
Chemical Products Corp 102 Old Mill Rd	Cartersville	GA	30120	770-382-2144	
TF Cust Svc: 877-210-9814 ■ *Web:* www.chemicalproductscorp.com					
Circle-Prosco Inc 401 N Gates Dr	Bloomington	IN	47404	812-339-3653	331-2566
Web: www.circleprosco.com					
Cormetech Inc 5000 International Dr	Durham	NC	27712	919-620-3000	620-3001
Web: www.cormetech.com					
Criterion Catalysts & Technologies 16825 Northchase Dr Ste 1000	Houston	TX	77060	281-874-2600	874-2641
Web: www.criterioncatalysts.com					
Dow Chemical Co 2030 Dow Ctr	Midland	MI	48674	989-636-1463	636-1830
NYSE: DOW ■ *TF Cust Svc:* 800-422-8193 ■ *Web:* www.dow.com					
DuPont Titanium Technologies 1007 Market St	Wilmington	DE	19898	302-774-1000	
TF: 800-441-7515 ■ *Web:* www.dupont.com					
Elementis Specialties Inc 469 Old Trenton Rd	East Windsor	NJ	08512	800-866-6800	443-2422*
**Fax Area Code:* 609 ■ *TF:* 800-866-6800 ■ *Web:* www.elementis.com					
Energy Research & Generation Inc 900 Stanford Ave	Oakland	CA	94608	510-658-9785	658-7428
Web: www.ergaerospace.com					
Enersul LP 7210 Blackfood Terr SE	Calgary	AB	T2H1M5	403-253-5969	259-2771
Web: www.enersul.com					
ExxonMobil Chemical Co 13501 Katy Fwy	Houston	TX	77079	281-870-6000	
Web: www.exxonmobilchemical.com					
Ferro Corp Electronic Materials Div 4150 E 56th St	Cleveland	OH	44105	216-641-8580	
Web: ferro.com					
FMC Corp 2929 Walnut St	Philadelphia	PA	19104	215-299-6000	299-5998
NYSE: FMC ■ *TF:* 888-548-4486 ■ *Web:* www.fmc.com					
Front Range Energy LLC 31375 Great Western Dr	Windsor	CO	80550	970-674-2910	
Web: www.frontrangeenergy.com					
Giles Chemical Corp 102 Commerce St	Waynesville	NC	28786	828-452-4784	452-4786
Web: www.gileschemical.com					
Green Plains Renewable Energy Inc 450 Regency Pkwy Ste 400	Omaha	NE	68114	402-884-8700	884-8776
NASDAQ: GPRE ■ *TF:* 877-886-2288 ■ *Web:* www.gpreinc.com					
Hawkins Inc 3100 E Hennepin Ave	Minneapolis	MN	55413	612-331-6910	331-5304
NASDAQ: HWKN ■ *TF:* 800-328-5460 ■ *Web:* www.hawkinsinc.com					
Horsehead Corp 4955 Steubenville Pk Ste 405	Pittsburgh	PA	15205	724-774-1020	
TF: 800-648-8897 ■ *Web:* www.horsehead.net					
Interstate Chemical Co Inc 2797 Freedland Rd	Hermitage	PA	16148	724-981-3771	981-8383
TF: 800-422-2436 ■ *Web:* www.interstatechemical.com					
Johnson Matthey Inc Catalysts & Chemicals Div 2001 Nolte Dr	West Deptford	NJ	08066	703-579-7222	384-7276*
**Fax Area Code:* 856 ■ *Web:* www.chemicals.matthey.com					
Jones Hamilton Co 30354 Tracy Rd	Walbridge	OH	43465	419-666-9838	666-1817
TF: 888-858-4425 ■ *Web:* www.jones-hamilton.com					
Kanto Corp 13424 N Woodrush Way	Portland	OR	97203	503-283-0405	240-0409
TF: 866-609-5571 ■ *Web:* www.kantocorp.com					
Keystone Aniline Corp 2501 W Fulton St	Chicago	IL	60612	312-666-2015	666-8530
TF: 800-522-4393 ■ *Web:* www.dyes.com					
LSB Industries Inc 16 S Pennsylvania Ave	Oklahoma City	OK	73107	405-235-4546	235-5067
NYSE: LXU ■ *Web:* www.lsbindustries.com					
Martin Marietta Magnesia Specialties Inc 8140 Corporate Dr Ste 220	Baltimore	MD	21236	410-780-5500	780-5777
TF: 800-648-7400 ■ *Web:* www.magnesiaspecialties.com					
Matheson Tri-Gas Inc 959 Rt 46 E	Parsippany	NJ	07054	973-257-1100	
Web: www.mathesongas.com					
Minerals Technologies Inc 622 Third Ave 38th Fl	New York	NY	10017	212-878-1831	
NYSE: MTX ■ *Web:* www.mineralstech.com					
Moravek Biochemicals Inc 577 Mercury Ln	Brea	CA	92821	714-990-2018	990-1824
Web: www.moravek.com					
NL Industries 16801 Greenspoint Pk Dr	Houston	TX	77060	281-423-3300	
NYSE: NL ■ *TF:* 800-866-5600 ■ *Web:* www.nl-ind.com					
Noah Technologies Corp of Texas 1 Noah Pk	San Antonio	TX	78249	210-691-2000	691-2600
Web: www.noahtech.com					
Nuclear Fuel Services Inc 1205 Banner Hill Rd	Erwin	TN	37650	423-743-9141	743-9025
Web: www.nuclearfuelservices.com					
Occidental Chemical Corp 5005 LBJ Fwy	Dallas	TX	75244	972-404-3800	
Web: www.oxy.com					
Old Bridge Chemicals Inc PO Box 175	Old Bridge	NJ	08857	732-727-2225	727-2653
TF: 800-275-3924 ■ *Web:* www.oldbridgechem.com					
Olin Corp Olin Chlor Alkali Products Div 490 Stuart Rd NE	Cleveland	TN	37312	423-336-4850	336-4876
Web: www.olinchloralkali.com/en-us					
OMYA Inc 39 Main St	Proctor	VT	05765	802-459-3311	459-6327
TF: 800-451-4468 ■ *Web:* www.omya.com/us-en					
Phibro Animal Health Corp 300 Frank W Burr Blvd Ste 21	Teaneck	NJ	07660	201-329-7300	329-7399
TF: 800-223-0434 ■ *Web:* www.phibrochem.com					
Plasticolors Inc 2600 Michigan Ave PO Box 816	Ashtabula	OH	44005	440-997-5137	992-3613
TF: 888-661-7675 ■ *Web:* www.chromaflo.com					
Potash Corp 1101 Skokie Blvd	Northbrook	IL	60062	847-849-4200	849-4695
TF: 800-667-0403 ■ *Web:* www.potashcorp.com					
Praxair Inc 39 Old Ridgebury Rd	Danbury	CT	06810	203-837-2000	
NYSE: PX ■ *TF:* 800-772-9247 ■ *Web:* www.praxair.com					
Rutgers Organics Corp (ROC) 201 Struble Rd	State College	PA	16801	814-238-2424	
TF: 888-469-2188 ■ *Web:* federalregister.gov					
Shepherd Chemical Co 4900 Beech St	Cincinnati	OH	45212	513-731-1110	731-1532
Web: www.shepchem.com					
Silberline Mfg Company Inc 130 Lincoln Dr PO Box B	Tamaqua	PA	18252	570-668-6050	668-0197
TF: 800-348-4824 ■ *Web:* www.silberline.com					
Solvay America Inc 3333 Richmond Ave	Houston	TX	77098	713-525-6000	525-7887
TF General: 800-365-6565 ■ *Web:* www.solvay.com					
Southern Ionics Inc 201 Commerce St	West Point	MS	39773	662-494-3055	495-2590
TF: 800-953-3585 ■ *Web:* www.southernionics.com					
Synalloy Corp 775 Spartan Blvd Ste 102 PO Box 5627	Spartanburg	SC	29304	864-585-3605	596-1501
NASDAQ: SYNL ■ *TF Orders:* 800-937-5449 ■ *Web:* www.synalloy.com					
Tanner Systems Inc PO Box 488	Saint Joseph	MN	56374	320-363-1800	
TF: 800-461-6454 ■ *Web:* www.tannersystems.com					
TETRA Technologies Inc 25025 I-45 N	The Woodlands	TX	77380	281-367-1983	364-4306
NYSE: TTI ■ *TF:* 800-327-7817 ■ *Web:* www.tetratec.com					
Texas United Corp 4800 San Felipe	Houston	TX	77056	713-877-2600	877-2664
TF: 800-554-8658 ■ *Web:* www.unitedsalt.com					
TOR Minerals International Inc 722 Burleson St	Corpus Christi	TX	78402	361-883-5591	883-7619
NASDAQ: TORM ■ *Web:* www.torminerals.com					
Tronox Inc 3301 NW 150th St	Oklahoma City	OK	73134	405-775-5000	
Web: www.tronox.com					
UOP LLC 25 E Algonquin Rd	Des Plaines	IL	60017	847-391-2000	391-2253
TF: 800-877-6184 ■ *Web:* www.uop.com					
Vulcan Materials Co 1200 Urban Ctr Dr PO Box 385014	Birmingham	AL	35238	205-298-3000	
NYSE: VMC ■ *TF:* 800-615-4331 ■ *Web:* www.vulcanmaterials.com					
Westlake Chemical Corp 2801 Post Oak Blvd Ste 600	Houston	TX	77056	713-960-9111	963-1562
NYSE: WLK ■ *TF:* 888-953-3623 ■ *Web:* www.westlakechemical.com					

144 CHEMICALS - INDUSTRIAL (ORGANIC)

	City	State	ZIP	Phone	Fax
Abengoa Bioenergy Corp 16150 Main Cir Dr Ste 300	Chesterfield	MO	63017	636-728-0508	728-1148
Web: www.abengoabioenergy.com					
AF Rx Inc 751 S Rose Ave	Oxnard	CA	93030	805-487-0696	483-6146
Web: www.agrx.com					
Altair Nanotechnologies Inc 204 Edison Way	Reno	NV	89502	775-856-2500	856-1619
NASDAQ: ALTI ■ *Web:* www.altairnano.com					
American Natural Soda Ash Corp 15 Riverside Ave	Westport	CT	06880	203-226-9056	227-1484
Web: www.ansac.com					
Ampacet Corp 660 White Plains Rd	Tarrytown	NY	10591	914-631-6600	631-7197
TF Cust Svc: 800-888-4267 ■ *Web:* www.ampacet.com					
Arizona Chemical Co Inc 4600 Touchton Rd E Ste 1200	Jacksonville	FL	32246	904-928-8700	
Web: www.arizonachemical.com					
Badger State Ethanol LLC 820 W 17th St PO Box 317	Monroe	WI	53566	608-329-3900	329-3866
Web: www.badgerstateethanol.com					
Bayer Corp 100 Bayer Rd	Pittsburgh	PA	15205	862-404-3000	777-3899*
**Fax Area Code:* 412 ■ *Web:* www.bayer.us					
Bayer Inc 77 Belfield Rd	Toronto	ON	M9W1G6	416-248-0771	
TF: 800-622-2937 ■ *Web:* www.bayer.ca					
BP PLC 28100 Torch Pkwy	Warrenville	IL	60555	800-333-3991	
NYSE: BP ■ *TF:* 800-333-3991 ■ *Web:* www.bp.com					
Cambrex Corp 1 Meadowlands Plz	East Rutherford	NJ	07073	201-804-3000	804-9852
NYSE: CBM ■ *TF:* 866-286-9133 ■ *Web:* www.cambrex.com					
Cardolite Corp 500 Doremus Ave	Newark	NJ	07105	800-322-7365	344-1197*
**Fax Area Code:* 973 ■ *TF:* 800-322-7365 ■ *Web:* www.cardolite.com					
Celanese Corp 1601 W LBJ Fwy	Dallas	TX	75234	972-443-4000	
NYSE: CE ■ *Web:* www.celanese.com					
Chemical Exchange Industries Inc 900 Clinton Dr PO Box 67	Galena Park	TX	77547	713-455-1206	455-8959
Web: texmark.com					
Chemstar Products Co 3915 Hiawatha Ave	Minneapolis	MN	55406	612-722-0079	722-2473
TF: 800-328-5037 ■ *Web:* www.chemstar.com					
Chevron Phillips Chemical Company LP 10001 Six Pines Dr	The Woodlands	TX	77380	832-813-4100	
TF: 800-231-1212 ■ *Web:* www.cpchem.com					
Colorcon Inc 415 Moyer Blvd	West Point	PA	19486	215-699-7733	661-2605
Web: www.colorcon.com					
CorsiTech 3200 SW Fwy Ste 2700 PO Box 27727	Houston	TX	77027	281-431-3628	623-4652*
**Fax Area Code:* 713 ■ *Web:* www.corsicanatech.com					
Dow Chemical Canada Inc (DCCI) 450 First St SW Ste 2100	Calgary	AB	T2P5H1	403-267-3500	267-3597
TF: 800-447-4369 ■ *Web:* www.dow.com					
Dow Chemical Co 2030 Dow Ctr	Midland	MI	48674	989-636-1463	636-1830
NYSE: DOW ■ *TF Cust Svc:* 800-422-8193 ■ *Web:* www.dow.com					
Dow Corning Corp PO Box 994	Midland	MI	48686	989-496-4000	496-1886*
**Fax:* Hum Res ■ *TF Cust Svc:* 800-248-2481 ■ *Web:* www.dowcorning.com					
DSM Chemicals North America Inc 1 Columbia Nitrogen Rd	Augusta	GA	30901	706-849-6600	849-6999*
**Fax:* Cust Svc ■ *TF:* 800-526-0189 ■ *Web:* www.dsm.com					
Eastman Chemical Co 200 S Wilcox Dr	Kingsport	TN	37660	423-229-2000	
NYSE: EMN ■ *TF Cust Svc:* 800-327-8626 ■ *Web:* www.eastman.com					
Elan Chemical Co 268 Doremus Ave	Newark	NJ	07105	973-344-8014	344-8014
Web: www.elan-chemical.com					
First Chemical Corp 1001 Industrial Rd	Pascagoula	MS	39581	228-762-0870	762-5213
TF: 877-243-6178 ■ *Web:* dupont.com					
Huntsman Corp 500 Huntsman Way	Salt Lake City	UT	84108	801-584-5700	584-5781
NYSE: HUN ■ *TF:* 888-490-8484 ■ *Web:* www.huntsman.com					
ICC Industries Inc 460 Pk Ave	New York	NY	10022	212-521-1700	521-1970
TF: 800-422-1720 ■ *Web:* www.iccchem.com					
Innospec Inc 8375 S Willow St	Littleton	CO	80124	303-792-5554	
NASDAQ: IOSP ■ *Web:* www.innospecinc.com					

Phone Fax

Inolex Chemical Co 2101 S Swanson St Philadelphia PA 19148 215-271-0800 271-6282*
*Fax: Cust Svc ■ *TF Cust Svc:* 800-521-9891 ■ *Web:* www.inolex.com

International Flavors & Fragrances Inc (IFF)
521 W 57th St New York NY 10019 212-765-5500 708-7132
NYSE: IFF ■ *Web:* www.iff.com

International Specialty Products Inc (ISP)
1361 Alps Rd Wayne NJ 07470 973-628-4000
TF: 800-622-4423 ■ *Web:* www.ashland.com

Lifeline Foods LLC 2811 S 11th St Rd Saint Joseph MO 64503 816-279-1651 279-1652
Web: www.lifeline-foods.com

Methanex Corp
1800 Waterfront Centre 200 Burrard St Vancouver BC V6C3M1 604-661-2600 661-2676
TSE: MX ■ *TF:* 800-661-8851 ■ *Web:* www.methanex.com

Mitsui Chemicals America Inc
800 Westchester Ave Rye Brook NY 10573 914-253-0777 253-0790*
*Fax: PR ■ *TF:* 800-972-7252 ■ *Web:* www.mitsuichemicals.com

National Enzyme Co Inc 15366 US Hwy 160 Forsyth MO 65653 417-546-4796 546-6433
TF: 800-825-8545 ■ *Web:* www.nationalenzyme.com

Niacet Corp 400 47th St Niagara Falls NY 14304 716-285-1474 285-1497
TF: 800-828-1207 ■ *Web:* www.niacet.com

Norquay Technology Inc
800 W Front St PO Box 468 Chester PA 19013 610-874-4330 874-3575
Web: www.norquaytech.com

Oakwood Products Inc
1741 Old Dunbar Rd West Columbia SC 29172 803-739-8800 739-6957
TF: 800-467-3386 ■ *Web:* www.oakwoodchemical.com

Pencco Inc 831 Bartlett Rd PO Box 600 San Felipe TX 77473 979-885-0005 885-3208
TF: 800-864-1742 ■ *Web:* www.pencco.com

Perstorp Polyols Inc 600 Matzinger Rd Toledo OH 43612 419-729-5448 729-3291
TF Cust Svc: 800-537-0280 ■ *Web:* www.perstorp.com

PMC Specialties Group Inc 501 Murray Rd Cincinnati OH 45217 513-242-3300 482-7315
TF: 800-543-2466 ■ *Web:* www.pmcsg.com

PPG Industries Inc 1 PPG Pl Pittsburgh PA 15272 412-434-3131 434-4291*
NYSE: PPG ■ *Fax: Hum Res ■ *Web:* www.ppg.com

RT Vanderbilt Company Inc 30 Winfield St Norwalk CT 06855 203-853-1400 853-1452
TF Cust Svc: 800-243-6064 ■ *Web:* www.rtvanderbilt.com

Sachem Inc 821 Woodward St Austin TX 78704 512-444-3626 445-5066
Web: www.sacheminc.com

Sasol North America Inc
900 Threadneedle St Ste 100 Houston TX 77079 281-588-3000
Web: www.sasolnorthamerica.com

Selee Corp 700 Shepherd St Hendersonville NC 28792 828-697-2411 693-1868
TF: 800-842-3818 ■ *Web:* www.selee.com

Shell Chemical Co 910 Louisiana St Houston TX 77002 713-241-6161
Web: www.shell.com

Shin-Etsu Silicones of America 1150 Damar Dr Akron OH 44305 330-630-9860 630-9855
TF: 800-544-1745 ■ *Web:* www.shinetsusilicones.com

Struktol Company of America Inc PO Box 1649 Stow OH 44224 330-928-5188 928-8726
TF: 800-327-8649 ■ *Web:* www.struktol.com

Sun Chemical Corp 35 Waterview Blvd Parsippany NJ 07054 973-404-6000 404-6001
TF: 800-543-2323 ■ *Web:* www.sunchemical.com

Sunoco Chemicals 1735 Market St Ste LL Philadelphia PA 19103 215-977-3000 977-3409
TF: 800-786-6261

Sunoco Inc 1735 Market St Ste LL Philadelphia PA 19103 215-977-3000 977-3409
NYSE: SUN ■ *TF:* 800-786-6261 ■ *Web:* sunoco.com

Synalloy Corp
775 Spartan Blvd Ste 102 PO Box 5627 Spartanburg SC 29304 864-585-3605 596-1501
NASDAQ: SYNL ■ *TF Orders:* 800-937-5449 ■ *Web:* www.synalloy.com

Tedia Company Inc 1000 Tedia Way Fairfield OH 45014 513-874-5340 874-5346
TF: 800-787-4891 ■ *Web:* www.tedia.com

Velsicol Chemical Corp
10400 W Higgins Rd Ste 700 Rosemont IL 60018 847-813-7888 768-3227
TF Cust Svc: 877-847-8351 ■ *Web:* www.velsicol.com

Vulcan Materials Co
1200 Urban Ctr Dr PO Box 385014 Birmingham AL 35238 205-298-3000
NYSE: VMC ■ *TF:* 800-615-4331 ■ *Web:* www.vulcanmaterials.com

Wacker Chemical Corp 3301 Sutton Rd Adrian MI 49221 517-264-8500 264-8246
TF: 888-922-5374 ■ *Web:* www.wacker.com

Waterworks America Inc
5005 Rockside Rd Crown Ctr 6th Fl Independence OH 44131 440-526-4815
Web: www.1water.com

Wausau Chemical Corp 2001 N River Dr Wausau WI 54403 715-842-2285 842-9059
TF: 800-950-6656 ■ *Web:* www.wausauchemical.com

Western Polymer Corp 32 Rd 'R' SE Moses Lake WA 98837 509-765-1803 765-0327
Web: www.westernpolymer.com

Wyoming Ethanol LLC 1919 E A St Torrington WY 82240 307-532-2449 532-8964

CHEMICALS - MEDICINAL

145 CHEMICALS - SPECIALTY

Phone Fax

ADA-ES Inc
9135 S Ridgeline Blvd Ste 200 Highlands Ranch CO 80129 303-734-1727 734-0330
NASDAQ: ADES ■ *TF:* 888-822-8617 ■ *Web:* www.adaes.com

Afton Chemical Corp 500 Spring St Richmond VA 23219 804-788-5800 788-5184
Web: www.aftonchemical.com

Airosol Company Inc 1206 Illinois St Neodesha KS 66757 620-325-2666 325-2602
TF: 800-633-9576 ■ *Web:* www.airosol.com

Akzo Nobel Chemicals Inc 10 Finderne Ave Bridgewater NJ 08807 888-331-6212 707-3664*
*Fax Area Code: 908 ■ *TF:* 888-331-6212 ■ *Web:* www.akzonobel.com

Alex C Fergusson LLC (AFCO)
5000 Letterkenny Rd Chambersburg PA 17201 800-345-1329 264-9182*
*Fax Area Code: 717 ■ *TF:* 800-345-1329 ■ *Web:* www.afcocare.us

Alfa Aesar Co 26 Parkridge Rd Ward Hill MA 01835 978-521-6300 322-4757*
*Fax Area Code: 800 ■ *TF:* 800-343-0660 ■ *Web:* www.alfa.com

AM Todd Co 1717 Douglas Ave Kalamazoo MI 49007 269-343-2603 343-3399
Web: www.wildflavors.com

American Pacific Corp (AMPAC)
3883 Howard Hughes Pkwy Ste 700 Las Vegas NV 89169 702-735-2200 735-4876
NASDAQ: APFC ■ *Web:* www.apfc.com

Phone Fax

American Polywater Corp 11222 60th St N Stillwater MN 55082 651-430-2270 430-3634
TF: 800-328-9384 ■ *Web:* www.polywater.com

American Radiolabeled Chemicals Inc (ARC)
101 ARC Dr Saint Louis MO 63146 314-991-4545 991-4692
TF: 800-331-6661 ■ *Web:* www.arc-inc.com

American Vanguard Corp
4695 MacArthur Ct Newport Beach CA 92660 949-260-1200
NYSE: AVD ■ *Web:* www.american-vanguard.com

Ameron International Corp
245 S Los Robles Ave Pasadena CA 91101 626-683-4000 683-4060
Web: www.nov.com

AMPAC Fine Chemicals (AFC)
MS 1007 PO Box 1718 Rancho Cordova CA 95741 916-357-6880 353-3523
TF: 800-311-9668 ■ *Web:* www.ampacfinechemicals.com

Anderson Chemical Co 325 S Davis Litchfield MN 55355 320-693-2477 693-8238
TF: 800-366-2477 ■ *Web:* www.accomn.com

Anderson Development Co 1415 E Michigan St Adrian MI 49221 517-263-2121 263-1000
Web: www.andersondevelopment.com

Angstrom Technologies Inc
7880 Foundation Dr Florence KY 41042 859-282-0020 282-8577
TF Cust Svc: 800-543-7358 ■ *Web:* www.angtech.com

Apollo Chemical Company LLC
1105 Southerland St Graham NC 27253 336-226-1161 226-7494
Web: www.apollochemical.com

Arch Chemicals Inc
1200 Old Lower River Rd PO Box 800 Charleston TN 37310 423-780-2724 780-2330
NYSE: ARJ ■ *TF:* 800-638-8174 ■ *Web:* lonza.com

Ashland Specialty Chemical Co
1745 Cottage St Ashland OH 44805 419-289-9588
Web: www.ashland.com

Athea Laboratories Inc 1900 W Cornell St Milwaukee WI 53209 800-743-6417 354-9219*
*Fax Area Code: 414 ■ *TF:* 800-743-6417 ■ *Web:* www.athea.com

Atlas Refinery Inc 142 Lockwood St Newark NJ 07105 973-589-2002 589-7377
Web: www.atlasrefinery.com

Baker Hughes Inc Baker Petrolite Div
12645 W Airport Blvd Sugar Land TX 77478 281-276-5400 275-7392*
*Fax: Hum Res ■ *TF:* 800-231-3606 ■ *Web:* www.bakerhughes.com

Barclay Water Management Inc 55 Chapel St Newton MA 02458 617-926-3400 924-5467
Web: www.barclaywm.com

Bedoukian Research Inc 21 Finance Dr Danbury CT 06810 203-830-4000 830-4010
Web: www.bedoukian.com

Berje Inc 700 Blair Rd Bloomfield NJ 07003 973-748-8980 680-9618
Web: www.berjeinc.com

Birchwood Laboratories Inc
7900 Fuller Rd Eden Prairie MN 55344 952-937-7900 937-7979
TF: 800-328-6156 ■ *Web:* www.birchwoodcasey.com

Blue Grass Chemical Specialties LP
895 Industrial Blvd New Albany IN 47150 812-948-1115 948-1561

Brulin & Company Inc
2920 Dr AJ Brown Ave Indianapolis IN 46205 317-923-3211 925-4596
TF: 800-776-7149 ■ *Web:* www.brulin.com

Buckman Laboratories Inc 1256 N McLean Blvd Memphis TN 38108 901-278-0330
TF: 800-282-5626 ■ *Web:* www.buckman.com

Cabot Corp 2 Seaport Ln Ste 1300 Boston MA 02210 617-345-0100 342-6103
NYSE: CBT ■ *TF:* 800-322-1236 ■ *Web:* www.cabotcorp.com

Cabot Microelectronics Corp 870 N Commons Dr Aurora IL 60504 630-375-6631 375-5539
NASDAQ: CCMP ■ *TF:* 800-811-2756 ■ *Web:* www.cabotcmp.com

Cabot Specialty Fluids Inc
Waterway Plaza Two 10001 Woodlock Forest Dr
Ste 275 The Woodlands TX 77380 281-298-9955 298-6190
TF: 800-322-1236 ■
Web: www.cabotcorp.com/solutions/products-plus/cesium-formate-brines

Cal-Pac Chemical Company Inc
6231 Maywood Ave Huntington Park CA 90255 323-585-2178
Web: cal-pac-chemicals.com

Cambridge Isotope Laboratories Inc
3 Highwood Dr Tewksbury MA 01876 978-749-8000 749-2768
TF: 800-322-1174 ■ *Web:* www.isotope.com

Chemtool Inc 801 W Rockton Rd Rockton IL 61072 815-459-1250
Web: www.chemtool.com

Chemtronics Inc 8125 Cobb Centre Dr Kennesaw GA 30152 770-424-4888
TF: 800-645-5244 ■ *Web:* www.chemtronics.com

Chippewa Valley Ethanol Company LLC
270 20th St NW Benson MN 56215 320-843-4813 843-4800
Web: www.cvec.com

CHT R Beitlich Corp 5046 Old Pineville Rd Charlotte NC 28217 704-523-4242

Citrus & Allied Essences Ltd
3000 Marcus Ave Ste 3E11 Lake Success NY 11042 516-354-1200 354-1262
Web: www.citrusandallied.com

Claire Manufacturing Co 1005 S Westgate Ave Addison IL 60101 630-543-7600 543-4310
TF Sales: 800-252-4731 ■ *Web:* www.clairemfg.com

Columbian Chemicals Co
1800 W Oak Commons Ct Marietta GA 30062 770-792-9400
TF: 800-235-4003 ■ *Web:* www.birlacarbon.com

Coral Chemical Co 1915 Industrial Ave Zion IL 60099 847-246-6666 246-6667
TF: 800-228-4646 ■ *Web:* www.coral.com

Cortec Corp 4119 White Bear Pkwy Saint Paul MN 55110 651-429-1100 429-1122
TF: 800-426-7832 ■ *Web:* www.cortecvci.com

CPC Aeroscience Inc 2700 SW 14th St Pompano Beach FL 33069 800-327-1835 977-7513*
*Fax Area Code: 954 ■ *TF Cust Svc:* 800-327-1835 ■ *Web:* cpcaeroscience.com

CRC Industries Inc 885 Louis Dr Warminster PA 18974 215-674-4300 674-2196
TF Cust Svc: 800-556-5074 ■ *Web:* www.crcindustries.com

Croda Inc 300 Columbus Cir Ste A Edison NJ 08837 732-417-0800 417-0804
Web: www.croda.com

Cytec Industries Inc 5 Garret Mtn Plz West Paterson NJ 07424 973-357-3100 357-3060
NYSE: CYT ■ *TF:* 800-652-6013 ■ *Web:* www.cytec.com

Delta Chemical Corp 2601 Cannery Ave Baltimore MD 21226 410-354-0100 354-1021
TF: 800-282-5322 ■ *Web:* www.usalco.com

Detrex Corp 24901 NW Hwy Ste 410 Southfield MI 48075 248-358-5800 799-7192
Web: www.detrex.com

Diversified Chemical Technologies Inc (DCT)
15477 Woodrow Wilson St Detroit MI 48238 313-867-5444 867-3831
TF: 800-243-1424 ■ *Web:* www.dchem.com

Company	City	State	Zip	Phone	Fax
Dober Chemical Group 11230 Katherine Crossing Ste 100 *TF:* 800-323-4983 ■ *Web:* www.dobergroup.com	Woodridge	IL	60517	630-410-7300	410-7444
Dover Chemical Corp 3676 Davis Rd NW *TF General:* 800-321-8805 ■ *Web:* www.doverchem.com	Dover	OH	44622	330-343-7711	365-3927
Dow Chemical Co, The 100 Independence Mall W *Web:* www.dow.com	Philadelphia	PA	19106	215-592-3000	
DSM Desotech Inc 1122 St Charles St **Fax:* Sales ■ *TF:* 800-222-7189 ■ *Web:* www.dsm.com	Elgin	IL	60120	847-697-0400	468-7785*
DuPont Chemical Solutions 1007 Market St *TF:* 800-441-7515 ■ *Web:* www.dupont.com	Wilmington	DE	19898	302-774-1000	355-4013
Dynaloy LLC 6445 Olivia Ln *TF:* 800-669-5709 ■ *Web:* www.dynaloy.com	Indianapolis	IN	46226	317-788-5694	788-5690
Elantas PDG Inc 5200 N Second St *TF:* 800-325-7492 ■ *Web:* www.elantas.com	Saint Louis	MO	63147	314-621-5700	436-1030
Enthone Inc 350 Frontage Rd *TF:* 800-431-2200 ■ *Web:* www.enthone.com	West Haven	CT	06516	203-934-8611	799-1513
Excelda Manufacturing Co 12785 Emerson Dr *TF:* 877-486-3801 ■ *Web:* www.excelda.com	Brighton	MI	48116	248-486-3800	486-3810
Foseco Metallurgical Inc 20200 Sheldon Rd *Web:* www.foseco.com	Cleveland	OH	44142	440-826-4548	243-7658
Frac Tech Services LLC 301 E 18th St *TF:* 866-877-1008 ■ *Web:* www.ftsi.com	Cisco	TX	76437	817-850-1008	
Freezetone Products Inc 7986 NW 14th St *Web:* www.freezetone-usa.com	Doral	FL	33126	305-640-0414	
Fremont Industries Inc 4400 Vly Industrial Blvd N PO Box 67 *TF:* 800-436-1238 ■ *Web:* www.fremontind.com	Shakopee	MN	55379	952-445-4121	496-3027
GE Betz 4636 Somerton Rd *TF Cust Svc:* 866-439-2837 ■ *Web:* www.gewater.com	Trevose	PA	19053	215-355-3300	
Genieco Inc 200 N Laflin St *TF:* 800-223-8217 ■ *Web:* gonesh.com	Chicago	IL	60607	312-421-2383	421-3042
GEO Specialty Chemicals Inc 401 S Earl Ave *Web:* www.geosc.com	Lafayette	IN	47904	765-448-9412	
Gold Eagle Co 4400 S Kildare Ave **Fax Area Code:* 773 ■ *TF:* 800-367-3245 ■ *Web:* www.goldeagle.com	Chicago	IL	60632	800-367-3245	376-5749*
Goulston Technologies Inc 700 N Johnson St *Web:* www.goulston.com	Monroe	NC	28110	704-289-6464	296-6400
Grace Davison 7500 Grace Dr *TF:* 800-638-6014 ■ *Web:* www.grace.com	Columbia	MD	21044	410-531-4000	531-4197
H Krevit & Company Inc 73 Welton St *Web:* www.hkrevit.com	New Haven	CT	06511	203-772-3350	
Harcros Chemicals Inc 5200 Speaker Rd *Web:* harcros.com	Kansas City	KS	66106	913-321-3131	621-7718
Hexion Specialty Chemicals Inc 180 E Broad St *Web:* www.momentive.com	Columbus	OH	43215	614-225-4000	
Hitachi Chemical Company America Ltd 10080 N Wolfe Rd Ste SW3-200 *Web:* www.hitachi-chemical.com	Cupertino	CA	95014	408-873-2200	873-2284
Honeywell 101 Columbia Rd *TF:* 800-822-7673 ■ *Web:* www.honeywell.com	Morristown	NJ	07960	973-455-2000	455-4807
Honeywell Fluorine Products 101 Columbia Rd *TF:* 800-951-1527 ■ *Web:* honeywell.com/pages/redirect.aspx?redirectid=179	Morristown	NJ	07962	973-455-2000	
Houghton Chemical Corp 52 Cambridge St *TF:* 800-777-2466 ■ *Web:* www.houghton.com	Allston	MA	02134	617-254-1010	
Hybrid Plastics 55 WL Runnels Industrial Dr *Web:* www.hybridplastics.com	Hattiesburg	MS	39401	601-544-3466	545-3103
I-K-I Mfg Company Inc 116 Swift St *Web:* www.ikimfg.com	Edgerton	WI	53534	608-884-3411	884-4712
ICC Chemicals 4660 Spring Grove Ave *Web:* www.icc-chemicals.com	Cincinnati	OH	45232	513-541-7100	541-6880
International Chemical Co 2628 N Mascher St *TF:* 888-225-5422 ■ *Web:* www.e-icc.com	Philadelphia	PA	19133	215-739-2313	423-7171
JM Huber Corp 499 Thornall St 8th Fl **Fax:* Hum Res ■ *TF:* 877-418-0038 ■ *Web:* www.huber.com	Edison	NJ	08837	732-549-8600	549-2239*
Kao Specialties Americas LLC 243 Woodbine St PO Box 2316 *TF:* 800-727-2214 ■ *Web:* chemical.kao.com	High Point	NC	27261	336-884-2214	884-8786
Kester Inc 800 W Thorndale Ave *TF:* 800-253-7837 ■ *Web:* www.kester.com	Itasca	IL	60143	630-616-4000	616-4044
KIK Custom Products 2730 Middlebury St *TF:* 800-479-6603 ■ *Web:* www.kikcorp.com	Elkhart	IN	46516	574-295-0000	296-1700
KIK Pool Additives Inc 5160 E Airport Dr *TF:* 800-745-4536 ■ *Web:* www.kem-tek.com	Ontario	CA	91761	909-390-9912	390-9911
King Industries Inc 1 Science Rd *TF:* 800-431-7900 ■ *Web:* www.kingindustries.com	Norwalk	CT	06852	203-866-5551	866-1268
KMCO LP 16503 Ramsey Rd *Web:* www.kmcoinc.com	Crosby	TX	77532	281-272-4100	328-9528
Kolene Corp 12890 Westwood Ave *TF:* 800-521-4182 ■ *Web:* www.kolene.com	Detroit	MI	48223	313-273-9220	273-5207
Koppers Inc 436 Seventh Ave *NYSE: KOP* ■ *TF:* 800-385-4406 ■ *Web:* www.koppers.com	Pittsburgh	PA	15219	412-227-2001	227-2333
Kronos Worldwide Inc 5430 LBJ Freeway Ste 1700 *NYSE: KRO* ■ *TF:* 800-866-5600 ■ *Web:* www.kronostio2.com	Houston	TX	75240	281-423-3300	423-3258
Leadership Performance Sustainability Laboratories 4647 Hugh Howell Rd **Fax Area Code:* 770 ■ *TF:* 800-241-8334 ■ *Web:* www.lpslabs.com	Tucker	GA	30084	800-241-8334	243-8899*
Lloyd Laboratories Inc 24 Fitch Ct *TF:* 800-361-6766	Wakefield	MA	01880	781-224-0083	
Lubrizol Corp 29400 Lakeland Blvd *NYSE: LZ* ■ *TF:* 800-380-5397 ■ *Web:* www.lubrizol.com	Wickliffe	OH	44092	440-943-4200	943-5337
MacDermid Inc 245 Freight St *Web:* www.macdermid.com	Waterbury	CT	06702	203-575-5700	
McGean-Rohco Inc 2910 Harvard Ave *TF Orders:* 800-932-7006 ■ *Web:* www.mcgean.com	Cleveland	OH	44105	216-441-4900	441-1377
Micro Powders Inc 580 White Plains Rd *Web:* www.micropowders.com	Tarrytown	NY	10591	914-793-4058	472-7098
Microchem Corp 90 Oak St *Web:* www.microchem.com	Newton	MA	02464	617-965-5511	965-5818
Milacron Inc 3010 Disney St *Web:* www.milacron.com	Cincinnati	OH	45209	513-487-5000	487-5086
Miller-Stephenson Chemical Co 55 Backus Ave *TF Tech Supp:* 800-992-2424 ■ *Web:* www.miller-stephenson.com	Danbury	CT	06810	203-743-4447	791-8702
Momar Inc 1830 Ellsworth Industrial Dr **Fax Area Code:* 800 ■ *TF:* 800-556-3967 ■ *Web:* www.momar.com	Atlanta	GA	30318	404-355-4580	849-5684*
Monroe Fluid Technology Inc 36 Draffin Rd *TF:* 800-828-6351 ■ *Web:* www.monroefluid.com	Hilton	NY	14468	585-392-3434	392-2691
Montana Sulphur & Chemical Co PO Box 31118 *Web:* www.montanasulphur.com	Billings	MT	59107	406-252-9324	252-8250
Montello Inc 6106 E 32nd Pl Ste 100 **Fax Area Code:* 918 ■ *TF:* 800-331-4628 ■ *Web:* www.montelloinc.com	Tulsa	OK	74135	800-331-4628	665-1480*
Moses Lake Industries Inc 8248 Randolph Rd NE *Web:* www.mlindustries.com	Moses Lake	WA	98837	509-762-5336	762-5981
Multisorb Technologies Inc 325 Harlem Rd *Web:* www.multisorb.com	Buffalo	NY	14224	716-824-8900	824-4128
Nalco Co 1601 W Diehl Rd *TF:* 800-288-0879 ■ *Web:* www.nalco.com	Naperville	IL	60563	630-305-1000	305-2900
Nanophase Technologies Corp 1319 Marquette Dr *OTC: NANX* ■ *Web:* www.nanophase.com	Romeoville	IL	60446	630-771-6700	771-0825
Northern Technologies International Corp (NTIC) 4201 Woodland Rd *NASDAQ: NTIC* ■ *Web:* natur-tec.com	Circle Pines	MN	55014	763-225-6600	
Nox-Crete Inc 1444 S 20th St *TF:* 800-669-2738 ■ *Web:* www.nox-crete.com	Omaha	NE	68108	402-341-2080	341-9752
OM Group Inc 811 Sharon Dr *NYSE: OMG* ■ *TF:* 800-519-0083	Westlake	OH	44145	440-899-2950	808-7114
OMNOVA Solutions Inc 175 Ghent Rd *NYSE: OMN* ■ *Web:* www.omnova.com	Fairlawn	OH	44333	330-869-4200	
OMNOVA Solutions Inc Performance Chemicals Div 165 S Cleveland Ave *TF:* 888-253-5454 ■ *Web:* www.omnova.com	Mogadore	OH	44260	330-628-6536	
Ortec Inc 505 Gentry Memorial Hwy PO Box 1469 *Web:* www.ortecinc.com	Easley	SC	29641	864-859-1471	859-8580
Pacific Ethanol Corp 400 Capitol Mall Ste 2060 *NASDAQ: PEIX* ■ *TF:* 866-508-4969 ■ *Web:* www.pacificethanol.net	Sacramento	CA	95814	916-403-2123	446-3937
Pavco Inc 1935 John Crosland Jr Dr *TF Orders:* 800-321-7735 ■ *Web:* www.pavco.com	Charlotte	NC	28208	704-496-6800	496-6810
Peach State Labs Inc (PSL) 180 Burlington Rd PO Box 1087 *TF:* 800-634-1653 ■ *Web:* www.peachstatelabs.com	Rome	GA	30162	706-291-8743	921-4888
Penford Corp 7094 S Revere Pkwy *NASDAQ: PENX*	Centennial	CO	80112	303-649-1900	649-1700
Peninsula Copper Industries Inc (PCI) 220 Calumet St *Web:* www.pencopper.com	Lake Linden	MI	49945	906-296-9918	296-9484
Penray Cos Inc 440 Denniston Ct *TF:* 800-373-6729 ■ *Web:* www.penray.com	Wheeling	IL	60090	847-459-5000	459-5043
PMC Global Inc 12243 Branford St *Web:* www.pmcglobalinc.com	Sun Valley	CA	91352	818-896-1101	686-2531
Precision Laboratories Inc 1429 S Shields Dr *TF:* 800-323-6280 ■ *Web:* www.precisionlab.com	Waukegan	IL	60085	847-596-3001	596-3017
Premier Colors Inc 100 Industrial Dr *TF:* 800-245-6944 ■ *Web:* www.premiercolorsinc.com	Union	SC	29379	864-427-0338	427-5824
PVS Chemicals Inc 10900 Harper Ave *TF:* 800-932-8860 ■ *Web:* www.pvschemicals.com	Detroit	MI	48213	313-921-1200	921-1378
Quaker Chemical Corp 901 Hector St *NYSE: KWR* ■ *TF:* 800-523-7010 ■ *Web:* quakerchem.com	Conshohocken	PA	19428	610-832-4000	832-8682
Qualitek International Inc 315 Fairbank St *Web:* www.qualitek.com	Addison	IL	60101	630-628-8083	628-6543
Radiator Specialty Co 1900 Wilkinson Blvd *TF:* 877-464-4865 ■ *Web:* www.gunk.com	Charlotte	NC	28208	704-688-2405	
Rentech Inc 10877 Wilshire Blvd 10th Fl *NASDAQ: RTK* ■ *Web:* www.rentechinc.com	Los Angeles	CA	90024	310-571-9800	571-9799
Rochester Midland Corp 333 Hollenbeck St *TF:* 800-836-1627 ■ *Web:* www.rochestermidland.com	Rochester	NY	14621	585-336-2200	467-4406
Roebic Laboratories Inc 25 Connair Rd PO Box 927 *Web:* www.roebic.com	Orange	CT	06477	203-795-1283	795-5227
Royal Chemical Co 1755 Enterprise Pkwy Ste 600	Twinsburg	OH	44087	330-467-1300	405-0975
SA Day Mfg Co Inc 1489 Niagara St *TF:* 800-747-0030 ■ *Web:* www.saday.com	Buffalo	NY	14213	716-881-3030	881-4353
Senomyx Inc 4767 Nexus Centre Dr *NASDAQ: SNMX* ■ *Web:* www.senomyx.com	San Diego	CA	92121	858-646-8300	404-0752
Sid Richardson Carbon & Energy Cos 201 Main St *Web:* www.sidrich.com	Fort Worth	TX	76102	817-390-8600	
Sigma-Aldrich Corp 3050 Spruce St *NASDAQ: SIAL* ■ **Fax Area Code:* 800 ■ *TF:* 800-325-3010 ■ *Web:* www.sigmaaldrich.com	Saint Louis	MO	63103	314-771-5765	325-5052*
Sika Corp 201 Polito Ave *TF:* 800-933-7452 ■ *Web:* www.usa.sika.com	Lyndhurst	NJ	07071	201-933-8800	
Solutek Corp 94 Shirley St *TF:* 800-403-0770 ■ *Web:* www.solutekcorporation.com	Boston	MA	02119	617-445-5335	445-9623
Spartan Chemical Company Inc 1110 Spartan Dr *TF:* 800-537-8990 ■ *Web:* www.spartanchemical.com	Maumee	OH	43537	419-531-5551	536-8423
Specco Industries Inc 13087 Main St *TF:* 800-441-6646 ■ *Web:* www.specco.com	Lemont	IL	60439	630-257-5060	257-9006
Spectra Gases Inc 1 Greenwich St *Web:* www.lindepremiumproducts.com	Stewartsville	NJ	08886	908-329-9700	329-9740
Sprayway Inc 1005 S Westgate Ave *TF:* 800-332-9000 ■ *Web:* www.spraywayinc.com	Addison	IL	60101	630-628-3000	543-7797
Stapleton Technologies Inc 1350 W 12th St *TF:* 800-266-0541 ■ *Web:* www.stapletontech.com	Long Beach	CA	90813	562-437-0541	437-8632

Phone Fax

Stepan Co 22 W Frontage Rd .... Northfield IL 60093 847-446-7500 501-2100
TF Cust Svc: 800-745-7837 ■ *Web:* www.stepan.com

Sunland Chemical & Research Corp
5447 San Fernando Rd W .... Los Angeles CA 90039 818-244-9600
Web: www.sunlandchemical.com

Symrise Inc 300 N St .... Teterboro NJ 07608 201-288-3200 462-2200
Web: www.symrise.com

Technic Inc 47 Molter St .... Cranston RI 02910 401-781-6100 781-2890
Web: www.technic.com

Technical Chemical Co 3327 Pipeline Rd .... Cleburne TX 76033 817-645-6088 556-0694
TF: 800-527-0885 ■ *Web:* www.technicalchemical.com

United Color Manufacturing Inc (UCM) PO Box 480 ... Newtown PA 18940 215-860-2165 860-8560
TF: 800-852-5942 ■ *Web:* www.unitedcolor.com

United Laboratories Inc 320 37th Ave .... Saint Charles IL 60174 800-323-2594 443-2087*
**Fax Area Code:* 630 ■ *TF:* 800-323-2594 ■ *Web:* www.unitedlabsinc.com

United Salt Corp 4800 San Felipe St .... Houston TX 77056 713-877-2600 877-2609
TF: 800-554-8658 ■ *Web:* www.unitedsalt.com

Univertical Corp 203 Weatherhead St .... Angola IN 46703 260-665-1500 665-1400
Web: www.univertical.com

Vertellus Specialties Inc
201 N Illinois St Ste 1800 .... Indianapolis IN 46204 317-247-8141 248-6402
TF: 800-777-3536 ■ *Web:* www.vertellus.com

Watcon Inc 2215 S Main St .... South Bend IN 46613 574-287-3397 287-2427
TF: 800-492-8266 ■ *Web:* www.watcon-inc.com

WestRock Co 5255 Virginia Ave .... North Charleston SC 29406 843-740-2300 740-2147
Web: www.mwv.com:80/en-us

WR Grace & Co 7500 Grace Dr .... Columbia MD 21044 410-531-4000 531-4367
NYSE: GRA ■ *TF:* 800-638-6014 ■ *Web:* www.grace.com

XL Brands 198 Nexus Dr .... Dalton GA 30721 706-272-5800 272-5801
TF: 800-367-4583 ■ *Web:* www.xlbrands.com

Zinkan Enterprises Inc 1919 Case Pkwy N .... Twinsburg OH 44087 800-229-6801 425-8202*
**Fax Area Code:* 330 ■ *TF:* 800-229-6801 ■ *Web:* www.zinkan.com

146 CHEMICALS & RELATED PRODUCTS - WHOL

Phone Fax

Advanced Polymers Inc
400 Paterson Plank Rd .... Carlstadt NJ 07072 201-933-0600
Web: www.advpolymer.com

Airgas Inc 259 N Radnor-Chester Rd Ste 100 .... Radnor PA 19087 610-687-5253 687-1052
NYSE: ARG ■ *TF:* 800-255-2165 ■ *Web:* www.airgas.com

Airgas Refrigerants Inc
2530 Sever Rd Ste 300 .... Lawrenceville GA 30043 770-717-2210
Web: www.airgasrefrigerants.com

Americas Styrenics LLC
24 Waterway Ave Ste 1200 .... Woodlands TX 77380 844-512-1212
TF: 844-512-1212 ■ *Web:* www.amstyrenics.com

Amfine Chemical Corp
10 Montnview Rd Ste 215N .... Upper Saddle River NJ 07458 201-818-0159 818-0259
Web: www.amfine.com

Anitox Corp 1055 Progress Cir .... Lawrenceville GA 30043 678-376-1055
Web: www.anitox.com

Aquatic Informatics Inc
570 Granville St Ste 1100 .... Vancouver BC V6C3P1 604-873-2782
TF: 877-870-2782 ■ *Web:* aquaticinformatics.com

Aramsco Inc 1480 Grandview Ave .... Paulsboro NJ 08086 856-686-7700
TF: 800-767-6933 ■ *Web:* www.aramsco.com

Ashland Distribution Co
5200 Blazer Pkwy PO Box 2219 .... Columbus OH 43216 614-790-3333
Web: www.ashland.com

Astro Chemicals Inc 126 Memorial Dr .... Springfield MA 01104 413-781-7240 781-7246
TF: 800-223-0776 ■ *Web:* www.astrochemicals.com

Austin Chemical Company Inc
1565 Barclay Blvd .... Buffalo Grove IL 60089 847-520-9600 520-9160
Web: www.austinchemical.com

Avchem Inc 5757 Phantom Dr Ste 300 .... Hazelwood MO 63042 314-880-2700
Web: www.avchem.com

B & b Medical Services Inc
5401 S Sheridan Rd Ste 204 .... Tulsa OK 74145 405-235-9548
Web: www.bandbmedical.com

B&P Process Equipment & Systems LLC
1000 Hess Ave .... Saginaw MI 48601 989-757-1300
Web: www.bpprocess.com

Barton Solvents Inc 1920 NE Broadway Ave .... Des Moines IA 50313 515-265-7998 265-0259
TF: 800-728-6488 ■ *Web:* www.barsol.com

Berryman Products Inc
3800 E Randol Mill Rd .... Arlington TX 76011 817-640-2376 640-4850
TF: 800-433-1704 ■ *Web:* www.berrymanproducts.com

Birko Corp 9152 Yosemite St .... Henderson CO 80640 303-289-1090
Web: www.birkocorp.com

Blendco Systems LLC 1 Pearl Buck Ct .... Bristol PA 19007 215-781-3600
Web: www.blendco.com

Boral Material Technologies Inc
45 NE Loop 410 Ste 700 .... San Antonio TX 78216 210-349-4069
Web: www.boralmti.com

Brandt Technologies Inc 231 W Grand Ave .... Bensenville IL 60106 630-787-1800
Web: www.brandttech.com

Brenntag Canada Inc 35 Vulcan St .... Rexdale ON M9W1L3 416-243-9615 243-9731
TF: 866-516-9707 ■ *Web:* www.brenntag.ca/en

Brenntag Mid-South Inc 1405 Hwy 136 W .... Henderson KY 42419 270-830-1200 827-3990*
**Fax:* Hum Res ■ *Web:* www.brenntagmid-south.com

Brenntag North America Inc
5083 Pottsville Pk PO Box 13786 .... Reading PA 19605 610-926-6100
Web: www.brenntag.com

Brenntag Northeast Inc 81 W Huller Ln .... Reading PA 19605 610-926-4151 926-4160
Web: www.brenntag.com/north-america/en/our-company/why-brenntag/regional-operating-companies/brenntag-northeast/index.jsp

Brenntag Southeast Inc 5083 Pottsville Pike .... Durham NC 27703 610-926-6100
Web: www.brenntagmid-south.com

Brenntag Southwest Inc 610 Fisher Rd .... Longview TX 75604 903-759-7151 759-3145
TF: 800-945-4528 ■
Web: www.brenntag.com/north-america/en/our-company/why-brenntag/regional-operating-companies/brenntag-southwest/index.jsp

Brown Machine LLC 330 N Ross St .... Beaverton MI 48612 989-435-7741
TF: 877-702-4142 ■ *Web:* www.brown-machine.com

Bulk Chemicals Inc 1074 Stinson Dr .... Reading PA 19605 610-926-4128
Web: www.bulkchemicals.com

Cal-Chlor Corp 627 Jefferson St .... Lafayette LA 70501 337-264-1449 264-9359
Web: www.cal-chlor.com

Callahan Chemical Co Broad St & Filmore Ave .... Palmyra NJ 08065 201-440-9000
Web: www.calchem.com

Canada Colors & Chemicals Ltd
175 Bloor St E Ste 1300 N Twr .... Toronto ON M4W3R8 416-443-5500 449-9039
Web: www.ccc-group.com

Canpotex Ltd
111 Second Ave S Ste 400 PO Box 1600 .... Saskatoon SK S7K3R7 306-931-2200 653-5505
Web: www.canpotex.com

Cardinal Color Inc 50 First Ave .... Paterson NJ 07524 973-684-1919 684-0865
Web: www.cardinalcolor.com

Centerchem Inc
20 Glover Ave Merritt On The River .... Norwalk CT 06850 203-822-9800
Web: www.centerchem.com

Charkit Chemical Corp 32 Haviland St Unit 1 .... Norwalk CT 06854 203-299-3220 299-1355
Web: www.charkit.com

Chempacific Corp 6200 Freeport Ctr .... Baltimore MD 21224 410-633-5771
Web: www.chempacific.com

Chemroy Canada Inc 106 Summerlea Rd .... Brampton ON L6T4X3 905-789-0701 789-7170
Web: www.chemroy.com

Chemsolv Inc 1140 Industry Ave SE .... Roanoke VA 24013 540-427-4000 427-3207
Web: www.chemsolv.com

Chemtura USA Corp 199 Benson Rd .... Middlebury CT 06749 203-573-2000
Web: chemtura.com

ClearTech Industries Inc
2302 Hanselman Ave .... Saskatoon SK S7L5Z3 306-664-2522
Web: www.cleartech.ca

Cole Chemical & Distributing Inc
1500 S Dairy Ashford St Ste 450 .... Houston TX 77077 713-465-2653 461-3462
Web: www.colechem.com

Connell Bros Co Ltd
345 California St 27th Fl .... San Francisco CA 94104 415-772-4000 772-4100
TF: 800-210-9839 ■ *Web:* www.connellbrothers.com

Coolant Control Inc 5353 Spring Grove Ave .... Cincinnati OH 45217 513-471-8770
TF: 800-535-3885 ■ *Web:* www.coolantcontrol.com

Dar-tech Inc 16485 Rockside Rd .... Cleveland OH 44137 216-663-7600 663-8007
TF: 800-228-7347 ■ *Web:* www.dar-tech.com

DB Becker Company Inc 46 Leigh St .... Clinton NJ 08809 908-730-6010 730-9118
TF: 800-394-3991 ■ *Web:* www.dbbecker.com

Denso North America Inc 9747 Whithorn Dr .... Houston TX 77095 281-821-3355
TF: 888-821-2300 ■ *Web:* www.densona.com

DM Figley Company Inc 10 Kelly Ct .... Menlo Park CA 94025 650-329-8700 329-0601
TF: 800-292-9919 ■ *Web:* www.dmfigley.com

Dorsett & Jackson Inc 3800 Noakes St .... Los Angeles CA 90023 323-268-1815 268-9082
TF: 800-871-8365 ■ *Web:* www.dorsettandjackson.com

Durr Marketing Assoc Inc PO Box 17600 .... Pittsburgh PA 15235 800-937-3877 829-7680*
**Fax Area Code:* 412 ■ *TF:* 800-937-3877 ■ *Web:* www.durrmarketing.com

Ellsworth Corp PO Box 1002 .... Germantown WI 53022 262-253-8600 253-8619
TF: 877-454-9224 ■ *Web:* www.ellsworth.com

EMCO Chemical Distributors Inc
2100 Commonwealth Ave .... North Chicago IL 60064 847-689-2200
Web: www.emcochem.com

ET Horn Co 16050 Canary Ave .... La Mirada CA 90638 714-523-8050 670-6851
TF: 800-442-4676 ■ *Web:* www.ethorn.com

Evonik Corp 299 Jefferson Rd .... Parsippany NJ 07054 973-929-8000
Web: corporate.evonik.us/region/north_america/en/pages/default.aspx

EW Kaufmann Co 140 Wharton Rd .... Bristol PA 19007 215-364-0240 364-4397
TF: 800-635-5358 ■ *Web:* www.ewkaufmann.com

Expo Chemical Company Inc
6807 Theall Rd Ste A .... Houston TX 77066 281-895-9200
Web: expochem.com

Expro Americas LLC 738 Hwy 6 S Ste 1000 .... Houston TX 77079 281-994-1158
Web: www.kinley.com

Fitz Chem Corp 450 E Devon Ave Ste 175 .... Itasca IL 60143 630-467-8383 467-1183
Web: www.fitzchem.com

Francis Drilling Fluids Ltd 240 Jasmine Rd .... Crowley LA 70526 337-783-8685
Web: www.fdfltd.com

FutureFuel Corp 8235 Forsyth Blvd 4th Fl .... Clayton MO 63105 805-565-9800
NYSE: FF ■ *Web:* www.futurefuelcorporation.com

Gallade Chemical Inc 1230 E St Gertrude Pl .... Santa Ana CA 92707 714-546-9901 546-2501
TF: 888-830-9092 ■ *Web:* www.galladechem.com

General Air Service & Supply Company Inc
1105 Zuni St .... Denver CO 80204 303-892-7003 595-9036
TF: 877-782-8434 ■ *Web:* www.generalair.com

George S Coyne Chemical Co 3015 State Rd .... Croydon PA 19021 215-785-3000 785-1585
TF: 800-523-1230 ■ *Web:* www.coynechemical.com

GJ Chemical Co 370-376 Adams St .... Newark NJ 07105 973-589-1450 589-5786
Web: www.gjchemical.com

Grignard Company LLC 505 Capobianco Plz .... Rahway NJ 07065 732-340-1111
Web: www.grignard.com

GTC Technology Inc
1001 S Dairy Ashford Ste 500 .... Houston TX 77077 281-597-4800
Web: gtctech.com

Hand Industries/Dirilyte Line 315 S Hand Ave .... Warsaw IN 46580 574-267-3525 267-7349
Web: www.handindustries.com

Harcros Chemicals Inc 5200 Speaker Rd .... Kansas City KS 66106 913-321-3131 621-7718
Web: harcros.com

Hardide Coatings Inc 440 Louisiana St .... Houston TX 77002 713-221-9020
Web: www.hardide.com

Haviland Enterprises Inc 421 Ann St NW .... Grand Rapids MI 49504 616-361-6691 361-9772
TF: 800-456-1134 ■ *Web:* www.havilandusa.com

Helm US Chemical Corp 1110 Centennial Ave .... Piscataway NJ 08854 732-981-1116 981-0528
Web: www.helmus.com

Company	City	State	ZIP	Phone	Fax
Hill Bros Chemical Co 1675 N Main St	Orange	CA	92867	714-998-8800	998-6310
TF: 800-994-8801 ■ *Web:* www.hillbrothers.com					
HM Royal Inc 689 Pennington Ave	Trenton	NJ	08618	609-396-9176	396-3185
TF: 800-257-9452 ■ *Web:* www.hmroyal.com					
Homax Products Inc 1835 Barkley Blvd	Bellingham	WA	98226	360-733-9029	
Web: www.homaxproducts.com					
Hubbard-Hall Inc 563 S Leonard St	Waterbury	CT	06708	203-756-5521	756-9017
TF: 800-331-6871 ■ *Web:* www.hubbardhall.com					
Hydrite Chemical Co 300 N Patrick Blvd	Brookfield	WI	53045	262-792-1450	792-8721
TF: 800-543-4560 ■ *Web:* www.hydrite.com					
ICC Chemical Corp 460 Pk Ave	New York	NY	10022	212-521-1700	521-1970
TF: 800-422-1720 ■ *Web:* www.iccchem.com					
Ideal Chemical & Supply Co 4025 Air Pk St	Memphis	TN	38118	901-363-7720	366-0864
TF: 800-232-6776 ■ *Web:* www.idealchemical.com					
Independent Chemical Corp 79-51 Cooper Ave	Glendale	NY	11385	718-894-0700	894-9224
TF: 800-892-2578 ■ *Web:* www.independentchemical.com					
Industrial Chemicals Inc 2042 Montreat Dr	Vestavia	AL	35216	205-823-7330	978-0485
TF Cust Svc: 800-476-2042 ■ *Web:* www.industrialchem.com					
Innophos Holdings Inc 259 Prospect Plains Rd	Cranbury	NJ	08512	609-495-2495	
NASDAQ: IPHS ■ *Web:* www.innophos.com					
InnoVactiv Inc 2 St-Germain St E Ste 200	Rimouski	QC	G5L8T7	418-721-2308	
Web: www.innovactiv.com					
INTERCAT Inc 2399 Hwy 34 Ramshorn Executive Ctr Ste C-1	Manasquan	NJ	08736	732-223-4644	
John R Hess & Company Inc 400 Stn St PO Box 3615	Cranston	RI	02910	401-785-9300	785-2510
TF: 800-828-4377 ■ *Web:* www.jrhessco.com					
John R White Company Inc PO Box 10043	Birmingham	AL	35202	205-595-8381	595-8386
TF: 800-245-1183 ■ *Web:* www.johnrwhite.com					
KA Steel Chemicals Inc 15185 Main St PO Box 729	Lemont	IL	60439	630-257-3900	257-3922
TF: 800-677-8335 ■ *Web:* www.kasteelchemicals.com					
KB International LLC 735 Broad St Ste 209	Chattanooga	TN	37402	423-266-6964	
Web: www.kbtech.com					
KMG-Bernuth Inc 9555 W Sam Houston Pkwy S Ste 600	Houston	TX	77099	713-600-3800	
Web: kmgchemicals.com					
Kraft Chemical Co 1975 N Hawthorne Ave	Melrose Park	IL	60160	708-345-5200	345-4005
TF: 800-345-5200 ■ *Web:* www.kraftchemical.com					
Kroff Inc 1 N Shore Ctr Ste 450 12 Federal St	Pittsburgh	PA	15212	412-321-9800	
Web: www.kroff.com					
Lambent Technologies Corp 3938 Porett Dr	Gurnee	IL	60031	847-244-3410	
Web: www.lambentcorp.com					
LidoChem Inc 20 Village Ct	Hazlet	NJ	07730	732-888-8000	264-2751
Web: www.lidochem.com					
LV Lomas Ltd 99 Summerlea Rd	Brampton	ON	L6T4V2	905-458-1555	458-0722
TF: 800-575-3382 ■ *Web:* www.lvlomas.com					
Maroon Inc 1390 Jaycox Rd	Avon	OH	44011	440-937-1000	937-1001
TF General: 877-627-6661 ■ *Web:* maroongroupllc.com/					
Mays Chemical Company Inc 5611 E 71st St	Indianapolis	IN	46220	317-842-8722	
Web: www.mayschem.com					
McCullough & Assoc 1746 NE Expy PO Box 29803	Atlanta	GA	30329	404-325-1606	329-0208
TF: 800-969-1606 ■ *Web:* www.mccanda.com					
Miles Chemical Co 12801 Rangoon St	Arleta	CA	91321	818-504-3355	
Web: www.mileschemical.com					
Milport Enterprises Inc 2829 S Fifth Ct	Milwaukee	WI	53207	414-769-7350	769-0167
Web: www.milport.com					
Mitsubishi International Corp 655 Third Ave	New York	NY	10017	212-605-2000	
Web: www.mitsubishicorp.com					
Mutchler Inc 20 Elm St	Harrington Park	NJ	07640	201-768-1100	
Web: mutchler.net					
Nagase America Holdings Inc 546 Fifth Ave 16th Fl	New York	NY	10036	212-703-1340	398-0687
Web: nagaseamerica.com					
Neutron Products Inc 22301 Mount Ephraim Rd	Dickerson	MD	20842	301-349-5001	
Web: neutronprod.com					
Nexeo Solutions LLC 3 Waterway Sq Pl Ste 1000	The Woodlands	TX	77380	281-297-0700	
Web: nexeosolutions.com					
Nisseki Chemical Texas Inc 10500 Bay Area Blvd	Pasadena	TX	77507	713-754-1000	
NuCo2 Inc 2800 SE Marketplace	Stuart	FL	34997	772-221-1754	781-3500
TF: 800-472-2855 ■ *Web:* www.nuco2.com					
Optima Chemical Group LLC 200 Willacoochee Hwy	Douglas	GA	31535	912-384-5101	
Web: www.optimachem.com					
Pain Enterprises Inc 101 Daniels Way	Bloomington	IN	47404	800-245-8583	330-1544*
**Fax Area Code:* 812 ■ *TF:* 800-245-8583 ■ *Web:* www.painenterprises.com					
Palmer Holland Inc 25000 Country Club Blvd Ste 444	North Olmsted	OH	44070	800-635-4822	686-2180*
**Fax Area Code:* 440 ■ *TF:* 800-635-4822 ■ *Web:* www.palmerholland.com					
Pidilite USA Inc 401 Maplewood Dr Ste 18	Jupiter	FL	33458	561-775-9600	622-1055
TF: 800-843-7813 ■ *Web:* www.cyclo.com					
Plaza Group Inc 10375 Richmond Ave Ste 1620	Houston	TX	77042	713-266-0707	266-8660
TF: 800-876-3738 ■ *Web:* www.theplazagrp.com					
Premier Performance LLC 278 E Dividend Dr	Rexburg	ID	83440	208-356-0106	
Web: www.wespeakdiesel.com					
Pride Solvents & Chemical Co of New York Inc 6 Long Island Ave	Holtsville	NY	11742	631-758-0200	758-0290
TF: 800-424-8802 ■ *Web:* www.pridesol.com					
Purity Cylinder Gases Inc PO Box 9390	Grand Rapids	MI	49509	616-532-2375	532-5626
Web: www.puritygas.com					
Quadra Chemicals Ltd 3901 Fixtessier	Vaudreuil-Dorion	QC	J7V5V5	450-424-0161	424-9458*
**Fax:* Hum Res ■ *TF:* 800-665-6553 ■ *Web:* www.quadra.ca					
Reagent Chemical & Research Inc 115 Rt 202	Ringoes	NJ	08551	908-284-2800	284-6090
TF: 800-231-1807 ■ *Web:* www.reagentchemical.com					
Ribelin Sales Inc 3857 Miller Pk Dr	Garland	TX	75042	972-272-1594	474-2354*
**Fax Area Code:* 877 ■ *TF:* 800-374-1594 ■ *Web:* www.ribelin.com					
Rowell Chemical Corp 15 Salt Creek Ln Ste 205	Hinsdale	IL	60521	630-920-8833	920-8994
TF: 888-261-7963 ■ *Web:* www.rowellchemical.com					
SARCOM Inc AEP Colloids Div 6299 Rt 9N	Hadley	NY	12835	518-696-9900	696-9997
TF: 800-848-0658 ■ *Web:* www.aepcolloids.com					
Sasol Wax North America Corp 21325-B Cabot Blvd	Hayward	CA	94545	510-783-9295	670-8659
Web: www.sasolwax.com					
Sessions Specialty Co 5090 Styers Ferry Rd	Lewisville	NC	27023	336-766-2880	723-0055*
**Fax Area Code:* 800 ■ *Web:* www.sessionsusa.com					
Shamrock Technologies Inc Foot Of Pacific St	Newark	NJ	07114	973-242-2999	
TF: 800-349-1822 ■ *Web:* www.shamrocktechnologies.com					
Solmax International Inc 2801 Marie-Victorin Blvd	Varennes	QC	J3X1P7	450-929-1234	
TF: 800-571-3904 ■ *Web:* www.solmax.com					
Solvents & Chemicals Inc 1904 Mykawa Rd	Pearland	TX	77581	281-485-5377	
TF: 800-622-3990 ■ *Web:* www.solvchem.com					
Special Materials Co 70 W 40th St 2nd Fl	New York	NY	10018	646-366-0400	
Web: www.smc-global.com					
Specified Technologies Inc 210 Evans Way	Somerville	NJ	08876	908-526-8000	526-9623
TF: 800-992-1180 ■ *Web:* www.stifirestop.com					
Spectra Colors Corp 25 Rizzolo Rd	Kearny	NJ	07032	201-997-0606	
TF: 800-527-8588 ■ *Web:* www.spectracolors.com					
Strem Chemicals Inc 7 Mulliken Way	Newburyport	MA	01950	978-499-1600	
TF: 800-647-8736 ■ *Web:* www.strem.com					
Sumitomo Chemical America Inc 335 Madison Ave Ste 830	New York	NY	10017	212-572-8200	572-8234
Web: www.sumitomo-chem.co.jp					
Sunbelt Chemicals Corp 71 Hargrove Grade	Palm Coast	FL	32137	386-446-4595	446-4627
Web: www.sunbeltchemicals.com					
Sweetlake Chemical Ltd 7402 Neuhaus St Ste A	Houston	TX	77061	713-827-8707	
SynCot Plastics Inc 350 Eastwood Dr	Cramerton	NC	28032	704-967-0010	
Web: www.syncot.com					
Tanner Industries Inc 735 Davisville Rd 3rd Fl	SouthHampton	PA	18966	215-322-1238	322-7791*
**Fax:* Sales ■ *TF:* 800-643-6226 ■ *Web:* www.tannerind.com					
Tarr LLC 2429 N Borthwick St	Portland	OR	97227	800-422-5069	288-0421*
**Fax Area Code:* 503 ■ *TF:* 800-422-5069 ■ *Web:* www.tarrllc.com					
TCR Industries 26 Centerpointe Dr Ste 120	La Palma	CA	90623	714-521-5222	521-1636
TF: 877-827-1444 ■ *Web:* www.tcrindustries.com					
Tilley Chemical Company Inc 501 Chesapeake Pk Plz	Baltimore	MD	21220	410-574-4500	391-6665
TF: 800-638-6968 ■ *Web:* tilleychem.com					
TM Deer Park Services LP 2525 Battleground Rd PO Box 1914	Deer Park	TX	77536	281-930-2525	930-2535
Web: www.texasmolecular.com					
TR International Trading Company Inc 1218 Third Ave Ste 2100	Seattle	WA	98101	206-505-3500	505-3501
Web: www.trichemicals.com					
TransChemical Inc 419 De Soto Ave	Saint Louis	MO	63147	314-231-6905	231-5851
TF: 888-873-6481 ■ *Web:* www.transchemical.com					
Tulstar Products Inc 5510 S Lewis Ave	Tulsa	OK	74105	918-749-9060	747-1444
Web: www.tulstar.com					
Ultra Clean Technologies Corp 1274 Hgwy 77	Bridgeton	NJ	08302	856-451-2176	
Web: ultracleantech.com					
Union Carbide Corp 1254 Enclave Pkwy	Houston	TX	77077	281-966-2016	
Web: www.unioncarbide.com					
Univar Canada Ltd 9800 Van Horne Way	Richmond	BC	V6X1W5	604-273-1441	
TF: 855-888-8648 ■ *Web:* www.univar.com					
Univar USA Inc 17425 NE Union Hill Rd	Redmond	WA	98052	425-889-3400	889-4100
TF: 855-888-8648 ■ *Web:* www.univar.com					
Van Horn Metz & Company Inc 201 E Elm St	Conshohocken	PA	19428	610-828-4500	
Web: www.vanhornmetz.com					
VanDeMark Chemical Inc 1 N Transit Rd	Lockport	NY	14094	716-433-6764	
Web: www.vandemarkinc.com					
Venture Mud L P 1305 W Illinois Ave	Midland	TX	79701	432-684-7101	
Web: www.venturemud.com					
Victory Petroleum Inc 2200 S Dixie Hwy Ste 601	Miami	FL	33133	305-255-4145	
Web: www.victorypetroleum.com					
Webb Chemical Service Corp 2708 Jarman St	Muskegon	MI	49444	231-733-2181	739-5454
Web: www.webbchemical.com					
Wego Chemical & Mineral Corp 239 Great Neck Rd	Great Neck	NY	11021	516-487-3510	487-3794
Web: www.wegochem.com					
Whitaker Oil Co 1557 Marietta Rd NW	Atlanta	GA	30318	404-355-8220	355-8217
TF: 888-895-3506 ■ *Web:* www.whitakeroil.com					
Wilshire Technologies Inc 318 Wall St	Princeton	NJ	08540	609-683-1117	
Web: www.wilshiretechnologies.com					
Wilson Industrial Sales Company Inc 201 S Wilson	Brook	IN	47922	219-275-7333	
TF: 800-633-5427 ■ *Web:* www.wilsonindustrial.com					

147 CHILD CARE MONITORING SYSTEMS - INTERNET

Company	City	State	ZIP	Phone	Fax
Jewish Child Care Assn of New York 120 Wall St Fl 12	New York	NY	10005	212-425-3333	425-9397
Web: www.jccany.org					
Mississippi Action For Progress Inc (MAP) 1751 Morson Rd	Jackson	MS	39209	601-923-4100	923-4114
TF: 800-924-4615 ■ *Web:* www.mapheadstart.org					

148 CHILDREN'S LEARNING CENTERS

Company	City	State	ZIP	Phone	Fax
Abrakadoodle Inc 46030 Manekin Pl Ste 110	Sterling	VA	20166	703-860-6570	
Web: www.abrakadoodle.com					

	City	State	ZIP	Phone	Fax
Abundant Life Christian Academy 1494 Banks Rd *Web:* www.alcapro.com	Margate	FL	33063	954-979-2665	
Adventure Guild L L C, The 3413 Hixson Pk *Web:* www.theadventureguild.com	Chattanooga	TN	37415	423-266-5709	
Alabama Christian Academy 4700 Wares Ferry Rd *Web:* www.alabamachristian.com	Montgomery	AL	36109	334-277-1985	
Alexandra Park Neighbourhood Learning Centre 707 Dundas St W *Web:* www.apnlc.org	Toronto	ON	M5T2W6	416-591-7384	
Asana Yoga Studio 16399 S Golden Rd Ste A *Web:* www.asanastudio.com	Golden	CO	80401	303-437-6666	
Autistic Treatment Center Inc 10503 Metric Dr *TF:* 877-666-2747 ■ *Web:* www.atcoftexas.org	Dallas	TX	75243	972-644-2076	
Beyond Yoga Inc 321 S Beverly Dr Ste N *Web:* www.beyondyoga.com	Beverly Hills	CA	90212	310-277-2030	
Bright Horizons Family Solutions LLC 200 Talcott Ave S *TF:* 800-324-4386 ■ *Web:* www.brighthorizons.com	Watertown	MA	02472	617-673-8000	673-8001
Bristow Academy Inc 365 Golden Knights Blvd *Web:* www.bristowgroup.com/about-bristow/bristow-academy	Titusville	FL	32780	321-385-2919	
Cape Christian Academy 10 Oyster Rd *Web:* capechristianacademy.com	Cape May Court House	NJ	08210	609-465-4132	
Centre for Skills Development & Training The 5151 New St *Web:* thecentre.on.ca	Burlington	ON	L7L1V3	905-333-3499	
Chase Collegiate School 565 Chase Pkwy *Web:* www.smmct.org	Waterbury	CT	06708	203-236-9500	
Child Care Links 6601 Owens Dr Ste 100 *Web:* www.childcarelinks.org	Pleasanton	CA	94588	925-417-8733	730-4942
Child Development Assoc Inc 678 Third Ave Ste 201 *TF:* 888-755-2445 ■ *Web:* www.cdasandiego.com	Chula Vista	CA	91910	619-427-4411	
Childcare Network Inc 3025 University Ave Ste B-2 *TF:* 866-521-5437 ■ *Web:* www.childcarenetwork.com	Columbus	GA	31907	706-562-8600	
Children's Home + Aid 125 S Wacker Dr 14th Fl *Web:* www.childrenshomeandaid.org	Chicago	IL	60606	312-424-0200	
Churchill School & Center, The 301 E 29th St *Web:* www.churchillschool.com	New York	NY	10016	212-722-0610	
College Internship Program Inc 18 Park St *Web:* www.cipworldwide.org	Lee	MA	01238	413-243-0710	
Collinsville Community 240 Regency Ctr *Web:* kahoks.org	Collinsville	IL	62234	618-343-2878	
Colonial Intermediate Unit 20 6 Danforth Rd *Web:* www.ciu20.org	Easton	PA	18045	610-252-5550	252-5740
Competency & Credentialing Institute 2170 S Parker Rd Ste 295 *Web:* www.cc-institute.org	Denver	CO	80231	303-369-9566	
Computer Explorers 12715 Telge Rd *TF:* 800-531-5053 ■ *Web:* www.computerexplorers.com	Cypress	TX	77429	800-531-5053	
Councel for Secular Humanism & Csicop 3965 Rensch Rd *Web:* www.centerforinquiry.net	Amherst	NY	14228	716-636-4869	
Da Vinci Academy 37w080 Hopps Rd *Web:* www.dvacademy.org	Elgin	IL	60124	847-841-7532	
DePelchin Children's Ctr 4950 Memorial Dr *TF:* 888-730-2335 ■ *Web:* www.depelchin.org	Houston	TX	77007	713-730-2335	802-3801
Derby Academy 56 Burditt Ave *Web:* derbyacademy.org	Hingham	MA	02043	781-749-0746	
Education Inc 2 Main St Ste 2A *Web:* www.educationinc.us	Plymouth	MA	02360	508-732-9101	
Elgin Academy 350 Park St *Web:* www.elginacademy.org	Elgin	IL	60120	847-695-0300	
Erskine Academy 309 Windsor Rd *Web:* erskineacademy.org	South China	ME	04358	207-445-2962	
FasTracKids International Ltd 6900 E Belleview Ave Ste 100 *TF:* 888-576-6888 ■ *Web:* fastrackids.com	Greenwood Village	CO	80111	303-224-0200	224-0222
Go Native Yacht Charters 1900 Purdy Ave *Web:* www.gnyc.com	Miami Beach	FL	33139	954-791-4692	
Goddard Systems Inc 1016 W Ninth Ave *TF:* 800-463-3273 ■ *Web:* www.goddardschool.com	King of Prussia	PA	19406	610-265-8510	
Golflogix Inc 15685 N Greenway-Hayden Loop Ste 100A *TF:* 877-977-0162 ■ *Web:* www.golflogix.com	Scottsdale	AZ	85260	877-977-0162	
Greater Holy Temple Christian Academy 5575 N 76th St *Web:* greaterholy.org	Milwaukee	WI	53218	414-265-4131	
Hansa Language Centre of Toronto Inc 51 Eglinton Ave E *Web:* www.hansacanada.com	Toronto	ON	M4P1G7	416-487-8643	
Head Start of Greater Dallas Inc 3954 Gannon Ln *Web:* www.hsgd.org	Dallas	TX	75237	972-283-6400	
Hill Country Christian School of Austin 12124 Ranch Rd 620 N *Web:* www.hillcountrychristianschool.org	Austin	TX	78750	512-331-7036	
Huntington Learning Centers Inc 496 Kinderkamack Rd *TF:* 800-653-8400 ■ *Web:* huntingtonhelps.com	Oradell	NJ	07649	201-261-8400	
J & L Self Defense Products Inc 70 Defense Dr *Web:* jldirect.com	Berkeley Springs	WV	25411	304-258-2900	
Jamaica Bay Riding Academy Inc 7000 Shore Pkwy *Web:* horsebackride.com	Brooklyn	NY	11234	718-531-8949	
Jivamukti Yoga Center Inc 841 Broadway Frnt 2 *Web:* www.jivamuktiyoga.com	New York	NY	10003	212-353-0214	
KinderCare Learning Centers Inc 650 NE Holladay St Ste 1400 PO Box 6760 **Fax Area Code:* 503 ■ *TF:* 800-633-1488 ■ *Web:* www.kindercare.com	Portland	OR	97232	800-633-1488	872-1427*
King Tiger Martial Arts Inc 13401 New Hampshire Ave *Web:* kingtigermartialarts.com	Colesville	MD	20904	301-989-2400	
Knowledge Universe 650 NE Holladay St Ste 1400 *Web:* www.kueducation.com/us	Portland	OR	97232	503-872-1300	
Kumon North America Inc 300 Frank W Burr Blvd Glenpointe Ctr E Ste 6 *TF:* 800-222-6284 ■ *Web:* www.kumon.com	Teaneck	NJ	07666	201-928-0444	928-0044
Lad Lake Inc W350s1401 Waterville Rd *TF:* 877-965-2131 ■ *Web:* www.ladlake.org	Dousman	WI	53118	262-965-2131	
Learning Care Group Inc 21333 Haggerty Rd Ste 300 *TF:* 877-817-3883 ■ *Web:* learningcaregroup.com	Novi	MI	48375	248-697-9000	697-9002
Literacy Kansas City 211 W Armour Blvd Fl 3 *Web:* literacykc.org	Kansas City	MO	64111	816-333-9332	
Marburn Academy 1860 Walden Dr *Web:* marburnacademy.org	Columbus	OH	43229	614-433-0822	
Marin Christian Academy 1370 S Novato Blvd. *Web:* visitmca.org	Novato	CA	94947	415-892-5713	
Matt Swanson's School of Golf 6224 Theall Rd *Web:* swingpure.com	Houston	TX	77066	713-413-4484	
Miami Valley Child Development Centers 215 Horace St *Web:* www.mvcdc.org	Dayton	OH	45402	937-226-5664	
Missionary Oblates 327 Oblate Dr *Web:* www.oblatemissions.com	San Antonio	TX	78216	210-349-1475	
Morgan Park Academy 2153 W 111th St *Web:* www.morganparkacademy.org	Chicago	IL	60643	773-881-6700	
Nacel Open Door Inc 380 Jackson St Ste 200 *Web:* www.nacelopendoor.org	St. Paul	MN	55101	651-686-0080	
Nardin Academy 795 Main St *Web:* www.frcdb.org	Buffalo	NY	14203	716-881-6262	
Naturebridge 28 Geary St Ste 650 *Web:* www.naturebridge.org	San Francisco	CA	94108	415-992-4700	
New Horizon Kids Quest Inc 3405 Annapolis Ln N Ste 100 **Fax Area Code:* 763 ■ *TF:* 800-941-1007 ■ *Web:* www.kidsquest.com	Plymouth	MN	55447	800-941-1007	383-6101*
Our Cooperative 525 Old Bellefonte Rd *Web:* www.oursc.k12.ar.us	Harrison	AR	72601	870-743-9100	
Pingree School 537 Highland St *Web:* pingree.org	South Hamilton	MA	01982	978-468-6232	
Pioneer Clubs 123 E Elk *TF:* 800-694-2582 ■ *Web:* www.pioneerclubs.org	Carol Stream	IL	60188	800-694-2582	
Planet Granite 815 Stewart Dr *Web:* planetgranite.com	Sunnyvale	CA	94085	408-991-9090	
Porter & Chester Institute Inc, The 670 Lordship Blvd *Web:* www.porterchester.com	Stratford	CT	06615	203-375-4463	
Potomac Appalachian Trail Club Inc, The 118 Park St Se *Web:* patc.net	Vienna	VA	22180	703-242-0965	
Primrose School Franchising Co 3660 Cedarcrest Rd *TF:* 800-745-0677 ■ *Web:* www.primroseschools.com	Acworth	GA	30101	770-529-4100	529-1551
Rejoice Church 13413 E 106th St N *Web:* www.rejoicechurch.com	Owasso	OK	74055	918-272-5291	
Rosedale Technical Institute 215 Beecham Dr Ste 2 *TF:* 800-521-6262 ■ *Web:* www.rosedaletech.org	Pittsburgh	PA	15205	412-521-6200	
Rural Resources Community Action 956 S Main St *TF:* 800-538-7659 ■ *Web:* www.ruralresources.org	Colville	WA	99114	509-684-8421	684-4740
Science Club for Girls Inc 136 Magazine St *Web:* scienceclubforgirls.org	Cambridge	MA	02139	617-372-4403	
Sivananda Yoga Vedanta Center 1185 Vicente St *Web:* www.sivananda.org	San Francisco	CA	94116	415-681-2731	
Sky Ranch 24657 CR 448 *TF:* 800-962-2267 ■ *Web:* www.skyranch.org	Van	TX	75790	903-266-3300	
Spirit Rock Meditation Center 5000 Sir Francis Drake Blvd *Web:* www.spiritrock.org	Woodacre	CA	94973	415-488-0164	
St. Raphael Academy 123 Walcott St *Web:* www.saintraphaelacademy.org	Pawtucket	RI	02860	401-723-8100	
Strake Jesuit College Preparatory Inc 8900 Bellaire Blvd *Web:* www.strakejesuit.org	Houston	TX	77036	713-774-7651	
Stride Learning Center 326 Parsley Blvd *Web:* www.stridekids.com	Cheyenne	WY	82007	307-632-2991	
Syracuse Academy of Science 1001 Park Ave *Web:* sascs.org	Syracuse	NY	13204	315-428-8997	
Talladega Clay Randolph Child Care Corp 925 N St E	Talladega	AL	35160	256-362-3852	
Tiger Schulmann's Karate Ctr 485 Blvd *TF:* 800-867-1218 ■ *Web:* tsk.com	Elmwood Park	NJ	07407	800-867-1218	
Tri Rivers Career Center 2222 Marion Mount Gilead Rd *Web:* www.tririvers.com	Marion	OH	43302	740-389-4681	
Voyager Academy 101 Hock Parc *Web:* www.voyageracademy.net	Durham	NC	27704	919-433-3301	
West Highland Christian Academy 1116 S Hickory Ridge Rd *Web:* www.whca-k12.org	Milford	MI	48380	248-887-6698	
Westford Riding Academy 22 Griffin Rd *Web:* www.westford-homesforsale.com	Westford	MA	01886	978-692-2894	

Phone Fax

Woodstock Academy 57 Academy Rd ... Woodstock CT 06281 860-928-6575
Web: www.woodstockacademy.org

World Wide Group LLC
5507 Nesconset Hwy Ste 10 ... Mount Sanai NY 11766 509-924-0955
Web: worldwidegrouptravel.com

Yeled V'yalda Early Childhood Ctr Inc
1312 38th St ... Brooklyn NY 11218 718-686-3700
Web: www.yeled.org

Zenya Yoga & Message Studio
101 Herman Melville Ave ... Newport News VA 23606 757-643-6900
Web: www.zenyayoga.com

149 CIRCUS, CARNIVAL, FESTIVAL OPERATORS

Phone Fax

Accent on Arrangements Inc
615 Baronne St Ste 303 ... New Orleans LA 70113 504-524-1227
Web: www.accent-dmc.com

Adrenaline Family Entertainment Inc
3325 French Park Dr Ste 6 ... Edmond OK 73034 405-340-9111
Web: www.afeparks.com

Big Apple Circus 1 Metrotech Ctr 3rd Fl ... Brooklyn NY 11201 212-268-2500 268-3163
TF: 800-922-3772 ■ *Web:* www.bigapplecircus.org

Chippendales USA LLC
4 ExpressWay Plz Ste 218 ... Roslyn Heights NY 11577 516-454-0981
TF: 866-244-7999 ■ *Web:* www.chippendales.com

Cirque du Soleil Inc 8400 Second Ave ... Montreal QC H1Z4M6 514-722-2324 722-3692
TF: 800-678-2119 ■ *Web:* www.cirquedusoleil.com

Crazy Horse Gentlemen's Club
980 Market St ... San Francisco CA 94102 415-658-9324
Web: www.crazyhorse-sf.com

Culpepper & Merriweather Circus PO Box 813 ... Hugo OK 74743 580-326-8833
Web: www.cmcircus.com

Encore Creative Inc 410 S Madison Dr ... Tempe AZ 85281 480-736-2800
Web: www.encorecreative.com

Extraordinary Events
13425 Ventura Blvd Ste 300 ... Sherman Oaks CA 91423 818-783-6112
Web: www.extraordinaryevents.net

Feld Entertainment Inc 8607 Westwood Ctr Dr ... Vienna VA 22182 703-448-4000
Web: www.feldentertainment.com

Green Tree Event Consultants 35 Storer St ... Saco ME 04072 207-781-2982
Web: www.nemadeshows.com

Maryland Renaissance Festival PO Box 315 ... Crownsville MD 21032 410-266-7304 573-1508
TF: 800-296-7304 ■ *Web:* www.marylandrenaissancefestival.com

Palace Cafe, The 139 S Murphy Ave ... Sunnyvale CA 94086 408-774-6111
Web: m.palacecafe.net

Pyrotek Special Effects Inc
7676 Woodbine Ave Ste 7 & 8 ... Markham ON L3R2N2 905-479-9991
Web: www.pyrotekfx.com

Raw Art Works Inc 37 Central Sq Ste 3 ... Lynn MA 01901 781-593-5515
Web: www.rawartworks.org

Ringling Bros & Barnum & Bailey Circus
8607 Westwood Ctr Dr ... Vienna VA 22182 703-448-4000
Web: www.ringling.com

Starkey International Institute for Household Management Inc, The
1350 Logan St ... Denver CO 80203 303-832-5510
TF: 800-888-4904 ■ *Web:* www.starkeyintl.com

Taikoproject 505 E 3rd St Ste 505 ... Los Angeles CA 90012 213-268-4011
Web: www.taikoproject.com

150 CLAY PRODUCTS - STRUCTURAL

See Also Brick, Stone, Related Materials p. 2094

Phone Fax

Acme Brick Co 3024 Acme Brick Plaza ... Fort Worth TX 76109 817-332-4101 821-3550*
**Fax Area Code:* 423 ■ *TF:* 866-430-2263 ■ *Web:* www.acmebrick.com

Belden Brick Company Inc 700 Tuscarawas St W ... Canton OH 44702 330-456-0031 456-2694
Web: www.beldenbrick.com

Boral Bricks Inc 9143 Bob Williams Pkwy ... Covington GA 30014 678-625-4051
TF: 800-526-7255 ■ *Web:* boralamerica.com

Bowerston Shale Co, The PO Box 199 ... Bowerston OH 44695 740-269-2921 269-5456
Web: www.bowerstonshale.com

Brampton Brick Ltd 225 Wanless Dr ... Brampton ON L7A1E9 905-840-1011 840-1535
TSE: BBLA ■ *Web:* www.bramptonbrick.com

Cherokee Brick & Tile Co Inc
3250 Waterville Rd ... Macon GA 31206 478-781-6800 781-8964
TF: 800-277-2745 ■ *Web:* www.cherokeebrick.com

Colloid Environmental Technologies Co (CETCO)
2870 Forbs Ave ... Hoffman Estates IL 60192 847-851-1899 527-9948*
**Fax Area Code:* 800 ■ *TF:* 800-527-9948 ■ *Web:* www.cetco.com

Cunningham Brick Co Inc 701 N Main St ... Lexington NC 27292 336-248-8541 472-2404
TF: 800-672-6181

Elgin-Butler Brick Co 2601 McHale Crt ... Austin TX 78758 512-453-7366
Web: www.elginbutler.com

Endicott Clay Products Co 57120 707 Rd ... Endicott NE 68350 402-729-3315 729-5804
Web: www.endicott.com

Endicott Tile LLC 57120 707 Rd ... Endicott NE 68350 402-729-3315 729-5804
Web: www.endicott.com

General Shale Products LLC
3015 Bristol Hwy ... Johnson City TN 37601 423-282-4661 952-4104
TF: 800-414-4661 ■ *Web:* www.generalshale.com

Glen-Gery Corp 1166 Spring St PO Box 7001 ... Wyomissing PA 19610 610-374-4011 374-1622
Web: www.glengery.com

Henry Brick Co Inc 3409 Water Ave ... Selma AL 36703 334-875-2600
TF: 800-218-3906 ■ *Web:* www.henrybrick.com

I-XL Industries Ltd 4900 102 Ave SE ... Calgary AB T2X2X8 403-526-5901
Web: ixlmasonry.com

International Chimney Corp
55 S Long St ... Williamsville NY 14221 800-828-1446 634-3983*
**Fax Area Code:* 716 ■ *TF:* 800-828-1446 ■ *Web:* www.internationalchimney.com

Phone Fax

Kansas Brick & Tile Inc 767 N US Hwy 281 ... Hoisington KS 67544 620-653-2157 653-7609
Web: www.kansasbrick.com

Kinney Brick Co
100 Prosperity Rd PO Box 1804 ... Albuquerque NM 87103 505-877-4550
TF: 800-464-4605 ■ *Web:* kinneybrickco.com

Lee Brick & Tile Co
3704 Hawkins Ave PO Box 1027 ... Sanford NC 27330 919-774-4800 774-7557
TF: 800-672-7559 ■ *Web:* www.leebrickonline.com

Logan Clay Products Co 201 S Walnut St ... Logan OH 43138 800-848-2141 385-9336*
**Fax Area Code:* 740 ■ *TF:* 800-848-2141 ■ *Web:* www.loganclaypipe.com

Ludowici Roof Tile Inc
4757 Tile Plant Rd PO Box 69 ... New Lexington OH 43764 740-342-1995 342-0025
TF Cust Svc: 800-945-8453 ■ *Web:* www.ludowici.com

Marion Ceramics Inc PO Box 1134 ... Marion SC 29571 843-423-1311 423-1515
TF: 800-845-4010 ■ *Web:* www.marionceramics.com

McNear Brick & Block
1 McNear BrickyaRd Rd PO Box 151380 ... San Rafael CA 94901 415-453-7702 453-3141
TF: 888-442-6811 ■ *Web:* www.mcnear.com

MCP Industries Inc Mission Clay Products Div
708 S Temescal St Ste 101 ... Corona CA 92879 951-736-1881 549-8280
Web: www.mcpind.com

Morin Brick Co 130 Morin Brick Rd PO Box 1510 ... Auburn ME 04210 207-784-9375 784-2013
Web: www.morinbrick.com

Mutual Materials Co 605 119th Ave NE ... Bellevue WA 98005 425-452-2300 454-7732
TF: 800-477-3008 ■ *Web:* www.mutualmaterials.com

Old Virginia Brick Co 2500 W Main St ... Salem VA 24153 540-389-2357 929-6411*
**Fax Area Code:* 434 ■ *TF:* 800-879-8227

Pacific Clay Products Inc
14741 Lake St ... Lake Elsinore CA 92530 951-674-2131 674-4909
Web: www.pacificclay.com

Palmetto Brick Co 3501 BrickyaRd Rd ... Wallace SC 29596 843-537-7861 537-4802
TF: 800-922-4423 ■ *Web:* www.palmettobrick.com

Pine Hall Brick Co 2701 Shorefair Dr ... Winston-Salem NC 27116 800-334-8689 725-3940*
**Fax Area Code:* 336 ■ *TF:* 800-334-8689 ■ *Web:* www.pinehallbrick.com

Potomac Valley Brick & Supply Co
15810 Indianola Dr Ste 100 ... Rockville MD 20855 301-309-9600 309-0929
Web: www.pvbrick.com

Redland Brick Inc 15718 Clear Spring Rd ... Williamsport MD 21795 301-223-7700
TF: 800-366-2742 ■ *Web:* redlandbrick.com

Richards Brick Co 234 Springer Ave ... Edwardsville IL 62025 618-656-0230 656-0944
Web: www.richardsbrick.com

Sioux City Brick & Tile Co
310 S Floyd Blvd ... Sioux City IA 51101 712-258-6571 252-3215
Web: www.siouxcitybrick.com

Statesville Brick Co 391 BrickyaRd Rd ... Statesville NC 28677 704-872-4123 872-4125
TF: 800-522-4716 ■ *Web:* www.statesvillebrick.com

Summitville Tiles Inc 15364 Ohio 644 ... Summitville OH 43962 330-223-1511 223-1414
Web: www.summitville.com

Superior Clay Corp 6566 Superior Rd SE ... Uhrichsville OH 44683 740-922-4122
TF: 800-848-6166 ■ *Web:* www.superiorclay.com

Taylor Clay Products Co
185 Peeler Rd PO Box 2128 ... Salisbury NC 28145 704-636-2411 636-2413
Web: taylorclaybrick.com/wp/index.php

Triangle Brick Co 6523 NC Hwy 55 ... Durham NC 27713 919-544-1796 544-3904
TF: 800-672-8547 ■ *Web:* www.trianglebrick.com

Whitacre Greer Fireproofing Inc
1400 S Mahoning Ave ... Alliance OH 44601 330-823-1610 823-5502
TF Cust Svc: 800-947-2837 ■ *Web:* www.wgpaver.com

Yankee Hill Brick & Tile
3705 S Coddington Ave ... Lincoln NE 68522 402-477-6663 477-2832
Web: www.yankeehillbrick.com

151 CLEANING PRODUCTS

See Also Brushes & Brooms p. 1877; Mops, Sponges, Wiping Cloths p. 2777

Phone Fax

ABC Compounding Company Inc & Acme Wholesale
6970 Jonesboro Rd ... Morrow GA 30260 770-968-9222 968-7281
TF: 800-795-9222 ■ *Web:* www.abccompounding.com

Abso-Clean Industries Inc 199 Wales Ave ... Tonawanda NY 14150 716-693-2111 693-2155

Adco Inc 1909 W Oakridge ... Albany GA 31707 800-821-7556
TF: 800-821-7556 ■ *Web:* www.adco-inc.com

AJ Funk & Co 1471 Timber Dr ... Elgin IL 60123 847-741-6760
Web: www.glasscleaner.com

American Cleaning Solutions
39-30 Review Ave ... Long Island NY 11101 718-392-8080 482-9366
TF: 888-929-7587 ■ *Web:* www.cleaning-solutions.com

Arrow-Magnolia International 2646 Rodney Ln ... Dallas TX 75229 972-247-7111 484-2896
TF: 800-527-2101 ■ *Web:* www.arrowmagnolia.com

Aztec International Inc 3010 Henson Rd ... Knoxville TN 37921 865-588-5357 538-2062*
**Fax Area Code:* 615 ■ *TF:* 800-369-5357 ■ *Web:* www.candlemaking.com

BAF Industries Inc 1451 Edinger Ave ... Tustin CA 92780 714-258-8055
TF: 800-437-9893 ■ *Web:* www.prowax.com

Buckeye International Inc
2700 Wagner Pl ... Maryland Heights MO 63043 314-291-1900 298-2850
TF: 800-321-2583 ■ *Web:* www.buckeyeinternational.com

Bullen Cos 1640 Delmar Dr PO Box 37 ... Folcroft PA 19032 610-534-8900 534-8912
TF: 800-444-8900 ■ *Web:* bullenonline.com

C & H Chemical Inc
13505 Industrial Park Blvd ... Plymouth MN 55441 763-582-1140 746-9235
Web: seacole.com

Camco Chemical Co 8145 Holton Dr ... Florence KY 41042 859-727-3200 727-1508
TF Cust Svc: 800-354-1001 ■ *Web:* www.camco-chem.com

Canberra Corp 3610 Holland Sylvania Rd ... Toledo OH 43615 419-841-6616 841-7597
TF: 800-832-8992 ■ *Web:* www.canberracorp.com

Carroll Co 2900 W Kingsley Rd ... Garland TX 75041 972-278-1304 840-0678
TF: 800-527-5722 ■ *Web:* www.carrollco.com

Cello Professional Products
1354 Old Post Rd ... Havre de Grace MD 21078 410-939-1234 939-3028
TF: 800-638-4850 ■ *Web:* www.cello-online.com

Phone | Fax

Champion Chemical Co 8319 S Greenleaf Ave .... Whittier CA 90602 800-424-9300 898-8064
TF: 800-424-9300 ■ *Web:* www.championchemical.com

Chemical Specialties Manufacturing Corp
901 N Newkirk St .... Baltimore MD 21205 410-675-4800 675-0038
TF Sales: 800-638-7370 ■ *Web:* www.chemspecworld.com

Church & Dwight Company Inc
469 N Harrison St.................................. Princeton NJ 08543 609-683-5900
NYSE: CHD ■ *Web:* www.churchdwight.com

Clorox Co 1221 Broadway.............................. Oakland CA 94612 510-271-7000 832-1463
NYSE: CLX ■ *TF Cust Svc:* 800-424-9300 ■ *Web:* www.thecloroxcompany.com

Copper Brite Inc
1482 E Valley Rd Ste 29 Ste 29 .... Santa Barbara CA 93108 805-565-1566 565-1394
Web: www.copperbrite.com

Correlated Products Inc
5616 Progress Rd.................................. Indianapolis IN 46242 317-243-3248 244-8461
TF: 800-428-3266 ■ *Web:* cpiroadsolutions.com

Crain Chemical Co 2624 Andjon Dr.................... Dallas TX 75220 214-358-3301 358-3304

Damon Industries Inc 12435 Rockhill Ave NE........... Alliance OH 44601 330-821-5310 821-6355
TF: 800-362-9850 ■ *Web:* www.damonq.com

Delta Carbona LP 376 Hollywood Ave Ste 208........... Fairfield NJ 07004 973-808-6260
TF: 888-746-5599 ■ *Web:* www.carbona.com

DeSoto LLC 6751 N. Sunset BLVD .... Glendale AZ 85305 815-727-4931 727-4333

Diamond Chemical Company Inc
Union Ave & Dubois St....................... East Rutherford NJ 07073 201-935-4300 935-6997
Web: www.diamondchem.com

Dreumex USA 3445 BoaRd Rd............................ York PA 17406 717-767-6881 767-6888
TF: 800-233-9382 ■ *Web:* www.dreumex.com/us

Dubois Chemicals 3630 E Kemper Rd .... Cincinnati OH 45241 800-438-2647 543-1720
TF: 800-438-2647 ■ *Web:* www.duboischemicals.com

Dura Wax Co 4101 W Albany St...................... McHenry IL 60050 815-385-5000 344-8056
TF: 800-435-5705 ■ *Web:* www.durawax.com

Elco Laboratories Inc
2545 Palmer Ave .... University Park IL 60484 708-534-3000
Web: elcolabs.com

Empire Cleaning Supply
12821 S Figueroa St........................... Los Angeles CA 90061 310-527-0132
Web: www.empirecleaningsupply.com

Emulso Corp 2750 Kenmore Ave .... Tonawanda NY 14150 716-854-2889 854-2809
Web: www.emulso.com

Falcon Safety Products Inc 25 Imclone Dr .... Branchburg NJ 08876 908-707-4900 707-8855
TF: 800-332-5266 ■ *Web:* www.falconsafety.com

Fine Organics Corp 420 Kuller Rd PO Box 2277 .... Clifton NJ 07015 973-478-1000 478-6120*
**Fax:* Sales ■ *TF:* 800-526-7480 ■ *Web:* www.fineorganicscorp.com

Frank B Ross Co 970-H New Brunswick Ave............. Rahway NJ 07065 732-669-0810 669-0814
Web: www.frankbross.com

Glissen Chemical Company Inc 1321 58th St......... Brooklyn NY 11219 718-436-4200

Goodwin Company Inc, The
12102 Industry St........................... Garden Grove CA 92841 714-894-0531 894-6293
Web: www.goodwininc.com

Granitize Products Inc 11022 Vulcan St............. South Gate CA 90280 562-923-5438 861-3475
Web: www.granitize.com

Heritage-Crystal Clean Inc 2175 Pt Blvd Ste 375 .... Elgin IL 60123 847-836-5670 836-5677
TF: 877-938-7948 ■ *Web:* www.crystal-clean.com

Hill Mfg Company Inc 1500 Jonesboro Rd SE............ Atlanta GA 30315 404-522-8364 522-9694
TF: 800-445-5123 ■ *Web:* www.hillmfg.com

Hillyard Chemical Company Inc
302 N Fourth St PO Box 909 .... Saint Joseph MO 64501 816-233-1321 861-0256*
**Fax Area Code:* 800 ■ *TF:* 800-365-1555 ■ *Web:* www.hillyard.com

Impact Products LLC 2840 Centennial Rd............... Toledo OH 43617 419-841-2891 841-7861
TF Cust Svc: 800-333-1541 ■ *Web:* www.impact-products.com

ITW Dymon 805 E Old 56 Hwy .... Olathe KS 66061 913-829-6296 397-8707
TF: 800-443-9536 ■ *Web:* itwprofessionalbrands.com

James Austin Co 115 Downieville Rd PO Box 827 .... Mars PA 16046 724-625-1535 625-3288
TF: 800-245-1942 ■ *Web:* www.jamesaustin.com

Kay Chemical Co 8300 Capital Dr.................. Greensboro NC 27409 336-668-7290 225-3098*
**Fax Area Code:* 651 ■ *TF:* 877-315-1115 ■ *Web:* www.ecolab.com

Koger/Air Corp PO Box 2098...................... Martinsville VA 24113 276-638-8821
TF: 800-368-2096 ■ *Web:* www.kogerair.com

Leadership Performance Sustainability Laboratories
4647 Hugh Howell Rd.................................... Tucker GA 30084 800-241-8334 243-8899*
**Fax Area Code:* 770 ■ *TF:* 800-241-8334 ■ *Web:* www.lpslabs.com

Lincoln Shoe Polish Co 172 Commercial St .... Sunnyvale CA 94086 408-732-5120 732-0659
Web: www.lincolnshoepolish.com

Lonn Mfg Co Inc 5450 W 84th St .... Indianapolis IN 46268 317-897-1440 898-4561
Web: www.lonn.net

Luseaux Laboratories Inc 16816 S Gramercy Pl......... Gardena CA 90247 310-324-1555
Web: luseaux.com

Madison Chemical Company Inc 3141 Clifty Dr .... Madison IN 47250 812-273-6000 273-6002
TF: 800-345-1915 ■ *Web:* madchem.com

Malco Products Inc
361 Fairview Ave PO Box 892....................... Barberton OH 44203 330-753-0361 753-2025
TF: 800-253-2526 ■ *Web:* www.malcopro.com

Matchless Metal Polish Co 840 W 49th Pl .... Chicago IL 60609 773-924-1515 924-5513
Web: www.matchlessmetal.com

Maxim Technologies Inc 1607 Derwent Way .... Delta BC V3M6K8 800-663-9925
TF: 800-663-9925 ■ *Web:* www.maxim-technologies.com

Meguiar's Inc 17991 Mitchell S .... Irvine CA 92614 949-752-8000 752-5784
TF Cust Svc: 800-347-5700 ■ *Web:* www.meguiars.com

Micro Care Corp 595 John Downey Dr.............. New Britain CT 06051 860-827-0626 827-8105
TF: 800-638-0125 ■ *Web:* www.microcare.com

Mission Laboratories 2433 Birkdale St............. Los Angeles CA 90031 323-223-1405 223-9968
Web: www.missionlabs.net

Morga-Gallacher Inc
8707 Millergrove Dr....................... Santa Fe Springs CA 90670 562-695-1232 699-8953
Web: www.morgan-gallacher.com

Mother's Polishes Waxes & Cleaners
5456 Industrial Dr........................ Huntington Beach CA 92649 714-891-3364 893-1827
TF: 800-221-8257 ■ *Web:* www.mothers.com

National Chemical Laboratories Inc
401 N Tenth St .... Philadelphia PA 19123 215-922-1200 922-5517
TF: 800-628-2436 ■ *Web:* www.nclonline.com

Phone | Fax

National Chemicals Inc
105 Liberty St PO Box 32............................ Winona MN 55987 507-454-5640 858-4141*
**Fax Area Code:* 877 ■ *TF Cust Svc:* 800-533-0027 ■ *Web:* www.nationalchemicals.com

NCH Corp 2727 Chemsearch Blvd........................ Irving TX 75062 972-438-0211 438-0186
TF: 800-527-9919 ■ *Web:* www.nch.com

New Pig Corp 1 Pork Ave.............................. Tipton PA 16684 814-684-0101 621-7447*
**Fax Area Code:* 800 ■ *TF:* 800-468-4647 ■ *Web:* www.newpig.com

Northern Labs Inc 5800 W Dr PO Box 850............ Manitowoc WI 54220 920-684-7137 684-4957
Web: www.northernlabs.com

Nuvite Chemical Compounds Corp
213 Freeman St .... Brooklyn NY 11222 718-383-8351 383-0008
TF: 800-394-8351 ■ *Web:* www.nuvitechemical.com

Ocean Bio-Chem Inc (OBCI)
4041 SW 47th Ave .... Fort Lauderdale FL 33314 954-587-6280 587-2813
NASDAQ: OBCI ■ *TF:* 800-327-8583 ■ *Web:* www.oceanbiochem.com

Paramount Chemical Specialties Inc
14750 NE 95th St .... Redmond WA 98052 425-882-2673
TF: 877-846-7826 ■ *Web:* www.kidsnpetsbrand.com

Prestige Brands International Inc
660 White Plains Rd Ste 250 .... Tarrytown NY 10591 914-524-6800 524-6815
Web: www.prestigebrandsinc.com

Prosoco Inc 3741 Greenway Cir..................... Lawrence KS 66046 800-255-4255 830-9797*
**Fax Area Code:* 785 ■ *TF:* 800-255-4255 ■ *Web:* www.prosoco.com

Reckitt Benckiser Inc
399 Interpace Pkwy PO Box 225................... Parsippany NJ 07054 973-404-2600
Web: www.rb.com

Safeguard Chemical Corp 411 Wales Ave .... Bronx NY 10454 718-585-3170 585-3657
TF: 800-536-3170 ■ *Web:* www.safeguardchemical.com

Safetec of America Inc 887 Kensington Ave............ Buffalo NY 14215 716-895-1822 895-2969
TF: 800-456-7077 ■ *Web:* www.safetec.com

SC Johnson & Son Inc 1525 Howe St .... Racine WI 53403 262-260-2154 260-6004
Web: www.scjohnson.com

Scott Fetzer Company Scot Laboratories Div
16841 Pk Cir Dr.............................. Chagrin Falls OH 44023 440-543-3033 543-1825
TF: 800-486-7268 ■ *Web:* scotstuffdirect.com

Scott's Liquid Gold Inc 4880 Havana St .... Denver CO 80239 303-373-4860
OTC: SLGD ■ *TF:* 800-447-1919 ■ *Web:* www.scottsliquidgold.com

Seventh Generation Inc 60 Lake St.................. Burlington VT 05401 802-658-3773 658-1771
TF: 800-456-1191 ■ *Web:* www.seventhgeneration.com

Share Corp 7821 N Faulkner Rd.................... Milwaukee WI 53224 414-355-4000 355-0516
TF: 800-776-7192 ■ *Web:* www.sharecorp.com

Simoniz USA 201 Boston Tpke.......................... Bolton CT 06043 800-227-5536 645-6070*
**Fax Area Code:* 860 ■ *TF:* 800-227-5536 ■ *Web:* www.simoniz.com

Snyder Manufacturing Corp
1541 W Cowles St .... Long Beach CA 90813 562-432-2038
Web: www.snydermanufacturing.com

State Industrial Products
3100 Hamilton Ave.................................. Cleveland OH 44114 216-861-7114
TF: 877-747-6986 ■ *Web:* www.stateindustrial.com

Stearns Packaging Corp 4200 Sycamore Ave.......... Madison WI 53714 608-246-5150 246-5149
TF: 800-655-5008 ■ *Web:* www.stearnspkg.com

Summit Industries Inc PO Box 7329................. Marietta GA 30065 800-241-6996
TF: 800-241-6996 ■ *Web:* www.summitinds.com

Sunshine Makers Inc
15922 Pacific Coast Hwy .... Huntington Harbour CA 92649 562-795-6000 592-3034
TF: 800-228-0709 ■ *Web:* www.simplegreen.com

Unit Chemical Corp 7360 Commercial Way........... Henderson NV 89015 702-564-6454 564-6629
TF: 800-879-8648 ■ *Web:* www.unitchemical.com

UNX Inc 707 E Arlington Blvd PO Box 7206 .... Greenville NC 27835 252-756-8616 756-2764
Web: www.unxinc.com

Warsaw Chemical Company Inc
Argonne Rd PO Box 858.................................. Warsaw IN 46580 574-267-3251 267-3884
TF: 800-548-3396 ■ *Web:* www.warsaw-chem.com

WD-40 Co 1061 Cudahy Pl........................ San Diego CA 92110 619-275-1400 275-5823
NASDAQ: WDFC ■ *TF:* 800-448-9340 ■ *Web:* www.wd40company.com

Webco Chemical Corp 420 W Main St .... Dudley MA 01571 508-943-9500 987-0366
Web: www.webco-chemical.com

West Penetone Corp 700 Gotham Pkwy .... Carlstadt NJ 07072 201-567-3000 510-3973
TF: 800-631-1652 ■ *Web:* www.penetone.com

Willert Home Products Inc 4044 Pk Ave .... Saint Louis MO 63110 314-772-2822 772-1409
Web: www.willert.com

ZEP Inc 1310 Seaboard Industrial Blvd NW................ Atlanta GA 30318 404-352-1680 603-7958
NYSE: ZEP ■ *TF:* 877-428-9937 ■ *Web:* www.zepinc.com

152 CLEANING SERVICES

See Also Bio-Recovery Services p. 1859; Building Maintenance Services p. 1877

Phone | Fax

1-800-Water Damage 1167 Mercer St.................. Seattle WA 98109 206-381-3041
TF: 800-928-3732 ■ *Web:* www.1800waterdamage.com

ABM Industries 600 Harrison St Ste 600 .... San Francisco CA 94107 415-351-4428
Web: locations.abm.com

BearCom Bldg Services 7022 S 400 W................. Midvale UT 84047 801-569-9500 569-8400
Web: bearcomservices.com

Boston's Best Chimney Sweep 76 Bacon St .... Waltham MA 02451 781-893-6611
TF Cust Svc: 800-660-6708 ■ *Web:* www.bestchimney.com

Braco Window Cleaning Service Inc
1 Braco International Blvd............................ Wilder KY 41076 859-442-6000 442-6001
Web: www.bracowindowcleaning.com

Clean Power LLC 124 N 121st St .... Milwaukee WI 53226 414-302-3000 302-3015
TF: 888-566-1717 ■ *Web:* www.cleanpower1.com

Clean-Tech Co 211 S Jefferson Ave .... Saint Louis MO 63103 314-652-2388
Web: www.cleantechcompany.com

Cleaning Authority 7230 Lee DeForest Dr............ Columbia MD 21046 410-740-1900 740-1906
TF: 888-658-0659 ■ *Web:* www.thecleaningauthority.com

CleanNet USA 9861 Brokenland Pkwy Ste 208 .... Columbia MD 21046 410-720-6444 720-5307
TF: 800-735-8838 ■ *Web:* www.cleannetusa.com

Coverall Cleaning Concepts
5201 Congress Ave Ste 275........................ Boca Raton FL 33487 866-296-8944 922-2423*
**Fax Area Code:* 561 ■ *TF:* 800-537-3371 ■ *Web:* www.coverall.com

Phone Fax

Diversified Maintenance Systems Inc
5110 Eisenhower Blvd Ste250 ..... Tampa FL 33634 813-383-0238
TF: 800-351-1557 ■ *Web:* www.diveinc.com

Duraclean International Inc
220 W Campus Dr ..... Arlington Heights IL 60004 847-704-7100 704-7101
TF: 800-862-5326 ■ *Web:* www.duraclean.com

Federal Bldg Services Inc
1641 Barclay Blvd ..... Buffalo Grove IL 60089 847-279-7360
TF: 800-982-9234 ■ *Web:* www.federalbuildingservice.com

Fish Window Cleaning Services Inc
200 Enchanted Pkwy ..... Manchester MO 63021 636-779-1500 530-7856
TF: 877-707-3474 ■ *Web:* www.fishwindowcleaning.com

GCA Services Group 1350 Euclid Ave Ste 1500 ..... Cleveland OH 44115 800-422-8760 583-0481*
**Fax Area Code:* 216 ■ *TF:* 800-422-8760 ■ *Web:* www.gcaservices.com

Healthcare Services Group Inc (HCSG)
3220 Tillman Dr Ste 300 ..... Bensalem PA 19020 215-639-4274
TF: 800-486-3289 ■ *Web:* www.hcsgcorp.com

Heaven's Best Carpet & Upholstery Cleaning
PO Box 607 ..... Rexburg ID 83440 208-359-1106 359-1236
TF: 800-359-2095 ■ *Web:* www.heavensbest.com

Ih Services Inc PO Box 5033 ..... Greenville SC 29606 864-297-3748 297-9219
Web: www.ihservices.com

Jan-Pro International Inc (JPI)
2520 Northwinds Pkwy Ste 375 ..... Alpharetta GA 30009 678-336-1780 336-1781
TF: 866-355-1064 ■ *Web:* www.jan-pro.com

Jani-King International Inc
16885 Dallas Pkwy ..... Addison TX 75001 972-991-0900 991-5723
TF: 800-526-4546 ■ *Web:* www.janiking.com

Linc Services Mid-Atlantic LLC
3701 Saunders Ave ..... Richmond VA 23227 804-254-5790
Web: www.lincservice.com

Maid Brigade USA/Minimaid Canada
4 Concourse Pkwy Ste 200 ..... Atlanta GA 30328 770-551-9630 391-9092
TF: 866-800-7470 ■ *Web:* www.maidbrigade.com

MaidPro Corp 180 Canal St ..... Boston MA 02114 617-742-8787 720-0700
TF: 888-624-3776 ■ *Web:* www.maidpro.com

Maids International 9394 W Dodge Rd Ste 140 ..... Omaha NE 68114 402-558-8600 558-4112
TF: 800-843-6243 ■ *Web:* www.maids.com

Merry Maids 3839 Forrest Hill-Irene Rd ..... Memphis TN 38125 800-798-8000 597-8140*
**Fax Area Code:* 901 ■ *TF:* 800-798-8000 ■ *Web:* www.merrymaids.com

MPW Industrial Services Group Inc
9711 Lancaster Rd SE ..... Hebron OH 43025 740-929-1614 928-8140
TF: 800-827-8790 ■ *Web:* mpwservices.com

Neighbors Stores Inc 1314 Old Hwy 601 S ..... Mount Airy NC 27030 336-789-5561 789-7067

OctoClean Franchising Systems
3357 Chicago Ave ..... Riverside CA 92507 951-683-5859
Web: www.octoclean.com

Platinum Maintenance Services Corp
120 Broadway 36th Fl ..... New York NY 10271 212-535-9700 480-2699
Web: www.platinummaintenance.com

Professional Contract Services Inc
718 W FM 1626 ..... Austin TX 78748 512-358-8887 358-8890
Web: www.pcsi.org

Professional Janitorial Service of Houston Inc
2303 Nance St ..... Houston TX 77020 713-850-0287 963-9420
Web: www.pjs.com

Rainbow International 1010 N University Pk Dr ..... Waco TX 76707 254-756-5463 745-2592
TF: 855-724-6269 ■ *Web:* www.rainbowintl.com

Serv-U-Clean 207 Edgeley Blvd ..... Concord ON L4K4B5 416-667-0696
Web: www.servuclean.com

Service Management Systems
7135 Charlotte Pike Ste 100 ..... Nashville TN 37209 615-399-1839 399-1438
Web: www.smsclean.com

ServiceMaster Clean
3839 Forrest Hill Irene Rd ..... Memphis TN 38125 800-245-4622 597-7600*
**Fax Area Code:* 901 ■ *TF General:* 844-319-5401 ■ *Web:* www.servicemasterclean.com/about-us/contact-us

Servpro Industries Inc 801 Industrial Blvd ..... Gallatin TN 37066 615-451-0600 451-0291
TF: 800-826-9586 ■ *Web:* www.servpro.com

Sharian Inc 368 W Ponce de Leon Ave ..... Decatur GA 30030 404-373-2274
Web: sharian.com

St. Moritz Bldg Services Inc
4616 Clairton Blvd ..... Pittsburgh PA 15236 412-885-2100 885-3953
TF: 800-218-9159 ■ *Web:* www.bsinc.com

Steam Bros Inc 2400 Vermont Ave ..... Bismarck ND 58504 701-222-1263 222-1372
TF: 800-767-5064 ■ *Web:* www.steambrothers.com

Steamatic Inc 3333 Quorum Dr Ste 280 ..... Fort Worth TX 76137 817-332-1575 796-1231
Web: www.steamatic.com

Support Services of America Inc
12440 Firestone Blvd Ste 312 ..... Norwalk CA 90650 562-868-3550 868-7811
TF: 888-564-0005 ■ *Web:* www.supportservicesamerica.com

Swisher Hygiene Co 4725 Piedmont Row Dr ..... Charlotte NC 28210 704-364-7707 444-4565*
**Fax Area Code:* 800 ■ *TF:* 800-444-4138 ■ *Web:* www.swsh.com

T.u.c.s. Cleaning Service Inc 166 Central Ave ..... Orange NJ 07050 973-673-0700
TF: 800-992-5998 ■ *Web:* www.tucscleaning.com

Vanguard Cleaning Systems Inc
655 Mariners Island Blvd Ste 303 ..... San Mateo CA 94404 650-287-2400 717-2082*
**Fax Area Code:* 479 ■ *Web:* www.vanguardcleaning.com

Venoco Inc 370 17th St Ste 3900 ..... Denver CO 80202 303-626-8300
NYSE: VQ ■ *TF:* 877-777-4778 ■ *Web:* www.venocoinc.com

Window Gang 405 Arendell St ..... Morehead City NC 28557 252-726-1463
TF: 877-946-4264 ■ *Web:* www.windowgang.com

153 CLOCKS, WATCHES, RELATED DEVICES, PARTS

Phone Fax

Borg Indak Inc 701 Enterprise Dr ..... Delavan WI 53115 262-728-5531
Web: www.borgindak.com

Bulova Corp Empire State Bldg 350 Fifth Ave ..... Woodside NY 10118 718-204-3300 204-3546
TF: 800-228-5682 ■ *Web:* www.bulova.com

Canterbury International
5632 W Washington Blvd ..... Los Angeles CA 90016 323-936-7111 936-7115
TF: 800-935-7111 ■ *Web:* www.canterburyintl.com

Phone Fax

Citizen Watch Co of America Inc
1000 W 190th St ..... Torrance CA 90502 800-321-1023
TF: 800-321-1023 ■ *Web:* www.citizenwatch.com

E Gluck Corp 60-15 Little Neck Pkwy ..... Little Neck NY 11362 718-784-0700
TF: 800-840-2933 ■ *Web:* www.armitron.com

Hamilton Watch Company Inc
1200 Harbor Blvd ..... Weehawken NJ 07086 201-271-4680
Web: www.hamiltonwatch.com

Howard Miller Clock Co 860 E Main Ave ..... Zeeland MI 49464 616-772-7277 772-1670
Web: www.howardmiller.com

Movado Group Inc 650 From Rd Ste 375 ..... Paramus NJ 07652 201-267-8000
NYSE: MOV ■ *Web:* www.movadogroupinc.com

Seiko Corp of America 1111 MacArthur Blvd ..... Mahwah NJ 07430 201-529-5730
TF Cust Svc: 800-545-2783 ■ *Web:* www.seikousa.com

Seiko Instruments USA Inc
21221 S Western Ave Ste 250 ..... Torrance CA 90501 310-517-7700 517-7709
TF Sales: 800-688-0817 ■ *Web:* www.seikoinstruments.com

Swatch Group 1200 Harbor Blvd 7th Fl ..... Weehawken NJ 07086 201-271-1400 981-8589*
**Fax Area Code:* 431 ■ *Web:* www.swatchgroup.com

Timex Group USA Inc
555 Christian Rd PO Box 310 ..... Middlebury CT 06762 203-346-5000 573-5143
TF: 800-448-4639 ■ *Web:* www.timex.com

Verdin Co, The 444 Reading Rd ..... Cincinnati OH 45202 800-543-0488 241-1855*
**Fax Area Code:* 513 ■ *TF:* 800-543-0488 ■ *Web:* www.verdin.com

Vulcan Inc 410 E Berry Ave ..... Foley AL 36535 888-846-2728 943-9270*
**Fax Area Code:* 251 ■ *TF:* 888-846-2728 ■ *Web:* www.vulcaninc.com

World of Watches 3701 Flamingo Rd Ste 100 ..... Miramar FL 33027 954-983-2181
TF: 866-961-8463 ■ *Web:* www.worldofwatches.com

154 CLOSURES - METAL OR PLASTICS

Phone Fax

AptarGroup Inc
475 W Terra Cotta Ave Ste E ..... Crystal Lake IL 60014 815-477-0424 477-0481
NYSE: ATR ■ *Web:* www.aptar.com

Caplugs LLC 2150 Elmwood Ave ..... Buffalo NY 14207 716-876-9855 874-1680
TF Cust Svc: 888-227-5847 ■ *Web:* www.caplugs.com

Carpin Manufacturing Inc 411 Austin Rd ..... Waterbury CT 06705 203-574-2556 753-8771
Web: www.carpin.com

Champion Container Corp
1455 N Michael Dr PO Box 90 ..... Wood Dale IL 60191 732-636-6700 855-8663
Web: www.championcontainer.com

Essentra PLC 3123 Stn Rd ..... Erie PA 16510 814-899-9263
TF: 800-847-0486 ■ *Web:* us.essentracomponents.com

Magenta Corp 3800 N Milwaukee Ave ..... Chicago IL 60641 773-777-5050 777-4055
Web: www.magentallc.com

Phoenix Closures Inc 1899 High Grove Ln ..... Naperville IL 60540 630-420-4750 420-4769
Web: www.phoenixclosures.com

Polytop Corp 110 Graham Dr ..... Slatersville RI 02876 401-767-2400 765-2694

Rexam Closures & Containers
3245 Kansas Rd ..... Evansville IN 47725 812-867-6671
Web: www.rexamcatalogue.com

Silgan Holdings Inc 4 Landmark Sq Ste 400 ..... Stamford CT 06901 203-975-7110 975-7902
NASDAQ: SLGN ■ *Web:* www.silganholdings.com

StockCap 123 Manufacturers Dr ..... Arnold MO 63010 636-282-6800 282-6888
TF: 800-827-2277 ■ *Web:* www.stockcap.com

Stull Technologies Inc 17 Veronica Ave ..... Somerset NJ 08873 732-873-5000 873-7131
Web: www.stulltech.com

Tipper Tie Inc 2000 Lufkin Rd ..... Apex NC 27502 919-362-8811 362-7058
TF: 800-331-2905 ■ *Web:* www.tippertie.com

Van Blarcom Closures Inc 156 Sandford St ..... Brooklyn NY 11205 718-855-3810 935-9855
Web: www.vbcpkg.com

Weatherchem Corp 2222 Highland Rd ..... Twinsburg OH 44087 330-425-4206 425-1385
TF: 800-316-0072 ■ *Web:* www.weatherchem.com

155 CLOTHING & ACCESSORIES - MFR

See Also Baby Products p. 1836; Clothing & Accessories - Whol p. 1945; Fashion Design Houses p. 2282; Footwear p. 2316; Leather Goods - Personal p. 2645; Personal Protective Equipment & Clothing p. 2926

155-1 Athletic Apparel

Phone Fax

Bristol Products Corp 700 Shelby St ..... Bristol TN 37620 423-968-4140 968-2084
TF Orders: 800-336-8775 ■ *Web:* www.bristolproducts.com

Choi Bros Inc 3401 W Div St ..... Chicago IL 60651 773-489-2800 489-3030
TF: 800-524-2464 ■ *Web:* www.choibrothers.com

Columbia Sportswear Co
14375 NW Science Pk Dr ..... Portland OR 97229 503-985-4125 985-5800
NASDAQ: COLM ■ *TF:* 800-622-6953 ■ *Web:* www.columbia.com

Cutter & Buck Inc 701 N 34th St Ste 400 ..... Seattle WA 98103 888-338-9944 448-0589*
**Fax Area Code:* 206 ■ *TF:* 800-713-7810 ■ *Web:* www.cutterbuck.com

Dodger Industries
2075 Stultz Rd PO Box 711 ..... Martinsville VA 24112 800-247-7879
TF Cust Svc: 800-247-7879 ■ *Web:* www.dodgerindustries.com

Elite Sportswear LP 2136 N 13th St ..... Reading PA 19604 610-921-1469 921-0208
TF Cust Svc: 800-345-4087 ■ *Web:* www.gkelite.com

Gear for Sports Inc 9700 Commerce Pkwy ..... Lenexa KS 66219 913-693-3200 689-1692
TF: 800-255-1065 ■ *Web:* www.gearforsports.com

MJ Soffe Co 1 Soffe Dr ..... Fayetteville NC 28312 888-257-8673 486-9030*
**Fax Area Code:* 910 ■ *TF:* 888-257-8673 ■ *Web:* www.soffe.com

No Fear Plaza Camino Real
2525 El Camino Real Ste 2525 ..... Carlsbad CA 92008 760-720-0189
Web: www.nofear.com

Powers Manufacturing Co
1340 Sycamore St PO Box 2157 ..... Waterloo IA 50704 319-233-6118 234-8048
Web: www.powersathletic.com

Phone Fax

Race Face Components Inc
100 Braid St — New Westminster BC V3L3P4 604-527-9996 527-9959
TF: 800-527-9244 ■ *Web:* www.raceface.com
Royal Textile Mills Inc 929 Firetower Rd — Yanceyville NC 27379 800-334-9361 934-9360
TF: 800-334-9361 ■ *Web:* www.dukeathletic-tactical.com
Russell Corp 755 Lee St — Alexander City AL 35010 256-500-4000
Scotty's Fashions Inc 636 Pen Argyl St — Pen Argyl PA 18072 610-863-6454
Web: www.scottysfashions.com
Volcom Inc 1740 Monrovia Ave — Costa Mesa CA 92627 949-646-2175 646-5247
Web: www.volcom.com

155-2 Belts (Leather, Plastics, Fabric)

Phone Fax

Circa Corp 1330 Fitzgerald Ave — San Francisco CA 94124 415-822-1600 822-1700
Gem Dandy Inc 200 W Academy St — Madison NC 27025 336-548-9624 427-7105
TF: 800-334-5101 ■ *Web:* www.gem-dandy.com
Max Leather Group Inc 1415 Redfern Ave — Far Rockaway NY 11691 718-471-3300 471-3707
Tandy Brands Accessories Inc
3631 W Davis St Ste A — Dallas TX 75211 214-519-5200
NASDAQ: TBAC

155-3 Casual Wear (Men's & Women's)

Phone Fax

Alps Sportswear Manufacturing Co
15 Union St — Lawrence MA 01840 978-683-2438 686-8051
Attraction Inc 672 Rue du Parc — Lac-Drolet QC G0Y1C0 819-549-2477 549-2734
TF: 800-567-6095 ■ *Web:* www.attraction.com
Badger Sportswear Inc 111 Badger Ln — Statesville NC 28625 704-871-0990
TF: 888-871-0990 ■ *Web:* www.badgersport.com
Big Dogs 519 Lincoln County Pkwy — Lincolnton NC 28092 800-244-3647
TF: 800-244-3647 ■ *Web:* www.bigdogs.com
Bobby Jones Retail Corp
1034 Windward Ridge Pkwy — Alpharetta GA 30005 888-776-0076
TF Cust Svc: 888-776-0076 ■ *Web:* www.bobbyjones.com
California Manufacturing Co
2270 Weldon Pkwy — Saint Louis MO 63146 314-567-4404 567-5062
Web: www.cmcbrands.com
Cherokee Inc 5990 Sepulveda Blvd Ste 600 — Sherman Oaks CA 91411 818-908-9868
NASDAQ: CHKE ■ *Web:* www.thecherokeegroup.com
Columbia Sportswear Co
14375 NW Science Pk Dr — Portland OR 97229 503-985-4125 985-5800
NASDAQ: COLM ■ *TF:* 800-622-6953 ■ *Web:* www.columbia.com
Crazy Shirts Inc 99-969 Iwaena St — Aiea HI 96701 808-487-9919
TF: 800-771-2720 ■ *Web:* www.crazyshirts.com
Deckers Outdoor Corp 495-A S Fairview Ave — Goleta CA 93117 805-967-7611 967-9722
NYSE: DECK ■ *TF:* 877-337-8333 ■ *Web:* www.deckers.com
Delta Apparel Inc 2750 Premier Pkwy Ste 100 — Duluth GA 30097 678-775-6900 775-6992
NYSE: DLA ■ *TF:* 800-285-4456 ■ *Web:* www.deltaapparel.com
Fruit of the Loom Inc
1 Fruit of the Loom Dr PO Box 90015 — Bowling Green KY 42102 270-781-6400 781-1754
TF: 888-378-4829 ■ *Web:* www.fruitactivewear.com
Fun-Tees 4735 Corporate Dr Ste 100 — Concord NC 28027 704-788-3003 795-9300
Web: www.funtees.com
Hamrick Inc 742 Peachoid Rd — Gaffney SC 29341 864-489-6095 489-9514
Web: www.hamricks.com
Harper Industries Inc 52 Virginia St — Lucedale MS 39452 601-947-2746 947-4739
L & L Manufacturing Co 815 N Nash St — El Segundo CA 90245 310-615-0000 615-4549
Ms. Bubbles Inc 2731 S Alameda St — Los Angeles CA 90058 323-544-0300 239-9709*
**Fax Area Code:* 213 ■ *Web:* www.msbubbles.com
Quiksilver Inc 15202 Graham St — Huntington Beach CA 92649 714-889-2200
NYSE: ZQK ■ *Web:* www.quiksilverinc.com
Rothschild & Company Inc 500 Seventh Ave — New York NY 10018 212-354-8550 382-1187
Sherry Mfg 3287 NW 65th St — Miami FL 33147 305-693-7000 691-6132
TF: 800-741-4750 ■ *Web:* www.sherrymfg.com
Sport-Haley Inc 200 Union Blvd Ste 400 — Denver CO 80228 303-320-8800
TF: 800-627-9211 ■ *Web:* www.sporthaley.com
Stussy Inc 17426 Daimler St — Irvine CA 92614 949-474-9255 474-8229
Web: www.stussy.com
Surf Line Hawaii Ltd 411 Puuhale Rd — Honolulu HI 96819 808-847-5985 841-5254
Web: www.jamsworld.com
Tonix Corp 40910 Encyclopedia Cir — Fremont CA 94538 510-651-8050 651-8052
TF: 800-227-2072 ■ *Web:* www.tonixteams.com
VF Corp 105 Corporate Ctr Blvd — Greensboro NC 27408 336-424-6000 424-7634
NYSE: VFC ■ *Web:* www.vfc.com
Whisper Knits Inc 175 E New Hampshire — Southern Pines NC 28387 910-246-0450 246-0550
Web: www.whisperknits.com
Wolf Manufacturing Co 1801 W Waco Dr PO Box 3100 — Waco TX 76707 254-753-7301 753-8919*
**Fax Area Code:* 257 ■ *TF:* 800-437-0940 ■ *Web:* www.wolfmfg.com

155-4 Children's & Infants' Clothing

Phone Fax

Byer California 66 Potrero Ave — San Francisco CA 94103 415-626-7844 245-0183*
**Fax Area Code:* 925 ■ *TF:* 844-628-4498 ■ *Web:* byerca.com
Candlesticks Inc 112 W 34th St Ste 901 — New York NY 10120 212-947-8900 643-9653
Devil Dog Mfg Company Inc 400 E Gannon Ave — Zebulon NC 27597 919-269-7485 269-5962
Donegal Industries Inc
860 Anderson Ferry Rd — Mount Joy PA 17552 717-653-4818
Florence Eiseman company LLC
1966 S Fourth St — Milwaukee WI 53204 800-558-9013
TF: 800-558-9013 ■ *Web:* www.florenceeiseman.com
Gerber Childrenswear Inc
7005 Pelham Rd Ste D — Greenville SC 29602 864-987-5200 987-5264
TF: 800-642-4452 ■ *Web:* www.gerberchildrenswear.com
Good Lad Apparel 431 E Tioga St — Philadelphia PA 19134 215-739-0200
Web: goodlad.com

Phone Fax

Happy Kids Inc 100 W 33rd St — New York NY 10001 212-239-4563 736-0397
Web: happykidspersonalized.com
IFG Corp 1372 Broadway — New York NY 10018 212-239-8615
Irwin Manufacturing Corp 398 Fitzgerald Hwy — Ocilla GA 31774 229-468-9481 468-9484
Kahn Lucas Lancaster Inc
112 W 34th St Ste 600 — New York NY 10120 212-244-4500 643-1345
Web: www.kahnlucas.com
LT Apparel Group 100 W 33rd St Ste 1012 — New York NY 10001 212-502-6000 268-5160
Web: www.lollytogs.com
Mayfair Infants Group 100 W 33rd St Ste 813 — New York NY 10001 212-279-3211
Web: tawil.com
New ICM LP PO Box 1060 — El Campo TX 77437 979-578-0543 578-0503
TF: 800-987-9008 ■ *Web:* www.newicm.com
Rare Editions for Girls 1250 Broadway — New York NY 10001 212-244-1390 967-4915
Web: www.rareeditionsoutlet.com/default.asp
Royal Park Uniforms Co 14139 Hwy 86 S — Prospect Hill NC 27314 336-562-3345 562-3832
S Schwab Co Inc
12101 Upper Potomac Industrial Pk St — Cumberland MD 21502 301-729-4488 722-4870
Web: times-news.com

155-5 Coats (Overcoats, Jackets, Raincoats, etc)

Phone Fax

Alpha Industries Inc
14200 Pk Meadow Dr Ste 110S — Chantilly VA 20151 703-378-1420 378-4910
TF General: 866-631-0719 ■ *Web:* www.alphaindustries.com
Essex Mfg Inc PO Box 92864 Ste 501 — Southlake TX 76092 212-239-0080
Web: www.baum-essex.com
G-III Apparel Group Ltd 512 Seventh Ave — New York NY 10018 212-403-0500 403-0551
NASDAQ: GIII ■ *Web:* www.giii.com
Helly Hansen US Inc 4104 C St NE Ste 200 — Auburn WA 98002 800-435-5901
TF: 800-435-5901 ■ *Web:* www.hellyhansen.com
Holloway Sportswear Inc 2633 Campbell Rd — Sidney OH 45365 800-331-5156 497-7337*
**Fax Area Code:* 937 ■ **Fax:* Cust Svc ■ *TF:* 800-331-5156 ■ *Web:* www.hollowayusa.com
Item House Inc 2920 S Steele St — Tacoma WA 98409 253-627-7168 627-1070
Web: itemhouseinc.com
London Fog 1615 Kellogg Dr — Douglas GA 31535 912-384-8189
TF: 877-588-8189 ■ *Web:* www.londonfog.com
MECA Sportswear 1120 Townline Rd — Tomah WI 54660 608-374-6450 374-6405
TF: 800-729-6322 ■ *Web:* www.mecasportswear.com
Pendleton Woolen Mills Inc 220 NW Broadway — Portland OR 97209 503-226-4801 535-5502
TF: 800-760-4844 ■ *Web:* www.pendleton-usa.com
RefrigiWear Inc 54 Breakstone Dr — Dahlonega GA 30533 706-864-5757 864-5898
TF Cust Svc: 800-645-3744 ■ *Web:* www.refrigiwear.com
Rennoc Corp 645 Pine St — Greenville OH 45331 800-372-7100 675-1727
TF: 800-372-7100 ■ *Web:* www.rennoc.com
Sport Obermeyer Ltd USA Inc 115 AABC — Aspen CO 81611 970-925-5060 925-9203
TF: 800-525-4203 ■ *Web:* www.obermeyer.com
Sport-Haley Inc 200 Union Blvd Ste 400 — Denver CO 80228 303-320-8800
TF: 800-627-9211 ■ *Web:* www.sporthaley.com
Standard Mfg Company Inc 750 Second Ave — Troy NY 12182 518-235-2200 235-2668
Web: www.sportsmaster.com
Woolrich Inc 2 Mill St — Woolrich PA 17779 570-769-6464 769-6234
TF: 800-995-1299 ■ *Web:* www.woolrich.com

155-6 Costumes

Phone Fax

Cleveland Costume & Display 1271 Pearl Rd — Brunswick OH 44212 440-846-9292
Web: clevelandcostume.com
Costume Gallery 4451 Rt 130 — Burlington NJ 08016 609-386-6601 386-0677
TF: 800-222-8125 ■ *Web:* www.costumegallery.net
Costume Specialists Inc 211 N Fifth St — Columbus OH 43215 614-464-2115 464-2114
TF: 800-596-9357 ■ *Web:* www.costumespecialists.com
Curtain Call Costumes 333 E Seventh Ave — York PA 17404 717-852-6910 839-1039*
**Fax Area Code:* 800 ■ *TF:* 888-808-0801 ■ *Web:* www.curtaincallcostumes.com
Disguise 12120 Kear Pl — Poway CA 92064 858-391-3600 391-3601
TF: 877-875-2557 ■ *Web:* www.disguise.com
Morris Costumes Inc 4300 Monroe Rd — Charlotte NC 28205 704-333-4653 348-3032
Web: morriscostumes.com
Sew Biz Industries 174 Cross St — Central Falls RI 02863 401-724-8410 726-9845
Stagecraft Costuming Inc
3950 Spring Grove Ave — Cincinnati OH 45223 513-541-7150 541-7159
Web: www.stagecraft.on-rev.com/stagecraft._inc./contact_information.html

155-7 Fur Goods

Phone Fax

Blum & Fink Inc 333 Seventh Ave — New York NY 10001 212-695-2606
Corniche Furs Inc 345 Seventh Ave 20th Fl — New York NY 10001 212-239-8655 239-1811
Web: www.nycfur.com
Goodman Couture 130 W 30th St — New York NY 10001 212-244-7422
Jerry Sorbara Furs Inc 39 W 32nd St Ste 1400 — New York NY 10001 212-594-3897
Web: sorbarafur.com
LA Rockler Fur Co 16 N Fourth St — Minneapolis MN 55401 612-332-8643 332-2926
Web: rocklerfur.com
Mohl Fur Company Inc 345 Seventh Ave 3rd Fl — New York NY 10001 212-736-7676 629-4832
Sekas International Ltd
345 Seventh Ave 19th Fl — New York NY 10001 212-629-6095 629-6097
Web: www.sekasinternational.com
Steve's Original Furs Inc
150 W 30th St 8th Fl — New York NY 10001 212-967-8007 967-3871
Web: stevesoriginalfurs.com

155-8 Gloves & Mittens

Phone Fax

Carolina Glove Co
116 Mclin Creek Rd PO Box 999 — Conover NC 28613 828-464-1132 485-2416
TF: 800-335-1918 ■ *Web:* www.carolinaglove.com

	City	State	Zip	Phone	Fax
Fowness Bros & Company Inc 16 E 34th St.	New York	NY	10016	212-683-0150	683-2832
TF All: 800-345-6837 ■ *Web:* urpowered.com					
Gloves Inc 1950 Collins Boulevard	Austell	MA	30106	770-944-9186	944-0012
TF: 800-476-4568 ■ *Web:* www.glovesinc.com/contacts					
Guard-Line Inc 215 S Louise St PO Box 1030	Atlanta	TX	75551	903-796-4111	796-7262*
**Fax:* Orders ■ *TF:* 800-527-8822 ■ *Web:* www.guardline.com					
Illinois Glove Co 3701 Commercial Ave	Northbrook	IL	60062	847-291-1700	291-7722
TF: 800-342-5458 ■ *Web:* www.illinoisglove.com					
Kinco International 4286 NE 185th Dr.	Portland	OR	97230	800-547-8410	536-4905
TF General: 800-547-8410 ■ *Web:* www.kinco.com					
Magid Glove & Safety Manufacturing Co 2060 N Kolmar Ave.	Chicago	IL	60639	773-384-2070	384-6677
TF: 800-444-8010 ■ *Web:* www.magidglove.com					
MCR Safety 5321 E Shelby Dr	Memphis	TN	38118	901-795-5810	999-3908*
**Fax Area Code:* 800 ■ **Fax:* Sales ■ *TF:* 800-955-6887 ■ *Web:* www.mcrsafety.com					
Midwest Quality Gloves Inc 835 Industrial Rd	Chillicothe	MO	64601	660-646-2165	646-6933
TF: 800-821-3028 ■ *Web:* www.midwestglove.com					
Montpelier Glove Co Inc 129 N Main St.	Montpelier	IN	47359	765-728-2481	
TF: 800-645-3931 ■ *Web:* www.montpeliergsp.com					
Nationwide Glove Co 925 Bauman Ln	Harrisburg	IL	62946	618-252-6303	
North Star Glove Co 2916 S Steele St.	Tacoma	WA	98409	253-627-7107	627-0597
TF: 800-423-1616 ■ *Web:* www.northstarglove.com					
Saranac Glove Co 999 LOmbardi Ave.	Green Bay	WI	54304	920-435-3737	435-7618
TF: 800-727-2622 ■ *Web:* www.saranacglove.com					
Slate Springs Glove Co 148 Vance St	Calhoun City	MS	38916	662-637-2222	637-2515
Southern Glove Mfg Company Inc 749 AC Little Dr	Newton	NC	28658	828-464-4884	464-7968
TF Cust Svc: 800-222-1113 ■ *Web:* www.southernglove.com					
Swany America Corp 115 Corp Dr	Johnstown	NY	12095	518-725-3333	725-2026
TF: 888-234-5450 ■ *Web:* www.swanyamerica.com					
Totes Isotoner Corp 9655 International Blvd.	Cincinnati	OH	45246	513-682-8200	
Web: www.totes-isotoner.com					
Wells Lamont Industry Group 6640 W Touhy Ave	Niles	IL	60714	800-247-3295	
TF: 800-247-3295 ■ *Web:* wellslamontindustrial.com					

155-9 Hats & Caps

	City	State	Zip	Phone	Fax
180s Inc 700 S Caroline St	Baltimore	MD	21231	410-534-6320	534-6321
TF: 877-725-4386 ■ *Web:* www.180s.com					
Ahead LLC 270 Samuel Barnet Blvd	New Bedford	MA	02745	508-985-9898	985-2371*
**Fax:* Cust Svc ■ *TF:* 800-282-2246 ■ *Web:* www.aheadweb.com					
American Needle Inc 1275 Busch Pkwy	Buffalo Grove	IL	60089	847-215-0011	
Web: www.shop.americanneedle.com					
Arlington Hat Co Inc 4725 34th St.	Long Island	NY	11101	718-361-3000	361-8713
Bollman Hat Co 110 E Main St	Adamstown	PA	19501	717-484-4361	484-2139
Web: www.bollmanhats.com					
F & M Hat Co Inc 103 Walnut St PO Box 40	Denver	PA	17517	717-336-5505	336-0501
TF: 800-953-4287 ■ *Web:* www.fmhat.com					
Greg Norman Collection 134 W 37th St Ste 4	New York	NY	10018	888-667-6264	
TF: 888-667-6264 ■ *Web:* gregnormancollection.com					
Julie Hat Co 5948 Industrial Blvd	Patterson	GA	31557	912-647-2031	
Korber Hats Inc 394 Kilburn St.	Fall River	MA	02724	508-672-7033	673-0762
TF Cust Svc: 800-428-9911 ■ *Web:* korberhats.com					
Kraft Hat Manufacturers Inc 725 Whittier St.	Bronx	NY	10474	845-735-6200	735-2299
Web: www.krafthat.com					
MPC Promotions 4300 Produce Rd PO Box 34336	Louisville	KY	40232	502-451-4900	451-8475*
**Fax Area Code:* 888 ■ *TF:* 800-331-0989 ■ *Web:* www.mpcpromotions.com					
New Era Cap Company Inc 160 Delaware Ave.	Buffalo	NY	14202	716-604-9000	
TF General: 877-632-5950 ■ *Web:* www.neweracap.com					
Paramount Apparel International Inc 1 Paramount Dr	Bourbon	MO	65441	573-732-4411	
TF: 866-274-4287 ■ *Web:* www.paramountapparel.com					
Stratton Hats Inc 3200 Randolph St.	Bellwood	IL	60104	708-544-5220	544-5243
TF: 877-453-3777 ■ *Web:* www.strattonhats.com					
Town Talk Inc 6310 Cane Run Rd	Louisville	KY	40258	502-736-2972	
TF: 800-626-2220 ■ *Web:* www.ttcaps.com					

155-10 Hosiery & Socks

	City	State	Zip	Phone	Fax
Acme-McCrary Corp 159 N St	Asheboro	NC	27203	336-625-2161	629-2263
Web: www.acme-mccrary.com					
Americal Corp 389 Americal Rd	Henderson	NC	27537	252-762-2000	762-0176
Berkshire General Store, The 25 Edison Dr.	Wayne	NJ	07470	973-696-6204	
Web: www.berkshiregeneralstore.com					
Bossong Hosiery Mills Inc 840 W Salisbury St.	Asheboro	NC	27203	336-625-2175	626-6607
Carolina Hosiery Mills Inc 710 Plantation Dr	Burlington	NC	27215	336-226-5581	
Commonwealth Hosiery Mills Inc 4964 Island Ford Rd	Randleman	NC	27317	336-498-2621	
Web: commonwealthhosiery.com					
Cooper Hosiery Mills Inc 4005 Gault Ave N	Fort Payne	AL	35967	256-845-1491	845-3554
Crescent Inc PO Box 669	Niota	TN	37826	423-568-2101	568-2104
Web: www.crescenthosiery.com					
Fox River Mills Inc 227 Poplar Stq PO Box 298	Osage	IA	50461	641-732-3798	732-5128
TF: 800-247-1815 ■ *Web:* www.foxsox.com					
Harriss & Covington Hosiery Mills Inc 1250 Hickory Chapel Rd	High Point	NC	27260	336-882-6811	889-2412
Web: www.harrissandcov.com					
Highland Mills Inc 340 E 16th St	Charlotte	NC	28206	704-375-3333	342-0391
Web: www.highlandmills.com					
Holt Hosiery Mills Inc 733 Koury Dr	Burlington	NC	27215	336-227-1431	227-8614
Web: holthosiery.com					
Jefferies Socks 2203 Tucker St	Burlington	NC	27215	336-226-7315	727-5502*
**Fax Area Code:* 800 ■ *TF:* 800-334-6831 ■ *Web:* www.jefferiessocks.com					
Jockey International Inc 2300 60th St PO Box 1417	Kenosha	WI	53140	800-562-5391	658-1812*
**Fax Area Code:* 262 ■ *TF:* 800-562-5391 ■ *Web:* www.jockey.com					
Keepers International Inc 9420 Eton Ave.	Chatsworth	CA	91311	818-407-5332	
Lea-wayne Knitting Mills Inc 5937 Commerce Blvd	Morristown	TN	37814	423-586-7513	586-6437
Lemco Mills Inc 766 Koury Dr	Burlington	NC	27215	336-226-5548	
Mayo Knitting Mills Inc 2204 Austin St PO Box 160	Tarboro	NC	27886	252-823-3101	823-0368
Web: mayoknitting.com					
Moretz Inc 514 W 21st St.	Newton	NC	28658	828-464-0751	
TF: 866-714-8486 ■ *Web:* www.goldtoe.com					
Renfro Corp 661 Linville Rd.	Mount Airy	NC	27030	336-719-8000	719-8215
TF: 800-334-9091 ■ *Web:* www.renfro.com					
Slane Hosiery Mills Inc 313 S Centennial St	High Point	NC	27261	336-883-4136	886-4543
Web: www.slanehosiery.com					
Tefron USA Inc 201 St Germain Ave SW	Valdese	NC	28690	828-879-6500	
Web: www.tefron.com					
Thor-Lo Inc 2210 Newton Dr	Statesville	NC	28677	704-872-6522	838-7010
TF: 888-846-7567 ■ *Web:* www.thorlo.com					
Trimfit Inc 1900 Frost Rd Ste 111	Bristol	PA	19007	215-781-0600	781-1803
Web: trimfit.com					
Twin City Knitting Company Inc (TCK) 104 Rock Barn Rd NE	Conover	NC	28613	828-464-4830	
TF: 800-438-6884 ■ *Web:* www.tcksports.com					
Wigwam Mills Inc 3402 Crocker Ave	Sheboygan	WI	53082	920-457-5551	
TF: 800-558-7760 ■ *Web:* www.wigwam.com					

155-11 Jeans

	City	State	Zip	Phone	Fax
Aalfs Mfg Co 1005 Fourth St.	Sioux City	IA	51101	712-252-1877	252-5205
Web: aalfs.com					
Ditto Apparel of California Inc 229 Webb Smith Dr	Colfax	LA	71417	318-627-3264	
Elk Brand Manufacturing Co 1601 County Hospital Rd PO Box 281287	Nashville	TN	37228	615-254-4300	
Web: www.elkbrand.com					
Flynn Enterprises Inc 2203 Walnut St.	Hopkinsville	KY	42240	270-886-0223	886-0573
Jordache Enterprises 1400 Broadway	New York	NY	10018	212-944-1330	768-5736
Web: www.jordache.com					
Lee Jeans 9001 W 67th St.	Merriam	KS	66202	913-384-4000	
TF Cust Svc: 800-453-3348 ■ *Web:* www.lee.com					
Levi Strauss & Co 1155 Battery St	San Francisco	CA	94111	415-501-6000	501-7112
TF: 866-290-6064 ■ *Web:* www.levistrauss.com					
Miller International Inc Rocky Mountain Clothing Company Div 8500 Zuni St.	Denver	CO	80260	303-428-5696	
Web: www.rockymountainclothing.com					
Reed Mfg Co Inc 1321 S Veterans Blvd	Tupelo	MS	38804	662-842-4472	237-5898*
**Fax Area Code:* 800 ■ *TF:* 800-466-1154 ■ *Web:* www.reedmanufacturing.com					
VF Corporation PO Box 21488	Greensboro	NC	27420	336-424-6000	283-3113*
**Fax Area Code:* 800 ■ *TF Orders:* 866-492-3370 ■ *Web:* www.vfc.com					

155-12 Men's Clothing

	City	State	Zip	Phone	Fax
After Six 118 W 20th St	New York	NY	10011	646-638-9600	
TF: 800-444-8304 ■ *Web:* www.aftersix.com					
American Apparel LLC 747 Warehouse St.	Los Angeles	CA	90021	213-488-0226	488-0334
TF: 888-747-0070 ■ *Web:* www.americanapparel.net					
Anniston Sportswear Corp PO Box 189	Anniston	AL	36201	256-236-1551	831-9414
TF: 866-814-9253 ■ *Web:* www.annistonstar.com					
Antigua Sportswear Inc 16651 N 84 Ave	Peoria	AZ	85382	623-523-6000	
TF: 800-528-3133 ■ *Web:* www.antigua.com					
Barry Better Menswear 125 John W Morrow Pkwy Ste 242B	Gainesville	GA	30501	770-534-7685	
Web: barrysmenswear.com					
Capital Mercury Apparel 1359 Broadway 19th Fl.	New York	NY	10018	212-704-4800	704-4830
David Peyser Sportswear Inc 90 Spence St.	Bay Shore	NY	11706	631-231-7788	435-8018
English American Tailoring Co 411 N Cranberry Rd	Westminster	MD	21157	410-857-5774	386-0417
Web: www.englishamericanco.com					
Fishman & Tobin Inc 4000 Chemical Rd Ste 500 Metroplex Corp Ctr-1	Plymouth Meeting	PA	19462	610-828-8400	
Web: www.fishmantobin.com					
Franklin Clothing Company Inc 208 Lurgan Ave	Shippensburg	PA	17257	717-532-4146	
Gitman & Co 2309 Chestnut St	Ashland	PA	17921	570-875-3100	
TF: 800-526-3929 ■ *Web:* www.gitman.com					
Gitman Bros Shirt Company Inc 2309 Chestnut St 19th Fl	Ashland	PA	10019	212-581-6968	
TF General: 800-526-3929 ■ *Web:* www.gitman.com					
Granite Knitwear Inc 805 S Salberry Ave Hwy 52S	Granite Quarry	NC	28072	704-279-5526	279-8205
TF Cust Svc: 800-476-9944 ■ *Web:* www.calcru.com					
Greg Norman Collection 134 W 37th St Ste 4	New York	NY	10018	888-667-6264	
TF: 888-667-6264 ■ *Web:* gregnormancollection.com					
H Freeman & Son Inc 411 N Cranberry Rd.	Westminster	MD	21157	410-857-5774	857-1560
TF: 800-876-7700 ■ *Web:* www.hfreemanco.com					
Haggar Clothing Co 11511 Luna Rd 2 Colinas Crossing	Dallas	TX	75234	214-352-8481	956-4367
TF: 877-841-2219 ■ *Web:* www.haggar.com					
Hardwick Clothes Inc 3800 Old Tasso Rd	Cleveland	TN	37312	800-251-6392	442-7394
TF: 800-251-6392 ■ *Web:* hardwick.com					
Hart Schaffner Marx (HSM) 1680 E Touhy Ave.	Des Plaines	IL	60018	800-327-4466	
TF: 800-327-4466 ■ *Web:* www.hartschaffnermarx.com					
Hickey Freeman 1155 N Clinton Ave	Rochester	NY	14621	585-467-7021	
TF Cust Svc: 844-755-7344 ■ *Web:* www.hickeyfreeman.com					

Phone Fax

Hugo Boss Fashions Inc 601 W 26th St 8th fl..........New York NY 10001 212-940-0600 940-0616
Web: www.hugoboss.com/us

Indiana Knitwear Corp 230 E Osage St.............. Greenfield IN 46140 317-462-4413 462-0994

Individualized Shirts Co 581 Cortland St .... Perth Amboy NJ 08861 732-826-8400
Web: individualizedshirts.com

Jos A Bank Clothiers 500 Hanover Pk.............. Hampstead MD 21074 410-239-2700
TF Cust Svc: 800-999-7472 ■ *Web:* www.josbank.com

Nautica Retail USA Inc 40 W 57th St Ste 7...........New York NY 10019 212-541-5757
Web: www.nautica.com

Oxford Industries Inc
999 Peachtree St NE Ste 688 ....Atlanta GA 30309 404-659-2424 653-1545
NYSE: OXM ■ *Web:* www.oxfordinc.com

Oxxford Clothes Inc 1220 W Van Buren St.............Chicago IL 60607 312-829-3600 829-6075
Web: www.oxxfordclothes.com

Phillips-Van Heusen Corp 200 Madison Ave ....New York NY 10016 212-381-3500
NYSE: PVH ■ *TF:* 888-203-1112 ■ *Web:* www.pvh.com

Scotty's Fashions Inc 636 Pen Argyl St ....Pen Argyl PA 18072 610-863-6454
Web: www.scottysfashions.com

Smart Apparel US Inc 1400 Broadway 10th Fl..........New York NY 10018 212-329-3400
Web: smartapparelus.com

Southwick Clothing LLC 20 Computer Dr............. Haverhill MA 01832 978-686-3833
Web: www.southwick.com

Tom James Co 263 Seaboard Ln......................Franklin TN 37067 615-771-0795
TF: 800-236-9023 ■ *Web:* www.tomjames.com

Weatherproof Garment Co
1071 Ave of the Americas..........................New York NY 10018 212-695-7716
Web: weatherproofgarment.com

155-13 Neckwear

Phone Fax

Burma Bibas Inc 597 Fifth Ave 10th Fl................New York NY 10017 212-750-2500
Web: www.burmabibas.com

Carolina Mfg 7025 Augusta Rd.................... Greenville SC 29605 864-299-0600 299-0603
TF: 800-845-2744 ■ *Web:* thebandannacompany.com

Carter & Holmes N1510 Geneva Ave .... Lake Geneva WI 53147 262-215-5494 248-1425
Web: www.carterholmes.com

Echo Design Group 10 E 40th St 16th Fl..............New York NY 10016 212-686-8771
TF General: 800-327-3896 ■ *Web:* www.echodesign.com

Mallory & Church LLC 676 S Industrial Way ....Seattle WA 98108 206-587-2100 587-2971

MMG Corp 1717 Olive St .... Saint Louis MO 63103 314-421-2182 421-4912

PVH Neckwear Inc 1735 S Santa Fe Ave ....Los Angeles CA 90021 213-688-7970
Web: www.pvh.com

Ralph Marlin & Co 1701 Pearl St Ste 4 .... Waukesha WI 53186 262-549-5100 549-5122

Robert Talbott Inc
2901 Monterey-Salinas Hwy.....................Camel Valley CA 93940 831-649-6000
Web: www.roberttalbott.com

155-14 Robes (Ceremonial)

Phone Fax

Academic Apparel 20644 Superior St .... Chatsworth CA 91311 818-886-8697 886-8743
TF: 800-626-5000 ■ *Web:* www.academicapparel.com

CM Almy Inc 1 Ruth Rd.......................... Pittsfield ME 04967 207-487-3232
TF: 800-225-2569 ■ *Web:* www.almy.com

Gaspard Inc 200 N Janacek Rd .... Brookfield WI 53045 262-784-6800 784-7567
TF: 800-784-6868 ■ *Web:* www.gaspardinc.com

Jostens Inc 3601 Minnesota Ave Ste 400 .... Minneapolis MN 55435 952-830-3300 830-3293*
**Fax:* Hum Res ■ *TF:* 800-235-4774 ■ *Web:* www.jostens.com

Oak Hall Industries 840 Union St...................... Salem VA 24153 540-387-0000 387-2034
TF: 800-223-0429 ■ *Web:* www.oakhalli.com

Thomas Creative Apparel Inc 1 Harmony Pl .... New London OH 44851 419-929-1506 929-0122
TF: 800-537-2575 ■ *Web:* www.thomasrobes.com

Willsie Cap & Gown Co 1220 S 13th St................Omaha NE 68108 402-341-6536
TF: 800-234-4696 ■ *Web:* www.willsieco.com

155-15 Sleepwear

Phone Fax

Isaco International Corp 5980 Miami Lakes Dr .... Miami FL 33014 305-594-4455 594-4496
Web: www.isaco.com

Milco Industries Inc 550 E Fifth St ....Bloomsburg PA 17815 570-784-0400 387-8433
Web: milcoind.com

Miss Elaine Inc 8430 Valcour Ave .... Saint Louis MO 63123 314-631-1900
TF: 800-458-1422 ■ *Web:* www.misselaine.com

Roytex Inc 16 E 34th St 17th Fl......................New York NY 10016 212-686-3500 686-4336
Web: www.roytex.com

Wormser Corp 150 Coolidge Ave....................Englewood NJ 07631 800-546-4040
TF: 800-546-4040 ■ *Web:* www.wormsercorp.com

155-16 Sweaters (Knit)

Phone Fax

Binghamton Knitting Co Inc 11 Alice St............Binghamton NY 13904 877-746-3368 722-4621*
**Fax Area Code:* 607 ■ *TF:* 877-746-3368 ■ *Web:* www.binghamtonknitting.com

Mamiye Bros Inc Group 1385 Broadway Ste 1385 ......New York NY 10018 212-279-4150 695-2659
Web: mamiye.com

155-17 Swimwear

Phone Fax

A & H Sportswear Company Inc
500 William St.....................................Pen Argyl PA 18072 610-863-4176

AH Schreiber Co 460 W 34th St Ste 1002..............New York NY 10001 212-564-2700 594-7234

Blue Sky Swimwear
729 E International Speedway Blvd...............Daytona Beach FL 32118 386-255-2590 253-5938
TF Orders: 800-799-6445 ■ *Web:* www.blueskyswimwear.com

Quiksilver Inc 15202 Graham St............. Huntington Beach CA 92649 714-889-2200
NYSE: ZQK ■ *Web:* www.quiksilverinc.com

TYR Sport 1790 Apollo Ct..........................Seal Beach CA 90740 714-897-0799
TF: 800-252-7878 ■ *Web:* tyr.com

Venus Swimwear 11711 Marco Beach Dr...........Jacksonville FL 32224 904-645-6000 648-0411*
**Fax Area Code:* 800 ■ *TF:* 800-366-7946 ■ *Web:* www.venus.com

155-18 Undergarments

Phone Fax

Alpha Distribution Solutions
350 Rte 61 S.............................. Schuylkill Haven PA 17972 570-385-0511 385-0467
Web: alphadistsol.com

Biflex Intimates Group
180 Madison Ave 6th Fl..........................New York NY 10016 212-532-8340
Web: biflex.com

Cupid Foundations Inc 475 Pk Ave S 17th Fl..........New York NY 10016 212-686-6224 481-9357
TF: 877-649-5283 ■ *Web:* cupidintimates.com

Delta Galil USA 1 Harmon Plz 5th Fl..................Secaucus NJ 07094 201-902-0055 902-0070
Web: www.deltagalil.com

Gelmart Industries Inc
136 Madison Ave 4th Fl..........................New York NY 10016 212-743-6900 725-7248
TF General: 800-746-0014 ■ *Web:* www.gelmart.com

Glamorise Foundations Inc 135 Madison Ave..........New York NY 10016 212-684-5025
Web: glamorise.com

Indera Mills Co 350 W Maple St PO Box 309..........Yadkinville NC 27055 336-679-4440 679-4475
TF: 800-334-8605 ■ *Web:* www.inderamills.com

Jockey International Inc
2300 60th St PO Box 1417....................... Kenosha WI 53140 800-562-5391 658-1812*
**Fax Area Code:* 262 ■ *TF:* 800-562-5391 ■ *Web:* www.jockey.com

Leading Lady 24050 Commerce Pk................ Beachwood OH 44122 216-464-5490
TF Cust Svc: 800-321-4804 ■ *Web:* www.leadinglady.com

Reliable of Milwaukee Inc
6737 W Washington Ste 3200 ....Milwaukee WI 53214 414-272-5084
Web: www.reliableofmilwaukee.com

Robinson Mfg Company Inc
798 Market St PO Box 338..........................Dayton TN 37321 423-775-2212
TF: 800-251-7286 ■ *Web:* www.robinsonmfg.com

Spencers Inc 290 Quarry Rd .... Mount Airy NC 27030 336-789-9111

Spirite Industries Inc 150 S Dean St...............Englewood NJ 07631 201-871-4910
Web: www.spirite.com

VF Corp 105 Corporate Ctr Blvd.................. Greensboro NC 27408 336-424-6000 424-7634
NYSE: VFC ■ *Web:* www.vfc.com

Wacoal America 50 Polito Ave.................... Lyndhurst NJ 07071 201-933-8400
TF: 800-922-6250 ■ *Web:* www.wacoal-america.com

Wacoal Europe 65 Sprague St.................... Hyde Park MA 02136 617-361-7559 361-7527
TF: 800-733-8964 ■ *Web:* www.wacoal-europe.com

155-19 Uniforms & Work Clothes

Phone Fax

A+ School Apparel 401 Knoss Ave................... Star City AR 71667 800-227-3215 628-9020*
**Fax Area Code:* 888 ■ *TF:* 800-227-3215 ■ *Web:* www.schoolapparel.com

Action Sports Systems Inc
617 Carbon City Rd PO Box 1442 ....Morganton NC 28655 828-584-8000
TF: 800-631-1091 ■ *Web:* www.actionsportsuniforms.com

Algy Team Collection 440 NE First Ave.............. Hallandale FL 33009 954-457-8100 928-2282*
**Fax Area Code:* 888 ■ *TF:* 800-458-2549 ■ *Web:* www.algyteam.com

American Uniform Co 4363 Ocoee St N Ste 3 .... Cleveland TN 37312 423-476-6561 479-6241

Anson Shirt Co Cloud Ave....................... Wadesboro NC 28170 704-694-5148

Barco Uniforms Inc 350 W Rosecrans Ave.............Gardena CA 90248 310-323-7315 324-5274*
**Fax:* Cust Svc ■ *TF:* 800-421-1874 ■ *Web:* www.barcouniforms.com

Berne Apparel Co 2210 Summit St................ New Haven IN 46774 260-469-3136
TF: 800-843-7657 ■ *Web:* www.berneapparel.com

Blauer Mfg Co Inc 20 Aberdeen St....................Boston MA 02215 617-536-6606 536-6948
TF: 800-225-6715 ■ *Web:* www.blauer.com

Blue Generation Div of M Rubin & Sons Inc
34-01 38th Ave................................Long Island NY 11101 718-361-2800 361-2680
TF: 888-336-4687 ■ *Web:* www.bluegeneration.com

Carhartt Inc 5750 Mercury Dr..................... Dearborn MI 48126 313-271-8460 271-3455
TF: 800-833-3118 ■ *Web:* www.carhartt.com

Choi Bros Inc 3401 W Div St........................Chicago IL 60651 773-489-2800 489-3030
TF: 800-524-2464 ■ *Web:* www.choibrothers.com

City Shirt Company Inc 10 City Shirt Rd.............Frackville PA 17931 570-874-4251

DeMoulin Bros & Company Inc
1025 S Fourth St .... Greenville IL 62246 618-664-2000 664-1712
TF: 800-228-8134 ■ *Web:* www.demoulin.com

Dennis Uniform Mfg Company Inc
135 SE Hawthorne Blvd ....Portland OR 97214 800-854-6951
TF: 800-854-6951 ■ *Web:* www.dennisuniform.com

Dickson Industries Inc 2425 Dean Ave.............Des Moines IA 50317 515-262-8061 262-1844
Web: www.dicksonindustries.com

Earl's Apparel Inc 908 S Fourth St....................Crockett TX 75835 936-544-5521 544-7973
TF: 800-527-3148 ■ *Web:* www.stanray.us

Elbeco Inc 4418 Pottsville Pk..........................Reading PA 19605 610-921-0651 921-8651
TF: 800-468-4654 ■ *Web:* www.elbeco.com

Encompass Group LLC 615 Macon Rd............. McDonough GA 30253 770-957-1211
TF: 800-284-4540 ■ *Web:* www.encompassgroup.net

Fechheimer Bros Company Inc
4545 Malsbary Rd .... Cincinnati OH 45242 513-793-5400 793-7819
TF: 800-543-1939 ■ *Web:* www.fechheimer.com

Gibson & Barnes 1900 Weld Blvd Ste 140 ....El Cajon CA 92020 619-440-6977 748-6694*
**Fax Area Code:* 800 ■ *TF Sales:* 800-748-6693 ■ *Web:* www.gibson-barnes.com

Golden Mfg Company Inc 125 Hwy 366 PO Box 390 ......Golden MS 38847 662-454-3428 454-9240

Howard Uniform Co 1915 Annapolis Rd...............Baltimore MD 21230 410-727-3086 727-3142
TF: 800-628-8299 ■ *Web:* www.howarduniform.com

Phone | Fax

I Spiewak & Sons Inc 463 Seventh Ave ... New York NY 10018 212-695-1620 629-4803
Web: www.spiewak.com

Integrated Textile Solutions Inc
865 Cleveland Ave ... Salem VA 24153 540-389-8113 387-5855
Web: www.intextile.com

Key Industries Inc 400 Marble Rd ... Fort Scott KS 66701 620-223-2000 223-5882
TF: 800-835-0365 ■ *Web:* www.keyapparel.com

Landau Uniforms Inc 8410 W Sandidge Rd ... Olive Branch MS 38654 662-895-7200
Web: www.landau.com

LC King Mfg Company Inc 24 Seventh St ... Bristol TN 37620 423-764-5188 764-6809
TF: 800-826-2510 ■ *Web:* lcking.com

Leventhal Ltd PO Box 564 ... Fayetteville NC 28302 800-847-4095 352-6635
TF General: 800-847-4095 ■ *Web:* www.leventhalltd.com

Lion Apparel Inc 7200 Poe Ave Ste 400 ... Dayton OH 45414 937-898-1949 898-2848*
**Fax:* Hum Res ■ *TF:* 800-548-6614 ■ *Web:* www.lionprotects.com

Nationwide Uniform Corp
235 Shepherdsville Rd ... Hodgenville KY 42748 270-358-4173 358-8255

Riverside Manufacturing Co 301 Riverside Dr ... Moultrie GA 31768 229-985-5210 890-2932
TF: 800-841-8677 ■ *Web:* www.riversideuniforms.com

Royal Park Uniforms Co 14139 Hwy 86 S ... Prospect Hill NC 27314 336-562-3345 562-3832

Rubin Bros Inc 2241 S Halsted St ... Chicago IL 60608 312-942-1111
Web: www.rubinbrothers.com

SCORE American Soccer Company Inc
726 E Anaheim St ... Wilmington CA 90744 800-626-7774
TF: 800-626-7774 ■ *Web:* www.scoresports.com

Scotty's Fashions Inc 636 Pen Argyl St ... Pen Argyl PA 18072 610-863-6454
Web: www.scottysfashions.com

Stanbury Uniforms Inc
108 Stanbury Industrial Dr PO Box 100 ... Brookfield MO 64628 660-258-2246 258-5781
TF: 800-826-2246 ■ *Web:* www.stanbury.com

Standard Textile Company Inc
1 Knollcrest Dr ... Cincinnati OH 45237 513-761-9255 761-0467
TF: 800-999-0400 ■ *Web:* www.standardtextile.com

Superior Uniform Group Inc
10055Seminole Blvd ... Seminole FL 33772 727-397-9611
NASDAQ: SGC ■ *TF Cust Svc:* 800-727-8643 ■ *Web:* superioruniformgroup.com

Topps Safety Apparel Inc
2516 E State Rd 14 ... Rochester IN 46975 574-223-4311 223-8622
TF: 800-348-2990 ■ *Web:* www.toppssafetyapparel.com

Universal Overall Co 1060 W Van Buren St ... Chicago IL 60607 312-226-3336 226-1986
TF Cust Svc: 800-621-3344 ■ *Web:* www.universaloverall.com

Wenaas AGS Inc
12211 Parc Crest Dr Bldg Ste 100 ... Stafford TX 77477 281-931-4300 931-4328
TF: 888-576-2668 ■ *Web:* www.wenaasusa.com

Williamson-Dickie Mfg Co
509 W Vickery Blvd ... Fort Worth TX 76104 866-411-1501
TF: 866-411-1501 ■ *Web:* www.dickies.com

155-20 Western Wear (Except Hats & Boots)

Phone | Fax

Darwood Manufacturing Co 620 W Railroad St S ... Pelham GA 31779 229-294-4932 294-9323
Web: www.darwoodmfg.com

Miller International Inc Rocky Mountain Clothing Company Div
8500 Zuni St ... Denver CO 80260 303-428-5696
Web: www.rockymountainclothing.com

Niver Western Wear Inc PO Box 101224 ... Fort Worth TX 76185 817-924-4299 924-4296
TF Orders: 800-433-5752

Rockmount Ranch Wear Manufacturing Co
1626 Wazee St ... Denver CO 80202 303-629-7777 629-5836
TF: 800-776-2566 ■ *Web:* www.rockmount.com

Sidran Inc 1050 Venture Ct Ste 100 ... Carrollton TX 75006 214-352-7979 352-0439
TF: 800-969-5015 ■ *Web:* www.sidraninc.com

155-21 Women's Clothing

Phone | Fax

Adrianna Papell 512 Seventh Ave 10th Fl ... New York NY 10018 212-695-5244
Web: www.adriannapapell.com

Alfred Angelo Inc 1301 Virginia Dr ... Fort Washington PA 19034 215-659-5300
TF: 888-218-0044 ■ *Web:* www.alfredangelo.com

Bari-Jay Fashions Inc 225 W 37th St 7th Fl ... New York NY 10018 212-921-1551 391-0165
Web: www.barijay.com

Basham Industries 10325 SR 56 ... Coalmont TN 37313 931-692-3218
Web: www.bashamindustries.com/contact.htm

bebe stores Inc 400 Valley Dr ... Brisbane CA 94005 415-715-3900
NASDAQ: BEBE ■ *TF:* 877-232-3777 ■ *Web:* www.bebe.com

Bernard Chaus Inc 530 Seventh Ave 18th Fl ... New York NY 10018 212-354-1280
Web: www.chausnewyork.com

Byer California 66 Potrero Ave ... San Francisco CA 94103 415-626-7844 245-0183*
**Fax Area Code:* 925 ■ *TF:* 844-628-4498 ■ *Web:* byerca.com

Carole Wren Inc 30-30 47th Ave ... Long Island NY 11101 718-552-3800
Web: www.carolewren.com

Christine Alexander Inc
34210 Ninth Ave S Ste 101 ... Federal Way WA 98003 253-874-5570
Web: www.christinealexander.com

Darue of California Inc 14102 S Broadway ... Los Angeles CA 90061 310-323-1350
TF: 877-693-2783 ■ *Web:* www.darue.com

Donna Karan International Inc
550 Seventh Ave ... New York NY 10018 212-789-1500 789-1820
TF General: 877-316-0975 ■ *Web:* www.donnakaran.com

Gator of Florida Inc 5002 N Howard Ave ... Tampa FL 33603 813-877-8267
Web: gatorofflorida.com

Graff Californiawear 1515 E 15th St ... Los Angeles CA 90021 213-749-0171 746-5754

JLM Couture Inc 525 Seventh Ave Ste 1703 ... New York NY 10018 212-221-8203
TF: 800-924-6475 ■ *Web:* www.jlmcouture.com

Jones Apparel Group Inc Jones New York Collection Div
1411 Broadway ... New York NY 10018 212-355-4449
TF: 800-999-1877 ■ *Web:* www.jny.com

Kellwood Co 600 Kellwood Pkwy ... Chesterfield MO 63017 314-576-3100 576-3434
Web: www.kellwood.com

Phone | Fax

Leon Max Inc 3100 New York Dr ... Pasadena CA 91107 626-797-9991 797-8555
TF: 888-334-4629 ■ *Web:* www.maxstudio.com

Scotty's Fashions Inc 636 Pen Argyl St ... Pen Argyl PA 18072 610-863-6454
Web: www.scottysfashions.com

Sunrise Brands 801 S Figueroa St Ste 2500 ... Los Angeles CA 90017 323-780-8250 881-0369
Web: www.sunrisebrands.com

Tama Mfg Company Inc 100 Cascade Dr ... Allentown PA 18109 610-231-3100 231-3180
Web: www.tamamfg.com

Tanner Cos LLC 581Rock Rd ... Rutherfordton NC 28139 828-287-4205 287-6196
TF: 877-872-4578

Ursula of Switzerland Inc 31 Mohawk Ave ... Waterford NY 12188 800-826-4041 237-3038*
**Fax Area Code:* 518 ■ *TF:* 800-826-4041 ■ *Web:* www.ursula.com

156 CLOTHING & ACCESSORIES - WHOL

Phone | Fax

Alternative Apparel Inc 700 Lake Ave ... Atlanta GA 30307 404-522-2665 460-1260
Web: www.iceboxcoolstuff.com

Crew Outfitters Inc 1001 Virginia Ave ... Atlanta GA 30354 888-345-5353
TF: 888-345-5353 ■ *Web:* www.crewoutfitters.com

Elastic Therapy Inc 718 Industrial Park Ave ... Asheboro NC 27205 336-625-0529
Web: www.elastictherapy.com

Foria International Inc
18689 Arenth Ave ... City of Industry CA 91748 626-912-6100 964-9933
Web: www.foria.com

Herman's Inc 2820 Blackhawk Rd ... Rock Island IL 61201 309-788-9568 786-8296
TF: 800-447-1295 ■ *Web:* hermansinc.com

Marmaxx Group 770 Cochituate Rd ... Framingham MA 01701 508-390-1000
Web: www.tjx.com

MediUSA L P 6481 Franz Warner Pkwy ... Whitsett NC 27377 336-449-4440
Web: www.mediusa.com

Noamex Inc 625 Wortman Ave ... Brooklyn NY 11208 718-342-2278 342-2258
Web: www.noamex.com

Smokin Joes Cigars LLC
2293 Saunders Settlement Rd ... Sanborn NY 14132 716-261-9327
Web: www.smokinjoes.com

Soex West USA LLC 3294 E 26th St ... Vernon CA 90058 323-264-8300 227-6845
Web: www.soexgroup.de

Topwin Corp 1808 Abalone Ave ... Torrance CA 90501 310-325-2255 325-1877
Web: www.topwin.co.jp

TSC Apparel LLC 12080 Mosteller Rd ... Cincinnati OH 45241 513-771-1138 248-1069*
**Fax Area Code:* 800 ■ *TF:* 800-543-7230 ■ *Web:* www.tscapparel.com

Tucker Rocky Distributing Inc
4900 Alliance Gateway Fwy ... Fort Worth TX 76177 817-258-9000
Web: www.tuckerrocky.com

William B Coleman Company Inc
4001 Earhart Blvd ... New Orleans LA 70125 504-822-1000 822-3152

World Wide Dreams LLC 4 W 33rd St ... New York NY 10001 212-244-4034

WS Emerson Co Inc 15 Acme Rd ... Brewer ME 04412 800-789-6120 989-8540*
**Fax Area Code:* 207 ■ *TF:* 800-789-6120 ■ *Web:* www.wsemerson.com

157 CLOTHING STORES

See Also Department Stores p. 2191

157-1 Children's Clothing Stores

Phone | Fax

Base Camp Franchising 170 S 1000 E ... Salt Lake City UT 84102 801-359-0071
Web: basecampfranchising.com

Children's Place Retail Stores Inc
500 Plz Dr ... Secaucus NJ 07094 201-558-2400
NASDAQ: PLCE ■ *TF:* 877-752-2387 ■ *Web:* www.childrensplace.com

Goldbug Inc 18245 E 40th Ave ... Aurora CO 80011 303-371-2535
TF: 800-942-9442 ■ *Web:* goldbuginc.com

Gymboree Corp 500 Howard St ... San Francisco CA 94105 415-278-7000 278-7100
NASDAQ: GYMB ■ *TF:* 877-449-6932 ■ *Web:* www.gymboree.com

Kid to Kid 1244 Township Line Rd ... Drexel Hill PA 19026 610-446-2544
Web: www.kidtokid.com

Stretch-O-Rama Inc 5 Paddock St ... Avenel NJ 07001 732-855-1400

Tween Brands Inc 8323 Walton Pkwy ... New Albany OH 43054 614-775-3500
Web: www.tooinc.com

Valor Brands LLC 960 N Point Pkwy Ste 100 ... Alpharetta GA 30005 770-346-9250
TF: 866-949-9098 ■ *Web:* www.valorbrands.com

Winmark Corp 605Hwy 169 N Ste 400 ... Minneapolis MN 55441 763-520-8500 520-8410
NASDAQ: WINA ■ *TF:* 877-536-1561 ■ *Web:* www.winmarkcorporation.com

157-2 Family Clothing Stores

Phone | Fax

Belvest USA Inc 5 E 57th St ... New York NY 10022 212-317-0460
Web: www.belvest.com

Blue Canoe Inc 390 Lk Benbow Dr ... Garberville CA 95542 707-923-1373
Web: www.bluecanoe.com

Bob's Stores Inc 160 Corporate Ct ... Meriden CT 06450 203-235-5775
TF: 866-333-2627 ■ *Web:* www.bobstores.com

Citi Trends Inc 104 Coleman Blvd ... Savannah GA 31408 912-236-1561
NASDAQ: CTRN ■ *Web:* www.cititrends.com

Dawahares Inc 1845 Alexandria Dr ... Lexington KY 40504 859-278-0422 514-3299
TF: 800-677-9108 ■ *Web:* www.dawahares.com

De Byle's Inc 20 N Brown St ... Rhinelander WI 54501 715-362-4406

Forman Mills
1070 Thomas Busch Memorial Hwy ... Pennsauken NJ 08110 856-486-1447
Web: formanmills.com

Foursome Inc 3570 Vicksveurg Ln N Ste 100 ... Plymouth MN 55447 763-473-4667 504-5555
TF: 888-368-7766 ■ *Web:* www.thefoursome.com

Genetic Los Angeles 2344 E 38th St ... Los Angeles CA 90015 213-747-3344
Web: geneticlosangeles.com

Halston LLC 1201 W Fifth St 11th fl ... Los Angeles CA 90017 844-425-7866
TF: 844-425-7866 ■ *Web:* www.halston.com

				Phone	Fax
Hammer's Store 1415 W Dinah Shore Blvd. *Web:* hammersstore.com	Winchester	TN	37398	931-967-2886	
Kittery Trading Post 301 US 1 *Fax Area Code: 207 ■ *TF:* 888-587-6246 ■ *Web:* www.kitterytradingpost.com	Kittery	ME	03904	603-334-1157	439-8001*
Madewell Inc 486 Broadway *Web:* www.madewell.com	New York	NY	10013	212-226-6954	
Marshalls Inc 770 Cochituate Rd *TF:* 800-627-7425 ■ *Web:* www.marshallsonline.com	Framingham	MA	01701	800-627-7425	
Name Brands Inc 7215 S Memorial Dr *Web:* www.halfofhalf.com	Tulsa	OK	74133	918-307-0289	
National Stores Inc 15001 S Figueroa St *Web:* www.fallasstores.net	Gardena	CA	90248	310-324-9962	856-0162
Palais Royal 10201 S Main St *TF:* 800-743-8730	Houston	TX	77025	713-667-5601	838-4494
Puritan of Cape Cod 408 Main St *TF:* 800-924-0606 ■ *Web:* www.puritancapecod.com	Hyannis	MA	02601	508-775-2400	
SDG, Inc 200 N Broadway St *Web:* www.sharpeclothing.com	Checotah	OK	74426	918-473-2233	
Thom Browne Inc 100 Hudson St *Web:* www.thombrowne.com	New York	NY	10013	212-633-1197	
TJ Maxx 770 Cochituate Rd *TF Cust Svc:* 800-926-6299 ■ *Web:* tjmaxx.tjx.com	Framingham	MA	01701	508-390-1000	
United Fashions of Texas LLC 4629 Macro Dr *Web:* melrosestore.com	San Antonio	TX	78218	210-662-7140	666-3211
Victor Talbots Inc 47 Glen Cove Rd *Web:* victortalbots.com	Greenvale	NY	11548	516-625-1787	
Wakefield's Inc 3100 McClellan Blvd Quintard Ave *TF:* 800-333-1552 ■ *Web:* www.wakefields.com	Anniston	AL	36201	256-237-9521	
Zumiez Inc 6300 Merrill Creek Pkwy Ste B *NASDAQ: ZUMZ* ■ *TF:* 877-828-6929 ■ *Web:* www.zumiez.com	Everett	WA	98203	425-551-1500	551-1555

157-3 Men's Clothing Stores

				Phone	Fax
Boyds Philadelphia 1818 Chestnut St *Web:* www.boydsphila.com	Philadelphia	PA	19103	215-564-9000	
Caplan's Mens Shops Inc 916 Third St *Web:* www.shopcaplans.com	Alexandria	LA	71301	318-427-7700	
Carroll & Co 425 N Canon Dr *TF:* 800-238-9400 ■ *Web:* www.carrollandco.com	Beverly Hills	CA	90210	310-273-9060	273-7974
Casual Male Retail Group Inc 555 Tpke St *NASDAQ: DXLG* ■ *Web:* casual-male-big-and-tall.destinationxl.com	Canton	MA	02021	781-828-9300	
Culwell & Son Inc 6319 Hillcrest Ave *Web:* www.culwell.com	Dallas	TX	75205	214-522-7000	
Dr. Denim Inc 1136 Market St *Web:* www.drdenimjeans.com/us	Philadelphia	PA	19107	215-564-5152	564-2984
JA Apparel Corp 650 Fifth Ave *Web:* www.josephabboud.com	New York	NY	10019	212-586-9140	
Jack O'Reilly Tuxedos LLC 2701 Fifth St Hwy *Web:* jackoreillytuxedos.com	Reading	PA	19605	610-929-9409	
Jos A Bank Clothiers 500 Hanover Pk *TF Cust Svc:* 800-999-7472 ■ *Web:* www.josbank.com	Hampstead	MD	21074	410-239-2700	
Kizan International Inc 100 W Hill Dr *Web:* www.louisraphael.com	Brisbane	CA	94005	415-468-7360	468-0444
Louis Boston 60 Northern Ave *Web:* www.louisboston.com	Boston	MA	02210	617-262-6100	
Men's Wearhouse Inc 6380 Rogerdale Rd *NYSE: MW* ■ *TF:* 877-986-9669 ■ *Web:* www.menswearhouse.com	Houston	TX	77072	281-776-7000	776-7038
Miltons Inc 250 Granite St *TF:* 888-645-8667 ■ *Web:* www.miltons.com	Braintree	MA	02184	781-848-1880	848-1090
Mitchells Family of Stores 270 Main St *Web:* mitchellstores.com	Huntington	NY	11743	631-423-1660	
Norton Ditto Company Inc 2425 W Alabama St *Web:* www.nortonditto.com	Houston	TX	77098	713-688-9800	621-3875
Patrick James Inc 780 W Shaw Ave *TF:* 888-427-6003 ■ *Web:* www.patrickjames.com	Fresno	CA	93704	559-224-5500	448-0601
Paul Fredrick Menstyle 223 W Poplar St *TF:* 800-247-1417 ■ *Web:* www.paulfredrick.com	Fleetwood	PA	19522	610-944-0909	944-6452
Rochester Big & Tall 700 Mission St *Web:* rochester-big-and-tall.destinationxl.com	San Francisco	CA	94103	415-982-6455	
Rubenstein Bros Inc 102 St Charles Ave *TF:* 800-725-7823 ■ *Web:* rubensteinsneworleans.com	New Orleans	LA	70130	504-581-6666	581-3305
Shaws Menswear Inc 1061 Village Park Dr Ste 204	Greensboro	GA	30642	706-454-5041	

157-4 Men's & Women's Clothing Stores

				Phone	Fax
Abercrombie & Fitch Co 6301 Fitch Pass *NYSE: ANF* ■ *Web:* www.abercrombie.com	New Albany	OH	43054	614-283-6500	
American Eagle Outfitters Inc 77 Hot Metal St *NYSE: AEO* ■ *TF Cust Svc:* 888-232-4535 ■ *Web:* www.ae.com	Pittsburgh	PA	15203	412-432-3300	
Barneys New York Inc 575 Fifth Ave *Fax: Hum Res ■ *Web:* www.barneys.com	New York	NY	10017	212-450-8700	450-8489*
Bergdorf Goodman Inc 754 Fifth Ave *TF Cust Svc:* 888-774-2424 ■ *Web:* www.bergdorfgoodman.com	New York	NY	10019	212-753-7300	
Buckle Inc 2407 W 24th St *NYSE: BKE* ■ *TF:* 800-626-1255 ■ *Web:* www.buckle.com	Kearney	NE	68845	308-236-8491	236-4493
Burberry Ltd (New York) 9 E 57th St *Web:* www.burberry.com	New York	NY	10022	212-407-7100	
Cohoes Fashions Inc 156 Hillside Rd Garden City Ctr	Cranston	RI	02920	401-946-7740	
Eddie Bauer LLC PO Box 7001 *TF Orders:* 800-426-8020 ■ *Web:* www.eddiebauer.com	Groveport	OH	43125	800-426-8020	
Gap Inc 2 Folsom St *NYSE: GPS* ■ *TF:* 800-333-7899 ■ *Web:* www.gapinc.com	San Francisco	CA	94105	650-952-4400	
J Crew Group Inc 770 Broadway *TF:* 800-562-0258 ■ *Web:* www.jcrew.com	New York	NY	10003	212-209-2500	209-2666
J McLaughlin 236250 Greenpoint Ave 2nd Fl *TF:* 844-532-5625 ■ *Web:* jmclaughlin.com	Brooklyn	NY	10021	212-879-9565	
Jack Henry Clothing Company Inc 612 W 47th St *Web:* kcclothiers.com	Kansas City	MO	64112	816-753-3800	
James Davis 400 S Grove Pk Rd *Web:* jamesdavisstore.com	Memphis	TN	38117	901-767-4640	
Joe's Jeans Inc 2340 S Eastern Ave *NASDAQ: JOEZ* ■ *TF:* 877-528-5637 ■ *Web:* www.joesjeans.com	Commerce	CA	90040	323-837-3700	
John B Malouf Inc 8201 Quaker Ave Ste 106 *TF:* 800-658-9500 ■ *Web:* www.maloufs.com	Lubbock	TX	79424	806-794-9500	
L Brands Inc 3 Limited Pkwy *NYSE: LTD* ■ *Web:* lb.com	Columbus	OH	43230	614-415-7000	
Maurices Inc 105 W Superior St *TF:* 866-977-1542 ■ *Web:* www.maurices.com	Duluth	MN	55802	218-727-8431	720-2102
Oak Hall Inc 6150 Poplar Ave Ste 146 *TF:* 844-625-4255 ■ *Web:* www.oakhall.com	Memphis	TN	38119	901-761-3580	761-5731
Pacific Sunwear of California Inc 3450 E Miraloma Ave *NASDAQ: PSUN* ■ *TF:* 800-444-6770 ■ *Web:* www.pacsun.com/on/demandware.store/sites-pacsun-site/default/default-start	Anaheim	CA	92806	714-414-4000	414-4251
Patagonia Inc 259 W Santa Clara St PO Box 150 *TF Cust Svc:* 800-638-6464 ■ *Web:* www.patagonia.com	Ventura	CA	93001	805-643-8616	648-8020
Paul Stuart Inc Madison Ave & 45th St *TF Orders:* 800-678-8278 ■ *Web:* www.paulstuart.com	New York	NY	10017	212-682-0320	
Plato's Closet 23021 Outer Dr *TF:* 800-592-8049 ■ *Web:* www.platoscloset.com	Allen Park	MI	48101	313-278-2300	
South Pole 222 Bridge Plz S *Web:* www.southpole-usa.com	Fort Lee	NJ	07024	201-242-5900	
Specialty Retailers Inc 10201 S Main St *TF:* 800-579-2302 ■ *Web:* www.stagestoresinc.com	Houston	TX	77025	800-579-2302	
Stanley Korshak 500 Crescent Ct Ste 100 *TF:* 855-749-9539 ■ *Web:* www.stanleykorshak.com	Dallas	TX	75201	214-871-3600	871-3617
TJX Cos Inc 770 Cochituate Rd *NYSE: TJX* ■ *TF:* 800-926-6299 ■ *Web:* www.tjx.com	Framingham	MA	01701	508-390-1000	
Town & County 2660 S Glenstone Ave	Springfield	MO	65804	417-883-6131	
Urban Outfitters Inc 30 Industrial Pk Blvd *TF:* 800-282-2200 ■ *Web:* www.urbanoutfitters.com	Trenton	SC	29847	800-282-2200	
Watch LA 1138 Wall St *Web:* www.watchla.com	Los Angeles	CA	90015	213-747-1838	747-2888

157-5 Specialty Clothing Stores

Specialty clothing stores are those which sell a specific type of clothing, such as Western wear, uniforms, etc.

				Phone	Fax
5.11 Inc 4300 Spyres Way *TF:* 866-451-1726 ■ *Web:* www.511tactical.com	Modesto	CA	95356	209-527-4511	527-1511
Aeropostale Inc 112 W 34th St Ste 22 *NYSE: ARO* ■ *Web:* www.aeropostale.com	New York	NY	10120	646-485-5410	
Alvin's Island - Tropical Department Stores 11400 NW 34rd St *Web:* www.alvinsisland.com	Doral	FL	33178	305-471-9394	
Carlen Enterprises Inc 1760 Apollo Ct *Web:* www.carlen.com	Seal Beach	CA	90740	562-296-1055	296-1052
Cavender's 2025 SW Loop 323 *Web:* www.cavenders.com	Tyler	TX	75701	903-561-2510	
Country Curtains PO Box 955 *TF:* 800-937-1237 ■ *Web:* www.countrycurtains.com	Stockbridge	MA	01262	413-243-1474	243-1067
Dunham's Sports 5000 Dixie Hwy *Web:* www.dunhamssports.com	Waterford	MI	48329	248-674-4975	
Hat World Corp 7555 Woodland Dr *TF:* 888-564-4287 ■ *Web:* www.lids.com	Indianapolis	IN	46278	888-564-4287	
HorseLoverZ com 254 N Cedar St *TF:* 877-804-7810 ■ *Web:* www.horseloverz.com	Hazleton	PA	18201	570-579-0054	
Hot Topic Inc 18305 E San Jose Ave *NASDAQ: HOTT* ■ *Web:* www.hottopic.com	City of Industry	CA	91748	626-839-4681	839-4686
Mark's Work Warehouse 30-1035 64th Ave SE *TF:* 800-663-6275 ■ *Web:* marks.com	Calgary	AB	T2H2J7	403-255-9220	255-6005
Mobile Nations 3151 E Thomas St *TF:* 888-599-8998	Inverness	FL	34453	352-400-4400	
Modell's Sporting Goods 498 Seventh Ave 20th Fl *TF:* 888-645-8667 ■ *Web:* www.modells.com	New York	NY	10018	800-275-6633	
Niver Western Wear Inc PO Box 101224 *TF Orders:* 800-433-5752	Fort Worth	TX	76185	817-924-4299	924-4296
Northwest Designs Ink Inc 13456 SE 27th Pl Ste 200 *Fax Area Code: 877 ■ *TF:* 800-925-9327 ■ *Web:* nwd.ink	Bellevue	WA	98005	800-925-9327	925-9327*
Overland Sheepskin Company Inc 2096 Nutmeg Ave *TF:* 800-683-7526 ■ *Web:* www.overland.com	Fairfield	IA	52556	641-472-8434	472-8474
Post & Nickel 144 N 14th St *TF:* 877-667-6107 ■ *Web:* www.postandnickel.com	Lincoln	NE	68508	402-476-3432	476-3454
Pro Image Sports 233 N 1250 W Ste 200 *Web:* www.proimagesports.com	Centerville	UT	84014	801-296-9999	296-1319
Sheplers Inc 6501 W Kellogg Dr *TF:* 888-835-4004 ■ *Web:* www.sheplers.com	Wichita	KS	67209	888-835-4004	
U S Cavalry Inc 2855 Centennial Ave *TF:* 866-286-1359 ■ *Web:* www.uscav.com	Radcliff	KY	40160	270-351-1164	352-0266
Watumull Bros Ltd 307 Lewers St Ste 600	Honolulu	HI	96815	808-971-8800	971-8824
Wilsons Leather Inc 7401 Boone Ave N *TF:* 800-967-6270 ■ *Web:* www.wilsonsleather.com	Brooklyn Park	MN	55428	763-391-4000	
Work 'n Gear Stores 2300 Crown Colony Dr Ste 300 *TF:* 800-987-0218 ■ *Web:* www.workngear.com	Quincy	MA	02169	800-987-0218	

157-6 Women's Clothing Stores

Company	City	State	Zip	Phone	Fax
A & E Stores Inc 1000 Huyler St *Web:* www.aestores.com	Teterboro	NJ	07608	201-393-0600	393-0233
A Nose For Clothes 14271 SW 120th St Ste 102 *Web:* www.anoseforclothes.com	Miami	FL	33186	305-253-8631	
A'Gaci LLC 12460 Network Blvd Ste 106 **Fax Area Code:* 702 ■ *TF:* 866-265-3036 ■ *Web:* www.agacistore.com	San Antonio	TX	78249	866-265-3036	258-8634*
ABS by Allan Schwartz 1231 Long Beach Ave *Web:* www.absstyle.com	Los Angeles	CA	90021	213-895-4400	
Altru Apparel 718 Gladys Ave Ste 2 *Web:* altruapparel.com	Los Angeles	CA	90021	213-622-0588	
Ann Inc 7 Times Sq *NYSE: ANN* ■ *TF:* 800-677-6788 ■ *Web:* www.anninc.com	New York	NY	10036	212-541-3300	541-3299
AnnTaylor Inc 7 Times Sq *TF:* 800-342-5266 ■ *Web:* www.anntaylor.com	New York	NY	10036	212-541-3300	
Avenue Stores Inc 365 W Passaic St *TF:* 888-843-2836 ■ *Web:* www.avenue.com	Rochelle Park	NJ	07662	201-845-0880	
Barbara Katz Sportswear Co 2240 SW 19th St Ste 601 *Web:* barbarakatz.com	Boca Raton	FL	33431	561-391-1066	391-5284
Big Girls Bras Etcetera Inc 3540 NW 56th St Ste 207 *TF:* 866-352-4494 ■ *Web:* www.biggerbras.com	Lauderdale	FL	33309	954-484-2701	
Big M Inc 12 Vreeland Ave *Web:* mandee.com	Totowa	NJ	07512	973-890-0021	
Bluefly Inc 42 W 39th St 9th Fl *NASDAQ: BFLY* ■ *TF Cust Svc:* 877-258-3359 ■ *Web:* www.bluefly.com	New York	NY	10018	212-944-8000	354-3400
Born Into It Inc 185 New Boston St *TF:* 800-560-2840 ■ *Web:* www.chowdaheadz.com	Woburn	MA	01801	781-491-0707	
Brioni Roman Style USA Corp 610 Fifth Ave Ste 404 *Web:* brioni.com	New York	NY	10020	212-332-6900	
C28 1180 Galleria At Tyler	Riverside	CA	92503	951-354-9777	
Canada Sportswear Corp 230 Barmac Dr *Web:* www.canadasportswear.com	North York	ON	M9L2Z3	416-740-8020	740-7106
Capsmith Inc 2240 Old Lk Mary Rd *TF:* 800-228-3889 ■ *Web:* capsmith.com	Sanford	FL	32771	407-328-7660	
Cato Corp, The 8100 Denmark Rd *TF:* 800-526-9169 ■ *Web:* www.catofashions.com	Charlotte	NC	28273	704-554-8510	
Ceri Linden LLC 180 Linden St *Web:* ceriboutique.com	Wellesley	MA	02482	781-416-0900	
Charlotte Russe Inc 5910 Pacific Center Blvd *TF:* 888-211-7271 ■ *Web:* www.charlotterusse.com	San Diego	CA	92121	888-211-7271	
Charming Shoppes Inc 933 MacArthur Blvd *NASDAQ: ASNA* ■ *Web:* www.ascenaretail.com	Mahwah	NJ	07430	551-777-6700	
Chico's FAS Inc 11215 Metro Pkwy *NYSE: CHS* ■ *TF:* 800-690-6903 ■ *Web:* www.chicosfas.com	Fort Myers	FL	33966	888-855-4986	
Christopher & Banks Corp 2400 Xenium Ln N *NYSE: CBK* ■ *Web:* www.christopherandbanks.com	Plymouth	MN	55441	763-551-5000	551-5198
Citizens of Humanity Inc 5715 Bickett St *Web:* www.citizensofhumanity.com	Huntington Park	CA	90255	323-923-1240	
Claire's Accessories 2400 W Central Rd *TF:* 800-252-4737 ■ *Web:* www.claires.co.uk	Hoffman Estates	IL	60192	847-765-1100	765-4676
Close To My Heart 1199 West 700 South *Web:* www.closetomyheart.com	Pleasant Grove	UT	84062	801-763-8395	
Clothes Minded Inc 1160 Sandhill Ave	Carson	CA	90746	310-638-9931	
Clothing Cove, The 414 N Main St	Milford	MI	48381	248-685-2500	
Cosabella 12186 SW 128th St	Miami	FL	33186	305-253-9904	
Daffodil 163 Pearl St	Essex Junction	VT	05452	802-879-0212	872-3221
David's Bridal Inc 1001 Washington St **Fax:* Cust Svc ■ *TF:* 844-400-3222 ■ *Web:* www.davidsbridal.com	Conshohocken	PA	19428	610-943-5000	642-7642*
Destination Maternity Corp 456 N Fifth St *NASDAQ: DEST* ■ *TF:* 800-466-6223 ■ *Web:* destinationmaternitycorp.com/home.asp	Philadelphia	PA	19123	215-873-2200	
DND Fashion Inc 10434 Rush St	South El Monte	CA	91733	626-442-1423	
Drapers & Damons 9 Pasteur Ste 200 *TF:* 800-843-1174 ■ *Web:* drapers.blair.com	Irvine	CA	92618	800-843-1174	
Edwards Lowell 8712 Wilshire Blvd	Beverly Hills	CA	90211	310-360-0466	
El Ad US Holding Inc 575 Madison Ave 22nd Fl *Web:* www.eladgroup.com	New York	NY	10022	212-213-8833	
Embry's 3361 Tates Creek Rd *Web:* embrys.com	Lexington	KY	40502	859-269-3390	
Express 1 Limited Pkwy *NYSE: EXPR* ■ *TF:* 888-397-1980 ■ *Web:* www.express.com	Columbus	OH	43230	888-397-1980	
Flemington Fur Co 8 Spring St *Web:* www.flemingtonfurs.com	Flemington	NJ	08822	908-782-2212	
Forever 21 Inc 2001 S Alameda St *TF Cust Svc:* 800-966-1355 ■ *Web:* www.forever21.com	Los Angeles	CA	90058	213-741-5100	
Fox's 80 Main St *Web:* www.foxs.com	Mineola	NY	11501	516-294-8321	
Frederick's of Hollywood Inc PO Box 2949 *TF:* 855-655-2514 ■ *Web:* www.fredericks.com	Phoenix	AZ	85062	800-323-9525	
Gartenhaus Furs 7101 Wisconsin Ave *Web:* www.fursbygartenhaus.com	Bethesda	MD	20814	301-656-2800	
GWK Enterprises 123 S Ctr St *Web:* fourseasonsdirect.com	Geneseo	IL	61254	309-944-4969	
Hemingway Apparel Manufacturing Inc 60 Apparel Dr *Web:* www.hemingwayapparel.com	Hemingway	SC	29554	843-558-2525	
Henig Inc 4135 Carmichael Rd *Web:* www.henigfurs.com	Montgomery	AL	36106	334-277-7610	
Henri Bendel Inc 712 Fifth Ave *TF:* 866-875-7975 ■ *Web:* lb.com	New York	NY	10019	212-247-1100	
Indice Mode 5401 Boul Des Galeries *Web:* lindicemode.com	Ville de Quebec	QC	G2K1N4	418-624-9330	
Irresistibles 7 Hawkes St *TF:* 800-555-9865 ■ *Web:* www.irresistibles.com	Marblehead	MA	01945	781-631-1248	
J Brand Holdings LLC 1214 E 18th St *Web:* www.jbrandjeans.com	Los Angeles	CA	90021	213-749-3500	
Jeans Warehouse Inc 2612 Waiwai Loop *Web:* jeanswarehousehawaii.com	Honolulu	HI	96819	808-839-2421	
Just For Wraps 5815 Smithway St *Web:* www.wrapper.com	Commerce	CA	90040	213-239-0503	
L & L Wings Inc 666 Broadway 2nd Fl *Web:* www.wingsbeachwear.com	New York	NY	10012	212-481-8299	481-8218
L Brands Inc 3 Limited Pkwy *NYSE: LTD* ■ *Web:* lb.com	Columbus	OH	43230	614-415-7000	
Lady Grace Stores Inc 139 Endicott St Ste 1 **Fax Area Code:* 800 ■ *TF:* 800-922-0504 ■ *Web:* www.ladygrace.com	Denvers	MA	01923	781-569-0727	437-9123*
Lane Bryant Inc 3344 Morse Crossing *TF Cust Svc:* 866-886-4731 ■ *Web:* www.lanebryant.com	Columbus	OH	43215	954-970-2205	
Lingerie Outlet Store 3720 S Santa Fe Ave	Vernon	CA	90058	323-588-6917	
Louis Vuitton NA Inc 1 E 57th St *TF Cust Svc:* 866-884-8866 ■ *Web:* louisvuitton.com	New York	NY	10022	212-758-8877	
Lovers Lane & Co 46750 Port St *Web:* www.loverslane.com	Plymouth	MI	48170	734-414-0010	
Maison Weiss 4500 I-55 at Highland Village *Web:* maisonweiss.com	Jackson	MS	39211	601-981-4621	981-4671
Mandee Shop 12 Vreeland Ave *TF Cust Svc:* 877-756-1958 ■ *Web:* www.mandee.com	Totowa	NJ	07512	973-890-0021	
Marla Junes Clothing Company Inc 207 Se Ct Ave *Web:* marlajunes.com	Pendleton	OR	97801	541-276-0778	
Marshall Retail Group 5385 Wynn Rd *Web:* www.marshallretailgroup.com	Las Vegas	NV	89118	702-385-5233	
Miken Sales Inc 539 S Mission Rd *Web:* mikenusa.com	Los Angeles	CA	90033	323-266-2560	266-2580
Motherhood Maternity 456 N Fifth St **Fax:* Cust Svc ■ *TF:* 800-291-7800 ■ *Web:* www.motherhood.com	Philadelphia	PA	19123	215-873-2200	625-3843*
New York & Co 330 W 34th St *TF:* 800-961-9906 ■ *Web:* www.nyandcompany.com	New York	NY	10001	800-961-9906	
NYDJ Apparel LLC 5401 S Soto St *TF:* 800-407-6001 ■ *Web:* www.nydj.com	Vernon	CA	90058	323-581-9040	
Paul's Boutique Inc 99 Rivington St	New York	NY	10002	646-805-0384	
Revolve Clothing Exchange 1620 E Seventh Ave *Web:* revolve.cx	Tampa	FL	33605	813-242-5970	
rue21 Inc 800 Commonwealth Dr Ste 100 *NASDAQ: RUE* ■ *Web:* www.rue21.com	Warrendale	PA	15086	724-776-9780	741-9020
Saks Jandel 5510 Wisconsin Ave *Web:* thebridalsalonatsaksjandel.com	Chevy Chase	MD	20815	301-652-2250	
Sherpa Adventure Gear Inc 7857 S 180th St *TF:* 877-724-8735 ■ *Web:* www.sherpaadventuregear.com	Kent	WA	98032	425-251-0760	
Sister Sam LLC 2150 E 10th St *Web:* www.bailey44.com	Los Angeles	CA	90021	213-228-1930	
Soft Surroundings 33 The Blvd *Web:* www.softsurroundings.com/FAQ/?faqId=133	Richmond heights	MO	63317	314-262-4949	
Stylexchange 1220 Belk Dr	Mount Pleasant	SC	29464	843-884-2244	
Swim 'n Sport Retail Inc 2396 NW 96th Ave *TF:* 800-497-2111 ■ *Web:* www.swimnsport.com	Miami	FL	33172	800-497-2111	
Sydneys Closet 11840 Dorsett Rd *TF:* 888-479-3639 ■ *Web:* www.sydneyscloset.com	Maryland Heights	MO	63043	314-344-5066	
Ulla Popken Ltd 12201 Long Green Pk *Web:* www.ullapopken.com	Glen Arm	MD	21057	410-592-9190	
Vanity Shop of Grand Forks Inc 2410 Great Northern Dr *TF:* 866-247-7920 ■ *Web:* www.vanity.com	Fargo	ND	58102	701-237-3330	
Victoria's Secret Stores 4 Limited Pkwy **Fax Area Code:* 614 ■ *TF:* 800-411-5116 ■ *Web:* www.victoriassecret.com	Reynoldsburg	OH	43068	800-411-5116	577-7844*
Wedding Shoppe Inc, The 1196 Grand Ave *TF:* 877-294-4991 ■ *Web:* www.weddingshoppeinc.com	Saint Paul	MN	55105	651-298-1144	
Western Glove Works Ltd 555 Logan Ave *Web:* westerngloveworks.ca	Winnipeg	MB	R3A0S4	204-788-4249	
Wet Seal Inc 26972 Burbank Ave *NASDAQ: WTSLA* ■ *TF:* 866-746-7938 ■ *Web:* www.wetseal.com	Foothill Ranch	CA	92610	949-699-3900	
White House/Black Market (WHBM) 11215 Metro Pkwy *TF:* 877-948-2525 ■ *Web:* www.whitehouseblackmarket.com	Fort Myers	FL	33966	239-277-6200	
Windsor Inc 4533 Pacific Blvd *TF:* 888-494-6376 ■ *Web:* www.windsorstore.com	Vernon	CA	90058	323-282-9000	973-4224

158 COAST GUARD INSTALLATIONS

Company	City	State	Zip	Phone	Fax
Barbers Point Coast Guard Air Station 1 Coral Sea Rd *Web:* www.uscg.mil	Kapolei	HI	96707	808-682-2771	
Borinquen Coast Guard Air Station 260 GuaRd Rd *Web:* www.uscg.mil/d7/airstaborinquen	Aguadilla	PR	00603	787-890-8400	
Cape Cod Coast Guard Air Station 2300 Wilson Blvd Ste 500 *TF:* 877-669-8724 ■ *Web:* uscg.mil/d1/airstacapecod	Arlington	VA	20598	202-372-4620	
Charleston Coast Guard Base 196 Tradd St *Web:* www.uscg.mil	Charleston	SC	29401	843-724-7600	
Coast Guard Sector Detroit 110 Mt Elliott Ave **Fax Area Code:* 313 ■ *Web:* www.uscg.mil	Detroit	MI	48207	206-220-7000	568-9469*
Coast Guard Sector Sault Sainte Marie 337 Water St *Web:* www.uscg.mil/d9/sectSaultSteMarie	Sault Sainte Marie	MI	49783	906-635-3217	
Corpus Christi Coast Guard Air Station 8930 Ocean Dr Hgr 41 *Web:* www.uscg.mil/history/stations/airsta_corpuschristi.asp	Corpus Christi	TX	78419	361-939-6393	

Phone | Fax

Houston Coast Guard Air Station
1178 Ellington Field ... Houston TX 77034 713-578-3000
Web: www.uscg.mil/d8/airstahouston

Integrated Support Command Miami Beach
100 MacArthur Cswy ... Miami Beach FL 33139 305-535-4300 535-4491
TF: 866-772-8724 ■ *Web:* www.uscg.mil/d7/sectmiami

Ketchikan Integrated Support Command
1300 Stedman St ... Ketchikan AK 99901 907-228-0340
Web: www.uscg.mil

Mayport Coast Guard Base
4200 Ocean St ... Atlantic Beach FL 32233 904-564-7500
Web: www.uscg.mil

Miami Coast Guard Air Station
Opa Locka Airport 14750 NW 44th Ct ... Opa Locka FL 33054 305-953-2130
Web: www.uscg.mil

Milwaukee Coast Guard Base
2420 S Lincoln Memorial Dr ... Milwaukee WI 53207 414-747-7100 747-7108
TF: 866-772-8724 ■ *Web:* www.uscg.mil

Port Angeles Coast Guard Air Station
Ediz Hook Rd ... Port Angeles WA 98362 360-417-5840
Web: www.uscg.mil

Sacramento Coast Guard Air Station
6037 Price Ave ... McClellan CA 95652 916-643-7659
Web: www.uscg.mil

United States Coast Guard/Personnel Services & Support Unit
400 Sand Island Pkwy ... Honolulu HI 96819 808-842-2062 842-2026
Web: www.uscg.mil

US Coast Guard Air Station Detroit
1461 N Perimeter Rd Selfridge ANGB ... Selfridge MI 48045 800-424-8802
TF: 800-424-8802 ■ *Web:* www.uscg.mil/d9/airstadetroit

US Coast Guard Air Station New Orleans
400 Russell Ave ... New Orleans LA 70143 504-393-6005
Web: uscg.mil

US Coast Guard Air Station Savannah
1297 N Lightning Rd Hunter AAF ... Savannah GA 31409 912-652-4646
Web: www.uscg.mil/d7/airstasavannah

159 COFFEE & TEA STORES

Phone | Fax

Bad Ass Coffee Co of Hawaii Inc
155 W Malvern Ave ... Salt Lake City UT 84115 239-213-0527 463-2606*
**Fax Area Code:* 801 ■ *Web:* badasscoffeestore.com

Caribou Coffee Company Inc
3900 Lakebreeze Ave N ... Minneapolis MN 55429 763-592-2200 592-2300
NASDAQ: CBOU ■ *TF Cust Svc:* 888-227-4268 ■ *Web:* www.cariboucoffee.com

Coffee Beanery Ltd, The 3429 Pierson Pl ... Flushing MI 48433 800-441-2255 733-1536*
**Fax Area Code:* 810 ■ *TF:* 800-441-2255 ■ *Web:* www.coffeebeanery.com

Coffee People Inc 33 Coffee Ln ... Waterbury VT 05676 831-633-6300

Dunkin' Donuts 130 Royall St ... Canton MA 02021 781-737-3000 737-4000
TF Cust Svc: 800-859-5339 ■ *Web:* www.dunkindonuts.com

Hawaii Coffee Company Inc 1555 Kalani St ... Honolulu HI 96817 808-847-3600
TF: 800-338-8353 ■ *Web:* hawaiicoffeecompany.com

McNulty's Tea & Coffee Company Inc
109 Christopher St ... New York NY 10014 212-242-5351
TF: 800-356-5200 ■ *Web:* www.mcnultys.com

Montana Coffee Traders Inc 5810 Hwy 93 S ... Whitefish MT 59937 406-862-7633 862-7680
TF: 800-345-5282 ■ *Web:* www.coffeetraders.com

Moxie Java International LLC
4990 W Chinden Blvd ... Boise ID 83714 208-322-7773
Web: moxiejava.com

Peet's Coffee & Tea Inc 1400 Pk Ave ... Emeryville CA 94608 510-594-2100
NASDAQ: GMCR ■ *TF Orders:* 800-999-2132 ■ *Web:* www.peets.com

Seattle's Best Coffee Co PO Box 3717 ... Seattle WA 98124 800-611-7793
TF: 800-611-7793 ■ *Web:* www.seattlesbest.com

Second Cup Ltd 6303 Airport Rd ... Mississauga ON L4V1R8 877-212-1818
TF: 877-212-1818 ■ *Web:* www.secondcup.com

Shefield Group 2265 W Railway St ... Abbotsford BC V2S2E3 604-859-1014 859-1711
Web: www.shefield.com

Starbucks Coffee Co 2401 Utah Ave S ... Seattle WA 98134 206-447-1575 318-3432
TF: 800-782-7282 ■ *Web:* www.starbucks.com

Tully's Coffee Corp 3100 Airport Way ... Seattle WA 98134 206-233-2070
Web: tullyscoffeeshops.com

VKI Technologies Inc 3200 2e rue ... Saint-hubert QC J3Y8Y7 450-676-0504
TF: 800-567-2951 ■ *Web:* www.vkitech.com

160 COLLECTION AGENCIES

Phone | Fax

A G Adjustments Ltd 740 Walt Whitman Rd ... Melville NY 11747 631-425-8800
Web: www.agaltd.com

A.R.M. Solutions Inc PO Box 2929 ... Camarillo CA 93011 888-772-6468
TF: 888-772-6468 ■ *Web:* www.armsolutions.com

AAA Collections Inc 3500 S First Ave Cir ... Sioux Falls SD 57105 605-339-1333
TF: 800-611-7371 ■ *Web:* www.aaa-coll.com

ABC-Amega Inc 1100 Main St ... Buffalo NY 14209 716-885-4444 878-2872
Web: www.abc-amega.com

acb American Inc 4351 Winston Ave ... Covington KY 41015 859-261-8745
Web: www.acbamerican.com

Access Credit Management Inc
11225 Huron Ln Ste 222 ... Little Rock AR 72211 501-664-2922
Web: www.arcollectors.com

Account Control Systems Inc
148 Veterans Dr Ste 4 ... Northvale NJ 07647 201-767-5300
Web: accountcontrolsystems.com

Accounts Management Center Inc
1976 E Grand Ave ... Hot Springs AR 71901 501-623-5594

ACE Recovery Inc 450 Blackbrook Rd ... Painesville OH 44077 440-856-7000
Web: www.acerecovery.com

Afni Inc 404 Brock Dr ... Bloomington IL 61702 309-828-5226
Web: www.afnicareers.com

Phone | Fax

AllianceOne Inc 4850 E St Rd Ste 300 ... Trevose PA 19053 215-354-5511 396-7255
TF: 866-405-7241 ■ *Web:* www.allianceoneinc.com

Allied International Credit Corp
16635 Young St Unit 26 ... Newmarket ON L3X1V6 877-451-2594
TF: 877-451-2594 ■ *Web:* www.aiccorp.com

American Accounts & Advisors
PO Box 250 ... Cottage Grove MN 55016 651-287-6100 287-6190
TF: 866-714-0489 ■ *Web:* www.amaccts.com

American Agencies Company Inc
21 E Ogden Ave Ste 201 ... Westmont IL 60559 630-493-1776 493-1781

Amsher Collection Services Inc
600 Beacon Pkwy W Ste 300 ... Birmingham AL 35209 205-322-4110
Web: www.amsher.com

Array Services Group Inc 200 14th Ave E ... Sartell MN 56377 320-253-7800
Web: www.arraysg.com

Arthur p Jones & Associates Inc
98 Cottage St ... Easthampton MA 01027 413-527-2388
Web: www.apjones.com

Asset Acceptance Capital Corp (AACC)
28405 Van Dyke Ave ... Warren MI 48093 586-939-9600
NASDAQ: AACC ■ *TF:* 800-545-9931 ■ *Web:* www.assetacceptance.com

Atlantic Credit & Finance Inc
2727 Franklin Rd ... Roanoke VA 24014 540-772-7800 772-7895
TF: 800-888-9419 ■ *Web:* www.atlanticcreditfinance.com

Berlin-Wheeler Inc 711 W McCarty St ... Jefferson City MO 65101 785-271-1000
Web: www.berlinwheeler.com

Bonneville Billing & Collection Inc
1186 East 4600 South Ste 100 ... Ogden UT 84403 801-621-7880
TF: 800-660-6138 ■ *Web:* www.bonncoll.com

Brennan & Clark LLC 721 E Madison Ste 200 ... Villa Park IL 60181 630-279-7600
TF: 800-858-7600 ■ *Web:* brennanclark.com

Carter Business Service Inc 150A Andover St ... Danvers MA 01923 781-246-4300
Web: carterbusiness.com

CBV Collections 1200-100 Sheppard Ave E ... Toronto ON M2N6N5 416-482-9323
TF: 866-877-9323 ■ *Web:* www.cbvcollections.com

CBY Systems Inc 33 S Duke St ... York PA 17401 717-843-8685
Web: www.cby.com

Cc Columbia Collectors Inc
1104 Main St Ste 311 ... Vancouver WA 98660 360-694-7585
TF: 800-694-7585 ■ *Web:* columbiacollectors.com

Cedars Business Services LLC
ÿ5230 Las Virgenes Rd ... Calabasas CA 91302 818-224-3800
Web: www.cedarfinancial.com

Client Services Inc
3451 Harry S Truman Blvd ... St Charles MO 63301 636-947-2321

CMI Credit Mediators Inc 414 Sansom St ... Upper Darby PA 19082 610-352-5151
Web: www.cmiweb.com

Coast Professional Inc 214 Expo Cir Ste 7 ... West Monroe LA 71292 318-807-4500
Web: www.coastprofessional.net

Coldebt Collection Systems
8 S Michigan Ave Ste 618 ... Chicago IL 60603 312-759-3804
Web: www.coldebtcollections.com

Collectcents Inc 1450 Meyerside Dr 2nd Fl ... Mississauga ON L5T2N5 905-670-7575
TF: 800-256-8964 ■ *Web:* www.collectcents.com

Collectcorp Corp 400 E Van Buren St Ste 700 ... Phoenix AZ 85004 602-443-2920 432-2923*
**Fax Area Code:* 888

Communications Credit & Recovery (CCR)
200 Garden City Plz Ste 200 ... Garden City NY 11530 516-294-6800 294-5682
Web: www.ccrcollect.com

Computer Credit Inc
470 W Hanes Mill Rd Ste 200 ... Winston-Salem NC 27105 336-761-1524 761-8852
TF: 800-942-2995

Conrad Acceptance Corp 476 W Vermont Ave ... Escondido CA 92025 760-735-5000
Web: www.payconrad.com

Consumer Adjustment Company Inc
4121 Union Rd Ste 201 ... St. Louis MO 63129 314-714-3880
Web: www.cacionline.net

Continental Service Group Inc
200 Cross Keys Office Pk ... Fairport NY 14450 585-421-1000
TF: 800-724-7500 ■ *Web:* www.conserve-arm.com

Credit Consulting Services Inc
201 John St Ste E ... Salinas CA 93901 831-424-0606
Web: www.creditconsultingservices.com

Credit Control Services Inc (CCS)
2 Wells Ave Ste 1 ... Newton MA 02459 617-965-2000 762-3035
TF: 800-526-0532 ■ *Web:* gsaadvantage.gov

Credit Management LP
4200 International Pkwy ... Carrollton TX 75007 800-377-7713 862-4440*
**Fax Area Code:* 972 ■ *TF:* 800-377-7713 ■ *Web:* www.thecmigroup.com

Creditors Adjustment Bureau-LC Financial (CABLCF)
14226 Ventura Blvd ... Sherman Oaks CA 91423 818-990-4800 780-3112
TF: 800-800-4523 ■ *Web:* www.cab-lcf.com

Creditors Financial Group LLC
3131 S Vaughn Way Ste 110 ... Aurora CO 80014 303-369-2345

Creditors Interchange Receivables Management LLC
80 Holtz Dr Airborne Business Park ... Cheektowaga NY 14225 716-614-7500
Web: www.creditorsinterchange.com

Creditors Service Bureau Inc
3410 Sw Van Buren St Ste 101 ... Topeka KS 66611 785-266-4567
Web: tbcsoftware.com

DataTicket Inc 4600 Campus Dr Ste 200 ... Newport Beach CA 92660 949-752-6937
Web: www.dataticket.com

Delmarva Collections Inc 820 E Main St ... Salisbury MD 21804 410-546-3742
Web: delmarvacollections.com

Denovus Corporation Ltd PO BOX 755 ... Ennis TX 75120 724-250-1970
Web: www.denovus.com

Diversified Collection Services Inc
1080 S Harlan Rd ... Lathrop CA 95330 209-858-3500

Dun & Bradstreet Receivable Management Services
103 JFK Pkwy ... Short Hills NJ 07078 973-921-5500
Web: www.dnb.com.hk

Dynamic Recovery Services Inc
4101 McEwen Rd Ste 150 ... Farmers Branch TX 75244 972-241-5611 484-3718
Web: www.drsinc.us

Phone Fax

Encore Capital Group Inc
3111 Camino Del Rio N Ste 300 .... San Diego CA 92108 858-560-2600
NASDAQ: ECPG ■ *TF:* 877-445-4581 ■ *Web:* www.encorecapital.com

Expert Global Solutions, Inc
507 Prudential Rd .... Horsham PA 19044 215-441-3000 441-3923
TF: 877-217-4423 ■ *Web:* www.ncogroup.com

Federated Adjustment Company Inc
7929 N Port Washington Rd .... Milwaukee WI 53217 414-228-0900
Web: facpaid.com

Fidelity Creditor Service Inc
216 S Louise St .... Glendale CA 91205 818-502-1981
Web: fcscollect.com

FMA Alliance Ltd 80 Garden Ctr Ste 3 .... Broomfield CO 80020 281-931-5050
TF: 800-955-5598 ■ *Web:* www.fmaalliance.com

Focus Receivables Management LLC
1130 Northchase Pkwy Ste 150 .... Marietta GA 30067 678-305-9606 228-0019
TF: 877-362-8766 ■ *Web:* www.focusrm.com

GB Collects LLC 145 Bradford Dr .... West Berlin NJ 08091 856-768-9995
Web: www.gbcollects.com

GC Services LP 6330 Gulfton St .... Houston TX 77081 713-777-4441 776-6641
TF: 800-756-6524 ■ *Web:* www.gcserv.com

General Collection Inc
310 N Walnut PO Box 1423 .... Grand Island NE 68802 308-381-1423
Web: www.generalcollection.com

General Revenue Corp 4660 Duke Dr Ste 300 .... Mason OH 45040 800-234-6258 469-7428*
**Fax Area Code:* 513 ■ *TF:* 800-234-6258 ■ *Web:* www.generalrevenue.com

General Service Bureau Inc 8429 Blondo St .... Omaha NE 68134 402-255-5025
Web: www.gsbcollect.com

Gulf Coast Collection Bureau Inc
5630 Marquesas Cir .... Sarasota FL 34233 941-927-6999 926-8872
TF: 866-991-7358 ■ *Web:* www.gulfcoastcollection.com

Harvard Collection Services Inc
4839 N Elston Ave .... Chicago IL 60630 773-283-7500
Web: www.harvardcollect.com

Hospital Billing & Collection Service Ltd
118 Lukens Dr .... New Castle DE 19720 302-552-8000 254-3750
TF: 877-254-9580 ■ *Web:* www.hbcs.org

I.C. System Inc 444 Hwy 96 E .... St. Paul MN 55127 651-481-6333
Web: www.icsystem.com

James, Stevens & Daniels Inc
1283 College Park Dr .... Dover DE 19904 302-735-4628
Web: www.jsdinc.net

Johnson & Rountree Premium Inc
12835 Point Del Mar Way .... Del Mar CA 92014 858-259-5846
Web: www.jrpremium.com

Keybridge Medical Revenue Management
2348 Baton Rouge Ave .... Lima OH 45805 419-879-4114
Web: www.keybridgemed.com

Kings Credit Services 510 N Douty St .... Hanford CA 93230 559-587-4200
Web: www.kingscredit.com

Lamont, Hanley & Associates Inc
1138 Elm St .... Manchester NH 03105 603-625-5547
Web: www.lhainc.com

M G Credit Inc 5115 San Juan Ave .... Jacksonville FL 32210 800-387-6503
TF: 800-387-6503 ■ *Web:* www.mgcredit.com

Matthews Pierce & Lloyd Inc
830 Walker Rd Ste 12 .... Dover DE 19904 302-678-5500
Web: mpli.net

Med Shield Inc 2424 E 55th St .... Indianapolis IN 46220 317-613-3700
TF: 800-272-5454 ■ *Web:* www.medshield.com

Medco Services Inc 6700 Odyssey Dr Ste 105 .... Huntsville AL 35805 256-665-9194
Web: www.extendedearlyout.com

Merchants & Medical Credit Corporation Inc
6324 Taylor Dr .... Flint MI 48507 810-239-3030
Web: www.mermed.com

MJ Altman Cos Inc 112 Se Ft King St .... Ocala FL 34471 352-732-1112
Web: mjaltman.com

Monarch Recovery Management Inc
10965 Decatur Rd .... Philadelphia PA 19154 215-281-7500
Web: monarchrm.com

Nationwide Credit Inc (NCI) PO Box 26314 Ste 600 .... Atlanta GA 30319 800-456-4729
TF: 800-456-4729 ■ *Web:* www.ncirm.com

Nationwide Recovery Systems Inc (NRS)
4635 McEwen Rd .... Dallas TX 75244 972-798-1000 798-1020
TF: 800-458-6357 ■ *Web:* www.nrs.us

Nelson Watson & Associates LLC
80 Merrimack St Ste 4 .... Haverhill MA 01830 978-416-2116
Web: www.nelsonwatson.com

Northland Group Inc 7831 Glenroy Rd Ste 250 .... Edina MN 55439 952-831-4005
Web: www.northlandgroup.com

NRA GROUP LLC 2491 Paxton St .... Harrisburg PA 17111 717-540-7636
Web: www.nationalrecovery.com

Payment America Systems Inc 450 10th Cir N .... Nashville TN 37203 615-255-9200
Web: www.paymentamerica.com

Penncro Associates Inc
95 James Way Ste 113 .... Southampton PA 18966 215-322-2438
Web: www.penncro.com

Pentagroup Financial LLC
5959 Corp Dr Ste 1400 .... Houston TX 77036 832-615-2100 615-2399
TF: 800-385-9060

Pioneer Credit Recovery Inc 26 Edward St .... Arcade NY 14009 585-492-1234
Web: www.pioneercreditrecovery.com

Portfolio Recovery Assoc LLC
120 Corporate Blvd
Ste 100 Reverside Commerce Ctr .... Norfolk VA 23502 888-772-7326
NASDAQ: PRAA ■ *TF:* 888-772-7326 ■ *Web:* www.portfoliorecovery.com

Premiere Credit of North America LLC
2002 Wellesley Blvd Ste 100 .... Indianapolis IN 46219 317-869-2621
Web: www.premierecredit.com

Quality Asset Recovery 7 Foster Ave Ste 101 .... Gibbsboro NJ 08026 856-925-1010
Web: www.qarcollect.com

Radius Global Solutions LLC 50 W Skippack Pk .... Ambler PA 19002 267-419-1111
Web: www.radiusgs.com

Receivable Management Inc
107 W Randol Mill Rd .... Arlington TX 76011 817-261-7534
Web: receivablemanagement.net

Recovery Partners LLC
4151 N Marshall Way Ste 12 .... Scottsdale AZ 85251 480-747-9888
Web: www.recoverypartners.com

Richmond North Assoc Inc 4232 Ridge Lea Rd .... Amherst NY 14226 716-832-5668 832-4236
Web: www.rnacollects.com

Roquemore & Roquemore Inc
329 Oaks Trl Ste 212 .... Garland TX 75043 972-226-9266
Web: www.roquemore.com

Rose, Snyder & Jacobs LLP
15821 Ventura Blvd Ste 490 .... Encino CA 91436 818-461-0600
Web: rsjcpa.com

Seattle Service Bureau Inc
18820 Aurora Ave Ste 205 .... Seattle WA 98133 206-533-0877
Web: www.nsbi.net

Sierra Receivables Management Inc
2500 Goodwater Ave .... Redding CA 96002 530-224-1360
Web: www.sierrareceivables.com

Stanislaus Credit Control Service Inc
914-14th St .... Modesto CA 95354 209-523-1813
Web: www.sccscollects.com

States Recovery Systems Inc
2951 Surrise Blvd Ste 100 .... Rancho Cordova CA 95742 916-631-7085
Web: www.statesrecovery.com

Stevens Business Service Inc 92 Bolt St Ste 1 .... Lowell MA 01852 978-458-2500
Web: www.sbs4money.com

Szabo Assoc Inc 3355 Lenox Rd NE Ste 945 .... Atlanta GA 30326 404-266-2464
Web: www.szabo.com

Todd, Bremer & Lawson Inc
560 S Herlong Ave .... Rock Hill SC 29732 803-323-5200
Web: www.tbandl.com

Total Credit Recovery Ltd 225 Yorkland Blvd .... Toronto ON M2J4Y7 416-774-4000
Web: www.totalcrediting.com

Transmodus Corp 500 Esplanade Dr Ste 700 .... Oxnard CA 93036 805-604-4472
Web: www.transmodus.net

Transworld Systems Inc PO Box 15618 .... Wilmington DE 19850 877-282-1250
TF: 888-446-4733 ■ *Web:* www.tsico.com

Tri-state Adjustments Inc
3439 East Ave S PO Box 3219 .... La Crosse WI 54602 608-788-8683
TF: 800-562-3906 ■ *Web:* www.wecollectmore.com

Tucker Albin & Assoc Inc
1702 N Collins Blvd .... Richardson TX 75080 469-424-3033
Web: tuckeralbin.net

Twenty-First Century Assoc 266 Summit Ave .... Hackensack NJ 07601 201-678-1144 678-9088
TF: 888-760-5052 ■ *Web:* www.tfc-associates.com

Union Adjustment Company Inc
3214 W Burbank Blvd .... Burbank CA 91505 818-566-8330
Web: www.unionadjustment.com

Unique Management Services Inc
119 E Maple St .... Jeffersonville IN 47130 812-285-0886
TF: 800-879-5453 ■ *Web:* www.unique-mgmt.com

United Collection Bureau Inc
5620 Southwyck Blvd .... Toledo OH 43614 419-866-6227
Web: ucbinc.com

United Recovery Systems LP 5800 N Course Dr .... Houston TX 77072 713-977-1234 977-0119
TF: 800-568-0399 ■ *Web:* www.unitedrecoverysystems.com

USCB Inc 3333 Wilshire Blvd .... Los Angeles CA 90010 213-387-6181
Web: www.uscbinc.com

Van Ru Credit Corp
1350 E Touhy Ave Ste 300E .... Des Plaines IL 60018 800-468-2678 673-5360*
**Fax Area Code:* 847 ■ *TF:* 800-468-2678 ■ *Web:* www.vanru.com

Vengroff Williams & Assoc Inc (VWA)
2099 S State College Bvld .... Anaheim CA 92806 866-737-4344
TF: 800-238-9655 ■ *Web:* www.vwinc.com

Williams & Fudge Inc 300 Chatham Ave .... Rock Hill SC 29730 803-329-9791
Web: wfcorp.com

Williams, Charles & Scott Ltd
2171 Jericho Tpke LL1 .... Commack NY 11725 631-462-1553
Web: www.wcscollects.com

161 COLLEGES - BIBLE

SEE ALSO

Phone Fax

Alaska Bible College 248 E Elmwood Ave .... Palmer AK 99645 907-822-3201
TF: 800-478-7884 ■ *Web:* www.akbible.edu

Allegheny Wesleyan College 2161 Woodsdale Rd .... Salem OH 44460 330-337-6403
TF: 800-292-3153 ■ *Web:* www.awc.edu

American Baptist College
1800 Baptist World Ctr Dr .... Nashville TN 37207 615-256-1463 226-7855
Web: www.abcnash.edu

Baptist Bible College 628 E Kearney St .... Springfield MO 65803 800-228-5754 268-6694*
**Fax Area Code:* 417 ■ **Fax:* Admissions ■ *TF:* 800-228-5754 ■ *Web:* gobbc.edu

Baptist University of the Americas
8019 S Pan Am Expy .... San Antonio TX 78224 210-924-4338 924-2701
TF: 800-721-1396 ■ *Web:* www.bua.edu

Barclay College 607 N Kingman St .... Haviland KS 67059 620-862-5252 862-5403
TF: 800-862-0226 ■ *Web:* www.barclaycollege.edu

Bethesda Christian University 730 N Euclid .... Anaheim CA 92801 714-517-1945
Web: buc.edu

Beulah Heights Bible College
892 Berne St SE PO Box 18145 .... Atlanta GA 30316 404-627-2681 627-0702*
**Fax:* Admissions ■ *TF:* 888-777-2422 ■ *Web:* www.beulah.org

Boise Bible College 8695 W Marigold St .... Boise ID 83714 208-376-7731 376-7743
TF: 800-893-7755 ■ *Web:* www.boisebible.edu

Calvary Bible College & Theological Seminary
15800 Calvary Rd .... Kansas City MO 64147 816-322-3960 331-4474*
**Fax:* Admissions ■ *TF:* 800-326-3960 ■ *Web:* www.calvary.edu

Central Christian College of the Bible
911 E Urbandale Dr .... Moberly MO 65270 660-263-3900 263-3936
TF: 888-263-3900 ■ *Web:* www.cccb.edu

Phone Fax

Cincinnati Christian University
2700 Glenway Ave . . . . . Cincinnati OH 45204 513-244-8100 244-8140
TF: 800-949-4228 ■ *Web:* www.ccuniversity.edu

Clear Creek Baptist Bible College
300 Clear Creek Rd. . . . . . Pineville KY 40977 606-337-3196 337-2372
TF: 866-340-3196 ■ *Web:* www.ccbbc.edu

College of Biblical Studies-Houston
7000 Regency Sq Blvd Ste 110. . . . . Houston TX 77036 713-785-5995 532-8150
TF: 844-227-9673 ■ *Web:* www.cbshouston.edu

Columbia International University
7435 Monticello Rd . . . . . Columbia SC 29203 803-754-4100 786-4209
TF: 800-777-2227 ■ *Web:* www.ciu.edu

Crossroads Bible College
601 N Shortridge Rd. . . . . Indianapolis IN 46219 317-352-8736
TF: 800-822-3119 ■ *Web:* www.crossroads.edu

Crossroads College 920 Mayowood Rd SW. . . . . Rochester MN 55902 507-288-4563 288-9046
TF: 800-456-7651 ■ *Web:* www.crossroadscollege.edu

Crown College 8700 College View Dr . . . . . Saint Bonifacius MN 55375 952-446-4100 446-4149
TF: 800-346-9252 ■ *Web:* www.crown.edu

Dallas Christian College 2700 Christian Pkwy . . . . . Dallas TX 75234 972-241-3371 241-8021
TF: 800-688-1029 ■ *Web:* www.dallas.edu

Davis College 400 Riverside Dr. . . . . Johnson City NY 13790 607-729-1581 729-2962
TF: 800-331-4137 ■ *Web:* www.davisny.edu

Ecclesia College 9653 Nations Dr . . . . . Springdale AR 72762 479-248-7236 248-1455
TF: 800-735-9926 ■ *Web:* ecollege.edu

Emmaus Bible College 2570 Asbury Rd . . . . . Dubuque IA 52001 563-588-8000 588-1216
TF: 800-397-2425 ■ *Web:* www.emmaus.edu

Faith Baptist Bible College 1900 NW Fourth St. . . . . Ankeny IA 50023 515-964-0601 964-1638
TF: 800-409-3305 ■ *Web:* www.faith.edu

Florida Christian College
1011 Bill Beck Blvd . . . . . Kissimmee FL 34744 407-847-8966 206-2007*
**Fax Area Code:* 321 ■ *TF:* 888-468-6322 ■ *Web:* johnsonu.edu/florida

Free Will Baptist Bible College
3606 W End Ave. . . . . Nashville TN 37205 615-844-5000 269-6028
TF: 888-979-3524 ■ *Web:* welch.edu

God's Bible School & College
1810 Young St . . . . . Cincinnati OH 45202 513-721-7944 721-1357
TF: 800-486-4637 ■ *Web:* www.gbs.edu

Grace Bible College
1011 Aldon St SW PO Box 910 . . . . . Grand Rapids MI 49509 616-538-2330 538-0599
TF: 800-968-1887 ■ *Web:* www.gbcol.edu

Grace University 1311 S Ninth St. . . . . Omaha NE 68108 402-449-2800 341-9587
TF: 800-383-1422 ■ *Web:* www.graceuniversity.edu

Great Lakes Christian College
6211 W Willow Hwy . . . . . Lansing MI 48917 517-321-0242 321-5902
TF Admissions: 800-937-4522 ■ *Web:* www.glcc.edu

Heritage Christian University
3625 Helton Dr PO Box HCU . . . . . Florence AL 35630 256-766-6610
TF: 800-367-3565 ■ *Web:* www.hcu.edu

Hobe Sound Bible College PO Box 1065 . . . . . Hobe Sound FL 33475 772-546-5534 545-1422
TF: 800-881-5534 ■ *Web:* www.hsbc.edu

Johnson University 7900 Johnson Dr . . . . . Knoxville TN 37998 865-573-4517 251-2337
TF: 800-827-2122 ■ *Web:* www.johnsonu.edu

Kentucky Mountain Bible College 855 Hwy 541 . . . . . Jackson KY 41339 606-693-5000
TF: 800-879-5622 ■ *Web:* www.kmbc.edu

King's College & Seminary 14800 Sherman Way. . . . . Van Nuys CA 91405 818-779-8500
Web: www.tku.edu

Kuyper College 3333 E Beltline Ave NE. . . . . Grand Rapids MI 49525 616-222-3000 222-3045
TF: 800-511-3749 ■ *Web:* www.kuyper.edu

Lancaster Bible College
901 Eden Rd PO Box 83403 . . . . . Lancaster PA 17608 717-569-7071 560-8213
TF: 800-544-7335 ■ *Web:* www.lbc.edu

Laurel University 1215 Eastchester Dr . . . . . High Point NC 27265 336-887-3000 889-2261
TF: 855-528-7358 ■ *Web:* www.laureluniversity.edu

Life Pacific College 1100 W Covina Blvd . . . . . San Dimas CA 91773 909-599-5433
TF: 877-886-5433 ■ *Web:* www.lifepacific.edu

Lincoln Christian College Seminary
100 Campus View Dr . . . . . Lincoln IL 62656 217-732-3168
TF: 888-522-5228 ■ *Web:* lincolnchristian.edu

Manhattan Christian College
1415 Anderson Ave . . . . . Manhattan KS 66502 785-539-3571 776-9251
TF: 877-246-4622 ■ *Web:* www.mccks.edu

Mid-Atlantic Christian Universit
715 N Poindexter St . . . . . Elizabeth City NC 27909 252-334-2070 334-2071
TF: 866-996-6228 ■ *Web:* www.macuniversity.edu

Moody Bible Institute 820 N La Salle St . . . . . Chicago IL 60610 312-329-4400 329-8955*
**Fax:* Admissions ■ *TF:* 800-967-4624 ■ *Web:* www.moody.edu

Multnomah University 8435 NE Glisan St . . . . . Portland OR 97220 503-255-0332 254-1268
TF: 800-275-4672 ■ *Web:* www.multnomah.edu

Oak Hills Christian College
1600 Oak Hills Rd SW . . . . . Bemidji MN 56601 218-751-8670 751-8825
TF: 888-751-8670 ■ *Web:* www.oakhills.edu

Ozark Christian College 1111 N Main St . . . . . Joplin MO 64801 417-624-2518 624-0090
TF: 800-299-4622 ■ *Web:* www.occ.edu

Rosedale Bible College 2270 Rosedale Rd. . . . . Irwin OH 43029 740-857-1311 857-1312*
**Fax Area Code:* 877 ■ *Web:* www.rosedale.edu

Saint Louis Christian College
1360 Grandview Dr. . . . . Florissant MO 63033 314-837-6777 837-8291
TF Admissions: 800-887-7522 ■ *Web:* www.slcconline.edu

Southeastern Baptist College 4229 Hwy 15 N . . . . . Laurel MS 39440 601-426-6346 426-6347
Web: www.southeasternbaptist.edu

Toccoa Falls College 107 Kincaid Dr . . . . . Toccoa Falls GA 30598 706-886-6831 282-6012
TF General: 800-868-3257 ■ *Web:* www.tfc.edu

Tri-State Bible College 506 Margaret St. . . . . South Point OH 45680 740-377-2520 377-0001
TF: 800-333-3243 ■ *Web:* www.tsbc.edu

Trinity Bible College 50 Sixth Ave N . . . . . Ellendale ND 58436 701-349-3621 349-5786
TF: 800-523-1603 ■ *Web:* www.trinitybiblecollege.edu

Trinity College of Florida 2430 Welbilt Blvd . . . . . Trinity FL 34655 727-376-6911 569-1410
TF: 800-388-0869 ■ *Web:* www.trinitycollege.edu

162 COLLEGES - COMMUNITY & JUNIOR

See Also Colleges - Fine Arts p. 1966; Colleges - Tribal p. 1967; Colleges & Universities - Four-Year p. 1968; Vocational & Technical Schools p. 3297
Institutions that offer academic degrees that can be transferred to a four-year college or university.

Alabama

Phone Fax

Central Alabama Community College
1675 Cherokee Rd . . . . . Alexander City AL 35010 256-234-6346 215-4244
TF: 800-643-2657 ■ *Web:* www.cacc.edu

Lurleen B Wallace Community College
Andalusia 1000 Dannelly Blvd PO Box 1418 . . . . . Andalusia AL 36420 334-222-6591 881-2201*
**Fax:* Admissions ■ *TF:* 877-382-4357 ■ *Web:* www.lbwcc.edu

Jefferson Davis Community College
Atmore 6574 Hwy 21 N . . . . . Atmore AL 36504 251-368-7610 368-7667
Web: www.jdcc.edu

Faulkner State Community College
Bay Minette 1900 Hwy 31 S. . . . . Bay Minette AL 36507 251-580-2111 580-2134
TF: 800-381-3722 ■ *Web:* www.faulknerstate.edu

Jefferson State Community College
2601 Carson Rd . . . . . Birmingham AL 35215 205-853-1200 856-6070*
**Fax:* Admissions ■ *TF:* 800-239-5900 ■ *Web:* www.jeffersonstate.edu

Snead State Community College
220 N Walnut St PO Box 734 . . . . . Boaz AL 35957 256-593-5120 593-7180*
**Fax:* Admissions ■ *Web:* www.snead.edu
Brewton 220 Alco Dr . . . . . Brewton AL 36426 251-867-4832 809-1596
Web: www.jdcc.edu
Childersburg 34091 US Hwy 280 . . . . . Childersburg AL 35044 256-378-5576 378-2027
Web: www.cacc.edu

Calhoun Community College PO Box 2216 . . . . . Decatur AL 35609 256-306-2500 306-2941
TF: 800-626-3628 ■ *Web:* www.calhoun.cc.al.us

Wallace Community College 1141 Wallace Dr. . . . . Dothan AL 36303 334-983-3521 983-6066*
**Fax:* Admissions ■ *TF:* 800-543-2426 ■ *Web:* www.wallace.edu

Enterprise State Community College (ESCC)
600 Plz Dr. . . . . Enterprise AL 36330 334-347-2623 393-6223
Web: www.escc.edu
Fairhope 440 Fairhope Ave . . . . . Fairhope AL 36532 251-990-0420 580-2285*
**Fax:* Admissions ■ *TF:* 800-231-3752 ■ *Web:* www.faulknerstate.edu

Bevill State Community College
2631 Temple Ave N . . . . . Fayette AL 35555 205-932-3221 932-3294*
**Fax:* Admissions ■ *TF:* 800-648-3271 ■ *Web:* www.bscc.edu

Gadsden State Community College
1001 George Wallace Dr PO Box 227. . . . . Gadsden AL 35902 256-549-8200 549-8205*
**Fax:* Admissions ■ *TF:* 800-226-5563 ■ *Web:* www.gadsdenstate.edu
Gulf Shores 3301 Gulf Shores Pkwy . . . . . Gulf Shores AL 36542 251-968-3101 968-3120
TF: 800-231-3752 ■ *Web:* www.faulknerstate.edu

Wallace State Community College
801 Main St . . . . . Hanceville AL 35077 256-352-8000 352-8129
TF: 866-350-9722 ■ *Web:* www.wallacestate.edu
Huntsville 102B Wynn Dr. . . . . Huntsville AL 35805 256-890-4701 890-4775*
**Fax:* Admissions ■ *TF:* 800-626-3628 ■ *Web:* www.calhoun.edu
Jasper 1411 Indiana Ave . . . . . Jasper AL 35501 205-387-0511 387-5191*
**Fax:* Admissions ■ *TF:* 800-648-3271 ■ *Web:* www.bscc.edu

Marion Military Institute 1101 Washington St. . . . . Marion AL 36756 334-683-2322
TF: 800-664-1842 ■ *Web:* www.marionmilitary.edu

Bishop State Community College 351 N Broad St . . . . . Mobile AL 36603 251-405-7000
Web: bishop.edu
Baker-Gaines Central 1365 Dr ML King Jr Ave . . . . . Mobile AL 36603 251-662-5400 405-4427
Web: bishop.edu
Southwest 925 Dauphin Island Pkwy . . . . . Mobile AL 36605 251-665-4100
Web: bishop.edu

Alabama Southern Community College
2800 S Alabama Ave. . . . . Monroeville AL 36461 251-575-3156 575-5356
TF: 866-901-1117 ■ *Web:* www.ascc.edu

Northwest-Shoals Community College
Muscle Shoals 800 George Wallace Blvd. . . . . Muscle Shoals AL 35661 256-331-5200 331-5366*
**Fax:* Admissions ■ *TF:* 800-645-8967 ■ *Web:* www.nwscc.edu

Southern Union State Community College
Opelika 1701 Lafayette Pkwy . . . . . Opelika AL 36801 334-745-6437 742-9418*
**Fax:* Admissions ■ *TF:* 800-707-0057 ■ *Web:* www.suscc.edu

Chattahoochee Valley Community College
2602 College Dr . . . . . Phenix City AL 36869 334-291-4900 291-4994*
**Fax:* Admissions ■ *Web:* www.cv.edu
Phil Campbell 2080 College Rd. . . . . Phil Campbell AL 35581 256-331-6200 331-6272*
**Fax:* Admissions ■ *TF:* 800-645-8967 ■ *Web:* www.nwscc.edu

Northeast Alabama Community College
PO Box 159 . . . . . Rainsville AL 35986 256-228-6001 228-6861
Web: www.nacc.edu
Redstone Arsenal 6250 Hwy 31 N . . . . . Tanner AL 35671 256-306-2500 306-2941
TF: 800-626-3628 ■ *Web:* www.calhoun.edu

Alabama Southern Community College
30755 Hwy 43 . . . . . Thomasville AL 36784 334-636-9642 636-1380
TF: 866-901-1117 ■ *Web:* www.ascc.edu

Shelton State Community College
9500 Old Greensboro Rd . . . . . Tuscaloosa AL 35405 205-391-2211 391-3910*
**Fax:* Admissions ■ *TF:* 877-211-7722 ■ *Web:* www.sheltonstate.edu
Valley 321 Fob James Dr. . . . . Valley AL 36854 334-756-4151 756-5183*
**Fax:* Admissions ■ *TF:* 800-707-0057 ■ *Web:* www.suscc.edu

Alaska

Phone Fax

University of Alaska Fairbanks
PO Box 757480 . . . . . Fairbanks AK 99775 907-474-7500 474-5379*
**Fax:* Admissions ■ *TF:* 800-478-1823 ■ *Web:* www.uaf.edu

University of Alaska Southeast Ketchikan
2600 Seventh Ave. . . . . Ketchikan AK 99901 907-225-6177 225-3624
TF: 877-465-6400 ■ *Web:* www.ketch.alaska.edu

Phone Fax

University of Alaska Anchorage Kodiak College
117 Benny Benson Dr. Kodiak AK 99615 907-486-4161 486-1264
TF: 800-486-7660 ■ *Web:* www.koc.alaska.edu
Northwest 400 E Front St PO Box 400. Nome AK 99762 907-443-2201 443-5602
TF: 800-478-2202 ■ *Web:* www.nwc.uaf.edu

University of Alaska Southeast Sitka
1332 Seward Ave. Sitka AK 99835 907-747-6653 747-7768
TF: 800-478-6653 ■ *Web:* www.uas.alaska.edu

University of Alaska Anchorage Kenai Peninsula College
156 College Rd. Soldotna AK 99669 877-262-0330 262-0322*
**Fax Area Code:* 907 ■ *TF:* 877-262-0330 ■ *Web:* www.kpc.alaska.edu

Alberta

Phone Fax

MacEwan College 10045 156 St NW. Edmonton AB T5P2P7 888-497-4622
TF: 888-497-4622 ■ *Web:* www.macewan.ca

Olds College 4500-50 St. Olds AB T4H1R6 403-556-8281
TF: 800-661-6537 ■ *Web:* www.oldscollege.ab.ca

Arizona

Phone Fax

Estrella Mountain Community College
3000 N Dysart Rd. Avondale AZ 85323 623-935-8000 935-8870*
**Fax:* Admissions ■ *Web:* www.emc.maricopa.edu

Mohave Community College
Bullhead City 3400 Hwy 95. Bullhead City AZ 86442 928-758-3926 704-9460
TF: 866-664-2832 ■ *Web:* www.mohave.edu

Chandler-Gilbert Community College
Pecos 2626 E Pecos Rd. Chandler AZ 85225 480-732-7000 732-7099*
**Fax:* Admissions ■ *Web:* www.cgc.maricopa.edu
Verde Valley 601 Black Hills Dr. Clarkdale AZ 86324 928-634-7501 634-6549*
**Fax:* Admissions ■ *TF:* 800-922-6787 ■ *Web:* www.yc.edu
North Mohave PO Box 980. Colorado City AZ 86021 928-875-2799 875-2831*
**Fax:* Admissions ■ *TF:* 800-678-3992 ■ *Web:* www.mohave.edu

Central Arizona College 8470 N Overfield Rd. Coolidge AZ 85228 520-494-5444 494-5083*
**Fax:* Admissions ■ *TF:* 800-237-9814 ■ *Web:* www.centralaz.edu

Cochise College 4190 W Hwy 80. Douglas AZ 85607 520-364-7943 417-4006*
**Fax:* Admissions ■ *TF:* 800-966-7943 ■ *Web:* cochise.edu

Coconino Community College
Lonetree 2800 S Lone Tree Rd. Flagstaff AZ 86001 928-527-1222 226-4110*
**Fax:* Admissions ■ *TF:* 800-350-7122 ■ *Web:* www.coconino.edu

Glendale Community College 6000 W Olive Ave. Glendale AZ 85302 623-845-3000 845-3303*
**Fax:* Admissions ■ *Web:* www2.gccaz.edu
North 5727 W Happy Vly Rd. Glendale AZ 85310 623-845-4000 845-4010
Web: www.gc.maricopa.edu/gccnorth

Northland Pioneer College PO Box 610. Holbrook AZ 86025 928-532-6111 536-3382*
**Fax:* Admissions ■ *TF:* 800-266-7845 ■ *Web:* www.npc.edu
Lake Havasu 1977 W Acoma Blvd. Lake Havasu City AZ 86403 928-855-7812 680-5955*
**Fax:* Admissions ■ *TF:* 866-664-2832 ■ *Web:* www.mohave.edu
Williams 7360 E Tahoe Ave. Mesa AZ 85212 480-988-8000 988-8993
Web: www.cgc.maricopa.edu

Mesa Community College 1833 W Southern Ave. Mesa AZ 85202 480-461-7000
TF: 866-532-4983 ■ *Web:* mesacc.edu
Red Mountain 7110 E McKellips Rd. Mesa AZ 85207 480-654-7200 654-7379
TF: 866-532-4983 ■ *Web:* mesacc.edu

GateWay Community College 108 N 40th St. Phoenix AZ 85034 602-286-8000 286-8072
TF: 888-994-4433 ■ *Web:* www.gatewaycc.edu

Paradise Valley Community College
18401 N 32nd St. Phoenix AZ 85032 602-787-6500 787-7025*
**Fax:* Admissions ■ *Web:* paradisevalley.edu

Phoenix College 1202 W Thomas Rd. Phoenix AZ 85013 602-285-7800 285-7700
Web: www.phoenixcollege.edu

South Mountain Community College
7050 S 24th St. Phoenix AZ 85042 602-243-8000 243-8199*
**Fax:* Admissions ■ *TF:* 855-622-2332 ■ *Web:* www.southmountaincc.edu

Yavapai College 1100 E Sheldon St. Prescott AZ 86301 928-445-7300 776-2151*
**Fax:* Admissions ■ *TF:* 800-922-6787 ■ *Web:* www.yc.edu

Scottsdale Community College
9000 E Chaparral Rd. Scottsdale AZ 85256 480-423-6000 423-6200*
**Fax:* Admissions ■ *TF:* 800-784-2433 ■ *Web:* www.scottsdalecc.edu
Sierra Vista 901 N Colombo Ave. Sierra Vista AZ 85635 520-515-0500 515-5452*
**Fax:* Admissions ■ *TF:* 800-966-7943 ■ *Web:* cochise.edu

Rio Salado College 2323 W 14Th St. Tempe AZ 85281 480-517-8000
TF: 855-622-2332 ■ *Web:* www.riosalado.edu

Eastern Arizona College 615 N Stadium Ave. Thatcher AZ 85552 928-428-8472 428-2578
TF: 800-678-3808 ■ *Web:* www.eac.edu

Pima Community College 401 N Bonita Ave. Tucson AZ 85709 520-206-2733 206-4790*
**Fax:* Admissions ■ *TF:* 800-860-7462 ■ *Web:* www.pima.edu
Desert Vista 5901 S Calle Santa Cruz. Tucson AZ 85709 520-206-5030 206-5050*
**Fax:* Admissions ■ *Web:* pima.edu
East 8181 E Irvington Rd. Tucson AZ 85709 520-206-7000 206-7875*
**Fax:* Admissions ■ *Web:* ecc.pima.edu
West 2202 W Anklam Rd. Tucson AZ 85709 520-206-6600 206-6728*
**Fax:* Admissions ■ *TF:* 800-860-7462 ■ *Web:* www.pima.edu

Arizona Western College 2020 S Ave 8 E. Yuma AZ 85366 928-317-6000 344-7543
TF: 888-293-0392 ■ *Web:* www.azwestern.edu

Arkansas

Phone Fax

NorthWest Arkansas Community College
1 College Dr. Bentonville AR 72712 479-636-9222 619-2229*
**Fax:* Admissions ■ *TF:* 800-995-6922 ■ *Web:* www.nwacc.edu

Arkansas Northeastern College
2501 S Div St PO Box 1109. Blytheville AR 72316 870-762-1020 763-1654*
**Fax:* Admissions ■ *Web:* www.anc.edu

South Arkansas Community College
PO Box 7010. El Dorado AR 71731 870-862-8131
TF: 800-955-2289 ■ *Web:* www.southark.edu

East Arkansas Community College
1700 Newcastle Rd. Forrest City AR 72335 870-633-4480 633-3840*
**Fax:* Admissions ■ *TF:* 877-797-3222 ■ *Web:* www.eacc.edu

North Arkansas College 1515 Pioneer Dr. Harrison AR 72601 870-743-3000 391-3339
TF: 800-679-6622 ■ *Web:* www.northark.edu

Phillips Community College PO Box 785. Helena AR 72342 870-338-6474 338-7542
Web: www.pccua.edu

National Park Community College
101 College Dr. Hot Springs AR 71913 501-760-4222 760-4236*
**Fax:* Admissions ■ *Web:* www.npcc.edu

Ouachita Technical College 1 College Cir. Malvern AR 72104 501-337-5000 337-9382
TF: 800-337-0266 ■ *Web:* coto.edu

Ozarka College 218 College Dr. Melbourne AR 72556 870-368-7371 368-2091
TF: 800-821-4335 ■ *Web:* www.ozarka.edu

Rich Mountain Community College 1100 College Dr. Mena AR 71953 479-394-7622
Web: www.rmcc.edu

Arkansas State University Mountain Home
1600 S College St. Mountain Home AR 72653 870-508-6100 508-6287
Web: www.asumh.edu

Arkansas State University Newport
7648 Victory Blvd. Newport AR 72112 870-512-7800 512-7825*
**Fax:* Admissions ■ *TF:* 800-976-1676 ■ *Web:* www.asun.edu

Pulaski Technical College
3000 W Scenic Dr. North Little Rock AR 72118 501-812-2200 771-2844
Web: www.pulaskitech.edu

Shorter College 604 N Locust St. North Little Rock AR 72114 501-374-6305 374-9333*

Crowley's Ridge College 100 College Dr. Paragould AR 72450 870-236-6901 236-7748*
**Fax:* Admissions ■ *TF:* 800-264-1096 ■ *Web:* www.crc.edu

Southeast Arkansas College 1900 Hazel St. Pine Bluff AR 71603 870-543-5900
TF: 888-732-7582

Black River Technical College
1410 Hwy 304 E. Pocahontas AR 72455 870-248-4000 248-4100
TF: 866-890-6933 ■ *Web:* www.blackrivertech.org

Mid-South Community College
2000 W Broadway. West Memphis AR 72301 870-733-6722 733-6719*
**Fax:* Admissions ■ *TF:* 866-733-6722 ■ *Web:* www.midsouthcc.edu

British Columbia

Phone Fax

Okanagan College 1000 KLO Rd. Kelowna BC V1Y4X8 250-762-5445
Web: www.okanagan.bc.ca

Justice Institute of British Columbia
715 McBride Blvd. New Westminster BC V3L5T4 604-525-5422
Web: www.jibc.bc.ca

Capilano University 2055 Purcell Way. North Vancouver BC V7J3H5 604-986-1911
Web: www.capilanou.ca

Ashton College 1190 Melville St. Vancouver BC V6E3W1 604-899-0803
Web: www.ashtoncollege.ca

Faculty of Education University of British Columbia
2125 Main Mall. Vancouver BC V6T1Z4 604-822-5242
Web: educ.ubc.ca

Langara College 100 W 49th Ave. Vancouver BC V5Y2Z6 604-323-5511
Web: langara.ca

Vancouver Community College
1155 E Broadway. Vancouver BC V5T4V5 604-871-7000
Web: www.vcc.ca

Camosun College 3100 Foul Bay Rd. Victoria BC V8P5J2 250-370-3018
Web: camosun.ca

California

Phone Fax

College of Alameda
555 Ralph Appezzato Meml Pkwy. Alameda CA 94501 510-522-7221 769-6019
Web: www.alameda.peralta.edu

Cabrillo College 6500 Soquel Dr. Aptos CA 95003 831-479-6100 479-5782*
**Fax:* Admitting ■ *TF:* 888-624-1139 ■ *Web:* www.cabrillo.edu

Bakersfield College 1801 Panorama Dr. Bakersfield CA 93305 661-395-4011 395-4500*
**Fax:* Admissions ■ *Web:* www.bakersfieldcollege.edu

Barstow College 2700 Barstow Rd. Barstow CA 92311 760-252-2411 252-1875
TF: 877-823-2378 ■ *Web:* barstow.edu

Berkeley City College 2050 Ctr St. Berkeley CA 94704 510-981-2800 841-7333
Web: berkeleycitycollege.edu

Cerro Coso Community College
Bishop 4090 W Line St. Bishop CA 93514 760-872-1565 872-5319*
**Fax:* Admissions ■ *TF:* 888-537-6932 ■ *Web:* www.cerrocoso.edu

Palo Verde College 1 College Dr. Blythe CA 92225 760-921-5500 921-3608*
**Fax:* Admissions ■ *Web:* www.paloverde.edu
San Elijo 3333 Manchester Ave. Cardiff CA 92007 760-944-4449 634-7875
TF: 888-201-8480 ■ *Web:* www.miracosta.cc.ca.us

Southwestern College 900 Otay Lakes Rd. Chula Vista CA 91910 619-421-6700 482-6489*
**Fax:* Admissions ■ *TF:* 866-262-9881 ■ *Web:* swccd.edu

West Hills College
Coalinga 300 Cherry Ln. Coalinga CA 93210 559-934-2000 935-3788*
**Fax:* Admissions ■ *TF:* 800-266-1114 ■ *Web:* www.westhillscollege.com
Compton Ctr 1111 E Artesia Blvd. Compton CA 90221 310-900-1600
Web: www.compton.edu

Orange Coast College
2701 Fairview Rd PO Box 5005. Costa Mesa CA 92628 714-432-0202
Web: orangecoastcollege.edu
Del Norte 883 W Washington Blvd. Crescent City CA 95531 707-465-2300 464-6867*
**Fax:* Admissions ■ *TF:* 800-641-0400 ■ *Web:* www.redwoods.edu

West Los Angeles College
9000 Overland Ave. Culver City CA 90230 310-287-4200 287-4327*
**Fax:* Admissions ■ *Web:* www.wlac.edu

DeAnza College 21250 Stevens Creek Blvd. Cupertino CA 95014 408-864-5678 864-8329*
**Fax:* Admissions ■ *Web:* www.deanza.edu

Cypress College 9200 Vly View St. Cypress CA 90630 714-484-7000 484-7446*
**Fax:* Admissions ■ *Web:* www.cypresscollege.edu
South Kern 140 Methusa Ave. Edwards AFB CA 93524 661-258-8644 258-0651*
**Fax:* Admissions ■ *TF:* 888-537-6932 ■ *Web:* www.cerrocoso.edu/sk

Cuyamaca College 900 Rancho San Diego Pkwy. El Cajon CA 92019 619-660-4000 660-4575*
**Fax:* Admissions ■ *TF:* 800-234-1597 ■ *Web:* www.cuyamaca.net

Grossmont College 8800 Grossmont College Dr. El Cajon CA 92020 619-644-7000 644-7933*
**Fax:* Admissions ■ *Web:* www.grossmont.edu

	City	State	Zip	Phone	Fax
College of the Redwoods 7351 Tompkins Hill Rd	Eureka	CA	95501	707-476-4100	476-4406*
**Fax:* Admissions ■ *TF:* 800-641-0400 ■ *Web:* www.redwoods.edu					
Solano Community College					
4000 Suisun Vly Rd	Fairfield	CA	94534	707-864-7171	864-7175*
**Fax:* Admissions ■ *Web:* www.solano.edu					
Mendocino Coast 440 Alger St	Fort Bragg	CA	95437	707-962-2600	961-0943
TF: 800-641-0400 ■ *Web:* www.redwoods.edu					
Coastline Community College					
11460 Warner Ave	Fountain Valley	CA	92708	714-546-7600	241-6288*
**Fax:* Admissions ■ *TF:* 866-422-2645 ■ *Web:* www.coastline.edu					
Ohlone College 43600 Mission Blvd.	Fremont	CA	94539	510-659-6000	659-7321*
**Fax:* Admissions ■ *Web:* www.ohlone.edu					
Queen of the Holy Rosary College					
43326 Mission Blvd	Fremont	CA	94539	510-657-2468	
Web: www.msjdominicans.org					
Fresno City College 1101 E University Ave	Fresno	CA	93741	559-442-4600	
TF: 866-245-3276 ■ *Web:* www.fresnocitycollege.edu					
State Center Community College District					
1525 e weldon ave	Fresno	CA	93704	559-226-0720	
Web: www.scccd.edu					
Fullerton College 321 E Chapman Ave.	Fullerton	CA	92832	714-992-7000	
Web: www.fullcoll.edu					
Gavilan College 5055 Santa Teresa Blvd.	Gilroy	CA	95020	408-847-1400	846-4940*
**Fax:* Admissions ■ *Web:* www.gavilan.edu					
Citrus College 1000 W Foothill Blvd.	Glendora	CA	91741	626-963-0323	914-8613*
**Fax:* Admissions ■ *Web:* www.citruscollege.edu					
Sierra College					
Nevada County 250 Sierra College Dr	Grass Valley	CA	95945	530-274-5300	274-5324*
**Fax:* Admissions ■ *TF:* 800-242-4004 ■ *Web:* www.sierracollege.edu					
Chabot College 25555 Hesperian Blvd	Hayward	CA	94545	925-485-5215	
Web: www.chabotcollege.edu					
Golden West College					
15744 Golden W St PO Box 2748.	Huntington Beach	CA	92647	714-892-7711	895-8960*
**Fax:* Admissions ■ *Web:* www.goldenwestcollege.edu					
Imperial Valley College					
380 E Atten Rd PO Box 158	Imperial	CA	92251	760-352-8320	355-2663*
**Fax:* Admissions ■ *Web:* www.imperial.edu					
Irvine Valley College 5500 Irvine Ctr Dr	Irvine	CA	92618	949-451-5100	
Web: www.ivc.edu					
Copper Mountain College 6162 Rotary Way.	Joshua Tree	CA	92252	760-366-3791	366-5255
TF: 866-366-3791 ■ *Web:* www.cmccd.edu					
College of Marin 835 College Ave	Kentfield	CA	94904	415-457-8811	460-0773*
**Fax:* Admissions ■ *Web:* www.marin.edu					
Kern River Valley					
5520 Lk Isabella Blvd.	Lake Isabella	CA	93240	760-379-5501	379-5547*
**Fax:* Admissions ■ *TF:* 888-537-6932 ■ *Web:* www.cerrocoso.edu					
Antelope Valley College 3041 W Ave K	Lancaster	CA	93536	661-722-6300	722-6531*
**Fax:* Admissions ■ *Web:* www.avc.edu					
Lemoore 555 College Ave	Lemoore	CA	93245	559-925-3000	924-1539
TF: 800-266-1114 ■ *Web:* www.westhillscollege.com					
Las Positas College 3033 Collier Canyon Rd	Livermore	CA	94551	925-424-1000	443-0742
Web: www.laspositascollege.edu					
Lompoc Valley 1 Hancock Dr.	Lompoc	CA	93436	805-735-3366	
Web: hancockcollege.edu					
Long Beach City College 4901 E Carson St	Long Beach	CA	90808	562-938-4111	938-4858*
**Fax:* Admissions ■ *TF:* 888-442-4551 ■ *Web:* www.lbcc.edu					
Foothill College 12345 El Monte Rd.	Los Altos Hills	CA	94022	650-949-7777	949-7048*
**Fax:* Admissions ■ *TF:* 800-234-1597 ■ *Web:* www.foothill.edu					
Los Angeles City College					
855 N Vermont Ave.	Los Angeles	CA	90029	323-953-4000	953-4013*
**Fax:* Admissions ■ *TF:* 800-207-1710 ■ *Web:* www.lacitycollege.edu					
Los Angeles Southwest College					
1600 W Imperial Hwy	Los Angeles	CA	90047	323-241-5225	
Web: www.lasc.edu					
Los Angeles Trade Technical College					
400 W Washington Blvd	Los Angeles	CA	90015	213-763-7000	763-5386*
**Fax:* Admissions ■ *Web:* www.lattc.edu					
Mount Saint Mary's University Doheny					
10 Chester Pl	Los Angeles	CA	90007	613-562-5353	477-2569*
**Fax Area Code:* 213 ■ **Fax:* Admissions ■ *Web:* www.bkstr.com					
Mammoth 101 College Pkwy PO Box 1865	Mammoth Lakes	CA	93546	760-934-2875	924-1613*
**Fax:* Admissions ■ *TF:* 888-537-6932 ■ *Web:* www.cerrocoso.edu					
Merced College 3600 M St.	Merced	CA	95348	209-384-6000	384-6339*
**Fax:* Admissions ■ *TF:* 800-784-2433 ■ *Web:* www.mccd.edu					
Saddleback College					
28000 Marguerite Pkwy	Mission Viejo	CA	92692	949-582-4500	347-8315*
**Fax:* Admissions ■ *Web:* www.saddleback.edu					
Modesto Junior College 435 College Ave.	Modesto	CA	95350	209-575-6550	575-6859*
**Fax:* Admissions ■ *Web:* www.mjc.edu					
Monterey Peninsula College 980 Fremont St	Monterey	CA	93940	831-646-4000	646-4015*
**Fax:* Admissions ■ *TF:* 877-663-5433 ■ *Web:* www.mpc.edu					
East Los Angeles College					
1301 Avenida Cesar Chavez	Monterey Park	CA	91754	323-265-8650	265-8688*
**Fax:* Admissions ■ *Web:* www.elac.edu					
Moorpark College 7075 Campus Rd	Moorpark	CA	93021	805-378-1400	378-1583*
**Fax:* Admissions ■ *Web:* moorparkcollege.edu					
Riverside Community College					
Moreno Valley 16130 Lasselle St.	Moreno Valley	CA	92551	951-571-6100	571-6188*
**Fax:* Admissions ■ *Web:* www.rcc.edu					
Napa Valley College 2277 Napa-Vallejo Hwy	Napa	CA	94558	707-256-7000	253-3064
TF: 800-826-1077 ■ *Web:* www.napavalley.edu					
Norco 2001 Third St	Norco	CA	92860	951-372-7000	
Web: www.rcc.edu					
Cerritos College 11110 Alondra Blvd	Norwalk	CA	90650	562-860-2451	467-5068*
**Fax:* Admitting ■ *Web:* www.cerritos.edu					
Indian Valley 1800 Ignacio Blvd.	Novato	CA	94949	415-883-2211	884-0429*
**Fax:* Admissions ■ *Web:* www.marin.edu					
Laney College 900 Fallon St	Oakland	CA	94607	510-834-5740	
Web: laney.edu					
Merritt College 12500 Campus Dr	Oakland	CA	94619	510-531-4911	
Web: www.merritt.edu					
MiraCosta College					
Oceanside 1 Barnard Dr Ste 7	Oceanside	CA	92056	760-757-2121	795-6626*
**Fax:* Admissions ■ *TF:* 888-201-8480 ■ *Web:* www.miracosta.edu					
Santiago Canyon College 8045 E Chapman Ave.	Orange	CA	92869	714-628-4900	628-4723*
**Fax:* Admissions ■ *Web:* www.sccollege.edu					
Butte College 3536 Butte Campus Dr	Oroville	CA	95965	530-895-2511	879-4313*
**Fax:* Admissions ■ *TF Hum Res:* 800-933-8322 ■ *Web:* www.butte.edu					
Oxnard College 4000 S Rose Ave	Oxnard	CA	93033	805-986-5800	986-5943*
**Fax:* Admissions ■ *Web:* www.oxnardcollege.edu					
College of the Desert					
43-500 Monterey Ave	Palm Desert	CA	92260	760-346-8041	862-1379*
**Fax:* Admissions ■ *Web:* www.collegeofthedesert.edu					
Pasadena City College 1570 E Colorado Blvd	Pasadena	CA	91106	626-585-7123	585-7915*
**Fax:* Admissions ■ *Web:* www.pasadena.edu					
William Carey International University					
1539 e howard st	Pasadena	CA	91104	626-797-1200	
Web: www.global-prayer-digest.com					
North County 2800 Buena Vista Dr	Paso Robles	CA	93446	805-591-6200	591-6370
Web: academic.cuesta.edu					
Los Medanos College 2700 E Leland Rd	Pittsburg	CA	94565	925-439-2181	427-1599
TF: 800-677-6337 ■ *Web:* www.losmedanos.edu					
Diablo Valley College 321 Golf Club Rd	Pleasant Hill	CA	94523	925-685-1230	609-8085
TF: 800-227-1060 ■ *Web:* www.dvc.edu					
Western University of Health Sciences					
309 E Second St	Pomona	CA	91766	909-623-6116	
TF: 800-346-1610 ■ *Web:* www.westernu.edu					
Porterville College 100 E College Ave	Porterville	CA	93257	559-791-2200	791-2349*
**Fax:* Admissions ■ *Web:* portervillecollege.edu					
Feather River College 570 Golden Eagle Ave	Quincy	CA	95971	530-283-0202	283-9961*
**Fax:* Admissions ■ *TF:* 800-442-9799 ■ *Web:* www.frc.edu					
Chaffey College 5885 Haven Ave	Rancho Cucamonga	CA	91737	909-652-6000	
Web: www.chaffey.edu					
Canada College 4200 Farm Hill Blvd	Redwood City	CA	94061	650-306-3100	306-3113*
**Fax:* Admissions ■ *Web:* www.canadacollege.edu					
Reedley College 995 N Reed Ave	Reedley	CA	93654	559-638-3641	638-5040
TF: 877-253-7122 ■ *Web:* reedleycollege.edu					
Indian Wells Valley					
3000 College Heights Blvd	Ridgecrest	CA	93555	760-384-6100	384-6377*
**Fax:* Admissions ■ *TF:* 888-537-6932 ■ *Web:* www.cerrocoso.edu					
Riverside 4800 Magnolia Ave	Riverside	CA	92506	951-222-8000	
Web: www.rcc.edu					
Sierra Community College 5000 Rocklin Rd.	Rocklin	CA	95677	916-624-3333	
TF: 800-242-4004 ■ *Web:* www.sierracollege.edu					
American River College					
4700 College Oak Dr	Sacramento	CA	95841	916-484-8011	484-8864*
**Fax:* Admissions ■ *Web:* www.arc.losrios.edu					
Cosumnes River College 8401 Ctr Pkwy.	Sacramento	CA	95823	916-691-7410	691-7467*
**Fax:* Admissions ■ *Web:* www.crc.losrios.edu					
Sacramento City College					
3835 Freeport Blvd	Sacramento	CA	95822	916-558-2351	558-2190*
**Fax:* Admissions ■ *Web:* www.scc.losrios.edu					
Hartnell College 156 Homestead Ave	Salinas	CA	93901	831-755-6700	759-6014*
**Fax:* Admissions ■ *TF:* 888-678-2871 ■ *Web:* www.hartnell.edu					
San Bernardino Valley College					
701 S Mt Vernon Ave	San Bernardino	CA	92410	909-384-4400	
Web: www.valleycollege.edu					
Skyline College 3300 College Dr	San Bruno	CA	94066	650-738-4100	
Web: www.skylinecollege.edu					
San Diego City College 1313 Pk Blvd	San Diego	CA	92101	619-388-3400	388-3241*
**Fax:* Admissions ■ *Web:* www.sdcity.edu					
San Diego Mesa College					
7250 Mesa College Dr	San Diego	CA	92111	619-388-2600	388-2960
Web: sdmesa.edu					
San Diego Miramar College					
10440 Black Mtn Rd	San Diego	CA	92126	619-388-7844	388-7915*
**Fax:* Admissions ■ *Web:* www.sdmiramar.edu					
City College of San Francisco					
50 Phelan Ave.	San Francisco	CA	94112	415-239-3000	239-3936*
**Fax:* Admissions ■ *TF:* 800-433-3243 ■ *Web:* www.ccsf.edu					
Mount San Jacinto College					
1499 N State St.	San Jacinto	CA	92583	951-487-6752	654-6738*
**Fax:* Admissions ■ *TF:* 800-624-5561 ■ *Web:* www.msjc.edu					
Evergreen Valley College					
3095 Yerba Buena Rd	San Jose	CA	95135	408-274-7900	223-9351*
**Fax:* Admissions ■ *Web:* www.evc.edu					
San Jose City College 2100 Moorpark Ave	San Jose	CA	95128	408-298-2181	298-1935*
**Fax:* Admissions ■ *Web:* www.sjcc.edu					
Cuesta College PO Box 8106	San Luis Obispo	CA	93403	805-546-3100	546-3975*
**Fax:* Admissions ■ *TF:* 800-675-2526 ■ *Web:* www.cuesta.edu					
Palomar College 1140 W Mission Rd.	San Marcos	CA	92069	760-744-1150	744-8123*
**Fax:* Admissions ■ *Web:* www.palomar.edu					
College of San Mateo 1700 W Hillsdale Blvd	San Mateo	CA	94402	650-574-6161	574-6506*
**Fax:* Admissions ■ *Web:* www.collegeofsanmateo.edu					
Contra Costa College 2600 Mission Bell.	San Pablo	CA	94806	510-235-7800	412-0769
Web: coast.contracosta.edu					
Santa Ana College 1530 W 17th St	Santa Ana	CA	92706	714-564-6000	564-6455*
**Fax:* Admissions ■ *Web:* www.sac.edu					
Santa Barbara City College					
721 Cliff Dr.	Santa Barbara	CA	93109	805-965-0581	963-7222*
**Fax:* Admissions ■ *TF:* 877-232-3919 ■ *Web:* www.sbcc.edu					
Mission College					
3000 Mission College Blvd	Santa Clara	CA	95054	408-988-2200	980-8980*
**Fax:* Admissions ■ *Web:* missioncollege.edu					
College of the Canyons					
26455 Rockwell Canyon Rd	Santa Clarita	CA	91355	661-259-7800	362-5566*
**Fax:* Admissions ■ *Web:* www.canyons.edu					
Allan Hancock College 800 S College Dr	Santa Maria	CA	93454	805-922-6966	922-3477*
**Fax:* Admissions ■ *TF:* 866-342-5242 ■ *Web:* hancockcollege.edu					
Santa Monica College 1900 Pico Blvd	Santa Monica	CA	90405	310-434-4000	434-3645*
**Fax:* Admissions ■ *Web:* www.smc.edu					
Santa Rosa Junior College					
1501 Mendocino Ave	Santa Rosa	CA	95401	707-527-4011	527-4798
TF: 800-564-7752 ■ *Web:* www.santarosa.edu					
West Valley College 14000 Fruitvale Ave	Saratoga	CA	95070	408-867-2200	
Web: www.westvalley.edu					
Columbia College 11600 Columbia College Dr	Sonora	CA	95370	209-588-5100	588-5104
TF: 888-722-2873 ■ *Web:* www.gocolumbia.edu					

Phone Fax

Lake Tahoe Community College
1 College Dr .... South Lake Tahoe CA 96150 530-541-4660 542-1781*
Fax: Admissions ■ *Web:* www.ltcc.edu

San Joaquin Delta College 5151 Pacific Ave .... Stockton CA 95207 209-954-5151 954-5769*
Fax: Admissions ■ *Web:* www.deltacollege.edu

Lassen Community College
478-200 Hwy 139 PO Box 3000 .... Susanville CA 96130 530-257-6181 257-8964*
Fax: Admissions ■ *Web:* www.lassencollege.edu

Los Angeles Mission College
13356 Eldridge Ave .... Sylmar CA 91342 818-364-7600 364-7806*
Fax: Admissions ■ *Web:* www.lamission.edu

Taft College 29 Emmons Pk Dr .... Taft CA 93268 661-763-7700 763-7758*
Fax: Admissions ■ *TF:* 800-379-6784 ■ *Web:* www.taftcollege.edu

El Camino College 16007 Crenshaw Blvd .... Torrance CA 90506 310-532-3670 660-3818
TF: 866-352-2646 ■ *Web:* www.elcamino.edu

Mendocino College 1000 Hensley Creek Rd .... Ukiah CA 95482 707-468-3000 468-3430*
Fax: Admissions ■ *Web:* www.mendocino.edu

Los Angeles Valley College
5800 Fulton Ave .... Valley Glen CA 91401 818-947-2600
Web: www.lavc.cc.ca.us

Ventura College 4667 Telegraph Rd .... Ventura CA 93003 805-654-6400
Web: www.venturacollege.edu

Victor Valley Community College
18422 Bear Valley Rd .... Victorville CA 92392 760-245-4271 245-9745
TF: 877-741-8532 ■ *Web:* www.vvc.edu

College of the Sequoias 915 S Mooney Blvd .... Visalia CA 93277 559-730-3700 737-4820*
Fax: Admissions ■ *Web:* www.cos.edu

Mount San Antonio College 1100 N Grand Ave .... Walnut CA 91789 909-594-5611
Web: www.mtsac.edu

College of the Siskiyous 800 College Ave .... Weed CA 96094 530-938-4461 938-5367*
Fax: Admissions ■ *TF:* 888-397-4339 ■ *Web:* www.siskiyous.edu

Rio Hondo College 3600 Workman Mill Rd .... Whittier CA 90601 562-692-0921 699-7386
Web: www.riohondo.edu

Los Angeles Harbor College
1111 Figueroa Pl .... Wilmington CA 90744 310-233-4000 233-4223
Web: www.lahc.cc.ca.us

Crafton Hills College 11711 Sand Canyon Rd .... Yucaipa CA 92399 909-794-2161 389-9141*
Fax: Admissions ■ *Web:* www.craftonhills.edu

Colorado

Phone Fax

Aspen 0255 Sage Way .... Aspen CO 81611 970-925-7740 925-6045
TF: 800-621-8559 ■ *Web:* www.coloradomtn.edu

Community College of Aurora
16000 E Centretech Pkwy .... Aurora CO 80011 303-360-4700 361-7432*
Fax: Admissions ■ *TF:* 844-493-8255 ■ *Web:* www.ccaurora.edu

Pikes Peak Community College
Centennial 5675 S Academy Blvd .... Colorado Springs CO 80906 719-502-2000
TF: 800-456-6847 ■ *Web:* www.ppcc.edu
Downtown Studio
100 W Pikes Peak Ave .... Colorado Springs CO 80903 719-502-2000
TF: 800-456-6847 ■ *Web:* www.ppcc.edu
Rampart Range 11195 Hwy 83 .... Colorado Springs CO 80921 719-502-2000
TF: 800-456-6847 ■ *Web:* www.ppcc.edu
Craig 50 College Dr .... Craig CO 81625 800-562-1105 824-1134*
Fax Area Code: 970 ■ *Fax:* Admissions ■ *TF:* 800-562-1105 ■ *Web:* www.cncc.edu

Community College of Denver 1111 E Colfax Ave .... Denver CO 80204 303-556-2600 556-2431
Web: www.ccd.edu
Larimer 4616 S Shields St .... Fort Collins CO 80526 970-226-2500 204-8484
TF: 888-800-9198 ■ *Web:* www.frontrange.edu
Fort Lupton 260 County Rd 29 1/2 .... Fort Lupton CO 80621 303-857-4022 352-5443*
Fax Area Code: 970 ■ *Web:* www.aims.edu

Morgan Community College 920 Barlow Rd .... Fort Morgan CO 80701 970-542-3100 867-6608
TF: 800-622-0216 ■ *Web:* www.morgancc.edu
Roaring Fork-Spring Valley
3000 County Rd 114 .... Glenwood Springs CO 81601 970-945-7481 928-9668
TF: 800-621-8559 ■ *Web:* www.coloradomtn.edu

Aims Community College 5401 W 20th St .... Greeley CO 80634 970-330-8008 506-6958*
Fax: Admissions ■ *TF:* 800-301-5388 ■ *Web:* www.aims.edu

Otero Junior College 1802 Colorado Ave .... La Junta CO 81050 719-384-6831 384-6933*
Fax: Admissions ■ *Web:* www.ojc.edu

Red Rocks Community College
13300 W Sixth Ave .... Lakewood CO 80228 303-914-6600 914-6666
Web: www.rrcc.edu

Lamar Community College 2401 S Main St .... Lamar CO 81052 719-336-2248 336-2400*
Fax: Admissions ■ *TF:* 800-968-6920 ■ *Web:* lamarcc.edu
Timberline 901 US Hwy 24 .... Leadville CO 80461 719-486-2015 486-3212
Web: www.coloradomtn.edu

Arapahoe Community College
5900 S Santa Fe Dr .... Littleton CO 80160 303-797-0100 797-5970*
Fax: Admissions ■ *TF:* 888-800-9198 ■ *Web:* www.arapahoe.edu

Front Range Community College (FRCC)
Boulder County 2190 Miller Dr .... Longmont CO 80501 303-678-3722 678-3699*
Fax: Admissions ■ *TF:* 888-800-9198 ■ *Web:* www.frontrange.edu

Pueblo Community College 900 W Orman Ave .... Pueblo CO 81004 719-549-3200
TF: 888-642-6017 ■ *Web:* www.pueblocc.edu

Colorado Northwestern Community College
500 Kennedy Dr .... Rangely CO 81648 970-675-3335 675-3343*
Fax: Admissions ■ *TF:* 800-562-1105 ■ *Web:* www.cncc.edu

Colorado Mountain College
Alpine 1330 Bob Adams Dr .... Steamboat Springs CO 80487 970-870-4444 870-4535*
Fax: Admissions ■ *TF:* 800-621-8559 ■ *Web:* www.coloradomtn.edu

Northeastern Junior College 100 College Ave .... Sterling CO 80751 970-521-6600 522-4664
TF: 800-626-4637 ■ *Web:* www.njc.edu

Trinidad State Junior College
600 Prospect St .... Trinidad CO 81082 719-846-5011 846-5620*
Fax: Admissions ■ *TF:* 800-621-8752 ■ *Web:* www.trinidadstate.edu
Westminster 3645 W 112th Ave .... Westminster CO 80031 303-404-5000 466-1623*
Fax: Admissions ■ *Web:* www.frontrange.edu

Connecticut

Phone Fax

Housatonic Community College
900 Lafayette Blvd .... Bridgeport CT 06604 203-332-5000 332-5123*
Fax: Admissions ■ *TF:* 866-733-2463 ■ *Web:* www.hctc.commnet.edu

Quinebaug Valley Community College
742 Upper Maple St .... Danielson CT 06239 860-774-1160 779-2998*
Fax: Admissions ■ *Web:* www.qvctc.commnet.edu

Asnuntuck Community College 170 Elm St .... Enfield CT 06082 860-253-3000 253-3014*
Fax: Admissions ■ *TF:* 800-501-3967 ■ *Web:* www.asnuntuck.edu

Tunxis Community College
271 Scott Swamp Rd .... Farmington CT 06032 860-773-1300
Web: tunxis.edu
Avery Point 1084 Shennecossett Rd .... Groton CT 06340 860-405-9019 405-9018
TF: 888-247-5556 ■ *Web:* www.averypoint.uconn.edu

Capital Community College 950 Main St .... Hartford CT 06103 860-906-5000 906-5129
TF: 800-894-6126 ■ *Web:* www.ccc.commnet.edu

Manchester Community College PO Box 1046 ...... Manchester CT 06045 860-512-2800 512-3221*
Fax: Admissions ■ *TF:* 888-999-5545 ■ *Web:* www.manchestercc.edu

Middlesex Community College
100 Training Hill Rd .... Middletown CT 06457 860-343-5800 344-7488*
Fax: Admissions ■ *TF:* 800-818-5501 ■ *Web:* mxcc.edu

Gateway Community College 60 Sargent Dr .... New Haven CT 06510 203-285-2000 285-2260*
Fax: Admissions ■ *TF:* 800-390-7723 ■ *Web:* www.gatewayct.edu

Norwalk Community College 188 Richards Ave .... Norwalk CT 06854 203-857-7060 857-3335*
Fax: Admissions ■ *TF:* 800-565-3036 ■ *Web:* www.ncc.commnet.edu

Three Rivers Community College Mohegan
574 New London Turnpike .... Norwich CT 06360 860-886-0177 885-1684*
Fax: Admissions ■ *Web:* www.trcc.commnet.edu

University of Connecticut
2131 Hillside Rd Unit 3088 .... Storrs CT 06269 860-486-2000 486-1476*
Fax: Admissions ■ *Web:* www.uconn.edu
Torrington 855 University Dr .... Torrington CT 06790 860-626-6800 626-6847
Web: www.torrington.uconn.edu

Naugatuck Valley Community College
750 Chase Pkwy .... Waterbury CT 06708 203-575-8040
Web: www.nv.edu
Waterbury 99 E Main St .... Waterbury CT 06702 203-236-9800 236-9805
Web: www.waterbury.uconn.edu
Greater Hartford 85 Lawler Rd .... West Hartford CT 06117 860-570-9214
Web: www.hartford.uconn.edu

Northwestern Connecticut Community College
Park Pl E .... Winsted CT 06098 860-738-6300 738-6437*
Fax: Admissions ■ *Web:* www.nwctc.commnet.edu

Florida

Phone Fax

South Florida Community College
600 W College Dr .... Avon Park FL 33825 863-453-6661 453-2365*
Fax: Admissions ■ *Web:* www.southflorida.edu

Palm Beach Community College
Belle Glade 1977 College Dr .... Belle Glade FL 33430 561-996-7222
Web: www.palmbeachstate.edu
Boca Raton 3000 St Lucie Ave .... Boca Raton FL 33431 561-862-4340 862-4350
Web: palmbeachstate.edu

Manatee Technical Institute East Campus
6305 State Rd 70 E .... Bradenton FL 34203 941-752-8100
Web: www.manateetechnicalinstitute.org

State College of Florida 5840 26th St W .... Bradenton FL 34207 941-752-5000 727-6380
Web: www.scf.edu
North 11415 Ponce de Leon Blvd .... Brooksville FL 34601 352-796-6726 797-5133
TF: 877-879-7422 ■ *Web:* phsc.edu
Levy County 114 Rodgers Blvd .... Chiefland FL 32626 352-493-9533 493-9994
Web: www.cf.edu
South Lake 1250 N Hancock Rd .... Clermont FL 34711 352-243-5722 243-0117
Web: lssc.edu

Brevard Community College (BCC)
Cocoa 1519 Clearlake Rd .... Cocoa FL 32922 321-632-1111 433-7357*
Fax: Admissions ■ *TF:* 888-747-2802 ■ *Web:* www.easternflorida.edu
North 1000 Coconut Creek Blvd .... Coconut Creek FL 33066 954-201-2240 201-2242*
Fax: Admissions ■ *TF:* 888-654-6482 ■ *Web:* www.broward.edu

Broward Community College
Central 3501 SW Davie Rd .... Davie FL 33314 954-201-7350
Web: www.broward.edu

Daytona Beach Community College
1200 W International Speedway Blvd .... Daytona Beach FL 32114 386-506-3000 506-3940
TF: 877-822-6669 ■ *Web:* www.daytonastate.edu
Downtown Ctr 111 E Las Olas Blvd .... Fort Lauderdale FL 33301 954-201-7350 201-7466*
Fax: Admissions ■ *TF:* 888-654-6482 ■ *Web:* www.broward.edu

Indian River State College (IRSC)
3209 Virginia Ave .... Fort Pierce FL 34981 772-462-4772 462-4699
TF: 866-792-4772 ■ *Web:* www.irsc.edu
North-Hialeah Ctr 1780 W 49th St .... Hialeah FL 33012 305-237-8700
Web: www.mdc.edu

Miami Dade College
Homestead 500 College Terr Rm A230 .... Homestead FL 33030 305-237-5555 237-5019*
Fax: Admissions ■ *Web:* www.mdc.edu/homestead

Florida Community College at Jacksonville
Downtown 101 State St W .... Jacksonville FL 32202 904-633-8100
TF: 877-633-5950 ■ *Web:* www.fscj.edu
Kent 3939 Roosevelt Blvd .... Jacksonville FL 32205 904-381-3400
Web: www.fccj.org
South 11901 Beach Blvd .... Jacksonville FL 32246 904-646-2111
Web: www.fccj.org

Florida State College at Jacksonville
North 4501 Capper Rd .... Jacksonville FL 32218 904-766-6500
Web: www.fccj.org

Florida Keys Community College
5901 College Rd .... Key West FL 33040 305-296-9081 292-5155*
Fax: Admissions ■ *TF:* 866-567-2665 ■ *Web:* www.fkcc.edu

	City	State	ZIP	Phone	Fax
Osceola 1800 Denn John Ln PO Box 3028	Kissimmee	FL	32802	407-299-5000	
Web: valenciacollege.edu					
Florida Gateway College 149 SE College Pl.	Lake City	FL	32025	386-752-1822	754-4594*
**Fax:* Admissions ■ *Web:* www.fgc.edu					
Lake Worth 4200 Congress Ave.	Lake Worth	FL	33461	561-868-3350	868-3584*
**Fax:* Admissions ■ *TF:* 866-576-7222 ■ *Web:* palmbeachstate.edu					
Central Florida Community College					
Citrus County 3800 S Lecanto Hwy	Lecanto	FL	34461	352-746-6721	249-1218
Web: www.cf.edu					
Lake-Sumter State College 9501 US Hwy 441	Leesburg	FL	34788	352-787-3747	
Web: www.lssc.edu					
North Florida Community College					
325 NW Turner Davis Dr.	Madison	FL	32340	850-973-2288	973-1696
TF: 877-501-0956 ■ *Web:* www.nfcc.edu					
Melbourne 3865 N Wickham Rd	Melbourne	FL	32935	321-632-1111	433-5770*
**Fax:* Admissions ■ *TF:* 888-747-2802 ■ *Web:* www.easternflorida.edu					
Kendall 11011 SW 104th St.	Miami	FL	33176	305-237-2000	
Web: www.mdc.edu/kendall					
Medical Ctr 950 NW 20th St	Miami	FL	33127	305-237-4100	237-4339
Web: www.mdc.edu/medical					
North 11380 NW 27th Ave.	Miami	FL	33167	305-237-1000	
Web: www.mdc.edu/north					
Wolfson 300 NE Second Ave	Miami	FL	33132	305-237-3000	
Web: www.mdc.edu/wolfson					
Pasco-Hernando Community College					
10230 Ridge Rd	New Port Richey	FL	34654	727-847-2727	816-3389*
**Fax:* Admissions ■ *TF:* 877-879-7422 ■ *Web:* phsc.edu					
Northwest Florida State College					
100 College Blvd	Niceville	FL	32578	850-678-5111	729-5273
Ocala 3001 SW College Rd	Ocala	FL	34474	352-237-2111	291-4450
Web: cf.edu					
Valencia Community College PO Box 3028	Orlando	FL	32802	407-299-5000	
Web: www.valenciacollege.edu					
East 701 N Econlockhatchee Trl	Orlando	FL	32825	407-299-5000	582-2621
Web: valenciacollege.edu					
Oviedo 2505 Lockwood Blvd	Oviedo	FL	32765	407-971-5000	971-5012
Web: seminolestate.edu					
Saint Johns River Community College					
5001 St Johns Ave	Palatka	FL	32177	386-312-4200	312-4048*
**Fax:* Admissions ■ *TF:* 888-757-2293 ■ *Web:* www.sjrstate.edu					
Palm Bay 250 Community College Pkwy	Palm Bay	FL	32909	321-632-1111	433-5325*
**Fax:* Admissions ■ *TF:* 888-747-2802 ■ *Web:* www.easternflorida.edu					
Palm Beach Gardens 3160 PGA Blvd.	Palm Beach Gardens	FL	33410	561-207-5340	
TF: 866-576-7222 ■ *Web:* www.palmbeachstate.edu					
Gulf Coast Community College					
5230 W Hwy 98	Panama City	FL	32401	850-769-1551	913-3308*
**Fax:* Admissions ■ *TF:* 800-311-3685 ■ *Web:* www.gulfcoast.edu					
Pines 16957 Sheridan St	Pembroke Pines	FL	33331	954-201-3601	201-3614
Web: www.broward.edu/locations/pines					
South 7200 Hollywood/Pines Blvd	Pembroke Pines	FL	33024	954-201-8835	201-8060*
**Fax:* Admissions ■ *Web:* www.broward.edu					
Pensacola Junior College 1000 College Blvd	Pensacola	FL	32504	850-484-1000	484-1829*
**Fax:* Admissions ■ *Web:* pensacolastate.edu					
Warrington 5555 W Hwy 98	Pensacola	FL	32507	850-484-2200	484-2375
TF: 888-897-3605 ■ *Web:* pensacolastate.edu					
Plant City 1206 N Pk Rd	Plant City	FL	33566	813-757-2102	757-2187
Web: www.hccfl.edu					
Edison College					
Charlotte 26300 Airport Rd	Punta Gorda	FL	33950	941-637-5629	637-3538*
**Fax:* Admissions ■ *TF:* 800-749-2322 ■ *Web:* fsw.edu					
Saint Augustine 2990 College Dr.	Saint Augustine	FL	32084	904-808-7400	
Web: sjrstate.edu					
Saint Petersburg College (SPC)					
PO Box 13489	Saint Petersburg	FL	33733	727-341-4772	
Web: www.spcollege.edu					
Seminole Community College 100 Weldon Blvd	Sanford	FL	32773	407-708-4722	
Web: seminolestate.edu					
Seminole State College					
2701 Boren Blvd PO Box 351	Sanford	FL	32773	405-382-9950	
TF: 877-738-6365 ■ *Web:* sscok.edu					
Seminole 9200 113th St N.	Seminole	FL	33772	727-394-6000	394-6132
Web: www.spcollege.edu/se/campus					
Sumter 1405 CR 526A	Sumterville	FL	33585	352-568-0001	568-7515
Web: lssc.edu					
Tallahassee Community College					
444 Appleyard Dr	Tallahassee	FL	32304	850-201-6200	201-8474*
**Fax:* Admissions ■ *Web:* www.tcc.fl.edu					
Hillsborough Community College (HCC)					
Brandon 10414 E Columbus Dr	Tampa	FL	33619	813-253-7801	
Web: www.hccfl.edu/campus/br					
Dale Mabry 4001 Tampa Bay Blvd	Tampa	FL	33614	813-253-7000	253-7400*
**Fax:* Admissions ■ *TF:* 866-253-7077 ■ *Web:* www.hccfl.edu					
Ybor City 2112 N 15th St PO Box 5096	Tampa	FL	33675	813-253-7602	
Web: www.hccfl.edu					
Titusville 1311 N US 1	Titusville	FL	32796	321-632-1111	433-5115
TF: 888-747-2802 ■ *Web:* www.easternflorida.edu					
Manatee Community College					
South 8000 S Tamiami Tr	Venice	FL	34293	941-408-1300	
Web: www.scf.edu					
Polk State College 999 Ave H NE	Winter Haven	FL	33881	863-297-1000	297-1060*
**Fax:* Admissions ■ *Web:* www.polk.edu					

Georgia

	City	State	ZIP	Phone	Fax
Darton College 2400 Gillionville Rd	Albany	GA	31707	229-430-6742	317-6607*
**Fax:* Admissions ■ *TF:* 866-775-1214 ■ *Web:* www.darton.edu					
Atlanta Metropolitan College					
1630 Metropolitan Pkwy SW	Atlanta	GA	30310	404-756-4000	756-4407*
**Fax:* Admissions ■ *Web:* www.atlm.edu					
Emory University Oxford College					
201 Dowman Dr PO Box 1418	Atlanta	GA	30322	404-727-6069	784-8359*
**Fax Area Code:* 770 ■ *TF:* 800-723-8328 ■ *Web:* www.emory.edu					
Morris Brown College					
643 Martin Luther King Jr Dr	Atlanta	GA	30314	404-739-1010	
Web: www.morrisbrown.edu					
Georgia Highlands College					
Cartersville 5441 Hwy 20 NE	Cartersville	GA	30121	678-872-8000	872-8013
TF: 800-332-2406 ■ *Web:* www.highlands.edu					
Georgia Perimeter College					
Clarkston 555 N Indian Creek Dr	Clarkston	GA	30021	678-891-3200	
Web: perimeter.gsu.edu					
Middle Georgia College 1100 Second St SE	Cochran	GA	31014	478-934-6221	
Web: www.mga.edu					
Andrew College 501 College St	Cuthbert	GA	39840	800-664-9250	
TF: 800-664-9250 ■ *Web:* www.andrewcollege.edu					
Decatur Campus 3251 Panthersville Rd	Decatur	GA	30034	678-891-2300	
Web: perimeter.gsu.edu					
Dunwoody 2101 Womack Rd	Dunwoody	GA	30338	770-274-5000	
Web: perimeter.gsu.edu					
Georgia Military College					
201 E Green St	Milledgeville	GA	31061	478-387-4900	445-6520*
**Fax:* Admissions ■ *TF:* 800-342-0413 ■ *Web:* www.gmc.edu					
Gainesville State College					
University of N Georgia Gainesville Campus					
3820 Mundy Mill Rd	Oakwood	GA	30566	678-717-3639	
Web: ung.edu/visitors/campuses/gainesville					
Floyd 3175 Cedartown Hwy	Rome	GA	30161	706-802-5000	295-6341
TF: 800-332-2406 ■ *Web:* www.highlands.edu					
East Georgia College 131 College Cir	Swainsboro	GA	30401	478-289-2000	289-2140*
**Fax:* Admissions ■ *TF:* 800-715-4255 ■ *Web:* www.ega.edu					
Abraham Baldwin Agricultural College					
2802 Moore Hwy ABAC 3	Tifton	GA	31793	229-391-5001	391-4931*
**Fax:* Admissions ■ *TF:* 800-733-3653 ■ *Web:* www.abac.edu					
Valdosta Technical College 4089 Val Tech Rd	Valdosta	GA	31602	229-333-2100	
Web: valdostatech.org					
Waycross College 2001 S Georgia Pkwy	Waycross	GA	31503	912-449-7600	
Web: sgsc.edu					
Young Harris College PO Box 116	Young Harris	GA	30582	706-379-3111	379-3108*
**Fax:* Admissions ■ *TF:* 800-241-3754 ■ *Web:* www.yhc.edu					

Hawaii

	City	State	ZIP	Phone	Fax
Hawaii Community College 200 W Kawili St	Hilo	HI	96720	808-934-2500	974-7692*
**Fax:* Admissions ■ *Web:* www.hawcc.hawaii.edu					
University of Hawaii					
Hilo 200 W Kawili St	Hilo	HI	96720	808-974-7414	933-0861*
**Fax:* Admissions ■ *TF Admissions:* 800-897-4456 ■ *Web:* hilo.hawaii.edu					
Honolulu Community College					
874 Dillingham Blvd	Honolulu	HI	96817	808-845-9129	847-9829*
**Fax:* Admissions ■ *Web:* www.honolulu.hawaii.edu					
Kapiolani Community College					
4303 Diamond Head Rd.	Honolulu	HI	96816	808-734-9000	734-9896
Web: www.kcc.hawaii.edu					
Maui Community College 310 W Kaahumanu Ave	Kahului	HI	96732	808-984-3267	242-9618*
**Fax:* Admissions ■ *TF:* 800-479-6692 ■ *Web:* www.maui.hawaii.edu					
Windward Community College					
45-720 Keaahala Rd.	Kaneohe	HI	96744	808-235-7400	247-5362*
**Fax:* Admissions ■ *Web:* windward.hawaii.edu					
Kauai Community College 3-1901 Kaumualii Hwy	Lihue	HI	96766	808-245-8311	245-8220
TF: 800-776-4816 ■ *Web:* www.kauai.hawaii.edu					
Leeward Community College 96-045 Ala Ike	Pearl City	HI	96782	808-455-0011	454-8804*
**Fax:* Admissions ■ *TF:* 888-442-4551 ■ *Web:* www.leeward.hawaii.edu					
Leeward Community College					
96-045 Ala Ike St.	Pearl City	HI	96782	808-455-0011	454-8804*
**Fax:* Admissions ■ *Web:* www.leeward.hawaii.edu					

Idaho

	City	State	ZIP	Phone	Fax
North Idaho College 1000 W Garden Ave.	Coeur d'Alene	ID	83814	208-769-3300	769-3399*
**Fax:* Library ■ *TF:* 877-404-4536 ■ *Web:* www.nic.edu					
College of Southern Idaho PO Box 1238	Twin Falls	ID	83303	208-733-9554	736-3014*
**Fax:* Admissions ■ *TF:* 800-680-0274 ■ *Web:* www.csi.edu					

Illinois

	City	State	ZIP	Phone	Fax
Southwestern Illinois College					
2500 Carlyle Ave	Belleville	IL	62221	618-235-2700	222-9768*
**Fax:* Admissions ■ *TF:* 800-222-5131 ■ *Web:* www.swic.edu					
Spoon River College (SRC) 23235 N County Hwy 22	Canton	IL	61520	309-647-4645	649-6393*
**Fax:* Admissions ■ *TF:* 800-334-7337 ■ *Web:* www.src.edu					
John A Logan College					
700 Logan College Rd	Carterville	IL	62918	618-985-2828	985-4433*
Kaskaskia College 27210 College Rd	Centralia	IL	62801	618-545-3090	
Web: kaskaskia.edu					
Parkland College 2400 W Bradley Ave	Champaign	IL	61821	217-351-2200	353-2640*
**Fax:* Admissions ■ *TF:* 888-467-6065 ■ *Web:* www.parkland.edu					
City Colleges of Chicago 226 W Jackson	Chicago	IL	60606	312-553-2500	553-3075*
**Fax:* Admissions ■ *TF:* 866-908-7582 ■ *Web:* www.ccc.edu					
Harry S Truman College 1145 W Wilson Ave	Chicago	IL	60640	773-878-1700	907-4464*
**Fax:* Admissions ■ *TF:* 877-863-6339 ■ *Web:* www.ccc.edu					
Kennedy-King College 6301 S Halsted St	Chicago	IL	60621	773-602-5000	
Web: www.ccc.edu/colleges/kennedy/pages/default.aspx					
Malcolm X College 1900 W Jackson	Chicago	IL	60612	312-850-7000	850-7092
TF: 877-542-0285 ■					
Web: www.ccc.edu/colleges/malcolm-x/Pages/default.aspx					
Olive-Harvey College 10001 S Woodlawn Ave.	Chicago	IL	60628	773-291-6100	291-6185
Web: www.ccc.edu/colleges/olive-harvey/pages/default.aspx					
Richard J Daley College 226 W Jackson	Chicago	IL	60606	312-553-2500	
Web: www.ccc.edu					
Saint Augustine College 1345 W Argyle St	Chicago	IL	60640	773-878-8756	878-0937*
**Fax:* Admissions ■ *Web:* www.staugustine.edu					

	City	State	ZIP	Phone	Fax
Universidad Popular 2801 S Hamlin Ave	Chicago	IL	60623	773-733-5055	
Web: www.universidadpopular.us					
Wilbur Wright College 4300 N Narragansett Ave	Chicago	IL	60634	773-777-7900	481-8185
Web: www.ccc.edu/colleges/wright/pages/default.aspx					
Prairie State College 202 S Halsted St	Chicago Heights	IL	60411	708-709-3500	709-3951*
**Fax:* Admissions ■ *TF:* 866-255-5437 ■ *Web:* www.prairiestate.edu					
Morton College 3801 S Central Ave	Cicero	IL	60804	708-656-8000	656-9592*
**Fax:* Admitting ■ *Web:* www.morton.edu					
McHenry County College 8900 US Hwy 14	Crystal Lake	IL	60012	815-455-3700	455-3766
TF: 888-977-4847 ■ *Web:* www.mchenry.edu					
Danville Area Community College 2000 E Main St	Danville	IL	61832	217-443-3222	443-8560*
**Fax:* Hum Res ■ *TF:* 877-342-3042 ■ *Web:* dacc.edu					
Richland Community College 1 College Pk	Decatur	IL	62521	217-875-7200	875-6965*
**Fax:* Hum Res ■ *Web:* www.richland.edu					
Oakton Community College 1600 E Golf Rd	Des Plaines	IL	60016	847-635-1600	635-1890*
**Fax:* Admissions ■ *Web:* www.oakton.edu					
Sauk Valley Community College 173 Illinois Rt 2	Dixon	IL	61021	815-288-5511	288-3190*
**Fax:* Admissions ■ *Web:* www.svcc.edu					
Elgin Community College 1700 Spartan Dr	Elgin	IL	60123	847-697-1000	608-5458*
**Fax:* Admissions ■ *TF:* 855-850-2525 ■ *Web:* www.elgin.edu					
Highland Community College 2998 W Pearl City Rd	Freeport	IL	61032	815-235-6121	235-6130*
**Fax:* Admissions ■ *Web:* www.highland.cc.il.us					
Carl Sandburg College 2400 Tom L Wilson Blvd	Galesburg	IL	61401	309-344-2518	344-3291
TF: 877-236-1862 ■ *Web:* www.sandburg.edu					
College of DuPage 425 Fawell Blvd	Glen Ellyn	IL	60137	630-858-2800	790-2686*
**Fax:* Admissions ■ *Web:* www.cod.edu					
Granite City 4950 Maryville Rd	Granite City	IL	62040	618-931-0600	931-1598
Web: www.swic.edu					
College of Lake County *Grayslake* 19351 W Washington St	Grayslake	IL	60030	847-223-6601	543-3061*
**Fax:* Admissions ■ *Web:* www.clcillinois.edu					
Southeastern Illinois College 3575 College Rd	Harrisburg	IL	62946	618-252-6376	252-3062*
**Fax:* Admissions ■ *TF:* 866-338-2742 ■ *Web:* www.sic.edu					
Rend Lake College 468 N Ken Gray Pkwy	Ina	IL	62846	618-437-5321	437-5677*
**Fax:* Admitting ■ *TF:* 800-369-5321 ■ *Web:* rlc.edu					
Joliet Junior College 1215 Houbolt Rd	Joliet	IL	60431	815-729-9020	280-2493*
**Fax:* Admissions ■ *Web:* www.jjc.edu					
North 1215 Houbolt Rd	Joliet	IL	60431	815-729-9020	886-4331
TF: 800-899-4722 ■ *Web:* www.jjc.edu					
Kankakee Community College 100 College Dr	Kankakee	IL	60901	815-802-8100	802-8101*
**Fax:* Admissions ■ *TF:* 800-526-0844 ■ *Web:* www.kcc.edu					
Black Hawk College *East* 1501 State Hwy 78	Kewanee	IL	61443	309-852-5671	856-6005*
**Fax:* Admissions ■ *TF:* 800-233-5671 ■ *Web:* www.bhc.edu					
Lincoln College 300 Keokuk St	Lincoln	IL	62656	217-732-3155	732-8859
TF: 800-569-0556 ■ *Web:* www.lincolncollege.edu					
Kishwaukee College 21193 Malta Rd	Malta	IL	60150	815-825-2086	825-2306
TF: 888-656-7329 ■ *Web:* www.kishwaukeecollege.edu					
Lake Land College 5001 Lk Land Blvd	Mattoon	IL	61938	217-234-5253	234-5390*
**Fax:* Admissions ■ *Web:* www.lakeland.cc.il.us					
Quad Cities 6600 34th Ave	Moline	IL	61265	309-796-5000	796-5209*
**Fax:* Admissions ■ *TF:* 800-334-1311 ■ *Web:* www.bhc.edu					
Heartland Community College 1500 W Raab Rd	Normal	IL	61761	309-268-8000	268-7992
Web: www.hcc.cc.il.us					
Illinois Valley Community College 815 N Orlando Smith Ave	Oglesby	IL	61348	815-224-2720	224-3033*
**Fax:* Admissions ■ *Web:* ivcc.edu					
Olney Central College 305 NW St	Olney	IL	62450	618-395-7777	395-1261*
**Fax:* Admissions ■ *TF:* 866-622-4322					
Harper College 1200 W Algonquin Rd	Palatine	IL	60067	847-925-6000	
Web: www.harpercollege.edu					
Moraine Valley Community College 9000 W College Pkwy	Palos Hills	IL	60465	708-974-4300	
Web: www.morainevalley.edu					
Pittsfield 1308 W Washington St	Pittsfield	IL	62363	217-285-5319	641-4192
Web: www.jwcc.edu					
John Wood Community College 1301 S 48th St	Quincy	IL	62305	217-224-6500	641-4192*
**Fax:* Admissions ■ *Web:* www.jwcc.edu					
Red Bud 500 W S Fourth St	Red Bud	IL	62278	618-282-6682	
Web: www.swic.edu					
Triton College 2000 N Fifth Ave	River Grove	IL	60171	708-456-0300	583-3147*
**Fax:* Admissions ■ *Web:* www.triton.edu					
Lincoln Trail College 11220 State Hwy 1	Robinson	IL	62454	618-544-8657	
TF: 866-582-4322 ■ *Web:* www.iecc.edu					
Rock Valley College 3301 N Mulford Rd	Rockford	IL	61114	815-921-7821	921-4269*
**Fax:* Admissions ■ *TF:* 800-973-7821 ■ *Web:* www.rockvalleycollege.edu					
Skokie Campus 7701 N Lincoln Ave	Skokie	IL	60077	847-635-1600	635-1497
Web: www.oakton.edu					
South Suburban College 15800 S State St	South Holland	IL	60473	708-596-2000	225-5806*
**Fax:* Admissions ■ *Web:* ssc.edu					
Lincoln Land Community College 5250 Shepherd Rd PO Box 19256	Springfield	IL	62794	217-786-2200	
TF: 800-727-4161 ■ *Web:* www.llcc.edu					
Springfield College in Illinois - Benedictine University 1500 N Fifth St	Springfield	IL	62702	217-525-1420	525-1497
TF: 800-635-7289 ■ *Web:* ben.edu					
Waubonsee Community College Rt 47 At Waubonsee Dr	Sugar Grove	IL	60554	630-466-7900	
Web: waubonsee.edu					
Shawnee Community College 8364 Shawnee College Rd	Ullin	IL	62992	618-634-3200	634-3300*
**Fax:* Admitting ■ *TF:* 800-481-2242 ■ *Web:* www.shawneecc.edu					
Lakeshore 33 N Genessee St	Waukegan	IL	60085	847-623-8686	543-2170*
**Fax:* Admissions ■ *Web:* www.clcillinois.edu					

Indiana

	City	State	ZIP	Phone	Fax
Jasper 850 College Ave	Jasper	IN	47546	812-482-3030	481-5960*
**Fax:* Admissions ■ *TF:* 800-809-8852 ■ *Web:* vujc.vinu.edu					
Vincennes University 1002 N First St	Vincennes	IN	47591	812-888-4313	888-5707*
**Fax:* Admissions ■ *TF:* 800-742-9198 ■ *Web:* my.vinu.edu/home					

Iowa

	City	State	ZIP	Phone	Fax
Des Moines Area Community College *Ankeny* 2006 S Ankeny Blvd	Ankeny	IA	50021	515-964-6200	964-6391*
**Fax:* Admissions ■ *TF:* 800-362-2127 ■ *Web:* go.dmacc.edu					
Scott Community College 500 Belmont Rd	Bettendorf	IA	52722	563-441-4001	441-4131*
**Fax:* Admissions ■ *TF:* 888-336-3907 ■ *Web:* www.eicc.edu					
Boone 1125 Hancock Dr	Boone	IA	50036	515-432-7203	433-5033*
**Fax:* Admissions ■ *TF:* 800-362-2127 ■ *Web:* go.dmacc.edu					
Northeast Iowa Community College *Calmar* 1625 Hwy 150 S PO Box 400	Calmar	IA	52132	563-562-3263	562-4369*
**Fax:* Admissions ■ *TF:* 800-728-2256 ■ *Web:* www.nicc.edu					
Carroll 906 N Grant Rd	Carroll	IA	51401	712-792-1755	792-6358
TF: 800-622-3334 ■ *Web:* go.dmacc.edu					
Kirkwood Community College 6301 Kirkwood Blvd SW	Cedar Rapids	IA	52404	319-398-5411	
TF: 800-332-2055 ■ *Web:* www.kirkwood.edu					
Iowa Western Community College *Clarinda* 923 E Washington St	Clarinda	IA	51632	712-542-5117	542-4608*
**Fax:* Admissions ■ *TF:* 800-521-2073 ■ *Web:* www.iwcc.cc.ia.us					
Clinton Community College 1000 Lincoln Blvd	Clinton	IA	52732	563-244-7001	244-7107*
**Fax:* Library ■ *TF:* 877-495-3320 ■ *Web:* www.eicc.edu					
Southwestern Community College 1501 W Townline St	Creston	IA	50801	641-782-7081	782-3312*
**Fax:* Admissions ■ *TF:* 800-247-4023 ■ *Web:* www.swcciowa.edu					
Urban/Des Moines 1100 Seventh St	Des Moines	IA	50314	515-244-4226	248-7253
TF: 800-622-3334 ■ *Web:* go.dmacc.edu					
Iowa Lakes Community College 300 S 18th St	Estherville	IA	51334	712-362-2604	362-8363*
**Fax:* Admissions ■ *TF:* 800-242-5106 ■ *Web:* www.iowalakes.edu					
Iowa Central Community College 2031 Quail Ave	Fort Dodge	IA	50501	515-576-7201	576-7724*
**Fax:* Admissions ■ *TF:* 800-362-2793 ■ *Web:* www.iccc.cc.ia.us					
Ellsworth Community College 1100 College Ave	Iowa Falls	IA	50126	641-648-4611	648-3128*
**Fax:* Admissions ■ *TF:* 800-322-9235 ■ *Web:* www.iavalley.cc.ia.us					
Southeastern Community College South 335 Messenger Rd	Keokuk	IA	52632	319-524-3221	524-8621*
**Fax:* Admissions ■ *TF:* 866-722-4692 ■ *Web:* scciowa.edu					
Marshalltown Community College 3700 S Ctr St	Marshalltown	IA	50158	641-752-7106	752-8149
TF: 866-622-4748 ■ *Web:* www.iavalley.cc.ia.us					
North Iowa Area Community College 500 College Dr	Mason City	IA	50401	641-423-1264	422-4385*
**Fax:* Admissions ■ *TF:* 888-466-4222 ■ *Web:* niacc.edu					
Muscatine Community College 152 Colorado St	Muscatine	IA	52761	563-288-6001	288-6104*
**Fax:* Admissions ■ *TF:* 888-336-3907 ■ *Web:* www.eicc.edu					
Indian Hills Community College 525 Grandview Ave	Ottumwa	IA	52501	641-683-5111	683-5741
TF: 800-726-2585 ■ *Web:* www.indianhills.edu					
Peosta 10250 Sundown Rd	Peosta	IA	52068	563-556-5110	557-0347*
**Fax:* Admissions ■ *TF:* 800-728-7367 ■ *Web:* www.nicc.edu					
Northwest Iowa Community College 603 W Pk St	Sheldon	IA	51201	712-324-5061	324-4136
TF: 800-352-4907 ■ *Web:* www.nwicc.edu					
Hawkeye Community College 1501 E Orange Rd	Waterloo	IA	50704	319-296-2320	296-2874*
**Fax:* Admissions ■ *TF:* 800-670-4769 ■ *Web:* www.hawkeyecollege.edu					
Southeastern Community College North 1500 W Agency Rd	West Burlington	IA	52655	319-752-2731	524-8621*
**Fax:* Admissions ■ *TF:* 866-722-4692					

Kansas

	City	State	ZIP	Phone	Fax
Cowley County Community College & Area Vocational-Technical School PO Box 1147	Arkansas City	KS	67005	620-442-0430	441-5350
TF: 800-593-2222 ■ *Web:* www.cowley.edu					
Neosho County Community College 800 W 14th St	Chanute	KS	66720	620-431-2820	431-0082*
**Fax:* Admissions ■ *Web:* www.neosho.edu					
Coffeyville Community College 400 W 11th St	Coffeyville	KS	67337	620-251-7700	252-7010*
Colby Community College 1255 S Range Ave	Colby	KS	67701	785-462-3984	460-4691*
**Fax:* Admissions ■ *TF:* 888-634-9350 ■ *Web:* www.colbycc.edu					
Cloud County Community College 2221 Campus Dr	Concordia	KS	66901	785-243-1435	
TF: 800-729-5101 ■ *Web:* www.cloud.edu					
Dodge City Community College 2501 N 14th Ave	Dodge City	KS	67801	620-225-1321	227-9277*
**Fax:* Admissions ■ *TF:* 800-367-3222 ■ *Web:* www.dc3.edu					
Butler Community College 901 S Haverhill Rd	El Dorado	KS	67042	316-321-2222	322-3316*
**Fax:* Admissions ■ *Web:* www.butlercc.edu					
Fort Scott Community College 2108 S Horton St	Fort Scott	KS	66701	620-223-2700	223-6530*
**Fax:* Admissions ■ *TF:* 800-874-3722 ■ *Web:* www.fortscott.edu					
Garden City Community College 801 N Campus Dr	Garden City	KS	67846	620-276-7611	276-9573
TF: 800-658-1696 ■ *Web:* www.gcccks.edu					
Barton County Community College 245 NE 30th Rd	Great Bend	KS	67530	620-792-2701	786-1160*
**Fax:* Admissions ■ *TF:* 800-722-6842 ■ *Web:* www.bartonccc.edu					

Phone | Fax

Hesston College 325 S College Dr PO Box 3000 Hesston KS 67062 620-327-4221 327-8300
TF: 800-995-2757 ■ *Web:* www.hesston.edu
Highland Community College (HCC) 606 W Main Highland KS 66035 785-442-6000 442-6106*
*Fax: Admissions ■ *Web:* www.highlandcc.edu
Hutchinson Community College & Area Vocational School
1300 N Plum St Hutchinson KS 67501 620-665-3500 728-8199*
*Fax: Admissions ■ *TF:* 800-289-3501 ■ *Web:* www.hutchcc.edu
Independence Community College
1057 W College Ave PO Box 708 Independence KS 67301 620-331-4100 331-0946*
*Fax: Admissions ■ *TF:* 800-842-6063 ■ *Web:* indycc.squarespace.com
Allen County Community College
1801 N Cottonwood St Iola KS 66749 620-365-5116 365-7406*
*Fax: Admissions ■ *TF:* 800-444-0535 ■ *Web:* www.allencc.edu
Donnelly College 608 N 18th St Kansas City KS 66102 913-621-6070 621-8734*
*Fax: Admissions ■ *TF:* 800-908-9946 ■ *Web:* www.donnelly.edu
Kansas City Kansas Community College
7250 State Ave Kansas City KS 66112 913-334-1100 288-7648*
*Fax: Admissions ■ *Web:* www.kckcc.edu
Seward County Community College
1801 N Campus Ave PO Box 1137 Liberal KS 67905 620-624-1951 629-2725
TF: 800-373-9951 ■ *Web:* www.sccc.edu
Manhattan Area Technical College
3136 Dickens Manhattan KS 66503 785-587-2800
TF: 800-352-7575 ■ *Web:* manhattantech.edu
Ottawa 226 S Beech St Ottawa KS 66067 785-242-2067 242-2068*
*Fax: Admissions ■ *TF:* 888-466-2588 ■ *Web:* www.neosho.edu
Johnson County Community College
12345 College Blvd Overland Park KS 66210 913-469-8500 469-2524
TF: 866-896-5893 ■ *Web:* www.jccc.edu
Labette Community College 200 S 14th St Parsons KS 67357 620-421-6700 421-0180*
*Fax: Admissions ■ *TF:* 888-522-3883 ■ *Web:* www.labette.cc.ks.us
Pratt Community College 348 NE SR-61 Pratt KS 67124 620-672-5641
TF: 800-794-3091 ■ *Web:* www.prattcc.edu

Kentucky

Phone | Fax

Ashland Community & Technical College
1400 College Dr Ashland KY 41101 606-326-2000 326-2192*
*Fax: Admissions ■ *TF:* 800-928-4256 ■ *Web:* www.ashland.kctcs.edu
Southeast Kentucky Community & Technical College
Cumberland 700 College Rd Cumberland KY 40823 606-589-2145 589-3175*
*Fax: Admissions ■ *TF:* 888-274-7322 ■ *Web:* southeast.kctcs.edu
Elizabethtown Community & Technical College
600 College St Rd Elizabethtown KY 42701 270-769-2371 769-0736
TF: 877-246-2322 ■ *Web:* www.elizabethtown.kctcs.edu
Hazard Community & Technical College
1 Community College Dr Hazard KY 41701 606-436-5721 439-2988
TF: 800-246-7521 ■ *Web:* www.hazcc.kctcs.edu
Hazard Campus 101 Vo Tech Dr Hazard KY 41701 606-436-5721 487-8417
TF: 800-246-7521 ■ *Web:* www.hazcc.kctcs.edu
Henderson Community College
2660 S Green St Henderson KY 42420 270-827-1867 831-9612*
*Fax: Admissions ■ *TF:* 800-696-9958 ■ *Web:* henderson.kctcs.edu
Hopkinsville Community College 720 N Dr Hopkinsville KY 42240 270-886-3921 886-0237*
*Fax: Admissions ■ *TF:* 866-534-2224 ■ *Web:* www.hopkinsville.kctcs.edu
Lees Campus 601 Jefferson Ave Jackson KY 41339 606-666-7521
TF: 800-246-7521 ■ *Web:* www.hazard.kctcs.edu
Bluegrass Community & Technical College
Cooper Campus 470 Cooper Dr Lexington KY 40506 859-246-6200 246-4666
TF: 866-774-4872 ■ *Web:* www.bluegrass.kctcs.edu
Ata Career Education
10180 Linn Sta Rd Ste A200 Louisville KY 40223 502-371-8330
Web: www.ata.edu
Jefferson Community & Technical College
109 E Broadway Louisville KY 40202 502-213-5333 213-2540*
*Fax: Admissions ■ *TF:* 855-246-5282 ■ *Web:* www.jefferson.kctcs.edu
Madisonville Community College
2000 College Dr Madisonville KY 42431 270-821-2250 824-1864*
*Fax: Admissions ■ *TF:* 866-227-4812 ■ *Web:* www.madisonville.kctcs.edu
Maysville Community & Technical College
1755 US 68 Maysville KY 41056 606-759-7141 759-5818
TF: 888-452-7322 ■ *Web:* www.maysville.kctcs.edu
Middlesboro 1300 Chichester Ave Middlesboro KY 40965 606-242-2145 248-3233
TF: 888-274-7322 ■ *Web:* southeast.kctcs.edu
West Kentucky Community & Technical College
4810 Alben Barkley Dr PO Box 7380 Paducah KY 42001 270-554-9200 554-6203*
*Fax: Admissions ■ *TF:* 855-469-5282 ■ *Web:* www.westkentucky.kctcs.edu
Mayo 513 Third St Paintsville KY 41240 606-789-5321 789-9753
Web: www.kctcs.net
Big Sandy Community & Technical College
1 Bert T Combs Dr Prestonsburg KY 41653 606-886-3863 886-6943*
*Fax: Admissions ■ *TF:* 888-641-4132 ■ *Web:* www.bigsandy.kctcs.edu
Saint Catharine College
2735 BaRdstown Rd Saint Catharine KY 40061 859-336-5082 336-5031*
*Fax: Admissions ■ *Web:* www.sccky.edu
Somerset Community College
808 Monticello St Somerset KY 42501 606-679-8501 676-9065
TF: 877-629-9722 ■ *Web:* www.somerset.kctcs.edu
Whitesburg 2 Long Ave Whitesburg KY 41858 606-633-0279 589-3377
TF: 888-274-7322 ■ *Web:* southeast.kctcs.edu

Louisiana

Phone | Fax

Louisiana State University
Alexandria 8100 US Hwy 71 S Alexandria LA 71302 318-445-3672 473-6418*
*Fax: Admissions ■ *TF Admissions:* 888-473-6417 ■ *Web:* www.lsua.edu
Baton Rouge Community College (BRCC)
201 Community College Dr Baton Rouge LA 70806 225-216-8000 216-8010
TF: 866-217-9823 ■ *Web:* www.mybrcc.edu
Delta College of Arts & Technology
7380 Exchange Pl Baton Rouge LA 70806 225-928-7770
Web: www.deltacollege.com
Bossier Parish Community College
6220 E Texas St Bossier City LA 71111 318-678-6000 678-6390
Web: www.bpcc.edu
Elaine P Nunez Community College
3710 Paris Rd Chalmette LA 70043 504-278-7497 278-7480
TF: 866-825-1954 ■ *Web:* www.nunez.edu
Eunice PO Box 1129 Eunice LA 70535 337-457-7311 550-1306*
*Fax: Admissions ■ *TF:* 888-367-5783 ■ *Web:* www.lsue.edu
Louisiana Delta Community College
7500 Millhaven Rd Monroe LA 71203 318-345-9000
TF: 866-500-5322 ■ *Web:* www.ladelta.edu

Maine

Phone | Fax

Washington County Community College
1 College Dr Calais ME 04619 207-454-1000 454-1092
Web: www.wccc.me.edu
Kennebec Valley Community College
92 Western Ave Fairfield ME 04937 207-453-5000 453-5010
TF: 800-528-5882 ■ *Web:* www.kvcc.me.edu
York County Community College 112 College Dr Wells ME 04090 207-646-9282 641-0837
TF: 800-580-3820 ■ *Web:* www.yccc.edu

Maryland

Phone | Fax

Baltimore City Community College
2901 Liberty Heights Ave Baltimore MD 21215 410-462-8000 462-8345*
*Fax: Admissions ■ *TF:* 888-203-1261 ■ *Web:* www.bccc.edu
Dundalk 7200 Sollers Pt Rd Baltimore MD 21222 410-282-6700 285-9903
Web: www.ccbcmd.edu
Essex 7201 Rossville Blvd Baltimore MD 21237 410-682-6000 840-2824*
*Fax Area Code: 443 ■ *Fax: Admissions ■ *TF:* 877-557-2575 ■ *Web:* ccbcmd.edu
Harford Community College 401 Thomas Run Rd Bel Air MD 21015 410-879-8920
Web: www.harford.edu
Community College of Baltimore County
Catonsville 800 S Rolling Rd Catonsville MD 21228 410-455-6050 719-6546*
*Fax: Admissions ■ *Web:* www.ccbcmd.edu
Howard Community College
10901 Little Patuxent Pkwy Columbia MD 21044 410-772-4800 876-8855*
*Fax: Admissions ■ *Web:* www.howardcc.edu
Allegany College of Maryland
12401 Willowbrook Rd SE Cumberland MD 21502 301-784-5000 784-5027*
*Fax: Admissions ■ *TF:* 800-974-0203 ■ *Web:* www.allegany.edu
Frederick Community College
7932 Opossumtown Pk Frederick MD 21702 301-846-2400
Web: www.frederick.edu
Hagerstown Community College
11400 Robinwood Dr Hagerstown MD 21742 301-790-2800 791-9165*
*Fax: Admissions ■ *Web:* www.hagerstowncc.edu
Hunt Valley 11101 McCormick Rd Hunt Valley MD 21031 410-771-6835
Web: www.ccbcmd.edu
College of Southern Maryland
La Plata 8730 Mitchell Rd PO Box 910 La Plata MD 20646 301-934-2251 870-3008
Web: www.csmd.edu
Prince George's Community College 301 Largo Rd Largo MD 20774 301-336-6000 322-0119*
*Fax: Admissions ■ *Web:* www.pgcc.edu
Leonardtown 22950 Hollywood Rd Leonardtown MD 20650 240-725-5300 725-5400*
*Fax: Admissions ■ *TF:* 800-933-9177 ■ *Web:* www.csmd.edu
Garrett College 687 Mosser Rd McHenry MD 21541 301-387-3000 387-3038*
*Fax: Admissions ■ *TF:* 866-554-2773 ■ *Web:* www.garrettcollege.edu
Cecil Community College 1 Seahawk Dr North East MD 21901 410-287-6060 287-1001*
*Fax: Admissions ■ *TF:* 866-966-1001 ■ *Web:* www.cecil.edu
Prince Frederick
115 J W Williams Rd Prince Frederick MD 20678 443-550-6000 550-6100
TF: 800-933-9177 ■ *Web:* www.csmd.edu
Montgomery College Rockville
51 Mannakee St Rockville MD 20850 301-279-5000
Web: cms.montgomerycollege.edu
Wor-Wic Community College 32000 Campus Dr Salisbury MD 21804 410-334-2800 334-2954*
*Fax: Admissions ■ *TF:* 800-735-2258 ■ *Web:* www.worwic.edu
Carroll Community College
1601 Washington Rd Westminster MD 21157 410-386-8000
TF: 888-221-9748 ■ *Web:* www.carrollcc.edu
Chesapeake College PO Box 8 Wye Mills MD 21679 410-758-1537 827-5878*
*Fax: Admissions ■ *Web:* www.chesapeake.edu

Massachusetts

Phone | Fax

Attleboro 11 Field St Attleboro MA 02703 508-226-2484 222-7638
Web: bristolcc.edu
Middlesex Community College 590 Springs Rd Bedford MA 01730 978-656-3370 280-3603*
*Fax Area Code: 781 ■ *Web:* www.middlesex.mass.edu
Bunker Hill Community College
Charlestown 250 New Rutherford Ave Boston MA 02129 617-228-2000 228-2082*
*Fax: Admissions ■ *TF:* 877-218-8829 ■ *Web:* www.bhcc.mass.edu
Fisher College 118 Beacon St Boston MA 02116 617-236-8800 236-5473*
*Fax: Admissions ■ *TF:* 866-266-6007 ■ *Web:* www.fisher.edu
Massasoit Community College
1 Massasoit Blvd Brockton MA 02302 508-588-9100 427-1255*
*Fax: Admissions ■ *Web:* www.massasoit.edu
Chelsea 175 Hawthorne St Bellingham Sq Chelsea MA 02150 617-228-2101 228-2106
Web: www.bhcc.mass.edu
North Shore Community College 1 Ferncroft Rd Danvers MA 01923 978-762-4000 762-4015*
*Fax: Admissions ■ *Web:* www.northshore.edu
Bristol Community College 777 Elsbree St Fall River MA 02720 508-678-2811 730-3255*
*Fax: Admissions ■ *Web:* www.bristol.mass.edu
New Bedford 777 Elsbree St Fall River MA 02720 508-678-2811
Web: www.bristolcc.edu

	Phone	Fax
Massachusetts Bay Community College		
Framingham 19 Flagg Dr. Framingham MA 01702	508-270-4000	872-4067
Web: www.massbay.edu		
County Regional Vocational Sch 147 Pond St. Franklin MA 02038	508-528-5400	
Web: www.tri-county.tc		
Dean College 99 Main St. Franklin MA 02038	508-541-1508	541-8726*
**Fax:* Admissions ■ *TF:* 877-879-3326 ■ *Web:* www.dean.edu		
Mount Wachusett Community College		
444 Green St. Gardner MA 01440	978-632-6600	630-9554*
**Fax:* Admissions ■ *Web:* mwcc.edu		
Greenfield Community College 1 College Dr. Greenfield MA 01301	413-775-1837	775-1827*
**Fax:* Admissions ■ *Web:* gcc.mass.edu		
Northern Essex Community College		
100 Elliott St. Haverhill MA 01830	978-556-3000	556-3729*
**Fax:* Admissions ■ *TF:* 800-422-4453 ■ *Web:* www.necc.mass.edu		
Holyoke Community College 303 Homestead Ave. Holyoke MA 01040	413-538-7000	552-2192*
**Fax:* Admissions ■ *TF:* 877-442-6222 ■ *Web:* www.hcc.edu		
Berkshire Community College 1350 W St. Pittsfield MA 01201	413-499-4660	447-7840
Web: www.berkshirecc.edu		
Plymouth 36 Cordage Pk Cir. Plymouth MA 02360	508-747-0400	
Web: www.quincycollege.edu		
Quincy College 1250 Hancock St. Quincy MA 02169	617-984-1700	984-1794
TF: 800-698-1700 ■ *Web:* www.quincycollege.edu		
Roxbury Community College		
1234 Columbus Ave. Roxbury Crossing MA 02120	617-541-5310	427-5316*
**Fax:* Admitting ■ *Web:* www.rcc.mass.edu		
Springfield Technical Community College		
1 Armory Sq PO Box 900. Springfield MA 01102	413-781-7822	746-0344*
**Fax:* Admissions ■ *TF:* 800-326-6142 ■ *Web:* www.stcc.edu		
Wellesley Hills 50 Oakland St. Wellesley Hills MA 02481	781-239-3000	239-1047
TF: 800-233-3182 ■ *Web:* www.massbay.edu		
Cape Cod Community College		
2240 Iyanough Rd. West Barnstable MA 02668	508-362-2131	375-4089*
**Fax:* Admissions ■ *TF:* 877-846-3672 ■ *Web:* www.capecod.edu		
Wall Street Horizon Inc		
400 W Cummings Park Ste 3650. Woburn MA 01801	781-994-3500	
Web: www.wallstreethorizon.com		
Quinsigamond Community College		
670 W Boylston St. Worcester MA 01606	508-853-2300	854-4357*
**Fax:* Admissions ■ *Web:* www.qcc.edu		

Michigan

	Phone	Fax
Alpena Community College (ACC) 665 Johnson St. Alpena MI 49707	989-356-9021	
TF: 888-468-6222 ■ *Web:* discover.alpenacc.edu		
Washtenaw Community College		
4800 E Huron River Dr PO Box 1610. Ann Arbor MI 48106	734-973-3300	677-5408*
**Fax:* Admissions ■ *Web:* www.wccnet.edu		
Auburn Hills 2900 Featherstone Rd. Auburn Hills MI 48326	248-232-4100	
Web: www.oaklandcc.edu		
Keweenaw Bay Ojibwa Community College		
111 Beartown Rd. Baraga MI 49908	906-353-4600	353-8107
Web: www.kbocc.org		
Kellogg Community College 450 N Ave. Battle Creek MI 49017	269-965-3931	966-4089*
**Fax:* Admissions ■ *Web:* kellogg.edu		
Lake Michigan College		
2755 E Napier Ave. Benton Harbor MI 49022	269-927-1000	927-6875*
**Fax:* Admissions ■ *Web:* www.lakemichigancollege.edu		
Oakland Community College		
2480 Opdyke Rd. Bloomfield Hills MI 48304	248-341-2000	341-2199
TF: 800-829-1040 ■ *Web:* www.oaklandcc.edu		
Southfield 2480 Opdyke Rd. Bloomfield Hills MI 48304	248-341-2000	233-2828*
**Fax:* Library ■ *TF:* 800-829-1040 ■ *Web:* www.oaklandcc.edu		
Bay Mills Community College		
12214 W Lakeshore Dr. Brimley MI 49715	906-248-3354	248-3351
TF: 800-844-2622 ■ *Web:* www.bmcc.edu		
Glen Oaks Community College		
62249 Shimmel Rd. Centreville MI 49032	269-467-9945	467-9068*
**Fax:* Admissions ■ *TF:* 888-994-7818 ■ *Web:* www.glenoaks.edu		
Macomb Community College		
Center 44575 Garfield Rd. Clinton Township MI 48038	586-445-7999	286-4787*
**Fax:* Admissions ■ *TF:* 866-622-6621 ■ *Web:* www.macomb.edu		
Henry Ford Community College		
5101 Evergreen Rd. Dearborn MI 48128	313-845-9600	845-9891*
**Fax:* Admissions ■ *TF:* 800-585-4322 ■ *Web:* www.hfcc.edu		
Downtown 1001 W Ft St. Detroit MI 48226	313-496-2758	961-9648
Web: www.wcccd.edu		
Eastern Campus 5901 Conner. Detroit MI 48213	313-922-3311	922-1104
Web: www.wcccd.edu		
Northwest 8200 W Outer Dr. Detroit MI 48219	313-943-4000	
Web: www.wcccd.edu		
Western Campus 801 W Fort St. Detroit MI 48226	734-699-7008	699-7152
Web: www.wcccd.edu		
Southwestern Michigan College (SMC)		
58900 Cherry Grove Rd. Dowagiac MI 49047	269-782-1000	782-1331
TF: 800-456-8675 ■ *Web:* www.swmich.edu		
Bay de Noc Community College		
2001 N Lincoln Rd. Escanaba MI 49829	906-786-5802	786-8515*
**Fax:* Admissions ■ *TF:* 800-221-2001 ■ *Web:* mybay.baycollege.edu		
Orchard Ridge 27055 OrchaRd Lake Rd. Farmington Hills MI 48334	248-522-3400	
Web: www.oaklandcc.edu		
Charles Stewart Mott Community College		
1401 E Ct St. Flint MI 48503	810-762-0200	762-5611
Web: www.mcc.edu		
Grand Rapids Community College		
143 Bostwick Ave NE. Grand Rapids MI 49503	616-234-4000	234-4107*
**Fax:* Admissions ■ *Web:* www.grcc.edu		
Mid Michigan Community College (MMCC)		
1375 S Clare Ave. Harrison MI 48625	989-386-6622	386-6613
Web: www.midmich.edu		
Hillsdale 3120 W Carleton Rd PO Box 712. Hillsdale MI 49242	517-437-3343	437-0232
TF: 888-522-7344 ■ *Web:* www.jccmi.edu		
Gogebic Community College E 4946 Jackson Rd. Ironwood MI 49938	906-932-4231	932-0868*
**Fax:* Admissions ■ *TF:* 800-682-5910 ■ *Web:* www.gogebic.cc.mi.us		
Jackson Community College 2111 Emmons Rd. Jackson MI 49201	517-787-0800	796-8631*
**Fax:* Admissions ■ *TF:* 888-522-7344 ■ *Web:* www.jccmi.edu		
Kalamazoo Valley Community College		
Arcadia Commons 202 N Rose St. Kalamazoo MI 49007	269-373-7800	373-7892
Web: kvcc.edu		
Texas Township 6767 W 'O' Ave. Kalamazoo MI 49003	269-488-4400	488-4161*
**Fax:* Admissions ■ *Web:* www.kvcc.edu		
Lansing Community College		
419 N Washington Sq. Lansing MI 48933	517-483-1957	483-9668
TF: 800-644-4522 ■ *Web:* www.lansing.cc.mi.us		
Schoolcraft College 18600 Haggerty Rd. Livonia MI 48152	734-462-4400	462-4553*
**Fax:* Admissions ■ *Web:* www.schoolcraft.edu		
Monroe County Community College		
1555 S Raisinville Rd. Monroe MI 48161	734-242-7300	242-9711*
**Fax:* Admissions ■ *TF:* 877-937-6222 ■ *Web:* www.monroeccc.edu		
Saginaw Chippewa Tribal College		
2274 Enterprise Dr. Mount Pleasant MI 48858	989-775-4123	775-4528
TF: 800-225-8172 ■ *Web:* www.sagchip.org		
Muskegon Community College		
221 S Quarterline Rd. Muskegon MI 49442	231-773-9131	777-0255*
**Fax:* Admissions ■ *TF:* 866-711-4622		
Bertrand Crossing 1905 Foundation Dr. Niles MI 49120	269-695-1391	695-2999
TF: 800-252-1562 ■ *Web:* www.lakemichigancollege.edu		
Niles Area 2229 US 12. Niles MI 49120	269-782-1233	
TF: 800-456-8675 ■ *Web:* www.swmich.edu		
North Central Michigan College		
1515 Howard St. Petoskey MI 49770	231-348-6605	
TF: 888-298-6605 ■ *Web:* www.ncmich.edu		
Kirtland Community College		
10775 N St Helen Rd. Roscommon MI 48653	989-275-5000	275-6789
TF: 866-632-9992 ■ *Web:* www.kirtland.edu		
Royal Oak 739 S Washington Ave. Royal Oak MI 48067	248-246-2400	
Web: www.oaklandcc.edu		
West Shore Community College PO Box 277. Scottville MI 49454	231-845-6211	845-3944*
**Fax:* Admissions ■ *TF:* 800-848-9722 ■ *Web:* www.westshore.edu		
Montcalm Community College 2800 College Dr. Sidney MI 48885	989-328-2111	328-2950*
**Fax:* Admissions ■ *Web:* www.montcalm.edu		
South Haven 125 Veterans Blvd. South Haven MI 49090	269-639-8442	
TF: 800-252-1562 ■ *Web:* www.lakemichigancollege.edu		
Wayne County Community College		
Downriver 21000 Northline Rd. Taylor MI 48180	734-946-3500	374-0240
Web: www.wcccd.edu		
Northwestern Michigan College		
1701 E Front St. Traverse City MI 49686	231-995-1000	995-1339*
**Fax:* Admissions ■ *TF:* 800-748-0566 ■ *Web:* www.nmc.edu		
Delta College 1961 Delta Rd. University Center MI 48710	989-686-9000	667-2202*
**Fax:* Admissions ■ *TF:* 888-636-4211 ■ *Web:* www.delta.edu		
South 14500 E 12-Mile Rd. Warren MI 48088	586-445-7000	445-7140*
**Fax:* Admissions ■ *TF:* 866-622-6621 ■ *Web:* www.macomb.edu		
Highland Lakes 7350 Cooley Lake Rd. Waterford MI 48327	248-942-3100	
TF: 800-829-1040 ■ *Web:* www.oaklandcc.edu		

Minnesota

	Phone	Fax
Riverland Community College 1900 Eigth Ave NW. Austin MN 55912	507-433-0600	433-0515
TF: 800-247-5039 ■ *Web:* www.riverland.edu		
Normandale Community College		
9700 France Ave S. Bloomington MN 55431	952-487-8200	
TF: 866-880-8740 ■ *Web:* www.normandale.edu		
Central Lakes College		
Brainerd 501 W College Dr. Brainerd MN 56401	218-855-8199	855-8057*
**Fax:* Admissions ■ *TF:* 800-933-0346 ■ *Web:* www.clcmn.edu		
North Hennepin Community College		
7411 85th Ave N. Brooklyn Park MN 55445	763-424-0702	424-0929*
**Fax:* Admissions ■ *TF:* 800-818-0395 ■ *Web:* www.nhcc.edu		
Cambridge 300 Polk St S. Cambridge MN 55008	763-433-1100	433-1841*
**Fax:* Admissions ■ *Web:* www.anokaramsey.edu		
Leech Lake Tribal College		
6945 Little Wolf Rd PO Box 180. Cass Lake MN 56633	218-335-4200	335-4209
TF: 866-676-2772 ■ *Web:* www.lltc.edu		
Fond du Lac Tribal & Community College		
2101 14th St. Cloquet MN 55720	218-879-0800	879-0814
TF: 800-657-3712 ■ *Web:* www.fdltcc.edu		
Anoka-Ramsey Community College		
11200 Mississippi Blvd NW. Coon Rapids MN 55433	763-433-1100	433-1521
TF: 800-627-3529 ■ *Web:* www.anokaramsey.edu		
Minnesota State Community & Technical College		
Detroit Lakes 900 Hwy 34E. Detroit Lakes MN 56501	218-846-3700	846-3794
TF: 800-492-4836 ■ *Web:* www.minnesota.edu		
Lake Superior College 2101 Trinity Rd. Duluth MN 55811	218-733-7600	733-5945*
**Fax:* Admissions ■ *TF:* 800-432-2884 ■ *Web:* lsc.edu		
East Grand Forks		
2022 Central Ave NE. East Grand Forks MN 56721	218-773-3441	793-2842
TF: 800-451-3441 ■ *Web:* www.northlandcollege.edu		
Vermilion Community College 1900 E Camp St. Ely MN 55731	218-365-7200	
TF: 800-657-3608 ■ *Web:* www.vcc.edu		
Mesabi Range Community & Technical College		
1100 Industrial Pk Dr PO Box 648. Eveleth MN 55734	218-741-3095	744-7466
TF: 800-657-3860 ■ *Web:* www.mr.mnscu.edu		
South Central College		
Faribault 1225 Third St. Faribault MN 55021	507-332-5800	332-5888
TF: 800-422-0391 ■ *Web:* www.southcentral.edu		
Fergus Falls 1414 College Way. Fergus Falls MN 56537	218-736-1500	736-1510*
**Fax:* Admissions ■ *TF:* 877-450-3322 ■ *Web:* www.minnesota.edu		
Itasca Community College		
1851 E Us Hwy 169. Grand Rapids MN 55744	218-327-4460	327-4350
TF: 800-996-6422 ■ *Web:* www.itascacc.edu		
Hibbing Community College 1515 E 25th St. Hibbing MN 55746	218-262-7200	262-6717*
**Fax:* Admissions ■ *TF:* 800-224-4422 ■ *Web:* www.hcc.mnscu.edu		

Phone | Fax

Rainy River Community College
1501 Hwy 71 .... International Falls MN 56649 218-285-7722 285-2239*
*Fax: Admissions ■ TF: 800-456-3996 ■ Web: www.rrcc.mnscu.edu
Inver Hills Community College
2500 80th St E .... Inver Grove Heights MN 55076 651-450-8500
TF: 866-576-0689 ■ Web: www.inverhills.edu
Minneapolis Community & Technical College
1501 Hennepin Ave .... Minneapolis MN 55403 612-659-6200 659-6210*
*Fax: Admissions ■ TF: 800-247-0911 ■ Web: www.minneapolis.edu
Moorhead 1900 28th Ave S .... Moorhead MN 56560 218-299-6500 299-6584*
*Fax: Admissions ■ TF: 800-426-5603 ■ Web: www.minnesota.edu
Mankato 1920 Lee Blvd .... North Mankato MN 56003 507-389-7200 388-9951
TF: 800-722-9359 ■ Web: www.southcentral.edu
Rochester Community & Technical College
851 30th Ave SE .... Rochester MN 55904 507-285-7210 280-3529*
*Fax: Admissions ■ TF: 800-247-1296 ■ Web: www.rctc.edu
Staples 1830 Airport Rd .... Staples MN 56479 218-894-5100 894-5185
TF: 800-247-6836 ■ Web: www.clcmn.edu
Northland Community & Technical College
1101 US Hwy 1 E .... Thief River Falls MN 56701 218-681-0701 681-0774*
*Fax: Admissions ■ TF: 800-959-6282 ■ Web: www.northlandcollege.edu
Century College 3300 Century Ave N .... White Bear Lake MN 55115 651-779-3300 773-1796*
*Fax: Admissions ■ TF: 800-228-1978 ■ Web: www.century.edu
Minnesota West Community & Technical College
1450 Collegeway .... Worthington MN 56187 507-372-3400 372-5803*
*Fax: Admissions ■ TF: 800-657-3966 ■ Web: www.mnwest.edu

Mississippi

Phone | Fax

Northeast Mississippi Community College
101 Cunningham Blvd .... Booneville MS 38829 662-728-7751 720-7405*
*Fax: Admissions ■ TF: 800-555-2154 ■ Web: www.nemcc.edu
East Central Community College PO Box 129 .... Decatur MS 39327 601-635-2111 635-4060*
*Fax: Admissions ■ TF: 877-462-3222 ■ Web: www.eccc.edu/transcripts.html
Jones County Junior College 900 S Ct St .... Ellisville MS 39437 601-477-4000 477-4258*
*Fax: Admissions ■ Web: jcjc.edu
Itawamba Community College
Fulton 602 W Hill St .... Fulton MS 38843 662-862-8000 862-8234*
*Fax: Admissions ■ TF: 800-433-3243 ■ Web: www.iccms.edu
Jackson County 2300 Hwy 90 PO Box 100 .... Gautier MS 39553 228-497-9602 497-7873
TF: 866-735-1122 ■ Web: www.mgccc.edu
Holmes Community College PO Box 399 .... Goodman MS 39079 662-472-2312
TF: 800-465-6374 ■ Web: holmescc.edu
Jefferson Davis 2226 Switzer Rd .... Gulfport MS 39507 228-896-3355 896-2520*
*Fax: Admissions ■ TF: 866-735-1122 ■ Web: www.mgccc.edu
Meridian Community College 910 Hwy 19 N .... Meridian MS 39307 601-483-8241 481-1305*
*Fax: Admissions ■ TF: 800-622-8431 ■ Web: www.mcc.cc.ms.us
Mississippi Delta Community College
PO Box 668 .... Moorhead MS 38761 662-246-6322
Web: www.msdelta.edu
Rankin 3805 Hwy 80 E .... Pearl MS 39208 601-932-5237
Web: www.hindscc.edu
Mississippi Gulf Coast Community College
51 Main St PO Box 548 .... Perkinston MS 39573 601-928-5211 928-6345*
*Fax: Admitting ■ TF: 866-735-1122 ■ Web: www.mgccc.edu
Pearl River Community College
101 Hwy 11 N .... Poplarville MS 39470 601-403-1000 403-1339*
*Fax: Admissions ■ TF: 877-772-2338 ■ Web: www.prcc.edu
Hinds Community College
501 E Main St PO Box 1100 .... Raymond MS 39154 601-857-5261 857-3539*
*Fax: Admissions ■ TF: 800-446-3722 ■ Web: www.hindscc.edu
East Mississippi Community College (EMCC)
1512 Kemper St .... Scooba MS 39358 662-476-8442
Web: www2.eastms.edu
Northwest Mississippi Community College
4975 Hwy 51 N .... Senatobia MS 38668 662-562-3200
Web: www.northwestms.edu
Southwest Mississippi Community College
1156 College Dr .... Summit MS 39666 601-276-2000 276-3888
Web: www.smcc.edu
Tupelo 2176 S Eason Blvd .... Tupelo MS 38804 662-620-5000
Web: www.iccms.edu
Copiah-Lincoln Community College PO Box 649 .... Wesson MS 39191 601-442-9111
Web: www.colin.edu
Natchez PO Box 649 .... Wesson MS 39191 601-442-9111
Web: www.colin.edu

Missouri

Phone | Fax

Jefferson College 1000 Viking Dr .... Hillsboro MO 63050 636-789-3951 789-5103*
*Fax: Admissions ■ Web: www.jeffco.edu
Metropolitan Community College Blue River
20301 E 78 Hwy .... Independence MO 64057 816-220-6500 220-6577*
*Fax: Admissions ■ Web: www.mcckc.edu
Maple Woods Community College
2601 NE Barry Rd .... Kansas City MO 64156 816-437-3000
Web: www.mcckc.edu
Metropolitan Community College Penn Valley
3201 SW Trafficway .... Kansas City MO 64111 816-759-4000 759-4161
TF: 866-676-6224 ■ Web: www.mcckc.edu
A.T. Still University of Health Sciences
800 W Jefferson St .... Kirksville MO 63501 660-626-2121
TF: 866-626-2878 ■ Web: www.atsu.edu
Metropolitan Community College Longview
500 SW Longview Rd .... Lees Summit MO 64081 816-672-2000
Web: www.mcckc.edu
Moberly Area Community College
101 College Ave .... Moberly MO 65270 660-263-4110 263-2406
TF: 800-622-2070 ■ Web: www.macc.edu
Crowder College 601 Laclede Ave .... Neosho MO 64850 417-451-3223 455-5731*
*Fax: Admissions ■ TF: 866-238-7788 ■ Web: www.crowder.edu

Phone | Fax

Watley Ctr 601 Laclede .... Neosho MO 64850 417-847-1706 847-1367
Web: www.crowder.edu
Cottey College 1000 W Austin Blvd .... Nevada MO 64772 417-667-8181 667-8103*
*Fax: Admissions ■ TF: 888-526-8839 ■ Web: www.cottey.edu
Mineral Area College
5270 Frat River Rd PO Box 1000 .... Park Hills MO 63601 573-431-4593 518-2166*
*Fax: Admissions ■ Web: www.mineralarea.edu
Three Rivers Community College
2080 Three Rivers Blvd .... Poplar Bluff MO 63901 573-840-9600
TF: 877-879-8722 ■ Web: www.trcc.edu
Saint Louis Community College (STLCC)
300 S Broadway .... Saint Louis MO 63102 314-539-5000 539-5170*
*Fax: Admissions ■ Web: www.stlcc.edu
Forest Park 5600 Oakland Ave .... Saint Louis MO 63110 314-644-9100 644-9375*
*Fax: Admissions ■ Web: www.stlcc.edu/fp
State Fair Community College 3201 W 16th St .... Sedalia MO 65301 660-530-5800
TF: 877-311-7322 ■ Web: www.sfccmo.edu
Ozarks Technical Community College
1001 E Chestnut Expy .... Springfield MO 65802 417-447-7500 447-6906*
*Fax: Admissions ■ Web: www.otc.edu
North Central Missouri College 1301 Main St .... Trenton MO 64683 660-359-3948 359-2211*
*Fax: Admissions ■ TF: 800-880-6180 ■ Web: www.ncmissouri.edu
East Central College 1964 Prairie Dell Rd .... Union MO 63084 636-583-5193 583-1897*
*Fax: Admissions ■ TF: 800-392-6848 ■ Web: www.eastcentral.edu

Montana

Phone | Fax

Dawson Community College 300 College Dr .... Glendive MT 59330 406-377-3396
TF: 800-821-8320 ■ Web: www.dawson.edu
Flathead Valley Community College
777 Grandview Dr .... Kalispell MT 59901 406-756-3822 756-3815
TF: 800-313-3822 ■ Web: www.fvcc.edu
Chief Dull Knife College PO Box 98 .... Lame Deer MT 59043 406-477-6215 477-6219
Web: www.cdkc.edu
Libby 225 Commerce Way .... Libby MT 59923 406-293-2721 293-5112*
*Fax: Admissions ■ Web: www.fvcc.edu
Miles Community College 2715 Dickinson St .... Miles City MT 59301 406-874-6100 874-6283*
*Fax: Admissions ■ TF: 800-541-9281 ■ Web: www.milescc.edu
Salish Kootenai College PO Box 70 .... Pablo MT 59855 406-275-4800 275-4801*
*Fax: Admissions ■ TF: 877-752-6553 ■ Web: www.skc.edu
Fort Peck Community College PO Box 398 .... Poplar MT 59255 406-768-6300 768-6301
Web: www.fpcc.edu

Nebraska

Phone | Fax

Southeast Community College
Beatrice 4771 W Scott Rd .... Beatrice NE 68310 402-228-3468 228-2218*
*Fax: Admissions ■ TF: 800-233-5027 ■ Web: www.southeast.edu
Central Community College
Columbus 4500 63rd St PO Box 1027 .... Columbus NE 68602 402-564-7132 562-1201*
*Fax: Admissions ■ Web: www.cccneb.edu
Elkhorn Valley 829 N 204th .... Elkhorn NE 68022 402-289-1200
Web: www.mccneb.edu
Grand Island 3134 W Hwy 34 PO Box 4903 .... Grand Island NE 68802 308-398-4222 398-7399*
*Fax: Admissions ■ TF: 877-222-0780 ■ Web: www.cccneb.edu
Hastings 550 Technical Blvd .... Hastings NE 68901 402-463-9811 461-2454
Web: www.cccneb.edu
Lincoln 8800 'O' St .... Lincoln NE 68520 402-471-3333 437-2404*
*Fax: Admissions ■ TF: 800-642-4075 ■ Web: www.southeast.edu
Nebraska Indian Community College PO Box 428 .... Macy NE 68039 402-837-5078 837-4183*
*Fax: Admissions ■ TF: 844-440-6422 ■ Web: www.thenicc.edu
McCook Community College 1205 E Third St .... McCook NE 69001 308-345-8100 345-8180*
*Fax: Admissions ■ TF: 800-658-4348 ■ Web: www.mpcc.edu
Northeast Community College
801 E Benjamin Ave PO Box 469 .... Norfolk NE 68702 402-371-2020 844-7396*
*Fax: Admissions ■ TF: 800-348-9033 ■ Web: www.northeast.edu
North Platte Community College
North 1101 Halligan Dr .... North Platte NE 69101 308-535-3601 534-5767*
*Fax: Admissions ■ TF: 800-658-4308 ■ Web: www.mpcc.edu
South 601 W State Farm Rd .... North Platte NE 69101 800-658-4348 535-3794*
*Fax Area Code: 308 ■ TF: 800-658-4348 ■ Web: www.mpcc.edu
Metropolitan Community College PO Box 3777 .... Omaha NE 68103 402-457-2400 457-2788*
*Fax: Admissions ■ TF: 800-228-9553 ■ Web: www.mccneb.edu
Western Nebraska Community College
1601 E 27th St .... Scottsbluff NE 69361 308-635-3606 635-6732
TF: 800-348-4435 ■ Web: www.wncc.net
Little Priest Tribal College
601 E College Dr PO Box 270 .... Winnebago NE 68071 402-878-2380 878-2355
Web: www.littlepriest.edu

Nevada

Phone | Fax

Fallon 160 Campus Way .... Fallon NV 89406 775-423-7565 423-8029
Web: www.wnc.edu/location/fallon
Henderson 700 College Dr .... Henderson NV 89002 702-651-3000 651-3509*
*Fax: Admissions ■ Web: csn.edu
Community College of Southern Nevada
West Charleston 6375 W Charleston Blvd .... Las Vegas NV 89146 702-651-5610
Web: www.csn.edu
Western Nevada Community College (WNC)
Douglas 1680 Bently Pkwy S .... Minden NV 89423 775-782-2413 782-2415
TF: 800-433-3243 ■ Web: www.wnc.edu
College of Southern Nevada
Cheyenne 3200 E Cheyenne Ave .... North Las Vegas NV 89030 702-651-4000
Web: www.csn.edu
Truckee Meadows Community College
7000 Dandini Blvd .... Reno NV 89512 775-673-7000 673-7028*
*Fax: Admissions ■ Web: www.tmcc.edu

New Hampshire

				Phone	Fax

White Mountains Community College (WMCC)
2020 Riverside Dr. Berlin NH 03570 603-752-1113 752-6335
TF: 800-445-4525 ■ *Web:* www.wmcc.edu

Community College System of New Hampshire (CCSNH)
26 College Dr Concord NH 03301 603-271-2722 271-2725
TF: 866-945-2255 ■ *Web:* www.ccsnh.edu

NHTI Concord's Community College
31 College Dr Concord NH 03301 603-271-6484 271-7139
TF: 800-247-0179 ■ *Web:* www.nhti.edu

Lakes Region Community College (LRCC)
379 Belmont Rd Laconia NH 03246 603-524-3207 524-8084
TF: 800-357-2992 ■ *Web:* www.lrcc.edu

Manchester Community College
1066 Front St Manchester NH 03102 603-206-8000 668-5354
TF: 800-924-3445 ■ *Web:* mccnh.edu

New Jersey

				Phone	Fax

Camden County College 200 College Dr Blackwood NJ 08012 856-227-7200 374-4917
TF: 888-228-2466 ■ *Web:* www.camdencc.edu

Camden City 200 N Broadway PO Box 200 Camden NJ 08102 856-338-1817
Web: www.camdencc.edu

Salem Community College
460 Hollywood Ave Carneys Point NJ 08069 856-299-2100 351-2763*
**Fax:* Admissions ■ *Web:* www.salemcc.edu

Union County College 1033 Springfield Ave Cranford NJ 07016 908-709-7000 709-7125*
**Fax:* Admissions ■ *TF:* 877-468-3229 ■ *Web:* www.ucc.edu

Middlesex County College
2600 Woodbridge Ave PO Box 3050 Edison NJ 08818 732-548-6000 906-7728*
**Fax:* Admissions ■ *TF:* 888-442-4551 ■ *Web:* middlesexcc.edu

Hudson County Community College
162 Sip Ave Jersey City NJ 07306 201-714-7200 714-2136*
**Fax:* Admissions ■ *Web:* www.hccc.edu

Brookdale Community College
765 Newman Springs Rd Lincroft NJ 07738 732-842-1900 224-2271*
**Fax:* Admissions ■ *TF:* 866-767-9512 ■ *Web:* www.brookdalecc.edu

Assumption College for Sisters
350 BernaRdsville Rd Mendham NJ 07945 973-543-6528 543-1738
Web: www.acs350.org

Essex County College 303 University Ave Newark NJ 07102 973-877-3000 877-3446*
**Fax:* Admissions ■ *Web:* www.essex.edu

Sussex County Community College
1 College Hill Rd Newton NJ 07860 973-300-2100 579-5226*
**Fax:* Admissions ■ *Web:* www.sussex.edu

Bergen Community College 400 Paramus Rd Paramus NJ 07652 201-447-7200 670-7973*
**Fax:* Admissions ■ *TF:* 877-612-5381 ■ *Web:* www.bergen.edu

Passaic County Community College
1 College Blvd Paterson NJ 07505 973-684-6800 684-6778*
**Fax:* Admissions ■ *Web:* www.pccc.cc.nj.us

Eastwick Colleges Inc 10 S Franklin Tpke Ramsey NJ 07446 201-327-8877
Web: www.eastwickcollege.edu

County College of Morris 214 Ctr Grove Rd Randolph NJ 07869 973-328-5000
TF: 888-726-3260 ■ *Web:* www.ccm.edu

Gloucester County College 1400 TanyaRd Rd Sewell NJ 08080 856-468-5000 468-8498*
**Fax:* Admissions ■ *Web:* www.gccnj.edu

Raritan Valley Community College
PO Box 3300 Somerville NJ 08876 908-526-1200 704-3442*
**Fax:* Admissions ■ *TF:* 888-326-4058 ■ *Web:* www.raritanval.edu

Ocean County College
College Dr PO Box 2001 Toms River NJ 08754 732-255-0400 255-0444
Web: www.ocean.edu

Mercer County Community College PO Box B Trenton NJ 08690 609-586-4800
TF: 800-982-9491 ■ *Web:* www.mccc.edu

Kerney Ctr N Broad & Academy St Trenton NJ 08608 609-586-4800
TF: 800-982-9491 ■ *Web:* www.mccc.edu

Cumberland County College 3322 College Dr Vineland NJ 08360 856-691-8600 691-3002*
**Fax:* Admissions ■ *TF:* 866-367-6232 ■ *Web:* www.cccnj.net

Warren County Community College
475 Rt 57 W Washington NJ 07882 908-835-9222
Web: www.warren.edu

West Essex 730 Bloomfield Ave West Caldwell NJ 07006 973-877-3175
Web: www.essex.edu

West Windsor 1200 Old Trenton Rd West Windsor NJ 08550 609-586-4800 570-3861*
**Fax:* Admissions ■ *TF:* 800-982-9491 ■ *Web:* www.mccc.edu

New Mexico

				Phone	Fax

Alamogordo (NMSU-A) 2400 N Scenic Dr Alamogordo NM 88310 575-439-3600 439-3760
Web: www.nmsua.edu

University of New Mexico (UNM)
1 University of New Mexico Albuquerque NM 87131 505-277-0111 277-6686
TF: 800-225-5866 ■ *Web:* www.unm.edu

Carlsbad 1500 University Dr Carlsbad NM 88220 505-234-9200
TF: 888-888-2199 ■ *Web:* carlsbad.nmsu.edu

Clovis Community College (CCC) 417 Schepps Blvd Clovis NM 88101 575-769-2811 769-4190*
**Fax:* Admissions ■ *TF:* 800-769-1409 ■ *Web:* www.clovis.edu

Northern New Mexico College
921 Paseo de Onate Espanola NM 87532 505-747-2100 747-5449
TF: 800-477-3632 ■ *Web:* www.nnmc.edu

San Juan College 4601 College Blvd Farmington NM 87402 505-326-3311 566-3500*
**Fax:* Admissions ■ *TF:* 866-426-1233 ■ *Web:* www.sanjuancollege.edu

Grants 1500 Third St Grants NM 87020 505-287-6678 287-2329*
**Fax:* Admissions ■ *Web:* www.grants.nmsu.edu

New Mexico Junior College 1 Thunderbird Cir Hobbs NM 88240 505-392-4510
TF: 800-657-6260 ■ *Web:* www.nmjc.edu

				Phone	Fax

Dona Ana Branch Community College (DACC)
2800 N Sonoma Ranch Blvd PO Box 30001 Las Cruces NM 88011 575-528-7000 528-7300*
**Fax:* Admissions ■ *TF:* 800-903-7503 ■ *Web:* dacc.nmsu.edu

New Mexico State University (NMSU)
MSC-3A PO Box 30001 Las Cruces NM 88003 575-646-3121 646-6330*
**Fax:* Admissions ■ *TF Admissions:* 800-662-6678 ■ *Web:* www.nmsu.edu

Luna Community College 366 Luna Dr Las Vegas NM 87701 505-454-2500 454-2519
TF: 800-588-7232 ■ *Web:* luna.edu

Los Alamos 4000 University Dr Los Alamos NM 87544 505-662-5919 661-4698*
**Fax:* Admissions ■ *Web:* losalamos.unm.edu

Valencia 280 La Entrada Los Lunas NM 87031 505-925-8580 925-8563*
**Fax:* Admissions ■ *TF:* 800-225-5866 ■ *Web:* www.unm.edu

Eastern New Mexico University Roswell
52 University Blvd PO Box 6000 Roswell NM 88202 800-243-6687 624-7144*
**Fax Area Code:* 505 ■ **Fax:* Admissions ■ *TF:* 800-243-6687 ■ *Web:* www.roswell.enmu.edu

Santa Fe Community College
6401 Richards Ave Santa Fe NM 87508 505-428-1000
Web: www.sfcc.edu

Mesalands Community College 911 S Tenth St Tucumcari NM 88401 575-461-4413
Web: www.mesalands.edu

New York

				Phone	Fax

Maria College 700 New Scotland Ave Albany NY 12208 518-438-3111 453-1366
Web: mariacollege.edu

College of Technology at Alfred
10 Upper College Dr Alfred NY 14802 607-587-4215 587-4299*
**Fax:* Admissions ■ *TF:* 800-425-3733 ■ *Web:* www.alfredstate.edu

Cayuga Community College 197 Franklin St Auburn NY 13021 315-255-1743 255-2117
TF: 866-598-8883 ■ *Web:* www.cayuga-cc.edu

Genesee Community College 1 College Rd Batavia NY 14020 585-343-0068 345-6810
TF: 866-225-5422 ■ *Web:* www.genesee.edu

Queensborough Community College
222-05 56th Ave Bayside NY 11364 718-631-6262 281-5189*
**Fax:* Admissions ■ *TF:* 877-253-7122 ■ *Web:* www.qcc.cuny.edu

Broome Community College 901 Front St Binghamton NY 13905 607-778-5000 778-5442*
**Fax:* Admissions ■ *TF:* 800-836-0689 ■ *Web:* www.sunybroome.edu

Grant 1001 Crooked Hill Rd Brentwood NY 11717 631-851-6700 851-6819*
**Fax:* Admissions ■ *TF:* 800-621-3362 ■ *Web:* www.sunysuffolk.edu

State University of New York
Brockport 350 New Campus Dr Brockport NY 14420 585-395-2751 395-5452
TF: 888-800-0029 ■ *Web:* www.brockport.edu

Bronx Community College 2155 University Ave Bronx NY 10453 718-289-5100 289-6003*
**Fax:* Admissions ■ *TF:* 866-888-8777 ■ *Web:* www.bcc.cuny.edu

Hostos Community College 500 Grand Concourse Bronx NY 10451 718-518-4444 518-4256*
**Fax:* Admissions ■ *TF:* 888-993-7650 ■ *Web:* www.hostos.cuny.edu

Kingsborough Community College
2001 Oriental Blvd Brooklyn NY 11235 718-368-5000 368-5356*
**Fax:* Admissions ■ *Web:* www.kbcc.cuny.edu

Erie Community College 121 Ellicott St Buffalo NY 14203 716-842-2770 851-1129
Web: www.ecc.edu

Trocaire College 360 Choate Ave Buffalo NY 14220 716-826-1200 828-6107*
**Fax:* Admissions ■ *Web:* www.trocaire.edu

Villa Maria College 240 Pine Ridge Rd Buffalo NY 14225 716-896-0700 896-0705
Web: www.villa.edu

Finger Lakes Community College
4340 Lakeshore Dr Canandaigua NY 14424 585-394-3500 394-5005
Web: www.fingerlakes.edu

Canton 34 Cornell Dr Canton NY 13617 315-386-7011 386-7929
TF: 800-388-7123 ■ *Web:* www.canton.edu

Corning Community College 1 Academic Dr Corning NY 14830 607-962-9251 962-9582*
**Fax:* Admissions ■ *Web:* www.corning-cc.edu

Delhi 2 Main St Delhi NY 13753 607-746-4000 746-4104
TF: 800-963-3544 ■ *Web:* www.delhi.edu

Tompkins Cortland Community College 170 N St Dryden NY 13053 607-844-8211 844-6541*
**Fax:* Admissions ■ *TF:* 888-567-8211 ■ *Web:* www.tc3.edu

Nassau Community College 1 Education Dr Garden City NY 11530 516-572-7500 572-9743
Web: www.ncc.edu

Herkimer County Community College
100 Reservoir Rd Herkimer NY 13350 315-866-0300 866-0062*
**Fax:* Admissions ■ *TF:* 844-464-4375 ■ *Web:* www.herkimer.edu

Columbia-Greene Community College 4400 Rt 23 Hudson NY 12534 518-828-4181 822-2015
TF: 888-668-4293 ■ *Web:* www.sunycgcc.edu

Jamestown Community College
525 Faulkner St PO Box 20 Jamestown NY 14702 716-338-1000
TF: 800-388-8557 ■ *Web:* www.sunyjcc.edu

Fulton-Montgomery Community College
2805 New York 67 Johnstown NY 12095 518-762-4651 762-4334
Web: www.fmcc.edu

Sullivan County Community College
112 College Rd Loch Sheldrake NY 12759 845-434-5750 434-0923*
**Fax:* Admissions ■ *Web:* www.sullivan.suny.edu

LaGuardia Community College
31-10 Thomson Ave Long Island NY 11101 718-482-5000 609-2033*
**Fax:* Admissions ■ *Web:* www.laguardia.edu/home

Orange County Community College 115 S St Middletown NY 10940 845-344-6222 342-8662
Web: www.sunyorange.edu

Bank Street College Library 610 W 112th St New York NY 10025 212-875-4595
Web: www.bankstreet.edu

Borough of Manhattan Community College
199 Chambers St Rm S-300 New York NY 10007 212-220-1265 220-2366
TF: 877-222-8387 ■ *Web:* www.bmcc.cuny.edu

Swedish Institute Inc 226 W 26th St Fl 5 New York NY 10001 212-924-5900
Web: www.swedishinstitute.edu

Three of Us Corp 39 W 19th St Fl 12 New York NY 10011 212-645-0030

Cattaraugus County 260 N Union St PO Box 5901 Olean NY 14760 716-376-7500 376-7020*
**Fax:* Admissions ■ *TF:* 800-388-9776 ■ *Web:* www.sunyjcc.edu

South 4041 Southwestern Blvd Orchard Park NY 14127 716-851-1003 851-1687*
**Fax:* Admissions ■ *Web:* www.ecc.edu

Clinton Community College
136 Clinton Pt Dr Plattsburgh NY 12901 518-562-4200 562-4158
TF: 800-552-1160 ■ *Web:* www.clinton.edu

Phone | Fax

Dutchess Community College
53 Pendell Rd .... Poughkeepsie NY 12601 845-431-8010 431-8605
Web: www.sunydutchess.edu
Adirondack Community College 640 Bay Rd .... Queensbury NY 12804 518-743-2200 745-1433
TF: 888-786-9235 ■ *Web:* www.sunyacc.edu
Eastern 121 Speonk-Riverhead Rd .... Riverhead NY 11901 631-548-2500 548-2504*
**Fax:* Admissions ■ *Web:* www.sunysuffolk.edu
Monroe Community College
1000 E Henrietta Rd .... Rochester NY 14623 585-292-2000 292-3860
Web: www.monroecc.edu
Niagara County Community College
3111 Saunders Settlement Rd .... Sanborn NY 14132 716-614-6222 614-6820*
**Fax:* Admissions ■ *TF:* 800-875-6269 ■ *Web:* www.niagaracc.suny.edu
North Country Community College
23 Santanoni Ave .... Saranac Lake NY 12983 518-891-2915 891-2915
TF: 888-879-6222 ■ *Web:* www.nccc.edu
Schenectady County Community College
78 Washington Ave .... Schenectady NY 12305 518-381-1200 381-1477
Web: www.sunysccc.edu
Suffolk County Community College
Ammerman 533 College Rd .... Selden NY 11784 631-451-4110
Web: www.sunysuffolk.edu
Ulster County Community College
Cottekill Rd .... Stone Ridge NY 12484 845-687-5000 687-5090
TF: 800-724-0833 ■ *Web:* www.sunyulster.edu
Rockland Community College 145 College Rd .... Suffern NY 10901 845-574-4000 574-4433
TF: 800-722-7666 ■ *Web:* www.sunyrockland.edu
Onondaga Community College 4941 Onondaga Rd .... Syracuse NY 13215 315-498-2622 498-2107
TF: 800-827-1000 ■ *Web:* www.sunyocc.edu
Hudson Valley Community College
80 Vandenburgh Ave .... Troy NY 12180 518-629-4822 629-4576*
**Fax:* Admissions ■ *TF:* 877-325-4822 ■ *Web:* www.hvcc.edu
Mohawk Valley Community College
1101 Sherman Dr .... Utica NY 13501 315-792-5400 792-5527
TF: 800-733-6822 ■ *Web:* www.mvcc.edu
Westchester Community College
75 Grasslands Rd .... Valhalla NY 10595 914-606-6600 606-6880*
**Fax:* Admissions ■ *TF:* 800-235-7267 ■ *Web:* www.sunywcc.edu
Jefferson Community College
1220 Coffeen St .... Watertown NY 13601 315-786-2200 786-2459
TF: 888-435-6522 ■ *Web:* www.sunyjefferson.edu
North 6205 Main St .... Williamsville NY 14221 716-634-0800 851-1429
Web: www.ecc.edu

North Carolina

Phone | Fax

Roanoke-Chowan Community College
109 Community College Rd .... Ahoskie NC 27910 252-862-1200 862-1355*
**Fax:* Admissions ■ *Web:* www.roanoke.cc.nc.us
Randolph Community College
629 Industrial Pk Ave .... Asheboro NC 27205 336-633-0200 629-4695
TF: 800-433-3243 ■ *Web:* www.randolph.edu
Asheville-Buncombe Technical Community College
340 Victoria Rd .... Asheville NC 28801 828-254-1921 251-6718*
**Fax:* Admissions ■ *Web:* www.abtech.edu
Brunswick Community College 50 College Rd .... Bolivia NC 28422 910-755-7300
TF: 800-754-1050 ■ *Web:* www.brunswickcc.edu
Transylvania 45 Oak Pk Dr .... Brevard NC 28712 828-883-2520
Web: www.blueridge.edu
Central Piedmont Community College
1201 Elizabeth Ave .... Charlotte NC 28204 704-330-2722 330-6136*
**Fax:* Admissions ■ *TF:* 877-530-8815 ■ *Web:* www.cpcc.edu
Cato 8120 Grier Rd PO Box 35009 .... Charlotte NC 28235 704-330-4801 330-4884*
**Fax:* Admissions ■ *Web:* www.cpcc.edu
Harper 315 W Hebron St .... Charlotte NC 28273 704-330-4400 330-4444
Web: www.cpcc.edu
Sampson Community College PO Box 318 .... Clinton NC 28329 910-592-8081 592-8048*
**Fax:* Admissions ■ *Web:* sampsoncc.edu
Haywood Community College 185 Freedlander Dr .... Clyde NC 28721 828-627-2821 627-4513*
**Fax:* Admissions ■ *TF:* 866-468-6422 ■ *Web:* www.haywood.edu
South 1531 Trinity Church Rd .... Concord NC 28027 704-216-7222
Web: rccc.edu
South PO Box 39 .... Creedmoor NC 27522 919-528-4737 528-1201*
**Fax:* Admissions ■ *TF:* 877-823-2378 ■ *Web:* www.vgcc.edu
Gaston College 201 Hwy 321-S .... Dallas NC 28034 704-922-6200 922-2344*
**Fax:* Admissions ■ *TF:* 800-634-7854 ■ *Web:* gaston.edu
Surry Community College 630 S Main St .... Dobson NC 27017 336-386-8121
Web: surry.edu
Bladen Community College PO Box 266 .... Dublin NC 28332 910-879-5556 879-5513
Web: www.bladencc.edu
Durham Technical Community College
1637 E Lawson St .... Durham NC 27703 919-686-3300 686-3669*
**Fax:* Admissions ■ *Web:* www.durhamtech.edu
College of the Albemarle PO Box 2327 .... Elizabeth City NC 27906 252-335-0821 335-2011*
**Fax:* Admissions ■ *TF:* 800-335-9050 ■ *Web:* www.albemarle.edu
Fayetteville Technical Community College
2201 Hull Rd .... Fayetteville NC 28303 910-678-8400 678-8407
TF: 877-245-5520 ■ *Web:* www.faytechcc.edu
Blue Ridge Community College
180 W Campus Dr .... Flat Rock NC 28731 828-694-1700 694-1690
Web: www.blueridge.edu
Wayne Community College
3000 Wayne Memorial Dr PO Box 8002 .... Goldsboro NC 27533 919-735-5151 736-9425*
**Fax:* Admissions ■ *TF:* 866-414-5064 ■ *Web:* www.waynecc.edu
Alamance Community College PO Box 8000 .... Graham NC 27253 336-578-2002 578-3964
TF: 877-667-7533 ■ *Web:* alamancecc.edu
Pamlico Community College PO Box 185 .... Grantsboro NC 28529 252-249-1851 249-2377*
**Fax:* Library ■ *Web:* www.pamlico.cc.nc.us
Richmond Community College PO Box 1189 .... Hamlet NC 28345 910-410-1700 582-7102*
**Fax:* Admissions ■ *TF:* 800-908-9946 ■ *Web:* www.richmondcc.edu
Vance-Granville Community College
200 Community College Rd .... Henderson NC 27537 252-492-2061 430-0460
Web: www.vgcc.edu

Phone | Fax

Catawba Valley Community College
2550 US Hwy 70 SE .... Hickory NC 28602 828-327-7000 327-7276
TF: 800-433-3243 ■ *Web:* www.cvcc.edu
Caldwell Community College & Technical Institute
2855 Hickory Blvd .... Hudson NC 28638 828-726-2200 726-2216*
**Fax:* Admissions ■ *Web:* www.caldwell.cc.nc.us
North 11930 Verhoeff Dr .... Huntersville NC 28078 704-330-4100 330-4113*
**Fax:* Admissions ■ *Web:* www.cpcc.edu/campuses/north
Coastal Carolina Community College
444 Western Blvd .... Jacksonville NC 28546 910-455-1221 455-7027*
**Fax:* Admissions ■ *Web:* coastalcarolina.edu
Guilford Technical Community College
601 Highpoint Rd PO Box 309 .... Jamestown NC 27282 336-334-4822 819-2022*
**Fax:* Admissions ■ *Web:* www.gtcc.edu
James Sprunt Community College
133 James Sprunt Dr .... Kenansville NC 28349 910-296-2400 296-1636*
**Fax:* Admissions ■ *Web:* jamessprunt.edu
Lenoir Community College PO Box 188 .... Kinston NC 28502 252-527-6223 233-6879
TF: 866-866-2362 ■ *Web:* www.lenoircc.edu
Davidson County Community College
PO Box 1287 .... Lexington NC 27293 336-249-8186 224-0240*
**Fax:* Admissions ■ *TF:* 800-233-4050 ■ *Web:* www.davidsonccc.edu
Louisburg College 501 N Main St .... Louisburg NC 27549 919-496-2521 496-1788*
**Fax:* Admissions ■ *TF:* 800-775-0208 ■ *Web:* www.louisburg.edu
Franklin 8100 Nc 56 Hwy .... Louisburg NC 27549 919-496-1567 496-6604
Web: www.vgcc.edu
Robeson Community College
5160 Fayetteville Rd PO Box 1420 .... Lumberton NC 28360 910-272-3700 272-3328
Web: robeson.edu
McDowell Technical Community College
54 College Dr .... Marion NC 28752 828-652-6021 652-1014*
**Fax:* Admissions ■ *Web:* mcdowelltech.edu
Madison 4646 US Hwy 25-70 .... Marshall NC 28753 828-649-2947 281-9859
Web: www.abtech.edu
Levine 2800 Campus Ridge Rd .... Matthews NC 28105 704-330-4200 330-4210
Web: cpcc.edu
Carteret Community College
3505 Arendell St .... Morehead City NC 28557 252-222-6000 222-6265
Web: www.carteret.edu
Western Piedmont Community College
1001 Burkemont Ave .... Morganton NC 28655 828-438-6000
Web: www.wpcc.edu
Tri-County Community College 21 Campus Cir .... Murphy NC 28906 828-837-6810 837-3266
Web: www.tricountycc.edu
Craven Community College 800 College Ct .... New Bern NC 28562 252-638-4131 638-4649*
**Fax:* Admissions ■ *Web:* www.cravencc.edu
Sandhills Community College
3395 Airport Rd .... Pinehurst NC 28374 910-692-6185 695-3981*
**Fax:* Admissions ■ *TF:* 800-338-3944 ■ *Web:* www.sandhills.edu
South Piedmont Community College 680 Hwy 74 .... Polkton NC 28135 704-272-5300 272-5303*
**Fax:* Admissions ■ *Web:* www.spcc.edu
Wake Technical Community College
9101 Fayetteville Rd .... Raleigh NC 27603 919-662-3500 661-0117*
**Fax:* Admissions ■ *Web:* www.waketech.edu
Nash Community College PO Box 7488 .... Rocky Mount NC 27804 252-443-4011 443-0828*
**Fax:* Admissions ■ *Web:* www.nashcc.edu
Piedmont Community College
1715 College Dr PO Box 1197 .... Roxboro NC 27573 336-599-1181 597-3817*
**Fax:* Admissions ■ *Web:* www.piedmont.cc.nc.us
Rowan-Cabarrus Community College
North
1333 Jake Alexander Blvd S PO Box 1595 .... Salisbury NC 28146 704-216-7222
Web: www.rccc.edu
Central Carolina Community College
1105 Kelly Dr .... Sanford NC 27330 919-775-5401 718-7380*
**Fax:* Admissions ■ *TF:* 800-682-8353 ■ *Web:* www.cccc.edu
Cleveland Community College 137 S Post Rd .... Shelby NC 28152 704-484-4000
Web: clevelandcc.edu
Johnston Community College 245 College Rd .... Smithfield NC 27577 919-934-3051 989-7862*
**Fax:* Admissions ■ *Web:* johnstoncc.edu
Isothermal Community College
286 ICC Loop Rd PO Box 804 .... Spindale NC 28160 828-286-3636 286-4014
Web: www.isothermal.edu
Mayland Community College
200 Mayland Dr PO Box 547 .... Spruce Pine NC 28777 828-765-7351 765-0728*
**Fax:* Admissions ■ *TF:* 800-462-9526 ■ *Web:* www.mayland.edu
Mitchell Community College
500 W Broad St .... Statesville NC 28677 704-878-3200 878-0872
Web: www.mitchellcc.edu
Southwestern Community College 447 College Dr .... Sylva NC 28779 828-339-4000 339-4613
TF: 800-447-4091 ■ *Web:* www.southwesterncc.edu
Warren County PO Box 207 .... Warrenton NC 27536 252-257-1900 257-3612*
**Fax:* Admissions ■ *TF:* 877-823-2378 ■ *Web:* www.vgcc.edu
Beaufort County Community College
5337 Hwy 264 E .... Washington NC 27889 252-946-6194 940-6393*
**Fax:* Admissions ■ *Web:* beaufortccc.edu
Halifax Community College 100 College Dr .... Weldon NC 27890 252-536-2551 536-4144
Web: www.halifaxcc.edu
Rockingham Community College
215 Wrenn Memorial Rd .... Wentworth NC 27375 336-342-4261 342-1809
Web: www.rockinghamcc.edu
Southeastern Community College PO Box 151 .... Whiteville NC 28472 910-642-7141 642-1267*
**Fax:* Admissions ■ *Web:* www.sccnc.edu
Wilkes Community College
1328 S Collegiate Dr PO Box 120 .... Wilkesboro NC 28697 336-838-6100 838-6277
TF: 866-222-1548 ■ *Web:* www.wilkescc.edu
Martin Community College
1161 Kehukee Pk Rd .... Williamston NC 27892 252-792-1521 792-0826
Web: www.martin.cc.nc.us
Cape Fear Community College
411 N Front St .... Wilmington NC 28401 910-362-7000 362-7080*
**Fax:* Admissions ■ *TF:* 800-487-5553 ■ *Web:* www.cfcc.edu
Pitt Community College
1986 Pitt Tech Rd PO Box 7007 .... Winterville NC 28590 252-493-7200 321-4401
Web: www.pittcc.edu

Phone *Fax*

Caswell County
331 Piedmont Dr PO Box 1150 .... Yanceyville NC 27379 336-694-5707 694-7086
Web: www.piedmont.cc.nc.us

North Dakota

Phone *Fax*

Turtle Mountain Community College
10145 BIA Rd 7 .... Belcourt ND 58316 701-477-7862 477-7892
TF: 800-827-1100 ■ *Web:* www.tm.edu

Bismarck State College 1500 Edwards Ave .... Bismarck ND 58501 701-224-5400 224-5643*
**Fax:* Admissions ■ *TF:* 800-445-5073 ■ *Web:* www.bismarckstate.edu

Minot State University Bottineau
105 Simrall Blvd. .... Bottineau ND 58318 701-228-5451 228-5499*
**Fax:* Admissions ■ *TF:* 800-542-6866 ■ *Web:* dakotacollege.edu

Lake Region State College
1801 College Dr N .... Devils Lake ND 58301 701-662-1514 662-1581*
**Fax:* Admissions ■ *TF:* 800-443-1313 ■ *Web:* www.lrsc.nodak.edu

Cankdeska Cikana Community College
PO Box 269 .... Fort Totten ND 58335 701-766-4415 766-4077
TF: 888-783-1463 ■ *Web:* www.littlehoop.edu

North Dakota State College of Science
800 Sixth St N .... Wahpeton ND 58076 701-671-2401 671-2201*
**Fax:* Admissions ■ *TF:* 800-342-4325 ■ *Web:* www.ndscs.edu

Williston State College
1410 University Ave PO Box 1326 .... Williston ND 58802 701-774-4200 774-4211*
**Fax:* Admissions ■ *TF:* 888-863-9455 ■ *Web:* willistonstate.edu

Ohio

Phone *Fax*

Ashtabula 3300 Lake Rd W .... Ashtabula OH 44004 440-964-3322 964-4269*
**Fax:* Admissions ■ *TF:* 800-988-5368 ■ *Web:* www.kent.edu/ashtabula

University of Cincinnati Clermont College
4200 Clermont College Dr .... Batavia OH 45103 513-732-5200 732-5303*
**Fax:* Admissions ■ *TF:* 866-446-2822 ■ *Web:* www.ucclermont.edu

Geauga 14111 Claridon-Troy Rd .... Burton OH 44021 440-834-4187 834-8846*
**Fax:* Admissions ■ *Web:* www.kent.edu/geauga

Wright State University Lake
7600 Lk Campus Dr .... Celina OH 45822 419-586-0300 586-0358*
**Fax:* Admissions ■ *TF:* 800-237-1477 ■ *Web:* lake.wright.edu

Cincinnati State Technical & Community College
3520 Central Pkwy .... Cincinnati OH 45223 513-569-1500 569-1562*
**Fax:* Admissions ■ *TF:* 877-569-0115 ■ *Web:* www.cincinnatistate.edu

University of Cincinnati
9555 Plainfield Rd .... Cincinnati OH 45236 513-745-5600 745-5768*
**Fax:* Admissions ■ *Web:* www.ucblueash.edu

Metropolitan 2900 Community College Ave ...... Cleveland OH 44115 216-987-4200
TF: 800-954-8742 ■ *Web:* www.tri-c.edu

Columbus State Community College
550 E Spring St .... Columbus OH 43215 614-287-2400 287-6019*
**Fax:* Admissions ■ *TF:* 800-621-6407 ■ *Web:* www.cscc.edu

Sinclair Community College 444 W Third St .... Dayton OH 45402 937-512-3000
TF: 800-315-3000 ■ *Web:* www.sinclair.edu

Lorain County Community College
1005 N Abbe Rd .... Elyria OH 44035 440-365-5222 366-4167
TF: 800-995-5222 ■ *Web:* www.lorainccc.edu

Owens Community College
Findlay 3200 Bright Rd .... Findlay OH 45840 800-466-9367
TF: 800-466-9367 ■ *Web:* www.owens.edu

Terra Community College 2830 Napoleon Rd. .... Fremont OH 43420 419-334-8400 334-9035
TF: 800-334-3886 ■ *Web:* www.terra.edu

Hamilton 1601 University Blvd .... Hamilton OH 45011 513-785-3000 785-3148*
**Fax:* Admissions ■ *Web:* www.ham.miamioh.edu

Cuyahoga Community College
Eastern 4250 Richmond Rd .... Highland Hills OH 44122 216-987-2024 987-2214*
**Fax:* Admissions ■ *TF:* 800-954-8742 ■ *Web:* www.tri-c.edu

Bowling Green State University Firelands
1 University Dr .... Huron OH 44839 419-433-5560 433-9696*
**Fax:* Admissions ■ *Web:* www.firelands.bgsu.edu

Kent State University
800 E. Summit St PO Box 5190 .... Kent OH 44242 330-672-2121 672-2499*
**Fax:* Admissions ■ *TF:* 800-988-5368 ■ *Web:* www.kent.edu

Lakeland Community College
7700 Clocktower Dr .... Kirtland OH 44094 440-525-7000 525-7651*
**Fax:* Admissions ■ *TF:* 800-589-8520 ■ *Web:* lakelandcc.edu

Washington State Community College
710 Colegate Dr .... Marietta OH 45750 740-374-8716 376-0257
Web: www.wscc.edu

Buckeye Career Center
545 University Dr Ne .... New Philadelphia OH 44663 330-339-2288
TF: 800-227-1665 ■ *Web:* www.buckeyecareercenter.org

University of Akron Wayne College
1901 Smucker Rd................................. Orrville OH 44667 330-683-2010 684-8989
TF: 800-221-8308 ■ *Web:* www.wayne.uakron.edu

Miami University 501 E High St .... Oxford OH 45056 513-529-1809 529-1550*
**Fax:* Admissions ■ *TF:* 866-426-4643 ■ *Web:* miamioh.edu

Western 11000 Pleasant Valley Rd. .... Parma OH 44130 216-987-2800 987-5071*
**Fax:* Admissions ■ *TF:* 800-954-8742 ■ *Web:* www.tri-c.edu

Toledo 30335 Oregon Rd.................... Perrysburg OH 43551 419-661-7000
TF: 800-466-9367 ■ *Web:* www.owens.edu

Edison Community College 1973 Edison Dr. .... Piqua OH 45356 937-778-8600 778-1920
TF: 888-442-4551 ■ *Web:* www.edisonohio.edu

South 12681 US Rt 62 .... Sardinia OH 45171 937-695-0307 695-8093*
**Fax:* Admissions ■ *TF:* 877-644-6562 ■ *Web:* www.sscc.edu

Clark State Community College
570 E Leffel Ln .... Springfield OH 45506 937-325-0691 328-6097
Web: www.clarkstate.edu

Southern State Community College
North 1850 Davids Dr .... Wilmington OH 45177 937-382-6645 383-1206*
**Fax:* Admissions ■ *TF:* 877-644-6562 ■ *Web:* www.sscc.edu

Oklahoma

Phone *Fax*

Western Oklahoma State College 2801 N Main St. .... Altus OK 73521 580-477-2000 477-7723
TF: 800-662-1113 ■ *Web:* www.wosc.edu

Redlands Community College
1300 S Country Club Rd. .... El Reno OK 73036 405-262-2552 422-1200*
**Fax:* Admissions ■ *TF:* 866-415-6367 ■ *Web:* www.redlandscc.edu

Northeastern Oklahoma A&M College 200 I St NE ...... Miami OK 74354 918-542-8441
Web: neo.edu

Rose State College 6420 SE 15th St .... Midwest City OK 73110 405-733-7372 736-0309*
**Fax:* Admissions ■ *TF:* 866-621-0987 ■ *Web:* www.rose.edu

Oklahoma City Community College
7777 S May Ave .... Oklahoma City OK 73159 405-682-1611 682-7521*
**Fax:* Admissions ■ *Web:* www.occc.edu

Oklahoma City 900 N Portland Ave .... Oklahoma City OK 73107 405-947-4421 945-9120*
**Fax:* Admissions ■ *TF:* 800-560-4099 ■ *Web:* www.osuokc.edu

Carl Albert State College 1507 S McKenna St........... Poteau OK 74953 918-647-1300
Web: www.carlalbert.edu

Rogers State University Pryor 421 S Elliott St. .... Pryor OK 74361 918-825-6117 825-6135*
**Fax:* Admissions ■ *TF:* 800-256-7511 ■ *Web:* www.rsu.edu

Southwestern Oklahoma State University Sayre
409 E Mississippi St. .... Sayre OK 73662 580-928-5533 928-1140*
**Fax:* Admissions ■ *Web:* www.swosu.edu/sayre

Oklahoma State University
219 Student Union Bldg .... Stillwater OK 74078 405-744-5000 744-7092
TF: 800-852-1255 ■ *Web:* www.okstate.edu

Murray State College 1 Murray Campus............ Tishomingo OK 73460 580-371-2371 371-9844*
**Fax:* Admissions ■ *TF:* 800-342-0698 ■ *Web:* www.mscok.edu

Northern Oklahoma College
1220 E Grand St PO Box 310 .... Tonkawa OK 74653 580-628-6200 628-6371*
**Fax:* Admissions ■ *Web:* noc.edu

Tulsa Community College
Metro 909 S Boston Ave .... Tulsa OK 74119 918-595-7000 595-7347*
**Fax:* Admissions ■ *TF:* 866-970-0233 ■ *Web:* www.tulsacc.edu

Northeast 3727 E Apache St. .... Tulsa OK 74115 918-595-7000 595-7594
Web: www.tulsacc.edu

Southeast 10300 E 81st St .... Tulsa OK 74133 918-595-7000 595-7748
Web: www.tulsacc.edu

West 7505 W 41st St .... Tulsa OK 74107 918-595-7000 595-8130
Web: www.tulsacc.edu

Connors State College 700 College Rd. .... Warner OK 74469 918-463-2931 463-6324
TF: 888-594-5171 ■ *Web:* connorsstate.edu

Eastern Oklahoma State College
1301 W Main St .... Wilburton OK 74578 918-465-2361 465-4417
Web: www.eosc.edu

Ontario

Phone *Fax*

Loyalist College Wallbridge-Loyalist Rd. .... Belleville ON K8N5B9 613-969-1913
Web: www.loyalistcollege.com

Mohawk College of Applied Arts & Technology
135 Fennell Ave W West Fifth St. .... Hamilton ON L8C1E9 905-575-1212
Web: www.mohawkcollege.ca

Queen's School of Business
Queen's University 143 Union St .... Kingston ON K7L3N6 613-533-2330
Web: smith.queensu.ca/index.php

Fleming College 200 Albert St S. .... Lindsay ON K9V5E6 705-324-9144
TF: 866-353-6464 ■ *Web:* flemingcollege.ca

Algonquin College of Applied Arts & Technology
1385 Woodroffe Ave .... Ottawa ON K2G1V7 613-727-4723
Web: www.algonquincollege.com

Willis College of Business & Technology
85 O'Connor St .... Ottawa ON K1P5M6 613-233-1128
TF: 877-233-1128 ■ *Web:* williscollege.com

Lambton College of Applied Arts & Technology, The
1457 London Rd .... Sarnia ON N7S6K4 519-542-7751
Web: www.lambton.on.ca

Sault College of Applied Arts & Technology, The
443 Northern Ave .... Sault Sainte Marie ON P6A5L3 705-759-6700
TF: 800-461-2260 ■ *Web:* www.saultcollege.ca

College of Nurses of Ontario
101 Davenport Rd .... Toronto ON M5R3P1 416-928-0900
TF: 800-387-5526 ■ *Web:* www.cno.org

Herzing College Toronto
220 Yonge St Eaton Centre Galleria Offices
Ste 202 .... Toronto ON M5B2H1 416-599-6996
Web: www.herzing.ca

Institute of Corporate Directors
602 - 40 University Ave .... Toronto ON M5J1T1 416-593-7741
TF: 877-593-7741 ■ *Web:* www.icd.ca

Niagara College of Applied Arts & Technology
300 Woodlawn Rd .... Welland ON L3C7L3 905-641-2252
Web: www.niagaracollege.ca

St. Clair College of Applied Arts & Technology, The
2000 Talbot Rd W................................... Windsor ON N9A6S4 519-966-1656
Web: www.stclairc.on.ca

Oregon

Phone *Fax*

Linn-Benton Community College
6500 Pacific Blvd SW .... Albany OR 97321 541-917-4999
Web: www.linnbenton.edu

Clatsop Community College 1653 Jerome Ave .... Astoria OR 97103 503-325-0910 325-5738
TF: 855-252-8767 ■ *Web:* www.clatsopcc.edu

Central Oregon Community College
2600 NW College Way .... Bend OR 97701 541-383-7700 383-7506*
**Fax:* Admissions ■ *Web:* www.cocc.edu

				Phone	Fax
Southwestern Oregon Community College					
1988 Newmark Ave	Coos Bay	OR	97420	541-888-2525	
TF: 800-962-2838 ■ *Web:* www.socc.edu					
Cottage Grove 1275 S River Rd	Cottage Grove	OR	97424	541-463-4202	942-5186
Web: www.lanecc.edu					
Lane Community College 4000 E 30th Ave	Eugene	OR	97405	541-463-3000	463-3995*
**Fax:* Admissions ■ *TF:* 800-321-2211 ■ *Web:* www.lanecc.edu					
Florence 3149 Oak St	Florence	OR	97439	541-997-8444	997-8448
TF: 800-222-3290 ■ *Web:* www.lanecc.edu					
Rogue Community College 3345 Redwood Hwy	Grants Pass	OR	97527	541-956-7500	471-3585*
**Fax:* Admissions ■ *TF:* 800-411-6508 ■ *Web:* www.roguecc.edu					
Mount Hood Community College					
26000 SE Stark St	Gresham	OR	97030	503-491-6422	491-7388*
**Fax:* Admissions ■ *Web:* www.mhcc.edu					
Klamath Community College					
7390 S Sixth St	Klamath Falls	OR	97603	541-882-3521	885-7758
Web: www.kcc.cc.or.us					
Riverside 117 S Central	Medford	OR	97501	541-245-7500	245-7648
Web: www.roguecc.edu					
Treasure Valley Community College					
650 College Blvd	Ontario	OR	97914	541-881-8822	881-2721*
**Fax:* Admissions ■ *TF:* 888-292-5247 ■ *Web:* www.tvcc.cc/index.cfm?					
Blue Mountain Community College					
2411 NW Carden Ave PO Box 100	Pendleton	OR	97801	541-276-1260	278-5871*
**Fax:* Admissions ■ *TF:* 888-441-7232 ■ *Web:* www.bluecc.edu					
Portland Community College					
Sylvania 12000 SW 49th Ave	Portland	OR	97219	503-244-6111	977-4740*
**Fax:* Admissions ■ *Web:* www.pcc.edu					
Umpqua Community College					
1140 Umpqva College Rd PO Box 967	Roseburg	OR	97470	541-440-4600	440-4612
TF: 800-820-5161 ■ *Web:* www.umpqua.edu					
Chemeketa Community College					
4000 Lancaster Dr NE PO Box 14007	Salem	OR	97305	503-399-5006	399-3918*
**Fax:* Admissions ■ *Web:* www.chemeketa.edu					
Tillamook Bay Community College					
4301 Third St	Tillamook	OR	97141	503-842-8222	
TF: 888-306-8222 ■ *Web:* www.tbcc.cc.or.us					

Pennsylvania

				Phone	Fax
NanoHorizons Inc					
270 Rolling Ridge Dr Ste 100	Bellefonte	PA	16823	814-355-4700	
TF: 866-584-6235 ■ *Web:* www.nanohorizons.com					
Northampton Community College					
3835 Green Pond Rd	Bethlehem	PA	18020	610-861-5300	861-4560*
**Fax:* Admissions ■ *TF:* 877-543-0998 ■ *Web:* www.northampton.edu					
Montgomery County Community College					
Central 340 DeKalb Pk	Blue Bell	PA	19422	215-641-6300	619-7188*
**Fax:* Admitting ■ *Web:* mc3.edu					
Bristol 1280 New Rodgers Rd	Bristol	PA	19007	215-781-3939	
Web: www.bucks.edu					
Harcum College 750 Montgomery Ave	Bryn Mawr	PA	19010	610-525-4100	526-6147*
**Fax:* Admissions ■ *TF:* 800-650-0035 ■ *Web:* www.harcum.edu					
Butler County Community College					
107 College Dr	Butler	PA	16002	724-287-8711	285-6047
TF: 888-826-2829 ■ *Web:* www.bc3.edu					
Downingtown 100 Bond Dr	Downingtown	PA	19335	484-237-6200	237-6305
Web: dccc.edu					
DuBois 1 College Pl	Du Bois	PA	15801	814-375-4700	375-4784*
**Fax:* Admissions ■ *TF:* 800-346-7627 ■ *Web:* www.ds.psu.edu					
Worthington Scranton 120 Ridge View Dr	Dunmore	PA	18512	570-963-2500	963-2524*
**Fax:* Admissions ■ *Web:* worthingtonscranton.psu.edu					
Pennsylvania Highlands Community College					
881 Hills Plz Dr Ste 450	Ebensburg	PA	15931	814-262-6446	262-6420
TF: 888-385-7325 ■ *Web:* www.pennhighlands.edu					
Lehigh Valley 8380 Mohr Ln PO Box 549	Fogelsville	PA	18051	610-285-5000	285-5220*
**Fax:* Admissions ■ *Web:* www.lv.psu.edu					
Us Health Connect Inc					
500 Office Ctr Dr	Fort Washington	PA	19034	800-889-4944	
TF: 800-889-4944 ■ *Web:* www.omniaeducation.com					
Gettysburg 731 Old Harrisburg Rd	Gettysburg	PA	17325	717-337-3855	337-3015*
**Fax:* Admissions ■ *TF:* 800-222-4222 ■ *Web:* www.hacc.edu					
Harrisburg Area Community College					
1 HACC Dr	Harrisburg	PA	17110	717-780-2300	231-7674*
**Fax:* Admissions ■ *TF:* 800-222-4222 ■ *Web:* www.hacc.edu					
Hazleton 76 University Dr	Hazleton	PA	18202	570-450-3000	450-3182*
**Fax:* Admissions ■ *TF:* 800-279-8495 ■ *Web:* www.hn.psu.edu					
Manor College 700 Fox Chase Rd	Jenkintown	PA	19046	215-885-2360	576-6564*
**Fax:* Admissions ■ *Web:* www.manor.edu					
Lebanon 735 Cumberland St	Lebanon	PA	17042	717-270-4222	270-6385
TF: 800-222-4222 ■ *Web:* www.hacc.edu					
Wilkes-Barre Old Rt 115 PO Box PSU	Lehman	PA	18627	570-675-2171	675-9113*
**Fax:* Admissions ■ *Web:* www.wb.psu.edu					
Fayette 2201 University Dr	Lemont Furnace	PA	15456	724-430-4100	430-4175*
**Fax:* Admissions ■ *TF:* 877-568-4130 ■ *Web:* www.fe.psu.edu					
Delaware County Community College					
901 Media Line Rd	Media	PA	19063	610-359-5000	359-5343
TF: 800-908-9946 ■ *Web:* www.dccc.edu					
Community College of Beaver County					
1 Campus Dr	Monaca	PA	15061	724-775-8561	728-7599*
**Fax:* Admissions ■ *TF:* 800-335-0222 ■ *Web:* www.ccbc.edu					
Beaver 100 University Dr	Monaca	PA	15061	724-773-3500	773-3578*
**Fax:* Admissions ■ *TF:* 877-564-6778 ■ *Web:* www.br.psu.edu					
Boyce 595 Beatty Rd	Monroeville	PA	15146	724-325-6614	
Web: www.ccac.edu					
Mont Alto 1 Campus Dr	Mont Alto	PA	17237	717-749-6000	749-6132*
**Fax:* Admissions ■ *TF:* 800-392-6173 ■ *Web:* www.ma.psu.edu					
Luzerne County Community College					
1333 S Prospect St	Nanticoke	PA	18634	800-377-5222	740-0238*
**Fax Area Code:* 570 ■ **Fax:* Admissions ■ *TF:* 800-377-5222 ■ *Web:* www.luzerne.edu					
New Kensington					
3550 Seventh St Rd Rt 780	New Kensington	PA	15068	724-334-5466	334-6111
Web: www.nk.psu.edu					
Bucks County Community College 275 Swamp Rd	Newtown	PA	18940	215-968-8000	968-8110*
**Fax:* Admissions ■ *Web:* www.bucks.edu					
Upper County 1 Hillendale Dr	Perkasie	PA	18944	215-258-7700	258-7749
Web: www.bucks.edu					
Community College of Philadelphia					
1700 Spring Garden St	Philadelphia	PA	19130	215-751-8000	751-8001*
**Fax:* Admissions ■ *Web:* www.ccp.edu					
Community College of Allegheny County					
Allegheny 808 Ridge Ave	Pittsburgh	PA	15212	412-237-2525	237-4581*
**Fax:* Admissions ■ *Web:* www.ccac.edu					
North 8701 Perry Hwy	Pittsburgh	PA	15237	412-366-7000	
Web: www.ccac.edu					
University of Pittsburgh 4227 Fifth Ave	Pittsburgh	PA	15260	412-624-4141	648-8815*
**Fax:* Admissions ■ *TF:* 877-999-3223 ■ *Web:* www.pitt.edu					
Pottstown 101 College Dr	Pottstown	PA	19464	610-718-1800	718-1999
Web: mc3.edu					
Berks PO Box 7009	Reading	PA	19610	610-396-6000	396-6077
Web: www.bk.psu.edu					
Reading Area Community College					
10 S Second St PO Box 1706	Reading	PA	19603	610-372-4721	607-6290*
**Fax:* Admissions ■ *TF:* 800-626-1665 ■ *Web:* www.racc.edu					
Lehigh Carbon Community College					
4525 Education Pk Dr	Schnecksville	PA	18078	610-799-2121	799-1527
TF General: 800-414-3975 ■ *Web:* www.lccc.edu					
Schuylkill 200 University Dr	Schuylkill Haven	PA	17972	570-385-6000	385-6272*
**Fax:* Admissions ■ *TF:* 800-243-2374 ■ *Web:* www.sl.psu.edu					
Lackawanna College 501 Vine St	Scranton	PA	18509	570-961-7810	
TF: 877-346-3552 ■ *Web:* facebook.com/lackawanna					
Shenango 147 Shenango Ave	Sharon	PA	16146	724-983-2803	983-2820*
**Fax:* Admissions ■ *TF:* 888-275-7009 ■ *Web:* www.shenango.psu.edu					
Southeast 2000 Elmwood Ave	Sharon Hill	PA	19079	610-957-5700	957-5787
Web: www.dccc.edu					
Morgan Ctr 234 High St	Tamaqua	PA	18252	570-668-6880	668-7296
TF: 800-424-2460 ■ *Web:* www.lccc.edu					
Monroe 3 Old Mill Rd	Tannersville	PA	18372	570-620-9221	620-9317
TF: 877-543-0998 ■ *Web:* www.northampton.edu					
Titusville 504 E Main St	Titusville	PA	16354	888-878-0462	827-4519*
**Fax Area Code:* 814 ■ **Fax:* Admissions ■ *TF:* 888-878-0462 ■ *Web:* www.upt.pitt.edu					
Pennsylvania State University					
201 Shields Bldg	University Park	PA	16802	814-865-4700	863-7590
Web: www.psu.edu					
McKeesport 201 Old Main	University Park	PA	16802	412-675-9000	
Web: www.psu.edu					
Valley Forge Military Academy & College					
1001 Eagle Rd	Wayne	PA	19087	610-989-1300	688-1545*
**Fax:* Admissions ■ *TF:* 800-234-8362 ■ *Web:* www.vfmac.edu					
South 1750 Clairton Rd Rt 885	West Mifflin	PA	15122	412-469-1100	469-6291*
**Fax:* Admissions ■ *Web:* www.ccac.edu					
York 1031 Edgecomb Ave	York	PA	17403	717-771-4000	771-4005*
**Fax:* Admissions ■ *TF:* 800-778-6227 ■ *Web:* www.yk.psu.edu					
Westmoreland County Community College					
145 Pavilion Ln	Youngwood	PA	15697	724-925-4000	
TF: 800-262-2103 ■ *Web:* wccc.edu					
Holland College 140 Weymouth St	Charlottetown	PE	C1A4Z1	902-566-9510	
Web: www.hollandc.pe.ca					

Quebec

				Phone	Fax
College De Rosemont 6400 16e Ave	Montreal	QC	H1X2S9	514-376-1620	
Web: www.crosemont.qc.ca					
Ecole des Hautes Etudes Commerciales de Montreal					
3000 chemin de la Cote-Sainte-Catherine	Montreal	QC	H3T2A7	514-340-6000	
Web: www.hec.ca					
Ecole Polytechnique de Montreal					
2900 Boul Edouard-Montpetit	Montreal	QC	H3T1J4	514-340-4711	
Web: www.polymtl.ca					
Institut De Tourisme & D'h?tellerie Du Qu?bec					
3535, rue Saint-Denis	Montreal	QC	H2X3P1	514-240-3984	
Web: www.ithq.qc.ca					
College Merici 755 Ch St-Louis	Quebec	QC	G1S1C1	418-683-1591	682-8938
TF: 800-208-1463 ■ *Web:* www.merici.ca					
Cegep De Sainte-Foy 2410 Ch Sainte-Foy	Sainte-foy	QC	G1V1T2	418-659-6600	
Web: www.cegep-ste-foy.qc.ca					
Cegep De Thetford					
671 Boul Frontenac O	Thetford Mines	QC	G6G1N1	418-338-8591	
Web: www.cegepthetford.ca					

Rhode Island

				Phone	Fax
Community College of Rhode Island					
Flanagan 1762 Louisquisset Pk	Lincoln	RI	02865	401-333-7000	333-7122*
**Fax:* Admissions ■ *Web:* www.ccri.edu					
Liston 1 Hilton St	Providence	RI	02905	401-455-6000	
Web: www.ccri.edu					
Knight 400 E Ave	Warwick	RI	02886	401-825-1000	825-2394*
**Fax:* Admissions ■ *Web:* www.ccri.edu					

Saskatchewan

				Phone	Fax
Saskatoon Business College Ltd					
221 Third Ave N	Saskatoon	SK	S7K2H7	306-244-6333	
TF: 800-679-7711 ■ *Web:* www.sbccollege.ca					

South Carolina

				Phone	Fax
Northeastern Technical College					
1201 Chesterfield Hwy	Cheraw	SC	29520	843-921-6900	537-6148
TF: 800-921-7399 ■ *Web:* www.netc.edu					

Phone Fax

Midlands Technical College PO Box 2408 .... Columbia SC 29202 803-738-1400 790-7524*
Fax: Admissions ■ *TF:* 800-922-8038 ■ *Web:* www.midlandstech.edu

University of South Carolina
1600 Hampton St .... Columbia SC 29208 803-777-7000 777-0101*
Fax: Admissions ■ *TF:* 800-868-5872 ■ *Web:* www.sc.edu

Aiken Technical College
2276 J Davis Hwy .... Graniteville SC 29829 803-593-9231 593-6526*
Fax: Admissions ■ *Web:* www.atc.edu

Greenville Technical College
Barton 506 S Pleasantburg Dr .... Greenville SC 29607 864-250-8000
TF All: 800-723-0673 ■ *Web:* www.gvltec.edu
Brashier PO Box 5616 .... Greenville SC 29606 864-250-8000
Web: www.greenvilletech.com

Williamsburg Technical College
601 MLK Jr Ave .... Kingstree SC 29556 843-355-4110 355-4289*
Fax: Admissions ■ *TF:* 800-768-2021 ■ *Web:* www.williamsburgtech.com

Orangeburg-Calhoun Technical College
3250 St Matthews Rd .... Orangeburg SC 29118 803-536-0311
Web: www.octech.edu

Clinton Junior College 1029 Crawford Rd .... Rock Hill SC 29730 803-327-7402 328-6318*
Fax: Admissions ■ *TF:* 877-837-9645

York Technical College 452 S Anderson Rd .... Rock Hill SC 29730 803-327-8000
TF: 800-922-8324 ■ *Web:* www.yorktech.com

Spartanburg Methodist College
1000 Powell Mill Rd .... Spartanburg SC 29301 864-587-4000 587-4355*
Fax: Admissions ■ *TF:* 800-772-7286 ■ *Web:* smcsc.edu
Greer 2522 Locust Hill Rd .... Taylors SC 29687 800-723-0673
TF: 800-723-0673 ■ *Web:* www.gvltec.edu/greer

North Greenville University
7801 N Tigerville Rd PO Box 1892 .... Tigerville SC 29688 864-977-7000 977-7177*
Fax: Admissions ■ *TF:* 800-468-6642 ■ *Web:* www.ngu.edu
Union 401 E Main St .... Union SC 29379 864-429-8728 427-3682
TF: 800-768-5566 ■ *Web:* uscunion.sc.edu

South Dakota

Phone Fax

Mitchell Technical Institute
821 N Capital St .... Mitchell SD 57301 800-684-1969 995-3083*
Fax Area Code: 605 ■ *TF:* 800-684-1969 ■ *Web:* www.mitchelltech.edu

Kilian Community College 300 E Sixth St .... Sioux Falls SD 57103 605-221-3100 336-2606*
Fax: Admissions ■ *TF:* 800-888-1147 ■ *Web:* www.kilian.edu

Sisseton Wahpeton College 12572 BIA Hwy 700 .... Sisseton SD 57262 605-698-3966 742-0394
Web: www.swc.tc

Lake Area Technical Institute
230 11th St NE PO Box 730 .... Watertown SD 57201 605-882-5284 882-6299
TF: 800-657-4344 ■ *Web:* lakeareatech.edu

Tennessee

Phone Fax

Chattanooga State Technical Community College
4501 Amnicola Hwy .... Chattanooga TN 37406 423-697-4400 697-4709*
Fax: Admissions ■ *TF:* 866-547-3733 ■ *Web:* www.chattanoogastate.edu

Cleveland State Community College
3535 Adkisson Dr .... Cleveland TN 37312 423-472-7141 478-6255
TF: 800-604-2722 ■ *Web:* clevelandstatecc.edu
Clifton 795 Main St .... Clifton TN 38425 931-676-6966 676-6941
Web: columbiastate.edu

Columbia State Community College
1665 Hampshire Pk .... Columbia TN 38401 931-540-2722 540-2830*
Fax: Admissions ■ *Web:* www.columbiastate.edu

Dyersburg State Community College
1510 Lake Rd .... Dyersburg TN 38024 731-286-3200 286-3325*
Fax: Admissions ■ *Web:* www.dscc.edu

Volunteer State Community College
1480 Nashville Pk .... Gallatin TN 37066 615-452-8600
TF: 888-335-8722 ■ *Web:* www.volstate.edu

Roane State Community College 276 Patton Ln .... Harriman TN 37748 865-354-3000 882-4562*
Fax: Admitting ■ *TF:* 800-343-9104 ■ *Web:* www.roanestate.edu

Jackson State Community College 2046 N Pkwy .... Jackson TN 38301 731-424-3520 425-9559*
Fax: Admissions ■ *Web:* www.jscc.edu

Pellissippi State Technical Community College
10915 HaRdin Vly Rd .... Knoxville TN 37933 865-694-6400 539-7217*
Fax: Admissions ■ *Web:* www.pstcc.edu
Lexington-Henderson Center 932 E Church St .... Lexington TN 38351 731-968-5722 968-1539
Web: www.jscc.edu

Motlow State Community College PO Box 8500 .... Lynchburg TN 37352 931-393-1500
TF: 800-654-4877 ■ *Web:* www.mscc.edu

Hiwassee College
225 Hiwassee College Dr .... Madisonville TN 37354 423-442-2001 442-8521*
Fax: Admissions ■ *TF:* 800-356-2187 ■ *Web:* www.hiwassee.edu

Southwest Tennessee Community College
PO Box 780 .... Memphis TN 38101 901-333-5000 333-4473
TF: 877-717-7822 ■ *Web:* www.southwest.tn.edu

Walters State Community College
500 S Davy Crockett Pkwy .... Morristown TN 37813 423-585-2600 585-6786*
Fax: Admissions ■ *TF:* 800-225-4770 ■ *Web:* www.ws.edu

Texas

Phone Fax

Abilene 717 E Industrial Blvd .... Abilene TX 79602 325-794-4400 442-5100*
Fax Area Code: 254 ■ *Web:* cisco.edu

Texas State Technical College (TSTC)
Abilene 650 E Hwy 80 .... Abilene TX 79601 325-672-7091 643-5987
TF: 800-852-8784 ■ *Web:* www.tstc.edu

Amarillo College 2201 S Washington St .... Amarillo TX 79109 806-371-5000 371-5066
Web: www.actx.edu

Smith System Driver Improvement Institute Inc
2301 E Lamar Blvd Ste 250 .... Arlington TX 76006 817-652-6969
TF: 800-777-7648 ■ *Web:* www.drivedifferent.com

Southeast 2100 SE Pkwy .... Arlington TX 76018 817-515-8223 515-3182*
Fax: Admissions ■ *Web:* www.tccd.edu

Trinity Valley Community College
Athens 100 Cardinal Dr .... Athens TX 75751 903-675-6200 675-6209*
Fax: Admissions ■ *TF:* 877-392-6433 ■ *Web:* www.tvcc.edu

Austin Community College (ACC)
5930 Middle Fiskville Rd .... Austin TX 78752 512-223-7000 223-7665*
Fax: Admissions ■ *TF:* 877-442-3522 ■ *Web:* www.austincc.edu
Cypress Creek 5930 Middle Fiskville Rd .... Austin TX 78752 512-223-4222 223-2048
Web: www.austincc.edu
Eastview 3401 Webberville Rd .... Austin TX 78702 512-223-5100 223-5900*
Fax: Admissions ■ *TF:* 888-626-1697 ■
Web: austincc.edu/locations/campuses/eastview-campus
Northridge 11928 Stonehollow Dr .... Austin TX 78758 512-223-4000 223-4651*
Fax: Admissions ■ *TF:* 877-990-0462 ■
Web: austincc.edu/locations/campuses/northridge-campus
Pinnacle 7748 Hwy 290 W .... Austin TX 78736 512-223-8001 223-8122
TF: 888-626-1697 ■
Web: austincc.edu/locations/campuses/pinnacle-campus
Rio Grande 1212 Rio Grande St .... Austin TX 78701 512-223-3000 223-3444*
Fax: Admissions ■ *TF:* 877-990-0462 ■
Web: austincc.edu/locations/campuses/rio-grande-campus
Riverside 1020 Grove Blvd .... Austin TX 78741 512-223-6000 223-6767*
Fax: Admissions ■ *TF:* 877-990-0462 ■
Web: austincc.edu/locations/campuses/riverside-campus

Mediatech Institute of Austin
4719 s congress ave .... Austin TX 78745 512-447-2002
TF: 866-498-1122 ■ *Web:* mediatech.edu

Lee College 200 Lee Dr .... Baytown TX 77520 281-427-5611 425-6555
Web: www.lee.edu

Coastal Bend College
Beeville 3800 Charco Rd .... Beeville TX 78102 361-358-2838 354-2254*
Fax: Admissions ■ *TF:* 866-722-2838 ■ *Web:* coastalbend.edu

Howard College 1001 Birdwell Ln .... Big Spring TX 79720 432-264-5000 264-5082*
Fax: Admissions ■ *TF:* 877-898-3833 ■ *Web:* www.howardcollege.edu
Southwest Collegiate Institute for the Deaf
3200 Ave C .... Big Spring TX 79720 432-264-3700 264-3707*
Fax: Admissions ■ *Web:* www.howardcollege.edu

Frank Phillips College (FPC) PO Box 5118 .... Borger TX 79008 806-457-4200
Web: www.fpctx.edu
Bowie 810 S Mill St .... Bowie TX 76230 940-872-4002 872-3065
Web: www.nctc.edu

Blinn College 902 College Ave .... Brenham TX 77833 979-830-4000 830-4110*
Fax: Admissions ■ *Web:* www.blinn.edu

Panola College 1109 W Panola St .... Carthage TX 75633 903-693-2000 693-2031*
Fax: Admissions ■ *Web:* www.panola.edu

Cisco Junior College 101 College Heights .... Cisco TX 76437 254-442-5000
Web: cisco.edu

Clarendon College
1122 College Dr PO Box 968 .... Clarendon TX 79226 806-874-3571 874-5080*
Fax: Admissions ■ *TF:* 800-687-9737 ■ *Web:* www.clarendoncollege.edu

Texas A&M Transportation Institute
3135 Tamu .... College Station TX 77843 979-845-1713
Web: tti.tamu.edu

Montgomery College 3200 College Pk Dr .... Conroe TX 77384 936-273-7000
Web: www.lonestar.edu

Del Mar College
East 101 Baldwin Blvd .... Corpus Christi TX 78404 361-698-1200 698-1595*
Fax: Admissions ■ *TF:* 800-652-3357 ■ *Web:* www.delmar.edu

Navarro College 3200 W Seventh Ave .... Corsicana TX 75110 903-874-6501 875-7353*
Fax: Admissions ■ *TF:* 800-628-2776 ■ *Web:* www.navarrocollege.edu

El Centro College 801 Main St .... Dallas TX 75202 214-860-2037 860-2233*
Fax: Admissions ■ *Web:* elcentrocollege.edu

Mountain View College 4849 W Illinois Ave .... Dallas TX 75211 214-860-8680 860-8570*
Fax: Admissions ■ *Web:* www.mountainviewcollege.edu/pages/default.aspx

Richland College 12800 Abrams Rd .... Dallas TX 75243 972-238-6100 238-6346*
Fax: Admissions ■ *Web:* richlandcollege.edu

Grayson County College 6101 Grayson Dr .... Denison TX 75020 903-465-6030 463-5284*
Fax: Admissions ■ *Web:* www.grayson.edu

El Paso Community College
Mission Del Paso 10700 Gateway E .... El Paso TX 79927 915-831-7017
Web: www.epcc.edu
Northwest 6701 S Desert Blvd .... El Paso TX 79932 915-831-8848
Web: www.epcc.edu
Valle Verde 919 Hunter Dr .... El Paso TX 79915 915-831-2000 831-2161*
Fax: Admissions ■ *TF:* 800-531-8292 ■ *Web:* www.epcc.edu

Brookhaven College 3939 Vly View Ln .... Farmers Branch TX 75244 972-860-4700 860-4886*
Fax: Admitting ■ *Web:* www.brookhavencollege.edu
Northwest 4801 Marine Creek Pkwy .... Fort Worth TX 76179 817-515-7100 515-7732*
Fax: Admissions ■ *TF:* 800-799-7233 ■ *Web:* www.tccd.edu
South 5301 Campus Dr .... Fort Worth TX 76119 817-515-8223 515-4110*
Fax: Admissions ■ *Web:* www.tccd.edu
Preston Ridge 9700 Wade Blvd .... Frisco TX 75035 972-377-1582 377-1723*
Fax: Admissions ■ *Web:* collin.edu

North Central Texas College
1525 W California St .... Gainesville TX 76240 940-668-7731 665-7075*
Fax: Admissions ■ *Web:* www.nctc.edu

Galveston College 4015 Ave Q .... Galveston TX 77550 409-763-6551 944-1501*
Fax: Admissions ■ *TF:* 866-483-4242 ■ *Web:* www.gc.edu
Harlingen 1902 N Loop 499 .... Harlingen TX 78550 956-364-4000 364-5117
TF: 800-852-8784 ■ *Web:* www.tstc.edu

Hill College 112 Lamar Dr PO Box 619 .... Hillsboro TX 76645 254-659-7500 582-7591*
Fax: Admissions ■ *Web:* www.hillcollege.edu

Houston Community College
Central College 1300 Holman .... Houston TX 77004 713-718-6000 718-7745
Web: central.hccs.edu
NortheastCollege 4638 Airline Dr .... Houston TX 77022 713-718-8100 718-7500
Web: www.hccs.edu

North Harris College 2700 WW Thorne Rd .... Houston TX 77073 281-618-5400 618-7141*
Fax: Admissions ■ *Web:* www.lonestar.edu
North 5800 Uvalde Rd .... Houston TX 77049 281-458-4050 459-7688*
Fax: Admissions ■ *Web:* www.sanjac.edu

Phone | Fax

South 13735 Beamer Rd ... Houston TX 77089 281-998-6150 922-3485
Web: www.sanjac.edu
Tarrant County College
Northeast 828 W Harwood Rd ... Hurst TX 76054 817-515-8223 515-6988*
**Fax:* Admissions ■ *TF:* 800-799-7233 ■
Web: www.tccd.edu/Campuses_and_Centers/Northeast_Campus.html
North Lake College 5001 N MacArthur Blvd ... Irving TX 75038 972-273-3000 273-3112*
**Fax:* Admissions ■ *Web:* www.northlakecollege.edu
Jacksonville College
105 BJ Albritton Dr ... Jacksonville TX 75766 903-586-2518 586-0743*
**Fax:* Admissions ■ *Web:* www.jacksonville-college.edu
Kilgore College 1100 Broadway ... Kilgore TX 75662 903-984-8531
Web: www.kilgore.edu
Central Texas College PO Box 1800 ... Killeen TX 76540 254-526-7161 526-1481
TF: 800-792-3348 ■ *Web:* www.online.ctcd.edu
Kingwood College 20000 Kingwood Dr ... Kingwood TX 77339 281-312-1600 312-1456
TF: 800-883-7939 ■ *Web:* www.lonestar.edu/kingwood.htm
Brazosport College 500 College Dr ... Lake Jackson TX 77566 979-230-3000 230-3443*
**Fax:* Admissions ■ *TF:* 877-717-7873 ■ *Web:* www.brazosport.edu
Cedar Valley College 3030 N Dallas Ave ... Lancaster TX 75134 972-860-8201
Web: www.dcccd.edu
Laredo Community College (LCC)
W End Washington St ... Laredo TX 78040 956-722-0521 721-5493
Web: www.laredo.edu
South Plains College 1401 S College Ave ... Levelland TX 79336 806-894-9611 897-3167*
**Fax:* Admissions ■ *Web:* www.southplainscollege.edu
Collin County Community College
Central Park 2200 W University Dr ... McKinney TX 75070 972-548-6790 548-6702*
**Fax:* Admissions ■ *Web:* collin.edu
Eastfield College 3737 Motley Dr ... Mesquite TX 75150 972-860-7100 860-8306
TF: 800-260-8000 ■ *Web:* eastfieldcollege.edu
Midland College 3600 N Garfield St ... Midland TX 79705 432-685-4500 685-6480*
**Fax:* Admissions ■ *TF:* 800-474-7164 ■ *Web:* www.midland.edu
Northeast Texas Community College
1735 Chapel Hill Rd ... Mount Pleasant TX 75455 903-572-1911 572-6712*
**Fax:* Admissions ■ *TF:* 800-870-0142 ■ *Web:* www.ntcc.edu
Odessa College 201 W University Blvd ... Odessa TX 79764 432-335-6400 335-6824
TF: 866-968-2862 ■ *Web:* www.odessa.edu
Lamar State College
Orange 410 Front St ... Orange TX 77630 409-883-7750 882-3055*
**Fax:* Admissions ■ *Web:* www.lsco.edu
Palestine PO Box 2530 ... Palestine TX 75802 903-729-0256 729-2325
TF: 866-882-2937 ■ *Web:* www.tvcc.edu
Paris Junior College 2400 Clarksville St ... Paris TX 75460 903-785-7661 782-0427*
**Fax:* Admissions ■ *TF:* 800-232-5804 ■ *Web:* www.parisjc.edu
San Jacinto College
Central 8060 Spencer Hwy ... Pasadena TX 77505 281-476-1501
Web: www.sanjac.edu
Spring Creek 2800 E Spring Creek Pkwy ... Plano TX 75074 972-881-5790 881-5174*
**Fax:* Admissions ■ *Web:* collin.edu
Port Arthur PO Box 310 ... Port Arthur TX 77641 409-983-4921 984-6025*
**Fax:* Admissions ■ *TF:* 800-477-5872 ■ *Web:* lamarpa.edu
Ranger College 1100 College Cir ... Ranger TX 76470 254-647-3234 647-3739*
**Fax:* Admissions ■ *TF:* 800-772-1213 ■ *Web:* www.rangercollege.edu
St. Mary's University San Antonio
1 Camino Santa Maria ... San Antonio TX 78228 210-436-3011
Web: www.rattlerbooks.com
Western Texas College 6200 College Ave ... Snyder TX 79549 325-573-8511 573-9321*
**Fax:* Admissions ■ *TF:* 888-468-6982 ■ *Web:* www.wtc.edu
Southwest College 9910 Cash Rd ... Stafford TX 77477 713-718-2000 718-7793
Web: southwest.hccs.edu
Sugar Land 14004 University Blvd ... Sugar Land TX 77479 281-243-8447 243-8583
TF: 800-561-9252 ■ *Web:* www.wcjc.edu
Sweetwater 300 Homer K Taylor Dr ... Sweetwater TX 79556 325-235-7300 235-7443
TF: 877-450-3595 ■ *Web:* www.tstc.edu
Temple College 2600 S First St ... Temple TX 76504 254-298-8300 298-8288*
**Fax:* Admissions ■ *TF Admissions:* 800-460-4636 ■ *Web:* www.templejc.edu
Texarkana College 2500 N Robison Rd ... Texarkana TX 75599 903-838-4541 832-5030*
**Fax:* Admissions ■ *TF:* 877-275-4377 ■ *Web:* www.texarkanacollege.edu
College of the Mainland 1200 N Amburn Rd ... Texas City TX 77591 409-938-1211
Web: www.com.edu
Tomball College 30555 Tomball Pkwy ... Tomball TX 77375 281-351-3300 351-3384*
**Fax:* Admissions ■ *Web:* www.lonestar.edu
Tyler Junior College PO Box 9020 ... Tyler TX 75711 903-510-2523 510-2161*
**Fax:* Admissions ■ *TF:* 800-687-5680 ■ *Web:* www.tjc.edu
Southwest Texas Junior College
2401 Garner Field Rd ... Uvalde TX 78801 830-278-4401 591-7396*
**Fax:* Admissions ■ *TF:* 888-886-8490 ■ *Web:* www.swtjc.net
Vernon College 4400 College Dr ... Vernon TX 76384 940-552-6291 553-1753
TF: 866-336-9371 ■ *Web:* www.vernoncollege.edu
Victoria College 2200 E Red River St ... Victoria TX 77901 361-573-3291 582-2525
Web: www.vc.cc.tx.us
McLennan Community College 1400 College Dr ... Waco TX 76708 254-299-8000 299-8694*
**Fax:* Admissions ■ *TF:* 866-339-5555 ■ *Web:* www.mclennan.edu
Waco 3801 Campus Dr ... Waco TX 76705 254-799-3611 867-3044
TF: 800-792-8784 ■ *Web:* www.waco.tstc.edu
Weatherford College 225 College Pk Dr ... Weatherford TX 76086 817-594-5471 598-6205*
**Fax:* Admissions ■ *TF:* 800-287-5471 ■ *Web:* www.wc.edu
Wharton County Junior College 911 Boling Hwy ... Wharton TX 77488 979-532-4560 532-6494*
**Fax:* Admissions ■ *TF:* 800-561-9252 ■ *Web:* www.wcjc.edu

Utah

Phone | Fax

San Juan 639 West 100 South ... Blanding UT 84511 435-678-2201 678-2220*
**Fax:* Admissions ■ *TF:* 800-395-2969 ■ *Web:* usueastern.edu
Snow College 150 College Ave PO Box 1037 ... Ephraim UT 84627 435-283-7000 283-7157*
**Fax:* Admissions ■ *TF:* 800-848-3399 ■ *Web:* www.snow.edu
Stevens Henager College 1890 South 1350 West ... Ogden UT 84401 800-622-2640 621-0853*
**Fax Area Code:* 801 ■ *TF:* 800-622-2640 ■ *Web:* www.stevenshenager.edu
Utah Valley State College 800 W University Pkwy ... Orem UT 84058 801-863-4636
TF: 800-952-8220 ■ *Web:* www.uvu.edu
College of Eastern Utah 451 E 400 N ... Price UT 84501 435-613-5000 613-5814*
**Fax:* Admissions ■ *TF:* 800-336-2381 ■ *Web:* usueastern.edu
Salt Lake Community College
Redwood 4600 S Redwood Rd ... Salt Lake City UT 84130 801-957-4111 957-4444
Web: www.slcc.edu
South City 1575 S State St ... Salt Lake City UT 84115 801-957-4111
Web: www.slcc.edu

Vermont

Phone | Fax

Community College of Vermont
Bennington 324 Main St ... Bennington VT 05201 802-447-2361 447-3246*
**Fax:* Admissions ■ *TF:* 800-431-0025 ■
Web: ccv.edu/event/bennington-center-2014-graduation-celebration
Brattleboro 70 Landmark Hill Ste 101 ... Brattleboro VT 05301 802-254-6370 257-2593
TF: 800-431-0025 ■
Web: ccv.edu/documents/2014/07/brattleboro-parking.pdf
Middlebury 10 Merchants Row Ste 223 ... Middlebury VT 05753 802-388-3032 388-4686*
**Fax:* Admissions ■ *TF:* 800-431-0025 ■ *Web:* www.ccv.edu
Montpelier PO Box 489 ... Montpelier VT 05602 802-828-4060
TF: 800-228-6686 ■ *Web:* www.ccv.edu
Morrisville 197 Harrell St Ste 2 ... Morrisville VT 05661 802-888-4258 888-2554*
**Fax:* Admissions ■ *TF:* 800-431-0025 ■ *Web:* www.ccv.edu
Newport 100 Main St Ste 150 ... Newport VT 05855 802-334-3387 334-5373*
**Fax:* Admissions ■ *TF:* 800-431-0025 ■ *Web:* ccv.edu/event/newport-open-house
Landmark College 1 River Rd S ... Putney VT 05346 802-387-6718
Web: landmark.edu
Rutland 60 W St ... Rutland VT 05701 802-786-6996 786-4980*
**Fax:* Admissions ■ *TF:* 800-228-6686 ■ *Web:* www.ccv.edu
Saint Albans 142 S Main St Ste 2 ... Saint Albans VT 05478 802-524-6541 524-5216*
**Fax:* Admissions ■ *Web:* www.ccv.edu
Saint Johnsbury 1197 Main St Ste 3 ... Saint Johnsbury VT 05819 802-748-6673 748-5014*
**Fax:* Admissions ■ *Web:* www.ccv.edu
Springfield 307 S St ... Springfield VT 05156 802-885-8360 885-8373
Web: www.ccv.edu
Upper Valley
145 Billings Farm Rd ... White River Junction VT 05001 802-295-8822 295-8862*
**Fax:* Admissions ■ *TF:* 800-431-0025 ■ *Web:* www.ccv.edu

Virginia

Phone | Fax

Virginia Highlands Community College
100 VHCC Dr PO Box 828 ... Abingdon VA 24212 276-739-2400
Web: www.vhcc.edu
Southside Virginia Community College
109 Campus Dr ... Alberta VA 23821 434-949-1000 949-7863
TF: 888-220-7822 ■ *Web:* www.southside.edu
Northern Virginia Community College
Alexandria 3001 N Beauregard St ... Alexandria VA 22311 703-845-6200 845-6046*
**Fax:* Admissions ■ *TF:* 855-259-1019 ■ *Web:* www.nvcc.edu
Annandale 8333 Little River Tpke ... Annandale VA 22003 703-323-3000
TF: 877-408-2028 ■ *Web:* www.nvcc.edu
Mountain Empire Community College
3441 Mtn Empire Rd ... Big Stone Gap VA 24219 276-523-2400 523-8297*
**Fax:* Admissions ■ *Web:* www.me.cc.va.us
Southwest Virginia Community College
724 Community College Rd ... Cedar Bluff VA 24609 276-964-2555 964-7716*
**Fax:* Admissions ■ *TF:* 855-877-3944 ■ *Web:* www.sw.edu
Piedmont Virginia Community College
501 College Dr ... Charlottesville VA 22902 434-977-3900 961-5425*
**Fax:* Admissions ■ *Web:* www.pvcc.edu
Tidewater Community College
Chesapeake 1428 Cedar Rd ... Chesapeake VA 23322 757-822-5100 822-5122
TF: 800-371-0898 ■ *Web:* www.tcc.edu
John Tyler Community College
13101 Jefferson Davis Hwy ... Chester VA 23831 804-796-4000 796-4362*
**Fax:* Admissions ■ *Web:* www.jtcc.edu
Dabney S Lancaster Community College
1000 Dabney Dr PO Box 1000 ... Clifton Forge VA 24422 540-863-2800 863-2915
TF: 887-773-7522 ■ *Web:* dslcc.edu
Danville Community College 1008 S Main St ... Danville VA 24541 434-797-2222 797-8541*
**Fax:* Admissions ■ *TF:* 800-560-4291 ■ *Web:* www.dcc.vccs.edu
New River Community College
5251 College PO Box 1127 ... Dublin VA 24084 540-674-3600 674-3644*
**Fax:* Admissions ■ *TF:* 866-462-6722 ■ *Web:* www.nr.edu
Paul D Camp Community College
100 N College Dr PO Box 737 ... Franklin VA 23851 757-569-6700 569-6795*
**Fax:* Admissions ■ *TF:* 855-877-3918 ■ *Web:* www.pdc.edu
Germanna Community College
Fredericksburg 10000 Germanna Pt Dr ... Fredericksburg VA 22408 540-891-3000 710-2092*
**Fax:* Admissions ■ *Web:* www.germanna.edu
Rappahannock Community College
Glenns 12745 College Dr ... Glenns VA 23149 804-758-6700 758-6830*
**Fax:* Admissions ■ *TF:* 800-836-9381 ■ *Web:* www.rappahannock.edu
Blue Ridge Community College Harrisonburg
160 N Mason St ... Harrisonburg VA 22802 540-432-3690
Web: www.brcc.edu
Locust Grove 2130 Germanna Hwy ... Locust Grove VA 22508 540-423-9030 727-3207
Web: www.germanna.edu
Central Virginia Community College
3506 WaRds Rd ... Lynchburg VA 24502 434-832-7600 832-7793*
**Fax:* Admissions ■ *Web:* cvcc.vccs.edu
Manassas 6901 Sudley Rd ... Manassas VA 20109 703-257-6600 257-6565*
**Fax:* Admitting ■ *TF:* 855-259-1019 ■ *Web:* www.nvcc.edu
Patrick Henry Community College
645 Patriot Ave PO Box 5311 ... Martinsville VA 24112 276-638-8777 656-0352*
**Fax:* Admissions ■ *TF:* 855-874-6692 ■ *Web:* www.ph.vccs.edu
Eastern Shore Community College
29300 Lankford Hwy ... Melfa VA 23410 757-789-1789 789-1737*
**Fax:* Admissions ■ *Web:* www.es.vccs.edu

	Phone	Fax
Middletown 173 Skirmisher Ln ... Middletown VA 22645 **Fax:* Admissions ■ *TF:* 800-906-5322 ■ *Web:* www.lfcc.edu	540-868-7000	868-7005*
Norfolk 121 College Pl. ... Norfolk VA 23510 *TF:* 800-371-0898 ■ *Web:* www.tcc.edu/welcome/locations/norfolk	757-822-1110	
Richard Bland College 11301 Johnson Rd ... Petersburg VA 23805 **Fax:* Admissions ■ *Web:* www.rbc.edu	804-862-6100	862-6490*
Portsmouth 7000 College Dr ... Portsmouth VA 23703 **Fax:* Admissions ■ *TF:* 800-371-0898 ■ *Web:* www.tcc.edu	757-822-2124	822-2002*
J Sargeant Reynolds Community College PO Box 85622 ... Richmond VA 23285 **Fax:* Admissions ■ *Web:* www.reynolds.edu	804-371-3000	371-3650*
Downtown 700 E Jackson St ... Richmond VA 23219 *Web:* www.jsr.vccs.edu	804-523-5455	371-3650
Virginia Western Community College 3094 Colonial Ave PO Box 14007 ... Roanoke VA 24038 **Fax:* Admissions ■ *TF:* 855-874-6690 ■ *Web:* www.virginiawestern.edu	540-857-8922	857-6102*
Hobbs Suffolk 271 Kenyon Rd ... Suffolk VA 23434 **Fax:* Admissions ■ *TF:* 855-877-3918 ■ *Web:* pdc.edu/about/hobbs-suffolk-campus	757-925-6300	925-6370*
Virginia Beach 1700 College Crescent ... Virginia Beach VA 23453 *TF:* 800-371-0898 ■ *Web:* www.tcc.edu	757-822-7100	822-7350
Lord Fairfax Community College *Fauquier* 6480 College St ... Warrenton VA 20187 **Fax:* Admissions ■ *Web:* www.lfcc.edu	540-351-1505	351-1530*
Warsaw 52 Campus Dr ... Warsaw VA 22572 **Fax:* Admissions ■ *TF:* 800-836-9381 ■ *Web:* www.rappahannock.edu	804-333-6700	333-0106*
Wytheville Community College 1000 E Main St ... Wytheville VA 24382 **Fax:* Admissions ■ *Web:* www.wcc.vccs.edu	276-223-4700	223-4860*

Washington

	Phone	Fax
Grays Harbor College 1620 Edward P Smith Dr ... Aberdeen WA 98520 **Fax:* Admissions ■ *TF:* 800-562-4830 ■ *Web:* www.ghc.edu	360-532-9020	538-4293*
Green River Community College 12401 SE 320th St ... Auburn WA 98092 **Fax:* Admissions ■ *Web:* www.greenriver.edu	253-833-9111	288-3454*
Bellevue Community College 3000 Landerholm Cir SE ... Bellevue WA 98007 **Fax:* Admissions ■ *Web:* www.bellevuecollege.edu	425-564-1000	564-4065*
Northwest Indian College 2522 Kwina Rd ... Bellingham WA 98226 **Fax:* Admissions ■ *TF:* 866-676-2772 ■ *Web:* www.nwic.edu	360-676-2772	392-4333*
Whatcom Community College 237 W Kellogg Rd ... Bellingham WA 98226 *TF:* 855-767-9003 ■ *Web:* www.whatcom.ctc.edu	360-676-2170	676-2171
Olympic College 1600 Chester Ave ... Bremerton WA 98337 **Fax:* Admissions ■ *TF:* 800-259-6718 ■ *Web:* www.olympic.edu	360-792-6050	475-7202*
Centralia College 600 W Locust St ... Centralia WA 98531 **Fax:* Admissions ■ *Web:* www.centralia.edu	360-736-9391	330-7503*
Everett Community College 2000 Tower St ... Everett WA 98201 **Fax:* Admissions ■ *TF:* 866-575-9027 ■ *Web:* www.everettcc.edu	425-388-9100	388-9129*
Grandview 500 W Main St ... Grandview WA 98930 *Web:* www.yvcc.edu	509-882-7000	882-7012
Clover Park Technical College 4500 Steilacoom Blvd SW ... Lakewood WA 98499 *Web:* www.cptc.edu	253-589-5800	
Pierce College 9401 Farwest Dr SW ... Lakewood WA 98498 **Fax:* Admissions ■ *Web:* www.pierce.ctc.edu	253-964-6500	964-6427*
Lower Columbia College 1600 Maple St PO Box 3010 ... Longview WA 98632 **Fax:* Admissions ■ *TF:* 866-900-2311 ■ *Web:* www.lowercolumbia.edu	360-442-2301	442-2379*
Edmonds Community College 20000 68th Ave W ... Lynnwood WA 98036 *TF:* 866-886-4854 ■ *Web:* www.edcc.edu	425-640-1500	640-1159
Big Bend Community College 7662 Chanute St ... Moses Lake WA 98837 **Fax:* Admissions ■ *TF:* 877-745-1212 ■ *Web:* www.bigbend.edu	509-793-2222	762-6243*
Skagit Valley College 2405 E College Way ... Mount Vernon WA 98273 **Fax:* Admissions ■ *TF:* 877-385-5360 ■ *Web:* www.skagit.edu	360-416-7600	416-7890*
South Puget Sound Community College 2011 Mottman Rd SW ... Olympia WA 98512 **Fax:* Admissions ■ *Web:* spscc.edu	360-754-7711	596-5709*
Omak 116 W Apple Ave PO Box 2058 ... Omak WA 98841 **Fax:* Admissions ■ *Web:* www.wvc.edu	509-422-7803	422-7801*
Columbia Basin College 2600 N 20th Ave ... Pasco WA 99301 *Web:* www.columbiabasin.edu	509-547-0511	546-0401
Peninsula College 1502 E Lauridsen Blvd ... Port Angeles WA 98362 **Fax:* Admissions ■ *Web:* www.pc.ctc.edu	360-452-9277	417-6581*
Puyallup 1601 39th Ave SE ... Puyallup WA 98374 **Fax:* Admissions ■ *TF:* 877-353-6763 ■ *Web:* www.pierce.ctc.edu	253-840-8400	840-8449*
Renton Technical College 3000 NE Fourth St ... Renton WA 98056 *Web:* www.rtc.edu	425-235-2352	235-7832
North Seattle Community College 9600 College Way N ... Seattle WA 98103 *TF:* 866-427-4747 ■ *Web:* www.northseattle.edu	206-527-3600	527-3671
South Seattle Community College 6000 16th Ave SW ... Seattle WA 98106 *Web:* www.southseattle.edu	206-764-5300	764-7947
Shelton 937 W Alpine Way ... Shelton WA 98584 **Fax:* Admissions ■ *TF:* 800-259-6718 ■ *Web:* www.olympic.edu	360-427-2119	432-5412*
Shoreline Community College 16101 Greenwood Ave N ... Shoreline WA 98133 *TF:* 866-427-4747 ■ *Web:* www.shoreline.edu	206-546-4101	546-5835
Spokane Community College 1810 N Greene St ... Spokane WA 99217 *TF:* 800-248-5644 ■ *Web:* www.scc.spokane.edu	509-533-7000	533-8181
Spokane Falls Community College 3410 W Ft George Wright Dr ... Spokane WA 99224 **Fax:* Admissions ■ *TF:* 888-509-7944 ■ *Web:* www.spokanefalls.edu	509-533-3500	533-3237*
Bates Technical College 1101 S Yakima Ave ... Tacoma WA 98405 **Fax:* Admissions ■ *Web:* www.bates.ctc.edu	253-680-7000	680-7001*
Tacoma Community College 6501 S 19th St ... Tacoma WA 98466 **Fax:* Admissions ■ *Web:* www.tacomacc.edu	253-566-5000	566-6011*
Clark College 1800 E McLoughlin Blvd ... Vancouver WA 98663 **Fax:* Admissions ■ *Web:* www.clark.edu	360-992-2000	992-2876*
Walla Walla Community College 500 Tausick Way ... Walla Walla WA 99362 **Fax:* Admissions ■ *TF:* 877-992-9922 ■ *Web:* www.wwcc.edu	509-522-2500	527-3661*
Wenatchee Valley College 1300 Fifth St ... Wenatchee WA 98801 **Fax:* Admissions ■ *TF:* 877-982-4968 ■ *Web:* www.wvc.edu	509-682-6800	682-6801*
Perry Technical Institute 2011 W Washington Ave ... Yakima WA 98903 *TF:* 888-528-8586 ■ *Web:* www.perrytech.edu	509-453-0374	
Yakima Valley Community College South 16th Ave & Nob Hill Blvd ... Yakima WA 98902 *Web:* www.yvcc.edu	509-574-4600	574-4649

West Virginia

	Phone	Fax
Potomac State College 101 Ft Ave ... Keyser WV 26726 **Fax:* Admissions ■ *TF:* 800-262-7332 ■ *Web:* www.potomacstatecollege.edu	304-788-6800	788-6939*
Eastern West Virginia Community & Technical College 316 Eastern Dr ... Moorefield WV 26836 *TF:* 877-982-2322 ■ *Web:* www.easternwv.edu	304-434-8000	434-7000
West Virginia University PO Box 6009 ... Morgantown WV 26506 *TF:* 800-344-9881 ■ *Web:* www.wvu.edu	304-293-2121	293-3080
Southern West Virginia Community & Technical College *Logan* 2900 Dempsey Branch Rd PO Box 2900 ... Mount Gay WV 25637 **Fax:* Admissions ■ *Web:* www.southernwv.edu	304-792-7098	792-7028*
Parkersburg 300 Campus Dr ... Parkersburg WV 26104 *TF:* 800-982-9887 ■ *Web:* www.wvup.edu	304-424-8000	424-8315
West Virginia Northern Community College 1704 Market St ... Wheeling WV 26003 *Web:* wvncc.edu	304-233-5900	232-8187

Wisconsin

	Phone	Fax
University of Wisconsin *Baraboo/Sauk County* 1006 Connie Rd ... Baraboo WI 53913 **Fax:* Admissions ■ *TF:* 800-621-7440 ■ *Web:* www.baraboo.uwc.edu	608-355-5200	355-5291*
Fond du Lac 400 University Dr ... Fond du Lac WI 54935 *Web:* www.fdl.uwc.edu	920-929-3600	
Lac Courte Oreilles Ojibwa Community College 13466 W Trepania Rd ... Hayward WI 54843 **Fax:* Admissions ■ *TF:* 888-526-6221 ■ *Web:* www.lco.edu	715-634-4790	634-5049*
Rock County 2909 Kellogg Ave ... Janesville WI 53546 *Web:* www.rock.uwc.edu	608-758-6523	758-6579
College of Menominee Nation PO Box 1179 ... Keshena WI 54135 **Fax:* Admissions ■ *TF:* 800-567-2344 ■ *Web:* www.menominee.edu	715-799-5600	799-4392*
Manitowoc 705 Viebahn St ... Manitowoc WI 54220 *TF:* 800-657-3866 ■ *Web:* www.manitowoc.uwc.edu	920-683-4700	683-4776
Marinette 750 W Bay Shore St ... Marinette WI 54143 **Fax:* Admissions ■ *Web:* www.marinette.uwc.edu	715-735-4300	735-4304*
Marshfield/Wood County 2000 W Fifth St ... Marshfield WI 54449 *TF:* 800-273-8255 ■ *Web:* www.marshfield.uwc.edu	715-389-6530	384-1718
Fox Valley 1478 Midway Rd ... Menasha WI 54952 *TF:* 800-273-8255 ■ *Web:* www.uwfox.uwc.edu	920-832-2600	832-2674
Barron County 1800 College Dr ... Rice Lake WI 54868 *TF:* 800-608-4578 ■ *Web:* www.barron.uwc.edu	715-234-8176	234-1975
Richland 1200 Hwy 14 W ... Richland Center WI 53581 **Fax:* Admissions ■ *TF:* 800-947-3529 ■ *Web:* richland.uwc.edu	608-647-6186	647-2275*
Sheboygan 1 University Dr ... Sheboygan WI 53081 **Fax:* Admissions ■ *Web:* sheboygan.uwc.edu	920-459-6600	459-6602*
Waukesha 1500 N University Dr ... Waukesha WI 53188 **Fax:* Admissions ■ *Web:* waukesha.uwc.edu	262-521-5200	521-5491*
Marathon County 518 S Seventh Ave ... Wausau WI 54401 *TF:* 888-367-8962 ■ *Web:* www.uwmc.uwc.edu	715-261-6100	261-6331
Washington County 400 S University Dr ... West Bend WI 53095 *TF:* 800-240-0276 ■ *Web:* washington.uwc.edu	262-335-5200	335-5220

Wyoming

	Phone	Fax
Casper College 125 College Dr ... Casper WY 82601 **Fax:* Admissions ■ *TF:* 800-442-2963 ■ *Web:* www.caspercollege.edu	307-268-2100	268-2611*
Laramie County Community College 1400 E College Dr ... Cheyenne WY 82007 **Fax:* Admissions ■ *TF:* 800-522-2993 ■ *Web:* www.lccc.cc.wy.us	307-778-5222	778-1350*
Gillette 300 W Sinclair St ... Gillette WY 82718 *TF:* 800-913-9139 ■ *Web:* www.sheridan.edu	307-686-0254	
Albany County 1125 Boulder Dr ... Laramie WY 82070 *TF:* 800-522-2993 ■ *Web:* www.lccc.wy.edu	307-721-5138	772-4266
Northwest College 231 W Sixth St ... Powell WY 82435 **Fax:* Admissions ■ *TF:* 800-560-4692 ■ *Web:* www.northwestcollege.edu	307-754-6000	754-6249*
Central Wyoming College 2660 Peck Ave ... Riverton WY 82501 *TF:* 800-735-8418 ■ *Web:* www.cwc.edu	307-855-2000	855-2092
Western Wyoming Community College 2500 College Dr ... Rock Springs WY 82901 **Fax:* Admissions ■ *TF:* 800-226-1181 ■ *Web:* www.wwcc.wy.edu	307-382-1600	382-1636*
Sheridan College 3059 Coffeen Ave PO Box 1500 ... Sheridan WY 82801 *TF:* 800-913-9139 ■ *Web:* www.sheridan.edu	307-674-6446	674-7205
Eastern Wyoming College 3200 W 'C' St ... Torrington WY 82240 **Fax:* Admissions ■ *TF:* 800-658-3195 ■ *Web:* new.ewc.wy.edu	307-532-8200	532-8222*

163 COLLEGES - CULINARY ARTS

	Phone	Fax
Arizona Culinary Institute 10585 N 114th St Ste 401 ... Scottsdale AZ 85259 *TF:* 866-294-2433 ■ *Web:* www.azculinary.edu	480-603-1066	603-1067

Phone | Fax

Baltimore International College
17 Commerce St. . . . . Baltimore MD 21202 410-752-4710 752-3730*
*Fax: Admissions ■ TF: 800-624-9926 ■ Web: www.stratford.edu

Cambridge School of Culinary Arts
2020 Massachusetts Ave . . . . Cambridge MA 02140 617-354-2020 576-1963
Web: www.cambridgeculinary.com

Capital Culinary Institute of Keiser College
Melbourne 900 S Babcock St. . . . . Melbourne FL 32901 321-409-4800 725-3766
TF: 877-636-3618 ■ Web: www.keiseruniversity.edu/melbourne

Cascade Culinary Institute 2600 NW College Way . . . . Bend OR 97701 541-383-7700
Web: www.cocc.edu

Chef John Folse Culinary Institute
PO Box 2099 . . . . Thibodaux LA 70310 985-449-7100
Web: www.nicholls.edu

Cook Street School of Fine Cooking
1937 Market St. . . . . Denver CO 80202 303-308-9300 308-9400
Web: www.cookstreet.com

Cooking & Hospitality Institute of Chicago
361 W Chestnut St . . . . Chicago IL 60610 312-944-0882 944-8557
TF Admissions: 877-828-7772 ■ Web: www.chefs.edu

Culinard-the Culinary Institute of Virginia College
436 Palisades Blvd. . . . . Birmingham AL 35209 205-802-1200
Web: www.culinard.com

Culinary Institute Alain & Marie LeNotre
7070 Allensby. . . . . Houston TX 77022 713-692-0077 692-7399
TF: 888-536-6873 ■ Web: www.culinaryinstitute.edu

Culinary Institute of America
1946 Campus Dr . . . . Hyde Park NY 12538 845-452-9430 451-1068
TF Admissions: 800-285-4627 ■ Web: www.ciachef.edu

Culinary Institute of America at Greystone
2555 Main St . . . . Saint Helena CA 94574 707-967-1100
Web: www.ciachef.edu

Culinary Institute of Charleston
7000 Rivers Ave . . . . Charleston SC 29406 843-574-6111
TF: 877-349-7184 ■ Web: www.tridenttech.edu

French Culinary Institute 462 Broadway . . . . New York NY 10013 888-324-2433
TF: 888-324-2433 ■ Web: www.internationalculinarycenter.com

Institute of Culinary Education
50 W 23rd St . . . . New York NY 10010 212-847-0700 847-0723
TF: 800-522-4610 ■ Web: www.ice.edu

JNA Institute of Culinary Arts
1212 S Broad St . . . . Philadelphia PA 19146 215-468-8800 468-8838
Web: www.culinaryarts.com

Kendall College 900 N North Branch St . . . . Chicago IL 60622 312-752-2000
TF: 888-905-3632 ■ Web: www.kendall.edu

Kitchen Academy 6370 W Sunset Blvd . . . . Hollywood CA 90028 866-548-2223
TF: 866-548-2223 ■ Web: www.chefs.edu

L'Academie de Cuisine Inc
16006 Industrial Dr. . . . . Gaithersburg MD 20877 301-670-8670 670-0450
TF: 800-664-2433 ■ Web: www.lacademie.com

Le Cordon Bleu College of Culinary Arts
Atlanta 1927 Lakeside Pkwy. . . . . Tucker GA 30084 770-938-4711
TF: 888-549-8222 ■ Web: www.chefs.edu
Las Vegas 1451 Ctr Crossing Rd. . . . . Las Vegas NV 89144 702-365-7690 365-7911
TF: 888-551-8222 ■ Web: www.chefs.edu
Suffield 8 PROGRESS DR . . . . Shelton CT 06484 203-929-0592
TF: 800-254-0547 ■ Web: www.lincolntech.edu

Louisiana Culinary Institute
10550 Airline Hwy . . . . Baton Rouge LA 70816 877-533-3198 769-8792*
*Fax Area Code: 225 ■ TF: 877-533-3198 ■ Web: lci.edu

New England Culinary Institute
56 College St . . . . Montpelier VT 05602 802-223-6324 225-3280
TF: 877-223-6324 ■ Web: www.neci.edu

Restaurant School at Walnut Hill College
4207 Walnut St. . . . . Philadelphia PA 19104 215-222-4200
TF: 877-925-6884 ■ Web: www.walnuthillcollege.edu

Robert Morris University Institute of Culinary Arts
401 S State St. . . . . Chicago IL 60605 312-935-4100 935-4182*
*Fax: Admissions ■ TF: 800-762-5960 ■ Web: www.robertmorris.edu/culinary

San Diego Culinary Institute (SDCI)
8024 La Mesa Blvd. . . . . La Mesa CA 91941 619-644-2100 644-2106
Web: sandiegoculinary.edu

Sclafani's Cooking School Inc
107 Gennaro Pl. . . . . Metairie LA 70005 504-833-7861
Web: www.sclafanicookingschool.com

Scottsdale Culinary Institute
8100 E Camelback Rd Ste 1001 . . . . Scottsdale AZ 85251 480-990-3773 990-0351
TF: 888-557-4222 ■ Web: www.chefs.edu

Star Career Academy 125 Michael Dr. . . . . Syosset NY 11791 516-364-4344 275-0549*
*Fax Area Code: 202 ■ Web: starcareer.edu
Manhattan 154 W 14th St . . . . New York NY 10011 212-675-6655
Web: starcareer.edu

Stratford University School of Culinary Arts
7777 Leesburg Pk. . . . . Falls Church VA 22043 703-821-8570 734-5339
TF: 800-444-0804 ■ Web: www.stratford.edu/?page=home_culinary

Tante Marie's Cooking School
271 Francisco St. . . . . San Francisco CA 94133 415-788-6699
Web: www.tantemarie.com

164 COLLEGES - FINE ARTS

See Also Colleges & Universities - Four-Year p. 1968; Vocational & Technical Schools p. 3297

Phone | Fax

American Academy of Art
332 S Michigan Ave 3rd Fl. . . . . Chicago IL 60604 312-461-0600 294-9570
TF: 888-461-0600 ■ Web: www.aaart.edu

American Academy of Dramatic Arts
120 Madison Ave . . . . New York NY 10016 212-686-9244
TF: 800-463-8990 ■ Web: aada.edu

Antonelli Institute 300 Montgomery Ave. . . . . Erdenheim PA 19038 215-836-2222 836-2794
TF: 800-722-7871 ■ Web: www.antonelli.edu

Art Academy of Cincinnati 1212 Jackson St . . . . Cincinnati OH 45202 513-562-6262 562-8778
TF: 800-323-5692 ■ Web: www.artacademy.edu

Art Ctr College of Design 1700 Lida St. . . . . Pasadena CA 91103 626-396-2200 795-0578
Web: www.artcenter.edu

Art Institute of Atlanta
6600 Peachtree Dunwoody Rd NE
100 Embassy Row . . . . Atlanta GA 30328 770-394-8300 394-0008
TF: 800-275-4242 ■ Web: www.artinstitutes.edu/atlanta

Art Institute of Boston at Lesley (AIB)
29 Everett St . . . . Cambridge MA 22138 617-585-6600
TF: 800-773-0494 ■ Web: www.lesley.edu

Art Institute of California
Inland Empire 674 E Brier Dr . . . . San Bernardino CA 92408 909-915-2100
TF: 800-353-0812 ■ Web: www.artinstitutes.edu/inland-empire
Los Angeles 2900 31st St . . . . Santa Monica CA 90405 310-752-4700 752-4708
TF: 888-646-4610 ■ Web: www.artinstitutes.edu/los-angeles
Orange County 3601 W Sunflower Ave . . . . Santa Ana CA 92704 714-830-0200 556-1923
Web: www.artinstitutes.edu
San Diego 7650 Mission Valley Rd . . . . San Diego CA 92108 858-598-1200 291-3206*
*Fax Area Code: 619 ■ TF: 888-624-0300 ■ Web: www.artinstitutes.edu/san-diego
San Francisco 1170 Market St. . . . . San Francisco CA 94102 415-865-0198 863-6344
TF: 888-493-3261 ■ Web: www.artinstitutes.edu/san-francisco

Art Institute of Charlotte
3 Lake Pointe Plz 3 LakePointe Plz. . . . . Charlotte NC 28217 704-357-8020 357-1133
TF: 800-872-4417 ■ Web: www.artinstitutes.edu

Art Institute of Colorado 1200 Lincoln St. . . . . Denver CO 80203 303-837-0825
TF: 800-275-2420 ■ Web: www.artinstitutes.edu/denver

Art Institute of Dallas 8080 Pk Ln Ste 100 . . . . Dallas TX 75231 214-692-8080 275-4243*
*Fax Area Code: 800 ■ TF: 800-275-4243 ■ Web: www.artinstitutes.edu

Art Institute of Fort Lauderdale
1799 SE 17th St . . . . Fort Lauderdale FL 33316 954-463-3000 728-8637
TF: 800-275-7603 ■ Web: www.artinstitutes.edu/fort-lauderdale

Art Institute of Houston 1900 Yorktown St. . . . . Houston TX 77056 713-623-2040 966-2700
TF: 800-275-4244 ■ Web: www.artinstitutes.edu

Art Institute of Indianapolis
3500 Depauw Blvd . . . . Indianapolis IN 46268 317-613-4800 613-4808
TF: 866-441-9031 ■ Web: www.artinstitutes.edu

Art Institute of Las Vegas
2350 Corporate Cir. . . . . Henderson NV 89074 702-369-9944 992-8458
TF: 800-833-2678 ■ Web: www.artinstitutes.edu

Art Institute of New York City
218-232 W 40th St. . . . . New York NY 10018 212-226-5500 625-6065
Web: www.artinstitutes.edu/new-york

Art Institute of Ohio
Cincinnati 8845 Covernor's Hill Dr Ste 100. . . . . . . Cincinnati OH 45249 513-833-2400 833-2411
TF: 866-613-5184 ■ Web: www.artinstitutes.edu

Art Institute of Philadelphia
1622 Chestnut St . . . . Philadelphia PA 19103 215-567-7080 405-6398
TF: 800-275-2474 ■ Web: www.artinstitutes.edu

Art Institute of Pittsburgh
420 Blvd of the Allies . . . . Pittsburgh PA 15219 412-263-6600 263-6667
TF: 800-275-2470 ■ Web: www.artinstitutes.edu

Art Institute of Portland 1122 NW Davis St . . . . Portland OR 97209 503-228-6528 227-1945*
*Fax: Admissions ■ TF: 888-228-6528 ■ Web: www.artinstitutes.edu

Art Institute of Seattle 2323 Elliott Ave . . . . Seattle WA 98121 206-448-0900 448-2501
TF: 800-275-2471 ■ Web: www.artinstitutes.edu

Art Institute of Tampa 4401 N Himes Ave Ste 150. . . . . Tampa FL 33614 813-873-2112 873-2171
TF: 866-703-3277 ■ Web: www.artinstitutes.edu

Art Institute of Washington
1820 N Ft Myer Dr . . . . Arlington VA 22209 703-358-9550 358-9759
TF: 877-303-3771 ■ Web: www.artinstitutes.edu/arlington

Art Institutes , The 15 S Ninth St. . . . . Minneapolis MN 55402 612-332-3361 332-3934
TF: 800-777-3643 ■ Web: www.artinstitutes.edu

California College of the Arts
Oakland 5212 Broadway . . . . Oakland CA 94618 510-594-3600
TF: 800-447-1278 ■ Web: www.cca.edu
San Francisco 1111 Eigth St . . . . San Francisco CA 94107 415-703-9500 703-9539
TF: 800-447-1278 ■ Web: www.cca.edu

California Institute of the Arts
24700 McBean Pkwy . . . . Valencia CA 91355 661-255-1050 253-7710
TF: 800-545-2787 ■ Web: www.calarts.edu

Cleveland Institute of Art 11141 E Blvd. . . . . Cleveland OH 44106 800-223-4700 754-3634*
*Fax Area Code: 216 ■ TF: 800-223-4700 ■ Web: www.cia.edu

Columbus College of Art & Design
60 Cleveland Ave . . . . Columbus OH 43215 614-224-9101 222-4040
TF: 877-997-2223 ■ Web: www.ccad.edu

Corcoran School of the Arts & Design
500 17th St NW . . . . Washington DC 20006 202-639-1800 639-1802
Web: corcoran.gwu.edu

Cornish College of the Arts 710 E Roy St . . . . Seattle WA 98121 206-323-1400 720-1011
TF: 800-726-2787 ■ Web: www.cornish.edu

Fashion Institute of Design & Merchandising
Los Angeles 919 S Grand Ave . . . . Los Angeles CA 90015 213-624-1200 624-4799
TF Admissions: 800-624-1200 ■ Web: fidm.edu
Orange County 17590 Gillette Ave. . . . . Irvine CA 92614 949-851-6200 851-6808
TF: 888-974-3436 ■ Web: fidm.edu
San Diego 350 Tenth Ave. . . . . San Diego CA 92101 619-235-2049 232-4322
TF: 800-243-3436 ■ Web: fidm.edu
San Francisco 55 Stockton St . . . . San Francisco CA 94108 415-675-5200 296-7299
TF: 800-422-3436 ■ Web: fidm.edu

Fashion Institute of Technology
227 W 27th St. . . . . New York NY 10001 212-217-7999
Web: www.fitnyc.edu

Florida School of the Arts 5001 St Johns Ave . . . . Palatka FL 32177 386-312-4300 312-4306
Web: floarts.org

Hussian School of Art
111 S Independence Mall E . . . . Philadelphia PA 19106 215-574-9600 574-9800
Web: www.hussianart.edu

Illinois Institute of Art
Chicago 350 N Orleans St Ste 136-L. . . . . Chicago IL 60654 312-280-3500 280-8562
TF: 800-351-3450 ■ Web: www.artinstitutes.edu
Schaumburg 1000 N Plz Dr . . . . Schaumburg IL 60173 847-619-3450 619-3064
TF: 800-314-3450 ■ Web: www.artinstitutes.edu

Institute of American Indian Arts (IAIA)
83 Avan Nu Po Rd . . . . Santa Fe NM 87508 505-424-2300 424-0505
TF: 800-804-6422 ■ Web: www.iaia.edu

				Phone	Fax
International Academy of Design & Technology					
Chicago 1 N State St Ste 500	Chicago	IL	60602	312-386-7681	
TF: 888-318-6111 ■ *Web:* www.iadt.edu					
Las Vegas 2495 Village View Dr	Henderson	NV	89074	702-990-0150	
TF: 866-400-4238 ■ *Web:* www.iadt.edu					
Kansas City Art Institute					
4415 Warwick Blvd	Kansas City	MO	64111	816-474-5224	802-3309
TF: 800-522-5224 ■ *Web:* www.kcai.edu					
Maine College of Art 522 Congress St	Portland	ME	04101	207-775-3052	772-5069
TF: 800-639-4808 ■ *Web:* www.meca.edu					
Maryland Institute College of Art					
1300 W Mt Royal Ave	Baltimore	MD	21217	410-669-9200	225-2337
Web: www.mica.edu					
Memphis College of Art 1930 Poplar Ave	Memphis	TN	38104	901-272-5100	272-5158
TF: 800-727-1088 ■ *Web:* www.mca.edu					
Miami International University of Art & Design					
1501 Biscayne Blvd	Miami	FL	33132	305-428-5700	374-5933
TF: 800-225-9023 ■ *Web:* www.artinstitutes.edu/miami					
Minneapolis College of Art & Design					
2501 Stevens Ave	Minneapolis	MN	55404	612-874-3760	874-3701
TF: 800-874-6223 ■ *Web:* www.mcad.edu					
Montclair Kimberley Academy, The					
201 Valley Rd	Montclair	NJ	07042	973-746-9800	
Web: www.mka.org					
Moore College of Art & Design					
20th St & the Pkwy	Philadelphia	PA	19103	215-965-4000	568-8017
TF: 800-523-2025 ■ *Web:* www.moore.edu					
New England Institute of Art					
10 Brookline Pl W	Brookline	MA	02445	617-582-4460	582-4500
TF: 800-903-4425 ■ *Web:* www.artinstitutes.edu					
New Hampshire Institute of Art					
148 Concord St	Manchester	NH	03104	603-623-0313	647-0658
TF: 866-241-4918 ■ *Web:* www.nhia.edu					
North Carolina School of the Arts					
1533 S Main St	Winston-Salem	NC	27127	336-770-3399	770-3370
Web: uncsa.edu					
Otis College of Art & Design					
9045 Lincoln Blvd	Los Angeles	CA	90045	310-665-6820	665-6821
TF: 800-527-6847 ■ *Web:* www.otis.edu					
Pennsylvania Academy of the Fine Arts					
School of Fine Arts 118 128 N Broad St	Philadelphia	PA	19102	215-972-7600	569-0153
TF: 800-799-7233 ■ *Web:* www.pafa.org					
Pennsylvania College of Art & Design					
204 N Prince St PO Box 59	Lancaster	PA	17608	717-396-7833	396-1339
Web: www.pcad.edu					
Rhode Island School of Design					
2 College St	Providence	RI	02903	401-454-6100	454-6309
TF: 800-364-7473 ■ *Web:* www.risd.edu					
Ringling College of Art & Design					
2700 N Tamiami Trl	Sarasota	FL	34234	941-351-5100	359-7517
TF: 800-255-7695 ■ *Web:* www.ringling.edu					
San Francisco Art Institute					
800 Chestnut St	San Francisco	CA	94133	415-771-7020	
TF: 800-345-7324 ■ *Web:* www.sfai.edu					
Savannah College of Art & Design					
342 Bull St PO Box 2072	Savannah	GA	31402	912-525-5100	525-5986
TF: 800-869-7223 ■ *Web:* www.scad.edu					
Atlanta 1600 Peachtree St PO Box 77300	Atlanta	GA	30357	404-253-2700	253-3466
TF: 877-722-3285 ■ *Web:* www.scad.edu					
School of Visual Arts 209 E 23rd St	New York	NY	10010	212-592-2000	592-2116
TF: 800-436-4204 ■ *Web:* www.sva.edu					
University of the Arts 320 S Broad St	Philadelphia	PA	19102	215-717-6049	717-6000
TF: 800-616-2787 ■ *Web:* www.uarts.edu					
Virginia Marti College of Art & Design					
11724 Detroit Ave	Lakewood	OH	44107	216-221-8584	221-2311
TF: 800-473-4350 ■ *Web:* vmcad.edu					
Watkins College of Art & Design					
2298 Rose Parks Blvd	Nashville	TN	37228	615-383-4848	383-4849
TF: 866-877-6395 ■ *Web:* watkins.edu					

165 COLLEGES - TRIBAL

See Also Colleges - Community & Junior p. 1950

Tribal Colleges generally serve geographically isolated American Indian populations that have no other means of accessing education beyond the high school level. They are unique institutions that combine personal attention with cultural relevance.

				Phone	Fax
Aaniiih Nakoda College					
269 Blackfeet Ave - Agency	Harlem	MT	59523	406-353-2607	353-2898*
**Fax:* Admissions ■ *Web:* ancollege.edu					
Anaheim University					
1240 S State College Blvd Rm 110	Anaheim	CA	92806	714-772-3330	
TF: 800-955-6040 ■ *Web:* www.anaheim.edu					
Ashland County West Holmes Career Center Jvs					
1783 State Rt 60	Ashland	OH	44805	419-289-3313	
Web: www.acwhcc-jvs.k12.oh.us					
Baker University 618 E Eighth St	Baldwin City	KS	66006	785-594-6451	
Web: www.bakeru.edu					
Bay Mills Community College					
12214 W Lakeshore Dr	Brimley	MI	49715	906-248-3354	248-3351
TF: 800-844-2622 ■ *Web:* www.bmcc.edu					
Briarcliffe College 1055 Stewart Ave	Bethpage	NY	11714	516-918-3600	
TF: 855-512-5333 ■ *Web:* www.briarcliffe.edu					
Buffalo Seminary 205 Bidwell Pkwy	Buffalo	NY	14222	716-885-6780	
Web: buffaloseminary.org					
Cankdeska Cikana Community College					
PO Box 269	Fort Totten	ND	58335	701-766-4415	766-4077
TF: 888-783-1463 ■ *Web:* www.littlehoop.edu					
Career Point Institute 485 Spencer Ln	San Antonio	TX	78201	210-732-3000	
Web: www.careerpointcollege.edu					
Cegep Andre Laurendeau 1111 Rue Lapierre	Lasalle	QC	H8N2J4	514-364-3320	
Web: www.claurendeau.qc.ca					
Cegep De L'outaouais					
333 Boul De La Cite-des-jeunes	Gatineau	QC	J8Y6M4	819-770-4012	
Cegep Marie-Victorin					
7000 rue Marie-Victorin	Montreal	QC	H1G2J6	514-325-0150	
Web: www.collegemv.qc.ca					
Chief Dull Knife College PO Box 98	Lame Deer	MT	59043	406-477-6215	477-6219
Web: www.cdkc.edu					
College De Maisonneuve					
3800 Rue Sherbrooke E	Montreal	QC	H1X2A2	514-251-1444	
Web: www.cmaisonneuve.qc.ca					
College De Valleyfield (cegep)					
169 Rue Champlain	Salaberry-de-valleyfield	QC	J6T1X6	450-373-9441	
Web: www.colval.qc.ca					
College of Menominee Nation PO Box 1179	Keshena	WI	54135	715-799-5600	799-4392*
**Fax:* Admissions ■ *TF:* 800-567-2344 ■ *Web:* www.menominee.edu					
College of Registered Nurses of Manitoba					
890 Pembina Hwy	Winnipeg	MB	R3M2M8	204-774-3477	
Web: www.crnm.mb.ca					
Earth & Ocean Sciences 6339 Stores Rd	Vancouver	BC	V6T1Z4	604-822-1697	
Web: www.eoas.ubc.ca					
Econcordia 1250 Guy	Montreal	QC	H3H2T4	514-848-8770	
Web: www.econcordia.com					
EDP University 560 Ave Ponce De Leon	San Juan	PR	00918	787-765-3560	
Fanshawe College 1460 Oxford St E	London	ON	N5Y5R6	519-452-4430	
Web: www.fanshawec.on.ca					
Fond du Lac Tribal & Community College					
2101 14th St	Cloquet	MN	55720	218-879-0800	879-0814
TF: 800-657-3712 ■ *Web:* www.fdltcc.edu					
Fort Peck Community College PO Box 398	Poplar	MT	59255	406-768-6300	768-6301
Web: www.fpcc.edu					
Grande Prairie Regional College					
10726 106 Ave	Grande Prairie	AB	T8V4C4	780-539-2911	
Web: www.gprc.ab.ca					
Haskell Indian Nations University					
155 Indian Ave PO Box 5031	Lawrence	KS	66046	785-749-8454	749-8429*
**Fax:* Admissions ■ *Web:* www.haskell.edu					
Hebrew Theological College 7135 Carpenter Rd	Skokie	IL	60077	847-982-2500	
Web: www.htc.edu					
Institute of American Indian Arts (IAIA)					
83 Avan Nu Po Rd	Santa Fe	NM	87508	505-424-2300	424-0505
TF: 800-804-6422 ■ *Web:* www.iaia.edu					
Keweenaw Bay Ojibwa Community College					
111 Beartown Rd	Baraga	MI	49908	906-353-4600	353-8107
Web: www.kbocc.org					
La Cite collegiale					
801 promenade de l'Aviation	Ottawa	ON	K1K4R3	613-742-2483	
Web: www.collegelacite.ca					
Lac Courte Oreilles Ojibwa Community College					
13466 W Trepania Rd	Hayward	WI	54843	715-634-4790	634-5049*
**Fax:* Admissions ■ *TF:* 888-526-6221 ■ *Web:* www.lco.edu					
Leech Lake Tribal College					
6945 Little Wolf Rd PO Box 180	Cass Lake	MN	56633	218-335-4200	335-4209
TF: 866-676-2772 ■ *Web:* www.lltc.edu					
Little Big Horn College					
8645 South Weaver Dr PO Box 370	Crow Agency	MT	59022	406-638-3100	638-3169
Web: www.lbhc.edu					
Little Priest Tribal College					
601 E College Dr PO Box 270	Winnebago	NE	68071	402-878-2380	878-2355
Web: www.littlepriest.edu					
Milwaukee Academy of Science					
2000 W Kilbourn Ave	Milwaukee	WI	53233	414-933-0302	
Web: milwaukeeacademyofscience.org					
Navajo Technical College PO Box 849	Crownpoint	NM	87313	505-786-4100	786-5644
Web: www.navajotech.edu					
Nebraska Indian Community College PO Box 428	Macy	NE	68039	402-837-5078	837-4183*
**Fax:* Admissions ■ *TF:* 844-440-6422 ■ *Web:* www.thenicc.edu					
Nicola Valley Institute of Technology					
4355 Mathissi Pl	Burnaby	BC	V5G4S8	604-602-9555	
Web: www.nvit.bc.ca					
Northeast Lakeview College					
1201 Kitty Hawk Rd	Universal City	TX	78148	210-486-5484	
Web: alamo.edu					
Northwest Indian College 2522 Kwina Rd	Bellingham	WA	98226	360-676-2772	392-4333*
**Fax:* Admissions ■ *TF:* 866-676-2772 ■ *Web:* www.nwic.edu					
O s u Center for Health Sciences					
1111 W 17th St	Tulsa	OK	74107	918-582-1972	
Web: www.healthsciences.okstate.edu					
Oglala Lakota College PO Box 629	Martin	SD	57551	605-455-6000	455-2787
Web: www.olc.edu					
Ontario Universities Application Centre					
170 Research Ln	Guelph	ON	N1G5E2	519-823-1940	
Web: www.ouac.on.ca					
Palmer College-chiropractic					
4705 S Clyde Morris Blvd	Port Orange	FL	32129	386-763-2709	
Web: palmer.edu					
Polaris Career Center 7285 Old Oak Blvd	Cleveland	OH	44130	440-891-7600	
Web: www.polaris.edu					
Robertson College 3-265 Notre Dame Ave	Winnipeg	MB	R3B1N9	204-943-5661	
Web: m.robertsoncollege.com					
Royal College of Dental Surgeons of Ontario					
6 Crescent Rd	Toronto	ON	M4W1T1	416-961-6555	
TF: 800-565-4591 ■ *Web:* rcdso.org					
Saginaw Chippewa Tribal College					
2274 Enterprise Dr	Mount Pleasant	MI	48858	989-775-4123	775-4528
TF: 800-225-8172 ■ *Web:* www.sagchip.org					
Salish Kootenai College PO Box 70	Pablo	MT	59855	406-275-4800	275-4801*
**Fax:* Admissions ■ *TF:* 877-752-6553 ■ *Web:* www.skc.edu					
Seneca College 1750 Finch Ave E	Toronto	ON	M2J2X5	416-491-5050	
Web: www.senecacollege.ca					
Sinte Gleska University					
101 Antelope Lk Cir Dr PO Box 105	Mission	SD	57555	605-856-8100	856-4194
Web: www.sintegleska.edu					
Sisseton Wahpeton College 12572 BIA Hwy 700	Sisseton	SD	57262	605-698-3966	742-0394
Web: www.swc.tc					

Phone *Fax*

Sitting Bull College 9299 Hwy 24 ... Fort Yates ND 58538 701-854-8000 854-3403*
**Fax:* Admissions ■ *Web:* www.sittingbull.edu

Southwestern Indian Polytechnic Institute
9169 Coors Blvd NW PO Box 10146 ... Albuquerque NM 87120 505-346-2306 346-2311
TF: 800-586-7474 ■ *Web:* www.sipi.edu

Stone Child College
8294 Upper Box Elder Rd ... Box Elder MT 59521 406-395-4875 395-4836*
**Fax:* Admissions ■ *Web:* www.stonechild.edu

Turtle Mountain Community College
10145 BIA Rd 7 ... Belcourt ND 58316 701-477-7862 477-7892
TF: 800-827-1100 ■ *Web:* www.tm.edu

United Tribes Technical College
3315 University Dr ... Bismarck ND 58504 701-255-3285 530-0640
Web: www.uttc.edu

Van Hoose Associates Inc 714 E Monument St ... Dayton OH 45402 937-531-6680
Web: www.vhainc.com

166 COLLEGES & UNIVERSITIES - FOUR-YEAR

See Also Colleges - Community & Junior p. 1950; Colleges - Fine Arts p. 1966; Colleges & Universities - Graduate & Professional Schools p. 1989; Colleges & Universities - Historically Black p. 1995; Military Service Academies p. 2771; Universities - Canadian p. 3278; Vocational & Technical Schools p. 3297

Alabama

Phone *Fax*

Alabama Agricultural & Mechanical University
4900 Meridian St PO Box 1087 ... Huntsville AL 35810 256-372-5000 372-5906
TF: 800-553-0816 ■ *Web:* www.aamu.edu

Alabama State University 915 S Jackson St ... Montgomery AL 36104 334-229-4100 229-4984*
**Fax:* Admissions ■ *TF Admissions:* 800-253-5037 ■ *Web:* www.alasu.edu

Amridge University 1200 Taylor Rd ... Montgomery AL 36117 334-387-3877 387-3878
TF: 888-790-8080 ■ *Web:* www.amridgeuniversity.edu

Auburn University
202 Mary Martin Hall ... Auburn University AL 36849 334-844-6425 844-6436*
**Fax:* Admissions ■ *TF Admissions:* 866-389-6770 ■ *Web:* www.auburn.edu
Montgomery 7440 E Dr ... Montgomery AL 36117 334-244-3000 244-3795
TF: 800-227-2649 ■ *Web:* www.aum.edu

Birmingham-Southern College
900 Arkadelphia Rd ... Birmingham AL 35254 205-226-4600 226-3074*
**Fax:* Admissions ■ *TF:* 800-523-5793 ■ *Web:* www.bsc.edu

Concordia College Selma 1712 Broad St ... Selma AL 36701 334-874-5700 874-5755

Faulkner University 5345 Atlanta Hwy ... Montgomery AL 36109 334-272-5820
TF: 800-879-9816 ■ *Web:* www.faulkner.edu

Huntingdon College 1500 E Fairview Ave ... Montgomery AL 36106 334-833-4497 833-4497*
**Fax:* Admissions ■ *TF Admissions:* 800-763-0313 ■ *Web:* www.huntingdon.edu

Jacksonville State University
700 Pelham Rd N ... Jacksonville AL 36265 256-782-5781 782-5953*
**Fax:* Admissions ■ *TF:* 800-231-5291 ■ *Web:* www.jsu.edu

Judson College 302 Bibb St ... Marion AL 36756 334-683-5110
TF Admissions: 800-447-9472 ■ *Web:* www.judson.edu

Ludwig Von Mises Institute 518 W Magnolia Ave ... Auburn AL 36832 334-321-2100
Web: www.mises.org

Miles College 5500 Myron Massey Blvd ... Fairfield AL 35064 205-929-1000 929-1627*
**Fax:* Admissions ■ *TF Admissions:* 800-445-0708 ■ *Web:* www.miles.edu

Oakwood College 7000 Adventist Blvd ... Huntsville AL 35896 256-726-7356 726-7154*
**Fax:* Admissions ■ *TF:* 800-824-5312 ■ *Web:* www.oakwood.edu

Samford University 800 Lakeshore Dr ... Birmingham AL 35229 205-726-3673 726-2171*
**Fax:* Admissions ■ *TF Admissions:* 800-888-7218 ■ *Web:* www.samford.edu

Selma University 1501 Lapsley St ... Selma AL 36701 334-872-2533
Web: selmauniversity.org

South University
Montgomery 5355 Vaughn Rd ... Montgomery AL 36116 334-395-8800 395-8859*
**Fax:* Admissions ■ *TF:* 866-629-2962 ■ *Web:* www.southuniversity.edu

Spring Hill College 4000 Dauphin St ... Mobile AL 36608 251-380-4000 460-2186*
**Fax:* Admissions ■ *TF Admissions:* 800-742-6704 ■ *Web:* badgerweb.shc.edu

Stillman College 3601 Stillman Blvd ... Tuscaloosa AL 35401 205-349-4240
TF: 800-841-5722 ■ *Web:* www.stillman.edu

Talladega College 627 W Battle St ... Talladega AL 35160 256-761-6100 362-0274*
**Fax:* Admissions ■ *TF:* 866-540-3956 ■ *Web:* talladega.brinkster.net

Troy University 600 University Ave ... Troy AL 36082 334-670-3100 670-3733*
**Fax:* Admissions ■ *TF:* 800-551-9716 ■ *Web:* www.troy.edu
Montgomery 231 Montgomery St PO Box 4419 . Montgomery AL 36104 888-357-8843
TF: 888-357-8843 ■ *Web:* troy.edu
Phenix City 1 University Pl ... Phenix City AL 36869 334-297-1007 448-5229*
**Fax:* Admissions ■ *Web:* troy.edu

Tuskegee University 1200 W Montgomery Rd ... Tuskegee AL 36088 334-727-8011 727-5750*
**Fax:* Admissions ■ *TF Admissions:* 800-622-6531 ■ *Web:* www.tuskegee.edu

United States Sports Academy, The
1 Academy Dr ... Daphne AL 36526 251-626-3303
Web: www.ussa.edu

University of Alabama PO Box 870132 ... Tuscaloosa AL 35487 205-348-6010 348-9046*
**Fax:* Admissions ■ *TF:* 800-933-2262 ■ *Web:* www.ua.edu
Birmingham 1530 Third Ave S THT 647 ... Birmingham AL 35294 205-996-6670 975-7114*
**Fax:* Admissions ■ *TF:* 800-421-8743 ■ *Web:* www.uab.edu
Huntsville 301 Sparkman Dr ... Huntsville AL 35899 256-824-1000 824-7780*
**Fax:* Admissions ■ *TF:* 800-824-2255 ■ *Web:* www.uah.edu

University of Mobile 5735 College Pkwy ... Mobile AL 36613 251-675-5990 442-2498*
**Fax:* Admissions ■ *TF:* 800-946-7267 ■ *Web:* www.umobile.edu

University of North Alabama
1 Harrison Plaza ... Florence AL 35632 256-765-4608
TF: 800-825-5862 ■ *Web:* www.una.edu

University of South Alabama 2500 Meisler Hall ... Mobile AL 36688 251-460-6141 460-7876
TF: 800-872-5247 ■ *Web:* www.usouthal.edu

University of West Alabama Station 200 ... Livingston AL 35470 205-652-3400 652-3522*
**Fax:* Admissions ■ *TF Admissions:* 800-621-8044

Alaska

Phone *Fax*

Alaska Pacific University
4101 University Dr ... Anchorage AK 99508 907-564-8248
TF: 800-252-7528 ■ *Web:* www.alaskapacific.edu

University of Alaska Anchorage
3211 Providence Dr ... Anchorage AK 99508 907-786-1800 786-4888*
**Fax:* Admissions ■ *TF:* 888-822-8973 ■ *Web:* www.uaa.alaska.edu

University of Alaska Fairbanks
PO Box 757480 ... Fairbanks AK 99775 907-474-7500 474-5379*
**Fax:* Admissions ■ *TF:* 800-478-1823 ■ *Web:* www.uaf.edu
Bristol Bay 527 Seward St PO Box 1070 ... Dillingham AK 99576 907-842-5109 842-5692*
**Fax:* Admissions ■ *TF:* 800-478-5109 ■ *Web:* www.uaf.edu

University of Alaska Southeast
11120 Glacier Hwy ... Juneau AK 99801 907-796-6000
TF: 877-465-4827 ■ *Web:* www.uas.alaska.edu

Wayland Baptist University Anchorage
7801 E 32 Ave ... Anchorage AK 99504 907-333-2277 337-8122
Web: www.wbu.edu

Arizona

Phone *Fax*

American Indian College of the Assemblies of God
10020 N 15th Ave ... Phoenix AZ 85021 602-944-3335 943-8299
TF: 800-621-7440 ■ *Web:* www.aicag.edu
East 7001 E Williams Field Rd ... Mesa AZ 85212 480-727-9911 965-3610
Web: campus.asu.edu/polytechnic
West PO Box 37100 ... Phoenix AZ 85069 602-543-5500 543-8312*
**Fax:* Admissions ■ *TF:* 855-278-5080 ■ *Web:* campus.asu.edu

Conservatory of Recording Arts & Sciences
2300 E Broadway Rd ... Tempe AZ 85282 480-858-9400
Web: www.audiorecordingschool.com

Embry-Riddle Aeronautical University Prescott
3700 Willow Creek Rd ... Prescott AZ 86301 928-777-3728
TF: 800-888-3728 ■ *Web:* www.erau.edu

Grand Canyon University 3300 W Camelback Rd ... Phoenix AZ 85017 602-639-7500
TF: 800-800-9776 ■ *Web:* www.gcu.edu

Indian Bible College 2918 N Aris Ave ... Flagstaff AZ 86004 928-774-3890 774-2655
TF: 866-503-7789 ■ *Web:* www.indianbible.org

International Baptist College
2211 W Germann Rd ... Chandler AZ 85286 480-245-7900 505-3299
TF General: 800-422-4858 ■ *Web:* www.tricityministries.org

Northern Arizona University PO Box 4084 ... Flagstaff AZ 86011 928-523-5511 523-6023*
**Fax:* Admissions ■ *TF Admissions:* 888-628-2968 ■ *Web:* www.nau.edu

Ottawa University Phoenix 10020 N 25th Ave ... Phoenix AZ 85021 602-371-1188 371-0035
TF: 800-235-9586 ■ *Web:* www.ottawa.edu

Prescott College 220 Grove Ave ... Prescott AZ 86301 877-350-2100 776-5242*
**Fax Area Code:* 928 ■ **Fax:* Admissions ■ *TF:* 877-350-2100 ■ *Web:* www.prescott.edu

University of Arizona PO Box 210300 ... Tucson AZ 85721 520-621-2211 621-9799*
**Fax:* Admissions ■ *Web:* www.arizona.edu

Western International University
9215 N Black Canyon Hwy ... Phoenix AZ 85021 602-943-2311
TF: 866-948-4636 ■ *Web:* west.edu

Arkansas

Phone *Fax*

Arkansas State University
PO Box 1630 ... State University AR 72467 870-972-3024 972-3406
TF: 800-382-3030 ■ *Web:* www.astate.edu

Central Baptist College 1501 College Ave ... Conway AR 72034 501-329-6872
TF: 800-205-6872 ■ *Web:* www.cbc.edu

Harding University 915 E. Market Ave ... Searcy AR 72149 501-279-4000 279-4129
TF: 800-477-4407 ■ *Web:* www.harding.edu

Henderson State University
1100 Henderson St ... Arkadelphia AR 71999 870-230-5000 230-5066*
**Fax:* Admissions ■ *TF:* 800-228-7333 ■ *Web:* www.hsu.edu

Hendrix College 1600 Washington Ave ... Conway AR 72032 501-329-6811 450-3843*
**Fax:* Admissions ■ *TF:* 800-277-9017 ■ *Web:* www.hendrix.edu

John Brown University
2000 W University St ... Siloam Springs AR 72761 479-524-9500 524-4196*
**Fax:* Admissions ■ *TF Admissions:* 877-528-4636 ■ *Web:* www.jbu.edu

Lyon College 2300 Highland Rd ... Batesville AR 72501 870-793-9813
Web: www.lyon.edu

Ouachita Baptist University
410 Ouachita St ... Arkadelphia AR 71998 870-245-5000 245-5500*
**Fax:* Admissions ■ *TF Admissions:* 800-342-5628 ■ *Web:* www.obu.edu

Philander Smith College
900 Daisy Bates Dr ... Little Rock AR 72202 501-370-5221 370-5225*
**Fax:* Admissions ■ *TF:* 800-446-6772 ■ *Web:* www.philander.edu

Southern Arkansas University
100 E University St ... Magnolia AR 71753 870-235-4000 235-5005*
**Fax:* Admissions ■ *TF:* 800-332-7286 ■ *Web:* web.saumag.edu

University of Arkansas
232 Silas Hunt Hall ... Fayetteville AR 72701 479-575-5346 575-7515*
**Fax:* Admissions ■ *TF Admissions:* 800-377-8632 ■ *Web:* www.uark.edu
Little Rock 2801 S University Ave ... Little Rock AR 72204 501-569-3000 569-8956
Web: www.ualr.edu
Monticello PO Box 3600 ... Monticello AR 71656 870-460-1026 460-1926*
**Fax:* Admissions ■ *TF:* 800-844-1826 ■ *Web:* www.uamont.edu
Pine Bluff 1200 N University Dr ... Pine Bluff AR 71601 870-575-8000 575-4608*
**Fax:* Admissions ■ *TF Admissions:* 800-264-6585 ■ *Web:* www.uapb.edu

University of Central Arkansas
201 Donaghey Ave ... Conway AR 72035 501-450-5000 450-5228*
**Fax:* Admissions ■ *TF Admissions:* 888-407-4747 ■ *Web:* www.uca.edu

University of the Ozarks
415 N College Ave ... Clarksville AR 72830 479-979-1227 979-1417*
**Fax:* Admissions ■ *TF Admissions:* 800-264-8636 ■ *Web:* www.ozarks.edu

Phone | Fax

Williams Baptist College
60 W Fulbright St . . . Walnut Ridge AR 72476 870-886-6741 886-3924*
Fax: Admissions ■ *TF:* 800-722-4434 ■ *Web:* www.wbcoll.edu

British Columbia

Phone | Fax

North Island College 2300 Ryan Rd . . . Courtenay BC V9N8N6 250-334-5000
Web: www.nic.bc.ca

Northern Lights College
11401 - Eigth St . . . Dawson Creek BC V1G4G2 250-782-5251 784-7549
Web: www.nlc.bc.ca

Pearson College 650 Pearson College Dr . . . Victoria BC V9C4H7 250-391-2411
Web: www.pearsoncollege.ca

Selkirk College 301 Frank Beinder Way . . . Castlegar BC V1N4L3 250-365-7292 365-6568
TF: 888-953-1133 ■ *Web:* www.selkirk.ca

California

Phone | Fax

Academy of Art University
79 New Montgomery St . . . San Francisco CA 94105 415-274-2200 618-6287
TF: 800-544-2787 ■ *Web:* www.academyart.edu

Alliant International University
10455 Pomerado Rd . . . San Diego CA 92131 858-635-4772 635-4555*
Fax: Admissions ■ *TF:* 866-825-5426 ■ *Web:* www.alliant.edu

American Career College Inc 151 Innovation Dr . . . Irvine CA 92617 949-783-4800
TF: 877-832-0790 ■ *Web:* americancareercollege.edu

Azusa Pacific University
901 E Alosta Ave PO Box 7000 . . . Azusa CA 91702 626-969-3434 812-3096
TF: 800-825-5278 ■ *Web:* www.apu.edu

Biola University 13800 Biola Ave . . . La Mirada CA 90639 562-903-6000 903-4709*
Fax: Admissions ■ *TF Admissions:* 800-652-4652 ■ *Web:* www.biola.edu

California Baptist University
8432 Magnolia Ave . . . Riverside CA 92504 951-689-5771 343-4525*
Fax: Admissions ■ *TF:* 877-228-8866 ■ *Web:* www.calbaptist.edu

California Christian College
4881 E University Ave . . . Fresno CA 93703 559-251-4215 251-4231
Web: www.calchristiancollege.edu

California Institute of Technology
1200 E California Blvd . . . Pasadena CA 91125 626-395-6811 683-3026*
Fax: Admissions ■ *TF:* 800-568-8324 ■ *Web:* www.caltech.edu

California International University
3130 Wilshire Blvd . . . Los Angeles CA 90010 213-381-3710 381-6990*
Fax: Admissions ■ *Web:* www.ciula.edu

California Lutheran University
60 W Olsen Rd . . . Thousand Oaks CA 91360 805-493-3135 493-3114
TF: 877-258-3678 ■ *Web:* www.callutheran.edu

California Maritime Academy
200 Maritime Academy Dr . . . Vallejo CA 94590 707-654-1330 654-1336*
Fax: Admissions ■ *TF:* 800-561-1945 ■ *Web:* www.csum.edu

California Pacific University
1017 E Grand Ave . . . Escondido CA 92025 760-739-7730
Web: www.cpu.edu

California Polytechnic State University
1 Grand Ave . . . San Luis Obispo CA 93407 805-756-1111 756-5400
TF: 800-424-6723 ■ *Web:* www.calpoly.edu

California State Polytechnic University Pomona
3801 W Temple Ave . . . Pomona CA 91768 909-869-7659 869-4555*
Fax: Admissions ■ *Web:* www.csupomona.edu

California State University
401 Golden Shore . . . Long Beach CA 90802 562-951-4000 951-4899
TF: 800-325-4000 ■ *Web:* www.calstate.edu

Bakersfield 9001 Stockdale Hwy . . . Bakersfield CA 93311 661-654-2011 654-3389*
Fax: Admissions ■ *Web:* auxiliary.calstate.edu

Channel Islands 1 University Dr . . . Camarillo CA 93012 805-437-8400 437-8509*
Fax: Admissions ■ *Web:* www.csuci.edu

Chico CSU Chico . . . Chico CA 95929 530-898-6321 898-6456*
Fax: Admissions ■ *TF Admissions:* 800-542-4426 ■ *Web:* www.csuchico.edu

Dominguez Hills 1000 E Victoria St . . . Carson CA 90747 310-243-3300 516-4573*
Fax: Admissions ■ *TF:* 888-545-6512 ■ *Web:* www.csudh.edu

East Bay 25800 Carlos Bee Blvd . . . Hayward CA 94542 510-885-3000 885-4059
TF: 877-829-5500 ■ *Web:* www.csueastbay.edu

Fresno 5241 N Maple Ave . . . Fresno CA 93740 559-278-4240 278-4812*
Fax: Admissions ■ *TF:* 800-700-2320 ■ *Web:* www.fresnostate.edu

Fullerton 800 N State College Blvd . . . Fullerton CA 92834 714-278-2011 278-2300
TF: 888-433-9406 ■ *Web:* www.fullerton.edu

Long Beach 1250 Bellflower Blvd . . . Long Beach CA 90840 562-985-4111 985-4973*
Fax: Admissions ■ *TF:* 800-663-1144 ■ *Web:* www.csulb.edu

Los Angeles 5151 State University Dr . . . Los Angeles CA 90032 323-343-3000 343-6306*
Fax: Admissions ■ *Web:* www.calstatela.edu

Monterey Bay 100 Campus Ctr . . . Seaside CA 93955 831-582-3000 582-3738*
Fax: Admissions ■ *Web:* www.csumb.edu

Northridge 18111 Nordhoff St . . . Northridge CA 91330 818-677-1200 677-3766
TF: 800-399-4529 ■ *Web:* www.csun.edu

Sacramento 6000 J St . . . Sacramento CA 95819 916-278-3901 278-7473
Web: www.csus.edu

San Bernardino 5500 University Pkwy . . . San Bernardino CA 92407 909-537-5188 537-7034
TF: 866-275-3772 ■ *Web:* www.csusb.edu

San Marcos 333 S Twin Oaks Valley Rd . . . San Marcos CA 92096 760-750-4000 750-3248*
Fax: Admissions ■ *TF:* 888-225-5427 ■ *Web:* www.csusm.edu

Stanislaus 1 University Cir . . . Turlock CA 95382 209-667-3152 667-3788
TF: 800-235-9292 ■ *Web:* www.csustan.edu

California State University Stanislaus
Library 1 University Cir . . . Turlock CA 95382 209-667-3234 667-3164
Web: library.csustan.edu

Stockton Ctr 612 E Magnolia St . . . Stockton CA 95202 209-467-5300 467-5333
Web: www.csustan.edu

Chapman University 1 University Dr . . . Orange CA 92866 714-997-6815 997-6713*
Fax: Admissions ■ *TF:* 888-282-7759 ■ *Web:* www.chapman.edu

Charles R Drew University of Medicine & Science
1731 E 120th St . . . Los Angeles CA 90059 323-563-4800 563-4957*
Fax: Admissions ■ *Web:* www.cdrewu.edu

Phone | Fax

Claremont McKenna College 500 E Ninth St . . . Claremont CA 91711 909-621-8088 621-8516
Web: www.cmc.edu

Cleveland Chiropractic College of Los Angeles Inc
590 N Vermont Ave . . . Los Angeles CA 90004 913-234-0600
Web: www.cleveland.edu

CODAN US Corp 3511 W Sunflower Ave . . . Santa Ana CA 92704 714-545-2111
Web: www.codanuscorp.com

Cogswell Polytechnical College
1175 Bordeaux Dr . . . Sunnyvale CA 94089 408-541-0100 747-0764*
Fax: Admissions ■ *TF:* 800-264-7955 ■ *Web:* www.cogswell.edu

Coleman College 8888 Balboa Ave . . . San Diego CA 92123 858-499-0202 499-0233
TF: 800-430-2030 ■ *Web:* www.coleman.edu

Columbia College Hollywood 18618 Oxnard St . . . Tarzana CA 91356 818-345-8414 345-9053
TF: 800-785-0585 ■ *Web:* www.columbiacollege.edu

Concordia University Irvine 1530 Concordia W . . . Irvine CA 92612 949-854-8002 854-6894
TF: 800-229-1200 ■ *Web:* www.cui.edu

Continuing Education of The Bar Sute 410
300 Frank H Ogawa Plz Ste 410 . . . Oakland CA 94612 510-302-2000
Web: www.ceb.com

Design Institute of San Diego
8555 Commerce Ave . . . San Diego CA 92121 858-566-1200 566-2711
TF: 800-619-4337 ■ *Web:* www.disd.edu

Dominican University of California
50 Acacia Ave . . . San Rafael CA 94901 415-457-4440 485-3214*
Fax: Admissions ■ *TF Admissions:* 888-323-6763 ■ *Web:* www.dominican.edu

Ex'pression College for Digital Arts
6601 Shellmound St . . . Emeryville CA 94608 510-654-2934
Web: www.expression.edu

Harvey Mudd College
301 Platt Blvd Kingston Hall . . . Claremont CA 91711 909-621-8011 607-7046*
Fax: Admissions ■ *TF:* 877-827-5462 ■ *Web:* www.hmc.edu

Hebrew Union College Los Angeles
3077 University Ave . . . Los Angeles CA 90007 213-749-3424 747-6128*
Fax: Admissions ■ *TF:* 800-899-0925 ■ *Web:* www.huc.edu

Holy Names University 3500 Mountain Blvd . . . Oakland CA 94619 510-436-1000 436-1325*
Fax: Admissions ■ *TF:* 800-430-1321 ■ *Web:* www.hnu.edu

Hope International University
2500 E Nutwood Ave . . . Fullerton CA 92831 714-879-3901 526-0231*
Fax: Admissions ■ *TF:* 866-722-4673 ■ *Web:* www.hiu.edu

Humboldt State University 1 Harpst St . . . Arcata CA 95521 707-826-3011 826-6190*
Fax: Admissions ■ *TF:* 866-850-9556 ■ *Web:* www.humboldt.edu

Humphreys College 6650 Inglewood Ave . . . Stockton CA 95207 209-478-0800 478-8721
TF: 800-433-3243 ■ *Web:* www.humphreys.edu

John F Kennedy University
100 Ellinwood Way . . . Pleasant Hill CA 94523 925-969-3300 969-3101*
Fax: Admissions ■ *TF:* 800-696-5358 ■ *Web:* www.jfku.edu

La Sierra University 4500 Riverwalk Pkwy . . . Riverside CA 92515 951-785-2000 785-2901
TF: 800-874-5587 ■ *Web:* www.lasierra.edu

Laguna College of Art & Design
2222 Laguna Canyon Rd . . . Laguna Beach CA 92651 949-376-6000 376-6009
TF: 800-255-0762 ■ *Web:* www.lcad.edu

Lee Strasberg Theatre Institute, The
7936 Santa Monica Blvd . . . West Hollywood CA 90046 323-650-7777
Web: www.strasberg.com

Lincoln University 401 15th St . . . Oakland CA 94612 510-628-8010 628-8012*
Fax: Admissions ■ *TF:* 888-810-9998 ■ *Web:* www.lincolnuca.edu

Loma Linda University 11234 Anderson St . . . Loma Linda CA 92354 909-558-1000
Web: www.llu.edu

Loyola Marymount University 1 LMU Dr . . . Los Angeles CA 90045 310-338-2700 338-2797
TF: 800-568-4636 ■ *Web:* www.lmu.edu

Master's College
21726 Placerita Canyon Rd . . . Santa Clarita CA 91321 661-259-3540 288-1037*
Fax: Admissions ■ *TF:* 800-568-6248 ■ *Web:* www.masters.edu

Menlo College 1000 El Camino Real . . . Atherton CA 94027 650-543-3753 543-4496
TF: 800-556-3656 ■ *Web:* www.menlo.edu

Mills College 5000 MacArthur Blvd . . . Oakland CA 94613 510-430-2135 430-3314*
Fax: Admissions ■ *TF Admissions:* 877-746-4557 ■ *Web:* www.mills.edu

Mount Saint Mary's University
12001 Chalon Rd . . . Los Angeles CA 90049 310-954-4250 954-4259*
Fax: Admissions ■ *TF Admissions:* 800-999-9893 ■ *Web:* www.msmc.la.edu

National Hispanic University 14271 Story Rd . . . San Jose CA 95127 408-254-6900 254-1369*
Fax: Admissions ■ *TF:* 877-762-9801 ■ *Web:* www.nhu.edu

National University 11255 N Torrey Pines Rd . . . La Jolla CA 92037 858-642-8000 642-8709
TF: 800-628-8648 ■ *Web:* www.nu.edu

Northwestern Polytechnic University
47671 Westinghouse Dr . . . Fremont CA 94539 510-592-9688 657-8975
TF: 877-878-8883 ■ *Web:* www.npu.edu

Notre Dame de Namur University
1500 Ralston Ave . . . Belmont CA 94002 650-508-3600 508-3426*
Fax: Admissions ■ *TF:* 800-263-0545 ■ *Web:* www.ndnu.edu

Occidental College 1600 Campus Rd . . . Los Angeles CA 90041 323-259-2700 341-4875*
Fax: Admissions ■ *TF Admissions:* 800-825-5262 ■ *Web:* www.oxy.edu

Pacific College Oriental Med Inc
7445 Mission Vly Rd Ste 105 . . . San Diego CA 92108 619-574-6909
TF: 800-729-0941 ■ *Web:* www.pacificcollege.edu

Pacific Oaks College 5 Westmoreland Pl . . . Pasadena CA 91103 877-314-2380
TF: 877-314-2380 ■ *Web:* www.pacificoaks.edu

Pacific States University
1516 S Western Ave . . . Los Angeles CA 90006 323-731-2383
TF: 888-200-0383 ■ *Web:* www.psuca.edu

Pacific Union College 1 Angwin Ave . . . Angwin CA 94508 707-965-6336 965-6432*
Fax: Admissions ■ *TF:* 800-862-7080 ■ *Web:* www.puc.edu

Pacifica Graduate Institute
249 Lambert Rd . . . Carpinteria CA 93013 805-969-3626
Web: www.pacifica.edu

Patten University 2433 Coolidge Ave . . . Oakland CA 94601 510-261-8500
TF: 888-370-7589 ■ *Web:* www.patten.edu

Pepperdine University 24255 Pacific Coast Hwy . . . Malibu CA 90263 310-506-4000 506-4861*
Fax: Admissions ■ *Web:* www.pepperdine.edu

Phillips Graduate Institute 5445 Balboa Blvd . . . Encino CA 91316 818-654-1721
Web: www.pgu.edu/index.php

Pitzer College 1050 N Mills Ave . . . Claremont CA 91711 909-621-8129 621-8770*
Fax: Admissions ■ *TF:* 800-748-9371 ■ *Web:* www.pitzer.edu

Phone Fax

Point Loma Nazarene University
3900 Lomaland Dr .... San Diego CA 92106 619-849-2200 849-2601*
*Fax: Admissions ■ *TF Admissions:* 800-733-7770 ■ *Web:* www.pointloma.edu

Pomona College 333 N College Way .... Claremont CA 91711 909-621-8134 621-8952*
*Fax: Admissions ■ *Web:* www.pomona.edu

Rudolf Steiner College 9200 Fair Oaks Blvd........... Fair Oaks CA 95628 916-961-8729
Web: www.steinercollege.edu

Ryokan College 11965 Venice Blvd Ste 304.......... Los Angeles CA 90066 310-390-7560 391-9756*
*Fax: Admissions ■ *TF:* 866-796-5261 ■ *Web:* www.ryokan.edu

Sage College 12125 Day St Ste L .... Moreno Valley CA 92557 951-781-2727
Web: www.sagecollege.edu

Saint Mary's College of California
1928 St Mary's Rd .... Moraga CA 94556 925-631-4000 376-7193*
*Fax: Admissions ■ *TF Admissions:* 800-800-4762 ■ *Web:* www.stmarys-ca.edu

Samuel Merritt College 370 Hawthorne Ave............ Oakland CA 94609 510-869-6576 869-6525*
*Fax: Admissions ■ *TF Admissions:* 800-607-6377 ■ *Web:* www.samuelmerritt.edu

San Diego Christian College
2100 Greenfield Dr .... El Cajon CA 92019 619-441-2200
TF: 800-676-2242 ■ *Web:* www.sdcc.edu

San Diego State University
5500 Campanile Dr............................. San Diego CA 92182 619-594-5200 594-1250*
*Fax: Admissions ■ *Web:* www.sdsu.edu
Imperial Valley 720 Heber Ave................. Calexico CA 92231 760-768-5520 768-5589*
*Fax: Admissions ■ *Web:* www.ivcampus.sdsu.edu

San Francisco Conservatory of Music
50 Oak St .... San Francisco CA 94102 415-864-7326 503-6299
TF: 800-999-8219 ■ *Web:* www.sfcm.edu

San Francisco State University
1600 Holloway Ave............................ San Francisco CA 94132 415-338-1111 338-7196*
*Fax: Admissions ■ *Web:* www.sfsu.edu

San Joaquin College of Law 901 Fifth St............... Clovis CA 93612 559-323-2100
Web: www.sjcl.edu

San Jose State University 1 Washington Sq........... San Jose CA 95192 408-924-1000 924-2050
TF: 800-273-8255 ■ *Web:* www.sjsu.edu

Santa Clara University
500 El Camino Real .... Santa Clara CA 95053 408-554-4000 554-5255
Web: www.scu.edu

Scripps College 1030 Columbia Ave................. Claremont CA 91711 909-621-8149 607-7508*
*Fax: Admissions ■ *TF:* 800-770-1333 ■ *Web:* scrippscollege.edu

Silicon Valley University
2160 Lundy Ave Ste 110.......................... San Jose CA 95131 408-435-8989
Web: www.svuca.edu

Simpson University 2211 College View Dr.............. Redding CA 96003 530-226-4606 226-4861*
*Fax: Admissions ■ *TF:* 888-974-6776 ■ *Web:* www.simpsonu.edu

Sonoma State University
1801 E Cotati Ave............................ Rohnert Park CA 94928 707-664-2880 664-2060*
*Fax: Admissions ■ *Web:* www.sonoma.edu

South Baylo University 1126 N Brookhurst St.......... Anaheim CA 92801 714-533-1495 533-6040
TF: 888-642-2956 ■ *Web:* www.southbaylo.edu

Southern California Institute of Architecture
960 E Third St................................ Los Angeles CA 90013 213-613-2200 613-2260*
*Fax: Admissions ■ *Web:* www.sciarc.edu

Southern California Seminary
2075 E Madison Ave................................ El Cajon CA 92019 888-389-7244 442-4510*
*Fax Area Code: 619 ■ *TF:* 888-389-7244 ■ *Web:* www.socalsem.edu

St. Mary Med Tech School 1050 Linden Ave........ Long Beach CA 90813 562-491-9000
Web: stmarymed.com

Stanford University 450 Serra Mall .... Stanford CA 94305 650-723-2091 725-2846
TF: 877-407-9529 ■ *Web:* www.stanford.edu

Thomas Aquinas College 10000 Ojai Rd........... Santa Paula CA 93060 805-525-4417 525-9342
TF: 800-634-9797 ■ *Web:* www.thomasaquinas.edu

Trinity Life Bible College
5225 Hillsdale Blvd .... Sacramento CA 95842 916-348-4689 334-2315*
*Fax: Admissions ■ *Web:* epic.edu

University of California (UCLA)
Berkeley 110 Sproul Hall MC Ste 5800 .... Berkeley CA 94720 510-642-6000 643-7333
TF: 866-740-1260 ■ *Web:* berkeley.edu
Davis 1 Shields Ave.............................. Davis CA 95616 530-752-1011 752-1280
Web: www.ucdavis.edu
Irvine 510 Aldrich Hall .... Irvine CA 92697 949-824-5011 824-2711
Web: www.uci.edu
Los Angeles 405 Hilgard Ave.................. Los Angeles CA 90095 310-825-4321 206-1206*
*Fax: Admissions ■ *Web:* www.ucla.edu
Merced PO Box 2039............................ Merced CA 95344 209-724-4400
TF: 866-270-7301 ■ *Web:* www.ucmerced.edu
Riverside
900 University Ave 1120 Hinderaker Hall .... Riverside CA 92521 951-827-3411 827-6344
TF: 800-426-2586 ■ *Web:* www.ucr.edu
San Diego 9500 Gilman Dr .... La Jolla CA 92093 858-534-2230 534-4831*
*Fax: Admissions ■ *Web:* www.ucsd.edu
San Francisco 505 Parnassus Ave........... San Francisco CA 94122 415-476-9000 353-3925
Web: www.ucsf.edu
Santa Barbara 1210 Cheadle Hall............ Santa Barbara CA 93106 805-893-8000 893-2676
TF: 888-488-8272 ■ *Web:* www.ucsb.edu
Santa Cruz 1156 High St Hahn Bldg Rm 150..... Santa Cruz CA 95064 831-459-2131
TF: 800-933-7584 ■ *Web:* www.ucsc.edu

University of California Irvine College of Health Sciences
1001 Health Science Rd .... Irvine CA 92697 949-824-9267 824-2118
Web: www.cohs.uci.edu

University of Judaism
15600 Mulholland Dr .... Los Angeles CA 90077 310-476-9777 471-3657*
*Fax: Admissions ■ *TF:* 888-853-6763 ■ *Web:* www.aju.edu

University of La Verne 1950 Third St .... La Verne CA 91750 909-593-3511
TF Admissions: 800-876-4858 ■ *Web:* laverne.edu

University of Redlands
1200 E Colton Ave PO Box 3080 .... Redlands CA 92373 909-793-2121 335-4089*
*Fax: Admissions ■ *TF:* 800-455-5064 ■ *Web:* www.redlands.edu

University of San Diego 5998 Alcala Pk .... San Diego CA 92110 619-260-4506 260-6836
TF: 800-248-4873 ■ *Web:* www.sandiego.edu

University of San Francisco
2130 Fulton St .... San Francisco CA 94117 415-422-5555 422-2217*
*Fax: Admissions ■ *TF Admissions:* 800-854-1385 ■ *Web:* www.usfca.edu

Phone Fax

University of Southern California
University Pk Campus .... Los Angeles CA 90089 213-740-2311 740-5229*
*Fax: Admissions ■ *Web:* www.usc.edu

University of the Pacific 3601 Pacific Ave........... Stockton CA 95211 209-946-2211 946-2413
TF: 800-959-2867 ■ *Web:* www.pacific.edu

Vanguard University of Southern California
55 Fair Dr .... Costa Mesa CA 92626 714-556-3610 966-5471*
*Fax: Admissions ■ *TF Admissions:* 800-722-6279 ■ *Web:* www.vanguard.edu

Weimar College 20601 W Paoli Ln PO Box 486.......... Weimar CA 95736 530-637-4111 422-7949
Web: weimar.edu

Westmont College 955 La Paz Rd .... Santa Barbara CA 93108 805-565-6000 565-6234*
*Fax: Admissions ■ *TF Admissions:* 800-777-9011 ■ *Web:* www.westmont.edu

Whittier College 13406 E Philadelphia St.............. Whittier CA 90608 562-907-4200 907-4870*
*Fax: Admissions ■ *Web:* www.whittier.edu

William Jessup University 333 Sunset Blvd........... Rocklin CA 95765 916-577-2200 577-2220*
*Fax: Admissions ■ *TF:* 800-355-7522 ■ *Web:* www.jessup.edu

Woodbury University 7500 Glenoaks Blvd.............. Burbank CA 91510 818-767-0888 767-7520
TF: 800-784-9663 ■ *Web:* www.woodbury.edu

World University 107 N Ventura St PO Box 1567............ Ojai CA 93024 805-646-1444 646-1217
TF: 888-370-7589 ■ *Web:* www.worldu.edu

Colorado

Phone Fax

Adams State College 208 Edgemont Blvd.............. Alamosa CO 81102 719-587-7712 587-7522
TF: 800-824-6494 ■ *Web:* www.adams.edu

Auraria Higher Education Ctr
1068 Ninth St Park .... Denver CO 80204 303-556-2400
Web: www.ahec.edu

Beth-El College of Nursing & Health Sciences
1420 Austin Bluffs Pkwy.................... Colorado Springs CO 80918 719-255-8227 262-4416
TF: 800-990-8227 ■ *Web:* uccs.edu/~bethel

Colorado Christian University
8787 W Alameda Ave .... Lakewood CO 80226 303-963-3200 963-3201
TF: 800-443-2484 ■ *Web:* www.ccu.edu
Loveland 3553 Clydesdale Pkwy Ste 300.......... Loveland CO 80538 970-669-8700 669-8701*
*Fax: Admissions ■ *TF:* 800-443-2484 ■ *Web:* www.ccu.edu

Colorado College
14 E Cache La Poudre St .... Colorado Springs CO 80903 719-389-6344 389-6816*
*Fax: Admissions ■ *TF:* 800-542-7214 ■ *Web:* www.coloradocollege.edu

Colorado School of Mines 1600 Maple St .... Golden CO 80401 303-273-3000 273-3509
TF: 800-446-9488 ■ *Web:* www.mines.edu

Colorado State University 200 W Lake St........... Fort Collins CO 80523 970-491-1101 491-7799*
*Fax: Admissions ■ *Web:* www.colostate.edu
Pueblo 2200 Bonforte Blvd .... Pueblo CO 81001 719-549-2100 269-7500*
*Fax Area Code: 814 ■ *TF:* 877-307-5678

Colorado Technical University
4435 N Chestnut St .... Colorado Springs CO 80907 719-598-0200
TF: 855-230-0555 ■ *Web:* www.coloradotech.edu

Fort Lewis College 1000 Rim Dr .... Durango CO 81301 970-247-7010 247-7179*
*Fax: Admissions ■ *TF:* 877-352-2656 ■ *Web:* www.fortlewis.edu

Johnson & Wales University Denver
7150 E Montview Blvd .... Denver CO 80220 303-256-9300 256-9333
TF: 877-598-3368 ■ *Web:* www.jwu.edu

Mesa State College 1100 N Ave .... Grand Junction CO 81501 970-248-1020 248-1973*
*Fax: Admissions ■ *TF:* 800-982-6372 ■ *Web:* coloradomesa.edu

Metropolitan State College of Denver
Student Success Bldg 890 Auraria Pkwy
Ste 140.. Denver CO 80204 303-556-3440 556-2720*
*Fax: Admissions ■ *Web:* www.msudenver.edu

Naropa University 2130 Arapahoe Ave................. Boulder CO 80302 303-444-0202 546-3536
TF: 800-772-6951 ■ *Web:* www.naropa.edu

National American University Colorado Springs
1915 Jamboree Dr Ste 185.................. Colorado Springs CO 80920 316-448-5400 590-8305*
*Fax Area Code: 719 ■ *TF:* 855-448-2318 ■ *Web:* www.national.edu

National American University Denver
1325 S Colorado Blvd Ste 100........................ Denver CO 80222 303-876-7100 876-7105*
*Fax: Admissions ■ *Web:* www.national.edu

Regis University 3333 Regis Blvd...................... Denver CO 80221 303-458-4100 964-5473
TF Admissions: 800-388-2366 ■ *Web:* www.regis.edu
Colorado Springs
7450 Campus Dr Ste 100 .... Colorado Springs CO 80920 800-568-8932 264-7095*
*Fax Area Code: 719 ■ *Fax: Admissions ■ *TF:* 800-568-8932 ■ *Web:* www.regis.edu

Springs Baptist Academy
3500 N Nevada Ave .... Colorado Springs CO 80907 719-593-7887 593-1798

University of Colorado
Boulder CB 552 .... Boulder CO 80309 303-492-1411 492-7115*
*Fax: Admissions ■ *Web:* www.colorado.edu
Colorado Springs PO Box 7150........... Colorado Springs CO 80933 719-262-3000 262-3116*
*Fax: Admissions ■ *TF:* 800-990-8227 ■ *Web:* www.uccs.edu

University of Colorado at Denver 1250 14th St .... Denver CO 80217 303-556-2400 556-4838
Web: www.ucdenver.edu/pages/ucdwelcomepage.aspx

University of Denver 2199 S University Blvd............ Denver CO 80210 303-871-2036 871-3301
TF: 800-525-9495 ■ *Web:* www.du.edu

University of Northern Colorado
501 20th St CB 92 .... Greeley CO 80639 970-351-2881 351-2984*
*Fax: Admissions ■ *TF Admissions:* 888-700-4862 ■ *Web:* www.unco.edu

US Air Force Academy (USAFA)
2304 Cadet Dr Ste 2300.................. Air Force Academy CO 80840 719-333-1110 333-3644
TF: 800-443-9266 ■ *Web:* www.usafa.af.mil

Western State College of Colorado
600 N Adams St................................ Gunnison CO 81231 970-943-2119 943-2363*
*Fax: Admissions ■ *TF Admissions:* 800-876-5309 ■ *Web:* www.western.edu

Women's College of the University of Denver
1901 E Asbury Ave .... Denver CO 80208 303-871-6848 871-6897
Web: www.womenscollege.du.edu

Yeshiva Toras Chaim Talmudical Seminary
1555 Stuart St....................................... Denver CO 80204 303-629-8200
Web: ytcdenver.org

Connecticut

Institution	City	State	Zip	Phone	Fax
Albertus Magnus College 700 Prospect St *Fax: Admissions ■ *TF Admissions:* 800-578-9160 ■ *Web:* www.albertus.edu	New Haven	CT	06511	203-773-8550	773-5248*
Briarwood College 2279 Mt Vernon Rd *Fax: Admissions ■ *TF:* 800-952-2444 ■ *Web:* www.lincolncollegene.edu	Southington	CT	06489	860-628-4751	628-6444*
Central Connecticut State University 1615 Stanley St *Web:* www.ccsu.edu	New Britain	CT	06050	860-832-2278	832-2295
Charter Oak State College 55 Paul J Manafort Dr *Web:* www.charteroak.edu	New Britain	CT	06053	860-832-3800	
Connecticut College 270 Mohegan Ave *Fax: Admissions ■ *TF:* 800-892-3363 ■ *Web:* www.conncoll.edu	New London	CT	06320	860-439-2000	439-4301*
Eastern Connecticut State University 83 Windham St *Fax: Admissions ■ *TF Admissions:* 877-353-3278 ■ *Web:* www.easternct.edu	Willimantic	CT	06226	860-465-5000	465-5544*
Fairfield University 1073 N Benson Rd *Fax: Admissions ■ *Web:* www.fairfield.edu	Fairfield	CT	06824	203-254-4000	254-4199*
Hartford Seminary 77 Sherman St *Fax: Admissions ■ *TF:* 877-860-2255 ■ *Web:* www.hartsem.edu	Hartford	CT	06105	860-509-9500	509-9509*
Holy Apostles College & Seminary 33 Prospect Hill Rd *Web:* www.holyapostles.edu	Cromwell	CT	06416	860-632-3077	
Lyme Academy College of Fine Arts 84 Lyme St *Web:* www.lymeacademy.edu	Old Lyme	CT	06371	860-434-5232	
Mitchell College 437 Pequot Ave *Fax: Admissions ■ *TF Admitting:* 800-443-2811 ■ *Web:* www.mitchell.edu	New London	CT	06320	860-701-5000	444-1209*
Paier College of Art Inc 20 Gorham Ave *Web:* www.paiercollegeofart.edu	Hamden	CT	06514	203-287-3031	287-3021
Post University 800 Country Club Rd *Fax: Admissions ■ *TF:* 800-345-2562 ■ *Web:* www.post.edu	Waterbury	CT	06723	203-596-4500	756-5810*
Quinnipiac University 275 Mt Carmel Ave *Fax: Admissions ■ *TF Admissions:* 800-462-1944 ■ *Web:* www.qu.edu	Hamden	CT	06518	203-582-8600	582-8906*
Sacred Heart University 5151 Pk Ave *Web:* www.sacredheart.edu	Fairfield	CT	06825	203-371-7999	365-7609
Southern Connecticut State University 501 Crescent St *TF:* 888-500-7278 ■ *Web:* www.southernct.edu	New Haven	CT	06515	203-392-5200	392-5727
St. Vincent's College 2800 Main St *Web:* www.stvincentscollege.edu	Bridgeport	CT	06606	203-576-5235	
University of Bridgeport 126 Pk Ave *Fax: Admissions ■ *TF:* 800-392-3582 ■ *Web:* www.bridgeport.edu	Bridgeport	CT	06604	203-576-4000	576-4941*
University of Connecticut 2131 Hillside Rd Unit 3088 *Fax: Admissions ■ *Web:* www.uconn.edu	Storrs	CT	06269	860-486-2000	486-1476*
Stamford 1 University Pl *Web:* www.stamford.uconn.edu	Stamford	CT	06901	203-251-8400	251-8556
University of Hartford 200 Bloomfield Ave *TF:* 800-947-4303 ■ *Web:* www.hartford.edu	West Hartford	CT	06117	860-768-4296	768-4961
University of New Haven 300 Boston Post Rd *Fax: Admissions ■ *TF:* 800-342-5864 ■ *Web:* www.newhaven.edu	West Haven	CT	06516	203-932-7319	931-6093*
University of Saint Joseph 1678 Asylum Ave *Web:* www.sjc.edu	West Hartford	CT	06117	860-232-4571	
US Coast Guard Academy 15 Mohegan Ave *TF:* 800-883-8724 ■ *Web:* www.cga.edu	New London	CT	06320	860-444-8500	701-6700
Wesleyan University 70 Wyllys Ave *Fax: Admissions ■ *Web:* www.wesleyan.edu	Middletown	CT	06459	860-685-3000	685-3001*
Western Connecticut State University 181 White St *TF:* 877-837-9278 ■ *Web:* wcsu.edu	Danbury	CT	06810	203-837-8200	837-8234
Yale University 38 Hill House Ave *Fax: Admissions ■ *Web:* www.yale.edu	New Haven	CT	06520	203-432-4771	432-9392*

Delaware

Institution	City	State	Zip	Phone	Fax
Delaware State University 1200 N DuPont Hwy *Fax: Admissions ■ *TF Admissions:* 800-845-2544 ■ *Web:* www.desu.edu	Dover	DE	19901	302-857-6351	857-6352*
Goldey Beacom College 4701 Limestone Rd *Fax: Admissions ■ *TF:* 800-833-4877 ■ *Web:* gbc.edu	Wilmington	DE	19808	302-998-8814	996-5408*
University of Delaware Hullihen Hall Rm 209 *Fax: Admissions ■ *Web:* www.udel.edu	Newark	DE	19716	302-831-2792	831-6905*
Wilmington University 320 N DuPont Hwy *Fax: Admissions ■ *TF Admissions:* 877-967-5464 ■ *Web:* www.wilmu.edu	New Castle	DE	19720	302-356-6739	328-5902*

District of Columbia

Institution	City	State	Zip	Phone	Fax
American University 4400 Massachusetts Ave NW *TF:* 800-829-1040 ■ *Web:* www.american.edu	Washington	DC	20016	202-885-1000	885-2558
Catholic University of America 620 Michigan Ave NE *Web:* www.cua.edu	Washington	DC	20064	202-319-5000	319-6533
Gallaudet University 800 Florida Ave NE *TF:* 800-995-0550 ■ *Web:* www.gallaudet.edu	Washington	DC	20002	202-651-5000	651-5744
George Washington University 2121 'I' St NW *TF:* 866-498-3382 ■ *Web:* www.gwu.edu	Washington	DC	20052	202-994-1000	994-9619
Mount Vernon College 2100 Foxhall Rd NW *Fax: Admissions ■ *TF:* 800-447-3765 ■ *Web:* www.gwu.edu	Washington	DC	20007	202-994-1000	994-0325*
Georgetown University 37th & 'O' Sts NW *Web:* www.georgetown.edu	Washington	DC	20057	202-687-3600	687-5084
Howard University 2400 Sixth St NW *Fax: Admissions ■ *TF:* 800-822-6363 ■ *Web:* www.howard.edu	Washington	DC	20059	202-806-6100	806-4465*
Potomac College 4000 Chesapeake St NW *Web:* potomac.edu	Washington	DC	20016	202-686-0876	
Strayer University 1133 15th St NW *TF:* 888-311-0355 ■ *Web:* www.strayer.edu	Washington	DC	20005	202-408-2400	
Takoma Park 6830 Laurel St NW *TF:* 888-311-0355 ■ *Web:* www.strayer.edu	Washington	DC	20012	202-722-8100	
Trinity University 125 Michigan Ave NE *Fax: Admissions ■ *TF Admissions:* 800-492-6882 ■ *Web:* www.trinitydc.edu	Washington	DC	20017	202-884-9000	884-9403*
University of the District of Columbia 4200 Connecticut Ave NW *Web:* www.udc.edu	Washington	DC	20008	202-274-5000	274-5552

Florida

Institution	City	State	Zip	Phone	Fax
American Intercontinental University South Florida 2250 N Commerce Pkwy *TF:* 855-377-1888 ■ *Web:* www.aiuniv.edu	Weston	FL	33326	954-446-6100	
Ave Maria University 5050 Ave Maria Blvd *Fax: Admissions ■ *TF:* 877-283-8648 ■ *Web:* avemaria.edu	Naples	FL	34119	239-280-2500	280-2556*
Baptist College of Florida 5400 College Dr *Fax: Admissions ■ *TF:* 800-328-2660 ■ *Web:* www.baptistcollege.edu	Graceville	FL	32440	850-263-3261	263-7506*
Barry University 11300 NE Second Ave *Fax: Admissions ■ *TF:* 800-756-6000 ■ *Web:* www.barry.edu	Miami Shores	FL	33161	305-899-3000	899-2971*
Orlando 1650 Sandlake Rd Ste 390 *Fax: Admissions ■ *TF:* 800-756-6000 ■ *Web:* barry.edu	Orlando	FL	32809	407-438-4150	438-9774*
Tallahassee 325 John Knox Rd Bldg A *Fax: Admissions ■ *TF:* 800-756-6000 ■ *Web:* barry.edu	Tallahassee	FL	32303	850-385-2279	385-7576*
Bethune-Cookman College 640 Dr Mary McLeod Bethune Blvd *Fax: Admissions ■ *TF Admissions:* 800-448-0228 ■ *Web:* www.cookman.edu	Daytona Beach	FL	32114	386-481-2900	481-2601*
Chipola College 3094 Indian Cir *Fax: Admissions ■ *Web:* www.chipola.edu	Marianna	FL	32446	850-526-2761	718-2287*
Clearwater Christian College 3400 Gulf to Bay Blvd *Web:* www.clearwater.edu	Clearwater	FL	33759	727-726-1153	
Columbia College Orlando 2600 Technology Dr Ste 100 *Fax: Admissions ■ *TF:* 800-231-2391 ■ *Web:* www.ccis.edu	Orlando	FL	32804	407-293-9911	293-8530*
Eckerd College 4200 54th Ave S *Fax: Admissions ■ *TF Admissions:* 800-456-9009 ■ *Web:* www.eckerd.edu	Saint Petersburg	FL	33711	727-867-1166	866-2304*
Embry-Riddle Aeronautical University *Daytona Beach* 600 S Clyde Morris Blvd *Fax: Admissions ■ *TF:* 800-862-2416 ■ *Web:* www.erau.edu	Daytona Beach	FL	32114	386-226-6000	226-7070*
Flagler College 74 King St *Fax: Admissions ■ *TF Admissions:* 800-304-4208 ■ *Web:* www.flagler.edu	Saint Augustine	FL	32084	904-829-6481	819-6466*
Florida A & M University 1700 Lee Hall Dr Rm G-7 Foote-Hilyer Administration Ctr *TF:* 866-642-1198 ■ *Web:* www.famu.edu	Tallahassee	FL	32307	850-599-3000	599-3069
Florida Atlantic University (FAU) 777 Glades Rd *Fax: Admissions ■ *TF Admissions:* 800-299-4328 ■ *Web:* www.fau.edu	Boca Raton	FL	33431	561-297-3000	297-2758*
Davie 3200 College Ave *TF:* 800-764-2222 ■ *Web:* www.fau.edu/broward/davie	Davie	FL	33314	954-236-1000	
Fort Lauderdale 111 E Las Olas Blvd *TF:* 800-764-2222	Fort Lauderdale	FL	33301	954-201-7350	
MacArthur 5353 Parkside Dr *Fax: Admissions ■ *TF:* 888-328-2586 ■ *Web:* www.fau.edu/jupiter	Jupiter	FL	33458	561-799-8500	799-8721*
Treasure Coast 777 Glades Rd *Fax: Admissions ■ *Web:* www.fau.edu	Boca Raton	FL	33431	772-873-3300	873-3304*
Florida College 119 N Glen Arven Ave *Fax: Admissions ■ *TF:* 800-326-7655 ■ *Web:* www.floridacollege.edu	Temple Terrace	FL	33617	813-988-5131	899-6772*
Florida College of Integrative Medicine 7100 Lk Ellenor Dr *Web:* www.fcim.edu	Orlando	FL	32809	407-888-8689	
Florida Institute of Technology 150 W University Blvd *Fax: Admissions ■ *TF:* 800-888-4348 ■ *Web:* www.fit.edu	Melbourne	FL	32901	321-674-8000	674-8004*
Florida International University 11200 SW Eigth St *TF:* 800-677-6337 ■ *Web:* www.fiu.edu	Miami	FL	33199	305-348-2000	348-3648
Florida Memorial University 15800 NW 42nd Ave *TF:* 800-822-1362 ■ *Web:* www.fmuniv.edu	Miami Gardens	FL	33054	305-626-3600	
Florida Southern College 111 Lk Hollingsworth Dr *Fax: Admissions ■ *TF Admissions:* 800-274-4131 ■ *Web:* www.flsouthern.edu	Lakeland	FL	33801	863-680-4131	680-4120*
Florida State University, The 600 W College Ave *Web:* www.fsu.edu	Tallahassee	FL	32306	850-644-4357	
Hodges University 2655 Northbrooke Dr *TF:* 800-466-8017 ■ *Web:* www.hodges.edu	Naples	FL	34119	239-513-1122	
Fort Myers 4501 Colonial Blvd *TF:* 800-466-0019 ■ *Web:* myhugo.hodges.edu	Fort Myers	FL	33966	239-938-7701	
Jacksonville University 2800 University Blvd N *Fax: Admissions ■ *TF:* 800-225-2027 ■ *Web:* www.ju.edu	Jacksonville	FL	32211	904-256-8000	256-7012*
Johnson & Wales University North Miami 1701 NE 127th St *Fax Area Code: 305 ■ *TF:* 866-598-3567 ■ *Web:* www.jwu.edu	North Miami	FL	33181	800-342-5598	892-7020*
Jones College 5353 Arlington Expy *TF:* 800-331-0176 ■ *Web:* www.jones.edu	Jacksonville	FL	32211	904-743-1122	
Logos Christian College 6620 Southpoint Dr S Ste 200 *TF:* 800-776-0127 ■ *Web:* www.logos.edu	Jacksonville	FL	32216	904-745-3311	
Lynn University 3601 N Military Trl *Fax: Admissions ■ *TF Admissions:* 800-888-5966 ■ *Web:* www.lynn.edu	Boca Raton	FL	33431	561-237-7900	237-7100*
New College of Florida 5800 Bay Shore Rd *Fax: Admissions ■ *TF:* 800-435-7352 ■ *Web:* www.ncf.edu	Sarasota	FL	34243	941-487-5000	487-5010*
Northwood University Florida 2600 N Military Trl *TF Admissions:* 800-458-8325 ■ *Web:* www.northwood.edu	West Palm Beach	FL	33409	561-478-5500	

Phone Fax

Nova Southeastern University
3301 College Ave .... Fort Lauderdale FL 33314 954-262-8000 262-3811*
*Fax: Admissions ■ TF: 800-541-6682 ■ Web: www.nova.edu

Palm Beach Atlantic University
PO Box 24708 .... West Palm Beach FL 33416 561-803-2000 803-2115*
*Fax: Admissions ■ TF: 888-468-6722 ■ Web: www.pba.edu

Pensacola Christian College 250 Brent Ln .... Pensacola FL 32503 850-478-8496 722-3355*
*Fax Area Code: 800 ■ TF: 800-722-4636 ■ Web: www.pcci.edu

Rollins College 1000 Holt Ave .... Winter Park FL 32789 407-646-2000 646-1502*
*Fax: Admissions ■ TF: 800-799-2586 ■ Web: www.rollins.edu

Rosenstiel School of Marine & Atmospheric Science University of Miami
4600 Rickenbacker Causeway Rosenstiel School .... Miami FL 33149 305-421-4000
Web: www.rsmas.miami.edu

Saint Leo University 33701 State Rd 52 .... Saint Leo FL 33574 352-588-8200 588-8257*
*Fax: Admissions ■ TF: 800-334-5532 ■ Web: www.saintleo.edu
Palatka Ctr 33701 State Rd 52 PO Box 6665 .... Saint Leo FL 33574 352-588-8200
TF: 800-334-5532 ■ Web: www.saintleo.edu

Saint Thomas University
16401 NW 37th Ave .... Miami Gardens FL 33054 305-628-6546 628-6591
TF: 800-367-9010 ■ Web: www.stu.edu

South University West Palm Beach
9801 Belvedere Rd University Ctr .... West Palm Beach FL 33411 561-273-6500
TF: 800-688-0932 ■ Web: www.southuniversity.edu

Southeastern University
1000 Longfellow Blvd .... Lakeland FL 33801 863-667-5000 667-5200
TF: 800-500-8760 ■ Web: seu.edu

Stetson University
421 N Woodland Blvd Unit 8378 .... DeLand FL 32723 386-822-7100 822-7112*
*Fax: Admissions ■ TF Admissions: 800-688-0101 ■ Web: www.stetson.edu

Trinity International University South Florida
8190 W SR 84 .... Davie FL 33324 954-382-6400 382-6420
TF: 800-822-3225 ■ Web: www.tiu.edu

University of Central Florida
4000 Central Florida Blvd PO Box 160000 .... Orlando FL 32816 407-823-2000 823-5625*
*Fax: Admissions ■ Web: www.ucf.edu

University of Florida
219 Grinter Hall PO Box 115500 .... Gainesville FL 32611 352-392-3261 392-2115*
*Fax: Admissions ■ TF: 866-876-4472 ■ Web: www.ufl.edu

University of Miami 1252 Memorial Dr .... Coral Gables FL 33146 305-284-4323 284-2507
Web: www.miami.edu

University of North Florida
4567 St Johns Bluff Rd S .... Jacksonville FL 32224 904-620-1000 620-2414
TF: 866-697-7150 ■ Web: www.unf.edu
Saint Petersburg 140 Seventh Ave S .... Saint Petersburg FL 33701 727-873-4135 873-4525
Web: www.usfsp.edu
Sarasota-Manatee 8350 N Tamiami Trail .... Sarasota FL 34243 941-359-4200 359-4236*
*Fax: Admissions ■ TF: 866-974-1222 ■ Web: usfsm.edu
Tampa 4202 E Fowler Ave .... Tampa FL 33620 813-974-2011 974-4346
TF: 800-299-2855 ■ Web: www.usf.edu

University of South Florida Polytechnic
Lakeland 3433 Winter Lake Rd .... Lakeland FL 33803 863-667-7000 667-7096*
*Fax: Admissions ■ TF: 800-873-5636

University of Tampa 401 W Kennedy Blvd .... Tampa FL 33606 813-253-3333 258-7398
Web: www.ut.edu

Warner Southern College 13895 Hwy 27 .... Lake Wales FL 33859 800-309-9563 949-7248*
*Fax: Admissions ■ TF: 800-309-9563 ■ Web: warner.edu

Webber International University
1201 N Scenic Hwy .... Babson Park FL 33827 800-741-1844 638-1591*
*Fax Area Code: 863 ■ *Fax: Admissions ■ TF: 800-741-1844

Georgia

Phone Fax

Agnes Scott College 141 E College Ave .... Decatur GA 30030 404-471-6000 471-6414*
*Fax: Admissions ■ TF: 800-868-8602 ■ Web: www.agnesscott.edu

Albany State University 504 College Dr Rd .... Albany GA 31705 229-430-4600 430-1614*

American InterContinental University
Atlanta
6600 Peachtree Dunwoody Rd
500 Embassy Row NE .... Atlanta GA 30328 404-965-6500
TF: 800-491-0182 ■ Web: www.aiuniv.edu
Dunwoody
6600 Peachtree-Dunwoody Rd 500 Embassy Row .... Atlanta GA 30328 404-965-6500 695-4538*
*Fax Area Code: 866 ■ *Fax: Admissions ■ TF: 855-377-1888 ■ Web: www.aiuniv.edu

Armstrong Atlantic State University
11935 Abercorn St .... Savannah GA 31419 800-633-2349
TF: 800-633-2349 ■ Web: www.armstrong.edu

Atlanta Christian College
2605 Ben Hill Rd .... East Point GA 30344 404-761-8861 214-0648*
*Fax: Admissions ■ Web: point.edu

Augusta State University 2500 Walton Way .... Augusta GA 30904 706-737-1632 667-4355
TF: 800-341-4373 ■ Web: www.augusta.edu

Berry College
2277 Martha Berry Hwy PO Box 490159 .... Mount Berry GA 30149 706-232-5374 290-2178*
*Fax: Admissions ■ TF: 800-237-7942 ■ Web: www.berry.edu

Brenau University 500 Washington St .... Gainesville GA 30501 770-534-6299 538-4701*
*Fax: Admissions ■ TF: 800-252-5119 ■ Web: www.brenau.edu

Brewton-Parker College
201 David-Eliza Fountain Cir Hwy 280
PO Box 197 .... Mount Vernon GA 30445 912-583-2241 583-3598*
*Fax: Admissions ■ TF: 800-342-1087 ■ Web: www.bpc.edu

Carver Bible College 3870 Cascade Rd .... Atlanta GA 30331 404-527-4520 527-4524
Web: www.carver.edu

Clark Atlanta University
223 James P Brawley Dr SW .... Atlanta GA 30314 404-880-8000 880-6174*
*Fax: Admissions ■ TF Admissions: 800-688-3228 ■ Web: www.cau.edu

Clayton State University
2000 Clayton State Blvd .... Morrow GA 30260 678-466-4000 466-4149*
*Fax: Admissions ■ Web: www.clayton.edu

Columbus State University
4225 University Ave .... Columbus GA 31907 706-507-8800
TF: 866-264-2035 ■ Web: columbusstate.edu

Covenant College 14049 Scenic Hwy .... Lookout Mountain GA 30750 706-820-1560 820-0893*
*Fax: Admissions ■ TF: 888-451-2683 ■ Web: www.covenant.edu

Phone Fax

Dalton State College 650 N College Dr .... Dalton GA 30720 706-272-4436 529-9266*
*Fax: Admissions ■ TF: 800-829-4436 ■ Web: www.daltonstate.edu

Emmanuel College 181 Spring St .... Franklin Springs GA 30639 706-245-7226 245-2876
TF: 800-860-8800 ■ Web: www.ec.edu

Emory University 201 Dowman Dr .... Atlanta GA 30322 404-727-6036 727-4303
TF Admissions: 800-727-6036 ■ Web: www.emory.edu

Fort Valley State University
1005 State University Dr .... Fort Valley GA 31030 478-825-6211
TF: 877-462-3878 ■ Web: www.fvsu.edu

Georgia College & State University
231 W Hancock St CB 23 .... Milledgeville GA 31061 478-445-5004 445-3653*
*Fax: Admissions ■ TF: 800-342-0471 ■ Web: www.gcsu.edu
Macon 433 Cherry St .... Macon GA 31206 478-752-4278 752-1064
TF: 800-342-0471 ■ Web: www.gcsu.edu/future-students/graduate

Georgia Institute of Technology 225 N Ave NW .... Atlanta GA 30332 404-894-2000 894-9511*
*Fax: Admissions ■ Web: www.gatech.edu

Georgia Southern University PO Box 8024 .... Statesboro GA 30460 912-478-5391
Web: www.georgiasouthern.edu

Georgia Southwestern State University
800 Gsw State University Dr .... Americus GA 31709 229-928-1273 931-2983
TF Admissions: 800-338-0082 ■ Web: www.gsw.edu

Georgia State University
33 Gilmer St SE Ste 200 .... Atlanta GA 30303 404-413-2000 413-2002
Web: www.gsu.edu

Gwinnett College of Business
4230 Lawrenceville Hwy Nw Ste 11 .... Lilburn GA 30047 770-381-7200
Web: www.gwinnettcollege.edu

Kennesaw State University 1000 Chastain Rd .... Kennesaw GA 30144 770-423-6000 420-4435*
*Fax: Admissions ■ TF: 888-875-3697 ■ Web: www.kennesaw.edu

LaGrange College 601 Broad St .... LaGrange GA 30240 706-880-8000 880-8010*
*Fax: Admissions ■ TF Admissions: 800-593-2885

Life University 1269 Barclay Cir .... Marietta GA 30060 770-426-2884
TF: 800-543-3203 ■ Web: www.life.edu

Luther Rice College & Seminary
3038 Evans Mill Rd .... Lithonia GA 30038 770-484-1204
Web: www.lru.edu

Macon State College 100 College Stn Dr .... Macon GA 31206 478-471-2700 471-5343*
*Fax: Admissions ■ TF: 800-272-7619 ■ Web: www.mga.edu
Warner Robins 100 University Blvd .... Warner Robins GA 31093 478-929-6700 929-6726
Web: www.mga.edu

Mercer University 1400 Coleman Ave .... Macon GA 31207 478-301-2650 301-2828*
*Fax: Admissions ■ TF: 800-637-2378 ■ Web: www.mercer.edu
Cecil B Day 3001 Mercer University Dr .... Atlanta GA 30341 678-547-6089 547-6367
TF: 800-840-8577 ■ Web: www.mercer.edu

Morehouse College 830 Westview Dr SW .... Atlanta GA 30314 404-681-2800 572-3668*
*Fax: Admissions ■ Web: www.morehouse.edu

Oglethorpe University 4484 Peachtree Rd,N.E. .... Atlanta GA 30319 404-364-8307 364-8491
TF: 800-428-4484 ■ Web: www.oglethorpe.edu

Paine College 1235 15th St .... Augusta GA 30901 706-821-8200
TF: 800-476-7703 ■ Web: www.paine.edu

Piedmont College 165 Central Ave .... Demorest GA 30535 706-776-0103 776-6635*
*Fax: Admissions ■ TF: 800-277-7020 ■ Web: www.piedmont.edu

Reinhardt College 7300 Reinhardt College Cir .... Waleska GA 30183 770-720-5526 720-5899*
*Fax: Admissions ■ TF: 877-346-4273 ■ Web: www.reinhardt.edu

Shorter University 315 Shorter Ave .... Rome GA 30165 706-233-7319 233-7224*
*Fax: Admissions ■ TF: 800-868-6980 ■ Web: www.shorter.edu

South University Savannah 709 Mall Blvd .... Savannah GA 31406 912-201-8000
TF: 800-688-0932 ■ Web: www.southuniversity.edu

Spelman College 350 Spelman Ln SW .... Atlanta GA 30314 404-681-3643 270-5201*
*Fax: Admissions ■ TF Admissions: 800-982-2411 ■ Web: www.spelman.edu

Thomas University 1501 Millpond Rd .... Thomasville GA 31792 229-226-1621
TF: 800-538-9784 ■ Web: www.thomasu.edu

Truett-McConnell College 100 Alumni Dr .... Cleveland GA 30528 706-865-2134
TF: 800-226-8621 ■ Web: www.truett.edu

University of West Georgia 1600 Maple St .... Carrollton GA 30117 678-839-5000 839-4747
Web: www.westga.edu

Valdosta State University
1500 N Patterson St .... Valdosta GA 31698 229-333-5800 333-5482*
*Fax: Admissions ■ TF: 800-618-1878 ■ Web: www.valdosta.edu

Wesleyan College 4760 Forsyth Rd .... Macon GA 31210 478-757-5219 757-4030*
*Fax: Admissions ■ TF: 800-447-6610 ■ Web: www.wesleyancollege.edu

Guam

Phone Fax

University of Guam
Unibetsed?t GuahanUOG Station .... Mangialo GU 96923 671-735-2910
Web: www.uog.edu

Hawaii

Phone Fax

Atlantic International University
900 Ft St Mall .... Honolulu HI 96813 808-924-9567
TF: 800-993-0066 ■ Web: www.aiu.edu

Brigham Young University Hawaii
55-220 Kulanui St .... Laie HI 96762 808-293-3211 293-3741*
*Fax: Admissions ■ Web: www.byuh.edu

Chaminade University 3140 Waialae Ave .... Honolulu HI 96816 808-735-4711 735-4735*
*Fax: Admissions ■ TF: 800-735-3733 ■ Web: www.chaminade.edu

Hawaii Pacific University
1164 Bishop St Ste 200 .... Honolulu HI 96813 808-544-0200 544-1136*
*Fax: Admissions ■ TF: 866-225-5478 ■ Web: www.hpu.edu
Windward Hawaii Loa 1164 Bishop St .... Honolulu HI 96813 808-544-0200
TF Admissions: 866-225-5478 ■ Web: www.hpu.edu

University of Hawaii
Hilo 200 W Kawili St .... Hilo HI 96720 808-974-7414 933-0861*
*Fax: Admissions ■ TF Admissions: 800-897-4456 ■ Web: hilo.hawaii.edu
Manoa 2600 Campus Rd Rm 001 .... Honolulu HI 96822 808-956-8975 956-4148*
*Fax: Admissions ■ TF Admissions: 800-823-9771 ■ Web: www.manoa.hawaii.edu
West Oahu 96-129 Ala Ike .... Pearl City HI 96782 808-454-4700 453-6075
TF: 866-299-8656 ■ Web: www.uhwo.hawaii.edu

Idaho

	City	State	Zip	Phone	Fax
Boise State University 1910 University Dr	Boise	ID	83725	208-426-1156	426-3765
TF: 800-824-7017 ■ *Web:* my.boisestate.edu					
Brigham Young University Idaho 525 S Ctr.	Rexburg	ID	83460	866-672-2984	496-1220*
*Fax Area Code: 208 ■ *Fax:* Admissions ■ *TF:* 866-672-2984 ■ *Web:* www.byui.edu					
College of Idaho 2112 Cleveland Blvd	Caldwell	ID	83605	208-459-5011	459-5757*
*Fax: Admissions ■ *TF Admissions:* 800-224-3246 ■ *Web:* www.collegeofidaho.edu					
Idaho State University 921 S Eigth Ave.	Pocatello	ID	83209	208-282-2475	282-4511*
*Fax: Admissions ■ *Web:* www.isu.edu					
Lewis-Clark State College 500 Eigth Ave.	Lewiston	ID	83501	208-792-5272	792-2210*
*Fax: Admissions ■ *TF:* 800-933-5272 ■ *Web:* www.lcsc.edu					
Northwest Nazarene University 623 Holly St	Nampa	ID	83686	208-467-8000	467-8645*
*Fax: Admissions ■ *TF Admissions:* 877-668-4968 ■ *Web:* www.nnu.edu					
University of Idaho 875 Perimeter Dr.	Moscow	ID	83844	208-885-6111	885-9119
TF: 888-884-3246 ■ *Web:* www.uidaho.edu					
Boise 322 E Front St Ste 190	Boise	ID	83702	208-334-2999	364-4035
TF: 866-264-7384 ■ *Web:* www.uidaho.edu					

Illinois

	City	State	Zip	Phone	Fax
Adler School of Professional Psychology					
65 E Wacker Pl Ste 2100	Chicago	IL	60601	312-201-5900	
Web: www.adler.edu					
American InterContinental University Los Angeles					
231 N Martingale Rd 6th Fl.	Schaumburg	IL	60173	877-701-3800	
TF: 877-701-3800 ■ *Web:* www.aiuniv.edu					
American Islamic College 640 W Irving Pk Rd.	Chicago	IL	60613	773-281-4700	281-8552*
*Fax: Admissions ■ *Web:* www.aicusa.edu					
Augustana College 639 38th St	Rock Island	IL	61201	309-794-7000	794-7174*
*Fax: Admissions ■ *TF:* 800-798-8100 ■ *Web:* www.augustana.edu					
Aurora University 347 S Gladstone Ave	Aurora	IL	60506	630-844-5533	844-5535
TF: 800-742-5281 ■ *Web:* www.aurora.edu					
Benedictine University 5700 College Rd	Lisle	IL	60532	630-829-6300	829-6301
TF: 888-829-6363 ■ *Web:* www.ben.edu					
Blackburn College 700 College Ave.	Carlinville	IL	62626	217-854-3231	854-3713*
*Fax: Admissions ■ *TF:* 800-233-3550 ■ *Web:* www.blackburn.edu					
Bradley University 1501 W Bradley Ave.	Peoria	IL	61625	309-676-7611	677-2797
TF Admissions: 800-447-6460 ■ *Web:* www.bradley.edu					
Chicago State University 9501 S King Dr.	Chicago	IL	60628	773-995-2513	995-3820*
*Fax: Admissions ■ *Web:* www.csu.edu					
Columbia College 600 S Michigan Ave 3rd Fl	Chicago	IL	60605	312-663-1600	344-8024*
*Fax: Admissions ■ *TF:* 866-705-0200 ■ *Web:* www.colum.edu					
Concordia University Chicago					
7400 Augusta St	River Forest	IL	60305	708-771-8300	
TF: 888-258-6773 ■ *Web:* www.cuchicago.edu					
DePaul University 1 E Jackson Blvd Ste 9100	Chicago	IL	60614	312-362-8300	362-5749
Web: www.depaul.edu					
Dominican University 7900 W Div St.	River Forest	IL	60305	708-366-2490	524-5990*
*Fax: Admissions ■ *TF:* 800-828-8475 ■ *Web:* www.dom.edu					
East-West University 816 S Michigan Ave	Chicago	IL	60605	312-939-0111	939-0083
TF: 877-398-9376 ■ *Web:* www.eastwest.edu					
Eastern Illinois University					
600 Lincoln Ave	Charleston	IL	61920	217-581-2223	581-7060*
*Fax: Admissions ■ *TF Admissions:* 800-252-5711 ■ *Web:* www.eiu.edu					
Elmhurst College 190 Prospect Ave	Elmhurst	IL	60126	630-617-3400	617-5501
TF: 800-697-1871 ■ *Web:* www.elmhurst.edu					
Eureka College 300 E College Ave	Eureka	IL	61530	309-467-6350	467-6576*
*Fax: Admissions ■ *TF Admissions:* 888-438-7352 ■ *Web:* www.eureka.edu					
Governors State University					
1 University Pkwy	University Park	IL	06048	708-534-5000	534-1640*
*Fax: Admissions ■ *TF:* 800-478-8478 ■ *Web:* www.govst.edu					
Greenville College 315 E College Ave	Greenville	IL	62246	618-664-7100	664-9841*
*Fax: Admissions ■ *TF:* 800-345-4440 ■ *Web:* www.greenville.edu					
Harrington College of Design					
200 W Madison St	Chicago	IL	60606	866-590-4423	
TF: 866-590-4423 ■ *Web:* www.harrington.edu					
Illinois College 1101 W College Ave.	Jacksonville	IL	62650	217-245-3030	245-3034*
*Fax: Admissions ■ *TF Admissions:* 866-464-5265 ■ *Web:* www.ic.edu					
Illinois Institute of Technology					
10 W 33rd St	Chicago	IL	60616	312-567-3025	567-6939*
*Fax: Admissions ■ *TF:* 800-448-2329 ■ *Web:* www.iit.edu					
Rice 201 E Loop Rd	Wheaton	IL	60189	630-682-6000	682-6010*
*Fax: Admissions ■ *Web:* www.iit.edu/rice					
Illinois State University					
North and School Streets Hovey Hall 201	Normal	IL	61790	309-438-2111	438-3932*
*Fax: Admissions ■ *TF Admissions:* 800-366-2478 ■ *Web:* illinoisstate.edu					
Illinois Wesleyan University 1312 Pk St	Bloomington	IL	61701	309-556-3031	556-3820*
*Fax: Admissions ■ *TF Admissions:* 800-332-2498 ■ *Web:* www.iwu.edu					
Judson University 1151 N State St.	Elgin	IL	60123	847-628-2500	628-2526*
*Fax: Admissions ■ *TF Admissions:* 800-879-5376 ■ *Web:* www.judsonu.edu					
Knox College 2 E S St	Galesburg	IL	61401	309-341-7000	341-7806*
*Fax: Admissions ■ *TF Admissions:* 800-678-5669 ■ *Web:* www.knox.edu					
Lake Forest College 555 N Sheridan Rd	Lake Forest	IL	60045	847-234-3100	735-6271
TF: 800-828-4751 ■ *Web:* www.lakeforest.edu					
Lakeview College of Nursing 903 N Logan Ave.	Danville	IL	61832	217-443-5238	
Web: www.lakeviewcol.edu					
Lewis University					
1 University Pkwy Unit 297	Romeoville	IL	60446	815-836-5250	836-5002
TF: 800-897-9000 ■ *Web:* www.lewisu.edu					
Loyola University Chicago					
Cudahy Library 1032 W Sheridan Rd.	Chicago	IL	60660	773-508-2632	
Web: libraries.luc.edu/cudahy					
Lake Shore 6525 N Sheridan Rd	Chicago	IL	60626	773-508-3075	508-8926
TF: 800-262-2373 ■ *Web:* www.luc.edu					
Water Tower 820 N Michigan Ave	Chicago	IL	60611	312-915-6500	915-7216*
*Fax: Admissions ■ *TF Admissions:* 800-262-2373 ■ *Web:* www.luc.edu					
MacMurray College 447 E College Ave	Jacksonville	IL	62650	217-479-7056	291-0702*
*Fax: Admissions ■ *TF:* 800-252-7485 ■ *Web:* www.mac.edu					
McKendree College 701 College Rd	Lebanon	IL	62254	618-537-4481	537-6496*
*Fax: Admissions ■ *TF:* 800-232-7228 ■ *Web:* www.mckendree.edu					
Millikin University 1184 W Main St.	Decatur	IL	62522	217-424-6211	
TF: 800-373-7733 ■ *Web:* www.millikin.edu					
Monmouth College 700 E Broadway Ave	Monmouth	IL	61462	309-457-2311	457-2141
TF: 888-827-8268 ■ *Web:* www.monmouthcollege.edu					
National University of Health Sciences					
200 E Roosevelt Rd.	Lombard	IL	60148	630-629-2000	889-6554
TF: 800-826-6285 ■ *Web:* www.nuhs.edu					
National-Louis University 1000 Capitol Dr.	Wheeling	IL	60090	847-947-5718	465-5730*
*Fax: Admissions ■ *TF:* 800-443-5522 ■ *Web:* www.nl.edu					
Chicago 122 S Michigan Ave.	Chicago	IL	60603	888-658-8632	465-5730*
*Fax Area Code: 847 ■ *Fax: Admissions ■ *TF:* 800-443-5522 ■ *Web:* www.nl.edu					
North Central College 30 N Brainard St.	Naperville	IL	60540	630-637-5800	637-5819*
*Fax: Admissions ■ *TF:* 800-411-1861 ■ *Web:* northcentralcollege.edu					
North Park University 3225 W Foster Ave	Chicago	IL	60625	773-244-5500	
TF: 800-888-6728 ■ *Web:* www.northpark.edu					
Northeastern Illinois University					
5500 N St Louis Ave	Chicago	IL	60625	773-442-4050	442-4020*
*Fax: Admissions ■ *TF:* 800-393-0865 ■ *Web:* www.neiu.edu					
Northern Illinois University					
1425 W Lincoln Hwy	DeKalb	IL	60115	815-753-1000	753-8312*
*Fax: Admissions ■ *TF:* 800-892-3050 ■ *Web:* www.niu.edu					
Northwestern University 1801 Hinman Ave	Evanston	IL	60208	847-491-7271	467-2331*
*Fax: Admissions ■ *TF:* 800-227-7368 ■ *Web:* www.northwestern.edu					
Olivet Nazarene University					
1 University Ave	Bourbonnais	IL	60914	815-939-5011	935-4998*
*Fax: Admissions ■ *TF:* 800-648-1463 ■ *Web:* www.olivet.edu					
Quincy University 1800 College Ave.	Quincy	IL	62301	217-222-8020	
TF: 866-703-4004 ■ *Web:* quhawks.com/index.aspx					
Robert Morris College					
Chicago 401 S State St	Chicago	IL	60605	312-935-6800	935-4182
TF: 800-762-5960 ■ *Web:* www.robertmorris.edu					
DuPage 905 Meridian Lk Dr.	Aurora	IL	60504	630-375-8100	375-8020*
*Fax: Admissions ■ *TF Admissions:* 800-762-5960 ■ *Web:* www.robertmorris.edu					
Orland Park 43 Orland Sq Dr	Orland Park	IL	60462	708-226-3800	226-5350
TF: 800-225-1520 ■ *Web:* www.robertmorris.edu					
Springfield 3101 Montvale Dr	Springfield	IL	62704	217-793-2500	793-4210*
*Fax: Admitting ■ *TF:* 800-762-5960 ■ *Web:* www.robertmorris.edu					
Rockford College 5050 E State St.	Rockford	IL	61108	815-226-4000	226-2822*
*Fax: Admissions ■ *TF:* 800-892-2984 ■ *Web:* www.rockford.edu					
Roosevelt University 430 S Michigan Ave.	Chicago	IL	60605	312-341-3500	
TF Admissions: 877-277-5978 ■ *Web:* www.roosevelt.edu					
Albert A Robin 1400 N Roosevelt Blvd.	Schaumburg	IL	60173	847-619-8600	619-8636*
*Fax: Admissions ■ *TF Admissions:* 877-277-5978 ■ *Web:* www.roosevelt.edu					
Rush University 600 S Paulina St	Chicago	IL	60612	312-942-7100	942-2219*
*Fax: Admissions ■ *Web:* www.rushu.rush.edu					
Saint Anthony College of Nursing					
5658 E State St	Rockford	IL	61108	815-395-5091	
Web: sacn.edu					
Saint Xavier University 3700 W 103rd St	Chicago	IL	60655	773-298-3000	298-3076*
*Fax: Admissions ■ *TF:* 800-462-9288 ■ *Web:* www.sxu.edu					
School of the Art Institute of Chicago					
36 S Wabash Ave	Chicago	IL	60603	312-629-6100	
TF Admissions: 800-232-7242 ■ *Web:* www.artic.edu					
Shimer College 3424 S State St	Chicago	IL	60616	312-235-3506	
TF: 800-215-7173 ■ *Web:* www.shimer.edu					
Southern Illinois University					
Edwardsville SR 157	Edwardsville	IL	62026	618-650-2000	650-5013*
*Fax: Admissions ■ *TF:* 888-328-5168 ■ *Web:* www.siue.edu					
Southern Illinois University Carbondale					
900 S Normal Ave Woody Hall MC 4716	Carbondale	IL	62901	618-536-7791	453-3250*
*Fax: Admissions ■ *Web:* gradschool.siu.edu					
Trinity Christian College					
6601 W College Dr	Palos Heights	IL	60463	708-597-3000	239-4826
Web: www.trnty.edu					
Trinity International University					
2065 Half Day Rd	Deerfield	IL	60015	847-945-8800	317-8097
TF: 800-822-3225 ■ *Web:* www.tiu.edu					
University of Chicago 5801 S Ellis Ave	Chicago	IL	60637	773-702-1234	702-4199*
*Fax: Admissions ■ *Web:* www.uchicago.edu					
University of Illinois					
Chicago 601 S Morgan	Chicago	IL	60607	312-996-7000	413-7628
Web: www.uic.edu					
Springfield 1 University Plz MS UHB 1080	Springfield	IL	62703	217-206-4847	206-6620*
*Fax: Admissions ■ *TF:* 888-977-4847 ■ *Web:* www.uis.edu					
Urbana-Champaign 901 W Illinois St	Urbana	IL	61801	217-333-0302	244-4614
Web: illinois.edu					
University of St Francis 500 Wilcox St	Joliet	IL	60435	800-735-7500	
TF: 800-735-7500 ■ *Web:* www.stfrancis.edu					
VanderCook College of Music					
3140 S Federal St	Chicago	IL	60616	312-225-6288	225-5211*
*Fax: Admissions ■ *Web:* www.vandercook.edu					
Western Illinois University 1 University Cir	Macomb	IL	61455	309-298-1414	298-3111*
*Fax: Admissions ■ *TF Admissions:* 877-742-5948 ■ *Web:* www.wiu.edu					
Quad Cities 3561 60th St.	Moline	IL	61265	309-762-9481	764-7172*
*Fax: Admissions ■ *TF:* 877-742-5948 ■ *Web:* www.wiu.edu					
Wheaton College 501 College Ave	Wheaton	IL	60187	630-752-5000	752-5285
TF: 800-222-2419 ■ *Web:* www.wheaton.edu					

Indiana

	City	State	Zip	Phone	Fax
American Conservatory of Music					
252 Wildwood Rd	Hammond	IN	46324	219-931-6000	
Web: www.americanconservatory.edu					
Anderson University 1100 E Fifth St	Anderson	IN	46012	765-649-9071	641-4091*
*Fax: Admissions ■ *TF Admissions:* 800-428-6414 ■ *Web:* www.anderson.edu					
Ball State University 2000 W University Ave.	Muncie	IN	47306	765-289-1241	285-1632*
*Fax: Admissions ■ *TF:* 800-382-8540 ■ *Web:* cms.bsu.edu					
Bethel College 1001 W McKinley Ave.	Mishawaka	IN	46545	574-807-7000	807-7000*
*Fax: Admissions ■ *TF Admissions:* 800-422-4101 ■ *Web:* www.bethelcollege.edu					

Phone *Fax*

Butler University 4600 Sunset Ave................Indianapolis IN 46208 317-940-8100 940-8150*
*Fax: Admissions ■ *TF:* 800-368-6852 ■ *Web:* www.butler.edu

Calumet College of Saint Joseph
2400 New York Ave ....Whiting IN 46394 219-473-4215 473-4336*
*Fax: Admissions ■ *TF:* 877-700-9100 ■ *Web:* www.ccsj.edu

DePauw University 101 E Seminary St.............Greencastle IN 46135 765-658-4006 658-4007*
*Fax: Admissions ■ *TF:* 800-447-2495 ■ *Web:* www.depauw.edu

Earlham College 801 National Rd W.................Richmond IN 47374 765-983-1600 983-1560*
*Fax: Admissions ■ *TF:* 800-327-5426 ■ *Web:* www.earlham.edu

Franklin College 101 Branigin Blvd ....Franklin IN 46131 317-738-8000 738-8274*
*Fax: Admissions ■ *TF:* 800-852-0232 ■ *Web:* www.franklincollege.edu

Goshen College 1700 S Main St.....................Goshen IN 46526 574-535-7000 535-7609*
*Fax: Admissions ■ *TF:* 800-348-7422 ■ *Web:* www.goshen.edu

Grace College 200 Seminary Dr ....Winona Lake IN 46590 574-372-5100 372-5120*
*Fax: Admissions ■ *TF:* 800-544-7223 ■ *Web:* www.grace.edu

Hanover College 484 Ball Dr.........................Hanover IN 47243 812-866-7000 866-7098
TF: 800-213-2178 ■ *Web:* www.hanover.edu

Holy Cross College 54515 SR 933 N ....Notre Dame IN 46556 574-239-8400 239-8323*
*Fax: Admissions ■ *Web:* www.hcc-nd.edu

Huntington University 2303 College Ave...........Huntington IN 46750 260-356-6000 358-3699*
*Fax: Admissions ■ *TF Admissions:* 800-642-6493 ■ *Web:* www.huntington.edu

Indiana State University
200 N Seventh St ....Terre Haute IN 47809 800-468-6478 237-8023*
*Fax Area Code: 812 ■ *TF:* 800-468-6478 ■ *Web:* www.indstate.edu

Indiana Tech 1600 E Washington Blvd ....Fort Wayne IN 46803 260-422-5561 422-7696
TF: 800-937-2448 ■ *Web:* www.indianatech.edu

Indiana University 300 N Jordan Ave..............Bloomington IN 47405 812-855-0661 855-5102
Web: www.indiana.edu

East 2325 Chester Blvd ....Richmond IN 47374 765-973-8208 973-8288*
*Fax: Admissions ■ *TF:* 800-959-3278 ■ *Web:* www.iue.edu

Kokomo 2300 S Washington St PO Box 9003......Kokomo IN 46904 765-455-9217 455-9537*
*Fax: Admissions ■ *TF:* 888-875-4485 ■ *Web:* www.iuk.edu

Northwest 3400 Broadway ....Gary IN 46408 219-980-6500 981-4219*
*Fax: Admissions ■ *TF:* 888-968-7486 ■ *Web:* www.iun.edu

South Bend 1700 Mishawaka Ave PO Box 7111 ..South Bend IN 46634 574-520-4870
TF: 877-462-4872 ■ *Web:* www.iusb.edu

Southeast 4201 Grant Line Rd ....New Albany IN 47150 812-941-2212 941-2595
TF: 800-852-8835 ■ *Web:* www.ius.edu

Indiana University-Purdue University
Columbus 4601 Central Ave ....Columbus IN 47203 812-348-7271 348-7257
Web: iupuc.edu

Fort Wayne 2101 E Coliseum Blvd.............Fort Wayne IN 46805 260-481-6100 481-6880*
*Fax: Hum Res ■ *TF:* 800-324-4739 ■ *Web:* www.ipfw.edu

Indianapolis 425 University Blvd ....Indianapolis IN 46202 317-274-5555 278-1862
Web: www.iupui.edu

Indiana Wesleyan University
4201 S Washington St ....Marion IN 46953 765-677-2138 677-2333*
*Fax: Admissions ■ *TF:* 800-332-6901 ■ *Web:* www.indwes.edu

Manchester College
604 E College Ave ....North Manchester IN 46962 260-982-5000 982-5239*
*Fax: Admissions ■ *TF Admissions:* 800-852-3648 ■ *Web:* www.manchester.edu

Marian University 3200 Cold Spring Rd.............Indianapolis IN 46222 317-955-6038 955-6401*
*Fax: Admissions ■ *TF Admissions:* 800-772-7264 ■ *Web:* www.marian.edu

Martin University 2171 Avondale Pl...............Indianapolis IN 46218 317-543-3235
Web: www.martin.edu

Oakland City University
138 N Lucretia St ....Oakland City IN 47660 812-749-4781 749-1433
TF: 800-737-5125 ■ *Web:* www.oak.edu

Purdue University
Schleman Hall 475 Stadium Mall Dr.............West Lafayette IN 47907 765-494-1776 494-0544*
*Fax: Admissions ■ *Web:* www.purdue.edu

Calumet 2200 169th St ....Hammond IN 46323 219-989-2400 989-2775*
*Fax: Admissions ■ *TF:* 800-447-8738 ■ *Web:* webs.purduecal.edu

North Central 1401 S US Hwy 421...............Westville IN 46391 219-785-5200 785-5538*
*Fax: Admissions ■ *Web:* www.pnc.edu

Rose-Hulman Institute of Technology
5500 Wabash Ave.............................Terre Haute IN 47803 812-877-1511 877-8941
TF Admissions: 800-248-7448 ■ *Web:* www.rose-hulman.edu

Saint Mary's College Le Mans Hall ....Notre Dame IN 46556 574-284-4587 284-4841*
*Fax: Admissions ■ *TF Admissions:* 800-551-7621 ■ *Web:* www.saintmarys.edu

Saint Mary-of-the-Woods College
3301 St Mary Rd....................Saint Mary Of The Woods IN 47876 812-535-5106 535-5010*
*Fax: Admissions ■ *TF:* 800-926-7692 ■ *Web:* www.smwc.edu

Taylor University 236 W Reade Ave ....Upland IN 46989 765-998-2751 998-4925*
*Fax: Admissions ■ *TF:* 800-882-3456 ■ *Web:* www.taylor.edu

Fort Wayne 915 W Rudisill Blvd ....Fort Wayne IN 46807 260-744-8790 745-4974
TF General: 800-882-3456 ■ *Web:* fw.taylor.edu

Tri-State University 1 University Blvd ....Angola IN 46703 781-800-5000
Web: tripadvisor.com

Trine University
4101 Edison Lakes Pkwy Ste 250...................Mishawaka IN 46545 574-243-0500
Web: www.trine.edu

Trinity College of The Bible & Trinity Theological Seminary
4233 Medwel Dr................................Newburgh IN 47630 812-853-0611
Web: www.trinitysem.edu

University of Evansville 1800 Lincoln Ave ....Evansville IN 47722 812-488-2000 488-4076*
*Fax: Admissions ■ *TF:* 800-423-8633 ■ *Web:* www.evansville.edu

University of Indianapolis
1400 E Hanna Ave ....Indianapolis IN 46227 317-788-3368 788-3300*
*Fax: Admissions ■ *TF:* 800-232-8634 ■ *Web:* www.uindy.edu

University of Notre Dame 220 Main Bldg...........Notre Dame IN 46556 574-631-7505 631-8665*
*Fax: Admissions ■ *Web:* www.nd.edu

University of Saint Francis-ft Wayne
2701 Spring St ....Fort Wayne IN 46808 260-399-7700
Web: www.sf.edu

University of Southern Indiana
8600 University Blvd ....Evansville IN 47712 812-464-1765 465-7154
TF: 800-467-1965 ■ *Web:* www.usi.edu

Valparaiso University 1700 Chapel Dr ....Valparaiso IN 46383 219-464-5011 464-6898*
*Fax: Admissions ■ *TF:* 888-468-2576 ■ *Web:* www.valpo.edu

Wabash College
410 W Wabash Ave PO Box 352...................Crawfordsville IN 47933 765-361-6225 361-6437*
*Fax: Admissions ■ *TF:* 800-345-5385 ■ *Web:* www.wabash.edu

Iowa

Phone *Fax*

Ashford University 400 N Bluff Blvd...................Clinton IA 52732 563-242-4023
TF: 800-242-4153 ■ *Web:* www.ashford.edu

Briar Cliff University 3303 Rebecca St ....Sioux City IA 51104 712-279-5321 279-1632*
*Fax: Admissions ■ *TF:* 800-662-3303 ■ *Web:* www.briarcliff.edu

Buena Vista University 610 W Fourth St............Storm Lake IA 50588 712-749-2253 749-2035
TF: 800-383-9600 ■ *Web:* www.bvu.edu

Central College 812 University St.........................Pella IA 50219 641-628-5285 628-5983*
*Fax: Admissions ■ *TF:* 877-462-3687 ■ *Web:* www.central.edu

Clarke College 1550 Clarke Dr ....Dubuque IA 52001 563-588-6300 588-6789*
*Fax: Admissions ■ *TF:* 888-825-2753 ■ *Web:* www.clarke.edu

Coe College 1220 First Ave NE ....Cedar Rapids IA 52402 319-399-8500 399-8816
TF: 877-225-5263 ■ *Web:* www.coe.edu

Cornell College 600 First St SW................Mount Vernon IA 52314 319-895-4215 895-4451*
*Fax: Admissions ■ *TF Admissions:* 800-747-1112 ■ *Web:* www.cornellcollege.edu

Divine Word College 102 Jacoby Dr SW ....Epworth IA 52045 563-876-3353 876-3407*
*Fax: Admissions ■ *TF:* 800-553-3321 ■ *Web:* www.dwci.edu

Dordt College 498 Fourth Ave NE ....Sioux Center IA 51250 712-722-6080 722-1198
TF: 800-343-6738 ■ *Web:* www.dordt.edu

Drake University 2507 University Ave..............Des Moines IA 50311 515-271-3181 271-2831
TF: 800-443-7253 ■ *Web:* www.drake.edu

Graceland University 1 University Pl..................Lamoni IA 50140 641-784-5000 784-5480*
*Fax: Admissions ■ *TF:* 800-859-1215 ■ *Web:* www.graceland.edu

Grand View College 1200 Grandview Ave ....Des Moines IA 50316 515-263-2800 263-2974*
*Fax: Admissions ■ *TF:* 800-444-6083 ■ *Web:* www.gvc.edu

Grinnell College 1115 8th Ave ....Grinnell IA 50112 641-269-3600 269-4800
TF: 800-247-0113 ■ *Web:* www.grinnell.edu

Iowa Braille & Sight Saving School 1002 G Ave ....Vinton IA 52349 319-472-5221
Web: www.iowa-braille.k12.ia.us

Iowa State Innovation System
2501 N Loop Dr Ste 1000.............................Ames IA 50010 515-296-7275
Web: www.isupark.org

Iowa State University 100 Alumni Hall ....Ames IA 50011 515-294-4111 294-2592*
*Fax: Admissions ■ *TF Admissions:* 800-262-3810 ■ *Web:* www.iastate.edu

Iowa Wesleyan College 601 N Main St..........Mount Pleasant IA 52641 800-582-2383 385-6240*
*Fax Area Code: 319 ■ *Fax: Admissions ■ *TF:* 800-582-2383 ■ *Web:* www.iwc.edu

Loras College 1450 Alta Vista St...................Dubuque IA 52001 563-588-7100 588-7119*
*Fax: Admissions ■ *TF:* 800-245-6727 ■ *Web:* www.loras.edu

Luther College 700 College Dr ....Decorah IA 52101 563-387-2000 387-2159*
*Fax: Admissions ■ *TF:* 800-458-8437 ■ *Web:* www.luther.edu

Maharishi University of Management
1000 N Fourth St ....Fairfield IA 52557 641-472-1110 472-1179
TF: 800-369-6480 ■ *Web:* www.mum.edu

Midwest Associates of Colleges Empl
100 E Grand Ave Ste 330 ....Des Moines IA 50309 515-243-2360
Web: www.nalmco.org

Morningside College 1501 Morningside Ave..........Sioux City IA 51106 712-274-5000 274-5101*
*Fax: Admissions ■ *TF:* 800-831-0806 ■ *Web:* www.morningside.edu

Mount Mercy College 1330 Elmhurst Dr NE ....Cedar Rapids IA 52402 319-368-6460 861-2390
TF: 800-248-4504 ■ *Web:* www.mtmercy.edu

Northwestern College 101 Seventh St SW ....Orange City IA 51041 712-707-7000 707-7164*
*Fax: Admissions ■ *TF:* 800-747-4757 ■ *Web:* www.nwciowa.edu

Saint Ambrose University 518 W Locust St ....Davenport IA 52803 563-333-6000 333-6243*
*Fax: Admissions ■ *TF Admissions:* 800-383-2627 ■ *Web:* www.sau.edu

Simpson College 701 N 'C' St........................Indianola IA 50125 515-961-6251 961-1870*
*Fax: Admissions ■ *TF:* 800-362-2454 ■ *Web:* www.simpson.edu

University of Dubuque 2000 University Ave ....Dubuque IA 52001 563-589-3000 589-3690*
*Fax: Admissions ■ *TF:* 800-722-5583 ■ *Web:* www.dbq.edu

University of Iowa 107 Calvin Hall....................Iowa City IA 52242 319-335-3847 335-1535
TF: 800-553-4692 ■ *Web:* www.uiowa.edu

University of Northern Iowa
1222 W 27th St.................................Cedar Falls IA 50614 319-273-2281 273-2885*
*Fax: Admissions ■ *TF Admissions:* 800-772-2037 ■ *Web:* www.uni.edu

Upper Iowa University
605 Washington St PO Box 1857.......................Fayette IA 52142 563-425-5200 425-5323*
*Fax: Admissions ■ *TF Admissions:* 800-553-4150 ■ *Web:* www.uiu.edu

Waldorf College 106 S Sixth St ....Forest City IA 50436 641-585-2450 585-8184*
*Fax: Admissions ■ *TF:* 800-292-1903 ■ *Web:* www.waldorf.edu

Wartburg College 100 Wartburg Blvd...................Waverly IA 50677 319-352-8264 352-8579*
*Fax: Admissions ■ *TF:* 800-772-2085 ■ *Web:* www.wartburg.edu

William Penn University 201 Trueblood Ave...........Oskaloosa IA 52577 800-779-7366 673-2113*
*Fax Area Code: 641 ■ *Fax: Admissions ■ *TF:* 800-779-7366 ■ *Web:* www.wmpenn.edu

Kansas

Phone *Fax*

Benedictine College 1020 N Second St...............Atchison KS 66002 913-367-5340 367-5462*
*Fax: Admissions ■ *TF:* 800-467-5340 ■ *Web:* www.benedictine.edu

Bethany College 335 E Swensson St ....Lindsborg KS 67456 785-227-3311 227-8993*
*Fax: Admissions ■ *TF Admissions:* 800-826-2281 ■ *Web:* www.bethanylb.edu

Bethel College 300 E 27th St ....North Newton KS 67117 316-283-2500 284-5286*
*Fax: Admissions ■ *TF:* 800-522-1887 ■ *Web:* www.bethelks.edu

Central Christian College PO Box 1403............McPherson KS 67460 620-241-0723 241-6032*
*Fax: Admissions ■ *TF:* 800-835-0078 ■ *Web:* www.centralchristian.edu

Emporia State University 1200 Commercial St..........Emporia KS 66801 620-341-1200 341-5599
TF: 877-468-6378 ■ *Web:* www.emporia.edu

Fort Hays State University 600 Pk St......................Hays KS 67601 785-628-4000
TF Admissions: 800-628-3478 ■ *Web:* www.fhsu.edu

Friends University 2100 University St ....Wichita KS 67213 316-295-5000
TF: 800-794-6945 ■ *Web:* www.friends.edu

Haskell Indian Nations University
155 Indian Ave PO Box 5031 ....Lawrence KS 66046 785-749-8454 749-8429*
*Fax: Admissions ■ *Web:* www.haskell.edu

Kansas State University 119 Anderson Hall..........Manhattan KS 66506 785-532-6250 532-6393*
*Fax: Admissions ■ *TF Admissions:* 800-432-8270 ■ *Web:* www.k-state.edu

Kansas State University-Salina
College of Technology & Aviation
2310 Centennial Rd ....Salina KS 67401 785-826-2640 532-7494*
*Fax: Admissions ■ *Web:* polytechnic.k-state.edu

Phone Fax

Kansas University
Edwards 12600 Quivira Rd. . . . Overland Park KS 66213 913-897-8400 897-8490*
**Fax:* Admissions ■ *Web:* www.edwardscampus.ku.edu

Kansas Wesleyan University 100 E Claflin Ave . . . Salina KS 67401 785-827-5541 827-0927*
**Fax:* Admissions ■ *TF:* 800-874-1154 ■ *Web:* www.kwu.edu

McPherson College PO Box 1402 . . . McPherson KS 67460 620-242-0400 241-8443*
**Fax:* Admissions ■ *TF:* 800-365-7402 ■ *Web:* www.mcpherson.edu

MidAmerica Nazarene University
2030 E College Way . . . Olathe KS 66062 913-782-3750 971-3481*
**Fax:* Admissions ■ *TF:* 800-800-8887 ■ *Web:* www.mnu.edu

Newman University 3100 McCormick Ave . . . Wichita KS 67213 316-942-4291 942-4483*
**Fax:* Admissions ■ *TF:* 877-639-6268 ■ *Web:* www.newmanu.edu

Ottawa University 1001 S Cedar St . . . Ottawa KS 66067 785-242-5200
TF Admissions: 800-755-5200 ■ *Web:* www.ottawa.edu

Pittsburg State University
1701 S Broadway St . . . Pittsburg KS 66762 620-235-4251 235-6003*
**Fax:* Admissions ■ *TF:* 800-854-7488 ■ *Web:* www.pittstate.edu

Southwestern College 100 College St. . . . Winfield KS 67156 620-229-6236 229-6344*
**Fax:* Admissions ■ *TF:* 800-846-1543 ■ *Web:* www.sckans.edu

Sterling College 125 W Cooper . . . Sterling KS 67579 620-278-2173 278-4418
TF: 800-346-1017 ■ *Web:* www.sterling.edu

Tabor College 400 S Jefferson St . . . Hillsboro KS 67063 620-947-3121 947-6276*
**Fax:* Admissions ■ *TF Admissions:* 800-822-6799 ■ *Web:* www.tabor.edu

University of Kansas 1502 Iowa St . . . Lawrence KS 66045 785-864-2700 864-5017
Web: www.ku.edu

University of Saint Mary
4100 S Fourth St . . . Leavenworth KS 66048 913-682-5151 758-6140*
**Fax:* Admissions ■ *TF:* 800-752-7043 ■ *Web:* www.stmary.edu

Washburn University 1700 SW College Ave . . . Topeka KS 66621 785-670-1010 670-1079
TF: 800-736-9060 ■ *Web:* www.washburn.edu

Wichita State University 1845 Fairmount St . . . Wichita KS 67260 316-978-3456 978-3174*
**Fax:* Admissions ■ *TF Admissions:* 800-362-2594 ■ *Web:* www.wichita.edu

Kentucky

Phone Fax

Alice Lloyd College 100 Purpose Rd . . . Pippa Passes KY 41844 606-368-6000
TF Admissions: 888-280-4252 ■ *Web:* www.alc.edu

Asbury College 1 Macklem Dr. . . . Wilmore KY 40390 859-858-3511 858-3921*
**Fax:* Admissions ■ *TF Admissions:* 800-888-1818 ■ *Web:* www.asbury.edu

Bellarmine University 2001 Newburg Rd. . . . Louisville KY 40205 502-272-8000
TF: 800-274-4723 ■ *Web:* www.bellarmine.edu

Berea College 101 Chestnut St . . . Berea KY 40403 859-985-3500 985-3512*
**Fax:* Admissions ■ *TF:* 800-326-5948 ■ *Web:* www.berea.edu

Brescia University 717 Frederica St. . . . Owensboro KY 42301 270-685-3131 686-4314*
**Fax:* Admissions ■ *TF Admissions:* 877-273-7242 ■ *Web:* brescia.edu

Campbellsville University
1 University Dr . . . Campbellsville KY 42718 270-789-5000 789-5071*
**Fax:* Admissions ■ *TF Admissions:* 800-264-6014 ■ *Web:* www.campbellsville.edu

Centre College 600 W Walnut St . . . Danville KY 40422 859-238-5350 238-5373
TF: 800-423-6236 ■ *Web:* www.centre.edu

Eastern Kentucky University
521 Lancaster Ave . . . Richmond KY 40475 859-622-2106 622-8024
TF: 800-465-9191 ■ *Web:* www.eku.edu

Georgetown College 400 E College St . . . Georgetown KY 40324 502-863-8000
TF Admissions: 800-788-9985 ■ *Web:* www.georgetowncollege.edu

Kentucky Christian University
100 Academic Pkwy . . . Grayson KY 41143 606-474-3000 474-3155*
**Fax:* Admissions ■ *TF Admissions:* 800-522-3181 ■ *Web:* www.kcu.edu

Kentucky State University 400 E Main St . . . Frankfort KY 40601 502-597-6000 597-5814*
**Fax:* Admissions ■ *TF Admissions:* 800-325-1716 ■ *Web:* www.kysu.edu

Kentucky Wesleyan College
3000 Frederica St . . . Owensboro KY 42301 270-852-3120 852-3133*
**Fax:* Admissions ■ *TF Admissions:* 800-999-0592 ■ *Web:* www.kwc.edu

Lindsey Wilson College
210 Lindsey Wilson St . . . Columbia KY 42728 270-384-2126 384-8591*
**Fax:* Admissions ■ *TF:* 800-264-0138 ■ *Web:* www.lindsey.edu

Louisville Bible College
8211 Restoration Dr . . . Louisville KY 40228 502-231-5221

Mid-Continent University 99 Powell Rd E . . . Mayfield KY 42066 270-247-8521 247-3115*
**Fax:* Admissions ■ *TF:* 888-628-4723 ■ *Web:* www.midcontinent.edu

Midway College 512 E Stephens St . . . Midway KY 40347 859-846-5346 846-5787*
**Fax:* Admissions ■ *TF:* 800-755-0031 ■ *Web:* midway.edu

Morehead State University
100 Admissions Ctr . . . Morehead KY 40351 606-783-2000 783-5038*
**Fax:* Admissions ■ *TF:* 800-585-6781 ■ *Web:* www.moreheadstate.edu

Murray State University 102 Curris Ctr . . . Murray KY 42071 270-809-3741 809-3780*
**Fax:* Admissions ■ *TF:* 800-272-4678 ■ *Web:* www.murraystate.edu
Hopkinsville 5305 Ft Campbell Blvd . . . Hopkinsville KY 42240 270-707-1525 707-1535*
**Fax:* Admissions ■ *TF:* 800-669-7654 ■ *Web:* murraystate.edu

Northern Kentucky University
Nunn Dr . . . Highland Heights KY 41099 859-572-5220 572-6665*
**Fax:* Admissions ■ *TF Admissions:* 800-637-9948 ■ *Web:* www.nku.edu

Pikeville College 147 Sycamore St . . . Pikeville KY 41501 606-218-5250 218-5255*
**Fax:* Admissions ■ *TF:* 866-232-7700 ■ *Web:* upike.edu

Spalding University 851 S Fourth St . . . Louisville KY 40203 502-585-9911 585-7158
TF: 800-896-8941 ■ *Web:* www.spalding.edu

Sullivan University 3101 BaRdstown Rd . . . Louisville KY 40205 502-456-6505
TF: 800-844-1354 ■ *Web:* www.sullivan.edu

Thomas More College
333 Thomas More Pkwy . . . Crestview Hills KY 41017 859-344-3332 344-3444
TF: 800-825-4557 ■ *Web:* www.thomasmore.edu

Transylvania University 300 N Broadway . . . Lexington KY 40508 859-233-8242 233-8797
TF: 800-872-6798 ■ *Web:* www.transy.edu

Union College 310 College St . . . Barbourville KY 40906 606-546-4151 546-1667*
**Fax:* Admissions ■ *TF:* 800-489-8646 ■ *Web:* www.unionky.edu

University of Kentucky 800 Rose St . . . Lexington KY 40536 859-257-9000 257-3823
TF: 866-900-4685 ■ *Web:* www.uky.edu

University of Louisville 2301 S Third St . . . Louisville KY 40292 502-852-5555 852-6526
TF: 800-334-8635 ■ *Web:* louisville.edu

University of the Cumberlands
6191 College Stn Dr . . . Williamsburg KY 40769 606-539-4201
TF: 800-343-1609 ■ *Web:* www.ucumberlands.edu

Phone Fax

Western Kentucky University
1906 College Heights Blvd . . . Bowling Green KY 42101 270-745-0111 745-6133*
**Fax:* Admissions ■ *TF Admissions:* 800-495-8463 ■ *Web:* www.wku.edu

Louisiana

Phone Fax

Centenary College of Louisiana
2911 Centenary Blvd . . . Shreveport LA 71104 318-869-5131 869-5005*
**Fax:* Admissions ■ *TF Admissions:* 800-234-4448 ■ *Web:* www.centenary.edu

Grambling State University 403 Main St . . . Grambling LA 71245 318-247-3811
TF: 800-569-4714 ■ *Web:* www.gram.edu

Louisiana College 1140 College Dr . . . Pineville LA 71359 318-487-7011 487-7550*
**Fax:* Admissions ■ *TF:* 800-487-1906 ■ *Web:* www.lacollege.edu

Louisiana State University
Alexandria 8100 US Hwy 71 S . . . Alexandria LA 71302 318-445-3672 473-6418*
**Fax:* Admissions ■ *TF Admissions:* 888-473-6417 ■ *Web:* www.lsua.edu
Baton Rouge 110 Thomas Boyd Hall . . . Baton Rouge LA 70803 225-578-3202 578-4433*
**Fax:* Admissions ■ *TF:* 888-846-6810 ■ *Web:* www.lsu.edu
Shreveport 1 University Pl . . . Shreveport LA 71115 318-797-5000 797-5286*
**Fax:* Admissions ■ *Web:* www.lsus.edu

Louisiana Tech University 305 Wisteria St . . . Ruston LA 71272 318-257-2000 257-2499*
**Fax:* Admissions ■ *TF Admissions:* 800-528-3241 ■ *Web:* www.latech.edu

Loyola University
Monroe Library 6363 St Charles Ave . . . New Orleans LA 70118 504-864-7111 864-7247
Web: library.loyno.edu
New Orleans 6363 St Charles Ave . . . New Orleans LA 70118 504-865-3240 865-3383*
**Fax:* Admissions ■ *TF Admissions:* 800-456-9652 ■ *Web:* www.loyno.edu

McNeese State University 4205 Ryan St . . . Lake Charles LA 70609 337-475-5000 475-5151*
**Fax:* Admissions ■ *TF:* 800-622-3352 ■ *Web:* www.mcneese.edu

Nicholls State University 906 E First St . . . Thibodaux LA 70310 985-446-0561 448-4929*
**Fax:* Admissions ■ *TF Admissions:* 877-642-4655 ■ *Web:* www.nicholls.edu

Northwestern State University
175 Sam Sibley Dr . . . Natchitoches LA 71497 318-357-4078 357-4660
TF: 800-767-8115 ■ *Web:* www.nsula.edu

Our Lady of Holy Cross College
4123 Woodland Dr . . . New Orleans LA 70131 504-394-7744 394-1182
TF: 800-259-7744 ■ *Web:* www.olhcc.edu

Our Lady of the Lake College
7434 Perkins Rd . . . Baton Rouge LA 70808 225-768-1700 768-1726*
**Fax:* Admissions ■ *TF Admissions:* 877-242-3509 ■ *Web:* www.ololcollege.edu

Southeastern Louisiana University
500 Western Ave . . . Hammond LA 70402 985-549-2062 549-5632*
**Fax:* Admissions ■ *TF:* 800-222-7358 ■ *Web:* www.southeastern.edu

Southern University & A & M College
156 Elton C Harrison Dr PO Box 9757 . . . Baton Rouge LA 70813 225-771-5180 771-4762*
**Fax:* Admissions ■ *TF Admissions:* 800-256-1531 ■ *Web:* www.subr.edu

Tulane University 6823 St Charles Ave . . . New Orleans LA 70118 504-865-5000 862-8715*
**Fax:* Admissions ■ *TF Admissions:* 800-873-9283 ■ *Web:* www.tulane.edu

Unitech Training Academy-houma
1227 Grand Caillou Rd . . . Houma LA 70363 985-223-1755
Web: www.unitechtrainingacademy.com

University of Louisiana
Lafayette 611 McKinley St . . . Lafayette LA 70504 337-482-1000 482-1317
TF: 800-752-6553 ■ *Web:* www.louisiana.edu
Monroe 700 University Ave . . . Monroe LA 71209 318-342-5430
TF Admissions: 800-372-5127 ■ *Web:* www.ulm.edu

University of New Orleans
Administrative Bldg Rm 103 Lakefront . . . New Orleans LA 70148 504-280-6000 280-5522
TF Admissions: 800-256-5866 ■ *Web:* www.uno.edu

Xavier University of Louisiana
1 Drexel Dr . . . New Orleans LA 70125 504-486-7411 520-7922
Web: www.xula.edu

Maine

Phone Fax

Bates College 2 Andrews Rd Ln Hall Rm1 . . . Lewiston ME 04240 207-786-6255 786-6025*
**Fax:* Admissions ■ *TF:* 888-522-8371 ■ *Web:* www.bates.edu

Bowdoin College 5000 College Stn . . . Brunswick ME 04011 207-725-3000 725-3101*
**Fax:* Admissions ■ *TF:* 800-829-1040 ■ *Web:* www.bowdoin.edu

Colby College 4800 Mayflower Hill . . . Waterville ME 04901 207-859-4800 859-4828*
**Fax:* Admissions ■ *TF Admissions:* 800-723-3032 ■ *Web:* www.colby.edu

College of the Atlantic 105 Eden St . . . Bar Harbor ME 04609 207-288-5015 288-4126*
**Fax:* Admissions ■ *TF Admissions:* 800-528-0025 ■ *Web:* www.coa.edu

Husson College 1 College Cir . . . Bangor ME 04401 207-941-7000 941-7935*
**Fax:* Admissions ■ *TF:* 800-448-7766 ■ *Web:* www.husson.edu

Maine Maritime Academy 66 Pleasant St . . . Castine ME 04420 207-326-4311 326-2515*
**Fax:* Admissions ■ *TF Admissions:* 800-464-6565 ■ *Web:* www.mainemaritime.edu

New England Bible College & Grace Evangelical Seminary
879 Sawyer St . . . South Portland ME 04106 207-799-5979
Web: www.nebc.edu

Saint Joseph's College of Maine
278 Whites Bridge Rd . . . Standish ME 04084 207-893-7746 893-7862*
**Fax:* Admissions ■ *TF Admissions:* 800-338-7057 ■ *Web:* www.sjcme.edu

Thomas College 180 W River Rd . . . Waterville ME 04901 207-859-1111 859-1114*
**Fax:* Admissions ■ *TF Admissions:* 800-339-7001 ■ *Web:* www.thomas.edu

Unity College 90 Quaker Hill Rd . . . Unity ME 04988 207-948-3131
TF: 800-624-1024 ■ *Web:* www.unity.edu

University of Maine 5713 Chadbourne Hall . . . Orono ME 04469 207-581-1110 581-1213*
**Fax:* Admissions ■ *TF Admissions:* 877-486-2364 ■ *Web:* www.umaine.edu
Augusta 46 University Dr . . . Augusta ME 04330 207-621-3000 621-3333*
**Fax:* Admissions ■ *TF:* 877-862-1234 ■ *Web:* www.uma.edu
Farmington 111 S St . . . Farmington ME 04938 207-778-7000 778-8182*
**Fax:* Admissions ■ *Web:* www.umf.maine.edu
Fort Kent 23 University Dr . . . Fort Kent ME 04743 207-834-7500 834-7609*
**Fax:* Admissions ■ *TF Admissions:* 888-879-8635 ■ *Web:* www.umfk.edu
Machias 116 O'Brien Ave . . . Machias ME 04654 207-255-1200
TF Admissions: 888-468-6866 ■ *Web:* machias.edu
Presque Isle 181 Main St . . . Presque Isle ME 04769 207-768-9400 768-9777*
**Fax:* Admissions ■ *Web:* www.umpi.maine.edu

Phone Fax

University of New England
11 Hills Beach Rd ... Biddeford ME 04005 207-283-0171
TF Admissions: 800-477-4863 ■ *Web:* www.une.edu
Westbrook College 716 Stevens Ave ... Portland ME 04103 207-797-7261
TF Admissions: 800-477-4863 ■ *Web:* www.une.edu

University of Southern Maine 96 Falmouth St ... Portland ME 04103 207-780-4141 780-5640
TF: 800-800-4876 ■ *Web:* www.usm.maine.edu
Gorham 37 College Ave ... Gorham ME 04038 207-780-5670 780-5640*
**Fax:* Admissions ■ *TF:* 800-800-4876 ■ *Web:* www.usm.maine.edu
Lewiston-Auburn College 51 Westminster St ... Lewiston ME 04240 207-753-6500 753-6555*
**Fax:* Admissions ■ *TF:* 800-800-4876 ■ *Web:* www.usm.maine.edu

Maryland

Phone Fax

Bowie State University 14000 Jericho Pk Rd ... Bowie MD 20715 301-860-4000 860-3518
TF: 877-772-6943 ■ *Web:* www.bowiestate.edu

Capitol Technology University
11301 Springfield Rd ... Laurel MD 20708 301-369-2800 953-1442*
**Fax:* Admissions ■ *TF:* 800-950-1992 ■ *Web:* www.captechu.edu

College of Notre Dame of Maryland
4701 N Charles St ... Baltimore MD 21210 410-435-0100 532-6287*
**Fax:* Admissions ■ *TF Admissions:* 800-753-3757 ■ *Web:* www.ndm.edu

Coppin State University 2500 W N Ave ... Baltimore MD 21216 410-951-3600 523-7351*
**Fax:* Admissions ■ *TF Admissions:* 800-635-3674 ■ *Web:* www.coppin.edu

Frostburg State University 101 Braddock Rd ... Frostburg MD 21532 301-687-4000 687-7074*
**Fax:* Admissions ■ *Web:* www.frostburg.edu

Goucher College 1021 Dulaney Vly Rd ... Towson MD 21204 410-337-6000 337-6354*
**Fax:* Admissions ■ *TF:* 800-468-2437 ■ *Web:* www.goucher.edu

Hood College 401 Rosemont Ave ... Frederick MD 21701 301-696-3400 696-3819*
**Fax:* Admissions ■ *TF:* 800-922-1599 ■ *Web:* www.hood.edu

Johns Hopkins University 3400 N Charles St ... Baltimore MD 21218 410-516-8000 516-6025
Web: www.jhu.edu

Loyola College 4501 N Charles St ... Baltimore MD 21210 410-617-5012 617-2176*
**Fax:* Admissions ■ *TF:* 800-221-9107 ■ *Web:* www.loyola.edu

McDaniel College 2 College Hill ... Westminster MD 21157 410-857-2230 857-2757*
**Fax:* Admissions ■ *TF Admissions:* 800-638-5005 ■ *Web:* www.mcdaniel.edu

Morgan State University
1700 E Cold Spring Ln ... Baltimore MD 21251 443-885-3333 885-8260*
**Fax:* Admissions ■ *TF:* 800-319-4678 ■ *Web:* www.morgan.edu

Mount Saint Mary's University
16300 Old Emmitsburg Rd ... Emmitsburg MD 21727 301-447-5214 447-5860*
**Fax:* Admissions ■ *TF Admissions:* 800-448-4347 ■ *Web:* www.msmary.edu

Peabody Institute of the Johns Hopkins University
Peabody Conservatory of Music
1 E Mt Vernon Pl ... Baltimore MD 21202 410-659-8110 659-8102
TF: 800-368-2521 ■ *Web:* www.peabody.jhu.edu

Saint Mary's College of Maryland
47645 College Dr ... Saint Marys City MD 20686 240-895-2000
TF Admissions: 800-492-7181 ■ *Web:* www.smcm.edu

Salisbury University 1200 Camden Ave ... Salisbury MD 21801 410-543-6000 546-6016*
**Fax:* Admissions ■ *TF:* 888-543-0148 ■ *Web:* www.salisbury.edu

Sojourner-Douglass College
200 N Central Ave ... Baltimore MD 21202 410-276-0306 675-1810
TF: 800-732-2630

Strayer University Prince George's
4710 Auth Pl Ste 100 ... Suitland MD 20746 888-311-0355
TF: 866-344-3297 ■ *Web:* www.strayer.edu

Towson University 8000 York Rd ... Towson MD 21252 410-704-2113 704-3030
TF: 866-301-3375 ■ *Web:* www.towson.edu

University of Baltimore 1420 N Charles St ... Baltimore MD 21201 410-837-4200 837-4793
TF Admitting: 877-277-5982 ■ *Web:* www.ubalt.edu

University of Maryland
7569 Baltimore Ave ... College Park MD 20742 301-405-1000 314-9693*
**Fax:* Admissions ■ *TF Admissions:* 800-422-5867 ■ *Web:* www.umd.edu
Baltimore County 1000 Hilltop Cir ... Baltimore MD 21250 410-455-1000 455-1094
TF: 800-810-0271 ■ *Web:* www.umbc.edu
Eastern Shore
30665 Student Services Ctr Ln ... Princess Anne MD 21853 410-651-2200 651-7922
Web: www.umes.edu

US Naval Academy 121 Blake Rd ... Annapolis MD 21402 410-293-1000 293-4348*
**Fax:* Admissions ■ *TF Admissions:* 888-249-7707 ■ *Web:* www.usna.edu

Villa Julie College
1525 Green Spring Valley Rd ... Stevenson MD 21153 410-486-7001 352-4440*
**Fax Area Code:* 443 ■ *TF:* 877-468-6852 ■ *Web:* stevenson.edu

Washington Adventist University
7600 Flower Ave ... Takoma Park MD 20912 301-891-4000 891-4167
TF: 800-835-4212 ■ *Web:* www.wau.edu

Washington College 300 Washington Ave ... Chestertown MD 21620 410-778-2800 778-7287
TF: 800-422-1782 ■ *Web:* www.washcoll.edu

Massachusetts

Phone Fax

American International College
1000 State St ... Springfield MA 01109 413-205-3201 205-3051*
**Fax:* Admissions ■ *TF Admissions:* 800-242-3142 ■ *Web:* www.aic.edu

Amherst College 220 S Pleasant St ... Amherst MA 01002 413-542-2000 542-2040*
**Fax:* Admissions ■ *TF:* 866-542-4438 ■ *Web:* www.amherst.edu

Anna Maria College 50 Sunset Ln ... Paxton MA 01612 800-344-4586
TF: 800-344-4586 ■ *Web:* www.annamaria.edu

Asian University for Women
1100 Massachusetts Ave Ste 3 ... Cambridge MA 02138 617-914-0500
Web: asian-university.org

Assumption College 500 Salisbury St ... Worcester MA 01609 508-767-7000 799-4412
TF: 888-882-7786 ■ *Web:* www.assumption.edu

Atlantic Union College 338 Main St ... South Lancaster MA 01561 978-368-2000 368-2517
TF: 800-282-2030 ■ *Web:* www.auc.edu

Babson College 231 Forest St ... Babson Park MA 02457 781-235-1200 239-4006*
**Fax:* Admissions ■ *TF Admissions:* 800-488-3696 ■ *Web:* www.babson.edu

Bay Path College 588 Longmeadow St ... Longmeadow MA 01106 800-782-7284
TF: 800-782-7284 ■ *Web:* www.baypath.edu

Phone Fax

Becker College 61 Sever St ... Worcester MA 01609 508-791-9241 890-1500*
**Fax:* Admissions ■ *TF:* 877-523-2537 ■ *Web:* www.becker.edu

Bentley College 175 Forest St ... Waltham MA 02452 781-891-2244 891-3414*
**Fax:* Admissions ■ *TF Admissions:* 800-642-7131 ■ *Web:* www.bentley.edu

Berklee College of Music 1140 Boylston St ... Boston MA 02215 617-747-2221 747-2047*
**Fax:* Admissions ■ *TF:* 800-421-0084 ■ *Web:* www.berklee.edu

Boston Baptist College 950 Metropolitan Ave ... Boston MA 02136 617-364-3510
TF: 888-235-2014 ■ *Web:* boston.edu

Boston College 140 Commonwealth Ave ... Chestnut Hill MA 02467 617-552-3100 552-0798
TF: 800-360-2522 ■ *Web:* www.bc.edu

Boston Conservatory of Music Dance & Theater
8 Fenway ... Boston MA 02215 617-536-6340 247-3159*
**Fax:* Admissions ■ *Web:* www.bostonconservatory.edu

Brandeis University 415 S St ... Waltham MA 02454 781-736-3500 736-3536
TF: 800-622-0622 ■ *Web:* www.brandeis.edu

Bridgewater State College 131 Summer St ... Bridgewater MA 02325 508-531-1000 531-1746*
**Fax:* Admissions ■ *Web:* www.bridgew.edu

Clark University 950 Main St ... Worcester MA 01610 508-793-7711 793-8821
TF: 800-462-5275 ■ *Web:* www.clarku.edu

College of the Holy Cross 1 College St ... Worcester MA 01610 508-793-2011 793-3888
TF: 800-442-2421 ■ *Web:* www.holycross.edu

Curry College 1071 Blue Hill Ave ... Milton MA 02186 617-333-2210 333-2114
TF: 800-669-0686 ■ *Web:* www.curry.edu

Eastern Nazarene College 23 E Elm Ave ... Quincy MA 02170 617-745-3000 745-3929
TF: 800-883-6288 ■ *Web:* www.enc.edu

ELMS College 291 Springfield St ... Chicopee MA 01013 413-592-3189
TF Admissions: 800-255-3567 ■ *Web:* www.elms.edu

Emerson College 10 Boylston Pl ... Boston MA 02116 617-824-8500 824-8609
TF: 888-627-7115 ■ *Web:* www.emerson.edu

Emmanuel College 400 Fenway ... Boston MA 02115 617-735-9715 735-9801
Web: www.emmanuel.edu

Endicott College 376 Hale St ... Beverly MA 01915 978-232-2021 232-2520*
**Fax:* Admissions ■ *TF Admissions:* 800-325-1114 ■ *Web:* www.endicott.edu

Framingham State College
100 State St PO Box 9101 ... Framingham MA 01701 508-620-1220 626-4017*
**Fax:* Admissions ■ *TF:* 866-361-8970 ■ *Web:* www.framingham.edu

Franklin W Olin College of Engineering
1000 Olin Way ... Needham MA 02492 781-292-2300 292-2210*
**Fax:* Admissions ■ *Web:* www.olin.edu

Gordon College 255 Grapevine Rd ... Wenham MA 01984 978-927-2300 867-4682*
**Fax:* Admissions ■ *TF:* 800-343-1379 ■ *Web:* www.gordon.edu

Hampshire College 893 W St ... Amherst MA 01002 413-549-4600 559-5631*
**Fax:* Admissions ■ *Web:* www.hampshire.edu

Harvard University 12 Holyoke St ... Cambridge MA 02138 617-495-1000 495-8821
Web: www.harvard.edu

Hellenic College-Holy Cross School of Theology
50 Goddard Ave ... Brookline MA 02445 617-731-3500 850-1460*
**Fax:* Admissions ■ *Web:* www.hchc.edu

Lasell College 1844 Commonwealth Ave ... Newton MA 02466 617-243-2225 243-2380*
**Fax:* Admissions ■ *TF Admissions:* 888-527-3554 ■ *Web:* www.lasell.edu

Lesley University 29 Everett St ... Cambridge MA 02138 617-868-9600 349-8313
TF: 800-999-1959 ■ *Web:* www.lesley.edu

Massachusetts College of Art
621 Huntington Ave ... Boston MA 02115 617-879-7222 879-7250
TF: 800-834-3242 ■ *Web:* www.massart.edu

Massachusetts College of Liberal Arts
375 Church St ... North Adams MA 01247 413-662-5000 662-5179
Web: www.mcla.edu

Massachusetts College of Pharmacy & Health Sciences
179 Longwood Ave ... Boston MA 02115 617-732-2850 732-2118
TF: 800-225-5506 ■ *Web:* www.mcphs.edu

Massachusetts Institute of Technology
77 Massachusetts Ave ... Cambridge MA 02139 617-253-1000 258-8304
Web: www.web.mit.edu

Massachusetts Maritime Academy
101 Academy Dr ... Buzzards Bay MA 02532 508-830-5000 830-5077*
**Fax:* Admissions ■ *TF Admissions:* 800-544-3411 ■ *Web:* www.maritime.edu

Merrimack College 315 Tpke St ... North Andover MA 01845 978-837-5000 837-5133*
**Fax:* Admissions ■ *Web:* www.merrimack.edu

MGH Institute of Health Professions Inc
Charlestown Navy Yard 36 First Ave ... Boston MA 02129 617-726-2947
Web: www.mghihp.edu

Montserrat College of Art
23 Essex St PO Box 26 ... Beverly MA 01915 978-921-4242 921-4241*
**Fax:* Admissions ■ *TF:* 800-836-0487 ■ *Web:* www.montserrat.edu

Mount Holyoke College 50 College St ... South Hadley MA 01075 413-538-2000 538-2409
TF: 800-642-4483 ■ *Web:* www.mtholyoke.edu

Mount Ida College 777 Dedham St ... Newton Center MA 02459 617-928-4500 928-4507*
**Fax:* Admissions ■ *Web:* www.mountida.edu

National Graduate School of Quality Management Inc, The
186 Jones Rd ... Falmouth MA 02540 508-457-1313
TF: 800-838-2580 ■ *Web:* www.ngs.edu

New England Conservatory 290 Huntington Ave ... Boston MA 02115 617-585-1100 585-1115*
**Fax:* Admissions ■ *Web:* necmusic.edu

Newbury College 129 Fisher Ave ... Brookline MA 02445 617-730-7000 731-9618*
**Fax:* Admitting ■ *TF:* 800-499-0143 ■ *Web:* www.newbury.edu

Nichols College 124 Ctr Rd ... Dudley MA 01571 508-213-1560 943-9885
TF: 800-470-3379 ■ *Web:* www.nichols.edu

Northeastern University 360 Huntington Ave ... Boston MA 02115 617-373-2000 373-8780*
**Fax:* Admissions ■ *TF:* 855-476-3391 ■ *Web:* www.northeastern.edu

Pine Manor College 400 Heath St ... Chestnut Hill MA 02467 617-731-7104 731-7102
TF: 800-762-1357 ■ *Web:* www.pmc.edu

Regis College 235 Wellesley St ... Weston MA 02493 781-768-7000 768-7071
TF: 866-438-7344 ■ *Web:* www.regiscollege.edu

Salem State College 352 Lafayette St ... Salem MA 01970 978-542-6000 542-6893
Web: www.salemstate.edu

School of the Museum of Fine Arts
230 The Fenway ... Boston MA 02115 617-369-3626 369-4264*
**Fax:* Admissions ■ *TF Admissions:* 800-643-6078 ■ *Web:* www.smfa.edu

Simmons College 300 The Fenway ... Boston MA 02115 617-521-2000 521-3190*
**Fax:* Admissions ■ *TF:* 800-345-8468 ■ *Web:* www.simmons.edu

	City	State	ZIP	Phone	Fax
Simon's Rock College of Bard 84 Alford Rd	Great Barrington	MA	01230	413-644-4400	528-7380*
*Fax: Admissions ■ *Web:* www.simons-rock.edu					
Smith College 7 College Ln.	NorthHampton	MA	01063	413-584-2700	585-2527
TF: 800-383-3232 ■ *Web:* www.smith.edu					
South Shore Educational Collaborative 75 Abington St	Hingham	MA	02043	781-749-7518	
Web: www.ssec.org					
Springfield College 263 Alden St.	Springfield	MA	01109	413-748-3136	748-3694*
*Fax: Admissions ■ *TF Admissions:* 800-343-1257 ■ *Web:* springfield.edu					
Stonehill College 320 Washington St.	Easton	MA	02357	508-565-1000	565-1545*
*Fax: Admissions ■ *Web:* www.stonehill.edu					
Suffolk University 8 Ashburton Pl	Boston	MA	02108	617-573-8460	557-1574
TF: 800-678-3365 ■ *Web:* www.suffolk.edu					
Tufts University 4 Colby St.	Medford	MA	02155	617-628-5000	627-4079
TF: 800-326-4001 ■ *Web:* www.tufts.edu					
University of Massachusetts					
Amherst 181 Presidents Dr	Amherst	MA	01003	413-545-0111	545-4312*
*Fax: Admissions ■ *Web:* www.umass.edu					
Boston 100 Morrissey Blvd Campus Ctr	Boston	MA	02125	617-287-6100	287-5999*
*Fax: Admitting ■ *Web:* www.umb.edu					
Dartmouth 285 Old Westport Rd	North Dartmouth	MA	02747	508-999-8000	999-8755*
*Fax: Admissions ■ *Web:* www.umassd.edu					
Lowell 1 University Ave	Lowell	MA	01854	978-934-4000	934-3086*
*Fax: Admissions ■ *Web:* www.uml.edu					
Wellesley College 106 Central St.	Wellesley	MA	02481	781-283-1000	283-3678*
*Fax: Admissions ■ *Web:* www.wellesley.edu					
Wentworth Institute of Technology 550 Huntington Ave	Boston	MA	02115	617-989-4590	989-4010*
*Fax: Admissions ■ *TF:* 800-556-0610 ■ *Web:* www.wit.edu					
Western New England College 1215 Wilbraham Rd	Springfield	MA	01119	413-782-3111	782-1777*
*Fax: Admissions ■ *TF:* 800-782-6665 ■ *Web:* wne.edu					
Westfield State University 577 Western Ave	Westfield	MA	01086	413-572-5300	572-0520*
*Fax: Admissions ■ *Web:* www.westfield.ma.edu					
Wheaton College 26 E Main St.	Norton	MA	02766	508-286-8200	286-8271
TF Admissions: 800-394-6003 ■ *Web:* wheatoncollege.edu					
Wheelock College 200 The Riverway	Boston	MA	02215	617-879-2206	879-2449
TF: 800-734-5212 ■ *Web:* www.wheelock.edu					
Williams College 880 Main St	Williamstown	MA	01267	413-597-3131	597-4052*
*Fax: Admissions ■ *TF:* 877-374-7526 ■ *Web:* www.williams.edu					
Worcester Polytechnic Institute 100 Institute Rd	Worcester	MA	01609	508-831-5000	831-5875*
*Fax: Admissions ■ *Web:* www.wpi.edu					

Michigan

	City	State	ZIP	Phone	Fax
Adrian College 110 S Madison St.	Adrian	MI	49221	517-265-5161	264-3331*
*Fax: Admissions ■ *TF Admissions:* 800-877-2246 ■ *Web:* www.adrian.edu					
Albion College 611 E Porter St	Albion	MI	49224	517-629-1000	629-0569
TF: 800-858-6770 ■ *Web:* www.albion.edu					
Alma College 614 W Superior St.	Alma	MI	48801	989-463-7139	463-7057
TF: 800-321-2562 ■ *Web:* www.alma.edu					
Andrews University 3976 Rose Dr.	Berrien Springs	MI	49103	269-471-7771	471-2670
TF: 800-253-2874 ■ *Web:* www.andrews.edu					
Baker College					
Auburn Hills 1500 University Dr	Auburn Hills	MI	48326	248-340-0600	340-0608*
*Fax: Admissions ■ *TF:* 888-429-0410 ■ *Web:* www.baker.edu					
Cadillac 9600 E 13th St	Cadillac	MI	49601	231-876-3100	876-3440
TF: 888-313-3463 ■ *Web:* www.baker.edu					
Clinton Township 34950 Little Mack Ave	Clinton Township	MI	48035	586-791-6610	
TF: 888-272-2842 ■ *Web:* www.baker.edu					
Flint 1050 W Bristol Rd	Flint	MI	48507	810-767-7600	766-4255*
*Fax: Admissions ■ *TF:* 800-964-4299 ■ *Web:* www.baker.edu					
Jackson 2800 Springport Rd	Jackson	MI	49202	517-788-7800	788-6187
TF: 888-343-3683 ■ *Web:* www.baker.edu					
Owosso 1020 S Washington St	Owosso	MI	48867	989-729-3350	729-3359*
*Fax: Admissions ■ *TF:* 800-879-3797 ■ *Web:* www.baker.edu					
Port Huron 3403 Lapeer Rd	Port Huron	MI	48060	810-985-7000	985-7066
TF: 888-262-2442 ■ *Web:* www.baker.edu					
Calvin College 3201 Burton St SE	Grand Rapids	MI	49546	616-526-6000	526-6777*
*Fax: Admissions ■ *TF:* 800-688-0122 ■ *Web:* www.calvin.edu					
Central Michigan University 102 Warriner Hall	Mount Pleasant	MI	48859	989-774-4000	774-7267*
*Fax: Admissions ■ *TF Admissions:* 888-292-5366 ■ *Web:* www.cmich.edu					
Chime Education Foundation 3300 Washtenaw Ave Ste 225	Ann Arbor	MI	48104	734-665-0000	
Web: chimecentral.org					
Concordia University Ann Arbor 4090 Geddes Rd	Ann Arbor	MI	48105	734-995-7322	995-4610
TF: 888-282-2338 ■ *Web:* www.cuaa.edu					
Cornerstone University 1001 E Beltline Ave NE	Grand Rapids	MI	49525	616-222-1426	222-1418*
*Fax: Admissions ■ *TF Admissions:* 800-787-9778 ■ *Web:* www.cornerstone.edu					
Davenport University					
Dearborn 4801 Oakman Blvd	Dearborn	MI	48126	313-581-4400	581-4480
TF: 800-585-1479 ■ *Web:* www.davenport.edu					
Flint 4318 Miller Rd Ste A	Flint	MI	48507	810-732-9977	732-9128*
*Fax: Admissions ■ *TF:* 800-727-1443 ■ *Web:* www.davenport.edu					
Lansing 220 E Kalamazoo St	Lansing	MI	48933	517-484-2600	484-1132*
*Fax: Admissions ■ *TF:* 800-686-1600 ■ *Web:* www.davenport.edu					
Lettinga Campus 6191 Kraft Ave SE.	Grand Rapids	MI	49512	616-698-7111	554-5214
TF: 866-925-3884 ■ *Web:* www.davenport.edu					
Saginaw 5300 Bay Rd	Saginaw	MI	48604	989-799-7800	799-9696*
*Fax: Admissions ■ *TF:* 800-968-8133 ■ *Web:* www.davenport.edu					
Warren 27650 Dequindre Rd	Warren	MI	48092	586-558-8700	558-7868*
*Fax: Admissions ■ *TF:* 800-724-7708 ■ *Web:* www.davenport.edu					
De La Salle Collegiate 14600 Common Rd.	Warren	MI	48093	586-778-2207	
Web: www.delasallehs.com					
Eastern Michigan University 1000 College Pl	Ypsilanti	MI	48197	734-487-1849	487-6559*
*Fax: Admissions ■ *TF:* 800-468-6368 ■ *Web:* www.emich.edu					
Ferris State University 1201 S State St.	Big Rapids	MI	49307	231-591-2000	591-3944*
*Fax: Admissions ■ *TF:* 800-433-7747 ■ *Web:* www.ferris.edu					
Traverse City 2200 Dendrinos Dr Ste 200H	Traverse City	MI	49684	231-995-1734	995-1736*
*Fax: Admissions ■ *TF:* 866-857-1954 ■ *Web:* www.ferris.edu					
Finlandia University 601 Quincy St.	Hancock	MI	49930	906-482-5300	487-7383*
*Fax: Admissions ■ *TF:* 800-682-7604 ■ *Web:* www.finlandia.edu					
Grand Valley State University 1 Campus Dr	Allendale	MI	49401	616-331-5000	331-2000
TF: 800-748-0246 ■ *Web:* www.gvsu.edu					
Hillsdale College 33 E College St.	Hillsdale	MI	49242	517-437-7341	437-3923*
*Fax: Admissions ■ *TF:* 888-886-1174 ■ *Web:* www.hillsdale.edu					
Hope College 69 E Tenth St PO Box 9000	Holland	MI	49422	616-395-7850	395-7130*
*Fax: Admissions ■ *TF Admissions:* 800-968-7850 ■ *Web:* www.hope.edu					
Kalamazoo College 1200 Academy St	Kalamazoo	MI	49006	269-337-7166	337-7390*
*Fax: Admissions ■ *TF Admissions:* 800-253-3602 ■ *Web:* www.kzoo.edu					
Kendall College of Art & Design of Ferris State University 17 Fountain St NW	Grand Rapids	MI	49503	616-451-2787	831-9689
TF: 800-676-2787 ■ *Web:* www.kcad.edu					
Kettering University 1700 University Ave	Flint	MI	48504	810-762-9500	762-9837
TF: 800-955-4464 ■ *Web:* www.kettering.edu					
Lake Superior State University 650 W Easterday Ave	Sault Sainte Marie	MI	49783	906-632-6841	635-6696*
*Fax: Admissions ■ *TF Admissions:* 888-800-5778 ■ *Web:* www.lssu.edu					
Lawrence Technological University 21000 W 10-Mile Rd	Southfield	MI	48075	248-204-3160	204-3188*
*Fax: Admissions ■ *TF:* 800-225-5588 ■ *Web:* www.ltu.edu					
Madonna University 36600 Schoolcraft Rd	Livonia	MI	48150	734-432-5339	432-5424
TF: 800-852-4951 ■ *Web:* www.madonna.edu					
Marygrove College 8425 W McNichols Rd	Detroit	MI	48221	313-927-1200	927-1399*
*Fax: Admissions ■ *TF Admissions:* 866-313-1927 ■ *Web:* www.marygrove.edu					
Michigan Jewish Institute 25401 Coolidge Hwy	Oak Park	MI	48237	248-414-6900	
TF: 888-463-6654 ■ *Web:* www.mji.edu					
Michigan State University 250 Hannah Admin Bldg.	East Lansing	MI	48824	517-355-1855	353-1647
Web: www.msu.edu					
Michigan Technological University 1400 Townsend Dr	Houghton	MI	49931	906-487-2335	487-2125*
*Fax: Admissions ■ *TF:* 888-688-1885 ■ *Web:* www.mtu.edu					
Northern Michigan University 1401 Presque Isle Ave	Marquette	MI	49855	906-227-2650	227-1747*
*Fax: Admissions ■ *TF:* 800-682-9797 ■ *Web:* www.nmu.edu					
Northwood University Michigan 4000 Whiting Dr	Midland	MI	48640	989-837-4200	837-4490*
*Fax: Admissions ■ *TF:* 800-622-9000 ■ *Web:* www.northwood.edu					
Oakland University 2200 Squirrel Rd	Rochester	MI	48309	248-370-2100	370-4462*
*Fax: Admissions ■ *TF Admissions:* 800-625-8648 ■ *Web:* www.oakland.edu					
Olivet College 320 S Main St	Olivet	MI	49076	269-749-7000	749-6617*
*Fax: Admissions ■ *TF:* 800-456-7189 ■ *Web:* www.olivetcollege.edu					
Rochester College 800 W Avon Rd	Rochester Hills	MI	48307	248-218-2011	218-2025*
*Fax: Admissions ■ *TF:* 800-521-6010 ■ *Web:* www.rc.edu					
Saginaw Valley State University 7400 Bay Rd	University Center	MI	48710	989-964-4200	790-0180
TF: 800-968-9500 ■ *Web:* www.svsu.edu					
Siena Heights University 1247 E Siena Heights Dr	Adrian	MI	49221	517-263-0731	264-7745
TF: 800-521-0009 ■ *Web:* www.sienaheights.edu					
Spring Arbor University 106 E Main St	Spring Arbor	MI	49283	517-750-1200	750-2745*
*Fax: Admissions ■ *TF Admissions:* 800-968-9103 ■ *Web:* saucougars.com					
University of Detroit Mercy 4001 W McNichols Rd	Detroit	MI	48221	313-993-1000	993-3326*
*Fax: Admissions ■ *TF Admissions:* 800-635-5020 ■ *Web:* www.udmercy.edu					
University of Detroit Mercy School of Dentistry *Corktown Campus* 2700 MLK Dr	Detroit	MI	48219	313-494-6611	
Web: www.udmercy.edu					
University of Michigan 515 E Jefferson St	Ann Arbor	MI	48109	734-764-1817	
Web: www.umich.edu					
Dearborn 4901 Evergreen Rd	Dearborn	MI	48128	313-593-5100	436-9167*
*Fax: Admissions ■ *Web:* umdearborn.edu					
Flint 303 E Kearsley St.	Flint	MI	48502	810-762-3000	762-3272
TF: 800-942-5636 ■ *Web:* www.flint.umich.edu					
Wayne State University 42 W Warren	Detroit	MI	48202	313-577-3577	577-7536*
*Fax: Admissions ■ *TF:* 877-978-4636 ■ *Web:* www.wayne.edu					
Western Michigan University 1903 W Michigan Ave	Kalamazoo	MI	49008	269-387-1000	387-2096*
*Fax: Admissions ■ *Web:* www.wmich.edu					

Minnesota

	City	State	ZIP	Phone	Fax
Apostolic Bible Institute Inc 6944 Hudson Blvd N	Saint Paul	MN	55128	651-739-7686	730-8669*
*Fax: Admissions ■ *Web:* www.apostolic.org					
Argosy University 1515 Central Pkwy.	Eagan	MN	55121	651-846-2882	994-7956*
*Fax: Admissions ■ *TF:* 888-844-2004 ■ *Web:* argosy.edu					
Augsburg College 2211 Riverside Ave	Minneapolis	MN	55454	612-330-1000	330-1590
TF: 800-788-5678 ■ *Web:* www.augsburg.edu					
Bemidji State University 1500 Birchmont Dr NE	Bemidji	MN	56601	218-755-2001	755-4048
TF Admissions: 800-475-2001 ■ *Web:* www.bemidjistate.edu					
Bethany Lutheran College 700 Luther Dr.	Mankato	MN	56001	507-344-7000	344-7376*
*Fax: Admissions ■ *TF:* 800-944-3066 ■ *Web:* www.blc.edu					
Bethel University 3900 Bethel Dr	Saint Paul	MN	55112	651-638-6400	635-1490*
*Fax: Admissions ■ *TF:* 800-255-8706 ■ *Web:* www.bethel.edu					
Carleton College 100 S College St.	Northfield	MN	55057	507-646-4000	646-4526*
*Fax: Admissions ■ *TF Admissions:* 800-995-2275 ■ *Web:* www.carleton.edu					
College of Saint Catherine 2004 Randolph Ave	Saint Paul	MN	55105	651-690-6000	
TF: 800-945-4599 ■ *Web:* www.stkate.edu					

Phone Fax

Minneapolis 601 25th Ave S ... Minneapolis MN 55454 651-690-7700 690-7849*
*Fax: Admissions ■ *TF:* 800-945-4599 ■ *Web:* www.stkate.edu

College of Saint Scholastica 1200 Kenwood Ave ... Duluth MN 55811 218-723-6046 723-5991*
*Fax: Admissions ■ *TF:* 800-447-5444 ■ *Web:* www.css.edu

Concordia College 901 Eigth St S ... Moorhead MN 56562 218-299-4000 299-4720
TF: 800-699-9897 ■ *Web:* www.concordiacollege.edu

Gustavus Adolphus College
800 W College Ave ... Saint Peter MN 56082 507-933-8000 933-7474
TF: 800-487-8288 ■ *Web:* www.gustavus.edu

Hamline University 1536 Hewitt Ave ... Saint Paul MN 55104 651-523-2207 523-2458
TF: 800-753-9753 ■ *Web:* www.hamline.edu

Macalester College 1600 Grand Ave ... Saint Paul MN 55105 651-696-6357 696-6724*
*Fax: Admissions ■ *TF Admissions:* 800-231-7974 ■ *Web:* www.macalester.edu

Martin Luther College 1995 Luther Ct ... New Ulm MN 56073 507-354-8221 354-8225*
*Fax: Admissions ■ *TF:* 877-652-1995 ■ *Web:* www.mlc-wels.edu

McNally Smith College of Music Foundation
19 Exchange St E ... Saint Paul MN 55101 651-361-3320
TF: 800-594-9500 ■ *Web:* www.mcnallysmith.edu

Metropolitan State University
700 E Seventh St ... Saint Paul MN 55106 651-793-1300 793-1310*
*Fax: Admissions ■ *TF:* 888-234-2690 ■ *Web:* www.metrostate.edu

Minnesota State University
Mankato 122 Taylor Ctr ... Mankato MN 56001 507-389-1822 389-1511
TF Admissions: 800-722-0544 ■ *Web:* www.mnsu.edu
Moorhead 1104 Seventh Ave S ... Moorhead MN 56563 218-477-2161
TF: 800-593-7246 ■ *Web:* www.mnstate.edu

North Central University
910 Elliot Ave S ... Minneapolis MN 55404 612-343-4460 343-4146*
*Fax: Admissions ■ *TF Admissions:* 800-289-6222 ■ *Web:* www.northcentral.edu

Northwestern College
3003 Snelling Ave N PO Box 130517 ... Saint Paul MN 55113 651-631-5100 631-5680
TF: 800-692-4020 ■ *Web:* www.unwsp.edu

Rasmussen College Inc
4400 W 78th St 6th Fl ... Bloomington MN 55345 952-545-2000
Web: www.rasmussen.edu

Saint Mary's University of Minnesota
700 Terr Heights ... Winona MN 55987 507-452-4430 457-1722*
*Fax: Admissions ■ *TF:* 800-635-5987 ■ *Web:* www.smumn.edu

Southwest Minnesota State University
1501 State St ... Marshall MN 56258 800-642-0684
TF: 800-642-0684 ■ *Web:* smsumustangs.com
Crookston 2900 University Ave 170 Owen Hall ... Crookston MN 56716 218-281-8569 281-8575*
*Fax: Admissions ■ *TF:* 800-862-6466 ■ *Web:* www.crk.umn.edu
Duluth 1049 University Dr ... Duluth MN 55812 218-726-8000 726-6394*
*Fax: Admissions ■ *TF:* 800-232-1339 ■ *Web:* www.d.umn.edu
Morris 600 E Fourth St ... Morris MN 56267 320-589-6035 589-1673*
*Fax: Admissions ■ *TF:* 800-992-8863 ■ *Web:* www.morris.umn.edu
Twin Cities
240 Williamson Hall 231 Pillsbury Dr SE ... Minneapolis MN 55455 612-625-2008 626-1693
TF: 800-752-1000 ■ *Web:* www.umn.edu

University of Saint Thomas
2115 Summit Ave ... Saint Paul MN 55105 651-962-5000 962-6160*
*Fax: Admissions ■ *TF:* 800-328-6819 ■ *Web:* www.stthomas.edu

Winona State University 175 W Mark St ... Winona MN 55987 507-457-5000 457-5620*
*Fax: Admissions ■ *TF:* 800-342-5978 ■ *Web:* www.winona.edu

Mississippi

Phone Fax

Belhaven College 1500 Peachtree St PO Box 153 ... Jackson MS 39202 601-968-5940 968-8946*
*Fax: Admissions ■ *TF:* 800-960-5940 ■ *Web:* www.belhaven.edu

Blue Mountain College PO Box 160 ... Blue Mountain MS 38610 662-685-4771 685-4776*
*Fax: Admissions ■ *TF:* 800-235-0136 ■ *Web:* www.bmc.edu

Delta State University 1003 W Sunflower Rd ... Cleveland MS 38733 662-846-4020 846-4684*
*Fax: Admissions ■ *TF:* 800-468-6378 ■ *Web:* www.deltastate.edu

Jackson State University
1400 John R Lynch St ... Jackson MS 39217 601-979-2121 979-3445*
*Fax: Admissions ■ *TF:* 800-848-6817 ■ *Web:* www.jsums.edu

Millsaps College 1701 N State St ... Jackson MS 39210 601-974-1000 974-1059*
*Fax: Admissions ■ *TF Admissions:* 800-352-1050 ■ *Web:* www.millsaps.edu

Mississippi College 200 S Capitol St ... Clinton MS 39056 601-925-3000 925-3950*
*Fax: Admissions ■ *TF:* 800-738-1236 ■ *Web:* www.mc.edu

Mississippi State University
PO Box 6305 ... Mississippi State MS 39762 662-325-2224 325-7360*
*Fax: Admissions ■ *Web:* www.msstate.edu

Mississippi University for Women
1100 College St MUW-1613 ... Columbus MS 39701 662-329-4750 241-7481*
*Fax: Admissions ■ *TF:* 877-462-8439 ■ *Web:* web3.muw.edu

Mississippi Valley State University
14000 Hwy 82 ... Itta Bena MS 38941 662-254-9041 254-3759
TF: 800-844-6885 ■ *Web:* www.mvsu.edu

Rust College 150 Rust Ave ... Holly Springs MS 38635 662-252-8000 252-2258*
*Fax: Admissions ■ *TF:* 888-886-8492 ■ *Web:* www.rustcollege.edu

Tougaloo College 500 W County Line Rd ... Tougaloo MS 39174 601-977-7700 977-4501*
*Fax: Admissions ■ *TF Admissions:* 888-424-2566 ■ *Web:* www.tougaloo.edu

University of Mississippi PO Box 1848 ... University MS 38677 662-915-7211 915-5869*
*Fax: Admissions ■ *Web:* www.olemiss.edu
Tupelo 1918 Briar Ridge Rd ... Tupelo MS 38804 662-844-5622 844-5625*
*Fax: Admissions ■ *TF:* 888-846-5622 ■ *Web:* www.outreach.olemiss.edu

University of Southern Mississippi
118 College Dr ... Hattiesburg MS 39406 601-266-1000 266-5148*
*Fax: Admissions ■ *TF:* 800-446-0892 ■ *Web:* www.usm.edu
Gulf Park 730 E Beach Blvd ... Long Beach MS 39560 228-865-4500
Web: www.usm.edu

William Carey University 498 Tuscan Ave ... Hattiesburg MS 39401 601-318-6051 318-6454*
*Fax: Admissions ■ *TF:* 800-962-5991 ■ *Web:* www.wmcarey.edu

Missouri

Phone Fax

Avila University 11901 Wornall Rd ... Kansas City MO 64145 816-501-2400 501-2453
TF: 866-943-5787 ■ *Web:* www.avila.edu

Central Methodist University
411 Central Methodist Sq ... Fayette MO 65248 660-248-3391 248-1872*
*Fax: Admissions ■ *TF:* 877-268-1854 ■ *Web:* www.centralmethodist.edu

Chamberlain College of Nursing
11830 Westline Industrial Ste 106 ... Saint Louis MO 63146 314-991-6200
TF: 888-556-8226 ■ *Web:* www.chamberlain.edu

College of the Ozarks
1 Industrial Dr PO Box 17 ... Point Lookout MO 65726 417-334-6411 335-2618*
*Fax: Admissions ■ *TF Admissions:* 800-222-0525 ■ *Web:* www.cofo.edu

Columbia College 1001 Rogers St ... Columbia MO 65216 573-875-8700 875-7209*
*Fax: Admissions ■ *TF:* 800-231-2391 ■ *Web:* www.ccis.edu

Columbia College Jefferson City
3314 Emerald Ln ... Jefferson City MO 65109 573-634-3250 634-8507
TF: 800-231-2391 ■ *Web:* ccis.edu/jeffcity

Columbia College Lake of the Ozarks
900 College Blvd ... Osage Beach MO 65065 573-348-6463 348-1791
TF: 800-231-2391 ■ *Web:* www.ccis.edu

Drury University 900 N Benton Ave ... Springfield MO 65802 417-873-7879 866-3873
TF: 800-922-2274 ■ *Web:* www.drury.edu

Evangel University 1111 N Glenstone Ave ... Springfield MO 65802 417-865-2815 865-9599
TF: 800-382-6435 ■ *Web:* evangel.edu

Graceland University Independence
1401 W Truman Rd ... Independence MO 64050 816-833-0524 833-2990*
*Fax: Admissions ■ *TF:* 800-833-0524 ■ *Web:* www.graceland.edu

Grantham University Inc 7200 NW 86th St ... Kansas City MO 64153 816-595-5759
Web: www.grantham.edu

Hannibal-LaGrange College 2800 Palmyra Rd ... Hannibal MO 63401 573-221-3675 221-6594
TF Admissions: 800-454-1119 ■ *Web:* www.hlg.edu

Harris-Stowe State University
3026 Laclede Ave ... Saint Louis MO 63103 314-340-3366 340-3555
Web: www.hssu.edu

Lincoln University
820 Chestnut St B-7 Young Hall ... Jefferson City MO 65102 573-681-5599 681-5889*
*Fax: Admissions ■ *TF Admissions:* 800-521-5052 ■ *Web:* www.lincolnu.edu

Lindenwood University
209 S Kingshighway ... Saint Charles MO 63301 636-949-2000 949-4989*
*Fax: Admissions ■ *TF:* 877-615-8212 ■ *Web:* www.lindenwood.edu

Missouri Baptist University
1 College Pk Dr ... Saint Louis MO 63141 314-434-1115 434-7596
TF: 877-434-1115 ■ *Web:* www.mobap.edu
Troy/Wentzville Extension
75 College Campus Dr ... Moscow Mills MO 63362 636-366-4363 356-4119*
*Fax: Admissions ■ *Web:* www.mobap.edu

Missouri Southern State University
3950 Newman Rd ... Joplin MO 64801 417-625-9300 659-4429
TF: 866-818-6778 ■ *Web:* www.mssu.edu

Missouri State University (MSU)
901 S National Ave ... Springfield MO 65897 417-836-5000 836-6334
TF: 800-492-7900 ■ *Web:* www.missouristate.edu

Missouri University of Science & Technology
Rolla 1870 Miner Cir G2 Parker Hall ... Rolla MO 65409 573-341-4111 341-4082*
*Fax: Admissions ■ *TF:* 800-522-0938 ■ *Web:* www.mst.edu

Missouri Valley College 500 E College St ... Marshall MO 65340 660-831-4000 831-4233*
*Fax: Admissions ■ *TF:* 800-999-8219 ■ *Web:* www.moval.edu

Missouri Western State University
4525 Downs Dr ... Saint Joseph MO 64507 816-271-4266 271-5833
TF: 800-662-7041 ■ *Web:* www.missouriwestern.edu

National American University Independence
3620 Arrowhead Ave ... Independence MO 64057 816-412-7700 412-7705
TF: 866-628-1288 ■ *Web:* www.national.edu

Northwest Missouri State University
800 University Dr ... Maryville MO 64468 660-562-1148 562-1821*
*Fax: Admissions ■ *TF:* 800-633-1175 ■ *Web:* www.nwmissouri.edu

Ozark Bible Institute & College
906 Summit St PO Box 398 ... Neosho MO 64850 417-451-2057 451-2059*
*Fax: Admissions ■ *Web:* obicollege.com

Park University 8700 NW River Pk Dr ... Parkville MO 64152 816-741-2000 741-9668
TF: 800-745-7275 ■ *Web:* www.park.edu

Principia College 13201 Clayton Rd ... St. Louis MO 63131 618-374-2131
TF: 800-277-4648 ■ *Web:* www.principia.edu

Rockhurst University 1100 Rockhurst Rd ... Kansas City MO 64110 816-501-4000 501-4241*
*Fax: Admissions ■ *TF:* 800-842-6776 ■ *Web:* www.rockhurst.edu

Saint Louis College of Pharmacy
4588 Parkview Pl ... Saint Louis MO 63110 314-367-8700 446-8304*
*Fax: Admissions ■ *TF:* 800-278-5267 ■ *Web:* www.stlcop.edu

Saint Louis University 221 N Grand Blvd ... Saint Louis MO 63103 314-977-7288 977-7136*
*Fax: Admissions ■ *TF:* 800-758-3678 ■ *Web:* www.slu.edu
Parks College of Engineering Aviation & Technology
3450 Lindell Blvd ... Saint Louis MO 63103 314-977-8203 977-8403
Web: parks.slu.edu

Southeast Missouri State University
1 University Plaza ... Cape Girardeau MO 63701 573-651-2000 651-5936*
*Fax: Admissions ■ *TF:* 866-562-6801 ■ *Web:* www.semo.edu

Southwest Baptist University
1600 University Ave ... Bolivar MO 65613 800-526-5859 328-1808*
*Fax Area Code: 417 ■ *Fax: Admissions ■ *TF:* 800-526-5859 ■ *Web:* www.sbuniv.edu

Stephens College 1200 E Broadway ... Columbia MO 65215 573-442-2211
Web: www.stephens.edu

Truman State University 100 E Normal St ... Kirksville MO 63501 660-785-4000 785-7456*
*Fax: Admissions ■ *TF:* 800-892-7792 ■ *Web:* www.truman.edu
Columbia 104 Jesse Hall ... Columbia MO 65211 573-882-6333 882-7887*
*Fax: Admissions ■ *TF:* 800-856-2181 ■ *Web:* www.missouri.edu
Kansas City 5100 Rockhill Rd ... Kansas City MO 64110 816-235-1000 235-5544
TF: 800-775-8652 ■ *Web:* www.umkc.edu
Saint Louis 1 University Blvd ... Saint Louis MO 63121 314-516-5000 516-5310*
*Fax: Admissions ■ *TF Admissions:* 888-462-8675 ■ *Web:* www.umsl.edu

Washington University in Saint Louis
Campus Box 1089 ... Saint Louis MO 63130 314-935-5000 935-4290
TF: 800-638-0700 ■ *Web:* www.wustl.edu

Westminster College 501 Westminster Ave ... Fulton MO 65251 573-592-5251 592-5255
TF Admissions: 800-475-3361 ■ *Web:* www.wcmo.edu

William Jewell College 500 College Hill WJC ... Liberty MO 64068 816-781-7700 415-5040
TF: 888-253-9355 ■ *Web:* www.jewell.edu

Phone Fax

William Woods University 1 University Ave . . . . Fulton MO 65251 573-592-4221 592-1146*
Fax: Admissions ■ *TF Admissions:* 800-995-3159 ■ *Web:* www.williamwoods.edu

Montana

Phone Fax

Academy of Nail Skin & Hair Inc
928 Broadwater Ave Ste C . . . . Billings MT 59101 406-252-3232
Web: academyofnailandskin.com

Carroll College 1601 N Benton Ave. . . . . Helena MT 59625 406-447-4300 447-4533
TF: 800-992-3648 ■ *Web:* www.carroll.edu

Montana State University
Billings 1500 University Dr . . . . Billings MT 59101 406-657-2011 657-2302*
Fax: Admissions ■ *TF:* 800-565-6782 ■ *Web:* www.msubillings.edu
Bozeman PO Box 172190 . . . . Bozeman MT 59717 406-994-2452 994-7360*
Fax: Admissions ■ *TF Admissions:* 888-678-2287 ■ *Web:* www.montana.edu
Northern PO Box 7751. . . . . Havre MT 59501 406-994-2452
TF: 800-662-6132 ■ *Web:* www.montana.edu

Montana Tech of the University of Montana
1300 W Pk St . . . . Butte MT 59701 406-496-4101 496-4710*
Fax: Admissions ■ *TF Admissions:* 800-445-8324 ■ *Web:* www.mtech.edu

Rocky Mountain College 1511 Poly Dr. . . . . Billings MT 59102 406-657-1000 657-1189*
Fax: Admissions ■ *TF:* 800-877-6259 ■ *Web:* www.rocky.edu

Student Assistance Foundation of Montana
2500 E Broadway St . . . . Helena MT 59601 406-495-7800
Web: www.trustudent.com

University of Great Falls 1301 20th St S . . . . Great Falls MT 59405 800-856-9544 791-5209*
Fax Area Code: 406 ■ *Fax:* Admissions ■ *TF Admissions:* 800-856-9544 ■ *Web:* www.ugf.edu

University of Montana 32 Campus Dr. . . . . Missoula MT 59812 406-243-6266 243-5711*
Fax: Admissions ■ *TF Admissions:* 800-462-8636 ■ *Web:* www.umt.edu
Western 710 S Atlantic St . . . . Dillon MT 59725 406-683-7011 683-7493*
Fax: Admissions ■ *TF Admissions:* 877-683-7331 ■ *Web:* www.umwestern.edu

Yellowstone Baptist College
1515 S Shiloh Rd . . . . Billings MT 59106 406-656-9950 656-3737*
Fax: Admissions ■ *TF:* 800-487-9950 ■ *Web:* yellowstonechristian.edu

Nebraska

Phone Fax

Bellevue University 1000 Galvin Rd S . . . . Bellevue NE 68005 402-293-2000 557-5438*
Fax: Admissions ■ *TF:* 800-756-7920 ■ *Web:* www.bellevue.edu

Chadron State College 1000 Main St . . . . Chadron NE 69337 308-432-6000 432-6229
TF: 800-242-3766 ■ *Web:* www.csc.edu

Clarkson College 101 S 42nd St. . . . . Omaha NE 68131 402-552-3100 552-6057*
Fax: Admissions ■ *TF:* 800-647-5500 ■ *Web:* www.clarksoncollege.edu

College of Saint Mary 7000 Mercy Rd. . . . . Omaha NE 68106 402-399-2400 399-2412*
Fax: Admissions ■ *TF:* 800-926-5534 ■ *Web:* www.csm.edu

Concordia University Nebraska
800 N Columbia Ave. . . . . Seward NE 68434 402-643-3651 643-4073*
Fax: Admissions ■ *TF:* 800-535-5494 ■ *Web:* www.cune.edu

Creighton University 2500 California Plz. . . . . Omaha NE 68178 402-280-2700 280-2685*
Fax: Admissions ■ *TF:* 800-282-5835 ■ *Web:* www.creighton.edu

Doane College 1014 Boswell Ave . . . . Crete NE 68333 402-826-2161 826-8600
TF: 800-333-6263 ■ *Web:* www.doane.edu
Grand Island 3180 W US Hwy 34. . . . . Grand Island NE 68801 308-398-0800 398-1726
TF: 800-333-6263 ■ *Web:* www.doane.edu
Lincoln 303 N 52nd St. . . . . Lincoln NE 68504 402-466-4774 466-4228
TF: 888-803-6263 ■ *Web:* www.doane.edu

Hastings College 710 N Turner Ave . . . . Hastings NE 68901 402-463-2402 461-7490*
Fax: Admissions ■ *TF:* 800-532-7642 ■ *Web:* www.hastings.edu

Midland University 900 N Clarkson St. . . . . Fremont NE 68025 402-941-6270 941-6513*
Fax: Admissions ■ *TF:* 800-642-8382 ■ *Web:* my.midlandu.edu

Nebraska Wesleyan University
5000 St Paul Ave . . . . Lincoln NE 68504 800-541-3818
TF: 800-541-3818 ■ *Web:* www.nebrwesleyan.edu

Peru State College 600 Hoyt St PO Box 10 . . . . Peru NE 68421 402-872-3815 872-2296*
Fax: Admissions ■ *TF:* 800-742-4412 ■ *Web:* www.peru.edu

Summit Christian College 2025 21st St . . . . Gering NE 69341 308-632-6933 632-8599
TF: 888-305-8083 ■ *Web:* www.summitcc.net

Union College 3800 S 48th St . . . . Lincoln NE 68506 402-486-2504 486-2566*
Fax: Admissions ■ *TF Admissions:* 800-228-4600 ■ *Web:* www.ucollege.edu

University of Nebraska
Kearney 905 W 25th St . . . . Kearney NE 68849 308-865-8441 865-8987*
Fax: Admissions ■ *TF:* 800-532-7639 ■ *Web:* www.unk.edu
Lincoln 1410 Q St . . . . Lincoln NE 68588 402-472-2023 472-0670*
Fax: Admissions ■ *TF:* 800-742-8800 ■ *Web:* www.unl.edu
Omaha 6001 Dodge St. . . . . Omaha NE 68182 402-554-2800 554-3472*
Fax: Admissions ■ *TF:* 800-858-8648 ■ *Web:* www.unomaha.edu

Wayne State College 1111 Main St. . . . . Wayne NE 68787 402-375-7000
TF: 800-228-9972 ■ *Web:* www.wsc.edu

York College 1125 E Eigth St. . . . . York NE 68467 402-363-5600 363-5623*
Fax: Admissions ■ *TF:* 800-950-9675 ■ *Web:* www.york.edu

Nevada

Phone Fax

Career College of Northern Nevada
1421 Pullman Dr . . . . Sparks NV 89434 775-856-2266
Web: www.ccnn.edu

Great Basin College 1500 College Pkwy . . . . Elko NV 89801 775-738-8493 753-2311*
Fax: Admissions ■ *TF:* 888-590-6726 ■ *Web:* www.gbcnv.edu

Morrison University
10315 Professional Cir Ste 201 . . . . Reno NV 89521 775-850-0700
Web: www.anthem.edu

Sierra Nevada College 999 Tahoe Blvd . . . . Incline Village NV 89451 775-831-1314
TF: 866-412-4636 ■ *Web:* www.sierranevada.edu

University of Nevada
Las Vegas 4505 S Maryland Pkwy . . . . Las Vegas NV 89154 702-895-3011 895-1118*
Fax: Admissions ■ *Web:* www.unlv.edu
Reno 1664 N Virginia St . . . . Reno NV 89557 775-784-1110 784-4283*
Fax: Admissions ■ *TF:* 866-263-8232 ■ *Web:* www.unr.edu

New Hampshire

Phone Fax

Colby-Sawyer College 541 Main St. . . . . New London NH 03257 603-526-3700 526-3452*
Fax: Admissions ■ *TF Admissions:* 800-272-1015 ■ *Web:* www.colby-sawyer.edu

Daniel Webster College 20 University Dr . . . . Nashua NH 03063 603-577-6000 577-6001
TF: 800-325-6876 ■ *Web:* www.dwc.edu

Dartmouth College 6016 McNutt Hall . . . . Hanover NH 03755 603-646-1110 646-1216
Web: www.dartmouth.edu

Franklin Pierce University
Concord 5 Chenell Dr . . . . Concord NH 03301 603-228-1155
TF: 800-437-0048 ■ *Web:* www.franklinpierce.edu
Keene 17 Bradco St . . . . Keene NH 03431 603-899-4000
TF: 800-325-1090 ■ *Web:* www.franklinpierce.edu
Lebanon 24 Airport Rd Ste 19 . . . . West Lebanon NH 03784 603-298-5549 899-1065*
Fax: Admissions ■ *TF:* 800-325-1090 ■ *Web:* www.franklinpierce.edu
Manchester 670 N Commercial St . . . . Manchester NH 03101 603-626-4972 626-4815
TF Admissions: 800-437-0048 ■ *Web:* www.franklinpierce.edu
Portsmouth 73 Corporate Dr . . . . Portsmouth NH 03801 603-433-2000 899-1067*
Fax: Admissions ■ *TF:* 800-325-1090 ■ *Web:* www.franklinpierce.edu
Rindge 40 University Dr. . . . . Rindge NH 03461 603-899-4000 899-4394*
Fax: Admissions ■ *TF Admissions:* 800-437-0048 ■ *Web:* www.franklinpierce.edu

Granite State College 8 Old Suncook Rd . . . . Concord NH 03301 603-228-3000 513-1389
TF: 888-228-3000 ■ *Web:* www.granite.edu
Berlin 25 Hall St Rm 144 . . . . Concord NH 03301 603-447-3970
TF: 855-472-4255 ■ *Web:* www.granite.edu
Portsmouth 51 International Dr . . . . Portsmouth NH 03801 603-332-8335
Web: www.granite.edu

Hesser College 3 Sundial Ave. . . . . Manchester NH 03103 603-668-6660 621-8994*
Fax: Admissions ■ *TF:* 888-971-2190 ■ *Web:* www.mountwashington.edu

Keene State College 229 Main St . . . . Keene NH 03435 603-352-1909 358-2767*
Fax: Admissions ■ *TF:* 800-572-1909 ■ *Web:* www.keene.edu

New England College 98 Bridge St . . . . Henniker NH 03242 603-428-2223
TF Admissions: 800-521-7642 ■ *Web:* www.nec.edu

Plymouth State University 17 High St . . . . Plymouth NH 03264 603-535-2237 535-2714*
Fax: Admissions ■ *TF:* 800-842-6900 ■ *Web:* www.plymouth.edu

Rivier College 420 S Main St . . . . Nashua NH 03060 603-888-1311 891-1799*
Fax: Admissions ■ *TF:* 800-447-4843 ■ *Web:* www.rivier.edu

Saint Anselm College 100 St Anselm Dr . . . . Manchester NH 03102 603-641-7500 641-7550
TF: 888-426-7356 ■ *Web:* www.anselm.edu

Southern New Hampshire University
2500 N River Rd . . . . Manchester NH 03106 603-668-2211 655-0236*
Fax Area Code: 802 ■ *TF:* 800-668-1249 ■ *Web:* www.snhu.edu

University of New Hampshire
3 Garrison Ave Grant House . . . . Durham NH 03824 603-862-1234 862-0077*
Fax: Admissions ■ *Web:* www.unh.edu
Manchester 400 Commercial St. . . . . Manchester NH 03101 603-641-4321 641-4305
TF: 800-287-9793 ■ *Web:* manchester.unh.edu

New Jersey

Phone Fax

Bloomfield College 467 Franklin St . . . . Bloomfield NJ 07003 973-748-9000 748-0916
TF: 800-848-4555 ■ *Web:* www.bloomfield.edu

Caldwell University 120 Bloomfield Ave . . . . Caldwell NJ 07006 973-618-3500 618-3600*
Fax: Admissions ■ *TF Admissions:* 888-864-9516 ■ *Web:* www.caldwell.edu

Centenary College 400 Jefferson St. . . . . Hackettstown NJ 07840 908-852-1400 852-3454*
Fax: Admissions ■ *TF Admissions:* 800-236-8679 ■ *Web:* www.centenarycollege.edu

College of New Jersey
2000 Pennington Rd PO Box 7718 . . . . Ewing NJ 08628 609-771-1855 637-5174*
Fax: Admissions ■ *TF:* 800-644-3562 ■ *Web:* tcnj.pages.tcnj.edu

College of Saint Elizabeth 2 Convent Rd . . . . Morristown NJ 07960 973-290-4700 290-4710*
Fax: Admissions ■ *TF Admissions:* 800-210-7900 ■ *Web:* www.cse.edu

Douglass College 100 George St . . . . New Brunswick NJ 08901 848-932-9500 932-8877*
Fax Area Code: 732 ■ *Web:* douglass.rutgers.edu

Drake College of Business
125 Broad St Fl 2 . . . . Elizabeth NJ 07201 908-352-5509

Drew University 36 Madison Ave . . . . Madison NJ 07940 973-408-3000 408-3068*
Fax: Admissions ■ *Web:* www.drew.edu

Fairleigh Dickinson University
285 Madison Ave . . . . Madison NJ 07940 973-443-8500 443-8088*
Fax: Admissions ■ *TF:* 800-338-8803 ■ *Web:* www.fdu.edu
Metropolitan 1000 River Rd . . . . Teaneck NJ 07666 201-692-2000 692-2560
TF: 800-338-8803 ■ *Web:* www.fdu.edu

Felician College 262 S Main St . . . . Lodi NJ 07644 201-559-6000 559-6138*
Fax: Admissions ■ *TF:* 888-442-4551 ■ *Web:* www.felician.edu
Rutherford 223 Montross Ave . . . . Rutherford NJ 07070 201-559-6000 559-3578
TF: 888-442-4551 ■ *Web:* www.felician.edu

Georgian Court University 900 Lakewood Ave . . . . Lakewood NJ 08701 800-458-8422 987-2000*
Fax Area Code: 732 ■ *Fax:* Admissions ■ *TF:* 800-458-8422 ■ *Web:* www.georgian.edu

Kean University 1000 Morris Ave Kean Hall . . . . Union NJ 07083 908-737-7100 737-7105*
Fax: Admissions ■ *TF:* 800-882-1037 ■ *Web:* www.kean.edu

Monmouth University 400 Cedar Ave . . . . West Long Branch NJ 07764 732-571-3456 263-5166*
Fax: Admissions ■ *TF:* 800-543-9671 ■ *Web:* www.monmouth.edu

Montclair State University 1 Normal Ave. . . . . Montclair NJ 07043 973-655-4000 655-7700*
Fax: Admissions ■ *TF Admissions:* 800-331-9205 ■ *Web:* www.montclair.edu

New Jersey City University 2039 JFK Blvd. . . . . Jersey City NJ 07305 201-200-2000 200-2044
TF: 888-441-6528 ■ *Web:* www.njcu.edu

New Jersey Institute of Technology
University Heights . . . . Newark NJ 07102 973-596-3000 596-3461
TF: 800-925-6548 ■ *Web:* www.njit.edu

Princeton University 33 Washington Rd . . . . Princeton NJ 08544 609-258-3000 258-6743*
Fax: Admissions ■ *TF:* 877-609-2273 ■ *Web:* www.princeton.edu

Ramapo College of New Jersey
505 Ramapo Vly Rd . . . . Mahwah NJ 07430 201-684-7500 684-7964*
Fax: Admissions ■ *Web:* www.ramapo.edu

Richard Stockton College of New Jersey
PO Box 195 . . . . Pomona NJ 08240 609-652-1776 748-5541*
Fax: Admissions ■ *Web:* intraweb.stockton.edu/eyos/page.cfm?siteID=164&pageID=7

Rider University 2083 Lawrenceville Rd . . . . Lawrenceville NJ 08648 609-896-5000 895-6645*
Fax: Admissions ■ *TF:* 800-257-9026 ■ *Web:* www.rider.edu

Phone Fax

Westminster Choir College 101 Walnut Ln .... Princeton NJ 08540 609-921-7100 921-2538*
*Fax: Admissions ■ *TF:* 800-962-4647 ■ *Web:* www.rider.edu
Rowan University 201 Mullica Hill Rd .... Glassboro NJ 08028 856-256-4200 256-4430*
*Fax: Admissions ■ *TF Admissions:* 877-787-6926 ■ *Web:* www.rowan.edu
Rutgers The State University of New Jersey
Camden 406 Penn St......................... Camden NJ 08102 856-225-6104 225-6498*
*Fax: Admissions ■ *Web:* www.camden.rutgers.edu
Newark 249 University Ave Rm 100............... Newark NJ 07102 973-353-5205 353-1440*
*Fax: Admissions ■ *Web:* www.newark.rutgers.edu
Rutgers University Foundation
7 College Ave Winants Hall .... New Brunswick NJ 08901 732-932-7777
Web: www.rutgers.edu
Seton Hall University 400 S Orange Ave .... South Orange NJ 07079 973-761-9332 275-2321*
*Fax: Admissions ■ *TF:* 800-992-4723 ■ *Web:* www.shu.edu
Stevens Institute of Technology
Castle Pt on the Hudson.......................... Hoboken NJ 07030 201-216-5194 216-8348*
*Fax: Admissions ■ *TF:* 800-458-5323 ■ *Web:* www.stevens.edu
Thomas Edison State College 101 W State St.......... Trenton NJ 08608 888-442-8372 984-8447*
*Fax Area Code: 609 ■ *Fax: Admissions ■ *TF:* 888-442-8372 ■ *Web:* www.tesu.edu
William Paterson University 300 Pompton Rd........... Wayne NJ 07470 973-720-2000 720-2910
TF: 877-978-3923 ■ *Web:* www.wpunj.edu

New Mexico

Phone Fax

College of Santa Fe 1600 St Michaels Dr .... Santa Fe NM 87505 505-473-6011
TF: 800-862-7759 ■ *Web:* mycollegeoptions.org
College of the Southwest 6610 N Lovington Hwy .... Hobbs NM 88240 575-392-6561 392-6006*
*Fax Area Code: 505 ■ *Fax: Admissions ■ *TF:* 800-530-4400 ■ *Web:* www.usw.edu
Eastern New Mexico University
1500 S Ave K Stn 6...................................Portales NM 88130 575-562-1011
TF: 800-367-3668 ■ *Web:* www.enmu.edu
Eastern New Mexico University-ruidoso
709 Mechem Dr ....Ruidoso NM 88345 575-257-2120
Web: www.ruidoso.enmu.edu
New Mexico Highlands University
901 University Ave .... Las Vegas NM 87701 505-425-7511 454-3552
TF: 877-850-9064 ■ *Web:* www.nmhu.edu
New Mexico Institute of Mining & Technology (NMT)
801 Leroy Pl......................................Socorro NM 87801 505-835-5434
TF Admissions: 800-428-8324 ■ *Web:* www.nmt.edu
New Mexico State University (NMSU)
MSC-3A PO Box 30001 .... Las Cruces NM 88003 575-646-3121 646-6330*
*Fax: Admissions ■ *TF Admissions:* 800-662-6678 ■ *Web:* www.nmsu.edu
Santa Fe University of Art & Design
1600 St Michaels Dr.................................. Santa Fe NM 87505 800-456-2673 473-6011*
*Fax Area Code: 505 ■ *Fax: Admissions ■ *TF:* 800-456-2673 ■ *Web:* www.santafeuniversity.edu
University of New Mexico (UNM)
1 University of New Mexico .... Albuquerque NM 87131 505-277-0111 277-6686
TF: 800-225-5866 ■ *Web:* www.unm.edu
Gallup 200 College Rd..............................Gallup NM 87301 505-863-7500 863-7610
TF: 800-225-5866 ■ *Web:* www.gallup.unm.edu
Western New Mexico University
1000 W College St PO Box 680 .... Silver City NM 88061 505-538-6011 538-6278*
*Fax Area Code: 575 ■ *TF Admissions:* 800-872-9668 ■ *Web:* www.wnmu.edu

New York

Phone Fax

Adelphi University PO Box 701 ....Garden City NY 11530 516-877-3050 877-3039*
*Fax: Admissions ■ *TF:* 800-233-5744 ■ *Web:* www.adelphi.edu
Manhattan Ctr 75 Varick St 2nd Fl............... New York NY 10013 212-965-8340 431-5161
TF: 800-233-5744 ■ *Web:* www.adelphi.edu
Albany College of Pharmacy (ACPHS)
106 New Scotland Ave ....Albany NY 12208 518-694-7221 694-7322*
*Fax: Admissions ■ *TF General:* 888-203-8010 ■ *Web:* www.acphs.edu
Albert A List College of Jewish Studies
3080 Broadway.....................................New York NY 10027 212-678-8832 280-6022*
*Fax: Admissions ■ *Web:* www.jtsa.edu/list-college
Bard College PO Box 5000 .... Annandale-on-Hudson NY 12504 845-758-7472 758-5208
TF: 800-872-7423 ■ *Web:* www.bard.edu
Barnard College Columbia University
3009 Broadway.....................................New York NY 10027 212-854-2014 854-6220*
*Fax: Admissions ■ *Web:* www.barnard.edu
Baruch College 55 Lexington Ave at 24th St............New York NY 10010 646-312-1000 312-1362
TF: 800-273-8255 ■ *Web:* www.baruch.cuny.edu
Binghamton University 4400 Vestal Pkwy E ....Binghamton NY 13902 607-777-2000 777-4445*
*Fax: Admissions ■ *TF:* 800-782-0289 ■ *Web:* www.binghamton.edu
Boricua College 3755 Broadway.......................New York NY 10032 212-694-1000 694-1015*
*Fax: Admissions ■ *Web:* www.boricuacollege.edu
Brooklyn College 2900 Bedford Ave................... Brooklyn NY 11210 718-951-5000 951-4506*
*Fax: Admissions ■ *Web:* www.brooklyn.cuny.edu
Buffalo State College 1300 Elmwood Ave...............Buffalo NY 14222 716-878-4000 878-6100*
*Fax: Admissions ■ *Web:* www.buffalostate.edu
Canisius College 2001 Main St ....Buffalo NY 14208 716-888-2200 888-3230*
*Fax: Admissions ■ *TF:* 800-843-1517 ■ *Web:* www.canisius.edu
Cazenovia College 8 Sullivan St.................... Cazenovia NY 13035 315-655-7208
TF: 800-654-3210 ■ *Web:* cazenovia.edu
City College of New York
138th St & Convent Ave ....New York NY 10031 212-650-6448 650-6417*
*Fax: Admissions ■ *TF Admissions:* 800-286-9937 ■ *Web:* www.ccny.cuny.edu
Clarkson University 10 Clarkson Ave.................. Potsdam NY 13699 315-268-6480 268-7647*
*Fax: Admissions ■ *TF Admissions:* 800-527-6577 ■ *Web:* www.clarkson.edu
Colgate University 13 Oak Dr.......................Hamilton NY 13346 315-228-1000 228-7544*
*Fax: Admissions ■ *Web:* www.colgate.edu
College of Mount Saint Vincent
6301 Riverdale Ave...............................Riverdale NY 10471 718-405-3304 405-3490*
*Fax: Admissions ■ *TF:* 800-722-4867 ■ *Web:* www.mountsaintvincent.edu
College of New Rochelle 29 Castle Pl ....New Rochelle NY 10805 914-654-5000
TF: 800-933-5923 ■ *Web:* www.cnr.edu
College of Saint Rose 432 Western Ave ....Albany NY 12203 518-454-5150 454-2013*
*Fax: Admissions ■ *TF:* 800-637-8556 ■ *Web:* www.strose.edu

Phone Fax

College of Staten Island
2800 Victory Blvd.................................... Staten Island NY 10314 718-982-2000 982-2500
TF: 888-442-4551 ■ *Web:* www.csi.cuny.edu
Columbia University 2960 Broadway.................New York NY 10027 212-854-1754
Web: www.columbia.edu
Concordia College New York
171 White Plains Rd............................. Bronxville NY 10708 914-337-9300 395-4636*
*Fax: Admissions ■ *TF Admissions:* 800-937-2655 ■ *Web:* www.concordia-ny.edu
Cooper Union for the Advancement of Science & Art
30 Cooper Sq.......................................New York NY 10003 212-353-4100 353-4327*
*Fax: Admissions ■ *TF:* 800-872-2777 ■ *Web:* www.cooper.edu
Cornell University 410 Thurston Ave ....Ithaca NY 14850 607-255-5241 254-5175*
*Fax: Admissions ■ *Web:* www.cornell.edu
D'Youville College 320 Porter Ave.....................Buffalo NY 14201 716-829-7600 829-7900*
*Fax: Admissions ■ *TF:* 800-777-3921 ■ *Web:* www.dyc.edu
Daemen College 4380 Main St.......................Amherst NY 14226 716-839-8225
TF: 800-462-7652 ■ *Web:* www.daemen.edu
Dominican College 470 Western Hwy .... Orangeburg NY 10962 845-359-7800 365-3150*
*Fax: Admissions ■ *TF:* 866-432-4636 ■ *Web:* www.dc.edu
Dowling College 150 Idle Hour Blvd.................. Oakdale NY 11769 631-244-3000 244-1059*
*Fax: Admissions ■ *TF:* 800-369-5464 ■ *Web:* www.dowling.edu
Elmira Business Institute-elmira Campus
303 N Main St .... Elmira NY 14901 607-733-7177
Web: www.ebi.edu
Elmira College 1 Pk Pl .... Elmira NY 14901 607-735-1724 735-1718*
*Fax: Admissions ■ *TF Admissions:* 800-935-6472 ■ *Web:* www.elmira.edu
Eugene Lang College 65 W 11th St...................New York NY 10011 212-229-5600 229-5355*
*Fax: Admissions ■ *Web:* www.newschool.edu/lang
Excelsior College 7 Columbia Cir .... Albany NY 12203 518-464-8500 464-8833*
*Fax: Admissions ■ *TF:* 888-647-2388 ■ *Web:* www.excelsior.edu
Farmingdale State University of New York
2350 Broadhollow Rd......................... Farmingdale NY 11735 631-420-2000 420-2633
Web: www.farmingdale.edu
Five Towns College 305 N Service Rd .... Dix Hills NY 11746 631-424-7000
Web: www.ftc.edu
Fordham University 441 E Fordham Rd ....Bronx NY 10458 718-817-3240 367-9404*
*Fax: Admissions ■ *TF:* 800-367-3426 ■ *Web:* www.fordham.edu
College at Lincoln Ctr 113 W 60th St............ New York NY 10023 212-636-6710 636-7002
TF: 800-367-3426 ■ *Web:* www.fordham.edu
Westchester 400 Westchester Ave ....West Harrison NY 10604 914-332-8295 817-3921*
*Fax Area Code: 718 ■ *TF:* 800-606-6090 ■ *Web:* www.fordham.edu
Fredonia State University of New York
Fredonia 280 Central Ave...................... Fredonia NY 14063 716-673-3111
Web: www.fredonia.edu
Hamilton College 198 College Hill Rd .... Clinton NY 13323 315-859-4421 859-4457*
*Fax: Admissions ■ *TF Admissions:* 800-843-2655 ■ *Web:* www.hamilton.edu
Hartwick College 1 Hartwick Dr......................Oneonta NY 13820 607-431-4150 431-4154*
*Fax: Admissions ■ *TF:* 888-427-8942 ■ *Web:* www.hartwick.edu
Hilbert College 5200 S Pk Ave .... Hamburg NY 14075 716-649-7900 649-1152
TF: 800-649-8003 ■ *Web:* www.hilbert.edu
Hobart & William Smith Colleges
300 Pulteney St .... Geneva NY 14456 315-781-3000 781-3914*
*Fax: Admissions ■ *TF Admissions:* 800-852-2256 ■ *Web:* www.hws.edu
Hofstra University 1000 Fulton Ave .... Hempstead NY 11549 516-463-6600 463-5100*
*Fax: Admissions ■ *TF:* 800-463-7872 ■ *Web:* www.hofstra.edu/home
Houghton College 1 Willard Ave PO Box 128.......... Houghton NY 14744 585-567-9200 567-9522*
*Fax: Admissions ■ *TF:* 800-777-2556 ■ *Web:* www.houghton.edu
Hunter College 695 Pk Ave Rm 1212W................New York NY 10065 212-772-4490 650-3472
Web: www.hunter.cuny.edu
Iona College 715 N Ave.........................New Rochelle NY 10801 914-633-2502 633-2486
TF: 800-264-6350 ■ *Web:* www.iona.edu
Ithaca College 953 Danby Rd...........................Ithaca NY 14850 607-274-3124 274-1900*
*Fax: Admissions ■ *TF Admissions:* 800-429-4274 ■ *Web:* www.ithaca.edu
Jewish Theological Seminary 3080 Broadway ....New York NY 10027 212-678-8832
Web: www.jtsa.edu
Keuka College 141 Central Ave.................... Keuka Park NY 14478 315-279-5254 536-5386*
*Fax: Admissions ■ *TF Admissions:* 866-632-9992 ■ *Web:* www.keuka.edu
Laboratory Institute of Merchandising
12 E 53rd St ....New York NY 10022 212-752-1530
TF: 800-677-1323 ■ *Web:* www.limcollege.edu
Le Moyne College 1419 Salt Springs Rd .... Syracuse NY 13214 315-445-4100 445-4711*
*Fax: Admissions ■ *TF Admissions:* 800-333-4733 ■ *Web:* www.lemoyne.edu
Lehman College 250 Bedford Pk Blvd W.................Bronx NY 10468 718-960-8000 960-8712*
*Fax: Admissions ■ *TF:* 800-311-5656 ■ *Web:* www.lehman.cuny.edu
Long Island University
Brentwood 100 Second Ave...................Brentwood NY 11717 631-273-5112 273-3155
Web: www.liunet.edu
Brooklyn 1 University Plz..................... Brooklyn NY 11201 718-488-1011 797-2399*
*Fax: Admissions ■ *TF:* 800-548-7526 ■ *Web:* www.liu.edu
Manhattan College 4513 Manhattan College Pkwy ....Bronx NY 10471 718-862-8000 862-8019*
*Fax: Admissions ■ *TF:* 800-622-9235 ■ *Web:* www.manhattan.edu
Manhattan School of Music 120 Claremont Ave ....New York NY 10027 212-749-2802 749-3025*
*Fax: Admissions ■ *Web:* www.msmnyc.edu
Manhattanville College 2900 Purchase St .... Purchase NY 10577 914-323-5464 694-1732
TF: 800-328-4553 ■ *Web:* www.mville.edu
Mannes College of Music 150 W 85th St.............New York NY 10024 212-580-0210 580-1738*
*Fax: Admissions ■ *Web:* www.newschool.edu
Marist College 3399 N Rd....................... Poughkeepsie NY 12601 845-575-3000 575-3215
TF: 800-436-5483 ■ *Web:* www.marist.edu
Marymount Manhattan College 221 E 71st St ....New York NY 10021 212-517-0400 517-0448
TF: 866-667-6572 ■ *Web:* www.mmm.edu
Medaille College 18 Agassiz Cir ....Buffalo NY 14214 716-880-2200 880-2007*
*Fax: Admissions ■ *TF:* 800-292-1582 ■ *Web:* www.medaille.edu
Medgar Evers College 1650 Bedford Ave .... Brooklyn NY 11225 718-270-4900 270-6411*
*Fax: Admissions ■ *TF:* 866-277-5719 ■ *Web:* www.mec.cuny.edu
Mercy College 555 Broadway ....Dobbs Ferry NY 10522 914-693-4500 674-7382*
*Fax: Admissions ■ *TF:* 800-637-2969 ■ *Web:* www.mercy.edu
Manhattan 66 W 35th St .... New York NY 10001 212-615-3300
TF: 800-637-2969 ■ *Web:* www.mercy.edu
White Plains 277 Martine Ave Ste 201.......... White Plains NY 10601 914-948-3666
TF: 888-464-6737 ■ *Web:* www.mercy.edu
Yorktown Heights 2651 Strang Blvd ...... Yorktown Heights NY 10598 914-245-6100 962-0931*
*Fax: Admissions ■ *TF:* 877-637-2946 ■ *Web:* www.mercy.edu

Phone Fax

Metropolitan College of New York
431 Canal St. New York NY 10013 212-343-1234 625-2072*
*Fax: Admissions ■ Web: www.metropolitan.edu

Molloy College
1000 Hempstead Ave PO Box 5002 Rockville Centre NY 11571 516-678-5000
TF Admissions: 888-466-5569 ■ Web: www.molloy.edu

Morrisville State College
80 Eaton St PO Box 901 Morrisville NY 13408 315-684-6000 684-6427*
*Fax: Admissions ■ TF Admissions: 800-258-0111 ■ Web: www.morrisville.edu

Mount Saint Mary College 330 Powell Ave Newburgh NY 12550 845-569-3248 562-6762
TF: 888-937-6762 ■ Web: www.msmc.edu

Nazareth College of Rochester 4245 E Ave. Rochester NY 14618 585-389-2525 389-2817
TF: 800-860-6942 ■ Web: www.naz.edu

New School 66 W 12th St. New York NY 10011 212-229-5600
Web: www.newschool.edu

New York City College of Technology
300 Jay St. Brooklyn NY 11201 718-260-5000 260-5504*
*Fax: Admissions ■ TF: 855-492-3633 ■ Web: www.citytech.cuny.edu

New York Institute of Technology
New York Institute of Technology Northern Blvd
PO Box 8000 Old Westbury NY 11568 516-686-1000
TF: 800-345-6948 ■ Web: www.nyit.edu
Islip PO Box 9029 Central Islip NY 11722 516-686-1000
TF: 800-345-6948 ■ Web: www.nyit.edu
Manhattan 1855 Broadway. New York NY 10023 212-261-1500 261-1505*
*Fax: Admissions ■ TF: 800-345-6948 ■ Web: www.nyit.edu

New York School of Interior Design
170 E 70th St New York NY 10021 212-472-1500 472-1867*
*Fax: Admissions ■ TF: 800-336-9743 ■ Web: www.nysid.edu

New York University 22 Washington Sq N. New York NY 10011 212-998-4500 995-4902*
*Fax: Admissions ■ TF: 888-243-2358 ■ Web: www.nyu.edu

Niagara University
5795 Lewiston Rd PO Box 2011 Niagara University NY 14109 716-286-8700 286-8710*
*Fax: Admissions ■ TF: 800-462-2111 ■ Web: www.niagara.edu

Northeastern Seminary at Roberts Wesleyan College
2265 Westside Dr. Rochester NY 14624 585-594-6800
Web: www.nes.edu

Nyack College 1 S Blvd. Nyack NY 10960 845-358-1710 358-3047*
*Fax: Admissions ■ TF Admissions: 800-336-9225 ■ Web: www.nyack.edu

Pace University 1 Pace Plz New York NY 10038 212-346-1200 346-1040*
*Fax: Admissions ■ TF: 866-722-3338 ■ Web: www.pace.edu
Pleasantville/Briarcliff
861 Bedford Rd Pleasantville NY 10570 914-773-3200 773-3851*
*Fax: Admissions ■ TF: 866-722-3338 ■ Web: www.pace.edu

Parsons New School for Design 65 Fifth Ave New York NY 10011 212-229-8989 229-8975*
*Fax: Admissions ■ TF Admissions: 800-252-0852 ■ Web: www.newschool.edu

Paul Smith's College
7833 New York 30 PO Box 265 Paul Smiths NY 12970 518-327-6227
TF Admissions: 800-421-2605 ■ Web: www.paulsmiths.edu

Polytechnic University
Long Island 105 Maxess Rd. Melville NY 11747 631-755-4300 755-4404*
*Fax: Admissions ■ TF Admissions: 877-503-7659 ■ Web: engineering.nyu.edu

Pratt Institute 200 Willoughby Ave. Brooklyn NY 11205 718-636-3669 636-3670
TF: 800-331-0834 ■ Web: www.pratt.edu

Purchase College 735 Anderson Hill Rd Purchase NY 10577 914-251-6000 251-6314*
*Fax: Admissions ■ TF: 800-553-8118 ■ Web: www.purchase.edu

Queens College 65-30 Kissena Blvd. Flushing NY 11367 718-997-5000 997-5617
TF: 888-888-0606 ■ Web: www.qc.cuny.edu

Rensselaer Polytechnic Institute 110 Eigth St. Troy NY 12180 518-276-6216 276-4072*
*Fax: Admissions ■ Web: www.rpi.edu

Roberts Wesleyan College 2301 Westside Dr Rochester NY 14624 585-594-6000 594-6371*
*Fax: Admissions ■ TF Admissions: 800-777-4792 ■ Web: www.roberts.edu

Rochester Institute of Technology
1 Lomb Memorial Dr Rochester NY 14623 585-475-2411 475-7424*
*Fax: Admissions ■ Web: www.rit.edu

Russell Sage College 45 Ferry St Troy NY 12180 518-244-2217 244-6880*
*Fax: Admissions ■ TF Admissions: 888-837-9724 ■ Web: www.sage.edu

Sage College of Albany 140 New Scotland Ave Albany NY 12208 518-292-1730 292-1912*
*Fax: Admissions ■ TF Admissions: 888-837-9724 ■ Web: www.sage.edu

Saint Francis College 180 Remsen St. Brooklyn Heights NY 11201 718-522-2300

Saint John's University 8000 Utopia Pkwy Queens NY 11439 718-990-2000 990-2096*
*Fax: Admissions ■ TF: 888-978-5646 ■ Web: www.stjohns.edu
Staten Island 300 Howard Ave Staten Island NY 10301 718-390-4500 390-4298*
*Fax: Admissions ■ Web: www.stjohns.edu

Saint Joseph's College
Brooklyn 245 Clinton Ave Brooklyn NY 11205 718-940-5300 636-8303*
*Fax: Admissions ■ Web: www.sjcny.edu

Saint Joseph's College NY
Suffolk 155 W Roe Blvd Patchogue NY 11772 631-687-5100
Web: www.sjcny.edu

Saint Lawrence University 23 Romoda Dr Canton NY 13617 315-229-5261 229-5818*
*Fax: Admissions ■ TF Admissions: 800-285-1856 ■ Web: www.stlawu.edu

Saint Thomas Aquinas College 125 Rt 340 Sparkill NY 10976 845-398-4000 398-4114
Web: www.stac.edu

Sarah Lawrence College 1 Meadway Bronxville NY 10708 800-888-2858 395-2515*
*Fax Area Code: 914 ■ *Fax: Admissions ■ TF: 800-888-2858 ■ Web: www.sarahlawrence.edu

Siena College 515 Loudon Rd. Loudonville NY 12211 518-783-2300 783-2436*
*Fax: Admissions ■ TF Admissions: 888-287-4362 ■ Web: www.siena.edu

Skidmore College 815 N Broadway Saratoga Springs NY 12866 518-580-5000 580-5584*
*Fax: Admissions ■ TF: 800-867-6007 ■ Web: www.skidmore.edu

State University of New York
Brockport 350 New Campus Dr Brockport NY 14420 585-395-2751 395-5452
TF: 888-800-0029 ■ Web: www.brockport.edu
College at Old Westbury, The
PO Box 210 Old Westbury NY 11568 516-876-3073 876-3307*
*Fax: Admissions ■ Web: www.oldwestbury.edu
College at Oneonta Ravine Pkwy Oneonta NY 13820 607-436-3500 436-3074*
*Fax: Admissions ■ Web: www.oneonta.edu
College of Agriculture & Technology at Cobleskill
Rt 7 Cobleskill NY 12043 518-255-5525 255-6769*
*Fax: Admissions ■ TF: 800-295-8988 ■ Web: www.cobleskill.edu
College of Environmental Science & Forestry
1 Forestry Dr Syracuse NY 13210 315-470-6500 470-6933*
*Fax: Admissions ■ TF Admissions: 800-777-7373 ■ Web: www.esf.edu
Cortland PO Box 2000 Cortland NY 13045 607-753-2011 753-5998*
*Fax: Admissions ■ Web: www.cortland.edu
Empire State College 1 Union Ave Saratoga Springs NY 12866 518-587-2100 587-9759*
*Fax: Admissions ■ TF: 800-847-3000 ■ Web: www.esc.edu
Geneseo 1 College Cir Geneseo NY 14454 585-245-5571 245-5550*
*Fax: Admitting ■ TF Admitting: 866-245-5211 ■ Web: www.geneseo.edu
Institute of Technology PO Box 3050. Utica NY 13504 315-792-7500 792-7837*
*Fax: Admissions ■ TF: 866-278-6948 ■ Web: sunypoly.edu
Maritime College 6 Pennyfield Ave Fort Schuyler Bronx NY 10465 718-409-7200 409-7465
TF: 888-800-0029 ■ Web: www.sunymaritime.edu
New Paltz 1 Hawk Dr New Paltz NY 12561 845-257-3212 257-3209*
*Fax: Admissions ■ TF: 877-696-7411 ■ Web: www.newpaltz.edu
Oswego 7060 SR 104 Oswego NY 13126 315-312-2500 312-3260*
*Fax: Admissions ■ Web: www.oswego.edu
Plattsburgh 101 Broad St. Plattsburgh NY 12901 518-564-2040 564-2045*
*Fax: Admissions ■ TF Admissions: 888-673-0012 ■ Web: www.plattsburgh.edu
Potsdam 44 Pierrpont Ave Potsdam NY 13676 315-267-2180 267-2163*
*Fax: Admissions ■ TF Admissions: 877-768-7326 ■ Web: www.potsdam.edu
University at Buffalo 12 Capen Hall Buffalo NY 14260 716-645-2450 645-6411*
*Fax: Admissions ■ TF: 888-822-3648 ■ Web: www.buffalo.edu

Stern College for Women of Yeshiva University
245 Lexington Ave New York NY 10016 212-340-7701 340-7788*
*Fax: Admissions ■ Web: www.yu.edu/stern

Stony Brook University 100 Nicolls Rd Stony Brook NY 11794 631-689-6000 632-9898
Web: www.stonybrook.edu

Syracuse University 900 S Crouse Ave Syracuse NY 13244 315-443-3611 443-4226*
*Fax: Admissions ■ TF: 800-782-5867 ■ Web: www.syr.edu

Touro College 27-33 W 23rd St. New York NY 10010 212-463-0400 627-9144
TF: 888-247-1387 ■ Web: www.touro.edu
Lander College for Men
75-31 150th St. Kew Gardens Hills NY 11367 718-820-4884 820-4838
Web: www.touro.edu

Tri-State College of Acupuncture
80 Eigth Ave Ste 400 New York NY 10011 212-242-2255
Web: www.tsca.edu

University at Albany 1400 Washington Ave. Albany NY 12222 518-442-3300 442-5383*
*Fax: Admissions ■ TF: 800-293-7869 ■ Web: www.albany.edu

University of Rochester
Wallace Hall PO Box 270251 Rochester NY 14627 585-275-2121 461-4595*
*Fax: Admissions ■ TF Admissions: 888-822-2256 ■ Web: www.rochester.edu

University of Saint Francis
180 Remsen St. Brooklyn Heights NY 11201 718-522-2300
TF: 800-356-8329 ■ Web: www.sfc.edu

US Merchant Marine Academy
300 Steamboat Rd Kings Point NY 11024 516-726-5800 773-5390*
*Fax: Admissions ■ TF: 866-546-4778 ■ Web: www.usmma.edu

US Military Academy
Admissions Bldg 606 3rd Fl. West Point NY 10996 845-938-4041 938-8121
Web: www.usma.edu

Utica College 1600 Burrstone Rd Utica NY 13502 315-792-3111 792-3003*
*Fax: Admissions ■ TF Admissions: 800-782-8884 ■ Web: www.utica.edu

Vassar College 124 Raymond Ave Poughkeepsie NY 12604 845-437-7000 437-7063
TF: 800-827-7270 ■ Web: www.vassar.edu

Vaughn College of Aeronautics & Technology
86-01 23rd Ave. East Elmhurst NY 11369 718-429-6600
TF: 866-682-8446 ■ Web: vaughn.edu

Wagner College 1 Campus Rd Staten Island NY 10301 718-390-3400 390-3105
TF Admissions: 800-221-1010 ■ Web: www.wagner.edu

Webb Institute 298 Crescent Beach Rd. Glen Cove NY 11542 516-671-2213 674-9838*
*Fax: Admissions ■ TF: 866-708-9322 ■ Web: webb.edu

Wells College 170 Main St Aurora NY 13026 315-364-3266 364-3227*
*Fax: Admissions ■ TF Admissions: 800-952-9355 ■ Web: www.wells.edu

Yeshiva University 500 W 185th St New York NY 10033 212-960-5400 960-0086*
*Fax: Admissions ■ Web: www.yu.edu

York College 94-20 Guy R Brewer Blvd. Jamaica NY 11451 718-262-2000 262-2601*
*Fax: Admissions ■ Web: www.york.cuny.edu

North Carolina

Phone Fax

Barton College PO Box 5000 Wilson NC 27893 252-399-6300 399-6572
TF: 800-345-4973 ■ Web: www.barton.edu

Belmont Abbey College
100 Belmont-Mt Holly Rd. Belmont NC 28012 704-461-6748
TF: 888-222-0110 ■ Web: www.belmontabbeycollege.edu

Bennett College 900 E Washington St Greensboro NC 27401 336-370-8624 517-2166*
*Fax: Admissions ■ TF Admissions: 800-413-5323 ■ Web: www.bennett.edu

Brevard College 1 Brevard College Dr Brevard NC 28712 828-883-8292 884-3790*
*Fax: Admissions ■ TF Admissions: 800-527-9090 ■ Web: www.brevard.edu

Campbell University
450 Leslie Campbell Ave PO Box 546 Buies Creek NC 27506 910-893-1290 893-1288*
*Fax: Admissions ■ TF: 800-334-4111 ■ Web: www.campbell.edu

Catawba College 2300 W Innes St Salisbury NC 28144 704-637-4111 637-4222*
*Fax: Admissions ■ TF: 800-228-2922 ■ Web: www.catawba.edu

Chowan University 1 University Pl Murfreesboro NC 27855 252-398-6439
TF Admissions: 888-424-6926 ■ Web: www.chowan.edu

Davidson College PO Box 7156 Davidson NC 28035 704-894-2000 894-2016*
*Fax: Admissions ■ TF: 800-768-0380 ■ Web: www.davidson.edu

Duke University 2138 Campus Dr PO Box 90586 Durham NC 27708 919-684-3214 681-8941*
*Fax: Admissions ■ Web: www.duke.edu

East Carolina University E Fifth St Greenville NC 27858 252-328-6131 328-6640
Web: www.ecu.edu

Elizabeth City State University
1704 Weeksville Rd Elizabeth City NC 27909 252-335-3400 335-3537*
*Fax: Admissions ■ TF Admissions: 800-347-3278 ■ Web: www.ecsu.edu

Elon University 100 Campus Dr Elon NC 27244 336-278-2000 278-7699
TF: 800-334-8448 ■ Web: www.elon.edu

Fayetteville State University
1200 Murchison Rd Fayetteville NC 28301 910-672-1371 672-1414*
*Fax: Admissions ■ TF Admissions: 800-222-2594 ■ Web: www.uncfsu.edu

Gardner-Webb University PO Box 817 Boiling Springs NC 28017 704-406-4498 406-4488*
*Fax: Admissions ■ TF: 800-253-6472 ■ Web: www.gardner-webb.edu

Name / Address	City	State	ZIP	Phone	Fax
Greensboro College 815 W Market St	Greensboro	NC	27401	336-272-7102	378-0154*
*Fax: Admissions ■ TF: 800-346-8226 ■ Web: greensboro.edu					
Guilford College 5800 W Friendly Ave	Greensboro	NC	27410	336-316-2000	316-2954*
*Fax: Admissions ■ TF Admissions: 800-992-7759 ■ Web: www.guilford.edu					
Heritage Bible College 1747 Bud Hawkins Rd PO Box 1628	Dunn	NC	28334	910-892-3178	892-1809
TF: 800-297-6351 ■ Web: www.heritagebiblecollege.edu					
High Point University 833 Montlieu Ave	High Point	NC	27262	336-841-9216	888-6382*
*Fax: Admissions ■ TF: 800-345-6993 ■ Web: www.highpoint.edu					
Johnson & Wales University Charlotte 801 W Trade St	Charlotte	NC	28202	980-598-1100	598-1111*
*Fax: Admissions ■ TF: 866-598-2427 ■ Web: www.jwu.edu					
Johnson C Smith University 100 Beatties Ford Rd	Charlotte	NC	28216	704-378-1000	378-1242*
*Fax: Admissions ■ TF Admissions: 800-782-7303 ■ Web: www.jcsu.edu					
King's College Library 322 Lamar Ave	Charlotte	NC	28204	704-372-0266	
TF: 800-768-2255 ■ Web: www.kingscollegecharlotte.edu					
Lees-McRae College 191 Main St W	Banner Elk	NC	28604	828-898-5241	
TF: 800-280-4562 ■ Web: www.lmc.edu					
Lenoir-Rhyne University 625 Seventh Ave NE	Hickory	NC	28601	828-328-7300	328-7378
TF: 800-277-5721 ■ Web: www.lr.edu					
Livingstone College 701 W Monroe St	Salisbury	NC	28144	704-216-6963	216-6215
TF: 800-835-3435 ■ Web: www.livingstone.edu					
Mars Hill College 100 Athletics St	Mars Hill	NC	28754	828-689-1219	
Web: marshilllions.com					
Meredith College 3800 Hillsborough St	Raleigh	NC	27607	919-760-8581	760-2348*
*Fax: Admissions ■ TF All: 800-637-3348 ■ Web: www.meredith.edu					
Methodist University 5400 Ramsey St	Fayetteville	NC	28311	910-630-7000	630-7285*
*Fax: Admissions ■ TF: 800-488-7110 ■ Web: www.methodist.edu					
Montreat College 310 Gaither Cir PO Box 1267	Montreat	NC	28757	828-669-8011	669-0120
TF: 800-622-6968 ■ Web: www.montreat.edu					
Mount Olive College 634 Henderson St	Mount Olive	NC	28365	919-658-2502	658-9816*
*Fax: Admissions ■ TF: 800-653-0854 ■ Web: umo.edu					
North Carolina A & T State University 1601 E Market St	Greensboro	NC	27411	336-334-7946	334-7478*
*Fax: Admissions ■ TF Admissions: 800-443-8964 ■ Web: www.ncat.edu					
North Carolina Central University 1801 Fayetteville St	Durham	NC	27707	919-530-6100	530-7625*
*Fax: Admissions ■ TF Admissions: 877-667-7533 ■ Web: www.nccu.edu					
North Carolina State University 2200 Hillsborough St	Raleigh	NC	27695	919-515-2011	515-5039*
*Fax: Admissions ■ TF: 800-662-7301 ■ Web: www.ncsu.edu					
North Carolina Wesleyan College 3400 N Wesleyan Blvd	Rocky Mount	NC	27804	252-985-5100	985-5295*
*Fax: Admissions ■ TF Admissions: 800-488-6292 ■ Web: www.ncwc.edu					
Pfeiffer University 48380 Hwy 52 N	Misenheimer	NC	28109	704-463-1360	463-1363*
*Fax: Admissions ■ TF: 800-338-2060 ■ Web: www.pfeiffer.edu					
Piedmont Baptist College 420 S Broad St	Winston-Salem	NC	27101	336-725-8344	725-5522*
*Fax: Admissions ■ TF Admissions: 800-937-5097 ■ Web: www.piedmontu.edu					
Queens University of Charlotte 1900 Selwyn Ave	Charlotte	NC	28274	704-337-2212	337-2403*
*Fax: Admissions ■ TF: 800-849-0202 ■ Web: www.queens.edu					
Saint Andrews Presbyterian College 1700 Dogwood Mile	Laurinburg	NC	28352	910-277-5555	277-5020*
*Fax: Admissions ■ TF: 800-763-0198 ■ Web: www.sa.edu					
Saint Augustine's College 1315 Oakwood Ave	Raleigh	NC	27610	919-516-4016	516-5805*
*Fax: Admissions ■ TF Admissions: 800-948-1126 ■ Web: www.st-aug.edu					
Salem College 601 S Church St	Winston-Salem	NC	27101	336-721-2600	917-5572*
*Fax: Admissions ■ TF Admissions: 800-327-2536 ■ Web: www.salem.edu					
Shaw University 118 E S St	Raleigh	NC	27601	919-546-8275	546-8271*
*Fax: Admissions ■ TF Admissions: 800-214-6683 ■ Web: www.shawu.edu					
University of North Carolina 910 Raleigh Rd PO Box 2688	Chapel Hill	NC	27515	919-962-1000	962-6725
Web: www.northcarolina.edu					
Asheville 1 University Heights CPO 1320	Asheville	NC	28804	828-251-6481	251-6482*
*Fax: Admissions ■ TF: 800-531-9842 ■ Web: www.unca.edu					
Chapel Hill Jackson Hall CB 2200	Chapel Hill	NC	27599	919-966-3621	962-3045*
*Fax: Admissions ■ Web: www.unc.edu					
Charlotte 9201 University City Blvd	Charlotte	NC	28223	704-687-2000	687-6483
Web: www.uncc.edu					
Greensboro 1400 Spring Garden St	Greensboro	NC	27412	336-334-5000	334-4180
TF: 877-862-4123 ■ Web: www.uncg.edu					
Pembroke PO Box 1510	Pembroke	NC	28372	910-521-6000	521-6497*
*Fax: Admissions ■ TF: 800-949-8627 ■ Web: www.uncp.edu					
Wilmington 601 S College Rd	Wilmington	NC	28403	910-962-3000	962-3038*
*Fax: Admissions ■ TF: 800-596-2880 ■ Web: uncw.edu					
Wake Forest University 1834 Wake Forest Rd	Winston-Salem	NC	27106	336-758-5255	758-4324*
*Fax: Admissions ■ Web: www.wfu.edu					
Warren Wilson College 701 Warren Wilson Rd	Swannanoa	NC	28778	828-298-3325	298-1440*
*Fax: Admissions ■ TF Admissions: 800-934-3536 ■ Web: www.warren-wilson.edu					
Western Carolina University (WCU) 1 University Dr	Cullowhee	NC	28723	828-227-7211	227-7319
TF: 877-928-4968 ■ Web: www.wcu.edu					
William Peace University 15 E Peace St	Raleigh	NC	27604	919-508-2000	508-2326*
*Fax: Admissions ■ TF: 800-732-2347 ■ Web: www.peace.edu					
Wingate University 220 N Camden Rd	Wingate	NC	28174	704-233-8000	233-8110
TF: 800-755-5550 ■ Web: www.wingate.edu					
Winston-Salem State University 601 S ML King Jr Dr 206 Thompson Ctr	Winston-Salem	NC	27110	336-750-2000	750-2079*
*Fax: Admissions ■ TF Admissions: 800-257-4052 ■ Web: www.wssu.edu					

North Dakota

Name / Address	City	State	ZIP	Phone	Fax
Dickinson State University 291 Campus Dr	Dickinson	ND	58601	701-483-2507	483-9959*
*Fax: Admissions ■ TF: 800-279-4295 ■ Web: www.dickinsonstate.edu					
Jamestown College 6000 College Ln	Jamestown	ND	58405	701-252-3467	253-4318
TF: 800-336-2554 ■ Web: www.uj.edu					
Mayville State University 330 Third St NE	Mayville	ND	58257	800-437-4104	788-4748*
*Fax Area Code: 701 ■ *Fax: Admissions ■ TF: 800-437-4104 ■ Web: leightoninteractive.com					
Minot State University 500 University Ave W	Minot	ND	58707	701-858-3000	858-3888
TF: 800-777-0750 ■ Web: www.minotstateu.edu					
North Dakota State University 1301 12th Ave N	Fargo	ND	58105	701-231-8643	231-8802*
*Fax: Admissions ■ TF: 800-488-6378 ■ Web: www.ndsu.edu					
University of Mary 7500 University Dr	Bismarck	ND	58504	701-255-7500	255-7687*
*Fax: Admissions ■ TF Admissions: 800-288-6279 ■ Web: www.umary.edu					
University of North Dakota PO Box 8357	Grand Forks	ND	58202	701-777-3000	
TF: 800-225-5863 ■ Web: und.edu					
Valley City State University 101 College St SW	Valley City	ND	58072	701-845-7990	845-7299
TF: 800-532-8641 ■ Web: www.vcsu.edu					

Ohio

Name / Address	City	State	ZIP	Phone	Fax
Ashland University 401 College Ave	Ashland	OH	44805	419-289-4142	289-5999
TF: 800-882-1548 ■ Web: www.ashland.edu					
Baldwin-Wallace College 275 Eastland Rd	Berea	OH	44017	440-826-2222	826-3830*
*Fax: Admissions ■ TF: 877-292-7759 ■ Web: www.bw.edu					
Bluffton University 1 University Dr	Bluffton	OH	45817	419-358-3000	358-3081*
*Fax: Admissions ■ TF: 800-488-3257 ■ Web: www.bluffton.edu					
Bowling Green State University 1001 E Wooster St	Bowling Green	OH	43403	419-372-2531	372-6955
TF: 866-246-6732 ■ Web: www.bgsu.edu					
Capital University College & Main St	Columbus	OH	43209	614-236-6101	236-6926*
*Fax: Admissions ■ TF: 866-544-6175 ■ Web: www.capital.edu					
Case Western Reserve University 2061 Cornell Rd	Cleveland	OH	44106	216-368-2000	368-5111
TF: 800-967-8898 ■ Web: www.case.edu					
Cedarville University 251 N Main St	Cedarville	OH	45314	937-766-7700	766-7575*
*Fax: Admissions ■ TF: 800-233-2784 ■ Web: www.cedarville.edu					
Central State University 1400 Brush Row Rd PO Box 1004	Wilberforce	OH	45384	937-376-6011	376-6648*
*Fax: Admissions ■ TF: 800-388-2781 ■ Web: www.centralstate.edu					
Cleveland Institute of Music 11021 E Blvd	Cleveland	OH	44106	216-791-5000	791-3063
Web: www.cim.edu					
Cleveland State University 2121 Euclid Ave	Cleveland	OH	44115	216-687-2000	687-9210*
*Fax: Admissions ■ TF: 888-278-6446 ■ Web: www.csuohio.edu					
College of Mount Saint Joseph 5701 Delhi Rd	Cincinnati	OH	45233	513-244-4200	244-4601
TF: 800-654-9314 ■ Web: www.msj.edu					
College of Wooster 1189 Beall Ave	Wooster	OH	44691	330-263-2000	263-2621
TF: 800-877-9905 ■ Web: www.wooster.edu					
Defiance College 701 N Clinton St	Defiance	OH	43512	419-784-4010	783-2468*
*Fax: Admissions ■ TF: 800-520-4632 ■ Web: www.defiance.edu					
Denison University 100 W College St	Granville	OH	43023	740-587-6394	587-8321*
*Fax: Admissions ■ TF: 800-336-4766 ■ Web: www.denison.edu					
Franklin University 201 S Grant Ave	Columbus	OH	43215	614-797-4700	
TF: 877-341-6300 ■ Web: www.franklin.edu					
Hebrew Union College Cincinnati 3101 Clifton Ave	Cincinnati	OH	45220	513-221-1875	221-0321*
*Fax: Admissions ■ Web: www.huc.edu					
Heidelberg University 310 E Market St	Tiffin	OH	44883	419-448-2000	448-2334
TF: 800-434-3352 ■ Web: www.heidelberg.edu					
Hiram College PO Box 67	Hiram	OH	44234	330-569-5169	569-5944*
*Fax: Admissions ■ TF Admissions: 800-362-5280 ■ Web: www.hiram.edu					
Hondros College 4140 Executive Pkwy	Westerville	OH	43081	888-466-3767	
TF: 888-466-3767 ■ Web: www.hondros.edu					
John Carroll University 20700 N Pk Blvd	Cleveland	OH	44118	216-397-1886	397-4981*
*Fax: Admissions ■ TF: 888-335-6800 ■ Web: www.jcu.edu					
Kent State University 800 E. Summit St PO Box 5190	Kent	OH	44242	330-672-2121	672-2499*
*Fax: Admissions ■ TF: 800-988-5368 ■ Web: www.kent.edu					
Ashtabula 3300 Lake Rd W	Ashtabula	OH	44004	440-964-3322	964-4269*
*Fax: Admissions ■ TF: 800-988-5368 ■ Web: www.kent.edu/ashtabula					
East Liverpool 400 E Fourth St	East Liverpool	OH	43920	330-385-3805	
Web: www.kent.edu					
Salem 2491 SR-45 S	Salem	OH	44460	330-332-0361	337-4122*
*Fax: Admissions ■ Web: www.kent.edu/columbiana					
Stark 6000 Frank Ave NW	North Canton	OH	44720	330-499-9600	499-0301*
*Fax: Admissions ■ TF: 800-988-5368 ■ Web: www.kent.edu/stark					
Trumbull Campus 4314 Mahoning Ave NW	Warren	OH	44483	330-847-0571	675-8888*
*Fax: Admissions ■ TF: 800-988-5368 ■ Web: www.kent.edu/trumbull					
Tuscarawas 330 University Dr NE	New Philadelphia	OH	44663	330-339-3391	339-3321*
*Fax: Admissions ■ TF: 800-988-5368 ■ Web: www.kent.edu/tusc					
Kenyon College 103 College Dr	Gambier	OH	43022	740-427-5000	427-5770
TF: 800-848-2468 ■ Web: www.kenyon.edu					
Lake Erie College 391 W Washington St	Painesville	OH	44077	440-375-7050	375-7005*
*Fax: Admissions ■ TF: 800-533-4996 ■ Web: www.lec.edu					
Lourdes College 6832 Convent Blvd	Sylvania	OH	43560	419-885-5291	882-3987*
*Fax: Admissions ■ TF: 800-878-3210 ■ Web: www.lourdes.edu					
Malone College 515 25th St NW	Canton	OH	44709	330-471-8100	471-8149*
*Fax: Admissions ■ TF: 800-521-1146 ■ Web: www.malone.edu					
Marietta College 215 Fifth St	Marietta	OH	45750	740-376-4000	376-8888*
*Fax: Admissions ■ TF Admissions: 800-331-7896 ■ Web: www.marietta.edu					
Miami University 501 E High St	Oxford	OH	45056	513-529-1809	529-1550*
*Fax: Admissions ■ TF: 866-426-4643 ■ Web: miamioh.edu					
Middletown 4200 E University Blvd	Middletown	OH	45042	513-727-3200	727-3223
TF: 877-898-4656 ■ Web: www.mid.muohio.edu					
Mount Union College 1972 Clark Ave	Alliance	OH	44601	330-823-2590	823-5097*
*Fax: Admissions ■ TF Admissions: 800-334-6682 ■ Web: mountunion.edu					
Mount Vernon Nazarene University 800 Martinsburg Rd	Mount Vernon	OH	43050	740-392-6868	
TF Admissions: 800-766-8206 ■ Web: www.mvnu.edu					
Muskingum College 163 Stormont St	New Concord	OH	43762	740-826-8211	826-8100*
*Fax: Admissions ■ TF Admissions: 800-752-6082 ■ Web: www.muskingum.edu					
Notre Dame College of Ohio 4545 College Rd	South Euclid	OH	44121	216-381-1680	
Web: www.ndc.edu					
Oberlin College 101 N Professor St	Oberlin	OH	44074	440-775-8121	775-6905
Web: home.oberlin.edu					

Institution	City	State	Zip	Phone	Fax
Ohio Business College 5202 Timber Commons Dr; *Web:* www.ohiobusinesscollege.edu	Sandusky	OH	44870	419-627-8345	
Ohio Dominican University 1216 Sunbury Rd; ***Fax:* Admissions ■ *TF:* 800-955-6446 ■ *Web:* www.ohiodominican.edu	Columbus	OH	43219	614-251-4500	251-0156*
Ohio Northern University 525 S Main St; **Fax:* Admissions ■ *TF Admissions:* 888-408-4668 ■ *Web:* www.onu.edu	Ada	OH	45810	419-772-2000	772-2313*
Ohio State University 154 W 12th Ave; **Fax:* Admissions ■ *TF:* 800-426-5046 ■ *Web:* www.osu.edu	Columbus	OH	43210	614-292-3980	292-4818*
Lima 4240 Campus Dr; *TF:* 800-228-1102 ■ *Web:* www.lima.osu.edu	Lima	OH	45804	419-995-8391	995-8483
Mansfield 1760 University Dr; *Web:* mansfield.osu.edu	Mansfield	OH	44906	419-755-4011	
Newark 1179 University Dr; **Fax:* Admissions ■ *TF:* 800-963-9275 ■ *Web:* newark.osu.edu	Newark	OH	43055	740-366-3321	364-9645*
Ohio University 120 Chubb Hall; **Fax:* Admissions ■ *TF:* 800-858-6843 ■ *Web:* www.ohio.edu	Athens	OH	45710	740-593-1000	593-0560*
Chillicothe 101 University Dr; *TF:* 877-462-6824 ■ *Web:* chillicothe.ohiou.edu	Chillicothe	OH	45601	740-774-7200	
Eastern 45425 National Rd; **Fax:* Admissions ■ *TF:* 800-648-3331 ■ *Web:* www.ohio.edu	Saint Clairsville	OH	43950	740-695-1720	695-7079*
Lancaster 1570 Granville Pike; **Fax:* Admissions ■ *TF:* 800-444-2910 ■ *Web:* www.ohio.edu	Lancaster	OH	43130	740-654-6711	687-9497*
Southern 1804 Liberty Ave; **Fax:* Admissions ■ *TF:* 800-626-0513 ■ *Web:* ohio.edu/southern	Ironton	OH	45638	740-533-4600	533-4632*
Zanesville 1425 Newark Rd; *Web:* www.ohio.edu	Zanesville	OH	43701	740-453-0762	453-6161
Ohio Wesleyan University 61 S Sandusky St Slocum Hall; **Fax:* Admissions ■ *TF:* 800-922-8953 ■ *Web:* www.owu.edu	Delaware	OH	43015	740-368-2000	368-3314*
Otterbein College 1 S Grove St; **Fax:* Admissions ■ *TF Admissions:* 800-488-8144 ■ *Web:* www.otterbein.edu	Westerville	OH	43081	614-823-1500	823-1200*
Shawnee State University 940 Second St; *TF:* 800-959-2778 ■ *Web:* www.shawnee.edu	Portsmouth	OH	45662	740-351-3221	351-3111
Tiffin University 155 Miami St; *TF:* 800-968-6446 ■ *Web:* www.tiffin.edu	Tiffin	OH	44883	419-447-6442	443-5006
Union Institute & University 440 E McMillan St; **Fax:* Admissions ■ *TF:* 800-486-3116 ■ *Web:* myunion.edu	Cincinnati	OH	45206	513-861-6400	861-0779*
University of Akron 277 E Buchtel Ave; *TF Admissions:* 800-655-4884 ■ *Web:* www.uakron.edu	Akron	OH	44325	330-972-7100	972-7022
University of Cincinnati 2600 Clifton Ave PO Box 210091; **Fax:* Admissions ■ *TF:* 866-397-3382 ■ *Web:* www.uc.edu	Cincinnati	OH	45221	513-556-1100	556-1105*
University of Dayton 300 College Pk; **Fax:* Admissions ■ *TF:* 800-837-7433 ■ *Web:* www.udayton.edu	Dayton	OH	45469	937-229-4411	229-4729*
University of Findlay 1000 N Main St; *TF:* 800-472-9502 ■ *Web:* www.findlay.edu	Findlay	OH	45840	419-422-8313	434-4822
University of Rio Grande 218 N College Ave; **Fax:* Admissions ■ *TF:* 800-282-7201 ■ *Web:* www.rio.edu	Rio Grande	OH	45674	740-245-5353	245-7260*
University of Toledo 2801 W Bancroft St; **Fax:* Admissions ■ *TF:* 800-586-5336 ■ *Web:* www.utoledo.edu	Toledo	OH	43606	419-530-4636	530-5745*
Ursuline College 2550 Lander Rd; **Fax:* Admissions ■ *TF:* 888-778-5463 ■ *Web:* www.ursuline.edu	Pepper Pike	OH	44124	440-449-4200	684-6138*
Walsh University 2020 E Maple St; **Fax:* Admissions ■ *TF Admissions:* 800-362-9846 ■ *Web:* www.walsh.edu	North Canton	OH	44720	330-499-7090	490-7165*
Wilberforce University 1055 N Bickett Rd PO Box 1001; **Fax:* Admissions ■ *TF Admissions:* 800-367-8568 ■ *Web:* www.wilberforce.edu	Wilberforce	OH	45384	937-376-2911	376-4751*
Wilmington College of Ohio 1870 Quaker Way; *TF:* 800-341-9318 ■ *Web:* www.wilmington.edu	Wilmington	OH	45177	937-382-6661	
Wittenberg University 200 W Ward St PO Box 720; **Fax:* Admissions ■ *TF:* 800-677-7558 ■ *Web:* www.wittenberg.edu	Springfield	OH	45501	937-327-6314	327-6379*
Wright State University 3640 Colonel Glenn Hwy; **Fax:* Admissions ■ *TF Admissions:* 800-247-1770 ■ *Web:* www.wright.edu	Dayton	OH	45435	937-775-5740	775-5795*
Xavier University 3800 Victory Pkwy; **Fax:* Admissions ■ *TF:* 800-344-4698 ■ *Web:* www.xavier.edu	Cincinnati	OH	45207	513-745-3000	745-4319*
Youngstown State University 1 University Plz; *TF Admissions:* 877-468-6978 ■ *Web:* www.ysu.edu	Youngstown	OH	44555	330-941-3000	

Oklahoma

Institution	City	State	Zip	Phone	Fax
Bacone College 2299 Old Bacone Rd; **Fax:* Admissions ■ *TF Admissions:* 888-682-5514 ■ *Web:* www.bacone.edu	Muskogee	OK	74403	918-683-4581	781-7416*
Cameron University 2800 W Gore Blvd; **Fax:* Admissions ■ *TF Admissions:* 888-454-7600 ■ *Web:* www.cameron.edu	Lawton	OK	73505	580-581-2289	581-5514*
East Central University 1100 E 14th St; *Web:* www.ecok.edu	Ada	OK	74820	580-332-8000	
Hillsdale Free Will Baptist College PO Box 7208; **Fax:* Admissions ■ *TF:* 800-460-6328 ■ *Web:* www.hc.edu	Moore	OK	73153	405-912-9000	912-9050*
Langston University 2013 Langston University PO Box 1500; **Fax Area Code:* 405 ■ *TF:* 877-466-2231 ■ *Web:* www.lunet.edu	Langston	OK	73050	877-466-2231	466-3271*
Mid-America Christian University 3500 SW 119th St; **Fax:* Admissions ■ *TF:* 888-888-2341 ■ *Web:* www.macu.edu	Oklahoma City	OK	73170	405-691-3800	692-3165*
Northeastern State University *Broken Arrow* 3100 E New Orleans; **Fax:* Admissions ■ *Web:* www.nsuba.edu	Broken Arrow	OK	74014	918-449-6000	449-6190*
Muskogee 2400 W Shawnee; *TF:* 800-722-9614 ■ *Web:* www.nsuok.edu	Muskogee	OK	74401	918-683-0040	458-2106
Tahlequah 600 N Grand Ave; *TF:* 800-722-9614 ■ *Web:* www.nsuok.edu	Tahlequah	OK	74464	918-456-5511	458-2342
Northwestern Oklahoma State University 709 Oklahoma Blvd; *Web:* nwosu.edu	Alva	OK	73717	580-327-1700	327-8699
Oklahoma Baptist University 500 W University St; *TF:* 800-654-3285 ■ *Web:* www.okbu.edu	Shawnee	OK	74804	405-275-2850	
Oklahoma Christian University PO Box 11000; **Fax:* Admissions ■ *TF:* 800-877-5010 ■ *Web:* www.oc.edu	Oklahoma City	OK	73136	405-425-5000	425-5069*
Oklahoma City University 2501 N Blackwelder Ave; **Fax:* Admissions ■ *TF Admissions:* 800-633-7242 ■ *Web:* www.okcu.edu	Oklahoma City	OK	73106	405-208-5050	208-5916*
Oklahoma Panhandle State University 323 Eagle Blvd; **Fax:* Admitting ■ *TF:* 800-664-6778 ■ *Web:* www.opsu.edu	Goodwell	OK	73939	580-349-2611	349-2302*
Oklahoma State University 219 Student Union Bldg; *TF:* 800-852-1255 ■ *Web:* www.okstate.edu	Stillwater	OK	74078	405-744-5000	744-7092
Tulsa 700 N Greenwood Ave; *TF:* 800-522-4002 ■ *Web:* www.osu-tulsa.okstate.edu	Tulsa	OK	74106	918-594-8000	594-8202
Oral Roberts University 7777 S Lewis Ave; **Fax:* Admissions ■ *TF:* 800-678-8876 ■ *Web:* www.oru.edu	Tulsa	OK	74171	918-495-6161	495-6222*
Rogers State University 1701 W Will Rogers Blvd; **Fax:* Admissions ■ *TF:* 800-256-7511 ■ *Web:* www.rsu.edu	Claremore	OK	74017	918-343-7546	343-7595*
Saint Gregory's University 1900 W MacArthur St; *TF Admissions:* 888-784-7347 ■ *Web:* www.stgregorys.edu	Shawnee	OK	74804	405-878-5100	878-5198
Southeastern Oklahoma State University 1405 N Fourth St; **Fax:* Admissions ■ *TF:* 800-435-1327 ■ *Web:* www.se.edu	Durant	OK	74701	580-745-2000	745-7502*
Southern Nazarene University 6729 NW 39th Expy; **Fax:* Admissions ■ *TF:* 800-648-9899 ■ *Web:* www.snu.edu	Bethany	OK	73008	405-789-6400	491-6320*
Southwestern Christian University 7210 NW 39th Expy PO Box 340; **Fax:* Admissions ■ *Web:* swcu.publishpath.com	Bethany	OK	73008	405-789-7661	495-0078*
Southwestern College 100 Campus Dr; *Web:* www.swosu.edu	Weatherford	OK	73096	580-772-6611	774-3795
University of Central Oklahoma 100 N University Dr; *Web:* www.uco.edu	Edmond	OK	73034	405-974-2000	
University of Oklahoma 1000 Asp Ave; *TF:* 800-234-6868 ■ *Web:* www.ou.edu	Norman	OK	73019	405-325-0311	325-7124
University of Oklahoma Health Sciences Center 1100 N Lindsay; *Web:* www.ouhsc.edu	Oklahoma City	OK	73104	405-271-4000	
University of Sciences & Arts of Oklahoma 1727 W Alabama Ave; **Fax:* Admissions ■ *TF:* 800-933-8726 ■ *Web:* www.usao.edu	Chickasha	OK	73018	405-224-3140	574-1220*
University of Tulsa 800 S Tucker Rd; **Fax:* Admissions ■ *TF:* 800-331-3050 ■ *Web:* www.utulsa.edu	Tulsa	OK	74104	918-631-2307	631-5003*

Ontario

Institution	City	State	Zip	Phone	Fax
Foundation for Montessori Education 291B Jane St; *Web:* www.montessori-ami.ca	Toronto	ON	M6S3Z3	416-769-7457	

Oregon

Institution	City	State	Zip	Phone	Fax
Concordia University Portland 2811 NE Holman St; **Fax:* Admissions ■ *TF:* 800-321-9371 ■ *Web:* www.cu-portland.edu	Portland	OR	97211	503-288-9371	280-8531*
Corban College 5000 Deer Pk Dr SE; *TF:* 800-845-3005 ■ *Web:* www.corban.edu	Salem	OR	97317	503-581-8600	585-4316
Eastern Oregon University 1 University Blvd; **Fax:* Admissions ■ *TF:* 800-452-8639 ■ *Web:* www.eou.edu	La Grande	OR	97850	541-962-3393	962-3418*
George Fox University 414 N Meridian St; **Fax:* Admissions ■ *TF:* 800-765-4369 ■ *Web:* www.georgefox.edu	Newberg	OR	97132	503-538-8383	554-3110*
Gutenberg College 1883 University St; *Web:* www.gutenberg.edu	Eugene	OR	97403	541-683-5141	683-6997
Lewis & Clark College 0615 SW Palatine Hill Rd; **Fax:* Admissions ■ *TF Admissions:* 800-444-4111 ■ *Web:* www.lclark.edu	Portland	OR	97219	503-768-7040	768-7055*
Linfield College 900 SE Baker St; **Fax:* Admissions ■ *TF Admissions:* 800-640-2287 ■ *Web:* www.linfield.edu	McMinnville	OR	97128	503-883-2213	883-2472*
Marylhurst University 17600 Pacific Hwy 43 PO Box 261; **Fax:* Admissions ■ *TF:* 800-634-9982 ■ *Web:* www.marylhurst.edu	Marylhurst	OR	97036	503-636-8141	635-6585*
Northwest Christian College 828 E 11th Ave; *TF:* 877-463-6622 ■ *Web:* www.nwcu.edu	Eugene	OR	97401	541-343-1641	684-7317
Oregon College of Art & Craft 8245 Sw Barnes Rd; *Web:* www.ocac.edu	Portland	OR	97225	503-297-5544	
Oregon Health & Science University Hospital 3181 SW Sam Jackson Pk Rd; *TF:* 800-292-4466 ■ *Web:* www.ohsu.edu	Portland	OR	97239	503-494-8311	494-3400
Oregon Institute of Technology 3201 Campus Dr; **Fax:* Admissions ■ *TF:* 800-422-2017 ■ *Web:* www.oit.edu	Klamath Falls	OR	97601	541-885-1150	885-1024*
Oregon State University 104 Kerr Admin Bldg; *TF:* 800-291-4192 ■ *Web:* www.oregonstate.edu	Corvallis	OR	97331	541-737-4411	737-2482
Pacific Northwest College of Art 1241 NW Johnson St; *TF:* 888-390-7499 ■ *Web:* www.pnca.edu	Portland	OR	97209	503-226-4391	821-8978
Pacific University 2043 College Way; **Fax:* Admissions ■ *TF Admissions:* 800-677-6712 ■ *Web:* www.pacificu.edu	Forest Grove	OR	97116	503-352-2007	352-2975*
Pioneer Pacific College 27501 Sw Pkwy Ave; *Web:* pioneerpacific.edu	Wilsonville	OR	97070	503-682-3903	
Portland State University 1825 SW Broadway PO Box 751; *TF:* 800-547-8887 ■ *Web:* www.pdx.edu	Portland	OR	97201	503-725-3000	725-5525

Phone Fax

Reed College 3203 SE Woodstock Blvd ... Portland OR 97202 503-777-7511 777-7553
TF Admissions: 800-547-4750 ■ *Web:* www.reed.edu

Southern Oregon University
1250 Siskiyou Blvd Britt Hall ... Ashland OR 97520 541-552-6411 552-8403*
*Fax: Admissions ■ *TF:* 800-482-7672 ■ *Web:* www.sou.edu

University of Oregon 1585 E 13th Ave ... Eugene OR 97403 541-346-1000 346-5815*
*Fax: Admissions ■ *TF Admissions:* 800-232-3825 ■ *Web:* www.uoregon.edu

University of Portland
5000 N Willamette Blvd ... Portland OR 97203 503-943-7147 943-7315*
*Fax: Admissions ■ *TF:* 888-627-5601 ■ *Web:* www.up.edu

Warner Pacific College 2219 SE 68th Ave ... Portland OR 97215 503-517-1020 517-1352
TF: 800-804-1510 ■ *Web:* www.warnerpacific.edu

Western Oregon University
345 Monmouth Ave N ... Monmouth OR 97361 503-838-8000 838-8067
TF Admissions: 877-877-1593 ■ *Web:* www.wou.edu

Willamette University 900 State St ... Salem OR 97301 503-370-6303 375-5363*
*Fax: Admissions ■ *TF:* 877-542-2787 ■ *Web:* www.willamette.edu

Pennsylvania

Phone Fax

Albright College 1621 N 13th St ... Reading PA 19604 610-921-2381 921-7294
TF: 800-252-1856 ■ *Web:* www.albright.edu

Allegheny College 520 N Main St ... Meadville PA 16335 814-332-4351
TF: 800-521-5293 ■ *Web:* www.allegheny.edu

Alvernia College 540 Upland Ave ... Reading PA 19611 610-796-8200 790-2873
TF: 888-258-3764 ■ *Web:* www.alvernia.edu

Arcadia University 450 S Easton Rd ... Glenside PA 19038 215-572-2900 881-8767*
*Fax: Admissions ■ *TF:* 877-272-2342 ■ *Web:* www.arcadia.edu

Automotive Training Center-warminster pa Campus
114 Pickering Way ... Exton PA 19341 610-363-6716
TF: 888-321-8992 ■ *Web:* www.autotraining.edu

Bloomsburg University 400 E Second St ... Bloomsburg PA 17815 570-389-3900 389-4795*
*Fax: Admissions ■ *TF:* 888-651-6117 ■ *Web:* www.bloomu.edu

Bryn Mawr College 101 N Merion Ave ... Bryn Mawr PA 19010 610-526-5000 526-7471*
*Fax: Admissions ■ *TF Admissions:* 800-262-2586 ■ *Web:* www.brynmawr.edu

Bucknell University 701 Moore Ave ... Lewisburg PA 17837 570-577-2000
Web: www.bucknell.edu

Cabrini College 610 King of Prussia Rd ... Radnor PA 19087 610-902-8552 902-8508*
*Fax: Acctg ■ *TF:* 800-848-1003 ■ *Web:* www.cabrini.edu

California University of Pennsylvania
250 University Ave ... California PA 15419 724-938-4000 938-4564
TF: 888-412-0479 ■ *Web:* calu.edu

Carlow University 3333 Fifth Ave ... Pittsburgh PA 15213 412-578-6000 578-6689
TF: 800-333-2275 ■ *Web:* www.carlow.edu

Carnegie Mellon University
5000 Forbes Ave ... Pittsburgh PA 15213 412-268-2000 268-7838*
*Fax: Admissions ■ *TF:* 844-625-4600 ■ *Web:* www.cmu.edu

Cedar Crest College 100 College Dr ... Allentown PA 18104 610-437-4471 606-4647*
*Fax: Admissions ■ *TF Admissions:* 800-360-1222 ■ *Web:* www.cedarcrest.edu

Chatham University 1 Woodland Rd ... Pittsburgh PA 15232 412-365-1100 365-1609
TF: 800-837-1290 ■ *Web:* www.chatham.edu

Chestnut Hill College
9601 Germantown Ave ... Philadelphia PA 19118 215-248-7001 248-7082*
*Fax: Admissions ■ *TF:* 800-248-0052 ■ *Web:* www.chc.edu

Cheyney University of Pennsylvania
1837 University Cir PO Box 200 ... Cheyney PA 19319 610-399-2275 399-2099*
*Fax: Admissions ■ *TF:* 800-243-9639 ■ *Web:* www.cheyney.edu

Clarion University of Pennsylvania
840 Wood St ... Clarion PA 16214 814-393-2306 393-2030*
*Fax: Admissions ■ *TF:* 800-672-7171 ■ *Web:* www.clarion.edu
Venango 1801 W First St ... Oil City PA 16301 814-676-6591 676-1348
TF: 800-672-7171 ■ *Web:* www.clarion.edu

Curtis Institute of Music
1726 Locust St ... Philadelphia PA 19103 215-893-5252 893-9065
TF: 800-640-4155 ■ *Web:* www.curtis.edu

Delaware Valley College 700 E Butler Ave ... Doylestown PA 18901 215-489-2211
TF: 800-233-5825 ■ *Web:* www.delval.edu

DeSales University 2755 Stn Ave ... Center Valley PA 18034 610-282-1100 282-0131
TF: 877-433-7253 ■ *Web:* www.desales.edu

Dickinson College PO Box 1773 ... Carlisle PA 17013 717-243-5121 245-1442*
*Fax: Admissions ■ *TF:* 800-644-1773 ■ *Web:* www.dickinson.edu

Drexel University 3141 Chestnut St ... Philadelphia PA 19104 215-895-2000 895-5939*
*Fax: Admissions ■ *TF Admissions:* 866-358-1010 ■ *Web:* www.drexel.edu

Duquesne University 600 Forbes Ave ... Pittsburgh PA 15282 412-396-6000 396-5779*
*Fax: Admissions ■ *TF:* 800-456-0590 ■ *Web:* www.duq.edu

East Stroudsburg University
200 Prospect St ... East Stroudsburg PA 18301 570-422-3542 422-3933*
*Fax: Admissions ■ *TF Admissions:* 877-230-5547 ■ *Web:* www.esu.edu

Eastern University 1300 Eagle Rd ... Wayne PA 19087 610-341-5800 341-1723*
*Fax: Admissions ■ *TF Admissions:* 800-452-0996 ■ *Web:* www.eastern.edu

Edinboro University of Pennsylvania
200 E Normal St ... Edinboro PA 16444 814-732-2761 732-2420*
*Fax: Admissions ■ *TF:* 888-846-2676 ■ *Web:* www.edinboro.edu

Elizabethtown College 1 Alpha Dr ... Elizabethtown PA 17022 717-361-1000 361-1365*
*Fax: Admissions ■ *Web:* www.etown.edu

Franklin & Marshall College PO Box 3003 ... Lancaster PA 17604 717-291-3951 291-4389*
*Fax: Admissions ■ *TF:* 877-678-9111 ■ *Web:* www.fandm.edu

Gannon University 109 University Sq ... Erie PA 16541 814-871-7000 871-5803
TF Admissions: 800-426-6668 ■ *Web:* www.gannon.edu

Geneva College 3200 College Ave ... Beaver Falls PA 15010 724-847-6500 847-6776*
*Fax: Admissions ■ *TF:* 800-847-8255 ■ *Web:* www.geneva.edu

Gettysburg College 300 N Washington St ... Gettysburg PA 17325 717-337-6000 337-6145*
*Fax: Admissions ■ *TF:* 800-431-0803 ■ *Web:* www.gettysburg.edu

Gratz College 7605 Old York Rd ... Melrose Park PA 19027 215-635-7300
TF: 800-475-4635 ■ *Web:* www.gratz.edu

Great Lakes Institute of Technology Toni & Guy Hairdressing Academy
5100 Peach St ... Erie PA 16509 814-864-6666
TF: 800-394-4548 ■ *Web:* www.glit.edu

Grove City College 100 Campus Dr ... Grove City PA 16127 724-458-2000 458-3395*
*Fax: Admissions ■ *Web:* www.gcc.edu

Gwynedd-Mercy College
1325 Sunneytown Pk PO Box 901 ... Gwynedd Valley PA 19437 215-646-7300 641-5556*
*Fax: Admissions ■ *TF Admissions:* 800-342-5462 ■ *Web:* gmercyu.edu

Harrisburg University of Science & Technology
215 Market St ... Harrisburg PA 17101 717-901-5100
Web: harrisburgu.edu

Haverford College 370 Lancaster Ave ... Haverford PA 19041 610-896-1000 896-1338
Web: www.haverford.edu

Holy Family University
9801 Frankford Ave ... Philadelphia PA 19114 215-637-7700
TF: 800-422-0010 ■ *Web:* holyfamily.edu

Immaculata University 1145 King Rd ... Immaculata PA 19345 610-647-4400 640-0836*
*Fax: Admissions ■ *TF:* 877-428-6329 ■ *Web:* www.immaculata.edu

Indiana University of Pennsylvania
1011 S Dr Sutton Hall Ste 117 ... Indiana PA 15705 724-357-2230 357-6281*
*Fax: Admissions ■ *TF:* 800-442-6830 ■ *Web:* www.iup.edu

Juniata College 1700 Moore St ... Huntingdon PA 16652 814-641-3000 641-3100*
*Fax: Admissions ■ *TF:* 877-586-4282 ■ *Web:* www.juniata.edu

Keystone College 1 College Green ... La Plume PA 18440 570-945-5141 945-7916*
*Fax: Admissions ■ *TF:* 800-824-2764 ■ *Web:* keystone.edu

King's College 133 N River St ... Wilkes-Barre PA 18711 570-208-5858 208-5971*
*Fax: Admissions ■ *TF:* 800-955-5777 ■ *Web:* www.kings.edu

Kutztown University 15200 Kutztown Rd ... Kutztown PA 19530 610-683-4000 683-1375
TF: 877-628-1915 ■ *Web:* www.kutztown.edu

La Roche College 9000 Babcock Blvd ... Pittsburgh PA 15237 412-367-9300
TF Admissions: 800-838-4572 ■ *Web:* www.laroche.edu

La Salle University 1900 W Olney Ave ... Philadelphia PA 19141 215-951-1500 951-1656*
*Fax: Admissions ■ *TF:* 800-328-1910 ■ *Web:* www.lasalle.edu

Lafayette College 730 High St ... Easton PA 18042 610-330-5000 330-5355*
*Fax: Admissions ■ *Web:* www.lafayette.edu

Lebanon Valley College 101 N College Ave ... Annville PA 17003 717-867-6181 867-6026*
*Fax: Admissions ■ *TF:* 866-582-4236 ■ *Web:* www.lvc.edu

Lincoln University
1570 Old Baltimore Pk PO Box 179 ... Lincoln University PA 19352 484-365-8000 365-8109*
*Fax: Admissions ■ *TF Admissions:* 800-790-0191 ■ *Web:* www.lincoln.edu

Lock Haven University 401 N Fairview St ... Lock Haven PA 17745 570-484-2011 484-2201*
*Fax: Admissions ■ *TF:* 800-233-8978 ■ *Web:* www.lhup.edu

Lycoming College 700 College Pl ... Williamsport PA 17701 570-321-4000 321-4317*
*Fax: Admissions ■ *TF:* 800-345-3920 ■ *Web:* www.lycoming.edu

Mansfield University Alumni Hall ... Mansfield PA 16933 570-662-4000 662-4121
TF Admissions: 800-577-6826 ■ *Web:* www.mansfield.edu

Mercyhurst College 501 E 38th St ... Erie PA 16546 814-824-2202 824-3634*
*Fax: Admissions ■ *TF:* 800-825-1926 ■ *Web:* www.mercyhurst.edu

Messiah College PO Box 3005 ... Grantham PA 17027 717-691-6000 796-5374*
*Fax: Admissions ■ *TF:* 800-233-4220 ■ *Web:* www.messiah.edu

Millersville University of Pennsylvania
PO Box 1002 PO Box 1002 ... Millersville PA 17551 717-872-3011 871-2147
TF: 800-682-3648 ■ *Web:* www.millersville.edu

Misericordia University 301 Lake St ... Dallas PA 18612 570-674-6400 675-2441*
*Fax: Admissions ■ *TF:* 866-262-6363 ■ *Web:* www.misericordia.edu

Moravian College 1200 Main St ... Bethlehem PA 18018 610-861-1300 625-7930*
*Fax: Admissions ■ *TF:* 800-441-3191 ■ *Web:* www.moravian.edu

Mount Aloysius College
7373 Admiral Perry Hwy ... Cresson PA 16630 814-886-6383 886-6441
TF: 888-823-2220 ■ *Web:* www.mtaloy.edu

Muhlenberg College 2400 Chew St ... Allentown PA 18104 484-664-3100 664-3234
Web: muhlenberg.edu

Neumann College 1 Neumann Dr ... Aston PA 19014 610-459-0905 361-5265*
*Fax: Admissions ■ *TF:* 800-963-8626 ■ *Web:* www.neumann.edu

Peirce College 1420 Pine St ... Philadelphia PA 19102 215-545-6400 670-9366*
*Fax: Admissions ■ *TF:* 888-467-3472 ■ *Web:* www.peirce.edu

Pennsylvania State University
201 Shields Bldg ... University Park PA 16802 814-865-4700 863-7590
Web: www.psu.edu
Abington College 1600 Woodland Rd ... Abington PA 19001 215-881-7300 881-7412*
*Fax: Admissions ■ *Web:* www.abington.psu.edu
Altoona 3000 Ivyside Pk ... Altoona PA 16601 814-949-5466 949-5564*
*Fax: Admissions ■ *TF:* 800-848-9843 ■ *Web:* www.altoona.psu.edu
Brandywine 25 Yearsley Mill Rd ... Media PA 19063 610-892-1200 892-1357*
*Fax: Admissions ■ *Web:* www.brandywine.psu.edu
Harrisburg 777 W Harrisburg Pk ... Middletown PA 17057 717-948-6250 948-6325*
*Fax: Admissions ■ *TF:* 800-222-2056 ■ *Web:* harrisburg.psu.edu

Pennsylvania State University at Erie
Behrend College 4701 College Dr ... Erie PA 16563 814-898-6000 898-6044
TF: 866-374-3378 ■ *Web:* psbehrend.psu.edu

Philadelphia University 4201 Henry Ave ... Philadelphia PA 19144 215-951-2800 951-2907*
*Fax: Admissions ■ *TF Admissions:* 800-951-7287 ■ *Web:* www.philau.edu

Point Park University 201 Wood St ... Pittsburgh PA 15222 412-391-4100 392-3902*
*Fax: Admissions ■ *TF Admissions:* 800-321-0129 ■ *Web:* www.pointpark.edu

Robert Morris University
6001 University Blvd ... Moon Township PA 15108 412-262-8200 397-2425
TF: 800-762-0097 ■ *Web:* www.rmu.edu

Rosemont College 1400 Montgomery Ave ... Rosemont PA 19010 610-527-0200 526-2971*
*Fax: Admissions ■ *TF Admissions:* 888-521-0983 ■ *Web:* www.rosemont.edu

Saint Francis University 117 Evergreen Dr ... Loretto PA 15940 814-472-3000
Web: www.francis.edu

Saint Joseph's University 5600 City Ave ... Philadelphia PA 19131 610-660-1000 660-1314*
*Fax: Admissions ■ *TF:* 888-232-4295 ■ *Web:* www.sju.edu

Saint Vincent College 300 Fraser Purchase Rd ... Latrobe PA 15650 724-532-6600 805-2953*
*Fax: Admissions ■ *TF:* 800-782-5549 ■ *Web:* www.stvincent.edu

Seton Hill University 1 Seton Hill Dr ... Greensburg PA 15601 724-838-4255 830-1294*
*Fax: Admissions ■ *TF:* 800-826-6234 ■ *Web:* www.setonhill.edu

Shippensburg University
1871 Old Main Dr ... Shippensburg PA 17257 717-477-1231 477-4016*
*Fax: Admissions ■ *TF:* 800-822-8028 ■ *Web:* www.ship.edu

Slippery Rock University 1 Morrow Way ... Slippery Rock PA 16057 724-738-9000 738-2913*
*Fax: Admissions ■ *TF:* 800-929-4778 ■ *Web:* www.sru.edu

South Hills School of Business & Technology
480 Waupelani Dr ... State College PA 16801 814-234-7755
Web: www.southhills.edu

Susquehanna University
514 University Ave ... Selinsgrove PA 17870 570-374-0101 372-2722
TF: 800-326-9672 ■ *Web:* www.susqu.edu

Phone Fax

Swarthmore College 500 College Ave . . . . Swarthmore PA 19081 610-328-8300 328-8580*
Fax: Admissions ■ *TF Admissions:* 800-667-3110 ■ *Web:* www.swarthmore.edu

Temple University 1801 N Broad St . . . . Philadelphia PA 19122 215-204-7000 204-5694
Web: www.temple.edu

Thiel College 75 College Ave . . . . Greenville PA 16125 724-589-2000 589-2013*
Fax: Admissions ■ *TF:* 800-248-4435 ■ *Web:* www.thiel.edu

Thomas Jefferson University
1020 Walnut St. . . . . Philadelphia PA 19107 215-955-6000 955-5151
TF: 800-533-3669 ■ *Web:* www.jefferson.edu

University of Pennsylvania
3451 Walnut St. . . . . Philadelphia PA 19104 215-898-5000 898-9670*
Fax: Admissions ■ *TF:* 800-537-5487 ■ *Web:* www.upenn.edu

University of Pittsburgh 4227 Fifth Ave . . . . Pittsburgh PA 15260 412-624-4141 648-8815*
Fax: Admissions ■ *TF:* 877-999-3223 ■ *Web:* www.pitt.edu

Bradford 300 Campus Dr. . . . . Bradford PA 16701 814-362-7555 362-5150
TF: 800-872-1787 ■ *Web:* www.upb.pitt.edu

Greensburg 150 Finoli Dr . . . . Greensburg PA 15601 724-837-7040 836-7160*
Fax: Admissions ■ *TF:* 888-843-4563 ■ *Web:* www.greensburg.pitt.edu

Johnstown 157 Blackington Hall . . . . Johnstown PA 15904 814-269-7050 269-7044
TF: 800-765-4875 ■ *Web:* www.upj.pitt.edu

University of Scranton
800 Linden St St Thomas Hall . . . . Scranton PA 18510 570-941-7400 941-5928*
Fax: Admissions ■ *TF:* 888-727-2686 ■ *Web:* scranton.edu

University of the Sciences in Philadelphia
600 S 43rd St . . . . Philadelphia PA 19104 215-596-8800 596-8821*
Fax: Admissions ■ *TF:* 888-857-6264 ■ *Web:* www.usciences.edu

Ursinus College
601 E Main St PO Box 1000 . . . . Collegeville PA 19426 610-409-3200 409-3662*
Fax: Admissions ■ *TF:* 877-448-3282 ■ *Web:* www.ursinus.edu

Valley Forge Christian College
1401 Charlestown Rd . . . . Phoenixville PA 19460 610-935-0450 917-2069*
Fax: Admissions ■ *TF:* 800-432-8322 ■ *Web:* www.vfcc.edu

Villanova University 800 Lancaster Ave. . . . . Villanova PA 19085 610-519-4500 519-6450
Web: www.villanova.edu

Washington & Jefferson College
60 S Lincoln St. . . . . Washington PA 15301 724-222-4400 223-6534*
Fax: Admissions ■ *TF:* 888-926-3529 ■ *Web:* www.washjeff.edu

Waynesburg College 51 W College St . . . . Waynesburg PA 15370 724-627-8191
TF Admissions: 800-225-7393 ■ *Web:* www.waynesburg.edu

West Chester University 700 S High St . . . . West Chester PA 19383 610-436-1000 436-2907
TF: 877-315-2165 ■ *Web:* www.wcupa.edu

Westminster College 319 S Market St. . . . . New Wilmington PA 16172 724-946-8761 946-6171*
Fax: Admissions ■ *TF:* 800-942-8033 ■ *Web:* www.westminster.edu

Widener University 1 University Pl. . . . . Chester PA 19013 610-499-4000 499-4676*
Fax: Admissions ■ *TF Admissions:* 888-943-3637 ■ *Web:* www.widener.edu

Wilkes University 84 W S St. Wilkes-Barre PA 18766 800-945-5378 408-4904*
Fax Area Code: 570 ■ *Fax:* Admissions ■ *TF:* 800-945-5378 ■ *Web:* www.wilkes.edu

Wilson College 1015 Philadelphia Ave . . . . Chambersburg PA 17201 717-264-4141 264-1578*
Fax: Admissions ■ *TF Admissions:* 800-421-8402 ■ *Web:* www.wilson.edu

York College of Pennsylvania
441 Country Club Rd . . . . York PA 17403 717-846-7788 815-6862*
Fax: Hum Res ■ *Web:* www.ycp.edu

Puerto Rico

Phone Fax

EDIC College Inc
Ave Rafael Cordero Calle Gnova Urb Caguas Norte
. . . . Caguas PR 00726 787-744-8519
Web: ediccollege.edu

Quebec

Phone Fax

John Abbott College
21275 Ch Lakeshore Bureau 2000
. . . . Sainte-anne-de-bellevue QC H9X3L9 514-457-6610 457-4730
Web: www.johnabbott.qc.ca

Marianopolis College 4873 Av Westmount . . . . Westmount QC H3Y1X9 514-931-8792
Web: www.marianopolis.edu

Rhode Island

Phone Fax

Brown University 45 Prospect St . . . . Providence RI 02912 401-863-2378 863-9300*
Fax: Admissions ■ *Web:* www.brown.edu

Bryant University 1150 Douglas Pk . . . . Smithfield RI 02917 401-232-6000 232-6741*
Fax: Admissions ■ *TF Admissions:* 800-622-7001 ■ *Web:* www.bryant.edu

Emma Pendleton Bradley Hospital
1011 Veterans Memorial Pkwy . . . . East Providence RI 02915 401-432-1000
Web: lifespan.org

Johnson & Wales University
Providence 8 Abbott Pk Pl . . . . Providence RI 02903 401-598-1000 598-4641
TF: 800-342-5598 ■ *Web:* www.jwu.edu

Providence College 1 Cunningham Sq . . . . Providence RI 02918 401-865-1000 865-2826*
Fax: Admissions ■ *TF Admissions:* 800-721-6444 ■ *Web:* www.providence.edu

Rhode Island College 600 Mt Pleasant Ave . . . . Providence RI 02908 401-456-8000 456-8817
TF: 800-669-5760 ■ *Web:* www.ric.edu

Roger Williams University 1 Old Ferry Rd . . . . Bristol RI 02809 401-254-3500 254-3557*
Fax: Admissions ■ *TF:* 800-458-7144 ■ *Web:* www.rwu.edu

Salve Regina University 100 Ochre Pt Ave . . . . Newport RI 02840 401-847-6650 848-2823*
Fax: Admissions ■ *TF:* 800-829-1040 ■ *Web:* www.salve.edu

University of Rhode Island (URI)
45 Upper College Rd . . . . Kingston RI 02881 401-874-1000 874-5523
Web: ww2.uri.edu

Feinstein Providence 80 Washington St. . . . . Providence RI 02903 401-277-5000
Web: ww2.uri.edu

South Carolina

Phone Fax

Allen University 1530 Harden St. . . . . Columbia SC 29204 803-376-5700 376-5733*
Fax: Mail Rm ■ *TF:* 877-625-5368 ■ *Web:* www.allenuniversity.edu

Benedict College 1600 Harden St . . . . Columbia SC 29204 803-253-5000
TF: 800-868-6598 ■ *Web:* www.benedict.edu

Bob Jones University
1700 Wade Hampton Blvd . . . . Greenville SC 29614 864-242-5100 232-9258*
Fax Area Code: 800 ■ *Fax:* Admissions ■ *TF Admissions:* 800-252-6363 ■ *Web:* www.bju.edu

Charleston Southern University
9200 University Blvd . . . . Charleston SC 29423 843-863-7050 863-7070
TF: 800-947-7474 ■ *Web:* www.csuniv.edu

Citadel, The 171 Moultrie St. . . . . Charleston SC 29409 843-953-5230 953-7036
TF: 800-868-1842 ■ *Web:* www.citadel.edu

Claflin University 400 Magnolia St. . . . . Orangeburg SC 29115 803-535-5000 535-5385
TF: 800-922-1276 ■ *Web:* www.claflin.edu

Clemson University 105 Sikes Hall . . . . Clemson SC 29634 864-656-3311 656-2464*
Fax: Admissions ■ *TF:* 800-640-2657 ■ *Web:* www.clemson.edu

Coastal Carolina University PO Box 261954 . . . . Conway SC 29528 843-349-2170 349-2127
TF: 800-277-7000 ■ *Web:* www.coastal.edu

Coker College 300 E College Ave . . . . Hartsville SC 29550 843-383-8000 383-8056*
Fax: Admissions ■ *TF:* 800-950-1908 ■ *Web:* www.coker.edu

College of Charleston 66 George St . . . . Charleston SC 29424 843-805-5507 953-6322
TF: 866-327-2400 ■ *Web:* www.cofc.edu

Columbia College 1301 Columbia College Dr . . . . Columbia SC 29203 803-786-3871 786-3674
TF: 800-277-1301 ■ *Web:* www.columbiasc.edu

Converse College 580 E Main St . . . . Spartanburg SC 29302 864-596-9000 596-9225*
Fax: Admissions ■ *TF Admissions:* 800-766-1125 ■ *Web:* www.converse.edu

Erskine College 2 Washington St . . . . Due West SC 29639 888-359-4358
TF Admissions: 888-359-4358 ■ *Web:* www.erskine.edu

Francis Marion University PO Box 100547 . . . . Florence SC 29501 843-661-1231 661-4635*
Fax: Admissions ■ *TF:* 800-368-7551 ■ *Web:* www.fmarion.edu

Furman University 3300 Poinsett Hwy . . . . Greenville SC 29613 864-294-2000 294-2018*
Fax: Admissions ■ *Web:* www.furman.edu

Lander University 320 Stanley Ave. . . . . Greenwood SC 29649 864-388-8307 388-8125*
Fax: Admissions ■ *TF Admissions:* 800-922-1117 ■ *Web:* www.lander.edu

Limestone College 1115 College Dr. . . . . Gaffney SC 29340 864-489-7151 488-8206*
Fax: Admissions ■ *TF:* 800-795-7151 ■ *Web:* www.limestone.edu

Medical University of South Carolina
41 Bee St MSC 203 . . . . Charleston SC 29425 843-792-3281 792-3764*
Fax: Admissions ■ *TF:* 800-424-6872 ■ *Web:* www.musc.edu

Morris College 100 W College St . . . . Sumter SC 29150 803-934-3200 773-8241*
Fax: Admissions ■ *TF Admissions:* 866-853-1345 ■ *Web:* www.morris.edu

Newberry College 2100 College St. . . . . Newberry SC 29108 803-276-5010 321-5138*
Fax: Admissions ■ *TF:* 800-845-4955 ■ *Web:* www.newberry.edu

Presbyterian College 503 S Broad St . . . . Clinton SC 29325 864-833-2820 833-8481*
Fax: Admissions ■ *TF:* 800-476-7272 ■ *Web:* www.presby.edu

South Carolina State University
300 College St NE PO Box 7127. . . . . Orangeburg SC 29117 803-536-7000 536-8990
TF Admissions: 800-260-5956 ■ *Web:* www.scsu.edu

South University Columbia 9 Science Ct . . . . Columbia SC 29203 803-799-9082 935-4382*
Fax: Admissions ■ *TF:* 800-688-0932 ■ *Web:* www.southuniversity.edu

Southern Wesleyan University 907 Wesleyan Dr. . . . . Central SC 29630 864-644-5000
TF: 800-282-8798 ■ *Web:* www.swu.edu

Technical College of the Lowcountry
921 Ribaut Rd. . . . . Beaufort SC 29902 843-525-8211
Web: www.tcl.edu

University of South Carolina
1600 Hampton St . . . . Columbia SC 29208 803-777-7000 777-0101*
Fax: Admissions ■ *TF:* 800-868-5872 ■ *Web:* www.sc.edu

Aiken 471 University Pkwy. . . . . Aiken SC 29801 803-648-6851 641-3727*
Fax: Admissions ■ *TF:* 866-254-2366 ■ *Web:* www.usca.edu

Beaufort 801 Carteret St. . . . . Beaufort SC 29902 843-521-4100 521-4198*
Fax: Admissions ■ *TF:* 866-455-4753 ■ *Web:* www.sc.edu

Sumter 200 Miller Rd. . . . . Sumter SC 29150 803-775-8727 775-2180*
Fax: Admissions ■ *TF:* 888-872-7868 ■ *Web:* www.uscsumter.edu

Upstate 800 University Way. Spartanburg SC 29303 864-503-5246 503-5727*
Fax: Admissions ■ *TF:* 800-277-8727 ■ *Web:* www.uscupstate.edu

Voorhees College 213 Wiggins Dr PO Box 678 . . . . Denmark SC 29042 803-780-1234
TF Admissions: 800-446-6250 ■ *Web:* www.voorhees.edu

Winthrop University 701 Oakland Ave . . . . Rock Hill SC 29733 803-323-2211 323-2137*
Fax: Admissions ■ *Web:* www.winthrop.edu

Wofford College 429 N Church St . . . . Spartanburg SC 29303 864-597-4000 597-4149*
Fax: Admissions ■ *Web:* www.wofford.edu

South Dakota

Phone Fax

Augustana College 2001 S Summit Ave. . . . . Sioux Falls SD 57197 605-274-0770 274-5518*
Fax: Admissions ■ *TF:* 800-727-2844 ■ *Web:* www.augie.edu

Black Hills State University
1200 University St Unit 9502 . . . . Spearfish SD 57799 605-642-6343 642-6254
TF: 800-255-2478 ■ *Web:* www.bhsu.edu

Dakota State University 820 N Washington Ave. . . . . Madison SD 57042 605-256-5139 256-5020
TF: 888-378-9988 ■ *Web:* www.dsu.edu

Dakota Wesleyan University
1200 W University Ave . . . . Mitchell SD 57301 605-995-2600 995-2699
TF: 800-333-8506 ■ *Web:* www.dwu.edu

Globe University 5101 S Broadband Ln . . . . Sioux Falls SD 57108 605-977-0705
Web: globeuniversity.edu

Mount Marty College 1105 W Eigth St . . . . Yankton SD 57078 605-668-1545 668-1508*
Fax: Admissions ■ *TF Admissions:* 800-658-4552 ■ *Web:* www.mtmc.edu

National American University
321 Kansas City St . . . . Rapid City SD 57701 605-394-4800 394-4871*
Fax: Admissions ■ *TF:* 800-843-8892 ■ *Web:* www.national.edu

Sioux Falls 5801 S Kiwanis Ave. . . . . Sioux Falls SD 57108 605-336-4600 336-4605*
Fax: Admissions ■ *TF:* 800-388-5430 ■ *Web:* www.national.edu

Northern State University 1200 S Jay St . . . . Aberdeen SD 57401 605-626-3011 626-2587*
Fax: Admissions ■ *TF:* 800-678-5330 ■ *Web:* www.northern.edu

				Phone	Fax
Oglala Lakota College PO Box 629	Martin	SD	57551	605-455-6000	455-2787
Web: www.olc.edu					
Presentation College 1500 N Main St	Aberdeen	SD	57401	605-225-1634	
TF: 800-437-6060 ■ Web: www.presentation.edu					
South Dakota School of Mines & Technology					
501 E St Joseph St	Rapid City	SD	57701	605-394-2414	394-1268
TF: 800-544-8162 ■ Web: www.sdsmt.edu					
South Dakota State University PO Box 2201	Brookings	SD	57007	605-688-4121	688-6891
TF: 800-952-3541 ■ Web: www.sdstate.edu					
University of Sioux Falls 1101 W 22nd St	Sioux Falls	SD	57105	605-331-6600	331-6615
TF: 800-888-1047 ■ Web: www.usiouxfalls.edu					
University of South Dakota 414 E Clark St	Vermillion	SD	57069	605-677-5341	677-6323*
*Fax: Admissions ■ TF: 877-269-6837 ■ Web: www.usd.edu					

Tennessee

				Phone	Fax
Aquinas College 4210 HaRding Rd	Nashville	TN	37205	615-297-7545	
TF Admissions: 800-649-9956 ■ Web: aquinascollege.edu					
Austin Peay State University					
601 College St	Clarksville	TN	37044	931-221-7661	221-6168*
*Fax: Admissions ■ TF Admissions: 800-844-2778 ■ Web: www.apsu.edu					
Belmont University 1900 Belmont Blvd	Nashville	TN	37212	615-460-6000	460-5434*
*Fax: Admissions ■ TF: 800-563-6765 ■ Web: www.belmont.edu					
Bethel University 325 Cherry Ave	McKenzie	TN	38201	731-352-4000	352-4241*
*Fax: Admissions ■ Web: www.bethelu.edu					
Bryan College 721 Bryan Dr PO Box 7000	Dayton	TN	37321	423-775-2041	775-7199
TF: 800-277-9522 ■ Web: www.bryan.edu					
Carson-Newman College					
1646 Russell Ave	Jefferson City	TN	37760	865-471-2000	471-3502*
*Fax: Admissions ■ TF: 800-678-9061 ■ Web: www.cn.edu					
Christian Bros University 650 E Pkwy S	Memphis	TN	38104	901-321-3000	321-3494*
*Fax: Admissions ■ TF Admissions: 800-288-7576 ■ Web: www.cbu.edu					
Cumberland University 1 Cumberland Sq	Lebanon	TN	37087	615-444-2562	444-2569
TF: 800-467-0562 ■ Web: www.cumberland.edu					
East Tennessee State University					
PO Box 70731	Johnson City	TN	37614	423-439-4213	439-4630
TF: 800-462-3878 ■ Web: www.etsu.edu					
Fisk University 1000 17th Ave N	Nashville	TN	37208	615-329-8500	329-8774
TF: 888-702-0022 ■ Web: www.fisk.edu					
Freed-Hardeman University 158 E Main St	Henderson	TN	38340	731-989-6651	989-6047
TF: 800-348-3481 ■ Web: www.fhu.edu					
King College 1350 King College Rd	Bristol	TN	37620	423-652-4861	
TF Admissions: 800-362-0014 ■ Web: www.king.edu					
Lambuth University 705 Lambuth Blvd	Jackson	TN	38301	731-427-4725	422-2169*
*Fax: Admissions ■ TF: 800-526-2305 ■ Web: memphis.edu					
Lane College 545 Ln Ave	Jackson	TN	38301	731-426-7500	426-7559*
*Fax: Admissions ■ TF Admissions: 800-960-7533 ■ Web: www.lanecollege.edu					
Lee University 1120 N Ocoee St	Cleveland	TN	37311	423-614-8000	614-8533*
*Fax: Admissions ■ TF: 800-533-9930 ■ Web: www.leeuniversity.edu					
Lincoln Memorial University					
6965 Cumberland Gap Pkwy	Harrogate	TN	37752	423-869-3611	
TF: 800-325-0900 ■ Web: www.lmunet.edu					
Lipscomb University 3901 Granny White Pk	Nashville	TN	37204	615-966-1000	966-1804*
*Fax: Admissions ■ TF: 800-333-4358 ■ Web: www.lipscomb.edu					
Martin Methodist College 433 W Madison St	Pulaski	TN	38478	931-363-9804	363-9803*
*Fax: Admissions ■ TF: 800-467-1273 ■ Web: www.martinmethodist.edu					
Maryville College					
502 E Lamar Alexander Pkwy	Maryville	TN	37804	865-981-8000	981-8005*
*Fax: Admissions ■ TF: 800-597-2687 ■ Web: www.maryvillecollege.edu					
Middle Tennessee State University					
1301 E Main St	Murfreesboro	TN	37132	615-898-2111	898-5478*
*Fax: Admissions ■ TF Admissions: 800-433-6878 ■ Web: www.mtsu.edu					
Milligan College PO Box 500	Milligan College	TN	37682	423-461-8730	461-8982*
*Fax: Admissions ■ TF: 800-262-8337 ■ Web: www.milligan.edu					
Nossi College of Art 590 Cheron Rd	Madison	TN	37115	615-514-2787	
TF: 888-986-2787 ■ Web: www.nossi.edu					
O'More College of Design 423 S Margin St	Franklin	TN	37064	615-794-4254	790-1662
TF: 888-662-1970 ■ Web: www.omorecollege.edu					
Oxford Graduate School Inc 500 Oxford Dr	Dayton	TN	37321	423-775-6596	
TF: 800-933-6188 ■ Web: www.ogs.edu					
Rhodes College 2000 N Pkwy	Memphis	TN	38112	901-843-3700	843-3631*
*Fax: Admissions ■ TF: 800-844-5969 ■ Web: www.rhodes.edu					
Southern Adventist University					
4881 Taylor Cir	Collegedale	TN	37315	423-236-2000	236-1000
TF: 800-768-8437 ■ Web: www.southern.edu					
Tennessee State University					
3500 John A Merritt Blvd PO Box 9609	Nashville	TN	37209	615-963-5000	963-5108
TF Admissions: 888-463-6878 ■ Web: www.tnstate.edu					
Tennessee Technological University					
1 William L J1s Dr	Cookeville	TN	38505	931-372-3888	372-6250
TF: 800-255-8881 ■ Web: www.tntech.edu					
Tennessee Temple University					
1815 Union Ave	Chattanooga	TN	37404	423-493-4100	493-4497*
*Fax: Admissions ■ TF: 800-553-4050 ■ Web: www.tntemple.edu					
Tennessee Wesleyan College 204 E College St	Athens	TN	37371	423-745-7504	744-9968
TF: 800-742-5892 ■ Web: www.tnwesleyan.edu					
Trevecca Nazarene University					
333 Murfreesboro Rd	Nashville	TN	37210	615-248-1200	248-7406*
*Fax: Admissions ■ TF: 888-210-4868 ■ Web: www.trevecca.edu					
Tusculum College 60 Shiloh Rd Hwy 107	Greeneville	TN	37743	423-636-7300	798-1622*
*Fax: Admissions ■ TF: 800-729-0256 ■ Web: www.tusculum.edu					
Union University 1050 Union University Dr	Jackson	TN	38305	731-661-5210	661-5589*
*Fax: Admissions ■ TF: 800-338-6466 ■ Web: www.uu.edu					
University of Tennessee (UTHSC)					
1331 Cir Pk Dr 320 Student Services Bldg	Knoxville	TN	37996	865-974-1000	974-3851*
*Fax: Admissions ■ Web: www.utk.edu					
Chattanooga 615 McCallie Ave	Chattanooga	TN	37403	423-425-4111	425-4157*
*Fax: Admissions ■ TF: 800-882-6627 ■ Web: www.utc.edu					
Health Science Ctr 920 Madison Ave	Memphis	TN	38163	901-448-5500	
Web: www.uthsc.edu					
Martin 544 University St	Martin	TN	38238	731-881-7020	881-7029
TF: 800-829-8861 ■ Web: www.utm.edu					
University of the South 735 University Ave	Sewanee	TN	37383	931-598-1238	598-3248*
*Fax: Admissions ■ TF: 800-522-2234 ■ Web: www.sewanee.edu					
Vanderbilt University 2201 W End Ave	Nashville	TN	37240	615-322-7311	343-7765
TF: 800-288-0432 ■ Web: www.vanderbilt.edu					

Texas

				Phone	Fax
Amberton University 1700 Eastgate Dr	Garland	TX	75041	972-279-6511	279-9773
Web: www.amberton.edu					
Angelina County Junior College District Texas					
3500 S First St	Lufkin	TX	75904	936-639-1301	
Web: www.angelina.edu					
Angelo State University					
2601 W Ave N ASU Stn 11014	San Angelo	TX	76909	325-942-2041	942-2078*
*Fax: Admissions ■ TF: 800-946-8627 ■ Web: www.angelo.edu					
Arlington Baptist College 3001 W Div St	Arlington	TX	76012	817-461-8741	274-1138*
*Fax: Admissions ■ Web: arlingtonbaptistcollege.edu					
Austin College 900 N Grand Ave	Sherman	TX	75090	903-813-3000	813-3197*
*Fax: Admissions ■ TF: 866-776-0056 ■ Web: www.austincollege.edu					
Austin Graduate School of Theology					
7640 Guadalupe St	Austin	TX	78752	512-476-2772	476-3919
TF: 866-287-4723 ■ Web: www.austingrad.edu					
Baylor University 1301 S University Parks Dr	Waco	TX	76798	254-710-3718	710-1066
TF: 800-229-5678 ■ Web: www.baylor.edu					
Concordia University Austin 3400 IH-35 N	Austin	TX	78705	512-486-2000	
TF: 800-865-4282 ■ Web: www.concordia.edu					
Criswell College 4010 Gaston Ave	Dallas	TX	75246	214-821-5433	
TF: 800-899-0012 ■ Web: www.criswell.edu					
Dallas Baptist University 3000 Mtn Creek Pkwy	Dallas	TX	75211	214-333-7100	333-5447*
*Fax: Admissions ■ TF: 800-460-1328 ■ Web: www.dbu.edu					
East Texas Baptist University					
1209 N Grove St	Marshall	TX	75670	903-935-7963	923-2001*
*Fax: Admissions ■ TF: 800-804-3828 ■ Web: www.etbu.edu					
Graduate Institute of Applied Linguistics Inc					
7500 W Camp Wisdom Rd	Dallas	TX	75236	972-708-7340	
Web: www.gial.edu					
Hardin-Simmons University 2200 Hickory St	Abilene	TX	79698	325-670-1206	671-2115*
*Fax: Admissions ■ TF: 877-464-7889 ■ Web: www.hsutx.edu					
Houston Baptist University 7502 Fondren Rd	Houston	TX	77074	281-649-3000	649-3217*
*Fax: Admissions ■ TF Admissions: 800-969-3210 ■ Web: www.hbu.edu					
Howard Payne University 1000 Fisk Ave	Brownwood	TX	76801	325-646-2502	
TF: 800-950-8465 ■ Web: www.hputx.edu					
Huston-Tillotson University 900 Chicon St	Austin	TX	78702	512-505-3000	505-3192*
*Fax: Admissions ■ TF: 877-487-8702 ■ Web: www.htu.edu					
Jarvis Christian College PO Box 1470	Hawkins	TX	75765	903-769-5700	769-1282*
*Fax: Admissions ■ Web: www.jarvis.edu					
Lamar University 4400 ML King Jr Pkwy	Beaumont	TX	77710	409-880-7011	880-8463
Web: www.lamar.edu					
LeTourneau University 2100 S Mobberly Ave	Longview	TX	75602	903-233-3000	233-4301*
*Fax: Admissions ■ TF: 800-759-8811 ■ Web: www.letu.edu					
Lubbock Christian University 5601 19th St	Lubbock	TX	79407	806-720-7151	720-7162*
*Fax: Admissions ■ TF: 800-933-7601 ■ Web: www.lcu.edu					
McMurry University					
1 McMurry University 1400 Sayles Blvd	Abilene	TX	79697	325-793-4700	
TF: 800-460-2392 ■ Web: www.mcm.edu					
Midwestern State University					
3410 Taft Blvd	Wichita Falls	TX	76308	940-397-4000	397-4672*
*Fax: Admissions ■ TF Admissions: 800-842-1922 ■ Web: www.mwsu.edu					
Northwood University					
Texas 1114 W FM 1382	Cedar Hill	TX	75104	972-291-1541	
TF: 800-927-9663 ■ Web: www.northwood.edu					
Our Lady of the Lake University					
411 SW 24th St	San Antonio	TX	78207	210-434-6711	431-4036*
*Fax: Admissions ■ TF: 800-436-6558 ■ Web: www.ollusa.edu					
Paul Quinn College 3837 Simpson Stuart Rd	Dallas	TX	75241	214-376-1000	
TF: 800-433-3243 ■ Web: www.pqc.edu					
Prairie View A & M University					
PO Box 519	Prairie View	TX	77446	936-857-2626	261-1079*
*Fax: Admissions ■ TF: 877-241-1752 ■ Web: www.pvamu.edu					
Rice University 6100 Main St	Houston	TX	77005	713-348-0000	348-5323*
*Fax: Admissions ■ TF: 866-294-4633 ■ Web: www.rice.edu					
Saint Mary's University					
1 Camino Santa Maria	San Antonio	TX	78228	210-436-3126	
TF Admissions: 800-367-7868 ■ Web: www.stmarytx.edu					
Sam Houston State University					
1903 University Ave	Huntsville	TX	77340	936-294-1111	294-3758*
*Fax: Admissions ■ TF: 866-232-7528 ■ Web: www.shsu.edu					
Schreiner University 2100 Memorial Blvd	Kerrville	TX	78028	830-792-7217	792-7226*
*Fax: Admissions ■ TF: 800-343-4919 ■ Web: www.schreiner.edu					
Southern Methodist University 6425 Boaz Ln	Dallas	TX	75205	214-768-2000	768-0202*
*Fax: Admissions ■ TF: 800-323-0672 ■ Web: www.smu.edu					
Southwestern Adventist University					
100 W Hillcrest Dr PO Box 567	Keene	TX	76059	817-645-3921	
TF Admissions: 888-732-7928 ■ Web: www.swau.edu					
Southwestern Assemblies of God University					
1200 Sycamore St	Waxahachie	TX	75165	972-937-4010	923-0006*
*Fax: Admissions ■ TF: 888-937-7248 ■ Web: www.sagu.edu					
Southwestern Christian College PO Box 10	Terrell	TX	75160	972-524-3341	563-7133
TF: 800-925-9357 ■ Web: www.swcc.edu					
Southwestern University PO Box 770	Georgetown	TX	78627	512-863-1200	863-9601*
*Fax: Admissions ■ TF: 800-252-3166 ■ Web: www.southwestern.edu					
Stephen F Austin State University					
1936 N St PO Box 13051	Nacogdoches	TX	75962	936-468-2504	468-3149*
*Fax: Admissions ■ Web: www.sfasu.edu					
Sul Ross State University E Hwy 90	Alpine	TX	79832	432-837-8011	837-8431*
*Fax: Admissions ■ TF: 888-722-7778 ■ Web: www.sulross.edu					
Tarleton State University					
1333 W Washington PO Box T-0030	Stephenville	TX	76402	254-968-9000	968-9951*
*Fax: Admissions ■ TF: 800-687-8236 ■ Web: www.tarleton.edu					
Texas A & M International University					
5201 University Blvd	Laredo	TX	78041	956-326-2001	326-2199
TF: 888-489-2648 ■ Web: www.tamiu.edu					

Phone Fax

Texas A & M University
Rudder Tower Ste 205 ... College Station TX 77843 979-845-8901 458-4617*
*Fax: Admissions ■ TF: 888-890-5667 ■ Web: www.tamu.edu
Corpus Christi 6300 Ocean Dr. ... Corpus Christi TX 78412 361-825-7024 825-5887*
*Fax: Admissions ■ Web: www.tamucc.edu
Galveston 200 Seawolf Pkwy Bldg 3026 ... Galveston TX 77553 409-740-4428 740-4731
TF: 877-322-4443 ■ Web: www.tamug.edu
Kingsville 700 University Blvd MSC 128 ... Kingsville TX 78363 361-593-2111 593-2195*
*Fax: Admissions ■ TF: 800-726-8192 ■ Web: www.tamuk.edu
Texarkana 7101 University Ave ... Texarkana TX 75503 903-223-3000 223-3140
TF: 866-791-9120 ■ Web: www.tamut.edu
Texas Christian University
TCU PO Box 297043 ... Fort Worth TX 76129 817-257-7490 257-7268
TF: 800-828-3764 ■ Web: www.tcu.edu
Texas College 2404 N Grand Ave ... Tyler TX 75702 903-593-8311
TF: 800-306-6299 ■ Web: www.texascollege.edu
Texas Lutheran University 1000 W Ct St ... Seguin TX 78155 830-372-8050 372-8096
TF: 800-771-8521 ■ Web: www.tlu.edu
Texas Southern University 3100 Cleburne St ... Houston TX 77004 713-313-7011 313-1859
TF: 800-252-5400 ■ Web: www.tsu.edu
Texas State University
San Marcos 601 University Dr ... San Marcos TX 78666 512-245-2340 245-8044*
*Fax: Admissions ■ TF Admissions: 866-294-0987 ■ Web: www.txstate.edu
Texas Tech University PO Box 45005 ... Lubbock TX 79409 806-742-1480 742-0062*
*Fax: Admissions ■ TF: 888-270-3369 ■ Web: www.ttu.edu
Texas Wesleyan University
1201 Wesleyan St ... Fort Worth TX 76105 817-531-4444
TF: 800-580-8980 ■ Web: txwes.edu
Texas Woman's University
304 Admin Dr PO Box 425589 ... Denton TX 76204 940-898-3188 898-3081*
*Fax: Admissions ■ TF: 866-809-6130 ■ Web: www.twu.edu
Trinity University 1 Trinity Pl ... San Antonio TX 78212 210-999-7011 999-8164*
*Fax: Admissions ■ TF: 800-874-6489 ■ Web: www.trinity.edu
University of Dallas 1845 E Northgate Dr ... Irving TX 75062 972-721-5266 721-5017*
*Fax: Admissions ■ TF Admissions: 800-628-6999 ■ Web: www.udallas.edu
University of Houston 4800 Calhoun Rd ... Houston TX 77004 713-743-1000 743-9665
Web: www.uh.edu
Clear Lake 2700 Bay Area Blvd ... Houston TX 77058 281-283-7600 283-2522*
*Fax: Admissions ■ Web: uhcl.edu
Victoria 3007 N Ben Wilson St ... Victoria TX 77901 361-570-4848 570-4114*
*Fax: Admissions ■ TF: 877-970-4848 ■ Web: www.uhv.edu
University of Mary Hardin-Baylor
900 College St PO Box 8004 ... Belton TX 76513 254-295-8642 295-5049*
*Fax: Admissions ■ TF: 800-727-8642 ■ Web: www.umhb.edu
University of North Texas PO Box 311277 ... Denton TX 76203 940-565-2681 565-2408*
*Fax: Admissions ■ TF: 800-868-8211 ■ Web: www.unt.edu
University of Saint Thomas
3800 Montrose Blvd ... Houston TX 77006 713-522-7911 525-3558*
*Fax: Admissions ■ TF: 800-856-8565 ■ Web: www.stthom.edu
University of Texas
Allied Health Sciences School
5323 Harry Hines Blvd ... Dallas TX 75390 214-648-3111 475-7641*
*Fax Area Code: 512
Austin 2400 Inner Campus Dr Mail Bldg Rm 7 ... Austin TX 78712 512-475-7399 475-7399*
*Fax: Admissions ■ Web: www.utexas.edu
Brownsville 80 Fort Brown St ... Brownsville TX 78520 956-882-8200
Web: opportunityequation.org
Dallas 800 W Campbell Rd Ste Be3204 ... Richardson TX 75080 972-883-2111 883-2599
TF: 800-889-2443 ■ Web: www.utdallas.edu
El Paso 500 W University Ave ... El Paso TX 79968 915-747-5000 747-8893*
*Fax: Admissions ■ TF Admissions: 800-551-0294 ■ Web: www.utep.edu
Pan American 1201 W University Dr ... Edinburg TX 78539 956-381-8872 381-2212
TF: 866-441-8872 ■ Web: www.utpa.edu
Permian Basin 4901 E University Blvd ... Odessa TX 79762 432-552-2020 552-3605*
*Fax: Admissions ■ TF Admissions: 866-552-8872 ■ Web: www.utpb.edu
San Antonio 6900 N Loop 1604 W ... San Antonio TX 78249 210-458-4011 458-7716*
*Fax: Admissions ■ TF: 800-669-0919 ■ Web: www.utsa.edu
Tyler 3900 University Blvd ... Tyler TX 75799 903-566-7000 566-7068*
*Fax: Admissions ■ TF: 800-888-9537 ■ Web: www.uttyler.edu
University of Texas Investment Management Co
401 Congress Ave Ste 2800 ... Austin TX 78701 512-225-1600
Web: www.utimco.org
University of the Incarnate Word
4301 Broadway St Ste 285 ... San Antonio TX 78209 210-829-6000 829-3921*
*Fax: Admissions ■ TF Admissions: 800-749-9673 ■ Web: www.uiw.edu
Wayland Baptist University
1900 W Seventh St ... Plainview TX 79072 806-291-1000 291-1973*
*Fax: Admissions ■ TF: 800-588-1928 ■ Web: www.wbu.edu
West Texas A & M University 2501 Fourth Ave ... Canyon TX 79016 806-651-2020 651-5285*
*Fax: Admissions ■ TF: 877-656-2065 ■ Web: www.wtamu.edu
Wiley College 711 Wiley Ave ... Marshall TX 75670 903-927-3300 927-3366*
*Fax: Admissions ■ TF Admissions: 800-658-6889 ■ Web: www.wileyc.edu

Utah

Phone Fax

Brigham Young University 730 E University Pkwy ... Provo UT 84604 801-422-7700
Dixie State University 225 S 700 E ... Saint George UT 84770 435-652-7500 656-4005*
*Fax: Admissions ■ TF: 855-628-8140 ■ Web: dixie.edu
Southern Utah University 351 W Ctr St ... Cedar City UT 84720 435-586-7700 865-8223*
*Fax: Admissions ■ Web: www.suu.edu
Uintah Basin Applied Technology College
1100 E Lagoon St ... Roosevelt UT 84066 435-722-6900
Web: ubatc.edu
University of Utah
201 South 1460 East Rm 250 S ... Salt Lake City UT 84112 801-581-7281
Web: www.utah.edu
Utah State University 1600 Old Main Hill ... Logan UT 84322 435-797-1116 797-1110
TF: 800-488-8108 ■ Web: www.usu.edu
Weber State University 3848 Harrison Blvd ... Ogden UT 84408 801-626-6000 626-6747
TF: 800-848-7770 ■ Web: www.weber.edu
Davis 2750 N University Pk Blvd ... Layton UT 84041 801-395-3473 395-3538*
*Fax: Admissions ■ TF: 800-848-7770 ■ Web: www.weber.edu

Phone Fax

Westminster College
1840 South 1300 East ... Salt Lake City UT 84105 801-832-2200 832-3101*
*Fax: Admissions ■ TF: 800-748-4753 ■ Web: www.westminstercollege.edu

Vermont

Phone Fax

Bennington College 1 College Dr ... Bennington VT 05201 802-442-5401 447-4269
TF: 800-833-6845 ■ Web: www.bennington.edu
Burlington College 351 N Ave ... Burlington VT 05401 800-862-9616 660-4331*
*Fax Area Code: 802 ■ TF: 800-862-9616 ■ Web: www.burlington.edu
Castleton State College 86 Seminary St ... Castleton VT 05735 802-468-5611 468-1476*
*Fax: Admissions ■ TF: 800-639-8521 ■ Web: www.csc.vsc.edu
Champlain College 163 S Willard St ... Burlington VT 05401 802-860-2700 860-2767
TF: 800-570-5858 ■ Web: www.champlain.edu
College of Saint Joseph in Vermont
71 Clement Rd ... Rutland VT 05701 802-773-5900
TF Admissions: 877-270-9998 ■ Web: www.csj.edu
Goddard College 123 Pitkin Rd ... Plainfield VT 05667 802-454-8311 454-1029*
*Fax: Admissions ■ TF: 800-468-4888 ■ Web: goddard.edu
Green Mountain College 1 Brennan Cir ... Poultney VT 05764 802-287-8000 287-8099
TF Admissions: 800-776-6675 ■ Web: www.greenmtn.edu
Johnson State College 337 College Hill ... Johnson VT 05656 802-635-2356 635-1230
TF: 800-635-2356 ■ Web: www.jsc.edu
Lyndon State College
1001 College Rd PO Box 919 ... Lyndonville VT 05851 802-626-6413 626-6335
TF: 800-225-1998 ■ Web: www.lyndonstate.edu
Marlboro College 2582 S Rd PO Box A ... Marlboro VT 05344 802-257-4333 451-7555
TF: 800-343-0049 ■ Web: www.marlboro.edu
Marlboro College Graduate Center
PO Box A PO Box A ... Marlboro VT 05344 802-258-9200
Web: www.marlboro.edu
Middlebury College 131 S Main St ... Middlebury VT 05753 802-443-3000 443-2056*
*Fax: Admissions ■ TF: 877-214-3330 ■ Web: www.middlebury.edu
Norwich University 158 Harmon Dr ... Northfield VT 05663 802-485-2001 485-2032
TF: 800-468-6679 ■ Web: www.norwich.edu
Saint Michael's College 1 Winooski Pk ... Colchester VT 05439 802-654-2000 654-2906
TF: 800-762-8000 ■ Web: www.smcvt.edu
School for International Training
1 Kipling Rd ... Brattleboro VT 05302 802-257-7751
Web: www.sit.edu
Southern Vermont College 982 Manison Dr ... Bennington VT 05201 802-442-5427 447-4695*
*Fax: Admissions ■ TF: 800-378-2782 ■ Web: www.svc.edu
University of Vermont 85 S Prospect St ... Burlington VT 05405 802-656-3131 656-8611
TF: 800-499-0113 ■ Web: www.uvm.edu

Virginia

Phone Fax

Bluefield College 3000 College Dr ... Bluefield VA 24605 276-326-3682 326-4395*
*Fax: Admissions ■ TF: 800-872-0175 ■ Web: www.bluefield.edu
Bridgewater College 402 E College St ... Bridgewater VA 22812 540-828-5375 828-5481
TF: 800-759-8328 ■ Web: www.bridgewater.edu
Christendom College 134 Christendom Dr ... Front Royal VA 22630 540-636-2900 636-1655*
*Fax: Admissions ■ TF: 800-877-5456 ■ Web: www.christendom.edu
Christopher Newport University
1 University Pl ... Newport News VA 23606 757-594-7015 594-7333*
*Fax: Admissions ■ TF Admissions: 800-333-4268 ■ Web: www.cnu.edu
College of William & Mary PO Box 8795 ... Williamsburg VA 23187 757-221-4000 221-1242*
*Fax: Admissions ■ Web: www.wm.edu
Eastern Mennonite University 1200 Pk Rd ... Harrisonburg VA 22802 540-432-4118 432-4444*
*Fax: Admissions ■ TF Admissions: 800-368-2665 ■ Web: www.emu.edu
Emory & Henry College PO Box 10 ... Emory VA 24327 276-944-4121 944-6935*
*Fax: Admissions ■ TF Admissions: 800-848-5493 ■ Web: www.ehc.edu
Ferrum College 215 Ferrum Mtn Rd ... Ferrum VA 24088 540-365-2121 365-4266
TF: 800-868-9797 ■ Web: www.ferrum.edu
George Mason University 4400 University Dr ... Fairfax VA 22030 703-993-1000 993-2392
TF: 888-627-6612 ■ Web: www.gmu.edu
Hampden-Sydney College PO Box 667 ... Hampden Sydney VA 23943 434-223-6120 223-6120*
*Fax: Admissions ■ TF Admissions: 800-755-0733 ■ Web: www.hsc.edu
Hampton University 100 E Queen St ... Hampton VA 23668 757-727-5000
TF: 800-624-3341 ■ Web: www.hamptonu.edu
Hollins University PO BOX 9707 ... Roanoke VA 24020 540-362-6401 362-6218*
*Fax: Admissions ■ TF Admissions: 800-456-9595 ■ Web: www.hollins.edu
James Madison University 800 S Main St ... Harrisonburg VA 22807 540-568-6211 568-3332*
*Fax: Admissions ■ Web: www.jmu.edu
Liberty University 1971 University Blvd ... Lynchburg VA 24502 434-582-2000 542-2311*
*Fax Area Code: 800 ■ *Fax: Admissions ■ TF: 800-543-5317 ■ Web: www.liberty.edu
Longwood University 201 High St ... Farmville VA 23909 434-395-2060 395-2332*
*Fax: Admissions ■ TF: 800-281-4677 ■ Web: www.longwood.edu
Lynchburg College 1501 Lakeside Dr ... Lynchburg VA 24501 434-544-8100 544-8653*
*Fax: Admissions ■ TF: 800-426-8101 ■ Web: www.lynchburg.edu
Mary Baldwin College
318 Prospect St PO Box 1500 ... Staunton VA 24401 540-887-7019 887-7292*
*Fax: Admissions ■ TF Admissions: 800-468-2262 ■ Web: www.mbc.edu
Marymount University 2807 N Glebe Rd ... Arlington VA 22207 703-522-5600 522-0349
TF: 800-548-7638 ■ Web: www.marymount.edu
Norfolk State University 700 Pk Ave ... Norfolk VA 23504 757-823-8600 823-2078*
*Fax: Admissions ■ TF: 800-274-1821 ■ Web: www.nsu.edu
Old Dominion University Rollins Hall ... Norfolk VA 23529 757-683-3685 683-3255*
*Fax: Admissions ■ TF: 800-348-7926 ■ Web: www.odu.edu
Peace Operations Training Institute Inc
1309 Jamestown Rd Ste 202 ... Williamsburg VA 23185 757-253-6933
Web: peaceopstraining.org
Radford University 801 E Main St ... Radford VA 24142 540-831-5371 831-5038*
*Fax: Admissions ■ TF Admissions: 800-890-4265 ■ Web: www.radford.edu
Randolph College 2500 Rivermont Ave ... Lynchburg VA 24503 434-947-8000 947-8996*
*Fax: Admissions ■ TF Admissions: 800-745-7692 ■ Web: www.randolphcollege.edu
Randolph-Macon College PO Box 5005 ... Ashland VA 23005 804-752-7200 752-4707*
*Fax: Admissions ■ TF: 800-888-1762 ■ Web: www.rmc.edu
Roanoke College 221 College Ln ... Salem VA 24153 540-375-2270 375-2267*
*Fax: Admissions ■ TF Admissions: 800-388-2276 ■ Web: www.roanoke.edu

Phone Fax

Saint Paul's College 115 College Dr. Lawrenceville VA 23868 434-848-3111 848-6407*

Shenandoah University 1460 University Dr. Winchester VA 22601 540-665-4581
TF: 800-432-2266 ■ *Web:* www.su.edu

Southern Virginia University
1 University Hill Dr. Buena Vista VA 24416 540-261-8400 261-8559
TF: 800-229-8420 ■ *Web:* www.svu.edu

Strayer University Alexandria
2730 Eisenhower Ave. Alexandria VA 22314 888-311-0355
TF: 888-311-0355 ■ *Web:* www.strayer.edu

Strayer University Arlington
2121 15th St N. Arlington VA 22201 703-892-5100 769-2677*
**Fax:* Admissions ■ *TF:* 888-478-7293 ■ *Web:* www.strayer.edu

Strayer University Fredericksburg
150 Riverside Pkwy Ste 100. Fredericksburg VA 22406 540-374-4300 301-1711*
**Fax:* Admissions ■ *TF:* 888-311-0355 ■ *Web:* www.strayer.edu

Strayer University Loudoun
45150 Russell Branch Pkwy Ste 200. Ashburn VA 20147 703-729-8800
Web: www.strayer.edu

Strayer University Manassas
9990 Battleview Pkwy. Manassas VA 20109 703-330-8400
Web: www.strayer.edu

Strayer University Woodbridge
13385 Minnieville Rd. Woodbridge VA 22192 703-878-2800
Web: www.strayer.edu

Sweet Briar College 134 Chappel Rd. Sweet Briar VA 24595 434-381-6100 381-6152*
**Fax:* Admissions ■ *TF Admissions:* 800-381-6142 ■ *Web:* www.sbc.edu

Swvhec PO Box 1987. Abingdon VA 24212 276-619-4302
Web: www.swcenter.edu

Tabernacle Baptist Bible College & Theological Seminary
717 N Whitehurst Landing Rd. Virginia Beach VA 23464 757-424-4673
Web: www.tbbcs.org

University of Mary Washington
1301 College Ave. Fredericksburg VA 22401 540-654-2000 654-1857*
**Fax:* Admissions ■ *TF Admissions:* 800-468-5614 ■ *Web:* www.umw.edu

University of Richmond 28 Westhampton Way. Richmond VA 23173 804-289-8000 287-6003
TF: 800-700-1662 ■ *Web:* www.richmond.edu
Westhampton College
28 Westhampton Way. University Of Richmond VA 23173 804-289-8000
TF: 800-700-1662 ■ *Web:* wc.richmond.edu

University of Virginia
Peabody Hall PO Box 400160. Charlottesville VA 22903 434-982-3200 924-3587*
**Fax:* Admissions ■ *Web:* www.virginia.edu

University of Virginia's College at Wise
1 College Ave. Wise VA 24293 276-328-0102
TF Admissions: 888-282-9324 ■ *Web:* www.uvawise.edu

Virginia Commonwealth University
910 W Franklin St. Richmond VA 23284 804-828-0100 828-1899
TF: 800-841-3638 ■ *Web:* www.vcu.edu

Virginia Intermont College 1013 Moore St. Bristol VA 24201 276-669-6101
TF: 800-451-1842 ■ *Web:* www.vic.edu

Virginia Military Institute
319 Letcher Ave. Lexington VA 24450 540-464-7211 464-7746*
**Fax:* Admissions ■ *TF:* 800-767-4207 ■ *Web:* www.vmi.edu

Virginia Polytechnic Institute & State University
112 Burruss Hall. Blacksburg VA 24061 540-231-6000 231-3242*
**Fax:* Admissions ■ *Web:* www.vt.edu

Virginia State University 1 Hayden Dr. Petersburg VA 23806 804-524-5000 524-5055
TF Admissions: 800-871-7611 ■ *Web:* www.vsu.edu

Virginia Union University
1500 N Lombardy St. Richmond VA 23220 804-342-3570 342-3511*
**Fax:* Admissions ■ *TF:* 800-368-3227 ■ *Web:* www.vuu.edu

Virginia University of Lynchburg - Community Development Corp
2058 Garfield Ave. Lynchburg VA 24501 434-528-5276
Web: vul.edu

Virginia Wesleyan College 1584 Wesleyan Dr. Norfolk VA 23502 757-455-3200 461-5238*
**Fax:* Admissions ■ *TF:* 800-737-8684 ■ *Web:* www.vwc.edu

Washington & Lee University
204 W Washington St. Lexington VA 24450 540-458-8710 458-8062*
**Fax:* Admissions ■ *TF:* 800-221-3943 ■ *Web:* www.wlu.edu

Weldon Cooper Ctr-Public Service
2400 Old Ivy Rd. Charlottesville VA 22903 434-982-5522
Web: www.coopercenter.org

Zamorano 9300 Lee Hwy Ste G130. Fairfax VA 22031 202-737-5580
Web: www.zamorano.edu

Washington

Phone Fax

Antioch University 2326 Sixth Ave. Seattle WA 98121 206-441-5352 268-4242
TF: 888-268-4477 ■ *Web:* www.antiochsea.edu

Central Washington University
400 E University Way. Ellensburg WA 98926 509-963-1111 963-3022*
**Fax:* Admissions ■ *TF Admissions:* 866-298-4968 ■ *Web:* www.cwu.edu

City University 11900 NE First St. Bellevue WA 98005 425-637-1010
TF Admissions: 800-426-5596 ■ *Web:* www.cityu.edu

Digipen Institute of Technology
5001 150th Ave Ne. Redmond WA 98052 425-558-0299
TF: 866-478-5236 ■ *Web:* www.digipen.edu

Eastern Washington University 526 Fifth St. Cheney WA 99004 509-359-6200 359-6692*
**Fax:* Admissions ■ *Web:* www.ewu.edu

Evergreen State College 2700 Evergreen Pkwy. Olympia WA 98505 360-867-6000 867-5114
TF: 888-492-9480 ■ *Web:* www.evergreen.edu

Gonzaga University 502 E Boone Ave. Spokane WA 99258 509-323-6572 323-5780*
**Fax:* Admissions ■ *TF:* 800-986-9585 ■ *Web:* www.gonzaga.edu

Heritage University 3240 Ft Rd. Toppenish WA 98948 509-865-8500 865-8659*
**Fax:* Admissions ■ *TF:* 888-272-6190 ■ *Web:* www.heritage.edu

Northwest University 5520 108th Ave NE. Kirkland WA 98033 425-822-8266 889-5224*
**Fax:* Admissions ■ *TF Admissions:* 800-669-3781 ■ *Web:* www.northwestu.edu

Pacific Lutheran University 1010 122nd St S. Tacoma WA 98444 253-531-6900
TF: 800-274-6758 ■ *Web:* www.plu.edu

Saint Martin's University 5300 Pacific Ave SE. Lacey WA 98503 360-438-4311 412-6189*
**Fax:* Admissions ■ *TF Admissions:* 800-368-8803 ■ *Web:* www.stmartin.edu

Seattle Pacific University 3307 Third Ave W. Seattle WA 98119 206-281-2000 281-2544*
**Fax:* Admissions ■ *TF:* 800-366-3344 ■ *Web:* www.spu.edu

Seattle University 901 12th Ave. Seattle WA 98122 206-296-6000 296-5656*
**Fax:* Admissions ■ *TF:* 800-426-7123 ■ *Web:* www.seattleu.edu

University of Puget Sound 1500 N Warner St. Tacoma WA 98416 253-879-3100
TF: 800-396-7191 ■ *Web:* www.pugetsound.edu

University of Washington 1410 NE Campus Pkwy. Seattle WA 98195 206-543-2100 685-3655*
**Fax:* Admissions ■ *Web:* www.washington.edu

Walla Walla University
204 S College Ave. College Place WA 99324 509-527-2327 527-2397
TF: 800-541-8900 ■ *Web:* www.wallawalla.edu

Washington State University PO Box 641040. Pullman WA 99164 509-335-3564 335-4902
TF: 888-468-6978 ■ *Web:* www.wsu.edu
Spokane 310 N Riverpoint Blvd PO Box 1495. Spokane WA 99210 509-358-7978 358-7538
TF: 800-233-3247 ■ *Web:* spokane.wsu.edu
Vancouver 14204 NE Salmon Creek Ave. Vancouver WA 98686 360-546-9788
Web: www.vancouver.wsu.edu

Western Washington University 516 High St. Bellingham WA 98225 360-650-3000 650-7369
Web: www.wwu.edu

Whitman College 345 Boyer Ave. Walla Walla WA 99362 509-527-5111 527-4967*
**Fax:* Admissions ■ *TF Admissions:* 877-462-9448 ■ *Web:* www.whitman.edu

Whitworth College 300 W Hawthorne Rd. Spokane WA 99251 509-777-1000 777-3758*
**Fax:* Admissions ■ *TF Admissions:* 800-533-4668 ■ *Web:* www.whitworth.edu

West Virginia

Phone Fax

Alderson-Broaddus College
101 College Hill Rd. Philippi WV 26416 304-457-1700 457-6239*
**Fax:* Admissions ■ *TF Admissions:* 800-263-1549 ■ *Web:* www.ab.edu

Bethany College 31 E Campus Dr. Bethany WV 26032 304-829-7000 829-7142*
**Fax:* Admissions ■ *TF:* 800-922-7611 ■ *Web:* www.bethanywv.edu

Bluefield State College 219 Rock St. Bluefield WV 24701 304-327-4000 325-7747*
**Fax:* Admissions ■ *TF:* 800-654-7798 ■ *Web:* bluefieldstate.edu

Concord University PO Box 1000. Athens WV 24712 304-384-3115 384-3218*
**Fax:* Admissions ■ *TF:* 800-344-6679 ■ *Web:* www.concord.edu

Davis & Elkins College 100 Campus Dr. Elkins WV 26241 304-637-1900 637-1800*
**Fax:* Admissions ■ *TF:* 800-624-3157 ■ *Web:* dewv.edu

Fairmont State University 1201 Locust Ave. Fairmont WV 26554 304-367-4892 367-4789*
**Fax:* Admissions ■ *TF Admissions:* 800-641-5678 ■ *Web:* www.fairmontstate.edu

Glenville State College 200 High St. Glenville WV 26351 304-462-7361 462-8619*
**Fax:* Admissions ■ *TF Admissions:* 800-924-2010 ■ *Web:* www.glenville.edu

Marshall University 1 John Marshall Dr. Huntington WV 25755 304-696-3170 696-3135*
**Fax:* Admissions ■ *TF:* 800-642-3463 ■ *Web:* www.marshall.edu

Ohio Valley University 1 Campus View Dr. Vienna WV 26105 304-865-6000

Salem International University 223 W Main St. Salem WV 26426 304-326-1109
TF: 800-283-4562 ■ *Web:* www.salemu.edu

Shepherd University 301 N King St. Shepherdstown WV 25443 304-876-5000 876-5165*
**Fax:* Admissions ■ *TF:* 800-344-5231 ■ *Web:* www.shepherd.edu

University of Charleston
2300 MacCorkle Ave SE. Charleston WV 25304 304-357-4800 357-4715*
**Fax:* Admissions ■ *TF Admissions:* 800-995-4682 ■ *Web:* www.ucwv.edu

West Virginia State University
117 Ferrell Hall PO Box 368. Institute WV 25112 304-766-3000
TF: 800-987-2112 ■ *Web:* www.wvstateu.edu

West Virginia University PO Box 6009. Morgantown WV 26506 304-293-2121 293-3080
TF: 800-344-9881 ■ *Web:* www.wvu.edu
Institute of Technology 405 Fayette Pk. Montgomery WV 25136 304-442-1000
TF: 888-554-8324 ■ *Web:* www.wvutech.edu

West Virginia Wesleyan College
59 College Ave. Buckhannon WV 26201 304-473-8000 473-8108*
**Fax:* Admissions ■ *TF Admitting:* 800-722-9933 ■ *Web:* www.wvwc.edu

Wheeling Jesuit University
316 Washington Ave. Wheeling WV 26003 304-243-2000 243-2397*
**Fax:* Admissions ■ *TF:* 800-624-6992 ■ *Web:* www.wju.edu

Wisconsin

Phone Fax

Alverno College PO Box 343922. Milwaukee WI 53234 414-382-6100
TF: 800-933-3401 ■ *Web:* www.alverno.edu

Bellin College of Nursing 3201 Eaton Rd. Green Bay WI 54311 920-433-6699 433-1922
TF: 800-236-8707 ■ *Web:* www.bellincollege.edu

Beloit College 700 College St. Beloit WI 53511 608-363-2500 363-2075*
**Fax:* Admissions ■ *TF Admissions:* 800-331-4943 ■ *Web:* www.beloit.edu

Cardinal Stritch University
6801 N Yates Rd. Milwaukee WI 53217 414-410-4000
TF: 800-347-8822 ■ *Web:* www.stritch.edu

Carroll University 100 NE Ave. Waukesha WI 53186 262-547-1211 951-3037*
**Fax:* Admissions ■ *TF:* 800-227-7655 ■ *Web:* www.carrollu.edu

Carthage College 2001 Alford Pk Dr. Kenosha WI 53140 262-551-8500 551-5762*
**Fax:* Admissions ■ *TF Admissions:* 800-351-4058 ■ *Web:* www.carthage.edu

Columbia College of Nursing (CCON)
4425 N Port Washington Rd. Glendale WI 53212 414-326-2330 326-2331
TF: 800-221-5573 ■ *Web:* www.ccon.edu

Concordia University Wisconsin
12800 N Lake Shore Dr. Mequon WI 53097 262-243-5700 243-4545*
**Fax:* Admissions ■ *TF Admissions:* 888-628-9472 ■ *Web:* www.cuw.edu

Edgewood College 1000 Edgewood College Dr. Madison WI 53711 608-663-2294 663-2214
TF: 800-444-4861 ■ *Web:* www.edgewood.edu

Immanuel Lutheran College Inc
501 Grover Rd. Eau Claire WI 54701 715-836-6636
Web: ilc.edu

Lakeland College PO Box 359. Sheboygan WI 53082 920-565-2111 565-1215*
**Fax:* Admissions ■ *TF:* 800-569-2166 ■ *Web:* www.lakeland.edu

Lawrence University 115 S Drew St. Appleton WI 54911 920-832-7000 832-6782
TF: 800-432-5427 ■ *Web:* www.lawrence.edu

Maranatha Baptist Bible College
745 W Main St. Watertown WI 53094 920-206-2330 261-9109*
**Fax:* Admissions ■ *TF:* 800-622-2947 ■ *Web:* mbu.edu

Marian University 45 S National Ave. Fond du Lac WI 54935 800-262-7426 923-8087*
**Fax Area Code:* 920 ■ *TF:* 800-262-7426 ■ *Web:* www.marianuniversity.edu

Marquette University 1217 W Wisconsin Ave. Milwaukee WI 53233 414-288-7302 288-3764*
**Fax:* Admissions ■ *TF Admissions:* 800-222-6544 ■ *Web:* www.marquette.edu

	Phone	Fax
Milwaukee Institute of Art & Design 273 E Erie St....Milwaukee WI 53202 *Fax: Admissions ■ TF: 888-749-6423 ■ Web: www.miad.edu	414-276-7889	291-8077*
Milwaukee School of Engineering 1025 N Broadway St....Milwaukee WI 53202 *Fax: Admissions ■ TF: 800-332-6763 ■ Web: www.msoe.edu	414-277-6763	277-7475*
Mount Mary College 2900 N Menomonee River Pkwy....Milwaukee WI 53222 *Fax: Admissions ■ TF Admissions: 800-321-6265 ■ Web: www.mtmary.edu	414-256-1219	256-0180*
Northland Baptist Bible College (NBBC) W10085 Pike Plains Rd....Dunbar WI 54119 Web: www.ni.edu	715-324-6900	
Northland College 1411 Ellis Ave....Ashland WI 54806 TF: 800-753-1840 ■ Web: www.northland.edu	715-682-1224	
Ripon College 300 Seward St PO Box 248....Ripon WI 54971 *Fax Area Code: 920 ■ *Fax: Admissions ■ TF Admissions: 800-947-4766 ■ Web: www.ripon.edu	800-947-4766	748-8335*
Saint Norbert College 100 Grant St....De Pere WI 54115 *Fax: Admissions ■ TF Admissions: 800-236-4878 ■ Web: www.snc.edu	920-403-3005	403-4072*
Silver Lake College 2406 S Alverno Rd....Manitowoc WI 54220 *Fax: Admissions ■ TF: 800-236-4752 ■ Web: www.sl.edu	920-686-6175	684-7082*
University of Wisconsin		
Baraboo/Sauk County 1006 Connie Rd....Baraboo WI 53913 *Fax: Admissions ■ TF: 800-621-7440 ■ Web: www.baraboo.uwc.edu	608-355-5200	355-5291*
Eau Claire 105 Garfield Ave PO Box 4004....Eau Claire WI 54701 *Fax: Admissions ■ TF: 800-473-2255 ■ Web: www.uwec.edu	715-836-2637	836-2409*
Green Bay 2420 Nicolet Dr....Green Bay WI 54311 *Fax: Admissions ■ TF: 800-465-4329 ■ Web: www.uwgb.edu	920-465-2000	465-5754*
La Crosse 1725 State St 115 Graff Main Hall....La Crosse WI 54601 TF: 800-382-2150 ■ Web: www.uwlax.edu	608-785-8000	785-6695
Madison 702 W Johnson St Ste 1101....Madison WI 53715 *Fax: Admissions ■ Web: www.wisc.edu	608-262-3961	262-7706*
Milwaukee PO Box 413....Milwaukee WI 53201 *Fax: Admissions ■ Web: www.uwm.edu	414-229-1122	229-6940*
Oshkosh 800 Algoma Blvd PO Box 2423....Oshkosh WI 54903 *Fax: Admissions ■ Web: www.uwosh.edu	920-424-0202	424-1207*
Parkside 900 Wood Rd....Kenosha WI 53141 *Fax: Admissions ■ Web: www.uwp.edu	262-595-2345	595-2008*
Platteville 1 University Plz....Platteville WI 53818 *Fax: Admissions ■ TF: 800-362-5515 ■ Web: www.uwplatt.edu	608-342-1125	342-1122*
River Falls 410 S Third St B3 E Hathorn Hall....River Falls WI 54022 TF: 800-852-5711 ■ Web: www.uwrf.edu	715-425-3911	425-0698
Stevens Point 2100 Main St....Stevens Point WI 54481 *Fax: Admissions ■ Web: www.uwsp.edu	715-346-0123	346-3296*
Stout 802 S Broadway....Menomonie WI 54751 *Fax: Admissions ■ TF Admissions: 800-447-8688 ■ Web: www.uwstout.edu	715-232-1232	232-1667*
Superior Belknap & Catlin PO Box 2000....Superior WI 54880 TF: 800-869-5088 ■ Web: www.uwsuper.edu	715-394-8101	394-8407
Whitewater 800 W Main St....Whitewater WI 53190 *Fax: Admissions ■ Web: www.uww.edu	262-472-1440	472-1515*
Viterbo University 900 Viterbo Dr....La Crosse WI 54601 *Fax: Admissions ■ TF: 800-848-3726 ■ Web: www.viterbo.edu	608-796-3000	796-3020*
Wisconsin Lutheran College 8800 W Bluemound Rd....Milwaukee WI 53226 *Fax: Admissions ■ Web: www.wlc.edu	414-443-8800	443-8514*

Wyoming

	Phone	Fax
University of Wyoming 1000 E University Ave Dept 3435....Laramie WY 82071 *Fax: Admissions ■ TF Admissions: 800-342-5996 ■ Web: www.uwyo.edu	307-766-5160	766-4042*

167 COLLEGES & UNIVERSITIES - GRADUATE &

	Phone	Fax
American Public University System (AMU) 111 W Congress St....Charles Town WV 25414 TF: 877-777-9081 ■ Web: www.amu.apus.edu	304-724-3700	
Cegep De Matane 25 Rte Du Parc....Sainte-anne-des-monts QC G4V2B9 Web: www.cegep-matane.qc.ca	418-763-7761	
College of Family Physicians of Canada The 2630 Skymark Ave....Mississauga ON L4W5A4 Web: www.cfpc.ca	905-629-0900	
Kern Community College District 2100 Chester Ave....Bakersfield CA 93301 Web: www.kccd.edu	661-336-5100	
Mirick O'Connell Demaillie & Lougee LLP 1700 Bank of Boston Tower 100 Frnt....Worcester MA 01608 Web: www.mirickoconnell.com	508-799-0541	
Trios College Business Technology Healthcare - London Campus 520 First St....London ON N5V3C6 Web: www.secondcareerontario.com	519-455-0551	

167-1 Law Schools

Law schools listed here are approved by the American Bar Association.

	Phone	Fax
Albany Law School of Union University (ALS) 80 New Scotland Ave....Albany NY 12208 TF: 800-448-3500 ■ Web: www.albanylaw.edu	518-445-2311	445-2369
American University Washington College of Law 4801 Massachusetts Ave NW....Washington DC 20016 TF: 800-995-6423 ■ Web: www.wcl.american.edu	202-274-4101	274-4107
Appalachian School of Law 1169 Edgewater Dr....Grundy VA 24614 TF: 800-895-7411 ■ Web: www.asl.edu	276-935-4349	935-8261
Sandra Day O'Connor College of Law PO Box 877906....Tempe AZ 85287 TF: 855-278-5080 ■ Web: www.law.asu.edu	480-965-6181	727-7930
Ave Maria University School of Law 1025 Commons Cir....Naples FL 34119 Web: www.avemarialaw.edu	239-687-5300	
Barry University Dwayne O Andreas School of Law 6441 E Colonial Dr....Orlando FL 32807 TF: 800-756-6000 ■ Web: www.barry.edu	321-206-5600	
Baylor University School of Law 1114 S University Parks Dr 1 Bear Pl 97288....Waco TX 76798 TF: 800-229-5678 ■ Web: baylor.edu	254-710-1911	710-2316
Benjamin N Cardozo School of Law Yeshiva University 55 Fifth Ave Brookdale Ctr....New York NY 10003 TF: 800-232-5463 ■ Web: www.cardozo.yu.edu	212-790-0200	790-0256
Boston College Law School 885 Centre St....Newton MA 02459 TF: 800-321-2211 ■ Web: www.bc.edu	617-552-8550	552-2615
Boston University School of Law 765 Commonwealth Ave....Boston MA 02215 TF: 800-321-2211 ■ Web: www.bu.edu/law	617-353-3100	353-0578
Brooklyn Law School 250 Joralemon St....Brooklyn NY 11201 *Fax: Admissions ■ Web: www.brooklaw.edu	718-780-7906	780-0395*
California Western School of Law 225 Cedar St....San Diego CA 92101 TF: 800-255-4252 ■ Web: www.cwsl.edu	619-239-0391	
Campbell University Norman Adrian Wiggins School of Law 113 Main St....Buies Creek NC 27506 *Fax Area Code: 910 ■ TF: 800-334-4111 ■ Web: www.law.campbell.edu	919-865-5991	893-1780*
Capital University Law School 303 E Broad St....Columbus OH 43215 TF: 800-362-2779 ■ Web: www.law.capital.edu	614-236-6500	236-6972
Case Western Reserve University School of Law 11075 E Blvd....Cleveland OH 44106 *Fax: Admissions ■ TF: 800-756-0036 ■ Web: law.case.edu	216-368-3600	368-1042*
Catholic University of America Columbus School of Law 3600 John McCormack Rd NE....Washington DC 20064 Web: www.law.edu	202-319-5140	319-4459
Chicago-Kent College of Law Illinois Institute of Technology 565 W Adams St....Chicago IL 60661 Web: www.kentlaw.iit.edu	312-906-5000	906-5280
City University of New York School of Law 65-21 Main St....Flushing NY 11367 *Fax: Admissions ■ Web: www.law.cuny.edu	718-340-4200	340-4435*
Cleveland State University Cleveland-Marshall College of Law 1801 Euclid Ave LB 138....Cleveland OH 44115 TF: 866-687-2304 ■ Web: www.law.csuohio.edu	216-687-2344	687-6881
Columbia University School of Law 435 W 116th St....New York NY 10027 Web: www.law.columbia.edu	212-854-2640	854-1109
Cornell Law School 226 Myron Taylor Hall....Ithaca NY 14853 Web: www.lawschool.cornell.edu	607-255-5141	255-7193
DePaul University College of Law 25 E Jackson Blvd....Chicago IL 60604 *Fax: Admissions ■ TF: 800-445-8667 ■ Web: www.law.depaul.edu	312-362-8701	362-5280*
Drake University School of Law 2507 University Ave....Des Moines IA 50311 TF: 800-443-7253 ■ Web: www.law.drake.edu	515-271-2824	271-1958
Duke University School of Law 201 Science Dr PO Box 90362....Durham NC 27708 TF: 888-529-2586 ■ Web: www.law.duke.edu	919-613-7006	
Emory University School of Law 1301 Clifton Rd....Atlanta GA 30322 *Fax: Admissions ■ Web: www.law.emory.edu	404-727-6816	727-6802*
Florida Coastal School of Law 8787 Bay Pine Rd....Jacksonville FL 32256 *Fax: Admissions ■ TF: 877-210-2591 ■ Web: www.fcsl.edu	904-680-7700	680-7692*
Florida State University College of Law 425 W Jefferson St....Tallahassee FL 32306 Web: www.law.fsu.edu	850-644-3400	644-5487
Fordham University School of Law 140 W 62nd St....New York NY 10023 *Fax: Admissions ■ Web: www.law.fordham.edu	212-636-6810	636-7984*
George Mason University School of Law 3301 N Fairfax Dr....Arlington VA 22201 Web: www.law.gmu.edu	703-993-8000	993-8088
George Washington University Law School 2000 H St NW....Washington DC 20052 *Fax: Admissions ■ Web: www.law.gwu.edu	202-994-6261	994-7230*
Georgetown University Law Ctr 600 New Jersey Ave NW....Washington DC 20001 *Fax: Admissions ■ Web: www.law.georgetown.edu	202-662-9000	662-9439*
Georgia State University College of Law 140 Decatur St....Atlanta GA 30303 *Fax: Admissions ■ Web: www.law.gsu.edu	404-651-2048	651-1244*
Golden Gate University School of Law 536 Mission St....San Francisco CA 94105 TF: 800-448-4968 ■ Web: law.ggu.edu	415-442-6600	442-6609
Gonzaga University School of Law 721 N Cincinnati St PO Box 3528....Spokane WA 99220 TF Admissions: 800-793-1710 ■ Web: www.law.gonzaga.edu	509-313-3700	
Howard University School of Law 2900 Van Ness St NW....Washington DC 20008 *Fax: Admissions ■ TF: 800-829-9019 ■ Web: www.law.howard.edu	202-806-8000	806-8162*
Indiana University School of Law Bloomington 211 S Indiana Ave....Bloomington IN 47405 Web: www.law.indiana.edu	812-855-7995	855-0555
Indiana University School of Law Indianapolis Lawrence W Inlow Hall 530 W New York St....Indianapolis IN 46202 Web: mckinneylaw.iu.edu	317-274-8523	274-3955
John Marshall Law School 315 S Plymouth Ct....Chicago IL 60604 TF: 800-285-2221 ■ Web: www.jmls.edu	312-427-2737	
Lewis & Clark Law School 10015 SW Terwilliger Blvd....Portland OR 97219 *Fax: Admissions ■ Web: www.lclark.edu	503-768-6600	768-6793*
Louis D Brandeis School of Law at the Univeristy of Louisville 2301 S Third St....Louisville KY 40208 Web: louisville.edu/law	502-852-6358	852-0862

	City	State	ZIP	Phone	Fax
Louisiana State University Paul M Hebert Law Ctr					
Paul M Hebert Law Ctr	Baton Rouge	LA	70803	225-578-8646	578-8647
Web: www.law.lsu.edu					
Loyola Marymount Law School					
919 Albany St	Los Angeles	CA	90015	213-736-1000	736-6523
Web: www.lls.edu					
Loyola University Chicago					
Cudahy Library 1032 W Sheridan Rd	Chicago	IL	60660	773-508-2632	
Web: libraries.luc.edu/cudahy					
School of Law 25 E Pearson St	Chicago	IL	60611	312-915-7120	915-7201
TF: 866-596-7890 ■ *Web:* www.luc.edu					
Loyola University New Orleans College of Law					
7214 St Charles Ave PO Box 901	New Orleans	LA	70118	504-861-5550	
Web: www.law.loyno.edu					
Marquette University Law School					
1215 W Michigan St	Milwaukee	WI	53233	414-288-7090	288-6403
Web: www.law.marquette.edu					
Michigan State University College of Law					
368 Law College Bldg	East Lansing	MI	48824	517-432-6810	432-0098*
**Fax:* Admissions ■ *TF:* 800-844-9352 ■ *Web:* www.law.msu.edu					
Mississippi College School of Law					
151 E Griffith St	Jackson	MS	39201	601-925-7100	925-7166*
**Fax:* Admissions ■ *Web:* www.law.mc.edu					
New England School of Law 154 Stuart St	Boston	MA	02116	617-451-0010	
Web: www.nesl.edu					
New York Law School 185 W Broadway	New York	NY	10013	212-431-2100	966-1522
TF: 877-937-6957 ■ *Web:* www.nyls.edu					
New York University School of Law					
110 W Third St	New York	NY	10012	212-998-6100	995-4527*
**Fax:* Admissions ■ *TF:* 800-522-0925 ■ *Web:* www.law.nyu.edu					
Northeastern University School of Law					
400 Huntington Ave	Boston	MA	02115	617-373-2395	373-8865
TF: 800-732-3400 ■ *Web:* www.northeastern.edu/law					
Northern Illinois University College of Law					
Swen Parson Hall	DeKalb	IL	60115	815-753-9655	753-4501
TF: 800-892-3050 ■ *Web:* law.niu.edu/law					
Northwestern University School of Law					
357 E Chicago Ave	Chicago	IL	60611	312-503-3100	503-0178*
**Fax:* Admissions ■ *TF:* 800-229-2032 ■ *Web:* www.law.northwestern.edu					
Notre Dame Law School					
University of Notre Dame					
1329 Biolchini Hall	Notre Dame	IN	46556	574-631-6627	631-4197
Web: www.law.nd.edu					
Nova Southeastern University Shepard Broad Law Ctr					
3305 College Ave	Fort Lauderdale	FL	33314	954-262-6100	262-3844*
**Fax:* Admissions ■ *TF:* 800-986-6529 ■ *Web:* www.nsulaw.nova.edu					
Ohio Northern University Claude W Pettit College of Law					
525 S Main St	Ada	OH	45810	419-772-2211	772-3042
TF: 877-452-9668 ■ *Web:* www.law.onu.edu					
Ohio State University Moritz College of Law					
55 W 12th Ave	Columbus	OH	43210	614-292-2631	292-1492
Web: www.moritzlaw.osu.edu					
Oklahoma City University School of Law					
2501 N Blackwelder Ave	Oklahoma City	OK	73106	405-208-5000	
TF: 800-230-3012 ■ *Web:* www.okcu.edu					
Pace University School of Law					
78 N Broadway	White Plains	NY	10603	914-422-4210	989-8714*
**Fax:* Admissions ■ *Web:* www.law.pace.edu					
Pennsylvania State University Dickinson School of Law					
150 S College St	Carlisle	PA	17013	717-240-5000	241-3503*
**Fax:* Admissions ■ *TF:* 800-840-1122 ■ *Web:* law.psu.edu					
Pepperdine University School of Law					
24255 Pacific Coast Hwy	Malibu	CA	90263	310-506-4631	506-7668*
**Fax:* Admissions ■ *Web:* www.law.pepperdine.edu					
Quinnipiac University School of Law					
275 Mt Carmel Ave	Hamden	CT	06518	203-582-3400	582-3339
TF: 800-462-1944 ■ *Web:* www.qu.edu					
Roger Williams University Ralph R Papitto School of Law					
10 Metacom Ave	Bristol	RI	02809	401-254-4500	254-4516*
**Fax:* Admissions ■ *TF:* 800-633-2727 ■ *Web:* www.law.rwu.edu					
Rutgers The State University of New Jersey					
Camden 406 Penn St	Camden	NJ	08102	856-225-6104	225-6498*
**Fax:* Admissions ■ *Web:* www.camden.rutgers.edu					
School of Law Camden 217 N Fifth St	Camden	NJ	08102	856-225-6375	
TF: 800-466-7561 ■ *Web:* www.camlaw.rutgers.edu					
Saint Louis University School of Law					
3700 Lindell Blvd	Saint Louis	MO	63108	314-977-2766	977-3333
TF: 800-758-3678 ■ *Web:* www.slu.edu					
Saint Thomas University School of Law					
16401 NW 37th Ave	Miami Gardens	FL	33054	305-623-2310	623-2357*
**Fax:* Admissions ■ *TF:* 800-245-4569 ■ *Web:* stu.edu/law					
Samford University Cumberland School of Law					
800 Lakeshore Dr	Birmingham	AL	35229	205-726-2400	726-2057
Web: cumberland.samford.edu					
Santa Clara University School of Law					
500 El Camino Real	Santa Clara	CA	95053	408-554-4361	554-5095*
**Fax:* Admissions ■ *Web:* www.scu.edu					
Seattle University School of Law					
901 12th Ave Sullivan Hall	Seattle	WA	98122	206-398-4000	398-4058*
**Fax:* Admissions ■ *Web:* www.law.seattleu.edu					
South Texas College of Law					
1303 San Jacinto St	Houston	TX	77002	713-659-8040	646-2906*
**Fax:* Admissions ■ *Web:* www.stcl.edu					
Southern Illinois University School of Law					
1209 W Chautauqua Rd	Carbondale	IL	62901	618-453-8858	453-8921*
**Fax:* Admissions ■ *TF:* 800-739-9187 ■ *Web:* www.law.siu.edu					
Southern Methodist University Dedman School of Law					
3300 University Blvd Ste 331	Dallas	TX	75205	214-768-2550	768-2549*
**Fax:* Admissions ■ *TF:* 888-768-5291 ■ *Web:* www.law.smu.edu					
Southern University Law Ctr					
2 Roosevelt Steptoe Dr	Baton Rouge	LA	70813	225-771-6297	771-2121
TF: 800-537-1135 ■ *Web:* www.sulc.edu					
Southwestern University School of Law					
3050 Wilshire Blvd	Los Angeles	CA	90010	213-738-6700	738-6899
Web: www.swlaw.edu					
Stanford University Law School					
559 Nathan Abbott Way Crown Quadrangle	Stanford	CA	94305	650-723-2465	723-0838*
**Fax:* Admissions ■ *Web:* www.law.stanford.edu					
Suffolk University Law School 120 Tremont St	Boston	MA	02108	617-573-8144	523-1367*
**Fax:* Admissions ■ *Web:* www.suffolk.edu					
Syracuse University College of Law					
950 Irving Ave	Syracuse	NY	13244	315-443-1962	443-9568
Web: www.law.syr.edu					
Temple University James E Beasley School of Law					
1719 N Broad St	Philadelphia	PA	19122	215-204-7861	204-1185
TF: 800-560-1428 ■ *Web:* www.law.temple.edu					
Texas Tech University School of Law					
1802 Hartford Ave	Lubbock	TX	79409	806-742-3990	742-1629
Web: www.law.ttu.edu					
Texas Wesleyan University School of Law					
1515 Commerce St	Fort Worth	TX	76102	817-212-4000	212-4141*
**Fax:* Admissions ■ *TF:* 800-733-9529 ■ *Web:* law.tamu.edu					
Thomas Jefferson School of Law					
1155 Island Ave	San Diego	CA	92101	619-297-9700	961-1382
TF: 877-318-6901 ■ *Web:* www.tjsl.edu					
Thomas M Cooley Law School 300 S Capitol Ave	Lansing	MI	48933	517-371-5140	
TF: 800-243-2586 ■ *Web:* www.cooley.edu					
Touro College Jacob D Fuchsberg Law Ctr					
225 Eastview Dr	Central Islip	NY	11722	631-421-2244	
Web: www.tourolaw.edu					
Tulane University Law School					
6329 Freret St Weinmann Hall	New Orleans	LA	70118	504-865-5930	865-6710*
**Fax:* Admissions ■ *TF:* 800-328-6819 ■ *Web:* www.law.tulane.edu					
University at Buffalo Law School					
John Lord O'Brian Hall	Buffalo	NY	14260	716-645-2052	645-2064
Web: www.law.buffalo.edu					
University of Akron School of Law					
150 University Ave	Akron	OH	44325	330-972-7331	258-2343
TF: 800-655-4884 ■ *Web:* www.uakron.edu					
University of Alabama PO Box 870132	Tuscaloosa	AL	35487	205-348-6010	348-9046*
**Fax:* Admissions ■ *TF Admissions:* 800-933-2262 ■ *Web:* www.ua.edu					
School of Law 101 Paul W Bryant Dr E	Tuscaloosa	AL	35401	205-348-5440	348-3971
Web: www.law.ua.edu					
University of Arizona James E Rogers College of Law					
1201 E Speedway Blvd PO Box 210176	Tucson	AZ	85721	520-621-1373	626-1839
Web: www.law.arizona.edu					
University of Arkansas at Little Rock William H Bowen School of Law					
1201 McMath Ave	Little Rock	AR	72202	501-324-9903	324-9909
Web: ualr.edu					
University of Arkansas School of Law					
1045 W Maple St	Fayetteville	AR	72701	479-575-5601	575-3937*
**Fax:* Admissions ■ *TF:* 800-295-9118 ■ *Web:* www.law.uark.edu					
University of California Berkeley School of Law					
2600 Bancroft Way 5 Boalt Hall	Berkeley	CA	94720	510-642-2274	643-6222*
**Fax:* Admissions ■ *Web:* www.law.berkeley.edu					
University of California Davis School of Law					
400 Mrak Hall Dr	Davis	CA	95616	530-752-0243	754-8371
Web: www.law.ucdavis.edu					
University of California Hastings College of the Law					
200 McAllister St	San Francisco	CA	94102	415-565-4600	581-8946*
**Fax:* Admissions ■ *Web:* www.uchastings.edu					
University of Chicago Law School					
1111 E 60th St	Chicago	IL	60637	773-702-9494	834-0942
Web: www.law.uchicago.edu					
University of Cincinnati College of Law					
2540 Clifton Ave	Cincinnati	OH	45221	513-556-6805	556-2391
Web: www.law.uc.edu					
University of Colorado School of Law					
2450 Kittredge Loop Rd	Boulder	CO	80309	303-492-8047	492-1757
Web: www.colorado.edu/law					
University of Connecticut School of Law					
45 Elizabeth St	Hartford	CT	06105	860-570-5100	570-5153*
**Fax:* Admissions ■ *TF:* 800-633-7867 ■ *Web:* www.law.uconn.edu					
University of Denver College of Law					
2255 E Evans Ave	Denver	CO	80208	303-871-6000	871-6378
Web: www.law.du.edu					
University of Detroit Mercy School of Law					
651 E Jefferson Ave	Detroit	MI	48226	313-596-0264	
TF: 888-726-6921 ■ *Web:* www.law.udmercy.edu					
University of Florida Fredric G Levin College of Law					
2500 SW Second Ave	Gainesville	FL	32611	352-273-0890	392-4087*
**Fax:* Admissions ■ *TF:* 877-429-1297 ■ *Web:* www.law.ufl.edu					
University of Georgia School of Law					
225 Herty Dr	Athens	GA	30602	706-542-5191	542-5556
Web: www.law.uga.edu					
University of Hawaii at Manoa					
Hamilton Library 2500 Campus Rd	Honolulu	HI	96822	808-956-6911	956-7109
Web: www.manoa.hawaii.edu					
William S Richardson School of Law					
2515 Dole St	Honolulu	HI	96822	808-956-7966	956-6402*
**Fax:* Admissions ■ *Web:* www.hawaii.edu					
University of Houston Law Ctr 100 Law Ctr	Houston	TX	77204	713-743-2100	743-2194*
**Fax:* Admissions ■ *TF:* 800-252-9690 ■ *Web:* www.law.uh.edu					
University of Idaho College of Law					
711 S Rayburn St	Moscow	ID	83844	208-885-4977	885-5709
TF: 888-884-3246 ■ *Web:* www.uidaho.edu					
University of Illinois College of Law					
504 E Pennsylvania Ave	Champaign	IL	61820	217-333-0930	244-1478
TF: 800-369-6151 ■ *Web:* www.law.illinois.edu					
University of Iowa College of Law					
130 Byington Rd	Iowa City	IA	52242	319-335-9034	335-9019
TF: 800-553-4692 ■ *Web:* www.law.uiowa.edu					
University of Kansas School of Law					
1535 W 15th St	Lawrence	KS	66045	785-864-4550	864-5054
TF: 877-404-5823 ■ *Web:* www.law.ku.edu					
University of Kentucky College of Law					
620 S Limestone St	Lexington	KY	40506	859-257-1678	323-1061
TF: 800-888-8189 ■ *Web:* www.law.uky.edu					

Phone | Fax

University of Maine School of Law
246 Deering Ave Portland ME 04102 207-780-4355 780-4239
Web: www.mainelaw.maine.edu

University of Memphis Cecil C Humphreys School of Law
3715 Central Ave Memphis TN 38152 901-678-2421 678-5210
TF: 800-872-3728 ■ *Web:* www.memphis.edu

University of Miami School of Law
1311 Miller Dr Coral Gables FL 33146 305-284-2339 284-3084*
**Fax:* Admissions ■ *Web:* www.law.miami.edu

University of Michigan Law School
625 S State St Ann Arbor MI 48109 734-764-1358 647-3218*
**Fax:* Admissions ■ *Web:* www.law.umich.edu

University of Minnesota Law School
229 19th Ave S Walter F Mondale Hall Minneapolis MN 55455 612-625-1000 626-1874*
**Fax:* Admissions ■ *Web:* www.law.umn.edu

University of Mississippi School of Law
301 Grove Loop PO Box 1848 University MS 38677 662-915-6870
Web: www.olemiss.edu

University of Missouri Columbia School of Law
203 Hulston Hall Columbia MO 65211 573-882-6487 882-4984
Web: www.law.missouri.edu

University of Missouri Kansas City School of Law
500 E 52nd St Kansas City MO 64110 816-235-1644 235-5276*
**Fax:* Admissions ■ *Web:* www.law.umkc.edu

University of Montana School of Law
32 Campus Dr Missoula MT 59812 406-243-4311 243-2576*
**Fax:* Admissions ■ *Web:* www.umt.edu/law

University of Nebraska College of Law
1875 N 42nd St Lincoln NE 68583 402-472-2161 472-5185
Web: www.unl.edu

University of Nevada Las Vegas William S Boyd School of Law
4505 Maryland Pkwy Las Vegas NV 89154 702-895-3671 895-1095
Web: www.law.unlv.edu

University of New Mexico School of Law
1117 Stanford Dr NE Albuquerque NM 87106 505-277-2146 277-0068

University of North Carolina School of Law
160 Ridge Rd Chapel Hill NC 27599 919-962-5106 843-7939
Web: www.law.unc.edu

University of North Dakota School of Law
264 Centennial Dr Stop 9003 Grand Forks ND 58202 701-777-2104
Web: law.und.edu

University of Oklahoma College of Law
300 Timberdell Rd Andrew M Coats Hall Norman OK 73019 405-325-4699 325-7474
Web: www.law.ou.edu

University of Oregon School of Law
1515 Agate St Eugene OR 97403 541-346-3852 346-1564
Web: www.law.uoregon.edu

University of Pennsylvania Law School
3400 Chestnut St Philadelphia PA 19104 215-898-7483 573-2025
Web: www.law.upenn.edu

University of Pittsburgh School of Law
3900 Forbes Ave Pittsburgh PA 15260 412-648-1400 648-2647
Web: www.law.pitt.edu

University of Richmond School of Law
28 W Hampton Way University of Richmond VA 23173 804-289-8740 289-8992
Web: www.law.richmond.edu

University of Saint Thomas School of Law
1000 LaSalle Ave Minneapolis MN 55403 651-962-4892 962-4876*
**Fax:* Admissions ■ *TF:* 800-328-6819 ■ *Web:* www.stthomas.edu

University of San Diego School of Law
5998 Alcala Pk San Diego CA 92110 619-260-4528 260-2218*
**Fax:* Admissions ■ *TF:* 800-248-4873 ■ *Web:* www.sandiego.edu/usdlaw

University of San Francisco School of Law
2130 Fulton St San Francisco CA 94117 415-422-6307 422-5442*
**Fax:* Admissions ■ *Web:* www.usfca.edu/law

University of South Carolina School of Law
701 S Main St Columbia SC 29208 803-777-6605 777-7751*
**Fax:* Admissions ■ *Web:* www.law.sc.edu

University of South Dakota School of Law
414 E Clark St Vermillion SD 57069 605-677-5443 677-5417
TF: 877-269-6837 ■ *Web:* www.usd.edu/law

University of Southern California Law School
699 Exposition Blvd Los Angeles CA 90089 213-740-7331

University of Tennessee College of Law
1505 Cumberland Ave Knoxville TN 37916 865-974-2521 974-6595
Web: www.law.utk.edu

University of Texas School of Law
727 E Dean Keeton St Austin TX 78705 512-471-5151 471-6988
Web: www.utexas.edu/law

University of the District of Columbia David A Clarke School of Law
4200 Connecticut Ave NW Washington DC 20008 202-274-7341 274-5583
Web: www.law.udc.edu

University of the Pacific McGeorge School of Law
3200 Fifth Ave Sacramento CA 95817 916-739-7105 739-7134*
**Fax:* Admissions ■ *Web:* www.mcgeorge.edu

University of Toledo College of Law
2801 W Bancroft MS 507 Toledo OH 43606 419-530-4131
Web: utoledo.edu/law

University of Utah SJ Quinney College of Law
332 South 1400 East Rm 101 Salt Lake City UT 84112 801-581-6833 581-6897
Web: www.law.utah.edu

University of Virginia School of Law
580 Massie Rd Charlottesville VA 22903 434-924-7354 924-7536
TF: 877-307-0158 ■ *Web:* www.law.virginia.edu

University of Washington School of Law
William H Gates Hall PO Box 353020 Seattle WA 98195 206-543-4078 543-5671
TF: 866-866-0158 ■ *Web:* www.law.uw.edu

University of Wisconsin Law School
975 Bascom Mall Madison WI 53706 608-262-2240 262-5485
TF: 866-301-1753 ■ *Web:* www.law.wisc.edu

Valparaiso University School of Law
651 College Ave Valparaiso IN 46383 219-465-7829 465-7808
TF: 888-825-7652 ■ *Web:* www.valpo.edu

Vanderbilt University Law School
131 21st Ave S Nashville TN 37203 615-322-2615 322-6631
Web: law.vanderbilt.edu

Vermont Law School
168 Chelsea St PO Box 96 South Royalton VT 05068 802-831-1239 763-7071
TF: 800-227-1395 ■ *Web:* www.vermontlaw.edu

Villanova University School of Law
299 N Spring Mill Rd Villanova PA 19085 610-519-7000 519-6291*
**Fax:* Admissions ■ *Web:* www1.villanova.edu

Wake Forest University School of Law
Worrell Professional Ctr
Wake Forest Rd Winston-Salem NC 27109 336-758-5435 758-3930*
**Fax:* Admissions ■ *Web:* www.law.wfu.edu

Washington & Lee University School of Law
Sydney Lewis Hall 4th Fl Lexington VA 24450 540-458-8502 458-8586*
**Fax:* Admissions ■ *Web:* www.law.wlu.edu

Washington University School of Law
1 Brookings Dr Anheuser-Busch Hall Saint Louis MO 63130 314-935-6400 935-8778*
**Fax:* Admissions ■ *Web:* law.wustl.edu

Wayne State University Law School
471 W Palmer St Detroit MI 48202 313-577-3937 993-8129*
**Fax:* Admissions ■ *Web:* www.law.wayne.edu

West Virginia University College of Law
PO Box 6130 Morgantown WV 26506 304-293-5301
Web: law.wvu.edu

Western State University College of Law
1111 N State College Blvd Fullerton CA 92831 714-459-1101 441-1748*
**Fax:* Admissions ■ *TF:* 800-978-4529 ■ *Web:* www.wsulaw.edu

Whittier Law School 3333 Harbor Blvd Costa Mesa CA 92626 714-444-4141 444-0250*
**Fax:* Admissions ■ *Web:* www.law.whittier.edu

Widener University Commonwealth Law School
3800 Vartan Way Harrisburg PA 17110 717-541-3900 541-3999
TF: 888-943-3637 ■ *Web:* www.law.widener.edu

Widener University School of Law Wilmington
4601 Concord Pk Wilmington DE 19803 302-477-2100 477-2224*
**Fax:* Admissions ■ *TF General:* 888-943-3637 ■ *Web:* law.widener.edu

Willamette University College of Law
245 Winter St SE Salem OR 97301 503-370-6282 370-6087*
**Fax:* Admissions ■ *TF:* 844-232-7228 ■ *Web:* www.willamette.edu/wucl

William & Mary Law School
613 S Henry St Williamsburg VA 23185 757-221-3800 221-3261*
**Fax:* Admissions ■ *Web:* www.wm.edu

William Mitchell College of Law
875 Summit Ave Saint Paul MN 55105 651-227-9171 290-6414
TF: 888-962-5529 ■ *Web:* mitchellhamline.edu

Yale Law School 127 Wall St New Haven CT 06511 203-432-4992 432-2112
Web: www.law.yale.edu

167-2 Medical Schools

Medical schools listed here are accredited, MD-granting members of the Association of American Medical Colleges. Accredited Canadian schools that do not offer classes in English are not included among these listings.

Phone | Fax

Albert Einstein College of Medicine of Yeshiva University
1300 Morris Pk Ave Bronx NY 10461 718-430-2000
Web: www.einstein.yu.edu

Baylor College of Medicine
1 Baylor Plz MS BCM365 Houston TX 77030 713-798-7766 798-1518
Web: www.bcm.edu

Boston University School of Medicine
715 Albany St Boston MA 02118 617-638-8000 638-5258*
**Fax:* Admissions ■ *Web:* www.bumc.bu.edu

Brody School of Medicine at East Carolina University
600 Moye Blvd Greenville NC 27834 252-744-1020 744-1926*
**Fax:* Admissions ■ *TF:* 800-722-3281 ■ *Web:* www.ecu.edu/med

Brown Medical School
222 Richmond St 1st Fl Providence RI 02912 401-863-2149 863-5096
Web: brown.edu

Case Western Reserve University School of Medicine (CWRU)
2109 Adelbert Rd Cleveland OH 44106 216-368-3450 368-6011
Web: case.edu/medicine

Cincinnati Children's Hospital Medical Ctr
3333 Burnet Ave Cincinnati OH 45229 513-636-4200 636-3733*
**Fax:* Admitting ■ *TF:* 800-344-2462 ■ *Web:* www.cincinnatichildrens.org

Dalhousie University Faculty of Medicine
1459 Oxford St Halifax NS B3H4R2 902-494-1874 494-6369*
**Fax:* Admissions ■ *Web:* www.medicine.dal.ca

Drexel University College of Medicine
2900 Queen Ln Philadelphia PA 19129 215-991-8202 843-1766
Web: www.drexel.edu/medicine

Duke University School of Medicine
Office of Admissions DUMC 3710 Durham NC 27710 919-684-2985 668-3714*
**Fax:* Admissions ■ *TF:* 888-275-3853 ■ *Web:* www.medschool.duke.edu

Eastern Virginia Medical School
700 W Olney Rd PO Box 1980 Norfolk VA 23501 757-446-5812 446-5896*
**Fax:* Admissions ■ *Web:* www.evms.edu

Emory University School of Medicine
1440 Clifton Rd NE Atlanta GA 30322 404-727-5660 727-5456*
**Fax:* Admissions ■ *Web:* www.med.emory.edu

Florida State University College of Medicine
1115 W Call St Tallahassee FL 32306 850-644-1855 645-2846*
**Fax:* Admissions ■ *Web:* www.med.fsu.edu

George Washington University School of Medicine & Health Sciences
2300 'I' St NW Ross Hall 716 Washington DC 20037 202-994-3506 994-1753
TF: 866-846-1107 ■ *Web:* smhs.gwu.edu

Georgetown University School of Medicine
3900 Reservoir Rd NW Washington DC 20057 202-687-1154 687-3079
Web: som.georgetown.edu

Harvard Medical School 25 Shattuck St Boston MA 02115 617-432-1550 432-3307*
**Fax:* Admissions ■ *TF:* 866-606-0573 ■ *Web:* www.hms.harvard.edu

Howard University College of Medicine
520 W St NW Washington DC 20059 202-806-6270 806-7934
Web: healthsciences.howard.edu/education/colleges/medicine

Indiana University School of Medicine
340 W Tenth St Ste 6200 Indianapolis IN 46202 317-274-8157
Web: www.medicine.iu.edu

Phone | Fax

Jefferson Medical College of Thomas Jefferson University
1015 Walnut St. . . . . . Philadelphia PA 19107 215-955-6983 955-5151
TF: 800-533-3669 ■ *Web:* jefferson.edu/university/jmc

Joan & Sanford Weill Medical College of Cornell University
445 E 69th St. . . . . . New York NY 10021 212-746-5454 746-8052*
*Fax: Admissions ■ *TF:* 800-422-0711 ■ *Web:* weill.cornell.edu

Joan C Edwards School of Medicine at Marshall University
1600 Medical Ctr Dr. . . . . . Huntington WV 25701 304-691-1700 691-1726
TF: 877-691-1600 ■ *Web:* jcesom.marshall.edu

Johns Hopkins University School of Medicine
601 N Caroline St. . . . . . Baltimore MD 21205 410-955-3080 955-0826
Web: www.hopkinsmedicine.org

Keck School of Medicine of the University of Southern California
1975 Zonal Ave KAM 100. . . . . . Los Angeles CA 90089 323-442-1100 442-2433*
*Fax: Admissions ■ *Web:* www.usc.edu

Loma Linda University School of Medicine
11175 Campus St. . . . . . Loma Linda CA 92350 909-558-4467 558-0359
TF: 800-422-4558 ■ *Web:* www.llu.edu/llu/medicine

Louisiana State University School of Medicine in New Orleans
433 Bolivar St. . . . . . New Orleans LA 70112 504-568-6262 568-7701
TF: 844-503-7283 ■ *Web:* www.medschool.lsuhsc.edu

Louisiana State University School of Medicine in Shreveport
1501 Kings Hwy PO Box 33932 . . . . . . Shreveport LA 71130 318-675-5069 675-5000
TF: 800-337-3627 ■ *Web:* www.sh.lsuhsc.edu

Loyola University Chicago Stritch School of Medicine
2160 S First Ave Bldg 120 Rm 200. . . . . . Maywood IL 60153 708-216-3229 216-9160*
*Fax: Admissions ■ *Web:* www.meddean.luc.edu

Mayo Medical School 200 First St SW . . . . . . Rochester MN 55905 507-284-2316 284-2634
Web: www.mayo.edu/mms

Medical College of Wisconsin
8701 Watertown Plank Rd. . . . . . . Milwaukee WI 53226 414-456-8296 456-6506
Web: www.mcw.edu

Medical University of South Carolina College of Medicine (MUSC)
171 Ashley Ave. . . . . . . Charleston SC 29425 843-792-1414
Web: academicdepartments.musc.edu

Michigan State University College of Human Medicine
965 Fee Rd Rm A-110 . . . . . . East Lansing MI 48824 517-353-1730 355-0342
Web: www.humanmedicine.msu.edu

Morehouse School of Medicine
720 Westview Dr SW . . . . . . Atlanta GA 30310 404-752-1500 752-1512*
*Fax: Admissions ■ *Web:* www.msm.edu

New Jersey Medical School
185 S Orange Ave Rm C-653 PO Box 1709 . . . . . . Newark NJ 07101 973-972-4631 972-7986
Web: njms.rutgers.edu

New York Medical College
40 Sunshine Cottage Rd. . . . . . . Valhalla NY 10595 914-594-4507
Web: www.nymc.edu

New York University School of Medicine
560 First Ave . . . . . . New York NY 10016 212-263-7300 263-0720
TF: 855-698-2220 ■ *Web:* www.med.nyu.edu

Northeast Ohio Medical University
4209 State Rt 44 PO Box 95 . . . . . . Rootstown OH 44272 330-325-2511
TF: 800-686-2511 ■ *Web:* neomed.edu

Northwestern University Feinberg School of Medicine
303 E Chicago Ave . . . . . . Chicago IL 60611 312-503-8649 503-6978
Web: www.feinberg.northwestern.edu

Ohio State University College of Medicine & Public Health
370 W Ninth Ave 155 Meiling Hall . . . . . . Columbus OH 43210 614-292-2220 247-7959*
*Fax: Admitting ■ *Web:* www.medicine.osu.edu

Oregon Health & Science University
Bone Marrow Transplant Program (OHSU)
3181 SW Sam Jackson Pk Rd . . . . . . Portland OR 97239 503-494-1617 494-7086
TF: 800-222-1222 ■ *Web:* www.ohsu.edu
School of Medicine
3181 SW Sam Jackson Pk Rd L-109. . . . . . . Portland OR 97239 503-494-7800 494-4629
TF: 800-775-5460 ■ *Web:* www.ohsu.edu

Pennsylvania State University College of Medicine
500 University Dr Rm C1805 . . . . . . Hershey PA 17033 717-531-4395 531-6225*
*Fax: Admissions ■ *Web:* www.pennstatehershey.org

Queen's University Faculty of Health Sciences
School of Medicine 68 Barrie St. . . . . . . Kingston ON K7L3N6 613-533-2542 533-3190
Web: healthsci.queensu.ca

Robert Wood Johnson Medical School
675 Hoes Ln. . . . . . . Piscataway NJ 08854 732-235-4576 235-5078
Web: www.rwjms.umdnj.edu

Rush Medical College of Rush University
600 S Paulina St. . . . . . . Chicago IL 60612 888-352-7874 942-2333*
*Fax Area Code: 312 ■ *Fax: Admissions ■ *TF:* 888-352-7874 ■ *Web:* www.rushu.rush.edu

Saint Louis University School of Medicine
1 North Grand. . . . . . . Saint Louis MO 63103 800-758-3678 977-9825*
*Fax Area Code: 314 ■ *TF:* 800-758-3678 ■ *Web:* www.slu.edu/colleges/med

Schulich School of Medicine & Dentistry
Western University . . . . . . London ON N6A5C1 519-661-3459 661-3797
Web: www.schulich.uwo.ca

Southern Illinois University School of Medicine
520 N Fourth St PO Box 19670 . . . . . . Springfield IL 62702 217-545-8000
TF: 800-342-5748 ■ *Web:* www.siumed.edu

Stanford University School of Medicine
291 Campus Dr Rm LK3C02 . . . . . . Stanford CA 94305 650-725-3900 725-7368
Web: med.stanford.edu

State University of New York Downstate Medical Ctr
450 Clarkson Ave. . . . . . . Brooklyn NY 11203 718-270-1000 270-7592
Web: www.downstate.edu

State University of New York Upstate Medical University
766 Irving Ave . . . . . . Syracuse NY 13210 315-464-4570 464-8867
TF: 800-736-2171 ■ *Web:* www.upstate.edu

Temple University School of Medicine
3500 N BRd St . . . . . . Philadelphia PA 19140 215-707-3656 707-6932
Web: www.temple.edu/medicine

Texas A & M University System Health Science Ctr
301 Tarrow St Fl 5 . . . . . . College Station TX 77840 979-458-7200
Web: www.tamhsc.edu
College of Medicine 8447 Hwy 47 3rd Fl. . . . . . . Bryan TX 77807 979-436-0237
Web: www.medicine.tamhsc.edu

Texas Tech University Health Sciences Ctr
Preston Smith Library of the Health Sciences
3601 Fourth St MS 7781 . . . . . . Lubbock TX 79430 806-743-2200 743-2218
Web: www.ttuhsc.edu/libraries/guides/lubbockguide.aspx#welcome
School of Medicine 3601 Fourth St MS 6207 . . . . . . Lubbock TX 79430 806-743-3000 743-3021
Web: www.ttuhsc.edu

Tufts University School of Medicine
136 Harrison Ave . . . . . . Boston MA 02111 617-636-7000 636-3805
Web: www.tufts.edu

Tulane University School of Medicine
1555 Poydras St Ste 1000 . . . . . . New Orleans LA 70118 504-988-5462
Web: tulane.edu

University at Buffalo School of Medicine & Biomedical Sciences
131 Biomedical Education Bldg . . . . . . Buffalo NY 14214 716-829-3466 829-3849*
*Fax: Admissions ■ *Web:* www.wings.buffalo.edu

University of Alberta Faculty of Medicine & Dentistry
2-45 Medical Sciences Bldg. . . . . . . Edmonton AB T6G2R3 780-492-6350 492-9531
Web: www.med.ualberta.ca

University of Arizona College of Medicine
1501 N Campbell Ave. . . . . . . Tucson AZ 85724 520-626-4555 626-6252
Web: www.medicine.arizona.edu

University of Arkansas for Medical Sciences
College of Medicine
4301 W Markham St Slot 551 . . . . . . Little Rock AR 72205 501-686-5354
Web: www.uams.edu/com

University of British Columbia Faculty of Medicine
317-2194 Health Sciences Mall . . . . . . Vancouver BC V6T1Z3 604-822-2421 822-6061
Web: www.med.ubc.ca

University of Calgary Faculty of Medicine
3330 Hospital Dr NW . . . . . . Calgary AB T2N4N1 403-220-7448
Web: cumming.ucalgary.ca/intranet

University of California Davis School of Medicine
4610 X St . . . . . . Sacramento CA 95817 916-734-2011
TF: 855-221-4673

University of California Irvine School of Medicine
1001 Health Sciences Rd 252 Irvine Hall . . . . . . Irvine CA 92697 949-824-6119
TF: 800-824-5388 ■ *Web:* www.som.uci.edu

University of California San Diego School of Medicine
9500 Gilman Dr MC 0602 . . . . . . La Jolla CA 92093 858-534-0830 534-6573
Web: som.ucsd.edu

University of Chicago Pritzker School of Medicine
924 E 57th St . . . . . . Chicago IL 60637 773-702-1939 702-2598

University of Cincinnati College of Medicine
231 Albert Sabin Way PO Box 670552 . . . . . . Cincinnati OH 45267 513-558-5575 558-1100
Web: www.med.uc.edu

University of Connecticut School of Medicine
263 Farmington Ave . . . . . . Farmington CT 06030 860-679-2000 679-1899*
*Fax: Admissions ■ *Web:* medicine.uconn.edu

University of Hawaii at Manoa
Hamilton Library 2500 Campus Rd . . . . . . Honolulu HI 96822 808-956-6911 956-7109
Web: www.manoa.hawaii.edu
John A Burns School of Medicine (JABSOM)
651 Ilalo St Medical Education Bldg . . . . . . Honolulu HI 96813 808-692-1000 692-1251
Web: www.jabsom.hawaii.edu

University of Illinois College of Medicine
808 S Wood St Rm 165 . . . . . . Chicago IL 60612 312-996-5635 996-6693*
*Fax: Admissions ■ *Web:* www.uic.edu/depts/mcam

University of Iowa Roy J & Lucille A Carver College of Medicine
200 CMAB . . . . . . Iowa City IA 52242 319-335-6707 335-8318
TF: 800-725-8460 ■ *Web:* www.medicine.uiowa.edu

University of Kentucky College of Medicine
Office of Medical Education MN 104 UKMC. . . . . . . Lexington KY 40536 859-323-6161 323-2076
TF: 800-273-8255 ■ *Web:* www.mc.uky.edu

University of Louisville School of Medicine
323 E Chestnut St. . . . . . . Louisville KY 40292 502-852-5193 852-0302
TF: 800-334-8635 ■ *Web:* www.louisville.edu/medschool

University of Manitoba Faculty of Medicine
727 McDermot Ave Rm 260 . . . . . . Winnipeg MB R3E3P5 204-789-3557 789-3928
Web: www.umanitoba.ca

University of Maryland School of Medicine
685 W Baltimore St
1-005 Bressler Research Bldg . . . . . . Baltimore MD 21201 410-706-7478 706-0467*
*Fax: Admissions ■ *Web:* www.medschool.umaryland.edu

University of Medicine & Dentistry of New Jersey
Graduate School of Biomedical Sciences (GSBS)
185 S Orange Ave MSB B640 . . . . . . Newark NJ 07107 973-972-4511
Web: rbhs.rutgers.edu

University of Minnesota Medical School Twin Cities
420 Delaware St SE Mayo MC 293. . . . . . . Minneapolis MN 55455 612-624-5100 626-4911
TF: 800-752-1000 ■ *Web:* www.health.umn.edu

University of Mississippi School of Medicine
2500 N State St. . . . . . . Jackson MS 39216 601-984-1080 984-1079
TF: 888-815-2005 ■ *Web:* www.umc.edu

University of Missouri-Kansas City School of Medicine
2411 Holmes St . . . . . . Kansas City MO 64108 816-235-1111 235-5277
TF: 800-735-2466 ■ *Web:* med.umkc.edu

University of Nebraska School of Medicine
985527 Nebraska Medical Ctr . . . . . . Omaha NE 68198 402-559-2259 559-6840
TF: 800-626-8431 ■ *Web:* www.unmc.edu

University of Nevada School of Medicine
1664 N Virginia St
Pennington Medical Education Bldg 357 . . . . . . Reno NV 89557 775-784-6063
Web: www.unr.edu

University of New Mexico School of Medicine
1 University of New Mexico . . . . . . Albuquerque NM 87131 505-272-4766 925-6031
TF: 877-977-2263 ■ *Web:* hsc.unm.edu/som

University of North Dakota School of Medicine & Health Sciences
501 N Columbia Rd . . . . . . Grand Forks ND 58203 701-777-5046 777-4942*
*Fax: Admissions ■ *TF:* 800-225-5863 ■ *Web:* www.med.und.edu

University of Oklahoma College of Medicine
PO Box 26901 . . . . . . Oklahoma City OK 73190 405-271-2265 271-3032
Web: www.oumedicine.com

University of Ottawa Faculty of Medicine
451 Smyth Rd. . . . . . . Ottawa ON K1H8M5 613-562-5700 562-5323
TF: 877-868-8292 ■ *Web:* www.uottawa.ca

				Phone	Fax
University of Pittsburgh School of Medicine					
3550 Terr St 518 Scaife Hall	Pittsburgh	PA	15261	412-648-9891	648-8768*
**Fax:* Admissions ■ *Web:* www.medschool.pitt.edu					
University of Rochester School of Medicine & Dentistry					
601 Elmwood Ave	Rochester	NY	14642	585-275-0017	756-5479*
**Fax:* Admissions ■ *TF:* 888-661-6162 ■ *Web:* www.urmc.rochester.edu/SMD					
University of South Alabama College of Medicine					
307 N University Blvd	Mobile	AL	36688	251-460-6101	460-6278
Web: www.southalabama.edu					
University of South Carolina School of Medicine					
6439 Garners Ferry Rd	Columbia	SC	29209	803-216-3300	733-3335
Web: www.med.sc.edu					
University of South Dakota School of Medicine					
414 E Clark St	Vermillion	SD	57069	605-677-5233	
University of South Florida College of Medicine (USF)					
12901 Bruce B Downs Blvd	Tampa	FL	33612	813-974-2229	974-4990
TF: 877-338-2577 ■ *Web:* health.usf.edu					
University of Tennessee Health Science Ctr College of Medicine					
920 Madison Ave	Memphis	TN	38163	901-448-5529	
Web: www.uthsc.edu					
University of Texas Medical Branch					
301 University Blvd	Galveston	TX	77555	409-772-2618	747-2909*
**Fax:* Admissions ■ *TF:* 800-228-1841 ■ *Web:* www.utmb.edu					
University of Texas Medical School at San Antonio					
7703 Floyd Curl Dr	San Antonio	TX	78229	210-567-4420	567-6962*
**Fax:* Admissions ■ *Web:* som.uthscsa.edu					
University of Texas Southwestern Medical Ctr Dallas					
Hematopoietic Cell Transplant Program					
2201 Inwood Rd 2nd Fl	Dallas	TX	75390	214-645-4673	
TF: 866-645-6455 ■ *Web:* www.utsouthwestern.edu					
Southwestern Medical School					
5323 Harry Hines Blvd	Dallas	TX	75390	214-648-3111	648-3289
TF: 866-648-2455 ■ *Web:* utsouthwestern.edu/education/medical-school					
University of Toronto Faculty of Medicine					
500 University Ave 2nd Fl	Toronto	ON	M5G1V7	416-978-6976	978-7144
Web: medicine.utoronto.ca					
University of Utah School of Medicine					
30 N 1900 E	Salt Lake City	UT	84132	801-581-7201	585-3300
TF: 844-988-7284 ■ *Web:* medicine.utah.edu					
University of Vermont College of Medicine					
89 Beaumont Ave E-126 Given Bldg	Burlington	VT	05405	802-656-2156	656-8577
TF: 800-571-0668 ■ *Web:* www.uvm.edu					
University of Virginia School of Medicine					
1300 Jefferson Pk Ave PO Box 800793	Charlottesville	VA	22908	434-924-5571	982-2586
Web: med.virginia.edu					
University of Washington School of Medicine					
A-300 Health Sciences Bldg PO Box 356340	Seattle	WA	98195	206-543-5560	616-3341
Web: www.uwmedicine.org					
University of Wisconsin Medical School					
750 Highland Ave Rm 2130	Madison	WI	53705	608-263-4925	262-4226*
**Fax:* Admissions ■ *Web:* www.med.wisc.edu					
Vanderbilt University School of Medicine					
215 Light Hall	Nashville	TN	37232	615-322-2145	343-8397
TF: 866-263-8263 ■ *Web:* medschool.vanderbilt.edu					
Virginia Commonwealth University School of Medicine					
1101 E Marshall St PO Box 980565	Richmond	VA	23298	804-828-9629	828-1246*
**Fax:* Admissions ■ *TF:* 800-332-8813 ■ *Web:* www.medschool.vcu.edu					
Wake Forest University School of Medicine					
Medical Ctr Blvd	Winston-Salem	NC	27157	336-716-4264	716-9593
TF: 800-445-2255 ■ *Web:* www.wakehealth.edu					
Washington University in Saint Louis School of Medicine					
660 S Euclid Ave	Saint Louis	MO	63110	314-362-5000	
Wayne State University School of Medicine					
540 E Canfield St 1310 Scott Hall	Detroit	MI	48201	313-577-1460	577-9420*
**Fax:* Admitting ■ *Web:* home.med.wayne.edu					
West Virginia University School of Medicine					
Medical Ctr Dr					
Health Sciences Ctr N Rm 1146	Morgantown	WV	26506	304-293-2408	293-7814
TF: 800-543-5650 ■ *Web:* www.hsc.wvu.edu/som					
Wright State University Boonshoft School of Medicine					
3640 Col Glenn Hwy	Dayton	OH	45435	937-775-2934	775-3322*
**Fax:* Admissions ■ *TF:* 800-338-4057 ■ *Web:* medicine.wright.edu					
Yale University School of Medicine					
333 Cedar St	New Haven	CT	06510	203-785-2643	785-3234
TF: 877-925-3637 ■ *Web:* medicine.yale.edu					

167-3 Theological Schools

Theological schools listed here are members of the Association of Theological Schools (ATS), an organization of graduate schools in the U.S. and Canada that conduct post-baccalaureate professional and academic degree programs to educate persons for the practice of ministry and for teaching and research in the theological disciplines. Listings include ATS accredited member schools, candidates for accredited membership, and associate member schools.

				Phone	Fax
Acadia Divinity College 38 Highland Ave	Wolfville	NS	B4P2R6	902-585-2210	
TF: 866-875-8975 ■ *Web:* www.acadiadiv.ca					
American Baptist Seminary of the West					
2606 Dwight Way	Berkeley	CA	94704	510-841-1905	841-2446
TF: 800-799-7233 ■ *Web:* www.absw.edu					
Anderson University 1100 E Fifth St	Anderson	IN	46012	765-649-9071	641-4091*
**Fax:* Admissions ■ *TF Admissions:* 800-428-6414 ■ *Web:* www.anderson.edu					
Andover Newton Theological School					
210 Herrick Rd	Newton Center	MA	02459	617-964-1100	
TF: 800-964-2687 ■ *Web:* www.ants.edu					
Andrews University Seventh-day Adventist Theological Seminary					
4145 E Campus Cir Dr					
Andrews University	Berrien Springs	MI	49104	269-471-3537	471-6202
TF: 800-253-2874 ■ *Web:* www.andrews.edu/sem					
Aquinas Institute of Theology					
23 S Spring Ave	Saint Louis	MO	63108	314-256-8800	256-8888
TF: 800-977-3869 ■ *Web:* www.ai.edu					
Asbury Theological Seminary					
204 N Lexington Ave	Wilmore	KY	40390	859-858-3581	
TF: 800-227-2879 ■ *Web:* www.asburyseminary.edu					
Ashland Theological Seminary 910 Ctr St	Ashland	OH	44805	419-289-5161	289-5969
Web: www.ashland.edu					
Assemblies of God Theological Seminary					
1435 N Glenstone Ave	Springfield	MO	65802	417-268-1000	268-1001
TF: 800-467-2487 ■ *Web:* www.agts.edu					
Associated Mennonite Biblical Seminary					
3003 Benham Ave	Elkhart	IN	46517	574-295-3726	
TF: 800-964-2627 ■ *Web:* www.ambs.edu					
Athenaeum of Ohio 6616 Beechmont Ave	Cincinnati	OH	45230	513-231-2223	231-3254
Web: www.mtsm.org					
Atlantic School of Theology 660 Francklyn St	Halifax	NS	B3H3B5	902-423-6939	492-4048
Web: www.astheology.ns.ca					
Austin Presbyterian Theological Seminary					
100 E 27th St	Austin	TX	78705	512-472-6736	479-0738
Web: www.austinseminary.edu					
Azusa Pacific University					
901 E Alosta Ave PO Box 7000	Azusa	CA	91702	626-969-3434	812-3096
TF: 800-825-5278 ■ *Web:* www.apu.edu					
Bangor Theological Seminary 159 State St	Portland	ME	04101	207-942-6781	990-1267
TF: 800-287-6781 ■ *Web:* www.bts.edu					
Baptist Missionary Assn Theological Seminary					
1530 E Pine St	Jacksonville	TX	75766	903-586-2501	586-0378
TF: 800-259-5673 ■ *Web:* www.bmats.edu					
Baptist Theological Seminary at Richmond					
8040 Villa Park Dr Ste 250	Richmond	VA	23227	804-355-8135	355-8182
TF: 888-345-2877 ■ *Web:* www.btsr.edu					
Barry University 11300 NE Second Ave	Miami Shores	FL	33161	305-899-3000	899-2971*
**Fax:* Admissions ■ *TF:* 800-756-6000 ■ *Web:* www.barry.edu					
Bethany Theological Seminary					
615 National Rd W	Richmond	IN	47374	765-983-1800	983-1840
TF: 800-287-8822 ■ *Web:* www.bethanyseminary.edu					
Bethel Seminary 3949 Bethel Dr	Saint Paul	MN	55112	651-638-6400	638-6002
TF: 800-255-8706 ■ *Web:* www.bethel.edu/seminary					
Bexley Hall Seminary 583 Sheridan Ave	Columbus	OH	43209	614-231-3095	
Web: www.bexleyseabury.edu					
Biblical Theological Seminary 200 N Main St	Hatfield	PA	19440	215-368-5000	368-2301
TF: 800-235-4021 ■ *Web:* www.biblical.edu					
Biola University 13800 Biola Ave	La Mirada	CA	90639	562-903-6000	903-4709*
**Fax:* Admissions ■ *TF Admissions:* 800-652-4652 ■ *Web:* www.biola.edu					
Blessed John XXIII National Seminary					
558 S Ave	Weston	MA	02493	781-899-5500	899-5500
Web: www.blessedjohnxxiii.edu					
Briercrest College & Seminary					
510 College Dr	Caronport	SK	S0H0S0	306-756-3200	756-5500
Web: www.briercrest.ca					
Byzantine Catholic Seminary of SS Cyril & Methodius					
3605 Perrysville Ave	Pittsburgh	PA	15214	412-321-8383	321-9936
Web: www.bcs.edu					
Calvin Theological Seminary					
3233 Burton St SE	Grand Rapids	MI	49546	616-957-6036	957-8621
TF: 800-388-6034 ■ *Web:* www.calvinseminary.edu					
Campbell University					
450 Leslie Campbell Ave PO Box 546	Buies Creek	NC	27506	910-893-1290	893-1288*
**Fax:* Admissions ■ *TF:* 800-334-4111 ■ *Web:* www.campbell.edu					
Canadian Southern Baptist Seminary					
200 Seminary View	Cochrane	AB	T4C2G1	403-932-6622	932-7049
TF: 877-922-2727 ■ *Web:* www.csbs.ca					
Carey Theological College 5920 Iona Dr	Vancouver	BC	V6T1J6	604-224-4308	224-5014
TF: 844-862-2739 ■ *Web:* www.carey-edu.ca					
Catholic Theological Union					
5416 S Cornell Ave	Chicago	IL	60615	773-324-8000	324-4360
Web: www.ctu.edu					
Catholic University of America					
620 Michigan Ave NE	Washington	DC	20064	202-319-5000	319-6533
Web: www.cua.edu					
Central Baptist Theological Seminary					
6601 Monticello Rd	Shawnee	KS	66226	913-667-5700	788-6510*
**Fax Area Code:* 412 ■ *TF:* 800-677-2287 ■ *Web:* www.cbts.edu					
Christ The King Seminary 711 Knox Rd	East Aurora	NY	14052	716-652-8900	652-8903
Web: www.cks.edu					
Christian Theological Seminary					
1000 W 42nd St	Indianapolis	IN	46208	317-924-1331	923-1961
TF: 800-585-0108 ■ *Web:* www.cts.edu					
Christian Witness Theological Seminary					
1975 Concourse Dr	San Jose	CA	95131	408-433-2280	676-5220*
**Fax Area Code:* 925 ■ *Web:* www.cwts.edu					
Church Divinity School of the Pacific					
2451 Ridge Rd	Berkeley	CA	94709	510-204-0700	644-0712
Web: www.cdsp.edu					
Cincinnati Christian University					
2700 Glenway Ave	Cincinnati	OH	45204	513-244-8100	244-8140
TF: 800-949-4228 ■ *Web:* www.ccuniversity.edu					
Claremont School of Theology					
1325 N College Ave	Claremont	CA	91711	909-447-2500	447-6389*
**Fax:* Admissions ■ *TF:* 800-733-5181 ■ *Web:* www.cst.edu					
Colgate Rochester Crozer Divinity School					
1100 S Goodman St	Rochester	NY	14620	585-271-1320	271-8013
TF: 888-937-3732 ■ *Web:* www.crcds.edu					
Columbia International University					
7435 Monticello Rd	Columbia	SC	29203	803-754-4100	786-4209
TF: 800-777-2227 ■ *Web:* www.ciu.edu					
Columbia Theological Seminary					
701 S Columbia Dr	Decatur	GA	30030	404-378-8821	377-9696
TF: 888-601-8916 ■ *Web:* www.ctsnet.edu					
Concordia Lutheran Seminary 7040 Ada Blvd	Edmonton	AB	T5B4E3	780-474-1468	479-3067
Web: www.concordiasem.ab.ca					
Concordia Seminary 801 Seminary Pl	Saint Louis	MO	63105	314-505-7000	
TF: 800-822-9545 ■ *Web:* www.csl.edu					
Concordia Theological Seminary					
6600 N Clinton St	Fort Wayne	IN	46825	260-452-2100	452-2121
TF: 800-481-2155 ■ *Web:* www.ctsfw.edu					
Cornerstone University					
1001 E Beltline Ave NE	Grand Rapids	MI	49525	616-222-1426	222-1418*
**Fax:* Admissions ■ *TF Admissions:* 800-787-9778 ■ *Web:* www.cornerstone.edu					

				Phone	*Fax*
Dallas Theological Seminary 3909 Swiss Ave. *Fax Area Code: 214 ■ TF: 800-992-0998 ■ Web: www.dts.edu	Dallas	TX	75204	800-387-9673	841-3664*
Denver Seminary 6399 S Santa Fe Dr. TF: 800-922-3040 ■ Web: www.denverseminary.edu	Littleton	CO	80120	303-761-2482	761-8060
Dominican House of Studies 487 Michigan Ave NE Web: www.dhs.edu	Washington	DC	20017	202-529-5300	
Dominican School of Philosophy & Theology 2301 Vine St. TF: 888-450-3778 ■ Web: www.dspt.edu	Berkeley	CA	94708	510-849-2030	849-1372
Drew University Theological School 36 Madison Ave Web: www.drew.edu	Madison	NJ	07940	973-408-3258	408-3068
Duke University Divinity School 407 Chapel Drive PO Box 90968 TF: 800-367-3853 ■ Web: www.divinity.duke.edu	Durham	NC	27708	919-660-3400	660-3473
Earlham School of Religion 228 College Ave. TF: 800-432-1377 ■ Web: www.esr.earlham.edu	Richmond	IN	47374	765-983-1423	983-1688
Eastern Mennonite University 1200 Pk Rd. *Fax: Admissions ■ TF Admissions: 800-368-2665 ■ Web: www.emu.edu	Harrisonburg	VA	22802	540-432-4118	432-4444*
Ecumenical Theological Seminary (ETS) 2930 Woodward Ave. Web: www.etseminary.org	Detroit	MI	48201	313-831-5200	
Eden Theological Seminary 475 E Lockwood Ave TF: 800-969-3627 ■ Web: www.eden.edu	Saint Louis	MO	63119	314-961-3627	918-2626
Episcopal Divinity School 99 Brattle St TF: 866-333-8742 ■ Web: www.eds.edu	Cambridge	MA	02138	617-868-3450	864-5385
Episcopal Theological Seminary of the Southwest (SSW) 501 E 32nd PO Box 2247 TF: 800-252-5400 ■ Web: www.ssw.edu	Austin	TX	78705	512-472-4133	472-3098
Erskine Theological Seminary 2 Washington St PO Box 338 TF: 888-359-4358 ■ Web: www.erskine.edu	Due West	SC	29639	864-379-8885	
Evangelical School of Theology 121 S College St. TF: 800-532-5775 ■ Web: www.evangelical.edu	Myerstown	PA	17067	717-866-5775	866-4667
Franciscan School of Theology 1712 Euclid Ave. TF: 855-355-1550 ■ Web: www.fst.edu	Berkeley	CA	94709	760-547-1800	547-1807
Fuller Theological Seminary 135 N Oakland Ave. TF: 800-235-2222 ■ Web: www.fuller.edu	Pasadena	CA	91182	626-584-5200	795-8767
Gardner-Webb University M Christopher White School of Divinity 110 S Main St PO Box 997 Web: gardner-webb.edu	Boiling Springs	NC	28017	704-406-4000	
General Theological Seminary 440 W 21st St. TF: 888-487-5649 ■ Web: gts.edu	New York	NY	10011	212-243-5150	727-3907
George Fox Evangelical Seminary 12753 SW 68th Ave TF: 800-493-4937 ■ Web: www.georgefox.edu	Portland	OR	97223	503-554-6150	554-6111
Golden Gate Baptist Theological Seminary 201 Seminary Dr. TF: 888-442-8701 ■ Web: www.ggbts.edu	Mill Valley	CA	94941	415-380-1300	380-1302
Gordon-Conwell Theological Seminary 130 Essex St. TF: 800-428-7329 ■ Web: www.gordonconwell.edu	South Hamilton	MA	01982	978-468-7111	468-6691
Grace Theological Seminary 200 Seminary Dr. TF: 800-544-7223 ■ Web: gts.grace.edu	Winona Lake	IN	46590	574-372-5100	372-5113
Graduate Theological Union 2400 Ridge Rd TF: 800-826-4488 ■ Web: www.gtu.edu	Berkeley	CA	94709	510-649-2400	649-1730
Harding University Graduate School of Religion 915 E Market Ave TF: 800-477-4407 ■ Web: harding.edu/bible/faculty	Searcy	AR	72143	501-279-4407	
Hartford Seminary 77 Sherman St *Fax: Admissions ■ TF: 877-860-2255 ■ Web: www.hartsem.edu	Hartford	CT	06105	860-509-9500	509-9509*
Hellenic College-Holy Cross School of Theology 50 Goddard Ave *Fax: Admissions ■ Web: www.hchc.edu	Brookline	MA	02445	617-731-3500	850-1460*
Hood Theological Seminary 1810 Lutheran Synod Dr. Web: www.hoodseminary.edu	Salisbury	NC	28144	704-636-7611	636-7699
Houston Graduate School of Theology 4300-C W Bellfort Blvd. Web: www.hgst.edu	Houston	TX	77035	713-942-9505	942-9506
Howard University School of Divinity 1400 Shepherd St NE TF: 800-822-6363 ■ Web: www.howard.edu	Washington	DC	20017	202-806-0500	806-0711
Iliff School of Theology 2201 S University Blvd TF: 800-678-3360 ■ Web: www.iliff.edu	Denver	CO	80210	303-744-1287	777-0164
Interdenominational Theological Ctr 700 Martin Luther King Jr Dr TF: 800-908-9946 ■ Web: www.itc.edu	Atlanta	GA	30314	404-527-7700	527-0901
Jesuit School of Theology at Berkeley 1735 LeRoy Ave TF: 800-824-0122 ■ Web: www.scu.edu	Berkeley	CA	94709	510-549-5000	841-8536
Kenrick-Glennon Seminary 5200 Glennon Dr. Web: www.kenrick.edu	Saint Louis	MO	63119	314-792-6100	792-6500
Knox College 59 St George St Web: www.utoronto.ca	Toronto	ON	M5S2E6	416-978-4500	971-2133
La Sierra University 4500 Riverwalk Pkwy TF: 800-874-5587 ■ Web: www.lasierra.edu	Riverside	CA	92515	951-785-2000	785-2901
Lancaster Theological Seminary 555 W James St TF: 800-393-0654 ■ Web: www.lancasterseminary.edu	Lancaster	PA	17603	717-393-0654	393-4254
Lexington Theological Seminary 631 S Limestone St TF: 866-296-6087 ■ Web: www.lextheo.edu	Lexington	KY	40508	859-252-0361	281-6042
Lincoln Christian College Seminary 100 Campus View Dr TF: 888-522-5228 ■ Web: lincolnchristian.edu	Lincoln	IL	62656	217-732-3168	
Lipscomb University 3901 Granny White Pk *Fax: Admissions ■ TF: 800-333-4358 ■ Web: www.lipscomb.edu	Nashville	TN	37204	615-966-1000	966-1804*
Logos Evangelical Seminary 9358 Telstar Ave. Web: www.logos-seminary.edu	El Monte	CA	91731	626-571-5110	571-5119
Louisville Presbyterian Theological Seminary 1044 Alta Vista Rd TF: 800-264-1839 ■ Web: www.lpts.edu	Louisville	KY	40205	502-895-3411	895-1096
Luther Seminary 2481 Como Ave. TF: 800-588-4373 ■ Web: www.luthersem.edu	Saint Paul	MN	55108	651-641-3456	641-3425
Lutheran School of Theology at Chicago 1100 E 55th St TF: 800-635-1116 ■ Web: www.lstc.edu	Chicago	IL	60615	773-256-0700	256-0782
Lutheran Theological Seminary 114 Seminary Crescent Web: www.usask.ca	Saskatoon	SK	S7N0X3	306-966-7850	966-7852
Lutheran Theological Seminary at Gettysburg 61 Seminary Ridge TF: 800-658-8437 ■ Web: www.ltsg.edu	Gettysburg	PA	17325	717-334-6286	334-3469
Lutheran Theological Seminary at Philadelphia 7301 Germantown Ave TF: 800-286-4616 ■ Web: www.ltsp.edu	Philadelphia	PA	19119	215-248-4616	248-4577
McCormick Theological Seminary 5460 S University Ave TF: 800-228-4687 ■ Web: www.mccormick.edu	Chicago	IL	60615	773-947-6300	288-2612
Meadville Lombard Theological School 5701 S Woodlawn Ave *Fax Area Code: 312 ■ TF: 800-848-0979 ■ Web: www.meadville.edu	Chicago	IL	60637	773-256-3000	327-7002*
Memphis Theological Seminary 168 E Pkwy S Web: www.memphisseminary.edu	Memphis	TN	38104	901-458-8232	452-4051
Mennonite Brethren Biblical Seminary 4824 E Butler Ave TF: 800-251-6227 ■ Web: www.fresno.edu/programs-majors/biblical-seminary	Fresno	CA	93727	559-453-2000	251-7212
Methodist Theological School in Ohio 3081 Columbus Pk. TF: 800-333-6876 ■ Web: www.mtso.edu	Delaware	OH	43015	740-363-1146	362-3135
Michigan Theological Seminary 41550 E Ann Arbor Trail TF: 800-356-6639 ■ Web: www.moody.edu	Plymouth	MI	48170	734-207-9581	207-9582
Mid-America Reformed Seminary 229 Seminary Dr. TF: 888-440-6277 ■ Web: www.midamerica.edu	Dyer	IN	46311	219-864-2400	864-2410
Midwestern Baptist Theological Seminary 5001 N Oak Trafficway TF: 800-944-6287 ■ Web: www.mbts.edu	Kansas City	MO	64118	816-414-3700	414-3799
Moravian Theological Seminary 1200 Main St. TF: 800-843-6541 ■ Web: www.moravianseminary.edu	Bethlehem	PA	18018	610-861-1516	861-1569
Mount Angel Seminary 1 Abbey Dr TF: 800-845-8272 ■ Web: www.mountangelabbey.org	Saint Benedict	OR	97373	503-845-3951	
Mount Saint Mary's University 16300 Old Emmitsburg Rd *Fax: Admissions ■ TF Admissions: 800-448-4347 ■ Web: www.msmary.edu	Emmitsburg	MD	21727	301-447-5214	447-5860*
Multnomah University 8435 NE Glisan St. TF: 800-275-4672 ■ Web: www.multnomah.edu	Portland	OR	97220	503-255-0332	254-1268
Nashotah House 2777 Mission Rd Web: www.nashotah.edu	Nashotah	WI	53058	262-646-6500	646-6504
Nazarene Theological Seminary 1700 E Meyer Blvd TF: 800-831-3011 ■ Web: www.nts.edu	Kansas City	MO	64131	816-333-6254	
New Brunswick Theological Seminary 35 Seminary Pl TF: 800-445-6287 ■ Web: www.nbts.edu	New Brunswick	NJ	08901	732-247-5241	249-5412
New Orleans Baptist Theological Seminary 3939 Gentilly Blvd TF: 800-662-8701 ■ Web: www.nobts.edu	New Orleans	LA	70126	504-282-4455	816-8023
New York Theological Seminary 475 Riverside Dr Ste 500 Web: nyts.edu	New York	NY	10115	212-870-1211	870-1236
Newman Theological College (NTC) 10012-84 St TF: 844-392-2450 ■ Web: www.newman.edu	Edmonton	AB	T6A0B2	780-392-2450	462-4013
North Park Theological Seminary 3225 W Foster Ave TF: 800-964-0101 ■ Web: www.northpark.edu	Chicago	IL	60625	773-244-6210	244-6244
Northern Seminary 660 E Butterfield Rd Web: www.seminary.edu	Lombard	IL	60148	630-620-2180	620-2190
Notre Dame Seminary 2901 S Carrollton Ave Web: nds.edu	New Orleans	LA	70118	504-866-7426	866-3119
NYACK 350 N Highland Ave TF: 800-541-6891 ■ Web: nyack.edu	Nyack	NY	10960	845-353-2020	
Oakland City University 138 N Lucretia St TF: 800-737-5125 ■ Web: www.oak.edu	Oakland City	IN	47660	812-749-4781	749-1433
Oblate School of Theology 285 Oblate Dr Web: www.ost.edu	San Antonio	TX	78216	210-341-1366	341-4519
Oral Roberts University 7777 S Lewis Ave *Fax: Admissions ■ TF: 800-678-8876 ■ Web: www.oru.edu	Tulsa	OK	74171	918-495-6161	495-6222*
Pacific Lutheran Theological Seminary 2770 Marin Ave TF: 800-235-7587 ■ Web: www.plts.edu	Berkeley	CA	94708	510-524-5264	524-2408
Pacific School of Religion 1798 Scenic Ave TF: 800-999-0528 ■ Web: www.psr.edu	Berkeley	CA	94709	510-848-0528	845-8948
Palmer Theological Seminary 588 N Gulph Rd TF: 800-220-3287 ■ Web: www.palmerseminary.edu	King Of Prussia	PA	19406	610-896-5000	649-3834
Payne Theological Seminary 1230 Wilberforce Clifton Rd TF: 888-816-8933 ■ Web: www.payne.edu	Wilberforce	OH	45384	937-376-2946	376-3330
Pentecostal Theological Seminary 900 Walker St NE TF: 800-228-9126 ■ Web: www.ptseminary.edu	Cleveland	TN	37311	423-478-1131	478-7711
Phillips Theological Seminary 901 N Mingo Rd TF: 800-843-4675 ■ Web: www.ptstulsa.edu	Tulsa	OK	74116	918-610-8303	610-8404
Phoenix Seminary 4222 E Thomas Rd Ste 400 TF: 888-443-1020 ■ Web: www.ps.edu	Phoenix	AZ	85018	602-850-8000	850-8080
Pittsburgh Theological Seminary 616 N Highland Ave TF: 800-451-4194 ■ Web: www.pts.edu	Pittsburgh	PA	15206	412-362-5610	363-3260

Institution	City	State	Zip	Phone	Fax
Pontifical College Josephinum 7625 N High St *TF:* 888-252-5812 ■ *Web:* www.pcj.edu	Columbus	OH	43235	614-885-5585	885-2307
Princeton Theological Seminary 64 Mercer St *TF:* 800-622-6767 ■ *Web:* www.ptsem.edu	Princeton	NJ	08540	609-921-8300	924-2973
Protestant Episcopal Theological Seminary in Virginia 3737 Seminary Rd *TF:* 800-941-0083 ■ *Web:* www.vts.edu	Alexandria	VA	22304	703-370-6600	370-6234
Providence College & Seminary 10 College Crescent *TF:* 800-668-7768 ■ *Web:* www.providenceuc.ca	Otterburne	MB	R0A1G0	204-433-7488	433-3046
Queen's College Faculty of Theology 210 Prince Philip Dr Ste 3000 *TF:* 877-753-0116 ■ *Web:* www.queenscollegemun.ca	Saint John's	NL	A1B3R6	709-753-0116	753-1214
Queen's Theological College Theological Hall 99 University Ave Rm 212 *Web:* www.queensu.ca	Kingston	ON	K7L3N6	613-533-2110	533-6879
Reformed Episcopal Seminary 826 Second Ave *Web:* www.reseminary.edu	Blue Bell	PA	19422	610-292-9852	292-9853
Reformed Presbyterian Theological Seminary 7418 Penn Ave *Web:* www.rpts.edu	Pittsburgh	PA	15208	412-731-6000	731-4834
Reformed Theological Seminary 5422 Clinton Blvd *TF:* 800-543-2703 ■ *Web:* www.rts.edu	Jackson	MS	39209	601-923-1600	923-1654
Regent College 5800 University Blvd *TF:* 800-663-8664 ■ *Web:* www.regent-college.edu	Vancouver	BC	V6T2E4	604-224-3245	224-3097
Regis College 15 St Mary St *Web:* www.regiscollege.ca	Toronto	ON	M4Y2R5	416-922-5474	922-2898
Roberts Wesleyan College 2301 Westside Dr **Fax:* Admissions ■ *TF Admissions:* 800-777-4792 ■ *Web:* www.roberts.edu	Rochester	NY	14624	585-594-6000	594-6371*
Sacred Heart School of Theology 7335 S Hwy 100 *Web:* shsst.edu	Franklin	WI	53132	414-425-8300	529-6999
Saint Bernard's School of Theology & Ministry 120 French Rd *Web:* www.stbernards.edu	Rochester	NY	14618	585-271-3657	271-2045
Saint Charles Borromeo Seminary 100 E Wynnewood Rd *Web:* www.scs.edu	Wynnewood	PA	19096	610-667-3394	
Saint John Vianney Theological Seminary 1300 S Steele St *Web:* www.sjvdenver.org	Denver	CO	80210	303-282-3427	
Saint John's Seminary 127 Lake St *Web:* www.sjs.edu	Brighton	MA	02135	617-254-2610	
Saint John's Seminary 5012 Seminary Rd *Web:* www.stjohnsem.edu	Camarillo	CA	93012	805-482-2755	
Saint Joseph's Seminary 201 Seminary Ave *Web:* www.archny.org	Yonkers	NY	10704	914-968-6200	
Saint Mary Seminary & Graduate School of Theology 28700 Euclid Ave *Web:* www.stmarysem.edu	Wickliffe	OH	44092	440-943-7600	943-7577
Saint Mary's Seminary & University 5400 Roland Ave *Web:* www.stmarys.edu	Baltimore	MD	21210	410-864-4000	
Saint Meinrad School of Theology 200 Hill Dr *Web:* www.saintmeinrad.edu	Saint Meinrad	IN	47577	812-357-6611	
Saint Patrick's Seminary & University 320 Middlefield Rd *Web:* www.stpsu.edu	Menlo Park	CA	94025	650-325-5621	323-5447
Saint Paul School of Theology 4370 W 109th St Ste 300 *TF:* 800-825-0378 ■ *Web:* www.spst.edu	Overland Park	KS	66211	800-825-0378	
Saint Peter's Seminary 1040 Waterloo St N *TF:* 888-548-9649 ■ *Web:* www.stpetersseminary.ca	London	ON	N6A3Y1	519-432-1824	432-0964
Saint Tikhon's Orthodox Theological Seminary St Tikhon's Rd PO Box 130 *Web:* www.stots.edu	South Canaan	PA	18459	570-561-1818	937-3100
Saint Vincent de Paul Regional Seminary 10701 S Military Trl *Web:* www.svdp.edu	Boynton Beach	FL	33436	561-732-4424	737-2205
Saint Vincent Seminary 300 Fraser Purchase Rd *Web:* www.saintvincentseminary.edu	Latrobe	PA	15650	724-532-6600	532-5052
Samford University 800 Lakeshore Dr **Fax:* Admissions ■ *TF Admissions:* 800-888-7218 ■ *Web:* www.samford.edu	Birmingham	AL	35229	205-726-3673	726-2171*
San Francisco Theological Seminary 105 Seminary Rd *TF:* 800-447-8820 ■ *Web:* www.sfts.edu	San Anselmo	CA	94960	415-451-2800	451-2851
Seminary of the Immaculate Conception 440 W Neck Rd *Web:* icseminary.edu	Huntington	NY	11743	631-423-0483	423-2346
Seton Hall University Immaculate Conception Seminary 400 S Orange Ave *TF:* 800-843-4255 ■ *Web:* www.shu.edu	South Orange	NJ	07079	973-761-9575	761-9577
Shaw University 118 E S St **Fax:* Admissions ■ *TF Admissions:* 800-214-6683 ■ *Web:* www.shawu.edu	Raleigh	NC	27601	919-546-8275	546-8271*
Sioux Falls Seminary 2100 S Summit *TF:* 800-440-6227 ■ *Web:* www.sfseminary.edu	Sioux Falls	SD	57105	605-336-6588	335-9090
Southeastern Baptist Theological Seminary 120 S Wingate St *TF:* 800-284-6317 ■ *Web:* www.sebts.edu	Wake Forest	NC	27587	919-556-3101	
Southern Baptist Theological Seminary 2825 Lexington Rd **Fax:* Admitting ■ *TF:* 800-626-5525 ■ *Web:* www.sbts.edu	Louisville	KY	40280	502-897-4011	897-4723*
Southwestern Baptist Theological Seminary PO Box 22740 *TF:* 877-467-9287 ■ *Web:* www.swbts.edu	Fort Worth	TX	76122	817-923-1921	921-8758
SS Cyril & Methodius Seminary 3535 Indian Trl *Web:* sscms.edu	Orchard Lake	MI	48324	248-683-0310	738-6735
Starr King School for the Ministry 2441 LeConte Ave *TF:* 866-727-4894 ■ *Web:* www.sksm.edu	Berkeley	CA	94709	510-845-6232	845-6273
Taylor University College & Seminary 11525 23rd Ave *TF:* 800-567-4988 ■ *Web:* www.taylor-edu.ca	Edmonton	AB	T6J4T3	780-431-5200	436-9416
Toronto School of Theology 47 Queen's Pk Crescent E *Web:* www.tst.edu	Toronto	ON	M5S2C3	416-978-4039	978-7821
Trinity Episcopal School for Ministry 311 11th St *TF:* 800-874-8754 ■ *Web:* tsm.edu	Ambridge	PA	15003	724-266-3838	266-4617
Trinity International University 2065 Half Day Rd *TF:* 800-822-3225 ■ *Web:* www.tiu.edu	Deerfield	IL	60015	847-945-8800	317-8097
Trinity Lutheran Seminary 2199 E Main St *TF:* 866-610-8571 ■ *Web:* tlsohio.edu	Columbus	OH	43209	614-235-4136	238-0263
Trinity Western University 7600 Glover Rd **Fax:* Admissions ■ *TF:* 888-468-6898 ■ *Web:* www.twu.ca	Langley	BC	V2Y1Y1	604-888-7511	513-2064*
Tyndale University College & Seminary 25 Ballyconnor Ct *TF:* 877-896-3253 ■ *Web:* www.tyndale.ca	Toronto	ON	M2M4B3	416-226-6380	226-6746
Union Theological Seminary 3041 Broadway *TF:* 800-251-9489 ■ *Web:* www.uts.columbia.edu	New York	NY	10027	212-662-7100	280-1416
Union Theological Seminary & Presbyterian School of Christian Education 3401 Brook Rd *TF:* 800-229-2990 ■ *Web:* upsem.edu	Richmond	VA	23227	804-355-0671	
United Theological Seminary 4501 Denlinger Rd *Web:* www.united.edu	Dayton	OH	45426	937-529-2201	
United Theological Seminary of the Twin Cities 3000 Fifth St NW *TF:* 800-937-1316 ■ *Web:* www.unitedseminary-mn.org	New Brighton	MN	55112	651-633-4311	633-4315
University of Dubuque Theological Seminary 2000 University Ave *TF:* 800-369-8387 ■ *Web:* udts.dbq.edu	Dubuque	IA	52001	563-589-3122	589-3110
University of Saint Mary of the Lake Mundelein Seminary 1000 E Maple Ave *Web:* www.usml.edu	Mundelein	IL	60060	847-566-6401	
University of Saint Michael's College Faculty of Theology 81 St Mary St *Web:* www.utoronto.ca	Toronto	ON	M5S1J4	416-926-1300	926-7276
University of Saint Thomas 2115 Summit Ave **Fax:* Admissions ■ *TF:* 800-328-6819 ■ *Web:* www.stthomas.edu	Saint Paul	MN	55105	651-962-5000	962-6160*
University of Saint Thomas School of Theology 9845 Memorial Dr *Web:* www.stthom.edu	Houston	TX	77024	713-686-4345	683-8673
University of Saskatchewan 1121 College Dr *TF:* 877-653-8501 ■ *Web:* www.usask.ca	Saskatoon	SK	S7N0W3	306-966-8970	966-8747
University of the South 735 University Ave **Fax:* Admissions ■ *TF:* 800-522-2234 ■ *Web:* www.sewanee.edu	Sewanee	TN	37383	931-598-1238	598-3248*
Urshan Graduate School of Theology 704 Howder Shell Rd *Web:* www.ugst.edu	Florissant	MO	63031	314-921-9290	921-9203
Vancouver School of Theology 6040 Iona Dr *TF:* 866-822-9031 ■ *Web:* www.vst.edu	Vancouver	BC	V6T2E8	604-822-9031	822-9212
Virginia Union University 1500 N Lombardy St **Fax:* Admissions ■ *TF:* 800-368-3227 ■ *Web:* www.vuu.edu	Richmond	VA	23220	804-342-3570	342-3511*
Wartburg Theological Seminary 333 Wartburg Pl *TF:* 800-225-5987 ■ *Web:* www.wartburgseminary.edu	Dubuque	IA	52003	563-589-0200	589-0333
Washington Baptist University 4302 Evergreen Ln *Web:* www.wbcs.edu	Annandale	VA	22003	703-333-5904	333-5906
Washington Theological Union 6896 Laurel St NW	Washington	DC	20012	202-726-8800	
Wesley Biblical Seminary 787 E Northside Dr *Web:* www.wbs.edu	Jackson	MS	39206	601-366-8880	366-8832
Wesley Theological Seminary 4500 Massachusetts Ave NW *TF:* 800-882-4987 ■ *Web:* wesleyseminary.edu	Washington	DC	20016	202-885-8600	885-8605
Western Seminary 5511 SE Hawthorne Blvd *TF:* 877-517-1800 ■ *Web:* www.westernseminary.edu	Portland	OR	97215	503-517-1800	517-1801
Western Theological Seminary 101 E 13th St *TF:* 800-392-8554 ■ *Web:* www.westernsem.edu	Holland	MI	49423	616-392-8555	392-7717
Westminster Theological Seminary 2960 Church Rd *TF:* 800-373-0119 ■ *Web:* www.wts.edu	Glenside	PA	19038	215-887-5511	887-5404
Westminster Theological Seminary in California 1725 Bear Vly Pkwy *TF:* 888-480-8474 ■ *Web:* www.wscal.edu	Escondido	CA	92027	760-480-8474	480-0252
Winebrenner Theological Seminary 950 N Main St *TF:* 800-992-4987 ■ *Web:* www.winebrenner.edu	Findlay	OH	45840	419-434-4200	434-4267
Yale Divinity School Admissions Office 409 Prospect St *TF:* 866-358-3806	New Haven	CT	06511	203-432-5360	777-6100

168 COLLEGES & UNIVERSITIES - HISTORICALLY BLACK

Historically Black Colleges & Universities (HBCUs) are colleges or universities that were established before 1964 with the intention of serving the African-American community. (Prior to 1964, African-Americans were almost always excluded from higher education opportunities at the predominantly white colleges and universities.)

Institution	City	State	Zip	Phone	Fax
Albany State University 504 College Dr Rd	Albany	GA	31705	229-430-4600	430-1614*
Allen University 1530 Harden St **Fax:* Mail Rm ■ *TF:* 877-625-5368 ■ *Web:* www.allenuniversity.edu	Columbia	SC	29204	803-376-5700	376-5733*
Benedict College 1600 Harden St *TF:* 800-868-6598 ■ *Web:* www.benedict.edu	Columbia	SC	29204	803-253-5000	
Bennett College 900 E Washington St **Fax:* Admissions ■ *TF Admissions:* 800-413-5323 ■ *Web:* www.bennett.edu	Greensboro	NC	27401	336-370-8624	517-2166*

Phone *Fax*

Bethune-Cookman College
640 Dr Mary McLeod Bethune Blvd . . . . .Daytona Beach FL 32114 386-481-2900 481-2601*
Fax: Admissions ■ *TF Admissions:* 800-448-0228 ■ *Web:* www.cookman.edu
Bishop State Community College 351 N Broad St . . . . . . .Mobile AL 36603 251-405-7000
Web: bishop.edu
Bluefield State College 219 Rock St. . . . . Bluefield WV 24701 304-327-4000 325-7747*
Fax: Admissions ■ *TF:* 800-654-7798 ■ *Web:* bluefieldstate.edu
Bowie State University 14000 Jericho Pk Rd . . . . Bowie MD 20715 301-860-4000 860-3518
TF: 877-772-6943 ■ *Web:* www.bowiestate.edu
Central State University
1400 Brush Row Rd PO Box 1004 . . . . .Wilberforce OH 45384 937-376-6011 376-6648*
Fax: Admissions ■ *TF:* 800-388-2781 ■ *Web:* www.centralstate.edu
Charles R Drew University of Medicine & Science
1731 E 120th St . . . . .Los Angeles CA 90059 323-563-4800 563-4957*
Fax: Admissions ■ *Web:* www.cdrewu.edu
Cheyney University of Pennsylvania
1837 University Cir PO Box 200. . . . . Cheyney PA 19319 610-399-2275 399-2099*
Fax: Admissions ■ *TF:* 800-243-9639 ■ *Web:* www.cheyney.edu
Claflin University 400 Magnolia St. . . . . .Orangeburg SC 29115 803-535-5000 535-5385
TF: 800-922-1276 ■ *Web:* www.claflin.edu
Clark Atlanta University
223 James P Brawley Dr SW . . . . .Atlanta GA 30314 404-880-8000 880-6174*
Fax: Admissions ■ *TF Admissions:* 800-688-3228 ■ *Web:* www.cau.edu
Clinton Junior College 1029 Crawford Rd. . . . . Rock Hill SC 29730 803-327-7402 328-6318*
Fax: Admissions ■ *TF:* 877-837-9645
Coppin State University 2500 W N Ave. . . . . .Baltimore MD 21216 410-951-3600 523-7351*
Fax: Admissions ■ *TF Admissions:* 800-635-3674 ■ *Web:* www.coppin.edu
Delaware State University 1200 N DuPont Hwy. . . . . .Dover DE 19901 302-857-6351 857-6352*
Fax: Admissions ■ *TF Admissions:* 800-845-2544 ■ *Web:* www.desu.edu
Elizabeth City State University
1704 Weeksville Rd . . . . .Elizabeth City NC 27909 252-335-3400 335-3537*
Fax: Admissions ■ *TF Admissions:* 800-347-3278 ■ *Web:* www.ecsu.edu
Fayetteville State University
1200 Murchison Rd . . . . Fayetteville NC 28301 910-672-1371 672-1414*
Fax: Admissions ■ *TF Admissions:* 800-222-2594 ■ *Web:* www.uncfsu.edu
Fisk University 1000 17th Ave N. . . . . .Nashville TN 37208 615-329-8500 329-8774
TF: 888-702-0022 ■ *Web:* www.fisk.edu
Florida A & M University
1700 Lee Hall Dr Rm G-7
Foote-Hilyer Administration Ctr . . . . Tallahassee FL 32307 850-599-3000 599-3069
TF: 866-642-1198 ■ *Web:* www.famu.edu
Florida Memorial University
15800 NW 42nd Ave. . . . . Miami Gardens FL 33054 305-626-3600
TF: 800-822-1362 ■ *Web:* www.fmuniv.edu
Fort Valley State University
1005 State University Dr. . . . . .Fort Valley GA 31030 478-825-6211
TF: 877-462-3878 ■ *Web:* www.fvsu.edu
Grambling State University 403 Main St . . . . Grambling LA 71245 318-247-3811
TF: 800-569-4714 ■ *Web:* www.gram.edu
Hampton University 100 E Queen St . . . . Hampton VA 23668 757-727-5000
TF: 800-624-3341 ■ *Web:* www.hamptonu.edu
Harris-Stowe State University
3026 Laclede Ave . . . . Saint Louis MO 63103 314-340-3366 340-3555
Web: www.hssu.edu
Hinds Community College
501 E Main St PO Box 1100. . . . . .Raymond MS 39154 601-857-5261 857-3539*
Fax: Admissions ■ *TF:* 800-446-3722 ■ *Web:* www.hindscc.edu
Howard University 2400 Sixth St NW. . . . . .Washington DC 20059 202-806-6100 806-4465*
Fax: Admissions ■ *TF:* 800-822-6363 ■ *Web:* www.howard.edu
Huston-Tillotson University 900 Chicon St . . . . Austin TX 78702 512-505-3000 505-3192*
Fax: Admissions ■ *TF:* 877-487-8702 ■ *Web:* www.htu.edu
Interdenominational Theological Ctr
700 Martin Luther King Jr Dr . . . . .Atlanta GA 30314 404-527-7700 527-0901
TF: 800-908-9946 ■ *Web:* www.itc.edu
Jackson State University
1400 John R Lynch St . . . . .Jackson MS 39217 601-979-2121 979-3445*
Fax: Admissions ■ *TF:* 800-848-6817 ■ *Web:* www.jsums.edu
Jarvis Christian College PO Box 1470 . . . . .Hawkins TX 75765 903-769-5700 769-1282*
Fax: Admissions ■ *Web:* www.jarvis.edu
Johnson C Smith University
100 Beatties Ford Rd . . . . Charlotte NC 28216 704-378-1000 378-1242*
Fax: Admissions ■ *TF Admissions:* 800-782-7303 ■ *Web:* www.jcsu.edu
Kentucky State University 400 E Main St . . . . Frankfort KY 40601 502-597-6000 597-5814*
Fax: Admissions ■ *TF Admissions:* 800-325-1716 ■ *Web:* www.kysu.edu
Lane College 545 Ln Ave. . . . . .Jackson TN 38301 731-426-7500 426-7559*
Fax: Admissions ■ *TF Admissions:* 800-960-7533 ■ *Web:* www.lanecollege.edu
Langston University
2013 Langston University PO Box 1500. . . . . .Langston OK 73050 877-466-2231 466-3271*
Fax Area Code: 405 ■ *TF:* 877-466-2231 ■ *Web:* www.lunet.edu
Lincoln University
820 Chestnut St B-7 Young Hall. . . . . .Jefferson City MO 65102 573-681-5599 681-5889*
Fax: Admissions ■ *TF Admissions:* 800-521-5052 ■ *Web:* www.lincolnu.edu
Lincoln University
1570 Old Baltimore Pk PO Box 179 . . . . .Lincoln University PA 19352 484-365-8000 365-8109*
Fax: Admissions ■ *TF Admissions:* 800-790-0191 ■ *Web:* www.lincoln.edu
Livingstone College 701 W Monroe St . . . . .Salisbury NC 28144 704-216-6963 216-6215
TF: 800-835-3435 ■ *Web:* www.livingstone.edu
Miles College 5500 Myron Massey Blvd. . . . . .Fairfield AL 35064 205-929-1000 929-1627*
Fax: Admissions ■ *TF Admissions:* 800-445-0708 ■ *Web:* www.miles.edu
Mississippi Valley State University
14000 Hwy 82 . . . . Itta Bena MS 38941 662-254-9041 254-3759
TF: 800-844-6885 ■ *Web:* www.mvsu.edu
Morehouse College 830 Westview Dr SW . . . . .Atlanta GA 30314 404-681-2800 572-3668*
Fax: Admissions ■ *Web:* www.morehouse.edu
Morehouse School of Medicine
720 Westview Dr SW . . . . .Atlanta GA 30310 404-752-1500 752-1512*
Fax: Admissions ■ *Web:* www.msm.edu
Morgan State University
1700 E Cold Spring Ln. . . . . .Baltimore MD 21251 443-885-3333 885-8260*
Fax: Admissions ■ *TF:* 800-319-4678 ■ *Web:* www.morgan.edu
Morris College 100 W College St . . . . .Sumter SC 29150 803-934-3200 773-8241*
Fax: Admissions ■ *TF Admissions:* 866-853-1345 ■ *Web:* www.morris.edu
Norfolk State University 700 Pk Ave. . . . . Norfolk VA 23504 757-823-8600 823-2078*
Fax: Admissions ■ *TF:* 800-274-1821 ■ *Web:* www.nsu.edu

North Carolina A & T State University
1601 E Market St . . . . .Greensboro NC 27411 336-334-7946 334-7478*
Fax: Admissions ■ *TF Admissions:* 800-443-8964 ■ *Web:* www.ncat.edu
North Carolina Central University
1801 Fayetteville St . . . . .Durham NC 27707 919-530-6100 530-7625*
Fax: Admissions ■ *TF Admissions:* 877-667-7533 ■ *Web:* www.nccu.edu
Oakwood College 7000 Adventist Blvd. . . . . Huntsville AL 35896 256-726-7356 726-7154*
Fax: Admissions ■ *TF:* 800-824-5312 ■ *Web:* www.oakwood.edu
Paine College 1235 15th St. . . . . .Augusta GA 30901 706-821-8200
TF: 800-476-7703 ■ *Web:* www.paine.edu
Paul Quinn College 3837 Simpson Stuart Rd. . . . . Dallas TX 75241 214-376-1000
TF: 800-433-3243 ■ *Web:* www.pqc.edu
Prairie View A & M University
PO Box 519 . . . . .Prairie View TX 77446 936-857-2626 261-1079*
Fax: Admissions ■ *TF:* 877-241-1752 ■ *Web:* www.pvamu.edu
Rust College 150 Rust Ave . . . . Holly Springs MS 38635 662-252-8000 252-2258*
Fax: Admissions ■ *TF:* 888-886-8492 ■ *Web:* www.rustcollege.edu
Saint Augustine's College 1315 Oakwood Ave. . . . . Raleigh NC 27610 919-516-4016 516-5805*
Fax: Admissions ■ *TF Admissions:* 800-948-1126 ■ *Web:* www.st-aug.edu
Saint Paul's College 115 College Dr . . . . .Lawrenceville VA 23868 434-848-3111 848-6407*
Selma University 1501 Lapsley St . . . . Selma AL 36701 334-872-2533
Web: selmauniversity.org
Shaw University 118 E S St. . . . . Raleigh NC 27601 919-546-8275 546-8271*
Fax: Admissions ■ *TF Admissions:* 800-214-6683 ■ *Web:* www.shawu.edu
Shelton State Community College
9500 Old Greensboro Rd . . . . Tuscaloosa AL 35405 205-391-2211 391-3910*
Fax: Admissions ■ *TF:* 877-211-7722 ■ *Web:* www.sheltonstate.edu
Shorter College 604 N Locust St. . . . . North Little Rock AR 72114 501-374-6305 374-9333*
South Carolina State University
300 College St NE PO Box 7127. . . . . .Orangeburg SC 29117 803-536-7000 536-8990
TF Admissions: 800-260-5956 ■ *Web:* www.scsu.edu
Southern University & A & M College
156 Elton C Harrison Dr PO Box 9757 . . . . Baton Rouge LA 70813 225-771-5180 771-4762*
Fax: Admissions ■ *TF Admissions:* 800-256-1531 ■ *Web:* www.subr.edu
Southwestern Christian College PO Box 10 . . . . Terrell TX 75160 972-524-3341 563-7133
TF: 800-925-9357 ■ *Web:* www.swcc.edu
Spelman College 350 Spelman Ln SW. . . . . .Atlanta GA 30314 404-681-3643 270-5201*
Fax: Admissions ■ *TF Admissions:* 800-982-2411 ■ *Web:* www.spelman.edu
Stillman College 3601 Stillman Blvd . . . . Tuscaloosa AL 35401 205-349-4240
TF: 800-841-5722 ■ *Web:* www.stillman.edu
Tennessee State University
3500 John A Merritt Blvd PO Box 9609 . . . . .Nashville TN 37209 615-963-5000 963-5108
TF Admissions: 888-463-6878 ■ *Web:* www.tnstate.edu
Texas College 2404 N Grand Ave . . . . Tyler TX 75702 903-593-8311
TF: 800-306-6299 ■ *Web:* www.texascollege.edu
Texas Southern University 3100 Cleburne St. . . . . .Houston TX 77004 713-313-7011 313-1859
TF: 800-252-5400 ■ *Web:* www.tsu.edu
Tougaloo College 500 W County Line Rd. . . . . .Tougaloo MS 39174 601-977-7700 977-4501*
Fax: Admissions ■ *TF Admissions:* 888-424-2566 ■ *Web:* www.tougaloo.edu
Trenholm State Technical College
1225 Air Base Blvd. . . . . Montgomery AL 36108 334-420-4200 420-4206
TF: 800-917-2081 ■ *Web:* www.trenholmstate.edu
Tuskegee University 1200 W Montgomery Rd. . . . . .Tuskegee AL 36088 334-727-8011 727-5750*
Fax: Admissions ■ *TF Admissions:* 800-622-6531 ■ *Web:* www.tuskegee.edu
University of the District of Columbia
4200 Connecticut Ave NW . . . . .Washington DC 20008 202-274-5000 274-5552
Web: www.udc.edu
Virginia State University 1 Hayden Dr . . . . .Petersburg VA 23806 804-524-5000 524-5055
TF Admissions: 800-871-7611 ■ *Web:* www.vsu.edu
Virginia Union University
1500 N Lombardy St. . . . . Richmond VA 23220 804-342-3570 342-3511*
Fax: Admissions ■ *TF:* 800-368-3227 ■ *Web:* www.vuu.edu
Voorhees College 213 Wiggins Dr PO Box 678 . . . . Denmark SC 29042 803-780-1234
TF Admissions: 800-446-6250 ■ *Web:* www.voorhees.edu
West Virginia State University
117 Ferrell Hall PO Box 368. . . . . Institute WV 25112 304-766-3000
TF: 800-987-2112 ■ *Web:* www.wvstateu.edu
Wilberforce University
1055 N Bickett Rd PO Box 1001. . . . . Wilberforce OH 45384 937-376-2911 376-4751*
Fax: Admissions ■ *TF Admissions:* 800-367-8568 ■ *Web:* www.wilberforce.edu
Wiley College 711 Wiley Ave. . . . . Marshall TX 75670 903-927-3300 927-3366*
Fax: Admissions ■ *TF Admissions:* 800-658-6889 ■ *Web:* www.wileyc.edu
Winston-Salem State University
601 S ML King Jr Dr 206 Thompson Ctr . . . . Winston-Salem NC 27110 336-750-2000 750-2079*
Fax: Admissions ■ *TF Admissions:* 800-257-4052 ■ *Web:* www.wssu.edu
Xavier University of Louisiana
1 Drexel Dr . . . . New Orleans LA 70125 504-486-7411 520-7922
Web: www.xula.edu

169 COMMODITY CONTRACTS BROKERS & DEALERS

See Also Investment Advice & Management p. 2597; Securities Brokers & Dealers p. 3163

Phone *Fax*

Advantage Futures LLC
231 S Lasalle St Ste 1400. . . . . .Chicago IL 60604 312-800-7000
Web: advantagefutures.com
Applied Research Co 53 W Jackson Blvd Ste 337. . . . . . . .Chicago IL 60604 312-922-7882
Web: www.appliedresearch.com
Basic Commodities Inc 863 S Orlando Ave. . . . . Winter Park FL 32789 407-629-2000
TF: 800-338-7006 ■ *Web:* basiccommodities.com
Cedar Petrochemicals Inc 110 Wall St 7th Fl . . . . .New York NY 10005 212-288-4320
ClearTrade Inc 5415 N Sheridan Rd Ste 5512 . . . . .Chicago IL 60640 773-561-9777
Web: www.cleartrade.com
Essex Futures Inc 8105 Irvine Ctr Dr Ste 840. . . . . Irvine CA 92618 949-450-8221
Web: www.essexfutures.com
GFI Group Inc 55 Water St . . . . .New York NY 10041 212-968-4100 968-2386
NYSE: GFIG ■ *TF:* 888-750-5884 ■ *Web:* www.gfigroup.com
Keeley Investment Corp
401 S La Salle St Ste 1201. . . . . .Chicago IL 60605 312-786-5000 786-5002
TF: 800-533-5344 ■ *Web:* www.keeleyfunds.com

Phone Fax

Koch Mineral Services LLC 4111 E 37th St N. . . . . Wichita KS 67220 316-828-5500 828-6997
TF: 800-750-5834

Koch Supply & Trading LP 4111 E 37th St N . . . . Wichita KS 67220 713-544-4123 828-5739*
**Fax Area Code:* 316 ■ *Web:* www.kochoil.com

Kolmar Americas Inc
10 Middle St Penthouse . . . . Bridgeport CT 06604 203-873-2051
Web: www.kolmargroup.com

Marubeni America Corp 375 Lexington Ave . . . . .New York NY 10017 212-450-0100 450-0700
Web: www.marubeni-usa.com

Mla General Contractor Inc PO Box 624 . . . . Fallbrook CA 92028 760-723-0210
Web: mlacontractor.com

OptionsXpress Inc 311 W Monroe Ste 1000 . . . . .Chicago IL 60606 312-630-3300 629-5256
TF: 888-280-8020 ■ *Web:* www.optionsxpress.com

Orion Futures 1905 W Busch Blvd. . . . . Tampa FL 33612 813-876-9662 876-5530

PS International Ltd
1414 Raleigh Rd Ste 205 . . . . Chapel Hill NC 27517 919-933-7400 933-7441
Web: www.psinternational.net

RJ O'Brien & Assoc
222 S Riverside Plz Ste 900 . . . . .Chicago IL 60606 312-373-5000 373-5238
TF: 866-438-7564 ■ *Web:* www.rjobrien.com

Rosenthal Collins Group LLC (RCG)
216 W Jackson Blvd Ste 400 . . . . .Chicago IL 60606 312-460-9200 795-7730*
**Fax:* Hum Res ■ *Web:* www.rcgdirect.com

Vestor Capital Corp
10 S Riverside Plz Ste 1400 . . . . .Chicago IL 60606 312-641-2400
Web: www.vestorcapital.com

Viridian Partners LLC
1745 Shea Ctr Dr Ste 190. . . . . .Highlands Ranch CO 80129 303-271-9114
Web: www.viridianpartners.com

Zaner Group LLC 150 S Wacker Dr Ste 2350. . . . . .Chicago IL 60606 312-277-0050 277-0150
TF: 800-621-1414 ■ *Web:* www.zaner.com

170 COMMUNICATIONS TOWER OPERATORS

See Also Communications Lines & Towers Construction p. 2075

Listed here are companies that own, operate, lease, maintain, and/or manage towers used by telecommunications services and radio broadcast companies, including free-standing towers as well as antenna systems mounted on monopoles or rooftops. Many of these companies also build their communications towers, but companies that only do the building are classified as heavy construction contractors.

Phone Fax

American Tower Corp 116 Huntington Ave 11th Fl . . . . .Boston MA 02116 617-375-7500 375-7575
NYSE: AMT ■ *TF:* 877-282-7483 ■ *Web:* www.americantower.com

Atlantic Tower Group of Cos Inc
6260 Pine Slash Rd . . . . Mechanicsville VA 23116 804-550-7490 559-6041
Web: www.atlantic-tower.com

CLS Group 609 S Kelly Ave Ste D . . . . .Edmond OK 73003 405-348-5460 551-8270
Web: www.clsgroup.com

Crown Castle International Corp
1220 Augusta Dr Ste 500 . . . . .Houston TX 77057 713-570-3000
NYSE: CCI ■ *TF:* 877-486-9377 ■ *Web:* www.crowncastle.com

Crown Castle USA Inc 2000 Corporate Dr . . . . .Canonsburg PA 15317 724-416-2000 416-2200
TF: 877-486-9377 ■ *Web:* crowncastle.com

LTS Wireless Inc 311 S LHS Dr . . . . .Lumberton TX 77657 409-755-4038 755-7409
TF: 800-255-5471 ■ *Web:* www.ltswireless.com

SBA Communications Corp
5900 Broken Sound Pkwy NW . . . . Boca Raton FL 33487 561-995-7670
NASDAQ: SBAC ■ *TF:* 800-487-7483 ■ *Web:* www.sbasite.com

Tower Innovations 3266 Tower Dr. Newburgh IN 47630 812-853-0595 853-6652
TF: 800-664-8222 ■ *Web:* www.centraltower.com

171 COMMUNITIES - ONLINE

See Also Internet Service Providers (ISPs) p. 2596

Phone Fax

America Online Inc (AOL) 22000 AOL Way. . . . . Dulles VA 20166 703-265-1000
Web: www.aol.com

AudienceScience Inc
1120 112th Ave NE Ste 400 . . . . .Bellevue WA 98004 425-201-3900
Web: www.audiencescience.com

Beliefnet Inc 999 Waterside Dr Ste 1900 . . . . Norfolk VA 23150 800-311-2458
TF: 800-311-2458 ■ *Web:* www.beliefnet.com

BlackPlanet.com 205 Hudson St 6th Fl. . . . . .New York NY 10013 212-431-4477 505-3478
Web: www.blackplanet.com

Internet Broadcasting Systems Inc
355 Randolph Ave . . . . Saint Paul MN 55102 651-365-4000
Web: www.ibsys.com

Knot Inc, The 462 Broadway 6th Fl. . . . . .New York NY 10013 212-219-8555 219-1929
Web: www.xogroupinc.com

Lawyers.com
Martindale-Hubbell 121 Chanlon Rd . . . . .New Providence NJ 07974 908-464-6800
TF: 800-526-4902 ■ *Web:* www.lawyers.com

Merit Network Inc 1000 Oakbrook Dr Ste 200. . . . . Ann Arbor MI 48104 734-764-9430 527-5790
Web: www.merit.edu

Military Advantage Inc
799 Market St Ste 700 . . . . San Francisco CA 94103 415-820-3434 820-0552
Web: www.military.com

Nominum Inc 800 Bridge Pkwy Ste 100. . . . . Redwood City CA 94065 650-381-6000
Web: www.nominum.com

One Call Concepts Inc 7223 Pkwy Dr Ste 210. . . . . .Hanover MD 21076 410-712-0082 712-0838
Web: www.occinc.com

QuinStreet Inc 950 Tower Ln 6th Fl . . . . .Foster City CA 94404 650-578-7700
Web: www.quinstreet.com

Salon.com 101 Spear St Ste 203 . . . . San Francisco CA 94105 415-645-9200
Web: www.salon.com

Sensitech Inc 800 Cummings Ctr Ste 258x . . . . Beverly MA 01915 978-927-7033 921-2112
TF: 800-843-8367 ■ *Web:* www.sensitech.com

SHRM Global Forum 1800 Duke St. . . . . Alexandria VA 22314 703-548-3440 535-6490
TF: 800-283-7476 ■ *Web:* www.shrm.org/global

Phone Fax

Spark Networks PLC
8383 Wilshire Blvd Ste 800 . . . . Beverly Hills CA 90211 323-836-3000
NYSE: LOV ■ *Web:* www.spark.net

Trinet Internet Solutions Inc
1423 Powhatan St Bldg 1 . . . . Alexandria VA 22314 703-548-8900
Web: trinetsolutions.com

WELL, The 1195 Park Ave Ste 206 . . . . Emeryville CA 94608 415-343-5731
Web: www.well.com

COMPRESSORS - AIR CONDITIONING & REFRIGERATION

See Air Conditioning & Heating Equipment - Commercial/Industrial p. 1720

172 COMPRESSORS - AIR & GAS

Phone Fax

A G Equipment Company Inc 3401 W Albany. . . . . . .Broken Arrow OK 74012 918-250-7386
Web: www.agequipmentcompany.com

Accessorie Air Compressor Systems Inc
1858 N Case St. . . . . .Orange CA 92865 714-634-2292
Web: accessorieair.com

Air Compressor Supply Inc
3916 S I-35 Service Rd. . . . . .Oklahoma City OK 73129 405-672-0382
Web: www.aircompressorsupplyinc.com

Air Relief Inc 32 E Powell Rd . . . . Mayfield KY 42066 270-247-0203
Web: airrelief.com

Airtek Inc PO Box 466 . . . . Irwin PA 15642 724-863-1350 864-7853
Web: www.airtek-inc.com

Ariel Corp 35 Blackjack Rd Ext. . . . . Mount Vernon OH 43050 740-397-0311
Web: www.arielcorp.com

Atlas Copco Comptec LLC 46 School Rd . . . . Voorheesville NY 12186 518-765-3344
Web: www.atlascopco.us

Bauer Compressors Inc 1328 Azalea Garden Rd . . . . Norfolk VA 23502 757-855-6006 855-6224
Web: www.bauercomp.com

Bitzer US Inc 4031 Chamblee Rd. Oakwood GA 30566 770-718-2900
Web: www.bitzer.de/us/us/?country=us

Blackhawk Equipment Co 6250 W 55th Ave. . . . . Arvada CO 80002 303-421-3000
Web: www.blackhawkequipment.com

Boss Industries Inc 1761 Genesis Dr. . . . . Laporte IN 46350 219-324-7776
Web: www.bossair.com

Brabazon Pumps & Compressor
2484 Century Rd. . . . . Green Bay WI 54303 920-498-6020
TF: 800-825-3222 ■ *Web:* www.brabazon.com

Cameron Turbocompressor 3101 Broadway. . . . . .Buffalo NY 14225 716-896-6603 896-1233
TF: 877-805-7911 ■ *Web:* cameron.slb.com

Champion A Gardner Denver Inc
1301 N Euclid Ave . . . . .Princeton IL 61356 815-875-3321
Web: www.gardnerdenver.com

Chapin International Inc 700 Ellicott St . . . . .Batavia NY 14021 585-343-3140 344-1775
Web: www.chapinmfg.com

Compressed Air Systems Inc 9303 Stannum St. . . . . Tampa FL 33619 813-626-8177 628-0187
TF: 800-626-8177 ■ *Web:* www.compressedairsystems.com

Compression Leasing Services Inc
1935 N Loop Ave . . . . .Casper WY 82601 307-265-3242
Web: www.compressionleasing.com

Compressor Engineering Corp (CECO)
5440 Alder Dr. . . . . .Houston TX 77081 713-664-7333 664-6444
TF: 800-879-2326 ■ *Web:* www.tryceco.com

Corken Inc 3805 NW 36th St . . . . .Oklahoma City OK 73112 405-946-5576 948-6664
TF: 800-631-4929 ■ *Web:* www.corken.com

CSI Compressor Systems Inc 3809 S FM 1788 . . . . .Midland TX 79706 432-563-1170 757-9604*
**Fax Area Code:* 903 ■ *Web:* www.csicompressco.com

Curtis Dyna-Fog Ltd 135 Region South Dr. . . . . .Westfield IN 46074 678-688-5601 896-3788*
**Fax Area Code:* 317 ■ *Web:* www.dynafog.com

Curtis-Toledo Inc 1905 Kienlen Ave. . . . . Saint Louis MO 63133 314-383-1300 383-1300
TF: 800-925-5431 ■ *Web:* us.fscurtis.com

Danfoss Scroll Technologies LLC
1 Scroll Dr . . . . .Arkadelphia AR 71923 870-246-0700
Web: www.scrolltech.com

Danmar Industries 2303 Oil Ctr Ct. . . . . .Houston TX 77073 281-230-1000 230-1010
Web: www.danmarind.com

Dearing Compressor & Pump Co
3974 Simon Rd. . . . . Youngstown OH 44512 330-783-2258
Web: www.dearingcomp.com

Dresser-Rand Co Paul Clark Dr PO Box 560. . . . . .Olean NY 14760 716-375-3000 375-3178
Web: www.dresser-rand.com

Dresser-Rand Co Reciprocating Products Div
100 Chemung St. . . . . Painted Post NY 14870 713-354-6100
Web: www.dresser-rand.com

Elliott Group 901 N Fourth St . . . . .Jeannette PA 15644 724-527-2811 600-8442
TF: 800-635-2208 ■ *Web:* www.elliott-turbo.com

Estis Compression LLC
545 Huey Lenard Loop . . . . .West Monroe LA 71292 318-397-5557
Web: www.estiscompression.com

Federal Equipment Co 5298 River Rd . . . . Cincinnati OH 45233 513-621-5260 621-0524
TF: 877-435-4723 ■ *Web:* www.federalequipment.com

Fountainhead Group Inc 23 Garden St . . . . New York Mills NY 13417 315-736-0037 768-4220
TF: 800-311-9903 ■ *Web:* www.thefountainheadgroup.com

FS-Elliott Company LLC 5710 Mellon Rd . . . . Export PA 15632 724-387-3200
Web: www.fs-elliott.com

Gardner Denver Inc 1800 Gardner Expy . . . . .Quincy IL 62305 217-222-5400 247-3506*
NYSE: GDI ■ **Fax Area Code:* 270 ■ *Web:* www.gardnerdenver.com

Gardner Denver Nash 1800 Gardner Expy . . . . .Quincy IL 62305 217-222-5400
TF: 800-637-5729 ■ *Web:* www.gardnerdenver.com

Gardner Denver Nash LLC
Alta Vista Business Park 200 Simko Blvd . . . . Charleroi PA 15022 724-239-1500
Web: www.gdnash.com

Gardner Denver Water Jetting Systems Inc
12300 N Houston Rosslyn . . . . .Houston TX 77086 281-448-5800 247-3506*
**Fax Area Code:* 270 ■ *Web:* www.gardnerdenver.com

Company	City	State	Zip	Phone	Fax
Gas Technology Energy Concepts LLC 401 William L Gaiter Pkwy Ste 4 — *TF:* 800-451-8294 ■ *Web:* www.gas-tec.com	Buffalo	NY	14215	800-451-8294	
Gast Mfg Inc 2300 M-139 Hwy PO Box 97 — *Web:* www.gastmfg.com	Benton Harbor	MI	49023	269-926-6171	925-8288
Guardair Corp 47 Veterans Dr — *TF:* 800-482-7324 ■ *Web:* www.guardair.com	Chicopee	MA	01022	413-594-4400	594-4884
Industrial Air Centers Inc 731 E Market St — *Web:* www.iacserv.com	Jeffersonville	IN	47130	812-280-7070	
Ingersoll Rand Air Solutions Group 800-D Beaty St — *TF:* 800-866-5457 ■ *Web:* company.ingersollrand.com	Davidson	NC	28036	800-866-5457	
Integrated Flow Systems LLC 43455 Osgood Rd	Fremont	CA	94539	510-659-4900	
ITW Industrial Finishing 195 International Blvd	Glendale Heights	IL	60139	630-237-5000	237-5011
Kaeser Compressors Inc PO Box 946 — *Web:* www.kaeser.com	Fredericksburg	VA	22404	540-898-5500	898-5520
Manchester Tank 1000 Corp Centre Dr Ste 300 — *TF:* 800-399-5628 ■ *Web:* www.mantank.com	Franklin	TN	37067	615-370-6300	370-6150
Master Mfg Co 747 N Yale Ave — *Fax Area Code: 320 ■ *TF:* 800-864-1649	Villa Park	IL	60181	630-833-7060	243-8030*
Mattson Spray Equipment 230 W Coleman St — *TF:* 800-877-4857 ■ *Web:* www.mattsonspray.com	Rice Lake	WI	54868	715-234-1617	236-7032
McGee Company Inc 1140 S Jason St — *Web:* www.mcgeecompany.com	Denver	CO	80223	303-777-2615	
Michigan Automotive Compressor Inc (MACI) 2400 N Dearing Rd — *Web:* www.michauto.com	Parma	MI	49269	517-622-7000	
Norwalk Compressor Co 1650 Stratford Ave — *TF:* 800-556-5001 ■ *Web:* www.norwalkcompressor.com	Stratford	CT	06615	203-386-1234	386-1300
Pristech Products Inc 6952 Fairgrounds Pkwy Ste 107 — *Web:* www.pristech.com	San Antonio	TX	78238	210-520-8051	509-7463
Puma Industries Inc 1992 Airways Blvd — *Web:* www.pumaairusa.com	Memphis	TN	38114	901-744-7979	
Quincy Compressor 3501 Wismann Ln — *Web:* www.quincycompressor.com	Quincy	IL	62305	217-222-7700	
Riley Industrial Services Inc 2615 San Juan Blvd PO Box 2014 — *Web:* www.rileyindustrial.com	Farmington	NM	87401	505-327-4947	326-0305
RIX Industries Inc 4900 Industrial Way — *Web:* www.rixindustries.com	Benicia	CA	94510	707-747-5900	
Rogers Machinery Company Inc 14650 SW 72nd Ave PO Box 230429 — *Web:* www.rogers-machinery.com	Portland	OR	97224	503-639-0808	
Sanden International (USA) Inc 601 S Sanden Blvd — *Web:* www.sanden.com	Wylie	TX	75098	972-442-8400	
Sauer Compressors USA Inc 64 Log Canoe Cir — *Web:* www.sauerusa.com	Stevensville	MD	21666	410-604-3142	
Saylor Beall Mfg Company Inc 400 N Kibbee St — *TF:* 800-248-9001 ■ *Web:* www.saylor-beall.com	Saint Johns	MI	48879	989-224-2371	224-8788
Scales Air Compressor Corp 110 Voice Rd — *TF:* 877-798-0454 ■ *Web:* www.scalesair.com	Carle Place	NY	11514	516-248-9096	248-9639
SCFM Compressor Systems 3701 S Maybelle Ave — *Web:* www.scfm.com	Tulsa	OK	74107	918-663-1309	
SIHI Pumps Inc 303 Industrial Blvd — *Web:* www.sihi-pumps.com	Grand Island	NY	14072	716-773-6450	773-2330
Spencer Turbine Co 600 Day Hill Rd — *TF:* 800-232-4321 ■ *Web:* www.spencerturbine.com	Windsor	CT	06095	860-688-8361	688-0098
Sullair Corp 3700 E Michigan Blvd — *Web:* www.sullair.com	Michigan City	IN	46360	219-879-5451	
Sullivan-Palatek Inc 1201 W US Hwy 20 — *TF:* 800-438-6203 ■ *Web:* www.palatek.com	Michigan City	IN	46360	219-874-2497	872-5043
Sulzer Metco US Inc 1101 Prospect Ave — *Fax: Sales ■ *TF:* 877-280-2342 ■ *Web:* www.sulzer.com	Westbury	NY	11590	516-334-1300	338-2414*
Technology General Corp 12 Cork Hill Rd — *Web:* www.iconservice.com	Franklin	NJ	07416	973-827-4143	
Tecumseh Products Co 1136 Oak Valley Dr — *NASDAQ: TECU* ■ *Web:* www.tecumseh.com	Ann Arbor	MI	48108	734-585-9500	352-3700
Thermionics Laboratory 1842 Sabre St — *TF:* 800-962-2310 ■ *Web:* www.thermionics.com	Hayward	CA	94545	510-538-3304	
Tuthill Vacuum Systems 4840 W Kearney St — *TF:* 800-634-2695 ■ *Web:* www.tuthill.com	Springfield	MO	65803	417-865-8715	865-2950
Wagner Spray Tech Corp 1770 Fernbrook Ln — *TF:* 800-328-8251 ■ *Web:* www.wagnerspraytech.com	Plymouth	MN	55447	763-553-7000	519-3563
Wittemann Company LLC, The 1 Industry Dr — *Web:* www.pureco2nfidence.com	Palm Coast	FL	32137	386-445-4200	
Zeks Compressed Air Solutions 1302 Goshen Pkwy — *TF:* 800-888-2323 ■ *Web:* www.zeks.com	West Chester	PA	19380	610-692-9100	692-9192

173 COMPUTER EQUIPMENT

See Also Automatic Teller Machines (ATMs) p. 1820; Business Machines - Mfr p. 1882; Calculators - Electronic p. 1889; Modems p. 1999; Computer Networking Products & Systems p. 2008; Flash Memory Devices p. 2287; Point-of-Sale (POS) & Point-of-Information (POI) Systems p. 2963

173-1 Computer Input Devices

Company	City	State	Zip	Phone	Fax
3M Touch Systems 501 Griffin Brook Dr — *TF:* 866-407-6666 ■ *Web:* www.3m.com	Methuen	MA	01844	978-659-9000	
Aten Technology Inc 23 Hubble — *TF:* 888-999-2836 ■ *Web:* www.aten-usa.com	Irvine	CA	92618	949-428-1111	428-1100
CH Products 970 Pk Ctr Dr — *Web:* www.chproducts.com	Vista	CA	92081	760-598-2518	598-2524
Chicony America Inc 53 Parker — *Web:* www.chicony.com.tw	Irvine	CA	92618	949-380-0928	380-8201
Cirque Corp 2463 South 3850 West — *TF:* 800-454-3375 ■ *Web:* www.cirque.com	Salt Lake City	UT	84120	801-467-1100	467-0208
Cortron Inc 59 Technology Dr — *Web:* www.cortroninc.com	Lowell	MA	01851	978-975-5445	975-0357
Elo TouchSystems Inc 301 Constitution Dr — *TF:* 800-557-1458 ■ *Web:* www.elotouch.com	Menlo Park	CA	94025	650-361-4700	361-4747
Esterline Interface Technologies 600 W Wilbur Ave — *TF:* 800-444-5923 ■ *Web:* www.esterline.com	Coeur d'Alene	ID	83815	208-765-8000	292-2275
Fujitsu Components America Inc 250 E Caribbean Dr — *Web:* www.fujitsu.com	Sunnyvale	CA	94089	408-745-4900	745-4970
GTCO CalComp Inc 7125 Riverwood Dr — *Web:* gtcocalcomp.com	Columbia	MD	21046	410-381-6688	
Gyration Inc 3601-B Calle Tecate — *Fax Area Code: 805 ■ *TF:* 888-340-0033 ■ *Web:* www.gyration.com	Camarillo	CA	93012	888-340-0033	987-6665*
Immersion Corp 30 Rio Robles — *NASDAQ: IMMR* ■ *Web:* www.immersion.com	San Jose	CA	95134	408-467-1900	467-1901
Interlink Electronics Inc 546 Flynn Rd — *OTC: LINK* ■ *Web:* interlinkelectronics.com	Camarillo	CA	93012	805-484-8855	484-8989
Kensington Computer Products Group 333 Twin Dolphin Dr 6th Fl — *TF:* 800-535-4242 ■ *Web:* www.kensington.com	Redwood Shores	CA	94065	650-572-2700	267-2800
Kinesis Corp 22030 20th Ave SE Ste 102 — *TF:* 800-454-6374 ■ *Web:* www.kinesis-ergo.com	Bothell	WA	98021	425-402-8100	402-8181
KYE Systems Corp 1301 NW 84th Ave Ste 127 — *TF:* 800-488-3111 ■ *Web:* www.geniusnet.com	Doral	FL	33126	305-468-9250	468-9251
Lite-On Trading USA Inc 720 S Hillview Dr — *Web:* www.us.liteon.com	Milpitas	CA	95035	408-946-4873	941-4597
Logitech Inc 6505 Kaiser Dr — *TF Sales:* 800-231-7717 ■ *Web:* www.logitech.com	Fremont	CA	94555	510-795-8500	792-8901
Macally USA Mace Group Inc 4601 E Airport Dr — *TF:* 800-644-1132 ■ *Web:* www.macally.com	Ontario	CA	91761	909-230-6888	230-6889
Mad Catz Interactive Inc 7480 Mission Vly Rd Ste 101 — *NYSE: MCZ* ■ *TF:* 800-659-2287 ■ *Web:* www.madcatz.com	San Diego	CA	92108	619-683-9830	683-9839
NaturalPoint Inc 33872 SE Eastgate Cir — *Web:* www.naturalpoint.com	Corvallis	OR	97333	541-753-6645	753-6689
NMB Technologies Corp 9730 Independence Ave — *Web:* www.nmbtc.com	Chatsworth	CA	91311	818-341-3355	341-8207
Numonics Corp 101 Commerce Dr PO Box 1005 — *TF:* 800-523-6716 ■ *Web:* interactivewhiteboards.com	Montgomeryville	PA	18936	215-362-2766	361-0167
PolyVision Corp 10700 Abbotts Bridge Rd Ste 100 — *TF:* 888-325-6351 ■ *Web:* www.polyvision.com	Johns Creek	GA	30097	678-542-3100	542-3200
SMART Modular Technologies Inc 39870 Eureka Dr — *NASDAQ: SMOD* ■ *TF:* 800-956-7627 ■ *Web:* www.smartm.com	Newark	CA	94560	510-623-1231	623-1434
SMART Technologies Inc 3636 Research Rd NW — *TSE: SMA* ■ *TF:* 888-427-6278 ■ *Web:* www.smarttech.com	Calgary	AB	T2L1Y1	403-245-0333	245-0366
Synaptics Inc 1251 McKay Dr — *NASDAQ: SYNA* ■ *Web:* www.synaptics.com	San Jose	CA	95131	408-904-1100	
TouchSystems Corp 220 Tradesmen Dr — *TF:* 800-320-5944 ■ *Web:* www.touchsystems.com	Hutto	TX	78634	512-846-2424	846-2425
Ultra Electronics Measurement Systems Inc 50 Barnes Pk N Ste 102 — *Web:* www.ultra-msi.com	Wallingford	CT	06492	203-949-3500	949-3598
Wacom Technology Corp 1311 SE Cardinal Ct — *TF:* 800-922-6613 ■ *Web:* www.wacom.com	Vancouver	WA	98683	360-896-9833	896-9724

173-2 Computers

Company	City	State	Zip	Phone	Fax
Aberdeen LLC 9130 Norwalk Blvd — *Fax: Sales ■ *TF:* 800-500-9526 ■ *Web:* www.aberdeeninc.com	Santa Fe Springs	CA	90670	562-699-6998	695-5570*
Acer America Corp 333 W San Carlos St Ste 1500 — *Fax: Sales ■ *TF:* 800-103-3311 ■ *Web:* www.acer.com	San Jose	CA	95110	408-533-7700	533-4574*
ACMA Computers Inc 1565 Reliance Way — *TF Sales:* 800-800-6328 ■ *Web:* www.acma.com	Fremont	CA	94539	510-651-8886	651-4119
ACME Portable Machines Inc 1330 Mtn View Cir — *Web:* www.acmeportable.com	Azusa	CA	91702	626-610-1888	610-1881
Amax Engineering Corp 1565 Reliance Way — *TF Cust Svc:* 800-889-2629 ■ *Web:* www.amax.com	Fremont	CA	94539	510-651-8886	651-4119
Apple Inc 1 Infinite Loop — *NASDAQ: AAPL* ■ *Fax: Mail Rm ■ *TF Cust Svc:* 800-275-2273 ■ *Web:* www.apple.com	Cupertino	CA	95014	408-996-1010	996-0275*
Azul Systems Inc 1600 Plymouth St — *TF:* 800-258-4199 ■ *Web:* www.azul.com	Mountain View	CA	94043	650-230-6500	230-6600
BlackBerry Ltd 295 Phillip St — *NASDAQ: BBRY* ■ *Web:* ca.blackberry.com	Waterloo	ON	N2L3W8	519-888-7465	888-7884
Bytespeed LLC 3131 24th Ave S — *TF:* 877-553-0777 ■ *Web:* www.bytespeed.com	Moorhead	MN	56560	218-227-0445	
Cemtrol Inc 3035 E La Jolla St — *Web:* www.cemtrol.com	Anaheim	CA	92806	714-666-6606	666-6616
CG Automation 60 Fadem Rd — *Web:* www.qeiinc.com	Springfield	NJ	07081	973-379-7400	379-2138
Chem USA Corp 38507 Cherry St — *TF:* 800-866-2436 ■ *Web:* www.chemusa.com	Newark	CA	94560	510-608-8818	608-8828
Comark Corp 93 W St — *TF:* 800-280-8522 ■ *Web:* www.comarkcorp.com	Medfield	MA	02052	508-359-8161	359-2267
Corvallis Microtechnology Inc 413 SW Jefferson Ave — *Web:* www.cmtinc.com	Corvallis	OR	97333	541-752-5456	752-4117
Cray Inc 901 Fifth Ave Ste 1000 — *NASDAQ: CRAY* ■ *Web:* www.cray.com	Seattle	WA	98164	206-701-2000	701-2500

				Phone	Fax
CSP Inc 43 Manning Rd	Billerica	MA	01821	978-663-7598	663-0150
NASDAQ: CSPI ■ *TF:* 800-325-3110 ■ *Web:* www.cspi.com					
CSS Laboratories Inc 1641 McGaw Ave.	Irvine	CA	92614	949-852-8161	852-0410
TF: 800-852-2680 ■ *Web:* www.csslabs.com					
Daisy Data Displays Inc 2850 Lewisberry Rd	York Haven	PA	17370	717-932-9999	932-8000
Web: www.makeitdaisy.com					
Datalux Corp 155 Aviation Dr	Winchester	VA	22602	540-662-1500	662-1682
TF: 800-328-2589 ■ *Web:* www.datalux.com					
Dedicated Computing N26 W23880 Commerce Cir	Waukesha	WI	53188	262-951-7200	523-2222
TF: 877-523-3301 ■ *Web:* www.dedicatedcomputing.com					
Dell Inc 1 Dell Way	Round Rock	TX	78682	512-338-4400	283-6161
NASDAQ: DELL ■ *TF:* 800-879-3355 ■ *Web:* www.dell.com					
Diversified Technology Inc 476 Highland Colony Pkwy	Ridgeland	MS	39157	601-856-4121	
Web: www.dtims.com					
Drive Thru Technology Inc 1755 N Main St	Los Angeles	CA	90031	323-576-1400	576-1470
TF: 800-933-8388 ■ *Web:* www.dttusa.com					
DRS Tactical Systems Inc 1110 W Hibiscus Blvd	Melbourne	FL	32901	850-302-3100	725-0496*
**Fax Area Code:* 321 ■ *Web:* drs.com					
Ectaco Inc 31-21 31st St	Long Island	NY	11106	718-728-6110	728-4023
TF: 800-710-7920 ■ *Web:* www.ectaco.com					
Electrovaya Inc 2645 Royal Windsor Dr	Mississauga	ON	L5J1K9	905-855-4610	822-7953
TSE: EFL ■ *TF:* 800-388-2865 ■ *Web:* www.electrovaya.com					
ENGlobal Corp 654 N Sam Houston Pkwy E Ste 400	Houston	TX	77060	281-878-1000	878-1010
NASDAQ: ENG ■ *Web:* www.englobal.com					
Equus Computer Systems Inc 5801 Clearwater Dr	Minnetonka	MN	55343	612-617-6200	
TF: 866-378-8727 ■ *Web:* www.equuscs.com					
Fujitsu America Inc 1250 E Arques Ave.	Sunnyvale	CA	94085	408-746-6200	746-6260
TF: 800-538-8460 ■ *Web:* www.fujitsu.com					
Gateway Inc 7565 Irvine Ctr Dr	Irvine	CA	92618	949-471-7040	471-7041
TF: 800-846-2000 ■ *Web:* www.gateway.com					
Granite Microsystems Inc 10202 N Enterprise Dr	Mequon	WI	53092	262-242-8800	242-8825
Web: www.granitemicrosystems.com					
Hewlett-Packard (Canada) Ltd (HP) 5150 Spectrum Way	Mississauga	ON	L4W5G1	905-206-4725	
TF: 888-447-4636 ■ *Web:* welcome.hp.com					
Hewlett-Packard Co 3000 Hanover St	Palo Alto	CA	94304	650-857-1501	857-5518
NYSE: HPQ ■ *TF Sales:* 800-752-0900 ■ *Web:* www.hp.com					
Immecor Corp 2351 Circadian Way	Santa Rosa	CA	95407	707-636-2550	636-2565
Web: www.immecor.com					
International Business Machines Corp (IBM) 1 New OrchaRd Rd	Armonk	NY	10504	914-499-1900	
NYSE: IBM ■ *TF:* 800-426-4968 ■ *Web:* www.ibm.com					
Keydata International Inc 201 Cir Dr N Ste 101	Piscataway	NJ	08854	732-868-0588	
Kontron Mobile Computing Inc 7631 Anagram Dr	Eden Prairie	MN	55344	952-974-7000	974-7199*
**Fax Area Code:* 612 ■ *TF:* 888-343-5396 ■ *Web:* kontron.com					
LXE Inc 125 Technology Pkwy	Norcross	GA	30092	770-447-4224	447-4405
TF: 800-664-4593 ■ *Web:* www.honeywellaidc.com					
MaxVision Corp 495 Production Ave.	Madison	AL	35758	256-772-3058	772-3078
TF: 800-533-5805 ■ *Web:* www.maxvision.com					
Micro Electronics Inc 4119 Leap Rd.	Hilliard	OH	43026	614-850-3000	850-3001
Web: www.microcenter.com					
Micro Electronics, Inc. 2701 Charter St Ste A	Columbus	OH	43228	614-326-8500	
TF: 877-636-9793 ■ *Web:* www.microcenter.com					
Micro Express Inc 8 Hammond Dr Ste 105	Irvine	CA	92618	949-460-9911	269-3070
TF: 800-989-9900 ■ *Web:* www.microexpress.net					
Micro/Sys Inc 3730 Pk Pl	Montrose	CA	91020	818-244-4600	244-4246
Web: www.embeddedsys.com					
Microtech Computers Inc 4921 Legends Dr.	Lawrence	KS	66049	785-841-9513	841-1809
Web: www.microtechcomp.com					
Microway Inc 12 RichaRds Rd.	Plymouth	MA	02360	508-746-7341	746-4678
Web: www.microway.com					
Myricom Inc 325 N Santa Anita Ave.	Arcadia	CA	91006	626-821-5555	821-5316
Web: www.myricom.com					
Panasonic Corporation of North America 2 Riverfront Plaza	Newark	NJ	07102	888-223-1012	
TF: 888-223-1012 ■					
Web: www.panasonic.com/business/toughbook/contact-toughbook.asp					
Pinnacle Data Systems Inc 6600 Port Rd Ste 100	Groveport	OH	43125	614-748-1150	748-1209
TF: 800-882-8282 ■ *Web:* www.avnetintegrated.com					
Quantum3D Inc 5225 Hellyer Ave Ste 220	Milpitas	CA	95138	408-600-2500	
TF: 888-747-1020 ■ *Web:* www.quantum3d.com					
Roper Mobile Technology 7450 S Priest Dr	Tempe	AZ	85283	480-705-4200	705-4216
Sharp Electronics Corp 1 Sharp Plz	Mahwah	NJ	07430	201-529-8200	529-8413
TF: 800-237-4277 ■ *Web:* www.sharpusa.com					
Sony Electronics Inc 1 Sony Dr.	Park Ridge	NJ	07656	201-930-1000	
TF Cust Svc: 800-222-7669 ■ *Web:* www.sony.com					
SRC Computers LLC 4240 N Nevada Ave	Colorado Springs	CO	80907	719-262-0213	262-0223
Stealth Computer Corp 530 Rowntree Dairy Rd Bldg 4	Woodbridge	ON	L4L8H2	905-264-9000	264-7440
TF: 888-783-2584 ■ *Web:* www.stealth.com					
Superchips Inc 1790 E Airport Blvd	Sanford	FL	32773	407-585-7000	585-1900
TF: 888-227-2447 ■ *Web:* www.superchips.com					
Systemax Inc 11 Harbor Pk Dr.	Port Washington	NY	11050	516-608-7000	608-7001
NYSE: SYX ■ *Web:* www.systemax.com					
Tangent Inc 191 Airport Blvd.	Burlingame	CA	94010	650-342-9388	342-9380
TF: 800-342-9388 ■ *Web:* www.tangent.com					
Technology Advancement Group Inc 22355 Tag Way	Sterling	VA	20166	703-406-3000	406-0305
TF: 800-824-7693 ■ *Web:* www.tag.com					
Toshiba America Inc 1251 Ave of the Americas Ste 4100	New York	NY	10020	212-596-0600	593-3875
TF: 800-457-7777 ■ *Web:* www.toshiba.com					
Toshiba America Information Systems Inc 9740 Irvine Blvd	Irvine	CA	92618	949-583-3000	
TF Cust Svc: 800-457-7777 ■ *Web:* www.toshiba.com					
TouchStar Solutions LLC *Touchstar Group* 5147 S Garnett Rd Ste D	Tulsa	OK	74146	918-307-7100	307-7190
Web: www.touchstargroup.com					
Transource Computers Corp 2405 W Utopia Rd	Phoenix	AZ	85027	623-879-8882	879-8887
TF: 800-486-3715 ■ *Web:* www.transource.com					
Twinhead Corp 48303 Fremont Blvd.	Fremont	CA	94538	800-995-8946	492-0820*
**Fax Area Code:* 510 ■ *TF Sales:* 800-995-8946 ■ *Web:* www.twinhead.com.tw					
Versalogic Corp 4211 W 11th Ave	Eugene	OR	97402	541-485-8575	485-5712
TF: 800-824-3163 ■ *Web:* www.versalogic.com					
Win Enterprises Inc 300 Willow St S	North Andover	MA	01845	978-688-2000	
Web: www.win-ent.com					
WYSE Technology Inc 3471 N First St.	San Jose	CA	95134	408-473-1200	473-2080
TF: 800-800-9973 ■ *Web:* www.wyse.com					

173-3 Modems

				Phone	Fax
ActionTec Electronics Inc 760 N Mary Ave	Sunnyvale	CA	94085	408-752-7700	541-9003
TF Tech Supp: 888-436-0657 ■ *Web:* www.actiontec.com					
Avocent Corp 4991 Corporate Dr.	Huntsville	AL	35805	256-430-4000	430-4030
TF: 866-286-2368 ■ *Web:* www.emersonnetworkpower.com					
Aztech Labs Inc 4005 Clipper Ct	Fremont	CA	94538	510-683-9800	683-9803
Web: www.aztech.com					
Best Data Products Inc 20740 Plummer St.	Chatsworth	CA	91311	818-773-9600	773-9619
Web: diamondmm.com					
Biscom Inc 321 Billerica Rd	Chelmsford	MA	01824	978-250-1800	250-4449
TF: 800-477-2472 ■ *Web:* www.biscom.com					
Canoga Perkins Corp 20600 Prairie St	Chatsworth	CA	91311	818-718-6300	718-6312
TF Tech Supp: 800-360-6642 ■ *Web:* www.canoga.com					
Cermetek Microelectronics Inc 374 Turquoise St	Milpitas	CA	95035	408-752-5000	942-1346
TF: 800-882-6271 ■ *Web:* www.cermetek.com					
Comtech EF Data Corp 2114 W Seventh St	Tempe	AZ	85281	480-333-2200	333-2540
Web: www.comtechefdata.com					
Copia International Ltd 1220 Iroquois Dr Ste 180	Naperville	IL	60563	630-778-8898	778-8848*
**Fax:* Sales ■ *TF Sales:* 800-689-8898 ■ *Web:* www.copia.com					
CXR Larus Corp 894 Faulstich Ct	San Jose	CA	95112	408-573-2700	
Web: www.cxr.com					
Data-Linc Group 3535 Factoria Blvd SE Ste 100	Bellevue	WA	98006	425-882-2206	867-0865
Web: www.data-linc.com					
Dataforth Corp 3331 E Hemisphere Loop	Tucson	AZ	85706	520-741-1404	741-0762
TF: 800-444-7644 ■ *Web:* www.dataforth.com					
Electronic Systems Technology Inc 415 N Quay St Bldg B-1	Kennewick	WA	99336	509-735-9092	783-5475
OTC: ELST ■ *Web:* www.esteem.com					
Encore Networks Inc 3800 Concorde Pkwy Ste 1500	Chantilly	VA	20151	703-318-7750	787-4625
Web: www.encorenetworks.com					
Engage Communications Inc 9565 Soquel Dr	Aptos	CA	95003	831-688-1021	688-1421
Web: www.engagecom.com					
FreeWave Technologies Inc 1880 S Flatiron Ct Ste F	Boulder	CO	80301	303-444-3862	786-9948
TF Cust Svc: 866-923-6168 ■ *Web:* www.freewave.com					
GRE America Inc 425 Harbor Blvd	Belmont	CA	94002	650-591-1400	591-2001
TF: 800-233-5973 ■ *Web:* www.greamerica.com					
Multi-Tech Systems 2205 Woodale Dr	Mounds View	MN	55112	763-785-3500	785-9874
TF Cust Svc: 800-328-9717 ■ *Web:* www.multitech.com					
Novatel Wireless Inc 9645 Scranton Rd Ste 205	San Diego	CA	92121	888-888-9231	812-3402*
NASDAQ: NVTL ■ **Fax Area Code:* 858 ■ *TF:* 888-888-9231 ■ *Web:* www.novatelwireless.com					
Phoebe Micro Inc 47606 Kato Rd.	Fremont	CA	94538	510-360-0800	360-0818
Web: www.phoebemicro.com					
Sierra Wireless Inc 13811 Wireless Way	Richmond	BC	V6V3A4	604-231-1100	231-1109
Web: www.sierrawireless.com					
Teldat Corp 1901 S Bascom Ave Ste 520	Campbell	CA	95008	408-892-9363	
Web: www.teldat.com					
Teletronics International Inc 2 Choke Cherry Rd	Rockville	MD	20850	301-309-8500	309-8851
Web: www.teletronics.com					
Unlimited Systems Corp Inc 9530 Padgett St.	San Diego	CA	92126	858-537-5010	550-7330
TF: 800-275-6354 ■ *Web:* www.konexx.com					
US Robotics Corp 1300 E Woodfield Dr Ste 506	Schaumburg	IL	60173	847-874-2000	874-2001
TF: 877-710-0884 ■ *Web:* www.usr.com					
Western Telematic Inc 5 Sterling	Irvine	CA	92618	949-586-9950	583-9514
TF: 800-854-7226 ■ *Web:* www.wti.com					
Wi-LAN Inc 303 Terry Fox Dr Ste 300	Ottawa	ON	K2K3J1	613-688-4900	688-4894
TSE: WIN ■ *Web:* www.wilan.com/home/default.aspx					
Works Computing Inc 1801 American Blvd E Ste 12	Bloomington	MN	55425	952-746-1580	746-1585
TF: 866-222-4077 ■ *Web:* www.workscomputing.com					
ZyXEL Communications Inc 1130 N Miller St.	Anaheim	CA	92806	714-632-0882	632-0858
TF: 800-255-4101 ■ *Web:* www.zyxel.com					

173-4 Monitors & Displays

				Phone	Fax
Aydin Displays Inc 1 Riga Ln	Birdsboro	PA	19508	610-404-7400	404-8190
TF: 866-367-2934 ■ *Web:* www.aydindisplays.com					
Barco Electronic Systems Pvt Ltd 11101 Trade Ctr Dr	Rancho Cordova	CA	95670	916-859-2500	859-2515
TF: 888-414-7226 ■ *Web:* barco.com					
BarcoView LLC 3059 Premiere Pkwy.	Duluth	GA	30097	678-475-8000	
Web: www.barco.com					
Conrac Inc 5124 Commerce Dr	Baldwin Park	CA	91706	626-480-0095	480-0077
TF: 800-451-5288 ■ *Web:* www.conrac.us					

Company	City	State	ZIP	Phone	Fax
Daisy Data Displays Inc 2850 Lewisberry Rd *Web:* www.makeitdaisy.com	York Haven	PA	17370	717-932-9999	932-8000
Daktronics Inc 201 Daktronics Dr *NASDAQ:* DAKT ■ *TF:* 800-325-8766 ■ *Web:* www.daktronics.com	Brookings	SD	57006	605-692-0200	697-4700
Dotronix Inc 160 First St SE *TF:* 800-720-7218 ■ *Web:* www.dotronix.com	New Brighton	MN	55112	651-633-1742	633-1065
Eizo Nanao Technologies Inc 5710 Warland Dr *TF:* 800-800-5202 ■ *Web:* www.eizo.com	Cypress	CA	90630	562-431-5011	431-4811
eMagin Corp 3006 Northup Way Ste 103 *NYSE: EMAN* ■ *Web:* www.emagin.com	Bellevue	WA	98004	425-284-5200	284-5201
Envision Peripherals Inc (EPI) 47490 Seabridge Dr *TF Tech Supp:* 888-838-6388 ■ *Web:* www.aocdisplay.com	Fremont	CA	94538	510-770-9988	770-1088
Futaba Corp of America 711 E State Pkwy *Web:* www.futaba.com	Schaumburg	IL	60173	847-884-1444	884-1635
General Digital Corp 8 Nutmeg Rd S *TF:* 800-952-2535 ■ *Web:* www.generaldigital.com	South Windsor	CT	06074	860-282-2900	282-2244
Gunze USA 2113 Wells Branch Pkwy Ste 5400 *Web:* www.gunzeusa.com	Austin	TX	78728	512-990-3400	252-1181
Hantronix Inc 10080 Bubb Rd *Web:* www.hantronix.com	Cupertino	CA	95014	408-252-1100	252-1123
ITUS Corp 12100 Wilshire Blvd Ste 1275 *OTC: COPY* ■ *Web:* ctipatents.com	Los Angeles	CA	90025	631-549-5900	
La Cie Ltd 22985 NW Evergreen Pkwy **Fax:* Mktg ■ *Web:* www.lacie.com	Hillsboro	OR	97124	503-844-4500	844-4508*
LG Electronics USA Inc 1000 Sylvan Ave *TF Tech Supp:* 800-243-0000 ■ *Web:* www.lg.com	Englewood Cliffs	NJ	07632	201-816-2000	
Lite-On Trading USA Inc 720 S Hillview Dr *Web:* www.us.liteon.com	Milpitas	CA	95035	408-946-4873	941-4597
NEC Corp of America 10850 Gold Ctr Dr Ste 200 *TF:* 800-632-4636 ■ *Web:* www.necam.com	Rancho Cordova	CA	95670	916-463-7000	
NEC Display Solutions of America Inc 500 Pk Blvd Ste 1100 **Fax:* Sales ■ *TF Cust Svc:* 800-632-4662 ■ *Web:* www.necdisplay.com	Itasca	IL	60143	630-467-3000	467-3010*
OSRAM Sylvania Inc 100 Endicott St *Web:* www.sylvania.com	Danvers	MA	01923	978-777-1900	750-2152
Pioneer Electronics (USA) Inc 1925 E Dominguez St *TF:* 800-421-1404 ■ *Web:* www.pioneerelectronics.com	Long Beach	CA	90810	310-952-2000	952-2402
Planar Systems Inc 1195 NW Compton Dr *NASDAQ: PLNR* ■ *TF:* 866-475-2627 ■ *Web:* www.planar.com	Beaverton	OR	97006	503-748-1100	748-1244
Sharp Electronics Corp 1 Sharp Plz *TF:* 800-237-4277 ■ *Web:* www.sharpusa.com	Mahwah	NJ	07430	201-529-8200	529-8413
Sharp Microelectronics of the Americas 5700 NW Pacific Rim Blvd *Web:* www.sharpsma.com	Camas	WA	98607	360-834-2500	834-8903
Sony Electronics Inc 1 Sony Dr *TF Cust Svc:* 800-222-7669 ■ *Web:* www.sony.com	Park Ridge	NJ	07656	201-930-1000	
Tatung Company of America Inc 2850 El Presidio St *TF:* 800-827-2850 ■ *Web:* www.tatungusa.com	Long Beach	CA	90810	310-637-2105	
Trans-Lux Corp 26 Pearl St *OTC: TNLX* ■ *TF:* 800-243-5544 ■ *Web:* www.trans-lux.com	Norwalk	CT	06850	203-853-4321	
Trans-Lux Fair-Play Inc 1700 Delaware Ave *TF:* 800-247-0265 ■ *Web:* www.fair-play.com	Des Moines	IA	50317	515-265-5305	265-3364
Video Display Corp 1868 Tucker Industrial Rd *NASDAQ: VIDE* ■ *TF Cust Svc:* 800-241-5005 ■ *Web:* www.videodisplay.com	Tucker	GA	30084	770-938-2080	493-3903
ViewSonic Corp 381 Brea Canyon Rd *TF:* 800-888-8583 ■ *Web:* ap.viewsonic.com	Walnut	CA	91789	909-444-8888	468-1240
Wells-Gardner Electronics Corp 9500 W 55th St Ste A *NYSE: WGA* ■ *TF:* 800-336-6630 ■ *Web:* www.wellsgardner.com	McCook	IL	60525	708-290-2100	290-2200

173-5 Multimedia Equipment & Supplies

Company	City	State	ZIP	Phone	Fax
Corsair Memory Inc 46221 Landing Pkwy *TF:* 888-222-4346 ■ *Web:* www.corsair.com	Fremont	CA	94538	510-657-8747	657-8748
Creative Labs Inc 1901 McCarthy Blvd *TF Cust Svc:* 800-998-1000 ■ *Web:* www.us.creative.com	Milpitas	CA	95035	408-428-6600	428-6611
Cyber Acoustics LLC 3109 NE 109th Ave *Web:* www.cyberacoustics.com	Vancouver	WA	98682	360-883-0333	883-4888
Kinyo Company Inc 14235 Lomitas Ave *TF:* 800-735-4696 ■ *Web:* www.kinyo.com	La Puente	CA	91746	626-333-3711	961-9114
Matrox Electronic Systems Ltd 1055 St Regis Blvd *TF:* 800-361-1408 ■ *Web:* www.matrox.com	Dorval	QC	H9P2T4	514-822-6000	822-6363
SpeakerCraft Inc 940 Columbia Ave *TF:* 800-448-0976 ■ *Web:* www.speakercraft.com	Riverside	CA	92507	951-787-0543	787-8747
VITEC 2200 Century Pkwy Ste 900 *Web:* vitec.com	Atlanta	GA	30345	404-320-0110	320-3132
Vocollect Inc 703 Rodi Rd *Web:* www.intermec.com	Pittsburgh	PA	15235	412-829-8145	829-0972

173-6 Printers

Company	City	State	ZIP	Phone	Fax
Addmaster Corp 225 Huntington Dr *Web:* www.addmaster.com	Monrovia	CA	91016	626-358-2395	358-2784
AMT Datasouth Corp 803 Camarillo Springs Rd Ste D *TF:* 800-215-9192 ■ *Web:* www.amtdatasouth.com	Camarillo	CA	93012	805-388-5799	484-5282
Citizen Systems America Corp 363 Van Ness Way Ste 404 *TF:* 800-421-6516 ■ *Web:* www.citizen-systems.com	Torrance	CA	90501	310-781-1460	781-9152
Craden Peripherals Corp 7860 Airport Hwy *Web:* www.craden.com	Pennsauken	NJ	08109	856-488-0700	488-0925
Datamax Corp 4501 Pkwy Commerce Blvd *TF:* 800-321-2233 ■ *Web:* www.datamaxcorp.com	Orlando	FL	32808	407-578-8007	578-8377
Digital Design Inc 67 Sand Pk Rd *TF:* 800-967-7746 ■ *Web:* www.genesisinkjet.com/ddiworldwide	Cedar Grove	NJ	07009	973-857-0900	857-9375
Eastman Kodak Co 343 State St *OTC: EKDKQ* ■ *Web:* www.kodak.com	Rochester	NY	14650	585-724-4000	
Epson America Inc 3840 Kilroy Airport Way *TF:* 800-463-7766 ■ *Web:* www.epson.com	Long Beach	CA	90806	562-981-3840	290-5220
Fujitsu Components America Inc 250 E Caribbean Dr *Web:* www.fujitsu.com	Sunnyvale	CA	94089	408-745-4900	745-4970
GCC Printers USA 209 Burlington Rd **Fax Area Code:* 800 ■ *Web:* www.gccprinters.de/en	Bedford	MA	01730	781-275-1115	442-2329*
Hewlett-Packard (Canada) Ltd (HP) 5150 Spectrum Way *TF:* 888-447-4636 ■ *Web:* welcome.hp.com	Mississauga	ON	L4W5G1	905-206-4725	
Hewlett-Packard Co 3000 Hanover St *NYSE: HPQ* ■ *TF Sales:* 800-752-0900 ■ *Web:* www.hp.com	Palo Alto	CA	94304	650-857-1501	857-5518
International Business Machines Corp (IBM) 1 New OrchaRd Rd *NYSE: IBM* ■ *TF:* 800-426-4968 ■ *Web:* www.ibm.com	Armonk	NY	10504	914-499-1900	
Konica Minolta Business Solutions USA Inc 100 Williams Dr *Web:* www.kmbs.konicaminolta.us	Ramsey	NJ	07446	201-825-4000	
Kroy LLC 3830 Kelley Ave *TF Cust Svc:* 888-888-5769 ■ *Web:* www.kroy.com	Cleveland	OH	44114	216-426-5600	426-5601
Lexmark International Inc 740 W New Cir Rd *NYSE: LXK* ■ *TF Cust Svc:* 800-539-6275 ■ *Web:* www.lexmark.com	Lexington	KY	40550	859-232-2000	
Mutoh America Inc 2602 S 47th St Ste 102 *TF:* 800-996-8864 ■ *Web:* www.mutoh.com	Phoenix	AZ	85034	480-968-7772	968-7990
NEC Corp of America 10850 Gold Ctr Dr Ste 200 *TF:* 800-632-4636 ■ *Web:* www.necam.com	Rancho Cordova	CA	95670	916-463-7000	
Oce-USA Inc 5450 N Cumberland Ave *TF:* 800-877-6232 ■ *Web:* csa.canon.com	Chicago	IL	60656	773-714-8500	693-7634
Oki Data Americas Inc 2000 Bishops Gate Blvd *TF Cust Svc:* 800-654-3282 ■ *Web:* www.okidata.com	Mount Laurel	NJ	08054	856-235-2600	222-5320
Pentax Imaging Co 633 17th St Ste 2600 *TF:* 800-877-0155 ■ *Web:* www.us.ricoh-imaging.com	Denver	CO	80202	303-799-8000	
Plastic Card Systems Inc 31 Pierce St *TF:* 800-742-2273 ■ *Web:* www.plasticard-systems.com	Northborough	MA	01532	508-351-6210	
Practical Automation Inc 45 Woodmont Rd *Web:* www.practicalautomation.com	Milford	CT	06460	203-882-5640	882-5648
Primera Technology Inc 2 Carlson Pkwy N Ste 375 *TF:* 800-797-2772 ■ *Web:* www.primera.com	Plymouth	MN	55447	763-475-6676	475-6677
Printek Inc 1517 Townline Rd *TF:* 800-368-4636 ■ *Web:* www.printek.com	Benton Harbor	MI	49022	269-925-3200	925-8539
Printronix Inc 14600 Myford Rd *TF:* 800-665-6210 ■ *Web:* www.printronix.com	Irvine	CA	92606	714-368-2300	368-2600
Ricoh Printing Systems America Inc 2390 Ward Ave Ste A *Web:* www.rpsa.ricoh.com	Simi Valley	CA	93065	805-578-4000	578-4001
RISO Inc 800 District Ave Ste 390 *TF General:* 800-942-7476 ■ *Web:* www.riso.com	Burlington	MA	01803	978-777-7377	777-2517
Roland DGA Corp 15363 Barranca Pkwy *TF:* 800-542-2307 ■ *Web:* www.rolanddga.com	Irvine	CA	92618	949-727-2100	727-2112
Sato America Inc 10350A Nations Ford Rd *TF:* 888-871-8741 ■ *Web:* www.satoamerica.com	Charlotte	NC	28273	704-644-1650	644-1662
Seiko Instruments USA Inc 21221 S Western Ave Ste 250 *TF Sales:* 800-688-0817 ■ *Web:* www.seikoinstruments.com	Torrance	CA	90501	310-517-7700	517-7709
Seiko Instruments USA Inc Business & Home Office Products Div (SII) 21221 S Western Ave Ste 250 *Web:* labelprinters.sii-thermalprinters.com	Torrance	CA	90501	310-517-7700	517-7779
Seiko Instruments USA Inc Micro Printer Div 2990 Lomita Blvd *TF:* 800-688-0817 ■ *Web:* labelprinters.sii-thermalprinters.com	Torrance	CA	90505	310-517-7778	
Sharp Electronics Corp 1 Sharp Plz *TF:* 800-237-4277 ■ *Web:* www.sharpusa.com	Mahwah	NJ	07430	201-529-8200	529-8413
SiPix Imaging Inc 47485 Seabridge Dr *Web:* www.eink.com	Fremont	CA	94538	510-743-2849	
Star Micronics America Inc 1150 King George's Post Rd **Fax:* Sales ■ *TF:* 800-782-7636 ■ *Web:* www.starmicronics.com	Edison	NJ	08837	732-623-5500	623-5590*
Stratix 4920 Avalon Ridge Pkwy *TF:* 800-883-8300 ■ *Web:* www.stratixcorp.com	Norcross	GA	30071	770-326-7580	326-7593
TallyGenicom 15345 Barranca Pkwy **Fax Area Code:* 703 ■ *TF:* 800-436-4266 ■ *Web:* www.tallygenicom.com	Irvine	CA	92618	714-368-2300	222-7629*
Telpar Inc 187 Crosby Rd Ste 100 *TF:* 800-872-4886 ■ *Web:* www.telpar.com	Dover	NH	03820	603-750-7237	742-9938
Toshiba America Inc 1251 Ave of the Americas Ste 4100 *TF:* 800-457-7777 ■ *Web:* www.toshiba.com	New York	NY	10020	212-596-0600	593-3875
TransAct Technologies Inc 1 Hamden Ctr 2319 Whitney Ave Ste 3B *NASDAQ: TACT* ■ *TF:* 800-243-8941 ■ *Web:* www.transact-tech.com	Hamden	CT	06518	203-859-6800	949-9048
Unimark Products 9818 Pflumm Rd *TF Cust Svc:* 800-255-6356 ■ *Web:* www.unimark.com	Lenexa	KS	66215	913-649-2424	649-5795
Xante Corp 2800 Dauphin St Ste 100 *TF:* 800-926-8839 ■ *Web:* xante.com	Mobile	AL	36606	251-473-6502	473-6503
Xerox Corp 45 Glover Ave PO Box 4505 *NYSE: XRX* ■ *TF:* 800-327-9753 ■ *Web:* www.xerox.com	Norwalk	CT	06856	203-968-3000	
Zebra Technologies Corp 475 Half Day Rd Ste 500 *NASDAQ: ZBRA* ■ *TF:* 800-423-0422 ■ *Web:* www.zebra.com	Lincolnshire	IL	60069	847-634-6700	913-8766

173-7 Scanning Equipment

Company	City	State	ZIP	Phone	Fax
Accu-Sort Systems Inc 511 School House Rd *TF:* 800-227-2633 ■ *Web:* www.datalogic.com	Telford	PA	18969	215-723-0981	721-5551
AirClic Inc 900 Northbrook Dr Ste 100 *TF:* 800-419-8495 ■ *Web:* www.airclic.com	Trevose	PA	19053	215-504-0560	504-0565
BenQ America Corp 15375 Barranca Ste A205 *TF:* 866-600-2367 ■ *Web:* www.benq.us	Irvine	CA	92618	949-255-9500	255-9600
BOWE Bell + Howell 760 S Wolf Rd **Fax Area Code:* 585 ■ *TF:* 800-220-3030 ■ *Web:* www.bellhowell.net	Wheeling	IL	60090	847-675-7600	340-8852*
CardScan Inc 25 First St Ste 107 *TF:* 800-942-6739 ■ *Web:* www.cardscan.com	Cambridge	MA	02141	617-492-4200	492-6659
Computerwise Inc 302 N Winchester Ln *TF:* 800-255-3739 ■ *Web:* www.computerwise.com	Olathe	KS	66062	913-829-0600	829-0810
Datalogic Scanning 959 Terry St *TF:* 800-695-5700 ■ *Web:* www.datalogic.com	Eugene	OR	97402	541-683-5700	345-7140
Eastman Kodak Co 343 State St *OTC: EKDKQ* ■ *Web:* www.kodak.com	Rochester	NY	14650	585-724-4000	
GTCO CalComp Inc 7125 Riverwood Dr *Web:* gtcocalcomp.com	Columbia	MD	21046	410-381-6688	
Hewlett-Packard Co 3000 Hanover St *NYSE: HPQ* ■ *TF Sales:* 800-752-0900 ■ *Web:* www.hp.com	Palo Alto	CA	94304	650-857-1501	857-5518
Hitachi Canada Ltd 5450 Explore Dr Ste 501 *TF:* 877-248-4237 ■ *Web:* www.hitachi.ca	Mississauga	ON	L4W5N1	905-629-9300	290-0141
iCAD Inc 98 Spit Brook Rd Ste 100 *NASDAQ: ICAD* ■ *TF:* 866-280-2239 ■ *Web:* www.icadmed.com	Nashua	NH	03062	603-882-5200	880-3843
InPath Devices 3610 Dodge St Ste 200 *TF:* 800-988-1914 ■ *Web:* www.inpath.com	Omaha	NE	68131	402-345-9200	
Microtek Lab Inc 10900 183rd St Ste 290 *Web:* www.microtekusa.com	Cerritos	CA	90703	310-687-5800	
Oce-USA Inc 5450 N Cumberland Ave *TF:* 800-877-6232 ■ *Web:* csa.canon.com	Chicago	IL	60656	773-714-8500	693-7634
Peripheral Dynamics Inc 5150 Campus Dr *TF:* 800-523-0253 ■ *Web:* www.pdiscan.com	Plymouth Meeting	PA	19462	610-825-7090	834-7708
Ricoh Electronics Inc 1100 Valencia Ave *Web:* www.rei.ricoh.com	Tustin	CA	92780	714-566-2500	
Roland DGA Corp 15363 Barranca Pkwy *TF:* 800-542-2307 ■ *Web:* www.rolanddga.com	Irvine	CA	92618	949-727-2100	727-2112
Scan-Optics Inc 169 Progress Dr *TF:* 800-543-8681 ■ *Web:* www.scanoptics.com	Manchester	CT	06042	860-645-7878	645-7995
Scantron Corp 34 Parker *TF:* 800-722-6876 ■ *Web:* www.scantron.com	Irvine	CA	92618	949-639-7500	639-7710
Stratix 4920 Avalon Ridge Pkwy *TF:* 800-883-8300 ■ *Web:* www.stratixcorp.com	Norcross	GA	30071	770-326-7580	326-7593
Techville Inc 11343 N Central Expwy *Web:* www.umax.com	Dallas	TX	75243	214-739-7033	
Videx Inc 1105 NE Cir Blvd *Web:* www.videx.com	Corvallis	OR	97330	541-738-5500	738-5501
Visioneer Inc 5673 Gibraltar Dr Ste 150 *Web:* www.visioneer.com	Pleasanton	CA	94588	925-251-6300	416-8600
Wizcom Technologies Inc Boston Post Rd W 33 Ste 320 *TF:* 888-777-0552 ■ *Web:* www.wizcomtech.com	Marlborough	MA	01752	508-251-5388	
ZBA Inc 94 Old Camplain Rd *TF:* 800-750-4239 ■ *Web:* www.zbaus.com	Hillsborough	NJ	08844	908-359-2070	595-0909

173-8 Storage Devices

Company	City	State	ZIP	Phone	Fax
Ampex Data Systems Corp 500 Broadway *Web:* www.ampex.com	Redwood City	CA	94063	650-367-2011	367-3106
Appro International Inc 901 Fifth Ave Ste 1000 *TF:* 800-950-2729 ■ *Web:* www.cray.com	Seattle	WA	98164	206-701-2000	299-9174
Apricorn Inc 12191 Kirkham Rd *TF:* 800-458-5448 ■ *Web:* www.apricorn.com	Poway	CA	92064	858-513-2000	513-2020
Atp Electronics Inc 750 N Mary Ave *Web:* www.atpinc.com	Sunnyvale	CA	94085	408-732-5000	732-5055
Avere Systems Inc 5000 Mcknight Rd Ste 404 *TF:* 888-882-8373 ■ *Web:* www.averesystems.com	Pittsburgh	PA	15237	412-894-2570	
BlueArc Corp 50 Rio Robles Dr *Web:* www.hds.com	San Jose	CA	95134	408-576-6600	576-6601
BridgeSTOR LLC 18060 Old Coach Dr *TF:* 800-280-8204 ■ *Web:* www.bridgestor.com	Poway	CA	92064	858-375-7076	
Cirrascale Corp 12140 Community Rd *TF:* 888-942-3800 ■ *Web:* www.cirrascale.com	Poway	CA	92064	858-874-3800	874-3838
CMS Peripherals Inc 12 Mauchly Unit E *TF:* 800-327-5773 ■ *Web:* www.cmsproducts.com	Irvine	CA	92618	714-424-5520	
Creative Labs Inc 1901 McCarthy Blvd *TF Cust Svc:* 800-998-1000 ■ *Web:* www.us.creative.com	Milpitas	CA	95035	408-428-6600	428-6611
CRU Acquisitions Group LLC 1000 SE Tech Ctr Dr Ste 160 *TF:* 800-260-9800 ■ *Web:* www.cru-inc.com	Vancouver	WA	98683	360-816-1800	816-1831
Cybernetics Inc 111 Cybernetics Way *Web:* www.cybernetics.com	Yorktown	VA	23693	757-833-9100	833-9300
DataDirect Networks 9351 Deering Ave *TF:* 800-837-2298 ■ *Web:* www.ddn.com	Chatsworth	CA	91311	818-700-7600	700-7601
Datalink Corp 8170 Upland Cir *NASDAQ: DTLK* ■ *TF:* 800-448-6314 ■ *Web:* www.datalink.com	Chanhassen	MN	55317	952-944-3462	
Digital Peripheral Solutions Inc 8015 E Crystal Dr **Fax Area Code:* 714 ■ *TF:* 877-998-3440 ■ *Web:* q-see.com	Anaheim	CA	92807	877-998-3440	692-5516*
Disc Makers 7905 N Rt 130 *TF:* 800-468-9353 ■ *Web:* www.discmakers.com	Pennsauken	NJ	08110	856-663-9030	661-3458
Dynamic Network Factory Inc 21353 Cabot Blvd *TF:* 800-947-4742 ■ *Web:* www.dnfstorage.com	Hayward	CA	94545	510-265-1122	265-1565
Edge Electronics Inc 75 Orville Dr *TF:* 800-647-3343 ■ *Web:* www.edgeelectronics.com	Bohemia	NY	11716	631-471-3343	471-3405
FlexPlay Technologies Inc 3350 Peachtree Rd One Capital City Plz Ste 1150 *Web:* www.flexplay.com	Atlanta	GA	30326	404-835-9900	
Fujitsu Computer Products of America Inc 1255 E Arques Ave *TF:* 800-626-4686 ■ *Web:* www.fujitsu.com	Sunnyvale	CA	94085	408-746-7000	746-6910
Fusion-io Inc 2855 E Cottonwood Pkwy Ste 100 *Web:* www.fusionio.com	Salt Lake City	UT	84121	801-424-5500	
Gridstore Inc 1975 W El Camino Real Ste 306 *TF:* 855-786-7065 ■ *Web:* www.gridstore.com	Mountain View	CA	94040	650-316-5515	
H Company Computer Products Inc 16812 Hale Ave *TF:* 800-726-2477 ■ *Web:* www.thinkcp.com	Irvine	CA	92606	949-833-3222	
Headway Technologies Inc 682 S Hillview Dr *Web:* headway.com	Milpitas	CA	95035	408-934-5300	
Hewlett-Packard (Canada) Ltd (HP) 5150 Spectrum Way *TF:* 888-447-4636 ■ *Web:* welcome.hp.com	Mississauga	ON	L4W5G1	905-206-4725	
Hewlett-Packard Co 3000 Hanover St *NYSE: HPQ* ■ *TF Sales:* 800-752-0900 ■ *Web:* www.hp.com	Palo Alto	CA	94304	650-857-1501	857-5518
Hie Electronics Inc 321 N Central Expy Ste 260 *TF:* 888-782-7937 ■ *Web:* www.hie-electronics.com	Mckinney	TX	75070	972-542-2327	
Hitachi America Ltd Computer Div 2000 Sierra Pt Pkwy **Fax Area Code:* 650 ■ *TF:* 800-448-2244 ■ *Web:* www.hitachi-america.us	Brisbane	CA	94005	800-448-2244	244-7776*
Hitachi Data Systems Corp 750 Central Expy *TF:* 877-437-3849 ■ *Web:* www.hds.com	Santa Clara	CA	95050	408-970-1000	727-8036
I/O Magic Corp 20512 Crescent Bay Dr Ste 106 *OTC: IOMG* ■ *Web:* www.iomagic.com	Lake Forest,	CA	92630	949-707-4800	855-3550
Idealstor LLC 12400 St Hwy 71 W Ste 350-364 *TF:* 888-864-3257 ■ *Web:* www.idealstor.com	Austin	TX	78738	512-279-4321	
Imation Corp 1 Imation Pl *NYSE: IMN* ■ *TF:* 888-466-3456 ■ *Web:* www.imation.com	Oakdale	MN	55128	651-704-4000	704-7100
Infortrend Corp 435 Lakeside Dr *Web:* www.infortrend.com	Sunnyvale	CA	94085	408-988-5088	
International Business Machines Corp (IBM) 1 New OrchaRd Rd *NYSE: IBM* ■ *TF:* 800-426-4968 ■ *Web:* www.ibm.com	Armonk	NY	10504	914-499-1900	
Kanguru Solutions 1360 Main St *TF Sales:* 888-526-4878 ■ *Web:* www.kanguru.com	Millis	MA	02054	508-376-4245	376-4462
La Cie Ltd 22985 NW Evergreen Pkwy **Fax:* Mktg ■ *Web:* www.lacie.com	Hillsboro	OR	97124	503-844-4500	844-4508*
LG Electronics USA Inc 1000 Sylvan Ave *TF Tech Supp:* 800-243-0000 ■ *Web:* www.lg.com	Englewood Cliffs	NJ	07632	201-816-2000	
Luminex Software Inc 871 Marlborough Ave *TF Sales:* 888-586-4639 ■ *Web:* www.luminex.com	Riverside	CA	92507	951-781-4100	781-4105
Microboards Technology LLC 8150 Mallory Ct PO Box 846 *TF:* 800-646-8881 ■ *Web:* www.microboards.com	Chanhassen	MN	55317	952-556-1600	556-1620
Mitsumi Electronics Corp 40000 Grand River Ave Novi Technology Ctr Ste 200 *Web:* www.mitsumi.com	Novi	MI	48375	248-426-8448	
NEC Corp of America 10850 Gold Ctr Dr Ste 200 *TF:* 800-632-4636 ■ *Web:* www.necam.com	Rancho Cordova	CA	95670	916-463-7000	
NexGen Storage Inc 361 Centennial Pkwy Ste 230 *Web:* nexgenstorage.com	Louisville	CO	80027	720-245-6300	
Perifitech of Ohio Inc 23108 Felch St *Web:* www.perifitech.com	Cleveland	OH	44128	216-332-0655	
Pexagon Technology Inc 14 Business Park Dr *Web:* www.pexagontech.com	Branford	CT	06405	203-458-3364	
Phoenix International 812 W Southern Ave *Web:* www.phenxint.com	Orange	CA	92865	714-283-4800	283-1169
Pioneer Electronics (USA) Inc 1925 E Dominguez St *TF:* 800-421-1404 ■ *Web:* www.pioneerelectronics.com	Long Beach	CA	90810	310-952-2000	952-2402
PURE Storage Inc 650 Castro St Ste 400 *TF:* 800-379-7873 ■ *Web:* www.purestorage.com	Mountain View	CA	94041	650-290-6088	
Qualstar Corp 3990-B Heritage Oak Ct *NASDAQ: QBAK* ■ *TF:* 800-468-0680 ■ *Web:* www.qualstar.com	Simi Valley	CA	93063	805-583-7744	583-7749
Quantum Corp 224 Airport Pkwy Ste 300 *NYSE: QTM* ■ *TF Tech Supp:* 800-677-6268 ■ *Web:* www.quantum.com	San Jose	CA	95110	408-944-4000	
Quantum/ATL 141 Innovation Dr *TF:* 800-677-6268 ■ *Web:* www.quantum.com	Irvine	CA	92617	949-856-7800	856-7799
Rimage Corp 7725 Washington Ave S *TF:* 800-553-8312 ■ *Web:* www.qumu.com	Minneapolis	MN	55439	952-944-8144	
SANBlaze Technology Inc 1 Monarch Dr Ste 204 *Web:* www.sanblaze.com	Littleton	MA	01460	978-679-1400	
Savage IO Inc 8 S Lyon St *Web:* www.savageio.com	Batavia	NY	14020	585-250-4216	
Seagate Technology LLC 10200 S De Anza Blvd *Web:* www.seagate.com	Cupertino	CA	95014	831-438-6550	
Shaffstall Corp 8531 Bash St *TF:* 800-357-6250 ■ *Web:* www.shaffstall.com	Indianapolis	IN	46250	317-842-2077	
Sony Electronics Inc 1 Sony Dr *TF Cust Svc:* 800-222-7669 ■ *Web:* www.sony.com	Park Ridge	NJ	07656	201-930-1000	
Tandberg Data 10225 Westmoor Dr Ste 125 *TF:* 800-392-2983 ■ *Web:* www.tandbergdata.com	Westminster	CO	80021	303-442-4333	
TDK USA Corp 525 RXR Plaza **Fax:* Sales ■ *Web:* www.tdk.com	Uniondale	NY	11556	516-535-2600	294-8318*

				Phone	Fax
TEAC America Inc 7733 Telegraph Rd ... Montebello *Web:* www.teac.com	CA	90640		323-726-0303	727-7656
Tegile Systems Inc 8000 Jarvis Ave. ... Newark *Web:* www.tegile.com	CA	94560		510-791-7900	
Themis Computer 47200 Bayside Pkwy ... Fremont *Web:* www.themis.com	CA	94538		510-252-0870	490-5529
Tintri Inc 2570 W El Camino Real ... Mountain View *TF:* 855-484-6874 ■ *Web:* www.tintri.com	CA	94040		650-209-3900	
Toshiba America Inc 1251 Ave of the Americas Ste 4100 ... New York *TF:* 800-457-7777 ■ *Web:* www.toshiba.com	NY	10020		212-596-0600	593-3875
Unitrends Software Corp 200 Wheeler Rd 2nd fl ... Burlington *TF:* 866-359-5411 ■ *Web:* www.unitrends.com	SC	01803		803-454-0300	
VeriStor Systems Inc 3308 Peachtree Industrial Blvd ... Duluth *Web:* www.veristor.com	GA	30096		678-990-1593	990-1597
Western Digital Corp 3355 Michelson Dr Ste 100 ... Irvine *NASDAQ: WDC* ■ *TF:* 800-832-4778 ■ *Web:* www.wdc.com	CA	92612		949-672-7000	672-5498

174 COMPUTER EQUIPMENT & SOFTWARE - WHOL

See Also Business Machines - Whol p. 1884; Electrical & Electronic Equipment & Parts - Whol p. 2217

			Phone	Fax
A.I.W. Inc 447 Tierra Verde Ln Ste 101 ... Winter Garden *Web:* www.aiwonline.net	FL	34787	407-521-4576	
AAA Digital Imaging Inc 5706 New Peachtree Rd ... Chamblee *Web:* www.aaadi.com	GA	30341	770-451-7861	
ABOL Software Inc 413 Creekstone Ridge ... Woodstock *Web:* www.iabol.com	GA	30188	678-494-3172	
Access Specialties International LLC 15230 Carrousel Way ... Rosemount *TF:* 800-332-1013 ■ *Web:* www.access-specialties.com	MN	55068	651-453-1283	
Addonics Technologies Inc 1918 Junction Ave ... San Jose *Web:* www.addonics.com	CA	95131	408-573-8580	
Advanced Clinical Services LLC 10 Pkwy N Ste 350 ... Deerfield *Web:* www.advancedclinical.com	IL	60015	847-267-1176	
Advanced Web Offset Inc 2260 Oak Ridge Way ... Vista *Web:* www.awoink.com	CA	92081	760-727-1700	
Ahearn & Soper Inc 100 Woodbine Downs Blvd ... Rexdale *TF:* 800-263-4258 ■ *Web:* www.ahearn.com	ON	M9W5S6	416-675-3999	675-3457
Alacritech Inc 1995 N First St Ste 200 ... San Jose *Web:* www.alacritech.com	CA	95112	408-287-9997	
Alexander Open Systems Inc 12851 Foster St ... Overland Park *TF:* 800-473-1110 ■ *Web:* www.aos5.com	KS	66213	913-307-2300	307-2380
Alexander's Print Advantage Co 245 South 1060 West ... Lindon *Web:* www.alexanders.com	UT	84042	801-224-8666	
Allied Group Inc, The 25 Amflex Dr ... Cranston *TF:* 800-556-6310 ■ *Web:* www.thealliedgrp.com	RI	02921	401-946-6100	
Altametrics Inc 3191 Red Hill Ave Ste 100 ... Costa Mesa *TF:* 800-676-1281 ■ *Web:* www.altametrics.com	CA	92626	800-676-1281	
Altruent Corp 1017 Passport Wayý ... Cary *Web:* www.altruent.com	NC	27804	919-828-4419	
Alvarez & Associates Llc 8601 Georgia Ave Ste 510 ... Silver Spring *Web:* www.alvarezassociates.com	MD	20910	301-565-3443	
American Portwell Technology Inc 44200 Christy St ... Fremont *TF:* 877-278-8899 ■ *Web:* www.portwell.com	CA	94538	510-403-3399	403-3184
Amex Inc 2724 Summer St NE ... Minneapolis *Web:* www.amexinc.com	MN	55413	612-331-3063	331-3180
Amnet Inc 219 W Colorado Ave Ste 200 ... Colorado Springs *Web:* www.amnet.net	CO	80903	719-442-6683	
APCON Inc 9255 SW Pioneer Ct ... Wilsonville *TF:* 800-624-6808 ■ *Web:* www.apcon.com	OR	97070	503-682-4050	
App-Techs Corp 505-B Willow Ln ... Lancaster *Web:* www.app-techs.com	PA	17601	717-735-0848	
Applied Ceramics Inc 48630 Milmont Dr ... Fremont *Web:* www.appliedceramics.net	CA	94538	510-249-9700	
Arbitech LLC 15330 Barranca Pkwy ... Irvine *Web:* www.arbitech.com	CA	92618	949-376-6650	
Arete Inc 65 S Main St Bldg E ... Pennington *Web:* www.areteinc.com	NJ	08534	609-737-1212	
Arrow Electronics Corp 7459 S Lima St ... Englewood *NYSE: ARW* ■ *Web:* www.arrow.com	CO	80112	303-824-4000	
Arrow Enterprise Computing Solutions 24 Inverness Pl E ... Englewood *Web:* www.arrowecs.com	CO	80112	303-824-7650	
ASA Tire Systems Inc 651 S Stratford Dr ... Meridian *TF:* 800-241-8472 ■ *Web:* www.asatire.com	ID	83642	208-855-0781	
ASE Technologies Inc 226 Lowell St ... Wilmington *Web:* www.ase-tech.com	MA	01887	978-658-0009	
Asentinel LLC 6410 Poplar Ave International Pl Tower 2 Ste 200 ... Memphis *Web:* www.asentinel.com	TN	38119	901-752-6200	
ASI Corp 48289 Fremont Blvd ... Fremont **Fax:* Sales ■ *TF:* 800-200-0274 ■ *Web:* www.asipartner.com	CA	94538	510-226-8000	226-8858*
ATEC Group 1762 Central Ave Ste 1 ... Albany	NY	12205	518-452-3700	
Aternity Inc 200 Friberg Pkwy Ste 1004 ... Westborough *Web:* www.aternity.com	MA	01581	508-475-0414	
Atlantix Global Systems 1 Sun Ct ... Norcross *TF:* 877-552-8526 ■ *Web:* www.atlantixglobal.com	GA	30092	770-248-7700	448-7726
Autostar Solutions Inc 1300 Summit Ave Ste 800 ... Fort Worth *TF:* 800-682-2215 ■ *Web:* www.autostarsolutions.com	TX	76102	800-682-2215	
AVAD Canada Ltd 205 Courtneypark Dr W ... Mississauga *TF:* 866-523-2823 ■ *Web:* ca.avad.com	ON	L5W0A5	866-523-2823	
Avnet Inc 2211 S 47th St ... Phoenix *NYSE: AVT* ■ *TF:* 888-822-8638 ■ *Web:* www.avnet.com	AZ	85034	480-643-2000	
Avnet Technology Solutions 8700 S Price Rd ... Tempe *TF:* 800-409-1483 ■ *Web:* www.ats.avnet.com	AZ	85284	480-794-6500	
Axiom Memory Solutions LLC 15 Chrysler ... Irvine *TF:* 888-658-3326 ■ *Web:* www.axiomupgrades.com	CA	92618	949-581-1450	
Barr Systems LLC 4500 NW 27th Ave ... Gainesville *Web:* www.barrsystems.com	FL	32606	352-491-3100	
Bay Technical Assoc Inc 5239 Ave A ... Long Beach Industrial Park *TF:* 800-523-2702 ■ *Web:* www.baytech.net	MS	39560	228-563-7334	
Big Huge Games Inc 1954 Greenspring Dr Ste 520 ... Timonium	MD	21093	410-842-0028	
Blueslice Networks Inc 1751 Richardson St Ste 7500 ... Montreal	QC	H3K1G6	514-935-9700	
BreezeGo Inc 3332 Southside Blvd ... Jacksonville *Web:* www.breezego.com	FL	32216	904-998-4066	
Burstek 12801 Westlinks Dr Ste 101 ... Fort Myers *TF:* 800-709-2551 ■ *Web:* www.burstek.com	FL	33913	239-495-5900	
Butler Technologies Inc 231 W Wayne St ... Butler *TF:* 800-494-6656 ■ *Web:* www.butlertechnologies.com	PA	16001	724-283-6656	
C Enterprises LP 2445 Cades Way ... Vista *Web:* www.copierdepot.com	CA	92081	760-599-5111	
Cabaret Systems Inc 8848 Red Oak Blvd ... Charlotte *Web:* cabaretsystems.com	NC	28217	704-333-1100	
CAD/CAM Consulting Services Inc (CCCS) 996 Lawrence Dr Ste 101 ... Newbury Park *TF:* 888-375-7676 ■ *Web:* www.cad-cam.com	CA	91320	805-375-7676	375-7678
Cadec Corp 645 Harvey Rd ... Manchester *Web:* www.cadec.com	NH	03103	603-668-1010	623-0604
Cakewalk Inc 268 Summer St 8th Fl ... Boston *Web:* www.cakewalk.com	MA	02210	617-423-9004	
Cash Management Solutions Inc 13921 Icot Blvd Ste 710 ... Clearwater *Web:* www.cashmgmt.com	FL	33760	727-524-1103	
CCT Technologies Inc 482 W San Carlos St ... San Jose *Web:* www.cland.com	CA	95110	408-519-3200	
Centered Networks Inc Pier 33 N ... San Francisco *Web:* www.centerednetworks.com	CA	94111	415-294-7776	
Central Florida Press Inc 4560 L B Mcleod Rd ... Orlando *Web:* www.printcfp.com	FL	32811	407-843-5811	
Champion Solutions Group 791 Pk of Commerce Blvd Ste 200 ... Boca Raton *TF:* 800-771-7000 ■ *Web:* www.championsg.com	FL	33487	561-997-2900	997-4043
Chief Architect Inc 6500 N Mineral Dr ... Coeur D'Alene *Web:* www.chiefarchitect.com	ID	83815	208-292-3400	
CHIPS Technology Group LLC 5 Aerial Way Ste 400 ... Syosset *Web:* www.chipscc.com	NY	11791	516-377-6585	
City Press Inc W238 N1650 Rockwood Dr ... Waukesha *Web:* www.citypressinc.com	WI	53188	262-523-3000	
Colorfx Inc 10776 Aurora Ave ... Des Moines *TF:* 800-348-9044 ■ *Web:* www.colorfxprint.com	IA	50322	800-348-9044	
Columbia Ultimate Business Systems Inc 4400 NE 77th Ave Ste 100 ... Vancouver *TF:* 800-488-4420 ■ *Web:* www.columbiaultimate.com	WA	98662	360-256-7358	260-1614
Columbus Productions Inc 4580 Cargo Dr ... Columbus *Web:* www.columbusproductionsinc.com	GA	31907	706-644-1595	
Column Technologies Inc 1400 Opus Pl Ste 110 ... Downers Grove *TF:* 866-265-8665 ■ *Web:* www.columnit.com	IL	60515	630-515-6660	271-1508
Comprehensive Traffic Systems Inc 4300 Harlan St ... Wheat Ridge *Web:* www.ctsworldwide.net	CO	80033	303-867-4039	
Computech International Inc 525 Northern Blvd ... Great Neck *Web:* www.cti-intl.com	NY	11021	516-487-0101	
Computer Aided Technology Inc 165 N Arlington Heights Rd Ste 101 ... Buffalo Grove *TF:* 888-308-2284 ■ *Web:* www.cati.com	IL	60089	888-308-2284	
Computer Connection of Central New York Inc 11206 Cosby Manor Rd ... Utica	NY	13502	315-724-2209	
Computer Crafts Inc 57 Thomas Rd ... Hawthorne *Web:* www.computer-crafts.com	NJ	07506	973-423-3500	
Computer Dynamics Inc 3030 Whitehall Pk Dr ... Charlotte **Fax Area Code:* 704 ■ *TF:* 866-599-6512 ■ *Web:* www.cdynamics.com	NC	28273	866-599-6512	583-9671*
Comstor Inc 14850 Conference Ctr Dr Ste 200 ... Chantilly *TF:* 800-955-9590 ■ *Web:* www.comstor.com	VA	20151	703-345-5100	
Configure Inc 1800 Hamilton Ave Ste 200 ... San Jose *Web:* www.configureinc.com	CA	95125	408-269-1122	
Cordoba Corp 1401 N Broadway ... Los Angeles *Web:* www.cordobacorp.com	CA	90012	213-895-0224	
Coridian Technologies Inc 1725 Lk Dr W ... Chanhassen *Web:* coridian.com	MN	55317	952-361-9980	
Cornell Mayo Assoc Inc 600 Lanidex Plz ... Parsippany *Web:* www.cornell-mayo.com	NJ	07054	973-887-3069	
Corporate Information Technologies Inc 14 Brick Walk Ln ... Farmington *Web:* www.corpit.com	CT	06032	860-676-2720	
Cpu Venturetech 401 E Collins Dr ... Casper *Web:* www.cpuventuretech.com	WY	82609	307-235-6212	
Cranel Inc 8999 Gemini Pkwy ... Columbus *TF General:* 800-288-3475 ■ *Web:* www.cranel.com	OH	43240	614-431-8000	431-8388
Crown Micro Inc 48351 Fremont Blvd ... Fremont *TF:* 800-963-7070 ■ *Web:* www.crownmicro.com	CA	94538	510-490-8187	
CS3 Technology 5272 S Lewis Ave Ste 100 ... Tulsa *Web:* www.crouchslavin.com	OK	74105	918-496-1600	
CSF International Inc 1629 Barber Rd ... Sarasota	FL	34240	941-379-0881	
D & H Distributing Company Inc 2525 N Seventh St ... Harrisburg *TF:* 800-340-1001 ■ *Web:* www.dandh.com	PA	17110	800-340-1001	340-1001

Company / Address	City	State	ZIP	Phone	Fax
Data Impressions 17418 Studebaker Rd.	Cerritos	CA	90703	562-207-9050	207-9053
TF: 800-777-6488 ■ *Web:* dataimpressions.com					
Data Sales Company Inc 3450 W Burnsville Pkwy.	Burnsville	MN	55337	952-890-8838	895-3369
TF: 800-328-2730 ■ *Web:* www.datasales.com					
Databit Inc 200 Route 17	Mahwah	NJ	07430	201-529-8050	
Web: www.databitinc.com					
Datamaxx Applied Technologies Inc 2001 Drayton Dr.	Tallahassee	FL	32311	850-558-8000	
Web: www.datamaxx.com					
Dataprobe Inc 1B Pearl Ct.	Allendale	NJ	07401	201-934-9944	
Web: www.dataprobe.com					
Daymark Solutions Inc 23 Third Ave.	Burlington	MA	01803	781-359-3000	
Web: www.daymarksi.com					
De Marque inc 400 Boul Jean-Lesage Bureau 540	Quebec	QC	G1K8W1	418-658-9143	
TF: 888-458-9143 ■ *Web:* www.demarque.com					
Deccan International 5935 Cornerstone Court W Ste 230	San Diego	CA	92121	858-764-8400	
Web: deccanintl.com					
Decision Academic Inc 411 Legget Dr Ste 501	Ottawa	ON	K2K3C9	613-254-9669	
Web: www.decisionacademic.com					
Dectrader 3547 Old Conejo Rd Unit 101	Newbury Park	CA	91320	805-480-1888	
Web: www.dectrader.com					
Delkin Devices Inc 13350 Kirkham Way	Poway	CA	92064	858-391-1234	
Web: www.delkin.com					
Dellas Graphics Inc 835 Canal St	Syracuse	NY	13210	315-474-4641	
Web: www.dellasgraphics.com					
Delta Computer Group Inc 4 Dubon Ct.	Farmingdale	NY	11735	631-845-0400	
Web: www.deltacomputergroup.com					
Desire2Learn Inc 151 Charles SW Ste 400.	Kitchener	ON	N2G1H6	519-772-0325	772-0324
TF: 888-772-0325 ■ *Web:* www.d2l.com					
Dieselpoint Inc 117 N Jefferson St	Chicago	IL	60661	773-528-1700	
Web: www.dieselpoint.com					
DigiLink Inc 840 S Pickett St	Alexandria	VA	22304	703-340-1800	
TF: 877-806-3444 ■ *Web:* www.digilink-inc.com					
Digital Storage Inc 7611 Green Meadows Dr	Lewis Center	OH	43035	740-548-7179	803-8030*
**Fax Area Code:* 800 ■ *TF:* 800-232-3475 ■ *Web:* www.digitalstorage.com					
Dirxion LLC 1859 Bowles Ave Ste 100	Fenton	MO	63026	636-717-2300	
TF: 888-391-0202 ■ *Web:* www.dirxion.com					
Dlt Solutions 13861 Sunrise Valley Dr Ste 400	Herndon	VA	20171	703-709-7172	709-8450
TF: 800-262-4358 ■ *Web:* www.dlt.com					
Documation LLC 1556 International Dr	Eau Claire	WI	54701	715-839-8899	
Web: documation.com					
DPC DATA Inc 103 Eisenhower Pkwy Ste 300	Roseland	NJ	07068	201-346-0701	
TF: 800-996-4747 ■ *Web:* www.dpcdata.com					
Dynamic Computer Corp 23400 Industrial Pk Ct	Farmington Hills	MI	48335	248-473-2200	473-2201
TF: 866-257-2111 ■ *Web:* www.dcc-online.com					
Dynamic Digital Depth Inc 2120 Colorado Ave Ste 100	Santa Monica	CA	90404	310-566-3340	
DYNAMIC SYSTEMS Inc 124 Maryland St	El Segundo	CA	90245	310-337-4400	
Web: www.dynamicsystemsinc.com					
E John Schmitz & Sons Inc 37 Loveton Cir.	Sparks	MD	21152	410-329-3000	
Web: www.schmitzpress.com					
e-TechServices.com Inc 5220 SW 91st Terrace	Gainesville	FL	32608	352-332-3200	
Web: web2.e-techservices.com					
Eastern Computer Exchange Inc 105 Cascade Blvd.	Milford	CT	06460	203-877-4334	
Web: www.ecei.com					
Eastern Data Inc 4386 Park Dr.	Norcross	GA	30093	770-279-8888	
Web: www.ediatlanta.com					
EDAC Systems Inc 10970 Pierson Dr	Fredericksburg	VA	22408	540-361-1580	
Web: www.edacsystems.com					
EDGAR Online Inc (EDGR) 55 Water St 11th Fl.	New York	NY	10004	212-658-5711	
TF: 888-870-2316 ■ *Web:* www.edgaronline.com					
Electronic Environments Corp 410 Forest St	Marlborough	MA	01752	508-229-1400	303-0579
TF: 800-342-5332 ■ *Web:* www.eecnet.com					
Eleven Wireless Inc 315 SW 11th Ave 3rd Fl	Portland	OR	97205	503-222-4321	
Web: www.elevenwireless.com					
Elk River Systems Inc 777 E Main Ste 108	Bozeman	MT	59715	406-632-4763	
TF: 888-771-0809 ■ *Web:* www.elkriversystems.com					
Enseo Inc 1680 Prospect Dr Ste 100	Richardson	TX	75081	972-234-2513	
Web: www.enseo.com					
Entre BTG Inc 6649-A Peachtree Industrial Blvd	Norcross	GA	30092	770-300-0256	
Web: www.entrebtg.com					
EON Reality Inc 39 Parker St Ste 100	Irvine	CA	92618	949-460-2000	
Web: www.eonreality.com					
Ergonomic Group Inc 609-3 Cantiague Rock Rd	Westbury	NY	11590	516-746-7777	
Web: www.ergogroup.com					
ESRI Canada Ltd 12 Concorde Pl Ste 900.	Toronto	ON	M3C3R8	416-441-6035	
TF: 866-625-4577 ■ *Web:* www.esri.ca					
EtherCom Corp 1409 Fulton Pl	Fremont	CA	94539	510-440-0242	
Web: www.ethercom.com					
ExtraView Corp 269 Mt Hermon Rd Ste 207	Scotts Valley	CA	95066	831-461-7100	
Web: www.extraview.com					
Exxact Corp 45445 Warm Springs Blvd.	Fremont	CA	94539	510-226-7366	
Web: www.exxactcorp.com					
Ficomp Inc 3015 Advance Ln.	Colmar	PA	18915	215-997-2600	
Flixster Inc 208 Utah St 4th Fl.	San Francisco	CA	94103	415-255-7215	
Web: www.flixster.com					
Floodgate Entertainment LLC 55 Moody St Ste 31	Waltham	MA	02453	781-893-3500	
Folgergraphics Inc 2339 Davis Ave.	Hayward	CA	94545	510-887-5656	
Web: www.folgergraphics.com					
Forquer Group Inc 100 State St Ste 310	Erie	PA	16507	814-453-3366	
Web: www.forquer.com					
FusionOps inc 707 California St	Mountain View	CA	94041	408-524-2222	
Web: www.fusionops.com					
Gamse Lithographing Company Inc 7413 Pulaski Hwy.	Baltimore	MD	21237	410-866-4700	
Web: www.gamse.com					
Gar Enterprises 418 E Live Oak Ave	Arcadia	CA	91006	626-574-1175	574-0553
Web: www.kgselectronics.com					
Gearbox Software LLC 101 E Park Blvd Ste 1200	Plano	TX	75074	972-312-8202	
Web: www.gearboxsoftware.com					
General Data Co Inc 4354 Ferguson Dr.	Cincinnati	OH	45245	513-752-7978	752-6947*
**Fax:* Sales ■ *TF:* 800-733-5252 ■ *Web:* www.general-data.com					
General Networks Corp 3524 Ocean View Blvd.	Glendale	CA	91208	818-249-1962	
Web: www.gennet.com					
Genius Jones Inc 49 NE 39th St	Miami	FL	33137	866-436-4875	
TF: 866-436-4875 ■ *Web:* www.geniusjones.com					
Global Computer Supplies Inc 11 Harbor Pk Dr	Port Washington	NY	11050	888-278-4437	
TF: 800-446-9662 ■ *Web:* www.tigerdirect.com					
Good Printers Inc 213 Dry River Rd	Bridgewater	VA	22812	540-828-4663	
TF: 800-296-3731 ■ *Web:* www.goodprinters.com					
Gotham Technology Group LLC 1 Paragon Dr Ste 200	Montvale	NJ	07645	201-474-4200	
Web: www.gothamtg.com					
Granite Business Solutions Inc 233 Technology Way Ste 4	Rocklin	CA	95765	916-577-2181	
Web: www.go-evolve.com					
Graphic Connections Group LLC 174 Chesterfield Industrial Blvd	Chesterfield	MO	63005	636-519-8320	
Web: www.gcfrog.com					
Graphic Management Specialty Products Inc 139 Evergreen Rd PO Box 408	Oconto	WI	54153	920-835-3299	
Web: www.gmsp.com					
Graphic Partners Inc 4300 Il Rt 173	Zion	IL	60099	847-872-9445	
Web: www.graphicpartners.com					
Graphic Products Inc PO Box 4030.	Beaverton	OR	97076	503-644-5572	646-0183
TF: 888-326-9244 ■ *Web:* www.graphicproducts.com					
GTC Systems Inc 504 W Mission Ave Ste 203	Escondido	CA	92025	858-560-5800	
Web: www.gtcsystems.com					
GTSI Corp 2553 Dulles View Dr Ste 100.	Herndon	VA	20171	703-502-2000	
NASDAQ: GTSI ■ *TF:* 800-999-4874 ■ *Web:* unicomgov.com					
Hamer Enterprises 4200-A N Bicentennial Dr	Mcallen	TX	78504	956-682-3466	
Web: hecorp.com					
Harding Poorman 4923 W 78th St	Indianapolis	IN	46268	317-876-3355	
Web: www.hardingpoorman.com					
Harwood International Corp 4713 Gann Store Rd 100 Northshore Office Park	Chattanooga	TN	37343	423-870-5500	
Web: www.harwood-intl.com					
Helmel Engineering Products Inc 6520 Lockport Rd.	Niagara Falls	NY	14305	716-297-8644	297-9405
TF: 800-237-8266 ■ *Web:* www.helmel.com					
HOBI International Inc 1202 Nagel Blvd	Batavia	IL	60510	630-761-0500	
Web: www.hobi.com					
Home Automated Living Inc 14401 Sweitzer Ln 6th Fl	Laurel	MD	20707	301-498-6000	
TF: 800-935-5313 ■ *Web:* www.automatedliving.com					
Horizon USA Data Supplies Inc 1595 Meadow Wood Ln Ste 1.	Reno	NV	89502	775-858-2300	
TF: 800-325-1199 ■ *Web:* www.horizonusa.com					
Hub Data Inc 70 Franklin St 7th Fl	Boston	MA	02110	617-530-1165	
Web: www.hubdata.com					
IAR Systems Software Inc 1065 E Hillsdale Blvd Century Plz	Foster City	CA	94404	650-287-4250	
Web: iar.com					
Iceptstechnology Group Inc 1301 Fulling Mill Rd.	Middletown	PA	17057	717-704-1000	704-1010
TF: 888-477-7989 ■ *Web:* www.icepts.com					
ICL Imaging Corp 51 Mellen St	Framingham	MA	01702	508-872-3280	
Web: www.icl-imaging.com					
Ideal Printers Inc 645 Olive St.	Saint Paul	MN	55130	651-855-1100	
Web: www.idealprint.com					
IndiSoft LLC 5550 Sterrett Pl Ste 311.	Columbia	MD	21044	410-730-0667	
Web: www.indisoft.us					
Industrios Software Inc 2150 Winston Park Dr Ste 214	Oakville	ON	L6H5V1	905-829-2525	
Web: www.industrios.com					
INETCO Systems Ltd 4664 Lougheed Hwy Ste 258.	Burnaby	BC	V5C5T5	604-451-1567	
Web: www.inetco.com					
Ingram Micro Inc 1600 E St Andrew Pl.	Santa Ana	CA	92705	714-566-1000	565-8899*
NYSE: IM ■ **Fax Area Code:* 716 ■ **Fax:* Cust Svc ■ *TF Sales:* 800-456-8000 ■ *Web:* www.ingrammicro.com					
InLine 600 Lakeshore Pkwy.	Birmingham	AL	35209	205-278-8100	
InnQuest Software Corp 5300 W Cypress Ste 160	Tampa	FL	33607	813-288-4900	
Web: www.innquest.com					
Inserts East Inc 7045 Central Hwy	Pennsauken	NJ	08109	856-663-8181	
Web: www.insertseast.com					
Intcomex Inc 3505 NW 107th Ave Ste 1	Miami	FL	33178	305-477-6230	477-5694
Web: www.intcomex.com					
Integral Networks Inc 4960 Rocklin Rd Ste 100	Rocklin	CA	95677	916-626-4000	
Web: www.integralnetworks.com					
Integrated Services Inc 15115 SW Sequoia Pkwy Ste 110.	Portland	OR	97224	503-968-8100	
Web: www.lubenet.com					
Intellicomm Inc 2701 Renaissance Blvd.	King Of Prussia	PA	19406	610-731-0400	
Web: www.intellicomm.com					
Intelligent Computer Solutions Inc 9350 Eton Ave	Chatsworth	CA	91311	818-998-5805	
TF: 888-994-4678 ■ *Web:* www.ics-iq.com					
InterTech Computer Products Inc 5225 S 39th St	Phoenix	AZ	85040	602-437-0035	
Web: www.allcovered.com					
Isc Kentucky 12305 Westport Rd Ste 1	Louisville	KY	40245	502-292-5097	
Web: iscky.com					

Company / Address	City	State	Zip	Phone	Fax
Island Computer Products Inc 20 Clifton Ave. *Web:* www.icpcorp.com	Staten Island	NY	10305	718-556-6700	
Itochu Technology Inc 3945 Freedom Cir Ste 350 *Web:* www.ctc-america.com	Santa Clara	CA	95054	408-727-8810	727-9391
Jack of All Games Inc 9271 Meridian Way *Web:* www.jackofallgames.com	West Chester	OH	45069	513-326-3020	
Journey Education Marketing Inc 13755 Hutton Dr Ste 500 *TF:* 800-874-9001 ■ *Web:* www.journeyed.com	Dallas	TX	75234	972-481-2000	245-3585
Kavi Corp 225 SE Main St *Web:* www.kavi.com	Portland	OR	97214	503-234-4220	
Kingdom Inc 719 Lambs Creek Rd *Web:* www.kingdom.com	Mansfield	PA	16933	570-662-7515	
Kirkwood Digital 55 Sixth Rd *Web:* kirkwooddigital.com	Woburn	MA	01801	781-938-6164	
Knowledge Reservoir LLC 1800 W Loop S Ste 1000 *Web:* www.knowledge-reservoir.com	Houston	TX	77027	713-586-5950	
Lake Cos Inc, The 2980 Walker Dr *Web:* www.lakeco.com	Green Bay	WI	54311	920-406-3030	406-3040
Las Vegas Color Graphics Inc 4265 W Sunset Rd *Web:* www.lasvegascolor.com	Las Vegas	NV	89118	702-617-9000	
Laser Pros International 1 International Ln *TF:* 888-558-5277 ■ *Web:* www.laserpros.com	Rhinelander	WI	54501	715-369-5995	369-5910
Leadman Electronic USA Inc 382 Laurelwood Dr *TF:* 877-532-3626 ■ *Web:* www.leadman.com	Santa Clara	CA	95054	408-738-1751	738-2620
Legacy Electronics Inc 1220 N Dakota St PO Box 348 *TF:* 888-466-3853 ■ *Web:* www.legacyelectronics.com	Canton	SD	57013	949-498-9600	
LendingTools.com Inc 200 N Broadway Ste 700 *Web:* www.lendingtools.com	Wichita	KS	67202	316-267-3200	
Lexy Pacific Corp 611 Vaqueros Ave *Web:* www.lexypacific.com	Sunnyvale	CA	94085	408-331-8818	
Lindsey & Company Inc 2302 Llama Dr *TF:* 800-890-7058 ■ *Web:* www.lindseysoftware.com	Searcy	AR	72143	501-268-5324	
LINQWARE Inc 6161 NE 175th St Ste 205 *Web:* www.lincware.com	Kenmore	WA	98028	585-563-1669	
Loeffler Randall Inc 525 Broadway 4th Fl *Web:* www.loefflerrandall.com	New York	NY	10012	212-226-8787	
Logical Choice Technologies Inc 1045 Progress Cir	Lawrenceville	GA	30043	770-564-1044	
Long View Systems Corp 3100 255 Fifth Ave SW *TF:* 866-515-6900 ■ *Web:* www.longviewsystems.com	Calgary	AB	T2P3G6	403-515-6900	
M & A Technology Inc 2045 Chenault Dr *TF:* 800-225-1452 ■ *Web:* www.macomp.com	Carrollton	TX	75006	972-490-5803	490-0616
MA Laboratories Inc 2075 N Capitol Ave *Web:* www.malabs.com	San Jose	CA	95132	408-941-0808	941-0909
MacPractice Inc 233 N Eighth St Ste 300 *TF:* 877-220-8418 ■ *Web:* www.macpractice.com	Lincoln	NE	68508	402-420-2430	
MasterGraphics Inc 2979 Triverton Pike Dr *TF:* 800-873-7238 ■ *Web:* www.mastergraphics.com	Madison	WI	53711	608-256-4884	
Max Group Corp 17011 Green Dr *TF:* 800-256-9040 ■ *Web:* www.maxgroup.com	City of Industry	CA	91745	626-935-0050	935-0056
MedInformatix Inc 5777 W Century Blvd Ste 1700 *Web:* www.medinformatix.com	Los Angeles	CA	90045	310-348-7367	
MeLLmo Inc 120 S Sierra Ave *Web:* www.roambi.com	Solana Beach	CA	92075	858-847-3272	
Merisel Inc 127 W 30th St 5th Fl *Web:* www.merisel.com	New York	NY	10001	212-594-4800	
Micro Technology Concepts (MTC) 17837 Rowland St *Web:* www.mtcusa.com	City Of Industry	CA	91748	626-839-6800	839-6899
Microland Electronics Corp 1883 Ringwood Ave *Web:* www.microlandusa.com	San Jose	CA	95131	408-441-1688	441-1767
Mimaki USA Inc 150 Satellite Blvd NE Ste A *Web:* www.mimakiusa.com	Suwanee	GA	30024	678-730-0170	
Minicomputer Exchange Inc 150A Charcot Ave	San Jose	CA	95131	408-733-4400	
MontaVista Software Inc 2929 Patrick Henry Dr *TF:* 888-624-4846 ■ *Web:* www.mvista.com	Santa Clara	CA	95054	408-572-8000	572-8005
MotionDSP Inc 700 Airport Blvd Ste 270 *Web:* www.motiondsp.com	Burlingame	CA	94010	650-288-1164	
Myriad Computer Solutions Inc 8040 Bryan Dairy Rd Ste F *Web:* www.myriadcs.com	Largo	FL	33777	727-541-6000	
Mythics Inc 1439 N Great Neck Rd *Web:* www.mythics.com	Virginia Beach	VA	23454	757-412-4362	
Ncs Global 32 Innovation Dr *Web:* www.newportcomputers.com	Rochester	NH	03867	603-926-4300	
neoSaej Corp 77 S Bedford St Ste 450 *Web:* www.neosaej.com	Burlington	MA	01803	781-272-1774	
NewWave Technologies Inc 4635 Wedgewood Blvd Ste 107 *Web:* www.newwavetech.com	Frederick	MD	21703	301-624-5300	
NinthDecimal Inc 150 Post St Ste 500 *Web:* www.ninthdecimal.com	San Francisco	CA	94108	415-821-8600	
Novarad Corp 752 East 1180 South Ste 200 *Web:* www.novarad.net	American Fork	UT	84003	801-642-1001	
NuMedics Inc 6950 SW Hampton Rd Ste 221 *Web:* www.numedics.com	Tigard	OR	97223	503-597-3861	
Office Systems of Texas 104 Lockhaven Dr *Web:* www.osot.com	Houston	TX	77073	281-443-2996	
One Touch Global Technologies Inc 1401 Dove St Ste 530 *Web:* www.onetouchgt.com	Newport Beach	CA	92660	949-270-0300	
Onix Networking Corp 18519 Detroit Ave *TF:* 800-664-9638 ■ *Web:* www.onixnet.com	Lakewood	OH	44107	800-664-9638	
Open Storage Solutions Inc 2 Castleview Dr *TF:* 800-387-3419 ■ *Web:* www.openstore.com	Toronto	ON	L6T5S9	905-790-0660	
Open Systems of Cleveland Inc 22999 Forbes Rd Ste A *TF:* 888-881-6660 ■ *Web:* www.osinc.com	Cleveland	OH	44146	440-439-2332	439-3794
OpenEye Scientific Software Inc 9 Bisbee Court Ste D *Web:* www.eyesopen.com	Santa Fe	NM	87508	505-473-7385	
Pact-One Solutions Inc 8215 S Eastern Ave Ste 101 *TF:* 866-722-8663 ■ *Web:* www.pact-one.com	Las Vegas	NV	89123	866-722-8663	
Palamida Inc 215 Second St 2nd Fl *Web:* palamida.com	San Francisco	CA	94105	415-777-9400	
Paragon Development Systems Inc 1823 Executive Dr *TF:* 800-966-6090 ■ *Web:* www.pdsit.net	Oconomowoc	WI	53066	800-966-6090	
Pathmaker Group LP 635 Fritz Dr Ste 110 *Web:* pathmaker-group.com	Coppell	TX	75019	817-704-3644	
Pc Treasures Inc 3720 Lapeer Rd *Web:* pctreasures.com	Auburn Hills	MI	48326	248-969-7800	
PCI Geomatics Inc 90 Allstate Pkwy Ste 501 *Web:* www.pcigeomatics.com	Markham	ON	L3R6H3	905-764-0614	
Peak Technologies Inc 10330 Old Columbia Rd *TF:* 800-926-9212 ■ *Web:* www.peak-ryzex.com	Columbia	MD	21046	800-926-9212	
PerfectForms Inc 1917 Palomar Oaks Way Ste 160 *Web:* www.perfectforms.com	Carlsbad	CA	92008	760-585-1870	
Pinneast Com Inc 5 Lk Carolina Blvd Ste 230 *Web:* www.pinneast.com	Columbia	SC	29229	803-926-9511	
Prism Color Corp 31 Twosome Dr *Web:* www.prismcolorcorp.com	Moorestown	NJ	08057	856-234-7515	
Professional Graphics Inc 25 Perry Ave *Web:* www.progi.net	Norwalk	CT	06850	203-846-4291	
Programmer's Paradise Inc 1157 Shrewsbury Ave Ste C *TF:* 800-441-1511 ■ *Web:* www.techxtend.com	Shrewsbury	NJ	07702	732-389-8950	389-0010
Promark Technology Inc 10900 Pump House Rd Ste B **Fax Area Code:* 301 ■ *TF:* 800-634-0255 ■ *Web:* www.promarktech.com	Annapolis Junction	MD	20701	240-280-8030	725-7869*
Prostar Computer Inc 837 Lawson St *TF:* 888-576-4742 ■ *Web:* www.pro-star.com	City of Industry	CA	91748	626-839-6472	
Provantage Corp 7249 Whipple Ave NW *TF:* 800-336-1166 ■ *Web:* www.provantage.com	North Canton	OH	44720	330-494-8715	494-5260
QBE LLC 15000 Washington St Ste 200 *Web:* www.qbe.net	Haymarket	VA	20169	571-248-7490	
Queen Beach Printers Inc 937 Pine Ave *Web:* www.qbprinters.com	Long Beach	CA	90813	562-436-8201	
Radiological Imaging Technology Inc 5065 List Dr *Web:* www.radimage.com	Colorado Springs	CO	80919	719-590-1077	
rain Technologies LP, The 11522 W Washington Blvd *Web:* www.thebrain.com	Los Angeles	CA	90066	310-751-5000	
Rave Computer Assn Inc 7171 Sterling Ponds Ct *TF:* 800-966-7283 ■ *Web:* www.rave.com	Sterling Heights	MI	48312	586-939-8230	939-7431
Real Asset Management Inc 309 Court Ave Ste 244 *Web:* www.realassetmgt.com	Des Moines	IA	50309	515-699-8564	
Real Solutions of Illinois Inc 100 N La Salle St Ste 1400 *Web:* www.realsolutions-us.com	Chicago	IL	60602	312-621-9100	
Real Time Consultants Inc 777 Corporate Dr Ste 1 *Web:* www.realtimenet.com	Mahwah	NJ	07430	201-512-1777	
Red Line Graphics Inc 6430 S Belmont Ave *Web:* www.redlinegroup.com	Indianapolis	IN	46217	317-784-3777	
Redline Trading Solutions Inc 18 Commerce Way Ste 6800 *Web:* www.redlinetrading.com	Woburn	MA	01801	781-995-3403	
Remcom Inc 315 S Allen St Ste 222 *Web:* www.remcom.com	State College	PA	16801	814-861-1299	
RemoteScan Corp 305 S Fourth St E Ste 200 *Web:* www.remote-scan.com	Missoula	MT	59801	406-721-0319	
Revana Inc 8123 S Hardy Dr *Web:* www.revana.com	Tempe	AZ	85284	480-902-5900	
Rippey Corp 5000 Hillsdale Cir *Web:* www.rippey.com	El Dorado Hills	CA	95762	916-939-4332	939-4338
Rorke Data Inc 7626 Golden Triangle Dr *TF:* 800-328-8147 ■ *Web:* support.rorke.com/legacy	Eden Prairie	MN	55344	952-829-0300	829-0988
Rpl Supplies Inc 141 Lanza Ave Bldg 3A *TF:* 800-524-0914 ■ *Web:* www.rplsupplies.com	Garfield	NJ	07026	973-767-0880	772-6601
Sanyo Denki America Inc 468 Amapola Ave *Web:* www.sanyo-denki.com	Torrance	CA	90501	310-783-5400	212-6545
ScanSource Inc 6 Logue Ct *NASDAQ: SCSC* ■ *TF:* 800-944-2432 ■ *Web:* www.scansource.com	Greenville	SC	29615	864-288-2432	
Scivantage Inc 499 Washington Blvd 11th Fl *TF:* 866-724-8268 ■ *Web:* www.scivantage.com	Jersey City	NJ	07310	646-452-0050	452-0049
SDV Solutions Inc 133 Waller Mill Rd Ste 100 *Web:* www.sdvsolutions.us	Williamsburg	VA	23185	757-903-2068	
SED International Inc 3505 Newpoint Pl Ste 450	Lawrenceville	GA	30043	770-243-1200	
Set Solutions Inc 550 Westcott St Ste 470 *Web:* www.setsolutions.com	Houston	TX	77007	713-956-6600	
SHI Corp 35W Broadway Ste 104 *TF:* 888-764-8888 ■ *Web:* www.shi-corp.com	Salt Lake City	UT	84101	888-764-8888	
SigmaTEK Systems LLC 1445 Kemper Meadow Dr *Web:* www.sigmanest.com	Cincinnati	OH	45240	513-674-0005	

Phone | Fax

Slam Dunk Networks Inc
2600 S El Camino Real San Mateo CA 94403 650-525-3902
Web: www.slamdunknetworks.com
Softmart Inc 450 Acorn Ln Downingtown PA 19335 610-518-4000 518-3000
TF Cust Svc: 800-328-1319 ■ *Web:* www.softmart.com
SofTouch Systems Inc 5601 NW 72nd St Oklahoma City OK 73132 405-728-1902
Web: www.rocketsoftware.com
Software House International (SHI)
290 Davidson Ave Somerset NJ 08873 888-764-8888
TF: 888-764-8888 ■ *Web:* www.shi.com
Solution Systems Inc
3201 Tollview Dr Rolling Meadows IL 60008 847-590-3000 590-0912
Web: www.solsyst.com
Soroc Technology Inc 607 Chrislea Rd Woodbridge ON L4L8A3 905-265-8000
Web: www.soroc.com
SouthWare Innovations Inc
1922 Professional Cir Auburn AL 36831 334-821-1108
Web: southware.com
Spruce Computer Systems Inc
9 Cornell Rd Latham New York NY 12110 518-777-8231
Web: www.sprucecomputer.com
St. Louis Lithographing Co 6880 Heege Rd St Louis MO 63123 314-352-1300
Stardock Systems Inc 15090 N Beck Rd Ste 300 Plymouth MI 48170 734-927-0677 927-0678
TF: 888-782-7362 ■ *Web:* www.stardock.com
Static Control Components Inc
3010 Lee Ave PO Box 152 Sanford NC 27331 919-774-3808 774-1287
TF: 800-488-2426 ■ *Web:* www.scc-inc.com
Stromberg Allen & Co 18504 W Creek Dr Tinley Park IL 60477 773-847-7131
Web: strombergallen.com
Symco Group Inc
5012 Bristol Industrial Way Ste 105 Buford GA 30518 770-451-8002
TF: 800-878-8002 ■ *Web:* www.symcogroup.com
Symmetry Software Corp
14350 N 87th St Ste 250 Scottsdale AZ 85260 480-596-1500
Web: www.symmetry.com
Synergy Resources Inc
3500 Sunrise Hwy Bldg 100 Ste 201 Great River NY 11739 631-665-2050
Web: www.synergyresources.net
SYNNEX Canada 200 Ronson Dr Etobicoke ON M9W5Z9 416-240-7012 240-2622*
**Fax:* Hum Res ■ *TF:* 800-268-1220 ■ *Web:* www.synnex.ca
Synnex Corp 44201 Nobel Dr Fremont CA 94538 510-656-3333 668-3777
NYSE: SNX ■ *TF Cust Svc:* 800-756-1888 ■ *Web:* www.synnex.com
Syntelli Solutions Inc
2440 Toringdon Way Ste 205 Charlotte NC 28277 704-927-5888
Web: www.syntelli.com
Tactical Communications Group LLC
2 Highwood Dr Bldg 2 Tewksbury MA 01876 978-654-4800
Web: g2tcg.com
Talari Networks Inc
20195 Stevens Creek Blvd Ste 220 Cupertino CA 95014 408-689-0400
Web: www.talari.com
Tanner Research Inc 825 S Myrtle Ave Monrovia CA 91016 626-471-9700
TF: 877-325-2223 ■ *Web:* www.tanner.com
Team-Linux Corp 314 Leo St Ste 200 Dayton OH 45404 937-443-2400
Web: www.team-linux.com
Tech Data Corp 5350 Tech Data Dr Clearwater FL 33760 727-539-7429
NASDAQ: TECD ■ *TF:* 800-237-8931 ■ *Web:* www.techdata.com
Tekla Inc 1075 Big Shanty Rd NW Ste 175 Kennesaw GA 30144 770-426-5105
TF: 877-835-5265 ■ *Web:* www.tekla.com
Telecorp Products Inc
2000 E Oakley Park Rd Ste 101 Walled Lake MI 48390 248-960-1000
Web: telecorpproducts.com
Teracai Corp 217 Lawrence Rd E North Syracuse NY 13212 315-883-3500
Web: www.teracai.com
Tharo Systems Inc 2866 Nationwide Pkwy Brunswick OH 44212 330-273-4408
Web: www.tharo.com
Think Computer Corp 3260 Hillview Ave Palo Alto CA 94304 415-670-9350
TF: 888-815-8599 ■ *Web:* www.thinkcomputer.com
Third Wave Systems Inc
7900 W 78th St Ste 300 Minneapolis MN 55439 952-832-5515
Web: www.thirdwavesys.com
TigerDirect Inc 7795 W Flagler St Ste 35 Miami FL 33144 800-800-8300
TF: 800-800-8300 ■ *Web:* www.tigerdirect.com
TKO Electronics Inc
31113 Via Colinas Westlake Village CA 91362 818-879-2233
Web: www.tkoelectronics.com
Topdek Inc 2926 NW 72nd Ave Miami FL 33122 305-599-0006
Web: www.topdek.com
Transcend Information Inc 1645 N Brian St Orange CA 92867 714-921-2000 921-2111
Web: www.transcend-info.com
Transim Technology Corp
433 NW Fourth Ave Ste 200 Portland OR 97209 503-450-1355
Web: www.transim.com
TransMagic Inc 11859 Pecos St Ste 310 Westminster CO 80234 303-460-1406
Web: transmagic.com
Transoft Solutions Inc
13575 Commerce Pkwy Ste 250 Richmond BC V6V2L1 604-244-8387 244-1770
TF: 888-244-8387 ■ *Web:* www.transoftsolutions.com
Tributary Systems Inc 3717 Commerce Pl Ste C Bedford TX 76021 817-354-8009
Web: www.tributary.com
UCI Communications LLC 500 St Michael St Mobile AL 36602 251-457-1404
Web: www.ucicom.com
Unified Systems Group Inc
1235 64th Ave SE Ste 4a Calgary AB T2H2J7 403-686-8088
TF: 866-892-8988 ■ *Web:* www.usg.ca
United Systems Inc 4335 N Classen Blvd Oklahoma City OK 73118 405-523-2162
Web: www.unitedsystemsok.com
Us Micro Corp 7000 Highlnds Pkwy SE Smyrna GA 30082 770-437-0706 437-0855
TF: 888-876-4276 ■ *Web:* www.usmicrocorp.com
Valve Corp 10500 NE 8th St Ste 1000 Bellevue WA 98004 425-889-9642
Web: www.valvesoftware.com
Vartek Services Inc 1785 S Metro Pkwy Dayton OH 45459 937-438-3550
TF: 800-954-2524 ■ *Web:* www.vartek.com

Phone | Fax

Vinoleo Solution & Services Corp
186 Bay 20th St Brooklyn NY 11214 718-837-2163
Web: www.vinoleoinc.com
Virginia Surety Company Inc
175 W Jackson Blvd 11th Fl Chicago IL 60604 312-356-3000
Virtucom Inc 6610 Bay Cir Ste E Norcross GA 30071 770-908-8100
Web: www.virtucom.com
Vivid Impact Corp 10116 Bunsen Way Louisville KY 40299 502-495-6900
Web: www.vividimpact.com
VLN Partners LLP 1212 E Carson St Pittsburgh PA 15203 412-381-0183
TF: 877-856-3311 ■ *Web:* www.vlnpartners.com
WDL Systems 220 Chatham Business Dr Pittsboro NC 27312 919-545-2500 545-2559
TF Sales: 800-548-2319 ■ *Web:* www.wdlsystems.com
WebQA Inc 900 S Frontage Rd Ste 110 Woodridge IL 60517 630-985-1300
Web: webqa.com
West-Com Nurse Call Systems Inc
2200 Cordelia Rd Fairfield CA 94534 707-428-5900
TF: 800-761-1180 ■ *Web:* www.westcall.com
Westcon Group Inc
520 White Plains Rd 2nd Fl Tarrytown NY 10591 914-829-7000 829-7137
TF: 800-527-9516 ■ *Web:* www.westconcomstor.com/global/en.html#home
Westcon Group, Inc
Westcon Convergence 520 White Plains Rd Ste 100 Omaha NE 68154 877-642-7750
TF: 877-642-7750 ■ *Web:* www.westconcomstor.com/global/en.html#home
Westham Trade Co Ltd 3620 NW 114th Ave Doral FL 33178 305-717-5400 593-0316
TF: 888-852-5000 ■ *Web:* www.wtrade.com
Whalley Computer Associates Inc
1 Whalley Way Southwick MA 01077 413-569-4200
Web: www.wca.com
Wheal-Grace Corp 300 Ralph St Belleville NJ 07109 973-450-8100
Web: www.wheal-grace.com
Wintec Industries Inc 675 Sycamore Dr Milpitas CA 95035 408-856-0500 856-0501
TF: 866-989-4683 ■ *Web:* www.wintecindustries.com
Wolf Colorprint Inc 111 Holmes Rd Newington CT 06111 860-666-1200
Woot Inc 4121 International Pkwy Carrollton TX 75007 972-417-3959 418-9245
TF: 866-551-6881 ■ *Web:* woot.com
WorldAPP Inc 220 Forbes Rd Braintree MA 02184 781-849-8118
Web: worldapp.com
Worth Higgins & Assoc Inc
8770 Park Central Dr Richmond VA 23227 804-264-2304
TF: 800-883-7768 ■ *Web:* worthhiggins.com
Zones Inc 1102 15th St SW Auburn WA 98001 253-205-3000 205-2655
Web: www.zones.com
Zuercher Technologies LLC
5121 S Solberg Ave Ste 150 Sioux Falls SD 57108 605-274-6061
TF: 877-229-2205 ■ *Web:* www.zuerchertech.com

COMPUTER & INTERNET TRAINING PROGRAMS

See Training & Certification Programs - Computer & Internet p. 3258

175 COMPUTER MAINTENANCE & REPAIR

Phone | Fax

24hourtek LLC 268 Bush St San Francisco CA 94104 415-294-4449
TF: 855-378-0787 ■ *Web:* www.24hourtek.com
Access Computers Inc 538 W Main St Lebanon OH 45036 513-932-5454
Web: www.accesscomputersinc.com
Accram Inc 2901 W Clarendon Ave Phoenix AZ 85017 800-786-0288
TF: 800-786-0288 ■ *Web:* www.accram.com
Acropolis Computers Inc 915 Whitelaw Ave Wood River IL 62095 618-254-8733
Web: www.acropolistech.com
Advantech Corp 3601 Rose Lk Dr Charlotte NC 28217 704-357-1450
Web: www.advantech.com
Adx Computer Services Inc
315 Arden Ave Ste 2 Glendale CA 91203 818-244-1121
Web: www.adxusa.com
Ah Computer Services Inc
7221 Aloma Ave Ste 300 Winter Park FL 32792 407-671-3557
Web: ahcomputers.net
Aim Computers 1819 Willow Pass Rd Concord CA 94520 925-687-2822
Web: www.aimcomp.com
Aixtek 1275 Fairfax Ave Ste 801 San Francisco CA 94124 415-282-1188
Web: www.eatonassoc.com
Allen-Myland Inc 515 Abbott Dr Broomall PA 19008 610-544-0571
Web: www.allenmyland.com
Arcomm Communications Corp 462 W Main St 3 Hillsboro NH 03244 603-464-4600
Web: arcomm1.com
Ariel Technologies 1980 E Lohman Ave Las Cruces NM 88001 877-524-6860
TF: 877-524-6860 ■ *Web:* arielusa.com
Ats Tech Solutions Inc
2550 Limestone Pky Ste F Gainesville GA 30501 770-538-2900
Web: www.atstech.net
Aura Advance Technologies Inc
1742 10th Ave SW Calgary AB T3C0J8 403-269-6123
Web: auraadvanced.com
Bde Computer Services LLC 399 Lakeview Ave Clifton NJ 07011 973-772-8507
TF: 877-233-4877 ■ *Web:* www.bdecomputer.com
BigByte Corp 47400 Seabridge Dr Fremont CA 94538 510-249-1100
Web: www.bigbytecorp.com
Bits & Bytes Computer Services
1987 Hendersonville Rd Ste B Asheville NC 28803 828-684-8953
Web: bitsbyte.com
Bocotek Inc 2420 Comanche Rd Ne Ste G1b Albuquerque NM 87107 505-237-0528
Web: bocotek.com
Brains II Canada Inc 165 Konrad Crescent Markham ON L3R9T9 905-946-8700
Web: www.brainsiisolutions.com
Brandon Business Machines Inc
505 W Robertson St Brandon FL 33511 813-689-1950
Web: www.bbmusa.com
Brentech Inc 9340 Carmel Mtn Rd Ste C San Diego CA 92129 858-484-7314
TF: 800-709-0440 ■ *Web:* www.brentech-inc.com

Phone Fax

Broken Acres Electronics 1005 E Strub Rd .... Sandusky OH 44870 419-621-8277
Web: www.brokenacres.com

Brooks-Jeffrey Computer Store
19 Medical Plz .... Mountain Home AR 72653 870-425-8064
TF: 800-506-8064 ■ *Web:* www.bjmweb.com

Brydan Solutions Inc
1500 E Tropicana Ave Ste 201a .... Las Vegas NV 89119 702-966-2774
Web: www.brydansolutions.com

Bryley Systems Inc 12 Main St .... Hudson MA 01749 978-562-6077
Web: www.bryley.com

Byte Right Support Inc 335 N Charles St .... Baltimore MD 21201 410-347-2983
Web: byterightsupport.com

C & e Computers 165 Ramona Ave .... South San Francisco CA 94080 650-872-6543
Web: cdgrp.com

C T S Services Inc 260 Maple St .... Bellingham MA 02019 508-528-7720
Web: www.ctsservices.com

C&W Enterprises Inc 2522 SE Federal Hwy .... Stuart FL 34994 772-287-5215
TF: 844-241-6442 ■ *Web:* www.cwnow.com

CAD & Graphic Supply Inc
2410 Luna Rd Ste 114 .... Carrollton TX 75006 972-409-7333
TF: 866-409-8211 ■ *Web:* www.cadgraphicsupply.com

Cascade Computer Maintenance Inc
3240 Commercial St SE .... Salem OR 97302 503-581-0081
Web: www.ccmaint.com

Cds - Networks & Services Inc
672 Stratford Blvd .... Kinston NC 28504 252-523-6664
Web: www.cdsnetworks.com

Chips Computer Services
14491 Forest Blvd N Apt 1b .... Hugo MN 55038 651-407-8555
Web: www.chipscs.com

ClickAway Corp 457 E McGlincy Ln Ste 1 .... Campbell CA 95008 408-626-9400
Web: www.clickaway.com

Cnic Inc 4418 Monroe Rd E .... Charlotte NC 28205 704-344-0090
Web: www.cnic-inc.com

Comp-u-sultants Inc 131 Waterford Rd .... Island Park NY 11558 516-897-8477
Web: www.comp-u-sultants.com

Compciti Business Solutions Inc
261 W 35th St Ste 603 .... New York NY 10001 212-594-4374
Web: www.compciti.com

Compro Computer Services Inc 105 E Dr .... Melbourne FL 32904 321-725-3624
Web: www.compro.net

Compu-Fix Inc 920 Thompson Run Rd .... West Mifflin PA 15122 412-464-0275
Web: compufix-inc.com

CompuCycle Inc 7700 Kempwood Dr .... Houston TX 77055 713-869-6700
Web: www.compucycle.net

Compudent Systems Inc 10345 Keele St Ste 6 .... Maple ON L6A3Y9 905-417-9345
Web: compudentinc.com

Computechnique 407 Stonebrook Dr .... Benton IL 62812 618-439-4000
Web: computechnique.com

Computer Centerline 1500 Broad St .... Greensburg PA 15601 724-838-0852
Web: cclprotech.com

Computer Clinic Center Inc
4427 Wisconsin Ave NW .... Washington DC 20016 202-362-9702
Web: www.cccits.com

Computer Equip Svces 261 W Main St .... Bay Shore NY 11706 631-666-1234
Web: netces.com

Computer Heaven 577 Oak Villa Blvd .... Baton Rouge LA 70815 225-923-0999
Web: computerheaven.com

Computer Repair & Sales 2930 W Main St .... Rapid City SD 57702 605-399-0278 342-6141
Web: www.computerrepair.org

Computer Specialists Inc
2101 Gaither Rd Ste 175 .... Rockville MD 20850 301-921-2111

Computer Troubleshooters USA
755 Commerce Dr Ste 605 .... Decatur GA 30030 800-877-0020
TF: 877-704-1702 ■ *Web:* www.dentsply.com

ComputerPlus Sales & Service Inc 5 Northway Ct .... Greer SC 29651 800-849-4426
TF: 800-849-4426 ■ *Web:* www.computer-plus.com

Comservco U S A Inc 141 Central Ave Ste W .... Farmingdale NY 11735 631-753-2000
Web: www.comservcousa.com

Comware Technical Services Inc
17922 Sky Park Cir Ste E .... Irvine CA 92614 949-851-9600
TF: 800-460-1970 ■ *Web:* comwaretech.com

CPT of South Florida Inc
2699 Stirling Rd Ste A 101 .... Fort Lauderdale FL 33312 954-963-2775 963-5781
Web: www.cpt-florida.com

Cross Consulting Group Office
405 Becker Ave N .... Sebeka MN 56477 218-837-6114
Web: www.cross-usa.com

CRSA Computer Rescue Inc
2434 Brockton St .... San Antonio TX 78217 210-366-4811
Web: www.computerrescuesa.com

Cru Solutions Inc 7261 Engle Rd Ste 305 .... Cleveland OH 44130 440-891-0330
Web: www.crusolutions.com

CRV Inc 3407 Northeast Pkwy Ste 170 .... San Antonio TX 78218 210-828-8552

Csj Technologies Inc
7322 Industrial Park Blvd .... Mentor OH 44060 440-269-8915
Web: www.imagecomputer.com

Dalton Computer Services Inc
1612 Cleveland Hwy .... Dalton GA 30721 706-259-3327
Web: www.daltoncomputer.com

Data Exchange Corp 3600 Via Pescador .... Camarillo CA 93012 805-388-1711 389-1726
TF: 800-237-7911 ■ *Web:* www.dex.com

Data Vista Inc 122 Burrs Rd Ste A .... Westampton NJ 08060 609-702-9300
Web: datavista.com

Dataserv Corp 8625 F St .... Omaha NE 68127 402-339-8700
TF: 888-901-8700 ■ *Web:* www.dataservcorp.com

Datatech Depot Inc 11390 Knott St Ste G .... Garden Grove CA 92841 714-908-5370
Web: www.dtdi.com

DBK Concepts Inc 12905 SW 129 Ave .... Miami FL 33186 305-596-7226 596-7222
TF: 800-725-7226 ■ *Web:* www.dbk.com

Decatur Computers Inc 1234 N Water St Ste B .... Decatur IL 62521 217-475-0226
TF: 800-429-7140 ■ *Web:* decaturcomputers.com

DecisionOne Corp 426 W Lancaster Ave .... Devon PA 19333 610-296-6000 296-2910
TF: 800-767-2876 ■ *Web:* decisionone.com

Desktop Consulting Services 43311 Joy Rd .... Canton MI 48187 888-600-2731
TF: 888-600-2731 ■ *Web:* dcs-mi.com

Dhc Communications Inc 607 Front St .... Nelson BC V1L4B6 250-352-0861
Web: www.dhc.bc.ca

Digirati Networks 9255 E River Rd Nw .... Coon Rapids MN 55433 763-784-3500
Web: www.digirati-networks.com

Digital Dot Systems Inc 13213 F St .... Omaha NE 68137 402-408-0115
Web: www.ddsine.com

Digital Rework Depot 1500 Soldiers Field Rd .... Brighton MA 02135 617-562-1444
Web: digitalrework.com

DP Solutions Inc 1508 S First St .... Lufkin TX 75901 936-637-7977
Web: www.dpsol.com

Eagle Haven Computers Inc
5860 Clearfield Woodland Hwy .... Clearfield PA 16830 814-765-5779
Web: www.eaglehaven.com

Eagle Networks Inc 2738 W Bullard Ave .... Fresno CA 93711 559-448-8877
Web: www.eaglenetworks.com

Electrosonics 17150 15 Mile Rd .... Fraser MI 48026 586-415-5555
TF: 800-858-8448 ■ *Web:* www.electrosonics.net

Elementum Solutions 2540 New Butler Rd .... New Castle PA 16101 724-656-8837
Web: www.elementumsolutions.com

Emf Inc 60 Foundry St .... Keene NH 03431 603-352-8400
TF: 800-992-3003 ■ *Web:* www.emfinc.com

Ener-Tel Services Inc 4512 Adobe Dr .... San Angelo TX 76903 325-658-8375
Web: www.ener-tel.com

Entre Computer Solutions
8900 N Second St .... Machesney Park IL 61115 815-399-5664
Web: www.entrerock.com

Essential Technologies Inc
1107 Hazeltine Blvd Ste 477 .... Chaska MN 55318 952-368-9001 368-3334
TF: 800-818-1125 ■ *Web:* www.essentialtechinc.com

Eventnet Usa 1129 Se Fourth Ave .... Fort Lauderdale FL 33316 954-467-9898
Web: www.eventnetusa.com

Everprint International Inc
18021 Cortney Ct .... City of Industry CA 91748 626-839-2569
TF: 800-984-5777

Ex-Cel Solutions Inc 14618 Grover St .... Omaha NE 68144 402-333-6541
Web: www.excels.com

Excalibur Data Systems
115 Sagamore Hill Rd .... Pittsburgh PA 15239 724-387-1331
Web: www.excaliburdata.com

Expert Laser Service
62 Pleasant St PO Box 744 .... Southbridge MA 01550 508-764-1413
Web: www.expertlaserservices.com

EZ Systems.com 3480 W Warner Ave Ste A .... Santa Ana CA 92704 714-662-4959
Web: www.ezsystems.com

Facet Computers 2103 Court St .... Pekin IL 61554 309-353-4727
Web: www.facettech.com

Falconwood Inc
1011 Camino Del Rio S Ste 610 .... San Diego CA 92108 619-297-9080
Web: www.falconwood.biz

Far Western Graphics Inc 1105 Kern Ave .... Sunnyvale CA 94085 408-481-9777
Web: fwgprinting.com

First Resource Computer Inc
590 Reservoir Ave .... Cranston RI 02910 401-941-2500
Web: www.frcomputers.com

Firsttech Corp
5675 E La Palma Ave Ste C .... Anaheim Hills CA 92807 714-777-5710
Web: cafishgrill.com

Fortress Computer Pros
11305 Rancho Bernardo Rd Ste 116 .... San Diego CA 92127 858-451-7020
Web: www.fortresscomputerpros.com

Ghostnet Inc 91 Sammy Mcghee Blvd Ste 109 .... Jasper GA 30143 706-253-1013
Web: www.ghostnetinc.com

Gtek Computers LLC 4111 FM 2986 .... Portland TX 78374 361-777-1400
Web: www.www.gtek.biz

Gtm Wholesale Liquidators Inc
2025 Gillespie Way Ste 108 .... El Cajon CA 92020 619-596-7486
Web: www.gtmstores.com

Hc & C Communications Inc
5427 Telegraph Ave Unit P .... Oakland CA 94609 510-655-1193
Web: www.hcccom.net

Helix Technologies Inc 8550 W Main St .... French Lick IN 47432 812-936-2525
Web: helixtec.net

Help Me Computers LLC 903 Austin Hwy .... San Antonio TX 78209 210-822-8817
Web: www.helpmecomputers.com

IIS Group LLC
1015 Virginia Dr Ste 1 W .... Fort Washington PA 19034 855-443-5777
TF: 855-443-5777 ■ *Web:* www.iisgroupllc.com

Ilink Technology Inc 9840 Willows Rd Ste 202 .... Redmond CA 98052 425-869-8104
Web: ilinktechnology.com

Insight Computing LLC 448 Ignacio Blvd Ste 490 .... Novato CA 94949 415-898-5411
TF: 800-380-8985 ■ *Web:* www.insight-computing.com

Intag Inc 11469 Olive Bld Ste 400 .... Saint Louis MO 63141 314-822-1102
Web: www.appliedws.com

Integranetics 325 Park Plz Dr 2b .... Owensboro KY 42301 270-685-6016
Web: integranetics.net

Integration Technologies Group Inc
2745 Hartland Rd Ste 200 .... Falls Church VA 22043 703-698-8282 698-0305
TF: 800-835-7823 ■ *Web:* www.itgonline.com

Integritech LLC 5267 Gender Rd .... Canal Winchester OH 43110 614-920-3366
Web: www.integritech.us

Integron Corp 35 Bermar Park .... Rochester NY 14624 585-426-6200
Web: www.integron.com

Inter-quest Corp 304 S Spring St .... Beaver Dam WI 53916 920-885-0141
Web: www.iqsvr.com

Interactive Services Group Inc
600 Delran Pkwy Ste C .... Delran NJ 08075 800-566-3310 824-9415*
*Fax Area Code: 856 ■ *TF:* 800-566-3310 ■ *Web:* isgtechnologies.com

Intermax Computer Associates Inc
242 Big Run Rd .... Lexington KY 40503 859-277-5453
Web: intermaxcomputer.com

Intraspek Inc 8707 Timber Oak Ln .... Laurel MD 20723 301-617-0521
Web: www.intraspek.com

Company / Address	City	State	Zip	Phone	Fax
Intratek Computer Inc 5431 Industrial Dr. *TF:* 800-892-8282 ■ *Web:* www.intrapc.com	Huntington Beach	CA	92649	800-892-8282	
J&S Electronic Business System Inc 878 Jefferson St *Web:* www.jselectronics.com	Burlington	IA	52601	319-752-5603	
Jadtec Computer Group 1520 W Yale Ave *Web:* www.jadtec.com	Orange	CA	92867	714-282-0828	
Jaguar Computer Systems Inc 4135 Indus Way *Web:* www.jaguar.net	Riverside	CA	92503	951-273-7950	734-5615
Just Service Inc 2940 N Clark St *Web:* www.justservice.com	Chicago	IL	60657	773-871-7171	
Just Solutions Inc 7300 Pittsford Palmyra Rd (RT 31) PO Box 118 *Web:* www.justinc.com	Fairport	NY	14450	585-203-8910	
Kam Companies Inc 3982 New Vision Dr. *Web:* kamcompanies.com	Fort Wayne	IN	46845	260-432-4432	
Kaplan Computers LLC 61 Tolland Tpke *Web:* kaplancomputers.com	Manchester	CT	06042	860-643-6474	
Kdt Solutions Inc 1256 Fifth St. *Web:* www.kdtsolutions.com	West Palm Beach	FL	33409	561-688-9399	
Kennewick Computer Co 2290 Robertson Dr *Web:* www.gopositive.com	Richland	WA	99354	509-371-0600	
Konicom Inc 1819 J St. *Web:* www.konicom.com	Sacramento	CA	95811	916-441-7373	
L. M. s Technical Services Inc 21 Grand Ave *Web:* www.lmstech.com	Farmingdale	NY	11735	631-694-2034	
Laser & Computer Options Inc 3758 E Grove St *Web:* www.laseroptionsinc.com	Phoenix	AZ	85040	480-968-8440	
Ledger Systems Inc 865 Laurel St *Web:* www.ledgersys.com	San Carlos	CA	94070	650-592-6211	
Lh Computer Services 12296 Wiles Rd *Web:* www.lhcomp.com	Coral Springs	FL	33321	954-752-5805	
Local.com Corp 7555 Irvine Ctr Dr *Web:* www.local.com	Irvine	CA	92618	949-784-0800	
M1 Networks Inc 6019 Mcpherson Rd Ste 4 *Web:* m1networks.net	Laredo	TX	78041	956-718-1005	
Markent Personnel Inc 121 E Conant St. *Web:* www.markentpersonnel.com	Portage	WI	53901	608-742-7300	
Masterit LLC 8024 Stage Hills Blvd Ste 101 *Web:* www.master-it.com	Memphis	TN	38133	901-377-7891	
Matthijssen Inc 14 Rt 10 *TF:* 800-845-2200 ■ *Web:* www.mattnj.com	East Hanover	NJ	07936	973-887-1100	887-2453
Maybank Systems 525 E Bay St Ste 201 *Web:* maybanksystems.com	Charleston	SC	29403	843-278-0339	
Mike Collins & Associates Inc 6048 Century Oaks Dr *Web:* www.mcollins.com	Chattanooga	TN	37416	423-892-8899	
Mri Technologies 17047 El Camino Real Ste 200 *Web:* mricompany.com	Houston	TX	77058	281-786-2004	
Murphy Mckay & Associates Inc 3468 Mt Diablo Blvd Ste B108 *Web:* www.murphymckay.com	Lafayette	CA	94549	925-283-9555	
Nations First Office Repair 1555 E Flamingo Rd Ste 202 *Web:* www.laptoprepairs.com	Las Vegas	NV	89119	702-699-5657	
NCE Computer Group 1866 Friendship Dr *Web:* www.ncegroup.com	El Cajon	CA	92020	619-212-3000	596-2881
Nettnetts Pc Llc 43 Grassy Plain St *Web:* www.nettnettspc.com	Bethel	CT	06801	203-512-1728	
Network Company of California 310 Via Vera Cruz *Web:* tncc.com	San Marcos	CA	92078	760-744-0442	
Network Experts 260 S Beverly Dr Ste 325 *Web:* www.networkexperts.la	Beverly Hills	CA	90212	310-275-1911	
Networks Made Simple Llc 64 Confederate Way *Web:* networksmadesimple.net	Stafford	VA	22554	540-657-5360	
Nexicore 4201 Guardian St. *Web:* www.avnetintegrated.com	Simi Valley	CA	93063	805-306-2500	
Noguska LLC 741 Countyline St. *Web:* www.noguska.com	Fostoria	OH	44830	419-435-0404	
Novastar Solutions Com LLC 35200 Plymouth Rd *Web:* www.novastar.net	Livonia	MI	48150	734-453-8003	
Npa Computers Inc 751 Coates Ave *TF:* 800-873-6724 ■ *Web:* www.npacomputers.com	Holbrook	NY	11741	631-467-2500	
Ockers Co 830 W Chestnut St *Web:* www.ockers.com	Brockton	MA	02301	508-586-4642	584-9180
Orion Communications Inc 7650 Standish Pl Ste 102 *Web:* www.oricomm.com	Rockville	MD	20855	301-921-9056	
Pacific Pharmacy Computers Inc 4167 N Golden State Bouelvard Ste 106 *Web:* www.goppc.com	Fresno	CA	93722	559-276-6168	
Palmer Computer Service Inc 230 New York Ave *Web:* palmer.net/pcsindex.htm	Huntington	NY	11743	631-300-1710	
Panurgy Inc 3 Wing Dr Ste 225 *Web:* www.panurgy.com	Cedar Knolls	NJ	07927	973-625-9686	
PC Doctors LLC 1257 N 8th St. *Web:* www.midwest-technologies.net	Medford	WI	54451	715-748-1911	
PC Innovations 1555 E Henrietta Rd *Web:* www.pcinnovations.com	Rochester	NY	14623	585-340-1555	
PC Professional Inc 1615 Webster St Ste *Web:* www.pcprofessional.com	Oakland	CA	94612	510-874-5864	
Pc Whizdom 297 Daniel Webster Hwy Ste 1 *Web:* www.pcwhizdom.com	Merrimack	NH	03054	603-424-1799	
Planetbids Inc 20929 Ventura Blvd. *Web:* home.planetbids.com	Woodland Hills	CA	91364	818-992-1771	
Portable CIO 172 Via Serena *Web:* www.theportablecio.com	Alamo	CA	94507	925-552-7953	
Precision Computer Services Inc (PCS) 175 Constitution Blvd S *TF:* 800-340-9890 ■ *Web:* www.precisiongroup.com	Shelton	CT	06484	203-929-0000	929-8800
Pride Computer Systems Inc 4006 S 3rd St S Regional Plz *Web:* www.pridecomputersystems.com	Jacksonville Beach	FL	32250	904-242-9522	
Prism Pointe Technologies LLC 4605 Coates Dr. *Web:* www.prismpoint.com	Fairburn	GA	30213	678-610-4900	
Pro-data Computer Services Inc 2809 S 160th St Ste 401 *TF:* 800-228-6318 ■ *Web:* www.prodatacomputer.com	Omaha	NE	68130	402-697-7575	
ProLender Solutions Inc 6050 Santo Rd Ste 160 *Web:* www.prolender.com	San Diego	CA	92124	619-258-3595	
Ptc Select LLC 2450 N Knoxville Ave *TF:* 800-225-2320 ■ *Web:* www.ptcselect.com	Peoria	IL	61604	309-685-8400	
Quick Electronics Inc 10800 76th Ct *Web:* www.quickelectronics.com	Largo	FL	33777	727-546-9299	
R-Cubed Service & Sales Inc 11126 Shady Trl *Web:* www.rcubed.com	Dallas	TX	75229	972-243-3830	
Ram Computers Inc 5500 N Western Ave Ste 101c *Web:* www.ramcomputersupply.com	Oklahoma City	OK	73118	405-842-9495	
Raven Computers 5952 Odana Rd *Web:* ravencomputers.com	Madison	WI	53719	608-661-1372	
Rb Technology Inc 860 Anburn Ct *Web:* www.rbtech-inc.com	Fremont	CA	94538	510-770-9922	
REACT Computer Services Inc 7654 Plz Ct	Willowbrook	IL	60527	630-323-6200	
Realistic Computing Inc 10461 Mill Run Cir *Web:* www.realistic-computing.com	Baltimore	MD	21117	410-744-8144	
Reboot Computer Services Inc 7011 Austin St Ste 3a *Web:* www.rebootcs.com	Forest Hills	NY	11375	718-897-7727	
Rescuecom Corp 2560 Burnet Ave **Fax Area Code:* 315 ■ *TF:* 800-737-2837 ■ *Web:* www.rescuecom.com	Syracuse	NY	13206	800-737-2837	433-5228*
Rockford It 419 N Mulford Rd Ste 2 *Web:* rockfordit.com	Rockford	IL	61107	815-316-7575	
Sanders Software Consulting Inc 3008 W 30th St. *Web:* www.sanderssoftware.com	Lawrence	KS	66047	785-865-5111	
Scanics 723 S Neil St Ste 101 *Web:* scanics.com	Champaign	IL	61825	217-403-4000	
Scot-tech 5608 6th Ave S *Web:* www.scot-tech.com	Seattle	WA	98108	206-763-7072	
Sentinel Technologies Inc 2550 Warrenville Rd *Web:* www.sentinel.com	Downers Grove	IL	60515	630-769-4300	
Service Express Inc 3854 Broadmoor Ave SE *Web:* www.seiservice.com	Grand Rapids	MI	49512	616-698-2221	
Shiloh Service Inc 85 Mtn View Pl *Web:* shilohservice.com	North Huntingdon	PA	15642	724-863-0190	
Simple Pc 101 Grace St	Greenwood	SC	29649	864-223-3344	
Smart Dolphins It Solutions Inc 3995 Quadra St Ste 303 *Web:* smartdolphins.com	Victoria	BC	V8X1J8	250-721-2499	
Smartware Computer Services 2821 S Bay St Ste B *Web:* scs3.com	Eustis	FL	32726	352-483-4350	
Spartan Computer Services Inc 350 W Phillips Rd. *Web:* www.spartancomputer.com	Greer	SC	29650	864-848-3810	
Systems Maintenance Services Inc (SMS) 10420 Harris Oaks Blvd Ste C *TF:* 877-405-0330 ■ *Web:* www.sysmaint.com	Charlotte	NC	28269	877-405-0330	
T&s Trading Co 1110 Ortega St. *Web:* tandstradingco.com	San Francisco	CA	94122	415-242-1551	
Team One Repair Inc 1911 Satellite Blvd Ste 100 *Web:* www.teamonerepair.com	Buford	GA	30518	678-985-0772	
tech guys inc 7913 Santa Fe Dr *Web:* www.techguys.com	Overland Park	KS	66204	913-381-5832	
Tech Team Solutions LLC 106 S Loudoun St *Web:* www.techteamsolutions.com	Winchester	VA	22601	540-667-2000	
Technicom Sales & Services Inc 1279 Sussex Dr *Web:* www.technicomcentral.com	North Lauderdale	FL	33068	954-597-9279	
Tecinfo Inc 601 N Deer Creek Dr E *Web:* tecinfo.net	Leland	MS	38756	662-686-9009	
Tecnet Canada Inc 3403 Seymour Pl. *Web:* www.tecnet.ca	Victoria	BC	V8X1W4	250-475-6066	
Telirite Technical Services Inc 2857 Lakeview Ct *Web:* www.telirite.com	Fremont	CA	94538	510-440-3888	
Throckmorten Enterprises 17433 Hwy 120 *Web:* throck.com	Big Oak Flat	CA	95305	209-962-7308	
Tracelogix Corp 3605 Knight Rd Ste 101 *Web:* www.tracelogix.com	Memphis	TN	38118	901-795-2777	
Trident Contract Management 2918 Marketplace Dr Ste 206 *Web:* www.trident-it.com	Madison	WI	53719	608-276-1900	
True Tech Systems Inc 24550 N River Rd *Web:* www.truetechsystems.com	Mt. Clemens	MI	48043	815-634-2881	
Tsg Networks 10462 San Pablo Ave *Web:* tsgnetworks.com	El Cerrito	CA	94530	510-525-6210	
Turner Techtronics Inc 3200 W Burbank Blvd *Web:* www.turnertech.com	Burbank	CA	91505	818-973-1060	
UCR LLC 1332 Woodman Dr *Web:* www.ucrnet.com	Dayton	OH	45432	937-253-8898	
V2 Systems Inc 9104 Manassas Dr Ste P *Web:* www.v2systems.com	Manassas	VA	20111	703-361-4606	

Phone | *Fax*

VideoBloom Inc
7350 E Progress Pl Ste 100 ... Greenwood Village CO 80111 303-694-7300
Web: videobloom.com

Vip Technology Solutions Group LLC
12149 S State Hwy 51 ... Coweta OK 74429 918-279-7000
Web: viptsg.com

Visual Net Design Lc 212 E Ramsey Rd ... San Antonio TX 78216 210-590-2734
TF: 800-590-2164 ■ *Web:* www.vndx.com

Vital Solutions International Llc
19 Leonberg Rd Ste 3 ... Cranberry Township PA 16066 724-776-6707
Web: www.vsint.com

VITEC Solutions LLC 455 Commerce Dr Ste 3 ... Amherst NY 14228 716-204-9200
Web: www.vitecsolutions.com

Voxtechnologies Com 301 S Sherman St ... Richardson TX 75081 972-234-4343
TF: 888-568-6224 ■ *Web:* www.voxtechnologies.com

W Dm Computer Services Inc
1900 Harrison St Ste 2 ... Quincy IL 62301 217-228-1950
Web: wdmquincy.com

Windstone Technology Services Inc
1645 E Missouri Ave Ste 320 ... Phoenix AZ 85016 602-248-9092
Web: windstonetech.com

WinSim Inc 14090 Southwest Fwy Ste 550 ... Sugar Land TX 77478 281-565-6700
Web: winsim.com

Wolf Technology Group Inc
1 Chick Springs Rd Ste 112 ... Greenville SC 29609 864-248-6316
Web: www.wolftg.com

Word-Tech Inc 5625 Foxridge Dr Ste 110 ... Mission KS 66202 913-722-3334
Web: www.wordtech.com

Wsb Computer Services Inc 21 Craft St ... Alamosa CO 81101 719-589-8940
Web: www.wsbcs.net

176 COMPUTER NETWORKING PRODUCTS & SYSTEMS

See Also Modems p. 1999; Systems & Utilities Software p. 2035; Telecommunications Equipment & Systems p. 3217

Phone | *Fax*

Accton Technology Corp
1200 Crossman Ave Ste 130 ... Sunnyvale CA 94089 408-747-0994 747-0982
Web: www.accton.com

Alcatel-Lucent 600 Mountain Ave ... Murray Hill NJ 07974 908-508-8080
Web: www.alcatel-lucent.com

Allied Telesyn International Corp
19800 N Creek Pkwy Ste 100 ... Bothell WA 98011 425-481-3895
TF: 800-424-4284 ■ *Web:* www.alliedtelesis.com

American Megatrends Inc (AMI)
5555 Oakbrook Pkwy Bldg 200 ... Norcross GA 30093 770-246-8600 246-8790
TF: 800-828-9264 ■ *Web:* www.ami.com

ASA Computers Inc 645 National Ave ... Mountain View CA 94043 650-230-8000 230-8090
TF: 800-732-5727 ■ *Web:* www.asacomputers.com

Avaya Inc 211 Mt Airy Rd ... Basking Ridge NJ 07920 908-953-6000
TF: 866-462-8292 ■ *Web:* www.avaya.com

Axis Communications Inc (ACI) 100 Apollo Dr ... Chelmsford MA 01824 978-614-2000 614-2100
TF: 800-444-2947 ■ *Web:* www.axis.com

Black Box Corp 1000 Pk Dr ... Lawrence PA 15055 724-746-5500 321-0746*
NASDAQ: BBOX ■ **Fax Area Code:* 800 ■ *TF:* 877-877-2269 ■ *Web:* www.blackbox.com

Blue Coat Systems Inc 420 N Mary Ave ... Sunnyvale CA 94085 408-220-2200 220-2250
NASDAQ: BCSI ■ *TF:* 866-302-2628 ■ *Web:* www.bluecoat.com

Brocade Communications Systems Inc
130 Holger Way ... San Jose CA 95134 408-333-8000 333-8101
NASDAQ: BRCD ■ *TF:* 800-752-8061 ■ *Web:* www.brocade.com

Cambex Corp 337 Tpke Rd ... Southborough MA 01772 508-281-0209 281-0214
OTC: CBEX ■ *TF:* 800-325-5565 ■ *Web:* www.cambex.com

Chatsworth Products Inc
31425 Agoura Rd ... Westlake Village CA 91361 818-735-6100 735-6199
TF: 800-834-4969 ■ *Web:* www.chatsworth.com

CIENA Corp Metro Transport Div
1185 Sanctuary Pkwy ... Alpharetta GA 30009 678-867-5100 867-5101
Web: www.ciena.com

Cisco Systems Inc 170 W Tasman Dr ... San Jose CA 95134 408-526-4000 526-4100
NASDAQ: CSCO ■ *TF:* 800-553-6387 ■ *Web:* www.cisco.com

Compex Inc 7918 Jones Branch Dr ... Mclean VA 22102 503-873-0188 482-0332*
**Fax Area Code:* 714 ■ **Fax:* Sales ■ *TF:* 800-279-8891 ■ *Web:* compextech.com

CompuCom Systems Inc 7171 Forest Ln ... Dallas TX 75230 972-856-3600
TF Cust Svc: 800-597-0555 ■ *Web:* www.compucom.com

Comtrol Corp 100 Fifth Ave NW ... Maple Grove MN 55112 763-494-4100 494-4199
TF: 800-926-6876 ■ *Web:* www.comtrol.com

Contemporary Control Systems Inc
2431 Curtiss St ... Downers Grove IL 60515 630-963-7070 963-0109
Web: www.ccontrols.com

Continental Resources Inc 175 Middlesex Tpke ... Bedford MA 01730 781-275-0850 275-6563
TF: 800-937-4688 ■ *Web:* www.conres.com

Coriant 220 Mill Rd ... Chelmsford MA 01824 978-250-2900 256-3434
Web: www.coriant.com/company/federal.asp/company/coriant-america.asp

Crossroads Systems Inc 8300 N MoPac Expy ... Austin TX 78759 512-349-0300
NASDAQ: CRDS ■ *TF:* 800-643-7148 ■ *Web:* www.crossroads.com

Crystal Group Inc 850 Kacena Rd ... Hiawatha IA 52233 319-378-1636 393-2338
TF: 877-279-7863 ■ *Web:* www.crystalrugged.com

Cubix Corp 2800 Lockheed Way ... Carson City NV 89706 775-888-1000
TF Sales: 800-829-0550 ■ *Web:* www.cubix.com

Cyberdata Corp 3 Justin Ct ... Monterey CA 93940 831-373-2601 373-4193
TF: 800-363-8010 ■ *Web:* www.cyberdata.net

D-Link Systems Inc
17595 Mt Herrmann St ... Fountain Valley CA 92708 714-885-6000 743-4905*
**Fax Area Code:* 866 ■ *TF:* 800-326-1688 ■ *Web:* www.dlink.com

Daly Computers Inc 22521 Gateway Ctr Dr ... Clarksburg MD 20871 301-670-0381 963-1516
TF: 800-955-3259 ■ *Web:* www.daly.com

Datacomm Management Sciences Inc
25 Van Zant St ... East Norwalk CT 06855 203-838-7183 838-1751

Dell Inc 1 Dell Way ... Round Rock TX 78682 512-338-4400 283-6161
NASDAQ: DELL ■ *TF:* 800-879-3355 ■ *Web:* www.dell.com

Digi International Inc 11001 Bren Rd E ... Minnetonka MN 55343 952-912-3444 912-4991
NASDAQ: DGII ■ *TF:* 877-912-3444 ■ *Web:* www.digi.com

Phone | *Fax*

Dot Hill Systems Corp 1351 S Sunset St ... Longmont CO 80501 303-845-3200 845-3655
NASDAQ: HILL ■ *TF:* 800-872-2783 ■ *Web:* www.dothill.com

Echelon Corp 550 Meridian Ave ... San Jose CA 95126 408-938-5200 790-3800
NASDAQ: ELON ■ *TF:* 888-324-3566 ■ *Web:* www.echelon.com

Egenera Inc 80 Central St ... Boxborough MA 01719 978-206-6300 206-6436
TF: 866-301-3117 ■ *Web:* www.egenera.com

Electronics for Imaging Inc
303 Velocity Way ... Foster City CA 94404 650-357-3500 357-3500
NASDAQ: EFII ■ *TF:* 888-334-8650 ■ *Web:* w3.efi.com

EMC Corp 176 S St ... Hopkinton MA 01748 508-435-1000
NYSE: EMC ■ *Web:* www.emc.com

Enterasys Networks Inc 50 Minuteman Rd ... Andover MA 01810 978-684-1000
Web: extremenetworks.com

eSoft Inc 295 Interlocken Blvd Ste 500 ... Broomfield CO 80021 303-444-1600
TF: 866-233-2296 ■ *Web:* untangle.com/esoft

Extreme Networks Inc 3585 Monroe St ... Santa Clara CA 95051 408-579-2800 579-3000
NASDAQ: EXTR ■ *TF:* 888-257-3000 ■ *Web:* www.extremenetworks.com

Ezenia! Inc 14 Celina Ave Ste 17 ... Nashua NH 03063 781-505-2100 880-4978*
**Fax Area Code:* 603 ■ *TF:* 800-966-2301 ■ *Web:* www.ezenia.com

F5 Networks Inc 401 Elliott Ave W ... Seattle WA 98119 206-272-5555 272-5556
NASDAQ: FFIV ■ *TF:* 888-882-4447 ■ *Web:* www.f5.com

Finisar Corp 1389 Moffett Pk Dr ... Sunnyvale CA 94089 408-548-1000 541-6129
NASDAQ: FNSR ■ *Web:* www.finisar.com

Fujitsu Computer Systems Corp
1250 E Arques Ave ... Sunnyvale CA 94085 408-746-6000
TF: 800-538-8460 ■ *Web:* solutions.us.fujitsu.com

Futurex Inc 864 Old Boerne Rd ... Bulverde TX 78163 830-980-9782 438-8782
TF: 800-251-5112 ■ *Web:* www.futurex.com

General DataComm Inc 6 Rubber Ave ... Naugatuck CT 06770 203-729-0271 723-2883
Web: www.gdc.com

High Point Solutions Inc 5 Gail Ct ... Sparta NJ 07871 973-940-0040 940-0041
Web: www.highpt.com

iGo Inc 17800 N Perimeter Dr Ste 200 ... Scottsdale AZ 85255 480-596-0061 596-0349
NASDAQ: IGOI ■ *TF:* 888-205-0093 ■ *Web:* www.igo.com

iLinc Communications Inc
2999 N 44th St Ste 650 ... Phoenix AZ 85018 602-952-1200 952-0544
TF: 800-767-9054 ■ *Web:* www.ilinc.com

IMC Networks Corp 19772 Pauling ... Foothill Ranch CA 92610 949-465-3000 465-3020
TF: 800-624-1070 ■ *Web:* bb-elec.com

Interphase Corp
4240 International Pkwy Ste 105 ... Carrollton TX 75007 214-654-5000 654-5500
NASDAQ: INPH ■ *TF:* 800-327-8638

Juniper Networks Inc 1194 N Mathilda Ave ... Sunnyvale CA 94089 408-745-2000 745-2100
NYSE: JNPR ■ *TF:* 888-586-4737 ■ *Web:* www.juniper.net

LightSand Communications Inc
101 E Pk Blvd Ste 600 ... Plano TX 75074 972-516-3740 516-3741
Web: www.lightsand.com

Link Computer Corp Inc PO Box 250 ... Bellwood PA 16617 814-742-7700 742-7900
Web: www.linkcorp.com

MAPSYS Inc 920 Michigan Ave ... Columbus OH 43215 614-224-5193 224-6048
Web: www.mapsysinc.com

Marvell Semiconductor Inc
5488 Marvell Ln ... Santa Clara CA 95054 408-222-2500
TF Cust Svc: 855-627-8355 ■ *Web:* www.marvell.com

Medical Knowledge Systems Inc
440 Burrough Ste 130 ... Detroit MI 48202 313-483-0955
Web: www.mksi.com

MTM Technologies Inc 1200 High Ridge Rd ... Stamford CT 06905 203-975-3700
OTC: MTMC ■ *Web:* www.mtm.com

NEC Corp of America
10850 Gold Ctr Dr Ste 200 ... Rancho Cordova CA 95670 916-463-7000
TF: 800-632-4636 ■ *Web:* www.necam.com

Netplanner Systems Inc
3145 Northwoods Pkwy Ste 800 ... Norcross GA 30071 770-662-5482 441-3773
TF: 800-795-1975 ■ *Web:* www.netplanner.com

Network Appliance Inc 495 E Java Dr ... Sunnyvale CA 94089 408-822-6000 822-4422
NASDAQ: NTAP ■ *TF Sales:* 800-443-4537 ■ *Web:* www.netapp.com

Network Dynamics Inc
640 Brooker Creek Blvd Ste 410 ... Oldsmar FL 34677 813-818-8597
TF: 877-818-8597 ■ *Web:* www.ndiwebsite.com

Network Equipment Technologies Inc
6900 Paseo Padre Pkwy ... Fremont CA 94555 510-713-7300 574-4000
NASDAQ: NWK

Overland Storage Inc 4820 Overland Ave ... San Diego CA 92123 858-571-5555 571-0982
NASDAQ: OVRL ■ *TF:* 800-729-8725 ■ *Web:* www.overlandstorage.com

OvisLink Technologies Corp
203 Lemon Creek Dr Ste C ... Walnut CA 91789 909-869-8666
Web: www.ovislink.com

Patton Electronics Co
7622 Rickenbacker Dr ... Gaithersburg MD 20879 301-975-1000 869-9293
Web: www.patton.com

Peak 10 752 Barret Ave ... Louisville KY 40204 502-315-6015
TF: 866-732-5836 ■ *Web:* www.peak10.com

Plaintree Systems Inc 110 Decosta St ... Arnprior ON K7S0B5 613-623-3434 623-4647
Web: www.plaintree.com

Polycom Inc 4750 Willow Rd ... Pleasanton CA 94588 800-765-9266
TF: 800-765-9266 ■ *Web:* www.polycom.com

PrimeArray Systems Inc 127 Riverneck Rd ... Chelmsford MA 01824 978-654-6250 654-6249
TF: 800-433-5133 ■ *Web:* www.primearray.com

Quantum Corp 11431 Willows Rd NE ... Redmond WA 98052 425-881-8004 297-3996*
**Fax Area Code:* 651 ■ *TF:* 800-284-5101 ■ *Web:* www.quantum.com

Quick Eagle Networks Inc 830 Maude Ave ... Mountain View CA 94043 650-962-8282

Raytheon Computer Products
1001 Boston Post Rd ... Marlborough MA 01752 781-522-3000
Web: www.raytheon.com

Ringdale Inc 101 Halmar Cove ... Georgetown TX 78628 512-288-9080 288-7210
TF: 888-288-9080 ■ *Web:* www.ringdale.com

Safari Circuits Inc 411 Washington St ... Otsego MI 49078 269-694-9471 692-2651
TF: 888-694-7230 ■ *Web:* www.safaricircuits.com

SafeNet Inc 4690 Millennium Dr ... Belcamp MD 21017 410-931-7500 931-7524
TF Sales: 800-533-3958 ■ *Web:* www.safenet-inc.com

Server Technology Inc 1040 Sandhill Dr ... Reno NV 89521 775-284-2000 284-2065
TF: 800-835-1515 ■ *Web:* www.servertech.com

Phone | Fax

Silicon Graphics Inc (SGI) 900 N McCarthy Blvd — Milpitas CA 95035 — 669-900-8000
Web: www.sgi.com

Skyline Network Engineering LLC
6956-F Aviation Blvd — Glen Burnie MD 21061 — 410-795-2700
Web: www.skylinenet.net

SOHOware Inc 1250 Oakmead Pkwy Ste 210 — Sunnyvale CA 94085 — 408-565-9888 565-9889
TF: 800-632-1118 ■ *Web:* www.sohoware.com

Solectek Corp 6370 Nancy Ridge Dr Ste 109 — San Diego CA 92121 — 858-450-1220 457-2681
TF: 888-299-8057 ■ *Web:* www.solectek.com

SonicWALL Inc 2001 Logic Dr — San Jose CA 95124 — 408-745-9600 745-9300
TF: 888-557-6642 ■ *Web:* www.sonicwall.com

Spectrum Communications Cabling Services Inc
226 N Lincoln Ave — Corona CA 92882 — 951-371-0549 270-3833

SteelCloud Inc 20110 Ashbrook Pl Ste 270 — Ashburn VA 20147 — 703-674-5500 674-5506
OTC: SCLD ■ *TF:* 800-296-3866 ■ *Web:* www.steelcloud.com

StoneFly Inc 21353 Cabot Blvd — Hayward CA 94545 — 510-265-1616 265-1565
TF: 888-786-6335 ■ *Web:* www.stonefly.com

Storage Engine Inc 1 Sheila Dr — Tinton Falls NJ 07724 — 732-747-6995 747-6542
TF: 866-734-8899 ■ *Web:* www.storageengine.com

Strictly Business Computer Systems Inc
848 Fourth Ave Ste 200 — Huntington WV 25701 — 888-529-0401 781-2590*
**Fax Area Code:* 304 ■ *TF:* 888-529-0401 ■ *Web:* www.sbcs.com

Systech Corp 16510 Via Esprillo — San Diego CA 92127 — 858-674-6500 613-2400
TF: 800-800-8970 ■ *Web:* www.systech.com

Systemax Inc 11 Harbor Pk Dr — Port Washington NY 11050 — 516-608-7000 608-7001
NYSE: SYX ■ *Web:* www.systemax.com

TalkPoint Communications Inc 100 William St — New York NY 10038 — 212-909-2900 909-2901
TF: 866-323-8660 ■ *Web:* talkpoint.com

Technology Integration Group (TIG)
7810 Trade St — San Diego CA 92121 — 858-566-1900 566-8794
TF: 800-858-0549 ■ *Web:* www.tig.com

Tekworks Inc 13000 Gregg St Ste B — Poway CA 92064 — 877-835-9675
TF: 877-835-9675 ■ *Web:* www.tekworks.com

Telebyte Inc 355 Marcus Blvd — Hauppauge NY 11788 — 631-423-3232 385-8184
TF: 800-835-3298 ■ *Web:* www.telebyteusa.com

TeleSoft International Inc
4029 S Capital of TX Hwy Ste 220 — Austin TX 78704 — 512-373-4224 788-5660
Web: www.telesoft-intl.com

Telkonet Inc 10200 W Innovation Dr Ste 300 — Milwaukee WI 53226 — 414-223-0473 258-8307
OTC: TKOI ■ *TF Sales:* 888-703-9398 ■ *Web:* www.telkonet.com

Transition Networks Inc 10900 Red Cir Dr — Minnetonka MN 55343 — 952-941-7600 941-2322
TF: 800-526-9267 ■ *Web:* www.transition.com

Transource Computers Corp 2405 W Utopia Rd — Phoenix AZ 85027 — 623-879-8882 879-8887
TF: 800-486-3715 ■ *Web:* www.transource.com

Trendware International Inc
20675 Manhattan Pl — Torrance CA 90501 — 310-961-5500 961-5511
TF: 888-326-6061 ■ *Web:* www.trendnet.com

Ultera Systems Inc
26081 Merit Cir Ste 125 — Laguna Hills CA 92653 — 949-367-8800 367-0758
TF: 877-462-7362 ■ *Web:* www.ultera.com

UNICOM 565 Brea Canyon Rd Ste A — Walnut CA 91789 — 626-964-7873 964-7880*
**Fax:* Mktg ■ *TF:* 800-346-6668 ■ *Web:* www.unicomlink.com

Unimark Products 9818 Pflumm Rd — Lenexa KS 66215 — 913-649-2424 649-5795
TF Cust Svc: 800-255-6356 ■ *Web:* www.unimark.com

US Robotics Corp
1300 E Woodfield Dr Ste 506 — Schaumburg IL 60173 — 847-874-2000 874-2001
TF: 877-710-0884 ■ *Web:* www.usr.com

ViewCast Corp 3701 W Plano Pkwy Ste 300 — Plano TX 75075 — 972-488-7200 488-7299
Web: www.viewcast.com

Virtela Technology Services Inc
5680 Greenwood Plz Blvd Ste 200 — Greenwood Village CO 80111 — 720-475-4000 475-4001
TF: 877-803-9629 ■ *Web:* www.virtela.net

Visara International Inc
2700 Gateway Centre Blvd Ste 600 — Morrisville NC 27560 — 919-882-0200
TF: 888-334-4380 ■ *Web:* www.visara.com

WatchGuard Technologies Inc
505 Fifth Ave S Ste 500 — Seattle WA 98104 — 206-613-6600 521-8342
TF Sales: 800-734-9905 ■ *Web:* www.watchguard.com

WAV Inc 2380 Prospect Dr — Aurora IL 60504 — 630-818-1000 818-4450
TF: 800-678-2419 ■ *Web:* www.wavonline.com

WideBand Corp 401 W Grand St — Gallatin MO 64640 — 660-663-3000 663-3736
TF: 888-663-3050 ■ *Web:* www.wband.com

Winchester Systems Inc
101 Billerica Ave Bldg 5 — North Billerica MA 01862 — 781-265-0200 265-0201
TF Cust Svc: 800-325-3700 ■ *Web:* www.winsys.com

Works Computing Inc
1801 American Blvd E Ste 12 — Bloomington MN 55425 — 952-746-1580 746-1585
TF: 866-222-4077 ■ *Web:* www.workscomputing.com

World Data Products Inc 121 Cheshire Ln — Minnetonka MN 55305 — 952-476-9000
TF: 888-210-7636 ■ *Web:* www.wdpi.com

ZT Group International Inc
350 Meadowlands Pkwy — Secaucus NJ 07094 — 201-559-1000 559-1004
TF: 888-984-8899 ■ *Web:* www.ztsystems.com

177 COMPUTER PROGRAMMING SERVICES - CUSTOM

See Also Computer Software p. 2026; Computer Systems Design Services p. 2039

Phone | Fax

2plus2 Partners Inc 5980 Horton St Ste 105 — Emeryville CA 94608 — 510-652-7700
Web: www.2plus2.com

3CLogic Inc 9201 Corporate Blvd Ste 470 — Rockville MD 20850 — 240-454-6347
Web: www.3clogic.com

4 Consulting Inc 1221 Abrams Rd — Richardson TX 75081 — 214-698-8633
Web: www.4ci-usa.com

4th Source Inc 2400 Veterans Blvd Ste 480 — Kenner LA 70062 — 855-875-4700
TF: 855-875-4700 ■ *Web:* www.4thsource.com

6k Systems Inc 44084 Riverside Pkwy Ste 340 — Leesburg VA 20176 — 703-724-1320
Web: www.6ksystems.com

7 Medical Systems LLC
651 Nicollet Mall Ste 501 — Minneapolis MN 55402 — 612-230-7700
Web: www.7medical.com

A L H Group Inc 880 Industrial Way — San Luis Obispo CA 93401 — 805-541-8739
Web: alh.alh-group.com

AB Controls Inc 188 Technology Dr Ste K — Irvine CA 92618 — 949-341-0977
Web: www.abcontrols.com

Abaris Inc 1255 Treat Blvd Ste 140 — Walnut Creek CA 94597 — 949-333-3500
Web: www.abaris-inc.com

Abila Inc 7901 Jones Branch Dr — Mclean VA 22102 — 703-506-7000
Web: www.abila.com/lp/avectra

AbleSys Corp 20954 Corsair Blvd — Hayward CA 94545 — 510-265-1883
Web: www.ablesys.com

ABSOFT Corp 2781 Bond St — Rochester Hills MI 48309 — 248-853-0050
Web: absoft.com

Abtech
17300 SW Upper Boones Ferry Rd Ste 110 — Portland OR 97224 — 503-924-1090
Web: www.abtech-pdx.com

AcademyOne Inc 601 Willowbrook Ln — West Chester PA 19382 — 610-436-5680
Web: www.academyone.com

Accelerated Technology Laboratories Inc
496 Holly Grove School Rd — West End NC 27376 — 910-673-8165
Web: www.atlab.com

Acceleware Ltd 435 10 Ave SE — Calgary AB T2G0W3 — 403-249-9099
Web: www.acceleware.com

Access Innovations Inc
4725 Indian School Rd NE Ste 100 — Albuquerque NM 87110 — 505-265-3591 256-1080
TF: 800-926-8328 ■ *Web:* www.accessinn.com

Access Softek Inc 727 Allston Way Ste C — Berkeley CA 94710 — 510-848-0606
Web: www.accessoftek.com

Acclaim Systems Inc
110 E Pennsylvania Blvd — Feasterville PA 19053 — 215-354-1420
Web: www.acclaimsystems.com

AccuCode Inc 6886 S Yosemite St Ste 100 — Centennial CO 80112 — 303-639-6111 639-6178
TF: 866-705-9879 ■ *Web:* www.accucode.com

Accumedic Computer Systems Inc
11 Grace Ave Ste 401 — Great Neck NY 11021 — 516-466-6800
TF: 800-765-9300 ■ *Web:* www.accumedic.com

Accumedscript LLP 1601 Bethel Rd — Columbus OH 43220 — 614-804-5656
Web: www.accumedscript.com

Accurate Computer Technology Inc
17821 Sky Park Cir Ste J — Irvine CA 92614 — 949-261-6677
Web: www.accuratecomputer.com

Accuzip 3216 El Camino Real — Atascadero CA 93422 — 805-461-7300
TF: 800-233-0555 ■ *Web:* www.accuzip.com

Ace Technologies Inc 2375 Zanker Rd Ste 250 — San Jose CA 95131 — 408-521-1139
Web: www.acetechnologies.com

Achieve IT Solutions Inc
640 Belle Terre Rd Bldg B — Port Jefferson NY 11777 — 631-543-3200
Web: www.achieveits.com

Acquidata Inc
6800 Gulfport Blvd S Ste 201-205 — St Petersburg FL 33707 — 860-910-4747
Web: www.acquidata.com

Actsoft Inc 8910 N Dale Mabry Hwy — Tampa FL 33614 — 813-936-2331 936-7541
TF: 888-732-6638 ■ *Web:* www.actsoft.com

Acuo Technologies LLC
8009 34th Ave S Riverview Office Tower
Ste 900 — Bloomington MN 55128 — 952-905-3440
Web: www.acuotech.com

Ad Astra Information Systems LLC
6900 W 80th St Ste 300 — Overland Park KS 66204 — 913-652-4100
Web: www.aais.com

Ad Solutions Group Inc
1200 Harger Rd Ste 203 — Oak Brook IL 60523 — 630-574-4545
Web: www.adsgroup.net

Ada Business Computers 1003 N Mississippi Ave — Ada OK 74820 — 580-436-2803
Web: www.adacomp.com

Adapt Software Applications
959 S Coast Dr Ste 100 — Costa Mesa CA 92626 — 714-389-1584
Web: www.adaptcrm.com

Adicio Inc
1 Carlsbad Research Ctr 2382 Faraday Ave
Ste 350 — Carlsbad CA 92008 — 760-602-9502
Web: www.adicio.com

Adino Inc 360 W Alden Ct — Chicago Heights IL 60411 — 708-481-1000
Web: www.adinoinc.com

ADMINS Inc 1035 Cambridge St — Cambridge MA 02141 — 617-494-5100
Web: www.admins.com

Ads Programming Services
1 Independence Plz Ste 820 — Birmingham AL 35209 — 205-803-2196
Web: www.adsprogramming.com

Advanced Chemistry Development Inc
110 Yonge St 14th Fl — Toronto ON M5C1T4 — 416-368-3435
TF: 800-304-3988 ■ *Web:* www.acdlabs.com

Advanced Computer Technologies LLC
101 Market Pl — Montgomery AL 36117 — 334-262-6882
Web: www.actinnovations.com

Advanced Computing Solutions Group Inc
19125 Northcreek Pkwy — Bothell WA 98011 — 425-609-3165
Web: www.acsgrp.com

Advanced Digital Data Inc 6 Laurel Dr — Flanders NJ 07836 — 973-584-4026 584-3205
TF: 800-922-0972 ■ *Web:* www.addsys.com

Advanced Health Media LLC (AHM)
420 Mountain Ave — New Providence NJ 07974 — 908-393-8700 393-8701
Web: www.ahmdirect.com

Advanced Solutions International Inc
901 N Pitt St Ste 200 — Alexandria VA 22314 — 703-739-3100 739-3218
Web: www.advsol.com

Advanced Systems Consultants Inc
4074 E Patterson Rd — Dayton OH 45430 — 937-429-1428
Web: ascsoftware.com

Advancedware Corp 13844 Alton Pkwy Ste 136 — Irvine CA 92618 — 949-609-1240
Web: advancedware.com

AdvanTech Inc 2661 Riva Rd Ste 1030 — Annapolis MD 21401 — 410-266-8000
Web: www.advantech-inc.com

Aeon Nexus Corp 174 Glen St — Glens Falls NY 12801 — 518-338-1551
Web: www.aeonnexus.com

Phone | Fax

Aequor Technologies Inc 377 Hoes Ln.... Piscataway NJ 08854 732-494-4999
Web: www.aequor.com

Ag Informaton Systems 306 Primrose Ln.... Mountville PA 17554 717-285-7105
Web: www.ag-is.com

Agb Investigative Services Inc
2033 W 95th St.... Chicago IL 60643 773-445-4300
Web: agbinvestigative.com

AgileAssets Inc 3001 Bee Caves Rd Ste 200.... Austin TX 78746 512-327-4200
Web: www.agileassets.com

Agiletics Inc
585 S Ronald Reagan Blvd Ste 113.... Longwood FL 32750 407-834-5115
Web: agiletics.com

Agilysys NV LLC 28925 Fountain Pkwy.... Solon OH 44139 770-810-7800
TF: 800-241-8768 ■ *Web:* www.agilysys.com

Agnik LLC 8840 Stanford Blvd Ste 1300.... Columbia MD 21045 410-290-0864
Web: www.agnik.com

Ahead Hum Res Inc/Prosoft LLC
2209 Heather Ln.... Louisville KY 40218 502-485-1000
TF: 888-749-1000 ■ *Web:* aheadhr.com

Airput Inc 3819 Germantown Pk.... Collegeville PA 19426 610-454-5100
Web: www.airput.com

Aisle7 215 NW Park Ave.... Portland OR 97209 503-234-4092
Web: aisle7.com

Alebra Technologies Inc
3810 Pheasant Ridge Dr NE Ste 100.... Minneapolis MN 55449 651-366-6140
TF: 888-340-2727 ■ *Web:* www.alebra.com

All of E Solutions 2510 W Sixth St.... Lawrence KS 66049 785-832-2900
Web: allofe.com

All Squared Web Design LLC
284 Susquehanna Trl.... Allentown PA 18104 610-351-5416
Web: allsquared.com

Alltech International Inc
8298-B Old Courthouse Rd Centennial Plz - Tysons Corner
.... Vienna VA 22182 703-506-1222
Web: www.alltech.net

Alpha Lex Systems Integration
11100 Bradner Pl.... Porter Ranch CA 91326 818-407-9200
Web: alphalex.com

Alpha Net Consulting LLC
3080 Olcott St Ste 235C.... Santa Clara CA 95054 408-330-0896
Web: anetcorp.com

Alphapoint Technology Inc
6371 Business Blvd Ste 200.... Sarasota FL 34240 941-907-8822
Web: new.alphapoint-us.net

Alphinat Inc Ste 680 2000 Peel.... Montreal QC H3A2W5 514-398-9799
Web: www.alphinat.com

Alr Systems & Software Inc 11707 M Cir.... Omaha NE 68137 402-891-1500
Web: www.alrsys.com

Alta Via Consulting LLC 127 ConKinnon Dr.... Lenoir City TN 37772 877-258-2842
TF: 877-258-2842 ■ *Web:* www.altavia.com

Altair Technology Inc 1116 W Blanco Rd.... San Antonio TX 78232 210-764-9900 497-1329
Web: www.altairtech.com

Altamira Technologies Corp
8201 Greensboro Dr Ste 800.... Mclean VA 22102 703-813-2100
Web: www.invertix.com

Altech Services Inc
1160 Parsippany Blvd Ste 202.... Parsippany NJ 07054 888-725-8324
TF: 888-725-8324 ■ *Web:* www.altechts.com

Altep Inc 7450 Remcon Cir.... El Paso TX 79912 915-533-8722
Web: www.altep.com

Altia Inc
7222 Commerce Ctr Dr Ste 240.... Colorado Springs CO 80919 719-598-4299
Web: www.altia.com

Alvarez Technology Group Inc
209 Pajaro St Ste A.... Salinas CA 93901 831-753-7677
Web: www.alvareztg.com

Amaram Technology Corp 2123 Mckay St Ste 445.... Vienna VA 22182 703-288-4113
Web: www.amaram.com

Ambasoft Inc 23505 Crenshaw Blvd Ste 153.... Torrance CA 90505 310-326-4160
Web: www.ambasoft.com

Amer Technology Inc 5717 Northwest Pkwy.... San Antonio TX 78249 210-256-7070
Web: www.amersolutions.com

American Hytech Corp
Headquarters 125 UPark Rd.... Pittsburgh PA 15238 412-826-3333
Web: ahc.net

American Technology Services Inc
2751 Prosperity Ave 6th Fl.... Fairfax VA 22031 703-876-0300
Web: www.networkats.com

AMS.NET Inc 502 Commerce Way.... Livermore CA 94550 925-245-6100
Web: www.ams.net

Amtex Enterprises Inc
4699 Old Ironsides Dr Ste 270.... Santa Clara CA 95054 408-734-4050
Web: www.amtexenterprises.com

Analytical Graphics Inc 220 Vly Creek Blvd.... Exton PA 19341 610-981-8000 981-8001
TF: 800-220-4785 ■ *Web:* www.agi.com

Analytical Mechanics Associates Inc
303 Butler Farm Rd Ste 104A.... Hampton VA 23666 757-865-0000
Web: www.ama-inc.com

Anchor Marketing Inc 2726 17th Ave S.... Grand Forks ND 58208 701-787-8230
Web: www.anchorwebsite.com

ANGOSS Software Corp Ste 200 111 George St.... Toronto ON M5A2N4 416-593-1122
Web: www.angoss.com

AnswerOn Inc 1707 Main St Ste 500.... Longmont CO 80501 720-684-4900
Web: www.answeron.com

Antares Development Corp
6243 W Ih 10 870.... San Antonio TX 78201 210-736-2220
Web: www.antares-corp.com

Aparaa Corp 14900 Landmark Blvd Ste 630.... Dallas TX 75254 888-441-2535
TF: 888-441-2535 ■ *Web:* www.aparaa.com

Apex Business Machines & Supplies
352 Riverside Dr.... Sudbury ON P3E1H7 705-674-4472
Web: apexbiz.com

Apex Information Management Consultants Inc
4515 Culver Rd Ste 310.... Rochester NY 14622 585-225-8430
Web: www.apeximc.com

Apex Innovations Inc 19951 W 162nd St.... Olathe KS 66062 913-254-0250
Web: www.apex-innovations.com

Apex Software Inc 37 Antrim Rd.... Pittston PA 18640 570-830-5893

APlus Technologies Inc
10015 Old Columbia Rd Ste B.... Columbia MD 21046 410-290-6233
Web: www.aplustechnologies.com

Apollo PACS Inc
7700 Leesburg Pike Ste 419.... Falls Church VA 22043 703-288-1474
Web: www.apolloei.com

APOS Systems Inc
100 Conestoga College Blvd Ste 1118.... Kitchener ON N2P2N6 519-894-2767
Web: www.apos.com

Appfluent Technology Inc
6001 Montrose Rd Tenth Fl Ste 1000.... Rockville MD 20852 301-770-2888
Web: www.appfluent.com

Applied Business Software
2847 Gundry Ave.... Signal Hill CA 90755 562-426-2188
TF: 800-833-3343 ■ *Web:* www.themortgageoffice.com

Applied Cad Knowledge Inc 18 Westech Dr.... Tyngsboro MA 01879 978-649-9800
Web: www.appliedcad.com

Applied Integrated Technologies Inc
6305 Ivy Ln Ste 520.... Greenbelt MD 20770 301-614-9700
Web: www.ait-i.com

Applied OLAP Inc
3322 Sw Memorial Pkwy Ste 647.... Huntsville AL 35801 256-885-4371
Web: www.appliedolap.com

Applied Performance Technologies Inc
400 W Wilson Bridge Rd Ste 250.... Worthington OH 43085 614-847-9600
Web: appliedperformance.com

Applied Software Inc
3919 National Dr Ste 200.... Burtonsville MD 20866 888-624-8439
TF: 888-624-8439 ■ *Web:* www.magview.com

Apprise Software Inc
3101 Emrick Blvd Ste 301.... Bethlehem PA 18020 610-991-3900
Web: www.apprise.com

Appsec Consulting Inc
6110 Hellyer Ave Ste 100.... San Jose CA 95138 408-224-1110
Web: www.appsecconsulting.com

AppTech Corp 2011 Palomar Airport Rd Ste 102.... Carlsbad CA 92011 877-720-0022
TF: 877-720-0022 ■ *Web:* apptechcorp.com

Apptricity Corp 5605 N Macarthur Blvd Ste 900.... Irving TX 75038 214-596-0601
Web: www.apptricity.com

Apriva Inc 8501 N Scottsdale Rd Ste 110.... Scottsdale AZ 85253 480-421-1210
TF: 877-277-0728 ■ *Web:* www.apriva.com

Aquarius Imaging LLC 3810 Inverrary Blvd.... Lauderhill FL 33319 954-777-2729
Web: www.aquariusimaging.com

Archibus Inc 18 Tremont St.... Boston MA 02108 617-227-2508 227-2509
Web: www.archibus.com

Archive-cd LLC 910 Beverly Way.... Jacksonville OR 97530 541-899-5704
TF: 800-323-1868 ■ *Web:* www.archive-cd.com

Archonix Systems LLC
30 Lk Ctr Executive Park 401 Rt 73 N Ste 105.... Marlton NJ 08053 856-787-0020
Web: www.archonixsystems.com

Archway Systems Inc
2134 Main St Ste 160.... Huntington Beach CA 92648 714-374-0440
Web: www.archwaysystems.com

Argo Data Resource Corp
1500 N Greenville Ave.... Richardson TX 75081 972-866-3300 866-3301
Web: www.argodata.com

Ariel Partners LLC 1501 BRdway 12th fl.... New York NY 10036 781-647-2425
Web: www.arielpartners.com

Aristatek Inc 710 E Garfield St Ste 220.... Laramie WY 82070 307-721-2126
TF: 877-912-2200 ■ *Web:* www.aristatek.com

Arkansas Data Services 27 Macarthur Dr.... Conway AR 72032 501-327-8000
Web: www.ark-data-services.com

Arnima Design 518 N Tampa St Ste 320.... Tampa FL 33602 813-341-3500
Web: arnima.com

Arowana Consulting Inc
1550 Park Ave Ste 202.... South Plainfield NJ 07080 732-412-3567
Web: www.arowanaconsulting.com

Arrayworks Inc 135 Wood Rd.... Braintree MA 02184 781-849-9797

Arrendale Associates Inc
20484 Chartwell Ctr Dr Ste G.... Cornelius NC 28031 704-895-8025
Web: www.aaita.com

Artemis Solutions Group Inc
2501 Coolidge Rd Ste 503.... East Lansing MI 48823 517-336-9925
Web: artemis-solutions.com

Artwork Conversion Software Inc
417 Ingalls St.... Santa Cruz CA 95060 831-426-6163
Web: www.artwork.com

Aruba Networks Inc 1344 Crossman Ave.... Sunnyvale CA 94089 408-227-4500 752-0626
NASDAQ: ARUN ■ *TF:* 800-943-4526 ■ *Web:* www.arubanetworks.com

Asa Solutions Inc
2155 W Pinnacle Peak Rd Ste 201.... Phoenix AZ 85027 480-922-9532
Web: www.asasolutions.com

Ascentive LLC 50 S 16th St Ste 3575.... Philadelphia PA 19102 215-320-6000
Web: www.ascentive.com

Aspect Consulting Inc
20140 Vly Forge Cir.... King Of Prussia PA 19406 610-783-0600
Web: www.aspect-consulting.com

Aspex Inc 1984 Isaac Newton Sq W.... Reston VA 20190 703-956-9343
Web: aspex.com

Assette LLC 1 Faneuil Hall 4th Fl.... Boston MA 02109 617-723-6161
Web: www.assette.com

Assist Cornerstone Technologies Inc
150 West Civic Ctr Dr Ste 601.... Sandy UT 84070 800-732-0136
TF: 800-732-0136 ■ *Web:* www.assistcornerstone.com

At-your-service Software Inc
450 Bronxville Rd.... Bronxville NY 10708 914-337-9030
Web: www.ayssoftware.com

				Phone	Fax
Atalasoft Inc 116 Pleasant St Ste 321 *Web:* www.atalasoft.com	Easthampton	MA	01027	413-572-4443	
Atigeo LLC 800 Bellevue Way NE Ste 600 *Web:* www.atigeo.com	Bellevue	WA	98004	425-635-3900	
Atlantic Software Technologies Inc 2435 Hwy 34 *Web:* www.astworld.com	Manasquan	NJ	08736	732-223-8810	
Atlas Systems Inc 5712 Cleveland St Ste 200 *TF:* 800-567-7401 ■ *Web:* www.atlas-sys.com	Virginia Beach	VA	23462	757-467-7872	
Atlatl Inc 3000 Croasdaile Dr *Web:* sehhey.com	Durham	NC	27705	919-384-0514	
Atomic Object LLC 941 Wealthy St SE *Web:* www.atomicobject.com	Grand Rapids	MI	49506	616-776-6020	
Austin Test Inc Dba Bridge 360 10415 Morado Cir	Austin	TX	78759	512-837-8798	
Authentech Software Developers In 11285 Palmer Ln *Web:* authentech.com	Twinsburg	OH	44087	330-425-4538	
Authentify Inc 8745 W Higgins Rd Ste 240 *Web:* www.authentify.com	Chicago	IL	60631	773-243-0300	
Auto Clerk Inc 936 Dewing Ave Ste G *Web:* www.autoclerk.com	Lafayette	CA	94549	925-284-1005	
Autologue Computer Systems Inc 8452 Commonwealth Ave *Web:* www.autologue.com	Buena Park	CA	90621	714-522-3551	
Automated Trading Desk LLC 11 eWall St *Web:* www.atdesk.com	Mount Pleasant	SC	29464	843-789-2000	
Avant Solution, The 22511 Telegraph Rd Ste 115 *Web:* avantsolution.com	Southfield	MI	48033	248-423-0052	
Avidian Technologies Inc 2053 152nd Ave NE *Web:* avidian.com	Redmond	WA	98052	206-686-3001	
Avilar Technologies Inc 6760 Alexander Bell Dr Ste 105 *Web:* www.avilar.com	Columbia	MD	21046	410-290-0008	
Avineon Inc 4825 Mark Ctr Dr Ste 700 *Web:* www.avineon.com	Alexandria	VA	22311	703-671-1900	671-1901
Avior Computing Corp Nashua Airport 11 Perimeter Rd *Web:* www.aviorcomputing.com	Nashua	NH	03063	603-886-8145	
Avtech Software Inc 16 Cutler St Cutler Mill *TF:* 888-220-6700 ■ *Web:* www.avtech.com	Warren	RI	02885	401-847-6700	
Avval Inc 1255 Windham Pkwy *Web:* www.avval.com	Romeoville	IL	60446	630-343-6860	
Axcient Inc 1161 San Antonio Rd *TF:* 800-715-2339 ■ *Web:* www.axcient.com	Mountain View	CA	94043	800-715-2339	
Axiom Software Ltd 400 Columbus Ave *TF:* 800-588-8805 ■ *Web:* www.axiomsw.com	Valhalla	NY	10595	914-769-8800	
AXIOM Systems Inc 241 E Fourth St Ste 200 *Web:* www.axiom-systems.com	Frederick	MD	21701	301-815-5220	
Axletree Solutions Inc 2 King Arthur Court Lakeside W Ste A-1 *Web:* www.axletrees.com	North Brunswick	NJ	08902	732-296-0001	
Axxiem Corp 578 Warburton Ave *Web:* www.axxiem.com	Hastings On Hudson	NY	10706	914-478-7600	
Axxis Inc 1295 Bandana Blvd Ste 120 *Web:* www.axxispetro.com	St. Paul	MN	55108	651-644-8280	
Aylus Networks Inc 6 Technology Park Dr *Web:* www.aylus.com	Westford	MA	01886	978-392-4730	
Azteca Systems Inc 11075 South State St Ste 24 *Web:* www.azteca.com	Sandy	UT	84070	801-523-2751	
B Sharp Technologies Inc 23 Lesmill Rd Ste 404 *TF:* 866-994-2499 ■ *Web:* www.bsharp.com	Toronto	ON	M3B3P6	416-445-7162	
B Swing Inc 700 Washington Ave N *Web:* www.bswing.com	Minneapolis	MN	55401	612-752-1160	
B&L Associates Inc 13 Tech Cir *Web:* www.bandl.com	Natick	MA	01760	508-651-1404	
Bachmann Software & Service 270 Sparta Ave Ste 104 *Web:* www.bachmannsoftware.com	Sparta	NJ	07871	973-729-9427	
BackOffice Associates LLC 940 Route 28 *Web:* www.boaweb.com	South Harwich	MA	02661	508-430-7100	
BAHAMA Consulting Corp 4651 Nicols Rd Ste 200 *Web:* bahama-consulting.com	Eagan	MN	55122	651-994-7900	
Bahwan CyberTek Inc 209 W Central St 312 *Web:* www.bahwancybertek.com	Natick	MA	01760	508-652-0001	
Baldwin Hackett & Meeks Inc 11602 W Ctr Rd *Web:* www.bhmi.com	Omaha	NE	68144	402-333-3300	
Bamboo Solutions Corp 11417 Sunset Hills Rd Ste 105 *Web:* www.bamboosolutions.com	Reston	VA	20190	703-964-2002	
Barcontrol Systems & Services Inc 113 Edinburgh Ct *TF:* 800-947-4362 ■ *Web:* www.barcontrol.com	Greenville	SC	29607	864-421-0050	
Bare Bones Software Inc 73 Princeton St Ste 206 *Web:* www.barebones.com	North Chelmsford	MA	01863	978-251-0500	
Basis Technology Corp 1 Alewife Center *Web:* www.basistech.com	Cambridge	MA	02140	617-386-2000	
BasWare Inc 60 Long Ridge Rd *Web:* www.basware.com	Stamford	CT	06902	203-487-7900	
Bay Computer Associates Inc 136 Frances Ave *Web:* www.baycomp.com	Cranston	RI	02910	401-461-1484	
Bayou Microsystems LLC 209 Abby Rd *Web:* www.bayoumicro.com	Thibodaux	LA	70301	985-414-3949	
BCNS Technologies 116 Highwood Ave *Web:* computernetworking-repair.com	Henderson	NV	89002	702-566-5321	
Bcs Engineering 25 Grosvenor St *Web:* www.bcsengineering.com	Athens	OH	45701	740-331-4481	
Beachhead Solutions Inc 1955 The Alameda *Web:* www.beachheadsolutions.com	San Jose	CA	95126	408-496-6936	
Bedrock Prime 1309 N Wilson Rd Ste A *TF:* 866-334-5914 ■ *Web:* www.bedrockprime.com	Radcliff	KY	40160	270-351-8043	
Behavior LLC 40 W 27th St Rm 1200 Ste 401 *Web:* www.behaviordesign.com	New York	NY	10001	212-532-4002	
Bellsoft Inc 3545 Cruise Rd Ste 102 *Web:* www.bellsoftinc.com	Lawrenceville	GA	30044	770-935-4152	
BEM Interactive Inc 416 Gallimore Dairy Rd Ste N *Web:* beminteractive.com	Greensboro	NC	27409	336-851-0040	
Bender Rbt Inc 17 Cardinale Ln *Web:* www.benderrbt.com	Queensbury	NY	12804	518-743-8755	
Benedict Group Inc 900 Small Dr *Web:* www.benedictgroup.com	Elizabeth City	NC	27909	252-330-4892	
Benefit Express Services LLC 1700 E Golf Rd Ste 1000 *Web:* www.benefitexpress.info	Schaumburg	IL	60173	847-637-1550	
Benelogic LLC 2118 Greenspring Dr *Web:* www.benelogic.com	Timonium	MD	21093	443-322-2494	
Bennet-Tec Information Systems Inc 50 Jericho Tpke *Web:* www.bennet-tec.com	Jericho	NY	11753	516-997-5596	
BeQuick Software Inc 4280 Professional Ctr Dr Ste 200 *Web:* www.bequick.com	Palm Beach Gardens	FL	33410	561-721-9600	
Berkeley Varitronics Systems Inc 255 Liberty St Liberty Corporate Park *Web:* www.bvsystems.com	Metuchen	NJ	08840	732-548-3737	
Berndt Group Ltd, The 3618 Falls Rd *Web:* www.berndtgroup.net	Baltimore	MD	21211	410-889-5854	
Betis Group Inc 6711 Lee Hwy *Web:* www.betis.com	Arlington	VA	22205	703-532-2008	
Bframe Data Systems Inc 3057 Peachtree Industrial Blvd Ste 200 *TF:* 800-833-1059 ■ *Web:* www.bframe.com	Duluth	GA	30097	678-387-0100	
Big Creek Software LLC 201 N Third St Ste E *Web:* www.bigcreek.com	Polk City	IA	50226	515-984-6243	
BigLever Software Inc 10500 Laurel Hill Cove *Web:* www.biglever.com	Austin	TX	78730	512-426-2227	
Bill.com Inc 1810 Embarcadero Rd *Web:* www.bill.com	Palo Alto	CA	94303	650-621-7700	
Billpro Management Systems Inc 30575 Euclid Ave *TF:* 800-736-0587 ■ *Web:* www.billpro.net	Wickliffe	OH	44092	440-516-3776	
BIPT Inc 5971 Cattleridge Blvd Ste 101 *Web:* focustechnologies.net	Sarasota	FL	34232	941-342-0077	
BIS Computer Solutions Inc 2428 Foothill Blvd *Web:* www.biscomputer.com	La Crescenta	CA	91214	818-248-5023	
Bit by Bit Computing 5233 Mccandlish Rd *Web:* bitbybitcomputing.com	Grand Blanc	MI	48439	810-694-7477	
BitWise Inc 1515 Woodfield Rd Ste 740 *Web:* www.bitwiseglobal.com	Schaumburg	IL	60173	847-969-1500	
Bizzuka Inc 105 Chapel Dr Ste 300 *Web:* www.bizzuka.com	Lafayette	LA	70506	337-216-4423	
Blackfin Technology Inc 1702 W Fairview Ave	Boise	ID	83702	208-338-1581	336-1795
Blue Chip Computer Systems 6733 S Sepulveda Blvd Ste 150 *Web:* www.bccs.com	Los Angeles	CA	90045	310-410-0126	
Blue Frog Solutions Inc 555 S Andrews Ave Ste 202	Pompano Beach	FL	33069	954-788-0700	
Blue Mountain Quality Resources Inc 1963 Cato Ave *Web:* coolblue.com	State College	PA	16801	814-234-2417	
Blueye Corp 1321 N Wood St *Web:* www.blueye.com	Chicago	IL	60622	773-342-1200	
Bluware Inc 16285 Park 10 Pl Ste 300 *Web:* www.bluware.com	Houston	TX	77084	713-335-1500	
BobCAD-CAM Inc 28200 US Hwy 19 N Ste E *Web:* www.bobcad.com	Clearwater	FL	33761	727-442-3554	
Bodhtree Solutions Inc 210 Hammond Ave *Web:* www.bodhtree.com	Fremont	CA	94539	408-954-8700	
Boingo Wireless Inc 10960 Wilshire Blvd Ste 800 *TF:* 800-880-4117 ■ *Web:* www.boingo.com	Los Angeles	CA	90024	310-586-5180	586-4060
Bond Consulting Services 3450 Spring St Ste 108 *Web:* www.bondconsultingservices.com	Long Beach	CA	90806	562-988-3451	
Boost Motor Group Inc 3080 Yonge St *TF:* 877-266-7841 ■ *Web:* www.boostmotorgroup.com	Toronto	ON	M4N3N1	416-487-7000	
Boston Logic Technology Partners Inc 81 Wareham St *Web:* www.bostonlogic.com	Boston	MA	02118	617-266-9166	
Boyer & Associates Inc 3525 Plymouth Blvd Ste 207 *Web:* www.boyerassoc.com	Plymouth	MN	55447	763-412-4300	
Bradford Technologies Inc 302 Piercy Rd *TF:* 866-445-8367 ■ *Web:* www.bradfordsoftware.com	San Jose	CA	95138	408-360-8520	
BrainX Inc 45 Rincon Dr Ste 103-3B *Web:* www.brainx.com	Camarillo	CA	93012	805-384-1001	
BTM Solutions Inc 572 Yorkville Rd E *Web:* www.btmsolutions.com	Columbus	MS	39702	662-328-2400	
BuildASign.com 11525B Stonehollow Dr Ste 220 *Web:* www.buildasign.com	Austin	TX	78758	512-374-9850	
Bullhorn Inc 33-41 Farnsworth St 5th Fl *Web:* www.bullhorn.com	Boston	MA	02210	617-478-9100	
Buscomm Inc 11696 Lilburn Park Rd *Web:* www.buscomminc.com	Saint Louis	MO	63146	314-567-7755	
Byrne Software Technologies Inc 16091 Swingley Ridge Rd Ste 200 *Web:* www.byrnesoftware.com	Chesterfield	MO	63017	636-537-2505	
Bytewyze 120 Iowa Ln Ste 101 *Web:* www.bytewyze.com	Cary	NC	27511	919-465-1916	

Company / Address	City	State	ZIP	Phone	Fax
C R I 8280 Greensboro Dr Ste 400 — *Web:* www.cri-solutions.com	Mc Lean	VA	22102	703-356-6956	
C-Sharp Technologies Inc 4700 Coolbrook Dr — *Web:* www.c-sharp.com	Hilliard	OH	43026	614-668-7182	
C2k 10555 Jefferson Blvd	Culver City	CA	90232	310-279-5530	
CAD Zone Inc, The 4790 SW Watson — *Web:* www.cadzone.com	Beaverton	OR	97005	503-641-1342	
Cake Development Corp 1785 E Sahara Ave Ste 490-423 — *Web:* www.cakedc.com	Las Vegas	NV	89104	702-425-5085	
Camcad Technologies Inc 5840 Red Bug Lake Rd Ste 175 — *Web:* www.camcadtech.com	Winter Springs	FL	32708	407-327-4975	
Canton Group, The 2920 Odonnell St — *Web:* cantongroup.com	Baltimore	MD	21224	410-675-5708	
Capstone Technology Corp 14300 SE 1st St — *Web:* www.capstonetechnology.com	Vancouver	WA	98684	360-619-5010	
Capstone Worldwide Inc 30 W Monroe St Ste 910 — *Web:* capstoneww.com	Chicago	IL	60603	312-854-7300	
CareEvolution Inc 320 Miller Ave Ste 195 — *Web:* careevolution.com	Ann Arbor	MI	48104	734-678-4788	
CareWatch Inc 3483 Satellite Blvd Ste 211 S — *Web:* www.carewatch.com	Duluth	GA	30096	770-409-0244	
Carillon Financials Corp 13601 Preston Rd Ste 550 — *Web:* www.carillon.us	Dallas	TX	75240	972-437-2230	
Carina Technology Inc 1300 Meridian St Ste A-13 — *TF:* 866-915-5464 ■ *Web:* www.carinatek.com	Huntsville	AL	35806	256-704-0422	
Carlson Software Inc 102 W Second St — *Web:* www.carlsonsw.com	Maysville	KY	41056	606-564-5028	
Carnegie Learning Inc 437 Grant St — *TF:* 888-851-7094 ■ *Web:* www.carnegielearning.com	Pittsburgh	PA	15219	412-690-6284	690-2444
Castellan Inc 16255 Ventura Blvd Ste 930 — *Web:* www.castellan.net	Encino	CA	91436	818-789-0088	
Catalpa Systems Inc 53 W Jackson Blvd # 552 — *Web:* www.catalpa-systems.com	Chicago	IL	60604	312-663-3658	
Cats Co 1607 E Big Beaver Rd Ste 110 — *Web:* www.catscompany.com	Troy	MI	48083	248-816-2287	
Cayuse Technologies LLC 72632 Coyote Rd — *Web:* www.cayusetechnologies.com	Pendleton	OR	97801	541-278-8200	
CDM Technologies Inc 2975 McMillan Ave Ste 272	San Luis Obispo	CA	93401	805-541-3750	
Celt Corp 65 Boston Post Rd W Ste 200 — *Web:* celtcorp.com	Marlborough	MA	01752	508-624-4474	
Cencotech Inc 141 Adelaide St W Ste 1600 — *Web:* www.cencotech.com	Toronto	ON	M5H3L5	416-861-1474	
Centriq University 8700 State Line Rd Ste 200 — *Web:* www.centriq.com	Leawood	KS	66206	913-322-7000	
Cepstral LLC 1801 E Carson St 2nd Fl — *Web:* www.cepstral.com	Pittsburgh	PA	15203	412-432-0400	
Channelnet 3 Harbor Dr Ste 206 — *Web:* www.channelnet.com	Sausalito	CA	94965	415-332-4704	332-1635
Chapman Location Systems 941 Clint Moore Rd — *Web:* c3ls.com	Boca Raton	FL	33487	561-995-9004	
Charles River Analytics Inc 625 Mt Auburn St Ste 3 — *TF:* 877-547-4600 ■ *Web:* www.cra.com	Cambridge	MA	02138	617-491-3474	868-0780
Cherryroad Technologies Inc 301 Gibraltar Dr Ste 2C — *TF:* 877-402-7804 ■ *Web:* www.cherryroad.com	Morris Plains	NJ	07950	973-402-7802	402-7808
Cimarron Software Services Inc 1115 Gemini — *Web:* www.cimarroninc.com	Houston	TX	77058	281-226-5100	226-5190
Cimetrics Inc 141 Tremont St Fl 11 — *Web:* www.cimetrics.com	Boston	MA	02111	617-350-7550	
Cipherspace LLC 376 Main St Ste 100 — *Web:* www.cipherspace.com	Bedminster	NJ	07921	973-630-1050	
Cistera Networks Inc 6509 Windcrest Dr Ste 160 — *Web:* web.cistera.com	Plano	TX	75024	972-381-4699	
Cisys Inc 8386 Six Forks Rd — *TF:* 844-494-9236 ■ *Web:* www.cisys.com	Raleigh	NC	27615	844-494-9236	
Citizant Inc 5180 Parkstone Dr Ste 100 — *TF:* 877-248-4926 ■ *Web:* citizant.com	Chantilly	VA	20151	703-667-9420	
Clairvia Inc 2525 Meridian Pkwy Ste 100 — *Web:* www.atstaff.com	Durham	NC	27713	919-382-8282	
Claricent Inc 22 Preserve way — *TF:* 888-325-6496 ■ *Web:* www.claricent.com	Sturbridge	MA	01566	888-325-6496	
Clarity Software Solutions Inc 92 Wall St Ste 1 — *Web:* www.clarityssi.com	Madison	CT	06443	203-453-3999	
ClearPoint Inc 89 Willow Ave Unit 1R — *Web:* www.clearpointlearning.com	Hoboken	NJ	07030	201-683-9944	
Clients First Business Solutions LLC 670 N Beers St Bldg 4 — *TF:* 866-677-6290 ■ *Web:* www.clientsfirst-us.com	Holmdel	NJ	07733	866-677-6290	
Clinicient Inc 708 SW Third Ave Ste 400 — *Web:* www.clinicient.com	Portland	OR	97204	503-525-0275	
ClioSoft Inc 39500 Stevenson Pl Ste 110 — *Web:* www.cliosoft.com	Fremont	CA	94539	510-790-4732	
CMA Consulting Services Inc 700 Troy Schenectady Rd — *TF:* 800-276-6101 ■ *Web:* www.cma.com	Latham	NY	12110	518-783-9003	783-5093
Coastal Software & Consulting Inc 1101 Se 182nd Ave — *Web:* www.coastalsoftware.com	Vancouver	WA	98683	360-891-6174	
Coaxis Inc 1515 SE Water Ave Ste 300 — *Web:* viewpoint.com	Portland	OR	97214	971-255-4800	
Code Green Networks Inc 385 Moffett Park Dr Ste 105 — *Web:* www.codegreennetworks.com	Sunnyvale	CA	94089	408-716-4200	
Code Red Inc 10 Milk St 10th Fl Ste 1050 — *Web:* www.coderedinc.com	Boston	MA	02108	617-330-4100	
CogniTech Corp 1060 East 100 South Ste 306 — *Web:* www.cognitech-ut.com	Salt Lake City	UT	84102	801-322-0101	
Cognitim Inc 455 N Whisman Rd Ste 400 — *Web:* www.cognitim.com	Mountain View	CA	94043	650-404-8000	
Coherent Solutions Inc 1600 Utica Ave S Ste 120 — *Web:* www.coherentsolutions.com	Minneapolis	MN	55416	612-279-6262	
CollabNet Inc 8000 Marina Blvd Ste 600 — *TF:* 888-532-6823 ■ *Web:* www.collab.net	Brisbane	CA	94005	650-228-2500	228-2501
College Health Services LLC 144 Turnpike Rd Ste 240 — *TF:* 866-636-8336 ■ *Web:* www.studenthealth101.com	Southborough	MA	01772	866-636-8336	
Collins Computing Inc 26050 Acero St — *Web:* www.collinscomputing.com	Mission Viejo	CA	92691	949-457-0500	
Commercial Programming Systems Inc 4400 Coldwater Canyon Ave — **Fax Area Code:* 818 ■ *TF:* 888-277-4562 ■ *Web:* www.cpsinc.com	Studio City	CA	91604	323-851-2681	301-1996*
COMPanion Corp 1831 Ft Union Blvd — *Web:* www.companioncorp.com	Salt Lake City	UT	84121	801-943-7277	
Companion Professional Services LLC 1301 Gervais St Ste 1700 — *TF:* 800-780-1170 ■ *Web:* www.tmfloyd.com	Columbia	SC	29201	803-765-1310	765-1431
Competitive Innovations LLC 2724 Dorr Ave Ste 100G — *Web:* www.cillc.com	Fairfax	VA	22031	703-698-5000	
Complete Innovations Inc 475 Cochrane Dr Ste 8 — *Web:* www.fleetcomplete.com	Markham	ON	L3R9R5	905-944-0863	
Complete Systems Support 2 Rosemar Cir Ste A — *Web:* www.cssiwv.com	Parkersburg	WV	26104	304-428-2143	
Compli 610 SW Broadway Ste 600 — *Web:* www.compli.com	Portland	OR	97205	503-294-2020	
Component Control Inc 1731 Kettner Blvd — *Web:* www.componentcontrol.com	San Diego	CA	92101	619-696-5400	
Compu-data International LLC 431 Nursery Rd Ste A300 — *TF:* 866-936-6069 ■ *Web:* www.cdlac.com	Spring	TX	77380	281-292-1333	
CompuPros Ltd 2 Bent Tree Twr 16479 Dallas Pkwy Ste 800 — *Web:* www.compupros.com	Addison	TX	75001	972-250-4504	
Compusearch Software Systems Inc 21251 Ridgetop Cir — **Fax Area Code:* 703 ■ *TF:* 855-817-2720 ■ *Web:* www.compusearch.com	Dulles	VA	20166	571-449-4000	481-3442*
Computech Corp 100 W Kirby St Ste 101 — *Web:* www.computechcorp.com	Detroit	MI	48202	248-594-6500	
Computek Inc 355 Crawford St Ste 214 — *Web:* www.e-computek.com	Portsmouth	VA	23704	757-399-0320	
Computer Aid Inc (CAI) 1390 Ridgeview Dr — *TF:* 877-432-7228 ■ *Web:* www.compaid.com	Allentown	PA	18104	610-530-5000	530-5298
Computer Analyst Service & Support 28116 Orchard Lk Rd — *Web:* www.cass-tech.com	Farmington Hills	MI	48334	248-538-7374	
Computer Arts Inc 320 SW Fifth Ave — *TF:* 800-365-9335 ■ *Web:* www.gocai.com	Meridian	ID	83642	208-385-9335	
Computer Frontiers Inc 5970 Frederick Crossing Ln Ste 101 — *Web:* www.computer-frontiers.com	Frederick	MD	21704	301-601-0624	
Computer Guidance Corp 15035 N 75th St — *TF:* 888-361-4551 ■ *Web:* www.computerguidance.com	Scottsdale	AZ	85260	480-444-7000	444-7001
Computer Office Solutions 7266 Sw 48th St — *Web:* www.snappydsl.com	Miami	FL	33155	305-663-8620	
Computer Parts Warehouse 4681 Calle Bolero — *Web:* www.thecpw.com	Camarillo	CA	93012	805-987-5882	
Computer Team Inc 1049 State St — *Web:* www.computerteam.com	Bettendorf	IA	52722	563-355-0426	
ComputerLogic Inc 4951 Forsyth Rd — *Web:* www.computerlogic.com	Macon	GA	31210	478-474-5593	
ComputerSmith Inc 457 Lazelle Rd — *Web:* computersmith.com	Westerville	OH	43081	614-436-0131	
Computerworks of Chicago Inc 5153 N Clark St — *TF:* 800-977-8212 ■ *Web:* www.booklog.com	Chicago	IL	60640	773-275-4437	
Computing Integrity Inc 60 Belvedere Ave — *Web:* cintegrity.com	Richmond	CA	94801	510-233-5400	
Computrition Inc 19808 Nordhoff Pl — **Fax Area Code:* 818 ■ *TF:* 800-222-4488 ■ *Web:* www.computrition.com	Chatsworth	CA	91311	800-222-4488	701-1702*
COMSO Inc 6303 Ivy Ln Ste 300 — *Web:* www.comso.com	Greenbelt	MD	20770	301-345-0046	
Comspark International Inc 3265 W Sarazens Cir Ste 201 — *Web:* www.comsparkint.com	Memphis	TN	38125	901-758-0261	
Concept Dynamics Ltd 5435 Bull Vly Rd Ste 306 — *Web:* cdlweb.net	Mchenry	IL	60050	815-344-1392	
Concurrent EDA LLC 5001 Baum Blvd Ste 640 — *Web:* www.concurrenteda.com	Pittsburgh	PA	15213	412-687-8800	
ConEst Software Systems Inc 592 Harvey Rd — *Web:* www.conest.com	Manchester	NH	03103	603-437-9353	
CoNetrix LLC 5214 68th St Ste 200 — *TF:* 800-356-6568 ■ *Web:* www.conetrix.com	Lubbock	TX	79424	806-687-8600	
CONIX Systems Inc 7252 Main St — *TF:* 800-332-1899 ■ *Web:* conix.com	Manchester Center	VT	05255	800-332-1899	
Construx Software 11820 Northup Way Ste E-200 — *TF:* 866-296-6300 ■ *Web:* www.construx.com	Bellevue	WA	98005	425-636-0100	636-0159
Consult Usa Inc 634 Alpha Dr — *TF:* 866-963-8621 ■ *Web:* consultusa.com	Pittsburgh	PA	15238	412-963-8621	
Contemporary Software Concepts Inc 455 Pennsylvania Ave Ste 205 — *Web:* www.consoftware.com	Fort Washington	PA	19034	610-687-6000	
Continuum Performance Systems Inc 634 Boston Post Rd — *Web:* www.continuumperformance.com	Madison	CT	06443	203-245-5000	

Phone Fax

Control Systems International Inc
8040 Nieman Rd. . . . Lenexa KS 66214 913-599-5010 599-5013

Corning Data Services Inc 139 Wardell St . . . Corning NY 14830 607-936-4241
Web: corningdata.com

Corporate Systems Engineering LLC
1215 Brookville Way. . . . Indianapolis IN 46239 317-375-3600
Web: www.corporatesystems.com

Corptax LLC 1751 Lk Cook Rd Ste 100 . . . Deerfield IL 60015 800-966-1639 236-8011*
**Fax Area Code:* 847 ■ *TF:* 800-966-1639 ■ *Web:* www.corptax.com

Coyote Software Corp
3425 Harvester Rd Ste 216. . . . Burlington ON L7N3N1 905-639-8533
Web: coyotecorp.com

Credant Technologies Inc
15303 Dallas Pkwy Ste 1420 . . . Addison TX 75001 972-458-5400 458-5454
TF: 800-929-8331

Crescendo Systems Corp 1600 Montgolfier . . . Laval QC H7T0A2 450-973-8029
TF: 800-724-2930 ■ *Web:* www.crescendo.com

CRM Innovation 8527 Bluejacket St . . . Lenexa KS 66214 913-492-2764
Web: www.crminnovation.com

Croop-LaFrance Inc 7647 Main St Fishers. . . . Victor NY 14564 585-869-6100
Web: www.croop-lafrance.com

Crowdstar Inc 330 Primrose Rd Ste 306. . . . Burlingame CA 94010 650-347-4166
Web: crowdstar.com

CRT Systems Inc 742 Anderson Rd N. . . . Rock Hill SC 29730 803-327-9030

CS Solutions Inc 3440 Federal Dr Ste 100 . . . Eagan MN 55122 651-603-8288
Web: www.cssolutionsinc.com

CSG Professional Services Inc
734 NW 14th Ave . . . Portland OR 97209 503-292-0859
Web: csgpro.com

CTE Solutions Inc 11 Holland Ave Ste 100. . . . Ottawa ON K1Y4S1 613-798-5353
TF: 800-699-4007 ■ *Web:* www.ctesolutions.com

CTH Technologies Inc
18w140 Butterfield Rd . . . Oakbrook Terrace IL 60181 331-684-9700
Web: www.cthtech.com

CTL Inc 375 Bridgeport Ave. . . . Shelton CT 06484 203-925-4266
Web: www.ctlinc.com

Culinary Software Services Inc
1900 Folsom St Ste 210. . . . Boulder CO 80302 303-447-3334
TF: 800-447-1466 ■ *Web:* www.culinarysoftware.com

Curl Inc 1 Cambridge Ctr 10th Fl . . . Cambridge MA 02142 617-761-1200
Web: curl.com

Customer Service Delivery Platform Corp
15615 Alton Pkwy Ste 310 . . . Irvine CA 92618 888-741-2737
TF: 888-741-2737 ■ *Web:* www.csdpcorp.com

Cutting Edge 1825 Gillespie Way Ste 100. . . . El Cajon CA 92020 619-258-7800
TF: 800-257-1666 ■ *Web:* www.cuttedge.com

Cyber-Ark Software Inc 60 Wells Ave. . . . Newton MA 02459 617-965-1544 965-1644
TF: 888-808-9005 ■ *Web:* cyberark.com

Cyberchrome Inc 3642 Main St . . . Stone Ridge NY 12484 845-687-2671
Web: cyberchromeusa.com

CyberMark International Inc
2222 W Parkside Ln Ste 116 . . . Phoenix AZ 85027 623-889-3380
Web: www.cybermark.com

Cybersoft North America Inc
1500 S Dairy Ashford St Ste 190 . . . Houston TX 77077 281-752-0600
Web: www.csnainc.com

CyberThink Inc 1125 US Hwy 22 Ste 1. . . . Bridgewater NJ 08807 908-429-8008 429-8004
Web: www.cyberthink.com

Cyberwolf Inc 1596 Pacheco St Ste 203 . . . Santa Fe NM 87505 505-983-6463
Web: www.cyberwolf.com

Cymbel Corp 154 Wells Ave. . . . Newton MA 02459 617-581-6633
Web: www.cymbel.com

D-Ta Systems Inc 2500 Lancaster Rd. . . . Ottawa ON K1B4S5 613-745-8713
TF: 877-382-3222 ■ *Web:* www.d-ta.com

Data Advantage Group Inc
604 Mission St. . . . San Francisco CA 94105 415-947-0400
Web: www.dag.com

Data Financial Inc 1100 Glen Oaks Ln. . . . Mequon WI 53092 262-243-5511
Web: www.datafinancial.com

Data Inc 72 Summit Ave. . . . Montvale NJ 07645 201-802-9800
Web: www.datainc.biz

Data Integrity Inc 228 Highland Ave . . . West Newton MA 02465 617-964-1977
Web: www.dii2000.com

Data Management Marketing 3225 Jordan Blvd. . . . Malabar FL 32950 321-725-8081
TF: 888-266-4127 ■ *Web:* www.dmm-marketing.com

Data Paradigm Inc 2323 Bryan St Ste 2600. . . . Dallas TX 75201 214-468-0200 722-1860
Web: dataparadigm.com

Data Select Systems Inc
2829 Townsgate Rd Ste 300. . . . Westlake Village CA 91361 805-446-2090
Web: www.clcsiii.com

Data Ventures 1475 Central Ave Ste 230 . . . Los Alamos NM 87544 505-662-6655
Web: www.dataventures.com

Data3 Corp 2448 E 81st St Ste 700 . . . Tulsa OK 74137 918-237-4400
Web: www.datathree.com

Databased Solutions Inc 1200 Route 22. . . . Bridgewater NJ 08807 908-314-0000
Web: www.dbsiservices.com

DataCeutics Inc 1610 Medical Dr Ste 300 . . . Pottstown PA 19464 610-970-2333
Web: www.dataceutics.com

Dataclarity Corp
7200 Falls Of Neuse Rd Ste 202. . . . Raleigh NC 27615 919-256-6700
Web: www.dataclaritycorp.com

Datacor Inc 25 Hanover Rd Ste 300B . . . Florham Park NJ 07932 973-822-1551
Web: www.datacorinc.com

Datafirst Corp 5124 Departure Dr . . . Raleigh NC 27616 919-876-6650
TF: 800-634-8504 ■ *Web:* www.datafirst.com

Dataflux Corp 940 NW Cary Pkwy Ste 201 . . . Cary NC 27513 919-447-3000 447-3100
TF: 800-727-0025

Datalink Software Consultants Inc
4745 N Seventh St Ste 200. . . . Phoenix AZ 85014 602-279-7788
Web: www.datalinksc.com

Datalogic Software Inc
1501 S 77 Sunshinestrip . . . Harlingen TX 78550 956-412-1424
Web: www.vesta.net

Phone Fax

DataMAX Software Group Inc, The
1101 Investment Blvd Ste 250 . . . El Dorado Hills CA 95762 916-939-4065
Web: www.datamaxsg.com

Dataprise Inc 9600 Blackwell Rd 4th Fl. . . . Rockville MD 20850 301-945-0700
Web: www.dataprise.com

DataWorks Plus LLC 728 N Pleasantburg Dr . . . Greenville SC 29607 864-672-2780
Web: www.dataworksplus.com

Davis Powers Inc 640 N La Salle Dr Ste 565 . . . Chicago IL 60654 312-654-9239
Web: davispowers.com

DAZ Systems Inc 880 Apollo St Ste 201 . . . El Segundo CA 90245 310-640-1300
Web: www.dazsi.com

Dealogic LLC 120 Broadway 8th Fl . . . New York NY 10271 212-577-4400
Web: www.dealogic.com

Debt Buyers Inc 3080 S Durango Dr Ste 208 . . . Las Vegas NV 89117 702-946-8440
Web: www.srcnv.com

deCarta Inc 4 N Second St Ste 950. . . . San Jose CA 95113 408-294-8400
Web: www.decarta.com

DecisionPoint Systems Inc
19655 Descartes . . . Foothill Ranch CA 92610 949-465-0065 215-9642
OTC: DPSI ■ *TF:* 800-336-3670 ■ *Web:* www.decisionpt.com

Decker Wright Corp 628 Shrewsbury Ave . . . Red Bank NJ 07701 732-747-9373
Web: www.deckerwright.com

Decurtis Corp 2314 Longmoore Ct . . . Orlando FL 32835 407-522-8722
Web: www.decurtis.com

Defined Logic LLC 116 Chestnut St . . . Red Bank NJ 07701 732-222-4310
Web: definedlogic.com

Dekker Ltd 3633 Inland Empire Blvd . . . Ontario CA 91764 909-384-9000 889-9163

Delta Data Software Inc
700 Brookstone Centre Pkwy . . . Columbus GA 31904 706-324-0855
Web: www.deltadatasoft.com

DeltaSoft Inc 624 Courtyard Dr. . . . Hillsborough NJ 08844 908-595-9777
Web: www.deltasoftinc.com

Demiurge Studios Inc 130 Prospect St 1st Fl . . . Cambridge MA 02139 617-354-7772
Web: demiurgestudios.com

DeNA Global Inc 1 Waters Park Dr Ste 165. . . . San Mateo CA 94403 650-638-1026
Web: dena.com/intl

Denim Group Ltd
1354 N Loop 1604 E Ste 110 . . . San Antonio TX 78232 844-572-4400
TF: 844-572-4400 ■ *Web:* www.denimgroup.com

Denodo Technologies 530 Lytton Ave Ste 301 . . . Palo Alto CA 94301 650-566-8833
Web: www.denodo.com

Desco Dental Systems LLC
5005 W Loomis Rd Ste 100 . . . Greenfield WI 53220 414-281-9192
TF: 800-392-7610 ■ *Web:* descodental.com

Design Hub Inc 600 W Michigan Ave Ste C. . . . Saline MI 48176 734-944-8705
Web: www.design-hub.com

Devicenet USA Inc 4000 Moorpark Ave Ste 116. . . . San Jose CA 95117 408-557-0413
Web: www.devicenet-usa.com

DeviceVM 1054 S De Anza Blvd Ste 200 . . . San Jose CA 95129 408-861-1088
Web: www.devicevm.com

Dh Web Inc 11377 Robinwood Dr Ste D. . . . Hagerstown MD 21742 301-733-7672
TF: 877-567-6599 ■ *Web:* www.dhwebsites.com

Diagnos Inc Ste 340 7005 Taschereau Blvd. . . . Brossard QC J4Z1A7 450-678-8882
Web: www.diagnos.ca

Digilabs Inc 1032 Elwell Ct Ste 245. . . . Palo Alto CA 94303 650-390-9749
Web: www.digilabs.com

Digital ChoreoGraphics PO Box 8268. . . . Newport Beach CA 92658 949-548-1969
TF: 800-548-1969 ■ *Web:* www.dcgfx.com

Digital Dogs Inc 16416 N 92nd St Ste 120. . . . Scottsdale AZ 85260 480-451-3647
Web: www.digitaldogs.com

Digital I-OIlc 1424 30th St. . . . San Diego CA 92154 619-423-4433
TF: 866-423-4433 ■ *Web:* www.digitalio.com

Digital Intelligence Systems Corp
8270 Greensboro Dr. . . . Chantilly VA 20151 703-752-7900
Web: www.disys.com

Digital Motorworks Inc
8601 RR 2222 Ste 400 Bldg I. . . . Austin TX 78730 512-349-9360
Web: www.digitalmotorworks.com

Digital Pictures 212 N Second St. . . . Minneapolis MN 55401 612-371-4515
Web: www.digitalpictures.com

Dino Software Corp
1912 Earldale Ct 200 PO Box 7105 . . . Alexandria VA 22306 703-768-2610
Web: www.dino-software.com

Discovery Information Technologies Inc
904 N Memorial Fwy . . . Nederland TX 77627 409-727-7080
Web: www.discoveryit.com

Distant Horizon 16612 W 159th St . . . Frankfort IL 60441 815-836-3410
Web: www.distanthorizon.com

Distek Integration Inc
1110 N County Rd 2350. . . . Carthage IL 62321 217-357-3100
Web: www.distek.com

DMI Technology Group 406 Kays Dr . . . Normal IL 61761 309-828-4439
Web: www.deskmic.com

Document Storage Systems Inc
12575 US Hwy 1 Ste 200-A . . . Juno Beach FL 33408 561-284-7000
Web: www.docstorsys.com

Donatech Corp 2094 185th St Ste 110 . . . Fairfield IA 52556 641-472-7474
Web: www.donatech.com

Dorian Business Systems Inc 1985 Forest Ln . . . Garland TX 75042 214-556-1912
Web: dorianbusinesssystems.com

Double Infinity Inc 14414 Detroit Ave . . . Lakewood OH 44107 216-228-7500
Web: www.doubleinfinity.com

DoubleCheck LLC
101 Gilbraltar Dr Ste 1E. . . . Morris Plains NJ 07950 973-984-2229
Web: www.doublechecksoftware.com

DrivenBI LLC 221 E Walnut St Ste 229. . . . Pasadena CA 91101 626-795-2088
Web: www.drivenbi.com

Droege Computing Services Inc
20 W Colony Pl Ste 120. . . . Durham NC 27705 919-403-9459
Web: droegecomputing.com

Droste Consultants Inc 140 Willow St . . . North Andover MA 01845 978-686-5775
Web: www.droste1.com

Phone *Fax*

DSD Business Systems Inc
5120 Shoreham Pl Ste 280 .... San Diego CA 92122 858-550-5900
Web: www.dsdinc.com

DSG Systems Inc 56 Inverness Dr E Ste 260 .... Englewood CO 80112 303-790-0453 790-0866
Web: www.dsgsys.com

Duley Hopkins & Assoc Inc
1200 Mtn Creek Rd .... Chattanooga TN 37405 423-877-1220
Web: dha-us.com

Dunn Solutions Group Inc
5550 W Touhy Ave Ste 400 .... Skokie IL 60077 847-673-0900
Web: www.dunnsolutions.com

Duo Consulting Inc 641 W Lk St Ste 301 .... Chicago IL 60661 312-529-3000
Web: www.duoconsulting.com

Dynaxys LLC 11911 Tech Rd .... Silver Spring MD 20904 301-622-0900
Web: www.dynaxys.com

E p Radiological Services Inc
8040 Remmet Ave Ste 1 .... Canoga Park CA 91304 818-313-9729
Web: www.epradinc.com

e3 Solutions Inc 50 Richmond St E Ste 200 .... Toronto ON M5C1N7 416-640-7033
Web: e3solutionsinc.com

EADOC 180 Grand Ave Ste 995 .... Oakland CA 94612 510-903-9658
Web: www.eadocsoftware.com

Eagle Applied Sciences LLC
1826 N Loop 1604 W Ste 350 .... San Antonio TX 78248 210-477-9242 581-8609
Web: www.eagle-app-sci.com

Eagle Technology Inc 11019 N Towne Sq Rd .... Mequon WI 53092 262-241-3845
Web: www.eaglecmms.com

ECCO Select Corp
4100 N Mulberry Dr Ste 400 .... Kansas City MO 64116 816-960-3800
Web: www.eccoselect.com

Ecd Systems Inc 2415 W Erie Dr .... Tempe AZ 85282 480-609-6300
Web: www.ecdsys.com

Echo Assoc Inc 933 Ridge Dr .... Mclean VA 22101 703-448-0633
Web: callecho.com

Echo Group Inc, The 15 Washington St .... Conway NH 03818 603-447-8600
Web: www.echoman.com

Edge Systems LLC 3S721 W Ave Ste 200 .... Warrenville IL 60555 630-810-9669 810-9228
TF Tech Supp: 800-352-3343 ■ *Web:* www.edge.com

Edgenet Inc 2948 Sidco Dr .... Atlanta GA 30326 615-371-3848
TF: 877-334-3638 ■ *Web:* www.edgenet.com

EdgeWave Inc 15333 Ave of Science .... San Diego CA 92128 858-676-2277
Web: www.edgewave.com

EdTek Services Inc 30 Wascana Ave .... Toronto ON M5A1V5 647-435-7133 827-1184*
**Fax Area Code:* 888 ■ *Web:* www.edtekservices.com

Education Management Systems Inc
4110 Shipyard Blvd .... Wilmington NC 28403 910-799-0121
TF: 800-541-8999 ■ *Web:* www.mealsplus.com

Effone Software Inc 1294 Kifer Rd Ste 709 .... Sunnyvale CA 94086 408-830-1010
Web: www.effone.com

eHire LLC 3565 Piedmont Rd NE Ste 300 .... Atlanta GA 30305 404-477-2680
Web: www.ehire.com

ElanTech Inc 7852 Walker Dr Ste 425 .... Greenbelt MD 20770 301-486-0600
Web: www.ameritas.com/wps/portal/corp

Electrocon International Inc
405 Little Lk Dr .... Ann Arbor MI 48103 734-761-8612
TF: 888-240-4044 ■ *Web:* www.electrocon.com

Elkco Corp 50 Dangelo Dr Ste 5 .... Marlborough MA 01752 508-842-2111
Web: www.elkco.com

Ellie Mae Inc 4155 Hopyard Rd Ste 200 .... Pleasanton CA 94588 925-227-7000
TF: 800-848-4904 ■ *Web:* elliemae.com

Ellkay 259 Cedar Ln .... Teaneck NJ 07666 201-791-0606
Web: www.ellkay.com

Emaint Enterprises LLC 438 N Elmwood Rd .... Marlton NJ 08053 856-810-2700
Web: emaint.com

Embedded Data Systems LLC
2019 Fortune Dr .... Lawrenceburg KY 40342 502-859-5490
Web: www.embeddeddatasystems.com

Emberex Inc 220 E 11th Ave Ste 6 .... Eugene OR 97401 541-687-5778
Web: www.emberex.com

Emfluence 106 W 11Th St Ste 2220 .... Kansas City MO 64105 816-472-5643
Web: www.emfluence.com

EmLogis Inc 9800 Richmond Ave Ste 235 .... Houston TX 77042 713-785-0960
Web: www.emlogis.com

Empower Financials Inc
305 E Eisenhower Ste 318 .... Ann Arbor MI 48108 734-747-9393
Web: empowerfin.com

Enabling Technologies Corp
12226 Long Green Pk .... Glen Arm MD 21057 443-625-5100
Web: www.enablingtechcorp.com

Endeavor Commerce Inc 13140 Coit Ste 450 .... Dallas TX 75240 214-736-7178
Web: endeavorcpq.com

Energent Inc 22 Frederick St Ste 1114 .... Kitchener ON N2H6M6 519-725-0906
Web: www.energent.com

Enfold Systems Inc 4617 Montrose Blvd .... Houston TX 77006 713-942-2377
Web: www.enfoldsystems.com

EngagePoint Inc 3901 Calverton Blvd Ste 110 .... Calverton MD 33309 301-388-7900
Web: www.consumerhealthtech.com

enherent Corp 6800 Jericho Turnpike Ste 116E .... Syosset NY 11791 732-321-1004
Web: www.enherent.com

Enilon Group 945 Foch St .... Fort Worth TX 76107 817-632-3200
Web: www.enilon.com

Enlightened Inc 1100 15th St N W Ste 300 .... Washington DC 20005 202-728-7190
Web: www.nlightened.com

Enounce Inc 2666 E Bayshore Rd .... Palo Alto CA 94303 650-494-6200
Web: www.enounce.com

Ensyte Energy Software International
770 S Post Oak Ln Ste 330 .... Houston TX 77056 713-622-2875
Web: www.ensyte.com

Enteo Software Inc
1150 Kelly Johnson Blvd Ste 102 .... Colorado Springs CO 80920 847-706-9400
Web: www.enteo.com

Entero Corp 1040 Seventh Ave SW Ste 500 .... Calgary AB T2P3G9 403-261-1820
TF: 877-261-1820 ■ *Web:* www.entero.com

Enterprise Computing Solutions Inc
26024 Acero .... Mission Viejo CA 92691 949-609-1980
Web: www.thinkecs.com

Enterprise Information Services Inc
1945 Old Gallows Rd Ste 500 .... Vienna VA 22182 703-749-0007
Web: www.goeis.com

Enthought Inc 515 Congress Ave Ste 2100 .... Austin TX 78701 512-536-1057
Web: www.enthought.com

Envision Technology Advisors LLC
999 Main St .... Pawtucket RI 02860 401-272-6688
Web: www.envisionsuccess.net

Epac Software Technologies Inc
42 Ladd St .... East Greenwich RI 02818 888-336-3722
TF: 888-336-3722 ■ *Web:* www.epacst.com

Ephibian Inc 3180 N Swan Rd .... Tucson AZ 85712 520-917-4747
Web: www.ephibian.com

Ephox Corp 2100 Geng Rd .... Palo Alto CA 94303 650-292-9659
Web: ephox.com

Epitec Inc 24800 Denso Dr Ste 150 .... Southfield MI 48033 248-353-6800
Web: epitec.com

Eportation LLC 401 S Second St Ste 305 .... Philadelphia PA 19147 215-627-2651
Web: www.eportation.com

Eric A. King 301 Grant St Ste 4300 .... Pittsburgh PA 15219 281-667-4200
TF: 888-742-2454 ■ *Web:* www.the-modeling-agency.com

eRIDE Inc
1 Letterman Drive Bldg C Ste 310 .... San Francisco CA 94129 415-848-7800
Web: www.eride.com

eROI Inc 505 NW Couch Ste 300 .... Portland OR 97209 503-221-6200
Web: www.eroi.com

Esprida Corp 5180 Orbitor Dr .... Mississauga ON L4W5L9 905-629-0455
Web: www.esprida.com

Et International 100 White Clay Ctr Ste 103 .... Newark DE 19711 302-738-1438
Web: etinternational.com

ETC ComputerLand 3206 Kochs Ln .... Quincy IL 62305 217-228-6180
Web: www.etccomputerland.com

ethosIQ LLC 17121 W Rd 201 .... Houston TX 77095 281-616-5711
Web: www.ethosiq.com

Eti-Net Inc 180 Rene Levesque E Ste 320 .... Montreal QC H2X1N6 514-395-1200
Web: www.etinet.com

Eureka Software Solutions Inc
3305 Northland Dr Ste 305 .... Austin TX 78731 512-459-9292
Web: www.eurekasoft.com

Eureka Technocrats Inc 1985 W Big Beaver Rd .... Troy MI 48084 248-816-1617
Web: www.eurekatek.com

Evans Caseload Inc 1915 Danforth Ave .... Toronto ON M4C1J5 416-762-0236
Web: caseload.com

Everest Consulting Group Inc
3840 Pk Ave Ste 203 .... Edison NJ 08820 732-548-2700 548-6200
Web: www.everestconsulting.net

Execusys Inc 6767 N Wickham Rd .... Melbourne FL 32940 321-253-0077
TF: 800-454-3081 ■ *Web:* execusys.com

Experts Exchange LLC PO Box 1062 .... San Luis Obispo CA 93406 805-787-0603
Web: www.experts-exchange.com

Experts Inc, The
2400 E Commercial Blvd Ste 614 .... Fort Lauderdale FL 33308 954-493-8040

Extensis 1800 SW First Ave Ste 500 .... Portland OR 97201 503-274-2020 274-0530
TF: 800-796-9798 ■ *Web:* www.extensis.com

Externetworks 10 Corporate Pl S .... Piscataway NJ 08854 732-465-0001
Web: www.externetworks.com

Eyefinity Inc
10875 International Dr Ste 200 .... Rancho Cordova CA 95670 877-448-0707
TF: 877-448-0707 ■ *Web:* www.eyefinity.com

Fabtrol Systems Inc 1025 Willamette St Ste 300 .... Eugene OR 97401 541-345-1494
Web: www.fabtrol.com

Fairway Technologies Inc
7825 Fay Ave Ste 100 .... La Jolla CA 92037 858-454-4471
Web: fairwaytech.com

Femme Comp Inc 14170 Newbrook Dr Ste 100 .... Chantilly VA 20151 703-961-1818
Web: www.femmecomp.com

FieldWorker Products Ltd
1092 Islington Ave Ste 202 .... Etobicoke ON M8Z4S1 416-483-3485
Web: www.fieldworker.com

FileTrail Inc 111 N Market St Ste 715 .... San Jose CA 95113 408-289-1300
Web: www.filetrail.com

Fillmore Group Inc, The
8501 La Salle Rd Ste 318 .... Towson MD 21286 410-465-6335
Web: www.thefillmoregroup.com

Financial Navigator Inc
883 N Shoreline Blvd Ste D-100 .... Mountain View CA 94043 650-962-0300
Web: www.finnav.com

Financial Software Systems Inc
100 Tournament Dr Ste 300 .... Horsham PA 19044 215-784-1100
Web: www.finsoftware.com

Fine Technology Solutions
7936 Grado El Tupelo .... Carlsbad CA 92009 760-274-2370
Web: www.fineonline.com

Fire Engine Red 700 Locust St Apt A4 .... Philadelphia PA 19106 215-829-1850
Web: fire-engine-red.com

First Insight Corp
22845 NW Bennett St Bldg B Ste 200 .... Hillsboro OR 97124 503-707-8600
Web: www.first-insight.com

Five K Computers & Internet Services
104 S Sixth Ave .... Yakima WA 98902 509-575-3600
Web: www.fivek.com

Fleet Advantage LLC
401 E Las Olas Blvd 17th Fl .... Fort Lauderdale FL 33301 954-615-4400
Web: www.fleetadvantage.net

Fm3 Systems Inc 20118 N 67th Ave Ste 110 .... Phoenix AZ 85023 602-288-1416
Web: fm3systems.com

Focus 360 Inc 27721 La Paz Rd .... Laguna Niguel CA 92677 949-234-0008
Web: www.focus360.com

Folderwave 238 Littleton Rd Ste 204 .... Westford MA 01886 978-392-2055
Web: www.folderwave.com

Phone Fax

Forcex Inc 2208 Charlotte Ave....... Nashville TN 37203 931-368-0111
Web: www.forcexinc.com
Foremost Media 1337 Excalibur Dr....... Janesville WI 53546 608-758-4841
Web: foremostmedia.com
Formotus Inc 9725 SE 36th St Ste 400....... Mercer Island WA 98040 206-973-5060
Web: www.formotus.com
Fortifire Inc 46560 Fremont Blvd Ste 119....... Fremont CA 94538 510-651-7770
Web: www.fortifire.com
Freedom Scientific Inc
11800 31st Court N....... St. Petersburg FL 33716 727-803-8000
TF: 800-444-4443 ■ *Web:* www.freedomscientific.com
Friedman Corp 1 Pkwy N Ste 400S....... Deerfield IL 60015 847-948-7180
Web: www.csisoftware.com
Fulcrum Technologies Inc 712 Aurora Ave N....... Seattle WA 98109 206-336-5656
Web: www.fulcrum.net
Full Spectrum Software 225 Tpke Rd....... Southborough MA 01772 508-620-6400
Web: www.fullspectrumsoftware.com
FusionOne Inc 11 N Roselle Rd....... Roselle IL 60172 408-282-1200
FusionStorm 2 Bryant St Ste 150....... San Francisco CA 94105 415-623-2626 623-2630
TF: 800-228-8324 ■ *Web:* www.fusionstorm.com
Futrend Technology Inc
8605 Westwood Ctr Dr Ste 502....... Vienna VA 22182 703-556-0016
TF: 866-388-7363 ■ *Web:* www.futrend.com
Future Computing Solutions Inc
23800 Via Del Rio....... Yorba Linda CA 92887 714-692-9120
Web: www.fcsinet.com
Future Tech Enterprise Inc 101-8 Colin Dr....... Holbrook NY 11741 631-472-5500 472-6599
Web: www.ftei.com
Future Visions Inc 3424 Stony Spring Cir....... Louisville KY 40220 502-499-6337
Web: futurevisions.com
G2 Software Systems Inc
4250 Pacific Hwy #125....... San Diego CA 92110 619-222-8025
Web: g2ss.com
Gallagher Systems Group Inc 2502 N Clark St....... Chicago IL 60614 773-348-5400
Gates Business Solutions LLC
2418 Crossroads Dr Ste 3600....... Madison WI 53718 608-661-0810
Gavel & Gown Software Inc 365 Bay St Ste 700....... Toronto ON M5H2V1 416-977-6633
Web: amicusattorney.com
Gcom Software Inc 24 Madison Ave Ext....... Albany NY 12203 518-869-1671
Web: www.gcomsoft.com
GDI Infotech Inc 3775 Varsity Dr....... Ann Arbor MI 48108 734-477-6900 477-7100
Web: www.gdii.com
GeBBS Healthcare Solutions Inc
560 Sylvan Ave Second Fl....... Englewood Cliffs NJ 07632 888-539-4282
TF: 888-539-4282 ■ *Web:* www.gebbs.com
Gene Codes Corp 775 Technology Dr....... Ann Arbor MI 48108 734-769-7249
TF: 800-497-4939 ■ *Web:* www.genecodes.com
Genesis Concepts & Consultants LLC
1777 Ne Loop 410 Ste 1009....... San Antonio TX 78217 210-451-5100
Web: www.genconcepts.com
Genesisfour Corp 7747 Ten Acre Rd....... Andrews SC 29510 843-461-4117 443-1303*
**Fax Area Code:* 978 ■ *TF:* 800-937-4364 ■ *Web:* www.service2k.com
Genova Technologies Inc
4250 River Ctr Court NE Ste A....... Cedar Rapids IA 52402 319-378-8455
Web: www.genovatech.com
Gevity Consulting Inc 375 Water St Ste 350....... Vancouver BC V6B5C6 604-608-1779
Web: www.global-village.net
GIDEON Informatics Inc
8721 Santa Monica Blvd Ste 234....... Los Angeles CA 90069 323-934-0000
Web: www.gideononline.com
Gilltek Systems Intl Inc 2409 S Rural Rd Ste C....... Tempe AZ 85282 480-831-5565
Web: www.gilltek.com
Gisbiz Inc 25 Century Blvd Ste 602....... Nashville TN 37214 615-465-8287
Web: www.gisbiz.com
Givenhansco Inc
2400 Corporate Exchange Dr Ste 103....... Columbus OH 43231 614-310-0060
Web: www.givenhansco.com
GL Communications Inc
818 W Diamond Ave 3rd Fl....... Gaithersburg MD 20878 301-670-4784
Web: www.gl.com
Glaser Technology Inc 123 W Madison St 1100....... Chicago IL 60602 312-578-0377
Web: www.glasertechnology.com
Glenbriar Technologies Inc 736-1100 8 Ave SW....... Calgary AB T2P1H4 403-233-7300
Web: www.glenbriar.com
Global Micro Solutions Inc
21250 Hawthorne Blvd Ste 540....... Torrance CA 90503 310-218-5678
Web: www.gmsnet.com
Global Nest LLC 281 State Rt 79 N Ste 208....... Morganville NJ 07751 732-333-5848
TF: 866-850-5872 ■ *Web:* www.globalnest.com
Global Reach Internet Productions LLC
2321 N Loop Dr Ste 101....... Ames IA 50010 515-996-0996
TF: 877-254-9828 ■ *Web:* www.globalreach.com
Global Solutions Network Inc
121 Congressional Ln Ste 302....... Rockville MD 20852 301-881-7012 881-7014*
**Fax Area Code:* 703 ■ *Web:* www.gsnhome.com
Gloto Corp 8171 Maple Lawn Blvd Ste 250....... Fulton MD 20759 301-317-9800
Web: gloto.com
Glu Mobile Inc 500 Howard St Ste 300....... San Francisco CA 94105 415-800-6100
Web: www.glu.com
Go 2 Group 138 N Hickory Ave....... Bel Air MD 21014 410-879-8102
TF: 877-442-4669 ■ *Web:* www.go2group.com
Good Design LLC 450 Industrial Park Rd....... Deep River CT 06417 860-526-1600
Web: gooddesignusa.com
Gorton Studios 4640 Nicols Rd Ste 205....... Saint Paul MN 55122 651-365-7891
Web: gortonstudios.com
Government Systems Technologies Inc
3159 Schrader Rd....... Dover NJ 07801 973-361-2627
Web: www.gstiusa.com
GP Solutions Inc 201 N Charles St Ste 2406....... Baltimore MD 21201 410-244-8548
Web: www.gpsonline.com
GPC Systems Inc 2108B Gallows Rd....... Vienna VA 22182 703-760-9700

Phone Fax

GPS Insight LLC
21803 N Scottsdale Rd Ste 220....... Scottsdale AZ 85255 480-663-9454
Web: www.gpsinsight.com
Grapnel Tech Services LLC
6905 Vista Dr....... West Des Moines IA 50266 515-953-5767
Web: www.grapneltech.com
Graycon Group Ltd 325 10th Ave SW....... Calgary AB T2R0A5 403-508-2255
Web: www.graycon.com
Great South Texas Corp 814 Arion Pkwy....... San Antonio TX 78216 210-369-0300
TF: 800-531-3858 ■ *Web:* www.comsoltx.com
Greenleaf Media 1917 Winnebago St Ste 100....... Madison WI 53704 608-240-9611
Web: greenleafmedia.com
Gregg Engineering Inc 403 Julie Rivers Dr....... Sugar Land TX 77478 281-494-8100
Web: www.greggeng.com
Grid Net Inc 126 S Park St Ste 501....... San Francisco CA 94107 415-872-5097
Web: www.grid-net.com
Grupo -sms 2525 Main St Ste 200....... Irvine CA 92614 949-223-9240
Web: www.grupo-sms.com
GSL Solutions Inc 1411 N W Shore Blvd Ste 204....... Tampa FL 33607 813-637-8535
Web: www.gslsolutions.com
Gst Information Technology Solutions
13043 166th St....... Cerritos CA 90703 562-345-8700 345-8701
TF: 800-833-0128 ■ *Web:* www.gstes.com
Guest-tek Ltd 240, 3030 - Third Ave N.E....... Calgary AB T2A6T7 403-509-1010
Web: www.guesttek.com
Gulo Solutions LLC 1467 N Elston Ave Ste 105....... Chicago IL 60642 773-276-8066
Web: www.gulosolutions.com
Gwynn Group 600 E Las Colinas Blvd Ste 150....... Irving TX 75039 214-485-5990
Web: www.gwynngroup.com
H & W Computer Systems Inc
6154 N Meeker Pl Ste 100....... Boise ID 83713 208-377-0336 377-0069
TF: 800-338-6692 ■ *Web:* www.hwcs.com
Hagerman Inc 510 W Washington Blvd....... Fort Wayne IN 46802 260-424-1470
Web: www.thehagermangroup.com
HAL Inc 11109 Cutten Rd Ste 200....... Houston TX 77066 281-260-8181
Web: www.hal-inc.com
Halden Group, The 5948 Harbour Park Dr....... Midlothian VA 23112 804-595-2295
Web: www.haldengroup.com
Hall Mark Global Technologies Inc
262 Chapman Rd Ste 101....... Newark DE 19702 302-366-8960
Web: www.hgtechinc.net
Halsted Communications Ltd
13 Commerce Dr....... Ballston Spa NY 12020 518-885-8590
Hammer Data Systems LLC 8138 Main St....... Garrettsville OH 44231 330-527-4018
Web: www.hammerdata.com
Hanson Information System
2433 W White Oaks Dr....... Springfield IL 62704 217-726-2400
TF: 888-245-8468 ■ *Web:* hansoninfosys.com
Harmonia Inc 2020 Kraft Dr Ste 1000....... Blacksburg VA 24060 540-951-5900
Web: www.harmonia.com
Harmonix Music Systems Inc
625 Massachusetts Ave....... Cambridge MA 02139 617-491-6144
Web: harmonixmusic.com
Harvey Software Inc
7050 Winkler Rd Ste 104....... Fort Myers FL 33919 800-231-0296
TF: 800-231-0296 ■ *Web:* www.harveysoft.com
Hawk Ridge Systems 5707 Redwood Rd Ste 18....... Oakland CA 94619 510-482-6110
Web: hawkridgesys.com
Hbm Integrated 600-1496 Bedford Hwy....... Bedford NS B4A1E5 902-835-9611
Web: www.hbmintegrated.com
HDF Group 1800 S Oak St Ste 203....... Champaign IL 61820 217-531-6100
Web: www.hdfgroup.org
Health Care Software Inc PO Box 2430....... Farmingdale NJ 07727 800-524-1038 938-5380*
**Fax Area Code:* 732 ■ *TF:* 800-524-1038 ■ *Web:* www.hcsinteractant.com
Health Information Designs Inc
391 Industry Dr....... Auburn AL 36832 334-502-3262
Healthcare Automation Inc 41 Sharpe Dr....... Cranston RI 02920 401-572-3040 572-3350
TF: 800-738-8850 ■ *Web:* www.healthcare-automation.com
Healthco Information Systems Inc
7657 Sw Mohawk St....... Tualatin OR 97062 503-612-1666
Web: www.healthcosystems.com
Helix Computer Systems Inc
2401 Hydraulic Rd....... Charlottesville VA 22901 434-963-4900
Web: www.helixsystems.com
Heller Consulting Inc
1736 Franklin St Ste 600....... Oakland CA 94611 510-841-4222
Web: www.teamheller.com
Henning Industrial Software Inc
102 First St Ste 211....... Hudson OH 44236 330-650-4212
Web: henningsoftware.com
Henschen & Associates Inc
432 W Gypsy Ln....... Bowling Green OH 43402 419-352-5454
Web: henschen.com
Hensley, Elam & Associates LLC
163 E Main St Ste 401....... Lexington KY 40507 859-389-8182
Web: www.hea.biz
Heuristic Park Inc 1512 Emory Rd Ne....... Atlanta GA 30306 404-373-7786
Web: www.heuristicpark.com
Hiasun Inc 5218 Atlantic Ave PO Box 785....... Mays Landing NJ 08330 609-625-0565
Web: hiasun.com
Higher One Inc 115 Munson St....... New Haven CT 06511 203-776-7776
Web: higherone.com
Highfleet Inc 3600 Odonnell St Ste 600....... Baltimore MD 21224 410-675-1201
Web: highfleet.com
Hitachi ID Systems Inc
500 1401 - First St SE Ste 500....... Calgary AB T2G2J3 403-233-0740
Web: www.hitachi-id.com
Hive Group Inc, The
2201 N Central Expy Ste 180....... Richardson TX 75080 972-808-0400
Web: www.hivegroup.com
Hobsons Digital Media Inc
1000 Broadway Ste 350....... Cincinnati OH 94607 513-891-5444
Web: www.hobsons.com

Name / Address	City	State	Zip	Phone	Fax
HolaDoctor Inc 30 Mansell Court Ste 215 *Web:* www.holadoctor.net	Roswell	GA	30076	770-649-0298	
Horizon Software International LLC 2915 Premier Pkwy Ste 300 *Web:* www.horizon-boss.com	Duluth	GA	30097	770-554-6353	
Horton Group 136 Rosa L Parks Blvd. *Web:* www.hortongroup.com	Nashville	TN	37203	615-292-8642	
HSMC Orizon 2007 E Prairie Cir. *Web:* hsmcorizon.com/technology-consulting-services	Olathe	KS	66062	816-525-9699	
HTC Global Services Inc 3270 W Big Beaver Rd *Web:* htcinc.com	Troy	MI	48084	248-786-2500	
Hubspan Inc 505 Fifth Ave S Ste 350	Seattle	WA	98104	206-838-5400	838-5449
Human Factors International Inc 410 W Lowe Ave. *TF:* 800-242-4480 ■ *Web:* www.humanfactors.com	Fairfield	IA	52556	641-472-4480	472-5412
Human Head Studios 1741 Commercial Ave Ste 200 *Web:* humanhead.com	Madison	WI	53704	608-440-8582	
Hx5 LLC 212 Eglin Pkwy Se *Web:* www.hxfive.com	Fort Walton Beach	FL	32548	850-362-6551	
HyperDisk Marketing Inc 18251 McDurmott W Ste A *TF:* 800-241-1210 ■ *Web:* www.hyperdisk.com	Irvine	CA	92614	949-442-9850	
I C S Solutions Inc 11964 Oak Creek Pkwy. *Web:* www.icss.com	Huntley	IL	60142	847-515-8000	
I. s Outsource Inc 19119 N Creek Pkwy Ste 200 *TF:* 800-240-2821 ■ *Web:* www.isoutsource.com	Bothell	WA	98011	206-374-0251	
iAdvantage Software Inc 404 E Chatham St. *Web:* www.iadvantagesoftware.com	Cary	NC	27511	919-469-3888	
Iars Systems Engineers 4121 Tytahun Cres Ste 200 *Web:* www.iars-syseng.com	West Vancouver	BC	V6N3N1	778-772-9419	
Idea Works Inc, The 100 W Briarwood Ln *TF:* 800-537-4866 ■ *Web:* www.ideaworks.com	Columbia	MO	65203	573-445-4554	
Ideal Software Systems Inc 4909 29th Ave *TF:* 800-964-3325 ■ *Web:* www.idealss.com	Meridian	MS	39305	601-693-1673	
IGEL Technology Inc 5353 NW 35th Ave *Web:* www.igel.com	Fort Lauderdale	FL	33309	954-739-9990	
Ignify Inc 200 Pine Ave 4th Fl *TF:* 888-599-4332 ■ *Web:* www.ignify.com	Long Beach	CA	90802	562-219-2000	
Ignite! Learning Inc 4030 W Braker Ln Ste 175 *Web:* www.ignitelearning.com	Austin	TX	78759	512-697-7000	
Illuminet Inc 4501 Intelco Loop SE *Web:* www.illuminet.com	Olympia	WA	98507	360-493-6000	
iLookabout Corp 383 Richmond St Ste 408 *TF:* 866-963-2015 ■ *Web:* www.ilookabout.com	London	ON	N6A3C4	519-963-2015	
Image API LLC 2002 Old St Augustine Rd Bldg D *TF:* 877-560-4274 ■ *Web:* www.imageapi.com	Tallahassee	FL	32301	850-222-1400	
Image Architects Inc 784 Morris Tpke *Web:* www.imagearch.com	Short Hills	NJ	07078	973-912-9334	
Imaginet Resources Corp 233 Portage Ave *TF:* 800-989-6022 ■ *Web:* imaginet.com	Winnipeg	MB	R3B2A7	204-989-6022	
Imec Technologies Inc 702 Bloomington Rd *Web:* www.imectechnologies.com	Champaign	IL	61820	217-643-7488	
Impact Interactive 5400 Laurel Springs Pkwy Ste 1003 *Web:* www.impact-interactive.com	Suwanee	GA	30024	678-679-6000	
implement.com Corp 701 N 36th St Ste 310 *Web:* www.implement.com	Seattle	WA	98103	206-547-8100	
Implementation & Consulting Services Inc 5066R W Chester Pk. *Web:* www.ics-corporate.com	Newtown Square	PA	19073	610-355-7750	
In-Touch Insight Systems Inc 400 March Rd *TF:* 800-263-2980 ■ *Web:* www.intouchinsight.com	Ottawa	ON	K2K3H4	800-263-2980	
Inclind Inc Web Development Services 208 W Market St. *Web:* www.inclind.com	Georgetown	DE	19947	302-856-2802	
Indigo BioSystems Inc 7820 Innovation Blvd Ste 250 *Web:* www.indigobio.com	Indianapolis	IN	46278	317-493-2400	
INDUS Corp 1951 Kidwell Dr. *Web:* www.induscorp.com	Vienna	VA	22182	703-506-6700	
Industrial Logic Inc 829 Bancroft Way *Web:* www.industriallogic.com	Berkeley	CA	94710	510-540-8336	
Infiniedge Software Inc 14320 Infiniedge Way *Web:* www.infiniedge.com	Prairieville	LA	70769	225-677-8902	
Infinite Campus Inc 4321 109th Ave NE *Web:* www.infinitecampus.com	Blaine	MN	55449	651-631-0000	
Info-Power International Inc 3345 Silverstone Dr *Web:* www.abw.com	Plano	TX	75023	972-424-4447	
Infoaccess.net LLC 8801 E Pleasant Vly Rd. *TF:* 800-255-0253 ■ *Web:* www.infoaccess.net	Cleveland	OH	44131	216-328-0100	
Infocrossing Inc 2 Christie Heights St *Web:* ww2.infocrossing.com	Leonia	NJ	07605	201-840-4700	
InfoExpress Inc 170 S Whisman Rd Ste B *Web:* www.infoexpress.com	Mountain View	CA	94041	650-623-0260	
Informant Technologies Inc 19 Jenkins Ave Ste 200 *TF:* 877-503-4636 ■ *Web:* www.informant-tech.com	Lansdale	PA	19446	215-412-9165	
Infosemantics 2605 Sagebrush Dr Ste 207 *Web:* www.infosemantics.com	Flower Mound	TX	75028	469-941-0266	
Infosilem Inc 99 Rue Emilien-marcoux *Web:* www.infosilem.com	Blainville	QC	J7C0B4	450-420-5565	
Infosource Inc 1300 City View Ctr *TF:* 800-393-4636 ■ *Web:* www.infosourcelearning.com	Oviedo	FL	32765	407-796-5200	796-5190
Infostretch Corp 2880 Lakeside Dr Ste 200 *Web:* infostretch.com	Santa Clara	CA	95054	408-727-1100	
Ingenuite Inc 7701 S Western Ave Ste 204 *Web:* ingenuite.com	Oklahoma City	OK	73139	405-636-1802	
Ingenuity Systems Inc 1700 Seaport Blvd 3rd Fl *Web:* www.ingenuity.com	Redwood City	CA	94063	650-381-5100	
inhouseIT 3193 Red Hill Ave *Web:* www.inhouseit.com	Costa Mesa	CA	92626	949-660-5655	
Inland Productivity Solutions Inc 1153 W Ninth St *Web:* www.inland-prod.com	Upland	CA	91786	909-981-4500	
Inmedius Inc 2247 Babcock Blvd. **Fax Area Code:* 412 ■ *TF:* 800-697-7110 ■ *Web:* www.inmedius.com	Pittsburgh	PA	15237	800-697-7110	459-0311*
Innography Inc 3900 N Capital Of Tx Hwy Ste 175	Austin	TX	78746	512-306-8688	
Innovasystems International LLC 2385 Northside Dr Ste 300 *Web:* www.innovasi.com	San Diego	CA	92108	619-955-5800	955-5801
InnovaTech Inc 1800 Diagonal Rd *Web:* www.innovateteam.com	Alexandria	VA	22314	703-418-3919	
Innovative Data Management Systems LLC 4006 W Azeele St *TF:* 866-706-4588 ■ *Web:* idmsystems.com	Tampa	FL	33609	813-207-2025	
Innovative Systems Group Inc 799 Roosevelt Rd *TF:* 800-739-2400 ■ *Web:* www.innovativesys.com	Glen Ellyn	IL	60137	630-858-8500	
inRESONANCE Inc 32 Industrial Dr E Ste 100 *Web:* www.inresonance.com	Northampton	MA	01060	413-587-0236	
Insequence Inc 750 Jim Parker Dr *Web:* www.insequence.com	Smyrna	TN	37167	615-459-8943	
Insight Technology Solutions Inc 17251 Melford Blvd Ste 100 *Web:* www.insighttsi.com	Bowie	MD	20715	301-860-1121	
Insurance Technology Consultants Inc (ITC) 2090 N Tustin Ave Ste 260 *Web:* www.itc-systems.com	Santa Ana	CA	92705	714-442-8702	
Insurity Inc 170 Huyshope Ave *TF:* 866-476-2606 ■ *Web:* insurity.com	Hartford	CT	06106	860-616-7721	
Integrated Alliances LLC 1777 Larimer St Ste 1905 *Web:* www.integratedalliances.com	Denver	CO	80202	303-683-9600	
Integrated Data Services Inc 2141 Rosecrans Ave Ste 2050 *Web:* www.idserve.com	El Segundo	CA	90245	631-265-7162	366-4317
Integrated Digital Technologies Corp 1501 S Brand Blvd *Web:* www.idt.edu	Glendale	CA	91204	818-396-3511	
Integrated Document Solutions Inc 3511 W Commercial Blvd *Web:* www.idssite.com	Fort Lauderdale	FL	33309	954-484-0969	
IntegriChain Inc 1628 JFK Blvd Ste 117 *Web:* www.integrichain.com	Philadelphia	PA	19103	609-806-5005	
Integrity Systems & Solutions LLC 1247 Highland Ave Ste 202 *TF:* 866-446-8797 ■ *Web:* www.integrityss.com	Cheshire	CT	06410	203-271-7971	
Intelligent Software Solutions Inc 5450 Tech Ctr Dr *Web:* www.issinc.com	Colorado Springs	CO	80919	719-452-7000	452-7001
Intellinetics 2190 Dividend Dr *Web:* www.intellinetics.com	Columbus	OH	43228	614-921-8170	
Intepros Consulting Inc 750 Marrett Rd *Web:* www.intepros.com	Lexington	MA	02421	781-761-1140	
Interdynamix 620-10180 101 St Nw *Web:* www.interdynamix.com	Edmonton	AB	T5J3S4	780-423-7005	
Intex Solutions Inc 110 A St *Web:* www.intex.com	Needham	MA	02494	781-449-6222	
Intrafinity Inc 60 ADELAIDE St E. *Web:* www.intrafinity.com	Toronto	ON	M5C3E4	416-848-9722	
InVision Software Inc 110 Lk Ave S Ste 35 *Web:* www.invisionsoft.com	Nesconset	NY	11767	631-360-3400	
IPextreme Inc 54 N Central Ave Ste 204 *Web:* www.ip-extreme.com	Campbell	CA	95008	408-540-0095	
IQMax Inc 15720 Brixham Hill Ave Ste 300 *Web:* iqmax.com	Charlotte	NC	28277	704-377-2202	
IQMS Inc 2231 Wisteria Ln *Web:* www.iqms.com	Paso Robles	CA	93446	805-227-1122	
iRise 2301 Rosecrans Ave Ste 4100 *Web:* www.irise.com	El Segundo	CA	90245	310-426-7800	
Ironspeed 2870 Zanker Rd #210 *Web:* ironspeed.com	San Jose	CA	95134	408-228-3400	
ISBX Corp 3415 S Sepulveda Blvd Ste 1250 *Web:* www.isbx.com	Los Angeles	CA	90034	310-437-8010	
Isc Sales Inc 4421 Tradition Trl. *TF:* 800-836-7472 ■ *Web:* www.iscenclosurecooling.com	Plano	TX	75093	972-964-2700	
isee systems Inc Wheelock Office Park 31 Old Etna Rd Ste 7N *Web:* www.iseesystems.com	Lebanon	NH	03766	603-448-4990	
Isis Papyrus America Inc 301 Bank St *Web:* www.isis-papyrus.com	Southlake	TX	76092	817-416-2345	416-1223
Island Key Computer Ltd 938 Howe St *Web:* www.islandkey.com	Vancouver	BC	V6Z1N9	604-669-8178	
Island Micro Solutions Inc 3375 Koapaka St Ste B282 *Web:* solutionshawaii.com	Honolulu	HI	96819	808-833-6048	
Island Technologies 17408 Chatsworth St Ste 200 *Web:* www.islandtechnologies.net	Granada Hills	CA	91344	818-832-2310	
ISR Info Way Inc 559 Donofrio Dr Ste 101 & 102 *Web:* www.isrinfo.com	Madison	WI	53719	608-827-7884	
ISTT Inc 846 Broadway Ave. *Web:* isttechnology.com	Bowling Green	KY	42101	270-781-5096	
It Doctors 2175 Northdale Blvd Nw *TF:* 888-472-2287 ■ *Web:* zinncorp.com	Minneapolis	MN	55433	763-267-6980	
Itology.com Ltd 214 - 11 Ave SE Ste 210 *TF:* 877-226-7726 ■ *Web:* www.itsportsnet.com	Calgary	AB	T2G0X8	403-226-3040	

Phone Fax

IV Most Consulting Inc 33 Park Dr Mt Kisco NY 10549 800-448-6678
TF: 800-448-6678 ■ *Web:* www.ivmost.com

Ivenuecom 9925 Painter Ave Ste A Whittier CA 90605 800-683-8314
TF: 800-683-8314 ■ *Web:* www.ivenue.com

Ivory Consulting Corp 325 Lennon Ln Walnut Creek CA 94598 925-926-1100
Web: www.ivorycc.com

Iyka Enterprises 3890 E Main St Saint Charles IL 60174 630-372-3900
Web: www.iyka.com

J L Patterson & Associates
725 W Town And Country Rd Ste 300 Orange CA 92868 714-835-6355
Web: www.jlpatterson.com

Jaas Systems Ltd 555 Lancaster Ave Reynoldsburg OH 43068 614-759-4167
Web: jaas.net

JBoss Inc 3340 Peachtree Rd Ste 1200 Atlanta GA 30326 404-467-8555
Web: www.redhat.com

JDi Data Corp
2400 E Commercial Blvd Ste 322 Fort Lauderdale FL 33308 954-938-9100
Web: www.jdidata.com

Jfw Enterprises Inc 3350 Pawtucket Ave Riverside RI 02915 401-438-3030
Web: www.wallace1.com

Jolera Inc 777 Richmond St W Unit 2 Toronto ON M6J0C2 416-410-1011
Web: www.jolera.com

JRI America Inc 277 Park Ave New York NY 10172 212-224-4200
Web: www.jri-america.com

JRL Enterprises Inc
1820 St Charles Ave Ste 203 New Orleans LA 70130 504-263-1380
Web: www.icanlearn.com

Jtl Technical Services LLC 113 Crosby Rd Ste 8 Dover NH 03820 603-834-6570
Web: www.jtltechnicalservices.com

Justia Inc 1380 Pear Ave Unit 2b Mountain View CA 94043 650-810-1990
Web: www.justia.com

Justice Systems Inc 4600 McLeod NE Albuquerque NM 87109 505-883-3987 883-2845
Web: www.justicesystems.com

Kallo Inc 15 Allstate Pkwy Ste 600 Markham ON L3R5B4 416-246-9997
Web: www.kalloinc.ca

Karpel Computer Systems Inc
770 Spirit of St Saint Louis MO 63005 314-892-6300
TF: 888-294-7886 ■ *Web:* www.karpel.com

KBACE Technologies Inc 6 Trafalgar Sq Nashua NH 03063 603-821-7000
TF: 800-334-4470 ■ *Web:* www.kbace.com

Keller Schroeder & Assoc Inc
4920 Carriage Dr Evansville IN 47715 812-474-6825
Web: kellerschroeder.com

Kelly Computer Systems
1060 La Avenida St Mountain View CA 94043 650-960-1010
Web: www.kelly.com

Kepware Inc 400 Congress St 4th Fl Portland ME 04101 207-775-1660
Web: www.kepware.com

Kestrel Labs Inc 3133 Indian Rd Ste K Boulder CO 80301 303-544-0660
Web: www.kestrellabs.com

Keycentrix LLC 2420 N Woodlawn Bldg 500 Wichita KS 67220 316-262-2231
Web: www.keycentrix.com

KEYW Corp 7740 Milestone Pkwy Ste 400 Hanover MD 21076 443-733-1600 733-1601
TF: 800-340-1001 ■ *Web:* www.keywcorp.com

Klein Systems Group Ltd 360-4400 Dominion St Burnaby BC V5G4G3 604-689-7117
TF: 877-689-7117 ■ *Web:* www.kleinsystems.com

Knowcean Consulting Inc
10605 Stapleford Hall Dr Potomac MD 20854 240-672-1699
Web: knowceanconsulting.com

Knowledge Relay LLC
5836 Corporate Ave Ste 130 Cypress CA 90630 714-761-6760
Web: www.knowledgerelay.com

Knowles - Mcniff
12862 Garden Grove Blvd Ste C Garden Grove CA 92843 800-820-5254
TF: 800-820-5254 ■ *Web:* www.knowles-mcniff.us

Koni Ameri Tech Services Inc 15 Serina Dr Plainsboro NJ 08536 732-226-0727
Web: www.katsi.com

Kord Technologies Inc
1101 Mcmurtrie Dr NW Bldg A Huntsville AL 35806 256-489-2346
Web: kordtechnologies.com

Kpit Infosystems Inc 33 Wood Ave S Ste 720 Iselin NJ 08830 732-321-0921
Web: www.kpit.com

Krillion Inc 607A W Dana St Mountain View CA 94041 949-784-0800 784-0880
TF: 877-784-0805

KSM Technology Partners LLC
2650 Eisenhower Ave Norristown PA 19403 610-628-0550
Web: ksmpartners.com

KUBRA Data Transfer Ltd 5050 Tomken Rd Mississauga ON L4W5B1 905-624-2220
Web: www.kubra.com

KVS Information Systems Inc
821 Maple Rd Williamsville NY 14221 716-626-1976
Web: www.kvsinfo.com

Kyyba Inc
28230 Orchard Lk Rd Ste 130 Farmington Hills MI 48334 248-813-9665
Web: www.kyyba.com

LAITEK Inc 18101 Martin Ave Homewood IL 60430 708-799-5000
Web: www.laitek.com

Lambda Research Corp 25 Porter Rd Littleton MA 01460 978-486-0766
Web: lambdares.com

Lancet Software Development Inc
11980 Portland Ave South Burnsville MN 55337 952-230-7360
Web: www.lancetdatasciences.com

Lancore Technologies 11211 Richmond Ave Houston TX 77082 281-493-5850
TF: 866-492-5800 ■ *Web:* www.lancoretech.com

LanXpert Corp 605 Market St Ste 410 San Francisco CA 94105 415-543-1033
Web: www.intivix.com

Laser App Software Inc
3190 Shelby St Ste D 100 Ontario CA 91764 909-985-2174
Web: www.laserapp.com

Lattice3d 582 Market St Ste 1215 San Francisco CA 94104 415-274-1670
Web: www.lattice3d.com

LBi Software Inc 7600 Jericho Tpke Woodbury NY 11797 516-921-1500
Web: www.lbisoftware.com

LCG Inc 6000 Executive Blvd Ste 410 Rockville MD 20852 301-984-4004
Web: lcgsystems.com

Lead Technologies Inc
1927 S Tryon St Ste 200 Charlotte NC 28203 704-332-5532
Web: www.leadtools.com

LeadScope Inc 1393 Dublin Rd Columbus OH 43215 614-675-3730
Web: www.leadscope.com

LeapFrog Systems Inc
1 International Pl 31st Fl Boston MA 02110 617-224-9700
Web: www.leapfrogsystems.com

Learnframe Inc 9551 S 700 E Draper UT 84020 801-523-8000 523-8012

Lease Harbor LLC 414 N Orleans St Ste 602 Chicago IL 60654 312-494-9470
Web: leaseharbor.com

Leaseteam Inc 4139 S 143rd Cir Omaha NE 68137 402-493-3445
Web: leaseteam.com

Lemko Corp 1 Pierce Place Ste 700 Itasca IL 60143 630-948-3025
Web: www.lemkocorp.com

Levelfield.com Inc 11675 Jollyville Rd Ste 207 Austin TX 78759 512-401-9200
Web: www.levelfield.com

Lexicon Technologies Inc 2195 Eastview Pkwy Conyers GA 30013 888-250-4075
TF: 888-250-4075 ■ *Web:* www.lexicontech.com

LGB & Associates Inc 10400 Eaton Pl Ste 130 Fairfax VA 22030 703-359-6950
Web: www.lgb-inc.com

LHS Productions Inc 260 Union St Northvale NJ 07647 201-767-2002
Web: www.videobankdigital.com

Lieberman Software Corp
1900 Ave of the Stars Ste 425 Los Angeles CA 90067 310-550-8575
TF: 800-829-6263 ■ *Web:* www.liebsoft.com

Life:WIRE Corp 131 Bloor St W Toronto ON M5S1R1 416-690-1516
Web: www.lifewiregroup.com

Liftoff LLC 1667 Patrice Cir Crofton MD 21114 410-419-1591
Web: www.liftofflearning.com

Lightwave Management Resources
4707 140th Ave N 316 Clearwater FL 33762 727-507-0983
Web: www.sycoretech.com

Link-Systems International Inc
4515 George Rd Ste 340 Tampa FL 33634 813-674-0660
Web: www.link-systems.com

Liquidframeworks 24 E Greenway Plz Houston TX 77046 713-552-9250
Web: liquidframeworks.com

Litera Corp 5000 Crossmill Rd Mcleansville NC 27301 336-375-2991
Web: www.litera.com

Loftware Inc 166 Corporate Dr Portsmouth NH 03801 603-766-3630
Web: www.loftware.com

Logic Choice Technologies LLC
950 E Haverford Rd Bryn Mawr PA 19010 610-525-1236
Web: www.logicchoice.com

Logical Images Inc 3445 Winton Pl Ste 240 Rochester NY 14623 585-427-2790
Web: www.logicalimages.com

Logical Innovations Inc
16902 El Camino Real Ste 3C Houston TX 77058 281-990-8560
Web: www.logical-i2.com

Logicorps 35015 Automation Dr Clinton Township MI 48035 586-792-9900
Web: www.logicorps.com

LogiSense Corp 278 Pinebush Rd Ste 102 Cambridge ON N1T1Z6 519-249-0508
Web: www.logisense.com

LogiSolve LLC 600 Inwood Ave N Ste 275 Oakdale MN 55128 763-383-1000
Web: www.logisolve.com

Logix Guru LLC 3821 Old William Penn Hwy Murrysville PA 15668 724-733-4500
Web: www.logixguru.com

Long Business Systems Inc
10749 Pearl Rd Ste 2A Strongsville OH 44136 440-846-8500
Web: www.lbsi.com

Lpit Solutions Inc
25 Commerce Ave Sw Ste 200 Grand Rapids MI 49503 616-632-2225
Web: www.lpitsolutions.com

Lucas Systems Inc 11279 Perry Hwy 4th Fl Wexford PA 15090 724-940-7000
Web: www.lucasware.com

LumenVox LLC 3615 Kearny Villa Rd San Diego CA 92123 858-707-7700
Web: www.lumenvox.com

LVM Systems Inc 4262 E Florian Ave Mesa AZ 85206 480-633-8200
Web: www.lvmsystems.com

Lymba Corp 1701 N Collins Blvd Richardson TX 75080 972-680-0800
Web: www.lymba.com

Lynx Media Inc
12501 Chandler Blvd Ste 202 Valley Village CA 91607 818-761-5859
TF: 800-451-5969 ■ *Web:* lynxmedia.com

Lyynks Inc 1812 W Burbank Blvd Unit 644 Burbank CA 91506 818-478-2260
Web: lyynks.com

M2M Data Corp 8668 Concord Ctr Dr Englewood CO 80112 303-768-0064
Web: www.m2mdatacorp.com

M2S Inc 12 Commerce Ave West Lebanon NH 03784 603-298-5509 298-5055
Web: www.m2s.com

Macdac Engineering 27 Quality Ave Somers CT 06071 860-749-5544
TF: 866-529-5078 ■ *Web:* www.macdac.com

Machinima Inc 8441 Santa Monica Blvd West Hollywood CA 90069 323-301-1529
Web: www.machinima.com

Macro Group Inc, The
1200 Washington Ave S Ste 350 Minneapolis MN 55415 612-332-7880
Web: www.macrogroup.net

Macro Solutions
800 Maryland Ave NE Ste 900 Washington DC 20002 703-527-9400
Web: www.macrosolutions.com

Magnatron Inc 225 S Peters Rd Knoxville TN 37923 865-769-2622
Web: magnatron.com

Mammography Reporting System Inc
19000 33rd Ave W Ste 130 Seattle WA 98115 206-633-6145
TF: 800-253-4827 ■ *Web:* www.mrsys.com

Management Analysis Inc 2070 Chain Bridge Rd Vienna VA 22182 703-506-0505
Web: www.mainet.com

Manifest Solutions Corp
2035 Riverside Dr Upper Arlington OH 43221 614-930-2800
Web: www.manifestsc.com

Company / Address	City	State	Zip	Phone	Fax
Marathon Digital Services 716 W Pennway St *TF:* 877-568-1122 ■ *Web:* www.mysmartplans.com	Kansas City	MO	64108	816-221-7881	
Marcole Enterprises Inc 2920 Camino Diablo Ste 200 *Web:* www.marcole.com	Walnut Creek	CA	94597	925-933-9792	
Marquis Software Development Inc 1611 Jaydell Cir Ste G *Web:* marquisware.com	Tallahassee	FL	32308	850-877-8864	
Mastermedia LLC 1908 Coney Island Ave Ste 200 *Web:* www.mastermediallc.com	Brooklyn	NY	11223	718-376-3700	504-4000
Maximum Insights Inc 17295 Chesterfield Airport Rd Ste 200 *Web:* www.maximuminsights.com	Chesterfield	MO	63005	314-878-8700	
MAXON COMPUTER Inc 2640 Lavery Ct Ste A *TF:* 877-264-6283 ■ *Web:* www.maxon.net	Newbury Park	CA	91320	805-376-3333	
MaxPoint Interactive Inc 3020 Carrington Mill Blvd Ste 300 *TF:* 800-916-9960 ■ *Web:* www.maxpoint.com	Morrisville	NC	27560	800-916-9960	
Maxwell Geoservices 1168 Hamilton St *Web:* maxwellgeoservices.com	Vancouver	BC	V6B2S2	604-678-3298	
McKissock LP 218 Liberty St *Web:* www.mckissock.com	Warren	PA	16365	814-723-6979	
McLeod Software Corporation Inc 2550 Acton Rd PO Box 43200 *Web:* www.mcleodsoftware.com	Birmingham	AL	35243	205-823-5100	
Media Excel Inc 8834 N Capital of Texas Hwy Ste 270 *Web:* www.mediaexcel.com	Austin	TX	78759	512-502-0034	502-0119
Medical Information Technology Inc 6423 City W Pkwy *Web:* meditech.com	Eden Prairie	MN	55344	952-941-1000	
Medivo Inc 55 Broad St 16th Fl *TF:* 888-362-4321 ■ *Web:* www.medivo.com	New York	NY	10004	888-362-4321	
MedMatica Consulting Associates 18 Barrington Ln *Web:* www.medmatica.com	Chester Springs	PA	19425	610-827-1356	
Mekanika Inc 3998 FAU Blvd Ste 210 *Web:* www.mekanika.com	Boca Raton	FL	33431	561-210-5671	
MembersFirst Inc 321 Commonwealth Rd *Web:* www.membersfirst.com	Wayland	MA	01778	508-653-3399	
MentorMate LLC 3036 Hennepin Ave *Web:* www.mentormate.com	Minneapolis	MN	55408	612-823-4000	
Menusoft Systems Corp 7370 Steel Mill Dr *Web:* www.digitaldining.com	Springfield	VA	22150	703-912-3000	
Merchants Building Maintenance 606 Monterey Pass Rd *Web:* www.mbmonline.com	Monterey Park	CA	91754	626-281-4882	
Meridian Technology Group Inc 12909 SW 68th Pkwy Ste 340 *TF:* 800-755-1038 ■ *Web:* www.meridiangroup.com	Portland	OR	97223	503-697-1600	697-8600
Mersoft Corp Corporate Woods Bldg 55 9300 W 110th St Ste 350 *Web:* www.mersoft.com	Overland Park	KS	66210	913-871-6200	
MetaLogix Inc 9789 Charlotte Hwy Ste 400-142 *Web:* www.metalogixinc.com	Fort Mill	SC	29707	704-543-1616	
MetroStar Systems Inc 1856 Old Reston Ave Ste 100 *Web:* www.metrostarsystems.com	Reston	VA	20190	703-481-9581	
Mi-Co LLC 4601 Creekstone Dr Ste 102 *Web:* www.mi-corporation.com	Durham	NC	27703	919-485-4819	
MI9 Business Intelligence Systems Inc 12000 Biscayne Blvd Ste 600 *Web:* mi9retail.com	Miami	FL	33181	416-491-1483	
Micro Performance Inc 2569 Housley Rd *Web:* www.microperformance.com	Annapolis	MD	21401	410-224-3100	
Micro Strategies Inc 85 Bloomfield Ave *Web:* www.microstrat.com	Denville	NJ	07834	973-625-7721	
Microintegration Inc 460 stull st Ste 200 *Web:* www.microintegration.net	South Bend	IN	46601	574-256-6777	
MicroPact Inc 12901 Worldgate Dr Ste 800 *Web:* www.micropact.com	Herndon	VA	20170	703-709-6110	
Microsmarts LLC 600 Holiday Plz Dr Ste 545 *Web:* microsmartsllc.com	Matteson	IL	60443	708-748-7558	
Midwest Medical Insurance Holding Co 7650 Edinborough Way Ste 400 *Web:* www.mmicgroup.com	Minneapolis	MN	55435	952-838-6700	
Mikal Corp 4382 Mount Carmel Tobasco *Web:* www.mikal.com	Cincinnati	OH	45244	513-528-5100	
Mil Corp 4000 Mitchellville Rd *TF:* 800-875-0867 ■ *Web:* www.milcorp.com	Bowie	MD	20716	301-805-8500	805-8505
Mil-Pac Technology 1672 Main St Ste E-254 *Web:* milpac.com	Ramona	CA	92065	760-788-3030	
Military Personnel Services Corp 6066 Leesburg Pk *Web:* www.mpscrc.com	Falls Church	VA	22041	571-481-4000	
Miller Energy Inc 3200 S Clinton Ave *Web:* www.millerenergy.com	South Plainfield	NJ	07080	908-755-6700	
Mimic Technologies Inc 811 First Ave Ste 408 *Web:* www.mimicsimulation.com	Seattle	WA	98104	206-923-3337	
MIMICS Inc 2620 Dakota NE *Web:* www.mimics.com	Albuquerque	NM	87110	505-332-9220	
Mindex Technologies Inc 3495 Winton Pl *Web:* mindex.com	Rochester	NY	14623	585-424-3590	
Mindfinders Inc 1200 18th St NW Ste 550 *Web:* www.themindfinders.com	Washington	DC	20036	202-772-4177	
MindTouch Inc 401 W A St *Web:* www.mindtouch.com	San Diego	CA	92101	619-795-8459	
Mintec Inc 3544 E Ft Lowell Rd *Web:* minesight.com	Tucson	AZ	85716	520-795-3891	
Minuteman Group Inc 35 Bedford St Ste 2 *Web:* www.minuteman-group.com	Lexington	MA	02420	781-861-7493	
Miria Systems Inc 2570 Blvd of the Generals Ste 222 *Web:* www.miriasystems.com	Norristown	PA	19403	484-446-3300	
MIS Training Institute LLC 153 Cordaville Rd Ste 200 *Web:* www.misti.com	Southborough	MA	01772	508-879-7999	
Mission Critical Technologies Inc 2041 Rosecrans Ave *Web:* www.mctinc.net	El Segundo	CA	90245	310-246-4455	246-9540
Misys International Banking Systems Inc 1180 Ave *Web:* www.misys.com	New York	NY	10036	212-898-9500	
MJ Partners Inc 1433 43rd Ave *Web:* www.mjpartnersinc.com	Kenosha	WI	53144	262-553-9696	
Modulant Inc 5600 Tennyson Pkwy Ste 355 *Web:* www.modulant.com	Plano	TX	75024	843-743-2888	
Mojo Interactive Inc 1080 Woodcock Rd Ste 108 *Web:* www.mojointeractive.com	Orlando	FL	32803	407-206-0700	
Momentummedia-mag Inc 31 Dutch Mill Rd *Web:* momentummedia.com	Ithaca	NY	14850	607-257-6970	
Money Market Directories Inc 401 E Market St PO Box 1608 *Web:* www.mmdwebaccess.com	Charlottesville	VA	22902	434-977-1450	
Money Tree Software Ltd 2430 NW Professional Wy *TF:* 877-421-9815 ■ *Web:* www.moneytree.com	Corvallis	OR	97330	541-754-3701	738-6522
Mortgageflex Systems Inc 1200 Riverplace Blvd Ste 650 *TF General:* 800-326-3539 ■ *Web:* www.mortgageflex.com	Jacksonville	FL	32207	904-356-2490	356-1099
MSI Data Systems 10033 N Port Washington Rd *Web:* www.msidata.com	Mequon	WI	53092	262-241-7800	
MTS Consulting Group Inc 25450 Friar Ln *Web:* www.mtsconsultinggroup.com	Southfield	MI	48033	248-875-7424	
Multisoft Corp 1723 SE 47th Ter *TF:* 888-415-0554 ■ *Web:* www.multisoft.com	Cape Coral	FL	33904	239-945-6433	
Mutare Software 2060 E Algonquin Rd *Web:* www.mutare.com	Rolling Meadows	IL	60008	847-496-2000	
Mutual Mobile Inc 206 E Ninth St Ste 1400 *TF:* 800-208-3563 ■ *Web:* www.mutualmobile.com	Austin	TX	78701	512-615-1800	
MWA Intelligence Inc 15990 N Greenway Hayden Loop Ste C400 *Web:* www.mwaintelligence.com	Scottsdale	AZ	85260	480-538-5900	
Mynah Technologies 504 Trade Ctr Blvd *Web:* www.mynah.com	Chesterfield	MO	63005	636-728-2000	
Nakisa Inc 733 Cathcart *Web:* www.nakisa.com	Montreal	QC	H3B1M6	514-228-2000	
Nanonation Inc 301 S 13th St Ste 700 *TF:* 866-843-6266 ■ *Web:* www.nanonation.net	Lincoln	NE	68508	402-323-6266	
Nasoft USA Inc 417 E Carmel St *Web:* www.nasoft.com	San Marcos	CA	92078	760-410-1210	
Nauticon Imaging Systems Inc 15878 Gaither Dr *Web:* www.nauticon.com	Gaithersburg	MD	20877	301-279-0123	
nCircle Network Security Inc 101 Second St Ste 400 *TF:* 866-897-8776 ■ *Web:* www.tripwire.com	San Francisco	CA	94105	503-276-7500	223-0182
Ndex Systems Inc 500 Saint-Jacques St Ste 400 *Web:* www.ndexsystems.com	Montreal	QC	H2Y1S1	514-288-0908	
NearSpace 5755 Long Prairie Rd Ste 240 *Web:* www.nearspace.com	Tillamook	OR	97141	707-795-1784	
Nelson Technology Assoc Inc 1051 Hill Meadow Pl *Web:* nelsontech.com	Danville	CA	94526	925-855-3610	
Neoris Inc 703 Waterford Way Ste 700 *Web:* www.neoris.com	Miami	FL	33126	305-728-6000	
Net Effect Technologies 730 E Cypress Ave *Web:* www.pay4music.com	Monrovia	CA	91016	626-930-0101	
Net Endeavor Inc 982 S Main St *Web:* net-endeavor.com	Pleasant Grove	UT	84062	801-796-5582	
Netcellent System Inc 4030 Valley Blvd *TF:* 888-595-3818 ■ *Web:* elliott.com	Walnut	CA	91789	909-598-9019	
Netcetera Consulting Inc ÿ205 - 828 Harbourside Dr *Web:* netcetera.ca	North Vancouver	BC	V7P3R9	604-980-2700	
Netlink Systems Inc 5959 Shallowford Rd PO Box 23054 *Web:* www.netlink-systems.com	Chattanooga	TN	37421	423-855-0065	
Netology LLC 1200 Summer St Ste 302 *Web:* www.netologyllc.com	Stamford	CT	06905	203-975-9630	
Nettempo Inc 130 Battery St Ste 500 *Web:* nettempo.com	San Francisco	CA	94111	415-992-4900	
Network Data Security Experts Inc 521 Branchway Rd *Web:* www.ndse.net	North Chesterfield	VA	23236	804-521-7946	
Network Dynamics Inc 640 Brooker Creek Blvd Ste 410 *TF:* 877-818-8597 ■ *Web:* www.ndiwebsite.com	Oldsmar	FL	34677	813-818-8597	
Networking Concepts Inc 9881 Broken Land Pkwy Ste 402 *Web:* www.networkingconcepts.com	Columbia	MD	21046	410-381-0100	
Neudesic LLC 8105 Irvine Ctr Dr *TF:* 800-805-1805 ■ *Web:* www.neudesic.com	Irvine	CA	92618	949-754-4500	754-6800
Neutral Tandem Inc 550 W Adams St Fl 9 *Web:* www.inteliquent.com	Chicago	IL	60661	312-384-8040	
New England Systems & Software Inc 33 Holly Ln *Web:* www.nessnetworks.com	Lake George	NY	12845	518-377-4057	
Newforma Inc 1750 Elm St *Web:* www.newforma.com	Manchester	NH	03104	603-625-6212	

	City	State	Zip	Phone	Fax
Newfound Technologies Inc					
1050 Kingsmill Pkwy	Columbus	OH	43229	614-318-5000	
Web: www.nfti.com					
Newgen Software Inc 1364 Beverly Rd Ste 300	Mclean	VA	22101	703-749-2855	
Web: newgen.net					
Nexenta Systems Inc 455 El Camino Real	Santa Clara	CA	95050	408-791-3300	
Web: www.nexenta.com					
Nexlan 28 W N St	Danville	IL	61832	217-431-7236	477-5731
TF: 877-263-9526 ■ *Web:* nexlan.com					
nextPoint Inc 4043 N Ravenswood Ave	Chicago	IL	60613	888-929-6398	
TF: 888-929-6398 ■ *Web:* www.nextpoint.com					
Nextware Technologies					
233 Wilshire Blvd Ste 400	Santa Monica	CA	90401	310-955-9919	
Web: www.nextwaretech.com					
Nimbleuser 656 Kreag Rd	Pittsford	NY	14534	585-586-4750	
Web: www.nimbleuser.com					
Nims & Associates 1445 Technology Ln Ste A8	Petaluma	CA	94954	707-781-6300	
TF: 877-454-3200 ■ *Web:* www.nimsassociates.com					
Nirvana Systems Inc 7000 N MoPac Ste 425	Austin	TX	78731	512-345-2545	
Web: www.omnitrader.com					
Nodus Technologies Inc					
2099 S State College Blvd Ste 250	Anaheim	CA	92806	909-482-4701	
Web: www.nodustech.com					
Noetix Corp 5010 148th Ave NE Ste 100	Redmond	WA	98052	425-372-2699	436-0406*
**Fax Area Code:* 866 ■ *TF:* 866-466-3849 ■ *Web:* www.noetix.com					
Noldus Information Technology Inc					
1503 Edwards Ferry Rd Ne Ste 201	Leesburg	VA	20176	703-771-0440	
Web: www.noldus.com					
Nomadix Inc 30851 Agoura Rd Ste 102	Agoura Hills	CA	91301	818-597-1500	597-1502
TF: 800-666-2349 ■ *Web:* www.nomadix.com					
Norman Technologies LLC					
630 Davidson Gateway Dr Ste 250	Davidson	NC	28036	704-896-0128	
Web: www.normantech.com					
Northwest Data Solutions LLC 2627 C St	Anchorage	AK	99503	907-227-1676	
TF: 800-544-0786 ■ *Web:* www.nwds-ak.com					
Not Rocket Science Inc 251 Hwy 21	Madisonville	LA	70447	985-845-2334	
TF: 888-785-8896 ■ *Web:* www.notrs.com					
Nova Development Corp					
23801 Calabasas Rd Ste 1018	Calabasas	CA	91302	818-591-9600	
Web: www.novadevelopment.com					
Nova Libra Inc 8609 W Bryn Mawr Ave Ste 208	Chicago	IL	60631	773-714-1441	
TF: 866-724-1807 ■ *Web:* novalibra.com					
Novani 900 Kearny St Ste 388	San Francisco	CA	94133	415-731-1111	
Web: www.novani.com					
November Research Group LLC					
2120 University Ave Ste 250	Berkeley	CA	94704	415-987-3313	
Web: www.novemberresearch.com					
Novex Software Developments Inc					
8743 Commercial St	New Minas	NS	B4N3C4	902-542-1813	
TF: 888-542-1813 ■ *Web:* novexsoftware.com					
Novosoft Inc 3803 Mount Bonnel Rd	Austin	TX	78731	512-454-1140	
Web: www.novosoft.us					
NOW Solutions Inc 101 W Renner Rd Ste 300	Richardson	TX	75082	972-437-3339	
Web: www.nowsolutions.com					
NowDocs International Inc					
1985 Lookout Dr	North Mankato	MN	56003	888-669-3627	
TF: 888-669-3627 ■ *Web:* www.nowdocs.com					
NuAxis LLC 8603 Westwood Ctr Dr Ste 340	Vienna	VA	22182	703-481-7400	
Web: nuaxis.com					
Nuesoft Technologies Inc					
1685 Terrell Mill Rd	Marietta	GA	30067	678-303-1140	
Web: www.nuemd.com					
Numeric Technologies Inc 4200 Cantera Dr	Warrenville	IL	60555	630-955-9060	
Web: www.ntsiinc.com					
Nylon Technology 350 Seventh Ave 10th fl	New York	NY	10001	212-691-1134	
Web: www.nylontechnology.com					
O P Solutions Inc 350 First Ave Ste MG	New York	NY	10010	212-979-1000	
Web: www.pattsy.com					
OA Systems Inc 10783 Edison Ct	Rancho Cucamonga	CA	91730	909-466-1605	
Web: www.oasite.com					
Oasis Computing Inc 1595 16th Ave	Richmond Hill	ON	L4B3N9	905-709-7456	
Web: www.oasiscomputing.com					
ObjectBuilders Inc					
20134 W Vly Forge Cir	King Of Prussia	PA	19406	610-783-7748	
Web: www.objectbuilders.com					
Objective Arts Inc 20 N Wacker Ave	Chicago	IL	60606	312-977-1150	
Web: objectivearts.com					
Objective Interface Systems Inc					
220 Spring St Ste 530	Herndon	VA	20170	703-295-6500	
Web: www.ois.com					
Objective Technologies Inc					
712 Heatherglen Dr	Southlake	TX	76092	817-251-6900	
ObjectRiver Inc 21 Pemberton Rd	Wayland	MA	01778	508-651-0767	
Web: www.objectriver.net					
Objectwin Technology Inc					
14800 St Mary's Ln Ste 100	Houston	TX	77079	713-782-8200	782-8283
Web: www.objectwin.com					
OC Systems Inc 9990 Fairfax Blvd Ste 270	Fairfax	VA	22030	703-359-8160	
Web: www.ocsystems.com					
Oculis Labs Inc 338 Clubhouse Rd	Hunt Valley	MD	21031	410-891-1701	
Web: www.oculislabs.com					
Oden Industries Inc					
301 E Vanderbilt Way Ste 425	San Bernardino	CA	92408	909-386-0310	
Web: www.odenindustries.com					
Oeconnection LLC 4205 Highlander Pkwy	Richfield	OH	44286	330-523-1830	523-1700
TF: 888-776-5792 ■ *Web:* www.oeconnection.com					
OfficeOps LLC 619 S Vulcan Ave Ste 106	Encinitas	CA	92024	504-405-0574	
Officepro Inc 8 Granite Pl Ste 26	Gaithersburg	MD	20878	301-468-3312	
Web: www.officeproinc.com					
Omega Airline Software 116 N Eighth St	Midlothian	TX	76065	972-775-3693	
Web: www.omegaair.com					
Omnitech Inc 5841 S Corporate Pl	Sioux Falls	SD	57108	605-336-0888	
Web: omnitech-inc.com					
On Center Software Inc					
8708 Technology Forest Pl Ste 175	The Woodlands	TX	77381	281-297-9000	
Web: www.oncenter.com					
One Point Solutions Inc 43422 W Oaks Dr Ste 294	Novi	MI	48377	248-887-8470	
Web: www.one-point.com					
One Web Systems Inc 6195 Barfield Rd Ste 170	Atlanta	GA	30328	404-252-5400	
Web: www.targetatlanta.com					
Oneshield Inc 62 Forest St	Marlborough	MA	01752	774-348-1000	
Web: oneshield.com					
ONRAD Inc 1770 Iowa Ave Ste 280	Riverside	CA	92507	951-786-0801	
Web: www.onradinc.com					
Onramp Access LLC 2916 Montopolis Dr Ste 300	Austin	TX	78741	512-322-9200	
Web: www.onr.com					
Ontario Systems Corp 1150 W Kilgore Ave	Muncie	IN	47305	765-751-7000	751-7099
Web: www.ontariosystems.com					
Open Dental Software					
Ste 110 3995 Fairview Industrial Dr SE	Salem	OR	97302	503-363-5432	
TF: 866-239-0469 ■ *Web:* www.opendental.com					
Openet Telecom Inc 1886 Metro Ctr Dr Ste 310	Reston	VA	20190	703-480-1820	
Web: www.openet.com					
OpenPeak Inc 1750 Clint Moore Rd	Boca Raton	FL	33487	561-893-7800	
Web: www.openpeak.com					
Operation Technology Inc 17 Goodyear Ste 100	Irvine	CA	92618	949-900-1000	
Web: etap.com					
OPSWAT Inc 398 Kansas St	San Francisco	CA	94103	415-590-7300	
Web: www.opswat.com					
Optical Image Technology Inc					
100 Oakwood Ave Ste 700	State College	PA	16803	814-238-0038	
Web: www.docfinity.com					
Optima Global Solutions Inc					
3131 Princeton Pike Ste 207	Lawrenceville	NJ	08648	609-586-8811	
Web: www.optimags.com					
Optimal Electronics Corp					
13915 Burnet Rd Ste 312	Austin	TX	78728	512-372-3415	
Web: www.optelco.com					
Optimum Solutions Corp 170 Earle Ave	Lynbrook	NY	11563	516-247-5300	
TF: 800-227-0672 ■ *Web:* www.oscworld.com					
Oracle Applications Users Group					
1 Piedmont Ctr Ste 400	Atlanta	GA	30305	404-240-0897	
Web: www.oaug.org					
Orasi Software Inc 114 TownPark Dr Ste 400	Kennesaw	GA	30144	678-819-5300	
Web: www.orasi.com					
Orchard Software Corp					
701 Congressional Blvd Ste 360	Carmel	IN	46032	317-573-2633	573-2633
TF: 800-856-1948 ■ *Web:* www.orchardsoft.com					
Orchestro Ste 350 1760 Old Meadow Rd	Mclean	VA	22102	703-640-3300	
Web: orchestro.com					
OriginLab Corp 1 Roundhouse Plz Ste 303	Northampton	MA	01060	413-586-2013	
Web: www.originlab.com					
Ortho Computer Systems Inc 1107 Buckeye Ave	Ames	IA	50010	515-233-1026	
Web: www.ortho2.com					
Other Firm LLC, The 618 NW Glisan St Ste 201	Portland	OR	97209	503-336-5359	
Web: www.theotherfirm.com					
Outa Knoware International 886 Salem Rd	Dracut	MA	01826	978-688-1388	
Web: outaknoware.com					
Overland Rentals Inc					
1901 N State Hwy 360 Ste 340	Grand Prairie	TX	75050	972-602-9819	
Web: www.point-of-rental.com					
Ox International Inc 13111 NW Fwy 5th Fl	Houston	TX	77040	713-895-6610	
Web: www.oxinternational.com					
P C Whip 4451 Henderson Rd	Hickory	PA	15340	724-356-4070	
Web: www.pcwhip.com					
Pace Computer Solutions Inc					
10480 Little Patuxent Pkwy Ste 760	Columbia	MD	21044	443-539-0290	
Web: www.pace-solutionsinc.com					
Pacific Tech Solutions LLC					
15530 Rckfeld Blvd Ste B4	Irvine	CA	92618	949-830-1623	
Web: www.pts1.com					
Paksys Software LLC 116 Salem Rd	North Brunswick	NJ	08902	732-297-8908	
Web: www.paksys.com					
Paladin Data Systems Corp					
19362 Powder Hill Pl NE	Poulsbo	WA	98370	360-779-2400	779-2600
TF: 800-532-8448 ■ *Web:* www.paladindata.com					
Palmetto GBA LLC 17 Technology Cir AG-905	Columbia	SC	29203	803-735-1034	
Web: www.palmettogba.com					
Panasas Inc 969 W Maude Ave	Sunnyvale	CA	94085	408-215-6800	215-6801
TF: 800-726-2727 ■ *Web:* www.panasas.com					
Pangaea Information Technologies Ltd					
219 W Chicago Ave	Chicago	IL	60654	312-337-5404	
Web: www.pangaeatech.com					
Pangolin Laser Systems Inc					
9501 Satellite Blvd Ste 109	Orlando	FL	32837	407-299-2088	
Web: pangolin.com					
Pangomedia Inc 3003 Minnesota Dr Ste 303	Anchorage	AK	99503	907-868-8092	
Web: pangomedia.com					
PaperThin Inc 300 Congress St Ste 303	Quincy	MA	02169	617-471-4440	
Web: www.paperthin.com					
PaperWise Inc 3171 E Sunshine	Springfield	MO	65804	417-886-7505	
Web: www.paperwise.com					
PAR Excellence Systems Inc					
11500 Northlake Dr	Cincinnati	OH	45249	513-936-9744	
Web: www.parexcellencesystems.com					
Paraben Corp 21690 Red Rum Dr Ste 137	Ashburn	VA	20147	801-796-0944	
Web: www.paraben.com					
Paragon Application Systems Inc					
326 Raleigh St	Holly Springs	NC	27540	919-567-9890	
Web: www.paragonedge.com					
Parity Computing Inc					
6160 Lusk Blvd Ste C205	San Diego	CA	92121	858-535-0516	
Web: www.paritycomputing.com					
Park Place Technologies Inc					
5910 Landerbrook Dr	Cleveland	OH	44124	877-778-8707	
TF: 877-778-8707 ■ *Web:* www.parkplacetechnologies.com					

Phone Fax

PASSUR Aerospace Inc 1 Landmark Sq Ste 1900 .... Stamford CT 06901 203-622-4086
Web: www.passur.com
Patel Consultants Corp 1525 Morris Ave .... Union NJ 07083 908-964-7575 964-3176
Web: www.patelcorp.com
Patriot Managed Care Solutions Inc
1800 Augusta Dr Ste 220 .... Houston TX 77057 713-346-6200
Web: www.patriotmcs.net
Patriot Technologies Inc
5108 Pegasus Ct Ste F .... Frederick MD 21704 301-695-7500 695-4711
TF: 888-417-9899 ■ *Web:* www.patriot-tech.com
Pattern Insight Inc
465 Fairchild Dr Ste 209 .... Mountain View CA 94043 866-582-2655
TF: 866-582-2655 ■ *Web:* patterninsight.com
Pc Focus Computer Co 7500 Mountain Ave .... Orangevale CA 95662 916-988-0404
Web: www.pcfocus.net
PC Scale Inc 119 S Fifth St .... Oxford PA 19363 610-932-4006
Web: www.pcscaletower.com
PCA Group Inc, The 455 Cayuga Rd Ste 200 .... Buffalo NY 14225 716-932-7830
Web: www.pcatechnologygroup.com
PCMS Datafit Inc
25 Merchant St Executive Centre 3 Ste 400 .... Cincinnati OH 45246 513-587-3100
Web: www.pcmsdatafit.com
Pen-Link Ltd 5944 VanDervoort Dr .... Lincoln NE 68516 402-421-8857
Web: www.penlink.com
Pepper Group, The 220 N Smith St Ste 406 .... Palatine IL 60067 847-963-0333
Web: www.peppergroup.com
Peppler & Associates Inc
22 E Dundee Rd Ste 26 .... Barrington IL 60010 847-382-6866
Web: peppler.com
Perforce Software Inc 2320 Blanding Ave .... Alameda CA 94501 510-864-7400
Web: perforce.com
Performance Software
2095 W Pinnacle Peak Rd Ste 120 .... Phoenix AZ 85027 623-780-1517 308-8688*
**Fax Area Code:* 602 ■ **Fax:* Sales ■ *Web:* www.psware.com
Performance Support Inc
5775 Carmichael Pkwy .... Montgomery AL 36117 334-244-9797
Web: www.at-psi.com
PERI Software Solutions Inc 570 Broad St. .... Newark NJ 07102 973-735-9500
Web: www.perisoftware.com
petroWEB Inc 1825 Blake St .... Denver CO 80202 303-308-9100
Web: www.petroweb.com
Petz Enterprises LLC 7575 W Linne Rd .... Tracy CA 95304 209-835-2720
Web: www.petzent.com
PFW Systems Corp 850 Medway Park Ct .... London ON N6G5C6 519-474-3300
Web: www.pfw.com
PharmaSys Inc 216 Towne Village Dr .... Cary NC 27513 919-468-2547
Web: www.pharma-sys.com
Phunware Inc 7800 Shoal Creek Blvd .... Austin TX 78757 855-521-8485
TF: 855-521-8485 ■ *Web:* www.phunware.com
PIC Business Systems Inc
5119 Beckwith Blvd Ste 106 .... San Antonio TX 78249 210-690-9106
TF: 800-742-7378 ■ *Web:* www.picbusiness.com
Picaboo Corp 1160 Chestnut St. .... Menlo Park CA 94025 650-326-3200
Web: www.picaboo.com
Pine River Capital Management LP
601 Carlson Pkwy Ste 330 .... Minnetonka MN 55305 612-238-3300
Web: www.pinerivercapital.com
Pipkins Inc
5 McBride & Son Ctr Dr Ste 140 .... Chesterfield MO 63005 314-469-6106
Web: www.pipkins.com
Pivot Systems Inc 2480 N First St Ste 150 .... San Jose CA 95131 408-435-1000
Web: www.pivotsys.com
Pixel Systems Inc 47 Greylynne Dr .... Princeton NJ 08540 609-945-3190
Web: www.pixelsystemsinc.com
Pixstar Inc 1515 Savannah Rd Ste 200 .... Lewes DE 19958 302-644-8650
PKMM Inc 265 E Main St Ste B .... Oceanport NJ 07757 732-935-1927
Web: pkmminc.com
Plan B Technologies Inc
16701 Melford Blvd Ste 150 .... Annapolis MD 21401 301-860-1006
TF: 888-925-1602
Pointwise Inc 213 S Jennings Ave .... Fort Worth TX 76104 817-377-2807
Web: www.pointwise.com
Polar Instruments Inc
18649 SW Farmington Rd .... Beaverton OR 97007 503-356-5270
Web: www.polarinstruments.com
Polaris Health Directions Inc
565 E Swedesford Rd Ste 200 .... Wayne PA 19087 215-359-3901
Web: www.polarishealth.com
Portable Technology Solutions LLC
221 David Ct. .... Calverton NY 11933 877-640-4152
TF: 877-640-4152 ■ *Web:* www.ptsmobile.com
Porter Lee Corp 1901 Wright Blvd .... Schaumburg IL 60193 847-985-2060
Web: www.porterlee.com
Portrait Displays Inc 6663 Owens Dr .... Pleasanton CA 94588 925-227-2700
Web: www.portrait.com
Pos Source 535 Harrison Ave. .... Panama City FL 32401 850-747-0581
TF: 800-232-1626 ■ *Web:* www.execu-tech.com
PowerServe International Inc
959 Broad St Ste 300 .... Augusta GA 30901 706-826-1506
Web: www.powerserve.net
Practice Technology Inc 1312 E Robinson St .... Orlando FL 32801 407-228-4400
Web: prevail.net
Prakat Solutions Inc 6016 Annandale Dr. .... Fort Worth TX 76132 817-846-7541
Web: www.prakat.com
Praxis Engineering Technologies Inc
135 National Business Pkwy. .... Annapolis Junction MD 20701 301-490-4299
Web: praxiseng.com
Predicate Logic Inc 6155 Cornerstone Ct E. .... San Diego CA 92121 858-715-0100
Web: www.predicate.com
Preferred Medical Marketing Corp
15720 Brixham Hill Ave Ste 460 .... Charlotte NC 28277 704-543-8103
TF: 800-543-8176 ■ *Web:* www.pmmconline.com
Preferred Strategies LLC 2425 Porter St Ste 20 .... Soquel CA 95073 831-465-7164
Web: www.preferredstrategies.com

Prelude Systems Inc 3911 Hartzdale Dr. .... Camp Hill PA 17011 717-441-2400
Web: preludeservices.com
Prenia Corp 16625 Redmond Way Ste M-418 .... Redmond WA 98052 425-999-4330
Web: www.prenia.com
PreViser Corp 20849 Cascade Ridge Dr .... Mount Vernon WA 98274 360-941-4715
Web: www.previser.com
Primal Fusion Inc 605-305 King St W .... Kitchener ON N2G1B9 519-741-1243
Web: www.primal.com
Prime Controls LP 1725 Lakepointe D .... Lewisville TX 75057 972-221-4849 420-4842
Web: www.prime-controls.com
Prince Software Inc 70 Hilltop Rd Ste 2400 .... Ramsey NJ 07446 201-934-0022
Web: www.princesoftware.com
Prism Microsystems Inc
8815 Centre Park Dr T Ste 300-A .... Columbia MD 21045 410-953-6776
Web: www.eventtracker.com
Prism Systems Inc 200 Virginia St. .... Mobile AL 36603 251-341-1140
Web: prismsystems.com
Pro-cad Software Ltd 12 Elbow River Rd. .... Calgary AB T3Z2V2 403-216-3375
TF: 888-477-6223 ■ *Web:* www.procad.com
Pro-Tek Manufacturing Inc
4849 Southfront Rd .... Livermore CA 94551 925-454-8100
Web: www.protekmfg.com
Procera Networks Inc 47448 Fremont Blvd. .... Fremont CA 94538 510-230-2777
Web: www.proceranetworks.com
Process Control Technology Inc
4335 Piedras Dr W Ste 175 .... San Antonio TX 78228 210-735-9141 735-9775
Web: www.gopct.com
ProcessMAP Corp 13450 W Sunrise Blvd Ste 160 .... Sunrise FL 33323 954-515-5040
Web: www.processmap.com
Productivity Apex Inc
11301 Corporate Blvd Ste 303 .... Orlando FL 32817 407-384-0800
Web: www.productivityapex.com
Profit Programming Inc
120 Cockysville Rd .... Hunt Valley MD 21030 410-316-1000
Web: www.profitprogramming.com
Profitsword LLC 9355 Cypress Cove Dr .... Orlando FL 32819 407-909-8822
TF: 866-930-6543 ■ *Web:* www.profitsword.com
Progeny Linux Systems Inc
9100 Keystone Ste 440 .... Indianapolis IN 46240 317-833-0313 833-0315
Progeny Software LLC
190 Congress Park Dr Ste 140 .... Delray Beach FL 33445 574-968-0822
Web: www.progenygenetics.com
Promiles Software Development
1900 Texas Ave .... Bridge City TX 77611 800-324-8588
TF: 800-324-8588 ■ *Web:* www.promiles.com
Promium LLC 3350 Monte Villa Pkwy Ste 220 .... Bothell WA 98021 425-286-9200
TF: 877-776-6486 ■ *Web:* www.promium.com
Proofpoint Systems Inc 1393 Oak Ave .... Los Altos CA 94024 650-968-7032
Web: proofpoint.net
Property Panorama Inc 9475 Pinecone Dr .... Mentor OH 44060 440-290-2200
TF: 877-299-6306 ■ *Web:* propertypanorama.com
ProSites Inc 27919 Jefferson Ave Ste 103 .... Temecula CA 92590 951-693-9101
Web: www.prosites.com
Prosync Technology Group LLC
6021 University Blvd Ste 300 .... Ellicott City MD 21043 410-772-7969
Web: www.prosync.com
Protech Systems Group 3350 Players Club Pkwy .... Memphis TN 38125 901-767-7550
TF: 800-459-5100 ■ *Web:* www.psgi.net
Proteus Technologies LLC
133 National Business Pkwy. .... Annapolis Junction MD 20701 443-539-3400
Web: proteus-technologies.com
Providge Consulting LLC
2207 Concord Pike Ste 537 .... Wilimington DE 19803 888-927-6583
TF: 888-927-6583 ■ *Web:* www.providge.com
Proware 7621 E Kemper Rd .... Cincinnati OH 45249 513-489-5477
Web: www.proware.com
Prowess Inc 1844 Clayton Rd .... Concord CA 94520 925-356-0360
Web: www.prowess.com
Proxibid Inc 4411 S 96 St .... Omaha NE 68127 402-505-7770
Web: www.proxibid.com
Proximex Corp 300 Santana Row Ste 200 .... San Jose CA 95128 408-215-9000
Web: www.proximex.com
Proximo Consulting Services Inc
2500 Plz Five .... Jersey City NJ 07311 800-236-9250
TF: 800-236-9250 ■ *Web:* www.proximo.com
Ps Websolutions Inc
906 Carriage Path Se Ste 106 .... Smyrna GA 30082 770-801-8866
Web: www.pswebsolution.com
Psychological Software Solutions Inc
4119 Montrose Blvd. .... Houston TX 77006 713-965-6941
Web: psiwaresolutions.com
Psychology Software Tools Inc
Sharpsburg Business Park 311 23rd St Ext
Ste 200 .... Sharpsburg PA 15215 412-271-5040
Web: www.pstnet.com
Psytech Solutions 1138 Stone Creek Dr. .... Hummelstown PA 17036 717-583-0349
Web: www.psytechsolutions.net
Public Systems Associates Inc
2431 S Acadian Thruway Ste 570 .... Baton Rouge LA 70808 225-346-0618
Web: publicsystems.org
Purvis Systems Inc 88 Silva Ln .... Middletown RI 02842 401-849-4750 849-0121
Web: purvis.com
Pyramid Software Development Inc
4008 Louetta Rd #404 .... Spring TX 77388 281-350-2535
Web: pyramidsdi.com
QFlow Systems LLC 9317 Manchester Rd. .... St. Louis MO 63119 314-968-9906
Web: www.qflowsystems.com
QHR Corp 1620 Dickson Ave Ste 300 .... Kelowna BC V1Y9Y2 250-448-7095
TF: 855-550-5004 ■ *Web:* www.qhrtechnologies.com
QSR Automations Inc
2301 Stanley Gault Pkwy .... Louisville KY 40223 502-297-0221
Web: www.qsrautomation.com
QStar Technologies Inc 8738 Ortega Park Dr .... Navarre FL 32566 850-243-0900
Web: www.qstar.com

Phone Fax

Quadramed Inc 12110 Sunset Hills Rd Ste 600 Reston VA 20190 703-709-2300
Web: www.quadramed.com
Qualnetics Corp 2183 Alpine Way Bellingham WA 98226 360-733-4151
Web: www.qualnetics.com
Quantros Inc 691 S Milpitas Blvd Ste 100 Milpitas CA 95035 408-957-3300
Web: www.quantros.com
Quantum Aviation Solutions Inc
1720 Epps Bridge Pkwy Ste 108 Number 304 Athens GA 30606 404-348-4839
Web: www.quantum.aero
Quantum Simulations Inc 5275 Sardis Rd Murrysville PA 15668 724-733-8603
Web: quantumsimulations.com
Questek Innovations LLC 1820 Ridge Ave Evanston IL 60201 847-328-5800
Web: www.questek.com
Questionmark Corp 5 Hillandale Ave Stamford CT 06902 203-358-3950
Web: www.questionmark.com
Quick Technologies Inc
2508 Highlander Way Ste 200 Carrollton TX 75006 214-631-6000
Web: www.qti.com
QuickCompliance Inc 8A Canal Ct Avon CT 06001 860-676-9400
Web: www.quickcompliance.net
QuickStart Intelligence Inc
16815 Von Karman Ave Ste 100 Irvine CA 92606 800-326-1044
TF: 866-991-3924 ■ *Web:* www.quickstart.com
Quorum Business Solutions Inc
811 Main St Ste 2000 Houston TX 77002 713-430-8601 430-8697
Web: www.qbsol.com
R Z Communications 1400 Smith Rd # B101 Austin TX 78721 512-386-7336
Web: www.rzaustin.com
R&D Logic Inc 1611 Borel Pl Ste 2 San Mateo CA 94402 650-571-5255
Web: www.rdlogic.com
Radiant Logic Inc 75 Rowland Way Ste 300 Novato CA 94945 415-209-6800
Web: www.radiantlogic.com
RADinfo Systems Inc 43676 Trade Ctr Pl Ste 100 Dulles VA 20166 703-713-3313
Web: www.radinfosystems.com
Radley Corp 23077 Greenfield Rd Ste 440 Southfield MI 48075 248-559-6858
Web: www.radley.com
RAF Technology Inc 15400 NE 90th St Ste 300 Redmond WA 98052 425-867-0700
Web: www.raf.com
Raintree Systems Inc 27307 Via Industria Temecula CA 92590 951-252-9400
Web: www.raintreeinc.com
RamQuest Software Inc
5801 Tennyson Pkwy Ste 500 Plano TX 75024 214-291-1600
Web: www.ramquest.com
Ramsoft Systems Inc
29777 Telegraph Rd Ste 2250 Southfield MI 48034 248-354-0100
Web: www.ramsoft.net
Ranch Santa Fe Technology
5961 Kearny Villa Rd San Diego CA 92123 858-565-7224
Rapid Insight Inc 53 Technology Ln Ste 112 Conway NH 03818 888-585-6511
TF: 888-585-6511 ■ *Web:* www.rapidinsightinc.com
Rapid Software Corp 3079 Parr Ln Grapevine TX 76051 817-251-0615
Web: www.rapidsw.com
Rata Associates LLC 1916 Boothe Cir Longwood FL 32750 407-831-7282
Web: www.rataassociates.com
Rave Wireless Inc 50 Speen St Framingham MA 01701 508-848-2484
Web: www.ravemobilesafety.com
Razorleaf Corp 3766 Fishcreek Rd Ste 291 Stow OH 44224 330-676-0022
Web: www.razorleaf.com
RBB Innovations 2-258 Queen St E Sault Sainte Marie ON P6A1Y7 705-942-9053
TF: 800-796-7864 ■ *Web:* rbbinnovations.com
RCI Technologies Inc 1133 Green St Iselin NJ 08830 732-382-3000
Web: www.rci-technologies.com
RDA Corp 303 International Cir Ste 340 Hunt Valley MD 21030 410-308-9300 308-9600
TF: 888-441-1278 ■ *Web:* www.rdacorp.com
Ready-to-run Software Inc 212 Cedar Cv Lansing NY 14882 607-533-4002
Web: www.rtr.com
ReadyGo Inc 1761 Pilgrim Ave Mountain View CA 94040 650-559-8990
Web: www.readygo.com
Real Time Information Services Inc
191 W Shaw Ave Ste 106 Fresno CA 93704 559-222-6456
Web: realtimeca.com
Real Vision Software Inc
3700 Jackson St Ste 203 Alexandria LA 71303 318-449-4579
Web: www.realvisionsoftware.com
Realdecoy Inc 205 Catherine St Ottawa ON K2P1C3 613-234-9330
Web: www.realdecoy.com
Rediker Software Inc 2 Wilbraham Rd Hampden MA 01036 413-566-3463 566-2274
TF: 800-213-9860 ■ *Web:* www.rediker.com
RedMane Technology LLC
8614 W Catalpa Ave Ste 1001 Chicago IL 60656 773-693-3919
Web: www.redmane.com
Redspin Inc 4690 Carpinteria Ave Ste B Carpinteria CA 93013 805-684-6858
Web: www.redspin.com
Referentia Systems Inc
155 Kapalulu Pl Ste 200 Honolulu HI 96819 808-840-8500
Web: www.referentia.com
Regional Economic Models Inc 433 W St Amherst MA 01002 413-549-1169 549-1038
Web: remi.com
REI Systems Inc 45335 Vintage Pk Plz Sterling VA 20166 703-480-9100 689-4680
Web: www.reisystems.com
ReleaseTEAM Inc 1400 W 122nd Ave Ste 202 Denver CO 80234 720-977-8010
Web: www.releaseteam.com
Reliable Software Resources Inc
22260 Haggerty Rd Ste 285 Northville MI 48167 248-477-3555
Web: www.rsrit.com
Renewable NRG Systems 110 Riggs Rd Hinesburg VT 05461 802-482-2255
Web: www.nrgsystems.com
RenoWorks Software Inc 2816 21 St NE Calgary AB T2E6Z2 403-296-3880
TF: 877-980-3880 ■ *Web:* www.renoworks.com
Rentfrow Inc 5675 Ralston St Ventura CA 93003 805-650-7677
Web: www.rentfrow.com
Reporting Systems Inc 851 Coho Way Ste 301 Bellingham WA 98225 360-647-6003
Web: www.emergencyreporting.com

Resolute Technology Solutions Inc
433 Main St Ste 600 Winnipeg MB R3B1B3 204-927-3520
Web: www.resoluts.com
Resort Data Processing Inc 211 Eagle Rd Avon CO 81620 970-845-1140
TF: 877-779-3717 ■ *Web:* www.resortdata.com
Resource & Financial Management Systems Inc
3073 Palisades Ct Tuscaloosa AL 35405 800-701-7367
TF: 800-701-7367 ■ *Web:* www.rfms.com
Resource Data Inc 560 E 34th Ave Ste 100 Anchorage AK 99503 907-563-8100
Web: www.resdat.com
Rethink Autism Inc 19 W 21st St Ste 403 New York NY 10010 646-257-2919
Web: www.rethinkfirst.com
RF Engineering Inc 13801 Bison Ct Silver Spring MD 20906 301-460-8374
Web: www.rfe-inc.com
Rfd & Associates Inc 401 Camp Craft Rd Austin TX 78746 512-347-9411
Web: www.rfdinc.com
Richter Media Inc 255 W 23rd St Apt 4ce New York NY 10011 212-802-8588
Web: www.richtermedia.com
Rina Group LLC
8180 Corporate Park Dr Ste 140 Cincinnati OH 45242 513-469-7462
Web: www.rinasystems.com
Rivet Software Inc 4340 S Monaco St 4th Fl Denver CO 80237 720-249-2100
Web: www.rivetsoftware.com
Robert Sharp & Associates Inc
3615 Canyon Lk Dr Ste 1 Rapid City SD 57702 605-341-5226
Web: www.robertsharpassociates.com
Robocast Inc 89 Fifth Ave New York NY 10003 212-620-0007
Web: robocast.com
Rochester Group Inc, The 600 Park Ave Rochester NY 14607 585-271-1110
Web: www.rochgrp.com
Rolands & Associates Corp
120 Del Rey Gardens Dr Del Rey Oaks CA 93940 831-373-2025
Web: www.rolands.com
Rooster Park 901 Thomas St Seattle WA 98109 206-801-0189
Web: www.roosterpark.com
Rose International
16401 Swingley Ridge Rd Ste 300 Chesterfield MO 63017 636-812-4000 812-0076
Web: www.roseit.com
Roshi Tech Inc 5 Castleton Ct Merrimack NH 03054 603-889-2211
Web: www.roshitech.com
Royal Cyber Inc 55 Shuman Blvd Ste 1025 Naperville IL 60563 630-355-6292
Web: www.royalcyber.com
RP Design Web Services
17 Meriden Ave Ste 2A Southington CT 06489 203-271-7991
TF: 800-847-3475 ■ *Web:* www.rpdesign.com
Rtz Associates Inc 150 Grand Ave Ste 200 Oakland CA 94612 510-986-6700
Web: www.rtzassociates.com
Rubicon Group Ltd, The
125 Windsor Dr Ste 118 Oak Brook IL 60523 630-574-7766
Web: www.rubgrp.com
Runner Technologies Inc
6530 W Rogers Cir Ste 31 Boca Raton FL 33487 561-395-9322
Web: runnertech.com
S2Tech 720 Spirit 40 Park Dr Chesterfield MO 63005 636-530-9286
Web: www.s2tech.com
S3 Ventures
6300 Bridgepoint Pkwy Bldg One Ste 405 Austin TX 78730 512-258-1759
Web: www.s3vc.com
Safe Banking Systems LLC
114 Old Country Rd Ste 320 Mineola NY 11501 631-547-5400
Web: www.safe-banking.com
Safe Passage International Inc
333 Metro Park Rochester NY 14623 585-292-4910
Web: www.safe-passage.com
SafeNet Consulting Inc 5810 Baker Rd Minnetonka MN 55345 952-930-3636
Web: www.safenetconsulting.com
SAFER Systems LLC 5284 Adolfo Rd Ste 100 Camarillo CA 93012 805-383-9711
Web: www.safersystemv10.com
Sagarsoft Inc 78 Eastern Blvd Glastonbury CT 06033 860-633-2025
Web: www.sagarsoft.com
Sage Computing Inc
11491 Sunset Hills Rd Ste 350 Reston VA 20190 703-742-7881
Web: sagecomputing.com
Sage Data Security LLC 2275 Congress St Portland ME 04102 207-879-7243
Web: www.sagedatasecurity.com
Sage Microsystems Inc 18 N Village Ave Exton PA 19341 610-524-1300
Web: www.sagemicrosystems.com
SageLogix Inc 9100 E Panorama Dr Ste 100 Englewood CO 80112 303-925-0100
Web: www.sagelogix.com
Sales Simplicity Software 325 E Elliot Rd Chandler AZ 85225 480-892-2500
Web: www.salessimplicity.net
Salford Systems Inc
9685 Via Excelencia Ste 208 San Diego CA 92126 619-543-8880
Web: www.salford-systems.com
Saltech Systems Inc 137 Lynn Ave Ste 200 Ames IA 50014 515-598-4347
Web: www.saltechsystems.com
SAMSA Inc 5560 Gratiot Ste D Saginaw MI 48638 989-790-0507
Web: www.samsa.com
SAP America Inc
1721 Moon Lake Blvd Ste 300 Hoffman Estates IL 60169 847-230-3800 230-3801
TF: 800-872-1727 ■ *Web:* www.sap.com
SAPIEN Technologies Inc 841 Latour Court Ste D Napa CA 94558 707-252-8700
Web: www.sapien.com
Satcom Direct Inc 1901 Hwy A1A Satellite Beach FL 32937 321-777-3000
Web: www.satcomdirect.com
Satcom Resources LLC 101 Eagle Rd Bldg 7 Avon CO 81620 970-748-3094
Web: www.satcomresources.com
Satmetrix Systems Inc 1100 Pk Pl San Mateo CA 94403 866-697-2103
TF: 866-697-2103 ■ *Web:* www.satmetrix.com
Satori Solutions 10901 W Toller Dr Ste 110 Littleton CO 80127 303-215-1921
Web: www.satorisolutions.com
Satuit Technologies Inc 100 Grossman Dr Braintree MA 02184 781-871-7788
Web: satuit.com

Company	City	State	Zip	Phone	Fax
Saturn Systems Inc 314 W Superior St Ste 1015 *TF:* 888-638-4335 ■ *Web:* www.saturnsys.com	Duluth	MN	55802	218-623-7200	
Saylent Technologies Inc 122 Grove St Ste 300 *Web:* www.saylent.com	Franklin	MA	02038	508-570-2161	
Scadaware Inc 1602 Rhodes Ln *Web:* www.scadaware.com	Bloomington	IL	61704	309-665-0135	
Scala Inc 350 Eagleview Blvd Ste 350 *Web:* www.scala.com	Exton	PA	19341	610-363-3350	
Scalability Experts Inc 1203 Crestside Dr *Web:* www.scalabilityexperts.com	Coppell	TX	75019	469-635-6200	
Scalar Decisions Inc 280 King St E 4th Fl *Web:* www.scalar.ca	Toronto	ON	M5A1K7	416-202-0020	
ScaleMP Inc 2175 Lemoine Ave Ste 401 *Web:* www.scalemp.com	Fort Lee	NJ	07024	201-429-9740	
Schedulicity Inc 424 E Main Ste 201 *Web:* www.schedulicity.com	Bozeman	MT	59715	406-582-0494	
ScholarOne Inc 375 Greenbrier Dr Ste 200 *Web:* ipscience.thomsonreuters.com/product/scholarone	Charlottesville	VA	22901	434-964-4000	
School Webmasters 2846 E Nora St *TF:* 888-750-4556 ■ *Web:* www.schoolwebmasters.com	Mesa	AZ	85213	602-750-4556	
SchoolCity Inc 2900 Lakeside Dr Ste 270 *Web:* www.schoolcity.com	Santa Clara	CA	95054	650-934-6123	
Scicom Infrastructure Services Inc 2250 N Druid Hills Rd Ne Ste 238 *Web:* www.scicominfra.com	Atlanta	GA	30329	404-636-9882	
SDK Software Inc 11320 86th Ave N *Web:* www.sdksoft.com	Maple Grove	MN	55369	763-657-1189	
SDN Global Inc 11101 Nations Ford Rd	Pineville	NC	28241	704-588-2233	
Seacoast Laboratory Data Systems Inc 195 New Hampshire Ave Ste 140 *Web:* www.sldsi.com	Portsmouth	NH	03801	603-431-4114	
Second Opinion Software LLC 3830 Del Amo Blvd 101 *Web:* www.2opinion.com	Torrance	CA	90503	310-538-2800	
SEDONA Corp 1003 W Ninth Ave 2nd Fl *Web:* www.sedonacorp.com	King Of Prussia	PA	19406	610-337-8400	
Seilevel Inc 3410 Far W Blvd *Web:* www.seilevel.com	Austin	TX	78731	512-527-9952	
Selbysoft Inc 8326 Woodland Ave E *TF:* 800-454-4434 ■ *Web:* www.selbysoft.com	Puyallup	WA	98371	253-770-2993	
Selltis LLC 3500 Hwy 190 Ste 200 *Web:* www.selltis.com	Mandeville	LA	70471	985-727-3455	
Selsoft Inc 303 S Jupiter Ste 110 *Web:* www.selsoftinc.com	Allen	TX	75002	217-721-3186	
Senscio Systems Inc 1740 Massachusetts Ave *Web:* www.sensciosystems.com	Boxborough	MA	01719	978-635-9090	
ServerLogic Corp 2800 Northup Way Ste 120 *Web:* www.serverlogic.com	Bellevue	WA	98004	425-803-0378	
Service Objects Inc 133 E de la Guerra St Ste 10 *Web:* www.serviceobjects.com	Santa Barbara	CA	93101	805-963-1700	
Shadow-soft LLC 185 Wentworth Ter *Web:* www.shadow-soft.com	Alpharetta	GA	30022	770-740-8030	
shared logic group inc, The 6904 Spring Vly Dr Ste 305 *TF:* 877-865-0083 ■ *Web:* www.sharedlogic.com	Holland	OH	43528	419-865-0083	
Shasta Qa 1538 Market St *Web:* www.shastaqa.com	Redding	CA	96001	530-242-5799	
Shaw Systems Assoc Inc 6200 Savoy Dr Ste 600 *Web:* www.shawsystems.com	Houston	TX	77036	713-782-7730	782-4158
Shelby Systems Inc 7345 Goodlett Farms Pkwy *Web:* www.shelbysystems.com	Cordova	TN	38016	901-757-2372	
Sherrill-Lubinski Corp 240 Tamal Vista Blvd *Web:* www.sl.com	Corte Madera	CA	94925	415-927-8400	
Shoreland Inc 933 N Mayfair Rd Ste 208 *Web:* www.shoreland.com	Milwaukee	WI	53226	414-290-1900	
Sibble Computer Consulting 1720 Venables St *Web:* pdscc.com	Vancouver	BC	V5L2H4	604-739-3709	
Sigma Systems Canada Inc 55 York St Ste 1100 *TF:* 888-782-6468 ■ *Web:* www.sigma-systems.com	Toronto	ON	M5J1R7	416-943-9696	
Signiant Inc 152 Middlesex Tpke *Web:* www.signiant.com	Burlington	MA	01803	781-221-4000	
Signifi Solutions Inc 2100 Matheson Blvd E Ste 100 *TF:* 877-744-6434 ■ *Web:* www.signifi.com	Mississauga	ON	L4W5E1	905-602-7707	
Silanis Technology Inc 8200 Decarie Blvd Ste 300 *Web:* www.esignlive.com	Montreal	QC	H4P2P5	514-337-5255	
Silk Software Corp 15440 Laguna Canyon Rd Ste 210 *Web:* www.silksoftware.com	Irvine	CA	92618	949-748-3700	
Silver Oven Studios Inc 953 Islington St *Web:* www.silveroven.com	Portsmouth	NH	03801	603-570-7300	
Simba Technologies Inc 938 W Eigth Ave *Web:* www.simba.com	Vancouver	BC	V5Z1E5	604-633-0008	
Simcrest Inc 700 Central Expy Ste 310 *Web:* www.simcrest.com	Allen	TX	75013	214-644-4000	
Simoncomputing Inc 5350 Shawnee Rd Ste 200 *Web:* simoncomputing.com	Alexandria	VA	22312	703-914-5454	
Simplesoft Inc 257 Castro St Ste 220 *Web:* www.smplsft.com	Mountain View	CA	94041	650-965-4515	
Sirsi Corp 3300 N Ashton Blvd Ste 500 *TF:* 800-288-8020 ■ *Web:* www.sirsidynix.com	Lehi	UT	84043	800-288-8020	
SiTime Corp 990 Almanor Ave *Web:* www.sitime.com	Sunnyvale	CA	94085	408-328-4400	
Skybox Security Inc 2099 Gateway Pl Ste 450 *Web:* www.skyboxsecurity.com	San Jose	CA	95110	408-441-8060	
Skyline Technologies Inc 1400 Lombardi Ave *Web:* skylinetechnologies.com	Green Bay	WI	54304	920-437-1360	
SmarterTools Inc 1903 W Parkside Ln Ste 106 *Web:* www.smartertools.com	Phoenix	AZ	85027	623-434-8050	
Smartronix Inc 44150 Smartronix Way *TF:* 866-442-7767 ■ *Web:* www.smartronix.com	Hollywood	MD	20636	301-373-6000	373-7171
Smooth Fusion Inc 5502 58th St Ste 500 *Web:* www.smoothfusion.com	Lubbock	TX	79414	806-771-3873	
Soft Science 3921 Oceanic Dr Ste 801 *Web:* www.softsciencetech.com	Oceanside	CA	92056	281-861-0832	
Softchalk LLC 22 S Auburn Ave *TF:* 877-638-2425 ■ *Web:* softchalk.com	Richmond	VA	23221	877-638-2425	
Softdocs Inc 920 Hemlock Dr *Web:* www.softdocs.com	Columbia	SC	29201	803-695-6044	
Softech Inc 28104 Orchard Lk Rd Ste 100 *Web:* dentech.com	Farmington Hills	MI	48334	248-855-6130	
Softek Service Inc 1101 14th St Nw Ste 850 *Web:* www.softekdc.com	Washington	DC	20005	202-747-5000	
Softeq Development Corp 14027 Memorial Dr Ste 302 *Web:* www.softeq.com	Houston	TX	77079	713-827-2228	
Softerware Inc 132 Welsh Rd Ste 140 *TF:* 800-220-8111 ■ *Web:* www.softerware.com	Horsham	PA	19044	215-628-0400	628-0585
Softman Products LLC 13470 Washington Blvd *Web:* www.buycheapsoftware.com	Marina Del Rey	CA	90292	310-305-3644	
Softplan Systems Inc 8118 Isabella Ln *TF:* 800-248-0164 ■ *Web:* www.softplan.com	Brentwood	TN	37027	615-370-1121	
Softplc Corp 25603 Red Brangus Rd *Web:* www.softplc.com	Spicewood	TX	78669	512-264-8390	
Softrisc Communication Solutions Inc 575 N Pastoria Ave *Web:* www.softrisc.com	Sunnyvale	CA	94085	408-333-9775	
SoftSol Resources Inc 46755 Fremont Blvd *Web:* www.softsol.com	Fremont	CA	94538	510-824-2000	
Softtec Inc 621 Wall St *Web:* host.softtec.com	Sevierville	TN	37862	865-428-2209	
Software & Services of Louisiana LLC 1120 S Pointe Pkwy *Web:* softwareservices.net	Shreveport	LA	71105	318-865-1505	
Software Methods Inc 770 E Market St *Web:* www.software-methods.com	West Chester	PA	19382	610-430-8956	
Software Professionals Inc 1029 Long Prairie Rd Ste A *Web:* www.spius.net	Flower Mound	TX	75022	972-518-0198	
Software Toolbox 148A E Charles St *Web:* www.softwaretoolbox.com	Matthews	NC	28105	704-849-2773	
Sohum Inc 1055 Minnesota Ave Ste 6 *Web:* www.sohum.biz	San Jose	CA	95125	408-265-2391	
Solai & Cameron Inc 2335 N Southport Ave *Web:* www.solcam.com	Chicago	IL	60614	773-506-2720	
Soleratec LLC 2430 Auto Park Way Ste 205 *Web:* www.soleratec.com	Escondido	CA	92029	760-743-7200	
Solers Inc 950 N Glebe Rd Ste 1100 *Web:* www.solers.com	Arlington	VA	22203	703-526-0001	908-9353
Soliant Consulting Inc 14 N Peoria St 2H *Web:* www.soliantconsulting.com	Chicago	IL	60607	312-850-3830	
Solix Technologies Inc 4701 Patrick Henry Dr Bldg 20 *Web:* www.solix.com	Santa Clara	CA	95054	408-654-6400	
Solutions Development Corp 12220 Charles St *Web:* www.sdc-world.com	La Plata	MD	20646	301-638-3040	
Sonatype Inc 12501 Prosperity Dr Ste 350 *Web:* www.sonatype.com	Silver Spring	MD	20904	301-684-8080	
Soniya Technology International 3130 De La Cruz Blvd Ste 98 *Web:* www.soniyatech.com	Santa Clara	CA	95054	408-493-0310	
Sonoma Wire Works 101 First St Ste 587 *Web:* www.sonomawireworks.com	Los Altos	CA	94022	650-948-2003	
Sophisticated Business Systems Inc 6600 LBJ Fwy Ste 210 *Web:* www.ateras.com	Dallas	TX	75240	972-664-9005	
Sotech Inc 12011 Guilford Rd	Annapolis Junction	MD	20701	301-470-7015	
Source Photonics Inc 20550 Nordhoff St *Web:* www.sourcephotonics.com	Chatsworth	CA	91311	818-773-9044	
South River Technologies Inc 1910 Towne Centre Blvd Ste 250 *Web:* www.southrivertech.com	Annapolis	MD	21401	410-266-0667	
Southeast Computer Solutions Inc 15165 Nw 77th Ave Ste 2009 *Web:* www.southeastcomputers.com	Miami	FL	33014	305-556-4697	
Southern Software Inc 150 Perry Dr *Web:* southernsoftware.com	Southern Pines	NC	28387	910-695-0005	
Space Ground System Solutions Inc 4343 Fortune Pl Ste C *Web:* www.sgss.com	Melbourne	FL	32904	321-956-8200	
SPARC LLC 2387 Clements Ferry Rd *Web:* www.sparcedge.com	Charleston	SC	29492	843-471-1231	
Sparta Systems Inc 2000 Waterview Dr Ste 300 *TF:* 888-261-5948 ■ *Web:* www.spartasystems.com	Holmdel	NJ	07733	609-807-5100	
Spartan Technology Solutions Inc 125 Venture Blvd Ste B *Web:* www.spartantechnology.com	Spartanburg	SC	29306	864-587-1386	
Spoken Translation Inc 1100 W View Dr *Web:* www.spokentranslation.com	Berkeley	CA	94705	510-843-9900	
Spud Software Inc 9468 S Saginaw Rd *Web:* www.spudsoftware.com	Grand Blanc	MI	48439	810-695-0001	
Sql Data Solutions Inc 43 Herkomer St *Web:* www.sqldatasolutionsinc.com	New Hyde Park	NY	11040	516-358-1998	
Square Root Inc 508 Oakland Ave *Web:* www.square-root.com	Austin	TX	78703	512-693-9232	

Phone Fax

Squarei Technologies Inc
1315 Oakridge Dr Ste 100 . . . . . Fort Collins CO 80525 970-377-0077
Web: www.squarei.com

Stackframe LLC 114 W First St Ste 246 . . . . . Sanford FL 32771 407-733-0885
Web: www.stackframe.com

Stantive Technologies Group Inc
61 Hyperion Ct Ste 8 . . . . . Kingston ON K7K1K7 613-887-2647
Web: www.stantive.com

StayinFront Inc 107 Little Falls Rd . . . . . Fairfield NJ 07004 973-461-4800
Web: stayinfront.com

Steadmantech 1153 Powderhouse Rd . . . . . Vestal NY 13850 866-772-0882
TF: 866-772-0882 ■ *Web:* www.steadmantech.com

Stellar Systems Inc 222 Ne Monroe St . . . . . Peoria IL 61602 309-677-7350
Web: www.ssinet.com

Stenograph LLC 1500 Bishop Ct . . . . . Mount Prospect IL 60056 847-803-1400 803-1089
TF: 800-323-4247 ■ *Web:* www.stenograph.com

StepOne Systems LLC
2801 Liberty Ave Ste 200 . . . . . Pittsburgh PA 15222 412-894-8698
Web: www.steponesystems.com

Sterling Resources Inc 6 Forest Ave . . . . . Paramus NJ 07652 201-843-6444
Web: sterlingnet.com

Stone Bond Technologies LP
1021 Main St Ste 1550 . . . . . Houston TX 77002 713-622-8798
Web: www.stonebond.com

Stone Design Corp
2400 Rio Grande Blvd Nw . . . . . Albuquerque NM 87104 505-345-4800
Web: www.stone.com

Stone Technologies Inc
550 Spirit of St Louis Blvd . . . . . Chesterfield MO 63005 636-530-7240
Web: www.stonetek.com

Stonebranch Inc 950 N Point Pkwy Ste 200 . . . . . Alpharetta GA 30005 678-366-7887
Web: www.stonebranch.com

Strafford Technology 1D Commons Dr . . . . . Londonderry NH 03053 603-434-2550
Web: www.strafford.com

Strand Management Solutions
61 Princeton Hightstown Rd . . . . . Princeton Junction NJ 08550 609-799-7715
Web: www.strandmanagement.com

Strata Decision Technology LLC
2001 S First St Ste 200 . . . . . Champaign IL 61820 217-359-8422
Web: www.stratadecision.com

Studsvik Scandpower Inc 1087 Beacon St Ste 301 . . . . . Newton MA 02459 617-965-7450
Web: www.studsvik.com

Subsystem Technologies Inc
2121 Crystal Dr Ste 680 . . . . . Arlington VA 22202 703-841-0071
Web: www.subsystem.com

Subx Inc 428 Fore St . . . . . Portland ME 04101 207-775-0808
Web: www.quantrix.com

Success Sciences Inc 17838 N US Hwy 4 . . . . . Tampa FL 33549 813-989-9900
Web: www.success-sciences.com

Sudjam 520 E Broadway Ste 202 . . . . . Glendale CA 91205 818-206-1145
Web: www.sudjam.com

Summa Technologies Inc 925 Liberty Ave . . . . . Pittsburgh PA 15222 412-258-3300
Web: www.summa.com

Sunplus Data Group Inc
3781 Presidential Pkwy Ste 132 . . . . . Atlanta GA 30340 770-455-3264
Web: www.sunplusdata.com

Support Group Inc, The 24 Prime Park Way . . . . . Natick MA 01760 508-653-8400
Web: www.supportgroup.com

Sureit Solutions Inc
1801 W Queen Creek Rd Ste 3 . . . . . Chandler AZ 85248 480-917-2000
Web: www.sureitinc.com

Surf Merchants 41 W St 5th Fl . . . . . Boston MA 02111 617-292-8008
Web: surfmerchants.com

Survey & Ballot Systems Inc
7653 Anagram Dr . . . . . Eden Prairie MN 55344 952-974-2300
Web: www.surveyandballotsystems.com

Sutisoft Inc 4984 El Camino Real Ste 200 . . . . . Los Altos CA 94022 650-969-7884
Web: www.sutisoft.com

Symitar Systems Inc 8985 Balboa Ave . . . . . San Diego CA 92123 619-542-6700
Web: www.symitar.com

Synergy Business Solutions Inc
16250 SW Upper Boones Ferry Rd . . . . . Portland OR 97224 503-601-4100
Web: www.synergybusiness.com

Synre Voice Technologies Inc 200 Cochrane Dr . . . . . Markham ON L3R8E7 905-946-8500
Web: www.synrevoice.com

Syntell Inc 2954 Boul Laurier . . . . . Quebec QC G1V4T2 418-266-0900
Web: www.syntell.com

Sysintelli Inc 9466 Black Mtn Rd Ste 140 . . . . . San Diego CA 92126 858-271-1600
Web: www.sysintelli.com

SysLogic Inc 375 Bishops Way Ste 105 . . . . . Brookfield WI 53005 262-780-0380
Web: www.syslogicinc.com

System Concepts Inc 15900 N 78th St . . . . . Scottsdale AZ 85260 480-951-8011
TF: 800-553-2438 ■ *Web:* www.foodtrak.com

Systems Application Engineering Inc
3655 Westcenter Dr . . . . . Houston TX 77042 713-783-6020
Web: www.saesystems.com

Systems Engineering Technologies Corp
6121 Lincolnia Rd Ste 200 . . . . . Alexandria VA 22312 703-941-7887
TF: 800-385-8977 ■ *Web:* www.sytechcorp.com

Systems Exchange Inc 26625 Carmel Ctr Pl . . . . . Carmel CA 93923 831-649-3800
Web: www.tfdg.com

Systems Integration & Management Inc
2611 Jefferson Davis Hwy . . . . . Arlington VA 22202 703-412-5068 412-5069

Systems Products & Solutions Inc (SPS)
307 Wynn Dr . . . . . Huntsville AL 35805 256-319-2135
Web: www.services-sps.com

Systems Resource Management Inc
42 Valley Rd . . . . . Middletown RI 02842 401-849-2913
Web: www.srminc.net

Systems Technology Group Inc
3155 W Big Beaver Rd . . . . . Troy MI 48084 248-643-9010 643-9250
Web: www.stgit.com

Systemtec Inc 246 Stoneridge Dr Ste 301 . . . . . Columbia SC 29210 803-806-8100
TF: 888-900-1655 ■ *Web:* systemtec.net

T.S.D. Inc 1620 Turnpike St N . . . . . Andover MA 01845 978-794-1400
Web: tsdweb.com

Table Trac Inc 6101 Baker Rd Ste 206 . . . . . Minnetonka MN 55345 952-548-8877
Web: www.tabletrac.com

TABLETmedia Inc 2468 Union St . . . . . San Francisco CA 94123 415-567-8100
Web: www.tabletmedia.com

Talent Logic Inc 2313 Timber Shadows . . . . . Kingwood TX 77339 281-358-1858
Web: talentlogic.com

Tallan Inc 175 Capital Blvd Ste 401 . . . . . Rocky Hill CT 06067 860-633-3693 513-4870
TF: 800-677-3693 ■ *Web:* www.tallan.com

Tamlin Software Developers Inc
5646 Milton St Ste 540 . . . . . Dallas TX 75206 214-739-6576
Web: www.tamlinsoftware.com

Tanager Inc
10010 Junction Dr Ste 120N . . . . . Annapolis Junction MD 20701 240-547-3150
Web: www.tanagerinc.com

Tangent Systems Inc
2155 Stnngton Ave . . . . . Hoffman Estates IL 60195 847-882-3833
Web: www.tangent-systems.com

Tangoe Inc 35 Executive Blvd . . . . . Orange CT 06477 203-859-9300 859-9427
NASDAQ: TNGO ■ *TF:* 877-571-4737 ■ *Web:* www.tangoe.com

Tapestry Solutions Inc 5643 Copley Dr . . . . . San Diego CA 92111 858-503-1990
Web: www.tapestrysolutions.com

Tarigma Corp 6161 Busch Blvd Ste 110 . . . . . Columbus OH 43229 614-436-3734
Web: www.tarigma.com

Tavant Technologies Inc
3101 Jay St Ste 101 . . . . . Santa Clara CA 95054 408-519-5400
Web: www.tavant.com

Taylor Data Systems Inc
181 E Evans St BTC 008 . . . . . Florence SC 29506 843-656-2084
Web: taylordata.com

TBS Communications Inc
1800 Peachtree St Ste 655 . . . . . Atlanta GA 30309 404-876-6989
Web: www.coolbluei.com

TC Net-Works 23610 Mohican St NW . . . . . St. Francis MN 55070 612-747-4357
Web: www.tcnet-works.com

Team Automation 2215 First St 104 . . . . . Simi Valley CA 93065 805-522-3875
Web: www.teamautomation.com

Teamwork Solutions 5005 Horizons Dr Ste 200 . . . . . Columbus OH 43220 614-457-7100
Web: www.teamsol.com

Tech Friends 1341 County Rd 759 . . . . . Jonesboro AR 72401 870-933-6386
Web: mytechfriends.com

Tech Heads Inc 7060 SW Beveland Rd . . . . . Tigard OR 97223 503-639-8542
Web: www.techeads.com

Tech Observer 40 Eisenhower Dr Ste 201 . . . . . Hackensack NJ 07652 201-489-7705
Web: www.tech-observer.com

Tech-X Corp 5621 Arapahoe Ave Ste A . . . . . Boulder CO 80303 303-448-0727
Web: www.cusys.edu

TechFlow Inc 6405 Mira Mesa Blvd Ste 250 . . . . . San Diego CA 92121 858-412-8000
Web: www.techflow.com

Techgene Solutions LLC 300 E Royal Ln Ste 109 . . . . . Irving TX 75039 972-580-0247
Web: techgene.com

Technical Differences
5256 S Mission Rd Ste 210 . . . . . Bonsall CA 92003 760-941-5800
Web: www.people-trak.com

Technical Empowerment Inc 141 Nevada St . . . . . El Segundo CA 90245 310-524-1700
Web: www.techempower.com

Technical Support Inc 11253 John Galt Blvd . . . . . Omaha NE 68137 402-331-4977
TF: 800-337-0283 ■ *Web:* www.techsi.com

Technical Toolboxes Ltd 3801 Kirby Dr Ste 520 . . . . . Houston TX 77098 713-630-0505
TF: 866-866-6766 ■ *Web:* www.ttoolboxes.com

Technosoft Corp 28411 NW Hwy Ste 640 . . . . . Southfield MI 48034 248-603-2600 603-2599
Web: www.technosoftcorp.com

Technotraining Inc
328 Office Sq Ln Ste 202 . . . . . Virginia Beach VA 23462 757-425-0728
Web: www.technotraining.net

Techone Inc 7901 Stoneridge Dr Ste 403 . . . . . Pleasanton CA 94588 408-894-8100
Web: www.techone.com

Techrecruiters Inc
675 N Brookfield Rd Ste 205 . . . . . Brookfield WI 53045 262-781-0920
Web: techrecruiters.biz

Tecplot Inc 3535 Factoria Blvd SE Ste 550 . . . . . Bellevue WA 98006 425-653-1200
Web: www.tecplot.com

Teksouth Corp 1420 Northbrook Dr Ste 220 . . . . . Birmingham AL 35071 205-631-1500
Web: www.teksouth.com

Tel Tech Plus Inc 393 Enterprise St . . . . . San Marcos CA 92078 760-510-1323
Web: www.ttp-us.com

Telemanager Technologies Inc
211 Warren St Ste 409 . . . . . Newark NJ 07103 973-679-7500
Web: www.pharmacyshopper.com

Telemessage Inc 468 Great Rd Ste 2 . . . . . Acton MA 01720 978-263-1015
Web: www.telemessage.com

Telenav Inc 950 De Guigne Dr . . . . . Sunnyvale CA 94085 408-245-3800
Web: telenav.com

Telenix Corp 9194 Red Branch Rd . . . . . Columbia MD 21045 410-772-3275
Web: www.telenix.com

TeleSecurity Sciences Inc
7391 Prairie Falcon Rd Ste 150-B . . . . . Las Vegas NV 89128 702-227-7327
Web: www.telesecuritysciences.com

TELESIS Corp 8300 Greensboro Dr Ste 600 . . . . . McLean VA 22102 240-241-5600
Web: www.telesishq.com

TeleVoice Inc
10497 Town & Country Way Ste 500 . . . . . Houston TX 77024 281-497-8000
Web: televoice.com

Tell Systems Inc 106 Bridge Ave . . . . . Bay Head NJ 08742 732-899-0202
Web: www.tellsystems.com

Telliant Systems LLC
3180 N Point Pkwy Ste 108 . . . . . Alpharetta GA 30005 678-892-2801
Web: www.telliant.com

Telosa Software Inc 610 Cowper St . . . . . Palo Alto CA 94301 650-853-1100
Web: www.telosa.com

Company / Address	City	State	Zip	Phone	Fax
Tempest Development Group Inc 8431 160 St Ste 103 *Web:* www.tempestdg.com	Surrey	BC	V4N0V6	604-597-2846	
Tempest Technologies LLC 38 S Last Chance Gulch st Ste 5a *Web:* tempest-av.com	Helena	MT	59601	425-996-0228	
Tenable Network Security Inc 7021 Columbia Gateway Dr Ste 500 *Web:* www.tenable.com	Columbia	MD	21046	410-872-0555	
Terasci Industries Inc 5362 Production Dr *Web:* www.terasci.com	Huntington Beach	CA	92649	714-896-0150	
TERiX Computer Service Inc 388 Oakmead Pkwy *Web:* www.terix.com	Sunnyvale	CA	94085	408-737-1455	
Terra Dotta LLC 501 W Franklin St Ste 105 *TF:* 877-368-8277 ■ *Web:* www.terradotta.com	Chapel Hill	NC	27516	877-368-8277	
Terracor Business Solutions 677 St Mary's Rd *TF:* 877-942-0005 ■ *Web:* terracor.ca	Winnipeg	MB	R2M3M6	204-477-5342	
Terranova International 3675 Nordstrom Ln *Web:* terranovabi.com	Lafayette	CA	94549	925-299-6833	
TerraSim Inc 420 Ft Duquesne Blvd One Gateway Ctr Ste 2050 *Web:* www.terrasim.com	Pittsburgh	PA	15222	412-232-3646	
Testware Associates Inc 21 E High St *Web:* www.testwareinc.com	Somerville	NJ	08876	908-526-2900	
Tetrad Computer Applications Ltd 1465 Slater Rd PO Box 5007 *Web:* www.tetrad.com	Vancouver	BC	V6G2T3	604-685-2295	
TEXbase Inc 895 Technology Blvd Ste 202 *Web:* www.texbase.com	Bozeman	MT	59718	406-582-8874	
Thermoanalytics Inc 23440 Airpark Blvd *Web:* www.thermoanalytics.com	Calumet	MI	49913	906-482-9560	
Thermoflow Inc 2 Willow St Ste 100 *Web:* www.thermoflow.com	southborough	MA	01745	978-579-7999	
Thinkmap Inc 599 Broadway 9th Fl *Web:* www.thinkmap.com	New York	NY	10012	212-285-8600	
Third Pillar Systems Inc 577 Airport Blvd 8th Fl *Web:* www.thirdpillar.com	Burlingame	CA	94010	650-372-1200	
Threespot Media LLC 3333 14th St NW *Web:* threespot.com	Washington	DC	20010	202-471-1000	
Tier1 Inc 2403 Sidney St Ste 225 *TF:* 888-284-0202 ■ *Web:* tier1inc.com	Pittsburgh	PA	15203	412-381-9201	
TIES 1667 Snelling Ave N *Web:* ties.k12.mn.us	St. Paul	MN	55108	651-999-6000	
Tietronix Software Inc 1331 Gemini Ave Ste 300 *Web:* www.tietronix.com	Houston	TX	77058	281-461-9300	
Tigerpaw Software Inc 2201 Thurston Cir *Web:* www.jamesfoxall.com	Bellevue	NE	68005	402-592-4544	
Tim Ivey Company Inc 1129 Riders Club Rd *Web:* timivey.com	Onalaska	WI	54650	608-738-8066	
Timberline Interactive Inc 5 Park St Ste 2 *Web:* www.timberlineinteractive.com	Middlebury	VT	05753	802-388-8377	
Time & Cents Consultants LLC 31 Deane Lane *Web:* www.timeandcents.com	Fairfield	CT	06824	203-254-7736	
Time Trak Systems Inc 933 Pine Grove *TF:* 888-484-6387 ■ *Web:* timetrak.com	Port Huron	MI	48060	810-984-1313	
TimeTECH Canada Inc 7420 Airport Rd Ste 101 *TF:* 877-816-8463 ■ *Web:* www.synerion.com	Mississauga	ON	L4T4E5	905-677-7009	
Timeware Inc 9329 Ravenna Rd Ste D *TF:* 866-936-2420 ■ *Web:* www.timewareinc.com	Twinsburg	OH	44087	330-963-2700	
Tips Inc 2402 Williams Dr *TF:* 800-242-8477 ■ *Web:* tipsweb.com	Georgetown	TX	78628	512-863-3653	863-5392
Titan Lenders Corp 5353 W Dartmouth Ave Ste 50 *TF:* 866-412-9180 ■ *Web:* www.titanlenderscorp.com	Denver	CO	80227	866-412-9180	
TIW Technology Inc 769 Youngs Hill Rd *Web:* www.tiwcorp.com	Easton	PA	18040	610-258-5161	
Tizbi Inc 800 Saint Mary's St Ste 402 *TF:* 888-729-0951 ■ *Web:* www.tizbi.com	Raleigh	NC	27605	888-729-0951	
Today's Business Computers 213 E Black Horse Pk *TF:* 800-371-5132 ■ *Web:* www.tbcusa.com	Pleasantville	NJ	08232	609-645-5132	
Tom Sawyer Software Corp 1997 El Dorado Ave *Web:* www.tomsawyer.com	Berkeley	CA	94707	510-208-4370	
Tone Software Inc 1735 S Brookhurst St *TF:* 800-833-8663 ■ *Web:* www.tonesoft.com	Anaheim	CA	92804	714-991-9460	
TopCoder Inc 95 Glastonbury Blvd *TF:* 866-867-2633 ■ *Web:* www.topcoder.com	Glastonbury	CT	06033	860-633-5540	657-4276
Torrid Technologies Inc 1860 Sandy Plains Rd Ste 204-129 *Web:* www.torrid-tech.com	Marietta	GA	30066	770-565-6405	
Total Cad Systems Inc 480 N Sam Houston Pkwy E Ste 234 *Web:* www.tcadsys.com	Houston	TX	77060	281-445-6161	
Total Computing Solutions of America Inc 23430 Hawthorne Blvd Skypark Office Ctr Bldg 3 Ste 300 *Web:* www.tcsamerica.com	Torrance	CA	90505	310-378-9100	
Total Solutions Inc 1626 County Line Rd *Web:* www.totalsolutions-inc.com	Madison	AL	35756	256-721-3987	
Touch Networks 2515 152nd Ave Ne *Web:* touchnetworks.com	Redmond	WA	98052	425-881-8806	
Towerstrides Inc 4229 Lafayette Ctr Dr Ste 1200 *Web:* www.towerstrides.com	Chantilly	VA	20151	703-953-1531	
Towerwall 615 Concord St *Web:* www.towerwall.com	Framingham	MA	01702	774-204-0700	
TrackAbout Inc 410 Rouser Rd Ste 400 *Web:* corp.trackabout.com	Moon Township	PA	15108	412-269-0446	
Tracorp Inc 5621 W Beverly Ln *Web:* www.tracorp.com	Glendale	AZ	85306	602-864-1385	
Trade Manage Capital Inc 299 Market St 4th Fl *TF:* 800-221-5676 ■ *Web:* www.yamner.com	Saddle Brook	NJ	07663	800-221-5676	
Transcendent LLC 1040 Cottonwood Ave Ste 300 *Web:* transcendent-llc.com	Hartland	WI	53029	262-953-2750	
TransGaming Inc 179 John St Ste 301 *Web:* www.transgaming.com	Toronto	ON	M5T1X4	416-979-9900	
Transpara Corp 4715 W Culpepper Dr Ste 100 *Web:* www.transpara.com	Pleasanton	CA	94566	925-218-6983	
Traveling Computers Inc 210 E Main St *Web:* www.tcinc.net	Riverton	WY	82501	307-856-8676	
Treehouse Software Inc 2605 Nicholson Rd Ste 230 *Web:* www.treehouse.com	Sewickley	PA	15143	724-759-7070	
TRG Networking 11436 Cronhill Dr Ste 4B *Web:* www.trgnetworking.com	Owings Mills	MD	21117	410-363-6980	
Tri-star Data Systems Inc 650 Sentry Pkwy Ste 1 *Web:* tristardatasystems.com	Blue Bell	PA	19422	610-941-2116	
Triad Interactive Inc 1100 H St Nw Ste 1201 *Web:* www.triadinteractive.com	Washington	DC	20036	202-347-0900	347-0930
Triangle MicroWorks Inc 2840 Plz Pl Ste 205 *Web:* www.trianglemicroworks.com	Raleigh	NC	27612	919-870-5101	
Triforce Consulting Svc Inc 650 N Cannon Ave *Web:* triforce-inc.com	Lansdale	PA	19446	215-362-2611	
Trifox Inc 3131 S Bascom Ave *Web:* www.trifox.com	Campbell	CA	95008	408-369-2300	
Trigyn Technologies Inc 100 Metroplex Dr Ste 101 *Web:* www.trigyn.com	Edison	NJ	08817	732-777-0050	
Trilog Group Inc 54 Cummings Park *Web:* www.triloggroup.com	Woburn	MA	01801	781-937-9963	
Triple Point Technology Inc 301 Riverside Ave *Web:* www.tpt.com	Westport	CT	06880	203-291-7979	
Triware Technologies Inc 76 Brookfield Rd *Web:* www.triware.ca	St John's	NL	A1E3T9	709-579-5000	
Trix Systems Inc 68 Smith St *Web:* www.trixsystems.com	Chelmsford	MA	01824	978-256-4445	
TriZetto Corporation 501 N Broadway 3rd Fl *TF:* 800-969-3666 ■ *Web:* www.trizettoprovider.com	Sacramento	CA	95814	800-969-3666	
Tropics Software Technologies Inc 7349 Merchant Crt *Web:* www.gotropics.com	Sarasota	FL	34240	941-955-1234	
Truckers Helper LLC, The 630 S Wickham Rd Ste 203 *Web:* www.truckershelper.com	Melbourne	FL	32904	321-956-7331	
True Solutions Inc 5001 Lyndon B Johnson Fwy Ste 125 *Web:* www.truesolutions.com	Dallas	TX	75244	972-770-0900	
Truepoint Solutions LLC 5714 Folsom Blvd Ste 236 *Web:* www.truepointsolutions.com	Sacramento	CA	95819	916-259-1293	
Trusant Technologies LLC 6011 University Blvd *Web:* trusant.com	Ellicott City	MD	21043	410-418-5400	
Trusted Integration Inc 525 Wythe St *Web:* www.trustedintegration.com	Alexandria	VA	22314	703-299-9171	
Trutek 1740 S Main St *Web:* www.trutek.com	Salt Lake City	UT	84115	801-486-6655	
Truven Holding Corp 777 E Eisenhower Pkwy *Web:* www.truvenhealth.com	Ann Arbor	MI	48108	734-913-3000	
TSA-Advet 4722 Campbells Run Rd *Web:* www.tsa.advet.com	Pittsburgh	PA	15205	412-787-0980	
Tucson Embedded Systems Inc 5620 N Kolb Rd *Web:* tucsonembedded.com	Tucson	AZ	85750	520-575-7283	575-5563
Turner Consulting Group Inc 306 Florida Ave NW *Web:* www.tcg.com	Washington	DC	20001	202-986-5533	
Twin Oaks Software Development Inc 1463 Berlin Tpke *TF:* 866-278-6750 ■ *Web:* www.healthclubsoftware.com	Berlin	CT	06037	860-829-6000	
Twin State Technical Services Ltd 3543 E Kimberly Rd *Web:* www.tsts.com	Davenport	IA	52807	563-441-1504	
Twinstar Inc 8703 Yates Dr Ste 115 *Web:* www.twinstarinc.net	Westminster	CO	80031	303-430-7101	
Tympani LLC 2001 Butterfield Rd Ste 250 *Web:* www.tympani.net	Downers Grove	IL	60515	630-981-5000	
Ultra Electronics Advanced Tactical Systems Inc 4101 Smith School Rd *Web:* www.ultra-ats.com	Austin	TX	78744	512-327-6795	327-8043
Unicentric Inc 3127 Penn Ave *TF:* 800-513-7745 ■ *Web:* www.unicentric.com	Pittsburgh	PA	15201	412-697-7200	
Unimax Systems Corporation Inc 430 First Ave N Ste 790 *Web:* www.unimax.com	Minneapolis	MN	55401	612-341-0946	
Unique Business Systems Corp 2901 Ocean Park Blvd # 215 *Web:* www.unibiz.com	Santa Monica	CA	90405	310-396-3929	
United e r p LLC 235 Closter Dock Rd Ste 503 *Web:* www.unitederp.com	Closter	NJ	07624	201-567-6315	
United Systems & Software Inc 300 Colonial Ctr Pkwy Ste 150 PO Box 958444 *TF:* 800-522-8774 ■ *Web:* www.ussisolutions.com	Lake Mary	FL	32746	407-875-2120	875-9600
Unity Technologies Inc 795 Folsom St Ste 200 *Web:* unity3d.com	San Francisco	CA	94107	415-539-3162	

Company / Address	City	State	Zip	Phone	Fax
Univeris Corp 111 George St 3rd Fl *Web:* www.univeris.com	Toronto	ON	M5A2N4	416-979-3700	
Unleaded Software Inc 2314 Broadway Unit B *Web:* www.unleadedsoftware.com	Denver	CO	80205	720-221-7126	
Unleashed Technologies 10005 Old Columbia Rd Ste L-261 *Web:* www.unleashed-technologies.com	Columbia	MD	21046	410-864-8980	
Unlimi-Tech Software Inc 1725 St Laurent Blvd Ste 205 *TF:* 877-327-9387 ■ *Web:* www.utechsoft.com	Ottawa	ON	K1G3V4	613-667-2439	
Unlimited Innovations Inc 180 N Riverview Dr Ste 320 *Web:* www.uius.com	Anaheim Hills	CA	92808	714-998-0866	
Untangle Inc 100 W San Fernando St Ste 565 *Web:* www.metavize.com	San Jose	CA	95113	408-598-4299	
US Networx Inc 6360 I 55 N Ste 310 *Web:* www.usnx.com	Jackson	MS	39211	601-956-4770	
USA Digital Solutions Inc 10835 N 25th Ave Ste 350 *Web:* digisolaz.com	Phoenix	AZ	85029	602-866-8199	
Usmax Corp 382 Gambrills Rd *Web:* www.usmax.com	Gambrills	MD	21054	301-912-1166	
Utilant LLC 475 Ellicott St Ste 5 *TF:* 888-884-5268 ■ *Web:* utilant.com	Buffalo	NY	14203	888-884-5268	
V2Soft Inc 300 Enterprise Ct Ste 100 *Web:* www.v2soft.com	Bloomfield Hills	MI	48302	248-904-1700	
Valco Data Systems Inc N57 W13652 Reichert Ave *Web:* valcodata.com	Menomonee Falls	WI	53051	262-781-7731	
Valid8 .com Inc 500 W Cummings Park Ste 6550 *TF:* 855-482-5438 ■ *Web:* valid8.com	Woburn	MA	01801	855-482-5438	
Valley Agricultural Software Inc 3950 S K St *Web:* www.vas.com	Tulare	CA	93274	559-686-9496	
Valley Scale Company LLC 751 W Kenwood Ave *Web:* www.thinkvsc.com	Clarksville	IN	47129	812-282-5269	
Valogix Inc 27 Division St Ste 2 *Web:* www.valogix.com	Saratoga Springs	NY	12866	518-450-0309	
ValueCheck Inc 8822 Ridgeline Blvd Ste 100 *Web:* www.valuecheckonline.com	Highlands Ranch	CO	80129	720-283-0737	
ValuSource LLC 4575 Galley Rd Ste 200E *Web:* www.valusource.com	Colorado Springs	CO	80915	719-548-4900	
Varen Technologies Inc 9801 Broken Land Pkwy Ste 100 *Web:* www.varentech.com	Columbia	MD	21046	410-290-8008	
Varite Inc 12 S First St Ste 404 *Web:* www.varite.com	San Jose	CA	95113	408-977-0700	
Vecna Technologies Inc 6404 Ivy Ln Ste 500 *Web:* www.vecna.com	Greenbelt	MD	20770	240-965-4500	
Vector Consulting 6455 E Johns Crossing *Web:* vectorconsulting.com	Duluth	GA	30097	770-246-0968	
Vector Planning & Services Inc 591 Camino De La Reina Ste 300 *TF:* 888-522-5491 ■ *Web:* myvpsi.com	San Diego	CA	92108	619-297-5656	
Vector Software Inc 1351 S County Trl Ste 310 *Web:* www.vectorcast.com	East Greenwich	RI	02818	401-398-7185	
VectorMAX Corp 4 Dubon Ct *Web:* www.vectormax.com	Farmingdale	NY	11735	212-937-7706	
Vektrex Electronic Systems Inc 10225 Barnes Canyon Rd *Web:* www.vektrex.com	San Diego	CA	92121	858-558-8282	
Vensiti Inc 1304 W Walnut Hill Ln Ste 212	Irving	TX	75038	972-887-7995	
Verecloud Inc 555 Eldorado Blvd Ste 200 *TF:* 877-300-2158	Broomfield	CO	80021	877-300-2158	
Verican Inc 1 Hallidie Plz Ste 404 *Web:* www.verican.com	San Francisco	CA	94102	415-296-7300	
Veridikal Inc 1541 E Hope St *Web:* www.veridikal.com	Mesa	AZ	85203	480-636-1830	
Verisource Services Inc 7600 W Tidwell Rd Ste 700 *Web:* www.verisource.com	Houston	TX	77040	713-647-6540	
Verisurf Software Inc 4907 E Landon Dr *Web:* www.verisurf.com	Anaheim	CA	92807	714-970-1683	
Veritas Medicine Inc 11 Cambridge Ctr *Web:* www.veritasmedicine.com	Cambridge	MA	02142	617-234-1500	
Verix Inc 339 S San Antonio Rd Ste 2G *Web:* www.verix.com	Los Altos	CA	94022	650-691-2700	
Veros Real Estate Solutions LLC 2333 N Broadway Ste 350 *TF:* 866-458-3767 ■ *Web:* www.veros.com	Santa Ana	CA	92706	714-415-6300	
Versonix Corp 1175 Saratoga Ave Ste 4 *Web:* versonix.com	San Jose	CA	95129	408-873-3131	
Vertex Software Corp 1515 S Cptl Of Tx Hwy 4 *Web:* www.vertex.com	Austin	TX	78746	512-328-3700	
Vertical Management Systems Inc 7 N Fair Oaks Ave 2nd Fl *TF:* 800-867-4357 ■ *Web:* www.vmshelp.com	Pasadena	CA	91103	800-867-4357	
Vertical Systems Inc 6462 City W Pkwy Ste 100 *Web:* www.vertsys.com	Eden Prairie	MN	55344	952-934-7533	
Viatron Systems Inc 18233 S Hoover St *Web:* www.viatron.com	Los Angeles	CA	90248	310-756-0610	
Vibration Research Corp 2385 Wilshere Dr # A *Web:* www.vibrationresearch.com	Jenison	MI	49428	616-669-3028	
VideoMining Corp 403 S Allen St Ste 101 *TF:* 800-898-9950 ■ *Web:* www.videomining.com	State College	PA	16801	800-898-9950	
Viget Labs LLC 400 S Maple Ave *Web:* viget.com	Falls Church	VA	22046	703-891-0670	
VirnetX Holding Corp 308 Dorla Court Ste 206 *Web:* virnetx.com	Zephyr Cove	NV	89448	831-438-8200	
Virtual Training Company Inc 5395 Main St *TF:* 888-316-5374 ■ *Web:* www.vtc.com	Stephens City	VA	22655	540-869-8686	
Viscira LLC 200 Vallejo St *Web:* www.viscira.com	San Francisco	CA	94111	415-848-8010	
Visibility Corp 200 Minuteman Rd *Web:* www.visibility.com	Andover	MA	01810	978-269-6500	269-6501
Vision Multimedia Technologies LLC 2031 Clipper Park Rd Ste 105	Baltimore	MD	21211	410-889-7770	
Vision Technologies Inc 530 McCormick Dr Ste G *TF:* 866-746-1122 ■ *Web:* www.visiontechnologiesinc.net	Glen Burnie	MD	21061	410-424-2183	424-2208
Visionary Legal Technologies LP 14677 Midway Rd Ste 118 *Web:* www.visionarylegaltechnologies.com	Addison	TX	75001	214-370-4359	
Visionsoft International Inc 1842 Old Norcross Rd Ste 100 *Web:* www.vsiiusa.com	Lawrenceville	GA	30044	770-682-2899	
Vistar Technologies Corp 11924 Forest Hill Blvd Ste 10-127 *Web:* vistartech.com	Wellington	FL	33414	561-792-6644	
Vistrian Inc 562 Valley Way *Web:* www.vistrian.com	Milpitas	CA	95035	408-719-0500	
Visual Learning Systems Inc PO Box 8226 *TF:* 866-968-7857 ■ *Web:* www.vls-inc.com	Missoula	MT	59807	866-968-7857	
Visual Purple LLC 75 Higuera St Ste 240 *Web:* www.visualpurple.com	San Luis Obispo	CA	93401	805-595-7579	
Visual Risk Technology 210 25th Ave N Ste 910 *Web:* www.vrisk.com	Nashville	TN	37203	615-321-4848	
Visualware Inc 937 Sierra Dr PO Box 668 *TF:* 866-847-9273 ■ *Web:* www.visualware.com	Turlock	CA	95380	209-262-3491	
Vitech Corp 2270 Kraft Dr Ste 1600 *Web:* www.vitechcorp.com	Blacksburg	VA	24060	540-951-3322	
Vivox Inc 2-4 Mercer Rd *Web:* www.vivox.com	Natick	MA	01760	508-650-3571	
Vocera Communications Inc 525 RACE St Ste 150 *Web:* www.vocera.com	San Jose	CA	95126	408-882-5100	
VoiceBox Technologies Inc 11980 NE 24th St Ste 100 *Web:* www.voicebox.com	Bellevue	WA	98005	425-968-7900	
Volare Systems Inc 4351 Canyonbrook Dr *Web:* volaresystems.com	Highlands Ranch	CO	80130	303-532-5838	
Volian Enterprises Inc 122 Kerr Rd *Web:* volian.com	New Kensington	PA	15068	724-335-3744	
Vortx Inc 2245 Ashland St *Web:* www.vortx.com	Ashland	OR	97520	541-201-9965	
VOSINC 2030 Arnold Dr *Web:* www.vosinc.com	Martinez	CA	94553	925-229-6600	
VPIsystems Corp 100 Davidson Ave Ste 203 *Web:* www.vpisystems.com	Somerset	NJ	08873	732-332-0233	469-7823
Vrp Consulting Inc 268 Bush St Ste 3836 *TF:* 855-545-3877 ■ *Web:* www.vrpinc.com	San Francisco	CA	94104	855-545-3877	
VSolvIT LLC 4171 Market St Ste 2 *Web:* www.vsolvit.com	Ventura	CA	93003	805-277-4705	
W a m s Inc 1800 E Lambert Ave Ste 155 *TF:* 800-421-7151 ■ *Web:* www.wamsinc.com	Brea	CA	92821	714-994-2811	
Wavecrest Computing Inc 2006 Vernon Pl *Web:* www.wavecrest.net	Melbourne	FL	32901	321-953-5351	
Wavefunction Inc 18401 Von Karman Ave *Web:* www.wavefun.com	Irvine	CA	92612	949-955-2120	
Wavelength Datacom LLC 1265 Oakmead Pkwy *Web:* www.wavdata.com	Sunnyvale	CA	94085	408-746-0200	
Web Advanced 36 Discovery Ste 100 *Web:* www.webadvanced.com	Irvine	CA	92618	949-453-1805	
Webaloo LLC 217 Second St N *Web:* www.webaloo.com	Stillwater	MN	55082	651-351-1041	
WebAssist.com Corp 227 N El Camino Real Ste 204 *Web:* www.webassist.com	Encinitas	CA	92024	760-633-4013	
WebEquity Solutions LLC 1010 N 102nd St Ste 100 *Web:* www.webequitysolutions.com	Omaha	NE	68114	402-344-5200	
Webmagic 87 N Raymond Ave Ste 850 *Web:* www.webmagic.com	Pasadena	CA	91103	626-794-5000	
WebNet Services Inc 247 Rt 100 *TF:* 866-923-4811 ■ *Web:* www.webnetservices.com	Somers	NY	10589	914-232-6900	232-6901
Weidenhammer Systems Corp 935 Berkshire Blvd *TF:* 866-497-2227 ■ *Web:* www.hammer.net	Reading	PA	19610	610-378-1149	378-9409
Weidt Group Inc, The 5800 Baker Rd Ste 100 *Web:* www.twgi.com	Minnetonka	MN	55345	952-938-1588	
Welligent Inc 5205 Colley Ave *TF:* 888-317-5960 ■ *Web:* www.welligent.com	Norfolk	VA	23508	888-317-5960	
Wellness Layers Inc 336 Atlantic Ave Ste 301 *Web:* www.wellnesslayers.com	East Rockaway	NY	11518	212-537-9498	
Wennsoft Inc 1970 S Calhoun Rd *Web:* www.wennsoft.com	New Berlin	WI	53151	262-821-4100	
Wescon Technology Inc 4655 Old Ironsides Dr *Web:* www.wescongroup.com	Santa Clara	CA	95054	408-727-8818	
West Gulf Maritime Association 1717 E Loop N Ste 200 *Web:* www.wgma.org	Houston	TX	77029	713-678-7655	
WetStone Technologies Inc 20 Thornwood Dr Ste 105 *Web:* www.wetstonetech.com	Ithaca	NY	14850	607-266-8086	
WhatIfSports.com Inc 10200 Alliance Rd *Web:* www.whatifsports.com	Cincinnati	OH	45242	513-333-0313	
White Ware Inc 22583 Park St *Web:* www.whiteware.com	Dearborn	MI	48124	313-792-1222	

				Phone	Fax
Whole Brain Group LLC, The 109 E Ann St. Web: www.thewholebraingroup.com	Ann Arbor	MI	48104	734-929-0431	
Winning Solutions Inc 1421 S Bell Ave Ste 105 Web: www.winningsolutionsinc.com	Ames	IA	50010	515-239-9900	
Winston Hospitality Inc 3701 National Dr Ste 120 Web: www.choate.com	Raleigh	NC	27612	919-334-6910	
Winware Inc 1955 W Oak Cir. TF: 888-419-1399 ■ Web: www.cribmaster.com	Marietta	GA	30062	770-419-1399	419-1968
Wiredrive 5340 Alla Rd Ste 109 Web: www.wiredrive.com	Los Angeles	CA	90066	310-823-8238	
WireSpring Technologies Inc 1901 W Cypress Creek Rd Ste 100 Web: wirespring.com	Fort Lauderdale	FL	33309	954-548-3300	
Wolfe Diversified Industries LLC 223 W Ninth St Web: www.wolfediversifiedindustries.com	Anderson	IN	46016	765-683-9374	
Wolfram Research Inc 100 Trade Ctr Dr TF: 800-965-3726 ■ Web: www.wolfram.com	Champaign	IL	61820	217-398-0700	398-0747
Work Technology Corp 255 Elm St Ste 300 Web: www.worktech.com	Somerville	MA	02144	617-625-5888	
Workshare Technology Inc 208 Utah St Ste 350 Web: www.workshare.com	San Francisco	CA	94103	415-975-3855	
Worthwhile 7 S Laurens St Ste 200 Web: worthwhile.com	Greenville	SC	29601	864-233-2552	
Wyant Data Systems Inc 245 Century Cir Ste 106 Web: www.wyantdata.com	Louisville	CO	80027	303-604-6254	
X-iss 2190 N Loop W Ste 415 Web: www.x-iss.com	Houston	TX	77018	713-862-9200	
X3O LLC 11810 Parklawn Dr Ste 208 Web: www.x3o.com	Rockville	MD	20852	301-816-9055	
Xcape Solutions Inc 207 Crystal Grove Blvd TF: 866-285-4899 ■ Web: www.xcapesolutions.net	Lutz	FL	33548	813-964-9101	
Xceltech Inc 2136 Gallows Rd Web: www.xceltech.com	Dunn Loring	VA	22027	703-208-9120	
Xelas Systems Engineering LLC 8111 Red Farm Ln Web: www.xelas-systems.com	Bowie	MD	20715	301-789-1162	
Xenex Enterprises Inc 155 Rexdale Blvd Ste 707 Web: www.xenex.ca	Toronto	ON	M9W5Z8	416-740-9704	
Xeno Media 18w100 22nd St Ste 128 Web: www.xenomedia.com	Oakbrook Terrace	IL	60181	630-599-1550	
Xiacon Inc 140 Fell Ct Ste 120 Web: www.xiaconinc.com	Hauppauge	NY	11788	631-300-3500	
Xlink Technology Inc 1546 Centre Pointe Dr. Web: www.xlink.com	Milpitas	CA	95035	408-263-8201	
XPAND Corp 1941 Roland Clarke Pl Web: www.xpandcorp.com	Reston	VA	20191	703-742-0900	
Xper2go 39120 Argonaut Way Ste 782 Web: www.xper2go.com	Fremont	CA	94538	510-585-2500	
Xrg Systems Inc 38 Lily Ct Ste 214 Web: xrgsystems.com	San Ramon	CA	94583	925-241-4995	
XSYS Inc 653 Steele Dr. Web: www.xsysinc.com	Valparaiso	IN	46385	219-477-4816	
Xytech Systems Corp 15451 San Fernando Mission Blvd Ste 400 Web: www.xytechsystems.com	Mission Hills	CA	91345	818-698-4900	
Y-Change 43575 Mission Blvd Web: www.y-change.com	Fremont	CA	94539	510-573-2205	
Yang Enterprises Inc 1420 Alafaya Trl Ste 200 Web: www.yangenterprises.com	Oviedo	FL	32765	407-365-7374	
Youngsoft Inc 49197 Wixom Tech Dr TF: 888-470-4553 ■ Web: www.youngsoft.com	Wixom	MI	48393	248-675-1200	675-1201
Z Option Inc 417 Oakbend Dr Ste 200 Web: www.zoption.com	Lewisville	TX	75067	972-315-8800	
Z-Law Software Inc 80 Upton Ave PO Box 40602 TF: 800-526-5588 ■ Web: www.z-law.com	Providence	RI	02940	401-331-3002	421-5334
Zasio Enterprises Inc 401 W Front St Ste 305 TF: 800-513-1000 ■ Web: www.zasio.com	Boise	ID	83702	800-513-1000	
Zeda Soft 2310 Gravel Dr Web: www.zedasoft.com	Fort Worth	TX	76118	817-616-1000	
Zenith Information Systems Inc 18757 Burbank Blvd Web: www.zis.com	Tarzana	CA	91356	310-826-8634	
Zenoss Inc 11305 Four Points Dr Bldg 1 Ste 300 Web: www.zenoss.com	Austin	TX	78726	410-990-0274	
Zentech Technical Services Inc 14800 Saint Marys Ln Ste 270 Web: www.zentech-usa.com	Houston	TX	77079	281-558-0290	
Zephyr-Tec Corp 9651 Business Ctr Dr Ste C TF: 877-493-7497 ■ Web: www.zephyr-tec.com	Rancho Cucamonga	CA	91730	909-481-9991	
Zethcon Corp 200 W 22nd St Ste 218 Web: zethcon.com	Lombard	IL	60148	847-318-0800	
Zinck Computer Group 131 Ilsley Ave Web: www.zcg.com	Dartmouth	NS	B3B1T1	902-468-2738	
Zirous Inc 1503 42nd St Ste 210 Web: www.zirous.com	West Des Moines	IA	50266	515-225-9015	
ZM Financial Systems Inc 5915 Farrington Rd Ste 201 Web: www.zmfs.com	Chapel Hill	NC	27517	919-493-0029	
Zombie Studios 420 Fourth Ave Web: www.zombie.com	Seattle	WA	98104	206-623-9655	
Zoomedia Inc 1620 Montgomery St. Web: hdmz.com	San Francisco	CA	94111	415-474-1192	
Zoot Enterprises Inc 555 Zoot Enterprises Ln Web: www.zootweb.com	Bozeman	MT	59718	406-586-5050	
Zotec Partners LLC 11460 N Meridian St Web: zotecpartners.com	Carmel	IN	46032	317-705-5050	

COMPUTER RESELLERS

See Computer Equipment & Software - Whol p. 2002

178 COMPUTER SOFTWARE

See Also Application Service Providers (ASPs) p. 1738; Computer Equipment & Software - Whol p. 2002; Computer Networking Products & Systems p. 2008; Computer Programming Services - Custom p. 2009; Computer Stores p. 2036; Computer Systems Design Services p. 2039; Educational Materials & Supplies p. 2205

				Phone	Fax
Calypso Technology Inc 595 Market St Ste 1800 Web: www.calypso.com	San Francisco	CA	94105	415-817-2400	284-1222
Williamson Law Book Co 790 Canning Pkwy TF: 800-733-9522 ■ Web: www.wlbonline.com	Victor	NY	14564	585-924-3400	924-4153

178-1 Business Software (General)

Companies listed here make general-purpose software products that are designed for use by all types of businesses, professionals, and, to some extent, personal users.

				Phone	Fax
1MAGE Software Inc 384 Inverness Pkwy Ste 206 *Fax Area Code: 303 ■ TF: 800-844-1468 ■ Web: www.1mage.com	Englewood	CO	80112	800-844-1468	796-0587*
4D Inc 3031 Tisch Way Ste 900 TF: 800-785-3303 ■ Web: www.4d.com	San Jose	CA	95128	408-557-4600	261-9879
ACI Worldwide 4965 Preston Pk Blvd Ste 800 TF: 877-238-3095 ■ Web: www.aciworldwide.com	Plano	TX	75093	972-599-5600	
ACOM Solutions Inc 2850 E 29th St. TF: 800-347-3638 ■ Web: www.acom.com	Long Beach	CA	90806	562-424-7899	424-8662
Actuate Corp 2207 Bridgepointe Pkwy Ste 500 NASDAQ: OTEX ■ TF Sales: 800-914-2259 ■ Web: www.actuate.com	San Mateo	CA	94404	650-645-3000	
Adexa Inc 5933 W Century Blvd 12th Fl. TF: 888-300-7692 ■ Web: www.adexa.com	Los Angeles	CA	90045	310-642-2100	338-9878
Adobe Systems Inc 345 Pk Ave NASDAQ: ADBE ■ TF: 800-833-6687 ■ Web: www.adobe.com	San Jose	CA	95110	408-536-6000	537-6000
AdStar Inc 4553 Glencoe Ave Ste 300 PINK: ADST	Marina del Rey	CA	90292	310-577-8255	577-8266
Advent Software Inc 600 Townsend St Ste 500 5th Fl. NASDAQ: ADVS ■ TF: 800-727-0605 ■ Web: www.advent.com	San Francisco	CA	94103	415-543-7696	543-5070
AgilQuest Corp 9407 Hull St Rd TF: 888-745-7455 ■ Web: www.agilquest.com	Richmond	VA	23236	804-745-0467	745-6243
Alpha Software Inc 70 BlanchaRd Rd Ste 206 Web: www.alphasoftware.com	Burlington	MA	01803	781-229-4500	272-4876
Alterian Inc 35 E Wacker Dr Ste 200 Web: www.sdl.com	Chicago	IL	60601	312-704-1700	704-1701
American Business Systems Inc 315 Littleton Rd *Fax Area Code: 978 ■ TF: 800-356-4034 ■ Web: www.abs-software.com	Chelmsford	MA	01824	800-356-4034	250-8027*
American Software Inc 470 E Paces Ferry Rd. NASDAQ: AMSWA ■ TF: 800-726-2946 ■ Web: www.amsoftware.com	Atlanta	GA	30305	404-261-4381	264-5206
Appian Corp 11955 Democracy Dr Ste 1700 Web: www.appian.com	Reston	VA	20190	703-442-8844	
APPX Software Inc 11363 San Jose Blvd Ste 301 TF: 800-879-2779 ■ Web: www.appx.com	Jacksonville	FL	32223	904-880-5560	880-6635
AquiTec International 547 W Jackson Blvd 9th Fl.	Chicago	IL	60661	312-264-1900	264-1991
Architecture Technology Corp (ATC) 9971 Vly View Rd Web: www.atcorp.com	Eden Prairie	MN	55344	952-829-5864	829-5868
Artemis International Solutions Corp 401 Congress Ave Ste 2650 Web: www.aisc.com	Austin	TX	78701	512-201-8222	874-8900
Astea International Inc 240 Gibraltar Rd NASDAQ: ATEA ■ TF: 800-878-4657 ■ Web: www.astea.com	Horsham	PA	19044	215-682-2500	682-2515
athenahealth Inc 311 Arsenal St NASDAQ: ATHN ■ TF: 800-981-5084 ■ Web: www.athenahealth.com	Watertown	MA	02472	617-402-1000	402-1099
AttachmateWRQ 1500 Dexter Ave N TF Sales: 800-872-2829 ■ Web: www.attachmate.com	Seattle	WA	98109	206-217-7500	217-7515
Attunity Inc 70 BlanchaRd Rd *Fax Area Code: 877 ■ TF: 866-288-8648 ■ Web: www.attunity.com	Burlington	MA	01803	781-730-4070	896-2760*
Avue Technologies Corp 3560 Bridgeport Way W Ste 3B Web: www.avuetech.com	University Place	WA	98466	253-573-1877	573-1876
Baudville Inc 5380 52nd St SE TF Orders: 800-728-0888 ■ Web: www.baudville.com	Grand Rapids	MI	49512	616-698-0889	698-0554
Blackbaud Inc 2000 Daniel Island Dr NASDAQ: BLKB ■ TF: 800-468-8996 ■ Web: www.blackbaud.com	Charleston	SC	29492	843-216-6200	216-6100
BMC Software Inc 2101 City W Blvd NASDAQ: BMC ■ TF: 800-841-2031 ■ Web: www.bmc.com	Houston	TX	77042	713-918-8800	918-8000
Bottomline Technologies 325 Corporate Dr. NASDAQ: EPAY ■ TF: 800-243-2528 ■ Web: www.bottomline.com	Portsmouth	NH	03801	603-436-0700	436-0300
Bradmark Technologies Inc 4265 San Felipe St Ste 700 TF: 800-621-2808 ■ Web: www.bradmark.com	Houston	TX	77027	713-621-2808	621-1639
Brady Identification Solutions 6555 W Good Hope Rd *Fax Area Code: 800 ■ *Fax: Cust Svc ■ TF Cust Svc: 800-537-8791 ■ Web: www.bradyid.com	Milwaukee	WI	53223	414-358-6600	292-2289*
Brainworks Software Inc 100 S Main St. TF: 800-755-1111 ■ Web: www.brainworks.com	Sayville	NY	11782	631-563-5000	563-6320

				Phone	Fax
BroadSoft Inc 9737 Washingtonian Blvd Ste 350 *NASDAQ: BSFT* ■ *Web:* www.broadsoft.com	Gaithersburg	MD	20877	301-977-9440	
Business Computer Design International Inc 1333 Burr Ridge Pkwy Ste 200 *Web:* www.bcdsoftware.com	Burr Ridge	IL	60527	630-986-0800	986-0926
CA Inc 1 CA Plz *NASDAQ: CA* ■ *TF:* 800-225-5224 ■ *Web:* www.ca.com	Islandia	NY	11749	631-342-6000	342-6800
CDC Trade Beam Inc 2 Waters Pk Dr Ste 100 *TF:* 888-311-1415 ■ *Web:* www.aptean.com	San Mateo	CA	94403	650-653-4800	
Cicero Inc 8000 Regency Pkwy Ste 542 *TF:* 866-538-3588 ■ *Web:* www.ciceroinc.com	Cary	NC	27518	919-380-5000	380-5121
Cincom Systems Inc 55 Merchant St *TF:* 800-224-6266 ■ *Web:* www.cincom.com	Cincinnati	OH	45246	513-612-2300	612-2000
Computing Technologies Inc 3028 Javier Rd Ste 400 *Web:* www.cots.com	Fairfax	VA	22031	703-280-8800	280-8804
Compuware Corp 1 Campus Martius St *NASDAQ: CPWR* ■ *TF:* 800-292-7432 ■ *Web:* www.compuware.com	Detroit	MI	48226	313-227-7300	
Current Analysis Inc 21335 Signal Hill Plz Ste 200 *TF:* 877-787-8947 ■ *Web:* www.currentanalysis.com	Sterling	VA	20164	703-404-9200	404-9300
Cyma Systems Inc 2330 W University Dr Ste 4 **Fax Area Code:* 480 ■ *TF:* 800-292-2962 ■ *Web:* www.cyma.com	Tempe	AZ	85281	800-292-2962	303-2969*
D&B Sales & Marketing Solutions 460 Totten Pond Rd *TF:* 866-473-3932 ■ *Web:* www.hoovers.com	Waltham	MA	02451	781-672-9200	
Data Direct Technologies 14100 SW Fwy	Sugar Land	TX	77478	281-491-4200	
Data Pro Acctg Software Inc 111 Second Ave NE Ste 1200 *TF:* 800-237-6377 ■ *Web:* www.dpro.com	Saint Petersburg	FL	33701	727-803-1500	803-1535
Datalogics Inc 101 N Wacker Dr Ste 1800 *Web:* www.datalogics.com	Chicago	IL	60606	312-853-8200	853-8282
Datamatics Management Services Inc 330 New Brunswick Ave *TF:* 800-673-0366 ■ *Web:* www.datamaticsinc.com	Fords	NJ	08863	732-738-9600	738-9603
Deltek Inc 13880 Dulles Corner Ln *NASDAQ: PROJ* ■ *TF:* 800-456-2009 ■ *Web:* www.deltek.com	Herndon	VA	20171	703-734-8606	734-0346
DeskNet Inc 10 Exchange Pl 20th Fl *Web:* www.desknetinc.com	Jersey City	NJ	07302	201-946-7080	
DLGL Ltd 850 Bd Michele Bohec *Web:* www.dlgl.com	Blainville	QC	J7C5E2	450-979-4646	
Drake Software 235 E Palmer St **Fax Area Code:* 828 ■ *TF:* 800-890-9500 ■ *Web:* www.drakesoftware.com	Franklin	NC	28734	800-890-9500	369-9928*
DST Systems Inc 333 W 11th St *NYSE: DST* ■ *Web:* www.dstsystems.com	Kansas City	MO	64105	816-435-1000	435-8630
E*Trade Financial Corp Corporate Services 4500 Bohannon Dr *TF:* 800-786-2575 ■ *Web:* us.etrade.com	Menlo Park	CA	94025	650-331-6000	331-6801
eCredit 777 Yamato Rd Ste 500 *TF:* 800-276-2321 ■ *Web:* www.cortera.com	Boca Raton	FL	33431	561-226-9000	
Edge Technologies Inc 3702 Pender Dr Ste 250 *TF:* 888-771-3343 ■ *Web:* www.edge-technologies.com	Fairfax	VA	22030	703-691-7900	691-4020
Elcom International Inc 50 Braintree Hill Park *OTC: ELCO*	Braintree	MA	02184	781-501-4000	
EMC Corp Documentum Div 6801 Koll Ctr Pkwy *Web:* www.emc.com	Pleasanton	CA	94566	925-600-6800	600-6850
EMC Document Sciences Corp 5958 Priestly Dr *Web:* emc.com/domains/docscience/index.htm	Carlsbad	CA	92008	760-602-1400	602-1450
Equitrac Corp 1000 S Pine Island Rd Ste 900 *Web:* www.equitrac.com	Plantation	FL	33324	954-888-7800	
eSignal 3955 Pt Eden Way *TF:* 800-815-8256 ■ *Web:* www.esignal.com	Hayward	CA	94545	510-266-6000	266-6100
Fidessa Financial Corp 17 State St 42nd Fl *Web:* fidessa.com	New York	NY	10004	212-269-9000	943-0353
FileMaker Inc 5201 Patrick Henry Dr **Fax:* Cust Svc ■ *TF Cust Svc:* 800-325-2747 ■ *Web:* www.filemaker.com	Santa Clara	CA	95054	408-987-7000	987-3932*
Fischer International Systems Corp 9045 Strada Stell Ct Ste 201 *TF Tech Supp:* 800-776-7258 ■ *Web:* www.fisc.com	Naples	FL	34109	239-643-1500	643-3772
FlexiInternational Software Inc 2 Enterprise Dr *OTC: FLXI* ■ *TF:* 800-353-9492 ■ *Web:* www.flexi.com	Shelton	CT	06484	203-925-3040	925-3044
Gemmar Systems International Inc 11450 Cote de Liesse *Web:* www.gsi.ca	Dorval	QC	H9P1A9	514-631-3336	
Gemstone Systems Inc 1260 NW Waterhouse Ave Ste 200 *TF:* 800-243-4772 ■ *Web:* www.gemstone.com	Beaverton	OR	97006	503-533-3000	629-8556
Global Shop Solutions Inc 975 Evergreen Cir *TF Sales:* 800-364-5958 ■ *Web:* www.globalshopsolutions.com	The Woodlands	TX	77380	281-681-1959	681-2663
Global Software Inc 3201 Beechleaf Ct Ste 170 *TF:* 800-326-3444 ■ *Web:* globalsoftwareinc.com	Raleigh	NC	27604	919-872-7800	876-8205
Glovia International Inc 2250 E Imperial Hwy Ste 200 *TF:* 888-245-6842 ■ *Web:* www.glovia.com	El Segundo	CA	90245	310-563-7000	563-7300
Grandite Inc PO Box 47133 *TF:* 866-808-3932 ■ *Web:* www.grandite.com	Quebec	QC	G1S4X1	581-318-2018	703-0924
GSE Systems Inc 1332 Londontown Blvd Ste 200 *NYSE: GVP* ■ *TF Cust Svc:* 800-638-7912 ■ *Web:* www.gses.com	Sykesville	MD	21784	410-970-7800	970-7997
Halogen Software 495 March Rd *TF:* 866-566-7778 ■ *Web:* www.halogensoftware.com	Kanata	ON	K2K3G1	613-270-1011	270-8311
HarrisData 13555 Bishops Ct Ste 300 *TF:* 800-225-0585 ■ *Web:* www.harrisdata.com	Brookfield	WI	53005	262-784-9099	784-5994
HighJump Software 5600 W 83rd St Ste 600 *TF:* 800-328-3271 ■ *Web:* www.highjump.com	Minneapolis	MN	55437	952-947-4088	
Hitachi Consulting Corp 14643 Dallas Pkwy Ste 800 *Web:* www.hitachiconsulting.com	Dallas	TX	75254	214-665-7000	665-7010
HK Systems Inc 2855 S James Dr *TF:* 800-424-7365 ■ *Web:* www.dematic.com	New Berlin	WI	53151	262-860-7000	860-7010
I-many Inc 1735 Market St 37th Fl *TF:* 877-774-2451 ■ *Web:* www.revitasinc.com	Philadelphia	PA	19103	215-344-1900	
IBM WebSphere Information Integration 26 Forest St *Web:* www.ibm.com/analytics/us/en/technology/data-integration	Marlborough	MA	01752	508-366-3888	
iCIMS Inc 90 Matawan Rd Pkwy 120 5th Fl *TF:* 800-889-4422 ■ *Web:* www.icims.com	Matawan	NJ	07747	732-847-1941	876-0422
Iconixx Software 3420 Executive Ctr Dr Ste 250 **Fax Area Code:* 512 ■ *TF:* 877-426-6499 ■ *Web:* iconixx.com	Austin	TX	78731	877-426-6499	651-3111*
IFS North America Inc 300 Pk Blvd Ste 555 *TF:* 888-437-4968 ■ *Web:* www.ifsworld.com	Chicago	IL	60143	888-437-4968	
Image Process Design 36800 Woodward Ave Ste 300 *Web:* www.ipdsolution.com	Bloomfield Hills	MI	48304	248-723-9733	203-2566
Infoglide Software 6500 River Pl Blvd Bldg 2 *Web:* www.infoglide.com	Austin	TX	78730	512-532-3500	532-3505
Informatica Corp 100 Cardinal Way *NASDAQ: INFA* ■ *TF:* 800-653-3871 ■ *Web:* www.informatica.com	Redwood City	CA	94063	650-385-5000	385-5500
Information & Computing Services Inc (ICS) 1650 Prudential Dr Ste 300 *TF:* 800-676-4427 ■ *Web:* www.icsfl.com	Jacksonville	FL	32207	904-399-8500	398-7855
InfoVista Corp 12950 Worldgate Dr Ste 250 *TF:* 866-921-9219 ■ *Web:* www.infovista.com	Herndon	VA	20170	703-435-2435	435-5122
Innovative Systems Inc 790 Holiday Dr Bldg 11 *TF:* 800-622-6390 ■ *Web:* www.innovativesystems.com	Pittsburgh	PA	15220	412-937-9300	937-9309
Inova Solutions Inc 110 Avon St *TF:* 800-637-1077 ■ *Web:* www.inovasolutions.com	Charlottesville	VA	22902	434-817-8000	817-8002
Inspiration Software Inc 6443 SW Beaverton Hillsdale Hwy Ste 370 *TF:* 800-877-4292 ■ *Web:* www.inspiration.com	Portland	OR	97221	503-297-3004	297-4676
Integrated Business Systems & Services Inc 1601 Shop Rd Ste E *TF:* 800-553-1038 ■ *Web:* www.ibss.net	Columbia	SC	29201	803-736-5595	
Integrated Decisions & Systems Inc 8500 Normandale Lk Blvd Ste 1200 *Web:* www.ideas.com	Minneapolis	MN	55437	952-698-4200	698-4299
Intellicorp Inc 2460 N 1st St Ste 260 *Web:* www.intellicorp.com	San Jose	CA	95131	408-454-3500	454-3529
International Business Machines Corp (IBM) 1 New OrchaRd Rd *NYSE: IBM* ■ *TF:* 800-426-4968 ■ *Web:* www.ibm.com	Armonk	NY	10504	914-499-1900	
InterraTech Corp PO Box 4 *TF:* 888-589-4889 ■ *Web:* www.interratech.com	Mount Ephraim	NJ	08059	856-854-5100	854-5102
InterSystems Corp 1 Memorial Dr *Web:* intersystems.com	Cambridge	MA	02142	617-621-0600	494-1631
Intuitive Research & Technology Corp 5030 Bradford Dr NW # 205 *Web:* www.irtc-hq.com	Huntsville	AL	35805	256-922-9300	922-1122
ISG Novasoft (ISGN) 600 A N John Rodes Blvd **Fax Area Code:* 321 ■ *TF:* 800-462-5545 ■ *Web:* www.isgn.com	Melbourne	FL	32934	800-939-8258	255-9366*
JDA Software Group Inc 1615 S Congress Ave Ste 200	Delray Beach	FL	33445	561-265-2700	
K-Systems Inc 2104 Aspen Dr *TF:* 800-221-0204 ■ *Web:* www.ksystemsinc.com	Mechanicsburg	PA	17055	717-795-7711	
Kalido 1 Wall St Ste 3 *TF:* 866-466-3849 ■ *Web:* www.kalido.com	Burlington	MA	01803	781-202-3200	202-3299
Levi Ray & Shoup Inc 2401 W Monroe St *Web:* www.lrs.com	Springfield	IL	62704	217-793-3800	787-3286
Logility Inc 470 E Paces Ferry Rd *TF:* 800-762-5207 ■ *Web:* www.logility.com	Atlanta	GA	30305	404-261-9777	264-5206
Longview Solutions 100 Matsonford Rd Ste 230 **Fax Area Code:* 484 ■ *TF:* 888-454-2549 ■ *Web:* www.longview.com	Radnor	PA	19087	610-977-0995	367-1153*
M2 Technology Inc 21702 Hardy Oak Ste 100 *TF:* 800-267-1760 ■ *Web:* www.m2ti.com	San Antonio	TX	78258	210-566-3773	566-3993
Malvern Systems Inc 81 Lancaster Ave Ste 219 *TF:* 800-296-9642 ■ *Web:* www.malvernsys.com	Malvern	PA	19355	800-296-9642	
Maverick Technologies 265 Admiral Trost Rd PO Box 470 *TF:* 888-917-9109 ■ *Web:* www.mavtechglobal.com	Columbia	IL	62236	618-281-9100	281-9191
Mayflowers Software 44 Stoneymeade Wy *Web:* www.maysoft.com	Acton	MA	01720	978-635-1700	371-1696
Mediagrif Interactive Technologies Inc 1111 St-Charles St W E Tower Ste 255 *TSE: MDF* ■ *TF:* 877-677-9088 ■ *Web:* www.mediagrif.com	Longueuil	QC	J4K5G4	450-449-0102	449-8725
Meridian Systems 1720 Prairie City Rd Ste 120 *TF:* 800-850-2660 ■ *Web:* www.meridiansystems.com	Folsom	CA	95630	916-294-2000	294-2001
Meridium Inc 207 Bullitt Ave SE *Web:* www.meridium.com	Roanoke	VA	24013	540-344-9205	345-7083
MicroBiz Corp 655 Oak Grove Ave Ste 493 Ste 493 *TF:* 800-937-2289 ■ *Web:* www.microbiz.com	Menlo Park	CA	94025	702-749-5353	
Microlink Enterprise Inc 20955 Pathfinder Rd Ste 100 *TF:* 800-829-3688 ■ *Web:* www.microlinkenterprise.com	Diamond Bar	CA	91765	562-205-1888	205-1886
Microsoft Corp 1 Microsoft Way *NASDAQ: MSFT* ■ *Web:* www.microsoft.com	Redmond	WA	98052	425-882-8080	936-7329
Microsoft Great Plains Business Solutions 3900 Great Plains Dr S *TF:* 888-477-7877 ■ *Web:* www.microsoft.com	Fargo	ND	58104	701-281-6500	
Microsystems 3025 Highland Pkwy Ste 450 *Web:* www.microsystems.com	Downers Grove	IL	60515	630-598-1100	
Milner Technologies Inc 5125 Peachtree Industrial Blvd *TF:* 800-592-3766 ■ *Web:* www.milnertechnologies.com	Norcross	GA	30092	770-734-5300	734-5379
Multi-Ad Inc 1720 W Detweiller Dr *TF:* 800-348-6485 ■ *Web:* www.multiad.com	Peoria	IL	61615	309-692-1530	692-6566
NetMotion Wireless Inc 701 N 34th St Ste 250 *TF:* 877-818-7626 ■ *Web:* www.netmotionwireless.com	Seattle	WA	98103	206-691-5500	691-5501
New Century Education Foundation PO Box 43052 **Fax Area Code:* 609 ■ *TF:* 866-326-1133 ■ *Web:* www.newcenturyeducation.org	Upper Montclair	NJ	07043	866-326-1133	586-8491*

				Phone	Fax
NewlineNoosh Inc 625 Ellis St Ste 300 .... Mountain View *TF:* 888-286-6674 ■ *Web:* noosh.com	CA	94043		650-637-6000	965-1377
North Atlantic Publishing Systems Inc 66 Commonwealth Ave........................... Concord *Web:* www.napsys.com	MA	01742		978-371-8989	371-5678
Novell Inc 1800 S Novell Pl............................Provo **Fax:* Sales ■ *TF:* 800-529-3400 ■ *Web:* www.novell.com	UT	84606		801-861-4272	861-3122*
Objectivity Inc 3099 N First St Ste 200................San Jose *TF:* 800-767-6259 ■ *Web:* www.objectivity.com	CA	95134		408-992-7100	992-7171
OMD Corp 3705 Missouri Blvd.................. Jefferson City *TF:* 866-440-8664 ■ *Web:* www.omdcorp.com	MO	65109		573-893-8930	893-3487
OneSCM 6805 Capital of Texas Hwy Ste 370 .... Austin *TF:* 800-324-5143 ■ *Web:* onescm.com	TX	78731		512-231-8191	231-0292
Open Systems Inc 4301 Dean Lakes Blvd..............Shakopee **Fax Area Code:* 952 ■ *TF Sales:* 800-328-2276 ■ *Web:* www.osas.com	MN	55379		800-328-2276	403-5870*
OpenLink Software Inc 10 Burlington Mall Rd Ste 265.....................Burlington *Web:* www.openlinksw.com	MA	01803		781-273-0900	229-8030
OpenText Corp 275 Frank Tompa Dr Ste 710 N.......... Waterloo *TF:* 800-499-6544 ■ *Web:* www.opentext.com	ON	N2L0A1		773-632-1400	
Oracle Corp 500 Oracle Pkwy.................. Redwood Shores *NYSE: ORCL* ■ *TF Sales:* 800-392-2999 ■ *Web:* www.oracle.com	CA	94065		650-506-7000	506-7200
Oracle Information Rights Management 500 Oracle Pkwy........................... Redwood Shores *Web:* www.oracle.com	CA	94065		650-506-7000	
Oracle USA 500 Oracle Pkwy .... Redwood Shores *TF:* 800-392-2999 ■ *Web:* www.oracle.com	CA	94065		650-506-7000	
Palisade Corp 798 Cascadilla St.............................Ithaca *TF:* 800-432-7475 ■ *Web:* www.palisade.com	NY	14850		607-277-8000	277-8001
Paperclip Software Inc 1 University Plz........... Hackensack **Fax:* Hum Res ■ *TF:* 800-929-3503 ■ *Web:* www.paperclip.com	NJ	07601		201-525-1221	525-1511*
Passport Corp 85 Chestnut Ridge Rd .... Montvale *TF:* 800-926-6736 ■ *Web:* www.passportcorp.com	NJ	07645		201-573-0038	573-0082
Payspan Inc 7751 Belfort Pkwy Ste 200 ....Jacksonville *TF:* 877-331-7154 ■ *Web:* www.payspan.com	FL	32256		877-331-7154	
PDI 3407 S 31st St................................. Temple *Web:* www.profdata.com	TX	76502		254-771-7100	771-7117
Pegasystems Inc 101 Main St ....Cambridge *NASDAQ: PEGA* ■ *Web:* www.pega.com	MA	02142		617-374-9600	374-9620
Pentagon 2000 Software Inc 15 W 34th St 5th Fl.................................New York *TF:* 800-643-1806 ■ *Web:* www.pentagon2000.com	NY	10001		212-629-7521	629-7513
PeopleStrategy Inc 5883 Glenridge Dr Ste 200...........Atlanta *TF:* 855-488-4100 ■ *Web:* www.peoplestrategy.com	GA	30328		855-488-4100	
Percussion Software Inc 600 Unicorn Pk Dr ....Woburn *TF:* 800-283-0800 ■ *Web:* www.percussion.com	MA	01801		781-438-9900	438-9955
Personnel Data Systems Inc (PDS) 470 Norriftown Rd Ste 202............................Blue Bell *TF:* 800-243-8737 ■ *Web:* www.pdssoftware.com	PA	19422		610-238-4600	238-4550
Pilgrim Quality Solutions 2807 W Busch Blvd ....Tampa *Web:* pilgrimquality.com	FL	33618		813-915-1663	915-1948
Pitney Bowes Group 1 Software 4200 Parliament Pl Ste 600 .... Lanham *TF:* 800-367-6950 ■ *Web:* www.g1.com	MD	20706		301-731-2300	
Planview Inc 12301 Research BlvdResearch Park Plz Ste 101........... Austin *TF:* 800-856-8600 ■ *Web:* www.planview.com	TX	78759		512-346-8600	346-9180
Platform Computing Inc 3760 14th Ave ....Markham *TF:* 877-528-3676 ■ *Web:* ibm.com	ON	L3R3T7		905-948-8448	948-9975
Print-O-Stat Inc 1011 W Market St.......................York *TF:* 800-711-8014 ■ *Web:* www.printostat.com	PA	17404		717-854-7821	846-4084
Process Control Technology Inc 4335 Piedras Dr W Ste 175 ....San Antonio *Web:* www.gopct.com	TX	78228		210-735-9141	735-9775
Progress Software Corp 14 Oak Pk................... Bedford *NASDAQ: PRGS* ■ *TF:* 800-477-6473 ■ *Web:* www.progress.com	MA	01730		781-280-4000	280-4095
QAD Inc 100 Innovation Pl .... Santa Barbara *NASDAQ: QADB* ■ *Web:* www.qad.com	CA	93108		805-566-6100	565-4202
Quest Software Inc 5 Polairis Way..................Aliso Viejo *NASDAQ: QSFT* ■ *TF:* 800-306-9329 ■ *Web:* www.quest.com	CA	92656		949-754-8000	754-8999
Quick Solutions Inc 440 Polaris Pkwy Ste 500.........................Westerville *Web:* www.quicksolutions.com	OH	43082		614-825-8000	825-8006
Quorum Business Solutions Inc 811 Main St Ste 2000...Houston *Web:* www.qbsol.com	TX	77002		713-430-8601	430-8697
Realtime Software Corp 24 Deane Rd............. Bernardston *TF:* 800-323-1143 ■ *Web:* www.realtimesw.com	MA	01337		847-803-1100	954-4764
Red Wing Software Inc 491 Hwy 19 ....Red Wing *TF:* 800-732-9464 ■ *Web:* www.redwingsoftware.com	MN	55066		651-388-1106	388-7950
Redemtech Inc 4115 Leap Rd.............................. Hilliard *TF:* 800-393-7627 ■ *Web:* www.arrowvaluerecovery.com	OH	43026		614-850-3366	
Rentrak Corp 7700 NE Ambassador Pl 3rd Fl............Portland *NASDAQ: RENT* ■ *TF:* 800-929-0070 ■ *Web:* www.rentrak.com	OR	97220		503-284-7581	
Sage Fixed Assets 2325 Dulles Corner Blvd Ste 700................... Herndon **Fax Area Code:* 703 ■ *TF:* 800-368-2405 ■ *Web:* www.sage.com	VA	20171		866-520-2519	793-2770*
Sand Technology Inc 8 Ave SW................... Westmount *NYSE: SNDTF* ■ *TF:* 877-468-2538 ■ *Web:* www.sand.com	QC	H3Z1B1		403-218-2010	
SAP 100 Consilium Pl .... Scarborough *TF:* 888-777-1727 ■ *Web:* www.sap.com	ON	M1H3E3		416-791-7100	791-7101
SAP America Inc 3999 W Chester Pk........... Newtown Square *Web:* www.sap.com	PA	19073		610-661-1000	
Sapphire International Inc 101 Merritt Blvd............ Trumbull	CT	06611		203-375-8668	375-1965
SAS Institute Inc 100 SAS Campus Dr.....................Cary *TF:* 800-727-0025 ■ *Web:* www.sas.com	NC	27513		919-677-8000	677-4444
Satori Software Inc 1301 5th Ave Ste 2200............ Seattle *TF:* 800-553-6477 ■ *Web:* www.satorisoftware.com	WA	98101		206-357-2900	357-2901
Sciforma Corp 985 University Ave Ste 5 .... Los Gatos *TF Sales:* 800-533-9876 ■ *Web:* www.sciforma.com	CA	95032		408-354-0144	354-0122
SDL International 2550 N First St Ste 301 .... San Jose *Web:* www.sdl.com	CA	95131		408-743-3600	743-3601
Selectica Inc 2121 S. El Camino Rl 10th Fl ....San Mateo *NASDAQ: SLTC* ■ **Fax Area Code:* 408 ■ *TF:* 877-712-9560	CA	94403		650-532-1500	570-9705*
SERENA Software Inc 2345 NW Amberbrook Dr Ste 200 ....Hillsboro *TF:* 800-457-3736 ■ *Web:* www.serena.com	OR	97006		650-481-3400	481-3700
Silvon Software Inc 900 Oakmont Ln Ste 400......... Westmont *TF:* 800-874-5866 ■ *Web:* www.silvon.com	IL	60559		630-655-3313	655-3377
Siwel Consulting Inc 71 W 23rd St Ste 1907...........New York *Web:* www.siwel.com	NY	10010		212-691-9326	929-6815
Skybridge Global Inc 161 Village Pkwy NE Ste 7.........................Marietta *Web:* www.skybridgeglobal.com	GA	30067		770-373-2300	953-8360
Soffront Software Inc 45437 Warm Springs Blvd ....Fremont *TF:* 800-763-3766 ■ *Web:* www.soffront.com	CA	94539		510-413-9000	413-9027
Software AG USA 11700 Plz America Dr Ste 700 ....Reston *TF:* 877-724-4965 ■ *Web:* www.softwareag.com	VA	20190		703-860-5050	391-6975
Sophos Inc 3 Van de Graaff Dr 2nd Fl ....Burlington **Fax Area Code:* 781 ■ *TF:* 866-866-2802 ■ *Web:* www.sophos.com	MA	01803		866-866-2802	494-5801*
Source Technologies 2910 Whitehall Pk Dr .... Charlotte *TF:* 800-922-8501 ■ *Web:* www.sourcetech.com	NC	28273		704-969-7500	969-7595
SP Systems Inc 7500 Greenway Ctr Dr Ste 850..........Greenbelt *TF:* 877-327-8732 ■ *Web:* www.sp-systems.com	MD	20770		301-614-1322	614-1328
Stamps.com Inc 1990 E Grand Ave................. El Segundo *NASDAQ: STMP* ■ *TF:* 855-889-7867 ■ *Web:* www.stamps.com	CA	90245		855-889-7867	
StrataCare Inc 17838 Gillette Ave...........................Irvine **Fax Area Code:* 949 ■ *TF:* 800-277-6512 ■ *Web:* www.stratacare.com	CA	92614		800-277-6512	743-1299*
Superior Software Inc 16055 Ventura Blvd Ste 650..........................Encino *TF:* 800-421-3264 ■ *Web:* www.superior-software.com	CA	91436		818-990-1135	783-5846
SYSPRO 959 S Coast Dr Ste 100............... Costa Mesa *TF:* 800-369-8649 ■ *Web:* www.syspro.com	CA	92626		714-437-1000	437-1407
Taleo Corp 4140 Dublin Blvd Ste 400 .... Dublin *NYSE: ORCL* ■ *TF:* 800-672-2531 ■ *Web:* www.oracle.com	CA	94568		925-452-3000	452-3001
TECSYS Inc 1 Pl Alexis Nihon Ste 800................. Montreal *TF:* 800-922-8649 ■ *Web:* www.tecsys.com	QC	H3Z3B8		514-866-0001	866-1805
Tenrox 401 Congress Avenue............................ Austin **Fax Area Code:* 626 ■ *TF:* 855-944-7526 ■ *Web:* uplandsoftware.com/tenrox	TX	78701		450-688-3444	796-6662*
Thomson Tax & Acctg 7322 Newman Blvd .... Dexter *TF Cust Svc:* 800-968-8900 ■ *Web:* tax.thomsonreuters.com/cs-professional-suite	MI	48130		800-968-8900	326-1040
TIBCO Software Inc 3303 Hillview Ave............. Palo Alto *NASDAQ: TIBX* ■ *Web:* www.tibco.com	CA	94304		650-846-1000	846-1005
Tribridge 4830 W Kennedy Blvd Ste 890 .... Tampa *TF:* 877-744-1360 ■ *Web:* www.tribridge.com	FL	33609		877-744-1360	
Trilogy Software Inc 401 Congress Ave Ste 2650......... Austin *Web:* www.trilogy.com	TX	78701		512-874-3100	
Trintech Inc 15851 Dallas Pkwy Ste 900................Addison *TF:* 800-416-0075 ■ *Web:* www.trintech.com	TX	75001		972-701-9802	701-9337
Tritek Solutions Inc 7617 Little River Tpke Ste 800 .... Annandale *Web:* www.perficient.com	VA	22003		703-333-3060	
Ultimate Software Group Inc 2000 Ultimate Way .... Weston *NASDAQ: ULTI* ■ *TF:* 800-432-1729 ■ *Web:* www.ultimatesoftware.com	FL	33326		954-331-7000	
Valiant Solutions Inc 110 Crossways Pk Dr .... Woodbury *Web:* www.valiant.com	NY	11797		516-390-1100	390-1111
Validar Inc 800 Maynard Ave S Ste 401 .... Seattle *TF:* 888-784-2929 ■ *Web:* www.validar.com	WA	98134		206-264-9151	
Versant Corp 255 Shoreline Dr Ste 450............ Redwood City *NASDAQ: VSNT* ■ *TF:* 888-446-4737 ■ *Web:* actian.com	CA	94065		650-232-2400	232-2401
Vertex Inc 1041 Old Cassatt Rd....................... Berwyn *TF:* 800-355-3500 ■ *Web:* www.vertexinc.com	PA	19312		610-640-4200	640-5892
VFA Inc 99 Bedford St.................................Boston *TF:* 800-693-3132 ■ *Web:* www.vfa.com	MA	02111		617-451-5100	350-7087
Vignette Corp 1301 S Mopac Expy Ste 100 .... Austin *TF:* 800-540-7292 ■ *Web:* www.opentext.com	TX	78746		512-741-4300	
Visible Systems Corp 201 Spring St .... Lexington *TF Sales:* 888-850-9911 ■ *Web:* www.visible.com	MA	02421		781-778-0200	778-0208
Vitria Technology Inc 945 Stewart Dr Ste 200.......................... Sunnyvale **Fax Area Code:* 408 ■ *TF:* 877-365-5935 ■ *Web:* www.vitria.com	CA	94085		877-365-5935	212-2720*
Wave Systems Corp 480 Pleasant St .... Lee *NASDAQ: WAVX* ■ *TF:* 800-928-3638 ■ *Web:* www.wave.com	MA	01238		413-243-1600	243-0045
Wizdom Systems Inc 1300 Iroquois Ave .... Naperville *Web:* www.wizdom.com	IL	60563		630-357-3000	357-3059
Worden Bros Inc 4905 Pine Cone Dr .... Durham *TF:* 800-776-4940 ■ *Web:* www.worden.com	NC	27707		919-408-0542	408-0545
Xaware Inc 3300 Irvine Ave Ste 261 .... Newport Beach *Web:* www.xaware.com	CA	92660		949-222-2287	
ZyLAB North America LLC 7918 Jones Branch Dr Ste 230.......................McLean **Fax Area Code:* 703 ■ *TF:* 866-995-2262 ■ *Web:* www.zylab.com	VA	22102		866-995-2262	991-2508*

178-2 Computer Languages & Development Tools

			Phone	Fax
Amzi! inc 83 Vance Crescent Ext .... Asheville *Web:* www.amzi.com	NC	28806	828-350-0350	
Applied Dynamics International Inc 3800 Stone School Rd .... Ann Arbor *TF:* 888-465-4329 ■ *Web:* www.adi.com	MI	48108	734-973-1300	668-0012
BSQUARE Corp 110 110th Ave NE.....................Bellevue *NASDAQ: BSQR* ■ *TF:* 888-820-4500 ■ *Web:* www.bsquare.com	WA	98004	425-519-5900	
Calypso Technology Inc 595 Market St Ste 1800 .... San Francisco *Web:* www.calypso.com	CA	94105	415-817-2400	284-1222
Data Access Corp 14000 SW 119th Ave................ Miami *TF:* 800-451-3539 ■ *Web:* www.dataaccess.com	FL	33186	305-238-0012	238-0012
DDC-I Inc 4600 E Shea Blvd Ste 102 ....Phoenix *Web:* www.ddci.com	AZ	85028	602-275-7172	252-6054
Diamond Edge Inc 661 W State St Ste A.......... Pleasant Grove *Web:* www.diamondedge.com	UT	84062	801-785-8473	

Company	City	State	Zip	Phone	Fax
Embarcadero Technologies Inc 100 California St 12th Fl. *Web:* www.embarcadero.com	San Francisco	CA	94111	415-834-3131	434-1721
Empress Software Inc 11785 Beltsville Dr *TF:* 866-626-8888 ■ *Web:* www.empress.com	Beltsville	MD	20705	301-220-1919	220-1997
FMS Inc 8150 Leesburg Pk Ste 600 *TF:* 866-367-7801 ■ *Web:* www.fmsinc.com	Vienna	VA	22182	703-356-4700	448-3861
Forth Inc 5959 W Century Blvd Ste 700 *TF:* 800-553-6784 ■ *Web:* www.forth.com	Los Angeles	CA	90045	310-999-6784	943-3806
Green Hills Software Inc 30 W Sola St *TF:* 800-765-4733 ■ *Web:* www.ghs.com	Santa Barbara	CA	93101	805-965-6044	965-6343
Instantiations Inc Officers Row Ste 1325B *TF:* 855-476-2558 ■ *Web:* www.instantiations.com	Vancouver	WA	98661	503-649-3836	649-3836
Integrated Computer Solutions Inc (ICS) 54 Middlesex Tpke Ste B *Web:* www.ics.com	Bedford	MA	01730	617-621-0060	621-9555
LANSA Inc 3010 Highland Pkwy Ste 275 *Web:* www.lansa.com	Downers Grove	IL	60515	630-874-7000	874-7001
Lattice Inc 1751 S Naperville Rd Ste 100 *TF Sales:* 800-444-4309 ■ *Web:* www.lattice.com	Wheaton	IL	60189	630-949-3250	949-3299
Mix Software Inc 1203 Berkeley Dr *TF:* 800-333-0330 ■ *Web:* www.mixsoftware.com	Richardson	TX	75081	972-231-0949	
NIS Inc 12995 Thomas Creek Rd. *Web:* nissoftware.net	Reno	NV	89511	775-852-0640	
Numara Software Inc 2202 NW Shore Blvd Ste 650 *TF Sales:* 855-834-7487 ■ *Web:* www.bmc.com	Tampa	FL	33607	813-227-4500	227-4501
Primus Software Corp 3061 Peachtree Industrial Blvd Ste 110 *Web:* www.primussoft.com	Duluth	GA	30097	770-300-0004	300-0005
Prolifics 5 Hanover Sqr Ste 2001 *TF:* 800-458-3313 ■ *Web:* www.prolifics.com	New York	NY	10004	212-267-7722	608-6753
Revelation Software 99 Kinderkamack Rd. *TF:* 800-262-4747 ■ *Web:* www.revelation.com	Westwood	NJ	07675	201-594-1422	722-9815
Rogue Wave Software Inc 5500 Flatiron Pkwy *TF:* 800-487-3217 ■ *Web:* www.roguewave.com	Boulder	CO	80301	303-473-9118	473-9137
SemWare Corp 730 Elk Cove Ct *Web:* www.semware.com	Kennesaw	GA	30152	678-355-9810	355-9812
Shaw Systems Assoc Inc 6200 Savoy Dr Ste 600 *Web:* www.shawsystems.com	Houston	TX	77036	713-782-7730	782-4158
SlickEdit Inc 3000 Aerial Ctr Pkwy Ste 120 *TF:* 800-934-3348 ■ *Web:* www.slickedit.com	Morrisville	NC	27560	919-473-0070	473-0080
Sunbelt Computer Systems Inc 13090 Swan Lake Rd CR 468 *Web:* www.sunbelt-plb.com	Tyler	TX	75704	903-881-0400	
Synactive Inc 950 Tower Ln Ste 750 *Web:* www.synactive.net	Foster City	CA	94404	650-341-3310	341-3610
Thoroughbred Software International Inc 285 Davidson Ave Ste 302 *TF:* 800-524-0430 ■ *Web:* www.thoroughbredsoftware.com	Somerset	NJ	08873	732-560-1377	560-1594
Zortec International 25 Century Blvd Ste 103 *TF:* 800-361-7005 ■ *Web:* www.zortec.com	Nashville	TN	37214	615-361-7000	361-3800

178-3 Educational & Reference Software

Company	City	State	Zip	Phone	Fax
Allen Communication Learning Services 55 West 900 South *TF:* 866-310-7800 ■ *Web:* www.allencomm.com	Salt Lake City	UT	84101	801-537-7800	537-7805
Atari Inc 417 Fifth Ave 8th Fl *Web:* www.atari.com	New York	NY	10016	212-726-6500	
Blackboard Inc 1899 L St NW 5th Fl *TF:* 800-424-9299 ■ *Web:* www.blackboard.com	Washington	DC	20036	202-463-4860	463-4863
CompassLearning Inc 203 Colorado St *TF:* 800-232-9556 ■ *Web:* www.compasslearning.com	Austin	TX	78701	512-478-9600	
Fuel Education LLC 2300 Corporate Park Dr *TF:* 800-222-2811	Herndon	VA	20171	844-251-4687	
Individual Software Inc 4255 HopyaRd Rd Ste 2 *TF:* 800-822-3522 ■ *Web:* www.individualsoftware.com	Pleasanton	CA	94588	925-734-6767	734-8337
Inscape Publishing Inc 6465 Wayzata Blvd Ste 800 *TF:* 877-735-8383 ■ *Web:* everythingdisc.com	Minneapolis	MN	55426	763-765-2222	765-2277
Inspiration Software Inc 6443 SW Beaverton Hillsdale Hwy Ste 370 *TF:* 800-877-4292 ■ *Web:* www.inspiration.com	Portland	OR	97221	503-297-3004	297-4676
Language Engineering Co 135 Beaver St Ste 204 *TF:* 888-366-4532 ■ *Web:* www.lec.com	Waltham	MA	02452	781-642-8900	
LDP Inc 75 Kiwanis Blvd PO Box O *TF:* 800-522-8413 ■ *Web:* www.leaderservices.com	West Hazleton	PA	18201	800-522-8413	
MindPlay Educational Software 440 S Williams Blvd Ste 206 *TF:* 800-221-7911 ■ *Web:* www.mindplay.com	Tucson	AZ	85711	520-888-1800	888-7904
Optimum Resource Inc 18 Hunter Rd	Hilton Head Island	SC	29926	843-689-8000	689-8008
Queue Inc 703 Post Rd *TF:* 800-232-2224 ■ *Web:* www.queueinc.com	Fairfield	CT	06824	800-232-2224	775-2729
Renaissance Learning Inc 2911 Peach St *TF:* 800-338-4204 ■ *Web:* renaissance.com	Wisconsin Rapids	WI	54494	715-424-3636	424-4242
Saba Software Inc 2400 Bridge Pkwy *OTC: SABA* ■ *TF:* 877-722-2101 ■ *Web:* www.saba.com	Redwood Shores	CA	94065	650-581-2500	696-1773
Scientific Learning Corp 300 Frank H Ogawa Plz Ste 600 *OTC: SCIL* ■ *TF:* 888-665-9707 ■ *Web:* www.scilearn.com	Oakland	CA	94612	510-444-3500	444-3580
Siboney Corp 325 N Kirkwood Rd	Saint Louis	MO	63122	314-822-3163	822-3197
TIBCO Software Inc 1700 Westlake Ave N Ste 500 *TF:* 866-247-8182 ■ *Web:* www.tibco.com	Seattle	WA	98109	206-283-8802	
Tom Snyder Productions Inc 100 Talcott Ave *TF:* 800-342-0236	Watertown	MA	02472	617-924-0938	926-6222
Transparent Language Inc 12 Murphy Dr **Fax Area Code: 603* ■ *TF:* 800-538-8867 ■ *Web:* www.transparent.com	Nashua	NH	03062	800-538-8867	262-6476*
Wordsmart Corp 10025 Mesa Rim Rd. *TF:* 800-858-9673	San Diego	CA	92121	858-565-8068	202-1820

178-4 Electronic Purchasing & Procurement Software

Company	City	State	Zip	Phone	Fax
Apptis Inc 4800 Westfields Blvd. *TF:* 888-277-8478	Chantilly	VA	20151	703-279-3000	745-1304
Ariba Inc 807 11th Ave *NASDAQ: ARBA* ■ *TF:* 866-772-7422 ■ *Web:* www.ariba.com	Sunnyvale	CA	94089	650-390-1000	
CA Inc 1 CA Plz *NASDAQ: CA* ■ *TF:* 800-225-5224 ■ *Web:* www.ca.com	Islandia	NY	11749	631-342-6000	342-6800
Covisint 1 Campus Martius Ste 700 *TF:* 800-229-4125 ■ *Web:* www.covisint.com	Detroit	MI	48226	800-229-4125	
Elavon 2 Concourse Pkwy Ste 300 **Fax Area Code: 865* ■ *TF:* 800-725-1243 ■ *Web:* www.elavon.com	Atlanta	GA	30328	678-731-5000	577-0661*
Fiserv Lending Solutions 455 S Gulph Rd Ste 125 *Web:* www.fiservlemans.com	King of Prussia	PA	19406	610-337-8686	337-7206
GXS Inc 9711 Washingtonian Blvd *TF:* 800-560-4347 ■ *Web:* www.gxs.com	Gaithersburg	MD	20878	301-340-4000	340-5299
International Business Machines Corp (IBM) 1 New OrchaRd Rd *NYSE: IBM* ■ *TF:* 800-426-4968 ■ *Web:* www.ibm.com	Armonk	NY	10504	914-499-1900	
MarketAxess Holdings Inc 299 Pk Ave 10th Fl *NASDAQ: MKTX* ■ *Web:* www.marketaxess.com	New York	NY	10171	212-813-6000	813-6390
SciQuest Inc 6501 Weston Pkwy Ste 200 *TF:* 888-638-7322 ■ *Web:* www.sciquest.com	Cary	NC	27513	919-659-2100	659-2199

178-5 Engineering Software

Company	City	State	Zip	Phone	Fax
Accelrys Inc 10188 Telesis Ct Ste 100 *NASDAQ: ACCL* ■ *TF:* 888-249-2284 ■ *Web:* www.accelrys.com	San Diego	CA	92121	858-799-5000	799-5100
Advanced Visual Systems Inc (AVS) 300 Fifth Ave. *OTC: AVSC* ■ *Web:* www.avs.com	Waltham	MA	02451	781-890-4300	890-8287
Altium Inc 2175 Salk Ave Ste 100 *TF Sales:* 800-544-4186 ■ *Web:* www.altium.com	Carlsbad	CA	92008	760-231-0760	231-0761
ANSYS Inc 275 Technology Dr *NASDAQ: ANSS* ■ *TF:* 800-937-3321 ■ *Web:* www.ansys.com	Canonsburg	PA	15317	724-746-3304	514-9494
Ashlar Inc 9600 Great Hills Trl Ste 150W-1625 *TF:* 800-877-2745 ■ *Web:* www.ashlar.com	Austin	TX	78759	512-250-2186	250-5811
Aspen Technology Inc 200 Wheeler Rd. *NASDAQ: AZPN* ■ *TF:* 888-996-7100 ■ *Web:* www.aspentech.com	Burlington	MA	01803	781-221-6400	
Autodesk Inc 111 McInnis Pkwy *NASDAQ: ADSK* ■ *TF Tech Supp:* 800-964-6432 ■ *Web:* www.autodesk.com	San Rafael	CA	94903	415-507-5000	507-5100
Bentley Systems Inc 685 Stockton Dr *TF:* 800-236-8539 ■ *Web:* www.bentley.com	Exton	PA	19341	610-458-5000	458-1060
Bohannan Huston Inc 7500 Jefferson St NE Courtyard 1 *TF:* 800-877-5332 ■ *Web:* www.bhinc.com	Albuquerque	NM	87109	505-823-1000	798-7988
CACI MTL Systems Inc 2685 Hibiscus Way *Web:* www.caci.com	Beavercreek	OH	45431	937-426-3111	
Cadalog Inc 1448 King St *Web:* www.cadalog-inc.com	Bellingham	WA	98229	360-647-2426	647-2890
Cadence Design Systems Inc 2655 Seely Ave *NASDAQ: CDNS* ■ *TF Cust Svc:* 800-746-6223 ■ *Web:* www.cadence.com	San Jose	CA	95134	408-943-1234	428-5001
CambridgeSoft Corp 100 CambridgePark Dr *TF:* 800-315-7300 ■ *Web:* www.cambridgesoft.com	Cambridge	MA	02140	617-588-9100	588-9190
Comarco Inc 25541 Commerce Ctr Dr. *OTC: CMRO* ■ *Web:* www.comarco.com	Lake Forest	CA	92630	949-599-7400	
CSA Inc 280 I- N Cir SE Ste 250 *Web:* www.csaatl.com	Atlanta	GA	30339	770-955-3518	956-8748
Data Description Inc 840 Hanshaw Rd 2nd Fl *Web:* www.datadesk.com	Ithaca	NY	14850	607-257-1000	
Direct Source Inc 8176 Mallory Ct *TF:* 800-934-8055 ■ *Web:* www.directsource.com	Chanhassen	MN	55317	952-934-8000	934-8030
Disk Software Inc 205 Ridgestone Dr. *Web:* www.disksoft.com	Murphy	TX	75094	972-423-7288	
DP Technology Corp 1150 Avenida Acaso *TF:* 800-627-8479 ■ *Web:* www.espritcam.com	Camarillo	CA	93012	805-388-6000	388-3085
Engineered Software Inc 4529 Intelco Loop SE *Web:* www.engsw.com	Lacey	WA	95803	336-299-4843	
Evolution Computing 7000 N 16th St Ste 120 514 *TF:* 800-874-4028 ■ *Web:* www.fastcad.com	Phoenix	AZ	85020	800-874-4028	
Geocomp Corp 1145 Massachusetts Ave. *TF Cust Svc:* 800-822-2669 ■ *Web:* www.geocomp.com	Boxborough	MA	01719	978-635-0012	635-0266
Gibbs & Assoc 323 Science Dr *TF Cust Svc:* 800-654-9399 ■ *Web:* gibbscam.com	Moorpark	CA	93021	805-523-0004	523-0006
Infinite Graphics Inc 4611 E Lake St *OTC: INFG* ■ *TF:* 800-679-0676 ■ *Web:* www.igi.com	Minneapolis	MN	55406	612-721-6283	721-3802
Intergraph Corp 19 Interpro Rd *TF:* 800-345-4856 ■ *Web:* www.intergraph.com	Madison	AL	35758	256-730-2000	730-2048
Kubotek USA 2 Mt Royal Ave Ste 500 *TF:* 800-372-3872 ■ *Web:* kubotek3d.com	Marlborough	MA	01752	508-229-2020	229-2121
LINDO Systems Inc 1415 N Dayton St. *TF Sales:* 800-441-2378 ■ *Web:* www.lindo.com	Chicago	IL	60622	312-988-7422	988-9065
Mathworks Inc 3 Apple Hill Dr *Web:* in.mathworks.com/	Natick	MA	01760	508-647-7000	647-7001
Mentor Graphics Corp 8005 SW Boeckman Rd *NASDAQ: MENT* ■ *TF:* 800-592-2210 ■ *Web:* www.mentor.com	Wilsonville	OR	97070	503-685-7000	685-1204
MSC.Software Corp 4675 MacArthur Crt *Web:* www.mscsoftware.com	Newport Beach	CA	92660	714-540-8900	784-4056
National Instruments Corp 11500 N Mopac Expy *NASDAQ: NATI* ■ *TF Cust Svc:* 800-433-3488 ■ *Web:* www.ni.com	Austin	TX	78759	512-794-0100	683-8411

Phone Fax

Numerical Control Computer Sciences
2600 Michelson Dr Ste 1700 Irvine CA 92612 949-852-3665 553-1911
Web: www.nccs.com

Parametric Technology Corp (PTC)
140 Kendrick St Needham MA 02494 781-370-5000 370-6000
NASDAQ: PTC ■ *TF:* 800-613-7535 ■ *Web:* www.ptc.com

Planit Solutions Inc 3800 Palisades Dr Tuscaloosa AL 35405 205-556-9199 556-9210
TF: 800-280-6932 ■ *Web:* www.verosoftware.com

PMS Systems Corp 2800 28th St Ste 109 Santa Monica CA 90405 310-450-2566 450-1311
TF: 800-755-3968 ■ *Web:* www.assetsmart.com

Science Application International Corp Inc (SAIC Inc)
1710 SAIC Dr McLean VA 22102 703-676-4300
TF: 866-400-7242 ■ *Web:* www.saic.com

Tripos Inc 1699 S Hanley Rd Saint Louis MO 63144 314-647-1099 647-9241
TF: 800-323-2960 ■ *Web:* certara.com

Triton Services Inc 2014 Industrial Dr Annapolis MD 21401 443-716-0600 716-0601
Web: www.tritonsvc.com

Zuken USA 238 Littleton Rd Ste 100 Westford MA 01886 978-692-4900 692-4725
TF: 800-447-7332 ■ *Web:* www.zuken.com

178-6 Games & Entertainment Software

Phone Fax

Abacus Software Inc
3413 Roger B Chaffee Memorial Blvd SE Grand Rapids MI 49546 616-241-3404
Web: www.abacuspub.com

Activision Inc 3100 Ocean Pk Blvd Santa Monica CA 90405 310-255-2000
Web: www.activision.com

Apogee Software Inc
1999 S Bascom Ave Ste 250 Campbell CA 95008 408-369-9001 369-9018
Web: www.apogee.com

Bethesda Softworks LLC
1370 Piccard Dr Ste 120 Rockville MD 20850 301-926-8300 926-8010
Web: www.bethsoft.com

Capcom USA Inc 800 Concar Dr Ste 300 San Mateo CA 94402 650-350-6500 350-6657
Web: www.capcom.com

Cyan Worlds Inc 14617 N Newport Hwy Mead WA 99021 509-468-0807 467-2209
Web: cyan.com

Disney Consumer Products
500 S Buena Vista St Burbank CA 91521 818-560-1000 553-5402*
**Fax Area Code:* 215 ■ **Fax:* Cust Svc ■ *TF PR:* 855-553-4763 ■ *Web:* thewaltdisneycompany.com

Electronic Arts Inc (EA)
209 Redwood Shores Pkwy Redwood City CA 94065 650-628-1500
NASDAQ: EA ■ *Web:* www.ea.com

Her Interactive Inc
1150 114th Ave SE Ste 200 Bellevue WA 98004 425-460-8787 460-8788
TF Orders: 800-461-8787 ■ *Web:* www.herinteractive.com

iEntertainment Network Inc
124 Quade Dr PO Box 3897 Cary NC 27519 919-238-4090 678-8302
OTC: IENT ■ *Web:* www.ient.com

Lucasfilm Ltd LucasArts Entertainment Div
1110 Gorgas St San Francisco CA 94129 415-746-8000
Web: starwars.com/games-apps

MakeMusic! Inc
7615 Golden Triangle Dr Ste M Eden Prairie MN 55344 952-937-9611 937-9760
NASDAQ: MMUS ■ *TF:* 800-843-2066 ■ *Web:* www.makemusic.com

Nintendo of America Inc 4820 150th Ave NE Redmond WA 98052 425-882-2040 882-3585
TF Cust Svc: 800-255-3700 ■ *Web:* www.nintendo.com

NovaLogic Inc 27489 Agoura Rd Agoura Hills CA 91301 818-880-1997 865-6405
Web: www.novalogic.com

Rovi Corp 2830 de la Cruz Blvd Santa Clara CA 95050 408-562-8400 567-1800
Web: www.rovicorp.com

SEGA of America Inc
350 Rhode Island St Ste 400 San Francisco CA 94103 415-701-6000 701-6001
Web: www.sega.com

Take-Two Interactive Software Inc
622 Broadway New York NY 10012 646-536-2842 536-2926
NASDAQ: TTWO ■ *Web:* www.take2games.com

THQ Inc 29903 Agoura Rd Agoura Hills CA 91301 818-871-5000 871-7400
NASDAQ: THQI ■ *Web:* thq.com

TreyArch 3420 Ocean Pk Blvd Ste 1000 Santa Monica CA 90405 310-581-4700 581-4702
Web: www.treyarch.com

WildTangent Inc
18578 NE 67th Ct Redmond E Office Complex
Bldg 5 Redmond WA 98052 425-497-4500 497-4501
Web: www.wildtangent.com

178-7 Internet & Communications Software

Phone Fax

@Comm Corp 150 Dow St Manchester NH 03101 650-375-8188 628-3140*
**Fax Area Code:* 603 ■ *TF:* 800-641-5400 ■ *Web:* www.atcomm.com

Activeworlds Inc 95 Parker St Newburyport MA 01950 978-499-0222 499-0221
Web: www.activeworlds.com

Adaptive Micro Systems Inc 7840 N 86th St Milwaukee WI 53224 414-357-2020 357-2029
TF: 800-558-4187 ■ *Web:* www.adaptivedisplays.com

Akamai Technologies Inc 150 Broadway Cambridge MA 02142 617-444-3000 444-3001
NASDAQ: AKAM ■ *TF:* 877-425-2624 ■ *Web:* www.akamai.com

Alexa Internet PO Box 29141 San Francisco CA 94129 415-561-6900 561-6795

Amcom Software Inc 10400 Yellow Cir Dr Eden Prairie MN 55343 952-230-5200 230-5510
TF: 800-852-8935 ■ *Web:* spok.com

Answers Corp 237 W 35th St Ste 1101 New York NY 10001 646-502-4778 502-4778
TF: 888-885-5008 ■ *Web:* www.answers.com

AnyDoc Software Inc 5404 Cypress Ctr Dr Ste 140 Tampa FL 33609 888-495-2638 222-0018*
**Fax Area Code:* 813 ■ *TF:* 888-495-2638 ■ *Web:* www.onbase.com/en/product/onbaseanydoc

Apex Voice Communications Inc
21700 Oxnard St Ste 1060 Woodland Hills CA 91367 818-379-8400 379-8410
TF: 800-727-3970 ■ *Web:* www.apexvoice.com

Ariba Inc 807 11th Ave Sunnyvale CA 94089 650-390-1000
NASDAQ: ARBA ■ *TF:* 866-772-7422 ■ *Web:* www.ariba.com

Phone Fax

Asure Softwar 110 Wild Basin Rd Austin TX 78746 512-437-2700 437-2365
NASDAQ: ASUR ■ *TF:* 888-323-8835 ■ *Web:* www.asuresoftware.com

AttachmateWRQ 1500 Dexter Ave N Seattle WA 98109 206-217-7500 217-7515
TF Sales: 800-872-2829 ■ *Web:* www.attachmate.com

Authorize.Net Corp PO Box 8999 San Francisco CA 94128 801-492-6450 492-6489
TF: 877-447-3938 ■ *Web:* www.authorize.net

Automation Technology Inc 2001 Gateway Pl San Jose CA 95110 408-350-7020 350-7021
Web: www.intertek.com

Avanquest Software USA 1333 W 120th Ave Westminster CO 80234 800-011-2312
TF: 800-011-2312 ■ *Web:* www.avanquest.com

Avistar Communications Corp
1855 S Grant St 4th Fl San Mateo CA 94402 650-525-3300 525-1360
OTC: AVSR ■ *TF:* 800-803-0153 ■ *Web:* www.avistar.com

Big Sky Technologies 9325 Sky Pk Ct Ste 120 San Diego CA 92123 858-715-5000 715-5010
TF: 800-736-2751 ■ *Web:* www.bigskytech.com

Blast Inc
220 Chatham Business Dr PO Box 818 Pittsboro NC 27312 919-533-0143 542-5955
TF: 800-242-5278 ■ *Web:* www.blast.com

Callware Technologies Inc 9100 S 500 W Sandy UT 84070 801-988-6800
TF: 800-888-4226 ■ *Web:* www.callware.com

ClickSoftware Inc 35 Corporate Dr Ste 400 Burlington MA 01803 781-272-5903 272-6409
NASDAQ: CKSW ■ *TF:* 888-438-3308 ■ *Web:* www.clicksoftware.com

Cothern Computer Systems Inc
1640 Lelia Dr Ste 200 Jackson MS 39216 601-969-1155 969-1184
TF: 800-844-1155 ■ *Web:* www.ccslink.com

Cykic Software Inc PO Box 3098 San Diego CA 92163 619-459-8799
Web: www.cykic.com

DataMotion Inc 35 Airport Rd Ste 120 Morristown NJ 07960 973-455-1245 455-0750
TF: 800-672-7233 ■ *Web:* datamotion.com

DealerTrack Holdings Inc
1111 Marcus Ave Ste M04 Lake Success NY 11042 516-734-3600
NASDAQ: TRAK ■ *TF:* 877-357-8725 ■ *Web:* www.dealertrack.com

Deerfield Communications Co 4241 Old US 27 S Gaylord MI 49735 989-732-8856 731-9299
Web: www.deerfield.com

Dynamic Instruments Inc
3860 Calle Fortunada San Diego CA 92123 858-278-4900 278-6700
TF: 800-793-3358 ■ *Web:* www.dynamicinst.com

eAcceleration Corp
1050 NE Hostmark St Ste 100-B Poulsbo WA 98370 360-779-6301 598-2450
TF Sales: 800-803-4588 ■ *Web:* www.eacceleration.com

Education Management Solutions Inc
436 Creamery Way Ste 300 Exton PA 19341 610-701-7002 653-1070*
**Fax Area Code:* 484 ■ *TF:* 877-367-5050 ■ *Web:* simulationiq.com

EXTOL International Inc
529 Terry Reiley Way Pottsville PA 17901 570-628-5500 628-6983
TF: 800-542-7284 ■ *Web:* www.extol.com

FutureSoft Inc 1660 Townhurst Dr Ste E Houston TX 77043 281-496-9400 496-1090
TF: 800-989-8908 ■ *Web:* www.futuresoft.com

GeoTrust Inc 350 Ellis St Bldg J Mountain View CA 94043 650-426-5010 237-8871
TF: 866-511-4141 ■ *Web:* www.geotrust.com

Grassroots Enterprise Inc
1875 Eye St NW Ste 900 Washington DC 20006 202-371-0200
Web: www.grassroots.com

Hilgraeve Inc 115 E Elm Ave Monroe MI 48162 734-243-0576 243-0645
TF Sales: 800-826-2760 ■ *Web:* www.hilgraeve.com

Hyland Software Inc 28500 Clemens Rd Westlake OH 44145 440-788-5000 788-5100
TF: 888-495-2638 ■ *Web:* onbase.com

Ikanos Communications 47669 Fremont Blvd Fremont CA 94538 510-979-0400 979-0500
NASDAQ: IKAN ■ *Web:* www.ikanos.com

Imecom Group 8 Governor Wentworth Hwy Wolfeboro NH 03894 603-569-0600 569-0609
TF: 800-329-9099 ■ *Web:* www.imecominc.com

InfoNow Corp 1875 Lawrence St Ste 1200 Denver CO 80202 303-293-0212 293-0213
TF: 855-524-3282 ■ *Web:* channelinsight.com

Information Builders Inc 2 Penn Plz New York NY 10121 212-736-4433 967-6406
TF: 800-969-4636 ■ *Web:* www.informationbuilders.com

IntelliNet Technologies Inc
1990 W New Haven Ave Ste 303 Melbourne FL 32904 321-726-0686 726-0683
TF: 888-726-0686 ■ *Web:* diametriq.com/intellinet-tech

Interact Inc 1225 L St Ste 600 Lincoln NE 68508 402-476-8786
Web: www.iivip.com

Interactive Intelligence Inc
7601 Interactive Way Indianapolis IN 46278 317-872-3000 872-3000
NASDAQ: ININ ■ *TF:* 800-267-1364 ■ *Web:* www.inin.com

InternetSafety.com Inc 3979 S Main St Ste 230 Acworth GA 30101 877-944-8080
TF: 877-944-8080 ■ *Web:* www.internetsafety.com

Ion Networks Inc
120 Corporate Blvd Ste A South Plainfield NJ 07080 908-546-3900 546-3901
TF: 800-722-8986 ■ *Web:* apitech.com

Jones Cyber Solutions Ltd
9697 E Mineral Ave Centennial CO 80112 303-784-3600 784-3797
Web: www.jonescyber.com

KANA Software Inc
840 W California Ave Ste 100 Sunnyvale CA 94086 650-614-8300 736-7613*
**Fax Area Code:* 408 ■ *Web:* www.kana.com

Keynote Systems Inc
777 Mariners Island Blvd San Mateo CA 94404 650-403-2400 403-5500
NASDAQ: KEYN ■ *TF:* 888-539-7978 ■ *Web:* www.keynote.com

Language Automation Inc (LAI)
1660 S Amphlett Blvd Ste 106 San Mateo CA 94402 650-571-7877
Web: www.lai.com

LassoSoft LLC PO Box 33 Manchester WA 98353 954-302-3526 302-3526
TF: 888-286-7753 ■ *Web:* www.lassosoft.com

LOGIKA Corp 3717 N Ravenswood Ave Chicago IL 60613 773-529-3482 529-3483
Web: www.logika.net

Mark/Space Softworks
1999 S Bascom Ave Ste 325 Campbell CA 95008 408-293-7299 293-7298
Web: www.markspace.com

Metric Stream Inc 2600 E Bayshore Rd Palo Alto CA 94303 650-620-2900 565-8542
Web: www.metricstream.com

Mirror Image Internet Inc 2 Highwood Dr Tewksbury MA 01876 781-376-1100 376-1110
TF: 800-353-2923 ■ *Web:* www.mirror-image.com

Mize Houser & Co 534 S Kansas Ave Ste 700 Topeka KS 66603 785-233-0536 233-1078
Web: www.mizehouser.com

Company	City	State	Zip	Phone	Fax
Moai Technologies Inc 100 First Ave 9th Fl *TF:* 800-814-1548 ■ *Web:* www.moai.com	Pittsburgh	PA	15222	412-454-5550	454-5555
Momentum Systems Ltd 41 Twosome Dr Ste 9 *TF:* 800-279-1384 ■ *Web:* www.momsys.com	Moorestown	NJ	08057	856-727-0777	273-3765
NetScout Systems Inc 310 Littleton Rd *NASDAQ: NTCT* ■ *TF:* 800-357-7666 ■ *Web:* www.netscout.com	Westford	MA	01886	978-614-4000	614-4004
NetVillage.com LLC 342 Main St *Web:* www.netvillage.com	Laurel	MD	20707	301-498-7797	498-8110
NICE Systems Inc 301 Rt 17 N 10th Fl *TF:* 800-994-4498 ■ *Web:* www.nice.com	Rutherford	NJ	07070	201-964-2600	964-2610
Northcore Technologies Inc 302 E Mall *NYSE: NTI*	Etobicoke	ON	M9B6C7	416-640-0400	
Nuance Communications Inc 1 Wayside Rd *NASDAQ: NUAN* ■ *TF:* 800-654-1187 ■ *Web:* www.nuance.com	Burlington	MA	01803	781-565-5000	
ObjectVideo Inc 11600 Sunrise Vly Dr Ste 290 *Web:* www.objectvideo.com	Reston	VA	20191	703-654-9300	654-9399
OmTool Ltd 6 Riverside Dr *OTC: OMTL* ■ *TF:* 800-886-7845 ■ *Web:* www.omtool.com	Andover	MA	01810	978-327-5700	659-1323
One Touch Systems Inc 2528 Qume Dr Unit 14 *TF:* 800-227-8862 ■ *Web:* www.onetouchsys.com	San Jose	CA	95131	408-436-4600	
Open Text Corp 275 Frank Tompa Dr *TSE: OTC* ■ *TF General:* 800-499-6544 ■ *Web:* www.opentext.com	Waterloo	ON	N2L0A1	519-888-7111	888-0677
Open Text Corp (USA) 100 Tri-State International Pkwy 3rd Fl *TSE: OTC* ■ *TF Sales:* 800-499-6544 ■ *Web:* www.opentext.com	Lincolnshire	IL	60069	847-267-9330	267-9332
OpenCon Systems Inc 377 Hoes Ln *Web:* www.opencon.com	Piscataway	NJ	08854	732-463-3131	463-3557
OpenConnect Systems Inc 2711 LBJ Fwy Ste 700 *TF:* 800-551-5881 ■ *Web:* www.oc.com	Dallas	TX	75234	972-484-5200	484-6100
OpenTV Corp 275 Sacramento St *Web:* www.nagra.com	San Francisco	CA	94111	415-962-5000	962-5300
Openwave Systems Inc 6201 College Blvd Ste 350 **Fax Area Code:* 650 ■ *Web:* owmobility.com	Overland Park	KS	66211	781-313-1400	480-8100*
Paloma Systems Inc 11250 Waples Mill Rd *Web:* www.palomasys.com	Fairfax	VA	22030	703-626-5024	591-0985
PartsRiver Inc 3155 Kearney St Ste 210 **Fax Area Code:* 510 ■ *TF:* 855-700-7278 ■ *Web:* www.partsriver.com	Fremont	CA	94538	855-700-7278	413-0079*
PCTEL Inc 471 Brighton Dr *NASDAQ: PCTI* ■ *Web:* www.pctel.com	Bloomingdale	IL	60108	630-372-6800	372-8077
Powersteering Software Inc 401 Congress Ave Ste 1850 *TF:* 866-390-9088 ■ *Web:* www.powersteeringsoftware.com	Austin	TX	78701	617-492-0707	492-9444
Propel Software Corp 1010 Rincon Cir *Web:* www.propel.com	San Jose	CA	95131	408-571-6300	577-1070
QSA ToolWorks LLC 3100 47th Ave *TF:* 800-784-7018 ■ *Web:* www.qsatoolworks.com	Long Island	NY	11101	516-935-9151	
Quadbase Systems Inc 275 Saratoga Ave Ste 105 *Web:* www.quadbase.com	Santa Clara	CA	95050	408-982-0835	982-0838
Qualcomm Inc 5775 Morehouse Dr *NASDAQ: QCOM* ■ *Web:* www.qualcomm.com	San Diego	CA	92121	858-587-1121	658-2100
Selectica Inc 2121 S. El Camino Rl 10th Fl *NASDAQ: SLTC* ■ **Fax Area Code:* 408 ■ *TF:* 877-712-9560	San Mateo	CA	94403	650-532-1500	570-9705*
Sendmail Inc 6475 Christie Ave Ste 350 *TF:* 888-594-3150 ■ *Web:* www.sendmail.com	Emeryville	CA	94608	510-594-5400	594-5429
Smith Micro Software Inc 51 Columbia St Ste 200 *NASDAQ: SMSI* ■ *Web:* www.smithmicro.com	Aliso Viejo	CA	92656	949-362-5800	362-2300
Support.com Inc 900 Chesapeake Dr 2nd Fl *NASDAQ: SPRT* ■ *TF:* 877-493-2778 ■ *Web:* www.support.com	Redwood City	CA	94063	650-556-9440	556-1195
Surety LLC 12020 Sunrise Vly Dr Ste 250 *TF:* 800-298-3115 ■ *Web:* www.surety.com	Reston	VA	20191	571-748-5800	748-5810
Symantec Corp 350 Ellis St *NASDAQ: SYMC* ■ *TF:* 800-441-7234 ■ *Web:* www.symantec.com	Mountain View	CA	94043	650-527-8000	527-8050
Symphony SMS 14881 Quorum Dr Ste 800 *Web:* www.tangoe.com	Dallas	TX	75254	972-581-7300	581-7301
Telenity Inc 755 Main St Ste 7 *Web:* www.telenity.com	Monroe	CT	06468	203-445-2000	268-1860
Transend Corp 225 Emerson St *Web:* www.transend.com	Palo Alto	CA	94301	650-324-5370	324-5377
UmeVoice Inc 20C Pimentel Ct Ste 1 *TF:* 888-230-3300 ■ *Web:* www.theboom.com	Novato	CA	94949	415-883-1500	
Vendio Services Inc 2800 Campus Dr Ste 150 *Web:* www.vendio.com	San Mateo	CA	94403	650-293-3500	
Verint Systems Inc 330 S Service Rd *Web:* www.verint.com	Melville	NY	11747	631-962-9600	962-9300
Vertical Communications Inc 3940 Freedom Cr Ste 110 *OTC: VRCC* ■ *TF Sales:* 800-914-9985 ■ *Web:* www.vertical.com	Santa Clara	CA	95054	408-404-1600	969-9601
Voxware Inc 300 American Metro Blvd Ste 155 *Web:* www.voxware.com	hamilton	NJ	08619	609-514-4100	514-4102
WaveLink Corp 1011 Western Ave Ste 601 *TF Tech Supp:* 888-697-9283 ■ *Web:* www.wavelink.com	Seattle	WA	98104	206-274-4280	652-2329
Websense Inc 10240 Sorrento Vly Rd *NASDAQ: WBSN* ■ *TF:* 800-723-1166 ■ *Web:* www.forcepoint.com/?utm_source=websense&utm_medium=redirect&utm_content=home	San Diego	CA	92121	858-320-8000	458-2950
Wexcel Inc 222 S Riverside Plz	Chicago	IL	60606	312-347-0955	347-0908
WorldFlash Software Inc 3853 Marcasel Ave *Web:* www.worldflash.com	Los Angeles	CA	90066	310-775-3633	
XAP Corp 3534 Hayden Ave *Web:* www.xap.com	Culver City	CA	90232	310-842-9800	
YellowBrix Inc 200 North Glebe Rd Ste 1025 *TF:* 888-325-9366	Arlington	VA	22203	703-548-3300	548-9151
Yodlee Inc 3600 Bridge Pkwy Ste 200 *Web:* yodlee.com	Redwood City	CA	94065	650-980-3600	
Zone Alarm 800 Bridge Pkwy *TF:* 877-966-5221 ■ *Web:* www.zonealarm.com	Redwood City	CA	94065	415-633-4500	633-4501

178-8 Multimedia & Design Software

Company	City	State	Zip	Phone	Fax
3D Systems Inc 333 Three D Systems Cir *TF:* 800-793-3669 ■ *Web:* www.3dsystems.com	Rock Hill	SC	29730	803-326-3900	
ACD Systems International Inc 129-1335 Bear Mtn Pkwy *Web:* www.acdsee.com	Victoria	BC	V9B6T9	250-419-6700	419-6742
Adobe Systems Inc 345 Pk Ave *NASDAQ: ADBE* ■ *TF:* 800-833-6687 ■ *Web:* www.adobe.com	San Jose	CA	95110	408-536-6000	537-6000
Apple Inc 1 Infinite Loop *NASDAQ: AAPL* ■ **Fax:* Mail Rm ■ *TF Cust Svc:* 800-275-2273 ■ *Web:* www.apple.com	Cupertino	CA	95014	408-996-1010	996-0275*
Auto FX Software 141 Village St Ste 2 *TF:* 800-839-2008 ■ *Web:* www.autofx.com	Birmingham	AL	35242	205-980-0056	980-1121
Autodessys Inc 2011 Riverside Dr *Web:* www.formz.com	Columbus	OH	43221	614-488-8838	488-0848
Avid Technology Inc 65-75 Network Dri *NASDAQ: AVID* ■ *TF:* 800-949-2843 ■ *Web:* www.avid.com	Burlington	MA	01803	978-640-6789	640-3366
Brilliant Digital Entertainment Inc 14011 Ventura Blvd Ste 501 *Web:* www.globalfileregistry.com	Sherman Oaks	CA	91423	818-386-2179	
Chyron Corp 5 Hub Dr *NASDAQ: CHYR* ■ *Web:* chyronhego.com	Melville	NY	11747	631-845-2000	
Concurrent 4375 River Green Pkwy Ste 100 *NASDAQ: CCUR* ■ *TF:* 877-978-7363 ■ *Web:* www.concurrent.com	Duluth	GA	30096	678-258-4000	258-4300
Corel Corp 1600 Carling Ave *TF Orders:* 800-772-6735 ■ *Web:* www.corel.com	Ottawa	ON	K1Z8R7	613-728-8200	761-9176
Dassault SystŠmes 166 Valley St *Web:* www.3ds.com/products-services/simulia	Providence	RI	02909	401-276-4400	276-4408
DeLorme 2 DeLorme Dr PO Box 298 **Fax Area Code:* 800 ■ *TF Sales:* 800-452-5931 ■ *Web:* www.delorme.com	Yarmouth	ME	04096	207-846-7000	561-5105*
Equilibrium Inc 100 Tamal Plz Ste 225 *TF:* 855-378-4542 ■ *Web:* equilibrium.com	Corte Madera	CA	94925	415-332-4343	331-8374
eWorkplace Solutions Inc 24461 Ridge Rt Dr Ste 210 *TF:* 888-477-7989 ■ *Web:* www.batchmaster.com	Laguna Hills	CA	92653	949-583-1646	271-4620
Fonthead Design Inc 3210 S Lansdowne Dr **Fax Area Code:* 866 ■ *Web:* www.fonthead.com	Wilmington	DE	19810	302-479-7922	806-1006*
HydroCAD Software Solutions LLC PO Box 477 *TF:* 800-927-7246 ■ *Web:* www.hydrocad.net	Chocorua	NH	03817	603-323-8666	323-7467
Image Labs International PO Box 1545 *TF:* 800-785-5995 ■ *Web:* www.imagelabs.com	Belgrade	MT	59714	406-585-7225	388-0998
Kofax PLC 15211 Laguna Canyon Rd *Web:* www.kofax.com	Irvine	CA	92618	949-783-1000	727-3144
La Cie Ltd 22985 NW Evergreen Pkwy **Fax:* Mktg ■ *Web:* www.lacie.com	Hillsboro	OR	97124	503-844-4500	844-4508*
Media 100 Inc 450 Donald Lynch Blvd *TF:* 888-772-6747 ■ *Web:* www.borisfx.com	Marlborough	MA	02210	508-460-1600	460-8627
MicroVision Development Inc 5541 Fermi Ct Ste 120 *TF:* 800-998-4555 ■ *Web:* www.mvd.com	Carlsbad	CA	92008	760-438-7781	438-7406
Minds-Eye-View Inc 103 Remsen St Ste 201 *Web:* www.ipix.com	Cohoes	NY	12047	518-237-1975	
Mitek Systems Inc 8911 Balboa Ave Ste B *Web:* www.miteksys.com	San Diego	CA	92123	858-503-7810	
Nemetschek North America 7150 Riverwood Dr *TF:* 888-646-4223 ■ *Web:* www.vectorworks.net	Columbia	MD	21046	410-290-5114	290-8050
NewTek Inc 5131 Beckwith Blvd *TF Cust Svc:* 800-862-7837 ■ *Web:* www.newtek.com	San Antonio	TX	78249	210-370-8000	370-8001
Octopus Media LLC 412 Eigth Ave	New York	NY	10001	212-967-5191	
Onyx Computing 10 Avon St *Web:* www.onyxtree.com	Cambridge	MA	02138	617-876-3876	
Overwatch Geospatial Operations 21660 Ridgetop Cir Ste 110 *TF:* 800-937-6881 ■ *Web:* textronsystems.com/company-overview/rebrand	Sterling	VA	20166	703-437-7651	437-0039
PaceWorks Inc 16780 Lark Ave *Web:* www.paceworks.com	Los Gatos	CA	95032	408-354-5711	884-2281
Patton & Patton Software Corp 1796 W Wimbledon Way *Web:* www.patton-patton.com	Tucson	AZ	85737	520-638-8738	
PC/Nametag 124 Horizon Dr **Fax Area Code:* 800 ■ *TF:* 877-626-3824 ■ *Web:* www.pcnametag.com	Verona	WI	53593	877-626-3824	233-9787*
Peerless Systems Corp 1055 Washington Blvd 8th Fl *NASDAQ: PRLS* ■ *Web:* www.peerless.com	Stamford	CT	06901	203-350-0040	
Prediction Systems Inc 309 Morris Ave Ste G *Web:* www.predictsys.com	Spring Lake	NJ	07762	732-449-6800	449-0897
Presagis 1301 W George Bush Fwy Ste 120 **Fax Area Code:* 469 ■ *TF:* 800-361-6424 ■ *Web:* www.presagis.com	Richardson	TX	75080	800-361-6424	467-4564*
Quark Inc 1800 Grant St *TF Cust Svc:* 800-676-4575 ■ *Web:* www.quark.com	Denver	CO	80203	800-676-4575	
RealNetworks Inc 2601 Elliott Ave Ste 1000 *NASDAQ: RNWK* ■ *TF Cust Svc:* 888-484-8256 ■ *Web:* www.realnetworks.com	Seattle	WA	98121	206-674-2700	674-2696
Scan-Optics Inc 169 Progress Dr *TF:* 800-543-8681 ■ *Web:* www.scanoptics.com	Manchester	CT	06042	860-645-7878	645-7995
Sigma Design 5521 Jackson St *TF Sales:* 888-990-0900 ■ *Web:* www.arriscad.com	Alexandria	LA	71303	318-449-9900	
Silicon Graphics Inc (SGI) 900 N McCarthy Blvd *Web:* www.sgi.com	Milpitas	CA	95035	669-900-8000	
SoftPress Systems Inc 3020 Bridgeway Ste 408 *TF:* 800-853-6454 ■ *Web:* www.softpress.com	Sausalito	CA	94965	415-331-4820	331-4824
Spatial Corp 310 Interlocken Pkwy Ste 200 *Web:* www.spatial.com	Broomfield	CO	80021	303-544-2900	544-3000
TechSmith Corp 2405 Woodlake Dr *TF:* 800-517-3001 ■ *Web:* www.techsmith.com	Okemos	MI	48864	517-381-2300	381-2336
Telestream Inc 848 Gold Flat Rd Ste 1 *TF:* 877-681-2088 ■ *Web:* www.telestream.net	Nevada City	CA	95959	530-470-1300	470-1301

Phone | Fax

Three D Graphics Inc
11340 W Olympic Blvd Ste 352 . . . Los Angeles CA 90064 310-231-3330 231-3303
TF: 800-913-0008 ■ *Web:* www.threedgraphics.com

Videotex Systems Inc 10255 Miller Rd . . . Dallas TX 75238 972-231-9200 231-2420
TF: 800-888-4336 ■ *Web:* www.videotexsystems.com

Worlds.com Inc 11 Royal Rd. . . . Brookline MA 02445 617-725-8900 975-3888
TF: 800-315-2580 ■ *Web:* www.worlds.com

178-9 Personal Software

Phone | Fax

Approva Corp 13454 Sunrise Vly Dr Ste 500 . . . Herndon VA 20171 703-956-8300 956-8350
Web: www.infor.com

Avery Dennison Corp 207 Goode Ave . . . Glendale CA 91203 626-304-2000
NYSE: AVY ■ *TF Cust Svc:* 888-567-4387 ■ *Web:* www.averydennison.com

Corel Corp 1600 Carling Ave . . . Ottawa ON K1Z8R7 613-728-8200 761-9176
TF Orders: 800-772-6735 ■ *Web:* www.corel.com

Equis International
90 South 400 West Ste 620 . . . Salt Lake City UT 84101 801-265-9996 265-3999
TF Sales: 800-882-3040 ■ *Web:* www.metastock.com

HowardSoft 7852 Ivanhoe Ave . . . La Jolla CA 92037 858-454-0121
TF: 800-248-2937 ■ *Web:* www.howardsoft.com

Intuit Inc 2632 Marine Way . . . Mountain View CA 94043 650-944-6000 944-5656
NASDAQ: INTU ■ *TF Cust Svc:* 800-446-8848 ■ *Web:* www.intuit.com

Logos Bible Software 1313 Commercial St . . . Bellingham WA 98225 360-527-1700
Web: www.logos.com

Micro Logic Corp 666 Godwin Ave . . . Midland Park NJ 07432 201-962-7510
Web: www.miclog.com

Microsoft Corp 1 Microsoft Way . . . Redmond WA 98052 425-882-8080 936-7329
NASDAQ: MSFT ■ *Web:* www.microsoft.com

MOTU Inc 1280 Massachusetts Ave . . . Cambridge MA 02138 617-576-2760 576-3609
Web: www.motu.com

Nolo.com 950 Parker St . . . Berkeley CA 94710 800-728-3555 645-0895
TF: 800-728-3555 ■ *Web:* www.nolo.com

Radialpoint 2050 Bleury St Ste 300 . . . Montreal QC H3A2J5 514-286-2636 286-0558
TF: 866-286-2636 ■ *Web:* www.radialpoint.com

Sony Creative Software 1617 Sherman Ave . . . Madison WI 53704 608-256-3133 250-1745
TF: 800-577-6642 ■ *Web:* www.sonycreativesoftware.com

Stevens Creek Software PO Box 2126 . . . Cupertino CA 95015 408-725-0424 366-1954
TF: 800-823-4279 ■ *Web:* www.stevenscreek.com

Symantec Corp 350 Ellis St . . . Mountain View CA 94043 650-527-8000 527-8050
NASDAQ: SYMC ■ *TF:* 800-441-7234 ■ *Web:* www.symantec.com

178-10 Professional Software (Industry-Specific)

Companies listed here manufacture software designed for specific professions or business sectors (i.e., architecture, banking, investment, physical sciences, real estate, etc.).

Phone | Fax

9Dots Management Corp
1100 E Hector St Ste 245 . . . Conshohocken PA 19428 610-684-6220

Access International Group Inc
248 Columbia Tpk . . . Florham Park NJ 07932 973-360-0750
Web: www.accessig.com

Acentia 3130 Fairview Pk Dr Ste 800 . . . Falls Church VA 22042 703-712-4000 712-4010
Web: acentia.com

ACI Worldwide Inc 6060 Coventry Dr . . . Elkhorn NE 68022 402-390-7600
NASDAQ: ACIW ■ *Web:* aciworldwide.com

Adacel Technologies Ltd 9677 Tradeport Dr . . . Orlando FL 32827 407-581-1560 581-1581
Web: www.adacelinc.com

AGFA HealthCare Corp 10 S Academy St . . . Greenville SC 29601 864-421-1600 421-1414
TF: 877-777-2432 ■ *Web:* www.agfahealthcare.com

AIMS Inc 235 Desiard St . . . Monroe LA 71201 318-323-2467 322-3472
TF: 800-729-2467 ■ *Web:* www.aims1.com

Algorithmics Inc 185 Spadina Ave . . . Toronto ON M5T2C6 416-217-1500 971-6100

Allot Communications 300 Tradecenter Ste 4680 . . . Woburn MA 01801 781-939-9300 939-9393
TF: 877-255-6826 ■ *Web:* www.allot.com

Allscripts Healthcare Solutions
222 Merchandise Mart Plz Ste 2024 . . . Chicago IL 60654 800-654-0889
NASDAQ: MDRX ■ *TF:* 800-654-0889 ■ *Web:* www.allscripts.com

Alternative System Concepts Inc
22 Haverhill Rd PO Box 128 . . . Windham NH 03087 603-437-2234 437-2722
Web: www.ascinc.com

Amdocs Ltd 1390 Timberlake Manor Pkwy . . . Chesterfield MO 63017 314-212-7000 212-7500
NYSE: DOX ■ *TF:* 866-426-8003 ■ *Web:* www.amdocs.com

American Traffic Solutions Inc
42 Oriental St . . . Providence RI 02908 401-274-5658 434-5807
OTC: NEST

Anchor Computer Inc 1900 New Hwy . . . Farmingdale NY 11735 631-293-6100 293-0891
TF: 800-728-6262 ■ *Web:* www.anchorcomputer.com

ARI Network Services Inc
10850 W Pk Pl Ste 1200 . . . Milwaukee WI 53224 414-973-4300 283-4357
TF: 877-805-0803 ■ *Web:* www.arinet.com

ASI DataMyte Inc 2800 Campus Dr Ste 60 . . . Plymouth MN 55441 763-553-1040 553-1041
TF: 800-207-5631 ■ *Web:* www.asidatamyte.com

Aspyra Inc 4360 Pk Terr Dr Ste 100 . . . Westlake Village CA 91361 800-437-9000 880-4398*
OTC: APYI ■ **Fax Area Code:* 818 ■ *TF:* 800-437-9000 ■ *Web:* www.aspyra.com

Avantus 15 W Strong St Ste 20A . . . Pensacola FL 32501 850-470-9336 600-2508*
**Fax Area Code:* 800 ■ *TF:* 800-600-2510 ■ *Web:* www.advantagecredit.com

Avaya Government Solutions Inc
12730 Fair Lakes Cir . . . Fairfax VA 22033 703-653-8000 653-8001
TF: 800-492-6769 ■ *Web:* www.avaya.com/avayagov

BatchMaster Software Inc
24461 Ridge Rt Dr Ste 210 . . . Laguna Hills CA 92653 949-583-1646 271-4620
TF: 800-359-0920 ■ *Web:* www.batchmaster.com

Baxter Planning Systems Inc
7801 N Capital of Texas Hwy Ste 250 . . . Austin TX 78731 512-323-5959 323-5354
Web: bybaxter.com

BenefitMall Inc 4851 LBJ Fwy Ste 1100 . . . Dallas TX 75244 469-791-3300 791-3313
TF: 888-338-6293 ■ *Web:* www.benefitmall.com

Phone | Fax

Brodart Co 500 Arch St . . . Williamsport PA 17701 570-326-2461
TF: 800-233-8467 ■ *Web:* www.brodart.com

C-Solutions Inc 1900 Folsom St Ste 205 . . . Boulder CO 80302 303-786-9461
Web: www.gmsworks.com

CACI MTL Systems Inc 2685 Hibiscus Way . . . Beavercreek OH 45431 937-426-3111
Web: www.caci.com

CAM Commerce Solutions Inc
17075 Newhope St Ste A . . . Fountain Valley CA 92708 714-241-9241 241-9893
TF: 800-726-3282 ■ *Web:* www.camcommerce.com

CareCentric Inc 20 Church St 12th Fl . . . Hartford CT 06103 800-808-1902
TF: 866-467-8263 ■ *Web:* www.carecentrix.com

Carousel Industries of North America Inc
659 S County Trl . . . Exeter RI 02822 800-401-0760 760-5236*
**Fax Area Code:* 860 ■ *TF:* 800-401-0760 ■ *Web:* www.carouselindustries.com

CCH Small Firm Services
225 Chastain Meadows Ct NW Ste 200 . . . Kennesaw GA 30144 866-345-4171 236-9168*
**Fax Area Code:* 706 ■ *TF Sales:* 866-345-4171 ■ *Web:* www.cchsfs.com

Cedara Software Corp
6303 Airport Rd Ste 500 . . . Mississauga ON L4V1R8 905-364-8000 364-8100
TF: 800-724-5970 ■ *Web:* www.merge.com

Charles River Development Inc
7 New England Executive Pk . . . Burlington MA 01803 781-238-0099 238-0088
Web: www.crd.com

Circa Information Technology
12001 Woodruff Ave . . . Downey CA 90241 562-803-1594
Web: www.circausa.com

CliniComp International 9655 Towne Ctr Dr . . . San Diego CA 92121 858-546-8202 546-1801
TF: 800-350-8202 ■ *Web:* www.clinicomp.com

Command Alkon Inc
1800 International Pk Dr Ste 400 . . . Birmingham AL 35243 205-879-3282 870-1405
TF: 800-624-1872 ■ *Web:* www.commandalkon.com

Community Computer Service Inc PO Box 980 . . . Auburn NY 13021 315-255-1751

Computac Inc 162 N Main St . . . West Lebanon NH 03784 603-298-5721 298-6189
Web: www.computac.com

Computers Unlimited 2407 Montana Ave . . . Billings MT 59101 406-255-9500 255-9595
TF: 800-763-0308 ■ *Web:* www.cu.net

Construction Software Technologies Inc
4500 W Lake Forest Drive Ste 502 . . . Cincinnati OH 45242 513-645-8004 645-8005
TF: 800-364-2059 ■ *Web:* www.isqft.com

Construction Systems Software Inc
494 Covered Bridge . . . Schertz TX 78154 210-979-6494
TF: 800-531-1035

CoStar Group Inc
2 Bethesda Metro Ctr 10th Fl . . . Bethesda MD 20814 301-215-8300
NASDAQ: CSGP ■ *TF:* 800-613-1303 ■ *Web:* www.costar.com

CSG Systems International 9555 Maroon Cir . . . Englewood CO 80112 303-796-2850 200-3333
NASDAQ: CSGS ■ *Web:* www.csgi.com

CSSC Inc 26 Mayfield Ave . . . Edison NJ 08837 732-225-5555 626-6035
Web: www.csscinc.com

Datatel Inc 4375 Fair Lakes Ct . . . Fairfax VA 22033 800-223-7036
TF: 800-223-7036 ■ *Web:* www.ellucian.com

DealerTrack Holdings Inc
1111 Marcus Ave Ste M04 . . . Lake Success NY 11042 516-734-3600
NASDAQ: TRAK ■ *TF:* 877-357-8725 ■ *Web:* www.dealertrack.com

Deltagen Inc 1900 S Norfolk St Ste 105 . . . San Mateo CA 94403 650-345-7602
Web: www.deltagen.com

Digineer 505 N Hwy 169 Ste 750 . . . Plymouth MN 55441 763-210-2300 210-2301
Web: www.digineer.com

Digital Harbor Inc 1934 Old Gallows Rd Ste 350 . . . Vienna VA 22182 703-635-3477
Web: www.digitalharbor.com

Digital Technology International
1180 N Mountain Springs Pkwy . . . Springville UT 84663 801-853-5000
Web: newscyclesolutions.com

DIS Corp 1315 Cornwall Ave . . . Bellingham WA 98225 360-733-7610 647-6921
TF Cust Svc: 800-426-8870 ■ *Web:* www.dis-corp.com

Document Security Systems Inc
200 Canal View Blvd Ste 300 . . . Rochester NY 14623 585-325-3610 325-2977
NYSE: DSS ■ *TF:* 877-407-8031 ■ *Web:* www.dsssecure.com

DynTek Inc 4440 Von Karman Ste 200 . . . Newport Beach CA 92660 949-271-6700
Web: www.dyntek.com

Eagle Point Software Corp 4131 Westmark Dr . . . Dubuque IA 52002 563-556-8392
TF: 800-678-6565 ■ *Web:* www.eaglepoint.com

Ellucian 4375 Fair Lakes Ct . . . Fairfax VA 22033 610-647-5930 968-4625*
**Fax Area Code:* 703 ■ *TF:* 800-223-7036 ■ *Web:* www.ellucian.com

Enghouse Systems Ltd 80 Tiverton Ct Ste 800 . . . Markham ON L3R0G4 905-946-3200 946-3201
TSE: ESL ■ *TF:* 866-206-0240 ■ *Web:* www.enghouse.com

Environmental Systems Research Institute Inc
380 New York St . . . Redlands CA 92373 909-793-2853 793-5953
TF Sales: 800-447-9778 ■ *Web:* www.esri.com

Envision Telephony Inc 901 Fifth Ave Ste 3300 . . . Seattle WA 98164 206-225-0800
Web: www.envisioninc.com

EPIQ Systems Inc 501 Kansas Ave . . . Kansas City KS 66105 913-621-9500
NASDAQ: EPIQ ■ *Web:* www.epiqsystems.com

Equis International
90 South 400 West Ste 620 . . . Salt Lake City UT 84101 801-265-9996 265-3999
TF Sales: 800-882-3040 ■ *Web:* www.metastock.com

eResearch Technology Inc
1818 Market St Ste 1000 . . . Philadelphia PA 19103 215-972-0420 972-0414
NASDAQ: ERT ■ *TF:* 800-704-9698 ■ *Web:* www.ert.com

Ericsson 1 Telcordia Dr . . . Piscataway NJ 08854 732-699-2000
TF: 800-521-2673 ■
Web: www.ericsson.com/ourportfolio/telcordia_landingpage

Final Draft Inc 26707 W Agoura Rd Ste 205 . . . Calabasas CA 91302 818-995-8995 995-4422
TF: 800-231-4055 ■ *Web:* www.finaldraft.com

Financial Engines Inc 1804 Embarcadero Rd . . . Palo Alto CA 94303 408-498-6000 565-4905*
NASDAQ: FNGN ■ **Fax Area Code:* 650 ■ *TF:* 888-443-8577 ■ *Web:* www.corp.financialengines.com

First DataBank Inc (FDB)
701 Gateway Blvd Ste 600 . . . South San Francisco CA 94080 800-633-3453
TF General: 800-633-3453 ■ *Web:* www.fdbhealth.com

Follett Software Co 1391 Corporate Dr . . . McHenry IL 60050 815-759-1700 344-8774
TF: 800-323-3397 ■ *Web:* www.follettlearning.com

FXCM Inc 32 Old Slip . . . New York NY 10005 212-897-7660 229-0004*
NYSE: FXCM ■ **Fax Area Code:* 877 ■ *TF:* 888-503-6739 ■ *Web:* www.fxcm.com

	City	State	Zip	Phone	Fax
General Dynamics C4 Systems					
400 John Quincy Adams Rd Bldg 80	Taunton	MA	02780	877-449-0600	
TF: 877-449-0600 ■ *Web:* www.gdc4s.com					
Geofields Inc 1201 W Peachtree St Ste 2450	Atlanta	GA	30309	404-253-1000	875-2442
Web: www.geofields.com					
GHG Corp 960 Clear Lk City Blvd	Webster	TX	77598	281-488-8806	488-1838
TF: 866-380-4146 ■ *Web:* www.ghg.com					
Glimmerglass Networks Inc					
26142 Eden Landing Rd	Hayward	CA	94545	510-723-1900	780-9851
TF: 877-723-1900 ■ *Web:* www.glimmerglass.com					
Global Turnkey Systems Inc 2001 US 46	Parsippany	NJ	07054	973-331-1010	
Web: www.gtsystems.com					
GoldenSource Corp 22 Cortlandt St	New York	NY	10007	212-798-7100	798-7238
Web: www.thegoldensource.com					
gomembers Inc 1155 Perimeter Center West	Atlanta	GA	30338	855-411-2783	
TF: 855-411-2783 ■ *Web:* www.aptean.com					
Guidance Software Inc					
215 N Marengo Ave 2nd Fl	Pasadena	CA	91101	626-229-9191	229-9199
TF: 866-229-9199 ■ *Web:* guidancesoftware.com					
HRsmart 2929 N Central Expwy Ste 110	Richardson	TX	75080	972-783-3000	853-5319*
**Fax Area Code:* 214 ■ *Web:* www.hrsmart.com					
IHS Energy Group 15 Inverness Way E	Englewood	CO	80112	303-736-3000	
TF: 800-447-2273 ■ *Web:* www.ihs.com					
ImageWare Systems Inc					
10815 Rancho BernaRdo Rd Ste 310	San Diego	CA	92127	858-673-8600	673-1770
Web: www.iwsinc.com					
Incyte Corp 1801 Augustine Cut-Off	Wilmington	DE	19803	302-498-6700	
NASDAQ: INCY ■ *Web:* www.incyte.com					
Info Tech Inc 5700 SW 34th St Ste 1235	Gainesville	FL	32608	352-381-4400	381-4444
TF: 888-352-2439 ■ *Web:* www.infotechfl.com					
Infor Global Solutions					
13560 Morris Rd Ste 4100	Alpharetta	GA	30004	678-319-8000	319-8682
TF: 866-244-5479 ■ *Web:* www.infor.com					
Innovative Technologies Corp (ITC)					
1020 Woodman Dr Ste 100	Dayton	OH	45432	937-252-2145	254-6853
TF: 800-745-8050 ■ *Web:* www.itc-1.com					
Input 1 LLC 6200 Canoga Ave Ste 400	Woodland Hills	CA	91367	818-713-2303	340-1261
TF: 888-882-2554 ■ *Web:* www.input1.com					
Insurance Information Technologies Inc (INSTEC)					
1811 Centre Pt Cir Ste 115	Naperville	IL	60563	630-955-9200	
Web: www.instec-corp.com					
Intradiem 3650 Mansell Rd Ste 500	Alpharetta	GA	30022	678-356-3500	
TF: 888-566-9457 ■ *Web:* www.intradiem.com					
IPC Systems Inc					
Harborside Financial Plz 10 15th Fl	Jersey City	NJ	07311	201-253-2000	253-2361
Web: www.ipc.com					
ISG Technology & Data Center 127 N Seventh St	Salina	KS	67401	785-823-1555	827-3310
Web: www.isgtech.com					
Island Pacific Inc 17310 Red Hill Ave Ste 320	Irvine	CA	92614	800-994-3847	
TF: 800-994-3847 ■ *Web:* www.islandpacific.com					
Ita Software Inc 141 Portland St	Cambridge	MA	02139	617-714-2100	621-3913
Web: www.itasoftware.com					
iWay Software 2 Penn Plz	New York	NY	10121	212-736-4433	967-6406
TF: 800-736-6130 ■ *Web:* www.informationbuilders.com					
JDA Software Group Inc 14400 N 87th St	Scottsdale	AZ	85260	480-308-3000	308-3001
NASDAQ: JDAS ■ *Web:* www.jda.com					
Jenzabar Inc 101 Huntington Ave Ste 2200	Boston	MA	02199	617-492-9099	492-9081
TF: 800-593-0028 ■ *Web:* www.jenzabar.com					
Kinaxis 700 Silver Seven Rd	Ottawa	ON	K2V1C3	613-592-5780	592-0584
TF General: 877-546-2947 ■ *Web:* www.kinaxis.com					
Knorr Assoc Inc 10 Pk Pl PO Box 400	Butler	NJ	07405	973-492-8500	492-0453
Web: www.knorrassociates.com					
Knovalent 3135 S State St Ste 300	Ann Arbor	MI	48108	734-996-8300	
Web: www.knovalent.com					
Labware Inc 3 Mill Rd Ste 102	Wilmington	DE	19806	302-658-8444	658-7894
Web: www.labware.com					
Land & Legal Solutions Inc					
300 S Hamilton Ave	Greensburg	PA	15601	724-853-8992	853-3221
TF: 800-245-7900					
Landacorp Inc 500 Orient St Ste 110	Chico	CA	95928	530-891-0853	891-8428
Web: www.landacorp.com					
Learnsomething Inc 2457 Care Dr	Tallahassee	FL	32308	850-385-7915	385-7964
Web: www.learnsomething.com					
Lumedx Corp 555 12th St Ste 2060	Oakland	CA	94607	510-419-1000	419-3699
TF: 800-966-0699 ■ *Web:* www.lumedx.com					
Luminex Molecular Diagnostics					
439 University Ave Ste 900	Toronto	ON	M5G1Y8	416-593-4323	593-1066
Web: www.luminexcorp.com					
LynuxWorks Inc 855 Embedded Way	San Jose	CA	95138	408-979-3900	979-3920
TF: 800-255-5969 ■ *Web:* lynx.com/index.php					
Management Information Control Systems Inc (MICS)					
2025 Ninth St	Los Osos	CA	93402	805-543-7000	543-0373
TF: 800-838-6427 ■ *Web:* www.bissoftware.com					
Managing Editor Inc 610 York Rd # 250	Jenkintown	PA	19046	215-886-5662	886-5681
Web: www.maned.com					
Manhattan Assoc Inc					
2300 Windy Ridge Pkwy 10th Fl	Atlanta	GA	30339	770-955-7070	955-0302
NASDAQ: MANH ■ *TF:* 877-756-7435 ■ *Web:* www.manh.com					
Market Scan Information Systems Inc					
811 Camarillo Springs Ste B	Camarillo	CA	93012	800-658-7226	
TF: 800-658-7226 ■ *Web:* www.marketscan.com					
Marshall & Swift					
777 S Figueroa St 12th Fl	Los Angeles	CA	90017	213-683-9000	683-9010
TF: 800-544-2678 ■ *Web:* www.marshallswift.com					
McKesson Information Solutions					
5995 Windward Pkwy	Alpharetta	GA	30005	404-338-6000	
TF: 800-981-8601 ■ *Web:* mckesson.com					
MDI Achieve					
10900 Hampshire Ave South Ste 100	Bloomington	MN	55438	952-995-9800	995-9735
TF: 800-869-1322 ■ *Web:* www.matrixcare.com					
MEDecision Inc 550 E Swedesford Rd Ste 220	Wayne	PA	19087	610-540-0202	540-0270
Web: www.medecision.com					
Media Cybernetics Inc 4340 E W Hwy Ste 400	Bethesda	MD	20814	301-495-3305	495-5964
TF Sales: 800-263-2088 ■ *Web:* www.mediacy.com					
Medical Information Technology Inc					
1 Meditech Cir	Westwood	MA	02090	781-821-3000	821-2199
Web: www.meditech.com					
MedPlus Inc 4690 Pkwy Dr	Mason	OH	45040	513-229-5500	229-5505
TF: 800-444-6235 ■					
Web: questdiagnostics.com/home/physicians/chartmaxx/mason-bu.html					
Megaputer Intelligence Inc					
1600 W Bloomfield Rd Ste E	Bloomington	IN	47403	812-330-0110	330-0150
Web: www.megaputer.com					
MicroBilt Corp 1640 Airport Rd Ste 115	Kennesaw	GA	30144	800-884-4747	218-4997*
**Fax Area Code:* 770 ■ *TF:* 800-884-4747 ■ *Web:* www.microbilt.com					
Midrange Software Inc 12716 Riverside Dr	Studio City	CA	91607	818-762-8539	762-6256
TF: 800-737-6766 ■ *Web:* www.midrangesoftware.com					
Minitab Inc					
Quality Plz 1829 Pine Hall Rd	State College	PA	16801	814-238-3280	238-1702
TF: 800-448-3555 ■ *Web:* www.minitab.com					
Mortgage Builders Software					
24370 NW Hwy Ste 200	Southfield	MI	48075	800-850-8060	
TF: 800-850-8060 ■ *Web:* www.mortgagebuilder.com					
Mzinga Inc 230 Third Ave	Waltham	MA	02451	781-577-8948	494-6555
TF: 888-694-6428 ■ *Web:* www.mzinga.com					
Navtech Inc 295 Hagey Blvd Ste 200	Waterloo	ON	N2L6R5	519-747-1170	747-1003
Web: www.navtechinc.com					
netGuru Inc 1240 N Van Buren St Ste 104	Anaheim	CA	92807	714-638-4878	414-0200
Web: www.netguru.com					
Netsol Technologies Inc					
23901 Calabasas Rd Ste 2072	Calabasas	CA	91302	818-222-9195	222-9197
NASDAQ: NTWK ■ *Web:* www.netsoltech.com					
New England Computer Services Inc					
168 Boston Post Rd Stes 6 & 7	Madison	CT	06443	203-245-3999	245-4513
TF Sales: 800-766-6327 ■ *Web:* www.necs.com					
NIC Inc 25501 W Valley Pkwy Ste 300	Olathe	KS	66061	877-234-3468	498-3472*
NASDAQ: EGOV ■ **Fax Area Code:* 913 ■ *TF:* 877-234-3468 ■ *Web:* www.egov.com					
Nissho Electronics USA Corp					
226 Airport Pkwy	San Jose	CA	95110	408-969-9700	969-9701
Web: www.nelco.com					
OATSystems Inc 309 Waverley Oaks Rd Ste 306	Waltham	MA	02452	781-907-6100	907-6098
TF: 877-628-7877 ■ *Web:* www.oatsystems.com					
Olson Research Assoc Inc					
10290 Old Columbia Rd	Columbia	MD	21046	410-290-6999	290-6726
TF: 888-657-6680 ■ *Web:* www.olsonresearch.com					
OpenTable Inc 1 Montgomery St 4th Fl	San Francisco	CA	94103	415-344-4200	
NASDAQ: OPEN ■ *TF:* 800-673-6822 ■ *Web:* www.opentable.com					
Opex Corp 305 Commerce Dr	Moorestown	NJ	08057	856-727-1100	727-1955
TF: 800-673-9288 ■ *Web:* www.opex.com					
OSI Software Inc 777 Davis St Ste 250	San Leandro	CA	94577	510-297-5800	357-8136
Web: www.osisoft.com					
OverDrive Inc 1 OverDr Wy Unit C	Cleveland	OH	44125	216-573-6886	573-6888
Web: www.overdrive.com					
Packet Design Inc 2455 Augustine Dr	Santa Clara	CA	95054	408-490-1000	562-0080
Web: www.packetdesign.com					
Pason Systems Inc 6130 Third St SE	Calgary	AB	T2H1K4	403-301-3400	301-3499
TSE: PSI ■ *TF:* 877-255-3158 ■ *Web:* www.pason.com					
Passport Health Communications Inc					
720 Cool Springs Blvd Ste 200	Franklin	TN	37067	615-661-5657	376-3552
TF: 888-661-5657 ■ *Web:* www.passporthealth.com					
PDF Solutions Inc					
333 W San Carlos St Ste 700	San Jose	CA	95110	408-280-7900	280-7915
NASDAQ: PDFS ■ *Web:* www.pdf.com					
Picis Inc 100 Quannapowitt Pkwy Ste 405	Wakefield	MA	01880	781-557-3000	557-3140
Web: picis.com					
PKC Corp 1 Mill St C13 Ste 355	Burlington	VT	05401	802-658-5351	658-3078
TF: 800-752-5351 ■ *Web:* www.pkc.com					
Planet Payment Inc 670 Long Beach Blvd	Long Beach	NY	11561	516-670-3200	670-3520
NYSE: PLPM ■ *Web:* www.planetpayment.com					
Pragmatics Inc 1761 Business Ctr Dr	Reston	VA	20190	703-761-4033	438-1779
Web: www.pragmatics.com					
ProCard Inc 1819 Denver W Dr Bldg 26 Ste 300	Lakewood	CO	80401	303-279-2255	279-2874
TF: 800-469-6578 ■ *Web:* www.procard.com					
Promodel Corp 3400 Bath Pike Ste 200	Bethlehem	PA	18017	801-223-4600	226-6046
TF: 888-900-3090 ■ *Web:* www.promodel.com					
Pros Holdings Inc 3100 Main St Ste 900	Houston	TX	77002	713-335-5151	335-8144
NYSE: PRO ■ *Web:* www.pros.com					
PSI International Inc 4000 Legato Rd Ste 850	Fairfax	VA	22033	703-621-5825	352-8236
Web: www.psiint.com					
QlikTech International AB					
150 N Radnor Chester Rd Ste E220	Radnor	PA	19087	888-828-9768	975-5987*
NASDAQ: QLIK ■ **Fax Area Code:* 610 ■ *TF:* 888-828-9768 ■ *Web:* qlik.com					
Quality Systems Inc (QSI)					
18111 Von Karman Ave Ste 600	Irvine	CA	92612	949-255-2600	255-2605
NASDAQ: QSII ■ *TF Cust Svc:* 800-888-7955 ■ *Web:* www.qsii.com					
QUMAS 66 York St	Jersey City	NJ	07302	973-805-8600	377-8687
TF Sales: 800-577-1545 ■ *Web:* www.qumas.com					
Qvidian Corp 175 Cabot St Ste 210	Lowell	MA	01854	513-631-1155	703-7631*
**Fax Area Code:* 978 ■ *TF:* 800-272-0047 ■ *Web:* www.qvidian.com					
RainMaker Software Inc 1777 Sentry Pkwy W	Blue Bell	PA	19422	610-567-3400	
TF: 800-336-0339					
Raytheon Co 10 Moulton St	Cambridge	MA	02138	617-873-8000	318-5041*
**Fax Area Code:* 703 ■ *TF:* 866-230-1307 ■ *Web:* www.raytheon.com/ourcompany/bbn					
Raytheon Solipsys 8170 Maple Lawn Blvd Ste 300	Fulton	MD	20759	240-554-8100	554-8101
Web: www.solipsys.com					
Red Wing Software Inc 491 Hwy 19	Red Wing	MN	55066	651-388-1106	388-7950
TF: 800-732-9464 ■ *Web:* www.redwingsoftware.com					
RESUMate Inc 2500 Packard St Ste 200	Ann Arbor	MI	48104	734-477-9402	
TF Cust Svc: 800-530-9310 ■ *Web:* www.resumate.com					
Retail Pro International LLC					
400 Plz Dr Ste 200	Folsom	CA	95630	916-605-7200	
OTC: RTPRQ ■ *TF:* 800-738-2457 ■ *Web:* www.retailpro.com					
Reynolds & Reynolds Co 1 Reynolds Way	Dayton	OH	45430	937-485-2000	
TF: 800-767-0080 ■ *Web:* www.reyrey.com					
Risk Management Solutions Inc					
7575 Gateway Blvd	Newark	CA	94560	510-505-2500	505-2501
Web: www.rms.com					

Phone Fax

RiskWatch (RWI) 1237 N Gulfstream Ave .... Sarasota Fl 34236 800-360-1898
TF: 800-360-1898 ■ *Web:* riskwatch.com/contact-us

Sapiens International Corp
4000 CentreGreen Way Ste 150 .... Cary NC 27513 919-405-1500 405-1700
NASDAQ: SPNS ■ *TF:* 888-281-1167 ■ *Web:* www.sapiens.com

Scantron Corp 34 Parker .... Irvine CA 92618 949-639-7500 639-7710
TF: 800-722-6876 ■ *Web:* www.scantron.com

Serendipity Systems Inc PO Box 10477 .... Sedona AZ 86339 928-282-6831 282-4383
Web: www.serendipsys.com

Siemens Product Lifecycle Management Software Inc
5800 Granite Pkwy Ste 600 .... Plano TX 75024 972-987-3000 987-3397
TF: 800-498-5351 ■ *Web:* www.plm.automation.siemens.com

Simulations Plus Inc 42505 Tenth St W .... Lancaster CA 93534 661-723-7723 723-5524
NASDAQ: SLP ■ *TF:* 888-266-9294 ■ *Web:* www.simulations-plus.com

SM & A 18400 Von Karman Ave Ste 500 .... Irvine CA 92612 949-975-1550 975-1624
Web: www.smawins.com

Snap-on Diagnostics 420 Barclay Blvd .... Lincolnshire IL 60069 847-478-0700
TF: 800-424-7226 ■ *Web:* www1.snapon.com

Snowbound Software
309 Waverley Oaks Rd Ste 401 .... Waltham MA 02452 617-607-2000 607-2002
Web: www.snowbound.com

Software Consulting Services LLC
630 Selvaggio Dr Ste 420 .... Nazareth PA 18064 610-746-7700 746-7900
Web: www.newspapersystems.com

SolidWorks Corp 300 Baker Ave .... Concord MA 01742 978-371-5011 371-7303
TF: 800-693-9000 ■ *Web:* www.solidworks.com

Spillman Technologies Inc
4625 Lake Pk Blvd .... Salt Lake City UT 84120 801-902-1200 902-1210
TF General: 800-860-8026 ■ *Web:* www.spillman.com

SQN Banking Systems 65 Indel Ave PO Box 423 .... Rancocas NJ 08073 609-261-5500 265-9517
Web: www.sqnsigs.com

StatSoft Inc 2300 E 14th St .... Tulsa OK 74104 918-749-1119 749-2217
Web: www.statsoft.com

SunGard Trust Systems Inc 5510 77 Ctr Dr .... Charlotte NC 28217 704-527-6300 527-9617
Web: www.sungard.com

Synergex International Corp
2330 Gold Meadow Way .... Rancho Cordova CA 95670 916-635-7300 635-6549
TF: 800-366-3472 ■ *Web:* www.synergex.com

Synopsys Inc 700 E Middlefield Rd .... Mountain View CA 94043 650-584-5000 965-8637
NASDAQ: SNPS ■ *TF:* 800-541-7737 ■ *Web:* www.synopsys.com

System Automation
7110 Samuel Morse Dr Ste 100 .... Columbia MD 21046 301-837-8000 837-8001
TF: 800-839-4729 ■ *Web:* www.systemautomation.com

System Innovators Inc
10550 Deerwood Pk Blvd Ste 700 .... Jacksonville FL 32256 800-963-5000 281-0075*
**Fax Area Code:* 904 ■ *TF:* 800-963-5000 ■ *Web:* systeminnovators.com

Tableau Software Inc 837 N 34th St Ste 400 .... Seattle WA 98103 206-633-3400 633-3004
Web: www.tableau.com

Thomson Elite
800 Corporate Pointe Ste 150 .... Los Angeles CA 90230 424-243-2100 642-5400*
**Fax Area Code:* 323 ■ *TF Cust Svc:* 800-354-8337 ■ *Web:* www.elite.com

TMW Systems Inc 21111 Chagrin Blvd .... Beachwood OH 44122 216-831-6606 831-3606
TF: 800-401-6682 ■ *Web:* www.tmwsystems.com

TradeStation Group Inc
8050 SW Tenth St Ste 2000 .... Plantation FL 33324 954-652-7000 652-7300
TF: 800-871-3577 ■ *Web:* www.tradestation.com

Transentric 1400 Douglas St Ste 0840 .... Omaha NE 68179 402-544-6000 501-2984
TF: 800-877-0328 ■ *Web:* www.transentric.com

TransWorks 9910 Dupont Cir Dr E Ste 200 .... Fort Wayne IN 46825 260-487-4400
TF: 800-435-4691 ■ *Web:* www.trnswrks.com

Tyler Technologies Inc 5949 Sherry Ln Ste 1400 .... Dallas TX 75225 800-431-5776 713-3741*
NYSE: TYL ■ **Fax Area Code:* 972 ■ *TF:* 800-431-5776 ■ *Web:* www.tylertech.com

US Dataworks Inc
1 Sugar Creek Ctr Blvd 5th Fl .... Sugar Land TX 77478 281-504-8000 565-2567
OTC: UDWK ■ *TF:* 888-254-8821 ■ *Web:* www.usdataworks.com

US Digital Corp 1400 NE 136th Ave .... Vancouver WA 98684 360-260-2468 260-2469
TF: 800-736-0194 ■ *Web:* www.usdigital.com

Vermont Systems Inc 12 Market Pl .... Essex Junction VT 05452 802-879-6993 879-5368
TF: 877-883-8757 ■ *Web:* www.vermontsystems.com

Vertafore Inc 7 Waterside Crossing .... Windsor CT 06095 800-444-4813 402-9569*
**Fax Area Code:* 425 ■ **Fax:* PR ■ *TF General:* 800-444-4813 ■ *Web:* www.vertafore.com

Viewlocity Technologies 5339 Alpha Rd Ste 170 .... Dallas TX 75240 972-715-0300
Web: www.viewlocity.com

ViPS Inc 1 W Pennsylvania Ave Ste 700 .... Towson MD 21204 410-832-8300
TF: 800-242-0230 ■
Web: gdit.com/capabilities/health/health-payer-solutions/customer-support

Vital Images Inc 5850 Opus Pkwy Ste 300 .... Minnetonka MN 55343 952-487-9500 487-9510
TF: 800-208-3005 ■ *Web:* www.vitalimages.com

VoltDelta Resources Inc
560 Lexington Ave 14th Fl .... New York NY 10022 212-827-2600
Web: www.voltdelta.com

Votenet Solutions Inc 1420 K St .... Washington DC 20005 202-737-2277 737-2283
Web: www.votenet.com

VT MAK 150 Cambridge Park Dr 3rd Fl .... Cambridge MA 02140 617-876-8085 876-9208
Web: www.mak.com

Wausau Financial Systems Inc
400 Wes2od Dr Ste 100 .... Wausau WI 54455 715-359-0427 241-2288
TF: 800-937-0017 ■ *Web:* www.wausaufs.com

Weather Services International
400 Minuteman Rd .... Andover MA 01810 978-983-6300 983-6400
TF: 800-872-2359

Wizsoft Inc 6800 Jericho Tpke Ste 120W .... Syosset NY 11791 516-393-5841 393-5842
Web: www.wizsoft.com

Wolters Kluwer Financial Services Inc
100 S Fifth St Ste 700 .... Minneapolis MN 55402 612-656-7700
TF: 800-552-9408 ■ *Web:* www.wolterskluwerfs.com

Wonderware Corp 26561 Rancho Pkwy S .... Lake Forest CA 92630 949-727-3200 727-3270
Web: software.schneider-electric.com/wonderware

Worksoft Inc 15851 Dallas Pkwy Ste 855 .... Addison TX 75001 214-239-0400 250-9900*
**Fax Area Code:* 972 ■ *TF:* 866-836-1773 ■ *Web:* www.worksoft.com

Xybernet Inc 10640 Scripps Ranch Blvd .... San Diego CA 92131 858-530-1900 530-1419
TF Cust Svc: 800-228-9026 ■ *Web:* www.xyber.net

178-11 Service Software

Phone Fax

Alorica Inc 5 Park Plaza Ste 1100 .... Irvine CA 92614 949-527-4600 606-7708*
**Fax Area Code:* 909 ■ *Web:* www.alorica.com

Applied Systems Inc 200 Applied Pkwy .... University Park IL 60466 708-534-5575 534-8016*
**Fax:* Hum Res ■ *TF Sales:* 800-999-5368 ■ *Web:* www.appliedsystems.com

Aptech Computer Systems Inc 135 Delta Dr .... Pittsburgh PA 15238 412-963-7440
TF: 800-245-0720 ■ *Web:* www.aptech-inc.com

ARINC Inc 2551 Riva Rd .... Annapolis MD 21401 410-266-4000 573-3300
TF: 866-321-6060 ■ *Web:* www.arinc.com

Aristotle Inc 205 Pennsylvania Ave SE .... Washington DC 20003 202-543-8345 543-6407*
**Fax:* Sales ■ *TF Sales:* 800-296-2747 ■ *Web:* www.aristotle.com

ASA International Ltd 10 Speen St .... Framingham MA 01701 508-626-2727 626-0645
Web: www.asaint.com

Automated Financial Systems Inc 123 Summit Dr .... Exton PA 19341 484-875-1250 524-7977*
**Fax Area Code:* 610 ■ *Web:* www.afsvision.com

Capital Growth Systems Inc
180 N LaSalle St Ste 2430 .... Chicago IL 60601 312-673-2400 673-2422
OTC: CGSYQ ■ *Web:* www.globalcapacity.com

CaseSoft Div
5000 Sawgrass Village Cir Ste 21 .... Ponte Vedra Beach FL 32082 904-273-5000 273-5001
Web: www.casesoft.com

Cerner Corp 2800 Rockcreek Pkwy .... North Kansas City MO 64117 816-221-1024
NASDAQ: CERN ■ *TF:* 888-827-7220 ■ *Web:* www.cerner.com

Datamann Inc 1994 Hartford Ave .... Wilder VT 05088 802-295-6600
TF: 800-451-4263 ■ *Web:* www.datamann.com

DHI Computing Service Inc
1525 West 820 North PO Box 51427 .... Provo UT 84601 801-373-8518 374-5316
TF: 800-992-1344 ■ *Web:* www.dhiprovo.com

Digital Solutions Inc 955 SE Olson Dr .... Waukee IA 50263 515-987-6227
TF Cust Svc: 888-464-8770 ■ *Web:* www.accesssystems.com

DPSI Inc 1801 Stanley Rd Ste 301 .... Greensboro NC 27407 336-854-7700 854-7715
TF: 800-897-7233 ■ *Web:* www.dpsi.com

Ebix Inc 5 Concourse Pkwy Ste 3200 .... Atlanta GA 30328 678-281-2020 281-2019
NASDAQ: EBIX ■ *TF:* 800-755-2326 ■ *Web:* www.ebix.com

Firstwave Technologies Inc
6263 N Scottsdale Rd Ste 180 .... Scottsdale AZ 85250 678-672-3112
TF: 800-540-6061 ■ *Web:* www.firstwave.com

Fiserv Mortgage Products
3575 Moreau Ct Ste 2 .... South Bend IN 46628 574-282-3300
Web: fiserv.com

Galaxy Hotel Systems LLC
15621 Red Hill Ave Ste 100 .... Tustin CA 92780 714-258-5800 258-5880
TF: 800-624-2953 ■ *Web:* www.galaxyhotelsystems.com

H & M Systems Software Inc
600 E Crescent Ave Ste 203 .... Upper Saddle River NJ 07458 201-934-3414 934-9206
Web: www.hm-software.com

IHS Inc 321 Inverness Dr S .... Englewood CO 80112 303-790-0600
NYSE: IHS ■ *TF:* 800-525-7052 ■ *Web:* www.ihs.com

Incontact Inc
7730 S Union Pk Ave Ste 500 .... Salt Lake City UT 84047 801-320-3200
NASDAQ: SAAS ■ *TF:* 800-363-6177 ■ *Web:* www.incontact.com

Insurance Data Processing Inc (IDP)
8101 Washington Ln .... Wyncote PA 19095 215-885-2150 887-4621
TF: 800-523-6745 ■ *Web:* www.idpnet.com

Jack Henry & Assoc Inc 663 W Hwy 60 PO Box 807 ...... Monett MO 65708 417-235-6652 235-8406
NASDAQ: JKHY ■ *TF:* 800-299-4222 ■ *Web:* www.jackhenry.com

Jobscope Corp 355 Woodruff Rd .... Greenville SC 29607 800-443-5794 458-3160*
**Fax Area Code:* 864 ■ *TF:* 800-443-5794 ■ *Web:* www.jobscope.com

Kalibrate Technologies PLC
25B Hanover Rd .... Florham Park NJ 07932 973-549-1850 549-1860
TF Cust Svc: 800-727-6774 ■ *Web:* www.kalibrate.com

Keane Care Inc 8383 158th Ave NE Ste 100 .... Redmond WA 98052 800-426-2675 307-2220*
**Fax Area Code:* 425 ■ *TF:* 800-426-2675 ■ *Web:* www.nttdataltc.com

Key Information Systems Inc
30077 Agoura Ct 1st fl .... Agoura Hills CA 91301 818-992-8950 992-8970
TF: 877-442-3249 ■ *Web:* www.keyisit.com

Kronos Inc 297 Billerica Rd .... Chelmsford MA 01824 978-250-9800 367-5900
TF: 888-293-5549 ■ *Web:* www.kronos.com

Liquent Inc 101 Gibraltar Rd .... Horsham PA 19044 215-328-4444 328-4360
Web: parexel.com/liquent

Management Technology America Ltd
4742 N 24th St Ste 410 .... Phoenix AZ 85016 602-381-5100 251-0903
Web: www.mtanet.com

Manatron Inc 510 E Milham Ave .... Portage MI 49002 269-567-2900 567-2930
TF Cust Svc: 866-471-2900 ■ *Web:* tax.thomsonreuters.com

MC Software LLC 2225 Washington Blvd .... Ogden UT 84401 801-621-3900

McCallie Assoc Inc 3906 Raynor Pkwy Ste 200 .... Bellevue NE 68123 402-291-2203 291-8221
Web: www.mccallie.com

Mediware Information Systems Inc
11711 W 79th St .... Lenexa KS 66214 913-307-1000 307-1111
NASDAQ: MEDW ■ *TF:* 800-255-0026 ■ *Web:* www.mediware.com

Metafile Information Systems Inc
2900 43rd St NW .... Rochester MN 55901 507-286-9232 286-9065
TF Sales: 800-638-2445 ■ *Web:* metaviewer.com

MicroMass Communications Inc
100 Regency Forest Dr Ste 400 .... Cary NC 27518 919-851-3182 851-3188
Web: www.micromass.com

MicroStrategy 1850 Towers Crescent Plz .... Tysons Corner VA 22182 703-848-8600 848-8610
NASDAQ: MSTR ■ *TF:* 888-266-0321 ■ *Web:* www.microstrategy.com

Mincron Software Systems
333 N Sam Houston Pkwy E Ste 1100 .... Houston TX 77060 281-999-7010 999-6329
Web: www.mincron.com

Narus Inc 570 Maude Ct .... Sunnyvale CA 94085 408-215-4300 215-4301

Netsmart Technologies Inc
3500 Sunrise Hwy Ste D-122 .... Great River NY 11739 631-968-2000 968-2123
TF: 800-421-7503 ■ *Web:* www.ntst.com

Newmarket International Inc
75 New Hampshire Ave .... Portsmouth NH 03801 603-436-7500 436-1826
TF: 888-829-8871 ■ *Web:* www.newmarketinc.com

				Phone	Fax
Parallels Holding 500 SW 39th St Ste 200 .... Renton *Web:* www.parallels.com	WA	98057		425-282-6400	282-6444
Radware Inc 575 Corporate Dr Lobby 2 .... Mahwah *TF:* 888-234-5763 ■ *Web:* www.radware.com	NJ	07430		201-512-9771	512-9774
Real Soft Inc 2540 Rt 130 N Ste 118 .... Cranbury *Web:* www.realsoftinc.com	NJ	08512		609-409-3636	409-3637
Sandata Technologies Inc 26 Harbor Pk Dr .... Port Washington *TF Sales:* 800-544-7263 ■ *Web:* www.sandata.com	NY	11050		516-484-4400	484-6084
SS & C Technologies Inc 80 Lamberton Rd .... Windsor *TF:* 800-234-0556 ■ *Web:* www.ssctech.com	CT	06095		860-298-4500	298-4900
Strictly Business Computer Systems Inc 848 Fourth Ave Ste 200 .... Huntington **Fax Area Code:* 304 ■ *TF:* 888-529-0401 ■ *Web:* www.sbcs.com	WV	25701		888-529-0401	781-2590*
Successfactors Inc 1500 Fashion Island Blvd Ste 300 .... San Mateo *NYSE: SFSF* ■ *TF:* 800-809-9920 ■ *Web:* www.successfactors.com	CA	94404		650-645-2000	645-2099
SunGard Pentamation Inc 1000 Business Ctr Dr .... Lake mary *TF Cust Svc:* 866-965-7732 ■ *Web:* www.sungardps.com	FL	32746		610-691-3616	
Symphony Technology Group LLC (STG) 2475 Hanover St .... Palo Alto *Web:* www.symphonytg.com	CA	94304		650-935-9500	935-9501
Synergistics Inc 9 Tech Cir Ste 2 .... Natick *TF:* 866-455-5222 ■ *Web:* www.millennium-groupinc.com	MA	01760		508-655-1340	651-2902
Technalysis Inc 7172 Waldemar Dr .... Indianapolis *Web:* www.technalysis.com	IN	46268		317-291-1985	291-7281
Teradata 900 E 96th St Ste 400 .... Indianapolis *Web:* teradata.com/teradata-applications	IN	46240		317-814-6465	
TimeValue Software 22 Mauchly .... Irvine *TF Sales:* 800-426-4741 ■ *Web:* www.timevalue.com	CA	92618		949-727-1800	727-3268
TMA Systems LLC 5100 E Skelly Dr Ste 900 .... Tulsa *TF:* 800-862-1130 ■ *Web:* www.tmasystems.com	OK	74135		918-858-6600	858-6655
Velos Inc 2201 Walnut Ave Ste 208 .... Fremont *Web:* www.velos.com	CA	94538		510-739-4010	739-4018
Xactware Solutions Inc 1100 West Traverse Pkwy .... Lehi *TF Sales:* 800-424-9228 ■ *Web:* www.xactware.com	UT	84043		801-764-5900	932-8013

178-12 Systems & Utilities Software

			Phone	Fax
ACCESS Systems Americas Inc 1188 E Arques Ave .... Sunnyvale *Web:* www.access-company.com	CA	94085	408-400-3000	400-1500
activePDF Inc 27405 Puerta Real Ste 100 .... Mission Viejo *TF:* 866-468-6733 ■ *Web:* www.activepdf.com	CA	92691	949-582-9002	582-9004
AEP Networks Inc 347 Elizabeth Ave Ste 100 .... Somerset	NJ	08873	732-764-8858	764-8862
Allen Systems Group Inc (ASG) 1333 Third Ave S .... Naples **Fax Area Code:* 800 ■ *TF:* 800-932-5536 ■ *Web:* www.asg.com	FL	34102	239-435-2200	325-2555*
Apex CoVantage LLC 198 Van Buren St 200 Presidents Plz .... Herndon *Web:* apexcovantage.com	VA	20170	703-709-3000	709-0333
Aspect Business Solutions 7550 IH-10 W 14th Fl .... San Antonio	TX	78229	210-298-5000	298-5001
Avatier Corp 2603 Camino Ramon Ste 110 .... San Ramon *TF:* 800-609-8610 ■ *Web:* www.avatier.com	CA	94583	925-217-5170	275-0853
Basis International Ltd 5901 Jefferson St NE .... Albuquerque *TF Orders:* 800-423-1394 ■ *Web:* www.basis.com	NM	87109	505-345-5232	345-5082
Beta Systems Software of North America Inc 8300 Greensboro Dr Ste L1-633 .... McLean *Web:* www.betasystems.com	VA	22102	703-889-1240	889-1241
Blue Lance Inc 410 Pierce St .... Houston *TF:* 800-856-2583 ■ *Web:* www.bluelance.com	TX	77002	713-255-4800	
bNimble Technologies 45987 Paseo Padre Pkwy Ste 7 .... Fremont	CA	94539	510-870-2312	445-0625
CA Inc 1 CA Plz .... Islandia *NASDAQ: CA* ■ *TF:* 800-225-5224 ■ *Web:* www.ca.com	NY	11749	631-342-6000	342-6800
CardLogix 16 Hughes Ste 100 .... Irvine *TF:* 866-392-8326 ■ *Web:* www.cardlogix.com	CA	92618	949-380-1312	380-1428
Certicom Corp 4701 Tahoe Blvd Bldg A .... Mississauga *TF:* 800-561-6100 ■ *Web:* www.certicom.com	ON	L4W0B5	905-507-4220	507-4230
Check Point Software Technologies Ltd 800 Bridge Pkwy .... Redwood City *NASDAQ: CHKP* ■ *TF:* 800-429-4391 ■ *Web:* www.checkpoint.com	CA	94065	650-628-2000	654-4233
Cincom Systems Inc 55 Merchant St .... Cincinnati *TF:* 800-224-6266 ■ *Web:* www.cincom.com	OH	45246	513-612-2300	612-2000
Citrix Systems Inc 851 W Cypress Creek Rd .... Fort Lauderdale *NASDAQ: CTXS* ■ *TF:* 800-393-1888 ■ *Web:* www.citrix.com	FL	33309	954-267-3000	267-9319
Columbia Data Products Inc 925 Sunshine Ln Ste 1080 .... Altamonte Springs *TF Sales:* 800-613-6288 ■ *Web:* cdp.com	FL	32714	407-869-6700	862-4725
Communication Intelligence Corp (CIC) 275 Shoreline Dr Ste 500 .... Redwood Shores *OTC: CICI* ■ *Web:* www.cic.com	CA	94065	650-802-7888	
CommuniGate Systems Inc 655 Redwood Hwy Ste 275 .... Mill Valley *TF:* 800-262-4722 ■ *Web:* www.stalker.com	CA	94941	415-383-7164	383-7461
ComponentOne LLC 201 S Highland Ave Third Fl 3rd Fl .... Pittsburgh *TF:* 800-858-2739 ■ *Web:* www.componentone.com	PA	15206	412-681-4343	681-4384
Condusiv Technologies 7590 N Glenoaks Blvd .... Burbank *TF Sales:* 800-829-6468	CA	91504	818-771-1600	252-5512
Crossmatch 720 Bay Rd Ste 100 .... Redwood City *TF:* 866-463-7792 ■ *Web:* www.crossmatch.com	CA	94063	650-474-4000	298-8313
CSI International Inc 8120 State Rt 138 .... Williamsport *TF:* 800-795-4914 ■ *Web:* www.csi-international.com	OH	43164	740-420-5400	333-7335
CSP Inc 43 Manning Rd .... Billerica *NASDAQ: CSPI* ■ *TF:* 800-325-3110 ■ *Web:* www.cspi.com	MA	01821	978-663-7598	663-0150
CYA Technologies Inc 4 Research Dr .... Shelton	CT	06484	203-513-3111	513-3139
DataViz Inc 612 Wheelers Farms Rd .... Milford *TF:* 800-733-0030 ■ *Web:* www.dataviz.com	CT	06460	203-874-0085	874-4345
Datawatch Corp 271 Mill Rd .... Chelmsford *NASDAQ: DWCH* ■ *TF:* 800-445-3311 ■ *Web:* www.datawatch.com	MA	01824	978-441-2200	441-1114
Descartes Systems Group Inc 120 Randall Dr .... Waterloo *TSE: DSG* ■ *TF:* 800-419-8495 ■ *Web:* www.descartes.com	ON	N2V1C6	519-746-8110	747-0082
Digicomp Research Corp 930 Danby Rd .... Ithaca	NY	14850	607-273-5900	273-8779
Digimarc Corp 9405 SW Gemini Dr .... Beaverton *NASDAQ: DMRC* ■ *TF:* 800-344-4627 ■ *Web:* www.digimarc.com	OR	97008	503-469-4800	
Distinct Corp 3315 Almaden Expy Ste 10 .... San Jose *Web:* www.distinct.com	CA	95118	408-445-3270	445-3274
Diversified International Sciences Corp 4550 Forbes Blvd Ste 300 .... Lanham	MD	20706	301-731-9070	731-9070
E-Net Corp 300 Valley St .... Sausalito *Web:* www.enet.com	CA	94965	415-332-6200	339-9592
eMag Solutions LLC 1120 Sanctuary Pkwy Ste 275 .... Alpharetta *TF:* 844-252-0113 ■ *Web:* www.emagsolutions.com	GA	30305	404-995-6060	872-8247
EMC Corp 2831 Mission College Blvd .... Santa Clara *TF Tech Supp:* 877-534-2867 ■ *Web:* www.emc.com	CA	95054	408-566-2000	
EMC Corp 176 S St .... Hopkinton *NYSE: EMC* ■ *Web:* www.emc.com	MA	01748	508-435-1000	
Empirix Inc 600 Technology Park Dr Ste 100 .... Billerica *Web:* www.empirix.com	MA	01821	978-313-7000	313-7001
Entrust Inc 5400 LBJ Fwy Ste 1340 .... Dallas *TF Sales:* 888-690-2424 ■ *Web:* www.entrust.com	TX	75240	972-728-0447	728-0440
Esker Inc 1212 Deming Way Ste 350 .... Madison *TF:* 800-368-5283 ■ *Web:* www.esker.com	WI	53717	608-828-6000	828-6001
Expert Choice Inc 1501 Lee Hwy Ste 302 .... Arlington *TF:* 888-259-6400 ■ *Web:* www.expertchoice.com	VA	22209	703-243-5595	243-5587
FalconStor Software Inc 2 Huntington Quad Ste 2S01 .... Melville *NASDAQ: FALC* ■ *Web:* www.falconstor.com	NY	11747	631-777-5188	501-7633
FileStream Inc 240 Glen Head Rd Ste 93 .... Glen Head *Web:* www.filestream.com	NY	11545	516-759-4100	759-3011
Heroix Corp 165 Bay State Dr .... Braintree *TF:* 800-229-6500 ■ *Web:* www.heroix.com	MA	02184	781-848-1701	843-3472
HID Global Corp 611 Center Ridge Dr .... Austin *TF:* 800-237-7769 ■ *Web:* www.hidglobal.com	TX	78753	512-776-9000	776-9930
Hitachi Data Systems Corp 750 Central Expy .... Santa Clara *TF:* 877-437-3849 ■ *Web:* www.hds.com	CA	95050	408-970-1000	727-8036
IMS Health 535 Legget Dr Twr C 7th Fl .... Kanata *NYSE: IMS* ■ *Web:* www.imshealth.com	ON	K2K3B8	613-599-0711	
Infosystems Technology Inc 4 Professional Dr Ste 118 .... Gaithersburg **Fax Area Code:* 301 ■ *Web:* www.rubix.com	MD	20879	202-412-0152	869-4667*
Innodata-Isogen Inc 3 University Plz Dr .... Hackensack *NASDAQ: INOD* ■ *TF:* 877-454-8400 ■ *Web:* www.innodata.com	NJ	07601	201-371-8000	
Innovative Security Systems Inc 1809 Woodfield Dr .... Savoy *Web:* gdc4s.com/pitbull	IL	61874	217-355-6308	
International Business Machines Corp (IBM) 1 New OrchaRd Rd .... Armonk *NYSE: IBM* ■ *TF:* 800-426-4968 ■ *Web:* www.ibm.com	NY	10504	914-499-1900	
InterTrust Technologies Corp 920 Stewart Dr Ste 100 .... Sunnyvale *TF:* 800-393-2272 ■ *Web:* www.intertrust.com	CA	94085	408-616-1600	616-1626
Intrusion Inc 1101 E Arapaho Rd .... Richardson *TF:* 888-637-7770 ■ *Web:* www.intrusion.com	TX	75081	972-234-6400	
Ipswitch Inc 83 Hartwell Ave .... Lexington *TF:* 800-793-4825 ■ *Web:* www.ipswitch.com	MA	02421	781-676-5700	676-5710
Kroll Ontrack Inc 9023 Columbine Rd .... Eden Prairie *TF:* 800-872-2599 ■ *Web:* www.krollontrack.com	MN	55347	952-937-5161	937-5750
LapLink Software Inc 600 108th Ave NE Ste 610 .... Bellevue *TF:* 800-343-8080 ■ *Web:* www.laplink.com	WA	98004	425-952-6000	952-6002
Lattice Inc 1751 S Naperville Rd Ste 100 .... Wheaton *TF Sales:* 800-444-4309 ■ *Web:* www.lattice.com	IL	60189	630-949-3250	949-3299
Lenel System International Inc 1212 Pittsford-Victor Rd .... Pittsford *Web:* www.lenel.com	NY	14534	585-248-9720	248-9185
Luminex Software Inc 871 Marlborough Ave .... Riverside *TF Sales:* 888-586-4639 ■ *Web:* www.luminex.com	CA	92507	951-781-4100	781-4105
Management Science Assoc Inc 6565 Penn Ave .... Pittsburgh *Web:* www.msa.com	PA	15206	412-362-2000	363-5598
McAfee Inc 2821 Mission College Blvd .... Santa Clara *TF Cust Svc:* 888-847-8766 ■ *Web:* www.mcafee.com	CA	95054	408-988-3832	970-9727
McCabe Software Inc 3300 N Ridge Rd .... Ellicott City *TF:* 800-638-6316 ■ *Web:* www.mccabe.com	MD	21043	410-381-3710	
Mediafour Corp 1101 Fifth St .... West Des Moines *Web:* www.mediafour.com	IA	50265	515-225-7409	225-6370
Micro Logic Corp 666 Godwin Ave .... Midland Park *Web:* www.miclog.com	NJ	07432	201-962-7510	
Microsoft Corp 1 Microsoft Way .... Redmond *NASDAQ: MSFT* ■ *Web:* www.microsoft.com	WA	98052	425-882-8080	936-7329
Mindjet Corp 1160 Battery St E 4th Fl .... San Francisco *TF:* 877-646-3538 ■ *Web:* www.mindjet.com	CA	94111	415-229-4200	229-4201
Mitem Corp 640 Menlo Ave .... Menlo Park *TF Sales:* 800-648-3660 ■ *Web:* www.mitem.com	CA	94025	650-323-1500	323-1511
MTI Systems Inc 59 Interstate D .... West Springfield *TF:* 800-644-4318 ■ *Web:* www.mtisystems.com	MA	01089	413-733-1972	739-9250
NetIQ Corp 1233 W Loop S .... Houston *TF Sales:* 888-323-6768 ■ *Web:* www.netiq.com	TX	77027	713-548-1700	548-1771
Network Appliance Inc 495 E Java Dr .... Sunnyvale *NASDAQ: NTAP* ■ *TF Sales:* 800-443-4537 ■ *Web:* www.netapp.com	CA	94089	408-822-6000	822-4422
New Year Tech Inc 12330 Pinecrest Rd Ste 100 .... Reston *TF:* 800-525-7767 ■ *Web:* www.nyt1.net	VA	20191	703-564-0290	564-0296
Norman Data Defense Systems Inc 9302 Lee Hwy .... Fairfax *Web:* www.norman.com	VA	22031	703-267-6109	934-6368
NovaStor Corp 29209 Canwood St .... Agoura Hills **Fax:* Sales ■ *Web:* www.novastor.com	CA	91301	805-579-6700	579-6710*

Company	City	State	Zip	Phone	Fax
NTP Software 20A NW Blvd Ste 136 *TF:* 800-226-2755 ■ *Web:* www.ntpsoftware.com	Nashua	NH	03063	603-622-4400	263-2375
Numara Software Inc 2202 NW Shore Blvd Ste 650 *TF Sales:* 855-834-7487 ■ *Web:* www.bmc.com	Tampa	FL	33607	813-227-4500	227-4501
Open Door Networks Inc 110 S Laurel St *Web:* www.opendoor.com	Ashland	OR	97520	541-488-4127	
Open Systems Management Inc 1511 Third Ave Ste 905 *Web:* www.osminc.com	Seattle	WA	98101	206-583-8373	
OPNET Technologies Inc 7255 Woodmont Ave. *NASDAQ: OPNT* ■ *Web:* riverbed.com/products-solutions/products/opnet.html?redirect=opnet	Bethesda	MD	20814	240-497-3000	497-3001
Optical Research Assoc 3280 E Foothill Blvd. *Web:* optics.synopsys.com	Pasadena	CA	91107	626-795-9101	795-9102
Oracle Corp 500 Oracle Pkwy. *NYSE: ORCL* ■ *TF Sales:* 800-392-2999 ■ *Web:* www.oracle.com	Redwood Shores	CA	94065	650-506-7000	506-7200
Perceptics Corp 9737 Cogdill Rd Ste 200 **Fax Area Code:* 865 ■ *TF:* 800-448-8544 ■ *Web:* www.perceptics.com	Knoxville	TN	37932	800-448-8544	966-9330*
Pervasive Software Inc 12365 Riata Trace Pkwy Bldg B *NASDAQ: PVSW* ■ *TF:* 800-287-4383 ■ *Web:* www.pervasive.com	Austin	TX	78727	512-231-6000	231-6010
Phoenix Technologies Ltd 915 Murphy Ranch Rd *TF:* 800-677-7305 ■ *Web:* www.phoenix.com	Milpitas	CA	95035	408-570-1000	570-1001
PKWare Inc 648 N Plankinton Ave Ste 220 *Web:* pkware.com/about-us	Milwaukee	WI	53203	414-289-9788	289-9789
Plex Systems Inc 1731 Harmon Rd *Web:* www.plex.com	Auburn Hills	MI	48326	248-391-8001	
Pragma Systems Inc 13809 Research Blvd Ste 675 *TF:* 800-224-1675 ■ *Web:* www.pragmasys.com	Austin	TX	78750	512-219-7270	219-7110
Process Software Corp 959 Concord St *TF:* 800-722-7770 ■ *Web:* www.process.com	Framingham	MA	01701	508-879-6994	879-0042
RadView Software Inc 991 Hgwy 22 W Ste 200 *TF:* 888-723-8439 ■ *Web:* www.radview.com	Bridgewater	NJ	08807	908-526-7756	
Raxco Software Inc 6 Montgomery Village Ave Ste 500 *TF Tech Supp:* 800-546-9728 ■ *Web:* www.raxco.com	Gaithersburg	MD	20879	301-527-0803	519-7711
RDKS Inc 17861 Cartwright Rd **Fax:* Sales ■ *Web:* www.litronic.com	Irvine	CA	92614	949-851-1085	851-8588*
Red Hat Inc 1801 Varsity Dr. *NYSE: RHT* ■ *TF:* 888-733-4281 ■ *Web:* www.redhat.com	Raleigh	NC	27606	919-754-3700	754-3701
Relais International 1690 Woodward Dr Ste 215 *TF:* 888-294-5244 ■ *Web:* www.relais-intl.com	Ottawa	ON	K2C3R8	613-226-5571	226-0998
Rhintek Inc 8835 Columbia 100 Pkwy Ste C *Web:* www.rhintek.com	Columbia	MD	21045	410-730-2575	
RSA Security Inc 174 Middlesex Tpke *TF:* 800-995-5095 ■ *Web:* www.rsa.com	Bedford	MA	01730	781-515-5000	515-5010
ScriptLogic Corp 6000 Broken Sound Pkwy NW *TF:* 800-306-9329 ■ *Web:* www.quest.com	Boca Raton	FL	33487	561-886-2400	886-2499
Serengeti Systems Inc 1108 Lavaca St Ste 120 PO Box 431 *TF:* 800-634-3122 ■ *Web:* www.serengeti.com	Austin	TX	78701	512-345-2211	480-8729
Silicon Graphics Inc (SGI) 900 N McCarthy Blvd *Web:* www.sgi.com	Milpitas	CA	95035	669-900-8000	
Simtrol Inc 520 Guthridge Ct Ste 250	Norcross	GA	30092	678-533-1200	
Skyward Inc 5233 Coye Dr *TF:* 800-236-0001 ■ *Web:* www.skyward.com	Stevens Point	WI	54481	715-341-9406	341-1370
Smart Card Integrators Inc (SCI) 2424 N Ontario St *Web:* www.sci-s.com	Burbank	CA	91504	818-847-1022	847-1454
SNMP Research International Inc 3001 Kimberlin Heights Rd *TF:* 877-644-5866 ■ *Web:* www.snmp.com	Knoxville	TN	37920	865-579-3311	579-6565
Software Engineering of America Inc (SEA) 1230 Hempstead Tpke *TF:* 800-272-7322 ■ *Web:* www.seasoft.com	Franklin Square	NY	11010	516-328-7000	354-4015
Software Pursuits Inc 1900 S Norfolk St *TF:* 800-367-4823 ■ *Web:* www.softwarepursuits.com	San Mateo	CA	94403	650-372-0900	372-2912
Stratus Technologies 111 Powdermill Rd *TF:* 800-787-2887 ■ *Web:* www.stratus.com	Maynard	MA	01754	978-461-7000	
Symantec Corp 350 Ellis St *NASDAQ: SYMC* ■ *TF:* 800-441-7234 ■ *Web:* www.symantec.com	Mountain View	CA	94043	650-527-8000	527-8050
Syncsort Inc 50 Tice Blvd *Web:* www.syncsort.com	Woodcliff Lake	NJ	07677	201-930-9700	882-8305
TeamQuest Corp 1 TeamQuest Way *TF:* 800-551-8326 ■ *Web:* www.teamquest.com	Clear Lake	IA	50428	641-357-2700	357-2778
TechSmith Corp 2405 Woodlake Dr *TF:* 800-517-3001 ■ *Web:* www.techsmith.com	Okemos	MI	48864	517-381-2300	381-2336
Tecsec Inc 12950 Worldgate Dr Ste 100 *Web:* www.tecsec.com	Herndon	VA	20170	571-299-4100	
Thales e-Security Inc 2200 N Commerce Pkwy Ste 200 *TF:* 888-744-4976 ■ *Web:* www.thales-esecurity.com	Weston	FL	33326	954-888-6200	888-6211
TigerLogic Corp 25-A Technology Dr *NASDAQ: TIGR* ■ *TF:* 800-367-7425 ■ *Web:* tigerlogic.com	Irvine	CA	92618	949-442-4400	250-8187
TrendMicro Inc 10101 N De Anza Blvd *TF:* 800-228-5651 ■ *Web:* www.trendmicro.com	Cupertino	CA	95014	408-257-1500	863-6526
Tripwire Inc 101 SW Main St Ste 1500 *TF General:* 800-874-7947 ■ *Web:* www.tripwire.com	Portland	OR	97204	503-276-7500	223-0182
TurboLinux Inc 600 Townsend St	San Francisco	CA	94103	415-503-4330	
UltraBac Software 15015 Main St Ste 200 *TF:* 866-554-8562 ■ *Web:* www.ultrabac.com	Bellevue	WA	98007	425-644-6000	644-8222
UniSoft Corp 10 Rollins Rd Ste 118 *Web:* www.unisoft.com	Millbrae	CA	94030	650-259-1290	259-1299
VanDyke Software Inc 4848 Tramway Ridge Dr NE Ste 101 *TF:* 800-952-5210 ■ *Web:* www.vandyke.com	Albuquerque	NM	87111	505-332-5700	332-5701
VCG LLC 1805 Old Alabama Rd *TF:* 800-318-4983 ■ *Web:* www.bond-us.com	Roswell	GA	30076	770-246-2300	449-3638
Vendant Inc 4845 Pearl E Cir Ste 101 *TF:* 800-714-4900 ■ *Web:* www.vedanthealth.com	Bouler	CO	80301	978-462-0737	462-4755
Vision Solutions Inc 15300 Barranca Pkwy *TF:* 800-683-4667 ■ *Web:* www.visionsolutions.com	Irvine	CA	92618	949-253-6500	253-6501
VisionAIR Inc 5601 Barbados Blvd *Web:* www.visionair.com	Castle Hayne	NC	28429	910-675-9117	
Visual Automation Inc 403 S Clinton St Ste 4 *Web:* www.visualautomation.com	Grand Ledge	MI	48837	517-622-1850	622-1761
Webroot Software Inc 2560 55th St *TF:* 800-772-9383 ■ *Web:* www.webroot.com	Boulder	CO	80301	303-442-3813	442-3846
Wilson WindowWare Inc 5421 California Ave SW *TF:* 800-762-8383 ■ *Web:* www.windowware.com	Seattle	WA	98136	206-938-1740	935-7129
Wind River Systems Inc 500 Wind River Way *TF:* 800-545-9463 ■ *Web:* www.windriver.com	Alameda	CA	94501	510-748-4100	749-2010
WinZip Computing Inc PO Box 540 *Web:* www.winzip.com	Mansfield	CT	06268	860-429-3542	429-3542
Xinet Inc 2560 Ninth St Ste 312 *Web:* www.northplains.com	Berkeley	CA	94710	510-845-0555	644-2680
XIOtech Corp 9950 Federal Dr Ste 100 *TF:* 866-472-6764 ■ *Web:* xiostorage.com	Colorado Springs	CO	80921	719-388-5500	
Yrrid Software Inc 507 Monroe St *Web:* www.yrrid.com	Chapel Hill	NC	27516	919-968-7858	968-7856
Zix Corp 2711 N Haskell Ave Ste 2300-LB *NASDAQ: ZIXI* ■ *TF:* 888-771-4049 ■ *Web:* www.zixcorp.com	Dallas	TX	75204	214-370-2000	370-2070
Zone Alarm 800 Bridge Pkwy *TF:* 877-966-5221 ■ *Web:* www.zonealarm.com	Redwood City	CA	94065	415-633-4500	633-4501

179 COMPUTER STORES

See Also Appliance & Home Electronics Stores p. 1736

Company	City	State	Zip	Phone	Fax
1 EDI Source Inc 31875 Solon Rd Ste 2 *Web:* www.1edisource.com	Solon	OH	44139	440-519-7800	
A Matter of Fax 105 Harrison Ave. *TF:* 800-433-3329 ■ *Web:* www.amatteroffax.com	Harrison	NJ	07029	973-482-3700	
Aberdeen LLC 9130 Norwalk Blvd **Fax:* Sales ■ *TF:* 800-500-9526 ■ *Web:* www.aberdeeninc.com	Santa Fe Springs	CA	90670	562-699-6998	695-5570*
Ablaze Wireless 4010 Moorpark Ave Ste 201 *Web:* www.ablazewireless.com	San Jose	CA	95117	408-615-0888	
Accordant Company LLC 365 S St Ste 100 *TF:* 800-363-1002 ■ *Web:* www.accordantco.com	Morristown	NJ	07960	973-887-8900	
Accounting Software Plus LLC 9125 39th Ave SW Ste 150 *Web:* www.acctsoft.com	Lakewood	WA	98499	253-952-6040	
ACCUCOM Technical Services Inc 660 N Glenville *Web:* www.accucom.com	Richardson	TX	75081	972-238-7502	
ADA Station Communication Inc 1079 Livingston Rd *Web:* www.adastation.com	Crossville	TN	38555	931-707-5389	
AFIX Technologies Inc 205 N Walnut St *Web:* www.afix.net	Pittsburg	KS	66762	620-232-6420	
Aim 2 Berkeley St Ste 403 *TF:* 866-645-2224 ■ *Web:* www.aim.ca	Toronto	ON	M5A4J5	416-594-9393	
Aktion Associates Inc 1687 Woodlands Dr. *Web:* www.aktion.com	Maumee	OH	43537	419-893-7001	
Aljex Software Inc 463 Union Ave *Web:* www.alcrest.com	Middlesex	NJ	08846	732-357-8700	
Allplus Computer Systems Corp 3075 NW 107th Ave *Web:* www.allpluscomputer.com	Doral	FL	33172	305-436-3993	
Amicus Technology 2118 Wilshire Blvd Ste 430 *Web:* www.amicustech.com	Santa Monica	CA	90403	310-670-4962	
Amika Mobile Corp 700 March Rd Ste 203 *Web:* www.amikamobile.com	Ottawa	ON	K2K2V9	613-599-4445	
Amptech Inc 201 Glocheski Dr *Web:* www.amptechinc.com	Manistee	MI	49660	231-464-5492	
Analynk Wireless LLC 790 Cross Pointe Rd *Web:* www.analynk.com	Columbus	OH	43230	614-755-5091	
Answer Co, The 200-4170 Still Creek Dr *Web:* www.theanswerco.com	Burnaby	BC	V5C6C6	604-473-9166	
Answer One Inc 2216 Young Dr Ste 3 *TF:* 800-517-7395 ■ *Web:* answerone.biz	Lexington	KY	40505	859-269-3482	
Applied Voice & Speech Technologies Inc 27042 Towne Centre Dr Ste 200 *Web:* www.avst.com	Foothill Ranch	CA	92610	949-699-2300	
Arbutus Software Inc 6450 Roberts St *TF:* 877-333-6336 ■ *Web:* www.arbutussoftware.com	Burnaby	BC	V5G4E1	604-437-7873	
ASAP Solutions Group LLC 3885 Holcomb Bridge Rd *Web:* www.myasap.com	Norcross	GA	30092	770-246-1718	
Ascendbridge Solutions 50 Acadia Ave. *Web:* www.ascendbridge.com	Markham	ON	L3R0B3	905-944-0047	
Aspyr Media Inc 1250 S Capital of Texas Hwy Ste 650 *Web:* www.aspyr.com	Austin	TX	78746	512-708-8100	708-9595
Atiwa Computer Leasing Exchange 6950 Portwest Dr Ste 100 *TF:* 800-428-2532 ■ *Web:* www.atiwa.com	Houston	TX	77024	713-467-9390	
Audcomp Computer Systems 611 Tradewind Dr Ste 100 *Web:* www.audcomp.com	Ancaster	ON	L9G4V5	905-304-1775	
Automated Medical Systems Inc 2310 N Patterson St Bldg H *TF:* 800-256-3240 ■ *Web:* automedical.com	Valdosta	GA	31602	800-256-3240	
Azar Computer Software Services Inc 1200 Regal Row *Web:* www.azarinc.com	Austin	TX	78748	512-476-5085	
BAASS Business Solutions BC Inc 305-9600 Cameron St *Web:* www.plus.ca	Burnaby	BC	V3J7N3	604-420-1099	

Company	City	State	ZIP	Phone	Fax
Balihoo Inc 404 S Eighth St Ste 300	Boise	ID	83702	866-446-9914	
TF: 866-446-9914 ■ *Web:* balihoo.com					
Barcoding Inc 2220 Boston St.	Baltimore	MD	21231	410-385-8532	385-8559
TF: 888-412-7226 ■ *Web:* www.barcoding.com					
Basic Software Systems 905 N Kings Hwy.	Texarkana	TX	75501	903-792-4421	
Web: www.basic-software.com					
BCS Prosoft Inc 2700 Lockhill Selma	San Antonio	TX	78230	210-308-5505	
Web: www.bcsprosoft.com					
Beacon Technologies Inc 1441 Donelson Pk.	Nashville	TN	37217	615-301-5020	
Web: beacontech.net					
Beb Software Systems					
1806 Swift Ave Ste 200	Kansas City	MO	64116	816-452-4222	
Web: www.bebsoft.com					
BEMAS Software Inc 7 The Pines Court Ste B	St. Louis	MO	63141	314-439-5300	
Best Choice Software Inc 2112 First St W	Bradenton	FL	34208	941-747-5858	
Web: www.bestchoicesoftware.com					
Bitlab LLC 1144 Parkwood Ave.	Park Ridge	IL	60068	847-823-5070	
Web: bitlab.com					
Bizco Technologies Inc 7950 "O" St.	Lincoln	NE	68510	402-323-4800	
Web: www.bizco.com					
BlueSun Inc 5500 N Service Rd Ste 1107	Burlington	ON	L7L6W6	905-333-3353	
Web: www.bluesun.ca					
Boston Electronics Corp 91 Boylston St.	Brookline	MA	02445	617-566-3821	
Web: www.boselec.com					
Bredy Consulting Services 50 Union St	Andover	MA	01810	978-482-2020	
Web: www.bnmc.net					
C-Team Systems Inc 38 Auriga Dr Unit 12.	Ottawa	ON	K2E8A5	613-727-8224	
Web: www.cteam.ca					
Canfield Scientific Inc 253 Passaic Ave	Fairfield	NJ	07004	973-276-0336	
Web: www.canfieldsci.com					
Cannon IV Inc 950 Dorman St.	Indianapolis	IN	46202	317-951-0500	
Web: www.cannon4.com					
Carrier IQ Inc 640 W California Ave Ste 100	Sunnyvale	CA	94086	650-625-5400	
Carrillo Business Technologies Inc					
750 The City Dr S Ste 225	Orange	CA	92868	888-241-7585	
TF: 888-241-7585 ■ *Web:* www.cbtechinc.com					
Caselle Inc 1656 South East Bay Blvd Ste 100	Provo	UT	84606	801-850-5000	
Web: www.caselle.com					
Cayuse Inc					
10700 SW Beaverton-Hillsdale Hwy					
Park Plz W Bldg III Ste 654	Beaverton	OR	97005	503-297-2108	
Web: cayuse.com					
CDW Corp 200 N Milwaukee Ave	Vernon Hills	IL	60061	847-465-6000	465-6800
TF: 800-800-4239 ■ *Web:* www.cdw.com					
Cendec Systems Inc Ste 315 1615 10th Ave SW	Calgary	AB	T3C0J7	403-215-9936	
Web: cendec.com					
CenterGate Research Group LLC 420 S Smith Rd.	Tempe	AZ	85281	480-804-8100	
Web: www.centergate.com					
Central Mass Web Design Inc 70 Snake Pond Rd	Gardner	MA	01440	978-632-5300	
Web: www.centralmasswebdesign.com					
Centric Business Systems Inc					
10702 Red Run Blvd.	Owings Mills	MD	21117	410-902-3300	
Web: www.centricbiz.com					
Cepeda Systems & Software Analysis Inc					
515 Sparkman Dr NW Ste 301	Huntsville	AL	35758	256-461-7985	
Web: www.cepedasystems.com					
Chenomx Inc 10230 Jasper Ave Ste 4350	Edmonton	AB	T5J4P6	780-432-0033	
Web: www.chenomx.com					
Colligo Networks Inc 400-1152 Mainland St.	Vancouver	BC	V6B4X2	604-685-7962	
TF: 866-685-7962 ■ *Web:* www.colligo.com					
Colonial Systems Inc					
326 Ballardvale St Ste 200	Wilmington	MA	01887	978-657-6508	
Web: colonialsystems.com					
Complete Solutions Technology Group LLC					
10701, Corporate Dr Ste 232	Stafford	TX	77477	832-886-4363	
Web: www.complete-solutions.com					
ComponentArt Inc 222 Bay St Ste 1201	Toronto	ON	M5K1E7	416-622-2923	
Comres Telecom 424 SW 12th Ave.	Deerfield Beach	FL	33442	954-462-9600	
Web: www.comresusa.com					
Concepts In Data Management Inc					
205 Oxford St E	London	ON	N6A5G6	800-668-8768	
TF: 800-668-8768 ■ *Web:* www.instanetsolutions.com					
Conference Group LLC, The					
254 Chapman Rd Topkis Bldg Ste 102	Newark	DE	19702	302-224-8255	
Web: confgroupinc.com					
ConnectWise Inc 4110 George Rd Ste 200.	Tampa	FL	33634	813-463-4700	
TF: 800-671-6898 ■ *Web:* www.connectwise.com					
CopperLeaf Technologies Inc					
4170 Still Creek Dr Ste 450	Burnaby	BC	V5C6C6	604-639-9700	
Web: www.copperleaf.com					
Crawford Technologies Inc					
45 St Clair Ave W Ste 102	Toronto	ON	M4V1K9	416-923-0080	
TF: 866-679-0864 ■ *Web:* www.crawfordtech.com					
CTrends Inc 27142 Burbank.	Foothill Ranch	CA	92610	949-472-9050	
Web: www.ctrends.com					
Datel Systems Inc 5636 Ruffin Rd	San Diego	CA	92123	858-571-3100	571-0452
Web: www.datelsys.com					
Db Technologies Inc					
3601 N First St PO Box 280	Bloomfield	NM	87413	505-632-7900	
Web: dbtechnm.com					
Ddi System LLC 75 Glen Rd Ste 204	Sandy Hook	CT	06482	877-599-4334	
TF: 877-599-4334 ■ *Web:* www.ddisystem.com					
Dehart Marine Electronics Inc					
134 W Carolina Ave	Memphis	TN	38103	901-523-0945	
TF: 800-523-4278 ■ *Web:* dehartmarine.com					
Devcare Solution Ltd 131 N High St Ste 640.	Columbus	OH	43215	614-221-2277	
Web: www.devcare.com					
Dexter & Chaney Inc 9700 Lk City Way NE	Seattle	WA	98115	206-364-1400	
Web: www.dexterchaney.com					
DMJ Technologies LLC 140 Henley Ave Ste 5	New Milford	NJ	07646	201-261-5560	
Web: www.dmjtechnologies.com					
DOVICO Software Inc 236 St George St Ste 119	Moncton	NB	E1C1W1	506-855-4477	
TF: 800-618-8463 ■ *Web:* www.dovico.com					

Company	City	State	ZIP	Phone	Fax
DTM Systems Inc 2323 Boundary Rd Unit 130	Vancouver	BC	V5M4V8	604-257-6700	
TF: 888-655-3282 ■ *Web:* www.dtm.ca					
Dynamic Business Solutions Inc					
30100 Telegraph Rd Ste 322	Bingham Farms	MI	48025	248-646-0093	
Web: www.qualitech.net					
East End Computers LLC 30 Long Island Ave	Sag Harbor	NY	11963	631-725-4000	
Web: www.eastendcomputer.com					
Echoworx Corp 4101 Yonge St Ste 708.	Toronto	ON	M2P1N6	416-226-8600	
Web: www.echoworx.com					
ElectSolve Technology Solutions & Services Inc					
4300 Youree Dr Bldg 1 Ste 520	Shreveport	LA	71105	318-221-2055	
Web: www.electsolve.com					
Employee Development Systems Inc					
7308 S Alton Way Ste 2J	Centennial	CO	80112	303-221-0710	
TF: 800-282-3374 ■ *Web:* www.employeedevelopmentsystems.com					
Envision Payment Solutions Inc					
3039 Premiere Pkwy Ste 600	Duluth	GA	30097	770-709-3000	
Web: envisionpayments.com					
EPLAN Software & Services LLC					
37000 Grand River Ave Ste 380	Farmington Hills	MI	48335	248-945-9204	
Web: www.eplan.de					
Erb's Business Machines Inc					
4935 Bowling St SW.	Cedar Rapids	IA	52404	319-364-5159	
Web: etsconnect.com					
Evident Point Software Corp					
160-3751 Shell Rd	Richmond	BC	V6X2W2	604-241-2711	
Web: www.evidentpoint.com					
Executech 12701 Marblestone Dr Ste 150.	Woodbridge	VA	22192	571-285-3331	
Web: www.esc-techsolutions.com					
Express Logic Inc 11423 W Bernardo Ct	San Diego	CA	92127	858-613-6640	
Web: www.expresslogic.com					
Eyelit Inc 5685 Whittle Rd	Mississauga	ON	L4Z3P8	905-502-6184	
Web: www.eyelit.com					
EyeSee360 Inc 300 Fleet St Ste 250	Pittsburgh	PA	15220	412-922-6002	
Web: eyesee360.com					
FatTail Inc 20969 Ventura Blvd Ste 209	Woodland Hills	CA	91364	818-615-0380	
Web: adserver.fattail.com					
FDM Software Ltd					
949 W Third St Ste 113	North Vancouver	BC	V7P3P7	604-986-9941	
Web: www.fdmsoft.com					
First Call Computer Solutions Inc					
616 S Higgins Ave	Missoula	MT	59801	406-721-4592	
Web: www.firstsolution.com					
FM Communications Inc 1914 Colvin Blvd.	Tonawanda	NY	14150	716-832-2026	
Web: www.fmcommunications.com					
Freeman Av 4545 W Davis St.	Dallas	TX	75211	214-623-1300	
Web: www.freeman.com					
GameStop Corp 625 Westport Pkwy	Grapevine	TX	76051	817-424-2000	424-2002
NYSE: GME ■ *TF:* 800-883-8895 ■ *Web:* www.gamestop.com					
Garza Enterprises Inc 840 W Rhapsody Dr	San Antonio	TX	78216	210-377-3500	
Web: www.costx.com					
Gateway Inc 7565 Irvine Ctr Dr	Irvine	CA	92618	949-471-7040	471-7041
TF: 800-846-2000 ■ *Web:* www.gateway.com					
Geeks.com 43195 Business Park Dr	Temecula	CA	92590	951-694-4335	726-7723*
**Fax Area Code:* 760 ■ *Web:* www.geeksstore.com/About_The_Geeks					
Georgian College of Applied Arts & Technology, The					
1 Georgian Dr	Barrie	ON	L4M3X9	705-728-1968	
Web: www.georgianc.on.ca					
Gold Key Solutions Inc					
18757 Burbank Blvd Ste 212	Los Angeles	CA	91301	818-865-0006	
Web: www.goldkeysolutions.com					
Gopher Electronics Company Inc					
222 Little Canada Rd	Saint Paul	MN	55117	651-490-4900	
Web: www.gopherelectronics.com					
Govconnection Inc 7503 Standish Pl	Rockville	MD	20855	800-998-0009	423-6192*
**Fax Area Code:* 603 ■ *TF:* 800-998-0009 ■ *Web:* www.govconnection.com					
Gts Communications & Cabling Co					
11953 Prospect Rd	Strongsville	OH	44149	440-878-8866	
TF: 877-487-8866 ■ *Web:* www.gtscommunications.com					
Hartco Inc 9393 Louis-H-Lafontaine	Montreal	QC	H1J1Y8	514-354-3810	354-1998
NYSE: HCI ■ *Web:* www.hartco.com					
Higher Gear Group Inc, The					
145 W Central Rd	Schaumburg	IL	60195	847-843-6800	
Web: www.onecommand.com/what-we-do-auto/highergear-crm					
Housing Data Systems					
750 W City Hwy 16 PO Box 883	West Salem	WI	54669	608-786-2366	
Web: www.housingdatasystems.com					
ICAM Technologies Corp					
21500 Nassr St.	Sainte-anne-de-bellevue	QC	H9X4C1	514-697-8033	
TF: 800-827-4226 ■ *Web:* www.icam.com					
imageTech Marketing Inc 10388 S Randall St.	Orange	CA	92869	714-639-5411	
Web: www.imagetechmarketing.com					
Indigo Rose Corp 123 Bannatyne Ave Ste 200	Winnipeg	MB	R3B0R3	204-946-0263	
TF: 800-665-9668 ■ *Web:* www.indigorose.com					
Ineo Technology LLC 3340-A Annapolis Ln.	Plymouth	MN	55447	612-236-2100	
Web: www.ineotechnology.com					
Innovative Information Solutions Inc					
61 I- Ln.	Waterbury	CT	06705	203-756-4243	
TF: 800-343-8121 ■ *Web:* www.innovativeis.com					
Insight Enterprises Inc 6820 S Harl Ave.	Tempe	AZ	85283	480-333-3000	
NASDAQ: NSIT ■ *TF:* 800-467-4448 ■ *Web:* www.insight.com					
Inspironix Inc 3400 Cottage Way.	Sacramento	CA	95825	916-488-3222	
Web: www.inspironix.com					
Intalio Inc 644 Emerson St Ste 200	Palo Alto	CA	94301	650-596-1800	249-0439
Web: www.intalio.com					
Intelex Technologies Inc					
905 King St West Ste 600.	Toronto	ON	M6K3G9	416-599-6009	
Web: www.intelex.com					
IPRO Tech Inc 6811 E Mayo Blvd Ste 350.	Phoenix	AZ	85054	602-324-4776	
Web: www.iprotech.com					
Janssen Consulting Inc					
1704 Mission Ave Ste 1	Carmichael	CA	95608	916-716-2326	
Web: www.janssenconsulting.com					

Phone | Fax

Jargon Software 708 N First St Minneapolis MN 55401 612-338-1175
Web: www.jargonsoft.com

Jencess Software & Technologies Inc
4509 - 101 St Edmonton AB T6E5C6 780-434-4444
Web: www.jencess.com

Jive Communications Inc
1275 West 1600 North Ste 100 Orem UT 84057 866-768-5429
TF: 866-768-5429 ■ *Web:* jive.com

Jonah Group Ltd, The 461 King St W 3rd Fl Toronto ON M5V1K4 416-304-0860
TF: 888-594-6260 ■ *Web:* www.jonahgroup.com

Karaman Communications Inc
4424 Bragg Blvd Ste 101 Fayetteville NC 28303 910-222-1234
Web: www.karamancom.com

Key Events Inc 657 Mission St Ste 202 San Francisco CA 94105 415-695-8000
Web: www.keyevents.com

Khemia Software Co 33080 Industrial Rd Livonia MI 48150 734-513-9940
Web: khemia.com

KLA Laboratories Inc 6800 Chase Rd Dearborn MI 48126 313-846-3800
Web: www.klalabs.com

KLJ Computer Solutions Inc
115 Joseph Zatzman Dr Dartmouth NS B3B1N3 888-455-5669
TF: 888-455-5669 ■ *Web:* www.venueclaims.com

Knowledge Information Solutions Inc
2877 Guardian Ln Ste 201 Virginia Beach VA 23452 757-463-0033 463-3971
TF: 877-547-7248 ■ *Web:* www.kisinc.net

L S Technologies LLC 4150 Rock Mtn Rd Fallbrook CA 92028 760-731-2320
Web: www.lstechnologies.com

Lanamark Inc 100 King St 56th Fl York ON M9N1L3 416-342-1960

Laser Tek Services Inc 205 19th St N Fargo ND 58102 701-239-4033
Web: www.lasertekservices.com

Launch Pad 18130 Jorene Rd Odessa FL 33556 888-920-3450
TF: 888-920-3450 ■ *Web:* www.launchpadonline.com

Lcptracker Inc 200 E Chapman Ave Ste D Orange CA 92866 714-669-0052
Web: www.lcptracker.com

LD Systems LP 407 Garden Oaks Houston TX 77018 713-695-9400
Web: www.ldsystems.com

Lieberman Group LLC, The
223 NW Second St Ste 300 Evansville IN 47708 812-434-6600
Web: www.ltnow.com

Loki Systems Inc 1258-13351 Commerce Pkwy Richmond BC V6V2X7 604-249-5050
TF: 800-378-5654 ■ *Web:* www.lokisys.com

London Computer Services 1007 Cottonwood Dr Loveland OH 45140 513-583-1482
TF: 800-669-0871 ■ *Web:* www.lcs.com

Lone Wolf Real Estate Technologies Inc
231 Shearson Crescent Ste 310 Cambridge ON N1T1J5 519-624-1236
Web: www.lwolf.com

M3 Technology Inc 58 Sawgrass Dr Bellport NY 11713 631-205-0005
Web: www.m3-tec.com

MACK Technologies Inc 27 Carlisle Rd Westford MA 01886 978-392-5500
Web: www.macktech.com

Macs at Work Inc 775 Hartford Tpke Shrewsbury MA 01545 508-845-0709
Web: www.macsatwork.com

MadCap Software Inc 7777 Fay Ave La Jolla CA 92037 858-320-0387
Web: www.madcapsoftware.com

Magitech Corp 1500 Don Mills Rd Ste 702 North York ON M3B3K4 416-441-1933
Web: www.ezgame.com

MailChannels Corp
142-757 W Hastings St Ste 612 Vancouver BC V6C1A1 604-685-7488
Web: www.mailchannels.com

Mainsaver Software LLC 10803 Thornmint Rd San Diego CA 92127 858-674-8700
Web: www.mainsaver.com

MC2 Inc 1106 S First St Milwaukee WI 53204 414-276-2200
Web: www.mc2wi.com

Medflow Inc 6739A Fairview Rd Charlotte NC 28210 704-927-9800
Web: medflow.com

Medical Priority Consultants Inc
139 E S Temple St Salt Lake City UT 84111 801-363-9127
Web: www.prioritydispatch.net

Medicat LLC
Sandy Springs 1100 Johnson Ferry Rd Ste LL75 Atlanta GA 30342 404-252-2295
Web: www.medicat.com

Medisys for Physicians Inc
7201 Halcyon Summit Dr Montgomery AL 36117 334-277-6201
Web: www.medisysinc.com

Meritech Inc 4577 Hinckley Industrial Pkwy Cleveland OH 44109 216-459-8333
Web: www.meritechinc.com

Messaging Architects 180 Peel St Ste 333 Montreal QC H3C2G7 514-392-9220
TF: 866-497-0101 ■ *Web:* www.netmail.com

Microdea Inc 85 Enterprise Blvd Ste 407 Markham ON L6G0B5 905-881-6071
Web: www.microdea.com

Momentum Healthware Inc
308-131 Provencher Blvd Winnipeg MB R2H0G2 204-231-3836
Web: www.momentumhealthware.com

Moore Oil Company Inc 4033 W Custer Ave Milwaukee WI 53209 414-462-3200
TF: 800-279-2976 ■ *Web:* mooreoil.com

Mphasis Corp 460 Pk Ave S Rm 1101 New York NY 10016 212-686-6655
Web: www.mphasis.com

NCX Inc 70 E Beaver Creek Rd Unit 2 Richmond Hill ON L4B3B2 905-370-7060
Web: www.ncxinc.ca

Netgain Networks Inc 8378 Attica Dr Riverside CA 92508 951-656-0194
TF: 855-667-2364 ■ *Web:* netgainnetworks.com

Network Depot LLC 12040 S Lakes Dr Ste 202 Reston VA 20191 703-264-7776
Web: www.networkdepot.com

Neuma Technology Inc 5450 Canotek Rd Ste 51 Ottawa ON K1J9G3 613-749-9450
Web: www.neuma.com

New Tech Solutions Inc 4179 Business Ctr Dr Fremont CA 94538 510-353-4070
Web: www.newtechsolutions.com

Newegg Inc 16839 E Gale Ave City of Industry CA 91745 626-271-9700 271-9403
TF: 800-390-1119 ■ *Web:* www.newegg.com

Nova Voice & Data Systems Inc
3909 Oceanic Dr Ste 401 Oceanside CA 92056 760-439-5200
TF: 800-558-6744 ■ *Web:* www.enova.us

Phone | Fax

Novus LLC 338 Commerce Dr Fairfield CT 06825 203-331-1112
Web: www.novusllc.com

Nuventive LLC 9800B McKnight Rd Ste 255 Pittsburgh PA 15237 412-847-0280
Web: www.nuventive.com

NuWave Technology Partners LLC 5268 Azo Ct Kalamazoo MI 49048 269-342-4400
Web: www.nuwavepartners.com

O P T 918 Mission Ave Oceanside CA 92054 760-722-3348
TF: 800-483-6287 ■ *Web:* www.optcorp.com

Office Solutions Inc 217 Mount Horeb Rd Warren NJ 07059 800-677-1778
TF: 800-677-1778 ■ *Web:* www.osi-technology.com

Omni-Med.com Inc 160 Pope St Cookshire QC J0B1M0 819-875-5411
Web: www.omnimed.com

Omnivex Corp 3300 Hwy 7 Ste 501 Concord ON L4K4M3 905-761-6640
TF: 800-745-8223 ■ *Web:* www.omnivex.com

Open Automation Software 5077 Bear Mtn Dr Evergreen CO 80439 303-679-0898
TF: 800-533-4994 ■ *Web:* www.opcsystems.com

Optessa Inc 5555 Calgary Trl NW Ste 1045 Edmonton AB T6H5P9 780-431-8426
Web: www.optessa.com

Optiwave Systems Inc 7 Capella Ct Ottawa ON K2E7X1 613-224-4700
Web: www.optiwave.com

Orion Industries Inc 1 Orion Park Dr Ayer MA 01432 978-772-6000
Web: www.orionindustries.com

P-Q Controls Inc 95 Dolphin Rd Bristol CT 06010 860-583-6994
Web: www.p-qcontrols.com

Palomino System Innovations Inc
533 College St Ste 404 Toronto ON M6G1A8 416-964-7333
TF: 866-360-0360 ■ *Web:* www.palominosys.com

ParetoLogic Inc 1827 Ft St Victoria BC V8R1J6 250-370-9229
Web: www.paretologic.com

Patriot Software Inc
2925 E 96th St Ste 100 Indianapolis IN 46240 317-573-5431
Web: patriotsoftware.net

PC Connection Inc 730 Milford Rd Rt 101A Merrimack NH 03054 603-683-2000 683-5766
NASDAQ: PCCC ■ *TF:* 888-213-0607 ■ *Web:* www.pcconnection.com

PC Connection Inc MacConnection Div
730 Milford Rd Rt 101A Merrimack NH 03054 888-213-0260
TF: 888-213-0260 ■ *Web:* www.macconnection.com

PC Mall Inc 2555 W 190th St Torrance CA 90504 310-354-5600
NASDAQ: PCMI ■ *TF:* 800-555-6255 ■ *Web:* www.pcm.com

Physmark Inc 101 E Pk Blvd Ste 600 Plano TX 75074 972-231-8000
TF: 800-922-7060 ■ *Web:* www.physmark.com

Pinnacle Corp, The 201A E Abram St Arlington TX 76010 817-795-5555
Web: www.pinncorp.com

Planet Technologies Inc
20400 Observation Dr Ste 107 Germantown MD 20876 301-721-0100
Web: go-planet.com

Pointon Communications 202 South Blvd Baraboo WI 53913 608-355-0257
Web: www.pointon.com

Points North Inc 371 Canal Park Dr Ste 210 Duluth MN 55802 218-726-1195
Web: www.points-north.com

PowerMed Corp 48 Free St Portland ME 04101 207-772-3920
Web: www.powermed.com

Primal Technologies Inc
3615 Laird Rd Ste 13 Mississauga ON L5L5Z8 416-548-3395
Web: www.primaltech.com

ProComp Software Consultants Inc
555 Cincinnati-Batavia Pk Cincinnati OH 45244 513-685-5245
Web: www.procompsoftware.com

Prolifiq Software Inc
8585 SW Watson Ave Ste 200 Beaverton OR 97008 503-684-1415
Web: prolifiq.com

Protis Computers 7212 Mcneil Dr Ste 202 Austin TX 78729 512-258-1282
Web: protis.com

PSI Software Inc 7326 Remcon Cir El Paso TX 79912 915-584-4100
Web: www.psisoftware.com

Qeh2 LLC 401 S Wilcox St Ste 202 Castle Rock CO 80104 303-688-7531
Web: www.qeh2.com

Quatro Systems Inc 231 Gibraltar Rd Horsham PA 19044 215-672-7100
Web: www.quatro.com

Questica Inc 980 Fraser Dr Ste 105 Burlington ON L7L5P5 877-707-7755
TF: 877-707-7755 ■ *Web:* www.questica.com

Radio Guys 2061 Fwy Dr Ste E Woodland CA 95776 530-406-0700
Web: www.theradioguys.com

Rainbow Computers Corp 6000 NW 97th Ave Ste 21 Doral FL 33178 305-592-2611
Web: www.rainbowcc.com

Recursion Software Inc
2591 Dallas Pkwy Ste 200 Frisco TX 75034 972-731-8800 731-8881
TF: 800-727-8674 ■ *Web:* www.recursionsw.com

RedSky Technologies Inc
925 W Chicago Ave Ste 300 Chicago IL 60642 312-432-4300
Web: www.redskye911.com

Regional Computer Recycling & Recovery LLC
7318 Victor Mendon Rd Victor NY 14564 585-924-3840
Web: www.ewaste.com

Repeated Signal Solutions Inc
7127 Hollister Ave Ste 109 Goleta CA 93117 805-685-6700
Web: www.repeatedsignal.com

RLM Communications Inc
1027 E Manchester Rd Spring Lake NC 28390 910-223-1350
TF: 877-223-1345 ■ *Web:* www.rlm-communications.com

Rushworks 800 Parker Sq Ste 200 Flower Mound TX 75028 469-293-1024
Web: www.rushworks.tv

Saffron Technology Inc
1000 CentreGreen Way Ste 160 Cary NC 27513 919-468-8201
Web: saffrontech.com

SDG Systems LLC 330 Perry Hwy Ste 200 Harmony PA 16037 724-452-9366
Web: www.sdgsystems.com

Sector Micro Computers Inc
399 Hoover Ave Ste 2 Bloomfield NJ 07003 973-429-1113
Web: sectormicro.com

Selectron Technologies Inc
12323 SW 66th Ave Portland OR 97223 503-443-1400
Web: www.selectrontechnologies.com

Phone | Fax

Service Communications Inc
10675 Willows Rd NE Ste 100 .... Redmond WA 98052 800-488-0468
TF: 800-488-0468 ■ *Web:* www.servicecommunications.com

Shamrock Office Solutions Inc
6908 Sierra Ct Ste A .... Dublin CA 94568 925-875-0480
Web: www.shamrockoffice.com

SHIELDS Electronics Supply Inc
4722 Middlebrook Pk .... Knoxville TN 37921 865-588-2421
Web: shieldselectronics.com

Side Effects Software Inc
123 Front St W Ste 1401 .... Toronto ON M5J2M2 416-504-9876
TF: 888-504-9876 ■ *Web:* www.sidefx.com

Silke Communications Inc 680 Tyler St .... Eugene OR 97402 541-687-1611
Web: www.silkecom.com

Silver Bullet Technology Inc
25 W Cedar St Ste 440 .... Pensacola FL 32502 850-437-5880
Web: www.sbullet.com

Smart Levels Media Inc 16 Hammond .... Irvine CA 92618 949-540-0500
Web: www.smartlevels.com

SoftCode Inc 33 Boston Post Rd W Ste 360 .... Marlborough MA 01752 774-348-3000

Softechnologies Inc
1504 W Northwest Blvd Ste C .... Spokane WA 99205 509-327-4624
Web: www.softechnologies.com

Software Development Forum
111 W Saint John Ste 200 .... San Jose CA 95113 408-414-5950
Web: www.sdforum.org

Software Enterprises Inc
5380 Twin Hickory Rd .... Glen Allen VA 23059 804-747-6436
Web: www.softent.com

Software Unlimited Inc
1314 Bedford Ave Ste 201 .... Baltimore MD 21208 410-602-9250
Web: medicalmastermind.com

SPLICE Software Inc 425 78 Ave SW .... Calgary AB T2H2L6 403-720-8326
Web: www.splicesoftware.com

STC Netcom Inc 11611 Industry Ave .... Fontana CA 92337 951-685-8181
Web: www.stcnetcom.com

Stealthbits Technologies
55 Harristown Rd Ste 106 .... Glen Rock NJ 07452 201-447-9300
Web: www.stealthbits.com

Stiehl Communications
W5361 County Rd Kk Ste A .... Appleton WI 54915 920-830-1116
Web: www.stiehlcommunications.com

Strata Health Solutions Inc
933 - 17 Ave SW Ste 600 .... Calgary BC T2T5R6 403-261-0616
Web: stratahealth.com

Strategy Companion Corp
3240 El Camino Real Ste 120 .... Irvine CA 92602 714-460-8398
Web: www.strategycompanion.com

Sunnking Inc 4 Owens Rd .... Brockport NY 14420 585-637-8365
Web: www.sunnking.com

Synergy Telcom Inc 8222 Indy Ln .... Indianapolis IN 46214 317-713-1652
Web: www.synergy-tel.com

Synetra Inc 8180 Lakeview Center .... Odessa TX 79765 432-561-7200
Web: www.synetra.com

System Solutions Inc 3630 Commercial Ave .... Northbrook IL 60062 847-272-6160
Web: www.thessi.com

Taurus Software Inc 420 Brewster Ave .... Redwood City CA 94063 650-482-2022
Web: taurus.com

Tech Depot 55 Corporate Dr Ste 5 .... Trumbull CT 06611 203-615-7000 251-4058*
**Fax Area Code:* 888 ■ **Fax:* Cust Svc

Techpeople Inc 5426 Guadalupe St Ste 211 .... Austin TX 78751 512-493-1400
Web: www.techpeopleinc.com

Tel-West Communications Inc
7311 E Broadway Ste B .... Spokane WA 99212 509-325-8500
Web: www.telwest.net

Telserv LLC 7 Progress Dr .... Cromwell CT 06416 860-740-3600
Web: www.telserv.com

TenAsys Corp 1400 NW Compton Dr Ste 301 .... Beaverton OR 97006 503-748-4720
Web: www.tenasys.com

Tetrasoft Inc
16647 Chesterfield Grove Rd Ste 120 .... Chesterfield MO 63005 636-530-7638
Web: www.tetrasoft.us

Ticoon Technology Inc
56 The Esplanade Ste 404 .... Toronto ON M5E1A7 416-513-9524
Web: www.ticoon.com

Tj Rock Enterprises Inc 5800 Genesis Ln .... Frederick MD 21703 301-831-4128
Web: tjrockcorp.com

Tlc Office Systems 500 N Chenango St Ste 314 .... Angleton TX 77515 979-848-8300
Web: tlcofficesystems.com

Top Producer Systems Inc
10651 Shellbridge Way Ste 155 .... Richmond BC V6X2W8 800-821-3657
TF: 800-821-3657 ■ *Web:* www.topproducer.com

Translations.com Inc 3 Pk Ave 39th Fl .... New York NY 10016 212-689-1616 685-9797
TF: 800-688-7205 ■ *Web:* www.translations.com

Triad Productions Inc 1910 Ingersoll Ave .... Des Moines IA 50309 515-243-2125
Web: www.triadav.com

Tricerat Inc 11500 Cronridge Dr Ste 100 .... Owings Mills MD 21117 410-715-4226
TF: 800-582-5167 ■ *Web:* www.tricerat.com

Trinium Technologies LLC 304 Tejon Pl .... Palos Verdes CA 90274 310-214-3118
Web: www.triniumtech.com

Tritech Software Systems 9860 Mesa Rim Rd .... San Diego CA 92121 858-799-7000 799-7010
Web: www.tritech.com

TriVium Systems Inc
1865 NW 169th Pl Ste 210 .... Beaverton OR 97006 503-439-9338
Web: www.triviumsys.com

Tukatech Inc 5527 E Slauson Ave .... Los Angeles CA 90040 323-726-3836 726-3866
Web: www.tukatech.com

TVL Inc 901 16th St W Ste 200 .... North Vancouver BC V7P1R2 604-983-2298
Web: www.tvl.com

Ultrasource Inc 22 Clinton Dr .... Hollis NH 03049 603-881-7799
Web: www.ultrasource.com

V-Soft Inc 888 Saratoga Ave Ste 203 .... San Jose CA 95129 408-342-1700
Web: v-softinc.com

V.L.S Systems Inc
4080 Lafayette Ctr Dr Ste 300 .... Chantilly VA 20151 703-953-3118
Web: www.vls-systems.com

Valley Office Systems 2050 First St .... Idaho Falls ID 83401 208-529-2777
Web: www.valleyofficesystems.com

Varay Systems LLC 201 E Main Dr Ste 700 .... El Paso TX 79901 915-496-8555
Web: www.varay.com

Vector Networks Inc 541 10th St Unit 123 .... Atlanta GA 30318 770-622-2850
Web: www.vector-networks.com

Vertex Systems Inc
440 Polaris Pkwy Ste 100 .... Westerville OH 43082 614-318-7100
Web: www.vertexsystems.com

Vertex Wireless LLC 500 Wegner Dr .... West Chicago IL 60185 630-293-6300
Web: www.vertexwireless.com

VistaVu Solutions Inc
30 Springborough Blvd SW Ste 214 .... Calgary AB T3H0N9 403-263-2727
Web: www.vistavusolutions.com

Vocantas Inc 750 Palladium Dr Ste 200 .... Ottawa ON K2V1C7 613-271-8853
TF: 877-271-8853 ■ *Web:* www.vocantas.com

Voice on the Go Inc 20 Amber St Ste 207 .... Markham ON L3R5P4 905-305-1355
TF: 877-977-0555 ■ *Web:* www.voiceonthego.com

Voyager Electronics Corp 3065 101st Ave NE .... Blaine MN 55449 763-571-7766
Web: www.voyagercorp.com

Web-Point Communications LLC
3801 Sunset Ave .... Rocky Mount NC 27804 252-557-0056
Web: www.wpc.net

WhiteLight Group LLC
N14 W24200 Tower Place Ste 203 .... Waukesha WI 53188 630-571-6705
Web: www.whitelightgrp.com

Winfund Software Corp 2 Gurdwara Rd Ste 206 .... Ottawa ON K2E1A2 613-526-1969
Web: www.winfund.com

World Recycling Co 5600 Columbia Park Rd .... Cheverly MD 20785 301-386-3010
Web: world-recycling.com

Worldlink Integration Group Inc
21076 Bake Pkwy Ste 106 .... Lake Forest CA 92630 949-861-2830
Web: www.worldlinkintegration.com

180 COMPUTER SYSTEMS DESIGN SERVICES

See Also Web Site Design Services p. 3306

Companies that plan and design computer systems that integrate hardware, software, and communication technologies.

Phone | Fax

1010data Inc 750 Third Ave 4th Fl .... New York NY 10017 212-405-1010
Web: www.1010data.com

30 Dps 118 N Tejon St 304 .... Colorado Springs CO 80903 719-380-9996
Web: www.30dps.com

3Gtms Inc 8 Progress Dr .... Shelton CT 06484 203-567-4610
Web: www.3gtms.com

3s Global Business Solutions
7923 Nita Ave .... Canoga Park CA 91304 818-453-4403
Web: www.3sgbs.com

3sharp LLC 14700 Ne 95th St Ste 210 .... Redmond WA 98052 425-882-1032
Web: www.3sharp.com

3T Systems
5990 Greenwood Pl Blvd Ste 350 .... Greenwood Village CO 80111 303-858-8800
Web: 3tsystems.com

3tech Corp 2828 W Parker Rd Ste B101 .... Plano TX 75075 972-490-4443
Web: www.3tech.com

42 Inc 2150 Allston Way Ste 300 .... Berkeley CA 94704 510-548-7948
Web: www.42inc.com

4Sight Group LLC
4001 Kennett Pk Ste 134-233 .... Wilmington DE 19807 800-490-2131
TF: 800-490-2131 ■ *Web:* www.4SightGroup.com

7strategy LLC 117 N Cooper St .... Olathe KS 66061 913-638-2130
TF: 888-231-3062 ■ *Web:* www.7strategy.com

A 2000 Network Solutions
237 Goolsby Blvd .... Deerfield Beach FL 33442 954-480-8430
Web: a2000ns.com

A Partner in Technology 105 Dresden Ave .... Gardiner ME 04345 207-582-0888
TF: 877-582-0888 ■ *Web:* www.apitechnology.com

A r C Informatique Inc 1776 Rue Mitis .... Chicoutimi QC G7K1H4 418-545-9224
Web: www.arcinformatique.com

AAE Systems Inc 642 N Pastoria Ave .... Sunnyvale CA 94085 408-732-1710
Web: www.aaesys.com

AAJ Technologies
6301 NW Fifth Way Ste 1700 .... Fort Lauderdale FL 33309 954-689-3984
Web: www.aajtech.com

Aasys Group 11301 N US Hwy 301 Ste 106 .... Thonotosassa FL 33592 813-246-4757
TF: 800-852-7091 ■ *Web:* www.aasysgroup.com

Abacus Business Solutions Inc
15301 Roosevelt Blvd Ste 303 .... Clearwater FL 33760 727-524-0177
Web: www.abacus-pos.com

Abacus Technology Corp
5454 Wisconsin Ave Ste 1100 .... Chevy Chase MD 20815 301-907-8500 907-8508
TF: 800-225-2135 ■ *Web:* www.abacustech.com

Acadiana Computer Systems Inc
324 Dulles Dr .... Lafayette LA 70506 337-981-2494
Web: www.acsmd.com

AccessIT Group Inc
2000 Vly Forge Cir Ste 106 .... King Of Prussia PA 19406 610-783-5200
Web: www.accessitgroup.com

Accs Inc 260 Oakhurst St .... Altamonte Springs FL 32701 407-767-5557
Web: www.accs.net

Acg Inc 7007 Corporate Way .... Dayton OH 45459 937-433-8122
TF: 800-890-5023 ■ *Web:* www.acgcbs.com

Achilles Guard Inc 4201 Spring Vly Rd Ste 1400 .... Dallas TX 75244 866-525-8680
TF: 866-525-8680 ■ *Web:* www.criticalwatch.com

ACI Consulting Corp 155 N Riverview Dr .... Anaheim Hills CA 92808 714-282-0378
Web: www.aciconsulting.com

Acranet 521 W Maxwell Ave Ste 209 .... Spokane WA 99201 800-304-1249
TF: 800-304-1249 ■ *Web:* www.acranet.com

				Phone	Fax
Acsis Inc 9 E Stow Rd *Web:* www.acsisinc.com	Marlton	NJ	08053	856-673-3000	
Activo Inc 161 Alden Rd Unit 6 *Web:* www.activo.ca	Markham	ON	L3R3W7	905-752-1900	
Acumen Solutions Inc 1660 International Dr Ste 500 *Web:* www.acumensolutions.com	McLean	VA	22102	703-600-4000	600-4001
Acxius Strategic Consulting LLC 500 Campus Dr Ste 300 *Web:* www.acxius.com	Morganville	NJ	07751	732-972-7970	
Adaptive Equipment Inc 2512 NE First Blvd Ste 700 *Web:* www.adaptivequipment.com	Gainesville	FL	32609	352-372-7821	
Adc Information Technologies Inc 950 Michigan Ave *Web:* www.ibswebsite.com	Columbus	OH	43215	614-240-5999	
Adjacent Technologies Inc 10415 Morado Cir Ste 120 Bldg 1 *Web:* www.adjacent-tech.com	Austin	TX	78759	512-388-1338	
Adroit Software Inc 23 Faulkner Rd *Web:* www.adroitgroup.com	Shrewsbury	MA	01545	508-755-5252	
AdTek Information Systems Inc 500 Fifth Ave Ste 2110 *Web:* www.adtek.com	New York	NY	10110	212-307-1115	
Advanced Data Systems Corp 15 Prospect St	Paramus	NJ	07652	201-368-2001	
Advanced Information Systems Group Inc 11315 Corporate Blvd Ste 210 *TF:* 800-593-8359 ■ *Web:* www.aisg.com	Orlando	FL	32817	407-581-2929	581-2935
Advanced Resource Technologies Inc 1555 King St Ste 400 *Web:* www.team-arti.com	Alexandria	VA	22314	703-682-4740	682-4820
Advent Global Solutions Inc 12777 Jones Rd Ste 445 *Web:* www.adventglobal.com	Houston	TX	77070	832-678-3889	
Aeroflex RAD Inc 5017 N 30th St *Web:* ams.aeroflex.com	Colorado Springs	CO	80919	719-531-0800	
AETEA Information Technology Inc 1445 Research Blvd Ste 300 *TF:* 888-772-3832 ■ *Web:* www.aetea.com	Rockville	MD	20850	301-721-4200	721-1730
Ag Connections Inc 1576 Killdeer Trl *Web:* www.agconnections.com	Murray	KY	42071	270-435-4369	
Agj Systems & Networks Inc 14257 Dedeaux Rd *Web:* www.agjsystems.com	Gulfport	MS	39503	228-392-7133	
AgniTEK LLC 214 N Main St *Web:* www.agnitek.com	Bryan	TX	77807	979-260-8324	
AGSI 3343 Peachtree Rd NE Ste 510 *TF:* 800-768-2474 ■ *Web:* www.agsi.com	Atlanta	GA	30326	404-816-7577	816-7578
Ahold Information Services 1200 Brookfield Blvd 1st Fl *Web:* aiscareers.aholdusa.com	Greenville	SC	29607	864-987-5600	
Aim Systems 350 Speedvale Ave W Unit 12 *Web:* www.aimsystems.ca	Guelph	ON	N1H7M7	519-837-1072	
AirSage Inc 1330 Spring St NW Ste 400 *Web:* www.airsage.com	Atlanta	GA	30309	404-809-2499	
Akins Consulting Inc 2915 Red Hill Ave *Web:* www.akinsconsulting.com	Costa Mesa	CA	92626	714-424-5151	
Alaska Computer Brokers 551 W Dimond Blvd *TF:* 866-261-4225 ■ *Web:* www.acbsolutions.net	Anchorage	AK	99515	907-267-4200	
Alexander & Tom Inc 3500 Boston St *Web:* alextom.com	Baltimore	MD	21224	410-327-7400	
Algo Design Inc 6455 Doris Lussier Ste 300 *Web:* www.algodesign.com	Boisbriand	QC	J7H0E8	450-681-2584	
ALI's Database Consultants 1151 Williams Dr *TF:* 866-257-8970 ■ *Web:* www.aliconsultants.com	Aiken	SC	29803	803-648-5931	
All Native Systems LLC 1 Mission Dr *Web:* www.allnativesystems.com	Winnebago	NE	68071	402-878-2700	
All Star Consulting Inc 1111 Oak St *Web:* www.all-stars.com	San Francisco	CA	94117	415-552-1400	
All Star Software Systems LLC 440 Smith St *Web:* www.allstarscanners.com	Middletown	CT	06457	860-613-1500	
All Systems Installation Inc 8300 10th Ave N Ste A *Web:* www.allsysinst.com	Golden Valley	MN	55427	763-593-1330	
Allstar Tech 1856 Angus St *Web:* allstartech.com	Regina	SK	S4T1Z4	306-522-7827	
Alpac Inc 5752 Cedar Ridge Dr *Web:* alpacinc.com	Ann Arbor	MI	48103	734-623-2866	
Alpha Engineering Associates Inc 716 Giddings Ave Ste 32 *Web:* www.alphaengr.com	Annapolis	MD	21401	410-295-9500	
AlphaKOR Group Inc 7800 Twin Oaks Dr *TF:* 877-944-6009 ■ *Web:* www.alphakor.com	Windsor	ON	N8N5B6	519-944-6009	
Alphaserve Technologies LLC 104 W 27th St *Web:* www.alphaserveit.com	New York	NY	10001	212-763-5500	
AlphaSoft Services Corp 2035 Lincoln Hwy Ste 1190	Edison	NJ	08817	925-952-6300	932-3743
Alpine Business Systems Inc 373 E Main St *Web:* alpinebiz.com	Somerville	NJ	08876	908-707-9696	
Alpine Consulting Inc 1100 E Wdfield Rd *Web:* www.alpineinc.com	Schaumburg	IL	60173	847-605-0788	
Alt-N Technologies Ltd 4550 State Hwy 360 Ste 100 *Web:* www.altn.com	Grapevine	TX	76051	817-601-3222	
Alta Computer Data Services LLC 8823 S Redwood Rd Ste D2 *Web:* alta-acs.com	West Jordan	UT	84088	801-233-0531	
AmberWave Inc 13 Garabedian Dr *Web:* www.amberwave.com	Salem	NH	03079	603-870-8700	870-8607
Amcom Data Processing Inc 2 Annabel Ln Ste 130 *Web:* www.amcom.biz	San Ramon	CA	94583	925-328-0322	
American Systems Corp 14151 Pk Meadow Dr Ste 500 *TF:* 800-733-2721 ■ *Web:* www.americansystems.com	Chantilly	VA	20151	703-968-6300	968-5151
Amgraf Inc 1501 Oak St *TF:* 800-304-4797 ■ *Web:* amgraf.com	Kansas City	MO	64108	816-474-4797	
Amnet Technology Solutions 26 Fahey St *Web:* www.amnetsystems.com	Stamford	CT	06907	203-355-2400	
Ampcus Inc 4530 Walney Rd Ste 203 *Web:* www.ampcus.com	Chantilly	VA	20151	703-637-7299	
Amtex Systems Inc 50 Broad St Ste 801 *Web:* www.amtexsystems.com	New York	NY	10004	212-269-6448	269-6458
Anakena Solutions Inc 5853 McDonie Ave *Web:* www.anakenasolutions.com	Woodland Hills	CA	91367	310-929-7869	
Analystik 1430 Rue Belanger *Web:* www.analystik.ca	Montreal	QC	H2G1A4	514-278-2727	
Animate Systems Inc 133 Richmond St W *Web:* www.animate.com	Toronto	ON	M5H2L3	416-535-2516	
Antares Technology Solutions Inc 8772 Quarters Lk Rd Bldg 13 *Web:* www.antaresnet.com	Baton Rouge	LA	70898	225-922-7748	
Appian Digital 3132 Commerce Pl # A2 *Web:* www.appiandigital.com	Burlington	NC	27215	336-538-4747	
Applied Data Trends Inc 107-A Clinton Ave *Web:* www.adt-it.com	Huntsville	AL	35801	256-319-0700	
Applied Minds LLC 2937 N Ontario St *Web:* appliedminds.com	Burbank	CA	91504	818-545-1400	
Applied Science Group Inc 4455 Genesee St Bldg 6 *Web:* www.appliedsciencesgroup.com	Buffalo	NY	14225	716-626-5100	
APPNET.COM 9649 NC Hwy 105 S *Web:* www.appnet.com	Banner Elk	NC	28604	828-963-7286	
Apprio Inc 425 Third St SW *Web:* www.apprioinc.com	Washington	DC	20024	202-684-8266	
Arcane Technologies Inc 918 Monticello Ave *TF:* 844-977-4890 ■ *Web:* www.arcanetech.com	Charlottesville	VA	22902	844-977-4890	
Architel Inc 8350 N Central Expy Ste 250 *TF:* 866-649-7571 ■ *Web:* www.architel.com	Dallas	TX	75206	214-550-2000	
Arcsoft Inc 46601 Fremont Blvd *Web:* arcsoft.com	Fremont	CA	94538	510-440-9901	
Ardham Technologies Inc 5411 Jefferson St NE Ste 200 *Web:* www.ardham.com	Albuquerque	NM	87109	505-872-9040	
Area Wide Technologies Inc 2110 Clearlake Blvd Ste 100 *Web:* areawidetech.com	Champaign	IL	61822	217-359-8041	
Argo Systems Inc 2964 Peachtree Rd *Web:* sintecmedia.com	Atlanta	GA	30305	404-869-4575	
Argos Computer Systems Inc 110 W 32nd St Fl 7 *Web:* www.argosnyc.com	New York	NY	10001	212-594-5400	
Arlington Computer Products Inc 851 Commerce Ct *TF Orders:* 800-548-5105 ■ *Web:* www.arlingtoncp.com	Buffalo Grove	IL	60089	847-541-6333	
Arrow Strategies LLC 27777 Franklin Rd Ste 1200 *Web:* www.arrowstrategies.com	Southfield	MI	48034	248-502-2500	502-2525
Art & Logic Inc 2 N Lk Ave Ste 1050 *Web:* www.artandlogic.com	Pasadena	CA	91101	818-500-1933	
Arx Networks LLC 581 Foster City Blvd Ste 210 *TF:* 800-972-2175 ■ *Web:* www.arxnetworks.com	Foster City	CA	94404	650-403-4279	
Ascend Quality Partners 20 Sunyside Ave Ste A195	Mill Valley	CA	94941	415-381-4400	
Ascent Services Group, The 3000 Oak Rd Ste 200 *Web:* www.ascentsg.com	Walnut Creek	CA	94597	925-627-4900	
Ashburn Consulting LLC 43848 Goshen Farm Ct *Web:* www.ashburnconsulting.com	Leesburg	VA	20176	703-652-9120	
ASI Computer Systems Inc 5250 Nordic Dr *Web:* www.asicomp.com	Cedar Falls	IA	50613	319-266-7688	
Asi Networks Inc 19331 E Walnut Dr N *TF:* 800-251-1336 ■ *Web:* www.asi-networks.com	City Of Industry	CA	91748	800-251-1336	
Aspen Networks Inc 3777 Stevens Creek Blvd *Web:* www.aspen-networks.com	Santa Clara	CA	95051	408-246-4059	
Asponte Technology Inc 11523 Palmbrush Trl Ste 137 *TF:* 888-926-9434 ■ *Web:* www.asponte.com	Lakewood Ranch	FL	34202	888-926-9434	
ASSETT Inc 11220 Assett Loop Ste 204 *Web:* www.assett.net	Manassas	VA	20109	703-365-8950	
ATC-NY Inc 33 Thornwood Dr Cornell Business & Technology Park Ste 500 *Web:* www.atc-nycorp.com	Ithaca	NY	14850	607-257-1975	
Athreya Inc 100 Jersey Ave Ste A 103 *Web:* athreyainc.com	New Brunswick	NJ	08901	732-246-2700	
Atlantic Webworks & Consulting Inc 331 S Swing Rd *Web:* www.atlanticwebworks.com	Greensboro	NC	27409	336-855-8572	
Attention Software Inc 2175 N Academy Cir Ste 100 *Web:* www.attentionsoftware.com	Colorado Springs	CO	80909	719-591-9110	
Attronica Computers Inc 15867 Gaither Dr *Web:* www.attronica.com	Gaithersburg	MD	20877	301-417-0070	
Aumtech Inc 710 Old Bridge Tpke *Web:* aumtech.com	East Brunswick	NJ	08816	732-254-1875	
Aurora Computer Technology Inc 6 Schubert St *Web:* auroracomputer.com	Staten Island	NY	10305	718-981-2363	

Company	City	State	ZIP	Phone	Fax
Autodraft Inc 2815 Baird Rd *Web:* www.adraft.com	Fairport	NY	14450	585-389-1900	
Automation Image Inc 2650 Vly View Ln Ste 100 *Web:* www.automationimage.com	Dallas	TX	75234	972-247-8816	243-2814
Automation Technologies Inc 8219 Leesburg Pk *Web:* www.ati4it.com	Vienna	VA	22182	703-883-1410	883-1435
Avant Systems Group 815-1661 Portage Ave *Web:* avant.ca	Winnipeg	MB	R3J3T7	204-789-9596	
AVF Consulting Inc 1220-A E Joppa Rd Ste 240 *Web:* www.avfconsulting.com	Baltimore	MD	21286	410-296-5100	
Avl Systems Design LLC 14901 Bristol Park Blvd *Web:* www.avl1.com	Edmond	OK	73013	405-749-1866	
AVS Installations LLC 400 Raritan Ctr Pkwy Ste D *Web:* www.avsillc.com	Edison	NJ	08837	732-634-7903	
AVT Inc 341 Bonnie Cir Ste 102 *TF:* 877-424-3663 ■ *Web:* www.autoretail.com	Corona	CA	92880	877-424-3663	
Axios Products Inc Ste 204 353 Veterans Hwy *Web:* www.axios.com	Commack	NY	11725	631-864-3666	
Axyz Automation Inc 2844 E Kemper Rd *TF:* 800-527-9670 ■ *Web:* www.axyz.com	Cincinnati	OH	45241	513-771-7444	
Ayoka LLC 1161 W Corporate Dr Ste 303 *Web:* www.ayokasystems.com	Arlington	TX	76006	817-210-4042	
Azure Horizons Inc 7115 N Ave Ste 185 *TF:* 877-494-6070 ■ *Web:* www.azure-horizons.com	Oak Park	IL	60302	877-494-6070	
Azure Solutions Inc 1010 W Hamlin Rd *Web:* azuresol.com	Rochester Hills	MI	48309	248-651-8210	
B Green Innovations Inc 750 Hwy 34 *TF:* 877-996-9333 ■ *Web:* bgreeninnovations.com	Matawan	NJ	07747	732-441-7700	
Banetti Inc 3451 NE 1st Ave M1008 *Web:* www.banetti.com	Miami	FL	33137	864-275-2282	
Banksys Management Inc 2750 Peachtree Industrial *Web:* www.banksys.net	Duluth	GA	30097	678-957-1234	
Banyan Medical Systems Inc 4106 S 87th St *TF:* 866-225-7790 ■ *Web:* www.banyanmedicalsystems.com	Omaha	NE	68127	402-403-4400	
Barcom Inc 400B Chickamauga Rd *Web:* www.barcominc.com	Chattanooga	TN	37421	423-855-1822	
Baroan Technologies 385 Falmouth Ave *Web:* www.baroan.com	Elmwood Park	NJ	07407	201-796-0404	
Barry Strock Consulting Associates Inc 154 Rosemont St *Web:* strock.com	Albany	NY	12206	518-459-4252	
Base One Technologies Inc 30 Church St Ste 28 *Web:* www.base-one.com	New Rochelle	NY	10801	914-633-0200	
Battle Medialab Inc 117 E Boca Raton Rd *Web:* battlemedialab.com	Boca Raton	FL	33432	561-395-1555	
Batuta Inc 1s450 Summit Ave Ste 210 *Web:* www.batuta.org	Oakbrook Terrace	IL	60181	630-827-2500	
Bay Microsystems Inc 2055 Gateway Pl Ste 650 *Web:* baymicrosystems.com	San Jose	CA	95110	408-437-0400	
Bay State Computers Inc 16901 Melford Blvd Ste 329 *Web:* www.bayst.com	Bowie	MD	20716	301-352-7878	352-6925
Bay State Integrated Technology Inc 22 Settlers Dr *Web:* www.baystatetechnology.com	Lakeville	MA	02347	508-947-1478	
Bazon Cox & Associates Inc 1244 Executive Blvd *TF:* 800-769-1763 ■ *Web:* www.bazcox.com	Chesapeake	VA	23320	757-410-2128	
BBH Solutions Inc 121 E 24th St *Web:* www.bbhinc.com	New York	NY	10010	212-475-7100	
Bec Legal Systems 175 Tri County Pkwy Ste 115 *Web:* www.beclegal.com	Springdale	OH	45246	513-948-1500	
Bek Business Solutions 723 Memorial Hwy *Web:* www.bekbusiness.com	Bismarck	ND	58504	701-255-2032	
Bell Techlogix 5777 Decatur Blvd **Fax Area Code: 888* ■ *TF:* 866-782-2355 ■ *Web:* www.belltechlogix.com	Indianapolis	IN	46241	317-333-7777	890-9494*
Bella Web Design Inc 3605 Sandy Plains Rd Ste 240-121 *Web:* www.bellawebdesign.com	Marietta	GA	30066	770-509-8797	
Benchmark Network Solutions Inc 1931 Evans Rd *Web:* www.benchmark-net.com	Cary	NC	27513	919-678-8595	
Bender Consulting Services Inc 3 Penn Ctr W Ste 223 *Web:* www.benderconsult.com	Pittsburgh	PA	15276	412-787-8567	
Beta Soft Systems Inc 42808 Christy St Ste 101 *Web:* www.betasoftsystems.com	Fremont	CA	94538	510-744-1700	
Bicitis Group Inc 426 Herrick Dr *Web:* www.bicitisgroup.com	Dover	NJ	07801	973-250-2394	
Bimsym Ebusiness Solutions 3466 Progress Dr Ste 218 *Web:* bimsym.com	Bensalem	PA	19020	215-639-7040	
Binovia Corp 8631 F St *Web:* www.binovia.com	Omaha	NE	68127	402-331-0202	
bitHeads Inc 1309 Carling Ave *TF:* 855-622-3232 ■ *Web:* www.bitheads.com	Ottawa	ON	K1Z7L3	613-722-3232	
Bits n Bytes Computer Systems 3201 Double C Dr *Web:* www.bnbtech.com	Norman	OK	73069	405-292-5408	
Bitworks LLC 126 Tower Rd *Web:* www.bitworksusa.net	Waterbury	CT	06710	203-756-9513	
BizNet Technology Inc 8125 S.W. 120th St *Web:* www.biznettechnology.com	Miami	FL	33156	305-256-2024	
BizSpeed Inc 3050 Royal Blvd S Ste 130 *Web:* www.bizspeed.com	Alpharetta	GA	30022	678-287-3310	
BlackBag Technologies Inc 300 Piercy Rd *Web:* www.blackbagtech.com	San Jose	CA	95138	408-844-8890	
Blast Advanced Media 950 Reserve Dr Ste 150 *TF:* 888-252-7866 ■ *Web:* www.blastam.com	Roseville	CA	95678	916-724-6701	
Blax Inc 6600 St-Urbain Ofc 33 *Web:* www.blax.ca	Montreal	QC	H2S3G8	514-523-4600	
Blough Tech Inc 119 S Broad St *Web:* www.bloughtech.com	Cairo	GA	39828	229-377-8825	
Blue Granite Inc 4664 Campus Dr Ste 100 *Web:* www.blue-granite.com	Kalamazoo	MI	49008	269-353-7512	
Blue Ion LLC 73 1/2 Wentworth St *Web:* www.blueion.com	Charleston	SC	29401	843-727-0310	
Blue Lotus Sidc Llc 509 Village Rd W *Web:* www.bluelotussidc.com	Princeton Junction	NJ	08550	609-716-4615	
Blue Tangerine Solutions Inc 1380 Sarno Rd Ste B *Web:* www.bluetangerinesolutions.com	Melbourne	FL	32935	321-309-6900	
Bluelock LLC 6325 Morenci Trl *TF:* 888-402-2583 ■ *Web:* www.bluelock.com	Indianapolis	IN	46268	888-402-2583	
Bluestorm Technologies Inc 455 Court St *Web:* www.bluestormtech.com	Binghamton	NY	13904	607-762-5401	
BlueView Inc 1325 E 15th St Ste 203 *Web:* www.blueviewagency.com	Tulsa	OK	74120	918-592-1400	
Blytheco LLC 23161 Mill Creek Dr *TF:* 800-425-9843 ■ *Web:* www.blytheco.com	Laguna Hills	CA	92653	949-583-9500	583-0649
BNL Inc 11760 Armistead Filler Ln *Web:* www.bnlinc.com	Lovettsville	VA	20180	540-822-5569	
Boldfocus Inc 1900 S Norfolk St Ste 350 *Web:* www.boldfocus.com	San Mateo	CA	94403	650-212-2653	
Book Systems Inc 4901 University Sq Ste 3 *Web:* www.booksys.com	Huntsville	AL	35816	256-533-9746	
Boston Systems & Solutions Llc 241 Winter St Ste 2 *Web:* www.bsscorp.com	Haverhill	MA	01830	978-469-0002	
Boxworks Technologies Inc 2065 Pkwy Blve *TF:* 877-495-2250 ■ *Web:* boxworks.com	Salt Lake City	UT	84119	801-214-6100	
Boyle Software Inc 42 W 24th St *Web:* www.boylesoftware.com	New York	NY	10010	212-691-0609	
Bradshaw Consulting Services Inc 2170 Woodside Exec Ct *Web:* www.bcs-gis.com	Aiken	SC	29803	803-641-0960	
Brave River Solutions Inc 875 Centerville Rd Bldg 3 *Web:* www.braveriver.com	Warwick	RI	02886	401-828-6611	
Breaker Group Inc, The 32 Mill St *Web:* www.breakergroup.com	Mount Holly	NJ	08060	609-267-1330	
Bredet Services Inc 1660 N Service Rd E Ste 105 *Web:* www.bredetservices.com	Oakville	ON	L6H7G3	905-337-7233	
BriarTek Inc 3129 Mount Vernon Ave *Web:* www.briartek.com	Alexandria	VA	22305	703-548-7892	
Bridgeline Digital 80 BlanchaRd Rd *TF:* 800-603-9936 ■ *Web:* www.bridgelinedigital.com	Burlington	MA	01803	781-376-5555	376-5033
Broadleaf Services Inc 10 Mall Rd *TF:* 866-337-7733 ■ *Web:* www.broadleafservices.com	Burlington	MA	01803	866-337-7733	
Bruno Enterprises Inc 379 Amherst St Ste 163 *Web:* www.bei.tc	Nashua	NH	03063	603-235-2624	
Buchanan Technologies Inc 1026 Texan Trl *TF:* 888-730-2774 ■ *Web:* www.buchanan.com	Grapevine	TX	76051	972-869-3966	
Buffalo Computer Graphics Inc 4185 Bayview Rd *Web:* www.buffalocomputergraphics.com	Blasdell	NY	14219	716-822-8668	
BUILDERadius Inc 16 Biltmore Ave Ste 300 *Web:* www.buildfax.com	Asheville	NC	28801	828-350-9950	
Bull HN Information Systems Inc 285 Billerica Rd *Web:* www.bull.com	Billerica	MA	01824	978-294-6000	244-0085
Burgiss Group LLC, The 111 River St Fl 10th *Web:* burgiss.com	Hoboken	NJ	07030	201-427-9600	
Burgundy Group Inc, The 2420 S Power Rd Ste 103 *Web:* www.tbginc.com	Mesa	AZ	85209	480-325-7700	
Burkhart Group Ltd, The 412 S Broadleigh Rd *Web:* burkhartgrp.com	Columbus	OH	43209	614-397-8788	
Burton Computer Resources Inc 400 N 16th Ave *Web:* www.burtoncomputer.com	Laurel	MS	39440	601-428-0205	
C-cube Consulting Inc 1238 Ridge Oak Ct *Web:* ccubeconsulting.net	San Jose	CA	95120	408-268-4886	
C-Double Web Development 5201 College Ave *Web:* c-double.com	Bakersfield	CA	93306	661-872-2738	
CACI International Inc 1100 N Glebe Rd *NYSE: CACI* ■ *TF:* 866-606-3471 ■ *Web:* www.caci.com	Arlington	VA	22201	703-841-7800	841-7882
Cad Technology Center 1000 Boone Ave N Ste 200 *TF:* 866-941-1181 ■ *Web:* www.cadtechnologycenter.com	Minneapolis	MN	55427	952-941-1181	
Cadence Technologies Inc 1075 Windward Ridge Pkwy Ste 100 *Web:* www.cadencetechnologies.com	Alpharetta	GA	30005	770-667-6250	
Cadnet Services 25 Sundial Ave *Web:* www.cadnetservices.com	Manchester	NH	03103	603-296-2376	
Cadnetics Inc 10 Bedford Sq Ste 300 *Web:* www.cadnetics.com	Pittsburgh	PA	15203	412-642-2701	
Cadre Computer Resources Co 201 E Fifth St Ste 1800 *TF:* 866-762-6700 ■ *Web:* www.ccr.com	Cincinnati	OH	45202	513-762-7350	762-6502
Cadsoft Consulting Inc 4578 N First Ave Ste 120 *Web:* cadsoft-consult.com	Tucson	AZ	85718	520-546-2233	
Cal Net Technology Group 9420 Topanga Canyon Blvd Ste 100 *Web:* www.calnettech.com	Chatsworth	CA	91311	818-701-5753	
Calibre Systems Inc 6354 Walker Ln Ste 300 Metro Pk *TF:* 888-225-4273 ■ *Web:* www.calibresys.com	Alexandria	VA	22310	703-797-8500	797-8501

Company	City	State	ZIP	Phone	Fax
Callisma Inc 1550 The Alameda The Garden Alameda Ste 305 *Web:* www.callisma.com	San Jose	CA	95126	408-882-0333	
Camadro Inc 508 Mohawk St Ste A *Web:* freearcade.com	Tecumseh	MI	49286	517-423-0523	
Camber Corp 670 Discovery Dr *TF:* 800-998-7988 ■ *Web:* www.camber.com	Huntsville	AL	35806	256-922-0200	922-3599
Canweb Internet Services 1086 Modeland Rd *TF:* 877-422-6932 ■ *Web:* www.canweb.ca	Sarnia	ON	N7S6L2	519-332-6900	
Capgemini US LLC 623 Fifth Ave # 33 *Web:* www.capgemini.com	New York	NY	10022	212-314-8000	
Capital Datacorp 3600 Madison Ave Ste 65 *Web:* www.capdata.com	North Highlands	CA	95660	916-529-4063	
CapitalSoft Inc 1702 N Collins Blvd Ste 211 *Web:* www.capitalsoft.com	Richardson	TX	75080	972-220-1560	
Capitol Computers Inc 151 Water St *Web:* www.capcomp.com	Augusta	ME	04330	207-623-2700	
CARA Group Inc, The Drake Oak Brook Plz 2215 York Rd Ste 300 *TF:* 866-401-2272 ■ *Web:* www.caracorp.com	Oak Brook	IL	60523	630-574-2272	
Carolina Computer Training Inc 33 Villa Rd Ste 100 *Web:* www.cctbusiness.com	Greenville	SC	29615	864-527-8100	
Caron Engineering Inc 1931 Sanford Rd *Web:* www.caroneng.com	Wells	ME	04090	207-646-6071	
Cascade Networks Inc 1111 - 11th Ave PO Box 887 *Web:* www.cni.net	Longview	WA	98632	360-414-5990	
Catapult Systems Inc 1221 S MoPac Expwy Ste 350 *TF:* 800-528-6248 ■ *Web:* www.catapultsystems.com	Austin	TX	78746	512-328-8181	328-0584
Cayman Technologies Inc 12954 Stonecreek Dr Ste E *TF:* 877-370-9470 ■ *Web:* www.caymantech.com	Pickerington	OH	43147	614-759-9461	
Cazarin Web Group 7064 E Fish Lk Rd *Web:* www.cazarin.com	Minneapolis	MN	55311	763-420-9992	
CBM of America Inc 1455 W Newport Ctr Dr *TF:* 800-881-8202 ■ *Web:* www.cbmusa.com	Deerfield Beach	FL	33442	954-698-9104	
Cbord Group Inc, The 61 Brown Rd	Ithaca	NY	14850	607-257-2410	257-1902
Cca Medical Inc 6 Southridge Ct *TF:* 800-775-2556 ■ *Web:* www.ccamedical.com	Greenville	SC	29607	864-233-2700	
CD Group Inc 5550 Triangle Pkwy *Web:* www.cdgroup.com	Norcross	GA	30092	678-268-2000	268-2001
CDMS Inc 550 Sherbrooke W West Tower Ste 250 *TF:* 866-337-2367 ■ *Web:* www.cdmsfirst.com	Montreal	QC	H3A1B9	514-286-2367	
Cdo Technologies Inc 5200 Sprngfeld St Ste 320 *TF:* 866-307-6616 ■ *Web:* www.cdotech.com	Dayton	OH	45431	937-258-0022	258-1614
Cdt Micrographics Inc 137 Water St *Web:* www.cdtmicrographics.com	Exeter	NH	03833	603-778-6140	
Centurion Data Systems N27w23957 Paul Rd Ste 102 *Web:* www.cendatsys.com	Pewaukee	WI	53072	262-524-9290	
Ceres Technology Group Inc 2985 Sterling Court Ste A *Web:* www.boulderpcs.com	Boulder	CO	80301	303-440-6963	
Certec Consulting Inc 4037 N Harvard Ave *Web:* www.certecconsulting.com	Arlington Heights	IL	60004	847-253-8968	
CGI Group Inc 1130 Sherbrooke St W 7th Fl *TSE: GIB/A* ■ *TF:* 800-828-8377 ■ *Web:* www.cgi.com	Montreal	QC	H3A2M8	514-841-3200	841-3299
CGS Technology Associates Inc 242 Old New Brunswick Rd Ste 420 *Web:* www.cgsonline.com	Piscataway	NJ	08854	732-750-4141	
Chameleon Consulting Inc 89 Falmouth Rd W *TF:* 866-903-7912 ■ *Web:* www.chamcon.com	Arlington	MA	02474	781-646-2272	
Chaney Systems Inc 5100 S Calhoun Rd *Web:* www.chaney.net	New Berlin	WI	53151	262-679-6000	
Cherokee Consulting LLC 5057 Bear Mtn Dr *Web:* www.cherokeeconsultingllc.com	Evergreen	CO	80439	303-674-4857	
Cherokee Information Services Inc 2850 Eisenhower Ave Ste 210 *Web:* www.cherokee-inc.com	Alexandria	VA	22314	703-416-0720	416-1045
Chi Corp 5265 Naiman Pkwy *Web:* www.chicorporation.com	Cleveland	OH	44139	440-498-2300	
Chris Young Consulting Co 83 N 64th St *Web:* chrisyoungconsulting.com	Harrisburg	PA	17111	717-561-9742	
CIBER Inc 6363 S Fiddler's Green Cir Ste 1400 *NYSE: CBR* ■ *TF:* 800-242-3799 ■ *Web:* www.ciber.com	Greenwood Village	CO	80111	303-220-0100	220-7100
Cigniti Inc 433 E Las Colinas Blvd Ste 1300 *Web:* www.cigniti.com	Irving	TX	75039	972-756-0622	
CIM Concepts Inc 100 W Commons Blvd Ste 101 *Web:* cimconcepts.com	New Castle	DE	19720	302-613-5400	
CIO Solutions 5425 Hollister Ave Ste 150 *Web:* www.ciosolutions.com	Santa Barbara	CA	93111	805-692-6700	
Citadel Information Services 4 Cornwall Dr Ste 225 *Web:* www.citadelinc.com	East Brunswick	NJ	08816	732-238-0072	
Ckc Laboratories Inc 5046 Sierra Pines Dr *Web:* www.ckc.com	Mariposa	CA	95338	209-966-5240	
CLAdirect Inc 8600 NW 17th St Ste 140 *Web:* cladirect.com	Miami	FL	33126	305-418-4253	
Clarkston Consulting 2655 Meridian Pkwy Ste 400 *TF:* 800-652-4274 ■ *Web:* www.clarkstonconsulting.com	Durham	NC	27713	919-484-4400	484-4450
Classy Llama Studios LLC 4064 S Lone Pine *Web:* www.classyllama.com	Springfield	MO	65804	417-866-8887	

Company	City	State	ZIP	Phone	Fax
ClearStory Systems Inc Suite 200B, One Research Dr *Web:* www3.clearstorysystems.com	Westborough	MA	01581	508-870-4000	
Clever Devices Ltd 300 Crossways Pk Dr *TF:* 800-872-6129 ■ *Web:* www.cleverdevices.com	Woodbury	NY	11797	516-433-6100	
CLICK-into Inc 160 Gibson Dr Ste 301 *Web:* www.click-into.com	Markham	ON	L3R9Y7	905-477-8853	
Clinton Rubin LLC Five Neshaminy Interplex Ste 205 *Web:* clintonrubin.com	Trevose	PA	19053	215-245-2212	
Clockwork 4120 Yonge St *Web:* www.clockwork.ca	North York	ON	M2P2B8	416-222-8990	
Cloud Creek Systems Inc 31255 Cedar Vly Dr Ste 319 *Web:* www.cloudcreek.com	Westlake Village	CA	91362	818-865-2800	
Cnc Consulting Inc 50 E Palisade Ave Ste 410 *Web:* www.cncconsult.com	Englewood	NJ	07631	201-541-9121	
CNP Technologies LLC 806 Tyvola Rd Ste 102 *Web:* www.cnp.net	Charlotte	NC	28217	704-927-6600	
Coalfire Systems Inc 361 Centennial Pkwy Ste 150 *Web:* www.coalfire.com	Louisville	CO	80027	303-554-6333	
Coaxis International 3411 Capital Medical Blvd *Web:* www.coaxis-asp.net	Tallahassee	FL	32308	850-201-0929	
Cognitive Technologies Inc 16333 S Great Oaks Dr Ste 201 *Web:* www.cog-ps.com	Round Rock	TX	78681	703-562-0600	
Cognizant Technology Solutions Corp 500 Frank W Burr Blvd *NASDAQ: CTSH* ■ **Fax:* Mktg ■ *TF:* 888-937-3277 ■ *Web:* www.cognizant.com	Teaneck	NJ	07666	201-801-0233	801-0243*
Colibri Ltd 419 E Crossville Rd Ste 102 *Web:* www.colibrilimited.com	Roswell	GA	30075	678-352-1001	
Collectiveview Inc 3333 S Bannock St Ste 425 *Web:* completenetwork.com	Englewood	CO	80110	303-268-3800	
COLSA Corp 6728 Odyssey Dr *Web:* www.colsa.com	Huntsville	AL	35806	256-964-5555	
Comet Micro System Inc 390 Swift Ave Ste 24 *Web:* www.cometmicro.com	South San Francisco	CA	94080	650-615-9123	
Comit Technologies 1325 Eraste Landry Rd *Web:* www.comittechnologies.com	Lafayette	LA	70506	337-326-5479	
Comlink Network Services 4009 S Meridian St *Web:* comlinkns.com	Indianapolis	IN	46217	317-786-3496	
Comm Source Data Inc 200 Waler Way Unit 2 *Web:* www.comm-source-data.com	Saint Augustine	FL	32086	904-829-8922	
Complex Technologies Corp 518 Old Post Rd Ste 7 *Web:* www.complextech.com	Edison	NJ	08817	732-709-5180	
Comport Consulting Corp 78 Orchard St *Web:* www.comport.com	Ramsey	NJ	07446	201-236-0505	
Compsys Inc 800 Wilcrest Ste 260	Houston	TX	77042	713-961-3999	
Comptron Data Inc 6164 S Hwy 92 *Web:* www.comptekinc.com	Hereford	AZ	85615	520-803-0800	
Compu-Cure New Orleans Inc 3528 Holiday Dr *Web:* compucure.com	New Orleans	LA	70114	504-486-7741	
CompuNet Consulting Group Inc 6535 Shiloh Rd Ste 300 *Web:* www.ccgi.net	Alpharetta	GA	30005	678-965-6500	
Compunite Computers Inc 39 US Hwy 46 Ste 803 *Web:* www.champion-workflow.com	Pine Brook	NJ	07058	973-227-6008	
Computan 3350 Merrittville Hwy *Web:* www.computan.com/	Thorold	ON	L2V4Y6	905-984-8388	
Computech Business Solutions 118 N. Conistor Ln., Ste B, #321 *Web:* www.ctbsonline.com	Liberty	MO	64068	816-880-0988	
Computech Inc 7735 Old Georgetown Rd *Web:* www.computechinc.com	Bethesda	MD	20814	301-656-4030	656-7060
Computek 9580 Commerce Center Dr *Web:* www.computek.com	Rancho Cucamonga	CA	91730	909-987-8515	
Computer Analytical Systems Inc (CASI) 1418 S Third St *TF:* 800-977-3475 ■ *Web:* www.c-a-s-i.com	Louisville	KY	40208	502-635-2019	
Computer Generated Solutions Inc 200 Vesey St Three World Financial Ctr 27th Fl *Web:* www.cgsinc.com	New York	NY	10281	212-408-3800	
Computer Horizons Corp 49 Old Bloomfield Ave *NYSE: CHZS*	Mountain Lakes	NJ	07046	973-299-4000	
Computer Power Solutions Inc 4644 Katella Ave *TF:* 800-444-1938 ■ *Web:* www.computerpowersolutions.com	Los Alamitos	CA	90720	562-493-4487	
Computer Pundits Corp 6515 Cecilia Cir *TF:* 888-786-3487 ■ *Web:* www.computerpundits.com	Bloomington	MN	55439	952-854-2422	
Computer Sciences Corp 2100 E Grand Ave *NYSE: CSC* ■ *TF:* 866-310-0950 ■ *Web:* www.csc.com	El Segundo	CA	90245	310-615-0311	
Computer Spectrum Inc 908 S 8th St Ste 100 *Web:* www.computerspectrum.com	Louisville	KY	40203	502-585-8866	
Computer Task Group Inc (CTG) 800 Delaware Ave *OTC: CTG* ■ *TF:* 800-992-5350 ■ *Web:* www.ctg.com	Buffalo	NY	14209	716-882-8000	887-7464
Computer Technology Assoc (CTA) 2033 San Elijo Ave Ste 330 *Web:* www.cta.com	Cardiff	CA	92007	301-581-3270	
Computers Visionaries Inc 1075 Oak St Ste 2 *Web:* crossvalley.com	Pittston	PA	18640	570-891-0220	
ComResource Inc 1159 Dublin Rd Ste 200 *Web:* www.comresource.com	Columbus	OH	43215	614-221-6348	

Company	City	State	ZIP	Phone	Fax
Comtech Network Systems Inc 1320 Lincoln Ave Ste 4 *Web:* www.comtechnetworks.com	Holbrook	NY	11741	631-981-2694	
Condortech Services Inc 6621-A Electronic Dr *Web:* www.condortech.com	Springfield	VA	22151	703-916-9200	
Conduit Corp 3212 W End Ave Ste 500 *Web:* www.conduitcorporation.com	Nashville	TN	37203	615-269-5710	
Connect Tech Inc 42 Arrow Rd. *TF:* 800-426-8979 ■ *Web:* www.connecttech.com	Guelph	ON	N1K1S6	519-836-1291	
CONNECT: The Knowledge Network Corp 5602 S Nevada St *Web:* www.xtivia.com	Littleton	CO	80120	303-730-7171	
Consult Dynamics Inc 1016 Delaware Ave. *Web:* www.dca.net	Wilmington	DE	19806	302-654-1019	
Contec Systems Industrial Corp 1566 Medical Dr Ste 310 *Web:* contecsystems.com	Pottstown	PA	19464	610-326-3235	
Context Creative Inc 317 Adelaide St W *Web:* contextcreative.com	Toronto	ON	M5V1P9	416-972-1439	
Continuum Worldwide Corp 3333 Farnam St Ste 1 *Web:* www.cwcsecurity.com	Omaha	NE	68131	402-916-1800	
Conventus Corporation Inc 809 N Racine Ste 300 *Web:* www.conventus-sei.com	Chicago	IL	60642	312-421-3270	
Convey Technology Inc 2 Campbell Dr. *Web:* www.conveytechnology.com	Somers	NY	10589	914-277-7502	
Convio Inc 11501 Domain Dr Ste 200 *Web:* www.convio.com	Austin	TX	78758	512-652-2600	
Cook Systems International Inc 6799 Great Oaks Rd Atrium II Ste 200 *Web:* www.cooksys.com	Memphis	TN	38138	901-757-8877	
Corbett Technology Solutions 4151 Lafeyette Ctr Dr Ste 700 *Web:* www.ctsi-usa.com	Chantilly	VA	20151	703-631-3377	
Corestar International Corp 1044 Sandy Hill Rd *Web:* www.corestar-corp.com	Irwin	PA	15642	724-744-4094	
Coretelligent LLC 75 Second Ave Ste 210 *Web:* coretelligent.com	Needham	MA	02494	781-247-4900	
Corstar Communications LLC 40 Saw Mill River Rd *Web:* www.corstar.com	Hawthorne	NY	10532	914-347-2700	
Corus Group LLC 130 Technology Pkwy *Web:* www.corus360.com	Norcross	GA	30092	770-300-4700	
Covansys Corp 32605 W 12 Mile Rd Ste 250 *TF:* 866-310-0950	Farmington Hills	MI	48334	248-488-2088	488-2089
Covestic Inc 5555 Lakeview Dr Ste 100 *Web:* www.covestic.com	Kirkland	WA	98033	425-803-9889	
Cr&t Management Inc 116 Mtn Way Dr *Web:* www.cr-t.com	Orem	UT	84058	801-222-0930	
Creation Engine 348 E Middlefield Rd *TF:* 800-431-8713 ■ *Web:* www.creationengine.com	Mountain View	CA	94043	650-934-0176	
Creative Logistics Solutions Inc 980 Mercantile Dr Ste J *TF:* 800-407-0280 ■ *Web:* www.creativelogistics.com	Hanover	MD	21076	410-793-0708	
CRI Advantage Inc 6149 N Meeker Pl Ste 200 *Web:* www.criadvantage.com	Boise	ID	83713	208-343-9192	
Cronin Business Solutions Inc 11720 SW 37th Ct Ste 300 *Web:* www.croninninc.com	Davie	FL	33330	954-243-3101	
Cronomagic Canada Inc 3333 boul Graham, Ste. 700 Ste *Web:* www.cronomagic.com	Mont-Royal	QC	H3R3L5	514-341-1579	
CSR Enterprise Networks 155 Academy St *Web:* www.csrinc.com	Williamsport	PA	17701	570-322-0590	
CSSI Inc 400 Virginia Ave SW Ste 210 *Web:* www.cssiinc.com	Washington	DC	20024	202-863-2175	
Custom Computer Specialists Inc (CCS) 70 Suffolk Ct *TF:* 800-598-8989 ■ *Web:* www.customonline.com	Hauppauge	NY	11788	631-864-6699	543-2512
Custom Consulting Associates LLC 1112 Sw 118th Pl *Web:* www.cca-llc.net	Oklahoma City	OK	73170	405-691-3417	
Custom Systems & Controls 132 Winter St *Web:* custom-sys.com	Framingham	MA	01702	508-879-4390	
CWPS Inc 14120 A Sullyfield Cir *TF:* 877-297-7472 ■ *Web:* www.cwps.com	Chantilly	VA	20151	877-297-7472	
Cyber Korp Inc 125 Fairfield Way Ste 380 *Web:* www.cyberkorp.com	Bloomingdale	IL	60108	630-980-4416	
Cyberbest Technology Inc 604 Ctland St Ste 121 *Web:* www.cyberbesttech.com	Orlando	FL	32804	407-732-6993	
CyberCore Technologies LLC 6605 Business Pkwy Meadowridge Business Park *Web:* www.cybercoretech.com	Elkridge	MD	21075	410-560-7177	
Cyberjaz Corp 2276 Todd Rd *Web:* www.cyberjaz.net	Aliquippa	PA	15001	412-922-2000	
Cybersoft 1958 Butler Pk Ste 100 *Web:* www.cybersoft.com	Conshohocken	PA	19428	610-825-6785	
Cybersoft Technologies Inc 4422 Cypress Creek Pkwy Ste 400 *Web:* www.cybersoftech.com	Houston	TX	77068	281-453-8500	
Cybertech Systems & Software Inc 3401 Quebec St Ste 3600 *Web:* www.cybertech.com	Denver	CO	80207	303-321-0592	321-0689
Cybrix Group Inc 4508 Oak Fair Blvd Ste 240 *Web:* www.cybrixgroup.com	Tampa	FL	33602	813-630-2744	
CYIOS Corporation Inc 1300 Pennsylvania Ave NW Ste 700 *Web:* www.cyios.com	Washington	DC	20004	202-204-3006	
Cypress Networks 4125 Walker Ave Ste C *TF:* 866-625-3502 ■ *Web:* www.cypressnetworks.net	Greensboro	NC	27407	336-841-3030	
Cyquent Inc 5410 Edson Ln Ste 210C *Web:* www.cyquent.com	Rockville	MD	20852	240-292-0230	
D G Consulting 295 Blohm Ave *Web:* dgconsult.com	Aromas	CA	95004	831-726-7060	
D V O Enterprises Inc 620 Windsor Ct *Web:* www.dvo.com	Alpine	UT	84004	801-492-1290	
Dallas Digital Services LLC 5316 Bransford Rd *Web:* www.ddserv.com	Colleyville	TX	76034	817-577-8794	
Data Computer Corporation of America 5310 Dorsey Hall Dr *Web:* www.dcca.com	Ellicott City	MD	21042	410-992-3760	
Data Consulting Group Inc 965 E Jefferson Ave *Web:* www.dcgroupinc.com	Detroit	MI	48207	313-963-7771	
Data Innovations Inc 120 Kimball Ave Ste 100 *Web:* www.datainnovations.com	South Burlington	VT	05403	802-658-2850	
Data Perceptions 174 Bridge St W *Web:* www.dataperceptions.com	Waterloo	ON	N2K1K9	519-749-9319	
Data Systems Analysts Inc (DSA) Eigth Neshaminy Interplex Ste 209 *TF:* 877-422-4372 ■ *Web:* www.dsainc.com	Trevose	PA	19053	215-245-4800	245-4375
Data-Quest Inc 4807 Jonestown Rd Ste 247 *Web:* www.dataquestinc.com	Harrisburg	PA	17109	717-545-2581	
Databranch Inc 132 N Union St Ste 108 *Web:* www.databranch.com	Olean	NY	14760	716-373-4467	
DataComm Networks Inc 6801 N 54th St *Web:* www.datacomm.com	Tampa	FL	33610	813-873-0674	
DataLink Interactive Inc 1120 Benfield Blvd Ste G *TF:* 888-565-3279 ■ *Web:* www.datalinktech.com	Millersville	MD	21108	410-729-0440	
Datamatrix Systems Inc 505 Lincoln Hwy *Web:* www.getdatamatrix.com	East Mckeesport	PA	15035	412-825-3600	
Datapro Inc 770 Ponce De Leon Blvd 2nd Fl *Web:* www.datapromiami.com	Coral Gables	FL	33134	305-374-0606	
Datapro Solutions Inc 6336 E Utah Ave *TF:* 888-658-6881 ■ *Web:* www.dataprosolutionsinc.com	Spokane	WA	99212	509-532-3530	
Dataskill Inc 5675 Ruffin Rd Ste 100 *Web:* www.dataskill.com	San Diego	CA	92123	858-755-3800	
Datatrend Technologies Inc 121 Cheshire Ln Ste 700 *Web:* www.datatrend.com	Minnetonka	MN	55305	952-931-1203	
Dataway Inc 255 Golden Gate Ave *Web:* www.dataway.com	San Francisco	CA	94102	415-882-8700	
Datroo Technologies LLC 1292 N 1st St Ste 707 *Web:* www.datroo.com	Abilene	TX	79601	325-675-8880	
Daugherty Systems Inc Three CityPl Ste 400 *Web:* www.daugherty.com	Saint Louis	MO	63141	314-432-8200	
Dayhuff Group LLC, The 740 Lakeview Plz Blvd Ste 300 *Web:* www.dayhuffgroup.com	Worthington	OH	43085	614-854-9999	
Dcs Netlink 1800 Macauley Ave *TF:* 877-327-6385 ■ *Web:* dcsnetlink.com	Rice Lake	WI	54868	715-236-7424	
Dcse Inc 95 Argonaut Ste 260 *Web:* www.dcse.com	Aliso Viejo	CA	92656	949-465-3400	
Decision Systems Plus Inc 248 Spring Lake Dr Ste 170 *TF:* 800-676-7374 ■ *Web:* www.motherg.com	Itasca	IL	60143	800-676-7374	
Decisive Business Systems Inc 7150 N Park Dr Ste 400 *TF:* 866-203-8948 ■ *Web:* www.decisivebiz.com	Pennsauken	NJ	08109	856-910-0900	
Decotech Systems Inc 2151 Salvio St Ste 260 *Web:* www.decotech.com	Concord	CA	94520	925-954-1520	
Delaney Computer Services 66 Orange Tpke *Web:* dcsny.com	Sloatsburg	NY	10974	845-753-5800	
Dell Perot Systems 370 Southpointe Blvd	Canonsburg	PA	15317	724-514-5000	
Delta Corporate Services Inc 129 Littleton Rd *TF:* 800-335-8220 ■ *Web:* www.deltacorp.com	Parsippany	NJ	07054	973-334-6260	331-0144
Denali Advance Integration (DAI) 17735 NE 65th St Ste 130 *TF:* 877-467-8008 ■ *Web:* www.denaliai.com	Redmond	WA	98052	425-885-4000	467-1127
Dental Systems Inc 5514 Decker Dr *Web:* www.iaplus.com	Baytown	TX	77520	281-838-3950	
Design Strategy Corp 805 Third Ave 11th Fl *TF:* 800-331-8726 ■ *Web:* www.designstrategy.com	New York	NY	10022	212-370-0000	949-3648
Detail Drafting and Design Inc 1090 216th Ave *Web:* ddd-services.com	East Bethel	MN	55011	763-434-2110	
Detroit Engineered Products Inc 850 East Long Lake Rd Ste 103 *Web:* www.depusa.com	Troy	MI	48085	248-269-7130	
Dew Software Inc 983 Corporate Way *Web:* www.dewsoftware.com	Fremont	CA	94539	510-490-9995	
Dexisive Inc 1840 Michael Faraday Drÿ Ste 310a *Web:* www.dexisive.com	Reston	VA	20190	703-935-0110	
Dialogic Inc 1504 Mccarthy Blvd *TF:* 800-755-4444 ■ *Web:* www.dialogic.com	Milpitas	CA	95035	408-750-9400	
Diamond Technology Inc 2309 Divisadero St 5 *Web:* www.diamondti.com	San Francisco	CA	94115	415-441-8916	
Digett 105 Falls Court Ste 300 *Web:* digett.com	Boerne	TX	78006	830-249-9494	
Digital Bungalow Inc 209 Essex St *Web:* www.digitalbungalow.com	Salem	MA	01970	978-565-0111	
Digital Celerity LLC 548 Market St Ste 22067 *TF:* 888-963-8876 ■ *Web:* www.digitalcelerity.com	San Francisco	CA	94104	888-963-8876	

				Phone	Fax
Digital Foundry Inc 1707 Tiburon Blvd *Web:* www.digitalfoundry.com	Belvedere Tiburon	CA	94920	415-789-1600	
Digital Measures 301 N Broadway 4th Fl *TF:* 866-348-5677 ■ *Web:* www.digitalmeasures.com	Milwaukee	WI	53202	866-348-5677	
Digital Ocean Corp 3701 Gillham Rd *Web:* www.digitaloceaninc.com	Kansas City	MO	64111	816-522-5764	
Digital Peach Web Design 1109 Russell Pkwy Ste B2 *Web:* www.digitalpeach.com	Warner Robins	GA	31088	478-922-1919	
Digital Video Networks LLC 9150 E Del Camino Ste 100 *Web:* www.digitalvideonetworks.com	Scottsdale	AZ	85258	480-588-3511	
Digium Inc 445 Jan Davis Dr NW *Web:* www.digium.com	Huntsville	AL	35806	256-428-6000	
Dini Communications 340 Campus Dr *Web:* dini.net	Edison	NJ	08837	732-225-4514	
Direct Services Miami Inc 10390 Usa Today Way *Web:* www.directservices.com	Miramar	FL	33025	954-433-9810	
Dirks Group, The 3802 Hummingbird Rd *TF:* 800-866-1486 ■ *Web:* www.dirksgroup.com	Wausau	WI	54401	715-848-9865	
Diverse Technology Solutions Inc 2949 Sunrise Hwy *Web:* www.diverse-technology.com	Islip Terrace	NY	11752	631-224-1200	
DLP Technologies Inc 8080 Reading Rd *Web:* www.netgainit.com	Cincinnati	OH	45237	513-232-7791	
DMC Technology Group Inc 7657 King's Pointe Rd *Web:* www.dmcconsulting.com	Toledo	OH	43617	419-535-2900	
Documentation Strategies Inc 15 Second Ave *Web:* www.docstrats.com	Rensselaer	NY	12144	518-432-1233	
Dominant Systems Corp 3850 Varsity Dr *Web:* domsys.com	Ann Arbor	MI	48108	734-971-1210	
Dowling Consulting Group Inc 32818 Walker Rd PO Box 176 *Web:* www.dowlinggroup.com	Avon Lake	OH	44012	440-348-9687	
Dp Guardian Inc 2270 W Chenango Ave Unit 300 *Web:* www.dpguardian.com	Littleton	CO	80120	303-783-0191	
DPE Systems Inc 425 Pontius Ave N Ste 430 *TF:* 800-541-6566 ■ *Web:* www.dpes.com	Seattle	WA	98109	206-223-3737	223-0859
Dr FirstCom Inc 9420 Key W Ave Ste 230 *Web:* drfirst.com	Rockville	MD	20850	301-231-9510	
Dr Tax Software Inc 3333 Graham Blvd Ste 222 *TF:* 800-663-7829 ■ *Web:* www.drtax.ca	Montreal	QC	H3R3L5	514-733-8355	
Drayton, Drayton & Lamar Inc 616 Ponder Pl Dr Ste 2 *Web:* www.ddlinc.com	Evans	GA	30809	706-854-1145	
Druide informatique Inc 1435 rue Saint-Alexandre Bureau 1040 *Web:* www.druide.com	Montreal	QC	H3A2G4	514-484-4998	
Durst Image Technology US LLC 50 Methodist Hill Dr Ste 100 *Web:* www.durstus.com	Rochester	NY	14623	585-486-0340	
Dxm Productions 472 S Shoreline Blvd *Web:* www.dxm.com	Mountain View	CA	94041	650-969-6580	
Dynacor Media 60 Ave Ste 9314 *Web:* dynacormedia.com	Edmonton	AB	T6E0C1	780-448-0093	
Dynamic Edge Inc 2245 S State St Ste 1200 *Web:* dynamic-edge.net	Ann Arbor	MI	48104	734-404-8061	
Dynamic Motion Control Inc 1333 N Kingsbury St *Web:* www.dmcinfo.com	Chicago	IL	60642	312-255-8757	
Dyonyx LP 1235 N Loop W *TF General:* 855-749-6758 ■ *Web:* www.dyonyx.com	Houston	TX	77008	713-485-7000	830-5909
Dytech Group 7201 Sandscove Ct Ste 4 *Web:* www.dytech.com	Winter Park	FL	32792	407-678-8300	
E & E It Consulting Services Inc 5026 Arthur Ave *Web:* ene-it-consulting.com	Mechanicsburg	PA	17050	717-975-1664	
E Innovative Com Inc 445 Poi Ct *Web:* www.innovative-e.com	Merritt Island	FL	32953	321-452-5905	
EA Consulting Inc 1024 Iron Point Rd *Web:* www.ea-inc.com	Folsom	CA	95630	916-357-6588	200-0368
Echomountain Llc 1483 Patriot Blvd *TF:* 877-311-1980 ■ *Web:* www.echomountain.com	Glenview	IL	60026	877-311-1980	
Echota Technologies Corp 3286 Northpark Blvd Ste A	Alcoa	TN	37701	865-273-1270	273-1277
Eck-mundy Associates Inc 450 E 11th Ave *Web:* www.eck-mundy.com	Jasper	IN	47546	812-634-8001	
Eco-Shift Power Corp 486 Leawood Cir *Web:* eco-shiftpower.com	Naples	FL	34104	519-650-9506	
Ecom Enterprises Inc 1230 Oakmead Pkwy Ste 318 *TF:* 877-955-3266 ■ *Web:* www.ecomenterprises.com	Sunnyvale	CA	94085	408-720-9194	
Ecom Solutions 7326 Yellowstone Blvd *Web:* www.ecomsolutions.net	Forest Hills	NY	11375	718-793-2828	
Edvance Research Inc 9901 W Interstate 10 Ste 1000 *Web:* edvanceresearch.com	San Antonio	TX	78230	210-558-1902	
EHD Technologies LLC 1600 Westgate Cir *Web:* www.ehdtech.com	Brentwood	TN	37027	615-953-1907	
Ekuber Ventures Inc 8300 Boone blvd Ste 512 Fl 5 *Web:* ekuber.com	Vienna	VA	22182	703-624-1473	
Elangeni Consulting Inc 115 Rt 46 W Bldg B Ste 13 *Web:* www.elangeni.com	Mountain Lakes	NJ	07046	973-541-1667	
Elara Systems 2880 Sunrise Blvd Ste 200 *Web:* www.elarasystems.com	Rancho Cordova	CA	95742	916-638-1658	
Electronic Warfare Assoc Inc (EWA Inc) 13873 Pk Ctr Rd Ste 500 *TF General:* 888-392-0002 ■ *Web:* www.ewa.com	Herndon	VA	20171	703-904-5700	904-5779
Elemco Software Integration Group Ltd 245 Atlantic St *Web:* www.elemcosoftware.com	Central Islip	NY	11722	631-234-3099	
Em Data Consultants Inc 42 Queen St S Ste 201 *Web:* www.emdci.com	Mississauga	ON	L5M1K4	905-858-8442	
EMA Design Automation Inc 225 Tech Park Dr *Web:* www.ema-eda.com	Rochester	NY	14623	585-334-6001	
eMagine Communications LLC 73 Stevens St *Web:* www.emagine.com	East Taunton	MA	02718	508-802-9577	
eMedia Music Corp 664 NE Northlake Way *TF:* 888-363-3424 ■ *Web:* www.emediamusic.com	Seattle	WA	98105	206-329-5657	
Emotion Studios 85 Liberty Ship Way *Web:* www.emotionstudios.com	Sausalito	CA	94965	415-331-6975	
Encompass Iowa LLC 1420 First Ave NE Ste 200 *Web:* www.encompassiowa.com	Cedar Rapids	IA	52402	319-862-0221	
End Point Corp 304 Park Ave S Ste 214 *Web:* www.endpoint.com	New York	NY	10010	212-929-6923	
Engenius Inc 31077 Schoolcraft Rd *Web:* www.engenius.com	Livonia	MI	48150	734-522-2120	
Engine Interactive 1415 10th Ave 4 *Web:* www.enginei.com	Seattle	WA	98122	206-709-1955	
Enginuiti Inc 8321 Old Cthouse Rd *Web:* www.enginuiti.com	Vienna	VA	22182	703-620-2266	
Enhanced Telecommunication Inc 6065 Atlantic Blvd *Web:* etisoftware.com	Norcross	GA	30071	770-242-3620	
enrich IT Inc 3655 Brookside Pkwy Ste 265 *Web:* www.enrichit.com	Alpharetta	GA	30022	770-667-0510	
Enscicon Corp 2420 W 26 Ave Ste 500 Bldg D *Web:* enscicon.com	Denver	CO	80211	303-832-8200	
Entre Solutions 51 W Fairmont Ave	Savannah	GA	31406	912-352-2046	
Eos Systems Inc 72 River Park St Ste 4 *TF:* 855-453-2600 ■ *Web:* www.eos-systems.com	Needham	MA	02494	855-453-2600	
Epc Consultants Inc 655 Davis St *Web:* www.epcconsultants.com	San Francisco	CA	94111	415-675-7580	
Epic Systems Corp 1979 Milky Way *Web:* epic.com	Verona	WI	53593	608-271-9000	
Epitomione 4502 Chews Vineyard *Web:* www.epitomione.com	Ellicott City	MD	21043	443-540-2230	
Epoch Online 324 W Pershing Blvd *Web:* www.epochonline.com	N Little Rock	AR	72114	501-907-7500	
Epsilon Management Systems Inc 151 Fairchild Ave Ste 2 *Web:* www.emscirc.com	Plainview	NY	11803	516-349-1440	
Epsilonium Systems Inc 201 E Southern Ave 205 *Web:* www.epsilonium.com	Tempe	AZ	85282	480-219-2629	
Esage Group LLC 605 1st Ave Ste 510 *Web:* www.esagegroup.com	Seattle	WA	98104	206-342-9981	
eSecurityToGo LLC 1109 Quail St *Web:* www.esecuritytogo.com	Newport Beach	CA	92660	949-261-5555	
Est Group LLC 1907 Ascension Blvd Ste 100 *Web:* www.est-grp.com	Arlington	TX	76006	817-382-8000	
Esti Consulting Services 812 Spadina Cres E *Web:* www.esti.ca	Saskatoon	SK	S7K3H4	306-242-2436	
Etrafficers 881 S Orem Blvd Ste 1 *Web:* www.etrafficers.com	Orem	UT	84058	801-221-9400	
Eventus Solutions Group 98 Inverness Dr E Ste 100 *Web:* www.eventusg.com	Englewood	CO	80112	303-376-6161	
eVerge Group Inc 4965 Preston Pk Blvd Ste 700 *TF:* 888-548-1973 ■ *Web:* www.evergegroup.com	Plano	TX	75093	972-608-1803	608-1893
Evolve Payment Systems 2974 Rice St *Web:* evolve-systems.com	Saint Paul	MN	55113	651-628-4000	
Exacta Corp 16595 W Bluemound Rd *Web:* exactacorp.com	Brookfield	WI	53005	262-796-0000	
Excedo Solutions Llc 44 Baldwin Dr *Web:* www.excedosolutions.com	Fredericksburg	VA	22406	703-725-3156	
Exceed Consulting 8259 Woodstone Dr SE *Web:* www.exceed-corp.com	Byron Center	MI	49315	616-698-1800	
Excel Computer Corp 6 Frost Dr *Web:* www.excelme.com	Bangor	ME	04401	207-990-3305	
Excel Technologies LLC 3701 Pender Dr *Web:* exceltechllc.com	Fairfax	VA	22030	703-246-9002	
Excella Consulting Inc 2300 Wilson Blvd Ste 630 *Web:* www.excella.com	Arlington	VA	22201	703-840-8600	
Exclamake! Inc PO Box 14310 *Web:* www.exclamake.net	Sn Luis Obisp	CA	93406	805-540-5114	
Exobase Corp 3150 De La Cruz Blvd *Web:* www.exobase.com	Santa Clara	CA	95054	408-235-8808	
Expert System Applications Inc 2681 Ashley Rd *Web:* www.expert-system.com	Shaker Heights	OH	44122	440-668-8184	
EZ Micro Solutions Inc 2670 Lehigh St *Web:* www.ezmicro.com	Whitehall	PA	18052	610-264-1232	
Facilite Informatique Canada Inc 5 Pl Ville-Marie Bureau 1045 *Web:* www.facilite.com	Montreal	QC	H3B2G2	514-284-5636	284-9529
Facility Gateway Corp 4920 Triangle St *Web:* www.facilitygateway.com	Mcfarland	WI	53558	608-838-6060	
Far Ridgeline Engagements Inc 285 W New York Ave *Web:* www.frleinc.com	Southern Pines	NC	28387	910-725-0303	
Federal Technology Solutions Inc 16 Hughes St Ste C106 *Web:* www.federalsales.com	Irvine	CA	92618	949-830-8858	

Phone Fax

FedTek Inc 12700 Black Forest Ln Ste 202 .... Woodbridge VA 22192 703-551-4718
Web: www.fedtek.com

Feith Systems & Software Inc
425 Maryland Dr. .... Ft Washington PA 19034 215-646-8000
Web: feith.com

FiberPlus Inc 8240 Preston Court Ste C .... Jessup MD 20794 301-317-3300
Web: www.fiberplusinc.com

Fifth Business Inc 24 Greenway Plz Ste 1200 .... Houston TX 77046 713-622-5423
Web: www.fifthbusiness.com

Figtree Consulting Inc
101 Gibraltar Dr Ste 3D .... Morris Plains NJ 07950 973-539-9311
Web: www.figtree.com

Finsoft Consultants Inc 545 8th Ave Ste 4 .... New York NY 10018 212-239-9191
Web: www.finsoftus.com

Firmwater 20 Maud St Ste 405 .... Toronto ON M5V2M5 416-815-1496
Web: www.firmwater.com

Flexible Business Systems 380 Oser Ave. .... Hauppauge NY 11788 631-756-0404
Web: www.flexiblesystems.com

Focus Technology Solutions Inc 93 Ledge Rd .... Seabrook NH 03874 603-766-0000
Web: www.focustsi.com

Focused Management Inc
6354 Walker Ln Ste 101 .... Franconia VA 22310 703-922-9600
Web: www.focusedmgmtinc.com

Folsom Technology Group Inc 440 Trowbridge Ln. ..... Folsom CA 95763 916-851-7330
Web: www.ftgroup.com

Force 3 Inc 2151 Priest Bridge Dr .... Crofton MD 21114 301-261-0204 721-5624*
**Fax Area Code:* 410 ■ *TF:* 800-391-0204 ■ *Web:* www.force3.com

Forgentum Inc 9312 W St .... Manassas VA 20110 703-906-8996
Web: www.forgentum.com

Formula Consultants Inc 100 S Anaheim Blvd .... Anaheim CA 92805 714-778-0123
Web: www.formula.com

Forward Thinking Systems
105 State Rt 101a Unit 21 .... Amherst NH 03031 603-882-8465
Web: forwardthinkingsys.com

FoxNet Solutions Inc 92 Erb St E .... Waterloo ON N2J1L6 519-886-8895
Web: www.foxnetsolutions.com

Friendly Solutions Corp 3837 N Panama Ave .... Chicago IL 60634 773-957-7800
Web: friendlysol.com

Frontier Computer Corp
1275 Business Pk Dr .... Traverse City MI 49686 231-929-1386
TF: 866-226-6344 ■ *Web:* www.frontiercomputercorp.com

Frontier Consulting Inc 10101 SW Fwy Ste 202 .... Houston TX 77074 713-778-0799
TF: 877-324-8729 ■ *Web:* www.frontier-consulting.com

Fujitsu Consulting 1250 E Arques Ave. .... Sunnyvale CA 94085 800-831-3183
TF: 800-831-3183 ■ *Web:* fujitsu.com

Fulcrum Group Inc, The
5751 Kroger Dr Ste 279 .... Fort Worth TX 76244 817-337-0300
Web: www.fulcrum.pro

Fultech Solutions Inc 7837 Bayberry Rd .... Jacksonville FL 32256 904-992-6624
Web: www.fultechsolutions.com

Fusionworks Inc
120 Condado Ave Pico Ctr Ste 102 .... San Juan PR 00907 787-721-1039
Web: www.fwpr.com

Future Com Ltd 807 Forest Rdg Dr Ste 105 .... Bedford TX 76022 817-510-1100
Web: www.myfuturecom.com

FYI Systems Inc 35 Waterview Blvd .... Parsippany NJ 07054 973-331-9050 331-9055
Web: www.fyisolutions.com

G&B Solutions Inc 1861 Wiehle Ave Ste 200 .... Reston VA 20190 703-883-1140 883-1143
Web: www.gbsolutionsinc.com

G2 Solutions Inc 35 Robinson St .... Newnan GA 30263 678-423-7744
Web: www.g2sinc.com

G2 Web Services LLC
1750 112th Ave NE Ste C101 .... Bellevue WA 98004 425-749-4040
TF: 888-788-5353 ■ *Web:* www.g2webservices.com

Gad Shaanan Design Inc 1260 Prospect St .... La Jolla CA 92037 858-729-9951
Web: www.gadshaanandesign.com

GadellNet Consulting Services LLC
1520 S Vandeventer .... St. Louis MO 63110 314-431-0358
Web: www.gadellnet.com

Garvin-Allen Solutions Ltd
Unit 12 155 Chain Lk Dr .... Halifax NS B3S1B3 902-453-3554
TF: 877-325-9062 ■ *Web:* www.garvin-allen.com

Gaslight Media 120 E Lake St .... Petoskey MI 49770 231-487-0692
Web: gaslightmedia.com

Gcas Inc 1531 Grand Ave Ste A .... San Marcos CA 92078 760-591-4227
Web: www.gcas.net

Gemini Computer Systems
1893 Daimler Rd Ste B .... Rockford IL 61112 815-227-5800
Web: geminicomputersystems.com

General Dynamics Information Technology
3211 Jermantown Rd .... Fairfax VA 22030 703-246-0200 995-6750
TF: 800-242-0230 ■ *Web:* www.gdit.com

Genesis Corp 950 Third Ave Fl 26 .... New York NY 10022 212-688-5522 421-6292
TF: 800-261-1776 ■ *Web:* www.genesis10.com

Geneva Consulting Group Inc
14 Vanderventer Ave Ste 250 .... Port Washington NY 11050 212-244-9595
Web: www.genevaconsulting.com

Genuitec LLC 2221 Justin Rd Ste 119-340 .... Flower Mound TX 75028 214-224-0461
Web: www.genuitec.com

Genwest Systems Inc PO Box 397 .... Edmonds WA 98020 425-771-2700
Web: www.genwest.com

GeoLogics Corp 5285 Shawnee Rd Ste 300 .... Alexandria VA 22312 703-750-4000 750-4010
TF: 800-684-3455 ■ *Web:* geologics.com

Geoscape International Inc 2100 W Flagler St .... Miami FL 33135 888-211-9353
TF: 888-211-9353 ■ *Web:* www.geoscape.com

Getnet Inc 333 E Indian School Rd .... Phoenix AZ 85012 602-264-7000
Web: www.getnet.net

GlassHouse Technologies Inc
200 Crossing Blvd .... Southborough MA 01772 508-879-5729
Web: www.glasshouse.com

Glencom Systems Inc 25 E Price St .... Linden NJ 07036 908-486-0420
Web: www.glen.com

Phone Fax

Global Consultants Inc 25 Airport Rd .... Morristown NJ 07960 973-889-5200 292-1643
TF: 877-264-6424 ■ *Web:* www.collabera.com

Global Help Desk Services Inc
2080 Silas Deane Hwy .... Rocky Hill CT 06067 800-770-1075
TF: 800-770-1075 ■ *Web:* www.ghdsi.com

Global Infotek Inc 1920 Association Dr Ste 200 .... Reston VA 20191 703-652-1600
Web: globalinfotek.com

Global Management Systems Inc (GMSI)
2201 Wisconsin Ave NW Ste 300 .... Washington DC 20007 202-471-4674 625-9016
Web: www.gmsi.com

Global Outsourcing Services Inc
40 Fleetwood Ct Ste 2 .... Ronkonkoma NY 11779 631-471-6798
Web: www.gostechnicalservices.com

Global Technology Resources Inc
990 S Bdwy Ste 300 .... Denver CO 80209 303-455-8800 803-6520*
**Fax Area Code:* 888 ■ *TF:* 877-603-1984 ■ *Web:* www.gtri.com

Globalspec Inc 350 Jordan Rd .... Troy NY 12180 518-880-0200 880-0250
TF: 800-261-2052 ■ *Web:* www.globalspec.com

Glotech 2551 Eltham Ave Ste A .... Norfolk VA 23513 757-499-3650
Web: glotech.net

GMD Studios 7057 University Blvd .... Winter Park FL 32792 407-657-8990
Web: www.gmdstudios.com

Gmp Networks Llc 4729 E Sunrise Dr Ste 121 .... Tucson AZ 85718 520-577-3891
Web: www.gmpnet.net

Gold Key Technology Solutions Inc
220 S Second St .... Temple TX 76501 254-774-9035
Web: goldkeytechnology.com

Goldbelt Raven LLC 14117 Robert Paris Ct .... Chantilly VA 20151 703-871-2091
Web: www.goldbeltraven.com

Goldberg Testa & Company Inc
6201 Ft Hamilton Pkwy .... Brooklyn NY 11219 718-748-4851

Good Dog Design 21 Corte Madera Ave Ste 2 .... Mill Valley CA 94941 415-383-0110
Web: gooddogdesign.com

GP Strategies Corp
11000 Broken Land Parkway Ste 200 .... Columbia MD 21044 443-367-9600
TF: 888-843-4784 ■ *Web:* www.gpstrategies.com

Granite Information Systems
1490 Union Lk Rd .... White Lake MI 48386 248-360-8400
Web: graniteinfosys.com

Grantek Systems Integration Inc
4480 Harvester Rd .... Burlington ON L7L4X2 905-634-0844
Web: grantek.com

Graphics Systems Corp. (GXSC)
W133 N5138 Campbell Dr .... Menomonee Falls WI 53051 262-790-1080
Web: www.gxsc.com

Green Technology Group, Llc, The
10619 Canterberry Rd .... Fairfax Station VA 22039 202-285-4748
Web: www.tgtgllc.com

Greenpages Inc 33 Badgers Island W .... Kittery ME 03904 207-439-7310 439-7334
TF: 888-687-4876 ■ *Web:* www.greenpages.com

Groupe Gsc 7800 Boul Metropolitain E .... Anjou QC H1K1A1 514-354-4222
Web: groupe-gsc.qc.ca

Groupe Informatique TechSolCom Inc
1450 City Councillors Ste 340 .... Montreal QC H3A2E6 514-392-9997
Web: www.techsolcom.ca

Groupe SYGIF Inc
120 Montee Industrielle-et-Commerciale .... Rimouski QC G5M1B1 418-721-5353
Web: groupesygif.ca

Gryphtech Inc 2595 Skymark Ave Ste 206 .... Mississauga ON L4W4L5 416-362-0543
Web: gryphtech.com

Gsat Inc 100 W Oak St Ste 200 .... Denton TX 76201 469-287-6771
TF: 866-977-4728 ■ *Web:* www.gsati.com

Harmonix Technologies Inc
4915 Paseo De Norte NE Ste A .... Albuquerque NM 87113 505-205-1585
Web: www.harmonixtechnologies.com

Harris Computer Systems Inc
1 Antares Dr Ste 400 .... Ottawa ON K2E8C4 613-226-5511
Web: www.harriscomputer.com

Harris Technology Services Inc
1603 Golf Course Rd SE Ste B .... Rio Rancho NM 87124 505-892-7364
Web: htsusa.com

Hartford Computer Group Inc
10440 Little Patuxent Pkwy 3rd Fl .... Columbia MD 21044 410-740-3020 740-8732
TF: 800-370-5849 ■ *Web:* www.hcgi.com

Hawk Isolutions Group Inc
6439 Plymouth Ave Ste 112 .... Saint Louis MO 63133 636-256-7534
Web: www.hawkisg.com

Hayden Technologies Inc
6075 Lk Forrest Dr Ste 150 .... Atlanta GA 30328 404-602-0471
Web: www.haydentechnologies.com

Hcl Global Systems Inc
24543 Indoplex Cir Ste 220 .... Farmington MI 48335 248-473-0720
Web: www.hclglobal.com

Hedrick Associates Inc
2360 Oak Industrial Dr Ne .... Grand Rapids MI 49505 616-454-1218
Web: hedrickassoc.com

Helios & Matheson North America Inc
350 Fifth Ave Ste 7520 .... New York NY 10018 212-979-8228
Web: www.tact.com

Henry A Bromelkamp & Co 106 E 24th St .... Minneapolis MN 55404 612-870-9087
TF: 877-767-6703 ■ *Web:* www.bromelkamp.com

Herrod Technology Inc Po Box 152495 .... Arlington TX 76015 214-202-0999
Web: herrodtech.com

Herzum Inc 175 N Franklin St Ste 301 .... Chicago IL 60606 312-602-1001
Web: www.herzum.com

Hexaware Technologies Inc 1095 Cranbury Rd .... Jamesburg NJ 08831 609-409-6950 409-6910
TF: 866-746-2133 ■ *Web:* www.hexaware.com

Hixardt Technologies Inc
119 W Intendencia St .... Pensacola FL 32502 850-439-3282
TF: 866-985-3282 ■ *Web:* www.hixardt.com

Hlb Systems Solutions 50 Malcolm Rd .... Guelph ON N1K1A9 519-822-3450
Web: www.hlbsolutions.com

Hln Consulting LLC 7072 Santa Fe Canyon Pl .... San Diego CA 92129 858-538-2220
Web: www.hln.com

Phone Fax

HMS Technologies Inc 1 Discovery Pl. Martinsburg WV 25403 304-596-5583
Web: www.hmstech.com

Holcomb Enterprises
25108 Marguerite Pkwy B-206 Mission Viejo CA 92692 949-458-0292
Web: www.holcombenterprises.com

Holman'S of Nevada Inc
4445 S Vly View Blvd Las Vegas NV 89103 702-222-1818
Web: www.holmansnv.com

Horizon Solutions LLC 175 Josons Dr Rochester NY 14623 585-424-7376
Web: hs-e.com

House of Brick Technologies LLC
9300 Underwood Ave Ste 300 Omaha NE 68114 402-445-0764
TF: 877-780-7038 ■ *Web:* www.houseofbrick.com

Houston Medical Records Inc
2211 Norfolk St Ste 950 Houston TX 77098 713-850-1190
Web: www.houmedicalbilling.com

Howard Systems International 2777 Summer St. Stamford CT 06905 800-326-4860 324-7722*
**Fax Area Code:* 203 ■ *TF:* 800-326-4860 ■ *Web:* www.howardsystems.com

HUB Technical Services
44 Norfolk Ave Ste 4 South Easton MA 02375 508-238-9887
TF: 877-482-8324 ■ *Web:* www.hubtechnical.com

Huber & Associates Inc
1400 Edgewood Dr Jefferson City MO 65109 573-634-5000
Web: www.teamhuber.com

Hurd It Communications 2106 Gallows Rd A Vienna VA 22182 703-442-3422
Web: www.hurdit.com

Hurdman Communications
1344 West 75 North Centerville UT 84014 801-292-7673
Web: hurdman.com

I-ology Inc 6900 E Camelback Rd Ste 450 Scottsdale AZ 85251 480-850-2800
Web: www.i-ology.com

I.M. Systems Group Inc
3206 Tower Oaks Blvd Ste 300 Rockville MD 20852 240-833-1889
Web: www.imsg.com

i4i Inc 116 Spadina Ave 5th Fl Toronto ON M5V2K6 416-504-0141
Web: www.i4i.com

Ibaset 27442 Portola Pkwy Foothill Ranch CA 92610 949-598-5200 598-2600
TF: 877-422-7381 ■ *Web:* www.ibaset.com

Icc 6406 Odana Rd Madison WI 53719 608-277-8000
Web: www.iccnow.com

Ice Technologies Inc 411 SE Ninth St Pella IA 50219 641-628-8724
TF: 877-754-8420 ■ *Web:* www.icetechnologies.com

Iconixx Software 3420 Executive Ctr Dr Ste 250 Austin TX 78731 877-426-6499 651-3111*
**Fax Area Code:* 512 ■ *TF:* 877-426-6499 ■ *Web:* iconixx.com

Iconomics Inc 1 Dundas St W Ste 2108 Toronto ON M5G1Z3 416-703-6547
Web: www.iconomics-inc.com

Ideal Integrations Inc 800 Regis Ave Pittsburgh PA 15236 412-349-6680
Web: www.idealintegrations.net

Idealogical Systems Inc 2900 John St Markham ON L3R5G3 905-474-0772
TF: 855-554-4332 ■ *Web:* www.idealogical.com

IdentityMine Inc 1015 A St Ste 1200 Tacoma WA 98104 253-779-8202
Web: www.identitymine.com

Idesign Solutions Inc 51 Roysun Rd Woodbridge ON L4L8P9 416-213-8445
Web: www.idesignsol.com

Ilan Systems 1107 Fair Oaks Ave South Pasadena CA 91030 800-678-3526
TF: 800-678-3526 ■ *Web:* www.ilan.com

Imaging Systems Technology Inc
4750 W Bancroft St Toledo OH 43615 419-536-5741
Web: www.isttouch.com

iMakeNews Inc 200 Fifth Ave Waltham MA 02451 781-890-4700 890-4701
TF: 866-964-6397 ■ *Web:* www.imninc.com

iModules Software Inc
5101 College Blvd Ste 300 Leawood KS 66211 913-888-0772
Web: www.imodules.com

Impact Makers Inc 1707 Summit Ave Ste 201 Richmond VA 23230 804-774-2600
Web: www.impactmakers.com

Impulse Point LLC 6810 New Tampa Hwy Ste 400 Lakeland FL 33815 863-802-3738
Web: www.impulse.com

In-Sys Solutions Inc
14048 W Petronella Dr Libertyville IL 60048 847-996-0400
Web: www.in-sys.com

Inc ommand Technologies Inc 21 W William St Corning NY 14830 607-936-5066
Web: incommandtechnologies.com

InCycle Software Inc
545 Promenade du Centropolis Ste 220 Laval QC H7T0A3 450-682-4777
TF: 800-565-0510 ■ *Web:* www.incyclesoftware.com

Indigo Dynamic Networks Llc
2413 W Algonquin Rd Algonquin IL 60102 888-464-6344
TF: 888-464-6344 ■ *Web:* www.indigodynamic.com

Indotronix International Corp (IIC)
331 Main St Poughkeepsie NY 12601 845-473-1137 473-1197
Web: www.iic.com

Indtai Inc 21525 Ridgetop Cir Ste 280 Sterling VA 20166 703-373-3188
Web: www.indtai.com

Indusa Technical Corp
1 TransAm Plz Dr Ste 350 Oakbrook Terrace IL 60181 630-424-1800
Web: www.indusa.com

Ineoquest Technologies Inc 170 Forbes Blvd Mansfield MA 02048 508-339-2497
Web: ineoquest.com

Inetsolution 250 Monroe NW Ste 400 Grand Rapids MI 49503 586-726-9490
TF: 855-728-5839 ■ *Web:* www.inetsolution.com

Infinity Software Development Inc
1901 Commonwealth Ln Tallahassee FL 32303 850-383-1011 383-1015
Web: www.infinity-software.com

Info-Link Technologies Inc
601 Pittsburgh Ave Mount Vernon OH 43050 740-393-3100
Web: www.infolinktechnologies.net

InfoGard Laboratories Inc
709 Fiero Ln Ste 25 San Luis Obispo CA 93401 805-783-0810
Web: www.infogard.com

Infolink 109 N Oregon St Ste 404c El Paso TX 79901 915-577-9466
Web: infolinksa.com

Inforeem Inc 1 Quality Pl Edison NJ 08820 732-494-4100
Web: www.inforeem.com

Phone Fax

Information Analysis Inc
11240 Waples Mill Rd Ste 201 Fairfax VA 22030 703-383-3000 293-7979
Web: www.infoa.com

Information Systems & Networks Corp (ISN)
10411 Motor City Dr Ste700 Bethesda MD 20817 301-469-0400 469-0767
Web: www.isncorp.com

Infosoft Group Inc 1123 N Water St Ste 400 Milwaukee WI 53202 414-278-0700
Web: www.milwaukeejobs.com

InfoSystems Inc 1317 Hickory Vly Rd Chattanooga TN 37421 423-624-6551
Web: www.infosystems.biz

Ingenium Corp
7474 Greenway Ctr Dr Maryland Trade Ctr II
Ste 800 Greenbelt MD 20770 301-883-9800
Web: www.ingenium.net

Innonet LLC 2 Huntley Rd Old Lyme CT 06371 860-395-0700
Web: www.innonetllc.com

Innosphere Systems Development Group Ltd
147 Wyndham St N Ste 306 Guelph ON N1H4E9 519-766-9726
Web: innosphere.ca

Innovasic Inc 5635 Jefferson St NE Ste A Albuquerque NM 87109 505-883-5263
Web: www.innovasic.com

Inovex Information Systems Inc
7240 Pkwy Dr Ste 140 Hanover MD 21076 443-782-1452
Web: www.inovexcorp.com

Insight Designs Web Solutions
2006 Broadway St 300 Boulder CO 80302 303-449-8567
Web: www.insightdesigns.com

Insite Computer Group Inc
8920 Woodbine Ave Ste 104 Markham ON L3R9W9 416-736-8386
Web: www.insite.ca

Insyst Inc 271 Rte 46 W Ste A201 Fairfield NJ 07004 973-227-6582
Web: www.insystus.com

Intecon LLC 1325 AeroPlz Dr Ste 105 Colorado Springs CO 80906 303-771-5337
Web: www.inteconusa.com

Integral Solutions LLC 450 Wofford St Spartanburg SC 29301 864-574-8161
Web: www.integralsg.com

Integrated Systems Analysts Inc
2001 N Beauregard St Ste 600 Alexandria VA 22311 703-824-0700 578-2626
TF: 800-929-1024 ■ *Web:* www.isa.com

Integration Partners Inc 12 Hayden Ave Lexington MA 02421 781-357-8100
Web: www.integrationpartners.com

Integri Net Solutions Inc
10020 W Fairview Ave 10 Boise ID 83704 208-376-0500
Web: www.insllc.net

Integridata Inc 7690 County 17 Blvd Cannon Falls MN 55009 507-263-9260
Web: www.integridata.com

Integrity Business Solutions Inc
9470 Annapolis Rd Lanham MD 20706 301-306-3100
Web: www.integritybsi.com

Integrity Tech Solutions
816 S Eldorado Rd Ste 4 Bloomington IL 61704 309-662-7723
Web: integrityts.com

Intelect Corp 4000 Dillon St Baltimore MD 21224 410-327-0020
Web: intelectcorp.com

Intelesys Corp 6797 Dorsey Rd Elkridge MD 21075 410-540-9755
Web: www.intelesyscorp.com

Intelli-Mine Inc 1200 Quail St Ste 270 Newport Beach CA 92660 949-486-2900
Web: www.intelli-mine.com

Intellicom Computer Consulting
1702 Second Ave Kearney NE 68847 308-237-0684
TF: 877-501-3375 ■ *Web:* www.intellicominc.com

Intelligent Decisions Inc
21445 Beaumeade Cir Ashburn VA 20147 703-554-1600
TF: 800-929-8331 ■ *Web:* www.intelligent.net

IntelliSoft Group LLC 61 Spit Brook Rd Nashua NH 03060 888-634-4464
TF: 888-634-4464 ■ *Web:* www.intellisoftgroup.com

Intelliswift Software Inc 2201 Walnut Ave Fremont CA 94538 510-490-9240
Web: www.intelliswift.com

Intellisys Technology LLC
1000 Jorie Blvd Ste 200 Oak Brook IL 60523 630-928-1111
Web: www.intellisystechnology.com

Intellys Corp 621 W College St Grapevine TX 76051 972-929-9000
Web: www.intellys.com

Interactive Business Systems Inc
2625 Butterfield Rd Oak Brook IL 60523 630-571-9100 571-2490
TF: 800-555-5427 ■ *Web:* www.ibs.com

Intercosmos Media Group Inc
650 Poydras St Ste 1150 New Orleans LA 70130 504-679-5170
Web: www.directnic.com

InterDev LLC
2650 Holcomb Bridge Rd Ste 310 Alpharetta GA 30022 770-643-4400
TF: 877-841-8069 ■ *Web:* www.interdev.com

InterNiche Technologies Inc
1999 S Bascom Ave Ste 700 Campbell CA 95008 408-540-1160
Web: www.iniche.com

InterRel Consulting Inc
The Rangers Ballpark in Arlington 1000 Ballpark Way
Ste 304 Arlington TX 76011 972-735-8716
Web: www.interrel.com

Intertech Training & Consulting Inc
25 Barcelona Ste 202 Irvine CA 92614 949-852-1165
Web: www.intertechconsulting.net

InterVision Systems Technologies Inc
2270 Martin Ave Santa Clara CA 95050 408-980-8550
TF: 800-787-6707 ■ *Web:* www.intervision.com

InterWorks Inc 1425 S Sangre Rd Stillwater OK 74074 405-624-3214
TF: 866-490-9643 ■ *Web:* www.interworks.com

Intraprisetechknowlogies LLC
3615 Harding Ave Ste 309 Honolulu HI 96816 808-735-8324
Web: www.intraprisetechknowlogies.com

IntraSystems Inc 3 Allied Dr Ste 103 Dedham MA 02026 781-986-1700
Web: www.intrasystems.com

Intrepid Control Systems Inc
5700 18 Mile Rd Sterling Heights MI 48314 586-731-7950
TF: 800-859-6265 ■ *Web:* www.intrepidcs.com

	City	State	Zip	Phone	Fax
Invizeon Corp 113 W Front St Ste 101 *Web:* www.invizeon.com	Missoula	MT	59802	406-543-4059	
Inyxa LLC 3501 W Algonguin Rd Ste 608 *Web:* inyxa.com	Rolling Meadows	IL	60008	224-325-4699	
IO Integration Inc 20480 Pacifica Dr Ste 1C *Web:* www.iointegration.com	Cupertino	CA	95014	408-996-3420	
IOActive Inc 701 Fifth Ave Ste 6850 *TF:* 866-760-0222 ■ *Web:* www.ioactive.com	Seattle	WA	98104	206-784-4313	
Iomer Internet Solutions 10110 107 St NW Ste 202 *Web:* www.iomer.com	Edmonton	AB	T5J1J4	780-424-3122	
IonIdea Inc 3913 Old Lee Hwy Ste 33B *Web:* www.ionidea.com	Fairfax	VA	22030	703-691-0400	
Ip Convergence Inc 416 Santa Fe Trl *Web:* www.ipcnv.com	Argyle	TX	76226	940-464-2900	
IP Network Solutions Inc 209 Elden St *Web:* www.ipnsinc.com	Herndon	VA	20170	703-787-0095	
Ipsmarx Technology Inc 11710 Plz America Dr Ste 2000 *Web:* www.ipsmarx.com	Reston	VA	20190	416-640-0375	
IQware Inc 5850 Coral Ridge Dr Ste 309 *TF:* 877-698-5151 ■ *Web:* www.iqwareinc.com	Coral Springs	FL	33076	954-698-5151	
Iris Software Inc 200 Metroplex Dr Ste 300 *Web:* www.irissoftware.com	Edison	NJ	08817	732-393-0034	393-0035
Irosoft 3100 Boul De La Cote-vertu *Web:* www.irosoft.com	Saint-laurent	QC	H4R2J8	514-920-0020	
ISG Prime LLC 12723 Mill Heights Ct *Web:* www.isgprime.com	Herndon	VA	20171	703-624-9409	
Isis It Inc 88 Vilcom Ctr Dr Ste 180 *TF:* 877-970-4747 ■ *Web:* www.isisit.com	Chapel Hill	NC	27514	919-932-6150	
Istech Inc 4691 Raycom Rd *Web:* www.istech-inc.com	Dover	PA	17315	717-764-5565	
IT Prophets LLC 3030 Woodbridge Ln *Web:* www.itprophets.com	Canton	GA	30114	770-335-1410	
IT Weapons 7965 Goreway Dr Unit 1 *Web:* www.itweapons.com	Brampton	ON	L6T5T5	905-494-1040	
Itcon Services Llc 3701 S George Mason Dr Unit 2502n *Web:* www.itcon-inc.com	Falls Church	VA	22041	703-671-6437	
Iteck Solutions Llc 4909 Morning Glory Ct *Web:* www.itecksolutions.com	Rockville	MD	20853	301-929-1852	
Itergy International Inc 2075 University Ste 700 *TF:* 866-522-5881 ■ *Web:* www.itergy.com	Montreal	QC	H3A2L1	514-845-5881	
ITSource Technology Inc 1401 Los Gamos Dr Ste 102 *TF:* 866-548-4911 ■ *Web:* www.itsourcetek.com	San Rafael	CA	94903	415-472-5700	
J K Datta Consultants Inc 711 W 40th St Ste 355 *Web:* www.datta-consultants.com	Baltimore	MD	21211	410-243-2882	
J4 Systems Inc 2521 Warren Dr Ste A *Web:* www.j4systems.com	Rocklin	CA	95677	916-303-7200	
Jacer Corp 10400 Eaton Pl Ste 501 *Web:* www.jacer.com	Fairfax	VA	22030	703-352-1964	
Jackson Technical LLC 427 S Boston Ave Ste 1010 *Web:* www.jacksontechnical.com	Tulsa	OK	74103	918-585-8324	
Jaekle Group Inc, The 1410 Highland Rd E *Web:* www.jaeklegroup.com	Macedonia	OH	44056	330-405-9353	
Jas Net Consulting Inc 2053 Grant Rd Ste 321 *Web:* jasnetconsulting.com	Los Altos	CA	94024	408-257-3279	
JASINT Consulting & Technologies LLC 6700 Alexander Bell Dr Ste 200 *Web:* www.jasint.com	Columbia	MD	21061	410-969-5573	
Jd Biggs & Associates Inc 12602 Bear Creek Ter *Web:* www.jdbiggs.com	Beltsville	MD	20705	410-322-8245	
Jibe Consulting Inc 5000 Meadows Rd Ste 300 *Web:* www.jibeconsulting.com	Lake Oswego	OR	97035	503-274-0788	
JKL Technologies Inc 501-I S Reno Rd Ste 355 *Web:* www.cos-jkl.com	Newbury Park	CA	91320	805-375-5820	
JMA Information Technology Inc 10551 Barkley Ste 400 *Web:* www.jmait.com	Overland Park	KS	66212	913-722-3252	
Jmk Systems Solutions Inc 20 Broadway Ave *Web:* www.jmkssi.com	Ipswich	MA	01938	978-356-8888	
Johnson-Laird Inc 850 NW Summit Ave *Web:* www.jli.com	Portland	OR	97210	503-274-0784	
Joint Technology Solution Inc 3919 Old Lee Hwy *Web:* jointtechnologysolution.net	Fairfax	VA	22030	703-218-0372	
Jonar Systems Inc 5645 Ch Saint-francois *Web:* www.jonar.com	Saint-laurent	QC	H4S1W6	514-335-5525	
Jrm Consultants Inc Po Box 90310 *Web:* www.jrmconsultants.com	Santa Barbara	CA	93190	805-564-3119	
Kanatek Technologies Inc 535 Legget Dr Ste 400 *TF:* 800-526-2821 ■ *Web:* www.kanatek.com	Kanata	ON	K2K3B8	613-591-1482	
KAP Project Services LTD 1200 Hwy 146 Ste 260 *Web:* www.kap.us.com	La Porte	TX	77571	281-842-8333	
Karabowicz & Associates 1215 Paramount Pkwy *Web:* karanet.com	Batavia	IL	60510	630-879-1360	
Karcher Group Inc 14221a Willard Rd Ste 1500 *Web:* www.karchergroup.com	Chantilly	VA	20151	703-631-6626	
Kemark Financial Services Inc 1 Blue Hill Plz 11th Fl *Web:* www.kemarkfinancial.com	Pearl River	NY	10965	845-620-9300	
Kemtah Group Inc 7601 Jefferson St NE Ste 120 *TF:* 877-753-6824 ■ *Web:* www.kemtah.com	Albuquerque	NM	87109	505-346-4900	
Kerrington Group Inc 24 S fifth St *Web:* www.kerringtongroup.com	Fernandina Beach	FL	32034	904-491-1411	
Key Software Systems LLC 5100 Belmar Blvd *Web:* www.keysoftwaresystems.com	Farmingdale	NJ	07727	732-409-6068	
Kezber i Solution 2685 Rue Hertel *Web:* www.kezber.com	Sherbrooke	QC	J1J2J4	819-566-6900	
KForce Government Soultions 2750 Prosperity Ave Ste 300 *TF:* 800-200-7465 ■ *Web:* www.kforcegov.com	Fairfax	VA	22031	703-245-7350	245-7560
Kinsey & Kinsey Inc 26 N Park Blvd *Web:* kinsey.com	Glen Ellyn	IL	60137	630-858-4866	
KiZan Technologies LLC 2900 Eastpoint Pkwy *Web:* www.kizan.com	Louisville	KY	40223	502-327-0333	
Kline Process Systems Inc 625 Spring St Ste 200 *Web:* www.kpsnet.com	Reading	PA	19610	610-371-0200	
KMP Designs Inc 7145 W Credit Ave Ste 101 *Web:* www.kmpdesigns.com	Mississauga	ON	L5N6J7	905-812-5635	
Kms Business Products Corp 3010 E Cervantes St *Web:* www.kmsbusiness.com	Pensacola	FL	32503	850-433-1131	
Knovation Inc 3630 Park 42 Dr Ste 170F *Web:* www.nettrekker.com	Cincinnati	OH	45241	513-731-4090	
Krove Corp 10180 Reflections Blvd *Web:* www.kroveonline.com	Sunrise	FL	33351	954-741-2972	
Kutir Corp 37600 Central Ct Ste 280 *Web:* www.kutirtech.com	Newark	CA	94560	510-402-4526	
Lafayette Data Systems Llc 605 S Buchanan St *Web:* www.lafayettedata.com	Lafayette	LA	70501	337-261-8999	
Lanair Group LLC 620 N Brand Blvd 6th Fl *Web:* www.lanairgroup.com	Glendale	CA	91203	323-512-7363	
Lancaster Systems Inc 411 Theodore Fremd Ave *Web:* www.lancastersys.com	Rye	NY	10580	914-967-5700	
Lantech LLC 1783 Tribute Rd Ste C *Web:* www.lantechllc.com	Sacramento	CA	95815	916-564-5455	
Launch Dynamic Media 292 Faust Rd *Web:* launchdm.com	Reading	PA	19608	610-898-1330	
Lauran Technology Corp 1 Hamilton Ave *Web:* www.laurantech.com	Cranford	NJ	07016	908-276-6262	
Lead IT Corp 1999 Wabash Ave Ste 210 *Web:* www.leaditgroup.com	Springfield	IL	62704	217-726-7250	
Leapfrog Services Inc 1605 Chantilly Dr Ste 300 *Web:* www.ribbit.net	Atlanta	GA	30324	404-870-2122	
Learning Worlds Inc 2647 Broadway Ste 5W *Web:* learningworlds.com	New York	NY	10025	212-725-0436	
Lectra USA Inc 889 Franklin Rd SE Bldg 100 *Web:* www.lectra.com	Marietta	GA	30067	770-422-8050	
Ledge Light Technologies Inc 88D Howard St Ste D *Web:* ledgelight.com	New London	CT	06320	860-444-0138	444-0274
Lek Technology Consultants Inc 12788 Gillard Rd *Web:* lekcomp.com	Winter Garden	FL	34787	407-877-6505	
Lextant Corp 580 N 4th St Ste 610 *Web:* www.lextant.com	Columbus	OH	43215	614-228-9711	
Lextech Inc 202 Wilson Downing Rd *Web:* www.lextechky.com	Lexington	KY	40517	859-278-9230	
Lightburn 325 E Chicago St Ste 301 *Web:* lightburn.co	Milwaukee	WI	53202	414-347-1866	
Lighthouse Computer Services Inc 6 Blackstone Valley Pl Ste 205 *TF:* 888-542-8030 ■ *Web:* www.lighthousecs.com	Lincoln	RI	02865	401-334-0799	334-0719
Linium LLC 187 Wolf Rd Ste 210 *Web:* www.linium.com	Albany	NY	12205	518-689-3198	
Link Medical Computing Inc 1208 B VFW Pkwy Ste 103 *Web:* www.linkmed.com	Boston	MA	02132	781-453-0300	
LinTech Global Inc 31600 W 13 Mile Rd Ste 122 *Web:* www.lintechglobal.com	Farmington Hills	MI	48334	248-851-8877	
Little Planet Learning 2963 Foster Creighton Dr Ste *Web:* www.littleplanet.com	Nashville	TN	37204	615-259-3733	
LiveTechnology Holdings Inc 16 Sterling Lk Rd LiveTechnology Park *Web:* www.livebuilder.com	Tuxedo Park	NY	10987	845-351-5100	
Livewire LLC 4900 W Clay St *Web:* www.getlivewire.com	Richmond	VA	23230	804-937-9001	
Locus Systems Inc 146 W Beaver Creek Rd Unit 1 *Web:* www.locussystems.com	Richmond Hill	ON	L4B1C2	905-948-0093	
Logic Solutions Inc 2929 Plymouth Rd Ste 207 *Web:* www.logicsolutions.com	Ann Arbor	MI	48105	734-930-0009	
Logicalis Inc 34505 W 12 Mile Rd Ste 210 *Web:* us.logicalis.com	Farmington Hills	MI	48331	248-957-5600	
Logicease Solutions Inc 1 Bay Plaza Ste 520 *TF:* 866-212-3273 ■ *Web:* complianceease.com	Burlingame	CA	94010	650-373-1111	
Logikal Solutions 3915 N 1800e Rd *Web:* www.logikalsolutions.com	Herscher	IL	60941	815-949-1593	
Login Consulting Services Inc 300 N Continental Blvd Ste 530 *Web:* www.loginconsult.com	El Segundo	CA	90245	310-607-9091	
Logistics Management Resources Inc 4300 Crossings Blvd *Web:* www.lmr-inc.com	Prince George	VA	23875	804-541-6193	541-2559
Look Matters 1815 Rae St Ste 202 *Web:* lookmatters.com	Regina	SK	S4T2E3	306-757-4686	

Company / Address	City	State	ZIP	Phone	Fax
Lucid Technology 1754 N Wilmot *Web:* www.lucidtec.com	Chicago	IL	60647	312-238-8976	
Lumtron Technologies Inc 820 E Terra Cotta Ave Ste 242 *Web:* www.lumtron.com	Crystal Lake	IL	60014	815-788-0088	
Lunar Cow 120 E Mill St Ste 415 *Web:* www.lunarcow.com	Akron	OH	44308	330-253-9000	
Lyniece Webstore Shopping 10201 W Pico Blvd *Web:* los-angeles.cylex-usa.com	Los Angeles	CA	90064	323-731-0220	
Lynx Computer Technologies Inc 7 Bristol Ct *TF:* 800-331-5969 ■ *Web:* lynxnet.com	Wyomissing	PA	19610	610-678-8131	
M Box Design 9234 Deering Ave *Web:* www.mboxdesign.com	Chatsworth	CA	91311	818-700-7770	
M R A Technologies 2502 Park Rd *Web:* www.mra-tech.com	Emerald Hills	CA	94062	650-361-8140	
M2ns Inc 6037 Frantz Rd Ste 103 *Web:* www.m2ns.com	Dublin	OH	43017	614-798-5177	
Maden Technologies 4601 N Fairfax Dr Ste 1030 *Web:* www.madentech.com	Arlington	VA	22203	703-940-3609	
Maestro Technologies Inc 1471 Boul Lionel Boulet *Web:* www.maestro.ca	Varennes	QC	J3X1P7	514-990-0864	
Magenium Solutions LLC 535 Pennsylvania Ave Ste 103 *Web:* www.magenium.com	Glen Ellyn	IL	60137	630-786-5900	
Mainline Information Systems Inc 1700 Summit Lk Dr *TF:* 866-490-6246 ■ *Web:* www.mainline.com	Tallahassee	FL	32317	850-219-5000	
MainSpring Inc 20010 Fisher Ave Ste E PO Box 505 *Web:* www.gomainspring.com	Poolesville	MD	20837	301-948-8077	
Mainstay Technologies 201 Daniel Webster Hwy *Web:* www.mstech.com	Belmont	NH	03220	603-524-4774	
Malaika Corp 3010 63rd Ave *Web:* www.malaikacorp.com	Hyattsville	MD	20785	240-235-6570	
Managed Business Solutions 12325 Oracle Blvd Ste 200 *Web:* www.thinkmbs.com	Colorado Springs	CO	80921	719-314-3400	314-3499
MANDEX Inc 12500 Fair Lakes Cir Ste 125 *Web:* www.mandex.com	Fairfax	VA	22033	703-227-0900	227-0910
Mandli Communications Inc 4801 Tradewinds Pkwy *TF:* 888-545-2214 ■ *Web:* mandli.com	Madison	WI	53718	608-835-3500	
Mantra Technologies LLC 1180 Arbor Creek Dr *Web:* www.mantrasys.com	Roswell	GA	30076	770-772-4678	
Marucco, Stoddard, Ferenbach & Walsh Inc 3445 Liberty Dr *Web:* www.msfw.com	Springfield	IL	62704	217-698-3535	
Mason Assocaites Inc 170 Us Rt 1 Ste 280 *Web:* www.masonassociates.com	Falmouth	ME	04105	207-347-3557	
Matricis Informatique Inc 1425 Rene-Levesque Blvd W Ste 240 *TF:* 866-394-0011 ■ *Web:* matricis.com	Montreal	QC	H3G1T7	514-394-0011	
Matrix Integration LLC 417 Main St *Web:* www.matrixintegration.com	Jasper	IN	47546	812-634-1550	
Matrix Technologies Inc 1760 Indian Wood Cir *Web:* matrixti.com	Maumee	OH	43537	419-897-7200	
Maverick Mesa Computer Specialties Inc 10814 W Orangewood Ave *Web:* mavmesa.com	Glendale	AZ	85307	623-872-1296	
Max It Group Inc 15 Rt 10 E Ste 205 *Web:* www.maxitgroupinc.com	Randolph	NJ	07869	973-343-2951	
Maximizer Software Inc 1090 W Pender St 10th Fl *Web:* www.maximizer.com	Vancouver	BC	V6E2N7	604-601-8000	
MCAD Technologies Inc 7450 W Alaska Dr *Web:* www.mcad.com	Lakewood	CO	80226	303-969-8844	
McCracken Financial Solutions Corp 8 Suburban Park Dr *Web:* www.mccrackenfs.com	Billerica	MA	01821	978-439-9000	
Mdl Enterprise Inc 9888 Southwest Fwy *TF:* 800-879-0840 ■ *Web:* www.mdlent.com	Houston	TX	77074	713-771-6350	
MediaPro Inc 20021 120th Ave NE Ste 102 *Web:* www.mediapro.com	Bothell	WA	98011	425-483-4700	
Medirect Inc 36380 Garfield Rd Ste 7 *Web:* www.medirectinc.com	Clinton Township	MI	48035	586-792-7777	
Medullan Inc 625 Mount Auburn St Ste 201 *Web:* www.medullan.com	Cambridge	MA	02138	617-547-0273	
Mentis Group 8330 Lyndon B Johnson Fwy Ste 450 *Web:* www.mentis-group.com	Dallas	TX	75243	214-691-7800	
Mercom Inc 313 Commerce Dr *TF:* 877-223-8330 ■ *Web:* www.mercomcorp.com	Pawleys Island	SC	29585	843-979-9957	979-9956
Merittech LLC 6700 Kirkville Rd Bldg B Ste 105	East Syracuse	NY	13057	315-234-4545	
Metters Industries Inc 8200 Greensboro Dr Ste 500 *Web:* www.metters.com	McLean	VA	22102	703-821-3300	821-3996
Micro Force Inc 505 Jericho Tpke *Web:* micro-force.com	Huntington Station	NY	11746	631-421-1030	
Micro Source Inc 655 Fairfield Ct *Web:* www.microsrc.com	Ann Arbor	MI	48108	734-669-8833	
Microserv Computer Techs Inc 1808 E 17th St *TF:* 866-988-7164 ■ *Web:* risebroadband.com	Idaho Falls	ID	83404	866-988-7164	
Microwest Software Systems Inc 10981 San Diego Mson Rd Ste 210 *Web:* www.microwestsoftware.com	San Diego	CA	92108	619-280-0440	
Microworks 359 Kent St Ste 301 *TF:* 877-232-3859 ■ *Web:* www.microworks.ca	Ottawa	ON	K2P0R6	613-232-3859	
Miles Technologies Inc 300 W Route 38 *TF:* 800-496-8001 ■ *Web:* www.milestechnologies.com	Moorestown	NJ	08057	856-439-0999	
Mills & Murphy Software Systems Inc 618 94th Ave N *Web:* www.millsmur.com	Saint Petersburg	FL	33702	727-577-1236	
MILVETS Systems Technology Inc 11825 High Tech Ave Ste 150 *Web:* www.milvets.com	Orlando	FL	32817	407-207-2242	
Mindwrap Inc 492 Blackwell Rd Ste 202 *Web:* www.mindwrap.com	Warrenton	VA	20186	540-347-2552	
Miragee Corp 2512 Merriwood Dr *Web:* www.miragee.com	Louisville	KY	40299	502-266-8768	
Mitchell and McCormick Inc 2165 W Park Ct Ste G *Web:* www.mandm.net	Stone Mountain	GA	30087	770-465-1511	
Mitchell-wayne Technologies 2901 3rd Ave N *Web:* www.mitchellwaynetech.com	Birmingham	AL	35203	205-313-7500	
Mobile Technical Services 70 Old Bloomfield Ave *Web:* mtsnj.com	Pine Brook	NJ	07058	973-808-2882	
Moc1 Solutions 2011 E Financial Way *Web:* moc1solutions.com	Glendora	CA	91741	626-610-1970	
Moment Design 13 Crosby St 6th Fl *Web:* www.momentnyc.com	New York	NY	10013	212-625-9744	
Moore Computing LLP 317 N 11th St Ste 200 *Web:* www.moorecomputing.com	Saint Louis	MO	63101	314-621-5585	
MorganFranklin Corp 1753 Pinnacle Dr Ste 1200 *Web:* www.morganfranklin.com	Mclean	VA	22102	703-564-7525	
Msi Tec Inc 8925 E Nichols Ave *Web:* www.msitec.com	Centennial	CO	80112	720-875-9835	
MSS Technologies Inc 1555 E Orangewood Ave *Web:* www.msstech.com	Phoenix	AZ	85020	602-387-2100	
Mtw Solutions LLC 3236 W Edgewood Dr Ste D *Web:* www.mtwsolutions.com	Jefferson City	MO	65109	573-893-7997	
Muller Systems Corp 926 Juliana Dr *Web:* www.mullersys.com	Woodstock	ON	N4V1B9	519-421-1800	
Multi Dimensional Integration 39 E Forrest Ave *Web:* www.mdiadvantage.com	Shrewsbury	PA	17361	717-227-1800	
Multicim Technologies Inc 16 Westminster ave N Ste 306C *Web:* www.multicim.com	Montreal West	QC	H4X1Z1	514-633-6401	
Multidev Technologies Inc 999 de Maisonneuve W Ste 1100 *Web:* chaindrive.com	Montreal	QC	H3A3L4	514-337-6465	
Multiple Media Inc 465 McGill St Office 1000 *Web:* www.multiplemedia.com	Montreal	QC	H2Y2H1	514-276-7660	
Mystikal Solutions LLC 431 Wolf Rd Ste 102	San Antonio	TX	78216	210-979-9300	
Mytech Partners Inc 2420 Long Lk Rd *Web:* www.mytech.com	Roseville	MN	55113	612-659-9800	
N Cell Systems Inc 1907 E Wayzata *Web:* ncell.com	Wayzata	MN	55391	952-746-5125	
N'Ware Technologies Inc 2885, 81e Rue *Web:* www.nwaretech.com	Saint-georges	QC	G6A0C5	418-227-4292	
Nbt Solutions LLC 188 State St Ste 200 *Web:* www.nbtsolutions.com	Portland	ME	04101	617-202-3088	
NCI Inc 11730 Plz America Dr Ste 700 *NASDAQ: NCIT* ■ *Web:* www.nciinc.com	Reston	VA	20190	703-707-6900	707-6901
Nebula Consulting Inc 207 Warwick Way *Web:* www.nebulaconsulting.com	North Wales	PA	19454	215-353-3141	
Nerd Force Inc 97 New Dorp Plz *Web:* www.nerdforce.com	Staten Island	NY	10306	718-370-6147	
NES Associates LLC 6400 Beulah St Ste 300 *Web:* www.nesassociates.com	Alexandria	VA	22310	703-224-2600	
Net Aspects 1499 Oliver Rd *Web:* netaspects.com	Fairfield	CA	94534	707-399-8060	
Netblaze Systems Inc 1299 Newell Hill Pl Ste 202 *Web:* www.netblaze.biz	Walnut Creek	CA	94596	925-932-1765	
Netcom Technologies Inc 313 N Berry St *Web:* netcomtechnologies.net	Brea	CA	92821	714-256-9229	
Netessentials Inc 705 Eighth St Ste 1000 *Web:* netess.net	Wichita Falls	TX	76301	940-767-6387	
Netgain Information Systems Co 220 Reynolds Ave *TF:* 855-651-7001 ■ *Web:* www.netgainis.com	Bellefontaine	OH	43311	937-593-7177	
Netlogix Inc 48 Court St *Web:* netlgx.com	Westfield	MA	01085	413-568-2777	
Netorian 98 S Main St *Web:* netorian.com	Allentown	NJ	08501	914-830-0629	
NetRate Systems Inc 3493 Woods Edge Dr *Web:* www.mcswin.com	Okemos	MI	48864	517-347-4900	
NetStandard Inc 2000 Merriam Ln *Web:* www.netstandard.com	Kansas City	KS	66106	913-262-3888	
Nettech LLC 1851 Hudson Ln *Web:* www.nettech.net	Monroe	LA	71201	318-387-0001	
NetVoyage Corp 2500 West Executive Pkwy Ste 350 *Web:* www.netdocuments.com	Lehi	UT	84043	801-226-6882	
Netway Solutions Inc 240 Palomino Dr *Web:* www.netwaysolutions.com	Salisbury	NC	28146	704-637-6155	
Netwize Inc 702 Confluence Ave *Web:* www.netwize.net	Salt Lake City	UT	84123	801-747-3200	
Network 2000 LLC 2100 N Nimitz Hwy *Web:* www.network2000-hi.com	Honolulu	HI	96819	808-848-0000	
Network America Inc 118 107th Ave *TF:* 877-624-8311 ■ *Web:* ldms.com	Treasure Island	FL	33706	877-624-8311	
Network Center Communications Inc 2536 West Main Ave *Web:* www.netcentersupply.com	Fargo	ND	58078	701-235-8100	

	Phone	Fax

Network Data Systems Inc
50 E Commerce Dr Ste 120 Schaumburg IL 60173 847-385-6700
Web: www.network-data.com

Network Directions PO Box 511466 Milwaukee WI 53203 414-269-2555
Web: www.net-directions.com

Network Insight LLC
10717 Sorrento Valley Rd Ste 100 San Diego CA 92121 858-450-1180
Web: www.centerbeam.com

Network Performance Inc
85 Green Mtn Dr South Burlington VT 05403 802-859-0808
TF: 800-639-6091 ■ *Web:* www.npi.net

Network Republic 639 Tully Rd San Jose CA 95111 408-993-1075
Web: www.networkrepublic.net

Network Specialty Group Inc
20251 Century Blvd Germantown MD 20874 301-208-9388
Web: www.nsgi-hq.com

Network Synergy Corp 126 Monroe Tpke Trumbull CT 06611 203-261-2201
Web: www.netsynergy.com

Network Vigilance LLC
10731 Treena St Ste 200 San Diego CA 92131 858-695-8676
Web: www.networkvigilance.com

Networks & More Inc 24 Highland Bnd Island Heights NJ 08732 732-929-1485
Web: andmore.com

Networks of Florida 111 N Baylen St Pensacola FL 32502 850-434-8600
Web: www.nof.com

Netwoven Inc 3837 Stone Pointe Way Pleasanton CA 94588 925-931-9390
Web: www.netwoven.com

Netx Llc 1602 Sibley Ct Sheboygan WI 53081 414-303-5503
Web: www.netxllc.com

NetXperts Inc 2680 Bishop Dr Ste 102 San Ramon CA 94583 925-806-0800
Web: www.netxperts.com

NetXposure Inc 735 SW First Ave 3rd Fl Portland OR 97204 503-499-4342
Web: netx.net

Netxusa Inc 231 Beverly Rd Greenville SC 29609 864-271-9868
Web: www.netxusa.com

Neuro Logic Systems Inc
451 Constitution Ave Camarillo CA 93012 805-389-5435
Web: www.nlsdisplays.com/index.html

Nevo Technologies Inc 26 Church St Cambridge MA 02138 617-354-6386
Web: www.nevo.com

New Age Technologies Inc
819 W Main St Ste 200 Louisville KY 40202 502-412-6681
Web: www.newat.com

New Target Inc 815 N Royal St Ste 100 Alexandria VA 22314 703-548-3433
Web: www.newtarget.com

New Technologies Inc 4380 Baldwin Rd Holly MI 48442 810-694-5426 694-1183
Web: www.newtechnologiesinc.com

New Wave Industries Inc 135 Day St Newington CT 06111 860-953-9283
Web: www.newwaveindustries.com

NewAgeSys Inc
231 Clarksville Rd Ste 200 Princeton Junction NJ 08550 609-919-9800 919-9830
TF: 888-863-9243 ■ *Web:* www.newagesys.com

Nex Computing Solutions Inc
7404 W Detroit St Ste 100 Chandler AZ 85226 480-838-0287
Web: www.nexedge.com

NexLevel Information Technology Inc
6829 Fair Oaks Blvd Ste 100 Carmichael CA 95608 916-692-2000
Web: www.nexlevelit.com

Next Eon Com 40 Meriam St Wakefield MA 01880 781-231-3200
Web: www.nexteon.com

NextGate Solutions Inc
3579 E Foothill Blvd Ste 587 Pasadena CA 91107 626-376-4100
Web: www.nextgate.com

Nintex USA LLC 10800 NE Eighth St Ste 400 Bellevue WA 98004 425-324-2400
Web: www.nintex.com

Nityo Infotech Corporation Inc
2652 Hidden Valley Dr Ste 303 Pittsburgh PA 15241 724-941-1067
Web: www.nityo.com

Nobel Systems Inc
436 E Vanderbilt Way San Bernardino CA 92408 909-890-5611
Web: www.nobel-systems.com

Northern Data Systems Inc 362 US Route One Falmouth ME 04105 207-781-3236
Web: www.ndsys.com

Northlan Solutions Inc 2370 County Rd J Saint Paul MN 55110 651-653-4866

NOTSOLDSEPARATELY.COM 2 Friends Ave Medford NJ 08055 856-727-8200
Web: www.notsoldseparately.com

Novacoast Inc 1505 Chapala St Santa Barbara CA 93101 800-949-9933
TF: 800-949-9933 ■ *Web:* www.novacoast.com

Novanis 3161 W White Oaks Dr Ste 100 Springfield IL 62704 217-698-0999
Web: www.novanis.com

NOVIPRO Inc 2055 Peel St Ste 701 Montreal QC H3A1V4 514-744-5353
TF: 866-726-5353 ■ *Web:* www.novipro.com

Novix Network Specialists Inc
2000 W Main St Ste J Saint Charles IL 60174 630-443-0036
Web: www.novixinc.com

Novo Solutions Inc
516 S Independence Blvd Virginia Beach VA 23452 757-687-6590
TF: 888-316-4559 ■ *Web:* www.novosolutions.com

Nowcom Corp 4751 Wilshire Blvd Ste 115 Los Angeles CA 90010 323-692-4040
Web: www.nowcom.com

nQueue Inc 7890 S Hardy Dr Ste 105 Tempe AZ 85284 800-299-5933
TF: 800-299-5933 ■ *Web:* www.nqueue.com

Ntegrity Networks 9652 Canberra Dr Littleton CO 80130 303-221-0738
Web: ntegritynetworks.com

Nth Generation Computing Inc
17055 Camino San Bernardo San Diego CA 92127 858-451-2383
Web: www.nth.com

NTT DATA, Inc 100 City Sq Boston MA 02129 800-745-3263 624-7940*
**Fax Area Code: 972* ■ *TF:* 800-745-3263 ■ *Web:* americas.nttdata.com

Numeric Computer Systems Inc 275 Oser Ave Hauppauge NY 11788 631-486-9000
Web: www.ncssuite.com

Nutech Information Systems
1010 Summer St Ste 406 Stamford CT 06905 203-961-8911
Web: www.nutechsoft.com

	Phone	Fax

Nutechs LLC
6785 Telegraph Rd Ste 350 Bloomfield Hills MI 48301 248-593-5700
Web: www.nutechs.com

nuTravel Technology Solutions LLC
181 Westchester Ave Ste 302 Port Chester NY 10573 914-848-4566
Web: www.nutravel.com

NuWare Technology Corp Inc
100 Wood Ave S Ste 122 Iselin NJ 08830 732-494-0550 494-4586
Web: www.nuware.com

Nvision Networking Inc 7450 N Thornydale Rd Tucson AZ 85741 520-219-6040
Web: nvisionnet.com

O'Neil Software Inc 11 Cushing Ste 100 Irvine CA 92618 949-458-1234
Web: oneilsoft.com

Oak Hill Technology Inc 12505-A Trl Dr St Austin TX 78737 512-288-0008
Web: www.oakhilltech.com

Oakland Consulting Group Inc
9501 Sheridan St Ste 200 Lanham MD 20706 301-577-4111
Web: www.ocg-inc.com

Oakwood Systems Group Inc
622 Emerson Rd Ste 350 Saint Louis MO 63141 314-824-3000
Web: www.oakwoodsys.com

Oar Net 1224 Kinnear Rd Columbus OH 43212 614-292-1956
TF: 800-627-6420 ■ *Web:* www.oar.net

Oasis Technology Inc 601 E Daily Dr Ste 226 Camarillo CA 93010 805-445-4833
Web: www.oasistechnology.com

Oculus VisionTech Inc
507 837 W Hastings St Vancouver BC V6C3N6 604-685-1017
Web: www.oculusvisiontech.com

ODIN Technologies Inc
21631 Red Rum Dr Ste 165 Ashburn VA 20147 703-968-0000
Web: www.ODINRFID.com

Odyssey Systems Consulting Group Ltd
201 Edgewater Dr Ste 270 Wakefield MA 01880 781-245-0111 245-5858
Web: www.odysseyconsult.com

Office Automation Technologies
11919 W. 1-70 Frontage Rd N Ste 123 Wheat Ridge CO 80033 303-202-5151
Web: www.oati1.com

Official Payments Corp 3550 Engineering Dr Norcross GA 30092 770-325-3100 325-3099
TF: 877-754-4413 ■ *Web:* www.officialpayments.com

Ohio Computer Aided Engineering Inc
1612 Georgetown Rd Hudson OH 44236 330-552-2301
Web: www.simutechgroup.com

Oic Group Inc 112 State St Ste Llb Peoria IL 61602 309-680-5600
Web: oicgroup.net

Okiok Data Ltd
655 Promenade du Centropolis Ste 230 Laval QC H7T0A3 450-681-1681
Web: www.okiok.com

Olmec Systems Inc 85 Bloomfield Ave Denville NJ 07834 973-586-6590
Web: www.olmec.com

Omni Data Llc 11 Research Dr Ste 1 Woodbridge CT 06525 203-747-7890
Web: www.omnianswers.net

Omni Information Systems Inc
1130 Hurricane Shoals Rd Ste 2600 Lawrenceville GA 30043 678-377-5560
Web: www.omni-info.com

Omnilogic Systems Inc 1420 Broad St Regina SK S4R1Y9 306-586-6116
Web: www.omnilogic.net

Omnistar Interactive Llc 9261 Red Cart Ct Columbia MD 21045 410-730-2188
Web: www.omnistaretools.com

Omnitech Labs Inc
215 Boul Du Seminaire S Saint-jean-sur-richelieu QC J3B8W1 450-359-0891
Web: www.omnitechlabs.net

Oncall Interactive LLC
216 Southfferson Ste 602 Chicago IL 60661 312-226-1259
Web: www.oncallinteractive.com

One Dot Systs Inc 5071 S State Rd 7 Ste 712 Davie FL 33314 954-327-1490
Web: www.onedotsystems.com

ONESPRING LLC
980 Birmingham Rd Ste 501-165 Alpharetta GA 30004 888-472-1840
TF: 888-472-1840 ■ *Web:* www.onespring.net

OnPath Business Solutions Inc
St Joseph's Bldg 1165 Kenaston St Ottawa ON K1B3N9 613-564-6565
Web: www.onpath.com

Open Technology Solutions LLC
8085 S Chester St Ste 100 Centennial CO 80112 303-708-7140
Web: www.open-techs.com

Oproma Inc 116 Av Gatineau Gatineau QC J8T4J6 819-568-4069
Web: www.oproma.com

Opsol Integrators Inc 1566 La Pradera Dr Campbell CA 95008 408-364-9915
TF: 800-996-7765 ■ *Web:* www.opsol.com

Optibase Inc 625 Ellis St Ste 102 Mountain View CA 94043 650-230-2400
Web: www.optibase.com

Optima Telecom Inc 4-20 Cachet Woods Court Markham ON L6C3G1 905-477-0987
Web: www.optimatele.com

Optimal Data Group Inc
251 Laurier Ave W Ste 900 Gloucester ON K1P5J6 613-566-7080
Web: www.optimal.ca

Oracular Inc 300 Ohio St Oshkosh WI 54902 920-303-0470
Web: www.oracular.com

Orlantech Inc 230 Lookout Pl Maitland FL 32751 407-228-7290
Web: www.orlantech.com

Osbee Industries Inc 99 Calvert St 100 Harrison NY 10528 914-777-6611
Web: osbee.com

OSHEAN Inc 6946 Post Rd Ste 402 North Kingstown RI 02852 401-398-7500
Web: www.oshean.org

Osprey Software & Systems Inc 13 Osprey Dr Berkley MA 02779 508-821-4486
Web: ospreyss.com

OUTSOURCEIT Inc 6810 Crain Hwy La Plata MD 20646 301-539-0200
Web: www.outsourceitcorp.com

P C Assistance Inc
3200 S Shackleford Rd Ste 9 Little Rock AR 72205 501-907-4722
Web: www.pcassistance.com

P3 Inc 621 Shrewsbury Ave Shrewsbury NJ 07702 732-530-0202
Web: www.pereless.com

Phone Fax

Pachyderm Consulting LLC
66 W 38th St Apt 11k Ste 33c....New York NY 10018 212-629-7600
Web: pachyderm.net

Pacific Software Publishing Inc
1404 140th Pl NE....Bellevue WA 98007 425-957-0808
Web: www.pspinc.com

Pacificad Inc 159 S Lincoln St....Spokane WA 99201 509-326-7789
Web: www.pacificad.com

Pandell Technology Corp
4838 Richard Rd SW Ste 400....Calgary AB T3E6L1 403-271-0701
Web: www.pandell.com

Paradata Financial Systems
640 Cepi Dr Ste B....Chesterfield MO 63005 636-530-4545
Web: paradatafinancial.com

Paradigm Software Technologies Inc
9 E 40th St 9th Fl....New York NY 10016 646-558-1950
Web: www.pdmtech.com

Paragon Data Systems Inc 2218 Superior Ave....Cleveland OH 44114 216-621-7571
Web: www.paragondatasystems.com

Paragus Strategic I T 112 Russell St....Hadley MA 01035 413-587-2666
Web: paragusit.com/

Parallel Edge Inc 126 E Beechtree Ln....Wayne PA 19087 610-293-0101
Web: www.paralleledge.com

Passageways LLC
1551 Win Hentschel Blvd....West Lafayette IN 47906 765-497-8829
Web: www.passageways.com

Pavliks Com 80 Bell Farm Rd....Barrie ON L4M5K5 705-726-2966
TF: 877-728-5457 ■ *Web:* www.pavliks.com

PC Care Inc 221 Parking Way....Lake Jackson TX 77566 979-297-1117
Web: www.pccare-inc.com

PC Guardian Anti-Theft Products Inc
2171 E Francisco Blvd Ste G....San Rafael CA 94901 415-259-3103
Web: www.pcguardian.com

PC Works Plus Inc 109 Stadium Dr PO Box 190....Bellwood PA 16617 814-742-9750
Web: www.pcworksplus.com

Pcm Networking
12995 Cleveland Ave Ste 216....Fort Myers FL 33907 239-334-1615
Web: www.pcmnetworking.com

PDX Inc & Affiliates 101 Jim Wright Fwy S....Fort Worth TX 76108 817-246-6760
Web: pdxinc.com

PEAK Resources Inc 2750 W Fifth Ave....Denver CO 80204 303-934-1200
Web: www.peakresources.com

Peaksware LLC 2770 Dagny Way Ste 212....Lafayette CO 80026 720-406-1839
Web: www.peaksware.com

Penguin Computing Inc 45800 Northport Loop W....Fremont CA 94538 415-954-2800
Web: www.penguincomputing.com

Phacil Inc 601 California St....San Francisco CA 94108 703-526-1800
Web: phacil.com

Phin Solutions Inc 18318 Joplin St NW....Elk River MN 55330 763-633-7007
Web: www.phinsolutions.com

Phoenix Integration Inc
1275 Drummers Ln One Glenhardie Corporate Ctr
Ste 105....Wayne PA 19087 610-971-9603
Web: www.phoenix-int.com

Phoinix Group Inc, The
16308 Calidonia Ste 100 - 105....Tampa FL 33624 813-962-4000
Web: www.phoinixgroup.com

Pi Tech 522 Shafor Blvd....Dayton OH 45419 937-272-1813

Pico Envirotec Inc 222 Snidercroft Rd....Concord ON L4K2K1 905-760-9512
Web: www.picoenvirotec.com

Pinnacle Technical Resources Inc
5501 Lyndon B Johnson Fwy....Dallas TX 75240 214-740-2424
Web: pinnacle1.com

PIREL Inc 1250 Nobel Ste 190....Boucherville QC J4B5H1 450-449-5199
TF: 800-449-7196 ■ *Web:* www.pirel.com

Pj Cook Web Designs Inc
2034 Rainbow Farms Dr....Safety Harbor FL 34695 727-712-9493
Web: pjcook.com

Planet Personal Agency Inc 55 Yonge St....Toronto ON M5E1J4 416-363-9888
Web: www.planet4it.com

Planned Systems International Inc
10632 Lttle Patuxent Pkwy....Columbia MD 21044 410-964-8000 964-8001
TF: 800-275-7749 ■ *Web:* www.plan-sys.com

Plaudit Design 2470 University Ave W....Saint Paul MN 55114 651-646-0696
Web: www.plauditdesign.com

Plexsys Interface Products Inc
4900 NW Camas Meadows Dr....Camas WA 98607 360-838-2500
Web: www.plexsys.com

Point Alliance Inc 20 Adelaide St E Ste 500....Toronto ON M5C2T6 416-943-0001
TF: 855-947-6468 ■ *Web:* www.pointalliance.com

Point of Sale System Services Inc
2 Shaker Rd Ste F100....Shirley MA 01464 978-425-3003
Web: pssmobilety.com

Pointe Technology Group Inc
7272 Pk Cir Dr Ste 200....Hanover MD 21076 410-712-9425
Web: www.pointetech.com

Pomeroy IT Solutions Inc 1020 Petersburg Rd....Hebron KY 41048 859-586-0600 586-4414
TF: 800-846-8727 ■ *Web:* www.pomeroy.com

Portland Webworks Inc 5 Milk St 2nd Fl....Portland ME 04101 207-773-6600
Web: www.portlandwebworks.com

Portola Systems Inc 7064 Corline Ct Ste B5....Sebastopol CA 95472 707-824-8800
Web: www.portolasystems.net

Potrero Media Corp 3043 Mission St....San Francisco CA 94110 415-974-1445
Web: www.potreromedia.com

PowerPhone Inc 1321 Boston Post Rd....Madison CT 06443 203-245-8911
Web: www.powerphone.com

PowerVision Inc 260 Harbor Blvd....Belmont CA 94002 650-620-9948
Web: powervisionlens.com

Practice Velocity LLC
8777 Velocity Dr....Machesney Park IL 61115 815-544-7480
Web: www.practicevelocity.com

Prairie Inc 1260 Iroquois Dr Ste 300....Naperville IL 60563 630-983-6400
Web: www.prairieinc.com

Preclick Corp 140 Ocean Blvd....Atlantic Highlands NJ 07716 732-291-7269
Web: www.preclick.com

Predictix Inc
1349 W Peachtree St NW Two Midtown Plz
Ste 1880....Atlanta GA 30309 404-478-2090
Web: www.predictix.com

Preferred Systems Solutions Inc
1945 Old Gallows Rd Ste 450....Vienna VA 22182 703-663-2777 663-2780
TF: 877-422-7149 ■ *Web:* www.pssfed.com

Premcom Corp 85 Northpointe Pkwy Ste 100....Amherst NY 14228 716-691-0791
Web: www.premcom.com

Premier Network Solutions Inc
5070 Oaklawn Dr....Cincinnati OH 45227 513-631-6381
Web: prenet.com

Prescient Infotech Inc 3930 Pender Dr Ste 160....Fairfax VA 22030 703-218-6233
Web: www.prescientinfotech.com

Presidio Networked Solutions Inc
7601 Ora Glen Dr Ste 100....Greenbelt MD 20770 301-313-2000 313-2400
TF: 800-452-6926 ■ *Web:* www.presidio.com

Presteligence Inc 8328 Cleveland Ave NW....Canton OH 44720 330-305-6960
Web: www.presteligence.com

Pro It Co 258 W 31st St....Chicago IL 60616 312-225-6847
Web: www.proitco.com

Proactive Networking 229 Marshall Rd....Platte City MO 64079 816-587-7878
TF: 800-255-6863 ■ *Web:* www.proactivekc.com

Procase Consulting 180 Caster Ave Unit 55....Woodbridge ON L4L5Y7 905-856-7479
Web: www.procaseconsulting.com

Process Data Control Corp
1803-A W Park Row Dr....Arlington TX 76013 817-459-4488
Web: www.pdccorp.com

Professional Software Engineering Inc
780 Lynnhaven Pkwy Ste 350....Virginia Beach VA 23452 757-431-2400 463-1071
TF: 800-924-1091 ■ *Web:* www.prosoft-eng.com

Progeny Systems Corp 9500 Innovation Dr....Manassas VA 20110 703-368-6107
Web: progeny.net

Progi-media Inc 1040 Boul Michele-bohec....Blainville QC J7C5E2 514-272-0599
Web: www.progi-media.com

Promedia Technology Services
535 Route 46....Little Falls NJ 07424 973-253-7600
Web: www.promedianj.com

Pronet Solutions Inc
4313 E Cotton Ctr Blvd Ste 120....Phoenix AZ 85040 602-650-1100
Web: www.pronetsol.com

Prophet Systems Innovations 214 N Spruce St....Ogallala NE 69153 308-284-3007
Web: www.rcsworks.com

Prosite Business Solutions
732 3rd St....New Martinsville WV 26155 304-455-5900
Web: www.probusinesstools.com

Protocol Networks Inc 15 Shore Dr....Johnston RI 02919 877-676-0146
TF: 877-676-0146 ■ *Web:* www.protocolnetworks.com

ProTrak International Inc
237 W 35th St Ste 507....New York NY 10001 212-265-9833
Web: www.protrak.com

Provade Inc 770 N Jefferson St Ste 230....Milwaukee WI 53202 414-395-8050
Web: www.provade.com

Psychological Services Inc
2950 N Hollywood Way Ste 200....Burbank CA 91505 818-847-6180
Web: corporate.psionline.com

Psychsoft PO Box 232....Quincy MA 02171 617-471-8733
Web: www.psych-soft.com

PTS Data Center Solutions Inc 16 Thornton Rd....Oakland NJ 07436 201-337-3833
Web: www.ptsdcs.com

Publish Or Perish Inc 825 E Roosevelt Rd....Lombard IL 60148 630-627-7227
Web: www.publishorperish.com

Punchcut LLC 170 Maiden Ln....San Francisco CA 94108 415-445-8855
Web: punchcut.com

Pup Group Inc Dba Enlighten, The
3027 Miller Rd....Ann Arbor MI 48103 734-668-6678 668-1883

Q.A. Technologies Inc 222 S 15th St Ste 1404....Omaha NE 68102 402-391-9200
Web: www.qat.com

QA Systems Inc 503 Oakland Ave....Austin TX 78703 713-396-0792
Web: www.qasystems.com

Qcera Inc 11041 Santa Monica Blvd Ste 818....Los Angeles CA 90025 310-473-7988
Web: www.qcera.com

Qdigital Corp 6037 S Ft Apache Rd Ste 100....Las Vegas NV 89148 702-360-9371
Web: www.qdigital.com

Quadrant 4 System Corp
1501 Woodfield Rd Ste 205....Rolling Meadows IL 60173 732-798-3000
Web: www.qfor.com

Quadrus Development Inc
640 - Eighth Ave SW Ste 400....Calgary AB T2P1G7 403-257-0850
Web: www.quadrus.com

Qualex Consulting Services Inc
4300 Biscayne Blvd....Miami FL 33137 877-887-4727
TF: 877-887-4727 ■ *Web:* www.qlx.com

Quikteks LLC 373 US 46....Fairfield NJ 07004 973-882-4644
Web: www.quikteks.com

QVS Software Inc 5950 Six Forks Rd....Raleigh NC 27609 919-676-1991
Web: qvssoftware.com

R & d Industries Inc 812 10th St....Milford IA 51301 712-338-2999
Web: www.rdi1.com

Radiant Networks Services Inc
13000 Middletown Industrial Blvd Ste D....Louisville KY 40223 502-379-4800
Web: www.radiant-networks.com

Radical Systems Solutions Inc
360 S Coyote Ln....Anaheim CA 92808 714-280-1619
Web: www.radicalsys.com

Ranac Computer Corp
4181 E 96th St Ste 280....Indianapolis IN 46240 317-844-0141
TF: 800-844-0141 ■ *Web:* ranac.com

Rapier Solutions Inc 3095 Senna Dr....Matthews NC 28105 704-321-2271
Web: www.rapiersolutions.com

RCO Systems Inc 251 James Jackson Ave....Cary NC 27513 919-319-3612
Web: www.rconet.com

Company	City	State	ZIP	Phone	Fax
Realized Financial Solutions Inc 17 Farmington Av Ste T4 *Web:* www.realizedfinancialsolutions.com	Plainville	CT	06062	860-747-0002	
Reb's Web Design & Computer Tech Support LLC 7965 Pipers Path *Web:* www.rebswebdesign.com	Glen Burnie	MD	21061	410-209-0285	
Redman Technologies Inc 10172-108 St *Web:* www.redmantech.com	Edmonton	AB	T5J1L3	780-425-6270	
Redondo Systems Inc 23326 Hawthorne Blvd *Web:* www.redondosystems.com	Torrance	CA	90505	310-375-9923	
Redwood Network Services 804 N Meadowbrook Dr Ste 135 *Web:* pendello.com	Olathe	KS	66062	913-254-1005	
RefurbUPS com Inc 379 Spook Rock Rd Bldg J *Web:* www.refurbups.com	Suffern	NY	10901	845-357-6911	
Relate Corp 900 Avenida Acaso Ste K *TF:* 800-428-3708 ■ *Web:* relate.com	Camarillo	CA	93012	805-482-7381	
Rembrandt Group LLC, The 2 N Rd Ste 3 *Web:* www.rembrandtgroup.com	Warren	NJ	07059	732-356-1600	
Remote Operations Co 200 Pakerland Dr *Web:* www.roccompany.com	Green Bay	WI	54303	920-437-4466	
Rendersoft Inc 5801 Christie Ave Ste 275 *Web:* www.rendersoftinc.com	Emeryville	CA	94608	510-652-3936	
Research Data Inc 3900 Carolina Ave *Web:* www.researchdata.com	Richmond	VA	23222	804-643-3468	
Resnet 1119 Brentfield Dr *Web:* www.resnet.org	Mc Lean	VA	22101	703-506-0203	
Revelex Corp 6405 Congress Ave Ste 120 *Web:* www.revelex.com	Boca Raton	FL	33487	561-988-5588	
Revision Technologies Inc 30 Richard Rd *Web:* www.revisiontek.com	Edison	NJ	08820	732-318-6175	
Rex Black Consulting Services Inc 31520 Beck Rd *TF:* 866-438-4830 ■ *Web:* www.rbcs-us.com	Bulverde	TX	78163	830-438-4830	
Rgen Solutions 4156 148th Ave Ne Bldg I *TF:* 800-745-0615 ■ *Web:* www.rgensolutions.com	Redmond	WA	98052	425-867-1350	
RhinoCorps Limited Co 1128 Pennsylvania St NE Ste 100 *Web:* www.rhinocorps.com	Albuquerque	NM	87110	505-323-9836	
River Run Computers Inc 2320 W Camden Rd *Web:* www.river-run.com	Milwaukee	WI	53209	414-228-7474	
Rivercrest Technologies Inc 3811 Creekside Ln *Web:* www.rcrest.com	Holmen	WI	54636	608-779-2000	
RiverPoint Group LLC 2200 E Devon Ave Ste 385 *TF:* 800-297-5601 ■ *Web:* www.riverpoint.com	Des Plaines	IL	60018	847-233-9600	233-9602
Rj Computer Networks Inc 13215 E Penn St Ste 210 *Web:* www.rjcomputers.com	Whittier	CA	90602	562-464-3644	
RJT Compuquest Inc 222 N Sepulveda Blvd Ste 2250 *Web:* rjtcompuquest.com	El Segundo	CA	90245	310-378-6666	
Rockport Technology Group Inc 5 Industrial Way Ste 2C *Web:* www.rockporttech.com	Salem	NH	03079	603-681-0333	
Rolta Tusc Inc 333 E Butterfield Rd Ste 900 *TF:* 800-755-8872 ■ *Web:* www.rolta.com	Lombard	IL	60148	630-960-2909	
Root Group Inc, The 1790 30th St Ste 140 *Web:* www.rootgroup.com	Boulder	CO	80301	303-447-8093	
Rophi Technical Services East 814 S Rosedale Ct *Web:* www.rophi.com	Grosse Pointe Woods	MI	48236	313-417-2021	
Royal Technocrats Inc 7447 Harwin Dr Ste 270 *Web:* royaltechnocrats.com	Houston	TX	77036	713-776-8300	
RTL Networks Inc 2460 W 26th Ave Ste 250 C *Web:* www.rtl-networks.com	Denver	CO	80211	303-757-3100	
RuleSpace LLC 1925 NW AmberGlen Pkwy Ste 210 *Web:* www.rulespace.com	Beaverton	OR	97006	503-290-5100	
Ryjac Computer Solutions Inc 18851 Bardeen Ave *Web:* www.ryjacsolutions.com	Irvine	CA	92612	949-253-9550	
Sabre Solution, The 200 East 31st St *TF:* 888-494-7200 ■ *Web:* www.sabre-tech.com	Savannah	OK	31401	912-355-7200	
Sagitec Solutions LLC 422 County Rd D E *Web:* sagitec.com	Little Canada	MN	55117	612-284-7130	
SAI Systems International Inc 12 Progress Dr *Web:* www.saisystems.com	Shelton	CT	06484	203-929-0790	
Sakki Computers Inc 22B Hempstead Tpke *Web:* www.sakki.com	Farmingdale	NY	11735	516-293-1609	
Sans Inc 10 White Wood Ln *Web:* www.sansinc.com	North Branford	CT	06471	203-488-0046	
Saturno Design 208 SW Stark St 4th Fl *Web:* www.saturnodesign.com	Portland	OR	97204	503-478-1830	
Saucon Technologies Inc 2455 Baglyos Cir *Web:* www.saucontds.com	Bethlehem	PA	18020	484-241-2500	
Sayers Group LLC 825 Corporate Woods Pkwy *TF:* 800-323-5357 ■ *Web:* www.sayers.com	Vernon Hills	IL	60061	800-323-5357	
Scanbuy Inc 10 E 39th St 10th Fl *Web:* www.scanbuy.com	New York	NY	10016	212-278-0178	
SCC Soft Computer Inc 5400 Tech Data Dr *TF:* 800-763-8352 ■ *Web:* www.softcomputer.com	Clearwater	FL	33760	727-789-0100	789-0124
Schuur Solutions 2500 E Imperial Hwy Ste 201 *Web:* schuur.com	Brea	CA	92821	714-986-9990	
Scorpion Design Inc 28480 Ave Stanford Ste 100 *TF:* 866-622-5648 ■ *Web:* www.scorpion.co	Valencia	CA	91355	866-622-5648	
Sda Consulting Inc 3011 183rd St # 377 *TF:* 800-823-2990 ■ *Web:* www.sdaci.com	Homewood	IL	60430	800-823-2990	
Securance LLC 6922 W Linebaugh Ave Ste 101 *TF:* 877-578-0215 ■ *Web:* www.securanceconsulting.com	Tampa	FL	33625	877-578-0215	
SecureInfo Corp 211 N Loop 1604 E Ste 200 *TF:* 888-677-9351 ■ *Web:* www.secureinfo.com	San Antonio	TX	78232	210-403-5600	
Seitel Leeds & Associates Inc 1200 Post Aly Ste 2 *Web:* www.sla.com	Seattle	WA	98101	206-832-2875	
Select Computing Inc 3001 Broadway St NE Ste 655 *Web:* www.selectcomputing.com	Minneapolis	MN	55413	612-331-5535	
Sendio Inc 4911 Birch St Ste 150 *Web:* www.sendio.com	Newport Beach	CA	92660	949-274-4375	
Sense Corp 2731 Sutton Blvd Ste 200 *Web:* www.sensecorp.com	Saint Louis	MO	63143	314-266-3700	
Sentari Technologies Inc 16775 Addison Rd Ste 600 *Web:* www.sentari.com	Addison	TX	75001	972-716-0893	
Servigistics Sns Inc 2300 Windy Ridge Pkwy 450 N Tower	Atlanta	GA	30339	770-565-2340	565-8767
Sgs Technologie LLC 6817 Southpoint Pkwy Ste 2104 *Web:* www.sgstechnologies.net	Jacksonville	FL	32216	904-332-4534	
Shadow Financial Systems Inc 1551 S Washington Ave *Web:* www.shadowfinancial.com	Piscataway	NJ	08854	732-225-6800	
ShareSquared Inc 2155 Verdugo Blvd Ste 33 *TF:* 800-445-1279 ■ *Web:* www.sharesquared.com	Montrose	CA	91020	800-445-1279	
Sharphat Inc 333 Sylvan Ave Ste 324 *Web:* sharphat.com	Englewood Cliffs	NJ	07632	201-503-0020	
SHINE Systems & Technologies 2216 Ivy Rd Ste 210 *Web:* www.shinesystech.com	Charlottesville	VA	22903	434-220-4717	
Simacor LLC 10700 Hwy 55 Ste 170 *TF:* 888-284-4415 ■ *Web:* www.simacor.com	Plymouth	MN	55441	763-544-4415	
Sitegoal LLC 2417 Ashdale Dr Ste B *Web:* www.sitegoals.com	Austin	TX	78757	512-474-2025	
Skeleton Key 3260 Hampton Ave Ste 200 *Web:* www.skeletonkey.com	Saint Louis	MO	63139	314-353-4300	
Skyline Ultd Inc 16333 S Great Ste 121 *Web:* www.skyline-ultd.com	Round Rock	TX	78681	703-671-9200	
Skyweb Networks 2710 State St *TF:* 866-575-9932 ■ *Web:* skywebonline.com	Saginaw	MI	48602	989-792-8681	
Smartech Systems Inc 500 E Brighton Ave *Web:* www.s2ieng.com	Syracuse	NY	13210	315-701-2316	
Smooth Solutions Inc 300-2 Route 17 South *Web:* smoothsolutions.com	Lodi	NJ	07644	973-249-6666	
SMS Data Products Group Inc 1751 Pinnacle Dr 12th Fl **Fax Area Code: 703* ■ *TF:* 800-331-1767 ■ *Web:* www.sms.com	McLean	VA	22102	800-331-1767	356-4831*
Snap Inc 4080 Lafayette Ctr Dr Ste 340 *TF:* 866-234-7627 ■ *Web:* www.snapinc.net	Chantilly	VA	20151	703-393-6400	
Social & Scientific Systems Inc 8757 Georgia Ave 12th Fl *Web:* www.s-3.com	Silver Spring	MD	20910	301-628-3000	628-3001
Society Consulting LLC 901 104th Ave Ne *Web:* societyconsulting.com	Bellevue	WA	98004	206-420-3500	
Soft-Con Enterprises Inc 6505 Belcrest Rd Ste 120 *Web:* www.softcon1.com	Hyattsville	MD	20782	301-429-0075	
Softassist Inc 700 American Ave *Web:* www.softassist.com	King Of Prussia	PA	19406	610-265-8484	
Softech & Associates Inc 1570 Corporate Dr Ste B *TF:* 877-638-3241 ■ *Web:* www.softechis.com	Costa Mesa	CA	92626	714-427-1122	
Softek International Inc 242 Old New Brunswick Rd Ste 320 *Web:* www.softekintl.com	Piscataway	NJ	08854	732-287-3337	
Softential Inc 607 Herndon Pkwy Ste 202 *Web:* www.softential.com	Herndon	VA	20170	703-650-0001	
Softrim Corp 9210 Estero Park Commons Blvd Ste 5 *Web:* www.softrim.com	Estero	FL	33928	239-449-4444	
Softsolutions Inc 325 Mtn Ave SW *Web:* www.softsolutionsit.com	Roanoke	VA	24016	540-345-1045	
Software Information Systems Inc (SIS) 165 Barr St *TF:* 800-337-6914 ■ *Web:* www.thinksis.com	Lexington	KY	40507	859-977-4747	977-4750
Software Technology Group 555 S 300 E *TF:* 888-595-1001 ■ *Web:* stgconsulting.com	Salt Lake City	UT	84111	801-595-1000	595-1080
Solar Technologies Inc 26180 Enterprise Way Bldg 100	Lake Forest	CA	92630	949-458-1080	458-1081
Solera Networks Inc 10713 S Jordan Gateway Ste 100 *Web:* www.soleranetworks.com	South Jordan	UT	84095	801-545-4100	
Solid Border Inc 1806 Turnmill St *Web:* www.solidborder.com	San Antonio	TX	78248	210-492-8125	
Solien Technology Inc 1411 5th St Ste 406 *Web:* www.solien.com	Santa Monica	CA	90401	310-576-2727	
Solomon Consulting Group LLC 6836 W 121st St Ste 2B *Web:* www.solomonbi.com	Overland Park	KS	66209	913-971-0082	
Solutia Consulting Inc 1241 Amundson Cir *Web:* www.solutia-consulting.com	Stillwater	MN	55082	651-351-0123	
Solution Beacon LLC 14419 Greenwood Ave N Ste 332 *Web:* www.solutionbeacon.com	Seattle	WA	98133	206-366-6606	
Solution Partners Inc 1770 N Park St Ste 100 *Web:* www.solpart.com	Naperville	IL	60563	630-416-1335	
SolutionsIQ Inc ÿ6801 185th Ave NE Ste 200 *Web:* www.solutionsiq.com	Redmond	WA	98052	425-451-2727	
Solvere LLC 69 Mcadenville Rd *Web:* www.solvere.net	Belmont	NC	28012	704-829-1015	
Somethingcool.com LLC 121a E High St *Web:* somethingcool.com	Potosi	MO	63664	573-436-2665	

				Phone	Fax
Sonit Systems LLC 130 W Field Dr *TF:* 800-296-0018 ■ *Web:* www.sonit.com	Archbold	OH	43502	419-446-2151	
Sonos Inc 223 E De La Guerra	Santa Barbara	CA	93101	805-965-3001	
SOS Security Inc 13333 Northwest Fwy Ste 600 *Web:* www.securesos.com	Houston	TX	77040	713-344-0630	
Southeastern Computer Consultants Inc 5166 Potomac Dr Ste 400 *Web:* www.teamscci.com	King George	VA	22485	301-695-5311	695-6101
Spaceflight Systems 47 Constitution Dr *Web:* ssc-nh.com	Bedford	NH	03110	603-472-4934	
SPAN Systems Corp 230 Sherman Ave Ste Nine *Web:* www.spansystems.com	Berkeley Heights	NJ	07922	908-665-9100	
Sparkhound Inc 11207 Proverbs Ave *TF:* 866-217-1500 ■ *Web:* www.sparkhound.com	Baton Rouge	LA	70816	225-216-1500	
Specific Impulse Inc 1060 Willow St Ste 6 *Web:* www.si9.com	San Jose	CA	95125	408-291-0070	
Spectraforce Technologies Inc 500 W Peace St *Web:* www.spectraforce.com	Raleigh	NC	27606	919-233-4466	
Spectro Associates Inc 734 Kent Oaks Way Ste 302 *Web:* www.spectrosales.com	Gaithersburg	MD	20878	410-321-7890	
Sphere 3D Corp 240 Matheson Blvd E *Web:* www.sphere3d.com	Mississauga	ON	L4Z1X1	416-749-5999	
Spherexx LLC 9142 S Sheridan *Web:* www.spherexx.com	Tulsa	OK	74133	918-491-7500	
Sprinklr Inc 29 W 35th St 8th Fl *Web:* www.sprinklr.com	New York	NY	10001	917-933-7800	
SQA LABS Inc 16880 N 73rd Ave *TF:* 855-477-2522 ■ *Web:* www.sqalabs.com	Peoria	AZ	85382	602-439-5500	
Squires Group Inc, The 608 Melvin Ave Ste 101 *Web:* www.squiresgroup.com	Annapolis	MD	21401	410-224-7779	
Ssinfotek Inc 9560 Research Dr *Web:* www.ssinfotek.com	Irvine	CA	92618	949-732-3100	
Staffing Technologies LLC 221 Roswell St Ste 200 *Web:* www.staffingtechnologies.com	Alpharetta	GA	30009	678-338-2040	
Starcare Systems Inc 107 S W St Ste 108	Alexandria	VA	22314	703-836-0331	
Starpoint Solutions 22 Cortlandt St Ste 14 *Web:* www.starpoint.com	New York	NY	10007	212-962-1550	962-7175
Startech Computing Inc 1755 Old W Main St *TF:* 888-385-0607 ■ *Web:* startech-comp.com	Red Wing	MN	55066	651-385-0607	
Statera Inc 6501 E Belleview Ave *Web:* statera.com	Englewood	CO	80111	720-346-0070	
STC Network Services Inc 4904 Oak Cir Dr N *TF:* 800-566-2453	Mobile	AL	36609	251-661-7130	
Stefanini TechTeam Inc 27335 W Eleven-Mile Rd *TF:* 800-522-4451 ■ *Web:* stefanini.com	Southfield	MI	48034	248-357-2866	357-2570
Stelvio Inc 430 Rue Sainte-helene *Web:* stelvio.com	Montreal	QC	H2Y2K7	514-281-8570	
Stg International Inc 4900 Seminary Rd Ste 1100 *TF:* 855-507-0660 ■ *Web:* www.stginternational.com	Alexandria	VA	22311	703-578-6030	578-4474
STI Computer Services Inc 2700 Van Buren Ave *Web:* sticomputer.com	Eagleville	PA	19403	610-650-9700	
Stockell Consulting Inc 15400 S Outer Forty Ste 105 *Web:* www.stockellconsulting.com	Chesterfield	MO	63017	636-537-9100	
Stottler Henke Associates Inc 1670 S Amphlett Blvd Ste 310 *Web:* www.stottlerhenke.com	San Mateo	CA	94402	650-931-2700	
Strata Information Group 3935 Harney St Ste 203 *Web:* sigcorp.com	San Diego	CA	92110	619-296-0170	
Stratacache Inc 2 Emmet St Ste 200 *Web:* www.stratacache.com	Dayton	OH	45405	937-224-0485	
Stratapult Inc 2650 Pilgrim Ct *TF:* 877-631-2900 ■ *Web:* www.inmar.com	Winston-salem	NC	27106	877-631-2900	
Strategic Network Consulting 520 Post Oak Blvd Ste 370 *Web:* www.snc.net	Houston	TX	77027	713-871-0011	
Sulaan Solutions Inc 410 N Roosevelt Ave Ste 106 *Web:* www.sulaan.com	Chandler	AZ	85226	480-626-4041	
Sumaria Systems Inc 99 Rosewood Dr *Web:* www.sumariasystems.com	Danvers	MA	01923	978-739-4200	739-4850
Summit 7 Systems Inc 300 Voyager Way Ste 300 *Web:* www.summit7systems.com	Huntsville	AL	35806	256-585-6868	
Sun Technologies Inc 3700 Mansell Rd Ste 125 *Web:* www.suntechnologies.com	Alpharetta	GA	30022	770-418-0434	
Sunquest Information Systems Inc 250 S Williams Blvd *Web:* www.sunquestinfo.com	Tucson	AZ	85711	520-570-2000	
Superior Access Solutions Inc 21037 Heron Way *Web:* www.sa-solutions.com	Lakeville	MN	55044	952-469-8874	
SupplyFrame Inc 51 W Dayton St Ste 100 *Web:* www.supplyframe.com	Pasadena	CA	91105	626-793-7732	
Surecomp Services Inc 2 Hudson Pl Fl 4 *Web:* www.surecomp.com	Hoboken	NJ	07030	201-217-1437	
Svam International Inc 233 E Shore Rd Ste 201 *TF:* 800-903-6716 ■ *Web:* www.svam.com	Great Neck	NY	11023	516-466-6655	466-8260
Swearingen Software Inc 7540 Pebble Beach Dr *Web:* www.swearingensoftware.com	Beaumont	TX	77707	713-849-2026	
Swinsoft Inc 13405 Folsom Blvd Ste 517 *Web:* www.swinsoft.com	Folsom	CA	95630	916-353-1963	

				Phone	Fax
Swip Systems Inc 1 Regency Plz Dr Ste 100 *Web:* swipsystems.com	Collinsville	IL	62234	618-346-8014	
Sykes Enterprises Inc 400 N Ashley Dr Ste 2800 *NASDAQ: SYKE* ■ *TF:* 800-867-9537 ■ *Web:* www.sykes.com	Tampa	FL	33602	813-274-1000	
Symmetrix Technologies LLC 106 N Denton Tap Rd Ste 210-262 *Web:* www.symmetrixtech.com	Coppell	TX	75019	972-599-1585	
Syncretic Software Inc 228 Philadelphia Pk *Web:* www.syncretic.com	Wilmington	DE	19809	302-762-2600	
Synergem Emergency Services L L C 1007 Warren St *Web:* www.synergemtech.com	Greensboro	NC	27403	336-808-0911	
Synergy 78474 Hwy 111 Ste A *Web:* www.synergyis.us	La Quinta	CA	92253	760-601-5244	
Synergy Associates LLC 550 Clydesdale Trl *TF:* 888-763-9920 ■ *Web:* www.synllc.com	Medina	MN	55340	888-763-9920	
Synergy Data Solutions Inc 1104 S State St Apt A *Web:* synergydata.com	Champaign	IL	61820	217-356-2522	
Syntel Inc 525 E Big Beaver Rd Ste 300 *NASDAQ: SYNT* ■ *Web:* www.syntelinc.com	Troy	MI	48083	248-619-2800	619-2888
SYSCOM Inc 400 E Pratt St Inner Harbor Ctr Ste 502 *Web:* www.syscom.com	Baltimore	MD	21202	410-539-3737	
Syscon Inc 94 Mcfarland Blvd *TF:* 888-797-2661 ■ *Web:* www.syscononline.com	Northport	AL	35476	205-758-2000	
Sysnet Technology Solutions Inc 4320 Stevens Creek Blvd Ste 229 *Web:* www.astirservices.net	San Jose	CA	95129	408-248-5000	
Sysorex Federal Inc 13800 Coppermine Rd Ste 300 *Web:* www.sysorex.com	Herndon	VA	20171	703-356-2900	
System Development Integration Inc (SDI) 33 W Monroe St Ste 400 *Web:* www.sdisolutions.com	Chicago	IL	60603	312-580-7500	580-7600
Systems Implementers Inc 350 S Williams Blvd *Web:* www.systemsimplementers.com	Tucson	AZ	85711	520-795-5729	
Systima Technologies Inc 1832 180th St SE *Web:* www.systima.com	Bothell	WA	98012	425-487-4020	
T-Base Communications Inc 885 Meadowlands Dr E Ste 401 *Web:* www.tbase.com	Ottawa	ON	K2C3N2	613-236-0866	
TAB Computer Systems Inc 29-31 Bissell St *Web:* tabinc.com	East Hartford	CT	06108	860-289-8850	
Tactix Consulting Group Inc 4424 Carver Woods Dr *Web:* www.tactixgroup.com	Cincinnati	OH	45242	513-333-4140	
Tammina Solutions LLC 11874 Sunrise Valley Dr *Web:* www.tammina.com	Reston	VA	20191	703-463-9429	
Tangible Solutions Inc 1320 Matthews Township Pkwy Ste 201 *TF:* 800-393-9886 ■ *Web:* www.tangible.com	Matthews	NC	28105	704-940-4200	
Tango Management Consulting LLC 5525 MacArthur Blvd Ste 450 *Web:* tangomc.com	Irving	TX	75038	817-291-8987	
Tbs Automation Systems Inc 122 Kings Hwy Ste 504 *Web:* tbsauto.com	Maple Shade	NJ	08052	856-424-3247	
TC Computer Service Inc 3303 FM1960 W Ste 100 *Web:* www.tccsi.com	Houston	TX	77068	713-686-2083	
Team Moose LLC 18702 N Creek Pkwy Ste 208 *Web:* www.virtualqube.com	Bothell	WA	98011	206-774-0619	
Tech Hero Of Central Florida LLC 4305 Vineland Rd., Ste G-12 *TF:* 800-900-8324 ■ *Web:* www.techhero.com	Orlando	FL	32811	800-900-8324	
Tech Mahindra Americas Inc 2140 Lk Park Blvd Ste 300 *Web:* techmahindra.com	Richardson	TX	75080	972-991-2900	
Tech-Pro Inc 3000 Centre Pointe Dr *Web:* www.tech-pro.com	Roseville	MN	55113	651-634-1400	
Techfusion 545 Concord Ln Ste 14 *Web:* www.techfusion.com	Cambridge	MA	02138	617-491-1001	
Technica Corp 22970 Indian Creek Dr Ste 500 *Web:* www.technicacorp.com	Dulles	VA	20166	703-662-2000	662-2001
Technoconseil Tc 1177 Boul Charest O *Web:* www.technoconseil.com	Quebec	QC	G1N2C9	418-687-9991	
Techspeed Inc 280 SW Moonridge Pl *Web:* www.techspeed.com	Portland	OR	97225	503-291-0027	
TecServ Inc 4602 E University Dr Ste 120 *Web:* www.tecservinc.com	Phoenix	AZ	85034	602-200-9841	
TECSys Development Inc 1600 10th St Ste B *Web:* www.tditechnologies.com	Plano	TX	75074	972-881-1553	
Teds Inc 235 Mtn Empire Rd *Web:* teds.com	Atkins	VA	24311	276-783-6991	
Tekmark Global Solutions LLC 100 Metroplex Dr Ste 102 *Web:* www.tekmark.com	Edison	NJ	08817	732-572-5400	
TeKONTROL Inc 711 W Amelia St *Web:* www.tekontrol.com	Orlando	FL	32805	407-398-6575	
Teksavers Inc 2120 Grand Ave Pkwy *TF:* 866-832-6188 ■ *Web:* teksavers.com	Austin	TX	78728	512-491-5304	233-2328
Telenet Communications Inc 16 Shenandoah Ave *Web:* www.telenetny.com	Staten Island	NY	10314	718-370-3900	
Telos Corp 19886 Ashburn Rd *OTC: TLSRP* ■ *Web:* www.telos.com	Ashburn	VA	20147	703-724-3800	
Tenlinks 300 Professional Ctr Dr *Web:* www.tenlinks.com	Novato	CA	94947	415-897-8800	
Tenplus Systems 500 Uwharrie Ct Ste C *Web:* www.tenplus.com	Raleigh	NC	27606	919-832-5799	

				Phone	Fax
TeraMach Technologies Inc 1130 Morrison Dr Ste 105 ... Ottawa	ON	K2H9N6		613-226-7775	
TF: 877-226-6549 ■ *Web:* www.teramach.com					
TFC.NET Corp 15211 Lk Maurine Dr ... Odessa	FL	33556		813-880-0909	
Web: www.tfc.net					
Tgo Consulting Inc 140 Renfrew Dr Ste 120 ... Markham	ON	L3R6B3		905-470-6830	
Web: www.tgo.ca					
Thaumaturgix Inc 2 W 45th St Ste 1408 ... New York	NY	10036		212-918-5000	
Web: www.tgix.com					
Thin Client Computing 34522 N Scottsdale Rd ... Scottsdale	AZ	85266		602-432-8649	
Web: www.thinclient.net					
Think Systems Inc 9103 Gardenia Rd ... Nottingham	MD	21236		443-725-5131	
Web: thinksi.com					
Thinklogic Llc 207 Hindry Ave ... Inglewood	CA	90301		310-337-6646	
Web: www.thinklogic.com					
ThruPoint Inc 1040 Ave of the Americas ... New York	NY	10018		646-562-6000	562-6100
Titan Consuting 3411 Preston Rd Ste C13 ... Frisco	TX	75034		972-377-3525	
Web: www.titanconsulting.net					
Titan Solutions Group Inc 11901 W Parmer Ln Ste 400 ... Cedar Park	TX	78613		512-345-4234	
Web: www.titansolutions.com					
TLX Inc 7944 E Beck Ln Ste 200 ... Scottsdale	AZ	85260		480-609-8888	
Web: www.tlxinc.com					
Tm Group Inc, The 34705 W Twelve Mile Rd Ste 371 ... Farmington Hills	MI	48331		248-489-0707	
Web: www.tmgroupinc.com					
TM Systems LLC 12711 Ventura Blvd Ste 270 ... Studio City	CA	91604		818-306-5300	
Web: www.tm-systems.com					
Toolworx Information Products Inc 7994 Grand River ... Brighton	MI	48114		810-220-5115	
Web: www.toolworx.com					
Toss Corp 1253 Worcester Rd Ste 304 ... Framingham	MA	01701		508-820-2990	
TF: 888-884-8677 ■ *Web:* www.toss.com					
Total Networx Inc 417 W Travelers Trail ... Burnsville	MN	55337		952-400-6500	
Web: www.totalnetworx.com					
Trace3 15326 Alton Pkwy ... Irvine	CA	92618		949-333-2300	
Web: www.trace3.com					
Tracy Time Systems Inc 230 32nd St SE ... Grand Rapids	MI	49548		616-241-1661	
Web: www.tracyinc.com					
Tratum Technologies Inc 950 Herndon Pkwy Ste 285 ... Herndon	VA	20170		703-456-7010	
Web: tratumtech.com					
TRI-COR Industries Inc 4403 Forbes Blvd ... Lanham	MD	20706		301-731-6140	306-6740
Web: www.tricorind.com					
Trianz Inc 3979 Freedom Cir Ste 210 ... Santa Clara	CA	95054		408-387-5800	
Web: www.trianz.com					
Tribridge 4830 W Kennedy Blvd Ste 890 ... Tampa	FL	33609		877-744-1360	
TF: 877-744-1360 ■ *Web:* www.tribridge.com					
Tricolor Inc 41 Margaret Dr Ste 202 ... Somerset	NJ	08873		732-873-0305	
Web: www.tricolor.com					
Trillium Teamologies Inc 219 S Main St Ste 300 ... Royal Oak	MI	48067		248-584-2080	
TF: 866-832-6884 ■ *Web:* www.trilliumteam.com					
Trimax Systems Inc 565 Explorer St ... Brea	CA	92821		714-255-8590	
Web: www.trimaxsystems.com					
Trinity Millennium Group Inc 2424 Babcock Rd Ste 300 ... San Antonio	TX	78229		210-615-1606	
Web: www.tringroup.com					
Trioro Inc 642 King St W ... Toronto	ON	M5V1M7		416-977-3333	
Web: www.trioro.com					
Trivalent Group Inc 3145 Prairie St SW Ste 101 ... Grandville	MI	49418		616-222-9200	
Web: www.trivalentgroup.com					
Trivalley Internet Inc 4713 First St Ste 110 ... Pleasanton	CA	94566		925-417-7600	
Web: www.trivalley.com					
Trivera Interactive N88 W16447 Main St Ste 400 ... Menomonee Falls	WI	53051		262-250-9400	
Web: www.trivera.com					
Trofholz Technologies Inc 2207 Plz Dr Ste 100 ... Rocklin	CA	95765		916-577-1903	
Web: www.trofholz.com					
Tsa Inc 2050 W Sam Houston Pkwy N ... Houston	TX	77043		713-935-1500	
Web: ww.tsa.com					
Turbotek Computer Corp 70 Zachary Rd Ste 3 ... Manchester	NH	03109		603-666-3062	
Web: turbotekcomputer.com					
Turn Key Distribution Systems Inc 450 Broadway ... Malden	MA	02148		781-322-3000	
Web: turnkey.com					
TuVox Inc 550 S Winchester Blvd, Ste. 300 Ste ... San Jose	CA	95128		408-625-1700	
Web: www.westinteractive.com					
Two Shea Consulting Inc 1009 Oak Hill Rd Ste 202 ... Lafayette	CA	94549		925-962-7432	
Web: www.twoshea.com					
Tygart Technology Inc 1543 Fairmont Ave ... Fairmont	WV	26554		304-363-6855	
Web: www.tygart.com					
Tylu Wireless Technology Llc Po Box 436900 ... Chicago	IL	60643		312-248-3134	
Web: www.tylu.com					
U r s Information Systems Inc 155 W St Ste 1 ... Wilmington	MA	01887		978-657-6100	
Web: www.ursinfo.ccm					
U2 Logic 8001 E 88th Ave ... Henderson	CO	80640		303-768-9601	
Web: www.u2logic.com					
Ultimate Technical Solutions Inc 651 Leson Ct ... Harvey	LA	70058		504-367-4957	
Web: www.utsi.us					
UNAPEN Inc 321 Research Pkwy Ste 201 ... Meriden	CT	06450		203-269-2111	
Web: unapen.com					
Ungerboeck Systems International Inc 100 Ungerboeck Park ... O'fallon	MO	63368		636-300-5606	
Web: www.ungerboeck.com					
UNICON International Inc 241 Outerbelt St ... Columbus	OH	43213		614-861-7070	
Web: www.unicon-intl.com					
Unified Field Inc 33 E 33rd St Ste 1107 ... New York	NY	10016		212-532-9595	
Web: www.unifiedfield.com					
Unlimited Technology Inc 20 Senn Dr ... Chester Springs	PA	19425		610-458-8901	
Web: www.utech-usa.com					
Upnorth Consulting Inc 331 Second Ave S Ste 202 ... Minneapolis	MN	55401		866-892-1758	
TF: 866-892-1758					
Uptime Solutions Professional Services Group Inc 3807 Gaskins Rd ... Richmond	VA	23233		804-836-1490	
Web: www.uptimesolutions.com					
Urban Insight Inc 3530 Wilshire Blvd Ste 1285 ... Los Angeles	CA	90010		213-792-2000	
Web: urbaninsight.com					
US Data Management LLC 1746-F S Victoria Ave ... Ventura	CA	93003		888-231-0816	
TF: 888-231-0816 ■ *Web:* www.usdm.com					
US-Analytics Solutions Group LLC 600 E Las Colinas Blvd Ste 2222 ... Irving	TX	75039		214-630-0081	630-0082
TF General: 877-828-8727 ■ *Web:* www.us-analytics.com					
Userful Corp 200-709 11th Ave SW ... Calgary	AB	T2R0E3		403-289-2177	
Web: www.userful.com					
USfalcon Inc 1 Copley Pkwy Ste 200 ... Morrisville	NC	27560		919-459-1956	
Web: www.usfalcon.com					
USWired Inc 2107 N First St Ste 250 ... San Jose	CA	95131		408-432-1144	
TF: 877-879-4733 ■ *Web:* www.uswired.com					
Utility Integration Solutions Inc 24 Benthill Ct ... Lafayette	CA	94549		925-939-0449	
Web: www.uisol.com					
Utopia Systems Inc 1172 Old Forge Rd ... New Castle	DE	19720		302-777-0772	
TF: 877-804-7421 ■ *Web:* www.utopiasystems.com					
V I Engineering Inc 27300 Haggerty Rd ... Farmington Hills	MI	48331		248-489-1200	
Web: viengineering.com					
Validata Computer & Research Corp 428 S Perry St ... Montgomery	AL	36104		334-834-2324	
Web: www.validata.com					
Valli Information Systems Inc 915 Main St Ste 100 ... Caldwell	ID	83605		208-459-3611	
Web: www.valli.com					
Valuemomentum Inc 3001 Hadley Rd Unit 8 ... South Plainfield	NJ	07080		908-755-0048	
Web: www.valuemomentum.com					
Vanguard Integrity Professionals Inc 6625 S Eastern Ave Ste 100 ... Las Vegas	NV	89119		702-794-0014	
TF: 877-794-0014 ■ *Web:* www.go2vanguard.com					
Vantix Systems 10119 97a Ave Nw ... Edmonton	AB	T5K2T3		780-421-0499	
Web: vantixsystems.com					
Vasc Alert LLC 3000 Kent Ave ... West Lafayette	IN	47906		765-775-2525	
Web: www.vasc-alert.com					
Vbeyond Corp 3 Skillman Close ... Hillsborough	NJ	08844		908-359-8416	
Web: www.vbeyond.com					
Velocity Partners Inc 15300 W Capitol Dr ... Brookfield	WI	53005		262-790-0800	
Web: www.velocitypartners.co.uk					
Ventera Corp 1881 Campus Commons Dr Ste 350 ... Reston	VA	20191		703-760-4600	390-1113
Web: www.ventera.com					
Ventraq Inc 817 E Gate Dr Ste 101 ... Mount Laurel	NJ	08054		856-866-1000	
Web: 1db088.campgn5.com/ventraq					
Ventura Technology Enterprises Ltd 94 547 Ukee St Ste 110 ... Waipahu	HI	96797		808-678-3900	
Web: www.venturatechnology.net					
Veriphyr Inc 703 Benvenue Ave ... Los Altos	CA	94024		650-384-0560	
Web: www.veriphyr.com					
Veritaaq Technology House Inc 2327 Saint-Laurent Blvd Ste 100 ... Ottawa	ON	K1G4J8		613-736-6120	
Web: www.veritaaq.ca					
Verity Three Inc 733 Ridgeview Dr ... Mchenry	IL	60050		815-385-4474	
Web: clients.veritythree.com					
Verma Systems Inc 4111 S Sherwood Forest Blvd ... Baton Rouge	LA	70816		225-296-0399	
Web: www.vermasystems.com					
Versacor Inc 340 Main St Ste 560 ... Worcester	MA	01608		508-757-9580	
Web: www.versacor.com					
Vertel Corp 21300 Victory Blvd Ste 700 ... Woodland Hills	CA	91367		818-227-1400	
Web: www.vertel.com					
Vertisoft 990 Boul Pierre-roux E ... Victoriaville	QC	G6T0K9		819-751-6660	
TF: 877-368-3241 ■ *Web:* www.vertisoftpme.com					
Victory Enterprises Inc 5200 30th St SW ... Davenport	IA	52802		563-884-4444	
Web: www.victoryenterprises.com					
Video Insight Inc 800 Gessner Rd Ste 700 ... Houston	TX	77024		713-621-9779	
Web: www.video-insight.com					
Viewsource 11841 Mason Montgomery Rd Ste C ... Cincinnati	OH	45249		513-671-6238	
Web: viewsource.com					
Viking Networks Inc 4655 Middle Rd B ... Columbus	IN	47203		812-372-0007	
Web: www.vikingnetworks.net					
Virtual Connect Technologies Inc 3089 S Hwy 14 ... Greer	SC	29650		864-288-9595	
Web: www.virtualconnect.net					
Virtual Education Software Inc 300 N Argonne Rd Ste 102 ... Spokane	WA	99212		509-891-7219	
Web: www.virtualeduc.com					
Virtual Enterprises Inc 12405 Grant St ... Thornton	CO	80241		303-301-3000	
Web: www.virtual.com					
Virtual IT Inc PO Box 1009 ... Moneta	VA	24121		540-345-6100	
Web: www.virtualitinc.com					
Virtual Matrix Corp 7200 France Ave S Ste 324 ... Minneapolis	MN	55435		952-835-6400	
Web: www.vmatrixcorp.com					
Virtually Better Inc 2450 Lawrenceville Hwy Ste 200 ... Decatur	GA	30033		404-634-3400	
Web: www.virtuallybetter.com					
Virtuit Systems Inc 101 Airport Executive Park ... Nanuet	NY	10954		845-371-3060	
Web: www.virtuitsystems.com					
Visionary Integration Professionals Inc 80 Iron Pt Cir Ste 100 ... Folsom	CA	95630		916-985-9625	985-9632
TF: 800-434-2673 ■ *Web:* trustvip.com					

Company	City	State	ZIP	Phone	Fax
Vistronix Inc 11091 Sunset Hills Rd Ste 700 *TF:* 800-483-2434 ■ *Web:* www.vistronix.com	Reston	VA	20190	703-463-2059	483-2500
Visual Retail Plus Inc 540 Hudson St *Web:* www.visualretailplus.com	Hackensack	NJ	07601	201-678-9888	
Vivid Solutions 2328 Government St *Web:* www.vividsolutions.com	Victoria	BC	V8T5G5	250-385-6040	
Voyager Systems Inc 360 Route 101 *Web:* www.voyagersystems.com	Bedford	NH	03110	603-472-5172	
Vvm Inc 5606 W Adams Ave *Web:* www.vvm.com	Temple	TX	76502	254-778-8028	
W-Industries Inc 11500 Charles Rd *Web:* www.w-industries.com	Houston	TX	77041	713-466-9463	
Wakelight Technologies Inc 155 Kapalulu Pl Ste 109 *Web:* www.wakelight.com	Honolulu	HI	96819	808-836-9253	
Walker Group Inc, The 20 Waterside Dr *Web:* www.walkersystemssupport.com	Farmington	CT	06032	860-678-3530	
Washington Consulting Group Inc 4915 Auburn Ave Ste 301 *Web:* www.washcg.com	Bethesda	MD	20814	301-656-2330	656-1996
Water Intelligence PLC 888 E Research Dr Ste 100 *Web:* www.waterintelligence.co.uk	Palm Springs	CA	92263	760-969-6830	
Watson SCS Inc 12157 W Linebaugh Ave Ste 381 *TF:* 866-805-6066 ■ *Web:* www.watsonscs.com	Tampa	FL	33626	866-805-6066	
Wavecode Inc 1651 N Collins Blvd *Web:* www.wavecode.com	Richardson	TX	75080	214-570-9559	
Waypoint Solutions Group LLC 9305 Monroe Rd Ste L *Web:* www.waypointsg.com	Charlotte	NC	28270	704-246-1717	
Web Creations & Consulting L L C 119 W Iron Ave 3rd Fl *Web:* www.wccit.com	Salina	KS	67401	785-823-7630	
Web Yoga Inc 938 Senate Dr *Web:* www.webyoga.com	Dayton	OH	45459	937-428-0000	
Webject Systems Inc 25 Central Sq Ste 2 *Web:* www.webject.com	Bridgewater	MA	02324	508-279-6562	
Western Digitech Inc 7312 SW 48th St *Web:* www.westerndigitech.com	Miami	FL	33155	305-669-0119	
White Sands Technology Inc 6737 Variel Ave Ste A *Web:* www.whitesands.com	Canoga Park	CA	91303	818-702-9200	
WidePoint Corp 7926 Jones Branch Dr Ste 124 **Fax Area Code:* 630 ■ *Web:* www.widepoint.com	Mclean	VA	22102	703-349-2577	629-7559*
Wimmer Solutions Corp 1341 N Northlake Way Ste 300 *Web:* www.wimmersolutions.com	Seattle	WA	98103	206-324-4594	
Winning Technologies Great Lakes LLC 147 Triad Ctr W *Web:* www.winningtech.com	O Fallon	MO	63366	636-379-8279	
Wiretree LLC 887 W Marietta St NW Ste 1 *Web:* www.wiretree.com	Atlanta	GA	30318	404-876-3835	
Wisdom Infotech Ltd 18650 W Corp Dr Ste 120 *Web:* www.wisdominfotech.com	Brookfield	WI	53045	262-792-0200	792-0202
WiseSoft LLC 5311 W 74th St *Web:* www.wise-soft.com	Edina	MN	55439	952-806-0015	
WISNET.COM 987 S Main St *Web:* www.wisnet.com	Fond Du Lac	WI	54935	920-921-8391	
WM Software Corp 3660 Ctr Rd Ste 371 *Web:* www.wmsoftware.com	Brunswick	OH	44212	330-558-0501	
Wmsvision Inc 1016 Copeland Oaks Dr *Web:* wmsvision.com	Morrisville	NC	27560	919-863-3388	
Wolcott Systems Group LLC 1684 Medina Rd Ste 204 *TF:* 866-965-2688 ■ *Web:* www.wolcottgroup.com	Medina	OH	44256	330-666-5900	666-5600
Wood Networks 10260 Robinson Dr *Web:* www.woodnetworks.com	Tyler	TX	75703	903-581-0922	
Working Machines Corp 2170 Dwight Way *TF:* 877-648-4808 ■ *Web:* www.workingmachines.com	Berkeley	CA	94704	510-704-1100	
Worksighted Inc 275 Hoover Blvd *Web:* www.worksighted.com	Holland	MI	49423	616-546-2691	
Worldcom Exchange Inc 43 NW Dr *Web:* www.wei.com	Salem	NH	03079	603-893-0900	
Worx Group LLC, The 18 Waterbury Rd *Web:* www.theworxgroup.com	Prospect	CT	06712	203-758-3311	
Wurldtech Security Technologies Inc 4 Bentall Ctr Ste 2000 *Web:* www.wurldtech.com	Vancouver	BC	V7X1J1	604-669-6674	
Wyde Corp 4660 Slater Rd Ste 222 *Web:* www.wyde.com	Eagan	MN	55122	651-882-2400	
Xcedex Inc 15600 Wayzata Blvd Ste 309 *Web:* www.xcedex.com	Wayzata	MN	55391	952-746-3036	
XEODesign Inc 5273 College Ave Ste 201 *Web:* www.xeodesign.com	Oakland	CA	94618	510-658-8077	
Xfer International Inc 39201 Schoolcraft Rd Ste B 9 *TF:* 800-438-9337 ■ *Web:* www.xfer.com	Livonia	MI	48150	734-927-6666	
Xoriant Corp 1248 Reamwood Ave *Web:* www.xoriant.com	Sunnyvale	CA	94089	408-743-4400	
XperNet Services Inc 22511 Katy Fwy *Web:* www.xpernet.com	Katy	TX	77450	281-392-5292	
Xtream It People Inc 50 Colvin Ave Ste 206 *Web:* www.xtreamit.com	Albany	NY	12206	518-437-0090	
Yaaman Inc 6376 Byron Ln *Web:* www.yaaman.com	San Ramon	CA	94582	408-625-7615	
Yaana Technologies LLC 542 Gibraltar Dr *Web:* www.yaanatech.com	Milpitas	CA	95035	408-719-9000	
Ydesigns Com Inc 35 Haywood St *Web:* www.fastpivot.com	Asheville	NC	28801	828-225-8883	
Yellow Dog Networks 9664 Marion Rd *Web:* www.yellowdognetworks.com	Kansas City	MO	64137	816-767-9364	
Yojna Inc 32605 W 12 Mile Rd Ste 275 *Web:* www.yojna.com	Farmington Hills	MI	48334	248-489-9650	
YouMail Inc 43 Corporate Park Ste 200 *TF:* 800-374-0013 ■ *Web:* www.youmail.com	Irvine	CA	92606	800-374-0013	
Zaphyr Technologies 628 State Rt 10 Ste 14 *Web:* www.zaphyr.net	Whippany	NJ	07981	973-560-9050	
ZeeWise 4920 Roswell Rd Ste 458 *Web:* www.zeewise.com	Atlanta	GA	30342	678-383-4040	
Zel Technologies LLC 54 Old Hampton Ln *Web:* zeltech.com	Hampton	VA	23669	757-722-5565	
Zenmonics Inc 125 Floyd Smith Office Park Dr Ste 220 *Web:* www.zenmonics.com	Charlotte	NC	28262	704-971-7315	
Zontec Inc 1389 Kemper Meadow Dr *TF:* 866-955-0088 ■ *Web:* www.zontec-spc.com	Cincinnati	OH	45240	513-648-9695	
ZyQuest Inc 1385 W Main Ave *TF:* 800-992-0533 ■ *Web:* www.zyquest.com	De Pere	WI	54115	920-499-0533	

181 CONCERT, SPORTS, OTHER LIVE EVENT PRODUCERS & PROMOTERS

Company	City	State	ZIP	Phone	Fax
Allstate Sugar Bowl 1500 Sugar Bowl Dr *Web:* www.allstatesugarbowl.org	New Orleans	LA	70112	504-828-2440	
AMS Entertainment 1120 Coast Village Cir *Web:* santabarbara.amsentertainment.com	Santa Barbara	CA	93108	805-899-4000	
Cinnabar California Inc 4571 Electronics Pl *Web:* www.cinnabar.com	Los Angeles	CA	90039	818-842-8190	842-0563
Contemporary Productions LLC 190 Carondelet Plz Ste 1111 *Web:* www.contemporaryproductions.com	Saint Louis	MO	63105	314-721-9090	
Culture Works 110 N Main St Ste 165 *Web:* cultureworks.org	Dayton	OH	45402	937-222-2787	
Dallas Fan Fares Inc 5485 Beltline Rd Ste 270 *Web:* www.fanfares.com	Dallas	TX	75254	972-239-9969	
Executive Visions Inc 7000 Miller Ct E *Web:* www.executivevisions.com	Norcross	GA	30071	770-416-6100	
Gilmore Entertainment Group 8901-A Business 17 N *TF:* 800-843-6779 ■ *Web:* thecarolinaopry.com	Myrtle Beach	SC	29572	843-913-4000	
Harlem Globetrotters International Inc 400 E Van Buren St Ste 300 *TF:* 800-641-4667 ■ *Web:* www.harlemglobetrotters.com	Phoenix	AZ	85004	602-258-0000	258-5925
House of Blues Entertainment Inc 7060 Hollywood Blvd *Web:* www.houseofblues.com	Hollywood	CA	90028	323-769-4600	769-4787
IMG Inc 1360 E Ninth St *Web:* img.com	Cleveland	OH	44114	216-522-1200	522-1145
JAM Productions Ltd 205 W Goethe *Web:* www.jamusa.com	Chicago	IL	60610	312-440-9191	
Lets Play Sports Inc 9606 Aero Dr Ste 1300 *Web:* www.letsplaysoccer.com	San Diego	CA	92123	858-637-5766	
Live Nation Inc 9348 Civic Ctr Dr *NYSE: LYV* ■ *Web:* www.livenation.com	Beverly Hills	CA	90210	310-867-7000	
Lotos Club, The 5 E 66th St *Web:* lotosclub.org	New York	NY	10065	212-737-7100	
Miss Universe LP 1370 Ave of the Americas 16th Fl *Web:* www.missuniverse.com	New York	NY	10019	212-373-4999	315-5378
Production Resource Group 300 Harvestore Dr *Web:* www.prg.com	DeKalb	IL	60115	815-756-9600	756-9377
Radio City Entertainment LLC 1260 Sixth Ave *Web:* www.radiocity.com	New York	NY	10020	212-485-7200	
Rockledge Hook & Ladder Social Hall Rentals 505 Huntingdon Pk *Web:* www.rockledgefireco.org	Rockledge	PA	19046	215-379-8373	
Speedway Motorsports Inc (SMI) 5555 Concord Pkwy S *NYSE: TRK* ■ *Web:* www.speedwaymotorsports.com	Concord	NC	28027	704-455-3239	
Top Rank Inc 3980 Howard Hughes Pkwy Ste 580 *Web:* www.toprank.com	Las Vegas	NV	89169	702-732-2717	
Willis & Woy Sports Group LLC 3030 Olive St Ste 520 *Web:* www.willis-woy.com	Dallas	TX	75219	214-969-7580	
Willy Bietak Productions Inc 1404 Third St Promenade Ste 200 *Web:* www.iceshows.com	Santa Monica	CA	90401	310-576-2400	
World Wrestling Entertainment Inc 1241 E Main St *NYSE: WWE* ■ *TF:* 866-993-7467	Stamford	CT	06902	203-352-8600	359-5151

182 CONCRETE - READY-MIXED

Company	City	State	ZIP	Phone	Fax
A Teichert & Son Inc 3500 American River Dr *Web:* www.teichert.com	Sacramento	CA	95864	916-484-3011	
AJ Walker Construction Co 421 S 21st St	Mattoon	IL	61938	217-235-5647	235-5939
Alamo Concrete Pavers 1008 Hoefgen *Web:* alamopavers.net	San Antonio	TX	78261	210-534-8821	534-8997
Allied Concrete Products LLC 3900 Shannon St	Chesapeake	VA	23324	757-494-5200	
Anderson Concrete Corp 400 Frank Rd *Web:* www.andersonconcrete.com	Columbus	OH	43207	614-443-0123	443-4001
Arizona Materials LLC 3636 S 43rd Ave *Web:* www.arizonamaterials.com	Phoenix	AZ	85009	602-278-4444	
AVR Inc 14698 Galaxy Ave *Web:* www.avrconcrete.com	Apple Valley	MN	55124	952-432-7132	

Phone Fax

Baccala Concrete Corp 100 Armento St . . . Johnston RI 02919 401-231-8300 232-3965
TF: 866-705-2382 ■ *Web:* baccalaconcrete.com

Baker Ready Mix & Building Materials
2800 Frenchmen St . . . New Orleans LA 70122 504-947-8081
Web: www.bakerreadymix.com

BARD Materials 2021 325th Ave PO Box 246 . . . Dyersville IA 52040 563-875-7145 875-7860
Web: bardmaterials.com

Bode Concrete 385 Mendell St . . . San Francisco CA 94124 415-920-7100
Web: www.bodegravel.com

Bonded Concrete Inc 303 Rt 155 . . . Watervliet NY 12189 518-273-5800
TF: 800-252-8589 ■ *Web:* www.bondedconcrete.com

Boston Sand & Gravel Company Inc
100 N Washington St . . . Boston MA 02114 617-227-9000
OTC: BSND ■ *TF:* 800-624-2724 ■ *Web:* www.bostonsand.com

Builders Redi-Mix Inc
30701 W 10 Mile Rd Ste 500
PO Box 2900 . . . Farmington Hills MI 48333 888-988-4400
TF: 888-988-4400 ■ *Web:* www.superiormaterialsllc.com

Building Products Corp 950 Freeburg Ave . . . Belleville IL 62220 618-233-4427 233-2031
TF: 800-233-1996 ■ *Web:* www.buildingproductscorp.com

CalPortland Co
5975 E Marginal Way S PO Box 1730 . . . Seattle WA 98134 206-764-3000
TF: 800-750-0123 ■ *Web:* www.calportland.com

Cemex USA 840 Gessner Ste 1400 . . . Houston TX 77024 713-650-6200 317-6047*
NYSE: CX ■ **Fax Area Code:* 212 ■ *TF:* 888-292-0070 ■ *Web:* www.cemex.com

Cemstone Products Co
2025 Centre Pt Blvd Ste 300 . . . Mendota Heights MN 55120 651-688-9292 688-0124
TF: 800-236-7866 ■ *Web:* www.cemstone.com

Centex Materials Inc
3019 Alvin Devane Blvd Ste 100 . . . Austin TX 78741 512-460-3003
Web: eaglematerials.com

Central Builders Supply Company Inc
125 Bridge Ave PO Box 152 . . . Sunbury PA 17801 570-286-6461 286-5108
TF: 800-326-9361 ■ *Web:* centralbuilderssupply.com

Central Concrete Supermix Inc 4300 SW 74th Ave . . . Miami FL 33155 305-262-3250 267-0698
Web: www.supermix.com

Central Concrete Supply Company Inc
755 Stockton Ave . . . San Jose CA 95126 408-293-6272 294-3162
TF: 866-404-1000 ■ *Web:* www.centralconcrete.com

Century Ready-Mix Corp
3250 Armand St PO Box 4420 . . . Monroe LA 71211 318-322-4444 322-7299
TF: 800-732-3969 ■ *Web:* centuryreadymix.com

Chandler Concrete Company Inc
1006 S Church St PO Box 131 . . . Burlington NC 27216 336-226-1181 226-2969
Web: www.chandlerconcrete.com

CJ Horner Company Inc 105 W Grand Ave . . . Hot Springs AR 71901 501-321-9600
Web: cjhornerinc.com

Clayton Cos, The PO Box 3015 . . . Lakewood NJ 08701 800-662-3044
TF: 800-662-3044 ■ *Web:* www.claytonco.com

Concrete Materials Corp (CMC) 106 Industry Rd . . . Richmond KY 40475 859-623-4238 623-4255
Web: www.concretematerialscompany.net

Conproco Corp 17 Production Dr . . . Dover NH 03820 603-743-5800
Web: www.conproco.com

Delta Concrete Products Co Inc
425 Florida Blvd . . . Denham Springs LA 70726 225-665-6103

Devine Bros Inc 38 Commerce St . . . Norwalk CT 06850 203-866-4421 857-4609
Web: www.devinebi.com

Dolese Bros Co 20 NW 13th St . . . Oklahoma City OK 73103 405-235-2311 297-8329
TF: 800-375-2311 ■ *Web:* dolese.com

Dragon Products Co 960 Ocean Ave . . . Portland ME 04103 207-774-6355

Dublin Construction Company Inc
305 S Washington St . . . Dublin GA 31021 478-272-0721
Web: www.dublinconstruction.com

Dunham Price Inc
210 Mike Hooks Rd PO Box 760 . . . Westlake LA 70669 337-433-3900 433-8895
Web: www.dunhamprice.com

Eagle Materials Inc
3811 Turtle Creek Blvd Ste 1100 . . . Dallas TX 75219 214-432-2000 432-2100
NYSE: EXP ■ *Web:* www.eaglematerials.com

Eastern Concrete Materials Inc
475 Market St . . . Elmwood Park NJ 07407 201-797-7979 791-9631*
**Fax:* Sales ■ *TF:* 800-822-7242 ■ *Web:* www.us-concrete.com

Eastern Industries Inc
4401 Camp Meeting Rd Ste 200 . . . Center Valley PA 18034 610-866-0932 867-1886
Web: www.eastern-ind.com

Ernst Enterprises Inc 3361 Successful Way . . . Dayton OH 45414 937-233-5555 233-9203
TF: 800-353-1555 ■ *Web:* ernstconcrete.com

Federal Materials Concrete
2425 Wayne Sullivan Dr . . . Paducah KY 42003 270-442-5496 443-6484
Web: www.fmc1.com

Garrott Bros Continous Mix Inc PO Box 419 . . . Gallatin TN 37066 615-452-2385
Web: www.garrottbros.com

Geiger Ready Mix Company Inc PO Box 50 . . . Leavenworth KS 66048 913-772-4010 772-8661
Web: www.geigerreadymix.com

Geneva Rock Products Inc 302 W 5400 S Ste 200 . . . Murray UT 84107 801-281-7900
TF: 855-614-6497 ■ *Web:* www.genevarock.com

Hardaway Concrete Co Inc 2001 Taylor St . . . Columbia SC 29204 803-254-4350

Hawaiian Cement 99-1300 Halawa Vly St . . . Aiea HI 96701 808-532-3400 532-3499
Web: www.hawaiiancement.com

Hempt Bros Inc 205 Creek Rd . . . Camp Hill PA 17011 717-737-3411 761-5019
Web: hemptbros.com

Hilltop Basic Resources Inc
1 W Fourth St Ste 1100 . . . Cincinnati OH 45202 513-651-5000 684-8222
Web: www.hilltopbasicresources.com

Ideal Ready Mix Company Inc
3902 W Mount Pleasant St . . . West Burlington IA 52655 319-754-4747
Web: www.idealrm.com

Ingram Readymix Inc 3580 Fm 482 . . . New Braunfels TX 78132 830-625-9156
Web: www.ingramreadymixinc.com

Irving Materials Inc (IMI) 8032 N SR-9 . . . Greenfield IN 46140 317-536-6650 326-3105
Web: www.irvmat.com

Irving Ready-Mix Inc 13415 Coldwater Rd . . . Fort Wayne IN 46845 260-637-3104

Jackson Ready Mix Concrete Inc
100 W Woodrow Wilson Dr . . . Jackson MS 39213 601-354-3801 292-3924
Web: delta-ind.com

Janesville Sand & Gravel Co (JSG)
1110 Harding St . . . Janesville WI 53547 608-754-7701
TF: 800-955-7702 ■ *Web:* www.jsandg.com

Jones & Sons Inc PO Box 2357 . . . Washington IN 47501 812-254-4731 254-3293
Web: www.jonesandsons.com

King's Material Inc 650 12th Ave SW . . . Cedar Rapids IA 52404 319-363-0233 366-0249
TF: 800-332-5298 ■ *Web:* www.kingsmaterial.com

Kirkpatrick Concrete Co
2000-A Southbridge Pkwy Ste 610 . . . Birmingham AL 35209 205-423-2600 621-0952
Web: nationalcement.com

Kloepfer Concrete & Paving Co
505 E Ellis PO Box 840 . . . Paul ID 83347 208-438-4525 438-5030
Web: www.kloepfer.com

Knife River Corp 1150 W Century Ave . . . Bismarck ND 58506 701-530-1400 530-1451
Web: www.kniferiver.com

Krehling Industries Inc 1399 Hagy Way . . . Harrisburg PA 17110 717-232-7936 236-8810
TF: 800-839-1654 ■ *Web:* www.krehlingcountertops.com

Kuert Concrete Inc 3402 Lincoln Way W . . . South Bend IN 46628 574-232-9911 232-9977
Web: www.kuert.com

Kuhlman Corp 1845 Indian Woods Cir . . . Maumee OH 43537 419-897-6000 897-6061
TF: 800-669-3309 ■ *Web:* www.kuhlman-corp.com

L & L Redi Mix 1939 Rt 206 . . . Southampton NJ 08088 609-859-2271
Web: www.llredimix.com

L Suzio Concrete Company Inc
975 Westfield Rd . . . Meriden CT 06450 203-237-8421 238-9177
TF: 888-789-4626 ■ *Web:* www.suzioyorkhill.com

Lafarge North America Inc
8700 W Bryn Mawr Ave Ste 300 . . . Chicago VA 60631 703-480-3600 480-3899
Web: www.lafarge-na.com

Loveland Ready Mix Concrete Inc
644 N County Rd 19 E . . . Loveland CO 80537 970-667-1108

Lycon Inc 1110 Harding St PO Box 427 . . . Janesville WI 53547 608-754-7701 754-8555
TF: 800-955-8758 ■ *Web:* www.lyconinc.com

Manitou Construction Company Inc
1260 Jefferson Rd . . . Rochester NY 14623 585-424-6040

Metro Ready Mix Concrete Inc
1136 Second Ave N . . . Nashville TN 37208 615-255-1900
Web: www.mrm1.com

Mid-Continent Concrete Co PO Box 3878 . . . Tulsa OK 74102 918-582-8111
Web: gccusa.com

MMC Materials Inc
1052 Highland Colony Pkwy Ste 201 . . . Ridgeland MS 39157 601-898-4000 898-4030
Web: www.mmcmaterials.com

National Cement Company of California Inc
15821 Ventura Blvd Ste 475 . . . Encino CA 91436 818-728-5200
Web: www.vicat.com

Ozark Ready Mix Company Inc
1115 Bluff Dr . . . Osage Beach MO 65065 573-348-1181
Web: www.ozarkreadymix.com

Pacific Concrete Industries 7170 Holz Rd . . . Lynden WA 98264 360-734-0910

Pennsy Supply Inc 1001 Paxton St . . . Harrisburg PA 17104 717-233-4511 238-7312
Web: www.pennsysupply.com

Pine Bluff Sand & Gravel Inc
1501 Heart Wood . . . white hall AR 71602 870-534-7120 534-2980
Web: pbsgc.applicantharbor.com

Prairie Group Inc 7601 W 79th St . . . Bridgeview IL 60455 708-458-0400 458-7626
TF Sales: 800-649-3690

Prestige Concrete Products
8529 S Pk Cr Ste 320 . . . Orlando FL 32819 407-802-3540 226-0359
Web: prestigeconcreteproducts.com

Ready Mixed Concrete Co 4315 Cuming St . . . Omaha NE 68131 402-556-3600 556-5171
Web: lymanrichey.com

RiverStone Group Inc 1701 Fifth Ave . . . Moline IL 61265 309-757-8250 757-8257
TF: 800-906-2489 ■ *Web:* www.riverstonegrp.com

RMX Holdings Inc 4602 E Thomas Rd . . . Phoenix AZ 85018 602-249-5814
Web: rmxholdings.com

Robar Enterprises Inc 17671 Bear Valley Rd . . . Hesperia CA 92345 760-244-5456 244-1819
Web: www.robarenterprises.com

Robertson's Ready Mix Concrete Inc
200 S Main St Ste 200 . . . Corona CA 92882 951-493-6500
Web: www.rrmca.com

Rockville Fuel & Feed Company Inc
14901 S Lawn Ln PO Box 1707 . . . Rockville MD 20849 301-762-3988 309-3894
Web: rockvilleconcrete.com

Roth Ready Mix Concrete Co 900 Kieley Pl . . . Cincinnati OH 45217 513-242-8400
Web: www.cincinnatireadymix.com

S & G Concrete Co 2110 Philadelphia Rd . . . Edgewood MD 21040 410-679-0500
Web: vulcanmaterials.com

Sequatchie Concrete Service Inc
406 Cedar Ave . . . South Pittsburg TN 37380 423-837-7913 837-7479
TF: 800-824-0824 ■ *Web:* www.seqconcrete.com

Shelby Materials
157 E Rampart St PO Box 242 . . . Shelbyville IN 46176 800-548-9516
TF: 800-548-9516 ■ *Web:* www.shelbymaterials.com

Silvi Concrete Products Inc
355 Newbold Rd . . . Fairless Hills PA 19030 215-295-0777
TF: 800-426-6273 ■ *Web:* www.silvi.com

Smith Ready Mix Inc 251 W Lincolnway . . . Valparaiso IN 46383 219-462-3191 465-4025
Web: www.smithreadymix.com

Speedway Redi Mix Inc 1201 N Taylor Rd . . . Garrett IN 46738 260-357-6885 357-0238
TF: 800-227-5649 ■ *Web:* www.speedwayredimix.com

Starvaggi Industries Inc
401 Pennsylvania Ave . . . Weirton WV 26062 304-748-1400 797-5208
Web: www.starvaggi.com

Stocker Concrete Co 7574 US Rt 36 . . . Gnadenhutten OH 44629 740-254-4626
Web: www.stockerconcrete.com

Superior Ready Mix Concrete LP
1508 Mission Rd . . . Escondido CA 92029 760-745-0556 740-9556
Web: superiorrm.com

Thomas Bennett & Hunter Inc 70 John St . . . Westminster MD 21157 410-848-9030 876-0733
Web: www.tbhconcrete.com

Company	City	State	Zip	Phone	Fax
Tilcon Connecticut Inc PO Box 1357	New Britain	CT	06050	860-224-6010	225-1865
TF: 888-845-2666 ■ *Web:* www.tilconct.com					
Titan America Inc 1151 Azalea Garden Rd	Norfolk	VA	23502	757-858-6500	855-7707
TF: 800-468-7622 ■ *Web:* www.titanamerica.com					
United Cos of Mesa County Inc 2273 River Rd	Grand Junction	CO	81505	970-243-4900	
Web: united-gj.com					
United Materials LLC The Woodlands Corporate Ctr E 3949 Forest Pkwy Ste 400	North Tonawanda	NY	14120	716-213-5832	213-5850
TF: 888-918-6483 ■ *Web:* www.unitedmaterialsllc.com					
US Concrete Inc 2925 Briarpark Dr Ste 1050	Houston	TX	77042	713-499-6200	499-6201
NASDAQ: USCR ■ *Web:* www.us-concrete.com					
VanDerVart Concrete Products 1436 S 15th St	Sheboygan	WI	53081	920-459-2400	459-2410
Web: vandervaartinc.com					
Westroc Inc 670 West 220 South	Pleasant Grove	UT	84062	801-785-5600	785-5600
WG Block Co 1414 Mississippi Blvd	Bettendorf	IA	52722	563-823-2080	823-2071
Willcan Inc PO Box 1357	Calhoun	GA	30703	706-629-2256	625-0587
Web: www.basicreadymix.com					

183 CONCRETE PRODUCTS - MFR

Company	City	State	Zip	Phone	Fax
A Duchini Inc 2550 McKinley Ave	Erie	PA	16503	814-456-7027	
TF: 800-937-7317 ■ *Web:* www.duchini.com					
Abresist Corp PO Box 38	Urbana	IN	46990	260-774-3327	
TF: 800-348-0717 ■ *Web:* www.abresist.com					
AC Miller Concrete Products Inc 31 E Bridge St PO Box 199	Spring City	PA	19475	610-948-4600	948-9750
Web: www.acmiller.com					
Accord Industries 4001 Forsyth Rd	Winter Park	FL	32792	407-671-6989	679-2297
TF General: 800-876-6989 ■ *Web:* www.universal100.com					
Acm Chemistries Inc 3190 Reps Miller Rd Ste 100	Norcross	GA	30071	770-417-3490	
Web: acmchem.com					
Acme Block & Brick Inc 248 Dayton Spur Rd	Crossville	TN	38555	931-484-8435	
Web: www.acmeblockandbrick.com					
Adams Products Co 5701 McCrimmon Pkwy PO Box 189	Morrisville	NC	27560	919-467-2218	469-0509
TF: 800-672-3131 ■ *Web:* www.adamsproducts.com					
Advanced Concrete Systems Inc 55 Advanced Ln	Middleburg	PA	17842	570-837-3955	
Web: www.yourbasement.com					
American Artstone Co 2025 N Broadway St	New Ulm	MN	56073	507-233-3700	
TF: 800-967-2076 ■ *Web:* www.american-artstone.com					
Ameron International Corp 245 S Los Robles Ave	Pasadena	CA	91101	626-683-4000	683-4060
Web: www.nov.com					
Amvic Inc 501 McNicoll Ave	Toronto	ON	M2H2E2	416-410-5674	
TF: 877-470-9991 ■ *Web:* www.amvicsystem.com					
Angelus Block Co Inc 11374 Tuxford St	Sun Valley	CA	91352	818-767-8576	768-3124
Web: www.angelusblock.com					
ARDEX Inc 400 Ardex Park Dr	Aliquippa	PA	15001	724-203-5000	
Web: www.ardex.com					
Arkansas Precast Corp 2601 Cory Dr	Jacksonville	AR	72076	501-982-1547	982-4001
Atlantic Concrete Products Inc 8900 Old Rt 13	Tullytown	PA	19007	215-945-5600	946-3102
TF: 800-988-7837 ■ *Web:* www.atlanticconcrete.com					
Basalite Concrete Products LLC 605 Industrial Way	Dixon	CA	95620	707-678-1901	678-6268
TF: 800-776-6690 ■ *Web:* www.basalite.com					
Bayshore Concrete Products Corp 1134 Bayshore Rd	Cape Charles	VA	23310	757-331-2300	331-2501
Web: www.usa.skanska.com					
Beavertown Block Company Inc 3612 Paxtonville Rd	Middleburg	PA	17842	570-837-1744	837-1591
Web: www.beavertownblock.net					
Black Diamond Paving Inc 41550 Boscell Rd	Fremont	CA	94538	510-770-1150	
Web: www.blackdiamondpaving.com					
Blakeslee Arpaia Chapman Inc 200 N Branford Rd	Branford	CT	06405	203-488-2500	
Web: bac-inc.com					
Blakeslee Prestress Inc Rt 139 McDermott Rd PO Box 510	Branford	CT	06405	203-481-5306	481-3562
Web: www.blakesleeprestress.com					
BNZ Materials Inc 6901 S Pierce St Ste 260	Littleton	CO	80128	303-978-1199	978-0308
TF: 800-999-0890 ■ *Web:* www.bnzmaterials.com					
Bomanite Corp 232 S Schnoor Ave	Madera	CA	93637	559-673-2411	
Web: www.bomanite.com					
Bonsal American Inc 8201 Arrowridge Blvd	Charlotte	NC	28273	704-525-1621	529-5261
TF: 800-424-9300 ■ *Web:* www.bonsalamerican.com/html/contact.html					
Buehner Block Co 2800 SW Temple	Salt Lake City	UT	84115	801-467-5456	467-0866
TF: 800-999-2565					
BuildBlock Building Systems LLC 9701 N Broadway Ext	Oklahoma City	OK	73114	405-840-3386	
Web: www.buildblock.com					
Burtco Inc 185 Rt 123	Westminster Station	VT	05159	802-722-3358	
Web: burtcoselfstorage.com					
By-Crete 517 King St	Lebanon	PA	17042	717-866-7690	
Web: www.bycrete.com					
Carr Concrete Corp Waverly Rd	Waverly	WV	26184	304-464-4013	
TF: 800-837-8918 ■ *Web:* www.carrconcrete.com					
Cary Concrete Products Inc 211 Dean St Ste 1D	Woodstock	IL	60098	815-338-2301	337-5801
Web: www.caryconcrete.com					
Cast Systems LLC 19400 Peachland Blvd	Port Charlotte	FL	33948	941-625-3474	
Web: www.castsystemsllc.com					
Cast-Crete Corp 6324 County Rd 579	Seffner	FL	33584	813-621-4641	
TF: 800-999-4641 ■ *Web:* www.castcrete.com					
Cement Industries Inc 2925 Hanson St PO Box 823	Fort Myers	FL	33902	239-332-1440	332-0370
TF: 800-332-1440 ■ *Web:* www.cementindustries.com					
Cement Products & Supply Co Inc 516 W Main St	Lakeland	FL	33815	863-686-5141	
Web: cementproducts.us					
Central Pre-Mix Concrete Co 5111 E Broadway	Spokane	WA	99212	509-534-6221	
Web: www.centralpremix.com					
Century Group Inc, The 1106 W Napoleon St PO Box 228	Sulphur	LA	70664	337-527-5266	527-8028
TF: 800-527-5232 ■ *Web:* www.centurygrp.com					
CERATECH Inc 1500 N Beauregard St Ste 320	Alexandria	VA	22311	703-894-1130	
Web: www.ceratechinc.com					
Champion Precast Inc 2441 N Hwy 61	Troy	MO	63379	573-384-5855	
Web: www.championprecast.com					
Chaney Enterprises 12480 Mattawoman Dr PO Box 548	Waldorf	MD	20604	301-932-5000	
TF: 888-244-0411 ■ *Web:* www.chaneyenterprises.com					
Ciment Quebec Inc 145 Blvd du Centenaire	St. Basile De Portneuf	QC	G0A3G0	418-329-2100	
Web: www.bcr.cc					
Cinder & Concrete Block Corp 10111 Beaver Dam Rd	Cockeysville	MD	21030	410-666-2350	666-8781
Web: cinderblockonline.com					
Clayton Block Co PO Box 3015	Lakewood	NJ	08701	800-662-3044	751-7618*
**Fax Area Code:* 732 ■ *TF:* 800-662-3044 ■ *Web:* www.claytonco.com					
Clayton Cos, The PO Box 3015	Lakewood	NJ	08701	800-662-3044	
TF: 800-662-3044 ■ *Web:* www.claytonco.com					
Coastal Concrete Southeast II LLC 2500 Cumberland Pkwy Ste 200	Atlanta	GA	30339	912-330-8990	
Web: www.coastalconcrete.com					
Colorado Precast Concrete Inc 1820 14th St SE	Loveland	CO	80537	970-669-0535	
Web: www.coloprecast.com					
Complete Home Concepts Inc 4380 Beljoum Blvd	Riverside	MO	64150	816-471-4663	
Web: www.completehomeconcepts.com					
Con Cast Pipe LP 299 Brock Rd S RR#3	Guelph	ON	N1H6H9	800-668-7473	
TF: 800-668-7473 ■ *Web:* www.concastpipe.com					
Con Forms 777 Maritime Dr	Port Washington	WI	53074	262-284-7800	284-7878
TF: 800-223-3676 ■ *Web:* www.conforms.com					
Concast Inc 1010 N Star Dr	Zumbrota	MN	55992	507-732-4095	
Web: www.concastinc.com					
Concrete Equipment Company Inc 237 N 13th St	Blair	NE	68008	402-426-4181	
Web: con-e-co.com					
Concrete Structures Inc 12100 NW 58 St	Miami	FL	33178	305-597-9393	
Web: www.concretestructures.net					
Concrete Technology Corp 1123 Port of Tacoma Rd PO Box 2259	Tacoma	WA	98401	253-383-3545	572-9386
Web: www.concretetech.com					
Concrete Tie Corp 130 E Oris St	Compton	CA	90222	310-886-1000	638-8363
Web: www.concretetie.net					
Construction Products Inc 1631 Ashport Rd	Jackson	TN	38305	731-668-7305	668-1361
TF: 800-238-8226 ■ *Web:* www.cpi-tn.com					
Cook Concrete Products Inc 5461 Eastside Rd	Redding	CA	96001	530-243-2562	243-6881
Web: www.cookconcreteproducts.com					
Coreslab Structures Inc 150 W Placentia Ave	Perris	CA	92571	951-943-9119	943-7571
Web: www.coreslab.com					
Cranesville Block Company Inc 1250 Riverfront Ctr	Amsterdam	NY	12010	518-684-6000	
Web: www.cranesville.com					
Creter Vault Corp 417 US Hwy 202	Flemington	NJ	08822	908-782-7771	
TF: 800-352-4890					
Cretex Concrete Products Wes 725 Bryan Stock Trail	Casper	WY	82601	307-265-3100	265-0013
Web: www.cretexwest.com					
Cretex Cos 311 Lowell Ave	Elk River	MN	55330	763-441-2121	441-3585
Web: cretexcompanies.com					
Crom Corp 250 SW 36th Terr	Gainesville	FL	32607	352-372-3436	372-6209
Web: www.cromgnv.com					
CXT Inc 3808 N Sullivan Rd Bldg 7	Spokane	WA	99216	509-921-8766	
Web: www.cxtinc.com					
David Kucera Inc 42 Steves Ln	Gardiner	NY	12525	845-255-1044	
Web: davidkucerainc.com					
DN Tanks 351 Cypress Ln	El Cajon	CA	92020	619-440-8181	
TF: 800-227-8181 ■ *Web:* www.dntanks.com					
Dolese Bros Co 20 NW 13th St	Oklahoma City	OK	73103	405-235-2311	297-8329
TF: 800-375-2311 ■ *Web:* dolese.com					
DuKane Precast Inc 1805 High Grove Ln	Naperville	IL	60540	630-355-8118	
Web: www.dukaneprecast.com					
Dura-Stress Inc 11325 County Rd 44	Leesburg	FL	34788	352-787-1422	787-0080
TF General: 800-342-9239 ■ *Web:* www.durastress.com					
Dutchland Inc PO Box 549	Gap	PA	17527	717-442-8282	442-9330
Web: www.dutchlandinc.com					
E Dillon & Co 2522 Swords Creek Rd PO Box 160	Swords Creek	VA	24649	276-873-6816	873-4208
TF: 800-234-8970 ■ *Web:* www.edillon.com					
Echo Rock Ventures 13620 Lincoln Way Ste 380	Auburn	CA	95603	530-823-9600	823-9650
Empire Blended Products Inc 250 Hickory Ln	Bayville	NJ	08721	732-269-4949	
Web: empireblended.com					
Entreprises Jf Faucher Inc 1100 Chemin De Saint-jean	La Prairie	QC	J5R2L5	450-659-2222	
Web: www.botanix.com					
EP Henry Corp 201 Pk Ave	Woodbury	NJ	08096	856-845-6200	845-0023
TF: 800-444-3679 ■ *Web:* www.ephenry.com					
Ernest Maier Inc 4700 Annapolis Rd	Bladensburg	MD	20710	301-927-8300	779-8924
TF: 888-927-8303 ■ *Web:* www.emcoblock.com					
F S Prestress LLC 190 Prestress Rd	Princeton	LA	71067	318-949-2444	
Web: www.fsprestress.com					
Fabcon Inc 6111 Hwy 13 W	Savage	MN	55378	952-890-4444	890-6657
TF: 800-727-4444 ■ *Web:* www.fabcon-usa.com					
Featherlite Bldg Products Corp 508 McNeil St	Round Rock	TX	78681	512-255-2573	255-2572
Web: www.featherlitetexas.com					

Company / Address	City	State	ZIP	Phone	Fax
Federal Block Corp 247 Walsh Ave *TF:* 800-724-1999 ■ *Web:* www.montfortgroup.com	New Windsor	NY	12553	845-561-4108	561-5344
Fencecrete America Inc 15089 Tradesman Dr *Web:* www.fencecrete.com	San Antonio	TX	78249	210-492-7911	
Fendt Builders Supply Inc 22005 Gill Rd *Web:* www.fendtproducts.com	Farmington Hills	MI	48335	248-474-3211	474-8110
Fibrebond Corp 1300 Davenport Dr. *Web:* www.fibrebond.com	Minden	LA	71055	318-377-1030	
Fin Pan Inc 3255 Symmes Rd *TF:* 800-833-6444 ■ *Web:* www.finpan.com	Hamilton	OH	45015	513-870-9200	
Finfrock Industries Inc 2400 Apopka Blvd *Web:* finfrock.com	Apopka	FL	32703	407-293-4000	297-0512
Fitzgerald Formliners Inc 1500 E Chestnut Ave *Web:* www.formliners.com	Santa Ana	CA	92701	714-547-6710	
Fizzano Bros Concrete Products Inc 1776 Chester Pk *Web:* www.fizzano.com	Crum Lynne	PA	19022	610-833-1100	833-5347
Flexicore of Texas PO Box 450049 *TF:* 888-359-4267 ■ *Web:* www.flexicoreoftexas.com	Houston	TX	77245	281-437-5700	437-8913
Florence Concrete Products Inc PO Box 5506 *Web:* www.florenceconcreteproducts.com	Florence	SC	29502	843-662-2549	667-0729
Fountain People Inc 4600 Hwy 123 *Web:* fountainpeople.com	San Marcos	TX	78666	512-392-1155	
Fritz Industries Inc 180 Gordon Dr Ste 113 **Fax Area Code:* 610 ■ *TF:* 800-345-6202 ■ *Web:* www.fritztile.com	Exton	PA	19341	800-345-6202	363-0735*
Gage Brothers Concrete Products Inc 4301 W 12th St *Web:* www.gagebrothers.com	Sioux Falls	SD	57106	605-336-1180	
Gary Merlino Construction Co 9125 Tenth Ave S	Seattle	WA	98108	206-762-9125	763-4178
General Shale Products LLC 3015 Bristol Hwy *TF:* 800-414-4661 ■ *Web:* www.generalshale.com	Johnson City	TN	37601	423-282-4661	952-4104
Geneva Pipe Inc 1465 West 400 North *Web:* www.genevapipe.com	Orem	UT	84057	801-225-2416	
George L Throop Co 444 N Fair Oaks Ave *TF:* 800-796-0285 ■ *Web:* www.throop.com	Pasadena	CA	91103	626-796-0285	
GFRC Cladding Systems LLC 118 N Shiloh Rd *Web:* www.gfrccladding.com	Garland	TX	75042	972-494-9000	494-1900
Giannini Garden Ornaments Inc 225 Shaw Rd *Web:* www.gianninigarden.com	South San Francisco	CA	94080	650-873-4493	
Glen-Gery Corp 1166 Spring St PO Box 7001 *Web:* www.glengery.com	Wyomissing	PA	19610	610-374-4011	374-1622
Grand Blanc Cement Products 10709 Ctr Rd *TF:* 800-875-7500 ■ *Web:* www.grandblanccement.com	Grand Blanc	MI	48439	810-694-7500	694-2995
Gulf Coast Pre-stress Inc 494 Market St	Pass Christian	MS	39571	228-452-9486	
H2 Pre-Cast Inc 3835 N Clemons *Web:* www.h2precast.com	East Wenatchee	WA	98802	509-884-6644	
Hancock Concrete Products Inc 17 Atlantic Ave *Web:* www.hancockconcrete.com	Hancock	MN	56244	320-392-5207	392-5155
Hanover Pavers Inc 240 Bender Rd *Web:* www.hanoverpavers.com	Hanover	PA	17331	717-637-0500	
Hastings Pavement Company LLC 200 Henry St *Web:* www.hastingsarchitectural.com	Lindenhurst	NY	11757	631-669-0600	669-8052
Heldenfels Enterprises Inc 5700 IH-35 S (Exit 199) *Web:* heldenfels.com	San Marcos	TX	78666	512-396-2376	396-2381
High Concrete Structures Inc 125 Denver Rd **Fax:* Sales ■ *TF:* 800-773-2278 ■ *Web:* www.highconcrete.com	Denver	PA	17517	717-336-9300	336-9301*
High Industries Inc 1853 William Penn Way *Web:* www.high.net	Lancaster	PA	17601	717-293-4444	293-4416
Hy-Grade Precast Concrete 2411 First St *TF:* 800-229-8568 ■ *Web:* www.hygradeprecast.com	St Catharines	ON	L2R6P7	905-684-8568	
Isabel Bloom LLC 736 Federal St Ste 2100 **Fax Area Code:* 563 ■ *TF:* 800-273-5436 ■ *Web:* www.ibloom.com	Davenport	IA	52803	800-273-5436	333-2044*
Jensen Precast 625 Bergin Way *TF:* 800-648-1134 ■ *Web:* www.jensenprecast.com	Sparks	NV	89431	775-359-6200	359-1038
Jersey Precast Corp 853 Nottingham Way *Web:* www.jerseyprecast.com	Hamilton Township	NJ	08638	609-689-3700	
Joseph P. Carrara & Sons Inc 167 N Shrewsbury Rd *Web:* www.jpcarrara.com	North Clarendon	VT	05759	802-775-2301	
JW Peters Inc 500 W Market St *TF:* 866-265-7888 ■ *Web:* journaltimes.com	Burlington	WI	53105	262-806-9009	763-2779
K & S Contractors Supply Company Inc 1971 Gunnville Rd	Lancaster	NY	14086	716-759-6911	759-2129
Kieft Bros Inc 837 S Riverside Dr *Web:* www.kieftbros.com	Elmhurst	IL	60126	630-832-8090	834-5765
King's Material Inc 650 12th Ave SW *TF:* 800-332-5298 ■ *Web:* www.kingsmaterial.com	Cedar Rapids	IA	52404	319-363-0233	366-0249
Kistner Concrete Products Inc 8713 Read Rd *TF:* 800-809-2801 ■ *Web:* www.kistner.com	East Pembroke	NY	14056	585-762-8216	762-8315
L M Scofield Co 6533 Bandini Blvd *TF:* 800-800-9900 ■ *Web:* www.scofield.com	Los Angeles	CA	90040	323-720-3000	
Lafarge North America Inc 8700 W Bryn Mawr Ave Ste 300 *Web:* www.lafarge-na.com	Chicago	VA	60631	703-480-3600	480-3899
Lakelands Concrete Products Inc 7520 E Main St *Web:* www.lakelandsconcrete.com	Lima	NY	14485	585-624-1990	
Landis Block Co 711 N County Line Rd PO Box 64418 *Web:* www.landisbc.com	Souderton	PA	18964	215-723-5506	723-5500
Leavcon Ii Inc 108 American Ave *Web:* www.leavcon.com	Lansing	KS	66043	913-351-1430	
Lombard Co 4245 W 123rd St *Web:* lombardcompany.com	Alsip	IL	60803	708-389-1060	389-7120
M-CON Products Inc 2150 Richardson Side Rd *TF:* 800-267-5515 ■ *Web:* www.mconproducts.com	Carp	ON	K0A1L0	613-831-1736	831-2048
Mack Industries Inc 1321 Industrial Pkwy N Ste 500 *Web:* www.mackconcrete.com	Brunswick	OH	44212	330-460-7005	
MantelsDirect 217 N Seminary St *TF:* 888-493-8898 ■ *Web:* www.mantelsdirect.com	Florence	AL	35630	888-493-8898	
Mathis-Akins Concrete Block Co Inc 130 Lower Elm St	Macon	GA	31206	478-746-5154	
Metromont Corp PO Box 2486 *TF:* 888-295-0383 ■ *Web:* www.metromont.com	Greenville	SC	29602	864-295-0295	295-0295
Midwest Cast Stone Inc 1610 State Ave *Web:* www.midwestcaststone.com	Kansas City	KS	66102	913-371-3300	
Midwest Tile & Concrete Products Inc 4309 Webster Rd *Web:* www.midwesttile.net	Woodburn	IN	46797	260-749-5173	493-2477
Millenium Products Inc 6346 Heron Pkwy *Web:* www.milleniumproducts.net	Clarkston	MI	48346	239-877-6811	
MMC Materials Inc 1052 Highland Colony Pkwy Ste 201 *Web:* www.mmcmaterials.com	Ridgeland	MS	39157	601-898-4000	898-4030
Modern Inc/Environmental & Wastewater 210 Durham Rd *TF:* 888-965-3227 ■ *Web:* www.modcon.com	Ottsville	PA	18942	610-847-5112	847-2468
Molin Concrete Products Co 415 Lilac St *TF:* 800-336-6546 ■ *Web:* www.molin.com	Lino Lakes	MN	55014	651-786-7722	786-0229
Montfort Bros Inc 44 Elm St *TF:* 800-724-1777 ■ *Web:* www.montfortgroup.com	Fishkill	NY	12524	845-896-6225	896-0021
Montfort Group, The 44 Elm St *TF:* 800-724-1777 ■ *Web:* www.montfortgroup.com	Fishkill	NY	12524	845-896-6225	896-0021
Mutual Materials Co 605 119th Ave NE *TF:* 800-477-3008 ■ *Web:* www.mutualmaterials.com	Bellevue	WA	98005	425-452-2300	454-7732
NAPCO Precast LLC 6949 Low Bid Ln *Web:* www.napcosa.com	San Antonio	TX	78250	210-509-9100	509-9111
National Concrete Products Co 939 S Mill St **Fax Area Code:* 281	Plymouth	MI	48170	734-453-8448	452-6506*
National Oilwell Varco (NOV) 7909 Parkwood Cir Dr *NYSE:* NOV ■ *TF:* 888-262-8645 ■ *Web:* www.nov.com	Houston	TX	77036	713-375-3700	
NC Products Corp 920 Withers Rd PO Box 27077 *TF:* 888-965-3227 ■ *Web:* oldcastleprecast.com	Raleigh	NC	27603	919-772-6301	772-1209
New Milford Block & Supply 574 Danbury Rd *TF:* 800-724-1888 ■ *Web:* www.montfortgroup.com	New Milford	CT	06776	860-355-1101	355-3772
Nitterhouse Concrete Products Inc 2655 Molly Pitcher Hwy *Web:* www.nitterhouse.com	Chambersburg	PA	17201	717-267-4505	267-4518
Northfield an Oldcastle Co 2200 S Main St *TF:* 800-227-6512 ■ *Web:* northfieldblock.com	West Bend	WI	53095	262-338-5700	
Norwalk Concrete Industries Inc 80 Commerce Dr *TF:* 800-733-3624 ■ *Web:* www.nciprecast.com	Norwalk	OH	44857	419-668-8167	
Oldcastle Precast Inc 7921 Southpark Pl Ste 200 *TF:* 800-642-3755 ■ *Web:* www.oldcastleprecast.com	Folsom	NJ	08037	800-642-3755	
Olson Precast Co (OPC) 2750 Marion Dr *TF:* 800-876-8374	Las Vegas	NV	89115	702-643-4371	643-4510
Orco Block Co Inc 11100 Beach Blvd *Web:* www.orco.com	Stanton	CA	90680	714-527-2239	895-4021
Phoenix Precast Products Inc 1856 E Deer Vly Rd *Web:* www.phoenixprecastproducts.com	Phoenix	AZ	85024	602-569-6090	
Pontchartrain Materials Corp 3819 France Rd *Web:* www.pontchartrain.com	New Orleans	LA	70126	504-949-7571	
Pre-Cast Specialties Inc 1380 NE 48th St *Web:* www.precastspecialties.com	Pompano Beach	FL	33064	954-781-4040	781-3539
Preload Inc 49 Wireless Blvd STE 200 *Web:* www.preload.com	Hauppauge	NY	11788	631-231-8100	231-8881
Premarc Corp 7505 E M 71	Durand	MI	48429	989-288-2661	288-6366
Premier Concrete Products 5102 Galveston Rd *Web:* www.premier-concrete.com	Houston	TX	77017	713-641-2727	641-1112
Prestress Engineering Corp 2220 Rt 176 *Web:* www.pre-stress.com	Prairie Grove	IL	60012	815-459-4545	459-6855
Prestress Services Inc 7855 NW Winchester Rd *Web:* www.prestressservices.com	Decatur	IN	46733	260-724-7117	724-3349
Prestressed Casting Co 1600 S Scenic Ave *Web:* www.prestressedcasting.com	Springfield	MO	65807	417-869-7350	
Puerto Rican Cement Company Inc PO Box 364487 *Web:* www.cemexpuertorico.com	San Juan	PR	00936	787-783-3000	
QUIKRETE Cos 3490 Piedmont Rd Ste 1300 *TF:* 800-282-5828 ■ *Web:* www.quikrete.com	Atlanta	GA	30305	404-634-9100	842-1424
Rancho Bldg Materials Co 4701 Wible Rd	Bakersfield	CA	93313	661-831-0831	831-0244
RCP Block & Brick Inc 8240 Broadway *TF:* 800-794-4727 ■ *Web:* www.rcpblock.com	Lemon Grove	CA	91945	619-460-7250	460-3926
Reading Precast Inc 5494 Pottsville Pike *TF:* 800-724-4881 ■ *Web:* www.readingprecast.com	Leesport	PA	19533	610-926-5000	926-0894
Reading Rock Inc 4600 Devitt Dr *TF:* 800-482-6466 ■ *Web:* www.readingrock.com	Cincinnati	OH	45246	513-874-2345	874-2520
RI Lampus Co 816 RI Lampus Ave PO Box 167 **Fax Area Code:* 724 ■ *Web:* www.lampus.com	Springdale	PA	15144	412-362-3800	274-2181*
Rinker Materials Corp Concrete Pipe Div 8311 W Carder Ct *TF:* 800-909-7763 ■ *Web:* www.rinkerpipe.com	Littleton	CO	80125	303-791-1600	791-1710
Rockwood Retaining Walls Inc 7200 Hwy 63 N **Fax Area Code:* 507 ■ *TF:* 800-535-2375 ■ *Web:* www.rockwoodwalls.com	Rochester	MN	55906	888-288-4045	529-2879*
Rolling Mix Management Ltd 7209 Railway St SE *Web:* www.rollingmix.com	Calgary	AB	T2H2V6	403-253-6426	

Phone *Fax*

Royal Concrete Pipe Inc
30622 Forest Blvd PO Box 430........................Stacy MN 55079 651-462-2130
Web: www.royalenterprises.net

SD Ireland Co 193 Industrial Ave....................Williston VT 05495 802-863-6222
TF: 800-339-4565 ■ *Web:* www.sdireland.com

Selkirk Canada Corp 375 Green Rd..............Stoney Creek ON L8E4A5 905-662-6600
Web: www.selkirkcorp.com

Seminole Precast Manufacturing Inc
331 Benson Junction Rd..........................Debary FL 32713 386-668-7323
Web: www.seminoleprecast.com

Sequatchie Concrete Service Inc
406 Cedar Ave............................South Pittsburg TN 37380 423-837-7913 837-7479
TF: 800-824-0824 ■ *Web:* www.seqconcrete.com

Silver State Materials LLC
4005 Dean Martin Dr..........................Las Vegas NV 89103 702-650-5000
Web: www.ssmaterials.com

Smith-Midland Corp 5119 Catlett Rd PO Box 300........Midland VA 22728 540-439-3266 439-1232
OTC: SMID ■ *Web:* www.smithmidland.com

Spancrete Industries Inc
N 16 W 23415 Stone Ridge Dr PO Box 828..........Waukesha WI 53187 414-290-9000
TF: 855-900-7726 ■ *Web:* www.spancrete.com

Specchem 444 Richmond Ave.....................Kansas City KS 66101 816-968-5600
Web: www.specchemllc.com

Speed Fab-Crete Corp International
PO Box 15580..................................Fort Worth TX 76119 817-478-1137 561-2544
Web: www.speedfab-crete.com

StressCrete Group 9200 Energy Ln.................Northport AL 35476 205-339-0711
Web: www.stresscretegroup.com

Stubbe's Precast 30 Muir Line.........................Harley ON N0E1E0 519-424-2183
Web: www.stubbesprecast.org

Superlite Block Co Inc 4150 W Turney Ave............Phoenix AZ 85019 602-352-3500 352-3813
TF: 800-366-7877 ■ *Web:* www.superliteblock.com

Terre Hill Silo Company Inc PO Box 10.............Terre Hill PA 17581 717-445-3100 445-3108
TF: 800-242-1509 ■ *Web:* www.terrehill.com

Texas Concrete Co 4702 N Vine St....................Victoria TX 77904 361-573-9145
Web: www.texasconcreteco.com

Tindall Corp 2273 Hayne St.......................Spartanburg SC 29301 864-576-3230 587-8828
TF: 800-849-4521 ■ *Web:* www.tindallcorp.com

Unistress Corp 550 Cheshire Rd....................Pittsfield MA 01201 413-499-1441 499-9930
Web: www.unistresscorp.com

Universal Concrete Products Corp
400 Old Reading Pk Ste 100..........................Stowe PA 19464 610-323-0700 323-4046
Web: www.universalconcrete.com

Utility Concrete Products 2495 Bungalow Rd...........Morris IL 60450 815-416-1000
Web: www.utilityconcrete.com

Valley Blox Inc 210 Stone Spring Rd.............Harrisonburg VA 22801 540-434-6725 434-6514*
**Fax: Acctg* ■ *TF:* 800-648-6725 ■ *Web:* valleybuildingsupply.com

Verti-Crete LLC 16500 South 500 West..............Bluffdale UT 84065 801-571-2028
Web: www.verti-crete.com

Walters & Wolf Precast 41777 Boyce Rd.............Fremont CA 94538 510-226-9800 226-0360
Web: www.waltersandwolf.com

Wausau Tile Inc PO Box 1520.......................Wausau WI 54402 715-359-3121 355-4627
TF: 800-388-8728 ■ *Web:* www.wausautile.com

Wells Concrete Products Inc
835 Hwy 109 NE PO Box 308...........................Wells MN 56097 507-553-3138 553-6089
TF: 800-658-7049 ■ *Web:* www.wellsconcrete.com

Western Architectural Services LLC
12552 South 125 West Ste B..........................Draper UT 84020 801-523-0393
Web: www.western-architectural.com

Wieser Concrete Products Inc
W3716 US Hwy 10..............................Maiden Rock WI 54750 715-647-2311 647-5181
TF: 800-325-8456 ■ *Web:* www.wieserconcrete.com

Wingra Stone Co 2975 Kapec Rd PO Box 44284........Madison WI 53744 608-271-5555 271-3142
TF: 800-249-6908 ■ *Web:* www.wingrastone.com

York Bldg Products Co 950 Smile Way..................York PA 17404 717-848-2831 854-9156
TF: 800-673-2408 ■ *Web:* www.yorkbuilding.com

184 CONFERENCE & EVENTS COORDINATORS

Phone *Fax*

Absolute Exhibits Inc 1382 Valencia Ave Ste H...........Tustin CA 92780 714-685-2800
Web: www.absoluteexhibits.com

Accent on Cincinnati 915 W Eigth St...............Cincinnati OH 45203 513-721-8687 721-1542
Web: www.accentcinti.com

Aim Meetings & Events 212 S Henry St Fl 2..........Alexandria VA 22314 703-549-9500
Web: www.aimmeetings.com

Amc Network LLC
708 Gravenstein Hwy N Ste 184...................Sebastopol CA 95472 707-829-9484
Web: www.amcnetwork.com

Arata Expositions Inc
15928 Tournament Dr.........................Gaithersburg MD 20877 301-921-0800
Web: www.arataexpo.com

ASD 6255 Sunset Blvd 19th Fl.....................Los Angeles CA 90028 323-817-2200 957-1131
TF: 800-421-4511 ■ *Web:* www.asdonline.com

Ashbury Images 1661 Tennessee St Ste 3G........San Francisco CA 94107 415-885-2742
Web: www.ashburyimages.org

Ashton Gardens Houston
21919 Inverness Forest Blvd.......................Houston TX 77073 281-362-0011
Web: www.ashtongardens.com

Ayers Meetings & Events Inc
19727 Whitewind Dr..................................Houston TX 77094 281-492-7272
Web: www.ayersme.com

Bell Trans 1900 Industrial Rd.......................Las Vegas NV 89102 702-739-7990
Web: www.airportshuttlelasvegas.com

Bixel & Co 8721 Sunset Blvd Ste 101...............Los Angeles CA 90069 310-854-3828
TF: 855-854-9830 ■ *Web:* www.bixelco.com

Briggs Inc 1501 Broadway..........................New York NY 10036 212-354-9440
Web: www.briggsnyc.com

Can-do Promotions Inc 6517 Wise Ave Nw.........North Canton OH 44720 330-494-3527
TF: 800-325-7981 ■ *Web:* www.candopromo.com

Phone *Fax*

Cappa & Graham Inc
401 Terry A Francois Blvd Ste 128...............San Francisco CA 94158 415-512-6967
Web: www.cappa-graham.com

Carlisle Productions Inc 1000 Bryn Mawr Rd..........Carlisle PA 17013 717-243-7855
Web: www.carlisleevents.com

Celebritees Inc 1014 Atlantic Ave....................Savannah GA 31401 912-233-9941
TF: 877-831-1005 ■ *Web:* www.celebritees.net

Centennial Conferences 908 Main St Ste 350.........Louisville CO 80027 303-499-2299 499-2599
Web: www.centennialconferences.com

COMCOR Event & Meeting Production
1040 Bayview Dr # 407......................Fort Lauderdale FL 33304 954-491-3233
Web: www.comcorevents.com

Conference & Logistics Consultants Inc
31 Old Solomans Island Rd.......................Annapolis MD 21401 410-571-0590 571-0592
Web: www.gomeeting.com

Conference & Travel 5655 Coventry Ln............Fort Wayne IN 46804 260-434-6600
TF: 800-346-9807 ■ *Web:* www.conftvl.com

Conference Consultants 445 El Escarpado.............Stanford CA 94305 650-324-1653 326-7751

Conference Group Inc 1580 Fishinger Rd...........Columbus OH 43221 614-488-2030 488-5747

Conference Hotels Unlimited 51 Harborview Rd...........Hull MA 02045 781-925-4000 925-2474
Web: conferencehotels.com

Conference Management Assoc Inc
45 Lyme Rd Ste 304..................................Hanover NH 03755 603-643-2325 643-1444

Conference Management Services PO Box 2506.....Monterey CA 93942 831-622-7772 622-0711
Web: www.conferencemanagement.net

Conference Solutions Inc
520 SW Yamhill St Ste 430..........................Portland OR 97204 503-244-4294 244-2401
Web: www.conferencesolutionsinc.com

Convention Consultants Historic Savannah Foundation
117 W Perry St......................................Savannah GA 31401 912-234-4088
Web: www.conventionconsultants.net

Copyworks 4837 First Ave Se Ste 103..............Cedar Rapids IA 52402 319-373-5335
Web: copyworks.com

Courtesy Assoc 2025 M St NW Ste 800.............Washington DC 20036 800-647-4689
TF: 800-647-4689 ■ *Web:* www.courtesyassociates.com

Creative Impact Group Inc
801 Skokie Blvd Ste 108...........................Northbrook IL 60062 847-945-7401
TF: 800-445-2171 ■ *Web:* www.creativeimpactgroup.com

Crescent City Consultants
1010 Common St Ste 3010.......................New Orleans LA 70112 504-561-1191 568-0783
Web: www.ccc-nola.com

CSI Worldwide Inc 40 Regency Plz..................Glen Mills PA 19342 610-558-4500
TF: 800-523-7118 ■ *Web:* www.csiworldwide.net

D & L Entertainment Services Inc 4120 Main St........Dallas TX 75226 214-634-0757
Web: dandlentertainment.com

Destination Resources 5435 Balboa Blvd Ste 106........Encino CA 91316 818-995-7915 990-6129
TF: 800-422-6524 ■ *Web:* www.destinationresources.com

Destination Services of Colorado Inc (DSC)
PO Box 3660...Avon CO 81620 970-476-6565
Web: www.dsc-co.com

Eagle Recognition 2706 Mtn Industrial Blvd.............Tucker GA 30084 770-985-0808
Web: www.eaglerecognition.com

Event Planning International Corp
10900 Granite St.....................................Charlotte NC 28273 980-233-3777 233-3800
TF: 800-940-2164 ■ *Web:* www.epicreg.com

Every Promotional Product
30401 Agoura Rd Ste 102.........................Agoura Hills CA 91301 818-597-9900
Web: www.everypromotionalproduct.com

Excel Decorators Inc 3748 Kentucky Ave...........Indianapolis IN 46221 317-856-1300
Web: lexusbadexperiences.com

Executive Arrangements
2460 Fairmount Blvd Ste 205........................Cleveland OH 44106 216-231-9311
Web: www.executivearrangements.com

Exhibit Concepts Inc 700 Crossroads Ct..............Vandalia OH 45377 800-324-5063
TF: 800-324-5063 ■ *Web:* www.exhibitconcepts.com

Exhibits Development Group LLC
Landmark Ctr 432 75 W Fifth St.....................Saint Paul MN 55102 651-222-1121
Web: www.exhibitsdevelopment.com

Experient Inc 2500 E Enterprise Pkwy................Twinsburg OH 44087 330-425-8333 425-3299
Web: www.experient-inc.com

Expo Group, The 5931 W Campus Cir Dr.................Irving TX 75063 972-580-9000 550-7877
TF: 800-736-7775 ■ *Web:* www.theexpogroup.com

ExpoMarketing LLC 2741 Dow Ave.......................Tustin CA 92780 949-250-3976
Web: www.expomarketing.com

Fotofest Inc 1113 Vine St Ste 101.....................Houston TX 77002 713-223-5522
Web: www.fotofest.org

Freddie Georges Production Group
15362 Graham St.....................................La Palma CA 92649 714-367-9260
Web: www.freddiegeorges.com

Freeman Cos 1600 Viceroy Ste 100.......................Dallas TX 75235 214-445-1000 445-0200
Web: www.freemanco.com

Gavel International Corp
300 Tri State International Ste 320................Lincolnshire IL 60069 847-945-8150 945-6569
TF: 800-544-2835 ■ *Web:* www.gavelintl.com

Genuity Concepts Inc 507 N Church St............Greensboro NC 27401 336-379-1850
Web: www.genuityconcepts.com

GES Exposition Services 7000 Lindell Rd............Las Vegas NV 89118 702-515-5500 515-5765
TF: 800-443-9767 ■ *Web:* www.ges.com

Gls Group Inc 27850 Detroit Rd.......................Westlake OH 44145 440-899-7770
TF: 800-955-9435 ■ *Web:* glsgroup.com

Graphic Creations Inc 213 E 4th Ave................Knoxville TN 37916 865-522-6221
Web: www.graphiccreations.com

Graylyn International Conference Center Inc
1900 Reynolda Rd..............................Winston-Salem NC 27106 336-758-2600
TF: 800-472-9596 ■ *Web:* graylyn.com

Great Events & TEAMS Inc
2170 S Parker Rd Ste 290...........................Denver CO 80231 303-394-2022 394-3450
TF: 866-706-7814 ■ *Web:* www.geteams.com

GT Consultants Inc 3050 Eagle Watch Dr...........Woodstock GA 30189 770-591-1343
Web: www.gtconsultantsinc.com

Gtcbio 635 W Foothill Blvd.........................Monrovia CA 91016 626-256-6405
Web: gtcbio.com

Hartford York 2615 Boeing Way.......................Stockton CA 95206 209-982-5462

				Phone	Fax
Health Connect Partners Inc					
65 Business Park Dr...Lebanon	TN	37090		615-449-6234	
Web: www.hlthcp.com					
Henry V Events 6360 NE ML K Jr Blvd...Portland	OR	97211		503-232-6666	
Web: www.henryvevents.com					
Holiday Models Convention Services					
3651 Lindell Rd Ste D140...Las Vegas	NV	89103		702-735-7353	796-5676
Web: www.holidaymodels.com					
Hughes Production 1625 Berger Ln PO Box 3556...Jackson	WY	83001		307-733-6505	733-0542
Web: www.hughesproduction.com					
Idegy 3990 Business Park Dr...Columbus	OH	43204		614-545-5000	
TF: 888-421-2288 ■ *Web:* idegy.com					
IDG World Expo 3 Speen St Ste 320...Framingham	MA	01701		508-879-6700	
Web: www.idgworldexpo.com					
Incentive Travel & Meetings (ITM)					
970 Clementstone Dr Ste 100...Atlanta	GA	30342		404-252-2728	252-8328
Web: www.usaitm.com					
International Meeting Managers Inc					
4550 Post Oak Pl Ste 342...Houston	TX	77027		713-965-0566	960-0488
TF: 800-423-7175 ■ *Web:* www.meetingmanagers.com					
International Trade Information Inc (ITI)					
900 Las Vegas Blvd S Unit 908...Las Vegas	NV	89101		818-591-2255	591-2289
Web: www.internationaltradeinformation.com					
Ivey Performance Marketing LLC					
5679 SE International Way...Portland	OR	97222		503-794-9800	
Web: www.ivey.com					
JBW Entertainment LLC					
2465 S Industrial Park Ave Ste 3...Phoenix	AZ	85282		623-434-8822	
Web: www.koolpartyrentals.com					
Kerry Group LLC, The 44 Soccer Park Rd...Fenton	MO	63026		636-203-5550	
Web: www.kerrygroup.net					
Key Event Group LLC, The 3815 Hilldale Dr...Nashville	TN	37215		615-352-6900	385-4976
Web: www.nashvilledmc.com					
LEO Events 265 S Front St...Memphis	TN	38103		901-766-1836	
Web: www.leoevents.com					
Lydon Co 143 St Clair Dr...Saint Simons Island	GA	31522		912-638-0901	638-2451
Lynnwood Convention Center 3711 196th St Sw...Lynnwood	WA	98036		425-778-7155	
Web: lynnwoodcc.com					
Management International Inc					
1828 SE First Ave...Fort Lauderdale	FL	33316		954-763-8003	425-1995*
*Fax Area Code: 800 ■ *Web:* www.currentreviews.com					
Maxcel Co 13601 Preston Rd E Twr Ste 935...Dallas	TX	75240		972-644-0880	680-2488
Web: www.maxcel.net					
Meeting Alliance LLC					
Bank Plz 14 Main St...Robbinsville	NJ	08691		609-208-1908	
Web: www.meetingalliance.com					
Meeting Connection Inc, The					
6373 Meadow Glen Dr N...Westerville	OH	43082		614-888-2568	
TF: 800-398-2568 ■ *Web:* www.the-meeting-connection.com					
Meeting Services Unlimited					
135 S Mitthoeffer Rd...Indianapolis	IN	46229		317-841-7171	
Web: www.conventionmanagers.com					
Meetings & Incentives Group					
21760 Stevens Creek Blvd...Cupertino	CA	95014		408-973-1915	
Web: www.migr.com					
Mirror Show Management Inc 855 Hard Rd...Webster	NY	14580		585-232-4020	
Web: www.mirrorshow.com					
MP Assoc Inc 1721 Boxelder St Ste 107...Louisville	CO	80027		303-530-4562	530-4334
Web: www.mpassociates.com					
National Trade Productions Inc					
313 S Patrick St...Alexandria	VA	22314		703-683-8500	836-4486
TF: 800-687-7469 ■ *Web:* www.ntpshow.com					
Nceca 4845 Pearl East Cir Ste 101...Boulder	CO	80301		303-828-2811	
Web: nceca.net					
Omnience Inc 1350 Center Dr Ste 100...Atlanta	GA	30338		770-399-3199	
Web: omnienceevents.com					
On the Scene 500 N Dearborn St Ste 550...Chicago	IL	60654		312-661-1440	
Web: www.onthescene.com/chicago-event-management-company					
Ones We Love Inc					
3901 Westerly Pl Ste 205...Newport Beach	CA	92660		714-658-1033	
Web: www.owlus.com					
Pacific Agenda 2425 NW Overton St...Portland	OR	97210		503-223-8633	
Paramount Convention Services Inc					
5015 Fyler Ave...Saint Louis	MO	63139		314-621-6677	
Web: www.paramountcs.com					
Pat Hoey Productions 167 Auburn St...Auburn	MA	01501		508-832-3300	
Web: www.thebostonhomeshow.com					
Paulette Wolf Events & Entertainment Inc					
1165 N Clark St Ste 613...Chicago	IL	60610		312-981-2600	
Web: www.pwe-e.com					
Pearson & Pipkin Inc					
1101 Pennsylvania Ave SE Ste 201...Washington	DC	20003		202-547-7177	
Pearson Group 904 Princess Anne St...Fredericksburg	VA	22401		540-373-4493	
Web: pearsonplanners.com					
Pittcon 300 Penn Ctr Blvd Ste 332...Pittsburgh	PA	15235		412-825-3220	
TF: 800-825-3221 ■ *Web:* www.pittcon.org					
Prestige Accommodations International					
1231 E Dyer Rd Ste 240...Santa Ana	CA	92705		714-957-9100	
TF: 800-321-6338 ■ *Web:* www.meetingplanners.com					
Productions USA Inc 1960 N Lincoln Pk W...Chicago	IL	60614		773-296-6200	296-6333
Web: www.productionsusa.com					
Proteus On-Demand Facilities LLC					
6727 Oak Ridge Commerce Way SW...Austell	GA	30168		770-333-1886	
Web: www.proteusondemand.com					
Recourse Communications Inc					
112 Intracoastal Pointe Dr...Jupiter	FL	33477		561-686-6800	
Web: www.rcirecruitmentsolutions.com					
Resource Connection Inc 161 S Main St...Middleton	MA	01949		978-777-9333	777-3360
TF: 800-649-5228 ■ *Web:* www.resource-connection.com					
Reverse Logistics Trends Inc					
441 West Main St Ste D...Lehi	UT	84043		801-331-8949	
Web: www.reverselogisticstrends.com					
Robustelli Corporate Services					
1717 Newfield Ave...Stamford	CT	06903		203-322-2790	912-6487
Web: www.rcsltd.com					
RX Worldwide Meetings Inc					
3060 Communications Pkwy Ste 200...Plano	TX	75093		214-291-2920	291-2930
TF: 800-562-1713 ■ *Web:* www.rx-worldwide.net					
S.A.F.E. Management LLC					
Arizona 1 Cardinals Dr...Glendale	AZ	85305		623-433-7300	
Web: www.safemanagement.net					
Sand Assoc 3560 Green St...Harrisburg	PA	17110		717-238-5558	238-4626
Web: www.sandassociates.com					
Schneider Group 5400 Bosque Blvd Ste 680...Waco	TX	76710		254-776-3550	776-3767
Web: www.sgmeet.com					
Seattle Hospitality Group					
16 W Harrison St 2nd Fl...Seattle	WA	98119		206-623-2090	623-2540
Web: www.shworldwide.com					
Secretariat PO Box 3509...Wilmington	DE	19807		302-654-4479	654-4117
Web: www.secevents.com					
Shepard Exposition Services					
1531 Carroll Dr NW...Atlanta	GA	30318		404-720-8600	720-8750
Web: www.shepardes.com					
Shreveport Convention Center 400 Caddo St...Shreveport	LA	71101		318-841-4000	
Web: shreveportcenter.com					
Splash!events Inc 210 Hillsdale Ave...San Jose	CA	95136		408-287-8600	
TF: 866-204-6000 ■ *Web:* www.splashevents.com					
Steven Restivo Event Services LLC					
805 Fourth St Ste 8...San Rafael	CA	94901		415-456-6455	
Web: www.sresproductions.com					
T3 Expo LLC					
8 Lakeville Business Park Unit 1...Lakeville	MA	02347		888-698-3397	
TF: 888-698-3397 ■ *Web:* www.t3expo.com					
TBA Global LLC 220 W 42nd St 10th Fl...New York	NY	10036		646-445-7000	445-7001
Transeair Travel LLC 2813 McKinley Pl NW...Washington	DC	20015		202-362-6100	362-7411
Web: www.transeairtravel.com					
Travizon Meeting Management					
275 Mishawum Rd Ste 300...Woburn	MA	01801		888-781-5200	
TF: 800-423-2500 ■ *Web:* www.travizon.com					
Universal Odyssey Inc					
1601 Dove St Ste 260...Newport Beach	CA	92660		949-263-1222	263-0983
Web: www.universalodyssey.com					
Van Winkle & Associates Inc					
1180 W Peachtree St Nw Ste 400...Atlanta	GA	30309		404-355-0126	
Web: www.vanwinkleassociates.com					
Vega Group 7220 Washington Ave...New Orleans	LA	70125		504-488-5222	
Web: www.vegagroup.com					
Vista Convention Services Inc					
6804 Delilah Rd...Egg Harbor Township	NJ	08234		609-485-2421	
Web: www.vistacs.com					
Westbury National Show Systems Ltd					
772 Warden Ave...Toronto	ON	M1L4T7		416-752-1371	
TF: 855-752-1372 ■ *Web:* www.westbury.com					
Weston & Assoc Inc 110 Thomas St...Winston-Salem	NC	27101		336-725-1147	725-0551
Web: www.westoninc.com					
Willwork Inc 23 Norfolk Ave...South Easton	MA	02375		508-230-3170	
Web: www2.willworkinc.com					
Wilsonwest Inc 1601 Dolores St...San Francisco	CA	94110		415-282-4560	
Web: www.wilsonwest.com					
Wings Unlimited Inc 455 Post Rd Ste 102...Darien	CT	06820		203-656-9591	656-1141
Web: www.wingsunlimited.net					

185 CONGLOMERATES

See Also Holding Companies p. 2464

A business conglomerate is defined here as a corporation that consists of many business units in different industries.

			Phone	Fax
3M Co 3M Ctr Bldg 225-3S-06...Saint Paul	MN	55144	651-733-1110	733-9973*
NYSE: MMM ■ *Fax:* Mail Rm ■ *TF:* 800-364-3577 ■ *Web:* www.3m.com				
Aerojet Rocketdyne Holdings Inc				
Hwy 50 & Aerojet Rd PO Box 537012...Rancho Cordova	CA	95742	916-355-4000	351-8667
NYSE: GY				
Alexander & Baldwin Inc 822 Bishop St...Honolulu	HI	96813	808-525-6611	525-6652
NYSE: ALEX ■ *TF:* 866-442-6551 ■ *Web:* www.alexanderbaldwin.com				
Alleghany Corp 1411 Broadway FL 34...New York	NY	10018	212-752-1356	
NYSE: Y ■ *Web:* www.alleghany.com				
Alticor Inc 7575 Fulton St E...Ada	MI	49355	616-787-1000	787-4764*
*Fax: Hum Res ■ *Web:* www.alticor.com				
Altria Group Inc 6601 W Broad St...Richmond	VA	23230	804-274-2200	
NYSE: MO ■ *Web:* www.altria.com				
AMERCO 1325 Airmotive Way Ste 100...Reno	NV	89502	775-688-6300	688-6338
NASDAQ: UHAL ■ *Web:* www.amerco.com				
Andersons Inc 480 W Dussel Dr...Maumee	OH	43537	419-893-5050	
NASDAQ: ANDE ■ *TF:* 800-537-3370 ■ *Web:* www.andersonsinc.com				
APi Group Inc 1100 Old Hwy 8 NW...New Brighton	MN	55112	800-223-4922	636-0312*
*Fax Area Code: 651 ■ *TF:* 800-223-4922 ■ *Web:* www.apigroupinc.com				
ARAMARK Corp 1101 Market St...Philadelphia	PA	19107	937-660-4708	
TF: 800-388-3300 ■ *Web:* www.aramark.com				
Archer Daniels Midland Co (ADM)				
4666 E Faries Pkwy...Decatur	IL	62526	217-424-5200	
NYSE: ADM ■ *TF:* 800-637-5843 ■ *Web:* www.adm.com				
Ashland Inc 50 E River Ctr Blvd PO Box 391...Covington	KY	41012	859-815-3333	
NYSE: ASH ■ *TF:* 877-546-2782 ■ *Web:* www.ashland.com				
Ball Corp 10 Longs Peak Dr...Broomfield	CO	80021	303-469-3131	
NYSE: BLL ■ *Web:* www.ball.com				
Berkshire Hathaway Inc 3555 Farnam St Ste 1440...Omaha	NE	68131	402-346-1400	346-3375
NYSE: BRK/A ■ *TF:* 800-223-2064 ■ *Web:* www.berkshirehathaway.com				
Berwind Group				
1500 Market St 3000 Ctr Sq W...Philadelphia	PA	19102	215-563-2800	575-2314
Web: www.berwind.com				
BFC Financial Corp				
401 E Las Olas Blvd Ste 800...Fort Lauderdale	FL	33301	954-940-4994	
OTC: BFCF ■ *Web:* www.bfcfinancial.com				

Company	City	State	ZIP	Phone	Fax
Brink's Inc 1801 Bayberry Ct PO Box 18100 NYSE: BCO ■ *Fax: Mail Rm ■ TF Sales: 800-274-6575 ■ Web: www.brinks.com/en	Richmond	VA	23226	804-289-9600	289-9770*
Brown-Forman Corp 850 Dixie Hwy PO Box 1080 NYSE: BFB ■ TF: 800-831-9146 ■ Web: www.brown-forman.com	Louisville	KY	40210	502-585-1100	774-7188
Canadian Tire Corp Ltd 2180 Yonge St PO Box 770 Stn K TSE: CTC ■ TF: 800-387-8803 ■ Web: www.corp.canadiantire.ca	Toronto	ON	M4P2V8	416-480-3000	544-7715
Carlson Cos Inc 701 Carlson Pkwy Web: www.carlson.com	Minnetonka	MN	55305	763-212-5000	
Chemed Corp 255 E Fifth St Ste 2600 NYSE: CHE ■ TF General: 800-982-7650 ■ Web: www.chemed.com	Cincinnati	OH	45202	513-762-6900	
Clorox Co 1221 Broadway NYSE: CLX ■ TF Cust Svc: 800-424-9300 ■ Web: www.thecloroxcompany.com	Oakland	CA	94612	510-271-7000	832-1463
CSX Corp 500 Water St 15th Fl NYSE: CSX ■ Web: csx.com	Jacksonville	FL	32202	904-359-3200	
Deere & Co 1 John Deere Pl NYSE: DE ■ Web: www.deere.com	Moline	IL	61265	309-765-8000	
Delaware North Cos Inc 40 Fountain Plz TF: 800-828-7240 ■ Web: www.delawarenorth.com	Buffalo	NY	14202	716-858-5000	858-5266
Deseret Management Corp 55 N 300 W Ste 800 Web: www.deseretmanagement.com	Salt Lake City	UT	84101	801-538-0651	517-4600
Dover Corp 3005 Highland Pkwy Ste 200 NYSE: DOV ■ Web: www.dovercorporation.com	Downers Grove	IL	60515	630-541-1540	743-2671
Dyson-Kissner-Moran Corp (DKM) 565 Fifth Ave 4th Fl Web: www.dkmcorp.com	New York	NY	10017	212-661-4600	986-7169
EBSCO Industries Inc 5724 Hwy 280 TF: 800-653-2726 ■ Web: www.ebscoind.com	Birmingham	AL	35242	205-991-6600	
Empire Company Ltd 115 King St TSE: EMP.A ■ Web: www.empireco.ca	Stellarton	NS	B0K1S0	902-755-4440	755-6477
Federal Signal Corp 1415 W 22nd St Ste 1100 NYSE: FSS ■ Web: www.federalsignal.com	Oak Brook	IL	60523	630-954-2000	954-2030
FirstService Corp 1140 Bay St 1st Service Bldg Ste 4000 TSE: FSV ■ Web: www.firstservice.com	Toronto	ON	M5S2B4	416-960-9500	960-5333
Fortune Brands Inc 520 Lk Cook Rd NYSE: FBHS ■ TF: 800-225-2719 ■ Web: www.fbhs.com	Deerfield	IL	60015	847-484-4400	
Griffon Corp 712 Fifth Ave 18th Fl NYSE: GFF ■ Web: www.griffon.com	New York	NY	10019	212-957-5000	957-5040
Hallwood Group Inc 3710 Rawlins St Ste 1500 NYSE: HWG ■ Web: www.hallwood.com	Dallas	TX	75219	214-528-5588	528-8855
Harris Teeter Inc PO Box 10100 NYSE: HTSI ■ TF: 800-432-6111 ■ Web: www.harristeeter.com	Mathews	NC	28106	704-844-3100	
Harsco Corp 350 Poplar Church Rd NYSE: HSC ■ TF: 866-470-3900 ■ Web: www.harsco.com	Camp Hill	PA	17011	717-763-7064	763-6424
Hitachi America Ltd 50 Prospect Ave TF: 800-448-2244 ■ Web: www.hitachi.com	Tarrytown	NY	10591	914-332-5800	332-5555
Holiday Cos 4567 American Blvd W PO Box 1224 TF: 800-745-7411 ■ Web: www.holidaystationstores.com	Bloomington	MN	55437	952-830-8700	
HT Hackney Co 502 S Gay St PO Box 238 TF: 800-406-1291 ■ Web: www.hthackney.com	Knoxville	TN	37901	865-546-1291	
IAC/InterActiveCorp 555 W 18th St NASDAQ: IACI ■ Web: www.iac.com	New York	NY	10011	212-314-7300	314-7309
iHeartMedia, Inc 200 E Basse Rd TF: 800-829-6551 ■ Web: www.iheartmedia.com	San Antonio	TX	78209	210-822-2828	
Jim Pattison Group 1067 W Cordova St Ste 1800 Web: www.jimpattison.com	Vancouver	BC	V6C1C7	604-688-6764	687-2601
Jordan Industries Inc (JII) 1751 Lake Cook Rd Ste 550	Deerfield	IL	60015	847-945-5591	945-5698
Kaman Corp PO Box 1 NYSE: KAMN ■ TF: 866-450-3663 ■ Web: www.kaman.com	Bloomfield	CT	06002	860-243-7100	
Kimball International Inc 1600 Royal St NASDAQ: KBAL ■ TF: 800-482-1616 ■ Web: www.kimball.com	Jasper	IN	47549	812-482-1600	
Kluge & Co 810 Seventh Ave Ste 29	New York	NY	10019	212-606-4400	606-4337
Koch Enterprises Inc 14 S 11th Ave Web: www.kochenterprises.com	Evansville	IN	47712	812-465-9800	465-9613
Koch Industries Inc PO Box 2256 Web: www.kochind.com	Wichita	KS	67201	316-828-3756	
Kohler Co Inc 444 Highland Dr *Fax: Mktg ■ TF: 800-456-4537 ■ Web: kohler.com	Kohler	WI	53044	920-457-4441	459-1826*
Kraus-Anderson Co (KA) 523 S Eigth St TF: 888-547-3983 ■ Web: www.krausanderson.com	Minneapolis	MN	55404	612-305-2934	332-0217
Lancaster Colony Corp 37 W Broad St NASDAQ: LANC ■ Web: www.lancastercolony.com	Columbus	OH	43215	614-224-7141	
Larry H Miller Group 9350 S 150 E Ste 1000 Web: www.lhm.com	Sandy	UT	84070	801-563-4100	264-3198
LDI Ltd 54 Monument Cir Ste 800 Web: www.ldiltd.com	Indianapolis	IN	46204	317-237-5400	237-2280
Leucadia National Corp 315 Pk Ave S 20th Fl NYSE: LUK ■ Web: www.leucadia.com	New York	NY	10010	212-460-1900	
LGL Group Inc, The 2525 Shader Rd NYSE: LGL ■ Web: www.lglgroup.com	Orlando	FL	32804	407-298-2000	
Loews Corp 667 Madison Ave Web: www.loews.com	New York	NY	10065	212-521-2000	
MacAndrews & Forbes Holdings Inc 35 E 62nd St Web: www.macandrewsandforbes.com	New York	NY	10065	212-572-8600	
Marmon Group LLC, The 181 W Madison St 26th Fl Web: www.marmon.com	Chicago	IL	60602	312-372-9500	845-5305
Mars Inc 6885 Elm St Web: www.mars.com	McLean	VA	22101	703-821-4900	448-9678
MAXXAM Inc 1330 Post Oak Blvd Ste 2000 OTC: MAXX ■ *Fax: Hum Res ■ Web: charleshurwitz.com	Houston	TX	77056	713-975-7600	267-3701*
McRae Industries Inc PO Box 1239 Web: www.mcraeindustries.com	Mount Gilead	NC	27306	910-439-6147	439-4190
MDU Resources Group Inc 1200 W Century Ave PO Box 5650 NYSE: MDU ■ TF: 866-760-4852 ■ Web: www.mdu.com	Bismarck	ND	58506	701-530-1000	
NACCO Industries Inc 5875 Landerbrook Dr Ste 300 NYSE: NC ■ TF: 877-756-5118 ■ Web: www.nacco.com	Cleveland	OH	44124	440-229-5151	
NESCO Inc 6140 Parkland Blvd Web: nescoresource.com	Mayfield Heights	OH	44124	440-461-6000	449-3111
Newell Rubbermaid Inc 3 Glenlake Pkwy NYSE: NWL ■ TF: 800-752-9677 ■ Web: www.newellbrands.com/pages/index.aspx?redirect=1	Atlanta	GA	30328	770-418-7000	677-8662
Olin Corp 190 Carondelet Plz Ste 1530 NYSE: OLN ■ Web: www.olin.com	Clayton	MO	63105	314-480-1400	
Onex Corp 161 Bay St PO Box 700 Web: www.onex.com	Toronto	ON	M5J2S1	416-362-7711	362-5765
Oxbow Corp 1601 Forum Pl Ste 1400 *Fax: Hum Res ■ Web: www.oxbow.com	West Palm Beach	FL	33401	561-697-4300	697-1876*
PepsiCo Inc 700 Anderson Hill Rd NYSE: PEP ■ TF PR: 800-433-2652 ■ Web: www.pepsico.com	Purchase	NY	10577	914-253-2000	
Procter & Gamble Co (PG) 1 Procter & Gamble Plaza NYSE: PG ■ Web: www.pg.com	Cincinnati	OH	45202	513-983-1100	
Raleigh Enterprises 5300 Melrose Ave 4th Fl Web: www.raleighenterprises.com	Hollywood	CA	90038	310-899-8900	899-8910
RB Pamplin Corp 805 SW Broadway Web: www.pamplin.org	Portland	OR	97205	503-248-1133	
Renco Group 1 Rockefeller Plaza # 29 Web: www.rencogroup.net	New York	NY	10020	212-541-6000	541-6197
Rowan Companies 2800 Postoak Blvd Ste 5450 NYSE: RDC ■ Web: www.rowan.com/home/default.aspx	Houston	TX	77056	713-621-7800	
Sammons Enterprises Inc 5949 Sherry Ln Ste 1900 Web: www.sammonsenterprises.com	Dallas	TX	75225	214-210-5000	210-5099
Seaboard Corp 9000 W 67th St NYSE: SEB ■ TF: 866-676-8886 ■ Web: www.seaboardcorp.com	Shawnee Mission	KS	66202	913-676-8800	676-8872
Siemens Corp 527 Madison Ave 8th Fl *Fax: Mktg ■ TF: 800-743-6367 ■ Web: www.usa.siemens.com	New York	NY	10022	212-258-4000	258-4099*
SPX Corp 13515 Ballantyne Corporate Pl NYSE: SPW ■ TF: 877-247-3797 ■ Web: www.spx.com	Charlotte	NC	28277	704-752-4400	
Sten Corp 10275 Wayzata Blvd S Ste 310 Web: www.stencorporation.com	Minnetonka	MN	55305	952-545-2776	
Tang Industries Inc 8960 Spanish Ridge Ave Web: nmlp.com	Las Vegas	NV	89148	702-734-3700	
TECO Energy Inc 702 N Franklin St NYSE: TE ■ Web: tecoenergy.com	Tampa	FL	33602	813-228-1111	228-1670
Teleflex Inc 155 S Limerick Rd NYSE: TFX ■ TF: 866-246-6990 ■ Web: www.teleflex.com	Limerick	PA	19468	610-948-5100	
Time Warner Inc 1 Time Warner Ctr NYSE: TWX ■ TF: 866-463-6899 ■ Web: www.timewarner.com	New York	NY	10019	212-484-8000	
Topa Equities Ltd 1800 Ave of the Stars Ste 1400 Web: www.topa.com	Los Angeles	CA	90067	310-203-9199	229-9788
Trinity Industries Inc 2525 Stemmons Fwy NYSE: TRN ■ TF: 800-631-4420 ■ Web: www.trin.net	Dallas	TX	75207	214-631-4420	589-8501
United Services Automobile Assn (USAA) 10750 McDermott Fwy TF: 800-531-8722 ■ Web: www.usaa.com	San Antonio	TX	78288	800-531-8722	531-5717
United Technologies Corp 1 Financial Plz NYSE: UTX ■ Web: www.utc.com	Hartford	CT	06103	860-728-7000	
Universal Corp 9201 Forest Hill Ave PO Box 25099 NYSE: UVV ■ Web: www.universalcorp.com	Richmond	VA	23260	804-359-9311	254-3582
Valhi Inc 5430 LBJ Fwy Ste 1700 3 Lincoln Ctr NYSE: VHI ■ *Fax: Acctg ■ Web: www.valhi.net	Dallas	TX	75240	972-233-1700	448-1445*
Viacom Inc 1515 Broadway 52nd Fl NASDAQ: VIAB ■ Web: www.viacom.com	New York	NY	10036	212-258-6000	
Viad Corp 1850 N Central Ave Ste 800 NYSE: VVI ■ Web: www.viad.com	Phoenix	AZ	85004	602-207-4000	
Walt Disney Co 500 S Buena Vista St NYSE: DIS ■ *Fax: Mail Rm ■ Web: thewaltdisneycompany.com	Burbank	CA	91521	818-560-1000	553-7210*
Watkins Associated Industries 1958 Monroe Dr NE	Atlanta	GA	30324	404-872-3841	
Wesco Financial Corp 301 E Colorado Blvd Ste 300 CVE: WSC ■ Web: www.wescofinancial.com	Pasadena	CA	91101	626-585-6700	449-1455
Weyerhaeuser Co 33663 Weyerhaeuser Way S NYSE: WY ■ TF: 800-525-5440 ■ Web: www.weyerhaeuser.com	Federal Way	WA	98003	253-924-2345	
Wirtz Corp 680 N Lk Shore Dr Ste 1900 Web: wirtzinsurance.com	Chicago	IL	60611	312-943-7000	943-9017

186 CONSTRUCTION - BUILDING CONTRACTORS - NON-RESIDENTIAL

Company	City	State	ZIP	Phone	Fax
1st Choice Facilities Services Corp 1941 Whitfield Park Loop TF: 866-241-0070 ■ Web: 1stchoicecorp.com	Sarasota	FL	34243	866-241-0070	
3LK Construction LLC 18401 Weaver St Web: www.3lkconstruction.com	Detroit	MI	48228	313-493-9101	
4 Sight Inc 135 Fifth Ave Web: www.4sightinc.com	New York	NY	10010	212-253-0525	
A & E Construction Co 152 Garrett Rd Web: www.aeconstruction.com	Upper Darby	PA	19082	610-449-3152	449-6325
A D Morgan Corp, The 716 N Renellie Dr Web: www.admorgan.com	Tampa	FL	33609	813-832-3033	831-9860
A J Martini Inc 5 Lowell Ave Web: www.ajmartini.com	Winchester	MA	01890	781-569-6900	
A Morton Thomas & Associates Inc 800 King Farm Blvd 4th Fl Web: www.amtengineering.com	Rockville	MD	20850	301-881-2545	
A R Mays Construction Inc 6900 E Indian School Rd Ste 200 Web: www.armays.com	Scottsdale	AZ	85251	480-850-6900	
A Ruiz Construction Company & Assoc Inc 1601 Cortland Ave Web: www.aruizconstruction.com	San Francisco	CA	94110	415-647-4010	

	City	State	Zip	Phone	Fax
A.O.W. Associates Inc 30 Essex St	Albany	NY	12206	518-482-3400	
Web: aowassoc.com					
AAPCO Southeast Inc 506 Webb Rd	Concord	NC	28025	704-784-2690	
Web: www.aapcogroup.com					
Abhe & Svoboda Inc 18100 Dairy Ln	Jordan	MN	55352	952-447-6025	
Web: www.abheonline.com					
Abide International Inc 561 First St W	Sonoma	CA	95476	707-935-1577	
Web: www.abideinternational.com					
Abrams Construction Inc 7 Kent St Ste 2	Brookline	MA	02445	617-566-9090	566-9098
Web: www.abrams-properties.com					
Absher Construction Company Inc					
1001 Shaw Rd	Puyallup	WA	98372	253-845-9544	841-0925
Web: absherco.com					
Accrete Construction LLC 801 Valley Ave NW	Puyallup	WA	98371	253-922-3399	
Web: www.bpci.net					
ACS Development Corporation Inc					
16148 Sand Canyon Ave	Irvine	CA	92618	949-263-1920	
Web: www.acsirvine.com					
Adamo Construction Inc					
11980 Woodside Ave Ste 5	Lakeside	CA	92040	619-390-6706	
Web: www.adamoconstruction.com					
Adler Group Inc 1400 NW 107 Ave	Miami	FL	33172	305-392-4000	
Web: www.adlergroup.com					
Adolfson & Peterson Construction Inc					
6701 W 23rd St	Minneapolis	MN	55426	952-544-1561	525-2333
Web: www.a-p.com					
Advanced Industrial Services Inc					
3250 Susquehanna Trial	York	PA	17406	717-764-9811	764-3144
TF: 800-544-5080 ■ *Web:* www.ais-york.com					
Aecon Buildings Inc 19020 33rd Ave W Ste 500	Lynnwood	WA	98036	425-774-2945	
Web: www.usa.aecon.com					
Aecon Group Inc 20 Carlson Ct Ste 800	Toronto	ON	M9W7K6	416-293-7004	
Web: www.aecon.com					
Aerie Inc 139 S Guild Ave Ste 101	Lodi	CA	95240	209-339-9751	
Web: www.aerieinc.com					
AIC International Inc					
736 S Chicago St PO Box 80925	Seattle	WA	98108	206-762-3340	
Web: www.aicconstruction.com					
Ajax Bldg Corp 1080 Commerce Blvd	Midway	FL	32343	850-224-9571	224-2496
Web: www.ajaxbuildingcorp.com					
AKEA Inc 25105 W Newberry Rd	Newberry	FL	32669	352-474-6124	
Web: www.akeainc.com					
Alan Shintani Inc 94-409 Akoki St	Waipahu	HI	96797	808-841-7631	
Web: www.alan-shintani.com					
Alan Utz & Assoc Inc (AU& A) PO Box 131857	Tyler	TX	75713	903-566-9797	566-9393
Web: www.auainc.com					
Albert C. Kobayashi Inc 94-535 Ukee St	Waipahu	HI	96797	808-671-6460	
Web: www.ack-inc.com					
Albert M Higley Co 2926 Chester Ave	Cleveland	OH	44114	216-861-2050	861-0038
Web: www.amhigley.com					
Albu & Associates Inc					
2711 W Fairbanks Ave	Winter Park	FL	32789	407-788-1450	
Web: www.albu.biz					
Alcamo Supply Corp 1152 Jericho Tpke	Commack	NY	11725	631-543-8820	
Web: www.alcamopools.com					
Alcan Electrical & Engineering Inc					
6670 Arctic Spur Rd	Anchorage	AK	99518	907-563-3787	562-6286
Web: www.alcanelectric.com					
Alex E. Paris Contracting Co					
1595 Smith Township State	Atlasburg	PA	15004	724-947-2235	947-3820
Web: www.alexparis.com					
All Pool & Spa Inc 905 Kalanianaole Hwy	Kailua	HI	96734	808-261-8991	
Web: www.allpoolandspa.com					
Allen Blasting & Coating Inc					
1668 Old Highway 61	Wever	IA	52658	319-367-5500	
Web: allenblastingandcoating.com					
Allen m p General Contractors Inc					
9807 Fair Oaks Blvd	Fair Oaks	CA	95628	916-904-5000	
Web: www.mpallen.com					
Alliance Construction Solutions LLC					
2725 Rocky Mtn Ave Ste 100	Loveland	CO	80538	970-663-9700	
Web: www.allianceconstruction.com					
AlliedCook Construction Corp					
8 US Route 1	Scarborough	ME	04074	207-772-2888	
Web: www.alliedcook.com					
Allstate Construction Inc 5718 Tower Rd	Tallahassee	FL	32303	850-514-1004	514-1206
Web: www.allstateconstruction.com					
Alpha Bldg Corp 24850 Blanco Rd	San Antonio	TX	78260	210-491-9925	491-9717
Web: www.alphabuilding.com					
Alten Construction Inc 720 12th St	Richmond	CA	94801	510-234-4200	
Web: www.altenconstruction.com					
Alvin H Butz Inc 840 W Hamilton St Ste 600	Allentown	PA	18101	610-395-6871	395-3363
Web: www.butz.com					
American Modular Systems Inc					
787 Spreckels Ave	Manteca	CA	95336	209-825-1921	
Web: www.americanmodular.com					
American Trademark Construction Services Inc					
200 Lau Pkwy	Englewood	OH	45315	937-832-8885	
Web: www.atcs-online.com					
Ameris Bank 24 Second Ave SE PO Box 3668	Moultrie	GA	31768	866-616-6020	
TF: 866-616-6020 ■ *Web:* www.amerisbank.com					
Anchor Construction Corp					
2254 25th Place NE	Washington	DC	20018	202-269-6694	
Web: www.anchorconst.com					
Anchor Tampa Inc 3907 W Osborne Ave	Tampa	FL	33614	813-879-8685	
TF: 800-879-8685 ■ *Web:* www.anchortampa.com					
Andersen Construction Company Inc					
6712 N Cutter Cir	Portland	OR	97217	503-283-6712	283-3607
Web: www.andersen-const.com					
Angeles Contractor Inc					
8461 Commonwealth Ave	Buena Park	CA	90621	714-443-3655	
Web: www.angelescontractor.com					
Ansco & Assoc LLC					
736 Park North Blvd Ste 100	Clarkston	GA	30021	336-852-3433	
Web: www.anscoinc.com					
Apex Homes Inc 7172 Rt 522	Middleburg	PA	17842	570-837-2333	837-2346
TF: 800-326-9524 ■ *Web:* www.apexhomesofpa.com					
Arch-Con Corp 1335 W Gray Ste 300	Houston	TX	77019	713-533-1900	
Web: www.arch-con.com					
Armada Hoffler					
222 Central Pk Ave Ste 2100	Virginia Beach	VA	23462	757-366-4000	
Web: www.armadahoffler.com					
Ashland Construction Co 4601 Atlantic Ave	Raleigh	NC	27604	919-872-7500	
Web: www.ashlandconstruction.com					
Ashton Company Inc, The					
2727 S Country Club Rd PO Box 26927	Tucson	AZ	85713	520-624-5500	791-9059
Web: www.ashtoncoinc.com					
Asi Constructors Inc					
1850 E Platteville Blvd	Pueblo West	CO	81007	719-647-2821	647-2890
Web: www.asiconstructors.com					
Atlas General Contractors LLC					
8218 E 121st St S	Bixby	OK	74008	918-369-3910	
Web: www.atlasgc.com					
Atmos Tech Industries L L C 1108 Pollack Ave	Ocean	NJ	07712	732-493-8400	
Web: www.atmostech.com					
Auld & White Constructors LLC					
4168 Southpoint Pkwy Ste 101	Jacksonville	FL	32216	904-296-2555	
Web: www.auld-white.com					
Ausland Builders Inc 3935 Highland Ave	Grants Pass	OR	97526	541-476-3788	
Web: auslandgroup.com					
Austin Co 6095 Parkland Blvd	Cleveland	OH	44124	440-544-2600	544-2661
Web: www.theaustin.com					
Austin Commercial Inc 3535 Travis Ste 300	Dallas	TX	75204	214-443-5700	443-5793*
**Fax:* Acctg ■ *Web:* www.austin-ind.com					
Auto Builders South Florida					
5715 Corporate Way	West Palm Beach	FL	33407	561-622-3515	
Web: www.questcontracting.com					
Aztec Building Systems Inc 3361 Deskin Dr	Norman	OK	73069	405-329-0255	
Web: www.aztecbuildingsystems.com					
B C & G Weithman Construction Company Inc					
2171 E Mansfield St	Bucyrus	OH	44820	419-562-8027	
B R Mcmillan & Associates Inc					
4030 Hwy 31 W	Cottontown	TN	37048	615-672-2996	
Web: www.brmcmillan.com					
B&B Contractors & Developers Inc					
2781 Salt Springs Rd	Youngstown	OH	44509	330-270-5020	270-5035
Web: www.bbcdonline.com					
B. H. Craig Construction Company Inc					
835 Wall St	Florence	AL	35630	256-766-3350	767-0367
Web: www.bhcraigconst.com					
Bachmann Construction Company Inc					
1201 S Stoughton Rd	Madison	WI	53716	608-222-8869	
Web: bachmannconstruction.net					
Baldwin & Shell Construction Co Inc					
1000 W Capitol PO Box 1750	Little Rock	AR	72201	501-374-8677	375-7649
Web: www.baldwinshell.com					
Balfour Beatty Construction (BBC)					
3100 McKinnon St 10th Fl	Dallas	TX	75201	214-451-1000	
Web: balfourbeattyus.com					
Balfour Beatty Construction					
7901 SW Sixth Ct Ste 200	Fort Lauderdale	FL	33324	954-585-4000	
Web: www.balfourbeattyus.com					
Bank of the Orient 233 Sansome St	San Francisco	CA	94104	415-338-0843	338-0619
TF: 877-275-3342 ■ *Web:* www.bankorient.com/home					
Barker-morrissey Contracting Inc					
3619 E Speedway Blvd Ste 101	Tucson	AZ	85716	520-323-3831	
Web: www.barkermorrissey.com					
Barlovento LLC 431 Technology Dr	Dothan	AL	36303	334-983-9979	983-9983
Web: barloventollc.com					
Barnhill Contracting Co					
4325 Pleasant Valley Rd	Raleigh	NC	27612	252-823-1021	823-0137
Web: www.barnhillcontracting.com					
Baron Sign Manufacturing 900 W 13th St	Riviera Beach	FL	33404	561-863-7446	
Web: www.baronsign.com					
Barr & Barr Inc 460 W 34th St	New York	NY	10001	212-563-2330	967-2297
Web: www.barrandbarr.com					
Barton Malow Enterprises Inc					
26500 American Dr	Southfield	MI	48034	248-436-5000	436-5001
Web: www.bartonmalow.com					
Batson-Cook Co 817 Fourth Ave PO Box 151	West Point	GA	31833	706-643-2500	643-2199
Web: www.batson-cook.com					
Bay Electric Company Inc 627 36th St	Newport News	VA	23607	757-595-2300	595-6112
Web: www.bayelectricco.com					
Baybutt Construction Corp 25 Avon St	Keene	NH	03431	603-352-6846	352-6633
Web: www.baybutt.com					
Bayland Buildings Inc PO Box 13571	Green Bay	WI	54307	920-498-9300	
Web: baylandbuildings.com					
Bayley Construction Co					
8005 SE 28th St Ste 100	Mercer Island	WA	98040	206-621-8884	343-7728
Web: www.bayley.net					
Baywood Homes 1140 Sheppard Ave W Unit 12	North York	ON	M3K2A2	416-633-7333	
BBL Construction Services Inc (BBL)					
302 Washington Ave Ext	Albany	NY	12203	518-452-8200	452-2897
Web: www.bblinc.com					
BE&K Building Group					
1031 S Caldwell St Ste 100	Charlotte	NC	28203	704-551-2700	551-2799
Web: www.bekbg.com					
Beauchamp Construction Co					
2100 Ponce De Leon Blvd Ste 825	Coral Gables	FL	33134	305-445-0819	447-0941
Web: www.beauchampco.com					
Beck & Hofer Construction Inc					
618 E Maple St	Sioux Falls	SD	57104	605-336-0118	
Web: beckandhofer.com					
Beck Group, The 1807 Ross Ave Ste 500	Dallas	TX	75201	214-303-6200	303-6300
Web: www.beckgroup.com					

Company	City	State	ZIP	Phone	Fax
Becker Arena Products Inc 6611 W Hwy 13 *TF:* 800-234-5522 ■ *Web:* www.beckerarena.com	Savage	MN	55378	952-890-2690	
Becker Bros Inc 401 Main St Ste 110 *Web:* bccinc.net	Peoria	IL	61602	309-674-1200	674-5454
Behlen Building Systems 102 W Fourth St *Web:* www.behlenbuildingsystems.com	Loveland	CO	80537	970-593-0596	
Beitzel Corp 12072 Bittinger Rd *Web:* www.beitzelcorp.com	Grantsville	MD	21536	301-245-4107	
Belrock Construction Ltd 185 Adesso Dr *Web:* www.belrock.com	Concord	ON	L4K3C4	905-669-9481	
Benaka Inc 7 Lawrence St *Web:* www.benakainc.com	New Brunswick	NJ	08901	732-246-7060	
Benchmark Construction Company Inc 4121 Oregon Pike PO Box 806 *Web:* www.benchmarkgc.com	Brownstown	PA	17508	717-626-9559	
Benjamin Development Company Inc 377 Oak St Ste 110 *Web:* www.benjamindevco.com	Garden City	NY	11530	516-745-0150	
Benning Construction Co Inc (BCC) 4695 S Atlanta Rd *Web:* www.benningnet.com	Atlanta	GA	30339	404-792-1911	792-2337
Bergenfield Public School District 225 W Clinton Ave *Web:* www.bergenfield.org	Bergenfield	NJ	07621	201-385-8801	
Berghammer Construction Corp 4750 N 132nd St *Web:* berghammer.com	Butler	WI	53007	262-790-4750	
Berkowsky & Associates Inc 2551 Us Hwy 130 Ste 2 *Web:* www.berkowsky.com	Cranbury	NJ	08512	609-655-2400	
Bernards Bros Inc 555 First St *Web:* www.bernards.com	San Fernando	CA	91340	818-898-1521	
Bethlehem Construction Inc 5505 Tichenal Rd *Web:* www.bethlehemconstruction.com	Cashmere	WA	98815	509-782-1001	
Bette & Cring LLC 22 Century Hill Dr Ste 201 *Web:* www.bettecring.com	Latham	NY	12110	518-213-1010	
Beyer Construction Ltd 3080 S Calhoun Rd *Web:* www.beyer.com	New Berlin	WI	53151	262-789-6040	
Bittenbender Consrtuction Lp 5 N. Columbus Blvd Pier 5 *Web:* www.bittenbenderconstruction.com	Philadelphia	PA	19106	215-925-8900	
BL Harbert International Inc 820 Shades Creek Pkwy Ste 3000 *Web:* blharbert.com	Birmingham	AL	35209	205-802-2800	802-2801
Blach Construction Co 469 El Cmino Real Ste 100 *Web:* www.blach.com	Santa Clara	CA	95050	408-244-7100	244-2220
Blaine Construction Corp 6510 Deane Hill Dr *Web:* www.blaineconstruction.com	Knoxville	TN	37919	865-693-8900	691-7606
BlueScope Construction Inc 1540 Genessee St *Web:* www.bluescopeconstruction.com	Kansas City	MO	64102	816-245-6000	245-6099
BNBuilders Inc 2601 Fourth Ave Ste 350 *Web:* www.bnbuilders.com	Seattle	WA	98121	206-382-3443	
Bockstael Construction (1979) Ltd 1505 Dugald Rd *Web:* www.bockstael.com	Winnipeg	MB	R2J0H3	204-233-7135	
Bognet Construction Associates Inc 1911 N Ft Myer Dr Ste 705 *Web:* www.bognet.com	Arlington	VA	22209	703-807-0007	
Bolton Construction & Service of WNC Inc 169 Elk Mtn Rd *Web:* boltonservicewnc.com	Asheville	NC	28804	828-253-3621	
Bond Bros Inc 145 Spring St *Web:* www.bondbrothers.com	Everett	MA	02149	617-387-3400	389-1412
Bondfield Construction Company Ltd 407 Basaltic Rd *Web:* www.bondfield.com	Concord	ON	L4K4W8	416-667-8422	
Bonnette Page & Stone Corp 91 Bisson Ave *Web:* www.bpsnh.com	Laconia	NH	03246	603-524-3411	524-4641
Boro Developers Inc 400 Feheley Dr *Web:* www.boroconstruction.com	King Of Prussia	PA	19406	610-272-7400	
Bosse Mattingly Constructors Inc 2116 Plantside Dr *Web:* www.bmconstructors.com	Louisville	KY	40299	502-671-0995	
Bowen & Watson Inc PO Box 877 *Web:* www.bowen-watson.com	Toccoa	GA	30577	706-886-3197	886-3010
Boyd Jones Construction Co 4360 Nicholas St *Web:* www.boydjones.biz	Omaha	NE	68131	402-553-1804	
Boyertown Area School District (BASD) 911 Montgomery Ave *Web:* www.boyertownasd.org	Boyertown	PA	19512	610-367-6031	369-7620
Brackett Builders Inc 185 Marybill Dr S *Web:* www.brackettbuilders.com	Troy	OH	45373	937-339-7505	
Bradbury & Stamm Construction Company Inc 7110 Second St NW *Web:* www.bradburystamm.com	Albuquerque	NM	87107	505-765-1200	842-5419
Branagh Inc 750 Kevin Ct *Web:* www.branaghinc.com	Oakland	CA	94621	510-638-6455	562-8371
Branch Group Inc 442 Rutherford Ave NE *Web:* www.branchgroup.com	Roanoke	VA	24016	540-982-1678	
Brannan Paving Coltd 111 Elk Dr PO Box 3403 *TF:* 800-626-7064 ■ *Web:* www.brannanpaving.com	Victoria	TX	77903	361-573-3130	573-6211
Brasfield & Gorrie LLC 3021 Seventh Ave S *TF:* 800-239-8017 ■ *Web:* www.brasfieldgorrie.com	Birmingham	AL	35233	205-328-4000	251-1304
Breiholz Construction Co 1527 Maine St *Web:* www.breiholz.com	Des Moines	IA	50309	515-288-6077	
Brice Bldg Company Inc 201 Sunbelt Pkwy	Birmingham	AL	35211	205-930-9911	918-1850
Briohn Building Corp 3885 N Brookfield Rd Ste 200 *Web:* www.briohn.com	Brookfield	WI	53045	262-790-0500	
Bristol Construction Services LLC 111 W 16th Ave Fl 3 *TF:* 877-563-0013 ■ *Web:* www.bristol-companies.com	Anchorage	AK	99501	907-563-0013	
Briston Construction LLC 309 E 10th Dr *Web:* www.bristonconstruction.com	Mesa	AZ	85210	480-776-5810	
Brookstone LP 3715 Dacoma St *Web:* www.brookstone-tx.com	Houston	TX	77092	713-683-8800	680-0088
Brycon Corp 134 Rio Rancho Blvd NE *Web:* www.brycon.com	Rio Rancho	NM	87124	505-892-6163	
Brytex Building Systems Inc 5610 97 St *Web:* www.brytex.com	Edmonton	AB	T6E3J1	780-437-7970	
BSI Constructors Inc 6767 SW Ave *Web:* www.bsistl.com	Saint Louis	MO	63143	314-781-7820	781-1354
BT Mancini Co Inc Brookman Div 876 S Milpitas Blvd *Web:* www.btmancini.com	Milpitas	CA	95035	408-942-7900	
Budreck Truck Lines Inc 8040 S Roberts Rd *TF:* 800-621-0013 ■ *Web:* www.budreck.com	Bridgeview	IL	60455	708-496-0522	496-0568
Buford-Thompson Co 1450 North Jim Wright Fwy Ft Worth *Web:* www.buford-thompson.com	White Settlement	TX	76108	817-467-4981	467-5619
BuilderGuru Contracting Inc 2124 Priest Bridge Dr Ste 14 *Web:* www.builderguru.com	Crofton	MD	21114	410-923-1379	
Building Bridges at Wilcat Way 1525 Ne Wildcat Way	Bentonville	AR	72712	479-254-5277	
Bullard Construction Inc PO Box 575 Ste 205 *Web:* www.bullardconstruction.com	Addison	TX	75001	972-661-8474	
Bulley & Andrews LLC 1755 W Armitage Ave *Web:* www.bulley.com	Chicago	IL	60622	773-235-2433	235-2471
Burrow Global LLC 6200 Savoy Dr Ste 800 *Web:* www.burrowglobal.com	Houston	TX	77036	713-963-0930	
Butler Brothers Supply Division Inc 2001 Lisbon St *Web:* www.butlerbros.com	Lewiston	ME	04240	207-784-6875	
Butters Construction & Development Inc 6820 Lyons Technology Ctr Ste 100 *Web:* www.butters.com	Coconut Creek	FL	33073	954-312-2415	570-8844
Bycor General Contractors Inc 6490 Marindustry Pl *Web:* www.bycor.com	San Diego	CA	92121	858-587-1901	
C Erickson & Sons Inc 2200 ARCH St Ste 200 *Web:* www.cerickson.com	Philadelphia	PA	19103	215-568-3120	496-9460
C F Evans & Company Inc 125 Regional Pkwy *Web:* www.cfevans.com	Orangeburg	SC	29118	803-536-6443	
C Overaa & Company Inc 200 Parr Blvd *Web:* www.overaa.com	Richmond	CA	94801	510-234-0926	237-2435
C T Earle Maintenance Co 7001 Gibsonton Dr	Gibsonton	FL	33534	813-677-7803	
C. Martin Company Inc 3395 W Cheyenne Ave *Web:* www.cmartin.com	North Las Vegas	NV	89032	702-656-8080	
C.a. Murren & Sons Co Inc 2275 Loganville Hwy *TF:* 866-912-8906 ■ *Web:* www.camurren.com	Grayson	GA	30017	770-682-2940	682-1802
C.t. Wilson Construction Co PO Box 2011 *Web:* www.ctwilson.com	Durham	NC	27702	919-383-2535	382-0044
C.W. Brown Inc 1 Labriola Ct *Web:* www.cwbrown.net	Armonk	NY	10504	914-741-1212	
C1S Group Inc 4231 Sigma Rd Ste 110 *Web:* www.c1sinc.com	Dallas	TX	75244	972-386-7005	
Ca Lindman Inc 10401 Guilford Rd *TF:* 877-737-8675 ■ *Web:* www.calindman.com	Jessup	MD	20794	301-470-4700	470-4708
Caddell Construction Co Inc 2700 Lagoon Pk Dr *Web:* www.caddell.com	Montgomery	AL	36109	334-272-7723	272-8844
Cadence Mcshane Corp 5057 Keller Springs Rd Ste 500 *Web:* www.cadencemcshane.com	Addison	TX	75001	972-239-2336	
Cahill Contractors Inc 425 California St Ste 2200 *Web:* www.cahill-sf.com	San Francisco	CA	94104	415-986-0600	
Caliber Construction Inc 240 N Orange Ave *Web:* www.caliberconstructioninc.com	Brea	CA	92821	714-255-2700	
Callahan Inc 80 First St *Web:* www.callahan-inc.com	Bridgewater	MA	02324	508-279-0012	
Camco Pacific Construction Company Inc 19712 MacArthur Blvd Ste 200 *Web:* www.camcopacific.com	Irvine	CA	92612	949-251-1300	
Camosy Construction Inc 43451 N US Hwy 41 *Web:* www.camosy.com	Zion	IL	60099	847-395-6800	395-6891
Capitol Construction Services Inc 10412 Allisonville Rd Ste 100 *Web:* www.capitolconstruct.com	Fishers	IN	46038	317-574-5488	
Carbondale Elementary School District 95 925 S Giant City Rd *Web:* www.ces95.org	Carbondale	IL	62902	618-457-3591	
Cardinal Construction Inc 531 Commercial St PO Box 897 *Web:* www.cardinalconst.com	Waterloo	IA	50704	319-232-5400	
Careage Development 4411 Point Fosdick Dr NW Ste 203 *Web:* www.careage.com	Gig Harbor	WA	98335	253-853-4457	853-5280
Carl Belt Inc 11521 Milnor Ave PO Box 1210 *Web:* www.thebeltgroup.com	Cumberland	MD	21502	301-729-8900	
Carmel Contractors Inc 8030 England St *Web:* www.carmelcontractors.com	Charlotte	NC	28273	704-552-2338	552-0397
Carroll County School District 605-9 Pine St *Web:* www.ccpsd.k12.va.us	Hillsville	VA	24343	276-730-3200	728-3195
Case Construction LLC 56 Midtown Park W Ste A	Mobile	AL	36606	251-338-2400	
Case Contracting Co 2311 Turkey Creek Rd *Web:* www.casecontracting.com	Plant City	FL	33566	813-754-3477	
Catamount Constructors Inc 1250 Bergen Pkwy Ste B200 *Web:* www.catamountinc.com	Evergreen	CO	80439	303-679-0087	

				Phone	Fax

Cavico Corp
17011 Beach Blvd Ste 1230 Huntington Beach CA 92647 714-843-5456 996-5818*
OTC: CAVO ■ **Fax Area Code:* 302 ■ *Web:* www.cavicocorp.com

CBS Construction Ltd
150 MacKay Crescent Fort Mcmurray AB T9H4W8 780-743-1810
Web: www.cbsconstruction.ca

CD Moody Construction Company Inc
6017 Redan Rd Lithonia GA 30058 770-482-7778 482-7727
Web: www.cdmoodyconstruction.com

CD Smith Construction Inc
889 E Johnson St Fond du Lac WI 54935 920-924-2900 924-2910
Web: www.cd-smith.com

CDI Contractors LLC 3000 Cantrell Rd Little Rock AR 72202 501-666-4300 666-4741
Web: www.cdicon.com

Cedar Grove Composting Inc
7343 E Marginal Way S Seattle WA 98108 206-832-3000 832-3030
TF: 888-832-3008 ■ *Web:* www.cedar-grove.com

Cello & Maudru Construction Company Inc
2505 Oak St Napa CA 94559 707-257-0454
Web: www.cello-maudru.com

Centerpoint Builders Ltd 5339 Alpha Rd Ste 250 Dallas TX 75240 972-220-0500

CenTex House Leveling 1120 E 52nd St Austin TX 78723 512-444-5438
TF: 888-425-5438 ■ *Web:* www.centexhouseleveling.com

Centrix Builders Inc
160 S Linden Ave
Ste 100 S San Francisco San Francisco CA 94080 650-876-9400
Web: www.centrixbuilders.com

Century Concrete Inc
1364 Air Rail Ave Virginia Beach VA 23455 757-460-5366 460-3296
Web: www.centuryconcreteinc.com

CF Jordan Construction LLC 7700 CF Jordan Dr El Paso TX 79912 915-877-3333 877-3999
Web: jordanfosterconstruction.com

CG Schmidt Inc 11777 W Lake Pk Dr Milwaukee WI 53224 414-577-1177 577-1155
TF: 800-248-1254 ■ *Web:* www.cgschmidt.com

Champion Site Prep LP 455 STATE Hwy 195 Georgetown TX 78633 512-863-3453
Web: www.idigdirt.com

Chanen Construction Company Inc
3300 N Third Ave Phoenix AZ 85013 602-266-3600
Web: www.srchanen.com

Channel Building Company Inc
355 Middlesex Ave Wilmington MA 01887 978-657-7300
Web: www.channelbuilding.com

Channel Systems Inc 74 98th Ave Oakland CA 94603 510-568-7170
Web: www.channelsystems.com

Charles C Brandt Construction Co
1505 N Sherman Dr Indianapolis IN 46201 317-375-1111 375-4321
Web: www.ccbrandt.com

Charles DeWeese Construction Inc
765 Industrial By Pass PO Box 504 Franklin KY 42135 270-586-9122
Web: www.charlesdeweeseconstruction.com

Charles N. White Construction Company Inc
613 Crescent Cir Ste 100 Ridgeland MS 39157 601-898-5180
Web: www.whiteconst.com

Charles Pankow Builders Ltd
199 S.Los Robles Ave Ste 300 Pasadena CA 91101 626-304-1190 696-1782
Web: www.pankow.com

Chasco Constructors Ltd LLP
2801 E Old Settlers Blvd Round Rock TX 78665 512-244-0600
Web: www.chasco.com

Chicago Records Management Inc
3815 Carnation St Franklin Park IL 60131 847-678-0002
Web: www.chicagorecords.com

Choate Construction Co
8200 Roberts Dr Ste 600 Atlanta GA 30350 678-892-1200 892-1202
Web: www.choateco.com

Chris Woods Construction Company Inc
8068 US Hwy 70 Memphis TN 38133 901-386-3182
Web: www.chriswoodsconstruction.com

Christa Construction LLC
119 Victor Heights Pkwy Victor NY 14564 585-924-3050
Web: www.christa.com

Christman Company Inc 208 N Capitol Ave Lansing MI 48933 517-482-1488 482-3520
Web: www.christmanco.com

Clancy & Theys Construction Co
516 W Cabarrus St Raleigh NC 27603 919-834-3601 834-2439
Web: www.clancytheys.com

Clarion Construction Inc
21067 Commerce Pointe Dr Walnut CA 91789 909-598-4060
Web: www.clarionconst.com

ClariPhy Communications Inc
7585 Irvine Ctr Dr Ste 100 Irvine CA 92618 949-861-3074
Web: www.clariphy.com

Claris Construction Inc 153 S Main St Newtown CT 06470 203-364-9460
Web: www.clarisconstruction.com

Clark & Sullivan Constructors Inc
905 Industrial Way Ste 26 Sparks NV 89431 775-355-8500
Web: www.clarksullivan.com

Clark Construction Group LLC
7500 Old Georgetown Rd Bethesda MD 20814 301-272-8100 272-1928
TF: 800-655-1330 ■ *Web:* www.clarkconstruction.com

Clark Transfer Inc 800A Paxton St Harrisburg PA 17104 717-238-0801
TF: 800-488-7585 ■ *Web:* www.clarktransfer.com

Clarksdale Municipal School District
101 McGuire St PO Box 1088 Clarksdale MS 38614 662-627-8500 627-8542
TF: 877-820-7831 ■ *Web:* www.cmsd.k12.ms.us

Cleary Building Corp
190 Paoli St PO Box 930220 Verona WI 53593 608-845-9700
Web: clearybuilding.com

Clemens Construction Company Inc
1435 Walnut St 7th Fl Philadelphia PA 19102 215-567-5757
Web: www.clemensconstruction.com

Climatec Inc 2851 W Kathleen Rd Phoenix AZ 85053 602-944-3330
Web: www.climatec.com

Clinton Fences Company Inc
2630 Old Washington Rd Waldorf MD 20601 301-645-8808
Web: fencesouthernmd.com

CM Company Inc 431 W McGregor Ct Boise ID 83705 208-384-0800
Web: www.cmcompany.com

Cm Construction Company Inc
12215 Nicollet Ave Burnsville MN 55337 952-895-8223
Web: www.cmconstructionco.com

Colaianni Construction Inc
2141 State Rt 150 Dillonvale OH 43917 740-769-2362
Web: www.colaianniconst.com

Coleman-Adams Construction Inc
1031 Performance Rd Forest VA 24551 434-525-4700
Web: www.coleman-adams.com

Comanco 4301 Sterling Commerce Dr Plant City FL 33566 813-988-8829 988-8779
Web: www.comanco.net

Commercial Air 601 Ransdell Rd Lebanon IN 46052 765-482-8121
Web: www.commercialair.com

Commodore Builders 80 Bridge St Newton MA 02458 617-614-3500 965-8354
Web: www.commodorebuilders.com

Complete Property Services Inc
140 Pine Ave S Oldsmar FL 34677 727-793-9777
Web: www.completeproperty.com

Con-Real Support Group LP
1900 Ballpark Way Ste 110 Arlington TX 76006 817-640-4420
Web: www.con-real.com

Concord Cos Inc 4215 E McDowell Rd Ste 201 Mesa AZ 85215 480-962-8080 962-0707
Web: www.concordinc.com

Condon-Johnson & Assoc Inc
480 Roland Way Ste 200 Oakland CA 94621 510-636-2100 568-9316
Web: www.condonjohnson.com

Condotte America Inc 10790 NW 127th St Medley FL 33178 305-670-7585 670-7462
Web: www.condotteamerica.com

Congleton Hacker Co PO Box 22640 Lexington KY 40522 859-254-6481
Web: www.congleton-hacker.com

Conlan Co, The 1800 Pkwy Pl Ste 1010 Marietta GA 30067 770-423-8000 423-8010
Web: www.conlancompany.com

Conlon Construction Company Inc
1100 Rockdale Rd Dubuque IA 52003 563-583-1724
Web: www.conlonco.com

Conrad Schmitt Studios Inc
2405 S 162nd St New Berlin WI 53151 262-786-3030
TF: 800-969-3033 ■ *Web:* www.conradschmitt.com

Consolidated Distribution Corp 1285 101st St Lemont IL 60439 630-972-9800
Web: www.cdcsupply.com

Construct Two Group 30 S Ivey Ln Orlando FL 32811 407-295-9812
Web: www.constructtwo.com

Construction Albert Jean Ltd
4045 Parthenais St Montreal QC H2K3T8 514-522-2121
Web: www.albertjean.com

Construction Outfitters International Inc
37450 Interstate 10 W Ste 101 Boerne TX 78006 830-816-2104
Web: www.coiworld.com

Cooper Brothers Construction Company Inc
3005 Citizens Pkwy Selma AL 36701 334-874-8267
Web: cooperbrothersconstruction.com

Cooper Pugeda Management Inc
65 Mccoppin St San Francisco CA 94103 415-543-6515
Web: www.cpmservices.com

CORE Construction Services of Arizona Inc
3036 E Greenway Rd Phoenix AZ 85032 602-494-0800
Web: www.coreconstruction.com

Corna/Kokosing Construction Co
6235 Westerville Rd Westerville OH 43081 614-901-8844 212-5599
Web: www.corna.com

Corporate Construction Ltd
8517 Excelsior Dr Ste 203 Madison WI 53717 608-827-6001 827-6066
Web: www.corporate-construction.com

Couvrette Building Systems
8665 Argent St Ste D Santee CA 92071 619-938-8000

Cox Schepp Construction Inc
2410 Dunavant St Charlotte NC 28203 704-716-2100
Web: www.coxschepp.com

CPM Constructors Inc 30 Bonney St PO Box B Freeport ME 04032 207-865-0000
Web: www.cpmconstructors.com

CR Meyer & Sons Co 895 W 20th Ave Oshkosh WI 54902 920-235-3350 235-3419
Web: www.crmeyer.com

Craftcorps Inc 3401 Manor Rd Austin TX 78723 512-476-8886
Web: www.craftcorps.com

Crawford Merz Anderson Construction Co
2316 Fourth Ave S Minneapolis MN 55404 612-874-9011
Web: www.cmacco.com

Creative Business Interiors
1535 S 101st St Milwaukee WI 53214 414-545-8500
Web: www.creativebusinessinteriors.com

Creative Times Dayschool Inc 2878 Commerce Way Ogden UT 84401 801-334-7250

Cresleigh Homes Corp
433 California St Ste 700 San Francisco CA 94104 415-982-7777
Web: hotelpurchase.com

Cressey Development Corp
555 W Eighth Ave Ste 200 Vancouver BC V5Z1C6 604-683-1256
Web: www.cressey.com

Crossland Construction Company Inc
PO Box 45 Columbus KS 66725 620-429-1414 429-1412
Web: www.crosslandconstruction.com

Crystal Steel Fabricators Inc - Acdbe
9317 Old Racetrack Rd Delmar DE 19940 302-846-0613
Web: www.crystalsteel.com

CSM Group Inc 444 W Michigan Ave Ste 100 Kalamazoo MI 49007 269-746-5600
Web: www.csmgroup.com

Culp Construction Co 2320 S Main St Salt Lake City UT 84115 801-486-2064
Web: www.culpco.com

Culpepper & Terpening Inc 2980 S 25th St Fort Pierce FL 34981 772-464-3537
Web: www.ct-eng.com

			Phone	Fax

Cutler Associates Inc 43 Harvard St ... Worcester MA 01609 508-757-7500
Web: cutlerdb.com

CW Driver General Contractors Inc
468 N Rosemead Blvd ... Pasadena CA 91107 626-351-8800 351-8880
Web: www.cwdriver.com

D & D Construction Services of Orlando Inc
2707 Rew Cir ... Ocoee FL 34761 407-654-7545
Web: www.ddconstructionservices.com

D'annunzio & Sons Inc 136 Central Ave Ste 102 ... Clark NJ 07066 732-574-1300 574-1244
Web: www.dannunziocorp.com

D.A.G. Construction Company Inc
4924 Winton Rd ... Cincinnati OH 45232 513-542-8597
Web: www.dag-cons.com

D.s.simmons Inc 112 W Chestnut St ... Goldsboro NC 27530 919-734-4700
Web: www.dssimmons.com

D4 Construction Services LLC 4121 Main St ... Rowlett TX 75088 972-463-0390
Web: www.d4cs.com

Da Pope Inc 1160 Chess Dr Ste 11 ... Foster City CA 94404 650-349-5086
Web: www.dapope.com

Danco Industrial Contractors Inc
1121 N Beverlye Rd ... Dothan AL 36303 334-792-3985
Web: www.dancoindustrial.com

Daniels Corp, The 20 Queen St W Ste 3400 ... Toronto ON M5H3R3 416-598-2129
Web: www.danielshomes.ca

Danis Bldg Construction Co
3233 Newmark Dr ... Miamisburg OH 45342 937-228-1225 228-7443
Web: www.danisbuilding.com

Daryl Flood Inc 450 Airline Dr Ste 100 ... Coppell TX 75019 972-471-1496 745-9629
TF: 800-325-9340 ■ *Web:* www.darylflood.com

Davenport Cos, The 20 N Main St ... South Yarmouth MA 02664 508-398-2293
Web: www.thedavenportcompanies.com

David Simpson Construction Company Inc
17177 Gillette Ave Unit A ... Irvine CA 92614 949-250-1348
Web: www.davidsimpsonconstruction.com

Davis & Assoc Inc 2852 N Webster Ave ... Indianapolis IN 46219 317-263-9947 238-9209
Web: www.davisassocindy.com

Daw Construction Group LLC
12552 South 125 West ... Draper UT 84020 801-553-9111
TF: 800-748-4778 ■ *Web:* www.dawcg.com

Dawson Construction Inc PO Box 30920 ... Bellingham WA 98225 360-756-1000 756-1001
Web: www.dawson.com

DE Harvey Builders Inc 3630 Westchase Dr ... Houston TX 77242 713-783-8710
Web: www.harveybuilders.com

De Jager Construction Inc 75-60th St SW ... Wyoming MI 49548 616-530-0060
Web: www.dejagerconstruction.com

Dean Kurtz Construction 1651 Rand Rd ... Rapid City SD 57702 605-343-6665
Web: www.deankurtzconstruction.com

Dean Snyder Construction Co 913 N 14th St ... Clear Lake IA 50428 641-357-2283 357-2232
Web: www.deansnyderconst.com

Deerfield Construction Company Inc
8960 Glendale Milford Rd ... Loveland OH 45140 513-984-4096 984-4180
Web: www.deerfieldconstruction.com

DEI Inc 1550 Kemper Meadow Dr ... Cincinnati OH 45240 513-825-5800
Web: www.dei-corp.com

Deig Bros Lumber & Construction Inc
2804 A St ... Evansville IN 47712 812-423-4201 421-5058
Web: www.deigbros.com

Deltec Homes Inc 69 Bingham Rd ... Asheville NC 28806 800-642-2508
TF: 800-642-2508 ■ *Web:* www.deltechomes.com

Demar Ltd 6200 Savoy Dr Ste 800 ... Houston TX 77036 713-963-0930 963-0941
Web: www.demar-ltd.com

DeMaria Bldg Company Inc
3031 W Grand Blvd Ste 624 ... Detroit MI 48202 313-870-2800 870-2810
Web: www.demariabuild.com

Denark Construction Inc
1635 Western Ave Ste 105 ... Knoxville TN 37921 865-637-1925
Web: www.denak.com

Denver Commercial Builders Inc (DCB)
909 E 62nd Ave ... Denver CO 80216 303-287-5525 287-3697
Web: www.dcb1.com

Desbuild Inc 4744 Baltimore Ave ... Hyattsville MD 20781 301-864-4095
Web: www.desbuild.com

Descor Builders
3164 Gold Camp Dr Ste 250 ... Rancho Cordova CA 95670 916-463-0191
Web: www.descorbuilders.com

Design Partnership, The
1629 Telegraph Ave Ste 500 ... Oakland CA 94612 415-777-3737
Web: www.dpsf.com

Designed Mobile Systems Industries
800 S Hwy 33 ... Patterson CA 95363 209-892-6298 892-5018

Devcon Construction Inc 690 Gibraltar Dr ... Milpitas CA 95035 408-942-8200 942-8200
Web: www.devcon-const.com

Devier Construction LLC
1932 Surgi Dr Ste F ... Mandeville LA 70448 985-626-3184
Web: www.devierconstruction.com

DEW Construction Corp
277 Blair Park Rd Ste 130 ... Williston VT 05495 802-872-0505
Web: www.dewcorp.com

Dick Anderson Construction Inc
3424 Hwy 12 East ... Helena MT 59601 406-443-3225 443-1537
Web: www.daconstruction.com

Dickinson Cameron Construction Company Inc
6184 Innovation Way ... Carlsbad CA 92009 760-438-9114
Web: www.dickinsoncameron.com

Diffenbaugh Inc 6865 Airport Dr ... Riverside CA 92504 951-351-6865 351-6880
TF: 800-394-5334 ■ *Web:* www.diffenbaugh.com

Dimeo Construction Co 75 Chapman St ... Providence RI 02905 401-781-9800 461-4580
Web: dimeo.com

Dineen Construction Corp 70 Disco Rd Ste 300 ... Toronto ON M9W1L9 416-675-7676
Web: www.dineen.com

DL Withers Construction LC 3220 E Harbour Dr ... Phoenix AZ 85034 602-438-9500 438-9600
Web: www.dlwithers.com

Dolan Construction Inc 401 S 13th St ... Reading PA 19602 610-372-4664
Web: www.dolanconstructioninc.com

Don Chapin Company Inc, The
560 Crazy Horse Canyon Rd ... Salinas CA 93907 831-449-4273 449-0700
Web: www.donchapin.com

Donahuefavret Contractors Inc
3030 E Causeway Approach ... Mandeville LA 70448 985-626-4431
Web: www.donahuefavret.com

Donohoe Cos Inc 2101 Wisconsin Ave NW ... Washington DC 20007 202-333-0880 342-3924
Web: www.donohoe.com

Doster Construction Co
2100 International Pk Dr ... Birmingham AL 35243 205-443-3800 951-2612
Web: www.dosterconstruction.com

Doug Hollyhand Construction Co
527 Main Ave ... Northport AL 35476 205-345-0955
Web: www.hollyhand.com

DPR Construction Inc 1450 Veterans Blvd ... Redwood City CA 94063 650-474-1450 474-1451
Web: www.dpr.com

Drahota Commercial LLC
4700 Innovation Dr Bldg C ... Fort Collins CO 80525 970-204-0100
Web: www.drahota.com

Drury Co 4072 State Hwy K ... Cape Girardeau MO 63701 573-334-8271

Drymalla Construction Company Ltd
608 Harbert St PO Box 698 ... Columbus TX 78934 979-732-5731
Web: www.drymalla.com

DSP Builders Inc 12000 E 47th Ave Ste 201 ... Denver CO 80239 303-289-0666
Web: www.dspbuilders.com

Duffield Aquatic 515 Concord Industrial Dr ... Seneca SC 29672 864-882-7900
Web: www.duffieldaquatics.com

Duffield Assoc Inc 5400 Limestone Rd ... Wilmington DE 19808 302-239-6634 239-8485
TF: 877-732-9633 ■ *Web:* duffnet.com

Dugan & Meyers 11110 Kenwood Rd ... Cincinnati OH 45242 513-891-4300 891-0704
Web: www.dugan-meyers.com

Dunlap & Company Inc 6325 E 100 South ... Columbus IN 47202 812-376-3021
Web: www.dunlapinc.com

Dunn Investment Co
3905 Messer Airport Hwy ... Birmingham AL 35222 205-592-8908
Web: dunnconstruction.com

Duplan Construction Inc 390 Industrial St ... Campbell CA 95008 408-866-6682
Web: duplanconstruction.com

Dyad Constructors Inc 8505 Holt St ... Houston TX 77054 713-799-9380 799-2021
TF: 800-803-9202 ■ *Web:* www.dyad-inc.com

E.R. Stuebner Construction Inc 227 Blair Ave ... Reading PA 19601 610-376-6625
Web: www.ersconstruction.com

Eagle Environmental Inc
891 West Robinson Dr Ste 4 ... North Salt Lake UT 84054 801-936-1155
Web: www.cnnct.com

Eagle River Homes LLC 21 S Groffdale Rd ... Leola PA 17540 717-656-2381
Web: www.eagleriverhomes.net

Eastern Construction Company Ltd
505 Consumers Rd Ste 1100 ... Toronto ON M2J5G2 416-497-7110
Web: www.easternconstruction.com

EBC Inc 1095 Valets St ... L'ancienne-lorette QC G2E4M7 418-872-0600
Web: www.ebcinc.com

EBCO General Contractor Ltd 305 W Gillis ... Cameron TX 76520 254-697-8516
Web: ebcogc.com

Ebert Inc 23350 County Rd 10 ... Loretto MN 55357 763-498-7844
Web: www.ebertconst.com

Ecological Restoration & Management Inc (ER&M)
9475 Deereco Rd Ste 406 ... Timonium MD 21093 410-337-4899 583-5678
Web: www.er-m.com

Ed Grush, General Contractor Inc
3236 E Willow St ... Signal Hill CA 90755 562-426-9526
Web: www.edgrush.com

Ed Taylor Construction South Inc
2713 N Falkenburg Rd ... Tampa FL 33619 813-623-3724 621-1439
Web: www.edtaylor.net

Edger Enterprises of Elmira Inc
330 E 14th St ... Elmira Heights NY 14903 607-733-9664
Web: www.edgerenterprises.com

Edifice Inc 1401 W Morehead St ... Charlotte NC 28208 704-332-0900
Web: www.edificeinc.com

EE Reed Construction LP
333 Commerce Green Blvd ... Sugar Land TX 77478 281-933-4000 933-4852
Web: www.eereed.com

EI Group Inc, The
2101 Gateway Centre Blvd Ste 200 ... Morrisville NC 27560 919-657-7500
Web: www.ei1.com

Ejh Construction Inc
30896 W 8 Mile Rd ... Farmington Hills MI 48336 248-478-1400
Web: ejhconstruction.com

Eklunds Inc 2860 Market Loop ... Southlake TX 76092 817-949-2030
Web: www.eklunds.com

Elder-Jones Inc 1120 E 80th St Ste 211 ... Minneapolis MN 55420 952-854-2854 854-2703
Web: www.elderjones.com

Eldor Contracting Corp 30 Corporate Dr ... Holtsville NY 11742 631-218-0010
Web: www.eldor.com

Eleven Western Builders Inc
2862 Executive Pl ... Escondido CA 92029 760-796-6346
Web: www.ewbinc.com

Elite Retails Services Inc PO Box 618 ... Lake Jackson TX 77566 979-285-0712 285-0714
Web: www.elite-construction.com

Ellis Stone Construction
3201 Stanley St PO Box 366 ... Stevens Point WI 54481 715-345-5000 345-5007
Web: www.elliswi.com

EllisDon Corp 2045 Oxford St ... London ON N5V2Z7 519-455-6770
Web: www.ellisdon.com

Emery Air Charter Inc 1 Airport Cir ... Rockford IL 61109 815-968-8287
TF: 800-435-8090 ■ *Web:* www.emeryair.net

EMJ Corp 2034 Hamilton Pl Blvd Ste 400 ... Chattanooga TN 37421 423-855-1550 855-6857
Web: www.emjcorp.com

Energy Services of America Corp
75 W third Ave ... Huntington WV 25701 304-399-6300 399-1096
OTC: ESOA ■ *Web:* www.energyservicesofamerica.com

	City	State	Zip	Phone	Fax
Engelberth Construction Inc 463 Mtn View Dr Ste 200 Second Fl *Web:* www.engelberth.com	Colchester	VT	05446	802-655-0100	
Engineering Economics Inc 8700 Monrovia St Ste 310 *Web:* www.eeiengineers.com	Lenexa	KS	66215	303-239-8700	
Environamics Inc 1401 Freedom Dr *Web:* www.environamics-inc.com	Charlotte	NC	28208	704-376-3613	
ERC Properties Inc 813 Ft St *Web:* www.erc.com	Barling	AR	72923	479-452-9950	
Erdman Co 1 Erdman Pl *Web:* www.erdman.com	Madison	WI	53717	608-410-8000	
ESA Construction Inc 645 El Molino Blvd Ste A *Web:* www.esaconstruction.com	Las Cruces	NM	88005	505-884-2171	888-3150
Eutaw Construction Company Inc 109 1/2 W Commerce St PO Box 36 *Web:* www.eutawconstruction.com	Aberdeen	MS	39730	662-369-8868	369-7770
Evergreen Engineering Portland LLC 7431 Nw Evergreen Pkwy Ste 210 *Web:* www.evergreenengineering.com	Hillsboro	OR	97124	503-439-8777	
Ewing Construction Company Inc PO Box 4235 *Web:* www.ewingcc.com	Corpus Christi	TX	78469	361-882-6525	882-8424
Express Construction Company Inc 355 118th Ave SE Ste 100 *Web:* www.expressconstruction.net	Bellevue	WA	98005	206-230-8500	
EXXCEL Project Management Inc 328 S Civic Ctr Dr *Web:* www.exxcel.com	Columbus	OH	43215	614-621-4500	
F&H Construction 1115 E Lockeford St *Web:* www.f-hconst.com	Lodi	CA	95240	209-931-3738	
FA Wilhelm Construction Co Inc 3914 Prospect St *Web:* www.fawilhelm.com	Indianapolis	IN	46203	317-359-5411	359-8346
Facility Construction Services Inc 8200 Lovett Ave *Web:* www.fcsdallas.com	Dallas	TX	75227	214-381-0101	275-4744
Facility Group Inc 2233 Lake Pk Dr *Web:* fdgatlanta.com	Smyrna	GA	30080	770-437-2700	437-3900
Fairfield Banchshares Inc 220 E Main St PO Box 429 *Web:* www.fairfieldnb.com	Fairfield	IL	62837	618-842-2107	842-5849
Faith Enterprises Inc 129 S Corona St *Web:* www.faithenterprisesinc.com	Colorado Springs	CO	80903	719-578-8281	
Fassberg Construction Co 17000 Ventura Blvd Ste 200 *Web:* www.fassbergconstruction.com	Encino	CA	91316	818-386-1800	
FBI Buildings Inc 3823 W 1800 S *Web:* www.fbibuildings.com	Remington	IN	47977	219-261-2157	
FCL Builders Inc 1150 Spring Lk Dr *Web:* www.fclbuilders.com	Itasca	IL	60143	630-773-0050	773-4030
Ferguson Construction Co 400 Canal St *Web:* www.ferguson-construction.com	Sidney	OH	45365	937-498-2381	498-1796
Findorff JH & Son Inc 300 S Bedford St *Web:* www.findorff.com	Madison	WI	53703	608-257-5321	257-5306
FIP Construction Inc 308 Farmington Ave *Web:* www.fipconstruction.com	Farmington	CT	06032	203-271-0356	
First Financial Bank PO Box 2122 PO Box 680 *Web:* first-online.com	Terre Haute	IN	47802	815-844-3171	842-2958
Fisher Development Inc 601 California St Ste 300 *Web:* www.fisherinc.com	San Francisco	CA	94108	415-228-3060	
Fite Building Company Inc 3116 Sexton Rd SE Ste A *Web:* www.fitebuilding.com	Decatur	AL	35603	256-353-5759	
Five Star Industries Inc 1308 Wells St Rd *Web:* www.5starind.com	Du Quoin	IL	62832	618-542-5421	
Flintco LLC 1624 W 21st St *TF:* 800-947-2828 ■ *Web:* www.flintco.com	Tulsa	OK	74107	918-587-8451	582-7506
Flow Construction Company Inc 3628 Trousdale Dr Ste E *Web:* flowconstruction.com	Nashville	TN	37204	615-832-0707	
Fluor Constructors International Inc 352 Halton Rd	Greenville	SC	29607	864-234-7335	234-5476
Fluor Daniel Inc 3 Polaris Way *Web:* www.fluor.com	Aliso Viejo	CA	92698	949-349-2000	349-2585
Ford Development Corp 11148 Woodward Ln *Web:* www.forddevelopment.com	Cincinnati	OH	45241	513-772-1521	772-1556
Forino Company LP 555 Mtn Home Rd *Web:* www.forino.com	Sinking Spring	PA	19608	610-670-2200	
Fort Hill Construction Inc 8118 Hollywood Blvd *Web:* www.forthill.com	Los Angeles	CA	90069	323-656-7425	
Fortney & Weygandt Inc 31269 Bradley Rd *Web:* www.fortneyweygandt.com	North Olmsted	OH	44070	440-716-4000	716-4010
Foushee & Assoc Inc 3260 118th Ave SE *Web:* www.foushee.com	Bellevue	WA	98005	425-746-1000	746-3737
Francis Tuttle Technology Ctr School District 21 12777 N Rockwell Ave *Web:* www.francistuttle.edu	Oklahoma City	OK	73142	405-717-7799	
Frank L. Blum Construction Co 830 E 25th St *Web:* www.flblum.com	Winston-Salem	NC	27105	336-724-5528	
Frank Rewold & Son Inc 333 E Second St *Web:* frankrewold.com	Rochester	MI	48307	248-651-7242	
Franklin Electric LP 916 Fulton St *Web:* www.franklinelectric.net	Pittsburgh	PA	15233	412-322-4477	
Fred Olivieri Construction Company Inc 6315 Promway Ave NW *Web:* www.fredolivieri.com	North Canton	OH	44720	330-494-1007	
Frederick Quinn Corp 103 S Church St *Web:* www.fquinncorp.com	Addison	IL	60101	630-628-8500	628-8595
Frize Corp 16605 Gale Ave *Web:* www.frizecorp.com	City Of Industry	CA	91745	626-369-6088	
Fuller Engineering Co 4135 W 99th St *Web:* www.fullerengineering.com	Carmel	IN	46032	317-228-5800	
Furino & Son Inc 66 Columbia Rd *Web:* www.furinoandsons.com	Branchburg	NJ	08876	908-756-7736	
Fusco Corp 555 Long Wharf Dr Long Wharf Maritime Ctr Ste 14 *Web:* www.fusco.com	New Haven	CT	06511	203-777-7451	
FutureNet Group Inc 12801 Auburn St *Web:* www.futurenetgroup.com	Detroit	MI	48223	313-544-7117	
G & D Transportation Inc 50 Commerce Dr *TF:* 800-451-6680 ■ *Web:* www.gdintegrated.com	Morton	IL	61550	800-451-6680	
G L Wilson Bldg Co 190 Wilson Pk Rd *Web:* www.glwilson.com	Statesville	NC	28625	704-872-2411	872-8281
G.M. Crisalli Associates Inc 843 Hiawatha Blvd W *Web:* gmca.com	Syracuse	NY	13204	315-454-0000	
Gaines Motor Lines Inc 2349 13th Ave SW PO Box 1549 *TF:* 800-438-7311 ■ *Web:* www.gainesml.com	Hickory	NC	28603	828-322-2000	324-7026
Galaxie Defense Marketing Services 5330 Napa St *TF:* 888-711-3427 ■ *Web:* www.galaxiemgmt.com	San Diego	CA	92110	619-299-9950	
Gamma Construction Co 2808 Joanel St *Web:* www.gammaconst.com	Houston	TX	77027	713-963-0086	963-0961
Ganneston Construction Corp 3025 N Belfast Ave *Web:* gannestonconstruction.com	Augusta	ME	04332	207-621-8505	
Ganther Construction & Architecture Inc 4825 County Rd A *Web:* www.ganther.com	Oshkosh	WI	54901	920-426-4774	
Garco Construction Inc 4114 E Broadway *Web:* www.garco.com	Spokane	WA	99202	509-535-4688	
Garling Construction Inc 1120 11th St *Web:* www.garlingconstruction.com	Belle Plaine	IA	52208	319-444-3409	444-2437
GE Johnson Construction Co 25 N Cascade Ave Ste 400 *Web:* www.gejohnson.com	Colorado Springs	CO	80903	719-473-5321	473-5324
Geis Cos, The 10020 Aurora Hudson Rd *Web:* www.buildgeis.com	Streetsboro	OH	44241	330-528-3500	528-0008
Geneva Construction Co (GCCO) 1350 Aurora Ave *Web:* www.genevaconstruction.net	Aurora	IL	60507	630-892-4357	892-7738
George J. Shaw Construction Co 1601 Bellefontaine Ave *Web:* georgeshawconstruction.com	Kansas City	MO	64127	816-231-8200	
George Sollitt Construction 790 N Central Ave *Web:* www.sollitt.com	Wood Dale	IL	60191	630-860-7333	
Gerace Construction Company Inc 4055 S Saginaw Rd *Web:* www.geraceconstruction.com	Midland	MI	48640	989-496-2440	496-2465
Gerald H Phipps 5995 Greenwood Florida Plaza Blvd Ste 100 *TF:* 866-487-2365 ■ *Web:* www.ghphipps.com	Greenwood Village	CO	80111	303-571-5377	629-7467
Gerardi Construction Inc 1604 N 19th St *Web:* www.gerardiconstruction.com	Tampa	FL	33605	813-248-4341	
Gerloff Company Inc 14955 Bulverde Rd *TF:* 800-486-3621 ■ *Web:* www.gerloffinc.com	San Antonio	TX	78247	210-490-2777	494-0610
Gibbs Construction LLC 5736 Citrus Blvd Ste 200 *Web:* www.gibbsconstruction.net	New Orleans	LA	70123	504-733-4336	
Gil Haugan Construction Inc 200 E 60th St N *Web:* www.gilhaugan.com	Sioux Falls	SD	57104	605-336-6082	
Gilbane Bldg Co New England Regional Office 7 Jackson Walkway *TF:* 800-445-2263 ■ *Web:* www.gilbaneco.com	Providence	RI	02903	401-456-5800	456-5936
Gilbane Bldg Company Mid-Atlantic Regional Office 7901 Sandy Spring Rd Ste 500 *TF:* 800-445-2263 ■ *Web:* www.gilbaneco.com	Laurel	MD	20707	410-649-1750	
Gilbane Bldg Company Southwest Regional Office 1331 Lamar St Ste 1170 *TF:* 800-445-2263 ■ *Web:* www.gilbaneco.com	Houston	TX	77010	713-209-1873	
Gilford Corp 4600 Powder Mill Rd Ste 350 *Web:* www.gilfordcorp.com	Beltsville	MD	20705	301-931-3900	
Gillis Gilkerson Inc 212 W Main St Ste 305 *Web:* www.gillisgilkerson.com	Salisbury	MD	21801	410-749-4821	
Giordano Construction Company Inc 1155 Main St *Web:* www.giordano-construction.com	Branford	CT	06405	203-488-7264	
Glenn H. Johnson Construction 1776 Winthrop Dr *Web:* www.ghjohnson.com	Des Plaines	IL	60018	847-297-4700	
Golden Sands General Contractors Inc 2500 NW 39 St *TF:* 888-994-4742 ■ *Web:* www.goldensandsgc.com	Miami	FL	33142	305-633-3336	
Gomez Construction Co 7100 SW 44th St *Web:* www.gomezconstruction.com	Miami	FL	33155	305-661-7660	661-0504
Gootee Construction Inc 2400 N Arnoult Rd *Web:* www.gootee.com	Metairie	LA	70001	504-831-1909	
Grae-Con Construction Inc PO Box 1778 *Web:* www.graecon.com	Steubenville	OH	43952	740-282-6830	282-6849
Granger Construction Co 6267 Aurelius Rd *Web:* www.grangerconstruction.com	Lansing	MI	48911	517-393-1670	393-1382
Gray Construction 10 Quality St *TF:* 800-814-8468 ■ *Web:* www.gray.com	Lexington	KY	40507	859-281-5000	252-5300
Green Acres Contracting Company Inc 703 Pennsylvania Ave *Web:* www.greenacrescontracting.com	Scottdale	PA	15683	724-887-8096	

Company	City	State	Zip	Phone	Fax
Greenway Enterprises Inc PO Box 5553 *Web:* www.greenwayent.com	Helena	MT	59604	406-458-9411	458-6516
GreenWood Inc 160 Milestone Way Ste A *Web:* www.gwood.com	Greenville	SC	29615	864-244-9669	
Greiner Construction Inc 625 Marquette Ave *Web:* www.greinerconstruction.biz	Minneapolis	MN	55402	612-338-1696	
Greystone Construction Co 500 S Marschall Rd Ste 300 *TF:* 888-742-6837 ■ *Web:* www.greystoneconstruction.com	Shakopee	MN	55379	952-496-2227	
Groupe Plombaction Inc 575 boul Pierre-Roux est *Web:* www.groupeplombaction.com	Victoriaville	QC	G6T1S7	819-752-6064	
Grunley Construction Company Inc 15020 Shady Grove Rd Ste 500 *Web:* www.grunley.com	Rockville	MD	20850	240-399-2000	399-2001
Gulf & Pacific Equities Corp 1300 Bay St Ste 300 *Web:* www.gpequities.com	Toronto	ON	M5R3K8	416-968-3337	
Gulf Seaboard General Contractors Inc 629 N Washington Hwy *Web:* www.gulfseaboard.com	Ashland	VA	23005	804-752-7600	
Gunda Corporation LLC 6161 Savoy Dr Ste 550 *Web:* www.gundacorp.com	Houston	TX	77036	713-541-3530	
Guntersville City Schools Board of Education 4200 Alabama 79 S	Guntersville	AL	35976	256-582-3159	582-6158
Gutierrez Co, The 1 Wall St *Web:* www.gutierrezco.com	Burlington	MA	01803	781-272-7000	272-3130
Gutknecht Construction Co 2280 Citygate Dr *Web:* www.gutknecht.com	Columbus	OH	43219	614-532-5410	
H & M Construction Company Inc 50 Security Dr *Web:* hmcompany.com	Jackson	TN	38305	731-664-6300	
H C Olsen Construction Company Inc 710 Los Angeles Ave *Web:* www.hcolsen.com	Monrovia	CA	91016	626-359-8900	
H.P. Cummings Construction Co 14 Prospect St PO Box 29 *Web:* www.hpcummings.com	Ware	MA	01082	413-967-6251	
Halbert Construction Company Inc 330 S Magnolia Ave Ste 203 *Web:* www.halbertco.com	El Cajon	CA	92020	619-593-3527	
Halco Products 100 Gordon St *Web:* www.halco-products.com	Elk Grove Village	IL	60007	847-956-1600	
Haley Construction Inc 900 Orange Ave *Web:* www.haleyconstruction.com	Daytona Beach	FL	32114	386-944-0470	
Haley-Greer Inc 2257 -C Lombardy Ln *Web:* www.haleygreer.com	Dallas	TX	75220	972-556-1177	556-1384
Halfacre Construction Co 7015 Professional Pkwy E *Web:* www.halfacreconstruction.com	Sarasota	FL	34240	941-907-9099	
Hammer & Hand Inc 1020 Se Harrison St *Web:* hammerandhand.com	Portland	OR	97214	503-232-2447	
Hanlin-Rainaldi Construction Corp 6610 Singletree Dr *Web:* www.hanlinrainaldi.com	Columbus	OH	43229	614-310-1466	
Hansen Company Inc, The 5665 Greendale Rd Ste A *Web:* www.hansencompany.com	Johnston	IA	50131	515-270-1117	270-3829
Harbour Contractors Inc 23830 W Main St *Web:* www.harbour-cm.com	Plainfield	IL	60544	815-254-5500	254-5505
Hardaway Group 615 Main St *Web:* www.hardaway.net	Nashville	TN	37206	615-254-5461	254-4518
Hardy Bros Inc 6406 Siloam Rd *Web:* www.hardybros.com	Siloam	NC	27047	336-374-5050	
Harkins Builders Inc 2201 Warwick Way *TF:* 800-227-2345 ■ *Web:* www.harkinsbuilders.com	Marriottsville	MD	21104	410-750-2600	480-4299
Harman Construction Inc 1633 Rogers Rd *Web:* harmanconstructioninc.net	Fort Worth	TX	76107	817-336-5780	336-5797
Harper Construction Company Inc 2241 Kettner Blvd Ste 300 *Web:* www.harperconstruction.com	San Diego	CA	92101	619-233-7900	
Harvey-Cleary Builders 207a Perry Pkwy Ste 1 *Web:* www.harveycleary.com	Gaithersburg	MD	20877	301-519-2288	
Haselden Construction LLC 6950 S Potomac St *Web:* www.haselden.com	Centennial	CO	80112	303-751-1478	751-1627
Haskell Co 111 Riverside Ave *TF:* 800-622-4326 ■ *Web:* haskell.com	Jacksonville	FL	32202	904-791-4500	791-4699
Haskell Corp PO Box 917 *Web:* www.haskellcorp.com	Bellingham	WA	98227	360-734-1200	734-5538
Hathaway Dinwiddie Construction Co 275 Battery St Ste 300 *Web:* www.hdcco.com	San Francisco	CA	94111	415-986-2718	956-5669
Hawkins Construction Co 2516 Deer Pk Blvd *Web:* www.hawkins1.com	Omaha	NE	68105	402-342-1607	
Haydon Building Corp 4640 E Cotton Gin Loop *Web:* www.haydonbc.com	Phoenix	AZ	85040	602-296-1496	
HBD Construction Inc 5517 Manchester Ave *Web:* www.hbdgc.com	Saint Louis	MO	63110	314-781-8000	
HBE Corp 11330 Olive Blvd *Web:* www.hbecorp.com	Saint Louis	MO	63141	314-567-9000	567-0602
Heartland Bldg Company Inc 117 William St	Middlesex	NJ	08846	732-302-9277	
Hedrick Brothers Construction Company Inc 2200 Centrepark W Dr Ste 100 *Web:* www.hedrickbrothers.com	West Palm Beach	FL	33409	561-689-8880	
Hellas Construction Inc 12710 Research Blvd Ste 240 *Web:* www.hellasconstruction.com	Austin	TX	78759	512-250-2910	
Henderson Corp 575New Jersey 28	Raritan	NJ	08869	908-685-1300	
Hennessy Construction Services Corp 2300 22nd St N *Web:* www.hcsfl.com	Saint Petersburg	FL	33713	727-821-3223	
Henning Construction Company Inc PO Box 394 *Web:* www.henningcompanies.com	Johnston	IA	50131	515-253-0943	253-0942
Hensel Phelps Construction Co 420 Sixth Ave PO Box 0 *Web:* www.henselphelps.com	Greeley	CO	80632	970-352-6565	352-9311
Herrero Brothers Inc 2100 Oakdale Ave *Web:* www.herrero.com	San Francisco	CA	94124	415-824-7675	
HG Reynolds Co Inc 113 Contract Dr	Aiken	SC	29801	803-641-1402	
HHI Corp 736 W Harrisville Rd *Web:* www.hhicorp.com	Ogden	UT	84404	385-333-4400	
Highland Partnership Inc 285 Bay Blvd *Web:* www.highlandpartnership.net	Chula Vista	CA	91910	619-498-2900	
Hilco Transport Inc 7700 Kenmont Rd *Web:* www.hilcotransport.com	Greensboro	NC	27409	336-273-9441	273-9701
Hinderliter Construction Inc 3601 N Saint Joseph Ave *Web:* www.hinderliterconstruction.com	Evansville	IN	47720	812-425-4137	
Hitt Contracting Inc 2900 Fairview Park Dr *Web:* www.hitt-gc.com	Falls Church	VA	22042	703-846-9000	846-9110
HJ Russell & Co 504 Fair St SW *Web:* www.hjrussell.com	Atlanta	GA	30313	404-330-1000	688-5179
Hoar Construction Inc 2 Metroplex Dr # 400 *Web:* www.hoar.com	Birmingham	AL	35209	205-803-2121	423-2323
HOF Construction Inc 3137 Jamieson Ave *Web:* www.hofconstruction.com	Saint Louis	MO	63139	314-645-2200	
Hoffman Construction Corp 805 SW Broadway Ste 2100 *Web:* www.hoffmancorp.com	Portland	OR	97205	503-221-8811	221-8934
Hoffman Planning, Design, & Construction Inc 122 E College Ave Ste 1G *Web:* www.hoffman.net	Appleton	WI	54911	920-731-2322	
Hohl Industrial Services Inc 770 Riverview Blvd *Web:* www.hohlind.com	Buffalo	NY	14150	716-332-0466	
Holder Construction Co 3333 Riverwood Pkwy Ste 400 *Web:* www.holderconstruction.com	Atlanta	GA	30339	770-988-3000	988-3042
Hollister Construction Co 4071 E. La Palma Ave Ste A *Web:* www.hollico.net	Anaheim	CA	92807	714-701-1400	
Holloman Corp 333 N Sam Houston Pkwy E Ste 600 *TF:* 800-521-2461 ■ *Web:* www.hollomancorp.com	Houston	TX	77060	281-878-2600	272-1227
Hood Construction Company Inc 1050 Shop Rd Ste A *Web:* www.hoodconstruction.com	Columbia	SC	29201	803-765-2940	
Horst Group Inc 320 Granite Run Dr PO Box 3330 *Web:* www.horstgroup.com	Lancaster	PA	17604	717-581-9800	581-9816
Hospitality Builders Inc 150 Knollwood Dr *Web:* www.hospitalitybuilders.com	Rapid City	SD	57401	605-791-3400	
Housley Communications Inc 3550 S Bryant Blvd *Web:* housleygroup.com	San Angelo	TX	76903	325-944-9905	944-1781
Howard Immel Inc 1820 Radisson St *Web:* www.immel-builds.com	Green Bay	WI	54302	920-468-8208	
Hunt Construction Group 2450 S Tibbs Ave *Web:* www.huntconstructiongroup.com	Indianapolis	IN	46241	317-227-7800	227-7810
Hunzinger Construction Co 21100 Enterprise Ave *Web:* www.hunzinger.com	Brookfield	WI	53045	262-797-0797	
Hutter Construction Corp 810 Turnpike Rd *Web:* hutterconstruction.com	New Ipswich	NH	03071	603-878-2300	
Hutton Construction Corp 2229 S W St *Web:* www.huttonconstruction.com	Wichita	KS	67213	316-942-8855	
Ideal Builders Inc 1406 Emil St *Web:* www.idealbuildersinc.com	Madison	WI	53713	608-271-8111	
Ideal Interiors Inc 450 Seventh Ave *Web:* www.ideal-interiors.com	New York	NY	10123	212-262-7005	262-7024
IMCO Carbide Tool Inc 28170 Cedar Park Blvd *Web:* www.imcousa.com	Perrysburg	OH	43551	419-661-6313	
Imco General Construction Inc 2116 Buchanan Loop *Web:* imcoconstruction.com	Ferndale	WA	98248	360-671-3936	
Industrial Contractors Inc (ICI) 401 NW First St **Fax Area Code: 812* ■ *Web:* www.usa.skanska.com	Evansville	IN	47708	973-753-3500	464-7255*
Industrial Resources Inc PO Box 2648 *Web:* www.indres.com	Fairmont	WV	26554	304-363-4100	
Inman-EMJ Construction 88 Union Ave Ste 400	Memphis	TN	38103	901-682-4100	682-0755
Inspec Group LLC 140 SW Arthur St *Web:* www.inspecgroup.com	Portland	OR	97201	503-595-6540	
Interface Construction Corp 8401 Wabash Ave *Web:* www.interfaceconstruction.com	Saint Louis	MO	63134	314-522-1011	522-1022
International Contractors Inc 977 S Rt 83 *Web:* www.iciinc.com	Elmhurst	IL	60126	630-834-8043	
IPAC Services Corp 8701 102 St *Web:* www.ipacservices.com	Clairmont	AB	T0H0W0	780-532-7350	
Irmscher Inc 1030 Osage St	Fort Wayne	IN	46808	260-422-5572	424-1487
Irwin Industries Inc 1580 W Carson St *Web:* www.irwinindustries.com	Long Beach	CA	90810	310-233-3000	834-9402
J D H Contracting 8109 Network Dr *Web:* www.jdhcontracting.com	Plainfield	IN	46168	317-839-0520	
J F C Construction Inc 4901 Pacheco Blvd *Web:* www.jfcconstruction.com	Martinez	CA	94553	925-228-0924	
J Kokolakis Contracting Inc 1500 Ocean Ave *Web:* www.jkokolakis.com	Bohemia	NY	11716	631-744-6147	744-6156
J L Wallace Inc 9111 W College Pointe Dr *Web:* www.jlwallaceinc.com	Fort Myers	FL	33919	239-437-1111	

Company	City	State	Zip	Phone	Fax
J R Roberts Corp 7745 Greenback Ln Ste 300 *Web:* www.jrroberts.com	Citrus Heights	CA	95610	916-729-5600	
J T Turner Construction Co Inc 2250 E Victory Dr Ste 104 *Web:* www.jttconst.com	Savannah	GA	31404	912-356-5611	356-5615
J.A. Street & Associates Inc 245 Birch St *Web:* www.jastreet.com	Blountville	TN	37617	423-323-8017	
J.I. Garcia Construction Co 4717 East Hedges Ave *Web:* www.jigarcia.com	Fresno	CA	93703	559-276-7726	
J.R. Abbot Construction Inc 3408 First Ave S *Web:* www.jrabbott.com	Seattle	WA	98134	206-467-8500	447-1885
J.W. Design & Construction Inc 3563 Sueldo St Ste I *Web:* www.jwdci.com	San Luis Obispo	CA	93401	805-544-3130	
JA Tiberti Construction Co 1806 Industrial Rd *Web:* www.tiberti.com	Las Vegas	NV	89102	702-248-4000	
Jackson Local Schools District (JLSD) 7602 Fulton Dr *Web:* jackson.stark.k12.oh.us	Massillon	OH	44646	330-830-8000	830-8008
Jacob White Construction Co 2000 W Parkwood Ste 100 *Web:* www.jacobwhitecc.com	Friendswood	TX	77546	281-286-6666	
James G Davis Construction Corp 12530 Parklawn Dr *Web:* www.davisconstruction.com	Rockville	MD	20852	301-881-2990	468-3918
Janus Corp 1081 Shary Cir *Web:* www.januscorp.com	Concord	CA	94518	925-969-9200	
Jasmine Engineering Inc 115 E Travis St Ste 1020 *Web:* www.jasmineengineering.com	San Antonio	TX	78205	210-227-3000	
Jayman MasterBUILT Inc 200 3132 - 118 Ave SE *Web:* www.jayman.com	Calgary	AB	T2Z3X1	403-258-3772	
Jaynes Corp 2906 Broadway NE **Fax Area Code:* 619 ■ *TF:* 800-393-6343 ■ *Web:* www.jaynescorp.com	Albuquerque	NM	87107	505-345-8591	233-4090*
JCN Construction Company Inc 155 Dow St *Web:* www.jcnconstruction.com	Manchester	NH	03101	603-624-7080	
JE Dunn Construction Co 1001 Locust St *Web:* www.jedunn.com	Kansas City	MO	64106	816-474-8600	460-2769
Jeffrey M. Brown Assoc LLC 2337 Philmont Ave *Web:* www.jmbassociates.com	Huntingdon Valley	PA	19006	215-938-5000	
Jendoco Construction Corp 2000 Lincoln Rd *Web:* www.jendoco.com	Pittsburgh	PA	15235	412-361-4500	
Jensen Builders Ltd 1175 S 32nd St *Web:* www.jensenbuilders.com	Fort Dodge	IA	50501	515-573-3292	
JESCO Inc 2020 McCullough Blvd *Web:* jescoinc.net	Tupelo	MS	38801	662-842-3240	
JGA-Beacon Inc 2200 Cook Dr *Web:* www.jgacorp.com	Atlanta	GA	30340	770-246-3400	
JLC Associates Inc 3198-A Airport Loop Dr *Web:* www.jlcassoc.com	Costa Mesa	CA	92626	714-241-4430	
John Burns Construction Company Inc 17601 Southwest Hwy *Web:* www.jbconstructionco.com	Orland Park	IL	60467	708-326-3500	
John Deklewa & Sons Inc 1273 Washington Pk	Bridgeville	PA	15017	412-257-9000	
John E Jones Oil Co Inc 1016 S Cedar PO Box 546 *TF:* 800-323-9821 ■ *Web:* www.jonesoil.net	Stockton	KS	67669	785-425-6746	425-6323
John Gallin & Son Inc 102 Madison Ave 9th Fl *Web:* www.gallin.com	New York	NY	10016	212-252-8900	
John S Clark Co Inc 210 Airport Rd *Web:* www.jsclark.com	Mount Airy	NC	27030	336-789-1000	789-7609
Joseph A Natoli Construction Corp 293 Changebridge Rd *Web:* www.jnatoli.com	Pine Brook	NJ	07058	973-575-1500	575-8216
Joseph Construction Company Inc 203 Letterman Rd *Web:* www.josephconst.com	Knoxville	TN	37919	865-584-3945	
K L House Construction Company Inc 6409 Acoma Rd SE *Web:* www.klhouse.com	Albuquerque	NM	87108	505-268-4361	268-9266
Kalamazoo Valley Plant Growers Cooperative Inc 8937 Krum Ave *Web:* www.kvpg.com	Galesburg	MI	49053	269-216-1200	
Kapp Construction Co 329 Mt Vernon Ave *Web:* www.kappconstruction.com	Springfield	OH	45501	937-324-0134	324-3406
Kaufman Lynn Construction Inc 4850 T-Rex Ave Ste 300 *Web:* www.kaufmanlynn.com	Boca Raton	FL	33431	561-361-6700	
Kcc Contractor Inc 2664 E Kearney St *Web:* www.killco.com	Springfield	MO	65803	417-883-1204	887-7338
KCI Construction Co 10315 Lk Bluff Dr *Web:* www.kciconstruction.com	St. Louis	MO	63123	314-894-8888	
Keating Bldg Corp 1600 Arch St Ste 300 *Web:* www.tutorperinibuilding.com	Philadelphia	PA	19103	610-668-4100	
Keating Daniel J Co 134 N Narberth Ave *Web:* www.djkeating.com	Narberth	PA	19072	610-664-2799	
Keller Inc N216 State Rd 55 *Web:* www.kellerbuilds.com	Kaukauna	WI	54130	920-766-5795	
Kelsey Construction Inc 306 E Princeton St *Web:* www.kelseyconstruction.com	Orlando	FL	32804	407-898-4101	
Kemp Bros. Construction Inc 10135 Geary Ave *Web:* www.kempbros.com	Santa Fe Springs	CA	90670	562-236-5000	
Ken Brady Construction Company Inc 4001 Turnagain Blvd *Web:* www.kenbrady.com	Anchorage	AK	99517	907-243-4604	
Kenmore Construction Co Inc 700 Home Ave *Web:* www.kenmorecompanies.com	Akron	OH	44310	330-762-9373	762-2135
Kenny Construction Co 2215 Sanders Rd Ste 400 **Fax Area Code:* 847 ■ *Web:* www.graniteconstruction.com	Northbrook	IL	60062	831-724-1011	272-5421*
Key Construction Inc 741 W Second *Web:* www.keyconstruction.com	Wichita	KS	67203	316-263-9515	
Kickerillo Cos 1306 S Fry Rd **Fax Area Code:* 281 ■ *Web:* www.kickerillo.com	Katy	TX	77450	713-951-0666	492-2018*
Kinco Constructors LLC 12600 Lawson Rd *Web:* www.kincoconstructors.com	Little Rock	AR	72210	501-225-7606	
Kinney Construction Services Inc 120 N Beaver St Ste 100 *Web:* www.kinneyconstruction.net	Flagstaff	AZ	86001	928-779-2820	
Kinsley Construction Inc 1110 E Princess St *Web:* www.kinsleyconstruction.com	York	PA	17403	717-741-3841	741-9054
Kirila Contractors Inc 505 Bedford Rd PO Box 179 *Web:* www.kirila.com	Brookfield	OH	44403	330-448-4055	
Kirtley-Cole Associates LLC 1010 SE Everett Mall Way Ste 102 *Web:* www.kirtley-cole.com	Everett	WA	98208	425-609-0400	
Kitchell Corp 1707 E Highland Ave **Fax:* Hum Res ■ *Web:* www.kitchell.com	Phoenix	AZ	85016	602-264-4411	364-6133*
Kiwi Ii Construction Inc 28177 Keller Rd *TF:* 877-465-4942 ■ *Web:* www.kiwiconstruction.com	Murrieta	CA	92563	951-301-8975	
Kjellstrom & Lee Inc 1607 Ownby Ln *Web:* www.kjellstromandlee.com	Richmond	VA	23220	804-288-0082	285-4288
Klassen Corp 2021 Westwind Dr *Web:* www.klassencorp.com	Bakersfield	CA	93301	661-324-3000	
Knutson Construction Services Inc 7515 Wayzata Blvd *Web:* www.knutsonconstruction.com	Minneapolis	MN	55426	763-546-1400	
Korte Co, The 9225 W Flamingo Rd Ste 100 *Web:* www.korteco.com	Las Vegas	NV	89147	702-228-9551	228-5852
Korth Companies Inc, The 9101 Gaither Rd *Web:* www.korthcos.com	Gaithersburg	MD	20877	301-921-9500	
KPRS Construction Services Inc 2850 Saturn St *Web:* www.kprsinc.com	Brea	CA	92821	714-672-0800	672-0871
Kraemer Bros Inc 925 Pk Ave *Web:* www.kraemerbrothers.com	Plain	WI	53577	608-546-2411	546-2509
Kreis Johnson Construction 160 Village St *Web:* www.johnsonkreis.com	Birmingham	AL	35242	205-981-9030	
Krusinski Construction Co 2107 Swift Dr *Web:* www.krusinski.com	Oak Brook	IL	60523	630-573-7700	
Kustom Fl LLC 265 Hunt Park Cv *TF:* 866-679-0699 ■ *Web:* www.kustom.us	Longwood	FL	32750	866-679-0699	
L Kelley Construction Co 2901 Falling Springs Rd *Web:* www.lkeeley.com	Sauget	IL	62206	314-421-5933	421-2266
L L Pelling Co 1425 W Penn St PO Box 230 *Web:* www.llpelling.com	North Liberty	IA	52317	319-626-4600	626-4605
La Habra City School District (LHCSD) 500 N Walnut St	La Habra	CA	90631	562-690-2305	
Lacy Construction Co 3356 W Old Hwy 30 P O Box 188 *Web:* www.lacygc.com	Grand Island	NE	68801	308-384-2866	
Ladco Company Ltd 200-40 Lakewood Blvd *Web:* www.ladco.mb.ca	Winnipeg	MB	R2J2M6	204-982-5900	
Lakeview Construction Inc 10505 Corp Dr Ste 200 *Web:* www.lvconstruction.com	Pleasant Prairie	WI	53158	262-857-3336	857-3424
Lampasas Isd 207 W Eigth St *Web:* www.lisdtx.org/index.cfm?	Lampasas	TX	76550	512-556-6224	556-8711
Landau Bldg Co 9855 Rinaman Rd *Web:* www.landau-bldg.com	Wexford	PA	15090	724-935-8800	935-6510
Landis Construction LLC 8300 Earhart Blvd Ste 300 PO Box 4278 *Web:* www.landisllc.com	New Orleans	LA	70118	504-833-6070	833-6662
Lanham Brothers General Contractors 2119 W 3rd St *Web:* www.lanhambros.com	Owensboro	KY	42301	270-683-4591	
Larson-Danielson Construction Company Inc 302 Tyler St *Web:* www.ldconstruction.com	La Porte	IN	46350	219-362-2127	
Lathrop Co 460 W Dussel Dr *Web:* www.turnerconstruction.com	Maumee	OH	43537	419-893-7000	
Law Company Inc, The 345 Riverview St *Web:* www.law-co.com	Wichita	KS	67203	316-268-0200	268-0210
Lease Crutcher Lewis 107 Spring St *Web:* www.lewisbuilds.com	Seattle	WA	98104	206-622-0500	
LeChase Construction Services LLC 300 Trolley Blvd *Web:* www.lechase.com	Rochester	NY	14606	585-254-3510	
Lee Kennedy Company Inc 122 Quincy Shore Dr *Web:* www.leekennedy.com	Quincy	MA	02171	617-825-6930	
Lee Lewis Construction Inc 7810 Orlando Ave *Web:* www.leelewis.com	Lubbock	TX	79423	806-797-8400	797-8492
Lehr Construction Company Inc 2115 Frederick Ave *Web:* www.lehrconstruction.com	Saint Joseph	MO	64501	816-232-4431	
Lend Lease Corp 200 Pk Ave 9th Fl *Web:* www.lendlease.com	New York	NY	10166	212-592-6800	592-6988
Leon D. DeMatteis Construction 820 Elmont Rd *Web:* www.dematteisorg.com	Elmont	NY	11003	516-285-5500	
Leonard S. Fiore Inc 5506 Sixth Ave Rear *Web:* www.lsfiore.com	Altoona	PA	16602	814-946-3686	
Leopardo Cos Inc 5200 Prairie Stone Pkwy *Web:* www.leopardo.com	Hoffman Estates	IL	60192	847-783-3000	783-3001
Letsos Co 8435 Westglen Dr PO Box 36927 *Web:* www.letsos.com	Houston	TX	77063	713-783-3200	972-7880

Company / Address	City	State	Zip	Phone	Fax
Lettire Construction Corp 334-336 E 110th St *Web:* lettire.com	New York	NY	10029	212-996-6640	
Levine Builders 42-09 235th St *Web:* www.levinebuilders.com	Douglaston	NY	11363	718-281-0550	
Lewis & Michael Inc 1827 Woodman Dr *TF:* 800-543-3524 ■ *Web:* atlaslm.com	Dayton	OH	45420	937-252-6683	
Lewis Contractors LLC 55 Gwynns Mill Ct *Web:* www.lewis-contractors.com	Owings Mills	MD	21117	410-356-4200	356-7732
Lightner Electronics Inc 1771 Beaver Dam Rd *TF:* 866-239-3888 ■ *Web:* www.lightnerelectronics.com	Claysburg	PA	16625	814-239-8323	
Linbeck Construction Corp 3900 Essex Ln Ste 1200 PO Box 22500 *Web:* www.linbeck.com	Houston	TX	77027	713-621-2350	
Lincoln Builders Inc 1809 Northpointe Ste 201 *Web:* www.lincolnbuilders.com	Ruston	LA	71270	318-255-3822	
Lippert Bros Inc 2211 E I-44 Service Rd PO Box 17450 *Web:* www.lippertbros.com	Oklahoma City	OK	73136	405-478-3580	478-3301
Llewelyn-davies Sahni International Inc 5120 Woodway Dr Ste 8010 *Web:* www.theldnet.com	Houston	TX	77056	713-850-1500	
Lloyd Bilyeu McLellan Construction Company Inc (LBM) 11421 Blankenbaker Access Dr *Web:* www.lbmconstructionco.com	Louisville	KY	40299	502-452-1151	454-0291
Loebl Schlossman & Hackl Inc 233 N Michigan Ave Ste 3000 *Web:* www.lshdesign.com	Chicago	IL	60601	312-565-1800	
Logan Trucking Inc 3224 Navarre Rd SW *TF:* 800-683-0142 ■ *Web:* www.logantrucking.com	Canton	OH	44706	330-478-1404	478-6706
Lombardi Contracting Corp 7744 Formula Pl	San Diego	CA	92121	858-566-0060	
Louis P Ciminelli Construction Corp 2421 Main St *Web:* www.lpciminelli.com	Buffalo	NY	14202	716-855-1200	854-6655
Loven Contracting Inc 1100 S Pinnacle St *Web:* www.lovencontracting.com	Flagstaff	AZ	86001	928-774-9040	
Luckett & Farley Architects Engineers & Construction Managers Inc 737 S Third St *Web:* www.luckett-farley.com	Louisville	KY	40202	502-585-4181	587-0488
Lueder Construction Co 9999 J St Ste B *Web:* www.lueder.com	Omaha	NE	68127	402-339-1000	
Lumber One Avon Inc 101 Second St NW PO Box 7 *Web:* www.lumber-one.com	Avon	MN	56310	320-356-7342	
Lusardi Construction Company Inc 1570 Linda Vista Dr *Web:* www.lusardi.com	San Marcos	CA	92078	760-744-3133	744-9064
Lydig Construction Inc 11001 E Montgomery St *Web:* www.lydig.com	Spokane	WA	99206	509-534-0451	535-6622
M.B. Kahn Construction Company Inc 101 Flintlake Rd *Web:* www.mbkahn.com	Columbia	SC	29223	803-736-2950	
M.J. Harris Construction Inc 1 Riverchase Rdg Ste 300 *Web:* www.mjharris.com	Birmingham	AL	35244	205-380-6800	
MA Angeliades Inc 5-44 47th Ave *Web:* www.ma-angeliades.com	Long Island	NY	11101	718-786-5555	786-4700
MA Mortenson Co 700 Meadow Ln N *Web:* www.mortenson.com	Minneapolis	MN	55422	763-522-2100	287-5430
Maas Bros Construction Company Inc 410 Water Tower Ct *Web:* www.maasbros.com	Watertown	WI	53094	920-261-1682	
MacDonald-Bedford LLC 2900 Main St Ste 200 *Web:* www.macdonaldbedford.com	Alameda	CA	94501	510-521-4020	
Magil Construction Corp 1655 rue De Beauharnois Ouest *Web:* www.magil.com	Montreal	QC	H4N1J6	514-341-9899	
Mak Design Build Inc 430 F St Ste B *Web:* www.makdesignbuild.com	Davis	CA	95616	530-750-2209	
Make It Right Inc 55 E Huntington Dr *Web:* www.makeitright.net	Arcadia	CA	91006	626-445-0366	
Mall Craft Inc 2225 N Windsor st *Web:* www.mallcraft.com	Altadena	CA	91001	626-398-3598	
Maloney & Bell General Contractors Inc 3117 Fite Cir Ste 101 *Web:* www.maloneyandbell.com	Sacramento	CA	95827	916-687-8779	756-2402
Mapp Construction LLC 344 Third St *Web:* mappconstruction.com	Baton Rouge	LA	70801	225-757-0111	
March Associates Inc 601 Hamburg Tpke *Web:* www.marchassociates.com	Wayne	NJ	07470	973-904-0213	
Marco Enterprises Inc 3504 Watkins Ave *Web:* www.marcoenterprises.com	Landover	MD	20785	301-773-5656	773-0422
Mark Cerrone Inc 2368 Maryland Ave *TF:* 855-250-7739 ■ *Web:* markcerrone.com	Niagara Falls	NY	14305	716-282-5244	
Market Contractors Ltd of Oregon 10250 NE Marx St *TF:* 800-793-1448 ■ *Web:* www.marketcontractors.com	Portland	OR	97220	503-255-0977	262-4280
Marlborough Public Schools (MPS) 17 Washington St *Web:* www.mps-edu.org	Marlborough	MA	01752	508-460-3509	
Marne Construction Inc 748 N Poplar St *Web:* www.marneconstruction.com	Orange	CA	92868	714-935-0995	
Martin Allgeier & Assoc Inc 7231 E 24th St *Web:* www.amce.com	Joplin	MO	64804	417-680-7200	
Martin-Harris Construction Co 3030 S Highland Dr *Web:* www.martinharris.com	Las Vegas	NV	89109	702-385-5257	474-8257
Mathiowetz Construction Co 30676 County Rd 24 *Web:* www.mathiowetzconst.com	Sleepy Eye	MN	56085	507-794-6953	794-3514
Matous Construction Ltd 8602 State Hwy 317 *Web:* www.matousconstruction.com	Belton	TX	76513	254-780-1400	780-2599
Matthews Construction Company Inc 210 First Ave S *Web:* www.matthewsconstruction.com	Conover	NC	28613	828-464-7325	465-6747
Max J. Kuney Co 120 N Ralph St PO Box 4008 *Web:* www.maxkuney.com	Spokane	WA	99220	509-535-0651	534-6828
MBA Construction 298 W Bridge St *Web:* www.mbaconstruction.net	Blackfoot	ID	83221	208-785-7171	
McBride Construction Resources Inc 224 Nickerson St *Web:* www.mcbrideconstruction.com	Seattle	WA	98109	206-283-7121	284-5670
McCarthy Bldg Cos Inc 1341 N Rock Hill Rd **Fax:* Mktg ■ *Web:* www.mccarthy.com	Saint Louis	MO	63124	314-968-3300	968-4642*
McGough Construction Co Inc 2737 Fairview Ave N *TF:* 800-552-7670 ■ *Web:* www.mcgough.com	Saint Paul	MN	55113	651-633-5050	633-5673
McIntyre Elwell & Strammer General Contractors Inc 1645 Barber Rd *Web:* www.mesgc.com	Sarasota	FL	34240	941-377-6800	
McKay-Cocker Construction Ltd 1665 Oxford St E *Web:* www.mckaycocker.com	London	ON	N5Y5R9	519-451-5270	
McPherson Concrete Storage Systems Inc 116 N Augustus St *Web:* www.mcphersonconcrete.com	Mcpherson	KS	67460	620-241-4362	
MDC Systems Inc 37 N Vly Rd 3 Sta Sq Ste 100 *TF:* 888-632-9977 ■ *Web:* www.mdcsystems.com	Paoli	PA	19301	610-640-9600	
MDS Builders of Texas Inc 3910 S IH 35 Frontage Rd Ste 110 *Web:* www.mdsbuilders.com	Austin	TX	78704	512-851-1133	
Mechanical Contractor 4165 Brunswick Rd *Web:* www.dmcmemphis.com	Memphis	TN	38133	901-730-4799	
Meehleis Modular Buildings Inc 1303 E Lodi Ave *Web:* www.meehleis.com	Lodi	CA	95240	209-334-4637	
Mehlville School District 3120 Lemay Ferry Rd *Web:* www.mehlvilleschooldistrict.com	Saint Louis	MO	63125	314-467-5000	467-5099
MEP Associates 2720 Arbor Ct *Web:* www.mepassociates.com	Eau Claire	WI	54701	715-832-5680	
MEP Consulting Engineers Inc 2928 Story Rd W Ste A *Web:* www.mepce.com	Las Colinas	TX	75038	972-870-9060	
Merced Irrigation District PO Box 2288 *TF:* 855-800-2267 ■ *Web:* mercedid.com	Merced	CA	95344	209-722-5761	722-6421
Mercer Construction Company Inc 42690 Rio Nedo Way Ste D *Web:* www.mercerconstruction.com	Temecula	CA	92590	951-296-0111	
Messer Construction Co 5158 Fishwick Dr *Web:* www.messer.com	Cincinnati	OH	45216	513-242-1541	242-6467
Met-Con Construction Inc 15760 Acorn Trl *Web:* www.met-con.com	Faribault	MN	55021	507-332-2266	
Metal Masters Inc 3825 Crater Lk Hwy *TF:* 800-866-9437 ■ *Web:* www.metalmasters-inc.com	Medford	OR	97504	541-779-1049	
Metropolitan Glass Inc 6400 Franklin St *Web:* www.metroglass.com	Denver	CO	80229	303-853-4527	
Meyer & Najem Inc 11787 Lantern Rd Ste 100 *TF:* 888-578-5131 ■ *Web:* www.meyer-najem.com	Fishers	IN	46038	317-577-0007	577-0286
MGM Mirage Design Group Inc 3260 Industrial Rd *TF:* 800-929-1111	Las Vegas	NV	89109	866-761-7111	
MGQ & Associates Inc 3104 N Armenia Ave Ste 4 *Web:* www.mgqassociates.com	Tampa	FL	33607	813-877-8895	
Mid Valley School District 52 Underwood Rd *Web:* www.mvsd.us	Throop	PA	18512	570-307-1150	307-1107
Midstate Construction Corp 1180 Holm Rd *Web:* www.midstateconstruction.com	Petaluma	CA	94954	707-762-3200	762-0700
Milan Engineering Inc 925 S Semoran Blvd Ste 100	Winter Park	FL	32792	407-678-2055	
Milender White Construction Co 12655 W 54th Dr *Web:* www.milenderwhite.com	Arvada	CO	80002	303-216-0420	
Miller-Davis Co 1029 Portage St *Web:* www.miller-davis.com	Kalamazoo	MI	49001	269-345-3561	
Millie & Severson Inc 3601 Serpentine Dr *Web:* www.mandsinc.com	Los Alamitos	CA	90720	562-493-3611	
Mine & Mill Industrial Supply Company Inc 2500 S Combee Rd **Fax Area Code:* 813 ■ *TF:* 800-282-8489 ■ *Web:* www.minemill.com	Lakeland	FL	33801	863-665-5601	623-6999*
Miron Construction Co Inc 1471 McMahon Dr *Web:* miron-construction.com	Neenah	WI	54956	920-969-7000	969-7393
Modular Connections LLC 1090 Industrial Blvd *TF:* 877-903-6335 ■ *Web:* www.modularconnections.com	Bessemer	AL	35022	205-980-4565	
Modular Genius Inc 1201 S Mountain Rd *TF:* 888-420-1113 ■ *Web:* www.modulargenius.com	Joppa	MD	21085	888-420-1113	
Momentum Engineering Company LLC 5225 Katy Fwy Ste 605 *Web:* momentumtx.com	Houston	TX	77007	713-910-8300	
Monarch Construction Company Inc PO Box 12249 *Web:* www.monarchconstruction.cc	Cincinnati	OH	45212	513-351-6900	351-0979
Montgomery Martin Contractors LLC 8245 Tournament Dr Ste 300 *Web:* www.montgomerymartin.com	Memphis	TN	38125	901-374-9400	374-9402
Moores Electrical & Mechanical PO Box 119 *TF:* 888-722-2712 ■ *Web:* www.mooreselectric.com	Altavista	VA	24517	434-369-4374	369-7402
Morcon Construction Company Inc 5905 Golden Vly Rd *Web:* www.morcon.com	Golden Valley	MN	55422	763-546-6066	
Morganti Group Inc 100 Mill Plain Rd 4th Fl **Fax:* Sales ■ *Web:* www.morganti.com	Danbury	CT	06811	203-743-2675	830-4478*
Morris Group Inc 3 Office Pk Cir Ste 302	Mountain Brook	AL	35223	205-871-3500	871-3963

Company	City	State	Zip	Phone	Fax
Moseley Architects PC 3200 Norfolk St *Web:* www.moseleyarchitects.com	Richmond	VA	23230	804-794-7555	355-5690
Mosser Construction 122 S Wilson Ave *Web:* www.mosserconstruction.com	Fremont	OH	43420	419-334-3801	
Motor Service Inc 130 Byassee Dr *TF:* 800-966-5080 ■ *Web:* www.motorserviceinc.net	Hazelwood	MO	63042	314-731-4111	731-1213
Multigon Industries Inc 525 Executive Boulevard *TF:* 800-289-6858 ■ *Web:* www.multigon.com	Yonkers	NY	10701	800-289-6858	
Munilla Construction Management LLC 6201 SW 70th St 2nd Fl *Web:* www.mcm-us.com	Miami	FL	33143	305-541-0000	541-9771
Murnane Bldg Contractors Inc 104 Sharron Ave *Web:* www.murnanebuilding.com	Plattsburgh	NY	12901	518-561-4010	561-5926
Murphy & Sons Inc 9148 Corporate Dr *Web:* www.murphyandsons.com	Southaven	MS	38671	662-393-3130	393-8111
Muse Concrete Contractors Inc 8599 Commercial Way *Web:* www.museconcrete.com	Redding	CA	96002	530-226-5151	
MYCON General Contractors Inc 208 E Louisiana Ste 200 *Web:* www.mycon.com	Mckinney	TX	75069	972-529-2444	
Nabholz Construction Corp PO Box 2090 *Web:* www.nabholz.com	Conway	AR	72033	501-505-5800	
Nastos Construction Inc 1421 Kenilworth Ave NE *Web:* www.nastos.com	Washington	DC	20019	202-398-5500	398-5501
National Fence Systems Inc 1033 Route One *Web:* www.nationalfencesystems.com	Avenel	NJ	07001	732-636-5600	
Near-Cal Corp 512 Chaney St *TF:* 800-969-3578 ■ *Web:* www.nearcal.com	Lake Elsinore	CA	92530	951-245-5400	
Neenan Co 2620 E Prospect Rd Ste 100 *Web:* neenan.com	Fort Collins	CO	80525	970-493-8747	493-5869
NeoCom Solutions Inc 10064 Main St *Web:* www.neocom.biz	Woodstock	GA	30188	678-238-1818	
Neumann Brothers Inc 1435 Ohio St *Web:* www.neumannbros.com	Des Moines	IA	50314	515-243-0156	
New Life Service Co. 39 W Fifth St *Web:* www.nlsco.com	Eureka	CA	95501	707-444-8222	
New Philadelphia City School District (NPCS) 248 Front Ave SW *Web:* www.npschools.org	New Philadelphia	OH	44663	330-364-0600	364-9310
NewGround Resources Inc 15450 S Outer Forty Dr Ste 300 *Web:* www.newground.com	Chesterfield	MO	63017	636-898-8100	
Nibbi Bros Inc 180 Hubbell St *Web:* www.nibbi.com	San Francisco	CA	94107	415-863-1820	863-1150
Nicholas & Associates 1001 Feehanville Dr *Web:* www.nicholasquality.com	Mount Prospect	IL	60056	847-394-6200	
Nooter Construction Co 1500 S Second St *Web:* www.nooterconstruction.com	Saint Louis	MO	63104	314-421-7600	
Nor-Son Inc 7900 Hastings Rd *TF:* 800-858-1722 ■ *Web:* www.nor-son.com	Baxter	MN	56425	218-828-1722	828-0487
Norcon Corp 5600 Municipal St *Web:* www.norconcorp.com	Schofield	WI	54476	715-359-5808	
Norfolk Dredging Co 110 Centervilless Tpke N *Web:* www.norfolkdredging.com	Chesapeake	VA	23320	757-547-9391	547-2833
NorSouth 2000 RiverEdge Pkwy Ste 450 *Web:* www.norsouth.com	Atlanta	GA	30328	770-850-8280	850-8230
North Salem Elementary School 140 Zion Hill Rd *Web:* www.sau57.org/northsalem/pages/home.aspx	Salem	NH	03079	603-893-7062	893-7062
Northern Trailer Ltd 3355 Sugarloaf Rd	Kamloops	BC	V2C6C3	250-828-2644	
Northstar Technology Corp 32 Mauchly Ste C *Web:* www.northstar-technology.com	Irvine	CA	92618	949-788-0738	
Norwood Co 375 Technology Dr *Web:* www.norwdco.com	Malvern	PA	19355	610-240-4400	
NRB Inc 115 S Service Rd W *Web:* www.nrb-inc.com	Grimsby	ON	L3M4G3	905-945-9622	
NTS Communications Inc 1220 Broadway *Web:* www.ntscom.com	Lubbock	TX	79401	806-771-0687	788-3398
Nujak Development Inc 711 N Kentucky Ave *TF:* 888-685-2526 ■ *Web:* www.nujak.com	Lakeland	FL	33801	863-686-1565	
Numega Solutions LLC 7426 Alban Sta Blvd Ste A104 *Web:* www.numegasolutions.com	Springfield	VA	22150	703-372-2200	
O & G Industries Inc 112 Wall St *Web:* www.ogind.com	Torrington	CT	06790	860-489-9261	489-9261
O'Connor Constructors Inc 45 Industrial Dr **Fax Area Code:* 781 ■ *Web:* www.oconnorconst.com	Canton	MA	02021	617-364-9000	828-8248*
O'Harrow Construction Co 4575 Ann Arbor Rd *Web:* www.oharrow.net	Jackson	MI	49202	517-764-4770	764-5564
O'Neal Construction Inc 525 W William *Web:* www.onealconstruction.com	Ann Arbor	MI	48103	734-769-0770	
Ocean Quest Pools Inc 10208 N Fm 620 *Web:* www.oceanquest.com	Austin	TX	78726	512-258-7379	
Oceanic Companies Inc 91-462 Komohana St *Web:* www.oceaniccompanies.com	Kapolei	HI	96707	808-682-0113	
Oceanside Unified School District (OUSD) 2111 Mission Ave *Web:* www.oside.k12.ca.us	Oceanside	CA	92058	760-966-4000	
Odebrecht Construction Inc 201 Alhambra Cir Ste 1000 *TF:* 800-771-0001 ■ *Web:* odebrecht.com	Coral Gables	FL	33134	305-341-8800	569-1500
Oliver & Company Inc 1300 S 51st St *Web:* www.oliverandco.net	Richmond	CA	94804	510-412-9090	
Oltmans Construction Co 10005 Mission Mill Rd *Web:* www.oltmans.com	Whittier	CA	90601	562-948-4242	695-5299
Omega Construction Inc 344 Shelleybrook Dr PO Box 250 *Web:* www.omegaconstruction.com	Pilot Mountain	NC	27041	336-368-5156	
Omni Construction Services Inc 533 Airport Blvd Ste 555 *Web:* www.clearkey.com	Burlingame	CA	94010	650-685-2490	
One Way Building Services Inc 6811 Washington Ave S *Web:* owbs.net	Minneapolis	MN	55439	952-942-0412	
Oneonta City School District 31 Ctr St *Web:* www.oneontacsd.org	Oneonta	NY	13820	607-433-8200	433-8290
Opechee Construction Corp 11 Corporate Dr *Web:* www.opechee.com	Belmont	NH	03220	603-527-9090	
Opp & Seibold General Construction Inc 1220 W Poplar St *Web:* www.oppseibold.com	Walla Walla	WA	99362	509-525-1373	
Opus Group of Cos 10350 Bren Rd W *Web:* www.opus-group.com	Minnetonka	MN	55343	952-656-4444	
Orcutt/Winslow 3003 N Central Ave *TF:* 800-331-5842 ■ *Web:* www.owp.com	Phoenix	AZ	85012	602-257-1764	257-9029
Orion Building Corp 9025 Overlook Blvd Ste 100 *Web:* www.orionbldg.com	Brentwood	TN	37027	615-321-4499	
Osborne Construction Company Inc 10602 NE 38th Pl Ste 100 *Web:* www.osborne.cc	Kirkland	WA	98033	425-827-4221	828-4314
Oscar J Boldt Construction Co 2525 N Roemer Rd *Web:* www.theboldtcompany.com	Appleton	WI	54911	920-739-6321	
OSI Inc 3950 Birmingham Hwy *Web:* www.osibuildings.com	Montgomery	AL	36108	334-834-3500	
Outside the Lines Inc 529 W Blueridge Ave *Web:* otl-inc.com	Orange	CA	92865	714-637-4747	
Owen-Ames-Kimball Co 300 Ionia Ave NW *Web:* www.owen-ames-kimball.com	Grand Rapids	MI	49503	616-456-1521	458-0770
Ozanne Construction Company Inc 1635 E 25th St *Web:* www.ozanne.com	Cleveland	OH	44114	216-696-2876	696-8613
P & C Construction Co 2133 NW York St *Web:* www.builtbypandc.com	Portland	OR	97210	503-665-0165	667-2565
P A Landers Inc 351 Winter St *TF:* 800-660-6404 ■ *Web:* www.palanders.com	Hanover	MA	02339	781-826-8818	829-8934
P.H. Hagopian Contractor Inc 778 W Town & Country Rd *Web:* www.phhagopian.com	Orange	CA	92868	714-543-4185	
Pacrim Engineering 233 W Cerritos Ave *Web:* www.pacrimengineering.com	Anaheim	CA	92805	714-683-0470	
Palace Construction Company Inc 7 S Galapago St *Web:* www.palaceconst.com	Denver	CO	80223	303-777-7999	777-5256
Pangere Corp 4050 W Fourth Ave *Web:* www.pangere.com	Gary	IN	46406	219-949-1368	944-3028
Paragon Supply Co 160 Reaser Ct *Web:* www.paragon-supply.com	Elyria	OH	44035	440-365-8040	
Parent Co, The PO Box 5036 *Web:* www.theparentco.com	Brentwood	TN	37024	615-221-7000	221-7013
Parkinson Construction Company Inc 3905 Perry St *Web:* www.parkinsonconstruction.com	Brentwood	MD	20722	301-985-6080	
Parkway Construction & Assoc LP 1000 Civic Cir *Web:* www.parkwayconstruction.com	Lewisville	TX	75067	972-221-1979	219-0061
Paul Hemmer Construction Co 250 Grandview Dr *Web:* www.paulhemmer.com	Fort Mitchell	KY	41017	859-341-8300	
PBG Builders Inc 1000 NorthChase Dr Ste 307 *Web:* www.pbgbuilders.com	Goodlettsville	TN	37072	615-256-2200	
PCL Construction Enterprises Inc 2000 S Colorado Blvd Tower 2 Ste 2-500 *Web:* www.pcl.com	Denver	CO	80222	303-365-6500	
PCL Construction Group Inc 5410 99th St NW *Web:* www.pcl.com	Edmonton	AB	T6E3P4	780-733-5000	
PDC Facilities Inc 700 Walnut Ridge Dr *TF:* 800-545-5998 ■ *Web:* www.pdcbiz.com	Hartland	WI	53029	262-367-7700	367-7744
Peacock Construction Inc 3421 Golden Gate Way *Web:* www.peacockconstruction.com	Lafayette	CA	94549	925-283-4550	
Peaklogix Inc 14409 Justice Rd *Web:* www.peaklogix.com	Midlothian	VA	23113	804-794-5700	
Pence Kelly Construction LLC 2747 Pence Loop SE *Web:* www.pencekelly.com	Salem	OR	97302	503-587-8129	
Penfield Fire Company Inc 1838 Penfield Rd *Web:* www.penfieldfire.org	Penfield	NY	14526	585-586-2413	
Pepper Construction 643 N Orleans St *Web:* www.pepperconstruction.com	Chicago	IL	60610	312-266-4700	266-2792
Peris Cos Inc 282 N Washington St *Web:* www.peris.com	Falls Church	VA	22046	703-533-4700	533-4710
Perma-Seal Waterproofing 513 Rogers St *TF:* 800-421-7325 ■ *Web:* www.permaseal.net	Downers Grove	IL	60515	630-512-0002	
Perry Construction Group Inc 1440 W 21st St *Web:* www.perryconst.com	Erie	PA	16502	814-459-8551	453-5653
Perspectiva 3401 Louisiana St Ste 270 *Web:* www.perspectiva.net	Houston	TX	77002	713-520-7580	
Petrini Corp 187 Rosemary St *Web:* www.petrinicorp.com	Needham	MA	02494	781-444-1963	
Pettus Mechanical Services 12647 Hwy 72 *Web:* www.pettushvac.com	Rogersville	AL	35652	256-389-8181	
Phipps Houses 902 Broadway 13th Fl *Web:* www.phippsny.org	New York	NY	10010	212-243-9090	
Phoenix Modular Inc 5139 N Tom Murray Ave *Web:* www.phoenixmodular.com	Glendale	AZ	85301	623-209-3300	
Phoenix Renovation & Restoration Inc 16250 Foster *Web:* www.kcphoenix.com	Overland Park	KS	66085	913-599-0055	

Company / Address	City	State	Zip	Phone	Fax
Piedmont Construction Group LLC (PCG) 107 Gateway Dr Ste B	Macon	GA	31210	478-405-8907	405-8908
Web: www.piedmontconstructiongroup.com					
Pierson Co 1200 W Harris St	Eureka	CA	95503	707-268-1800	268-1801
Web: www.piersoncompany.com					
Pierson Construction Inc 4500 N Route E	Columbia	MO	65202	573-445-8493	
Web: www.piersonconstruction.net					
Pinkard Construction Co 9195 W Sixth Ave	Lakewood	CO	80215	303-986-4555	985-5050
Web: www.pinkardcc.com					
Pinkerton & Laws Inc 1165 N Chase Pkwy Ste 100	Marietta	GA	30067	770-956-9000	618-8688
Web: pinkerton-laws.com					
Pinner Construction Company Inc 1255 S Lewis St	Anaheim	CA	92805	714-490-4000	
Web: www.pinnerconstruction.com					
Pioneer Construction Company Inc 550 Kirtland St SW	Grand Rapids	MI	49507	616-247-6966	247-0186
Web: www.pioneerinc.com					
Pioneer Contract Services Inc 8090 Kempwood Dr	Houston	TX	77055	713-464-8200	464-7100
Web: www.pioneercontract.com					
Pizzagalli Construction Co 193 Tilley Dr	South Burlington	VT	05403	802-658-4100	
Web: www.pcconstruction.com					
PKC Construction 7802 Barton St	Lenexa	KS	66214	913-782-4646	
Plant Process Equipment Inc 280 Reynolds Ave	League City	TX	77573	281-333-7850	332-6280
Web: www.plant-process.com					
Plasteak Inc 3563 Copley Rd	Copley	OH	44321	330-668-2587	
TF: 800-320-1841 ■ *Web:* www.plasteak.com					
Plath & Company Inc 1575 Francisco Blvd E	San Rafael	CA	94901	415-460-1575	
Web: plathco.com					
PM Construction Co Inc PO Box 728	Saco	ME	04072	207-282-7697	
TF: 800-646-0068 ■ *Web:* www.pmconstruction.com					
PMG Project Management Group LLC 2723 Houston Ave	Houston	TX	77009	713-880-2626	
Web: www.pmgunited.com					
Pointe General Contractors LLC 1209 Pointe Ctr Dr Ste 105	Chattanooga	TN	37421	423-755-0844	
Web: www.pointecentre.com					
Polaris Engineering Inc 212 Pine St	Lake Charles	LA	70601	337-497-0652	
Web: www.polarisengr.com					
Polhemus Savery DaSilva Architects Builders 157 Brewster-Chatham Rd (Rt 137)	East Harwich	MA	02645	508-945-4500	945-9803
Web: www.psdab.com					
Port Jervis City School District 9 Thompson St	Port Jervis	NY	12771	845-858-3100	856-1885
Web: www.pjschools.org					
Porta-King Building Systems 4133 Shoreline Dr	Earth City	MO	63045	800-284-5346	
TF: 800-284-5346 ■ *Web:* www.portaking.com					
Portable Buildings Inc 3235 Bay Rd	Milford	DE	19963	302-335-1300	
TF: 800-205-5030 ■ *Web:* www.portablebuildingsinc.com					
Power Construction Company LLC 8750 W Bryn Mawr Ave Ste 500	Chicago	IL	60631	312-596-6960	925-1372*
**Fax Area Code:* 847 ■ *Web:* www.powerconstruction.net					
Powers & Sons Construction Company Inc 2636 W 15th Ave	Gary	IN	46404	219-949-3100	949-5906
Web: www.powersandsons.com					
Prava Construction Services Inc 2032 Corte Del Nogal Ste 100	Carlsbad	CA	92011	760-929-9787	
Web: www.pravacsi.com					
Premiere Concrete Inc 11332 Red Lion Rd	White Marsh	MD	21162	410-344-1604	
Web: premierconcrete.biz					
Primary Integration LLC 8180 Greensboro Dr Ste 700	Mclean	VA	22102	703-356-2200	
Web: www.primaryintegration.com					
Prime Contractors Inc 525 N Sam Houston Pkwy E	Houston	TX	77060	281-999-0875	999-0885
Primus Builders Inc 8294 Hwy 92 Ste 210	Woodstock	GA	30189	770-928-7120	928-6548
Web: www.primusbuilders.com					
Prince George County Public Schools 6410 Cts Dr	Prince George	VA	23875	804-733-2700	733-2737
Web: www.pgs.k12.va.us					
Prismatic Development Inc 60 Route 46	Fairfield	NJ	07004	973-882-1133	
Web: www.prisdev.com					
PRO Building Systems Inc 3678 N Peachtree Rd	Atlanta	GA	30341	770-455-1791	
Web: www.probldgsystems.com					
Progressive Contracting Company Inc 10 N Ritters Ln	Owings Mills	MD	21117	410-356-9096	356-9098
Web: www.progressivecci.com					
Promac Inc 1153 Timber Dr	Elgin	IL	60123	847-695-8181	
Web: www.promac.com					
Prosser Wilbert Construction Inc 13730 W 108th St	Lenexa	KS	66215	913-906-0104	
Web: www.prosserwilbert.com					
Provident Construction Inc 12424 E Weaver Pl	Centennial	CO	80111	720-482-0200	
Web: www.providentconstruction.com					
Quadrants Inc 49132 Wixom Tech Dr	Wixom	MI	48393	248-960-3900	960-9867
Quandel Group Inc 3003 N Front St Ste 203	Harrisburg	PA	17110	717-657-0909	652-6282
Web: www.quandel.com					
Quantum Crossings LLC 111 E Wacker Dr Ste 990	Chicago	IL	60601	312-467-0065	
Web: www.quantumcrossings.com					
Quorex Construction Ltd 142 Cardinal Crescent	Saskatoon	SK	S7L6H6	306-244-3717	
Web: www.quorex.ca					
R & O Construction Co 933 Wall Ave	Ogden	UT	84404	801-627-1403	
Web: www.randoco.com					
R A Burch Construction Company Inc 405 Maple St Bldg B	Ramona	CA	92065	760-788-0800	
Web: www.raburch.com					
R F Stearns Inc 4000 Kruse Way Pl Bldg 3 Ste 100	Lake Oswego	OR	97035	503-601-8700	
Web: www.rfstearns.com					
R W Mercer Co 2322 Brooklyn Rd PO Box 180	Jackson	MI	49204	517-787-2960	787-8111
TF: 877-763-7237 ■ *Web:* www.rwmercer.com					
R Zoppo Corp 160 Old Maple St	Stoughton	MA	02072	781-344-8822	344-7382
Web: www.zoppo.com					
R&h Construction Co 1530 SW Taylor St	Portland	OR	97205	503-228-7177	
Web: www.rhconst.com					
Ra-lin & Associates Bldg Contr 101 Parkwood Cir	Carrollton	GA	30117	770-834-4884	
Web: www.ra-lin.com					
Raco General Contractors 1401 Dalon Rd NE	Atlanta	GA	30306	404-873-3567	876-1394
Web: www.racogc.com					
Rafn Co 1721 132nd Ave NE	Bellevue	WA	98005	425-702-6600	
Web: www.rafn.com					
Ragnar Benson Construction LLC 250 S NW Hwy	Park Ridge	IL	60068	847-698-4900	692-9320
Web: www.ragnarbenson.com					
Ramtech Bldg Systems Inc 1400 Hwy 287 S	Mansfield	TX	76063	800-568-9376	473-3485*
**Fax Area Code:* 817 ■ *TF:* 855-887-1888 ■ *Web:* www.ramtechmodular.com/index.html					
Rand Construction Co 1428 W Ninth St	Kansas City	MO	64101	816-421-4143	421-4144
Web: www.randsc.com					
Randolph & Son Builders Inc PO Box 410283	Charlotte	NC	28241	704-588-7116	588-8280
Web: www.randolphbuilders.com					
Ray Angelini Inc 105 Blackwood-Barnsboro Rd	Sewell	NJ	08080	856-228-5566	
Web: www.raiservices.com					
RD Olson Construction 2955 Main St 3rd Fl	Irvine	CA	92614	949-474-2001	474-1534
Web: www.rdolson.com					
Renaissance Cos, The 8925 E Pima Ctr Pkwy Ste 205	Scottsdale	AZ	85258	480-967-0880	
Web: www.renaissancecos.com					
Renfrow Bros Inc 855 Gossett Rd	Spartanburg	SC	29307	864-579-0558	
TF: 800-260-8412 ■ *Web:* www.renfrowbros.com					
Renier Construction Corp 2164 Citygate Dr	Columbus	OH	43219	614-866-4580	
Web: www.renier.com					
Reno Contracting Inc 1450 Frazee Rd Ste 100	San Diego	CA	92108	619-220-0224	220-0229
Web: renocon.com					
Rentenbach Constructors Inc 2400 Sutherland Ave	Knoxville	TN	37919	865-546-2440	546-3414
Web: www.rentenbach.com					
Richard & Richard Construction Company Inc 234 Venture St Ste 100	San Marcos	CA	92078	760-759-2260	
Web: www.rrconstruction.com					
Ricks Barbecue Inc 2367 Hwy 43 S	Leoma	TN	38468	931-852-2324	
TF: 800-544-5864 ■ *Web:* www.ricksbbq.com					
Riddleberger Bros Inc (RBI) 6127 S Valley Pk	Mount Crawford	VA	22841	540-434-1731	432-1691
Web: www.rbiva.com					
Riley Construction Company Inc 5301 99th Ave	Kenosha	WI	53144	262-658-4381	
Web: www.rileycon.com					
Ringland-Johnson Construction PO Box 5165	Rockford	IL	61125	815-332-8600	332-8411
Web: www.ringland.com					
River City Construction LLC 101 Hoffer Ln	East Peoria	IL	61611	309-694-3120	694-1332
Web: www.rcclic.com					
Robert E. Porter Construction Company Inc 1720 W Lincoln St	Phoenix	AZ	85007	602-253-4911	
Web: robertporterconstruction.com					
Robins & Morton Group 400 Shades Creek Pkwy Ste 200	Birmingham	AL	35209	205-870-1000	871-0906
Web: www.robinsmorton.com					
Roche Constructors Inc 361 71st Ave	Greeley	CO	80634	970-356-3611	356-3619
Web: www.rocheconstructors.com					
Rochon Corp 3650 Annapolis Ln N Ste 101	Plymouth	MN	55447	763-559-9393	559-8101
Web: www.rochoncorp.com					
Rockdale Pipeline Inc PO Box 1157	Conyers	GA	30012	770-922-4123	
Web: www.rockdalepipeline.com					
Roebbelen Construction Inc 1241 Hawks Flight Ct	El Dorado Hills	CA	95762	916-939-4000	939-4028
Web: www.roebbelen.com					
Rogers-O'Brien Construction USA 1901 Regal Row	Dallas	TX	75235	214-962-3000	962-3001
Web: www.rogers-obrien.com					
Rough Brothers Inc 5513 Vine St	Cincinnati	OH	45217	513-242-0310	
Web: www.roughbros.com					
Roy Anderson Corp 11400 Reichold Rd	Gulfport	MS	39503	228-896-4000	896-4078
TF: 800-688-4003 ■ *Web:* www.rac.com					
Roy Kirby & Sons Inc 1403 Rome Rd	Baltimore	MD	21227	410-536-0808	536-0799
Web: www.roykirby.com					
RSH Architects 363 Vanadium Rd Ste 200	Pittsburgh	PA	15243	412-429-1555	279-7285
Web: www.rsharc.com					
Rudolph & Sletten Inc 1600 Seaport Blvd Ste 350	Redwood City	CA	94063	650-216-3600	599-9112
Web: www.rsconstruction.com					
Ruhlin Company Inc PO Box 190	Sharon Center	OH	44274	330-239-2800	239-1828
Web: www.ruhlin.com					
Ruscilli Construction Co Inc 5000 Arlington Ctr Blvd Ste 300	Columbus	OH	43220	614-876-9484	876-0253
Web: www.ruscilli.com					
Russo Corp 1421 Mims Ave SW	Birmingham	AL	35211	205-923-4434	
Web: www.russocorp.com					
Rust Orling Architecture Inc 1215 Cameron St	Alexandria	VA	22314	703-836-3205	
Web: www.rustorling.com					
RW Allen LLC 1015 Broad St	Augusta	GA	30901	706-733-2800	733-3879
Web: www.rwallen.com					
RW Setterlin Bldg Co 560 Harmon Ave	Columbus	OH	43223	614-459-7077	
Web: www.setterlin.com					
Ryan Cos US Inc 50 S Tenth St Ste 300	Minneapolis	MN	55403	612-492-4000	492-3000
Web: www.ryancompanies.com					
Rycon Construction Inc 2525 Liberty Ave	Pittsburgh	PA	15222	412-392-2525	392-2526
TF: 800-883-1901 ■ *Web:* www.ryconinc.com					

Company / Address	City	State	Zip	Phone	Fax
S C & A Construction Inc 3411 Silverside Rd Shipley Bldg Ste 200 *Web:* www.scaconstructs.com	Wilmington	DE	19810	302-478-6030	
S D Deacon Corp 17681 Mitchell N Ste 100 *Web:* www.deacon.com	Irvine	CA	92614	949-222-9060	222-0596
Sain Construction Co 713 Vincent St *Web:* www.sainconstruction.com	Manchester	TN	37355	931-728-7644	
Sambe Construction Company Inc 1650 Hylton Rd	Pennsauken	NJ	08110	856-663-7751	663-5859
Samet Corp 309 Gallimore Dairy Rd Ste 102 PO Box 8050 *Web:* www.sametcorp.com	Greensboro	NC	27409	336-544-2600	544-2638
Samuels Group Inc 311 Financial Way St 300 *Web:* www.samuelsgroup.net	Wausau	WI	54401	715-842-2222	
Satterfield & Pontikes Construction Inc 11000 Equity Dr Ste 100 *Web:* www.satpon.com	Houston	TX	77041	713-996-1300	996-1400
Saugus Union School, The 24930 Ave Stanford *Web:* www.saugususd.org	Santa Clarita	MA	91355	661-294-5300	
Saunders Construction Inc 6950 S Jordan Rd *Web:* www.saundersci.com	Centennial	CO	80112	303-699-9000	680-7448
Saxon Group Inc, The 790 Brogdon Rd	Suwanee	GA	30024	770-271-2174	271-2176
SBBI Inc 3282 State Hwy 82 PO Box 770 *Web:* www.sbbiaz.com	Sonoita	AZ	85637	520-455-5983	
SBCC Inc 1711 Dell Ave *Web:* www.sbci.com	Campbell	CA	95008	408-379-5500	
SC Anderson Inc PO Box 81747 *Web:* www.scanderson.com	Bakersfield	CA	93308	661-392-7000	391-9999
Sc Builders Inc 910 Thompson Pl *Web:* www.scbuildersinc.com	Sunnyvale	CA	94085	408-328-0688	
Scharine Group, The 4213 N Scharine Rd *TF:* 800-472-2880 ■ *Web:* www.thescharinegroup.com	Whitewater	WI	53190	608-883-2880	
Schimenti Construction Co 650 Danbury Rd *Web:* www.schimenti.com	Ridgefield	CT	06877	914-244-9100	244-9103
Schmidt Bros. Inc 420 N Hallett Ave *TF:* 800-200-7318 ■ *Web:* www.schmidtbrosinc.com	Swanton	OH	43558	419-826-3671	
Schneider Electric Buildings LLC 1354 Clifford Ave *TF:* 888-444-1311 ■ *Web:* www.schneider-electric.com	Loves Park	IL	61111	888-444-1311	
Scott Builders Inc 8105 - 49 Ave Close *Web:* www.scottbuilders.com	Red Deer	AB	T4P2V5	403-343-7270	346-4310
Scott Swimming Pools Inc 75 Washington Rd *Web:* www.scottpools.com	Woodbury	CT	06798	203-263-2108	
SCR Construction Company Inc 5420 FM 2218 Rd *Web:* www.scrconstruction.net	Richmond	TX	77469	281-344-0700	344-0099
SDB Inc 810 W 1st St *Web:* www.sdb.com	Tempe	AZ	85281	480-967-5810	967-5841
SDV Construction Inc 6436 Edith Blvd Ne *Web:* www.sdvconstruction.com	Albuquerque	NM	87107	505-883-3176	
Sedalco Inc 2554 E Long Ave *Web:* www.sedalco.com	Fort Worth	TX	76137	817-831-2245	831-2248
Sellen Construction Co Inc 227 Westlake Ave N *Web:* www.sellen.com	Seattle	WA	98109	206-682-7770	623-5206
Septagon Construction 113 E Third St *TF:* 800-733-5999 ■ *Web:* www.septagon.com	Sedalia	MO	65301	660-827-2115	826-8058
Sfcc Inc 2410 Squire Pl Ste B *Web:* www.sfccinc.net	Dallas	TX	75234	972-484-2480	
Shales McNutt Construction 425 Renner Dr *Web:* www.shalesmcnutt.com	Elgin	IL	60123	847-622-1214	
Shaw Construction Company LLC 300 Kalamath St *Web:* www.shawconstruction.net	Denver	CO	80223	303-825-4740	825-6403
Shawmut Design & Construction 560 Harrison Ave *Web:* www.shawmut.com	Boston	MA	02118	617-622-7000	622-7001
Sherrick Aerospace 307 Emery Dr *Web:* www.sherrickco.com	Nashville	TN	37214	615-872-1050	
Shiel Sexton Company Inc 902 N Capitol Ave *Web:* www.shielsexton.com	Indianapolis	IN	46204	317-423-6000	423-6300
Shingobee Builders Inc PO Box 8 *Web:* www.shingobee.com	Loretto	MN	55357	763-479-1300	479-3267
Shioi Construction Inc 98-724 Kuaho Pl *Web:* shioihawaii.com	Pearl City	HI	96782	808-487-2441	
Shoemaker Construction Co 100 Front St Ste 365 *Web:* www.shoemakerco.com	West Conshohocken	PA	19428	610-941-5500	941-5525
Sigal Construction Corp 2231 Crystal Dr Ste 200 *Web:* www.sigal.com	Arlington	VA	22202	703-302-1500	302-1520
Sigma Associates Inc 535 Griswold St Ste 500 *Web:* www.sigmaassociates.com	Detroit	MI	48226	313-963-9700	
Signal Point Systems Inc 1270 Shiloh Rd Ste 100 *Web:* sigpoint.com	Kennesaw	GA	30144	770-499-0439	
Singer Group Inc, The 12915 Dover Rd *Web:* www.singergrp.com	Reisterstown	MD	21136	410-561-7561	
Sjostrom & Sons Inc PO Box 5766 *Web:* www.sjostromconstruction.com	Rockford	IL	61125	815-226-0330	226-8868
Skanska USA Inc 1616 Whitestone Expy *Web:* www.skanska.com	Whitestone	NY	11356	718-767-2600	767-2663
Skyline Construction 731 Sansome St 4th Fl *Web:* www.skylineconstruction.build	San Francisco	CA	94111	415-908-1020	
Sletten Construction Company Inc 1000 25th St N *Web:* www.slettencompanies.com	Great Falls	MT	59401	406-761-7920	761-0923
SLR Contracting & Service Company Inc 260 Michigan Ave *Web:* www.slrcontracting.com	Buffalo	NY	14203	716-896-8148	
Small Mine Development LLC 967 E Parkcenter Blvd *Web:* www.undergroundmining.com	Boise	ID	83706	208-338-8880	338-8881
Smith Tank & Steel Inc 42422 Hwy 30 *Web:* www.smith-tank.net	Gonzales	LA	70737	225-644-8747	
Smoot Construction Co 1907 Leonard Ave *Web:* www.smootconstruction.com	Columbus	OH	43219	614-253-9000	
Snyder Langston Inc 17962 Cowan St *Web:* www.snyder-langston.com	Irvine	CA	92614	949-863-9200	863-1087
Sordoni Construction Co 409 Main St *Web:* sordonionline.com	Chester	NJ	07930	908-879-1130	
Sordoni Construction Services Inc 45 Owen St *Web:* www.sordoni.com	Forty Fort	PA	18704	570-287-3161	287-0298
South Brunswick Public Schools 231 Black Horse Ln PO Box 181 *Web:* www.sbschools.org	Monmouth Junction	NJ	08852	732-297-7800	
South Coast Construction Services 8935 Knight Rd *Web:* www.sccsi.net	Houston	TX	77054	713-222-2308	
Southeast Connections LLC 2720 Dogwood Dr SE *Web:* www.seconnections.com	Conyers	GA	30013	404-659-1422	
Speed Fab-Crete Corp International PO Box 15580 *Web:* www.speedfab-crete.com	Fort Worth	TX	76119	817-478-1137	561-2544
SPS Corp 3502 Independence Dr *Web:* www.spscorporation.com	Fort Wayne	IN	46808	260-482-3702	
Stanker & Galetto Inc 317 W Elmer Rd *Web:* www.stankergaletto.com	Vineland	NJ	08360	856-692-8098	
Star Consultants Inc 1910 Bethel Rd *Web:* starconsultants.org	Columbus	OH	43235	614-538-8445	538-8446
Stella May Contracting Inc 1512 Edgewood Rd *Web:* stellamay.com	Edgewood	MD	21040	410-679-8306	
Stellar Group 2900 Hartley Rd **Fax:* Sales ■ *TF:* 800-488-2900 ■ *Web:* stellar.net	Jacksonville	FL	32257	904-260-2900	268-4932*
Stenstrom Cos Ltd 2420 20th St PO Box 5866 *Web:* www.rstenstrom.com	Rockford	IL	61125	815-398-2420	398-0041
Sterling Construction Company Inc 20810 Fernbush Ln *NASDAQ: STRL* ■ *Web:* strlco.com	Houston	TX	77073	281-821-9091	821-2995
Stevens Construction Corp PO Box 7726 *Web:* www.stevensconstruction.com	Madison	WI	53707	608-222-5100	222-5930
Stidham Trucking Inc PO Box 308 *TF:* 800-827-9500 ■ *Web:* www.stidhamtrucking.com	Yreka	CA	96097	530-842-4161	842-2047
Stiles Construction Co 301 E Las Olas Blvd *Web:* www.stiles.com	Fort Lauderdale	FL	33301	954-627-9300	627-9288
Story Construction Co 300 S Bell Ave *Web:* www.storycon.com	Ames	IA	50010	515-232-4358	232-0599
Streeter Assoc Inc 101 E Woodlawn Ave PO Box 118 *TF:* 866-493-1640 ■ *Web:* www.streeterassociates.com	Elmira	NY	14902	607-734-4151	732-2952
Structura Inc 9208 Waterford Centre Blvd Ste 100 *Web:* www.structurainc.com	Austin	TX	78758	512-495-9702	495-9712
Structure Tone Inc 770 Broadway 9th Fl *Web:* www.structuretone.com	New York	NY	10003	212-481-6100	685-9267
Suffolk Construction 65 Allerton St *Web:* www.suffolk.com	Boston	MA	02119	617-445-3500	541-2128
Sullivan & McLaughlin Companies Inc 74 Lawley St *Web:* www.sullymac.com	Boston	MA	02122	617-474-0500	
Sun Builders Co 5870 6 N Hwy Ste 206 *Web:* www.sunbuildersco.com	Houston	TX	77084	281-815-1020	
Sun Eagle Corp 461 N Dean Ave *Web:* www.suneaglecorporation.com	Chandler	AZ	85226	480-961-0004	940-0160
Sun State Builders Inc 1050 W Washington St Ste 214 *Web:* www.sunstatebuilders.com	Tempe	AZ	85281	480-894-1286	
Sundt Construction Inc 2015 W River Rd Ste 101 *TF:* 800-467-5544 ■ *Web:* www.sundt.com	Tucson	AZ	85704	520-750-4600	
Sunpeak Construction Inc 1401 Quail St Ste 105 *Web:* www.sunpeak.com	Newport Beach	CA	92660	949-474-0501	
Swanson Construction Co 3400 Towne Pointe Dr *Web:* swansonbuilt.com	Bettendorf	IA	52722	563-332-4859	
Swinerton Builders 260 Townsend St *Web:* www.swinerton.com	San Francisco	CA	94107	415-421-2980	984-1292
T&G Constructors Inc 8623 Commodity Cir *Web:* www.t-and-g.com	Orlando	FL	32819	407-352-4443	352-0778
Taggart Global LLC 4000 Town Ctr Blvd Ste 200 *Web:* www.taggartglobal.com	Canonsburg	PA	15317	724-754-9800	
Taisei Construction Corp 6261 Katella Ave Ste 200	Cypress	CA	90630	714-886-1530	886-1550
Talladega City Schools 501 S St E PO Box 946 *Web:* www.talladega-cs.net	Talladega	AL	35160	256-315-5600	315-5606
Tanglewood Conservatories 15 Engerman Ave *Web:* www.tanglewoodconservatories.com	Denton	MD	21629	410-479-4700	
Tarlton Corp 5500 W Pk Ave *Web:* www.tarltoncorp.com	Saint Louis	MO	63110	314-633-3300	647-1940
Tbi Construction & Construction Management Inc 1960 the Alameda Ste 100 *Web:* strategic-cm.com	San Jose	CA	95126	408-246-3691	241-9983
TCI Architects/Engineers/Contractors Inc 1718 State Rd 16	La Crosse	WI	54601	608-781-5700	781-5705
TCS Communications LLC 2045 W Union Ave Bldg E *Web:* www.tcscomm.com	Englewood	CO	80110	303-377-3800	377-8300
Technology Site Planners Inc 8188 Business Way *Web:* www.techsiteplan.com	Plain City	OH	43064	614-873-7800	

Company	City	State	ZIP	Phone	Fax
Tedco Construction Corp Tedco Pl. *Web:* www.tedco.com	Carnegie	PA	15106	412-276-8080	276-6804
Telecon Inc 13 500 boul Metropolitain E. *TF:* 800-465-0349 ■ *Web:* www.telecon.ca	Montreal	QC	H1A3W1	514-644-2333	
Tepsco 2909 Aaron St. *Web:* www.tepsco.com	Deer Park	TX	77536	281-604-0309	930-0788
Theatre Projects Consultants Inc 47 Water St. *Web:* www.theatreprojects.com	South Norwalk	CT	06854	203-299-0830	
Thomas & Marker Construction Co 2084 US 68 S PO Box 250 *Web:* www.thomasmarker.com	Bellefontaine	OH	43311	937-599-2160	
Thompson Thrift Construction Inc 901 Wabash Ave Ste 300 *Web:* www.thompsonthrift.com	Terre Haute	IN	47807	812-235-5959	235-8122
ThompsonBrooks Inc 151 Vermont St Ste 9 *Web:* thompsonbrooks.com	San Francisco	CA	94103	415-581-2600	
THS Constructors 150 Executive Ctr Dr Ste B108 *Web:* www.thsconstructors.com	Greenville	SC	29615	864-254-6066	
Tiger Construction Ltd 6280 Everson Goshen Rd *Web:* www.hub-4.com	Everson	WA	98247	360-966-7252	
Tilden-Coil Constructors Inc 3612 Mission Inn Ave. *Web:* www.tilden-coil.com	Riverside	CA	92501	951-684-5901	
Tilton Asset Management 510 Boston Post Rd *Web:* tiltonasset.com	Weston	MA	02493	781-373-2244	
TN Ward Co 129 Coulter Ave *Web:* www.tnward.com	Ardmore	PA	19003	610-649-0400	
Tom Rectenwald Construction Inc 330A Perry Hwy *Web:* www.tomrectenwald.com	Harmony	PA	16037	724-452-8801	
Toney Construction Services Inc 14031 Huffmeister Rd. *Web:* www.toneyconstruction.com	Cypress	TX	77429	281-304-1778	
Top Shop Inc, The 5740 Logan St *Web:* www.tshopinc.com	Denver	CO	80216	303-996-6026	
Torcon Inc 328 Newman Springs Rd *Web:* www.torcon.com	Red Bank	NJ	07701	732-704-9800	704-9810
Torti Gallas & Partners Inc 1300 Spring St Ste 400 *Web:* www.tortigallas.com	Silver Spring	MD	20910	301-588-4800	650-2255
Tower Lighting of Texas 1251 Rolling Creek Rd *Web:* www.navacomm.com	Spring Branch	TX	78070	830-228-4594	
Tredyffrin-Easttown School District (TESD) 940 W Valley Rd Ste 1700 *Web:* www.tesd.net/	Wayne	PA	19087	610-240-1900	
Trehel Corp PO Box 1707 *TF:* 800-319-7006 ■ *Web:* www.trehel.com	Clemson	SC	29633	864-654-6582	654-7788
Tri-C Construction Company Inc 1765 Merriman Rd *Web:* www.tricc.com	Akron	OH	44313	330-836-2722	869-8373
Tri-state Design Construction Inc 7401 Old York Rd *Web:* www.tristatedesign.net	Elkins Park	PA	19027	215-782-8200	782-8282
Tribalco LLC 4915 St Elmo Ave Ste 501 *Web:* www.tribalco.com	Bethesda	MD	20814	301-652-8450	
Tribble & Stephens Construction Ltd 8588 Katy Fwy Ste 100 *Web:* www.tribblestephens.com	Houston	TX	77024	713-465-8550	973-7107
Trotter & Morton Ltd 5711 - First St SE *Web:* www.trotterandmorton.com	Calgary	AB	T2H1H9	403-255-7535	
Turelk Inc 3700 Santa Fe Ave Ste 200 *Web:* www.turelk.com	Long Beach	CA	90810	310-835-3736	835-5909
Turner Construction Co 375 Hudson St **Fax:* Mktg ■ *Web:* www.turnerconstruction.com	New York	NY	10014	212-229-6000	229-6390*
Turner Universal 336 James Record Rd *Web:* www.turnerconstruction.com	Huntsville	AL	35824	256-461-6700	
Tutor Perini Corp 15901 Olden St *Web:* www.tutorperini.com	Sylmar	CA	91342	508-628-2000	
Tutor-Saliba Corp 15901 Olden St *Web:* www.tutorsaliba.com	Sylmar	CA	91342	818-362-8391	367-5379
TWC Construction Inc 431 Eastgate Rd 3rd Fl. *Web:* www.twcconstruction.com	Henderson	NV	89011	702-597-3444	
Tyler 2 Construction Inc 5400 Old Pineville Rd. *Web:* www.tyler2construction.com	Charlotte	NC	28217	704-527-3031	
U S Government Absentee Shawnee Tribe of Oklahoma 2025 Gordon Cooper Dr *Web:* www.astribe.com	Shawnee	OK	74801	405-275-4030	
U S Group Inc 100 Executive Ctr Dr Ste 217 *Web:* www.usgroupinc.com	Columbia	SC	29210	803-798-1420	798-1450
Ukpeagvik Inupiat Corp 1250 Agvik St PO Box 890 *Web:* www.ukpik.com	Barrow	AK	99723	907-852-4460	852-4459
Unit Company Inc 620 E Whitney Rd *Web:* www.unitcompany.com	Anchorage	AK	99501	907-349-6666	
Universal Construction Company Inc 11200 W 79th St. *Web:* www.universalconstruction.net	Lenexa	KS	66214	913-342-1150	342-1151
University Moving & Storage Co 23305 Commerce Dr *TF:* 800-448-6683 ■ *Web:* www.universitymoving.com	Farmington Hills	MI	48335	248-615-7000	615-8515
USM Inc 1880 Markley St *TF:* 800-355-4000 ■ *Web:* www.usmservices.com	Norristown	PA	19401	610-278-9000	275-8023
USS Cal Builders Inc 8051 Main St *Web:* www.usscalbuilders.com	Stanton	CA	90680	714-828-4882	
UW Marx Inc 20 Gurley Ave *Web:* www.uwmarx.com	Troy	NY	12182	518-272-2541	272-1196
Valley Construction Co 3610 - 78th Ave W *Web:* www.valleyconstruction.com	Rock Island	IL	61201	309-787-0292	787-7048
Van Hoose Construction 101 NE 70th St *Web:* www.vhcon.com	Oklahoma City	OK	73105	405-848-0415	848-3911
Vandervert Construction Inc 608 E Holland Ave *Web:* www.vandervertconstruction.com	Spokane	WA	99218	509-467-6654	
Vaughn Construction 10355 Westpark Dr *Web:* www.vaughnconstruction.com	Houston	TX	77042	713-243-8300	243-8350
VCI Telcom Inc 1921 W 11th St *Web:* www.vcicom.com	Upland	CA	91786	909-946-0905	
Veit & Company Inc 14000 Veit Pl. *Web:* www.veitusa.com	Rogers	MN	55374	763-428-2242	
Vesta Properties Ltd 9770 196A St Ste 101A *Web:* www.vestaproperties.com	Langley	BC	V1M2X5	604-888-7869	
Vinco Inc PO Box 907 *Web:* www.vinco-inc.com	Forest Lake	MN	55025	651-982-4642	
Virtexco Corp 977 Norfolk Sq *TF:* 800-766-1082 ■ *Web:* www.virtexco.com	Norfolk	VA	23502	757-466-1114	466-1115
Vissering Construction Co 175 Benchmark Industrial Dr *Web:* www.vissering.com	Streator	IL	61364	815-673-5511	
VJS Construction Services W233 N2847 Roundy Cir W *Web:* www.vjscs.com	Pewaukee	WI	53072	262-542-9000	
Vratsinas Construction (VCC) 216 Louisiana St PO Box 2558 *Web:* www.vccusa.com	Little Rock	AR	72203	501-376-0017	376-4145
VRH Construction Corp 320 Grand Ave *Web:* www.vrhcorp.com	Englewood	NJ	07631	201-871-4422	
W E O'Neil Construction Co 2751 N Clybourn Ave *Web:* www.weoneil.com	Chicago	IL	60614	773-755-1611	
W. L. Butler Construction Inc 204 Franklin St *Web:* www.wlbutler.com	Redwood City	CA	94063	650-361-1270	361-8657
W. Rogers Co 649 Bizzell Dr *Web:* www.wrogers.com	Lexington	KY	40510	859-231-6290	233-2066
WA Klinger LLC 2015 E Seventh St PO Box 8800 *Web:* www.waklinger.com	Sioux City	IA	51102	712-277-3900	
Wakefield Corp, The 10646 Dutchtown Rd *Web:* www.thewakefieldcorp.com	Knoxville	TN	37932	865-675-1550	675-1582
Walbridge Aldinger Co 777 Woodward Ave #300 *Web:* www.walbridge.com	Detroit	MI	48226	313-963-8000	963-8150
Walker Industries Holdings Ltd 2800 Thorold Townline Rd *TF:* 866-694-9360 ■ *Web:* www.walkerind.com	Niagara Falls	ON	L2E6S4	905-227-4142	
Wallick Construction Company Inc PO Box 1023 *Web:* www.wallickcos.com	Columbus	OH	43216	614-863-4640	863-1725
Walsh Construction Co 2905 SW First Ave *Web:* www.walshconstructionco.com	Portland	OR	97201	503-222-4375	274-7676
Walsh Group Inc 929 W Adams St *TF:* 800-957-1842 ■ *Web:* walshgroup.com	Chicago	IL	60607	312-563-5400	563-5466
Walton County Board of Education 200 Double Springs Church Rd *Web:* www.walton.k12.ga.us	Monroe	GA	30656	770-266-4520	
Wantman Group Inc 2035 Vista Pkwy Ste 100 *Web:* www.wantmangroup.com	West Palm Beach	FL	33411	561-687-2220	
Wanzek Construction Inc 2028 2nd Ave NW *Web:* www.wanzek.com	West Fargo	ND	58078	701-282-6171	282-6166
Ware County Board of Education 1301 Bailey St *TF:* 800-419-3191 ■ *Web:* www.ware.k12.ga.us	Waycross	GA	31501	912-283-8656	283-8698
Warfel Construction Co 1110 Enterprise Rd *Web:* www.warfelcc.com	East Petersburg	PA	17520	717-299-4500	299-4628
Warren Paving Inc 562 Elks Lk Rd PO Box 572 *Web:* www.warrenpaving.com	Hattiesburg	MS	39403	601-544-7811	544-2005
Washington Local Schools 3505 W Lincolnshire Blvd *TF:* 800-462-3589 ■ *Web:* www.washloc.k12.oh.us	Toledo	OH	43606	419-473-8251	473-8247
Washtenaw County Road Commission 555 N Zeeb Rd *Web:* www.wcroads.org	Ann Arbor	MI	48103	734-761-1500	761-3239
Waterbury Public School District (WPSD) 236 Grand St Ste 1 *Web:* www.waterbury.k12.ct.us	Waterbury	CT	06702	203-574-8000	574-8010
Weaver Cooke Construction LLC 8401 Key Blvd *Web:* www.weavercooke.com	Greensboro	NC	27409	336-378-7900	378-7901
Weber Group Inc 5233 Progress Way *Web:* webergroupinc.com	Sellersburg	IN	47172	812-246-2100	246-2109
Weis Builders Inc 2227 Seventh St NW *Web:* www.weisbuilders.com	Rochester	MN	55901	507-288-2041	
Weitz Company Inc 5901 Thornton Ave *Web:* www.weitz.com	Des Moines	IA	50321	515-246-4700	
Weitz/Cohen Construction Co 4725 S Monaco St Ste 100 *Web:* www.weitz.com	Denver	CO	80237	303-860-6600	860-6698
Welbro Bldg Corp 2301 Maitland Ctr Pkwy Ste 250 *Web:* www.welbro.com	Maitland	FL	32751	407-475-0800	475-0801
Welch & Rushe Inc 391 Prince George's Blvd *TF:* 800-683-3852 ■ *Web:* www.welchandrushe.com	Upper Marlboro	MD	20774	301-430-6000	
Wesely-thomas Enterprises Inc 250 Lombard St Ste 1 *Web:* www.wtei.com	Thousand Oaks	CA	91360	805-379-2365	
West Bay Builders Inc 250 Bel Marin Keys Blvd *Web:* www.westbaybuilders.com	Novato	CA	94949	415-456-8972	

Phone Fax

West Coast Construction
9021 Rancho Park Ct .... Rancho Cucamonga CA 91730 909-982-6979
Web: www.wccsinc.com

West Construction Inc
318 S Dixie Hwy Ste 4-5.......... Lake Worth FL 33460 561-588-2027
Web: www.westconstructioninc.net

Western Builders of Amarillo Inc
700 S Grant St .... Amarillo TX 79101 806-376-4321
Web: www.wbamarillo.com

Western Summit Constructors Inc
9780 Mt Pyramid Ct Ste 100 .... Englewood CO 80112 303-298-9500 325-0304
Web: www.westernsummit.com

WG Yates & Sons Construction Co Inc
1 Gulley Ave .... Philadelphia MS 39350 601-656-5411 656-8958
Web: www.wgyates.com

Whiting-Turner Contracting Co 300 E Joppa Rd.......... Towson MD 21286 410-821-1100 337-5770
Web: www.whiting-turner.com

Wichman Construction 5029 W Grace St .... Tampa FL 33607 813-282-1179
Web: www.wichmanconstruction.com

Wild Bldg Contractors Inc
225 W First N St Ste 102 .... Morristown TN 37814 423-581-5639 587-4037
Web: www.wildbuilding.com

William A Randolph Inc 820 Lakeside Dr Ste 3.......... Gurnee IL 60031 847-856-0123
Web: www.warandolph.com

William Blanchard Co 199 Mountain Ave .... Springfield NJ 07081 973-376-9100 376-9154
Web: wmblanchard.com

Williams Company of Orlando Inc
2301 Silver Star Rd.......... Orlando FL 32804 407-295-2530 297-0459
Web: www.williamsco.com

Windstar Lines Inc 1903 US Hwy 71 N .... Carroll IA 51401 712-792-4221 792-9615
TF: 888-494-6378 ■ *Web:* www.gowindstar.com

Winter Construction Co 191 Peachtree St NE.......... Atlanta GA 30303 404-588-3300
Web: winter-construction.com

Winter Park Construction Co 221 Cir Dr.......... Maitland FL 32751 407-644-8923 645-1972
Web: www.wpc.com

WM Brode Co 100 Elizabeth St PO Box 299.......... Newcomerstown OH 43832 740-498-5121 498-8553
Web: www.wmbrode.com

WM Jordan Company Inc
11010 Jefferson Ave.......... Newport News VA 23601 757-596-6341 596-7425
Web: www.wmjordan.com

Wolverine Bldg Group Inc 4045 Barden SE.......... Grand Rapids MI 49512 616-949-3360 949-6211
Web: www.wolvgroup.com

Woodfield Inc 3161 Hwy 376 S.......... Camden AR 71701 870-231-6020 231-6070
TF: 800-501-6020 ■ *Web:* www.woodfieldinc.com

Worth Construction Company Inc 24 Taylor Ave .... Bethel CT 06801 203-797-8788 791-2515
Web: www.worthconstruction.com

Wright Construction Corp
5811 Youngquist Rd.......... Fort Myers FL 33912 239-481-5000 481-2448
Web: www.wrightconstructioncorp.com

Wright Construction Western Inc
2919 Cleveland Ave .... Saskatoon SK S7K8A9 306-934-0440
Web: www.wrightconstruction.ca

Wright Process Systems 88 Commerce St .... Lodi CA 95240 209-369-2795
Web: www.wrightps.com

WS Bellows Construction Corp 1906 Afton St.......... Houston TX 77055 713-680-2132 680-2614
Web: www.wsbellows.com

WS Cumby Inc 938 Lincoln Ave.......... Springfield PA 19064 610-328-5353
Web: www.cumby.com

Wurzel Builders Ltd 8721 S First St.......... Austin TX 78748 512-282-9488
Web: wurzelbuilders.com

Yeargin Potter Shackelford Construction Inc
121 Edinburgh Ct.......... Greenville SC 29607 864-232-1491
Web: www.ypsconst.com

Yellowridge Construction Ltd
2605 Clarke St Ste 200.......... Port Moody BC V3H1Z4 604-936-2605
Web: yellowridge.ca

Zachry Group 527 Logwood Ave .... San Antonio TX 78221 210-588-5000 588-5060
Web: www.zachrygroup.com

Zeeland Public Schools (ZPS)
183 W Roosevelt Ave .... Zeeland MI 49464 616-748-3000 748-3033
Web: www.zps.org

Ziolkowski Construction Inc
4050 Ralph Jones Dr .... South Bend IN 46628 574-287-1811
Web: www.zbuild.com

187 CONSTRUCTION - BUILDING CONTRACTORS - RESIDENTIAL

Phone Fax

A2 Inc 22 W 19th St 5th Fl.......... New York NY 10011 212-807-8772
Web: www.a2inc.com

Agbayani Construction Corp 88 Dixon Ct .... Daly City CA 94014 415-221-2065 665-9470
Web: www.agbayani.com

Air Contact Transport Inc PO Box 570.......... Budd Lake NJ 07828 800-765-2769 691-0127*
**Fax Area Code:* 973 ■ *TF:* 800-765-2769 ■ *Web:* actovernight.com

Alcan Electrical & Engineering Inc
6670 Arctic Spur Rd.......... Anchorage AK 99518 907-563-3787 562-6286
Web: www.alcanelectric.com

Alexander Company Inc, The
145 E Badger Rd Ste 200 .... Madison WI 53713 608-258-5580 258-5599
Web: www.alexandercompany.com

Alliance Construction Solutions LLC
2725 Rocky Mtn Ave Ste 100.......... Loveland CO 80538 970-663-9700
Web: www.allianceconstruction.com

Alpha Ten Technologies Inc
2720 Loker Ave W Ste K.......... Carlsbad CA 92010 760-438-9144
Web: www.alphaten.com

Alps Construction Inc 15745 Annico Dr.......... Lockport IL 60441 708-301-3366
Web: www.alpsconstruction.com

Arthur Rutenberg Homes Inc
13922 58th St N.......... Clearwater FL 33760 727-536-5900
TF: 800-274-6637 ■ *Web:* www.arthurrutenberghomes.com

Aui Contractors LLC 4775 N Fwy.......... Fort Worth TX 76106 817-926-4377 926-4387
Web: www.auigc.com

Phone Fax

Ball Homes LLC 3609 Walden Dr.......... Lexington KY 40517 859-268-1191 268-9093
TF: 888-268-1101 ■ *Web:* www.ballhomes.com

Bar None Auction Inc 4751 Power Inn Rd.......... Sacramento CA 95826 866-372-1700 383-6865*
**Fax Area Code:* 916 ■ *TF:* 866-372-1700 ■ *Web:* www.barnoneauction.com

Beals-Martin & Associates Inc
2596 Bay Rd Ste A.......... Redwood City CA 94063 650-364-8141
Web: www.bealsmartin.com

Big Sky Construction Company Inc
507 Exposition Ave.......... Dallas TX 75226 972-226-4704
Web: www.bigskyconstruction.com

Bob Schmitt Homes Inc
9095 Gatestone Rd.......... North Ridgeville OH 44039 440-327-9495
Web: www.bobschmitthomes.com

Bobo Construction Inc 9728 Kent St .... Elk Grove CA 95624 916-685-2285
Web: www.boboconstructioninc.com

Boller Construction Company Inc
3045 Washington St.......... Waukegan IL 60085 847-662-5566
Web: www.bollerconstruction.com

Bozzuto Group 7850 Walker Dr Ste 400.......... Greenbelt MD 20770 301-220-0100 220-3738
TF General: 866-698-7513 ■ *Web:* www.bozzuto.com

Braxton Design Group
1622 Beckoning Ridge Rd .... Charlottesville VA 22901 434-977-7999
Web: braxtondesigngroup.com

Breeden Homes Inc 366 E 40th Ave.......... Eugene OR 97405 541-686-9431 686-0918

Broadmoor LLC 2740 N Arnoult Rd.......... Metairie LA 70002 504-885-5400
Web: www.broadmoorllc.com

Brooks and Freund LLC
5661 Independence Cir Ste 1.......... Fort Myers FL 33912 239-939-5251
Web: www.brooksandfreund.com

Burnsteads, The 11980 NE 24th St Ste 200.......... Bellevue WA 98005 425-454-1900
Web: www.burnstead.com

Bush Construction Corp
4029 Ironbound Rd Ste 200.......... Williamsburg VA 23188 757-220-2874 229-2542

Calcon Constructors Inc 2270 W Bates Ave.......... Englewood CO 80110 303-762-1554
Web: www.calconci.com

Chrisanntha Construction Corp
4661 Dewey Ave PO Box 165.......... Gorham NY 14461 585-526-6376
Web: www.chrisanntha.com

Churchill Development Corp
5 Choke Cherry Rd Ste 360 .... Rockville MD 20850 240-243-1000
Web: www.churchillbuilders.com

City Dash 949 Laidlaw Ave.......... Cincinnati OH 45237 513-562-2000
Web: www.citydash.com

Clark-Pacific Corp 1980 S River Rd.......... West Sacramento CA 95691 916-371-0305 372-0323
Web: www.clarkpacific.com

Coakley & Williams Construction Inc
16 S Summit Ave Ste 300.......... Gaithersburg MD 20877 301-963-5000
Web: www.coakleywilliams.com

Colson & Colson Construction Co
2260 McGilchrist St SE .... Salem OR 97302 503-586-7401
Web: www.colson-colson.com

Conrad Bros Inc 800 Industrial Ave .... Chesapeake VA 23324 757-543-3521
Web: www.conradbrothersinc.com

Construction Enterprises Inc (CEI)
325 Seaboard Ln Ste 170.......... Franklin TN 37067 615-332-8880 771-0818
Web: www.constructionenterprises.com

Crossgates Inc 3555 Washington Rd .... McMurray PA 15317 724-941-9240 941-4339
Web: www.crossgatesinc.com

Cynergy Systems Inc 1851 Chespark Dr.......... Gastonia NC 28052 704-864-2999
Web: www.cynergysystemsinc.com

Damuth Trane 1100 Cavalier Blvd.......... Chesapeake VA 23323 757-558-0200 558-9715
Web: www.damuth.com

Dot-Line Transportation PO Box 8739.......... Fountain Valley CA 92728 323-780-9010 780-1552
TF: 800-423-3780 ■ *Web:* www.dotline.net

Drees Co 211 Grandview Dr .... Fort Mitchell KY 41017 859-578-4200 578-4200
TF: 866-265-2980 ■ *Web:* www.dreeshomes.com

DuBois Area School District Inc
500 Liberty Blvd.......... Du Bois PA 15801 814-371-2700
Web: www.dasd.k12.pa.us

Eastforest Homes Ltd 155 Washburn Dr .... Kitchener ON N2R1S1 519-742-2846
Web: www.eastforesthomes.com

Eid-Co Homes 1701 32nd Ave S .... Fargo ND 58103 701-237-0510
Web: www.eid-co.com

Elan Construction Limited
3639-27 St NE Ste 100.......... Calgary AB T1Y5E4 403-291-1165
Web: www.elanconstruction.com

Excel Homes Inc 10642 S Susquehanna Trail.......... Liverpool PA 17045 717-444-3395 444-7577

Eyde Co 4660 S Hagadorn Ste 660.......... East Lansing MI 48823 517-351-2480 351-3946
TF: 800-422-3933 ■ *Web:* www.eyde.com

F D Rich Co 222 Summer St.......... Stamford CT 06901 203-359-2900 328-7980
Web: www.fdrich.com

Fandor Homes 68 Romina Dr.......... Vaughan ON L4K4Z7 905-669-5820
Web: fandorhomes.com

Farmington School District R-7
1022 Ste Genevieve Ave.......... Farmington MO 63640 573-701-1300 701-1309
Web: www.farmington.k12.mo.us

FH Martin Constructors 28740 Mound Rd .... Warren MI 48092 586-558-2100 558-2921
Web: www.fhmartin.com

Fish Enterprises 905 S Fair Oaks Ave.......... Pasadena CA 91105 626-773-8800 773-8820
Web: www.fishenterprises.com

Forbes Homes Inc 470 Cayuga Rd .... Cheektowaga NY 14225 716-688-5597 688-6674
Web: www.forbeshomes.com

Franklin Development Co
21260 Gathering Oak Ste 101.......... San Antonio TX 78260 210-694-2223
Web: franklincompanies.com

Fulton Homes Corp 9140 S Kyrene Rd Ste 202 .... Tempe AZ 85284 480-753-6789 753-5554
Web: www.fultonhomes.com

Galaxy Builders Ltd 4729 College Pk.......... San Antonio TX 78249 210-493-0550 493-1238
Web: thegalaxycompanies.com

Gioffre Cos Inc 6262 Eiterman Rd.......... Dublin OH 43016 614-764-0032 764-1620
Web: www.gioffreconstruction.com

Green Valley Corp 777 N First St 5th Fl.......... San Jose CA 95112 408-287-0246 998-1737
Web: www.barryswensonbuilder.com

	City	State	Zip	Phone	Fax
Grupe Co 3255 W March Ln Ste 400 *TF:* 877-984-7873 ■ *Web:* www.grupe.com	Stockton	CA	95219	209-473-6000	473-6001
Hardaway Group 615 Main St *Web:* www.hardaway.net	Nashville	TN	37206	615-254-5461	254-4518
Harkins Builders Inc 2201 Warwick Way *TF:* 800-227-2345 ■ *Web:* www.harkinsbuilders.com	Marriottsville	MD	21104	410-750-2600	480-4299
Harper Corp General Contractors 35 W Ct St Ste 400 *Web:* www.harpercorp.com	Greenville	SC	29601	864-527-2500	527-2536
Hasbrouck Heights Board of Education 379 Blvd *Web:* www.hhschools.org	Hasbrouck Heights	NJ	07604	201-288-6150	
Hawaii Modular Space Inc 91-282 Kalaeloa Blvd *Web:* www.hawaiimodularspace.com	Kapolei	HI	96707	808-682-5559	682-5199
Haywood County School District 900 E Main St *Web:* www.haywoodschools.com	Brownsville	TN	38012	731-772-9613	772-3275
Hernandez Cos Inc 3734 E Anne St *Web:* www.hernandezcompanies.com	Phoenix	AZ	85040	602-438-7825	438-6558
Hitt Contracting Inc 2900 Fairview Park Dr *Web:* www.hitt-gc.com	Falls Church	VA	22042	703-846-9000	846-9110
Hovnanian Enterprises Inc 1806 S Highland Ave *Web:* khov.com	Lombard	IL	60148	630-953-2222	
Icon West Inc 520 S La Fayette Park Pl Ste 503 *Web:* www.icon-west.com	Los Angeles	CA	90057	213-385-0027	
James A Cummings Inc 3575 NW 53rd St *Web:* www.jamesacummings.com	Fort Lauderdale	FL	33309	954-733-4211	485-9688
JB Sandlin Cos 5137 Davis Blvd *TF:* 800-821-4663 ■ *Web:* sandlinhomes.com	Fort Worth	TX	76180	817-281-3509	656-0719
John Cannon Homes Inc 6710 Professional Pkwy W *Web:* www.johncannonhomes.com	Sarasota	FL	34240	941-924-5935	924-4129
Jokake Construction Co 5013 E Washington St Ste 100 *Web:* www.jokake.com	Phoenix	AZ	85034	602-224-4500	667-5500
Joseph J. Henderson & Son Inc 4288 Old Grand Ave PO Box 9 *Web:* www.jjhenderson.com	Gurnee	IL	60031	847-244-3222	244-9572
Kablooe Design 9162 Davenport St NE *Web:* www.kablooe.com	Minneapolis	MN	55449	763-785-9595	
Kalian Cos 225 Hwy 35 Navesink N *Web:* www.kalian.com	Red Bank	NJ	07701	732-741-0054	741-3404
Kickerillo Cos 1306 S Fry Rd **Fax Area Code:* 281 ■ *Web:* www.kickerillo.com	Katy	TX	77450	713-951-0666	492-2018*
Kopf Builders Inc 420 Avon Belden Rd *TF:* 888-933-5673 ■ *Web:* www.kopf.net	Avon Lake	OH	44012	440-933-6908	933-6956
LAS Enterprises Inc 2413 L & A Rd *TF:* 800-264-1527 ■ *Web:* lashome.com	Metairie	LA	70001	504-887-1515	832-0036
Lewis Builders Inc 54 Sawyer Ave *Web:* www.lewisbuilders.com	Atkinson	NH	03811	603-362-5333	362-4936
Lizardos Engineering Assoc Pc 200 Old Country Rd Ste 670 *Web:* www.leapc.com	Mineola	NY	11501	516-484-1020	484-0926
M e Group Inc 2820 N 48th St Ste 200 *Web:* www.megroup.com	Lincoln	NE	68504	402-464-3833	
McBride & Son Inc 16091 Swingley Ridge Rd Ste 300 *Web:* www.mcbridehomes.com	Chesterfield	MO	63005	636-537-2000	537-2546
Mercy Housing Inc 1999 Broadway Ste 1000 *TF:* 866-338-0557 ■ *Web:* www.mercyhousing.org	Denver	CO	80202	303-830-3300	
Michaels Group LLC 10 Blacksmith Dr Ste 1 *Web:* www.michaelsgroup.com	Malta	NY	12020	518-899-6311	899-6260
Morgan Group Inc 5606 S Rice Ave *Web:* www.morgangroup.com	Houston	TX	77081	713-361-7200	361-7299
Nordaas American Homes Company Inc 10091 State Hwy 22 *TF:* 800-658-7076 ■ *Web:* nordaashomes.com	Minnesota Lake	MN	56068	507-462-3331	462-3211
Norris School District 6940 Calloway Dr *TF:* 800-877-8339 ■ *Web:* www.norris.k12.ca.us	Bakersfield	CA	93312	661-387-7000	399-9750
NVR Inc 11700 Plz America Dr Ste 500 *NYSE:* NVR ■ *Web:* nvrinc.com	Reston	VA	20190	703-956-4000	
O'Harrow Construction Co 4575 Ann Arbor Rd *Web:* www.oharrow.net	Jackson	MI	49202	517-764-4770	764-5564
Ole South Properties Inc 201 E Main St Ste 300 *Web:* www.olesouth.com	Murfreesboro	TN	37130	615-896-0019	896-9380
Olgoonik Development LLC 3201 C St Ste 700 *TF:* 855-763-2613 ■ *Web:* www.olgoonik.com	Anchorage	AK	99503	907-562-8728	562-8751
Olympus Homes Inc PO Box 2999 *Web:* www.olympushomes.com	Westerville	OH	43086	614-523-2000	
Perry Homes PO Box 34306 *TF:* 800-247-3779 ■ *Web:* www.perryhomes.com	Houston	TX	77234	713-948-7700	
Prince Telecom Inc 551 Mews Dr Ste A *Web:* www.princetelecom.com	New Castle	DE	19720	302-324-1800	324-0428
Providence Homes Inc 4901 Belfort Rd Ste 140 *TF:* 866-836-0981 ■ *Web:* www.providencehomesinc.com	Jacksonville	FL	32256	904-262-9898	262-9861
Purcell Construction Inc 277 Dennis St *Web:* www.purcellc.com	Humble	TX	77338	281-548-1000	548-2998
Pyramid Construction Inc 275 N Franklin Tpke *Web:* www.pyramidgroup.biz	Ramsey	NJ	07446	201-327-1919	327-0054
R L Turner Corp 1000 W Oak St *Web:* www.rlturner.com	Zionsville	IN	46077	317-873-2712	873-1262
Reimers & Jolivette Inc 2344 NW 24th Ave *Web:* reimersandjolivette.com	Portland	OR	97210	503-228-7691	228-2721
Rio Verde Development Inc 25609 N Danny Ln *TF:* 800-233-7103 ■ *Web:* www.theverdes.com	Rio Verde	AZ	85263	480-471-1962	471-0107
Rockford Homes Inc 999 Polaris Pkwy Ste 200 *Web:* www.rockfordhomes.net	Columbus	OH	43240	614-785-0015	785-9181
Rohde Construction Company Inc 4087 Brockton Dr *Web:* rohdeconstruction.com	Kentwood	MI	49512	616-698-0880	698-1850
Royal American Construction Co Inc 1002 W 23rd St Ste 400 *Web:* royalamericanconstruction.com	Panama City	FL	32405	850-769-8981	
RS Mowery & Sons Inc 1000 Bent Creek Blvd *Web:* www.rsmowery.com	Mechanicsburg	PA	17050	717-506-1000	506-1010
Russell Construction Company Inc 4600 E 53rd St *Web:* www.russellco.com	Davenport	IA	52807	563-459-4600	
Rust Constructors Inc 2 Perimeter Pk S Ste 300 W *Web:* rustconstructors.azurewebsites.net	Birmingham	AL	35243	205-995-7171	995-3873
Schneider Homes Inc 6510 Southcenter Blvd *Web:* www.schneiderhomes.com	Tukwila	WA	98188	206-248-2471	242-4209
Selmer Co 2200 Woodale Ave *Web:* theboldtcompany.com	Green Bay	WI	54313	920-434-0230	
Shaw Construction Company LLC 300 Kalamath St *Web:* www.shawconstruction.net	Denver	CO	80223	303-825-4740	825-6403
Shreve Land Company Inc 624 Travis St Ste 100 *Web:* www.shreveland.com	Shreveport	LA	71101	318-226-0056	226-0064
Shugart Enterprises LLC 221 Jonestown Rd *Web:* www.shugartenterprises.com	Winston-Salem	NC	27104	336-765-9661	765-1295
Simpson County School District 176 W Ct St PO Box 127 *Web:* www.simpsoncounty.biz	Mendenhall	MS	39114	601-847-2375	847-2380
Skogman Construction Company Inc 411 First Ave *Web:* www.skogman.com	Cedar Rapids	IA	52401	319-363-8285	366-7257
Smith Bros Construction 444 S Cedros Ave *Web:* www.smithbrothersconstruction.com	Solana Beach	CA	92075	858-350-1445	
Southern California Boiler Inc 5331 Business Dr *TF:* 800-775-2645 ■ *Web:* www.californiaboiler.com	Huntington Beach	CA	92649	714-891-0701	
SS Steele & Company Inc 4951 Government Blvd *Web:* www.steelehomes.cc	Mobile	AL	36693	251-661-9600	
Stabile Cos Inc 20 Cotton Rd Ste 200 *Web:* www.stabilecompanies.com	Nashua	NH	03063	603-889-0318	595-2571
Stanmar Inc 321 Commonwealth Rd Ste 201 *Web:* www.stanmar-inc.com	Wayland	MA	01778	508-310-9922	
Staples Construction Company Inc 1501 Eastman Ave *TF:* 800-881-4650 ■ *Web:* www.staplesconstruction.com	Ventura	CA	93003	805-658-8786	658-8785
Star Signs LLC 801 E Ninth St *Web:* www.starsignsllc.com	Lawrence	KS	66046	785-842-2881	
Structural Component Systems Inc (SCS) 1255 Front St *TF:* 800-844-5622 ■ *Web:* www.scstruss.com	Fremont	NE	68026	402-721-5622	721-6170
Sunset Development Co 1 Annabel Ln Ste 201 *Web:* www.bishopranch.com	San Ramon	CA	94583	925-866-0100	866-1330
T&G Constructors Inc 8623 Commodity Cir *Web:* www.t-and-g.com	Orlando	FL	32819	407-352-4443	352-0778
T. Gerding Construction Co PO Box 1082 *Web:* www.tgerding.com	Corvallis	OR	97339	541-753-2012	
TH Properties 345 Main St *TF Sales:* 800-225-5847 ■ *Web:* www.thproperties.com	Harleysville	PA	19438	215-513-4270	511-3202
Thompson Realty Corp 2505 N Plano Rd Ste 3000 *Web:* www.thompson-realty.com	Richardson	TX	75082	972-644-2400	
Thor Construction Inc 5400 Main St NE Ste 203 *Web:* www.thorcon.net	Minneapolis	MN	55421	763-571-2580	571-2631
Traton Corp 720 Kennesaw Ave NW *Web:* www.tratonhomes.com	Marietta	GA	30060	770-427-9064	
Triple Crown Corp 5351 Jaycee Ave *TF:* 877-822-4663 ■ *Web:* www.triplecrowncorp.com	Harrisburg	PA	17112	717-657-5729	657-8125
True Homes LLC 2649 Breckenridge Ctr Dr Ste 104 *Web:* truehomesusa.com	Monroe	NC	28110	704-238-1229	238-1150
Trustmark Construction Corp 841 Sweetwater Ave *Web:* www.trustmarkcorp.com	Florence	AL	35630	256-760-9624	760-0902
Tuttle Construction Inc 880 Shawnee Rd *Web:* www.tuttlenet.com	Lima	OH	45805	419-228-6262	229-7414
Tyler Construction Company Inc 433 Rabon Rd *Web:* www.tyler-construction.com	Columbia	SC	29223	803-865-1404	
United-Bilt Homes Inc 8500 Line Ave *TF:* 800-551-8955 ■ *Web:* www.ubh.com	Shreveport	LA	71106	318-861-4572	869-0132
Urban Concrete Contractors Ltd 24114 Blanco Rd *Web:* www.urbanconcrete.com	San Antonio	TX	78258	210-490-0090	490-1505
Vantage Homes 1710 Jet Stream Dr Ste 200 *Web:* www.vhco.com	Colorado Springs	CO	80921	719-534-0984	
Vendini Inc 660 Market St *TF:* 800-901-7173 ■ *Web:* www.vendini.com	San Francisco	CA	94104	800-901-7173	
Venture Express Inc 131 Industrial Blvd *Web:* www.ventureexpress.com	La Vergne	TN	37086	615-793-9500	793-9267
Village Green Cos 30833 NW Hwy *TF:* 800-521-2220 ■ *Web:* www.villagegreen.com	Farmington Hills	MI	48334	248-851-9600	851-6161
Voorhees International Inc 575 Rudder Rd Ste 109 *Web:* www.voorheesintl.com	Fenton	MO	63026	636-349-1555	349-5130
Wallick Construction Company Inc PO Box 1023 *Web:* www.wallickcos.com	Columbus	OH	43216	614-863-4640	863-1725
Walsh Group Inc 929 W Adams St *TF:* 800-957-1842 ■ *Web:* walshgroup.com	Chicago	IL	60607	312-563-5400	563-5466

	City	State	ZIP	Phone	Fax
Walter Toebe Construction Co 29001 Wall St PO Box 930129 *Web:* www.toebe-construction.com	Wixom	MI	48393	248-349-7500	349-4870
Weavertown Environmental Group 2 Dorrington Rd *TF:* 800-746-4850 ■ *Web:* www.weavertown.com	Carnegie	PA	15106	724-746-4850	
Wermers Multi-Family Corp 5120 Shoreham Pl Ste 150 *Web:* www.wermerscompanies.com	San Diego	CA	92122	858-535-1475	535-0171
Western Water Constructors Inc 707 Aviation Blvd *Web:* www.westernwater.com	Santa Rosa	CA	95403	707-540-9640	540-9641
Wexford Homes 135 Keveling Dr. *Web:* www.wexfordhomes.com	Saline	MI	48176	734-470-6647	
Wheeler Construction Inc 3255 E Gulf to Lake Hwy *Web:* www.citrusbuilder.com	Inverness	FL	34453	352-726-0973	637-4959
Wildish Land Co Inc 3600 Wildish Ln PO Box 40310 *Web:* www.wildish.com	Eugene	OR	97408	541-485-1700	683-7722
William Lyon Homes 4695 MacArthur Ct 8th Fl *Web:* www.lyonhomes.com	Newport Beach	CA	92660	949-833-3600	476-2178
Winchester Homes Inc 6905 Rockledge Dr Ste 800 *Web:* yourhomeyourway.com/winchester	Bethesda	MD	20817	301-803-4800	474-1609
Wohlsen Construction Co 548 Steel Way PO Box 7066 *Web:* www.wohlsenconstruction.com	Lancaster	PA	17604	717-299-2500	299-3419

188 CONSTRUCTION - HEAVY CONSTRUCTION CONTRACTORS

	City	State	ZIP	Phone	Fax
Allen & Shariff Corp 7061 Deepage Dr *Web:* www.allenshariff.com	Columbia	MD	21045	410-381-7100	
Apac-ks Wilkerson Crane Rental 12790 E 36th St N *Web:* www.wilkersoncranerental.com	Tulsa	OK	74116	918-437-9500	
Bo-mac Contractors Ltd 1020 Lindbergh Dr. *TF:* 800-526-6221 ■ *Web:* www.bomaccontractors.com	Beaumont	TX	77707	409-842-2125	
Borek Construction Ltd 9690 Rd 223 PO Box 870 *Web:* www.borekltd.com	Dawson Creek	BC	V1G4H8	250-782-5561	
Broda Construction Ltd 4271 - Fifth Ave E. *Web:* www.brodagroup.com	Prince Albert	SK	S6V7V6	306-764-5337	
Capitol Tunneling Inc 2216 Refugee Rd *Web:* www.capitoltunneling.com	Columbus	OH	43207	614-444-0255	
Castle Contracting LLC 760 S 2nd St *Web:* www.castlecontracting.com	St. Louis	MO	63102	314-421-0042	
Chet Morrison Contractors LLC 9 Bayou Dularge Rd *Web:* www.chetmorrison.com	Houma	LA	70363	985-868-1950	
Comer Industries Inc 12730 Virkler Dr *Web:* www.comerindustries.com	Charlotte	NC	28273	704-588-8400	
Currier Construction Inc 36 N 56th St *Web:* www.currierinc.com	Phoenix	AZ	85034	602-274-4370	
Dcr Business Solutions Inc PO Box 297 *Web:* www.dcrservices.com	Mulberry	FL	33860	863-904-1077	428-9027
Elkhorn Construction Inc 71 Allegiance Cir PO Box 809 *Web:* www.elkhornconstruction.com	Evanston	WY	82930	307-789-1595	
Fagor Automation Corp 2250 Estes Ave *Web:* www.fagorautomation.com	Elk Grove Village	IL	60007	847-981-1500	
Floating Island International Inc 10052 Floating Island Way *Web:* www.floatingislandinternational.com	Shepherd	MT	59079	406-373-5200	
Geo-Solutions Inc 1250 Fifth Ave *Web:* www.geo-solutions.com	New Kensington	PA	15068	724-335-7273	
Golf Creations 18250 Beck Rd *Web:* lohmann.com	Marengo	IL	60152	815-923-1868	
Gulf Engineering LLC 611 Hill St. *TF:* 800-347-4749 ■ *Web:* www.gulfengineering.com	Jefferson	LA	70121	504-733-4868	
Halmar International LLC 421 E Route 59 Nanuet *Web:* www.halmarinternational.com	New York	NY	10954	845-735-3511	
Harbor Rail Services of California Inc 1550 W Colorado Blvd	Pasadena	CA	91105	626-398-4065	
LandTek Group Inc, The 235 County Line Rd *Web:* www.landtekgroup.com	Amityville	NY	11701	631-691-2381	
Larkin Enterprises Inc 317 W Broadway PO Box 405 *TF:* 800-990-5418 ■ *Web:* larkinent.com	Lincoln	ME	04457	207-794-8700	
Lone Star Railroad Contractors Inc 4201 S Interstate 45 *Web:* www.lonestarrailroad.com	Ennis	TX	75119	972-878-9500	
McNally International Inc 1855 Barton St E. *Web:* www.mcnallycorp.com	Hamilton	ON	L8H2Y7	905-549-6561	
Norair Engineering Corp 337 Brightseat Rd Ste 200 *Web:* www.norair.com	Landover	MD	20785	301-499-2202	
Oman Systems Inc 3334 Powell Ave. *TF:* 800-541-0803 ■ *Web:* www.omanco.com	Nashville	TN	37204	615-385-2500	
Pala Group LLC 16347 Old Hammond Hwy *Web:* www.palagroup.com	Baton Rouge	LA	70895	225-272-5194	
Pease & Sons Inc 10601 Waller Rd E. *Web:* www.peaseandsons.com	Tacoma	WA	98448	253-531-7700	
Pinck & Company Inc 98 Magazine St. *Web:* pinck-co.com	Boston	MA	02119	617-445-3555	
PNR RailWorks Inc 2595 Deacon St PO Box 2280 *Web:* www.pnrail.com	Abbotsford	BC	V2T4X2	604-850-9166	
Power Grid Engineering LLC 5744 Canton Cove Ste 110 *TF:* 877-819-1171 ■ *Web:* www.powergridengineering.com	Winter Springs	FL	32708	321-244-0170	
R&R Contracting Inc 5201 N Washington St. *TF:* 800-872-5975 ■ *Web:* www.rrcontracting.net	Grand Forks	ND	58203	701-772-7667	
RealEnergy LLC 1500 Soscol Ferry Rd *Web:* realenergy.com	Napa	CA	94558	707-944-2400	
Tecon Services Inc 515 Garden Oaks Blvd *TF:* 800-245-1728 ■ *Web:* www.teconservices.com	Houston	TX	77018	713-691-2700	
Thompson Brothers (Construction) LP 411 S Ave PO Box 4300 *Web:* www.thompsonbros.com	Spruce Grove	AB	T7X3B4	780-962-1030	
Utilipath Inc 136 Corporate Pk Dr Ste G	Mooresville	NC	28117	704-948-1005	658-3929
Vancouver Pile Driving Ltd 20 Brooksbank Ave *Web:* www.vanpile.com	North Vancouver	BC	V7J2B8	604-986-5911	
Voice Construction Ltd 7545 52 St. *Web:* www.voiceconst.com	Edmonton	AB	T6B0A7	780-469-1351	
Watts Constructors LLC 737 Bishop St Ste 2900 *Web:* www.wattsconstructors.com	Honolulu	HI	96813	808-543-5201	
White Construction Inc 3900 E White Ave *Web:* www.whiteconstruction.com	Clinton	IN	47842	765-832-8526	
Zellner Construction Services LLC 2926 Ridgeway Rd *Web:* www.zellnerconstruction.com	Memphis	TN	38115	901-794-1100	794-9141

188-1 Communications Lines & Towers Construction

	City	State	ZIP	Phone	Fax
Black & Veatch 11401 Lamar Ave *Web:* www.bv.com	Overland Park	KS	66211	913-458-2000	
Cellcom Services Inc 11301 W 218th St.	Peculiar	MO	64078	816-779-5660	
CLS Group 609 S Kelly Ave Ste D *Web:* www.clsgroup.com	Edmond	OK	73003	405-348-5460	551-8270
CommStructures Inc 101 E Roberts Rd *Web:* www.commstructures.com	Pensacola	FL	32534	850-968-9293	968-9283
Fluor Daniel Inc 3 Polaris Way *Web:* www.fluor.com	Aliso Viejo	CA	92698	949-349-2000	349-2585
Malouf Engineering International Inc 17950 Preston Rd Ste 720 *Web:* www.maloufengineering.com	Dallas	TX	75252	972-783-2578	783-2583
MasTec Inc 800 Douglas Rd 12th Fl *NYSE: MTZ* ■ *TF:* 800-531-5000 ■ *Web:* www.mastec.com	Coral Gables	FL	33134	305-599-1800	406-1960
NAT-COM Inc 2622 Audubon Rd *Web:* www.nat-com.com	Eagleville	PA	19403	610-666-7947	
Quanta Services Inc 1360 Post Oak Blvd Ste 2100 *NYSE: PWR* ■ *Web:* www.quantaservices.com	Houston	TX	77056	713-629-7600	629-7676
Seacomm Erectors Inc 32527 SR 2 PO Box 1740 *Web:* www.seacomm.com	Sultan	WA	98294	360-793-6564	793-4402
Utility Services Inc 400 N Fourth St *TF:* 800-638-3278 ■ *Web:* www.montana-dakota.com	Bismarck	ND	58501	701-222-7900	

188-2 Foundation Drilling & Pile Driving

	City	State	ZIP	Phone	Fax
Berkel & Co Contractors Inc PO Box 335 *Web:* www.berkelandcompany.com	Bonner Springs	KS	66012	913-422-5125	441-0402
Case Foundation Co 1325 W Lake St. *TF:* 800-999-4087 ■ *Web:* www.casefoundation.com	Roselle	IL	60172	630-529-2911	529-2995
LG Barcus & Sons Inc 1430 State Ave *TF:* 800-255-0180 ■ *Web:* www.barcus.com	Kansas City	KS	66102	913-621-1100	621-3288
Malcolm Drilling Co Inc 3503 Breakwater Ct *TF:* 800-523-2200 ■ *Web:* www.malcolmdrilling.com	Hayward	CA	94545	510-780-9181	780-9167
WM Brode Co 100 Elizabeth St PO Box 299 *Web:* www.wmbrode.com	Newcomerstown	OH	43832	740-498-5121	498-8553

188-3 Golf Course Construction

	City	State	ZIP	Phone	Fax
Barbaron Inc 107 NE Fourth St *Web:* www.barbaron.com	Crystal River	FL	34429	352-795-9010	
Formost Construction Co PO Box 559 *Web:* www.formostconstruction.com	Temecula	CA	92593	951-698-7270	698-6170
Golf Development Construction Inc PO Box 197249 *Web:* www.golfdev.com	Louisville	KY	40259	502-894-8916	
Golf Visions LLC 344 E Lyndale Ave *Web:* golfvisions.net	Northlake	IL	60164	708-562-5247	
Golf Works Inc 3660 Stone Ridge Rd	Austin	TX	78746	512-327-8089	327-8169
Harris Miniature Golf 141 W Burk Ave *TF:* 888-294-6530 ■ *Web:* www.harrisminigolf.com	Wildwood	NJ	08260	609-522-4200	729-0100
Johnson Golf Course Builders 497 Golf Rd	South Sioux City	NE	68776	402-494-4687	494-0816
Landscapes Unlimited LLC 1201 Aries Dr *Web:* www.landscapesunlimited.com	Lincoln	NE	68512	402-423-6653	423-4487
MacCurrach Golf Construction Inc 3501 Faye Rd *Web:* www.maccurrachgolf.com	Jacksonville	FL	32226	904-646-1581	
Niebur Golf Inc 1230 Tenderfoot Hill Rd Ste 100 *Web:* www.nieburdevelopment.com	Colorado Springs	CO	80906	719-527-0313	
Prince Contracting LLC 10210 Highland Manor Dr Ste 110 *Web:* www.princecontracting.com	Tampa	FL	33610	813-699-5900	699-5901
Ryan Inc Central 2700 E Racine St *Web:* www.ryancentral.com	Janesville	WI	53545	608-754-2291	754-3290

Phone Fax

Shapemasters Inc PO Box 11128 ... Southport NC 28461 910-278-1434 278-1944
Web: www.shapemasters.com
Total Golf Construction Inc 4045 43rd Ave ... Vero Beach FL 32960 772-562-1177 562-2773
Web: www.totalgolfconstruction.com
Wadsworth Golf Construction Co
13941 Van Dyke Rd ... Plainfield IL 60544 815-436-8400 436-8404
Web: www.wadsworthgolf.com

188-4 Highway, Street, Bridge, Tunnel Construction

Phone Fax

A Teichert & Son Inc
3500 American River Dr ... Sacramento CA 95864 916-484-3011
Web: www.teichert.com
Ace Asphalt & Paving Co 115 S Averill Ave ... Flint MI 48506 810-238-1737 238-4326
Web: aceasphaltpaving.com
Adams Construction Co 523 Rutherford Ave NE ... Roanoke VA 24016 540-982-2366 982-2942
TF: 800-237-6060 ■ *Web:* www.adamspaving.com
Ajax Paving Industries Inc 1957 Crooks Rd Ste A ... Troy MI 48084 248-244-3300 574-8334*
**Fax Area Code:* 813 ■ *TF:* 888-468-5489 ■ *Web:* www.ajaxpaving.com
Allan A Myers Inc 1805 Berks Rd PO Box 1340 ... Worcester PA 19490 610-222-8800 222-3300
TF: 800-596-6118 ■ *Web:* www.allanmyers.com
Allen Company Inc 525 Burbank St ... Broomfield CO 80020 303-469-1857 466-7437
TF: 800-876-8600 ■ *Web:* www.allencompany.net
American Bridge Co
1000 American Bridge Way ... Coraopolis PA 15108 412-631-1000 631-2000*
**Fax:* Acctg ■ *Web:* www.americanbridge.net
American Civil Constructors Inc
4901 S Windemere St ... Littleton CO 80120 303-795-2582 347-1844
Web: www.accbuilt.com
American Paving Company Inc
315 N Thorne PO Box 4348 ... Fresno CA 93706 559-268-9886
Web: www.americanpavingco.com
Anderson Bros Construction Company Inc
11325 Hwy 210 E PO Box 668 ... Brainerd MN 56401 218-829-1768 829-7607
Web: www.andersonbrothers.com
Anderson Columbia Co Inc
871 NW Guerdon St PO Box 1829 ... Lake City FL 32056 386-752-7585 755-5430
Web: www.andersoncolumbia.com
Angelo Iafrate Construction Co
26300 Sherwood Ave ... Warren MI 48091 586-756-1070 756-0467
Web: www.iafrate.com
Arrow Road Construction Co
3401 S Busse Rd ... Mount Prospect IL 60056 847-437-0700 437-0779
Web: www.arrowroad.com
Austin Bridge & Road Inc
6330 Commerce Dr Ste 150 ... Irving TX 75063 214-596-7300 596-7395
Web: www.austin-ind.com
Autostrade International of Virginia
45305 Catalina Ct Ste 102 ... Sterling VA 20166 703-904-8001
Balfour Beatty Inc
999 Peachtree St NE Ste 200 ... Atlanta GA 30309 404-875-0356 607-1784
Web: www.balfourbeatty.com
Barber Bros Contracting Company LLC
2636 Dougherty Dr ... Baton Rouge LA 70805 225-355-5611 355-5615
Web: www.barber-brothers.com
Barnhill Contracting Co
4325 Pleasant Valley Rd ... Raleigh NC 27612 252-823-1021 823-0137
Web: www.barnhillcontracting.com
Barrett Industries Corp
3 Becker Farm Rd Ste 307 ... Roseland NJ 07068 973-533-1001 533-1020
Web: www.barrettpaving.com
Barriere Construction Co LLC
1 Galleria Blvd Ste 1650 ... Metairie LA 70001 504-581-7283 581-2270
TF: 866-645-3060 ■ *Web:* www.barriere.com
Basic Resources Inc 928 12th St Ste 700 ... Modesto CA 95354 209-521-9771 579-9502
Blythe Construction Inc 2911 N Graham St ... Charlotte NC 28206 704-375-8474 375-7814
Web: www.blytheconstruction.com
Boh Bros Construction Co LLC
730 S Tonti St ... New Orleans LA 70119 504-821-2400 821-0714
TF: 800-284-3377 ■ *Web:* www.bohbros.com
Border States Paving Inc 4101 N 32nd St ... Fargo ND 58102 701-237-4860 237-0233
Web: borderstatespaving.com
Borderland Construction Company Inc
400 E 38 St ... Tucson AZ 85713 520-623-0900 623-0232
Web: borderland-inc.com
BR Amon & Sons Inc W 2950 State Rd 11 ... Elkhorn WI 53121 262-723-2547 723-2666
Branch Highways Inc 442 Rutherford Ave ... Roanoke VA 24016 540-982-1678 982-4216
Web: www.branchhighways.com
Brechan Enterprises Inc 2705 Mill Bay Rd ... Kodiak AK 99615 907-486-3215 486-4889
Web: www.brechanconstructionllc.com
Brox Industries Inc 1471 Methuen St ... Dracut MA 01826 978-454-9105 805-9720
Web: www.broxindustries.com
C.A Rasmussen Inc 28548 Livingston Ave ... Valencia CA 91355 661-367-9040 367-9099
Web: www.carasmussen.com
Cardi Corp 400 Lincoln Ave ... Warwick RI 02888 401-739-8300
Web: www.cardi.com
CC Myers Inc 3286 Fitzgerald Rd ... Rancho Cordova CA 95742 916-635-9370 635-8961
Web: www.ccmyers.com
Central Allied Enterprises Inc
1243 Raff Rd SW ... Canton OH 44710 330-477-6751 477-1660
Web: www.central-allied.com
Cessford Construction Co PO Box 160 ... Le Grand IA 50142 641-479-2695 479-2003
Web: omgmidwest.com
Cherry Hill Construction Inc
8211 Washington Blvd ... Jessup MD 20794 410-799-3577 799-5483
Web: www.cherryhillconstruction.com
Cianbro Corp 335 Hunnewell Ave ... Pittsfield ME 04967 866-242-6276
TF: 866-242-6276 ■ *Web:* www.cianbro.com
Civil Constructors Inc 2283 US Hwy 20 E ... Freeport IL 61032 815-235-2200
Web: www.helmgroup.com
CJ Mahan Construction Co 3400 SW Blvd ... Grove City OH 43123 614-875-8200 875-1175
Web: www.cjmahan.com

Phone Fax

Clark Construction Group LLC
7500 Old Georgetown Rd ... Bethesda MD 20814 301-272-8100 272-1928
TF: 800-655-1330 ■ *Web:* www.clarkconstruction.com
Clarkson Construction Co
4133 Gardner Ave ... Kansas City MO 64120 816-483-8800 241-6823
Web: clarksonconstruction.com
Concrete General Inc
8000 Beechcraft Ave ... Gaithersburg MD 20879 301-948-4450 948-8273
Web: www.concretegeneral.com
Concrete Materials Inc 1201 W Russell St ... Sioux Falls SD 57118 605-357-6000 334-6221
Web: www.concretematerialscompany.com
Constructors Inc 1815 Y St ... Lincoln NE 68508 402-434-1764 434-1799
Web: www.constructorslincoln.com
Crowder Construction Company Inc
PO Box 30007 ... Charlotte NC 28230 704-372-3541 376-3573
TF: 800-849-2966 ■ *Web:* www.crowdercc.com
CS McCrossan Inc PO Box 1240 ... Maple Grove MN 55311 763-425-4167 425-1255
Web: www.mccrossan.com
Cummins Construction Company Inc
1420 W Chestnut Ave ... Enid OK 73702 580-233-6000
TF: 800-375-6001 ■ *Web:* www.cumminsasphalt.com
Curran Contracting Company Inc
286 Memorial Ct ... Crystal Lake IL 60014 815-455-5100 455-7894
Web: www.currancontracting.com
Curran Group Inc 286 Memorial Ct ... Crystal Lake IL 60014 815-455-5100 455-7894
Web: www.currangroup.com
Cutler Repaving Inc 921 E 27th St ... Lawrence KS 66046 785-843-1524 843-3942
Web: www.cutlerrepaving.com
CW Matthews Contracting Company Inc
1600 Kenview Dr ... Marietta GA 30061 770-422-7520 422-1068
Web: www.cwmatthews.com
D & J Enterprises Inc 3495 Lee Rd 10 ... Auburn AL 36832 334-821-1249
Web: www.djenterprises.net
D'Ambra Construction Co Inc
800 Jefferson Blvd ... Warwick RI 02886 401-737-1300
Web: www.d-ambra.com
DA Collins Construction Co Inc 269 Ballard Rd ... Wilton NY 12831 518-664-9855
Web: www.dacollins.com
David A Bramble Inc 705 Morgnec Rd ... Chestertown MD 21620 410-778-3023 778-3427
Web: www.davidabrambleinc.com
David Nelson Construction Co
3483 Alternate 19 ... Palm Harbor FL 34683 727-784-7624 786-8894
Web: www.nelson-construction.com
Dean Word Company Ltd
1245 River Rd PO Box 310330 ... New Braunfels TX 78131 830-625-2365 606-5008
TF: 800-683-3926 ■ *Web:* www.deanword.com
Delta Cos Inc 114 S Silver Springs Rd ... Cape Girardeau MO 63703 573-334-5261 334-9576
Web: www.deltacos.com
Delta Railroad Construction Inc
2648 W Prospect Rd PO Box 1398 ... Ashtabula OH 44004 440-992-2997 992-1311
Web: www.deltarr.com
Dement Construction Co PO Box 1812 ... Jackson TN 38302 731-424-6306 424-5308
Web: www.dementconstruction.com
DH Blattner & Sons Inc 392 County Rd 50 ... Avon MN 56310 320-356-7351 356-7392
Web: www.dhblattner.com
Dondlinger & Sons Construction Company Inc
2656 S Sheridan ... Wichita KS 67217 316-945-0555 945-9009
Web: dondlinger.biz
Driggs Co LLC 8700 Ashwood Dr ... Capitol Heights MD 20743 301-350-4000
Web: www.driggs.net
Duininck Inc 408 Sixth St PO Box 208 ... Prinsburg MN 56281 800-328-8949
TF General: 800-328-8949 ■ *Web:* www.duininckcompanies.com
Dunn Roadbuilders LLC 411 W Oak St PO Box 6560 ... Laurel MS 39441 601-649-4111 425-4644
Web: www.dunnroadbuilders.com
ECCO III Enterprises Inc
201 Saw Mill River Rd ... Yonkers NY 10701 914-963-3600 963-3989
Web: www.eccoiii.com
Edward Kraemer & Sons Inc 1 Plainview Rd ... Plain WI 53577 608-546-2311 546-2130
Web: www.edkraemer.com
Elam Construction Inc
556 Struthers Ave ... Grand Junction CO 81501 970-242-5370 245-7716
TF: 800-675-4598 ■ *Web:* www.elamconstruction.com
English Construction Co Inc 615 Church St ... Lynchburg VA 24504 434-845-0301 845-0306
Web: www.englishconst.com
Evans & Assoc Construction Company Inc
3320 N 14th St ... Ponca City OK 74601 580-765-6693
Web: evans-assoc.com
F H Paschen S N Nielsen Inc
8725 W Higgins Rd Ste 200 ... Chicago IL 60631 773-444-3474 693-0064
Web: www.fhpaschen.com
Facchina Construction Co Inc
102 Centennial St Ste 201 ... La Plata MD 20646 240-776-7000 776-7001
Web: www.facchina.com/ContactUs.aspx
FCI Constructors Inc
3070 I-70 Business Loop # A ... Grand Junction CO 81504 970-434-9093 434-7583
Web: www.fciol.com
Flatiron Constructors Inc
10090 E I25 Frontage Rd ... Longmont CO 80504 303-485-4050 485-3922
Web: www.flatironcorp.com
Fluor Constructors International Inc
352 Halton Rd ... Greenville SC 29607 864-234-7335 234-5476
FNF Construction Inc 115 S 48th St ... Tempe AZ 85281 480-784-2910 829-8607
Web: www.fnfinc.com
Fox Contractors Corp
5430 W Ferguson Rd Ste B ... Fort Wayne IN 46809 260-747-7461 747-7717
Web: www.foxcontractors.com
Francis O Day Construction Company Inc
850 E Gude Dr ... Rockville MD 20850 301-652-2400 340-6592
Web: www.foday.com
Fred Weber Inc
2320 Creve Coeur Mill Rd ... Maryland Heights MO 63043 314-344-0070 344-0970
TF: 866-739-8855 ■ *Web:* www.fredweberinc.com
Gallagher & Burk Inc 344 High St ... Oakland CA 94601 510-261-0466
Web: www.gallagherandburk.com

Company	City	State	ZIP	Phone	Fax
Gallagher Asphalt Corp 18100 S Indiana Ave	Thornton	IL	60476	708-877-7160	877-5222
TF: 800-536-7160 ■ *Web:* www.gallagherasphalt.com					
George & Lynch Inc 150 Lafferty Ln	Dover	DE	19901	302-736-3031	734-9743
Web: www.geolyn.com					
George Harms Construction Co Inc PO Box 817	Farmingdale	NJ	07727	732-938-4004	938-2782
Web: www.ghcci.com					
Gilbert Southern Corp 3555 Farnam St	Omaha	NE	68131	402-342-2052	271-2829*
**Fax:* Hum Res ■ *Web:* www.kiewit.com					
Glasgow Inc 104 Willow Grove Ave	Glenside	PA	19038	215-884-8800	884-1465
TF: 877-222-5514 ■ *Web:* www.glasgowinc.com					
Godbersen-Smith Construction Company Inc 5784 Iowa 175	Ida Grove	IA	51445	712-364-3388	364-4301
Gohmann Asphalt & Construction Inc PO Box 2428	Clarksville	IN	47131	812-282-1349	288-2168
Gowan Construction Inc PO Box 228	Oslo	MN	56744	701-699-5171	699-3400
Web: www.gowanconstruction.com					
Granite Construction Inc 585 W Beach St	Watsonville	CA	95076	831-724-1011	722-9657
NYSE: GVA ■ *Web:* www.graniteconstruction.com					
Gray & Sons Inc 430 W Padonia Rd	Timonium	MD	21093	410-771-4311	771-8125
TF: 800-254-0752 ■ *Web:* www.graynson.com					
Great Lakes Construction Co 2608 Great Lakes Way	Hinckley	OH	44233	330-220-3900	220-7670
Web: greatlakesway.com					
Gulf Asphalt Corp 4116 US Hwy 231	Panama City	FL	32404	850-785-4675	769-3456
Web: www.gaccontractors.com					
Halverson Construction Company Inc 620 N 19th St	Springfield	IL	62702	217-753-0027	753-1904
Web: www.halversonconstruction.com					
Hardrives of Delray Inc 2101 S Congress Ave	Delray Beach	FL	33445	561-278-0456	278-2147
Web: www.hardrivespaving.com					
Harper Co 1648 Petersburg Rd	Hebron	KY	41048	859-586-8890	586-8891
Web: harperco.com					
Harper Industries Inc 616 Northview St	Paducah	KY	42001	270-442-2753	443-9154
Web: www.harper1.com					
Hempt Bros Inc 205 Creek Rd	Camp Hill	PA	17011	717-737-3411	761-5019
Web: hemptbros.com					
Herzog Contracting Corp 600 S Riverside Rd	Saint Joseph	MO	64507	816-233-9001	233-9881
TF: 800-541-7846 ■ *Web:* www.herzog.com					
Hi-Way Paving Inc 4343 Weaver Ct N	Hilliard	OH	43026	614-876-1700	876-1899
Web: www.hiwaypaving.com					
Hinkle Contracting Corp 395 N Middletown Rd	Paris	KY	40361	859-987-3670	987-0727
Web: www.hinklecontracting.com					
Hoover Construction Co Inc PO Box 1007	Virginia	MN	55792	218-741-3280	741-6804
TF: 800-741-0970 ■ *Web:* www.hooverconstruction.biz					
HRI Inc 1750 W College Ave	State College	PA	16801	814-238-5071	238-0131
TF: 877-474-9999 ■ *Web:* www.hrico.com					
Hubbard Construction Co 1936 Lee Rd	Winter Park	FL	32789	407-645-5500	623-3865
Web: www.hubbard.com					
Hudson River Construction Co 1800 Church	Albany	NY	12202	518-434-6677	
Web: www.hudsonriverconstruction.com					
Hughes Group Inc 6200 E Hwy 62	Jeffersonville	IN	47130	812-282-4393	283-0142
Web: hughesdevelopmentllc.com					
Hunter Contracting Co 701 N Cooper Rd	Gilbert	AZ	85233	480-892-0521	892-4932
TF: 877-992-0521 ■ *Web:* www.huntercontracting.com					
Hutchens Construction Co 1007 Main St	Cassville	MO	65625	417-847-2489	847-5561
TF: 888-728-3482 ■ *Web:* www.hutchensconstruction.com					
India Globalization Capital Inc 4336 Montgomery Ave	Bethesda	MD	20814	301-983-0998	465-0273*
NYSE: IGC ■ **Fax Area Code:* 240 ■ *Web:* www.indiaglobalcap.com					
J Reese Construction Inc 10805 Thornmint Rd Ste 200	San Diego	CA	92127	858-592-6500	
Web: www.debinc.com					
Jack B Parson Cos 2350 South 1900 West	Ogden	UT	84401	801-731-1111	
TF: 888-672-7766 ■ *Web:* www.stakerparson.com					
James D Morrissey Inc 9119 Frankford Ave	Philadelphia	PA	19114	215-357-5505	338-3225
TF: 877-536-6857 ■ *Web:* www.jdm-inc.com					
James H Drew Corp 8701 Zionsville Rd	Indianapolis	IN	46268	317-876-3739	876-3829
Web: jameshdrew.com					
James McHugh Construction Co 1737 S Michigan Ave	Chicago	IL	60616	312-986-8000	431-8518
Web: www.mchughconstruction.com					
James W Glover Ltd 248 Sand Island Access Rd	Honolulu	HI	96819	808-591-8977	
Web: www.gloverltd.com					
Jay Dee Contractors Inc 38881 Schoolcraft Rd	Livonia	MI	48150	734-591-3400	464-6868
Web: www.jaydee.us					
JB Coxwell Contracting Inc 6741 Lloyd Rd W	Jacksonville	FL	32254	904-786-1120	783-2970
Web: www.jbcoxwell.com					
JD Abrams LP 111 Congress Ave Ste 2400	Austin	TX	78701	512-322-4000	322-4018
Web: www.jdabrams.com					
JF Shea Construction Inc 655 Brea Canyon Rd	Walnut	CA	91789	909-594-9500	883-3371
TF: 888-779-7333 ■ *Web:* www.jfshea.com					
JF White Contracting Co 10 Burr St	Framingham	MA	01701	508-879-4700	558-0460*
**Fax Area Code:* 617 ■ *TF:* 866-539-4400 ■ *Web:* www.jfwhite.com					
JLB Contracting LP 7151 Randol Mill Rd	Fort Worth	TX	76120	817-261-2991	261-3044
John Carlo Inc 20848 Hall Rd	Clinton Township	MI	48038	586-741-5362	
John R Jurgensen Co 11641 Mosteller Rd	Cincinnati	OH	45241	513-771-0820	771-2678
Web: www.jrjnet.com					
Johnson Bros Corp 5476 Lithia Pinecrest Rd	Lithia	FL	33547	813-685-5101	685-5939
Web: www.johnson-bros.com					
K-Five Construction Corp 13769 Main St	Lemont	IL	60439	630-257-5600	257-6788
Web: k-five.com					
Kamminga & Roodvoets Inc 3435 Broadmoor Ave SE	Grand Rapids	MI	49512	616-949-0800	949-1894
Kankakee Valley Construction Company Inc 4356 W SR 17	Kankakee	IL	60901	815-937-8700	937-0402
Web: www.kvcci.com					
KF Jacobsen & Co 4315 SE McLoughlin Blvd	Portland	OR	97202	503-239-5532	
Kiewit Corp 3555 Farnam St	Omaha	NE	68131	402-342-2052	271-2829*
**Fax:* Hum Res ■ *Web:* www.kiewit.com					
Kiska Construction Corp USA 10-34 44th Dr	Long Island	NY	11101	718-943-0400	943-0401
Web: www.kiskagroup.com					
Knife River Corp 1150 W Century Ave	Bismarck	ND	58506	701-530-1400	530-1451
Web: www.kniferiver.com					
Kokosing Construction Company Inc 17531 Waterford Rd PO Box 226	Fredericktown	OH	43019	740-694-6315	694-1481
TF: 800-800-6315 ■ *Web:* www.kokosing.biz					
Koss Construction Co 5830 SW Drury Ln	Topeka	KS	66604	785-228-2928	228-2927
Web: kossconstruction.com					
Lake Erie Construction Co 25 S Norwalk Rd	Norwalk	OH	44857	419-668-3302	
Web: lec-co.com					
Lakeside Industries Inc 6505 226th Pl SE # 200	Issaquah	WA	98027	425-313-2600	313-2620
Web: www.lakesideind.com					
Lane Construction Company Inc 1 Indian Rd	Denville	NJ	07834	973-586-2700	586-2965
Web: www.thelanegroup.us					
Lane Construction Corp 90 Fieldstone Ct	Cheshire	CT	06410	203-235-3351	237-4260
Web: www.laneconstruct.com					
Las Vegas Paving Corp 4420 S Decatur Blvd	Las Vegas	NV	89103	702-251-5800	251-1968
Web: www.lasvegaspaving.com					
Lawrence Construction Company Inc 9002 N Moore Rd	Littleton	CO	80125	303-791-5642	791-5647
Web: lawrence-construction.com					
LC Whitford Company Inc 164 N Main St	Wellsville	NY	14895	585-593-3601	593-1876
Web: www.lcwhitford.com					
Lee Construction Co PO Box 7667	Charlotte	NC	28241	704-588-5272	588-1535
Web: www.leecarolinas.com					
Lehigh Asphalt Paving & Construction Co Inc PO Box 549	Tamaqua	PA	18252	570-668-4303	668-5910
TF: 877-222-5514 ■ *Web:* www.glasgowinc.com/subsidiaries.aspx					
LH Lacy Co 1880 Crown Dr Ste 1200	Dallas	TX	75234	214-357-0146	350-0662
Web: www.lhlacy.com					
Lunda Construction Company Inc 620 GebhaRdt Rd	Black River Falls	WI	54615	715-284-9491	284-9146
Web: www.lundaconstruction.com					
Manatt's Inc 1775 Old 6 Rd	Brooklyn	IA	52211	641-522-9206	522-5594
TF: 800-532-1121 ■ *Web:* www.manatts.com					
Markham Contracting Company Inc 22820 N 19th Ave	Phoenix	AZ	85027	623-869-9100	869-9400
Web: www.markhamcontracting.com					
Martin K. Eby Construction Co 610 N Main Ste 500 Ste 500	Wichita	KS	67203	316-268-3500	268-3649
Web: www.ebycorp.com					
Mathy Construction Co Inc 920 Tenth Ave N	Onalaska	WI	54650	608-783-6411	783-4311
TF: 800-822-5246 ■ *Web:* mathy.com					
Matich Corp 1596 Harry Sheppard Blvd	San Bernardino	CA	92408	909-382-7400	382-0191
TF: 800-404-4975 ■ *Web:* www.matichcorp.com					
Maymead Inc 1995 Roan Creek Rd	Mountain City	TN	37683	423-727-2000	
Web: www.maymead.com					
McCarthy Improvement Company Inc 5401 Victoria Ave	Davenport	IA	52807	563-359-0321	344-3740
Web: www.mccarthyimprovement.com					
McCourt Equipment Company Inc 60 K St Ste 2	Boston	MA	02127	617-269-2330	
Web: www.mccourtconstruction.com					
MCM Construction Inc 6413 32nd St PO Box 620	North Highlands	CA	95660	916-334-1221	334-8355
Web: www.mcmconstructioninc.com					
McMurry Ready Mix Co 5684 Old W Yellowstone Hwy	Casper	WY	82604	307-473-9581	235-0144
Web: www.mcmurryreadymix.com					
Meadow Valley Corp 4602 E Thomas	Phoenix	AZ	85018	602-437-5400	437-1681
Web: www.meadowvalley.com					
Merco Inc 1117 Rt 31 S	Lebanon	NJ	08833	908-730-8622	730-6472
Web: www.mercoinc.com					
Mica Corp 5750 N Riverside Dr	Fort Worth	TX	76137	817-847-6121	847-6831
Michael Baker Corp 100 Airsite Dr Airsite Business Pk	Moon Township	PA	15108	412-269-6300	463-0503*
NYSE: BKR ■ **Fax Area Code:* 757 ■ *TF:* 800-553-1153 ■ *Web:* www.mbakercorp.com					
Michigan Paving & Materials Co 1100 Market Ave SW	Grand Rapids	MI	49503	616-459-9545	
Web: www.michiganpaving.com					
Mid Valley School District 52 Underwood Rd	Throop	PA	18512	570-307-1150	307-1107
Web: www.mvsd.us					
Milestone Contractors LP 3410 S 650 E	Elizabethtown	IN	47232	812-579-5248	579-6703
TF: 800-377-7727 ■ *Web:* www.milestonelp.com					
Mountain States Constructors Inc 3601 Pan American Rd NE	Albuquerque	NM	87107	505-292-0108	790-1503*
**Fax Area Code:* 303					
NAB Construction Corp 112-20 14th Ave	College Point	NY	11356	718-762-0001	961-3789
Web: www.nabconstruction.com					
Nagle Paving Co 39525 W 13 Mile Rd 300	Novi	MI	48377	248-553-0600	553-0669
Web: www.naglepaving.com					
Nesbitt Contracting Company Inc 100 S Price Rd	Tempe	AZ	85281	480-423-7600	423-7680
Web: www.nesbitts.com					
Newell Roadbuilders Inc 13266 US Hwy 31	Hope Hull	AL	36043	334-288-2702	288-2721
Northern Improvement Co 4000 12th Ave NW	Fargo	ND	58108	701-277-1225	277-1516
Web: www.nicnd.com/nic/nic1.html					
Oakgrove Construction Inc 6900 Seneca St	Elma	NY	14059	716-652-2200	655-3919
TF: 866-435-1499 ■ *Web:* www.oakgroveconst.com					
Odebrecht Construction Inc 201 Alhambra Cir Ste 1000	Coral Gables	FL	33134	305-341-8800	569-1500
TF: 800-771-0001 ■ *Web:* odebrecht.com					
Oldcastle Materials Inc 900 Ashwood Pkwy Ste 700	Atlanta	GA	30338	770-522-5600	522-5608
Web: www.apac.com					
P Flanigan & Sons Inc 2444 Loch Raven Rd	Baltimore	MD	21218	410-467-5900	467-3127
Web: www.pflanigan.com					
Palmer Paving Corp 25 Blanchard St	Palmer	MA	01069	413-283-8354	289-1939
TF: 800-244-8354 ■ *Web:* www.palmerpaving.com					
Parsons Corp 100 W Walnut St	Pasadena	CA	91124	626-440-2000	440-2630
Web: www.parsons.com					

Phone Fax

Pavex Inc 4400 Gettysburg Rd Camp Hill PA 17011 717-761-1502 761-0329
Web: pavexinc.com
PCiRoads LLC 14123 42nd St NE Saint Michael MN 55376 763-497-6100 497-6101
Web: www.pciroads.com
Peckham Industries Inc 20 Haarlem Ave White Plains NY 10603 914-949-2000 949-2075
Web: www.peckham.com
Perry Engineering Company Inc 1945 Millwood Pk Winchester VA 22602 540-667-4310 667-7618
Web: www.perryeng.com
Peter Baker & Son Co 1349 Rockland Rd Lake Bluff IL 60044 847-362-3663 362-0707
Web: www.peterbaker.com
Petricca Industries Inc 550 Cheshire Rd Pittsfield MA 01201 413-442-6926 499-9930
Web: unistresscorp.com
Phillips Contracting Co PO Box 2069 Columbus MS 39704 662-328-6250 329-3291
Web: www.phillipscontracting.com
Pike Industries Inc 3 Eastgate Pk Rd Belmont NH 03220 603-527-5100 527-5101
TF: 800-283-0803 ■ *Web:* pikeindustries.com
PJ Keating Co 998 Reservoir Rd Lunenburg MA 01462 978-582-5200 582-7130
TF: 800-441-4119 ■ *Web:* www.pjkeating.com
PKF-Mark III Inc 17 Black Smith Rd ste 101 Newtown PA 18940 215-968-5031 968-3829
Web: www.pkfmarkiii.com
Plote Inc 1100 Brandt Dr Hoffman Estates IL 60192 847-695-9300 695-9317
Web: www.plote.com
Prince Contracting LLC 10210 Highland Manor Dr Ste 110 Tampa FL 33610 813-699-5900 699-5901
Web: www.princecontracting.com
Pulice Construction Inc 2033 W Mountain View Rd Phoenix AZ 85021 602-944-2241 944-8861
Web: www.pulice.com
Ranger Construction Industries Inc 101 Sansbury's Way West Palm Beach FL 33411 561-793-9400 790-4332
TF: 800-969-9402 ■ *Web:* www.rangerconstruction.com
Ray Bell Construction Company Inc 255 Wilson Pake Cir Brentwood TN 37027 615-373-4343 373-9224
Reeves Construction Co Inc 101 Sheraton Ct Macon GA 31210 478-474-9092 474-9192
TF: 800-743-0593 ■ *Web:* www.reevescc.com
Reilly Construction Co Inc PO Box 99 Ossian IA 52161 563-532-9211 532-9759
Web: www.reilly-construction.com
Reliable Contracting Co Inc 2410 Evergreen Rd Ste 200 Gambrills MD 21054 410-987-0313
TF: 800-492-4357 ■ *Web:* www.reliablecontracting.com
Richard F Kline Inc 7700 Grove Rd Frederick MD 21704 301-662-8211 662-0041
Web: www.rfkline.com
Rieth-Riley Construction Co Inc 3626 Elkhart Rd PO Box 477 Goshen IN 46526 574-875-5183 875-8405
Web: rieth-riley.com
Rifenburg Construction Inc 159 Brick Church Rd Troy NY 12180 518-279-3265 279-4260
Web: www.rifenburg.com
Rogers Group Inc 421 Great Cir Rd Nashville TN 37228 615-242-0585
Web: www.rogersgroupincint.com
Royal Contracting Company Ltd 677 Ahua St Honolulu HI 96819 808-839-9006 839-7571
Web: www.royalcontracting.com
RS Audley Inc 1113 Route 3A Bow NH 03304 603-224-7724 225-7614
Web: www.audleyconstruction.com
Ruhlin Company Inc PO Box 190 Sharon Center OH 44274 330-239-2800 239-1828
Web: www.ruhlin.com
Sargent Corp 378 Bennoch Rd Stillwater ME 04489 207-827-4435 827-6150
TF: 800-533-1812 ■ *Web:* www.sargent-corp.com
Schiavone Construction Company Inc 150 Meadowlands Pkwy 3rd Fl Secaucus NJ 07094 201-867-5070 866-6132
Web: www.schiavoneconstruction.com
Scott Construction Inc 560 Munroe Ave Lake Delton WI 53940 608-254-2555 254-2249
TF: 800-843-1556 ■ *Web:* www.scottconstruct.com
Scruggs Company Inc PO Box 2065 Valdosta GA 31604 229-242-2388 242-7109
TF: 800-230-7263 ■ *Web:* scruggscompany.com
Shelly Co 80 Pk Dr Thornville OH 43076 740-246-6315 246-4715
Web: www.shellyco.com
Sherwood Construction Company Inc 3219 W May St Wichita KS 67213 316-943-0211 943-3772
Web: www.sherwoodcompanies.com
Shirley Contracting Corp 8435 Backlick Rd Lorton VA 22079 703-550-8100 550-7897
Web: www.shirleycontracting.com
Sioux Falls Construction Company Inc 800 S Seventh Ave Sioux Falls SD 57101 605-336-1640 334-9342
Web: journeyconstruction.com
Skanska USA Inc 1616 Whitestone Expy Whitestone NY 11356 718-767-2600 767-2663
Web: www.skanska.com
Skanska USA Inc 295 Bendix Rd Virginia Beach VA 23452 757-420-4140
Web: skanska.com
Sletten Construction Company Inc 1000 25th St N Great Falls MT 59401 406-761-7920 761-0923
Web: www.slettencompanies.com
Sloan Construction Co Inc 250 Plemmons Rd Duncan SC 29334 864-968-2250 968-2255
Web: www.sloan-construction.com
Staker Parson Cos 2350 South 1900 West Ogden UT 84401 801-731-1111
TF: 888-672-7766 ■ *Web:* stakerparson.com
Standard Concrete Products Inc (SCP) PO Box 1360 Columbus GA 31902 706-322-3274 322-7856
Web: www.standardconcrete.net
Steve P Rados Inc 2002 E McFadden Ave Ste 200 PO Box 15128 Santa Ana CA 92705 714-835-4612 835-2186
Web: www.radoscompanies.com
Suburban Grading & Utilities Inc 1190 Harmony Rd Norfolk VA 23502 757-461-1800
Web: www.suburbangrading.com
Sukut Construction Inc 4010 W Chandler Ave Santa Ana CA 92704 714-540-5351 545-2438
TF: 888-785-8801 ■ *Web:* www.sukut.com
Sully-Miller Contracting Co Inc 135 S State Collage Blvd Ste 400 Brea CA 92821 714-578-9600 578-2850*
**Fax:* Hum Res ■ *Web:* sully-miller.com
Summers-Taylor Inc 300 W Elk Ave Elizabethton TN 37643 423-543-3181
Web: summerstaylor.com
Sundt Construction Inc 2015 W River Rd Ste 101 Tucson AZ 85704 520-750-4600
TF: 800-467-5544 ■ *Web:* www.sundt.com

Superior Construction Company Inc 2045 E Dunes Hwy PO Box 64888 Gary IN 46401 219-886-3728 885-4328
Web: www.superior-construction.com
Sweeping Services of Texas LP 3324 Roy Orr Blvd Grand Prairie TX 75050 817-268-4100
Web: wastepartners.com
TJ Lambrecht Construction Inc 10 Gougar Rd Joliet IL 60432 815-727-9211 727-6421
Tony Angelo Cement Construction Co 46850 Grand River Ave Novi MI 48374 248-344-4000 344-4048
Traylor Bros Inc 835 N Congress Ave Evansville IN 47715 812-477-1542 474-3223
TF: 866-895-1491 ■ *Web:* www.traylor.com
Trumbull Corp 1020 Lebanon Rd West Mifflin PA 15122 412-462-9300
Web: www.trumbullcorp.com
Tutor Perini Corp 15901 Olden St Sylmar CA 91342 508-628-2000
Web: www.tutorperini.com
United Contractors Midwest Inc PO Box 13420 Springfield IL 62791 217-546-6192 546-1904
Web: www.ucm.biz
Vecellio & Grogan Inc 2251 Robert C Byrd Dr Beckley WV 25802 304-252-6575 252-4131
TF: 800-255-6575 ■ *Web:* www.vecelliogrogan.com
Walsh Group Inc 929 W Adams St Chicago IL 60607 312-563-5400 563-5466
TF: 800-957-1842 ■ *Web:* walshgroup.com
Washington Corp PO Box 16630 Missoula MT 59808 406-523-1300 523-1399
Web: www.washcorp.com
WE Blain & Sons Inc 98 Pearce Rd Mount Olive MS 39119 601-797-4551
Web: blain-co.com
WG Yates & Sons Construction Co Inc 1 Gulley Ave Philadelphia MS 39350 601-656-5411 656-8958
Web: www.wgyates.com
Williams Bros Construction Company Inc 3800 Milam St Houston TX 77006 713-522-9821 520-5247
Web: www.wbctx.com
Windsor Service 2415 Kutztown Rd Reading PA 19605 610-929-0716
Web: www.windsorstore.com
Winzinger Inc 1704 Marne Hwy PO Box 537 Hainesport NJ 08036 609-267-8600 267-4079
Web: www.winzinger.com
WM Brode Co 100 Elizabeth St PO Box 299 Newcomerstown OH 43832 740-498-5121 498-8553
Web: www.wmbrode.com
Yantis Co 3611 Paesano's Pkwy Ste 300 San Antonio TX 78231 210-655-3780 655-8526
Web: www.yantiscompany.com
Yonkers Contracting Company Inc 969 Midland Ave Yonkers NY 10704 914-965-1500 378-8885
Web: www.yonkerscontractingco.com
Zachry Holdings Inc 527 Logwood Ave San Antonio TX 78221 210-588-5000
Web: www.zachrygroup.com

188-5 Marine Construction

Phone Fax

Anderson-Tully 1725 N Washington St Vicksburg MS 39183 601-629-3283 629-3284
Web: www.andersontully.com
Andrie Inc 561 E Western Ave Muskegon MI 49442 231-728-2226 726-6747
TF: 800-722-2421 ■ *Web:* www.andrietg.com
Bellingham Marine Industries Inc 1001 C St Bellingham WA 98225 360-676-2800 734-2417
TF: 800-733-5679 ■ *Web:* www.bellingham-marine.com
Choctaw Transportation Co Inc 1311 E Ct Dyersburg TN 38025 731-286-0012
Web: choctawtrans.com
Civil Constructors Inc 2283 US Hwy 20 E Freeport IL 61032 815-235-2200
Web: www.helmgroup.com
Corey Delta Inc 261 Arthur Rd PO Box 637 Martinez CA 94553 707-747-7500
Web: www.coreydelta.com
DeSilva Gates Construction Inc 11555 Dublin Blvd Dublin CA 94568 925-829-9220 803-4268
Web: www.desilvagates.com
Dot-Line Transportation PO Box 8739 Fountain Valley CA 92728 323-780-9010 780-1552
TF: 800-423-3780 ■ *Web:* www.dotline.net
Frontier-Kemper Constructors Inc 1695 Allen Rd Evansville IN 47710 812-426-2741 428-0337
TF: 877-554-8600 ■ *Web:* www.frontierkemper.com
Granite Construction Inc 585 W Beach St Watsonville CA 95076 831-724-1011 722-9657
NYSE: GVA ■ *Web:* www.graniteconstruction.com
Great Lakes Dredge & Dock Co 2122 York Rd Oak Brook IL 60523 630-574-3000 574-2909
NASDAQ: GLDD ■ *Web:* www.gldd.com
Hawaiian Dredging & Construction Co 201 Merchant St Honolulu HI 96813 808-735-3211 735-7416
Web: www.hdcc.com
James Steele Construction Co 1410 Sylvan St Saint Paul MN 55117 651-488-6755 488-4787
Web: www.jamessteeleconstruction.com
JR Filanc Construction Company Inc 740 N Andreasen Dr Escondido CA 92029 760-941-7130 941-3969
TF: 877-225-5428 ■ *Web:* www.filanc.com
Lane Construction Corp 90 Fieldstone Ct Cheshire CT 06410 203-235-3351 237-4260
Web: www.laneconstruct.com
Luhr Bros Inc 250 W Sand Bank Rd Columbia IL 62236 618-281-4106 281-4288
Web: www.luhr.com
Manson Construction Co 5209 E Marginal Way S Seattle WA 98134 206-762-0850 764-8590
Web: www.mansonconstruction.com
Massman Construction Co 8901 State Line Rd Ste 240 PO Box 8458 Kansas City MO 64114 816-523-1000 333-2109
Web: www.massman.net
McDermott International Inc 757 N Eldridge Pkwy Houston TX 77079 281-870-5000
NYSE: MDR ■ *Web:* www.mcdermott.com
Norris School District 6940 Calloway Dr Bakersfield CA 93312 661-387-7000 399-9750
TF: 800-877-8339 ■ *Web:* www.norris.k12.ca.us
P Gioioso & Sons Inc 50 Sprague St Hyde Park MA 02136 617-364-5800 364-9462
Web: www.pgioioso.com
Skanska USA Inc 295 Bendix Rd Virginia Beach VA 23452 757-420-4140
Web: skanska.com

				Phone	Fax
TG Construction Inc 139 Nevada St *Web:* www.tgconst.com	El Segundo	CA	90245	310-640-0220	640-2907
Washington Corp PO Box 16630 *Web:* www.washcorp.com	Missoula	MT	59808	406-523-1300	523-1399
Weeks Marine Inc 4 Commerce Dr *Web:* www.weeksmarine.com	Cranford	NJ	07016	908-272-4010	272-4740

188-6 Mining Construction

				Phone	Fax
AME Inc 2467 Coltharp Rd PO Box 909 *TF:* 800-849-7766 ■ *Web:* www.ameonline.com	Fort Mill	SC	29716	803-548-7766	548-7448
Frontier-Kemper Constructors Inc 1695 Allen Rd *TF:* 877-554-8600 ■ *Web:* www.frontierkemper.com	Evansville	IN	47710	812-426-2741	428-0337
Sundt Construction Inc 2015 W River Rd Ste 101 *TF:* 800-467-5544 ■ *Web:* www.sundt.com	Tucson	AZ	85704	520-750-4600	

188-7 Plant Construction

				Phone	Fax
Angelo Iafrate Construction Co 26300 Sherwood Ave *Web:* www.iafrate.com	Warren	MI	48091	586-756-1070	756-0467
Bancroft Construction Co 1300 N Grant Ave Ste 110 *Web:* www.bancroftconstruction.com	Wilmington	DE	19806	302-655-3434	655-4599
Barton Malow Enterprises Inc 26500 American Dr *Web:* www.bartonmalow.com	Southfield	MI	48034	248-436-5000	436-5001
Bechtel North America 3000 Post Oak Blvd *Web:* www.bechtel.com	Houston	TX	77056	713-235-2000	960-9031
Bechtel Petroleum & Chemical 3000 Post Oak Blvd *Web:* www.bechtel.com	Houston	TX	77056	713-235-2000	
Big-D Construction Corp 404 West 400 South *Web:* www.big-d.com	Salt Lake City	UT	84101	801-415-6000	415-6900
Black & Veatch 11401 Lamar Ave *Web:* www.bv.com	Overland Park	KS	66211	913-458-2000	
Bowen Engineering Corp 8802 N Meridian St *Web:* www.bowenengineering.com	Indianapolis	IN	46260	317-842-2616	841-4257
Brasfield & Gorrie LLC 3021 Seventh Ave S *TF:* 800-239-8017 ■ *Web:* www.brasfieldgorrie.com	Birmingham	AL	35233	205-328-4000	251-1304
Brinderson 3330 Harbor Blvd Ste 100 *Web:* www.brinderson.com	Costa Mesa	CA	92626	714-466-7100	466-7320
Cajun Constructors Inc 15635 Airline Hwy *TF:* 877-401-5911 ■ *Web:* cajunusa.com	Baton Rouge	LA	70817	225-753-5857	751-9777
CCC Group Inc 5797 Dietrich Rd *Web:* www.cccgroupinc.com	San Antonio	TX	78219	210-661-4251	661-6060
Cianbro Corp 335 Hunnewell Ave *TF:* 866-242-6276 ■ *Web:* www.cianbro.com	Pittsfield	ME	04967	866-242-6276	
Cives Corp 1825 Old Alabama Rd Ste 200 *Web:* www.cives.com	Roswell	GA	30076	770-993-4424	998-2361
Civil Constructors Inc 2283 US Hwy 20 E *Web:* www.helmgroup.com	Freeport	IL	61032	815-235-2200	
Clark Construction Co 3535 Moores River Dr *Web:* www.clarkcc.com	Lansing	MI	48911	517-372-0940	372-0668
Clark Construction Group LLC 7500 Old Georgetown Rd *TF:* 800-655-1330 ■ *Web:* www.clarkconstruction.com	Bethesda	MD	20814	301-272-8100	272-1928
Day & Zimmermann Group Inc 1818 Market St *TF:* 877-319-0270 ■ *Web:* www.dayzim.com	Philadelphia	PA	19130	215-299-8000	
English Construction Co Inc 615 Church St *Web:* www.englishconst.com	Lynchburg	VA	24504	434-845-0301	845-0306
Fluor Daniel Inc 3 Polaris Way *Web:* www.fluor.com	Aliso Viejo	CA	92698	949-349-2000	349-2585
Forcum Lannom Contractors LLC 350 US Hwy 51 Bypass S *Web:* www.forcumlannom.com	Dyersburg	TN	38024	731-287-4700	287-4701
Gilbane Bldg Co 7 Jackson Walkway *TF:* 800-445-2263 ■ *Web:* www.gilbaneco.com	Providence	RI	02903	401-456-5800	
Gray Construction 10 Quality St *TF:* 800-814-8468 ■ *Web:* www.gray.com	Lexington	KY	40507	859-281-5000	252-5300
H & M Construction Company Inc 50 Security Dr *Web:* hmcompany.com	Jackson	TN	38305	731-664-6300	
Haskell Co 111 Riverside Ave *TF:* 800-622-4326 ■ *Web:* haskell.com	Jacksonville	FL	32202	904-791-4500	791-4699
Hoffman Construction Corp 805 SW Broadway Ste 2100 *Web:* www.hoffmancorp.com	Portland	OR	97205	503-221-8811	221-8934
Hunt Construction Group 2450 S Tibbs Ave *Web:* www.huntconstructiongroup.com	Indianapolis	IN	46241	317-227-7800	227-7810
Hunter Contracting Co 701 N Cooper Rd *TF:* 877-992-0521 ■ *Web:* www.huntercontracting.com	Gilbert	AZ	85233	480-892-0521	892-4932
JF White Contracting Co 10 Burr St **Fax Area Code:* 617 ■ *TF:* 866-539-4400 ■ *Web:* www.jfwhite.com	Framingham	MA	01701	508-879-4700	558-0460*
Johnson Bros Corp 5476 Lithia Pinecrest Rd *Web:* www.johnson-bros.com	Lithia	FL	33547	813-685-5101	685-5939
Koch Specialty Plant Services 12221 E Sam Houston Pkwy N *TF:* 800-765-9177 ■ *Web:* www.kochservices.com	Houston	TX	77044	713-427-7700	427-7747
Louis P Ciminelli Construction Corp 2421 Main St *Web:* www.lpciminelli.com	Buffalo	NY	14202	716-855-1200	854-6655
MECS Inc 14522 S Outer 40 Rd *Web:* www.mecsglobal.com	Chesterfield	MO	63017	314-275-5700	275-5701
Northeast Remsco Construction Inc 1433 Hwy 34 S Bldg B1 *TF:* 800-879-8204 ■ *Web:* www.northeastconstruction.org	Farmingdale	NJ	07727	732-557-6100	736-8900
Parsons Corp 100 W Walnut St *Web:* www.parsons.com	Pasadena	CA	91124	626-440-2000	440-2630
Performance Contractors Inc 9901 Pecu Ln *Web:* www.performance-br.com	Baton Rouge	LA	70810	225-751-4156	751-8409
Pizzagalli Construction Co 193 Tilley Dr *Web:* www.pcconstruction.com	South Burlington	VT	05403	802-658-4100	
Powell Technologies 3622 Bristol Hwy *Web:* powell-tech.com	Johnson City	TN	37601	423-282-0111	282-1541
Rudolph & Sletten Inc 1600 Seaport Blvd Ste 350 *Web:* www.rsconstruction.com	Redwood City	CA	94063	650-216-3600	599-9112
Sargent Corp 378 Bennoch Rd *TF:* 800-533-1812 ■ *Web:* www.sargent-corp.com	Stillwater	ME	04489	207-827-4435	827-6150
Shook Construction 4977 Northcutt Pl *Web:* www.shookconstruction.com	Dayton	OH	45414	937-276-6666	276-6676
SJ Amoroso Construction Co Inc 390 Bridge Pkwy *Web:* www.sjamoroso.com	Redwood Shores	CA	94065	650-654-1900	654-9002
Skanska USA Bldg Inc 389 Interpace Pkwy 5th Fl *Web:* www.usa.skanska.com	Parsippany	NJ	07054	973-753-3500	753-3499
Skanska USA Inc 1616 Whitestone Expy *Web:* www.skanska.com	Whitestone	NY	11356	718-767-2600	767-2663
Todd & Sargent Inc 2905 SE Fifth St *Web:* www.tsargent.com	Ames	IA	50010	515-232-0442	232-0682
Turner Industries Group LLC 8687 United Plaza Blvd **Fax:* Mail Rm ■ *TF:* 800-288-6503 ■ *Web:* www.turner-industries.com	Baton Rouge	LA	70809	225-922-5050	922-5055*
Ventech Engineers Inc 1149 Ellsworth Dr *Web:* www.ventech-eng.com	Pasadena	TX	77506	713-477-0201	477-2420
Walbridge Aldinger Co 777 Woodward Ave #300 *Web:* www.walbridge.com	Detroit	MI	48226	313-963-8000	963-8150
Walsh Group Inc 929 W Adams St *TF:* 800-957-1842 ■ *Web:* walshgroup.com	Chicago	IL	60607	312-563-5400	563-5466
WG Yates & Sons Construction Co Inc 1 Gulley Ave *Web:* www.wgyates.com	Philadelphia	MS	39350	601-656-5411	656-8958
Whiting-Turner Contracting Co 300 E Joppa Rd *Web:* www.whiting-turner.com	Towson	MD	21286	410-821-1100	337-5770
Zachry Holdings Inc 527 Logwood Ave *Web:* www.zachrygroup.com	San Antonio	TX	78221	210-588-5000	

188-8 Railroad Construction

				Phone	Fax
Acme Construction Co Inc 7695 Bond St *Web:* www.acmerrinc.com	Cleveland	OH	44139	440-232-7474	232-7477
Atlas Railroad Construction LLC 1370 Washington Pike Ste 202 **Fax Area Code:* 585 ■ *Web:* gwrr.com	Bridgeville	PA	15017	412-677-2020	785-6206*
Campbell Earl Construction Co 6060 Armour Dr	Houston	TX	77020	713-673-6208	672-9614
Parsons Corp 100 W Walnut St *Web:* www.parsons.com	Pasadena	CA	91124	626-440-2000	440-2630
RailWorks Corp 5 Penn Plz *Web:* www.railworks.com	New York	NY	10001	212-502-7900	
RW Summers Railroad Contractor Inc 3693 E Gandy Rd *Web:* www.rwsummers.net	Bartow	FL	33830	863-533-8107	533-8100
Snelson Company Inc 601 W State St *Web:* www.snelsonco.com	Sedro Woolley	WA	98284	360-856-6511	856-5816
Swanson Contracting Co 11701 S Mayfield Ave *Web:* www.swansoncontracting.com	Alsip	IL	60803	708-388-0623	388-9986
Trac-Work Inc 3801 N Ste 1-45 *Web:* www.trac-work.com	Ennis	TX	75119	972-878-2232	
Tutor-Saliba Corp 15901 Olden St *Web:* www.tutorsaliba.com	Sylmar	CA	91342	818-362-8391	367-5379
WE Yoder Inc 41 S Maple St *TF:* 800-889-5149 ■ *Web:* www.weyoderinc.com	Kutztown	PA	19530	610-683-7383	683-8638

188-9 Refinery (Petroleum or Oil) Construction

				Phone	Fax
ARB Inc 26000 Commercentre Dr *Web:* www.arbinc.com	Lake Forest	CA	92630	949-598-9242	454-7190
Austin Industrial Inc 2801 E 13th S PO Box 87888 *TF:* 866-308-2592 ■ *Web:* www.austin-ind.com	La Porte	TX	77571	713-641-3400	641-2424
Bechtel North America 3000 Post Oak Blvd *Web:* www.bechtel.com	Houston	TX	77056	713-235-2000	960-9031
Bechtel Petroleum & Chemical 3000 Post Oak Blvd *Web:* www.bechtel.com	Houston	TX	77056	713-235-2000	
Fluor Daniel Inc 3 Polaris Way *Web:* www.fluor.com	Aliso Viejo	CA	92698	949-349-2000	349-2585
McDermott International Inc 757 N Eldridge Pkwy *NYSE:* MDR ■ *Web:* www.mcdermott.com	Houston	TX	77079	281-870-5000	
Oscar J Boldt Construction Co 2525 N Roemer Rd *Web:* www.theboldtcompany.com	Appleton	WI	54911	920-739-6321	
Parsons Corp 100 W Walnut St *Web:* www.parsons.com	Pasadena	CA	91124	626-440-2000	440-2630
Ref-Chem LP 1128 S Grandview PO Box 2588 *Web:* www.ref-chem.com	Odessa	TX	79761	432-332-8531	332-3325
Snelson Company Inc 601 W State St *Web:* www.snelsonco.com	Sedro Woolley	WA	98284	360-856-6511	856-5816

Phone Fax

Turner Industries Group LLC
8687 United Plaza Blvd. Baton Rouge LA 70809 225-922-5050 922-5055*
*Fax: Mail Rm ■ TF: 800-288-6503 ■ Web: www.turner-industries.com

Underground Construction Company Inc
5145 Industrial Way Benicia CA 94510 707-746-8800 746-1314
TF: 800-227-2314 ■ Web: www.undergrnd.com

Zachry Holdings Inc 527 Logwood Ave San Antonio TX 78221 210-588-5000
Web: www.zachrygroup.com

188-10 Water & Sewer Lines, Pipelines, Power Lines Construction

Phone Fax

Amzak Corp 1 N Federal Hwy Ste 400 Boca Raton FL 33432 561-953-4164 338-7677
Web: www.amzak.com

Angelo Iafrate Construction Co
26300 Sherwood Ave Warren MI 48091 586-756-1070 756-0467
Web: www.iafrate.com

Argonaut Constructors Inc
1236 Central Ave PO Box 639 Santa Rosa CA 95402 707-542-4862 542-3210
Web: www.argonautconstructors.com

Aubrey Silvey Enterprises Inc
371 Hamp Jones Rd Carrollton GA 30117 770-834-0738 834-1055
Web: www.silvey.com

B Frank Joy LLC 5355 Kilmer Pl Hyattsville MD 20781 301-779-9400 699-6013
TF: 800-992-3569 ■ Web: www.bfjoy.com

Balfour Beatty Inc
999 Peachtree St NE Ste 200 Atlanta GA 30309 404-875-0356 607-1784
Web: www.balfourbeatty.com

Bancker Construction Corp
218 Blydenburgh Rd Islandia NY 11749 631-582-8880 582-3698
Web: www.bancker.com

Barnard Construction Company Inc PO Box 99 Bozeman MT 59771 406-586-1995 586-3530
Web: www.barnard-inc.com

Bechtel North America 3000 Post Oak Blvd Houston TX 77056 713-235-2000 960-9031
Web: www.bechtel.com

BRB Contractors Inc 3805 NW 25th St Topeka KS 66618 785-232-1245 235-8045
TF: 800-722-3145 ■ Web: www.brbcontractors.com

Cajun Constructors Inc 15635 Airline Hwy Baton Rouge LA 70817 225-753-5857 751-9777
TF: 877-401-5911 ■ Web: cajunusa.com

Callas Contractors Inc
10549 Downsville Pk Hagerstown MD 21740 301-739-8400 739-7065
Web: www.callascontractors.com

Cianbro Corp 335 Hunnewell Ave Pittsfield ME 04967 866-242-6276
TF: 866-242-6276 ■ Web: www.cianbro.com

Cives Corp 1825 Old Alabama Rd Ste 200 Roswell GA 30076 770-993-4424 998-2361
Web: www.cives.com

Contractors Northwest Inc
3731 N Ramsey Rd Coeur d'Alene ID 83815 208-667-2456 667-6388
Web: www.contractorsnorthwest.com

CW Wright Construction Company Inc
11500 Iron Bridge Rd Chester VA 23831 804-768-1054 768-6057
Web: www.cwwright.com

EE Cruz & Co Inc
165 Ryan St The Cruz Bldg South Plainfield NJ 07080 908-462-9600 946-7592*
*Fax Area Code: 732 ■ Web: eecruz.com

Elkins Constructors Inc
6104 S Gazebo Pk Jacksonville FL 32257 904-353-6500
TF: 800-772-1213 ■ Web: www.elkinsconstructors.com

Facchina Construction Co Inc
102 Centennial St Ste 201 La Plata MD 20646 240-776-7000 776-7001
Web: www.facchina.com/ContactUs.aspx

FCI Constructors Inc
3070 I-70 Business Loop # A Grand Junction CO 81504 970-434-9093 434-7583
Web: www.fciol.com

Frontier-Kemper Constructors Inc
1695 Allen Rd Evansville IN 47710 812-426-2741 428-0337
TF: 877-554-8600 ■ Web: www.frontierkemper.com

Garney Cos Inc 1333 NW Vivion Rd Kansas City MO 64118 816-741-4600 741-4488
Web: www.garney.com

Global Industries Ltd 8000 Global Dr Sulphur LA 70665 208-992-9226 583-5100*
*Fax Area Code: 337 ■ Web: lake-charles.gopickle.com

Granite Construction Inc 585 W Beach St Watsonville CA 95076 831-724-1011 722-9657
NYSE: GVA ■ Web: www.graniteconstruction.com

GSE Construction Company Inc
6950 Preston Ave Livermore CA 94551 925-447-0292 447-0962
Web: www.gseconstruction.com

Hall Contracting Corp 6415 Lakeview Rd Charlotte NC 28269 704-598-0818 598-3855
Web: hallcontracting.com

Henkels & McCoy Inc 985 Jolly Rd Blue Bell PA 19422 215-283-7600 283-7659
TF: 888-436-5357 ■ Web: www.henkels.com

Hood Corp 3166 Horseless Carriage Rd Norco CA 92860 951-520-4282 520-4385
Web: www.hoodcorp.com

Hubbard Construction Co 1936 Lee Rd Winter Park FL 32789 407-645-5500 623-3865
Web: www.hubbard.com

Insituform Technologies Inc
17988 Edison Ave St. Louis MO 63005 636-530-8000 519-8010
TF Cust Svc: 800-234-2992 ■ Web: www.insituform.com

Irish Construction Inc 2641 River Ave Rosemead CA 91770 626-288-8530 573-5136
Web: www.irishteam.com

James White Construction Company Inc
4156 Freedom Way Weirton WV 26062 304-748-8181 748-8183
Web: jameswhiteconstruction.com

Jay Dee Contractors Inc 38881 Schoolcraft Rd Livonia MI 48150 734-591-3400 464-6868
Web: www.jaydee.us

JC Evans Construction Company Inc
11230 Gold Express Dr Ste 310-325 Gold River CA 95670 512-244-1400 244-1900
Web: jc-evans.com

JF Shea Construction Inc 655 Brea Canyon Rd Walnut CA 91789 909-594-9500 883-3371
TF: 888-779-7333 ■ Web: www.jfshea.com

JF White Contracting Co 10 Burr St Framingham MA 01701 508-879-4700 558-0460*
*Fax Area Code: 617 ■ TF: 866-539-4400 ■ Web: www.jfwhite.com

Phone Fax

JH Berra Construction Company Inc
5091 Baumgartner Rd Saint Louis MO 63129 314-487-5617
Web: www.jhberra.com

John F Otto Inc 1717 Second St Sacramento CA 95811 916-441-6870 441-6138
Web: www.ottoconstruction.com

Johnson Bros Corp 5476 Lithia Pinecrest Rd Lithia FL 33547 813-685-5101 685-5939
Web: www.johnson-bros.com

JR Filanc Construction Company Inc
740 N Andreasen Dr Escondido CA 92029 760-941-7130 941-3969
TF: 877-225-5428 ■ Web: www.filanc.com

Kankakee Valley Construction Company Inc
4356 W SR 17 Kankakee IL 60901 815-937-8700 937-0402
Web: www.kvcci.com

Kimmins Contracting Corp 1501 Second Ave Tampa FL 33605 813-248-3878 579-1081
Web: www.kimmins.com

Kip Inc 25740 Washington Ave Murrieta CA 92562 951-698-7890
Web: www.kipincorporated.com

Kiska Construction Corp USA
10-34 44th Dr Long Island NY 11101 718-943-0400 943-0401
Web: www.kiskagroup.com

Koch Specialty Plant Services
12221 E Sam Houston Pkwy N Houston TX 77044 713-427-7700 427-7747
TF: 800-765-9177 ■ Web: www.kochservices.com

Landmark Structures LP 1665 Harmon Rd Fort Worth TX 76177 817-439-8888 439-9001
TF: 800-888-6816 ■ Web: www.teamlandmark.com

Lane Construction Corp 90 Fieldstone Ct Cheshire CT 06410 203-235-3351 237-4260
Web: www.laneconstruct.com

Latex Construction Co PO Box 917 Conyers GA 30012 770-760-0820 760-0852
Web: www.latexconstruction.com

Layne 4520 N State Rd 37 Orleans IN 47452 812-865-3232 865-3075
TF All: 855-529-6301 ■ Web: www.layne.com

MasTec Inc 800 Douglas Rd 12th Fl Coral Gables FL 33134 305-599-1800 406-1960
NYSE: MTZ ■ TF: 800-531-5000 ■ Web: www.mastec.com

McLean Contracting Co 6700 McLean Way Glen Burnie MD 21060 410-553-6700 553-6718
Web: mcleancont.com

Mears Group Inc 4500 N Mission Rd Rosebush MI 48878 989-433-2929 433-2199
TF: 800-632-7727 ■ Web: www.mears.net

Michels Corp 817 W Main St Brownsville WI 53006 920-583-3132 583-3429
TF: 877-297-8663 ■ Web: www.michels.us

Miller Pipeline Corp
8850 Crawfordsville Rd Indianapolis IN 46234 317-293-0278 293-8502
TF: 800-428-3742 ■ Web: www.millerpipeline.com

Miron Construction Co Inc 1471 McMahon Dr Neenah WI 54956 920-969-7000 969-7393
Web: miron-construction.com

Montana Construction Corp Inc 80 Contant Ave Lodi NJ 07644 973-478-5200 478-7604
Web: www.montanaconstructioninc.com

Mountain Cascade Inc PO Box 5050 Livermore CA 94551 925-373-8370
Web: www.mountaincascade.com

New River Electrical Corp PO Box 70 Cloverdale VA 24077 540-966-1650 966-1699
Web: www.newriverelectrical.com

Northeast Remsco Construction Inc
1433 Hwy 34 S Bldg B1 Farmingdale NJ 07727 732-557-6100 736-8900
TF: 800-879-8204 ■ Web: www.northeastconstruction.org

Oldcastle Materials Inc
900 Ashwood Pkwy Ste 700 Atlanta GA 30338 770-522-5600 522-5608
Web: www.apac.com

P Gioioso & Sons Inc 50 Sprague St Hyde Park MA 02136 617-364-5800 364-9462
Web: www.pgioioso.com

Penn Line Service Inc 300 Scottdale Ave Scottdale PA 15683 724-887-9110 887-0545
Web: www.pennline.com

Phylway Construction LLC 1074a Hwy 1 Thibodaux LA 70301 985-446-9644
Web: www.phylway.com

Quanta Services Inc
1360 Post Oak Blvd Ste 2100 Houston TX 77056 713-629-7600 629-7676
NYSE: PWR ■ Web: www.quantaservices.com

RH White Construction Company Inc
41 Central St Auburn MA 01501 508-832-3295 832-7084
Web: www.rhwhite.com

River City Construction LLC
101 Hoffer Ln East Peoria IL 61611 309-694-3120 694-1332
Web: www.rccllc.com

Satellite Store 7412 Preston Hwy Louisville KY 40219 502-966-0045
Web: www.thesatellitestore.com

Shaw Constructors Inc 36445 Perkins Rd Prairieville LA 70769 225-673-4606
Web: cbi.com

Sheehan Pipe Line Construction Co
2431 E 61st St Ste 700 Tulsa OK 74136 918-747-3471 747-9888
Web: www.sheehanpipeline.com

Siciliano Inc 3601 Winchester Rd Springfield IL 62707 217-585-1200 585-1211
Web: www.sicilianoinc.com

Sletten Construction Company Inc
1000 25th St N Great Falls MT 59401 406-761-7920 761-0923
Web: www.slettencompanies.com

Snelson Company Inc 601 W State St Sedro Woolley WA 98284 360-856-6511 856-5816
Web: www.snelsonco.com

Spiniello Cos 354 Eisenhower Pkwy Livingston NJ 07039 973-808-8383 808-9591
Web: www.spiniello.com

Stuart C Irby Co 815 S President St Jackson MS 39201 713-476-0788
TF: 866-687-4729 ■ Web: www.irby.com

Suburban Grading & Utilities Inc
1190 Harmony Rd Norfolk VA 23502 757-461-1800
Web: www.suburbangrading.com

Sumter Utilities Inc 1151 N Pike W Sumter SC 29153 803-469-8585 469-4600
Web: www.sumter-utilities.com

TA Loving Company Inc 400 Patetown Rd Goldsboro NC 27530 919-734-8400 731-7538
Web: www.taloving.com

TJ Lambrecht Construction Inc 10 Gougar Rd Joliet IL 60432 815-727-9211 727-6421

Tri Dal Ltd 540 Commerce St Southlake TX 76092 817-481-2886 481-8195
Web: www.tridal.com

Underground Construction Company Inc
5145 Industrial Way Benicia CA 94510 707-746-8800 746-1314
TF: 800-227-2314 ■ Web: www.undergrnd.com

Utility Services Inc 400 N Fourth St Bismarck ND 58501 701-222-7900
TF: 800-638-3278 ■ Web: www.montana-dakota.com

	City	State	Zip	Phone	Fax
Walbridge Aldinger Co 777 Woodward Ave #300	Detroit	MI	48226	313-963-8000	963-8150
Web: www.walbridge.com					
Welded Construction LP 26933 Eckel Rd	Perrysburg	OH	43551	419-874-3548	874-4883
Web: www.welded-construction.com					
West Valley Construction Company Inc 580 McGlincey Ln	Campbell	CA	95008	800-588-5510	371-3604*
**Fax Area Code:* 408 ■ *TF:* 800-588-5510 ■ *Web:* www.westvalleyconstruction.com					
Wharton-Smith Inc 750 Monroe Rd	Sanford	FL	32771	407-321-8410	321-4368
Web: www.whartonsmith.com					
Whitesell-Green Inc 3881 N Palafox St	Pensacola	FL	32505	850-434-5311	434-5315
Web: www.whitesell-green.com					
Willbros Engineers Inc 2087 E 71st St	Tulsa	OK	74136	918-496-0400	491-9436
Web: www.willbros.com					
Yantis Co 3611 Paesano's Pkwy Ste 300	San Antonio	TX	78231	210-655-3780	655-8526
Web: www.yantiscompany.com					
Yates Construction Company Inc 9220 NC Hwy 65	Stokesdale	NC	27357	336-379-8131	
Web: www.yatesconstruction.com					

189 CONSTRUCTION - SPECIAL TRADE CONTRACTORS

See Also Swimming Pools p. 3213

189-1 Building Equipment Installation or Erection

	City	State	Zip	Phone	Fax
AWC Commercial Window Coverings Inc 825 Williamson Ave	Fullerton	CA	92832	714-879-3880	879-8419
TF: 800-252-2280 ■ *Web:* www.awc-cwc.com					
Baltimore Rigging Company Inc, The 6601 Tributary St	Baltimore	MD	21224	443-696-4001	696-4006
TF: 800-626-2150 ■ *Web:* www.baltimorerigging.com					
Bigge Crane & Rigging Company Inc 10700 Bigge St PO Box 1657	San Leandro	CA	94577	510-638-8100	639-4053
TF: 888-337-2444 ■ *Web:* bigge.com					
Chicago Elevator Co 3260 W Grand Ave	Chicago	IL	60651	773-227-0737	
Web: www.chicagoelevator.com					
Columbia Elevator Products Company Inc 380 Horace St	Bridgeport	NY	06610	888-858-1558	937-9181*
**Fax Area Code:* 914 ■ *TF:* 888-858-1558 ■ *Web:* www.columbiaelevator.com					
Commercial Contracting Corp 4260 N Atlantic Blvd	Auburn Hills	MI	48326	248-209-0500	209-0501
Web: www.cccnetwork.com					
Don R Fruchey Inc 5608 Old Maumee Rd	Fort Wayne	IN	46803	260-749-8502	749-6337
Web: www.donrfruchey.com					
DW Nicholson Corp 24747 Clawiter Rd	Hayward	CA	94545	510-887-0900	783-9948
Web: www.dwnicholson.com					
Elward Construction Co 680 Harlan St	Lakewood	CO	80214	303-239-6303	239-8719
TF: 800-933-5339 ■ *Web:* www.elward.com					
Fenton Rigging & Contracting Inc 2150 Langdon Farm Rd	Cincinnati	OH	45237	513-631-5500	631-4361
Web: fenton1898.com					
George W Auch Co 735 S Paddock St PO Box 430719	Pontiac	MI	48341	248-334-2000	334-3404
Web: www.auchconstruction.com					
Integral Automation Inc 16w171 Shore Ct	Burr Ridge	IL	60527	630-654-4300	654-8519
Web: www.premiertool.com					
International Industrial Contracting Corp 35900 Mound Rd	Sterling Heights	MI	48310	586-264-7070	264-7088
Web: www.iiccusa.com					
James Machine Works LLC 1521 Adams St	Monroe	LA	71201	318-322-6104	388-4245
TF: 800-259-6104 ■ *Web:* www.jmwinc.net					
PS Marcato Elevator Co 4411 11th St	Long Island	NY	11101	718-392-6400	
Web: www.psmarcato.com					
Rigging International 1210 Marina Village Pkwy	Alameda	CA	94501	510-865-2400	865-9450
Web: www.sarens.com					
Sand Steel Bldg Co 101 Browell St PO Box 129	Emerado	ND	58228	701-594-4435	594-4438
Schindler Elevator Corp 20 Whippany Rd	Morristown	NJ	07960	973-397-6500	397-3619*
**Fax:* Mail Rm ■ *TF:* 800-225-3123 ■ *Web:* www.schindler.com					
SCI Global Structural Contours Inc PO Box 4970	Greenwich	CT	06830	203-531-4400	531-4403
Web: www.sciglobal.com					
W & H Systems Inc 120 Asia Pl	Carlstadt	NJ	07072	201-933-7840	933-2144
TF: 800-966-6993 ■ *Web:* www.whsystems.com					
Wales Industrial Service Inc PO Box 21628	Waco	TX	76702	254-772-3310	772-3420
Web: www.walesindustrial.com					
Wyatt Field Service Co 15415 Katy Fwy Ste 800	Houston	TX	77094	281-675-1300	675-1390
Web: www.wyattfieldservice.com					

189-2 Carpentry & Flooring Contractors

	City	State	Zip	Phone	Fax
ACMAT Corp 233 Main St	New Britain	CT	06051	860-229-9000	
OTC: ACMT ■ *Web:* www.acmatcorp.com					
Archadeck 2924 Emerywood Pkwy Ste 101	Richmond	VA	23294	804-353-6999	
TF: 800-722-4668 ■ *Web:* www.archadeck.com					
Associated Floors 32 Morris Ave	Springfield	NJ	07081	800-800-4320	
TF: 800-800-4320 ■ *Web:* www.assocint.com					
Bonitz Contracting Company Inc 645 Rosewood Dr PO Box 82	Columbia	SC	29202	803-799-0181	748-9223
Web: www.bonitz.us					
Carpenter Contractors of America Inc 3900 Ave D NW	Winter Haven	FL	33880	863-294-6449	299-9940
TF: 800-959-8806 ■ *Web:* www.carpentercontractors.com					
Cincinnati Floor Company Inc 5162 Broerman Ave	Cincinnati	OH	45217	513-641-4500	482-4204
TF: 800-886-4501 ■ *Web:* www.cincifloor.com					
Covington Flooring Co Inc 709 First Ave N	Birmingham	AL	35203	205-328-2330	328-2496
Web: www.covington.com					
Custom Stone 2999 Teagarden St	San Leandro	CA	94577	510-667-0099	667-0099
Web: www.customstoneusa.com					
E&K Companies 343 Carol Ln	Elmhurst	IL	60126	630-530-9001	
TF: 800-365-5760 ■ *Web:* www.e-kco.com					
Frank Novak & Sons Inc 23940 Miles Rd	Cleveland	OH	44128	216-475-5440	475-2802
Interior Construction Services Ltd 2930 Market St	Saint Louis	MO	63103	314-534-6664	534-6663
Web: www.ics-stl.com					
John H Hampshire Inc 320 W 24th St	Baltimore	MD	21211	410-366-8900	467-7391
Web: www.jhhampshire.com					
Kalman Floor Company Inc 1202 Bergen Pkwy Ste 110	Evergreen	CO	80439	303-674-2290	674-1238
TF: 800-525-7840 ■ *Web:* kalmanfloor.com					
Meyer & Lundahl 2345 W Lincoln St	Phoenix	AZ	85009	602-254-9286	
Web: www.meyerandlundahl.com					
Overhead Door Company of Sacramento Inc 6756 Franklin Blvd	Sacramento	CA	95823	916-421-3747	
TF: 800-929-3667 ■ *Web:* www.overheaddoor.com					
Rock-Tred Corp 405 Oakwood Ave	Waukegan	IL	60085	847-673-8200	679-6665*
**Fax:* Cust Svc ■ *Web:* www.rocktred.com					
Sundt Construction 2620 S 55th St	Tempe	AZ	85282	480-293-3000	
TF: 800-280-3000 ■ *Web:* www.sundt.com					
Tribco Construction Services 200 S Michigan Ave Ste 200	Chicago	IL	60604	312-341-0303	341-1534
Turner-Brooks Inc 28811 John R Rd	Madison Heights	MI	48071	248-548-3400	548-9213
Web: turnerbrooks.com					

189-3 Concrete Contractors

	City	State	Zip	Phone	Fax
Alex E. Paris Contracting Co 1595 Smith Township State	Atlasburg	PA	15004	724-947-2235	947-3820
Web: www.alexparis.com					
Allied Contractors Inc 204 E Preston St	Baltimore	MD	21202	410-539-6727	332-4594
Web: alliedcontractor.com					
Asphalt Specialists Inc 1780 Highwood E	Pontiac	MI	48340	248-334-4570	334-4135
Web: www.asipaving.com					
Aurora Blacktop Inc 1065 Sard Ave	Montgomery	IL	60538	630-892-9389	554-3306
Baker Concrete Construction Inc 900 N Garver Rd	Monroe	OH	45050	513-539-4000	539-4380
TF: 800-359-3935 ■ *Web:* www.bakerconcrete.com					
Barnard Construction Company Inc PO Box 99	Bozeman	MT	59771	406-586-1995	586-3530
Web: www.barnard-inc.com					
Berglund Construction 8410 S Chicago Ave	Chicago	IL	60617	773-374-1000	374-0701
Web: www.berglundco.com					
Bi-Con Services Inc 10901 Clay Pike Rd	Derwent	OH	43733	740-685-2542	685-3863
Web: www.biconservices.com					
Blair Concrete Services 1410-B Diggs Dr	Raleigh	NC	27603	919-833-9088	560-7828*
**Fax Area Code:* 804 ■ *Web:* www.donleyinc.com					
Bomel Construction Company Inc 8195 E Kaiser Blvd	Anaheim Hills	CA	92808	714-921-1660	921-1943
Web: www.bomelconstruction.com					
Bowen Engineering Corp 8802 N Meridian St	Indianapolis	IN	46260	317-842-2616	841-4257
Web: www.bowenengineering.com					
Ceco Concrete Construction LLC 9135 Barton	Overland Park	KS	66214	913-362-1855	
Web: www.cecoconcrete.com					
Cleveland Cement Contractors Inc 4823 Van Epps Rd	Cleveland	OH	44131	216-741-3954	741-9278
Web: www.clevelandcement.com					
Colorado Asphalt Services Inc 3700 E 56th Ave	Commerce	CO	80022	303-292-3434	292-6267
Web: www.coloradoasphalt.com					
Culbertson Enterprises Inc (CEI) 600A Snyder Ave	West Chester	PA	19382	610-436-6400	
TF: 800-382-2685					
Damon G Douglas Co 26 Worlds Fair Dr Suite A	Somerset,	NJ	08873	908-272-0100	560-0305*
**Fax Area Code:* 732 ■ *Web:* www.dgdco.com					
Dance Bros Inc 825C Hammonds Ferry Rd	Linthicum	MD	21090	410-789-8200	636-3663
Web: dancebrothers.com					
Donley's Inc 5430 Warner Rd	Cleveland	OH	44125	216-524-6800	642-3216
Web: www.donleyinc.com					
Dywidag Systems International 320 Marmon Dr	Bolingbrook	IL	60440	630-739-1100	739-5517
TF: 800-457-7633 ■ *Web:* www.dywidag-systems.com					
Egizii Electric Inc (EEI) 700 N MacArthur Blvd	Springfield	IL	62702	217-528-4001	528-1677
Francis O Day Construction Company Inc 850 E Gude Dr	Rockville	MD	20850	301-652-2400	340-6592
Web: www.foday.com					
Harris Cos Inc 909 Montreal Cir	Saint Paul	MN	55102	651-602-6500	602-6699
Web: www.hmcc.com					
Healy Long & Jevin Inc 2000 Rodman Rd	Wilmington	DE	19805	302-654-8039	654-8153
Web: www.healylongjevin.com					
Hubbard Construction Co 1936 Lee Rd	Winter Park	FL	32789	407-645-5500	623-3865
Web: www.hubbard.com					
John Rohrer Contracting Company Inc 2820 Roe Ln Bldg S	Kansas City	KS	66103	913-236-5005	236-7291
Web: www.johnrohrercontracting.com					
Kalman Floor Company Inc 1202 Bergen Pkwy Ste 110	Evergreen	CO	80439	303-674-2290	674-1238
TF: 800-525-7840 ■ *Web:* kalmanfloor.com					
Landavazo Bros Inc 29280 Pacific St	Hayward	CA	94544	510-581-7104	581-7423
Larson Contracting Inc 508 West Main St	Lake Mills	IA	50450	641-592-5800	592-8610
TF: 800-765-1426 ■ *Web:* www.larsoncontracting.com					
Lindblad Construction Co 717 E Cass St	Joliet	IL	60432	815-726-6251	723-4907
Web: www.lindbladconstruction.com					
Manafort Bros Inc 414 New Britain Ave	Plainville	CT	06062	860-229-4853	747-4861
Web: www.manafort.com					

Company	City	State	Zip	Phone	Fax
Miller & Long Concrete Construction Inc 4824 Rugby Ave *Web:* www.millerandlong.com	Bethesda	MD	20814	301-657-8000	657-8610
Musselman & Hall Contractors LLC 4922 E Blue Banks PO Box 300858 *TF:* 800-257-4255 ■ *Web:* www.musselmanandhall.com	Kansas City	MO	64130	816-861-1234	861-1237
Oldcastle Precast Bldg Systems Div 1401 Trimble Rd **Fax Area Code:* 410 ■ *TF:* 800-523-9144 ■ *Web:* oldcastleprecast.com	Edgewood	MD	21040	800-523-9144	612-1214*
Otto Baum Company Inc 866 N Main St *Web:* www.ottobaum.com	Morton	IL	61550	309-266-7114	263-1050
Proshot Concrete Inc 4158 Musgrove Dr *TF:* 800-633-3141 ■ *Web:* www.proshotconcrete.com	Florence	AL	35630	256-764-5941	764-5946
Richard Goettle Inc 12071 Hamilton Ave *Web:* www.goettle.com	Cincinnati	OH	45231	513-825-8100	825-8107
SB Ballard Construction Co 2828 Shipps Corner Rd *Web:* www.sbballard.com	Virginia Beach	VA	23453	757-440-5555	451-2873
Seretta Construction Inc 2604 Clark St *Web:* www.seretta.com	Apopka	FL	32703	407-290-9440	290-9372
Smock Fansler Corp 2910 W Minnesota St *Web:* www.smockfansler.com	Indianapolis	IN	46241	317-248-8371	244-4507
Suncoast Post-Tension LP 509 N Sam Houston Pkwy Ste 400 E *TF:* 800-847-8886 ■ *Web:* www.suncoast-pt.com	Houston	TX	77060	281-668-1840	668-1862
Superior Gunite Inc 12306 Van Nuys Blvd *Web:* www.shotcrete.com	Lakeview Terrace	CA	91342	818-896-9199	896-6699
TAS Commercial Concrete Construction LLC 19319 Oil Ctr Blvd *Web:* www.tasconcrete.com	Houston	TX	77073	281-230-7500	230-7664
Treviicos Corp 38 Third Ave *Web:* www.treviicos.com	Charlestown	MA	02129	617-241-4800	737-5810
Weaver-Bailey Contractors Inc PO Box 60 *TF:* 800-253-3385 ■ *Web:* www.weaverbailey.com	El Paso	AR	72045	501-796-2301	796-2372

189-4 Electrical Contractors

Company	City	State	Zip	Phone	Fax
A E C Group Inc, The 1735 Fifth Ave *Web:* www.aecgroup.com	McKeesport	PA	15132	412-678-1440	
A. M. Ortega Construction Inc 10125 Ch Rd *TF:* 800-909-1988 ■ *Web:* www.amortega.com	Lakeside	CA	92040	619-390-1988	390-1941
AC Corp 301 Creek Ridge Rd *TF:* 800-422-7378 ■ *Web:* www.accorporation.com	Greensboro	NC	27406	336-273-4472	765-0416
AC Electric Co 2921 Hangar Way PO Box 81977 *Web:* www.a-celectric.com	Bakersfield	CA	93308	661-410-0000	410-0400
Aldridge Electric Inc 844 E Rockland Rd *Web:* www.aldridgegroup.com	Libertyville	IL	60048	847-680-5200	680-5298
Allan Briteway Electrical Contractors Inc 130 Algonquin Pkwy *Web:* www.allanbriteway.com	Whippany	NJ	07981	973-781-0022	781-1744
Althoff Industries Inc 8001 S Rt 31 **Fax:* Sales ■ *TF:* 800-225-2443 ■ *Web:* www.althoffind.com	Crystal Lake	IL	60014	815-455-7000	455-9375*
Anderson Electric Inc PO Box 758 *Web:* www.anderson-electric.com	Springfield	IL	62705	217-529-5471	529-0412
Anixter Inc 2301 Patriot Blvd *TF:* 800-492-1212 ■ *Web:* www.anixter.com	Glenview	IL	60026	224-521-8000	521-8100
Arrow Electric Company Inc 317 Wabasso Ave *TF:* 888-999-5591 ■ *Web:* www.arrowelectric.com	Louisville	KY	40209	502-367-0141	361-8613
Aschinger Electric Co 877 Horan Dr *Web:* www.aschinger.com	Fenton	MO	63026	636-343-1211	343-9658
Athena Engineering Inc 456 E Foothill Blvd *TF:* 877-777-4778 ■ *Web:* www.athenaengineering.net	San Dimas	CA	91773	909-599-0947	599-5018
B & I Contractors Inc 2701 Prince St *Web:* bandiflorida.com	Fort Myers	FL	33916	239-332-4646	332-5928
Baker Electric Inc 111 Jackson Ave *Web:* www.bakerelectric.com	Des Moines	IA	50315	515-288-6774	288-2226
Barth Electric Company Inc 1934 N Illinois St *TF:* 800-666-6226 ■ *Web:* www.barthelectric.com	Indianapolis	IN	46202	317-924-6226	923-6938
Bell Electrical Contractors Inc 128 Millwell Dr **Fax Area Code:* 800 ■ *TF:* 800-717-2355 ■ *Web:* www.bellelectrical.com	Maryland Heights	MO	63043	314-739-7744	717-2355*
Bergelectric Corp 5650 W Centinela Ave *Web:* www.bergelectric.com	Los Angeles	CA	90045	310-337-1377	337-2663
Berger Engineering Co 10900 Shady Trl *Web:* www.berger-engr.com	Dallas	TX	75220	214-358-4451	351-2954
Berwick Electric Co 3450 N Nevada Ave Ste 100 *Web:* www.berwickelectric.com	Colorado Springs	CO	80907	719-632-7683	471-9660
Brink Constructors Inc 2950 N Plz Dr *Web:* www.brinkred.com	Rapid City	SD	57702	605-342-6966	342-5905
Broadway Electric Service Company Inc 1800 N Central St *Web:* besco.com	Knoxville	TN	37917	865-524-1851	546-2104
Broadway Electrical Company Inc 295 Freeport St *Web:* www.broadelec.com	Boston	MA	02122	617-288-7900	288-4169
Brothers Inc 1000 Sussex Blvd *TF:* 866-276-7462 ■ *Web:* www.brotherselectric.com	Broomall	PA	19008	610-328-0670	328-6218
Bruce & Merrilees Electric Co 930 Cass St *TF:* 800-652-5560 ■ *Web:* www.bruceandmerrilees.com	New Castle	PA	16101	724-652-5566	652-8290
Cache Valley Electric Inc 875 N 1000 W *TF:* 888-558-0600 ■ *Web:* www.cve.com	Logan	UT	84321	435-752-6405	752-9111
Campbell Alliance Group Inc 8045 Arco Corporate Dr Ste 500 *TF:* 888-297-2001 ■ *Web:* www.campbellalliance.com	Raleigh	NC	27617	919-844-7100	844-7560
Cannon & Wendt Electric Co 4020 N 16th St *Web:* www.cannon-wendt.com	Phoenix	AZ	85016	602-279-1681	230-8464
Capital Electric Construction Company Inc 600 Broadway Ste 600 *Web:* www.capitalelectric.com	Kansas City	MO	64105	816-472-9500	421-4244
Center Line Electric Inc 26554 Lawrence *Web:* www.centerline-elec.com	Center Line	MI	48015	586-757-5505	759-2453
Church & Murdock Electric Inc 5709 Wattsburg Rd *Web:* www.churchandmurdock.com	Erie	PA	16509	814-825-3456	825-4043
Cleveland Group Inc 1281 Fulton Industrial Blvd *Web:* www.clevelandelectric.com	Atlanta	GA	30336	404-696-4550	505-7792
Cochran Electric Company Inc 12500 Aurora Ave N *Web:* www.cochraninc.com	Seattle	WA	98133	206-367-1900	
Collins Electric Co Inc 53 Second Ave *TF:* 877-553-2810 ■ *Web:* www.collinselectricco.com	Chicopee	MA	01020	413-592-9221	592-4157
Commander Electric Inc 500 Johnson Ave PO Box 526	Bohemia	NY	11716	631-563-3223	563-8322
Commonwealth Electric Co of Midwest PO Box 80638 *Web:* www.commonwealthelectric.com	Lincoln	NE	68501	402-474-1341	474-0114
Contemporary Electrical Services Inc 1954 Isaac Newton Sq W *Web:* www.cont-elec.com	Reston	VA	20190	703-255-9226	
Continental Electric Company Inc 9501 E Fifth Ave PO Box 2710 *Web:* www.continentalelectric.com	Gary	IN	46403	219-938-3460	938-3469
Cupertino Electric Inc 1132 N Seventh St *Web:* www.cei.com	San Jose	CA	95112	408-808-8000	275-8575
Custom Cable Industries Inc 3221 Cherry Palm Dr *TF:* 800-552-2232 ■ *Web:* www.mflightwave.com	Tampa	FL	33619	813-623-2232	623-3534
Daidone Electric Inc 200 Raymond Blvd *Web:* daidoneelectric.com	Newark	NJ	07105	973-690-5216	344-3645
Dashiell Corp 12301 Kurland Dr Ste 400 *Web:* www.dashiell.com	Houston	TX	77034	713-558-6600	558-6694
Davis H Elliot Co Inc 1920 Progress Dr SE *Web:* www.davishelliot.com	Roanoke	VA	24013	540-427-5459	
Decker Electric Company Inc 1282 Folsom St	San Francisco	CA	94103	415-552-1622	861-4257
Del Monte Electric Company Inc 6998 Sierra Ct *Web:* www.delmonteelectric.com	Dublin	CA	94568	925-829-6000	829-6033
Divane Bros Electric Co 2424 Rose St *Web:* www.divanebros.com	Franklin Park	IL	60131	847-455-7143	
Dorey Electric Co PO Box 10158 *Web:* www.doreyelectric.com	Norfolk	VA	23513	757-855-3381	
Ducci Electrical Contractors Inc 427 Goshen Rd *Web:* duccielectrical.com	Torrington	CT	06790	860-489-9267	489-7980
Dycom Industries Inc 11770 US Hwy 1 Ste 101 *NYSE:* DY ■ *Web:* www.dycomind.com	Palm Beach Gardens	FL	33408	561-627-7171	
Dynalectric Corp 4462 Corporate Ctr Dr **Fax Area Code:* 866 ■ **Fax:* Acctg ■ *TF:* 866-890-7794 ■ *Web:* www.kdc-systems.com	Los Alamitos	CA	90720	714-828-7000	890-7794*
E-J Electric Installation Co 46-41 Vernon Blvd *Web:* www.ej1899.com	Long Island	NY	11101	718-786-9400	937-9120
EC Co PO Box 10286 *TF:* 800-462-3370 ■ *Web:* www.e-c-co.com	Portland	OR	97296	800-659-3511	
EC Ernst Inc 132 Log Canoe Cir *TF:* 800-683-7770 ■ *Web:* www.ecernst.com	Stevensville	MD	21666	301-350-7770	499-0933
Edwin L Heim Co 1918 Greenwood St *TF:* 800-692-7316 ■ *Web:* www.edwinlheim.com	Harrisburg	PA	17104	717-233-8711	233-8619
Egizii Electric Inc (EEI) 700 N MacArthur Blvd	Springfield	IL	62702	217-528-4001	528-1677
ElDeCo Inc 5751 Augusta Rd *Web:* www.eldecoinc.com	Greenville	SC	29605	864-277-9088	277-2811
Electric Resource Contractors Inc 4024 Washington Ave N *Web:* eganco.com	Minneapolis	MN	55412	612-522-6511	
Electrical Contractors Inc 3510 Main St *Web:* www.ecincorporated.com	Hartford	CT	06120	860-549-2822	549-7948
Electrical Corp of America 7320 Arlington Ave *Web:* www.ecahq.com	Raytown	MO	64133	816-737-3206	356-0731
Electronic Contracting Co 6501 N 70th St *TF:* 800-366-5320 ■ *Web:* www.eccoinc.com	Lincoln	NE	68507	402-466-8274	466-0819
EMCOR Construction Services Inc 1420 Spring Hill Rd Ste 500 *Web:* www.emcorgroup.com	McLean	VA	22102	703-556-8000	556-0890
EMCOR Group Inc 301 Merritt 7 6th Fl *NYSE:* EME ■ *TF:* 866-890-7794 ■ *Web:* www.emcorgroup.com	Norwalk	CT	06851	203-849-7800	849-7900
EMCOR Hyre Electric Co 2655 Garfield Ave *Web:* www.emcorhyre.com	Highland	IN	46322	219-923-6100	838-3631
Engineered Protection Systems Inc 750 Front Ave NW *TF:* 800-966-9199 ■ *Web:* www.epssecurity.com	Grand Rapids	MI	49504	616-459-0281	459-0553
Enterprise Electric Co 4204 Shannon Dr *Web:* www.eecompany.com	Baltimore	MD	21213	410-488-8200	488-6639
Ermco Inc 1625 W Thompson Rd *Web:* www.ermco.com	Indianapolis	IN	46217	317-780-2923	780-2853
Ferndale Electric Company Inc 915 E Drayton Ave *Web:* www.ferndale-electric.com	Ferndale	MI	48220	248-545-4404	545-8140
Ferran Services & Contracting 530 Grand St *Web:* www.ferran-services.com	Orlando	FL	32805	407-422-3551	648-0961
Fisk Electric Co 111 TC Jester Blvd *Web:* www.fiskcorp.com	Houston	TX	77007	713-868-6111	880-2918
Forest Electric Corp 1375 BRdway *Web:* www.forestelectric.net	New York	NY	10018	212-318-1500	318-1518
Foshay Electric Company Inc 7676 Engineer Rd *Web:* www.foshayelectric.com	San Diego	CA	92111	858-277-7676	
Fox Electric Ltd 1104 Colorado Ln *Web:* www.foxelectric.com	Arlington	TX	76015	817-461-2571	261-7311

Company	City	State	ZIP	Phone	Fax
Fox Valley Fire & Safety Company Inc 2730 Pinnacle Dr *Web:* www.foxvalleyfire.com	Elgin	IL	60124	847-695-5990	695-3699
G & M Electrical Contractors Co 1746 N Richmond St *Web:* www.gm-electric.com	Chicago	IL	60647	773-278-8200	278-8038
Gardner-Zemke Company Inc 6100 Indian School Rd NE *Web:* gardnerzemke.com	Albuquerque	NM	87110	505-881-0555	
Gaylor Electric 5750 Castle Creek Pkwy N Dr Ste 400 *TF:* 800-878-0577 ■ *Web:* www.gaylor.com	Indianapolis	IN	46250	317-843-0577	848-0364
Gibson Electric Company Inc 3100 Woodcreek Dr *Web:* www.gibsonelec.com	Downers Grove	IL	60515	630-288-3800	743-2100
Gill-Simpson Inc 11620 Red Run Blvd	Reisterstown	MD	21136	410-467-3335	366-4557
Goldfield Corp 1684 W Hibiscus Blvd *NYSE: GV* ■ *Web:* www.goldfieldcorp.com	Melbourne	FL	32901	321-724-1700	
GR Sponaugle & Sons Inc 4391 Chambers Hill Rd *Web:* www.grsponaugle.com	Harrisburg	PA	17111	717-564-1515	564-3675
Grand-Kahn Electric (GK) 2455 W Grand Ave *Web:* www.grandkahn.com	Chicago	IL	60612	312-298-1500	298-1501
Gregory Electric Company Inc 2124 College St *Web:* www.gregoryelectric.com	Columbia	SC	29205	803-748-1122	748-1102
GSL Electric 8540 S Sandy Pkwy *Web:* www.gslelectric.com	Sandy	UT	84070	801-565-0088	565-0099
Guarantee Electrical Co 3405 Bent Ave *Web:* www.geco.com	Saint Louis	MO	63116	314-772-5400	772-9261
Gulf Electric Company Inc of Mobile PO Box 2385 *Web:* www.gulfelec.com	Mobile	AL	36652	251-666-0654	666-6323
H & H Group Inc 2801 Syene Rd *Web:* www.hhindustries.com	Madison	WI	53713	608-273-3434	273-9654
Hargrove Electric Company Inc 1522 Market Ctr Blvd *Web:* www.hargroveelectric.com	Dallas	TX	75207	214-742-8665	744-0846
Hatzel & Buehler Inc 3600 Silverside Rd *Web:* www.hatzelandbuehler.com	Wilmington	DE	19803	302-478-4200	478-2750
HB Frazer Co 514 Shoemaker Rd *Web:* hbfrazer.com	King of Prussia	PA	19406	610-768-0400	992-5070
Hi-Tech Electric Inc 11116 W Little York Rd Bldg 8 *Web:* www.hitechelectric.com	Houston	TX	77041	832-243-0345	467-0132
Highlines Construction Company Inc 701 Bridge City Ave	Westwego	LA	70096	504-436-3961	
Hilscher Clarke Electric Co 519 Fourth St NW *Web:* www.hilscher-clarke.com	Canton	OH	44703	330-452-9806	452-5867
Honshy Electric Company Inc 7345 SW 41st St *Web:* www.honshyelectric.com	Miami	FL	33155	305-264-5500	266-3159
Hooper Corp 2030 Pennsylvania Ave *TF:* 877-630-7554 ■ *Web:* www.hoopercorp.com	Madison	WI	53704	608-249-0451	249-7360
Howe Electric Inc 4682 E Olive Ave *Web:* www.howe-electric.com	Fresno	CA	93702	559-255-8992	255-9745
Hunt Electric Corp 7900 Chicago Ave S *Web:* www.huntelec.com	Bloomington	MN	55420	651-646-2911	643-6575
Industrial Contractors Inc 701 Ch Dr *TF:* 800-467-3089 ■ *Web:* www.icinorthdakota.com	Bismarck	ND	58501	701-258-9908	258-9988
Industrial Power & Lighting Corp 60 Depost St Ste 500 *TF:* 800-639-3702 ■ *Web:* www.iplcorp.com	Buffalo	NY	14206	716-854-1811	854-1828
Industrial Specialty Contractors LLC 20480 Highland Rd *Web:* www.iscgrp.com	Baton Rouge	LA	70817	225-756-8001	
Inglett & Stubbs LLC 5200 Riverview Rd *Web:* www.inglett-stubbs.com	Mableton	GA	30126	404-881-1199	872-3101
Integrated Electrical Services Inc (IES) 5433 Westheimer Rd Ste 500 *NASDAQ: IESC* ■ *Web:* ies-corporate.com	Houston	TX	77056	713-860-1500	
Intermountain Electric Inc (IME) 5050 Osage St Ste 500 *Web:* imelect.com	Denver	CO	80221	303-733-7248	722-2410
Interstates Construction Services Inc 1520 N Main Ave *TF:* 800-827-1662 ■ *Web:* www.interstates.com	Sioux Center	IA	51250	712-722-1662	722-1667
J & M Brown Company Inc 267 Amory St *Web:* www.jmbco.com	Jamaica Plain	MA	02130	617-522-6800	522-6422
JF Electric Inc 100 Lakefront Pkwy PO Box 570 *Web:* www.jfelectric.com	Edwardsville	IL	62025	618-797-5353	797-5354
John A Penney Company Inc 270 Sidney St	Cambridge	MA	02139	617-547-7744	547-4332
Jordano Electric Company Inc 200 Hudson St *Web:* www.jordanoelectric.com	Hackensack	NJ	07601	201-489-4800	489-5071
Kearney Electric Inc 3609 E Superior Ave *Web:* www.kearneyaz.com	Phoenix	AZ	85040	602-437-0235	
Kelso-Burnett Co 5200 Newport Dr *Web:* www.kelso-burnett.com	Rolling Meadows	IL	60008	847-259-0720	259-0839
Kirby Electric Inc 415 Northgate D *Web:* www.kirbyelectricinc.com	Warrendale	PA	15086	724-772-1800	772-2227
Kleinknecht Electric Company Inc 252 W 37th St Ste 1402 *Web:* www.kecny.com	New York	NY	10018	212-728-1800	
Koontz-Wagner Electric Company Inc 3801 Voorde Dr *TF:* 800-345-2051 ■ *Web:* www.koontz-wagner.com	South Bend	IN	46628	574-232-2051	
Lake Erie Electric Inc 25730 First St *Web:* www.lakeerieelectric.com	Westlake	OH	44145	440-835-5565	835-5688
Linder & Assoc Inc 840 N Main St PO Box 1202 *Web:* www.linderandassociates.com	Wichita	KS	67201	316-265-1616	265-8097
LK Comstock & Company Inc 83 Central Ave 12th Fl *Web:* www.railworks.com	East Farmingdale	NY	11735	212-502-7900	502-1865
Ludvik Electric Co 3900 S Teller St *Web:* www.ludvik.com	Lakewood	CO	80235	303-781-9601	783-6349
Marathon Electrical Contractors Inc 614 38th St S *Web:* www.marathonelectrical.com	Birmingham	AL	35222	205-323-8500	
Marrs Electric Inc PO Box 690296 *Web:* www.marrselectric.com	Tulsa	OK	74169	918-437-5802	438-3563
Matco Electric Corp 3913 Gates Rd *Web:* www.matcoelectric.com	Vestal	NY	13850	607-729-4921	729-0932
Mayers Electric Company Inc 4004 Erie Ct *Web:* www.mayerselectric.com	Cincinnati	OH	45227	513-272-2900	272-2904
Meade Electric Company Inc 9550 W 55th St Ste A *Web:* www.meadeelectric.com	Countryside	IL	60525	708-588-2500	588-2501
Meisner Electric Inc 220 NE First St *Web:* www.mei.cc	Delray Beach	FL	33444	561-278-8362	278-8397
Merit Electric Company Inc 6520 125th Ave N *TF:* 800-330-5945 ■ *Web:* www.meritelectricco.com	Largo	FL	33773	727-536-5945	536-9014
Merit Electrical Inc 17723 Airline Hwy *Web:* www.meritelectrical.com	Prairieville	LA	70769	225-673-8850	673-8838
Metropower Inc PO Box 5228 *Web:* www.metropower.com	Albany	GA	31706	229-432-7345	436-3869
Mid-City Electrical Construction 1099 Sullivant Ave *Web:* www.midcityelectric.com	Columbus	OH	43223	614-221-5153	
Miller Electric Co 2251 Rosselle St *TF Sales:* 877-540-2160 ■ *Web:* www.mecojax.com	Jacksonville	FL	32204	904-513-2818	389-8653
Miller Engineering Co 1616 S Main St *Web:* mecogroup.com	Rockford	IL	61102	815-963-4878	
MJ Electric Inc PO Box 686 *Web:* www.mjelectric.com	Iron Mountain	MI	49801	906-774-8000	779-4217
MMR Group Inc 15961 Airline Hwy *TF:* 800-880-5090 ■ *Web:* www.mmrgrp.com	Baton Rouge	LA	70817	225-756-5090	753-7012
Mojave Electric Inc 3755 W Hacienda Ave	Las Vegas	NV	89118	702-798-2970	798-3740
Mona Electric Group Inc 7915 Malcolm Rd *Web:* www.getmona.com	Clinton	MD	20735	301-868-8400	868-4178
Morrow-Meadows Corp 231 Benton Ct *Web:* www.morrow-meadows.com	City of Industry	CA	91789	909-598-7700	598-3907
Morse Electric Inc 500 W S St *Web:* www.themorsegroup.com	Freeport	IL	61032	815-266-4200	266-8900
Motor City Electric Co 9440 Grinnell St *Web:* www.mceco.com	Detroit	MI	48213	313-921-5300	921-5310
Msf Electric Inc 10455 Fountaingate Dr *TF:* 866-366-7943 ■ *Web:* www.msfelectric.com	Stafford	TX	77477	281-494-4700	
Muska Electric Co 1985 Oakcrest Ave *Web:* www.muskaelectric.com	Roseville	MN	55113	651-636-5820	
Muth Electric Inc 1717 N Sanborn PO Box 1400 *TF:* 800-888-1597 ■ *Web:* www.muthelectric.com	Mitchell	SD	57301	605-996-3983	996-2203
Mutual Telecom Services Inc 250 First Ave Ste 301 **Fax Area Code:* 781 ■ *TF:* 800-687-2848 ■ *Web:* www.blackbox.com	Needham	MA	02494	800-687-2848	449-1996*
MYR Group 1701 W Golf Rd Twr 3 Ste 1012 *Web:* www.myrgroup.com	Rolling Meadows	IL	60008	847-290-1891	290-1892
Netsville Inc 72 Cascade Dr *TF:* 888-638-7845 ■ *Web:* www.netsville.com	Rochester	NY	14614	585-232-5670	232-4512
Network Infrastructure Corp 8945 S Harl Ave Ste 102 *TF:* 866-456-4422 ■ *Web:* www.us.logicalis.com	Tempe	AZ	85284	480-850-5050	
New Com Electric 4035 Flossmoor St	Las Vegas	NV	89115	702-876-1116	
Newtron Group, The 8183 W El Cajon Dr *Web:* www.thenewtrongroup.com	Baton Rouge	LA	70815	225-927-8921	
O'Connell Electric Co 830 Phillips Rd *Web:* www.oconnellelectric.com	Victor	NY	14564	585-924-2176	924-4973
Operational Security Systems Inc 1231 Collier Rd NW Ste D *Web:* www.ossatl.com	Atlanta	GA	30318	404-352-0025	
Palmer Electric & Showcase Lighting 875 Jackson Ave *Web:* www.palmer-electric.com	Winter Park	FL	32789	407-646-8700	647-8951
Parsons Electric LLC 5960 Main St NE *TF:* 800-403-4832	Minneapolis	MN	55432	763-571-8000	571-7210
PayneCrest Electric & Communications 10411 Baur Blvd *Web:* www.payneelectric.com	Saint Louis	MO	63132	314-996-0400	996-0500
Peoples Electric Company Inc 277 E Fillmore Ave *Web:* www.peoplesco.com	Saint Paul	MN	55107	651-227-7711	
Perlectric 2711 Prosperity Ave *Web:* perlectric.com	Fairfax	VA	22031	703-352-5151	352-5155
Perreca Electric Co 520 Broadway *Web:* www.perreca.com	Newburgh	NY	12550	845-562-4080	
Phillips Bros Electrical Contractors Inc 235 Sweet Spring Rd *TF:* 800-220-5051 ■ *Web:* www.philipsbrothers.com	Glenmoore	PA	19343	610-458-8578	458-8438
Pieper Electric Inc 5070 N 35th St *TF:* 800-424-8802 ■ *Web:* www.pieperpower.com	Milwaukee	WI	53209	414-462-7700	462-7711
Pike Electric Corp 100 Pike Way PO Box 868 *NYSE: PIKE* ■ *TF:* 800-424-7453	Mount Airy	NC	27030	336-789-2171	
Power City Electric Inc 3327 E Olive Ave *Web:* www.powercityelectric.com	Spokane	WA	99202	509-535-8500	535-4665
Premier Electrical Corp 4401 85th Ave N *Web:* www.premiercorp.net	Brooklyn Park	MN	55443	763-424-6551	424-5225
Pritchard Electric Company Inc 2425 Eigth Ave *Web:* www.pritchardelectric.com	Huntington	WV	25703	304-529-2566	529-2567
R K Electric Inc 42021 Osgood Rd *TF:* 800-400-4418 ■ *Web:* www.rkelectric.com	Fremont	CA	94539	510-770-5660	770-5684
R2W Inc 5957 McLeod Dr *Web:* www.r2west.com	Las Vegas	NV	89120	702-434-6500	

Company / Address	City	State	ZIP	Phone	Fax
Ready Electric Company Inc 3300 Gilmore Industrial Blvd *Web:* www.readyelec.com	Louisville	KY	40213	502-893-2511	893-2519
Rex Moore Electrical Contractors & Engineers 6001 Outfall Cir *TF:* 800-266-1922 ■ *Web:* www.rexmoore.com	Sacramento	CA	95828	916-372-1300	372-4013
RFI Communications & Security Systems 360 Turtle Creek Ct. *TF:* 800-341-9292 ■ *Web:* www.rfi.com	San Jose	CA	95125	408-298-5400	882-4401
Riggs Distler Company Inc 9411 Philadelphia Rd Ste M *Web:* www.riggsdistler.com	Baltimore	MD	21237	410-633-0300	633-2119
Roman Electric Company Inc 640 S 70th St *Web:* www.romanelectric.com	Milwaukee	WI	53214	414-771-5400	471-8693
Romanoff Electric Company LLC 5570 Enterprise Blvd *Web:* quebe.com	Toledo	OH	43612	419-726-2627	726-5406
Rosendin Electric Inc 880 N Mabury Rd **Fax:* Hum Res ■ *Web:* www.rosendin.com	San Jose	CA	95133	408-286-2800	793-5001*
Rydalch Electric Inc 250 Plymouth Ave *Web:* www.rydalchelectric.com	Salt Lake City	UT	84115	801-265-1813	
Salem Electric Company Inc 3933 Westpoint Blvd PO Box 26784 *Web:* www.salemelectriccoinc.com	Winston-Salem	NC	27114	336-765-0221	765-7286
SASCO Electric 2750 Moore Ave. *Web:* www.sasco.com	Fullerton	CA	92833	714-870-0217	738-3571
Schenectady Hardware & Electric Company Inc PO Box 338 *Web:* www.sheinc.com	Schenectady	NY	12301	518-346-2369	372-7549
Schmidt Electric Coy L P 9701 FM 1625 *Web:* www.schmidt-electric.com	Austin	TX	78747	512-243-1450	
Sesco Lighting Inc 1133 W Morse Blvd Ste 100 *Web:* www.sescolighting.com	Winter Park	FL	32789	407-629-6100	629-6168
Shambaugh & Son LP 7614 Opportunity Dr *TF:* 866-890-7794 ■ *Web:* www.shambaugh.com	Fort Wayne	IN	46825	260-487-7777	487-7701
Shaw Electric Co 22100 Telegraph Rd *Web:* www.shawelectric.com	Southfield	MI	48033	248-228-2000	228-2080
Shawver & Son Inc 144 NE 44th St *Web:* www.shawver.net	Oklahoma City	OK	73105	405-525-9451	525-6136
Shelley Electric Inc 3619 W 29th St S. *Web:* www.shelleyelectric.com	Wichita	KS	67217	316-945-8311	
Smith & Keene Electric Service Inc 833 Live Oak Dr *Web:* www.smithandkeene.com	Chesapeake	VA	23320	757-420-1231	420-5340
Southern Air Inc 2655 Lakeside Dr *TF:* 800-743-1214 ■ *Web:* www.southern-air.com	Lynchburg	VA	24501	434-385-6200	385-9081
Spg Solar Inc 1039 N McDowell Blvd	Petaluma	CA	94954	415-883-7657	
Sprig Electric Co 1860 S Tenth St *Web:* www.sprigelectric.com	San Jose	CA	95112	408-298-3134	298-2132
Staff Electric Company Inc W 133 N 5030 Campbell Dr *Web:* staffelectric.com	Menomonee Falls	WI	53051	262-781-8230	
Staley Inc 8101 Fourche Rd *TF:* 877-616-0661 ■ *Web:* www.staleyinc.com	Little Rock	AR	72209	501-565-3006	565-9674
Starr Electric Company Inc 6 Battleground Ct *Web:* www.starrelectric.net	Greensboro	NC	27408	336-275-0241	273-0734
Steiny & Company Inc 221 N Ardmore Ave PO Box 74901 *Web:* www.steinyco.com	Los Angeles	CA	90004	213-382-2331	381-6781
Stoner Electric Inc 1904 SE Ochoco St *Web:* www.stonergroup.com	Milwaukie	OR	97222	503-462-6500	659-4968
Sturgeon Electric Company Inc 12150 E 112th Ave *Web:* www.myrgroup.com	Henderson	CO	80640	303-286-8000	
Sunwest Electric Inc 3064 E Miraloma Ave. *Web:* www.sunwestelectric.net	Anaheim	CA	92806	714-630-8700	630-8740
Super Electric Construction Co 4300 W Chicago Ave *Web:* www.superelec.com	Chicago	IL	60651	773-489-4400	235-1455
System Electric Co 1278 Montalvo Way *Web:* www.systemelectric.com	Palm Springs	CA	92262	760-327-7847	323-7247
T & J Electrical Corp 636 Second Ave. *Web:* www.tandjelectric.com	Troy	NY	12182	518-237-1893	
Taft Electric Co 1694 Eastman Ave *Web:* taftelectric.com	Ventura	CA	93003	805-642-0121	644-6488
TEC Corp 2300 Seventh St *Web:* www.tec-corp.com	Sioux City	IA	51105	712-252-4275	
Teknon Corp 15443 NE 95th St *TF:* 800-338-6142 ■ *Web:* www.teknon.com	Redmond	WA	98052	425-895-8535	895-0535
Tennessee Associated Electric 7511 Taggart Ln *Web:* www.tn-associated.com	Knoxville	TN	37938	865-524-3686	522-1553
Terry's Electric Inc 600 N Thacker Ave Ste A *Web:* www.terryselectric.com	Kissimmee	FL	34741	407-572-2100	
Totem Electric of Tacoma Inc 2332 Jefferson Ave *Web:* www.totemelectric.com	Tacoma	WA	98402	253-383-5022	272-5214
Tri-City Electrical Contractors Inc 430 W Dr *TF:* 800-768-2489 ■ *Web:* tcelectric.com	Altamonte Springs	FL	32714	407-788-3500	682-7353
Triangle Electric Co 29787 Stephenson Hwy *Web:* www.trielec.com	Madison Heights	MI	48071	248-399-2200	399-2612
Van Ert Electric Company Inc 7019 Stewart Ave. *Web:* www.vanert.com	Wausau	WI	54401	715-845-4308	848-3671
Vaughn Industries LLC 1201 E Findlay St *Web:* www.vaughnindustries.com	Carey	OH	43316	419-396-3900	
WA Chester LLC 4390 Parliament Pl Ste Q *Web:* wachester.com	Lanham	MD	20706	240-487-1940	487-1941
Wasatch Electric 2455 W 1500 S Ste A *Web:* www.wasatchelectric.com	Salt Lake City	UT	84104	801-487-4511	487-5032
Watson Electrical 1500 Charleston St *Web:* www.watsonelec.com	Wilson	NC	27893	252-237-7511	243-1607
Wayne J Griffin Electric Inc 116 Hopping Brook Rd **Fax Area Code:* 508 ■ *TF:* 800-421-0151 ■ *Web:* www.waynejgriffin.com	Holliston	MA	01746	800-421-0151	429-7825*
Wellington Power Corp 40th & Butler Sts *Web:* www.wellingtonpower.com	Pittsburgh	PA	15201	412-681-0103	681-0109
Welsbach Electric Corp 111-01 14th Ave. *TF:* 866-890-7794 ■ *Web:* www.welsbachelectric.com	College Point	NY	11356	718-670-7900	670-7999
West-Fair Electric Contractors Inc 200 Brady Ave *Web:* www.west-fair.com	Hawthorne	NY	10532	914-769-8050	769-7451
White Electrical Construction Co 1730 Chattahoochee Ave *TF:* 888-519-4483 ■ *Web:* white-electrical.com	Atlanta	GA	30318	404-351-5740	355-5823
Williard Limbach 175 Titus Ave Ste 100. **Fax:* Cust Svc ■ *Web:* www.limbachinc.com	Warrington	PA	18976	215-488-9700	488-9699*
York River Electric Inc 108 Production Dr *Web:* www.yorkriverelectric.com	Yorktown	VA	23693	757-369-3673	369-3680
Zwicker Electrical Company Inc 360 Pk Ave S 4th Fl *Web:* www.zwicker-electric.com	New York	NY	10010	212-477-8400	995-8469

189-5 Excavation Contractors

Company / Address	City	State	ZIP	Phone	Fax
Allied Contractors Inc 204 E Preston St *Web:* alliedcontractor.com	Baltimore	MD	21202	410-539-6727	332-4594
Aman Environmental Construction Inc 614 E Edna Pl *Web:* www.amanenvironmental.com	Covina	CA	91723	626-967-4287	332-1877
Anastasi Trucking & Paving Inc 4430 Walden St *Web:* www.anastasitrucking.com	Lancaster	NY	14086	716-683-5003	683-5045
Andrews Excavating Inc 5 W Willow Rd *Web:* andrewsexcavating.com	Willow Street	PA	17584	717-464-3329	464-4963
B & B Wrecking & Excavating Inc 4510 E 71st St Ste 6 *Web:* www.bbwrecking.net	Cleveland	OH	44105	216-429-1700	429-1717
Barnard Construction Company Inc PO Box 99 *Web:* www.barnard-inc.com	Bozeman	MT	59771	406-586-1995	586-3530
Berkel & Co Contractors Inc PO Box 335 *Web:* www.berkelandcompany.com	Bonner Springs	KS	66012	913-422-5125	441-0402
Bi-Con Services Inc 10901 Clay Pike Rd *Web:* www.biconservices.com	Derwent	OH	43733	740-685-2542	685-3863
Borderland Construction Company Inc 400 E 38 St. *Web:* borderland-inc.com	Tucson	AZ	85713	520-623-0900	623-0232
BR Kreider & Son Inc 63 Kreider Ln. *Web:* www.brkreider.com	Manheim	PA	17545	717-898-7651	569-8074
Carl Bolander & Sons Company Inc 251 Starkey St *Web:* www.bolander.com	Saint Paul	MN	55107	651-224-6299	223-8197
Case Foundation Co 1325 W Lake St. *TF:* 800-999-4087 ■ *Web:* www.casefoundation.com	Roselle	IL	60172	630-529-2911	529-2995
CP Ward Inc PO Box 900 *Web:* www.cpward.com	Scottsville	NY	14546	585-889-8800	889-6008
Dywidag Systems International 320 Marmon Dr *TF:* 800-457-7633 ■ *Web:* www.dywidag-systems.com	Bolingbrook	IL	60440	630-739-1100	739-5517
Feutz Contractors Inc 1120 N Main St PO Box 130 *Web:* www.feutzcontractors.com	Paris	IL	61944	217-465-8402	463-2256
Foundation Constructors Inc 81 Big Break Rd PO Box 97 *TF:* 800-841-8740 ■ *Web:* www.foundationpiledriving.com	Oakley	CA	94561	925-754-6633	625-5783
Francis O Day Construction Company Inc 850 E Gude Dr *Web:* www.foday.com	Rockville	MD	20850	301-652-2400	340-6592
Geo-Con Inc 1250 Fifth Ave *Web:* www.geocon.net	New Kensington	PA	15235	412-856-7700	373-3357
George J Igel & Company Inc 2040 Alum Creek Dr *Web:* www.igelco.com	Columbus	OH	43207	614-445-8421	445-8205
Harry C. Crooker & Sons Inc PO Box 5001 *Web:* www.crooker.com	Topsham	ME	04086	207-729-5511	725-4025
Hayward Baker Inc 1130 Annapolis Rd Ste 202 *TF:* 800-456-6548 ■ *Web:* www.haywardbaker.com	Odenton	MD	21113	410-551-8200	551-1900
HT Sweeney & Son Inc 308 Dutton Mill Rd *Web:* htsweeney.com	Brookhaven	PA	19015	610-872-8896	874-6730
Independence Excavating Inc 5720 Schaaf Rd *TF:* 800-524-3478 ■ *Web:* www.indexc.com	Independence	OH	44131	216-524-1700	524-1701
J Fletcher Creamer & Son Inc 101 E Broadway *TF:* 800-835-9801 ■ *Web:* www.jfcson.com	Hackensack	NJ	07601	201-488-9800	488-2901
Kamminga & Roodvoets Inc 3435 Broadmoor Ave SE.	Grand Rapids	MI	49512	616-949-0800	949-1894
Luburgh Inc 4174 E Pk.	Zanesville	OH	43701	740-452-3668	454-7225
M Rondano Inc 49 E Ave *Web:* www.rondano.com	Norwalk	CT	06851	203-846-1577	846-9564
Manafort Bros Inc 414 New Britain Ave *Web:* www.manafort.com	Plainville	CT	06062	860-229-4853	747-4861
Markham Contracting Company Inc 22820 N 19th Ave. *Web:* www.markhamcontracting.com	Phoenix	AZ	85027	623-869-9100	869-9400
McAninch Corp 4001 Delaware Ave *Web:* www.mcaninchcorp.com	West Des Moines	IA	50313	515-267-2500	267-2550
McGowan-Stauffer Inc 1400 Stn St. *Web:* www.mcgowan-stauffer.com	Coraopolis	PA	15108	412-264-3500	
Merlyn Contractors Inc PO Box 917 *Web:* www.merlyn.us	Novi	MI	48376	248-349-3800	

				Phone	Fax
Moretrench American Corp 100 Stickle Ave *Web:* www.moretrench.com	Rockaway	NJ	07866	973-627-2100	627-3950
Nicholson Construction Co 12 McClane St *TF:* 800-388-2340 ■ *Web:* www.nicholsonconstruction.com	Cuddy	PA	15031	412-221-4500	221-3127
Noralco Corp 1920 Lincoln Rd *Web:* www.noralco.com	Pittsburgh	PA	15235	412-361-6678	361-6535
Oldcastle Materials Inc 900 Ashwood Pkwy Ste 700 *Web:* www.apac.com	Atlanta	GA	30338	770-522-5600	522-5608
Ortiz Enterprises Inc 6 Cushing Way Ste 200 *Web:* www.ortizent.com	Irvine	CA	92618	949-753-1414	
Park Construction Company Inc 1481 81st Ave NE *Web:* www.parkconstructionco.com	Minneapolis	MN	55432	763-786-9800	786-2952
Pavex Inc 4400 Gettysburg Rd *Web:* pavexinc.com	Camp Hill	PA	17011	717-761-1502	761-0329
Perry Engineering Company Inc 1945 Millwood Pk *Web:* www.perryeng.com	Winchester	VA	22602	540-667-4310	667-7618
Phillips & Jordan Inc 6621 Wilbanks Rd *TF:* 800-955-0876 ■ *Web:* www.pandj.com	Knoxville	TN	37912	865-688-8342	688-8369
PT Ferro Construction Co 700 Rowell Ave *Web:* www.ptferro.com	Joliet	IL	60433	815-726-6284	726-5614
Raymond Excavating Co Inc 800 Gratiot Blvd *TF:* 800-837-6770 ■ *Web:* www.raymondexcavating.com	Marysville	MI	48040	810-364-6881	
Richard Goettle Inc 12071 Hamilton Ave *Web:* www.goettle.com	Cincinnati	OH	45231	513-825-8100	825-8107
Ruttura & Sons Construction Co Inc 200 Cabot St *Web:* www.ruttura.com	West Babylon	NY	11704	631-454-0291	454-8804
Ryan Inc Central 2700 E Racine St *Web:* www.ryancentral.com	Janesville	WI	53545	608-754-2291	754-3290
Seubert Excavators Inc 604 King St	Cottonwood	ID	83522	208-962-3501	
Shoosmith Bros Inc 11800 Lewis Rd *Web:* www.shoosmith.com	Chester	VA	23831	804-748-5823	748-8482
Sierrita Mining & Ranching Company Inc 9333 White Hills Loop	Sahuarita	AZ	85629	520-625-1204	
Soil Engineering Construction Inc 927 Arguello St *Web:* soilengineeringconstruction.com	Redwood City	CA	94063	650-367-9595	367-8139
Stroer & Graff Inc 1830 Phillips Ln	Antioch	CA	94509	925-778-0200	778-6766
Subsurface Constructors Inc 110 Angelica St *Web:* www.subsurfaceconstructors.com	Saint Louis	MO	63147	314-421-2460	421-2479
Super Excavators Inc N 59 W 14601 Bobolink Ave *Web:* www.superexcavators.com	Menomonee Falls	WI	53051	262-252-3200	252-8079
Terra Engineering & Construction Corp 2201 Vondron Rd *Web:* whyterra.com	Madison	WI	53718	608-221-3501	221-4075
TJ Lambrecht Construction Inc 10 Gougar Rd	Joliet	IL	60432	815-727-9211	727-6421
Union Engineering Company Inc 3658 N Ventura Ave	Ventura	CA	93001	805-648-3373	
Urban Foundation/Engineering LLC 32-33 111th St *TF:* 877-395-5459	East Elmhurst	NY	11369	718-478-3021	899-4967
Velting Contractors Inc 3060 Breton Rd SE *Web:* www.velting.com	Kentwood	MI	49512	616-949-6660	949-8168

189-6 Glass & Glazing Contractors

				Phone	Fax
Benson Industries LLC 1650 NW Naito Pkwy Ste 250 *Web:* www.bensonglobal.com	Portland	OR	97209	503-226-7611	226-0070
Cartner Glass Systems Inc 2508 Westinghouse Blvd	Charlotte	NC	28273	704-588-1976	588-9440
Culbertson Enterprises Inc (CEI) 600A Snyder Ave *TF:* 800-382-2685	West Chester	PA	19382	610-436-6400	
Enclos Corp 2770 Blue Water Rd *TF:* 888-234-2966 ■ *Web:* www.enclos.com	Eagan	MN	55121	651-796-6100	994-6360
General Glass Company Inc 5797 MacCorkle Ave SE	Charleston	WV	25304	304-925-2171	925-8915
Giroux Glass Inc 850 W Washington Blvd *TF:* 800-684-5277 ■ *Web:* www.girouxglass.com	Los Angeles	CA	90015	213-747-7406	747-8778
Karas & Karas Glass Company Inc 455 Dorchester Ave *TF:* 800-888-1235 ■ *Web:* www.karasglass.com	Boston	MA	02127	617-268-8800	269-0536
Lafayette Glass Company Inc 2841 Teal Rd *Web:* www.lafayetteglass.com	Lafayette	IN	47905	765-474-1402	
Lee & Cates Glass Inc 5355 Shawland Rd *TF:* 888-844-1989 ■ *Web:* www.leeandcatesglass.com	Jacksonville	FL	32254	904-358-8555	358-8777
Lynbrook Glass & Architectural Metals Corp 941 Motor Pkwy *Web:* www.lynbrookglass.com	Hauppauge	NY	11788	631-582-3060	582-3974
Masonry Arts Inc 2105 Third Ave N *Web:* www.masonryarts.com	Bessemer	AL	35020	205-428-0780	
National Glass & Metal Company Inc 1424 Easton Rd Ste 400 *Web:* www.ngmco.com	Horsham	PA	19044	215-938-8880	938-7028
Sashco Inc 720 S Rochester Ave Ste D *TF:* 800-600-3232 ■ *Web:* www.sashcoinc.com	Ontario	CA	91761	909-937-8222	937-8223
Sound Glass Sales Inc 5501 75th St W *TF:* 800-468-9949 ■ *Web:* www.soundglass.com	Tacoma	WA	98499	253-473-7477	473-0849
Waltek & Company Ltd 2130 Waycorss Rd *Web:* www.walteklttd.com	Cincinnati	OH	45240	513-577-7980	577-7990
Walters & Wolf 41450 Boscell Rd *Web:* www.waltersandwolf.com	Fremont	CA	94538	510-490-1115	651-7172

189-7 Masonry & Stone Contractors

				Phone	Fax
Bruns-Gutzwiller Inc 305 John St *Web:* www.bruns-gutzwiller.com	Batesville	IN	47006	812-934-2105	934-2107
Caretti Inc 4590 Industrial Pk Rd PO Box 1301 *Web:* www.carettimasonry.com	Camp Hill	PA	17011	717-737-6759	737-6880
Culbertson Enterprises Inc (CEI) 600A Snyder Ave *TF:* 800-382-2685	West Chester	PA	19382	610-436-6400	
Dee Brown Inc (DBI) 4101 S Shiloh Rd PO Box 570335 **Fax:* Tech Supp ■ *Web:* www.deebrowncompanies.com	Dallas	TX	75357	214-321-6443	328-1039*
Design Masonry Inc 20703 Santa Clara St *Web:* www.designmasonry.com	Canyon Country	CA	91351	661-298-1013	298-0117
Edgar Boettcher Mason Contractors Inc Yard 3803 N Euclid *Web:* www.boettchermasonry.com	Bay City	MI	48706	989-684-4807	684-4824
Evans-Mason Inc 1021 S Grand Ave E *Web:* evans-mason.com	Springfield	IL	62703	217-522-3396	522-3190
Gallegos Corp PO Box 821 *TF:* 800-425-5346 ■ *Web:* www.gallegoscorp.com	Vail	CO	81658	970-926-3737	926-3727
International Chimney Corp 55 S Long St **Fax Area Code:* 716 ■ *TF:* 800-828-1446 ■ *Web:* www.internationalchimney.com	Williamsville	NY	14221	800-828-1446	634-3983*
JD Long Masonry Inc 7044 Colchester Park Dr PO Box 1457 *Web:* www.jdlongmasonry.net/gallery.htm	Manassas	VA	20112	703-550-8880	730-5210
John J Smith Masonry Co 9200 Green Pk Rd *Web:* www.smithmasonry.com	Saint Louis	MO	63123	314-894-9500	894-1172
Kauai Builders Ltd 3988 Halau St	Lihue	HI	96766	808-245-2911	245-1769
Kretschmar & Smith Inc 6293 Pedley Rd *Web:* kandsmasonry.com	Riverside	CA	92509	951-361-1405	
Leonard Masonry Inc 5925 Fee Fee Rd *Web:* www.leonardmasonry.com	Hazelwood	MO	63042	314-731-5500	731-3366
Lindblad Construction Co 717 E Cass St *Web:* www.lindbladconstruction.com	Joliet	IL	60432	815-726-6251	723-4907
Manganaro Corp New England 52 Cummings Pk *Web:* www.manganaro.com	Woburn	MA	01801	781-937-8880	937-8882
Masonry Arts Inc 2105 Third Ave N *Web:* www.masonryarts.com	Bessemer	AL	35020	205-428-0780	
MB Haynes Corp 187 Deaverview Rd *Web:* www.mbhaynes.com	Asheville	NC	28806	828-254-6141	253-8136
Mid-Continental Restoration Company Inc 401 E Hudson Rd PO Box 429 *TF:* 800-835-3700 ■ *Web:* www.midcontinental.com	Fort Scott	KS	66701	620-223-3700	223-5052
Montana Stone Gallery LLC 6900 Kestrel Dr *Web:* www.montanastonegallery.com	Missoula	MT	59808	406-541-7625	
Otto Baum Company Inc 866 N Main St *Web:* www.ottobaum.com	Morton	IL	61550	309-266-7114	263-1050
Pyramid Masonry Contractors Inc 2330 Mellon Ct *Web:* pyramidmasonry.net	Decatur	GA	30035	770-987-4750	981-7142
Ron Kendall Masonry Inc 101 Benoist Farms Rd *TF:* 866-844-1404 ■ *Web:* www.ronkendallmasonry.com	West Palm Beach	FL	33411	561-793-5924	795-2621
Schiffer Mason Contractors Inc 2190 Delhi St NE PO Box 250 *Web:* www.schiffermasonry.com	Holt	MI	48842	517-694-2566	
Seedorff Masonry Inc 408 W Mission St *Web:* www.seedorff.com	Strawberry Point	IA	52076	563-933-2296	933-4114
Snow Jr & King Inc 2415 Church St *Web:* www.snowjrandking.com	Norfolk	VA	23504	757-627-8621	
Sun Valley Masonry Inc 10828 N Cave Creek Rd *Web:* www.svmasonry.com	Phoenix	AZ	85020	602-943-6106	997-6857
Treviicos Corp 38 Third Ave *Web:* www.treviicos.com	Charlestown	MA	02129	617-241-4800	737-5810
WASCO Inc 1122 Second Ave N Ste B *Web:* www.wascomasonry.com	Nashville	TN	37208	615-244-9090	726-2643

189-8 Painting & Paperhanging Contractors

				Phone	Fax
Ascher Bros Company Inc 3033 W Fletcher St *Web:* www.ascherbrothers.com	Chicago	IL	60618	773-588-0001	588-5350
Askins Family LTP 208 S Blanding St	Lake City	SC	29560	843-394-8555	394-8333
Avalotis Co 400 Jones St *Web:* www.avalotis.com	Verona	PA	15147	412-828-9666	
Benise-Dowling & Assoc Inc 5068 Snapfinger Woods Dr *Web:* www.benise-dowling.com	Decatur	GA	30035	770-981-4237	593-0342
Borbon Inc 7312 Walnut Ave *Web:* www.borbon.net	Buena Park	CA	90620	714-994-0170	994-0641
Brock Services LLC 1675 Spindletop Rd *TF:* 800-600-9675 ■ *Web:* www.brockgroup.com	Beaumont	TX	77705	409-833-7571	839-4705
CertaPro Painters Ltd 150 Green Tree Rd Ste 1003 **Fax Area Code:* 610 ■ *TF:* 800-689-7271 ■ *Web:* www.certapro.com	Oaks	PA	19456	800-689-7271	650-9997*
E Caligari & Son Inc 1333 Ingleside Rd *Web:* www.ecaligariandson.com	Norfolk	VA	23502	757-853-4511	
F D Thomas Inc 217 Bateman Dr *Web:* www.fdthomas.com	Central Point	OR	97502	541-664-3010	664-1105
George E Masker Inc 887 71st Ave *Web:* www.maskerpainting.com	Oakland	CA	94621	510-568-1206	638-2530
Goodman Decorating Co 3400 Atlanta Industrial Pkwy NW *Web:* www.goodman-decorating.com	Atlanta	GA	30331	404-965-3626	965-2558

	City	State	Zip	Phone	Fax
Hartman-Walsh Painting Co 7144 N Market St *Web:* www.hartmanwalsh.com	Saint Louis	MO	63133	314-863-1800	863-6964
Hess Sweitzer Inc 2805 S 160th St *Web:* www.hesssweitzerpainting.com	New Berlin	WI	53151	262-641-9100	
JP Carroll Company Inc 310 N Madison Ave *Web:* myhomepro.org	Los Angeles	CA	90004	323-660-9230	
K2 Industrial Services 5233 Hohman Ave *TF:* 866-524-6387 ■ *Web:* www.k2industrial.com	Hammond	IN	46320	219-933-5300	933-5301
Long Painting Co 21414 68th Ave S *TF:* 800-678-5664 ■ *Web:* www.longpainting.com	Kent	WA	98032	253-234-8050	234-0034
Madias Bros Inc 12850 Evergreen Rd	Detroit	MI	48223	313-272-5330	272-5345
Midwest Pro Painting Inc 12845 Farmington Rd *TF:* 800-860-6757 ■ *Web:* www.mpp-inc.com	Livonia	MI	48150	734-427-1040	427-0209
ML McDonald LLC 50 Oakland St PO Box 315 *TF:* 800-733-6243 ■ *Web:* www.mlmcdonald.com	Watertown	MA	02471	617-923-0900	926-8418
National Services Group Inc 1682 Langley Ave *TF:* 800-394-6000 ■ *Web:* www.nationalservicesgroup.com	Irvine	CA	92614	714-564-7900	564-8725
NLP Enterprises Inc PO Box 349 *Web:* www.nlpentinc.com	Owings Mills	MD	21117	410-356-7500	356-7525
Peter King Corp 11040 N 19th Ave *Web:* petekingaz.com	Phoenix	AZ	85029	602-944-4441	943-4876
Specialty Finishes Inc 1545 Marietta Blvd NW *Web:* www.specialtyfinishes.com	Atlanta	GA	30318	404-351-1062	351-0535
TMI Coatings Inc 3291 Terminal Dr *TF:* 800-328-0229 ■ *Web:* www.tmicoatings.com	Saint Paul	MN	55121	651-452-6100	452-0598
Vulcan Painters Inc PO Box 1010 *Web:* www.vulcan-group.com	Bessemer	AL	35021	205-428-0556	424-2267

189-9 Plastering, Drywall, Acoustical, Insulation Contractors

	City	State	Zip	Phone	Fax
Acousti Engineering Co of Florida Inc 4656 34th St SW *TF:* 800-434-3467 ■ *Web:* www.acousti.com	Orlando	FL	32811	407-425-3467	425-5108
Allied Construction Services & Color Inc 2122 Fleur Dr PO Box 937 *TF:* 800-365-4855 ■ *Web:* www.alliedconst.com	Des Moines	IA	50304	515-288-4855	288-2069
Anning Johnson Company Inc 1959 Anson Dr *Web:* www.anningjohnson.com	Melrose Park	IL	60160	708-681-1300	681-1310
API Construction Co 1100 Old Hwy 8 NW *TF:* 800-223-4922 ■ *Web:* www.apiconst.com	New Brighton	MN	55112	651-636-4320	636-0312
Baker Triangle 401 Highway 80 E *TF:* 800-458-3480 ■ *Web:* www.bakerdrywall.com	Mesquite	TX	75150	972-289-5534	
Bayside Interiors Inc 3220 Darby Common *Web:* www.baysideinteriors.com	Fremont	CA	94539	510-438-9171	438-9375
BHN Corp 435 Madison Ave *Web:* www.bhncorp.com	Memphis	TN	38103	901-521-9500	521-9507
Burnham Industrial Contractors Inc 3229 Babcock Blvd *Web:* www.burnhamindustrial.net	Pittsburgh	PA	15237	412-366-6622	366-7540
Cannon Constructors Inc 17000 Ventura Blvd Ste 301 *Web:* www.cannongroup.com	Encino	CA	91316	818-906-6200	906-6220
CE Thurston & Sons Inc 3335 Croft St *TF:* 800-444-7713 ■ *Web:* www.cethurston.com	Norfolk	VA	23513	757-855-7700	
Central Ceilings Inc 36 Norfolk Ave *Web:* www.centralceilings.com	South Easton	MA	02375	508-238-6985	238-2191
Circle B Company Inc 5636 S Meridian St *Web:* circlebco.com	Indianapolis	IN	46217	317-787-5746	780-2654
Circle Group, The 1275 Alderman Dr *Web:* www.thecirclegroup.com	Alpharetta	GA	30005	678-356-1000	
Cleveland Construction Inc 8620 Tyler Blvd *Web:* www.clevelandconstruction.com	Mentor	OH	44060	440-255-8000	205-1138
Davenport Insulation Inc 7400 Gateway Ct *TF:* 855-626-6459 ■ *Web:* www.truteam.com/davenportmanassas	Manassas	VA	20109	703-631-7744	631-8730
Daw Technologies Inc 1600 West 2200 South Ste 201 *Web:* www.dawtech.com	Salt Lake City	UT	84119	801-977-3100	973-6640
Drywall Contractors Inc 2920 N Arlington Ave *Web:* www.drywallpartners.com	Indianapolis	IN	46218	317-546-6605	
E&K Companies 343 Carol Ln *TF:* 800-365-5760 ■ *Web:* www.e-kco.com	Elmhurst	IL	60126	630-530-9001	
Entrx Corp 800 Nicollet Mall Ste 2690	Minneapolis	MN	55402	612-333-0614	338-7332
FL Crane & Sons Inc 508 S Spring St PO Box 428 *TF:* 800-748-9523 ■ *Web:* www.flcrane.com	Fulton	MS	38843	662-862-2172	862-2649
Group Builders Inc 511 Mokauea St *Web:* www.groupbuilders.net	Honolulu	HI	96819	808-832-0888	
Henderson-Johnson Co Inc 918 Canal St *Web:* www.hjcoinc.com	Syracuse	NY	13210	315-479-5561	479-5585
Interior Construction Services Ltd 2930 Market St *Web:* www.ics-stl.com	Saint Louis	MO	63103	314-534-6664	534-6663
Irex Contracting Group 120 N Lime St *TF:* 800-487-7255 ■ *Web:* www.irexcontracting.com	Lancaster	PA	17608	800-487-7255	
ISI Insulation Specialties Inc 2142 Rheem Dr Ste A **Fax Area Code:* 410	Pleasanton	CA	94588	925-846-7990	439-3769*
Jacobson & Company Inc 1079 E Grand St PO Box 511 *Web:* www.jacobsoncompany.com	Elizabeth	NJ	07207	908-355-5200	355-8680
KHS & S Contractors Inc 5422 Bay Ctr Dr Ste 200 *TF:* 866-991-7277 ■ *Web:* www.khss.com	Tampa	FL	33609	813-628-9330	628-4339
Kramig Insulation 323 S Wayne Ave *TF:* 888-579-0079 ■ *Web:* www.kramiginsulation.com	Cincinnati	OH	45215	513-761-4010	
Land Coast Insulation Inc 4017 Second St *TF:* 800-333-9424 ■ *Web:* www.landcoast.com	New Iberia	LA	70560	337-367-7741	367-7744
Lotspeich Co 16101 NW 54th Ave *Web:* www.lotspeich.com	Miami	FL	33014	305-624-7777	624-4517
Luse Holdings Inc 3990 Enterprise Ct *Web:* luse.com	Aurora	IL	60504	630-862-2600	862-2674
M Ecker & Co 9525 W Bryn Mawr Ave Ste 900	Rosemont	IL	60018	847-994-6000	233-9715
Manganaro Corp New England 52 Cummings Pk *Web:* www.manganaro.com	Woburn	MA	01801	781-937-8880	937-8882
Marek Bros Co 3701 Piney Woods *Web:* www.marekbros.com	Houston	TX	77018	713-681-9213	681-0446
Midwest Drywall Company Inc 1351 S Reca Ct *Web:* www.mwdw.com	Wichita	KS	67209	316-722-9559	722-9682
ML McDonald LLC 50 Oakland St PO Box 315 *TF:* 800-733-6243 ■ *Web:* www.mlmcdonald.com	Watertown	MA	02471	617-923-0900	926-8418
National Acoustics Inc 515 W 36th St *Web:* nationalacoustics.com	New York	NY	10001	212-695-1252	695-4539
Paul J Krez Co 7831 N Nagle Ave *Web:* www.krezgroup.com	Morton Grove	IL	60053	847-581-0017	965-7841
Precision Walls Inc 1230 NE MaynaRd Rd *TF:* 800-849-9255 ■ *Web:* www.precisionwalls.com	Cary	NC	27513	919-832-0380	839-1402
Shields Inc 2625 Hope Church Rd *Web:* www.shieldsinc.com	Winston-Salem	NC	27103	336-765-9040	765-3715
South Valley Drywall Inc 12362 Dumont Way *Web:* www.southvalleydrywall.com	Littleton	CO	80125	303-791-7212	470-0116
Spectrum Interiors Inc 2652 Crescent Springs Rd *Web:* www.spectruminterior.com	Crescent Springs	KY	41017	859-331-2696	331-4322
Thorne Assoc Inc 1450 W Randolph St *Web:* www.thorneassociates.com	Chicago	IL	60607	312-738-5230	738-5249
TJ McCartney Inc 3 Capitol St Ste 1 *Web:* www.tjminc.com	Nashua	NH	03063	603-889-6380	880-0770
Turner-Brooks Inc 28811 John R Rd *Web:* turnerbrooks.com	Madison Heights	MI	48071	248-548-3400	548-9213
Waco Inc 5450 Lewis Rd PO Box 829 *Web:* www.wacoinc.net	Sandston	VA	23150	804-222-8440	226-3241
Walldesign Inc 5940 Key Ct	Loomis	CA	95650	916-660-0102	
Western Partitions Inc 8300 SW Hunziker Rd *TF:* 800-783-0315 ■ *Web:* www.westernpartitions.com	Tigard	OR	97223	503-620-1600	624-5781
Wyatt Inc 4545 Campbells Run Rd *Web:* www.wyattinc.com	Pittsburgh	PA	15205	412-787-5800	787-5845

189-10 Plumbing, Heating, Air Conditioning Contractors

	City	State	Zip	Phone	Fax
A & B Mechanical Contractors Inc 272 West 3620 South *Web:* abmechanicalcontractors.com	Salt Lake City	UT	84115	801-263-1700	
AC Corp 301 Creek Ridge Rd *TF:* 800-422-7378 ■ *Web:* www.accorporation.com	Greensboro	NC	27406	336-273-4472	765-0416
Accent Plumbing Inc 21101 Fm 685	Pflugerville	TX	78660	512-251-2819	
ACCO Engineered Systems 6265 San Fernando Rd *TF Cust Svc:* 800-998-2226 ■ *Web:* www.accoair.com	Glendale	CA	91201	818-243-1727	247-6533
Action Inc 1308 Church St *Web:* action-mechanical.com	Barling	AR	72923	479-452-5723	
Adkins & Kimbrough Mechanical 4415 Turin Dr *Web:* jadkinsmechanical.com	Bessemer	AL	35020	205-432-4000	
Adrian L Merton Inc 9011 E Hampton Dr *Web:* almertoninc.com	Capitol Heights	MD	20743	301-336-2700	
Advance Mechanical Contractors 1301 E Burnett St *Web:* advancemechanicalcontractors.com	Signal Hill	CA	90755	562-426-1725	
Advance Mechanical Systems Inc 425 Algonquin Rd *Web:* www.jfahern.com	Arlington Heights	IL	60005	847-593-2510	593-2536
Air Comfort Corp 2550 Braga Dr *TF:* 800-466-3779 ■ *Web:* www.aircomfort.com	Broadview	IL	60155	708-345-1900	345-2730
Air Con Refrigeration & Heating Inc 123 Lake St	Waukegan	IL	60085	847-336-4128	336-4949
Air Controls Bozeman Inc 7510 Shedhorn Dr *Web:* aircontrolsbozeman.com	Bozeman	MT	59718	406-587-6292	
Aire Serv Heating & Air Conditioning Inc 1020 N University Parks Dr Ste 101 *TF:* 855-259-2280 ■ *Web:* www.aireserv.com	Waco	TX	76707	254-523-3600	
Airtrol Inc 3960 N St *Web:* airtrolmechanical.com	Baton Rouge	LA	70806	225-383-2617	343-7986
AJ Perri Inc 1138 Pine Brook Rd *Web:* ajperri.com	Tinton Falls	NJ	07724	732-982-8700	
Al Gordon Plumbing & Heating LC 3855 W Airline Hwy *Web:* algordonplumbing.com	Waterloo	IA	50703	319-233-3991	
Alaka'i Mechanical Corp 2655 Waiwai Loop *TF:* 800-600-1085 ■ *Web:* www.alakaimechanical.com	Honolulu	HI	96819	808-834-1085	834-1800
Albert Arno Inc 5000 Claxton Ave *Web:* albertarnostl.com	St Louis	MO	63120	314-383-2700	
Aldag Honold Mechanical Inc 3509 S Business Dr *Web:* www.aldaghonold.com	Sheboygan	WI	53082	920-458-5558	458-3750
All Hvac Service Company Inc 9030 Ft Hamilton Pkwy *Web:* allhvac.com	Brooklyn	NY	11209	718-833-0148	
Allen'S Tri-State Mechanical 404 S Hayden St *Web:* allenstristate.com	Amarillo	TX	79101	806-376-8345	
Allied Fire Protection LP PO Box 2842 *TF:* 800-604-2600 ■ *Web:* www.alliedfireprotection.com	Pearland	TX	77588	281-485-6803	412-9668
Allied Mechanical Services Inc 145 N Plains Industrial Rd *TF:* 888-237-3017 ■ *Web:* www.alliedmechanical.com	Wallingford	CT	06492	269-344-0191	
ALLPoints Inc 909 Lunt Ave *Web:* allpointsinc.net	Schaumburg	IL	60193	847-585-0160	
Althoff Industries Inc 8001 S Rt 31 **Fax:* Sales ■ *TF:* 800-225-2443 ■ *Web:* www.althoffind.com	Crystal Lake	IL	60014	815-455-7000	455-9375*

Company / Address	City	State	Zip	Phone	Fax
American Mechanical Services 13300 Mid Atlantic Blvd *Web:* www.amsofusa.com	Laurel	MD	20708	301-206-5070	206-2520
American Residential Services LLC 9010 Maier Rd Ste 105 *TF:* 866-399-2885 ■ *Web:* www.ars.com	Laurel	MD	20723	901-271-9700	
Anderson Rowe & Buckley Inc 2833 Third St	San Francisco	CA	94107	415-282-1625	282-0752
Anron Air Systems Inc 440 Wyandanch Ave *Web:* anronac.com	West Babylon	NY	11704	631-643-3433	491-6983
AO Reed & Co 4777 Ruffner St. *Web:* www.aoreed.com	San Diego	CA	92111	858-565-4131	292-6958
Arden Engineering Constructors LLC 505 Narragansett Pk Dr. *Web:* www.ardeneng.com	Pawtucket	RI	02861	401-727-3500	727-3540
Armistead Mechanical Inc 168 Hopper Ave. *TF:* 800-587-5267 ■ *Web:* www.armisteadmechanical.com	Waldwick	NJ	07463	201-447-6740	447-6744
Arnold Refrigeration Inc 1122 N Cherry *TF:* 800-441-1170 ■ *Web:* arnoldrefrigeration.com	San Antonio	TX	78202	210-225-5493	225-2605
ASA Controls Inc 10051 Simonson Rd Ste 8 *Web:* asacontrols.com	Harrison	OH	45030	513-353-3101	
Atlantic Constructors Inc 1401 Battery Brooke Pkwy *Web:* www.atlanticconstructors.com	Richmond	VA	23237	804-222-3400	222-6638
Atlas Welding & Boiler Repair Inc 2373 Tiebout Ave	Bronx	NY	10458	718-365-6600	367-5658
Atmac Mechanical Services LP 1201 Summit Ave *Web:* www.atmac.com	Plano	TX	75074	214-428-1544	
August Arace & Sons Inc 642 Third Ave.	Elizabeth	NJ	07202	908-354-1626	
Azco Inc PO Box 567 *Web:* www.azco-inc.com	Appleton	WI	54912	920-734-5791	734-7432
B & I Contractors Inc 2701 Prince St *Web:* bandiflorida.com	Fort Myers	FL	33916	239-332-4646	332-5928
B-G Mechanical Service Inc 12 Second Ave *TF:* 800-992-7386 ■ *Web:* www.bgmechanical.com	Chicopee	MA	01020	413-888-1500	594-2983
Baker Group 4224 Hubbell Ave *TF:* 855-262-4000 ■ *Web:* www.thebakergroup.com	Des Moines	IA	50317	515-262-4000	266-1025
Barry Assoc Inc 17 Halls Mill Rd	Preston	CT	06365	860-889-8943	
Baumann & De Groot Inc 116 E Lakewood Blvd *Web:* baumannanddegroot.com	Holland	MI	49424	616-355-6550	
Bay Mechanical Inc 2696 Reliance Dr Ste 200 *TF:* 888-229-6324 ■ *Web:* www.baymechanical.com	Virginia Beach	VA	23452	757-468-6700	468-0377
BC Plumbing Co 1215 S Seventh St *Web:* bcplumbing.net	Louisville	KY	40203	502-634-9725	
BCH Mechanical Inc 6354 118th Ave N *Web:* www.bchmechanical.com	Largo	FL	33773	727-546-3561	545-1801
Beasley Heating & Air 57 Wc Beasley Ln	Coats	NC	27521	919-894-4248	
Benjamin Plumbing Inc 5396 King James Way *Web:* benjaminplumbing.com	Madison	WI	53719	608-271-7071	
Bernhard Mechanical Contractors Inc 10321 Airline Hwy *Web:* www.bernhardmechanical.com	Baton Rouge	LA	70816	225-293-2791	
Beutler Air Conditioning Service 855 National Dr Ste 109 **Fax Area Code:* 916 ■ *TF:* 866-559-0108 ■ *Web:* www.beutler.com	Sacramento	CA	95834	866-559-0108	646-2200*
Biggs Plumbing Co 1615 Dungan Ln *Web:* biggsplumbing.com	Austin	TX	78754	512-837-5955	
BMW Constructors Inc 1740 W Michigan St *Web:* www.bmwcnstrs.com	Indianapolis	IN	46222	317-267-0400	267-0459
Bradham Bros Inc 6128 Rozzelles Ferry Rd *Web:* bradhambrothers.com	Charlotte	NC	28214	704-392-8056	
Bradley Plumbing & Heating Inc 431 Hackel Dr	Montgomery	AL	36117	334-271-0700	
Bratcher Heating & Air Conditioning Inc 1210 Ft Jesse Rd *Web:* bratchercomfort.com	Normal	IL	61761	309-454-1611	
Brewer-Garrett Company (Inc) 6800 Eastland Rd *Web:* www.brewer-garrett.com	Cleveland	OH	44130	440-243-3535	243-9993
Brown Sprinkler Corp 4705 Pinewood Rd **Fax Area Code:* 580 ■ *Web:* www.brownsprinkler.com	Louisville	KY	40218	502-968-6274	625-4398*
Btu Management Inc 534 La Crosse St *Web:* btumanagement.com	Mauston	WI	53948	608-847-4600	
Butcher Air Conditioning Company Inc 101 Boyce St *Web:* butcherac.com	Broussard	LA	70518	337-837-2000	
Butters-Fetting Company Inc 1669 S First St *TF:* 800-361-6154 ■ *Web:* www.buttersfetting.com	Milwaukee	WI	53204	414-645-1535	645-7622
C & R Mechanical 12825 Pennridge Dr *TF:* 800-524-3828 ■ *Web:* www.crmechanical.com	Bridgeton	MO	63044	314-739-1800	739-1721
Calvert Plumbing & Heating Company Inc 5806 York Rd *Web:* calvertinc.com	Baltimore	MD	21212	410-323-5400	
Campito Plumbing & Heating Inc 3 Hemlock St	Latham	NY	12110	518-785-0994	785-0769
Cape Coral Plumbing Inc 5812 Enterprise Pkwy *Web:* capecoralplumbing.com	Fort Myers	FL	33905	239-693-4714	
Capron Company Inc 411 N Stonestreet Ave *Web:* capron.com	Rockville	MD	20850	301-424-9500	
Cattrell Cos Inc 906 Franklin St *Web:* cattrell.com	Toronto	OH	43964	740-537-2481	
CCI Mechanical Inc 758 S Redwood Rd *Web:* ccimechanical.com	Salt Lake City	UT	84104	801-973-9000	975-7204
Central Air Conditioning Inc 3435 W Harry St *Web:* www.centralairco.com	Wichita	KS	67213	316-945-0797	
Central Heating And 2317 Nc Hwy 11 N *Web:* centralheataircondltioning.com	Kinston	NC	28501	252-527-6676	
Central Mechanical Construction Company Inc 631 Pecan Cir *Web:* www.centralmechanical.com	Manhattan	KS	66502	785-537-2437	537-2491
Central Systems Htg & A/C Inc 2857 Wbound 40 Hwy	Blue Springs	MO	64015	816-228-2022	
Chad Stephens Inc Dba Comfort Solutions 1470 Wall Ave	Ogden	UT	84404	801-393-2206	
Champion Industrial Contractors Inc 1420 Coldwell Ave PO Box 4399 *Web:* championindustrial.com	Modesto	CA	95350	209-524-6601	524-6931
Chapman Corp 331 S Main St *Web:* www.chapmancorporation.com	Washington	PA	15301	724-228-1900	228-4311
Charles P. Blouin Inc 203 New Zealand Rd *Web:* www.cpblouin.com	Seabrook	NH	03874	603-474-3400	474-7118
Chas Roberts Heating & Air Conditioning Inc 9828 N 19th Ave *Web:* www.chasroberts.com	Phoenix	AZ	85021	602-331-2686	997-0068
Chilmar Corp 5724 Belair Rd *Web:* chilmar.com	Baltimore	MD	21206	410-426-5482	
Christianson Air Conditioning & Plumbing 1950 Louis Henna Blvd *Web:* www.christiansonco.com	Round Rock	TX	78664	512-246-5200	246-5201
Cinfab Mechanical Inc 5240 Lester Rd *Web:* www.cinfab.com	Cincinnati	OH	45213	513-396-6100	396-7574
Clima-Tech 200 Bilmar Dr Ste 180 *Web:* clima-tech.com	Pittsburgh	PA	15205	208-377-9755	
Climate Design Air ConditioningIn 12530 47th Way N *TF:* 888-572-7245 ■ *Web:* climatedesign.com	Clearwater	FL	33762	888-572-7245	
Climate Engineers Inc 3005 Robins Rd *Web:* climate-engr.com	Hiawatha	IA	52233	319-364-1569	
Coastal Mechanical Services LLC 394 E Dr *TF:* 866-584-9528 ■ *Web:* www.coastalmechanical.com	Melbourne	FL	32904	321-725-3061	984-0718
Cobb Mechanical Contractors 2906 W Morrison *Web:* www.cobbmechanical.com	Colorado Springs	CO	80904	719-471-8958	389-0127
Collins Plumbing Inc 8130 Commercial St *Web:* collinsplumbing.com	La Mesa	CA	91942	619-469-0800	
ColonialWebb Contractors Co 2820 Ackley Ave *TF:* 877-208-3894 ■ *Web:* www.colonialwebb.com	Richmond	VA	23228	804-916-1400	264-5083
Comfort Group Inc, The 659 Thompson Ln *Web:* www.thecomfortgroup.com	Nashville	TN	37204	615-263-2900	
Comfort Systems USA 9745 Bent Oak Dr **Fax Area Code:* 713	Houston	TX	77040	832-590-5700	856-9720*
Comfort Systems USA Inc 675 Bering Ste 400 *NYSE:* FIX ■ *TF:* 800-723-8431 ■ *Web:* www.comfortsystemsusa.com	Houston	TX	77057	713-830-9600	830-9696
Correct Temp Inc 268 Hampstead Rd *Web:* correcttemp.com	Methuen	MA	01844	978-688-8700	
Corrigan Co 3545 Gratiot St *Web:* www.corriganco.com	Saint Louis	MO	63103	314-771-6200	771-8537
Cox Engineering Co 35 Industrial Dr *Web:* coxengineering.com	Canton	MA	02021	781-302-3300	302-3444
Critchfield Mechanical Inc 1901 Junction Ave *Web:* www.cmihvac.com	San Jose	CA	95131	408-437-7000	437-7199
Cullum Mechanical Construction Inc 3325 Pacific Ave *Web:* www.culluminc.com	North Charleston	SC	29418	843-554-6645	
CW Plumbing & Design Inc 41683 Date St	Murrieta	CA	92562	951-894-7703	
D J Heating & Air Conditioning Inc 1409 Rt 9W	Marlboro	NY	12542	845-236-4436	
Dauenhauer & Son Plumbing & Piping Company Inc 3416 Robards Ct *Web:* www.dauenhauerplumbing.com	Louisville	KY	40218	502-451-2882	
Dave Droegkamp Heating Air Conditioning & Sheet Metal Inc 540 Norton Dr *Web:* davedroegkamp.com	Hartland	WI	53029	262-367-2820	
Davis Contractors Ltd 5205 Fm 236	Cuero	TX	77954	361-275-5721	
Dean Custom Air LLC 120 Logan Rd *Web:* deancustomair.com	Bluffton	SC	29909	843-706-2850	
DeBra-Kuempel 3976 Southern Ave *TF:* 800-395-5741 ■ *Web:* www.debra-kuempel.com	Cincinnati	OH	45227	513-271-6500	271-4676
Dee Plumbing Inc 3828 W 128th Pl *Web:* deeplumbing.com	Alsip	IL	60803	708-389-8075	
Dehart Plumbing Heating & Air Inc 311 Bitritto Way *Web:* dehartinc.com	Modesto	CA	95356	209-523-4578	
Delta Fire Sprinklers Inc 111 Tech Dr *Web:* delta-fire.com	Sanford	FL	32771	407-328-3000	
Delta Technology Corp 1223 Valentine Ave Se	Pacific	WA	98047	253-863-8415	
Dmi Corp PO Box 53 *Web:* www.deckermechanical.com	Cedar Hill	TX	75104	972-291-9907	299-6437
Doody Mechanical Inc 7450 Flying Cloud Dr *Web:* www.metromech.com	Eden Prairie	MN	55344	952-941-7010	
Dorvin D Leis Company Inc 202 Lalo St *Web:* www.leisinc.com	Kahului	HI	96732	808-877-3902	
Downey Inc 2203 W Michigan St	Milwaukee	WI	53233	414-933-3123	
Downing Heating & Air Conditioning Inc 3070 Kerner Blvd Ste K *Web:* downinghvac.com	San Rafael	CA	94901	415-485-1011	
Dunbar Mechanical Inc 2806 N Reynolds Rd *TF:* 800-719-2201 ■ *Web:* www.dunbarmechanical.com	Toledo	OH	43615	419-537-1900	537-8840
Dupree Plumbing Company Inc 869 Worley Dr *Web:* www.dupreeplumbing.com	Marietta	GA	30066	770-428-2291	
E Mitchell Inc 1580 Indiana St	San Francisco	CA	94107	415-826-2929	
Eastern Mechanical Services Inc 3 Starr St *Web:* emsinc.us	Danbury	CT	06810	203-792-7668	748-0385
Edward J Meloney Inc 22 Madison Ave.	Lansdowne	PA	19050	610-626-4900	
Elliott & Bradley Plumbing Inc 10030 Windisch Rd *Web:* elliottandbradley.com	West Chester Township	OH	45069	513-772-0050	
EM Duggan Inc 140 Will Dr *Web:* emduggan.com	Canton	MA	02021	781-828-2292	828-0991
EMCOR Group Inc 301 Merritt 7 6th Fl *NYSE:* EME ■ *TF:* 866-890-7794 ■ *Web:* www.emcorgroup.com	Norwalk	CT	06851	203-849-7800	849-7900

Company	City	State	Zip	Phone	Fax
Engineering & Refrigeration Inc 56 Baldwin Ave. *Web:* dupont.com	Jersey City	NJ	07306	201-333-4200	
Enting Water Conditioning Inc 3211 Dryden Rd *Web:* enting.com	Dayton	OH	45439	937-294-5100	
ERP Group Inc 88 Farwell St	West Haven	CT	06516	203-931-0490	
EW Tompkins Company Inc 126 Sheridan Ave *Web:* www.thetompkinsgroup.com	Albany	NY	12210	518-462-6577	462-6570
Fagan Co 3125 Brinkerhoff Rd PO Box 15238 *Web:* www.faganco.com	Kansas City	KS	66115	913-621-4444	621-1735
Farmer & Irwin Corp 3300 Ave K *Web:* www.fandicorp.com	Riviera Beach	FL	33404	561-842-5316	842-5999
FE Moran 2265 Carlson Dr *Web:* femoran.com	Northbrook	IL	60062	847-498-4800	498-9091
Ferran Services & Contracting 530 Grand St *Web:* www.ferran-services.com	Orlando	FL	32805	407-422-3551	648-0961
Fisher Air Heating & Air Conditioning Services 239 Viking Ave *Web:* fisherair.com	Brea	CA	92821	714-529-9600	
Fisher Container Corp 1111 Busch Pkwy *TF:* 800-837-2247 ■ *Web:* www.fishercontainer.com	Buffalo Grove	IL	60089	847-541-0000	541-0075
Fitzgerald Contractors Inc 7103 St Vincent Ave *TF:* 800-259-3264 ■ *Web:* www.fitzgeraldcontractors.com	Shreveport	LA	71106	318-869-3262	865-9640
Foulk Bros Plumbing & Heating Co 322 W Seventh St *Web:* www.foulkbrothers.com	Sioux City	IA	51103	712-258-3388	
Fountain Construction Co 5655 Hwy 18 W *Web:* www.fountainconstruction.com	Jackson	MS	39209	601-373-4162	373-4300
Fox Service Co PO Box 19047 *TF:* 866-668-4749 ■ *Web:* www.foxservice.com	Austin	TX	78760	512-442-6782	
Frank Lill & Son Inc 785 Old Dutch Rd *Web:* www.franklillandson.com	Victoriaville	NY	14564	585-265-0490	265-1842
Frank M Booth Inc 222 Third St *Web:* www.frankbooth.com	Marysville	CA	95901	530-742-7134	742-8109
FW Spencer & Son Inc 99 S Hill Dr *Web:* www.fwspencersoninc.com	Brisbane	CA	94005	415-468-5000	468-4579
G E Tignall & Company Inc 14 Mccann Ave *Web:* getignall.com	Cockeysville	MD	21030	410-666-3000	
Gay WW Mechanical Contractor Inc 524 Stockton St *Web:* wwgmc.com	Jacksonville	FL	32204	904-388-2696	389-4901
General Hydronics Inc 1001 Zuni Dr	Alamogordo	NM	88310	575-437-6512	
George H Wilson Inc 250 Harvey W Blvd *Web:* www.geohwilson.com	Santa Cruz	CA	95060	831-423-9522	423-9903
Getzschman Heating LLC 1700 E 23rd St *Web:* getzschman.com	Fremont	NE	68025	402-721-6301	
Gillette Air Conditioning Company Inc 1215 San Francisco *Web:* www.gillette-ac.com	San Antonio	TX	78201	210-735-9235	736-1932
Godwin Plumbing Inc 3703 Division Ave *Web:* godwinplumbing.com	Grand Rapids	MI	49548	616-243-3131	
Gold Mechanical Inc 4735 W Division St *TF:* 877-873-9770 ■ *Web:* goldmechanical.com	Springfield	MO	65802	417-873-9770	
Gowan Inc 5550 Airline Dr *Web:* www.gowaninc.com	Houston	TX	77076	713-696-5400	695-1726
Goyette Mechanical Co 3842 Gorey Ave *TF:* 877-469-3883 ■ *Web:* www.goyettemechanical.com	Flint	MI	48501	810-743-6883	743-9090
GR Sponaugle & Sons Inc 4391 Chambers Hill Rd *Web:* www.grsponaugle.com	Harrisburg	PA	17111	717-564-1515	564-3675
Grant Supply Company Inc 901 Joyce Kilmer Ave *Web:* grantsupply.com	North Brunswick	NJ	08902	732-545-1018	
Green Mechanical Construction Inc 322 W Main St *Web:* gmci.com	Glasgow	KY	42141	270-651-8978	
Greg'S Heating & Air Cond Inc 2115 Pacific Blvd Se *Web:* gregsheating.com	Albany	OR	97321	541-926-8950	
Griffith ID Inc 735 S Market St *Web:* www.idgriffith.com	Wilmington	DE	19801	302-656-8253	656-8268
Grunau Company Inc 1100 W Anderson Ct *TF:* 800-365-1920 ■ *Web:* www.grunau.com	Oak Creek	WI	53154	414-216-6900	768-7950
H & H Group Inc 2801 Syene Rd *Web:* www.hhindustries.com	Madison	WI	53713	608-273-3434	273-9654
H & R Mechanical Contractors Inc 106 Demand Ct *Web:* hrmech.com	Georgetown	KY	40324	502-863-4955	
HACI Mechanical Contractors Inc 2108 W Shangri La Rd *Web:* www.hacimechanical.com	Phoenix	AZ	85029	602-944-1555	678-0266
Hampshire Fire Protection Company Inc 8 N Wentworth Ave *Web:* www.hampshirefire.com	Londonderry	NH	03053	603-432-8221	
Hanna Plumbing & Supply Co 643 S Santa Fe Ave	Vista	CA	92083	760-726-2002	
Harder Mechanical Contractors Inc 2148 NE M L King Blvd *Web:* www.harder.com	Portland	OR	97212	503-281-1112	287-5284
Hardy Corp 350 Industrial Dr *TF:* 800-289-4822 ■ *Web:* www.hardycorp.com	Birmingham	AL	35211	205-252-7191	326-6268
Harford Refrigeration Company Inc 7915 Philadelphia Rd *Web:* harfordrefrigeration.com	Rosedale	MD	21237	410-698-1076	
Harold G Butzer Inc 730 Wicker Ln *TF:* 800-769-1065 ■ *Web:* hgbutzer.com	Jefferson City	MO	65109	573-636-4115	636-7053
Harris & Hart Inc 1759 West 1200 South	Ogden	UT	84404	801-731-0577	
Harry Grodsky & Company Inc 33 Shaws Ln *Web:* www.grodsky.com	Springfield	MA	01104	413-785-1947	737-9870
Haslett Heating & Cooling Inc 920 King Ave *Web:* haslettmechanical.com	Columbus	OH	43212	614-299-2133	
Haury Plumbing & Heating Inc 1816 N Market St	Sparta	IL	62286	618-443-2416	
HE Neumann Inc 100 Middle Creek Rd *TF:* 800-627-5312 ■ *Web:* www.heneumann.com	Triadelphia	WV	26059	304-232-3040	232-7858
Heating & Plumbing Engineers Inc 407 Fillmore Pl *Web:* www.hpeinc.com	Colorado Springs	CO	80907	719-633-5414	633-4031
Heide & Cook Ltd 1714 Kanakanui St *Web:* www.heidecook.com	Honolulu	HI	96819	808-841-6161	841-4889
Heritage Mechanical Services Inc 305 Suburban Ave **Fax Area Code:* 631 ■ *Web:* www.heritagemech.com	Deer Park	NY	11729	516-558-2000	667-8613*
Herman Goldner Co Inc 7777 Brewster Ave *TF:* 800-355-5997 ■ *Web:* www.goldner.com	Philadelphia	PA	19153	215-365-5400	492-6486
High Purity Systems Inc 8432 Quarry Rd *Web:* www.highpurity.com	Manassas	VA	20110	703-330-5094	
Hill Mechanical Group 11045 Gage Ave *Web:* www.hillgrp.com	Franklin Park	IL	60131	847-451-5000	451-5011
HiMEC Mechanical 1400 Seventh St NW *Web:* www.himec.com	Rochester	MN	55901	507-281-4000	281-5206
Holaday-Parks Inc 4600 S 134 Pl *Web:* www.holadayparks.com	Seattle	WA	98168	206-248-9700	248-8700
Hooper Corp 2030 Pennsylvania Ave *TF:* 877-630-7554 ■ *Web:* www.hoopercorp.com	Madison	WI	53704	608-249-0451	249-7360
Horwitz/NSI 4401 Quebec Ave N *Web:* www.horwitzinc.com	New Hope	MN	55428	763-533-1900	235-9810
Hubbard & Drake General Mechanical Contractors Inc PO Box 1867 *TF:* 800-353-9245 ■ *Web:* www.hubbarddrake.com	Decatur	AL	35602	256-353-9244	350-5043
Humphrey Company Ltd 4439 W 12th St *Web:* www.humphreyltd.com	Houston	TX	77055	713-686-8606	
Hurckman Mechanical Industries Inc PO Box 10977 *TF:* 844-499-8771 ■ *Web:* www.hurckman.com	Green Bay	WI	54307	920-499-8771	
I & M Heating & Appliance Service Inc 1628 S Michigan St *Web:* iandmheatingandcooling.com	South Bend	IN	46613	574-288-3351	
IHP Industrial Inc 1701 S Eigth St PO Box 578 *Web:* ihpindustrial.com	Saint Joseph	MO	64502	816-364-1581	232-4473
IMCOR-Interstate Mechanical Corp 1841 E Washington St *TF:* 800-628-0211 ■ *Web:* www.imcor-az.com	Phoenix	AZ	85034	602-257-1319	271-0674
Independent Mechanical Industries Inc 4155 N Knox Ave *Web:* www.independentmech.com	Chicago	IL	60641	773-282-4500	282-2046
Industrial Air Inc 428 Edwardia Dr PO Box 8769 *Web:* www.industrialairinc.com	Greensboro	NC	27409	336-292-1030	855-7763
Industrial Contractors Inc 701 Ch Dr *TF:* 800-467-3089 ■ *Web:* www.icinorthdakota.com	Bismarck	ND	58501	701-258-9908	258-9988
Industrial Piping Inc 800 Culp Rd *TF:* 800-951-0988 ■ *Web:* www.goipi.com	Pineville	NC	28134	704-588-1100	588-5614
Interstate Mechanical Contractors Inc 3200 Henson Rd *Web:* interstatemechanical.com	Knoxville	TN	37921	865-588-0180	602-4124
J A Sauer Co 4559 Peoples Rd *Web:* jasauerco.com	Pittsburgh	PA	15237	412-931-7200	
J F Jacobs Inc 31523 W 8 Mile Rd *Web:* jfjacobsinc.net	Livonia	MI	48152	248-476-7888	
J J Plumbing LLC 4210 B ST NW Ste K *Web:* jjplumbingllc.com	Auburn	WA	98001	253-939-1390	
J Lawrence Hall Company Inc 17 Progress Ave *Web:* jlawrencehall.com	Nashua	NH	03062	603-882-2021	
J-Berd Mechanical Contractors Inc 3308 Southway Dr *Web:* j-berd.com	St Cloud	MN	56301	320-656-0847	
Jack Laurence Corp 12831 W Golden Ln	San Antonio	TX	78249	210-696-0273	
Jackson & Blanc Inc 7929 Arjons Dr *Web:* www.jacksonandblanc.com	San Diego	CA	92126	858-831-7900	527-1502
Jacobs Mechanical Inc 1366 Hopple St *Web:* jacobsmech.com	Cincinnati	OH	45225	513-681-6800	
Jamar Co 4701 Mike Colalillo Dr *Web:* www.jamarcompany.com	Duluth	MN	55807	218-628-1027	628-1174
James Craft & Son Inc 2780 York Haven Rd PO Box 8 *Web:* www.jamescraftson.com	York Haven	PA	17370	717-266-6629	266-6623
James E Conner Jr Plumbing 505 Rt 168 Stes B And C *Web:* jameseconnerjrplumbing.com	Turnersville	NJ	08012	856-784-0004	
Janazzo Services Corp 140 Norton St Rt 10 PO Box 469 *TF:* 800-297-3931 ■ *Web:* www.janazzo.com	Milldale	CT	06467	860-621-7381	621-7529
JC Higgins Corp 70 Hawes Way *Web:* www.jchigginscorp.com	Stoughton	MA	02072	781-341-1500	344-6075
JF Ahern Co 855 Morris St *TF:* 800-532-0155 ■ *Web:* www.jfahern.com	Fond du Lac	WI	54935	920-921-9020	921-8632
JH Kelly 821 Third Ave *Web:* www.jhkelly.com	Longview	WA	98632	360-423-5510	423-9170
John Bouchard & Sons Co 1024 Harrison St *Web:* www.jbouchard.com	Nashville	TN	37203	615-256-0112	256-2427
John E Green Co 220 Victor Ave *Web:* www.johnegreen.com	Highland Park	MI	48203	313-868-2400	868-0011
John Hoadley & Sons Inc 672 Union St *Web:* hoadleyandsons.com	Rockland	MA	02370	781-878-8098	
John W Danforth Co 300 Colvin Woods Pkwy *TF:* 800-888-6119 ■ *Web:* www.jwdanforth.com	Tonawanda	NY	14150	716-832-1940	832-2388
Johnson Contracting Company Inc 2750 Morton Dr *Web:* www.jccinc.com	East Moline	IL	61244	309-755-0601	
Joy Equipment Protection Inc 5690 Casitas Pass Rd *Web:* joyequipment.com	Carpinteria	CA	93014	805-684-0805	
JR Barto Heating/Air- Conditioning/Sheet Metal Inc 300 N G St *Web:* jrbarto.com	Lompoc	CA	93436	805-736-5160	

				Phone	Fax
JR Pierce Plumbing Co 14481 Wicks Blvd	San Leandro	CA	94577	510-483-5473	
Web: jrpierceplumbing.com					
Kaiser Air Cond & Sheet Metal Inc 600 Pacific Ave	Oxnard	CA	93030	805-988-1800	
Web: kaiserac.com					
Karls Mechanical Contractors Inc 954 Forward Ave	Chilton	WI	53014	920-849-2050	
Web: karlsmechanical.com					
Kenron Industrial A/C Inc 299 Gregory St	Rochester	NY	14620	585-442-5600	
Web: kenron.com					
Kings Aire Inc 1035 Kessler Dr	El Paso	TX	79907	915-592-2997	
Web: kingsaire.com					
Kinseth Plumbing & Heating Inc 148 E Main St	Belmond	IA	50421	641-444-4428	
Web: kinsethplumbing.com					
KLM Mechanical Service Inc PO Box 35121	Louisville	KY	40232	502-955-2062	
TF: 866-466-4438 ■ *Web:* klm-mechanical.com					
Kreider Ayers & Assoc Inc 1130 Patterson Ave SW	Roanoke	VA	24016	540-343-7612	
Kuhlman Inc N 56 W 16865 Ridgewood Dr	Menomonee Falls	WI	53051	262-252-9400	252-9401
Web: www.kuhlmaninc.com					
Lawman Heating & Cooling Inc PO Box 599	Sackets Harbor	NY	13685	315-646-2919	
Web: www.lawmanhc.com					
Lawson Mechanical Contractors 6090 S Watt Ave	Sacramento	CA	95829	916-381-5000	381-5073
Web: www.lawsonmechanical.com					
Leardon Boiler Works Inc 479 Walton Ave	Bronx	NY	10451	718-585-5314	
Lee Co Inc 331 Mallory Stn Rd	Franklin	TN	37067	615-567-1000	
Web: www.leecompany.com					
Lightfoot Air Conditioning & Refrigeration 1414 W Oak	Palestine	TX	75801	903-723-2665	
Web: lightfootair.com					
Limbach Facility Services LLC 31 35th St	Pittsburgh	PA	15201	412-359-2100	359-2235
Web: www.limbachinc.com					
Long Building Technologies Inc 5001 S Zuni St	Littleton	CO	80120	303-975-2100	
Web: long.com					
Lutz Frey Corp 1195 Ivy Dr	Lancaster	PA	17601	717-898-6808	898-3421
TF: 800-280-6794 ■ *Web:* www.freylutz.com					
MA Ogg Heating & Air Conditioning 4721 Arrow Hwy Ste B	Montclair	CA	91763	909-624-8608	
MacDonald-Miller Facility Solutions Inc 7717 Detroit Ave SE	Seattle	WA	98106	206-763-9400	767-6773
TF: 800-962-5979 ■ *Web:* www.macmiller.com					
Mallory & Evans Inc 646 Kentucky St	Scottdale	GA	30079	404-297-1000	297-1075
Web: www.malloryandevans.com					
Mared Mechanical Contractors Corp 4230 W Douglas Ave	Milwaukee	WI	53209	414-536-0411	
Web: maredmechanical.com					
Martin Petersen Company Inc 9800 55th St	Kenosha	WI	53144	262-658-1326	658-1048
Web: mpcmech.com					
Martz Plumbing & Heating Inc 216 W Fifth St	Waynesboro	PA	17268	717-762-6115	
McCarl's Inc 1413 Ninth Ave	Beaver Falls	PA	15010	724-843-5660	843-3180
Web: www.mccarl.com					
McClure Co 4101 N Sixth St	Harrisburg	PA	17110	717-232-9743	236-5239
TF: 800-382-1319 ■ *Web:* www.mcclureco.com					
McCrea Equipment Company Inc 4463 Beech Rd	Temple Hills	MD	20748	301-423-4585	
TF: 800-597-0091 ■ *Web:* mccreaway.com					
McKenney's Inc 1056 Moreland Industrial Blvd SE	Atlanta	GA	30316	404-622-5000	624-8665
TF: 877-440-4204 ■ *Web:* www.mckenneys.com					
McKinstry Co 5005 Third Ave S	Seattle	WA	98134	206-762-3311	762-2624
TF: 800-669-6223 ■ *Web:* www.mckinstry.com					
McNutt Service Group Inc 39 Loop Rd	Arden	NC	28704	828-212-4292	
Web: www.mcnuttservicegroup.com					
Meccon Industries Inc 2703 Bernice Rd	Lansing	IL	60438	708-474-8300	474-9550
Web: www.meccon.com					
Mechancial Service Corp 41 S Jefferson Rd	Whippany	NJ	07981	973-884-5000	
Web: mscnj.com					
Mechanical Construction Company LLC 3001 17th St	Metairie	LA	70002	504-833-8291	831-4760
Web: www.bernhardmcc.com					
Mechanical Inc 2283 US Rt 20 E	Freeport	IL	61032	815-235-2200	
Web: www.helmgroup.com					
Merit Electrical Inc 17723 Airline Hwy	Prairieville	LA	70769	225-673-8850	673-8838
Web: www.meritelectrical.com					
Mid-State Contracting LLC 2001 County Hwy U	Wausau	WI	54402	715-675-2388	675-6971
Web: www.midstatecontracting.com					
Midwest Mechanical Group 801 Parkview Blvd	Lombard	IL	60148	630-850-2300	655-0730
TF: 800-214-3680 ■ *Web:* www.midwestmech.com					
Miller Engineering Co 1616 S Main St	Rockford	IL	61102	815-963-4878	
Web: mecogroup.com					
Mitchell Plumbing & Heating Company Inc 801 N Rowley St 1328	Mitchell	SD	57301	605-996-7583	
MJ Flaherty Co 1 Gateway Ctr Ste 450	Newton	MA	02458	617-969-1492	964-0176
Web: www.mjflaherty-hvac.com					
MJ Mechanical Services Inc 2040 Military Rd	Tonawanda	NY	14150	716-874-9200	
Web: tonawandaboilerrepair.com					
MM Comfort Systems 18103 NE 68th St	Redmond	WA	98052	425-881-7920	
Web: mmcomfortsystems.com					
MMC Corp 10955 Lowell Ste 350	Overland Park	KS	66210	913-469-0101	469-8780
Web: mmccorp1932.com					
Mock Plumbing & Mechanical Inc PO Box 22456	Savannah	GA	31403	912-232-1104	232-6284
Web: www.mocksavannah.com					
Mollenberg-Betz Inc 300 Scott St	Buffalo	NY	14204	716-614-7473	
Web: www.mollenbergbetz.com					
Monterey Mechanical Co 8275 San Leandro St	Oakland	CA	94621	510-632-3173	632-0732
Web: www.montmech.com					
Moore J & Co 118 Naylon Ave	Livingston	NJ	07039	973-992-6970	992-8860
Web: www.jmoore.com					
Morrison Construction Co 1834 Summer St	Hammond	IN	46320	219-932-5036	933-7302
Web: www.mcco.com					
Mountain Air Conditioning & Heating Corp 735 S Broadway	Hicksville	NY	11801	516-935-0149	
Mr Rooter Corp 1010 N University Parks Dr	Waco	TX	76707	800-583-8003	745-2501*
**Fax Area Code:* 254 ■ *TF:* 877-766-8305 ■ *Web:* www.mrrooter.com					
Multiple Ventilation Products Inc 1313 Bigley Ave	Charleston	WV	25302	304-720-8686	
Web: mvphvac.net					
Murphy & Miller Inc 600 W Taylor St	Chicago	IL	60607	312-427-8900	427-0324
Web: www.murphymiller.com					
Murphy Co Mechanical Contractors & Engineers 1233 N Price Rd	Saint Louis	MO	63132	314-997-6600	997-4536
TF: 888-838-4038 ■ *Web:* www.murphynet.com					
MYR Group 1701 W Golf Rd Twr 3 Ste 1012	Rolling Meadows	IL	60008	847-290-1891	290-1892
Web: www.myrgroup.com					
Nagelbush Mechanical Inc 1800 NW 49th St Ste 110	Fort Lauderdale	FL	33309	954-736-3000	748-7881
Web: www.nagelbush.com					
National HVAC Service Ltd 101 Bradford Rd Ste 340	Wexford	PA	15090	724-935-9390	935-9533
TF: 800-281-3608 ■ *Web:* www.nationalhvacservice.com					
Nitro Electric Co LLC 4300 First Ave 2nd Fl	Nitro	WV	25143	304-722-7701	757-1213*
**Fax:* Acctg ■ *Web:* www.nitro-electric.com					
NV Heathorn Co 1155 Beecher St	San Leandro	CA	94577	510-569-9100	569-9106
Web: www.nvheathorn.com					
Oak Brook Mechanical Services Inc 961 S Rt 83	Elmhurst	IL	60126	630-941-3555	941-0294
Web: omshvac.com					
Oasis Air Conditioning Heating & Sheet Metal Inc 1931 Grimes St	Fallon	NV	89406	775-423-5258	
Oregon Equipment Service Corpora 180 NE Irving Ave	Bend	OR	97701	541-388-2235	
Web: oregonequipmentservice.com					
Ouellette Plumbing & Heating 36 Dorset Ln	Williston	VT	05495	802-878-6004	
P & D Mechanical Inc 627 Old Hartford Rd	Colchester	CT	06415	860-537-0617	
P1 Group Inc 2151 Haskell Ave Bldg 1	Lawrence	KS	66046	785-843-2910	
TF: 800-376-2911 ■ *Web:* www.p1group.com					
Pace Mechanical Services Inc 301 Merritt Seven	Norwalk	CT	06851	203-849-7800	849-7900
TF: 866-890-7794 ■ *Web:* www.emcorgroup.com					
Pacific Mechanical Corp 2501 Annalisa Dr	Concord	CA	94520	925-827-4940	827-0519
Web: www.pmcorporation.com					
Palmer & Sicard Inc 140 Epping Rd	Exeter	NH	03833	603-778-1841	
Web: palmerandsicard.com					
Par Plumbing Company Inc 60 N Prospect Ave	Lynbrook	NY	11563	516-887-4000	
Web: www.parplumbing.com					
PC Godfrey Inc 1816 Rozzells Ferry Rd	Charlotte	NC	28208	704-334-8604	376-5186
Web: pcgodfreyservice.com					
PC Jackson Plumbing 3908 Corporation Cir	Charlotte	NC	28216	704-391-1017	
Penguin Air Conditioning Corp 26 W St	Brooklyn	NY	11222	718-706-6500	706-2536
Web: www.penguinac.com					
Performance Contracting Group Inc 16400 College Blvd	Lenexa	KS	66219	913-888-8600	492-8723
TF: 800-255-6886 ■ *Web:* www.pcg.com					
Piedmont Mechanical Inc 116 John Dodd Rd PO Box 4925	Spartanburg	SC	29305	864-578-9114	578-5314
Web: www.piedmontmechanical.com					
Pierce Assoc Inc 4216 Wheeler Ave PO Box 9050	Alexandria	VA	22304	703-751-2400	751-2479
Web: www.pierceassociates.com					
Pipco Cos Ltd, The 1409 W Altorfer Dr	Peoria	IL	61615	309-692-4060	
Pleune Service Co 750 Himes Se	Grand Rapids	MI	49548	616-243-6374	
Web: pleuneservice.com					
Plyler Construction 3505 Texoma Pkwy PO Box 912406	Sherman	TX	75091	903-893-6393	892-3523
Web: www.plylerbuilds.com					
Poole & Kent Corp 4530 Hollins Ferry Rd	Baltimore	MD	21227	410-247-2200	247-2331
Web: www.poole-kent.com					
Postler & Jaeckle Corp 615 S Ave	Rochester	NY	14620	585-546-7450	546-4316
TF: 800-724-4252 ■ *Web:* www.postlerandjaeckle.com					
Power Piping Co 436 Butler St	Pittsburgh	PA	15223	412-323-6200	323-6334
Web: powerpipingcompany.com					
Power Process Piping Inc 45780 Port St	Plymouth	MI	48170	734-451-0130	451-0763
Web: www.ppphq.com					
Precision Piping & Mechanical Inc 5201 Middle Mt Vernon Rd	Evansville	IN	47712	812-425-5052	425-5067
Web: www.ppmiconstruction.com					
Pritchett Controls Inc 6980 Muirkirk Meadows Dr	Beltsville	MD	20705	301-470-7300	
TF: 877-743-2363 ■ *Web:* pritchettcontrols.com					
Pro-Tec Refrigeration Inc 3640 N 39th Ave	Phoenix	AZ	85019	602-222-9881	
Web: protecref.com					
Process Construction Inc 1421 Queen City Ave	Cincinnati	OH	45214	513-251-2211	
Web: www.processconstruction.com					
PSF Industries Inc 65 S Horton St	Seattle	WA	98134	206-622-1252	682-1070
TF General: 800-426-1204 ■ *Web:* www.psfindustries.com					
Questec Constructors Inc 1390 Boone Industrial Dr Ste 260	Columbia	MO	65202	573-875-0260	
Web: questec.us					
Ralph Warner & Sons Inc Plumbing & Heating 161 Berlin St	Southington	CT	06489	860-628-6826	
Ray L Hellwig Plumbing & Heating Inc 1301 Laurelwood Rd	Santa Clara	CA	95054	408-727-5612	
Web: www.rlhellwig.com					
Reedy Industries Inc 2440 Ravine Way Ste 200	Glenview	IL	60025	847-729-9450	729-0558
Web: www.reedyindustries.com					
Regional Heating & Air Conditioning Inc 2525 Won Rd	Colorado Springs	CO	80910	719-392-6171	
Reigel Plumbing & Heating Inc 1701 S Galvin Ave	Marshfield	WI	54449	715-387-3411	
Web: reigelplumbing.com					

Company	City	State	Zip	Phone	Fax
Remco Inc 195 Hempt Rd *Web:* remcopa.com	Mechanicsburg	PA	17050	717-697-0389	
Riggs Distler Company Inc 9411 Philadelphia Rd Ste M *Web:* www.riggsdistler.com	Baltimore	MD	21237	410-633-0300	633-2119
RJH Air Conditioning & Refrige 12232 Distribution Pl *Web:* rjhhvacr.com	Beltsville	MD	20705	301-776-7270	
RK Mechanical Inc 3800 Xanthia St *TF:* 877-576-9696 ■ *Web:* www.rkmi.com	Denver	CO	80238	303-355-9696	355-8666
Robert Gibb & Sons Inc 205 SW 40th St *Web:* www.robertgibb.com	Fargo	ND	58103	701-282-5900	281-0819
Robert Jones Plumbing Inc 6071 SR- 128 *Web:* robertjonesplumbing.com	Cleves	OH	45002	513-353-2230	353-2247
Rock Hill Mechanical Corp 524 Clark Ave *Web:* www.rhmcorp.com	Saint Louis	MO	63122	314-966-0600	966-3679
Roth Bros Inc PO Box 4209 *TF:* 800-872-7684 ■ *Web:* www.rothbros.com	Youngstown	OH	44515	330-793-5571	
Roth Heating Company Inc 400 W Drexel Ave *Web:* rothheating.com	Oak Creek	WI	53154	414-764-4700	
Roto-Rooter Inc 255 E Fifth St 2500 Chemed Ctr *TF:* 800-768-6911 ■ *Web:* www.rotorooter.com	Cincinnati	OH	45202	513-762-6690	
RW Warner Inc 217 Monroe Ave *Web:* www.rwwarner.com	Frederick	MD	21701	301-662-5387	698-0451
Saber Plumbing Co 325 Market Pl *Web:* saberplumbing.com	Escondido	CA	92029	760-480-5716	
Sauer Inc 11223 Phillips Pkwy Dr E *Web:* www.sauer-inc.com	Jacksonville	FL	32256	904-262-6444	
SB Ballard Construction Co 2828 Shipps Corner Rd *Web:* www.sbballard.com	Virginia Beach	VA	23453	757-440-5555	451-2873
Schambach Plumbing & Heating Inc 40W899 Russell Rd	Elgin	IL	60124	847-464-5373	
Schoppe Company Inc 352 Van Buren Ave *Web:* schoppe.net	Salt Lake City	UT	84115	801-467-5466	
Schweizer Dipple Inc 7227 Div St *Web:* www.schweizer-dipple.com	Oakwood Village	OH	44146	440-786-8090	786-8099
Shambaugh & Son LP 7614 Opportunity Dr *TF:* 866-890-7794 ■ *Web:* www.shambaugh.com	Fort Wayne	IN	46825	260-487-7777	487-7701
Shaw-Winkler Inc 4910 Dawn Ave *Web:* shawwinkler.com	East Lansing	MI	48823	517-351-5720	
Shook & Fletcher Mechanical Contractors Inc 2915 Richard Arrington Jr Blvd N *Web:* shook-fletcher.com	Birmingham	AL	35203	205-252-9400	252-9407
Sigman Heating & Air Conditioning 6200 Old Saint Louis Rd *Web:* sigmanhvacr.com	Belleville	IL	62223	618-234-4343	
Silvertip Inc 600 St Mary St *Web:* silvertip-inc.com	Lewisburg	PA	17837	570-523-1206	
Smith & Oby Co 7676 Northfield Rd *Web:* www.smithandoby.com	Walton Hills	OH	44146	440-735-5333	735-5334
Sojam LLC Dba Martin J Braun Co 6325 Erdman Ave	Baltimore	MD	21205	410-488-3990	
Southern Air Inc 2655 Lakeside Dr *TF:* 800-743-1214 ■ *Web:* www.southern-air.com	Lynchburg	VA	24501	434-385-6200	385-9081
Southern Industrial Constructors Inc 6101 Triangle Dr *TF:* 866-890-7794 ■ *Web:* www.southernindustrial.com	Raleigh	NC	27617	919-782-4600	782-2935
Southland Industries 7421 Orangewood Ave *Web:* www.southlandind.com	Garden Grove	CA	92841	714-901-5800	
Spengler Company Inc 1402 Frontage Rd *Web:* spenglerco.com	Ofallon	IL	62269	618-632-4433	
Stratz Heating & Cooling Inc 20960 19 Mile Rd *Web:* stratzheatingandcooling.com	Big Rapids	MI	49307	231-796-3717	
Stromberg Sheet Metal Works Inc 6701 Distribution Dr *Web:* www.strombergmetals.com	Beltsville	MD	20705	301-931-1000	931-1020
Sturdevant Refrigeration & Air Conditioning Inc 475 Hukilike St *Web:* www.sturdevantair.com	Kahului	HI	96732	808-871-6404	
Sturm Heating Inc 1112 N Nelson St *Web:* sturmheating.com	Spokane	WA	99202	509-325-4505	
SubZero Constructors Inc 30055 Comercio *Web:* www.szero.com	Rancho Santa Margarita	CA	92688	949-216-9500	216-9539
Summers Heating & Air Conditio 6031 Rising Sun Ave *Web:* summersquality.com	Philadelphia	PA	19111	215-722-3716	
Systems Contracting Corp 214 N Washington Ave Ste 700 *Web:* tsg.bz	El Dorado	AR	71730	870-862-1315	
TA Caid Industries Inc 2275 E Ganley Rd *Web:* www.caid.com	Tucson	AZ	85706	520-294-3126	294-8180
Tatro Plumbing Company Inc 1285 Acraway Ste 300 *TF:* 888-828-7648 ■ *Web:* tatroplumbing.com	Garden City	KS	67846	620-277-2167	
TDIndustries 13850 Diplomat Dr *Web:* www.tdindustries.com	Dallas	TX	75234	972-888-9500	
Telgian Corp 10505 Sorrento Valley Rd Ste 450 *TF:* 877-835-4426 ■ *Web:* www.telgian.com	San Diego	CA	92121	858-795-1000	
Thorpe Heating & Cooling Inc 8402 Us Hwy 98 N *TF:* 855-858-2577 ■ *Web:* thorpeac.com	Lakeland	FL	33809	863-858-2577	
Tom Rostron Co Inc 2490 Tiltons Corner Rd *Web:* tomrostron.com	Wall Township	NJ	07719	732-223-8221	
Trautman & Shreve Inc 4406 Race St *Web:* www.trautman-shreve.com	Denver	CO	80216	303-295-1414	295-0324
Trouble Free Plumbing Inc 802 Willow St *Web:* troublefreeinc.com	Pekin	IL	61554	309-347-5309	
University Mechanical & Engineering Contractors Inc 1168 Fesler St *Web:* www.umec.com	El Cajon	CA	92020	619-956-2500	956-2300
US Engineering Co 3433 Roanoke Rd *Web:* www.usengineering.com	Kansas City	MO	64111	816-753-6969	931-5773
US Home Services 9260 Marketplace Dr *Web:* directenergy.com	Miamisburg	OH	45342	937-898-0826	
Vals Plumbing & Heating Inc 413 Front St *Web:* valsplumbing.com	Salinas	CA	93901	831-424-1633	
Vasey Commercial Heating & Air Company Nditioning Inc 10830 Andrade Dr *Web:* www.vasey.com	Zionsville	IN	46077	317-873-2512	
Vermont Heating & Ventilating Company Inc 16 Tigan St *Web:* www.vhv.com	Winooski	VT	05404	802-655-8805	655-8809
Victoria Air Conditioning Ltd 513 Profit Dr *Web:* victoriaair.com	Victoria	TX	77901	361-578-5241	
Viglione Heating & Cooling Inc 259 Commerce St *Web:* viglione.biz	East Haven	CT	06512	203-787-8588	
Walter N Yoder & Sons Inc 16200 McMullen Hwy SW PO Box 1337 *Web:* wnyoder.com	Cumberland	MD	21502	301-729-0610	729-1517
Ward Systems & Services Inc 2121 Cee Gee	San Antonio	TX	78217	210-824-7683	
Warwick Plumbing & Heating Corp 11048 Warwick Blvd *Web:* www.wphcorp.com	Newport News	VA	23601	757-599-6111	595-9739
Way Engineering Ltd 5308 Ashbrook Dr *Web:* wayeng.com	Houston	TX	77081	713-666-3541	
Wayne Crouse Inc 3370 Stafford St *Web:* www.waynecrouse.com	Pittsburgh	PA	15204	412-771-5176	771-2357
WB Guimarin & Co Inc 1124 Bluff Industrial Blvd *Web:* www.wbguimarin.com	Columbia	SC	29202	803-256-0515	252-8239
WB Wallis & Co 540 Kentucky St *Web:* wbwallis.com	Scottdale	GA	30079	404-294-1722	
WD Manor Mechanical Contractors Inc 1838 N 23rd Ave *Web:* www.wdmanor.com	Phoenix	AZ	85009	602-253-0703	253-3659
Weather Champions Ltd 158 Dikeman St *Web:* wechamps.com	Brooklyn	NY	11231	718-522-0300	
Webb Heating & Air Conditioning 170 Webb Way *Web:* webbhvac.com	Advance	NC	27006	336-998-2121	
Weeks Service Co 1306 Hwy 3 S *Web:* weeksservicecompany.com	League City	TX	77573	281-332-9555	332-9558
Wellington Power Corp 40th & Butler Sts *Web:* www.wellingtonpower.com	Pittsburgh	PA	15201	412-681-0103	681-0109
Western Air & Refrigeration Co 15914 S Avalon Blvd *Web:* www.limbachinc.com	Compton	CA	90220	310-327-4400	
WG Tomko Inc 2559 Rt 88 *Web:* www.wgtomko.com	Finleyville	PA	15332	724-348-2000	348-7001
William E Walter Inc 1917 Howard Ave *TF:* 800-681-3320 ■ *Web:* www.williamewalter.com	Flint	MI	48503	810-232-7459	232-8698
Williard Limbach 175 Titus Ave Ste 100 **Fax:* Cust Svc ■ *Web:* www.limbachinc.com	Warrington	PA	18976	215-488-9700	488-9699*
Worth & Company Inc 6263 Kellers Church Rd *TF:* 800-220-5130 ■ *Web:* www.worthandcompany.com	Pipersville	PA	18947	267-362-1100	362-1130
Yearout Mechanical & Engineering Inc 8501 Washington St NE *Web:* www.yearout.com	Albuquerque	NM	87113	505-884-0994	883-5073
Young Plumbing & Heating Co 750 S Hackett Rd *Web:* www.youngphc.com	Waterloo	IA	50701	319-234-4411	234-4540

189-11 Remodeling, Refinishing, Resurfacing Contractors

Company	City	State	Zip	Phone	Fax
A J Johns Inc 3225 Anniston Rd *Web:* www.ajjohns.com	Jacksonville	FL	32246	904-641-2055	641-2102
Bathcrest Inc 265E 3900 S *TF:* 800-826-6790 ■ *Web:* www.bathcrest.com	Salt Lake City	UT	84107	801-957-1400	
California Closet Co 610A DuBois St *TF General:* 888-336-9707 ■ *Web:* www.californiaclosets.com	San Rafael	CA	94901	415-256-8500	256-8501
Closet Factory 12800 S Broadway *TF:* 800-838-7995 ■ *Web:* www.closetfactory.com	Los Angeles	CA	90061	310-516-7000	516-8065
DreamMaker Bath & Kitchen by Worldwide 510 N Valley Mills Dr Ste 304 *TF:* 800-583-2133 ■ *Web:* www.dreammaker-remodel.com	Waco	TX	76710	800-583-2133	
Handyman Connection Inc 11115 Kenwood Rd *TF:* 800-884-2639 ■ *Web:* www.handymanconnection.com	Cincinnati	OH	45242	513-771-3003	771-6439
Kitchen Tune-Up Inc 813 Cir Dr *TF:* 800-333-6385 ■ *Web:* www.kitchentuneup.com	Aberdeen	SD	57401	605-225-4049	
Miracle Method US Corp 4239 N Nevada Ave Ste 115 *TF:* 800-444-8827 ■ *Web:* www.miraclemethod.com	Colorado Springs	CO	80907	719-594-9091	594-9282
Perma-Glaze Inc 1638 Research Loop Rd Ste 160 *TF:* 800-332-7397 ■ *Web:* www.permaglaze.com	Tucson	AZ	85710	520-722-9718	296-4393
Re-Bath LLC 16879 N 75th Ave Ste 101 *TF:* 800-426-4573 ■ *Web:* rebath.com	Peoria	AZ	85382	800-426-4573	

189-12 Roofing, Siding, Sheet Metal Contractors

Company	City	State	Zip	Phone	Fax
A Zahner Sheet Metal Company Inc 1400 E Ninth St *Web:* www.azahner.com	Kansas City	MO	64106	816-474-8882	474-7994
AC Dellovade Inc 108 Cavasina Dr *Web:* www.acdellovade.com	Canonsburg	PA	15317	724-873-8190	873-8187

				Phone	Fax
All-South Subcontractors Inc 2678 Queenstown Rd *TF:* 800-873-8110 ■ *Web:* www.allsouthsub.com	Birmingham	AL	35210	205-836-8111	836-4227
Anson Industries Inc 1959 Anson Dr *Web:* www.ansonindustries.com	Melrose Park	IL	60160	708-681-1300	681-1310
B & M Roofing of Colorado Inc 3768 Eureka Way *Web:* www.bmroofing.com	Frederick	CO	80516	303-443-5843	938-9642
Baker Roofing Co 517 Mercury St *TF:* 800-849-4096 ■ *Web:* www.bakerroofing.com	Raleigh	NC	27603	919-828-2975	828-9352
Beldon Enterprises Inc PO Box 13380 *TF:* 800-688-7663 ■ *Web:* www.beldon.com	San Antonio	TX	78213	210-341-3100	341-2959
BHW Sheet Metal Co 113 Johnson St *Web:* bhwsm.com	Jonesboro	GA	30236	770-471-9303	478-7923
Birdair Inc 65 Lawrence Bell Dr Ste 100 *TF:* 800-622-2246 ■ *Web:* www.birdair.com	Amherst	NY	14221	716-633-9500	633-9850
Bonland Industries Inc 50 Newark-Pompton Tpke *TF:* 800-232-6600 ■ *Web:* www.bonlandhvac.com	Wayne	NJ	07470	973-694-3211	628-1120
Brazos Urethane Inc 1031 Sixth St N *TF:* 866-527-2967 ■ *Web:* www.brazosurethane.com	Texas City	TX	77590	409-965-0011	948-1511
Centimark Corp 12 Grandview Cir **Fax Area Code:* 724 ■ *TF:* 800-558-4100 ■ *Web:* www.centimark.com	Canonsburg	PA	15317	800-558-4100	743-7770*
Charles F Evans Company Inc 800 Canal St *Web:* evansroofingcompany.com	Elmira	NY	14901	607-734-8151	733-5422
Commercial Siding & Maintenance Co, The 8059 Crile Rd *TF:* 800-229-4276 ■ *Web:* www.commercialsiding.com	Painesville	OH	44077	440-352-7800	352-7048
Construction Services Inc 2214 S Lincoln St	Amarillo	TX	79109	806-373-1732	373-9472
Crown Corr Inc 7100 W 21st Ave *Web:* www.crowncorr.com	Gary	IN	46406	219-949-8080	944-9922
DC Taylor Co 312 29th St NE *TF:* 800-876-6346 ■ *Web:* www.dctaylorco.com	Cedar Rapids	IA	52402	319-363-2073	363-8311
Dee Cramer Inc 4221 E Baldwin Rd *TF:* 888-342-6995 ■ *Web:* www.deecramer.com	Holly	MI	48442	810-579-5000	579-2664
Dix Corp 4024 S Grove Rd *Web:* www.dixcorp.com	Spokane	WA	99224	509-838-4455	838-4464
Douglass Colony Group Inc 5901 E 58th Ave *TF:* 877-288-0650 ■ *Web:* www.douglasscolony.com	Commerce	CO	80022	303-288-2635	
Elmsford Sheet Metal Work Inc 23 Arlo Ln *Web:* www.elmsfordsheetmetal.com	Cortlandt Manor	NY	10567	914-739-6300	739-1285
Enterprise Roofing & Sheet Metal Co 1021 Irving St *Web:* www.enterpriserfg.com	Dayton	OH	45419	937-298-8664	
Fort Roofing & Sheet Metal Works Inc 14 W Oakland Ave *Web:* www.fortroofing.com	Sumter	SC	29150	803-773-9391	773-7711
Gowan Inc 5550 Airline Dr *Web:* www.gowaninc.com	Houston	TX	77076	713-696-5400	695-1726
Hahnel Bros Co (HBC) 46 Strawberry Ave PO Box 1160 *Web:* www.hahnelbrosco.com	Lewiston	ME	04243	207-784-6477	
Heidler Roofing Services Inc 2120 Alpha Dr *TF:* 866-792-3549 ■ *Web:* www.heidlerroofing.com	York	PA	17408	717-792-3549	792-4660
Henry C Smither Roofing Company Inc 6850 E 32nd St PO Box 26057 *Web:* www.smitherroofing.com	Indianapolis	IN	46226	317-545-1304	546-4764
IG Inc 720 S Sara Rd *TF:* 800-654-8433 ■ *Web:* www.igok.com	Mustang	OK	73064	405-376-9393	376-3933
Jamar Co 4701 Mike Colalillo Dr *Web:* www.jamarcompany.com	Duluth	MN	55807	218-628-1027	628-1174
John J Campbell Company Inc 6012 Resources Dr *Web:* www.campbellroofing.com	Memphis	TN	38134	901-372-8400	
Johnson Contracting Company Inc 2750 Morton Dr *Web:* www.jccinc.com	East Moline	IL	61244	309-755-0601	
Jottan Inc PO Box 166 *TF:* 800-364-4234 ■ *Web:* www.jottan.com	Florence	NJ	08518	609-447-6200	447-6200
Ketcher & Co Inc 1717 E 5th *Web:* ketcherco.com	North Little Rock	AR	72114	501-372-5216	
LE Schwartz & Son Inc 279 Reid St *Web:* www.leschwartz.com	Macon	GA	31206	478-745-6563	745-2711
M Gottfried Roofing Inc 89 Research Dr *Web:* www.mgottfried.com	Stamford	CT	06906	203-323-8173	
Midland Engineering 52369 SR 933 N *Web:* www.midlandengineering.com	South Bend	IN	46637	574-272-0200	272-7400
Miller-Thomas-Gyekis Inc 3341 Stafford St	Pittsburgh	PA	15204	412-331-4610	331-8871
National International Roofing Corp 11317 Smith Dr *TF:* 800-221-7663 ■ *Web:* www.nir.com	Huntley	IL	60142	847-669-3444	669-3173
North American Roofing Services Inc 41 Dogwood Rd *TF:* 800-551-5602 ■ *Web:* www.naroofing.com	Asheville	NC	28806	828-687-7767	687-1230
Olsson Roofing Company Inc 740 S Lake St *Web:* www.olssonroofing.com	Aurora	IL	60506	630-892-0449	892-1556
Orndorff & Spaid Inc 11722 Old Baltimore Pk *Web:* www.osroofing.com	Beltsville	MD	20705	301-937-5911	
R.A. Smith National Inc 16745 W Bluemound Rd Ste 200 *Web:* www.rasmith.com	Brookfield	WI	53005	262-781-1000	781-8466
RD Herbert & Sons Company Inc 1407 Third Ave N *Web:* www.rdherbert.com	Nashville	TN	37208	615-242-3501	256-4056
Schreiber Corp 29945 Beck Rd *TF:* 800-558-2706 ■ *Web:* www.schreiberroofing.com	Wixom	MI	48393	248-926-1500	926-1788
Schust Engineering Inc 701 North St *TF:* 800-686-9297 ■ *Web:* www.schustengineering.com	Auburn	IN	46706	800-686-9297	
Sechrist-Hall Co 102 Omaha	Corpus Christi	TX	78408	361-884-5264	
Silktown Roofing Inc 27 Pleasant St *Web:* www.silktownroofing.com	Manchester	CT	06040	860-647-0198	
Snyder Roofing & Sheet Metal Inc 12650 SW Hall Blvd *Web:* snyder-builds.com	Tigard	OR	97223	503-620-5252	684-3310
Standard Roofing Co 516 N McDonough St PO Box 1309 *TF:* 800-239-5705 ■ *Web:* www.standardtaylor.com	Montgomery	AL	36102	334-265-1262	834-3004
Superior Roofing & Sheet Metal Co Inc 3405 S 500 W *Web:* www.superior-roof.l7marketing.com	Salt Lake City	UT	84115	801-266-1473	266-1522
TDIndustries 13850 Diplomat Dr *Web:* www.tdindustries.com	Dallas	TX	75234	972-888-9500	
Tecta America Co 15002 Wicks Blvd *Web:* www.tectaamerica.com	San Leandro	CA	94577	510-686-4951	
Tri-State Roofing & Sheet Metal Group 101 South Meadville Rd *Web:* www.tri-stateservicegroup.com	Davisville	WV	26142	304-295-3311	295-6991
Turner Roofing & Sheet Metal Inc 1200 E Memphis St *Web:* www.turnerroofing.com	Broken Arrow	OK	74012	918-258-2585	
US Industries Inc 1701 First Ave *TF:* 800-456-8721	Evansville	IN	47710	812-425-2428	
Western Fireproofing Company of Kansas Inc 1501 Westport Rd *Web:* www.westernfireproofing.com	Kansas City	MO	64111	816-561-7667	

189-13 Sprinkler System Installation (Fire Sprinklers)

				Phone	Fax
Active Fire Sprinkler Corp 63 Flushing Ave	Brooklyn	NY	11205	718-834-8300	
Advance Fire Protection Company Inc 1451 W Lambert Rd *Web:* firesprinkleradvisoryboard.org	La Habra	CA	90631	562-691-0918	691-5482
All-South Subcontractors Inc 2678 Queenstown Rd *TF:* 800-873-8110 ■ *Web:* www.allsouthsub.com	Birmingham	AL	35210	205-836-8111	836-4227
August Winter & Sons Inc 2323 N Roemer Rd *TF:* 800-236-8882 ■ *Web:* www.augustwinter.com	Appleton	WI	54911	920-739-8881	739-2230
Brendle Sprinkler Co Inc 3635 S Montgomery St **Fax Area Code:* 334 ■ *TF:* 800-392-8021	Tacoma	WA	98409	800-392-8021	277-7967*
Cosco Fire Protection Inc 1075 W Lambert Rd Bldg D *TF:* 800-485-3795 ■ *Web:* www.coscofire.com	Brea	CA	92821	714-989-1800	989-1801
Crisp-Ladew Fire Protection Co 5201 Saunders Rd *Web:* crisp-ladew.com	Fort Worth	TX	76119	817-572-3663	
FE Moran 2265 Carlson Dr *Web:* femoran.com	Northbrook	IL	60062	847-498-4800	498-9091
Fire Protection Co 12828 S Ridgeway Ave	Alsip	IL	60803	708-371-4300	371-4340
Fire Protection Systems Inc 22 Industrial Pk Dr *Web:* www.fireprotectionsys.com	Hendersonville	TN	37075	615-822-3600	822-3427
Firetrol Protection Systems Inc 3696 West 900 South Ste A *Web:* www.firetrol.net	Salt Lake City	UT	84104	801-485-6900	485-6902
Geo M Robinson & Co 1461 Atteberry Ln	San Jose	CA	95131	408-432-6264	
High Point Sprinkler Inc 2 Regency Industrial Blvd	Thomasville	NC	27360	336-475-6181	
JF Ahern Co 855 Morris St *TF:* 800-532-0155 ■ *Web:* www.jfahern.com	Fond du Lac	WI	54935	920-921-9020	921-8632
John E Green Co 220 Victor Ave *Web:* www.johnegreen.com	Highland Park	MI	48203	313-868-2400	868-0011
McDaniel Fire Systems 1055 W Joliet Rd **Fax Area Code:* 800 ■ *Web:* www.mcdanielfire.com	Valparaiso	IN	46385	219-462-0571	611-2907*
National Automatic Sprinkler Industries 8000 Corporate Dr *TF:* 800-638-2603 ■ *Web:* www.nasifund.org	Landover	MD	20785	301-577-1700	429-4709
Oliver Fire Protection & Security 501 Feheley Dr *Web:* www.oliverfps.com	King of Prussia	PA	19406	610-277-1331	277-2837
Patti & Sons Inc 8 Berry St	Brooklyn	NY	11249	718-963-3700	388-8671
SA Comunale Company Inc 2900 Newpark Dr *TF:* 800-776-7181 ■ *Web:* www.sacomunale.com	Barberton	OH	44203	330-706-3040	861-0860
Security Fire Protection Co Inc 4495 Mendenhall Rd S *TF:* 888-274-8595 ■ *Web:* www.securityfire.com	Memphis	TN	38141	901-362-6250	366-7869
Tyco Fire & Security 6600 Congress Ave *Web:* www.tyco.com	Boca Raton	FL	33487	561-912-6000	
Viking Automatic Sprinkler Co 301 York Ave *Web:* www.vikingsprinkler.com	Saint Paul	MN	55130	651-558-3300	558-3310
Wayne Automatic Fire Sprinklers Inc 222 Capital Ct *Web:* www.waynefire.com	Ocoee	FL	34761	407-656-3030	656-8026
Western States Fire Protection Co 7020 S Tucson Way *Web:* www.wsfp.com	Centennial	CO	80112	303-792-0022	790-3875
Wiginton Fire Systems 699 Aero Ln *Web:* www.wiginton.net	Sanford	FL	32771	407-585-3200	585-3280

189-14 Structural Steel Erection

				Phone	Fax
Adams & Smith Inc 1380 W Ctr St *Web:* www.adamsandsmith.com	Lindon	UT	84042	801-785-6900	785-6400
Advance Tank & Construction Co 3700 E County Rd 64 PO Box 219 *Web:* www.advancetank.com	Wellington	CO	80549	970-568-3444	568-3435
Albach Company Inc 301 E Prosper St *Web:* www.albachco.com	Chalmette	LA	70043	504-271-1113	
Albany Steel Inc 566 Broadway *TF:* 800-342-9317 ■ *Web:* www.albanysteel.net	Albany	NY	12204	518-436-4851	436-1458

	Phone	Fax
Allstate Steel Company Inc 130 S Jackson Ave . . . Jacksonville FL 32220 *Web:* www.allstatesteel.com	904-781-6040	
Arben Group LLC 175 Marble Ave . . . Pleasantville NY 10570 *Web:* arbengroup.com	914-741-5459	741-2923
Area Erectors Inc 2323 Harrison Ave . . . Rockford IL 61104 *Web:* www.areaerectors.com	815-398-6700	398-6787
Ben Hur Construction Co 3783 Rider Trail S . . . Saint Louis MO 63045 *Web:* www.benhurconstruction.com	314-298-8007	298-9671
Bosworth Steel Erectors Inc 4001 Jaffee St . . . Dallas TX 75216 *Web:* www.bosworthsteel.com	214-371-3700	371-1020
Bratton Corp 2801 E 85th St . . . Kansas City MO 64132 *Web:* www.brattonsteel.com	816-363-1014	361-8021
Brunton Enterprises Inc 8815 Sorensen Ave . . . Santa Fe Springs CA 90670 *Web:* www.plas-tal.com	562-945-0013	696-7620
Canron Construction Inc 4600 NE 138th Ave . . . Portland OR 97230 *Web:* supremegroup.com	503-255-8634	253-3907
CBI Services Inc 14105 S Route 59 . . . Plainfield IL 60544 *TF:* 866-235-5687 ■ *Web:* www.cbi.com	302-325-8400	
CE Toland & Son 5300 Industrial Way . . . Benicia CA 94510 *Web:* cetoland.com	707-747-1000	747-5300
Central Maintenance & Welding Inc (CMW) 2620 E Keysville Rd . . . Lithia FL 33547 *TF:* 877-704-7411 ■ *Web:* www.cmw.cc	813-737-1402	737-1820
Century Steel Erectors Co 210 Washington Ave . . . Dravosburg PA 15034 *TF:* 888-601-8801 ■ *Web:* www.centurysteel.com	412-469-8800	469-0813
Chicago Bridge & Iron Co 6001 Rogerdale Rd . . . Houston TX 77072 *NYSE: CBI* ■ *TF General:* 866-235-5687 ■ *Web:* www.cbi.com	713-485-1000	
Dix Corp 4024 S Grove Rd . . . Spokane WA 99224 *Web:* www.dixcorp.com	509-838-4455	838-4464
Fenton Rigging & Contracting Inc 2150 Langdon Farm Rd . . . Cincinnati OH 45237 *Web:* fenton1898.com	513-631-5500	631-4361
Fought & Company Inc 14255 SW 72nd Ave . . . Tigard OR 97224 *Web:* www.fought.org	503-639-3141	
High Industries Inc 1853 William Penn Way . . . Lancaster PA 17601 *Web:* www.high.net	717-293-4444	293-4416
High Steel Structures Inc 1915 Old Philadelphia Pike PO Box 10008 . . . Lancaster PA 17605 *Web:* www.highsteel.com	717-390-4270	399-4102
Highland Tank & Manufacturing Co 1 Highland Rd . . . Stoystown PA 15563 *Web:* www.highlandtank.com	814-893-5701	893-6126
Lafayette Steel Erector Inc 313 Westgate Rd . . . Lafayette LA 70506 *TF:* 877-234-9435 ■ *Web:* www.l-s-e.com	337-234-9435	234-0217
Midwest Steel & Equipment Company Inc 9825 Moers Rd . . . Houston TX 77075 *Web:* www.midwest-steel.com	713-991-7843	991-4745
Midwest Steel Inc 2525 E Grand Blvd . . . Detroit MI 48211 *Web:* www.midweststeel.com	313-873-2220	873-2222
Pittsburg Tank & Tower Co Inc 1 Watertank Pl . . . Henderson KY 42420 **Fax:* Sales ■ *TF:* 800-222-5555 ■ *Web:* www.watertank.com	270-826-9000	827-4417*
Rebar Engineering Inc 10706 Painter Ave . . . Santa Fe Springs CA 90670	562-946-2461	941-7740
Ryan Iron Works Inc 1830 Broadway . . . Raynham MA 02767 *Web:* www.ryanironworks.net	508-822-8001	823-1359
Schuff Steel Co 420 S 19th Ave . . . Phoenix AZ 85009 *TF:* 800-435-8528 ■ *Web:* www.schuff.com	602-252-7787	452-4465
Shurtleff & Andrews Corp 1875 West 500 South . . . Salt Lake City UT 84104 *Web:* www.shurtleff-slc.com	801-973-9096	
Southeastern Construction & Maintenance Company Inc 1150 Pebbledale Rd PO Box 1055 . . . Mulberry FL 33860 *Web:* www.southeasternconst.com	863-428-1511	428-1110
Sure Steel Inc 7528 Cornia Dr . . . South Weber UT 84405	801-917-5800	917-5799
Tampa Steel Erecting Co 5127 Bloomingdale Ave . . . Tampa FL 33619 *Web:* tampasteelerecting.com	813-677-7184	677-8364
Walden Structures Inc 801 Opal Ave . . . Mentone CA 92359 *Web:* www.waldenstructures.com	909-389-9100	
Waldinger Corp 2601 Bell Ave . . . Des Moines IA 50321 *TF:* 800-473-4934 ■ *Web:* www.waldinger.com	515-284-1911	323-5150
Washington Ornamental Iron Works Inc 17926 S Broadway . . . Gardena CA 90248 *Web:* washingtoniron.com	310-327-8660	
Williams Industries Inc 8624 JD Reading Dr . . . Manassas VA 20109 *OTC: WMSI* ■ *Web:* www.wmsi.com	703-335-7800	335-7802
WO Grubb Steel Erection Inc 5120 Jefferson Davis Hwy . . . Richmond VA 23234 *TF:* 866-964-7822 ■ *Web:* www.wogrubb.com	804-271-9471	271-2539
Zimkor Industries Inc 7011 W Titan Rd . . . Littleton CO 80125 *Web:* www.zimkor.com	303-791-1333	791-1340

189-15 Water Well Drilling

	Phone	Fax
Alsay Inc 6615 Gant St . . . Houston TX 77066 *TF:* 800-833-5969 ■ *Web:* alsaywater.com	281-444-6960	444-7081
Kelley Dewatering & Construction Co 5175 Clay Ave SW . . . Wyoming MI 49548 *Web:* www.kelleydewatering.com	616-538-8010	538-0708
Ohio Drilling Co 2405 Bostic Blvd SW . . . Massillon OH 44647 *Web:* ohiodrilling.com	330-832-1521	
Ots-Nj LLC (OTS) 340 Bismark Rd . . . Jackson NJ 08527	732-833-0600	833-1169
Raba-Kistner Consultants Inc 12821 W Golden Ln . . . San Antonio TX 78249 *TF:* 866-722-2547 ■ *Web:* www.rkci.com	210-699-9090	699-6426
Rosencrantz-Bemis Water Well Co 1105 Hwy 281 Bypass . . . Great Bend KS 67530 *TF:* 800-466-2467 ■ *Web:* kansaswaterwelldrilling.com	620-793-5512	
Tri-State Drilling Inc 16940 Hwy 55 W . . . Plymouth MN 55446 *TF:* 800-383-1033 ■ *Web:* www.tristatedrilling.com	763-553-1234	553-9778
Water Resources International Inc 1100 Alakea St Ste 2900 . . . Honolulu HI 96813 *Web:* www.brninc.com	808-531-8422	531-7181

189-16 Wrecking & Demolition Contractors

	Phone	Fax
Allied Erecting & Dismantling Company Inc 2100 Poland Ave . . . Youngstown OH 44502 *TF:* 800-624-2867 ■ *Web:* www.aed.cc	330-744-0808	744-3218
Barnard Construction Company Inc PO Box 99 . . . Bozeman MT 59771 *Web:* www.barnard-inc.com	406-586-1995	586-3530
Bi-Con Services Inc 10901 Clay Pike Rd . . . Derwent OH 43733 *Web:* www.biconservices.com	740-685-2542	685-3863
Bierlein Cos Inc 2000 Bay City Rd . . . Midland MI 48642 *TF:* 800-336-6626 ■ *Web:* www.bierlein.com	989-496-0066	496-0144
Cherry Demolition 6131 Selinsky Rd . . . Houston TX 77048 *TF:* 800-444-1123 ■ *Web:* www.cherrycompanies.com	713-987-0000	987-0629
Dustrol Inc 1200 E Main PO Box 309 . . . Towanda KS 67144 *Web:* www.dustrol.com	316-536-2262	536-2789
Edgerton Contractors Inc 545 W Ryan Rd PO Box 901 . . . Oak Creek WI 53154 *Web:* edgerton.us	414-764-4443	764-9788
Ferma Corp 1265 Montecito Ave . . . Mountain View CA 94043 *TF:* 877-337-6211 ■ *Web:* www.fermacorp.com	650-961-2742	968-3945
James White Construction Company Inc 4156 Freedom Way . . . Weirton WV 26062 *Web:* jameswhiteconstruction.com	304-748-8181	748-8183
Kimmins Contracting Corp 1501 Second Ave . . . Tampa FL 33605 *Web:* www.kimmins.com	813-248-3878	579-1081
Kipin Industries Inc 4194 Green Garden Rd . . . Aliquippa PA 15001 *TF:* 800-782-8050	724-495-6200	495-2219
Manafort Bros Inc 414 New Britain Ave . . . Plainville CT 06062 *Web:* www.manafort.com	860-229-4853	747-4861
Mercer Wrecking Recycling Corp 1519 Calhoun St . . . Trenton NJ 08638 *Web:* mercergroup.com	609-393-6775	
Midwest Steel & Equipment Company Inc 9825 Moers Rd . . . Houston TX 77075 *Web:* www.midwest-steel.com	713-991-7843	991-4745
National Wrecking Co 2441 N Leavitt St . . . Chicago IL 60647 *Web:* www.nationalwrecking.com	773-384-2800	384-0403
NCM 404 N Berry St . . . Brea CA 92821 *TF:* 800-283-2933 ■ *Web:* ncmgroup.com	714-672-3500	
Noralco Corp 1920 Lincoln Rd . . . Pittsburgh PA 15235 *Web:* www.noralco.com	412-361-6678	361-6535
O'Rourke Wrecking Co 660 Lunken Pk Dr . . . Cincinnati OH 45226 *TF:* 800-354-9850 ■ *Web:* www.orourkewrecking.com	513-871-1400	871-1313
Patuxent Cos 2124 Priest Bridge Dr Ste 18 . . . Crofton MD 21114 *TF:* 800-628-4942 ■ *Web:* www.patuxentcompanies.com	410-793-0181	
Plant Reclamation 912 Harbour Way S . . . Richmond CA 94804 *Web:* www.plantreclamation.com	510-233-6552	237-6739
Robinette Demolition Inc 0 S 560 Hwy 83 . . . Oakbrook Terrace IL 60181 *Web:* www.rdidemolition.com	630-833-7997	833-8047
Siciliano Inc 3601 Winchester Rd . . . Springfield IL 62707 *Web:* www.sicilianoinc.com	217-585-1200	585-1211
US Dismantlement LLC 2600 S Throop St . . . Chicago IL 60608 *Web:* www.usdllc.com	312-328-1400	328-1477

190 CONSTRUCTION MACHINERY & EQUIPMENT

See Also Industrial Machinery, Equipment, & Supplies p. 2559; Material Handling Equipment p. 2732

	Phone	Fax
Acco Material Handling Solutions LLC 76 Acco Dr PO Box 792 . . . York PA 17405 *Web:* www.accolifting.com	717-741-4863	
Allen Engineering Corp 819 S Fifth St . . . Paragould AR 72450 *Web:* www.alleneng.com	870-236-7751	
Allied Construction Products LLC 3900 Kelley Ave . . . Cleveland OH 44114 *TF Cust Svc:* 800-321-1046 ■ *Web:* www.alliedcp.com	216-431-2600	431-2601
Allis Roller LLC 9800 S 60th St . . . Franklin WI 53132 *Web:* www.allis-roller.com	414-423-9000	
Altec Industries Inc 210 Inverness Ctr Dr . . . Birmingham AL 35242 *Web:* altec.com	205-991-7733	408-8601
Ashland Industries Inc 1115 Rail Dr PO Box 717 . . . Ashland WI 54806 *Web:* www.ashlandind.com	715-682-4622	
Asphalt Drum Mixers Inc (ADM) 1 ADM Pkwy . . . Huntertown IN 46748 *Web:* www.admasphaltplants.com	260-637-5729	637-3164
Astec Industries Inc 1725 Shepherd Rd . . . Chattanooga TN 37421 *NASDAQ: ASTE* ■ *Web:* www.astecindustries.com	423-899-5898	899-4456
Atlantic Construction Fabrics Inc 2831 CaRdwell Rd . . . Richmond VA 23234 *TF:* 800-448-3636 ■ *Web:* www.acfenvironmental.com	804-271-2363	743-7779
Automation Engineering LLC 1100 W Grand Ave . . . Salina KS 67401 *Web:* www.bcd.com	785-309-0505	
Bandit Industries Inc 6750 W Millbrook Rd . . . Remus MI 49340 *TF:* 800-952-0178 ■ *Web:* www.banditchippers.com	989-561-2270	561-2273
Barnhart Crane & Rigging Co 1701 Dunn Ave . . . Memphis TN 38106 *TF:* 800-727-0149 ■ *Web:* www.barnhartcrane.com	901-775-3000	
Bay Shore Systems Inc 14206 N Ohio St . . . Rathdrum ID 83858 *TF:* 888-569-3745 ■ *Web:* eventbrite.com/e	208-687-3311	

Company	City	State	Zip	Phone	Fax
Bid-Well Corp PO Box 97	Canton	SD	57013	800-843-9824	987-2605*
*Fax Area Code: 605 ■ TF: 800-843-9824 ■ Web: www.terex.com					
Bihler of America Inc 85 Industrial Rd	Phillipsburg	NJ	08865	908-213-9001	329-9111
Web: www.bihler.com					
Boart Longyear Co 2640 W 1700 S	Salt Lake City	UT	84104	801-972-6430	977-3374
TF: 800-453-8740 ■ Web: www.boartlongyear.com					
Bomag Americas Inc 2000 Kentville Rd	Kewanee	IL	61443	309-853-3571	852-0350
TF: 800-782-6624 ■ Web: www.bomag.com					
BradenCarco Gearmatic Paccar Winch Div 800 E Dallas St	Broken Arrow	OK	74012	918-251-8511	259-1575
Web: www.paccarwinch.com					
Burns Power Tools 350 Mariano Bishop Blvd	Fall River	MA	02721	508-675-0381	
Web: www.burnstools.com					
Caron Compactor Co 1204 Ullrey Ave	Escalon	CA	95320	209-838-2062	838-1404
TF: 800-542-2766 ■ Web: www.caroncompactor.com					
Caterpillar Engine Systems Inc 100 NE Adams St	Peoria	IL	61629	309-675-1000	
Caterpillar Inc 100 NE Adams St	Peoria	IL	61629	309-675-1000	
NYSE: CAT ■ Web: www.cat.com					
Cemen Tech Inc 1700 N 14th St	Indianola	IA	50125	515-961-7407	961-7409
TF: 800-247-2464 ■ Web: www.cementech.com					
Central Mine Equipment Company Inc 4215 Rider Trl N	Earth City	MO	63045	314-291-7700	291-4880
TF: 800-325-8827 ■ Web: www.cmeco.com					
Centurion Industries Inc 1107 N Taylor Rd	Garrett	IN	46738	260-357-6665	357-6761
TF: 888-832-4466 ■ Web: www.centurionind.com					
Charles Machine Works Inc PO Box 66	Perry	OK	73077	580-336-4402	
TF Cust Svc: 800-654-6481 ■ Web: www.ditchwitch.com					
Chemgrout Inc 805 E 31st St	La Grange Park	IL	60526	708-354-7112	354-3881
Web: www.chemgrout.com					
Chicago Slitter Company Inc, The 1025 W Thorndale Ave	Itasca	IL	60143	630-875-9800	
Web: www.therdigroup.com					
Clm Equipment Company Inc 3135 Hwy 90 E	Broussard	LA	70518	337-837-6693	
TF: 800-256-0490 ■ Web: www.clmequipment.com					
Contractors Equipment Supply Company Inc 2000 E Overland Rd	Meridian	ID	83642	208-888-3337	
Web: www.cescoequip.com					
Crane Carrier (Canada) Ltd 11523 186 St	Edmonton	AB	T5S2W6	780-443-2493	
Web: pacifictruck.com					
CRC Evans Pipeline International Inc 10700 E Independence St	Tulsa	OK	74116	918-438-2100	
TF: 800-664-9224 ■ Web: www.crc-evans.com					
DB & S Lumber Co 78 Accord Park Dr	Norwell	MA	02061	781-878-3345	
Web: www.dbslumber.com					
Deep South Crane & Rigging 15324 Airline Hwy	Baton Rouge	LA	70817	225-753-4371	
Web: www.deepsouthcrane.com					
Deepwell Services LLC 719 W New Castle St	Zelienople	PA	16063	724-473-0687	
Web: deepwellservices.com					
Demag Cranes & Components 29201 Aurora Rd	Solon	OH	44139	440-248-2400	
TF: 866-920-3000 ■ Web: www.demagcranes.us					
DENIS CIMAF Inc 188 de l'Eglise	Roxton Falls	QC	J0H1E0	450-548-7007	548-7008
Web: www.deniscimaf.com					
Derr & Gruenewald Construction Co (DGCC) 11100 E 108th Ave	Brighton	CO	80601	303-287-3456	287-3459
Web: www.dgccsteel.com					
E-Z Trench Manufacturing Inc 2315 Hwy 701 S	Loris	SC	29569	843-756-6444	
Web: www.eztrench.com					
Eagle Iron Works 129 E Holcomb Ave	Des Moines	IA	50313	515-243-1123	243-8214
Web: www.eagleironworks.com					
ED Etnyre & Co 1333 S Daysville Rd	Oregon	IL	61061	815-732-2116	732-7400
TF: 800-995-2116 ■ Web: www.etnyre.com					
Elgin National Industries Inc 2001 Butterfield Rd	Downers Grove	IL	60515	630-434-7200	434-7272
Web: www.elginindustries.com					
Enventure Global Technology LLC 15995 N Barkers Landing Ste 350	Houston	TX	77079	281-552-2200	
Web: www.enventuregt.com					
Erie Strayer Co 1851 Rudolph Ave	Erie	PA	16502	814-456-7001	452-3422
Web: www.eriestrayer.com					
Esco Corp 2141 NW 25th Ave	Portland	OR	97210	503-228-2141	226-8071
TF: 800-523-3795 ■ Web: www.escocorp.com					
F&M Mafco Inc PO Box 11013	Cincinnati	OH	45211	513-367-2151	367-0363
TF: 800-333-2151 ■ Web: www.fmmafco.com					
Flint Equipment Company - West Columbia 3464 Sunset Blvd	West Columbia	SC	29169	803-794-9340	
Web: www.flintequipco.com					
Gencor Industries Inc 5201 N Orange Blossom Trail	Orlando	FL	32810	407-290-6000	578-0577*
NASDAQ: GENC ■ *Fax: Sales ■ TF General: 888-887-1266 ■ Web: www.gencor.com					
GES Global Energy Services Inc 3220 Cypress Creek Pkwy	Houston	TX	77068	888-523-6797	
TF: 888-523-6797 ■ Web: www.global-energy.ca					
Gradall Industries Inc 406 Mill Ave SW	New Philadelphia	OH	44663	330-339-2211	339-8468
TF: 800-382-8302 ■ Web: www.gradall.com					
Gulf Crane Services Inc 73413 Bollfield Dr	Covington	LA	70435	985-892-0056	
Web: www.gulfcraneservices.com					
Guntert & Zimmerman Construction Div Inc 222 E Fourth St	Ripon	CA	95366	209-599-0066	
TF: 800-733-2912 ■ Web: www.guntert.com					
Gyrodata Inc 23000 Northwest Lk Dr	Houston	TX	77095	281-213-6300	
TF: 800-348-6063 ■ Web: www.gyrodata.com					
H & E Equipment Services Inc 11100 Mead Rd	Baton Rouge	LA	70809	225-298-5200	
NASDAQ: HEES ■ TF: 866-467-3682 ■ Web: www.he-equipment.com					
H&R Agri-Power Inc 4900 Eagle Way	Hopkinsville	KY	42240	270-886-3918	
Web: www.hragripower.com					
Harlo Corp 4210 Ferry St SW	Grandville	MI	49468	616-538-0550	
Web: www.harlocorporation.com					
Henke Manufacturing Corp 3070 Wilson Ave	Leavenworth	KS	66048	913-682-9000	
Web: www.henkemfg.com					
Hensley Industries Inc 2108 Joe Field Rd PO Box 29779	Dallas	TX	75229	972-241-2321	241-0915*
*Fax: Cust Svc ■ TF: 888-406-6262 ■ Web: www.hensleyind.com					
Highway Equipment Co 1330 76th Ave SW	Cedar Rapids	IA	52404	319-363-8281	286-3350
Web: www.highwayequipment.com					
Hunter Heavy Equipment Inc 2829 Texas Ave	Texas City	TX	77590	409-945-2382	945-9145
TF: 800-562-7368 ■ Web: www.hunterheavyequipment.com					
Hunting Energy Services Inc 24 Waterway Ste 700	The Woodlands	TX	77380	281-442-7382	
Web: www.huntingplc.com					
Inquipco 2730 N Nellis Blvd	Las Vegas	NV	89115	702-644-1700	
TF: 800-598-3465 ■ Web: www.inquipco.com					
J J Curran Crane Co 865 S Ft St	Detroit	MI	48217	313-842-1700	
Web: www.jjcurran.com					
Jakes Crane & Rigging Inc 6109 Dean Martin Dr	Las Vegas	NV	89118	702-872-5253	
TF: 800-872-5253 ■ Web: www.jakescrane.com					
James E Roberts-obayashi Corp 20 Oak Ct	Danville	CA	94526	925-820-0600	
Web: www.jerocorp.com					
Jennmar Corp 258 Kappa Dr	Pittsburgh	PA	15238	412-963-9071	963-9767
Web: www.jennmar.com					
Jensen Mixers International Inc 5354 S Garnett Rd	Tulsa	OK	74146	918-627-5770	
Web: jensenmixer.net					
JH Fletcher & Co Inc 402 High St	Huntington	WV	25705	304-525-7811	525-3770
TF: 800-327-6203 ■ Web: www.jhfletcher.com					
JLG Industries Inc 1 JLG Dr	McConnellsburg	PA	17233	717-485-5161	485-6417
Web: www.jlg.com					
John Deere Construction & Forestry 1515 Fifth Ave	Moline	IL	61265	309-765-0227	748-0117*
*Fax: Cust Svc ■ Web: deere.com					
Joy Global Inc 177 Thorn Hill Rd	Warrendale	PA	15086	724-779-4500	779-4509
Web: www.joyglobal.com					
Kawasaki Construction Machinery Copr of America 60 Amlajack Blvd	Newnan	GA	30265	770-499-7000	
Web: www.kcmcorp.com					
Kor-it Inc 1964 Auburn Blvd	Sacramento	CA	95815	888-727-4560	
TF: 888-727-4560 ■ Web: www.kor-it.com					
Kress Corp 227 W Illinois St	Brimfield	IL	61517	309-446-3395	446-9625
Web: www.kresscarrier.com					
LA Pipeline Rental & Industrial Supply LLC 3210 E Napoleon St	Sulphur	LA	70663	337-533-8184	
Web: www.lapipelinerentals.com					
Liebherr-America Inc 4100 Chestnut Ave	Newport News	VA	23607	757-245-5251	928-8700
Web: liebherr.com					
Link-Belt Construction Equipment Co 2651 Palumbo Dr	Lexington	KY	40583	859-263-5200	
Web: www.linkbelt.com					
Liquid Waste Technology LLC 1750 Madison Ave	New Richmond	WI	54017	715-246-2888	
Web: www.lwtpithog.com					
Machine Maintenance Inc 2300 Cassens Dr	Fenton	MO	63026	636-343-9970	
TF: 800-325-3322 ■ Web: www.lubyequipment.com					
Man Lift Mfg Co 5707 S Pennsylvania Ave	Cudahy	WI	53110	414-486-1760	
Web: manliftmfg.com					
Manitowoc Company Inc 2400 S 44th St	Manitowoc	WI	54220	920-684-4410	
NYSE: MTW ■ Web: www.manitowoc.com					
Mayville Engineering Company Inc 715 S St	Mayville	WI	53050	920-387-4500	387-2682
Web: www.mecinc.com					
McLellan Equipment Inc 251 Shaw Rd	South San Francisco	CA	94080	650-873-8100	589-7398
TF: 800-848-8449 ■ Web: mclellanindustries.com					
Meyer Products 18513 Euclid Ave	Cleveland	OH	44112	216-486-1313	486-1321*
*Fax: Sales ■ Web: www.meyerproducts.com					
Mi-Jack Products Inc 3111 W 167th St	Hazel Crest	IL	60429	708-596-5200	
Web: www.mi-jack.com					
Midland Machinery Company Inc 101 Cranbrook Ext	Tonawanda	NY	14150	716-692-1200	692-1206
Web: www.midlandmachinery.com					
Midwestern Industries Inc 915 Oberlin Rd SW	Massillon	OH	44647	330-837-4203	837-4210
TF Cust Svc: 877-474-9464 ■ Web: www.midwesternind.com					
Millcraft Industries Inc 95 W Beau St Ste 600	Washington	PA	15301	724-229-8800	229-8800
Web: www.millcraftinv.com					
Mixer Systems Inc 190 Simmons Ave	Pewaukee	WI	53072	262-691-3100	
Web: www.mixersystems.com					
Mr Crane Inc 647 N Hariton St	Orange	CA	92868	714-633-2100	
TF: 800-598-3465 ■ Web: www.mrcrane.com					
Nexgen Enterprises Inc 1099 Greenleaf Ave	Elk Grove Village	IL	60007	847-303-9800	303-9801
Web: gonexgen.com					
Nordco Inc 245 W Forest Hill Ave	Oak Creek	WI	53154	414-766-2180	766-2379
Web: www.nordco.com					
North American Equipment Upfitters Inc 6 Sutton Cir	Hooksett	NH	03106	603-624-6288	
Web: www.naeuinc.com					
Pace Engineering Inc 4800 Beidler Rd	Willoughby	OH	44094	440-942-1234	
Web: www.paceparts.net					
Palmer Steel Supplies Inc 4300 Acapulco Ave	Mcallen	TX	78503	956-686-6575	686-7022
Web: www.palmersteel.com					
Pengo Corp 500 E Hwy 10	Laurens	IA	50554	712-845-2540	845-2497
TF Cust Svc: 800-599-0211 ■ Web: www.pengoattachments.com					
Pennsylvania Crusher Corp 600 Abbott Dr	Broomall	PA	19008	610-544-7200	543-0190
Web: terrasource.com					
Peri Formwork Systems Inc 7135 Dorsey Run Rd	Elkridge	MD	21075	410-712-7225	
Web: www.peri-usa.com					
Pettibone Corp 2626 Warrenville Rd	Downers Grove	IL	60515	630-353-5000	353-5026
Web: pettibonellc.com					
Pierce Pacific Manufacturing Inc 4424 NE 158th PO Box 30509	Portland	OR	97294	503-808-9110	808-9111
TF: 800-760-3270 ■ Web: www.piercepacific.com					

Phone Fax

Precision Husky Corp 850 Markeeta Spur Rd ....Moody AL 35004 205-640-5181 640-1147
Web: www.precisionhusky.com

Prime Systems Inc 416 Mission St ....Carol Stream IL 60188 630-681-2100
Web: www.primeuv.com

Putzmeister America 1733 90th St ....Sturtevant WI 53177 800-553-3414
TF: 800-553-3414 ■ *Web:* www.putzmeister.com

Radwell International Inc
111 Mt Holly Bypass ....Lumberton NJ 08048 609-288-9393
Web: www.radwellinternational.com

Ramsey Winch Company Inc 1600 N Garnett Rd ....Tulsa OK 74116 918-438-2760 438-6688
TF: 800-777-2760 ■ *Web:* www.ramsey.com

Reco Equipment Inc 41245 Reco Rd ....Belmont OH 41245 740-782-1314 782-1020
TF: 800-686-7326 ■ *Web:* www.recoequip.com

REED LLC 13822 Oaks Ave ....Chino CA 91710 909-287-2100
Web: www.reedmfg.com

Richland LLC 1905 Mines Rd.........................Pulaski TN 38478 931-424-3900
Web: www.richlandllc.com

RKI Inc 2301 Central Pkwy ....Houston TX 77092 713-688-4414 688-8982
TF: 800-346-8988 ■ *Web:* www.rki-us.com

Roadtec Inc
800 Manufacturers Rd PO Box 180515.............Chattanooga TN 37405 423-265-0600 267-7104
TF: 800-272-7100 ■ *Web:* www.roadtec.com

Robertson Transformer Co
13611 Thornton Rd............................Blue Island IL 60406 708-388-2315 388-2420
TF: 800-323-5633 ■ *Web:* www.robertsontransformer.com

Rotary Drilling Tools USA LP
9022 Vincik Ehlert PO Box 73.......................Beasley TX 77417 979-387-3223
Web: www.rdt-usa.co

Rotochopper Inc 217 W St PO Box 295 ....Saint Martin MN 56367 320-548-3586
Web: www.rotochopper.com

Rovibec Inc 475 Rte du Port ....Nicolet QC J3T1M5 819-289-5005 289-2203
Web: rovibecagrisolutions.com

Sauber Manufacturing Co 10 N Sauber Rd...............Virgil IL 60151 630-365-6600
Web: www.saubermfg.com

Scomi Oiltools Inc 6818 N Sam Houston Pkwy W ....Houston TX 77064 281-260-6016
Web: www.scomigroup.com.my

Shamokin Filler Company Inc PO Box 568 ....Shamokin PA 17872 570-644-0437
TF: 800-577-8008 ■ *Web:* www.shamokinfiller.com

Shelby Industries Inc 175 McDaniels Rd.............Shelbyville KY 40065 502-633-2040 633-2186
Web: www.shelbyindustries.com

Shimpo 1701 Glenlake Ave ....Itasca IL 60143 630-924-7138
TF: 800-842-1479 ■ *Web:* www.nidec-shimpo.com

Simco Drilling Equipment Inc PO Box 448 ....Osceola IA 50213 641-342-2166 342-6764
TF: 855-222-8570 ■ *Web:* www.simcodrill.com

Star Su Company LLC
5200 Prairie Stone Pkwy Ste 100 ....Hoffman Estates IL 60192 847-649-1450
Web: www.star-su.com

Stephens Manufacturing Co
711 W Fourth St............................Tompkinsville KY 42167 270-487-6774
Web: www.stephensmfg.com

Superwinch Inc 359 Lake Rd.........................Dayville CT 06241 860-928-7787 928-1143
TF: 800-323-2031 ■ *Web:* www.superwinch.com

Swenson Spreader Co 127 Walnut St ....Lindenwood IL 61049 815-393-4455 393-4964
TF: 888-825-7323 ■ *Web:* www.swensonproducts.com

Terex Corp 200 Nyala Farm Rd.......................Westport CT 06880 203-222-7170 222-7976
NYSE: TEX ■ *Web:* www.terex.com

Terex Roadbuilding
8236 W I-40 Service Rd ....Oklahoma City OK 73128 405-787-6020
Web: www.terex.com

Test Mark Industries Inc
995 N Market St ....East Palestine OH 44413 330-426-2200
TF: 800-783-3227 ■ *Web:* www.testmark.net

Thermal Technologies Inc
130 Northpoint Ct............................Blythewood SC 29016 803-691-8000
Web: www.thermaltechnologies.com/index.html

Thrustmaster of Texas Inc PO Box 840189 ....Houston TX 77041 713-937-6295 937-7962
Web: thrustmaster.net

Treeline Well Services Inc
750 333 - 11th Ave SW ....Calgary AB T2R1L9 403-266-2868
TF: 844-344-7447 ■ *Web:* www.treelinewell.com

Tulsa Winch Group 11135 S James Ave................Jenks OK 74037 918-298-8300 298-8301
Web: www.team-twg.com

United Rotary Brush Corp 15607 W 100th Ter ....Lenexa KS 66219 913-888-8450
Web: www.united-rotary.com

Varel International
1625 W Crosby Dr Ste 124........................Carrollton TX 75006 972-242-1160 242-8770
TF: 800-827-3526 ■ *Web:* www.varelintl.com

Volvo Construction Equipment of North America Inc
312 Volvo Way ....Shippensburg PA 17257 717-532-9181
Web: www.volvoce.com

VT LeeBoy Inc
500 Lincoln County Pkwy Extention ....Lincolnton NC 28092 704-966-3300
Web: www.leeboy.com

Wacker Neuson
N 92 W 15000 Anthony Ave ....Menomonee Falls WI 53051 262-255-0500 822-0710*
**Fax Area Code: 800* ■ *TF:* 800-770-0957 ■ *Web:* products.wackerneuson.com

Web Equipment 464 Central Rd ....Fredericksburg VA 22401 540-657-5855
TF: 800-225-3858 ■ *Web:* www.webequipment.com

Wenzel Downhole Tools Ltd
5920 Macleod Trail SW Ste 504.......................Calgary AB T2H0K2 403-262-3050
Web: www.downhole.com

Western Products Inc 7777 N 73rd St...............Milwaukee WI 53223 414-354-2310 354-2310*
**Fax: Cust Svc* ■ *Web:* www.westernplows.com

Wilco Marsh Buggies & Draglines Inc
1304 Macarthur Ave ....Harvey LA 70058 504-341-3409
TF: 800-253-0869 ■ *Web:* www.wilcomarshbuggies.com

Wingenback Inc
Bay F Century Park 707 Barlow Trl....................Calgary AB T2E8C2 403-221-8120 291-5114
Web: www.wingenback.com

Xcaliber LP 5051 Fm 2920 ....Spring TX 77388 281-219-8100
TF: 866-620-8586 ■ *Web:* www.xcaliberlp.com

Young Corp 3231 Utah Ave S.........................Seattle WA 98134 206-624-1071 682-6881
TF: 800-321-9090 ■ *Web:* www.youngcorp.com

Phone Fax

Ziebell Water Service Products
2001 Pratt Blvd............................Elk Grove Village IL 60007 847-364-0670
Web: www.ziebellproducts.com

Zimmerman Industries Inc 196 Wabash Rd ....Ephrata PA 17522 717-733-6166
Web: www.zimmermanindustries.com

191 CONSTRUCTION MATERIALS

See Also Home Improvement Centers p. 2479

191-1 Brick, Stone, Related Materials

Phone Fax

Accent Marble & Granite Inc
21609 N 12th Ave Ste 800 ....Phoenix AZ 85027 623-582-1501
Web: accentmarblegranite.com

AHI Supply Inc PO Box 884......................Friendswood TX 77549 281-331-0088 331-9813
TF: 800-873-5794 ■ *Web:* www.ahi-supply.com

All Tile Inc 1201 Chase Ave...................Elk Grove Village IL 60007 847-979-2500
TF: 877-255-8453 ■ *Web:* www.alltile.com

Allen Refractories Co (Inc)
131 Shackelford Rd ....Pataskala OH 43062 740-927-8000 927-9404
Web: www.allenrefractories.com

Alley-Cassetty Cos Inc 2 Oldham St.................Nashville TN 37213 615-244-0440
Web: www.alley-cassetty.com

Architectural Ceramics Inc
800 E Gude Dr Ste F..............................Rockville MD 20850 301-762-4140 762-2497
Web: www.architecturalceramics.net

Arley Wholesale Inc 700 N S Rd ....Scranton PA 18504 570-344-9874
Web: www.arleywholesale.com

Atlas Construction Supply Inc
4640 Brinnell St ....San Diego CA 92111 858-277-2100 277-0585
TF: 877-588-2100 ■ *Web:* www.atlasform.com

Bedrock International LLC 9929 Lackman Rd ....Lenexa KS 66219 913-438-7625
Web: www.kcstone.com

Bierschbach Equipment & Supply Co
PO Box 1444 ....Sioux Falls SD 57101 605-332-4466 332-4522
TF: 800-843-3707 ■ *Web:* bierschbach.com

Castelli Marble Inc 3958 Superior Ave E.............Cleveland OH 44114 216-361-1222 361-1797
Web: castellimarbleinc.com

Century Roof Tile 23135 Saklan Rd ....Hayward CA 94545 510-780-9489
TF: 888-233-7548 ■ *Web:* www.centuryrooftile.com

ClarkWestern Dietrich Building Systems LLC
9100 Centre Pointe Dr Ste 210..................West Chester OH 45069 513-870-1100
Web: www.clarkdietrich.com

Clay Ingels Company LLC 914 Delaware Ave ....Lexington KY 40505 859-252-0836
Web: www.clay-ingels.com

Colonial Materials of Fayetteville Inc
570 Belt Blvd ....Fayetteville NC 28301 910-485-5099
Web: colonialmaterials.com

Commercial Ready Mix Products Inc PO Box 189.......Winton NC 27986 252-358-5461 358-4912
Web: www.crmpinc.com

Consolidated Brick & Bldg Supls Inc
127 W 24th St Fl 3 ....New York NY 10011 212-645-6700
Web: www.consolidatedbrick.com

Contempo Ceramic Tile Corp
3732 South 300 West.........................Salt Lake City UT 84115 801-262-1717
Web: contempotile.com

Corriveau-Routhier Inc 266 Clay St ....Manchester NH 03103 603-627-3805 627-3805
Web: www.corriveaurouthier.com

CSC Home & Hardware 1580 Earl L Core Rd........Morgantown WV 26505 304-292-1340
Web: www.wvcsc.com

E-Z Mix Inc 11450 Tuxford St.......................Sun Valley CA 91352 818-768-0568
Web: www.ezmixinc.com

East Coast Sales Company Inc
554 N State Rd ....Briarcliff Manor NY 10510 914-923-5000
Web: www.ecsceramics.com

Engler Meier & Justus Inc
1030 Vandustrial Dr ....Westmont IL 60559 630-852-4600
Web: www.westmontint.com

FAYBLOCK Materials Inc
130 Builders Blvd.............................Fayetteville NC 28302 910-323-9198
TF: 800-326-9198 ■ *Web:* www.fayblock.com

FG Wilson Inc 10431 N Commerce Pkwy ....Miramar FL 33025 954-433-2212
Web: www.fgwilsonmiami.com

Foothill Ready Mix Inc 11415 State Hwy 99W ....Red Bluff CA 96080 530-527-2565
Web: foothillreadymix.com

Foundation Technologies Inc
1400 Progress Industrial Blvd ....Lawrenceville GA 30043 678-407-4640
TF: 800-773-2368 ■ *Web:* www.foundationtechnologies.com

Frank Thompson Transport Inc PO Box 1876........El Dorado AR 71731 870-862-5426

Fullen Dock & Warehouse Inc 382 Klinke Rd.........Memphis TN 38127 901-358-9544 357-2879
TF: 800-467-7104 ■ *Web:* www.fullendock.com

Fyfe Co LLC 3940 Ruffin Rd Ste C ....San Diego CA 92123 858-642-0694 444-2982
Web: www.fyfeco.com

Garden State Tile Distributors Inc
5001 Industrial Rd ....Farmingdale NJ 07727 732-938-6675
Web: www.gstile.com

Gerrity Stone Inc 225 Merrimac St...................Woburn MA 01801 781-938-1820
Web: www.gerritystone.com

Granicor Inc
300 Rue De Rotterdam ....Saint-augustin-de-desmaures QC G3A1T4 418-878-3530 878-3208
Web: www.granicor.com

Granite Construction Inc 585 W Beach St ....Watsonville CA 95076 831-724-1011 722-9657
NYSE: GVA ■ *Web:* www.graniteconstruction.com

Graniterock Co
350 Technology Dr PO Box 50001.................Watsonville CA 95077 831-768-2000 768-2201
TF: 888-762-5100 ■ *Web:* www.graniterock.com

Guaranteed Supply Company of South Carolina Inc
1211 Rotherwood Rd ....Greensboro NC 27406 336-273-6140
Web: www.guaranteedsupply.com

Gypsum Supply Company Inc 859 74th St.........Byron Center MI 49315 616-583-9300
Web: www.gypsum-supply.com

Company	City	State	ZIP	Phone	Fax
Henry Products Inc 302 S 23rd Ave *TF:* 800-525-5533 ■ *Web:* www.henryproducts.com	Phoenix	AZ	85009	602-253-3191	254-2325
Hudson Liquid Asphalts Inc 89 Ship St	Providence	RI	02903	401-274-2200	274-2220
Iberia Tiles Corp 2975 NW 77 Ave *Web:* www.iberiatiles.com	Miami	FL	33122	305-591-3880	
In-O-Vate Technologies Inc 810 Saturn St Ste 21 *TF:* 888-443-7937 ■ *Web:* www.dryerbox.com	Jupiter	FL	33477	561-743-8696	
Indital USA Ltd 7947 Mesa Dr *Web:* www.indital.com	Houston	TX	77028	713-694-6065	
Inter Tile 2300 Polvorosa Ave *Web:* www.intertile.com	San Leandro	CA	94577	760-773-1001	
Intrepid Enterprises Inc 1848 Industrial Blvd *Web:* intrepidstone.com	Harvey	LA	70058	504-348-2861	340-7018
Jaeckle Wholesale Inc 4101 Owl Creek Dr *TF:* 800-236-7225 ■ *Web:* www.jaeckledistributors.com	Madison	WI	53718	608-838-5400	
Jarco Supply LLC 100 Ag Dr *Web:* jarcosupply.com	Youngsville	NC	27596	919-562-0123	
Jeffrey Court Inc 620 Parkridge Ave *Web:* www.jeffreycourt.com	Norco	CA	92860	951-340-3383	
Kamco Supply Corp of Boston 181 New Boston St *Web:* www.kamcoboston.com	Woburn	MA	01801	781-938-0909	
Kencove Farm Fence Inc 344 Kendall Rd *Web:* www.charleskendall.com	Blairsville	PA	15717	724-459-8991	
L Thorn Co Inc 6000 Grant Line Rd *TF:* 800-662-4594 ■ *Web:* www.lthorn.com	New Albany	IN	47150	812-246-4461	246-2678
Lang Stone Co Inc 707 Short St *Web:* www.langstone.com	Columbus	OH	43215	614-235-4099	
Lyman-Richey Corp 4315 Cuming St *Web:* www.lymanrichey.com	Omaha	NE	68131	402-558-2727	556-5171
Lynx Brand Fence Products 4330 76 Ave SE *TF:* 800-665-5969 ■ *Web:* www.lynxfence.com	Calgary	AB	T2C2J2	403-273-4821	
Marble Systems Inc 2737 Dorr Ave *Web:* www.marblesystems.com	Fairfax	VA	22031	703-204-1818	
Materials Mktg Ltd 120 W Josephine St *Web:* www.mstoneandtile.com	San Antonio	TX	78212	210-731-8453	
Meadow Burke LLC 531 S Us Hwy 301 *Web:* www.meadowburke.com	Tampa	FL	33619	813-248-1944	
Merrimac Tile Company Inc 18 Tsienneto Rd *Web:* www.merrimactile.com	Derry	NH	03038	603-432-2544	
Mixcor Aggregates Inc 6303 43 St *Web:* www.mixcor.ca	Leduc	AB	T9E0G8	780-986-6721	
Nemo Tile Co 17702 Jamaica Ave *Web:* www.nemotile.com	Jamaica	NY	11432	718-291-5969	
Patene Building Supplies Ltd 641 Speedvale Ave W *TF:* 800-265-8319 ■ *Web:* www.patene.com	Guelph	ON	N1K1E6	519-822-1890	
Potvin & Bouchard Inc 3900 Rue Colbert St-Jean Cp550 *Web:* www.potvinbouchard.qc.ca	Jonquiere	QC	G7X7W4	418-547-4752	
Preferred Sands LLC 100 Matsonford Rd One Radnor Corporate Ctr *Web:* preferredsands.com	Radnor	PA	19087	610-834-1969	
PRL Glass Systems Inc 251 Mason Way *TF:* 800-433-7044 ■ *Web:* www.prlglass.com	City Of Industry	CA	91746	626-961-5890	
Quick Crete Products 731 Parkridge Ave *TF:* 866-703-3434 ■ *Web:* www.quickcrete.com	Norco	CA	92860	866-703-3434	
Reimers-kaufman Concrete Prods 6200 Cornhusker Hwy *Web:* www.reimerskaufman.com	Lincoln	NE	68507	402-434-1855	434-1877
Rio Grande Co 201 Santa Fe Dr *Web:* www.riograndeco.com	Denver	CO	80223	303-825-2211	629-0417
Robert F Henry Tile Company Inc 1008 Lagoon Business Loop *Web:* www.henrytile.com	Montgomery	AL	36117	334-269-2518	
Saf-t-co Supply 1300 E Normandy Pl *Web:* www.saftco.com	Santa Ana	CA	92705	714-547-9975	
Safety Seal 8100 Belvedere Rd	West Palm Beach	FL	33411	561-790-5801	
Stone Connection Inc 3045 Business Park Dr *Web:* www.stoneconnection.com	Norcross	GA	30071	770-662-0188	
Stone Source LLC 215 Pk Ave S *Web:* www.stonesource.com	New York	NY	10003	212-979-6400	979-6989
Superior Concrete Block Company Inc 401 Mckinzie St S *Web:* www.cencrete.com	Mankato	MN	56001	507-387-7068	
Synergy Ceramics Gp LLC 5200 Tennyson Pkwy Ste 400 *Web:* synergyceramics.com	Plano	TX	75024	972-608-0515	
Terrazzo & Marble Supply Company of Illinois 77 Wheeling Rd *Web:* www.tmsupply.com	Wheeling	IL	60090	847-353-8000	353-8001
Tri-State Brick & Stone of New York Inc 333 Seventh Ave 5th Fl *Web:* btsbm.com	New York	NY	10001	212-686-3939	686-4387
United Marble & Granite Inc 2163 Martin Ave *Web:* www.umgslabs.com	Santa Clara	CA	95050	408-347-3300	
Universal Minerals International Inc 4620 S Coach Dr *Web:* www.mrrinc.com	Tucson	AZ	85714	520-748-9362	
Vimco Inc 300 Hansen Access Rd *TF Cust Svc:* 888-468-4626 ■ *Web:* www.vimcoinc.com	King Of Prussia	PA	19406	610-768-0500	768-0586
WF Saunders & Sons Inc PO Box A *Web:* www.saundersconcrete.com	Nedrow	NY	13120	315-469-3217	469-3940
Zeiser Wilbert Vault Inc 750 Howard St *TF:* 800-472-4335 ■ *Web:* zeiserwilbertvault.com	Elmira	NY	14904	607-733-0568	
Zircoa Inc 31501 Solon Rd *Web:* www.zircoa.com	Solon	OH	44139	440-248-0500	

191-2 Construction Materials (Misc)

Company	City	State	ZIP	Phone	Fax
Alliance Wood Group Engineering LP 330 Barker Cypress Rd *TF:* 866-313-0052	Houston	TX	77094	281-828-6000	647-9701
American Fence Inc 2502 N 27th Ave *TF:* 888-691-4565 ■ *Web:* www.americanfence.com	Phoenix	AZ	85009	602-272-2333	734-0580
Arabel Inc 16301 NW 49th Ave *TF Sales:* 800-759-5959 ■ *Web:* www.arabel.com	Hialeah	FL	33014	305-623-8302	624-0714
Basic Components Inc 1201 S Second Ave *TF:* 800-452-1780 ■ *Web:* www.basiccomp.com	Mansfield	TX	76063	817-473-7224	473-3388
Brooks Construction Company Inc 6525 Ardmore Ave *Web:* www.brooks1st.com	Fort Wayne	IN	46809	260-478-1990	747-7086
Buchheit Inc 33 Perry County Rd 540 *Web:* www.buchheitonline.com	Perryville	MO	63775	573-547-1010	547-1001
Builders Hardware & Specialty Company Inc 2002 W 16th St **Fax Area Code:* 412 ■ *Web:* www.builders-hardware.net	Erie	PA	16505	814-453-4736	488-8909*
Chemung Supply Corp PO Box 527 *TF:* 800-733-5508 ■ *Web:* www.chemungsupply.com	Elmira	NY	14903	607-733-5506	732-5379
Clyde Cos Inc 730 North 1500 West *Web:* www.clydeinc.com	Orem	UT	84057	801-802-6900	802-6906
Concrete Materials Inc 1201 W Russell St *Web:* www.concretematerialscompany.com	Sioux Falls	SD	57118	605-357-6000	334-6221
CR Laurence Company Inc 2503 E Vernon Ave PO Box 58923 **Fax Area Code:* 800 ■ *TF:* 800-421-6144 ■ *Web:* www.crlaurence.com	Los Angeles	CA	90058	323-588-1281	262-3299*
DS Brown Co 300 E Cherry St *TF:* 800-848-1730 ■ *Web:* www.dsbrown.com	North Baltimore	OH	45872	419-257-3561	257-2200
Eastern Wholesale Fence Co Inc 274 Middle Island Rd *TF:* 800-339-3362 ■ *Web:* www.easternfence.com	Medford	NY	11763	631-698-0900	698-6408
Empire Bldg Materials Inc PO Box 220 **Fax Area Code:* 406 ■ *TF:* 800-332-4577 ■ *Web:* www.empireinc.com	Bozeman	MT	59771	800-548-8201	587-3144*
Fargo Glass & Paint Company Inc 1801 Seventh Ave N *Web:* fargoglass.com	Fargo	ND	58102	701-235-4441	235-3435
Gossen /Corp 2030 W Bender Rd *TF:* 800-558-8984 ■ *Web:* www.gossencorp.com	Milwaukee	WI	53209	414-228-9800	228-9077
H Myers John & Son Inc 2200 Monroe St *Web:* www.jhmson.com	York	PA	17404	717-792-2500	792-5115
J O Galloup Co 3838 Clay Ave SW *TF:* 888-755-3110 ■ *Web:* www.galloup.com	Wyoming	MI	49548	269-965-4005	965-3263
Kuriyama of America Inc 360 E State Pkwy *TF:* 800-800-0320 ■ *Web:* www.kuriyama.com	Schaumburg	IL	60173	847-755-0360	885-0996
Lummus Supply Co 1554 Bolton Rd NW *Web:* www.lummus-supply.com	Atlanta	GA	30331	404-794-1501	794-4519
Penrod Co 2809 S Lynnhaven Rd Ste 350 *TF:* 800-537-3497 ■ *Web:* www.thepenrodcompany.com	Virginia Beach	VA	23452	757-498-0186	498-1075
Powers Products Co 2695 W Third Ave *Web:* www.powersproducts.com	Denver	CO	80219	307-634-5190	
Robert N Karpp Company Inc 480 E First St *TF:* 800-244-5886 ■ *Web:* www.karpp.com	Boston	MA	02127	617-269-5880	269-2387
Rose & Walker Supply Lafayette Inc (RWS) 3565 US Hwy 52 S *Web:* www.roseandwalkersupply.com	Lafayette	IN	47905	765-471-7070	474-7507
Spates Fabricators 85435 Middleton *Web:* www.spates.com	Thermal	CA	92274	760-397-4122	397-4724
Star Sales & Distributing Corp 29 Commerce Way *TF:* 800-222-8118 ■ *Web:* www.starsales.com	Woburn	MA	01801	781-933-8830	933-2145
T H Rogers Lumber Co, The PO Box 5770 *Web:* www.throgers.com	Edmond	OK	73083	405-330-2181	

191-3 Lumber & Building Supplies

Company	City	State	ZIP	Phone	Fax
84 Lumber Co 1019 Rt 519 *TF:* 800-664-1984 ■ *Web:* www.84lumber.com	Eighty Four	PA	15330	724-228-8820	
Alamo Lumber Co 10800 Sentinel Dr *TF:* 855-828-9792 ■ *Web:* alamo.doitbest.com	San Antonio	TX	78217	210-352-1300	
Allied Bldg Products Corp 15 E Union Ave *TF:* 800-541-2198 ■ *Web:* www.alliedbuilding.com	East Rutherford	NJ	07073	201-507-8400	507-3855
Alpine Lumber Co 1120 W 122nd Ave Ste 301 *TF:* 800-499-1634 ■ *Web:* www.alpinelumber.com	Denver	CO	80234	303-451-8001	451-5232
American Direct Procurement Inc 11000 Lakeview Ave *Web:* www.americandirectco.com	Lenexa	KS	66219	913-677-5588	
American International Forest Products LLC (AIFP) 5560 SW 107th Ave *TF:* 800-366-1611 ■ *Web:* www.lumber.com	Beaverton	OR	97005	503-641-1611	641-2800
Arnold Lumber Co 251 Fairgrounds Rd *TF:* 800-339-0116 ■ *Web:* www.arnold.myeshowroom.com	West Kingston	RI	02892	401-783-2266	792-3610
Auburn Corp 10490 164th Pl *TF:* 800-393-1826 ■ *Web:* www.auburncorp.com	Orland Park	IL	60467	708-349-7676	
Babcock Lumber Company Inc 2220 Palmer St PO Box 8348 *TF:* 800-553-4441 ■ *Web:* www.babcocklumber.com	Pittsburgh	PA	15218	412-351-3515	351-1522
Baille Lumber Co 4002 Legion Dr PO Box 6 *TF:* 800-950-2850 ■ *Web:* www.baillie.com	Hamburg	NY	14075	716-649-2850	649-2811
Banner Supply Co 7195 NW 30th St *TF:* 888-511-4004 ■ *Web:* www.bannersupply.com	Miami	FL	33122	305-593-2946	477-2775
Bayer Built Woodworks Inc 24614 Hwy 71 *Web:* www.bayerbuilt.com	Belgrade	MN	56312	320-254-3651	254-3601
Beavertooth Oak Inc 401 S Fir St *TF:* 800-306-1942 ■ *Web:* www.beavertooth.net	Medford	OR	97501	541-779-1942	776-0944

Company	City	State	Zip	Phone	Fax
Bender Lumber Company Inc 3120 Brock Ln *Web:* www.benderlumber.com	Bedford	IN	47421	812-279-9737	
Big C Lumber Inc 50860 Princess Way PO Box 176 *TF:* 888-297-0010 ■ *Web:* www.bigclumber.com	Granger	IN	46530	574-277-4550	271-3823
Big Creek Lumber 3564 Hwy 1 *Web:* www.big-creek.com	Davenport	CA	95017	831-457-5015	423-2800
Birmingham International Forest Products LLC 300 Riverhills Business Pk *TF:* 800-767-2437 ■ *Web:* www.bifp.com	Birmingham	AL	35242	205-972-1500	972-1461
Britton Lumber Company Inc 7 Ely Rd PO Box 389 *TF:* 800-343-5300 ■ *Web:* www.brittonlumber.com	Fairlee	VT	05045	802-333-4388	333-4295
Brookside Lumber & Supply Co 500 Logan Rd PO Box 327 *Web:* www.brooksidelumber.com	Bethel Park	PA	15102	412-835-7610	835-8672
Buckeye Pacific LLC 4386 SW Macadam Ave Ste 200 *TF:* 800-767-9191 ■ *Web:* www.buckeyepacific.com	Portland	OR	97207	503-274-2284	274-2284
Builders FirstSource Inc 2001 Bryan St Ste 1600 *NASDAQ: BLDR* ■ *Web:* www.bldr.com	Dallas	TX	75201	214-880-3500	880-3599
Builders General Supply Co 15 Sycamore Ave **Fax Area Code: 732* ■ *TF:* 800-570-7227 ■ *Web:* www.buildersgeneral.com	Little Silver	NJ	07739	800-570-7227	741-1095*
Campbellsport Bldg Supply Inc 227 W Main St PO Box 510 *Web:* www.drexelteam.com	Campbellsport	WI	53010	920-533-4412	533-4333
Causeway Lumber Co 3318 SW Second Ave *Web:* www.causewaylumber.com	Fort Lauderdale	FL	33315	954-763-1224	
Champion Lumber Co 1313 Chicago Ave Ste 100 *Web:* www.championlumber.net	Riverside	CA	92507	951-684-5670	275-0825
Chelsea Lumber Co 1 Old Barn Cir *TF:* 800-875-9126 ■ *Web:* www.chelsealumber.com	Chelsea	MI	48118	734-475-9126	475-7320
Chicago Lumber Company of Omaha, The 1324 Pierce St PO Box 3487 *TF:* 800-642-8210 ■ *Web:* www.clc-omaha.com	Omaha	NE	68103	402-342-0840	344-8323
Cleary Millwork Company Inc 235 Dividend Rd *TF:* 800-486-7600 ■ *Web:* www.clearymillwork.com	Rocky Hill	CT	06067	860-721-0520	
CNC Assoc Ny Inc 101 Kentile Rd *Web:* www.cncassociates.com	South Plainfield	NJ	07080	718-416-3853	
Counter Pro Inc 210 Lincoln St *TF:* 800-899-2444 ■ *Web:* counterproincusa.com	Manchester	NH	03103	603-647-2444	647-6770
Coventry Lumber Inc 2030 Nooseneck Hill Rd *TF:* 800-390-0919 ■ *Web:* www.coventrylumber.com	Coventry	RI	02816	401-821-2800	828-2870
Creative Pultrusions Inc 214 Industrial Ln *TF:* 888-274-7855 ■ *Web:* www.creativepultrusions.com	Alum Bank	PA	15521	814-839-4186	839-4276
Custom Builder Supply Company Inc PO Box 413 *Web:* www.custombuildersupply.com	Williamsburg	VA	23187	757-229-5150	253-7568
Doka USA Ltd 214 Gates Rd *TF:* 877-365-2872 ■ *Web:* www.doka.com	Little Ferry	NJ	07643	201-329-7839	641-6254
Door Systems Inc PO Box 511 *TF:* 800-545-3667 ■ *Web:* doorsys.com	Framingham	MA	01704	508-875-3508	
Falmouth Lumber Inc 670 Teaticket Hwy *Web:* www.falmouthlumber.com	East Falmouth	MA	02536	508-548-6868	457-0649
Forest City Trading Group LLC 10250 SW Greenburg Rd Ste 300 *TF:* 800-767-3284 ■ *Web:* www.fctg.com	Portland	OR	97223	503-246-8500	246-1116
Forest Products Group Inc, The 1033 Dublin Rd *Web:* www.forestproductsgroup.com	Columbus	OH	43215	614-488-9743	
Foxworth-Galbraith Lumber Co 4965 Preston Pk Blvd Ste 400 *TF:* 800-688-8082 ■ *Web:* www.foxgal.com	Plano	TX	75093	972-665-2400	454-4251
Frank Miller Lumber Company Inc 1690 Frank Miller Rd *TF:* 800-345-2643 ■ *Web:* www.frankmiller.com	Union City	IN	47390	765-964-3196	964-6618
Frank Paxton Lumber Co 7455 Dawson Rd **Fax:* Sales ■ *TF:* 800-325-9800 ■ *Web:* www.paxtonwood.com	Cincinnati	OH	45243	513-984-8200	984-9060*
Genesee Reserve Supply Inc 200 Jefferson Rd *Web:* www.geneseereserve.com	Rochester	NY	14623	585-292-7040	292-7046
Gerretsen Bldg Supply Co 1900 NE Airport Rd *Web:* www.gerretsen.com	Roseburg	OR	97470	541-672-2636	
Great Lakes Gypsum & Supply 33900 Concord Rd	Livonia	MI	48150	734-421-1170	421-5237
Great Lakes Veneer Inc 222 S Parkview Ave PO Box 476 *Web:* www.greatlakesveneer.com	Marion	WI	54950	715-754-2501	754-2582
Guardian Building Products (GBPD) 979 Batesville Rd *TF:* 800-569-4262 ■ *Web:* guardianbp.com	Greer	SC	29651	864-297-6101	281-3558
H. W. Culp Lumber Co PO Box 235 *Web:* www.culplumber.com	New London	NC	28127	704-463-7311	463-4100
Hagle Lumber Company Inc 3100 Somis Rd PO Box 120 *Web:* www.haglelumber.com	Somis	CA	93066	805-987-3887	987-7564
Hatch & Bailey Company Inc 1 Meadow St Ext *Web:* www.hatchandbailey.com	Norwalk	CT	06854	203-866-5515	854-1712
Hawaii Planing Mill Ltd (HPM) 16-166 Melekahiwa St *TF:* 877-841-7633 ■ *Web:* www.hpmhawaii.com	Keaau	HI	96749	808-966-5693	966-7564
Holt & Bugbee Co 1600 Shawsheen St *TF:* 800-325-6010 ■ *Web:* www.holtandbugbee.com	Tewksbury	MA	01876	978-851-7201	851-3941
Howard Lumber Co 475 Columbia Industrial Blvd *Web:* howardlumbercompany.com	Evans	GA	30809	706-868-8400	
Hutchison Inc 7460 Hwy 85 PO Box 1158 *TF:* 800-525-0121 ■ *Web:* www.hutchison-inc.com	Adams City	CO	80022	303-287-2826	289-3286
Huttig Bldg Products Inc (HBP) 555 Maryville University Dr Ste 400 *OTC: HBPI* ■ *TF:* 800-325-4466 ■ *Web:* www.huttig.com	Saint Louis	MO	63141	314-216-2600	216-2601
Idaho Pacific Lumber Co (IdaPac) 7255 Franklin Rd *TF:* 800-231-2310 ■ *Web:* www.idapac.com	Boise	ID	83709	208-375-8052	375-3054
Jb Wholesale Roofing & Bldg Supplies Inc 21524 Nordhoff St *Web:* www.jbroofing.com	Chatsworth	CA	91311	818-998-0440	
Jewett-Cameron Trading Company Ltd 32275 NW Hillcrest PO Box 1010 *NASDAQ: JCTCF* ■ *TF:* 800-547-5877 ■ *Web:* www.jewettcameron.com	North Plains	OR	97133	503-647-0110	647-2272
Kight Home Ctr 5521 Oak Grove Rd *Web:* www.kighthomecenter.com	Evansville	IN	47715	812-479-8281	
Kimal Lumber Co 400 Riverview Dr *Web:* www.kimallumber.com	Nokomis	FL	34275	941-484-9721	484-9593
Kleet Lumber Company Inc 777 Pk Ave *TF:* 800-696-5533 ■ *Web:* www.kleet.com	Huntington	NY	11743	631-427-7060	427-4384
Lumbermen's Merchandising Corp 137 W Wayne Ave **Fax Area Code: 484* ■ *Web:* www.lmc.net	Wayne	PA	19087	610-293-7000	293-7098*
Lyman Lumber Co 520 Third St Ste 200 *Web:* www.lymanlumber.com	Excelsior	MN	55331	952-470-3600	470-3670
Lyon & Billard Co, The 38 Gypsy Ln	Meriden	CT	06451	203-235-4487	235-9736
Magbee Contractors Supply 1065 Bankhead Hwy *Web:* www.magbee.com	Winder	GA	30680	678-425-2600	425-2602
Magnolia Forest Products Inc 13252 I- 55 S PO Box 99 **Fax Area Code: 601* ■ *TF:* 800-366-6374 ■ *Web:* www.magnoliaforest.com	Terry	MS	39170	800-366-6374	878-2590*
Markraft Cabinets Inc 2705 Castle Creek Ln *Web:* www.markraft.com	Wilmington	NC	28401	910-762-1986	762-1985
Matheus Lumber Company Inc 15800 Woodinville-Redmond Rd NE PO Box 2260 *TF:* 800-284-7501 ■ *Web:* www.matheuslumber.com	Woodinville	WA	98072	425-489-3000	822-4028
Matt's Building Materials 404 E Expy 83 *Web:* www.mattsbuildingmaterials.com	Pharr	TX	78577	956-787-5561	
Mattingly Lumber & Millwork Inc 410 E St *Web:* www.mattinglylumber.com	Madison	IL	62040	636-343-3877	
McCray Lumber Co 10741 El Monte Ln *Web:* www.mccraylumber.com	Overland Park	KS	66211	913-341-6900	341-1881
Mead Clark Lumber Co Hearn Ave & Dowd Dr PO Box 529 *TF:* 800-585-9663 ■ *Web:* www.meadclark.com	Santa Rosa	CA	95402	707-576-3333	523-0350
MID-AM Bldg Supply Inc 1615 Omar Bradley Dr PO Box 645 *TF:* 800-892-5850 ■ *Web:* www.midambuilding.com	Moberly	MO	65270	660-263-2140	263-7892
Mid-South Bldg Supply Inc 7940 Woodruff Ct *Web:* www.msbs.net	Springfield	VA	22151	703-321-8500	321-9308
Millard Lumber Inc 12900 I St PO Box 45445 *TF:* 800-228-9260 ■ *Web:* millardlumber.com	Omaha	NE	68145	402-896-2800	896-2865
Milliken Millwork Inc 172 Plummer Rd *TF:* 800-452-0251 ■ *Web:* www.millikenmillwork.com	Sidman	PA	15955	800-452-0251	
Musser Lumber Company Inc 200 Shoal Ridge Dr *Web:* www.musserlumber.com	Rural Retreat	VA	24368	276-686-5113	686-5169
Nalco Real Estate Corp 24595 Groesbeck Hwy	Warren	MI	48089	586-775-8200	775-4110
National Industrial Lumber Co 1 Chicago Ave **Fax Area Code: 412* ■ *TF:* 800-289-9352 ■ *Web:* www.nilco.net/about-us/locations	Elizabeth	PA	15037	800-289-9352	384-3955*
Ohio Valley Supply Co 3512 Spring Grove Ave *TF:* 800-696-5608 ■ *Web:* www.ovsco.com	Cincinnati	OH	45223	513-681-8300	853-3307
Omega Products International 1681 California Ave *TF:* 800-600-6634 ■ *Web:* www.omega-products.com	Corona	CA	92881	951-737-7447	520-2594
Orgain Building Supply Co 65 Commerce St *Web:* www.orgainbuilding.com	Clarksville	TN	37040	931-647-1567	
Pacific Source Inc PO Box 2323 *TF:* 888-343-1515 ■ *Web:* www.pacsource.com	Woodinville	WA	98072	888-343-1515	
Pacific Wood Laminates Inc 885 Railroad Ave PO Box 820 *Web:* www.pacificwoodlaminates.com	Brookings	OR	97415	541-469-4177	
Palmer-Donavin Manufacturing Co 1200 Steelwood Rd *TF:* 800-589-4412 ■ *Web:* www.palmerdonavin.com	Columbus	OH	43212	614-486-9657	486-5073
Park Avenue Building & Roofing Supplies LLC 2120 Atlantic Ave *Web:* www.parkavebenmoore.com	Brooklyn	NY	11233	718-403-0100	596-5085
Parker Lumber Co Inc 2192 Eastex Fwy *Web:* www.parkersbuildingsupply.com	Beaumont	TX	77703	409-898-7000	347-0942
Parker Lumber Co of Port Arthur Inc 2948 Gulfway Dr *TF:* 855-828-9792 ■ *Web:* www.parkersbuildingsupply.com	Port Arthur	TX	77642	409-983-2745	983-3993
Parksite Inc 1563 Hubbard Ave *TF:* 800-338-3355 ■ *Web:* www.parksite.com	Batavia	IL	60510	630-761-9490	761-6820
Product Distributors Inc 4200 Beach Dr Ste 2 Ste 2 *Web:* www.forpd.com	Rapid City	SD	57702	605-341-6500	341-1976
Pyramid Interiors Distributors Inc PO Box 181058 *TF:* 800-456-0592 ■ *Web:* www.pyramidinteriors.com	Memphis	TN	38181	901-375-4197	
Quality Plywood Specialties Inc 4500 110th Ave N *TF:* 888-722-1181 ■ *Web:* www.qualityplywoodspec.com	Clearwater	FL	33762	727-572-0500	571-3623
Quality Wholesale Bldg Inc 11701 KinaRd Rd	North Little Rock	AR	72117	501-945-3442	945-0506
Raymond Bldg Supply Corp 7751 Bayshore Rd *TF:* 877-731-7272 ■ *Web:* www.rbsc.net	North Fort Myers	FL	33917	239-731-8300	731-3299
Reliable Wholesale Lumber Inc 7600 Redondo Cir *TF:* 877-795-4638 ■ *Web:* www.rwli.net	Huntington Beach	CA	92648	714-848-8222	847-1605
Richmond International Forest Products Inc 4050 Innslake Dr Ste 100 *TF:* 800-767-0111 ■ *Web:* www.rifp.com	Glen Allen	VA	23060	804-747-0111	270-4547

Company	City	State	Zip	Phone	Fax
Ridout Lumber Co 125 Henry Farrar Dr. *Web:* www.ridoutlumber.com	Searcy	AR	72143	501-268-3929	
Rigidply Rafters Inc 701 E Linden St. *Web:* www.rigidply.com	Richland	PA	17087	717-866-6581	
Riverhead Bldg Supply Corp 1093 Pulaski St. *TF:* 800-378-3650 ■ *Web:* www.rbscorp.com	Riverhead	NY	11901	631-727-3650	727-7713
Riverside Forest Products Inc 2912 Professional Pkwy *TF:* 888-855-8733 ■ *Web:* www.riversideforest.com	Augusta	GA	30907	706-855-5500	863-3362
RP Lumber Company Inc 514 E Vandalia St *Web:* www.rplumber.com	Edwardsville	IL	62025	618-656-1514	656-6785
Russin Lumber Corp 21 Leonards Dr *TF:* 800-724-0010 ■ *Web:* www.russinlumber.com	Montgomery	NY	12549	845-457-4000	457-4010
Schoeneman Bros Co 4000 S Western Ave *Web:* www.schoenemans.com	Sioux Falls	SD	57103	605-339-0745	
Seaboard International Forest Products LLC 22F Cotton Rd *TF:* 800-669-6800 ■ *Web:* www.sifp.com	Nashua	NH	03063	603-881-3700	598-2280
Seigle's 1331 Davis Rd. *Web:* www.seigles.com	Elgin	IL	60123	847-742-2000	697-6521
Service Construction Supply Inc PO Box 13405 *TF:* 866-729-4968 ■ *Web:* www.serviceconstructionsupply.com	Birmingham	AL	35202	205-252-3158	252-5720
Solar Industries Inc PO Box 27337 *TF:* 800-449-2323 ■ *Web:* www.solarindustriesinc.com	Tucson	AZ	85726	520-519-8258	
Spellman Hardwoods Inc 4645 N 43rd Ave. **Fax Area Code:* 623 ■ *TF:* 800-624-5401 ■ *Web:* www.spellmanhardwoods.com	Phoenix	AZ	85031	602-272-2313	930-7668*
Sprenger Midwest Inc 700 S Fourth Ave. *Web:* www.sprengermidwest.com	Sioux Falls	SD	57104	605-334-7705	334-5205
Stevenson Lumber 501 Division	Adrian	MI	49221	517-265-5151	265-5534
Stock Bldg Supply 8020 Arco Corporate Dr *Web:* www.stockbuildingsupply.com	Raleigh	NC	27617	919-431-1000	431-1700
Stock Building Supply 8020 Arco Corporate Dr. *Web:* www.stockbuildingsupply.com/stock	Raleigh	NC	27617	919-431-1000	
Sunderland Bros Co 9700 J St *Web:* www.sunderlands.com	Omaha	NE	68127	402-339-2220	339-4455
Timber Products Co 305 S Fourth St PO Box 269 *TF:* 800-547-9520 ■ *Web:* www.timberproducts.com	Springfield	OR	97477	541-747-4577	744-4296
Timberline Forest Products LLC PO Box 1568 *Web:* www.timberlineforestproducts.com	Sherwood	OR	97140	503-590-5485	590-7421
Tischler Und Sohn 6 Suburban Ave *Web:* www.tischlerwindows.com	Stamford	CT	06901	203-674-0600	674-0601
Tri-state Forest Products Inc 2105 Sheridan Ave *TF:* 800-949-6325 ■ *Web:* www.tsfpi.com	Springfield	OH	45505	937-323-6325	323-6888
Tulnoy Lumber Inc 1620 Webster Ave *Web:* www.tulnoylumber.com	Bronx	NY	10457	718-901-1700	299-8920
US Lumber Group Inc 2160 Satellite Blvd Ste 450 *Web:* www.uslumber.com	Duluth	GA	30097	678-474-4577	474-4575
Verhalen Inc 500 Pilgrim Way *TF:* 800-895-0071 ■ *Web:* www.verhaleninc.com	Green Bay	WI	54304	920-431-8900	431-8901
Viking Forest Products LLC 7615 Smetana Ln *TF:* 800-733-3801 ■ *Web:* www.vikingforest.com	Eden Prairie	MN	55344	952-941-6512	941-4633
VNS Corp 325 Commerce Loop PO Box 1659 *Web:* www.vnscorp.com	Vidalia	GA	30475	912-537-8964	537-4839
Warren Trask Co 1481 Central St *Web:* www.wtrask.com	Stoughton	MA	02072	781-341-2426	341-3522
Western Lumber Cy LLC 2240 Tower E Ste 200 *TF:* 800-633-5554 ■ *Web:* www.westernlumber.com	Medford	OR	97504	541-779-5121	779-0155
Wheeler Lumber LLC 9330 James Ave S *TF:* 800-328-3986 ■ *Web:* www.wheeler-con.com	Bloomington	MN	55431	952-929-7854	929-2909
White Cap Industries Inc 1723 S Ritchie St *TF:* 800-944-8322 ■ *Web:* www.whitecap.com	Santa Ana	CA	92705	714-258-3300	258-3289
Wilson Lumber Co Inc 4818 Meridian St *Web:* www.wilsonlumber.net	Huntsville	AL	35811	256-852-7411	851-9904
Window Rama Enterprises Inc 71 Heartland Blvd *TF:* 800-897-7262 ■ *Web:* www.windowrama.com	Edgewood	NY	11717	631-667-8088	
Wright Do-it Ctr 1306 N Market *Web:* www.wrightdoit.com	Sparta	IL	62286	618-443-5335	687-1030
WT Harvey Lumber Co 800 15th St PO Box 310 *Web:* www.harveylumber.com	Columbus	GA	31902	706-322-8204	323-2433
Zeeland Lumber & Supply Co 146 E Washington *TF:* 888-772-2119 ■ *Web:* www.zeelandlumber.com	Zeeland	MI	49464	616-772-2119	772-6409

191-4 Roofing, Siding, Insulation Materials

Company	City	State	Zip	Phone	Fax
ABC Seamless 3001 Fiechtner Dr *TF:* 800-732-6577 ■ *Web:* www.abcseamless.com	Fargo	ND	58103	701-293-5952	
ABC Supply Company Inc 1 ABC Pkwy *TF:* 800-738-7477 ■ *Web:* www.abcsupply.com	Beloit	WI	53511	608-362-7777	
B & L Wholesale Supply Inc 70 Hartford St *Web:* www.blwholesale.com	Rochester	NY	14605	585-546-6616	546-7326
Beacon Roofing Supply Inc 1 Lakeland Pk Dr *NASDAQ: BECN* ■ *TF:* 877-645-7663 ■ *Web:* www.beaconroofingsupply.com	Peabody	MA	01960	978-535-7668	
Best Distributing Company Inc PO Box 128 *Web:* www.bestdistributing.com	Goldsboro	NC	27533	919-735-1651	
Brunswick Floors 3550 Darien Hwy *Web:* www.brunswickfloors.com	Brunswick	GA	31525	912-265-0222	
Burbank Roofing Supply Inc 700 N Victory Blvd *Web:* www.roofingdealer.com	Burbank	CA	91502	818-840-8851	
Carlisle Cos Inc 13925 Ballantyne Corporate Pl Ste 400 *NYSE: CSL* ■ *TF:* 800-248-5995 ■ *Web:* www.carlisle.com	Charlotte	NC	28277	704-501-1100	501-1190
Carlisle SynTec 1285 Ritner Hwy PO Box 7000 *TF:* 800-479-6832 ■ *Web:* www.carlislesyntec.com	Carlisle	PA	17013	717-245-7000	245-7053
Crane Composites Inc 23525 W Eames St **Fax:* Hum Res ■ *TF:* 800-435-0080 ■ *Web:* www.cranecomposites.com	Channahon	IL	60410	815-467-8600	467-8666*
E O Wood Company Inc PO Box 7416 *Web:* www.eowood.com	Fort Worth	TX	76111	817-834-8811	831-0834
Fire Brick Engineers Co 2400 S 43rd St *Web:* www.firebrickengineers.com	Milwaukee	WI	53219	414-383-6000	
Frank Roberts & Sons Inc 1130 Robertsville Rd *TF:* 800-262-8955 ■ *Web:* frankrobertsandsons.com	Punxsutawney	PA	15767	814-938-5000	938-0880
General Insulation Company Inc 278 Mystic Ave Ste 209 *TF:* 800-229-9148 ■ *Web:* www.generalinsulation.com	Medford	MA	02155	781-391-2070	391-3094
Harvey Industries Inc 1400 Main St **Fax Area Code:* 781 ■ *TF:* 800-598-5400 ■ *Web:* www.harveybp.com	Waltham	MA	02451	800-598-5400	398-7715*
Howred Corp 7887 San Felipe St Ste 122 *TF:* 800-535-5053 ■ *Web:* www.howred.com	Houston	TX	77063	713-781-3980	784-3985
James Hardie Bldg Products 26300 La Alameda Ave Ste 400 *TF:* 888-542-7343 ■ *Web:* www.jameshardie.com	Mission Viejo	CA	92691	949-348-1800	367-1294
Jenkins Brick & Tile Company LLC 201 Sixth St N *Web:* www.jenkinsbrick.com	Montgomery	AL	36104	334-834-2210	
JPS Industries Inc 55 Beattie Pl # 1510 *Web:* jps-industries.com	Greenville	SC	29601	864-239-3900	
Lansing Bldg Products 8501 Sanford Dr *TF:* 800-768-5762 ■ *Web:* lansingbp.com	Richmond	VA	23228	804-266-8771	266-0166
MacArthur Co 2400 Wycliff St *TF:* 800-777-7507 ■ *Web:* www.macarthurco.com	Saint Paul	MN	55114	651-646-2773	642-9630
McClure-Johnston Co 201 Corey Ave *TF:* 800-232-0018 ■ *Web:* www.cassadymcclure.com	Braddock	PA	15104	412-351-4300	351-1480
Norandex Bldg Materials Distribution Inc 1 ABC Pkwy Ste 100 *Web:* www.norandex.com	Beloit	WA	53511	330-656-8809	
North Carolina Foam Industries Inc 1515 Carter St *TF:* 800-346-8229 ■ *Web:* www.ncfi.com	Mount Airy	NC	27030	336-789-9161	789-9586
Oberfields LLC 1165 Alum Creek Dr *TF:* 800-845-7644 ■ *Web:* www.oberfields.com	Columbus	OH	43209	614-252-0955	
Olympia Tile International Inc 1000 Lawrence Ave W *TF:* 800-268-1613 ■ *Web:* www.olympiatile.com	Toronto	ON	M6A1C6	416-785-6666	
Onduline North America Inc 4900 Ondura Dr *TF:* 800-777-7663 ■ *Web:* www.ondura.com	Fredericksburg	VA	22407	540-898-7000	898-4991
Owens Corning 1 Owens Corning Pkwy *NYSE: OC* ■ *Web:* www.owenscorning.com	Toledo	OH	43659	419-248-8000	325-1538
Pacific Coast Bldg Products Inc 10600 White Rock Rd Bldg B Ste 100 *Web:* www.paccoast.com	Rancho Cordova	CA	95670	916-631-6500	631-6685
Pfister Maintenance Inc 80 E Fifth St *Web:* www.pfisterroofing.com	Paterson	NJ	07524	973-569-9330	
Philadelphia Reserve Supply Co 200 Mack Dr *TF:* 800-347-7726 ■ *Web:* www.prsco.org	Croydon	PA	19021	215-785-3141	
Plastatech Engineering Ltd 725 Morley Dr *TF:* 800-892-9358 ■ *Web:* www.plastatech.com	Saginaw	MI	48601	989-754-6500	754-1626
Roofing & Insulation Supply Inc 12221 Merit Dr Ste 1015 *Web:* www.risris.com	Dallas	TX	75251	972-239-8309	239-8310
Roofing Products & Bldg Supply Company Inc 4955 River Rd *Web:* www.rfgproducts.com	Jefferson	LA	70121	504-733-0404	733-0360
Roofing Supply Group 8319 N Lamar Blvd *Web:* rsgroof.com	Austin	TX	78753	512-834-4347	834-4352
Roofing Wholesale Co Inc 1918 W Grant St *TF Cust Svc:* 800-528-4532 ■ *Web:* www.rwc.org	Phoenix	AZ	85009	602-258-3794	256-0932
SG Wholesale Roofing Supplies Inc 1101 E Sixth St *Web:* www.sgroof.com	Santa Ana	CA	92701	714-568-1906	568-1915
Shook & Fletcher Insulation Co 4625 Valleydale Rd *TF:* 888-829-2575 ■ *Web:* www.shookandfletcher.com	Birmingham	AL	35242	205-991-7606	991-7745
Spec Bldg Materials Inc 4300 W Ave *TF:* 800-588-3892 ■ *Web:* speccorp.com	San Antonio	TX	78213	210-342-2727	340-0688
Specialty Products & Insulation Co (SPI) 1650 Manheim Pk Ste 202 *TF:* 800-788-7764 ■ *Web:* www.spi-co.com	Lancaster	PA	17601	717-569-3900	519-4046
Standard Roofings Inc 100 Pk Rd *Web:* www.abcsupply.com	Tinton Falls	NJ	07724	732-542-5200	389-4982
Supreme Systems Inc 1355 N Walton Walker Blvd *Web:* www.supremeroofing.com	Dallas	TX	75211	214-330-8913	
Toitures GGR Inc 34 Trudel Cp 333 *TF:* 800-043-7760 ■ *Web:* www.toituresggr.com	Amos	QC	J9T3A7	819-727-3348	
Variform Inc 5020 Weston Pkwy Ste 400 **Fax Area Code:* 816 ■ *TF:* 800-800-2244 ■ *Web:* www.plygem.com/wps/portal/home/brands/variform	Cary	NC	27513	888-975-9436	903-6942*
Warko Roofing Company Inc 18 Morgan Dr *Web:* www.thewarkogroup.com	Reading	PA	19608	610-796-4545	796-4547
Wesco Cedar Inc PO Box 520 *TF:* 800-547-2511 ■ *Web:* www.wescocedar.com	Creswell	OR	97426	541-688-5020	688-5024

192 CONSULTING SERVICES - ENVIRONMENTAL

See Also Recyclable Materials Recovery p. 3056; Remediation Services p. 3059; Waste Management p. 3304

Company	City	State	Zip	Phone	Fax
A & A Maintenance Enterprise Inc 965 Midland Ave *TF:* 800-280-0601 ■ *Web:* www.aamaintenance.com	Yonkers	NY	10704	914-969-0009	
A G Miller Company Inc 53 Batavia St *Web:* www.agmiller.com	Springfield	MA	01109	413-732-9297	734-1236
Aadfw Inc 2161 Regal Pkwy *Web:* www.aadfwinc.com	Euless	TX	76040	817-540-0153	

Company	City	State	Zip	Phone	Fax
Aarcher 910 Commerce Rd *Web:* www.aarcherinc.com	Annapolis	MD	21401	410-897-9100	
Abitibi Geophysique Ltd 1740 ch Sullivan 1400 *Web:* www.ageophysics.com	Val-d'or	QC	J9P7H1	819-874-8800	
ACS Manufacturing Inc 1601 Commerce Blvd *Web:* www.acsmanufacturing.com	Denison	TX	75020	903-462-2001	
adaptiveARC Inc P.O. Box 5568 *Web:* www.adaptivearc.com	Oceanside	CA	92052	215-676-7876	
AirTek Indoor Air Solutions Inc 9424 Chesapeake Dr *TF:* 877-858-6213 ■ *Web:* www.air-tek.net	San Diego	CA	92123	877-858-6213	
All Waste Inc 143 Murphy Rd *Web:* www.allwaste.com	Hartford	CT	06114	860-724-4575	
Ameresco Inc 111 Speen St Ste 410 *TF:* 866-263-7372 ■ *Web:* www.ameresco.com	Framingham	MA	01701	508-661-2200	661-2201
AmeriPark LLC 3200 Cobb Galleria Pkwy Ste 299 *Web:* www.ameripark.com	Atlanta	GA	30339	678-303-5962	
Arcadis 630 Plz Dr Ste 200 *Web:* www.arcadis.com//en/united-states/cookie-wall	Highlands Ranch	CO	80129	720-344-3500	344-3535
ARISE Technologies Corp 65 Northland Rd *Web:* www.arisetech.com	Waterloo	ON	N2V1Y8	519-725-2244	
Arizona Energy Masters 219 W Lone Cactus *Web:* www.arizonaenergymasters.com	Phoenix	AZ	85027	602-427-0007	
Ash Creek Associates Inc 3015 Southwest First Ave *Web:* www.ashcreekassociates.com	Portland	OR	97201	503-924-4704	
Ashbrook Simon-Hartley LP 11600 E Hardy *Web:* www.alfalaval.com/as-h	Houston	TX	77093	281-449-0322	
Avogadro Group LLC, The 2825 Verne Roberts Cir *Web:* www.avogadrogroup.com	Antioch	CA	94509	925-680-4300	
Badger Express LLC 181 Quality Ct *TF:* 800-972-0084 ■ *Web:* www.badgerexpress.com	Fall River	WI	53932	920-484-5808	
Basic Systems Inc 9255 Cadiz Rd *Web:* www.basic-systems.com	Cambridge	OH	43725	740-432-3001	
Beary Landscaping Inc 15001 W 159th St *Web:* bearylandscaping.com	Lockport	IL	60491	708-349-1500	
Blade Energy Partners Ltd 2600 Network Blvd Ste 550 *TF:* 800-849-1545 ■ *Web:* www.blade-energy.com	Frisco	TX	75034	972-712-8407	712-8408
BlazeTech Corp 29B Montvale Ave *Web:* www.blazetech.com	Woburn	MA	01801	781-759-0700	
Blue Pillar Inc 9025 N River Rd Ste 150 *TF:* 888-234-3212 ■ *Web:* bluepillar.com	Indianapolis	IN	46240	888-234-3212	
BP Environmental Inc 1103 S Talbot St Ste D *Web:* www.bpenvironmental.net	St. Michaels	MD	21663	410-745-0919	
BPI Inc 612 S Trenton Ave *Web:* www.bpiminerals.com	Pittsburg	PA	15221	412-334-8554	
Brighter Planet Inc 36 Main St *Web:* brighterplanet.com	Middlebury	VT	05753	802-458-0441	
Brightergy LLC 1617 Main St 3rd Fl *Web:* brightergy.com	Kansas City	MO	64108	816-866-0555	
Broad Oak Energy II LLC 1707 Market Pl Ste 320 *Web:* www.broadoakenergy.com	Irving	TX	75063	972-444-8808	
Burnaby Lake Greenhouses Ltd 17250 80 Ave *Web:* www.burlake.com	Surrey	BC	V4N6J6	604-576-2088	
Buzas Greenhouses 3927 Newburg Rd *Web:* buzasgreenhouseandfarm.com	Easton	PA	18045	610-252-5289	
C. F. Bean LLC 619 Engineers Rd *Web:* www.cfbean.com	Belle Chasse	LA	70037	504-587-8700	
C12 Energy LLC 2054 University Ave Ste 400 *Web:* www.c12energy.com	Berkeley	CA	94704	617-674-2478	
C2I LLC 4243 Jackson St *Web:* www.c2invest.net	The Plains	VA	20198	540-253-2500	
Cantu Pest Control 323 Industrial Blvd Ste C *Web:* cantupestcontrol.com	Mckinney	TX	75069	972-562-9999	
Caravan Facilities Management LLC 1400 Weiss St *TF:* 855-211-7450 ■ *Web:* www.caravanfm.com	Saginaw	MI	48602	855-211-7450	
Cardinal Group Inc, The 406 King St E *Web:* www.cardinalgroup.ca	Toronto	ON	M5A1L4	416-971-4494	
Carr Environmental Group Inc 504 Spring Hill Dr Ste 300 Spring *Web:* www.ceg-group.com	Houston	TX	77386	281-872-9300	
CH2M Hill Cos Ltd 9191 S Jamica St **Fax Area Code:* 720 ■ *Web:* www.ch2m.com	Englewood	CO	80112	303-771-0900	286-9250*
Chicago Parking Meters LLC 2735 N Ashland Ave *Web:* www.chicagometers.com	Chicago	IL	60614	773-935-2178	
Chicanos Por La Causa Inc 1112 E Buckeye Rd *Web:* www.cplc.org	Phoenix	AZ	85034	602-257-0700	256-2740
Clear Comfort Water LLC 4888 Pearl E Cir Ste 250 *Web:* clearcomfort.com	Boulder	CO	80301	303-872-4477	
Climate Registry, The 523 W Sixth St Ste 445 *TF:* 866-523-0764 ■ *Web:* www.theclimateregistry.org	Los Angeles	CA	90014	866-523-0764	
CoaLogix Inc 11707 Steele Creek Rd	Charlotte	NC	28273	704-827-8933	
COCAT LLC 4905 Lima St *Web:* www.cocat.com	Denver	CO	80239	303-333-0392	
Compaction Technologies Inc 1171 Northland Dr Ste 121 *TF:* 877-860-6900 ■ *Web:* www.compactiontechnologies.com	Mendota Heights	MN	55120	877-860-6900	
Covino Environmental Assoc Inc 300 Wildwood Ave *Web:* www.covinoinc.com	Woburn	MA	01801	781-933-2555	932-9402
Cox Mclain Environmental Consulting Inc 6010 Balcones Dr Ste 210 *Web:* www.coxmclain.com	Austin	TX	78731	512-338-2223	
Cramer Fish Sciences 300 Se Arrow Creek Ln *Web:* www.fishsciences.net	Gresham	OR	97030	503-491-9577	
Crop Quest Inc 1204 W Frntview ST, *Web:* www.cropquest.com	Dodge City	KS	67801	620-225-2233	
Direct Supply Inc 6767 N Industrial Rd *Web:* www.directsupply.com	Milwaukee	WI	53223	414-358-2805	358-7411
Divisions Maintenance Group Inc 1 RiverFrnt Pl Ste 510 *TF:* 877-448-9730 ■ *Web:* www.divisionsinc.com	Newport	KY	41071	877-448-9730	
Doef's Greenhouses RR Site one Box 14 Ste 3 *Web:* www.doefsgreenhouses.com	Lacombe	AB	T4L2N3	403-782-2704	
DPRA Inc 200 Research Dr *Web:* www.dpra.com	Manhattan	KS	66503	785-539-3565	537-0272
Draper Aden Assoc Inc 2206 S Main St *Web:* www.daa.com	Blacksburg	VA	24060	540-552-0444	552-0291
Durisol Inc 67 Frid St *Web:* www.armtec.com	Hamilton	ON	L8P4M3	905-521-0999	
e4Sciences LLC 27 Glen Rd N Entrance *Web:* www.e4sciences.com	Sandy Hook	CT	06482	203-270-8100	
Earth Networks Inc 12410 Milestone Ctr Dr Ste 300 *Web:* www.earthnetworks.com	Germantown	MD	20876	301-250-4000	
Earth Resource Systems LLC 16285 Laconia Ln *Web:* www.earthresourcesystems.com	Milton	GA	30004	404-513-5429	
Earth Systems Services Inc 895 Aerovista Pl Ste 102 *TF:* 866-781-0112 ■ *Web:* www.earthsystems.com	San Luis Obispo	CA	93401	805-781-0112	781-0180
Earthcon Consultants Inc 1880 W Oak Pkwy Bldg 100 Ste 106 *Web:* www.earthcon.com	Marietta	GA	30062	770-973-2100	
Eastern Janitorial Services Inc 23 N Michigan Ave *Web:* www.easternjs.com	Kenilworth	NJ	07033	908-298-8120	
ECMS Inc 9437 Elm Ave *Web:* www.ecms.com	Orangevale	CA	95662	916-988-0867	
Ecology & Environment Inc 368 Pleasant View Dr *NASDAQ: EEI* ■ *Web:* www.ene.com	Lancaster	NY	14086	716-684-8060	684-0844
EHS Support Inc 110 Kentzel Rd *Web:* www.ehs-support.com	Pittsburgh	PA	15237	412-855-3047	
Ehs-International Inc 13228 NE 20th St Ste 100 *Web:* www.ehsintl.com	Bellevue	WA	98005	425-455-2959	
Energy Worldnet 1210 S Bus Hwy 81/287 Decatur *Web:* www.energyworldnet.com	Decatur	TX	76234	940-626-1941	
EnerNex Corp 620 Mabry Hood Rd Ste 300 *Web:* www.enernex.com	Knoxville	TN	37932	865-218-4600	
Entact LLC 3129 Bass Pro Dr *Web:* www.entact.com	Grapevine	TX	76051	972-580-1323	550-7464
Entec Services Inc 30 Monroe Dr *Web:* www.entecservices.com	Pelham	AL	35124	205-358-1011	
Entomos 4445 SW 35th Ter *Web:* www.entomos.com	Gainesville	FL	32608	352-371-6490	
Enviro Clean Services LLC 11717 N Morgan Rd *Web:* www.envirocleanps.com	Yukon	OK	73099	405-373-4545	
Environmental & Safety Designs Inc 5724 Summer Trees Dr *TF:* 800-588-7962 ■ *Web:* www.ensafe.com	Memphis	TN	38134	901-372-7962	372-2454
Environmental Standards Inc 1140 Vly Forge Rd *Web:* www.envstd.com	Valley Forge	PA	19482	610-935-5577	
Envirotest Corp 200 Day Hill Rd Ste 210 *Web:* www.etest.com	Windsor	CT	06095	860-607-2120	
EnviroTrac Ltd 5 Old Dock Rd *Web:* www.envirotrac.com	Yaphank	NY	11980	631-924-3001	
ESE Solutions LLC 2131 Homestead Blvd Ste *Web:* www.esesolutions.com	Westborough	MA	01581	857-540-2679	
Eureka Resources LLC 419 Second St *Web:* www.eureka-resources.com	Williamsport	PA	17701	570-323-2535	
Fauske & Assoc LLC 16w070 83rd St *TF:* 877-328-7531 ■ *Web:* www.fauske.com	Burr Ridge	IL	60527	630-323-8750	986-5481
First Environment Inc 91 Fulton St *TF:* 800-486-5869 ■ *Web:* www.firstenvironment.com	Boonton	NJ	07005	973-334-0003	334-0928
Fishbio Environmental LLC 180 E 4th St Ste 160 *Web:* www.fishbio.com	Chico	CA	95928	530-892-9686	
G D G Environment Group Ltd 430, rue St-Laurent *Web:* www.gdg.ca	Trois-RiviŠres	QC	G8T6H3	819-373-3097	
Ganaraska Region Conservation 2216 28 Hwy *Web:* www.grca.on.ca	Port Hope	ON	L1A3V8	905-885-8173	
GEEP Ecosys Inc 220 John St *Web:* www.geepecosys.com	Barrie	ON	L4N2L2	705-725-1919	
Gershman, Brickner & Bratton Inc 8550 Arlington Blvd Ste 304 *TF:* 800-573-5801 ■ *Web:* www.gbbinc.com	Fairfax	VA	22031	703-573-5800	
Gestion P R Maintenance Inc 639 King St W Ste 203 *Web:* www.prmaintenance.com	Kitchener	ON	N2G1C7	905-304-8300	
Giant Resource Recovery Company Inc 654 Judge St PO Box 352 *TF:* 800-637-4023 ■ *Web:* www.grr-giant.com	Harleyville	SC	29488	803-496-2200	
Gilman & Pastor LLP 63 Atlantic Ave 3rd Fl *TF:* 877-428-7374 ■ *Web:* www.gilmanlawllp.com	Boston	MA	02110	617-742-9700	
Glacial Energy 2701 N Dallas Pkwy Ste 120 *TF:* 877-569-2841 ■ *Web:* www.glacialenergy.com	Plano	TX	75093	877-569-2841	
GLE Associates Inc 5405 Cypress Center Dr Ste 110 *TF:* 888-453-4531 ■ *Web:* www.gleassociates.com	Tampa	FL	33609	813-241-8350	
Great Ecology 315 W 36th St 10th fl *Web:* www.greatecology.com	New York	NY	10018	212-579-6800	
Green Seal Environmental Inc 114 State Rd Bldg B *Web:* www.gseenv.com	Sagamore Beach	MA	02562	508-888-6034	

Name / Address	City	State	ZIP	Phone	Fax
GREENandSAVE LLC Greater Philadelphia 204 Old Lancaster Rd Ste *Web:* www.greenandsave.com	Devon	PA	19333	610-628-1300	
Greene Lyon Group Inc 14 Schooner Rdg. *Web:* www.greenelyon.com	Marblehead	MA	01945	617-290-2276	
GreenerU Inc 1 Moody St *Web:* greeneru.com	Waltham	MA	02453	781-891-3750	
Greenland International Consulting Ltd 120 Hume St. *Web:* www.grnland.com	Collingwood	ON	L9Y1V5	705-444-8805	
Groundwater & Environmental Services Inc 1340 Campus Pkwy Bldg B *Web:* www.gesonline.com	Neptune	NJ	07753	732-919-0100	
Growth Energy 777 N Capitol St NE Ste 805 *Web:* www.growthenergy.org	Washington	DC	20002	202-545-4000	
Heath Consultants Inc 9030 Monroe Rd *TF:* 800-432-8487 ■ *Web:* www.heathus.com	Houston	TX	77061	713-844-1300	844-1309
Hemet, California 445 E Florida Ave *Web:* www.cityofhemet.org	Hemet	CA	92543	951-765-2330	
Hilltop Enterprises Inc 1157 Phoenixville Pk Ste 102 *Web:* www.hilltopenterprises.com	West Chester	PA	19380	610-430-6920	
HKA Enterprises Inc 337 Spartangreen Blvd *TF:* 800-825-5452 ■ *Web:* www.hkaa.com	Duncan	SC	29334	864-661-5100	
Hotel Cleaning Services Inc 9609 N 22nd Ave *Web:* www.hotelcleaningservices.com	Phoenix	AZ	85021	602-588-0864	
Hydrozonix LLC 8940 Gall Blvd *Web:* www.hydrozonix.com	Zephyrhills	FL	33541	813-780-4380	
IESI NY Corp 325 Casanova St *Web:* progressivewaste.com	Bronx	NY	10474	718-542-5659	
IHI Environmental Inc 640 E Wilmington Ave *Web:* www.ihi-env.com	Salt Lake City	UT	84106	801-466-2223	
Inland Technologies Inc 14 Queen St PO Box 253 *TF:* 877-633-5263 ■ *Web:* www.inlandgroup.ca	Truro	NS	B2N5C1	902-895-6346	
Interra Energy Inc 6456 Osler St. *Web:* interraenergy.us	San Diego	CA	92111	858-412-0738	
ISN Global Enterprises Inc Po Box 1391 *TF:* 877-376-4476 ■ *Web:* isnglobal.com	Claremont	CA	91711	909-670-0601	
J Frank Schmidt & Son Company Inc 9500 SE 327th Ave *Web:* www.jfschmidt.com	Boring	OR	97009	503-663-4128	
JM Sorge Inc 57 Fourth St. *Web:* www.jmsorge.com	Somerville	NJ	08876	908-218-0066	
John Holmlund Nursery LLC 29285 SE Hwy 212 *Web:* www.jhnsy.com	Boring	OR	97009	503-663-6650	
Joseph Freedman Co Inc 115 Stevens St Ste *Web:* www.josephfreedmanco.com	Springfield	MA	01104	413-781-4444	
Karbone Inc 130 W 42nd St 9th Fl. *TF:* 800-728-2056 ■ *Web:* www.karbone.com	New York	NY	10036	646-291-2900	219-7168
KB Environmental Sciences Inc 9500 Koger Blvd N Ste 211 *Web:* www.kbenv.com	Saint Petersburg	FL	33702	727-578-5152	
Keen Technical Solutions LLC 800 Cottageview Dr Ste 1042 *TF:* 888-675-7772 ■ *Web:* www.keen-minds.com	Traverse City	MI	49684	888-675-7772	
Kellermeyer Bergensons Services LLC 1575 Henthorne Dr *Web:* www.kbs-clean.com	Maumee	OH	43537	419-867-4300	
Kemron Environmental Services Inc 8521 Leesburg Pike Ste 175 *TF:* 888-429-3516 ■ *Web:* kemron.com	Vienna	VA	22182	703-893-4106	893-1741
KERAMIDA Inc 401 N College Ave *Web:* keramida.com	Indianapolis	IN	46202	317-685-6600	
Klean Industries Inc 349 W Georgia St Ste 3038 *Web:* www.kleanindustries.com	Vancouver	BC	V6B3X5	604-637-9609	
KRK Capital Partners LLP 621 5Th St NE *Web:* www.krkcapitalpartners.com	Washington	DC	20002	202-747-6565	
Leo Gentry Wholesale Nursery Inc 11251 Southeast 232nd Ave. *Web:* leogentrynursery.com	Gresham	OR	97080	503-658-5181	
LG Chem Power Inc 1857 Technology Dr *Web:* www.lgcpi.com	Troy	MI	48083	248-307-1800	
Liesch Associates Inc 13400 15th Ave N *Web:* www.liesch.com	Minneapolis	MN	55441	763-489-3100	
Logees Greenhouses Ltd 141 N St *TF:* 888-330-8038 ■ *Web:* www.logees.com	Danielson	CT	06239	860-774-8038	
Los Alamos Technical Assoc Inc 999 Central Ave Ste 300 *TF:* 800-888-1745 ■ *Web:* www.lata.com	Los Alamos	NM	87544	505-662-9080	662-1757
LP Amina Inc 13850 Ballantyne Corporate Pl Ste 125 *Web:* www.lpamina.com	Charlotte	NC	28277	704-944-5425	
Lucas Newman Science & Technologies Inc 5403 Bluebird Trl *Web:* artlucas.org	Stillwater	OK	74074	502-409-7231	
Lynn Water & Sewer Commission 400 Parkland Ave *Web:* www.lynnwatersewer.org	Lynn	MA	01905	781-596-2400	
Maxymillian Technologies Inc 1801 E St *Web:* www.maxymillian.com	Pittsfield	MA	01201	413-499-3050	443-0511
Medallion Laboratories 9000 Plymouth Ave N. *TF:* 800-245-5615 ■ *Web:* www.medallionlabs.com	Minneapolis	MN	55427	763-764-4453	764-4010
Micah Group 389 Waller Ave Ste 210 *TF:* 877-260-7760 ■ *Web:* www.micahgroup.com	Lexington	KY	40504	859-260-7760	
Micromidas Inc 930 Riverside Pkwy Ste 10 *Web:* www.micromidas.com	West Sacramento	CA	95605	916-231-9329	
Mondre Energy Inc 1800 John F Kennedy Blvd Ste 1504 *Web:* www.mondreenergy.com	Philadelphia	PA	19103	215-988-0577	
Moran Environmental Recovery LLC 75-D York Ave *Web:* www.moranenvironmental.com	Randolph	MA	02368	781-815-1100	
MPS Group Inc 2920 Scotten St **Fax Area Code:* 248 ■ *Web:* www.mpsgrp.com	Detroit	MI	48210	313-841-7588	489-0653*
MWD 583 San Ysidro Rd *Web:* www.montecitowater.com/	Santa Barbara	CA	93108	805-969-2271	
Mwh Global Inc 380 Interlocken Crescent Ste 200 *TF:* 866-257-5984 ■ *Web:* www.mwhglobal.com	Broomfield	CO	80021	303-533-1900	533-1901
MyClean Inc 247 W 35th 9th Fl *Web:* www.myclean.com	New York	NY	10018	646-912-8473	
Nal Property Inspection 10416 Investment Cir *TF:* 800-774-9555 ■ *Web:* www.nal1.com	Rancho Cordova	CA	95670	916-361-0555	
Native Environmental LLC 3250 S 35th Ave *Web:* www.nativeaz.com	Phoenix	AZ	85009	602-254-0122	
Navarro Research & Engineering Inc 669 Emory Valley Rd *TF:* 866-681-5265 ■ *Web:* www.navarro-inc.com	Oak Ridge	TN	37830	865-220-9650	220-9651
Neal Mast & Son Inc Greenhouses 1780 4 Mile Rd Nw *TF:* 800-311-6278 ■ *Web:* www.nealmastgreenhouses.com	Grand Rapids	MI	49544	616-784-3323	
Neo Corp 289 Silkwood Dr *TF:* 800-822-1247 ■ *Web:* www.neocorporation.com	Canton	NC	28716	800-822-1247	
Norman Scott Company Inc 126 29th St Dr SE *Web:* www.in-tolerance.com	Cedar Rapids	IA	52403	319-363-8561	363-2106
Normandeau Assoc Inc 25 Nashua Rd *Web:* www.normandeau.com	Bedford	NH	03110	603-472-5191	472-7052
North Wind Inc 1425 Higham St *Web:* northwindgrp.com	Idaho Falls	ID	83402	208-528-8718	
NTS Inc 526 Chestnut St *Web:* www.netechnical.com	Virginia	MN	55792	218-741-4290	
Nuka Research & Planning Group LLC 1451 N Boone Ln *Web:* www.nukaresearch.com	Seldovia	AK	99663	907-234-7821	
Oil Mop LLC 131 Keating Dr *Web:* www.oilmop.com	Belle Chasse	LA	70037	504-394-6110	
Olive Hill Greenhouses Inc 3508 Olive Hill Rd *Web:* olivehill.net	Fallbrook	CA	92028	760-728-4596	
Omaha Public Power District 444 S 16th St Mall *Web:* www.oppd.com	Omaha	NE	68102	402-636-2000	
Omni Environmental LLC 321 Wall St Research Park *Web:* www.omnienvironmental.com	Princeton	NJ	08540	609-924-8821	
Onsite Energy Corp 2701 Loker Ave W Ste 107 *Web:* www.onsitenergy.com	Carlsbad	CA	92010	760-931-2400	
Ontario Clean Water Agency 1 Yonge St *TF:* 800-515-2759 ■ *Web:* www.ocwa.com	Toronto	ON	M5E1E5	416-314-5600	314-8300
P E La Moreaux & Assoc Inc PO Box 2310 *TF:* 800-682-6338 ■ *Web:* www.pela.com	Tuscaloosa	AL	35403	205-752-5543	752-4043
Parsons Infrastructure & Technology 100 W Walnut St. **Fax Area Code:* 256 ■ *Web:* www.parsons.com	Pasadena	CA	91124	626-440-4000	830-0287*
Partner Assessment Corp 2154 Torrance Blvd Ste 200 *TF:* 800-419-4923 ■ *Web:* www.partneresi.com	Torrance	CA	90501	800-419-4923	
Paul Davis Systems Canada Ltd 38 Crockford Blvd. *Web:* pauldavis.ca	Toronto	ON	M1R3C2	416-299-8890	
PEER Consultants PC 888 17th St NW Ste 850 *Web:* www.peercpc.com	Washington	DC	20006	202-478-2060	
Pegasus Sustainability Solutions Inc 2693 Research Park Dr Ste 201 *TF:* 888-681-9616 ■ *Web:* www.pegasus-sustainability.com	Fitchburg	WI	53711	888-681-9616	
PERC Water Corp 17862 Georgetown Ln *Web:* www.percwater.com	Huntington Beach	CA	92647	714-375-5338	
Perma-Fix Environmental Services Inc 8302 Dunwoody Pl Ste 250 *NASDAQ: PESI* ■ *TF:* 800-365-6066 ■ *Web:* www.perma-fix.com	Atlanta	GA	30350	770-587-9898	587-9937
PermaTreat Inc 505 Lafayette Blvd *Web:* www.permatreat.com	Fredericksburg	VA	22401	540-373-6655	
PharmEcology Associates LLC 12229 W N Ave Ste 2 *Web:* www.pharmecology.com	Wauwatosa	WI	53226	414-292-3959	
Pinchin Group, The 2470 Milltower Ct. *Web:* www.thepinchingroup.com	Mississauga	ON	L5N7W5	905-363-0678	
PlantIt Wise Inc 10010 Creekwood Path *Web:* www.planetwiseinc.com	Spring Branch	TX	78070	210-241-3666	
Portage Inc 1075 S Utah Ave Ste 200 *Web:* www.portageinc.com	Idaho Falls	ID	83402	208-528-6608	523-8860
Potesta & Associates Inc 7012 MacCorkle Ave SE *Web:* potesta.com	Charleston	WV	25304	304-342-1400	
Prestige Maintenance USA Ltd 1808 10th St Ste 300 *Web:* www.prestigeusa.net	Plano	TX	75074	972-578-9801	
Pro Park America Inc 1 Union Pl. *Web:* www.propark.com	Hartford	CT	06103	860-527-2378	
PSC 5151 San Felipe Ste 1100 **Fax Area Code:* 713 ■ *TF:* 800-726-1300 ■ *Web:* www.pscnow.com	Houston	TX	77056	800-726-1300	985-5318*
Pure Strategies Inc 47R Englewood Rd *Web:* www.purestrategies.com	Gloucester	MA	01930	978-525-2214	
Quest Recycling Services LLC 6175 Main St Ste 420 *Web:* www.questrecycling.com	Frisco	TX	75034	972-464-0004	
R E I Consultants Inc PO Box 286 *TF:* 800-999-0105 ■ *Web:* www.reiclabs.com	Beaver	WV	25813	304-255-2500	255-2572
Ramboll Environ 4350 N Fairfax Dr Ste 300 *Web:* www.ramboll-environ.com	Arlington	VA	22203	703-516-2300	516-2345
Ran-Pro Farms Inc 2618 County Rd Ste 1149 *Web:* www.ranprofarms.com	Tyler	TX	75704	903-593-7381	

Phone | Fax

Randys Environmental Services
4351 US Hwy 12 SE PO Box 169 ...... Delano MN 55328 763-972-3335 972-6042
Web: www.randysenvironmentalservices.com

RECON Environmental Inc 1927 Fifth Ave. ...... San Diego CA 92101 619-308-9333
Web: www.recon-us.com

Red Oak Greenhouses Inc 401 W Coolbaugh St. ...... Red Oak IA 51566 712-623-5191
Web: redoakgreenhouse.com

Red River Sanitors Inc 1522 Corporate Dr ...... Shreveport LA 71107 318-222-6070
Web: www.sanitors.com

Reliance Trading Corporation of America
55 Watermill Ln ...... Great Neck NY 11021 516-466-6240
Web: beautysilk.com

RJN Group Inc 200 W Front St. ...... Wheaton IL 60187 630-682-4700 682-4754
TF: 800-227-7838 ■ *Web:* www.rjn.com

RPS JD Consulting Inc 404 Camp Craft Rd. ...... Austin TX 78746 512-347-7588
Web: www.jdconsult.com

S & ME Inc 3201 Spring Forest Rd. ...... Raleigh NC 27616 919-872-2660 876-3958
TF Cust Svc: 800-849-2517 ■ *Web:* www.smeinc.com

Sabre Companies LLC, The
1891 New Scotland Rd ...... Slingerlands NY 12159 518-514-1572
Web: www.thesabrecompanies.com

Sage Environmental Consulting LP
4611 Bee Caves Rd Ste 100 ...... Austin TX 78746 512-327-0288
Web: www.sageenvironmental.com

Sanexen Environmental Services Inc
1471 Lionel-Boulet Blvd Ste 32 ...... Varennes QC J3X1P7 450-652-9990
Web: www.sanexen.com

SCS Aquaterra 7311 W 130th St Ste 100 ...... Overland Park KS 66213 913-681-0030
Web: www.aquaterra-env.com

Shalewater Solutions Inc
37 Grande Meadows Dr Ste 201 ...... Bridgeport WV 26330 304-592-2794
Web: www.shalewater.com

SHIFT Energy Inc 75 Prince William St. ...... Saint John NB E2L2B2 506-642-9422
Web: www.shiftenergy.com

SNC-Lavalin Operations & Maintenance Inc
304 The E Mall Ste 900 ...... Toronto ON M9B6E2 416-207-4700
TF: 800-397-2458 ■ *Web:* www.snclavalinom.com

Source Intelligence LLC
1921 Palomar Oaks Way Ste 205 ...... Carlsbad CA 92008 877-916-6337
TF: 877-916-6337 ■ *Web:* www.sourceintelligence.com

Southern Landscape Professionals Inc
8625 Mount Pleasant Church Rd ...... Willow Spring NC 27592 919-552-1156
Web: www.southernlandscapepros.com

Southwest Hazard Control Inc 1953 W Grant Rd. ...... Tucson AZ 85745 520-622-3607
Web: swhaz.com

Spherix Inc 6430 Rockledge Dr Ste 503. ...... Bethesda MD 20817 301-897-2540 897-2567
NASDAQ: SPEX ■ *TF:* 855-816-0624 ■ *Web:* www.spherix.com

SpotHero Inc 200 S Wacker Dr ...... Chicago IL 60606 312-566-7768
Web: spothero.com

Stella Group Ltd, The
1616 H St NW Ste 1020 ...... Washington DC 20006 202-347-2214
Web: www.thestellagroupltd.com

Sunora Energy Solutions 2342 E University Dr. ...... Phoenix AZ 85034 602-772-5220
Web: sunoraenergy.com

Sustainable Resources Group Inc
440 Creamery Way Ste 150 ...... Exton PA 19341 610-840-9200
Web: www.sustainableresourcesgroup.com

SWCA Inc 3033 N Central Ave Ste 145. ...... Phoenix AZ 85012 602-274-3831 274-3958
TF: 800-828-8517 ■ *Web:* www.swca.com

Team Industrial Services Inc
25 Bodrington Ct ...... Markham ON L6G1B6 905-940-9334
Web: www.teamcleaningsolutions.com

TechLaw Inc 14500 Avion Pkwy Ste 300. ...... Chantilly VA 20151 703-818-1000
Web: www.techlawinc.com

Tetra Tech EC Inc 1000 the American Rd. ...... Morris Plains NJ 07950 973-630-8000 980-3539*
**Fax Area Code:* 303 ■ *Web:* www.tteci.com

Tetra Tech Geo
21335 Signal Hill Plaza Ste 100 ...... Sterling VA 20164 703-444-7000
Web: www.geotransinc.com

Tetra Tech Inc 3475 E Foothill Blvd ...... Pasadena CA 91107 626-351-4664 351-5291
NASDAQ: TTEK ■ *Web:* www.tetratech.com

Tidewater Environmental Services Inc
38 Romney St Ste 202 ...... Charleston SC 29403 843-762-3750
Web: www.tidewaterenvironmental.com

TITAN Engineering Inc
2801 Network Blvd Ste 200 ...... Frisco TX 75034 469-365-1100
Web: www.titanengineering.com

Toronto And Region Conservation Authority
5 Shoreham Dr ...... Toronto ON M3N1S4 416-661-6600
Web: www.trca.on.ca

TRC Cos Inc 21 Griffin Rd N. ...... Windsor CT 06095 860-298-9692 298-6399
Web: www.trcsolutions.com

Tyree Organization Ltd, The
3000 Midlantic Dr Ste 105 ...... Mount Laurel NJ 08054 856-898-6800
Web: www.tyreeorg.com

U.S. Facilities Inc 30 N 41 St Ste 400 ...... Philadelphia PA 19104 800-236-6241
TF: 800-236-6241 ■ *Web:* usfacilities.com

USA Synthetic Fuel Corp
Ste 1600 312 Walnut St Ste 1600. ...... Cincinnati OH 45202 513-762-7870
Web: www.usasfc.com

Utility Service Company Inc
535 Courtney Hodges Blvd. ...... Perry GA 31069 478-987-0303
TF: 855-526-4413 ■ *Web:* www.utilityservice.com

Vela Environmental 503 2ND St N.E. ...... Washington DC 20002 202-544-8200
Web: velaenvironmental.com

Vertex Engineering Services Inc
400 Libbey Pkwy ...... Weymouth MA 02189 781-952-6000 335-3543
TF: 888-298-5162 ■ *Web:* vertexeng.com

Vivint Solar Inc 4931 North 300 West. ...... Provo UT 84604 877-404-4129
TF: 877-404-4129 ■ *Web:* www.vivintsolar.com

Waste Strategies LLC 1290 Bay Dale Dr Ste 290. ...... Arnold MD 21012 202-302-8370
Web: www.wastestrategies.com

Western Technologies Inc 3737 E Broadway Rd ...... Phoenix AZ 85040 602-437-3737 470-1341
TF: 800-580-3737 ■ *Web:* www.wt-us.com

Whitman Strategy Group LLC, The
PO Box 1621 ...... New Brunswick NJ 08903 646-330-4850
Web: www.whitmanstrategygroup.com

Woolpert Inc 4454 Idea Ctr Blvd ...... Dayton OH 45430 937-461-5660 461-0743
Web: www.woolpert.com

WorleyParsons Corp 6330 W Loop S. ...... Bellaire TX 77401 713-407-5000 350-1300
Web: www.worleyparsons.com

WSP Environment & Energy LLC
4840 Pearl E Cir W Ste 30 ...... Boulder Co 80301 703-709-6500
Web: www.wsp-pb.com

XENCO Laboratories Inc
4143 Greenbriar Dr Ste I. ...... Stafford TX 77477 281-240-4200
Web: www.xenco.com

Yardmaster Inc 1447 N Ridge Rd ...... Painesville OH 44077 440-357-8400
Web: www.yardmaster.com

YPSILANTI Michigan Community Utilities Authority
2777 State Rd ...... Ypsilanti MI 48198 734-484-4600
Web: www.ycua.org

Zerowait Corp 707 Kirkwood Hwy ...... Wilmington DE 19805 302-996-9408 738-4302
TF: 888-811-0808 ■ *Web:* www.zerowait.com

Zia Engineering & Environmental Consultants LLC
755 S Telshor Blvd Ste F-201. ...... Las Cruces NM 88011 575-532-1526
Web: www.ziaeec.com

193 CONSULTING SERVICES - HUMAN RESOURCES

See Also Professional Employer Organizations (PEOs) p. 2989

Phone | Fax

180 Business Solutions
1000 W Wilshire Blvd Ste 203 ...... Oklahoma City OK 73116 405-840-4180
Web: 180business.com

A.S.G. Staffing Inc
231 W Grand Ave Ste 102. ...... Bensenville IL 60106 630-787-6150
Web: www.asgstaffing.com

Aasgard Summit Management Services Inc
4017 13th Ave W ...... Seattle WA 98119 206-284-0475
Web: aasgardsummit.net

Abacus Group LLC 14 Penn Plz. ...... New York NY 10122 212-812-8444
Web: www.abacusgrpllc.com

ACRT Inc 1333 Home Ave. ...... Akron OH 44310 330-945-7500 945-7200
TF: 800-622-2562 ■ *Web:* www.acrtinc.com

Administrative Resource Options Inc
200 W Adams St Ste 2000 ...... Chicago IL 60606 312-634-0300
Web: www.aroptions.com

Advantage Sci LLC
222 N Sepulveda Blvd Ste 1780 ...... El Segundo CA 90245 310-536-9876
Web: www.advantagesci.com

Adventium Llc 320 E 35th St Apt 5b ...... New York NY 10016 212-481-9576
Web: www.adventium.net

Aegis Group 41451 W 11 Mile Rd ...... Novi MI 48375 248-344-1450
Web: www.aegis-group.com

Afterburner Inc
55 Ivan Allen Junior Blvd Ste 525. ...... Atlanta GA 30308 404-835-3500
Web: www.afterburnerseminars.com

Alliance For Employee Growth & Development Inc, The
80 Cottontail Ln Ste 320. ...... Somerset NJ 08873 800-323-3436
TF: 800-323-3436 ■ *Web:* www.employeegrowth.com

American Tcb 7560 Lindbergh Dr ...... Gaithersburg MD 20879 301-216-1500
Web: wll.com

Applied Clinical Intelligence LLC
251 St Asaphs Rd 3 Bala Plz W Ste 402 ...... Bala Cynwyd PA 19004 484-429-7200
Web: www.aciclinical.com

Arcus LLC 8170 Adams Dr ...... Hummelstown PA 17036 717-703-3200
Web: www.arcus.net

Ard Group Inc 116 John St Apt 602 ...... New York NY 10038 212-571-1111
Web: www.ardcareers.com

Arthur J Gallagher & Co 2 Pierce Pl ...... Itasca IL 60143 630-773-3800 285-4000
NYSE: AJG ■ *TF:* 888-285-5106 ■ *Web:* www.ajg.com

Ashtead Technology Inc 19407 Pk Row Ste 170 ...... Houston TX 77084 281-398-9533
TF: 800-242-3910 ■ *Web:* www.ashtead-technology.com

Assess It 12137 Travertine Ct. ...... Poway CA 92064 949-491-1269
Web: assessit.com

Atfocus 394 Old Orchard Grove ...... Toronto ON M5M2E9 416-485-4220
Web: atfocus.ca

Atlantic Personnel Search Inc
9624 Pennsylvania Ave. ...... Upper Marlboro MD 20772 301-599-2108
TF: 877-229-5254 ■ *Web:* www.atlanticpersonnel.com

B. E. Smith Inc 9777 Ridge Dr ...... Lenexa KS 66219 800-467-9117
TF: 800-467-9117 ■ *Web:* www.besmith.com

Bader Group Inc, The 4615 48th St. ...... San Diego CA 92115 619-501-9586
Web: www.badergroup.com

BayGroup International
2200 Larkspur Landing Cir. ...... Larkspur CA 94939 415-464-4400
Web: www.baygroup.com

Bci Staffing Inc
11800 Northfall Ln Ste 1405. ...... Alpharetta GA 30009 678-393-8536
Web: www.bci-it.com

Bedford Consulting Group Inc
145 Adelaide St W Ste 400 ...... Toronto ON M5H4E5 416-963-9000
Web: www.bedfordgroup.com

Benz Communications LLC
209 Mississippi St ...... San Francisco CA 94107 888-550-5251
TF: 888-550-5251 ■ *Web:* www.benzcommunications.com

Berkhemer Clayton Inc
241 S Figueroa St Ste 300 ...... Los Angeles CA 90012 213-621-2300
Web: www.berkhemerclayton.com

Berks & Beyond Employment Services Inc
926 Penn Ave. ...... Wyomissing PA 19610 610-376-9675
Web: www.berksandbeyond.com

Bessire & Associates Inc
7621 Little Ave Ste 106. ...... Charlotte NC 28226 704-341-1423
TF: 800-797-7355 ■ *Web:* bessire.com

Phone | Fax

Biko Ltd Co 3920 Ravens Crest Dr .... Plainsboro NJ 08536 617-910-0160
Web: www.bikotech.biz

Blackwell Consulting Services Inc
100 S Wacker Dr .... Chicago IL 60606 312-553-0730 553-0745
Web: www.bcsinc.com

Bosch & Associates LLC 111 Beach Rd .... Fairfield CT 06824 203-255-8700
Web: www.boschllc.com

Brace Management Group Inc
9500 Arena Dr Ste 250 .... Upper Marlboro MD 20774 301-772-7600
Web: www.bracemgmt.com

Buyer Advertising Inc 189 Wells Ave .... Newton MA 02459 617-969-4646
Web: www.buyerads.com

C f a Staffing 543 W N St .... Lima OH 45801 419-224-0035
Web: www.cfainc.us

Cadmus Group Inc 100 Fifth Ave Ste 100 .... Waltham MA 02451 617-673-7000 673-7001
Web: www.cadmusgroup.com

Caldwell Partners International Inc, The
165 Ave Rd .... Toronto ON M5R3S4 416-920-7702
Web: www.caldwellpartners.com

Caliper Corporation Inc
506 Carnegie Ctr Ste 300 .... Princeton NJ 08543 609-524-1400
Web: www.calipercorp.com

Capitol Employee Benefits Inc
224 Web Foot Ln .... Stevensville MD 21666 410-604-6488
Web: capitolbenefits.com

Career Co 15880 Rose Ave .... Los Gatos CA 95030 408-354-1964
Web: www.careercompany.com

Carlsen Resources 312 W Riverwoods Dr .... New Hope PA 18938 215-862-5610
Web: www.carlsenresources.com

Carnow Conibear & Assoc Ltd
600 W Van Buren Ste 500 .... Chicago IL 60607 312-782-4486 782-5145
TF: 800-860-4486 ■ *Web:* www.ccaltd.com

CarterBaldwin Inc 200 Mansell Court E Ste 450 .... Roswell GA 30076 678-448-0000
Web: www.carterbaldwin.com

Cedarstone Partners Inc 209 E Liberty Dr .... Wheaton IL 60187 630-580-5750
Web: www.cedarstonepartners.com

CEO Inc 412 Louise Ave .... Charlotte NC 28204 704-372-4701
Web: ceoinc.com

Certus International Inc 9 Cedarwood Dr Ste 8 .... Bedford NH 03110 603-627-1212
Web: www.certusintl.com

Challenger Gray & Christmas Inc
150 S Wacker Dr Ste 2800 .... Chicago IL 60606 312-332-5790 332-4843
TF: 855-242-3424 ■ *Web:* www.challengergray.com

Chernoff Diamond & Company LLC
725 RXR Plz E Tower .... Uniondale NY 11556 516-683-6100
Web: www.chernoffdiamond.com

Citystaff Inc 1701 K St Nw Ste 500 .... Washington DC 20006 202-861-4200
Web: www.citystaffdc.com

Clark Consulting 2100 Ross Ave .... Dallas TX 75201 214-871-8717 720-6050
Web: www.clarkconsulting.com

Coleman Lew & Associates Inc
326 W Tenth St .... Charlotte NC 28202 704-377-0362
Web: www.colemanlew.com

Collaborative Consulting LLC
70 BlanchaRd Rd Ste 500 .... Burlington MA 01803 781-565-2600 565-2700
TF: 877-376-9900 ■ *Web:* collaborative.com

Comcentric Inc
10463 Park Meadows Dr Ste 208 .... Lone Tree CO 80124 303-805-4700
Web: www.comcentric.com

Concepts 3 Marketing and Management Inc
309 N Waterview Dr .... Richardson TX 75080 972-690-8412
Web: www.concepts3inc.com

Conspectus Inc 222 Purchase St .... Rye NY 10580 914-925-0600
Web: www.conspectusinc.com

CONTAX Inc 893 Yonge St .... Toronto ON M4W2H2 416-927-1913
Web: www.contax.com

Courtland Associates Inc
22500 Orchard Lk Rd .... Farmington MI 48336 248-888-3535

CoveyLink Worldwide LLC
175 W Canyon Crest Rd Ste 100 .... Alpine UT 84004 801-756-2700
Web: www.coveylink.com

CPE HR Inc 9000 Sunset Blvd Ste 900 .... West Hollywood CA 90064 310-734-4222
Web: www.cpehr.com

Creative Group Inc 619 N Lynndale Dr .... Appleton WI 54914 920-739-8550
Web: www.creativegroupinc.com

Crown Advisors Inc
100 McKnight Park Dr Ste 110 .... Pittsburgh PA 15237 412-348-1540
Web: www.crownsearch.com

CyberCoders Inc 6591 Irvine Ctr Dr Ste 200 .... Irvine CA 92618 949-885-5151
Web: www.cybercoders.com

Davies Park 10060 Jasper Ave Nw .... Edmonton AB T5J3R8 780-420-9900
Web: www.daviespark.com

DB Consulting Group Inc
8403 Colesville Rd .... Silver Spring MD 20910 301-589-4020
Web: www.dbconsultinggroup.com

Ddj Myers Ltd 4455 E Camelback Rd Ste C138 .... Phoenix AZ 85018 602-840-9595
Web: ddjmyers.com

Demand Planning LLC 10g Roessler Rd Ste 508 .... Woburn MA 01801 781-995-0685
Web: demandplanning.net

Development Dimensions International
1225 Washington Pike .... Bridgeville PA 15017 412-257-0600 220-2942
TF Mktg: 800-933-4463 ■ *Web:* www.ddiworld.com

dicentra Inc 161 Bay St 27th Fl .... Toronto ON M5R1B2 416-361-3400
Web: www.dicentra.com

Digital Action Inc
8 E Germantown Pk .... Plymouth Meeting PA 19462 610-941-0700
Web: digital-action.com

DuffyGroup Inc 4727 E Union Hills Dr Ste 200 .... Phoenix AZ 85050 602-861-5840
Web: www.duffygroupinc.com

E3 Services Conseils Inc
19 Le Royer St W Ste 304 .... Montreal QC H2Y1W4 514-281-1737
Web: e3sc.com

Phone | Fax

Ecology and Environment Inc
368 Pleasant View Dr .... Lancaster NY 14086 716-684-8060 684-0844
Web: www.ene.com

Eda Staffing Inc 371 Forest Ave Ste 2 .... Portland ME 04101 207-775-2577
Web: www.edastaffing.com

EdgeLink LLC 2525 SW 1st Ave Ste 110 .... Portland OR 97201 503-246-3989
Web: www.edgelink.com

EDI Specialists Inc 31 Bellows Rd .... Raynham MA 02767 508-821-4644
Web: www.edispecialists.com

EGGers Consulting Company Inc
11272 Elm St Eggers Plz .... Omaha NE 68144 402-333-3480
Web: www.eggersconsulting.com

Emergo Group Inc 816 Congress Ave Ste 1400 .... Austin TX 78701 512-327-9997
Web: www.emergogroup.com

Employer Plan Services Inc
2180 N Loop W Ste 400 .... Houston TX 77018 713-351-3500
Web: www.epsibenefitsinc.com

EnergX LLC 1000 B Clearview Ct .... Oak Ridge TN 37830 865-483-9288
Web: www.energxllc.com

Engineering Services Network Inc
2450 Crystal Dr Ste 1015 .... Arlington VA 22202 703-412-3640
Web: www.esncc.com

Entium Technology Partners Llc
1288 Valley Forge Rd Ste 50 .... Valley Forge PA 19482 610-415-7200
Web: entium.com

Er Marketing 512 Delaware St .... Kansas City MO 64105 816-471-1400
Web: www.ermarketing.net

Essential Personnel Inc
3415 W State St Ste B .... Grand Island NE 68803 308-381-4400
Web: www.essentialpersonnelinc.com

Estrada Strategies Franchise Inc
3400 Inland Empire Blvd Ste 101 .... Ontario CA 91764 909-917-1771
Web: www.estradastrategies.com

Et Search Inc 1712 Valdes Dr .... La Jolla CA 92037 858-459-3443

Exceed Resources Inc 294 New Rd .... Monmouth Junction NJ 08852 732-329-2742
Web: www.exceedresourcesinc.com

Exceed Staffing LLC
363 N Sam Houston Pkwy E Ste 1100 .... Houston TX 77550 409-770-9000
TF: 866-609-2884 ■ *Web:* www.exceedstaffing.com

Excel Staffing Companies
1700 Louisiana Boulvard NE Ste 210 .... Albuquerque NM 87110 505-262-1871
Web: www.excelstaff.com

Executive Resources International LLC
63 Atlantic Ave .... Boston MA 02110 617-742-8970
Web: erisearch.net

Findley Davies 1 Seagate # 2050 .... Toledo OH 43604 419-255-1360 259-5685
Web: www.findleydavies.com

Floyd Browne Group 3875 Embassy Parkway .... Akron OH 44333 330-375-0800 665-0620
TF General: 800-362-2764 ■ *Web:* ctconsultants.com

FPMI Solutions Inc
1033 N Fairfax St Ste 200 .... Alexandria VA 22314 888-644-3764
TF: 888-644-3764 ■ *Web:* www.fpmi.com

Frederic W Cook & Co 90 Pk Ave 35th Fl .... New York NY 10016 212-986-6330 986-3836
Web: www.fwcook.com

G K Partners 401 E 74th St Apt 18h .... New York NY 10021 212-535-5617
Web: gk-partners.com

Gabriel Roeder Smith & Co
1 Towne Sq Ste 800 .... Southfield MI 48076 248-799-9000 799-9020
TF: 800-521-0498 ■ *Web:* www.gabrielroeder.com

Gaming Laboratories International Inc
600 Airport Rd .... Lakewood NJ 08701 732-942-3999 942-0043
Web: www.gaminglabs.com

Genesis Global Group Inc 28 Highland Rd .... Westport CT 06880 203-222-1795
Web: www.g3global.com

Geomet Technologies LLC
20251 Century Blvd .... Germantown MD 20874 301-428-9898 428-9482
TF: 877-407-8033 ■ *Web:* www.geomet.com

Global Organization and Planning Services Llc
1 Mapes Ave Apt 2f .... Newark NJ 07112 973-374-6637
Web: globalorganizationplanning.com

Global Search Network Inc 118 S Fremont Ave .... Tampa FL 33606 813-832-8300
TF: 800-254-3398 ■ *Web:* www.globalsearchnetwork.com

Globe Consultants Inc 3112 Porter St Ste D .... Soquel CA 95073 800-208-0663
TF: 800-208-0663 ■ *Web:* www.globeconsultants.com

Goodwill Industries of Akron Ohio Inc, The
570 E Waterloo Rd .... Akron OH 44319 330-724-6995
TF: 800-989-8428 ■ *Web:* www.goodwillakron.org

GRA Inc 2317 Falling Creek Rd .... Silver Spring MD 20904 215-884-7500

Gravett & Associates 4054 Sandstone Ct .... Cincinnati OH 45245 513-753-8870
Web: www.gravett.com

H r Office Inc, The
2437 Commercial Blvd Ste 5 .... State College PA 16801 814-238-3750
Web: www.thehrofficeinc.com

Hanley Wood Market Intelligence
555 Anton Blvd Ste 950 .... Costa Mesa CA 92626 714-540-8500 452-0833*
**Fax Area Code:* 480 ■ *TF:* 800-938-8839 ■ *Web:* www.metrostudy.com

Harrington Group, The 873 Inverness Cir .... Spartanburg SC 29306 864-585-5850
Web: harringtongroup.net

Hay Group Inc 1650 Arch St Ste 2300 .... Philadelphia PA 19107 215-861-2000 861-2111
TF: 800-716-4429 ■ *Web:* www.haygroup.com

Hayes & Wiesel Independent Solutions Inc
78365 United States Hwy 111 Ste 316 .... La Quinta CA 92253 760-347-5505
Web: www.hwisolutions.com

Hire Dynamics LLC 1845 Satellite Blvd Ste 800 .... Duluth GA 30097 678-482-0200
Web: www.hiredynamics.com

Hire Profile Inc 2225 Laurel Mill Way .... Roswell GA 30076 770-992-3434
Web: www.hire-profile.com

Hobbs & Towne Inc
1288 Vly Forge Rd PMB 269 PO Box 987 .... Valley Forge PA 19482 610-783-4600
Web: hobbstowne.com

Hsa Lps 1520 S Beverly Glen Blvd Ste 305 .... Los Angeles CA 90024 310-286-2722
Web: www.hsa-lps.com

Hudson RPO 10 S Wacker Dr Ste 2600 .... Chicago IL 60606 312-795-4275 795-4288
NASDAQ: HSON ■ *Web:* us.hudson.com

Listing	City	State	Zip	Phone	Fax
Impact Management Services 29792 Telegraph Rd Ste 150 *Web:* www.theimpactanswer.com	Southfield	MI	48034	248-262-5200	
Impact Science & Technology Inc 85 NW Blvd	Nashua	NH	03063	603-459-2255	
Independent Roofing Consultants 2901 Tullman St *Web:* www.irctech.com	Santa Ana	CA	92705	949-476-8626	476-9810
Indiggo Associates Inc 4600 E W Hwy Ste 875 *Web:* www.indiggoassociates.com	Bethesda	MD	20814	240-314-0533	
InfoMart Inc 1582 Terrell Mill Rd *TF:* 800-800-3774 ■ *Web:* www.infomart-usa.com	Marietta	GA	30067	770-984-2727	
Infusive Solutions Inc 411 Fifth Ave Rm 702 *Web:* www.infusivesolutions.com	New York	NY	10016	212-566-1400	
Inglewood Associates LLC 160 Inglewood Dr *Web:* www.inglewoodassociates.com	Pittsburgh	PA	15228	216-839-6700	
Innolect Inc 1004 Palmyra Dr *Web:* innolectinc.com	Tega Cay	SC	29708	803-396-8500	
Insight 444 Scott Dr *TF:* 800-467-4448 ■ *Web:* www.insight.com	Bloomingdale	IL	60108	800-467-4448	
Insight Global Inc (IGI) 4170 Ashford Dunwoody Rd Ste 250 *TF:* 888-336-7463 ■ *Web:* www.insightglobal.net	Atlanta	GA	30319	404-257-7900	257-1004
Intelisearch Inc 60 Long Ride Rd Ste 304 *Web:* www.isimpact.com	Stamford	CT	06902	203-325-1389	
Iowa Employment Solutions 430 E Grand Ave *Web:* www.iowaemploymentsolutions.com	Des Moines	IA	50309	515-281-9700	
Ipsos Understanding UnLtd 615 Elsinore Pl 3rd Fl *Web:* www.understanding-unltd.com	Cincinnati	OH	45202	513-871-4644	
ITAC Solutions LLC 700 Montgomery Hwy Ste 148 *Web:* www.itacsolutions.com	Birmingham	AL	35216	205-326-0004	
ITR Group Inc 2520 Lexington Ave S Ste 500 *TF:* 866-290-3423 ■ *Web:* www.itrgroupinc.com	Saint Paul	MN	55120	866-290-3423	
JC Jones & Associates LLC One Lockwood Dr Ste 310 *Web:* www.jcjones.com	Pittsford	NY	14534	585-899-4072	
Johnson, Grossnickle & Associates LLC 29 S Park Blvd *Web:* www.jgacounsel.com	Greenwood	IN	46143	317-215-2400	
Jon Harvey Associates Inc 1300 N Federal Hwy Ste 104 *Web:* www.jonharvey.com	Boca Raton	FL	33432	561-368-5900	
K2 Partnering 475 Sansome St Ste 1720 *Web:* k2partnering.com	San Francisco	CA	94111	415-391-3804	
Kazak Composites Inc 10f Gill St *Web:* plasan-na.com	Woburn	MA	01801	781-932-5667	
Kelchner Inc 50 Advanced Dr *Web:* www.kelchner.com	Springboro	OH	45066	937-704-9890	
Ken Clark International Inc 2000 Lenox Dr Ste 200 *Web:* www.kenclark.com	Lawrenceville	NJ	08648	609-308-5200	
Ken Leiner Associates Inc 11510 Georgia Ave Ste 105 *Web:* www.kla-inc.com	Silver Spring	MD	20902	301-933-8800	
Kerton Group 8032 Canyon Creek Cir *Web:* kertongroup.com	Pleasanton	CA	94588	408-935-8702	
Kimmel & Associates Inc 25 Page Ave *Web:* www.kimmel.com	Asheville	NC	28801	828-251-9900	
Kincannon & Reed LLC 40 Stoneridge Dr Ste 101 *Web:* www.krsearch.com	Waynesboro	VA	22980	540-941-3460	
Lanmark Staffing Co 1002 Green Ave *Web:* lanmarkstaffing.com	Orange	TX	77630	409-886-7676	
Leaderpoint Llc 6045 Martway St Ste 108 *Web:* www.leaderpoint.biz	Mission	KS	66202	913-384-3212	
Lee Hecht Harrison LLC 50 Tice Blvd *TF:* 800-611-4544 ■ *Web:* www.lhh.com	Woodcliff Lake	NJ	07677	800-611-4544	
LifeCourse Associates Inc 9080 Eaton Park Rd *TF:* 866-537-4999 ■ *Web:* www.lifecourse.com	Great Falls	VA	22066	866-537-4999	
Linder Associates 7 E 14th St Apt 817 *Web:* www.srlinder.com	New York	NY	10003	212-645-7598	
LJ Kushner & Associates LLC 36 W Main St Ste 302 *Web:* ljkushner.com	Freehold	NJ	07728	732-577-8100	
Longnecker & Associates 11011 Jones Rd Ste 200 *Web:* www.longnecker.com	Houston	TX	77070	281-378-1350	
LSA Assoc Inc 20 Executive Pk Ste 200 *Web:* lsa.net	Irvine	CA	92614	949-553-0666	553-8076
Lux 5 Events 4060 Campus Dr Ste 110 *Web:* lux5events.com	Newport Beach	CA	92660	714-505-0050	
Magellan Search Group Inc 620 W Germantown Pike Ste 300 *Web:* www.magellangroup.com	Plymouth Meeting	PA	19462	610-941-0100	
Magis Group LLC, The 106 Brinker Rd *Web:* themagisgroup.com	Barrington	IL	60010	847-756-4200	
Mandrake Management Consultants 55 St Clair Ave W Ste 401 *Web:* www.mandrake.ca	Toronto	ON	M4V2Y7	416-922-5400	
Martin Partners LLC 224 S Michigan Ave Ste 620 *Web:* www.martinpartners.com	Chicago	IL	60604	312-922-1800	
Mb Consulting Group Inc 225 S Meramec Ave Ste 621t *Web:* www.contactmb.com	Saint Louis	MO	63105	314-725-3584	
Mc2 Executive Search Inc P.O. Box 452 *Web:* www.mc2execsearch.com	Washington Crossing	PA	18977	215-504-5488	
Med Pro Health Care Staffing 5608 Princeton Ave *Web:* www.medprostaffing.com	Columbus	GA	31904	706-322-7085	

Listing	City	State	Zip	Phone	Fax
Medicus Healthcare Solutions LLC 7 Industrial Way Unit 5 *TF:* 855-301-0563 ■ *Web:* www.medicushcs.com	Salem	NH	03079	855-301-0563	
Mercer LLC 400 W Market St *TF:* 800-333-3070 ■ *Web:* www.mercer.com	Louisville	KY	40202	502-561-4500	561-4747
Mice Groups Inc, The 1730 S Amphlett Blvd Ste 100 *Web:* www.micegroups.com	San Mateo	CA	94402	650-655-4800	
Michael C. Fina Corporate Sales 3301 Hunters Point Ave *TF:* 800-999-3462 ■ *Web:* www.mcfrecognition.com	Long Island	NY	11101	800-999-3462	
Mid-Michigan Industries Inc (MMI) 2426 Pkwy Dr *Web:* www.mmionline.com	Mount Pleasant	MI	48858	989-773-6918	773-1317
Mission Benefits Inc 256 Gibraltar Dr Ste 104 *Web:* www.missionbenefits.com	Sunnyvale	CA	94089	408-734-0438	
Mission Search International Inc 2203 N Lois Ave Ste 1225 *Web:* www.missionsearch.com	Tampa	FL	33607	813-870-9500	
Modern Management Inc 253 Commerce Dr Ste 105 *TF:* 800-323-1331 ■ *Web:* www.modernmanagement.com	Grayslake	IL	60030	847-945-7400	
Montgomery County Intermediate Unit 23 1605 W Main St Ste B *Web:* www.mciu.org	Norristown	PA	19403	610-539-8550	
Morehead Associates Inc 700 E Morehead St Ste 200 *Web:* www.moreheadassociates.com	Charlotte	NC	28202	704-522-0776	
Moresatile Global Mktng Llc 4110 Milano Way *Web:* www.moresatile.com	Oceanside	CA	92057	760-757-7676	
Morgan Samuels Co 6420 Wilshire Blvd Ste 1100 *Web:* morgansamuels.com	Los Angeles	CA	90048	310-205-2200	
Msys Inc 140 Iowa Ln Ste 201 *Web:* www.msysinc.com	Cary	NC	27511	919-380-9783	
National Ctr for Retirement Benefits Inc 666 Dundee Rd Ste 1200 **Fax Area Code:* 847 ■ *TF:* 800-666-1000 ■ *Web:* www.ncrb.com	Northbrook	IL	60062	800-666-1000	564-4944*
NPAworldwide 1680 Viewpond Dr SE *Web:* www.npaworldwide.com	Grand Rapids	MI	49508	616-455-6555	
Nurse Staffing LLC 1700 Route 23 N Ste 100 *Web:* www.nursesapply.com	Wayne	NJ	07470	973-709-1009	
Ocius LLC 651 W Washington Ste 200 *Web:* ocius.net	Chicago	IL	60661	312-850-3500	
Onesmartworld Inc 79 Simcoe St *Web:* www.onesmartworld.com	Collingwood	ON	L9Y1M3	705-444-1234	
Options Group Inc 121 E 18th St *Web:* www.optionsgroup.com	New York	NY	10003	212-982-0900	
Pacific Firm The 2501 Ninth St Ste 102 *Web:* www.pacfirm.com	Berkeley	CA	94710	510-647-1000	
Parker Remick Inc 1106 Harris Ave Ste 201 *Web:* www.parkerremick.com	Bellingham	WA	98225	360-527-2555	
Pembrooke Occupational Health Inc 2307 N Parham Rd *Web:* www.pembrooke.com	Richmond	VA	23229	804-346-1010	
PerformTech Inc 810 King St	Alexandria	VA	22314	703-548-0320	
Point B Communications 750 N Orleans Ste 550 *Web:* pointbcommunications.com	Chicago	IL	60654	312-867-7750	
Premium Retail Services Inc 618 Spirit Dr *Web:* www.premiumretail.com	Chesterfield	MO	63005	636-728-0592	
Prescott Legal Search Inc 3900 Essex Ln Ste 1110 *Web:* www.prescottlegal.com	Houston	TX	77027	713-439-0911	
Pridestaff Inc 7535 N Palm Ave Ste 101 *Web:* www.pridestaff.com	Fresno	CA	93711	559-432-7780	
Prima Worldwide Inc 22 El Paseo *Web:* www.primaworldwide.com	Santa Barbara	CA	93101	805-695-0070	
Principia Partners 604 Gordon Dr *TF:* 800-378-8330 ■ *Web:* www.principiaconsulting.com	Exton	PA	19341	800-378-8330	
PSTG Consulting 72 Scollard St *Web:* www.pstgconsulting.com	Toronto	ON	M5R1G2	416-593-0000	
Purcell International Group 500 S Kraemer Blvd Ste 102 *Web:* www.purcellintl.com	Brea	CA	92821	714-524-0640	
Qualigence Inc 35200 Schoolcraft Rd *Web:* www.qualigence.com	Livonia	MI	48150	734-432-6300	
Quantus Software 32-62 Scurfield Blvd *TF:* 866-478-1308	Winnipeg	MB	R3Y1M5	866-478-1308	
Raia & Associates Inc 930 Bunty Station Rd *Web:* www.raia-assoc.com	Delaware	OH	43015	740-369-6882	
Rapid Response Marketing LLC 7500 W Lk Mead Blvd Ste 9463 *Web:* www.xy7.com	Las Vegas	NV	89128	702-631-9714	
Razorfish Platforms 7750 Paragon Rd *Web:* technologyplatforms.razorfish.com	Dayton	OH	45459	937-723-2300	
Real Time Strategy LLC 40 S St Ste 300 *Web:* www.realtimestrategy.com	Marblehead	MA	01945	781-990-0962	
Recruitech International Inc 120 Gibraltar Rd Ste 120 *Web:* www.recruitech.com	Horsham	PA	19044	215-293-1300	
Resources Unlimited Co 7931 Nw 54th Ave *Web:* www.resourcesunlimited.com	Johnston	IA	50131	515-270-0694	
Ricklin-Echikson Assoc 374 Millburn Ave *TF:* 800-544-2317 ■ *Web:* www.r-e-a.com	Millburn	NJ	07041	973-376-2020	
Right Management Consultants Inc 1600 John F Kennedy Blvd Ste 610 *TF:* 800-237-4448 ■ *Web:* www.right.com	Philadelphia	PA	19103	215-972-7277	
Riviera Advisors Inc P.O. Box 41446 *TF:* 800-635-9063 ■ *Web:* www.rivieraadvisors.com	Long Beach	CA	90853	800-635-9063	
Rjr Innovations 1400 St Laurent Blvd *Web:* www.rjrinnovations.com	Ottawa	ON	K1K4H4	613-233-1915	

Phone | Fax

RLR Management Consulting Inc
78-010 Main St Ste 200 La Quinta CA 92253 760-771-5036
Web: www.rlrmgmt.com
Roger Grace Associates LLC 109 Greenfield Ct Naples FL 34110 239-596-8738
Web: www.rgrace.com
Roux Assoc Inc 209 Shafter St Islandia NY 11749 631-232-2600 232-9898
TF: 800-322-7689 ■ *Web:* www.rouxinc.com
Runzheimer International Runzheimer Pk Rochester WI 53167 262-971-2200 971-2254
TF: 800-558-1702 ■ *Web:* www.runzheimer.com
Searchlogix Group, The
2950 Cherokee St Nw Ste 1000 Kennesaw GA 30144 770-517-2660
Web: searchlogixgroup.com
Searchwide Inc 320 Myrtle St W Stillwater MN 55082 651-275-1370
TF: 888-386-6390 ■ *Web:* searchwide.com
Seaton Companies, The 860 W Evergreen Ave Chicago IL 60642 312-915-0700
Web: www.seatoncorp.com
Segal Co 333 W 34th St New York NY 10001 212-251-5000 365-3243*
**Fax Area Code: 646* ■ *Web:* www.segalco.com
Selection Management Systems Inc
155 Tri County Pkwy Ste 150 Cincinnati OH 45246 513-522-8764
Web: www.selection.com
Senior Housing Management Inc
208 35th St Dr SE Ste 500 Cedar Rapids IA 52403 319-363-6094
Web: www.seniorhousingcompanies.com
Sharp Sky Partners
520 Baker Bldg 706 Second Ave South Minneapolis MN 55402 612-339-3444
Web: www.sharpsky.com
Sierra Hr Partners Inc
7112 N Fresno St Ste 450 Fresno CA 93720 559-431-8090
Web: sierrahr.com
Solenture Inc 2 Gateway Ctr Ste 1600 Pittsburgh PA 15222 412-281-5472
Web: www.solenture.com
Source Group Inc, The
3478 Buskirk Ave Ste 100 Pleasant Hill CA 94523 925-944-2856
Web: www.thesourcegroup.net
Staffing Services Inc
1045 Gateway Loop Ste D Springfield OR 97477 541-345-9675
Web: www.staffingoregon.com
Stanley Hunt DuPree & Rhine Inc (SHDR)
7701 Airport Ctr Dr Greensboro NC 27409 800-768-4873
TF: 888-999-4701 ■ *Web:* www.shdr.com/shdr/shdr/start.page
Stewart Daly Inc 1134 Ballena Blvd Ste 18 Alameda CA 94501 510-521-8586
Web: www.stewartdaly.com
Summit Business-Consulting Inc 679 Norbury Dr Hudson OH 44236 330-656-0495
Web: www.summit-business.com
Superior Environmental Corp 1128 Franklin Ct Marne MI 49435 616-667-4000 667-3668
TF: 877-667-4142 ■ *Web:* www.superiorenvironmental.com
Synechron Inc 15 Maiden Ln Ste 1100 New York NY 10038 212-619-5200
Web: www.synechron.com
Talent Function Group LLC
11346 Middle Ridge Ter San Diego CA 92128 858-748-3136
Web: www.talentfunction.com
TalentQuest Inc 1275 Peachtree St NE Ste 400 Atlanta GA 30309 404-266-9368
Web: www.talentquest.com
Tct Computing Group Inc Po Box 402 Bel Air MD 21014 410-893-5800
TF: 866-828-6372 ■ *Web:* www.tctcomputing.com
Tech Center Inc 265 S Main St Akron OH 44308 330-762-6212
Web: www.techcenterinc.com
TerraFirma 600 Grant St Ste 700 Denver CO 80203 303-861-0388 923-1191*
**Fax Area Code: 602*
Think Resources Inc 225 Scientific Dr Norcross GA 30092 770-390-9888
Web: www.thinkresources.com
Thornmark Asset Management Inc
119 Spadina Ave Ste 701 Toronto ON M5V2L1 416-204-6200
TF: 877-204-6201 ■ *Web:* www.thornmark.com
Threshold Placement Services
35 W Pine St, Ste 213 Orlando FL 32801 407-296-4370
Web: www.thresholdplacement.com
Tier 3 Inc 106 E Chestnut St Stillwater MN 55082 651-334-7810
Web: www.tier3-inc.com
Tosan Inc 2209 Larimer St Unit A Denver CO 80205 303-832-7606
Web: www.tosaninc.com
Total Resource Management Inc
510 King St Ste 200 Alexandria VA 22314 703-548-4285 548-3641
TF: 877-548-5100 ■ *Web:* www.trmnet.com
TRACOM Group, The 6675 S Kenton St Ste 118 Centennial CO 80111 303-470-4900
Web: www.tracomcorp.com
Transhire
3601 W Commercial Blvd Ste 12 Fort Lauderdale FL 33309 954-484-5401
Web: www.transhiregroup.com
Trendtec Inc 2381 Zanker Rd San Jose CA 95131 408-435-9500
Web: www.trendtec.com
TriCore Inc 117 N Gold Dr Bldg 1 Robbinsville NJ 08691 609-918-2668
Web: www.tricore.com
Union Resource Marketing 12301 Rosewood Dr Leawood KS 66209 913-322-2702
Web: www.unionresourcemarketing.com
United Way of Central Md Inc, The
100 S Charles St PO Box 1576 Baltimore MD 21203 410-547-8000 547-8289
TF: 800-429-0618 ■ *Web:* www.uwcm.org
Uptime Group Inc, The 200 Violet St Ste 150 Golden CO 80401 303-757-4611
Vantige Inc 100 W Rd Ste 300 Towson MD 21204 410-337-4774
Web: www.vantigeinc.com
Venue Management Services Inc
500 N 1st Ave Ste 4 Arcadia CA 91006 626-445-6000
Web: www.venueservices.com
Weinberg Group Inc, The
1220 Nineteenth St NW Ste 300 Washington DC 20036 202-833-8077
Web: www.weinberggroup.com
Whitaker Medical Ltd
1200 Enclave Pkwy Ste 200 Houston TX 77077 281-870-1000
Wilcox Miller & Nelson
100 Howe Ave Ste 155 N Sacramento CA 95825 916-977-3700
Web: www.wilcoxcareer.com

Phone | Fax

workforcetactix Inc 954 Ridgebrook Rd Ste 200 Sparks MD 21152 443-212-1540
Web: www.workforcetactix.com
ZE PowerGroup Inc 130 - 5920 No Two Rd Richmond BC V7C4R9 604-244-1469
TF: 866-944-1469 ■ *Web:* www.ze.com

194 CONSULTING SERVICES - MANAGEMENT

See Also Association Management Companies p. 1748; Management Services p. 2710

Phone | Fax

1secureaudit LLC 1600 Tysons Blvd Fl 8 Mc Lean VA 22102 424-220-8940
TF: 800-321-0706 ■ *Web:* www.1secureaudit.com
3 Kings Environmental Inc
1311 SE Grace Ave Battle Ground WA 98604 360-666-5464
Web: www.3kingsenvironmental.com
360 Press Solutions 2009 Windy Ter Cedar Park TX 78613 512-381-2360
Web: www.360presssolutions.com
360 Solutions LLC 2114 Austin Ave Waco TX 76701 254-755-7000
TF: 800-374-2879 ■ *Web:* www.360solutions.com
3plus Logistics Co
20250 S Alameda St Rancho Dominguez CA 90221 310-667-5160
Web: e3pl.com
89 Degrees Inc 25 Mall Rd Burlington MA 01803 781-221-5400
Web: www.89degrees.com
A C e International Company Inc
85 Independence Dr Taunton MA 02780 508-884-9600
TF: 800-223-4685 ■ *Web:* www.aceintl.com
a i Solutions Inc 10001 Derekwood Ln Ste 215 Lanham MD 20706 301-306-1756 306-1754
Web: www.ai-solutions.com
A Y R Consulting Group 3708 Rodale Way Ste 200 Dallas TX 75287 972-820-8400
Web: ayrconsulting.com
A1 Roof Trusses Ltd Co
4451 Saint Lucie Blvd Fort Pierce FL 34946 772-409-1010
Web: www.a1truss.com
Abacus Automation Inc 264 Shields Dr Bennington VT 05201 802-442-3662
Web: abacusautomation.com
Abacus Planning Group Inc 2500 Devine St Columbia SC 29205 803-933-0054
Web: www.abacusplanninggroup.com
ABACUS Project Management Inc
3030 N Central Ave Ste 1207 Phoenix AZ 85012 602-265-6870
Web: www.abacuspm.com
Abba Technologies Inc
1501 San Pedro Dr NE Albuquerque NM 87110 505-889-3337 889-3338
TF: 888-222-2832 ■ *Web:* www.abbatech.com
ABeam Consulting (USA) Ltd
8445 Freeport Pkwy 4th Fl Irving TX 75063 972-929-3130
Web: www.abeam.com
Abrams Consulting Group Inc
3020 Wchester Ave Ste 307 Purchase NY 10577 914-696-5100
Web: www.abramsconsulting.com
ABS Group of Cos Inc
Abs Plz 16855 Northchase Dr Houston TX 77060 281-673-2800
Web: www.abs-group.com
AC Group Inc 118 Lyndsey Dr Montgomery TX 77316 281-413-5572
Web: www.acgroup.org
AC Lordi Corp 101 Lindenwood Dr Ste 201 Malvern PA 19355 610-738-0100
Web: www.aclordi.com
AC Square Inc 371 Foster City Blvd Foster City CA 94404 650-293-2730
Academic Keys LLC 1066 Storrs Rd Ste D Storrs CT 06268 860-429-0218
Web: www.academickeys.com
Academy Leadership LLC
10120 Vly Forge Cir King Of Prussia PA 19406 610-783-0630
Web: www.academyleadership.com
Acadia Enviromental Technology 48 Free St Portland ME 04101 207-780-1230
Web: www.acadiaenvironmental.com
Acai Solutions LLC
1285 Ave Of Americas 35th Fl New York NY 10019 212-554-4460
Web: www.acaisolutions.com
ACC Environmental Consultants Inc
7977 Capwell Dr Ste 100 Oakland CA 94621 510-638-8400
Web: www.accenv.com
Accelero Health Partners LLC
380 Southpointe Blvd Plz II Ste 400 Canonsburg PA 15317 724-743-3760
Web: www.accelerohealth.com
Accenture Inc 5450 Explorer Dr Ste 400 Mississauga ON L4W5M1 416-641-5000 641-5099
Web: www.accenture.com
Access Highway Inc 96 Carleton Ave Central Islip NY 11722 631-232-9119
Acclivus Corp 14500 Midway Rd Dallas TX 75244 972-385-1277 386-6720
Web: www.acclivus.com
Accucom Consulting Inc 250 Post Rd E Westport CT 06880 203-221-1212 221-1946
Web: accucomci.com
Accumyn LLC 1415 Congress St Ste 200 Houston TX 77002 713-800-2550
Web: www.accumyn.com
Accuvoice Inc 343 Wainwright Dr Northbrook IL 60062 847-559-7272
Achievement Incentives & Meetings
64 River Rd East Hanover NJ 07936 973-386-9500
TF: 800-454-1424 ■ *Web:* www.aimtrav.com
ACM Capital Partners LLC
200 S Biscayne Blvd 7th Fl Miami FL 33131 305-960-8851
Web: www.acmcapitalpartners.com
Acorn Consulting 803 Curtis St Menlo Park CA 94025 650-329-8923
Web: www.acorn-od.com
Acquest International 909 Third Ave 27th Fl New York NY 10022 212-719-1500
Web: www.acquestinternational.com
ACS Assoc Inc 2145 Edge Hill Rd Huntingdon Valley PA 19006 215-784-0661
Action Learning Systems Inc
135 S Rosemead Blvd Pasadena CA 91107 626-744-5344
Web: www.actionlearningsystems.com
Active Environmental Technologies Inc
203 Pine St Mount Holly NJ 08060 609-702-1500
Web: www.active-env.com

Phone | Fax

Acumentra Health Inc
2020 SW Fourth Ave Ste 520 .... Portland OR 97201 503-279-0100
Web: www.acumentra.org

AcuTech Group Inc 1919 Gallows Rd Ste 900 .... Vienna VA 22182 703-676-3180
Web: www.acutech-consulting.com

Adaptek Systems Inc 14224 Plank St .... Fort Wayne IN 46818 260-637-8660
Web: www.adapteksystems.com

adaQuest Inc 14450 NE 29th Pl Ste Ste 220 .... Bellevue WA 98007 425-284-7800
Web: www.adaquest.com

Addx Corp 4900 Seminary Rd Ste 570 .... Alexandria VA 22311 703-933-7637 933-7638
Web: www.addxcorp.com

Adiligy LLC 845 Third Ave 6th Fl .... New York NY 10022 646-290-5288
Web: www.adiligy.com

Adizes 6404 Via Real .... Carpinteria CA 93013 805-565-2901
Web: www.adizes.com

Administrative Controls Management Inc
525 Avis Dr Ste 2 .... Ann Arbor MI 48108 734-995-9640
Web: www.acmpm.com

Advanced Analytical Consulting Group Inc
211 Congress St .... Boston MA 02110 617-338-2224
Web: www.aacg.com

Advanced Electronics
2601 Manhattan Beach Blvd .... Redondo Beach CA 90278 310-725-0410
TF: 800-750-7234 ■ *Web:* www.advancedelectronics.com

Advanced Energy Corp
909 Capability Dr Ste 2100 .... Raleigh NC 27606 919-857-9000
TF: 800-869-8001 ■ *Web:* www.advancedenergy.org

Advanced Recovery Service
5434 King Ave Ste 200 .... Pennsauken NJ 08109 856-488-8860
Web: www.advancedrecoveryservice.com

Advancement LLC 32200 Solon Rd .... Solon OH 44139 440-248-8550
TF: 866-364-3370 ■ *Web:* www.advancementllc.com

Advantage Consulting Inc
7611 Little River Tpke Ste 204 W .... Annandale VA 22003 703-642-5153
Web: www.acibiz.com

Advantage Performance Group Inc
700 Larkspur Landing Cir .... Larkspur CA 94939 415-925-6832 925-9512
TF: 800-494-6646 ■ *Web:* www.advantageperformance.com

Adventive Mktg Inc
417 S Arlington Heights Rd .... Arlington Heights IL 60005 847-590-1110
Web: www.adventivemarketing.com

Advisory Board Co, The 2445 M St NW .... Washington DC 20037 202-266-5600 672-5700
NASDAQ: ABCO ■ *Web:* www.advisory.com

Advus Corp 16 E 34th St 15th Fl .... New York NY 10016 212-400-7922
Web: www.advus.com

AFC Industries Inc 13-16 133rd Pl .... College Point NY 11356 718-747-0237
TF: 800-663-3412 ■ *Web:* www.afcindustries.com

Affect Strategies Inc 60 W 38th St 4th Fl .... New York NY 10018 212-398-9680
Web: www.affectstrategies.com

Affiliated Power Purchasers International LLC
224 Phillip Morris Dr Ste 402 .... Salisbury MD 21804 800-520-6685
TF: 800-520-6685 ■ *Web:* www.appienergy.com

Affinitas Corp 1015 N 98th St Ste 100 .... Omaha NE 68114 402-505-5000
TF: 800-369-6495 ■ *Web:* www.affinitas.net

Affinity Consultants Inc 222 N Canal St .... Canal Fulton OH 44614 330-854-9066
Web: www.affinityconsultants.com

Affinity Management Group LLC
10205 Westheimer Rd Ste 460 .... Houston TX 77042 713-452-3100
Web: www.affinity-mgt.com

Affinity Wealth Management Inc
1702 Lovering Ave .... Wilmington DE 19806 302-652-6767
TF: 800-825-8399 ■ *Web:* www.affinitywealth.com

AFIMAC Inc 8160 Parkhill Dr .... Milton ON L9T5V7 905-693-0746
Web: afimacglobal.com

AFrame Digital Inc
1889 Preston White Dr Ste 101 .... Reston VA 20191 571-308-0147
Web: www.aframedigital.com

AFYA Inc 8101 Sandy Spring Rd Ste 301 .... Laurel MD 20707 301-957-3040
Web: www.afyainc.com

Agcall Inc 251 Midpark Blvd SE .... Calgary AB T2X1S3 403-256-1229 254-2371
TF: 877-273-4333 ■ *Web:* www.agcall.com

Ageatia Technology Consultancy Services Inc
850 E Higgins Rd Ste 125 .... Schaumburg IL 60173 847-517-8415
TF: 855-243-4842 ■ *Web:* www.ageatia.com

Airbus North America Holdings
198 Van Buren St Ste 300 .... Herndon VA 20170 703-834-3400 834-3593
TF: 888-340-2375 ■ *Web:* www.airbus.com

AirStar International Inc
5273 N Commerce Ave Unit 11 .... Moorpark CA 93021 805-553-9996
Web: www.airstarintl.com

AK Capital LLC 445 Park Ave Fl 9 .... New York NY 10022 212-333-8634
Web: www.akcapital.com

Alan Davis & Assoc Inc 538 Main Rd .... Hudson QC J0P1J0 450-458-3535
Web: www.alandavis.com

Alaska Permanent Capital Management Co
900 W Fifth Ave Ste 601 .... Anchorage AK 99501 907-272-7575
Web: www.apcm.net

Alba Spectrum Technologies 1715 Wabansia .... Chicago IL 60622 773-384-9264
Web: www.albaspectrum.com

Albert Moving & Storage Inc
4401 Barnett Rd .... Wichita Falls TX 76310 940-696-7000
Web: www.albertmovingandstorage.com

Albright Stonebridge Group
555 Thirteenth St NW Ste 300 W .... Washington DC 20004 202-637-8600
Web: www.albrightstonebridge.com

ALCO Sales & Service Co
6851 High Grove Blvd .... Burr Ridge IL 60527 630-655-1900
TF: 800-323-4282 ■ *Web:* www.alcosales.com

Alego Health 24651 Center Ridge Rd., Ste 400 .... Westlake OH 44145 440-918-4570
TF: 855-918-4570 ■ *Web:* www.alegohealth.com

Aleut Management Services LLC
5540 Tech Ctr Dr Ste 100 .... Colorado Springs CO 80919 719-531-9090
Web: www.aleutmgt.com

Phone | Fax

Alexander Street Press LLC 3212 Duke St .... Alexandria VA 22314 703-212-8520
Web: alexanderstreet.com

Alia Conseil Inc
Place Iberville III 2960 Laurier Blvd Ste 214 .... Quebec QC G1V4S1 418-652-1737
Web: www.aliaconseil.com

Alimansky Capital Group Inc 12 E 44th St Ph .... New York NY 10017 212-832-7300
Web: www.alimansky.com

Aliron International Inc
5231 Massachusetts Ave .... Bethesda MD 20816 301-229-1900
Web: www.aliron.com

All4 Inc 2393 Kimberton Rd .... Kimberton PA 19442 610-933-5246
Web: www.all4inc.com

Allant Group Inc, The
2056 Westings Ave Ste 500 .... Naperville IL 60563 800-367-7311 355-3090*
**Fax Area Code:* 630 ■ *TF:* 800-367-7311 ■ *Web:* www.allantgroup.com

Alliance Geotechnical Group Inc
3228 Halifax St .... Dallas TX 75247 972-444-8889
Web: www.aggengr.com

Alliance Solutions Group Inc
11838 Rock Landing Dr Oyster Point Business Park
Ste 207 .... Newport News VA 23606 757-223-7233
Web: www.asg-inc.org

Alliant Co-op Data Solutions LLC
301 Fields Ln N Ctr .... Brewster NY 10509 845-617-5500
Web: alliantinsight.com

Allied Business Consulting
295 Durham Ave Ste 212 .... South Plainfield NJ 07080 908-222-7015 834-0930
Web: www.abcincus.com

ALLogistx International, Inc.
2130 Huntington Dr Ste 205 .... South Pasadena CA 91030 323-254-9550
Web: allogistx.com

Allsup Inc 300 Allsup Pl .... Belleville IL 62223 800-854-1418 236-5778*
**Fax Area Code:* 618 ■ *TF:* 800-854-1418 ■ *Web:* www.allsup.com

AllTek Staffing & Resource Group Inc
600 Davidson Rd .... Pittsburgh PA 15239 412-573-0077
Web: www.alltekstaffing.com

Almaco 99 M Ave .... Nevada IA 50201 515-382-3506
Web: www.almaco.com

Alpha & Omega Financial Management Consultants Inc
8580 La Mesa Blvd Ste 100 .... La Mesa CA 91942 800-755-5060
TF: 800-755-5060 ■ *Web:* www.alpha-omega-inc.com

Alpha Corp 21351 Ridgetop Cir Ste 200 .... Dulles VA 20166 703-450-0800 450-0043
Web: www.alphacorporation.com

Alpha Investment Consulting Group LLC
111 E Kilbourn Ave Ste 1600 .... Milwaukee WI 53202 414-319-4100
Web: www.alpha-investment.com

Alphamicron Inc 1950 SR- 59 Ste 100 .... Kent OH 44240 330-676-0648 676-0649
Web: www.alphamicron.com

Alphaport Inc 18013 Cleveland Pkwy Ste 170 .... Cleveland OH 44135 216-619-2400
Web: www.alpha-port.com

Alpine Innovations 275 North 950 East .... Lehi UT 84043 801-766-4994
TF: 866-489-6788 ■ *Web:* www.alpineproducts.com

Alster Communications 3062 N Cir .... Anchorage AK 99507 907-344-9674
Web: alster.com

Altair Customer Intelligence
341 Cool Springs Blvd Ste 450 .... Franklin TN 37067 615-468-6800
TF: 800-241-6631 ■ *Web:* www.altairci.com

Altair Engineering Inc 1820 E Big Beaver Rd .... Troy MI 48083 248-614-2400 614-2411
TF: 888-222-7822 ■ *Web:* www.altair.com

Altamont Environmental Inc 231 Haywood St .... Asheville NC 28801 828-281-3350
Web: www.altamontenvironmental.com

AltaTerra Ltd 530 Lytton Ave 2nd Fl .... Palo Alto CA 94301 650-362-0440

AltEnergy LLC 137 Rowayton Ave .... Rowayton CT 06853 203-299-1400
Web: www.altenergyllc.com

Altfest Personal Wealth Management
425 Park Ave 24th Fl .... New York NY 10022 212-406-0850
Web: www.altfest.com

Altman Weil Inc PO Box 625 .... Newtown Square PA 19073 610-359-9900 359-0467
TF: 866-886-3600 ■ *Web:* www.altmanweil.com

Altoros Systems 830 Stewart Dr Ste 119 .... Sunnyvale CA 94085 650-395-7002
TF: 855-258-6767 ■ *Web:* www.altoros.com

Altus Alliance LLC
719 Second Ave The Millennium Tower 14th Fl .... Seattle WA 98104 206-438-1890
Web: www.altusalliance.com

Alvarez & Marsal Holdings LLC
600 Lexington Ave 6th Fl .... New York NY 10022 212-759-4433 759-5532
Web: www.alvarezandmarsal.com

Ambit Consulting 310-1847 Broadway W .... Vancouver BC V6J1Y6 604-662-3130
Web: ambit-consulting.com

Amerex Energy Services LLC
1 Sugar Creek Ctr Blvd Ste 700 .... Sugar Land TX 77478 281-340-5200
Web: www.amerexenergy.com

American Cybersystems Inc (ACS)
2400 Meadowbrook Pkwy .... Duluth GA 30096 770-493-5588 270-6248*
**Fax Area Code:* 877 ■ *Web:* www.acsicorp.com

American Executive Management Inc
30 Federal St .... Salem MA 01970 978-744-5923
Web: www.americanexecutive.us

American Geothermal Systems Inc
8650 Spicewood Springs Rd .... Austin TX 78759 512-219-1465
Web: www.amgeosystems.com

American Journal of Pathology
9650 Rockville Pk .... Bethesda MD 20814 301-634-7130
Web: www.asip.org

American Mktg Services & Consultant
939 Tower Rd .... Mundelein IL 60060 847-566-4545
Web: amscinc.com

American National Logistics Inc
202 N San Jacinto St .... Rockwall TX 75087 972-772-3132
Web: www.anlinc.com

American Partners Inc 1005 Main St Ste 2205 .... Pawtucket RI 02860 401-312-4262
Web: www.americanpartnersinc.com

Americorp Financial LLC 877 S Adams Rd .... Birmingham MI 48009 248-723-4500
Web: www.eamericorp.com

Phone Fax

Amherst Capital Partners LLC
Brown St Centre 255 E Brown St Ste 120 .... Birmingham MI 48009 248-642-5660

Ami Adini & Assoc Inc 4609 Russell Ave .... Los Angeles CA 90027 323-913-4073
TF: 888-400-4260 ■ *Web:* www.amiadini.com

Amino Transport Inc 223 NE Loop 820 Ste 101 .... Hurst TX 76053 800-304-3360
TF: 800-304-3360 ■ *Web:* www.aminotransport.com

Amirit Technologies Inc
271 Us Hwy 46 Ste C103 .... Fairfield NJ 07004 973-575-7557 828-0205
Web: amirit.com

Ammunition Group
1500 Sansome St RoundHouse 1 .... San Francisco CA 94111 415-632-1170
Web: www.ammunitiongroup.com

Amotec Inc 1701 E 12th St Ste 103 .... Cleveland OH 44114 440-250-4600
Web: www.amotecinc.com

AMVC Management Services LLC 508 Market St ...... Audubon IA 50025 712-563-2080
Web: www.amvcms.com

AnaJet LLC 3050 Redhill Ave .... Costa Mesa CA 92626 714-662-3200
Web: www.anajet.com

Analysis Group Inc 111 Huntington Ave 10th Fl .... Boston MA 02199 617-425-8000 425-8001
Web: www.analysisgroup.com

Anchor Benefit Consulting Inc
2400 Maitland Ctr Pkwy Ste 111 .... Maitland FL 32751 407-667-8766
TF: 800-845-7629 ■ *Web:* anchorbenefit.com

Anchor QEA LLC 720 Olive Way Ste 1900 .... Seattle WA 98101 206-287-9130 287-9131
Web: www.anchorqea.com

Anderson LeNeave & Co
6000 Fairview Rd Ste 625 .... Charlotte NC 28210 704-552-9212
Web: www.andersonleneave.com

Andrews Logistics Inc
2445 E Southlake Blvd .... Southlake TX 76092 817-527-2770
TF: 866-536-1234 ■ *Web:* www.andrewslogistics.com

Ann Mcgee-cooper & Assoc Inc 4236 Hockaday Dr ...... Dallas TX 75229 214-357-8550
Web: www.amca.com

Another 9 LLC 777 Old Saw Mill River Rd .... Tarrytown NY 10591 914-909-1800
Web: www.another9.com

Answerport Inc 241 N Broadway Ste 401 .... Milwaukee WI 53202 414-289-9100
Web: www.answerport.com

Antaean Solutions LLC
11700 Preston Rd Ste 600-213 .... Dallas TX 75230 214-987-3439
Web: www.antaeans.com

Antarctica Asset Management Ltd
57 E 11th St .... New York NY 10003 212-925-1419
Web: www.antarcticaam.com

Anthem Mktg Corp 549 W Randolph Ste 700 .... Chicago IL 60661 312-441-0382
Web: www.anthemedge.com

APN Consulting Inc 475 Wall St .... Princeton NJ 08540 609-924-3400
Web: www.apnconsultinginc.com

Apple Spice Junction West Valley
2235 South 1300 West Ste A .... Salt Lake City UT 84119 801-359-8821
Web: www.applespice.com

Apples of Gold Center for Learning
604 Liberty St Ste 123 .... Pella IA 50219 641-620-1160

Applied Educational Systems Inc 208 Bucky Dr .... Lititz PA 17543 717-627-7710
Web: www.aeseducation.com

Applied Energy Group Inc
1377 Motor Pkwy Ste 401 .... Islandia NY 11749 631-434-1414
Web: www.appliedenergygroup.com

Aqua Finance Inc 1 Corporate Dr Ste 300 .... Wausau WI 54401 715-848-5425
Web: www.aquafinance.com

Aquantia Corp 700 Tasman Dr .... Milpitas CA 95035 408-228-8300
Web: www.aquantia.com

Archimede Gruden USA Inc 51 Newark St Ste 302 ...... Hoboken NJ 07030 201-798-0222

Ardent Sound Inc 33 S Sycamore St .... Mesa AZ 85202 480-649-1806
Web: www.ardentsound.com

Ardmore Banking Advisors Inc
44 E Lancaster Ave Second Fl
44 E Lancaster Ave Second Fl .... Ardmore PA 19003 610-649-4643
Web: www.ardmoreadvisors.com

ARG Recovery LLC 3308 Preston Rd Ste 350-215 .... Plano TX 75093 972-335-2090
Web: www.argrecovery.com

Argent Wealth Management 404 Wyman St Ste 375 .... Waltham MA 02451 781-290-4900
Web: www.argentwm.com

Ariel Group Inc, The
1050 Waltham St Ste 600 .... Lexington MA 02421 781-761-9000
Web: www.arielgroup.com

Arlington Capital Management Inc
21 S Evergreen Ave Ste 210 .... Arlington Heights IL 60005 847-670-4030
TF: 855-471-5796 ■ *Web:* www.arlington-capital.com

Armortex Inc 5926 Corridor Pkwy .... Schertz TX 78154 210-661-8306 661-8308
Web: www.armortex.com

Arthur D Little Inc 1 Federal St Ste 2810 .... Boston MA 02110 617-532-9550 261-6630
Web: www.adlittle.com

Arthur Langhus Layne LLC 1718 S Cheyenne .... Tulsa OK 74119 918-382-7581
Web: www.all-llc.com

Arthur W Wood Company Inc
50 Congress St Ste 300 .... Boston MA 02109 617-542-0500
Web: www.arthurwood.com

Artifex Technology Consulting Inc
614 George Washington Hwy .... Lincoln RI 02865 401-723-6644
TF: 888-278-4339 ■ *Web:* www.artifextech.com

Ascend Advisory Group LLC 6760 Perimeter Dr .... Dublin OH 43016 614-784-6000
Web: www.ascendadvisory.com

Ascent Capital Management LLC
2796 NW Clearwater Dr Ste 200 .... Bend OR 97703 541-382-4847
Web: www.ascentcap.com

Asian American Business Development Center Inc
80 Wall St Ste 418 .... New York NY 10005 212-966-0100
Web: www.aabdc.com

Asian Inc Social Svc Crdntr
1167 Mission St Fl 4 .... San Francisco CA 94103 415-928-5910
Web: www.asianinc.org

Aspen Environmental Group
5020 Chesebro Rd Ste 200 .... Agoura Hills CA 91301 818-597-3407
Web: www.aspeneg.com

ASR Analytics LLC 1389 Canterbury Way .... Potomac MD 20854 301-738-9502
Web: www.asranalytics.com

ASR Constructors Inc 5230 Wilson St .... Riverside CA 92509 951-779-6580
Web: asrconstructors.com

Asset Based Lending Consultant
1641 NW 71st Ter .... Hollywood FL 33024 954-962-0099
Web: www.ablc.net

Associated Industries Management Services Inc
1206 N Lincoln Ste 200 .... Spokane WA 99201 509-326-6885
Web: www.aiin.com

Astek Corp 5055 Corporate Plz Dr .... Colorado Springs CO 80919 719-260-1625
Web: www.simtek.com

ASU Group, The 2120 University Park Dr .... Okemos MI 48805 517-349-2212
Web: www.asugroup.com

AT Kearney Inc 227 W Adams St Ste 2500 .... Chicago IL 60606 312-648-0111 223-6200
Web: www.atkearney.com

Atlanta International Consulting Group (aicg)
1401 Peachtree St Ne Ste 500 .... Atlanta GA 30309 404-872-4884
Web: www.aicginc.com

Atlas Brown Investment Advisors Inc
333 E Main St - 400 .... Louisville KY 40202 502-271-2900
TF: 866-871-0334 ■ *Web:* www.atlasbrown.com

Atlas Scientific Technologies Inc
2430 University Blvd W .... Jacksonville FL 32217 904-731-0241
Web: www.atlasscitech.com

Audax Labs 101 Huntington Ave .... Boston MA 02199 617-859-1500
Web: www.audaxgroup.com

Audio Advisor 3427 Kraft Ave SE .... Grand Rapids MI 49512 616-254-8870 254-8875
TF: 800-942-0220 ■ *Web:* www.audioadvisor.com

Audio Visual Dynamics 424 Sand Shore Rd .... Morristown NJ 07960 973-993-8500
Web: avdusa.com

Audit Integrity Inc
11111 Santa Monica Blvd Ste 220 .... Los Angeles CA 90025 310-444-8820

August Mack Environmental Inc
1302 N Meridian St Ste 300 .... Indianapolis IN 46202 317-916-8000
Web: www.augustmack.com

Auroros Inc 5809 Vly Mist Ct .... Raleigh NC 27613 919-841-0553
Web: www.aurorosinc.com

Aurotech Inc 6909 Timber Creek Ct .... Clarksville MD 21029 301-854-1326
Web: www.aurotechcorp.com

Austin Ribbon & Computer Supplies Inc (ARC)
9211 Waterford Centre Blvd Ste 202 .... Austin TX 78758 512-452-0651 452-0691
TF: 800-783-7459 ■ *Web:* arc-is.com

Automation & Control Technology Inc
6141 Avery Rd .... Dublin OH 43016 614-495-1120
Web: www.autocontroltech.com

Automotive Quality & Logistics Inc
14744 Jib St .... Plymouth MI 48170 734-459-1670
Web: www.aql-inc.com

Avanti Corp 6621 Richmond Hgwy Ste 200 .... Alexandria VA 22306 703-916-1660
Web: www.avanticorporation.com

Avanti Environmental Inc
10842 Noel St Ste 108 .... Los Alamitos CA 90720 714-730-3320
Web: www.avantienvironmental.com

Avenger Aircraft & Services LLC
103 N Main St Ste 106 .... Greenville SC 29601 864-232-8073
Web: www.avengeraircraft.com

Avery Point Mktg Solutions 244 Upton Rd .... Colchester CT 06415 860-537-2440

Avoca Group 179 Nassau St Ste 3a .... Princeton NJ 08542 609-252-9020 252-9022
Web: www.theavocagroup.com

Avs Group 3120 S Ave .... La Crosse WI 54601 608-787-8101
Web: www.avsgroup.com

Award Solutions Inc 2100 Lakeside Blvd .... Richardson TX 75082 972-664-0727 664-0729
TF: 877-472-9273 ■ *Web:* awardsolutions.com

Axiom Resource Management Inc
5203 Leesburg Pk Ste 300 .... Falls Church VA 22041 703-208-3000
TF: 800-566-9305 ■ *Web:* www.axiom-rm.com

Axios Inc 528 Fourth St NW .... Grand Rapids MI 49504 616-949-2525
Web: www.axiosincorporated.com

Axis Teknologies
8800 Roswell Rd Bldg A Ste 265 .... Sandy Springs GA 30350 678-441-0260

Azavar Technologies 55 E Jackson Ste 2100 .... Chicago IL 60604 312-583-0100
Web: www.azavar.com

Aztec Energy Partners Inc
1951 Honey Creek Commons .... Conyers GA 30013 770-760-1100
Web: aztec-energy.com

B Ma Media Group 4091 Erie St .... Willoughby OH 44094 440-975-4262
Web: www.bmamedia.com

B27 Resources 1417 Gables Ct .... Plano TX 75075 214-473-8580
Web: www.b27resources.com/b27//gp.nsf/viewsub?openform&page=B27Locations

Baa Indianapolis LLC
2500 S High School Rd Ste 100 .... Indianapolis IN 46241 317-487-5025
Web: www.indianapolisairport.com

Bad Boy Inc 102 Industrial Dr .... Batesville AR 72501 870-698-0090
Web: www.badboymowers.com

BAE Systems Analytical Solutions Inc
308 Voyager Way .... Huntsville AL 35806 256-890-8000
Web: www.mevatec.com

Bain & Co 131 Dartmouth St .... Boston MA 02116 617-572-2000 572-2427
Web: www.bain.com

Banda Group International LLC
1799 E Queen Creek Rd Ste 1 .... Chandler AZ 85286 480-636-8734
Web: www.bandagroupintl.com

Bankers Business Management Services Inc
8121 Georgia Ave Ste 950 .... Silver Spring MD 20910 301-565-0601
Web: www.bankersbms.com

Bar Green Inc 619 E Winghouse Blvd .... Charlotte NC 28273 704-552-6483 552-1403
Web: www.bargreeninc.com

Barnes & Conti Assoc Inc
940 Dwight Way Ste 15 .... Berkeley CA 94710 510-644-0911
Web: www.barnesconti.com

Barnes Communications Inc 1 Yonge St Ste 1504 .... Toronto ON M5E1E5 416-367-5000 367-5390
Web: www.barnesir.com

Phone | Fax

Bay Area Economics 1285 66th St. Emeryville CA 94608 510-547-9380
Web: www.bae1.com

Bay Dynamics Inc 595 Market St Ste 920 San Francisco CA 94105 415-912-3130
Web: www.baydynamics.com

BC One Call Ltd 4259 Canada Way Ste 222 Burnaby BC V5G1H1 604-257-1900
Web: www.bconecall.bc.ca

BCS Inc 8920 Stephens Rd Ste 200 Laurel MD 20723 410-997-7778
Web: www.bcs-hq.com

Beachwood Systems Consulting Inc
13315 Broadway Ave Cleveland OH 44125 216-823-1800
Web: www.beachsys.com

Beacon Assoc Inc 900-A S Main St Ste 102 Bel Air MD 21014 410-638-7279 638-7662
TF: 877-846-5046 ■ *Web:* www.beaconassociates.net

Beacon Financial Partners
25800 Science Park Dr Ste 100 Beachwood OH 44122 216-910-1850
TF: 866-568-3951 ■ *Web:* www.beaconplanners.com

Beacon Occupational Health & Safety Services Inc
800 Cordova St. Anchorage AK 99501 907-222-7612
Web: www.beaconohss.com

Beacon Partners Inc 97 Libbey Pkwy Ste 310 Weymouth MA 02189 781-982-8400

Beam 24 School St Boston MA 02108 617-254-3800
Web: www.beamland.com

BeamPines Inc 232 Madison Ave 10th Fl New York NY 10016 212-476-4100
Web: www.beampines.com

Becker''s ASC Review 77 Wacker Chicago IL 60611 312-750-6016
TF: 800-417-2035 ■ *Web:* www.beckersasc.com

Becton Healthcare Resources Inc
5674 Stoneridge Dr Ste 116 Pleasanton CA 94588 925-520-0005
Web: www.bhrcorp.org

Beeson & Assoc Inc 7711 Cambridge Ct. Crestwood KY 40014 502-241-8460

Behavioral Science Technology Inc
417 Bryant Cir Ojai CA 93023 805-646-0166
TF: 800-548-5781 ■ *Web:* www.bstsolutions.com

Bekker Compliance Consulting Partners LLC
19360 Rinaldi St Ste 453 Porter Ranch CA 91326 818-836-1291
Web: www.bccp-llc.com

Benchmark Technologies International Inc
411 Hackensack Ave Fl 8 Hackensack NJ 07601 201-996-0077
TF: 800-265-8254 ■ *Web:* www.btiworld.com

Benedetto Guitars Inc 10 Mall Ter Ste A Savannah GA 31406 912-692-1400
Web: benedettoguitars.com

Benefitdecisions Inc 125 S Wacker Ste 2075 Chicago IL 60606 312-606-4800
Web: www.benefitdecisions.com

Benemax Inc 7 W Mill St Medfield MA 02052 800-528-1530
TF: 800-528-1530 ■ *Web:* www.benemax.com

Benjamin Schlesinger & Assoc LLC
3 Bethesda Metro Ctr Ste 700 Bethesda MD 20814 301-951-7266
Web: www.bsaenergy.com

Benson Mktg Group
2700 Napa Vly Corporate Dr Ste H Napa CA 94558 707-254-9292
Web: www.bensonmarketing.com

Berkeley Communications Corp 1321 67th St Emeryville CA 94608 510-644-1599
TF: 877-237-5266 ■ *Web:* www.berkcom.com

Bernzott Capital Advisors
888 W Ventura Blvd Ste B Camarillo CA 93010 805-389-9445
Web: www.bernzott.com

Bertling Logistics Inc 19054 Kenswick Dr Humble TX 77338 281-774-2300
Web: www.bertling.com

Beta-tech Consulting Inc 1553 Markham Way Sacramento CA 95818 916-443-0300
Web: beta-techconsulting.com

Betacom Inc 9331 E Fowler Ave Ste F Thonotosassa FL 33592 813-985-4097
Web: www.betacominc.com

BGR Holding LLC
The Homer Bldg Eleventh Fl S 601 Thirteenth St NW
Washington DC 20005 202-333-4936
Web: www.bgrdc.com

BIA Financial Network Inc
15120 Enterprise Ct Chantilly VA 20151 703-818-2425
TF: 800-331-5086 ■ *Web:* www.bia.com

Biggins Lacy Shapiro & Company LLC
47 Hulfish St Ste 400 Princeton NJ 08542 609-924-9775
Web: www.blsstrategies.com

Bingham Osborn & Scarborough LLC
345 California St Ste 1100 San Francisco CA 94104 415-781-8535
Web: www.bosinvest.com

BIO Analytics 65 Broad St Stamford CT 06901 203-327-0800
Web: www.bio4analytics.com

Bioline USA Inc 305 Constitution Dr Taunton MA 02780 508-880-8990
Web: www.bioline.com

Biondo Investment Advisors LLC
540 Routes 6 & 209 Milford PA 18337 570-296-5525
Web: www.thebiondogroup.com

Biostat International Inc
14506 University Point Pl Ste A Tampa FL 33613 813-979-1619
Web: biostatinternational.com

BioXcel Corp 780 E Main St Branford CT 06405 203-433-4086
Web: www.bioxcel.com

Bizfin 50 Mclaughlin Dr Greensburg PA 15601 724-836-6827
Web: www.bizfin.com

Bizphyx Inc 1910 Poplar Dr Wylie TX 75098 972-429-5560
Web: www.bizphyx.com

Black Letter Discovery Inc
33 New Montgomery St Ste 950 San Francisco CA 94105 415-946-2470
Web: www.blackletterdiscovery.com

Blaine Tech Services Inc 1680 Rogers Ave San Jose CA 95112 408-573-0555
TF: 800-545-7558 ■ *Web:* www.blainetech.com

Blanton & Assoc Inc
5 Lakeway Centre Ct Ste 200 Austin TX 78734 512-264-1095 264-1531
TF: 888-863-5881 ■ *Web:* www.blantonassociates.com

Blood Group Alliance Inc
1300 Division Rd Ste 102 West Warwick RI 02893 401-381-0600

Blue Door Consulting 21 W New York Ave. Oshkosh WI 54901 920-230-2583
Web: www.bluedoorconsulting.com

Blue Garnet Assoc LLC
8055 W Manchester Ave Ste 430 Playa Del Rey CA 90293 310-439-1930
Web: www.bluegarnet.net

Blue Magnet Partners LLC
11030 Jones Bridge Rd Ste 206 Alpharetta GA 30022 770-265-9858
Web: www.bluemagnetpartners.com

Blue Ridge Grain & Mktg Inc
2545 Flintridge Rd Ste 120 Gainesville GA 30501 770-535-2864

Blue Ridge Partners Management Consulting LLC
1350 Beverly Rd Ste 115 Mclean VA 22101 703-448-1881
Web: www.blueridgepartners.com

Blue Tent Mktg 218 E Valley Rd Ste 205 Carbondale CO 81623 970-704-3240
Web: bluetent.com

Bluepoint Leadership Development Ltd
25 Whitney Dr. Milford OH 45150 513-683-4702
TF: 888-221-8685 ■ *Web:* www.bluepointleadership.com

Blumberg Capital 501 Folsom St Ste 400 San Francisco CA 94105 415-905-5000
Web: www.blumbergcapital.com

BlumbergExcelsior Inc 16 Court St 14th Fl. Brooklyn NY 11241 212-431-5000
Web: www.blumberg.com

Boa Technology Inc 1760 Platte St Denver CO 80202 303-455-5126
TF: 844-203-1297 ■ *Web:* www.boatechnology.com

Bob Hart Consulting LLC
5126 W Evans Creek Rd Rogue River OR 97537 541-582-8890

Bockorny Group Inc
1101 16th St Northwest Ste 500 Washington DC 20036 202-659-9111
Web: www.bockornygroup.com

Bollard Group LLC, The 1 Joy St Boston MA 02108 617-720-5800
Web: www.bollard.com

Bon Secours Virginia HealthSource Inc
7229 Forest Ave Ste 208 Richmond VA 23226 804-673-2727
Web: richmond.bonsecours.com

Bonanza Trade & Supply
6853 Lankershim Blvd North Hollywood CA 91605 818-765-6577
TF: 888-965-6577 ■ *Web:* www.stonetooling.com

Boomer Consulting 610 Humboldt St. Manhattan KS 66502 785-537-2358
TF: 800-739-9998 ■ *Web:* www.boomer.com

Boomer Project 2601 Floyd Ave Richmond VA 23220 804-358-8981
Web: www.boomerproject.com

Boomtown Internet Group Inc
111 Rosemary Ln Glenmoore PA 19343 888-454-3330
TF: 888-454-3330 ■ *Web:* www.boomtownig.com

Booz Allen Hamilton Inc 8283 Greensboro Dr McLean VA 22102 703-902-5000 902-3333
TF: 866-390-3908 ■ *Web:* www.boozallen.com

Bordercomm Partners LP 6842 Industrial Ave El Paso TX 79915 915-779-3000
Web: bordercomm.com

Bortz Media & Sports Group Inc
5105 DTC Pkwy Ste 200 Greenwood Village CO 80111 303-893-9902 893-9913
Web: www.bortz.com

Boston Consulting Group Inc 53 State St 6th Fl. Boston MA 02109 617-973-1200
Web: www.bcg.com

Boston Event Guide.com
475 Hillside Ave Needham Heights MA 02494 781-444-7771
Web: www.bostoneventguide.com

Boston Market Strategies Inc
500 Cummings Ctr Ste 3150 Beverly MA 01915 781-245-7773
Web: www.bmsi3.com

Boundless Network Inc 200 E Sixth St Ste 300 Austin TX 78701 512-472-9200 472-9204
Web: www.boundlessnetwork.com

Boykin Management Co
8015 W Kenton Cir Ste 220 Huntersville NC 28078 704-896-2880
Web: www.boykin.com

Brakke Consulting Inc 2735 Villa Creek Ste 140 Dallas TX 75234 972-243-4033
TF: 877-399-6354 ■ *Web:* www.brakkeconsulting.com

Brand Advisor 512 Union St San Francisco CA 94133 415-393-0800
Web: www.brandadvisors.com

Brand Electric Inc 6274 E 375 S Lafayette IN 47905 765-296-3437
Web: www.brandelectric.com

Brand Integrity 60 Park Ave Rochester NY 14607 585-442-5404
Web: www.brandintegrity.com

Brattle Group Inc, The 44 Brattle St Cambridge MA 02138 617-864-7900
Web: www.brattle.com

Braverman Financial Associates
2173 Embassy Dr Lancaster PA 17603 717-399-4030
Web: www.bravermanfinancial.com

Bread Loaf Corp 1293 Rt 7 S Middlebury VT 05753 802-388-9871 388-3815
Web: breadloaf.com

Breakthrough Management Group Inc
1200 17th St Ste 180 Denver CO 80202 303-827-0010
TF: 800-467-4462 ■ *Web:* www.bmgi.com

Brokers Logistics Ltd 1000 Hawkins Blvd. El Paso TX 79915 915-778-7751 778-1358
Web: www.brokerslogistics.com

Brookstone Capital Management
1745 S. Naperville Rd Ste 200 Wheaton IL 60189 630-653-1400
Web: www.brookstonecm.com

Brownlie & Braden LLC
2820 Ross Tower 500 N Akard Dallas TX 75201 214-219-4650
TF: 888-339-4650 ■ *Web:* www.brownliebraden.com

Bryn Mawr Capital Management Inc
1 Town Pl Ste 200 Bryn Mawr PA 19010 484-380-8100
Web: www.brynmawrcap.com

BTAS Inc 3572 Dayton-Xenia Rd Ste 210 Beavercreek OH 45432 937-431-9431
Web: www.btas.com

BTS USA Inc 300 Stamford Pl Ste 425 Stamford CT 06902 203-316-2740
TF: 800-445-7089 ■ *Web:* www.bts.com

Bucher & Christian Consulting Inc
10 W Market St Ste 1300 Indianapolis IN 46204 317-423-8980
TF: 866-363-1132 ■ *Web:* www.bcforward.com

Building Performance Institute Inc
107 Hermes Rd Ste 210 Malta NY 12020 518-899-2727
TF: 877-274-1274 ■ *Web:* www.bpihomeowner.org

Bull & Bear Capital Advisors Inc
8659 Nathans Cove Ct Jacksonville FL 32256 904-363-3600
Web: www.bullbearcapital.com

Company / Address	City	State	Zip	Phone	Fax
Bull Mktg Group LLC 79 S Milwaukee Ave *Web:* bullmarketinggroup.com	Wheeling	IL	60090	847-520-1182	
Bulldawg Mktg Inc 115 Eastbend Ct *Web:* www.bulldawgmarketing.com	Mooresville	NC	28117	704-660-6441	
Bullseye Database Mktg LLC 5546 S 104th E Ave *Web:* www.bullseyedm.com	Tulsa	OK	74146	918-587-1731	
Bullseye Strategy LLC 1700 E Las Olas Blvd Ste 301 *Web:* www.bullseyestrategy.com	Fort Lauderdale	FL	33301	954-591-8999	
Bundy Group 24 Walnut Ave *Web:* bundygroup.com	Roanoke	VA	24016	540-342-2151	
Burchfield Group Inc, The 1295 Northland Dr Ste 350 *TF:* 800-778-1359 ■ *Web:* www.burchfieldgroup.com	St Paul	MN	55120	651-389-5640	
Burdeshaw Associates Ltd 4701 Sangamore Rd Ste N100 *Web:* www.burdeshaw.com	Bethesda	MD	20816	301-229-5800	
Burl Capital LLC 1 International Pl 7th Fl *Web:* www.burlcapital.com	Boston	MA	02110	617-936-3358	
Burnham Nationwide Inc The Burnham Ctr 111 W Washington St Ste 450 *Web:* burnhamnationwide.com	Chicago	IL	60602	312-407-7990	
Burton-Taylor International Consulting LLC 1319 Thornapple Dr Mezzanine Level *Web:* www.burton-taylor.com	Osprey	FL	34229	646-201-4152	
Busek Company Inc 11 Tech Cir *Web:* www.busek.com	Natick	MA	01760	508-655-5565	
Bush Consulting Group 136 S Broadway Ave 2nd Fl *Web:* bushconsultinggroup.com	Salem	OH	44460	330-337-6104	
Business Advancement Inc 178 Sycamore Terr *Web:* www.businessadvance.com	Glen Rock	NJ	07452	201-612-1228	
Business Leaders for Michigan 600 Renaissance Ctr Ste 1760 *Web:* www.businessleadersformichigan.com	Detroit	MI	48243	313-259-5400	
Business Resource Group (BRG) 10440 N Central Expy Ste 1150 *TF:* 888-391-9166 ■ *Web:* www.brg.com	Dallas	TX	75231	214-777-5100	777-5101
Business Training Library Inc 285 Chesterfield Business Pkwy *Web:* www.bizlibrary.com	Chesterfield	MO	63005	636-534-1000	
BusinessBroker Network LLC 375 Northridge Rd Ste 475 *Web:* www.businessbroker.net	Atlanta	GA	30350	770-391-5061	
Businesspersons Between Jobs Inc 601 Claymont Dr *Web:* bbj.org	Ballwin	MO	63011	636-394-1440	
BUSlink Media 440 Cloverleaf Dr *Web:* www.buslink.com	Baldwin Park	CA	91706	626-336-1888	
C & C Reservoirs Inc 13831 NW Fwy Ste 450 *Web:* www.ccreservoirs.com	Houston	TX	77040	713-776-3872	
C Myers Corp 8222 S 48th St Ste 275 *TF:* 800-238-7475 ■ *Web:* www.cmyers.com	Phoenix	AZ	85044	602-840-0606	
C4 Planning Solutions LLC 4914 Deans Bridge Rd *Web:* www.c4plans.com	Blythe	GA	30805	706-592-1520	
Cabot Advisory Group LLC, The 90 Washington Vly Rd	Bedminster	NJ	07921	908-719-8966	
California Primary Care Association 1231 I St Ste 400 *Web:* www.cpca.org	Sacramento	CA	95814	916-440-8170	
Callahan Financial Planning Co 3157 Farnam St Ste 7112 *Web:* callahanplanning.com	Omaha	NE	68131	402-341-2000	
Calliope Learning 1581H Hillside Ave *Web:* www.calliopelearning.com	Victoria	BC	V8T2C1	250-213-6239	
Callisto Integration 635 Fourth Line Ste 16 *TF:* 800-387-0467 ■ *Web:* www.aseco.net	Oakville	ON	L6L5B3	905-339-0059	
CALMAC Manufacturing Corp 3-00 Banta Pl *Web:* www.calmac.com	Fair Lawn	NJ	07410	201-797-1511	
Calnet Inc 12359 Sunrise Vly Dr Ste 270 *TF General:* 877-322-5638 ■ *Web:* www.calnet.com	Reston	VA	20191	703-547-6800	547-6806
Cambay Group Inc, The 2999 Oak Rd Ste 400 *Web:* www.cambaygroup.com	Walnut Creek	CA	94597	925-933-1405	
Cambria Consulting Inc 1 Bowdoin Sq *Web:* www.cambriaconsulting.com	Boston	MA	02114	617-523-7500	
Cambria Solutions Inc 1050 20th St Ste 275 *Web:* www.cambriasolutions.com	Sacramento	CA	95811	916-326-4446	
Cambridge Financial Services Group Inc 83 Mason St *Web:* www.cambridgegroup.net	Greenwich	CT	06830	203-869-0033	
Cambridge Meridian Group Inc 50 Church St Ste 50 *Web:* www.cambridgemeridian.com	Cambridge	MA	02138	617-876-7400	
Campaign Consultation Inc 2819 Saint Paul St *Web:* www.campaignconsultation.com	Baltimore	MD	21218	410-243-7979	
Canadian Enerdata Ltd 86 Ringwood Dr Ste 201 *Web:* www.enerdata.com	Stouffville	ON	L4A1C3	905-642-8167	
Canadian Urban Institute 555 Richmond St W *Web:* www.canurb.com	Toronto	ON	M5T3A3	416-365-0816	
Canaudit Inc 2139 Tapo St Ste 206 *Web:* www.canaudit.com	Simi Valley	CA	93063	805-583-3723	
Cape Fox Corp PO Box 8558 *Web:* www.capefoxcorp.com	Ketchikan	AK	99901	907-225-5163	
CapGen Financial Grou 120 W 45th St Ste 1010 *Web:* www.capgen.com	New York	NY	10036	212-542-6868	
Capital Advisors Ltd LLC 20600 Chagrin Blvd *TF:* 888-295-7908 ■ *Web:* www.capitaladvisorsltd.com	Shaker Heights	OH	44122	216-295-7900	
Capital Consulting Corp 2810 Old Lee Hwy Ste 304 *Web:* www.capconcorp.com	Fairfax	VA	22031	703-876-0400	
Capital Investment Advisors Inc 200 Sandy Springs Pl Ne Ste 300 *TF:* 888-531-0018 ■ *Web:* www.yourwealth.com	Atlanta	GA	30328	404-531-0018	
Capitol Archives & Record Storage Inc 133 Laurel St *TF:* 800-381-2277 ■ *Web:* www.capitolarchives.com	Hartford	CT	06106	860-951-8981	
Capri Capital Partners LLC 875 N Michigan Ave Ste 3430 *Web:* www.capricap.com	Chicago	IL	60611	312-573-5300	
Capstrat Inc 1201 Edwards Mill Rd 4th Fl *Web:* capstrat.com	Raleigh	NC	27607	919-828-0806	
Carana Corp 4350 Fairfax Dr Ste 900 *Web:* www.carana.com	Arlington	VA	22203	703-243-1700	
Cardiosolutions Inc 75 Mill St *Web:* www.cardiosolutionsinc.com	Stoughton	MA	02072	781-344-0801	
Carepro Health Services 1014 Fifth Ave SE *TF:* 800-575-8810 ■ *Web:* www.careprohs.com	Cedar Rapids	IA	52403	800-575-8810	
Carlisle & Company Inc 30 Monument Sq Ste 225 *Web:* www.carlisle-co.com	Concord	MA	01742	978-318-0500	
Carlson Capital Management Inc 11 Bridge Sq *Web:* carlsoncap.com	Northfield	MN	55057	507-645-8887	
Carolina Financial Group 185 W Main St *Web:* www.carofin.com	Brevard	NC	28712	828-393-0088	
Carroll County Economic Development 111 N Mason St	Carrollton	MO	64633	660-542-8760	
Carter Express Inc 4020 W 73rd St *TF:* 800-738-7705 ■ *Web:* www.carter-express.com	Anderson	IN	46011	800-738-7705	
CartwrightDownes Inc 950 Lee St Ste 110 *TF:* 800-323-2049 ■ *Web:* www.cartwrightdownes.com	Des Plaines	IL	60016	847-685-2700	
Cascade Financial Management Inc 950 17th St Ste 950 *TF:* 800-353-0008 ■ *Web:* www.cascade-inc.com	Denver	CO	80202	800-353-0008	
Catalyst Mktg Design Inc 930 S Calhoun St *Web:* catalystgetsit.com	Fort Wayne	IN	46802	260-422-4888	
Catalytic Combustion Corp 709 21st Ave *Web:* www.catalyticcombustion.com	Bloomer	WI	54724	715-568-2882	
Catapult Direct Mktg LLC 300 Orchard City Dr Ste 131 *Web:* www.catapultdata.com	Campbell	CA	95008	408-369-8111	
Cato Research Ltd 4364 S Alston Ave *Web:* www.cato.com	Durham	NC	27713	919-361-2286	361-2290
Cavalier Logistics Management Inc 45085 Old Ox Rd *Web:* www.cavlog.com	Dulles	VA	20166	703-733-4010	
Caxton Growth Partners 5755 Granger Rd Ste 100	Independence	OH	44131	216-867-9780	
CBI Group LLC Casho Mill Professional Ctr 1501 Casho Mill Rd Ste 9 *Web:* www.thecbigroup.com	Newark	DE	19711	302-266-0860	
CBI Research Inc 600 Unicorn Park Dr *TF:* 800-817-8601 ■ *Web:* www.cbinet.com	Woburn	MA	01801	339-298-2100	
CCG Facilities Integration Inc 1500 S Edgewood St *Web:* www.ccgfacilities.com	Baltimore	MD	21227	410-525-0010	
Cedar Management Consulting International LLC 250 Park Ave 7th Fl *Web:* www.cedar-consulting.com	New York	NY	10177	212-572-6314	
Ceeva Inc 643 First Ave Ste 300 *TF:* 866-233-8248 ■ *Web:* www.ceeva.com	Pittsburgh	PA	15219	412-690-2300	
Cenergistic Inc 5950 Sherry Ln Ste 900 *TF:* 888-782-7937 ■ *Web:* www.cenergistic.com	Dallas	TX	75225	214-346-5950	
Center for Civic Education 5145 Douglas Fir Rd *TF:* 800-350-4223 ■ *Web:* www.civiced.org	Calabasas	CA	91302	818-591-9321	
Center for Collaborative 33 Harrison Ave # 6 *Web:* cce.org	Boston	MA	02111	617-421-0134	
Center for Cultural Interchange 746 N La Salle Dr *TF:* 866-224-0061 ■ *Web:* www.cci-exchange.com	Chicago	IL	60654	312-944-2544	
Center for Professional 1 Liberty Blvd *Web:* www.cfpie.com	Malvern	PA	19355	610-688-1708	
Centris Consulting Inc 800 James Ave *Web:* www.centrisconsulting.com	Scranton	PA	18510	570-963-1136	
Century Health Solutions Inc 2951 SW Woodside Dr *TF:* 800-227-0089 ■ *Web:* www.century-health.com	Topeka	KS	66614	785-233-1816	
CFI Group 625 Avis Dr *Web:* www.cfigroup.com	Ann Arbor	MI	48108	734-930-9090	930-0911
CFM Partners Inc 4435 Macomb St NW *Web:* www.cfmpartners.com	Washington	DC	20016	202-364-2380	
CFO Strategies LLC 2221 Arbutus St	Newport Beach	CA	92660	949-338-9394	
CGLA Infrastructure Inc 1827 Jefferson Pl NW *Web:* www.cg-la.com	Washington	DC	20036	202-776-0990	
Cgn & Assoc Inc 415 SW Washington St *TF:* 888-746-4246 ■ *Web:* www.cgnglobal.com	Peoria	IL	61602	309-495-2100	495-2370
ChaCha Search Inc 14550 Clay Terr Blvd Ste 130 *TF:* 800-224-2242 ■ *Web:* www.chacha.com	Carmel	IN	46032	317-660-6680	
Chambers Group Inc 5 Hutton Centre Dr Ste 750 *Web:* www.chambersgroupinc.com	Santa Ana	CA	92707	949-261-5414	
Champion College Services Inc 7776 S Pointe Pkwy W Ste 250 *TF:* 800-761-7376 ■ *Web:* www.championcollegeservices.com	Tempe	AZ	85044	480-947-7375	
Chao & Company Ltd 8460 Tyco Rd Ste E *Web:* www.chaoco.com	Vienna	VA	22182	703-847-4380	
Charter Trust Co 90 N Main St *Web:* www.chartertrust.com	Concord	NH	03301	603-224-1350	
CHC Consulting 1845 W Orangewood Ave Ste 300 *Web:* chcconsulting.com	Orange	CA	92868	949-250-0004	

Name / Address	City	State	Zip	Phone	Fax
Checchi & Company Consulting Inc 1899 L St NW Ste 800 *Web:* www.checchiconsulting.com	Washington	DC	20036	202-452-9700	466-9070
Chem Space Assoc Inc 655 William Pitt Way *Web:* www.lcms.com	Pittsburgh	PA	15238	412-828-3191	
ChemADVISOR Inc 811 Camp Horne Rd Stone Quarry Crossing Ste 220 *Web:* www.chemadvisor.com	Pittsburgh	PA	15237	412-847-2000	
Chemonics International Inc 1717 H St NW *Web:* www.chemonics.com	Washington	DC	20006	202-955-3300	
Chief Manufacturing Inc 6436 City W Pkwy Ste 700 *Web:* www.chiefmfg.com	Prairie	MN	55378	952-894-6280	
Children's Educational Network Inc 283 S Escondido Blvd *Web:* www.childrenseducationalnetwork.com	Escondido	CA	92025	760-233-2863	
Childrens Education Connection Inc 6301 Hwy 39 *Web:* childrenseducationconnection.com	Meridian	MS	39305	601-485-2856	
CHP & Assoc Consulting Engineers Inc 7660 Woodway Dr Ste 400 *Web:* buryinc.com/news/detail/bury-acquires-chp-and-associates	Houston	TX	77063	713-977-3430	
Christensen Roberts Solutions 60 Pond St *Web:* www.crsol.com	Milford	CT	06460	203-389-4440	
Chrysalis Consulting LLC 11711 N Pennsylvania St *Web:* www.chrysalisglobal.com	Carmel	IN	46032	317-844-1400	
CIMdata Inc 3909 Research Park Dr *Web:* www.cimdata.com	Ann Arbor	MI	48108	734-668-9922	
Cinetic Media Inc 555 W 25th St 4th Fl *Web:* www.cineticmedia.com	New York	NY	10001	212-204-7979	
Cipher Systems LLC 2661 Riva Rd Ste 1000 *TF:* 888-899-1523 ■ *Web:* www.cipher-sys.com	Annapolis	MD	21401	410-412-3326	897-1066
CipherMax Inc 3 Results Way	Cupertino	CA	95014	408-861-3697	861-3650
Circadian Technologies Inc 2 Main St Ste 310 *TF:* 800-284-5001 ■ *Web:* www.circadian.com	Stoneham	MA	02180	781-439-6300	439-6399
Cirrus Assoc LLC 11757 Katy Fwy Ste 1300 *Web:* www.cirrusassociates.com	Houston	TX	77079	281-854-2383	
City of New Westminster 511 Royal Ave *Web:* www.newwestcity.ca	New Westminster	BC	V3L1H9	604-527-4605	
CL Services Inc 600 S Central Ave Ste 300 *Web:* www.clservicesinc.com	Atlanta	GA	30354	678-686-0933	
Claritee Group LLC 196 W Ashland St *Web:* www.clariteegroup.com	Doylestown	PA	18901	267-338-3300	
Clark & Wamberg LLC 102 S Wynstone Park Dr	North Barrington	IL	60010	847-304-5800	
Clarus Mktg Group LLC 500 Enterprise Dr 2nd Fl	Rocky Hill	CT	06067	860-358-9198	
Classroom Inc 245 Fifth Ave 20th Fl *Web:* www.classroominc.org	New York	NY	10016	212-545-8400	
Clear Blue Skies Communications 2 Thatcher St	Hyde Park	MA	02136	617-361-3229	
ClearBridge Compensation Group LLC 515 Madison Ave 32nd Fl *Web:* www.clearbridgecomp.com	New York	NY	10022	212-886-1022	
ClearCreek Partners 1743 Wazee St Ste 375 *Web:* www.clearcreekpartners.com	Denver	CO	80202	303-383-1100	
Clearedge Mktg LLC 415 N Lasalle St Ste 202 *Web:* www.clearedgemarketing.com	Chicago	Il	60654	312-731-3149	
CLEAResult 4301 Westbank Dr Ste 300 *Web:* www.clearesult.com	Austin	TX	78746	512-327-9200	
Client Mktg Systems Inc 880 Price St	Pismo Beach	CA	93449	805-773-7981	
Client Success Group Inc 5166 Sunny Creek Dr *Web:* www.clientsuccessgroup.com	San Jose	CA	95135	408-531-1907	
Cliffwater LLC 4640 Admiralty Way Ste 1101 Marina Twr *Web:* www.cliffwater.com	Marina Del Rey	CA	90292	310-448-5000	
Cline Resource & Development Co 430 Harper Park Dr *Web:* www.clineres.com	Beckley	WV	25801	304-255-7458	
CLX Logistics LLC 1777 Sentry Pkwy W Abington Hall Ste 300 *Web:* www.clxlogistics.com	Blue Bell	PA	19422	215-461-3805	
CMF Associates LLC 325 Chestnut St Ste 410 *Web:* www.cmfassociates.com	Philadelphia	PA	19106	215-531-7500	
CMS Innovative Consultants 8 Fletcher Pl *Web:* www.cmsav.com	Melville	NY	11747	631-425-3000	
Co-Sales Co 2700 N Third St Ste 1000 *Web:* www.co-sales.com	Phoenix	AZ	85004	602-254-5555	
Coalesce Mktg & Design Inc 4321 W College Ave Ste 250 *Web:* www.coalescemarketing.com	Appleton	WI	54914	920-380-4444	
Coastal Logistics Group Inc 50 Sonny Perdue Dr *Web:* www.clg-sav.com	Garden City	GA	31408	912-964-0707	
Coates Field Service Inc 4800 N Santa Fe *Web:* www.coatesfieldservice.com	Oklahoma City	OK	73118	405-528-5676	
Cogenix Consulting Ltd 401-50 Burnhamthorpe Rd W	Mississauga	ON	L5B3C2	905-803-9132	
Cogistics Inc 2485 Drane Field Rd *Web:* www.cogistics.com	Lakeland	FL	33811	863-647-9389	
Cohasset Assoc Inc 505 N Lk Shore Dr Apt 3806 *Web:* www.cohasset.com	Chicago	IL	60611	312-527-1550	
Cohen Asset Management Inc 1900 Ave of the Stars Ste 500 *Web:* www.cohenasset.com	Los Angeles	CA	90067	310-860-0598	
Coles Mktg Communications Inc 3950 Priority Way S Dr Ste 106 *Web:* www.colesmarketing.com	Indianapolis	IN	46240	317-571-0051	
Collins Consulting 630 Woofter Ave *Web:* collins.net	Colby	KS	67701	785-462-8352	
Colony Group LLC, The 2 Atlantic Ave *Web:* www.thecolonygroup.com	Boston	MA	02110	617-723-8200	
Colt International Inc 300 Flint Ridge Rd *Web:* www.coltinternational.com	Webster	TX	77598	281-280-2100	
Command Consulting Group LLC 1919 M St NW STE 200 *Web:* www.commandcg.com	Washington	DC	20036	202-207-2930	
Communispond Inc 12 Barns Ln. *TF:* 800-529-5925 ■ *Web:* www.communispond.com	East Hampton	NY	11937	631-907-8010	
Community Care Inc 1555 S Layton Blvd. *TF:* 866-992-6600 ■ *Web:* www.communitycareinc.org	Milwaukee	WI	53215	414-385-6600	
Compass Career Management Solutions LLC 8509 Crown Crescent Ct *Web:* www.compasscareer.com	Charlotte	NC	28227	704-849-2500	
Compass Mktg Solutions LLC 808 P St Ste 300 *Web:* compassventures.com	Lincoln	NE	68508	402-438-3222	
Compensation Resources Inc 310 Rt 17 N *TF:* 877-934-0505 ■ *Web:* www.compensationresources.com	Upper Saddle River	NJ	07458	201-934-0505	934-0737
Compensia Inc 1731 Technology Dr Ste 810 *Web:* www.compensia.com	San Jose	CA	95110	408-876-4025	
Complete Healthcare Communications Inc 1 Dickinson Dr Ste 200 *Web:* www.thechcgroup.com	Chadds Ford	PA	19317	610-358-3600	
Compliance Corp 21617 S Essex Dr Ste 34 *Web:* www.compliancecorporation.com	Lexington Park	MD	20653	301-863-8070	863-8290
Compliance Professional Resources LLC 11 Hanover Sq Ste 501 *Web:* www.complianceprofessionalresources.com	New York	NY	10005	212-257-6500	
Compliance Services Group Inc 7619 University Ave *Web:* www.csg.net	Lubbock	TX	79423	806-748-0040	748-0030
Comprehensive Consulting Group 1800 Walt Whitman Rd *Web:* www.ccg1800.com	Melville	NY	11747	631-249-0500	
Comprehensive Financial Planning Inc 1075 Main Ave Ste 216 *TF:* 877-901-5227 ■ *Web:* www.compfinancial.com	Durango	CO	81301	970-385-5227	
Comprehensive Loss Management Inc 15800 32nd Ave N Ste 106 *Web:* www.clmi-training.com	Minneapolis	MN	55447	763-551-1022	
Comprehensive Pharmacy Services Inc (CPS) 6409 N Quail Hollow Rd *TF:* 800-968-6962 ■ *Web:* www.cpspharm.com	Memphis	TN	38120	901-748-0470	748-4069
Compu- Vision Consulting Inc 2050 SR- 27 Ste 202 *Web:* www.compuvis.com	North Brunswick	NJ	08902	732-422-1500	
Computech Consulting Inc 707 West 700 South Ste 201 *Web:* www.i4.net	Woods Cross	UT	84087	801-294-6400	
Computer Management Technologies Inc 731 Gratiot Ave *Web:* www.cmtonline.com	Saginaw	MI	48602	989-791-4860	791-4928
Computer Resource Solutions 1 Pierce Pl *Web:* www.crscorp.com	Itasca	IL	60143	630-467-1010	
Computer Training Systems 200 W Douglas Ave Ste 230 *Web:* www.ctsys.com	Wichita	KS	67202	316-265-1585	
Computerized Assessments & Learning LLC 1202 E 23rd St Ste B *Web:* www.caltesting.org	Lawrence	KS	66046	785-856-3850	
Comspec Corp 822 N Elm St *Web:* www.comspeccorp.com	Greensboro	NC	27401	336-370-1456	
Comtel 750 Ensminger Rd Ste 100 *Web:* www.comtel.us	Tonawanda	NY	14150	716-874-5500	
Concensus Consulting LLC 103 Fox Trot Dr *Web:* concensus.com	Mars	PA	16046	724-898-1888	
Concentric Energy Advisors Inc 293 Boston Post Rd W Ste 500 *Web:* www.ceadvisors.com	Marlborough	MA	01752	508-263-6200	
Condor Capital Management Inc 1973 Washington Vly Rd *Web:* www.condorcapital.com	Martinsville	NJ	08836	732-356-7323	
Condor Earth Technologies Inc 21663 Brian Ln *TF:* 800-800-0490 ■ *Web:* www.condorearth.com	Sonora	CA	95370	209-532-0361	532-0773
Consolidated Chassis Management LLC 500 International Dr *Web:* www.ccmpool.com	Budd Lake	NJ	07828	973-298-8900	
Consolidated Construction Management Services Inc 9 Professional Cir Ste 204 *Web:* www.ccmscorp.com	Colts Neck	NJ	07722	732-303-1997	
Consortia Consulting Inc 233 S 13th St Ste 1225 *Web:* www.consortiaconsulting.com	Lincoln	NE	68508	402-441-4315	
Constat Corp 1860 Blake St Ste 650 *Web:* constat.com	Denver	CO	80202	303-572-1051	
Consultants & Builders Inc 3850 Peachtree Industrial Blvd *Web:* www.consultantsandbuilders.com	Duluth	GA	30096	770-729-8183	
Consumer Sales Solutions 537 Douglas Ave *Web:* bk.com	Dunedin	FL	34698	727-733-8700	
Container Consulting Service Inc 455 Mayock Rd *Web:* www.ccs-packaging.com	Gilroy	CA	95020	408-842-1919	
Contemporary Benefits Design Inc 1956 Wellness Blvd	Monroe	NC	28110	704-847-1007	
Continental Shelf Assoc Inc 8502 SW Kansas Ave *Web:* www.conshelf.com	Stuart	FL	34997	772-219-3000	219-3010

Phone Fax

Contoural Inc 5150 El Camino Real Ste D-30 .... Los Altos CA 94022 650-390-0800
Web: www.contoural.com
Contract Land Staff LLC
2245 Texas Dr Ste 200 .... Sugar Land TX 77479 281-240-3370 240-5009
TF: 800-874-4519 ■ *Web:* www.contractlandstaff.com
Conway MacKenzie Inc
401 S Old Woodward Ave Ste 340 .... Birmingham MI 48009 248-433-3100
Web: www.conwaymackenzie.com
Cook & Co 12 Masterton Rd .... Bronxville NY 10708 914-779-4838
Web: www.cook-co.com
Coradix Technology Consulting Ltd
151 Slater St .... Ottawa ON K1P5H3 613-234-0800 234-0988
Web: www.coradix.com
CoreTech 550 American Ave Ste 301 .... King of Prussia PA 19406 800-220-3337
TF: 800-220-3337 ■ *Web:* xsellresources.com
Cornelius & Assoc Inc 631 Harden St Ste G .... Columbia SC 29205 803-779-3354
Web: www.collegiateproject.com
Corner Alliance Inc 1620 L St NW Ste 200 .... Washington DC 20036 202-754-8120
Web: www.corneralliance.com
Cornerstone Consulting & Technology
44 Montgomery St Ste 3360 .... San Francisco CA 94104 415-705-7800
Web: www.cornerstoneconcilium.com
Cornerstone Systems Inc
3250 Players Club Pkwy .... Memphis TN 38125 901-842-0660
TF: 800-278-7677 ■ *Web:* www.cornerstone-systems.com
Corporate Dynamics Inc 1630 W Diehl Rd .... Naperville IL 60563 630-778-9991
Web: www.corpdyn.com
Corporate Executive Board Co
1919 N Lynn St .... Arlington VA 22209 571-303-3000 303-3100
NYSE: CEB ■ *TF:* 866-913-2632 ■ *Web:* www.cebglobal.com
Corporate Finance Group Inc 15 Broad St 5th Fl .... Boston MA 02109 617-531-8270
Web: www.cfgi.com
Corporate Ink Public Relations Ltd
90 Washington St .... Newton MA 02458 617-969-9192
Web: www.corporateink.com
Corridor Capital LLC
12400 Wilshire Blvd Ste 645 .... Los Angeles CA 90025 310-442-7000
Web: www.corridorcapital.com
Corridor Group Inc, The
6405 Metcalf Ste 108 .... Overland Park KS 66202 913-362-0600
Web: www.corridorgroup.com
Corybant PO Box 19136 .... Boulder CO 80308 303-447-1988
Web: www.corybant.com
Coskata Inc 4575 Weaver Pkwy Ste 100 .... Warrenville IL 60555 630-657-5800
Cosmos Consulting Group Inc 212 E Ohio St .... Chicago IL 60611 312-222-0700
Cosmos Sports 1690 Bonhill Rd .... Mississauga ON L5T1C8 905-564-4660 564-4881
Web: www.cosmossports.com
Country Aircheck 1102 17th Ave S Ste 205 .... Nashville TN 37212 615-320-1450
Web: countryaircheck.com
COVELLO GROUP Inc, The
1660 Olympic Blvd Ste 300 .... Walnut Creek CA 94596 925-933-2300
Web: www.covellogroup.com
Cowin & Company Inc 301 Industrial Dr .... Birmingham AL 35219 205-945-1300
Web: www.cowin-co.com
CRA International Inc
200 Clarendon St Ste T-33 .... Boston MA 02116 617-425-3000 425-3132
NASDAQ: CRAI ■ *Web:* www.crai.com
Cradlerock Group LLC, The 65 High St 402 .... Stamford CT 06905 203-324-0088
Web: www.cradlerock.com
Crandall Engineering Ltd
1077 St. George Blvd .... Moncton NB E1E4C9 506-857-2777 857-2753
TF: 866-857-2777 ■ *Web:* www.crandallnb.com
Crane Metamarketing Ltd
831 Christopher Robin Rd .... Alpharetta GA 30005 770-642-2082
Web: www.cranesnest.com
Creative Advantage Inc 246 W End Ave Ste 9G .... New York NY 10023 212-475-9300
Web: www.creativeadvantage.com
Creative Assoc International Inc
5301 Wisconsin Ave NW Ste 700 .... Washington DC 20015 202-966-5804 363-4771
Web: www.creativeassociatesinternational.com
Creative Educational Concepts
1792 Alysheba Way Ste 100 .... Lexington KY 40509 859-260-1717
Web: www.ceconcepts.net
Creative Energy Options Inc
45 Country Pl Ln .... White Haven PA 18661 570-636-3858
Web: www.retreatpa.com
Creative Management Services LLC
3 Alpine Ct .... Chestnut Ridge NY 10977 845-639-8600
Web: www.mc-2online.com
Crescendo Consulting Group
48 Free St Ste 206 .... Portland ME 04101 207-774-2345
Web: www.crescendocg.com
CRG Consulting 301 Moodie Dr Ste 325 .... Ottawa ON K2H9C4 613-596-2910 820-4718
TF: 888-215-5147 ■ *Web:* www.thecrg.com
Critical Path Strategies Inc 33 Fm 474 .... Boerne TX 78006 830-249-1977
Web: criticalpathstrategies.com
Cross X Platform LLC
2570 Blvd Of The Generals Ste X .... Audubon PA 19403 610-539-2297
Web: www.crossxplatform.com
Crosscheck Compliance LLC
810 W Washington Blvd .... Chicago IL 60607 312-346-4600
Web: www.crosscheckcompliance.com
CSBA 1667 K St Nw Ste 900 .... Washington DC 20006 202-331-7990
Web: www.csbaonline.org
CSI Latina Financial Inc 2100 Coral Way Ste 706 .... Miami FL 33145 305-860-1616
Web: www.csilatina.com
Cso Insights 36 Tamal Vista Blvd .... Corte Madera CA 94925 415-924-3500
Web: www.csoinsights.com
CTI Consulting
9711 Washingtonian Blvd Ste 550 .... Gaithersburg MD 20878 301-528-8591
Web: www.countertech.com
CU America Financial Services
200 W 22nd St Ste 2800 .... Lombard IL 60148 630-620-5200
Web: www.cuamerica.com

Phone Fax

Culturalink Inc 922 E Wayne St .... South Bend IN 46617 574-233-3700
Curbstone Financial Management Corp
741 Chestnut St .... Manchester NH 03104 603-624-8462
TF: 800-370-2872 ■ *Web:* www.curbstonefinancial.com
Cyon Research Corp 8220 Stone Trail Dr .... Bethesda MD 20817 301-365-9085 365-4586
Web: www.cyonresearch.com
D & S Mktg Systems Inc 1205 38th St .... Brooklyn NY 11218 718-633-8383
Web: dsmarketing.com
D Hilton Assoc Inc 9450 Grogans Mill Rd .... Spring TX 77380 281-292-5088
TF: 800-367-0433 ■ *Web:* www.dhilton.com
D2M Inc 935 Benecia Ave .... Sunnyvale CA 94085 650-567-9995
Web: www.d2m-inc.com
DA Kreuter Assoc Inc 555 N Ln Ste 5020 .... Conshohocken PA 19428 610-834-1100 834-7722
Web: www.dakassociates.com
Daland Corp 9313 Eat 34th St N Ste 100 .... Wichita KS 67226 316-681-1081
Web: www.dalandcorp.com
DANSR Inc 818 W Evergreen Ave .... Chicago IL 60642 312-475-0464
Web: www.dansr.com
Danville Signal Processing Inc
38570 100th Ave .... Cannon Falls MN 55009 507-263-5854
TF: 877-230-5629 ■ *Web:* www.danvillesignal.com
Danya International Inc
8737 Colesville Rd Ste 1100 .... Silver Spring MD 20910 301-565-2142
Web: www.danya.com
Data Communication Solutions Inc
10125 Crosstown Cir Ste 235 .... Eden Prairie MN 55344 952-941-5466
Web: www.dcs-is-edi.com
Data Mktg Network Inc 701 Murfreesboro Pk .... Nashville TN 37210 615-313-7000
Web: dnicorp.com
Data Partners Inc 12857 Banyan Creek Dr .... Fort Myers FL 33908 239-267-8762
TF: 866-423-1818 ■ *Web:* www.data-partners.com
Data Stream Mobile Technologies
11531 Interchange Cir S .... Miramar FL 33025 954-271-1240
Web: www.dswltech.net
Data Technology Services
1300 N Berard St .... Breaux Bridge LA 70517 337-332-4347
Web: www.dtscom.com
Datanomics 991 US Hwy 22 W Ste 301 .... Bridgewater NJ 08807 908-707-8200
Web: www.datanomics.com
Datatime Consulting 109 Forrest Ave .... Narberth PA 19072 610-668-9640
Web: www.datatimeconsult.com
David Allen Co 407 Bryant Cir Ste H .... Ojai CA 93023 805-646-8432
Web: gettingthingsdone.com
David Kurlan & Assoc Inc 114 Turnpike Rd .... Westborough MA 01581 508-389-9350
Web: www.salesdevelopmentspecialists.com
David Powell Inc 3190 Clearview Way Ste 100 .... San Mateo CA 94402 650-357-6000
Web: www.davidpowell.com
Davies Consulting Inc
6935 Wisconsin Ave Ste 600 .... Chevy Chase MD 20815 301-652-4535 907-9355
TF: 800-811-8336 ■ *Web:* www.daviescon.com
Dawnbreaker Inc 3161 Union St .... North Chili NY 14514 585-594-0025
Web: www.dawnbreaker.com
Dawson Logistics Inc 431 N Vermilion .... Danville IL 61832 217-442-7036
Web: www.dawsonlogistics.com
Day Enterprises Inc 1912 S Ridge Ave .... Kannapolis NC 28083 704-933-2218
Web: www.carfare.com
DB Root & Company Inc
436 Seventh Ave Ste 2800 .... Pittsburgh PA 15219 412-227-2800
TF: 888-227-0913 ■ *Web:* www.dbroot.com
dbaDIRECT Inc 7310 Turfway Rd Ste 300 .... Florence KY 41042 859-283-2520
Web: www.dbadirect.com
dBrn Assoc Inc 189 Curtis Rd .... Hewlett Neck NY 11598 516-569-4557
Web: www.dbrnassociates.com
Dcc Lee Enterprises dba McDonald's
12276 San Jose Blvd Ste 601 .... Jacksonville FL 32223 904-288-6750
Web: www.mcdjax.com
DDF CPA Group 107A Edwards Rd .... Starke FL 32091 904-964-7404
Web: www.ddfcpa.com
Dean & Co 8065 Leesburg Pk Ste 500 .... Vienna VA 22182 703-506-3900 506-3905
Web: www.dean.com
Deca Aviation Engineering Ltd
7050 Telford Way .... Mississauga ON L5S1V7 905-405-1371
Web: deca-aviation.com
Decca Design 476 S 1st St .... San Jose CA 95113 408-947-1411
Web: www.decdesign.com
Dechert-Hampe & Co (DHC)
33332 Valle Rd .... San Juan Capistrano CA 92675 949-429-1999
Web: www.dechert-hampe.com
Deegit Inc 1111 Plz Dr Ste 370 .... Schaumburg IL 60173 847-330-1985
Web: www.deegit.com
DeFoe Corp 800 S Columbus Ave .... Mount Vernon NY 10550 914-699-7440
Web: www.defoecorp.com
DeHayes Consulting Group
2999 Douglas Blvd Ste 320 .... Roseville CA 95661 916-782-8321
Web: www.dcgcorp.com
Dell 8270 Willow Oaks Corporate Dr Ste 300 .... Fairfax VA 22031 703-289-8000
Web: www.dell.com
Deloitte Consulting LLP 25 Broadway 3rd Fl .... New York NY 10004 212-618-4000 850-1485*
**Fax Area Code: 866* ■ *Web:* www.deloitte.com
Deprince Race & Zollo Inc
250 Pk Ave S Ste 250 Ste 250 .... Winter Park FL 32789 407-420-9903 841-8778
Web: www.drz-inc.com
Desert Whale Jojoba Company Inc
2101 E Beverly Dr .... Tucson AZ 85719 520-882-4195
Web: www.desertwhale.com
DevTech Systems Inc
1700 N Moore St Ste 1720 .... Arlington VA 22209 703-312-6038 312-6039
Web: www.devtechsys.com
DG Capital Management Inc
800 Boylston St 16th Fl .... Boston MA 02199 857-453-6705
Web: www.dgcap.com
Dimension Capital Management
1221 Brickell Ave Ste 2450 .... Miami FL 33131 305-371-2776
Web: www.dimensioncapital.com

Company / Address	City	State	Zip	Phone	Fax
Direct Mktg Solutions Inc 8534 NE Alderwood Rd *Web:* www.resultsdm.com	Portland	OR	97220	503-281-1400	
Diversicare Leasing Corp 1621 Galleria Blvd *Web:* www.advocat.com	Brentwood	TN	37027	615-771-7575	
Diversified Lenders Inc 5607 S Ave Q *TF:* 800-288-3024 ■ *Web:* www.diversifiedlenders.com	Lubbock	TX	79412	800-288-3024	
DK Consultants LLC 1307 Carpers Farm Way *Web:* www.dkconsult.net	Vienna	VA	22182	703-438-3648	
DM Transportation Management Services Inc 740 Reading Ave *TF:* 888-399-0162 ■ *Web:* www.dmtrans.com	Boyertown	PA	19512	610-367-0162	369-0270
DME-Direct Inc 28486 Westinghouse Pl Ste 120 *TF:* 877-721-7701 ■ *Web:* www.dme-direct.com	Valencia	CA	91355	877-721-7701	
Dock Street Asset Management Inc 263 Glenville Rd *Web:* www.dockstreet.net	Greenwich	CT	06831	203-532-9470	
Dodge Communications Inc 11675 Rainwater Dr Ste 300 *Web:* www.dodgecommunications.com	Alpharetta	GA	30009	770-998-0500	
Doherty Enterprises Inc 7 Pearl Ct *Web:* www.dohertyinc.com	Allendale	NJ	07401	201-818-4669	
Domus Inc 123 Ave Of The Arts Ste 1980 *Web:* www.domusinc.com	Philadelphia	PA	19109	215-772-2805	
Douglas Wilson Cos Inc 450 B St Ste 1900 *Web:* www.douglaswilson.com	San Diego	CA	92101	619-641-1141	
Drew Wireless 459 Collindale Ave Nw *Web:* www.drewwireless.com	Grand Rapids	MI	49504	616-453-7200	
DrugLogic Inc 11490 Commerce Park Dr Ste 540 *Web:* www.druglogic.com	Reston	VA	20191	703-821-3200	
DWQ Assoc Ltd 38 N Ct St *Web:* www.dwqassociates.com	Providence	RI	02903	401-273-5220	
Eagle Financial Management Services LLC 400 Travis St Ste 518 *Web:* www.eaglefms.net	Shreveport	LA	71101	318-675-0826	
EagleOne Case Management Solutions Inc 80 Burr Ridge Pkwy Ste 121 *Web:* www.eagleonecms.com	Burr Ridge	IL	60527	630-655-0800	
EAI Inc Environmental Management Service 50 Prescott St *TF:* 800-886-3241 ■ *Web:* www.eaienviro.com	Jersey City	NJ	07304	201-395-0010	
EBA Engineering Consultants Ltd 14940-123 Ave *Web:* www.eba.ca	Edmonton	AB	T5V1B4	780-451-2130	454-5688
ECG Management Consultants Inc 1111 Third Ave Ste 2700 *TF:* 800-729-7635 ■ *Web:* www.ecgmc.com	Seattle	WA	98101	206-689-2200	689-2209
Echo Global Logistics Inc 600 W Chicago Ave Ste 725 *TF:* 800-354-7993 ■ *Web:* www.echo.com	Chicago	IL	60654	800-354-7993	
Eckler Ltd 110 Sheppard Ave E Ste 900 *Web:* www.eckler.ca	Toronto	ON	M2N7A3	416-429-3330	
Edge Biosystems Inc 201 Perry Pkwy Ste 5 *Fax Area Code: 800 ■ *Web:* www.edgebio.com	Gaithersburg	MD	20877	301-990-2685	326-2685*
Edgewood Management LLC 535 Madison Ave 15th Fl *Web:* www.edgewood.com	New York	NY	10022	212-652-9100	
EDS Manufacturing Inc 765 N Target Range Rd *Web:* www.edsmanufacturing.com	Nogales	AZ	85621	520-287-9711	
Effective Training Inc 14143 Farmington Rd *Web:* www.etinews.com	Livonia	MI	48154	734-744-5940	
eHDL Inc 3106 Commerce Pkwy *Web:* www.ehdl.com	Miramar	FL	33025	954-331-6500	
Ehlers & Assoc Inc 3060 Centre Pointe Dr *TF:* 800-552-1171 ■ *Web:* www.ehlers-inc.com	Roseville	MN	55113	651-697-8500	
ElectroChem Inc 400 W Cummings Pk *Web:* www.fuelcell.com	Woburn	MA	01801	781-938-5300	
Eltrex Industries 65 Sullivan St	Rochester	NY	14605	585-454-6100	
EMC Corp Documentum Div 6801 Koll Ctr Pkwy *Web:* www.emc.com	Pleasanton	CA	94566	925-600-6800	600-6850
Employees Only Inc 3256 University Dr Ste 25 *Web:* www.employeesonly.net	Auburn Hills	MI	48326	248-276-0950	
Encore Consumer Capital 111 Pine St Ste 1825 *Web:* www.encoreconsumercapital.com	San Francisco	CA	94111	415-296-9850	
Energy & Resource Solutions Inc 120 Water St Ste 350 *Web:* www.ers-inc.com	North Andover	MA	01845	978-521-2550	
Energy Automation Systems Inc 145 Anderson Ln *Web:* www.energyautomation.com	Hendersonville	TN	37075	615-822-7250	
EnerVision Inc 4170 Ashford Dunwoody Rd Ste 550 *TF:* 888-999-8840 ■ *Web:* www.enervision-inc.com	Atlanta	GA	30319	678-510-2900	
England Logistics Inc 1325 South 4700 West *TF:* 800-848-7810 ■ *Web:* www.englandlogistics.com	Salt Lake City	UT	84104	801-656-4500	
EnSolve Biosystems Inc 5805 Departure Dr Ste B *Web:* www.ensolve.com	Raleigh	NC	27616	919-954-6196	
Envision Group 990 W 190th St Ste 220 *Web:* www.envisiongroup.com	Torrance	CA	90502	310-523-2000	
EP Wealth Advisors Inc 21515 Hawthorne Blvd Ste 1200 *TF:* 800-272-2328 ■ *Web:* www.epwealth.com	Torrance	CA	90503	310-543-4559	
EQUIS Hospitality Management LLC 1034 S Brentwood Blvd Ste 2020 *Web:* www.equishospitality.com	St. Louis	MO	63144	314-932-3200	
Equity Communications LLC 1512 Grand Ave Ste 200 *Web:* www.equitycommunications.com	Santa Barbara	CA	93103	805-897-1880	
Eskridge & Assocs 595 Round Rock W Dr Ste 406	Round Rock	TX	78681	512-244-7023	
Essex Radez LLC 440 S LaSalle St Ste 1111 *Web:* www.essexradez.com	Chicago	IL	60605	312-212-1815	
eStrategy Solutions Inc 6601 Vaught Ranch Rd Ste 100 *Web:* www.esslearning.com	Austin	TX	78730	512-451-0100	
Ethis Communications Inc 44 Church St Ste 200 *Web:* www.ethiscommunications.com	White Plains	NY	10601	212-791-1440	
Eubel Brady & Suttman Asset Management Inc 10100 Innovation Dr Ste 410 *TF:* 800-391-1223 ■ *Web:* www.ebs-asset.com	Dayton	OH	45342	937-291-1223	
Evensky & Katz LLC 4000 Ponce de Leon Boulevard Ste 850 *TF:* 800-448-5435 ■ *Web:* www.evensky.com	Coral Gables	FL	33146	305-448-8882	
ExaDigm Inc 2871 Pullman St *TF:* 800-933-0064 ■ *Web:* www.exadigm.com	Santa Ana	CA	92705	949-486-0320	
Extra Mile Mktg Inc 12600 SE 38th St Ste 205 *TF:* 866-907-1753 ■ *Web:* www.extramilemarketing.com	Bellevue	WA	98006	425-746-1572	
Fagen Inc 501 W Hwy 212 PO Box 159 *Web:* www.fageninc.com	Granite Falls	MN	56241	320-564-3324	
Fairview Advisors LLC 3838 Tamiami Trl N Ste 416 *Web:* www.fairviewadvisors.com	Naples	FL	34103	239-213-1107	
Fairway Consulting Group 300 Merrick Rd Ste 404 *Web:* fcgsearch.com	Lynbrook	NY	11563	516-596-2800	
Far Hills Group LLC 1180 Ave Of The Americas 18th Fl *Web:* www.farhills.com	New York	NY	10036	212-840-7779	
Farrar Scientific LLC 30765 State Rt 7 *Web:* www.farrarscientific.com	Marietta	OH	45750	740-374-8300	
Faulk & Winkler LLC 6811 Jefferson Hwy *TF:* 800-927-6811	Baton Rouge	LA	70806	225-927-6811	
FCG Advisors LLC 1 Main St Ste 202 *Web:* www.fcgadvisors.com	Chatham	NJ	07928	973-635-7374	
FemmePharma Inc 37 W Ave 2nd Fl *Web:* www.femmepharma.com	Wayne	PA	19087	610-995-0801	
Ferrell Capital Management LLC 4 Greenwich Office Park *Web:* www.ferrellcapital.com	Greenwich	CT	06831	203-862-9500	
Financial Advisory Service Inc 4747 W 135th St *TF:* 888-700-9230 ■ *Web:* www.faskc.com	Leawood	KS	66224	913-239-2300	
Financial Management Professionals Inc 6034 W Courtyard Dr Ste 380 *Web:* www.fmprofessionals.com	Austin	TX	78730	512-329-5174	
Fine Furniture Design & Mktg LLC 1107 N Main St *Web:* www.ffdm.com	High Point	NC	27262	336-883-9918	
Fingerpaint Mktg Inc 395 Broadway *Web:* fingerpaintmarketing.com	Saratoga Springs	NY	12866	518-693-6960	
FinSer Corp 1 Alamo Ctr 106 S St Mary'S St Ste 600 *Web:* www.finser.com	San Antonio	TX	78205	210-224-5492	
First Clinical Research LLC 2249 Sutter St *Web:* www.firstclinical.com	San Francisco	CA	94115	650-465-0119	
First Command Financial Services Inc 1 FirstComm Plz *TF:* 800-443-2104 ■ *Web:* www.firstcommand.com	Fort Worth	TX	76109	817-731-8621	
First Financial Equity Corp 7373 N Scottsdale Rd Ste D-120 *Web:* www.ffec.com	Scottsdale	AZ	85253	480-951-0079	
First Manhattan Consulting Group 90 Pk Ave 18th Fl *Web:* www.fmcg.com	New York	NY	10016	212-557-0500	338-9296
First Niagara RISK Management 1215 Manor Dr *TF:* 800-421-0004 ■ *Web:* www.firstniagara.com	Mechanicsburg	PA	17055	717-795-8666	
Fisher & Arnold Inc 9180 Crestwyn Hills Dr *TF:* 888-583-9724 ■ *Web:* www.fisherarnold.com	Memphis	TN	38125	901-748-1811	
Fisher International Inc 50 Water St *Web:* www.fisheri.com	Norwalk	CT	06854	203-854-5390	854-5070
Flex-Pay Business Services Inc 723 Coliseum Dr Ste 200 *TF:* 800-457-2143 ■ *Web:* www.flex-pay.com	Winston-Salem	NC	27106	336-773-0128	
FlexEnergy Inc 30 New Hampshire Ave *Web:* www.flexenergy.com	Portsmouth	NH	03801	603-430-7000	
Fluor Corp 6700 Las Colinas Blvd *TF:* 800-405-6637 ■ *Web:* www.fluor.com	Irving	TX	75039	469-398-7000	398-7255
FMI Corp 5171 Glenwood Ave Ste 200 *TF General:* 800-669-1364 ■ *Web:* www.fminet.com	Raleigh	NC	27612	919-787-8400	785-9320
Food Management Associates Inc 22349 La Palma Ave Ste 115 *Web:* www.foodmgt.com	Yorba Linda	CA	92887	714-694-2828	
Foodbuy LLC 1105 Lakewood Pkwy *Web:* www.foodbuy.com	Alpharetta	GA	30009	678-256-8000	
Franchoice Inc 7500 Flying Cloud Dr *TF:* 877-396-4238 ■ *Web:* www.franchoice.com	Eden Prairie	MN	55344	952-345-8400	
Frazier & Deeter LLC 600 Peachtree St Ste 1900 *Web:* www.frazierdeeter.com	Atlanta	GA	30308	404-253-7500	
Front Runner Consulting LLC 6850 O'Bannon Bluff *TF:* 877-328-3360 ■ *Web:* www.frontrunnerconsulting.com	Loveland	OH	45140	513-697-6850	
FST Logistics Inc 2040 Atlas St *Web:* www.fstlogistics.com	Columbus	OH	43228	614-529-7900	
Fulcrum International Ltd 280 Railroad Ave *Web:* www.fulcrum-intl.com	Greenwich	CT	06830	203-869-8181	
Fulenwider Enterprises Inc 104 Mull St *Web:* www.fulenwider.net	Morganton	NC	28655	828-437-8000	

Company / Address	City	State	Zip	Phone	Fax
Fusion Solutions Inc 16901 N Dallas Pkwy Ste 114 *TF:* 888-817-1951 ■ *Web:* www.fusionsolutionsinc.com	Dallas	TX	75001	972-764-1708	
GA Repple & Co 101 Normandy Rd *Web:* www.garepple.com	Casselberry	FL	32707	407-339-9090	
Galtere Ltd 515 Madison Ave 35th Fl *Web:* www.galtere.com	New York	NY	10022	212-598-1837	
Garcia & Assoc Inc 1 Saunders Ave *Web:* www.garciaandassociates.com	San Anselmo	CA	94960	415-458-5803	
Gargiulo Inc 15000 Old 41 N *Web:* www.gargiulo.com	Naples	FL	34110	239-597-3131	
Garnett & Helfrich Capital 1200 Park Pl Ste 330 *Web:* www.garnetthelfrich.com	San Mateo	CA	94403	650-234-4200	
Gateway Communications Services 220 Log Canoe Cir *Web:* www.gatewaycsi.com	Stevensville	MD	21666	410-670-4399	
Gavin de Becker & Assoc 11684 Ventura Blvd Ste 440 *Web:* www.gavindebecker.com	Studio City	CA	91604	818-760-4213	506-0426
Genesys Venture Inc 4-1250 Waverley St *Web:* www.genesysventure.com	Winnipeg	MB	R3T6C6	204-487-2328	
Geneva Capital LLC 522 Broadway St Ste 4 *TF:* 800-408-9352 ■ *Web:* www.gogc.com	Alexandria	MN	56308	800-408-9352	
Geneva Venture Group 101 California St Ste 2710 *Web:* www.genevagroup.com	San Francisco	CA	94111	415-433-4646	
Genex Services Inc 440 E Swedesford Rd Ste 1000 *TF:* 888-464-3639 ■ *Web:* www.genexservices.com	Wayne	PA	19087	610-964-5100	964-1919
Geocom Inc 366 Madison Ave 10th Fl *Web:* www.geocom-inc.com	New York	NY	10017	212-949-0712	
GEOSYS Inc 3030 Harbor Ln *Web:* www.geosys.com	Plymouth	MN	55447	763-557-0092	
Gerken Capital Associates 110 Tiburon Blvd Ste 5 *Web:* gerkencapital.com	Mill Valley	CA	94941	415-383-1464	
GESD Capital Partners 50 Francisco St Ste 235 *Web:* www.gesd.net	San Francisco	CA	94133	415-477-8200	
Ginac Group Inc, The 8834 N Capital of Texas Hwy Ste 200	Austin	TX	78759	512-943-6801	
Global Change Assoc Inc 2576 Broadway *Web:* www.global-change.com	New York	NY	10025	212-316-0223	
Global Equity Capital LLC 6260 Lookout Rd *Web:* www.globalequitycap.com	Boulder	CO	80301	303-531-1000	
Global Experiences Inc 209 W St *Web:* www.globalexperiences.com	Annapolis	MD	21401	410-267-7306	
Global Inventures Inc 2400 Camino Ramon Bishop Ranch 6 Ste 375 *Web:* www.inventures.com	San Ramon	CA	94583	925-275-6690	
Global Mktg Group Worldwide LLC 704 Executive Blvd Ste I *Web:* www.gmgww.com	Valley Cottage	NJ	10989	201-475-7755	
Global Public Affairs Inc 50 O'Connor St Ste 901 *Web:* globalpublicaffairs.ca	Ottawa	ON	K1P6L2	613-782-2336	
Global SATCOM Technology Inc 9141 Arbuckle Dr *Web:* www.globalsatcom.com	Gaithersburg	MD	20877	301-963-0088	
Global Stock Trends Corp 1 Park Place 621 NW 53rd St Ste 240 *Web:* www.globalstocktrends.com	Boca Raton	FL	33487	401-885-4606	
Global Strategy Group LLC 895 Broadway 5th Fl *Web:* www.globalstrategygroup.com	New York	NY	10003	212-260-8813	
Global Ventures Inc 2106 145th Ave SE *Web:* www.globalventuresinc.com	Bellevue	WA	98007	206-292-1428	
GlobalPhone Corp 137 N Washington St *Web:* www.gphone.com	Falls Church	VA	22046	703-533-2122	
Globe Mktg Services Inc 133 NW 122nd St *Web:* globeontheweb.com	Oklahoma City	OK	73114	405-755-8282	
Globe Tax Services Inc 90 Broad St 16th Fl *Web:* www.globetax.com	New York	NY	10004	212-747-9100	
Goldin Associates LLC 350 Fifth Ave The Empire State Bldg *Web:* www.goldinassociates.com	New York	NY	10118	212-593-2255	
Goodman Networks Inc 6400 International Ste 1000 *Web:* www.goodmannetworks.com	Plano	TX	75093	972-406-9692	406-9291
Gordon L Seaman Inc 29 Old Dock Rd *Web:* www.gordonlseaman.com	Yaphank	NY	11980	631-567-8000	
Gradient Corp 20 University Rd *Web:* www.gradientcorp.com	Cambridge	MA	02138	617-395-5000	395-5001
Grande Communications Networks LLC 401 Carlson Cir *Web:* mygrande.com	San Marcos	TX	78666	512-878-4000	
Grant Thornton LLP 175 W Jackson Blvd 20th Fl *Web:* www.grantthornton.com	Chicago	IL	60604	312-856-0200	602-8099
Great Plains Tribal Chairmen's Health Board 1770 Rand Rd *TF:* 800-745-3466 ■ *Web:* www.aatchb.org	Rapid City	SD	57702	605-721-1922	
Great Point Partners LLC 165 Mason St 3rd Fl *Web:* www.greatpointpartnersllc.com	Greenwich	CT	06830	203-971-3300	
Greater Ny Dental Meeting 518 Fifth Ave Fl 3 *TF:* 844-797-7469 ■ *Web:* www.gnydm.com	New York	NY	10036	212-398-6922	
Greek Peak Mountain Resort 2000 NYS Rt 392 *Web:* www.greekpeak.net	Cortland	NY	13045	607-835-6300	
Greenwich Assoc LLC 6 High Ridge Pk *TF:* 800-704-1027 ■ *Web:* www.greenwich.com	Stamford	CT	06905	203-629-1200	629-1229
GREYHAWK North America LLC 260 Crossways Park Dr *Web:* www.greyhawk.com	Woodbury	NY	11797	516-921-1900	
Gries Financial LLC 1801 E Ninth St Ste 1600 *Web:* www.gries.com	Cleveland	OH	44114	216-861-1148	
Groton Partners LLC 640 Fifth Ave Ste 1700 *Web:* www.grotonpartners.com	New York	NY	10019	212-430-1800	
Groupe Sante Sedna Inc 1010 Sherbrooke W Ste 2405 *Web:* www.groupesedna.ca	Montreal	QC	H3A2R7	514-844-8760	
GrowthForce LLC 800 Rockmead Ste 200 *Web:* growthforce.com	Kingwood	TX	77339	281-358-2007	
Guttman Development Strategies Inc 400 Valley Rd Ste 103 *Web:* www.guttmandev.com	Mt. Arlington	NJ	07856	973-770-7177	
GW & Wade LLC 93 Worcester St *Web:* www.gwwade.com	Wellesley	MA	02481	781-239-1188	
Haitian American Community Development 181 NE 82 St Ste 2 *Web:* www.haitianamericancdc.org	Miami	FL	33138	305-759-2542	
Harrison Scott Publications Inc 5 Marine View Plz Ste 301 *Web:* www.hspnews.com	Hoboken	NJ	07030	201-659-1700	
Hart Hotels Inc 617 Dingens St *Web:* www.harthotels.com	Buffalo	NY	14206	716-893-6551	
Hatch Ltd 2800 Speakman Dr *Web:* www.hatch.com	Mississauga	ON	L5K2R7	905-855-7600	855-8270
Hay Group Inc 1650 Arch St Ste 2300 *TF:* 800-716-4429 ■ *Web:* www.haygroup.com	Philadelphia	PA	19107	215-861-2000	861-2111
Hazmat Environmental Group Inc 60 Commerce Dr *Web:* www.hazmatinc.com	Buffalo	NY	14218	716-827-7200	827-7217
Health Dimensions Group 4400 Baker Rd Ste 100 *Web:* www.healthdimensionsgroup.com	Minneapolis	MN	55343	763-537-5700	
Health Integrated Inc 10008 N Dale Mabry Hwy *Web:* www.healthintegrated.com	Tampa	FL	33618	813-388-4000	
Health Management Services Inc 9100 Southwest Fwy Ste 114 *Web:* www.hmssleep.com	Houston	TX	77074	713-541-2727	
Healthcare Analytics 125-310 Village Blvd	Princeton	NJ	08540	609-452-2488	452-2668
Healthcasts Meded 55 E Ninth St Apt 7I	New York	NY	10003	212-533-1111	
Healthforce Partners Inc 18323 Bothell Everett Hwy *TF:* 877-437-2497 ■ *Web:* www.healthforcepartners.com	Bothell	WA	98012	425-806-5700	806-5701
HealthInsight Inc 756 E Winchester St Ste 200 *Web:* www.healthinsight.org	Salt Lake City	UT	84107	801-892-0155	
Healthy Companies International Inc 2101 Wilson Blvd Ste 1002 *Web:* healthycompanies.com	Arlington	VA	22201	703-351-9901	
Hefren - Tillotson Inc 308 Seventh Ave *Web:* www.hefren.com	Pittsburgh	PA	15222	412-434-0990	
Helix Enterprises Inc 4300 Forbes Blvd Ste 140 *Web:* helixenterprises.com	Lanham	MD	20706	301-429-0880	
HELIX Environmental Planning Inc 7578 El Cajon Blvd Ste 200 *Web:* www.helixepi.com	La Mesa	CA	91942	619-462-1515	
Herbal Magic Inc 1867 Yonge St Ste 700 *Web:* www.herbalmagic.ca	Toronto	ON	M4S1Y5	416-487-7009	
Heritage Financial Consultants LLC 307 International Cir Ste 390 *Web:* heritageconsultants.com	Hunt Valley	MD	21030	410-785-0033	
Herman Weissker Inc 1645 Brown Ave *Web:* www.hermanweissker.com	Riverside	CA	92509	951-826-8800	
Hicaps Inc 600 N Regional Rd *Web:* www.hicaps.com	Greensboro	NC	27409	336-665-1234	
High Ridge Partners 140 S Dearborn Ste 420 *Web:* www.high-ridge.com	Chicago	IL	60603	312-456-5636	
HighVista Strategies LLC 200 Clarendon St John Hancock Tower 50th Fl *Web:* www.highvistastrategies.com	Boston	MA	02116	617-406-6500	
Homrich & Berg Inc 3060 Peachtree Rd Ste 830 *Web:* www.homrichberg.com	Atlanta	GA	30305	404-264-1400	
Horan Capital Management LLC 230 Schilling Cir Ste 234 *Web:* www.horancm.com	Hunt Valley	MD	21031	410-494-4380	
Human Resource Development Press Inc 22 Amherst Rd *TF:* 800-822-2801 ■ *Web:* www.hrdpressonline.com	Amherst	MA	01002	413-253-3488	
Huntington Hotel Group LLC 105 Decker Ct Ste 500 *Web:* www.huntingtonhotelgroup.com	Irving	TX	75062	972-510-1200	
I-Behavior Inc 2051 Dogwood St Ste 220 *Web:* www.i-behavior.com	Louisville	CO	80027	303-228-5000	
IBCC Industries Inc 3200 S Third St *Web:* www.ibccind.com	Milwaukee	WI	53207	414-486-5460	
IBT Enterprises LLC 1770 Indian Trail Rd Ste 300 *TF:* 877-242-8428 ■ *Web:* www.ibtenterprises.com	Norcross	GA	30093	770-381-2023	381-2123
ICF International Inc 9300 Lee Hwy *NASDAQ: ICFI* ■ *Web:* www.icfi.com	Fairfax	VA	22031	703-934-3000	934-3740
Idaho Innovation Center Inc 2300 N Yellowstone Hwy Ste 100 *Web:* www.iictr.com	Idaho Falls	ID	83401	208-523-1026	
Ideal Innovations Inc 950 N Glebe Rd Ste 800 *Web:* www.idealinnovations.com	Arlington	VA	22203	703-528-9101	528-1913
In-Store Broadcasting Network LLC 175 S Main St Ste 220 *Web:* instoreaudionetwork.com	Salt Lake City	UT	84111	801-596-9344	
Inca Engineers Inc 400 112th Ave NE Ste 400 *TF:* 800-825-4622	Bellevue	WA	98004	425-635-1000	635-1150

Company / Address	City	State	ZIP	Phone	Fax
Independent Equipment Co 2471 McMullen Booth Rd Ste 309	Clearwater	FL	33759	727-796-7733	
Web: www.iecvalue.com					
Independents Service Co 2710 Market St.	Hannibal	MO	63401	573-221-4615	
Web: www.isco.net					
Indiana Health Information Exchange Inc 846 N Senate Ave Ste 300	Indianapolis	IN	46202	317-644-1750	
Web: www.ihie.org					
Infodata Corp 181 Waukegan Rd Ste 300	Northfield	IL	60093	847-486-0000	386-7166
Web: www.infodatacorp.com					
Informa Research Services Inc 26565 Agoura Rd Ste 300	Calabasas	CA	91302	818-880-8877	
Web: informaresearchservices.com					
Initiative for a Competitive Inner City 200 High St Fl 3	Boston	MA	02110	617-292-2363	
Web: www.icic.org					
Innovation Capital LLC 222 N Sepulveda Blvd Ste 1300	El Segundo	CA	90245	310-335-9333	
Web: www.innovation-capital.com					
Innovative Resources Consultant Group Inc 1 Pk Plz Ste 600	Irvine	CA	92614	949-252-0590	252-0592
Web: www.ircginc.com					
Insight Environmental Consultants Inc 5500 Ming Ave Ste 360	Bakersfield	CA	93309	661-282-2200	
Web: www.insenv.com					
Integrated Decisions & Systems Inc 8500 Normandale Lk Blvd Ste 1200	Minneapolis	MN	55437	952-698-4200	698-4299
Web: www.ideas.com					
Integrated Health Management Services LLC 2632 E Thomas Rd Ste 103	Phoenix	AZ	85016	602-522-3240	
Web: www.ihmsllc.com					
Integrated Mktg Services Inc 279 Wall St Research Pk	Princeton	NJ	08540	609-683-9055	
Web: www.imsworld.com					
Integrated Title Insurance Services LLC 1092 E S Union Ave	Midvale	UT	84047	801-307-0160	
Web: www.itstitle.com					
Integrity Interactive Corp 51 Sawyer Rd Ste 510	Waltham	MA	02453	781-891-9700	
Intellex Consulting Services Inc 4 Apple Row	Kennett Square	PA	19348	610-388-3939	
Web: www.intellexinc.com					
Intellimed International Corp 1825 E Northern Ave Ste 175	Phoenix	AZ	85020	602-230-0333	
Web: www.intellimed.com					
Interaction Assoc 70 Fargo St Ste 908	Boston	MA	02210	617-234-2700	234-2727
TF: 800-347-8352 ■ *Web:* www.interactionassociates.com					
Interactive Motion Technologies Inc 80 Coolidge Hill Rd	Watertown	MA	02472	617-926-4800	
Web: www.interactive-motion.com					
Investment Management & Consulting Group 97A Exchange St	Portland	ME	04101	207-774-6552	
Web: www.imcgrp.com					
Investor Group Services LLC 855 Boylston St 10th Fl	Boston	MA	02116	617-371-4000	
Web: www.igsboston.com					
IQ BackOffice LLC 2121 Rosecrans Ave Ste 3350	El Segundo	CA	90245	310-322-2311	
Web: www.iqbackoffice.com					
Iridian Asset Management LLC 276 Post Rd W	Westport	CT	06880	203-341-7800	
Web: www.iridian.com					
Irvine Technology Corp 201 E Sandpointe Ave Ste 300	Santa Ana	CA	92707	866-322-4482	434-8869*
**Fax Area Code:* 714 ■ *TF:* 866-322-4482 ■ *Web:* www.irvinetechcorp.com					
IVG Energy Ltd 20 E Greenway Pl Ste 400	Houston	TX	77046	713-554-3700	
Web: www.ivgenergy.com					
iWay Software 2 Penn Plz	New York	NY	10121	212-736-4433	967-6406
TF: 800-736-6130 ■ *Web:* www.informationbuilders.com					
iXP Corp Princeton Forrestal Village 103 Main St	Princeton	NJ	08540	609-759-5100	
Web: www.ixpcorp.com					
Jadoo Power Systems Inc 181 Blue Ravine Rd Ste 120	Folsom	CA	95630	916-608-9044	
Web: www.jadoopower.com					
Janson Media Inc 118 Main St	Tappan	NJ	10983	845-359-8488	
Web: www.janson.com					
JANUS Research Group Inc 600 Ponder Pl Dr	Evans	GA	30809	706-364-9100	
Web: janusresearch.com					
Jay Cashman Inc 549 S St	Quincy	MA	02269	617-890-0600	
Web: www.jaycashman.com					
JB&A Inc 5203 Leesburg Pk Ste 1401	Falls Church	VA	22041	703-399-2850	
Web: www.jb-a-inc.com					
JBCStyle Inc 108 W 39th St 7th Fl	New York	NY	10018	212-355-3197	
Web: www.jbcstyle.com					
Jeff Zell Consultants Inc 1031 Fourth Ave	Coraopolis	PA	15108	412-262-2022	
Web: www.jeffzell.com					
Jeffrey Slocum & Assoc Inc 43 Main St S E Ste 148	Minneapolis	MN	55414	612-338-7020	
Web: www.jslocum.com					
Jet Support Services Inc 180 N Stetson 29th Fl	Chicago	IL	60601	312-644-4444	
Web: www.jetsupport.com					
JH Technology Inc 5107 Lena Rd Unit 111	Bradenton	FL	34211	941-758-7710	
TF: 800-808-0300 ■ *Web:* www.jhtechnology.com					
JJDS Environmental Inc 40 Woodview Dr	Doylestown	PA	18901	267-880-2325	
Web: www.jjdsenvironmental.com					
JM Search & Company Inc 1045 First Ave Ste 110	King Of Prussia	PA	19406	610-964-0200	
Web: www.jmsearch.com					
John Snow Inc 44 Farnsworth St	Boston	MA	02210	617-482-9485	482-0617
Web: www.jsi.com					
Johnson Rice & Company LLC 639 Loyola Ave Ste 2775	New Orleans	LA	70113	504-525-3767	
Web: www.jrco.com					
Julie Morgenstern Enterprises LLC 850 Seventh Ave	New York	NY	10019	212-586-8084	
Web: www.juliemorgenstern.com					
Kaiser Assoc 1615 L St NW 13th Fl	Washington	DC	20036	202-454-2000	
Web: www.kaiserassociates.com					
KAMedData.com Inc 4400 Bayou Blvd Ste 12	Pensacola	FL	32503	850-477-2475	
Web: www.kameddata.com					
Kamsky Assoc Inc 563 Park Ave	New York	NY	10065	212-317-1116	
Web: www.kamsky.com					
Kaya Assoc Inc 101 Quality Cir Ste 120	Huntsville	AL	35806	256-382-8084	382-8089
Web: www.kayacorp.com					
KCB Management 117 E Colorado Blvd Ste 400	Pasadena	CA	91105	626-356-0944	
Web: www.kcbm.com					
Keel Point Advisors LLC 8065 Leesburg Pk Ste 300	Vienna	VA	22182	703-807-2020	
Web: www.keelpoint.com					
Ken Blanchard Companies Inc, The 125 State Pl	Escondido	CA	92029	760-839-8070	
Web: www.kenblanchard.com					
Kepner-Tregoe Inc PO Box 704	Princeton	NJ	08542	609-921-2806	497-0130
TF: 800-537-6378 ■ *Web:* www.kepner-tregoe.com					
Kessler & Assoc Inc 31800 NW Hwy	Farmington Hills	MI	48334	248-855-4224	855-4405
Web: www.kesslercpa.com					
Keystone Equities Group, The 1003 B Egypt Rd	Oaks	PA	19456	610-415-6300	
TF: 800-715-9905 ■ *Web:* www.keystoneequities.com					
Keystone Fruit Marketing Inc 820 Park Row 636 PO Box 189	Salinas	PA	93901	717-597-2112	597-4096
Web: www.keystonefruit.com					
Kimley-Horn & Associates Inc 3001 Weston Pkwy	Cary	NC	27513	919-677-2000	
Web: www.kimley-horn.com					
King Chapman & Broussard Consulting Group Inc 3355 W Albama St Ste 1255	Houston	TX	77098	713-223-7233	
Web: www.kcbcg.com					
Kinsight LLC 600 University Park Pl Ste 501	Birmingham	AL	35209	205-871-3334	
TF: 866-871-3334 ■ *Web:* www.kinsight.com					
Kipp Foundation 135 Main St Ste 1700	San Francisco	CA	94105	415-399-1556	
TF: 866-345-5477 ■ *Web:* www.kipp.org					
Kline & Company Inc 35 Waterview Blvd Ste 305	Parsippany	NJ	07424	973-435-6262	435-6291
TF: 800-290-5214 ■ *Web:* www.klinegroup.com					
Kmea 964 Fifth Ave	San Diego	CA	92101	619-342-7377	
Web: www.kmea.net					
Knight Electronics Inc 10557 Metric Dr	Dallas	TX	75243	214-340-0265	
TF: 800-323-2439 ■ *Web:* www.orionfans.com					
Knight Facilities Management Inc 5360 Hampton Pl	Saginaw	MI	48604	989-793-8820	399-9096
Web: www.knightfm.com					
Knowledge Anywhere Inc 3015 112th Ave NE Ste 210	Bellevue	WA	98004	425-454-4454	
Web: www.knowledgeanywhere.com					
KnowledgeBank Inc 1481 Chain Bridge Rd Ste 201	Mclean	VA	22101	703-448-8070	
Web: www.knowledgebank.us.com					
Kozeny-Wagner Inc 951 W Outer Rd	Arnold	MO	63010	636-296-2012	
Web: www.kozenywagner.com					
KPMG LLP 333 Base St Ste 4600	Toronto	ON	M5H2S5	416-777-8500	777-8818
Web: www.kpmg.com					
KPMG LLP US 3 Chestnut Ridge Rd	Montvale	NJ	07645	201-307-7000	307-7575
Web: www.kpmg.com					
Kraus Manning Inc 7233 Lk Ellenor Dr	Orlando	FL	32809	407-251-0085	
Web: www.kraus-manning.com					
Kroll Inc 600 Third Ave	New York	NY	10016	212-593-1000	593-2631
TF: 800-675-3772 ■ *Web:* www.kroll.com					
Krueger-Gilbert Health Physics Inc 1118 Baldwin Mll Rd PO Box 410	Jarrettsville	MD	21084	410-692-9806	
Web: kruegergilbert.com					
Kurt Salmon Assoc Inc 1355 Peachtree St NE Ste 900	Atlanta	GA	30309	404-892-0321	898-9590
Web: www.kurtsalmon.com					
L E Peabody & Assoc Inc 1501 Duke St Ste 200	Alexandria	VA	22314	703-836-0100	836-0285
Web: www.lepeabody.com					
La Jolla Sports Club Inc 7825 Fay Ave	La Jolla	CA	92037	858-456-2595	
Web: www.lajollasportsclub.com					
Lachman Consultant Services Inc 1600 Stewart Ave Ste 604	Westbury	NY	11590	516-222-6222	
Web: www.lachmanconsultants.com					
Lamont Engineers 548 Main St	Cobleskill	NY	12043	518-234-4028	234-4613
TF: 800-882-9721 ■ *Web:* www.lamontengineers.com					
Lang Asset Management Inc 171 Village Pkwy NE Bldg 8A	Marietta	GA	30067	404-256-4100	256-1473
Web: www.langasset.com					
Larrabee Ventures Inc 15165 Ventura Blvd Ste 450	Sherman Oaks	CA	91403	818-789-6020	
Web: www.larrabeeventures.com					
Latigo Partners LP 450 Park Ave Ste1200	New York	NY	10022	212-754-1610	
Web: www.latigopartners.com					
Lavista Assoc Inc 3105 Northwoods Pl	Norcross	GA	30071	770-448-6400	
Web: www.lavista.com					
Leehar Distributors Inc 701 Emerson Rd Ste 301	Creve Coeur	MO	63141	314-652-3121	
Web: www.ldirx.com					
Legacy Capital LLC 433 Metairie Rd Ste 405	Metairie	LA	70005	504-837-3450	
Web: legacycapital.com					
Legacy Financial Partners LLC 1912 21st Ave S	Nashville	TN	37212	615-292-5351	
Web: www.legacy-fp.com					
Legend Group Inc, The 4600 E Park Dr Ste 300	Palm Beach Gardens	FL	33410	561-694-0110	
Web: www.legendgroup.com					
LEK Consulting 28 State St 16th Fl	Boston	MA	02109	617-951-9500	951-9392
TF: 800-929-4535 ■ *Web:* www.lek.com					
Leopard Communications Inc 555 17th St Ste 300	Denver	CO	80202	303-527-2900	530-3480
Web: www.leopard.com					

				Phone	Fax
Leuthold Weeden Capital Management LLC 33 S Sixth St Ste 4600 *Web:* www.leutholdfunds.com	Minneapolis	MN	55402	612-332-9141	
Lewin Group 3130 Fairview Pk Dr Ste 800 *TF:* 877-227-5042 ■ *Web:* www.lewin.com	Falls Church	VA	22042	703-269-5500	269-5501
Lewtan Technologies Inc 410 Totten Pond Rd 4th Fl *Web:* www.lewtan.com	Waltham	MA	02451	781-895-9800	890-3684
Lexipol LLC 6B Liberty Ste 200 *Web:* www.lexipol.com	Aliso Viejo	CA	92656	949-484-4444	
LifePlans Inc 51 Sawyer Rd Ste 340 *Web:* www.lifeplansinc.com	Waltham	MA	02453	781-893-7600	647-3552
LifeSafe Services LLC 5971 Powers Ave Ste 108 *Web:* www.lifesafeservices.com	Jacksonville	FL	32217	904-730-4800	
Limited Management 1230 Pottstown Pike Ste 6 *Web:* www.ltdmgmt.com	Glenmoore	PA	19343	610-715-3710	458-8039
Line Systems Inc 1645 W Chester Pk *Web:* www.linesystems.com	West Chester	PA	19382	610-355-9700	
Liquidhub Inc 500 E Swedesford Rd Ste 300 *Web:* www.liquidhub.com	Wayne	PA	19087	484-654-1400	654-1401
Liquidia Technologies Inc 419 Davis Dr Ste 100 *Web:* www.liquidia.com	Morrisville	NC	27560	919-328-4400	
Livingstone Partners LLC 443 N Clark Ste 200 *Web:* www.livingstonepartners.com	Chicago	IL	60654	312-670-5900	
Lochridge Group 420 Boylston St	Boston	MA	02116	617-267-5959	
Lockwood International Inc 10203 Wallisville Rd *Web:* www.lockwoodint.com	Houston	TX	77013	713-675-8186	675-2733
Loftus Engineering Inc 233 S Mccrea St Ste 700 *Web:* www.applied-e-s.com	Indianapolis	IN	46225	317-352-5822	
Logical Automation Inc 1011 Alcon St *Web:* www.logicalautomation.com	Pittsburgh	PA	15220	412-444-0400	
Logile Inc 1333 Corporate Dr Ste 310 *Web:* www.logile.com	Irving	TX	75038	972-550-6000	
Long International 10029 Whistling Elk Dr *Web:* www.long-intl.com	Littleton	CO	80127	303-972-2443	972-6980
Loring Ward International Ltd 3055 Olin Ave Ste 2000 *Web:* www.loringward.com	San Jose	CA	95128	408-260-3100	
Lucas Engineering & Management Services Inc 1201 Jadwin Ave Ste 102 *Web:* www.lucasinc.com	Richland	WA	99352	509-942-1080	
Lynda.com Inc 6410 Via Real *TF:* 888-335-9632 ■ *Web:* www.lynda.com	Carpinteria	CA	93013	805-477-3900	
M Floyd John & Assoc Inc (JMFA) 125 N Burnett Dr **Fax Area Code:* 281 ■ *TF:* 800-809-2307 ■ *Web:* www.jmfa.com	Baytown	TX	77520	800-809-2307	424-8864*
M&N Trading LLC 952 W Lake St *Web:* www.mntrading.com	Chicago	IL	60607	312-568-5000	568-5010
Mac Pizza Management Inc 3104 Texas Ave S *Web:* www.macpizzamgmt.com	College Station	TX	77845	979-695-9912	
Macadam Capital Partners 4800 SW Macadam Ave Ste 311 *Web:* www.macadamcapital.com	Portland	OR	97239	503-225-0889	
Mahoney Assoc Inc 2455 E Sunrise Blvd Ste 300 *Web:* www.mahoneyandassociates.com	Fort Lauderdale	FL	33304	954-564-4300	
Maine Pointe LLC 470 Atlantic Ave 4th Fl *Web:* www.mainepointe.com	Boston	MA	02210	617-273-8450	
Manchester Capital Management LLC 3657 Main St PO Box 416 *Web:* www.mcmllc.com	Manchester	VT	05254	802-362-4410	
Manex Resource Group Inc 1100 - 1199 W Hastings St *TF:* 888-456-1112 ■ *Web:* www.manexresourcegroup.com	Vancouver	BC	V6E3T5	604-684-9384	
Mariner Wealth Advisors 1 Giralda Farms Ste 130 *TF:* 800-364-2468	Madison	NJ	07940	800-364-2468	
Market Metrics Inc 53 State St Ste 6 *Web:* www.marketmetrics.com	Boston	MA	02109	617-376-0550	
Marketing Werks Inc 130 E Randolph St *Web:* www.marketingwerks.com	Chicago	IL	60601	312-228-0800	228-0801
Mars & Co 124 Mason St *Web:* www.marsandco.com	Greenwich	CT	06830	203-629-9292	629-9432
Marsh Berry & Company Inc 4420 Sherwin Rd *TF:* 800-426-2774 ■ *Web:* www.marshberry.com	Willoughby	OH	44094	440-354-3230	
Marshall & Stevens Inc 355 S Grand Ave Ste 1750 *TF:* 800-950-9588 ■ *Web:* www.marshall-stevens.com	Los Angeles	CA	90071	213-612-8000	612-8010
Marshall Communications Corp 20098 Ashbrook Pl Ste 260 *Web:* www.marshallcomm.com	Ashburn	VA	20147	571-223-2010	
Marvin F Poer & Company Inc 12700 Hillcrest Rd Ste 125 *Web:* www.mfpoer.com	Dallas	TX	75230	972-770-1100	
Maryland Health Enterprises Inc 3300 N Ridge Rd Ste 390 *Web:* www.lorienhealth.com	Ellicott City	MD	21043	410-750-7500	
MAXIMUS Inc 11419 Sunset Hills Rd *NYSE: MMS* ■ *TF:* 800-629-4687 ■ *Web:* www.maximus.com	Reston	VA	20190	703-251-8500	251-8240
Mazars Harel Drouin LLP 215 Saint Jacques Bureau 1200 *Web:* www.mazars.ca	Montreal	QC	H2Y1M6	514-845-9253	
Mazzone & Associates Inc 75 Fourteenth St NE Office Tower at the Four Seasons Ste 2800 *Web:* www.globalmna.com	Atlanta	GA	30309	404-931-8545	
MBL International Corp 4 H Constitution Way *TF:* 800-200-5459 ■ *Web:* www.mblintl.com	Woburn	MA	01801	781-939-6964	
McBee Assoc Inc 997 Old Eagle School Rd Ste 205 *TF:* 800-767-6203 ■ *Web:* www.mcbeeassociates.com	Wayne	PA	19087	610-964-9680	964-7987
McDonald Information Service Inc 215 14th St *Web:* www.callmis.com	Jersey City	NJ	07310	201-659-2600	
McDonald Partners LLC 959 W St Clair Ave *Web:* www.mcdonald-partners.com	Cleveland	OH	44113	216-912-0567	
McKinsey & Company Inc 55 E 52nd St *Web:* www.mckinsey.com	New York	NY	10022	212-446-7000	446-8575
McManus Wealth Building & Management 1930 17th St Ste 210 *Web:* www.mcmanusandyou.com	Boulder	CO	80302	303-544-0355	
MedExpert International Inc 1300 Hancock St *Web:* www.medexpert.com	Redwood City	CA	94063	650-326-6000	
Media Breakaway LLC 1490 W 121st Ave Ste 201 *Web:* www.mediabreakaway.com	Westminster	CO	80234	303-464-8164	464-8218
Medical Communications Media Inc 17 Blacksmith Rd Ste 100 *Web:* cmecorner.com	Newtown	PA	18940	267-364-0556	
Medical Doctor Assoc Inc 145 Technology Pkwy NW **Fax Area Code:* 770 ■ *TF:* 800-780-3500 ■ *Web:* www.mdainc.com	Norcross	GA	30092	800-780-3500	246-0882*
Medifit Corporate Services Inc 25 Hanover Rd *TF:* 866-848-5577 ■ *Web:* www.medifit.com	Florham Park	NJ	07932	973-593-9000	593-9007
MediLodge Group, The 64500 Van Dyke *Web:* www.lcsnet.com	Washington	MI	48095	586-752-5008	
Medlink Corp 10393 San Diego Mission Rd Ste 120 *Web:* www.medlink.com	San Diego	CA	92108	619-640-4660	
Medweb California LLC 667 Folsom St *Web:* www.medweb.com	San Francisco	CA	94107	415-541-9980	
MEMdata LLC 1601 Sebesta *Web:* www.memdata.com	College Station	TX	77845	979-695-1950	695-1954
Mercer Inc 1166 Ave of the Americas *Web:* www.mercer.com	New York	NY	10036	212-345-5000	345-7414
MGT of America Inc 2123 Centre Pt Blvd *Web:* www.mgtamer.com	Tallahassee	FL	32308	850-386-3191	385-4501
MilesTek Corp 1506 Interstate 35 W *TF:* 800-958-5173 ■ *Web:* www.milestek.com	Denton	TX	76207	940-484-9400	
Milliman USA 1301 Fifth Ave Ste 3800 **Fax:* Mktg ■ *Web:* in.milliman.com	Seattle	WA	98101	206-624-7940	340-1380*
Mindlance Inc 80 River St Fl 4 *Web:* www.mindlance.com	Hoboken	NJ	07030	201-386-5400	386-0553
Miratek Corp Inc 8201 Lockheed Dr Ste 218 *Web:* miratek.us	El Paso	TX	79925	915-772-2852	772-1764
Mitsubishi Power Systems Inc 100 Colonial Ctr Pkwy *TF:* 800-445-9723 ■ *Web:* www.mpshq.com	Lake Mary	FL	32746	407-688-6201	688-6481
MMC Group LLC 105 Decker Ct Ste 1100 *Web:* www.careerxroads.com	Irving	TX	75062	732-821-6652	
Mobile Video Services Ltd 1620 I St NW Ste 1000 10th Fl *Web:* www.mobilevideo.net	Washington	DC	20006	202-331-8882	
Modspace Financial Services Canada Ltd 2300 N Park Dr *Web:* www.modspace.com/en-ca	Brampton	ON	L6S6C6	905-794-3900	
Mojix Inc 11075 Santa Monica Blvd Ste 350 *Web:* www.mojix.com	Los Angeles	CA	90025	310-479-9021	
Monarch Dental Corp 7989 Belt Line Rd Ste 90 *Web:* www.monarchdental.com	Dallas	TX	75248	972-702-9017	
Mongoose Atlantic Inc 61 Broadway Rm 3024	New York	NY	10006	212-968-0196	
Monroe Financial Partners Inc 100 N Riverside Plz Ste 1620 *TF:* 800-766-5560 ■ *Web:* www.monroefp.com	Chicago	IL	60606	312-327-2530	327-2540
Monsoon Capital LLC 4720 Montgomery Ln Ste 410 *Web:* www.monsooncapital.com	Bethesda	MD	20814	301-222-8000	
Morgan Creek Capital Management LLC 301 W Barbee Chapel Rd Ste 200 *Web:* www.morgancreekcap.com	Chapel Hill	NC	27517	919-933-4004	
Morley Company Inc 2717 Schust *TF:* 800-323-1492 ■ *Web:* www.morleycompanies.com/travel	Saginaw	MI	48603	989-791-2565	497-1874
Morton Consulting LLC 4701 Cox Rd *Web:* www.mortonconsulting.com	Glen Allen	VA	23060	804-290-4272	
Motivano Inc 5810 W Cypress St Ste H *TF:* 866-664-4621 ■ *Web:* www.motivano.com	Tampa	FL	33607	866-664-4621	
Mount Hood Equity Partners LP 4800 SW Meadows Rd Ste 300	Lake Oswego	OR	97035	503-639-0915	
Mount Yale Capital Group LLC 8000 Norman Ctr Dr Ste 630 *Web:* www.mtyale.com	Minneapolis	MN	55437	952-897-5390	
MultiLingual Solutions Inc 11 N Washington St Ste 300 *Web:* www.mlsolutions.com	Rockville	MD	20850	301-424-7444	
Musselman Hotels LLC 2912 Eastpoint Pkwy *Web:* www.musselmanhotels.com	Louisville	KY	40223	502-426-3006	
Mx Group, The 7020 High Grove Blvd **Fax Area Code:* 630 ■ *TF:* 800-827-0170 ■ *Web:* www.themxgroup.com	Burr Ridge	IL	60527	800-827-0170	654-0302*
Mzinga 10 Burlington Mall Rd Ste 111 **Fax Area Code:* 781 ■ *TF:* 888-694-6428 ■ *Web:* www.mzinga.com	Burlington	MA	01803	888-694-6428	494-6555*
NANA Development Corp 909 W Ninth Ave *Web:* www.nana-dev.com	Anchorage	AK	99501	907-265-4100	
Nathan Assoc Inc 2101 Wilson Blvd Ste 1200 *Web:* www.nathaninc.com	Arlington	VA	22201	703-516-7700	351-6162
National Economic Research Assoc Inc 1166 Ave of the Americas 29th Fl *Web:* www.nera.com	New York	NY	10036	914-448-4000	448-4040
National Product Services Inc 105 Decker Ct Ste 700	Irving	TX	75062	972-373-9484	

Company / Address	City	State	Zip	Phone	Fax
Navigant Consulting Inc 30 S Wacker Dr Ste 3100 *NYSE: NCI* ■ **Fax:* Mktg ■ *TF:* 800-621-8390 ■ *Web:* www.navigant.com	Chicago	IL	60606	312-583-5700	583-5701*
Navigy Inc 4800 Deerwood Campus Pkwy DCC9-1 *Web:* www.navigy.net	Jacksonville	FL	32246	904-363-5490	
Navitaire Inc 333 S Seventh St Ste 500 *TF:* 877-216-6787 ■ *Web:* www.navitaire.com	Minneapolis	MN	55402	612-317-7000	317-7575
Neace Lukens Inc 2305 River Rd *TF:* 888-499-8092 ■ *Web:* www.neacelukens.com	Louisville	KY	40206	502-894-2100	894-8602
Neshaminy Constructors Inc 1839 Bustleton Pk *Web:* www.nci3.com	Feasterville	PA	19053	215-322-2700	
Netspeed Learning Solutions 3016 Ne Blakeley St Ste 100 *TF:* 877-517-5271 ■ *Web:* www.netspeedlearning.com	Seattle	WA	98105	206-517-5271	
Network Innovations Inc 4424 Manilla Rd SE *TF:* 888-466-2772 ■ *Web:* www.networkinv.com	Calgary	AB	T2G4B7	403-287-5000	
Newbn Inc 14240 Proton Rd *Web:* www.newbenefits.com	Dallas	TX	75244	972-404-8192	
Newport Real Estate Services Inc 3184 Airway Ave Ste H *Web:* www.nres.net	Costa Mesa	CA	92626	714-850-0085	
Newton & Associates Inc 1806 Rocky River Rd *Web:* www.newtonandassociates.com	Charlotte	NC	28213	704-597-4384	
Nexant Inc 44 S Broadway 5th Fl *Web:* www.nexant.com	White Plains	NY	10601	914-609-0300	609-0399
NextMark Inc 33 S Main St 3rd Fl *Web:* www.nextmark.com	Hanover	NH	03755	603-643-1307	
North Central Pennsylvania Regional Planning & Development Commission 651 Montmorenci Rd *TF:* 800-942-9467 ■ *Web:* www.ncentral.com	Ridgway	PA	15853	814-773-3162	772-7045
Northern Management Services Inc 607 Church St *Web:* www.nmsinc.com	Sandpoint	ID	83864	208-263-1363	
Northern Oak Capital Management Inc 555 E Wells St Ste 1625 *TF:* 888-283-1884 ■ *Web:* www.northern-oak.com	Milwaukee	WI	53202	414-278-0590	
Novotus LLC 5508 Parkcrest Dr Ste 100 **Fax Area Code:* 866 ■ *TF:* 800-856-0143 ■ *Web:* www.novotus.com	Austin	TX	78731	512-733-2244	540-1074*
Nth Degree Financial Solutions 1500 Noyes St *Web:* www.nthdegreefinancial.com	Evanston	IL	60201	847-328-0907	
O M V Medical Inc 6940 Carroll Ave *Web:* www.omvmedical.com	Takoma Park	MD	20912	301-270-9212	270-9335
O'Brien & Company Inc 710 Second Ave Ste 925 *Web:* www.obrienandco.com	Seattle	WA	98104	206-621-8626	
O'Neill & Assoc LLC 31 New Chardon St *TF:* 866-989-4321 ■ *Web:* www.oneillandassoc.com	Boston	MA	02114	617-646-1000	
Oak Creek Energy Systems Inc 500 La Terraza Blvd *Web:* www.oces.com	Escondido	CA	92025	760-975-0910	
Oakwood Capital Management LLC 12121 Wilshire Blvd Ste 1250 *TF:* 800-586-0600 ■ *Web:* www.oakwoodcap.com	Los Angeles	CA	90025	310-772-2600	
Occupational Health Dynamics 197 Cahaba Vly Pkwy *Web:* www.ohdusa.com	Pelham	AL	35124	205-980-0180	
Oleet & Co LLC 452 5th Ave *Web:* www.oleet.com	New York	NY	10018	212-235-2200	
Omniture Inc 250 Brannan St *Web:* www.adobe.com	San Francisco	CA	94107	408-536-6000	
Onsite Occupational Health & Safety Inc 101 N Hart St *Web:* www.onsiteohs.com	Princeton	IN	47670	812-770-4480	
Ontility LLC 3403 N Sam Houston Pkwy Ste 300 *Web:* www.ontility.com	Houston	TX	77086	281-854-1400	
Optima Group Inc 2150 Post Rd *Web:* www.optimagroupinc.com	Fairfield	CT	06824	203-255-1066	
Organizational Dynamics Inc 790 Boston Rd Ste 201 *TF:* 800-634-4636 ■ *Web:* www.orgdynamics.com	Billerica	MA	01821	978-671-5454	671-5005
Orion Development Group 177 Beach 116th St Ste 4 *Web:* www.odgroup.com	Rockaway Park	NY	11694	718-474-4600	
Orion Mobility LLC 4 Mountainview Terrace Ste 101 *TF:* 800-476-7787 ■ *Web:* www.orionmobility.com	Danbury	CT	06810	203-762-0365	834-9625
Orr Group, The 110 S Stratford Rd Ste 402 *Web:* www.theorrgroup.com	Winston-salem	NC	27104	336-722-7881	
Ortloff Engineers Ltd 415 W Wall Ave Ste 2000 *Web:* www.ortloff.com	Midland	TX	79701	432-685-0277	685-0258
Osi Consulting Inc 5950 Canoga Ave Ste 300 *Web:* www.osius.com	Woodland Hills	CA	91367	818-992-2700	992-8700
OSS.Net Inc PO Box 369 *Web:* www.oss.net	Oakton	VA	22124	703-266-6390	
OZ Systems Inc 2001 Ne Green Oaks Blvd *Web:* www.spassociates.com	Arlington	TX	76006	817-385-0390	
Pacific Material Handling Solutions Inc 3428 Arden Rd *Web:* www.pmhsi.com	Hayward	CA	94545	510-786-0215	
Pacrim Hospitality Services Inc 30 Damascus Rd *TF:* 877-680-7666 ■ *Web:* www.pacrimhospitality.com	Bedford	NS	B4A0C1	902-404-7474	
Palladium Group Inc 55 Old Bedford Rd Ste 100 *TF:* 800-773-2399 ■ *Web:* www.thepalladiumgroup.com	Lincoln	MA	01773	781-259-3737	259-3389
Palmaz Scientific Inc 3065 Skyway Ct Ste 1700 *Web:* www.palmazscientific.com	Fremont	CA	94539	214-520-9292	
Panthera Global Inc 155 N Wacker Dr 42nd Fl	Chicago	IL	60606	312-214-4660	
Paradigm Learning Inc 2701 N Rocky Pt Dr *Web:* www.paradigmlearning.com	Tampa	FL	33607	813-287-9330	
Paric Corp 77 Westport Plz Ste 250 *Web:* www.paric.com	St. Louis	MO	63146	636-561-9500	
Parsec Financial Management Inc 6 Wall St *TF:* 888-877-1012 ■ *Web:* www.parsecfinancial.com	Asheville	NC	28801	828-255-0271	
PathGroup Inc 5301 Virginia Way *TF:* 877-456-6706 ■ *Web:* www.pathgroup.com	Brentwood	TN	37027	615-221-4500	
Patten & Patten Inc 520 Lookout St *TF:* 800-757-3480 ■ *Web:* www.patteninc.com	Chattanooga	TN	37403	423-756-3480	
PDM Healthcare 24700 Ctr Ridge Rd Ste 110 *Web:* www.pdmhealthcare.com	Cleveland	OH	44145	440-871-1721	
Pencor Inc 1361 13th Ave S Ste 250 *Web:* www.pencor-inc.com	Jacksonville Beach	FL	32250	904-242-4245	242-0521
Pension Consulting Alliance Inc 514 NW 11th Ave Ste 203 *Web:* www.pensionconsulting.com	Portland	OR	97209	503-226-1050	
Penske Vehicle Services Inc 1225 E Maple Rd *TF:* 877-210-5290 ■ *Web:* penskevehicleservices.com	Troy	MI	48083	248-729-5400	
Performance Indicator LLC 116 John St/South Mill 1st Fl *Web:* www.performanceindicator.com	Lowell	MA	01852	978-459-4500	
Permedion Inc 350 Worthington Rd Ste H *Web:* hmspermedion.com	Westerville	OH	43082	614-895-9900	
Perry Johnson Registrars Inc 26555 Evergreen Rd Ste 1340 *Web:* www.pjr.com	Southfield	MI	48076	248-358-3388	
Persimmon Group, The 11 E Fifth St Ste 300 *Web:* www.thepersimmongroup.com	Tulsa	OK	74103	918-592-4121	
PharmaSeq Inc 11 Deer Park Dr Ste 104 *Web:* www.pharmaseq.com	Monmouth Junction	NJ	08852	732-355-0100	355-0102
Philip Crosby Assoc 306 Dartmouth St *TF:* 877-276-7295 ■ *Web:* www.philipcrosby.com	Boston	MA	02116	877-276-7295	
Phillips Financial Management LLC 6920 Pointe Inverness Way Ste 230 *Web:* www.1phillips.com	Fort Wayne	IN	46804	260-420-7732	
Pindler & Pindler Inc 11910 Poindexter Ave *TF:* 800-669-6002 ■ *Web:* www.pindler.com	Moorpark	CA	93021	805-531-9090	
Pinnacle Management Systems Inc 8500 North Stemmons Freeway Ste 6010 **Fax Area Code:* 888 ■ *TF:* 888-975-1119 ■ *Web:* www.pinnaclemanagement.com	Dallas	TX	75247	703-382-9161	975-9991*
Pinnacle Performance Improvement Worldwide (PPIW) 101 Main St *TF:* 800-368-3408 ■ *Web:* www.pinnaclecg.com	Pepperell	MA	01463	978-925-9797	925-9798
Pinney Assoc Inc 4800 Montgomery Ln Ste 400 *Web:* www.pinneyassociates.com	Bethesda	MD	20814	301-718-8440	718-0034
Pipitone Group 3933 Perrysville Ave *Web:* pipitonegroup.com	Pittsburgh	PA	15214	412-321-0879	
Plan Administrators Inc 1300 Enterprise Dr *Web:* www.pai.com	De Pere	WI	54115	920-339-2974	
Plank Enterprises Inc 4404 Anderson Dr *Web:* www.plankenterprises.com	Eau Claire	WI	54703	715-839-1225	
Plastic Technologies Inc 1440 Timberwolf Dr *Web:* www.plastictechnologies.com	Holland	OH	43528	419-867-5400	
Platinum Systems Specialists Inc 4715 Yender Ave *Web:* www.platinum-universe.com	Lisle	IL	60532	630-375-6800	375-9069
PM Environmental Inc 3340 Ranger Rd *Web:* www.pmenv.com	Lansing	MI	48906	517-321-3331	
Pma Consultants LLC 1 Woodward Ave Ste 1400 *Web:* www.pmaconsultants.com	Detroit	MI	48226	313-963-8863	963-8918
Pollock Planning Assoc Inc 232 Juniper Way *Web:* www.pollockplanning.com	Mountainside	NJ	07092	908-789-4226	
Porter Henry & Company Inc 455 E 86th St *Web:* www.porterhenry.com	New York	NY	10028	212-953-5544	
PPI Construction Management Inc 8200 NW 15th Pl Ste B	Gainesville	FL	32606	352-331-1141	
Pragmatek Consulting Group 8500 Normandale Lake Blvd Ste 1060 *TF:* 800-833-3164 ■ *Web:* www.pragmatek.com	Bloomington	MN	55437	612-333-3164	378-2914
Prairie Cardiovascular Consultants Ltd 619 E Mason St *Web:* www.prairiecardiovascular.com	Springfield	IL	62701	217-788-0706	
Precision Automation Company Inc 1841 Old Cuthbert Rd *Web:* www.precisionautomationinc.com	Cherry Hill	NJ	08034	856-428-7400	
Presidio Group Inc, The 5295 South 300 West Ste 550 *TF:* 800-924-1404 ■ *Web:* www.presidio-group.com	Salt Lake City	UT	84107	801-924-1400	
Press Ganey Associates Inc 404 Columbia Pl *TF:* 800-232-8032 ■ *Web:* www.pressganey.com	South Bend	IN	46601	800-232-8032	
Primesource Staffing LLC 5250 Leetsdale Dr Ste 101 *Web:* www.primesourcestaffing.com	Denver	CO	80246	303-869-2990	869-2997
Princeton Capital Management Inc 47 Hulfish St Ste 500 *Web:* www.pcminvest.com	Princeton	NJ	08542	609-924-6867	
PRISM Mktg Services Inc 222 W College Ave Ste 2A *Web:* www.prism-mktg.com	Appleton	WI	54911	920-380-2380	
Pritchett LLC 8150 N Central Expy Ste 1350 *TF:* 800-992-5922 ■ *Web:* www.pritchettnet.com	Dallas	TX	75206	214-239-9600	239-9650
Proactive Communications Inc 100 E Whitestone Blvd Ste 148 *Web:* www.proactivecommo.com	Cedar Park	TX	78613	254-699-0067	
Professional Bank Services Inc 6200 Dutchmans Ln Ste 305 *TF:* 800-523-4778 ■ *Web:* www.probank.com	Louisville	KY	40205	502-451-6633	451-6755
Professional Research Consultants Inc 11326 P St *TF:* 800-428-7455 ■ *Web:* www.prccustomresearch.com	Omaha	NE	68137	402-592-5656	592-3019

				Phone	Fax
Profile Mktg Research Inc 4020 S 57th Ave Ste 101 . . . . Lake Worth *Web:* radius-global.com		FL	33463	561-965-8300	
Program Planning Professionals 1340 Eisenhower Pl . . . . Ann Arbor *TF:* 877-728-2331 ■ *Web:* www.pcubed.com		MI	48108	734-741-7770	741-1343
Progressive Mktg Products Inc 3130 E Miraloma Ave . . . . Anaheim *TF:* 800-368-9700 ■ *Web:* www.mounts.com		CA	92806	714-632-7100	
Projects Plus Inc 254 W 29th St 5th Fl . . . . New York *Web:* www.projectsplusinc.com		NY	10001	212-997-0100	
ProManage LLC 150 N Michigan Ave Ste 2930. . . . Chicago *Web:* www.promanageplan.com		IL	60603	312-456-0665	
Promontory Financial Group LLC 1201 Pennsylvania Ave NW Ste 617. . . . Washington *Web:* www.promontory.com		DC	20004	202-384-1200	
Promontory Point Capital 322 E Michigan St Ste 500. . . . Milwaukee *Web:* www.promontorypointcapital.com		WI	53202	414-225-0484	
Prophet Equity LLC 1460 Main St Ste 200. . . . South Lake *Web:* www.prophetequity.com		TX	76092	817-898-1500	
Protected Investors of America Inc 235 Montgomery St Ste 1050. . . . San Francisco *TF:* 800-786-2559 ■ *Web:* www.protectedinvestors.com		CA	94104	800-786-2559	
PsyMax Solutions LLC 25550 Chagrin Blvd Ste 100. . . . Cleveland *TF:* 866-774-2273 ■ *Web:* www.psymaxsolutions.com		OH	44122	216-896-9991	
Public Consulting Group Inc 148 State St . . . . Boston **Fax Area Code:* 617 ■ *TF:* 800-210-6113 ■ *Web:* www.publicconsultinggroup.com		MA	02109	800-210-6113	426-4632*
Public Resources Advisory Group Inc 39 Broadway Ste 1210 . . . . New York *Web:* www.pragadvisors.com		NY	10006	212-566-7800	
Purple Cows Inc 3210 N Canyon Rd Ste 307 . . . . Provo *Web:* www.purplecows.com		UT	84604	801-344-8532	
Q Analysts LLC 5201 Great America Pkwy. . . . Santa Clara *Web:* www.qanalysts.com		CA	95054	408-907-8500	
QSL Print Communications Inc 3000 Pierce Pkwy. . . . Springfield *Web:* www.qslprinting.com		OR	97477	541-687-1184	
Quadel Consulting 1200 G St NW Ste 700. . . . Washington *TF:* 866-640-1019 ■ *Web:* www.quadel.com		DC	20005	202-789-2500	898-0632
Quality Built LLC 401 SE 12th St Ste 200. . . . Fort Lauderdale *Web:* www.qualitybuilt.com		FL	33316	954-358-3500	
Quality Business Solutions Inc 280 Hindman Rd. . . . Travelers Rest *Web:* qualitybsolutions.net		SC	29690	952-564-3088	
Quality Group Inc, The 5825 Glenridge Dr Ste 3-101 . . . . Atlanta *Web:* www.thequalitygroup.net		GA	30328	404-843-9525	
Quest Turnaround Advisors LLC 800 Westchester Ave Ste S-520 . . . . Rye Brook *Web:* www.qtadvisors.com		NY	10573	914-253-8100	
Questor 700 E Maple Rd 2nd Fl . . . . Birmingham *Web:* questor.com		MI	48009	248-593-1930	723-3907
Quorum Health Resources LLC 105 Continental Pl . . . . Brentwood *Web:* www.qhr.com		TN	37027	615-371-7979	
R L Hulett & Company Inc 8000 Maryland Ave Ste 245 . . . . St Louis *Web:* www.rlhulett.com		MO	63105	314-721-0607	
R W Rog & Company Inc 630 Johnson Ave Ste 103 . . . . Bohemia *TF:* 877-218-0085 ■ *Web:* www.rwroge.com		NY	11716	631-218-0077	
Radiant Communication Inc 5512 Merrick Rd. . . . Massapequa		NY	11758	516-798-0465	
Radio Communications Co 8035 Chapel Hill Rd . . . . Cary *TF:* 800-508-7580 ■ *Web:* www.rccws.com		NC	27513	919-467-2421	
Rapid Ratings Pty Ltd 86 Chambers St Ste 701 . . . . New York *Web:* www.rapidratings.com		NY	10007	646-233-4600	
Rath & Strong Inc 1666 Massachusetts Ave PO Box 170 . . . . Lexington *TF:* 800-622-2025 ■ *Web:* www.rathstrong.com		MA	02420	781-861-1700	861-1424
Raytheon Professional Services LLC 1200 S Jupiter Rd. . . . Garland *Web:* raytheon.com/ourcompany/rps		TX	75042	972-205-5100	
Raytrans Management Inc 1501 Reedsdale St Ste 3001. . . . Pittsburgh *Web:* www.raytrans.com		PA	15233	412-321-0100	
RCI Consultants Inc 17314 State Hwy 249 Ste 350. . . . Houston *Web:* www.rcigroup.us		TX	77064	281-970-4221	970-4241
Red Level Networks LLC 24371 Catherine Industrial Dr Ste 223 . . . . Novi *Web:* www.redlevelnetworks.com		MI	48375	248-412-8200	
Redmond Co, The W228 N745 Westmound Dr. . . . Waukesha *Web:* www.theredmondco.com		WI	53186	262-549-9600	
Reed Group Ltd 10155 Westmoor Dr Ste 210 . . . . Westminster *Web:* www.reedgroup.com		CO	80021	303-247-1860	247-1863
Regency Hotel Management LLC 3211 W Sencore Dr . . . . Sioux Falls *Web:* www.regency-mgmt.com		SD	57107	605-334-2371	
Renewable Choice Energy Inc 4775 Walnut St Ste 230 . . . . Boulder *Web:* www.renewablechoice.com		CO	80301	303-468-0405	
Resort Parks International 2901 Cherry Ave. . . . Signal Hill *Web:* resortparks.com		CA	90755	562-595-8818	
Resources For Living Ltd 4407 Monterey Oaks Blvd. . . . Austin *Web:* www.resourcesforliving.com/login.aspx		TX	78749	512-358-8400	
Respira Medical Inc 521 Progress Dr BWI Tech Park Ste A - C . . . . Linthicum *Web:* www.respiramedical.com		MD	21090	443-200-0055	
RETax Funding LP 14785 Preston Rd Ste 495 . . . . Dallas *Web:* www.retaxfunding.com		TX	75254	972-855-3550	

				Phone	Fax
Revere Group, The 325 N LaSalle Ste 325. . . . Chicago *TF:* 800-745-3263 ■ *Web:* americas.nttdata.com		IL	60654	213-228-2500	
RGBS Enterprises 2842 Richmond Ter . . . . Staten Island *Web:* www.rgbse.com		NY	10303	718-981-0734	
RHR International LLP 233 S Wacker Dr 95th Fl . . . . Chicago *Web:* rhrinternational.com		IL	60606	312-924-0800	924-0801
RINET Company LLC 101 Federal St 14th Fl. . . . Boston *Web:* www.rinetco.com		MA	02110	617-488-2700	
Rippe Keane Mktg Inc 5950 Seminole Centre Ct Ste 220. . . . Madison *Web:* www.rippekeane.com		WI	53711	608-277-9097	
Rising Tide Capital Inc 334 Martin Luther King Dr . . . . Jersey City *Web:* risingtidecapital.org		NJ	07305	201-432-4316	
Risk Management Services Co (RMSC) 9100 Marksfield Rd . . . . Louisville **Fax Area Code:* 888 ■ *Web:* www.rmsc.com		KY	40222	502-326-5900	326-5909*
RM Strategic Marketing 800 W End Ave . . . . New York *Web:* www.rmstrategicmarketing.com		NY	10025	212-961-1120	
Robert E Nolan Company Inc 92 Hopmeadow St . . . . Weatogue *TF:* 800-653-1941 ■ *Web:* www.renolan.com		CT	06089	860-658-1941	651-3465
Robert Group Inc, The 3108 Los Feliz Blvd . . . . Los Angeles *Web:* www.therobertgroup.com		CA	90039	323-669-9100	
Robinson & Maites Inc 35 E Wacker Dr Ste 3500. . . . Chicago *Web:* radiant-1.com		IL	60601	312-372-9333	
Robson Forensic Inc 354 N Prince St . . . . Lancaster *TF:* 800-813-6736 ■ *Web:* www.robsonforensic.com		PA	17603	717-293-9050	
Rodheim Mktg Group 125 E Baker St Ste 143 . . . . Costa Mesa		CA	92626	714-557-5100	
Roff Enterprises Inc 438 N Frederick Ave . . . . Gaithersburg *Web:* www.hhcgroup.com		MD	20877	301-963-0762	
Roland Berger & Partners 230 Pk Ave Ste 112 . . . . New York *Web:* www.rolandberger.com		NY	10017	212-651-9660	756-8750
Romar Learning Solutions LLC 28420 Hardy Toll Rd Ste 150 . . . . Spring *Web:* www.romarlearning.com		TX	77373	281-292-5508	
Roscoe Medical Inc 21973 Commerce Pkwy. . . . Strongsville *Web:* www.roscoemedical.com		OH	44149	440-572-1962	
Rose Displays Ltd 35 Congress St . . . . Salem *TF:* 800-631-9707 ■ *Web:* www.rosedisplays.com		MA	01970	978-219-8100	
RoseRyan Inc 35473 Dumbarton Ct. . . . Newark *Web:* www.roseryan.com		CA	94560	510-456-3056	
Round Table Wealth Management 319 Lenox Ave . . . . Westfield *Web:* roundtablewealth.com		NJ	07090	908-789-7310	
Roy Jorgensen Assoc Inc 3735 Buckeystown Pk. . . . Buckeystown *Web:* www.royjorgensen.com		MD	21717	301-831-1000	
Royal Paper Corp 10232 Palm Dr. . . . Santa Fe Springs *Web:* www.royal-paper.com		CA	90670	562-903-9030	944-6000
Royce Associates A LP 35 Carlton Ave. . . . East Rutherford *Web:* www.royceintl.com		NJ	07073	201-438-5200	
RSI Logistics Inc 2419 Science Pkwy. . . . Okemos *Web:* www.rsilogistics.com		MI	48864	517-349-7713	
RTD Financial Advisors Inc 30 S 17th St United Plz Ste 1620 . . . . Philadelphia *Web:* www.rtdfinancial.com		PA	19103	215-557-3800	
Ruhof Corp, The 393 Sagamore Ave. . . . Mineola *Web:* www.ruhof.com		NY	11501	516-294-5888	
Ryan Group Inc, The 14110 Dallas Pkwy. . . . Dallas *Web:* www.ryangroupinc.com		TX	75254	972-385-7781	
Sage Financial Group 300 Barr Harbor Dr Five Tower Bridge Ste 200. . . . West Conshohocken *Web:* www.sagefinancial.com		PA	19428	484-342-4400	
SageView Advisory Group LLC 1920 Main St Ste 800. . . . Irvine *Web:* www.sageviewadvisory.com		CA	92614	949-955-1395	
SAK Management Services LLC 1 Northfield Plz Ste 210 . . . . Northfield *Web:* www.sakmgmt.com		IL	60093	773-202-0000	
Sambatek Inc 12800 Whitewater Dr Ste 300. . . . Minnetonka *Web:* www.sambatek.com		MN	55343	763-476-6010	
Sanli Pastore & Hill Inc Sanli Pastore & Hill 1990 S Bundy Dr Ste 800. . . . Los Angeles *Web:* www.sphvalue.com		CA	90025	310-571-3400	
Sapient Corp 131 Dartmouth St 3rd Fl. . . . Boston *NASDAQ: SAPE* ■ *TF:* 866-796-6860 ■ *Web:* www.sapient.com		MA	02116	617-621-0200	621-1300
Savage & Assoc Inc 4427 Talmadge Rd. . . . Toledo *Web:* www.savageandassociates.com		OH	43623	419-475-8665	
Savant Capital LLC 190 Buckley Dr . . . . Rockford *Web:* www.savantcapital.com		IL	61107	815-227-0300	
Savino Del Bene USA Inc 1905 S Mt Prospect Rd Ste D. . . . Des Plaines *Web:* www.savinodelbene.com		IL	60018	847-390-3600	
SBW Consulting Inc 2820 Northup Way Ste 230 . . . . Bellevue *Web:* www.sbwconsulting.com		WA	98004	425-827-0330	
Scalable Display Technologies Inc 585 Massachusetts Ave 4th Fl . . . . Cambridge *Web:* www.scalabledisplay.com		MA	02139	617-864-9300	
Schaffer Consulting 707 Summer St. . . . Stamford *Web:* www.schafferresults.com		CT	06901	203-322-1604	316-0591
Schahet Hotels Inc 9333 N Meridian St. . . . Indianapolis *Web:* www.schahethotels.com		IN	46260	317-848-9000	
Schweppe Inc 376 W N Ave (Route 64). . . . Lombard *Web:* www.chefsaver.com		IL	60148	630-627-3550	
Scorelogix LLC 2 Reads Way Ste 226 . . . . New Castle *Web:* www.scorelogix.com		DE	19720	302-328-1210	
Scott Madden & Assoc Inc 2626 Glenwood Ave Ste 480. . . . Raleigh *TF:* 888-473-6748 ■ *Web:* www.scottmadden.com		NC	27608	919-781-4191	

Company	City	State	Zip	Phone	Fax
SCP Construction LLC 5340 W Luke Ave *Web:* www.scpaz.com	Glendale	AZ	85301	623-931-9131	
SeaMates International Inc 316 Main St PO Box 436 *Web:* www.seamates.com	East Rutherford	NJ	07073	201-896-8899	
Secova Inc 5000 Birch St W Tower Ste 1400 *TF:* 800-257-0011 ■ *Web:* www.secova.com	Newport Beach	CA	92660	714-384-0530	384-0600
Sedlak Management Consultants Inc Metropolitan Plz 22901 Millcreek Blvd Ste 600 *Web:* www.jasedlak.com	Highland Hills	OH	44122	216-206-4700	206-4840
Selerix Systems Inc 2851 Craig Dr Ste 300 *Web:* www.selerix.com	Mckinney	TX	75070	469-452-7076	
Self Opportunity Inc 808 Office Park Cir *TF:* 800-594-7036 ■ *Web:* www.selfopportunity.com	Lewisville	TX	75057	214-222-1500	
Selling Source LLC 325 E Warm Springs Rd Ste 200 *TF:* 800-251-6147 ■ *Web:* sellingsource.com	Las Vegas	NV	89119	702-407-0707	407-0711
Seneca Partners Inc 300 Park St Ste 400 *Web:* www.senecapartners.com	Birmingham	MI	48009	248-723-6650	
Sequent Energy Management LP 1200 Smith St Ste 900 *Web:* www.sequentenergy.com	Houston	TX	77002	832-397-1700	397-1722
SES Advisors Inc 10 Shurs Ln Ste 102 *Web:* www.sesadvisors.com	Philadelphia	PA	19127	215-508-1600	
Setpoint Systems Inc 2835 Commerce Way *Web:* www.setpointusa.com	Ogden	UT	84401	801-621-4117	
Sharkey Howes & Javer Inc 720 S Colorado Blvd Ste 600 S Twr *TF:* 800-557-9380 ■ *Web:* www.shwj.com	Denver	CO	80246	303-639-5100	
Shenkman Capital Management Inc 461 Fifth Ave 22nd Fl *Web:* www.shenkmancapital.com	New York	NY	10017	212-867-9090	
Sherman International Corp 367 Mansfield Ave *Web:* www.shermaninternational.com	Pittsburgh	PA	15220	412-928-2880	
Shoreline Partners LLC 6310 Greenwich Dr Ste 120 *Web:* www.shoreline.com	San Diego	CA	92122	858-587-9800	
Sierra Group, The 588 N Gulph Rd # 110 *Web:* www.thesierragroup.com	King Of Prussia	PA	19406	610-992-0288	
SigmaBleyzer 123 N Post Oak Ln Ste 410 *Web:* www.sigmableyzer.com	Houston	TX	77024	713-621-3111	
Signature Inc 5115 Parkcenter Ave *TF:* 800-398-0518 ■ *Web:* signatureworldwide.com	Dublin	OH	43017	614-766-5101	
Simply Healthcare Plans Inc 1701 Ponce De Leon Blvd Ste 300 *TF:* 877-577-9042 ■ *Web:* www.simplyhealthcareplans.com	Coral Gables	FL	33134	305-408-5890	
Sirius Solution LLC 1233 W Loop S *Web:* www.sirsol.com	Houston	TX	77027	713-888-0488	888-0235
SiriusDecisions Inc 187 Danbury Rd *Web:* www.siriusdecisions.com	Wilton	CT	06897	203-665-4000	
Skillman Corp, The 3834 S Emerson Ave Bldg A *Web:* www.skillman.com	Indianapolis	IN	46203	317-783-6151	
Social Communications Co 380 Altair Wy Ste 100 *Web:* www.sococo.com	Sunnyvale	CA	94086	650-425-7801	
Solving International 1755 The Exchange Ste 380	Atlanta	GA	30339	770-988-2600	988-2626
Sorrento Pacific Financial LLC 10150 Meanley Dr 1st Fl *Web:* www.mybd.com	San Diego	CA	92131	858-805-7900	
Specialty Construction Management Inc 1314 Eigth St Nw *Web:* www.specialtyconstruction.net	Washington	DC	20001	202-832-7250	
Specialty Sales & Mktg Inc 6725 Millcreek Dr Ste 5 *Web:* www.specialtysales.ca	Mississauga	ON	L5N5V3	905-816-0011	
Spectrum Financial System Inc 163 McKenzie Rd *TF:* 800-525-0555 ■ *Web:* www.spectrumfinancialinc.com	Mooresville	NC	28115	704-663-4466	663-0611
SpenDifference LLC 12015 E 46th Ave Ste 300 *Web:* www.spendifference.com	Denver	CO	80239	303-531-2680	
Ssci 3065 Kent Ave *TF:* 800-375-2179 ■ *Web:* www.ssci-inc.com	West Lafayette	IN	47906	765-463-0112	463-4722
Stablex Canada Inc 760 Blvd Industriel *Web:* www.stablex.com	Blainville	QC	J7C3V4	450-430-9230	430-4642
Staff Management Group LLC 172 New St	New Brunswick	NJ	08901	732-246-0099	
Standing Dog Interactive 6060 N Central Expy Ste 350 *Web:* www.standingdog.com	Dallas	TX	75206	214-696-9600	
Stanley-Laman Group Ltd 1235 Westlakes Dr Ste 295 *Web:* www.stanleylaman.com	Berwyn	PA	19312	610-993-9100	
Starbridge Media Group Inc 6723 Whittier Ave Ste 307	Mclean	VA	22101	703-760-0051	
Stelera Wireless LLC 13431 Bdwy Extn Ste 102	Oklahoma City	OK	73114	405-751-3525	
Stem International Inc 4692 Millennium Dr Ste 400 *Web:* www.stemint.com	Belcamp	MD	21017	410-272-9080	272-9085
Stertil-Koni USA Inc 200 Log Canoe Cir *Web:* www.stertil-koni.com	Stevensville	MD	21666	410-643-9001	
Stewart Environmental Consultants LLC 3801 Automation Way Ste 200 *TF:* 800-373-1348 ■ *Web:* www.stewartenv.com	Fort Collins	CO	80525	970-226-5500	
Stockbridge Risk Management Inc 40 Cutter Mill Rd *Web:* www.stockbridgerisk.com	Great Neck	NY	11021	516-499-5678	487-1146
Stone House Consulting LLC 126 Thornton Rd *Web:* www.stonehouseconsulting.com	Thornton	PA	19373	610-358-1791	

Company	City	State	Zip	Phone	Fax
Storm Technologies Inc 411 N Depot St *Web:* www.stormeng.com	Albemarle	NC	28002	704-983-2040	
Strategic Advisors Inc 400 Southpointe Blvd Plz I Ste 440 *Web:* www.strategicad.com	Canonsburg	PA	15317	724-743-5800	
Strategic Decisions Group 745 Emerson St *Web:* www.sdg.com	Palo Alto	CA	94301	650-475-4400	475-4401
Strategic Employee Services Inc 11410 Kingston Pk Ste 100 *Web:* www.seshr.com	Knoxville	TN	37934	865-671-0534	675-0186
Strategic Public Partners Inc 88 E Broad St Ste 1770 *Web:* www.1spp.com	Columbus	OH	43215	614-222-8490	
Strategic Resources Inc 7927 Jones Branch Dr *Web:* www.sri-hq.com	McLean	VA	22102	703-749-3040	749-3046
Straw Hat Cooperative Corp 18 Crow Canyon Ct Ste 270 *Web:* www.strawhatpizza.com	San Ramon	CA	94583	925-837-3400	
Sullivan- Bille & Co 600 Clark Rd 4th Fl *Web:* www.sullivanbillepc.com	Tewksbury	MA	01876	978-970-2900	
Summit Envirosolutions Inc 1217 Bandana Blvd N *Web:* www.summite.com	St Paul	MN	55108	651-644-8080	
Summit Health Inc 27175 Haggerty Rd *Web:* www.summithealth.com	Novi	MI	48377	248-799-8303	
Summit Publications Inc 404 S Jefferson St *Web:* www.bestlocalsearch.com	Kearney	MO	64060	816-628-5492	
Sumnicht & Associates W6240 Communication Ct Ste 1 *Web:* www.sumnicht.com	Appleton	WI	54914	920-731-4455	
Sunrise Labs Inc 5 Dartmouth Dr *Web:* www.sunriselabs.com	Auburn	NH	03032	603-644-4500	
SYMMEDRx LLC 10955 Lowell Ave Ste 600 *Web:* www.symmedrx.com	Overland Park	KS	66210	913-338-4900	
Syndicated Capital Inc 1299 Ocean Ave Ste 210 *Web:* www.computercafe.com	Santa Monica	CA	90401	310-255-4490	
Synectic Solutions Inc 1701 Pacific Ave Ste 260 *Web:* www.synecticsolutions.com	Oxnard	CA	93033	805-483-4800	
Sysorex Global Holding Corporation 405 Clyde Ave *Web:* www.sysorex.com	Mountain View	CA	94043	650-967-2200	
Systech Solutions Inc 500 N Brand Blvd Ste 1900 *Web:* www.systechusa.com	Glendale	CA	91203	818-550-9690	550-9692
System of Systems Analytics Inc 11250 Waples Mill Rd Ste 300 *Web:* www.sosacorp.com	Fairfax	VA	22030	703-349-7057	
System Planning Corp (SPC) 3601 Wilson Blvd *Web:* www.sysplan.com	Arlington	VA	22201	703-351-8200	
Talemed Inc 6279 Tri Ridge Blvd Ste 110 *Web:* www.talemed.com	Loveland	OH	45140	513-774-7300	
Tata Consultancy Services Ltd (TCS) 101 Pk Ave 26th Fl *Web:* www.tcs.com	New York	NY	10178	212-557-8038	867-8652
Tbm Consulting Group Inc 4400 Ben Franklin Blvd *TF:* 800-438-5535 ■ *Web:* www.tbmcg.com	Durham	NC	27704	919-471-5535	471-5135
Tech Usa Inc 8334 Veterans Hwy *TF:* 888-584-8181 ■ *Web:* www.techusa.net	Millersville	MD	21108	410-729-4328	987-9080
Technology & Business Integrators 136 Summit Ave Ste 205 *Web:* www.tbicentral.com	Montvale	NJ	07645	201-573-0400	
Technology Commercialization Group LLC 1009 Slater Rd Ste 450 *Web:* www.t-c-group.com	Durham	NC	27703	919-941-0700	
Technomic Inc 300 S Riverside Plaza Ste 1200 *Web:* www.technomic.com	Chicago	IL	60606	312-876-0004	876-1158
Techsico Enterprise Solutions Inc 910 S Hudson Ave *Web:* www.techsico.com	Tulsa	OK	74112	918-585-2347	
Tel-Adjust Inc 29000 Inkster Rd Ste 115 *Web:* www.teladjust.com	Southfield	MI	48034	248-208-1600	208-0805
Tele-Measurements Inc 145 Main Ave *TF:* 800-223-0052 ■ *Web:* www.telemeasurements.com	Clifton	NJ	07014	973-473-8822	
Telesoft Corp 1661 E Camelback Rd Ste 300 *Web:* www.telesoft.com	Phoenix	AZ	85016	602-308-2100	308-1300
Tenera Environmental 971 Dewing Ave Ste 101 *Web:* www.tenera.com	Lafayette	CA	94549	925-962-9769	
Terra Nova Asset Management LLC 777 Third Ave *Web:* www.terranovausa.com	New York	NY	10017	212-355-1234	
Terrahealth Inc 5710 W Hausman Ste 108 *Web:* www.terrahealth.com	San Antonio	TX	78249	210-475-9881	475-9397
Tessada & Associates Inc 8001 Forbes Pl Ste 310	Springfield	VA	22151	703-564-1210	
Testmax 927 Lincoln Rd Ste 209 *Web:* www.testmax.net	Miami Beach	FL	33139	305-673-5728	
TheraTogs Inc 305 Society Dr Ste 3-C *Web:* www.theratogs.com	Telluride	CO	81435	970-728-7078	
Thomson ISI ResearchSoft 2141 Palomar Airport Rd Ste 350 *TF:* 800-722-1227 ■ *Web:* www.refman.com	Carlsbad	CA	92009	760-438-5526	
Thyssen Krupp Hearn 59 I- Dr *TF:* 877-854-7178 ■ *Web:* www.tkmna.com	Wentzville	MO	63385	636-332-1772	
Tidal Basin Holdings Inc 675 N Washington St *Web:* www.tidalbasingroup.com	Alexandria	VA	22314	703-683-8551	
Tom McCall & Assoc Inc 20180 Governors Hwy Ste 100 *TF:* 800-715-5474 ■ *Web:* www.tmccall.com	Olympia Fields	IL	60461	708-747-5707	747-5890
Tompkins International 6870 Perry Creek Rd *TF:* 800-789-1257 ■ *Web:* tompkinsinc.com	Raleigh	NC	27616	919-876-3667	872-9666

				Phone	Fax
Total Technology Ventures LLC 1230 Peachtree St Ne Ste 1150 *Web:* ttvcapital.com	Atlanta	GA	30309	404-347-8400	
Traffic Management Inc 8862 W 35W Service Dr NE Ste 270 *Web:* www.trafficmgmt.com	Minneapolis	MN	55449	763-544-3455	
Transition Partners Co 11732 Bowman Green Dr *Web:* www.tpco.us	Reston	VA	20190	703-736-0550	
Transportation Management Services Inc 16600 Table Mtn Pkwy *Web:* www.imagitas.com	Golden	CO	80403	303-287-8600	
Travelclick 7 Times Sq 38th Fl *TF:* 866-674-4549 ■ *Web:* www.travelclick.com	New York	NY	10036	212-817-4800	
Treesdale Partners LLC 1325 Ave of the Americas Ste 2302 *Web:* www.treesdalellc.com	New York	NY	10019	212-299-5525	
TrestleTree Inc 3715 Business Dr Ste 202 *Web:* www.trestletree.com	Fayetteville	AR	72703	479-582-0777	
Triage Consulting Group 221 Main St Ste 1100 *Web:* www.triageconsulting.com	San Francisco	CA	94105	415-512-9400	512-9404
TrialCard Inc 6501 Weston Pkwy Ste 370 *Web:* corp.trialcard.com	Cary	NC	27513	919-845-0774	
Tribal Solutions Inc 10875 John W Elliott Dr Ste 400 *Web:* www.tribalsolutionsinc.com	Frisco	TX	75033	972-984-1000	
Triumph Enterprises Inc 8000 W park Drive Ste 600 *Web:* www.triumph-enterprises.com	McLean	VA	22102	703-563-4400	
Troon Golf LLC 15044 N Scottsdale Rd Ste 300 *Web:* www.troongolf.com	Scottsdale	AZ	85254	480-606-1000	
Trotter Wellness Ltd 2124 Kohler Memorial Dr Ste 300 *Web:* www.trotterwellness.com	Sheboygan	WI	53081	920-457-3036	
Trout & Partners Ltd 8 Wahneta Rd *Web:* www.troutandpartners.com	Old Greenwich	CT	06870	203-637-7001	637-7071
True Partners Consulting LLC 225 W Wacker Dr Ste 1600 *Web:* www.tpctax.com	Chicago	IL	60606	312-235-3300	
Tunnell Consulting 900 E Eigth Ave Ste 106 *Web:* www.tunnellconsulting.com	King of Prussia	PA	19406	610-337-0820	337-1884
Tunstall Consulting Inc 13153 N Dale Mabry Hwy Ste 200 *Web:* www.tunstallconsulting.com	Tampa	FL	33618	813-968-4461	961-2315
UcompassCom Inc 3019 Shannon Lakes N Ste 203 *Web:* www.ucompass.com	Tallahassee	FL	32309	850-297-1800	
ULC Robotics Inc 88 Arkay Dr *Web:* www.ulcrobotics.com	Hauppauge	NY	11788	631-667-9200	
UMS Group Inc 300 Interpace Pkwy Ste C380 *Web:* www.umsgroup.com	Parsippany	NJ	07054	973-335-3555	335-7738
United Rebar Inc 8301 Galena Ave *Web:* unitedrebar.com	Sacramento	CA	95828	916-379-9900	379-9909
University Research Company LLC 7200 Wisconsin Ave Ste 600 *Web:* www.urc-chs.com	Bethesda	MD	20814	301-654-8338	941-8427
Urban Science 400 Renaissance Ctr Ste 2900 *TF:* 800-321-6900 ■ *Web:* www.urbanscience.com	Detroit	MI	48243	313-259-9900	259-9901
Urology Healthcare Group Inc 720 Cool Springs Blvd Ste 500 *Web:* www.cimplify.net	Franklin	TN	37067	615-261-6700	
Utility Technologies International Corp 4700 Homer Ohio Ln *Web:* www.uti-corp.com	Groveport	OH	43125	614-482-8080	
V2 Capital LLC 2700 Patriot Blvd Ste 420	Glenview	IL	60026	847-201-3620	
Validation Systems Inc 988 San Antonio Rd *Web:* www.validationsystems.com	Palo Alto	CA	94303	650-856-4874	
Vanport Manufacturing Inc 28590 Se Wally Rd *Web:* vanport-international.com/en	Boring	OR	97009	503-663-4466	
VARIS LLC 9245 Sierra College Blvd *Web:* www.varis1.com	Roseville	CA	95661	916-294-0860	
Vawter Financial Ltd 1161 Bethel Rd Ste 304 *TF:* 800-955-1575 ■ *Web:* www.vawterfinancial.com	Columbus	OH	43220	614-451-1002	
VCFO Holdings Inc 6836 Austin Ctr Blvd Bldg 1 Ste 280 *Web:* www.vcfo.com	Austin	TX	78731	512-345-9441	
VCNA Prairie Inc 7601 W 79th St PO Box 1123 *Web:* www.prairie.com	Bridgeview	IL	60455	708-458-0400	
VDC Research Group Inc 679 Worcester Rd Ste 2 *Web:* www.vdcresearch.com	Natick	MA	01760	508-653-9000	653-9836
Veber Partners LLC 605 N W 11th Ave *Web:* www.veber.com	Portland	OR	97209	503-229-4400	
Verity International Ltd 200 King St W Ste 1301 *TF:* 877-623-2396 ■ *Web:* www.verityintl.com	Toronto	ON	M5H3T4	416-862-8422	
Vermillion Financial Advisors Inc 16 Executive Ct Ste 3 *Web:* www.vermillionfinancial.com	South Barrington	IL	60010	847-382-9999	
Vermont Composites Inc 25 Performance Dr *Web:* www.vtcomposites.com	Bennington	VT	05201	802-442-9964	445-2921
Vesta Hospitality LLC 900 Washington St Ste 760 *Web:* www.vestahospitality.com	Vancouver	WA	98660	360-737-0442	
Viatech Systems Inc 1749 Old Meadow Rd 650 *Web:* www.viatech-systems.net	McLean	VA	22102	703-917-0550	917-0558
Viccs Inc 11821 Parklawn Dr Ste 224 *Web:* www.viccs.com	Rockville	MD	20852	301-984-1355	984-1360
Virginia Society of Professional Engineers 5301 Creek H8s Dr *Web:* www.vspe.org	Midlothian	VA	23112	804-364-0505	
Virtu Financial Inc 645 Madison Ave *Web:* www.virtu.com	New York	NY	10022	212-418-0100	
Vital Mktg LLC 115 E 23rd St 10th Fl *Web:* www.vitalmarketing.com	New York	NY	10010	212-995-9525	
Vital Wave Consulting 555 Bryant St Ste 226 *Web:* vitalwave.com	Palo Alto	CA	94301	650-964-1316	
VoiceAge Corp 750 Lucerne Rd Ste 250 *Web:* www.voiceage.com	Montreal	QC	H3R2H6	514-737-4940	
Wainscot Media LLC 110 Summit Ave *Web:* www.wainscotmedia.com	Montvale	NJ	07645	201-571-2244	
Wakely Consulting Group Inc 17757 US 19 Ste 310 *Web:* www.wakely.com	Clearwater	FL	33764	727-507-9858	507-9658
Waller Financial Planning Group Inc 941 Chatham Ln Ste 212 *Web:* www.waller.com	Columbus	OH	43221	614-457-7026	
Walsh Brothers Inc 210 Commercial St *Web:* www.walshbrothers.com	Boston	MA	02109	617-878-4800	
Walter Greenblatt & Associates LLC 430 Nassau St *Web:* www.wgreenblatt.com	Princeton	NJ	08540	609-497-1282	
Washington Group Consultants LLC PO Box A *Web:* www.washingtongroup.com	Fairfax	VA	22031	703-591-6600	591-6602
Watermark Capital Partners LLC 272 E Deerpath Rd Ste 320 *Web:* www.watermarkcap.com	Lake Forest	IL	60045	847-482-8600	
Watermark Learning Inc 7300 Metro Blvd Ste 207 *TF:* 800-646-9362 ■ *Web:* www.watermarklearning.com	Minneapolis	MN	55439	952-921-0900	
WCD Consultants LLC 23 Rt 31 N Ste B26 *Web:* www.wcdgroup.com	Pennington	NJ	08534	609-730-0007	730-0011
WealthTrust LLC 8434 E Shea Blvd *Web:* www.wealthtrust.com	Scottsdale	AZ	85260	480-339-5221	
Weeden & Company LP 145 Mason St *TF:* 800-843-9333 ■ *Web:* www.weedenco.com	Greenwich	CT	06830	203-861-7670	
Welocalize Inc 241 E Fourth St Ste 207 *TF:* 800-370-9515 ■ *Web:* www.welocalize.com	Frederick	MD	21701	301-668-0330	668-0335
West Coast Asset Management Inc 1205 Coast Village Rd	Montecito	CA	93108	805-653-5333	
West Coast Dental Services Inc 12121 Wilshire Blvd Ste 1111 *Web:* www.westcoastdental.com	Los Angeles	CA	90025	310-820-9933	
West Coast Financial LLC 1525 State St Ste 104 *Web:* www.wcfinc.com	Santa Barbara	CA	93101	805-962-9131	
West Monroe Partners LLC 222 W Adams St *TF:* 800-828-6708 ■ *Web:* www.westmonroepartners.com	Chicago	IL	60606	312-602-4000	
Westcare Management Inc 3155 River Rd S Ste 100 *TF:* 800-541-3732 ■ *Web:* www.westcaremgt.com	Salem	OR	97302	800-541-3732	
Westport Resources Management Inc 55 Greens Farms Rd *Web:* www.westportresources.com	Westport	CT	06880	203-226-0222	
Whimsy Inc 1901 S Busse Rd *Web:* www.whimsytrucking.com	Mount Prospect	IL	60056	847-690-1246	
White Oaks Wealth Advisors Inc 80 S Eighth St IDS Ctr Ste 1725 *Web:* www.whiteoakswealth.com	Minneapolis	MN	55402	612-455-6900	
White Shield Inc 320 N 20th Ave *Web:* www.whiteshield.com	Pasco	WA	99301	509-547-0100	
Whitsons Food Service Corp 1800 Motor Pkwy *Web:* www.whitsons.com	Islandia	NY	11749	631-424-2700	
Wildlands Inc 3855 Atherton Rd *Web:* www.wildlandsinc.com	Rocklin	CA	95765	916-435-3555	
Wind River Financial Inc 18500 W Corporate Dr *Web:* www.windriverfinancial.com	Brookfield	WI	53045	262-792-1119	
Windmill International Inc 12 Murphy Dr Ste 200 *Web:* www.windmill-intl.com	Nashua	NH	03062	603-888-5502	888-5512
Witzenmann USA LLC 2200 Centerwood Dr *Web:* www.witzenmann-usa.com	Warren	MI	48091	586-756-1900	
Wk Dickson & Co Inc 616 Colonnade Dr *Web:* www.wkdickson.com	Charlotte	NC	28205	704-334-5348	334-0078
WM Smith Securities Inc 1700 Lincoln St Ste 2545 *Web:* www.wmsmith.com	Denver	CO	80203	303-831-9696	
Wolgast Corp 4835 Towne Centre Rd Ste 203 *Web:* www.wolgastcorporation.com	Saginaw	MI	48604	989-790-9120	
Women's Mktg Inc 1221 Post Rd E Ste 201 *Web:* www.womensmarketing.com	Westport	CT	06880	203-256-0880	
WorkCare.com 300 S Harbor Blvd Ste 600 *TF:* 800-455-6155 ■ *Web:* www.workcare.com	Anaheim	CA	92805	800-455-6155	
Worldtech International LLC 2331 Mill Rd Ste 100 *Web:* www.worldtech-int.com	Alexandria	VA	22314	703-778-5444	
XMaLpha Technologies LLC 935 Arbogast St *Web:* www.xmalpha.com	Shoreview	MN	55126	651-484-0471	
Zachary Scott & Co 1200 Fifth Ave Ste 1500 *Web:* www.zacharyscott.com	Seattle	WA	98101	206-224-7380	
Zeiders Enterprises Inc 2750 Killarney Dr Ste 100 *Web:* www.zeiders.com	Woodbridge	VA	22192	703-496-9000	580-6339

195 CONSULTING SERVICES - MARKETING

				Phone	Fax
1-2-1 Marketing Services Group Inc 20195 S Diamond Lk Rd Ste 700 *Web:* www.121msg.com	Rogers	MN	55374	763-428-8123	
2020 Companies LLC 3575 Lone Star Cir Ste 200 *Web:* www.2020companies.com	Fort Worth	TX	76177	817-490-0100	

Company / Address	City	State	Zip	Phone	Fax
220 Marketing 3405 Kenyon St Ste 501	San Diego	CA	92110	877-220-6584	
TF: 877-220-6584 ■ *Web:* www.220marketing.com					
3 Media Web Solutions Inc 1900 W Park Dr Ste 280	Westborough	MA	01581	508-845-8900	
Web: www.3mediaweb.com					
360 Bc Group Inc 25562 Gloriosa Dr	Mission Viejo	CA	92691	949-916-9120	
Web: 360-biz.com/					
451 Marketing LLC 21 School St	Boston	MA	02108	617-259-1605	
Web: www.451marketing.com					
5th Business 5100 Orbitor Dr Ste 100	Mississauga	ON	L4W4Z4	905-275-2220	
TF: 866-875-2220 ■ *Web:* www.5thbusiness.com					
6s Marketing 1120 Hamilton St.	Vancouver	BC	V6B2S2	604-642-6765	
TF: 888-642-6765 ■ *Web:* www.6smarketing.com					
7Summits LLC 1110 Old World Third St Ste 500	Milwaukee	WI	53203	866-705-6372	
TF: 866-705-6372 ■ *Web:* www.7summitsagency.com					
87AM Holdings LLC 321 W 44Th St Ste 703	New York	NY	10036	646-695-4723	
Web: www.87am.com					
8fold LLC 58 Mackenzie Rd.	Morristown	NJ	07960	973-380-0070	
Web: www.8foldworks.com					
919 Marketing Company Inc 102 Avent Ferry Rd	Holly Springs	NC	27540	919-557-7890	
Web: www.919marketing.com					
A.D.D. Marketing Inc 6600 Lexington Ave	Los Angeles	CA	90038	323-790-0500	
Web: www.addmarketing.com					
Accelerant Sales Group LLC 39 E Hanover Ave Ste C3	Morris Plains	NJ	07950	973-331-0600	
Web: www.accelerantsales.com					
Ace Ranking 211 Sutter St Ste 400	San Francisco	CA	94108	415-536-3929	
Web: www.acerankings.com					
Achieve LLC 233 McCrea St Ste 200	Indianapolis	IN	46225	317-637-3000	
Web: www.achieveguidance.com					
Aci Event Group 652 Hayes St	San Francisco	CA	94102	415-553-7880	
Web: www.acieventgroup.com					
Acme Merchandise and Apparel Inc 46 Blackburn Ctr Ste 47	Gloucester	MA	01930	978-282-4800	
Web: www.acmeapparel.com					
AcrobatAnt LLC 1336 E 15th St.	Tulsa	OK	74120	918-938-7901	
Web: www.acrobatant.us					
Action Lead Solutions 2232 N Clybourn Ave Ste 300	Chicago	IL	60614	773-661-1570	
Web: actionleadsolutions.com					
ACTON Marketing LLC 3401 NW 39th St	Lincoln	NE	68524	402-470-2909	
Web: www.acton.com					
AD-EX International Inc 1301 Glendale-Milford Rd	Cincinnati	OH	45215	513-771-2339	
Web: www.adex-intl.com					
Adams & Associates of Nevada Inc 10395 Double R Blvd	Reno	NV	89521	775-348-0900	
Web: www.adamsaai.com					
Adams Addressing Assoc Inc 39 Faranella Dr	East Hanover	NJ	07936	973-887-3409	
Web: www.adamsdms.com					
Adams Group Inc, The 925 Gervais St	Columbia	SC	29201	803-765-1223	
Web: www.adamsgroup.com					
Adams Unlimited 80 Broad St Ste 3202	New York	NY	10004	212-956-5900	
Web: adams-pr.com					
Add3 LLC 500 E Pk St 2nd Fl	Seattle	WA	98122	206-568-3772	
Web: www.add3.com					
Adex Media Inc 883 N Shoreline Blvd Ste A200	Mountain View	CA	94943	650-967-3040	
Web: www.adex.com					
Adfirmative LLC 11416 Hollister Dr Ste	Austin	TX	78739	866-966-9968	
TF: 866-966-9968 ■ *Web:* adfirmative.com					
Adrian Miller Direct Mktg 43 Park Ave	Port Washington	NY	11050	516-767-9288	
Web: adrianmiller.com					
Advisors Excel LLC 1300 SW Arrowhead Rd Ste 200	Topeka	KS	66604	866-363-9595	
TF: 866-363-9595 ■ *Web:* www.advisorsexcel.com					
Aerotronics Marketing Inc 5331 Derry Ave Ste O	Agoura Hills	CA	91301	818-735-6633	
Web: www.aerotronics.net					
AgileCat LLC 1818 Market st Ste 220	Philadelphia	PA	19127	215-508-2082	
Web: www.agilecat.com					
aimClear 525 S Lk Ave Ste 320	Duluth	MN	55812	218-727-4325	
Web: www.aimclearblog.com					
AIS RealTime 4440 Bowen Blvd SE	Grand Rapids	MI	49508	877-314-1100	
TF: 877-314-1100 ■ *Web:* www.aisservice.com					
Albert Risk Management Consultants 72 River Park St	Needham Heights	MA	02494	781-449-2866	
Web: www.albertrisk.com					
Albion International Services 2520 Nw 97th Ave Ste 110	Miami	FL	33172	305-406-1000	
Web: www.albionstaffing.com					
Alcott Whitney LLC 414 Bridge St	Franklin	TN	37064	615-790-9155	
Web: www.alcottwhitney.com					
Alipes CME Inc 175 Portland St Fifth Fl	Boston	MA	02114	617-303-1045	
Web: www.alipescme.com					
All Terrain 2675 W Grand Ave	Chicago	IL	60612	312-421-7672	
Web: www.allterrain.net					
Allout Marketing Inc 1905 Wayzata Blvd Ste 130	Wayzata	MN	55391	952-404-0800	
Web: www.alloutsuccess.com					
Alpha Marketing Inc 343 E Six Forks Rd Ste 360	Raleigh	NC	27609	919-836-2169	
Web: www.alphamarketing.com					
Alpha Strategies Investment Consulting Inc 10 David St.	Ladera Ranch	CA	92694	949-429-7129	
Web: asinvestmentgroup.com					
Altitude Marketing 417 State Rd 2nd Fl	Emmaus	PA	18049	610-421-8601	
Web: altitudemarketing.com					
Americhip Inc 19032 S Vermont Ave.	Los Angeles	CA	90248	310-323-3697	
Web: www.americhip.com					
Amerivon Holdings LLC 2815 Townsgate Rd Ste 225	Westlake Village	CA	91361	805-719-4800	
Web: www.amerivon.com					
AMPERAGE Marketing 6711 Chancellor Dr	Cedar Falls	IA	50613	319-268-9151	
Web: www.amperagemarketing.com/?ref=meandv					
Analytical Group Inc, The 16638 N 90th St	Scottsdale	AZ	85260	480-483-7505	
Web: www.analyticalgroup.com					
Angie Brewer & Associates LC 9104 58th Dr E	Bradenton	FL	34202	941-757-4300	
Web: www.angiebrewer.com					
Answers Systems Inc 4029 Tampa Rd	Oldsmar	FL	34677	813-818-9299	
Web: www.afsi.com					
Aperio Insights LLC 6057 Preston Haven Dr	Dallas	TX	75230	469-363-0109	
Web: aperioinsights.com					
Apex Asset Management LLC 2501 Oregon Pike Ste 201	Lancaster	PA	17601	717-519-1780	
TF: 888-592-2149 ■ *Web:* www.apexasset.com					
Applied Marketing Research Inc 420 W 98th St.	Kansas City	MO	64114	816-442-1010	
Web: www.appliedmr.com					
Applied Skills & Knowledge 100 W Hanover Ave	Cedar Knolls	NJ	07927	973-631-1607	
Web: www.appliedskills.com					
Archie McPhee and Co 2428 NW Market St	Seattle	WA	98113	425-349-3009	
Web: mcphee.com					
Argo Marketing Group 64 Lisbon St	Lewiston	ME	04240	207-514-0744	
Web: argomarketing.com					
Armstrong Partnership LP 23 Prince Andrew Pl	Toronto	ON	M3C2H2	416-444-3050	
Web: www.armstrongpartnership.com					
Arrowhead Promotion & Fulfillment Company Inc 1105 SE Eighth St.	Grand Rapids	MN	55744	218-327-1165	
Web: www.apfco.com					
Asen Marketing & Advertising Inc 2210 Sutherland Ave Ste 115	Knoxville	TN	37919	865-769-0006	
Web: www.asenmarketing.com					
ASL Marketing 2 Dubon Ct	Farmingdale	NY	11735	516-248-6100	
Web: www.aslmarketing.com					
Aspasie Inc 221 Saint-Georges	Saint-barnabe-nord	QC	G0X2K0	819-379-2157	
Web: www.aspasie.com					
ASTONE Inc 2300 Tulare St Ste 210	Fresno	CA	93721	559-375-7100	
Atomic Design 277 Alexander St Ste 208	Rochester	NY	14607	585-271-8661	
Web: atomicdesigninc.net					
Atomic Leads Inc 4926 Windy Hill Dr	Raleigh	NC	27609	919-439-4900	
Web: www.atomicleads.com					
Attema Marketing Inc 3105 W 135th St	Burnsville	MN	55337	952-890-1843	
Web: www.attemamarketing.com					
Augeo Affinity Marketing Inc 2561 Territorial Rd	St. Paul	MN	55114	651-917-9143	
Web: www.augeomarketing.com					
Aura 360 Ventures 28 DanFth St	Portland	ME	04101	207-699-2360	
Web: aura360.com					
Auto Internet Marketing Inc 2495 Enterprise Rd Ste 201	Clearwater	FL	33763	727-791-0825	
Web: www.autointernetmarketing.com					
autograph Inc 999 N NorthLk Way	Seattle	WA	98103	425-445-2742	
Web: www.autograph.me					
Autopacific Inc 2991 Dow Ave	Tustin	CA	92780	714-838-4234	
Web: www.autopacific.com					
Autotegrity Inc 198 Broadway 2nd Fl	Cambridge	MA	02139	617-208-4420	
Web: www.autotegrity.com					
Avala Marketing Group Inc 1078 Headquarters Park	Fenton	MO	63026	636-343-9988	
Web: www.avalamarketing.com					
Avant Strategies LLC 913 W McDowell Rd	Phoenix	AZ	85007	480-788-8230	
Web: avantstrategies.net					
Avideon Corp PO Box 4830	Baltimore	MD	21211	443-957-1986	
Web: www.avideon.com					
Axcept Media LLC 411 N Washington Ave Ste 208	Minneapolis	MN	55401	612-279-1310	
Web: axceptmedia.com					
Axiom Marketing Inc 624 E Park Ave	Libertyville	IL	60048	847-362-5656	
Web: www.axmarketing.com					
Azul Partners Inc 421 W Melrose Ste 10C	Chicago	IL	60657	773-525-7406	
Web: www.azulpartners.com					
Backus Turner International 3116 N Federal Hwy	Pompano Beach	FL	33064	305-573-9996	
Web: www.backusturner.com					
Baesman Group Inc 274 Marconi Blvd	Columbus	OH	43215	614-771-2300	
Web: www.baesman.com					
Bailey House Inc 180 Christopher St	New York	NY	10014	212-337-3000	
Web: www.baileyhouse.org					
Ballantine and Company Inc PO Box 805	Carlisle	MA	01741	978-369-1772	
Web: www.ballantine-inc.com					
Ballard Direct 7000 W Palmetto Park Rd Ste 210	Boca Raton	FL	33433	914-262-6951	
Web: www.ballarddirect.com					
Band Digital Inc 150 N Michigan Ave Ste 300	Chicago	IL	60601	312-981-6000	
Web: banddigital.com					
Bates Communications Inc 40 Grove St Ste 310	Wellesley	MA	02482	781-235-8239	
Web: www.bates-communications.com					
Bay MarketForce LLC 2410 S Main St Ste C	West Bend	WI	53095	262-355-5612	
Web: www.baymarketforce.com					
BDS Marketing Inc 10 Holland	Irvine	CA	92618	949-472-6700	
Web: www.bdsmktg.com					
Becker Media 2633 Telegraph Ave Ste 110	Oakland	CA	94607	510-465-6200	
Web: www.beckermedia.net					
Beezley Management LLC 23632 Calabasas Rd Ste 105	Calabasas	CA	91302	818-591-8555	
Web: www.beezleymanagement.com					
Bellomy Research Inc 175 Sunnynoll Ct.	Winston-Salem	NC	27106	800-443-7344	
TF: 800-443-7344 ■ *Web:* www.bellomyresearch.com					

	City	State	Zip	Phone	Fax
Benevity Social Ventures Inc 1110 First St SW *Web:* www.benevity.com	Calgary	AB	T2R0V1	403-237-7875	
Best Image Marketing Inc 2222 Park Pl Blvd. *Web:* connect.homes.com	Clearlake	CA	95422	707-995-5050	
Beverage Marketing Corp 850 Third Ave 18th Fl *TF:* 800-275-4630 ■ *Web:* www.beveragemarketing.com	New York	NY	10022	212-688-7640	826-1255
Big Idea Group Inc 175 Canal St, 5B *Web:* www.bigideagroup.net	Manchester	NH	03101	603-641-5955	
BIGEYE DIRECT Inc 13864 Redskin Dr. *Web:* www.bigeyedirect.com	Herndon	VA	20171	703-955-3020	
Bill Good Marketing Inc 6891 S 700 W *Web:* www.billgoodmarketing.com	Midvale	UT	84040	801-572-1480	
BioVid Corp 10 Canal St Ste 136 *Web:* biovid.com	Bristol	PA	19007	609-750-1400	
Birthday In A Box Inc 7951 Cessna Ave *Web:* www.birthdayinabox.com	Gaithersburg	MD	20879	301-956-1616	
Blane Canada Ltd PO Box 4408 *Web:* www.blanecanada.com	Wheaton	IL	60189	630-462-9222	
Blaze Marketing Solutions Ltd 1000 Windmill Rd Ste 32 *Web:* blazemarketing.com	Dartmouth	NS	B3B1L7	902-468-0537	
Blue Lotus Creative 7971 Columbia St *Web:* www.bluelotuscreative.com	Vancouver	BC	V5Z2X5	604-306-8701	
Blue Telescope 236 W 30 St 7th Fl *Web:* www.blue-telescope.com	New York	NY	10001	212-675-7702	
Blue Wave Marketing and Promotion 180 Canal St Ste 300 *Web:* www.bluewavemarketing.com	Boston	MA	02114	617-948-5000	
Bluedog Design LLC 403 N Carpenter St *Web:* www.bluedogdesign.com	Chicago	IL	60642	312-243-1101	
BlueHornet Networks Inc 2355 Northside Dr Ste B250 *Web:* www.bluehornet.com	San Diego	CA	92108	619-295-1856	
BlueKai Inc 20883 Stevens Creek Blvd, Ste 200 *Web:* www.bluekai.com	Cupertino	CA	95014	408-200-8300	
BlueRush Media Group Corp 75 Sherbourne St *Web:* www.bluerush.com/en	Toronto	ON	M5A2P9	416-203-0618	
BMA Communications LLC 115 Trolley Ct *Web:* www.bmacommunications.com	Pittsburgh	PA	15237	412-391-4332	
Boomers & Beyond Inc 1998 Ruffin Mill Rd *TF:* 800-958-8324 ■ *Web:* www.firststreetonline.com	Colonial Heights	VA	23834	804-524-9888	524-9889
Boost Rewards 811 E Fourth St Ste B *TF:* 800-324-9756 ■ *Web:* www.boostrewards.com	Dayton	OH	45402	800-324-9756	
Booth Bay Marketing 1220 Valley Forge Rd Ste 45 *Web:* www.boothbay.com	Phoenixville	PA	19460	610-933-5112	
BQ6 Media Group 110 Gibraltar Rd Ste 100, *Web:* www.bq6media.com	Horsham	PA	19044	267-965-2000	
Brains On Fire Inc 148 River St *Web:* www.brainsonfire.com	Greenville	SC	29601	864-676-9663	
Brand Iron 821 22nd St *Web:* brandiron.net	Denver	CO	80205	303-534-1901	
Brand Protection Agency LLC 2700 Fairmount St *TF:* 866-339-5657 ■ *Web:* brandprotectionagency.com	Dallas	TX	75201	866-339-5657	
Brand Sense Partners LLC 10441 Jefferson Blvd Ste 100 *Web:* bsp.com	Culver City	CA	90232	310-867-7222	
Brandamplitude Llc 3467 Notre Dame Path *Web:* brandamplitude.com	Stevensville	MI	49127	269-429-6526	
Brd Solutions 101 Trenton Cir *Web:* www.brdsolutions.net	Canonsburg	PA	15317	724-941-6375	
Bridgz Marketing Group 7831 E Bush Lk Rd *Web:* www.bridgz.com	Minneapolis	MN	55439	952-841-6200	
Brighter Collective 12115 W Bluff Creek Dr *Web:* www.brightercollective.com	Los Angeles	CA	90094	310-857-2900	
BrightHouse LLC 790 Marietta St *Web:* www.thinkbrighthouse.com	Atlanta	GA	30318	404-240-2500	
Britto Agency The 234 W 56th St Fl 5 *Web:* thebrittoagency.com	New York	NY	10019	212-977-6772	
Broadway Marketing Ltd 80 Fuller Rd *Web:* www.broadwaymarketing.com	Albany	NY	12205	518-489-3226	
Brogan & Partners Advertising Consultancy Inc 800 N Old Woodward Ave Ste 100 *Web:* www.brogan.com	Birmingham	MI	48009	248-341-8200	
Bromley Group LLC, The 15 W 26th St 3rd Fl *Web:* tbg-world.com	New York	NY	10010	212-696-1100	
Brooks Group, The 15 W 37th St 16th Fl *Web:* www.brookspr.com	New York	NY	10018	212-768-0860	
BSM Media Inc 2335 E Atlantic Blvd Ste 300 *Web:* www.bsmmedia.com	Fort Lauderdale	FL	33062	954-943-2322	
Builder Homesite Inc 11900 Ranch Rd 620 N *Web:* www.builderhomesite.com	Austin	TX	78750	512-371-3800	
Bullseye Marketing Group 125 E Main St Ste 205 *Web:* www.bullseyegroup.biz	Mount Kisco	NY	10549	914-242-8288	
Burnham Marketing LLC 1 Amber Ridge Rd *Web:* www.burnhammarketing.com	Chestnut Ridge	NY	10977	917-204-6999	
Business Efficacy 6130 Blue Cir Dr Ste 100 *Web:* www.businessefficacy.com	Minneapolis	MN	55343	952-217-0425	
Business-to-Business Marketing Communications Inc 900 Ridgefield Dr Ste 270 *Web:* www.btbmarketing.com	Raleigh	NC	27609	919-872-8172	872-8875
Buzz Marketing Group 1018 Laurel Oak Rd Ste 1 *Web:* buzzmg.com	Voorhees	NJ	08043	856-346-3456	
C-4 Analytics LLC 999 Broadway Ste 500 *Web:* www.c-4analytics.com	Saugus	MA	01906	617-250-8888	
C.J. Driscoll & Associates 2636 Via Carrillo *Web:* www.cjdriscoll.com	Palos Verdes Estates	CA	90274	310-544-5046	
Cadence Marketing Llc 509 Lk Ct *Web:* www.cadencemarketingllc.com	Basalt	CO	81621	970-927-0377	
Cadmium Cd LLC 19 Newport Dr Ste 101 *TF:* 877-426-6323 ■ *Web:* www.cadmiumcd.com	Forest Hill	MD	21050	410-638-9239	
Calmare Therapeutics Inc 1375 Kings Hwy *Web:* calmaretherapeutics.com	Fairfield	CT	06824	203-368-6044	368-5399
Calmetto 883 Ne Main St Ste 2 *Web:* www.siia.org	Simpsonville	SC	29681	864-962-2201	
Campus Special LLC, The 3575 Koger Blvd Ste 300 *TF:* 800-365-8520	Duluth	GA	30096	800-365-8520	
Canary Marketing Inc 600 San Ramon Vly Blvd Ste 200 *Web:* www.canarymarketing.com	Danville	CA	94526	925-314-1888	
Cannella Response Television LLC 492 N Pine St *Web:* www.drtv.com	Burlington	WI	53105	262-763-4810	
Car People Marketing Inc 1020 W International Spee *Web:* www.carpeoplemarketing.com	Daytona Beach	FL	32114	386-761-3131	
Carey Color Inc 6835 Ridge Rd *Web:* careyweb.com	Wadsworth	OH	44281	330-239-1835	
Cargo Management Systems Llc 827 E Main St *TF:* 855-484-9235 ■ *Web:* www.cmscargo.com	Richmond	KY	40475	855-484-9235	
Cdr Assessment Group Inc 1644 S Denver Ave *TF:* 888-406-0100 ■ *Web:* cdrassessmentgroup.com	Tulsa	OK	74119	918-488-0722	
CellTrust Corp 14822 N 73rd St Bldg B Ste 113 *Web:* www.celltrust.com	Scottsdale	AZ	85260	480-515-5200	
Centrus Group Inc 1653 Merriman Rd Ste 211 *Web:* centrusgroup.com	Akron	OH	44313	330-864-5800	
Ceridian Benefits Services Inc 3201 34th St South *Web:* www.ceridian-benefits.com	St. Petersburg	FL	33711	727-864-3300	
Channel Partners LLC 10 Holland Dr *Web:* www.channelpartners.com	Irvine	CA	92618	949-472-6711	
Cheshire Marketing Inc 3209 Guess Rd Ste 108 *TF:* 800-495-4633 ■ *Web:* www.cheshiremarketing.com	Durham	NC	27705	919-479-2008	
Chisano Marketing Communications Inc 2000 Byers Rd *Web:* www.chisano.com	Miamisburg	OH	45342	937-866-4914	
Cibo Global LLC 649 Frnt St *Web:* www.cibosf.com	San Francisco	CA	94111	415-233-6606	
Classical Marketing LLC 150 N Martingale Rd Ste 800 *TF:* 800-613-3489 ■ *Web:* classicalmarketing.com	Schaumburg	IL	60173	847-969-1696	
Clear Link Technologies LLC 5202 W Douglas Corrigan Way Ste 300 *Web:* www.clear-link.com	Salt Lake City	UT	84116	801-424-0018	
Client Focused Media Inc 100 Festival Park Ave *Web:* cfmedia.net	Jacksonville	FL	32202	904-232-3001	
Clientize com Inc 160 W Camino Real Ste 250 *Web:* www.clientize.com	Boca Raton	FL	33432	561-417-5533	
Coalesce Corp 447 Miller Ave Ste E *Web:* www.coalesce.com	Mill Valley	CA	94941	415-384-3040	
Coefficient Inc 509 Altaloma Ave *Web:* www.intandem.io	Orlando	FL	32803	303-513-2124	
Cohn 2434 W Caithness Pl *Web:* www.cohnmarketing.com	Denver	CO	80211	303-839-1415	
Colletti-fiss Llc 8423 E Charter Oak Dr *Web:* collettifiss.com	Scottsdale	AZ	85260	480-483-1480	
Common Interest Management Services Inc 315 Diablo Rd Ste 221 *Web:* www.commoninterest.com	Danville	CA	94526	925-743-3080	
ComNet Marketing Group Inc 1214 Stowe Ave *TF:* 877-581-2565 ■ *Web:* www.comnetmarketing.com	Medford	OR	97501	877-581-2565	
CompAnalysis Inc 725 Washington St Ste 302 *Web:* www.companalysis.com	Oakland	CA	94607	510-763-3774	
Competitrack Inc 36-36 33rd St *Web:* www.competitrack.com	Long Island City	NY	11106	718-482-4200	
Compu-Mail LLC 3235 Grand Island Blvd *Web:* compu-mail.com	Grand Island	NY	14072	716-775-8001	
Computech Systems Inc 400 C SouthLk Blvd *Web:* computechsystemsinc.com	North Chesterfield	VA	23236	804-897-7917	
ComStar Networks LLC 1820 NE Jensen Beach Blvd Ste 564 *TF:* 800-516-1595 ■ *Web:* www.comstarnetwork.net	Jensen Beach	FL	34957	800-516-1595	
Concept Studio LLC, The 165 Kings Hwy N *Web:* www.tcspromo.com	Westport	CT	06880	203-227-7444	
Content Firm LLC, The 26 Academy Dr E *Web:* evanschuman.com	Whippany	NJ	07981	973-993-8098	
Cooper Thomas LLC 923 V St Nw *Web:* cooperthomas.com	Washington	DC	20001	202-387-8366	
Cortac Group Inc 29512 Baycrest Dr *Web:* www.cortacgroup.com	Rancho Palos Verdes	CA	90275	310-377-2085	
Creor Group LLC Po Box 110398 *TF:* 877-774-4312 ■ *Web:* creorgroup.com	Campbell	CA	95011	408-248-4822	
Crimson Consulting Group 4970 El Camino Real Ste 200 *Web:* crimsonmarketing.com	Los Altos	CA	94022	650-960-3600	960-3737
Crossfire Media Inc 1940 Commerce St *Web:* www.crossfiremedia.com	Yorktown Heights	NY	10598	914-302-2900	
Crossmark Inc 5100 Legacy Dr *TF:* 877-699-6275 ■ *Web:* www.crossmark.com	Plano	TX	75024	469-814-1000	814-1355

Company / Address	City	State	Zip	Phone	Fax
Crowded Ocean Inc 148 Castro St Ste B1 *Web:* www.crowdedocean.com	Mountain View	CA	94041	650-455-4191	
Crucial Interactive Inc 21 Camden St 5th Fl *TF:* 877-244-6562 ■ *Web:* www.crucialinteractive.com	Toronto	ON	M5V1V2	416-645-0135	
Crunch Brands 1 First Ave Bldg 34 *Web:* crunchbrands.com	Charlestown	MA	02129	617-241-5553	
Culture22 Communications LLC 935B N Plum Grove Rd *Web:* www.culture22.com	Schaumburg	IL	60173	847-517-9022	
Customer Elation Inc 9065 Lyndale Ave South *Web:* www.customerelation.com	Bloomington	MN	55420	952-653-0801	
D A Crowley & Associates Inc 3 Overlook Dr *Web:* www.dacrowley.com	Amherst	NH	03031	603-673-7050	
D Side Advisors 12601 Easton Dr *Web:* dside.com	Saratoga	CA	95070	408-255-4620	
D.Trio Marketing Group 401 N Third St Ste 480 *Web:* www.dtrio.com	Minneapolis	MN	55401	612-436-0323	
D3Logic Inc 89 Commercial Way *Web:* www.d3logic.com	East Providence	RI	02914	401-435-4300	
d50 Media Inc 93 Worcester St Ste 101 *Web:* www.d50media.com	Wellesley	MA	02481	781-446-4370	
Dane Media LLC 385 Sylvan Ave Ste 24 *TF:* 888-233-2863 ■ *Web:* www.danemedia.com	Englewood Cliffs	NJ	07632	888-233-2863	
Data Banque Ltd 5500 Brooktree Rd Ste 200 *Web:* www.databanque.com	Wexford	PA	15090	412-548-1030	
Datamart Direct Inc 6405 Muirfield Dr	Hanover Park	IL	60133	630-307-7100	
Davis Brand Capital LLC 1180 Peachtree St Ste 2605 *Web:* davisbrandcapital.com	Atlanta	GA	30309	404-347-7778	
Day Vision Marketing 2222 S 12th St Ste D *Web:* www.dayvision.com	Allentown	PA	18103	610-403-3999	
Daymon Assoc Inc 700 Fairfield Ave *Web:* www.daymon.com	Stamford	CT	06902	203-352-7500	352-7947
DCI Marketing Inc 2727 W Good Hope Rd *Web:* www.dci-artform.com	Milwaukee	WI	53209	414-228-7000	228-4366
dDirect Inc 2707 Peachtree Sq *Web:* www.ddirect.com	Atlanta	GA	30360	678-530-0034	
De Kadt Marketing and Research Inc 162 Danbury Rd *Web:* dekadt.com	Ridgefield	CT	06877	203-431-1212	
Decision Counsel Inc 1912 Bonita Ave *Web:* decisioncounsel.com	Berkeley	CA	94704	510-883-9830	
Delaney Meeting & Event Planning 1 Mill St Ste 315 *Web:* www.delaneymeetingevent.com	Burlington	VT	05401	802-865-5202	
Deloitte Digital 837 N 34th St Ste 100 *Web:* www.deloittedigital.com/us	Seattle	WA	98103	206-633-1167	
Delta Marketing Dynamics 205 S Salina St Ste 400 *Web:* deltamarketingdynamics.com	Syracuse	NY	13202	315-492-2905	
Demonstrating To Win 7150 Campus Dr Ste 330 *Web:* www.demo2win.com	Colorado Springs	CO	80920	719-594-9959	
Deniro Marketing LLC 6777 Embarcadero Dr Ste 3 *TF:* 877-752-1458 ■ *Web:* www.deniromarketing.com	Stockton	CA	95219	209-477-7676	
Design Compendium Inc, The 155 20th St *Web:* www.designcompendium.com	Brooklyn	NY	11232	718-499-7722	
Deskey 120 E Eighth St *Web:* www.deskey.com	Cincinnati	OH	45202	513-721-6800	
Directives West Inc 110 E 9th St Ste A525 *Web:* www.directiveswest.com	Los Angeles	CA	90079	213-627-5921	
Djs Marketing Group Inc 2398 S Dixie Hwy *Web:* www.djs-marketing.com	Miami	FL	33133	305-640-5939	
DMI Music & Media Solutions 35 W Dayton St *Web:* www.dmimusic.com	Pasadena	CA	91105	626-795-0432	
Do My Own Pest Control 4260 Communications Dr *Web:* www.domyownpestcontrol.com	Norcross	GA	30093	770-840-8831	
Doneger Group, The 463 Seventh Ave *Web:* www.doneger.com	New York	NY	10018	212-564-1266	
Dreamspan Product Innovation LLC 11645 N Cave Creek Rd *Web:* www.dreamspan.com	Phoenix	AZ	85020	602-354-7640	
Driveline Holdings Inc 700 Freeport Pkwy Ste 100 *TF:* 888-123-4567 ■ *Web:* www.drivelineretail.com	Coppell	TX	75019	888-123-4567	
Duffy & Partners LLC 710 Second St S Ste 602 *Web:* www.duffy.com	Minneapolis	MN	55401	612-548-2333	
Dunn Group Inc, The 999 Riverview Dr Ste 302 *Web:* dunngrp.com	Totowa	NJ	07511	973-237-9500	
Dymun & Co 200 1st Ave Ste 400 *Web:* dymun.com	Pittsburgh	PA	15222	412-281-2345	
E-power Marketing Inc 111 N Main St Ste 405 *Web:* www.epower.com	Oshkosh	WI	54901	920-303-1244	
East Tennessee Human Resource Agency Inc 9111 Cross Park Dr Ste A-250 *Web:* www.ethra.org	Knoxville	TN	37923	865-691-2551	
ebQuickstart 3000 S IH 35 Ste 320 *Web:* ebq.com	Austin	TX	78704	512-637-9696	
Ecity Interactive Inc 136 S 15th St *Web:* ecityinteractive.com	Philadelphia	PA	19102	215-557-0767	
Eclipse Marketing Services Inc 240 Cedar Knolls Rd Ste 100 *TF:* 800-837-4648 ■ *Web:* www.eclipsemarketingservices.com	Cedar Knolls	NJ	07927	800-837-4648	
Economic Consulting Services LLC 2001 L St NW *Web:* www.economic-consulting.com	Washington	DC	20036	202-466-7720	466-2710
Edgar Dunn & Co Hills Plz Two Harrison St Ste 310 *Web:* www.edgardunn.com	San Francisco	CA	94105	415-977-1870	
Edge Training Systems 9710 Farrar Ct Ste P *Web:* www.edgetrainingsystems.com	North Chesterfield	VA	23236	804-272-0333	
EdgeCore LLC 1025 Technology Pkwy Ste A *Web:* www.edgecore.com	Cedar Falls	IA	50613	319-277-3700	
edufficient com 14 Vervalen St *Web:* www.edufficient.com	Closter	NJ	07624	201-297-7424	
eGumBall Inc 8687 Research Dr Ste 200 *TF:* 800-890-8940 ■ *Web:* www.egumball.com	Irvine	CA	92618	800-890-8940	
Eire Direct Marketing 720 N Franklin St Ste 310 *Web:* www.eiredirect.com	Chicago	IL	60654	312-640-4000	
Emarketingwerx Inc 5335 W 138th St *Web:* www.emarketingwerx.com	Hawthorne	CA	90250	310-686-2314	
EMC Creative 175 N California Blvd Ste 440 *Web:* www.emccreative.com	Walnut Creek	CA	94596	925-837-9380	
Emerald Hospitality Associates Inc 2001 Crocker Rd Ste 300 *Web:* www.emeraldhospitality.com	Westlake	OH	44145	440-239-9848	
EnSys Energy & Systems Inc 1775 Massachussets Ave *Web:* www.ensysenergy.com	Lexington	MA	02420	781-274-8454	
Entegral Energy Marketing Inc 1228 Kensington Rd NW Ste 205 *Web:* www.entegralenergy.com	Calgary	AB	T2N3P3	403-283-1133	
Environics Analytics Group Ltd 33 Bloor St E Ste 400 *TF:* 888-339-3304 ■ *Web:* www.environicsanalytics.ca	Toronto	ON	M4W3H1	416-969-2733	
Envision Marketing Inc 26941 Cabot Rd Ste 121 *Web:* www.envisionmarketing.net	Laguna Hills	CA	92653	949-367-7818	
Epic Research LLC 300 Centennial Cir *Web:* www.epicresearch.net	Greenville	DE	19807	302-467-5445	
Ernst-Van Praag Inc 433 Plaza Real Ste 275 *Web:* www.evpconsulting.com	Boca Raton	FL	33432	561-447-0557	
ESN Interactive 440 Seaton St Ste 301 *Web:* www.edusearch.com	Los Angeles	CA	90013	323-337-0600	
Ethos Marketing & Design 907 Main St *Web:* ethos-marketing.com	Westbrook	ME	04092	207-856-2610	
EtQ Management Consultants Inc 399 Conklin St Ste 208 *Web:* www.etq.com	Farmingdale	NY	11735	516-293-0949	
Eventsful Inc 305 E 40th St Apt 6f *Web:* www.eventsful.com	New York	NY	10016	212-682-8405	
Eview 360 Corp 39255 Country Club Dr Ste B-1 *Web:* www.eview360.com	Farmington Hills	MI	48331	248-306-5191	
Evviva Brands LLC 2403 Mira Vista Dr *Web:* evvivabrands.com	El Cerrito	CA	94530	510-215-2783	
Excell Marketing L C 5501 Park Ave *Web:* www.excellmktg.com	Des Moines	IA	50321	515-244-0300	
Exclaimit Inc 3825 Misty Landing Dr *Web:* www.exclaimit.com	Valrico	FL	33594	813-731-8718	
Experience Corp, The 127A E 71st St *Web:* richardattiasassociates.com	New York	NY	10021	212-794-8801	
Extole Inc 350 Sansome St Ste 700 *Web:* www.extole.com	San Francisco	CA	94104	415-625-0411	
Eyeball Digital Inc 187 Lafayette St *Web:* www.eyeballnyc.com	New York	NY	10013	212-431-5324	
Eze Castle Integration Inc 260 Franklin St 12th Fl *TF:* 800-752-1382 ■ *Web:* www.eci.com	Boston	MA	02110	617-217-3000	217-3001
F & H. Solutions Group LLC 1300 19th St Nw Ste 420 *Web:* fhsolutionsgroup.com	Washington	DC	20036	202-719-2000	
Faith Popcorn's BrainReserve 55 E 59th St 18th Fl *Web:* www.faithpopcorn.com	New York	NY	10022	212-772-7778	
FarmLink Marketing Solutions Inc Suite 110-93 Lombard Ave *TF:* 877-376-5465 ■ *Web:* www.farmlinksolutions.ca	Winnipeg	MB	R3B3B1	877-376-5465	
Fast Horse 240 Ninth Ave N *Web:* www.fasthorseinc.com	Minneapolis	MN	55401	612-746-4610	
Felder Communications Group 50 Louis NW Trade Ctr Ste 600 *Web:* www.felder.com	Grand Rapids	MI	49503	616-459-1200	
FGI Seattle LLC 229 8th St S *Web:* www.fgi.com	Kirkland	WA	98033	206-734-3750	
FinCo Management LLC 18 Doaks Ln	Marblehead	MA	01945	781-639-6000	
Find & Convert 36181 E Lk Rd Ste 188 *Web:* www.findandconvert.com	Palm Harbor	FL	34685	727-234-0952	
Finity Communications Inc 1314 Nw Irving St Apt 710 *Web:* www.finity.com	Portland	OR	97209	503-808-9240	
Fitch Inc 585 S Front St Ste 50 *Web:* www.fitch.com	Columbus	OH	43215	614-885-3453	885-4289
FiveStars Loyalty Inc 321 11th St *Web:* www.fivestars.com	San Francisco	CA	94103	860-578-2770	
Fixation Marketing Inc 4340 East-West Hwy Ste 200 *Web:* www.fixation.com	Bethesda	MD	20814	240-207-2009	
Flashman Studios LLC 4280 26Th St *Web:* www.flashmanstudios.com	San Francisco	CA	94131	415-826-7654	
Flexi Display Marketing Inc 24669 Halsted Rd Ste *Web:* www.flexidisplay.com	Farmington Hills	MI	48335	248-987-6400	
Forward Branding & Identity 34 May St *Web:* www.forwardbranding.com	Webster	NY	14580	585-872-9222	
Fourandhalf Inc 3581 Sneath Ln *Web:* fourandhalf.com	San Bruno	CA	94066	650-871-5808	
FourCubed LLC 509 First Ave NE *Web:* fourcubed.com	Minneapolis	MN	55413	612-454-1509	

Company	City	State	Zip	Phone	Fax
Fransmart Inc 320 King St Ste 250 *Web:* www.fransmart.com	Alexandria	VA	22314	703-549-5332	
Frantz Group Inc, The 1245 Cheyenne Ave *TF:* 800-707-0064 ■ *Web:* www.thefrantzgroup.com	Grafton	WI	53024	262-204-6000	
Fresh Consulting LLC 914 140th Ave NE Ste 300 *Web:* www.freshconsulting.com	Bellevue	WA	98006	425-516-7597	
FuelFX LLC 5205 Spruce St *TF:* 877-255-2543 ■ *Web:* www.fuelfx.com	Bellaire	TX	77401	877-255-2543	
Fulcrum Analytics Inc 70 W 40th St 10th Fl *Web:* www.fulcrumanalytics.com	New York	NY	10018	212-651-7000	651-7049
Fusion Risk Management Inc 3601 W Algonquin Rd Ste 510 *Web:* www.fusionriskmgmt.com	Rolling Meadows	IL	60008	847-632-1002	
Futuredontics Inc 6060 Ctr Dr 7th Fl *Web:* www.futuredontics.com	Los Angeles	CA	90045	310-215-6400	
G Sp Group Inc 1343 Boswall Dr *Web:* gspgroup.com	Worthington	OH	43085	614-888-7502	
G3 Communications 411 State Rt 17 S Ste 410 *TF:* 888-603-3626 ■ *Web:* gthreecom.com	Hasbrouck Heights	NJ	07604	888-603-3626	
Gams Communications LLC 308 W Erie St Ste 4 *Web:* www.gamscom.com	Chicago	IL	60654	312-280-2740	
Gannett Offset 7950 Jones Branch Dr. *Web:* www.gannett.com	McLean	VA	22107	703-750-8673	
GasPedal LLC 333 W N Ave Ste 500 *Web:* www.gaspedal.com	Chicago	IL	60610	312-932-9000	
Gc Marketing Services 10 E 23rd St Ste 300 *Web:* www.gcmarketingservices.com	New York	NY	10010	212-780-5200	
George P. Johnson Co 3600 Giddings Rd *Web:* www.gpj.com	Auburn Hills	MI	48326	248-475-2500	
Gifting Services LLC 7494-B Santa Monica Blvd *Web:* www.giftingservices.com	West Hollywood	CA	90046	323-874-4156	
GLS Companies Inc 6845 Winnetka Cir *Web:* glsprecisionmarketing.com	Brooklyn Park	MN	55428	763-535-7277	
GoalLine Solutions 3115 Harvester Rd Ste 200 *TF:* 866-788-4625 ■ *Web:* www.goallinesolutions.com	Burlington	ON	L7N3H8	866-788-4625	
Gold Stars Speakers Bureau 7478 N La Cholla Blvd *TF:* 800-844-4384 ■ *Web:* www.goldstars.com	Tucson	AZ	85741	520-742-4384	
Goldense Group Inc 1346 South St *Web:* www.goldensegroupinc.com	Needham	MA	02492	781-444-5400	
Gorilla Marketing 4100 Flat Rock Dr Ste A *Web:* www.gorillamarketing.net	Riverside	CA	92505	951-353-8133	
Grace Marketing Mount Vernon Sq Bldg 6700 Beta Dr, 3rd Fl *Web:* www.gracemarketingco.com	Mayfield Village	OH	44143	440-442-7000	
Gravity Group 107 E Water St *Web:* www.gravitygroup.com	Harrisonburg	VA	22801	540-433-3071	
Grayrose Marketing Group 9631 Ne Colfax St *Web:* www.grayrose.com	Portland	OR	97220	503-281-1922	
Great Falls Marketing LLC 121 Mill St *TF:* 800-221-8895 ■ *Web:* www.greatfallsmarketing.com	Auburn	ME	04210	800-221-8895	
Green Leads LLC 16 Haverhill St *Web:* www.greenleads.com	Andover	MA	01810	978-633-3233	
Group for Organizational Effectiveness Inc, The 727 Waldens Pond Rd *Web:* groupoe.com	Albany	NY	12203	518-456-7738	
Group Iii Marketing of Plymouth Inc 1907 Wayzata Blvd Ste 200 *Web:* www.group3marketing.com	Wayzata	MN	55391	952-475-3269	
Growthpoint Inc 926 76th Ave S *Web:* growthpoint-inc.com	Fargo	ND	58104	701-235-1600	
GSI Interactive Inc 1075 First Ave *Web:* trueaction.com	King Of Prussia	PA	19406	610-491-7100	
GY&K Antler 181 S St *Web:* gykantler.com	Boston	MA	02111	617-423-0011	
Haley Marketing Group 6028 Sheridan Dr *Web:* www.haleymarketing.com	Buffalo	NY	14221	716-631-8981	
Hanapin Marketing LLC 501 N Morton St Ste 212 *Web:* www.hanapinmarketing.com	Bloomington	IN	47404	812-330-3134	
Hansa GCR LLC 308 SW First Ave *TF:* 800-755-7683 ■ *Web:* www.hansagcr.com	Portland	OR	97204	503-241-8036	
Harrison Group A YouGov Co 21 W Main St One Exchange Pl Fl 5 *Web:* research.yougov.com	Waterbury	CT	06702	203-573-0400	
HatchBeauty Agency LLC 1715 18th St *TF:* 877-428-2424 ■ *Web:* hatchbeauty.com	Santa Monica	CA	90404	877-428-2424	
Hcpro Inc 75 Sylvan St Ste A-10 *TF:* 800-650-6787 ■ *Web:* www.hcpro.com	Danvers	MA	01923	800-650-6787	
Healthmark Services 217 Lakewood Rd	Van Buren	AR	72956	479-471-9797	
Heinzeroth Marketing Group 415 Y Blvd Ste 3 *Web:* www.heinzeroth.com	Rockford	IL	61107	815-967-0929	
Hero Media Group LLC 65 State Rt 4 E *Web:* www.heromediagroup.com	River Edge	NJ	07661	201-880-0675	
High Tide Creative 208 Bridge St PO Box 1714 *Web:* www.hightidecreative.com	Bridgeton	NC	28560	252-671-7087	
Holden Advisors Corp 35 Forest Ridge Ste 160 *Web:* www.holdenadvisors.com	Concord	MA	01742	978-405-0020	
Hollis Marketing 2130 Brenner St *TF:* 866-797-3301 ■ *Web:* hollismarketing.com	Saginaw	MI	48602	989-797-3300	
Holsted Marketing Inc 112 W 34th St Ste 1405 *Web:* www.holstedmarketing.com	New York	NY	10120	212-686-8537	
Home Team Marketing LLC 812 Huron Rd E Ste 205 *Web:* www.hometeammarketing.com	Cleveland	OH	44115	216-566-8326	
Hr Alliance LLC 580 W Main St *Web:* hralliancewithyou.com	Wytheville	VA	24382	276-223-1718	
Hr Answers Inc 7659 SW Mohawk St *Web:* www.hranswers.com	Tualatin	OR	97062	503-885-8614	
Hr Consultants Inc 160 Jari Dr Ste 180 *Web:* www.hrconsults.com	Johnstown	PA	15904	814-266-3818	
HRinterax Inc 61 Interstate Ln *Web:* www.hr411.com	Waterbury	CT	06705	203-575-1330	
Huka Productions LLC 924 Valmont St Ste 103 *TF:* 888-512-7469 ■ *Web:* www.hukaentertainment.com	New Orleans	LA	70115	888-512-7469	
Hunter Business Group LLC 4650 N Port Washington Rd *Fax Area Code: 414 ■ *TF:* 800-423-4010 ■ *Web:* www.hunterbusiness.com	Milwaukee	WI	53212	800-423-4010	203-8225*
Hype Agency Llc, The 155 Main St Frnt 1 *Web:* thehypeagency.com	Salem	NH	03079	603-328-9019	
ICiDigital Inc 4000 Westchase Blvd Ste 280 *Web:* www.icidigital.com	Raleigh	NC	27607	919-883-9467	
ICS Marketing Services Inc 4225 Legacy Pkwy *TF:* 888-394-1890 ■ *Web:* www.icshq.com	Lansing	MI	48911	517-394-1890	
Image Matters LLC 201 Loudoun St SW *Web:* www.imagemattersllc.com	Leesburg	VA	20175	703-669-5510	
Impact Planning Group 11 Grumman Hill Rd *Web:* www.impactplan.com	Wilton	CT	06897	203-854-1011	
Impaq Corp 9000 W Sunset Blvd Ste 525 *Web:* impaqcorp.com	Los Angeles	CA	90069	310-275-0055	
Impatto Custom Marketing Inc 23235 Telegraph Rd *Web:* impatto.com	Southfield	MI	48033	248-415-5000	
In Touch Marketing Inc 2793 Deerhaven Dr *Web:* intouchmarketinginc.net	Cincinnati	OH	45244	513-474-6317	
Infinia Group LLC 515 W 20th St 6th Fl *Web:* www.infiniagroup.com	New York	NY	10011	212-463-5100	
Infinity Marketing Team Inc 6525 W Sunset Blvd Ste Gs2 *Web:* www.infinitymarketingteam.com	Los Angeles	CA	90028	323-962-4784	
Infomax Shelf Management Inc 1000 Nevada Hwy Ste 204 *Web:* infomaxshelfmgmt.com	Boulder City	NV	89005	702-293-3407	
Informed Sources Inc 88 Sunnysd Blvd Ll012 *Web:* www.informed-sources.com	Plainview	NY	11803	516-576-0246	
Initial Outfitters Inc 209 Alabama St *Web:* www.initialoutfitters.com	Auburn	AL	36832	334-887-1856	
INPUT Inc 11720 Plz America Dr Ste 1200 *Web:* www.input.com	Reston	VA	20190	703-707-3500	
Inquiry Systems Inc 1195 Goodale Blvd *TF:* 800-508-1116 ■ *Web:* www.inquirysys.com	Columbus	OH	43212	614-464-3800	
Insider Marketing 10801 E Northwest Hwy *Web:* www.insidermarketing.com	Dallas	TX	75238	214-348-4350	
Insight Marketing Design Inc 401 E Eighth St Ste 304 *Web:* insightmarketingdesign.com	Sioux Falls	SD	57103	605-275-0011	
Insights in Marketing LLC 444 Skokie Blvd Ste 200 *Web:* www.insightsinmarketing.com	Wilmette	IL	60091	847-853-0500	
Insigniam Performance 1205 N Coast Hwy Ste D *Web:* insigniam.com	Laguna Beach	CA	92651	949-494-4553	
inStream Media Inc 40 Walnut St Ste 401 *Web:* www.instreamglobal.com	Wellesley	MA	02481	781-419-6575	
Integrity Marketing Solutions 7111 W 151st St Ste 216 *Web:* www.integritymarketingsolutions.com	Overland Park	KS	66223	913-402-8434	
Intela LLC 929 Pearl St Ste 200 *Web:* www.intela.com	Boulder	CO	80302	303-473-0000	
Intellimar Inc 7560 Main St *Web:* www.intellimar.com	Sykesville	MD	21784	410-552-9940	552-9939
IntelliShop LLC 2025 Michael Owens Way *Web:* www.intelli-shop.com	Perrysburg	OH	43551	419-872-5103	
Intersect Media Solutions 766 N Sun Dr Ste 2000 *TF:* 866-404-5913 ■ *Web:* www.printplacement.com	Lake Mary	FL	32746	866-404-5913	
InTouch Inc 2 Pine Tree Dr Ste 307 *Web:* www.startwithalead.com	Arden Hills	MN	55112	651-255-7700	
Intrinzic Inc 1 Levee Way Ste 3121 *Web:* intrinzicbrands.com	Newport	KY	41071	859-261-2200	
Invenio Marketing Solutions Inc 2201 Donley Dr Ste 200 *TF:* 800-926-1754 ■ *Web:* www.inveniomarketing.com	Austin	TX	78758	512-990-2000	
InVision Communications Inc 1280 Civic Dr 3rd Fl *Web:* www.iv.com	Walnut Creek	CA	94596	925-944-1211	
iORMYX Inc 1100-D Elden St Ste 304 *Web:* www.iormyx.com	Herndon	VA	20170	703-456-7010	
Ipsenault Co, The 3791 River Rd N Ste F *TF:* 866-240-7032 ■ *Web:* ipsenault.com	Keizer	OR	97303	503-390-8968	
Ivie & Associates Inc 601 Silveron Blvd Ste 200 *Web:* www.ivieinc.com	Flower Mound	TX	75028	972-899-5000	
IWCO Direct Holdings Inc 7951 Powers Blvd. *Web:* www.iwco.com	Chanhassen	MN	55317	952-470-6460	
J C Marketing Associates Inc 467 Main St PO Box 289 *Web:* jcmarketingassociates.com	Wakefield	MA	01880	781-245-7070	
J Carter Marketing Inc 205 Smithtown Blvd *Web:* www.jcartermarketing.com	Nesconset	NY	11767	631-979-5620	
J Hl Mail Marketing 3100 Borham Ave *TF:* 800-236-0581 ■ *Web:* www.jhl.com	Stevens Point	WI	54481	715-341-0581	
J-dak Inc 6257 Hwy 76 E *Web:* jdak.com	Springfield	TN	37172	615-382-5651	
J. Knipper & Company Inc 1 Healthcare Way *TF:* 888-564-7737 ■ *Web:* www.knipper.com	Lakewood	NJ	08701	732-905-7878	
J. Stokes & Associates Inc 1444 N Main St *Web:* jstokes.com	Walnut Creek	CA	94596	925-933-1624	

Company	City	State	Zip	Phone	Fax
James Gutheim & Associates Inc 16400 Ventura Blvd Ste 312 *Web:* gutheim.com	Encino	CA	91436	818-784-7189	
JD Events LLC 5520 Park Ave Ste 305 *Web:* www.jdevents.com	Trumbull	CT	06611	203-371-6322	
Jms Elite 5900 Som Ctr Rd Ste 12 *Web:* www.jmselite.com	Willoughby	OH	44094	440-943-9200	
Jooven8 Marketing & Consulting Inc 2390 Crenshaw Blvd Ste 219 *Web:* www.jooven8.com	Torrance	CA	90501	310-530-0650	
Jordan Education Media Inc 19105 Hilltop Rd *Web:* www.jordaneducationmedia.com	Lake Oswego	OR	97034	503-638-9200	
JP Marketing 7690 N Palm Ave Ste 105 *Web:* jpmktg.com	Fresno	CA	93711	559-438-2180	
kabookaboo Marketing LLC 396 Alhambra Cir Ste 700 *Web:* www.kabookaboo.com	Coral Gables	FL	33134	305-569-9154	
Kahler Slater Inc 111 W Wisconsin Ave *Web:* www.kahlerslater.com	Milwaukee	WI	53203	414-272-2000	
KARMA Media Labs LLC 10215 Santa Monica Blvd *Web:* www.karmamedialabs.com	Los Angeles	CA	90067	310-722-7027	
Karo Group Inc 308-611 Alexander St *Web:* www.karo.com	Vancouver	BC	V6A1E1	604-255-6100	
KELYN Group LLC, The 137 Stone Root Ln Ste 1 *Web:* www.thekelyngroup.com	Concord	MA	01742	978-369-7000	
Kempton Group, The 2 Garfield Pl Ste 1501 *Web:* tkg-marketing.com	Cincinnati	OH	45202	513-651-5556	
Ken Creative Inc 1500 Park Ave Ste 200 *Web:* kencreative.com	Emeryville	CA	94608	510-879-7977	
Kenneth Clark Company Inc 10264 Baltimore National Pk *Web:* www.kennethclark.com	Ellicott City	MD	21042	410-480-2582	
Kern Organization Inc 20955 Warner Ctr Ln *Web:* kernagency.com	Woodland Hills	CA	91367	818-703-8775	
Kesselman Jones 3411 Candelaria Rd Ne Ste G *TF:* 866-219-4582 ■ *Web:* www.kessjones.com	Albuquerque	NM	87107	505-266-3461	
Keystone Marketing Company Inc 709 N Main St *Web:* www.keystonemarketing.net	Winston-salem	NC	27101	333-407-6063	
Keyword Connects LLC 241 Crescent St *Web:* www.keywordconnects.com	Waltham	MA	02453	781-899-3675	
Khong Guan Corp 30068 Eigenbrodt Way *TF:* 877-889-8968 ■ *Web:* kgcusa.squarespace.com	Union City	CA	94587	510-487-7800	487-0301
KLM Creative Inc 520 Townsend St *Web:* klmcreative.com	San Francisco	CA	94103	415-503-4150	
Kollabra 2422 Lindbergh St *Web:* www.kollabra.net	Auburn	CA	95602	530-887-1258	
Kombi Ltd 6 Thompson Dr *Web:* www.kombicanada.com	Essex Junction	VT	05452	802-879-3369	
Kotler Marketing Group 925 15th St Nw Ste 400 *Web:* www.kotlermarketing.com	Washington	DC	20005	202-331-0555	
Krt Marketing Inc 3685 Mt Diablo Blvd Ste 255 *Web:* www.krtmarketing.com	Lafayette	CA	94549	925-284-0444	
KSL Media Inc 387 Park Ave S *Web:* www.kslmedia.com	New York	NY	10016	212-352-5800	
Kuczmarski & Assoc 2001 N Halsted Ste 201 *Web:* www.kuczmarski.com/contact-2	Chicago	IL	60614	312-988-1539	
Ky-ani Sun Inc 1070 Riverwalk Dr Ste 350 *Web:* www.kyani.net	Idaho Falls	ID	83402	208-529-9872	
L b L Strategies Ltd 6321 N Avondale Ave Ste 214 *Web:* lblstrategies.com	Chicago	IL	60631	773-774-0240	
L-K Marketing Group LLC 2421 Richards Dr *Web:* www.lksupport.com	Waco	TX	76710	254-741-1570	
Landajob Advertising & Marketing Talent 222 W Gregory Blvd Ste 304 *TF:* 800-931-8806 ■ *Web:* www.landajobnow.com	Kansas City	MO	64114	816-523-1881	
Landor Assoc Ltd 1001 Front St *TF:* 888-252-6367 ■ *Web:* www.landor.com	San Francisco	CA	94111	415-365-1700	365-3190
Lansberg, Gersick & Associates LLC 100 Whitney Ave Apt 1 *Web:* www.lgassoc.com	New Haven	CT	06510	203-497-8855	
Launch 2 W 45th St Fl 9 *Web:* www.321launch.com	New York	NY	10036	212-845-5800	
Laurdan Associates Inc 10220 River Rd Ste 201 *Web:* www.laurdan.com	Potomac	MD	20854	301-299-4117	
LaVERDAD Hispanic Marketing Solutions 7817 Cooper Rd *Web:* www.laverdadmarketing.com	Cincinnati	OH	45242	513-891-1430	
Lawgical Inc 11693 San Vicente Blvd Ste 910 *TF:* 800-811-4458 ■ *Web:* corp.lawgical.com	Los Angeles	CA	90049	800-811-4458	
Lawrimore Communications Inc 1320 Fillmore Ave Unit 312 *Web:* www.lciweb.com	Charlotte	NC	28203	704-332-4344	
LBi US LLC 11 W 19th St Fl 3 *Web:* www.lbi.com	New York	NY	10011	212-274-0470	
LeadCreations com LLC 605 Lincoln Rd Ste 460 *Web:* www.leadcreations.com	Miami Beach	FL	33139	305-831-0999	
Leader Graphic Design Inc 5410 Newport Dr Ste 44 *Web:* www.leadergraphics.com	Rolling Meadows	IL	60008	847-564-5409	
LeadMD Inc 9383 E Bahia Dr Ste 225 *Web:* www.leadmd.com	Scottsdale	AZ	85260	480-278-7205	
Left Brain DGA 3130 Alpine Rd Ste 288-154 *Web:* www.leftbraindga.com	Portola Valley	CA	94028	650-561-3435	
Legendary Marketing 3729 S Lecanto Hwy *TF:* 800-827-1663 ■ *Web:* www.legendarymarketing.com	Lecanto	FL	34461	352-527-3553	
Leisure and Recreation Concepts Inc 2151 Ft Worth Ave *Web:* larcinc.com/	Dallas	TX	75211	214-942-4474	
Lever Interactive Inc 701 Warrenville Rd Ste 200 *Web:* www.leverinteractive.com	Lisle	IL	60532	630-435-6400	
LeveragePoint Media Corp 111 Water St *Web:* www.leveragepointmedia.com	East Dundee	IL	60118	847-437-5300	
Lexicon Branding Inc 30 Liberty Ship Way Ste 3360 *Web:* www.lexiconbranding.com	Sausalito	CA	94965	415-332-1811	332-2528
Libby Perszyk Kathman Holdings Inc 19 Garfield Pl *Web:* www.lpk.com	Cincinnati	OH	45202	513-241-6330	
Licensing Resource Group LLC 442 Century Ln Ste 100 *Web:* learfieldlicensing.com	Holland	MI	49423	616-395-0676	
Lift Agency Inc 205 Industrial Pkwy N Unit 1 *Web:* www.getlift.com	Aurora	ON	L4G4C4	647-684-3242	
Linick Group Inc, The 7 Putter Ln Linick Bldg *Web:* www.andrewlinickdirectmarketing.com	Middle Island	NY	11953	631-924-3888	
Lionshare Marketing Inc 7830 Barton St *Web:* www.lionsharemarketing.com	Overland Park	KS	66214	913-631-8400	
Liquid Agency Inc 448 S Market St *Web:* www.liquidagency.com	San Jose	CA	95113	408-850-8800	
Lloyd Schuh Advertising Inc 2207 Cantrell Rd *TF:* 866-572-6584 ■ *Web:* www.lscmarketing.com	Little Rock	AR	72202	501-374-2332	
Lmd 14409 Greenview Dr Ste 200 *Web:* www.lmdagency.com	Laurel	MD	20708	301-498-6656	
LOC Enterprises LLC 7575 E Kemper Rd *TF:* 888-963-6320 ■ *Web:* www.locenterprisesllc.com	Cincinnati	OH	45249	888-963-6320	
LocBox 400 Second St Ste 400 *TF:* 855-256-2269 ■ *Web:* app.locbox.com	San Francisco	CA	94107	855-256-2269	
lonelybrand LLC 118 W Kinzie St Fl 2 *Web:* www.lonelybrand.com	Chicago	IL	60654	312-880-7506	
Loop Consulting Group 9485 Sw 72nd St Ste A204 *Web:* loopconsulting.com	Miami	FL	33173	305-271-9915	
LoyaltyExpress Inc 53 Commerce Way *Web:* www.loyaltyexpress.com	Woburn	MA	01801	781-938-1175	
LRG Marketing Communications Inc 48 Burd St Ste105 *Web:* lrgmarketing.com	Nyack	NY	10960	845-358-1801	
M & p Export Management Corp 2329 Hwy 34 Ste 204 *Web:* mpexport.com	Manasquan	NJ	08736	732-223-0160	
M45 Marketing Services Inc 524 W Stephenson St *Web:* m45.com	Freeport	IL	61032	815-297-0166	
MacroSoft Inc 2 Sylvan Way 3rd Fl *Web:* www.macrosoftinc.com	Parsippany	NJ	07054	973-889-0500	
Magic Logix Inc 16610 Dallas Pkwy Ste 2200 *Web:* www.magiclogix.com	Dallas	TX	75248	214-694-2162	
Magicomm LLC 15 Alexander Rd *Web:* www.magicomm.biz	Billerica	MA	01821	978-964-1900	
Magnani & Associates Advertising Inc 200 S Michigan Ave Ste 500 *Web:* www.magnani.com	Chicago	IL	60604	312-957-0770	
Magnets Usa 817 Connecticut Ave NE *TF:* 800-869-7562 ■ *Web:* www.magnetsusa.com	Roanoke	VA	24012	800-869-7562	
Mail Sort Inc 2005 Newpoint Pkwy Ste 100 *Web:* www.mailsortinc.com	Lawrenceville	GA	30043	770-717-5500	
Maker Studios Inc 13428 Maxella Ave Ste 525 *Web:* www.makerstudios.com	Los Angeles	CA	90016	310-606-2182	
Mallett Group Inc, The 566 Danbury Rd Ste 6 *Web:* www.mallettgroup.com	New Milford	CT	06776	860-350-0809	
Mannix Mktg Inc 11 Broad St 3rd Fl *Web:* www.mannixmarketing.com	Glens Falls	NY	12801	518-743-9424	
Mapping Analytics LLC 120 Allens Creek Rd Ste 15 *Web:* www.mappinganalytics.com	Rochester	NY	14618	585-271-6490	
MARC Promotions 7172 Lkview Pkwy W Dr *Web:* www.marcpromotions.com	Indianapolis	IN	46268	317-290-3516	
Marcom Gurus 2083 Louise Ln *Web:* marcomgurus.com	Los Altos	CA	94024	650-564-0011	
Market Connections Inc 46 Haywood St Ste 340 *Web:* www.mktconnections.com	Asheville	NC	28801	828-254-9737	
MarketBridge Inc 4350 East-West Hwy 6th Fl **Fax Area Code:* 301 ■ *TF:* 888-468-6658 ■ *Web:* www.market-bridge.com	Bethesda	MD	20814	240-752-1800	907-3282*
Marketing General Inc 625 N Washington St Ste 450 *Web:* www.marketinggeneral.com	Alexandria	VA	22314	703-739-1000	
Marketing Management Group Inc 561 Seventh Ave 17th Fl *Web:* www.mmgus.com	New York	NY	10018	212-768-9660	
Marketing Results 2900 W Horizon Ridge Pkwy Ste 200 *Web:* www.marketingresults.net	Henderson	NV	89052	702-361-3850	
MarketingProfs LLC 419 N Larchmont Blvd #295 *TF:* 866-557-9625 ■ *Web:* www.marketingprofs.com	Los Angeles	CA	90004	866-557-9625	
MarketWise Solutions Inc 4843 W 106th St *Web:* www.marketwisesolutions.com	Zionsville	IN	46077	317-873-6976	
Markitects Inc 107 W Lancaster Ave Ste 203 *Web:* www.markitects.com	Wayne	PA	19087	610-687-2200	
Marnell Companies LLC 222 Via Marnell Way *Web:* www.marnellcompanies.com	Las Vegas	NV	89119	702-739-2000	

Company	City	State	ZIP	Phone	Fax
Martin Group LLC, The 477 Main St *Web:* tmgbrandfuel.com	Buffalo	NY	14203	716-853-2757	
Martin Investment Management LLC 1560 Sherman Ave Ste 1250 *Web:* www.martin-investments.com	Evanston	IL	60201	847-424-9124	
MASCARI Sales & Marketing LLC 32823 W Twelve Mile Rd *Web:* www.cmascari.com	Farmington Hills	MI	48334	248-488-1110	
Mass Connections Inc 13131 E 166th St	Cerritos	CA	90703	562-365-0200	
Massini Group 1323 NE Orenco Stn Pkwy Ste 300 *Web:* www.massini-group.com	Hillsboro	OR	97124	503-640-9800	
Massive Prints Inc 2035 Vista Bella Way Rancho Dominguez *Web:* www.massiveinc.com	Compton	CA	90220	310-667-8991	
Maturehealth Communications 502 Centennial Ave *Web:* www.maturehealth.com	Cranford	NJ	07016	908-709-8080	
Mcdaniels Marketing Communications 11 Olt Ave *TF:* 866-431-4230 ■ *Web:* www.mcdanielsmarketing.com	Pekin	IL	61554	309-346-4230	
McDill Associates 4800 Leapfrog Ln *Web:* jacobsheart.org	Soquel	CA	95073	831-462-3198	
Mcdowell Group Inc 9360 Glacier Hwy Ste 201 *Web:* www.mcdowellgroup.net	Juneau	AK	99801	907-586-6126	
Mcelroy & Associates Inc 1164 George Ln *Web:* www.mcelroyassociates.net	Naperville	IL	60540	630-355-3151	
Mckinley Marketing Partners Inc 111 Franklin St *Web:* mckinleymarketingpartners.com	Alexandria	VA	22314	703-836-8578	
Mclellan Creative 695 Mistletoe Rd Ste M2 *Web:* www.mclellancreative.com	Ashland	OR	97520	541-488-2270	
MedeliaCommunications LLC 2029 Taft St *Web:* www.medelia.com	Hollywood	FL	33020	954-922-0846	
Mediplay Inc 526 Pylon Dr *Web:* mediplay.com	Raleigh	NC	27606	919-341-8582	
Menasha Rand Group 3 Ethel Rd Ste 301 *Web:* www.rand-div.com	Edison	NJ	08817	732-287-2525	
Meridia Audience Response 5207 Militia Hill Rd Ste 100 *Web:* www.meridiaars.com	Plymouth Meeting	PA	19462	610-260-6800	
Meridian One Corp 5775 General Washington Dr *Web:* www.meridianone.com	Alexandria	VA	22312	703-461-5200	
Merit Marketing Inc 741 S Campbell Ave *Web:* meritmarketinginc.com	Tucson	AZ	85719	520-624-8211	
Merkle Inc 50 Chestnut Ridge Rd Ste. 120 *Web:* www.merkleinc.com	Montvale	NJ	07645	201-571-2000	
Metrix Marketing Inc 40 Wildbriar Rd *Web:* www.metrix-marketing.com	Rochester	NY	14623	585-334-0890	
MFR Consultants Inc 128 Chestnut St *Web:* www.mfrconsultants.com	Philadelphia	PA	19106	215-238-9270	
Michael Allen Co 9 Old Kings Hwy South *Web:* www.michaelallencompany.com	Darien	CT	06820	203-662-5100	
Midlantic Marketing 117 Commons Ct *Web:* www.midlantic.net	Chadds Ford	PA	19317	610-361-0500	
Military Sales & Service Co 5301 S Westmoreland Rd *Web:* mssco.com	Dallas	TX	75237	214-330-4621	330-1740
Mill33 Inc 848 Elm St Ste 301 *TF:* 888-603-2336 ■ *Web:* www.mill33.com	Manchester	NH	03101	888-603-2336	
Miller Heiman Inc 10509 Professional Cir Ste 100 *Web:* www.mhiglobal.com	Reno	NV	89521	775-827-4411	
Millstone Medical Outsourcing LLC 580 Commerce Dr *Web:* www.millstonemedical.com	Fall River	MA	02720	508-679-8384	679-8414
Missouri Enterprise 1706 E 10th St *TF:* 800-956-2682 ■ *Web:* www.missourienterprise.org	Rolla	MO	65401	800-956-2682	
Mitchell Group The Consltnt 1816 11th St Nw *Web:* www.the-mitchellgroup.com	Washington	DC	20001	202-745-1919	
Mizzen Marketing Resources LLC 8195 Bramble Creek Ct *Web:* www.mizzenmarketing.com	Mansfield	TX	76063	817-477-1991	
MMI Associates Inc 7406 Chapel Hill Rd Ste H *Web:* www.mmipublicrelations.com	Raleigh	NC	27607	919-233-6600	
Mobiquity Networks Inc 600 Old Country Rd Ste 541 *Web:* www.mobiquitynetworks.com	Garden City	NY	11530	516-256-7766	
ModernThink LLC 4519 Weldin Rd *Web:* www.modernthink.com	Wilmington	DE	19803	302-764-4477	
Mood Media Corp 1703 W Fifth St Ste 600 *Web:* www.moodmedia.com	Austin	TX	78703	512-380-8500	
Moosylvania Marketin LC 7303 Marietta Ave *Web:* www.moosylvania.com	St. Louis	MO	63143	314-644-7900	
Morgan Marketing and Communications 690 Mill Hill Ter *Web:* morganmarketcomm.com	Southport	CT	06890	203-255-4686	
Morris & Mcdaniel Inc Consultants 117 S Saint Asaph St *Web:* www.morrisandmcdaniel.com	Alexandria	VA	22314	703-836-3600	
Morrison Agency Inc, The 3365 Piedmont Rd Ste 1400 Tower Walk at Tower Pl *Web:* www.morrisonagency.com	Atlanta	GA	30305	404-233-3405	261-8384
Mosteller & Associates 2433 Morgantown Rd Ste 100 *Web:* www.mostellerhr.com	Reading	PA	19607	610-779-3870	
Motive 620 16th St Ste 200 *Web:* thinkmotive.com	Denver	CO	80202	303-302-2100	
Mpell Solutions LLC 3142 Tiger Run Ct Ste 108 *Web:* www.mpellsolutions.com	Carlsbad	CA	92010	760-477-9261	

Company	City	State	ZIP	Phone	Fax
Mrv Marketing Llc 31877 Del Obispo St Ste 203 *Web:* mrvdairysolutions.com	San Juan Capo	CA	92675	949-487-0550	
Murdoch Marketing 217 E 24th St Ste 220 *Web:* www.murdochmarketing.com	Holland	MI	49423	616-392-4893	
N.A.Williams Co 2900 A Paces Ferry Rd *Web:* www.nawilliams.com	Atlanta	GA	30339	770-433-2282	
Nancy Bailey & Associates Inc 1403 Macy Dr *Web:* www.baileylicensing.com	Roswell	GA	30076	678-352-1000	
National Food Laboratory Inc 6363 Clark Ave *Web:* www.thenfl.com	Dublin	CA	94568	925-828-1440	833-9239
NCompass International Inc 8223 Santa Monica Blvd *Web:* www.ncompassonline.com	West Hollywood	CA	90046	323-785-1700	
Nelson Ink 330 Second St N *Web:* nelsonink.com	Middle River	MN	56737	218-222-3831	
Net Impact LLC, The 1415 Elbridge Payne Rd Ste 165 *Web:* www.thenetimpact.com	Chesterfield	MO	63017	636-458-7772	
Nethawk Interactive Inc 1255 Park Ave Ste D *Web:* www.nethawk.net	Emeryville	CA	94608	510-595-2220	
Netmark.com 1930 N Woodruff Ave *TF:* 800-935-5133 ■ *Web:* www.netmark.com	Idaho Falls	ID	83401	800-935-5133	
Netsertive Inc 2400 Perimeter Park Dr Ste 100 *TF:* 800-940-4351 ■ *Web:* www.netsertive.com	Research Triangle Region	NC	27560	800-940-4351	
New Angle Media 2601 E Thomas Rd Ste 235 *Web:* www.newanglemedia.com	Phoenix	AZ	85016	602-840-5530	
New Product Insights Inc 433 Ward Pkwy *Web:* www.npinpi.com	Kansas City	MO	64112	816-582-8700	
newBrandAnalytics Inc 1250 23rd St NW Ste 450 *Web:* www.newbrandanalytics.com	Washington	DC	20037	202-800-7850	
Nex 21 Llc 1400 Urban Ctr Dr Ste 100 *Web:* www.nex21.com	Vestavia	AL	35242	205-520-9916	
NexAge Technologies USA Inc 75 Lincoln Hwy Ste 101 *Web:* www.nexageusa.com	Iselin	NJ	08830	732-494-4944	
Nexsales Corp 20660 Stevens Creek Blvd Ste 129 *Web:* www.nexsales.com	Cupertino	CA	95104	408-831-3800	
Next Marketing Inc 2820 Peterson Pl *Web:* www.nextmarketing.com	Norcross	GA	30071	770-225-2200	
Next Steps Marketing 1 Polk St Fl 2 *Web:* www.nextstepsmarketing.com	San Francisco	CA	94102	415-773-1841	
Nielsen Media Research Ltd 160 McNabb St *Web:* www.nielsenmedia.ca	Markham	ON	L3R4B8	905-475-9595	
Niven Marketing Group, The 955 Kimberly Dr *Web:* www.niven.net	Carol Stream	IL	60188	630-580-6000	580-5690
NKP Medical Marketing Inc 10220 Culver Blvd Ste 208 *TF:* 888-274-8383 ■ *Web:* www.nkpmedical.com	Culver City	CA	90232	888-274-8383	
NMV The Marketing Firm Inc 11300 Coloma Rd Ste B-14 *Web:* www.nmvinc.com	Gold River	CA	95670	916-852-7716	
Nordis Direct 4401 NW 124th Ave *Web:* www.nordisdirect.com	Coral Springs	FL	33065	954-323-5500	
Northern Response International Ltd 50 Staples Ave Richmond Hill *Web:* www.northernresponse.com	Toronto	ON	L4B0A7	905-737-6698	
Notions Marketing Corp 1500 Buchanan Ave Sw *Web:* notions-marketing.com	Grand Rapids	MI	49507	616-243-8424	
nParallel LLC 13120 County Rd 6 *Web:* www.nparallel.com	Minneapolis	MN	55441	763-231-4800	
Nu Image Marketing 1271 N Tustin Ave *Web:* nimarketing.com	Anaheim	CA	92807	714-575-8947	
NuGrowth Solutions LLC 4181 ArlingGate Plz *Web:* www.nugrowthsolutions.com	Columbus	OH	43228	614-219-6550	
Obi Creative 2920 Farnam St *Web:* www.obicreative.com	Omaha	NE	68131	402-493-7999	
Oglethorpe Inc 18302 Highwoods Preserve Pkwy Ste 114 *Web:* www.oglethorpeinc.com	Tampa	FL	33647	813-978-1933	
Ohana Companies LLC, The 1405 Foulk Rd Foulkstone Plz Ste 200 *Web:* www.everybodywins.com	Wilmington	DE	19803	302-225-5505	
Oil Can Henry's 19150 Sw 90th Ave *Web:* www.oilcanhenry.com	Tualatin	OR	97062	503-783-3888	
Omelet LA 8673 Hayden Pl *Web:* omeletla.com	Culver City	CA	90232	213-427-6400	
Omgeo LLC 55 Thomson Pl *TF:* 866-496-6436 ■ *Web:* www.omgeo.com	Boston	MA	02210	866-496-6436	
On Track Marketing Inc 1910 W N Ave *Web:* www.otmarketing.com	Chicago	IL	60622	773-235-0017	
OnIt Digital LLC 684 S Mountain Rd *Web:* www.onitdigital.com	New York	NY	10956	212-655-9632	
onramp Branding LLC 111 N Chestnut St Ste 200 *Web:* www.onrampbranding.com	Winston-salem	NC	27101	336-397-5333	
Optimum System Products 5061 Fwy Dr E *Web:* www.optimumcompanies.com	Columbus	OH	43229	614-885-4464	
Opus Events Agency 9309 SW Nimbus Ave *Web:* www.opuseventsagency.com	Beaverton	OR	97008	971-223-0777	
OrangeSoda Inc 732 E Utah Vly Dr *Web:* www.orangesoda.com	American Fork	UT	84003	801-610-2500	
Orbit Design 2560 Sheridan Blvd Ste 4 *Web:* www.orbit-design.com	Denver	CO	80214	303-433-1616	
OutboundEngine Inc 200 E 6th, Ste 205 *TF:* 800-562-7315 ■ *Web:* www.outboundengine.com	Austin	TX	78701	800-562-7315	

Phone Fax

P W Feats Inc 3 E Read St ... Baltimore MD 21202 410-727-5575
Web: www.featsinc.com

P4 Performance Management Inc 105 Brooks Ave ... Raleigh NC 27607 800-431-0648
TF: 800-431-0648 ■ *Web:* www.p4performance.com

Padulo Integrated Inc 1 St Clair Ave W ... Toronto ON M4V1K7 416-515-0119
Web: www.padulo.ca

Page Group Inc, The
8905 Fairview Rd Ste 401 ... Silver Spring MD 20910 301-565-4020
Web: www.pagegroup.com

Painweek 6 Erie St ... Montclair NJ 07042 973-415-5100
Web: www.painweek.org

Paradowski Creative Inc 1928 Locust St ... St. Louis MO 63103 314-241-2150
Web: paradowski.com

Parks Productions Ltd 2250 Pontiac Rd ... Auburn Hills MI 48326 248-370-9200
Web: www.parkspro.com

Patpatia & Associates Inc
1803 Sixth St Ste A ... Berkeley CA 94710 510-559-7140
Web: patpatia.com

Patrona Corp 1919 S Eads St Ste 202 ... Arlington VA 22202 571-255-4707
Web: www.patronacorp.com

Paulsen Marketing Inc
3510 S First Ave Cir ... Sioux Falls SD 57105 605-336-1745
Web: www.paulsen.ag

PayStream Advisors Inc
2923 S Tryon St Ste 240 ... Charlotte NC 28203 704-523-7357
Web: www.paystreamadvisors.com

PDI Inc
300 Interpace Pkwy
Morris Corp Ctr 1 Bldg A ... Parsippany NJ 07054 800-242-7494
NASDAQ: PDII ■ *TF:* 800-242-7494 ■ *Web:* www.pdi-inc.com

Peak Sales & Marketing Inc
4751 Lindle Rd Ste 128 ... Harrisburg PA 17111 717-986-0301
Web: www.peaksalesmkt.com

Pedowitz Group, The 810 Mayfield Rd ... Milton GA 30009 855-738-6584
TF: 855-738-6584 ■ *Web:* www.pedowitzgroup.com

PeerDirect Corp 14 Oak Park ... Bedford MA 01730 781-280-4080
Web: www.peerdirect.com

Pelerei Inc 2379 Broad Run Ct ... Jefferson MD 21755 301-371-7100
Web: www.pelerei.com

Penny Group Inc, The 1328 Harding Pl ... Charlotte NC 28204 704-372-1400
Web: thepennygroup.com

Pentera Inc 8650 Commerce Park Pl Ste G ... Indianapolis IN 46268 317-875-0910
Web: www.pentera.com

Peppers & Rogers Group 901 Main Ave # 212 ... Norwalk CT 06851 203-642-5121 642-5126
Web: www.1to1media.com

Peritus Partners Inc 703 Briar Ranch Ln ... San Jose CA 95120 408-910-4362
Web: www.peritusp.com

PharmaCentra LLC 3000 Northwoods Pkwy ... Norcross GA 30071 770-395-0088
Web: www.pharmacentra.com

PharMethod Inc 1170 Wheeler Way ... Langhorne PA 19047 215-354-1212
Web: www.pharmethod.com

Piranha Marketing Inc 4440 S Rural Rd Bldg F ... Tempe AZ 85282 480-858-0008
Web: joepolish.com

Planogramming Solutions Inc
9080 Golfside Dr ... Jacksonville FL 32256 904-448-0834
Web: www.planogrammingsolutions.com

PNT Marketing Services Inc
2420 Jackson Ave ... Long Island City NY 11101 718-433-4053
Web: www.pntmarketingservices.com

Points International Ltd 171 John St 5th Fl ... Toronto ON M5T1X3 416-595-0000
Web: www.points.com

Polygenesis Corp
4260 Us Hwy 1 Ste 5 ... Monmouth Junction NJ 08852 732-355-1001
Web: www.polygenesis.com

Populus Group LLC 850 Stephenson Hwy Ste 500 ... Troy MI 48083 248-581-1100 581-1170
Web: www.populusgroup.com

Practical Imagination Enterprising
18 Losey Rd ... Ringoes NJ 08551 908-237-2246
Web: www.practical-imagination.com

Pragma Corp, The 116 E Broad St ... Falls Church VA 22046 703-237-9303
Web: www.pragmacorp.com

Pragmatic Marketing Inc
8910 E Raintree Dr ... Scottsdale AZ 85260 480-515-1411
Web: www.pragmaticmarketing.com

Premier Direct Marketing Inc
7725 National Tpke Unit 100 ... Louisville KY 40214 502-367-6441
TF: 800-737-0205 ■ *Web:* premierdm.net

PrestoBox Inc 1030 NW 12th Ave Ste 324 ... Portland OR 97209 503-387-3459
Web: prestobox.com

Pricing Advisor Inc 3535 Roswell Rd Ste 59 ... Marietta GA 30062 770-509-9933
Web: pricingsociety.com

Prime Concepts Group Inc
1807 S Eisenhower St ... Wichita KS 67209 316-942-1111
TF: 800-946-7804 ■ *Web:* www.primeconcepts.com

PrimeQ Solutions Inc
26035 Acero Ste 100 ... Mission Viejo CA 92691 949-707-8500
Web: www.primeq.com

Printfection LLC 3700 Quebec St Unit 100-136 ... Denver CO 80207 866-459-7990
TF: 866-459-7990 ■ *Web:* www.printfection.com

Pro-mail Associates Inc 22404 66th Ave S ... Kent WA 98032 206-282-2400
TF: 855-867-5081 ■ *Web:* www.pmadm.com

Proficient Learning LLC
1508 Military Cutoff Rd Ste 304 ... Wilmington NC 28403 910-509-0104
Web: www.proficientlearning.com

Projectline Services Inc 506 2nd Ave Ste 400 ... Seattle WA 98104 206-382-2025
Web: www.projectlineinc.com

Pronto Post Inc 5300 NW 163 St ... Miami Gardens FL 33014 305-621-7900
Web: www.prontopost.com

ProOrbis LLC 112 Moores Rd Ste 400 ... Malvern PA 19355 610-240-0200
Web: www.proorbis.com

Prospectiv Direct Inc
40 Harvard Mill Sq Ste 1 ... Wakefield MA 01880 781-305-2100
Web: www.prospectiv.com

Phone Fax

Potential 6805 Hobson Valley Dr Ste 106 ... Woodridge IL 60517 630-724-0578
Web: www.protential.com

PSD Global LLC 505 N Mansfield St ... Alexandria VA 22304 703-531-8773
Web: www.psdglobal.com

Public Impact 504 Dogwood Dr ... Carrboro NC 27510 919-240-7955
Web: www.publicimpact.com

Public Policy Institute 1231 Lincoln Dr ... Carbondale IL 62901 618-453-4009
Web: www.siu.edu

Punch Media 7151 Sprague St 3rd Fl ... Philadelphia PA 19119 215-621-6024
Web: www.punchmedia.biz

Punchkick Interactive Inc
22 W Ontario St 4th Fl ... Chicago IL 60654 216-526-1544
Web: www.punchkickinteractive.com

Pursuit Group, The 2528 Wembley Ter N ... Toledo OH 43617 866-478-7783
TF: 866-478-7783 ■ *Web:* www.thepursuitgroup.com

Quala-Tel Enterprises
9925 Business Park Ave Ste A ... San Diego CA 92131 858-577-2900
Web: www.qualatel.com

Quintevents LLC
9300 Harris Corners Pkwy Ste 120 ... Charlotte NC 28269 248-961-0725
Web: www.quintevents.com

Quixote Group Research Marketing
3107 Brassfield Rd Ste 100 ... Greensboro NC 27410 336-605-0363
Web: www.quixotegroup.com

R M Kaul & Associates Inc 10 Bennett Ave ... New York NY 10033 646-706-1807
Web: www.rmkaul.com

Rainmaker Marketing Corp 15519 Dawnbrook Dr ... Houston TX 77068 281-537-1200
Web: www.rainmakermarketing.com

Ramapo Sales & Marketing Inc
4760 Goer Dr Ste F ... North Charleston SC 29406 800-866-9173
TF: 800-866-9173 ■ *Web:* www.ramapoglass.com

Rassak Experience 972 Mission St 5th fl ... San Francisco CA 94103 415-621-4300
Web: rassak.com

Raven One to One Marketing 1020 Airport Rd ... Allentown PA 18109 484-240-6500
TF: 866-577-4121 ■ *Web:* raven121.com

RAZR Marketing Inc 10590 Wayzata Blvd ... Minnetonka MN 55305 763-404-6100
Web: www.razrmarketing.com

Red Cloud Promotions
1600 Sawtelle Blvd Ste 108 ... Los Angeles CA 90025 310-444-5583
Web: redcloudpromotions.com

Red Feather Marketing Group Inc 332 Main St ... Madison NJ 07940 973-966-1399
Web: www.red-feather.com

Reese Military Sales Inc
2820 Bransford Ave ... Nashville TN 37204 615-298-5774
Web: reesemilitarysales.com

Regalix Inc 1121 San Antonio Rd Ste B200 ... Palo Alto CA 94303 650-331-1167
Web: www.regalix.com

Rely Services Inc
2354 Hassell Rd Ste B ... Hoffman Estates IL 60169 847-310-8750
TF: 866-735-9328 ■ *Web:* relyservices.com

Rennhack Marketing Services Inc
752 Port America Pl ... Grapevine TX 76051 817-481-6516

Revolve Marketing 330 Waymont Ct Ste 100 ... Lake Mary FL 32746 407-804-2710
Web: www.revolvemarketing.com

REVShare Corp 32836 Wolf Store Rd ... Temecula CA 92592 951-302-2091
Web: www.revshare.com

Ries & Ries 2195 River Cliff Dr ... Roswell GA 30076 770-643-0880
Web: www.ries.com

Rimm-Kaufman Group LLC
701 E Water St ... Charlottesville VA 22902 434-970-1010
Web: www.rimmkaufman.com

Riovida Networks 2133 Clinton Ave ... Alameda CA 94501 510-693-0166

RMI Direct Marketing Inc 42 Old Ridgebury Rd ... Danbury CT 06810 203-798-0448
Web: www.rmidirect.com

Rocket Media Inc 3335 E Baseline Rd ... Gilbert AZ 85234 480-699-2579
Web: www.rocketmedia.com

Rome Group Inc, The 3120 locust ... Saint Louis MO 63103 314-533-0930
Web: www.theromegroup.com

Ronin Corp 2 Research Way Ste 203 ... Princeton NJ 08540 609-452-0060 452-0091
Web: ronin.com

Ross Marketing Inc 2214 Main St Ste A ... Cedar Falls IA 50613 319-266-5881
Web: rossmarketing.net

RPM Direct LLC 24 Arnett Ave Ste 100 ... Lambertville NJ 08530 609-566-7150
Web: www.rpmdirectllc.com

RS Consulting USA 39 S LaSalle St ... Chicago IL 60603 312-368-0800
Web: www.rsconsulting-usa.com

RTC Inc 2800 Golf Rd ... Rolling Meadows IL 60008 847-640-2400
Web: www.rtc.com

Rymax Corp 19 Chapin Rd Bldg B ... Pine Brook NJ 07058 973-808-4066
Web: www.rymaxinc.com

S. Emerson Group Inc 407 E Lancaster Ave ... Wayne PA 19087 610-971-9600
Web: www.emersongroup.com

S.H. Hirth & Associates Inc
36 W 44th St Ste 610 ... New York NY 10036 212-997-1187
Web: www.shhirthandassociates.com

Sales Evolution LLC 2837 Dogwood Ln ... Broomall PA 19008 610-353-8686
Web: www.salesevolution.com

Sales Readiness Group Inc
8015 SE 28th St Ste 206 ... Mercer Island WA 98040 800-490-0715
TF: 800-490-0715 ■ *Web:* www.salesreadinessgroup.com

Salt Branding LLC
1265 Battery St Fl 2 Ste 120 ... San Francisco CA 94111 415-616-1500
Web: saltbranding.com

Scarsin Corp 2 Brock St W Ste 201 ... Uxbridge ON L9P1P2 905-852-0086
Web: www.scarsin.com

Schmidt Consulting Services Inc
405 McKnight Park Dr ... Pittsburgh PA 15237 412-367-1226
Web: www.schmidtcs.com

School Photo Marketing 35 Vanderburg Rd ... Marlboro NJ 07746 732-431-0440
TF: 877-543-9745 ■ *Web:* www.schoolphotoonline.com

Scientia Global Inc 2210 Front St Ste 204 ... Melbourne FL 32901 321-733-1971
Web: www.scientiaglobal.com

Name / Address	City	State	ZIP	Phone	Fax
Scott Yaw Associates LLC 1074 Park Ave *Web:* www.scottyaw.com	Wycombe	PA	18980	215-598-9977	
Sebring Software Inc 1400 Cattlemen Rd Ste A *Web:* www.sebringsoft.com	Sarasota	FL	34232	941-377-0715	
Seevibes 3414 Park Ave Ste 308 *Web:* seevibes.com	Montreal	QC	H2X2H5	514-439-6909	
Selling Simplified Inc 7400 E Orchard Rd Ste 350S *Web:* sellingsimplified.com	Greenwood Village	CO	80111	720-638-8500	
Senior Marketing Specialist 801 Gray Oak Dr *TF:* 800-689-2800 ■ *Web:* www.smsteam.net	Columbia	MO	65201	800-689-2800	
Serendipity Interactive LLC 301 McCullough Dr 4th Fl *Web:* www.serendipityinteractive.com	Charlotte	NC	28262	704-775-8212	
Seroka & Associates 200 S Executive Dr *Web:* www.seroka.com	Waukesha	WI	53005	262-523-3740	
Sharks Success Marketing Ent 1532 Pickwood Ave *Web:* www.sharkssuccess.com	Fern Park	FL	32730	407-260-9780	
Sherpa Marketing 8448 Maourer Rd *Web:* www.sherpamarketing.net	Lenexa	KS	66219	646-567-8305	
Shopping Channel Direct, The 59 Ambassador Dr *Web:* theshoppingchanneldirect.com	Mississauga	ON	L5T2P9	647-201-3448	
Shoptology Inc 7800 N Dallas Pkwy Ste 160 *Web:* www.goshoptology.com	Plano	TX	75024	479-871-9663	
Sid Factor 7 Inc 1827 Pearl St Ste 1 *Web:* sidfactor.com	Boulder	CO	80302	303-449-5323	
Sid Lee Inc 75 Rue Queen Bureau 1400 *Web:* www.sidlee.com	Montreal	QC	H3C2N6	514-282-2200	
Signet Inc 1801 Shelby Oaks Dr N Ste 12 *TF:* 800-654-3889 ■ *Web:* www.gosignet.com	Memphis	TN	38134	901-387-5555	
Silicon Alley Group 1 Austin Ave Fl 2	Iselin	NJ	08830	732-326-1600	
SilverTech Inc 196 Bridge St *Web:* www.silvertech.com	Manchester	NH	03104	603-669-6600	
Simply Ideas LLC 5348 SW 34th Way *Web:* www.simplyideas.com	Hollywood	FL	33312	954-391-7123	
Sitkins Group Inc 6700 Winkler Rd Ste 4 *Web:* www.sitkinselect.com	Fort Myers	FL	33919	239-337-2555	
Sixth Sense Media 4220 NC Hwy 55 Ste 340 *Web:* www.sixthsensemedia.com	Durham	NC	27713	919-484-2442	
Sixth Star Entertainment & Marketing Inc 21 NW Fifth St *Web:* www.sixthstar.com	Fort Lauderdale	FL	33301	954-462-6760	
Skillpath Seminars 6900 Squibb Rd *Web:* www.skillpath.com	Mission	KS	66201	913-362-3900	
Sky High Marketing 6000 S Eastern Ave Ste 5D *TF:* 800-246-7447 ■ *Web:* www.skyhighmarketing.com	Las Vegas	NV	89119	800-246-7447	
Smartsearch Marketing 4450 Arapahoe Ave Ste 100 *Web:* smartsearchmarketing.com	Boulder	CO	80303	303-444-3134	
Smithgeiger LLC 31365 Oak Crest Dr Ste 150 *Web:* smithgeiger.com	Westlake Village	CA	91361	818-874-2000	
Sms Direct Inc 7540 Mason King Ct *Web:* www.smsdirect.com	Manassas	VA	20109	703-392-0123	
Snipp Interactive Inc 6708 Tulip Hill Ter *Web:* www.snipp.com	Bethesda	MD	20816	604-718-5454	
SOAP Group, The PO Box 7828 *Web:* www.thesoapgroup.com	Portland	ME	04112	207-772-0066	
Softresources LLC 11411 Ne 124th St Ste 270 *Web:* www.softresources.com	Kirkland	WA	98034	425-216-4030	
Somerset Management Group LLC 1215 Livingston Ave Ste 306 *Web:* somersetmgmt.com	New Jersey	NJ	08902	732-228-8200	
Sonawane Webdynamics Inc 44031 Pipeline Plz Ste 305 *Web:* www.sonawane.com	Ashburn	VA	20147	703-723-9191	
Sound Impressions Music Marketing L.L.C 14290 Gillis Rd Ste A *TF:* 888-512-9119 ■ *Web:* www.fancorps.com	Dallas	TX	75244	888-512-9119	
Special Audience Marketing Inc 6700 Manchaca Rd *Web:* specialaudience.com	Austin	TX	78745	512-441-6484	
Spencer Hall Inc 11321 Terwilligerscreek Dr *TF:* 888-883-4332 ■ *Web:* www.spencerhall.com	Cincinnati	OH	45249	513-683-9724	
Splash Omnimedia 711 E Main St Ste J2 *Web:* www.splashomnimedia.com	Lexington	SC	29072	803-785-5656	
St. Meyer & Hubbard Inc 10N865 Williamsburg Dr *Web:* www.stmeyerandhubbard.com	Elgin	IL	60124	847-717-4328	
Stafford Communications Group Inc 309 South St Ste 3 *TF:* 877-694-7547 ■ *Web:* www.staffcom.com	New Providence	NJ	07974	908-464-7740	
Stage 4 Solutions inc 4701 Patrick Henry Dr Bldg 19 *Web:* www.stage4solutions.com	Santa Clara	CA	95054	408-868-9739	
Starmark International Inc 210 S Andrews Ave *TF:* 888-280-9630 ■ *Web:* www.starmark.com	Fort Lauderdale	FL	33301	954-874-9000	874-9010
Stevens & Tate Inc 1900 S Highland Ave Ste 200 *Web:* www.stevens-tate.com	Lombard	IL	60148	630-627-5200	
Stevenson & Vestal 2347 W Hanford Rd *TF:* 800-535-3636 ■ *Web:* www.stevensonvestal.com	Burlington	NC	27215	800-535-3636	
Stone Coast Fund Services LLC 2 Portland Sq *Web:* www.stone-coast.com	Portland	ME	04101	207-699-2680	
Stoptech Ltd 365 Industrial Dr *TF:* 800-537-0102 ■ *Web:* stoptechltd.com	Harrison	OH	45030	513-202-5500	
Stratton Gilmore Group 37 Old Shore Rd *Web:* strattongilmoregroup.com	Madison	WI	53704	608-249-3610	
Street Fighter Marketing Inc 467 Waterbury Ct *Web:* www.streetfighter.com	Gahanna	OH	43230	614-337-7474	
Strider Marketing 6-6150 Hwy 7 Ste 400 *TF:* 800-314-8895 ■ *Web:* striderseo.com	Woodbridge	ON	L4H0R6	800-314-8895	
StringCan Interactive LLC 7525 E Camelback Rd Ste 201 *Web:* www.stringcaninteractive.com	Scottsdale	AZ	85251	480-612-0360	
Strottman International Inc 46 Corporate Park Ste 200 *Web:* www.strottman.com	Irvine	CA	92606	949-852-1166	
Stuart Maue Mitchell & James Ltd 3850 Mckelvey Rd *TF:* 800-291-9940 ■ *Web:* www.smmj.com	St. Louis	MO	63044	314-291-3030	
Suarez Corp Industries 7800 Whipple Ave NW *TF:* 800-764-0008 ■ *Web:* www.suarez.com	North Canton	OH	44720	330-494-5504	
Success Associates LLC 26 Kings Vly Ct *Web:* www.successassociates.com	Damascus	MD	20872	301-391-6161	
Summit Direct Mail Inc 1655 Terre Colony Ct *TF:* 877-247-0993 ■ *Web:* www.summitdm.com	Dallas	TX	75212	469-916-5170	
Summit Resources LLC 410 Peachtree Pkwy *Web:* summitresourcesland.com/	Cumming	GA	30041	720-439-4770	
Sunbelt Sales & Marketing Associates Inc 170 Ottley Dr *Web:* www.filmloc.com	Atlanta	GA	30324	404-892-8778	
Sundog Inc 2000 44th St SW Fl 6 *TF:* 888-978-6364 ■ *Web:* www.sundoginteractive.com	Fargo	ND	58103	701-235-5525	
Suss Consulting 801 Old York Rd Noble Plz Ste 305 *TF:* 888-984-5900 ■ *Web:* www.sussconsulting.com	Jenkintown	PA	19046	215-884-5900	884-1637
Swatchcraft 516 Townsend Ave *Web:* www.swatchcraft.com	High Point	NC	27263	336-434-5095	
Swiss Knife Shop 10 Northern Blvd Ste 8 *TF:* 866-438-7947 ■ *Web:* www.swissknifeshop.com	Amherst	NH	03031	603-732-0069	
Symblaze Inc 9229 Sunset Blvd Ste 422 *Web:* www.symblaze.com	Los Angeles	CA	90069	310-859-6100	
Symbolist 1090 Texan Trl *TF:* 800-498-6885 ■ *Web:* www.symbolist.com	Grapevine	TX	76051	800-498-6885	
Symetri Internet Marketing 6520 Airport Ctr Dr Ste 208 *Web:* www.symetri.com	Greensboro	NC	27409	336-285-0940	
Syndyne Corp 12109 Ne 95th St *Web:* syndyne.com	Vancouver	WA	98682	360-256-8466	
Synergy Direct Response 130 E Alton Ave *TF:* 888-902-6166 ■ *Web:* www.synergydr.com	Santa Ana	CA	92707	714-754-5733	
Tactician Corp 305 N Main St *Web:* www.tactician.com	Andover	MA	01810	978-475-4475	
Tahzoo LLC 3128 M St Nw *Web:* www.tahzoo.com	Washington	DC	20007	202-621-7160	
Tartan Marketing 10467 93rd Ave N Maple Grove *Web:* www.tartanmarketing.com	Osseo	MN	55369	763-391-7575	
TASC Technical Services LLC 73 Newton Rd *TF:* 877-304-8272 ■ *Web:* www.tasctech.com	Plaistow	NH	03865	877-304-8272	
TDA Group, The Four Main St Ste 100 *Web:* www.tdagroup.com	Los Altos	CA	94022	650-948-3140	
TDH Marketing & Communications Inc 8153 Garnet Dr *Web:* www.tdh-marketing.com	Dayton	OH	45458	937-438-3434	
Team Epic LLC 230 East Ave *Web:* www.teamvelocity.com	Westport	CT	06880	203-831-2100	
Team Marketing Inc 6810 N State Rd 7 *Web:* www.teaminc.net	Coconut Creek	FL	33073	561-995-0690	
Tech-Trek Ltd 1015 Matheson Blvd E Unit 6 *Web:* www.tech-trek.com	Mississauga	ON	L4W3A4	905-238-0366	
Techniart Inc 41 Bridge St *Web:* techniart.com	Collinsville	CT	06019	860-693-8697	
Technical Communities Inc 1000 Cherry Ave Ste 100 *TF:* 888-665-2765 ■ *Web:* www.technicalcommunities.com	San Bruno	CA	94066	650-624-0525	624-0535
Techno Source USA Inc 20 W 22nd St Ste 1101 *Web:* www.technosourcehk.com	New York	NY	10010	212-929-5200	
TechnoPlanet Productions Inc 7030 Woodbine Ave Fl 5 *Web:* www.technoplanet.com	Markham	ON	L3R6G2	905-839-0603	
TechSearch International Inc 4801 Spicewood Springs Rd Ste 150 *Web:* www.techsearchinc.com	Austin	TX	78759	512-372-8887	
Telescope Inc 11845 W Olympic Blvd Ste 695 *Web:* www.telescope.tv	Los Angeles	CA	90064	424-270-2900	
Televerde Inc 4636 E University Dr Ste 150 *Web:* www.televerde.com	Phoenix	AZ	85034	480-736-8137	
Tenet Partners 122 W 27th St 9th Fl *Web:* tenetpartners.com	New York	NY	10001	212-329-3030	329-3031
Text My Market Inc 350 North 500 West *Web:* www.textmymarket.info	Lehi	UT	84043	801-331-5580	
Think Reliability 2225 County Rd 90 *Web:* www.thinkreliability.com	Pearland	TX	77584	281-412-7766	
Thobe Group Inc 2727 Raintree Dr *TF:* 888-462-3477 ■ *Web:* www.thobe.com	Carrollton	TX	75006	972-418-1163	
Thompson Murray Inc 605 West Lkview Dr *Web:* wmurraythompson.com	Springdale	AR	72764	479-575-0200	
Three Deep Marketing 289 5th St E 2nd Fl *Web:* www.threedeepmarketing.com	Saint Paul	MN	55101	651-789-7701	
Three Ships Media 111 E Hargett St Ste 200 *Web:* www.three-ships.com	Raleigh	NC	27601	919-612-8319	
Through Smoke Creative Inc 480 Gate 5 Rd Studio 340 *Web:* www.throughsmoke.com	Sausalito	CA	94965	415-289-7500	
Tompkins Research & Management Consulting Inc 203 Redstone Hill *Web:* www.trmc.com	Plainville	CT	06062	860-747-0497	

				Phone	Fax
TOP Marketing U.S.A. LLC 1332 Baur Blvd Web: www.topmarketingusa.com	St. Louis	MO	63132	314-262-8550	
Topps Digital Services 1524 Cloverfield Blvd Ste G Web: www.gmg-entertainment.com	Santa Monica	CA	90404	310-566-1420	
Total Assault Llc 3272 Motor Ave Ste G Web: www.totalassault.com	Los Angeles	CA	90034	310-280-3777	
TOTAL Marketing Inc 8000 Carrick St Web: www.totalmktg.com	Fort Worth	TX	76116	817-560-3970	
TowerData Inc 379 Park Ave S 5th Fl Web: www.towerdata.com	New York	NY	10016	646-742-1771	
TR Design Inc 115 Tucker Farm Rd Web: www.trdesign.com	North Andover	MA	01845	978-470-1444	
Traffic Jam Events LLC 704 Hickory Ave TF: 800-922-8109 ■ Web: www.trafficjamevents.com	Harahan	LA	70123	800-922-8109	
Transcosmos America Inc 879 W 190th St Ste 1050 Web: www.transcosmos.net	Gardena	CA	90248	310-630-0072	
Triax Data Inc 800 S Gay St Ste 650 Web: www.triaxdata.com	Knoxville	TN	37929	865-971-4333	
Trident Marketing 1930 N Poplar St Web: www.tridentmarketing.com	Southern Pines	NC	28387	910-693-3000	
Trio Solutions Inc 505 Belle Hall Pkwy Unit 202 Web: triohrsolutions.com	Mount Pleasant	SC	29464	414-870-9896	
Triton Technologies Inc 115 Plymouth St Web: www.tritontechnology.com	Mansfield	MA	02048	508-230-7300	
Truebridge Inc 105 Beach St Ste 3 Web: www.truebridge.com	Boston	MA	02111	617-956-5020	
TSYS Loyalty Inc 5897 Windward Pkwy Web: www.tsysloyalty.com	Alpharetta	GA	30005	678-297-4350	
Tvc Marketing 3200 W Wilshire Blvd Web: www.tvcmatrix.com	Oklahoma City	OK	73116	405-843-2722	
Twin City Sales & Marketing 361 W End Blvd Web: www.twincitysam.com	Winston-salem	NC	27101	336-685-1501	
TWOBOLT Marketing Technologies Inc 1110 Central Ave Web: www.twobolt.com	Pawtucket	RI	02861	401-724-7600	
Umbrella Entertainment Group 6385 Rose Ln Ste A Web: www.umbrellaent.com.au	Carpinteria	CA	93013	613-902-5130	
United Marketing Group LLC 929 N Plum Grove Rd *Fax Area Code: 630 ■ TF: 800-513-7000	Schaumburg	IL	60173	847-240-2005	438-5788*
Up Right Mktg Inc 305 S Grant St Web: www.uprightmarketing.com	San Mateo	CA	94401	650-375-1388	
Upp Entertainment Marketing Inc 3401 Winona Ave Web: www.upp.net	Burbank	CA	91504	818-526-0111	
Uproar Communications 2144 State St Ste C Web: uproarcom.com	Ann Arbor	MI	48104	734-975-8888	
Upword Search Marketing Llc 10 Milk St Ste 306 Web: www.upwordsem.com	Boston	MA	02108	617-956-4025	
V12 Group Inc 141 W Front St Ste 410 Web: www.v12groupinc.com	Red Bank	NJ	07701	732-842-1001	
Valuewise Corp 662 Plank Rd Ste C Web: www.valuewisecorp.com	Clifton Park	NY	12065	518-383-0409	
Vanguard Management Group 9300 N 16th St Web: www.vanguardmanagementgroup.com	Tampa	FL	33612	813-930-8036	
Velocity Sales & Marketing 1700 Parkes Dr Web: newenglandoutdoorreps.com	Broadview	IL	60155	708-681-1601	
Venture Solutions Inc 1170 Grey Fox Rd Web: www.venturesolutions.com	Arden Hills	MN	55112	651-494-1740	
VeraData.com LLC 1910 Park Meadows Dr Ste 200 Web: www.veradata.com	Fort Myers	FL	33907	239-204-5000	
Verequest 127 Peters Dr Web: www.verequest.com	Fredericton	NB	E3G0G7	416-362-6777	
ViewCentral 900 E Hamilton Ave OTC: RMKR ■ TF: 888-322-5169 ■ Web: www.rainmakersystems.com	Campbell	CA	95008	408-626-3800	369-0910
Vikus Corp 2255 Center St Ste 107 Web: www.vikus.com	Chattanooga	TN	37421	423-954-3378	
Vip Sports Marketing Inc 3319 N Elston Ave Web: www.vipsm.com	Chicago	IL	60618	312-951-0700	
Virtual Edge Institute LLC 340 Mullin Ct Web: www.virtualedgeinstitute.com	Pleasanton	CA	94566	925-600-1001	
Vistex Inc 2300 Barrington Rd Ste 550 Web: www.vistex.com	Hoffman Estates	IL	60169	847-490-0420	
Vistra Communications LLC 15436 N Florida Ave Ste 160 Web: www.consultvistra.com	Tampa	FL	33613	813-961-4700	
Volume 9 Inc 1660 S Albion St Ste 800 Web: www.v9seo.com	Denver	CO	80222	303-955-5228	
W Ca Logistics 643 Bodey Cir Unit A Web: www.wcalogistics.com	Urbana	OH	43078	937-653-6382	
Waife & Associates Inc 62 Warren St Web: www.waife.com	Needham	MA	02492	781-449-7032	
Waldbillig & Besteman Inc 8001 Excelsior Dr Ste 110 Web: www.nelsonschmidt.com	Madison	WI	53717	608-829-0900	
Wasabi Rabbit Inc 19 Fulton St Ste 307 Web: www.wasabirabbit.com	New York	NY	10038	646-366-0000	
Wayne Reaves Software & Websites Inc 6211 Thomaston Rd Web: www.waynereaves.com	Macon	GA	31220	478-474-8779	
Web Clients LLC 2300 Vartan Way Ste 100 Web: www.webclients.net	Harrisburg	PA	17110	717-346-3600	
Web Decisions LLC 303 Pisgah Church Rd Ste 2A Web: www.webdecisions.com	Greensboro	NC	27455	336-545-7817	
Web Talent Marketing 322 N Arch St Ste 120 Web: www.webtalentmarketing.com	Lancaster	PA	17603	717-283-4045	
WebiMax LLC 6000 Commerce Pkwy Ste A TF: 866-832-3638 ■ Web: www.webimax.com	Mount Laurel	NJ	08054	866-832-3638	
Wellness International Network Ltd 5800 Democracy Dr *Fax Area Code: 800	Plano	TX	75024	972-312-1100	430-4674*
Wendy Soucie Consulting Llc 218 S Main St Ste B Web: www.wendysoucie.com	Lodi	WI	53555	608-225-1985	
West Park Direct 2728 Euclid Ave Fl 2	Cleveland	OH	44115	216-589-0200	
Westland Financial Services Inc 1717 Kettner Blvd Ste 200 Web: westlandinc.com	San Diego	CA	92101	619-238-8144	
Wiken Promotion & Advertising Inc 901 12 Oaks Ctr Dr Web: www.wiken.com	Wayzata	MN	55391	952-476-2002	
Wilde Agency 201 Summer St Web: www.wildeagency.com	Holliston	MA	01746	508-893-0223	
Wilkin Guge Marketing 3237 E Guasti Rd Ste 220 Web: www.wilkinguge.com	Ontario	CA	91761	909-390-1239	
Willems Marketing 120 N Morrison St Ste 200 Web: www.willemsmarketingandevents.com	Appleton	WI	54911	920-831-6580	
Wilson Marketing Group Inc 17015 13th Ave N Web: www.wilsonconsultants.com	Plymouth	MN	55447	763-476-2216	
Windjammer Promotions Inc 1112 Main St Web: windjammerpromotions.com	Osterville	MA	02655	508-428-2099	
Winn Technology Group Inc 523 Palm Harbor Blvd Web: www.winntech.net	Palm Harbor	FL	34683	727-789-0006	
Wise Technical Marketing Inc 1430 Cherokee Rd Web: wisetechnical.com	Louisville	KY	40204	502-473-8300	
Workbook LLC 6762 Lexington Ave Web: www.workbook.com	Los Angeles	CA	90038	323-856-0008	
World Steel Dynamics Inc 456 Sylvan Ave Web: www.worldsteeldynamics.com	Englewood Cliffs	NJ	07632	201-503-0900	
WSI Internet 5580 Explorer Dr Ste 600 TF: 888-678-7588 ■ Web: www.wsicorporate.com	Mississauga	ON	L4W4Y1	905-678-7588	678-7242
Xenium Resources 7401 Sw Washo Ct Ste 200 Web: www.xeniumhr.com	Tualatin	OR	97062	503-612-1555	
yourDealer 420 E 55th St Ste 8H TF: 866-847-7502 ■ Web: www.yourdealer.net	New York	NY	10022	866-847-7502	
ZGM Collaborative Marketing Inc 1324 17th Ave SW Ste 500 Web: www.zgm.ca	Calgary	AB	T2T5S8	403-770-2250	
Zionist Organization of America Inc 4 E 34th St 3rd Fl Web: zoa.org	New York	NY	10016	212-481-1500	
Zonic Design & Imaging Llc 2565 3rd St Ste 324 Web: www.zonicdesign.com	San Francisco	CA	94107	415-643-3700	
ZS Assoc 1800 Sherman Ave Ste 700 Web: www.zsassociates.com	Evanston	IL	60201	847-492-3600	864-6280

196 CONSULTING SERVICES - TELECOMMUNICATIONS

				Phone	Fax
110 Technologies Inc 190 WildfLwr Ln Web: 110technology.com	Hillsborough	NJ	08844	908-431-7899	
2020 Exhibits Inc 10550 S Sam Huston Pkwy W TF: 800-856-6659 ■ Web: www.2020exhibits.com	Houston	TX	77071	713-354-0900	
2ndEdison Inc 11 El Gavilan Rd Web: www.2ndedison.com	Orinda	CA	94563	925-253-1002	
3 e Consulting Services 6 Dickinson Dr Ste 111 Web: 3econsultingservices.com	Chadds Ford	PA	19317	610-358-5950	
352-MEDIA 133 SW 130th Way Ste D Web: www.352inc.com	Newberry	FL	32669	352-374-9657	
360 Cloud Solutions LLC 14350 N 87th St Ste 165 Web: www.360cloudsolutions.com	Scottsdale	AZ	85260	480-295-3420	
360 Networx LLC 668 N 44th St Ste 300 Web: networx360.com	Phoenix	AZ	85008	480-497-7000	
3E Company Inc 3207 Grey Hawk Ct Web: www.3ecompany.com	Carlsbad	CA	92010	760-602-8700	
4patientcare 100 Oceangate Ste 1200 Web: 4patientcare.com	Long Beach	CA	90802	562-861-1800	
6th Street Consulting 250 N. Harbor Dr. Ste. 321 Ste Web: www.6sc.com	Redondo Beach	CA	90277	310-694-3844	
9g Products Inc 222 Oak St Web: www.9gproducts.com	Bonner Springs	KS	66012	913-422-7400	
A G Wassenaar Inc 2180 S Ivanhoe St Ste 5	Denver	CO	80222	303-759-8100	
A3 Communications Inc 1038 Kinley Rd Bldg B Web: a3communications.com	Irmo	SC	29063	803-744-5000	
Aacom Inc 201 Stuyvesant Ave TF: 800-273-3719 ■ Web: www.aacomnj.com	Lyndhurst	NJ	07071	201-438-2244	
Ab Ovo Inc 2320-H Walsh Ave TF: 866-549-0782 ■ Web: www.abovoinc.com	Santa Clara	CA	95051	408-567-9090	
Abc Quality Consulting Services 1115 Grand Cyn Web: abcquality.com	Brea	CA	92821	714-256-0223	
Absolute Mgic Cmpters Internet Po Box 10226 Web: www.absolutemagic.com	Westminster	CA	92685	714-899-8154	
Acceles Inc 1616 Westgate Cir Web: www.acceles.com	Brentwood	TN	37027	615-771-3774	
Accent Information Systems Inc 585 Sunbury Rd Web: www.accentservices.com	Delaware	OH	43015	740-548-7378	
Accupro Trademark Services Llp 401 W Georgia St Ste 702 Web: accuprotm.com	Vancouver	BC	V6B5A1	604-661-9292	

Phone | Fax

Accuscreen Systems 1038 Main St Baton Rouge LA 70802 225-343-8378
Web: www.accuscreensystems.com
ACME Business Consulting LLC
249 NW Park Ave Portland OR 97209 503-232-1416
Web: www.acmebusinessconsulting.com
Acorn Environmental Consultants Inc
8040 Stevens Ave S Ste Minneapolis MN 55420 952-888-4901
Web: www.acornenvironmental.com
Actionlink Llc 4100 Embassy Pkwy Akron OH 44333 330-665-1660
Web: www.actionlink.com
Actuarial Research Corp
6928 Little River Tpke Ste E Annandale VA 22003 703-941-7400
Web: www.aresearch.com
Acuity Audio Visual 11301 Industrial Rd Manassas VA 20109 703-361-6080
Web: www.acuityav.com
Acuity Inc 12930 Worldgate Dr Ste 100 Herndon VA 20170 703-766-0977
Web: www.myacuity.com
Adaptiva Corp 3005 112th Ave NE, Ste 250 Bellevue WA 98015 425-823-4500
Web: www.adaptiva.com
ADB Consulting & CRO Inc
8569 Pines Blvd Ste 215 Pembroke Pines FL 33024 954-517-1970
Web: www.adbccro.com
Adelphi Consulting Group Inc
8209 Sw Cirrus Dr Beaverton OR 97008 503-641-3501
Web: adelphigroup.net
Adept Consulting Services Inc 408 W Main St Lansdale PA 19446 215-855-3610
Web: www.adeptusa.com
Adhere Solutions Inc
3105 N Ashland Ave Ste 267 Chicago IL 60657 312-618-8600
Web: www.adheresolutions.com
Adistec 7620 NW 25 St Unit 7 Miami FL 33122 786-221-2300
Web: www.adistec.com
Advance Communications & Consulting Inc
8803 Swigert Ct Unit A Bakersfield CA 93311 661-664-0177
Web: www.advancecomm.net
Adventace 2166 Chardonnay Cir Gibsonia PA 15044 724-443-2383
Web: www.adventace.com
Aerial Innovations Inc 3703 W Azeele St Tampa FL 33609 813-254-7339
TF: 800-223-1701 ■ *Web:* www.flythis.com
Aether Consulting Inc 8369 Windstone Ct Goodrich MI 48438 586-939-8028
Web: aetherconsulting.com
Affinion Loyalty Group Inc 7814 Carousel Ln Richmond VA 23294 804-217-8090
Web: affinion.com
Affinity 2600 N Mayfair Rd Ste 400 Milwaukee WI 53226 414-258-0200
Web: www.affinityit.com
AHC Inc 2230 N Fairfax Dr Ste 100 Arlington VA 22201 703-486-0626
Web: www.ahcinc.org
Ahec 1200 N Elam Ave Greensboro NC 27401 336-832-8025
Web: gahec.org
AIG Technologies Inc 2 Peach Tree Hill Rd Livingston NJ 07039 973-533-3200
Web: www.aigtechnologies.net
Air Chek Inc 1936 Butler Bridge Rd Mills River NC 28759 828-684-0893
TF: 800-247-2435 ■ *Web:* www.radon.com
Air-Transport IT Services Inc
5950 Hazeltine National Dr Ste 210 Orlando FL 32822 407-370-4664
Web: www.airit.com
Ajilon Communications
970 Peachtree Industrial Blvd Ste 200 Suwanee GA 30024 678-482-5103 482-8849
TF: 800-843-6910
Alacrinet Inc 530 Lytton Ave 2nd Fl Palo Alto CA 94301 650-646-2670
Web: www.alacrinet.com
Alchemic Dream Inc 442 Ave Willow Shawinigan QC G9N1X2 819-840-9607
Web: www.alchemicdream.com
Alevistar Group Presidential Blvd Bala Cynwyd PA 19004 610-617-7800
Web: www.alevistar.com
Alidade Technology Inc 111 Knoll Dr Collegeville PA 19426 877-265-1581
TF: 877-265-1581 ■ *Web:* alidadetech.com
Allegro Consultants Ltd
9800 JEB Stuart Pkwy Ste 106 Glen Allen VA 23059 804-553-1130
Web: www.allegroconsultants.com
Allied Consultants Inc 1304 W Ave Austin TX 78701 512-236-8535
Web: www.alliedconsultants.com
Alltech Consulting Services Inc
258 Wall St Princeton NJ 08540 609-945-2590
Web: www.alltechconsultinginc.com
Alogic US LLC 1845 Ferguson Rd Allison Park PA 15101 412-635-2500
Web: www.alogic-us.com
Alonso Consulting Inc 204 Passaic Ave Fl 1 Fairfield NJ 07004 973-575-1414
Web: www.alonso.com
Alpha I Marketing Corp 65 W Red Oak Ln White Plains NY 10604 914-697-5300
Web: www.alpha1marketing.com
Altamont Capital Partners
400 Hamilton Ave Ste 230 Palo Alto CA 94301 650-264-7750
Web: www.altamontcapital.com
AltaRock Energy Inc
2320 Marinship Way Ste 300 Sausalito CA 94965 415-331-0130
Web: www.altarockenergy.com
Alto Consulting & Training
7210 Metro Blvd Minneapolis MN 55439 952-831-6604
Web: www.altoconsulting.com
Amcest Nationwide Monitoring 1017 Walnut St Roselle NJ 07203 800-631-7370
TF: 800-631-7370 ■ *Web:* www.amcest.com
American Ecotech LLC 100 Elm St Factory D Warren RI 02885 877-247-0403
TF: 877-247-0403 ■ *Web:* www.americanecotech.com
Americtraining Inc 4315 Brook Rd Nw Lancaster OH 43130 740-756-7461
Web: www.ameritraining.com
AMITA Corp 2650 Queensview Dr Ste 250 Ottawa ON K2B8H6 613-742-6482
Web: www.amita.com
AMTEL 900 Lafayette St Ste 506 Santa Clara CA 95050 408-615-0522
Web: www.amtelnet.com
Anacom Inc 3000 Tasman Dr Santa Clara CA 95054 408-519-2062
Web: www.anacominc.com

Ananke Inc 14 Imperial Pl Ste 202 Providence RI 02906 401-331-2780
Web: www.ananke.com
AndPlus LLC 1881 Worcester Rd Ste 201 Framingham MA 01701 508-425-7533
Web: www.andplus.com
ANEXIO Technology Services Inc
1 Bank of America Plz 421 Fayetteville St Raleigh NC 27601 941-556-3410
TF: 844-208-6512 ■ *Web:* www.anexio.com
Angarai International Inc
9111 Edmonston Rd Ste 305 Greenbelt MD 20770 410-472-5000
Web: www.angarai-intl.com
Anthony Wayne Business Exchange
3508 Stellhorn Rd Ste Fort Wayne IN 46815 219-485-1990
Web: www.anthonywayne.com
Aok Networking LLC 820 Clark St Oviedo FL 32765 407-249-1989
Web: www.aoknetworking.com
Aperion Information Technologies Inc
90 S Washington St Oxford MI 48371 248-969-9791
Web: www.aperion.com
Apex Computer Systems Inc
13875 Cerritos Corp Dr Ste A Cerritos CA 90703 562-926-6820
Web: www.acsi2000.com
Applied Broadband Inc
1881 9th St Canyon Ctr Ste 125 Boulder CO 80302 303-449-2033
Web: www.appliedbroadband.com
Applied Power Technologies Inc
470 Vandell Way Ste A Campbell CA 95008 408-342-0790
Web: www.apt4power.com
Approach Information Technology Inc
2027 Blue Heron Dr Melbourne FL 32940 321-242-6760
Web: www.approachit.com
Aquascape Environmental 605 Mauldin Dr Woodstock GA 30188 678-445-0077
Web: www.aquascape.net
Aquaterra Technologies Inc PO Box 774 West Chester PA 19381 610-431-5733
Web: aquaterra-tech.com
Aquilent Inc 1100 W St Laurel MD 20707 301-939-1000
Web: www.aquilent.com
Arbor Solutions Inc
1345 Monroe Ave NW Ste 309 Grand Rapids MI 49505 616-451-2500
Web: www.arbsol.com
Arc Aspicio LLC 1725 I St NW Ste 300 Washington DC 20006 703-465-2060
Web: www.arcaspicio.com
Arcadia Solutions LLC
20 Blanchard Rd Unit 10 Burlington MA 01803 781-202-3600
Web: www.arcadiasolutions.com
Arclyte Technologies Inc 953 S Meridian Alhambra CA 91803 626-281-2220
Web: www.arclytetech.com
Arctic Wolf Networks Inc
440 Wolfe Rd Mail Stop 147 Sunnyvale CA 94085 888-272-8429
TF: 888-272-8429 ■ *Web:* arcticwolf.com
Area Wide Communication 3850 Broadway St Portsmouth VA 23703 757-638-3327
Web: areawidecomm.com
Arganteal Corp 9226 Knoll Crest Loop Austin TX 78759 512-801-6729
Web: www.arganteal.com
Argos Security Services Inc
1183 Park Oak Ct Milpitas CA 95035 408-829-6544
Web: www.argossecurity.com
Arxis Technology Inc 2468 Tapo Canyon Rd Simi Valley CA 93063 805-306-7800
Web: www.arxistechnology.com
ASCC Inc 15 Ogle View Rd Cranberry Township PA 16066 724-772-2722
Web: asccinc.com
Ascendum Solutions LLC 10290 Alliance Rd Cincinnati OH 45242 513-792-5100
Web: www.ascendum.com
Asm Consulting Services
22 Sunnyhill Rd Emerald Hills CA 94062 650-780-9321
Web: www.consultingasm.com
Associated Communications & Research Services Inc (ACRS)
817 NE 63rd St Oklahoma City OK 73105 405-843-9966
Astatech Inc 2525 Pearl Buck Rd Bristol PA 19007 215-785-2656
TF: 800-387-2269 ■ *Web:* www.astatechinc.com
Atlantic Prsnnel Tnant Scrning
3780 Burns Rd Ste 6 Palm Beach Gardens FL 33410 561-776-1804
Web: www.atlanticscreening.com
Atrion Networking Corp 30 Service Ave Warwick RI 02886 401-736-6400 633-6766
TF: 800-890-4526 ■ *Web:* www.atrion.net
ATS Group LLC 1200 Atwater Dr Ste 170 Malvern PA 19355 484-320-4302
Web: www.theatsgroup.com
Attac Consulting Group
301 E Liberty St Ste 605 Ann Arbor MI 48104 734-214-2990
Web: attacconsulting.com
Autoscan Inc 4040 23rd Ave W Seattle WA 98199 206-282-1616
Web: www.autoscaninc.com
Avaleris Inc 1400-45 O'Connor St Ottawa ON K1P1A4 613-237-9695
Web: www.avaleris.com
Avalon Consulting LLC
5600 Tennyson Pkwy Ste 230 Plano TX 75024 469-424-3449
Web: www.avalonconsult.com
Avancent Consulting Corp
1896 Kentucky Ave Winter Park FL 32789 407-897-8664
Web: www.avancent.com
Avani Media Inc 80 Liberty Ship Way Ste 25 Sausalito CA 94965 415-331-2150
Web: www.avanimedia.com
Avant! LLC 4667 Mission St San Francisco CA 94112 415-349-4840
Web: avantexperience.com
Avantia Inc 9655 Sweet Vly Dr Valley View OH 44125 216-901-9366
Web: www.avantia-inc.com
Avantica Technologies
2680 Bayshore Pkwy Ste 416 Mountain View CA 94043 650-248-9678
TF: 877-372-1955 ■ *Web:* www.avantica.net
Avesta Computer Services Ltd
1 Executive Dr Ste 120 Somerset NJ 08873 201-369-9400
TF: 888-283-7821 ■ *Web:* www.avestacs.com
AXIA Consulting LLC 1391 W Fifth Ave Ste 320 Columbus OH 43212 614-675-4050
TF: 866-937-5550 ■ *Web:* www.axiaconsulting.net

Company	City	State	ZIP	Phone	Fax
Axian Inc 9600 Sw Nimbus Ave *Web:* www.axian.com	Beaverton	OR	97008	503-644-6106	
Axim Systems Inc 15 Diamond Rd. *Web:* www.axim.com	Lexington	MA	02420	781-497-0942	
Axiom Technology Group Inc 2077 Miner St, Ste 204 *Web:* axiomtechgroup.com	Des Plaines	IL	60016	630-861-1000	
Axsess Energy Group Llc 18 Sawmill Dr *Web:* www.axsessgroup.com	Northborough	MA	01532	508-351-9050	
Aztech Technologies Inc 5 McCrea Hill Rd *Web:* www.aztechtech.com	Ballston Spa	NY	12020	518-885-5385	
Azurea Inc 365 Gus Hipp Blvd *Web:* www.dragonpoint.com	Rockledge	FL	32955	321-631-0610	
B C L of Texas 2212 S Congress Ave *Web:* www.bcloftexas.org	Austin	TX	78704	512-912-9884	
B D N Industrial Hygiene Consultants Inc 8105 Valleywood Ln *TF:* 800-968-0123 ■ *Web:* bdnihc.com	Portage	MI	49024	269-329-1237	
B e p Consulting Inc 1006 W Lk St *Web:* bepinc.com	Chicago	IL	60607	312-850-3140	
B i d Designs 1525 Perimeter Pkwy Nw Ste 125 *Web:* bid-designs.com	Huntsville	AL	35806	256-489-2815	
B2 Environmental Inc 10838 Old Mill Rd Ste A *Web:* www.b2environmental.com	Omaha	NE	68154	402-330-0763	
BACM Consultants Inc 6601 SW 56th St *Web:* www.bacmconsultants.com	Davie	FL	33314	754-581-4153	
Bailiwick Data Systems Inc 4260 Norex Dr *Web:* www.bailiwick.com	Chaska	MN	55318	952-556-5502	
BairesDev 1999 S. Bascom Ave, Ste 700 *Web:* www.bairesdev.com	Campbell	CA	95008	408-600-1331	
Baka Communications Inc 630 The East Mall *TF:* 866-884-3329 ■ *Web:* www.baka.ca	Etobicoke	ON	M9B4B1	416-641-2800	
Balance Consulting 1050 Highland Dr Ste F *Web:* balanceconsult.com	Ann Arbor	MI	48108	734-668-1099	
BalancePoint Inc 9201 Ward Pkwy Ste 200 *Web:* www.balancepointcorp.com	Kansas City	MO	64114	816-268-1400	
Bank Advisory Group LLC, The 15100 Gebron Dr *Web:* www.bankadvisory.com	Austin	TX	78734	512-263-8800	
Banks com Inc Suite 2200, 425 Market St *Web:* www.banks.com	SAN FRANCISCO	CA	94105	415-962-9700	
Barbaricum LLC 819 Seventh St NW *Web:* barbaricum.com	Washington	DC	20001	202-393-0873	
Bard Consulting Llc 100 Pine St Ste 2420 *Web:* www.bardconsulting.com	San Francisco	CA	94111	415-421-2822	
Barrio Logan College Institute 1625 Newton Ave Ste 200 *Web:* blci.org	San Diego	CA	92113	619-232-4686	
Beckmill Research Llc 108 Deer Dr *Web:* beckmill.com	Lexington	VA	24450	540-463-6200	
Becterm Inc 4780 Boul Henri-bourassa *Web:* becterm.com	Quebec	QC	G1H3A7	418-622-6777	
Benefitvision Inc 4522 RFD *TF:* 800-810-2200 ■ *Web:* www.benefitvision.com	Long Grove	IL	60047	800-810-2200	
Bensinger Consulting 625 W Deer Vly Rd Ste 103 *Web:* www.bensingerconsulting.com	Phoenix	AZ	85027	602-237-8500	
BestIT.com Inc 3724 N Third St. *Web:* www.bestit.com	Phoenix	AZ	85012	602-667-5613	
Bestmark Inc 5500 Feltl Rd Ste 200 *Web:* www.bestmark.com	Minnetonka	MN	55343	952-922-3890	
Betach Solutions Inc 12 Manning Close NE *Web:* www.betach.com	Calgary	AB	T2E7N6	403-984-2473	
Beyond Roi Inc 4185 Truman Dr *Web:* getbeyondroi.com	Frisco	TX	75034	214-872-1100	
Big Bang ERP Inc 105 De Louvain W *TF:* 844-361-4408 ■ *Web:* www.bigbangerp.com	Montreal	QC	H2N1A3	514-360-4408	
Bio Medware 3526 W Liberty Rd Ste 100 *Web:* www.biomedware.com	Ann Arbor	MI	48103	734-913-1098	
Bio Rem Usa Inc 2496 W Royalton Rd *Web:* biorem.com	Broadview Heights	OH	44147	440-230-9542	
Bio-west Inc 1063 West 1400 North *Web:* bio-west.com	Logan	UT	84321	435-752-4202	
Biodiversity Research Institute 276 Canco Rd *Web:* www.briloon.org	Portland	ME	04103	207-839-7600	
Biota Pacific Environmental Sciences Inc 10516 E Riverside Dr *Web:* connectory.com	Bothell	WA	98011	425-402-6887	
BITS 3190 Fairview Park Dr Ste 350 *Web:* www.thebitsgroup.com	Falls Church	VA	22042	703-822-0970	
BizTech Inc 1150 First Ave Ste 320 *Web:* www.biztech.com	King Of Prussia	PA	19406	610-592-0600	
Blue Skies Consulting LLC 100 Blue Skies Dr Belen Alexander Airport (E80) *Web:* www.blueskies.aero	Belen	NM	87002	505-864-3700	
Bluecube Information Technology 10521 S Parker Rd, Ste F *Web:* www.bluecubeit.com	Parker	CO	80134	720-463-3800	
Bluemetal Architects Inc 44 Pleasant St *TF:* 866-252-0111 ■ *Web:* www.bluemetal.com	Watertown	MA	02472	866-252-0111	
Bokanyi Consulting Inc 800 Town & Country Blvd Ste 300 *Web:* www.bokanyiconsulting.com	Houston	TX	77024	281-809-0110	
Bolder Technology Inc 4740 Hancock Dr. *Web:* bolder.com	Boulder	CO	80303	303-447-8677	
Borek Business Solutions 1144 Willagillespie Rd Ste 28 *Web:* www.borekbusinesssolutions.com	Eugene	OR	97401	541-345-3883	
Borenson and Associates 330 Schantz Rd *Web:* borenson.com	Allentown	PA	18104	610-398-6908	
Bossa Nova Technologies LLC 606 Venice Blvd Ste B *Web:* www.bossanovatech.com	Venice	CA	90291	310-577-8113	
Botnay Bay Computer 177 Bartlett St. *Web:* botnaybay.com	Portsmouth	NH	03801	603-436-6035	
Brad Montgomery Productions Inc 6574 S Zeno Ct. *Web:* www.bradmontgomery.com	Aurora	CO	80016	303-691-0726	
Bradford & Galt Inc 11457 Olde Cabin Rd Ste 200 *Web:* bradfordandgalt.com	Saint Louis	MO	63141	314-997-4644	
Bradley Mj and Associates Inc 47 Jct Sq Dr *Web:* www.mjbradley.com	Concord	MA	01742	978-369-5533	
Bradley-Sciocchetti Inc 4420 N Crescent Blvd *Web:* www.bsihvac.com	Pennsauken	NJ	08109	856-663-3022	
Braxton Technologies LLC 6 N Tejon St Ste 220 *Web:* www.braxtontech.com	Colorado Springs	CO	80903	719-380-8488	
Brazos Telecommunications Inc 109 N Ave D *Web:* www.brazosnet.com	Olney	TX	76374	940-564-5659	
Bridgeforce Inc 101 Ponds Edge Dr Ste 100 *Web:* www.bridgeforce.com	Chadds Ford	PA	19317	302-325-7100	
BrightMove Inc 320 High Tide Dr # 201 *TF:* 877-482-8840 ■ *Web:* www.brightmove.com	Saint Augustine	FL	32080	877-482-8840	
Brimtek Inc 21660 Red Rum Dr Ste 105 *Web:* www.brimtek.com	Ashburn	VA	20147	571-918-4921	
Broadband Specialists Inc 1700 Peachtree Rd *Web:* bsicable.com	Balch Springs	TX	75180	972-329-1280	
Brook Consulting Services Inc 2 Quimby Ln. *Web:* brookconsultingservice.com	Flemington	NJ	08822	908-284-9836	
Brookman LLC 61 Rhode Island Ave NW *Web:* www.brookman.com	Washington	DC	20001	301-515-0450	
Brubaker & Associates Inc 7626 Hammerly Blvd *Web:* www.brubakerandassociates.com	Houston	TX	77055	713-464-4666	
Bryant Christie Inc 500 Union St Ste 701 *Web:* www.bryantchristie.com	Seattle	WA	98101	206-292-6340	
BTI Group 4 N 2nd St Ste 560 *Web:* www.btigroupma.com	San Jose	CA	95113	408-246-1102	
Bts Consulting Group Ltd 355 Glen Arms Dr. *Web:* btsconsultinggroup.com	Danville	CA	94526	925-837-1730	
Bugcrowd Inc 921 Front St 1st Fl *TF:* 888-361-9734 ■ *Web:* bugcrowd.com	San Francisco	CA	94111	650-260-8443	
BusinessGenetics Inc 9605 S Kingston Ct Ste 290 *Web:* www.businessgenetics.net	Englewood	CO	80112	720-266-1024	
C p Environmental Group Inc 1092 Fifth Ave	New Kensington	PA	15068	724-594-1900	
Cadence Environmental Energy Inc 401 Cadence Park Plz. *Web:* www.cadencerecycling.com	Michigan City	IN	46360	219-879-0371	
Cage Inc 6440 N Beltline Rd Ste 125 *Web:* www.cage-inc.com	Irving	TX	75063	972-550-1001	
CAI Hosting Inc 55 State St *Web:* www.creativeapproachesinc.com	East Bloomfield	NY	14443	585-657-6379	
Caiman Consulting Corp 15127 NE 24th St Ste 547 *Web:* www.caimanconsulting.com	Redmond	WA	98052	425-214-4598	
Caine Real Estate Group 111 Williams St. *Web:* www.cbcaine.com	Greenville	SC	29601	864-250-2850	
Cait Llc 799 Cromwell Park Dr Ste F *Web:* caitllc.net	Glen Burnie	MD	21061	410-863-4601	
Calder Bateman 10241 109 St Nw *Web:* www.calderbateman.com	Edmonton	AB	T5J1N2	780-426-3610	
Cale Parking Systems USA Inc 13808 Monroes Business Park *Web:* www.caleparkingusa.com	Tampa	FL	33635	813-405-3900	
Calibre Computer Solutions LLC 318 W Glendale St *Web:* www.calibreforhome.com	Princeton	IN	47670	812-386-8919	
Cam Consulting Group Llc 10 Tudor Ct *Web:* cam4consulting.com	Chesterfield	NJ	08515	609-291-1937	
Cameron-cole LLC 200 E Government St Ste 100 *Web:* www.cameron-cole.com	Pensacola	FL	32502	850-434-1011	
Campaign Services Inc 117 N Saint Asaph St *Web:* campaignsolutions.com	Alexandria	VA	22314	703-684-3435	
Campos Market Research 216 Blvd Of The Allies *Web:* www.campos.com	Pittsburgh	PA	15222	412-471-8484	
Canadian Professional Sales Association 310 Front St W Ste 800 *TF:* 888-267-2772 ■ *Web:* www.cpsa.com	Toronto	ON	M5V3B5	416-408-2685	
Candoris Technologies LLC 9 E Main St *Web:* www.candoris.com	Annville	PA	17003	717-228-1600	
Canidium LLC 3801 Kirby Dr, S456 *TF:* 877-651-1837 ■ *Web:* www.canidium.com	Houston	TX	77024	877-651-1837	
Canon Information Technology Services Inc 850 Greenbrier Cir *Web:* www.consumerusa.cannon.com	Chesapeake	VA	23320	757-579-7100	
CAP Index Inc 150 John Robert Thomas Dr The Commons at Lincoln Center *Web:* capindex.com	Exton	PA	19341	610-903-3000	
Capital Hill Group 45 O'Connor St Ste 1540 *Web:* capitalhillgroup.ca	Ottawa	ON	K1P1A4	613-235-0221	
Cardiff Park Advisors 2257 Vista La Nisa *TF:* 888-332-2238 ■ *Web:* www.cardiffpark.com	Carlsbad	CA	92009	760-635-7526	

Phone Fax

Cardinal Point Solutions LLC
935 N 3rd Ave St. Charles IL 60174 630-584-7851
Web: www.cardinalpointsolutions.com

Cardwell Group 24481 Detroit Rd Ste 300 Cleveland OH 44145 440-892-1410
Web: www.connectionsonline.net

CareWorks Technologies Ltd 5555 Glendon Ct Dublin OH 43016 614-336-4680
Web: www.careworkstech.com

Carnegie East House For Seniors
1844 Second Ave New York NY 10128 212-410-0033
TF: 888-410-0033 ■ *Web:* carnegieeast.org

Casey, Quirk & Associates LLC
17 Old King's Hwy S Ste 200 Darien CT 06820 203-899-3000
Web: www.caseyquirk.com

Cash Flow Solutions Inc
5166 College Corner Pk Oxford OH 45056 800-736-5123
TF: 800-736-5123 ■ *Web:* www.followthefrog.com

Cask LLC 5151 Shoreham Pl Ste 140 San Diego CA 92122 858-458-9951
Web: www.caskllc.com

Casson-Mark Corp 10515 Markison Rd Dallas TX 75238 214-340-0880
Web: www.cmarkcorp.com

Catalyst IT Services Inc 502 S Sharp St Baltimore MD 21201 410-385-2500
Web: catalystdevworks.com

Catamount Energy Corp 71 Allen St Ste 101 Rutland VT 05701 802-773-6684
Web: www.duke_energy.com

Cautela-Solutions Ltd 201 Lawrence Dr PMB 104 Heath TX 75032 972-772-8020
Web: www.cautela-solutions.com

Cc Coaching & Consulting Inc
5595 S Sycamore St Littleton CO 80120 303-984-9000
Web: www.cccandc.com

CCS Presentation Systems Inc
17350 N Hartford Dr Scottsdale AZ 85255 480-348-0100
Web: www.ccsprojects.com

Celerity Consulting Group Inc
2 Gough St Ste 300 San Francisco CA 94103 415-986-8850
TF: 866-224-4333 ■ *Web:* www.celerityconsulting.net

Celigo LLC 230 Twin Dolphin Dr Ste A Redwood City CA 94065 650-579-0210
Web: www.celigo.com

Cella Consulting LLC 4350 E W Hwy Ste 307 Bethesda MD 20814 301-280-0313
Web: www.cellaconsulting.com

Centra Consulting Inc 413 W Idaho St Ste 302 Boise ID 83702 208-338-9400
Web: www.centrainc.com

CFC Technology Corporation LLC
6110 Blue Cir Dr Ste 110 Minnetonka MN 55343 763-235-5300
Web: www.cfctechnology.com

CGI Federal Inc 12601 Fair Lks Cir Fairfax VA 22033 703-227-6000
Web: www.cgifederal.com

Chameleon Group LLC 951 Islington St Portsmouth NH 03801 603-570-4300
Web: www.chameleonsales.com

Chamness Technology Inc
2255 Little Wall Lk Rd Blairsburg IA 50034 515-325-6133
Web: www.chamnesstechnology.com

Chaney & Associates 230 Highview Ave Pittsburgh PA 15238 412-767-0307
Web: www.chaneyassociates.com

Change Companies, The 5221 Sigstrom Dr Carson City NV 89706 775-885-2610
TF: 888-889-8866 ■ *Web:* www.changecompanies.net

Channel Solutions LLC
3145 E Chandler Blvd Ste 110 Phoenix AZ 85048 866-501-9690
TF: 866-501-9690 ■ *Web:* www.cscorp-us.com

Chase & Associates Cpas PC
9293 Corporate Cir Manassas VA 20110 703-361-7114
Web: www.chaseadvisors.com

Chase Enterprises Inc 6509 W Reno Ave Oklahoma City OK 73127 405-495-1722
Web: www.chappellsupply.com

Cherokee Crc Llc 916 W 23rd St Tulsa OK 74107 918-582-9110
Web: cherokee-crc.com

Chetan Sharma Consulting LLC
1778 12th Ave NE Issaquah WA 98029 425-657-0555
Web: www.chetansharma.com

Chevo Consulting LLC
2275 Research Blvd Ste 100 Rockville MD 20850 301-309-0040
Web: www.chevoconsulting.com

Chlopak Leonard Schechter & Associates Inc
1850 M St, NW Ste 550 Washington DC 20036 202-289-5900
Web: www.clsdc.com

Choice Telecommunications Inc
7640 Dixie Hwy Ste 150 Clarkston MI 48346 248-922-1151
Web: www.choicetel.com

CHP International Inc 1040 N Blvd Ste 220 Oak Park IL 60301 708-848-9650
TF: 800-449-2614 ■ *Web:* www.chpinternational.com

CHR Solutions Inc 9700 Bissonnet Ste 2800 Houston TX 77036 713-995-4778
Web: www.chrsolutions.com

Chuck Schubert & Associates
17197 N Laurel Park Dr Ste 114 Livonia MI 48152 734-953-5600
Web: csasoftware.com

Cibola Systems Corp 180 S Cypress St Orange CA 92866 714-480-0272
Web: www.cibolasystems.com

Ciris Energy Inc
9155 E Nichols Ave Ste 200 Centennial CO 80112 303-649-2000
Web: www.cirisenergy.com

Cirro 31920 Del Obispo Ste 260 San Juan Capistrano CA 92675 949-900-4567
Web: www.cirro.com

Civic Resource Group LLC
915 Wilshire Blvd Ste 1680 Los Angeles CA 90017 213-225-1170
TF: 800-771-0026 ■ *Web:* www.civicresource.com

CJ Brown Energy PC 4245 Union Rd Ste 204b Buffalo NY 14225 716-565-9190
Web: www.cjbrownenergy.com

Clarite Consulting 20 Tower Hill Rd Mountain Lakes NJ 07046 973-541-0051
Web: www.clariteconsulting.com

Clear North Technologies Inc
10300 Valley View Rd Ste 111 Eden Prairie MN 55344 952-828-9434
Web: www.clearnorthtech.com

Clear Resolution Consulting LLC
5523 Research Park Dr Ste 240 Baltimore MD 21228 443-543-5260
Web: www.crctoday.com

Phone Fax

ClearConnex Inc 1021 Main Campus Rd Ste 300 Raleigh NC 27606 760-845-4028
Web: www.clearconnex.com

ClearEdge IT Solutions LLC
10620 Guilford Rd Ste 200 Jessup MD 20794 443-212-4700
Web: www.clearedgeit.com

Clearview International LLC
6606 LBJ Fwy Ste 135 Dallas TX 75240 972-419-5991
Web: www.clearviewfocus.com

Click Optimize Creative Group
700 Blue Ridge Rd Ste 107 Raleigh NC 27606 919-301-8406
Web: cocg.co

Clinical Meeting Management Inc 313 Cedar St Bastrop TX 78602 512-303-6610
Web: www.cmmglobal.com

Cloud 9 Living 4999 Pearl E Cir Ste 102 Boulder CO 80301 866-525-6839
TF: 866-525-6839 ■ *Web:* www.cloud9living.com

CMS Operations LLC 1850 Borman Ct St. Louis MO 63146 314-432-6688
Web: www.cms-group.com

Coact Associates Ltd 2748 Centennial Rd Toledo OH 43617 866-646-4400
TF: 866-646-4400 ■ *Web:* teamcoact.com

Coastal Healthcare Consulting Inc
6808 220th St SW Ste 204 Mountlake Terrace WA 98043 206-324-6540
Web: www.coastalhealthcare.com

Code for America Labs Inc 1070 Warfield Ave Oakland CA 94610 510-645-9626
Web: www.codeforamerica.org

Coeur Business Group Inc
18 Hawk Ridge Dr Ste 150 Lake Saint Louis MO 63367 636-561-2455
Web: www.coeurgroup.com

Cohesion Corp 5151 Pfeiffer Rd Ste 105 Cincinnati OH 45242 513-306-4888
Web: www.cohesion.com

Cokeva Inc 9000 Foothils Blvd Roseville CA 95747 916-462-6000
Web: www.cokeva.com

Coleman Hines Inc 20830 N Tatum Blvd Ste 330 Phoenix AZ 85050 480-346-5800
Web: colemanhines.com

Colocenters Inc 2001 Sixth Ave Ste 1800 Seattle WA 98121 206-777-7600
Web: www.colocenters.com

Comaintel Inc 121 Second Ave Ste 100 Grand-mere QC G9T7G1 819-538-6583
Web: www.comaintel.com

Comnexia Corp 590 W Crssvlle Rd Roswell GA 30075 678-323-5000
Web: www.comnexia.com

Compass Computer Group Inc 9408 Ravenna Rd Twinsburg OH 44087 330-963-0800
Web: www.compasscomputergroup.com

Complete Network Management 649 Enterprise Dr Houma LA 70360 985-580-3040
Web: completenetwork.com

Compqsoft Inc 505N Sam Houston Pkwy E Ste 682 Houston TX 77060 281-914-4428
Web: www.compqsoft.com

CompuOne Corp
9888 Carroll Centre Rd Ste 201 San Diego CA 92126 858-404-7000
TF: 888-226-6781 ■ *Web:* www.compuone.com

Compusoft Integrated Solutions Inc
31500 W 13 Mile Rd Ste 200 Farmington Hills MI 48334 248-538-9494
Web: www.compusoft-is.com

ComSci LLC 485B Rt 1 S Ste 100 Iselin NJ 08830 732-632-8000 632-1830
Web: uplandsoftware.com/comsci

Comvox Systems LLC
5570-403 Florida Mining Blvd S Jacksonville FL 32257 904-538-9899
Web: www.comvoxsystems.com

Concepts of Independence Inc
120 Wall St 9th Fl New York NY 10005 212-293-9999
Web: www.coiny.org

Concepts to Operations Inc 12502 Trelawn Terr Bowie MD 20721 410-224-8911
Web: www.concepts2ops.com

Conde Group Inc 4141 Jutland Dr Ste 130 San Diego CA 92117 800-838-0819
TF: 800-838-0819 ■ *Web:* www.condegroup.com

ConSova Corp 1536 Cole Blvd Ste 350 Lakewood CO 80401 303-565-5124
Web: www.consova.com

Consumers Marine Electronics Inc
1758 State Hwy 34 N PO BOX 1319 Wall NJ 07719 732-681-9025
Web: www.consumermarinesupply.com

Contava Inc 4103 97 St Nw Edmonton AB T6E6E9 780-434-7564
Web: www.contava.com

Contex Americas Inc 15737 Crabbs Branch Way Derwood MD 20855 240-399-5600
Web: www.contex.com

Copperstone Connect Inc
3308 Cindy Cres Ste 200 Mississauga ON L4Y3J6 416-849-2320
Web: www.copperstoneconnect.com

Cordev Inc 146 B Hillwood Ave Ste 146 B Falls Church VA 22046 703-237-2802
Web: www.cordev.net

Core Management Resources Group Inc
515 Mulberry St Macon GA 31201 478-741-3521
TF: 888-741-2673 ■ *Web:* www.corehealthbenefits.com

Core Mississippi Operations LLC
12091 Bricksome Ave Ste B Baton Rouge LA 70816 225-756-2673
Web: www.coreoccupational.com

Core Vision IT Solutions 1266 NW Hwy Palatine IL 60067 855-788-5835
TF: 855-788-5835 ■ *Web:* www.cvits.com

Corporate It Solutions Inc 661 Pleasant St Norwood MA 02062 888-521-2487
TF: 888-521-2487 ■ *Web:* www.corpitsol.com

Corporate West Computer Systems
1610 Dell Ave Ste F Campbell CA 95008 408-374-4655
Web: www.corpwest.com

Cost Control Associates Inc 310 Bay Rd Queensbury NY 12804 518-798-4437
TF: 800-836-3787 ■ *Web:* www.costcontrolassociates.com

Covetrix It Consulting Group
18333 Preston Rd Ste 550 Dallas TX 75252 214-575-9583

Craig Roberts Assoc Inc
4230 Avondale Ave Ste 202 Dallas TX 75219 214-526-6470
Web: www.craigroberts.com

Credent Technologies LLC
30 Brookfield St Ste A South Windsor CT 06074 860-436-6391
Web: www.credenttech.com

Crescent Services LLC 5721 NW 132nd St Oklahoma City OK 73142 405-603-1200
Web: www.crescentservices.net

	City	State	Zip	Phone	Fax
CRM Dynamics Inc 5800 Ambler Dr, Unit 106 *TF:* 866-740-2424 ■ *Web:* www.crmdynamics.ca	Mississauga	ON	M4N2A5	866-740-2424	
CrossRealms Inc 55 W Monroe St Ste 3330 *Web:* www.crossrealms.com	Chicago	IL	60603	312-278-4445	
Crunchy Logistics 189 S Orange Ave Ste 2000 *Web:* crunchy.co	Orlando	FL	32801	407-476-2044	
Crystal Communications Ltd 1525 Lakeville Dr Ste 230 *TF:* 888-949-6603 ■ *Web:* www.crystalcomltd.com	Kingwood	TX	77339	281-361-5199	
Crystal Technologies Group Inc 1566 Mcdaniel Dr *Web:* crystaltechnologies.com	West Chester	PA	19380	610-430-2005	
CS Consulting Group LLC 11491 Raedene Way *Web:* www.csconsultinggroup.com	San Diego	CA	92131	858-530-8250	
Cs&S Computer Systems Inc 1440 W University Dr *Web:* www.css-computers.com	Tempe	AZ	85281	480-968-8585	
CSI Group Inc, The 11 Farview Ter *Web:* thecsigroup.com	Paramus	NJ	07652	201-587-1400	
CT Solutions Inc 12700 Fair Lakes Cir Ste 160 *Web:* www.ctsols.com	Fairfax	VA	22033	703-289-1560	
Cura Hospitality Inc 2970 Corporate Court Ste 5 *Web:* www.curahospitality.com	Orefield	PA	18069	610-530-7300	
Customized Energy Solutions Ltd 1528 Walnut St 22nd Fl *Web:* ces-ltd.com	Philadelphia	PA	19102	215-875-9440	
Cyber City Inc 224 W 30th St Rm 1100 *Web:* cybercityinc.com	New York	NY	10001	212-633-0649	
Cybersearch Ltd 800 E Northwest Hwy Ste 950 *Web:* www.cybsearch.com	Palatine	IL	60074	847-357-0200	
Cycom Canada Corp 31 Prince Andrew Pl Ste 1 *Web:* www.cycom.com	North York	ON	M3C2H2	416-494-5040	
Cygnus Corporation Inc 5640 Nicholson Ln Ste 300 *Web:* www.cygnusc.com	Rockville	MD	20852	301-231-7537	
Cygnus Systems Inc 25650 Goddard Rd *Web:* cygnus-sys.com	Taylor	MI	48180	313-291-4900	
Cynergy Solutions LLC 543 Country Club Dr Ste 538 *TF:* 877-296-3749 ■ *Web:* www.cynergysolutions.net	Simi Valley	CA	93065	805-416-1610	
Dakota Analytics Inc 205 Fifth Ave SW Ste 600 *Web:* www.dakotaanalytics.com	Calgary	AB	T2P2V7	403-264-6999	
Dalby, Wendland & Company PC 201 Centennial St Ste 300 PO Box 1150 *Web:* dalbycpa.com	Glenwood Springs	CO	81601	970-243-1921	
Daman Consulting Inc 1250 S Capial Of Texas Hw *Web:* damaninc.com	Austin	TX	78746	512-329-6646	
Dan's Excavating Inc 12955 23 Mile Rd *Web:* www.dansexc.com	Shelby	MI	48315	586-254-2040	
Data Concepts LLC 4405 Cox Rd *Web:* www.dataconcepts-inc.com	Glen Allen	VA	23060	804-968-4700	
Data Path 318 McHenry Ave *TF:* 888-693-2827 ■ *Web:* mydatapath.com	Modesto	CA	95354	209-521-0055	
DataMentors LLC 2319-104 Oak Myrtle Ln *Web:* www.datamentors.com	Wesley Chapel	FL	33544	813-960-7800	
Datascan LP 2210 Hutton Dr Ste 100 *Web:* www.datascan.com	Carrollton	TX	75006	214-351-4848	
Datashield LLC 1440 Show Berry St *TF:* 855-328-2744 ■ *Web:* www.datashieldprotect.com	Park City	UT	84098	855-328-2744	
Datatel Solutions Inc 875 Laurel Dr *Web:* www.datatelsolutions.com	Roseville	CA	95678	916-825-2267	
David Horowitz Freedom Center 14148 Magnolia Blvd Ste 103 *Web:* www.horowitzfreedomcenter.org	Sherman Oaks	CA	91423	818-849-3470	
Davidson Institute for Talent Development 9665 Gateway Dr *Web:* www.davidsongifted.org	Reno	NV	89521	775-852-3483	
DCR Workforce Inc 7815 NW Beacon Sq Blvd Ste 224 *TF:* 888-327-4867 ■ *Web:* www.dcrworkforce.com	Boca Raton	FL	33487	888-327-4867	
dcVAST Inc 1319 Butterfield Rd Ste 504 *Web:* www.dcvast.com	Downers Grove	IL	60515	630-964-6060	
Decisionwise Inc 1971 N State St *Web:* www.decision-wise.com	Provo	UT	84604	801-515-6500	
Decypher Technologies Ltd 200 Concord Plz Dr *Web:* www.decypherpsigov.com	San Antonio	TX	78216	210-735-9900	
DelaGet LLC 6608 Flying Cloud Dr *TF:* 866-264-5050 ■ *Web:* www.delaget.com	Eden Prairie	MN	55344	866-264-5050	
Delaware Power Systems Corp 11782 Hammersmith Way Ste 118 *Web:* www.delpowersys.com	Richmond	BC	V7A5E2	604-247-2800	
Delcom Group LP 2525B E SH 121 Ste 400 *Web:* www.delcomgroup.com	Lewisville	TX	75056	214-389-5500	
Delta Risk LLC 106 S St Mary's St Ste 428 *Web:* www.delta-risk.net	San Antonio	TX	78205	210-293-0707	
Dennis & Schisler Inc 206 S Mulberry St Ste 1128 *Web:* dennisandschisler.com	Mount Vernon	OH	43050	740-397-1721	
Denver Cyber Security 8100 E Union Ave Ste 2008 *Web:* www.denvercybersecurity.com	Denver	CO	80237	303-997-5506	
Designhammer Media Group LLC 1912 E Nc Hwy 54 Ste 201 *Web:* designhammer.com	Durham	NC	27713	919-544-0086	
Detechtion Technologies 1100-8th Ave SW Ste 277 *Web:* www.detechtion.com	Calgary	AB	T2P3T8	403-250-9220	
DIGICON Corp 7361 Calhoun Pl Ste 430 *Web:* www.digicon.com	Rockville	MD	20855	301-721-6300	
Digicorp Inc 3315 N 124th St Ste E *Web:* digicorp-inc.com	Brookfield	WI	53005	262-402-6100	
Digital Evidence Group Inc 1730 M St NW Ste 812 *Web:* www.digitalevidencegroup.com	Washington	DC	20036	202-232-0646	
Digitek Software Inc 650 Radio Dr 43035 *Web:* www.digiteksoftware.com	Lewis Center	OH	43035	614-764-8875	
Dimension Consulting Inc 2620 Second Ave Ste 9D *TF:* 855-222-6444 ■ *Web:* www.dimcon.com	San Diego	CA	92103	703-636-0933	
Directec Corp 1650 Lyndon Farm Ct Ste 202 *TF:* 800-588-7800 ■ *Web:* www.directec.com	Louisville	KY	40223	502-357-5000	
Distant Focus Corp 4114b Fieldstone Rd *Web:* distantfocus.com	Champaign	IL	61822	217-351-2655	
Distributors Solutions LLC 978 Cook St *Web:* www.distributorssolutions.com	Denver	CO	80206	303-277-3359	
DMR Consulting Inc 7946 Front Beach Rd *Web:* www.dmrcinc.com	Panama City Beach	FL	32407	850-230-3767	
Domital Corp 8858 NW 18th Terrace *Web:* www.domital.com	Doral	FL	33172	305-594-0873	
Donnell Systems Inc 130 S Main St Ste 375 *Web:* www.ocie.net	South Bend	IN	46601	574-232-3784	
Donriver Inc 2633 McKinney Ave Ste 130-101 *TF:* 866-733-1684 ■ *Web:* www.donriver.com	Dallas	TX	75204	866-733-1684	
DPM Consulting Services Inc 507 E Maple Rd *Web:* www.dpmcs.com	Troy	MI	48083	248-740-8735	
DRT Strategies Inc 4245 N Fairfax Dr Ste 800 *Web:* www.drtstrategies.com	Arlington	VA	22203	571-482-2500	
Due North Consulting Inc 105 Owens Pkwy Ste C *TF:* 800-899-2676 ■ *Web:* duenorthmedia.com	Birmingham	AL	35244	205-989-9394	
Dvp Technologies LLC 123 Hillcrest Dr *Web:* www.dvptech.com	Southbury	CT	06488	203-262-6005	
Dynamics Edge Inc 2635 N First St Ste #148 *TF:* 800-453-5961 ■ *Web:* www.dynamicsedge.com	San Jose	CA	95134	800-453-5961	
Dynamis Inc 3707 Henson Rd *Web:* dynamis-inc.com	Knoxville	TN	37921	865-588-5422	
e Learning Guild, The 375 E St Ste 200 *Web:* www.elearningguild.com	Santa Rosa	CA	95404	707-566-8990	
E Pluribus Partners Consultant 104 Brookside Dr Fl 2 *Web:* www.epluribuspartners.com	Greenwich	CT	06831	203-422-6511	
E R O Resources Corp 1842 Clarkson St *Web:* www.eroresources.com	Denver	CO	80218	303-830-1188	
e-Zsigma (Canada) Inc 1 Dundas St W Ste 2500 *Web:* www.ezsigmagroup.com	Toronto	ON	M5G1Z3	416-593-8026	
Earthbalance Corp 2579 N Toledo Blade Blvd *Web:* www.earthbalance.com	North Port	FL	34289	941-426-7878	
Eastex Environmental Lab Inc 1119 S University Dr PO Box 631375 *TF:* 800-525-0508 ■ *Web:* www.eastexlabs.com	Nacogdoches	TX	75961	936-569-8879	
EB Computing 19 Piping Rock Dr *Web:* www.eb-computing.com	Ossining	NY	10562	914-523-8142	
EBI Consulting Inc 21 B St *Web:* www.ebiconsulting.com	Burlington	MA	01803	781-273-2500	
eBusinessDesign 111 W St. John St Ste 1100 *Web:* www.ebusinessdesign.com	San Jose	CA	95113	408-654-7900	
Ecg Consulting Group Inc 40 British American Blvd Ste 7 *Web:* www.ecgconsulting.com	Latham	NY	12110	518-220-9100	
Echo Technology Solutions 216 11th St *Web:* www.echots.com	San Francisco	CA	94103	415-857-3246	
Eclipse Energy Systems Inc 2345 Anvil St N *Web:* www.eclipsethinfilms.com	Saint Petersburg	FL	33710	727-344-7300	
ECS & R 3237 Us Hwy 19 *TF:* 866-815-0016 ■ *Web:* www.ecsr.net	Cochranton	PA	16314	814-425-7773	
Edify Technologies Inc 2200 S Main St Ste 306 *Web:* www.edifytech.com	Lombard	IL	60148	630-932-9308	
Edtec Central LLC 22620 Woodward Ave Ste C *Web:* edtec.net	Ferndale	MI	48220	248-582-8100	
Eduworks Corp 136 Sw Washington Ave Ste 203 *Web:* eduworks.com	Corvallis	OR	97333	541-753-0844	
Edwards Industries LLC 6085 Marshalee Dr Ste 140 *TF:* 800-556-2506 ■ *Web:* www.edwps.com	Elkridge	MD	21075	443-561-0180	
Efk Group LLC 1027 S Clinton Ave *Web:* www.efkgroup.com	Trenton	NJ	08611	609-393-5838	
eFulgent Datawarehousing Solutions 3404 W Cheryl Dr Ste A290 *Web:* www.efulgent.com	Phoenix	AZ	85051	602-439-5503	
Egen Solutions Inc 40 Shuman Blvd Ste 302 *Web:* egen.solutions	Naperville	IL	60563	630-870-1935	
Egroup Inc 482 Wando Park Blvd *Web:* www.egroup-us.com	Mount Pleasant	SC	29464	843-284-0146	
Eh Krohl Consulting Inc 3704 Duxford Dr *Web:* www.fdacompliance.com	Raleigh	NC	27614	919-676-4801	
Ekm Metering Inc 363 Berkeley Way *Web:* www.ekmmetering.com	Santa Cruz	CA	95062	831-425-7371	
Elan Technologies 5143 Kennedy Ave *Web:* elantech.net	Cincinnati	OH	45213	513-322-0463	
Electroline Data Communications Inc N779 Communication Dr *Web:* www.edci.com	Appleton	WI	54912	920-733-0303	
ELI Inc 2675 Paces Ferry Rd Se Ste 470 *TF:* 800-497-7654 ■ *Web:* www.eliinc.com	Atlanta	GA	30339	770-319-7999	
Elk Environmental Services 1420 Clarion St *TF:* 800-851-7156 ■ *Web:* www.elkenv.com	Reading	PA	19601	610-372-4760	

				Phone	Fax
Ellis Management Services Inc 4324 N Beltine Rd. TF: 888-988-3767 ■ Web: www.epmsonline.com	Irving	TX	75038	972-256-3767	
Ellumen Inc 1401 Wilson Blvd Ste 1200 Web: www.ellumen.com	Arlington	VA	22209	703-253-5555	
Elm Consulting 26741 Portola Pkwy Ste 1E#494 Web: www.elmgroup.com	Foothill Ranch	CA	92610	678-200-5220	
Embience Inc 6450 Lusk Blvd E202203 Web: www.embience.com	San Diego	CA	92121	858-366-0415	
Emgence Technologies Inc 11440 W Bernardo Ct Web: www.emgence.com	San Diego	CA	92127	858-753-1985	
Emission Monitoring Service Inc 400 S Hwy 146 Web: www.emsi-air.com	Baytown	TX	77520	281-428-1140	
EMMsphere 102 W Third St Ste 1200 Web: www.marketspheremarketing.com	Winston-salem	NC	27101	336-608-3060	
Empathylogic.com 15732 Los Gatos Blvd #434 Web: www.empathylogic.com	Los Gatos	CA	95032	408-940-3951	
Employee Resource Systems Inc 29 E Madison St Ste 1600 Web: ers-eap.com	Chicago	IL	60602	312-269-0287	
Encari LLC 250 Pkwy Dr Ste 150 Web: www.encari.com	Lincolnshire	IL	60069	847-947-8448	
Endsight 1440 Fourth St Ste B Web: www.endsight.net	Berkeley	CA	94710	510-280-2000	
Endurance IT Services 4646 Princess Anne Rd Ste 104 Web: www.endurance-it.com	Virginia Beach	VA	23462	757-216-3671	
Energy Market Innovations 83 Columbia St Ste 400 Web: emiconsulting.com	Seattle	WA	98104	206-621-1160	
Enform 1538 25 Ave Ne Web: www.enform.ca	Calgary	AB	T2E8Y3	403-250-9606	
Enterforce Inc 626 W Moreland Blvd. Web: www.enterforce.com	Waukesha	WI	53188	262-542-2218	
Entre Technology Service 1501 14th St W Ste 201 Web: www.entremt.com	Billings	MT	59102	406-256-5700	
EntryPoint Consulting LLC 4700 Rockside Rd Summit Office Park Bldg 1 Ste 625 Web: www.entrypointconsulting.com	Independence	OH	44131	216-674-9070	
Enviroapplications Inc 2831 Camino Del Rio S Ste 214 Web: www.enviroapplications.com	San Diego	CA	92108	619-291-3636	
Envirosafe Services of Ohio Inc 876 Otter Creek Rd Web: www.envirosafeservices.com	Oregon	OH	43616	419-698-3500	
Envirosep Fluid & Heat Recovery Systems 31 Aviation Blvd Web: www.envirosep.com	Georgetown	SC	29440	843-546-7400	
EnviroServe JV 5502 Schaaf Rd Web: www.enviroserve.com	Cleveland	OH	44131	216-642-1311	
Envirosure Solutions Llc 1979 E Broadway Rd Ste 2 Web: envirosure.com	Tempe	AZ	85282	480-784-4621	
Envirotech Financial Inc 500 N State College Ste 1100 Web: etfinancial.com	Orange	CA	92868	714-532-2731	
Epicom Corp 211 E Seventh St Ste 110 Web: www.epicom.com	Austin	TX	78701	512-481-9000	
Epitome Networks LLC 3532 Mayland Ct Web: www.epitomenetworks.com	Richmond	VA	23233	804-419-8300	
Equity Methods LLC 15300 N 90th St Ste 400 Web: www.equitymethods.com	Scottsdale	AZ	85260	480-428-3344	
Ergos Technology Partners Inc 3831 Golf Dr Web: www.ergos.com	Houston	TX	77018	713-621-9220	
Erick Nielsen Enterprises Inc 4453 County Rd Mm # O Web: www.eneinc.com	Orland	CA	95963	530-865-9409	
Ericsson 1 Telcordia Dr TF: 800-521-2673 ■ Web: www.ericsson.com/ourportfolio/telcordia_landingpage	Piscataway	NJ	08854	732-699-2000	
ERP International LLC 603 Seventh St Ste 203 Web: www.erpinternational.com	Laurel	MD	20707	301-490-0080	
ESI Information Technologies 1550 Metcalfe St Ste 1100 Web: www.esitechnologies.com	Montreal	QC	H3A1X6	514-745-3311	
Essdack 1500 E 11th Ave Ste 200 Web: www.essdack.org	Hutchinson	KS	67501	620-663-9566	
Etek It Services Inc 830 E Higgins Rd Ste 102 Web: etekit.com	Schaumburg	IL	60173	847-969-0200	
Etelint Consulting Inc 1683 Moongate Cres Web: www.etelintconsulting.com	Mississauga	ON	L5M4T2	905-826-3977	
Etera Consulting 1100 17th St NW Ste 605 Web: www.eteraconsulting.com	Washington	DC	20036	202-349-0177	
Eurogentec North America 3347 Industrial Ct Ste A Web: www.eurogentec.com	San Diego	CA	92121	858-793-2661	
Evantage Consulting LLC 12 Third Ave N Ste 40 Web: www.evantageconsulting.com	Minneapolis	MN	55401	612-677-0640	
Eventive LLC 817 W Superior St Ste 1 Web: www.eventivellc.com	Chicago	IL	60642	312-997-2393	
Events Forum Inc 2 Oxford Xing Ste 4 Web: www.eventsforum.net	New Hartford	NY	13413	315-792-7600	
Eventus Group 15280 N W 79th Ct Ste 100 Web: www.eventusgroup.com	Miami Lakes	FL	33016	305-557-4443	
Everglades Technologies 1 Union Sq W 3rd Fl Web: www.etny.net	New York	NY	10003	212-741-0000	
Evogi Group Inc, The 20645 N Pima Rd Bldg N Ste 130 TF: 888-277-5573	Scottsdale	AZ	85255	888-277-5573	
Evoke Research & Consulting LLC 1000 Wilson Blvd Ste 2500 Web: www.evokeconsulting.com	Arlington	VA	22209	703-415-1007	
Evoke Technologies 7106 Corporate Way Web: www.evoketechnologies.com	Dayton	OH	45459	937-660-4925	
Exalt Integrated Technologies 401 Bombay Ln Web: www.exaltit.com	Roswell	GA	30076	770-217-4688	
Excalibur Technology Corp 700 Fox Glen Lowr Level Web: www.excaltech.com	Barrington	IL	60010	847-842-9570	
Excel Management Systems Inc 691 N High St 2nd Fl Web: www.emsi.com	Columbus	OH	43215	614-224-4007	
Eyak Technology LLC 360 W Benson Blvd Ste 210 Web: www.eyaktek.com	Anchorage	AK	99501	907-276-4472	
Facility Programming & Consulting Inc 100 W Houston St Ste 1100 Web: www.facilityprogramming.com	San Antonio	TX	78205	210-228-9600	
Faneuil Inc 2 Eaton St Ste 1002 Web: www.faneuil.com	Hampton	VA	23669	757-722-3235	
Fdr and Cp Services Llc 2503 Tabor Rd Web: www.fdrservices.com	Bryan	TX	77803	979-778-0333	
Federal It 2806 Pinnacle Dr Web: www.federalit.com	Burleson	TX	76028	817-484-2771	
Fentress Inc 945 Sunset Vly Dr Web: www.fentress.com	Sykesville	MD	21784	301-854-4885	
Fineline Technologies Inc 3145 Medlock Bridge Rd Web: www.finelinetech.com	Norcross	GA	30071	678-969-0835	
Fitt Telecommunications Inc 1740 W Sam Houston Pkwy N Web: fittcom.com	Houston	TX	77043	281-497-8181	
Fleming-Lee Shue Inc 226 W 26th St 9th Fl Web: www.flemingleeshue.com	New York	NY	10001	212-675-3225	
Flight Trak Inc 1872 Dover St Web: www.flighttrak.com	Broomfield	CO	80020	303-438-8640	
Florance & Associates Consulting 1011 Hampshire Ln Ste 200 Web: floranceandassociates.com	Richardson	TX	75080	972-690-1909	
Focus IP Inc 609 W Main St Ste 202 Web: www.appdetex.com	Boise	ID	83702	208-794-5788	
Formatech It Services 3263 Claremont Way # B Web: www.formatech-it.com	Napa	CA	94558	707-258-1492	
Fortin Consulting Inc 215 Hamel Rd TF: 844-273-3117 ■ Web: www.fortinconsulting.com	Hamel	MN	55340	763-478-3606	
Fortistar LLC 1 N Lexington Ave Web: www.fortistar.com	White Plains	NY	10601	914-421-4900	
Fortrust LLC 4300 Brighton Blvd Web: www.fortrustdatacenter.com	Denver	CO	80216	720-264-2000	
Foxboro Consulting Inc 17 Crowne Pond Ln PO Box 646 Web: www.foxboro.net	Wilton	CT	06897	203-761-4901	
FPT USA Corp 155 Bovet Rd Ste 303 Web: fpt-software.com	San Mateo	CA	94402	650-349-5000	
Frank Lynn & Associates Inc 500 Park Blvd Ste 1300 TF: 800-245-5966 ■ Web: www.franklynn.com	Itasca	IL	60143	312-263-7888	
FranNet LLC 10302 Brookridge Village Blvd Ste 201 Web: www.frannet.com	Louisville	KY	40291	502-753-2380	
Frayman Group Inc, The 128 Brighton Beach Ave Ste 400 P.O. Box 299 Web: www.fraymangroup.com	Brooklyn	NY	11235	718-648-7700	
Frecom 435 W Baltimore Pk Web: frecominc.com	West Grove	PA	19390	610-869-3307	
Freed & Associates 412 Yale Ave Web: www.freedassociates.com	Berkeley	CA	94708	510-525-1853	
FreshAddress Inc 36 Crafts St Web: www.freshaddress.com	Newton	MA	02458	617-965-4500	
Friedman Group, The 5759 Uplander Way Web: www.thefriedmangroup.com	Culver City	CA	90230	310-590-1248	
fuseproject LLC 528 Folsom St Web: www.fuseproject.com	San Francisco	CA	94105	415-908-1492	
Futureproof LLC 2374 St Claude Ave Web: www.futureproofnola.com	New Orleans	LA	70119	504-822-8995	
G Stephens Inc 133 N Summit St Web: www.gstephensinc.com	Akron	OH	44304	330-762-1386	
G Tj Consulting 20100 Cornillie Dr Web: gtjonline.com	Roseville	MI	48066	586-293-9600	
GameChanger Products LLC 2207 Harbor Bay Pkwy Web: gamechanger.net	Alameda	CA	94502	510-521-7985	
Gantec Corp 1111 Plz Dr Ste 310 Web: www.gantecusa.com	Schaumburg	IL	60173	847-885-7655	
Genesys Engineering PC 629 Fifth Ave Bldg 3 Web: www.genesysengineering.net	Pelham	NY	10803	914-251-0540	
Gentech Systems Management LLC PO Box 3426 Web: www.gentech.com	Trenton	NJ	08619	609-890-2522	
Geo-Comm Inc 601 W St. Germain St Web: www.geo-comm.com	St. Cloud	MN	56301	320-240-0040	
Geostat Environmental LLC 115 E Marlin St Web: www.geostatenvironmental.com	Mcpherson	KS	67460	620-241-6090	
Gh Package Product & Testing Consulting Inc 4090 Thunderbird Ln Web: www.ghtesting.com	Fairfield	OH	45014	513-870-0080	
Gila River Telecommunications Inc 7065 W Allison Dr Web: www.gilanet.net	Chandler	AZ	85226	520-796-3333	

Phone *Fax*

Gladstein Neandross & Associates LLC
3015 Main St Ste 300 ... Santa Monica CA 90405 310-314-1934
Web: www.gladstein.org

Global Cloud Limited
901 Adams Xing Unit 2 ... Cincinnati OH 45202 513-333-0450
Web: www.globalcloud.net

Global Environment & Technology Foundation
2900 S Quincy St Ste 375 ... Arlington VA 22206 703-379-2713
Web: www.getf.org

Global Inflight Products 8918 152nd Ave Ne ... Redmond WA 98052 425-558-2778
Web: www.gipusa.com

Global IT Communications Inc
6720 Bright Ave ... Whittier CA 90601 562-698-2500
Web: globalit.com

Global Productivity Solutions LLC
19176 Hall Rd Ste 250 ... Clinton Township MI 48038 586-412-9609
Web: globalproductivitysolutions.com

Global-Z International Inc 395 Shields Dr ... Bennington VT 05201 802-445-1011
Web: www.globalz.com

Globex International Inc
ў570 Lexington Ave 15th Fl ... New York NY 10022 203-256-1475
Web: www.globexusa.com

GMarie Group Inc, The
1050 E Ray Rd Ste A5-31 ... Chandler AZ 85225 602-795-8374
Web: www.gmariegroup.com

GNC Consulting Inc 21195 S LaGrange Rd ... Frankfort IL 60423 815-469-7255
Web: www.gnc-consulting.com

Go Pro Management Inc 22 Cynthia Rd ... Needham MA 02494 781-444-5753
Web: www.gopromanagement.com

Gopa It Consultants Inc 247 N San Mateo Dr ... San Mateo CA 94401 408-725-7168
Web: www.novigo.com

Grade A 9 Slack Rd Ste 200 ... Ottawa ON K2G0B7 613-721-3331
Web: www.gradea.ca

Greenbusch Group Inc
1900 W Nickerson St Ste 201 ... Seattle WA 98119 206-378-0569
TF: 855-476-2874 ■ *Web:* www.greenbusch.com

Greene Consulting Associates LLC
Waterstone Bldg 4751 Best Rd Ste 450 ... Atlanta GA 30337 404-324-4600
Web: www.greeneconsults.com

Greening of Detroit 1418 Michigan Ave ... Detroit MI 48216 313-237-8733
Web: greeningofdetroit.com

Greenstar Environmental Solutions LLC
6 Gellatly Dr ... Wappingers Falls NY 12590 845-223-9944
Web: www.greenstarsolutions.com

Greenview Data Inc 8178 Jackson Rd ... Ann Arbor MI 48103 734-426-7500
TF: 800-458-3348 ■ *Web:* www.greenviewdata.com

Greenwood King Properties 2 Inc
1616 S Voss Rd Ste 900 ... Houston TX 77057 713-784-0888
TF: 800-403-0888 ■ *Web:* www.greenwoodking.com

GreyCastle Security LLC 500 Federal St Ste 540 ... Troy NY 12180 518-274-7233
Web: www.greycastlesecurity.com

Greystone Healthcare Management Corp
4042 Park Oaks Blvd Ste 300 ... Tampa FL 33610 813-635-9500
Web: www.greystonehealth.com

Grisham Consulting Services
3514 E Tropicana Ave Ste 2 ... Las Vegas NV 89121 702-450-6523
Web: grishamconsultingservices.com

Groff NetWorks LLC 11 State St ... Troy NY 12180 518-320-8906
Web: www.groffnetworks.com

GSPANN Technologies Inc 362 Fairview Way ... Milpitas CA 95035 408-263-3435
Web: www.gspann.com

GSS Infotech Inc 1699 Wall St Ste 201 ... Mt. Prospect IL 60056 847-640-3700
Web: www.gssinfotech.com

Guidant Partners 1410 Donelson Pike Ste B5 ... Nashville TN 37217 615-327-9111
Web: www.guidantpartners.com

Guide Productions LLC 30589 Monarch Ct ... Evergreen CO 80439 604-669-0500
Web: www.guideproductions.com

Gurus Information Technology Services LLC
517 Georges Rd ... North Brunswick NJ 08902 732-247-7747
Web: www.gurusit.com

Gvnw Consulting
2270 La Montana Way Ste 200 ... Colorado Springs CO 80918 719-594-5800
Web: gvnw.com

H I M on Call Inc 1033 Hamilton St ... Allentown PA 18101 610-435-5724
Web: www.himoncall.com

H2O Consulting Inc 5870 Hwy 6 N Ste 215 ... Houston TX 77084 281-861-6215
Web: h2oconsulting.net

H3 Solutions Inc 10432 Balls Ford Rd Ste 230 ... Manassas VA 20109 703-335-2311
Web: www.h3s-inc.com

Haberfeld Associates Inc
206 S 13th St Ste 1500 ... Lincoln NE 68508 402-475-1191
Web: www.haberfeld.com

Hanover Research 1700 K St NW 8th Fl ... Washington DC 20006 202-559-0050
Web: www.hanoverresearch.com

Hardware Com LLC 7667 Cahill Rd Ste 400 ... Minneapolis MN 55439 952-697-6069
Web: us.hardware.com

Harris Miller Miller & Hanson Inc
77 S Bedford St Ste 120 ... Burlington MA 01803 781-229-0707
Web: www.hmmh.com

Harvey Hohauser & Associates
5600 New King Dr Ste 355 ... Troy MI 48098 248-641-1400
Web: www.hohauser.com

Hays Financial Consulting LLC
Atlanta Financial Ctr 3343 Peachtree Rd
Ste 200 ... Atlanta GA 30326 404-926-0060
Web: haysconsulting.net

Hazmateam Inc 12 Kimball Hill Rd ... Hudson NH 03051 603-882-6247
Web: www.hazmateam.com

HBS Consulting Inc 53 Golden Aster Ste ... Brisbane CA 94005 415-508-1541
Web: www.hbsconsult.com

HCI Group, The
6440 Southpoint Pkwy Ste 300 ... Jacksonville FL 32216 904-337-6300
TF: 866-793-2484 ■ *Web:* thehcigroup.com

Phone *Fax*

HCL America Inc 330 Potrero Ave ... Sunnyvale CA 94085 408-733-0480
Web: www.hcl.com

Head in the Cloud Inc
220A Twin Dolphin Dr ... Redwood Shores CA 94065 650-234-7100
Web: www.hitcloud.com

Helix Commerce International Inc
117 Melrose Ave ... Toronto ON M5M1Y8 647-477-6254
Web: www.helixcommerce.com

Heritage Global Solutions Inc
230 N Maryland Ave ... Glendale CA 91206 818-547-4474
TF: 800-915-4474 ■ *Web:* www.heritageglobalsolutions.com

Hernandez Consulting LLC 3221 Tulane Ave ... New Orleans LA 70119 504-305-8571
Web: www.hernandezconsulting.com

HFS Chicago Scholars 1074 W Taylor St Ste 201 ... Chicago IL 60607 312-421-4070
Web: www.hfschicagoscholars.com

Hicks & Company Inc 1504 W Fifth St ... Austin TX 78703 512-478-0858
Web: hicksenv.com

Hile Group 1100 Beech St Bldg 15 ... Normal IL 61761 309-888-4453
Web: www.hilegroup.com

Himebaugh Consulting Inc
4940 Munson St Nw Ste 2100 ... Canton OH 44718 330-493-9700
Web: www.hcd.net

Hoop Group, The 1930 Heck Ave Bldg 3 ... Neptune NJ 07753 732-502-2255
Web: www.hoopgroup.com

Hope Foundation Inc 1252 N Loesch Rd ... Bloomington IN 47404 812-355-6000
Web: www.hopefoundation.org

Horizon Consulting Inc
44135 Woodridge Pkwy Ste 100 ... Lansdowne VA 20176 703-726-6430
Web: horizon-inc.com

Horsley Witten Group Inc 90 Route 6A Unit 1 ... Sandwich MA 02563 508-833-6600
Web: www.horsleywitten.com

HPM Inc 3231 Osgood Common ... Fremont CA 94539 510-353-0770
Web: www.hpmnetworks.com

HR Focal Point LLC 5151 Headquarters Dr Ste 135 ... Plano TX 75024 855-464-4737
TF: 855-464-4737 ■ *Web:* www.hrfocalpoint.com

Hr Strategies & Solutions
49663 Draper Cir Ste 200 ... Plymouth MI 48170 734-455-1185
Web: www.yourhrteam.net

HR&A Advisors Inc 99 Hudson St 3rd Fl ... New York NY 10013 212-977-5597
Web: www.hraadvisors.com

Hrd Consulting Services 2310 Wineberry Ter ... Baltimore MD 21209 410-466-9023
Web: www.hrdconsultingservices.com

Hrd Discount Book Society
2002 Renaissance Blvd ... King Of Prussia PA 19406 610-279-2002
TF: 800-633-4533 ■ *Web:* www.hrdqstore.com

Hunt Conference Group Inc
611 S Main St Ste 410 ... Grapevine TX 76051 817-410-4660
Web: www.huntconferencegroup.com

Hunter Benefits Consulting Group Inc
119 E Palatine Rd Ste 104 ... Palatine IL 60067 847-776-2125
Web: hunterbenefits.com

Hybrid Design Services 2479 Elliott Dr ... Troy MI 48083 313-730-1800
Web: hybriddesignservices.com

Hydro Geo Chem Inc
6340 E Thomas Rd Ste 224 ... Scottsdale AZ 85251 480-421-1501
Web: www.hgcinc.com

I Macc 900 E Diehl Rd Ste 110 ... Naperville IL 60563 630-527-9052
Web: imacc.net

i SOLUTIONS Midwest
4741 Central St Ste 202 ... Kansas City MO 64112 816-304-6344
Web: www.isolutionsmidwest.com

I T S Corp 300 E Esplanade Dr Ste 1450 ... Oxnard CA 93036 805-604-9191
Web: www.itscorporation.com

I.T. Blueprint Solutions Consulting Inc
170-422 Richards St ... Vancouver BC V6B2Z4 866-261-8981
TF: 866-261-8981 ■ *Web:* www.itblueprint.ca

Iccg Capital Inc 906 18th St Ste 122 ... Plano TX 75074 972-424-5600
Web: www.iccgcapital.com

ICI Services Corp
500 Viking Dr Ste 400 ... Virginia Beach VA 23452 757-340-6970
Web: www.icisrvcs.com

Icreon Tech Inc 433, 5th Ave 4th Fl ... New York NY 10016 212-706-6023
Web: www.icreon.us

Ideal Consulting Services Inco
521 American Legion Hwy ... Westport MA 02790 508-636-6615
Web: idealconsultingservices.com

IDT|RPM Consulting Services
1009 W Hawthorn Dr ... Itasca IL 60143 630-875-1100
TF: 877-722-6438 ■ *Web:* www.idt-inc.com

IeSmart Systems LLC 15200 E Hardy Rd ... Houston TX 77032 281-447-6278
TF: 866-437-6278 ■ *Web:* www.iesmartsystems.com

Ifocus Consulting Inc 100 39th St Ste 201 ... Astoria OR 97103 503-338-7443
TF: 888-308-6192 ■ *Web:* ifocus-consulting.com

ikaSystems Corp 134 Turnpike Rd ... Southborough MA 01772 508-229-0600
Web: www.ikasystems.com

Illuminous Enterprises Inc
3129 S Hacienda Blvd Ste 691 ... Hacienda Heights CA 91745 626-600-2087
Web: www.illuminousinc.com

Imagenation Systems
3029 Stony Brook Dr Ste 104 ... Raleigh NC 27604 919-876-6833
Web: www.isav.biz

Imanami Corp 2301 Armstrong St Ste 211 ... Livermore CA 94551 925-371-3000
Web: imanami.com

iMethods LLC
10748 Deerwood Park Blvd Ste 150 ... Jacksonville FL 32256 888-306-2261
TF: 888-306-2261 ■ *Web:* www.imethods.com

iMomentous 20 Gibraltar Rd Ste 109 ... Horsham PA 19044 888-985-7755
TF: 888-985-7755 ■ *Web:* www.imomentous.com

IMPRES Technology Solutions Inc
10330 Pioneer Blvd Ste 280 ... Santa Fe Springs CA 90670 562-298-4030
TF: 800-652-9686 ■ *Web:* www.imprestechnology.com

Improve Group Inc, The
1385 Mendota Heights Rd Ste 200b ... Mendota Heights MN 55120 877-467-7847
TF: 877-467-7847 ■ *Web:* www.theimprovegroup.com

Phone Fax

Inbound Call Experts LLC
700 Banyan Trl Ste 200 .... Boca Raton FL 33431 561-705-0700
Web: www.inboundcallexperts.com

Indus Instruments 721 Tristar Dr Ste C .... Webster TX 77598 281-286-1130
Web: www.indusinstruments.com

Info X Distribution LLC 3 Aspen Dr Ste 1 .... Randolph NJ 07869 973-386-1411
Web: www.info-x.com

Infogrow Corp 2140 Front St .... Cuyahoga Falls OH 44221 800-897-9807
TF: 800-897-9807 ■ *Web:* www.infogrowcorp.com

Infoquest Consulting Group Inc
68 Culver Rd Ste 106 .... Monmouth Junction NJ 08852 609-409-5151
Web: www.infoquestgroup.com

Infosmart Systems Inc
5850 Town and Country Blvd Ste 1102 .... Frisco TX 75034 972-267-5900
Web: www.infosmartsys.com

Infotex Inc 2366 W Blvd .... Kokomo IN 46902 765-236-2323
Web: www.infotex.com

Infotier 7 Century Dr .... Parsippany NJ 07054 973-538-2600
Web: infotier.com

InfoZen Inc 6700A Rockledge Dr Ste 300 .... Bethesda MD 20817 301-605-8000
Web: www.infozen.com

Ingk Labs LLC 101 Fifth Ave .... New York NY 10003 646-350-3004
Web: ingk.com

Inog-ps Llc 13346 Nw 14th St .... Pembroke Pines FL 33028 954-441-2744
Web: www.inog-ps.com

Insight Analytics Group 313 Gordon Dr .... Exton PA 19341 610-363-6353
Web: www.insight-analytics.com

InSys Consulting Services Inc
395 W Passaic St 4th Fl .... Rochelle Park NJ 07662 201-621-4797
Web: www.insysus.com

Intact Info Solutions LLC
1370 Vly Vista Dr Ste 265 .... Diamond Bar CA 91765 909-396-9200
TF: 888-986-7736 ■ *Web:* www.intactinfo.com

Intega IT 210-1900 Merivale Rd .... Ottawa ON K2G4N4 613-260-1114
Web: www.intega.ca

Integra Information Technologies Inc
101 South 27th St .... Boise ID 83702 208-336-2720
TF: 800-444-8688 ■ *Web:* www.integrainfotech.com

integraSoft Inc 2547 Tech Dr .... Bettendorf IA 52722 563-332-5030
TF: 877-630-7960 ■ *Web:* integrasoft.com

Intelestream Inc 27 N Wacker Dr Ste 370 .... Chicago IL 60606 312-244-3774
Web: www.intelestream.net

Interact One Inc 4665 Cornell Rd Ste 255 .... Cincinnati OH 45241 513-469-7042
Web: www.interactone.com

InterBase Corp
22485 La Palma Ave Ste 200D .... Yorba Linda CA 92887 714-701-3600
Web: www.interbasecorp.com

Interboro Systems Corp 206 San Jorge St .... San Juan PR 00926 787-641-7777
Web: www.interboropr.com

Intervoice Inc 17811 Waterview Pkwy .... Dallas TX 75252 972-454-8000
Web: www.intervoice.com

Intone Networks Inc 10 Austin Ave Ste A7 .... Iselin NJ 08830 732-721-3002
Web: www.intonenetworks.com

IntraEdge Inc 80 N McClintock Dr Ste 2 .... Chandler AZ 85226 480-240-5240
Web: www.intraedge.com

Intrinium Inc
1521 N Argonne Rd Ste C 328 .... Spokane Valley WA 99212 509-340-3323
Web: www.intrinium.com

Investigator Support Services
1320 N Milwaukee Ave Fl 2 .... Chicago IL 60622 773-278-1567
Web: www.researchsite.net

INW Solutions
4500 Holland Office Park Ste #301 .... Virginia Beach VA 23452 757-563-3572
Web: www.inwsolutions.com

Iomosaic Corp 93 Stiles Rd .... Salem NH 03079 603-893-7009
TF: 844-466-6724 ■ *Web:* www.iomosaic.com

IPC Technologies Inc
7200 Glen Forest Dr Ste 100 .... Richmond VA 23226 804-622-7288
TF: 877-947-2835 ■ *Web:* www.ipctech.com

iStreet Solutions LLC
1075 Triangle Ct Ste 130 .... West Sacramento CA 95605 916-792-3762
Web: www.istreetsolutions.com

IT America Inc 100 Metroplex Dr Ste 207 .... Edison NJ 08817 732-985-5100
Web: www.itamerica.com

IT Company LLC, The
10208 Murdock Rd Ste 101 .... Knoxville TN 37932 865-862-6053
Web: www.theitco.net

Itech Consulting Partners LLC
30 Church Hill Rd Ste 7 .... Newtown CT 06470 203-270-0051
Web: www.itechcp.com

itelligence Inc 10856 Reed Hartman Hwy .... Cincinnati OH 45242 513-956-2000
Web: itelligencegroup.com

ITERA International Energy Corp
9995 Gate Pkwy N Ste 400 .... Jacksonville FL 32246 904-996-8800

Ito Consulting Group Llc 90 Federal St .... Belchertown MA 01007 413-323-8785
Web: www.itoconsultinggroup.com

ITSqc LLC 3945 Forbes Ave Ste 422 .... Pittsburgh PA 15213 412-436-5212
Web: www.itsqc.org

Ivar Jacobson Consulting Llc
211 N Union St Ste 100 .... Alexandria VA 22314 703-836-3628
Web: www.ivarjacobson.com

J C Hanlon Consulting Inc
52611 Jessie Dr .... Chesterfield MI 48051 586-435-6231
Web: www.jchci.com

J K Consulting 990 E Ninth St .... Lockport IL 60441 815-588-4530
TF: 866-634-9633 ■ *Web:* www.jkconsulting.net

J L A Consulting 1013 N Causeway Blvd .... Metairie LA 70001 504-835-9639
Web: www.jlaconsulting.net

J Wda 2359 Fourth Ave Ste 300 .... San Diego CA 92101 619-233-6777
Web: www.jwdainc.com

Janalent Corp
7582 Las Vegas Blvd. S. Ste. 580 Ste .... Las Vegas NV 89123 888-290-4870
TF: 888-290-4870 ■ *Web:* www.janalent.com

Phone Fax

Janus Consulting Inc 14408 Ashleigh Greene Rd .... Boyds MD 20841 301-515-9113
Web: janusconsulting.com

JCG Technologies Inc 50 S Belcher Rd .... Clearwater FL 33765 727-461-3776
Web: jcgtech.com

Jcms Inc 1741 Whitehorse Mercerville Rd .... Mercerville NJ 08619 609-631-0700
Web: www.jcms.com

Jdk Consulting 4924 Balboa Blvd Ste 487 .... Encino CA 91316 818-705-8050
TF: 855-535-7877 ■ *Web:* www.jdkconsulting.com

Jet Logistics Inc 2610 W Terminal Blvd .... Raleigh NC 27623 919-840-0555
Web: www.jetlogisticsinc.com

JMP IT Services 535 W 152 St .... New York NY 10031 646-397-8117
Web: www.jmpits.com

John Leslie Consulting 20 Souhegan St .... Milford NH 03055 603-673-6132
Web: www.jlc.net

Jones Environmental Inc
708 Milam St Ste 100 .... Shreveport LA 71101 318-226-8444
TF: 877-345-4534 ■ *Web:* www.jonesenvironmentalinc.com

JVKellyGroup Inc 145 E Main St .... Huntington NY 11743 631-427-2888
Web: www.jvkg.com

Jzanus Healthcare Financial Service
170 Jericho Tpke .... Floral Park NY 11001 516-326-0808
Web: www.artlink.net

K r Consulting Group Ltd 287 Burnside Ave .... Lawrence NY 11559 516-837-0335
Web: krgroupny.com

K&R Negotiation Associates LLC
908 Ethan Allen Hwy .... Ridgefield CT 06877 203-431-7693
Web: www.negotiators.com

K-Four Systems LLC 1660 Washington St .... Holliston MA 01746 774-233-0697
Web: kfoursystems.com

K.D. Analytical Consulting Inc
4460 Linglestown Rd .... Harrisburg PA 17112 717-343-2984
Web: www.kdanalytical.com

Kaava Consulting Inc 15190 Sw 136th St Ste 24 .... Miami FL 33196 305-255-5151
Web: kaavainc.com

Kalba International Inc 116 McKinley Ave .... New Haven CT 06515 203-397-2199
Web: www.kalbainternational.com

KAMM Consulting Inc
1407 W Newport Ctr Dr .... Deerfield Beach FL 33442 954-949-2200
Web: www.kammconsulting.com

Kaseya Corp 400 Totten Pond Rd Ste 200 .... Waltham MA 02451 877-926-0001
TF: 877-926-0001 ■ *Web:* www.kaseya.com

KBTS Technologies Inc 41461 W 11 Mile Rd .... Novi MI 48375 248-374-1230
Web: kbtstech.com

KDC Technologies 27201 Tourney Rd Ste 201 .... Valencia CA 91355 877-532-1112
TF: 877-532-1112 ■ *Web:* www.kdctechnologies.com

Kenton Groupcom LLC
4454 Fairway Oaks Dr Ste 400 .... Mulberry FL 33860 651-451-3465
Web: www.kentongroup.com

KEOGH Consulting Inc
10217 Brecksville Rd Ste 101 .... Brecksville OH 44141 440-526-2002
Web: www.keogh-consulting.com

Keres Consulting Inc 5600 Wymng Blvd 225 .... Albuquerque NM 87109 505-837-2104
Web: www.keresnm.com

Keysource Group Inc, The
1920 Georgetown Rd Ste C .... Hudson OH 44236 330-342-4630
Web: www.thekeysource.com

Kingery Construction Co 201 N 46th St .... Lincoln NE 68503 402-465-4400
Web: www.kccobuilders.com

Kingsley Consulting Group Ltd
701 Papworth Ave Ste 207 .... Metairie LA 70005 504-834-6484
Web: kingsleygroup.com

Kinsbursky Brothers Inc 125 E Commercial .... Anaheim CA 92801 714-738-8516
Web: www.kinsbursky.com

Kinsley & Associates
5401 S Prince St Ste 107 .... Littleton CO 80120 303-798-3664
Web: kinsleyassociates.com

Kinzelman Art Consulting Llc 3909 Main St .... Houston TX 77002 713-533-9923
Web: www.kinzelmanart.com

Kln Klein Product Development Inc
19787 56 Ave .... Langley BC V3A3X8 604-530-1491
Web: klnklein.com

Kms Consulting Services Inc
92 Broadway Ste 206 .... Greenlawn NY 11740 631-912-0200
Web: kmssolutions.com

Knack Systems LLC 1 Woodbridge Ctr Ste 335 .... Woodbridge NJ 07095 732-596-0110
Web: www.knacksystems.com

Know It All Background Research Services Inc
1950 St Rd Ste 402 .... Bensalem PA 19020 215-245-1975
Web: www.screenmyapplicants.com

Koers-turgeon Consulting Service Inc
2000 Ridgeview Rd .... Salina KS 67401 785-825-8192
Web: beef4u.com

Korn Consulting Group Inc
151 E 83rd St Apt 4ab .... New York NY 10028 212-734-6200
Web: www.kornconsulting.com

KRAMER aerotek Inc 580 Utica Ave .... Boulder CO 80304 303-247-1762
Web: www.krameraerotek.com

Krell Institute 1609 Golden Aspen Dr .... Ames IA 50010 515-956-3696
Web: www.krellinst.org

KRW Consulting Group LLC
1881 Commerce Dr Ste 111 .... Elk Grove Village IL 60007 847-734-0128
Web: www.krweng.com

Kwame Building Group Inc, The
1204 Washington Ave 200 .... Saint Louis MO 63103 314-862-5344
Web: www.kwamebuildinggroup.com

Kyra InfoTech Inc 4454 Florida National Dr .... Lakeland FL 33813 863-686-2271
Web: kyrasolutions.com/index.htm

L D Reeves & Associates Inc
1889 Manzana Ave .... Punta Gorda FL 33950 941-575-3555
Web: www.ldreeves.com

Labat-Anderson Inc 8000 Westpark Dr Ste 400 .... Mclean VA 22102 703-506-9600
Web: www.labat.com

Phone | Fax

Lakeview Professional Services Inc
104 S Maple St — Corona CA 92880 — 951-371-3390
Web: www.lakeviewpro.com

Lambert Consulting Group Inc
8699 Craigston Ct — Dublin OH 43017 — 614-792-6582
Web: lambertconsultinggroup.com

Laminar Consulting Services 424 S Olive St — Orange CA 92866 — 888-531-9995
TF: 888-531-9995 ■ *Web:* www.laminarconsulting.com

Lane Group LLC, The 14-25 Plz Rd — Fair Lawn NJ 07410 — 201-398-9230
Web: www.tlgmeetings.com

Lanlogic Inc 248 Rickenbacker Cir — Livermore CA 94551 — 925-273-2300
Web: www.lanlogic.com

LANSolutions LLC 6359 Nancy Ridge Dr — San Diego CA 92121 — 858-587-8000
Web: www.lansolutions.net

Larta Institute 606 S Olive St Ste 650 — Los Angeles CA 90014 — 213-694-2826
Web: www.larta.org

LAURUS Systems Inc
3460 Ellicott Ctr Dr Ste 101 — Ellicott City MD 21043 — 410-465-5558
Web: www.laurussystems.com

Lawrence Behr Assoc Inc 3400 Tupper Dr — Greenville NC 27834 — 252-757-0279 — 752-9155
TF: 800-522-4464 ■ *Web:* www.lbagroup.com/associates

Layer 3 Technologies Inc
1645 Lyell Ave Ste 200 — Rochester NY 14606 — 585-254-1966
Web: layer3direct.com

Lazorpoint LLC 812 Huron Rd E Ste 800 — Cleveland OH 44115 — 216-325-5200
Web: www.lazorpoint.com

Le Groupe Genitique Inc
2655 Blvd du Royaume Faubourg Sagamie
Ste 480 — Jonquiere QC G7S4S9 — 418-548-4626
Web: www.genitique.com

LED Supply Co 747 Sheridan Blvd Unit 8E — Lakewood CO 80214 — 877-595-4769
TF: 877-595-4769 ■ *Web:* ledsupplyco.com

Leeds Consulting Group Llc
1381 Bellewood Ln — Freeland WA 98249 — 360-331-5745
Web: www.leedscg.com

Les Solutions Victrix Inc
630 Sherbrooke St W Ste 1100 — Montreal QC H3A1E4 — 514-879-1919
Web: www.victrix.ca

Levementum Inc 55 N Arizona Place# 203 — Chandler AZ 85225 — 480-320-2500
Web: www.levementum.com

Lew Edwards Group, The 5454 Broadway — Oakland CA 94618 — 510-594-0224
Web: lewedwardsgroup.com

Lewis & Ellis Inc
2929 N Central Expy Ste 200 — Richardson TX 75080 — 972-850-0850
Web: www.lewisellis.com

Lightopia LLC 1043 N Coast Hwy — Laguna Beach CA 92651 — 949-715-5575
Web: www.lightopiaonline.com

Linguagraphics 194 Park Pl — Brooklyn NY 11238 — 718-789-2782
Web: www.linguagraphics.com

Liquid Networx Inc 415 N Main Ave — San Antonio TX 78205 — 210-516-1023
Web: www.liquidnetworx.com

Lloyd's Register Americas Inc
1330 Enclave Pkwy Ste 200 — Houston TX 77077 — 281-675-3100
Web: www.cdlive.lr.org

Lme Consulting 4625 Ladera Way — Carmichael CA 95608 — 916-601-1961
Web: www.lmeconsulting.net

Loblolly Consulting Llc 506 Carolyn Ave — Austin TX 78705 — 512-320-5421
Web: loblollyconsulting.com

Lochbridge One Campus Martius — Detroit MI 48226 — 313-227-2621
Web: www.lochbridge.com

Loffler Companies Inc
1101 E 78th St Ste 200 — Bloomington MN 55420 — 952-925-6800
Web: www.loffler.com

Lohfeld Consulting Group Inc
940 S River Landing Rd — Edgewater MD 21037 — 410-336-6264
Web: www.lohfeldconsulting.com

Lomax Consulting Group Llc The
1435 N Rt 9 — Cape May Court House NJ 08210 — 609-465-9857
Web: lomaxconsulting.com

Loyalty Factor LLC
579 Sagamore Ave Unit 109 — Portsmouth NH 03801 — 603-334-3401
Web: www.loyaltyfactor.com

LRA Worldwide Inc 300 Welsh Rd Bldg 1 Ste 200 — Horsham PA 19044 — 215-957-1999
Web: www.lraworldwide.com

Lucidview LLC 80 Rolling Links Blvd. — Oak Ridge TN 37830 — 865-220-8440
TF: 888-582-4384 ■ *Web:* www.lucidview.com

Lundquist Consulting Inc
111 Anza Blvd Ste 310 — Burlingame CA 94010 — 650-342-9486
Web: www.lundquistconsulting.com

Luther Consulting LLC
10435 Commerce Dr Ste 140 — Carmel IN 46032 — 317-636-0282
TF: 866-517-6570 ■ *Web:* www.lutherconsulting.com

Lyceum Kennedy French & American School
1 Cross Rd — Ardsley NY 10502 — 914-479-0722
Web: lyceumkennedy.org

Lylab Technology Solutions Inc
526 Cumberland St. — Lebanon PA 17042 — 717-279-8595
Web: www.lylab.net

Lyle Co 3140 Gold Camp Dr Ste 30 — Rancho Cordova CA 95670 — 916-266-4581
Web: www.lyleco.com

MAC Source Communications Inc
701 Erie Blvd W — Syracuse NY 13204 — 315-362-9200
Web: www.macsourceinc.com

Mach 1 Development LLC
525 K E Market St Ste 296 — Leesburg VA 20176 — 703-349-1461
Web: www.mach1development.com

Magnolia Consulting LLC
5135 Blenheim Rd — Charlottesville VA 22902 — 434-984-5540
TF: 855-984-5540 ■ *Web:* www.magnoliaconsulting.org

Makarios Consulting Llc
2837 Westerham Rd Ste — Downingtown PA 19335 — 610-380-8735
Web: makariosconsulting.com

Making Waves Education Program 200 24th St — Richmond CA 94804 — 510-237-3434
Web: www.making-waves.org

Makor Solutions LLC 7430 W 27th St — St. Louis Park MN 55426 — 952-922-2975
Web: recyclingmanager.com

Malibu Technologies Inc
48700 Structural Dr — Chesterfield MI 48051 — 586-598-9900
Web: www.malibutech.com

Management Network Group Inc (TMNG)
7300 College Blvd Ste 302 — Overland Park KS 66210 — 913-345-9315
NASDAQ: CRTN ■ *Web:* cartesian.com

Maple Lake Ltd 60 Columbia Way Ste 502 — Markham ON L3R0C9 — 905-513-7480
Web: www.txtgroup.com

Mar-kee Consulting Group Inc 26248 Equity Dr — Daphne AL 36526 — 251-621-7010
Web: www.markeegroup.com

Market Creation Group LLC
910 Santa Fe Dr Studio 11 — Denver CO 80204 — 303-325-7423
Web: www.marketcreationgroup.com

Market Force Information Inc
371 Centennial Pkwy Ste 210 — Louisville CO 80027 — 303-402-6920
Web: www.marketforce.com

Marks Group P C 45 E city ave — Bala Cynwyd PA 19004 — 610-842-2400
Web: www.marksgroup.net

Marlin Environmental Inc
3935 Commerce Dr — Saint Charles IL 60174 — 630-444-1933
Web: marlinenv.com

Marlo Plastic Products Inc
289 State Route 33 Ste 12 — Manalapan Township NJ 07726 — 732-792-1988
Web: marloplasticproducts.com

Marston Keyser Associates Inc
160 Pacific Ave Ste 204 — San Francisco CA 94111 — 415-398-3050
Web: www.keysermarston.com

Marvin Huffaker Consulting Inc
1311 W Chandler Blvd Ste 160 — Chandler AZ 85224 — 480-988-7215
TF: 888-690-0013 ■ *Web:* www.redjuju.com

Matasano Security LLC 39 W 14th St Ste 202 — New York NY 10011 — 888-677-0666
TF: 888-677-0666 ■ *Web:* matasano.com

Math Teachers Press Inc
4850 Park Glen Rd — St Louis Park MN 55416 — 952-545-6535
Web: www.movingwithmath.com

Mather Economics LLC
43 Woodstock St Historic Roswell District — Roswell GA 30075 — 770-993-4111
Web: www.mathereconomics.com

Matrix Risk Consultants Inc
3130 S Tech. Blvd — Miamisburg OH 45342 — 937-886-0000
Web: www.matrixrc.com

Matt Construction Corp
9814 Norwalk Blvd Ste 100 — Santa Fe Springs CA 90670 — 562-903-2277
Web: www.mattconstruction.com

Max Environmental Technologies Inc
1815 Washington Rd — Pittsburgh PA 15241 — 412-343-4900
TF: 800-851-7845 ■ *Web:* www.maxenvironmental.com

Max Technical Training 4900 Pkwy Dr Ste 160 — Mason OH 45040 — 513-322-8888
TF: 866-595-6863 ■ *Web:* www.maxtrain.com

MayStreet LLC 154 Grand St — New York NY 10013 — 646-801-2354
Web: www.maystreet.com

mcaConnect LLC
7720 E Belleview Ave Ste B-300 — Greenwood Village CO 80111 — 303-407-8330
Web: www.mcaconnect.net

Mccann Systems LLC 290 Fernwood Ave — Edison NJ 08837 — 732-346-9600
Web: www.mccannsystems.com

Mcdermott & Miller Pc 404 E 25th St Ste 1 — Kearney NE 68847 — 308-234-5565
Web: www.mmcpas.com

McKing Consulting Corp
2810 Old Lee Hwy Ste 250 — Fairfax VA 22031 — 703-204-2385
Web: www.mcking.com

MCM Services Group 1300 Corporate Ctr Curve — Eagan MN 55121 — 888-507-6262
TF: 888-507-6262 ■ *Web:* www.mcmservicesgroup.com

Mcmahon Group Inc
670 Mason Ridge Ctr Dr Ste 220 — Saint Louis MO 63141 — 314-744-5040
Web: www.mcmahongroup.com

McVeigh Associates Ltd 275 Dixon Ave — Amityville NY 11701 — 631-789-8833
Web: www.mcveigh.com

Measurement Group LLC, The
5757 Uplander Way Ste 200 — Culver City CA 90230 — 310-216-1800
Web: www.themeasurementgroup.com

Med Legal Consulting Source Inc
201 S Santa Fe Ave Ste 100 — Los Angeles CA 90012 — 213-347-0203
Web: elevateservices.com

Medical Learning Inc 287 E Sixth St Ste 400 — St. Paul MN 55101 — 651-292-3400
Web: www.medlearn.com

Medical Specialties Managers Inc
1 City Blvd W Ste 1100 — Orange CA 92868 — 714-571-5000
Web: www.msmnet.com

MediRevv Inc 2600 University Pkwy — Coralville IA 52241 — 888-665-6310
TF: 888-665-6310 ■ *Web:* www.medirevv.com

Medisolv Inc
10420 Little Patuxent Pkwy Ste 400 — Columbia MD 21044 — 443-539-0505
Web: www.medisolv.com

Medmart Inc 10780 Reading Rd — Cincinnati OH 45241 — 888-260-4430
TF: 888-260-4430 ■ *Web:* www.medmartonline.com

Meeting Masters 107 Oakmont Rd — Mount Laurel NJ 08054 — 856-787-9590
Web: meetingmastersinc.com

Megaplexus Corp 214 California St — Newton MA 02458 — 617-244-4405
Web: www.megaplexus.com

Meltmedia 1255 W Rio Salado Pkwy Ste 209 — Tempe AZ 85281 — 602-340-9440
Web: www.meltmedia.com

Menlo Scientific Ltd 5161 Rain Cloud Dr — Richmond CA 94803 — 510-758-9014
Web: www.sysid-labs.com

Mercury Z 1150 Se Maynard Rd Ste 140 — Cary NC 27511 — 877-548-4052
TF: 877-548-4052 ■ *Web:* www.mercuryz.com

Meridian Associates Inc 1 E Erie St Ste 240 — Chicago IL 60611 — 312-335-8050
Web: www.meridianai.com

Meridian Institute 105 Village Pl — Dillon CO 80435 — 970-513-8340
Web: www.merid.org

			Phone	Fax
Merit Solutions Inc 1749 S Naperville Rd Ste 200 .... Wheaton *Web:* meritsolutions.com	IL	60189	630-614-7133	
Meta Solutions Inc 63 Grove St .... Somerville *Web:* www.metasol.com	NJ	08876	908-791-1900	
MetaOption LLC 574 Newark Ave Ste 210 .... Jersey City *Web:* www.metaoption.com	NJ	07306	201-377-3150	
Michael Brandman Associates 220 Commerce Ste 200 .... Irvine *TF:* 888-826-5814 ■ *Web:* www.firstcarbonsolutions.com	CA	92602	714-508-4100	
Michell Consulting Group Inc 8240 NW 52nd Ter Ste 410 .... Doral *TF:* 800-442-5011 ■ *Web:* www.michellgroup.net	FL	33166	305-592-5433	
Midego Inc 4710 Olley Ln .... Fairfax *Web:* midego.publishpath.com	VA	22032	571-331-4158	
Midrange Solutions Inc 20 Hillside Ave .... Springfield *Web:* www.midrangeusa.com	NJ	07081	973-912-7050	
Mind Drivers LLC The Mill 381 Brinton Lk Rd .... Thornton	PA	19373	610-361-1000	
MindSpark International Inc 1205 Peachtree Pkwy Ste 1204 .... Cumming *TF:* 888-820-3616 ■ *Web:* www.mindsparkit.com	GA	30041	888-820-3616	
Miramar Hospitality Consulting 153 2nd St Ste 105 .... Los Altos *Web:* www.miramarhospitality.com	CA	94022	650-941-5202	
MIRUS Restaurant Solutions 820 Gessner Rd Ste 1600 .... Houston *Web:* www.mirus.com	TX	77024	713-468-7300	
MIS Inc 222 W Highland Dr .... Lakeland *Web:* www.mis-inc.net	FL	33813	863-669-1100	
Mit Professionals Inc 523 Lovett Blvd .... Houston *Web:* www.mitprof.com	TX	77006	713-934-9700	
MOBI Wireless Management LLC 6100 W 96th St Ste 150 .... Indianapolis *TF:* 855-259-6624 ■ *Web:* mobiwm.com	IN	46278	855-259-6624	
Montie Design 2106 Jerimouth Dr .... Apex *Web:* www.montie.com	NC	27502	919-481-1845	
Moran Technology Consulting Llc 1215 Hamilton Ln Ste 200 .... Naperville *TF:* 888-699-4440 ■ *Web:* www.morantechnology.com	IL	60540	888-699-4440	
More Effective Consulting LLC 10 Chestnut Cir .... Mont Vernon *Web:* www.moreeffective.com	NH	03057	603-801-3923	
MoreDirect Inc 1001 Yamato Rd Ste 200 .... Boca Raton *Web:* www.moredirect.com	FL	33431	561-237-3300	
Morphix Business Consulting PO Box 5217 Stn A .... Calgary *TF:* 866-680-2503 ■ *Web:* www.morphix.biz	AB	T2H1X3	403-520-7710	
Morris Energy Group LLC 36 Corbett Way .... Eatontown *Web:* www.morrisenergy.com	NJ	07724	732-542-2454	
Mosaic Event Management Inc 67 Haight St .... San Francisco *Web:* www.mosaicevents.com	CA	94102	415-908-2650	
Mr.Copy Inc 5657 Copley Dr .... San Diego *Web:* www.mrc360.com	CA	92111	858-573-6300	
MTE Consultants Inc 520 Bingemans Centre Dr .... Kitchener *Web:* www.mte85.com	ON	N2B3X9	519-743-6500	
MultiLing Corp 180 N University Ave 6th Fl .... Provo *Web:* www.multiling.com	UT	84601	801-377-2000	
MX Consulting Services Inc 544 Paramount Dr Ste 1 .... Raynham *Web:* www.mxcsi.com	MA	02767	508-821-5855	
Mxi Environmental Services Llc 26319 Old Trail Rd .... Abingdon *Web:* www.mxiinc.com	VA	24210	276-628-6636	
Mxn Corp 1025 Rose Creek Dr Ste 620 .... Woodstock *Web:* mxncorp.com	GA	30189	770-926-1884	
MYTA Corp 4905 Del Ray Ave, Ste 507 .... Bethesda *Web:* www.myta.com	MD	20814	301-656-6982	
MYTecSoft Inc 989 Knox Abbott Dr Ste 291 .... Cayce *Web:* www.mytecsoft.com	SC	29033	803-244-0255	
N & b Team Consulting Inc 3625 Nw 82nd Ave Ste 207 .... Doral *Web:* nbteamconsulting.com	FL	33166	305-514-2404	
Nation Consulting LLC 5027 W N Ave .... Milwaukee *Web:* www.nationconsulting.com	WI	53208	414-344-1733	
Native Seeds-search 3584 E River Rd .... Tucson *TF:* 866-622-5561 ■ *Web:* www.nativeseeds.org	AZ	85718	520-622-0830	
Natl Elevator Industrial Educational Program 11 Larsen Way .... Attleboro *Web:* www.neiep.org	MA	02763	508-699-2200	
NavCom Technology Inc 20780 Madrona Ave .... Torrance *Web:* www.navcomtech.com	CA	90503	310-381-2000	
Navigant Healthcare Cymetrix 2875 Michelle Dr Ste 250 .... Irvine *Web:* www.cymetrix.com	CA	92606	714-361-6800	
Necando Solutions Inc 620 St-Jacques Ste 500 .... Montreal *Web:* necando.com	QC	H3C1C7	514-360-4000	
Nei Turner Media Group 91 W Geneva St .... Williams Bay *Web:* www.ntmediagroup.com	WI	53191	262-245-1000	
Neko Industries Inc 3017 Douglas Blvd Ste 300 .... Roseville *Web:* www.nekoind.com	CA	95661	916-774-7125	
Nelrod Co 3109 Lubbock Ave .... Fort Worth *TF:* 866-448-0961 ■ *Web:* www.nelrod.com	TX	76109	817-922-9000	
Neltner Billing & Consulting Services inc 6463 Taylor Mill Rd .... Independence *TF:* 888-635-8637 ■ *Web:* neltnerbilling.com	KY	41051	888-635-8637	
Nennie & Associates 340 W Exchange St .... Sycamore *Web:* www.nenniandassoc.com	IL	60178	815-899-9421	
Neos LLC 20 Church St .... Hartford *Web:* www.neosllc.com	CT	06103	860-519-5601	
Neotelis Inc 4802 Verdun St Ste 1 .... Montreal *Web:* www.neotelis.com	QC	H4G1N1	514-281-1211	

			Phone	Fax
Net Matrix Solutions 10235 W Little York Rd Ste 435 .... Houston *Web:* www.netmatrixsolutions.com	TX	77040	281-598-2600	
Net Source Inc 8020 Shaffer Pkwy .... Littleton *Web:* www.netsourcestorage.com	CO	80127	303-948-3360	
Net World Technology Corp 65 S College St .... Carlisle *Web:* networldtechnology.com	PA	17013	717-249-7232	
NetForecast Inc 955 Emerson Dr .... Charlottesville *Web:* www.netforecast.com	VA	22901	434-249-1310	
Netlink Software Group America Inc 999 Tech Row .... Madison Heights *TF:* 800-485-4462 ■ *Web:* netlink.com	MI	48071	800-485-4462	
Netwood Communications 12655 Henri-Fabre Blvd Ste 201 .... Mirabel *Web:* www.obds.aero	QC	J7N1E1	450-476-1420	
Network Designs Integration Services Inc 103 Hammond Ave Ste 101 .... Fremont *Web:* www.network-designs.com	CA	94539	510-249-9549	
Network Frontiers LLC 244 Lafayette Cir .... Lafayette *Web:* www.netfrontiers.com	CA	94549	510-931-6611	
Neutron Inc 220 Reese Rd .... State College *TF:* 800-813-4218 ■ *Web:* www.neutronet.com	PA	16801	814-237-0902	
Nevada Crystal Premium LLC 6185 S Vly View Blvd .... Las Vegas *Web:* nevadacrystalpremium.com	NV	89118	702-892-0535	
Newdea Inc 4B Inverness Court E Ste 110 .... Englewood *Web:* www.newdea.com	CO	80112	720-249-3030	
Next Step Partners 1730 Vallejo St Apt 5 .... San Francisco *Web:* www.nextsteppartners.com	CA	94123	415-762-0148	
NextRidge Inc 12 Elmwood Rd .... Albany *Web:* www.nextridgeinc.com	NY	12204	518-292-6505	
Nextrio LLC 4803 E Fifth St .... Tucson *Web:* www.nextrio.com	AZ	85711	520-545-7100	
Nfocus Consulting Inc 1594 Hubbard Dr .... Lancaster *Web:* www.n-focus.com	OH	43130	740-654-5809	
Nicomm Llc 2235 Gateway Dr .... Sycamore *Web:* www.nicomm.net	IL	60178	815-758-0661	
Ninety Five 5 LLC 1767 Lakewood Ranch Blvd Ste 209 .... Bradenton *Web:* www.nf5.com	FL	34211	484-323-2413	
Nordisk Systems Inc 13475 SE Johnson Rd .... Milwaukie *TF:* 800-676-2777 ■ *Web:* nordisksystems.com	OR	97222	503-353-7555	
North Fork Crow River Wsd 311 Brighton Ave Ste C .... Buffalo *Web:* crowriver.org	MN	55313	320-346-2869	
Northspan Group Inc, The 221 W First St .... Duluth *TF:* 800-232-0707 ■ *Web:* www.ardc.org	MN	55802	218-722-5545	
Norwin Technologies Corp 10 Prince Pl .... Newburyport *Web:* www.norwintechnologies.com	MA	01950	978-462-0909	
Nova Corp 1445 Sheffler Dr Ste 201 .... Chambersburg *Web:* www.nova-dine.com	PA	17201	717-262-9750	
Nova Partners Inc 201 Moffett Blvd Ste 307 .... Mountain View *Web:* www.novapartners.com	CA	94043	650-324-5324	
Novotech Technologies Corp 57 Iber Rd Unit 2 .... Ottawa *Web:* www.novotech.com	ON	K2S1E7	613-280-1900	
Noxent Inc 6400 Boul Taschereau Bur 220 .... Brossard *TF:* 800-268-4364 ■ *Web:* www.noxent.com	QC	J4W3J2	800-268-4364	
npm Inc 200 Frank H Ogawa Plz 5th Fl Ste 500 .... Oakland *Web:* www.npmjs.com	CA	94612	619-339-2014	
NUBE Inc 16238 Ranch Rd Ste F-108 .... Austin *TF:* 888-400-3133 ■ *Web:* www.nube.us.com	TX	78717	888-400-3133	
Nurego Inc 812 2nd Ave Ste 800 .... Seattle *Web:* www.nurego.com	WA	98005	425-891-3468	
Nuvue Business Solutions 2913 London Bell Dr .... Raleigh *Web:* www.nuvue.com	NC	27614	919-562-5599	
Oasis Ranch Management 86235 Ave 52 .... Coachella *Web:* seaviewsales.com	CA	92236	760-398-8850	
Object Edge Inc 315 Lennon Ln .... Walnut Creek *Web:* www.objectedge.com	CA	94598	925-943-5558	
Object Systems Group Inc 8600 Freeport Pkwy Ste 400 .... Irving *Web:* www.osgcorp.com	TX	75063	972-650-2026	
Objectiva Software Solutions Inc 505 Lomas Santa Fe Dr Ste 170 .... Solana Beach *Web:* www.objectivasoftware.com	CA	92075	760-230-6607	
Oceanus Partners 16540 Pointe Village Dr Ste 208 .... Lutz *TF:* 888-496-1117 ■ *Web:* www.oceanuspartners.com	FL	33558	888-496-1117	
Old Town IT LLC 2312 Mount Vernon Ave Ste 201 .... Alexandria *Web:* www.oldtownit.com	VA	22301	703-579-6930	
Omnia Group Inc, The 601 S Blvd .... Tampa *Web:* www.omniagroup.com	FL	33602	813-254-9449	
Omnikron Systems 20920 Warner Center Ln Ste A .... Woodland Hills *Web:* www.omnikron.com	CA	91367	818-591-7890	
OmniPoint Inc 3111 W Dr Martin Luther King Jr. Blvd Ste 100 .... Tampa *Web:* www.omnipointinc.com	FL	33607	813-574-3841	
Omnipress 2600 Anderson St .... Madison *Web:* omnipress.com	WI	53704	608-246-2600	
OmniVue Business Solutions LLC 1355 Windward Concourse Ste 200 .... Alpharetta *Web:* www.omnivue.net	GA	30005	770-587-0095	
One Consulting Group Inc 977 Ponce De Leon Pl Ne Ste 3 .... Atlanta *Web:* onecginc.com	GA	30306	404-815-8005	
One Eighty Consulting Inc 413 N Meridian St .... Tallahassee *Web:* 180consultinginc.com	FL	32301	850-412-0300	
One Source Safety & Health Inc 140 S Village Ave Ste 130 .... Exton *Web:* 1ssh.com	PA	19341	610-524-5525	

Phone / Fax

OneRoof Inc 1 Maritime Plz Ste 1100 San Francisco CA 94111 415-391-0556
Web: www.oneroof.com

Opal Financial Group Inc 10 E 38th St 4th Fl New York NY 10016 212-532-9898
Web: www.opalgroup.net

Open Spatial Inc 13575 58th St N Ste 180 Clearwater FL 33760 800-696-1238
TF: 800-696-1238 ■ *Web:* www.openspatial.com

Optimal Satcom Inc
11180 Sunrise Vly Dr Ste 200 Reston VA 20191 703-657-8800
Web: optimalsatcom.com

Optimal Strategix Group Inc
Ste 118 140 Terry Dr Newtown PA 18940 215-867-1880
Web: www.optimalstrategix.com

Optimus Solutions LLC 22 Technology Park S Norcross GA 30092 770-447-1951
Web: www.softchoice.com

OPTIO LLC 390 Spaulding Ave SE Ada MI 49301 888-981-3282
TF: 888-981-3282 ■ *Web:* www.optiodata.com

ORR Associates Inc 2801 M St NW Washington DC 20007 202-338-6100
Web: www.oai-usa.com

Osage LLC 302 S Cheyenne Ste 112 Tulsa OK 74103 918-582-5633
Web: www.osagellc.com

Osi Environmental Inc 3300 E 83rd Pl Merrillville IN 46410 219-942-4886
Web: osienv.com

Otb Solutions Group Llc 5727 17Th Ave NE Seattle WA 98105 206-528-3757
Web: www.otbsolutions.com

Overture Partners LLC 57 Wells Ave # 22 Newton MA 02459 617-614-9600
Web: www.overturepartners.com

P i Incentive 220 Duncan Mill Rd Ste 315 Toronto ON M3B3J5 416-383-0766
Web: www.piincentives.com

P3 North America Inc
ÿ25650 W Eleven Mile Rd Ste 300 Troy MI 48034 248-792-2277
Web: www.p3-group.com

Paciello Group LLP, The 88 Temple St Nashua NH 03060 603-882-4122
Web: www.paciellogroup.com

Pacotech Inc 1739 Nina Lee Ln Houston TX 77018 713-688-0404
Web: www.pacotech.com

Palitto Consulting Services Inc
600 Weber Dr Wadsworth OH 44281 330-335-7271
Web: www.palittoconsulting.com

Palo Alto Consulting Group, The
502 Waverley St Palo Alto CA 94301 650-326-1784
Web: www.paloaltocg.com

Palo Alto Networks Inc
4401 Great America Pkwy Santa Clara CA 95054 408-753-4000
Web: www.paloaltonetworks.com

Pams Inc 3361 Pomona Blvd Pomona CA 91768 909-869-7267
Web: www.pamsinc.com

Panorama Consulting Solutions
8200 S Quebec Ste A3-315 Centennial CO 80112 303-974-7171
Web: www.panorama-consulting.com

Parallax Consulting LLC 325 Wood Rd Ste 107 Braintree MA 02184 781-535-6004
Web: parallax-consulting.com

Parallax Press 2236 Sixth St Berkeley CA 94710 510-540-6411
Web: www.parallax.org

Partner Harvard Medical International Inc
131 Dartmouth St 5th Fl Boston MA 02116 617-535-6400
Web: www.phmi.partners.org

Pathway Health Services Inc
2025 Fourth St White Bear Lake MN 55110 651-407-8699
Web: www.pathwayhealth.com

Patricia Egen Consulting LLC
803 Creek Overlook Chattanooga TN 37415 423-875-2652
Web: www.egenconsulting.com

PayneGroup Inc 719 2nd Ave Ste 850 Seattle WA 98104 206-344-8966
Web: www.thepaynegroup.com

Peak Environmental Inc 74 Main St 2nd Fl Woodbridge NJ 07095 732-326-1010
Web: www.peak-environmental.com

Peduzzi Associates Ltd 221 S Alfred St Alexandria VA 22314 703-836-7990
Web: www.pal-aerospace.com

Penn Systems Group 5068 W Chester Pk Ste Edgemont PA 19028 610-353-3800
Web: www.pennsys.com

Penncomp 2050 N Loop West Ste 200 Houston TX 77018 713-669-0965
Web: www.penncomp.com

Persimmon Technologies Corp
200 Harvard Mill Sq Ste 110 Wakefield MA 01880 781-587-0677
Web: www.persimmontech.com

Personnel Systems Associates Inc
7551 E Moonridge Ln Anaheim CA 92808 714-281-8337
Web: personnelsystems.com

Pervasive Solutions 117 Victor Heights Pkwy Victor NY 14564 585-300-0440
Web: www.pervasivesolutions.net

Pete Fowler Construction Services
931 Calle Negocio Ste J San Clemente CA 92673 949-240-9971
Web: www.petefowler.com

PFI Tech 5761 Rickenbacker Rd Commerce CA 90040 310-824-1800
Web: www.pfitech.com

PhishLabs PO Box 20877 Charleston SC 29413 843-628-3368
TF: 877-227-0790 ■ *Web:* www.phishlabs.com

Pilat (North America) Inc
460 US Hwy 22 W Ste 408 Whitehouse Station NJ 08889 908-823-9417
Web: pilat.com

Pistachio Consulting Inc 67 Maple St Milton MA 02186 800-747-1941
TF: 800-747-1941 ■ *Web:* www.pistachioconsulting.com

Plan First Technologies Inc 120 Groton Ave Cortland NY 13045 607-756-9347
Web: www.p1tech.net

Planaxis Inc
505 de Maisonneuve Blvd W Ste 200 Montreal QC H3A3C2 514-878-2295
Web: www.planaxis.com

Plasco Energy Group Inc 515 Legget D Ste 100 Kanata ON K2K3G4 613-287-3127
Web: www.plascoenergy.com

Platinum Vault Inc
10554 Norwalk Blvd Santa Fe Springs CA 90670 562-903-1494
TF: 888-671-2888 ■ *Web:* www.hartleymedical.com

PlusOne Solutions Inc
3501 Quadrangle Blvd Ste 120 Orlando FL 32817 407-359-5929
TF: 877-943-0100 ■ *Web:* www.plusonesolutions.net

PMOLink LLC 2001 Lakeshore Dr Mandeville LA 70448 985-674-5968
Web: www.pmolink.com

Pneumex Inc 2605 N. Boyer Ave Sandpoint ID 83864 208-265-4105
Web: www.pneumex.com

Pollution Control Corp
500 W Country Club Rd Chickasha OK 73018 800-966-1265
TF: 800-966-1265 ■ *Web:* www.pollutioncontrolcorp.com

Portable Church Industries Inc 1923 Ring Dr Troy MI 48083 248-585-9540
TF: 800-939-7722 ■ *Web:* www.portablechurch.com

Potomac Communications Group Inc
1133 20th St Nw Ste 400 Washington DC 20036 202-466-7391
Web: www.pcgpr.com

Potomac Healthcare Solutions LLC
1549 Old Bridge Rd Ste 201 Woodbridge VA 22192 703-436-9009
Web: www.potomachealthcare.com

PotomacWave Consulting Inc
107 S W St Ste 770 Alexandria VA 22314 703-623-5144
Web: www.potomacwave.com

Power Depot Inc 3553 NW 78th Ave Miami FL 33122 305-592-7100
Web: www.powerdepot.com

PowerBeam Inc 441 Clyde Ave Mountain View CA 94043 650-336-1193
Web: www.powerbeam.biz

Practice Management Consultants Inc
6115 Is Park Ct Fort Myers FL 33908 239-267-5444
Web: www.ehrpmc.com

Praemittias Group Inc
8871 Ridgeline Blvd Highlands Ranch CO 80129 720-344-0611
Web: www.praemittias.com

Praxis Data Systems Inc 4 Foster Ave Ste C Gibbsboro NJ 08026 856-679-2256
Web: www.praxisnet.com

Preclinomics Inc 7918 Zionsville Rd Indianapolis IN 46268 317-872-6001
Web: www.preclinomics.com

PremierComm LLC 415 N Prince St Ste 200 Lancaster PA 17603 717-431-7100
Web: www.premiercommllc.com

Pretium Partners Inc 3240 Henderson Rd Ste A Columbus OH 43220 614-457-1726
Web: www.pretiumpartners.com

Prism Consulting Inc 1150 Hancock St Ste 400 Quincy MA 02169 617-328-9896
Web: www.prismconsultinginc.com

Proactive Management Consulting LLC
2700 Cumberland Pkwy SE Atlanta GA 30339 770-319-7468
TF: 877-319-2198 ■ *Web:* www.proactive-management.com

Procon Consulting Llc
2300 N Pershing Dr Ste 305 Arlington VA 22201 703-527-7059
Web: www.proconconsulting.com

Procurri LLC 5825 Peachtree Corners E Ste A Norcross GA 30092 770-817-9092
Web: www.procurri.com

Product Safety Consulting Inc
605 Country Club Dr Ste I Bensenville IL 60106 630-238-0188
TF: 877-804-3066 ■ *Web:* productsafetyinc.com

Profit Recovery Partners LLC
18231 W McDurmott Irvine CA 92614 949-851-2777
Web: www.prpllc.com

Project Consulting Services Inc
3300 W Esplanade Ave S Ste 500 Metairie LA 70002 504-833-5321
TF: 855-468-7473 ■ *Web:* www.projectconsulting.com

Project X Ltd 25 Rumsey Rd Toronto ON M4G1N7 416-422-8900
Web: www.pxltd.ca

ProSource Solutions LLC
4199 Kinross Lakes Pkwy Ste 150 Richfield OH 44286 866-549-0279
TF: 866-549-0279 ■ *Web:* www.prosource-corp.com

Prosper Advisors Llc 20 Bedford Rd Armonk NY 10504 914-730-3500
Web: www.prosperadv.com

Psa Constructors Inc 1516 E Hillcrest St Orlando FL 32803 407-898-9119
Web: www.psaonline.com

Public Data Works Inc 2720 Reynolda Rd Winston-salem NC 27106 336-725-4456
Web: www.publicdataworks.com

Public Sector Consultants Inc
600 W Saint Joseph St Ste 10 Lansing MI 48933 517-484-4954
Web: www.pscinc.com

Pulsar It Consulting Inc
9200 Worthington Rd Ste 101 Westerville OH 43082 614-781-3787
Web: gammillgroup.com

PV-Tron Inc 8810 Blvd Langelier Saint-Leonard QC H1P3H2 514-723-2131
Web: www.pvtron.com

Pyramid Healthcare Solutions Inc
14141 46th St N Ste 1212 Clearwater FL 33762 727-431-3000
Web: www.pyramidhs.com

Qsoft Consulting 38 Baldwin Ln Glastonbury CT 06033 860-777-9022
Web: www.qsoftconsultingllc.com

Quadlogic Controls Corp
3300 Northern Blvd Fl 2 Fl 2 Long Island NY 11101 212-930-9300
TF: 877-797-6347 ■ *Web:* www.quadlogic.com

Quality Management Solutions LLC
146 Lowell St Ste 300B Wakefield MA 01889 800-645-6430
TF: 800-645-6430 ■ *Web:* www.qmsinc.com

QualPro Inc 3117 Pellissippi Pkwy Knoxville TN 37931 865-927-0491
Web: www.qualproinc.com

Quantum Information Systems Solutions Inc
2805 Pontiac Lk Rd Ste 2C Waterford MI 48328 248-393-3621
Web: www.qinfosys.com

Quartech Systems Ltd
2160 Springer Ave Ste 200 Burnaby BC V5B3M7 604-291-9686
Web: www.quartech.com

Quasius Investment Corp
4805 Independence Pkwy Ste 100 Tampa FL 33634 813-249-2514
Web: www.gca.net

Qubera Solutions Inc
220 Twin Dolphin Dr Ste C Redwood City CA 94065 650-294-4460
Web: www.quberasolutions.com

				Phone	Fax
R2 Unified Technologies 980 N Federal Hwy Ste 410 TF: 866-464-7381 ■ Web: www.r2ut.com	Boca Raton	FL	33432	561-515-6800	
Rader Solutions Ltd 537 Cajundome Blvd Ste 209 Web: radersolutions.com	Lafayette	LA	70506	337-205-4652	
Radgov Inc 6750 N Andrews Ave Ste 200 Web: www.radgov.com	Fort Lauderdale	FL	33309	954-938-2800	
Raffa Consulting Economists Inc 17 S Osceola Ave Ste 200 Web: raffaconsulting.com	Orlando	FL	32801	407-648-5141	
Rage Administrative & Marketing Services Inc 1313 N Webb Rd Ste 200 Web: www.rage-inc.com	Wichita	KS	67206	316-634-1888	
Rally Education LLC 22 Railroad Ave Web: www.rallyeducation.com	Glen Head	NY	11545	516-671-0700	
Rational Energies LLC 12200 Middleset Rd Ste 300 Web: rationalenergies.com	Eden Prairie	MN	55344	952-807-0080	
RDS Solutions LLC 99 Grayrock Rd TF: 888-473-7435 ■ Web: www.rdssolutions.com	Clinton	NJ	08809	888-473-7435	
Red Path Consulting Group 1011 Washington Ave S Ste 350 Web: redpathcg.com	Minneapolis	MN	55415	612-843-3360	
Redapt Inc 12226 134th CT NE Bldg D Web: www.redapt.com	Redmond	WA	98052	425-882-0400	
Redhawk Network Security LLC 62958 Layton Ave Ste One Web: www.redhawksecurity.com	Bend	OR	97701	541-382-4360	
RedLegg 100 Illinois St Ste 200 TF: 877-811-5040 ■ Web: www.redlegg.com	St. Charles	IL	60174	877-811-5040	
ReelGrobman 96 N 2nd St Web: www.reelgrobman.com	San Jose	CA	95113	408-288-7833	
Relevant Media Group 100 S Lk Destiny Dr Web: www.relevantmagazine.com	Orlando	FL	32810	407-660-2997	
Reliable Lighting & Energy Concepts Inc 5144 N Commerce Ave Ste F Web: www.reliablelighting.net	Moorpark	CA	93021	805-517-1717	
Remedi Consulting Co 96 Northwoods Blvd Ste A2 Web: www.remedi.com	Columbus	OH	43235	614-436-4040	
Research into Action Inc 3934 Ne Mlking Jr Blvd Ste 300 TF: 888-492-9100 ■ Web: researchintoaction.com	Portland	OR	97212	503-287-9136	
Resolve Inc 1255 23rd St NW Ste 275 Web: www.resolv.org	Washington	DC	20037	202-944-2300	
Response Design Corp 5541 Simpson Ave TF: 888-204-3833 ■ Web: www.responsedesign.com	Ocean City	NJ	08226	888-204-3833	
Results Media Group 725 W Mcdowell Rd Web: www.laneterralever.com	Phoenix	AZ	85007	602-257-0007	
Reunion Power LLC 310 Hudson St Ste 2A-B Web: www.reunionpower.com	Hackensack	NJ	07601	201-546-7722	
Revention Inc 1315 W Sam Houston Pkwy North Ste 100 TF: 877-738-7444 ■ Web: www.revention.com	Houston	TX	77043	877-738-7444	
Rhein Consulting Laboratories 4475 Sw Scholls Ferry Rd Ste 101 Web: www.rheinlabs.com	Portland	OR	97225	503-292-1988	
RhinoDox Document Storage Chicago 1200 Humbracht Cir Web: www.rhinodoxdocumentstoragechicago.com	Bartlett	IL	60103	630-372-8861	
Ria Compliance Consultants Inc 11640 Arbor St Ste 100 Web: www.ria-compliance-consultants.com	Omaha	NE	68144	402-345-4034	
Richard Carlton Consulting Inc 1941 Rollingwood Dr Web: www.rcconsulting.com	Fairfield	CA	94534	707-422-4053	
Ridgeline Consulting Group Inc 1110 Winchester Trl Ste Web: ridgelineconsulting.com	Downingtown	PA	19335	610-518-1430	
Rigel Networks LLC 1500 Quail St Ste 280 Web: www.rigelnetworks.com	Newport Beach	CA	92660	949-891-2571	
Rimkus Consulting Group Inc 8 Greenway Plz Ste 500 Web: www.rimkus.com	Houston	TX	77046	713-621-3550	
Ris Corp 5905 Weisbrook Ln Ste 101 Web: www.ris-corp.com	Knoxville	TN	37909	865-588-4456	
RISC Networks Inc 1 Rankin Ave Second Fl TF: 866-808-1227 ■ Web: www.riscnetworks.com	Asheville	NC	28801	866-808-1227	
Risetime Inc 130 S Jefferson St Ste 100 Web: www.risetime.com	Chicago	IL	60610	312-362-9930	
Rjc Designs Inc 1916 Crain Hwy S Ste 10 Web: rjcdesigns.com	Glen Burnie	MD	21061	410-760-7712	
RJK Partners LLC 1756 Forest Oaks Dr Web: www.rjkpartners.com	Hudson	OH	44236	330-414-8705	
Rjm Wireless Consulting Services Inc 12300 Perry Hwy Ste 206 Web: rjmwireless.com	Wexford	PA	15090	724-934-1055	
Rls Logistics 2260 Industrial Way Web: www.rlslogistics.com	Vineland	NJ	08360	856-691-2040	
RMG Financial Consulting Inc 813 E Ballard Ave Web: www.rmgfinancial.com	Colbert	WA	99005	509-468-2956	
Robert Frances Group 46 Kent Hills Ln Ste 201 Web: www.rfgonline.com	Wilton	CT	06880	203-429-8951	
Robert Rippe & Associates Inc 6117 Blue Cir Dr Web: www.robertrippe.com	Minnetonka	MN	55343	952-933-0313	
Roi Communications Inc 5274 Scotts Vly Dr Web: www.roico.com	Scotts Valley	CA	95066	831-430-0170	
Roi Consulting Ll Llc 176 Logan St TF: 866-465-6470 ■ Web: www.roillc.net	Noblesville	IN	46060	866-465-6470	
Rook Consulting 5537 Makati Cir TF: 888-712-9531 ■ Web: www.rookconsulting.net	San Jose	CA	95123	888-712-9531	
Root Inc 5470 Main St TF: 800-852-1315 ■ Web: www.rootinc.com	Sylvania	OH	43560	800-852-1315	
Ropes Associates Inc 333 N New River Dr 3rd Fl Web: www.ropesassociates.com	Ft. Lauderdale	FL	33301	954-525-6600	
Rose Shattuck & Associates LLC 4505 Fair Meadows Ln Ste 205 Web: shattuckconsulting.com	Raleigh	NC	27607	919-256-1675	
Rouis & Company LLP 51 Sullivan St Web: www.rouiscpas.com	Wurtsboro	NY	12790	845-888-5656	
Rouse Consulting Group Inc 422 16th St Web: www.go2rcg.com	Moline	IL	61265	309-762-3589	
Rrk Assoc 14044 W Petronella Dr Ste 5 Web: www.rrkassociates.net	Libertyville	IL	60048	847-680-0866	
Rsi Corp 543 Main St TF: 888-830-5648 ■ Web: www.rsicorp.com	Kiowa	KS	67070	620-825-4600	
Rstn Consulting Llc 1035 Pearl St Lbby 4 Web: www.rstn.com	Boulder	CO	80302	303-447-6878	
RTP Technology Corp 95 N Rte 17 Web: www.rtptech.com	Paramus	NJ	07652	201-796-2266	
Rue & Associates Inc 7264 Hanover Green Dr Web: www.rueassociates.com	Mechanicsville	VA	23111	804-730-7455	
Rulesware LLC 10 N Martingale Rd Ste 400 Web: www.rulesware.com	Schaumburg	IL	60173	312-224-8501	
Ryad Consulting Inc 4876 Township Trce Web: ryadconsulting.com	Marietta	GA	30066	770-650-8468	
Ryan Public Safety Solutions Inc 12119 Us Hwy 431 Web: www.rpss911.com	Guntersville	AL	35976	256-279-0082	
Rybar Group Inc, The 3150 Owen Rd Web: therybargroup.com	Fenton	MI	48430	810-750-6822	
S & L International 150 E Colorado Blvd Ste 203 Web: www.slinternational.com	Pasadena	CA	91105	626-405-0999	
S1 Corp 705 Westech Dr705 Westech Dr Ste Web: www.s1.com	NORCROSS	GA	30092	404-923-3500	
S3 Integrity LLC 12912 Water Point Blvd Web: www.s3integrity.com	Windermere	FL	34786	407-876-1200	
Sabertooth Technologies 5944 Coral Ridge Dr # 215 Web: www.stooth.net	Coral Springs	FL	33076	954-635-5545	
Sabio Information Technologies Inc 8200 NW 27th St Ste 116 Web: www.sabioit.com	Miami	FL	33122	305-499-9088	
Sabretech Consulting LLC 154 Lewis St TF: 800-267-1715 ■ Web: www.sabretechllc.com	Hillsdale	MI	49242	517-437-7150	
Safari Micro Inc 2185 W Pecos Rd TF: 888-446-4770 ■ Web: www.safarimicro.com	Chandler	AZ	85224	888-446-4770	
Safety Center Inc 3909 Bradshaw Rd Web: www.safetycenter.org	Sacramento	CA	95827	916-366-7233	
Safeway Industrial Services LLC 308 E Air Depot Rd Web: www.safewayind.com	Glencoe	AL	35905	256-492-3704	
Salem Associates Inc 7074 Peachtree Indus Blvd Web: www.salemassociates.com	Norcross	GA	30071	770-729-8089	
SandPoint Consulting Inc 2716 Colonial Way Web: www.sandpointc.com	Bloomfield Hills	MI	48304	248-481-2072	
SatisfYd 47 E Chicago Ave Ste 310 TF: 800-562-9557 ■ Web: satisfyd.com	Naperville	IL	60540	800-562-9557	
Saturn Infotech Inc 1120 Welsh Rd Ste 110 Web: saturninfotech.com	North Wales	PA	19454	267-337-6779	
Savis Inc 9 N Wabash Ave Ste 102 Web: www.savis-inc.com	Chicago	IL	60602	847-797-8857	
SBP Consulting Inc 3406 78th St Web: www.sbpcorp.com	Moline	IL	61265	732-631-0002	
Scheig Associates PO Box 2628 Web: www.scheig.com	Gig Harbor	WA	98332	253-858-3534	
School Loop Inc 49 Powell St Web: www.schoolloop.com	San Francisco	CA	94102	650-351-5060	
Scireg Inc 12733 Directors Loop Web: www.scireg.com	Woodbridge	VA	22192	703-494-6500	
Score a Goal in The Classroom 819 Penn St Web: scoreagoal.org	Fort Worth	TX	76102	817-429-4024	
Scribe Inc 842 S Second St Web: scribenet.com	Philadelphia	PA	19147	215-336-5094	
SDLC Partners LP 2790 Mosside Blvd Ste 705 Web: www.sdlcpartners.com	Monroeville	PA	15146	412-373-1950	
Sea Shepherd Conservation Society 1225 Wold Rd Web: www.seashepherd.org	Friday Harbor	WA	98250	360-370-5650	
Selection Resource Inc 3231 Central Park W Ste 109	Toledo	OH	43617	310-824-8999	
Selectus Consulting LLC 17875 Kandel Rd Web: selectusconsulting.com	Marysville	OH	43040	937-644-8562	
SemiTorr Inc 10655 Manhasset Dr Web: www.semitorrinc.com	Tualatin	OR	97062	503-682-7052	
Senes Oak Ridge Center for Risk Analysis Inc 102 Donner Dr Web: senes.com	Oak Ridge	TN	37830	865-483-6111	
Sequel Data Systems Inc 11824 Jollyville Rd Ste 400 Web: www.sequeldata.com	Austin	TX	78759	512-918-8841	
Sera-Brynn LLC 5806 Harbour View Blvd Ste 204 Web: sera-brynn.com	Suffolk	VA	23435	757-243-1257	
Sererra Consulting Group LLC 5430 Trabuco Rd Ste 150 TF: 877-276-3774 ■ Web: www.sererra.com	Irvine	CA	92620	877-276-3774	

Phone *Fax*

Serti Informatique Inc 7555 Beclard St ... Montreal QC H1J2S5 514-493-1909
TF: 800-361-6615 ■ *Web:* www.serti.com

ServerLift Corp 17453 N 25th Ave ... Phoenix AZ 85023 602-254-1557
Web: www.serverlift.com

Service Technologies Inc 1284 Logan Cir NW ... Atlanta GA 30318 404-355-6262
Web: servicetechnologies.net

ServIT Inc 3721 Cherokee St ... Kennesaw GA 30144 770-499-6300
Web: www.servit.net

Sevatec Inc 3112 Fairview Park Dr ... Falls Church VA 22042 571-766-1300
Web: www.sevatec.com

Seven Degrees 891 Laguna Canyon Rd ... Laguna Beach CA 92651 949-376-1555
Web: www.seven-degrees.com

Shearer & Associates Inc
4960 Corporate Dr Ste 100 ... Huntsville AL 35805 256-830-1031
Web: shearerassociates.us

Shelko Consulting Llc 545 N Maple Ave ... Ridgewood NJ 07450 201-444-2089
Web: www.shelko.com

Sierra Business Council 10116 Jibboom St ... Truckee CA 96161 530-582-4800
Web: sierrabusiness.org

Sigma Resources LLC 7950 Saltsburg Rd ... Pittsburgh PA 15239 412-712-1070
Web: www.sigma-resources.com

Sign Biz Inc 24681 La Plz Ste 270 ... Dana Point CA 92629 949-234-0408
TF: 800-633-5580 ■ *Web:* www.signbiz.com

Signal Securities Inc 700 Throckmorton St ... Fort Worth TX 76102 817-877-4256
Web: www.signalsecurities.com

Signal-Tech 4985 Pittsburgh Ave ... Erie PA 16509 814-835-3000
TF: 877-547-9900 ■ *Web:* www.signal-tech.com

Silicon Engines Ltd
3550 W Salt Creek Ln ... Arlington Heights IL 60005 847-637-1180

Silver State Gaming Inc
6145 S. Rainbow Ste 100 ... Las Vegas NV 89118 702-255-1777
Web: www.silverstategaminginc.com

Simon Consulting LLC
3200 N Central Ave Ste 2460 ... Phoenix AZ 85012 602-279-7500
Web: www.simonconsulting.net

Simple Computer Repair LLC
10525 S Eastern Ave Ste 140 ... Henderson NV 89052 702-614-3186
Web: www.simplecomputerrepair.com

Simplicity Consulting Inc
11250 Kirkland Way Ste 203 ... Kirkland WA 98033 888-252-0385
TF: 888-252-0385 ■ *Web:* www.simplicityci.com

Simplion Technologies Inc
1525 McCarthy Blvd Ste 228 ... Milpitas CA 95035 408-935-8686
Web: www.simplion.com

Sims & Steele Consulting
44 Merrimon Ave Ste 3a ... Asheville NC 28801 828-254-9004
Web: simsandsteele.com

SinglePoint Solutions Inc
9710 Park Plz Ave Ste 201 ... Louisville KY 40241 502-212-4017
Web: www.sptsolutions.com

SiteTuners com Inc
2535 Kettner Blvd Ste 3A3 ... San Diego CA 92101 619-223-8020
Web: www.sitetuners.com

Sivad Business Solutions LLC
2021 Aldbury Ln ... Woodstock GA 30189 678-215-1705
Web: www.sivadsolutions.com

Skidata Inc 1 Harvard Way Ste 5 ... Hillsborough NJ 08844 908-243-0000
Web: www.skidata.com

Skipping Stone Inc 83 Pine St Ste 101 ... West Peabody PA 01960 978-717-6100
Web: www.skippingstone.com

Sky I T Group LLC 330 Seventh Ave ... New York NY 10001 212-868-7800
TF: 866-641-6017 ■ *Web:* www.skyitgroup.com

Skygone Inc 1000 New York St Ste 107 ... Redlands CA 92374 888-759-4471
TF: 888-759-4471 ■ *Web:* www.skygoneinc.com

SlickData 252 Nassau St 2nd Fl ... Princeton NJ 08542 609-736-0036
Web: www.slickdata.com

Smart Safety Group
2535 Camino Del Rio S Ste 125 ... San Diego CA 92108 619-491-3099
TF: 877-345-7627 ■ *Web:* www.smartsafetygroup.com

SmarTek21 LLC 12910 Totem Lk Blvd NE Ste 200 ... Kirkland WA 98034 425-242-3786
Web: www.smartek21.com

Smith Management Group
1860b Williamson Ct ... Louisville KY 40223 502-587-6482
Web: www.smithmanage.com

Smithlain Enterprises Inc
1300 Meridian St Ste 15 ... Huntsville AL 35801 256-704-7880
Web: www.smithlain.com

SOAProjects Inc
495 N Whisman Rd Ste 100 ... Mountain View CA 94043 650-960-9900
Web: soaprojects.com

SoftNice Inc 5050 Tilghman St Ste 115 ... Allentown PA 18104 610-871-0400
Web: www.softnice.com

Solutions Plus 35583 Atlantic Ave ... Millville DE 19967 864-967-6782
Web: www.splus.net

Solvera Solutions Inc 201 - 1853 Hamilton St ... Regina SK S4P2C1 306-757-3510
Web: www.solvera.ca

Somerset Consulting Group Inc
PO Box 180344 Ste 120 ... Austin TX 78718 512-327-0090
Web: www.somersetcg.com

Sonas Consulting 8233 Brittany Dr ... Dublin CA 94568 650-619-4853
Web: www.sonasconsulting.com

Sonoma Technical Support Services
8840 210th St Ste 342 ... Langley BC V1M2Y2 866-898-3123
TF: 866-898-3123 ■ *Web:* www.sonomaservices.com

Soundearth 2811 Fairview Ave E ... Seattle WA 98102 206-306-1900
Web: www.soundearthinc.com

Soundview Executive Book Summaries
10 Lacrue Ave ... Concordville PA 19331 484-785-1304
Web: www.summary.com

Source Data Products Inc
18350 Mount Langley St ... Fountain Valley CA 92708 714-593-0387
TF: 800-333-2669 ■ *Web:* www.source-data.com

Source One Technical Solutions LLC
1952 Route 22 E ... Bound Brook NJ 08805 732-748-8643
Web: www.source1tek.com

SourceN Inc 4848 San Filipe Rd #150 116 ... San Jose CA 95135 831-297-2838
Web: sourcen.com

Sousa Court Reporters 1013 Garces Ave ... Las Vegas NV 89101 702-765-7100
Web: www.sousa.com

South Alabama Regional Planning Commission
110 Beauregard St ... Mobile AL 36633 251-433-6541
Web: www.sarpc.org

Southland Safety LLC 1409 Kilgore Dr ... Henderson TX 75652 903-657-8669
TF: 866-723-3719 ■ *Web:* southlandsafety.com

Southwest Networks Inc
19020 N Indian Ave Ste 2B ... Desert Hot Springs CA 92240 760-288-2200
Web: www.southwest-networks.com

Sovereign Systems LLC 705 Clubside Dr ... Roswell GA 30076 404-549-5272
Web: www.sovsystems.com

Spader Business Management
2101 W 41st St Ste 49 ... Sioux Falls SD 57105 800-772-3377
TF: 800-772-3377 ■ *Web:* www.spader.com

Spatial Data Inc 4545 Fuller Dr Ste 416 ... Irving TX 75038 972-791-0911
Web: www.spatial-data.com

Spd Foundation
5655 S Yosemite St Ste 305 ... Greenwood Village CO 80111 303-794-1182
Web: spdfoundation.net

Spearhead Staffing LLC
991 Route 22 W Ste 200 Third Fl ... Bridgewater NJ 08807 908-864-8081
Web: www.spearheadstaffing.com

Spectral Sciences Inc 4 4th Ave ... Burlington MA 01803 781-273-4770
Web: www.spectral.com

Spire Consulting Group LLC
114 W Seventh St Ste 1300 ... Austin TX 78701 512-637-0845
TF: 855-216-0812 ■ *Web:* www.spireconsultinggroup.com

Spire Technologies Inc
2140 SW Jefferson St Ste 300 ... Portland OR 97201 503-222-3086
Web: www.spiretech.com

Spokane Neighborhood Action Programs
212 W Second Ave ... Spokane WA 99201 509-744-3370
Web: www.snapwa.org

SQL Star International Inc
8820 Kenamar Dr Ste 506 ... San Diego CA 92121 650-204-9490
Web: www.sqlstar.com

Sri Quality Sys
300 Northpointe Cir Ste 304 ... Seven Fields PA 16046 724-934-9000
TF: 800-549-6709 ■ *Web:* www.sriregistrar.com

Ssg Ltd 801 E Campbell Rd Ste 350 ... Richardson TX 75081 214-333-2000
Web: www.ssglimited.com

Staffcentrix LLC 33 Woodstock Meadows ... Woodstock CT 06281 860-928-6969
Web: www.staffcentrix.com

Stahl Consulting Group PA 8626 N Himes Ave ... Tampa FL 33614 813-936-0313
Web: www.stahlconsulting.com

Stanard & Associates Inc
309 W Washington St Ste 1000 ... Chicago IL 60606 312-553-0213
Web: stanard.com

Stanfield Systems Inc 718 Sutter St Ste 108 ... Folsom CA 95630 916-608-8006
Web: www.www.stanfieldsystems.com

Star Trax Inc 1200 Woodwards Heights ... Ferndal MI 48220 248-263-6300
Web: startrax.com

Starnet Data Design Inc
2659 Townsgate Rd Ste 227 ... Westlake Village CA 91361 805-371-0585
Web: www.starnetdata.com

Sterliteusa 1117 Lake St ... Oak Park IL 60301 708-383-4003
Web: sterliteusa.com

Stillmeadow Inc 12852 Park One Dr ... Sugar Land TX 77478 281-240-8828
Web: www.stillmeadow.com

Stohl Environmental LLC
4169 Allendale Pkwy 100 ... Blasdell NY 14219 716-312-0070
Web: www.stohlenvironmental.com

Stored Technology Solutions Inc
5 Sagamore St Ste A ... Glens Falls NY 12801 518-793-1111
Web: www.storedtech.com

storyminers Inc 1862 Wilkenson Crossing ... Marietta GA 30066 770-425-9830
Web: www.mikewittenstein.com

StrateGen Consulting LLC
2150 Allston Way Ste 210 ... Berkeley CA 94704 510-665-7811
Web: strategen.com

Strategic Development Solutions LLC
11150 W Olympic Blvd Ste 910 ... Los Angeles CA 90064 310-914-5333
Web: www.sdsgroup.com

Street Solutions Inc 2930 Plz Five ... Jersey City NJ 07311 201-763-9500
Web: www.streetsolutions.com

Stria Inc 4300 Resnik Ct ... Bakersfield CA 93313 661-617-6601
Web: www.stria.com

Strickland General Agency Inc
2963 Gulf To Bay Blvd ... Clearwater FL 33759 727-669-8886
Web: www.sgainfl.com

Stroudwater Associates Inc
50 Sewall St Ste 102 ... Portland ME 04102 207-221-8250
Web: www.stroudwater.com

Sts Consulting Services LLC
434 E Loop 281 Ste 105 ... Longview TX 75605 903-247-1787
Web: ststx.com

Summit Environmental Consultants Inc
640 Main St ... Lewiston ME 04240 207-795-6009
Web: www.summitenv.com

Superior Communications Inc 704 E Gude Dr ... Rockville MD 20850 301-762-7878
Web: www.scicommo.com

Company / Address	City	State	ZIP	Phone	Fax
Superna Business Consulting Inc 104 Schneider Rd *Web:* www.superna.net	Kanata	ON	K2K1Y2	613-729-1100	
Surfrider Foundation 942 Calle Negocio Ste 350 *Web:* www.surfrider.org	San Clemente	CA	92673	949-492-8170	
Surrex Solutions Corp 300 N Sepulveda Blvd Ste 1020 *TF:* 866-308-2628 ■ *Web:* www.surrex.com	El Segundo	CA	90245	866-308-2628	
Survival Strategies Inc 335 N Third St. *Web:* www.survivalstrategies.com	Burbank	CA	91502	818-276-1000	
Swedenborg Foundation Inc 320 N Church St. *Web:* swedenborg.com	West Chester	PA	19380	610-430-3222	
Switchfast Technologies 4043 N Ravenswood Ste 203 *Web:* www.switchfast.com	Chicago	IL	60613	773-241-3007	
Symbolic Systems Inc 25 Chatham Rd. *Web:* www.symbolic.com	Summit	NJ	07901	908-665-5940	
Synercomm Inc 3265 Gateway Rd Ste 650 *Web:* www.synercomm.com	Brookfield	WI	53045	262-860-4220	
Synertel 80 Tanforan Ave Ste 14. *Web:* www.synertel.com	San Francisco	CA	94080	415-970-0100	
SyNet Technology Solutions Inc 205 Hallene Rd Ste 101 *Web:* www.synetinc.com	Warwick	RI	02886	401-736-6450	
Syntegrity Network Inc 9500 Braddock Rd *Web:* www.syntegritynet.com	Fairfax	VA	22032	703-425-3078	
System Improvements Inc 238 S Peters Rd Ste 301. *Web:* www.taproot.com	Knoxville	TN	37923	865-539-2139	
Systems Plus Computers Inc 12 Centerra Pkwy Ste 20. *TF:* 800-388-8486 ■ *Web:* www.spci.com	Lebanon	NH	03766	603-643-5800	
Syvantis Technologies LLC 13822 Bluestem Ct Ste. *TF:* 800-450-8908 ■ *Web:* www.syvantis.com	Baxter	MN	56425	800-450-8908	
Talent Plus Inc 1 Talent Plus Way *Web:* www.talentplus.com	Lincoln	NE	68506	402-489-2000	
TalentSmart Inc 11526 Sorrento Vly Rd. *Web:* www.talentsmart.com	San Diego	CA	92121	858-509-0582	
Tallgrass Restoration LLC 2221 Hammond Dr. *TF:* 877-699-8300 ■ *Web:* www.tallgrassrestoration.com	Schaumburg	IL	60173	847-925-9830	
Tandem Select 113 S College Ave *Web:* www.premieress.com	Fort Collins	CO	80524	970-491-9655	
Tango Consulting Group LLC 31 James Vincent Dr. *TF:* 877-567-6045 ■ *Web:* www.tangoconsulting.com	Clinton	CT	06413	877-567-6045	
TayganPoint Consulting Group Inc 243 N Union St Ste 210 *Web:* www.tayganpoint.com	Lambertville	NJ	08530	609-460-4211	
Tcs of America Enterprises Llc 2 Mcdaniels Dr. *Web:* www.tcsofamerica.com	Brookline	NH	03033	603-249-3367	
Te21 Inc 1184 Clements Ferry Rd Ste G. *TF:* 866-982-8321 ■ *Web:* www.te21.com	Charleston	SC	29492	843-579-2520	
Teachers' Curriculum Institute 3735 Bradview Dr Ste 100 *Web:* teachtci.com	Sacramento	CA	95827	916-366-3686	
Team Work Consulting Inc 22550 Mccauley Rd *Web:* www.teamworkconsulting.com	Shaker Heights	OH	44122	216-360-1790	
Tech Allies Consulting LLC 300 E Business Way Ste 200 *TF:* 866-321-0101 ■ *Web:* www.techalliesconsulting.com	Cincinnati	OH	45241	866-321-0101	
Techblocks Inc 399 Applewood Crescent Ste 400 *Web:* tblocks.com	Vaughan	ON	L4K4J3	416-775-1919	
Techforce Inc 3445 Breckinridge Blvd *TF:* 866-837-3783 ■ *Web:* www.techforce.net	Duluth	GA	30096	678-597-2300	
Technical Assurance Inc 38112 Second St *TF:* 866-953-3147 ■ *Web:* www.technicalassurance.com	Willoughby	OH	44094	440-953-3147	
Technolab International Corp 2020 NE 163 St *TF:* 888-382-2851 ■ *Web:* www.technolabcorp.com	Miami	FL	33162	305-433-2973	
Technology Futures Inc (TFI) 13740 Research Blvd (N Hwy 183) Ste C-1 *TF:* 800-835-3887 ■ *Web:* www.tfi.com	Austin	TX	78750	512-258-8898	258-0087
Technomedia Solutions LLC 4545 36th St. *Web:* www.gotechnomedia.com	Orlando	FL	32811	407-351-0909	
Technossus LLC 17885 Von Karman Ave Ste 410. *Web:* www.technossus.com	Irvine	CA	92614	949-769-3500	
Techorbit Inc 1303 W Walnut Hill Ln Ste 300 *Web:* www.techorbit.com	Irving	TX	75038	214-276-1379	
Techwave Consulting Inc 1 E Uwchlan Ave *Web:* techwavenet.com	Exton	PA	19341	484-872-8707	
TekScape 247 W 30th St *Web:* tekscapeit.com	New York	NY	10001	917-398-1437	
Tel Tec Security Systems Inc 5020 Lisa Marie Ct. *TF:* 800-292-9227 ■ *Web:* www.tel-tec.com	Bakersfield	CA	93313	661-397-5511	
TELCOR Inc 7101 A St *Web:* www.telcor.com	Lincoln	NE	68510	402-489-1207	
Teledyne Controls 1365 Corporate Ctr Curv *Web:* www.teledynecontrols.com	Eagan	MN	55121	651-994-1000	
Telephone Doctor Inc 30 Hollenberg Ct *TF:* 800-882-9911 ■ *Web:* www.telephonedoctor.com	Bridgeton	MO	63044	314-291-1012	
Telesolv Consulting LLC 1210 Florida Ave Ne. *Web:* telesolvconsulting.com	Washington	DC	20002	202-558-5639	
Telnet Inc 7630 Standish Pl. *Web:* www.telnet-inc.com	Rockville	MD	20855	301-840-7110	
TelServ Communications Inc 1011 1st Ave SE. *Web:* solo.telserv.com	Aberdeen	SD	57401	605-229-1050	
Tenzing Consulting LLC 607 E Dr *Web:* tenzingconsulting.com	Sewickley	PA	43617	412-259-7920	
thinkASG 15265 Alton Pkwy Ste 300 *TF:* 800-991-9274 ■ *Web:* www.thinkasg.com	Irvine	CA	92618	800-991-9274	
Thinkwrap Commerce Inc 303 Moodie Dr Ste 200. *Web:* www.thinkwrap.com	Ottawa	ON	K2H9R4	613-751-4441	
Third Sky Inc 2601 Blanding Ave Ste C362 *Web:* www.thirdsky.com	Alameda	CA	94501	415-272-4262	
ThriveOn Inc 210 S 20th St. *TF:* 855-767-2571 ■ *Web:* www.thriveon.co	New Ulm	MN	56073	855-767-2571	
Tiburon Strategic Advisors LLC 1735 Tiburon Blvd *Web:* www.tiburonadvisors.com	Tiburon	CA	94920	415-789-2540	
Tiburon Technologies Inc 176 South St.	Hopkinton	MA	01748	216-520-3100	
Tierra Right of Way Services Ltd 1575 E River Rd Ste 201. *TF:* 800-887-0847 ■ *Web:* www.tierra-row.com	Tucson	AZ	85718	520-319-2106	
Tilson Technology Management 245 Commercial St Ste 203 *Web:* www.tilsontech.com	Portland	ME	04101	207-591-6427	
Todd Herman & Associates PA 620 Green Vly Rd Ste 104. *Web:* www.toddherman.com	Greensboro	NC	27408	336-297-4200	
Tom Hopkins International Inc 465 E Chilton Dr Ste 4 *Web:* www.tomhopkins.com	Chandler	AZ	85255	480-949-0786	
TopLine Strategies 11333 N. Scottsdale Rd Ste 240 , *Web:* toplinestrategies.com	Scottsdale	AZ	85254	480-503-8584	
Total Event Resources 1920 Thoreau Dr N Ste 105 *Web:* www.total-event.com	Schaumburg	IL	60173	847-397-2200	
Totalis Consulting Group 402 Park Dr *Web:* totalis.com	Warner Robins	GA	31088	478-328-0901	
ToxServices LLC 1367 Connecticut Ave Nw Ste 300 *Web:* toxservices.com	Washington	DC	20036	202-429-8787	
Trace Environmental Systems Inc 7 Park Lk Rd Ste 9 *Web:* www.traceenv.com	Sparta	NJ	07871	973-383-3550	
Tradescape Inc 520 S El Camino Real Ste 640. *TF:* 800-697-6068 ■ *Web:* www.tradescape.biz	San Mateo	CA	94402	800-697-6068	
Training Modernization Group Inc 9737 Peppertree Rd *TF:* 866-855-6449 ■ *Web:* www.tmgva.com	Spotsylvania	VA	22553	540-295-9313	
Tri-Basin Natural Resources District 1723 Burlington St. *TF:* 877-995-6688 ■ *Web:* tribasinnrd.org	Holdrege	NE	68949	877-995-6688	
Tri-com Consulting Group LLC, The 333 Industrial Park Rd *Web:* www.tricomgroup.com	Middletown	CT	06457	860-635-9600	
Trilliant Technology Group Inc 1602 Lynnview *Web:* www.trilliant.net	Houston	TX	77055	713-263-9200	
Trincon Group LLC 1683 Old Henderson Rd. *Web:* trincon.com	Columbus	OH	43220	614-442-0590	
Trinity Systems Technologies Inc 5885 Cumming Hwy Ste 108-273 *TF:* 888-828-5655 ■ *Web:* www.trinitysystemstech.com	Sugar Hill	GA	30518	888-828-5655	
Trio Media Group LLC 182 Hilderbrand Dr Ste 100 *Web:* triomediagroup.com	Atlanta	GA	30328	404-255-1970	
Triple-I Corp, The 6330 Lamar Ave Ste 230. *Web:* www.triplei.com	Overland Park	KS	66202	913-563-7200	
Triton Environmental Inc 385 Church St Ste 201. *Web:* www.tritonenvironmental.com	Guilford	CT	06437	203-458-7200	
TriVista Business Group Inc 15 Enterprise Ste 410. *Web:* www.trivista.com	Aliso Viejo	CA	92656	949-218-4830	
TRM Technologies Inc 280 Albert St Ste 1000 10th Fl *Web:* www.trm.ca	Ottawa	ON	K1P5G8	613-722-8843	
True North Strategic Advisors LLC 347 W Berry St Ste 100 *Web:* www.truenorthsa.com	Fort Wayne	IN	46802	260-420-5050	
TrueCloud 2147 E Baseline Rd. *TF:* 866-990-8783 ■ *Web:* www.truecloud.com	Tempe	AZ	85283	866-990-8783	
TruMethods LLC 66 East Main St Ste H *Web:* www.trumethods.com	Moorestown	NJ	08057	856-316-4900	
TSPI Inc 20 Pidgeon Hill Dr Ste 106 *TF:* 877-455-8774 ■ *Web:* www.tspi.net	Sterling	VA	20165	877-455-8774	
Turning Point Inc, The 1835 W State Rt 89A Ste 4 *Web:* www.turningpoint.com	Sedona	AZ	86336	928-203-9711	
Twin Eagle Consulting LLC 7300 S Alton Way Unit 5A *Web:* www.twineagleconsulting.com	Centennial	CO	80112	832-770-4300	
Twin Technologies LLC 6360 French's Hollow Rd *Web:* www.twintechs.com	Altamont	NY	12009	518-391-2663	
U S Energy Services Inc 605 N Hwy 169 Ste 1200 *Web:* www.usenergyservices.com	Plymouth	MN	55441	763-543-4600	
Unicard Systems Inc 5340 Alpha Rd. *Web:* www.worldgiftcard.com	Dallas	TX	75240	972-385-4000	
Unintech Consulting Engineers Inc 2431 E Evans Rd. *Web:* www.unintech.com	San Antonio	TX	78259	210-641-6003	

Company	City	State	Zip	Phone	Fax
Unison Systems Inc 6130 Greenwood Plz Blvd Ste 100 *Web:* www.unisonsystems.com	Greenwood Village	CO	80111	303-623-8800	
Unisys Corp 801 Lakeview Dr Ste 100 *Web:* www.unisys.com	Blue Bell	PA	19422	215-986-4011	
Upgrade It Consulting Services Inc 3030 Royal Blvd S Ste 220 *Web:* www.upgradeitcs.com	Alpharetta	GA	30022	770-345-3173	
Urban Strategies LLC 2341 Ninth St S PO Box 41408 *Web:* www.urbanstrategies.us	Arlington	VA	22204	202-368-3408	
Ursa Institute 390 Fourth St Fl 1 *Web:* www.cus-united.org	San Francisco	CA	94107	415-777-1922	
Us Tank Alliance Inc 7400 Skyline Dr E Ste A *Web:* www.USTankWeb.com	Columbus	OH	43235	614-923-0154	
USA Consulting Inc 701 E Plano Pkwy Ste 300 *Web:* www.usaci.com	Plano	TX	75074	972-673-0333	
USAS Technologies LLC 293 State Rt 18 Ste 242 E Brunswick *Web:* usastechnologies.com	New York City	NJ	08816	646-216-8114	
USC Consulting Group LLC 3000 Bayport Dr Ste 1010 *Web:* www.usccg.com	Tampa	FL	33607	813-636-4004	
Usman Trade 11018 Watson Mill Ct Ste 103 *Web:* usmantrade.com	Sugar Land	TX	77478	281-933-7200	
Utility Sales Assoc Inc 930 E Oak St *Web:* www.utilitysales.net	Lake In The Hills	IL	60156	847-658-8965	
Utilityone Inc 268 W Beaver St Ste 105 *Web:* getutilityone.com	Hallam	PA	17406	717-840-4200	
Utiliworks Consulting LLC 8000 GSRI Ave LBTC Bldg Ste 245 *Web:* www.utiliworks.com	Baton Rouge	LA	70820	225-578-0080	
V 2 It Services Inc 2340 E Trinity Mills Rd Ste 300 *TF:* 877-400-0293 ■ *Web:* www.itservices2.com	Carrollton	TX	75006	877-400-0293	
V t i Valtronics Inc 3463 Double Springs Rd *Web:* www.val-tronics.com	Valley Springs	CA	95252	209-754-0707	
V2Solutions Inc 2340 Dr Walsh Ave *Web:* www.v2solutions.com	Santa Clara	CA	95051	408-550-2340	
VAC-TRON Equipment LLC 27137 S Hwy 33 *Web:* www.vactron.com	Okahumpka	FL	34762	352-728-2222	
VAE Inc 12005 Sunrise Vly Dr Ste 202 *Web:* www.vaeit.com	Reston	VA	20191	703-942-6727	
Vales Consulting Group LLC 125 Wappanocca Ave *Web:* www.valesconsulting.com	Rye	NY	10580	914-967-3200	
Valicom Corp 5940 Seminole Centre Ct Ste 300 *Web:* www.valicomcorp.com	Madison	WI	53711	608-274-3515	
Valor Development LLC 757 N Broadway Ste 400 *Web:* www.valordevelopment.com	Milwaukee	WI	53202	414-220-9370	
Value Consulting LLC 23475 Rock Haven Way Ste 200 *Web:* www.valconusa.com	Sterling	VA	20166	703-723-0100	
VCOMP Solutions 1919 S Highland Ave Ste 200D *TF:* 888-978-2667 ■ *Web:* www.vcompsolutions.com	Lombard	IL	60148	888-978-2667	
Velocite Systems Inc 810 Cromwell Park Dr Ste K *Web:* www.velocitesystems.com	Glen Burnie	MD	21061	443-572-0015	
Venice Consulting Group 501 Milwood Ave *Web:* www.veniceconsulting.com	Venice	CA	90291	310-450-7937	
Vensai Technologies 2450 Atlanta Hwy Ste 1002 *TF:* 866-849-4057 ■ *Web:* www.vensaiinc.com	Cumming	GA	30040	770-888-4804	
Verde Pr & Consulting 1485 Florida Rd Ste 202c *Web:* verdepr.com	Durango	CO	81301	970-259-3555	
Verinon Technology Solutions Ltd 3395 N Arlington Heights Rd *Web:* www.verinon.com	Arlington Heights	IL	60004	847-577-5256	
Verologix LLC 18100 Von Karman Ave *TF:* 800-403-8041 ■ *Web:* www.verologix.com	Irvine	CA	90623	800-403-8041	
Verteks Consulting Inc 2102 SW 20th Pl Ste 602 *Web:* www.verteks.com	Ocala	FL	34471	352-401-0909	
Vertisys Corp 821-B Livingston Ct *Web:* www.vertisys.com	Marietta	GA	30067	770-955-1755	
Vested Group, The 1001 E 15th St Ste 200 *Web:* thevested.com	Plano	TX	75074	972-429-9025	
Veteran Corps of America 220 E State St Ste 2F *Web:* www.veterancorps.com	O'fallon	IL	62269	703-691-8385	
Victor J Rauch Consulting 3410 Mission Ave Unit 3 *Web:* www.vicrauch.com	Carmichael	CA	95608	916-485-1579	
Vintage IT Services 1210 W Fifth St *Web:* www.vintageits.com	Austin	TX	78703	512-481-1117	
Vision One It Consulting Inc 7112 Ofc Park Dr *Web:* www.v1corp.com	West Chester	OH	45069	513-892-0027	
Vision-It Inc 2502 Iron Forge Rd *Web:* www.vitinc.net	Herndon	VA	20171	703-668-0717	
Visitec Marketing Associates Inc 2020 Dean St Unit H *Web:* www.visitec.com	St. Charles	IL	60174	630-762-0300	
Vista Projects Ltd 330-4000 4thÿSt SEÿ Ste B29 *Web:* www.vistaprojects.com	Calgary	AB	T2G2W3	403-255-3455	
ViWo Inc 10801 National blvd 410 *TF:* 888-898-4787 ■ *Web:* www.viwoinc.com	Los Angeles	CA	90064	877-958-5174	
Vode Lighting LLC 1206 E Macarthur St Ste 3 *Web:* vode.com	Sonoma	CA	95476	707-996-9898	
W D Communications 227 E Bergen Pl Ste 6 *Web:* wdcommunications.com	Red Bank	NJ	07701	732-530-2076	
WAC Consulting Inc 367 W Main St *Web:* www.wacinc.com	Northborough	MA	01532	508-393-7731	
Wainhouse Research LLC 34 Duckhill Ter *Web:* www.wainhouse.com	Duxbury	MA	02332	781-934-6165	
Wakensys Corp 505 N Lk Shore Dr Ste 222 *Web:* www.wakensys.com	Chicago	IL	60611	773-754-3230	
WALZ Postal Solutions Inc 27398 Via Industria *Web:* www.walzgroup.com	Temecula	CA	92590	951-491-6800	
Warner Consulting Inc 5106 Berryessa St *Web:* warner-consulting.com	Oceanside	CA	92056	760-806-7722	
Warrior Consultant Group 3463 Daisy Ct *Web:* warriorgroup.com	Brunswick	OH	44212	330-225-5120	
Waterfall Mobile Inc 1132 Howard St *Web:* www.waterfallmobile.com	San Francisco	CA	94103	415-487-1200	
Watershed Co, The 750 Sixth St S *Web:* www.watershedco.com	Kirkland	WA	98033	425-822-5242	
Watson Institute, The 301 Campmeeting Rd *Web:* www.thewatsoninstitute.org	Sewickley	PA	15143	412-741-1958	
Wcm Group Inc, The 110 S Bender Ave *Web:* wcmgroup.com	Humble	TX	77338	281-446-7070	
WebeDoctor 471 W Lambert Rd Ste 102 *Web:* webedoctor.com	Brea	CA	92821	714-990-3999	
Welch Global Consulting 10084 Oak Knoll Ter *Web:* www.welchgc.com	Colorado Springs	CO	80920	970-292-6600	
West Side Telecommunications 1449 Fairmont Rd *Web:* westsidetelecommunications.net	Morgantown	WV	26501	304-983-2211	
Western Reserve Partners LLC 200 Public Sq Ste 3750 *Web:* wesrespartners.com	Cleveland	OH	44114	216-589-0900	
Whetstone Group Llc 3934 Murphy Canyon Rd Ste B200 *Web:* www.whetstonegroup.com	San Diego	CA	92123	858-627-0726	
Whitney, Bradley & Brown Inc 11790 Sunrise Vly Dr *Web:* www.wbbinc.com	Reston	VA	20191	703-448-6081	
Wi-fi Guys LLC 7265 Hwy 1 *Web:* www.wi-figuys.com	Finland	MN	55603	218-353-7798	
William Ives Consulting Inc 320 S Tryon St Ste 213 *Web:* www.wicusa.com	Charlotte	NC	28202	704-376-5600	
Wilogic Inc 15896 Manufacture Ln *Web:* www.wilogic.com	Huntington Beach	CA	92649	714-230-8487	
Wilson Consulting Group 100 Old Schoolhouse Rd *Web:* wcg-pc.com	Mechanicsburg	PA	17055	717-591-3070	
Windfall Assoc 981 Chestnut St *Web:* www.windfall-assoc.com	Newton Upper Falls	MA	02464	617-969-1790	969-1777
WingSwept 800 Benson Rd *Web:* www.wingswept.com	Garner	NC	27529	919-779-0954	
Wipro Inc 1300 Crittenden Ln Ste 200 *Web:* www.wipro.com	Mountain View	CA	94043	650-316-3555	
Wirehead Security LLC The Atrium Bldg 2501 Blue Ridge Rd Ste 250 *Web:* www.wireheadsecurity.com	Raleigh	NC	27607	919-863-4373	
Wizard Computer Services Inc 421 Page St *Web:* www.wizardcpu.com	Stoughton	MA	02072	781-341-2222	
Wlh Consulting Inc 1417 Capri Ln *Web:* www.wlhconsulting.com	Weston	FL	33326	954-385-0770	
WOG LLC 23 S Harrison St *Web:* www.whiteoak-group.com	Easton	MD	21601	410-690-3511	
Wolf Consulting Inc 3875 Franklin Towne Court Ste 110 *Web:* www.wolfconsulting.com	Murrysville	PA	15668	724-325-2900	
Woodbury Technologies Inc 1725 East 1450 South *TF:* 800-408-8857 ■ *Web:* www.woodburytech.com	Clearfield	UT	84015	800-408-8857	
Wostmann & Associates Inc 105 S Seward St Ste 301 *Web:* www.wostmann.com	Juneau	AK	99801	907-586-6167	
Writers' Express, The 271 Cambridge St Ste 303 *Web:* www.amplify.com	Cambridge	MA	02141	617-844-1003	
Xantrion Inc 651 20th St *Web:* www.xantrion.com	Oakland	CA	94612	510-272-4701	
Xp3 Corp 525 Carswell Ave Unit L *Web:* xp3hornet.com	Holly Hill	FL	32117	330-562-8490	
xRM3 Inc 2604-b El Camino Real Ste 251 *Web:* xrmcubed.com	Carlsbad	CA	92008	760-585-4250	
Y Tech Solutions Inc 5706 Benjamin Ctr Dr Ste 116 *Web:* www.y-tech.com	Tampa	FL	33634	813-880-0800	
YASH Technologies Inc 605-17th Ave *Web:* www.yash.com	East Moline	IL	61244	309-755-0433	
Yellow Pencil Inc 503 10158 - 103 St *Web:* yellowpencil.com	Edmonton	AB	T5J0X6	780-423-5917	
YourAmigo Inc 4708 Del Valle Pkwy *Web:* www.youramigo.com	Pleasanton	CA	94566	510-813-1355	
Yoush Consulting Inc 7481 Woodbine Ave Ste 204 *Web:* www.youshconsulting.com	Markham	ON	L3R2W1	905-307-6263	
Youth Frontiers Inc 6009 Excelsior Blvd *TF:* 888-992-0222 ■ *Web:* www.youthfrontiers.org	Minneapolis	MN	55416	952-922-0222	
Yuxi Pacific Group LLC 517 Britton Dr *Web:* www.yuxipacific.com	King Of Prussia	PA	19406	610-616-3966	
Z-tech Associates 181 Bedford St Ste 2 *Web:* www.ztechnet.com	Lexington	MA	02420	781-863-8884	

Phone Fax

ZapThink LLC 108 Woodlawn Rd Ste 2A .... Baltimore VA 21210 781-207-0203
Web: www.zapthink.com

Zarinkelk Engineering Services Inc
3033 Chimney Rock Rd .... Houston TX 77056 832-242-2426
Web: www.zarinkelk.com

Zbeta Consulting Inc 851 Irwin St Ste 305 .... San Rafael CA 94901 415-259-0422
Web: www.zbetaconsulting.com

zedSuite 210 Water St Ste 400 .... St. John's NL A1C1A9 709-722-7213
TF: 877-722-1177 ■ *Web:* www.zedsuite.com

Zencos Consulting LLC
1400 Crescent Green Ste 140 .... Cary NC 27518 919-459-4600
Web: www.zencos.com

Zestron Corp 11285 Assett Loop .... Manassas VA 20109 703-393-9880
Web: www.zestron.com

197 CONSUMER INFORMATION RESOURCES - GOVERNMENT

Phone Fax

Afterschool.gov 370 L'Enfant Promenade SW .... Washington DC 20447 202-401-9215 205-9688
Web: www.acf.hhs.gov

Alzheimer's Disease Education & Referral Ctr
PO Box 8250 .... Silver Spring MD 20907 301-495-1080 495-3334
TF: 800-438-4380 ■ *Web:* www.nia.nih.gov/alzheimers

Centers for Disease Control & Prevention (CDC)
1600 Clifton Rd NE .... Atlanta GA 30333 404-639-7000 639-7111
Web: www.cdc.gov

National Center for Immunization & Respiratory Diseases
1600 Clifton Rd NE MS E-05 .... Atlanta GA 30333 800-232-4636
TF: 800-232-4636 ■ *Web:* www.cdc.gov/vaccines

Travelers Health 1600 Clifton Rd NE .... Atlanta GA 30333 800-232-4636 232-3299*
**Fax Area Code:* 888 ■ *TF:* 800-232-4636 ■ *Web:* wwwnc.cdc.gov/travel

Consumer Product Safety Commission (CPSC)
4340 E W Hwy Ste 502 .... Bethesda MD 20814 301-504-7923 504-0051
TF: 800-638-2772 ■ *Web:* www.cpsc.gov

Corp for National & Community Service
AmeriCorps USA 1201 New York Ave NW .... Washington DC 20525 202-606-5000
TF: 800-833-3722 ■ *Web:* www.nationalservice.gov

Learn & Serve America
1201 New York Ave NW .... Washington DC 20525 202-606-5000
TF: 800-833-3722 ■ *Web:* www.nationalservice.gov

Education Resource Information Ctr (ERIC)
c/o CSC 655 15th St NW Ste 500 .... Washington DC 20005 800-538-3742
TF: 800-538-3742 ■ *Web:* www.usa.gov

Eldercare Locator
1730 Rhode Island Ave NW Ste 1200 .... Washington DC 20036 800-677-1116 872-0057*
**Fax Area Code:* 202 ■ *TF:* 800-677-1116 ■ *Web:* www.eldercare.gov

Energy Efficiency & Renewable Energy Information Ctr
1000 Independence Ave SW .... Washington DC 20585 202-586-4849 236-2023*
**Fax Area Code:* 360 ■ *TF:* 877-337-3463 ■ *Web:* energy.gov

FedWorld.gov
National Technical Information Service
5285 Port Royal Rd .... Alexandria VA 22312 703-605-6000
TF: 800-553-6847 ■ *Web:* fedworld.ntis.gov

Foster Grandparent Program c/o Senior Corps
1201 New York Ave NW .... Washington DC 20525 202-606-5000
TF: 800-424-8867 ■ *Web:* www.nationalservice.gov

Grants.gov
Dept of Health & Human Services
200 Independence Ave SW HHH Bldg .... Washington DC 20201 800-518-4726
TF: 800-518-4726 ■ *Web:* www.grants.gov

Homeland Security Information Ctr
National Technical Information Service
5301 Shawnee Rd .... Alexandria VA 22312 703-605-6000 487-4639
Web: www.ntis.gov

National Clearinghouse for Alcohol & Drug Information
11426 Rockville Pk PO Box 2345 .... Rockville MD 20847 800-729-6686
TF: 800-729-6686 ■ *Web:* samhsa.gov

National Institute for Literacy (NIFL)
1775 'I' St NW Ste 730 .... Washington DC 20006 202-233-2025 233-2050
TF: 800-228-8813 ■ *Web:* www.lincs.ed.gov

National Institutes of Health (NIH)
9000 Rockville Pike .... Bethesda MD 20892 301-496-4000
Web: www.nih.gov

National Mental Health Information Ctr
PO Box 42557 .... Washington DC 20015 800-487-4889 747-5470*
**Fax Area Code:* 240 ■ *TF:* 800-487-4889 ■ *Web:* www.samhsa.gov

National Women's Health Information Ctr
200 Independence Ave S.W .... Washington DC 20201 800-994-9662
TF: 800-994-9662 ■ *Web:* www.womenshealth.gov

President's Council on Physical Fitness Sports & Nutrition
1101 Wootton Pkwy Ste 560 .... Rockville MD 20852 240-276-9567 276-9860
Web: www.fitness.gov

Project Safe Neighborhoods
Office of Justice Programs
810 Seventh St NW .... Washington DC 20531 202-616-6500 305-1367
TF: 888-744-6513 ■ *Web:* www.bja.gov

PubMed
US National Library of Medicine
8600 Rockville Pike .... Bethesda MD 20894 888-346-3656 402-1384*
**Fax Area Code:* 301 ■ *TF:* 888-346-3656 ■ *Web:* www.ncbi.nlm.nih.gov

Recreation.gov 1849 C St NW .... Washington DC 20240 202-208-4743
TF: 877-444-6777 ■ *Web:* www.recreation.gov

Retired & Senior Volunteer Program (RSVP)
1201 New York Ave NW .... Washington DC 20525 202-606-5000
TF: 800-833-3722 ■ *Web:* www.nationalservice.gov

Senior Corps 1201 New York Ave NW .... Washington DC 20525 202-606-5000
TF: 800-833-3722 ■ *Web:* www.nationalservice.gov

US Dept of Labor Women's Bureau
200 Constitution Ave NW Rm S-3002 .... Washington DC 20210 202-693-6710 693-6710
TF: 800-827-5335 ■ *Web:* www.dol.gov/wb

Phone Fax

US General Services Administration
1800 F St NW .... Washington DC 20405 800-488-3111
TF: 800-488-3111 ■ *Web:* www.usa.gov

USA Freedom Corps 1201 New York Ave NW .... Washington DC 20005 202-606-5000
TF: 800-833-3722 ■ *Web:* www.nationalservice.gov

USDA Ctr for Nutrition Policy & Promotion
3101 Pk Ctr Dr .... Alexandria VA 22302 703-305-7600 305-3300
Web: www.fns.usda.gov

198 CONTAINERS - METAL (BARRELS, DRUMS, KEGS)

Phone Fax

Actron Steel Inc 2866 Cass Rd .... Traverse City MI 49685 231-947-3981

American Metal Crafters LLC 695 High St .... Middletown CT 06457 860-343-1960
Web: www.americanmetalcraftersllc.com

Berenfield Containers Inc
4555 Lk Forest Dr Ste 205 .... Blue Ash OH 45242 513-618-3780 618-3781
Web: www.berenfield.com

C&C Fabrication Company Inc
30 Fabrication Dr .... Lacey's Spring AL 35754 256-881-7300
TF: 888-485-5130 ■ *Web:* www.ccfab.com

Cendrex Inc 11303 26th Ave .... Montreal QC H1E6N6 514-493-1489
Web: www.cendrex.com

Champion Co 400 Harrison St .... Springfield OH 45505 937-875-9235 324-2397
Web: www.championspd.com

Champion Container Corp
1455 N Michael Dr PO Box 90 .... Wood Dale IL 60191 732-636-6700 855-8663
Web: www.championcontainer.com

Chicago Steel Container Corp
1846 S Kilbourn Ave .... Chicago IL 60623 773-277-2244 277-1585
Web: chicagosteelcontainer.com

Columbia Metal Spinning Company Inc
4351 N Normandy Ave .... Chicago IL 60634 773-685-2800
Web: www.cmspinning.com

Conco Inc 4000 Oaklawn Dr .... Louisville KY 40219 502-969-1333 962-2190
Web: www.concocontainers.com

Container Research Corp (CRC)
1 Hollow Hill Rd .... Glen Riddle PA 19037 610-459-2160
TF: 844-220-9574 ■ *Web:* www.crc-flex.com

Csi Industries Inc 6910 W Ridge Rd .... Fairview PA 16415 814-474-9353 474-5797
TF: 800-937-9033 ■ *Web:* www.flo-bin.com

DeWys Manufacturing Inc 15300 Eigth Ave .... Marne MI 49435 616-677-5281
Web: www.dewysmfg.com

Ductmate Industries Inc 210 Fifth St .... Charleroi PA 15022 724-258-0500
Web: www.ductmate.com

Erie Engineered Products Inc
3949 Walden Ave .... Lancaster NY 14086 716-206-0204
Web: www.containers-cases.com

Fabricated Metals LLC 6300 Kenjoy Dr .... Louisville KY 40214 502-363-2625
Web: www.fabricatedmetals.com

Fiba Technologies Inc
1535 Grafton Rd PO Box 360 .... Millbury MA 01527 508-887-7100 754-2254
Web: www.fibatech.com

Gardner Manufacturing Inc 1201 W Lake St .... Horicon WI 53032 920-485-4303
Web: www.gardnermfg.com

General Steel Drum LLC 4500 S Blvd .... Charlotte NC 28209 704-525-7160
Web: www.generalsteeldrum.com

Geometrica Inc 12300 Dundee Ct Ste 200 .... Cypress TX 77429 832-220-1200 482-0879
Web: www.geometrica.com

Greentree Toyota Scion 87 Federal Rd .... Danbury CT 06811 203-730-4040
Web: www.greentree.com

Greif Inc 425 Winter Rd .... Delaware OH 43015 740-549-6000 657-6592
NYSE: GEF ■ *TF:* 877-781-9797 ■ *Web:* www.greif.com

Harper Motors Inc 200 Hwy 531 .... Minden LA 71055 318-377-0395
TF: 800-259-0395 ■ *Web:* www.harperminden.com

Highlands Diversified Services Inc
250 Westinghouse Dr .... London KY 40741 606-878-1856
Web: www.hds-usa.com

Imperial Industries Inc
505 Industrial Pk Ave .... Rothschild WI 54474 715-359-0200 355-5349
TF: 800-558-2945 ■ *Web:* www.imperialind.com

Impulse Manufacturing Inc
55 Impulse Industrial Dr .... Dawsonville GA 30534 706-216-1700
Web: www.impulsemfg.com

Industrial Container Services
7152 First Ave S .... Seattle WA 98108 206-763-2345
TF: 800-273-3786 ■ *Web:* www.iconserv.com

Innovative Fluid Handling Systems
3300 E Rock Falls Rd .... Rock Falls IL 61071 815-626-1018 626-1438
TF: 800-435-7003 ■ *Web:* www.ifhgroup.com

Justrite Manufacturing Co
2454 E Dempster St Ste 300 .... Des Plaines IL 60016 847-298-9250 298-9261
TF: 800-798-9250 ■ *Web:* www.justritemfg.com

Klune Industries Inc
7323 Coldwater Canyon Ave .... North Hollywood CA 91605 818-503-8100
Web: www.klunev.com

Lebus International Inc 215 Industrial Dr .... Longview TX 75602 903-758-5521 757-7782
Web: www.lebus-intl.com

McKey Perforating Company Inc
3033 S 166th St .... New Berlin WI 53151 262-786-2700
Web: www.mckeyperforatedmetal.com

Meyer Steel Drum Inc 3201 S Millard Ave .... Chicago IL 60623 773-376-8376 376-7060
Web: www.meyersteeldrum.com

Mi-T-M Corp 8650 Enterprise Dr .... Peosta IA 52068 563-556-7484
Web: www.mitm.com

Mid-America Steel Drum Co Inc
8570 S Chicago Rd .... Oak Creek WI 53154 414-762-1114 762-1623
Web: www.midamericasteeldrum.com

Midwest Products & Engineering Inc
10597 W Glenbrook Ct .... Milwaukee WI 53224 414-355-0310
Web: www.mpe-inc.com

Company	City	State	Zip	Phone	Fax
Modern Aire Manufacturing Corp 7319 Lankershim Blvd *TF:* 866-731-2007 ■ *Web:* www.modernaire.com	North Hollywood	CA	91605	818-765-9870	
Myers Container Corp 8435 NE Killingsworth *TF:* 800-406-9377 ■ *Web:* www.myerscontainer.com	Portland	OR	97220	503-501-5830	501-5831
North Coast Container Corp 8806 Crane Ave *Web:* www.ncc-corp.com	Cleveland	OH	44105	216-441-6214	441-6239
Northwest Chevrolet 2516 Duss Ave *Web:* www.wrightcars.com	Ambridge	PA	15003	724-266-3380	
Norton Packaging Inc 20670 Cosair Blvd *Web:* www.nortonpackaging.com	Hayward	CA	94545	510-786-3445	782-5329
Packaging Specialties Inc 300 Lake Rd *TF:* 800-344-9271 ■ *Web:* www.packspec.com	Medina	OH	44256	330-723-6000	725-8180
PCI Industries Inc 5101 Blue Mound Rd *Web:* www.pci-industries.com	Fort Worth	TX	76106	817-509-2300	
Penn Metal Fabricators Inc 2103 New Germany Rd *Web:* www.pennmetalfab.com	Ebensburg	PA	15931	814-472-6000	
Quadra Tech Inc 864 E Jenkins Ave *Web:* www.quadra-techinc.com	Columbus	OH	43207	614-443-0630	
R&M Manufacturing Company LLC 200 Centennial Dr *Web:* www.rmmco.com	Buffalo	MN	55313	763-574-9225	
Rice Motor Company LLC 2630 Battleground Ave *Web:* ricetoyota.com	Greensboro	NC	27408	336-288-1190	
Self Industries Inc 3491 Mary Taylor Rd *Web:* selfindustries.com	Birmingham	AL	35235	205-655-3284	655-3288
Skolnik Industries Inc 4900 S Kilbourn Ave *TF:* 800-441-8780 ■ *Web:* www.skolnik.com	Chicago	IL	60632	773-735-0700	
Smith Industries Inc 2781 Gunter Park Dr E *Web:* www.jrsmith.com	Montgomery	AL	36109	334-277-8520	
Stackbin Corp 29 Powderhill Rd *TF Sales:* 800-333-1603 ■ *Web:* www.stackbin.com	Lincoln	RI	02865	401-333-1600	333-1952
Stainless Metals Inc 60-01 31 Ave *Web:* www.stainlessmetals.com	Woodside	NY	11377	718-784-1454	
Textainer Equipment Management Ltd 650 California St Fl 16 *Web:* www.textainer.com	San Francisco	CA	94108	415-434-0551	434-0599
United Skys 702 Magna Dr *Web:* unitedskys.com	Round Lake	IL	60073	847-546-7776	
USA Container Company Inc 1776 S Second St *TF:* 888-752-7722 ■ *Web:* www.usacontainer.com	Piscataway	NJ	08854	732-752-7722	
Von Duprin Inc 2720 Tobey Dr *TF:* 800-999-0408 ■ *Web:* us.allegion.com	Indianapolis	IN	46219	800-999-0408	
Westmor Industries LLC 3 Development Dr *Web:* westmor-ind.com	Morris	MN	56267	320-589-2100	
Worthington Dealership Group 5548 Paseo Del Norte *Web:* www.calworthington.com	Carlsbad	CA	92008	760-431-1222	
Wrobel Engineering Company Inc 154 Bodwell St *Web:* www.wrobeleng.com	Avon	MA	02322	508-586-8338	
Young Bros Stamp Works Inc 1415 Howard Ave *Web:* mw-radio.com	Muscatine	IA	52761	563-263-3575	

199 CONTAINERS - PLASTICS (DRUMS, CANS, CRATES, BOXES)

Company	City	State	Zip	Phone	Fax
Akro-Mils Inc 1293 S Main St **Fax Area Code:* 330 ■ *TF:* 800-253-2467 ■ *Web:* www.akro-mils.com	Akron	OH	44301	800-253-2467	761-6348*
Beden-Baugh Products Inc 105 Lisbon Rd *TF:* 866-598-5794 ■ *Web:* www.naclsolutions.com	Laurens	SC	29360	864-682-3136	
Belco Mfg Company Inc 2303 Taylors Vly Rd *TF:* 800-251-8265 ■ *Web:* www.belco-mfg.com	Belton	TX	76513	254-933-9000	939-2644
Berry Plastics Corp PO Box 959 *Web:* www.berryplastics.com	Evansville	IN	47706	812-424-2904	
Berry Plastics Corp 101 Oakley St *TF:* 877-662-3779 ■ *Web:* www.berryplastics.com	Evansville	IN	47710	812-424-2904	424-0128
Brentwood Industries Inc 500 Spring Ridge Dr *Web:* www.brentwoodindustries.com	Reading	PA	19610	610-374-5109	
Buckhorn Inc 55 W Techne Ctr Dr *TF:* 800-543-4454 ■ *Web:* www.buckhorninc.com	Milford	OH	45150	513-831-4402	831-5474
Case Design Corp 333 School Ln *TF:* 800-847-4176 ■ *Web:* www.casedesigncorp.com	Telford	PA	18969	215-703-0130	703-0139
Champion Container Corp 1455 N Michael Dr PO Box 90 *Web:* www.championcontainer.com	Wood Dale	IL	60191	732-636-6700	855-8663
Chem-Tainer Industries Inc 361 Neptune Ave *TF:* 800-275-2436 ■ *Web:* www.chemtainer.com	West Babylon	NY	11704	631-661-8300	661-8209
Comar Inc 1 Comar Pl *TF:* 800-962-6627 ■ *Web:* www.comar.com	Buena	NJ	08310	856-692-6100	692-9251
Custom-Pak Inc 1131 Roosevelt St *Web:* www.custom-pak.com	Clinton	IA	52732	563-242-1801	244-5362
ECS Composites Inc 3560 Rogue River Hwy *Web:* www.ecscase.com	Grants Pass	OR	97527	541-476-8871	474-2479
Fibrenetics Inc 2 Cutters Dock Rd *Web:* www.fibglass.com	Woodbridge	NJ	07095	732-636-5670	636-6624
Fort Recovery Industries Inc 2440 Ohio 49 *Web:* www.fortrecoveryindustries.com	Fort Recovery	OH	45846	419-375-4121	375-4194
Gatekeeper Systems Inc 8 Studebaker *TF:* 888-808-9433 ■ *Web:* www.gatekeepersystems.com	Irvine	CA	92618	949-453-1940	453-8148
Handley Industries Inc 2101 Brooklyn Rd *TF:* 800-870-5088 ■ *Web:* www.handleyind.com	Jackson	MI	49203	517-787-8821	787-3946
Hedwin Corp 1600 Roland Heights Ave **Fax:* Cust Svc ■ *TF:* 800-638-1012 ■ *Web:* www.hedwin.com	Baltimore	MD	21211	410-467-8209	889-5189*
HGI Skydyne 100 River Rd *TF:* 800-428-2273 ■ *Web:* www.skydyne.com	Port Jervis	NY	12771	800-428-2273	
Iroquois Products of Chicago 2220 W 56th St *TF:* 800-453-3355 ■ *Web:* www.iroquoisproducts.com	Chicago	IL	60636	800-453-3355	
Jewel Case Corp 110 Dupont Dr *TF:* 800-441-4447 ■ *Web:* www.jewelcase.com	Providence	RI	02907	401-943-1400	943-1426
McConkey Co 1615 Puyallup St PO Box 1690 *TF:* 800-426-8124 ■ *Web:* www.mcconkeyco.com	Sumner	WA	98390	253-863-8111	863-5833
Menasha Corp 1645 Bergstrom Rd *TF:* 800-558-5073 ■ *Web:* www.menasha.com	Neenah	WI	54956	920-751-1000	751-1236
Molded Fiber Glass Tray Co 6175 US Hwy 6 *TF Sales:* 800-458-6050 ■ *Web:* www.mfgtray.com	Linesville	PA	16424	814-683-4500	683-4504
Myers Industries Inc 1293 S Main St *NYSE: MYE* ■ **Fax:* Acctg ■ *Web:* www.myersindustries.com	Akron	OH	44301	330-253-5592	761-6156*
ORBIS Corp 1055 Corporate Ctr Dr *TF:* 800-999-8683 ■ *Web:* www.orbiscorporation.com	Oconomowoc	WI	53066	262-560-5000	560-5841
Owens-Illinois Inc 1 Michael Owens Way *NYSE: OI* ■ *Web:* www.o-i.com	Perrysburg	OH	43551	567-336-5000	
Paragon Mfg Company Inc 2001 N 15th Ave *Web:* www.paragonmanufacturing.com	Melrose Park	IL	60160	708-345-1717	345-1721
Pelican Products Inc 147 N Main St *TF:* 800-542-7344 ■ *Web:* www.pelican.com	South Deerfield	MA	01373	413-665-2163	665-4801
Plano Molding Co 431 E S St *TF:* 800-226-9868 ■ *Web:* www.planomolding.com	Plano	IL	60545	630-552-3111	
Plas-Tanks Industries Inc 39 Standen Dr *TF:* 800-247-6709 ■ *Web:* www.plastanks.com	Hamilton	OH	45015	513-942-3800	942-3993
Plastic Enterprises Company Inc 401 SE Thomson Dr *Web:* ipl-plastics.com/afficher.aspx?section=313&langue=en	Lees Summit	MO	64082	816-246-8200	246-8119
Plastic Forming Company Inc 20 S Bradley Rd *TF:* 800-732-2060 ■ *Web:* www.pfccases.com	Woodbridge	CT	06525	203-397-1338	389-0420
Plastican Inc 101 Lillian Dr PO Box 868 *Web:* www.bwaycorp.com	Macon	GA	31217	978-537-4911	537-6376
Plastics Research Corp 1400 S Campus Ave *Web:* www.prccal.com	Ontario	CA	91761	909-391-2006	391-2205
Rehrig Pacific Co 4010 E 26th St *TF:* 800-421-6244 ■ *Web:* www.rehrigpacific.com	Los Angeles	CA	90023	323-262-5145	269-8506
River Bend Industries 2421 16th Ave S *TF:* 800-365-3070 ■ *Web:* www.riverbendind.com	Moorhead	MN	56560	218-236-1818	
Rocket Box Inc 125 E 144th St *TF:* 800-762-5521 ■ *Web:* www.rocketbox.com	Bronx	NY	10451	718-292-5370	
Rotonics Manufacturing Inc 6770 Brighton Blvd *Web:* www.snyderplasticsolutions.com	Commerce	CO	80022	303-227-9300	
RPM Industries Inc 26 Aurelius Ave *TF:* 800-669-3676 ■ *Web:* www.rpmindustriesinc.com	Auburn	NY	13021	315-255-1105	252-1167
Schaefer Systems International Inc 10021 Westlake Dr *TF:* 800-876-6000 ■ *Web:* ssi-schaefer.us	Charlotte	NC	28241	704-944-4500	588-1862
Snyder Industries Inc 4700 Fremont St *Web:* www.snydernet.com	Lincoln	NE	68504	402-467-5221	465-1220
Specialty Plastic Fabricators Inc 9658 196th St *TF:* 800-747-9509 ■ *Web:* www.spfinc.com	Mokena	IL	60448	708-479-5501	479-5598
Stack-On Products Co 1360 N Old Rand Rd *TF:* 800-323-9601 ■ *Web:* www.stack-on.com	Wauconda	IL	60084	847-526-1611	526-6599
Toter Inc PO Box 5338 *TF:* 800-424-0422 ■ *Web:* www.toter.com	Statesville	NC	28677	704-872-8171	878-0734
Tulip Corp 714 E Keefe Ave *Web:* www.tulipcorp.com	Milwaukee	WI	53212	414-963-3120	
Tulip Corp 3125 Highland Ave *Web:* www.tulipcorp.com	Niagara Falls	NY	14305	716-282-1261	285-6075
Unifuse LLC 2092 New York 9G *Web:* www.unifuse.com	Staatsburg	NY	12580	845-889-4000	889-4002
US Plastic Corp 1390 Newbrecht Rd *TF:* 800-537-9724 ■ *Web:* www.usplastic.com	Lima	OH	45801	419-228-2242	228-5034
Xerxes Corp 7901 Xerxes Ave S *Web:* www.xerxes.com	Minneapolis	MN	55431	952-887-1890	887-1870

200 CONTAINERS - WOOD

See Also Pallets & Skids p. 2866

Company	City	State	Zip	Phone	Fax
Abbot & Abbot Box Corp 37-11 Tenth St **Fax Area Code:* 718 ■ *TF:* 888-525-7186 ■ *Web:* www.abbotbox.com	Long Island	NY	11101	888-525-7186	392-8439*
Associated Pallets Inc 71 Premium Dr *Web:* www.associatedpallet.com	South Carrollton	KY	42374	270-754-4087	
Bonsai Artransport Inc 509 Mccormick Dr Ste O *Web:* www.bonsai-finearts.com	Glen Burnie	MD	21061	410-768-2787	
Buckeye Diamond Logistics Inc 15 Sprague Rd *Web:* www.buckeyediamond.com	South Charleston	OH	45368	937-462-8361	
Case Crating & Packing 3340A Greens Rd Ste 900 *Web:* www.casecratingandpacking.com	Houston	TX	77032	713-862-7283	
Commercial Lumber & Pallet Co 135 Long Ln *TF:* 800-252-4968 ■ *Web:* www.clcpallets.com	City Of Industry	CA	91746	800-252-4968	
Demptos Napa Cooperage 1050 Soscol Ferry Rd *Web:* www.demptos.fr	Napa	CA	94558	707-257-2628	257-1622
Dove Manufacturing Plant 1 2525 N Sixth St *TF:* 866-444-3272 ■ *Web:* knoxcountyarccom	Vincennes	IN	47591	812-886-4312	
Elberta Crate & Box Co 606 Dothan Hwy *Web:* www.elberta.net	Bainbridge	GA	39818	229-246-2266	246-0387
Franklin Crates Inc 311 NE Bay sixth Ave	Micanopy	FL	32667	352-466-3141	466-0708

Phone Fax

Greif Inc 425 Winter Rd Delaware OH 43015 740-549-6000 657-6592
NYSE: GEF ■ *TF:* 877-781-9797 ■ *Web:* www.greif.com

Independent Stave Company Inc
1078 S Jefferson PO Box 104 Lebanon MO 65536 417-588-4151 588-3344
Web: independentstavecompany.com

Johnston's Trading Inc 11 N Pioneer Ave Woodland CA 95776 530-661-6152
Web: johnstontrading.com

Liberty Bell Equipment Corp
3201 S 76th St Philadelphia PA 19153 215-492-6700
Web: www.medcotool.com

Maine Bucket Co 21 Fireslate Pl Lewiston ME 04240 207-784-6700
TF: 800-231-7072 ■ *Web:* mainebucket.com

Mele & Co 2007 Beechgrove Pl Utica NY 13501 315-733-4600 733-3183
TF: 800-635-6353 ■ *Web:* www.melejewelrybox.com

Monte Package Company Inc
3752 Riverside Rd Riverside MI 49084 269-849-1722 849-0185
TF: 800-653-2807 ■ *Web:* www.montepkg.com

Northwest Pallet Supply Co 3648 Morreim Dr Belvidere IL 61008 815-544-6001
Web: www.northwestpallet.com

Pallet Factory Inc, The 3740 Arnold Rd Memphis TN 38118 901-795-8300
Web: www.thepalletfactory.com

Pallet Services Inc
12926 Farm to Market Rd Mount Vernon WA 98273 800-769-2245 627-5119*
**Fax Area Code:* 253 ■ *TF:* 800-769-2245 ■ *Web:* www.palletservices.com

Pomona Box Co 301 W Imperial Hwy PO Box 536 La Habra CA 90631 714-871-0932
Web: www.pomonabox.com

Southwest Forest Products Inc
2828 S 35th Ave Ste 720 Phoenix AZ 85009 602-278-3493
Web: www.southwestforestproducts.com

Stearnswood Inc 320 Third Ave NW Hutchinson MN 55350 320-587-2137 587-7646
Web: www.stearnswood.com

Texas Basket Co 100 Myrtle Dr Jacksonville TX 75766 903-586-8014 586-0988
TF: 800-657-2200 ■ *Web:* www.texasbasket.com

TKV Containers Inc 4582 E Harvey Ave Fresno CA 93702 559-251-5551

Wisconsin Box Company Inc 929 Townline Rd Wausau WI 54402 715-842-2248 842-2240
TF: 800-876-6658 ■ *Web:* www.wisconsinbox.com

201 CONTROLS - INDUSTRIAL PROCESS

Phone Fax

3D Instruments LP 2900 E White Star Ave Anaheim CA 92806 714-399-9200
Web: www.3dinstruments.com

3PS Inc 1300 Arrow Point Dr Cedar Park TX 78613 512-610-5200
Web: www.3psinc.com

ADA-ES Inc
9135 S Ridgeline Blvd Ste 200 Highlands Ranch CO 80129 303-734-1727 734-0330
NASDAQ: ADES ■ *TF:* 888-822-8617 ■ *Web:* www.adaes.com

ADS Environmental Services
4940 Research Dr Huntsville AL 35805 256-430-3366 430-6633
TF: 800-633-7246 ■ *Web:* www.adsenv.com

Advanced Systems Integrators
45 Craig Dr Apt 4S West Springfield MA 01108 413-230-5010
Web: www.asiopen.com

AeroControlex Group 313 Gillett St Painesville OH 44077 440-352-6182 354-2912
Web: www.aerocontrolex.com

Air Logic Power Systems LLC
1745 S 38th St Ste 100 Milwaukee WI 53215 414-671-3332
Web: www.alpsleak.com

ALL-TEST Pro LLC 123 Spencer Plain Rd Old Saybrook CT 06475 860-399-4222
TF: 800-952-8776 ■ *Web:* www.alltestpro.com

Alpha Technologies Services LLC
3030 Gilchrist Rd Akron OH 44305 330-745-1641 848-7326
TF: 800-356-9886 ■ *Web:* www.alpha-technologies.com

Altech Environment USA Corp 2623 Kaneville Ct Geneva IL 60134 630-262-4400
Web: www.altechusa.com

AMETEK Automation & Process Technologies
1080 N Crooks Clawson MI 48017 248-435-0700 435-8120
TF: 800-635-0289 ■ *Web:* www.ametekapt.com

AMETEK Power Instruments 50 Fordham Rd Wilmington MA 01887 978-988-4903 988-4944*
**Fax:* Cust Svc ■ *Web:* www.ametekpower.com

AMETEK Process & Analytical Instruments THERMOX Div
150 Freeport Rd Pittsburgh PA 15238 412-828-9040 826-0399
Web: www.ametekpi.com

Amot Controls Corp 8824 Fallbrook Dr Houston TX 77064 281-940-1800 559-9419*
**Fax Area Code:* 713 ■ *Web:* www.amotusa.com

Applied Microstructures Inc 2381 Bering Dr San Jose CA 95131 408-907-2885
TF: 877-683-2678 ■ *Web:* www.appliedmst.com

Arcet Equipment Company Inc
1700 Chamberlayne Ave Richmond VA 23222 800-388-0302
TF: 800-388-0302 ■ *Web:* arc3gases.com

ARi Industries Inc 381 Ari Ct Addison IL 60101 630-953-9100
TF: 800-237-6725 ■ *Web:* www.ariindustries.biz

Arzel Zoning Technology Inc
4801 Commerce Pkwy Cleveland OH 44128 216-831-6068
TF: 800-611-8312 ■ *Web:* www.arzelzoning.com

ASCO Valve Inc 50-60 Hanover Rd Florham Park NJ 07932 973-966-2000
Web: www.asco.com/en-us

Athena Controls Inc 5145 Campus Dr Plymouth Meeting PA 19462 610-828-2490 828-7084
TF: 800-782-6776 ■ *Web:* www.athenacontrols.com

ATI Industrial Automation Export Co
1031 Goodworth Dr Apex NC 27539 919-772-0115 772-8259
Web: www.ati-ia.com

Auburn Systems LLC 8 Electronics Ave Danvers MA 01923 978-777-2460
TF: 800-255-5008 ■ *Web:* www.auburnsys.com

Automation Nth 491 Waldron Rd La Vergne TN 37086 615-793-7704
Web: www.automationnth.com

Automation Products Group Inc (APG)
1025 West 1700 North Logan UT 84321 435-753-7300 753-7490
TF: 888-525-7300 ■ *Web:* www.apgsensors.com

Automation Service 13871 Parks Steed Dr Earth City MO 63045 314-785-6600 785-6610
TF: 800-325-4808 ■ *Web:* www.automationservice.com

Automation Systems Interconnect Inc
4700 Wport Dr Ste 500 Mechanicsburg PA 17055 717-249-5581
Web: www.asi-ez.com

Azonix Corp 900 Middlesex Tpke Bldg 6 Billerica MA 01821 978-670-6300 670-8855
TF: 800-967-5558 ■ *Web:* www.azonix.com

Bacharach Inc 621 Hunt Vly Cir New Kensington PA 15068 724-334-5000 334-5001
TF: 800-736-4666 ■ *Web:* www.bacharach-inc.com

Barksdale Inc 3211 Fruitland Ave Los Angeles CA 90058 323-589-6181 589-3463
TF: 800-835-1060 ■ *Web:* www.barksdale.com

BECS Technology Inc
9487 Dielman Rock Island Industrial Dr Saint Louis MO 63132 314-567-0088
Web: www.becs.com

Bio-Chem Fluidics Inc 85 Fulton St Boonton NJ 07005 973-263-3001
Web: www.biochemfluidics.com

Blue-White Industries Ltd
5300 Business Dr Huntington Beach CA 92649 714-893-8529 894-9492
Web: www.bluwhite.com

Brookfield Engineering Lab Inc
11 Commerce Blvd Middleboro MA 02346 508-946-6200 946-6262
TF: 800-628-8139 ■ *Web:* www.brookfieldengineering.com

Brooks Instrument 250 Andrews Rd Trevose PA 19053 215-357-0893
Web: www.keyinstruments.com

Budzar Industries Inc
38241 Willoughby Pkwy Willoughby OH 44094 440-918-0505
Web: www.budzar.com

Buhler Inc 13105 12th Ave N Plymouth MN 55441 763-847-9900 847-9911
TF: 800-722-7483 ■ *Web:* www.buhlergroup.com

Cal-Bay Systems Inc 3070 Kerner Blvd Ste B San Rafael CA 94901 415-258-9400

Campbell Scientific Inc 815 West 1800 North Logan UT 84321 435-753-2342 750-9540
Web: www.campbellsci.com

Canfield Connector Div 8510 Foxwood Ct Youngstown OH 44514 800-554-5071
TF: 800-554-5071 ■ *Web:* www.canfieldconnector.com

Cec Controls Co Inc 14555 Barber Ave Warren MI 48088 586-779-0222 779-0266
TF: 877-924-0303 ■ *Web:* www.ceccontrols.com

Celesco Transducer Products Inc
20630 Plummer St Chatsworth CA 91311 818-701-2750
TF: 800-423-5483 ■ *Web:* www.celesco.com

Celtech Corp 1300 Terminal Dr Carlsbad NM 88220 575-887-2044
Web: www.aseholdings.com

Cephasonics Inc 160 Saratoga Ave Ste 180 Santa Clara CA 95051 408-249-4629
Web: www.cephasonics.com

Cincinnati Test Systems Inc 5555 Dry Fork Rd Cleves OH 45002 513-367-6699 367-5426
TF: 800-850-3189 ■ *Web:* www.cincinnati-test.com

Clearsign Combustion Corp
12870 Interurban Ave S Seattle WA 98168 206-673-4848
Web: www.clearsign.com

Cleveland Electric Labortories
1776 Enterprise Pkwy Twinsburg OH 44087 330-425-4747
Web: www.clevelandelectriclabs.com

Colloidal Dynamics Pty Ltd
5150 Palm Vly Rd Ste 303 Ponte Vedra Beach FL 32082 904-686-1536
Web: www.colloidal-dynamics.com

Compressor Controls Corp 4725 121st St Des Moines IA 50323 515-270-0857 270-1331
Web: www.cccglobal.com

Conax Buffalo Technologies LLC
2300 Walden Ave Buffalo NY 14225 716-684-4500 684-7433
TF: 800-223-2389 ■ *Web:* www.conaxtechnologies.com

Control Gaging Inc 5200 Venture Dr Ann Arbor MI 48108 734-668-6750
Web: www.controlgaging.com

Cooper Atkins Corp 33 Reeds Gap Rd Middlefield CT 06455 860-349-3473 349-8994
TF Sales: 800-835-5011 ■ *Web:* cooper-atkins.com/default.asp

Corelis Inc
Alondra Corporate Ctr 13100 Alondra Blvd Cerritos CA 90703 562-926-6727
Web: www.corelis.com

Crane Company Dynalco Controls Div
3690 NW 53rd St Fort Lauderdale FL 33309 954-739-4300 484-3376
TF: 800-368-6666 ■ *Web:* www.dynalco.com

Crest Semiconductors Inc
2001 Gateway Pl 610 W San Jose CA 95110 408-441-0303
Web: www.slicex.com

Cresta Technology Corp
3900 Freedom Cir Ste 201 Santa Clara CA 95054 408-486-5610
Web: www.crestatech.com

CUES Inc 3600 Rio Vista Ave Orlando FL 32805 407-849-0190
TF: 800-327-7791 ■ *Web:* www.cuesinc.com

Custom Control Manufacturer of Kansas Inc
5601 Merriam Dr Merriam KS 66203 913-722-0343
Web: www.customcontrolmfr.com

Custom Control Sensors Inc
21111 Plummer St Chatsworth CA 91311 818-341-4610 709-0426
Web: www.ccsdualsnap.com

Custom Sensors & Technologies (CST)
14401 Princeton Ave Moorpark CA 93021 805-552-3599
Web: www.cstsensors.com

Daniel Measurement & Control Inc
5650 Brittmoore Rd Houston TX 77041 713-467-6000 827-3880
TF: 800-518-1623 ■ *Web:* www.emersonprocess.com

Davidson Instruments Inc
9391 Grogan's Mill Rd The Woodlands TX 77380 281-362-4900
Web: www.davidson-instruments.com

Daytronic Corp 2566 Kohnle Dr Miamisburg OH 45342 937-293-2566
Web: www.daytronic.com

Del Mar Scientific Acquisition Ltd
4951 Airport Pkwy Ste 803 Addison TX 75001 972-661-5160
TF: 800-722-4270 ■ *Web:* www.delmarscientific.com

DENT Instruments Inc 925 SW Emkay Dr Bend OR 97702 541-388-4774
Web: www.dentinstruments.com

Dexter Research Center Inc
7300 Huron River Dr Dexter MI 48130 734-426-3921
Web: www.dexterresearch.com

Dickson Co 930 S Westwood Ave Addison IL 60101 630-543-3747 543-0498
TF: 800-757-3747 ■ *Web:* www.dicksondata.com

Digalog Systems Inc 3180 S 166th St New Berlin WI 53151 262-797-8000
Web: www.digalogsystems.com

Phone | Fax

Dwyer Instruments Inc
102 Indiana Hwy 212 PO Box 373 . . . Michigan City IN 46360 219-879-8000 872-9057
Web: www.dwyer-inst.com

Eico Inc 1054 Yosemite Dr . . . Milpitas CA 95035 408-945-9898
Web: www.eico.net

Eldridge Products Inc 2700 Garden Rd Bldg A . . . Monterey CA 93940 831-648-7777
TF: 800-321-3569 ■ *Web:* www.epiflow.com

Electro Optical Industries Inc
859 Ward Dr . . . Santa Barbara CA 93111 805-964-6701 967-8590
Web: www.electro-optical.com

Emerson Process Management
8100 W Florissant Ave Annex K . . . Saint Louis MO 63136 314-553-1847 553-1982
Web: www.emersonprocess.com

Emulation Technology Inc 759 Flynn Rd . . . Camarillo CA 93012 805-383-8480
TF: 800-232-7837 ■ *Web:* www.emulation.com

Encoder Products Co 464276 Hwy 95 S PO Box 249 . . . Sagle ID 83860 208-263-8541 263-0541
TF: 800-366-5412 ■ *Web:* www.encoder.com

Endress+Hauser Inc 2350 Endress Pl . . . Greenwood IN 46143 317-535-7138 535-8498
TF: 888-363-7377 ■ *Web:* www.us.endress.com

Enerac Inc 67 Bond St . . . Westbury NY 11590 516-997-2100
TF: 800-695-3637 ■ *Web:* www.enerac.com

Enmetric Systems Inc 617 Mtn View Ave Ste 5 . . . Belmont CA 94002 650-762-5757
Web: www.enmetric.com

ERDCO Engineering Corp 721 Custer Ave . . . Evanston IL 60202 847-328-0550
Web: www.erdco.com

Fairchild Industrial Products Co
3920 Westpoint Blvd . . . Winston-Salem NC 27103 336-659-3400 659-9323*
**Fax:* Sales ■ *TF:* 800-334-8422 ■ *Web:* www.fairchildproducts.com

Fast Heat Inc 776 Oaklawn Ave . . . Elmhurst IL 60126 630-833-5400 833-2040
TF: 877-747-8575 ■ *Web:* www.fastheat.com

Fluid Components International
1755 La Costa Meadows Dr . . . San Marcos CA 92078 760-744-6950 736-6250
TF: 800-863-8703 ■ *Web:* www.fluidcomponents.com

Forney Corp 16479 N Dallas Pkwy Ste 600 . . . Addison TX 75001 972-458-6100 458-6650
TF Cust Svc: 800-356-7740 ■ *Web:* www.forneycorp.com

Fred Knapp Engraving Company Inc
5102 Douglas Ave . . . Racine WI 53402 262-639-9035
Web: www.air-logic.com

FTI Flow Technology Inc 8930 S Beck Ave Ste 107 . . . Tempe AZ 85284 480-240-3400
Web: www.ftimeters.com

GainSpan Corp 3590 N First St Ste 300 . . . San Jose CA 95134 408-627-6500
Web: www.gainspan.com

Galvanic Applied Sciences USA Inc
41 Wellman St . . . Lowell MA 01851 978-848-2701
TF: 866-252-8470 ■ *Web:* www.galvanic.com

GE Infrastructure Sensing
1100 Technology Pk Dr . . . Billerica MA 01821 978-437-1000
TF: 800-833-9438 ■ *Web:* www.ge-mcs.com

Gefran ISI Inc 8 Lowell Ave . . . Winchester MA 01890 781-729-5249
TF: 888-888-4474 ■ *Web:* www.gefran.com

Gems Sensors Inc 1 Cowles Rd . . . Plainville CT 06062 860-747-3000 747-4244
TF: 800-378-1600 ■ *Web:* www.gemssensors.com

General Devices Company Inc
1410 S Post Rd . . . Indianapolis IN 46239 317-897-7000
TF: 800-821-3520 ■ *Web:* www.generaldevices.com

Geotech Environmental Equipment Inc
2650 E 40th Ave . . . Denver CO 80205 303-320-4764 322-7242
TF: 800-833-7958 ■ *Web:* www.geotechenv.com

Geotest - Marvin Test Systems Inc
1770 Kettering . . . Irvine CA 92614 949-263-2222
Web: marvintest.com

GF Piping Systems 3401 Aero Jet Ave . . . El Monte CA 91731 626-571-2770 573-2057
Web: www.gfps.com

GfG Instrumentation Inc
1194 Oak Vly Dr Ste 20 . . . Ann Arbor MI 48108 734-769-0573
TF: 800-959-0329 ■ *Web:* www.gfg-inc.com

Greenvity Communications Inc
673 S Milpitas Blvd Ste 204 . . . Milpitas CA 95035 408-935-9434
Web: www.greenvity.com

Guided Wave Inc 3033 Gold Canal Dr . . . Rancho Cordova CA 95670 916-638-4944
Web: www.guidedwave.com

Halma Holdings Inc
11500 Northlake Dr Ste 306 . . . Cincinnati OH 45249 513-772-5501
Web: www.halma.com

Hammond Manufacturing Company Ltd
394 Edinburgh Rd N . . . Guelph ON N1H1E5 519-822-2960
Web: www.hammfg.com

Harco Laboratories Inc 186 Cedar St . . . Branford CT 06405 203-483-3700
Web: www.harcolabs.com

Harding Instruments 7741 Wagner Rd NW . . . Edmonton AB T6E5X7 780-462-7100
TF: 888-792-1171 ■ *Web:* www.harding.ca

Hart Scientific Inc 799 E Utah Vly Dr . . . American Fork UT 84003 801-763-1600 763-1010
TF: 800-438-4278 ■ *Web:* us.flukecal.com

Healthspace USA Inc 4860 Cox Rd Ste 200 . . . Glen Allen VA 23060 804-935-8532
TF: 866-860-4224 ■ *Web:* www.healthspace.ca

Heraeus Electro-Nite Co 1 Summit Sq Ste 1 . . . Langhorne PA 19047 215-944-9000 944-9000
Web: www.heraeus-electro-nite.com

HO Trerice Co 12950 W Eight-Mile Rd . . . Oak Park MI 48237 248-399-8000 399-7246
TF: 888-873-7423 ■ *Web:* www.trerice.com

Hoffland Environmental Inc
10391 Silver Springs Rd . . . Conroe TX 77303 936-856-4515
Web: www.hoffland.net

Honeywell Automation & Control Solutions
11 W Spring St . . . Freeport IL 61032 815-235-5500
Web: www.honeywell.com

HSQ Technology 26227 Research Rd . . . Hayward CA 94545 510-259-1334 259-1391
TF: 800-486-6684 ■ *Web:* www.hsq.com

Industrial Scientific Corp
7848 Steubenville Pk . . . Oakdale PA 15071 412-788-4353 788-8353
TF: 800-338-3287 ■ *Web:* www.indsci.com

INFICON Inc 2 Technology Pl . . . East Syracuse NY 13057 315-434-1100 437-3803
Web: www.inficon.com

Intelligent Instrumentation Inc
3529 N Williams Ave . . . Portland OR 97227 503-928-3188
Web: www.instrument.com

Invisa Inc 1800 Second St Ste 965 . . . Sarasota FL 34236 941-870-3950
Web: www.invisa.com

IO Industries Inc 1510 Woodcock St . . . London ON N6H5S1 519-663-9570 663-9571
Web: www.ioindustries.com

IO Semiconductor Inc
4350 Executive Dr Ste 200 . . . San Diego CA 92121 858-373-0440
Web: www.iosemi.com

ISCO Inc 4700 Superior St PO Box 82531 . . . Lincoln NE 68501 402-464-0231 465-3022*
**Fax:* Cust Svc ■ *TF:* 800-228-4250 ■ *Web:* www.isco.com

ITT Industries Inc 1133 Westchester Ave . . . White Plains NY 10604 914-641-2000 696-2950
NYSE: ITT ■ *TF:* 800-254-2823 ■ *Web:* www.itt.com

JMS Southeast Inc 105 Temperature Ln . . . Statesville NC 28677 704-873-1835
Web: www.jms-se.com

Keller America Inc
813 Diligence Dr Ste 120 . . . Newport News VA 23606 757-596-6680
Web: www.kelleramerica.com

King Instrument Company Inc
12700 Pala Dr . . . Garden Grove CA 92841 714-891-0008
Web: www.kinginstrumentco.com

Kistler-Morse Corp 150 Venture Blvd . . . Spartanburg SC 29306 864-574-2763 574-8063
TF: 800-426-9010 ■ *Web:* www.kistlermorse.com

Lake Shore Cryotronics 575 McCorkle Blvd . . . Westerville OH 43082 614-891-2243 818-1600
TF: 877-969-0010 ■ *Web:* www.lakeshore.com

LaMotte Co 802 Washington Ave . . . Chestertown MD 21620 410-778-3100 778-6394
TF: 800-344-3100 ■ *Web:* www.lamotte.com

Larson Davis Inc 3425 Walden Ave . . . Depew NY 14043 716-926-8243
Web: www.larsondavis.com

Lime Instruments LLC 1187 Brittmoore Rd . . . Houston TX 77043 713-781-1883
Web: www.limeinst.net

Linear Laboratories 42025 Osgood Rd . . . Fremont CA 94539 510-226-0488 226-1112
TF: 800-536-0262 ■ *Web:* www.linearlabs.com

Liquid Controls LLC 105 Albrecht Dr . . . Lake Bluff IL 60044 847-295-1050
Web: www.lcmeter.com

Lynntech Inc
2501 Earl Rudder Fwy S Ste 100 . . . College Station TX 77845 979-764-2200
Web: www.lynntech.com

Magnetrol International Inc
5300 Belmont Rd . . . Downers Grove IL 60515 630-969-4000 969-9489
TF: 800-624-8765 ■ *Web:* magnetrol.com

Mahr Federal Inc 1144 Eddy St . . . Providence RI 02905 401-784-3100 784-3246
TF Orders: 800-343-2050 ■ *Web:* www.mahrfederal.com

Malema Engineering Corp 1060 S Rogers Cir . . . Boca Raton FL 33487 561-995-0595 995-0622
TF: 800-637-6418 ■ *Web:* www.malema.com

MAMAC Systems Inc 8189 Century Blvd . . . Minneapolis MN 55317 952-556-4900
TF: 800-843-5116 ■ *Web:* www.mamacsys.com

Mark-10 Corp 11 Dixon Ave . . . Copiague NY 11726 631-842-9200
Web: www.mark-10.com

Marsh Bellofram Corp 8019 Ohio River Blvd . . . Newell WV 26050 304-387-1200 387-1212
TF: 800-727-5646 ■ *Web:* www.marshbellofram.com

Maxcess International Corp
222 W Memorial Rd . . . Oklahoma City OK 73114 405-755-1600
Web: www.maxcessintl.com

Maxitrol Co 23555 Telegraph Rd PO Box 2230 . . . Southfield MI 48033 248-356-1400 356-0829
Web: www.maxitrol.com

McCrometer Inc 3255 W Stetson Ave . . . Hemet CA 92545 951-652-6811 652-3078
TF: 800-220-2279 ■ *Web:* www.mccrometer.com

Measurement Technology Northwest Inc
4211 24th Ave W . . . Seattle WA 98199 206-634-1308
Web: www.mtnw-usa.com

Mensor Corp 201 Barnes Dr . . . San Marcos TX 78666 512-396-4200 396-1820
Web: www.mensor.com

Metron Inc 1505 W Third Ave . . . Denver CO 80223 303-592-1903 534-1947
Web: www.metroninc.com

Micro Lithography Inc 1257 Elko Dr . . . Sunnyvale CA 94089 408-747-1769
Web: www.mliusa.com

Micro Motion Inc 7070 Winchester Cir . . . Boulder CO 80301 303-530-8400
TF: 800-522-6277 ■
Web: www2.emersonprocess.com/en-us/brands/micromotion

MicroMod Automation Inc 75 Town Centre Dr . . . Rochester NY 14623 585-321-9200
TF: 800-480-1975 ■ *Web:* www.micmod.com

Minco Products Inc 7300 Commerce Ln NE . . . Minneapolis MN 55432 763-571-3121 571-0927*
**Fax:* Sales ■ *Web:* www.minco.com

MKS Instruments Inc 2 Tech Dr Ste 201 . . . Andover MA 01810 978-645-5500 557-5100
TF: 800-428-9401 ■ *Web:* www.mksinst.com

Mocon Inc 7500 Mendelssohn Ave N . . . Minneapolis MN 55428 763-493-6370 493-6358
NASDAQ: MOCO ■ *Web:* www.mocon.com

Monarch Instrument Inc 15 Columbia Dr . . . Amherst NH 03031 603-883-3390
Web: www.monarchinstrument.com

Moore Industries International Inc
16650 Schoenborn St . . . North Hills CA 91343 818-894-7111 891-2816
TF: 800-999-2900 ■ *Web:* www.miinet.com

NDC Infrared Engineering
5314 N Irwindale Ave . . . Irwindale CA 91706 626-960-3300 939-3870
Web: www.ndc.com

Nearfield Systems Inc 19730 Magellan Dr . . . Torrance CA 90502 310-525-7000
TF: 800-334-7384 ■ *Web:* www.nearfield.com

Noren Products Inc 1010 Obrien Dr . . . Menlo Park CA 94025 650-322-9500 324-1348
Web: www.norenproducts.com

Noshok Inc 1010 W Bagley Rd . . . Berea OH 44017 440-243-0888 243-3472
Web: www.noshok.com

NRD LLC 2937 Alt Blvd PO Box 310 . . . Grand Island NY 14072 716-773-7634 773-7744
TF: 800-525-8076 ■ *Web:* www.nrdstaticcontrol.com

Octasic Inc 4101 Molson St Ste 300 . . . Montreal QC H1Y3L1 514-282-8858
Web: www.octasic.com

Omega Engineering Inc 1 Omega Dr PO Box 4047 . . . Stamford CT 06907 203-359-1660 359-7700*
**Fax:* Cust Svc ■ *TF:* 800-826-6342 ■ *Web:* www.omega.com

ONICON Inc 11451 Belcher Rd S . . . Largo FL 33773 727-447-6140
Web: www.onicon.com

Onset Computer Corp PO Box 3450 . . . Pocasset MA 02559 508-759-9500 759-9100
TF: 800-564-4377 ■ *Web:* www.onsetcomp.com

				Phone	Fax
Opto 22 Inc 43044 Business Park Dr *Web:* www.opto22.com	Temecula	CA	92590	951-695-3000	
OPW Fuel Management Systems 6900 Santa Fe Dr **Fax:* Cust Svc ■ *TF:* 800-547-9393 ■ *Web:* www.opwglobal.com	Hodgkins	IL	60525	708-485-4200	485-4630*
Orange Research Inc 140 Cascade Blvd *TF:* 800-989-5657 ■ *Web:* www.orangeresearch.com	Milford	CT	06460	203-877-5657	
Orion Instruments LLC 2105 Oak Villa Blvd *TF:* 866-556-7466 ■ *Web:* www.orioninstruments.com	Baton Rouge	LA	70815	225-906-2343	906-2344
PakSense Inc 6223 N Discovery Pl *TF:* 877-832-0720 ■ *Web:* www.paksense.com	Boise	ID	83713	208-489-9010	
Palmer Wahl Instrumentation Group 234 Old Weaverville Rd *Web:* www.palmerwahl.com	Asheville	NC	28804	828-658-3131	
Paper Machine Components 11 Old Sugar Hollow Rd *TF:* 800-869-5747 ■ *Web:* www.pmc1.com	Danbury	CT	06810	203-792-8686	
Parker Hannifin Corp 6035 Parkland Blvd *Web:* parker.com	Cleveland	OH	44124	216-896-3000	514-6738
Parker Hannifin Corp Veriflo Div 250 Canal Blvd *TF:* 800-272-7537 ■ *Web:* parker.com	Richmond	CA	94804	510-235-9590	232-7396
PdMA Corp 5909-C Hampton Oaks Pkwy *TF:* 800-476-6463 ■ *Web:* www.pdma.com	Tampa	FL	33610	813-621-6463	
Pearpoint Inc 72055 Corporate Way *TF:* 800-688-8094 ■ *Web:* spx.com/en/pearpoint	Thousand Palms	CA	92276	760-343-7350	
Pentair 7433 Harwin Dr *TF:* 800-545-6258 ■ *Web:* pentairthermal.com	Houston	TX	77036	800-545-6258	
Photon Dynamics Inc 5970 Optical Ct	San Jose	CA	95138	408-226-9900	
Portage Electric Products Inc 7700 Freedom Ave NW *TF:* 888-464-7374 ■ *Web:* www.pepiusa.com	North Canton	OH	44720	330-499-2727	499-1853
Porter Instrument Company Inc 245 Township Line Rd PO Box 907 *TF:* 888-723-4001 ■ *Web:* www.porterinstrument.com	Hatfield	PA	19440	215-723-4000	723-2199
Potter Electric Signal Company Inc 5757 Phantom Dr Ste 125 *TF:* 800-325-3936 ■ *Web:* www.pottersignal.com	Hazelwood	MO	63042	314-878-4321	595-6999
Pressure Profile Systems Inc 5757 Century Blvd Ste 600 *TF:* 888-249-2464 ■ *Web:* www.pressureprofile.com	Los Angeles	CA	90045	310-641-8100	
Proportion-Air Inc 8250 N 600 W PO Box 218 *Web:* www.proportionair.com	Mccordsville	IN	46055	317-335-2602	
Proteus Industries 340 Pioneer Way *Web:* www.proteusind.com	Mountain View	CA	94041	650-964-4163	
Pyromation Inc 5211 Industrial Rd *Web:* www.pyromation.com	Fort Wayne	IN	46825	260-484-2580	482-6805
Q-Lab Corp 800 Canterbury Rd *Web:* www.q-lab.com	Westlake	OH	44145	440-835-8700	
Qualitrol Company LLC 1385 Fairport Rd *Web:* www.qualitrolcorp.com	Fairport	NY	14450	585-586-1515	377-0220
Quantenna Communications Inc 3450 W Warren Ave *Web:* www.quantenna.com	Fremont	CA	94538	510-743-2260	
RACO Mfg & Engineering Company Inc 1400-62nd St *Web:* www.racoman.com	Emeryville	CA	94608	510-658-6713	
Radian Research Inc 3852 Fortune Dr *Web:* www.radianresearch.com	Lafayette	IN	47905	765-449-5500	
RAE Systems 3775 N First St *TF:* 877-723-2878 ■ *Web:* www.raesystems.com	San Jose	CA	95134	408-952-8200	952-8480
Raven Industries Inc 205 E Sixth St *NASDAQ: RAVN* ■ *TF:* 800-243-5435 ■ *Web:* www.ravenind.com	Sioux Falls	SD	57104	605-336-2750	335-0268
Raytheon Network Centric Systems (NCS) 2501 W University Dr *Web:* www.raytheon.com	McKinney	TX	75071	781-522-3000	
Red Lion Controls Inc 20 Willow Springs Cir *Web:* www.redlion.net	York	PA	17406	717-767-6511	
Renco Encoders Inc 26 Coromar Dr *Web:* www.renco.com	Goleta	CA	93117	847-490-1191	
REOTEMP Instrument Corp 10656 Roselle St *Web:* www.reotemp.com	San Diego	CA	92121	858-784-0710	
Research Inc 7128 Shady Oak Rd *Web:* pcscontrols.com	Eden Prairie	MN	55344	952-941-3300	941-3628
Restek Corp 110 Benner Cir *Web:* www.restek.com	Bellefonte	PA	16823	814-353-1300	
Robertshaw Industrial Products 1602 Mustang Dr *TF:* 800-228-7429 ■ *Web:* www.robertshawindustrial.com	Maryville	TN	37801	865-981-3100	981-3168
Rochester Gauges Inc of Texas 11616 Harry Hines Blvd *TF:* 800-821-1829 ■ *Web:* www.rochestergauges.com	Dallas	TX	75229	972-241-2161	620-1403
Ronan Engineering Co 21200 Oxnard St **Fax Area Code:* 818 ■ *TF:* 800-327-6626 ■ *Web:* www.ronan.com	Woodland Hills	CA	91367	800-327-6626	992-6435*
Rosemount Analytical Inc Process Analytical Div 6565 P Davis Industrial Pkwy **Fax Area Code:* 330 ■ *TF:* 800-433-6076 ■ *Web:* www.emersonprocess.com	Solon	OH	44139	440-914-1261	684-4434*
RTP Corp 1834 SW Second St *Web:* www.rtpcorp.com	Pompano Beach	FL	33069	954-974-5500	975-9815
Sabina Motors & Controls Inc 1440 N Burton Pl *Web:* www.sabinadrives.com	Anaheim	CA	92806	714-956-0480	956-0486
Sable Systems International Inc 6000 S Ea Ste 1 *TF:* 800-330-0465 ■ *Web:* www.sablesys.com	Las Vegas	NV	89119	702-269-4445	
Santa Barbara Infrared Inc 30 S Calle Cesar Chavez Ste D *Web:* www.sbir.com	Santa Barbara	CA	93103	805-965-3669	
Scienscope Inc 5751 Schaefer Ave *Web:* www.scienscope.com	Chino	CA	91710	909-590-7273	
Scully Signal Co 70 Industrial Way *TF:* 800-272-8559 ■ *Web:* www.scully.com	Wilmington	MA	01887	617-692-8600	692-8620
See Water Inc 121 N Dillon St *TF:* 888-733-9283 ■ *Web:* www.seewaterinc.com	San Jacinto	CA	92583	951-487-8073	487-0557
Sensidyne Inc 16333 Bay Vista Dr *TF:* 800-451-9444 ■ *Web:* www.sensidyne.com	Clearwater	FL	33760	727-530-3602	539-0550
Sensory Analytics LLC 4413-C W Market St *Web:* www.sensoryanalytics.com	Greensboro	NC	27407	336-315-6090	315-6030
Sensus USA Inc 8601 Six Forks Rd Stes 300 & 700 *TF:* 800-638-3748 ■ *Web:* www.sensus.com	Raleigh	NC	27615	919-845-4000	
Siemens Milltronics Process Instruments Inc 1954 Technology Dr *Web:* w3.siemens.com/mcms/automation/en/pages/automation-technology.aspx	Peterborough	ON	K9J6X7	705-745-2431	
Sierra Instruments Inc 5 Harris Ct Bldg L *TF:* 800-866-0200 ■ *Web:* www.sierrainstruments.com	Monterey	CA	93940	831-373-0200	373-4402
Signature Control Systems Inc 25 Manzanita *Web:* www.signaturecontrol.com	Littleton	CO	80127	720-641-1131	
SJE-Rhombus 22650 County Hwy 6 PO Box 1708 *TF:* 800-746-6287 ■ *Web:* www.sjerhombus.com	Detroit Lakes	MN	56502	218-847-1317	847-4617
SOR Inc 14685 W 105th St *TF:* 800-676-6794 ■ *Web:* sorinc.com	Lenexa	KS	66215	913-888-2630	888-0767
SpectraSensors Inc 4333 W Sam Houston Pkwy N *Web:* www.spectrasensors.com	Houston	TX	77043	713-300-2700	
Spectronics Corp 956 Brush Hollow Rd *TF:* 800-274-8888 ■ *Web:* www.spectroline.com	Westbury	NY	11590	800-274-8888	491-6868
Spectrum Controls Inc PO Box 5533 *Web:* www.spectrumcontrols.com	Bellevue	WA	98006	425-746-9481	641-9473
Spirax Sarco Inc 1150 Northpoint Blvd *TF:* 800-883-4411 ■ *Web:* www.spiraxsarco.com/us	Blythewood	SC	29016	803-714-2000	714-2222
Sterling Inc 2900 S 160th St *TF Cust Svc:* 800-783-7835 ■ *Web:* www.acscorporate.com/sterling	New Berlin	WI	53151	262-641-8600	641-8653
Sutron Corp 22400 Davis Dr *NASDAQ: STRN* ■ *Web:* www.sutron.com	Sterling	VA	20164	703-406-2800	406-2801
Taylor Precision Products LLC 2220 Entrada del Sol Ste A *TF:* 866-843-3905 ■ *Web:* www.taylorusa.com	Las Cruces	NM	88001	866-843-3905	
Teledyne Advanced Pollution Instrumentation 9480 Carroll Pk Dr *TF:* 800-324-5190 ■ *Web:* www.teledyne-api.com	San Diego	CA	92121	858-657-9800	657-9816
Teledyne Monitor Labs Inc (TML) 35 Inverness Dr E *TF:* 800-422-1499 ■ *Web:* www.monitorlabs.com	Englewood	CO	80112	303-792-3300	799-4853
Temptime Corp 116 American Rd *Web:* www.temptimecorp.com	Morris Plains	NJ	07950	973-984-6000	
Tevet LLC 85 Spring St S *TF:* 866-886-8527 ■ *Web:* www.tevetllc.com	Mosheim	TN	37818	678-905-1300	
Thermo Fisher Scientific Inc 81 Wyman St *NYSE: TMO* ■ *TF:* 800-678-5599 ■ *Web:* www.thermofisher.com	Waltham	MA	02454	781-622-1000	622-1207
Thermo Probe Inc 112-A Jetport Dr *Web:* www.thermoprobe.net	Pearl	MS	39208	601-939-1831	
Tiger Optics LLC 250 Titus Ave *Web:* www.tigeroptics.com	Warrington	PA	18976	215-343-6600	
Titan Logix Corp 4130 - 93 St *TF:* 877-462-4085 ■ *Web:* www.titanlogix.com	Edmonton	AB	T6E5P5	780-462-4085	450-8369
Transcat Inc 35 Vantage Pt Dr *NASDAQ: TRNS* ■ *TF:* 800-800-5001 ■ *Web:* www.transcat.com	Rochester	NY	14624	585-352-9460	352-1486
Tritech Group Ltd 5413 - 271 St *Web:* www.tritechgroup.ca	Langley	BC	V4W3Y7	604-607-8878	
Troxler Electronic Laboratories Inc 3008 E Cornwallis Rd PO Box 12057 *TF:* 877-876-9537 ■ *Web:* www.troxlerlabs.com	Research Triangle Park	NC	27709	919-549-8661	549-0761
TSI Inc 500 CaRdigan Rd *TF:* 800-874-2811 ■ *Web:* www.tsi.com	Shoreview	MN	55126	651-483-0900	490-3824
Unicontrol Inc 1111 Brookpark Rd *Web:* www.unicontrolinc.com	Cleveland	OH	44109	216-398-4414	
United Electric Controls Co 180 Dexter Ave *Web:* www.ueonline.com	Watertown	MA	02472	617-926-1000	926-2568
Uson LP 8640 N Eldridge Pkwy *Web:* www.uson.com	Houston	TX	77041	281-671-2000	671-2001
Vacuum Instrument Corp 2099 Ninth Ave *Web:* www.vicleakdetection.com	Ronkonkoma	NY	11779	631-737-0900	
Veeder-Root 125 Powder Forest Dr *TF:* 888-262-7539 ■ *Web:* www.veeder.com	Simsbury	CT	06070	860-651-2700	651-2719
Venture Measurement Company LLC 150 Venture Blvd *Web:* www.venturemeasurement.com	Spartanburg	SC	29306	864-574-8960	578-7308
VIEW Micro-Metrology Inc 1711 W 17th St *Web:* www.viewmm.com	Tempe	AZ	85281	480-295-3150	
Visualant Inc 500 Union St Ste 420 *Web:* www.visualant.net	Seattle	WA	98101	206-903-1351	
Weed Instrument Company Inc 707 Jeffrey Way *Web:* ultra-nspi.com	Round Rock	TX	78665	512-434-2900	
Wika Instrument Corp 1000 Wiegand Blvd *TF:* 888-945-2872 ■ *Web:* www.wika.us	Lawrenceville	GA	30043	770-513-8200	338-5118
Wilmington Instrument Company Inc 332 N Fries Ave *TF:* 800-544-2843 ■ *Web:* www.calcert.com	Wilmington	CA	90744	310-834-1133	
Wilmington Research & Development Corp 50 Parker St *Web:* www.wrdcorp.com	Newburyport	MA	01950	978-499-0100	
Winland Electronics Inc 1950 Excel Dr *NYSE: WEX* ■ *TF:* 800-635-4269 ■ *Web:* www.winland.com	Mankato	MN	56001	507-625-7231	387-2488
World Energy Alternatives LLC 2 Constitution Ctr *TF:* 800-829-3676 ■ *Web:* www.worldenergy.net	Boston	MA	02129	617-889-7300	
World Energy Labs (2) Inc 365 E Middlefield Rd	Mountain View	CA	94043	650-900-4600	
XiTRON Technologies Inc 7507 Convoy Ct *Web:* www.xitrontech.com	San Diego	CA	92111	858-530-8099	
Yokogawa Corp of America 12530 W Airport Blvd *TF:* 800-888-6400 ■ *Web:* www.yokogawa.com/us	Sugar Land	TX	77478	281-340-3800	340-3838

Phone | Fax

YSI Inc 1700-1725 Brannum Ln .... Yellow Springs OH 45387 937-767-7241 767-9353
TF Cust Svc: 800-765-4974 ■ *Web:* www.ysi.com

ZK Celltest Inc 256 Gibraltar Dr Ste 109 .... Sunnyvale CA 94089 408-752-0449
TF: 800-837-8235 ■ *Web:* www.zk.com

Zolo Technologies Inc 4946 N 63rd St .... Boulder CO 80301 303-604-5800
Web: www.zolotech.com

ZTEC Instruments Inc 7715 Tiburon St Ne. .... Albuquerque NM 87109 505-342-0132
Web: www.ztecinstruments.com

202 CONTROLS - TEMPERATURE - RESIDENTIAL & COMMERCIAL

Phone | Fax

Alerton 6670 185th Ave NE. .... Redmond WA 98052 425-869-8400 869-8445
Web: www.alerton.com

APCOM Inc 125 SE Pkwy .... Franklin TN 37064 615-794-5574 791-0660
Web: www.apcom-inc.com

Automated Logic Corp 1150 Roberts Rd N .... Kennesaw GA 30144 770-429-3000 429-3001
Web: www.automatedlogic.com

Azonix Corp 900 Middlesex Tpke Bldg 6 .... Billerica MA 01821 978-670-6300 670-8855
TF: 800-967-5558 ■ *Web:* www.azonix.com

CAPP/USA 201 Marple Ave .... Clifton Heights PA 19018 610-394-1100 237-3292*
**Fax Area Code:* 800 ■ **Fax:* Sales ■ *TF:* 800-356-8000 ■ *Web:* www.cappusa.com

Channel Products Inc
7100 Wilson Mills Rd. .... Chesterland OH 44026 440-423-0113 423-1502
Web: www.channelproducts.com

Clean Coal Technologies Inc
12th Fl 295 Madison Ave .... New York NY 10017 646-710-3549
Web: www.cleancoaltechnologiesinc.com

Cooper Atkins Corp 33 Reeds Gap Rd .... Middlefield CT 06455 860-349-3473 349-8994
TF Sales: 800-835-5011 ■ *Web:* cooper-atkins.com/default.asp

DeltaTRAK Inc PO Box 398 .... Pleasanton CA 94566 925-249-2250 249-2251
TF: 800-962-6776 ■ *Web:* www.deltatrak.com

Emerson Climate Technologies - Retail Solutions
1065 Big Shanty Rd NW Ste 100 .... Kennesaw GA 30144 770-425-2724 425-9319
TF: 800-829-2724 ■ *Web:* www.emersonclimate.com

Eurotherm USA 44621 Guilford Dr Ste 100 .... Ashburn VA 20147 703-724-7300 724-7301
Web: www.eurotherm.com

Hallcrest Inc 1820 Pickwick Ln. .... Glenview IL 60026 847-998-8580 998-6866
Web: www.hallcrest.com

Hansen Technologies Corp
6827 High Grove Blvd .... Burr Ridge IL 60527 630-325-1565 325-1572
TF: 800-426-7368 ■ *Web:* www.hantech.com

HSQ Technology 26227 Research Rd .... Hayward CA 94545 510-259-1334 259-1391
TF: 800-486-6684 ■ *Web:* www.hsq.com

Johnson Controls Systems
9410 Bunsen Pkwy Ste 100-B .... Louisville KY 40220 502-671-7300
TF: 800-765-7773 ■ *Web:* www.johnsoncontrols.com

Kidde-Fenwal Inc 400 Main St. .... Ashland MA 01721 508-881-2000
TF Hum Res: 800-872-6527 ■ *Web:* www.kidde-fenwal.com

KMC Controls Inc 19476 Industrial Dr .... New Paris IN 46553 574-831-5250 831-5252
TF: 877-444-5622 ■ *Web:* www.kmc-controls.com

Nailor Industries of Texas Inc
4714 Winfield Rd .... Houston TX 77039 281-590-1172 590-3086
Web: www.nailor.com

Novar Controls Corp
6060 Rockside Woods Blvd Ste 400. .... Cleveland OH 44131 800-348-1235 682-1614*
**Fax Area Code:* 216 ■ *TF:* 800-348-1235 ■ *Web:* www.novar.com

Phoenix Controls Corp 75 Discovery Way .... Acton MA 01720 978-795-1285 795-1111
Web: www.phoenixcontrols.com

Portage Electric Products Inc
7700 Freedom Ave NW .... North Canton OH 44720 330-499-2727 499-1853
TF: 888-464-7374 ■ *Web:* www.pepiusa.com

Prentke Romich Co 1022 Heyl Rd .... Wooster OH 44691 330-262-1984 263-4829
TF: 800-848-8008 ■ *Web:* www.prentrom.com

Residential Control Systems
11481 Sunrise Gold Cir Ste 1 .... Rancho Cordova CA 95742 916-635-6784 635-7668
TF: 888-727-4822 ■ *Web:* www.rcstechnology.com

Sabine River Authority of Texas PO Box 579 .... Orange TX 77631 409-746-2192 746-3780
Web: www.sra.dst.tx.us

Siemens Bldg Technologies Inc
1000 Deerfield Pkwy .... Buffalo Grove IL 60089 847-215-1000 215-1093
TF General: 800-877-7545 ■ *Web:* www.buildingtechnologies.siemens.com

Taylor Precision Products LLC
2220 Entrada del Sol Ste A .... Las Cruces NM 88001 866-843-3905
TF: 866-843-3905 ■ *Web:* www.taylorusa.com

Therm-O-Disc Inc 1320 S Main St .... Mansfield OH 44907 419-525-8500 525-8344*
**Fax:* Sales ■ *Web:* www.thermodisc.com

WAKO Electronics USA Inc
2105 Production Dr .... Louisville KY 40299 502-429-8866 429-8869
Web: www.wako-usa.com

Watlow Winona 1241 Bundy Blvd. .... Winona MN 55987 507-454-5300 452-4507
TF: 800-928-5692 ■ *Web:* www.watlow.com

Weiss Instruments Inc 905 Waverly Ave. .... Holtsville NY 11742 631-207-1200 207-0900
Web: www.weissinstruments.com

Xylem 8200 N Austin Ave .... Morton Grove IL 60053 847-966-3700 983-5954
Web: unitedstates.xylemappliedwater.com

203 CONTROLS & RELAYS - ELECTRICAL

Phone | Fax

ABB SSAC 8242 Loop Rd .... Baldwinsville NY 13027 315-638-1300 638-0333
TF Tech Supp: 800-377-7722 ■ *Web:* www.ssac.com

Absolute Electronics Inc
W137 N8589 Landover Ct .... Menomonee Falls WI 53051 262-250-1151
Web: www.absoluteelectronics.net

Allied Controls Inc 150 E Aurora St .... Waterbury CT 06708 203-757-4200
TF: 800-788-0955 ■ *Web:* alliedcontrols.com

American Relays Inc 15537 S Blackburn Ave .... Norwalk CA 90650 562-944-0447 944-0590
Web: www.americanrelays.com

American Zettler Inc 75 Columbia .... Aliso Viejo CA 92656 949-831-5000 831-8642
Web: www.azettler.com

Phone | Fax

AMETEK National Controls Corp
1725 Western Dr. .... West Chicago IL 60185 630-231-5900 231-1377
TF: 800-323-2593 ■ *Web:* ameteknCC.com

AMX Corp 3000 Research Dr .... Richardson TX 75082 469-624-8585
TF: 855-269-8585 ■ *Web:* www.amx.com

Anaheim Automation 910 E Orangefair Ln. .... Anaheim CA 92801 714-992-6990 992-0471
TF Sales: 800-345-9401 ■ *Web:* www.anaheimautomation.com

Artisan Controls Corp
111 Canfield Ave Bldg B15-18 .... Randolph NJ 07869 973-598-9400
Web: www.artisancontrols.com

Automation & Control Services Inc
2440 Ontario St .... Schererville IN 46375 219-558-2060
Web: www.automationcontrolservices.com

Balboa Instruments Inc 1382 Bell Ave .... Tustin CA 92780 714-384-0382
Web: www.balboainstruments.com

Barantec Inc 777 Passaic Ave Fl 4 .... Clifton NJ 07012 973-779-8774 779-8768
Web: www.barantec.com

Basler Electric Co 12570 SR- 143 PO Box 269 .... Highland IL 62249 618-654-2341 654-2351
Web: www.basler.com

Bright Image Corp 2830 S18th Ave .... Broadview IL 60155 888-449-5656 449-1155*
**Fax Area Code:* 708 ■ *TF:* 888-449-5656 ■ *Web:* www.touchandglow.com

Bus-tech Inc 26 Crosby Dr .... Bedford MA 01710 800-284-3172
TF: 800-284-3172

Cambridge Viscosity Inc 101 Stn Landing .... Medford MA 02155 303-893-0552

Cleveland Motion Controls Inc
7550 Hub Pkwy .... Cleveland OH 44125 216-524-8800 642-2199
TF: 800-321-8072 ■ *Web:* www.cmccontrols.com

Connor-Winfield Corp 2111 Comprehensive Dr. .... Aurora IL 60505 630-851-4722
Web: www.conwin.com

Contrex Inc 8900 Zachary Ln N .... Maple Grove MN 55369 763-424-7800
TF: 800-342-4411 ■ *Web:* www.contrexinc.com

Control Masters Inc 5235 Katrine Ave. .... Downers Grove IL 60515 630-968-2390 968-3260
Web: www.controlmasters.com

Control Resources Inc 11 Beaver Brook Rd. .... Littleton MA 01460 978-486-4160
Web: controlresources.com

Converteam Inc 610 Epsilon Dr .... Pittsburgh PA 15238 412-967-0765
Web: www.gepowerconversion.com

Coto Technology USA 66 Whitecap Dr. .... North Kingstown RI 02852 401-943-2686 942-0920
Web: www.cotorelay.com

Crydom Inc
2320 Paseo de las Americas Ste 201 .... San Diego CA 92154 619-210-1550
Web: www.crydom.com

Datacom Systems Inc 9 Adler Dr. .... East Syracuse NY 13057 315-463-9541
Web: www.datacomsystems.com

Digi-Data Corp 11101 W 120th Ave Ste 350 .... Broomfield CO 80021 303-604-9020 604-9017
Web: www.digidata.com

Digital Control Systems Inc
7401 SW Capitol Hwy. .... Portland OR 97219 503-246-8110
Web: www.dcs-inc.net

DST Controls 651 Stone Rd .... Benicia CA 94510 707-745-5117
TF: 800-251-0773 ■ *Web:* www.dstcontrols.com

Ducommun Inc 23301 Wilmington Ave. .... Carson CA 90745 310-513-7280 513-7279
NYSE: DCO ■ *TF:* 800-522-6645 ■ *Web:* www.ducommun.com

Duct-O-Wire Co 345 Adams Cir. .... Corona CA 92882 951-735-8220 735-2372
TF: 800-752-6001 ■ *Web:* www.ductowire.com

Durex Industries Inc 190 Detroit St .... Cary IL 60013 847-639-5600 639-2199
Web: www.durexindustries.com

Easter Owens Electric Co 6692 Fig St .... Arvada CO 80004 303-431-0111
TF: 866-204-3707 ■ *Web:* www.easter-owens.com

Eaton Corp 1111 Superior Ave Eaton Ctr .... Cleveland OH 44114 216-523-5000
Web: www.eaton.com

ELCON Inc 600 Twin Rail Dr .... Minooka IL 60447 815-467-9500
Web: www.elconinc.net

Electric Motor & Contracting Co Inc
3703 Cook Blvd .... Chesapeake VA 23323 757-487-2121 487-5983
Web: www.emc-co.com

Electric Regulator Corp 6189 El Camino Real .... Carlsbad CA 92009 760-438-7873 438-0437
TF: 800-458-6566 ■ *Web:* www.electricregulator.com

Electrical & Electronics 3881 Danbury Rd. .... Brewster NY 10509 914-769-5000 769-3641
Web: www.eecontrols.com

Electrical Design & Control Co
2200 Stephenson Hwy .... Troy MI 48083 248-743-2400
Web: www.edandc.com

Electro-Matic Products Co 2235 N Knox Ave .... Chicago IL 60639 773-235-4010 235-7317
Web: www.em-chicago.com

Electroid Co 45 Fadem Rd. .... Springfield NJ 07081 973-467-8100 467-2606
Web: www.electroid.com

Electronic Theatre Controls Inc
3031 Pleasantview Rd. .... Middleton WI 53562 608-831-4116 836-1736
TF: 800-688-4116 ■ *Web:* www.etcconnect.com

Enercon Engineering Inc 201 Altorfer Ln .... East Peoria IL 61611 309-694-1418 694-3703
TF: 800-218-8831 ■ *Web:* www.enercon-eng.com

Energy Conversion Technologies Inc
1271 Denison St Unit 56-59 Unit 56-59. .... Markham ON L3R4B5 905-947-4300
Web: www.energyconversiontech.com

FSI Technologies Inc 668 E Western Ave .... Lombard IL 60148 630-932-9380 932-0016
TF: 800-468-6009 ■ *Web:* www.fsinet.com

Fujitsu Components America Inc
250 E Caribbean Dr .... Sunnyvale CA 94089 408-745-4900 745-4970
Web: www.fujitsu.com

FXC Corp 3410 S Susan St. .... Santa Ana CA 92704 714-556-7400 641-5093
Web: www.pia.com

G & L Motion Control Inc
672 S Military Rd .... Fond Du Lac WI 54935 920-921-7100
Web: kdn.kollmorgen.com/content/gl-support-downloads-and-documentation

Genesis International Inc
1040 Fox Chase Industrial Dr. .... Arnold MO 63010 636-282-0011
Web: www.genesis-international.com

Gentec Inc 2625 Dalton .... Quebec QC G1P3S9 418-651-8000
TF: 800-463-4480 ■ *Web:* gentec.ca

GET Engineering Corp 9350 Bond Ave. .... El Cajon CA 92021 619-443-8295 443-8613
TF: 877-494-1820 ■ *Web:* www.getntds.com

	City	State	ZIP	Phone	Fax
Glendinning Marine Products 740 Century Cir *TF:* 800-500-2380 ■ *Web:* www.glendinningprods.com	Conway	SC	29526	843-399-6146	399-5005
Globe Electronic Hardware Inc 34-24 56th St *TF:* 800-221-1505 ■ *Web:* www.globelectronics.com	Woodside	NY	11377	718-457-0303	457-7493
Governors America Corp 720 Silver St *Web:* www.governors-america.com	Agawam	MA	01001	413-786-5600	
Guardian Electric Mfg Company Inc 1425 Lake Ave *TF:* 800-762-0369 ■ *Web:* www.guardian-electric.com	Woodstock	IL	60098	815-334-3600	337-0377
Hamlin Electronics Inc 612 E Lake St *Web:* www.hamlin.com	Lake Mills	WI	53551	920-648-3000	648-3001
Harold Beck & Sons Inc 11 Terry Dr *Web:* www.haroldbeck.com	Newtown	PA	18940	215-968-4600	
Hasco Relays & Electronics International Corp 906 Jericho Tpke *Web:* www.hascorelays.com	New Hyde Park	NY	11040	516-328-9292	
HF scientific Inc 3170 Metro Pkwy *Web:* www.hfscientific.com	Fort Myers	FL	33916	239-337-2116	
High Country Tek Inc 208 Gold Flat Ct *Web:* www.highcountrytek.com	Nevada City	CA	95959	530-265-3236	
Honeywell Automation & Control Solutions 11 W Spring St *Web:* www.honeywell.com	Freeport	IL	61032	815-235-5500	
Honeywell Sensing & Control 11 W Spring St *TF Cust Svc:* 800-537-6945 ■ *Web:* www.honeywell.com	Freeport	IL	61032	815-235-5500	
Hubbell Industrial Controls 4301 Cheyenne Dr *Web:* www.hubbell-icd.com	Archdale	NC	27263	336-434-2800	434-2803
Hydrolevel Co 83 Water St *TF:* 800-654-0768 ■ *Web:* www.hydrolevel.com	New Haven	CT	06511	203-776-0473	
Icm Controls Corp 7313 William Barry Blvd *TF:* 800-365-5525 ■ *Web:* www.icmcontrols.com	North Syracuse	NY	13212	315-233-5266	233-5276
IDEC Corp 1175 Elko Dr *TF:* 800-262-4332 ■ *Web:* www.idec.com	Sunnyvale	CA	94089	408-747-0550	744-9055
Imperial Irrigation District (IID) PO Box 937 *TF:* 800-303-7756 ■ *Web:* www.iid.com	Imperial	CA	92251	760-482-9600	482-9611
Inertia Dynamics Inc 31 Industrial Pk Rd *TF:* 800-800-6445 ■ *Web:* www.idicb.com	New Hartford	CT	06057	860-482-4444	
Infitec Inc 6500 Badgley Rd *Web:* www.infitec.com	East Syracuse	NY	13057	315-433-1150	
Intermatic Inc 7777 Winn Rd *Web:* www.intermatic.com	Spring Grove	IL	60081	815-675-7000	675-7001
Jennings Technology Co 970 McLaughlin Ave *Web:* www.jenningstech.com	San Jose	CA	95122	408-292-4025	286-1789
JR Merritt Controls Inc 55 Sperry Ave *Web:* www.jrmerritt.com	Stratford	CT	06615	203-381-0100	
K/E Electric Supply Co 146 N Groesbeck Hwy *Web:* www.keelectric.com	Mount Clemens	MI	48043	586-469-3005	469-3006
KB Electronics Inc 12095 NW 39th St *TF:* 800-221-6570 ■ *Web:* www.kbelectronics.com	Coral Springs	FL	33065	954-346-4900	346-3377
KEMCO Industries LLC 70 Keyes Ct *Web:* www.kemco.com	Sanford	FL	32773	407-322-1230	
Keytroller LLC 3907 W Martin Luther King Blvd *Web:* www.keytroller.com	Tampa	FL	33614	813-877-4500	
Kobelt Manufacturing Company Ltd 8238 129th St *Web:* www.kobelt.com	Surrey	BC	V3W0A6	604-572-3935	590-8313
Leach International Corp 6900 Orangethorpe Ave *TF:* 800-232-7700 ■ *Web:* www.esterline.com	Buena Park	CA	90622	714-736-7598	739-1713
Lutron Electronics Company Inc 7200 Suter Rd *TF Tech Supp:* 800-523-9466 ■ *Web:* www.lutron.com	Coopersburg	PA	18036	610-282-6280	282-6253
Mac Products Inc 60 Pennsylvania Ave PO Box 469 *Web:* www.macproducts.net	Kearny	NJ	07032	973-344-0700	344-5368
Magnet Schultz of America Inc 401 Plaza Dr *Web:* www.magnet-schultz.com	Westmont	IL	60559	630-789-0600	789-0614
MagneTek Inc N49 W13650 Campbell Dr *NASDAQ: MAG* ■ *TF:* 800-288-8178 ■ *Web:* www.magnetek.com	Menomonee Falls	WI	53051	800-288-8178	298-3503
Marquardt Switches Inc 2711 US 20 *Web:* us.marquardt.com	Cazenovia	NY	13035	315-655-8050	655-8042
Martin Automatic Inc 1661 Northrock Ct *Web:* www.martinauto.com	Rockford	IL	61103	815-654-4800	654-4810
Maxcess International, Inc. 222 W Memorial Rd PO Box 26508 *TF:* 800-333-3433	Oklahoma City	OK	73114	405-755-1600	755-8425
McDade-Woodcock Inc 2404 Claremont Ave NE PO Box 11592 *Web:* mwieic.com	Albuquerque	NM	87107	505-884-0155	884-6073
Moog Inc Jamison Rd *NYSE: MOG/A* ■ *TF:* 800-336-2112 ■ *Web:* www.moog.com	East Aurora	NY	14052	716-652-2000	687-4457
Mosebach Manufacturing Co 1417 Mclaughlin Run Rd *Web:* www.mosebachresistors.com	Pittsburgh	PA	15241	412-220-0200	
Networks Electronic Co 9750 De Soto Ave *Web:* www.networkselectronic.com	Chatsworth	CA	91311	818-341-0440	718-7133
Novaspect Inc 1124 Tower Rd *Web:* www.novaspect.com	Schaumburg	IL	60173	847-956-8020	885-8200
OEM Controls Inc 10 Controls Dr *Web:* www.oemcontrols.com	Shelton	CT	06484	203-929-8431	929-3867
OMRON Corp 1 Commerce Dr *TF:* 800-556-6766 ■ *Web:* www.omron247.com	Schaumburg	IL	60173	847-843-7900	843-7787
OMRON Scientific Technologies Inc 6550 Dumbarton Cir *TF:* 888-510-4357 ■ *Web:* www.sti.com	Fremont	CA	94555	510-608-3400	744-1440
Ormec Systems Corp 19 Linden Pk *TF:* 800-656-7632 ■ *Web:* www.ormec.com	Rochester	NY	14625	585-385-3520	385-5999
Panasonic Electric Works Corp of America 629 Central Ave *TF:* 800-276-6289 ■ *Web:* www.pewa.panasonic.com	New Providence	NJ	07974	908-464-3550	464-4128

	City	State	ZIP	Phone	Fax
Parker Hannifin Corp Electromechanical Automation Div 5500 Business Pk Dr *TF:* 800-358-9068 ■ *Web:* www.parkermotion.com	Rohnert Park	CA	94928	707-584-7558	584-8015
Parker McCrory Manufacturing Co 2000 Forest Ave *TF:* 800-662-1038 ■ *Web:* www.parmakusa.com	Kansas City	MO	64108	816-221-2000	221-9879
Payne Engineering Co Rt 29 PO Box 70 *TF Orders:* 800-331-1345 ■ *Web:* www.payneng.com	Scott Depot	WV	25560	304-757-7353	757-7305
Peerless Instrument Company Inc 1966-D Broadhollow Rd *Web:* www.peerless.cwfc.com	Farmingdale	NY	11735	631-396-6500	396-6555
Pepperl Fuchs Inc 1600 Enterprise Pkwy *Web:* www.pepperl-fuchs.us	Twinsburg	OH	44087	330-425-3555	425-4607
Phasetronics Inc 1600 Sunshine Dr *Web:* www.phasetronics.com	Clearwater	FL	33765	727-573-1819	
Pine Instrument Co 101 Industrial Dr *Web:* www.pineinst.com	Grove City	PA	16127	724-458-6391	458-4648
Polytron Corp 4400 Wyland Dr *TF:* 888-228-0246 ■ *Web:* www.polytron-corp.com	Elkhart	IN	46516	574-522-0246	522-0457
Precision Governors Inc 2322 Seventh Ave *Web:* www.pgcontrols.com	Rockford	IL	61104	815-229-5300	
Precision Multiple Controls Inc 33 Greenwood Ave *Web:* pmcontrols.com	Midland Park	NJ	07432	201-444-0600	445-8575
Premier System Integrators Inc 140 Weakley Ln *Web:* www.premier-system.com	Smyrna	TN	37167	615-355-7200	355-7210
PVA Tepla America Inc 251 Corporate Terr *TF Sales:* 800-527-5667 ■ *Web:* pvateplaamerica.com	Corona	CA	92879	951-371-2500	
RAM Industrial Services Inc 5460B Pottsville Pk *Web:* www.rammotors.com	Leesport	PA	19533	610-916-8000	
RCI Custom Products 801 NE St Ste 2A *TF:* 800-546-4724 ■ *Web:* www.rcicustom.com	Frederick	MD	21701	301-620-9130	620-9103
Relay Specialties Inc 17 Raritan Rd *TF:* 800-526-5376 ■ *Web:* www.relayspec.com	Oakland	NJ	07436	201-337-1000	
Rockford Systems Inc 4620 Hydraulic Rd **Fax:* Sales ■ *TF Cust Svc:* 800-922-7533 ■ *Web:* www.rockfordsystems.com	Rockford	IL	61109	815-874-7891	874-6144*
Sendec Corp 72 Perinton Pkwy *TF:* 800-295-8000 ■ *Web:* apitech.com	Fairport	NY	14450	585-425-3390	425-3392
Sequence Controls Inc 150 Rosamond St *TF:* 800-663-1833 ■ *Web:* www.sequencecontrols.com	Carleton	ON	K7C1V2	613-257-7356	
Snaptron Inc 960 Diamond Valley Dr *Web:* www.snaptron.com	Windsor	CO	80550	970-686-5682	
SOR Inc 14685 W 105th St *TF:* 800-676-6794 ■ *Web:* sorinc.com	Lenexa	KS	66215	913-888-2630	888-0767
South/Shore Controls Inc 4485 N Ridge Rd *Web:* www.southshorecontrols.com	Perry	OH	44081	440-259-2500	259-2500
Sparton 27 Hale Spring Rd *TF:* 800-443-4132 ■ *Web:* sparton.com	Plaistow	NH	03865	603-382-3840	
Spectra Precision Inc 10355 Westmoor Dr Ste 100 *Web:* www.spectraprecision.com	Westminster	CO	80021	720-587-4700	
Sprecher + Schuh 15910 International Plaza Dr *TF:* 877-721-5913 ■ *Web:* www.sprecherschuh.com	Houston	TX	77032	281-442-9000	442-1570
SSI Technologies Inc PO Box 5011 *Web:* www.ssitechnologies.com	Janesville	WI	53547	608-757-2000	
Statek Corp 512 N Main St *Web:* www.statek.com	Orange	CA	92868	714-639-7810	997-1256
Static Controls Corp 30460 S Wixom Rd *Web:* www.scccontrols.com	Wixom	MI	48393	248-926-4400	
Struthers-Dunn 407 E Smith St Ste B *Web:* www.struthers-dunn.com	Timmonsville	SC	29161	843-346-4427	346-4465
Sturdy Corp 1822 Carolina Beach Rd *TF:* 800-721-3282 ■ *Web:* www.sturdycorp.com	Wilmington	NC	28401	910-763-2500	763-2650
Super Talent Technology Corp 2077 N Capitol Ave *Web:* www.supertalent.com	San Jose	CA	95132	408-934-2560	
Systems East Inc 30 Basil Sawyer Dr *TF:* 800-230-8734 ■ *Web:* systemseastinc.com	Hampton	VA	23666	757-766-8400	
Systems Machines Automation Components Corp 5807 Van Allen Way *Web:* www.smac-mca.com	Carlsbad	CA	92008	760-929-7575	929-7588
Tech/Ops Sevcon Inc 155 Northboro Rd *NASDAQ: SEV* ■ *Web:* www.techopssevcon.com	Southborough	MA	01772	508-281-5500	
Time Mark Corp 11440 E Pine St *TF:* 800-862-2875 ■ *Web:* www.time-mark.com	Tulsa	OK	74116	918-438-1220	437-7584
Time-O-Matic Inc 1015 Maple St *TF:* 800-637-2645 ■ *Web:* www.watchfiresigns.com	Danville	IL	61832	217-442-0611	442-1020
Tornatech Inc 7075, Place Robert-Joncas Ste 132 *TF:* 800-363-8448 ■ *Web:* www.tornatech.com	Saint-laurent	QC	H4M2Z2	514-334-0523	334-5448
Transdyn Inc 4256 Hacienda Dr # 100 *Web:* kapsch.net/ktc	Pleasanton	CA	94588	925-225-1600	225-1610
Triumph Controls Inc 205 Church Rd *TF:* 800-322-2885 ■ *Web:* triumphgroup.com	North Wales	PA	19454	215-699-4861	699-2595
Trombetta 8111 N 87th St *Web:* www.trombetta.com	Milwaukee	WI	53224	414-410-0300	355-3882
Unico Inc 3725 Nicholson Rd *Web:* www.unicous.com	Franksville	WI	53126	262-886-5678	504-7396
Ventek Inc 4030 W First St Ste 100 *Web:* www.ventek-inc.com	Eugene	OR	97402	541-344-5578	
Wago Corp N120 W19129 Freistadt Rd **Fax Area Code:* 262 ■ *TF:* 800-346-7245 ■ *Web:* www.wago.us	Germantown	WI	53022	800-346-7245	255-3232*
Whitepath Fab Tech Inc 16402 Hwy 515 N *Web:* www.whitepath.com	Ellijay	GA	30540	706-276-2511	276-2524
Whittaker Controls Inc 12838 Saticoy St *Web:* www.whittakercontrols.com	North Hollywood	CA	91605	818-765-8160	759-2190
Woodward Controls Inc 6250 W Howard St *Web:* www.woodward.com	Niles	IL	60714	847-967-7730	
X-COM Systems LLC 12345-B Sunrise Vly Dr *TF:* 800-342-8408 ■ *Web:* www.xcomsystems.com	Reston	VA	20191	703-390-1087	

Phone *Fax*

Yaskawa America Inc 2121 Norman Dr S Waukegan IL 60085 847-887-7000 887-7310*
Fax: Mktg ■ *TF:* 800-927-5292 ■ *Web:* www.yaskawa.com

204 CONVENIENCE STORES

See Also Gas Stations p. 2349; Grocery Stores p. 2444

Phone *Fax*

7-Eleven Inc 1722 Routh Ste 100 Dallas TX 75221 703-255-1800
TF: 800-255-0711 ■ *Web:* www.7-eleven.com
A & E Stores Inc 1000 Huyler St Teterboro NJ 07608 201-393-0600 393-0233
Web: www.aestores.com
Cafepress.com Inc 1850 Gateway Dr Ste 300 Foster City CA 94404 650-655-3120 240-0260
TF: 877-809-1659 ■ *Web:* www.cafepress.com
Casey's General Stores Inc 1 Convenience Blvd Ankeny IA 50021 515-965-6100
NASDAQ: CASY ■ *Web:* www.caseys.com
Cracker Barrel Convenience Stores Inc
12221 Industriplex Blvd Baton Rouge LA 70809 225-753-3200 753-3200
TF: 800-547-4151 ■ *Web:* crackerbarrelcstores.com
Crown Coco Inc 1717 Broadway St Minneapolis MN 55413 612-331-9344
Dairy Barn Stores Inc 544 Elwood Rd East Northport NY 11731 631-368-8050 266-2547
Web: www.dairybarn.com
Dixie Gas & Oil Corp 229 Lee Hwy P O Box 900 Verona VA 24482 540-248-6273
Web: www.dixiegas.com
E-Z Mart Stores
602 W Falvey Ave PO Box 1426 Texarkana TX 75501 903-832-6502 832-3731
Web: www.ezmart.com
Fkg Oil Co 721 W Main Belleville IL 62220 618-233-6754 233-1327
TF: 800-873-3546 ■ *Web:* www.mymotomart.com
Go-Mart Inc 915 Riverside Dr Gassaway WV 26624 304-364-8000
Web: gomart.com
Heathco'S Pizza & Variety 375 Court St Auburn ME 04210 207-689-9175
Web: heathcos.com
Heritage Dairy Stores Inc 376 Jessup Rd Thorofare NJ 08086 856-845-2855 845-8392
Web: www.heritages.com
Holiday Stationstores
4567 American Blvd W Bloomington MN 55437 952-830-8700
TF: 800-745-7411 ■ *Web:* www.holidaystationstores.com
Hollar Co 2012 Rainbow Dr Gadsden AL 35901 256-547-1644
Web: shell.com
Jet Food Stores of Georgia
1106 S Harris St Sandersville GA 31082 478-552-2588 552-8758
JFM Inc 4276 Lakeland Dr Flowood MS 39232 601-664-7177 664-7272
Web: www.jfminc.net
Johnny Quick Food Stores 96 Shaw Ave Ste 240 Clovis CA 93612 559-297-6830
Web: www.johnnyquik.com
Krause Gentle Corp 6400 Westown Pkwy West Des Moines IA 50266 515-226-0128 457-0178
Web: www.kumandgo.com
Kwik Trip Inc 1626 Oak St PO Box 2107 La Crosse WI 54602 608-781-8988 781-7517
Web: www.kwiktrip.com
Lassus BROS Handy Dandy 1800 Magnavox Way Fort Wayne IN 46804 260-436-1415 436-0340
Web: www.lassus.com
Leading Market Technologies Inc
58 Winter St 5th Fl Boston MA 02108 617-494-4747
Web: www.lmtech.com
Li'l Thrift Food Marts Inc
1007 Arsenal Ave Fayetteville NC 28305 910-433-4490
Web: www.shortstopfoodmarts.com
Loaf N' Jug Mini Mart 442 Keeler Pkwy Pueblo CO 81001 719-948-3071
Web: www.loafnjug.com
Love's Travel Stops & Country Stores Inc
10601 N Pennsylvania Ave Oklahoma City OK 73120 800-388-0983
TF: 800-388-0983 ■ *Web:* www.loves.com
Mac's Convenience Stores Inc
305 Milner Ave Ste 400 4th Fl Toronto ON M1B3V4 800-268-5574 291-4947*
Fax Area Code: 416 ■ *TF:* 800-268-5574 ■ *Web:* www.macs.ca
Maverik Inc 880 W Center St North Salt Lake UT 84054 801-936-5557 885-3832*
Fax Area Code: 307 ■ *TF Cust Svc:* 800-789-4455 ■ *Web:* www.maverik.com
Miller & Holmes Inc 2311 O'Neil Rd Hudson WI 54016 715-377-1730
Web: mhgas.com
Open Pantry Food Marts
10505 Corporate Dr Ste 101 Pleasant Prairie WI 53158 262-857-1156 857-9667
TF: 800-242-3358 ■ *Web:* www.openpantry.com
Pantry Inc 305 Gregson Dr Cary NC 27511 919-774-6700
NASDAQ: PTRY
Plaid Pantries Inc 10025 SW Allen Blvd Beaverton OR 97005 503-646-4246 646-3071
TF: 800-677-5243 ■ *Web:* www.plaidpantry.com
Presto Food Stores Inc
1513 James L Redman Pkwy Plant City FL 33563 813-754-3511 752-5494
Quik Stop Markets Inc 4567 Enterprise St Fremont CA 94538 510-657-8500
Web: quikstop.com
QuikTrip Corp 4705 S 129th E Ave Tulsa OK 74134 918-615-7700 615-7377
TF: 800-441-0253 ■ *Web:* www.quiktrip.com
Rocky Top Markets LLC 1324 Lawnville Rd Kingston TN 37763 865-717-0700
Scaffs Inc 134 Se Colburn Ave Lake City FL 32025 386-752-7344
Web: scaffs.com
Seven-Eleven Hawaii Inc 1755 Nuuanu Ave Honolulu HI 96817 808-526-1711
Sheetz Inc 5700 Sixth Ave Altoona PA 16602 814-941-5106 941-5105
TF: 800-487-5444 ■ *Web:* www.sheetz.com
Speedway LLC 500 Speedway Dr Enon OH 45323 937-864-3001
TF Cust Svc: 800-643-1948 ■ *Web:* www.speedway.com
Stop In Food Stores Inc 3000 Ogden Rd Roanoke VA 24018 540-772-4700
Stripes Convenience Stores
4525 Ayers St Corpus Christi TX 78415 361-884-2464 884-2494
NYSE: SUSS ■ *TF:* 800-569-3585 ■ *Web:* stripesstores.com/index.cms
Tedeschi Food Shops Inc 14 Howard St Rockland MA 02370 781-878-8210 878-0476
Web: www.tedeschifoodshops.com
Tom Thumb Food Stores Inc 97 W Okeechobee Rd Hialeah FL 33010 305-885-5451
Web: tomthumb.com
Uppy's Convenience Stores Inc
4710 Williamsburg Rd Richmond VA 23231 804-204-1534
Valdak Corp 1149 36th Ave S Grand Forks ND 58201 701-746-8371 772-9464
Web: www.valleydairy.com

Phone *Fax*

Wawa Inc 260 W Baltimore Pike Media PA 19063 610-358-8000 358-8808*
Fax: Hum Res ■ *TF:* 800-444-9292 ■ *Web:* www.wawa.com
Xtramart 221 Quinebaug Rd North Grosvenordale CT 06255 800-243-6366
TF: 800-243-6366 ■ *Web:* www.xtramart.com

205 CONVENTION CENTERS

See Also Performing Arts Facilities p. 2912; Stadiums & Arenas p. 3204
Listings are alphabetized by city names within state groupings.

Alabama

Phone *Fax*

Birmingham-Jefferson Convention Complex
2100 Richard Arrington Jr Blvd N Birmingham AL 35203 205-458-8400 328-8523
Web: www.bjcc.org
Von Braun Ctr 700 Monroe St Huntsville AL 35801 256-533-1953 551-2203
Web: www.vonbrauncenter.com

Alaska

Phone *Fax*

William A Egan Civic & Convention Ctr
555 W Fifth Ave Anchorage AK 99501 907-263-2800 263-2858
Web: www.anchorageconventioncenters.com
Carlson Ctr 2010 2nd Ave Fairbanks AK 99701 907-451-7800 451-1195
Web: www.carlson-center.com
Centennial Hall Convention Ctr 101 Egan Dr Juneau AK 99801 907-586-5283 586-1135
TF: 800-478-4176 ■ *Web:* www.juneau.org

Arizona

Phone *Fax*

Glendale Civic Ctr 5750 W Glenn Dr Glendale AZ 85301 623-930-4300 930-4319
Web: www.glendaleciviccenter.com
Mesa Convention Ctr 263 N Ctr St Mesa AZ 85201 480-644-2178 644-2617
Web: mesaaz.gov/business/mesa-convention-center
Phoenix Convention Ctr 100 N Third St Phoenix AZ 85004 602-262-6225
TF: 800-282-4842 ■ *Web:* www.phoenixconventioncenter.com
Tucson Convention Ctr 260 S Church Ave Tucson AZ 85701 520-791-4101 791-5572
Web: tucsonaz.gov
Yuma Civic Ctr 1440 W Desert Hills Dr Yuma AZ 85365 928-373-5040 344-9121
TF: 866-966-0220 ■ *Web:* www.yumaaz.gov

Arkansas

Phone *Fax*

Fort Smith Convention Ctr 55 S Seventh St Fort Smith AR 72901 479-788-8932
Web: www.fortsmith.org
Hot Springs Convention Ctr (HSCVB)
134 Convention Blvd PO Box 6000 Hot Springs AR 71902 501-321-2277 955-2600
TF: 800-625-7576 ■ *Web:* www.hotsprings.org
Statehouse Convention Ctr
426 W Markham PO Box 3232 Little Rock AR 72203 501-376-4781
TF: 800-844-4781 ■ *Web:* littlerockmeetings.com/convention-center

British Columbia

Phone *Fax*

Vancouver Convention & Exposition Centre (VCEC)
1055 Canada Pl Vancouver BC V6C0C3 604-689-8232 647-7232
TF: 866-785-8232 ■ *Web:* www.vancouverconventioncentre.com

California

Phone *Fax*

Anaheim Convention Ctr 800 W Katella Ave Anaheim CA 92802 714-765-8950 765-8965
Web: www.anaheim.net/1117/anaheim-convention-center-arena
Rabobank Arena Theater & Convention Ctr
1001 Truxtun Ave Bakersfield CA 93301 661-852-7300 861-9904
Web: rabobankarena.com
Carson Ctr 801 E Carson St Carson CA 90745 310-835-0212 835-0160
Web: www.carsoncenter.com
Cow Palace 2600 Geneva Ave Daly City CA 94014 415-404-4100 404-4111
Web: www.cowpalace.com
Fresno Convention Ctr 848 M St Fresno CA 93721 559-445-8100 445-8110
Web: www.fresnoconventioncenter.com
Bren Events Ctr 100 Bren Events Ctr Irvine CA 92697 949-824-5050 824-5097
Web: www.ucirvinesports.com/bren/index
Long Beach Convention & Entertainment Ctr
300 E Ocean Blvd Long Beach CA 90802 562-436-3636 436-9491
Web: www.longbeachcc.com
California Market Ctr 110 E Ninth St Los Angeles CA 90079 213-630-3600 630-3708
TF: 800-225-6278 ■ *Web:* www.californiamarketcenter.com
Los Angeles Convention Ctr
1201 S Figueroa St Los Angeles CA 90015 213-741-1151
Web: www.lacclink.com
Shrine Auditorium & Exposition Ctr
665 W Jefferson Blvd Los Angeles CA 90007 213-748-5116
Web: www.shrineauditorium.com
Modesto Centre Plaza 1000 L St Modesto CA 95354 209-577-6444 544-6729
Web: www.modestogov.com/prnd/facilities/mcp
Monterey Conference Ctr 1 Portola Plz Monterey CA 93940 831-646-3770 646-3777
TF Sales: 800-742-8091 ■ *Web:* www.montereyconferencecenter.com
WLA Investments Inc
1301 Dove St Ste 1080 Newport Beach CA 92660 949-851-2020
Web: www.wlainvestments.com
Oakland Convention Ctr 1001 Broadway Oakland CA 94607 510-451-4000 835-3466
TF: 800-228-9290 ■ *Web:* marriott.com

Phone | Fax

Ontario Convention Ctr
2000 E Convention Ctr Way ... Ontario CA 91764 909-937-3000 937-3080
TF: 800-455-5755 ■ *Web:* www.ontariocc.org

Palm Springs Convention Ctr
277 N Avenida Caballeros ... Palm Springs CA 92262 760-325-6611 778-4102
TF: 800-898-7256 ■ *Web:* www.palmspringscc.com

Sacramento Convention Ctr 1400 J St ... Sacramento CA 95814 916-808-5291 808-7687
Web: www.sacramentoconventioncenter.com

NOS Events Ctr 689 SE St ... San Bernardino CA 92408 909-888-6788
Web: www.nosevents.com

San Diego Convention Ctr 111 W Harbor Dr ... San Diego CA 92101 619-525-5000 525-5005
TF: 800-525-7322 ■ *Web:* visitsandiego.com

Moscone Ctr 747 Howard St ... San Francisco CA 94103 415-974-4000 974-4073
Web: www.moscone.com

Nob Hill Masonic Ctr
1111 California St ... San Francisco CA 94108 415-776-7457
Web: www.sfmasoniccenter.com

San Jose Convention Center (SJC)
150 W San Carlos St ... San Jose CA 95110 408-792-4194 277-3535
TF: 800-726-5673 ■
Web: www.sanjose.org/plan-a-meeting-event/venues/convention-center

Santa Clara Convention Ctr
5001 Great America Pkwy ... Santa Clara CA 95054 408-748-7000
Web: www.santaclara.org

Santa Monica Civic Auditorium
1855 Main St ... Santa Monica CA 90401 310-458-8551
TF: 866-728-3229 ■ *Web:* smgov.net/departments/ccs/civicauditorium

Visalia Convention Ctr 303 E Acequia Ave ... Visalia CA 93291 559-713-4000 713-4804
TF: 800-640-4888 ■ *Web:* www.ci.visalia.ca.us

Colorado

Phone | Fax

Colorado Springs City Auditorium
221 E Kiowa St ... Colorado Springs CO 80903 719-385-5969 385-6584
TF: 800-888-4748 ■ *Web:* www.springsgov.com

Colorado Convention Ctr 700 14th St ... Denver CO 80202 303-228-8000 228-8103
Web: www.denverconvention.com

Equitable Building 730 17th St Ste 200 ... Denver CO 80202 303-893-5456
Web: www.stcharlestown.com

Two Rivers Convention Ctr 159 Main St ... Grand Junction CO 81501 970-263-5700 263-5720
Web: www.tworiversconvention.com

Connecticut

Phone | Fax

XL Ctr 1 Civic Ctr Plz ... Hartford CT 06103 860-249-6333
Web: www.xlcenter.com

District of Columbia

Phone | Fax

Washington Convention Ctr Authority
801 Mt Vernon Pl NW ... Washington DC 20001 202-249-3000
TF: 800-368-9000 ■ *Web:* www.dcconvention.com

Florida

Phone | Fax

Ocean Ctr 101 N Atlantic Ave ... Daytona Beach FL 32118 386-254-4500 254-4512
TF: 800-858-6444 ■ *Web:* www.oceancenter.com

Greater Fort Lauderdale-Broward County Convention Ctr
1950 Eisenhower Blvd ... Fort Lauderdale FL 33316 954-765-5900
Web: www.ftlauderdalecc.com

Harborside Event Ctr 1375 Monroe St ... Fort Myers FL 33901 239-321-8110
Web: www.fmharborside.com

Accesso Partners LLC
1140 E Hallandale Beach Blvd ... Hallandale Beach FL 33009 954-454-4665
Web: www.accessopartners.com

Prime Osborn Convention Ctr
1000 Water St ... Jacksonville FL 32204 904-630-4000 630-4029
Web: www.jaxevents.com/primeosbornconventioncenter

Lakeland Ctr 701 W Lime St ... Lakeland FL 33815 863-834-8100 834-8101
Web: www.thelakelandcenter.com

Miami Beach Convention Ctr
1901 Convention Ctr Dr ... Miami Beach FL 33139 305-673-7311 673-7435
Web: www.miamibeachconvention.com

Orange County Convention Ctr (OCCC)
9800 International Dr ... Orlando FL 32819 407-685-9800 685-9876
TF: 800-345-9845 ■ *Web:* www.occc.net

Manatee Convention Ctr 1 Haben Blvd ... Palmetto FL 34221 941-722-3244 729-1820
TF: 800-822-2017 ■ *Web:* www.bradentongulfislands.com

Turnbull Conference Ctr
555 W Pensacola St
FSU Ctr for Professional Development ... Tallahassee FL 32306 850-644-3801 644-2589
Web: alwayslearning.fsu.edu

Tampa Convention Ctr 333 S Franklin St ... Tampa FL 33602 813-274-8511 274-7430
TF: 866-790-4111 ■ *Web:* www.tampagov.net

Palm Beach County Convention Ctr
650 Okeechobee Blvd ... West Palm Beach FL 33401 561-366-3000 366-3001
Web: www.palmbeachfl.com

Georgia

Phone | Fax

AmericasMart 240 Peachtree St NW Ste 2200 ... Atlanta GA 30303 404-220-3000
TF: 800-285-6278 ■ *Web:* www.americasmart.com

Cobb Galleria Centre 2 Galleria Pkwy ... Atlanta GA 30339 770-955-8000
Web: www.cobbgalleria.com

Georgia World Congress Ctr
285 Andrew Young International Blvd NW ... Atlanta GA 30313 404-223-4200 223-4211
Web: www.gwcc.com

Georgia International Convention Ctr
2000 Convention Ctr Concourse ... College Park GA 30337 770-997-3566 994-8559
TF: 888-331-4422 ■ *Web:* www.gicc.com

Columbus Georgia Convention & Trade Ctr
801 Front Ave ... Columbus GA 31901 706-327-4522
Web: www.columbusga.org/tradecenter

Northwest Georgia Trade & Convention Ctr
2211 Dug Gap Battle Rd ... Dalton GA 30720 706-272-7676
Web: www.visitdaltonga.com

Georgia Mountains Ctr
301 Main St SW PO Box 2496 ... Gainesville GA 30501 770-534-8420
Web: www.gainesville.org

Jekyll Island Convention Ctr
1 N Beachview Dr ... Jekyll Island GA 31527 912-635-5203
Web: www.jekyllisland.com

Meadows & Ohly LLC Two Sun Ct Ste 350 ... Norcross GA 30092 678-282-0220
Web: www.meadowsandohly.com

Savannah International Trade & Convention Ctr
1 International Dr ... Savannah GA 31421 912-447-4000 447-4722*
**Fax:* Sales ■ *TF:* 888-644-6822 ■ *Web:* www.savtcc.com

Hawaii

Phone | Fax

Hawaii Convention Ctr 1801 Kalakaua Ave ... Honolulu HI 96815 808-943-3500 943-3599
TF: 800-295-6603 ■ *Web:* www.meethawaii.com

Idaho

Phone | Fax

Boise Centre on the Grove 850 W Front St ... Boise ID 83702 208-336-8900 336-8803
Web: www.boisecentre.com

Illinois

Phone | Fax

DataCo LLC
85 W Algonquin Rd Ste 360 ... Arlington Heights IL 60005 847-290-0636
Web: www.datacosolutions.com

McCormick Place 2301 S Lk Shore Dr ... Chicago IL 60616 312-791-7000 791-6543
Web: www.mccormickplace.com

Merchandise Mart
222 Merchandise Mart Plz Ste 470 ... Chicago IL 60654 312-527-4141
TF: 800-677-6278 ■ *Web:* www.merchandisemart.com/mmart

Navy Pier 600 E Grand Ave ... Chicago IL 60611 312-595-7437
TF: 800-595-7437 ■ *Web:* www.navypier.com

Gateway Ctr 1 Gateway Dr ... Collinsville IL 62234 618-345-8998 345-9024
TF: 800-289-2388 ■ *Web:* gatewaycenter.com

Exposition Gardens 1601 W Northmoor Rd ... Peoria IL 61614 309-691-6332 691-2372
Web: www.expogardensinc.com

Oakley-Lindsay Ctr 300 Civic Ctr Plaza Ste 237 ... Quincy IL 62301 217-223-1000 223-1330
TF: 800-978-4748 ■ *Web:* www.oakleylindsaycenter.com

Quad City Conservation Alliance Expo Ctr
2621 Fourth Ave ... Rock Island IL 61201 309-788-5912 788-9619
Web: www.qccaexpocenter.com

Donald E Stephens Convention Ctr
5555 N River Rd ... Rosemont IL 60018 847-692-2220 696-9700
Web: www.rosemont.com

Prairie Capital Convention Ctr (PC3)
1 Convention Ctr Plz ... Springfield IL 62701 217-788-8800 788-0811
Web: springfieldpc3.com

Indiana

Phone | Fax

Bloomington Monroe County Convention Ctr
302 S College Ave ... Bloomington IN 47403 812-336-3681 349-2981
Web: www.bloomingtonconvention.com

Grand Wayne Convention Ctr
120 W Jefferson Blvd ... Fort Wayne IN 46802 260-426-4100 420-9080
Web: www.grandwayne.com

Indiana Convention Ctr & Lucas Oil Stadium (ICCLOS)
100 S Capitol Ave ... Indianapolis IN 46225 317-262-3400 262-3685
Web: www.icclos.com

Horizon Convention Ctr 401 S High St ... Muncie IN 47305 765-288-8860 751-9190
TF: 888-288-8860 ■ *Web:* www.horizonconvention.com

Century Ctr 120 S St Joseph St ... South Bend IN 46601 574-235-9711 235-9185
Web: www.centurycenter.org

Iowa

Phone | Fax

Venuworks Inc 4611 Mortensen Rd Ste 111 ... Ames IA 50014 515-232-5151
Web: www.venuworks.com

US Cellular Ctr 370 First Ave E ... Cedar Rapids IA 52401 319-398-5211
TF: 800-745-3000 ■ *Web:* www.uscellularcenter.com

RiverCenter Adler Theatre 136 E Third St ... Davenport IA 52801 563-326-8500 326-8505
Web: www.riverctr.com

Polk County Convention Complex
730 Third St ... Des Moines IA 50309 515-564-8001 564-8001
Web: www.iowaeventscenter.com

Sioux City Convention Ctr 801 Fourth St ... Sioux City IA 51101 712-279-4800 279-4900
TF: 800-593-2228 ■ *Web:* www.visitsiouxcity.org/convention-center

Tyson Events Ctr 401 Gordon Dr ... Sioux City IA 51101 712-279-4850 279-4903
TF: 800-593-2228 ■ *Web:* www.tysoncenter.com

Kansas

Phone | Fax

Kansas Expocentre 1 Expocentre Dr ... Topeka KS 66612 785-235-1986 235-2967
TF: 800-745-3000 ■ *Web:* www.ksexpo.com

				Phone	Fax
Century II Performing Arts & Convention Ctr 225 W Douglas Ave *Web:* www.century2.org	Wichita	KS	67202	316-264-9121	

Kentucky

				Phone	Fax
Frankfort Convention Ctr 405 Mero St *Web:* www.frankfortconventioncenter.com	Frankfort	KY	40601	502-564-5335	564-3310
Lexington Convention Ctr 430 W Vine St *Web:* www.lexingtoncenter.com	Lexington	KY	40507	859-233-4567	253-2718
Kentucky International Convention Ctr 221 S Fourth St *TF:* 800-701-5831 ■ *Web:* www.kyconvention.org	Louisville	KY	40202	502-595-4381	584-9711

Louisiana

				Phone	Fax
Baton Rouge River Ctr 275 S River Rd *Web:* www.brrivercenter.com	Baton Rouge	LA	70802	225-389-3030	389-4954
Bossier Civic Ctr 620 Benton Rd *Web:* www.bossiercity.org	Bossier City	LA	71111	318-741-8900	741-8910
Pontchartrain Ctr 4545 Williams Blvd *TF:* 800-745-3000 ■ *Web:* www.pontchartraincenter.com	Kenner	LA	70065	504-465-9985	468-6692
Cajundome & Convention Ctr 444 Cajundome Blvd *Web:* www.cajundome.com	Lafayette	LA	70506	337-265-2100	265-2311
Monroe Civic Ctr 401 Lea Joyner Expy *Web:* ci.monroe.la.us	Monroe	LA	71201	318-329-2225	329-2548
Ernest N Morial Convention Ctr 900 Convention Ctr Blvd *Web:* www.mccno.com	New Orleans	LA	70130	504-582-3023	582-3088
Festival Plaza 101 Crockett St *TF:* 888-458-4748 ■ *Web:* www.shreveportla.gov	Shreveport	LA	71101	318-673-5100	673-5105

Maine

				Phone	Fax
Augusta Civic Ctr 16 Cony St *Web:* www.augustamaine.gov	Augusta	ME	04330	207-626-2405	626-5968
Cross Insurance Center 515 Main St *TF:* 800-745-3000 ■ *Web:* www.crossinsurancecenter.com	Bangor	ME	04401	207-561-8300	

Maryland

				Phone	Fax
Baltimore Convention Ctr 1 W Pratt St *Web:* www.bccenter.org	Baltimore	MD	21201	410-649-7000	649-7008

Massachusetts

				Phone	Fax
Boston Convention & Exhibition Ctr 415 Summer St *Web:* massconvention.com	Boston	MA	02210	617-954-2000	954-2299
Exchange Conference Ctr 212 Northern Ave *Web:* www.exchangeconferencecenter.com	Boston	MA	02210	617-790-1900	790-1922
John B Hynes Veterans Memorial Convention Ctr 900 Boylston St *TF:* 800-392-6089 ■ *Web:* massconvention.com	Boston	MA	02115	617-954-2000	954-2299
MassMutual Ctr 1277 Main St *Web:* www.massmutualcenter.com	Springfield	MA	01103	413-787-6610	787-6645
DCU Ctr 50 Foster St *Web:* www.dcucenter.com	Worcester	MA	01608	508-755-6800	929-0111

Michigan

				Phone	Fax
Cobo Conference & Exhibition Ctr 1 Washington Blvd *Web:* www.cobocenter.com	Detroit	MI	48226	313-877-8777	877-8577
DeVos Place 303 Monroe Ave *Web:* www.devosplace.org	Grand Rapids	MI	49503	616-742-6500	742-6590
Lansing Ctr 333 E Michigan Ave *Web:* www.lansingcenter.com	Lansing	MI	48933	517-483-7400	483-7439
Horizons Conference Ctr 6200 State St *Web:* www.horizonscenter.com	Saginaw	MI	48603	989-799-4122	799-4188

Minnesota

				Phone	Fax
Duluth Entertainment Convention Ctr 350 Harbor Dr *TF:* 800-628-8385 ■ *Web:* www.decc.org	Duluth	MN	55802	218-722-5573	722-4247
Earle Brown Heritage Ctr 6155 Earle Brown Dr *Web:* www.earlebrown.com	Minneapolis	MN	55430	763-569-6300	
Minneapolis Convention Ctr 1301 Second Ave S *Web:* www.minneapolis.org	Minneapolis	MN	55403	612-335-6000	335-6757
Mayo Civic Ctr 30 Civic Ctr Dr SE *TF:* 800-422-2199 ■ *Web:* www.mayociviccenter.com	Rochester	MN	55904	507-328-2220	328-2221
Saint Paul RiverCentre 175 W Kellogg Blvd *Web:* www.rivercentre.org	Saint Paul	MN	55102	651-265-4800	265-4899

Mississippi

				Phone	Fax
Mississippi Coast Coliseum & Convention Ctr 2350 Beach Blvd *TF:* 800-726-2781 ■ *Web:* mscoastcoliseum.com	Biloxi	MS	39531	228-594-3700	594-3812
James M Trotter Convention Ctr 402 Second Ave N	Columbus	MS	39701	662-328-4164	329-5166
Natchez Convention Ctr 211 Main St *TF:* 888-475-9144 ■ *Web:* www.natchezconventioncenter.org	Natchez	MS	39120	601-442-5880	

Missouri

				Phone	Fax
Jack Lawton Webb Convention Ctr 5300 S Range Line Rd	Joplin	MO	64804	417-781-4000	623-7400
Kansas City Convention & Entertainment Centers 301 W 13th St *TF:* 800-767-7700 ■ *Web:* visitkc.com/convention-center/index.aspx	Kansas City	MO	64105	816-513-5000	
Nrccua 3651 Ne Ralph Powell Rd *Web:* www.nrccua.org	Lees Summit	MO	64064	816-525-2201	
America's Ctr Convention Ctr 701 Convention Plz Ste 300 *TF:* 800-325-7962 ■ *Web:* www.explorestlouis.com/americascenter/public.asp	Saint Louis	MO	63101	314-342-5036	342-5040
Saint Louis Executive Conference Ctr 701 Convention Plz *TF:* 800-325-7962 ■ *Web:* www.explorestlouis.com	Saint Louis	MO	63101	314-342-5050	
Springfield Exposition Ctr 635 E St Louis St *Web:* www.upspringfield.com	Springfield	MO	65806	417-522-3976	864-3077
Koch Development Co 222 S Central Ave Ste 1100 *Web:* www.kochdevelopment.com	St. Louis	MO	63105	314-333-5624	

Montana

				Phone	Fax
MetraPark 308 6th Ave N *TF:* 800-366-8538 ■ *Web:* www.metrapark.com	Billings	MT	59101	406-256-2400	
City of Great Falls PO Box 5021 Great Falls Civic Ctr *Web:* www.greatfallsmt.net	Great Falls	MT	59403	406-771-0885	
Helena Civic Ctr 340 Neill Ave *Web:* www.helenaciviccenter.com	Helena	MT	59601	406-447-8481	447-8480

Nebraska

				Phone	Fax
Pershing Ctr 226 Centennial Mall S	Lincoln	NE	68508	402-441-8744	441-7913
Lied Lodge & Conference Center 2700 Sylvan Rd *Web:* liedlodge.org	Nebraska City	NE	68410	402-873-8733	

Nevada

				Phone	Fax
Elko Convention & Visitors Authority 700 Moren Way *TF:* 800-248-3556 ■ *Web:* www.elkocva.com	Elko	NV	89801	775-738-4091	738-2420
Henderson Convention Ctr 200 S Water St *TF:* 877-775-5252 ■ *Web:* www.visithenderson.com	Henderson	NV	89015	702-267-2171	
Sands Expo & Convention Ctr 201 Sands Ave *Web:* www.sandsexpo.com	Las Vegas	NV	89169	702-733-5556	733-5568
Reno-Sparks Convention Ctr 4590 S Virginia St *TF:* 800-367-7366 ■ *Web:* www.visitrenotahoe.com	Reno	NV	89502	775-827-7600	827-7701

New Jersey

				Phone	Fax
New Jersey Convention & Exposition Ctr 97 Sunfield Ave *TF:* 800-367-0070 ■ *Web:* www.njexpocenter.com	Edison	NJ	08837	732-417-1400	
Meadowlands Exposition Ctr 355 Plaza Dr *Web:* www.mecexpo.com	Secaucus	NJ	07094	201-330-7773	330-1172
Garden State Exhibit Ctr 50 Atrium Dr *Web:* www.gsec.com	Somerset	NJ	08873	732-469-4000	
Wildwoods Convention Ctr 4501 Boardwalk *TF:* 800-992-9732 ■ *Web:* www.wildwoodsnj.com	Wildwood	NJ	08260	609-729-9000	846-2631

New Mexico

				Phone	Fax
Albuquerque Convention Ctr 401 Second St NW *Web:* www.albuquerquecc.com	Albuquerque	NM	87102	505-768-4575	768-3239

New York

				Phone	Fax
Office of General Services Corning Tower 41st Fl Empire State Plz *TF:* 877-426-6006 ■ *Web:* ogs.ny.gov	Albany	NY	12242	518-474-3899	457-3081
Buffalo Niagara Convention Ctr 153 Franklin St Convention Ctr Plz *TF:* 800-995-7570 ■ *Web:* www.buffaloconvention.com	Buffalo	NY	14202	716-855-5555	855-3158
Enstoa Inc 12 W 31st St Fl 8 *Web:* www.enstoa.com	New York	NY	10001	212-913-0870	
Jacob K Javits Convention Ctr 655 W 34th St *Web:* www.javitscenter.com	New York	NY	10001	212-216-2000	216-2588
Rochester Riverside Convention Ctr 123 E Main St *Web:* www.rrcc.com	Rochester	NY	14604	585-232-7200	232-1510
Saratoga Springs City Ctr 522 Broadway *Web:* saratogacitycenter.org	Saratoga Springs	NY	12866	518-584-0027	584-0117

Oncenter Complex 800 S State St .... Syracuse NY 13202 315-435-8000 435-8099
TF: 800-776-7548 ■ *Web:* www.oncenter.org

North Carolina

Phone Fax

Asheville Civic Ctr 87 Haywood St .... Asheville NC 28801 828-259-5743 259-5777
TF: 888-464-4218 ■ *Web:* www.ashevillenc.gov

Charlotte Convention Ctr 501 S College St .... Charlotte NC 28202 704-339-6000 339-6024
Web: www.charlotteconventionctr.com

Metrolina Expo Trade Ctr
7100 Statesville Rd .... Charlotte NC 28269 704-596-4650 295-1983
Web: www.metrolinatradeshowexpo.com

Park Expo & Conference Ctr, The
800 Briar Creek Rd .... Charlotte NC 28205 704-333-7709
Web: theparkexponc.com

Greensboro Coliseum Complex 1921 W Lee St ...... Greensboro NC 27403 336-373-7400 373-2170
Web: www.greensborocoliseum.com

International Home Furnishings Ctr
210 E Commerce Ave .... High Point NC 27260 336-888-3700 882-1873

Raleigh Convention Ctr 500 S Salisbury St .... Raleigh NC 27601 919-996-8500
Web: www.raleighconvention.com

Benton Convention Ctr 301 W Fifth St .... Winston-Salem NC 27101 336-727-2976
Web: twincityquarter.com

North Dakota

Phone Fax

Bismarck Civic Ctr 315 S Fifth St .... Bismarck ND 58504 701-355-1370 222-6599

Fargo Civic Ctr 207 N Fourth St .... Fargo ND 58102 701-241-1480 241-1483
Web: www.cityoffargo.com

Alerus Ctr 1200 42nd St S .... Grand Forks ND 58201 701-792-1200 746-6511
Web: www.aleruscenter.com

Ohio

Phone Fax

John S Knight Ctr 77 E Mill St .... Akron OH 44308 330-374-8900 374-8971
TF: 800-245-4254 ■ *Web:* www.johnsknightcenter.org

Duke Energy Ctr 525 Elm St .... Cincinnati OH 45202 513-419-7300 419-7327
Web: www.duke-energycenter.com

International Exposition Ctr 1-X Ctr Dr .... Cleveland OH 44135 216-676-6000
TF: 855-436-8683 ■ *Web:* www.ixcenter.com

Franklin County Veterans Memorial
300 W Broad St .... Columbus OH 43215 614-221-4341 221-8422

Greater Columbus Convention Ctr
400 N High St .... Columbus OH 43215 614-827-2500 221-7239
TF: 800-626-0241 ■ *Web:* www.columbusconventions.com

Dayton Convention Ctr 22 E Fifth St .... Dayton OH 45402 937-333-4700 333-4711
Web: www.daytonconventioncenter.com

Sharonville Convention Ctr
11355 Chester Rd .... Sharonville OH 45246 513-771-7744 772-5745
TF: 800-294-3179 ■ *Web:* www.sharonvilleconventioncenter.com

SeaGate Convention Centre 401 Jefferson Ave .... Toledo OH 43604 419-255-3300 255-7731
Web: www.toledo-seagate.com

Oklahoma

Phone Fax

Cherokee Strip Conference Ctr 123 W Maine St .... Enid OK 73701 580-234-1919

Cox Business Services Convention Ctr
1 Myriad Gardens .... Oklahoma City OK 73102 405-602-8500 602-8505
Web: www.coxconventioncenter.com

Expo Square 4145 E 21st St .... Tulsa OK 74114 918-744-1113 744-8725
TF: 877-781-2660 ■ *Web:* www.exposquare.com

Tulsa Convention Ctr 100 Civic Ctr .... Tulsa OK 74103 918-894-4350
Web: www.coxcentertulsa.com

Ontario

Phone Fax

Mckenna Distribution & Warehousing
1260 Lkshore Rd E .... Mississauga ON L5E3B8 905-274-1234
Web: www.mckennalogistics.ca

Chair-man Mills Inc 501 Consumers Rd .... Toronto ON M2J5E2 416-391-0400
Web: www.chairmanmills.com

Metro Toronto Convention Centre
255 Front St W .... Toronto ON M5V2W6 416-585-8000 585-8262*
**Fax:* Hum Res ■ *Web:* www.mtccc.com

Oregon

Phone Fax

Lane Events Ctr 796 W 13th Ave .... Eugene OR 97402 541-682-4292 682-3614
Web: www.atthefair.com

Florence Events Ctr 715 Quince St .... Florence OR 97439 541-997-1994 902-0991
TF: 888-968-4086 ■ *Web:* www.ci.florence.or.us

City of Pendleton 500 SW Dorion Ave .... Pendleton OR 97801 541-966-0201 966-0251
TF: 800-238-5355 ■ *Web:* www.pendleton.or.us

Oregon Convention Ctr
777 NE Martin Luther King Jr Blvd .... Portland OR 97232 503-235-7575 235-7417
TF: 800-791-2250 ■ *Web:* www.oregoncc.org

Portland Metropolitan Exposition Ctr
2060 N Marine Dr .... Portland OR 97217 503-736-5200 736-5201
Web: www.expocenter.org

Oregon State Fair & Expo Ctr 2330 17th St NE .... Salem OR 97301 503-947-3247 947-3206
Web: oregonstatefair.org

Salem Conference Ctr 200 Commercial St SE .... Salem OR 97301 503-589-1700 589-1715
TF Sales: 877-589-1700 ■ *Web:* salemconventioncenter.org

Seaside Civic & Convention Ctr 415 First Ave .... Seaside OR 97138 503-738-8585 738-0198
TF: 800-394-3303 ■ *Web:* www.seasideconvention.com

Pennsylvania

Phone Fax

Valley Forge Convention Ctr
1160 First Ave .... King of Prussia PA 19406 610-768-3215
Web: www.vfconventioncenter.com

Hampton Inn Philadelphia Ctr City-Convention Ctr
1301 Race St .... Philadelphia PA 19107 215-665-9100 665-9200
TF: 800-426-7866 ■ *Web:* www3.hilton.com

Pennsylvania Convention Ctr
1101 Arch St .... Philadelphia PA 19107 215-418-4700
TF: 800-428-9000 ■ *Web:* www.paconvention.com

David L Lawrence Convention Ctr
1000 Ft Duquesne Blvd .... Pittsburgh PA 15222 412-565-6000 565-6008
Web: www.pittsburghcc.com

Stetson Convention Services Inc
2900 Stayton St .... Pittsburgh PA 15212 412-223-1090 223-1094
Web: www.stetsonexpo.com

Quebec

Phone Fax

Ivanhoe Cambridge Inc
1001 Sq Victoria bureau C-500 .... Montreal QC H2Z2B5 514-841-7600
Web: www.ivanhoecambridge.com

Rhode Island

Phone Fax

Rhode Island Convention Ctr 1 Sabin St .... Providence RI 02903 401-458-6000 458-6500
Web: www.riconvention.com

South Carolina

Phone Fax

Charleston Area Convention Ctr Complex (CACC)
5001 Coliseum Dr .... Charleston SC 29418 843-529-5000 529-5010
Web: www.charlestonconventioncenter.com

Myrtle Beach Convention Ctr
2101 N Oak St .... Myrtle Beach SC 29577 843-918-5000 918-1243
TF: 800-537-1690 ■ *Web:* www.sheratonmyrtlebeach.com

South Dakota

Phone Fax

Rushmore Plaza Civic Ctr
444 Mt Rushmore Rd N .... Rapid City SD 57701 605-394-4115 394-4119
TF: 800-468-6463 ■ *Web:* www.gotmine.com

Tennessee

Phone Fax

Chattanooga Convention Ctr
1150 Carter St PO Box 6008 .... Chattanooga TN 37402 423-756-0001
TF: 800-962-5213 ■ *Web:* www.chattconvention.org

Knoxville Convention Ctr 701 Henley St .... Knoxville TN 37902 865-522-5669 329-0422
Web: www.kccsmg.com

Memphis Cook Convention Ctr
3205 Elvis Presley Blvd .... Memphis TN 38116 901-543-5333
Web: www.memphistravel.com

Nashville Convention Ctr 601 Commerce St .... Nashville TN 37203 615-742-2000 742-2014
Web: www.nashvilleconventionctr.com

Texas

Phone Fax

Amarillo Civic Ctr 401 S Buchanan St .... Amarillo TX 79101 806-378-4297 378-4234
Web: amarillociviccenter.com

Arlington Convention Ctr 1200 Ballpark Way .... Arlington TX 76011 817-459-5000 459-5091
Web: webapps.arlingtontx.gov/tmp/acc

Austin Convention Ctr 500 E Cesar Chavez St .... Austin TX 78701 512-404-4000 404-4416
Web: www.austinconventioncenter.com

Palmer Events Ctr 900 Barton Springs Rd .... Austin TX 78704 512-404-4500 404-4422
Web: www.austinconventioncenter.com

Beaumont Civic Ctr Complex 701 Main St .... Beaumont TX 77701 409-838-3435 838-3715
TF: 800-782-3081 ■ *Web:* www.discoverbeaumont.com

Bell County Expo Ctr 301 W Loop 121 .... Belton TX 76513 254-933-5353 933-5354
Web: www.bellcountyexpo.com

American Bank Ctr
1901 N Shoreline Blvd .... Corpus Christi TX 78401 361-826-4700 826-4905
Web: www.americanbankcenter.com

Dallas Convention Ctr 650 S Griffin St .... Dallas TX 75202 214-939-2750 939-2700
TF: 877-850-2100 ■ *Web:* www.dallasconventioncenter.com

Dallas Market Ctr 2100 Stemmons Fwy Ste 113 .... Dallas TX 75207 214-655-6100 749-5479
TF: 800-325-6587 ■ *Web:* www.dallasmarketcenter.com

Rolex Watch Usa Inc 2651 N Harwood St Ste 600 .... Dallas TX 75201 214-871-0500
Web: www.rolex.com

El Paso Convention & Performing Arts Ctr
1 Civic Ctr Plz .... El Paso TX 79901 915-534-0600 534-0687
TF: 800-351-6024 ■ *Web:* www.visitelpaso.com

Fort Worth Convention Ctr 1201 Houston St .... Fort Worth TX 76102 817-392-6338 392-2756
TF: 866-630-2588 ■ *Web:* fortworthtexas.gov

Moody Gardens Convention Ctr 7 Hope Blvd .... Galveston TX 77554 409-741-8484
TF: 888-388-8484 ■ *Web:* www.moodygardenshotel.com

Grapevine Convention Ctr, The
1209 S Main St .... Grapevine TX 76051 817-410-3459 410-3090
TF: 866-782-7897 ■ *Web:* www.grapevinetexasusa.com

George R Brown Convention Ctr
1001 Avenida de Las Americas .... Houston TX 77010 713-853-8000 853-8090
TF: 800-427-4697 ■ *Web:* www.grbhouston.com

	City	State	Zip	Phone	Fax
Maude Cobb Convention Ctr 100 Grand Blvd PO Box 1952 *Web:* www.longviewtexas.gov/2345/convention-activity-complex	Longview	TX	75604	903-237-1230	
Lubbock Memorial Civic Ctr 1501 MacDavis Ln *Web:* www.mylubbock.us/departmental-websites/departments/civic-center/home	Lubbock	TX	79401	806-775-2242	775-3240
Plano Centre 2000 E Springcreek Pkwy. *TF:* 800-613-3222 ■ *Web:* plano.gov	Plano	TX	75074	972-422-0296	424-0002
Robert A "Bob" Bowers Civic Ctr 3401 Cultural Ctr Dr *Web:* www.portarthur.net	Port Arthur	TX	77642	409-985-8801	
San Angelo Convention Ctr Coliseum & Auditorium 500 Rio Concho Dr. *Web:* cosatx.us	San Angelo	TX	76903	325-653-9577	
Henry B Gonzalez Convention Ctr 200 E Market St *TF:* 877-504-8895 ■ *Web:* www.sahbgcc.com	San Antonio	TX	78205	210-207-8500	223-1495
South Padre Island Convention Centre 7355 Padre Blvd *TF:* 800-657-2373 ■ *Web:* www.sopadre.com	South Padre Island	TX	78597	956-761-3000	761-3024
Frank W Mayborn Civic & Convention Ctr 3303 N Third St *Web:* ci.temple.tx.us	Temple	TX	76501	254-298-5720	298-5388
Oil Palace, The 10408 Hwy 64 E *Web:* www.oilpalace.com	Tyler	TX	75707	903-566-2122	566-4206
MPEC (Multi-Purpose Events Ctr) 1000 Fifth St. *Web:* www.wfmpec.com	Wichita Falls	TX	76301	940-716-5500	

Utah

	City	State	Zip	Phone	Fax
Golden Spike Event Ctr 1000 North 1200 West *Web:* www.goldenspikeeventcenter.com	Ogden	UT	84404	801-399-8798	
Ogden Eccles Conference Ctr 2415 Washington Blvd *TF:* 866-472-4627 ■ *Web:* oeccutah.com	Ogden	UT	84401	801-689-8600	689-8651
Salt Palace Convention Ctr 100 W Temple *Web:* www.visitsaltlake.com/salt-palace-convention-center	Salt Lake City	UT	84101	801-534-4777	

Virginia

	City	State	Zip	Phone	Fax
Greater Richmond Convention Ctr 403 N Third St *Web:* www.richmondcenter.com	Richmond	VA	23219	804-783-7300	

Washington

	City	State	Zip	Phone	Fax
Meydenbauer Ctr 11100 NE Sixth St *Web:* www.meydenbauer.com	Bellevue	WA	98004	425-637-1020	637-0166
Three Rivers Convention Ctr & Coliseum 7016 W Grandbridge Blvd *Web:* www.threeriversconventioncenter.com	Kennewick	WA	99336	509-737-3700	
Ocean Shores Convention Ctr 120 W Chance a La Mer Ave. *TF:* 800-874-6737 ■ *Web:* www.oceanshoresconventioncenter.com	Ocean Shores	WA	98569	360-289-4411	289-4412
Bell Harbor International Conference Ctr 2211 Alaskan Way Pier 66 *TF:* 888-772-4422 ■ *Web:* www.bellharbor.com	Seattle	WA	98121	206-441-6666	441-6665
Washington State Convention 800 Convention Pl *Web:* wscc.com	Seattle	WA	98101	206-694-5000	694-5399
Spokane Ctr 720 W Mallon Ave. *Web:* www.spokanecenter.com	Spokane	WA	99201	509-279-7000	279-7050
Greater Tacoma Convention & Trade Ctr 1500 Broadway *TF:* 800-745-3000 ■ *Web:* www.tacomaconventioncenter.com	Tacoma	WA	98402	253-830-6601	573-2363
Yakima Convention Ctr 10 N Eigth St *TF:* 800-221-0751 ■ *Web:* www.visityakima.com	Yakima	WA	98901	509-575-6062	575-6252

West Virginia

	City	State	Zip	Phone	Fax
Charleston Civic Ctr & Coliseum 200 Civic Ctr Dr *Web:* www.charlestonwvciviccenter.com	Charleston	WV	25301	304-345-1500	345-3492

Wisconsin

	City	State	Zip	Phone	Fax
Green Lake Conference Center W2511 State Rd 23 *Web:* www.glcc.org	Green Lake	WI	54941	920-294-3323	
La Crosse Ctr 300 Harborview Plz *Web:* www.lacrossecenter.com	La Crosse	WI	54601	608-789-7400	789-7444
Alliant Energy Ctr of Dane County 1919 Alliant Energy Ctr Way *Web:* www.alliantenergycenter.com	Madison	WI	53713	608-267-3976	267-0146
Monona Terrace Community & Convention Ctr 1 John Nolen Dr *Web:* www.mononaterrace.com	Madison	WI	53703	608-261-4000	261-4049
Frontier Airlines Ctr 400 W Wisconsin Ave *TF:* 800-745-3000 ■ *Web:* wisconsincenter.org	Milwaukee	WI	53203	414-908-6000	908-6010

Wyoming

	City	State	Zip	Phone	Fax
Casper Events Ctr 1 Events Dr *TF:* 800-442-2256 ■ *Web:* www.casperwy.gov	Casper	WY	82601	307-235-8441	

206 CONVENTION & VISITORS BUREAUS

See Also Travel & Tourism Information - Canadian p. 3267; Travel & Tourism Information - Foreign Travel p. 3267

Listings are alphabetized by city names.

	City	State	Zip	Phone	Fax
Aberdeen Convention & Visitors Bureau 10 Railroad Ave SW PO Box 78 *TF:* 800-645-3851 ■ *Web:* www.visitaberdeensd.com	Aberdeen	SD	57401	605-225-2414	225-3573
Abilene Convention & Visitors Bureau 1101 N First St *TF:* 800-727-7704 ■ *Web:* www.abilenevisitors.com	Abilene	TX	79601	325-676-2556	676-1630
Abilene Convention & Visitors Bureau 201 NW Second St *TF:* 800-569-5915 ■ *Web:* www.abilenecityhall.com	Abilene	KS	67410	785-263-2231	263-4125
Abingdon Convention & Visitors Bureau 335 Cummings St. *TF:* 800-435-3440 ■ *Web:* visitabingdonvirginia.com	Abingdon	VA	24210	276-676-2282	
Akron/Summit County Convention & Visitors Bureau 77 E Mill St. *TF:* 800-245-4254 ■ *Web:* www.visitakron-summit.org	Akron	OH	44308	330-374-8900	374-7626
Albany County Convention & Visitors Bureau 25 Quackenbush Sq *TF:* 800-258-3582 ■ *Web:* www.albany.org	Albany	NY	12207	518-434-1217	434-0887
Albany Visitors Assn 300 Second Ave SW *TF:* 800-526-2256 ■ *Web:* www.albanyvisitors.com	Albany	OR	97321	541-928-0911	926-1500
Albuquerque Convention & Visitors Bureau 20 First Plz Ste 601 *TF:* 800-733-9918 ■ *Web:* visitalbuquerque.org	Albuquerque	NM	87102	505-842-9918	247-9101
Alexandria Convention & Visitors Assn 221 King St. *TF:* 800-388-9119 ■ *Web:* www.visitalexandriava.com	Alexandria	VA	22314	703-746-3301	
Alexandria/Pineville Area Convention & Visitors Bureau (APACVB) 707 Main St PO Box 1070 *TF:* 800-551-9546 ■ *Web:* alexandriapinevillela.com	Alexandria	LA	71301	318-442-9546	443-1617
Allegan County Tourist & Recreational Council 3255 122nd Ave Ste 103 *TF:* 888-425-5342 ■ *Web:* www.visitallegancounty.com	Allegan	MI	49010	269-686-9088	673-0454
Lehigh Valley Visitor Ctr 840 Hamilton St Ste 200 *TF:* 800-747-0561 ■ *Web:* www.discoverlehighvalley.com	Allentown	PA	18101	610-882-9200	
Alpena Area Convention & Visitors Bureau 235 W Chisholm St *TF:* 800-425-7362 ■ *Web:* www.visitalpena.com	Alpena	MI	49707	989-354-4181	356-3999
Alton Regional Convention & Visitors Bureau (ARCVB) 200 Piasa St *TF:* 800-258-6645 ■ *Web:* www.visitalton.com	Alton	IL	62002	618-465-6676	465-6151
Amana Colonies Convention & Visitors Bureau 622 46th Ave *TF:* 800-579-2294 ■ *Web:* www.amanacolonies.com	Amana	IA	52203	319-622-7622	
Amarillo Convention & Visitor Council 1000 S Polk St *TF:* 800-692-1338 ■ *Web:* www.visitamarillo.com	Amarillo	TX	79101	806-374-1497	373-3909
Lorain County Visitors Bureau 8025 Leavitt Rd *TF:* 800-334-1673 ■ *Web:* www.visitloraincounty.com	Amherst	OH	44001	440-984-5282	984-7363
Anaheim/Orange County Visitor & Convention Bureau 800 W Katella Ave *TF:* 855-405-5020 ■ *Web:* visitanaheim.org	Anaheim	CA	92802	714-765-8888	991-8963
Anchorage Convention & Visitors Bureau 524 W Fourth Ave *TF:* 800-478-6657 ■ *Web:* www.anchorage.net	Anchorage	AK	99501	907-276-4118	
Anderson/Madison County Visitors & Convention Bureau 6335 S Scatterfield Rd *TF:* 800-533-6569 ■ *Web:* www.visitandersonmadisoncounty.com	Anderson	IN	46013	765-643-5633	643-9083
Steuben County Tourism Bureau 430 N Wayne St Ste 1B *TF:* 888-665-5668 ■ *Web:* www.lakes101.org	Angola	IN	46703	260-665-5386	
Ann Arbor Area Convention & Visitors Bureau 120 W Huron St *TF:* 800-888-9487 ■ *Web:* www.visitannarbor.org	Ann Arbor	MI	48104	734-995-7281	995-7283
Southernmost Illinois Tourism Bureau PO Box 378 *TF:* 800-248-4373 ■ *Web:* www.southernmostillinois.com	Anna	IL	62906	618-833-9928	
Annapolis & Anne Arundel County Conference & Visitors Bureau (AAACCVB) 26 W St. *TF:* 888-302-2852 ■ *Web:* www.visitannapolis.org	Annapolis	MD	21401	410-280-0445	263-9591
Fox Cities Convention & Visitors Bureau 3433 W College Ave *TF:* 800-236-6673 ■ *Web:* www.foxcities.org	Appleton	WI	54914	920-734-3358	734-1080
Arkansas City Convention & Visitors Bureau 106 S Summit St PO Box 795 *Web:* www.arkcity.org	Arkansas City	KS	67005	620-442-0230	
Arlington Convention & Visitors Bureau 1905 E Randol Mill Rd *TF:* 800-433-5374 ■ *Web:* www.arlington.org	Arlington	TX	76011	817-265-7721	265-5640
Aspen Chamber Resort Assn 425 Rio Grande Pl *TF:* 800-670-0792 ■ *Web:* www.aspenchamber.org	Aspen	CO	81611	970-925-1940	920-1173
Athens Convention & Visitors Bureau 300 N Thomas St *TF:* 800-653-0603 ■ *Web:* www.visitathensga.com	Athens	GA	30601	706-357-4430	546-8040
Athens County Convention & Visitors Bureau 667 E State St *TF:* 800-878-9767 ■ *Web:* www.athensohio.com	Athens	OH	45701	740-592-1819	593-7365
Atlanta Convention & Visitors Bureau 233 Peachtree St NE Ste 1400 *Web:* www.atlanta.net	Atlanta	GA	30303	404-521-6600	
Cobb Travel & Tourism 1 Galleria Pkwy *TF:* 800-451-3480 ■ *Web:* www.travelcobb.org	Atlanta	GA	30339	678-303-2622	303-2625
Atlantic City Convention & Visitors Authority 2314 Pacific Ave *TF:* 888-228-4748 ■ *Web:* www.atlanticcitynj.com	Atlantic City	NJ	08401	609-348-7100	
Auburn-Opelika Tourism Bureau 714 E Glenn Ave *TF:* 866-880-8747 ■ *Web:* www.aotourism.com	Auburn	AL	36830	334-887-8747	821-5500

Name / Address	City	State	Zip	Phone	Fax
Augusta Metropolitan Convention & Visitors Bureau 1450 Greene St Ste 560 *TF:* 800-726-0243 ■ *Web:* visitaugusta.com	Augusta	GA	30901	706-823-6600	823-6609
Aurora Area Convention & Visitors Bureau 43 W Galena Blvd *TF:* 800-477-4369 ■ *Web:* www.enjoyaurora.com	Aurora	IL	60506	630-897-5581	
Austin Convention & Visitors Bureau 301 Congress Ave Ste 200 *TF:* 800-926-2282 ■ *Web:* www.austintexas.org	Austin	TX	78701	512-474-5171	583-7282
Catalina Island Visitors Bureau 1 Green Pier PO Box 217 *TF:* 877-854-1125 ■ *Web:* www.catalinachamber.com	Avalon	CA	90704	310-510-1520	510-7607
Vail Valley Tourism Bureau 101 Fawcett Rd Ste 240 *Web:* www.visitvailvalley.com	Avon	CO	81620	970-476-1000	
Baker County Visitors & Convention Bureau 490 Campbell St *TF:* 800-523-1235 ■ *Web:* www.visitbaker.com	Baker City	OR	97814	541-523-3356	523-9187
Greater Bakersfield Convention & Visitors Bureau 515 Truxtun Ave *TF:* 866-425-7353 ■ *Web:* www.visitbakersfield.com	Bakersfield	CA	93301	661-852-7282	325-7074
Baltimore Area Convention & Visitors Assn (BACVA) 100 Light St 12th Fl *TF:* 877-225-8466 ■ *Web:* www.baltimore.org	Baltimore	MD	21202	410-659-7300	727-2308
Bandera County Convention & Visitors Bureau 126 State Hwy 16 S PO Box 171 *TF:* 800-364-3833 ■ *Web:* www.banderacowboycapital.com	Bandera	TX	78003	830-796-3045	
Greater Bangor Convention & Visitors Bureau 40 Harlow St *TF:* 800-916-6673 ■ *Web:* www.visitbangormaine.com	Bangor	ME	04401	207-947-5205	
Clermont County Convention & Visitors Bureau (CCCVB) 410 E Main St PO Box 100 *TF:* 800-796-4282 ■ *Web:* www.visitclermontohio.com	Batavia	OH	45103	513-732-3600	
Baton Rouge Convention & Visitors Bureau 359 Third St *TF:* 800-527-6843 ■ *Web:* www.visitbatonrouge.com	Baton Rouge	LA	70801	225-383-1825	
Battle Creek/Calhoun County Convention & Visitors Bureau 77 E Michigan Ave Ste 100 *TF:* 800-397-2240 ■ *Web:* www.battlecreekvisitors.org	Battle Creek	MI	49017	269-962-2240	
Beaumont Convention & Visitors Bureau 505 Willow St *TF:* 800-392-4401 ■ *Web:* www.beaumontcvb.com	Beaumont	TX	77701	409-880-3749	880-3750
Greene County Convention & Visitors Bureau 1221 Meadowbridge Dr *TF:* 800-733-9109 ■ *Web:* www.greenecountyohio.org	Beavercreek	OH	45434	937-429-9100	429-7726
Washington County Visitors Assn 12725 SW Millikan Way Ste 210 *TF:* 800-537-3149 ■ *Web:* tualatinvalley.org	Beaverton	OR	97005	503-644-5555	644-9784
Southern West Virginia Convention & Visitors Bureau 1406 Harper Rd *TF:* 800-847-4898 ■ *Web:* www.visitwv.com	Beckley	WV	25801	304-252-2244	
Bedford County Visitors Bureau 131 S Juliana St *TF:* 800-765-3331 ■ *Web:* www.visitbedfordcounty.com	Bedford	PA	15522	814-623-1771	623-1671
Gaston County Travel & Tourism 620 N Main St *TF:* 800-849-9994 ■ *Web:* www.gastongov.com	Belmont	NC	28012	704-825-4044	
Beloit Convention & Visitors Bureau 500 Public Ave *TF:* 800-423-5648 ■ *Web:* www.visitbeloit.com	Beloit	WI	53511	608-365-4838	365-6850
Bucks County Conference & Visitors Bureau (BCCVB) 3207 St Rd *TF:* 800-836-2825 ■ *Web:* www.visitbuckscounty.com	Bensalem	PA	19020	215-639-0300	642-3277
Southwestern Michigan Tourism Council 2300 Pipestone Rd *Web:* www.swmichigan.org	Benton Harbor	MI	49022	269-925-6301	925-7540
Greater Big Rapids Convention & Visitors Bureau 246 N State St *Web:* www.bigrapids.org	Big Rapids	MI	49307	231-796-7640	796-0832
Big Spring Convention & Visitor Bureau 215 W Third St PO Box 3359 *TF:* 866-222-7100 ■ *Web:* www.bigspringtx.com	Big Spring	TX	79720	432-264-6032	264-6047
Billings Convention & Visitors Bureau 815 S 27th St PO Box 31177 *TF:* 800-735-2635 ■ *Web:* www.visitbillings.com	Billings	MT	59107	406-245-4111	245-7333
Mississippi Gulf Coast Convention & Visitors Bureau 2350 Beach Blvd Ste A *TF:* 888-467-4853 ■ *Web:* www.gulfcoast.org	Biloxi	MS	39531	228-896-6699	896-6788
Greater Binghamton Convention 49 Ct St Second Fl PO Box 995 *Web:* greaterbinghamtonchamber.com	Binghamton	NY	13902	607-772-8860	722-4513
Greater Birmingham Convention & Visitors Bureau 2200 Ninth Ave N *TF:* 800-458-8085 ■ *Web:* birminghamal.org	Birmingham	AL	35203	205-458-8000	458-8086
Bismarck-Mandan Convention & Visitors Bureau 1600 Burnt Boat Dr *TF:* 800-767-3555 ■ *Web:* www.discoverbismarckmandan.com	Bismarck	ND	58503	701-222-4308	222-0647
Bloomington Convention & Visitors Bureau (BCVB) 7900 International Dr Ste 990 *TF:* 800-346-4289 ■ *Web:* www.bloomingtonmn.org	Bloomington	MN	55425	952-858-8500	858-8854
Bloomington-Normal Area Convention & Visitors Bureau 3201 CIRA Dr Ste 201 *TF:* 800-433-8226 ■ *Web:* www.visitbn.org	Bloomington	IL	61704	309-665-0033	661-0743
Bloomington/Monroe County Convention & Visitors Bureau 2855 N Walnut St *TF:* 800-800-0037 ■ *Web:* www.visitbloomington.com	Bloomington	IN	47404	812-334-8900	334-2344
Columbia-Montour Visitors Bureau 121 Papermill Rd *TF:* 800-847-4810 ■ *Web:* www.itourcolumbiamontour.com	Bloomsburg	PA	17815	570-784-8279	
Mercer County Convention & Visitors Bureau 621 Commerce St *TF:* 800-221-3206 ■ *Web:* www.visitmercercounty.com	Bluefield	WV	24701	304-325-8438	324-8483
Boise Convention & Visitors Bureau 250 S Fifth St Ste 300 *TF:* 800-635-5240 ■ *Web:* www.boise.org	Boise	ID	83702	208-344-7777	
North Carolina High Country Host 1700 Blowing Rock Rd *TF:* 800-438-7500 ■ *Web:* www.highcountryhost.com	Boone	NC	28607	828-264-1299	265-0550
Greater Boston Convention & Visitors Bureau (GBCVB) 2 Copley Pl Ste 105 *TF:* 888-733-2678 ■ *Web:* www.bostonusa.com	Boston	MA	02116	617-536-4100	424-7664
Bottineau Convention & Visitor Bureau 519 Main St Ste 1 *Web:* www.bottineau.com	Bottineau	ND	58318	701-228-3849	228-5130
Boulder Convention & Visitors Bureau 2440 Pearl St *TF:* 800-444-0447 ■ *Web:* www.bouldercoloradousa.com	Boulder	CO	80302	303-442-2911	938-2098
Brenham/Washington County Convention & Visitor Bureau 314 S Austin St *TF:* 888-273-6426 ■ *Web:* www.brenhamtexas.com	Brenham	TX	77833	979-836-3695	836-2540
Greater Bridgeport Conference & Vistors Ctr 164 W Main St *TF:* 800-368-4324 ■ *Web:* www.greater-bridgeport.com	Bridgeport	WV	26330	304-842-7272	
Aquinex Services Llc 991 Us Hwy 22 Ste 200 *Web:* aquinex.com	Bridgewater	NJ	08807	201-633-3208	
Minneapolis Northwest 6200 Shingle Creek Pkwy Ste 130 *TF:* 800-541-4364 ■ *Web:* www.minneapolisnorthwest.com	Brooklyn Center	MN	55430	763-852-7500	
Northwest Pennsylvania's Great Outdoors Visitors Bureau 2801 Maplevale Rd *TF:* 800-348-9393 ■ *Web:* www.visitpago.com	Brookville	PA	15825	814-849-5197	849-1969
Brownsville Convention & Visitors Bureau 650 Ruben M Torres Sr Blvd *TF:* 800-626-2639 ■ *Web:* brownsville.org	Brownsville	TX	78521	956-546-3721	
Brunswick & The Golden Isles of Georgia Visitors Bureau 4 Glynn Ave *TF:* 800-933-2627 ■ *Web:* www.goldenisles.com	Brunswick	GA	31520	912-265-0620	265-0629
Buena Park Convention & Visitors Office 6601 Beach Blvd **Fax Area Code:* 714 ■ *TF:* 800-541-3953 ■ *Web:* www.visitbuenapark.com	Buena Park	CA	90621	800-541-3953	522-3319*
Buffalo Niagara Convention & Visitors Bureau 403 Main St Ste 630 *TF:* 800-283-3256 ■ *Web:* www.visitbuffaloniagara.com	Buffalo	NY	14203	716-852-2356	852-0131
San Mateo County Convention & Visitors Bureau 111 Anza Blvd Ste 410 *TF:* 800-288-4748 ■ *Web:* www.smccvb.com	Burlingame	CA	94010	650-348-7600	348-7687
Burlington/Alamance County Convention & Visitors Bureau 200 S Main St PO Box 519 *TF:* 800-637-3804 ■ *Web:* www.visitalamance.com	Burlington	NC	27216	336-570-1444	228-1330
Vermont Convention Bureau 60 Main St Ste 100 *TF:* 877-264-3503 ■ *Web:* www.vermont.org	Burlington	VT	05401	802-860-0606	863-1538
Cadillac Area Visitors Bureau 201 N Mitchell St *TF:* 800-225-2537 ■ *Web:* www.cadillacmichigan.com	Cadillac	MI	49601	231-775-0657	779-5933
Tourism Calgary 200 238 11th Ave SE *TF:* 800-661-1678 ■ *Web:* www.visitcalgary.com	Calgary	AB	T2G0X8	403-263-8510	262-3809
Cambridge Office for Tourism Inc 4 Brattle St Ste 208 *Web:* www.cambridgeusa.org	Cambridge	MA	02138	617-441-2884	
Finger Lakes Visitors Connection 25 Gorham St *TF:* 877-386-4669 ■ *Web:* www.visitfingerlakes.com	Canandaigua	NY	14424	585-394-3915	
Canton/Stark County Convention & Visitors Bureau 222 Market Ave N *TF:* 800-552-6051 ■ *Web:* www.visitcanton.com	Canton	OH	44702	330-454-1439	456-3600
Cape Girardeau Convention & Visitors Bureau 400 Broadway Ste 100 *TF:* 800-777-0068 ■ *Web:* www.visitcape.com	Cape Girardeau	MO	63701	573-335-1631	334-6702
Carlsbad Convention & Visitors Bureau 400 Carlsbad Village Dr *TF:* 800-227-5722 ■ *Web:* www.visitcarlsbad.com	Carlsbad	CA	92008	760-434-6093	434-6056
Hamilton County Convention & Visitors Bureau Inc 37 E Main St *TF:* 800-776-8687 ■ *Web:* www.visithamiltoncounty.com	Carmel	IN	46032	317-848-3181	848-3191
Carrington Convention & Visitors Bureau City Hall 103 10th Ave N PO Box 501 *TF:* 800-641-9668 ■ *Web:* www.cgtn-nd.com	Carrington	ND	58421	701-652-2524	652-2391
Casper Area Convention & Visitors Bureau 992 N Poplar St *TF:* 800-852-1889 ■ *Web:* visitcasper.com	Casper	WY	82601	307-234-5362	261-9928
Cedar City-Brian Head Tourism & Convention Bureau 581 N Main St *TF:* 800-354-4849 ■ *Web:* www.scenicsouthernutah.com	Cedar City	UT	84721	435-586-5124	586-4022
Cedar Rapids Area Convention & Visitors Bureau 87 16th Ave Ste 200 *TF:* 800-735-5557 ■ *Web:* www.gocedarrapids.com	Cedar Rapids	IA	52404	319-398-5009	398-5089
Champaign County Convention & Visitors Bureau 108 S Neil St *TF:* 800-369-6151 ■ *Web:* www.visitchampaigncounty.org	Champaign	IL	61820	217-351-4133	
Chapel Hill/Orange County Visitors Bureau 501 W Franklin St **Fax Area Code:* 919 ■ *TF:* 888-968-2060 ■ *Web:* www.visitchapelhill.org	Chapel Hill	NC	27516	888-968-2060	968-2062*
Charleston Area Convention & Visitors Bureau 423 King St *TF:* 800-868-8118 ■ *Web:* www.charlestoncvb.com	Charleston	SC	29403	843-853-8000	853-0444
Charleston Convention & Visitors Bureau 601 Morris St Ste 204 *Web:* www.charlestonwv.com	Charleston	WV	25301	304-344-5075	
Charlotte Convention & Visitors Bureau 500 S College St Ste 300 *TF:* 800-722-1994 ■ *Web:* www.charlottesgotalot.com	Charlotte	NC	28202	704-334-2282	342-3972
Chattanooga Area Convention & Visitors Bureau 215 Broad St *TF:* 800-322-3344 ■ *Web:* www.chattanoogafun.com	Chattanooga	TN	37402	423-756-8687	265-1630
Chautauqua County Visitors Bureau Chautauqua Main Gate Rt 394 PO Box 1441 *TF:* 800-242-4569 ■ *Web:* www.tourchautauqua.com	Chautauqua	NY	14722	716-357-4569	357-2284

Name / Address	City	State	ZIP	Phone	Fax
Cherokee Tribal Travel & Promotions 498 Tsali Blvd. *TF:* 877-440-9990	Cherokee	NC	28719	828-359-6492	554-6475
Chesapeake Conventions & Tourism Bureau (CCT) 860 Greenbrier Cir Ste 101 *TF:* 888-889-5551 ■ *Web:* www.visitchesapeake.com	Chesapeake	VA	23320	757-502-4898	502-8016
Randolph County Tourism Committee 1 Taylor St Courthouse *Web:* www.randolphco.org	Chester	IL	62233	618-826-5000	826-3750
Cheyenne Area Convention & Visitors Bureau 121 W 15th St Ste 202 *TF:* 800-426-5009 ■ *Web:* www.cheyenne.org	Cheyenne	WY	82001	307-778-3133	778-3190
Chicago Convention & Tourism Bureau 2301 S Lk Shore Dr McCormick Complex Lakeside Ctr *Web:* www.choosechicago.com	Chicago	IL	60616	312-567-8500	
Chicago Office of Tourism & Culture 78 E Washington St 4th Fl *TF:* 888-871-5311 ■ *Web:* www.choosechicago.com	Chicago	IL	60602	312-744-2400	
Chula Vista Convention & Visitors Bureau 233 Fourth Ave *Web:* www.chulavistaconvis.com	Chula Vista	CA	91910	619-426-2882	420-1269
Greater Cincinnati Convention & Visitors Bureau 525 Vine St Ste 1500 *TF:* 800-543-2613 ■ *Web:* www.cincyusa.com	Cincinnati	OH	45202	513-621-2142	621-5020
Pickaway County Visitors Bureau 325 W Main St *TF:* 800-283-4678 ■ *Web:* www.pickaway.com	Circleville	OH	43113	740-474-3636	420-9181
Clarksville/Montgomery County Tourist Commission 25 Jefferson St Ste 300 *TF:* 800-530-2487 ■ *Web:* www.clarksvillepartnership.com	Clarksville	TN	37040	931-647-2331	645-1574
Clear Lake Convention & Visitors Bureau 205 Main Ave PO Box 188 *TF:* 800-285-5338 ■ *Web:* www.clearlakeiowa.com	Clear Lake	IA	50428	641-357-2159	357-8141
Visit St Petersburg Clearwater 13805 58th St N Ste 2-200 *TF:* 877-352-3224 ■ *Web:* www.visitstpeteclearwater.com	Clearwater	FL	33760	727-464-7200	
Clinton Convention & Visitors Bureau 721 S Second St *Web:* www.clintoniowatourism.com	Clinton	IA	52732	563-242-5702	
Brevard County Tourism Development 430 Brevard Ave Ste 150 *TF:* 877-572-3224 ■ *Web:* brevardcounty.us	Cocoa Village	FL	32922	321-433-4470	433-4476
Park County Travel Council (PCTC) 836 Sheridan Ave PO Box 2454 *TF:* 800-393-2639 ■ *Web:* www.yellowstonecountry.org	Cody	WY	82414	307-587-2297	527-6228
Ranch at Ucross, The 1701 Sheridan Ave PO Box 30 *Web:* blairhotels.com	Cody	WY	82835	307-737-2281	
Colby Convention & Visitors Bureau 350 S Range Ste 10 *TF:* 800-611-8835 ■ *Web:* www.oasisontheplains.com	Colby	KS	67701	785-460-7643	460-4509
Bryan/College Station Convention & Visitors Bureau (BCSCVB) 715 University Dr E *TF:* 800-777-8292 ■ *Web:* www.visitaggieland.com	College Station	TX	77840	979-260-9898	260-9800
Colorado Springs Convention & Visitors Bureau 515 S Cascade Ave *TF:* 800-888-4748 ■ *Web:* www.visitcos.com	Colorado Springs	CO	80903	719-635-7506	635-4968
Columbia Convention & Visitors Bureau 300 S Providence Rd *TF:* 800-652-0987 ■ *Web:* www.visitcolumbiamo.com	Columbia	MO	65203	573-875-1231	443-3986
Columbia Metropolitan Convention & Visitors Bureau 1101 Lincoln St PO Box 15 *TF:* 800-264-4884 ■ *Web:* www.columbiacvb.com	Columbia	SC	29202	803-545-0000	545-0013
Columbus Area Visitors Ctr 506 Fifth St *TF:* 800-468-6564 ■ *Web:* www.columbus.in.us	Columbus	IN	47201	812-378-2622	372-7348
Columbus Convention & Visitors Bureau 900 Front Ave *TF:* 800-999-1613 ■ *Web:* www.visitcolumbusga.com	Columbus	GA	31901	706-322-1613	322-0701
Columbus Convention & Visitors Bureau PO Box 789 *TF:* 800-327-2686 ■ *Web:* visitcolumbusms.org	Columbus	MS	39703	662-329-1191	329-8969
Greater Columbus Convention & Visitors Bureau 277 W Nationwide Blvd Ste 125 *TF:* 866-397-2657 ■ *Web:* www.experiencecolumbus.com	Columbus	OH	43215	614-221-6623	221-5618
Polk County Travel & Tourism 20 E Mills St PO Box 308 *TF:* 800-440-7848 ■ *Web:* www.nc-mountains.org	Columbus	NC	28722	828-894-2324	
New Hampshire Div of Travel & Tourism Development 172 Pembroke Rd PO Box 1856 *TF:* 800-262-6660 ■ *Web:* www.visitnh.gov	Concord	NH	03302	603-271-2665	271-6870
Coos Bay-North Bend Visitor & Convention Bureau 50 Central Ave *TF:* 800-824-8486 ■ *Web:* www.oregonsadventurecoast.com	Coos Bay	OR	97420	541-269-0215	269-2861
Iowa City/Coralville Area Convention & Visitors Bureau 900 First Ave Hayden Fry Way *TF:* 800-283-6592 ■ *Web:* www.iowacitycoralville.org	Coralville	IA	52241	319-337-6592	337-9953
Corinth Area Convention & Visitors Bureau 215 N Fillmore St *TF:* 800-748-9048 ■ *Web:* www.corinth.net	Corinth	MS	38834	662-287-8300	286-0102
Corpus Christi Convention & Visitors Bureau 101 N Shoreline Blvd Ste 430 *TF:* 800-678-6232 ■ *Web:* www.visitcorpuschristitx.org	Corpus Christi	TX	78401	361-881-1888	887-9023
Corvallis Tourism 420 NW Second St *TF:* 800-334-8118 ■ *Web:* www.visitcorvallis.com	Corvallis	OR	97330	541-757-1544	753-2664
Council Grove/Morris County Chamber of Commerce & Tourism 207 W Main St *Web:* www.councilgrove.com	Council Grove	KS	66846	620-767-5413	
Northern Kentucky Convention & Visitors Bureau (NKYCVB) 50 E RiverCenter Blvd Ste 200 *TF:* 877-659-8474 ■ *Web:* meetnky.com	Covington	KY	41011	859-261-4677	261-5135
Montgomery County Visitors & Convention Bureau 218 E Pike St *TF:* 800-866-3973 ■ *Web:* www.visitmoco.com	Crawfordsville	IN	47933	765-362-5200	362-5215
Crescent City-Del Norte County Chamber of Commerce (CCDNCVB) 1001 Front St *TF:* 800-343-8300 ■ *Web:* delnorte.org	Crescent City	CA	95531	707-464-3174	464-3561
Dallas Convention & Visitors Bureau 325 N St Paul St Ste 700 *TF:* 800-232-5527 ■ *Web:* www.visitdallas.com	Dallas	TX	75201	214-571-1000	571-1000
Central Florida Visitors & Convention Bureau 101 Adventure Ct *TF:* 800-828-7655 ■ *Web:* www.visitcentralflorida.org	Davenport	FL	33837	863-420-2586	420-2593
Tucker County Convention & Visitors Bureau 410 William Ave *TF:* 800-782-2775 ■ *Web:* www.canaanvalley.org	Davis	WV	26260	304-259-5315	
Dayton/Montgomery County Convention & Visitors Bureau 1 Chamber Plz Ste A *TF:* 800-221-8235 ■ *Web:* daytoncvb.com	Dayton	OH	45402	937-226-8211	226-8294
Decatur Area Convention & Visitors Bureau 202 E N St *TF:* 800-331-4479 ■ *Web:* www.decaturcvb.com	Decatur	IL	62523	217-423-7000	423-7455
Decatur/Morgan County Convention & Visitors Bureau (DMCCVB) 719 Sixth Ave SE PO Box 2349 *TF:* 800-232-5449 ■ *Web:* www.decaturcvb.org	Decatur	AL	35602	256-350-2028	
Wicomico County Convention & Visitors Bureau 8480 Ocean Hwy *TF:* 800-332-8687 ■ *Web:* www.wicomicotourism.org	Delmar	MD	21875	410-548-4914	
Denver Metro Convention & Visitors Bureau 1555 California St Ste 300 *TF:* 800-480-2010 ■ *Web:* www.denver.org	Denver	CO	80202	303-892-1112	
Greater Des Moines Convention & Visitors Bureau 400 Locust St Ste 265 *TF:* 800-451-2625 ■ *Web:* www.catchdesmoines.com	Des Moines	IA	50309	515-286-4960	244-9757
Detroit Metropolitan Convention & Visitors Bureau 211 W Fort St Ste 1000 *TF:* 877-424-5554 ■ *Web:* www.visitdetroit.com	Detroit	MI	48226	313-202-1800	202-1833
Dickinson Convention & Visitors Bureau 72 E Museum Dr *TF:* 800-279-7391 ■ *Web:* www.visitdickinson.com	Dickinson	ND	58601	701-483-4988	483-9261
Dothan Area Convention & Visitors Bureau 3311 Ross Clark Cir *TF:* 888-449-0212 ■ *Web:* www.dothanalcvb.com	Dothan	AL	36301	334-794-6622	
Kent County & Greater Dover Delaware Convention & Visitors Bureau 435 N DuPont Hwy *TF:* 800-233-5368 ■ *Web:* www.visitdover.com	Dover	DE	19901	302-734-1736	734-0167
DuQuoin Tourism Commission 20 N Chestnut St PO Box 1037 *TF:* 800-455-9570 ■ *Web:* www.duquointourism.org	Du Quoin	IL	62832	618-542-8338	
Dublin Convention & Visitors Bureau 9 S High St *TF:* 800-245-8387 ■ *Web:* www.irishisanattitude.com	Dublin	OH	43017	614-792-7666	760-1818
Duluth Convention & Visitors Bureau 21 W Superior St Ste 100 *TF:* 800-438-5884 ■ *Web:* www.visitduluth.com	Duluth	MN	55802	218-722-4011	722-1322
Durango Area Tourism Office 111 S Camino del Rio *TF:* 800-525-8855 ■ *Web:* www.durango.org	Durango	CO	81301	970-247-3500	
Durham Convention & Visitors Bureau 101 E Morgan St *TF:* 800-446-8604 ■ *Web:* durham-nc.com	Durham	NC	27701	919-687-0288	683-9555
Eagan Convention & Visitors Bureau 1501 Central Pkwy *TF:* 866-324-2620 ■ *Web:* www.eaganmn.com	Eagan	MN	55121	651-675-5546	
Talbot County Tourism Office 11 S Harrison St *Web:* www.tourtalbot.org	Easton	MD	21601	410-770-8000	770-8057
Visit Eau Claire 4319 Jeffers Rd *TF:* 888-523-3866 ■ *Web:* www.visiteauclaire.com	Eau Claire	WI	54703	715-831-2345	
Effingham Convention & Visitors Bureau 201 E Jefferson Ave *TF:* 800-772-0750 ■ *Web:* www.effinghamil.com	Effingham	IL	62401	217-342-5305	342-2746
Elgin Area Convention & Visitors Bureau 60 S Grove Ave *TF:* 800-217-5362 ■ *Web:* www.northernfoxrivervalley.com	Elgin	IL	60120	847-695-7540	695-7668
Elkhart County Convention & Visitors Bureau 219 Caravan Dr *TF:* 800-262-8161 ■ *Web:* www.amishcountry.org	Elkhart	IN	46514	574-262-8161	262-3925
Howard County Tourism Council 8267 Main St Side Entrance *TF:* 866-313-6300 ■ *Web:* www.howardcountymd.gov	Ellicott City	MD	21043	410-313-1900	
Grays Harbor Tourism PO Box 1229 *TF:* 800-621-9625 ■ *Web:* visitgraysharbor.com	Elma	WA	98541	360-482-2651	
VisitErie 208 E Bayfront Pkwy Ste 103 *TF:* 800-524-3743 ■ *Web:* www.visiteriepa.com	Erie	PA	16507	814-454-1000	459-0241
Eugene Cascades Coast 754 Olive St *TF:* 800-547-5445 ■ *Web:* www.eugenecascadescoast.org	Eugene	OR	97440	541-484-5307	343-6335
Humboldt County Convention & Visitors Bureau 1034 Second St *TF:* 800-346-3482 ■ *Web:* www.redwoods.info	Eureka	CA	95501	707-443-5097	443-5115
Evansville Convention & Visitors Bureau 401 SE Riverside Dr *TF:* 800-433-3025 ■ *Web:* www.visitevansville.com	Evansville	IN	47713	812-421-2200	421-2207
Fairbanks Convention & Visitors Bureau 101 Dunkel St Ste 111 *TF:* 800-327-5774 ■ *Web:* www.explorefairbanks.com	Fairbanks	AK	99701	907-456-5774	459-3757
Jefferson County Visitor's Bureau PO Box 274 *Web:* www.visitoregontrail.org	Fairbury	NE	68352	402-729-3000	
Fairfax County Convention & Visitors Bureau (FXVA) 3702 Pender Dr Ste 420 *TF:* 800-732-4732 ■ *Web:* www.fxva.com	Fairfax	VA	22030	703-790-0643	
Convention & Visitors Bureau of Marion County 1000 Cole St Ste A *TF:* 800-834-7365 ■ *Web:* www.marioncvb.com	Fairmont	WV	26554	304-368-1123	
Fairmont Convention & Visitors Bureau 323 E Blue Earth Ave *TF:* 800-657-3280 ■ *Web:* visitfairmontmn.com	Fairmont	MN	56031	507-235-8585	
Fargo-Moorhead Convention & Visitors Bureau 2001 44th St S *TF:* 800-235-7654 ■ *Web:* www.fargomoorhead.org	Fargo	ND	58103	701-282-3653	282-4366

Phone Fax

Farmington Convention & Visitors Bureau
3041 E Main St Farmington NM 87402 505-326-7602
TF: 800-448-1240 ■ *Web:* www.farmingtonnm.org

Fayetteville Area Convention & Visitors Bureau (FACVB)
245 Person St Fayetteville NC 28301 910-483-5311 484-6632
TF: 800-255-8217 ■ *Web:* www.visitfayettevillenc.com

Flagstaff Convention & Visitors Bureau
323 W Aspen Ave Flagstaff AZ 86001 928-779-7611 556-1305
TF: 800-217-2367 ■ *Web:* www.flagstaffarizona.org

Florence Convention & Visitors Bureau
3290 W Radio Dr Florence SC 29501 843-664-0330 665-9480
TF General: 800-325-9005 ■ *Web:* www.visitflo.com

Tropical Everglades Visitor Assn
160 US Hwy Ste 1 Florida City FL 33034 305-245-9180
Web: www.tropicaleverglades.com

Fond du Lac Convention & Visitors Bureau
171 S Pioneer Rd Fond du Lac WI 54935 920-923-3010 929-6846
TF: 800-937-9123 ■ *Web:* www.fdl.com

Fort Collins Convention & Visitors Bureau
19 Old Town Sq Ste 137 Fort Collins CO 80524 970-232-3840 232-3841
TF: 800-274-3678 ■ *Web:* www.visitftcollins.com

Greater Fort Lauderdale Convention & Visitors Bureau
100 E Broward Blvd Ste 200 Fort Lauderdale FL 33301 954-765-4466 765-4467
TF: 877-272-5465 ■ *Web:* www.sunny.org

Fort Madison 614 Ninth St Fort Madison IA 52627 319-372-5471 372-6404
TF: 800-210-8687 ■ *Web:* fortmadison.com

Lee County Visitors & Convention Bureau
2201 Second St Ste 600 Fort Myers FL 33901 239-338-3500 334-1106
TF: 800-237-6444 ■ *Web:* www.fortmyers-sanibel.com

Fort Smith Convention & Visitors Bureau
2 N 'B' Fort Smith AR 72901 479-783-8888 784-2421
TF: 800-637-1477 ■ *Web:* www.fortsmith.org

Fort Wayne/Allen County Convention & Visitors Bureau
927 S Harrison St Fort Wayne IN 46802 260-424-3700 424-3914
TF: 800-767-7752 ■ *Web:* www.visitfortwayne.com

Fort Worth Convention & Visitors Bureau
111 W Fourth St Ste 200 Fort Worth TX 76102 817-336-8791 698-7823
TF: 800-433-5747 ■ *Web:* www.fortworth.com

Frankenmuth Convention & Visitors Bureau
635 S Main St Frankenmuth MI 48734 989-652-6106 652-3841
TF: 800-386-8696 ■ *Web:* www.frankenmuth.org

Frankfort/Franklin County Tourist & Convention Commission
100 Capitol Ave Frankfort KY 40601 502-875-8687
TF: 800-960-7200 ■ *Web:* www.visitfrankfort.com

Williamson County Convention & Visitors Bureau
400 Main St Ste 200 Franklin TN 37064 615-791-7554
Web: www.visitwilliamson.com

Tourism Council of Frederick County Inc
151 S East St Frederick MD 21701 301-600-2888
TF: 800-999-3613 ■ *Web:* www.visitfrederick.org

Fredericksburg Chamber of Commerce
302 E Austin St Fredericksburg TX 78624 830-997-6523 997-8588
TF: 888-997-3600 ■ *Web:* www.fredericksburg-texas.com

Dodge County Convention & Visitors Bureau
338 N Main St Fremont NE 68025 402-753-6414 721-1511
Web: www.fremontne.org

Fremont/Sandusky County Convention & Visitors Bureau
712 N St Ste 102 Fremont OH 43420 419-332-4470 332-4359
TF: 800-255-8070 ■ *Web:* www.sanduskycounty.org

Fresno & Clovis Convention & Visitors Bureau
1550 E Shaw Ave Ste 101 Fresno CA 93710 559-981-5500 445-0122
TF: 800-788-0836 ■ *Web:* www.playfresno.org

Alachua County Visitors & Convention Bureau
30 E University Ave Gainesville FL 32601 352-374-5260 338-3213
TF: 866-778-5002 ■ *Web:* www.visitgainesville.com

Galena/Jo Daviess County Convention & Visitors Bureau (GJDCCVB)
101 Bouthillier St Galena IL 61036 815-777-3557 777-3566
TF General: 800-747-9377 ■ *Web:* www.galena.org

Galesburg Area Convention & Visitors Bureau
2163 E Main St Galesburg IL 61401 309-343-2485
TF: 800-916-3330 ■ *Web:* www.visitgalesburg.com

Finney County Convention & Visitors Bureau
1511 E Fulton Terr Garden City KS 67846 620-275-1900 276-3290
TF: 866-267-4638 ■ *Web:* www.gardencity.net

Georgetown Convention & Visitors Bureau
1101 N College St Georgetown TX 78626 512-930-3545 930-3697
TF: 800-436-8696 ■ *Web:* www.visit.georgetown.org

Gettysburg Convention & Visitors Bureau
571 W Middle St Gettysburg PA 17325 717-334-6274 334-1166
TF: 800-337-5015 ■ *Web:* destinationgettysburg.com/index.asp

Greater Grand Forks Convention & Visitors Bureau
4251 Gateway Dr Grand Forks ND 58203 701-746-0444 746-0775
TF: 800-866-4566 ■ *Web:* www.visitgrandforks.com

Grand Junction Visitors & Convention Bureau
740 Horizon Dr Grand Junction CO 81506 970-244-1480 243-7393
TF: 800-962-2547 ■ *Web:* www.visitgrandjunction.com

Grand Rapids/Kent County Convention & Visitors Bureau
171 Monroe Ave NW Ste 700 Grand Rapids MI 49503 616-459-8287
TF: 800-678-9859 ■ *Web:* www.experiencegr.com

Grants Pass Visitors & Convention Bureau
1995 NW Vine St Grants Pass OR 97526 541-476-7574 476-9574
TF: 800-547-5927 ■ *Web:* travelgrantspass.com

Houma Area Convention & Visitors Bureau
114 Tourist Dr Gray LA 70359 985-868-2732
TF: 800-688-2732 ■ *Web:* www.houmatravel.com

Greeley Convention & Visitors Bureau
902 Seventh Ave Greeley CO 80631 970-352-3567 352-3572
TF: 800-449-3866 ■ *Web:* www.greeleychamber.com

Packer Country Visitor & Convention Bureau
1901 S Oneida St Green Bay WI 54304 920-494-9507 405-1271
TF: 888-867-3342 ■ *Web:* www.greenbay.com

Greensboro Area Convention & Visitors Bureau
2200 Pinecroft Rd Ste 200 Greensboro NC 27407 336-274-2282 230-1183
TF: 800-344-2282 ■ *Web:* visitgreensboronc.com

Phone Fax

Greater Greenville Convention & Visitors Bureau
148 River St Ste 222 Greenville SC 29601 864-421-0000 421-0005
TF: 800-351-7180 ■ *Web:* www.visitgreenvillesc.com

Greenville-Pitt County Convention & Visitors Bureau (GPCCVB)
417 Cotanche St Ste 100 Greenville NC 27858 252-329-4200 329-4205
TF: 800-537-5564 ■ *Web:* www.visitgreenvillenc.com

Greenwood Convention & Visitors Bureau
111 E Market St Greenwood MS 38930 662-453-9197 453-5526
TF: 800-748-9064 ■ *Web:* www.gcvb.com

Alabama Gulf Coast Convention & Visitors Bureau
3150 Gulf Shores Pkwy PO Box 457 Gulf Shores AL 36547 251-968-7511
TF: 800-745-7263 ■ *Web:* www.gulfshores.com

Lake County Convention & Visitors Bureau
5465 W Grand Ave Ste 100 Gurnee IL 60031 847-662-2700 662-2702
TF: 800-525-3669 ■ *Web:* www.visitlakecounty.org

Hagerstown/Washington County Convention & Visitors Bureau
16 Public Sq Hagerstown MD 21740 301-791-3246 791-2601
TF: 888-257-2600 ■ *Web:* www.visithagerstown.com

Hampton Conventions & Visitors Bureau
1919 Commerce Dr Ste 290 Hampton VA 23666 757-722-1222 896-4600
TF: 800-487-8778 ■ *Web:* visithampton.com

Hannibal Convention & Visitors Bureau
505 N Third St Hannibal MO 63401 573-221-2477 221-6999
TF: 866-263-4825 ■ *Web:* www.visithannibal.com

Jefferson County Convention & Visitors Bureau
37 Washington Ct Harpers Ferry WV 25425 304-535-2627
TF: 866-435-5698 ■ *Web:* www.discoveritallwv.com

Hershey Harrisburg Region Visitors Bureau
3211 N Front St Ste 301-A Harrisburg PA 17110 717-231-7788
TF: 877-727-8573 ■ *Web:* www.visithersheyharrisburg.org

Positively Cleveland Visitors Ctr
2207 Forest Hills Rd Ste 100 Harrisburg PA 17112 216-875-6680
TF: 800-321-1001 ■ *Web:* thisiscleveland.com

Long Island Convention & Visitors Bureau & Sports Commission
330 Motor Pkwy Ste 203 Hauppauge NY 11788 877-386-6654 951-3439*
**Fax Area Code:* 631 ■ *TF:* 877-386-6654 ■ *Web:* www.discoverlongisland.com

Hays Convention & Visitors Bureau
2700 Vine St PO Box 490 Hays KS 67601 785-628-8202 628-1471
TF: 800-569-4505 ■ *Web:* www.haysusa.com

Alpine Helen/White County Convention & Visitors Bureau
726 Bruckenstrasse PO Box 730 Helen GA 30545 706-878-2181
TF: 800-858-8027 ■ *Web:* www.helenga.org

Henderson County Tourist Commission
101 N Water St Ste B Henderson KY 42420 270-826-3128 826-0234
TF: 800-648-3128 ■ *Web:* www.hendersonky.org

Henderson County Travel & Tourism
201 S Main St Hendersonville NC 28792 828-693-9708 697-4996
TF: 800-828-4244 ■ *Web:* www.historichendersonville.org

Huntingdon County Visitors Bureau
6993 Seven Pt Rd Ste 2 Hesston PA 16647 814-658-0060 658-0068
TF: 888-729-7869 ■ *Web:* www.raystown.org

Hickory Metro Convention & Visitors Bureau
1960 13th Ave Dr SE Hickory NC 28602 828-322-1335 322-8983
TF: 800-509-2444 ■ *Web:* www.hickorymetro.com

High Point Convention & Visitors Bureau
300 S Main St High Point NC 27260 336-884-5255
TF: 800-720-5255 ■ *Web:* www.highpoint.org

Hilton Head Island Visitors & Convention Bureau
1 Chamber Dr PO Box 5647 Hilton Head Island SC 29938 843-785-3673 785-7110
TF: 800-523-3373 ■ *Web:* www.hiltonheadisland.org

Holland Area Convention & Visitors Bureau
76 E Eigth St Holland MI 49423 616-394-0000 394-0122
TF: 800-506-1299 ■ *Web:* www.holland.org

Hawaii Visitors & Convention Bureau
2270 Kalakaua Ave Ste 801 Honolulu HI 96815 800-464-2924
TF: 800-464-2924 ■ *Web:* www.gohawaii.com

Hot Springs Convention & Visitors Bureau
134 Convention Blvd Hot Springs AR 71901 501-321-2277
TF: 800-543-2284 ■ *Web:* www.hotsprings.org

Greater Houston Convention & Visitors Bureau
901 Bagby St Ste 100 Houston TX 77002 713-437-5200
TF: 800-446-8786 ■ *Web:* www.visithoustontexas.com

Cabell-Huntington Convention & Visitors Bureau
PO Box 347 Huntington WV 25708 304-525-7333 525-7345
TF: 800-635-6329 ■ *Web:* www.wvvisit.org

Huntington County Visitors & Convention Bureau
407 N Jefferson St Huntington IN 46750 260-359-8687
TF: 800-848-4282 ■ *Web:* www.visithuntington.org

Huntington Beach Marketing & Visitors Bureau
301 Main St Ste 208 Huntington Beach CA 92648 714-969-3492
TF: 800-729-6232 ■ *Web:* www.surfcityusa.com

Huntsville/Madison County Convention & Visitor's Bureau
500 Church St Ste 1 Huntsville AL 35801 256-551-2230 551-2324
TF: 800-843-0468 ■ *Web:* www.huntsville.org

Huron Chamber & Visitors Bureau
1725 Dakota Ave S Huron SD 57350 605-352-0000 352-8321
TF: 800-487-6673 ■ *Web:* www.huronsd.com

Hurricane Convention & Visitors Bureau
3255 Teays Vly Rd PO Box 1086 Hurricane WV 25526 304-562-5896 562-5858
Web: www.hurricanewv.com

Putnam County Convention & Visitors Bureau
3744 Teays Valley Rd Ste 209 Hurricane WV 25526 304-757-7282
Web: www.putnamcountycvb.com

Greater Hutchinson Convention & Visitors Bureau
117 N Walnut St PO Box 519 Hutchinson KS 67504 620-662-3391 662-2168
TF: 800-691-4262 ■ *Web:* www.hutchchamber.com

Incline Village/Crystal Bay Visitors Bureau
969 Tahoe Blvd Incline Village NV 89451 775-832-1606 832-1605
TF: 800-468-2463 ■ *Web:* www.gotahoenorth.com

Indiana County Tourist Bureau
2334 Oakland Ave Ste 68 Indiana PA 15701 724-463-7505 465-3819
TF: 877-746-3426 ■ *Web:* www.visitindianacountypa.org

Indianapolis Convention & Visitors Assn
200 S Capitol Ave Ste 300 Indianapolis IN 46225 317-262-3000
TF: 800-862-6912 ■ *Web:* www.visitindy.com

Phone | Fax

Western Upper Peninsula Convention & Visitor Bureau
405 N Lake St PO Box 706 ... Ironwood MI 49938 906-932-4850
TF: 800-522-5657 ■ *Web:* www.explorewesternup.com

Irving Convention & Visitors Bureau
500 W Las Colinas Blvd ... Irving TX 75039 972-252-7476
TF: 800-247-8464 ■ *Web:* www.irvingtexas.com

Ithaca/Tompkins County Convention & Visitors Bureau
904 E Shore Dr ... Ithaca NY 14850 607-272-1313 272-7617
TF: 800-284-8422 ■ *Web:* www.visitithaca.com

Jackson County Convention & Visitors Bureau
141 S Jackson St ... Jackson MI 49201 517-764-4440 780-3688
TF: 800-245-5282 ■ *Web:* www.experiencejackson.com

Metro Jackson Convention & Visitors Bureau
111 E Capitol St Ste 102 ... Jackson MS 39202 601-960-1891 960-1827
TF: 800-354-7695 ■ *Web:* www.visitjackson.com

Jacksonville Convention & Visitors Bureau
310 E State St ... Jacksonville IL 62650 217-243-5678
TF: 800-593-5678 ■ *Web:* www.jacksonvilleil.org

Onslow County Tourism
1099 Gum Branch Rd ... Jacksonville NC 28540 800-932-2144 347-4705*
**Fax Area Code:* 910 ■ *TF:* 800-932-2144 ■ *Web:* www.onlyinonslow.com

Visit Jacksonville 208 N Laura St Ste 1 ... Jacksonville FL 32202 904-798-9111
TF: 800-733-2668 ■ *Web:* www.visitjacksonville.com

Jamestown Promotions & Tourism Ctr
404 Louis L'Amour Ln ... Jamestown ND 58401 701-251-9145 251-9146
TF: 800-222-4766 ■ *Web:* discoverjamestownnd.com

Jefferson City Convention & Visitors Bureau
700 E Capitol Ave ... Jefferson City MO 65101 573-632-2820 638-4892
TF: 800-769-4183 ■ *Web:* www.visitjeffersoncity.com

Clark-Floyd Counties Convention & Tourism Bureau
315 Southern Indiana Ave ... Jeffersonville IN 47130 812-282-6654 282-1904
TF: 800-552-3842 ■ *Web:* www.sunnysideoflouisville.org

Greater Johnstown/Cambria County Convention & Visitors Bureau
111 Roosevelt Blvd Ste A ... Johnstown PA 15906 814-536-7993 539-3370
TF: 800-237-8590 ■ *Web:* www.visitjohnstownpa.com

Heritage Corridor Convention & Visitors Bureau
339 W Jefferson St ... Joliet IL 60435 815-727-2323 727-2324
TF: 800-926-2262 ■ *Web:* www.heritagecorridorcvb.com

Joplin Convention & Visitors Bureau
222 W Third St ... Joplin MO 64801 417-625-4789 624-7948
Web: www.visitjoplinmo.com

Juneau Convention & Visitors Bureau
101 Egan Dr ... Juneau AK 99801 907-586-1737 586-6304
TF: 888-581-2201 ■ *Web:* www.traveljuneau.com

Kalamazoo County Convention & Visitors Bureau
141 E Michigan Ave Ste 100 ... Kalamazoo MI 49007 269-488-9000 488-0050
TF: 800-888-0509 ■ *Web:* www.discoverkalamazoo.com

Flathead Convention & Visitors Bureau
15 Depot Pk ... Kalispell MT 59901 406-756-9091 257-2500
TF: 800-543-3105 ■ *Web:* www.fcvb.org

Cabarrus County Convention & Visitors Bureau
3003 Dale Earnhardt Blvd ... Kannapolis NC 28083 704-782-4340 782-4333
TF: 800-848-3740 ■ *Web:* www.visitcabarrus.com

Kansas City Convention & Visitors Assn
1100 Main St Ste 2200 ... Kansas City MO 64105 816-221-5242
TF: 800-767-7700 ■ *Web:* www.visitkc.com

Kansas City Kansas Convention & Visitors Bureau Inc
901 N Eigth St PO Box 171517 ... Kansas City KS 66117 913-321-5800
TF: 800-264-1563 ■ *Web:* www.visitkansascityks.com

Chester County Tourist Bureau
300 Greenwood Rd ... Kennett Square PA 19348 484-770-8550 770-8557
Web: www.brandywinevalley.com

Tri-Cities Visitor & Convention Bureau
7130 W Grandridge Blvd Ste B ... Kennewick WA 99336 509-735-8486 783-9005
TF: 800-254-5824 ■ *Web:* www.visittri-cities.com

Kenosha Area Convention & Visitors Bureau
812 56th St ... Kenosha WI 53140 262-654-7307 654-0882
TF: 800-654-7309

Kerrville Convention & Visitors Bureau
2108 Sidney Baker St ... Kerrville TX 78028 830-792-3535 792-3230
TF: 800-221-7958 ■ *Web:* www.kerrvilletexascvb.com

Ketchikan Visitors Bureau 131 Front St ... Ketchikan AK 99901 907-225-6166 225-4250
TF: 800-770-3300 ■ *Web:* www.visit-ketchikan.com

Key West Visitors Ctr 510 Greene St 1st Fl ... Key West FL 33040 305-294-2587 294-7806
TF General: 800-533-5397 ■ *Web:* www.keywestchamber.org

Monroe County Tourist Development Council
1201 White St Ste 102 ... Key West FL 33040 305-296-1552 296-6962
TF: 800-242-5229 ■ *Web:* www.fla-keys.com

Killeen Civic & Conference Ctr & Visitors Bureau
3601 S WS Young Dr ... Killeen TX 76542 254-501-3888
Web: www.visitkilleen.com

Valley Forge Convention & Visitors Bureau
1000 First Ave Ste 101 ... King of Prussia PA 19406 610-834-1550 834-0202
TF General: 888-847-4883 ■ *Web:* www.valleyforge.org

Kingsport Convention & Visitors Bureau (KCVB)
400 Clinchfield St Ste 100 ... Kingsport TN 37660 423-392-8820 392-8833
TF: 800-743-5282 ■ *Web:* www.visitkingsport.com

Armstrong County Tourist Bureau
125 Market St Ste 2 ... Kittanning PA 16201 724-543-4003 545-3119
TF: 888-265-9954 ■ *Web:* www.armstrongcounty.com

Discover Klamath 205 Riverside Dr Ste B ... Klamath Falls OR 97601 541-882-1501 850-0125
TF: 800-445-6728 ■ *Web:* www.meetmeinklamath.com

Knoxville Tourism & Sports Corp
301 S Gay St ... Knoxville TN 37902 865-523-7263
TF: 800-727-8045 ■ *Web:* visitknoxville.com

Lake Barkley Tourist Commission
82 Days Inn Dr ... Kuttawa KY 42055 270-388-5300 388-5301
TF: 800-355-3885 ■ *Web:* www.lakebarkley.org

La Crosse Area Convention & Visitors Bureau
410 Veterans Memorial Dr ... La Crosse WI 54601 608-782-2366 782-4082
TF: 800-658-9424 ■ *Web:* www.explorelacrosse.com

Lafayette Convention & Visitors Commission
1400 NW Evangeline Thwy ... Lafayette LA 70501 337-232-3737 232-0161
TF: 800-346-1958 ■ *Web:* www.lafayettetravel.com

Phone | Fax

Lafayette-West Lafayette Convention & Visitors Bureau
301 Frontage Rd ... Lafayette IN 47905 765-447-9999 447-5062
TF: 800-872-6648 ■ *Web:* www.homeofpurdue.com

Laguna Beach Visitors & Conference Bureau
381 Forest Ave ... Laguna Beach CA 92651 949-497-9229
TF: 800-877-1115 ■ *Web:* visitlagunabeach.com

Southwest Louisiana Convention & Visitors Bureau
1205 N Lakeshore Dr ... Lake Charles LA 70601 337-436-9588
TF: 800-456-7952 ■ *Web:* www.visitlakecharles.org

Seminole County Convention & Visitors Bureau
1515 International Pkwy Ste 1013 ... Lake Mary FL 32746 407-665-2900 665-2920
TF: 800-800-7832 ■ *Web:* www.visitseminole.com

Lake Placid Convention & Visitors Bureau
2608 Main St ... Lake Placid NY 12946 518-523-2445 523-2605
TF: 800-447-5224 ■ *Web:* www.lakeplacid.com

Chicago Southland Convention & Visitors Bureau
2304 173rd St ... Lansing IL 60438 708-895-8200 895-8288
TF: 888-895-8233 ■ *Web:* www.cscvb.com

Greater Lansing Convention & Visitors Bureau
500 E Michigan Ave Ste 180 ... Lansing MI 48912 517-487-0077 487-5151
TF: 888-252-6746 ■ *Web:* www.lansing.org

Prince George's County Conference & Visitors Bureau
9200 Basil Ct Ste 101 ... Largo MD 20774 301-925-8300 925-2053
Web: www.visitprincegeorges.com

Las Cruces Convention & Visitors Bureau
211 N Water St ... Las Cruces NM 88001 575-541-2444 541-2164
TF: 800-429-9488 ■ *Web:* www.lascrucescvb.org

Las Vegas Convention & Visitors Authority
3150 Paradise Rd ... Las Vegas NV 89109 702-892-0711 837-0315
TF: 877-847-4858 ■ *Web:* www.lvcva.com

Leavenworth Convention & Visitors Bureau
100 N fifth St Rm 104 ... Leavenworth KS 66048 913-682-4113
Web: www.visitleavenworthks.com

Boone County Convention & Visitors Bureau
PO Box 644 ... Lebanon IN 46052 765-484-8572
Web: www.boonecvb.com

Lenexa Convention & Visitors Bureau
11180 Lackman Rd ... Lenexa KS 66219 913-888-1414 888-3770
Web: www.lenexa.org

Greenbrier County Convention & Visitors Bureau
200 W Washington St ... Lewisburg WV 24901 304-645-1000 647-3001
TF: 800-833-2068 ■ *Web:* www.greenbrierwv.com

Lexington Convention & Visitors Bureau
301 E Vine St ... Lexington KY 40507 859-233-7299 254-4555
TF: 800-845-3959 ■ *Web:* www.visitlex.com

Laurel Highlands Visitors Bureau
120 E Main St ... Ligonier PA 15658 724-238-5661 238-3673
TF: 800-333-5661 ■ *Web:* www.laurelhighlands.org

Lima/Allen County Convention & Visitors Bureau
144 S Main St Ste 101 ... Lima OH 45801 419-222-6075 222-0134
TF: 888-222-6075 ■ *Web:* www.lima-allencvb.com

Abraham Lincoln Tourism Bureau of Logan County
1555 Fifth St ... Lincoln IL 62656 217-732-8687
Web: tourlogancounty.com

Lincoln Convention & Visitors Bureau
1135 M St Ste 300 ... Lincoln NE 68508 402-434-5335 436-2360
TF: 800-423-8212 ■ *Web:* www.lincoln.org

Lincoln City Visitor & Convention Bureau
801 SW Hwy 101 Ste 401 ... Lincoln City OR 97367 541-996-1274 994-2408
TF: 800-452-2151 ■ *Web:* www.oregoncoast.org

Lisle Convention & Visitors Bureau
925 Burlington Ave ... Lisle IL 60532 630-769-1000 769-1006
TF: 800-733-9811 ■ *Web:* stayinlisle.com

Western CT Convention & Visitors Bureau
PO Box 968 ... Litchfield CT 06759 860-567-4506 567-5214
Web: www.northwestct.com

Little Rock Convention & Visitors Bureau
426 W Markham St PO Box 3232 ... Little Rock AR 72203 501-376-4781 374-2255
TF: 800-844-4781 ■ *Web:* www.littlerock.com

Lodi Conference & Visitors Bureau
115 S School St ... Lodi CA 95240 209-365-1195
TF: 800-798-1810 ■ *Web:* www.visitlodi.com

London/Laurel County Tourist Commission
140 Faith Assembly Church Rd ... London KY 40741 606-878-6900 877-1689
TF: 800-348-0095 ■ *Web:* www.laurelkytourism.com

Long Beach Convention & Visitors Bureau
301 E Ocean Blvd ... Long Beach CA 90802 562-436-3645 435-5653
TF: 800-452-7829 ■ *Web:* www.visitlongbeach.com

Cowlitz County Tourism 1900 Seventh Ave ... Longview WA 98632 360-577-3137
Web: www.visitmtsthelens.com

Los Angeles Convention & Visitors Bureau
333 S Hope St 18th Fl ... Los Angeles CA 90071 213-624-7300
Web: www.discoverlosangeles.com

Louisville & Jefferson County Convention & Visitors Bureau
401 W Main St Ste 2300 ... Louisville KY 40202 502-584-2121 584-6697
TF: 800-626-5646 ■ *Web:* www.gotolouisville.com

Greater Merrimack Valley Convention & Visitors Bureau
40 French St 2nd Fl ... Lowell MA 01852 978-459-6150 459-4595
TF: 800-443-3332 ■ *Web:* www.merrimackvalley.org

Lubbock Convention & Visitors Bureau
1500 Broadway St 6th Fl ... Lubbock TX 79401 806-747-5232 747-1419
TF: 800-692-4035 ■ *Web:* www.visitlubbock.org

Lumberton Area Visitors Bureau
3431 Lackey St ... Lumberton NC 28360 910-739-9999
TF: 800-359-6971 ■ *Web:* www.lumberton-nc.com

Mackinaw Area Visitors Bureau
10800 US 23 ... Mackinaw City MI 49701 231-436-5664 436-5991
TF: 800-666-0160 ■ *Web:* www.mackinawcity.com

Macomb Area Convention & Visitors Bureau
201 S Lafayette St ... Macomb IL 61455 309-833-1315 833-3575
Web: www.makeitmacomb.com

Macon-Bibb County Convention/Visitors Bureau
450 Martin Luther King Jr Blvd ... Macon GA 31201 478-743-1074 745-2022
TF: 800-768-3401 ■ *Web:* www.maconga.org

				Phone	Fax

Greater Madison Convention & Visitors Bureau
615 E Washington Ave .... Madison WI 53703 608-255-2537 258-4950
TF: 800-373-6376 ■ *Web:* www.visitmadison.com

Madison Convention & Visitors Bureau
118 N Main St .... Madison GA 30650 706-342-4454
Web: www.madisonga.org

Saint Tammany Parish Tourist & Convention Commission
68099 Hwy 59 .... Mandeville LA 70471 985-892-0520 892-1441
TF: 800-634-9443 ■ *Web:* www.louisiananorthshore.com

Manhattan Convention & Visitors Bureau
501 Poyntz Ave .... Manhattan KS 66502 785-776-8829 776-0679
TF: 800-759-0134 ■ *Web:* www.manhattancvb.org

Manitowoc Area Visitor & Convention Bureau
4221 Calumet Ave .... Manitowoc WI 54221 800-627-4896
TF: 800-627-4896 ■ *Web:* www.manitowoc.info

Greater Mankato Growth 1961 Premier Dr .... Mankato MN 56001 507-385-6640 345-4451
TF: 800-697-0652 ■ *Web:* www.greatermankato.com

Mansfield/Richland County Convention & Visitors Bureau
124 N Main St .... Mansfield OH 44902 419-525-1300 524-7722
TF: 800-642-8282 ■ *Web:* www.mansfieldtourism.com

Outer Banks Visitors Bureau 1 Visitor Ctr Cir .... Manteo NC 27954 252-473-2138 473-5777
TF: 877-629-4386 ■ *Web:* www.outerbanks.org

Marion-Grant County Convention & Visitors Bureau
428 S Washington St Ste 261 .... Marion IN 46953 765-668-5435 668-5424
TF: 800-662-9474 ■ *Web:* www.showmegrantcounty.com

Williamson County Tourism Bureau
1602 Sioux Dr .... Marion IL 62959 618-997-3690 997-1874
TF General: 800-433-7399 ■ *Web:* www.visitsi.com

Marquette Country Convention & Visitors Bureau
337 W Washington St .... Marquette MI 49855 906-228-7749
TF: 800-544-4321 ■ *Web:* www.travelmarquettemichigan.com

Marshall Area Convention & Visitors Bureau
317 W Main St .... Marshall MN 56258 507-532-4484 532-4485
Web: www.marshall-mn.org

Marshfield Convention & Visitors Bureau
700 S Central Ave PO Box 868 .... Marshfield WI 54449 715-384-3454 387-8925
TF: 800-422-4541 ■ *Web:* www.marshfieldchamber.com

Mason City Convention & Visitors Bureau
2021 Fourth St SW Hwy 122 W .... Mason City IA 50401 641-422-1663
TF: 800-423-5724 ■ *Web:* www.visitmasoncityiowa.com

Melbourne Regional Chamber of East Central Florida
1005 E Strawbridge Ave .... Melbourne FL 32901 321-724-5400 725-2093
Web: melbourneregionalchamber.com

Memphis Convention & Visitors Bureau
47 Union Ave .... Memphis TN 38103 901-543-5300 543-5350
TF: 888-633-9099 ■ *Web:* www.memphistravel.com

Merced Conference & Visitors Bureau (MCVB)
710 W 16th St .... Merced CA 95340 209-384-2791
TF: 800-446-5353 ■ *Web:* visitmerced.travel

Meridian/Lauderdale County Tourism Bureau
212 Constitution Ave .... Meridian MS 39301 601-482-8001 486-4988
TF: 888-868-7720 ■ *Web:* www.visitmeridian.com

Greater Miami Convention & Visitors Bureau
701 Brickell Ave Ste 2700 .... Miami FL 33131 305-539-3000 530-5859
TF: 800-933-8448 ■ *Web:* www.miamiandbeaches.com

LaPorte County Convention & Visitors Bureau
4073 S Franklin St .... Michigan City IN 46360 219-872-5055 872-3660
TF: 800-634-2650 ■ *Web:* www.michigancitylaporte.com

Middletown Convention-Visitors (MCVB)
4935 Riverview Ave .... Middletown OH 45042 513-422-3030
Web: gettothebc.com

Midland County Convention & Visitors Bureau
300 Rodd St Ste 101 .... Midland MI 48640 989-839-0340 835-3701
TF: 800-444-9979 ■ *Web:* gogreat.com

Visit Milledgeville 200 W Hancock St .... Milledgeville GA 31061 478-452-4687 453-4440
TF: 800-653-1804 ■ *Web:* www.visitmilledgeville.org

Greater Milwaukee Convention & Visitors Bureau
648 N Plankinton Ave Ste 425 .... Milwaukee WI 53203 414-273-7222 273-5596
TF: 800-554-1448 ■ *Web:* www.visitmilwaukee.org

Meet Minneapolis
250 Marquette Ave Ste 1300 .... Minneapolis MN 55401 612-767-8000
TF: 800-445-7412 ■ *Web:* www.minneapolis.org

Minot Convention & Visitors Bureau
1020 S Broadway .... Minot ND 58701 701-857-8206 857-8228
TF: 800-264-2626 ■ *Web:* www.visitminot.org

Modesto Convention & Visitors Bureau
1150 Ninth St Ste C .... Modesto CA 95354 209-526-5588 526-5586
TF: 888-640-8467 ■ *Web:* www.visitmodesto.com

Quad Cities Convention & Visitors Bureau
1601 River Dr Ste 110 .... Moline IL 61265 309-277-0937 764-9443
TF: 800-747-7800 ■ *Web:* www.visitquadcities.com

Monterey County Convention & Visitors Bureau
PO Box 1770 .... Monterey CA 93942 831-657-6400 648-5373
TF: 888-221-1010 ■ *Web:* www.seemonterey.com

Montgomery Area Chamber of Commerce Convention & Visitor Bureau
300 Water St .... Montgomery AL 36104 334-261-1100
TF: 800-240-9452 ■ *Web:* www.visitingmontgomery.com

Montrose Visitor & Convention Bureau
107 S Cascade Ave .... Montrose CO 81401 970-249-5000 964-4073
TF: 888-212-8294 ■ *Web:* www.visitmontrose.com

Greater Morgantown Convention & Visitors Bureau
68 Donley St .... Morgantown WV 26501 304-292-5081 291-1354
TF: 800-458-7373 ■ *Web:* www.tourmorgantown.com

Knox County Convention & Visitors Bureau
107 S Main St .... Mount Vernon OH 43050 740-392-6102 392-7840
TF: 800-837-5282 ■ *Web:* www.visitknoxohio.org

Mount Vernon Convention & Visitors Bureau
1100 Main St .... Mount Vernon IL 62864 618-242-3151 242-6849
TF: 800-252-5464 ■ *Web:* www.mtvernon.com

Muncie Visitors Bureau 3700 S Madison St .... Muncie IN 47302 765-284-2700 284-3002
TF: 800-568-6862 ■ *Web:* visitmuncie.org/muncie-sports-plex

Muskegon County Convention & Visitors Bureau
610 W Western Ave .... Muskegon MI 49440 231-724-3100 724-1398
TF: 800-250-9283 ■ *Web:* www.visitmuskegon.org

Nacogdoches Convention & Visitors Bureau
200 E Main St .... Nacogdoches TX 75961 936-564-7351 462-7688
TF: 888-653-3788 ■ *Web:* www.visitnacogdoches.org

Napa Valley Conference & Visitors Bureau
600 Main St .... Napa CA 94559 707-251-5895
TF: 855-847-6272 ■ *Web:* www.visitnapavalley.com

Greater Naples Marco Island Everglades Convention & Visitors Bureau
2800 Horseshoe Dr .... Naples FL 34104 239-252-2384 252-2404
TF: 800-688-3600 ■ *Web:* www.paradisecoast.com

Brown County Convention & Visitors Bureau
10 N Van Buren St PO Box 840 .... Nashville IN 47448 812-988-7303 988-1070
TF: 800-753-3255 ■ *Web:* www.browncounty.com

Nashville Convention & Visitors Bureau (NCVB)
150 Fourth Ave N Ste G250 .... Nashville TN 37219 615-259-4730 259-4126
TF: 800-657-6910 ■ *Web:* www.visitmusiccity.com

Natchez Convention & Visitors Bureau
640 S Canal St .... Natchez MS 39120 601-446-6345
TF: 800-647-6724 ■ *Web:* www.visitnatchez.org

Craven County Convention & Visitors Bureau
203 S Front St .... New Bern NC 28560 252-637-9400 637-0250
TF: 800-437-5767 ■ *Web:* www.visitnewbern.com

Greater New Braunfels Chamber of Commerce Inc, The
390 S Seguin Ave PO Box 311417 .... New Braunfels TX 78130 830-625-2385 625-7918
TF: 800-572-2626 ■ *Web:* innewbraunfels.com

Lawrence County Tourist Promotion Agency
229 S Jefferson St .... New Castle PA 16101 724-654-8408 654-2044
TF: 888-284-7599 ■ *Web:* www.visitlawrencecounty.com

New Orleans Metropolitan Convention & Visitors Bureau
2020 St Charles Ave .... New Orleans LA 70130 504-566-5011 566-5046
TF: 800-672-6124 ■ *Web:* www.neworleanscvb.com

NYC & Co 810 Seventh Ave 3rd Fl .... New York NY 10019 212-484-1200 397-1931
Web: www.nycgo.com

Newberry Area Tourism Assn, The PO Box 308 .... Newberry MI 49868 906-293-5562
TF: 800-831-7292 ■ *Web:* www.newberrytourism.com

Newport County Convention & Visitors Bureau
23 America's Cup Ave .... Newport RI 02840 401-849-8048
Web: discovernewport.org

Newport Beach Conference & Visitors Bureau
1200 Newport Ctr Dr Ste 120 .... Newport Beach CA 92660 949-719-6100
TF: 800-216-1598 ■ *Web:* www.visitnewportbeach.com

Newport News Tourism Development Office
700 Town Ctr Dr Ste 320 .... Newport News VA 23606 757-926-1400 926-1441
TF: 888-493-7386 ■ *Web:* www.newport-news.org

Newton Convention & Visitor Bureau
300 E 17th St S Ste 400 .... Newton IA 50208 641-792-0299
TF: 800-798-0299 ■ *Web:* www.visitnewton.com

Niagara Tourism & Convention Corp
10 Rainbow Blvd .... Niagara Falls NY 14303 716-282-8992 285-0809
TF: 877-325-5787 ■ *Web:* www.niagara-usa.com

Nome Convention & Visitors Bureau 301 Front St .... Nome AK 99762 907-443-6624 443-5832
Web: www.visitnomealaska.com

Norfolk Area Chamber of Commerce
405 Madison Ave .... Norfolk NE 68701 402-371-4862 371-0182
Web: www.norfolk.ne.us

Norfolk Convention & Visitors Bureau
232 E Main St .... Norfolk VA 23510 757-664-6620 622-3663
TF: 800-368-3097 ■ *Web:* www.visitnorfolktoday.com

Norman Convention & Visitors Bureau
309 E Main St .... Norman OK 73069 405-366-8095
TF: 800-767-7260 ■ *Web:* www.visitnorman.com

Lincoln County Convention & Visitor's Bureau
315 W Eugene Ave .... North Platte NE 69101 308-532-4729 532-5914
Web: www.visitnorthplatte.com

North Ridgeville Visitors Bureau
34845 Lorain Rd .... North Ridgeville OH 44039 440-327-3737 327-1474
Web: www.nrchamber.com

DuPage Convention & Visitors Bureau
915 Harger Rd Ste 240 .... Oak Brook IL 60523 630-575-8070 575-8078
TF: 800-232-0502 ■ *Web:* www.discoverdupage.com

Oak Park Area Convention & Visitors Bureau
1118 Westgate .... Oak Park IL 60301 708-524-7800 524-7473
TF: 888-625-7275 ■ *Web:* www.visitoakpark.com

Yosemite Sierra Visitors Bureau
40637 Hwy 41 .... Oakhurst CA 93644 559-683-4636
Web: www.yosemitethisyear.com

Oakland Convention & Visitors Bureau
481 Water St .... Oakland CA 94607 510-839-9000
Web: www.visitoakland.org

Ocean City Convention & Visitors Bureau
4001 Coastal Hwy .... Ocean City MD 21842 410-289-8181
TF: 800-626-2326 ■ *Web:* www.ococean.com

Oconomowoc Convention & Visitors Bureau
174 E Wisconsin Ave .... Oconomowoc WI 53066 262-569-2186 569-2164
TF: 888-936-7463 ■ *Web:* www.oconomowoc-wi.gov

Odessa Convention & Visitors Bureau
700 N Grant Ave Ste 200 .... Odessa TX 79761 432-333-7871 333-7858
TF: 800-780-4678 ■ *Web:* www.odessacvb.com

Ogden/Weber Convention & Visitors Bureau
2438 Washington Blvd .... Ogden UT 84401 801-778-6250 399-0783
TF: 800-255-8824 ■ *Web:* www.visitogden.com

Oklahoma City Convention & Visitors Bureau
123 Pk Ave .... Oklahoma City OK 73102 405-297-8912 297-8888
TF: 800-225-5652 ■ *Web:* www.visitokc.com

McDowell County Tourism Development Authority
91 S Catawba Ave .... Old Fort NC 28762 828-668-4282 668-4924
TF: 888-233-6111 ■ *Web:* blueridgetravelers.com

Olympia Lacey Tumwater Visitor & Convention Bureau
103 Sid Snyder Ave SW .... Olympia WA 98501 360-704-7544 704-7533
TF: 877-704-7500 ■ *Web:* www.visitolympia.com

Greater Omaha Convention & Visitors Bureau
1001 Farnam St Ste 200 .... Omaha NE 68102 402-444-4660 444-4511
TF: 866-937-6624 ■ *Web:* www.visitomaha.com

Ontario Area Chamber of Commerce
251 SW 9th St .... Ontario OR 97914 541-889-8012 889-8331
TF: 866-989-8012 ■ *Web:* www.ontariochamber.com

Phone Fax

Ontario Convention & Visitors Bureau
2000 E Convention Ctr Way . . . . . Ontario CA 91764 909-937-3000 937-3080
TF: 800-455-5755 ■ *Web:* www.ontarioocc.org

Orlando/Orange County Convention & Visitors Bureau Inc
6700 Forum Dr Ste 100 . . . . . Orlando FL 32821 407-363-5872
TF: 800-972-3304 ■ *Web:* www.visitorlando.com

Lake of the Ozarks Convention & Visitors Bureau
5815 Hwy 54 PO Box 1498 . . . . . Osage Beach MO 65065 573-348-1599 348-2293
TF: 800-386-5253 ■ *Web:* www.funlake.com

Ottawa Tourism & Convention Authority
150 Elgin St Ste 1405 . . . . . Ottawa ON K2P1L4 613-237-5150 237-7339
TF: 800-363-4465 ■ *Web:* www.ottawatourism.ca

Ottawa Visitors Ctr 106 W Lafayette St . . . . . Ottawa IL 61350 815-434-2737 434-4530
TF: 888-688-2924 ■ *Web:* pickusottawail.com

Overland Park Convention & Visitors Bureau
9001 W 110th St Ste 100 . . . . . Overland Park KS 66210 913-491-0123 491-0015
TF: 800-262-7275 ■ *Web:* www.visitoverlandpark.com

Owensboro-Davies County Tourist Commission
215 E Second St . . . . . Owensboro KY 42303 270-926-1100
TF: 800-489-1131 ■ *Web:* www.visitowensboro.com

Oxford Convention & Visitors Bureau
102 Ed Perry Blvd . . . . . Oxford MS 38655 662-232-2367
TF: 800-758-9177 ■ *Web:* visitoxfordms.com

Oxnard Convention & Visitors Bureau
1000 Town Ctr Dr Ste 130 . . . . . Oxnard CA 93036 805-385-7545 385-7571
TF: 800-269-6273 ■ *Web:* www.visitoxnard.com

Panama City Beach Convention & Visitors Bureau
17001 Panama City Beach Pkwy . . . . . Panama City Beach FL 32413 850-233-5070
TF: 800-722-3224 ■ *Web:* www.visitpanamacitybeach.com

Park City Chamber of Commerce/Convention & Visitors Bureau
1850 Sidewinder Dr Ste 320 . . . . . Park City UT 84060 435-649-6100
TF: 800-453-1360 ■ *Web:* www.visitparkcity.com

Greater Parkersburg Convention & Visitors Bureau
350 Seventh St . . . . . Parkersburg WV 26101 304-428-1130 428-8117
TF: 800-752-4982 ■ *Web:* www.greaterparkersburg.com

Pasadena Convention & Visitors Bureau
300 E Green St . . . . . Pasadena CA 91101 626-795-9311 795-9656
TF: 800-307-7977 ■ *Web:* www.visitpasadena.com

Pensacola Convention & Visitors Bureau
1401 E Gregory St . . . . . Pensacola FL 32502 850-434-1234 432-8211
TF: 800-874-1234 ■ *Web:* www.visitpensacola.com

Peoria Area Convention & Visitors Bureau
456 Fulton St Ste 300 . . . . . Peoria IL 61602 309-676-0303 676-8470
TF: 800-747-0302 ■ *Web:* www.peoria.org

Perry Area Convention & Visitors Bureau
101 Gen Courtney Hodges Blvd PO Box 1609 . . . . . Perry GA 31069 478-988-8000 988-8005
Web: www.perryga.com

Petoskey Area Visitors Bureau
401 E Mitchell St . . . . . Petoskey MI 49770 231-348-2755 348-1810
TF: 800-845-2828 ■ *Web:* www.petoskeyarea.com

Philadelphia Convention & Visitors Bureau
1700 Market St Ste 3000 . . . . . Philadelphia PA 19103 215-636-3300 636-3327
Web: www.discoverphl.com

Greater Phoenix Convention & Visitors Bureau
400 E Van Buren St Ste 600 . . . . . Phoenix AZ 85004 602-254-6500 253-4415
TF: 877-225-5749 ■ *Web:* www.visitphoenix.com

Pigeon Forge Dept of Tourism
PO Box 1390 . . . . . Pigeon Forge TN 37868 865-453-8574
TF: 800-251-9100 ■ *Web:* www.mypigeonforge.com

Pine Bluff Convention & Visitors Bureau (PBCVB)
1 Convention Ctr Plz . . . . . Pine Bluff AR 71601 870-536-7600 850-2105
TF: 800-536-7660 ■ *Web:* www.pinebluffcvb.org

Greater Pittsburgh Convention & Visitors Bureau
120 Fifth Ave 5th Ave Pl, 1st Level . . . . . Pittsburgh PA 15222 412-281-7711 644-5512
TF: 800-359-0758 ■ *Web:* www.visitpittsburgh.com

Plano Convention & Visitors Bureau
2000 E Spring Creek Pkwy . . . . . Plano TX 75074 972-941-5840 424-0002
TF: 800-817-5266 ■ *Web:* www.visitplano.com

Ponca City Tourism
420 E Grand Ave PO Box 1109 . . . . . Ponca City OK 74602 580-765-4400 765-2798
TF: 866-763-8092 ■ *Web:* visitponcacity.com

North Olympic Peninsula Visitor & Convention Bureau
338 W First St Ste 104 PO Box 670 . . . . . Port Angeles WA 98362 360-452-8552 452-7383
TF: 800-942-4042 ■ *Web:* www.olympicpeninsula.org

Port Arthur Convention & Visitors Bureau
3401 Cultural Ctr Dr . . . . . Port Arthur TX 77642 409-985-7822
TF: 800-235-7822 ■ *Web:* www.portarthurtexas.com

Lake Erie Shores & Islands Welcome Ctr
770 SE Catawba Rd . . . . . Port Clinton OH 43452 419-734-4386 734-9798
TF: 800-441-1271 ■ *Web:* www.shoresandislands.com

Indiana Dunes the Casual Coast
1215 N State Rd 49 . . . . . Porter IN 46304 219-926-2255 929-5395
TF: 800-283-8687 ■ *Web:* www.indianadunes.com

Greater Portland Convention & Visitors Bureau
94 Commercial St Ste 300 . . . . . Portland ME 04101 207-772-4994 874-9043
Web: www.visitportland.com

Travel Portland
Pioneer Courthouse Square
701 S.W. Sixth Ave. . . . . . Portland OR 97205 503-275-9750
TF: 877-678-5263 ■ *Web:* www.travelportland.com

Providence Warwick Convention & Visitors Bureau
10 Memorial Blvd . . . . . Providence RI 02903 401-456-0200 351-2090
TF: 800-233-1636 ■ *Web:* www.goprovidence.com

Utah Valley Convention & Visitors Bureau
111 S University Ave . . . . . Provo UT 84601 801-851-2100 851-2109
TF: 800-222-8824 ■ *Web:* www.utahvalley.com

Plumas County Visitors Bureau 550 Crescent St . . . . . Quincy CA 95971 530-283-6345
TF: 800-326-2247 ■ *Web:* www.plumascounty.org

Quincy Area Convention & Visitors Bureau (QACVB)
532 Gardner Expy . . . . . Quincy IL 62301 217-214-3700
TF: 800-978-4748 ■ *Web:* www.seequincy.com

Greater Raleigh Convention & Visitors Bureau
421 Fayetteville St Mall Ste 1505 . . . . . Raleigh NC 27602 919-834-5900 831-2887
TF: 800-849-8499 ■ *Web:* www.visitraleigh.com

Palm Springs Desert Resorts Convention & Visitors Authority
70-100 Hwy 111 . . . . . Rancho Mirage CA 92270 760-770-9000
TF: 800-967-3767 ■ *Web:* www.visitgreaterpalmsprings.com

Rapid City Convention & Visitors Bureau
444 Mt Rushmore Rd N . . . . . Rapid City SD 57701 605-718-8484 348-9217
TF: 800-487-3223 ■ *Web:* www.visitrapidcity.com

Reading & Berks County Visitors Bureau
2525 N 12th St Ste 101 . . . . . Reading PA 19605 610-375-4085 375-9606
TF: 800-443-6610 ■ *Web:* www.gogreaterreading.com

Rehoboth Beach Convention Ctr
229 Rehoboth Ave . . . . . Rehoboth Beach DE 19971 302-227-4641 227-4643
TF: 888-743-3628 ■ *Web:* www.cityofrehoboth.com

Reno-Sparks Convention & Visitors Authority
PO Box 837 . . . . . Reno NV 89504 775-827-7600 827-7678
TF: 800-443-1482 ■ *Web:* www.visitrenotahoe.com

Richardson Convention & Visitors Bureau
411 W Arapaho Rd Ste 105 . . . . . Richardson TX 75080 972-744-4034 744-5834
TF: 888-690-7287 ■ *Web:* www.richardsontexas.org

Richmond Metropolitan Convention & Visitors Bureau
401 N Third St . . . . . Richmond VA 23219 804-782-2777
TF: 800-370-9004 ■ *Web:* visitrichmondva.com

Richmond/Wayne County Convention & Tourism Bureau
5701 National Rd E . . . . . Richmond IN 47374 765-935-8687 935-0440
TF: 800-828-8414 ■ *Web:* www.visitrichmond.org

Ridgecrest Area Convention & Visitors Bureau (RACVB)
643 N China Lake Blvd Ste C . . . . . Ridgecrest CA 93555 760-375-8202 375-9850
TF: 800-847-4830 ■ *Web:* racvb.com

Rising Sun/Ohio County Convention Tourism & Visitors Commission
100 S Walnut St . . . . . Rising Sun IN 47040 812-438-4933
Web: www.enjoyrisingsun.com

Riverside Convention & Visitors Bureau
3750 University Ave Ste 175 . . . . . Riverside CA 92501 951-222-4700
TF: 888-748-7733 ■ *Web:* www.riversidecvb.com

Roanoke Valley Convention & Visitors Bureau
101 Shenandoah Ave NE . . . . . Roanoke VA 24016 540-342-6025 342-7119
TF: 800-635-5535 ■ *Web:* www.visitroanokeva.com

Tunica MS 13625 Hwy 61 N . . . . . Robinsonville MS 38664 888-488-6422
TF: 888-488-6422 ■ *Web:* www.tunicatravel.com

Rochester Convention & Visitors Bureau
30 Civic Ctr Dr SE Ste 200 . . . . . Rochester MN 55904 507-288-4331 288-9144
TF: 800-634-8277 ■ *Web:* www.rochestercvb.org

Visit Rochester 45 E Ave Ste 400 . . . . . Rochester NY 14604 585-279-8300 232-4822
TF: 800-677-7282 ■ *Web:* www.visitrochester.com

Rockhill-York County Convention & Visitors Bureau
452 S Anderson Rd . . . . . Rock Hill SC 29730 803-329-5200 329-0145
TF: 888-702-1320 ■ *Web:* www.visityorkcounty.com

Rockford Area Convention & Visitors Bureau
102 N Main St . . . . . Rockford IL 61101 815-963-8111 963-4298
TF: 800-521-0849 ■ *Web:* www.gorockford.com

Conference & Visitors Bureau of Montgomery County MD Inc
111 Rockville Pk Ste 800 . . . . . Rockville MD 20850 240-777-2060 777-2065
TF: 877-789-6904 ■ *Web:* www.visitmontgomery.com

Greater Rome Convention & Visitors Bureau
402 Civics Ctr Dr . . . . . Rome GA 30161 706-295-5576
TF: 800-444-1834 ■ *Web:* www.romegeorgia.org

Big Ten Conference 5440 Park Pl . . . . . Rosemont IL 60018 847-696-1010
Web: bigten.org

Rosemont Convention Bureau
9301 Bryn Mawr Ave . . . . . Rosemont IL 60018 847-823-2100 696-9700
Web: www.rosemont.com

Sacramento Convention & Visitors Bureau
1608 'I' St . . . . . Sacramento CA 95814 916-808-7777 808-7788
TF: 800-292-2334 ■ *Web:* visitsacramento.com

Greater Saint Charles Convention & Visitors Bureau
230 S Main St . . . . . Saint Charles MO 63301 636-946-7776 949-3217
TF: 800-366-2427 ■ *Web:* www.historicstcharles.com

Saint Cloud Area Convention & Visitors Bureau
525 Hwy 10 S Ste 1 . . . . . Saint Cloud MN 56304 320-251-4170 656-0401
TF: 800-264-2940 ■ *Web:* www.granitecountry.com

Saint Joseph Convention & Visitors Bureau
109 S Fourth St . . . . . Saint Joseph MO 64501 816-233-6688 233-9120
TF: 800-785-0360 ■ *Web:* www.stjomo.com

Auglaize & Mercer Counties Convention & Visitors Bureau
900 Edgewater Dr . . . . . Saint Marys OH 45885 419-394-1294
TF: 800-860-4726 ■ *Web:* www.seemore.org

Saint Paul RiverCentre Convention & Visitors Authority
175 W Kellogg Blvd . . . . . Saint Paul MN 55102 651-265-4800
Web: www.rivercentre.org

City Of Salem 101 S Broadway . . . . . Salem IL 62881 618-548-2222 548-5330
Web: www.salemil.us

Salem Convention & Visitors Assn
181 High St NE . . . . . Salem OR 97301 503-581-4325 581-4540
TF: 800-874-7012 ■ *Web:* www.travelsalem.com

North of Boston Convention & Visitors Bureau (NBCVB)
I-95 Southbound Exit 60 PO Box 5193 . . . . . Salisbury MA 01952 978-465-6555
Web: www.northofboston.org

Rowan County Convention & Visitors Bureau
204 E Innes St Ste 120 . . . . . Salisbury NC 28144 704-638-3100 642-2011
TF: 800-332-2343 ■ *Web:* www.visitsalisburync.com

Visit Salt Lake 90 SW Temple . . . . . Salt Lake City UT 84101 801-534-4900 541-4955*
**Fax Area Code:* 800 ■ *TF:* 800-541-4955 ■ *Web:* www.visitsaltlake.com

San Angelo Chamber of Commerce
418 W Ave B . . . . . San Angelo TX 76903 325-655-4136 658-1110
TF: 800-252-1381 ■ *Web:* www.sanangelo.org

San Antonio Convention & Visitors Bureau
203 S St Marys St Ste 200 . . . . . San Antonio TX 78205 210-207-6700 207-6768
TF: 800-447-3372 ■ *Web:* www.visitsanantonio.com

San Bernardino Convention & Visitors Bureau
1955 Hunts Ln . . . . . San Bernardino CA 92408 909-891-1151
Web: www.san-bernardino.org

San Diego Convention & Visitors Bureau
2215 India St . . . . . San Diego CA 92101 619-232-3101 696-9371
Web: www.sandiego.org

	City	State	ZIP	Phone	Fax
San Francisco Convention & Visitors Bureau 201 Third St Ste 900 *TF:* 855-847-6272 ■ *Web:* www.sanfrancisco.travel	San Francisco	CA	94103	415-974-6900	227-2602
San Jose Convention & Visitors Bureau 408 Almaden Blvd *TF:* 800-726-5673 ■ *Web:* www.sanjose.org	San Jose	CA	95110	408-295-9600	277-3535
Puerto Rico Convention Bureau 100 Convention Blvd *TF:* 800-875-4765 ■ *Web:* www.prconvention.com	San Juan	PR	00907	787-725-2110	725-2133
Marin Convention & Visitors Bureau 1 Mitchell Blvd Ste B *TF:* 866-925-2060 ■ *Web:* www.visitmarin.org	San Rafael	CA	94903	415-925-2060	925-2063
Santa Barbara Visitors Bureau & Film Commission 1601 Anacapa St *TF:* 800-676-1266 ■ *Web:* www.santabarbaraca.com	Santa Barbara	CA	93101	805-966-9222	966-1728
Santa Clara Convention/Visitors Bureau 1850 Warburton Ave *TF:* 800-272-6822 ■ *Web:* www.santaclara.org	Santa Clara	CA	95050	408-244-9660	244-9202
Santa Cruz County Conference & Visitors Council 303 Water St Ste 100 *TF:* 800-833-3494 ■ *Web:* www.santacruz.org	Santa Cruz	CA	95060	831-425-1234	425-1260
Santa Fe Convention Ctr 201 W Marcy St *TF:* 800-777-2489 ■ *Web:* www.santafe.org	Santa Fe	NM	87501	505-955-6200	955-6222
Santa Monica Convention & Visitors Bureau 1920 Main St Ste B *TF:* 800-544-5319 ■ *Web:* www.santamonica.com	Santa Monica	CA	90405	310-319-6263	319-6273
Visit Sarasota County 1777 Main St Ste 302 *TF:* 800-522-9799 ■ *Web:* www.visitsarasota.org	Sarasota	FL	34236	941-955-0991	
Saratoga Convention & Tourism Bureau 60 Railroad Pl Ste 301 *TF:* 855-424-6073 ■ *Web:* www.discoversaratoga.org	Saratoga Springs	NY	12866	518-584-1531	584-2969
Sault Sainte Marie Convention & Visitors Bureau 225 E Portage Ave *TF:* 800-647-2858 ■ *Web:* www.saultstemarie.com	Sault Sainte Marie	MI	49783	906-632-3366	
Savannah Area Convention & Visitors Bureau 101 E Bay St *Web:* www.visitsavannah.com	Savannah	GA	31401	912-661-2662	644-6499
Greater Woodfield Convention & Visitors Bureau 1375 E Woodfield Rd Ste 120 *TF:* 800-847-4849 ■ *Web:* www.chicagonorthwest.com	Schaumburg	IL	60173	847-490-1010	490-1212
Scottsdale Convention & Visitors Bureau 4343 N Scottsdale Rd Ste 170 *TF:* 800-782-1117 ■ *Web:* www.experiencescottsdale.com	Scottsdale	AZ	85251	480-421-1004	421-9733
Lackawanna County Convention & Visitors Bureau 99 Glenmaura National Blvd *TF:* 800-229-3526 ■ *Web:* www.visitnepa.org	Scranton	PA	18507	570-496-1701	
Seattle's Convention & Visitors Bureau 701 Pike St Ste 800 *TF:* 866-732-2695 ■ *Web:* www.visitseattle.org	Seattle	WA	98101	206-461-5800	461-5855
Seward Convention & Visitors Bureau 2001 Seward Hwy *Web:* seward.com	Seward	AK	99664	907-224-8051	224-5353
Visit MercerCounty PA 50 N Water Ave *TF:* 800-637-2370 ■ *Web:* www.visitmercercountypa.com	Sharon	PA	16146	724-346-3771	346-0575
Shelby County Office of Tourism 315 E Main St *TF:* 800-874-3529 ■ *Web:* www.lakeshelbyville.com	Shelbyville	IL	62565	217-774-2244	
Shepherdsville-Bullitt County Tourist & Convention Commission 395 Paroquet Springs Dr *TF:* 800-526-2068 ■ *Web:* www.travelbullitt.org	Shepherdsville	KY	40165	502-543-8687	543-4889
Shipshewana/LaGrange County Convention & Visitors Bureau 350 S Van Buren St Ste H *TF:* 800-254-8090 ■ *Web:* visitshipshewana.org	Shipshewana	IN	46565	260-768-4008	768-4091
Shreveport-Bossier Convention & Tourist Bureau 629 Spring St *TF:* 800-551-8682 ■ *Web:* www.shreveport-bossier.org	Shreveport	LA	71101	318-222-9391	222-0056
Sioux City Tourism Bureau 801 Fourth St *TF:* 800-593-2228 ■ *Web:* www.visitsiouxcity.org	Sioux City	IA	51101	712-279-4800	279-4900
Sioux Falls Convention & Visitors Bureau 200 N Phillips Ave Ste 102 *TF:* 800-333-2072 ■ *Web:* visitsiouxfalls.com	Sioux Falls	SD	57104	605-336-1620	336-6499
Sitka Convention & Visitors Bureau 303 Lincoln St Ste 4 *TF:* 800-557-4852 ■ *Web:* www.sitka.org	Sitka	AK	99835	907-747-5940	
Skagway Visitor Information 245 Broadway PO Box 1029 *TF:* 888-762-1898 ■ *Web:* www.skagway.com	Skagway	AK	99840	907-983-2855	983-3854
Johnston County Convention & Visitors Bureau 235 E Market St *TF:* 800-441-7829 ■ *Web:* www.johnstoncountync.org	Smithfield	NC	27577	919-989-8687	989-6295
South Bend/Mishawaka Convention & Visitors Bureau 401 E Colfax Ave Ste 310 *TF:* 800-519-0577 ■ *Web:* www.visitsouthbend.com	South Bend	IN	46617	800-519-0577	
Lake Tahoe Visitors Authority 3066 Lk Tahoe Blvd *TF:* 800-288-2463 ■ *Web:* www.tahoesouth.com	South Lake Tahoe	CA	96150	530-544-5050	
South Padre Island Convention & Visitors Bureau 7355 Padre Blvd *TF:* 800-767-2373 ■ *Web:* www.sopadre.com	South Padre Island	TX	78597	956-761-6433	
South Sioux City Convention & Visitors Bureau 4401 Dakota Ave *TF:* 866-494-1307 ■ *Web:* visitsouthsiouxcity.com	South Sioux City	NE	68776	402-494-1307	
Convention & Visitors Bureau-Village of Pinehurst Southern Pines Aberdeen Area 10677 Hwy 15-501 *TF:* 800-346-5362 ■ *Web:* www.homeofgolf.com	Southern Pines	NC	28387	910-692-3330	692-2493
Spartanburg Convention & Visitors Bureau 298 Magnolia St *Web:* www.visitspartanburg.com	Spartanburg	SC	29306	864-594-5050	
Spokane Convention & Visitors Bureau 801 W Riverside Ste 301 *TF:* 800-662-0084 ■ *Web:* www.visitspokane.com	Spokane	WA	99201	509-624-1341	623-1297
Central Illinois Tourism Development Office 700 E Adams St *Web:* visitlandoflincoln.com	Springfield	IL	62701	217-525-7980	
Greater Springfield Convention & Visitors Bureau 1441 Main St *TF:* 800-723-1548 ■ *Web:* www.valleyvisitor.com	Springfield	MA	01103	413-787-1548	781-4607
Greater Springfield Convention & Visitors Bureau 20 S Limestone St Ste 100 *TF:* 800-803-1553 ■ *Web:* www.greaterspringfield.com	Springfield	OH	45502	937-325-7621	325-8765
Springfield Convention & Visitors Bureau 109 N Seventh St *TF:* 800-545-7300 ■ *Web:* www.visitspringfieldillinois.com	Springfield	IL	62701	217-789-2360	544-8711
Springfield Missouri Convention & Visitors Bureau 815 E St Louis St Ste 100 *TF:* 800-678-8767 ■ *Web:* www.springfieldmo.org	Springfield	MO	65806	417-881-5300	881-2231
Data Connectors LLC 12620 Lamplighter Sq *Web:* www.dataconnectors.com	St. Louis	MO	63128	314-525-7140	
Centre County Convention & Visitors Bureau 800 E Pk Ave *TF:* 800-358-5466 ■ *Web:* www.visitpennstate.org	State College	PA	16803	814-231-1400	231-8123
Stevens Point Area Convention & Visitors Bureau 340 Div St N *Web:* www.stevenspointarea.com	Stevens Point	WI	54481	715-344-2556	344-5818
Pocono Mountains Vacation Bureau 1004 Main St *TF:* 800-722-9199 ■ *Web:* www.poconomountains.com	Stroudsburg	PA	18360	570-421-5791	421-6927
Racine County Convention & Visitors Bureau 14015 Washington Ave *TF:* 800-272-2463 ■ *Web:* realracine.com	Sturtevant	WI	53177	262-884-6400	
Central Oregon Visitors Association 57100 Beaver Dr Bldg 6 Ste 130 *TF:* 800-800-8334 ■ *Web:* www.visitcentraloregon.com	Sunriver	OR	97707	800-800-8334	
Superior/Douglas County Convention & Visitors Bureau 305 Harborview Pkwy *TF:* 800-942-5313 ■ *Web:* www.superiorchamber.org	Superior	WI	54880	715-392-7151	
Tourism Bureau Southwestern Illinois 4387 N. Illinois St Ste 200 *TF:* 800-442-1488 ■ *Web:* www.thetourismbureau.org	Swansea	IL	62226	618-257-1488	
Tacoma Regional Convention & Visitor Bureau 1516 Commerce St *TF:* 800-272-2662 ■ *Web:* www.traveltacoma.com	Tacoma	WA	98402	253-627-2836	
North Lake Tahoe Resort Assn 100 N Lake Blvd *TF:* 800-468-2463 ■ *Web:* www.gotahoenorth.com	Tahoe City	CA	96145	530-581-6900	581-1686
North Lake Tahoe Visitors & Convention Bureau PO Box 1757 *TF:* 800-462-5196 ■ *Web:* www.gotahoenorth.com	Tahoe City	CA	96145	530-581-6900	581-1686
Chambers of Commerce / Tourism 106 E Jefferson St *TF:* 800-628-2866 ■ *Web:* www.visittallahassee.com	Tallahassee	FL	32301	850-606-2305	606-2301
Tampa Bay & Co 401 E Jackson St Ste 2100 *TF:* 877-230-0078 ■ *Web:* www.visittampabay.com	Tampa	FL	33602	813-223-1111	229-6616
Tempe Tourism Office 222 South Mill Ave Ste 120 *TF:* 866-914-1052 ■ *Web:* www.tempetourism.com	Tempe	AZ	85281	480-894-8158	968-8004
Terre Haute Convention & Visitors Bureau 5353 E Margaret Dr *TF:* 800-366-3043 ■ *Web:* www.terrehaute.com	Terre Haute	IN	47803	800-366-3043	
Thief River Falls Convention & Visitors Bureau (TRFCVB) 102 Main Ave N *TF:* 800-657-3700 ■ *Web:* www.visittrf.org	Thief River	MN	56701	218-686-9785	
City of Thomasville Tourism Authority 144 E Jackson St *TF:* 800-533-4587 ■ *Web:* www.thomasvillega.com	Thomasville	GA	31792	229-226-3424	228-4188
Three Lakes Information Bureau 1704 Superior St PO Box 268 *TF:* 800-972-6103 ■ *Web:* www.threelakes.com	Three Lakes	WI	54562	715-546-3344	
River Country Tourism Bureau PO Box 214 *TF:* 800-447-2821 ■ *Web:* www.rivercountry.com	Three Rivers	MI	49093	800-447-2821	
Greater Toledo Convention & Visitors Bureau 401 Jefferson Ave *TF:* 800-243-4667 ■ *Web:* www.dotoledo.org	Toledo	OH	43604	419-321-6404	
Tomah Convention & Visitors Bureau 901 Kilbourn Ave PO Box 625 *TF:* 800-948-6624 ■ *Web:* www.tomahwisconsin.com	Tomah	WI	54660	608-372-2166	372-2167
Travel Industry Assn of Kansas 919 S Kansas Ave *Web:* www.tiak.org	Topeka	KS	66612	785-233-9465	
Visit Topeka Inc 618 S Kansas Ave *TF:* 800-235-1030 ■ *Web:* www.visittopeka.com	Topeka	KS	66603	785-234-1030	234-8282
Toronto Convention & Visitors Assn 207 Queen's Quay W Ste 405 PO Box 126 *TF:* 800-499-2514 ■ *Web:* www.seetorontonow.com	Toronto	ON	M5J1A7	416-203-2600	203-6753
Smoky Mountain Visitors Bureau 7906 E Lamar Alexander Pkwy *TF:* 800-525-6834 ■ *Web:* www.smokymountains.org	Townsend	TN	37882	865-448-6134	
Baltimore County Visitor Ctr 400 Washington Ave *Web:* www.enjoybaltimorecounty.com	Towson	MD	21204	410-887-2849	
Traverse City Convention & Visitors Bureau 101 W Grandview Pkwy *TF:* 800-940-1120 ■ *Web:* www.traversecity.com	Traverse City	MI	49684	231-947-1120	947-2621
Atlanta's DeKalb Convention & Visitors Bureau 1957 Lakeside Pkwy Ste 510 *TF:* 800-999-6055 ■ *Web:* www.visitatlantasdekalbcounty.com	Tucker	GA	30084	770-492-5000	492-5033
Metropolitan Tucson Convention & Visitors Bureau 100 S Church Ave *TF:* 800-638-8350 ■ *Web:* www.visittucson.org	Tucson	AZ	85701	520-624-1817	884-7804
Tulsa Convention & Visitors Bureau 1 W Third St Ste 100 *TF:* 800-558-3311 ■ *Web:* www.visittulsa.com	Tulsa	OK	74103	800-558-3311	
Turlock Convention & Visitors Bureau 115 S Golden State Blvd *Web:* www.visitturlock.org	Turlock	CA	95380	209-632-2221	
Colbert County Tourism & Convention Bureau 719 Hwy 72 W PO Box 740425 *TF:* 800-344-0783 ■ *Web:* www.colbertcountytourism.org	Tuscumbia	AL	35674	256-383-0783	

	City	State	ZIP	Phone	Fax
Tyler Convention & Visitors Bureau (TCVB) 315 N Broadway *TF:* 800-235-5712 ■ *Web:* www.visittyler.com	Tyler	TX	75702	903-592-1661	592-1268
Oneida County Convention & Visitors Bureau PO Box 551 *TF:* 800-426-3132 ■ *Web:* www.oneidacountytourism.com	Utica	NY	13503	315-724-7221	724-7335
Vallejo Convention & Visitors Bureau 289 Mare Island Way *TF General:* 866-921-9277 ■ *Web:* www.visitvallejo.com	Vallejo	CA	94590	707-642-3653	644-2206
Greater Vancouver Convention & Visitors Bureau 200 Burrard St *Web:* www.tourismvancouver.com	Vancouver	BC	V6C3L6	604-682-2222	682-1717
Southwest Washington Convention & Visitors Bureau 1220 Main S Ste 220 *TF:* 877-600-0800 ■ *Web:* www.visitvancouverusa.com	Vancouver	WA	98660	360-750-1553	750-1553
Ventura Visitors & Convention Bureau 101 S California St *TF:* 800-333-2989 ■ *Web:* visitventuraca.com	Ventura	CA	93001	805-648-2075	648-2150
Iron Range Tourism Bureau 403 N First St *TF:* 800-777-8497 ■ *Web:* www.ironrange.org	Virginia	MN	55792	218-749-8161	
Virginia Beach Convention & Visitor Bureau (VBCVB) 2101 Parks Ave Ste 500 *TF:* 800-700-7702 ■ *Web:* www.visitvirginiabeach.com	Virginia Beach	VA	23451	757-385-4700	437-4747
Visalia Convention & Visitors Bureau PO Box 2734 *TF:* 800-524-0303 ■ *Web:* www.visitvisalia.org	Visalia	CA	93279	559-334-0141	713-4800
Waco Convention & Visitors Bureau 100 Washington Ave *TF:* 800-321-9226 ■ *Web:* www.wacoheartoftexas.com	Waco	TX	76701	254-750-5810	750-5801
Kallman Worldwide Inc 4 N St Ste 800 *TF:* 877-492-7028 ■ *Web:* kallman.com	Waldwick	NJ	07463	201-251-2600	
Warren County Visitors Bureau 22045 Rt 6 *TF:* 800-624-7802 ■ *Web:* www.wcvb.net	Warren	PA	16365	814-726-1222	726-7266
Kosciusko County Convention & Visitors Bureau (KOSCVB) 111 Capital Dr *TF:* 800-800-6090 ■ *Web:* www.koscvb.org	Warsaw	IN	46582	574-269-6090	269-2405
Washington DC Convention & Tourism Corp 901 Seventh St NW 4th Fl *TF:* 800-422-8644 ■ *Web:* washington.org	Washington	DC	20001	202-789-7000	
Waterloo Convention & Visitor Bureau 500 Jefferson St *TF:* 800-728-8431 ■ *Web:* www.travelwaterloo.com	Waterloo	IA	50701	319-233-8350	233-2733
Wausau Central Wisconsin Convention & Visitors Bureau (CWCVB) 219 Jefferson St Ste B *TF:* 888-948-4748 ■ *Web:* www.visitwausau.com	Wausau	WI	54403	715-355-8788	359-2306
Tioga County Visitors Bureau 2053 Rt 660 *TF:* 888-846-4228 ■ *Web:* www.visittiogapa.com	Wellsboro	PA	16901	570-724-0635	
West Branch Area Chamber of Commerce 422 W Houghton Ave *TF:* 800-755-9091 ■ *Web:* wbacc.com	West Branch	MI	48661	989-345-2821	
West Hollywood Convention & Visitors Bureau 8687 Melrose Ave Ste M38 *TF:* 800-368-6020 ■ *Web:* www.visitwesthollywood.com	West Hollywood	CA	90069	310-289-2525	
Monroe-West Monroe Convention & Visitors Bureau 601 Constitution Dr PO Box 1436 *TF:* 800-843-1872 ■ *Web:* www.monroe-westmonroe.org	West Monroe	LA	71292	318-387-5691	324-1752
Palm Beach County Convention & Visitors Bureau 1555 Palm Beach Lakes Blvd Ste 800 *TF:* 800-554-7256 ■ *Web:* www.palmbeachfl.com	West Palm Beach	FL	33401	561-233-3000	233-3009
Wheeling Convention & Visitors Bureau 1401 Main St *TF:* 800-828-3097 ■ *Web:* www.wheelingcvb.com	Wheeling	WV	26003	304-233-7709	
Westchester County Tourism & Film 148 Martine Ave Ste 104 *Web:* westchestergov.com	White Plains	NY	10601	914-995-8500	995-8505
Wichita Convention & Visitors Bureau 515 Main St Ste 115 *TF:* 800-288-9424 ■ *Web:* www.visitwichita.com	Wichita	KS	67202	316-265-2800	265-0162
Williamsburg Destination Marketing Committee 421 N Boundary St PO Box 3495 *TF:* 800-368-6511 ■ *Web:* www.visitwilliamsburg.com	Williamsburg	VA	23187	757-229-6511	
Martin County Travel & Tourism Authority 100 E Church St PO Box 382 *TF:* 800-776-8566 ■ *Web:* www.visitmartincounty.com	Williamston	NC	27892	252-792-6605	
Cape Fear Coast Convention & Visitors Bureau 505 Nutt St Unit A *TF:* 877-406-2356 ■ *Web:* www.wilmingtonandbeaches.com	Wilmington	NC	28401	910-341-4030	341-4029
Greater Wilmington Convention & Visitors Bureau 100 W Tenth St Ste 20 **Fax Area Code:* 302 ■ *TF:* 800-489-6664 ■ *Web:* www.visitwilmingtonde.com	Wilmington	DE	19801	800-489-6664	652-4726*
Wilson Visitors Bureau 209 Broad St *TF:* 800-497-7398 ■ *Web:* www.wilson-nc.com	Wilson	NC	27893	252-243-8440	243-7550
Winnemucca Convention & Visitors Authority 50 W Winnemucca Blvd *TF:* 800-962-2638 ■ *Web:* www.winnemucca.nv.us	Winnemucca	NV	89445	775-623-5071	623-5087
Winona Convention & Visitors Bureau 160 Johnson St *TF:* 800-657-4972 ■ *Web:* visitwinona.com	Winona	MN	55987	507-452-0735	454-0006
Winston-Salem Convention & Visitors Bureau 200 Brookstown Ave *TF:* 866-728-4200 ■ *Web:* www.visitwinstonsalem.com	Winston-Salem	NC	27101	336-728-4200	728-4220
Wisconsin Dells Visitors & Convention Bureau 701 Superior St PO Box 390 *TF:* 800-223-3557 ■ *Web:* www.wisdells.com	Wisconsin Dells	WI	53965	608-254-8088	254-4293
Wayne County Convention & Visitors Bureau 428 W Liberty St *TF:* 800-362-6474 ■ *Web:* wccvb.com	Wooster	OH	44691	330-264-1800	
Worcester County Convention & Visitors Bureau 91 Prescott St *TF:* 866-755-7439 ■ *Web:* www.centralmass.org	Worcester	MA	01605	508-755-7400	
Mahoning County Convention & Visitors Bureau 21 W Boardman St *TF:* 800-447-8201 ■ *Web:* www.youngstownlive.com	Youngstown	OH	44503	330-740-2130	740-2144
Ypsilanti Area Convention & Visitors Bureau 106 W Michigan Ave *Web:* www.ypsilanti.org	Ypsilanti	MI	48197	734-483-4444	
Yuma Convention & Visitors Bureau 201 N Fourth Ave *TF:* 800-293-0071 ■ *Web:* www.visityuma.com	Yuma	AZ	85364	928-783-0071	783-1897

207 CONVEYORS & CONVEYING EQUIPMENT

See Also Material Handling Equipment p. 2732

	City	State	ZIP	Phone	Fax
Airfloat LLC 2230 Brush College Rd *TF:* 800-888-0018 ■ *Web:* www.airfloat.com	Decatur	IL	62526	217-423-6001	422-1049
Alba Manufacturing Inc 8950 Seward Rd *Web:* www.albamfg.com	Fairfield	OH	45011	513-874-0551	
Allied Uniking Corporation Inc 4750 Cromwell Ave	Memphis	TN	38118	901-365-7240	
Allor Manufacturing Inc 12534 Emerson Dr *TF:* 888-382-6300 ■ *Web:* allorplesh.com	Brighton	MI	48116	248-486-4500	
AMF Bakery Systems 2115 W Laburnum Ave *TF:* 800-225-3771 ■ *Web:* www.amfbakery.com	Richmond	VA	23227	804-355-7961	355-1074
Arrowhead Conveyor Corp 3255 Medalist Dr PO Box 2408 *Web:* www.arrowheadconveyor.com	Oshkosh	WI	54903	920-235-5562	
Automated Conveyor Systems Inc 3850 Southland Dr *Web:* www.automatedconveyors.com	West Memphis	AR	72301	870-732-5050	732-5191
Automatic Systems Inc 9230 E 47th St *TF:* 800-366-3488 ■ *Web:* www.asi.com	Kansas City	MO	64133	816-356-0660	356-5730
Automation & Modular Components Inc 10301 Enterprise Dr *Web:* www.amcautomation.com	Davisburg	MI	48350	248-922-4740	
Automation Tool Co 101 Mill Dr *Web:* www.automationtool.com	Cookeville	TN	38501	931-528-5417	
Automotion Inc 11000 Lavergne Ave *Web:* www.automotionconveyors.com	Oak Lawn	IL	60453	708-229-3700	229-3799
Beltservice Corp 4143 Rider Trl N *TF:* 800-727-2358 ■ *Web:* www.beltservice.com	Earth City	MO	63045	314-344-8500	344-8511
Bilt-Rite Conveyors 735 Industrial Loop Rd *TF:* 800-558-3616 ■ *Web:* www.bilt-rite.com	New London	WI	54961	920-982-6600	982-7750
BW Container Systems 1305 Lakeview Dr *TF:* 800-527-0494 ■ *Web:* www.bwcontainersystems.com	Romeoville	IL	60446	630-759-6800	759-2299
C & M Conveyor 4598 SR 37 *TF:* 800-551-3195 ■ *Web:* www.cmconveyor.com	Mitchell	IN	47446	812-849-5647	
Caddy Corp of America 509 Sharptown Rd *Web:* www.caddycorp.com	Bridgeport	NJ	08014	856-467-4222	467-5511
Cambelt International Corp 2820 West 1100 South *TF:* 855-226-2358 ■ *Web:* www.cambelt.com	Salt Lake City	UT	84104	801-972-5511	972-5522
Cambridge International 105 Goodwill Rd *TF:* 800-638-9560 ■ *Web:* www.cambridge-intl.com	Cambridge	MD	21613	410-901-4979	901-4979
Can Lines Engineering 9839 Downey Norwalk Rd PO Box 7039 *Web:* www.canlines.com	Downey	CA	90241	562-861-2996	869-5293
Carrier Vibrating Equipment Inc 3400 Fern Vly Rd *TF:* 800-547-7278 ■ *Web:* www.carriervibrating.com	Louisville	KY	40213	502-969-3171	969-3172
Chantland-Pvs Co, The PO Box 69 *Web:* www.chantlandpulley.com	Humboldt	IA	50548	515-332-4040	332-4923
Christianson Systems Inc 20421 15th St SE PO Box 138 *TF:* 800-328-8896 ■ *Web:* www.christianson.com	Blomkest	MN	56216	320-995-6141	995-6145
CIGNYS 68 Williamson St	Saginaw	MI	48601	989-753-1411	753-4386
Co-Op Country Farmers Elevator 340 Dupont Ave NE *Web:* www.coopcountry.com	Renville	MN	56284	320-329-8377	
Con-Vey Keystone 526 NE Chestnut Roseburg *Web:* www.con-vey.com	Roseburg	OR	97470	541-672-5506	672-2513
Conveyor Components Co 130 Seltzer Rd *TF Cust Svc:* 800-233-3233 ■ *Web:* www.conveyorcomponents.com	Croswell	MI	48422	810-679-4211	679-4510
Conveyor Engineering & Manufacturing Co 1345 76th Ave SW *Web:* www.conveyoreng.com	Cedar Rapids	IA	52404	319-364-5600	
Conveyor Technologies Inc 5313 Womack Rd *Web:* www.conveyor-technologies.com	Sanford	NC	27330	919-776-7227	
Conveyors Inc 620 S Fourth Ave *Web:* www.conveyorsinc.net	Mansfield	TX	76063	817-473-4645	473-3024
Cyclonaire Corp 2922 N Division Ave *TF:* 800-445-0730 ■ *Web:* www.cyclonaire.com	York	NE	68467	402-362-2000	362-2001
Daifuku North American Holdings Co 6700 Tussing Rd *Web:* www.daifuku.com	Reynoldsburg	OH	43068	614-863-1888	
Dakota Fabricating Inc 12111 W Northern Ave *Web:* www.dakotafab.com	Glendale	AZ	85307	623-935-7805	
Dearborn Mid-West Conveyor Co (DMWCC) 20334 Superior Rd *Web:* www.dmwcc.com	Taylor	MI	48180	734-288-4400	288-1914
Dematic 507 Plymouth Ave NE **Fax Area Code:* 616 ■ *TF Cust Svc:* 877-725-7500 ■ *Web:* www.dematic.com	Grand Rapids	MI	49505	877-725-7500	913-7701*
Dynamic Air Inc 1125 Willow Lk Blvd *Web:* www.dynamicair.com	Saint Paul	MN	55110	651-484-2900	484-7015
Engineered Products Inc 500 Furman Hall Rd *TF:* 888-301-1421 ■ *Web:* www.engprod.com	Greenville	SC	29609	864-234-4888	234-4860
Eriez Manufacturing Company Inc 2200 Asbury Rd *Web:* www.eriez.com	Erie	PA	16506	814-835-6000	
Essmueller Co 334 Ave A PO Box 1966 *Web:* www.essmueller.com	Laurel	MS	39440	601-649-2400	649-4320
Evana Automation 5825 Old Boonville Hwy *TF:* 800-468-6774 ■ *Web:* www.evanaautomation.com	Evansville	IN	47715	812-479-8246	

	Phone	Fax

Fame Industries Inc 51100 Grand River Ave ....Wixom MI 48393 248-348-7760 348-2120
Web: www.fameind.com

FATA Automation Inc
6050 Nineteen Mile Rd.......................Sterling Heights MI 48314 586-323-9400
Web: www.fatainc.com

Feeco International Inc 3913 Algoma Rd............Green Bay WI 54311 920-468-1000 469-5110
TF: 800-373-9347 ■ *Web:* www.feeco.com

Flexible Steel Lacing Co
2525 Wisconsin Ave.........................Downers Grove IL 60515 630-971-0150 971-1180
TF: 800-323-3444 ■ *Web:* www.flexco.com

Fred D Pfening Co 1075 W Fifth Ave ....Columbus OH 43212 614-294-5361
Web: www.pfening.com

Garvey Corp 208 S Rt 73 ....Blue Anchor NJ 08037 609-561-2450 561-2328
TF: 800-257-8581 ■ *Web:* www.garvey.com

General Kinematics Corp 5050 Rickert Rd ....Crystal Lake IL 60014 815-455-3222 455-2285
Web: generalkinematics.com

Grasan Equipment Co 440 S Illinois Ave.............Mansfield OH 44907 419-526-4440 524-2176
Web: www.grasan.com

Hansen Manufacturing Corp 5100 W 12th St ....Sioux Falls SD 57107 605-332-3200
TF: 800-328-1785 ■ *Web:* www.hiroller.com

Hapman 6002 E N Ave ....Kalamazoo MI 49048 269-343-1675 349-2477
TF: 800-427-6260 ■ *Web:* www.hapman.com

Hohl Machine & Conveyor Company Inc
1580 Niagara St ....Buffalo NY 14213 716-882-7210
Web: www.hohlmachine.com

Horsley Co, The
1630 South 4800 West Ste D ....Salt Lake City UT 84104 801-401-5500
Web: www.horsleyco.com

Hustler Conveyor Co 4101 Crusher Dr.................O'fallon MO 63368 636-441-8600
Web: www.ampulverizer.com

Hytrol Conveyor Company Inc 2020 Hytrol St........Jonesboro AR 72401 870-935-3700 852-3233*
**Fax Area Code:* 800 ■ *Web:* www.hytrol.com

I J White Corp 20 Executive Blvd..................Farmingdale NY 11735 631-293-2211
Web: www.ijwhite.com

Illinois Crane Inc 1621 W Chanute Rd ....Peoria IL 61615 309-692-0856
Web: www.illinoiscrane.com

Industrial Kinetics Inc
2535 Curtiss St.............................Downers Grove IL 60515 630-655-0300
Web: www.iki.com

Intelligrated Products
475 E High St PO Box 899 ....London OH 43140 513-701-7300
TF: 866-936-7300 ■ *Web:* www.intelligrated.com

Interroll Corp 3000 Corporate Dr...................Wilmington NC 28405 910-799-1100 830-9679*
**Fax Area Code:* 800 ■ *Web:* www.interroll.es

Intralox LLC 8715 Bollman Pl ....Savage MD 20763 301-575-2200
Web: www.intralox.com

IPS Group Inc 4343 Easton Rd...................Saint Joseph MO 64503 816-233-1800
Web: www.continentalscrew.com

Jorgensen Conveyors Inc 10303 N Baehr Rd ....Mequon WI 53092 262-242-3089 242-4382
TF: 800-325-7705 ■ *Web:* www.jorgensenconveyors.com

Joy Global Inc
177 Thorn Hill Rd Thorn Hill Industrial Park
.....................................Warrendale PA 15086 724-779-4500
Web: www.joyglobal.com

Kice Industries Inc 5500 N Mill Heights Dr.............Wichita KS 67219 316-744-7151 744-7355
TF: 877-289-5423 ■ *Web:* www.kice.com

Knight Global 2705 Commerce Pkwy ....Auburn Hills MI 48326 248-377-4950 377-2135
Web: www.knight-ind.com

KWS Mfg Company Ltd 3041 Conveyor Dr ....Burleson TX 76028 817-295-2247 447-8528
TF: 800-543-6558 ■ *Web:* www.kwsmfg.com

Laitram LLC 200 Laitram Ln..........................Harahan LA 70123 504-733-6000 733-2143
TF: 800-535-7631 ■ *Web:* www.laitram.com

LEWCO Inc 706 Lane St ....Sandusky OH 44870 419-625-4014

Martin Engineering 1 Martin Pl.....................Neponset IL 61345 309-594-2384 594-2432
TF: 800-544-2947 ■ *Web:* www.martin-eng.com

Master Solutions Inc 20 Wolf Bridge Rd ....Carlisle PA 17013 717-243-6849
Web: www.mastersi.com

Mayfran International Inc 6650 Beta Dr.............Cleveland OH 44143 440-461-4100 461-5565
Web: www.mayfran.com

Metzgar Conveyor Co Inc
901 Metzgar Dr NW ....Comstock Park MI 49321 616-784-0930 784-4100
TF: 888-266-8390 ■ *Web:* www.metzgarconveyors.com

Millard Manufacturing Corp 10602 Olive St ....Omaha NE 68128 402-331-8010
Web: www.millardmfg.com

Miller Transfer 3833 State Rt 183...................Rootstown OH 44272 330-325-2521
Web: www.millertransfer.com

Multi-fab Products LLC
N90 W14507 Commerce Dr ....Menomonee Falls WI 53051 262-502-1707
Web: www.multi-fab.com

Nercon Engineering & Manufacturing Inc
3972 S US Hwy 45 ....Oshkosh WI 54902 920-233-3268 233-3159
Web: www.nerconconveyors.com

Nol-tec Systems Inc 425 Apollo Dr ....Circle Pines MN 55014 651-780-8600 780-4400
Web: www.nol-tec.com

Nordstrong Equipment Ltd 5 Chester Ave.............Winnipeg MB R2L1W5 204-667-1553
Web: www.nordstrongequipment.com

Novi Precision Products Inc
11777 E Grand River Ave ....Brighton MI 48116 810-227-1024 227-6160
Web: www.noviprecision.com

Overhead Conveyor Co 1330 Hilton Rd ....Ferndale MI 48220 248-547-3800 547-8344
Web: www.occ-conveyor.com

Pflow Industries 6720 N Teutonia Ave ....Milwaukee WI 53209 414-352-9000
Web: www.pflow.com

Prab Inc 5944 E Kilgore Rd..........................Kalamazoo MI 49048 269-382-8200 349-2477
TF: 800-968-7722 ■ *Web:* www.prab.com

Price Rubber Corp 2733 Gunter Park Dr W ....Montgomery AL 36109 334-277-5470
Web: www.pricerubber.com

Railex Corp 89-02 Atlantic Ave ....Ozone Park NY 11416 718-845-5454 738-1020
Web: www.railexcorp.com

Ralphs-pugh Company Inc 3931 Oregon St ....Benicia CA 94510 707-745-6363
Web: www.ralphs-pugh.com

Rapat Corp 919 Odonnel St..........................Hawley MN 56549 218-483-3344 483-3535
TF: 800-325-6377 ■ *Web:* www.rapat.com

Rapid Industries 4003 Oaklawn Dr..................Louisville KY 40219 502-968-3645 968-6331
TF: 800-727-4381 ■ *Web:* www.rapidindustries.com

Renold Jeffrey 2307 Maden Dr....................Morristown TN 37813 423-586-1951 581-2399
TF: 800-251-9012 ■ *Web:* www.renoldjeffrey.com

Richards-Wilcox Inc 600 S Lake St ....Aurora IL 60506 800-253-5668 897-6994*
**Fax Area Code:* 630 ■ *TF:* 800-253-5668 ■ *Web:* www.richardswilcox.com

Roll-A-Way Conveyor Inc 2335 N Delaney Rd...........Gurnee IL 60031 847-336-5033 336-6542
TF: 800-747-9024 ■ *Web:* www.roll-away.com

Ryson International Inc 300 Newsome Dr ....Yorktown VA 23692 757-898-1530 898-1580
Web: www.ryson.com

Schroeder Industries LLC 580 W Pk Rd ....Leetsdale PA 15056 724-318-1100 318-1200
TF: 800-722-4810 ■ *Web:* www.schroederindustries.com

Screw Conveyor Corp 700 Hoffman St...............Hammond IN 46327 219-931-1450 931-0209
Web: www.screwconveyor.com

Shick Tube Veyor Corp 4346 Clary Blvd ....Kansas City MO 64130 816-861-7224 921-1901
TF: 877-744-2587 ■ *Web:* www.shickusa.com

Shuttleworth Inc 10 Commercial Rd...............Huntington IN 46750 260-356-8500 359-7810
TF: 800-444-7412 ■ *Web:* www.shuttleworth.com

Southern Systems Inc 4101 Viscount Ave............Memphis TN 38118 901-362-7340 360-8002
Web: www.ssiconveyors.com

Stewart Systems 808 Stewart Ave.......................Plano TX 75074 972-422-5808 509-8734
TF: 800-966-5808 ■ *Web:* www.stewart-systems.com

Superior Industries LLC
315 E State Hwy 28 PO Box 684.......................Morris MN 56267 320-589-2406
Web: www.superior-ind.com

Sweet Mfg Company Inc 2000 E Leffel Ln...........Springfield OH 45505 937-325-1511 322-1963
TF Cust Svc: 800-334-7254 ■ *Web:* www.sweetmfg.com

Swisslog 10825 E 47th Ave ....Denver CO 80239 303-371-7770 373-7870
TF: 800-525-1841 ■ *Web:* www.swisslog.com

T K F Inc 726 Mehring Way ....Cincinnati OH 45203 513-241-5910
Web: www.tkf.com

Tekno Inc 1 Wall St ....Cave City KY 42127 270-773-4181
Web: www.tekno.com

TGW-Ermanco Inc 6870 Grand Haven Rd............Spring Lake MI 49456 231-798-4547 798-8322
Web: www.tgw-group.com

Thomas Conveyor Co 555 N Burleson Blvd ....Burleson TX 76028 817-295-7151 447-3840
TF: 800-433-2217 ■ *Web:* www.thomasconveyor.com

Trans-Global Solutions Inc
11811 East Fwy Ste 630..............................Houston TX 77029 713-453-0341 453-2756
Web: www.tgsgroup.com

Transco Industries Inc 5534 NE 122nd Ave ....Portland OR 97230 503-256-1955 256-0723
TF: 800-545-9991 ■ *Web:* www.transco-ind.com

Uni-Pak Corp 1015 N Ronald Reagan Blvd ....Longwood FL 32750 407-830-9300 830-4106
Web: www.unipak.com

United Conveyor Corp 2100 Norman Dr W ....Waukegan IL 60085 847-473-5900 473-5959
Web: www.unitedconveyor.com

Unitrak Corporation Ltd 299 Ward St ....Port Hope ON L1A3W4 905-885-8168
Web: www.unitrak.com

Universal Industries Inc 5800 Nordic Dr ....Cedar Falls IA 50613 319-277-7501 277-2318
TF: 800-553-4446 ■ *Web:* www.universalindustries.com

VAC-U-MAX 69 William St..........................Belleville NJ 07109 973-759-4600
TF: 800-822-8629 ■ *Web:* www.aeromechanical.com

W & H Systems Inc 120 Asia Pl ....Carlstadt NJ 07072 201-933-7840 933-2144
TF: 800-966-6993 ■ *Web:* www.whsystems.com

Warehouse Systems Inc 601 Academy Dr...........Northbrook IL 60062 847-562-9526
Web: www.warehousesys.com

WASP Inc PO Box 249 ....Glenwood MN 56334 320-634-5126 634-5881
Web: www.waspinc.com

Webb-Stiles Co
675 Liverpool Dr PO Box 464......................Valley City OH 44280 330-225-7761 225-5532
Web: www.webb-stiles.com

Webster Industries Inc 325 Hall St...................Tiffin OH 44883 419-447-8232 448-1618
TF: 800-243-9327 ■ *Web:* www.websterchain.com

Western Pneumatics Inc PO Box 21340..............Eugene OR 97402 541-461-2600 461-2606
Web: www.westernp.com

Westfalia Technologies Inc 3655 Sandhurst Dr ....York PA 17406 717-764-1115 764-1118
TF: 800-673-2522 ■ *Web:* www.westfaliausa.com

Westmont Industries
10805 Painter Ave ....Santa Fe Springs CA 90670 562-944-6137 946-5299
Web: www.westmont.com

Whirl Air Flow Corp 20055 177th St.................Big Lake MN 55309 763-262-1200 262-1212
TF: 800-373-3461 ■ *Web:* www.whirlair.com

White Conveyors Inc 10 Boright Ave.................Kenilworth NJ 07033 908-686-5700
Web: www.white-conveyors.com

White Systems Inc 30 Boright Ave...................Kenilworth NJ 07033 908-272-6700
Web: www.whitesystems.com

Wire Belt Company of America
154 Harvey Rd ....Londonderry NH 03053 603-644-2500 644-3600
TF Cust Svc: 800-922-2637 ■ *Web:* www.wirebelt.com

WPS Industries Inc 228 Industrial St ....West Monroe LA 71292 318-812-2800
Web: www.wpsindustries.com

Young Industries Inc 16 Painter St ....Muncy PA 17756 570-546-3165 546-1888
TF: 800-546-3165 ■ *Web:* www.youngInds.com

208 CORD & TWINE

	Phone	Fax

40-Up Tackle Co 16 Union Ave PO Box 442...........Westfield MA 01086 413-562-0385
Web: www.40uptackleco.com

Algoma Net Co 1525 Mueller St ....Algoma WI 54201 920-487-5577 487-2852
Web: www.algomanet.com

All Line Inc
16851 E Parkview Ave Unit 2 ....Fountain Hills AZ 85268 480-306-6001 306-6001
Web: www.alllinerope.com

Ashaway Line & Twine Manufacturing Co
24 Laurel St ....Ashaway RI 02804 401-377-2221 377-9091
TF: 800-556-7260 ■ *Web:* www.ashawayusa.com

Atkins & Pearce Inc 1 Braid Way.................Covington KY 41017 859-356-2001 356-2395
TF: 800-837-7477 ■ *Web:* www.atkinsandpearce.com

Bridon Cordage LLC 909 E 16th St..................Albert Lea MN 56007 507-377-1601
TF: 800-533-6002 ■ *Web:* www.bridoncordage.com

	Phone	Fax
Brownell & Company Inc 423 E Haddam-Moodus Rd . . . . Moodus CT 06469 *Web:* www.brownellco.com	860-873-8625	873-1944
Carron Net Company Inc 1623 17th St PO Box 177 . . . . Two Rivers WI 54241 *TF:* 800-558-7768 ■ *Web:* www.carronnet.com	920-793-2217	793-2122
Cortland Line Company Inc 3736 Kellogg Rd. . . . . Cortland NY 13045 *Web:* www.cortlandline.com	607-756-2851	753-8835
Flow Tek Inc PO Box 2018 . . . . Boulder CO 80306 *Web:* www.monic.com	303-530-3050	
Gladding Braided Products LLC 110 Country Rd . . . . South Otselic NY 13155 *Web:* gladdingbraid.com	315-653-7211	653-4492
I & I Sling Inc PO Box 2423. . . . . Aston PA 19014 *TF:* 800-874-3539 ■ *Web:* www.slingmax.com	610-485-8500	494-5835
James Thompson & Company Inc 381 Pk Ave S # 718 . . . . New York NY 10016 *Web:* www.jamesthompson.com	212-686-4242	686-9528
New England Ropes Inc 848 Airport Rd. . . . . Fall River MA 02720 *TF:* 800-333-6679 ■ *Web:* www.neropes.com	508-678-8200	679-2363
Pacific Fibre & Rope Company Inc 903 Flint St. . . . . Wilmington CA 90744 *TF:* 800-825-7673 ■ *Web:* www.pacificfibre.com	310-834-4567	
Pelican Rope Works Inc 4001 W Carriage Dr . . . . Santa Ana CA 92704 *TF:* 800-464-7673 ■ *Web:* www.pelicanrope.com	714-545-0116	545-7673
PlymKraft Inc 479 Export Cir. . . . . Newport News VA 23601 *TF:* 800-992-0854 ■ *Web:* www.plymkraft.com	757-595-0364	595-3993
Puget Sound Rope Corp 1012 Second St . . . . Anacortes WA 98221 *TF:* 888-525-8488 ■ *Web:* www.cortlandcompany.com	360-293-8488	293-8480
Rockford Manufacturing Co 3901 Little River Rd . . . . Rockford TN 37853	865-970-3131	
Rocky Mount Cord Co 381 N Grace St. . . . . Rocky Mount NC 27804 *TF Orders:* 800-342-9130 ■ *Web:* www.rmcord.com	252-977-9130	977-9123
Samson Rope Technologies Inc 2090 Thornton Rd. . . . . Ferndale WA 98248 **Fax Area Code:* 800 ■ *TF Cust Svc:* 800-227-7673 ■ *Web:* www.samsonrope.com	360-384-4669	299-9246*

209 CORK & CORK PRODUCTS

See Also Office & School Supplies p. 2844

	Phone	Fax
Amorim Cork Composites 26112 110th St . . . . Trevor WI 53179 *Web:* www.amorimcorkcomposites.com/index.php	262-862-2311	
Expanko Inc 180 Gordon Dr Ste 113 . . . . Exton PA 19341 **Fax Area Code:* 610 ■ *TF:* 800-345-6202 ■ *Web:* www.expanko.com	800-345-6202	363-0735*
Manton Industrial Cork Products Inc 415 Oser Ave Unit U . . . . Hauppauge NY 11788 *TF:* 800-663-1921 ■ *Web:* www.mantoncork.com	631-273-0700	273-0038
Maryland Cork Co Inc 505 Blue Ball Rd PO Box 126 . . . . Elkton MD 21922 *TF:* 800-662-2675 ■ *Web:* www.marylandcork.com	410-398-2955	392-9433

210 CORPORATE HOUSING

	Phone	Fax
Alikar Gardens Resort, The 1123 Verde Dr . . . . Colorado Springs CO 80910 *Web:* www.alikar.com	719-475-2564	
Churchill Corporate Services 56 Utter Ave . . . . Hawthorne NJ 07506 *TF:* 800-941-7458 ■ *Web:* www.furnishedhousing.com	973-636-9400	636-0179
Cincinnati Metropolitan Housing Authority 16 W Central Pkwy . . . . Cincinnati OH 45202 *Web:* www.cintimha.com	513-421-2642	
Coast to Coast Corporate Housing 10773 Los Alamitos Blvd . . . . Los Alamitos CA 90720 *TF:* 800-451-9466 ■ *Web:* www.ctchousing.com	562-795-0250	795-0251
ExecSuite Third Ave SW Ste 702 . . . . Calgary AB T2P3B4 *TF:* 800-667-4980 ■ *Web:* www.execsuite.ca	403-294-5800	294-5959
Klein & Company Corporate Housing Services Inc 914 Washington Ave. . . . . Golden CO 80401 *TF:* 800-208-9826 ■ *Web:* www.kleinandcompany.com	303-796-2100	796-2101
ExecuStay Corp 2222 Corinth Ave . . . . Los Angeles CA 90064 *TF:* 800-990-9292 ■ *Web:* www.execustay.com	800-990-9292	
Oakwood Crystal City 400 15th St S . . . . Arlington VA 22202 *TF:* 877-902-0832 ■ *Web:* www.oakwood.com	703-920-9550	
Oakwood Worldwide 2222 Corinth Ave . . . . Los Angeles CA 90064 *TF:* 800-888-0808 ■ *Web:* www.oakwood.com	310-478-1021	444-2210
SuiteAmerica 4970 Windplay Dr Ste C-1 . . . . El Dorado Hills CA 95762 *TF:* 800-410-4305 ■ *Web:* www.suiteamerica.com	916-941-7970	941-7989
Windsor Corporate Suites 3516 Stearns Hills Rd. . . . . Waltham MA 02451 *Web:* www.windsorcommunities.com	781-899-5100	

211 CORRECTIONAL & DETENTION MANAGEMENT (PRIVATIZED)

See Also Correctional Facilities - Federal p. 2162; Correctional Facilities - State p. 2163; Juvenile Detention Facilities p. 2616

	Phone	Fax
Colorado Correctional Industries 4999 Oakland St. . . . . Denver CO 80239 *TF Cust Svc:* 800-685-7891 ■ *Web:* www.coloradoci.com	719-226-4206	226-4220
Corrections Corp of America 10 Burton Hills Blvd . . . . Nashville TN 37215 *NYSE: CXW* ■ *TF:* 800-624-2931 ■ *Web:* www.cca.com	615-263-3000	263-3000
Youth Services International 6000 Cattleridge Dr Ste 200. . . . . Sarasota FL 34232 *Web:* www.youthservices.com	941-953-9199	953-9198

212 CORRECTIONAL FACILITIES - FEDERAL

See Also Correctional & Detention Management (Privatized) p. 2162; Correctional Facilities - State p. 2163; Juvenile Detention Facilities p. 2616

	Phone	Fax
Federal Bureau of Prisons 320 First St NW . . . . Washington DC 20534 *Web:* www.bop.gov	202-307-3198	514-6620
Administrative-Maximum US Penitentiary *Florence* PO Box 8500 . . . . Florence CO 81226 *TF:* 877-623-8426 ■ *Web:* www.bop.gov/locations/institutions/flm	719-784-9464	784-5290
Federal Correctional Complex		
Beaumont 5830 Knauth Rd . . . . Beaumont TX 77705 *Web:* www.bop.gov	409-727-0101	720-5000
Coleman 846 NE 54th Terr. . . . . Coleman FL 33521 *TF:* 877-623-8426 ■ *Web:* www.bop.gov	352-689-5000	689-5027
Federal Correctional Institution (FCI)		
Bastrop 1341 Hwy 95 N PO Box 730 . . . . Bastrop TX 78602 *Web:* www.bop.gov	512-321-3903	304-0117
Big Spring 1900 Simler Ave. . . . . Big Spring TX 79720 *Web:* www.bop.gov/locations/institutions/big	432-466-2300	466-2576
Butner Old NC Hwy 75 PO Box 1000 . . . . Butner NC 27509 *TF:* 877-623-8426 ■ *Web:* www.bop.gov	919-575-4541	575-5023
Cumberland 14601 Burbridge Rd SE . . . . Cumberland MD 21502 **Fax:* Hum Res ■ *Web:* www.bop.gov	301-784-1000	784-1008*
Edgefield 501 Gary Hill Rd PO Box 723 . . . . Edgefield SC 29824 *Web:* www.bop.gov	803-637-1500	637-9840
El Reno PO Box 1000. . . . . El Reno OK 73036 *Web:* fedcrimlaw.com	405-262-4875	
Englewood 9595 W Quincy Ave . . . . Littleton CO 80123 *TF:* 877-623-8426 ■ *Web:* www.bop.gov	303-985-1566	763-2553
Fairton 655 Fairton-Millville Rd PO Box 280 . . . . Fairton NJ 08320 *TF:* 877-623-8426 ■ *Web:* www.bop.gov	856-453-1177	453-4015
Florence 5880 State Hwy 67 S . . . . Florence CO 81226 *Web:* usmarshals.gov	719-784-9100	
Forrest City 1400 Dale Bumpers Rd . . . . Forrest City AR 72335 *TF:* 877-623-8426 ■ *Web:* www.bop.gov	870-630-6000	494-4496
Jesup 2600 Hwy 301 S . . . . Jesup GA 31599 *Web:* bop.gov	912-427-0870	427-1125
Loretto 772 St Joseph St . . . . Loretto PA 15940 *TF:* 877-623-8426 ■ *Web:* www.bop.gov	814-472-4140	472-6046
Manchester 805 Fox Hollow Rd PO Box 4000 . . . . Manchester KY 40962 *TF:* 877-623-8426 ■ *Web:* www.bop.gov	606-598-1900	599-4115
McKean 6975 Rt 59 PO Box 8000 . . . . Lewis Run PA 16738 *TF:* 877-623-8426 ■ *Web:* www.bop.gov	814-362-8900	363-6821
Milan PO Box 9999 . . . . Milan MI 48160 *Web:* www.bop.gov/locations/institutions/mil	734-439-1511	439-0949
Morgantown 446 Greenbag Rd . . . . Morgantown WV 26501 *Web:* www.bop.gov	304-296-4416	284-3613
Oxford PO Box 500 . . . . Oxford WI 53952 *Web:* www.bop.gov	608-584-5511	584-6371
Pekin 2600 S Second St . . . . Pekin IL 61554 *Web:* bop.gov	309-346-8588	477-4685
Phoenix 37900 N 45th Ave . . . . Phoenix AZ 85086	623-465-9757	465-5199
Ray Brook 128 Ray Brook Rd PO Box 300 . . . . Ray Brook NY 12977 *Web:* www.bop.gov	518-897-4000	897-4216
Safford 1529 W Hwy 366 PO Box 9000 . . . . Safford AZ 85546 *Web:* www.bop.gov	928-428-6600	348-1331
Talladega 565 E Renfroe Rd. . . . . Talladega AL 35160 *Web:* www.bop.gov/locations	256-315-4100	315-4495
Tallahassee 501 Capital Cir NE . . . . Tallahassee FL 32301 *Web:* federalprisoncalls.net	850-878-2173	
Terminal Island 1299 Seaside Ave. . . . . San Pedro CA 90731 *Web:* www.bop.gov	310-831-8961	732-5335
Yazoo City 2225 Haley Barbour Pkwy PO Box 5050 . . . . Yazoo City MS 39194 *TF:* 877-623-8426 ■ *Web:* www.bop.gov	662-751-4800	751-4958
Federal Detention Ctr (FDC)		
Honolulu 351 Elliot St . . . . Honolulu HI 96820 *Web:* www.bop.gov	808-838-4200	838-4510
Houston 1200 Texas Ave . . . . Houston TX 77002	713-221-5400	
Oakdale PO Box 5060 . . . . Oakdale LA 71463 *Web:* www.bop.gov	318-335-4466	215-2046
Philadelphia PO Box 572 . . . . Philadelphia PA 19106 *Web:* www.bop.gov	215-521-4000	521-7220
SeaTac PO Box 13901 . . . . Seattle WA 98198 *TF:* 877-623-8426 ■ *Web:* www.bop.gov/locations/institutions/set/index.jsp	206-870-5700	870-5717
Federal Medical Ctr		
Butner Old N Carolina Hwy 75 . . . . Butner NC 27509 *Web:* www.bop.gov	919-575-3900	575-4801
Lexington 3301 Leestown Rd. . . . . Lexington KY 40511 *Web:* bop.gov	859-255-6812	253-8821
Federal Prison Camp (FPC)		
Bryan 1100 Ursuline Ave PO Box 2147 . . . . Bryan TX 77805 **Fax:* Warden ■ *Web:* www.bop.gov	979-823-1879	821-3316*
Duluth 6902 Airport Rd PO Box 1400 . . . . Duluth MN 55814 *TF:* 877-623-8426 ■ *Web:* www.bop.gov	218-722-8634	733-4701
Montgomery Maxwell AFB. . . . . Montgomery AL 36112 *TF:* 877-623-8426 ■ *Web:* www.bop.gov/locations/institutions/mon	334-293-2100	293-2326
Medical Ctr for Federal Prisoners Springfield 1900 W Sunshine St. . . . . Springfield MO 65807 *TF:* 877-623-8426 ■ *Web:* www.bop.gov	417-862-7041	837-1717
Metropolitan Correctional Ctr		
Chicago 71 W Van Buren St. . . . . Chicago IL 60605 *TF:* 877-623-8426 ■ *Web:* www.bop.gov	312-322-0567	322-1120
New York 150 Pk Row . . . . New York NY 10007 *Web:* www.bop.gov/locations/institutions/nym/index.jsp	646-836-6300	836-7751

Phone | Fax

US Penitentiary (USP)
Allenwood PO Box 3500 .... White Deer PA 17887 570-547-0963 547-9201
Web: www.bop.gov/locations/institutions/alp
Atwater 1 Federal Way PO Box 019001 .... Atwater CA 95301 209-386-0257 386-4635
TF: 877-623-8426 ■ *Web:* www.bop.gov/locations/institutions/atw
Lewisburg 2400 Robert Miller Dr................Lewisburg PA 17837 570-523-1251 522-7745
Pollock 1000 Airbase Rd PO Box 1000............Pollock LA 71467 318-561-5300 561-5391
Web: bop.gov

213 CORRECTIONAL FACILITIES - STATE

See Also Correctional & Detention Management (Privatized) p. 2162; Correctional Facilities - Federal p. 2162; Juvenile Detention Facilities p. 2616

Alabama

Phone | Fax

Bibb Country Correctional Facility 565 Bibb Ln .... Brent AL 35034 205-926-5252 926-9928
Web: doc.alabama.gov
Bullock County Correctional Facility
104 Bullock Dr PO Box 5107 ....Union Springs AL 36089 334-738-5625 738-5020
Web: alabama.gov
Elmore Correctional Ctr
3520 Marion Spillway Rd...........................Elmore AL 36025 334-567-1460 567-1804
Web: www.doc.state.al.us
Holman Correctional Facility
866 Ross Rd PO Box 3700..........................Atmore AL 36503 251-368-8173 368-1095
Web: www.doc.state.al.us
Kilby Correctional Facility
12201 Wares Ferry Rd .... Montgomery AL 36117 334-215-6600
Web: doc.alabama.gov
Limestone Correctional Facility
28779 Nick Davis Rd .... Harvest AL 35749 256-233-4600 233-1930
Saint Clair Correctional Facility
1000 St Clair Rd...............................Springville AL 35146 205-467-6111 467-2474
Staton Correctional Facility
2690 Marion Spillway Rd PO Box 56.................Elmore AL 36025 334-567-2221
Web: doc.state.al.us
Tutwiler Prison for Women 8966 US Hwy 231........Wetumpka AL 36092 334-567-4369 514-6576
Web: doc.state.al.us
Ventress Correctional Facility
Hwy 239 N PO Box 767 .... Clayton AL 36016 334-775-3331
Web: alabama.gov
William E Donaldson Facility 100 Warrior Ln ....Bessemer AL 35023 205-436-3681 436-3399
Web: doc.state.al.us

Alaska

Phone | Fax

Anchorage Correctional Complex
1400 E Fourth Ave ....Anchorage AK 99501 907-269-4100 269-4208
Web: www.correct.state.ak.us
Anvil Mountain Correctional Ctr
1810 Ctr Creek Rd PO Box 730 ....Nome AK 99762 907-443-2241 443-5195
Web: www.correct.state.ak.us
Fairbanks Correctional Ctr 1931 Eagan Ave ....Fairbanks AK 99701 907-458-6700 458-6751
TF: 877-741-0741 ■ *Web:* correct.state.ak.us
Hiland Mountain Correctional Ctr Library
9101 Hesterberg Rd .... Eagle River AK 99577 907-694-9511 694-4507
Web: correct.state.ak.us
Ketchikan Correctional Ctr
1201 Schoenbar Rd ....Ketchikan AK 99901 907-228-7350 225-7031
Web: www.correct.state.ak.us
Lemon Creek Correctional Ctr
2000 Lemon Creek Rd ....Juneau AK 99801 907-465-6200 465-6224
Web: www.correct.state.ak.us
Palmer Correctional Ctr PO Box 919 ....Palmer AK 99645 907-745-5054 746-1574
TF: 877-741-0741 ■ *Web:* www.correct.state.ak.us/institutions/palmer
Spring Creek Correctional Ctr 3600 Bette Cato......... Seward AK 99664 907-224-8200 224-8062
Web: www.correct.state.ak.us/corrections
Wildwood Correctional Ctr 10 Chugach Ave ....Kenai AK 99611 907-260-7200 260-7208
Web: www.correct.state.ak.us
Yukon-Kuskokwim Correctional Ctr
1000 Chief Eddie Hoffman Hwy PO Box 400 .... Bethel AK 99559 907-543-5245 543-3097
Web: www.correct.state.ak.us

Arizona

Phone | Fax

Arizona State Prison Complex-Douglas
6911 N BDI Blvd PO Box 3867.......................Douglas AZ 85607 520-364-7521 364-7445
Arizona State Prison Complex-Eyman
4374 E Butte Ave PO Box 3500........................ Florence AZ 85132 520-868-0201 868-0276
TF: 866-333-2039 ■ *Web:* corrections.az.gov
Arizona State Prison Complex-Florence
1305 E Butte Ave PO Box 629.......................... Florence AZ 85132 520-868-4011 868-5333
Web: corrections.az.gov
Arizona State Prison Complex-Lewis
26700 S Hwy 85 PO Box 70..........................Buckeye AZ 85326 623-386-6160 386-7332
Web: corrections.az.gov/location/98/lewis
Arizona State Prison Complex-Perryville
2105 N Citrus Rd ....Goodyear AZ 85395 623-853-0304 853-0425
Arizona State Prison Complex-Phoenix
2500 E Van Buren PO Box 52109......................Phoenix AZ 85072 602-685-3100 685-3124
Web: corrections.az.gov/location/105/phoenix
Arizona State Prison Complex-Safford
896 S Crook Rd ....Safford AZ 85546 928-428-4698 428-3235
Web: corrections.az.gov
Arizona State Prison Complex-Winslow
2100 S Hwy 87 .... Winslow AZ 86047 928-289-9551 289-2951
Web: az.gov

Phone | Fax

Arizona State Prison Complex-Yuma
7125 E Juan Sanchez Blvd .... San Luis AZ 85349 928-627-8871 627-6703
Web: corrections.az.gov

Arkansas

Phone | Fax

Arkansas Department of Correction
302 Wackenhut Way...............................Newport AR 72112 870-523-2639 523-6202
Web: www.adc.arkansas.gov
Arkansas Dept of Corrections Cummins Unit
Hwy 388 PO Box 500 ....Grady AR 71644 870-850-8899 850-8861
Web: adc.arkansas.gov
Arkansas Dept of Corrections Delta Regional Unit
425 W Capitol Ave Ste 1620...................... Little Rock AR 72201 501-324-8900
Web: www.arkansas.gov
Arkansas Dept of Corrections East Arkansas Regional Unit
326 Lee 601 PO Box 180 ....Brickeys AR 72320 870-295-4700 295-6564
Web: adc.arkansas.gov/pages/default.aspx
Arkansas Dept of Corrections Maximum Security Unit
2501 State Farm Rd .... Tucker AR 72168 501-842-3800 842-1977
TF: 866-801-3435 ■ *Web:* www.arkansas.gov
Arkansas Dept of Corrections North Central Unit
10 Prison Cir HC 62 PO Box 300..................Calico Rock AR 72519 870-297-4311 297-4322
Web: adc.arkansas.gov
Arkansas Dept of Corrections Tucker Unit
2400 State Farm Rd PO Box 240 .... Tucker AR 72168 501-842-2519 842-3958
TF: 800-682-7377 ■ *Web:* adc.arkansas.gov
Arkansas Dept of Corrections Varner Unit
Hwy 388 PO Box 600...............................Grady AR 71644 870-575-1800 479-3803
Web: adc.arkansas.gov
Arkansas Dept of Corrections Wrightsville Unit
PO Box 1000 ....Wrightsville AR 72183 501-897-5806 897-5716
Web: adc.arkansas.gov

California

Phone | Fax

Avenal State Prison 1 Kings Hwy PO Box 39............. Avenal CA 93204 559-386-0587 386-0907
Web: cdcr.ca.gov
California Correctional Institution
24900 Hwy 202 PO Box 1031...................... Tehachapi CA 93581 661-822-4402 823-5020
Web: www.cdcr.ca.gov
California Men's Colony (CMC)
Hwy 1 PO Box 8101 .... San Luis Obispo CA 93409 805-547-7900
Web: www.cdcr.ca.gov
California State Prison Corcoran
4001 King Ave PO Box 8800 ....Corcoran CA 93212 559-992-8800 386-7461
Web: www.cdcr.ca.gov
California State Prison Los Angeles County
44750 60th St W.................................Lancaster CA 93536 661-729-2000 729-6930
Web: cdcr.ca.gov
California State Prison Solano
2100 Peabody Rd PO Box 4000 .... Vacaville CA 95696 707-451-0182 454-3200
Calipatria State Prison 7018 Blair Rd................Calipatria CA 92233 760-348-7000 348-7188
Web: cdcr.ca.gov
Centinela State Prison
2302 Brown Rd PO Box 731.........................Imperial CA 92251 760-337-7900 337-7692
Web: cdcr.ca.gov
Central California Women's Facility (CCWF)
23370 Rd 22 PO Box 1501 .... Chowchilla CA 93610 559-665-5531
Web: www.cdcr.ca.gov/facilities_locator/ccwf.html
Chuckawalla Valley State Prison (CVSP)
19025 Wiley's Well Rd PO Box 2289 .... Blythe CA 92226 760-922-5300 922-6855
Web: cdcr.ca.gov
Folsom State Prison 300 Prison Rd.................. Represa CA 95671 916-985-2561 351-3010
Web: cdcr.ca.gov
High Desert State Prison (HDSP)
475-750 Rice Canyon Rd PO Box 750 .... Susanville CA 96127 530-251-5100
Web: www.cdcr.ca.gov
Ironwood State Prison
19005 Wiley's Well Rd PO Box 2229 .... Blythe CA 92225 760-921-3000
Web: www.cdcr.ca.gov/facilities_locator/isp.html
Mule Creek State Prison 4001 Hwy 104...................Ione CA 95640 209-274-4911 274-4861
TF: 877-256-6877 ■ *Web:* cdcr.ca.gov
Pelican Bay State Prison (PBSP)
5905 Lake Earl Dr PO Box 7000..................Crescent City CA 95531 707-465-1000 465-4376
TF: 877-256-6877 ■ *Web:* www.cdcr.ca.gov
Pleasant Valley State Prison
24863 W Jayne Ave PO Box 8500 .... Coalinga CA 93210 559-935-4900 386-7461
TF: 877-256-6877 ■ *Web:* www.cdcr.ca.gov
RJ Donovan Correctional Facility at Rock Mountain
480 Alta Rd.................................. San Diego CA 92179 619-661-6500 661-6253
TF: 877-256-6877 ■ *Web:* cdcr.ca.gov
Salinas Valley State Prison 31625 Hwy 101 N ....Soledad CA 93960 831-678-5500 678-5503
Web: cdcr.ca.gov
Valley State Prison for Women
21633 Ave 24 PO Box 99 .... Chowchilla CA 93610 559-665-6100
Web: cdcr.ca.gov

Colorado

Phone | Fax

Arkansas Valley Correctional Facility (AVCF)
12750 Colorado 96 PO Box 1000....................Crowley CO 81033 719-267-3520 267-5024
Web: www.doc.state.co.us
Delta Correctional Ctr 4102 Saw Mill Mesa Rd .... Delta CO 81416 970-874-7614 874-7614
Denver Women's Correctional Facility
3600 Havana St ....Denver CO 80239 303-371-4804
Fremont Correctional Facility (FCF)
E US Hwy 50 Evans Blvd PO Box 999.............. Canon City CO 81215 719-269-5002 269-5020
Web: www.colorado.gov/pacific/cdoc/address-and-phone-number-information
Limon Correctional Facility 49030 State Hwy 71......... Limon CO 80826 719-775-9221 775-7607
Web: www.colorado.gov/pacific/cdoc/search/site/Limon%20Correctional%20Facility

				Phone	Fax
Rifle Correctional Ctr 200 County Rd 219	Rifle	CO	81650	970-625-1700	625-1706
Sterling Correctional Facility 12101 Hwy 61	Sterling	CO	80751	970-521-5010	

Connecticut

				Phone	Fax
Brooklyn Correctional Institution 59 Hartford Rd *Web:* ct.gov	Brooklyn	CT	06234	860-779-2600	779-2394
Corrections Dept 1106 N Ave *Web:* ct.gov	Bridgeport	CT	06606	203-579-6131	579-6693
Corrigan Correctional Institution 986 Norwich-New London Tpke *Web:* www.ct.gov	Uncasville	CT	06382	860-848-5700	848-5821
Enfield Correctional Institution 289 Shaker Rd PO Box 1500 *Web:* www.ct.gov	Enfield	CT	06082	860-763-7300	
Garner Correctional Institution 50 Nunnawauk Rd *Web:* ct.gov	Newtown	CT	06470	203-270-2800	270-1826
Gates Correctional Institution 131 N Bridebrook Rd *Web:* www.ct.gov	Niantic	CT	06357	860-691-4700	691-4745
Hartford Correctional Ctr 177 Weston St *Web:* ct.gov	Hartford	CT	06120	860-240-1800	566-2725
MacDougall Correctional Institution 1153 E St S *Web:* ct.gov	Suffield	CT	06080	860-627-2100	627-2144
New Haven Correctional Ctr 245 Whalley Ave	New Haven	CT	06511	203-974-4111	974-4167
Northern Correctional Institution 287 Bilton Rd *Web:* ct.gov	Somers	CT	06071	860-763-8600	763-8651
Willard-Cybulski Correctional Institution 391 Shaker Rd *Web:* ct.gov	Enfield	CT	06082	860-763-6100	763-6111
York Correctional Institution 201 W Main St *Web:* www.ct.gov	Niantic	CT	06357	860-451-3001	451-3200

Delaware

				Phone	Fax
Baylor Women's Correctional Institution 660 Baylor Blvd	New Castle	DE	19720	302-577-3004	577-7099
Sussex Corrections Institution 23203 Dupont Blvd PO Box 500	Georgetown	DE	19947	302-856-5280	

Florida

				Phone	Fax
Apalachee Correctional Institution 35 Apalachee Dr *Web:* dc.state.fl.us	Sneads	FL	32460	850-718-0688	593-6445
Avon Park Correctional Institution County Rd 64 E PO Box 1100 *Web:* dc.state.fl.us	Avon Park	FL	33826	863-453-3174	453-1511
Baker Correctional Institution 20706 US Hwy 90 *Web:* myflorida.com	Sanderson	FL	32087	386-719-4500	758-5759
Bay Correctional Facility 5400 Bayline Dr *Web:* dc.state.fl.us	Panama City	FL	32404	850-769-1455	769-1942
Brevard Correctional Institution 855 Camp Rd *Web:* dc.state.fl.us	Cocoa	FL	32927	321-634-6000	634-6066
Calhoun Correctional Institution 19562 SE Institutional Dr Unit 1 *Web:* dc.state.fl.us	Blountstown	FL	32424	850-237-6500	237-6508
Charlotte Correctional Institution 33123 Oil Well Rd *Web:* dc.state.fl.us	Punta Gorda	FL	33955	941-833-2300	575-5747
Corrections Department 16415 Spring Hill Dr	Brooksville	FL	34604	352-754-6715	544-2307
Cross City Corrections Dept 568 NE 255 St *Web:* dc.state.fl.us	Cross City	FL	32628	352-498-4444	
Desoto Correctional Institution 13617 SE Hwy 70 *Web:* dc.state.fl.us	Arcadia	FL	34266	863-494-3727	494-1740
Florida Department of Corrections 8784 W US 27 **Fax Area Code:* 904	Mayo	FL	32066	386-294-4500	829-4534*
Florida State Prison 7819 NW 228 St *Web:* dc.state.fl.us	Raiford	FL	32026	904-368-2500	368-2732
Gainesville Correctional Institution 2845 NE 39th Ave	Gainesville	FL	32609	352-955-2001	334-1675
Gulf Correctional Institution 500 Ike Steele Rd *Web:* dc.state.fl.us	Wewahitchka	FL	32465	850-639-1100	639-1182
Hamilton Correctional Institution 10650 SW 46th St	Jasper	FL	32052	386-792-5151	
Jackson Correctional Institution 5563 Tenth St *Web:* dc.state.fl.us	Malone	FL	32445	850-569-5260	569-5996
Lake City Correctional Facility 7906 E US Hwy 90 *Web:* www.cca.com	Lake City	FL	32055	386-755-3379	752-7202
Lake Correctional Institution 19225 US Hwy 27 *Web:* dc.state.fl.us	Clermont	FL	34711	352-394-6146	
Lancaster Correctional Institution 3449 SW SR 26 *Web:* dc.state.fl.us	Trenton	FL	32693	352-463-4100	463-3476
Liberty Correctional Institution 11064 NW Dempsey Barron Rd *Web:* dc.state.fl.us	Bristol	FL	32321	850-643-9400	643-9412
Lowell Correctional Institution-Women's Unit 11120 NW Gainesville Rd *Web:* dc.state.fl.us	Ocala	FL	34482	352-401-5301	401-5331
Madison Correctional Institution 382 SW MCI Way *Web:* dc.state.fl.us	Madison	FL	32340	850-973-5300	973-3666
Moore Haven Correctional Facility 1282 E SR 78 NW PO Box 718501 *Web:* dc.state.fl.us	Moore Haven	FL	33471	863-946-2420	946-3437
New River West Correctional Institution 7819 NW 228th St *Web:* dc.state.fl.us	Raiford	FL	32026	904-368-3000	368-2732
Okaloosa Correctional 3189 Little Silver Rd *Web:* dc.state.fl.us	Crestview	FL	32539	850-682-0931	689-7803
Okeechobee Correctional Institution 3420 NE 168th St *TF:* 800-574-5729 ■ *Web:* dc.state.fl.us	Okeechobee	FL	34972	863-462-5400	462-5402
Putnam Correctional Institution 128 Yelvington Rd *Web:* www.myflorida.com	East Palatka	FL	32131	386-326-6800	312-2219
Quincy Correctional Institution 2225 Pat Thomas Pkwy *Web:* dc.state.fl.us	Quincy	FL	32351	850-627-5400	875-3572
Santa Rosa Correctional Institution 5850 E Milton Rd *Web:* dc.state.fl.us	Milton	FL	32583	850-983-5800	983-5907
South Bay Correctional Facility 600 US Hwy 27 S *TF:* 800-574-5729 ■ *Web:* dc.state.fl.us	South Bay	FL	33493	561-992-9505	992-9551
Sumter Correctional Institution 9544 County Rd 476 B *Web:* dc.state.fl.us	Bushnell	FL	33513	352-793-2525	793-3542
Taylor Correctional Institution 8501 Hampton Springs Rd *Web:* dc.state.fl.us	Perry	FL	32348	850-838-4000	838-4024
Tomoka Correctional Institution 3950 Tiger Bay Rd *Web:* dc.state.fl.us	Daytona Beach	FL	32124	386-323-1070	323-1006
Union Correctional Institution 7819 NW 228th St *Web:* dc.state.fl.us	Raiford	FL	32026	386-431-2000	431-2010
Zephyrhills Correctional Institution 2739 Gall Blvd	Zephyrhills	FL	33541	813-782-5521	780-0134

Georgia

				Phone	Fax
Baldwin State Prison Laying Farm Rd PO Box 218 *Web:* dcor.state.ga.us	Hardwick	GA	31034	478-445-5218	445-6507
Calhoun State Prison 27823 Main St PO Box 249 *Web:* www.dcor.state.ga.us	Morgan	GA	39866	229-849-5000	849-5017
Dooly State Prison 1412 Plunkett Rd PO Box 750	Unadilla	GA	31091	478-627-2000	627-2140
Hancock State Prison 701 Prison Blvd PO Box 339 *Web:* dcor.state.ga.us	Sparta	GA	31087	706-444-1000	444-1137
Lee Arrendale State Prison 2023 Gainesville Hwy *Web:* dcor.state.ga.us	Alto	GA	30510	706-776-4700	
Lee State Prison 153 Pinewood Rd *Web:* dcor.state.ga.us	Leesburg	GA	31763	229-759-6453	759-3065
Phillips State Prison 2989 W Rock Quarry Rd *Web:* dcor.state.ga.us	Buford	GA	30519	770-932-4500	932-4544
Pulaski State Prison Upper River Rd Rt 2 PO Box 839 *Web:* www.dcor.state.ga.us	Hawkinsville	GA	31036	478-783-6000	783-6008
Rogers State Prison 1978 Georgia Hwy 147	Reidsville	GA	30453	912-557-7771	557-7051
Rutledge State Prison 7175 Manor Rd	Columbus	GA	31907	706-568-2340	568-2126
Smith State Prison 9676 Hwy 301 N PO Box 726 *Web:* www.dcor.state.ga.us	Glennville	GA	30427	912-654-5000	654-5131
Valdosta State Prison 3259 Valtech Rd PO Box 310 *Web:* www.dcor.state.ga.us	Valdosta	GA	31603	229-333-7900	333-5387
Walker State Prison 97 Kevin Lake PO Box 98 *Web:* www.dcor.state.ga.us	Rock Spring	GA	30739	706-764-3600	764-3613
Ware State Prison 3620 N Harris Rd *Web:* dcor.state.ga.us	Waycross	GA	31501	912-285-6400	287-6520
West Central State Prison 4600 Fulton Mill Rd *Web:* www.dcor.state.ga.us	Macon	GA	31208	478-471-2908	471-2068

Hawaii

				Phone	Fax
Waiawa Correctional Facility 94-560 Kamehameha Hwy *Web:* hawaii.gov	Waipahu	HI	96797	808-677-6150	

Idaho

				Phone	Fax
Idaho Maximum Security Institution (IMSI) PO Box 51 *Web:* www.idoc.idaho.gov	Boise	ID	83707	208-338-1635	
Idaho State Correctional Institution PO Box 14 *Web:* idoc.idaho.gov	Boise	ID	83707	208-336-0740	334-2748
North Idaho Correctional Institution 236 Radar Rd	Cottonwood	ID	83522	208-962-3276	962-7119
Pocatello Women's Correctional Ctr 1451 Fore Rd *Web:* idoc.idaho.gov	Pocatello	ID	83204	208-236-6360	236-6362

Illinois

Facility	City	State	ZIP	Phone	Fax
Big Muddy River Correctional Ctr 251 N Hwy 37 PO Box 1000 *Web:* illinois.gov	Ina	IL	62846	618-437-5300	437-5627
Centralia Correctional Ctr 9330 Shattuc Rd PO Box 1266 *Web:* www2.illinois.gov	Centralia	IL	62801	618-533-4111	533-4112
Danville Correctional Ctr 3820 E Main St *Web:* www2.illinois.gov	Danville	IL	61834	217-446-0441	
Dixon Correctional Ctr 2600 N Brinton Ave.	Dixon	IL	61021	815-288-5561	288-0118
East Moline Correctional Ctr 100 Hillcrest Rd *Web:* www.illinois.gov/idoc/facilities/pages/eastmolinecorrectionalcenter.aspx	East Moline	IL	61244	309-755-4511	755-2589
Graham Correctional Ctr 12078 Illinois Rt 185 PO Box 499 *Web:* www2.illinois.gov	Hillsboro	IL	62049	217-532-6962	532-6799
Hill Correctional Ctr 600 S Linwood Rd	Galesburg	IL	61401	309-343-4212	
Jacksonville Correctional Ctr 2268 E Morton Ave. *Web:* illinois.gov	Jacksonville	IL	62650	217-245-1481	
Lincoln Correctional Ctr 1098 1350th St PO Box 549 *Web:* illinois.gov	Lincoln	IL	62656	217-735-5411	735-5381
Logan Correctional Ctr 1096 1350th St *Web:* www.illinois.gov/idoc/facilities/pages/logancorrectionalcenter.aspx	Lincoln	IL	62656	217-735-5581	735-1077
Menard Correctional Ctr 711 Kaskaskia St.	Menard	IL	62259	618-826-5071	
Pinckneyville Correctional Ctr 5835 SR- 154 *Web:* illinois.gov	Pinckneyville	IL	62274	618-357-9722	357-2083
Pontiac Correctional Ctr 700 W Lincoln St *Web:* www.illinois.gov/idoc/facilities/Pages/pontiaccorrectionalcenter.aspx	Pontiac	IL	61764	815-842-2816	842-3420
Robinson Correctional Ctr 13423 E 1150th Ave *Web:* www2.illinois.gov	Robinson	IL	62454	618-546-5659	544-2166
Shawnee Correctional Ctr 6665 SR 146 E *Web:* www.illinois.gov/idoc/facilities/pages/shawneecorrectionalcenter.aspx	Vienna	IL	62995	618-658-8331	658-8822
Southwestern Correctional Ctr 950 Kings Hwy *Web:* www.illinois.gov/idoc/facilities/pages/southwesternillinoiscorrectionalcenter.aspx	East Saint Louis	IL	62203	618-394-2200	394-2228
Stateville Correctional Ctr 16830 S Broadway St PO Box 112 *Web:* www.illinois.gov	Joliet	IL	60434	815-727-3607	727-5511
Taylorville Correctional Ctr 1144 Illinois Rt 29 PO Box 1000 *Web:* illinois.gov	Taylorville	IL	62568	217-824-4004	824-4042
Vandalia Correctional Ctr Rt 51 N PO Box 500 *Web:* www.illinois.gov	Vandalia	IL	62471	618-283-4170	283-9147
Vienna Correctional Ctr 6695 SR 146 E Ste 146	Vienna	IL	62995	618-658-8371	658-3609
Western Illinois Correctional Ctr 2500 Illinois 99 *Web:* www.illinois.gov	Mount Sterling	IL	62353	217-773-4441	

Indiana

Facility	City	State	ZIP	Phone	Fax
Henryville Correctional Facility PO Box 148 *Web:* www.in.gov/idoc/2398.htm	Henryville	IN	47126	812-294-4372	294-1523
Indiana State Prison 1 Pk Row	Michigan City	IN	46360	219-874-7258	
Indiana Women's Prison 2596 N Girls School Rd *Web:* in.gov	Indianapolis	IN	46214	317-244-3387	244-4670
Madison Correctional Facility 800 MSH Busstop Dr *Web:* in.gov	Madison	IN	47250	812-265-6154	265-2142
Miami Correctional Facility 3038 W 850 S *Web:* in.gov	Bunker Hill	IN	46914	765-689-8920	689-7479
New Castle Correctional Facility 1000 Van Nuys Rd	New Castle	IN	47362	765-593-0111	778-3395
Plainfield Correctional Facility 727 Moon Rd *Web:* in.gov	Plainfield	IN	46168	317-839-2513	837-1875
Putnamville Correctional Facility 1946 W Hwy 40 **Fax:* Warden ■ *Web:* in.gov	Greencastle	IN	46135	765-653-8441	653-7461*
Rockville Correctional Facility 811 W 50 N *Web:* in.gov	Rockville	IN	47872	765-569-3178	569-3178
Wabash Valley Correctional Facility PO Box 1111 *Web:* www.in.gov/idoc/2409.htm	Carlisle	IN	47838	812-398-5050	398-5065

Iowa

Facility	City	State	ZIP	Phone	Fax
Clarinda Correctional Facility 1800 N 16th St Ste 1 *Web:* www.doc.state.ia.us	Clarinda	IA	51632	712-542-5634	542-4844
Fort Dodge Correctional Facility 1550 L St *Web:* www.doc.state.ia.us/InstitutionDescriptions	Fort Dodge	IA	50501	515-574-4700	
Iowa Correctional Institution for Women 420 Mill St SW *Web:* mitchellvilleprison.org	Mitchellville	IA	50169	515-725-5042	725-5015
Iowa State Penitentiary Ave E & 1st St PO Box 409 *TF:* 800-382-0019 ■ *Web:* iaprisonind.com	Fort Madison	IA	52627	319-372-1908	372-2856
Newton Correctional Facility 307 S 60th Ave W *Web:* doc.state.ia.us	Newton	IA	50208	641-792-7552	791-1683

Kansas

Facility	City	State	ZIP	Phone	Fax
El Dorado Correctional Facility 1737 SE Hwy 54 PO Box 311 *Web:* www.dc.state.ks.us	El Dorado	KS	67042	316-321-7284	321-5349
Hutchinson Correctional Facility PO Box 1568 *Web:* www.doc.ks.gov/facilities/hcf	Hutchinson	KS	67504	620-662-2321	662-8662
Topeka Correctional Facility 815 SE Rice Rd *TF:* 888-317-8204 ■ *Web:* dc.state.ks.us	Topeka	KS	66603	785-296-3317	
Winfield Correctional Facility 1806 Pine Crest Cir *Web:* dc.state.ks.us	Winfield	KS	67156	620-221-6660	221-9229

Kentucky

Facility	City	State	ZIP	Phone	Fax
Blackburn Correctional Complex 3111 Spurr Rd *Web:* corrections.ky.gov	Lexington	KY	40511	859-246-2366	246-2376
Eastern Kentucky Correctional Complex 200 Rd to Justice *Web:* www.corrections.ky.gov	West Liberty	KY	41472	606-743-2800	743-2811
Green River Correctional Complex 1200 River Rd *Web:* corrections.ky.gov	Central City	KY	42330	270-754-5415	
Kentucky Correctional Institution for Women 3000 Ash Ave *TF:* 877-687-6818 ■ *Web:* corrections.ky.gov	Pewee Valley	KY	40056	502-241-8454	243-0079
Kentucky State Reformatory 3001 W Hwy 146 *Web:* corrections.ky.gov	LaGrange	KY	40032	502-222-9441	222-8115
Luther Luckett Correctional Complex Dawkins Rd PO Box 6 *TF:* 800-511-1670 ■ *Web:* www.corrections.ky.gov	LaGrange	KY	40031	502-222-0363	222-8112
Western Kentucky Correctional Complex 374 New Bethel Church Rd *Web:* corrections.ky.gov	Fredonia	KY	42411	270-388-9781	388-0031

Louisiana

Facility	City	State	ZIP	Phone	Fax
Allen Correctional Ctr 3751 Lauderdale Woodyard Rd *Web:* doc.la.gov	Kinder	LA	70648	337-639-2942	639-2944
Avoyelles Correctional Ctr 1630 Prison Rd *Web:* doc.la.gov	Cottonport	LA	71327	318-876-2891	876-4220
Catahoula Correctional Ctr 499 Columbia Rd *Web:* lasallecorrections.com	Harrisonburg	LA	71340	318-744-2121	744-2126
David Wade Correctional Ctr 670 Bell Hill Rd	Homer	LA	71040	318-927-9631	
Dixon Correctional Institute 5568 Hwy 68 *Web:* doc.louisiana.gov	Jackson	LA	70748	225-634-1200	634-4543
Louisiana State Penitentiary 17544 Tunica Trace *Web:* doc.la.gov	Angola	LA	70712	225-655-4411	
Vernon Correctional Facility 2294 Slagle Rd	Leesville	LA	71446	337-238-4522	238-4208

Maine

Facility	City	State	ZIP	Phone	Fax
Downeast Correctional Dept 64 Base Rd	Machiasport	ME	04655	207-255-1100	255-1176
Maine Correctional Ctr 17 Mallison Falls Rd *Web:* maine.gov	Windham	ME	04062	207-893-7000	893-7001

Maryland

Facility	City	State	ZIP	Phone	Fax
Eastern Correctional Institution 30420 Revells Neck Rd	Westover	MD	21890	410-845-4000	845-4055
Jessup Correctional Institution 7804 House of Correction Rd	Jessup	MD	20794	410-799-0100	
Maryland Correctional Adjustment Ctr 401 E Madison St	Baltimore	MD	21202	410-539-5445	332-4561
Maryland Correctional Institution for Women (MCI-W) 7943 Brockbridge Rd	Jessup	MD	20794	410-379-3800	799-6146
Maryland Correctional Institution-Hagerstown 18601 Roxbury Rd *Web:* msa.maryland.gov	Hagerstown	MD	21746	301-733-2800	797-2872
Maryland Correctional Training Ctr 18800Roxbury Rd. *Web:* dbm.maryland.gov	Hagerstown	MD	21746	301-791-7200	797-8574
Roxbury Correctional Institution 18701 Roxbury Rd **Fax Area Code:* 301	Hagerstown	MD	21746	240-420-3000	797-0795*
Western Correctional Institution 13800 McMullen Hwy	Cumberland	MD	21502	301-729-7000	729-7063

Massachusetts

Facility	City	State	ZIP	Phone	Fax
Bay State Correctional Ctr 28 Clark St. *Web:* mass.gov	Norfolk	MA	02056	508-668-1687	668-1687
Massachusetts Correctional Institution-Cedar Junction 2405 Main St *Web:* www.mass.gov	Walpole	MA	02071	508-668-2100	
Massachusetts Correctional Institution-Framingham PO Box 9007 *Web:* www.mass.gov	Framingham	MA	01704	508-532-5100	

Phone Fax

Massachusetts Correctional Institution-Plymouth (MCI)
1 Bumps Pond Rd. . . . . South Carver MA 02366 508-291-2441
Web: www.mass.gov

North Central Correctional Institution at Gardner
500 Colony Rd . . . . . Gardner MA 01440 978-632-2000 630-6040

Old Colony Correctional Ctr 1 Admin Rd . . . . . Bridgewater MA 02324 508-279-6000 279-6754
Web: mass.gov

Souza-Baranowski Correctional Ctr
PO Box 8000 . . . . . Shirley MA 01464 978-514-6500 514-6529
Web: www.mass.gov

Michigan

Phone Fax

Alger Correctional Facility
N 6141 Industrial Pk Dr . . . . . Wetmore MI 49895 906-387-5000
Web: www.michigan.gov/corrections

Baraga Correctional Facility 13924 Wadaga Rd . . . . . Baraga MI 49908 906-353-7070
Web: www.michigan.gov/corrections

Carson City Correctional Facility
10274 Boyer Rd . . . . . Carson City MI 48811 989-584-3941
Web: www.michigan.gov/corrections

Central Michigan Correctional Facility
320 N Hubbard. . . . . Saint Louis MI 48880 989-681-6668
Web: www.michigan.gov/corrections

Charles E Egeler Correctional Facility
3855 Cooper St . . . . . Jackson MI 49201 517-780-5600 780-5814
TF: 855-444-3911 ■ *Web:* www.michigan.gov/corrections

Chippewa Correctional Facility 4269 W M-80. . . . . Kincheloe MI 49784 906-495-2275
Web: www.michigan.gov/corrections

Cooper Street Correctional Facility
3100 Cooper St . . . . . Jackson MI 49201 517-780-6175
Web: www.michigan.gov/corrections

Earnest C Brooks Correctional Facility
2500 S Sheridan Dr . . . . . Muskegon Heights MI 49444 231-773-9200
Web: www.michigan.gov/corrections

G Robert Cotton Correctional Facility
3500 N Elm Rd. . . . . Jackson MI 49201 517-780-5000 780-5100
TF: 855-444-3911 ■ *Web:* www.michigan.gov/corrections

Gus Harrison Correctional Facility
2727 E Beecher St . . . . . Adrian MI 49221 517-265-3900
Web: www.michigan.gov

Hiawatha Correctional Facility
4533 W Industrial Pk Dr. . . . . Kincheloe MI 49786 906-495-5661
Web: www.michigan.gov

Huron Valley Correctional Facility
3201 Bemis Rd. . . . . Ypsilanti MI 48197 734-572-9900 572-9499
TF: 855-444-3911 ■ *Web:* www.michigan.gov

Ionia Maximum Correctional Facility
1576 W Bluewater Hwy. . . . . Ionia MI 48846 616-527-6331 527-6863
Web: www.michigan.gov/corrections

Kinross Correctional Facility
16770 S Watertower Dr. . . . . Kincheloe MI 49788 906-495-2282
Web: www.michigan.gov/corrections

Lakeland Correctional Facility
141 First St. . . . . Coldwater MI 49036 517-278-6942
Web: www.michigan.gov/corrections

Macomb Correctional Facility
34625 26th Mile Rd . . . . . New Haven MI 48048 586-749-4900
Web: michigan.gov

Marquette Branch Prison 1960 US Hwy 41 S . . . . . Marquette MI 49855 906-226-6531 226-6557
Web: www.michigan.gov/corrections

Michigan Reformatory 1727 Bluewater Hwy. . . . . Ionia MI 48846 616-527-2510
Web: www.michigan.gov/corrections

Mound Correctional Facility 17601 Mound Rd. . . . . Detroit MI 48212 313-368-8300 368-8972
Web: www.michigan.gov/corrections

Muskegon Correctional Facility
2400 S Sheridan Dr . . . . . Muskegon MI 49442 517-335-1426
Web: www.michigan.gov/corrections

Newberry Correctional Facility
13747 E County Rd 428 . . . . . Newberry MI 49868 906-293-6200
Web: www.michigan.gov/corrections

Oaks Correctional Facility
1500 Caberfae Hwy. . . . . Manistee MI 49660 231-723-8272
Web: www.michigan.gov/corrections

Richard A Handlon Correctional Facility
1728 Bluewater Hwy . . . . . Ionia MI 48846 616-527-3100
Web: www.michigan.gov/corrections

Riverside Correctional Facility
777 W Riverside Dr. . . . . Ionia MI 48846 616-527-0110
Web: www.michigan.gov

Saginaw Correctional Facility
9625 Pierce Rd. . . . . Freeland MI 48623 989-695-9880
Web: www.michigan.gov

Saint Louis Correctional Facility
8585 N Croswell Rd . . . . . Saint Louis MI 48880 989-681-6444
Web: www.michigan.gov

Thumb Correctional Facility
3225 John Conley Dr . . . . . Lapeer MI 48446 810-667-2045 667-2048
TF: 855-444-3911 ■ *Web:* www.michigan.gov

Minnesota

Phone Fax

Minnesota Correctional Facility-Fairbault
1101 Linden Ln . . . . . Faribault MN 55021 507-334-0700 332-4538*
**Fax:* Warden ■ *TF:* 800-657-3830 ■ *Web:* www.doc.state.mn.us

Minnesota Correctional Facility-Lino Lakes
7525 Fourth Ave. . . . . Lino Lakes MN 55014 651-717-6100

Minnesota Correctional Facility-Moose Lake
1000 Lk Shore Dr. . . . . Moose Lake MN 55767 218-485-5000 485-5010

Minnesota Correctional Facility-Rush City
7600 525th St. . . . . Rush City MN 55069 320-358-0400 358-0538

Minnesota Correctional Facility-Shakopee
1010 W Sixth Ave. . . . . Shakopee MN 55379 952-496-4440 496-4476
Web: www.doc.state.mn.us

Minnesota Correctional Facility-Stillwater
970 Picket St N. . . . . Bayport MN 55003 651-779-2700 351-3600

Mississippi

Phone Fax

Central Mississippi Correctional Facility
3794 Hwy 468 . . . . . Pearl MS 39208 601-932-2880 932-6202
Web: mdoc.state.ms.us

Issaquena County Correctional Facility
PO Box 220 . . . . . Mayersville MS 39113 662-873-2153 873-2956
Web: www.mdoc.ms.gov/institutions/pages/regional-facilities.aspx

Marion/Walthall Correctional Facility
503 S Main St. . . . . Columbia MS 39429 601-736-3621 736-4473
Web: mdoc.state.ms.us

Marshall County Correctional Facility
833 W St. . . . . Holly Springs MS 38635 662-274-0225

Mississippi State Penitentiary
Hwy 49 W PO Box 1057. . . . . Parchman MS 38738 662-745-6611 745-8912
TF: 800-844-0898

South Mississippi Correctional Institution
22689 Hwy 63 N PO Box 1419. . . . . Leakesville MS 39451 601-394-5600 394-4451
Web: mdoc.state.ms.us

Wilkinson County Correctional Ctr
2999 US 61 N. . . . . Woodville MS 39669 601-888-3199
Web: www.cca.com

Winston County Correctional Facility
PO Box 1437 . . . . . Louisville MS 39339 662-773-2528 773-4989
Web: www.mdoc.ms.gov/pages/facility-locations.aspx

Missouri

Phone Fax

Algoa Correctional Ctr
8501 No More Victims Rd . . . . . Jefferson City MO 65102 573-751-3911 526-1385*
**Fax:* Warden ■ *TF:* 800-392-1111 ■ *Web:* mo.gov

Boonville Correctional Ctr
1216 E Morgan St. . . . . Boonville MO 65233 660-882-6521 882-7825*
**Fax:* Warden ■ *TF:* 800-392-8486 ■ *Web:* doc.mo.gov

Central Missouri Correctional Ctr
2600 Hwy 179 . . . . . Jefferson City MO 65109 573-751-2053

Chillicothe Correctional Ctr
3151 Litton Rd . . . . . Chillicothe MO 64601 660-646-4032 646-1217
TF: 800-392-8486 ■ *Web:* doc.mo.gov

Farmington Correctional Ctr
1012 W Columbia St . . . . . Farmington MO 63640 573-218-7100
Web: mo.gov

Jefferson City Correctional Ctr
8200 No More Victims Rd . . . . . Jefferson City MO 65101 573-751-3224
Web: mo.gov

Missouri Eastern Correctional Ctr
18701 Old Hwy 66 . . . . . Pacific MO 63069 636-257-3322 257-5296
Web: mo.gov

Moberly Correctional Ctr 5201 S Morley. . . . . Moberly MO 65270 660-263-3778
Web: www.doc.mo.gov

Northeast Correctional Ctr
13698 County Rd 46. . . . . Bowling Green MO 63334 573-324-9975 324-5183
Web: mo.gov

Ozark Correctional Ctr 929 Honor Camp Ln . . . . . Fordland MO 65652 417-767-4491

Potosi Correctional Ctr
11593 State Hwy O. . . . . Mineral Point MO 63660 573-438-6000 438-6006
Web: mo.gov

Tipton Correctional Ctr 619 N Osage Ave. . . . . Tipton MO 65081 660-433-2031
Web: doc.mo.gov

Western Missouri Correctional Ctr
609 E Pence Rd . . . . . Cameron MO 64429 816-632-1390 632-2562
Web: mo.gov

Montana

Phone Fax

Montana State Prison 400 Conley Lk Rd . . . . . Deer Lodge MT 59722 406-846-1320
TF: 888-739-9122 ■ *Web:* www.cor.mt.gov

Montana Women's Prison 701 S 27th St . . . . . Billings MT 59101 406-247-5100 247-5161
Web: mt.gov

Nebraska

Phone Fax

Lincoln Correctional Ctr
3216 W Van Dorn St PO Box 22800. . . . . Lincoln NE 68522 402-479-6175
Web: www.corrections.nebraska.gov

Nebraska Correctional Ctr for Women
1107 Recharge Rd . . . . . York NE 68467 402-362-3317 362-3892
TF: 877-634-8463 ■ *Web:* www.corrections.nebraska.gov

Nebraska State Penitentiary 4201 S 14th St. . . . . Lincoln NE 68502 402-471-3161 471-4326
TF: 877-634-8463 ■ *Web:* www.corrections.nebraska.gov

Omaha Correctional Ctr 2323 Ave J PO Box 11099 . . . . . Omaha NE 68110 402-595-3963 595-2227

Nevada

Phone Fax

Ely State Prison 4569 NV-90 . . . . . Ely NV 89301 775-289-8800 684-3399
Web: doc.nv.gov

Lovelock Correctional Ctr 1200 Prison Rd. . . . . Lovelock NV 89419 775-273-1300 273-4277
Web: doc.nv.gov

Northern Nevada Correctional Ctr
1721 Snyder Dr PO Box 7000. . . . . Carson City NV 89702 775-887-9297
Web: doc.nv.gov

Facility	City	State	ZIP	Phone	Fax
Warm Springs Correctional Ctr 3301 E Fifth St PO Box 7007 *Web:* doc.nv.gov	Carson City	NV	89702	775-684-3000	

New Hampshire

Facility	City	State	ZIP	Phone	Fax
New Hampshire State Prison 281 N State St PO Box 14 *Web:* www.nh.gov/nhdoc/facilities/concord.html	Concord	NH	03302	603-271-1801	
New Hampshire State Prison for Women 317 Mast Rd *TF:* 800-639-1122	Goffstown	NH	03045	603-668-6137	679-5869
Northern New Hampshire Correctional Facility 138 E Milan Rd *Web:* nh.gov	Berlin	NH	03570	603-752-2906	752-0405

New Jersey

Facility	City	State	ZIP	Phone	Fax
Bayside State Prison 4293 Rt 47 *Web:* state.nj.us	Leesburg	NJ	08327	856-785-0040	785-2559
East Jersey State Prison 1100 Woodbridge Ave Lock Bag R *Web:* state.nj.us	Rahway	NJ	07065	732-499-5010	499-5022
New Jersey State Prison PO Box 861 *Web:* www.state.nj.us	Trenton	NJ	08625	609-292-9700	
South Woods State Prison 215 Burlington Rd S *Web:* state.nj.us	Bridgeton	NJ	08302	856-459-7000	459-7140
Southern State Correctional Facility 4295 N Delsea Dr	Delmont	NJ	08314	856-785-1300	785-1236

New Mexico

Facility	City	State	ZIP	Phone	Fax
Central New Mexico Correctional Facility 1525 Morris Rd	Los Lunas	NM	87031	505-865-1622	383-3510
Guadalupe County Correctional Facility S Hwy 54 PO Box 520 *Web:* geogroup.com	Santa Rosa	NM	88435	575-472-1001	
New Mexico Women's Correctional Facility 1700 Old US Hwy PO Box 800 *Web:* cd.nm.gov	Grants	NM	87020	505-287-2941	285-6828
Roswell Correctional Ctr 578 W Chickasaw Rd **Fax Area Code:* 505 ■ *Web:* cd.nm.gov/apd/rcc.html	Hagerman	NM	88232	575-625-3100	625-3190*
Southern New Mexico Correctional Facility 1983 Joe R Silva Blvd *Web:* cd.nm.gov/apd/snmcf.html	Las Cruces	NM	88004	575-523-3200	523-3349
Torrance County Detention Ctr 209 E Allen Ayers	Estancia	NM	87016	505-384-2711	

New York

Facility	City	State	ZIP	Phone	Fax
Adirondack Correctional Facility 196 Ray Brook Rd PO Box 110 *Web:* www.doccs.ny.gov	Ray Brook	NY	12977	518-891-1343	
Albion Correctional Facility 3595 State School Rd *Web:* nicic.gov	Albion	NY	14411	585-589-5511	
Altona Correctional Facility 555 Devil Den Rd *Web:* www.doccs.ny.gov/faclist.html	Altona	NY	12910	518-236-7841	
Arthur Kill Correctional Facility 2911 Arthur Kill Rd *Web:* metro.org	Staten Island	NY	10309	718-356-7333	
Attica Correctional Facility 639 Exchange St PO Box 149 *Web:* www.doccs.ny.gov/faclist.html	Attica	NY	14011	585-591-2000	
Auburn Correctional Facility 135 State St PO Box 618 *Web:* www.doccs.ny.gov/faclist.html	Auburn	NY	13021	315-253-8401	
Bare Hill Correctional Facility 181 Brand Rd	Malone	NY	12953	518-483-8411	483-8411
Bayview Correctional Facility 550 W 20th St *Web:* doccs.ny.gov	New York	NY	10011	212-255-7590	
Bedford Hills Correctional Facility 247 Harris Rd *Web:* www.doccs.ny.gov/faclist.html	Bedford Hills	NY	10507	914-241-3100	
Camp Georgetown Correctional Facility 3191 Crumbhill Rd	Georgetown	NY	13072	315-837-4446	
Cape Vincent Correctional Facility 36560 New York 12E	Cape Vincent	NY	13618	315-654-4100	654-4103
Cayuga Correctional Facility 2202 State Rt 38A PO Box 1150 *Web:* www.doccs.ny.gov	Moravia	NY	13118	315-497-1110	
Chateaugay Correctional Facility 7874 SR 11 PO Box 320 *Web:* doccs.ny.gov	Chateaugay	NY	12920	518-497-3300	
Clinton Correctional Facility 1156 Cook St *Web:* www.doccs.ny.gov/faclist.html	Dannemora	NY	12929	518-492-2511	
Collins Correctional Facility Middle Rd PO Box 490 *Web:* www.doccs.ny.gov	Collins	NY	14034	716-532-4588	
Coxsackie Correctional Facility 11260 Rt 9W PO Box 200 *Web:* www.doccs.ny.gov	Coxsackie	NY	12051	518-731-2781	
Eastern Correctional Facility 30 Institution Rd PO Box 338 *Web:* doccs.ny.gov	Napanoch	NY	12458	845-647-7400	
Elmira Correctional Facility 1879 Davis St *Web:* doccs.ny.gov	Elmira	NY	14901	607-734-3901	
Franklin Correctional Facility 62 Bare Hill Rd PO Box 10	Malone	NY	12953	518-483-6040	
Fulton Correctional Facility 1511 Fulton Ave	Bronx	NY	10457	718-583-8000	
Gouverneur Correctional Facility 112 Scotch Settlement Rd	Gouverneur	NY	13642	315-287-7351	287-7351
Gowanda Correctional Facility S Rd PO Box 350 *Web:* www.doccs.ny.gov	Gowanda	NY	14070	716-532-0177	
Great Meadow Correctional Facility 11739 SR 22 PO Box 51 *Web:* www.doccs.ny.gov/faclist.html	Comstock	NY	12821	518-639-5516	
Green Haven Correctional Facility 594 Rt 216 *Web:* www.doccs.ny.gov	Stormville	NY	12582	845-221-2711	
Greene Correctional Facility 165 Plank Rd PO Box 8 *Web:* www.doccs.ny.gov	Coxsackie	NY	12051	518-731-2741	
Lakeview Shock Incarceration Ctr 9300 Lake Ave PO Box T *Web:* ncjrs.gov	Brocton	NY	14716	716-792-7100	
Lincoln Correctional Facility 31-33 W 110th St *Web:* doccs.ny.gov	New York	NY	10026	212-860-9400	860-2099
Livingston Correctional Facility 7005 Sonyea Rd *Web:* doccs.ny.gov	Sonyea	NY	14556	585-658-3710	
Lyon Mountain Correctional Facility 3864 SR 374	Lyon Mountain	NY	12952	518-735-4546	
Marcy Correctional Facility 9000 Old River Rd	Marcy	NY	13403	315-768-1400	
Mid-State Correctional Facility PO Box 216 *Web:* www.prisontalk.com	Marcy	NY	13403	315-768-8581	
Moriah Shock Incarceration Correctional Facility 75 Burhart Ln PO Box 999 *Web:* www.doccs.ny.gov	Mineville	NY	12956	518-942-7561	
Oneida Correctional Facility 6100 School Rd	Rome	NY	13440	315-339-6880	
Orleans Correctional Facility 3531 Gaines Basin Rd	Albion	NY	14411	585-589-6820	
Riverview Correctional Facility 1110 Tibbits Dr PO Box 158 *Web:* doccs.ny.gov	Ogdensburg	NY	13669	315-393-8400	
Rochester Correctional Facility 470 Ford St	Rochester	NY	14608	585-454-2280	
Sing Sing Correctional Facility 354 Hunter St *Web:* www.doccs.ny.gov	Ossining	NY	10562	914-941-0108	
Southport Correctional Facility 236 Bob Masia Dr PO Box 2000 *Web:* www.doccs.ny.gov	Pine City	NY	14871	607-737-0850	
Sullivan Correctional Facility 325 Riverside Dr PO Box 116 *Web:* www.doccs.ny.gov	Fallsburg	NY	12733	845-434-2080	
Summit Correctional Facility 137 Eagle Heights Rd	Summit	NY	12175	518-287-1721	
Taconic Correctional Facility 250 Harris Rd **Fax Area Code:* 718 ■ *Web:* doccs.ny.gov	Bedford Hills	NY	10507	914-241-3010	722-6220*
Ulster Correctional Facility 750 Berme Rd	Napanoch	NY	12458	845-647-1670	
Upstate Correctional Facility 309 Bare Hill Rd PO Box 2000 *Web:* doccs.ny.gov	Malone	NY	12953	518-483-6997	
Wallkill Correctional Facility 50 McKendrick Rd *Web:* www.doccs.ny.gov/faclist.html	Wallkill	NY	12589	845-895-2021	
Washington Correctional Facility 72 Lock 11 Rd *Web:* www.doccs.ny.gov/faclist.html	Comstock	NY	12821	518-639-4486	
Watertown Correctional Facility 23147 Swan Rd	Watertown	NY	13601	315-782-7490	
Wende Correctional Facility 3040 Wende Rd PO Box 1187 *Web:* www.doccs.ny.gov/faclist.html	Alden	NY	14004	716-937-4000	
Wyoming Correctional Facility 3203 Dunbar Rd PO Box 501 *Web:* www.doccs.ny.gov/faclist.html	Attica	NY	14011	585-591-1010	

North Carolina

Facility	City	State	ZIP	Phone	Fax
Avery/Mitchell Correctional Ctr 600 Amity Pk Rd *Web:* doc.state.nc.us	Spruce Pine	NC	28777	828-765-0229	765-0946
Brown Creek Correctional Institution 248 Prison Camp Rd PO Box 310 *Web:* www.doc.state.nc.us	Polkton	NC	28135	704-694-2622	694-2709
Buncombe Correctional Ctr 2988 Riverside Dr *Web:* www.doc.state.nc.us	Asheville	NC	28804	828-645-7630	
Carteret Correctional Facility 1084 Orange St PO Box 220 *Web:* www.doc.state.nc.us	Newport	NC	28570	252-223-5100	223-3069
Catawba Correctional Ctr 1347 Prison Camp Rd	Newton	NC	28658	828-466-5521	466-5523
Central Prison 1300 Western Blvd *Web:* www.ncdps.gov/index2.cfm?a=000003,002240,002381,002252	Raleigh	NC	27606	919-733-0800	715-2645
Craggy Correctional Ctr 2992 Riverside Dr *Web:* ncdps.gov	Asheville	NC	28804	828-645-5315	658-2183
Davidson Correctional Ctr 1400 Thomason St *Web:* www.doc.state.nc.us	Lexington	NC	27292	336-249-7528	249-6962
Durham Correctional Ctr 3900 Guess Rd	Durham	NC	27705	919-477-2314	471-2257
Eastern Correctional Institution 2821 Hwy 903 N PO Box 215	Maury	NC	28554	252-747-8101	747-8260
Franklin Correctional Ctr 5918 NC 39 Hwy S PO Box 155 *Web:* www.ncdps.gov/index2.cfm?a=000003,002240,002381,002253	Bunn	NC	27508	919-496-6119	496-6032
Gaston Correctional Ctr 520 Justice Ct *Web:* www.doc.state.nc.us	Dallas	NC	28034	704-922-3861	922-1491

Facility	City	State	ZIP	Phone	Fax
Greene Correctional Institution 2699 Hwy 903 N PO Box 39 *Web:* doc.state.nc.us	Maury	NC	28554	252-747-3676	747-4432
Harnett Correctional Institution 1210 McNeil St. *Web:* www.ncdps.gov/index2.cfm?a=000003,002391,002934	Lillington	NC	27546	910-893-2751	893-6432
Hoke Correctional Institution 243 Old Hwy 211 *Web:* www.doc.state.nc.us	Raeford	NC	28376	910-944-7612	944-4752
Hyde Correctional Ctr 620 Prison Rd PO Box 278 *Web:* www.doc.state.nc.us	Swanquarter	NC	27885	252-926-1810	926-2306
Johnston Correctional Institution 2465 US 70 W	Smithfield	NC	27577	919-934-8386	934-9150
Lumberton Correctional Institution 75 Legend Rd *Web:* www.ncdps.gov	Lumberton	NC	28359	910-618-5574	
Nash Correctional Institution 2869 US 64 Alt PO Box 600 *Web:* www.ncdps.gov/Search.cfm?q=Nash+Correctional+Institution	Nashville	NC	27856	252-459-4455	459-7728
Neuse Correctional Institution 701 Stevens Mill Rd	Goldsboro	NC	27530	919-731-2023	
New Hanover Correctional Ctr 330 Div Dr. *Web:* www.doc.state.nc.us	Wilmington	NC	28402	910-251-2666	251-2670
North Carolina Correctional Institution for Women 1034 Bragg St. *Web:* doc.state.nc.us	Raleigh	NC	27610	919-733-4340	733-8031
North Piedmont Correctional Ctr for Women 1420 Raleigh Rd *Web:* www.doc.state.nc.us	Lexington	NC	27292	336-242-1259	
Odom Correctional Institution 485 Odom Prison Rd	Jackson	NC	27845	252-534-5611	574-2011
Orange Correctional Ctr 2110 Clarence Walters Rd	Hillsborough	NC	27278	919-732-9301	644-1395
Pasquotank Correctional Institution 527 Commerce Dr *Web:* ncdps.gov	Elizabeth City	NC	27906	252-331-4881	331-4866
Pender Correctional Institution 906 Penderlea Hwy *Web:* www.ncdps.gov	Burgaw	NC	28425	910-259-8735	
Raleigh Correctional Ctr for Women 1201 S State St.	Raleigh	NC	27610	919-733-4248	733-9737
Randolph Correctional Ctr 2760 US Hwy 220	Asheboro	NC	27205	336-625-2578	625-5717
Robeson Correctional Ctr 803 NC Hwy 711	Lumberton	NC	28359	910-618-5535	618-5532
Rowan Correctional Ctr 4750 S Main St PO Box 1207 *Web:* www.ncdps.gov	Salisbury	NC	28147	919-838-4000	733-8272
Rutherford Correctional Ctr 549 Ledbetter Rd *Web:* www.doc.state.nc.us	Spindale	NC	28160	828-286-4121	286-9285
Sampson Correctional Institution 700 NW Blvd Hwy 421N *Web:* www.ncdps.gov	Clinton	NC	28328	910-592-2151	592-2543
Sanford Correctional Ctr 417 Prison Camp Rd. *Web:* www.ncdps.gov/index2.cfm?a=000003,002240,002381,002297	Sanford	NC	27330	919-776-4325	774-1866
Southern Correctional Institution 272 Glen Rd PO Box 786 *Web:* www.ncdps.gov	Troy	NC	27371	910-572-3784	
Wake Correctional Ctr 1000 Rock Quarry Rd *TF:* 866-719-0108 ■ *Web:* ncdps.gov	Raleigh	NC	27610	919-733-7988	733-9166
Warren Correctional Institution 379 Collins Rd *TF:* 866-719-0108	Manson	NC	27553	252-456-3400	456-4300
Wilkes Correctional Ctr 404 Statesville Rd *Web:* wilkesprisonministry.org	North Wilkesboro	NC	28659	336-667-4533	

Ohio

Facility	City	State	ZIP	Phone	Fax
Allen Correctional Institution 770 W BRd St *Web:* www.drc.state.oh.us	Columbus	OH	43222	419-224-8000	224-5828
Dayton Correctional Institution 4104 Germantown St PO Box 17399 *Web:* www.drc.ohio.gov	Dayton	OH	45417	937-263-0060	263-1322
Grafton Correctional Institution 2500 S Avon Beldon Rd *Web:* drc.ohio.gov	Grafton	OH	44044	440-748-1161	748-2521
Lebanon Correctional Institution 3791 State Rt 63 PO Box 56 *Web:* www.drc.ohio.gov/public/leci.htm	Lebanon	OH	45036	513-932-1211	932-1320
London Correctional Institution 1580 SR 56 *Web:* www.drc.ohio.gov	London	OH	43140	740-852-2454	852-4854
Lorain Correctional Institution 2075 Avon Belden Rd *TF:* 888-988-4768 ■ *Web:* drc.ohio.gov	Grafton	OH	44044	440-748-1049	748-2191
Madison Correctional Institution 1851 State Rt 56 PO Box 740 *Web:* www.drc.ohio.gov	London	OH	43140	740-852-9777	852-3666
Mansfield Correctional Institution 1150 N Main St PO Box 788 *Web:* www.drc.ohio.gov	Mansfield	OH	44901	419-525-4455	524-8022
Marion Correctional Institution PO Box 57 *Web:* ohio.gov	Marion	OH	43302	740-382-5781	382-0595
Noble Correctional Institution 15708 McConnelsville Rd *Web:* drc.ohio.gov	Caldwell	OH	43724	740-732-5188	732-2651
North Central Correctional Institution 670 Marion Williamsport PO Box 1812 *Web:* www.drc.ohio.gov/public/ncci.htm	Marion	OH	43302	740-387-7040	387-5575
Ohio Reformatory for Women 1479 Collins Ave *Web:* drc.ohio.gov	Marysville	OH	43040	937-642-1065	642-7603
Ohio State Penitentiary 878 Coitsville HubbaRd Rd. *Web:* drc.ohio.gov	Youngstown	OH	44505	330-743-0700	742-5144
Pickaway Correctional Institution PO Box 209 *Web:* www.drc.ohio.gov	Orient	OH	43146	614-877-4362	877-4514
Richland Correctional Institution 1001 Olivesburg Rd *Web:* ohio.gov	Mansfield	OH	44905	419-526-2100	521-2810
Ross Correctional Institution 16149 SR 104 PO Box 7010 *Web:* drc.ohio.gov	Chillicothe	OH	45601	740-774-7050	774-7065
Southeastern Correctional Institution 5900 B I S Rd *Web:* ohio.gov	Lancaster	OH	43130	740-653-4324	653-0779
Southern Ohio Correctional Facility 1724 SR 728 PO Box 45699 *Web:* drc.ohio.gov	Lucasville	OH	45699	740-259-5544	259-2882
Toledo Correctional Institution 2001 E Central Ave PO Box 80033 *Web:* drc.ohio.gov	Toledo	OH	43608	419-726-7977	726-7157
Trumbull Correctional Institution 5701 Burnett Rd *Web:* drc.ohio.gov	Leavittsburg	OH	44430	330-898-0820	898-0848
Warren Correctional Institution 5787 S Rt 63 PO Box 120 *Web:* www.drc.ohio.gov	Lebanon	OH	45036	513-932-3388	933-0150

Oklahoma

Facility	City	State	ZIP	Phone	Fax
Cimarron Correctional Facility 3200 S Kings Hwy *Web:* www.cca.com	Cushing	OK	74023	918-225-3336	225-3363
Davis Correctional Facility 6888 E 133Rd Rd *Web:* cca.com	Holdenville	OK	74848	405-379-6400	379-6496
Great Plains Correctional Facility 700 Sugar Creek Dr *Web:* www.geogroup.com	Hinton	OK	73047	405-542-3711	
Howard McLeod Correctional Ctr 1970 E Whippoorwill Ln *Web:* www.ok.gov	Atoka	OK	74525	580-889-6651	889-2264
James Crabtree Correctional Ctr 216 N. Murray St *Web:* www.ok.gov	Helena	OK	73741	580-852-3221	
Jess Dunn Correctional Ctr PO Box 316 *Web:* www.ok.gov	Taft	OK	74463	918-682-7841	682-4372
John Lilley Correctional Ctr 105150 N 3670 Rd PO Box 407971 *Web:* www.ok.gov	Boley	OK	74829	918-667-3381	667-3959
Joseph Harp Correctional Ctr 16161 Moffat Rd PO Box 548 *Web:* www.ok.gov	Lexington	OK	73051	405-527-5593	527-4841
Lawton Correctional Facility 8607 SE Flower Mound Rd	Lawton	OK	73501	580-351-2778	351-2641
Mabel Bassett Correctional Ctr 29501 Kickapoo Rd	McLoud	OK	74851	405-964-3020	964-3014
Oklahoma State Penitentiary Corner of W & Stonewall PO Box 97 *Web:* www.ok.gov	McAlester	OK	74502	918-423-4700	423-3862
Oklahoma State Reformatory 1700 E First St PO Box 514 *Web:* www.ok.gov	Granite	OK	73547	580-480-3700	480-3997

Oregon

Facility	City	State	ZIP	Phone	Fax
Coffee Creek Correctional Facility 24499 SW Grahams Ferry Rd *Web:* www.oregon.gov	Wilsonville	OR	97070	503-570-6400	570-6417
Columbia River Correctional Institution 2575 Ctr St NE *Web:* www.oregon.gov	Salem	OR	97301	503-280-6646	280-6012
Oregon State Correctional Institution 3405 Deer Pk Dr SE *Web:* www.oregon.gov/doc/ops/prison/pages/osci.aspx	Salem	OR	97310	503-373-0101	378-8919
Oregon State Penitentiary 2575 Ctr St NE *Web:* oregon.gov	Salem	OR	97301	503-378-2453	378-3897
Powder River Correctional Facility 3600 13th St *Web:* oregon.gov	Baker City	OR	97814	541-523-6680	523-6678
Snake River Correctional Institution 777 Stanton Blvd *Web:* www.oregon.gov	Ontario	OR	97914	541-881-5000	881-5009
South Fork Forest Camp (SFFC) 48300 Wilson River Hwy *Web:* www.oregon.gov	Tillamook	OR	97317	503-842-2811	842-7943
Two Rivers Correctional Institution 82911 Beach Access Rd *Web:* oregon.gov	Umatilla	OR	97882	541-922-2001	

Pennsylvania

Facility	City	State	ZIP	Phone	Fax
Quehanna Motivational Boot Camp 4395 Quehanna Hwy Staff. *Web:* www.portal.state.pa.us/portal/server.pt/community/hide_quehanna/11404	Karthaus	PA	16845	814-263-4125	
SCI-Coal Township 1 Kelley Dr. *TF:* 800-322-4472	Coal Township	PA	17866	570-644-7890	
SCI-Dallas 1000 Follies Rd. *Web:* www.cor.pa.gov/facilities/stateprisons/pages/dallas.aspx#.v3tgxfnr_iu	Dallas	PA	18612	570-675-1101	820-4842
SCI-Graterford PO Box 246 **Fax Area Code: 484* ■ *Web:* www.portal.state.pa.us	Graterford	PA	19426	610-489-4151	961-7907*

	City	State	Zip	Phone	Fax
SCI-Greene 169 Progress Dr Staff	Waynesburg	PA	15370	724-852-2902	
Web: www.portal.state.pa.us/portal/server.pt/community/hide_greene/11373					
SCI-Greensburg 165 SCI Ln	Greensburg	PA	15601	724-837-4397	
Web: www.portal.state.pa.us					
SCI-Houtzdale PO Box 1000	Houtzdale	PA	16698	814-378-1000	
Web: www.portal.state.pa.us					
SCI-Huntingdon 1100 Pike St	Huntingdon	PA	16652	814-643-2400	946-7380
SCI-Mahanoy 301 Morea Rd	Frackville	PA	17932	570-773-2158	
SCI-Muncy PO Box 180	Muncy	PA	17756	570-546-3171	
Web: www.portal.state.pa.us					
SCI-Pittsburgh 3001 Beaver Rd	Pittsburgh	PA	15233	412-761-1955	766-8225
Web: www.cor.pa.gov/Facilities/CommunityCorrections/Pages/RegionIIIFacilities.aspx#.Vd7L7Ha1Gko					
SCI-Retreat 660 SR 11	Hunlock Creek	PA	18621	570-735-8754	733-1041
Web: portal.state.pa.us					
SCI-Rockview 1 Rockview Pl PO Box A	Bellefonte	PA	16823	814-355-4874	355-6026
Web: www.portal.state.pa.us					
SCI-Smithfield 1120 Pike St PO Box 999	Huntingdon	PA	16652	814-643-6520	
Web: www.portal.state.pa.us					
SCI-Somerset 1590 Walters Mill Rd	Somerset	PA	15510	814-443-8100	443-8137
SCI-Waymart PO Box 256 Ste 6	Waymart	PA	18472	570-488-5811	
Web: www.portal.state.pa.us/portal/server.pt/community/hide_waymart/11432					
State Correctional Institution of Albion 10745 Rt 18	Albion	PA	16475	814-756-5778	756-9737
Web: portal.state.pa.us					

Rhode Island

	City	State	Zip	Phone	Fax
Donald W Wyatt Detention Facility 950 High St	Central Falls	RI	02863	401-729-1190	729-1194
Web: www.wyattdetention.com					

South Carolina

	City	State	Zip	Phone	Fax
Allendale Correctional Institution 1057 Revolutionary Trl PO Box 1151	Fairfax	SC	29827	803-632-2561	632-2498
Web: doc.sc.gov					
Broad River Correctional Institution 4460 Broad River Rd	Columbia	SC	29210	803-896-2234	
Web: www.doc.sc.gov					
Evans Correctional Institution 610 Hwy 9 W	Bennettsville	SC	29512	843-479-4181	896-4977*
**Fax Area Code:* 803 ■ *Web:* doc.sc.gov					
Goodman Correctional Institution 4556 Broad River Rd	Columbia	SC	29210	803-896-8565	896-1671
TF: 866-230-7761 ■ *Web:* doc.sc.gov					
Kershaw Correctional Institution 4848 Gold Mine Hwy	Kershaw	SC	29067	803-896-3301	
Web: www.doc.sc.gov					
Kirkland Correctional Institution 4344 Broad River Rd	Columbia	SC	29210	803-896-1521	896-1766
Web: doc.sc.gov					
Leath Correctional Institution 2809 Airport Rd	Greenwood	SC	29649	864-229-5709	896-1766*
**Fax Area Code:* 803 ■ *Web:* doc.sc.gov					
Lee Correctional Institution 990 Wisacky Hwy	Bishopville	SC	29010	803-428-2800	896-1766
TF: 877-846-3472					
Lieber Correctional Institution PO Box 205	Ridgeville	SC	29472	843-875-3332	
Web: www.doc.sc.gov/institutions/lieber.jsp					
MacDougall Correctional Institution 1516 Old GilliaRd Rd	Ridgeville	SC	29472	843-688-5251	688-4047
Web: doc.sc.gov					
McCormick Correctional Institution 386 Redemption Way	McCormick	SC	29899	864-443-2114	443-2114
Web: doc.sc.gov					
Stevenson Correctional Institution 4546 Broad River Rd	Columbia	SC	29210	803-896-8575	896-1222
Web: doc.sc.gov					
Trenton Correctional Institution 84 Greenhouse Rd	Trenton	SC	29847	803-896-3000	
Web: www.doc.sc.gov					
Turbeville Correctional Institution PO Box 252	Turbeville	SC	29162	843-659-4800	
Web: www.doc.sc.gov/institutions/turbeville.jsp					
Walden Correctional Institution 4340 Broad River Rd	Columbia	SC	29210	803-896-8580	896-1225
Web: doc.sc.gov					
Women's Correctional Institution 4450 Broad River Rd	Columbia	SC	29210	803-896-8590	896-1226

South Dakota

	City	State	Zip	Phone	Fax
Jameson Annex 1600 N Dr PO Box 5911	Sioux Falls	SD	57117	605-367-5051	367-5585
Web: www.doc.sd.gov					
Mike Durfee State Prison 1412 Wood St	Springfield	SD	57062	605-369-2201	369-2813
TF: 800-537-0025 ■ *Web:* doc.sd.gov					
South Dakota State Penitentiary 1600 N Dr PO Box 5911	Sioux Falls	SD	57117	605-367-5051	367-5038
Web: doc.sd.gov					

Tennessee

	City	State	Zip	Phone	Fax
Hardeman County Correctional Facility 2520 Union Springs Rd PO Box 549	Whiteville	TN	38075	731-254-6000	254-6060
Web: www.cca.com					
Northeast Correctional Complex 5249 Hwy 67 W PO Box 5000	Mountain City	TN	37683	423-727-7387	727-5415
Web: tn.gov					
Northwest Correctional Complex 960 SR 212	Tiptonville	TN	38079	731-253-5000	253-5150
Web: tn.gov					
Riverbend Maximum Security Institution 7475 Cockrill Bend Blvd	Nashville	TN	37243	615-350-3100	350-3400
TF: 800-770-8277 ■ *Web:* tn.gov					
South Central Correctional Facility 555 Forest Ave PO Box 279	Clifton	TN	38425	931-676-5372	676-5104
Web: www.state.tn.us					
Tennessee Prison for Women 3881 Stewarts Ln	Nashville	TN	37243	615-741-1255	
Web: tn.gov					
Wayne County Boot Camp PO Box 182	Clifton	TN	38425	931-676-3345	
TF: 855-876-7283 ■ *Web:* www.tennessee.gov					
West Tennessee State Penitentiary 480 Green Chapel Rd PO Box 1150	Henning	TN	38041	731-738-5044	
Web: www.tn.gov					

Texas

	City	State	Zip	Phone	Fax
Bartlett State Jail 1018 Arnold Dr	Bartlett	TX	76511	254-527-3300	527-4489
Bradshaw State Jail 3900 W Loop 571 N PO Box 9000	Henderson	TX	75653	903-655-0880	655-0500
Web: www.cca.com					
Cole State Jail 3801 Silo Rd	Bonham	TX	75418	903-583-1100	583-7903
Web: tdcj.state.tx.us					
Criminal Justice Department 3901 State Jail Rd	El Paso	TX	79938	915-856-0046	849-4795
Dominguez State Jail 6535 Cagnon Rd	San Antonio	TX	78252	210-675-6620	677-0316
Web: tdcj.state.tx.us					
Hutchins State Jail 1500 E Langdon Rd	Dallas	TX	75241	972-225-1304	
Web: tdcj.state.tx.us					
Kegans State Jail 707 Top St	Houston	TX	77002	713-224-6584	224-6212
Web: tdcj.state.tx.us					
Lindsey State Jail 1620 FM 3344	Jacksboro	TX	76458	940-567-2272	567-2292
Web: tdcj.state.tx.us					
Lopez State Jail 1203 El Cibolo Rd	Edinburg	TX	78542	956-316-3810	316-7447
Web: tdcj.state.tx.us					
Lychner State Jail 2350 Atascocita Rd	Humble	TX	77396	281-454-5036	454-4163
Plane State Jail 904 FM 686	Dayton	TX	77535	936-258-2476	257-4449
Web: tdcj.state.tx.us					
Travis County State Jail 8101 FM 969	Austin	TX	78724	512-926-4482	
Web: tdcj.state.tx.us					
Willacy County State Jail 1695 S Buffalo Dr	Raymondville	TX	78580	956-689-4900	689-4001
Woodman State Jail 1210 Coryell City Rd	Gatesville	TX	76528	254-865-9398	
Web: tdcj.state.tx.us					

Utah

	City	State	Zip	Phone	Fax
Central Utah Correctional Facility 255 East 300 North	Gunnison	UT	84634	435-528-6000	528-6051
Web: corrections.utah.gov					
Iron County Utah State Correctional Facility 2136 N Main St	Cedar City	UT	84721	435-867-7555	
Web: ironsheriff.net					
Utah State Prison 14425 Bitterbrush Ln	Draper	UT	84020	801-576-7000	
Web: corrections.utah.gov					

Vermont

	City	State	Zip	Phone	Fax
Chittenden Regional Correctional Facility 7 Farrell St	South Burlington	VT	05403	802-863-7356	863-7473
Web: www.doc.state.vt.us					
Northeast Regional Correctional Facility 1270 W Rt 5	Saint Johnsbury	VT	05819	802-748-8151	748-6604
Northern State Correctional Facility 2559 Glen Rd	Newport	VT	05855	802-334-3364	334-3367
Web: vermont.gov					
Northwest State Correctional Facility 3649 Lower Newton Rd	Swanton	VT	05488	802-524-6771	527-7534
Web: doc.state.vt.us					
Southeast State Correctional Facility 546 State Farm Rd	Windsor	VT	05089	802-674-6717	674-2249
Web: www.doc.state.vt.us					

Virginia

	City	State	Zip	Phone	Fax
Augusta Correctional Ctr 1821 Estaline Vly Rd	Craigsville	VA	24430	540-997-7000	997-7017
Web: vadoc.virginia.gov					
Bland Correctional Ctr 256 Bland Farm Rd	Bland	VA	24315	276-688-3341	
Web: vadoc.virginia.gov					
Buckingham Correctional Ctr 1349 Correctional Ctr Rd	Dillwyn	VA	23936	434-391-5980	983-1752
Web: vadoc.virginia.gov					
Deep Meadow Correctional Ctr 3500 Woods Way	State Farm	VA	23160	804-598-5503	
Web: vadoc.virginia.gov					
Deerfield Correctional Ctr 21360 Deerfield Dr	Capron	VA	23829	434-658-4368	850-8488*
**Fax Area Code:* 870 ■ *TF:* 800-560-4292					
Greensville Correctional Ctr 901 Corrections Way	Jarratt	VA	23870	434-535-7000	535-7640
Web: vadoc.virginia.gov					

Phone | Fax

Haynesville Correctional Ctr
421 Barnfield Rd PO Box 129 ... Haynesville VA 22472 804-333-3577
Web: www.vadoc.virginia.gov
Lawrenceville Correctional Ctr
1607 Planters Rd ... Lawrenceville VA 23868 434-848-9349 848-0232
Web: vadoc.virginia.gov
Lunenburg Correctional Ctr
690 Falls Rd PO Box 1424 ... Victoria VA 23974 434-696-2045
Web: vadoc.virginia.gov
Nottoway Correctional Ctr
2892 Schutt Rd PO Box 488 ... Burkeville VA 23922 434-767-5543
Web: vadoc.virginia.gov
Red Onion State Prison
10800 H Jack Rose Hwy PO Box 970 ... Pound VA 24279 276-796-7510
Web: vadoc.virginia.gov
Saint Brides Correctional Ctr
701 Sanderson Rd ... Chesapeake VA 23322 757-421-6600
Sussex I State Prison 24414 Musselwhite Dr ... Waverly VA 23891 804-834-9967 834-9995
Web: vadoc.state.va.us
Sussex II State Prison 24427 Musselwhite Dr ... Waverly VA 23891 804-834-2678 834-4073
Web: vadoc.state.va.us
Virginia Department of Corrections
12352 Coffeewood Dr ... Mitchells VA 22729 540-829-6483
Web: vadoc.state.va.us
Wallens Ridge State Prison
272 Dogwood Dr PO Box 759 ... Big Stone Gap VA 24219 276-523-3310
Web: vadoc.virginia.gov

Washington

Phone | Fax

Airway Heights Corrections Ctr
11919 W Sprague Ave PO Box 1899 ... Airway Heights WA 99001 509-244-6700 244-6710
Web: www.doc.wa.gov
Cedar Creek Correctional Ctr
12200 Bordeaux Rd PO Box 37 ... Littlerock WA 98556 360-359-4100
Web: www.doc.wa.gov/facilities/prison/cccc
Clallam Bay Corrections Ctr
1830 Eagle Crest Way ... Clallam Bay WA 98326 360-963-2000 963-3292
Web: doc.wa.gov
Coyote Ridge Corrections Ctr
1301 N Ephrata St ... Connell WA 99326 509-543-5800 543-5801
Web: www.doc.wa.gov
Hawaii Health Matters PO Box 88900 ... Steilacoom WA 98388 253-512-6600
Web: www.hawaiihealthmatters.org
Larch Corrections Ctr 15314 NE Dole Vly Rd ... Yacolt WA 98675 360-260-6300 686-3892
Web: doc.wa.gov
Olympic Corrections Ctr 11235 Hoh Mainline ... Forks WA 98331 360-374-6181
Web: doc.wa.gov
Washington Corrections Ctr for Women
9601 Bujacich Rd NW ... Gig Harbor WA 98332 253-858-4200 858-4289
Washington State Penitentiary
1313 N 13th Ave ... Walla Walla WA 99362 509-525-3610
Web: doc.wa.gov
Washington State Reformatory
16550 177th Ave SE PO Box 777 ... Monroe WA 98272 360-794-2600
Web: www.doc.wa.gov

West Virginia

Phone | Fax

Denmar Correctional Ctr HC 64 PO Box 125 ... Hillsboro WV 24946 304-653-4201 653-4855
Web: wvdoc.com
Mount Olive Correctional Complex
1 Mtnside Way ... Mount Olive WV 25185 304-442-7213 442-7225
Northern Regional Correctional Facility
112 Northern Regional Correctional Dr ... Moundsville WV 26041 304-843-4067 843-4073
TF: 866-984-8463 ■ *Web:* www.wvdoc.com
Pruntytown Correctional Ctr PO Box 159 ... Grafton WV 26354 304-265-6111 265-6120
Web: www.wvdoc.com
Saint Mary's Correctional Ctr
2880 N Pleasants Hwy ... Saint Marys WV 26170 304-684-5500 684-5506
Web: www.wvdoc.com/wvdoc/prisonsandfacilities/saintmaryscorrectionalcenter/tabid/56/default.aspx

Wisconsin

Phone | Fax

Columbia Correctional Institution
2925 Columbia Dr PO Box 950 ... Portage WI 53901 608-742-9100 742-9111
Web: doc.wi.gov
Fox Lake Correctional Institution
PO Box 147 ... Fox Lake WI 53933 920-928-3151 928-6929
Web: doc.wi.gov
Green Bay Correctional Institution
2833 Riverside Dr ... Green Bay WI 54307 920-432-4877 432-5388
Web: doc.wi.gov
Kettle Moraine Correctional Institution
PO Box 31 ... Plymouth WI 53073 920-526-3244 526-3989
Web: doc.wi.gov
Oakhill Correctional Institution
5212 County Hwy M PO Box 140 ... Oregon WI 53575 608-835-3101 835-6082
Web: doc.wi.gov/familiesvisitors/findfacility/oakhillcorrectionalinstitution
Oshkosh Correctional Institution
1730 W Snell Rd PO Box 3530 ... Oshkosh WI 54903 920-231-4010 236-2615
Web: doc.wi.gov
Prairie du Chien Correctional Institution
500 E Parrish St ... Prairie du Chien WI 53821 608-326-7828 326-5960
Web: doc.wi.gov
Racine Correctional Institution
2019 Wisconsin St ... Sturtevant WI 53177 262-886-3214 886-3514
Web: doc.wi.gov
Taycheedah Correctional Institution (WWCS)
751 County Rd PO Box 1947 ... Fond Du Lac WI 54935 920-929-3800 929-2946
Web: doc.wi.gov
Waupun Correctional Institution
200 S Madison St ... Waupun WI 53963 920-324-5571 324-7250
Web: doc.wi.gov/familiesvisitors/findfacility/waupuncorrectionalinstitution
Wisconsin Secure Program Facility
1101 Morrison Dr ... Boscobel WI 53805 608-375-5656 375-5595

Wyoming

Phone | Fax

Honor Conservation Camp 40 Pippin Rd ... Newcastle WY 82701 307-746-4436 746-9316
Wyoming Honor Farm 40 Honor Farm Rd ... Riverton WY 82501 307-856-9578 856-2505
Wyoming State Penitentiary 2900 S Higley Rd ... Rawlins WY 82301 307-328-1442
Wyoming Women's Ctr 1000 W Griffith PO Box 300 ... Lusk WY 82225 307-334-3693 334-2254
Web: doc.state.wy.us

214 COSMETICS, SKIN CARE, AND OTHER PERSONAL CARE PRODUCTS

See Also Perfumes p. 2926

Phone | Fax

AHAVA North America 330 7th Avenue ... New York NY 10001 800-366-7254
TF: 800-366-7254 ■ *Web:* www.ahavaus.com
Aire-Master of America Inc 1821 N State Hwy Cc ... Nixa MO 65714 417-725-2691 725-5737
TF: 800-525-0957 ■ *Web:* www.airemaster.com
Apothecary Products
11750 12th Ave S Burnsville ... Burnsville MN 55337 800-328-2742 328-1584
TF: 800-328-2742 ■ *Web:* www.apothecaryproducts.com
Arizona Natural Resources
2525 E BeaRdsley Rd ... Phoenix AZ 85050 602-569-6900 569-9697
Web: www.arizonanaturalresources.com
At Last Naturals Inc 401 Columbus Ave ... Valhalla NY 10595 800-527-8123 747-3791*
**Fax Area Code:* 914 ■ *TF:* 800-527-8123 ■ *Web:* www.atlastnaturals.com
Autumn Harp Inc 26 Thompson Dr ... Essex Junction VT 05452 802-857-4600 857-4601
Web: www.autumnharp.com
Aveda Corp 4000 Pheasant Ridge Dr ... Blaine MN 55449 763-951-4000 783-4110
TF: 800-644-4831 ■ *Web:* www.aveda.com
Avon Products Inc 1345 Ave of the Americas ... New York NY 10017 212-282-7000
NYSE: AVP ■ *TF Cust Svc:* 800-367-2866 ■ *Web:* www.avon.com
Bath & Body Works 7 Limited Pkwy E ... Reynoldsburg OH 43068 800-395-1001
TF: 800-395-1001 ■ *Web:* www.bathandbodyworks.com
Bath-and-Body.com 1073 Exchange St ... Boise ID 83716 208-345-5136
BeautiControl Inc
2121 Midway Rd PO Box 815189 ... Carrollton TX 75006 800-232-8841 960-7923*
**Fax Area Code:* 972 ■ **Fax:* Sales ■ *TF:* 800-232-8841 ■ *Web:* shop.beauticontrol.com
Belcam Inc Delagar Div 27 Montgomery St ... Rouses Point NY 12979 518-297-3366 297-3366
TF: 800-328-3006 ■ *Web:* www.belcamshop.com
BeneFit Cosmetics 225 Bush St ... San Francisco CA 94104 415-781-8153
TF Cust Svc: 800-781-2336 ■ *Web:* www.benefitcosmetics.com
Body Shop, The 5036 One World Way ... Wake Forest NC 27587 919-554-4900
Web: www.thebodyshop.in
Borghese Inc 3 E 54th St 20th Fl ... New York NY 10022 212-659-5300
Web: www.borghese.com
Bradford Soap Works Inc
200 Providence St ... West Warwick RI 02893 401-821-2141 821-1660
Web: www.bradfordsoap.com
Bronner Bros Inc 2141 Powers Ferry Rd ... Marietta GA 30067 770-988-0015 953-0848
TF: 800-241-6151 ■ *Web:* www.bronnerbros.com
CBI Laboratories 4201 Diplomacy Rd ... Fort Worth TX 76155 972-241-7546 352-1094*
**Fax Area Code:* 800 ■ *TF:* 800-822-7546 ■ *Web:* www.cbiskincare.com
CCA Industries Inc
200 Murray Hill Pkwy ... East Rutherford NJ 07073 201-935-3232
NYSE: CAW ■ *TF Cust Svc:* 800-524-2720 ■ *Web:* www.ccaindustries.com
Chattem Inc 1715 W 38th St PO Box 2219 ... Chattanooga TN 37409 423-821-4571 821-0395
Web: www.chattem.com
Church & Dwight Company Inc
469 N Harrison St ... Princeton NJ 08543 609-683-5900
NYSE: CHD ■ *Web:* www.churchdwight.com
Clinique Laboratories Inc
767 Fifth Ave 37th Fl ... New York NY 10153 212-572-3983
TF: 800-419-4041 ■ *Web:* www.clinique.com
Color Factory, The 11312 Penrose St ... Sun Valley CA 91352 818-767-2889 767-4062
Combe Inc 1101 Westchester Ave ... White Plains NY 10604 914-694-5454
TF: 800-431-2610 ■ *Web:* www.combe.com
Cosmetic Essence Inc 2182 Hwy 35 ... Holmdel NJ 07733 732-888-7788 888-6086
Web: www.cosmeticessence.com
Cosmolab Inc 1100 Garrett Pkwy ... Lewisburg TN 37091 931-359-6253 359-8465
Cosrich Group Inc 12243 Branford St ... Sun Valley CA 91352 818-686-2500 897-7590
Web: www.ouchiesonline.com
Coty Inc 2 Pk Ave 17th Fl ... New York NY 10016 212-389-7300
Web: www.coty.com
Crabtree & Evelyn Ltd 102 Peake Brook Rd ... Woodstock CT 06281 860-928-2761 928-1296
TF: 800-272-2873 ■ *Web:* www.crabtree-evelyn.com
DEB Inc 2815 Coliseum Centre Dr Ste 600 ... Charlotte NC 28217 704-263-4240 263-9601
TF: 800-248-7190 ■ *Web:* www.debgroup.com
Farouk Systems Inc 250 Pennbright Dr ... Houston TX 77090 281-876-2000
TF: 800-237-9175 ■ *Web:* www.farouk.com
Forever Living Products International Inc
7501 E McCormick Pkwy ... Scottsdale AZ 85258 480-998-8888 905-8451
TF: 888-440-2563 ■ *Web:* www.foreverliving.com
Fruit of The Earth Inc
3101 High Rver Rd Ste 175 ... Fort Worth TX 76155 972-790-0808 790-1322
Web: www.fote.com
GOJO Industries Inc 1 GOJO Plz Ste 500 ... Akron OH 44311 330-255-6000 329-4656*
**Fax Area Code:* 800 ■ *TF:* 800-321-9647 ■ *Web:* www.gojo.com
Guest Supply Inc
4301 US Hwy 1 PO Box 902 ... Monmouth Junction NJ 08852 609-514-9696 514-2692
TF Cust Svc: 800-446-7819 ■ *Web:* www.guestsupply.com
Gurwitch Products LLC 8 Greenway Plz Ste 7 ... Houston TX 77046 281-275-7000
TF: 888-637-2437 ■ *Web:* www.gurwitchproducts.com
H2O Plus Inc 845 W Madison St ... Chicago IL 60607 312-850-9283 633-1440
TF Cust Svc: 800-242-2284 ■ *Web:* www.h2oplus.com

Phone Fax

Hillshire Brands 2200 W Don Tyson Pkwy ....Springdale AR 72762 479-290-6397
TF: 800-323-7117 ■ *Web:* www.tysonfoods.com/hillshire-brands.aspx
Imperial Distributors Inc 33 Sword St .... Auburn MA 01501 508-756-5156 756-0085
Web: www.imperialdist.com
Jafra Cosmetics International
2451 Townsgate Rd .... Westlake Village CA 91361 805-449-3000 449-3253
TF: 800-551-2345 ■ *Web:* www.jafra.com
Jan Marini Skin Research Inc
6951 Via Del Oro .... San Jose CA 95119 408-362-0130 362-0140
TF: 800-347-2223 ■ *Web:* www.janmarini.com
John Amico Haircare Products
4731 W 136th St..................................Crestwood IL 60445 708-824-4000
TF: 800-676-5264 ■ *Web:* www.johnamico.com
John Paul Mitchell Systems
1888 Century Park E ste 1600 ....Los Angeles CA 90067 800-793-8790
TF Cust Svc: 800-793-8790 ■ *Web:* www.paulmitchell.com
Johnson & Johnson Consumer Products Co
199 Grandview Rd .... Skillman NJ 08558 908-874-1000
TF: 866-565-2229 ■ *Web:* www.johnsonsbaby.com
Johnson & Johnson Inc 7101 Notre-Dame E........... Montreal QC H1N2G4 514-251-5100
TF: 800-361-8990 ■ *Web:* www.jnjcanada.com
Key West Aloe 13095 N Telecom Pkwy.................... Tampa FL 33637 800-445-2563
TF: 800-445-2563 ■ *Web:* www.keywestaloe.com
Kolmar Laboratories Inc 20 W King St..............Port Jervis NY 12771 845-856-5311 856-0640
Web: www.kolmar.com
L Brands Inc 3 Limited Pkwy .... Columbus OH 43230 614-415-7000
NYSE: LTD ■ *Web:* lb.com
L'Oreal USA 575 Fifth Ave ....New York NY 10017 212-818-1500
TF: 800-322-2036 ■ *Web:* www.lorealusa.com
Lee Pharmaceuticals Inc
1434 Santa Anita Ave .... South El Monte CA 91733 626-442-3141 442-6994
OTC: LPHM
Luster Products Inc 1104 W 43rd St ....Chicago IL 60609 773-579-1800 579-1912
TF: 800-621-4255 ■ *Web:* www.lusterproducts.com
Mana Products Inc 32-02 Queens Blvd .... Long Island NY 11101 718-361-2550 786-3204
Web: www.manaproducts.com
Markwins International Corp
22067 Ferrero Pkwy ....Walnut CA 91789 909-595-8898
Web: www.markwins.com
Mary Kay Inc PO Box 799045 .... Dallas TX 75379 972-687-6300 687-1608*
**Fax:* Cust Svc ■ *TF Cust Svc:* 800-627-9529 ■ *Web:* www.marykay.com
Maybelline New York
575 Fifth Ave PO Box 1010.........................New York NY 10017 800-944-0730
TF: 800-944-0730 ■ *Web:* www.maybelline.com
Merle Norman Cosmetics Inc
9130 Bellanca Ave ....Los Angeles CA 90045 310-641-3000 641-7144
TF: 800-421-6648 ■ *Web:* www.merlenorman.com
Neutrogena Corp 5760 W 96th St..................Los Angeles CA 90045 310-642-1150
TF: 800-582-4048 ■ *Web:* www.neutrogena.com
Nutramax Laboratories Inc
2208 Lakeside Blvd .... Edgewood MD 21040 410-776-4000
TF: 800-925-5187 ■ *Web:* www.nutramaxlabs.com
Obagi Medical Products Inc
3760 Kilroy Airport Way Ste 500 .... Long Beach CA 90806 562-628-1007 628-1008
TF: 800-636-7546 ■ *Web:* www.obagi.com
Origins Natural Resources Inc 767 Fifth Ave..........New York NY 10153 800-674-4467
TF Cust Svc: 800-674-4467 ■ *Web:* www.origins.com
Orly International Inc 7710 Haskell Ave ....Los Angeles CA 91406 818-994-1001 994-1144
Web: www.orlybeauty.com
Paramount Cosmetics Inc 93 Entin Rd Ste 4 .... Clifton NJ 07014 973-472-2323 472-5005
TF: 800-522-9880 ■ *Web:* www.paramountcosmetics.net
Person & Covey Inc 616 Allen Ave.................. Glendale CA 91201 800-423-2341 547-9821*
**Fax Area Code:* 818 ■ *TF:* 800-423-2341 ■ *Web:* www.personandcovey.com
Personal Products Co
1 Johnson & Johnson Plaza.................. New Brunswick NJ 08933 732-524-0400
Web: www.jnj.com/our_company/family_of_companies
Peter Thomas Roth Labs LLC
460 Pk Ave 16th Fl.................................New York NY 10022 212-581-5800 581-5810
Web: www.peterthomasroth.com
Pfizer Inc 235 E 42nd St..........................New York NY 10017 212-733-2323 573-7851
NYSE: PFE ■ *TF:* 800-879-3477 ■ *Web:* www.pfizer.com
Philosophy Inc 3809 E Watkins.......................Phoenix AZ 85034 800-568-3151 736-0600*
**Fax Area Code:* 480 ■ *TF:* 800-568-3151 ■ *Web:* www.philosophy.com
Prescriptives Inc 767 Fifth Ave ....New York NY 10153 866-290-6471
TF: 866-290-6471 ■ *Web:* www.prescriptives.com
Prestige Brands International Inc
660 White Plains Rd Ste 250 .... Tarrytown NY 10591 914-524-6800 524-6815
Web: www.prestigebrandsinc.com
Prestige Cosmetics Corp 1601 Green Rd....... Pompano Beach FL 33064 954-480-9202 480-9220
Web: www.prestigecosmetics.com
Qosmedix 2002 Orville Dr N..................... Ronkonkoma NY 11779 631-242-3270 242-3291
Web: www.qosmedix.com
Revlon Consumer Products Corp
1501 Williamsboro St............................... Oxford NC 27565 212-527-4000
TF: 800-473-8566 ■ *Web:* www.revlon.com
Rozelle Cosmetics 4260 Loop Rd .... Westfield VT 05874 802-744-2270 744-2236
TF: 800-451-4216 ■ *Web:* www.rozelle.com
Scolding Locks Corp 1520 W Rogers Ave .... Appleton WI 54914 920-733-5561
Sebastian International Inc
6109 DeSoto Ave .... Woodland Hills CA 91367 818-999-5112
Web: wellainteractive.com
sephora.com Inc
525 Market St 1st Market Twr 32nd Fl .... San Francisco CA 94105 415-284-3300
TF Cust Svc: 877-737-4672 ■ *Web:* www.sephora.com
SkinMedica Inc 5770 Armada Dr .... Carlsbad CA 92008 760-448-3600
Sothys USA Inc 1500 NW 94th Ave........................ Miami FL 33172 305-594-4222 592-5785
TF: 800-325-0503 ■ *Web:* www.sothys-usa.com
Star Nail Products Inc 29120 Ave Paine ....Valencia CA 91355 661-257-7827 257-5856
TF: 800-762-6245 ■ *Web:* www.starnail.com
Tom's of Maine Inc 302 Lafayette Ctr.............. Kennebunk ME 04043 800-985-3874
TF: 800-367-8667 ■ *Web:* www.tomsofmaine.com
Twincraft Inc 2 Tigan St ....Winooski VT 05404 802-655-2200
Web: www.twincraft.com

Phone Fax

ULTA Beauty 1000 Remington Blvd Ste 120 ....Bolingbrook IL 60440 630-410-4800 226-8210
TF: 866-983-8582 ■ *Web:* www.ulta.com
Urban Decay 833 W 16th St.................... Newport Beach CA 92663 949-631-4504
TF: 800-784-8722 ■ *Web:* www.urbandecay.com
Vi-Jon Labs Inc 8515 Page Ave.................... Saint Louis MO 63114 314-427-1000 427-1010
Web: www.vijon.com
Victoria Vogue Inc 90 Southland Dr .... Bethlehem PA 18017 610-865-1500 865-6089
Web: businessfinder.lehighvalleylive.com
Wahl Clipper Corp 2900 Locust St .... Sterling IL 61081 800-767-9245 625-0091*
**Fax Area Code:* 815 ■ *TF:* 800-767-9245 ■ *Web:* www.wahl.com
WE Bassett Co 100 Trap Falls Rd Ext .... Shelton CT 06484 203-929-8483 929-8963
Web: www.trim.com
Wella Corp 6109 DeSoto Ave.................. Woodland Hills CA 91367 818-999-5112
TF: 800-829-4422 ■ *Web:* www.wella.com
Zotos International Inc 100 Tokeneke Rd .... Darien CT 06820 203-655-8911 656-7784
TF: 888-242-4247 ■ *Web:* www.zotos.com

215 CREDIT CARD PROVIDERS & RELATED SERVICES

Companies listed here include those that issue credit cards as well as companies that provide services to these companies (i.e., rewards programs, theft prevention, etc.).

Phone Fax

Advanta Medical Solutions LLC
10830 Guilford Rd Ste 312................. Annapolis Junction MD 20701 240-554-1200
Web: www.advantamedicalsolutions.com
American Advisors Group
3800 W Chapman Ave 3rd Fl.........................Orange CA 92868 949-724-1707
Web: www.aag.com
American Express Company Inc
World Financial Ctr 200 Vesey St....................New York NY 10285 212-640-2000 640-0404
NYSE: AXP ■ *TF:* 800-528-4800 ■ *Web:* www.americanexpress.com
Applied Card Systems 50 Applied Card Way.......... Glen Mills PA 19342 866-227-5627 840-2758*
**Fax Area Code:* 484 ■ *TF:* 866-227-5627 ■ *Web:* www.appliedcard.com
Bank of America Card Services
1 Commercial Pl 2nd Fl .... Norfolk VA 23510 757-441-4770
TF: 800-732-9194 ■ *Web:* locators.bankofamerica.com
Capital One Financial Corp
1680 Capital One Dr................................McLean VA 22102 800-926-1000 290-7335*
NYSE: COF ■ **Fax Area Code:* 877 ■ *TF:* 800-655-2265 ■ *Web:* www.capitalone.com
Celtic Financial Group LLC
60 Cutter Mill Rd Ste 402.........................Great Neck NY 11021 516-466-0550
Web: www.celticfinancial.com
Chevron Texaco Credit Card Ctr PO Box P........... Concord CA 94524 800-243-8766 827-6367*
**Fax Area Code:* 925 ■ *TF:* 800-243-8766 ■ *Web:* www.chevrontexacocards.com
Diners Club International 111 W Monroe..............Chicago IL 60603 800-234-6377
TF: 800-234-6377 ■ *Web:* www.dinersclubus.com
Discover Financial Services
2500 Lk Cook Rd .... Riverwoods IL 60015 224-405-0900
Web: www.discoverfinancial.com
Green Dot Corp 3465 E Foothill Blvd..................Pasadena CA 91107 626-765-2000
Web: www.greendot.com
Intersections Inc 3901 Stonecroft Blvd .... Chantilly VA 20151 703-488-6100
NASDAQ: INTX ■ *TF:* 800-695-7536 ■ *Web:* www.intersections.com
Loan Science 9600 Great Hills Trail E Ste 200 .... Austin TX 78759 866-311-9450
TF: 866-311-9450 ■ *Web:* www.loanscience.com
MasterCard Inc 2000 Purchase St .... Purchase NY 10577 914-249-2000
NYSE: MA ■ *TF:* 800-100-1087 ■ *Web:* www.mastercard.us/en-us.html
Moneris Solutions Corp 3300 Bloor St W.............. Toronto ON M8X2X2 416-734-1000
Web: www.moneris.com
Rewards Network 2 N Riverside Plaza Ste 200...........Chicago IL 60606 866-559-3463
TF: 866-844-3753 ■ *Web:* www.rewardsnetwork.com
Saks Inc 12 E 49th St..............................New York NY 10017 212-940-5305
Web: www.saksincorporated.com
Transaction Network Services Inc.
10740 Parkridge Blvd Ste 100 .... Reston VA 20191 703-453-8300
TF: 866-523-0661 ■ *Web:* www.tnsi.com
Unifund CCR Partners Inc
10625 Techwoods Cir............................ Cincinnati OH 45242 513-489-8877
Web: www.unifund.com
Vesta Corp 11950 SW Garden PL ....Portland OR 97223 503-790-2500 790-2525
Web: www.trustvesta.com
Visa Inc PO Box 8999....................... San Francisco CA 94128 415-932-2100
NYSE: V ■ *TF:* 866-765-9644 ■ *Web:* www.visa.co.in
Wright Express Corp 97 Darling Ave .... South Portland ME 04106 207-773-8171
NYSE: WEX ■ *TF:* 800-761-7181 ■ *Web:* www.wexinc.com

216 CREDIT & FINANCING - COMMERCIAL

See Also Banks - Commercial & Savings p. 1839; Credit & Financing - Consumer p. 2172

Phone Fax

AFCO Credit Corp 14 Wall St ....New York NY 10005 212-401-4400 401-4436
TF: 800-288-6901 ■ *Web:* afco.com
Ag Georgia Farm Credit PO Box 1820.................... Perry GA 31069 478-987-8300
Web: www.aggeorgia.com
Alexander Capital Corp
900 W Castleton Rd Ste 200.....................Castle Rock CO 80104 303-814-0475
Amada Capital Corp 7025 Firestone Blvd .... Buena Park CA 90621 714-739-2111 739-4099
Web: www.amadacapital.com
American AgCredit (ACA) PO Box 1120 .... Santa Rosa CA 95402 707-545-1200
TF: 800-800-4865 ■ *Web:* www.agloan.com
American Capital Strategies Ltd
2 Bethesda Metro Ctr 14th Fl .... Bethesda MD 20814 301-951-6122 654-6714
NASDAQ: ACAS ■ *Web:* www.americancapital.com
AMRESCO Commercial Finance LLC
412 E Parkcenter Blvd................................Boise ID 83706 208-333-2000 333-2050
Web: www.amresco.com
Arkansas Capital Corp Group
200 S Commerce St Ste 400....................... Little Rock AR 72201 501-374-9247 374-9425
TF: 800-216-7237 ■ *Web:* www.arcapital.com

Phone | Fax

ATEL Capital Group
600 California St 6th Fl ... San Francisco CA 94108 415-989-8800 989-3796
TF: 800-543-2835 ■ *Web:* www.atel.com

Automotive Finance Corp (AFC)
13085 Hamilton Crossing Blvd ... Carmel IN 46032 865-384-8250
TF: 888-335-6675 ■ *Web:* www.afcdealer.com

AutoStar 114 Ave of the Americas Ste 39 ... New York NY 10036 212-930-9400
TF: 800-288-6782

Bank of America Business Capital
1 Bryant Park ... New York NY 10036 860-659-3200
Web: www.bofaml.com/content/boaml/en_us/home.html#home_trending

BMO Financial Corp
1 First Canadian Place 11th Fl ... Toronto ON M5X1A1 416-359-4440
TF: 800-553-0332 ■ *Web:* www.bmo.com

Bombardier Capital Group
261 Mountain View Dr 4th Fl ... Colchester VT 05446 802-764-5232 764-5244*
**Fax:* Sales ■ *TF:* 800-949-5568 ■ *Web:* www.bombardier.com

BTM Capital Corp 111 Huntington Ave ... Boston MA 02199 617-573-9000 345-5153

Capital Business Credit LLC
1700 Broadway 19th Fl ... New York NY 10019 212-887-7900 887-7968
Web: www.capitalbusinesscredit.com

Cascade Federal Credit Union 18020 80th Ave S ... Kent WA 98032 425-251-8888 251-0299
TF: 800-562-2853 ■ *Web:* www.cascadefcu.org

CDC Small Business Finance Corp
2448 Historic Decatur Rd Ste 200 ... San Diego CA 92106 619-291-3594
TF: 800-611-5170 ■ *Web:* cdcloans.com

CIT Group Inc 505 Fifth Ave ... New York NY 10017 212-771-0505
NYSE: CIT ■ *Web:* www.cit.com

CIT Group Inc 1 CIT Dr ... Livingston NJ 07039 973-740-5000
NYSE: CIT ■ *Web:* www.cit.com

Co-op Finance Assn Inc, The
10100 N Ambassador Dr Ste 315
PO Box 901532 ... Kansas City MO 64153 816-214-4200 214-4221
TF: 877-835-5232 ■ *Web:* www.cfafs.com

Colonial Farm Credit Aca
7104 Mechanicsville Tpke PO Box 727 ... Mechanicsville VA 23111 804-746-4581
TF: 800-777-8908 ■ *Web:* www.colonialfarmcredit.com

Connell Finance Company Inc
200 Connell Dr ... Berkeley Heights NJ 07922 908-673-3700 673-3800
Web: connellco.com

CSA Financial Corp 343 Commercial St ... Boston MA 02109 617-357-1700
Web: www.csafinancial.com

Dexia CLF 445 Pk Ave 7th Fl ... New York NY 10022 212-515-7000 753-5522
Web: www.dexia.com

DLL 1111 Old Eagle School Rd ... Wayne PA 19087 610-386-5000
Web: www.dllgroup.com

Equity Funding 12505 Bel-Red Rd Ste 200 ... Bellevue WA 98005 425-283-1040 283-1054
TF: 866-332-3863 ■ *Web:* www.equity-funding.com

Farm Credit Leasing (FCL)
600 Hwy 169 S Ste 300 ... Minneapolis MN 55426 952-417-7800 417-7801
TF: 800-444-2929 ■ *Web:* www.farmcreditleasing.com

Farm Credit Of Central Florida Aca
115 S Missouri Ave Ste 400 ... Lakeland FL 33815 863-682-4117 688-9364
TF: 800-533-2773 ■ *Web:* www.farmcreditcfl.com

Farm Credit Of Northwest Florida Aca
5052 Hwy 90 ... Marianna FL 32446 850-526-4910 482-6597
TF: 800-527-0647 ■ *Web:* www.farmcredit-fl.com

Financial Pacific Co
3455 S 344th Way Ste 300 ... Federal Way WA 98001 800-447-7107 447-7106
TF: 800-447-7107 ■ *Web:* www.finpac.com

First Carolina Corporate Credit Union
7900 Triad Ctr Dr Ste 410 ... Greensboro NC 27409 800-585-4317 299-7842*
**Fax Area Code:* 336 ■ *TF:* 800-585-4317 ■ *Web:* www.firstcarolina.org

First Community Financial Corp (FCFC)
4000 N Central Ave Ste 100 ... Phoenix AZ 85012 602-265-7715 577-7907*
OTC: FMFP ■ **Fax Area Code:* 312 ■ *TF:* 877-777-4778 ■ *Web:* capitalsource.com

Ford Motor Credit Co 1 American Rd ... Dearborn MI 48121 313-322-3000
TF: 800-727-7000 ■ *Web:* credit.ford.com

GE Healthcare Financail Services
500 W Monroe ... Chicago IL 60661 312-697-3999
Web: www.gehcfinance.com

GE Vendor Financial Services
1719 Rt 10 E Ste 306 ... Parsippany NJ 07054 203-373-2039
TF: 800-626-2000

Grandbridge Real Estate Capital LLC
271 17th St NW Ste 750 ... Atlanta GA 30363 704-332-4454 332-1931
Web: www.gbrecap.com

Greenstone Farm Credit Services Aca
3515 West Rd ... East Lansing MI 48823 800-968-0061
TF: 800-444-3276 ■ *Web:* www.greenstonefcs.com

Imh Financial Corp
7001 N Scottsdale Rd Ste 2050 ... Scottsdale AZ 85253 480-840-8400
TF: 800-510-6445 ■ *Web:* www.imhfc.com

Imperial PFS (UPAC) 8245 Nieman Rd ... Lenexa KS 66214 913-894-6150
TF: 800-877-7848

iStar Financial Inc
1114 Ave of the Americas 39th Fl ... New York NY 10036 212-930-9400
NYSE: STAR ■ *TF:* 888-603-5847 ■ *Web:* www.istarfinancial.com

Jackson Purchase Ag Credit Assn PO Box 309 ... Mayfield KY 42066 270-247-5613
TF: 877-422-4203 ■ *Web:* rivervalleyagcredit.com

John Deere Credit Co 6400 NW 86th St ... Johnston IA 50131 515-267-3000 267-3292
TF: 800-275-5322 ■ *Web:* www.deere.com/en_us/jdc

Key Equipment Finance 1000 S McCaslin Blvd ... Superior CO 80027 888-301-6238
TF: 888-301-6238 ■ *Web:* www.keyequipmentfinance.com

Marquette Commercial Finance
1600 W 82nd St Ste 250 ... Bloomington MN 55431 952-703-7474
Web: www.marqcfi.com

Marquette Financial Cos
60 S Sixth St Ste 3800 ... Minneapolis MN 55402 952-703-7474
Web: www.marqtransfinance.com

Medallion Financial Corp
437 Madison Ave 38th Fl ... New York NY 10022 212-328-2100 328-2121*
NASDAQ: TAXI ■ **Fax:* PR ■ *TF:* 877-633-2554 ■ *Web:* www.medallionfinancial.com

MicroFinancial Inc
16 New England Executive Pk Ste 200 ... Burlington MA 01803 781-994-4800 994-4938
NASDAQ: MFI ■ *TF:* 877-868-3800 ■ *Web:* www.microfinancial.com

New York Business Development Corp (NYBDC)
50 Beaver St Ste 500 ... Albany NY 12207 518-463-2268 463-0240
TF: 800-923-2504 ■ *Web:* www.nybdc.com

ORIX USA Corp 1717 Main St Ste 900 ... Dallas TX 75201 214-237-2000 237-2018
Web: www.orix.com

PACCAR Financial Corp 777 106th Ave NE ... Bellevue WA 98004 425-468-7100 468-8220
Web: www.paccarfinancial.com

Park Community Federal Credit Union
PO Box 18630 ... Louisville KY 40261 502-968-3681 964-6704
TF: 800-626-2870 ■ *Web:* www.parkcommunity.com

PDS Gaming Corp 6280 Annie Oakley Dr ... Las Vegas NV 89120 702-736-0700 740-8692
TF: 800-479-3612 ■ *Web:* www.pdsgaming.com

Phoenix American Inc 2401 Kerner Blvd ... San Rafael CA 94901 866-895-5050 485-4891*
**Fax Area Code:* 415 ■ *TF:* 866-895-5050 ■ *Web:* www.phxa.com

Phoenix Growth Capital Corp
2401 Kerner Blvd ... San Rafael CA 94901 866-895-5050
TF: 866-895-5050 ■ *Web:* www.phxa.com

Phoenix Leasing Inc 2401 Kerner Blvd ... San Rafael CA 94901 866-895-5050
TF: 866-895-5050 ■ *Web:* www.phxa.com

Pinnacle Business Finance Inc
615 Commerce St Ste 101 ... Tacoma WA 98402 253-284-5600 821-5903*
**Fax Area Code:* 800 ■ *TF:* 800-566-1993 ■ *Web:* www.pinnaclecap.com

Pioneer Credit Co 1870 Executive Pk NW ... Cleveland TN 37312 423-476-6511 559-8439
Web: www.pioneercredit.net

PMC Commercial Trust 17950 Preston Rd Ste 600 ... Dallas TX 75252 972-349-3200 349-3265
NASDAQ: CMCT ■ *TF:* 800-486-3223 ■ *Web:* cimgroup.com/pmc

Priority Capital Inc 174 Green St ... Melrose MA 02176 781-321-8778 321-4108
TF: 800-761-2118 ■ *Web:* prioritycapital.com

Private Export Funding Corp
280 Pk Ave 4th Fl W ... New York NY 10017 212-916-0300 286-0304
Web: www.pefco.com

Puerto Rico Farm Credit Aca PO Box 363649 ... San Juan PR 00936 787-753-0579
TF: 800-981-3323 ■ *Web:* prfarmcredit.com

Republic Financial Corp
5251 DTC Pkwy Ste 300 ... Greenwood Village CO 80111 303-751-3501
TF: 800-596-3608 ■ *Web:* www.republic-financial.com

Schroder Investment Management North America Inc (SIMNA)
875 Third Ave 22nd Fl ... New York NY 10022 800-730-2932 632-2954*
**Fax Area Code:* 212 ■ *TF:* 800-730-2932 ■ *Web:* www.schroders.com/us

Siemens Financial Services Inc 170 Wood Ave S ... Iselin NJ 08830 732-590-6500
TF: 800-327-4443 ■ *Web:* finance.siemens.com

Snap-on Credit LLC
950 Technology Way Ste 301 ... Libertyville IL 60048 877-777-8455 777-9375
TF: 877-777-8455 ■ *Web:* www.snaponcredit.com

Southgroup & Financial Services Inc
795 Woodlands Pkwy Ste 101 ... Ridgeland MS 39157 601-914-3220
TF: 855-744-6777 ■ *Web:* www.southgroup.net

Sta International
1400 Old Country Rd Ste 411 ... Westbury NY 11590 516-997-2400 997-2632
TF: 866-970-9882 ■ *Web:* www.stacollect.com

Taycor LLC 6065 Bristol Pkwy ... Culver City CA 90230 310-895-7704 568-9922
TF: 800-322-9738 ■ *Web:* www.taycor.com

Textron Financial Corp 40 Westminster St ... Providence RI 02903 401-621-4200
Web: www.textronfinancial.com

Tyndall Federal Credit Union Inc
PO Box 59760 ... Panama City FL 32412 850-769-9999 747-4215
TF: 888-896-3255 ■ *Web:* tyndall.org

Verizon Credit Inc 201 N Tampa St ... Tampa FL 33602 813-229-6000
TF: 800-483-7988 ■ *Web:* www.verizon.com

Wells Fargo 420 Montgomery St ... San Francisco CA 94104 800-877-4833
NYSE: WFC ■ *TF:* 800-877-4833 ■ *Web:* www.wellsfargo.com

Wells Fargo Equipment Finance Inc
733 Marquette Ave Ste 700 ... Minneapolis MN 55402 612-667-9876 667-9711
TF: 877-322-8228 ■
Web: www.wellsfargo.com/com/financing/equipment-financing

Western Agcredit PO Box 95850 ... South Jordan UT 84095 801-571-9200 576-0600
TF: 800-824-9198 ■ *Web:* www.westernagcredit.com

Winthrop 11100 Wayzata Blvd Ste 800 ... Minneapolis MN 55305 952-936-0226
Web: www.winthropresources.com

Xerox Financial Services Inc
800 Long Ridge Rd ... Stamford CT 06904 203-968-3000
TF: 800-275-9376 ■ *Web:* xerox.com

217 CREDIT & FINANCING - CONSUMER

See Also Banks - Commercial & Savings p. 1839; Credit & Financing - Commercial p. 2171; Credit Unions p. 2174

Phone | Fax

Acacia Capital Corp
101 S Ellsworth Ave Ste 300 ... San Mateo CA 94401 650-372-6400
Web: www.acacia-capital.com

Allied Home Mortgage Capital Corp
6110 Pinemont Dr ... Houston TX 77092 713-353-0400

Atlantic Bay Mortgage Group
596 Lynnhaven Pkwy Ste 102 ... Virginia Beach VA 23452 757-213-1660
TF: 866-877-3143 ■ *Web:* www.atlanticbay.com

Budget Finance Co 1849 Sawtelle Blvd ... Los Angeles CA 90025 310-696-4050
TF: 800-225-6267 ■ *Web:* www.bfcloans.com

Capital Access Group
150 California St Ste 250 ... San Francisco CA 94111 415-217-7600
Web: www.capitalaccess.com

Collegiate Funding Services LLC
10304 Spotsylvania Ave ... Fredericksburg VA 22408 540-374-1600
Web: htyp.org

Continental Currency Services Inc (CCS)
PO Box 10970 ... Santa Ana CA 92711 714-667-6699 569-0882
Web: www.ccurr.com

Corpfinance International Ltd 229 Niagara St ... Toronto ON M6J2L5 416-364-6191
Web: www.corpfinance.ca

	City	State	Zip	Phone	Fax
Credit Acceptance Corp 25505 W 12 Mile Rd *TF:* 800-634-1506 ■ *Web:* www.credaccept.com	Southfield	MI	48034	248-353-2700	
DAS Acquisition Company LLC 12140 Woodcrest Executive Dr Ste 150 *Web:* www.usa-mortgage.com	St Louis	MO	63141	314-628-2000	
Dent-A-Med Inc 203 E Emma Ave	Springdale	AR	72764	479-750-6700	
DHI Mortgage Co Ltd 10700 Pecan Park Blvd Ste 450 *TF:* 800-315-8434 ■ *Web:* www.dhimortgage.com	Austin	TX	78750	512-502-0545	502-0031
Dollar Loan Ctr LLC 6122 W Sahara Ave *TF:* 866-550-4352 ■ *Web:* www.dontbebroke.com	Las Vegas	NV	89146	702-693-5626	364-5627
Enerbank USA Inc 1245 E Brickyard Rd Ste 600 *TF:* 888-390-1220 ■ *Web:* www.enerbank.com	Salt Lake City	UT	84106	888-390-1220	
Farm Credit of The Virginias Aca 106 Sangers Ln *TF:* 800-559-1016 ■ *Web:* www.farmcreditofvirginias.com	Staunton	VA	24401	540-886-3435	886-3437
Farm Credit West 1478 Stone Pt Dr Ste 450 *Web:* www.farmcreditwest.com	Roseville	CA	95661	860-741-4380	
Finance Factors Ltd 1164 Bishop St *TF:* 800-648-7136 ■ *Web:* www.financefactors.com	Honolulu	HI	96813	808-548-4940	548-5148
Finance of America Mortgage 300 Welsh Rd Bldg 5 *Web:* www.financeofamerica.com	Horsham	PA	19044	215-591-0222	
First Insurance Funding Corp 450 Skokie Blvd Ste 1000 *TF:* 800-837-3707 ■ *Web:* www.firstinsurancefunding.com	Northbrook	IL	60062	800-837-3707	837-3709
Ford Motor Credit Co 1 American Rd *TF:* 800-727-7000 ■ *Web:* credit.ford.com	Dearborn	MI	48121	313-322-3000	
Franklin American Mortgage Company Inc 501 Corporate Centre Dr Ste 400 *Web:* www.franklinamerican.com	Franklin	TN	37067	615-778-1000	
Franklin Credit Management Corp 101 Hudson St *TF:* 800-255-5897 ■ *Web:* www.franklincredit.com	Jersey City	NJ	07302	201-604-1800	839-4512
Gateway Mortgage Group LLC 6910 E 14th St *TF:* 877-406-8109 ■ *Web:* www.gatewayloan.com	Tulsa	OK	74112	918-712-9000	
General Motors Acceptance Corp (GMAC) 200 Renaissance Ctr **Fax Area Code:* 800 ■ *TF:* 800-200-4622 ■ *Web:* www.ally.com	Detroit	MI	48265	877-320-2559	428-4622*
Guaranteed Rate Inc 3940 N Ravenswood *TF:* 866-934-7283 ■ *Web:* www.guaranteedrate.com	Chicago	IL	60613	773-290-0505	
Harley-Davidson Financial Services Inc PO Box 21489 *TF:* 888-691-4337 ■ *Web:* www.harley-davidson.com	Carson City	NV	89721	888-691-4337	
iMortgage Services Inc 2570 Boyce Plz Rd Boyce Plz Iii *TF:* 888-575-8555 ■ *Web:* www.imortgageservices.com	Pittsburgh	PA	15241	412-220-7330	
MCAP Financial Corp 1140 W Pender St Ste 1400 *TF:* 800-977-5877 ■ *Web:* mcap.com	Vancouver	BC	V6E4G1	604-681-8805	
Mercedes-Benz Financial Services USA LLC PO Box 685 **Fax Area Code:* 877 ■ *TF:* 800-654-6222 ■ *Web:* www.mbfs.com	Roanoke	TX	76262	800-654-6222	267-6745*
Ministry Partners Investment Company LLC 915 W Imperial Hwy Ste 120 *Web:* www.ministrypartners.org	Brea	CA	92821	714-671-5720	
Mortgage Intelligence Inc 5770 Hurontario St Ste 600 *Web:* www.mortgageintelligence.ca	Mississauga	ON	L5R3G5	905-283-3600	
Nationwide Title Clearing Inc 2100 Alternate 19 N *Web:* www.nationwidetitleclearing.com	Palm Harbor	FL	34683	727-771-4000	
Nelnet Inc 121 S 13th St Ste 204 *NYSE: NNI* ■ *TF:* 888-486-4722 ■ *Web:* www.nelnet.com	Lincoln	NE	68508	402-458-2370	
New York City Housing Development Corp 110 William St *Web:* www.nychdc.com	New York	NY	10038	212-227-5500	227-6865
Nicholas Financial Inc 2454 McMullen Booth Rd Bldg C *NASDAQ: NICK* ■ *TF:* 800-237-2721 ■ *Web:* nicholasfinancial.com	Clearwater	FL	33759	727-726-0763	726-2140
Ontario Centres of Excellence Inc 156 Front St W Ste 200 *TF:* 866-759-6014 ■ *Web:* www.oce-ontario.org	Toronto	ON	M5J2L6	416-861-1092	
Paramount Equity Mortgage Inc 8781 Sierra College Blvd *Web:* www.paramountequity.com	Roseville	CA	95661	916-290-9999	
PreCash Inc 5120 Woodway Dr Ste 6001 *TF:* 800-773-2274 ■ *Web:* www.precash.com	Houston	TX	77056	713-600-2267	
Prestige Financial Services Inc 1420 S 500 W *TF:* 888-822-7422 ■ *Web:* www.gopfs.com	Salt Lake City	UT	84115	801-844-2100	844-2600
Prime Rate Premium Finance Corp 2141 Enterprise Dr PO Box 100507 *TF Cust Svc:* 800-777-7458 ■ *Web:* www.primeratepfc.com	Florence	SC	29501	843-669-0937	292-1080
Redwood Credit Union PO Box 6104 *TF:* 800-479-7928 ■ *Web:* www.redwoodcu.org	Santa Rosa	CA	95406	707-545-4000	
Regional Acceptance Corp 1424 E Fire Tower Rd *TF:* 877-722-7299 ■ *Web:* www.regionalacceptance.com	Greenville	NC	27858	252-321-7700	353-1852
Republic Finance 7031 Commerce Cir *Web:* www.republicfinance.com	Baton Rouge	LA	70809	225-927-0005	
Rpm Mortgage Inc 3240 Stone Vly Rd W *Web:* rpm-mtg.com	Alamo	CA	94507	925-295-9300	
Sallie Mae 12061 Bluemont Way **Fax Area Code:* 800 ■ *TF Cust Svc:* 888-272-5543 ■ *Web:* www.salliemae.com	Reston	VA	20190	703-810-3000	848-1949*
Security Finance Corp 181 Security Plc *TF All:* 800-395-8195 ■ *Web:* www.security-finance.com	Spartanburg	SC	29307	864-582-8193	
Select Portfolio Servicing Inc 3815 SW Temple *TF:* 800-258-8602 ■ *Web:* www.spservicing.com	Salt Lake City	UT	84115	800-258-8602	
SLM Corp 12061 Bluemont Way *NASDAQ: SLM* ■ *TF Cust Svc:* 888-272-5543 ■ *Web:* www.salliemae.com	Reston	VA	20190	703-810-3000	
Standard Management Co 6151 W Century Blvd Ste 300 *Web:* standardmanagement.com	Los Angeles	CA	90045	310-410-2300	
Stann Financial LLC 4021 N Saint Peters Pkwy *Web:* www.stannfinancial.com	St Peters	MO	63304	636-447-8770	
Toyota Financial Services 19001 S Western Ave *TF Cust Svc:* 800-874-8822 ■ *Web:* www.toyotafinancial.com	Torrance	CA	90501	212-715-7386	
Triad Financial Services Inc 4336 Pablo Oaks Ct *TF:* 800-522-2013 ■ *Web:* www.triadfs.com	Jacksonville	FL	32224	800-522-2013	
United Finance Co 515 E Burnside St *Web:* www.unitedfinance.com	Portland	OR	97214	503-232-5153	238-6453
Wallick & Volk Mortgage 222 E 18th St *TF:* 800-280-8655 ■ *Web:* www.wvmb.com	Cheyenne	WY	82001	307-634-5941	
Watson Mortgage Corp 6206 Atlantic Blvd Ste 1 *Web:* watsonmortgagecorp.com	Jacksonville	FL	32211	904-645-7111	
WebBank Corp 215 S State St Ste 1000 *TF:* 888-881-3789 ■ *Web:* www.webbank.com	Salt Lake City	UT	84111	801-456-8350	
Wells Fargo Education Financial Services PO Box 5185 *TF:* 800-658-3567 ■ *Web:* www.wellsfargo.com	Sioux Falls	SD	57117	800-658-3567	456-0561
Wells Fargo Financial Inc 800 Walnut St *TF:* 800-735-3008 ■ *Web:* wellsfargo.com	Des Moines	IA	50309	515-280-7741	
Western Funding Inc PO Box 94858 *TF:* 888-434-3122 ■ *Web:* www.westernfundinginc.com	Las Vegas	NV	89193	702-434-1990	
WFS Financial Inc 23 Pasteur *Web:* www.wellsfargodealerservices.com	Irvine	CA	92618	949-753-3866	

218 CREDIT REPORTING SERVICES

	City	State	Zip	Phone	Fax
Advantage Credit Inc 32065 Castle Ct Ste 300 *TF:* 800-670-7993 ■ *Web:* www.advcredit.com	Evergreen	CO	80439	303-670-7993	
Argus Research Co 61 Broadway Ste 1910 *Web:* www.argusresearch.com	New York	NY	10006	212-425-7500	
Baltimore Credit & Collection Services Inc 6400 Baltimore National Pk Ste 469 *Web:* www.bccs2.com	Catonsville	MD	21228	410-549-6444	
Building Industry Credit Association 2351 W Third St *Web:* www.bica.com	Los Angeles	CA	90057	213-251-1100	
CBCInnovis Inc 250 E Town St *Web:* www.cbcinnovis.com	Columbus	OH	43215	614-222-4343	
Coface Services North America Inc 50 Millstone Rd *TF:* 877-626-3223 ■ *Web:* www.coface-usa.com	East Windsor	NJ	08520	609-469-0400	490-1582
Community Bankers Merchant Services Inc 908 S Old Missouri Rd *Web:* www.merchantprocessing.com	Springdale	AZ	72764	479-725-1000	
Constellation Technology Corp 7887 Bryan Dairy Rd Ste 100 *TF:* 800-335-7355 ■ *Web:* www.contech.com	Largo	FL	33777	727-547-0600	
Credit Bureau of Connecticut Inc, The 600 Saw Mill Rd *Web:* www.avantus.com	West Haven	CT	06516	203-931-2000	
Creditors Bureau Associates 420 College St *TF:* 866-949-4213 ■ *Web:* www.cbamacon.com	Macon	GA	31201	478-750-1111	
Data Facts Inc 8520 Macon Rd Ste 2 *Web:* www.datafacts.com	Cordova	TN	38018	901-685-7599	
Equifax Credit Marketing Services 1550 Peachtree St NW *NYSE: EFX* ■ *TF Sales:* 800-660-5125 ■ *Web:* www.equifax.com	Atlanta	GA	30309	404-885-8000	
Equifax Inc 1550 Peachtree St NW *NYSE: EFX* ■ *TF Sales:* 888-202-4025 ■ *Web:* www.equifax.com	Atlanta	GA	30309	404-885-8000	
Experian Information Solutions Inc 475 Anton Blvd *TF Cust Svc:* 888-397-3742 ■ *Web:* www.experian.com	Costa Mesa	CA	92626	714-830-7000	
Fitch Ratings Inc 1 State St Plz *TF:* 800-753-4824 ■ *Web:* www.fitchratings.com	New York	NY	10004	212-908-0500	
Holloway Credit Solutions LLC 1286 Carmichael Way *Web:* hollowaycredit.com	Montgomery	AL	36106	334-396-1200	
Incharge Institute of America Inc 5750 Major Blvd *Web:* www.incharge.org	Orlando	FL	32819	407-291-7770	
Kroll Factual Data Inc 5200 Hahns Peak Dr **Fax Area Code:* 800 ■ *TF:* 800-929-3400 ■ *Web:* www.krollfactualdata.com	Loveland	CO	80538	970-663-5700	929-3297*
Merchants Credit Bureau 955 Green St *TF:* 800-426-5265 ■ *Web:* www.mcbusa.com	Augusta	GA	30901	706-823-6246	823-6253
Moody's Corp 250 Greenwich St 7 World Trade Ctr *NYSE: MCO* ■ *Web:* www.moodys.com	New York	NY	10007	212-553-0300	
NACM South Texas Inc 10887 S Wilcrest Dr *TF:* 866-252-6226 ■ *Web:* www.nacmsouthtexas.org	Houston	TX	77099	281-228-6100	
Screeningone Inc 2233 W 190th St *TF:* 888-327-6511 ■ *Web:* www.screeningone.com	Torrance	CA	90504	888-327-6511	
Strategic Information Resources Inc 155 Brookdale Dr *Web:* www.backgrounddecision.com	Springfield	MA	01104	413-736-4511	
Tele-Track 5550 Peach Tree Pkwy Ste 600 *TF:* 800-729-6981 ■ *Web:* www.corelogic.com	Norcross	GA	30092	770-449-8809	
TENA Companies Inc 251 W Lafayette Frontage Rd *Web:* www.tenaco.com	Saint Paul	MN	55107	651-293-1234	
TransUnion LLC 555 W Adams St *TF:* 866-922-2100 ■ *Web:* www.transunion.com	Chicago	IL	60661	866-922-2100	
Trudiligence LLC 3190 S Wadsworth Blvd Ste 260 *TF:* 800-580-0474 ■ *Web:* www.trudiligence.com	Lakewood	CO	80227	303-692-8445	

Phone Fax

219 CREDIT UNIONS

Phone Fax

1st Advantage Federal Credit Union
110 Cybernetics Way .... Yorktown VA 23693 757-877-2444
Web: 1stadvantage.org

1st Midamerica Credit Union
731 E Bethalto Dr .... Bethalto IL 62010 618-258-3168
Web: 1stmidamerica.org

66 Federal Credit Union PO Box 1358 .... Bartlesville OK 74005 918-336-7662
TF: 800-897-6991 ■ *Web:* www.truitycu.org

Affinity Federal Credit Union
73 Mountain View Blvd PO Box 621 .... Basking Ridge NJ 07920 800-325-0808
TF: 800-325-0808 ■ *Web:* www.affinityfcu.com

Air Force Federal Credit Union
1560 Cable Ranch Rd Ste 200 .... San Antonio TX 78245 210-673-5610 673-5102
TF: 800-227-5328 ■ *Web:* www.airforcefcu.com

Alabama Credit Union 220 Paul Bryant Dr E .... Tuscaloosa AL 35401 205-348-5944
Web: alabamacu.com

Alabama One Credit Union
1215 Veterans Memorial Pkwy .... Tuscaloosa AL 35404 205-759-1595
Web: alabamaone.org

Alaska USA Federal Credit Union
4000 Credit Union Dr PO Box 196613 .... Anchorage AK 99503 907-563-4567 561-0773
TF: 800-525-9094 ■ *Web:* www.alaskausa.org

Allegacy Federal Credit Union
1691 Westbrook Plaza Dr .... Winston-Salem NC 27103 336-774-3400 774-3475
TF: 800-782-4670 ■ *Web:* www.allegacyfcu.org

America First Credit Union
1344 West 4675 South .... Ogden UT 84405 801-627-0900 778-8079*
**Fax:* Hum Res ■ *TF:* 800-999-3961 ■ *Web:* www.americafirst.com

American Airlines Employees Federal Credit Union
4151 Amon Carter Blvd PO Box 155489 .... Fort Worth TX 76155 817-952-4500
TF: 800-533-0035 ■ *Web:* www.aacreditunion.org

American Eagle Federal Credit Union
417 Main St .... East Hartford CT 06118 860-568-2020 568-2020
TF: 800-842-0145 ■ *Web:* www.americaneagle.org

Americo Federal Credit Union 4101 Main St .... Erie PA 16511 814-899-6608
Web: americofcu.com

Americu Credit Union 1916 Black River Blvd .... Rome NY 13440 315-356-3000
Web: americu.org

Amoco Federal Credit Union PO Box 889 .... Texas City TX 77592 409-948-8541
TF: 800-231-6053 ■ *Web:* www.amocofcu.org

Andrews Federal Credit Union (AFCU)
5711 Allentown Rd .... Suitland MD 20746 301-702-5500 702-5330
TF: 800-487-5500 ■ *Web:* www.andrewsfcu.org

ANG Federal Credit Union PO Box 170204 .... Birmingham AL 35217 205-841-4525 841-4545
TF: 800-237-6211 ■ *Web:* www.angfcu.org

APCO Employees Credit Union 750 17th St N .... Birmingham AL 35203 205-257-3601
TF: 800-249-2726 ■ *Web:* www.apcocu.org

Apple Federal Credit Union 4029 Ridge Top Rd .... Fairfax VA 22030 703-788-4800
Web: applefcu.org

Argentine Santa Fe Industries Credit Union
4150 Kansas Ave .... Kansas City KS 66106 913-342-9039 342-1517

Arizona Federal Credit Union PO Box 60070 .... Phoenix AZ 85082 602-683-1000
TF: 800-523-4603 ■ *Web:* www.arizonafederal.org

Arkansas Federal Credit Union
2424 Marshall Rd .... Jacksonville AR 72076 501-982-1000
Web: afcu.org

Ascend Federal Credit Union
520 Airpark Dr PO Box 1210 .... Tullahoma TN 37388 931-455-5441
TF: 800-342-3086 ■ *Web:* www.ascendfcu.org

Ascentra Credit Union 1710 Grant St .... Bettendorf IA 52722 563-355-0152
TF: 800-426-5241 ■ *Web:* ascentra.org

Atlanta Postal Credit Union
501 Pulliam St SW Ste 350 .... Atlanta GA 30312 404-768-4126 768-0815
TF: 800-849-8431 ■ *Web:* www.apcu.com

Autotruck Federal Credit Union
3611 Newburg Rd .... Louisville KY 40218 502-459-8981 458-0371
TF: 800-459-2328 ■ *Web:* www.autotruckfcu.org

Bank-Fund Staff Federal Credit Union
PO Box 27755 .... Washington DC 20038 202-458-4300 522-1528
TF: 800-923-7328 ■ *Web:* www.bfsfcu.org

BayPort Credit Union Inc
3711 Huntington Ave .... Newport News VA 23607 757-928-8850 380-8127
TF: 800-928-8801 ■ *Web:* www.bayportcu.org/home.html

Beacon Credit Union PO Box 627 .... Wabash IN 46992 260-563-7443
TF: 800-762-3136 ■ *Web:* www.beaconcu.org

Bellco First Federal Credit Union
7600 E OrchaRd Rd Ste 400N .... Greenwood Village CO 80111 303-689-7800
TF: 800-235-5261 ■ *Web:* www.bellco.org

Bethpage Federal Credit Union
899 S Oyster Bay Rd .... Bethpage NY 11714 800-628-7070 349-6828*
**Fax Area Code:* 516 ■ *TF:* 800-628-7070 ■ *Web:* www.bethpagefcu.com

BlueCross BlueShield of Tennessee Inc
1 Cameron Hill Cir .... Chattanooga TN 37402 423-755-5600
TF: 800-848-0298 ■ *Web:* www.bcbst.com

Bramco Inc 1801 Watterson Trl .... Louisville KY 40232 502-493-4300
Web: www.bramco.com

Campus Federal Credit Union PO Box 98036 .... Baton Rouge LA 70898 225-769-8841 659-2197*
**Fax Area Code:* 602 ■ *TF:* 888-769-8841 ■ *Web:* www.campusfederal.org

Campus USA Credit Union PO Box 147029 .... Gainesville FL 32614 352-335-9090
TF: 800-367-6440 ■ *Web:* www.campuscu.com

Caribe Federal Credit Union 195 Oneil St .... San Juan PR 00918 787-474-5147
Web: caribefederal.com

CFCU Community Credit Union 1030 Craft Rd .... Ithaca NY 14850 607-257-8500
TF: 800-428-8340 ■ *Web:* mycfcu.com

Chartway Federal Credit Union
160 Newtown Rd .... Virginia Beach VA 23462 757-552-1000 671-7691*
**Fax:* Hum Res ■ *TF:* 800-678-8765 ■ *Web:* www.chartway.com

Phone Fax

Chicago Patrolmen'S Federal Credit Union
1407 W Washington Blvd .... Chicago IL 60607 312-726-8814
Web: cpdfcu.com

Citadel Federal Credit Union
520 Eagleview Blvd .... Exton PA 19341 610-380-6000 380-6070
TF: 800-666-0191

Citizens Equity First Credit Union
5401 W Dirksen Pkwy .... Peoria IL 61607 309-633-7000
TF Cust Svc: 800-633-7077 ■ *Web:* www.cefcu.com

Class Act Federal Credit Union
3620 Fern Vly Rd .... Louisville KY 40219 502-964-7575 966-2061
TF: 800-292-2960 ■ *Web:* www.classact.org

Coast Central Credit Union Inc
2650 Harrison Ave .... Eureka CA 95501 707-445-8801 442-2532
TF: 800-974-9727 ■ *Web:* www.coastccu.org

Coastal Federal Credit Union
1000 St Albans Dr .... Raleigh NC 27609 919-420-8000
TF: 800-868-4262 ■ *Web:* www.coastal24.com

Collins Community Credit Union
1150 42nd St Ne .... Cedar Rapids IA 52402 319-393-9000
Web: collinscu.org

Commonwealth Credit Union PO Box 978 .... Frankfort KY 40602 502-564-4775
TF: 800-228-6420 ■ *Web:* www.ccuky.org

Community America Credit Union (CACU)
9777 Ridge Dr .... Lenexa KS 66219 913-905-7000 905-7111
TF: 800-892-7957 ■ *Web:* www.communityamerica.com

Community Resource Federal Credit Union
20 Wade Rd .... Latham NY 12110 518-783-2211 783-2266
TF: 888-783-2211 ■ *Web:* www.communityresource.coop

Communitywide Federal Credit Union
1555 W Western Ave .... South Bend IN 46619 574-239-2700
Web: www.comwide.com

Coors Credit Union 816 Washington Ave .... Golden CO 80401 303-279-6414 279-6336
TF: 800-770-6414 ■ *Web:* www.coorscu.org

Coosa Pines Federal Credit Union
17591 Plant Rd .... Childersburg AL 35044 256-378-5559 378-3881
TF: 800-237-9789 ■ *Web:* www.coosapinesfcu.org

CP Federal Credit Union 1100 Clinton Rd .... Jackson MI 49202 517-784-7101
Web: cpfederal.com

Credit Union Acceptance Company LLC
9601 Jones Rd Ste 108 .... Houston TX 77065 281-970-2822
TF: 866-970-2822 ■ *Web:* www.cuac.net

Credit Union of Southern California
PO Box 200 .... Whittier CA 90608 562-698-8326 990-5492*
**Fax Area Code:* 714 ■ *TF:* 866-287-6225 ■ *Web:* www.cusocal.org

Credit Union of Texas PO Box 517028 .... Dallas TX 75251 972-263-9497 301-1980
TF: 800-314-3828 ■ *Web:* www.cutx.org

Credit.com Inc 160 Spear St Ste 1020 .... San Francisco CA 94105 415-901-1550
Web: www.credit.com

Dearborn Federal Credit Union
400 Town Ctr Dr .... Dearborn MI 48126 313-336-2700 336-2700
TF: 888-336-2700 ■ *Web:* www.dfcufinancial.com

Deer Valley Federal Credit Union
16215 N 28th Ave .... Phoenix AZ 85053 602-375-7300 375-7333
TF: 800-579-5051 ■ *Web:* deervalleycu.org

Delta Employees Credit Union
1025 Virginia Ave .... Atlanta GA 30354 404-715-4725 677-4776
TF: 800-544-3328 ■ *Web:* www.deltacommunitycu.com

Denver Fire Dept Federal Credit Union (DFDFCU)
2201 Federal Blvd .... Denver CO 80211 303-228-5300 228-5333
TF: 866-880-7770 ■ *Web:* www.dfdfcu.com

Desert Schools Federal Credit Union
148 N 48th St .... Phoenix AZ 85034 602-433-7000 634-2993
TF: 800-456-9171 ■ *Web:* www.desertschools.org

Digital Employees' Federal Credit Union
220 Donald Lynch Blvd .... Marlborough MA 01752 508-263-6700 263-6392
TF: 800-328-8797 ■ *Web:* www.dcu.org

Direct Federal Credit Union PO Box 9123 .... Needham MA 02494 781-455-6500 455-9922
Web: www.direct.com

Dover Federal Credit Union 1075 Silver Lk Blvd .... Dover DE 19904 302-678-8000
Web: doverfcu.com

Dow Chemical Employees' Credit Union
600 E Lyon Rd .... Midland MI 48640 989-835-7794 832-4883
Web: www.dcecu.org

Duca Financial Services Credit Union Ltd
5290 Yonge St .... Toronto ON M2N5P9 416-223-8502
TF: 866-900-3822 ■ *Web:* duca.com

Dupaco Community Credit Union
3999 Pennsylvania Ave .... Dubuque IA 52002 563-557-7600
TF: 800-373-7600 ■ *Web:* dupaco.com

Educational Employees Credit Union
PO Box 5242 .... Fresno CA 93755 559-437-7700 451-0198
TF: 800-538-3328 ■ *Web:* www.myeecu.org

Educators Credit Union (ECU)
1400 N Newman Rd PO Box 081040 .... Racine WI 53406 262-886-5900 884-7233
TF: 800-236-5898 ■ *Web:* www.ecu.com

Eglin Federal Credit Union
838 Eglin Pkwy NE .... Fort Walton Beach FL 32547 850-862-0111 862-0111
TF: 800-367-6159 ■ *Web:* eglinfcu.org

Ent Federal Credit Union
7250 Campus Dr .... Colorado Springs CO 80920 719-574-1100 388-9065
TF: 800-525-9623 ■ *Web:* www.ent.com

Evansville Teachers Federal Credit Union
PO Box 5129 .... Evansville IN 47716 812-477-9271 473-9704
TF: 800-800-9271 ■ *Web:* www.etfcu.org

FAA Credit Union PO Box 26406 .... Oklahoma City OK 73126 405-682-1990
TF: 800-448-1990 ■ *Web:* www.faaecu.org

Faa Federal Credit Union 3920 Whitebrook Dr .... Memphis TN 38118 901-366-0066
TF: 800-346-0069 ■ *Web:* faafcu.org

Fairwinds Federal Credit Union
3087 N Alafaya Trl .... Orlando FL 32826 407-277-5045 658-7937*
**Fax:* Acctg ■ *TF:* 800-443-6887 ■ *Web:* www.fairwinds.org

Fedchoice Federal Credit Union
10001 Willowdale Rd .... Lanham MD 20706 301-699-6100
Web: fedchoice.org

Phone Fax

Finance Ctr Federal Credit Union
PO Box 26501 .... Indianapolis IN 46226 317-916-7700
TF: 800-473-2328 ■ *Web:* www.fcfcu.com
Financial Partners Credit Union PO Box 7005 .... Downey CA 90241 562-923-0311
TF: 800-950-7328 ■ *Web:* www.fpcu.org
Firefighters Community Credit Union Inc
2300 St Clair Ave NE .... Cleveland OH 44114 216-621-4644 694-3600
TF: 800-621-4644 ■ *Web:* www.ffcommunity.com
First Community Credit Union (FCCU)
PO Box 1030 .... Chesterfield MO 63006 636-728-3333
TF: 800-767-8880 ■ *Web:* www.firstcommunity.com
First Florida Credit Union
500 W First St. .... Jacksonville FL 32202 904-359-6800
Web: firstflorida.org
Fort Knox Federal Credit Union PO Box 900 .... Radcliff KY 40159 502-942-0254
TF: 800-756-3678 ■ *Web:* www.fortknoxfcu.org
Fort Worth City Credit Union
PO Box 100099 .... Fort Worth TX 76185 817-732-2803 377-7966
TF: 888-732-3085 ■ *Web:* www.fwccu.org
Fort Worth Community Credit Union
1905 Forest Ridge Dr PO Box 210848 .... Bedford TX 76021 817-835-5000 835-5235
TF: 800-817-8234 ■ *Web:* www.ftwccu.org
Forum Credit Union PO Box 50738 .... Indianapolis IN 46250 317-558-6000
TF: 800-382-5414 ■ *Web:* www.forumcu.com
Founders Federal Credit Union
607 N Main St .... Lancaster SC 29720 803-289-5927
TF Tech Supp: 888-918-7403 ■ *Web:* www.foundersfcu.com
Fox Communities Credit Union
3401 E Calumet St .... Appleton WI 54915 920-993-9000
Web: foxcu.org
Georgia Cu Affiliates
6705 Sugarloaf Pkwy Ste 200 .... Duluth GA 30097 770-476-9625
TF: 800-768-4282 ■ *Web:* gcua.org
Georgia's Own Credit Union
1155 Peachtree St NE Ste 400 .... Atlanta GA 30309 404-874-1166 881-2950
TF: 800-533-2062 ■ *Web:* www.georgiasown.org
Gesa Credit Union 51 Gage Blvd PO Box 500 .... Richland WA 99352 509-946-1611
TF: 888-946-4372 ■ *Web:* www.gesa.com
Greater Texas Federal Credit Union
6411 N Lamar Blvd .... Austin TX 78752 512-458-2558
Web: gtfcu.org
Greylock Federal Credit Union 150 W St .... Pittsfield MA 01201 413-236-4000 443-0292
TF: 800-207-5555 ■ *Web:* greylock.org
GTE Federal Credit Union PO Box 172599 .... Tampa FL 33672 813-871-2690
TF: 888-871-2690 ■ *Web:* www.gtefinancial.org
Guadalupe Credit Union 3601 Mimbres Ln .... Santa Fe NM 87507 505-982-8942 216-0497
TF: 800-540-5382 ■ *Web:* www.guadalupecu.org
Guardian Credit Union
4501 W Greenfield Ave .... West Milwaukee WI 53214 414-546-7450
Web: guardiancu.org
Hamilton City Employees Federal Credit Union
309 Ct St .... Hamilton OH 45011 513-868-5881 867-7339
TF: 800-264-5578 ■ *Web:* www.allwealth.org
Harbor Credit Union 800 Weise St .... Green Bay WI 54302 920-431-6688
TF: 800-827-4645 ■ *Web:* harborcu.com
HarborOne Credit Union 770 Oak St PO Box 720 .... Brockton MA 02301 508-895-1000
TF: 800-244-7592 ■ *Web:* www.harborone.com
Hilco Federal Credit Union 120 Texas Dr .... Kerrville TX 78028 830-257-8238
Web: hilcocu.com
Holley Credit Union 1107 Mineral Wells Ave .... Paris TN 38242 731-644-9031
Web: holleycreditunion.org
Hoosier Hills Credit Union 630 Lincoln Ave .... Bedford IN 47421 812-279-6644
Web: hoosierhillscu.org
Horizon Credit Union
13224 E Mansfield Ste 300 .... Spokane Valley WA 99216 800-808-6402
TF: 800-808-6402 ■ *Web:* hzcu.org
Hudson Valley Federal Credit Union
159 Barnegat Rd .... Poughkeepsie NY 12601 845-463-3011 463-3613
TF: 800-468-3011 ■ *Web:* www.hvfcu.org
Hughes Federal Credit Union Inc PO Box 11900 .... Tucson AZ 85734 520-794-8341
TF: 866-760-3156 ■ *Web:* www.hughesfcu.org
I B M Southeast Employees Federal Credit Union
PO Box 5090 .... Boca Raton FL 33431 561-982-4700
TF: 888-567-8688 ■ *Web:* www.ibmsecu.org
Indiana Credit Union League
5975 Castle Creek Parkway N Ste 300 .... Indianapolis IN 46250 317-594-5300
TF: 800-285-5300 ■ *Web:* icul.org
Indiana Members Credit Union (IMCU)
7110 W Tenth St .... Indianapolis IN 46214 317-248-8556
TF: 800-556-9268 ■ *Web:* www.imcu.com
Interra Credit Union 300 W Lincoln Ave .... Goshen IN 46526 574-534-2506
Web: interracu.com
Island Federal Credit Union 120 Motor Pkwy .... Hauppauge NY 11788 631-851-1100
TF: 800-475-5263 ■ *Web:* www.islandfcu.com
Keesler Federal Credit Union PO Box 7001 .... Biloxi MS 39534 228-385-5500 385-5535
TF: 888-533-7537 ■ *Web:* www.kfcu.org
Kern Schools Federal Credit Union
PO Box 9506 .... Bakersfield CA 93389 661-833-7900
TF: 800-221-3311 ■ *Web:* www.ksfcu.org
KeyPoint Credit Union 2805 Bowers Ave .... Santa Clara CA 95051 408-731-4100 731-4485
TF: 888-255-3637 ■ *Web:* www.kpcu.com
Kinecta Federal Credit Union
1440 Rosecrans Ave PO Box 10003 .... Manhattan Beach CA 90266 310-643-5400 643-8350*
**Fax:* Hum Res ■ *TF:* 800-854-9846 ■ *Web:* www.kinecta.org
L & N Federal Credit Union
9265 Smyrna Pkwy .... Louisville KY 40229 502-368-5858
TF: 800-443-2479 ■ *Web:* www.lnfcu.com
La Capitol Federal Credit Union
PO Box 3398 .... Baton Rouge LA 70821 225-342-5055 342-9135
TF: 800-522-2748 ■ *Web:* www.lacapfcu.org
Lafayette Federal Credit Union (Inc)
3535 University Blvd W .... Kensington MD 20895 301-929-7990
TF: 800-888-6560 ■ *Web:* www.lfcu.org

Phone Fax

Landmark Credit Union
5445 S Westridge Dr PO Box 510910 .... New Berlin WI 53151 262-796-4500 782-3422
TF: 800-801-1449 ■ *Web:* www.landmarkcu.com
Langley Federal Credit Union
1055 W Mercury Blvd .... Hampton VA 23666 757-827-7200 825-7557
TF: 800-826-7490 ■ *Web:* www.langleyfcu.org
Leominster Credit Union 20 Adams St .... Leominster MA 01453 978-537-8021
TF: 800-649-4646 ■ *Web:* www.leominstercu.com
Local Government Federal Credit Union
323 W Jones St Ste 600 .... Raleigh NC 27603 919-857-2150 755-0193
TF: 888-732-8562 ■ *Web:* www.lgfcu.org
Lockheed Federal Credit Union (LFCU)
2340 Hollywood Way .... Burbank CA 91505 818-565-2020
TF: 800-328-5328 ■ *Web:* logixbanking.com
Los Angeles Federal Credit Union
PO Box 53032 .... Los Angeles CA 90053 818-242-8640 242-5812
TF: 877-695-2328 ■ *Web:* www.lafcu.org
Los Angeles Police Federal Credit Union
PO Box 10188 .... Van Nuys CA 91410 818-787-6520
TF: 877-695-2732 ■ *Web:* www.lapfcu.org
Matanuska Valley Fcu 1020 S Bailey St .... Palmer AK 99645 907-745-4891
Web: mvfcu.coop
Mazuma Credit Union 9300 Troost Ave .... Kansas City MO 64131 816-361-4194
Web: mazuma.org
Member One Federal Credit Union
202 Fourth Ne .... Roanoke VA 24016 540-982-8811
Web: memberonefcu.com
Members Group Inc, The 1500 NW 118th St .... Des Moines IA 50325 800-268-1884
TF: 800-268-1884 ■ *Web:* www.tmg.global
Meriwest Credit Union PO Box 530953 .... San Jose CA 95153 877-637-4937 363-3330*
**Fax Area Code:* 408 ■ *TF:* 877-637-4937 ■ *Web:* www.meriwest.com
Michigan Schools & Government Credit Union
40400 Garfield Rd .... Clinton Township MI 48038 586-263-8800
Midwest America Federal Credit Union
1104 Medical Pk Dr .... Fort Wayne IN 46825 260-482-3334 423-8298
TF: 800-348-4738 ■ *Web:* www.mwafcu.org
Miramar Federal Credit Union
9494 Miramar Rd .... San Diego CA 92196 858-695-9494 271-1537
TF: 800-640-1228 ■ *Web:* www.miramarfcu.com
Mission City Federal Credit Union
1391 Franklin St .... Santa Clara CA 95050 408-244-5818
Web: missioncityfcu.org
Mission Federal Credit Union PO Box 919023 .... San Diego CA 92121 858-524-2850
TF: 800-500-6328 ■ *Web:* www.missionfed.com
Missoula Federal Credit Union
3600 Brooks St .... Missoula MT 59801 406-523-3300
Web: missoulafcu.org
Mountain America Credit Union
PO Box 9001 .... West Jordan UT 84084 801-325-6228
TF: 800-748-4302 ■ *Web:* www.macu.com
Municipal Credit Union PO Box 3205 .... New York NY 10007 212-693-4900
TF: 866-512-6109 ■ *Web:* www.nymcu.org
Mutual Savings Credit Union Inc
2040 Valleydale Rd .... Birmingham AL 35244 205-682-1100
Web: www.mutualsavings.org
Nassau Financial Federal Credit Union
1325 Franklin Ave Ste 500 .... Garden City NY 11530 516-742-4900
TF: 800-216-2328 ■ *Web:* www.nassaufinancial.org
Neighbors Federal Credit Union
PO Box 2831 .... Baton Rouge LA 70821 225-819-2178 819-8923
TF: 866-819-2178 ■ *Web:* www.neighborsfcu.org
New England Federal Credit Union
PO Box 527 .... Williston VT 05495 802-879-8790
TF: 800-400-8790 ■ *Web:* www.nefcu.com
New Orleans Firemens Federal Credit Union
PO Box 689 .... Metairie LA 70004 504-889-9090 889-9082
TF: 800-647-1689 ■ *Web:* www.noffcu.org
North American Van Lines Inc
5001 US Hwy 30 W .... Fort Wayne IN 46818 260-429-2511
Web: www.northamerican.com
North Country Federal Credit Union Inc
69 Swift St Ste 100 .... South Burlington VT 05403 802-657-6847 864-9849
TF: 800-660-3258 ■ *Web:* www.northcountry.org
North Island Credit Union 5898 Copley Dr .... San Diego CA 92111 619-656-6525 656-4050
TF Cust Svc: 800-848-5654 ■ *Web:* www.northislandcu.com
NuUnion Credit Union 501 S Capitol Ave .... Lansing MI 48933 517-267-7200
TF: 888-267-7200 ■ *Web:* www.laketrust.org
Odjfs Federal Credit Union 4020 E Fifth Ave .... Columbus OH 43219 614-466-3416
Web: www.odjfscu.com
Oil Capital Community Credit Union
4132 E 51st St .... Tulsa OK 74135 918-743-4080
Web: www.oilcapital.com
Oklahoma Federal Credit Union
517 NE 36th St .... Oklahoma City OK 73105 405-524-6467 524-1067
TF: 800-522-8510 ■ *Web:* okfcu.com
Orange County's Credit Union PO Box 11777 .... Santa Ana CA 92711 714-755-5900
TF: 888-354-6228 ■ *Web:* orangecountyscu.org
Owensboro Federal Credit Union
717 Harvard Dr PO Box 1189 .... Owensboro KY 42302 270-683-1054 685-3987
TF: 800-264-1054 ■ *Web:* www.ofcuonline.com
Pacific Marine Credit Union
M C X Complex .... Camp Pendleton CA 92055 760-430-7511
TF: 800-736-4500 ■ *Web:* www.pmcu.com
Pacific NW Federal Credit Union (PNWFCU)
12106 NE Marx St .... Portland OR 97220 503-256-5858 253-5858
TF: 866-692-8669 ■ *Web:* www.pnwfcu.org
Pacific Service Federal Credit Union
PO Box 8191 .... Walnut Creek CA 94596 925-296-6200
TF: 888-858-6878 ■ *Web:* www.pacificservice.org
Partners 1St Federal Credit Union
1330 Directors Row .... Fort Wayne IN 46808 260-471-8336
Web: partners1stcu.org
Pawtucket Credit Union 1200 Central Ave .... Pawtucket RI 02861 401-722-2212
Web: pcu.org

	City	State	Zip	Phone	Fax
Pearl Harbor Federal Credit Union (PHFCU) 94-449 Ukee St. — *Fax Area Code: 808 ■ TF: 800-987-5583 ■ Web: www.phfcu.com	Waipahu	HI	96797	800-987-5583	218-6299*
Pennsylvania State Employees Credit Union 1 Credit Union Pl — TF: 800-237-7328 ■ Web: www.psecu.com	Harrisburg	PA	17110	717-234-8484	772-2272
Pentagon Federal Credit Union 2930 Eisenhower Ave — TF: 800-247-5626 ■ Web: www.penfed.org	Alexandria	VA	22314	800-247-5626	253-6589
People First Federal Credit Union 2141 Downyflake Ln — Web: peoplefirstcu.org	Allentown	PA	18103	610-797-7440	
Pine Bluff Cotton Belt Federal Credit Union 1703 River Pines Blvd — TF: 888-249-1904 ■ Web: www.pbcottonbeltfcu.coop	Pine Bluff	AR	71601	870-535-6365	535-0765
Pittsford Federal Cu 1321 Pittsford Mendon Rd — Web: pittsfordfcu.org	Mendon	NY	14506	585-624-7474	
Police & Fire Federal Credit Union 901 Arch St. — TF: 800-228-8801 ■ Web: www.pffcu.org	Philadelphia	PA	19107	215-931-0300	
Portland Teachers Credit Union PO Box 3750 — TF: 800-527-3932 ■ Web: www.onpointcu.com	Portland	OR	97208	503-228-7077	273-2698
Premier America Credit Union 19867 Prairie St PO Box 2178 — TF: 800-772-4000 ■ Web: www.premieramerica.com	Chatsworth	CA	91313	818-772-4000	772-4175
Premier Members Federal Credit Union 5495 Arapahoe Ave. — *Fax Area Code: 307 ■ TF: 800-468-0634 ■ Web: www.pmfcu.org	Boulder	CO	80303	303-657-7000	777-7252*
Prime Financial Credit Union 5656 S Packard Ave — Web: primefinancialcu.org	Cudahy	WI	53110	414-486-4500	
Primeway Federal Credit Union 12811 Northwest Fwy — Web: primewayfcu.com	Houston	TX	77040	713-799-6200	
Provident Central Credit Union 303 Twin Dolphin Dr — TF: 800-632-4600 ■ Web: www.providentcu.org	Redwood City	CA	94065	650-508-0300	508-7202
Randolph-Brooks Federal Credit Union PO Box 2097 — TF: 800-580-3300 ■ Web: www.rbfcu.org	Universal City	TX	78148	210-945-3300	
Red Canoe Credit Union 1418 15th Ave — Web: redcanoecu.com	Longview	WA	98632	360-425-2130	
Redstone Federal Credit Union 220 Wynn Dr NW — *Fax: Cust Svc ■ TF: 800-234-1234 ■ Web: www.redfcu.org	Huntsville	AL	35893	256-837-6110	722-3655*
Rhode Island State Employees Credit Union 160 Francis St — TF: 855-322-7428 ■ Web: www.ricreditunion.org	Providence	RI	02903	401-751-7440	331-5907
Rockland Federal Credit Union 241 Union St — TF: 800-562-7328 ■ Web: www.rfcu.com	Rockland	MA	02370	781-878-0232	792-3866
Rogue Credit Union 1370 Center Dr — Web: www.roguecu.org	Medford	OR	97501	541-858-7328	
RTN Federal Credit Union 600 Main St. — TF: 800-338-0221 ■ Web: www.rtn.org	Waltham	MA	02452	781-736-9900	736-9856
SAC Federal Credit Union (SAFCU) 11515 S 39th St — TF: 800-228-0392 ■ Web: www.sacfcu.com	Bellevue	NE	68123	402-292-8000	829-0149
Safe 1 Credit Union PO Box 2203 — TF: 800-322-4529 ■ Web: www.safe1.org	Bakersfield	CA	93303	661-327-3818	
SAFE Credit Union 3720 Madison Ave — TF: 800-733-7233 ■ Web: www.safecu.org	North Highlands	CA	95660	916-979-7233	
Safeamerica Credit Union 6001 Gibraltar Dr — TF: 800-972-0999 ■ Web: www.safeamerica.com	Pleasanton	CA	94588	925-734-4111	
San Antonio Federal Credit Union PO Box 1356 — TF: 800-234-7228 ■ Web: www.sacu.com	San Antonio	TX	78295	210-258-1234	258-1543
San Diego County Credit Union 6545 Sequence Dr — *Fax Area Code: 858 ■ TF: 877-732-2848 ■ Web: www.sdccu.com	San Diego	CA	92121	877-732-2848	597-6509*
San Francisco Federal Credit Union 770 Golden Gate Ave — TF: 800-852-7598 ■ Web: www.sanfranciscofcu.com	San Francisco	CA	94102	415-775-5377	775-5340
Sb1 Federal Credit Union PO Box 7480 — TF: 800-806-9465 ■ Web: www.sb1fcu.org	Philadelphia	PA	19101	215-569-3700	
Schools Financial Credit Union 1485 Response Rd Ste 126 — TF: 800-962-0990 ■ Web: www.schools.org	Sacramento	CA	95815	916-569-5400	
Secure First Credit Union 3000 Winewood Rd — TF: 877-520-2115	Birmingham	AL	35215	205-520-2115	520-2110
Security Service Federal Credit Union 16211 La Cantera Pkwy — TF: 800-527-7328 ■ Web: www.ssfcu.org	San Antonio	TX	78256	210-476-4000	444-3000
Selco Community Credit Union 299 E 11th Ave. — TF: 800-445-4483 ■ Web: www.selco.org	Eugene	OR	97401	541-686-8000	686-4367
Seven Seventeen Credit Union Inc 3181 Larchmont Ave NE — Web: www.sscu.net	Warren	OH	44483	330-372-8100	372-8337
Sharefax Credit Union Inc 1147 Old SR- 74 — Web: sharefax.org	Batavia	OH	45103	513-753-2440	
Solarity Credit Union 110 N Fifth Ave — Web: solaritycu.org	Yakima	WA	98902	509-248-1720	
South Carolina Federal Credit Union PO Box 190012 — TF: 800-845-0432 ■ Web: www.scfederal.org	North Charleston	SC	29419	843-797-8300	
Space Coast Credit Union 8045 N Wickham Rd PO Box 419001 — TF: 800-447-7228 ■ Web: www.sccu.com	Melbourne	FL	32941	321-752-2222	723-3716
St. Anne's Credit Union of Fall River 286 Oliver St. — Web: www.stannes.com	Fall River	MA	02724	508-324-7300	673-1542
Stanford Federal Credit Union 1860 Embarcadero Rd — *Fax Area Code: 866 ■ TF: 888-723-7328 ■ Web: www.sfcu.org	Palo Alto	CA	94303	650-723-2509	579-9764*
Star One Federal Credit Union PO Box 3643 — TF: 866-543-5202 ■ Web: www.starone.org	Sunnyvale	CA	94088	408-543-5202	543-5203
State Employees Credit Union of Maryland Inc 971 Corporate Blvd. — TF: 800-879-7328 ■ Web: www.secumd.org	Linthicum	MD	21090	410-487-7328	
State Employees Federal Credit Union 700 Patroon Creek Blvd Patroon Creek Corporate Ctr. — TF: 800-727-3328 ■ Web: www.sefcu.com	Albany	NY	12206	518-452-8234	
State Employees' Credit Union (SECU) PO Box 29606 — TF: 888-732-8562 ■ Web: www.ncsecu.org	Raleigh	NC	27626	919-857-2150	857-2000
Sunstate Federal Credit Union (Inc) PO Box 1162 — TF: 877-786-7828 ■ Web: www.sunstatefcu.org	Gainesville	FL	32627	352-381-5200	
Teachers Credit Union (TCU) PO Box 1395 — TF: 800-552-4745 ■ Web: www.tcunet.com	South Bend	IN	46624	574-284-6247	
Teachers Federal Credit Union (TFCU) 2410 N Ocean Ave — TF: 800-341-4333 ■ Web: www.teachersfcu.org	Farmingville	NY	11738	631-698-7000	
Tech Credit Union 10951 Broadway — TF: 800-276-8324 ■ Web: www.techcu.org	Crown Point	IN	46307	219-663-5120	662-4384
Telcoe Federal Credit Union 820 Lousiana St — TF: 800-482-9009 ■ Web: telcoe.com	Little Rock	AR	72201	501-375-5321	375-6233
Texans Credit Union 777 E Campbell Rd — TF: 800-843-5295 ■ Web: www.texanscu.org	Richardson	TX	75081	972-348-2000	348-2200
Texas Dow Employees Credit Union (TDECU) 1001 FM 2004 — TF: 800-839-1154 ■ Web: www.tdecu.org	Lake Jackson	TX	77566	979-297-1154	299-0212
Tower Federal Credit Union 7901 Sandy Spring Rd — *Fax: Cust Svc ■ TF: 800-787-8328 ■ Web: www.towerfcu.org	Laurel	MD	20707	301-497-7000	497-8930*
Transwest Credit Union 37 West 1700 South — Web: transwestcu.com	Salt Lake City	UT	84115	801-487-1692	
Travis Federal Credit Union 1 Travis Way — TF: 800-877-8328 ■ Web: www.traviscu.org	Vacaville	CA	95687	707-449-4000	
Trugrocer Federal Credit Union 501 E Highland St. — Web: trugrocer.com	Boise	ID	83706	208-385-5200	
Truliant Federal Credit Union 3200 Truliant Way — TF: 800-822-0382 ■ Web: www.truliantfcu.org	Winston-Salem	NC	27103	336-659-1955	659-3540
Tulsa Federal Credit Union 9323 E 21st St — Web: tulsafederalcu.org	Tulsa	OK	74129	918-610-0200	
Tyco Electronics Federal Credit Union PO Box 3449 — *Fax Area Code: 800 ■ TF: 888-673-3288 ■ Web: www.reachcu.coop	Redwood City	CA	94064	888-673-3288	280-8926*
U S Employees O C Federal Credit Union PO Box 44000 — TF: 800-227-6366 ■ Web: www.usecreditunion.org	Oklahoma City	OK	73144	405-685-6200	
Ukrainian National Federal Credit Union 215 Second Ave PO Box 160 — TF: 866-859-5848 ■ Web: www.ukrnatfcu.org	New York	NY	10003	212-533-2980	995-5204
Union Special Corp 1 Union Special Plz. — Web: www.unionspecial.com	Huntley	IL	60142	847-669-5101	
United Nations Federal Credit Union (UNFCU) 24-01 44th Rd Ct Sq Pl — TF: 800-891-2471 ■ Web: www.unfcu.org	Long Island	NY	11101	347-686-6000	686-6400
Unitus Community Credit Union PO Box 1937 — TF: 800-452-0900 ■ Web: www.unituscu.com	Portland	OR	97207	503-227-5571	423-8345
University & State Employees Credit Union 10120 Pacific Heights Blvd Ste 100 — TF: 866-873-2448 ■ Web: www.usecu.org	San Diego	CA	92121	858-795-6100	795-6007
University of Hawaii Federal Credit Union PO Box 22070 — TF: 800-927-3397 ■ Web: www.uhfcu.com	Honolulu	HI	96823	808-983-5500	
University of Hawaii Foundation, The 2444 Dole St Bachman Hall 105 — TF: 866-846-4262 ■ Web: www.uhfoundation.org	Honolulu	HI	96822	808-956-8849	
US Alliance Federal Credit Union 600 Midland Ave — *Fax Area Code: 914 ■ TF: 800-431-2754 ■ Web: usalliance.org	Rye	NY	10580	800-431-2754	881-3464*
US New Mexico Federal Credit Union (USNMFCU) 3939 Osuna Rd NE PO Box 129 — TF: 888-342-8766 ■ Web: useaglefcu.org	Albuquerque	NM	87109	505-342-8888	342-8975
Valley First Credit Union PO Box 1411 — TF: 877-549-4567 ■ Web: www.valleyfirstcu.org	Modesto	CA	95353	209-549-8500	524-1741
Vantage Credit Union (VCU) PO Box 4433 — TF: 800-522-6009 ■ Web: www.vcu.com	Bridgeton	MO	63044	314-298-0055	
Verity Credit Union PO Box 75974 — TF: 800-444-4589 ■ Web: www.veritycu.com	Seattle	WA	98175	206-440-9000	361-5300
Vermont Federal Credit Union 84 Pine St — Web: vermontfederal.org	Burlington	VT	05402	802-658-0225	
Virginia Credit Union 7500 Boulders View Dr — TF: 800-285-5051 ■ Web: www.vacu.org	Richmond	VA	23225	804-323-6000	608-8619
Visions Federal Credit Union (VFUC) 24 McKinley Ave. — TF: 800-242-2120 ■ Web: www.visionsfcu.org	Endicott	NY	13760	607-754-7900	786-1718
Vons Employees Federal Credit Union 4455 Arden Dr PO Box 8023 — Web: vonsefcu.org	El Monte	CA	91731	626-444-1972	350-5850
Vystar Credit Union 1802 Kernan Blvd S — TF: 800-445-6289 ■ Web: vystarcu.org	Jacksonville	FL	32246	904-777-6000	
Washington State Employees Credit Union 330 Union Ave SE — TF: 800-562-0999 ■ Web: www.wsecu.org	Olympia	WA	98501	360-943-7911	
Wescom Credit Union 123 S Marengo Ave PO Box 7058 — TF: 888-493-7266 ■ Web: www.wescom.org	Pasadena	CA	91101	626-535-1000	
Westby Co-op Credit Union 501 N Main St — Web: www.wccucreditunion.coop	Westby	WI	54667	608-634-3118	
Westconsin Credit Union 3333 Schneider Ave Se — Web: westconsincu.org	Menomonie	WI	54751	715-235-3403	

			Phone	Fax
Westerra Credit Union 3700 E Alameda Ave ... Denver	CO	80209	303-321-4209	
White River Credit Union 1499 Garrett St ... Enumclaw *Web:* www.whiterivercu.com	WA	98022	360-825-4833	
Whitehall Credit Union 5025 E Main St ... Columbus *Web:* whitehallcu.org	OH	43213	614-866-5025	
Williams Lake & District Credit Union 139 N Third Ave ... Williams Lake *Web:* www.wldcu.com	BC	V2G2A5	250-392-4135	
Wings Financial Credit Union 14985 Glazier Ave Ste 100 ... Apple Valley *TF:* 800-692-2274 ■ *Web:* www.wingsfinancial.com	MN	55124	952-997-8000	997-8124
Workers' Credit Union 815 Main St PO Box 900 ... Fitchburg *TF:* 800-221-4020 ■ *Web:* www.wcu.com	MA	01420	978-345-1021	343-5825
Wright-Patt Credit Union Inc 2455 Executive Pk Blvd PO Box 286 ... Fairborn *TF:* 800-762-0047 ■ *Web:* www.wpcu.coop	OH	45324	937-912-7000	912-8002
Y-12 Federal Credit Union 501 Lafayette Dr ... Oak Ridge *TF:* 800-482-1043 ■ *Web:* www.y12fcu.org	TN	37830	865-482-1043	
Yolo Federal Credit Union 266 W Main St ... Woodland *TF:* 877-965-6328 ■ *Web:* yolofcu.org	CA	95695	530-668-2700	

220 CRUISE LINES

See Also Casinos p. 1894; Cruises - Riverboat p. 2177; Ports & Port Authorities p. 2965; Travel Agencies p. 3264

			Phone	Fax
Baja Expeditions Inc 3096 Palm St ... San Diego *TF:* 800-843-6967 ■ *Web:* www.bajaex.com	CA	92104	858-581-3311	
Blount Small Ship Adventures 461 Water St ... Warren *TF:* 800-556-7450 ■ *Web:* blountsmallshipadventures.com	RI	02885	401-247-0955	
Bluewater Adventures Ltd 252 E First St Ste 3 ... North Vancouver *TF:* 888-877-1770 ■ *Web:* www.bluewateradventures.ca	BC	V7L1B3	604-980-3800	980-1800
Carnival Cruise Lines 3655 NW 87th Ave ... Miami *TF:* 800-764-7419 ■ *Web:* carnival.com	FL	33178	305-599-2600	
China Ocean Shipping Co Americas Inc (COSCO) 100 Lighting Way ... Secaucus *TF:* 800-242-7354 ■ *Web:* www.cosco-usa.com	NJ	07094	201-422-0500	422-8956
Costa Cruise Lines 200 S Pk Rd Ste 200 ... Hollywood **Fax:* Hum Res ■ *TF:* 800-462-6782 ■ *Web:* www.costacruise.com	FL	33021	954-266-5600	266-5880*
Cruise West 3826 18th Ave W ... Seattle *TF:* 888-862-8881 ■ *Web:* www.un-cruise.com	WA	98119	206-283-9322	
Crystal Cruises Inc 11755 Wilshire Blvd. Ste 900 ... Los Angeles *Web:* www.crystalcruises.com	CA	90025	310-785-9300	
Cunard Line Ltd 24303 Town Ctr Dr Ste 200 ... Valencia *TF:* 800-728-6273 ■ *Web:* www.cunard.com	CA	91355	661-753-1000	
Discovery Cruises Inc 1775 NW 70th Ave ... Miami *TF:* 800-866-8687	FL	33126	305-477-2867	
Great Lakes Cruise Co 3270 Washtenaw Ave ... Ann Arbor **Fax Area Code:* 734 ■ *TF:* 888-891-0203 ■ *Web:* www.greatlakescruising.com	MI	48104	888-891-0203	677-1428*
Holland America Line 300 Elliott Ave W ... Seattle *TF:* 800-426-0327 ■ *Web:* www.hollandamerica.com	WA	98119	206-281-3535	281-7110
Hurtigruten 405 Pk Ave ... New York *TF:* 866-552-0371	NY	10022	212-319-1300	
Lindblad Expeditions 96 Morton St 9th Fl ... New York *TF:* 800-397-3348 ■ *Web:* www.expeditions.com	NY	10014	212-765-7740	265-3770
Maine Windjammer Cruises PO Box 617 ... Camden *TF:* 800-736-7981 ■ *Web:* www.mainewindjammercruises.com	ME	04843	207-236-2938	236-3229
MSC Cruises USA Inc 6750 N Andrews Ave Ste 100 ... Fort Lauderdale *Web:* www.msccruisesusa.com/en-us/homepage.aspx	FL	33309	954-772-6262	
Oceania Cruises Inc 8300 NW 33rd St Ste 308 ... Miami *TF:* 800-531-5619 ■ *Web:* www.oceaniacruises.com	FL	33122	305-514-2300	514-2222
Princess Cruises 24844 Rockefeller Ave ... Santa Clarita **Fax:* Sales ■ *TF:* 800-774-6237 ■ *Web:* www.princess.com	CA	91355	661-753-0000	284-4771*
Rockport Schooner Cruises PO Box 272 ... Belfast *TF:* 866-732-2473 ■ *Web:* www.wanderbirdcruises.com	ME	04915	207-338-3088	
Royal Caribbean International 1050 Caribbean Way ... Miami *TF:* 800-327-6700 ■ *Web:* www.royalcaribbean.com	FL	33132	305-539-6000	
Sea Cloud Cruises Inc 282 Grand Ave Ste 3 ... Englewood *TF:* 888-732-2568 ■ *Web:* www.seacloud.com	NJ	07631	201-227-9404	227-9424
SeaDream Yacht Club 601 Brickell Key Dr Ste 1050 ... Miami *TF:* 800-707-4911 ■ *Web:* www.seadream.com	FL	33131	305-631-6110	631-6110
Star Clippers Inc 760 NW 107th Ave ... Miami *TF Resv:* 800-442-0556 ■ *Web:* www.starclippers.com	FL	33172	305-442-0550	
Travel Dynamics International 132 E 70th St ... New York *TF:* 800-257-5767 ■ *Web:* traveldynamics.com	NY	10021	212-517-7555	774-1560
Windstar Cruises 2101 Fourth Ave Ste 210 ... Seattle *TF Resv:* 800-258-7245 ■ *Web:* www.windstarcruises.com	WA	98121	206-292-9606	733-2790
World, The 1551 Sawgrass Corporate Pkwy Ste 200 ... Fort Lauderdale *TF:* 800-394-2255 ■ *Web:* www.aboardtheworld.com	FL	33323	954-538-8449	431-7151

221 CRUISES - RIVERBOAT

See Also Casinos p. 1894; Cruise Lines p. 2177

			Phone	Fax
American Cruise Lines 741 Boston Post Rd Ste 200 ... Guilford *TF:* 800-814-6880 ■ *Web:* www.americancruiselines.com	CT	06437	203-453-6800	453-0417
Englund Marine & Industrial Supply Company Inc 95 Hamburg Ave PO Box 296 ... Astoria *TF:* 800-228-7051 ■ *Web:* www.englundmarine.com	OR	97103	503-325-4341	325-6421
French Country Waterways Ltd 24 Bay Rd ... Duxbury *TF:* 800-222-1236 ■ *Web:* www.fcwl.com	MA	02332	781-934-2454	
Gateway Clipper Fleet 350 W Stn Sq Dr ... Pittsburgh *Web:* www.gatewayclipper.com	PA	15219	412-355-7980	355-7987
Spirit of Dubuque 500 E Third St ... Dubuque *Web:* www.dubuqueriverrides.com	IA	52001	563-583-8093	585-0634
Uniworld 17323 Ventura Blvd ... Encino *TF:* 800-733-7820 ■ *Web:* www.uniworld.com/en	CA	91316	818-382-7820	
Victoria Cruises Inc 57-08 39th Ave ... Woodside *TF Cust Svc:* 800-348-8084 ■ *Web:* www.victoriacruises.com	NY	11377	212-818-1680	818-9889
Viking River Cruises 5700 Canoga Ave Ste 200 ... Woodland Hills *TF Cust Svc:* 877-668-4546 ■ *Web:* www.vikingrivercruises.com	CA	91367	818-227-1234	227-1237

222 CUTLERY

See Also Silverware p. 3186

			Phone	Fax
Atlanta Cutlery Corp 2147 Gees Mill Rd ... Conyers *TF:* 800-883-0300 ■ *Web:* www.atlantacutlery.com	GA	30013	770-922-3700	760-8993
Buck Knives Inc 660 S Lochsa St ... Post Falls *TF:* 800-326-2825 ■ *Web:* www.buckknives.com	ID	83854	208-262-0500	262-0555
Crescent Manufacturing Co 1310 Majestic Dr ... Fremont *TF:* 800-537-1330 ■ *Web:* www.crescentblades.com	OH	43420	419-332-6484	332-6564
Cutco Corp 1116 E State St ... Olean *TF:* 800-828-0448 ■ *Web:* www.cutco.com	NY	14760	716-372-3111	
Dexter-Russell Inc 44 River St ... Southbridge *TF:* 800-343-6042 ■ *Web:* www.dexter1818.com	MA	01550	508-765-0201	764-2897
Douglas/Quikut Co 118 E Douglas Rd ... Walnut Ridge **Fax Area Code:* 870 ■ *TF:* 800-982-5233 ■ *Web:* www.douglasquikut.com	AR	72476	800-982-5233	886-2911*
Fiskars Brands Inc 2537 Daniels St ... Madison *TF:* 866-348-5661 ■ *Web:* www2.fiskars.com	WI	53718	866-348-5661	
Gerber Legendary Blades Inc 14200 SW 72nd Ave ... Portland *Web:* gerbergear.com	OR	97224	503-639-6161	
KA-BAR Knives Inc 200 Homer St ... Olean *TF:* 800-282-0130 ■ *Web:* www.kabar.com	NY	14760	716-372-5952	790-7188
KAI USA ltd 18600 SW Teton Ave ... Tualatin *Web:* kershaw.kaiusaltd.com	OR	97062	503-682-1966	682-7168
Lamson & Goodnow Mfg Co 45 Conway St ... Shelburne Falls *TF:* 800-872-6564 ■ *Web:* www.lamsonsharp.com	MA	01370	413-625-0201	
Master Cutlery Inc 700 Penhorn Ave ... Secaucus *TF:* 888-271-7229 ■ *Web:* www.mastercutlery.com	NJ	07094	201-271-7600	271-7666
Midwest Tool & Cutlery Co Inc 1210 Progress St PO Box 160 ... Sturgis *TF:* 800-782-4659 ■ *Web:* www.midwestsnips.com	MI	49091	269-651-7964	651-4412
Millers Forge Inc 1411 Capital Ave ... Plano *Web:* www.millersforge.com	TX	75074	972-422-2145	881-0639
Ontario Knife Co 26 Empire St ... Franklinville **Fax Area Code:* 800 ■ *TF:* 800-222-5233 ■ *Web:* www.ontarioknife.com	NY	14737	716-676-5527	299-2618*
Pacific Handy Cutter Inc 17819 Gillette Ave ... Irvine *TF Cust Svc:* 800-229-2233 ■ *Web:* www.pacifichandycutter.com	CA	92614	714-662-1033	662-7595
Professional Cutlery Direct LLC 242 Branford Rd ... North Branford *TF:* 800-792-6650	CT	06471	800-792-6650	296-8039
Queen Cutlery Co 507 Chestnut St ... Titusville **Fax Area Code:* 716 ■ *TF Sales:* 800-222-5233 ■ *Web:* www.queencutlery.com	PA	16354	814-827-3673	676-5535*
Rada Manufacturing Co PO Box 838 ... Waverly *TF:* 800-311-9691 ■ *Web:* www.radacutlery.com	IA	50677	319-352-5454	352-0770
Swiss Army Brands Inc 7 Victoria Dr PO Box 1212 ... Monroe *TF Cust Svc:* 800-442-2706 ■ *Web:* www.victorinox.com	CT	06468	203-929-6391	
Wenger North America Inc 15 Corporate Dr ... Orangeburg *TF Cust Svc:* 800-431-2996 ■ *Web:* www.wengerna.com	NY	10962	845-365-3500	425-4700
WR Case & Sons Cutlery Co 50 Owens Way PO Box 4000 ... Bradford **Fax Area Code:* 814 ■ *TF:* 800-523-6350 ■ *Web:* www.wrcase.com	PA	16701	800-523-6350	368-1736*
Zippo Manufacturing Co 33 Barbour St ... Bradford *Web:* www.zippo.com	PA	16701	814-368-2700	

223 CYLINDERS & ACTUATORS - FLUID POWER

See Also Automotive Parts & Supplies - Mfr p. 1830

			Phone	Fax
Advance Automation Company Inc 3526 N Elston Ave ... Chicago *Web:* www.advanceautomationco.com	IL	60618	773-539-7633	539-7299
American Cylinder Company Inc 481 S Governors Hwy ... Peotone *Web:* www.americancylinder.com	IL	60468	708-258-3935	258-3980
Atlas Cylinder Corp 500 S Wolf Rd ... Des Plaines *Web:* parker.com	IL	60016	847-298-2400	294-2655
Beaver Aerospace & Defense Inc 11850 Mayfield St ... Livonia *Web:* www.beaver-online.com	MI	48150	734-853-5003	853-5043
BEI Technologies 2470 Coral St ... Vista *Web:* www.beikimco.com	CA	92081	760-597-6300	
Best Metal Products Co 3570 Raleigh Dr SE ... Grand Rapids *Web:* www.bestmetalproducts.com	MI	49512	616-942-7141	942-0949
Bosch Rexroth Corp 5150 Prairie Stone Pkwy ... Hoffman Estates *TF:* 800-860-1055 ■ *Web:* www.boschrexroth.com/en/us	IL	60192	847-645-3600	645-6201
Clippard Instrument Lab 7390 Colerain Ave ... Cincinnati *TF:* 877-245-6247 ■ *Web:* www.clippard.com	OH	45239	513-521-4261	521-4464
Columbus Hydraulics Co PO Box 250 ... Columbus *Web:* www.columbushydraulics.com	NE	68601	402-564-8544	564-0129
Commercial Honing Co Inc 8608 Sultana Ave ... Fontana *Web:* www.commercialhoning.com	CA	92335	909-829-1211	829-7631
Control Line Equipment Inc 14750 Industrial Pkwy ... Cleveland *TF:* 888-895-1440 ■ *Web:* www.control-line.com	OH	44135	216-433-7766	
Cunningham Manufacturing Co 318 S Webster St ... Seattle *TF:* 800-767-0038 ■ *Web:* www.cunninghamcylinders.com	WA	98108	206-767-3713	762-3457

Phone | Fax

Dynex Rivett Inc 770 Capitol Dr ... Pewaukee WI 53072 262-691-0300 691-0312
Web: www.dynexhydraulics.com

Eckel Mfg Company Inc 8035 N County Rd W ... Odessa TX 79764 432-362-4336 362-1827
TF: 800-654-4779 ■ *Web:* www.eckel.com

Energy Mfg Co Inc 204 Plastic Ln ... Monticello IA 52310 319-465-3537 465-5279
Web: www.energymfg.com

Fabco-Air Inc 3716 NE 49th Ave ... Gainesville FL 32609 352-373-3578 375-8024
Web: www.fabco-air.com

Galland Henning Nopak Inc
1025 S 40th St ... West Milwaukee WI 53215 414-645-6000 645-6048
Web: www.nopak.com

General Engineering Co
26485 Hillman Hwy PO Box 549 ... Abingdon VA 24212 276-628-6068 628-4311
Web: generalengr.com

Great Bend Industries Inc 8701 Sixth St ... Great Bend KS 67530 620-792-4368 792-3935
Web: www.greatbendindustries.com

Hader/Seitz Inc 15600 W Lincoln Ave ... New Berlin WI 53151 877-388-2101
TF: 877-388-2101 ■ *Web:* www.haderind.com/seitz.htm

Hannon Hydraulics LLC 625 N Loop 12 ... Irving TX 75061 972-438-2870 554-4047
TF: 800-333-4266 ■ *Web:* www.hannonhydraulics.com

Helac Corp 225 Battersby Ave ... Enumclaw WA 98022 360-825-1601 825-1603
TF: 800-327-2589 ■ *Web:* www.helac.com

Hol-Mac Corp 2730-A Hwy 15 PO Box 349 ... Bay Springs MS 39422 601-764-4121 764-3438
TF: 800-844-3019 ■ *Web:* www.hol-mac.com

Humphrey Products Co
5070 E N Ave PO Box 2008 ... Kalamazoo MI 49048 269-381-5500 381-4113
TF: 800-477-8707 ■ *Web:* www.humphrey-products.com

Hydac Technology Corp
2260-2280 City Line Rd ... Bethlehem PA 18017 610-266-0100
Web: www.hydac-na.com/sites/hydac-na

ITT Industries Inc Engineered Valves Div
33 Centerville Rd ... Lancaster PA 17603 717-509-2200 509-2336
TF: 800-366-1111 ■ *Web:* www.engvalves.com

JARP Industries Inc 1051 Pine St PO Box 923 ... Schofield WI 54476 715-359-4241 355-4960
Web: www.jarpind.com

Linak Us Inc 2200 Stanley Gault Pkwy ... Louisville KY 40223 502-253-5595 253-5596
Web: www.linak-us.com

Luxfer Gas Cylinders 3016 Kansas Ave ... Riverside CA 92507 951-684-5110 328-1117
TF: 800-764-0366 ■ *Web:* luxfer.com

Lynair Inc 3515 Scheele Dr ... Jackson MI 49202 517-787-2240 787-4521
Web: www.lynair.com

Micromatic LLC 525 Berne St ... Berne IN 46711 260-589-2136 589-8966
TF: 800-333-5752 ■ *Web:* www.micromaticllc.com

Moog Flo-Tork Inc 1701 N Main St PO Box 68 ... Orrville OH 44667 330-682-0010 683-6857
Web: flotork.com

Motion Systems Corp 600 Industrial Way W ... Eatontown NJ 07724 732-222-1800 389-9191
Web: actuator.com

Norris Cylinder Co 4818 W Loop 281 ... Longview TX 75603 903-757-7633 237-7654
TF: 800-527-8418 ■ *Web:* www.norriscylinder.com

Parker Hannifin Corp Automation Actuator Div
135 Quadral Dr ... Wadsworth OH 44281 330-336-3511 334-3335
TF: 800-272-7537 ■ *Web:* www.parker.com

Parker Hannifin Corp Cylinder Div
500 S Wolf Rd ... Des Plaines IL 60016 847-298-2400 294-2655
TF: 800-272-7537 ■ *Web:* parker.com

Parker Hannifin Corp Oildyne Div
5520 Hwy 169 N ... Minneapolis MN 55428 763-533-1600 533-0082
Web: parker.com

Parker Instrumentation Group
6035 Parkland Blvd ... Cleveland OH 44124 216-896-3000 896-4022
TF: 800-272-7537 ■ *Web:* parker.com

PHD Inc 9009 Clubridge Dr ... Fort Wayne IN 46809 260-747-6151 747-6754
TF: 800-624-8511 ■ *Web:* www.phdinc.com

Quincy Ortman Cylinders
3501 Wismann Ln PO Box C-2 ... Quincy IL 62305 217-277-0321 222-1773
TF: 844-759-4922 ■ *Web:* www.ortmanfluidpower.com

Sargent Controls & Aerospace
5675 W Burlingame Rd ... Tucson AZ 85743 520-744-1000 744-9494
TF: 800-230-0359 ■ *Web:* www.sargentaerospace.com

Seabee Corp 712 First St NW ... Hampton IA 50441 641-456-4871 456-2387
Web: www.seabeecylinders.com

Sheffer Corp 6990 Cornell Rd ... Cincinnati OH 45242 513-489-9770 489-3034*
*Fax: Sales ■ *Web:* www.sheffercorp.com

Southwestern Controls
6720 Sands Point Dr Ste 100 ... Houston TX 77074 713-777-2626 988-1750
Web: www.swcontrols.com

Standex International Corp Custom Hoists Div
771 County Rd 30A W PO Box 98 ... Hayesville OH 44838 419-368-4721 368-4209
TF: 800-837-4668 ■ *Web:* www.customhoists.com

Tactair Fluid Controls Inc 4806 W Taft Rd ... Liverpool NY 13088 315-451-3928 451-8919
Web: www.tactair.com

Texas Hydraulics Inc PO Box 1067 ... Temple TX 76503 254-778-4701 774-9940
Web: www.texashydraulics.com

Tol-O-Matic Inc 3800 County Rd 116 ... Hamel MN 55340 763-478-8000 478-8080
TF: 800-328-2174 ■ *Web:* www.tolomatic.com

Wabash Technologies
1375 Swan St PO Box 829 ... Huntington IN 46750 260-355-4100 355-4265*
*Fax: Sales ■ *TF:* 800-487-6865

224 DATA COMMUNICATIONS SERVICES FOR WIRELESS DEVICES

Companies listed here deliver data such as customized news or stock information, other personalized content, and/or multimedia, audio, and video from the Internet to wireless devices (cellular phones, Personal Digital Assistants, pagers, laptop computers).

Phone | Fax

2lemetry Inc 1321 15th St Ste 200 ... Denver CO 80202 720-606-2646
Web: 2lemetry.com

4comm Inc 40 Burt Dr Ste 4 ... Deer Park NY 11729 631-254-1000
Web: 4commny.com

7thOnline Inc 24 W 40th St 11th Fl ... New York NY 10018 212-997-1717
Web: www.7thonline.com

Accel Networks LLC 4905 34th StS #227 ... St. Petersburg FL 33711 877-406-8585
TF: 877-406-8585 ■ *Web:* www.accel-networks.com

Addictive Mobility Inc 72 Fraser Ave Ste 201 ... Toronto ON M6K3J7 416-535-0706
Web: addictivemobility.com

ADEX Corp 1035 Windward Ridge Pkwy Ste 500 ... Alpharetta GA 30005 678-393-7900
Web: www.adextelecom.com

Advanced C4 Solutions Inc
4017 W Dr Martin Luther King Junior Blvd ... Tampa FL 33614 813-282-3031
Web: www.ac4s.com

Air2Web Inc 1230 Peachtree St NE ... Atlanta GA 30309 404-942-5300 815-7708

AirRoamer Inc Adelaide St W Ste 354 - 157 ... Toronto ON M5H4E7 647-258-6589
Web: www.airroamer.com

AldeaVision Solutions Inc
8550 Cote de Liesse Blvd Ste 200 ... Saint-Laurent QC H4T1H2 514-344-5432
Web: www.aldeavision.com

All Communications Network Of Canada Co
1100 Ave. des Canadiens-de-Montr?al Ste 450 ... Montreal QC H3B2S2 514-390-2525
Web: acncanada.ca

Alligato Inc 202 - 4555 Kingsway ... Burnaby BC V5H4T8 778-383-7570
Web: www.alligatomobile.com

Altius Broadband Inc
3314 Papermill Rd Ste 100 ... Phoenix MD 21131 410-667-1638
Web: www.altiuscomm.com

Ansatel Communications Inc 940 Kingsway ... Vancouver BC V5V3C4 604-872-6500
Web: ansatel.com

AOL Canada Inc 99 Spadina Ave Ste 200 ... Toronto ON M5V3P8 416-263-8100
TF: 888-265-6306 ■ *Web:* www.aol.ca

Archi-Tech Systems Inc
275 Phillips Blvd Ste 140 ... Ewing NJ 08618 609-882-2447
Web: www.archi-tech.com

Argent Associates Inc 140 Fieldcrest Ave ... Edison NJ 08837 732-512-9009
Web: www.argentassociates.com

Ascedia Inc 161 S First St ... Milwaukee WI 53204 414-292-3200
Web: www.ascedia.com

Audience Communication Inc
174 Spadina Rd Ste 101 ... Toronto ON M5T2C2 416-703-3737
Web: www.audienceinc.ca

Authenex Inc 1413 Grant Rd ... Mountain View CA 94040 650-641-1198
Web: www.authenex.com

Auto Data Direct Inc
1379 Cross Creek Cir ... Tallahassee FL 32301 850-877-8804
TF: 866-923-3123 ■ *Web:* www.add123.com

Avotus Corp 409 Matheson Blvd E ... Mississauga ON L4Z2H2 905-890-9199
Web: www.avotus.com

Awecomm Technologies L L C
165 Kirts Blvd Ste 400 ... Troy MI 48084 248-404-9910
Web: www.awecomm.com

Azimuth Systems Inc 35 Nagog Pk ... Acton MA 01720 978-263-6610 263-5352
Web: www.azimuthsystems.com

B2B2C Inc 1575 Henri-Bourassa Blvd W Ste 255 ... Montreal QC H3M3A9 514-908-5420
Web: www.b2b2c.ca

BestTransport.com Inc
400 W Wilson Bridge Rd Ste 100 ... Columbus OH 43085 614-888-2378
Web: www.besttransport.com

BlackBerry 2200 University Ave E Ste 200 ... Waterloo ON N2L3X2 519-888-7465
TF: 877-255-2377 ■ *Web:* www.blackberry.net

Blast Communications Inc
1444 N Farnsworth Ave Ste 304 ... Aurora IL 60505 630-375-9600
Web: www.blastcomm.com

Broadcast Microwave Services Inc (BMS)
12367 Crosthwaite Cir ... Poway CA 92064 858-391-3050 391-3049
TF: 800-669-9667 ■ *Web:* bms-inc.com

Broadcast Technical Services Inc
7219 Gessner Dr ... Houston TX 77040 832-467-0002
Web: www.btshouston.com

Buyatab Online Inc 204 - 576 Seymour St ... Vancouver BC V6B3K1 888-267-0447
TF: 888-267-0447 ■ *Web:* www.buyatab.com

C5 Group Inc 1329 Bay St ... Toronto ON M5R2C4 416-927-0718
Web: www.c5groupinc.com

Calpop Com Inc 600 W Seventh St ... Los Angeles CA 90017 866-467-8846
TF: 866-467-8846

Carousel Industries of North America Inc
659 S County Trl ... Exeter RI 02822 800-401-0760 760-5236*
*Fax Area Code: 860 ■ *TF:* 800-401-0760 ■ *Web:* www.carouselindustries.com

Catalyst Communications Technologies Inc
2107 Graves Mill Rd Mail Stop D ... Forest VA 24551 434-582-6146
Web: www.catcomtec.com

CaTECH Systems Ltd 201 Whitehall Dr Unit 4 ... Markham ON L3R9Y3 905-944-0000
Web: catechsystems.com

CBOSS Inc 7332 Southern Blvd Sutton Ctr Plz ... Boardman OH 44512 330-726-0429
Web: www.cboss.com

CHARGED.fm 10 Jay St ... Brooklyn NY 11201 646-490-2700
Web: www.charged.fm

Chatr Wireless 333 Bloor St E 8th Fl ... Toronto ON M4W1G9 800-485-9745
TF: 800-485-9745 ■ *Web:* www.chatrwireless.com

Cirrus9 Inc 15 Market Sq ... Saint John NB E2L1E8 855-643-6691
TF: 855-643-6691 ■ *Web:* www.cirrus9.net

Clevest Solutions Inc
13911 Wireless Way Ste 100 ... Richmond BC V6V3B9 604-214-9700
TF: 866-915-0088 ■ *Web:* www.clevest.com

CodeExcellence.com Inc 3553 31 St NW ... Calgary AB T2L2K7 403-800-2071
Web: www.codeexcellence.com

Cognify PO Box 69337 ... Oro Valley AZ 85737 888-264-6439
TF: 888-444-7992 ■ *Web:* www.cognify.com

Colba.Net Telecom Inc
6465 TransCanada Hwy Ville St-Laurent ... Montreal QC H4T1S3 514-856-3500
Web: www.colba.net

Cologix Inc 2300 15th St Ste 300 ... Denver CO 80202 720-230-7000
Web: www.cologix.com

Com-Net Services Inc 7786 S Commerce Ave ... Baton Rouge LA 70815 225-928-1231
TF: 800-676-2137 ■ *Web:* www.comnetserv.com

ComCanada Communications Inc
232-1027 Davie St ... Vancouver BC V6E4L2 604-998-4500
Web: www.comcanada.ca

Phone Fax

Commerx Computer Systems Inc
2880 Argentia Rd Unit 1........................ Mississauga ON L5N7X8 905-542-9400
Web: www.commerx.ca

Commodity Systems Inc
200 W Palmetto Park Rd Ste 200................. Boca Raton FL 33432 561-392-8663
Web: www.csidata.com

Condo Control Central 10 St Mary Stÿ Ste 200.......... Toronto ON M5X1C7 888-762-6636
TF: 888-762-6636 ■ *Web:* www.condocontrolcentral.com

Conxxus LLC 330 W Ottawa.......................... Paxton IL 60957 217-379-2026
Web: www.conxxus.com

CoopTel coop de t?l?communication
5521, chemin de l?A?roport......................... Valcourt QC J0E2L0 450-532-2667
Web: www.cooptel.qc.ca

Copper Valley Telephone Cooperative Inc
329 Fairbanks Dr.................................. Valdez AK 99686 907-835-2231
Web: www.cvinternet.net

Coranet Corp 2 Washington St Ste 701...............New York NY 10004 212-635-2770
Web: coranet.com

Cti Communication Technologies
18110 chesterfield airport rd...................... Chesterfield MO 63005 636-537-7200
Web: www.cti-stl.com

Data Conversion Laboratory Inc
61-18 190th St Ste 205 .... Fresh Meadows NY 11365 718-357-8700
Web: dclab.com

Dataware LLC 2900 W 11th St Ste 102............. Sioux Falls SD 57104 605-336-0820
Web: www.datawareservices.com

Despegar com Inc 14 NE, 1st Ave Ste 516............. Miami FL 33132 305-577-4919
Web: www.despegar.com

Dial800 LLC 9911 Pico Blvd Ste 1200...............Los Angeles CA 90035 800-342-5800
TF: 800-700-1987 ■ *Web:* www.dial800.com

Digital Map Products Inc
18831 Von Karman Ave Ste 200........................ Irvine CA 92612 949-333-5111
Web: www.digitalmapproducts.com

Digital Networks Group Inc
100 Columbia Ste 100............................. Aliso Viejo CA 92656 949-428-6333
Web: www.digitalnetworksgroup.com

Discover Communications Inc
30 Victoria Crescent.............................. Brampton ON L6T1E4 905-455-5600
TF: 888-456-8989 ■ *Web:* www.getconnected.ca

Dissolve Inc 425 78 Ave SW......................... Calgary AB T2V5K5 650-450-9048
Web: www.dissolve.com

Dot VN Inc 9449 Balboa Ave Ste 114................. San Diego CA 92123 858-571-2007
Web: www.dotvn.com

Doublehorn Communications 1802 W Sixth St.......... Austin TX 78703 214-283-1400
TF: 855-618-6423 ■ *Web:* www.doublehorn.com

Dovetail Communications Inc
30 E Beaver Creek Rd Ste 202 .... Richmond Hill ON L4B1J2 905-886-6640
Web: dvtail.com

dPi Teleconnect LLC 1330 Capital Pkwy............. Carrollton TX 75006 972-488-5500

DriverDO LLC 734 Massachusetts St.................. Lawrence KS 66044 844-366-6837
TF: 844-366-6837 ■ *Web:* www.driverdo.com

Dtreds LLC 1329 Shepard Dr Ste 2.................... Sterling VA 20164 877-694-7766
TF: 877-694-7766 ■ *Web:* www.dtreds.com

DXStorm.com Inc 824 Winston Churchill Blvd........... Oakville ON L6J7X2 905-842-8262
TF: 877-397-8676 ■ *Web:* www.dxstorm.com

Dynamic Mobile Data Systems Inc
285 Davidson Ave Ste 501......................... Somerset NJ 08873 732-537-0016 302-9558

EDge Interactive Inc 67 Mowat Ave Ste 533............ Toronto ON M6K3E3 416-494-3343
TF: 800-211-5577 ■ *Web:* www.edgeip.com

EDULINX Canada Corp
2 Robert Speck Pkwy 14th Fl.................... Mississauga ON L4Z1H8 905-306-2995
Web: www.studentaid.alberta.ca

Emergency Communications for SW British Columbia Inc
3301 E Pender St................................ Vancouver BC V5K5J3 604-215-5000
Web: www.ecomm911.ca

Ensource Inc 7970 Bayberry Rd Ste 5...............Jacksonville FL 32256 904-448-6901
Web: www.ensource.net

Everbridge Inc 500 N Brand Blvd Ste 1000............ Glendale CA 91203 818-230-9700
Web: www.everbridge.com

Execulink Telecom Inc 619 Main St N............. Burgessville ON N0J1C0 866-706-1994
TF: 866-706-1994 ■ *Web:* www.execulink.com

Fibernetics Corp 605 Boxwood Dr.................. Cambridge ON N3E1A5 519-489-6700
TF: 866-973-4237 ■ *Web:* www.fibernetics.ca

Fibre Noire Internet Inc
550 Ave Beaumont Ste 320......................... Montreal QC H3N1V1 877-907-3002
TF: 877-907-3002 ■ *Web:* m.fibrenoire.ca

First Growth Holdings Ltd
4388 Still Creek Dr Unit 235...................... Vancouver BC V5C6C6 604-688-9588
Web: firstgrowthholdings.com

FONEX Data Systems Inc
5400 Ch St-Francois .... St-Laurent QC H4S1P6 514-333-6639
Web: www.fonex.com

FreshGrade Inc 301-1447 Ellis St.................... Kelowna BC V1Y2A3 877-957-7757
TF: 877-957-7757 ■ *Web:* www.freshgrade.com

FundThrough Inc 260 Spadina Ave Ste 400.............. Toronto ON M5T2E4 800-766-0460
TF: 800-766-0460 ■ *Web:* www.fundthrough.com

Gabriels Technology Solutions Inc
250 Hudson St Rm 1002 .... New York NY 10013 212-741-0700
Web: www.gabriels.net

Giles Craig Communications Inc
504 Snidow St.................................... Pembroke VA 24136 540-544-2288
Web: www.pemtel.com

Gistics Inc 4171 Piedmont Ave Ste 210................ Oakland CA 94611 510-450-9999
Web: gistics.com

Glint Inc 808 Winslow St...................... Redwood City CA 94063 650-817-7240
Web: www.glintinc.com

Global Relay Communications Inc
220 cambie St.................................... Vancouver BC V6B2M9 604-484-6630
TF: 866-484-6630 ■ *Web:* www.globalrelay.com

GreenSky Trade Credit LLC
1797 Northeast Expy Ste 100........................ Atlanta GA 30329 866-936-0602
TF: 866-936-0602 ■ *Web:* www.greenskycredit.com

Groupe Maskatel Inc
3455 Blvd Choquette......................... Saint-Hyacinthe QC J2S7Z8 450-250-5050
Web: www.maskatel.ca

Handy Networks LLC 1801 Calif St Ste 240.............. Denver CO 80202 303-414-6910
Web: www.handynetworks.com

Hay Communications 72863 Blind Line PO Box 99........ Zurich ON N0M2T0 519-236-4333
Web: www.hay.net

HiBeam Internet & Voice
400 S Woods Mill Rd Ste 305 .... Chesterfield MO 63017 636-203-9400

Hookflash Solutions Inc 6679 1A Ave Unit 1............. Delta BC V4M3B3 604-628-9688
Web: www.hookflash.ca

Hotwire Communications LLC
1 Belmont Ave Ste 1100........................ Bala Cynwyd PA 19004 800-409-4733
TF: 800-355-5668 ■ *Web:* hotwirecommunications.com

Hover Networks Inc
40 Gardenville Pkwy Ste 102......................... Buffalo NY 14224 716-650-5650
Web: www.hovernetworks.com

Huxley Communications Cooperative
102 n main ave...................................... Huxley IA 50124 515-597-2212
TF: 800-231-4922 ■ *Web:* www.huxcomm.net

iLeads.com LLC
567 San Nicolas Dr Ste 180................... Newport Beach CA 92660 877-245-3237
TF: 877-245-3237 ■ *Web:* www.ileads.com

Immediatek Inc(NDA) 3301 Airport Fwy Ste 200......... Bedford TX 76021 888-661-6565
TF: 888-661-6565 ■ *Web:* www.immediatek.com

InfoSearch Media Inc 6041 Bristol Pkwy........... Culver City CA 90230 310-437-7380
Web: www.infosearchmedia.com

Inspire Communications Inc 1414 Montauk Ct.......... Bartlett IL 60103 630-233-1331
Web: inspiredcom.com

Interlinc Direct Corp 1-65 Superior Blvd........... Mississauga ON L5T2X9 905-677-2620
Web: www.interlincdirect.com

Intermec Technologies Corp 6001 36th Ave W.......... Everett WA 98203 425-348-2600 355-9551
TF Sales: 800-934-3163 ■ *Web:* www.intermec.com

InterStar Communications Inc 102 Sampson St........ Clinton NC 28329 910-564-4638
Web: www.starcom.net

iTalkBB Canada Inc
109 - 235 Yorkland Blvd........................... North York ON M2J4Y8 877-482-5522
TF: 877-482-5522 ■ *Web:* www.italkbb.com

Ituran USA Inc
1700 NW 64th St Ste 100..................... Fort Lauderdale FL 33309 954-484-3806
Web: www.ituranusa.com

Itx Corp 1169 Pittsford Victor Rd Ste 100................ Pittsford NY 14534 585-899-4888
TF: 800-600-7785 ■ *Web:* www.itx.com

Jatom Systems Inc 99 Michael Cowpland Dr............. Kanata ON K2M1X3 613-591-5910

JM Eventsonline ca Inc 155 Colonnade Rd Ste 17....... Ottawa ON K2E7K1 866-638-3687
TF: 866-638-3687 ■ *Web:* secure.eventsonline.ca

JumpStart Wireless Corp
566 SW 20th Ct Ste B.......................... Delray Beach FL 33445 561-243-4700
Web: www.jumpstartwireless.com

Kin Communications Inc
736 Granville St Ste 100........................... Vancouver BC V6Z1G3 604-684-6730
TF: 866-684-6730 ■ *Web:* www.kincommunications.com

Koplar Communications International Inc
50 Maryland Dr Ste 300.......................... Saint Louis MO 63108 314-345-1000
Web: www.koplar.com

Kuboo Inc Ste 101 7740 E Evans Rd................. Scottsdale AZ 85260 480-385-3893
Web: www.safecom.net

Larson Data Communications Inc
220 S. Kimball St PO Box 96 .... Mitchell SD 57301 605-996-5521
Web: larsondata.com

Laurel Highland Total Communications Inc
4157 Main St..................................... Stahlstown PA 15687 724-593-2411
Web: www.lhtc.co

Lead Intelligence Inc 201 S Maple Ave Ste 150.......... Ambler PA 19002 267-460-7287
Web: www.leadid.com

Lemieux Bedard Communications Inc
2665 King W Ste 315 .... Sherbrooke QC J1L2G5 819-823-0850
Web: www.lemieuxbedard.com

LemonStand eCommerce Inc
912-525 Seymour St .... Vancouver BC V6B3H7 604-558-0555
TF: 855-332-0555 ■ *Web:* lemonstand.com

Lesic & Camper Communications
172 E State St Ste 410 .... Columbus OH 43215 614-224-7755
Web: www.lesiccamper.com

Link America Inc 3002 Century Dr.................... Rowlett TX 75088 972-463-0050
Web: www.linkam.com

Loft Communications & Events Inc
27 Atlantic Ave..................................... Toronto ON M6K3E7 416-699-5638
Web: loftcommunications.com

Lpi Communications Group Inc
253 62 Ave Se Ste 101.............................. Calgary AB T2H0R5 403-735-0655
Web: www.lpi-group.com

Lytro 1300 Terra Bella Ave..................... Mountain View CA 94043 650-316-8888
Web: www.lytro.com

Marketingworks Inc
7000 Romaine St Ste 200........................ Los Angeles CA 90038 323-436-2000
Web: www.marketingworksagency.com

MarketQuiz Inc
12500 San Pedro Ave Ste 657 .... San Antonio TX 78216 210-494-7770

Masergy Communications Inc
2740 N Dallas Pkwy Ste 260............................ Plano TX 75093 214-442-5700 442-5756
TF: 866-588-5885 ■ *Web:* www.masergy.com

MediaCore Inc 26 Bastion Sq Ste 205 .... Victoria BC V8W1H9 250-590-9394
TF: 877-682-6655 ■ *Web:* mediacore.com

MedTel.com Inc 353 Third Ave Ste 19 ....New York NY 10010 212-777-7722
Web: www.medtel.com

Metalink Technologies Inc
417 Wayne Ave PO Box 1124....................... Defiance OH 43512 419-782-3472
TF: 888-999-8002 ■ *Web:* www.metalink.net

Meteorcomm LLC 1201 SW Seventh St .... Renton WA 98057 253-872-2521 872-7662
Web: www.meteorcomm.com

Metro 1 120 NE 27 St Ste 200 .... Miami FL 33137 305-571-9991 571-9661
Web: www.metro1.com

				Phone	Fax
MFour Mobile Research Inc 3525 Hyland Ave Ste 240 *Web:* mfour.com	Costa Mesa	CA	92626	714-754-1234	
Mig Communications 800 Hearst Ave *Web:* www.migcom.com	Berkeley	CA	94710	510-845-7549	
Mob4Hire Inc 918?16th Ave NW Ste 90 *Web:* www.mob4hire.com	Calgary	AB	T2M0K3	403-399-4589	
Mobilicity 101 Exchange Ave *TF:* 877-866-2458 ■ *Web:* www.mobilicity.ca	Vaughan	ON	L4K5R6	877-866-2458	
Modulis Inc 6250 Blvd Monk *Web:* www.modulis.com	Montreal	QC	H4E3H7	514-284-2020	
Mojio Inc 1080 Howe St 9th Fl *TF:* 855-556-6546 ■ *Web:* www.moj.io	Vancouver	BC	V6Z2T1	855-556-6546	
Mornington Communications Co-operative Ltd 16 Mill St E *Web:* mornington.ca	Milverton	ON	N0K1M0	519-595-8331	
MTS Communications Inc 333 Main St *Web:* www.mts.ca	Winnipeg	MB	R3C3V6	204-225-5687	
Namecheap Inc 11400 W Olympic Blvd Ste 200 *Web:* www.namecheap.com	Los Angeles	CA	90064	661-310-2107	
Netfast Communications Inc 989 Ave of the Americas 4th Fl *Web:* www.netfast.com	New York	NY	10018	212-792-5200	
Netkrom Technologies Inc 2134 Nw 99th Ave *Web:* www.netkrom.com	Miami	FL	33172	305-418-2232	
NetLine Corp 750 University Ave Ste 200 *Web:* www.netline.com	Los Gatos	CA	95032	408-340-2200	
Network Earth Inc 14 Cambridge Ct *TF:* 888-201-5160 ■ *Web:* www.netearth.com	Wappingers Falls	NY	12590	888-201-5160	
NetWorth Services Inc 1661 E Camelback Rd Ste 200 *Web:* www.networthservices.com	Phoenix	AZ	85016	602-222-6380	
Nitel Inc 1101 W Lk St 6th Fl *TF:* 888-450-2100 ■ *Web:* www.nitelusa.com	Chicago	IL	60607	888-450-2100	
NKTelco Inc 301 W S St PO Box 219 *TF:* 888-658-3526 ■ *Web:* www.nktelco.net	New Knoxville	OH	45871	419-753-2457	
Nonfiction Studios Inc 450, 318 - 11th Ave SE *Web:* www.nonfiction.ca	Calgary	AB	T2G0Y2	403-686-8887	
NTG Clarity Networks Inc 2820 Fourteenth Ave Ste 202 *Web:* www.ntgclarity.com	Markham	ON	L3R0S9	905-305-1325	
NthGen Software Inc 4711 Yonge St Ste 506 *Web:* www.nthgensoftware.com	Toronto	ON	M2N6K8	416-900-0941	
Oil-Law Records Corp 8 N W 65th St *TF:* 888-464-5529 ■ *Web:* www.oil-law.com	Oklahoma City	OK	73116	405-840-1631	
Okanjo Partners Inc 220 E Buffalo St Ste 303 *Web:* www.okanjo.com	Milwaukee	WI	53202	414-810-1760	
Omnis Network LLC 3655 Torrance Blvd Ste 230 *Web:* www.omnis.com	Torrance	CA	90503	310-316-9600	
Ontario Research and Innovation Optical Network (ORION), The 360 Bay St 7th Fl *Web:* www.orano.on.ca	Toronto	ON	M5H2V6	416-507-9860	
Ontash & Ermac Inc 876 Kndrkamak Rd Ste 201 *Web:* www.ontash.com	River Edge	NJ	07661	201-265-2189	
Optical & Telecommunication Solutions Inc 16835 Addison Rd Ste 105 *Web:* www.optelsol.com	Addison	TX	75001	972-931-0360	
Optimum Computer Solutions Inc 780 Westridge Rd *Web:* www.ocscorp.com	The Woodlands	TX	77380	281-364-0539	
Outreach Communications 2801 Glenda St *TF:* 800-982-3760 ■ *Web:* www.outreachcom.com	Haltom City	TX	76117	817-288-7200	
Ovation Data Services Inc 14199 Westfair E Dr *Web:* www.ovationdata.com	Houston	TX	77040	713-464-1300	
Oxford Media Group 70 Wellington St S *Web:* oxfordmediagroup.com	Woodstock	ON	N4S3H6	519-539-9762	
Pa-Go Mobile Inc 150 NE 95th St Ste 307 *TF:* 877-425-2196 ■ *Web:* www.pa-gomobile.com	Seattle	WA	98115	877-425-2196	
Permabit Technology Corp 10 Canal Park 3rd Fl *Web:* www.permabit.com	Cambridge	MA	02141	617-252-9600	
Pilar Services Inc 13910 Laurel Lakes Ave *Web:* www.pilarservices.net	Laurel	MD	20707	301-362-1569	
Pinger Inc 97 S Second St Ste 210 *Web:* www.pinger.com	San Jose	CA	95113	408-271-5700	
Piquniq Management Corp 6613 Brayton Dr *Web:* www.alaska.net	Anchorage	AK	99507	907-522-5234	
PocketiNet Communications Inc 45 Terminal Loop Rd Ste 210 *Web:* www.pocketinet.com	Walla Walla	WA	99362	509-526-5026	
Powered By Search Inc 505 Consumers Rd Ste 507 *TF:* 866-611-5535 ■ *Web:* www.poweredbysearch.com	Toronto	ON	M2J4V8	416-840-9044	
PUC Telecom Inc 765 Queen E *Web:* www.ssmpuc.com	Sault Ste Marie	ON	P6A2A8	705-759-6500	
Pure Brand Communications LLC 2401 Larimer St *Web:* www.pure-brand.com	Denver	CO	80205	303-625-1085	
Purple Forge Corp 900 Greenbank Rd Ste 315 *Web:* www.purpleforge.com	Ottawa	ON	K2J4P6	613-216-2148	
Radixx Solutions International Inc 6310 Hazeltine National Dr *Web:* www.radixx.com	Orlando	FL	32822	407-856-9009	
Redline Communications Inc 302 Town Centre Blvd 3rd Fl *TF:* 866-633-6669 ■ *Web:* rdlcom.com	Markham	ON	L3R0E8	905-479-8344	
Remote Dynamics Inc 400 Chisholm Pl Ste 411 *Web:* citysearch.com/guide/dallas-tx-metro	Plano	TX	75075	214-440-5200	440-5208
Rhiza Inc 5850 Ellsworth Ave Ste 200 *Web:* rhiza.com	Pittsburgh	PA	15232	412-488-0600	
RightsTrade LLC 11846 Ventura Blvd Ste 120 *Web:* www.rightstrade.com	Studio City	CA	91604	818-766-2607	
Rightway Gate Inc 5858 Edison Pl *Web:* www.rwgusa.com	Carlsbad	CA	92008	760-736-3700	
RigNet Inc 1880 S Dairy Ashford Rd Ste 300 *Web:* www.rig.net	Houston	TX	77077	281-674-0100	
Ringgold Telephone Company Inc 200 Evitt Pkwy PO Box 869 *Web:* www.rtctel.com	Ringgold	GA	30736	706-965-2345	
RIWI Corp, The 459 Bloor St W Ste 200 *Web:* riwi.com	Toronto	ON	M5S1X9	416-205-9984	
Roam Mobility Inc 400 - 311 Water St *TF:* 888-762-6487 ■ *Web:* www.roammobility.com	Vancouver	BC	V6B1B8	888-762-6487	
Rockynet.com Inc 1919 Fourteenth St Ste 617 *Web:* www.rockynet.com	Boulder	CO	80302	303-444-7052	
S t & p Communications Inc 320 Springside Dr Ste 150 *Web:* www.stpinc.com	Fairlawn	OH	44333	330-668-1932	
Sandler Partners 1200 Artesia Blvd Ste 305 *Web:* www.sandlerpartners.com	Hermosa Beach	CA	90254	310-796-1393	
Satellite Management Services Inc 4529 E Bwy Rd *TF:* 800-788-8388 ■ *Web:* www.smstv.com	Phoenix	AZ	85040	602-386-4444	
SharedReviews com Inc 1938 Bloor St W *Web:* sharedreviews.com	Toronto	ON	M6P4J2	416-619-0992	
SimpleSignal Inc 34232 Pacific Coast Hwy *Web:* www.simplesignal.com	Dana Point	CA	92629	949-487-3333	
Single Digits Inc 4 Bedford Farms Dr Ste 210 *Web:* www.singledigits.com	Bedford	NH	03110	603-580-1539	
Siren Telephone Company Inc 7723 W Main St *Web:* sirentel.com	Siren	WI	54872	715-349-2224	
Skycasters LLC 1520 S Arlington St # 100 *Web:* www.skycasters.com	Akron	OH	44306	330-785-2100	
Skyway West 555 W Hastings St *Web:* www.skywaywest.com	Vancouver	BC	V0N2W2	604-482-1225	
Skyy Consulting Inc 1335 Fourth St Ste 200 *Web:* www.callfire.com	Santa Monica	CA	90401	213-221-2289	
Smart Cabling Solutions Inc 1250 N Winchester St *TF:* 877-390-9501 ■ *Web:* www.thinkscs.com	Olathe	KS	66061	913-390-9501	
Soleo Communications Inc WillowBrook Office Park 300 WillowBrook Dr *Web:* www.soleo.com	Fairport	NY	14450	585-641-4300	
SpeedInfo Inc 100 Park Ctr Plz Ste 590 *Web:* speedinfo.com	San Jose	CA	95113	408-446-7660	
Spin Games LLC 100 Washington St Ste 100 & 250 *Web:* www.spingames.net	Reno	NV	89501	775-420-3550	
SPROUT Wellness Solutions Inc 366 Adelaide St W Ste 301 *TF:* 866-535-5027 ■ *Web:* www.sproutatwork.com	Toronto	ON	M5V1R9	866-535-5027	
SSI Micro Ltd 356B Old Airport Rd *Web:* www.ssimicro.com	Yellowknife	NT	X1A3T4	867-669-7500	
StockCharts.com Inc 11241 Willows Rd Ste 140 *Web:* www.stockcharts.com	Redmond	WA	98052	425-881-2606	
Subex Inc 12101 Airport Way Ste 300 *Web:* www.subexworld.com	Broomfield	CO	80021	303-301-6200	
Superheat Fgh Services Inc 313 Garnet Dr *TF:* 888-508-3226 ■ *Web:* www.superheatfgh.com	New Lenox	IL	60451	888-508-3226	
Synchronoss Technologies Inc 200 Crossing Blvd *NASDAQ: SNCR* ■ *TF:* 866-620-3940 ■ *Web:* www.synchronoss.com	Bridgewater	NJ	08807	866-620-3940	
Talena Inc 830 Hillview Ct *Web:* www.talena-inc.com	Milpitas	CA	95035	408-649-6338	
TBayTel Inc 1060 Lithium Dr *Web:* www.tbaytel.net	Thunder Bay	ON	P7B6G3	807-623-4400	
Telaurus Communications LLC 210 Malapardis Rd *Web:* www.telaurus.com	Cedar Knolls	NJ	07927	973-889-8990	
Telebroad LLC 452 Broadway *Web:* www.telebroad.com	Brooklyn	NY	11211	212-444-9911	
Telebyte Communications Inc 6816 50 Ave *Web:* www.telebyte.ca	Red Deer	AB	T4N4E3	403-346-9966	
Teleco 5221 Oleander Dr *Web:* www.teleco-ilm.com	Wilmington	NC	28403	910-791-7000	
TeleCommunication Systems Inc 275 W St Ste 400 *NASDAQ: TSYS* ■ *TF:* 800-810-0827 ■ *Web:* www.telecomsys.com	Annapolis	MD	21401	410-263-7616	263-7617
TELUS Mobility 200 Consilium Pl Ste 1600 *Web:* mobility.telus.com	Scarborough	ON	M1H3J3	604-291-2355	
TELUS Quebec 6 Rue Jules-A-Brillant *TF:* 866-558-2273 ■ *Web:* www.telusquebec.com	Rimouski	QC	G5L7E4	866-558-2273	
TeraGo Networks Inc 55 Commerce Vly Dr W Ste 800 *TF:* 866-837-2461 ■ *Web:* www.terago.ca	Thornhill	ON	L3T7V9	866-837-2461	
TextureMedia Inc 6604 N Lamar Blvd *Web:* www.naturallycurly.com	Austin	TX	78752	512-371-7545	
Thescore Inc 500 King St W 4th Fl *Web:* mobile.thescore.com	Toronto	ON	M5V1L9	416-479-8812	
Threshold Communications Inc 16541 Redmond Way Ste 245C *TF:* 844-844-1382 ■ *Web:* www.thresholdcommunications.com	Redmond	WA	98052	206-812-6200	
Tierzero 700 Wilshire Blvd 6th Fl *Web:* www.tierzero.com	Los Angeles	CA	90017	213-784-1400	
Totelcom Communications LLC 6100 Hwy 16 S PO Box 290 *Web:* totelcom.net	De Leon	TX	76444	254-893-1000	
Trade Service Company LLC 15092 Ave of Science *TF:* 800-854-1527 ■ *Web:* www.tradeservice.com	San Diego	CA	92128	800-854-1527	
Transtelco Inc 500 W Overland Ave Ste 310 *Web:* www.transtelco.net	El Paso	TX	79901	915-534-8100	

Phone Fax

Trojan Professional Services Inc
14410 Cerritos Ave ... Los Alamitos CA 90720 800-451-9723
TF: 800-451-9723 ■ *Web:* www.trojanonline.com

Trulioo Inc 300 - 420 W Hastings St ... Vancouver BC V6B1L1 888-773-0179
TF: 888-773-0179 ■ *Web:* www.trulioo.com

Underline Communications LLC
12 W 27th St 14th Fl ... New York NY 10001 212-994-4340
Web: www.underlinecom.com

Uniserve Communications Corp
Ste 330 333 Terminal Ave ... Vancouver BC V6A4C1 604-924-8118
Web: www.uniserve.com

UniteU Technologies Inc 12 Pine Cone Dr ... Pittsford NY 14534 866-386-4838
TF: 866-386-4838 ■ *Web:* www.uniteu.com

Upstream Communications Gp LLC
1609 shoal creek blvd Ste 203 ... Austin TX 78748 512-583-7134
Web: getupstream.com

US Online com Inc
25 N Wenatchee Ave Ste 207B ... Wenatchee WA 98801 509-663-6031
Web: www.usonline.com

Usablenet Inc 142 W 57th St 7th Fl ... New York NY 10019 212-965-5388
Web: www.usablenet.com

USBid Inc 2320 Commerce Park Dr ... Palm Bay FL 32905 321-725-9565
Web: www.usbid.com

Used-Car-Parts.com Inc 1980 Highland Pk ... Fort Wright KY 41017 859-344-1925
Web: www.car-part.com

V-Empower Inc 6800 Willow Creek Rd ... Bowie MD 20720 301-805-9194
Web: www.v-empower.com

Visionpoint LLC 152 Rockwell Rd ... Newington CT 06111 860-436-9673
Web: www.visionpointllc.com

Vistanet Communications
6804 Villa Hermosa Dr ... El Paso TX 79912 915-587-1500
Web: vistanetworks.com

Vitac Corp 101 Hillpointe Dr ... Canonsburg PA 15317 724-514-4000
Web: www.vitac.com

Vitelity Communications LLC
7900 E Union Ave Ste 1100 ... Denver CO 80237 720-257-5400
Web: www.vitelity.com

Vorsite Corp 1201 Western Ave Ste 450 ... Seattle WA 98101 206-781-1797
Web: www.vorsite.com

Weblink Solutions 23950 Craftsman Rd ... Calabasas CA 91302 866-296-1977
TF: 866-296-1977 ■ *Web:* www.weblinkcorp.com

WebsiteBox Corp 245 Fairview Mall Dr Ste 401 ... Toronto ON M2J4T4 416-907-6981
Web: www.websitebox.com

Westman Communications Group 1906 Park Ave ... Brandon MB R7B0R9 204-725-4300
Web: www.westmancom.com

Whitecourt Communications 4214 42 Ave ... Whitecourt AB T7S0A3 780-778-3778
Web: whitecourtcommunications.ca

WIND Mobile
207 Queens Quay W Ste 710 PO Box 114 ... Toronto ON M5J1A7 877-946-3184
TF: 877-946-3184 ■ *Web:* www.windmobile.ca

Wireless Analytics LLC 230 N St Ste 4 ... Danvers MA 01923 888-588-5550
TF: 888-588-5550 ■ *Web:* www.wirelessanalytics.com

XipLink Inc 3981 St Laurent Blvd Ste 800 ... Montreal QC H2W1Y5 514-848-9640
Web: www.xiplink.com

Xittel telecommunications Inc
1100, Pl du Technoparc Ste 301 ... Trois-RiviŠres QC G9A0A9 819-370-3232
Web: www.xittel.net

ZapTel Corp 1440 Hicks Rd ... Rolling Meadows IL 60008 847-342-2000
Web: www.zaptel.com

Zerigo Inc 810 W Maude Ave ... Sunnyvale CA 94085 720-210-5439
Web: www.zerigo.com

Zimmerman Associates Inc
10600 Arrowhead Dr Ste 325 ... Fairfax VA 22030 703-883-0506
Web: www.zai-inc.com

Zingle Inc 5235 Avenida Encinas Ste A ... Carlsbad CA 92008 877-946-4536
TF: 877-946-4536 ■ *Web:* www.zingle.me

Zone Communication Group LLC
911 W Eighth St ... Cincinnati OH 45203 859-816-8681
Web: www.zonecg.com

Zyme Solutions Inc
240 Twin Dolphin Dr Ste D ... Redwood Shores CA 94065 650-294-4700
TF: 888-200-6629 ■ *Web:* www.zyme.com

225 DATA PROCESSING & RELATED SERVICES

See Also Electronic Transaction Processing p. 2230; Payroll Services p. 2911

Phone Fax

1Cloud 25 Lowell St Ste 407 ... Manchester NH 03101 603-296-0760
Web: 1cloudbusiness.com

360 Services Inc 12623 Newburgh Rd ... Livonia MI 48150 734-591-9360

5280 Solutions Inc
8740 Lucent Blvd Ste 400 ... Highlands Ranch CO 80129 303-696-5280
Web: www.5280solutions.com

A T Secure Net 2001 Columbus St ... Bakersfield CA 93305 661-872-4807
Web: atsecure.net

Aboundi Inc 4 Bud Way Unit 10 ... Nashua NH 03063 603-889-8188
Web: www.aboundi.com

Abtronics Inc 211 Dixon Ave ... Molalla OR 97038 503-829-6100
Web: www.abtronics.com

Accretive Technologies Inc
330 Research Ct Ste 250 ... Norcross GA 30092 678-328-2440
Web: www.accretive.com

Accura Engineering
3342 International Park Dr Se ... Atlanta GA 30316 404-241-8722
Web: www.accuraengineering.com

Ace Mailing Corp 2757 16th St ... San Francisco CA 94103 415-863-4223
Web: www.acemailingsf.com

ACH Payment Solutions Inc 6919 Treymore Ct ... Sarasota FL 34243 941-360-8859
Web: www.achpaymentsolutions.com

ACI Communications
5115 Douglas Fir Rd Ste A ... Calabasas CA 91302 818-223-3600 223-3609
Web: www.acicommunications.com

ACI Merchant Services Inc
136 E Watson Ave Ste 204 ... Langhorne PA 19047 215-741-6970
Web: acimerchant.com

Acroamatics Inc 5385 Holli Ste 105 ... Santa Barbara CA 93111 805-967-9909
Web: www.acroamatics.com

ActForex Inc 110 Wall St 7th Fl ... New York NY 10005 212-425-7111
Web: www.actforex.com

ActiFi Inc 3030 Harbor Ln Ste 216 ... Plymouth MN 55447 763-550-0223
Web: www.actifi.com

ActiveStrategy Inc
620 W Germantown Pk ... Plymouth Meeting PA 19462 484-690-0700

ADEC Solutions USA 10 Monument St ... Deposit NY 13754 607-467-4600 467-4632
Web: www.adecsolutions-usa.com

Advansoft International Inc
415 W Golf Rd Ste 55 ... Arlington Heights IL 60005 847-952-0000
Web: www.adso.com

Advantis Medical Inc
2121 Southtech Dr Ste 600 ... Greenwood IN 46143 317-859-2300
Web: www.advantismedical.com

Adxstudio Inc 200 - 1445 Park St ... Regina SK S4N4C5 306-569-6500
TF: 800-508-7811 ■ *Web:* www.adxstudio.com

Affinigent Inc 4 Kent Rd Ste 200 ... York PA 17402 717-600-0033
TF: 800-932-3380 ■ *Web:* www.affinigent.com

AG Dealer Ltd 44 Byward Market Sq ... Ottawa ON K1N7A2 613-596-8022
Web: www.agdealer.com

Allegiance Consultinginc 2601 Blake St Ste 110 ... Denver CO 80205 720-947-9201
Web: www.acinow.net

Allison Royce & Associates Inc
PO BOX 790010 Ste 760 ... San Antonio TX 78279 210-564-7000 564-7001
Web: allisonroyce.com

Altapacific Technology Group Inc
1525 E Shaw Ave Ste 201 ... Fresno CA 93710 559-439-5700
Web: www.altapacific.com

Ambient Consulting LLC
5500 Wayzata Blvd Ste 1250 ... Minneapolis MN 55416 763-582-9000 582-7901
Web: www.ambientconsulting.com

Amec Foster Wheeler 1002 Walnut St Ste 200 ... Boulder CO 80302 303-443-7839
Web: www.amecfw.com

Ameritox Ltd 300 E Lombard St Ste 1610 ... Baltimore MD 21201 443-220-0115
Web: www.ameritox.com

AMSplus Inc 400 Washington St ... Braintree MA 02184 781-843-1223
Web: www.amsplus.com

Annese & Associates Inc
747 Pierce Rd Ste 2 ... Clifton Park NY 12065 518-371-9000
Web: www.annese.com

Applicantpro 3688 campus dr Ste 150 ... Eagle Mountain UT 84005 801-766-0174
Web: www.applicantpro.com

Applied Imaging Inc 5282 E Paris SE ... Grand Rapids MI 49512 616-554-5200
Web: www.appliedimaging.com

Applied Innovations Corp
6401 N Congress Ave Ste 200 ... Boca Raton FL 33487 561-981-8196
Web: www.appliedi.net

Applied Services & Information Systems Inc
209 Business Park Dr ... Virginia Beach VA 23462 757-498-0100
Web: www.asisinfo.net

Apperfect Corp
20065 Stevens Creek Blvd Ste 2A ... Cupertino CA 95014 408-252-4100
Web: www.apperfect.com

Apx Power Markets Inc
224 Airport Pkwy Ste 600 ... San Jose CA 95110 408-517-2100 517-2985
Web: www.apx.com

ARCON Corp 260 Bear Hill Rd Ste 200 ... Waltham MA 02451 781-890-3330
Web: www.arcon.com

Argos Systems Inc 19 Crosby Dr ... Bedford MA 01730 781-271-9111
Web: www.argos.com

Argus Connection Inc
1111 W N Carrier Pkwy Ste 300 ... Grand Prairie TX 75050 469-471-0035
Web: www.argusx.com

Armed Forces Financial Network LLC
11601 Roosevelt Blvd TA-94 ... Saint Petersburg FL 33716 727-227-2880
Web: www.affn.org

Artbeats Software Inc 1405 N Myrtle Rd ... Myrtle Creek OR 97457 541-863-4429
Web: www.artbeats.com

Aspen Group Inc, The
1100 Wayne Ave Ste 1200 ... Silver Spring MD 20910 301-650-6200
Web: www.theaspengroupinc.com

Assessment Technology Inc
6700 E Speedway Blvd ... Tucson AZ 85710 520-323-9033
TF: 800-367-4762 ■ *Web:* www.ati-online.com

AtHomeNet Inc PO Box 1405 ... Suwanee GA 30024 770-904-7930
Web: www.athomenet.com

Atlantech Online Inc
1010 Wayne Ave Ste 630 ... Silver Spring MD 20910 301-589-3060
TF: 800-256-1612 ■ *Web:* www.atlantech.net

AtNetPlus Inc 1000 Campus Dr Ste 700 ... Stow OH 44224 330-945-5685
Web: www.atnetplus.com

Audiokinetic Inc 409 St-Nicolas St Ste 300 ... Montreal QC H2Y2P4 514-499-9100
Web: www.audiokinetic.com

Augmentum Inc
1065 E Hillsdale Blvd Ste 413 ... Foster City CA 94404 650-578-9221
Web: augmentum.com

Automatic Data Processing Inc (ADP) 1 ADP Blvd ... Roseland NJ 07068 800-225-5237
NASDAQ: ADP ■ *TF:* 800-225-5237 ■ *Web:* www.adp.com

AutoVision Wireless Inc
360 Deerhide Crescent ... Toronto ON M9M2Y6 416-747-4444 747-4443
TF: 866-514-8030 ■ *Web:* www.autovisionwireless.com

Axis Technical Group Inc 300 S Ahrbor Blvd ... Anaheim CA 92805 714-491-2636
Web: axistechnical.com

Ayalogic Inc 530 S Main St Ste 1731 ... Akron OH 44311 330-253-2700

Bankcard Central Inc 1321 Burlington St ... Kansas City MO 64116 816-221-1133
Web: www.bankcardcentral.com

Phone Fax

Baracci Solutions Inc 24 Boul De La Concorde E .... Laval QC H7G4X2 450-662-8700
Web: www.baracci.com

Beanstalk Data 656 michael wylie dr .... Charlotte NC 28217 800-892-3997
TF: 800-892-3997 ■ *Web:* beanstalkdata.com

Beanstream Internet Commerce Inc
1803 Douglas St Ste 200 .... Victoria BC V8T5C3 250-472-2326 472-2330
TF: 888-472-0811 ■ *Web:* www.beanstream.com

Beasley Direct Marketing Inc
15227 Perry Ln............................ Morgan Hill CA 95037 408-782-0046
Web: www.beasleydirect.com

Believe Wireless LLC
9722 Groffs Mill Dr Ste 112 .... Owings Mills MD 21117 410-902-0070
Web: www.believewireless.com

Belwave Communications 4132 Edgehill Rd .... Fort Worth TX 76116 817-737-3124

Berkadia Commercial Mortgage LLC
118 Welsh Rd............................... Horsham PA 19044 215-328-3200
Web: www.berkadia.com

Bing Design 126 E Ctr College St.............. Yellow Springs OH 45387 937-767-2521
Web: www.bingdesign.com

Biobridges LLC 167 Worcester St Ste 211............ Wellesley MA 02481 781-416-0909
Web: www.biobridges.com

BlackInk IT 277 E 12th St .... Indianapolis IN 46202 317-472-8000
Web: www.integrate.net

Blade Technologies Inc
10820 Sunset Office Dr Ste 101 .... St. Louis MO 63127 314-752-7999
Web: www.bladetechinc.com

Blekko Inc 130 Marine Pkwy Ste 200 .... Redwood City CA 94065 650-631-3845
Web: blekko.com

Blizzard Internet Marketing Inc
50629 Hwy 6 .... Glenwood Springs CO 81601 970-928-7875
TF: 888-840-5893 ■ *Web:* www.blizzardinternet.com

Blue Fountain Media Inc
102 Madison Ave 2nd Fl........................... New York NY 10016 212-260-1978
Web: www.bluefountainmedia.com

Blue Mine Group 12626 High Bluff Dr Ste 450......... San Diego CA 92130 858-792-2633

Blue Rock Technologies 800 Kirts Blvd .... Troy MI 48084 248-786-6100
TF: 866-390-8200 ■ *Web:* www.bluerocktech.com

Bluechip Athletic Solutions LLC
5885 Glenridge Dr Ste 115......................... Atlanta GA 30328 404-941-2510
Web: bas-llc.net

Bluegrassnet Development Corp
321 E Breckinridge St........................... Louisville KY 40203 502-589-4638
Web: www.bluegrass.net

BlueTie Inc 2480 Browncroft Blvd Ste 2b .... Rochester NY 14625 585-586-2000 586-2268
TF: 800-258-3843 ■ *Web:* www.bluetie.com

BNSF Logistics LLC
4700 S Thompson Ste A202........................ Springdale AR 72764 888-285-4514
TF: 888-285-4514 ■ *Web:* www.bnsflogistics.com

Borer Financial Communication LLC
615 Fifth St Ste 210 .... Carlstadt NJ 07072 201-939-9297
Web: borerfinancial.com

BP Logix Inc 410 S Melrose Dr Ste 100.................. Vista CA 92081 760-643-4121
Web: www.bplogix.com

Brainstorm Internet Inc 640 Main Ave Ste 201......... Durango CO 81301 970-247-1442
Web: www.gobrainstorm.net

Brandx Internet LLC 927 Sixth St Apt 4 .... Santa Monica CA 90403 310-395-5500
Web: www.brandx.net

Brewster Technology 1591 Rt 22 Bldg 1............. Brewster NY 10509 845-279-9400
Web: www.brewstertech.net

Brilliant Store Inc 933 Corporate Way .... Fremont CA 94539 510-668-0398
Web: www.brilliant-electronics.com

Broadjam Inc 6401 Odana Rd .... Madison WI 53719 608-271-3633
Web: www.broadjam.com

Browsersoft Inc 450 Navajo Ln.............. Shawnee Mission KS 66217 913-851-2453
Web: browsersoft.com

Btm Global Consulting
330 S Second Ave Ste 450..................... Minneapolis MN 55401 612-238-8800
Web: www.btmglobal.com

BusinessEdge Solutions Inc
1 Tower Ctr Blvd.......................... East Brunswick NJ 08816 732-828-3200
Web: emc.com/domains/businessedge/index.htm

C7 Data Centers Inc
14870 S Pony Express Rd Ste 200.................. Bluffdale UT 84065 801-822-5300
Web: www.c7.com

Cadence Group Inc 1095 Zonolite Rd Ste 105 .... Atlanta GA 30306 404-874-0544
Web: www.cadence-group.com

Cambey & West Inc 120 N Route 9W.................. Congers NY 10920 845-267-3490
Web: www.cambeywest.com

Capax Global LLC 590 Headquarters Plaza .... Morristown NJ 07960 973-401-0660
TF: 888-682-8900 ■ *Web:* www.capaxglobal.com

Capricorn Systems Inc 3569 Habersham At N........... Tucker GA 30084 678-514-1080 514-1081
Web: www.capricornsys.com

Carahsoft Technology Corp
12369 Sunrise Vly Dr Ste D2 .... Reston VA 20191 703-871-8500 871-8505
TF: 888-662-2724 ■ *Web:* www.carahsoft.com

Cardtronics GP Inc 3110 Hayes Rd Ste 300............ Houston TX 77082 281-596-9988
Web: www.cardtronics.com

Casher Assoc Inc 110 Pond Brook Rd .... Newton MA 02467 617-527-3927
Web: www.casherassociates.com

Cass Information Systems Inc
13001 Hollenberg Dr .... Bridgeton MO 63044 314-506-5500 506-5560
NASDAQ: CASS ■ *Web:* www.cassinfo.com

Castles Information Network 301 Alamo Dr .... Vacaville CA 95688 707-455-3401
Web: www.castles.com

Catylist Inc 211 W Upper Wacker Dr Ste 450 .... Chicago IL 60606 312-499-2000

CBE Technologies Inc 215 N Brow St.......... East Providence RI 02914 401-453-1234
Web: www.cbetech.com

CCC Information Services Inc
222 Merchandise Mart Plz .... Chicago IL 60654 800-621-8070
TF: 800-621-8070 ■ *Web:* www.cccis.com

Central Service Assn 93 S Coley Rd .... Tupelo MS 38801 662-842-5962 840-1329
TF: 877-842-5962 ■ *Web:* www.csa1.com

Central Valley Broadband LLC
1624 Santa Clara Dr Ste 250 .... Roseville CA 95661 530-852-0318
Web: www.calwisp.com

Centurion Service Group LLC
1400 N 25th Ave............................. Melrose Park IL 60160 708-761-6655
Web: www.centurionservice.com

Certain Affinity
3107 oak creek dr PO Box 302799..................... Austin TX 78727 512-524-8510
Web: www.certainaffinity.com

Chelsio Communications Inc
370 San Aleso Ave Ste 100........................ Sunnyvale CA 94085 408-962-3600
Web: www.chelsio.com

Chrisian Inc 17561 Hillside Ave...................... Jamaica NY 11432 718-465-9151
Web: www.chrisian.com

Churchill & Harriman LLC 239 Wall St .... Princeton NJ 08540 609-921-3551
Web: chus.com

Ciao Systems Inc 4326 Lorcom Ln................... Arlington VA 22207 703-524-9356
Web: www.ciaosoftware.com

CitiusTech Inc 2 Research Way...................... Princeton NJ 08540 877-248-4871
TF: 877-248-4871 ■ *Web:* www.citiustech.com

Claimsnet.com Inc 14860 Montfort Dr Ste 250 .... Dallas TX 75254 972-458-1701 458-1737
TF: 800-356-1511 ■ *Web:* www.claimsnet.com

Claris Networks LLC 6100 Lonas Dr .... Knoxville TN 37909 865-251-5555
Web: clarisnetworks.com

Clear Government Solutions Inc
11850 Baltimore Ave .... Beltsville MD 20705 301-289-3030
Web: www.cleargovsolutions.com

Clear Wireless LLC 4400 Carillon Point................ Kirkland WA 98033 425-216-7600
Web: www.clear.com

CNC Software Inc 671 Old Post Rd.................... Tolland CT 06084 860-875-5006
TF: 800-228-2877 ■ *Web:* www.mastercam.com

Cogeco Data Services LP 413 Horner Ave .... Toronto ON M8W4W3 416-599-3282
Web: www.cogecopeer1.com/en

Collective Technologies LLC 9433 Bee Caves Rd .... Austin TX 78733 512-263-5500 263-0606
TF: 800-994-1640 ■ *Web:* www.colltech.com

Colosseum Online Inc 800 Petrolia Rd .... Toronto ON M3J3K4 416-739-7873
TF: 877-739-7873 ■ *Web:* www.colosseum.com

Commercial Computer Service Inc
2916 W Sixth St .... Fort Worth TX 76107 817-335-6411
Web: minimaxgolf.com

Communication Data Services 1901 Bell Ave .... Des Moines IA 50315 515-246-6837 246-6687
TF: 866-897-7987 ■ *Web:* www.cds-global.com

Compact Information Systems Inc
7120 185th Ave NE Ste 150 .... Redmond WA 98052 425-869-1379
Web: www.compactlists.com

Complete Data Solutions LLC
7115 Leesburg Pk Ste 317 .... Falls Church VA 22043 703-536-3282
Web: know-your-data.com

Computer Engineering 509 NW 5th St............ Blue Springs MO 64014 816-228-2976
Web: www.thinkcei.com

Computer Fulfillment 24 Cook St .... Billerica MA 01821 978-671-0440 671-0450
Web: www.computerfulfillment.com

Computer Services Inc 3901 Technology Dr........... Paducah KY 42001 270-442-7361
OTC: CSVI ■ *TF:* 800-545-4274 ■ *Web:* www.csiweb.com

Comtech Mobile Datacom Corp
20430 Century Blvd .... Germantown MD 20874 240-686-3300
Web: www.comtechmobile.com

Concord Document Services Inc
1321 W 12th St................................ Los Angeles CA 90015 213-745-3175
Web: www.copying.la

Conenza Inc 810 Third Ave Ste 220..................... Seattle WA 98104 206-792-4247
Web: www.conenza.com

Connecticut On-Line Computer Ctr Inc
135 Darling Dr .... Southington CT 06489 860-678-0444 677-1169
Web: www.cocc.com

Continental Graphics Corp
4060 N Lakewood Blvd Bldg 801 5th Fl .... Long Beach CA 90808 714-503-4200 827-5111
TF: 800-862-5691 ■ *Web:* www.cdgnow.com

Convergence LLC 6 Journey Ste 160 .... Aliso Viejo CA 92656 949-716-8322
Web: www.convergence.net

Coon Valley Telecommunications
105 Central Ave .... Coon Valley WI 54623 608-452-3101
Web: www.coonvalleytel.com

Cornwell Data Services Inc 352 Evelyn St........... Paramus NJ 07652 201-261-1050
TF: 866-981-1050 ■ *Web:* cornwelldirect.com

Cott Systems Inc
2800 Corporate Exchange Dr Ste 300............... Columbus OH 43231 614-847-4405
Web: www.cottsystems.com

CPT Group Inc 16630 Aston St .... Irvine CA 92606 949-852-8240
Web: www.cptgroup.com

Creative Breakthroughs Inc
2075 W Big Beaver Rd Ste 700......................... Troy MI 48084 248-519-4000
Web: www.cbihome.com

Crispin Corp 600 Wade Ave......................... Raleigh NC 27605 919-845-7744
Web: www.crispincorp.com

Critical Mention Inc 521 Fifth Ave 16th Fl............ New York NY 10175 212-398-1141
Web: www.criticalmention.com

Cross Circuit Electronics Inc
3020 Scott Blvd .... Santa Clara CA 95054 408-654-9637
Web: www.cross-circuit.com

Crosscom National LLC
900 Deerfield Pkwy.......................... Buffalo Grove IL 60089 847-520-9200 419-4884
TF: 888-471-6050 ■ *Web:* www.crosscomnational.com

CrossView Inc 505 Millennium Dr Allen .... Allen TX 75013 408-748-1410
Web: www.crossview.com

Cst Data 10725 John Price Rd .... Charlotte NC 28273 704-927-3282
TF: 866-383-3282 ■ *Web:* cstdata.com

CU*Answers 6000 28th St SE Ste 100............. Grand Rapids MI 49546 616-285-5711
TF: 800-327-3478 ■ *Web:* www.cuanswers.com

Custom Processing Services Inc
2 Birchmont Dr................................. Reading PA 19606 610-779-7001
Web: www.customprocessingservices.com

Company	City	State	Zip	Phone	Fax
Customer Paradigm Inc 5353 Manhattan Cir Ste 103	Boulder	CO	80303	303-499-9318	
TF: 888-772-0777 ■ *Web:* www.customerparadigm.com					
Cyber Pro Systems Inc 1 World Trade Ctr Ste 2400	Long Beach	CA	90831	562-256-3800	
Web: www.mdxnet.com					
Cyberonic Internet Communications Inc 544 Pleasant St.	Worcester	MA	01602	508-751-4801	
Web: www.cyberonic.com					
Cyberspace Solutions LLC 12015 Lee Jackson Hwy Ste 400	Fairfax	VA	22033	703-472-5715	
Web: www.cspacesol.com					
D K Global 420 Missouri Ct	Redlands	CA	92373	909-747-0201	
TF: 866-375-2214 ■ *Web:* www.dkglobal.net					
D Net Internet Service 208 E Palmer St.	Franklin	NC	28734	828-349-3638	
TF: 877-601-3638 ■ *Web:* www.dnet.net					
Dantom Systems Inc 29241 Beck Rd	Wixom	MI	48393	248-567-7300	
TF: 866-536-2376 ■ *Web:* www.dantomsystems.com					
Dark Field Technologies Inc 70 Robinson Blvd.	Orange	CT	06477	203-298-0731	
Web: www.darkfield.com					
Dash Inc W176 N9830 Rivercrest Dr.	Germantown	WI	53022	262-345-5600	
Web: dashdev.com					
Data Dash Inc 3928 Delor St.	Saint Louis	MO	63116	314-832-5788	
TF: 800-211-5988 ■ *Web:* www.datadash.com					
Data Dimensions Corp 400 Midland Ct	Janesville	WI	53546	608-757-1100	
Web: datadimensions.com					
Data Lab 7333 N Oak Pk Ave	Niles	IL	60714	847-647-6678	
Web: www.data-lab.com					
Data Reduction Systems Corp 1323 Burnet Ave	Union	NJ	07083	908-687-5636	
Web: www.drscorp.com					
Data Services Inc 31516 Winterplace Pkwy	Salisbury	MD	21804	410-546-2206	
TF: 800-432-4066 ■ *Web:* www.dataservicesinc.com					
Data Supplies Inc 11300 Lakefield Dr	Duluth	GA	30097	770-476-4455	
Web: datasuppliesinc.com					
Dataflo Corp 2722 S 87th Ave	Omaha	NE	68124	402-861-9454	
Web: www.mydataflo.com					
Datamark Inc 123 W Mills Ave Ste 400.	El Paso	TX	79901	800-477-1944	
TF: 800-477-1944 ■ *Web:* www.datamark.net					
DataSite Northwest Inc 21086 24th Ave S Ste 120	Seatac	WA	98198	206-859-2800	
Web: www.datasitenw.com					
Datasoft Inc 700 Plz Dr	Secaucus	NJ	07094	201-319-0494	
Web: tradeblazer.com					
Datavalet Technologies Inc 5275 ch Queen-Mary	Montreal	QC	H3W1Y3	514-385-4448	
Web: www.datavalet.com					
Dataxport 10950 Pellicano Dr Ste C4.	El Paso	TX	79935	915-771-9090	
Web: www.dataxport.net					
Datex Billing Services Inc 2333 N Sheridan Way	Mississauga	ON	L5K1A7	905-822-2300	
Web: www.datex.ca					
Datrose Inc 660 Basket Rd.	Webster	NY	14580	585-265-1780	
Web: datrose.com					
Davissa Telephone Systems Inc 23800 Commerce Park	Cleveland	OH	44122	216-464-6633	
Web: www.davissa.com					
DAZ Productions Inc 12637 South 265 West Ste 300	Draper	UT	84020	801-495-1777	
Web: www.daz3d.com					
Dbnet Systems Inc 3602 Keenland Dr	Marietta	GA	30062	770-509-3638	
Web: www.dbnetsystems.com					
Decentrix Inc 1200 17th St Ste 770	Denver	CO	80202	303-899-4000	
Web: www.decentrix.net					
Delvinia Inc 370 King St West 5th Fl.	Toronto	ON	M5V1J9	416-364-1455	
Web: www.delvinia.com					
Desert Dog Marketing LLC 4641 N 12th St Ste 200	Phoenix	AZ	85014	800-506-0398	
TF: 800-506-0398 ■ *Web:* www.pinnaclecart.com					
Destiny Solutions Inc 40 Holly St	Toronto	ON	M4S3C3	416-480-0500	
TF: 866-403-0500 ■ *Web:* www.destinysolutions.com					
Devtopia Digital 220 King St W Ste 300.	Toronto	ON	M5H1K4	416-239-4826	
Web: www.devtopia.com					
Dexrex LLC 6 University Dr Ste 201	Amherst	MA	01002	413-461-3031	
Digital Footprints International LLC 1142 Broadway Ste 400	Tacoma	WA	98402	253-590-4100	
Web: www.internetidentity.com					
Dini Group, The 7469 Draper Ave	La Jolla	CA	92037	858-454-3419	
Web: www.dinigroup.com					
Direct Online Marketing 4727 Jacob St	Wheeling	WV	26003	304-214-4850	
TF: 800-979-3177 ■ *Web:* www.directom.com					
Directory One Inc 9135 Katy Fwy Ste 204	Houston	TX	77024	713-465-0051	
TF: 800-477-1324 ■ *Web:* www.directoryone.com					
DirectWest Corp 2550 Sandra Schmirler Way Ste 200	Regina	SK	S4W1A1	306-777-0333	
TF: 800-667-8201 ■ *Web:* www.directwest.com					
Discovery Research Group 6975 Union Pk Ctr Ste 150	Midvale	UT	84047	800-678-3748	748-2784*
**Fax Area Code:* 801 ■ *TF:* 800-678-3748 ■ *Web:* www.discoveryresearchgroup.com					
Doc 2 E-file Inc 4500 S Wayside Dr Ste 102	Houston	TX	77087	713-649-2006	
TF: 888-649-2006 ■ *Web:* www.doc2e-file.com					
Docufree Corp 1175 Northmeadow Pkwy Ste 140	Roswell	GA	30076	770-643-2900	
TF: 877-220-4350					
DOmedia LLC 274 Marconi Blvd One Marconi Pl Ste 400	Columbus	OH	43215	614-324-2583	
Web: domedia.com					
Dominknow Learning Systems 40 Sunset Blvd	Perth	ON	K7H2Y4	613-264-0096	
Web: www.dominknow.com					
Doon Technologies Inc 200 Middlesex-Essex Tpke Ste 309	Iselin	NJ	08830	732-404-1334	
Web: www.doontec.com					
Dovetail Internet Technologies LLC 40 Southbridge St Ste 210	Worcester	MA	01608	508-845-6465	
Web: www.dovetailinternet.com					
DoxTek Inc 264 W Center St	Orem	UT	84057	877-705-7226	
TF: 877-705-7226 ■ *Web:* www.doxtek.com					
DPF Data Services Group Inc 1990 Swarthmore Ave.	Lakewood	NJ	08701	732-370-8840	370-1751
TF: 800-431-4416 ■ *Web:* www.dpfdata.com					
Dundee Internet Service Inc 168 Riley St	Dundee	MI	48131	734-529-5331	
TF: 888-222-8485 ■ *Web:* dundee.net					
DuVoice Corp 608 State St S Ste 100	Kirkland	WA	98033	425-889-9790	
TF: 800-888-1057 ■ *Web:* www.duvoice.com					
DWS Inc 102 Kimball Ave Ste 2	South Burlington	VT	05403	802-861-6004	
Web: www.dwsincorporated.com					
E Commerce Partners Dotnet Corp 59 Franklin St	New York	NY	10013	212-334-3390	
Web: www.ecommercepartners.net					
E Ink Holdings Inc 733 Concord Ave	Cambridge	MA	02138	617-499-6000	499-6200
Web: www.eink.com					
E-cubed Media Synthesis Ltd 3807 William St	Burnaby	BC	V5C3J1	604-294-1556	
Web: www.e-cubed.net					
Ease Technologies Inc 10320 Little Patuxent Pkwy Ste 1104	Columbia	MD	21044	301-854-0010	
Web: www.easetech.com					
East Coast Datacom Inc 245 Gus Hipp Blvd Ste 3	Rockledge	FL	32955	321-637-9980	
Web: www.ecdata.com					
Easy Dynamics Inc 2003 11th st nw	Washington	DC	20001	202-558-7275	
Web: www.easydynamics.com					
EasyStreet Online Services Inc 9705 SW Sunshine Ct	Beaverton	OR	97005	503-646-8400	
Web: www.easystreet.com					
Ebix BPO 151 N Lyon Ave	Hemet	CA	92543	951-658-4000	
Web: www.certsonline.com					
eBlox Inc 404 W 30th St Ste A	Austin	TX	78705	512-867-1001	
Web: www.eblox.com					
eDaptive Systems 400 Red Brook Blvd Ste 120	Owings Mills	MD	21117	410-327-3366	
Web: www.edaptivesys.com					
Edcor Data Services Corp 3310 W Big Beaver Ste 305	Troy	MI	48084	248-530-4200	
Web: www.edcor.com					
EDGE Technology Services Inc 116 Washington Ave 2nd Fl	North Haven	CT	06473	860-635-3342	
Web: edgets.com					
Effective Data Inc 1515 E Wdfield Rd	Schaumburg	IL	60173	847-969-9300	
TF: 877-825-5233 ■ *Web:* effective-data.com					
Efficient Forms LLC 10394 W Chatfield Ave Bldg 3 Ste 109	Littleton	CO	80127	303-785-8600	
Web: www.efficientforms.com					
eGov Strategies LLC 233 S Mccrea St Ste 600	Indianapolis	IN	46225	317-634-3468	
Web: www.egovstrategies.com					
Electric Pulp Inc 4901 S Isabel Pl Ste 200	Sioux Falls	SD	57108	605-988-0177	
Web: electricpulp.com					
Electric Rain 3100 Carbon Pl Ste 102	Boulder	CO	80301	303-543-8233	
Web: www.erain.com					
Elkhartnet 401 E Colfax Ave	South Bend	IN	46617	574-524-1000	
Web: www.elkhart.net					
Elysium Inc 100 Galleria Officentre Ste 426	Southfield	MI	48034	248-799-9800	
Web: www.elysiuminc.com					
Enhanced Software Products Inc 1811 N Hutchinson Rd	Spokane	WA	99212	509-534-1514	
TF: 800-456-5750 ■ *Web:* www.espsolution.net					
Entap Inc 136 E Market St	Indianapolis	IN	46204	317-634-9523	
Web: www.entap.com					
Envision Online Media Inc 1150 Morrison Dr Ste 201	Ottawa	ON	K2H8S9	613-594-2804	
Web: www.envisiononline.ca					
EPIQ Technologies Inc 4711 Viewridge Ave Ste 230	San Diego	CA	92123	858-467-9961	
Web: www.epiqtech.com					
Equifax Inc 1550 Peachtree St NW	Atlanta	GA	30309	404-885-8000	
NYSE: EFX ■ *TF Sales:* 888-202-4025 ■ *Web:* www.equifax.com					
Essentialtalk Network 1289 Highfield Cres Se	Calgary	AB	T2G5M2	403-537-9690	
Web: www.essentialtalk.com					
eWomenNetwork Inc 14900 Landmark Blvd Ste 540	Dallas	TX	75254	972-620-9995	
Web: www.ewomennetwork.com					
Examination Management Services Inc 15333 N Pima Rd Ste 330	Scottsdale	AZ	85260	214-689-3600	689-3644
Web: www.emsinet.com					
Exceed Technologies Inc 2605 Cleda Dr	Columbus	MS	39701	662-328-8333	
Web: www.exceedtech.net					
Fair Isaac Corp 2665 Long Lake Rd Bldg C	Roseville	MN	55113	612-758-5200	758-5201
NYSE: FICO ■ *TF Cust Svc:* 888-342-6336 ■ *Web:* www.fico.com					
Fakhoury Law Group Pc 3290 w big beaver rd	Troy	MI	48084	248-643-4900	
Web: www.employmentimmigration.com					
Federico Consulting Inc 333 W Shaw Ave	Fresno	CA	93704	559-224-5922	
Web: www.federico.net					
Financial Services Inc 21 Harristown Rd	Glen Rock	NJ	07452	201-652-6000	
FinditQuick.com Inc 1817 Saunders Settlement Rd.	Niagara Falls	NY	14304	716-297-5292	
Web: www.finditquick.com					
First Class Solutions Inc 11426 Dorsett Rd	Maryland Heights	MO	63043	314-209-7800	
Web: www.firstclasssolutions.com					
Flight Landata Inc 250 Clark St	North Andover	MA	01845	978-682-7767	
Web: www.flightlandata.com					
Flightline Data Services Inc 138 Peachtree Ct	Fayetteville	GA	30215	770-487-3482	
Web: www.flightline.com					
Flightpath Inc 36 W 25Th St 9th Fl.	New York	NY	10010	212-674-5600	
Web: www.flightpath.com					
Flw International 1147 W Ohio St	Chicago	IL	60642	312-239-2174	
Web: www.flwint.net					

Phone *Fax*

Flynn Systems Corp 74 Northeastern Blvd Nashua NH 03062 603-598-4444
Web: www.flynn.com

Forte Data Systems Inc 3330 Paddock Pkwy Suwanee GA 30024 678-208-0206
TF: 800-571-8702 ■ *Web:* www.fortedata.com

FotoKem Industries Inc 2801 W Alameda Ave Burbank CA 91505 818-846-3101
Web: www.fotokem.com

Fpweb.net LC 1714 Gilsinn Ln Fenton MO 63026 636-600-8960
Web: www.fpweb.net

Fractal Analytics Ltd
951 Mariners Island Ste 307 San Mateo CA 94404 650-378-1284
Web: www.fractalanalytics.com

Fred Flare Inc 300f Kingsland Ave Brooklyn NY 11222 718-599-9221

Freedom Consulting Group Inc
9891 Broken Land Pkwy Ste 300 Columbia MD 21046 410-290-9035
Web: freedomconsultinggroup.com

Freight Security Net Inc
7501 N Capital of Texas Hwy Ste A-140 Austin TX 78731 512-225-6490
Web: www.freightwatchintl.com

Fusionist LLC 438 Amapola Ave Ste 225 Torrance CA 90501 310-787-7877
Web: www.fusionist.com

Gage E Services LLC
601 S Phillips Ave Ste 100 Sioux Falls SD 57104 605-332-1242
Web: www.geshosting.com

Gaggle Net 1319 n veterans pkwy Bloomington IL 61704 309-665-0572
Web: www.gaggle.net

Galatea Associates LLC
20 Holland St Ste 405 Somerville MA 02144 617-623-5466
Web: www.galatea-associates.com

GenArts Inc 955 Massachusetts Ave Cambridge MA 02139 617-492-2888
Web: www.genarts.com

Genetec Inc 2280 Alfred-Nobel Blvd Ste 400 Montreal QC H4S2A4 514-332-4000
TF: 866-684-8006 ■ *Web:* www.genetec.com

GEOSPAN Corp 10900 73rd Ave N Ste 136 Minneapolis MN 55369 763-493-9320
TF: 800-436-7726 ■ *Web:* www.geospan.com

Geotrace Technologies Inc
12141 Wickchester Ln Ste 200 Houston TX 77079 281-497-8440
Web: www.geotrace.com

Giact Systems Inc 700 Central Expy S Allen TX 75013 214-644-0450
Web: www.motio.com

GigaCrete Inc 6775 Speedway Blvd Ste M105 Las Vegas NV 89115 702-643-6363
Web: www.gigacrete.com

Glance Networks Inc 1167 Massachusetts Ave Arlington MA 02476 781-646-8505
TF: 877-452-6236 ■ *Web:* www.glance.net

Global Data Consultants LLC
1144 Kennebec Dr Chambersburg PA 17201 717-262-2080
Web: gdcitsolutions.com

Global Geophysical Services Inc
13927 S Gessner Rd Missouri City TX 77489 713-972-9200 972-1008
NYSE: GGS ■ *Web:* www.globalgeophysical.com

Global Graphics Software Inc
31 Nagog Pk Ste 315 Acton MA 01720 978-849-0011
Web: www.globalgraphics.com

Global Health Care Exchange LLC (GHX)
1315 W Century Dr Louisville CO 80027 720-887-7000 887-7200
TF: 800-968-7449 ■ *Web:* www.ghx.com

Globat LLC 11684 Ventrura Blvd Ste 825 Studio City CA 91604 323-874-9000
Web: www.globat.com

Goold Health Systems Inc PO Box 1090 Augusta ME 04332 207-622-7153
TF: 800-832-9672 ■ *Web:* www.ghsinc.com

Grant Street Group Inc
339 Sixth Ave Ste 1400 Pittsburgh PA 15222 412-391-5555
Web: www.grantstreet.com

Green Idea 950 page st San Francisco CA 94117 415-863-2157
Web: www.greenidea.com

GreenGeeks LLC 5739 Kanan Rd Ste 300 Agoura Hills CA 91301 310-496-8946
TF: 877-326-7483 ■ *Web:* www.greengeeks.com

Greystar Development & Construction LP
750 Bering Dr Ste 400 Houston TX 77057 713-966-5000
Web: www.greystar.com

Grid Dynamics Consulting Services Inc
4600 Bohannon Dr Ste 220 Menlo Park CA 94025 650-523-5000
Web: www.griddynamics.com

Gtess Corp 2435 N Central Expwy Ste 500 Richardson TX 75080 972-792-5500
Web: www.banctec.com

Habanero Consulting Group Inc
510-1111 Melville St Vancouver BC V6E3V6 604-709-6201
TF: 866-841-6201 ■ *Web:* www.habaneroconsulting.com

Halfaker & Associates LLC
2900 S Quincy St Ste 410 Arlington VA 22206 703-434-3900
Web: www.halfakerandassociates.com

Hartley Data Service Inc (HDS)
1807 Glenview Rd Ste 201 Glenview IL 60025 847-724-9280 729-2199
Web: hartleydata.com

Haug Communications Inc 622 Neptune Dr Seneca KS 66538 785-336-3579
Web: www.bbwi.net

Havanet Communications
1190 Sw 170th Ave Unit 101 Beaverton OR 97006 503-531-9048
Web: www.hevanet.com

Health Management Systems Inc 401 Pk Ave S New York NY 10016 212-857-5000 857-5004
TF: 877-357-3268 ■ *Web:* www.hms.com

Healthbridge 11300 Cornell Park Dr Ste 360 Blue Ash OH 45242 513-469-7222
Web: www.healthbridge.org

Healthcare Administrative Partners LLC
112 Chesley Dr Media PA 19063 610-892-8889
Web: www.hapusa.com

Healthpac Computer Systems Inc
1010 E Victory Dr Savannah GA 31405 912-341-7420
Web: www.healthpac.net

Hidden Variable Studios LLC
1800 S Brand Blvd Ste 204 Glendale CA 91204 818-985-4263
Web: www.hiddenvariable.com

Hiebing Group, The 315 Wisconsin Ave Madison WI 53703 608-256-6357
Web: www.hiebing.com

Phone *Fax*

High Standards Technology
17000 El Camino Real Houston TX 77058 281-990-9422
Web: www.weredown.com

Hillcraft Ltd 2202 Advance Rd Madison WI 53718 608-221-3220
Web: hillcraft.com

Hivelocity Ventures Corp
8010 Woodland Ctr Blvd Ste 700 Tampa FL 33614 813-471-0355
TF: 888-869-4678 ■ *Web:* www.hivelocity.net

Hme Providers Inc
1410 White Dr PO Box 411985 Titusville FL 32780 321-267-7576
Web: www.hmeproviders.com

HomeAway.com Inc 1011 W Fifth St Ste 300 Austin TX 78703 512-782-0805
Web: www.homeaway.com

HUGE Inc 45 Main St 2nd Fl Brooklyn NY 11201 718-625-4843
Web: www.hugeinc.com

Hyperion Inc 1660 Intl Dr Mclean VA 22102 703-848-8850
Web: www.hyperioninc.com

I Sc International 9700 W Bluemound Rd Milwaukee WI 53226 414-476-7755
Web: www.iscinternational.com

i4DM 8227 Cloverleaf Dr Ste 312 Millersville MD 21108 410-729-7920
Web: www.i4dm.com

Icio Inc 1373 Ridge Commons Blvd Hanover MD 21076 410-903-4166
Web: www.icioinc.com

ICON Laboratories Inc 123 Smith St Farmingdale NY 11735 631-777-8833
Web: iconplc.com

ICTV Brands Inc 489 Devon Park Dr Ste 315 Wayne PA 19087 484-598-2300
Web: ictvbrands.com

Icvm Group Inc 50 Love Ln Mattituck NY 11952 631-298-5505
Web: www.icvmgroup.com

Idm Computer Solutions Inc 5559 Eureka Dr Hamilton OH 45011 513-892-8600
Web: idmcomp.com

Image Data Inc 18 Petra Ln Albany NY 12205 518-862-2740
Web: www.imgdata.com

Imagecat Inc 400 Oceangate Ste 1050 Long Beach CA 90802 562-628-1675
Web: www.imagecatinc.com

Imagenet LLC 6411 S 216th St Kent WA 98032 253-395-0110
Web: www.imagenet.com

ImageSource Inc 612 Fifth Ave SW Olympia WA 98501 360-943-9273
Web: www.imagesourceinc.com

IMC Inc 6354 walker lane Ste 300 Virginia VA 22310 703-871-8700
Impact Solutions Consulting Inc
1300 Ridenour Blvd NW Ste 210 Kennesaw GA 30152 770-795-9525
Web: www.impactsc.com

Impatica Inc 2430 Don Reid Dr Ste 200 Ottawa ON K1H1E1 613-736-9982
TF: 800-548-3475 ■ *Web:* www.impatica.com

Incontrol Technology Inc 1651 e main st El Cajon CA 92021 619-270-1260
TF: 888-508-1288 ■ *Web:* incontroltechnology.com

Infi Net Solutions Inc 6430 S 84th St Omaha NE 68127 402-895-5777
Web: www.omahait.com

Influxis 28110 Ave Stanford Unit D Valencia CA 91355 661-775-3936
Web: www.influxis.com

InfoMine Inc 580 Hornby St Ste 900 Vancouver BC V6C3B6 604-683-2037
TF: 888-683-2037 ■ *Web:* www.infomine.com

Infosec Inc 14001c Saint Germain Dr Centreville VA 20121 703-825-1202
Web: www.infosecinc.com

Infotech Global Inc 371 Hoes Ln Piscataway NJ 08854 732-271-0600
Web: www.igiusa.com

Infutor Data Solutions Inc 2017 S Rte 59 Plainfield IL 60586 312-348-7900
Web: www.infutor.com

IngletBlair LLC 6207 Bee Cave Rd Ste 110 Austin TX 78746 512-732-0498
Web: www.ingletblair.com

Inmediata Health Group Corp
342 Calle San Luis Ste 203 San Juan PR 00920 787-774-0606
Web: www.inmediata.com

Innotap 200 North Warner Rd Ste 210 King of Prussia PA 19406 855-438-4666
TF: 855-438-4666 ■ *Web:* innotap.com

Innovasium Inc 55 Albert St Ste 200 Markham ON L3P2T4 905-479-5555
Web: www.innovasium.com

Input Solutions Inc 9250 Gaither Rd Gaithersburg MD 20877 301-948-6620
Web: www.inputsolutions.com

Inspired eLearning Inc
613 NW Loop 410 Ste 530 San Antonio TX 78216 210-579-0224
TF: 800-631-2078 ■ *Web:* www.inspiredelearning.com

INTEG Process Group Inc
2919 E Hardies Rd 1st Fl Gibsonia PA 15044 724-933-9350
Web: www.integpg.com

Integrated Solution Group Inc, The
10 Cedar St Woburn MA 01801 781-938-0712
Web: www.intsolgrp.com

IntelliStance LLC 213 Court St Middletown CT 06457 860-704-6381
Web: www.marketstance.com

Interactive Tracking Systems Inc
820 51st St E Ste 150 Saskatoon SK S7K0X8 306-665-5026
Web: www.itracks.com

Interface Multimedia Inc
8505 Fenton St Silver Spring MD 20910 301-585-0068
Web: www.ifmm.com

International Procurement Agency Inc
4322 Avondale Ln Nw Canton OH 44708 330-477-5020
Web: www.usaipa.com

Internet Applications Group
999 Commercial St Ste 210 Palo Alto CA 94303 650-424-0496
Web: inapp.com

Internet Creations Inc
2000 Waterview Dr Ste 100 Hamilton NJ 08691 609-570-7200
Web: www.internetcreations.com

Internet Employment Linkage Inc
1010 Lk St Ste 611 Oak Park IL 60301 708-848-4351
Web: www.ielinc.net

Internet Nebraska Inc
1719 N Cotner Blvd Ste B Lincoln NE 68505 402-434-8680
TF: 800-438-4638 ■ *Web:* www.inebraska.com

Company / Address	City	State	Zip	Phone	Fax
introNetworks Inc 1482 E Valley Rd Ste 446 *Web:* www.intronetworks.com	Santa Barbara	CA	93108	805-722-1040	
inXile entertainment Inc 2727 Newport Blvd *Web:* www.inxile-entertainment.com	Newport Beach	CA	92663	949-675-3690	
Iostudio LLC 565 Marriott Dr Ste 700 *Web:* www.iostudio.com	Nashville	TN	37214	615-256-6282	
IP Fabrics Inc 3720 SW 141st Ave Ste 201 *Web:* www.ipfabrics.com	Beaverton	OR	97005	503-444-2400	
IPS Worldwide LLC 265 Clyde Morris Blvd Ste 100 *Web:* www.ipsww.com	Ormond Beach	FL	32174	386-672-7727	
Iqr Consulting Inc 1915 gardenview cir *Web:* iqrconsulting.com	Santa Rosa	CA	95403	707-921-7071	
IRA Services Trust Co 1160 Industrial Rd Ste 1 *Web:* www.ierinc.com	San Carlos	CA	94070	650-593-2221	
ISD Inc 2500 W Higgins Rd Ste 250 *Web:* www.isdinc.com	Hoffman Estates	IL	60169	847-519-1150	
ISS Software Solutions Inc 5 Great Vly Pkwy Ste 110 *Web:* www.intsoftinc.com	Malvern	PA	19355	610-560-4300	
IT-Lifeline Inc 23403 E Mission Ave *Web:* www.itlifeline.net	Liberty Lake	WA	99019	509-984-1600	
ITRenew Inc 8356 Central Ave *Web:* www.itrenew.com	Newark	CA	94560	408-744-9600	
Ives Group Inc 9 Main St Ste 2F *Web:* www.ivesinc.com	Sutton	MA	01590	508-476-7007	
Ivision Inc 1430 W Peachtree St NW *Web:* ivision.com	Atlanta	GA	30309	678-999-3002	
iWeb Group Inc 20 Place du Commerce *Web:* iweb.com	Montreal	QC	H3E1Z6	514-286-4242	
Jacquette Consulting Inc 710 Providence Rd *Web:* www.jacquette.com	Malvern	PA	19355	610-644-4485	
Jdm Systems Consultants Inc 33117 Hamilton Ct *Web:* www.jdmconsulting.com	Farmington Hills	MI	48334	248-324-1937	
JP Digital Imaging Inc 230 Polaris Ave *Web:* www.jpdigital.com	Mountain View	CA	94043	650-965-0803	
K2 Communications 880 Apollo St Ste 239 *Web:* k2communications.com	El Segundo	CA	90245	310-524-9100	
K2Share LLC 1005 University Dr E *Web:* k2share.com	College Station	TX	77840	979-260-0030	
Keane Inc 210 Porter Dr Ste 315 **Fax Area Code:* 617	San Ramon	CA	94583	925-838-8600	241-9507*
Kell Partners 303 camp craft rd *Web:* www.kellpartners.com	Austin	TX	78746	512-850-5355	
Kelser Corp 111 Roberts St Ste D *TF:* 800-647-5316 ■ *Web:* www.kelsercorp.com	East Hartford	CT	06108	860-528-9819	291-9088
Key Computing 85 Sea Ln *Web:* keycomputing.com	Farmingdale	NY	11735	631-264-0660	
Keycom Communications 1144 Solana Ave *Web:* www.keycom.net	Winter Park	FL	32789	407-949-0600	
Keylogic Systems Inc 3168 Collins Ferry Rd *Web:* keylogic.com	Morgantown	WV	26505	304-296-9100	
Keystone Information Systems 1000 S Lenola Rd *Web:* www.keyinfosys.com	Maple Shade	NJ	08052	856-722-0700	
Kinsail Corp 1420 Beverly Rd Ste 150 *Web:* www.kinsail.com	Mclean	VA	22101	703-994-4194	
Kirtley Technology Corp 9s531 Wilmette Ave *TF:* 888-757-0778 ■ *Web:* kirtleytech.com	Darien	IL	60561	630-512-0213	
Klein Managment Systems Inc 259 S Middletown Rd *Web:* kleinmgmt.com	Nanuet	NY	10954	845-623-7778	
Koniag Services Inc 4100 Lafayette Dr Ste 303 *Web:* www.ksikoniag.com	Chantilly	VA	20151	703-488-9300	
Krueger Associates Inc 105 Commerce Dr *Web:* www.nfsrv.com	Aston	PA	19014	610-532-4700	
L & E Meridan 7400 Fullerton Rd *Web:* www.l-e.com	Springfield	VA	22153	703-913-0300	
L Tech Network Services Inc 9926 Pioneer Blvd Ste 101 *Web:* www.ltechnet.com	Santa Fe Springs	CA	90670	562-222-1121	
La Touraine Inc 625 Broadway Ste 700 *TF:* 800-893-8871 ■ *Web:* latouraineinc.com	San Diego	CA	92101	800-893-8871	
Lake Data Center Inc 800 Lloyd Rd *Web:* www.lakedata.com	Wickliffe	OH	44092	440-944-2020	
Learning Enhancement Corp 200 S Wacker Dr Ste 3100 *TF:* 877-272-4610 ■ *Web:* www.mybrainware.com	Chicago	IL	60606	312-455-1758	
Leatherup Com 955 Venice Blvd *TF:* 800-846-6010 ■ *Web:* www.leatherup.com	Los Angeles	CA	90015	213-763-6185	
Lifeline Data Centers LLC 401 N Shadeland Ave *Web:* www.lifelinedatacenters.com	Indianapolis	IN	46219	317-423-2591	
LifePics Inc 5777 Central Ave Ste 120 *Web:* www.lifepics.com	Boulder	CO	80301	303-413-9500	
Light Styles Internet LLC 1843 S Broadway Ave Ste 104 *Web:* www.lightingshowroom.com	Boise	ID	83706	208-433-3900	
Listengage.com 5 Edgell Rd Ste 30a *Web:* www.listengage.com	Framingham	MA	01701	508-935-2275	
Little Apple Technologies 112 S Broadway *Web:* littleappletech.com	Manhattan	MT	59741	406-284-3174	
Livesmart 360 LLC 6311 Porter Rd Ste 11	Sarasota	FL	34240	941-371-1010	
LoganBritton Inc 1700 Park St Ste 111 *TF:* 800-362-4352 ■ *Web:* www.loganbritton.com	Naperville	IL	60563	800-362-4352	
Login Inc 4003 E Speedway Blvd *Web:* www.login.com	Tucson	AZ	85712	520-618-3000	
Long Lines LLC 501 Fourth St PO Box 67 *Web:* www.longlines.com	Sergeant Bluff	IA	51054	712-271-4000	
Lord Whalen LLC 371 Van Ness Way Ste 110 *Web:* www.institutionalriskanalytics.com	Torrance	CA	90501	310-676-3300	
Lowe-Martin Company Inc 400 Hunt Club Rd *TF:* 866-521-9871 ■ *Web:* www.lmgroup.com	Ottawa	ON	K1V1C1	613-741-0962	
Lumension Security Inc 8660 E Hartford Dr Ste 300 **Fax Area Code:* 480 ■ *TF:* 888-725-7828 ■ *Web:* www.lumension.com	Scottsdale	AZ	85255	888-725-7828	970-6323*
Lunarline Inc 3300 N Fairfax Dr Ste 308 *Web:* www.lunarline.com	Arlington	VA	22201	571-481-9300	
MaddenCo Inc 4847 E Virginia Ste G *Web:* www.maddenco.com	Evansville	IN	47715	812-474-6245	
Magmic Inc 126 York St *Web:* www.magmic.com	Ottawa	ON	K1N5T5	613-241-3571	
MajescoMastek 105 Fieldcrest Ave Ste 208 *Web:* www.majesco.com	Edison	NJ	08837	732-590-6400	
Makro Technologies Inc 1 Washington Pk Ste 1502 *Web:* www.makrotech.com	Newark	NJ	07102	973-481-0100	
marblemedia Inc 74 Fraser Ave Ste 100 *Web:* www.marblemedia.com	Toronto	ON	M6K3E1	416-646-2711	
Marketware Inc 7070 Union Park Ctr Ste 300 *Web:* marketware.com	Midvale	UT	84047	801-944-4230	
Mass Media Inc 883 Patriot Dr *Web:* www.massmedia.com	Moorpark	CA	93021	805-531-9399	
Mathtech Inc 6402 Arlington Blvd Ste 1200 *Web:* mathtechinc.com	Falls Church	VA	22042	703-875-8866	
Mcf Technology Solutions LLC 30400 Detroit Rd *Web:* www.mcftech.com	Westlake	OH	44145	440-201-6050	
MecSoft Corp 18019 Sky Park Cir Ste KL *Web:* www.mecsoft.com	Irvine	CA	92614	949-654-8163	
MediConnect Global Inc 10897 South Riverfront Pkwy Ste 500 *Web:* www.mediconnect.net	South Jordan	UT	84095	801-545-3700	
MedPricer.com Inc 2351 Boston Post Rd Ste 208 *Web:* www.medpricer.com	Guilford	CT	06437	203-453-4554	
MegaPath Inc 6800 Koll Ctr Pkwy Ste 200 *Web:* www.megapath.com	Pleasanton	CA	94566	925-201-2500	
Melissa DATA Corp 22382 Avenida Empresa *Web:* www.melissadata.com	Rancho Santa Margarita	CA	92688	949-858-3000	
Memorial Hermann Health Network Providers Inc 7737 SW Fwy Ste C98 *Web:* mhmd.memorialhermann.org	Houston	TX	77074	713-338-6464	
Meridian Midwest Payment 402 S Patterson Ave *Web:* meridian-midwest.com	Joplin	MO	64801	887-916-1846	
MeriTec Services Inc 12770 Cimarron Path Ste 118 *Web:* www.meritecservices.com	San Antonio	TX	78249	210-694-4635	
Merritt Technical Associates Inc 114 Saint Johns Rd *Web:* www.merritt-tech.com	Wilton	CT	06897	203-834-0010	
MessageSolution Inc 1851 McCarthy Blvd Ste 105 *Web:* www.messagesolution.com	Milpitas	CA	95035	408-383-0100	
Metasense Inc 403 Commerce Ln Ste 5 *Web:* www.metasenseusa.com	West Berlin	NJ	08091	856-873-9950	
MIB Inc 50 Braintree Hill Park *Web:* www.mib.com	Braintree	MA	02184	781-329-4500	
Microwave Applications Group 3030 Industrial Pkwy *Web:* magsmx.com	Santa Maria	CA	93455	805-928-5711	
Mid America Computer Corp PO Box 700 *TF:* 800-622-2502 ■ *Web:* www.maccnet.com	Blair	NE	68008	402-426-6222	533-5369
Mile High Shooting Accessories LLC 3731 Monarch St *TF:* 877-871-9990 ■ *Web:* milehighshooting.com	Erie	CO	80516	303-255-9999	
Mod43 Inc 7946 N Lilley Rd *Web:* mod43.com	Canton	MI	48187	734-416-1009	
Modern Earth 449 Provencher Blvd *TF:* 866-766-7640 ■ *Web:* www.modernearth.net	Winnipeg	MB	R2J0B8	204-885-2469	
Moja Inc 7010 Infantry Ridge Rd *Web:* www.moja.net	Manassas	VA	20109	703-369-4339	
Momentum Capital Partners 1227 W Magnolia Ave Ste 300 *Web:* www.mocappartners.com	Fort Worth	TX	76104	817-920-7599	
Moog Animatics 3200 Patrick Henry Dr *Web:* www.animatics.com	Santa Clara	CA	95054	408-748-8721	
Mudiam Inc 7100 regency Sq blvd *TF:* 888-306-2062 ■ *Web:* www.mudiaminc.com	Houston	TX	77036	713-484-7266	
Murphy Industries Inc 1650 Cascade Dr *Web:* www.acc-net.com	Marion	OH	43302	740-387-7890	
Musictoday LLC 5400 Three Notched Rd *Web:* www.musictoday.com	Crozet	VA	22932	434-205-7049	
N-Dimension Solutions Inc 9030 Leslie St Unit 300 *TF:* 866-837-8884 ■ *Web:* www.n-dimension.com	Richmond Hill	ON	L4B1G2	905-707-8884	
Nakina Systems Inc 80 Hines Rd Ste 200 *TF:* 877-625-4627 ■ *Web:* www.nakinasystems.com	Ottawa	ON	K2K2T8	613-254-7351	
Natel Telecommunications Lc 907 W Burlington Ave *Web:* www.natel.net	Fairfield	IA	52556	641-469-6220	
NeST Technologies Corp 44901 Falcon Pl Ste 116 *Web:* www.nesttech.com	Sterling	VA	20166	703-653-1100	
Net Solutions Technology Center 38 Sams Point Rd Ab	Beaufort	SC	29907	843-525-6469	
Netcom Systems Inc 200 Metroplex Dr *Web:* www.netcom-sys.com	Edison	NJ	08817	732-393-6100	

Company / Address	City	State	Zip	Phone	Fax
NetQuest Corp 523 Fellowship Rd Ste 205 *Web:* www.netquestcorp.com	Mt Laurel	NJ	08054	856-866-0505	
Network Magic Unlimited 1723 21st St *Web:* www.netmagicu.com	Santa Monica	CA	90404	310-449-1411	
NeuCo Inc 12 Post Office Sq 4th Fl *Web:* www.neuco.net	Boston	MA	02109	617-587-3100	
Nevada Automotive Test Center 605 Ft Churchill Rd *Web:* www.natc-ht.com	Silver Springs	NV	89429	775-629-2000	
New West Technologies Inc 4606 SE Division St *Web:* www.newestech.com	Portland	OR	97206	503-235-4656	
Nexcess.net LLC 21700 Melrose Ave *TF:* 866-639-2377 ■ *Web:* www.nexcess.net	Southfield	MI	48075	866-639-2377	
nexDimension Technology Solutions LLC 10060 Medlock Bridge Rd Ste 100 *Web:* www.nexdimension.net	Johns Creek	GA	30097	770-475-1575	
NexTalk Inc 10757 River Front Pkwy Ste 290 *Web:* www.nextalk.com	South Jordan	UT	84095	801-274-6001	
Nextpage Inc 13997 S Minuteman Dr Ste 300	Draper	UT	84020	801-748-4400	748-4410
Nexxus Marketing Group LLC, The 85 Sam Fonzo Dr *Web:* www.thenexxusgroup.com	Beverly	MA	01923	978-762-3900	
Nimble Assessment Systems Inc 3 Bridge St Ste B101	Newton	MA	02458	617-431-4441	
Nimbus Design 2363 Broadway St *Web:* www.nimbusdesign.com	Redwood City	CA	94063	650-365-7568	
Nourtek Services Corp 100 decker ct Ste 191 *Web:* www.nourtek.com	Irving	TX	75062	972-717-2700	
Novaces LLC Poydras Ctr 650 Poydras St Ste 2320 *Web:* www.novaces.com	New Orleans	LA	70130	504-544-6888	
Novologix Inc 10400 Viking Dr	Eden Prairie	MN	55344	952-826-2500	
O'neil Data Systems Inc 12655 Beatrice St *Web:* www.oneildata.com	Los Angeles	CA	90066	310-448-6400	
Oasis Systems Inc 24 Hartwell Ave *Web:* www.oasissystems.com	Lexington	MA	02421	781-676-7333	676-7353
Objectstream Inc 7725 W Reno Ave Ste 307 *Web:* www.objectstream.com	Oklahoma City	OK	73127	405-942-4477	
Observera Inc 3856 Dulles S Court Ste I *Web:* www.observera.com	Chantilly	VA	20151	703-378-3153	
Oly Penn. Inc 245 E Washington St *Web:* startpage.olypen.com	Sequim	WA	98382	360-683-1456	
Omeda Communications 555 Huehl Rd *Web:* omeda.com	Northbrook	IL	60062	847-564-8900	
One Technologies LP 8144 Walnut Hill Ln Ste 600 *TF:* 888-550-8471 ■ *Web:* www.onetechnologies.net	Dallas	TX	75231	888-550-8471	
Online Business Applications Inc 9018 Heritage Pkwy Ste 600 *Web:* www.irmsonline.com	Woodridge	IL	60517	630-243-9810	
onShore Networks LLC 1407 W Chicago Ave *Web:* www.onshore.com	Chicago	IL	60642	312-850-5200	
Opal Soft 1288 Kifer Rd # 201 *Web:* www.opalsoft.com	Sunnyvale	CA	94086	408-267-2211	
Open Logic Corp 28345 Beck Rd Ste 308 *Web:* www.open-logix.com	Wixom	MI	48393	248-869-0080	
Openface Inc 3445 Park Ave *TF:* 800-865-8585 ■ *Web:* www.openface.com	Montreal	QC	H2X2H6	514-281-8585	
Opinion Access Corp 47-10 32nd Pl *TF:* 888-489-3282 ■ *Web:* www.opinionaccess.com	Long Island	NY	11101	718-729-2622	
Optimetra Inc 1710 Chapel Hills Dr *TF:* 800-758-9710 ■ *Web:* www.optimetra.com	Colorado Springs	CO	80920	800-758-9710	
Orchid Suites Inc 1309 Emerson St NW *TF:* 877-255-4300	Washington	DC	20011	877-255-4300	
Original Media LLC 38 E 29th St 5th Fl *Web:* www.originalmedia.com	New York	NY	10016	212-683-3086	
Oristech Inc Po Box 310069 *Web:* www.oristech.com	New Braunfels	TX	78131	830-620-7422	
Oski Technology Inc 2513 E Charleston Rd Ste 203 *Web:* www.oskitechnology.com	Mountain View	CA	94043	408-216-7728	
Ovation Networks Inc 222 Third Ave Se Ste 276 *Web:* www.ovationnetworks.com	Cedar Rapids	IA	52401	319-365-6200	
Overture Technologies Inc 6900 Wisconsin Ave Ste 200 *Web:* home.overturecorp.com	Bethesda	MD	20815	301-492-2140	
P K W Associates Inc 705 E Ordnance Rd Ste 108 *TF:* 888-358-3900 ■ *Web:* www.pkwassoc.com	Baltimore	MD	21226	443-773-1000	
P Murphy & Assoc Inc 2301 W Olive Ave *Web:* www.pmurphy.com	Burbank	CA	91506	818-841-2002	
P2i Inc 1236 Main St *Web:* www.p2ionline.com	Hellertown	PA	18055	610-814-0550	
Palm Pictures LLC 110 E 25th St *Web:* www.palmpictures.com	New York	NY	10010	646-790-1211	
PASCO Inc 1140 Terex Rd *Web:* pasco-group.com	Hudson	OH	44236	330-655-7000	
Passport Online Inc 9786 Sw Nimbus Ave *Web:* www.passportonlineinc.com	Beaverton	OR	97008	503-626-7766	
PCC Technology Group LLC 2 Barnard Ln	Bloomfield	CT	06002	860-242-3299	
PenTeleData 540 Delaware Ave PO Box 197 *TF:* 800-281-3564 ■ *Web:* www.penteledata.net	Palmerton	PA	18071	800-281-3564	
Peraso Technologies Inc 144 Front St W Ste 685 *Web:* www.perasotech.com	Toronto	ON	M5J2L7	416-637-1048	
Photo Den Vision & Sound 315 SE Seventh St *Web:* photoden.com	Grants Pass	OR	97526	541-479-1833	
Photodex Corp 11100 Metric Blvd Ste 400 *Web:* www.photodex.com	Austin	TX	78758	512-419-7000	
Pinnacle Business Systems Inc 3824 S Blvd St Ste 200 *TF:* 800-311-0757 ■ *Web:* www.pbsnow.com	Edmond	OK	73013	800-311-0757	444-3439
Pinpoint Data 339 Somerset St *TF:* 866-974-6764 ■ *Web:* www.couponchek.com	North Plainfield	NJ	07060	908-756-9400	
Pipeline Interactive Inc 941 Cumberland St *Web:* www.pipelineinteractive.com	Lebanon	PA	17042	717-273-5665	
Pixeled Business Systems Inc 350 W Ninth Ave Ste 106 *Web:* www.pixeled.com	Escondido	CA	92025	858-566-6060	
PlasmaNet Inc 420 Lexington Ave Ste 2435 *Web:* freelotto.com	New York	NY	10170	212-931-6760	
Poka Lambro Telephone Cooperative Inc 560 US Hwy 87 *Web:* www.poka.com	Wilson	TX	79381	806-924-7234	
Pool 4 Tool America LLC 34119 W 12 Mile Rd Ste 320 *Web:* www.pool4tool.com	Farmington Hills	MI	48331	248-244-0851	
PowerMetal Technologies Inc 2726 Loker Ave W *Web:* www.powermetalinc.com	Carlsbad	CA	92010	760-607-0404	
Premier Management Corp 8894 Stanford Blvd Ste 405 *Web:* premgtcorp.com	Columbia	MD	21045	443-656-3550	
Presentek Inc 987 University Ave Ste 11 *Web:* www.presentek.com	Los Gatos	CA	95032	408-354-1264	
Pricon Inc 1831 W Lincoln Ave *Web:* www.pricon.com	Anaheim	CA	92801	714-758-8832	
Prime Care Technologies Inc 6650 Sugarloaf Pkwy Ste 400 *Web:* primecaretech.com	Duluth	GA	30097	770-870-2888	
Printco Graphics Inc 14112 Industrial Rd *TF:* 888-593-1080 ■ *Web:* www.printcographics.com	Omaha	NE	68144	402-593-1080	
Printmail Systems Inc 23 Friends Ln *TF:* 800-910-4844 ■ *Web:* www.printmailsolutions.com	Newtown	PA	18940	215-860-4250	860-2204
Prism Visual Software Inc 1 Sagamore Hl Dr Ste 2B *Web:* www.prismvs.com	Port Washington	NY	11050	516-944-5920	
PRISMHR 50 Resnik Rd Ste 200 *TF:* 877-837-4311 ■ *Web:* www.prismhr.com	Plymouth	MA	02360	508-747-7261	
Pro Net Communications Inc 1152 Mainland St Ste 230 *Web:* www.pro.net	Vancouver	BC	V6B5L1	604-606-0660	
ProducersWEB Inc 8 Penn Ctr 1628 John F Kennedy Blvd Ste 1850 *Web:* www.producersweb.com	Philadelphia	PA	19103	215-561-2686	
Projectools Company Inc 4099 Hwy 36 N *Web:* www.projectools.com	Bellville	TX	77418	713-371-9840	
Prologic Technology Systems Inc 10801-1 N Mopac Expy Ste 120 *Web:* www.ptsteams.com	Austin	TX	78759	512-328-9496	
Prospection Inc 1750 Av De Vitre *Web:* www.prospection.qc.ca	Quebec	QC	G1J1Z6	418-521-2248	
Protogate Inc 12225 World Trade Dr *TF:* 877-473-0190 ■ *Web:* www.protogate.com	San Diego	CA	92128	858-451-0865	
PRWT Services Inc 1835 Market St 8th Fl *Web:* www.prwt.com	Philadelphia	PA	19103	215-569-8810	569-9893
Puppet Labs 308 SW Second Ave 5th Fl *Web:* puppet.com	Portland	OR	97204	503-575-9775	
Pyramid Consulting Inc 11100 Atlantis Pl *TF:* 877-248-0024 ■ *Web:* www.pyramidci.com	Alpharetta	GA	30022	678-514-3500	
QC Data International Inc 8000 E Maplewood Ave Ste 300 *Web:* www.qcdata.com	Greenwood Village	CO	80111	303-783-8888	
Qlan Corp 23232 Peralta Dr 117 *Web:* www.griffinoptometric.com	Laguna Hills	CA	92653	949-597-8560	
QUESTAR LLC 2905 W Service Rd *Web:* questarweb.com	Eagan	MN	55121	651-688-0089	
Radius Technology Group Inc 804 Pershing Dr Ste 1 *Web:* www.radius360.net	Silver Spring	MD	20910	301-565-3400	
Rally Software Development Corp 3333 Walnut St *Web:* rallydev.com	Boulder	CO	80301	303-565-2800	
Ramco Systems Corp 3150 Brunswick Pk Ste 130 *TF:* 800-472-6261 ■ *Web:* www.ramco.com	Lawrenceville	NJ	08648	609-620-4800	
Ramius Corp 201-227 Rue Montcalm *Web:* www.ramius.net	Gatineau	QC	J8Y3B9	613-230-3808	
Randr Inc 3764 Ninth St *Web:* www.randrinc.com	Riverside	CA	92501	951-369-3427	
Rangam Consultants Inc 370 Campus Dr Ste 103 **Fax Area Code: 877* ■ *TF:* 877-583-7054 ■ *Web:* www.rangam.com	Somerset	NJ	08873	908-704-8843	606-6587*
Raptr Inc 701 N Shoreline Blvd *Web:* raptr.com	Mountain View	CA	94043	650-215-1328	
Rassai 500 Throckmorton St Ste 375	Fort Worth	TX	76102	817-332-0069	
Raven Software Corp 8496 Greenway Blvd *Web:* www.ravensoftware.com	Middleton	WI	53562	608-833-5791	
Ray Allen Inc 400 W Erie St Ste 400 *Web:* www.rayalleninc.com	Chicago	IL	60654	312-895-0222	
RCF Information Systems Inc 4200 Colonel Glenn Hwy Glenn Tech Ctr Ste 100 *Web:* rcfinfo.com	Beavercreek	OH	45431	937-427-5680	
Real Intent Inc 990 Almanor Ave Ste 220 *Web:* www.realintent.com	Sunnyvale	CA	94085	408-830-0700	
Reality Technology Inc 2444 Washington St Ste 201 *Web:* www.reality-technology.com	Denver	CO	80205	303-757-1107	

Phone | Fax

Reallygreatrate Inc
423 S Pacific Coast Hwy Ste 202 .... Redondo Beach CA 90277 310-540-8900
Web: www.reallygreatrate.com

Red Clay Interactive
22 Buford Village Way Ste 221 .... Buford GA 30518 770-297-2430
TF: 866-251-2800 ■ *Web:* www.redclayinteractive.com

Red Storm Entertainment Inc
2000 Centregreen Way Ste 300 .... Cary NC 27513 919-460-1776
Web: www.redstorm.com

RedTail Solutions Inc 69 Milk St Ste 100 .... Westborough MA 01581 508-983-1900
TF: 866-764-7601 ■ *Web:* redtailsolutions.com

Reed Technology & Information Services Inc
7 Walnut Grove Dr .... Horsham PA 19044 215-441-6400
Web: www.reedtech.com

REGEN Energy Inc 15 Belfield Rd Ste 5 .... Toronto ON M9W1E8 416-934-1040
Web: www.regenenergy.com

Renesys Corp 1155 Elm St Ste 510 .... Manchester NH 03101 603-643-9300
Web: dyn.com/performance-assurance

Renew Data Corp 9500 Arboretum Blvd .... Austin TX 78759 512-276-5500 276-5555
TF: 888-811-3789 ■ *Web:* www.renewdata.com

RESOLUTE Partners LLC
37 W Center St Ste 301 .... Southington CT 06489 860-628-6800
Web: www.resolutepartners.com

Resource Technology Management Inc
251 Maitland Av Ste 215 .... Maitland FL 32701 407-998-8000
Web: www.rtm-inc.com

Respondus Inc
8201 164th Ave NE Ste 200 PO Box 3247 .... Redmond WA 98052 425-497-0389
Web: www.respondus.com

Richweb Inc 4235 Innslake Dr Ste 201 .... Glen Allen VA 23060 804-747-8592
Web: www.richweb.com

Right Systems Inc 2600 Willamette Dr NE Ste C .... Lacey WA 98516 360-956-0414 956-0336
TF: 800-571-1717 ■ *Web:* www.rightsys.com

Riverbed Technology Inc 199 Fremont St .... San Francisco CA 94105 415-247-8800 247-8801
NASDAQ: RVBD ■ *Web:* www.riverbed.com

Ross Group Inc 2730 Indian Ripple Rd .... Dayton OH 45440 937-427-3069
Web: www.rossgroupinc.com

Rugged Systems Inc 13000 Danielson St Q .... Poway CA 92064 858-391-1006
TF: 888-584-2673 ■ *Web:* www.coresystemsusa.com

Rurbanc Data Services Inc 7622 N SR- 66 .... Defiance OH 43512 419-783-8800
Web: www.rdsiweb.com

Ryantech Inc 1794 Olympic Pkwy Ste 250 .... Park City UT 84098 435-647-0118
Web: www.ryantechinc.com

Ryte Byte Inc s4125a rocky point rd .... Baraboo WI 53913 608-356-6822
Web: www.rytebyteinc.com

Sable Networks Inc 3171 Jay St .... Santa Clara CA 95054 408-727-5514
Web: www.sablenetworks.com

Saepio Technologies Inc
4601 Madison Ave 4th Fl .... Kansas City MO 64112 816-777-2100
TF: 877-468-7613 ■ *Web:* www.saepio.com

Safe Systems Inc 11395 Old Roswell Rd .... Alpharetta GA 30009 770-752-0550
Web: www.safesystems.com

Sagerock.com 15 Broad St .... Akron OH 44305 330-379-9000
Web: www.sagerock.com

SalePoint Inc 9909 Huennekens St Ste 205 .... San Diego CA 92121 858-546-9400
Web: www.salepoint.com

Scicom Data Services Ltd 10101 Bren Rd E .... Minnetonka MN 55343 952-933-4200 936-4132
TF: 800-488-9087

Screenz 5212 N Clark St .... Chicago IL 60640 773-912-1565
Web: screenz.com

Seagull Scientific Inc 1616 148th Ave Se .... Bellevue WA 98007 425-641-1408
Web: seagullscientific.com

SecureOne Data Solutions LLC
2801 N 33rd Ave Ste 1 .... Phoenix AZ 85009 602-415-1111
Web: www.datacenteraz.com

Seguin Services Inc 3100 S Central Ave .... Cicero IL 60804 708-222-4250
Web: www.seguin.org

SevenTwenty Strategies
1220 19th St NW Ste 300 .... Washington DC 20036 202-962-3955
Web: www.720strategies.com

SHAZAM Inc 6700 Pioneer Pkwy .... Johnston IA 50131 515-288-2828
Web: www.shazam.net

Shipcom Wireless Inc
11200 Richmond Ave Ste 552 .... Houston TX 77082 281-558-5252
Web: www.shipcomwireless.com

Shop Floor Automations Inc 5360 Jackson Dr .... La Mesa CA 91942 619-461-4000
TF: 877-611-5825 ■ *Web:* www.shopfloorautomations.com

Sigma Solutions Inc 422 E Ramsey Rd .... San Antonio TX 78216 210-348-9876
TF: 800-567-5964 ■ *Web:* www.sigmasolinc.com

SILVACO Inc 4701 Patrick Henry Dr Bldg 2 .... Santa Clara CA 95054 408-567-1000
Web: www.silvaco.com

Simplifile LC 4844 North 300 West Ste 202 .... Provo UT 84604 801-373-0151
TF: 800-460-5657 ■ *Web:* simplifile.com

Six Red Marbles LLC
10 City Sq 3rd Fl Charlestown .... Boston MA 02129 857-588-9000
Web: www.sixredmarbles.com

Skybank Financial Services Corp
1444 Biscayne Blvd Ste 309 .... Miami FL 33132 800-617-9980
TF: 800-617-9980 ■ *Web:* www.skybankfinancial.com

Smart Web Concepts Inc
701 Riverside Ave Ste 3 .... Roseville CA 95678 916-782-2288
Web: boostlogics.com

Smartorg Inc 855 oak grove ave .... Menlo Park CA 94025 650-328-1612
Web: www.smartorg.com

Smilebox Inc 15809 Bear Creek Pkwy .... Redmond WA 98052 360-797-5269
Web: www.smilebox.com

Societe Grics 5100 Rue Sherbrooke E .... Montreal QC H1V3R9 514-251-3700
Web: grics.ca

Sof Tec Solutions Inc
384 Inverness Pkwy # 211 .... Englewood CO 80112 303-662-1010 662-1060
TF: 888-376-3832 ■ *Web:* www.softecinc.com

Softcom Technology Consulting Inc 10 Bay St .... Toronto ON M5J2R8 416-957-7400
Web: softcom.com

Softlayer Technologies Inc 4849 Alpha Rd .... Dallas TX 75244 214-442-0600 442-0601
TF Sales: 866-398-7638 ■ *Web:* www.softlayer.com

Sorteo Games Inc 6725 Mesa Ridge Rd Ste 202 .... San Diego CA 92121 858-554-0297
Web: www.sorteogames.com

SourceMedical Solutions Inc
100 Grandview Pl Ste 400 .... Birmingham AL 35243 866-245-8093
TF: 866-245-8093 ■ *Web:* www.sourcemed.net

South Point Systems Inc 1019 Us Hwy 431 .... Boaz AL 35957 256-593-1337
Web: www.southpoint.net

Southern Data Systems Inc
1245 Land O Lakes Dr .... Roswell GA 30075 770-993-7103
TF: 888-425-6151 ■ *Web:* www.southern-data.com

Spectrum Data Inc 131 N Third St .... Oregon IL 61061 815-732-6567
TF: 800-733-6567 ■ *Web:* www.spectrumdata.org

Splashdot Inc 609 Hastings St W .... Vancouver BC V6B4W4 604-899-0597
Web: www.splashdot.com

SportsDirect Inc 211 Horseshoe Lk Dr .... Halifax NS B3S1E1 902-835-3320
TF: 866-756-9771 ■ *Web:* www.sportsdirectinc.com

SQAD Inc 303 S Broadway Ste 130 .... Tarrytown NY 10591 914-524-7600
Web: www.sqad.com

SRA OSS Inc 5300 Stevens Creek Blvd Ste 460 .... San Jose CA 95129 408-855-8200
Web: www.sraoss.com

SRB Education Solutions Inc
200 Town Centre Blvd Ste 400 .... Markham ON L3R8G5 905-943-7706 943-7713
Web: www.srbeducationsolutions.com

Standard Data Corp 26 Journal Sq .... Jersey City NJ 07306 201-533-4433 533-8236
Web: www.standarddata.com

Stark Services
12444 Victory Blvd 3rd Fl .... North Hollywood CA 91606 818-985-2003
Web: www.starkservices.com

Statco 8870 Business Park Dr .... Austin TX 78759 512-795-5000
Web: www.statco.com

Steadfast Networks Inc
350 E Cermak Rd Ste 240 .... Chicago IL 60616 312-602-2689
Web: www.steadfast.net

Storm Internet Services Inc
1760 Courtwood Crescent .... Ottawa ON K2C2B5 613-567-6585 567-3227
TF: 866-257-8676 ■ *Web:* www.storm.ca

Stratagem Inc 10922 N Cedarburg Rd .... Mequon WI 53092 262-532-2700
Web: www.stratagemconsulting.com

Strategic Power Systems Inc
11016 Rushmore Dr Frenette Bldg Ste 275 .... Charlotte NC 28277 704-544-5501
Web: www.spsinc.com

StreamingEdge (USA) Inc 75 Park Pl 4-th Fl .... New York NY 10007 212-791-6026
Web: www.streamingedge.com

Strictly Technology LLC
5381 nw 33rd ave .... Fort Lauderdale FL 33309 954-606-5440
Web: www.strictlyeducation.com

SunGard Data Systems Inc 680 E Swedesford Rd .... Wayne PA 19087 416-646-5932
TF: 866-264-4829 ■ *Web:* www.sungard.com

Sunhillo Corp 444 Kelley Dr .... West Berlin NJ 08091 856-767-7676
Web: www.sunhillo.com

Sunrise Systems Inc 16 Pearl St Ste 101 .... Metuchen NJ 08840 732-603-2200
Web: www.sunrisesys.com

SupraNet Communications Inc
8000 Excelsior Dr .... Madison WI 53717 608-836-0282
Web: www.supranet.net

Syclone Designs Inc
32 Jack Heard Dr Ste 200 .... Dawsonville GA 30534 706-265-4394
Web: syclone.net

Symplr 616 Cypress Creek Pkwy Ste 800 .... Houston TX 77090 281-863-9500
Web: www.symplr.com

Synergon Solutions Inc 1335 Gateway Dr .... Melbourne FL 32901 321-728-2674
Web: www.synergon.net

Synergy Networks Inc
10970 S Cleveland Ave Ste 406 .... Fort Myers FL 33907 239-790-7000
Web: www.snworks.com

Systems House, The 1033 Rte 46 East Ste A202 .... Clifton NJ 07013 973-777-8050
TF: 800-637-5556 ■ *Web:* tshinc.com

Systems Insight Inc 514 Madison Ave 200 .... Covington KY 41011 859-291-9026
Web: www.systemsinsight.com

Systemsmith Inc 18436 Hawthorne Blvd #208 .... Torrance CA 90504 310-921-2735
Web: cognistix.com

TAG Online Inc 6 Prospect Village Plz 1st Fl .... Clifton NJ 07013 973-783-5583
Web: www.tagonline.com

Talario LLC 815 Medary Ave .... Brookings SD 57006 605-692-9877
Web: www.talario.com

Tango Media Group 326 Carlaw Ave .... Toronto ON M4M3N8 416-204-6269
Web: www.tangomediagroup.com

Taskstream LLC 71 W 23rd St .... New York NY 10010 212-868-2700
TF: 800-311-5656 ■ *Web:* taskstream.com

Tax Management Associates Inc
2225 Coronation Blvd .... Charlotte NC 28227 704-847-1234
TF: 800-951-5350 ■ *Web:* www.tma1.com

TDEC 8120 Woodmont Ave Ste 550 .... Bethesda MD 20814 301-718-0703 718-1615
Web: www.tdec.com

TechSkills LLC 108 Wild Basin Rd Ste 150 .... Austin TX 78746 512-328-4235
Web: www.techskills.edu

Techsmart Solutions Inc
328 Air Park Dr Ste 200 .... Fort Collins CO 80524 970-498-0808
Web: onlinepchelp.com

Techsol4u Inc 95 w 11th st .... Tracy CA 95376 209-833-3212
Web: www.techsolglobalit.com

Techware Distribution Inc 7720 W 78th St .... Minneapolis MN 55439 952-944-0083
TF: 800-295-0083 ■ *Web:* www.techwaredist.com

Tecnicard Inc 3191 Coral Way Ste 800 .... Miami FL 33145 305-442-0018 442-9937
TF: 800-317-6020 ■ *Web:* www.tecnicard.com

Telecom Ottawa Ltd 100 Maple Grove Rd .... Ottawa ON K2V1B8 613-225-4631

Telehouse International Corporation of America Inc
The Teleport 7 Teleport Dr .... Staten Island NY 10311 718-355-2500
Web: telehouse.com

Telesto Group LLC 1060 State Rd Ste 102 .... Princeton NJ 08540 609-503-4201
Web: www.telestogroup.com

				Phone	Fax
Telogical Systems LLC 7900 Westpark Dr. *Web:* telogicalsystems.com	Mclean	VA	22102	703-734-7776	
Teradata Corp 10000 Innovation Dr *NYSE:* TDC ■ *TF:* 866-548-8348 ■ *Web:* in.teradata.com	Dayton	OH	45342	866-548-8348	
TigerLead Solutions LLC 30700 Russell Ranch Rd Ste 102 *TF:* 888-844-3744 ■ *Web:* www.tigerlead.com	Westlake Village	CA	91362	888-844-3744	
Total Immersion Software Inc 1 Enterprise Pkwy Ste 330	Hampton	VA	23666	757-224-6250	
Townsend Security 724 columbia st nw *TF:* 800-357-1019 ■ *Web:* townsendsecurity.com	Olympia	WA	98501	360-359-4400	
TPG Marine Enterprises LLC 1341 N Capitol Ave *Web:* www.tpgmarine.com	Indianapolis	IN	46202	317-631-0234	
Trend 660 American Ave Ste 203 *TF:* 877-330-9900 ■ *Web:* www.trendmls.com	King Of Prussia	PA	19406	610-783-4650	
Tribal Nova Inc 4200 Boul Saint-Laurent Ste 1203 *Web:* www.tribalnova.com	Montreal	QC	H2W2R2	514-598-0444	
TriTech Enterprise Systems Inc 1869 Brightseat Rd *Web:* www.tritechenterprise.com	Hyattsville	MD	20785	301-918-8250	
Triton-Tek Inc 445 W Erie St Ste 208 *TF:* 866-387-4866 ■ *Web:* www.triton-tek.com	Chicago	IL	60654	312-467-9201	
Triveni Digital Inc 40 Washington Rd *Web:* www.trivenidigital.com	Princeton Junction	NJ	08550	609-716-3500	716-3503
UDP Inc 2426 Cee Gee *Web:* udp.com	San Antonio	TX	78217	210-828-6171	
Ultra Logistics Inc 17-17 Rt 208 N Ste 160 *Web:* www.ultralogistics.com	Fair Lawn	NJ	07410	201-703-5110	
Unicon Group Ltd 1734 Gilsinn Ln *Web:* www.unicongl.com	St. Louis	MO	63026	636-394-2012	
UniFocus LP 2455 McIver Ln *Web:* www.unifocus.com	Carrollton	TX	75006	972-512-5000	
UnitedLayer Inc 200 Paul Ave Ste 110 *Web:* www.unitedlayer.com	San Francisco	CA	94124	415-349-2100	
Uptick Marketing Inc 201 Summit Pkwy *Web:* www.infomedia.com	Birmingham	AL	35209	205-823-4440	
Urban Web Design 102-19 Dallas Rd *TF:* 877-889-2573 ■ *Web:* urbanweb.net	Victoria	BC	V8V5A6	250-380-1296	
US Alliance Group Inc 30052 Aventura Ste B *Web:* www.usag-inc.com	Rancho Santa Margarita	CA	92688	949-888-4408	
US Internet Corp 12450 Wayzata Blvd Ste 224 *Web:* www.usinternet.com	Minnetonka	MN	55305	952-253-3262	
V-fluence Interactive Public Realtions Inc 7770 Regents Rd *TF:* 877-835-8362 ■ *Web:* www.v-fluence.com	San Diego	CA	92122	877-835-8362	
Valley Techlogic Inc 261 Business Park Way *Web:* www.valleytechlogic.com	Atwater	CA	95301	209-384-8324	
Vam USA LLC 19210 Hardy Rd *TF:* 888-863-5204 ■ *Web:* www.vam-usa.com	Houston	TX	77041	713-479-3200	
Vangent Inc 4250 N Fairfax Dr	Arlington	VA	22203	703-284-5600	284-5628
VEITS Group LLC 425 Metro Pl N Ste 330 *Web:* www.veitsgroup.com	Dublin	OH	43017	614-467-5414	
Versasuite 13401 Pond Springs Rd *TF:* 800-903-8774 ■ *Web:* versasuite.com	Austin	TX	78729	512-249-8774	
Versatile Systems Inc 4900 Ritter Rd Ste 100 *NYSE:* CVE ■ **Fax Area Code:* 425 ■ *TF:* 800-262-1622 ■ *Web:* www.versatile.com	Mechanicsburg	PA	17055	800-262-1622	778-8577*
Vertafore Inc 11724 NE 195th St *TF:* 800-444-4813 ■ *Web:* www.vertafore.com	Bothell	WA	98011	425-402-1000	402-9569
Virtual Technology Services LLC 806 W Curtis Dr *Web:* www.vts-llc.com	Midwest City	OK	73110	405-733-3500	
Visicom Media Inc 6200 Blvd Taschereau Ste 304 *Web:* www.vmn.net	Brossard	QC	J4W3J8	450-672-0401	
Visionet Systems Inc 4 Cedarbrook Dr Bldg B *Web:* www.visionetsystems.com	Cranbury	NJ	08512	609-452-0700	
Visp.net 301 NE Sixth St *Web:* www.visp.net	Grants Pass	OR	97526	541-955-6900	
VITAL Network Services Inc 14520 McCormick Dr *Web:* www.vital-ns.com	Tampa	FL	33626	813-818-5100	
WAND Inc 2170 S Parker Rd Ste 295 *Web:* www.wandinc.com	Denver	CO	80231	303-623-1200	
Web Age Solutions Inc 439 University Ave Ste 820 *TF:* 866-206-4644 ■ *Web:* www.webagesolutions.com	Toronto	ON	M5G1Y8	866-206-4644	
Web Direct Brands Inc 13100 State Rd 54 *Web:* www.webdirectbrands.com	Odessa	FL	33556	813-920-7259	
Web Full Circle Inc 1000 NC Music Factory Blvd Ste B9 *Web:* www.webfullcircle.com	Charlotte	NC	28206	980-322-0518	
Web Your Business Inc 226 Saxony Rd *Web:* www.webyourbusiness.com	Johnstown	CO	80534	970-593-6260	
WebLinc LLC 22 S Third St 2nd Fl *Web:* weblinc.com	Philadelphia	PA	19106	215-925-1800	
WebLink International Inc 3905 W Vincennes Rd Ste 210 *Web:* www.weblinkinternational.com	Indianapolis	IN	46268	317-872-3909	
WebmasterWorld Inc 3801 N Capital of Texas Hwy e240-181 *Web:* www.webmasterworld.com	Austin	TX	78746	512-231-8107	
WebRing Inc 500 A St Ste 2 *Web:* www.webring.com	Ashland	OR	97520	541-488-9895	
WebWisdom.com Inc Syracuse Technology Garden 235 Harrison St Ste 303 *Web:* www.collabworx.com	Syracuse	NY	13202	315-579-4330	
Welsh Consulting 31 Milk St Ste 805 *Web:* www.welsh.com	Boston	MA	02109	617-695-9800	
Wesucceed Solutions Inc 175 Olde Haof Day *Web:* www.wesucceed.com	Lincolnshire	IL	60069	847-229-8130	
WiBand Communications Corp 187 Commerce Dr **Fax Area Code:* 780 ■ *Web:* www.wiband.com	Winnipeg	MB	R3P1A2	204-633-6333	430-4079*
Williams Records Management 1925 E Vernon Ave *TF Cust Svc:* 888-478-3453 ■ *Web:* www.williamsdatamanagement.com	Los Angeles	CA	90058	323-234-3453	233-5451
Winbeam Inc 302 W Otterman St *Web:* www.winbeam.com	Greensburg	PA	15601	724-219-0400	
WinterGreen Research Inc 6 Raymond St *Web:* www.wintergreenresearch.com	Lexington	MA	02421	781-863-5078	
WisdomTools LLC 501 N Morton St Indiana University Research Pk Ste 206 *Web:* www.wisdomtools.com	Bloomington	IN	47404	812-856-4202	
Wisetek Providers Inc 11211 Waples Mill Rd *Web:* www.wisepro.com	Fairfax	VA	22030	703-766-8850	
WMW Communications Inc 135 N Magnolia Ave Ste D *Web:* www.ao.net	Orlando	FL	32801	407-895-1200	
Woodberry Graphics 11110 Pepper Rd Ste J	Hunt Valley	MD	21031	410-584-9790	
Woodwing Usa 615 Griswold St Ste 520 *Web:* www.woodwing.com	Detroit	MI	48226	313-962-0542	
Worldwide Revenue Solutions Inc 555 Republic Dr Ste 440 *Web:* www.wrsol.com	Plano	TX	75074	972-424-2200	
Wrightsoft Corp 131 Hartwell Ave *TF:* 800-225-8697 ■ *Web:* www.wrightsoft.com	Lexington	MA	02421	800-225-8697	
XE.com Inc 1145 Nicholson Rd Ste 200 *TF:* 877-932-6640 ■ *Web:* www.xe.com	Newmarket	ON	L3Y9C3	416-214-5606	
Xiologix 8215 SW Tualatin Sherwood *TF:* 888-492-6843 ■ *Web:* xiologix.com	Tualatin	OR	97062	503-691-4364	
Yakabod Inc 2 N Market St Ste 300 *Web:* www.yakabod.com	Frederick	MD	21701	301-662-4554	
Z3 Technologies Inc 11400 W Bluemond Rd *Web:* www.z3tech.com	Wauwatosa	WI	53226	414-607-9767	
Z57 Internet Solutions 10045 Mesa Rim Rd **Fax Area Code:* 858 ■ *TF:* 800-899-8148 ■ *Web:* www.z57.com	San Diego	CA	92121	800-899-8148	869-9931*
Zapata Technology Inc 1450 Greene St Ste 500 *Web:* www.zapatatechnology.com	Augusta	GA	30901	706-955-4809	
Zedo Inc 850 Montgomery St Ste 150 *Web:* zedo.com	San Francisco	CA	94133	415-348-1975	
Zedx Inc 369 Rolling Ridge Dr *Web:* www.zedxinc.com	Bellefonte	PA	16823	814-357-8490	
Zion Software LLC 2842 Main St Ste 325 *Web:* www.zionsoftware.com	Glastonbury	CT	06033	860-432-6258	
ZirMed Inc 888 W Market St. Ste 400 *Web:* public.zirmed.com	Louisvill	KY	40202	502-473-7709	

226 DATING SERVICES

				Phone	Fax
50000 Feet Inc 1700 W Irving Park Rd Ste 110 *Web:* www.50000feet.com	Chicago	IL	60613	773-529-6760	
A Total Tan 1400 Teal Rd Ste 4 *Web:* atotaltan.net	Lafayette	IN	47905	765-474-1514	
Adventure Quest Laser Tag 1200 S Clearview Pkwy Ste 1106 *Web:* www.lasertagnola.com	New Orleans	LA	70123	504-207-4444	
Aloha United Way Inc 200 N Vineyard Blvd Ste 700 *Web:* www.auw.org	Honolulu	HI	96817	808-536-1951	
Art Craft Display Inc 500 Business Centre Dr *TF:* 800-878-0710 ■ *Web:* artcraftdisplay.com	Lansing	MI	48917	517-485-2221	
ASA Entertainment LLC 201 N Riverside Dr Ste C *Web:* www.asaentertainment.com	Indialantic	FL	32903	321-722-9300	
Ashley Madison Agency, The 2300 Yonge St *TF:* 866-742-2218 ■ *Web:* www.ashleymadison.com	Toronto	ON	M4P1E4	866-742-2218	
Atom Group LLC, The 125 Brewery Ln Ste 6 *Web:* www.theatomgroup.com	Portsmouth	NH	03801	603-501-0003	
Austin Enviro Group 6802 Manzanita St *Web:* www.aegaustin.com	Austin	TX	78759	512-913-0077	
Balnea Spa 319 chemin du Lac Gale *TF:* 866-734-2110 ■ *Web:* www.balnea.ca	Bromont	QC	J2L2S5	450-534-0604	
Beckers Tax Service & Financial Management Company Inc 5625 Cypress Creek Pkwy Ste 321 *Web:* tenfortyplus.com	Houston	TX	77069	281-397-7777	
Bhargava Wealth Management 609 White Pine Rd *Web:* www.bhargavacapital.com	Franklin Lakes	NJ	07417	201-897-0085	
Bliss Triune Enterprises Llc 4595 Mount Vernon Dr *Web:* blisstriune.com	Los Angeles	CA	90043	323-291-6607	
Boswell's Party Supplies Danville 1901 Cam Ramon *Web:* www.boswells-party.com	Danville	CA	94526	925-866-1644	
Buffalo Design Collaborative Group, The 443 Delaware Ave *Web:* www.schneiderdesign.com	Buffalo	NY	14202	716-923-7000	
Caledon Laboratories Ltd 40 Armstrong Ave *TF:* 877-225-3366 ■ *Web:* www.caledonlabs.com	Georgetown	ON	L7G4R9	905-877-0101	
Cambridge Credit Counseling Corp 67 Hunt St *Web:* www.cambridge-credit.org	Agawam	MA	01001	413-821-8900	
Cantey Hanger LLP 600 W Sixth St Ste 300 *Web:* www.canteyhanger.com	Fort Worth	TX	76102	817-877-2863	
Carbon Design Systems Inc 125 Nagog Park *Web:* www.carbondesignsystems.com	Acton	MA	01720	978-264-7300	
Career Training Education 970 Klamath Ln *Web:* www.sutter.k12.ca.us	Yuba City	CA	95993	530-822-5120	

Phone | Fax

Cfj Manufacturing 5001 N Fwy Ste E Fort Worth TX 76106 817-625-9559
Web: www.cfjmanufacturinglp.com
Chakshu Research Inc 130 Knowles Dr Ste A Los Gatos CA 95032 408-871-1002
Web: www.chakshu.com
Cirion Technologies Inc 33 Nottingham Rd Grafton MA 01519 508-839-6121
Web: www.ciriontech.com
Clinic of Distinctive 638 11 Ave Sw Calgary AB T2R0E2 403-294-0036
Web: distinctivetherapy.com
Clink Events LLC 3006 Bee Cave Rd Ste C-250 Austin TX 78746 512-236-0264
Web: www.clinkevents.com
Cmrg Business Solutions 2401 Trinity Ln Mckinney TX 75070 888-828-8097
TF: 888-828-8097 ■ *Web:* www.cmrgsolutions.com
Cornerstar Inc 10145 Nw Ash St Portland OR 97229 503-546-0500
Web: www.cornerstar.com
Corvallis Peter Productions
2200 N Interstate Ave Portland OR 97227 503-222-1665
Web: www.petercorvallis.com
Counterparts LLC 2012 N 117th Ave Ste 105 Omaha NE 68164 402-932-2220
Web: www.mycounterparts.com
Creative Monograms 122 N 30th St Billings MT 59101 406-259-9925
Web: www.creativemonograms.com
Credit Plus Inc 31550 WinterPl Pkwy Salisbury MD 21804 410-742-9551
Web: www.creditplus.com
Des Moines Golf & Country Club Educational Corp
1600 Jordan Creek Pkwy West Des Moines IA 50266 515-440-7500
Web: www.dmgcc.org
Design Space Mdlar Bldings Inc
29336 Airport Rd Eugene OR 97402 541-461-9122
Web: www.dsmbi.com
Digimap Data Services Inc
40 Kodiak Cres Unit 13 Toronto ON M3J3G5 416-633-2213
Web: www.digimap.com
Digiscribe International LLC
150 Clearbrook Rd Ste 125 Elmsford NY 10523 800-686-7577
TF: 800-686-7577 ■ *Web:* www.digiscribe.info
Eharmony.com Inc 2401 Colorado Ave Santa Monica CA 90404 424-258-1199
Web: www.eharmony.com
Elle K Associates Inc 11900 Castlegate Ct Rockville MD 20852 301-984-4494
Web: ellekassociates.com
Epic Companies 1841 Enterprise Dr Ste 200 Harvey LA 70058 504-340-5252
Web: epiccompanies.com
Equal Vision Records 136 Fuller Rd Albany NY 12205 518-458-8250
Web: www.equalvision.com
Express Immigration & Paralegal Services
10143 Sepulveda Blvd Mission Hills CA 91345 818-894-4611
Fandango Productions LLC
4601 Hollins Ferry Rd Baltimore MD 21227 410-539-7236
Fine Hospitality Group LLC
545 W Lambert Rd Ste D Brea CA 92821 714-990-8800
Web: www.finehospitality.com
Forest Preserve Dist of Dupage County
1717 31st St Oak Brook IL 60523 630-616-8424
TF: 800-526-0857 ■ *Web:* www.dupageforest.com
FreeRealTime com Inc
22365 El Toro Rd Ste 224 Lake Forest CA 92630 949-458-6935
Web: www2.freerealtime.com
Friendfinder Network Inc
6800 Broken Sound Pkwy Ste 200 Boca Raton FL 33487 561-912-7000
TSE: FFN ■ *TF:* 888-575-8383 ■ *Web:* ffn.com
Gloria Ferrer Caves & Vineyards
23555 Arnold Dr Sonoma CA 95476 707-996-7256
Web: www.gloriaferrer.com
Great Expectations 14180 Dallas Pkwy Ste 100 Dallas TX 75254 972-448-7900 448-7969
Group Health Solutions Inc
148 Madison Ave Fl 15 New York NY 10016 212-779-4158
Web: www.grouphealthsolutions.com
Hartmann Studios Inc 100 W Ohio Ave Richmond CA 94804 510-970-3297
Web: www.hartmannstudiosproductions.com
Herlache Enterprises 6417 W 87th St Ste 3 Oak Lawn IL 60453 888-446-8854
TF: 888-446-8854 ■ *Web:* telassist.com
Hgs Financial Services 680 Craig Rd Saint Louis MO 63141 314-432-5341
Web: www.hgsfinancialservices.com
Hr Resolutions 2033 Linglestown Rd Harrisburg PA 17110 717-329-1107
Web: www.hrresolutions.com
Hudson Community Enterprises
68-70 Tuers Ave Jersey City NJ 07306 201-434-3303
Web: www.hudsoncommunity.org
iGov Technologies Inc
9211 Palm River Rd Ste 110 Tampa FL 33619 813-612-9470
TF: 800-777-9375 ■ *Web:* www.igov.com
Inpa System 22 Great Oaks Blvd San Jose CA 95119 408-362-1541
Web: www.inpasystems.com
Intersyn Technologies LP 2736 Albans Houston TX 77005 713-866-4808
Web: www.intersyn.com
It's Just Lunch! Inc 101 W Grand Ave Ste 502 Chicago IL 60611 312-644-9999
Web: www.itsjustlunch.com
Jepson Technologies Inc
14900 Ventura Blvd Ste 210 Sherman Oaks CA 91403 818-990-0601
Web: jepsontech.com
Joester Loria Group Inc, The
30 Irving Pl 10th Fl New York NY 10003 212-683-5150
Web: joesterloriagroup.com
Jsr Power Systems International Llc
5563 De Zavala Rd Ste 200 San Antonio TX 78249 210-558-1943
Web: jsrpsi.com
LesConcierges Inc 77 Maiden Ln 6th Fl San Francisco CA 94108 415-905-0922
Web: www.lesconcierges.com
Lexicon Group, The 1721 De La Vina St Santa Barbara CA 93101 805-898-1943
Web: www.lexicongroup.com
M Eg Enterprises 262 W Broadway Waukesha WI 53186 262-522-3220
MaxVal Group Inc 2251 Grant Rd Los Altos CA 94024 650-472-0644
Web: www.maxval.com
MEMStaff Inc 8 Pine St Newburyport MA 01950 617-996-9263
Web: www.memstaff.com

MerlinOne Inc 17 Whitney Rd Quincy MA 02169 617-328-6645
Web: www.merlinone.com
Metro Property Group 600 W 138th St New York NY 10031 212-924-3905
Web: www.mymetroproperty.com
Momentum Inc 1520 Fourth Ave Ste 300 Seattle WA 98101 206-267-1900
Web: www.momentumbuilds.com
Murphy Harpst Children's Centers
338 W Third St Sw Rome GA 30165 706-232-5663
Web: murphyharpst.org
Nexus Business Solutions
157 S Kalamazoo Mall Dr Ste 105 Kalamazoo MI 49007 269-373-1500
Web: www.nexusbusiness.com
Niche Business Solutions 2300 Ctr Ave Ste 4 New Bern NC 28562 252-514-4177
Web: nichebusinesssolutions.com
Noerr Programs Corp, The 6632 Fig St Arvada CO 80004 303-642-7147
Web: www.noerrprograms.com
Nvms Inc 9255 Center St Ste 200 Manassas VA 20110 703-361-6262
Web: www.nvms.com
Ohio Hispanic Coalition
3556 Sullivant Ave Ste 203 Columbus OH 43204 614-275-1755
Web: ohiohispaniccoalition.org
Olympic Paint Co 6804 Enterprise Dr Louisville KY 40214 502-361-2681
Web: www.porterpaints.com
Omni Cubed Inc 1390 Broadway Ste B155 Placerville CA 95667 877-311-1976
TF: 877-311-1976 ■ *Web:* omnicubed.com
Ownersite Technologies LLC
1425 Market Blvd Ste 330-179 Roswell GA 30076 404-402-7117
Web: www.ownersite.com
PAYjr Inc 4717 Worth St Appartment 2 Dallas TX 75246 214-823-5200
Web: www.payjr.com
People Skills International 2910 Baily Ave San Diego CA 92105 619-262-9951
Promocentric Inc 5 Forbes Rd Hampton NH 03842 603-758-6377
Web: www.promocentric.net
Psychic Readings by Sylvia 546 Rogers St Lowell MA 01852 978-937-0998
Web: www.sylviaspsychicreadings.com
Real Time Risk Systems Llc
80 Wall St Ste 500 New York NY 10005 212-425-3705
Web: realtimerisksystems.com
Realhome.com Inc 1100 Summer St Stamford CT 06905 203-323-7715
Web: www.ahahome.com
Red Lodge Mountain Resort 305 Ski Run Rd Red Lodge MT 59068 406-446-2610
Web: m.redlodgemountain.com
Red Sky Solutions Llc
3600 Birch St Ste 100 Newport Beach CA 92660 949-273-2639
Web: redskysolutions.com
Secure Resolutions Inc
1921 S Alma School Rd Ste 201 Mesa AZ 85210 480-491-7016
Web: www.secureresolutions.com
Seva Technologies LLC
1618 Mahan Ctr Blvd Tallahassee FL 32308 850-391-4832
Web: www.sevatechnologies.com
Siena Engineering Group Inc
50 Mall Rd Ste 203 Burlington MA 01803 781-221-8400
Web: sienaengineeringgroup.com
Smi Travel Inc 1170 Nikki View Dr Brandon FL 33511 813-315-9840
Web: smitrav.com
Solomon Group 825 Girod St New Orleans LA 70113 504-252-4500
Web: www.solomongroup.com
Spa Douce Heure 110 338 Rte Les Coteaux QC J7X1A2 450-267-4949
Web: www.spadouceheure.com
Spark Networks PLC
8383 Wilshire Blvd Ste 800 Beverly Hills CA 90211 323-836-3000
NYSE: LOV ■ *Web:* www.spark.net
Spring Meadows Golf Cntry Clb 59 Lewiston Rd Gray ME 04039 207-657-2586
Web: www.springmeadowsgolf.com
Stainlesslux Inc 3736 Fallon Rd Ste 408 Dublin CA 94568 925-271-7700
Web: www.stainlesslux.com
Stoelt Productions
1962 S La Cienega Blvd Los Angeles CA 90034 323-463-3700
Web: www.stoeltproductions.com
Sunrise Wood Designs 720 107th St Arlington TX 76011 817-701-4101
Web: sunrisewooddesigns.com
SVM LP 200 E Howard Ave Ste 220 Des Plaines IL 60018 877-300-1786
TF: 877-300-1786 ■ *Web:* www.svmcards.net
Synch-Solutions Inc 211 W Wacker Dr Ste 300 Chicago IL 60606 312-252-3700
Web: www.synch-solutions.com
Tarrytown House Estate & Conference Center
49 E Sunnyside Ln Tarrytown NY 10591 914-591-8200
TF: 800-553-8118 ■ *Web:* www.tarrytownhouseestate.com
Tauber-Arons Inc 13848 Ventura Blvd Sherman Oaks CA 91423 323-851-2008
Web: www.tauberaronsinc.com
Thomas Computer Solutions LLC
7915 Westpark Dr Mclean VA 22102 703-839-8700
Web: www.tcstranslations.com
Twisted Networks Inc 1528 Evans St Ste N Greenville NC 27834 252-321-8974
Web: www.twistednetworx.com
U.S. Claims Services Inc
3801 Pegasus Dr Ste 101 Bakersfield CA 93308 661-399-1108
Web: www.usclaimsservices.com
Unique Home Design Inc 17510 S Dixie Hwy Miami FL 33157 305-255-1114
Web: www.uniquehomedesign.com
United Human Capital Solutions
1 Centerpointe Dr Ste 580 Lake Oswego OR 97035 503-443-6008
Web: www.uhcsolutions.com
Up by Seven 16 Rennie Dr Andover MA 01810 978-475-8200
Web: www.upbyseven.com
Veer Right Management Group Inc
3195 Airport Blvd Nw Ste D Wilson NC 27896 252-237-5900
Vology Corp 281 E Water St Rockland MA 02370 781-384-2023
Web: www.vology.com
Vulcan Value Partners LLC
3 Protective Ctr 2801 Hwy 280 S Ste 300 Birmingham AL 35223 205-803-1582
Web: www.vulcanvaluepartners.com

Phone | Fax

Wedding Experience
2307 Douglas Rd Ste 400........................Coral Gables FL 33145 305-421-1260
TF: 866-223-9672 ■ *Web:* www.theweddingexperience.com
Wharfedale Technologies Inc
2850 Brunswick Pk............................Lawrenceville NJ 08648 609-791-9387
Web: wftus.com
William Charles Executive Search Partners
5550 Cascade Rd Se Ste 200....................Grand Rapids MI 49546 616-464-4355
Web: www.william-charles.com
World Class Incentives
426 N Rand Rd............................North Barrington IL 60010 847-381-1800
Web: www.worldclassincentives.com

227 DENTAL ASSOCIATIONS - STATE

See Also Health & Medical Professionals Associations p. 1789

Phone | Fax

Alabama Dental Assn 836 Washington Ave.........Montgomery AL 36104 334-265-1684 262-6218
Web: www.aldaonline.org
Alaska Dental Society
9170 Jewel Lake Rd Ste 203......................Anchorage AK 99502 907-563-3003 563-3009
Web: www.akdental.org
Arizona Dental Assn
3193 N Drinkwater Blvd..........................Scottsdale AZ 85251 480-344-5777 344-1442
TF: 800-866-2732 ■ *Web:* www.azda.org
Arkansas State Dental Assn 7480 Hwy 107..........Sherwood AR 72120 501-834-7650 834-7657
TF: 800-501-2732 ■ *Web:* www.arkansasdentistry.org
California Dental Assn 1201 K St.................Sacramento CA 95853 916-443-0505 443-2943
TF: 800-736-7071 ■ *Web:* www.cda.org
Colorado Dental Assn
8301 E Prentice Ave Ste 400................Greenwood Village CO 80111 303-740-6900 740-7989
TF: 866-777-4771 ■ *Web:* www.cdaonline.org
Delaware State Dental Society
200 Continental Dr Ste 111..........................Newark DE 19713 302-368-7634 368-7669
Web: www.delawarestatedentalsociety.org
District of Columbia Dental Society
2025 M St NW Ste 800..........................Washington DC 20036 202-367-1163
Web: www.dcdental.org
Florida Dental Assn 1111 E Tennessee St...........Tallahassee FL 32308 850-681-3629 561-0504
TF: 800-877-9922 ■ *Web:* www.floridadental.org
Georgia Dental Assn
7000 Peachtree Dnwdy Rd NE Ste 200 Bldg 17...........Atlanta GA 30328 404-636-7553 633-3943
TF: 800-432-4357 ■ *Web:* www.gadental.org
Hawaii Dental Assn
1345 S Beretania St Ste 301.....................Honolulu HI 96814 808-593-7956 593-7636
TF: 800-359-6725 ■ *Web:* www.hawaiidentalassociation.net
Idaho State Dental Assn 1220 W Hays St................Boise ID 83702 208-343-7543
Web: theisda.org
Illinois State Dental Society
1010 S Second St..............................Springfield IL 62704 217-525-1406 525-8872
TF: 888-286-2447 ■ *Web:* www.isds.org
Indiana Dental Assn 401 W Michigan St............Indianapolis IN 46202 317-634-2610 634-2612
TF: 800-562-5646 ■ *Web:* www.indental.org
Iowa Dental Assn 8797 NW 54th Ave Ste 100..........Johnston IA 50131 515-331-2298 334-8007
TF: 800-828-2181 ■ *Web:* www.iowadental.org
Louisiana Dental Assn
7833 Office Pk Blvd...........................Baton Rouge LA 70809 225-926-1986 926-1886
TF: 800-388-6642 ■ *Web:* www.ladental.org
Maine Dental Assn 29 Assn Dr..................Manchester ME 04351 207-622-7900
Web: www.medental.org
Maryland State Dental Assn 6410 Dobbin Rd.........Columbia MD 21045 410-964-2880 964-0583
Web: www.msda.com
Massachusetts Dental Society
2 Willow St Ste 200..........................Southborough MA 01745 508-480-9797 480-0002
TF: 800-342-8747 ■ *Web:* www.massdental.org
Michigan Dental Assn 3657 Okemos Rd Ste 200........Okemos MI 48864 517-372-9070 372-0008*
**Fax:* PR ■ *TF:* 800-589-2632 ■ *Web:* www.smilemichigan.com
Minnesota Dental Assn
1335 Industrial Blvd Ste 200.....................Minneapolis MN 55413 612-767-8400 767-8500
TF: 800-950-3368 ■ *Web:* www.mndental.org
Mississippi Dental Assn
439 B katherine Dr Ste C...........................Flowood MS 39232 601-664-9691
TF: 866-982-0442 ■ *Web:* www.msdental.org
Missouri Dental Assn
3340 American Ave............................Jefferson City MO 65109 573-634-3436 635-0764
TF: 800-688-1907 ■ *Web:* www.modental.org
Montana Dental Assn
17 1/2 S Last Chance Gulch PO Box 1154...............Helena MT 59624 406-443-2061 443-1546
TF: 800-257-4988 ■ *Web:* www.mtdental.com
Nebraska Dental Assn 7160 S 29th St Ste 1.............Lincoln NE 68516 402-476-1704 476-2641
TF: 888-789-2614 ■ *Web:* www.nedental.org
Nevada Dental Assn
8863 W Flamingo Rd Ste 102......................Las Vegas NV 89147 702-255-4211 255-3302
TF: 800-962-6710 ■ *Web:* www.nvda.org
New Hampshire Dental Society 23 S State St.........Concord NH 03301 603-225-5961 226-4880
Web: www.nhds.org
New Jersey Dental Assn
1 Dental Plaza PO Box 6020.................North Brunswick NJ 08902 732-821-9400 821-1082
Web: www.njda.org
New Mexico Dental Assn
9201 Montgomery Blvd NE Ste 601..............Albuquerque NM 87111 505-294-1368 294-9958
TF: 888-787-1722 ■ *Web:* www.nmdental.org
New York State Dental Assn
20 Corporate Woods Blvd #602.......................Albany NY 12211 518-465-0044 465-3219
TF: 800-255-2100 ■ *Web:* www.nysdental.org
North Carolina Dental Society 1600 Evans Rd...............Cary NC 27513 919-677-1396 677-1397
TF: 800-662-8754 ■ *Web:* www.ncdental.org
North Dakota Dental Assn PO Box 1332..............Bismarck ND 58501 701-223-8870 223-0855
TF: 800-444-1330 ■ *Web:* www.nddental.com
Ohio Dental Assn 1370 Dublin Rd..................Columbus OH 43215 614-486-2700 486-0381
TF: 800-497-6076 ■ *Web:* www.oda.org
Oklahoma Dental Assn 317 NE 13th St...........Oklahoma City OK 73104 405-848-8873 848-8875
TF: 800-876-8890 ■ *Web:* www.okda.org

Phone | Fax

Oregon Dental Assn PO Box 3710.................Wilsonville OR 97070 503-218-2010 218-2009
TF: 800-452-5628 ■ *Web:* www.oregondental.org
Pennsylvania Dental Assn 3501 N Front St..........Harrisburg PA 17110 717-234-5941 232-7169
Web: www.padental.org
Riverside Dental Group 7251 Magnolia Ave..........Riverside CA 92504 951-689-5031
Web: www.riversidedentalgroup.com
South Carolina Dental Assn 120 Stonemark Ln........Columbia SC 29210 803-750-2277 750-1644
TF: 800-327-2598 ■ *Web:* www.scda.org
South Dakota Dental Assn
804 N Euclid Ave Ste 103.............................Pierre SD 57501 605-224-9133 224-9168
TF: 866-551-8023 ■ *Web:* www.sddental.org
Tennessee Dental Assn (TDA)
660 Bakers Bridge Ave Ste 300......................Franklin TN 37067 615-628-0208
Web: www.tenndental.org
Texas Dental Assn 1946 S IH-35 Ste 400................Austin TX 78704 512-443-3675 443-3031
TF: 800-832-1145 ■ *Web:* www.tda.org
Utah Dental Assn
1151 East 3900 South Ste 160..................Salt Lake City UT 84124 801-261-5315 261-1235
Virginia Dental Assn (VDA)
3460 Mayland Ct Ste 110..........................Richmond VA 23233 804-288-5750 288-1880
TF: 877-726-0850 ■ *Web:* www.vadental.org
West Virginia Dental Assn
2016 1/2 Kanawha Blvd E.........................Charleston WV 25311 304-344-5246 344-5316
Web: www.wvdental.org
Wisconsin Dental Assn
6737 W Washington St Ste 2360...................West Allis WI 53214 414-276-4520 864-2997*
**Fax Area Code:* 800 ■ *TF:* 800-364-7646 ■ *Web:* www.wda.org
Wyoming Dental Assn (WYDA) 259 S Ctr Ste 201.........Casper WY 82601 307-237-1186 237-1186
Web: www.wyda.org

228 DENTAL EQUIPMENT & SUPPLIES - MFR

Phone | Fax

3D Medical Manufacturing Inc
1006 W 15th St................................Riviera Beach FL 33404 561-842-7175
Web: www.3dmedicalmfg.com
3M ESPE Dental Products Div
3M Ctr Bldg 0275-02-SE-03.......................Saint Paul MN 55144 651-575-5144 733-2481
TF: 800-634-2249 ■ *Web:* 3m.com
3M Unitek 2724 Peck Rd..........................Monrovia CA 91016 800-634-5300
TF: 800-634-5300 ■ *Web:* www.3m.com
A-dec Inc 2601 Crestview Dr........................Newberg OR 97132 503-538-7478 538-0276
TF Cust Svc: 800-547-1883 ■ *Web:* a-dec.com/en
Accutron Inc 1733 Parkside Ln.....................Phoenix AZ 85027 623-780-2020
TF: 800-531-2221 ■ *Web:* www.accutron-inc.com
ACTEON North America Inc
124 Gaither Dr Ste 140........................Mount Laurel NJ 08054 856-222-9988
Web: www.acteongroup.com
AdDent Inc 43 Miry Brook Rd........................Danbury CT 06810 203-778-0200
Web: www.addent.com
Air Techniques Inc 1295 Walt Whitman Rd............Melville NY 11747 516-433-7676
TF: 888-247-8481 ■ *Web:* www.airtechniques.com
Alfa Medical Equipment Specialists Inc
59 Madison Ave................................Hempstead NY 11550 516-489-3855
Web: www.sterilizers.com
Align Technology Inc 2560 Orchard Pkwy............San Jose CA 95131 408-470-1000 470-1010
NASDAQ: ALGN ■ *Web:* www.aligntech.com
Alpha Pro Tech Ltd 60 Centurian Dr.................Markham ON L3R9R2 905-479-0654
TF: 800-749-1363 ■ *Web:* www.alphaprotech.com
Am-Touch Dental 28703 Industry Dr.................Valencia CA 91355 661-294-1213
TF: 800-350-4568 ■ *Web:* www.amtouch.com
American Medical Technologies Inc
5655 Bear Ln..................................Corpus Christi TX 78405 361-289-1145
OTC: ADLI
American Orthodontics Corp
1714 Cambridge Ave.............................Sheboygan WI 53081 920-457-5051 457-1485
TF: 800-558-7687 ■ *Web:* www.americanortho.com
Argen Corp, The 5855 Oberlin Dr...................San Diego CA 92121 858-455-7900
Web: www.argen.com
Arges Imaging Inc 129 N Hill Ave..................Pasadena CA 91106 626-529-3766
Aribex Inc 744 South 400 East........................Orem UT 84097 801-226-5522
TF: 866-340-5522 ■ *Web:* aribex.com
Barnhardt Mfg Co 1100 Hawthorne Ln................Charlotte NC 28205 800-277-0377 342-1892*
**Fax Area Code:* 704 ■ *TF:* 800-277-0377 ■ *Web:* www.barnhardt.net
Bicon LLC 501 Arborway..........................Boston MA 02130 617-524-4443
TF: 800-882-4266 ■ *Web:* www.bicon.com
BlueLight analytics inc
24-2625 Joseph Howe Dr..............................Halifax NS B3L4G4 902-407-4242
Web: curingresin.com
Brasseler USA 1 Brasseler Blvd..................Savannah GA 31419 800-841-4522 927-8671*
**Fax Area Code:* 912 ■ *TF:* 800-841-4522 ■ *Web:* www.brasselerusa.com
Buffalo Dental Manufacturing Company Inc
159 Lafayette Dr.................................Syosset NY 11791 516-496-7200
TF: 800-828-0203 ■ *Web:* www.buffalodental.com
Centrix Inc 770 River Rd..........................Shelton CT 06484 203-929-5582
TF: 800-235-5862 ■ *Web:* www.centrixdental.com
Closure Medical Corp 5250 Greens Dairy Rd...........Raleigh NC 27616 919-876-7800 790-1041
Web: www.closuremed.com
Coltene/Whaledent Inc 235 Ascot Pkwy.........Cuyahoga Falls OH 44223 330-916-8800 916-7077
TF: 800-221-3046 ■ *Web:* www.coltene.com
Darby Group Cos Inc 300 Jericho Quad...............Jericho NY 11753 516-683-1800 688-2880
DCI International 305 N Springbrook Rd.............Newberg OR 97132 503-538-8343
Web: www.dcionline.com
Den-Mat Corp 2727 Skyway Dr....................Santa Maria CA 93455 805-922-8491 922-6933
TF: 800-433-6628 ■ *Web:* www.denmat.com
DEN-TAL-EZ Group Inc 2 W Liberty Blvd Ste 160.........Malvern PA 19355 610-725-8004 725-9898
TF: 866-383-4636 ■ *Web:* dentalez.com
DEN-TAL-EZ Inc Equipment Div
2500 Hwy 31 S..................................Bay Minette AL 36507 251-937-6781 937-0461
TF: 800-383-4636 ■ *Web:* dentalez.com
DENTCA Inc 3608 Griffith Ave....................Los Angeles CA 90011 323-232-7505
Web: www.dentca.com

Phone | Fax

DenTek Oral Care Inc 307 Excellence Way .... Maryville TN 37801 865-983-1300
Web: www.dentek.com

Dentsply Caulk 38 W Clarke Ave. .... Milford DE 19963 302-422-4511 422-3480*
*Fax: Acctg ■ TF: 800-532-2855 ■ Web: www.dentsply.com

DENTSPLY International
221 W Philadelphia St PO Box 872 ....York PA 17405 717-845-7511
TF: 800-800-2888 ■ Web: www.dentsply.com

Dentsply International Inc
221 W Philadelphia St PO Box 872 ....York PA 17405 717-845-7511 849-4762
NASDAQ: XRAY ■ TF: 800-877-0020 ■ Web: www.dentsply.com

Dentsply International Inc Tulsa Dental Div
5100 E Skelly Dr Ste 300 .... Tulsa OK 74135 918-493-6598 493-6599
TF: 800-662-1202 ■
Web: www.dentsply.com/content/dentsply/en_us-global/endodontics.html

Dexta Corp 962 Kaiser Rd .... Napa CA 94558 707-255-2454
Web: www.dexta.com

Essential Dental Systems Inc
89 Leuning St Ste 8 .... South Hackensack NJ 07606 201-487-9090
Web: www.edsdental.com

G & H Wire Company Inc 2165 Earlywood Dr ....Franklin IN 46131 317-346-6655
TF: 800-526-1026 ■ Web: www.ghorthodontics.com

GC America Inc 3737 W 127th St .... Alsip IL 60803 708-597-0900 371-5103*
*Fax: Cust Svc ■ TF Cust Svc: 800-323-7063 ■ Web: www.gcamerica.com

Great Lakes Orthodontic Laboratories Div
200 Cooper Ave .... Tonawanda NY 14150 800-828-7626
TF: 800-828-7626 ■ Web: www.greatlakesortho.com

Heraeus 300 Heraeus Way .... South Bend IN 46614 800-431-1785 522-1545
TF General: 800-431-1785 ■ Web: heraeus-kulzer-us.com

Heraeus Kulzer LLC 99 Business Park Dr. .... Armonk NY 10504 914-219-9000
Web: heraeus-kulzer-us.com

Hu-Friedy Mfg Company Inc 3232 N Rockwell St. ....Chicago IL 60618 773-975-6100
TF: 800-483-7433 ■ Web: www.hu-friedy.com

Hygenic Corp 1245 Home Ave. ....Akron OH 44310 330-633-8460 633-9359
TF: 800-321-2135 ■ Web: www.hygenic.com

Inter-Med Inc 2200 Northwestern Ave. .... Racine WI 53404 262-636-9755
Web: www.vista-dental.com

Isolite Systems 111 Castilian Dr. .... Santa Barbara CA 93117 805-560-9888
TF: 800-560-6066 ■ Web: www.isolitesystems.com

Issaquah Dental Lab Inc 640 NW Gilman Blvd .... Issaquah WA 98027 425-392-5125
Web: www.issaquah-dl.com

Keystone Dental Inc 144 Middlesex Tpke .... Burlington MA 01803 781-328-3490
TF: 866-902-9272 ■ Web: www.keystonedental.com

Kinetic Instrument Inc 17 Berkshire Blvd .... Bethel CT 06801 203-743-0080
TF: 800-233-2346 ■ Web: www.kineticinc.com

Lancer Orthodontics Inc
1493 Poinsettia Bldg 143 .... Vista CA 92081 760-744-5585 598-0418
NYSE: LANZ ■ TF Cust Svc: 800-854-2896 ■ Web: www.lancerortho.com

Lang Dental Manufacturing Co 175 Messner Dr. ...... Wheeling IL 60090 847-215-6622
TF: 800-222-5264 ■ Web: www.langdental.com

LifeCore Biomedical LLC 3515 Lyman Blvd .... Chaska MN 55318 952-368-4300 368-3411
TF Cust Svc: 800-348-4368 ■ Web: www.lifecore.com

M & M Innovations 7424 Blythe Island Hwy. .... Brunswick GA 31523 912-265-7110
TF: 800-688-3384 ■ Web: www.drgeorges.com

Metrex Research Corp 1717 W Collins Ave ....Orange CA 92867 714-516-7788
Web: www.metrex.com

Microbrush International Ltd
1376 Cheyenne Ave .... Grafton WI 53024 262-375-4011
Web: www.microbrush.com

Midwest Dental Equipment Services & Supplies
2700 Commerce St. .... Wichita Falls TX 76301 800-766-2025 551-3514*
*Fax Area Code: 888 ■ TF: 800-766-2025 ■ Web: www.mwdental.com

Miltex Inc 589 Davies Dr ....York PA 17402 717-840-9335
Web: www.miltex.com

Myotronics-noromed Inc 5870 S 194th St ....Kent WA 98032 206-243-4214
TF: 800-426-0316 ■ Web: www.myotronics.com

Nasseo Inc 13660 N 94th Dr Bldg D .... Peoria AZ 85381 858-633-6503
Web: nasseo.com

Net32 Inc 250 Towne Village Dr. ....Cary NC 27513 919-468-1177
TF: 800-517-1997 ■ Web: www.net32.com

Nobel Biocare USA Inc
22715 Savi Ranch Pkwy .... Yorba Linda CA 92887 714-282-4800 998-9236
TF: 800-993-8100 ■ Web: www.nobelbiocare.com

Novalab Group Inc 2350 Power St .... Drummondville QC J2C7Z4 819-474-2580
Web: www.novadent.com

ORMCO Corp 1717 W Collins Ave ....Orange CA 92867 714-516-7400 317-6012*
*Fax Area Code: 800 ■ TF Cust Svc: 800-854-1741 ■ Web: www.ormco.com

OrthoAccel Technologies Inc
8275 El Rio St Ste 100 ....Houston TX 77054 832-631-1660
Web: www.acceledent.com

Pentron Clinical Technologies LLC
53 N Plains Industrial Rd .... Wallingford CT 06492 800-243-3969
TF: 800-243-3969 ■ Web: www.pentron.com

Practicon Inc 1112 Sugg Pkwy. .... Greenville NC 27834 252-752-5183
TF: 800-959-9505 ■ Web: www.practicon.com

Premier Dental Products Co
1710 Romano Dr PO Box 4500. .... Plymouth Meeting PA 19462 610-239-6000 239-6171
TF: 888-773-6872 ■ Web: www.premusa.com

PRIMUS Sterilizer Company LLC 6565 S 118th St. .... Omaha NE 68137 402-344-4200
Web: www.primus-sterilizer.com

Quantum Dental Technologies Inc
748 Briar Hill Ave .... Toronto ON M6B1L3 866-993-9910
TF: 866-993-9910 ■ Web: www.thecanarysystem.com

Rocky Mountain Orthodontics Inc (RMO Inc)
650 W Colfax Ave ....Denver CO 80204 303-592-8200 592-8200*
*Fax: Hum Res ■ TF: 800-525-6375 ■ Web: www.rmortho.com

S s White Burs Inc 1145 Towbin Ave .... Lakewood NJ 08701 732-905-1100
Web: www.sswhitedental.com

Sirona Dental Systems LLC
4835 Sirona Dr Ste 100 .... Charlotte NC 28273 704-587-0453
TF: 800-659-5977 ■
Web: cereconline.com/ecomaxl/index.php?site=cerec_20_years

Southern Implants Inc 5 Holland Bldg 209 .... Irvine CA 92618 949-273-8505
TF: 866-700-2100 ■ Web: www.southernimplants.us

Phone | Fax

Stern Empire Dental Lab 1805 W 34th St. ....Houston TX 77018 713-688-1301
TF: 800-229-0214 ■ Web: www.sternempire.com

Sterngold Dental LLC 23 Frank Mossberg Dr. .... Attleboro MA 02703 508-226-5660
Web: www.sterngold.com

Sunstar Americas Inc 4635 W Foster Ave ....Chicago IL 60630 888-777-3101 553-2014*
*Fax Area Code: 800 ■ TF: 888-777-3101 ■ Web: www.gumbrand.com

Therapeutic Solutions International Inc
4093 Oceanside Blvd Ste B. .... Oceanside CA 92056 760-295-7208
Web: www.therapeuticsolutionsint.com

TP Orthodontics Inc 100 Ctr Plz ....La Porte IN 46350 219-785-2591 324-3029
TF: 800-348-8856 ■ Web: www.tportho.com

Trident Labs Inc 12000 Aviation Blvd. .... Hawthorne CA 90250 310-915-9121
Web: www.tridentlab.com

Water Pik Inc 1730 E Prospect Rd .... Fort Collins CO 80553 800-525-2774
TF: 800-525-2774 ■ Web: www.waterpik.com

Whip Mix Corp
361 Farmington Ave PO Box 17183 .... Louisville KY 40217 502-637-1451
Web: www.whipmix.com

Young Dental Manufacturing LLC
13705 Shoreline Court E .... Earth City MO 63045 314-344-0010
Web: www.youngdental.com

Zest Anchors LLC 2061 Wineridge Pl .... Escondido CA 92029 760-743-7744
Web: www.zestanchors.com

Zimmer Orthopaedic Surgical Products Inc
200 W Ohio Ave ....Dover OH 44622 330-343-8801
Web: zimmer.com

229 DEPARTMENT STORES

Phone | Fax

Ammar's Inc 710 S College Ave. .... Bluefield VA 24605 276-322-4686 326-1060
Web: www.magicmartstores.com

Ann & Hope Inc 1 Ann & Hope Way ....Cumberland RI 02864 877-228-7824
TF: 877-228-7824 ■ Web: www.curtainandbathoutlet.com

Apex Co 100 Main St .... Pawtucket RI 02860 401-729-7200
Web: www.theapexcompanies.com

Beall's Inc 1806 38th Ave E. .... Bradenton FL 34208 941-747-2355 746-1171
Web: www.beallsinc.com

Belk Inc 2801 W Tyvola Rd. .... Charlotte NC 28217 704-357-1000
OTC: BLKIB ■ Web: www.belk.com

Bloomingdale's 1000 Third Ave .... New York NY 10022 212-705-2000 705-2805
TF: 800-950-0047 ■ Web: www.bloomingdales.com

Bob's Sporting Goods 1111 Hudson St .... Longview WA 98632 360-425-3870 636-4334
TF: 800-292-5551 ■ Web: www.bobsmerch.com

Bon-Ton Stores Inc 2801 E Market St ....York PA 17402 717-757-7660
NASDAQ: BONT ■ TF: 800-945-4438 ■ Web: www.bonton.com

BootBarn Inc 620 Pan American Dr. .... Livingston TX 77351 936-327-2405
Web: www.bootbarn.com

Boscov's Dept Stores 4500 Perkiomen Ave. .... Reading PA 19606 610-779-2000
Web: www.boscovs.com

Boston Store Inc 2400 N Mayfair Rd .... Milwaukee WI 53226 414-453-7500
Web: news.bonton.com/ecommupgrade/siteupgrade_bos.html

Bracker's Dept Store 68 N Morley Ave .... Nogales AZ 85621 520-287-3631 287-7137

Browning Arms Co 1 Browning Pl. .... Morgan UT 84050 801-876-2711
Web: www.browning.com

Century 21 Dept Stores 22 Cortlandt St ....New York NY 10007 212-227-9092 267-4271*
*Fax: Hum Res ■ Web: www.c21stores.com

Cookies The Kids Department Store
510 Fulton St .... Brooklyn NY 11201 718-797-3300
TF: 877-942-6654 ■ Web: www.cookieskids.com

Diesel USA Inc 923 N Rush St. ....Chicago IL 60611 312-255-0157
Web: www.diesel.com

Dillard's Inc 1600 Cantrell Rd .... Little Rock AR 72201 501-376-5200
NYSE: DDS ■ Web: www.dillards.com

DTLR Holding Inc 1300 Mercedes Dr ....Hanover MD 21076 410-850-5911
Web: www.dtlr.com

Fred's Inc 4300 New Getwell Rd. .... Memphis TN 38118 901-365-8880
NASDAQ: FRED ■ TF: 800-374-7417 ■ Web: www.fredsinc.com

Glik Co 3248 Nameoki Rd .... Granite City IL 62040 618-876-1065 876-7819
Web: www.gliks.com

Good's Store 1338 Main St .... East Earl PA 17519 717-354-4026
Web: www.goodsstores.com

Gordman 12100 W Ctr Rd. .... Omaha NE 68144 402-691-4000 691-4269
TF: 855-290-6454 ■ Web: www.gordmans.com

JC Penney Co Inc 6501 Legacy Dr .... Plano TX 75024 972-431-1000 431-9140*
NYSE: JCP ■ *Fax: Cust Svc ■ Web: www.jcpenney.com

Jones & Jones Inc 4500 N Tenth St Ste 90 ....McAllen TX 78504 956-687-1171 631-3345

Kohl's Corp
N 56 W 17000 Ridgewood Dr. .... Menomonee Falls WI 53051 262-703-7000
NYSE: KSS ■ TF: 855-564-5705 ■ Web: www.kohls.com

Lancaster Sales Co
1375 Old Logan Rd Rt 33S .... Lancaster OH 43130 740-653-5334 653-2783

Langstons Co 2034 NW Seventh St. .... Oklahoma City OK 73106 405-235-9536
TF: 800-658-2831 ■ Web: www.langstons.com

Lord & Taylor 424 Fifth Ave. ....New York NY 10018 212-391-3344 391-3262
TF: 800-223-7440 ■ Web: www.lordandtaylor.com

Macy's 400 Fifth Ave .... Pittsburgh PA 15219 513-573-7912
TF: 877-884-3751 ■ Web: www.macys.com

Macy's 151 W 34th St. ....New York NY 10001 212-695-4400
Web: www.macys.com

Macy's 111 N State St. ....Chicago IL 60602 312-781-1000
Web: www.macys.com

Macy's Inc 7 W 7th St .... Cincinnati OH 45202 513-579-7000 579-7555
NYSE: M ■ TF: 800-261-5385 ■ Web: www.federated-fds.com

Marine Corps Community Services
3044 Catlin Ave .... Quantico VA 22134 703-784-3809
Web: www.usmc-mccs.org

Mast General Store & Annex Nc
3565 Nc Hwy 194 S .... Banner Elk NC 28604 828-963-6511
Web: www.mastgeneralstore.com

Masters Inc 5741 NW Cornelius Pass Rd .... Hillsboro OR 97124 503-531-3308 531-9153
TF: 877-652-5656

Phone Fax

Mc-Caulou's Inc 3512 Mount Diablo Blvd .... Lafayette CA 94549 925-283-3380
Web: www.mccaulous.com

MH King Co 1032 Idaho Ave .... Burley ID 83318 208-678-7181
Web: kingsdiscount.com

Neiman Marcus Group Inc 1618 Main St .... Dallas TX 75201 214-743-7600 573-5320
Web: neimanmarcuscareers.com

Pants Store, The 8029 Parkway Dr .... Leeds AL 35094 205-699-6166
Web: www.pantsstore.com

Peebles Inc 1 Peebles St .... South Hill VA 23970 800-743-8730
TF: 800-723-4548 ■ *Web:* www.stage.com/store/?brand=peebles

Proffitt & Goodson Inc
Old Kingston Pl 4800 Old Kingston Pk
Ste 200 .... Knoxville TN 37919 865-584-1850
TF: 866-776-3355 ■ *Web:* www.proffittgoodson.com

Reitmans (Canada) Ltd 250 Sauve St W .... Montreal QC H3L1Z2 514-384-1140
TSE: RET.A ■ *Web:* www.reitmans.com

RH Reny Inc 731 Rt 1 .... Newcastle ME 04553 207-563-3177 563-5681
Web: www.renys.com

Sav-Mart Co 1729 N Wenatchee Ave .... Wenatchee WA 98801 509-663-1671
Web: www.savemart.com/contact-us-163

Sears Canada Inc 290 Yonge St Ste 700 .... Toronto ON M5B2C3 416-362-1711
TSE: SCC ■ *TF:* 877-987-3277 ■ *Web:* www.sears.ca

Sears Roebuck & Co 3333 Beverly Rd .... Hoffman Estates IL 60179 847-286-2500
Web: www.sears.com

Shopko LLC 700 Pilgrim Way .... Green Bay WI 54304 920-429-2211
Web: www.shopko.com

Sierra Trading Post Inc 5025 Campstool Rd .... Cheyenne WY 82007 307-775-8050
Web: www.sierratradingpost.com

SmartBargains Inc 101 S State Rd 7 Ste 201 .... Hollywood FL 33023 877-222-6660
TF: 877-222-6660 ■ *Web:* www.smartbargains.com

Stein Mart Inc 1200 Riverplace Blvd .... Jacksonville FL 32207 904-346-1500
NASDAQ: SMRT ■ *Web:* www.steinmart.com

Target Corp 1000 Nicollet Mall .... Minneapolis MN 55403 612-304-6073 304-6073*
NYSE: TGT ■ **Fax:* Hum Res ■ *TF Cust Svc:* 800-440-0680 ■ *Web:* www.target.com

Tongass Trading Co 201 Dock St .... Ketchikan AK 99901 907-225-5101 247-0481
TF: 800-235-5102 ■ *Web:* www.tongasstrading.com

Trading Union Inc 401 N Nordic Dr .... Petersburg AK 99833 907-772-3881
Web: acehardware.com

Von Maur Inc 6565 Brady St .... Davenport IA 52806 563-388-2200 388-2242
Web: www.vonmaur.com

Wal-Mart Puerto Rico Inc PO Box 4960 .... Caguas PR 00726 787-653-7777
Web: www.walmartpr.com

Wal-Mart Stores Inc 702 SW Eigth St .... Bentonville AR 72716 479-273-4000
NYSE: WMT ■ *TF Cust Svc:* 800-925-6278 ■ *Web:* corporate.walmart.com

Walmart.com 1919 Davis St .... San Leandro CA 94577 800-925-6278
TF: 800-925-6278 ■ *Web:* www.walmart.com

230 DEVELOPMENTAL CENTERS

Residential facilities for the developmentally disabled.

Phone Fax

Altoona Ctr 1020 Green Ave .... Altoona PA 16601 814-946-2700 946-1420
Web: www.myaltoonacenterfornursingcare.com

Caswell Developmental Ctr 2415 W Vernon Ave .... Kinston NC 28504 252-208-4000
Web: caswellcenter.org

Central Virginia Training Ctr
521 Colony Rd .... Madison Heights VA 24572 434-947-6000
Web: www.cvtc.dbhds.virginia.gov

Development Counsellors International Ltd (DCI)
215 Pk Ave S 14th Fl .... New York NY 10003 212-725-0707 725-2254
Web: www.aboutdci.com

Glenwood Resource Ctr 711 S Vine St .... Glenwood IA 51534 712-527-4811 527-2329
Web: dhs.iowa.gov

Lanterman Developmental Ctr 3530 Pomona Blvd .... Pomona CA 91769 909-595-1221 598-4352
Web: www.dds.ca.gov

Parsons State Hospital & Training Ctr
2601 Gabriel St .... Parsons KS 67357 620-421-6550 421-3623
Web: kdads.ks.gov

Porterville Developmental Ctr (PDC)
26501 Ave 140 PO Box 2000 .... Porterville CA 93258 559-782-2222 784-5630
Web: www.dds.ca.gov/Porterville/Index.cfm

Productive Alternatives Inc
1205 N Tower Rd .... Fergus Falls MN 56537 218-998-5630 736-2541
TF: 800-627-3529 ■ *Web:* www.paiff.org

Sonoma Developmental Ctr 15000 Arnold Dr .... Eldridge CA 95431 707-938-6000 938-3605*
**Fax:* Admitting ■ *TF:* 800-862-0007 ■ *Web:* www.dds.ca.gov

Woodward Resource Ctr 1251 334th St .... Woodward IA 50276 515-438-2600
TF: 888-229-9223 ■ *Web:* dhs.iowa.gov

231 DIAGNOSTIC PRODUCTS

See Also Biotechnology Companies p. 1859; Medicinal Chemicals & Botanical Products p. 2748; Pharmaceutical Companies p. 2934; Pharmaceutical Companies - Generic Drugs p. 2936

Phone Fax

3-V Biosciences Inc 1050 Hamilton Ct .... Menlo Park CA 94025 650-561-8600
Web: www.3vbio.com

A & A Pharmachem Inc 4-77 Auriga Dr .... Ottawa ON K2E7Z7 613-228-2600
Web: www.aapharmachem.com

A & Z Pharmaceutical Inc 180 Oser Ave .... Hauppauge NY 11788 631-952-3802 952-3900
Web: www.azpharmaceutical.com

A & Z Pharmaceutical LLC
2275 Swallow Hill Rd Bldg 1200 .... Pittsburgh PA 15220 412-279-8000
Web: www.azpharm.com

Abaxis Inc 3240 Whipple Rd .... Union City CA 94587 510-675-6500 441-6150
NASDAQ: ABAX ■ *TF:* 800-822-2947 ■ *Web:* www.abaxis.com

Abbott Laboratories Abbott Diagnostics Div
100 Abbott Pk Rd .... Abbott Park IL 60064 847-937-6100
TF: 800-387-8378 ■ *Web:* www.abbottdiagnostics.com

Phone Fax

Acceleron Pharma Inc 128 Sidney St .... Cambridge MA 02139 617-649-9200
Web: www.acceleronpharma.com

ACCU-BREAK Pharmaceuticals Inc
1000 S Pine Island Rd Ste 430 .... Plantation FL 33324 954-236-7351
Web: www.accubreakpharmaceuticals.com

Accurate Chemical & Scientific Corp
300 Shames Dr .... Westbury NY 11590 516-333-2221 997-4948
TF: 800-645-6264 ■ *Web:* www.accuratechemical.com

Actinobac Biomed Inc 15 Pelham Rd .... Kendall Park NJ 08824 732-371-2694
Web: www.actinobac.com

ADH Health Products Inc 215 N Rt 303 .... Congers NY 10920 845-268-0027 268-2988
Web: www.adhhealth.com

Advanced Biotechnologies Inc (ABI)
9108 Guilford Rd .... Columbia MD 21046 410-792-9779 497-9773*
**Fax Area Code:* 301 ■ *TF:* 800-426-0764 ■ *Web:* www.abionline.com

Advanced Distribution Systems Inc
105-107 Stonehurst Ct .... Northvale NJ 07647 201-767-7350
Web: www.ads-outsource.com

Advanced Vision Research Inc 660 Main St .... Woburn MA 01801 781-932-8327
Web: www.theratears.com

Adynxx Inc 731 Market St Ste 420 .... San Francisco CA 94103 415-512-7740
Web: www.adynxx.com

Aerial BioPharma LLC
9001 Aerial Ctr Pkwy Aerial Ctr Executive Pk
Ste 110 .... Morrisville NC 27560 919-460-9500
Web: www.aerialbio.com

Aerpio Therapeutics Inc
9987 Carver Rd Ste 420 .... Cincinnati OH 45242 513-985-1920
Web: www.aerpio.com

Afferent Pharmaceuticals Inc
2929 Campus Dr Ste 230 .... San Mateo CA 94403 650-286-1276
Web: www.afferentpharma.com

Akers Biosciences Inc 201 Grove Rd .... Thorofare NJ 08086 856-848-8698
Web: www.akersbio.com

Akorn Inc 1925 W Field Ct .... Lake Forest IL 60045 847-279-6100 279-6123
NASDAQ: AKRX ■ *TF:* 800-932-5676 ■ *Web:* www.akorn.com

Alder Biopharmaceuticals Inc
11804 N Creek Pkwy S .... Bothell WA 98011 425-205-2900
Web: www.alderbio.com

ALerCHEK Inc 15 Oak St Ste 302 .... Springvale ME 04083 207-490-2266 490-2210
TF: 877-282-9542 ■ *Web:* www.alerchek.com

Alere Inc 51 Sawyer Rd Ste 200 .... Waltham MA 02453 781-647-3900
TF: 877-441-7440 ■ *Web:* www.alere.com

Alere San Diego Inc 9975 Summers Ridge Rd .... San Diego CA 92121 781-647-3900
TF: 866-284-3684 ■ *Web:* alere.com

Alinea Pharmaceuticals Inc
1 Memorial Dr Ste 1225 .... Cambridge MA 02142 617-914-0123

Alk - Abello Pharmaceuticals Inc
35-151 Brunel Rd .... Mississauga ON L4Z2H6 905-290-9952
TF: 800-663-0972 ■ *Web:* www.alk-abello.com

Allermed Laboratories Inc 7203 Convoy Ct .... San Diego CA 92111 800-221-2748
TF: 800-221-2748 ■ *Web:* www.allermed.com

Alnara Pharmaceuticals Inc 840 Memorial Dr .... Cambridge MA 02139 617-349-3690

Aloha Medicinals Inc 2300 Arrowhead Dr .... Carson City NV 89706 775-886-6300
TF: 877-835-6091 ■ *Web:* www.alohamedicinals.com

Alphora Research Inc
2395 Speakman Dr Ste 2001 .... Mississauga ON L5K1B3 905-403-0477
Web: www.alphoraresearch.com

Altheus Therapeutics Inc
755 Research Pkwy Ste 435 .... Oklahoma City OK 73104 405-319-8180

AMAG Pharmaceuticals Inc 61 Mooney St .... Cambridge MA 02138 617-497-2070
AMEX: AVM

American Qualex Scientific Products (AQSP)
920-A Calle Negocio .... San Clemente CA 92673 949-492-8298
Web: www.aqsp.com

Amresco Inc 6681 Cochran Rd .... Solon OH 44139 440-349-1313 349-3255
TF: 800-448-4442 ■ *Web:* www.amresco-inc.com

AnaSpec Inc 34801 Campus Dr .... Fremont CA 94555 510-791-9560 791-9572
TF: 800-452-5530 ■ *Web:* www.anaspec.com

AntiCancer Inc 7917 Ostrow St .... San Diego CA 92111 858-654-2555 268-4175
TF: 800-511-2555 ■ *Web:* www.anticancer.com

Ardelyx Inc 34175 Ardenwood Blvd .... Fremont CA 94555 510-745-1700
Web: www.ardelyx.com

Ascend Laboratories 180 Summit Ave Ste 200 .... Montvale NJ 07645 201-476-1977
Web: www.ascendlaboratories.com

Ascend Therapeutics Inc
607 Herndon Pkwy Ste 110 .... Herndon VA 20170 703-471-4744
TF: 888-412-5751 ■ *Web:* www.ascendtherapeutics.com

Ascenta Therapeutics Inc
101 Lindenwood Dr Ste 405 .... Malvern PA 19355 610-408-0301 725-1515

Ash Stevens Inc 5861 John C Lodge Fwy .... Detroit MI 48202 313-872-6400
Web: www.ashstevens.com

Athena Diagnostics Inc
377 Plantation St 2nd Fl .... Worcester MA 01605 508-756-2886 753-5601
TF: 800-394-4493 ■ *Web:* www.athenadiagnostics.com

Avid Radiopharmaceuticals Inc
3711 Market St 7th Fl .... Philadelphia PA 19104 215-298-0700
Web: www.avidrp.com

AxioMx Inc 688 E Main St .... Branford CT 06405 203-208-1918
Web: www.axiomxinc.com

Aylward Enterprises Inc 401 Industrial Dr .... New Bern NC 28562 252-633-5757
Web: www.aylward.com

Azevan Pharmaceuticals Inc 116 Research Dr .... Bethlehem PA 18015 610-419-1057
Web: www.azevan.com

Bachem-Peninsula Laboratories Inc
305 Old County Rd .... San Carlos CA 94070 650-801-6090 595-4071
TF: 800-922-1516 ■ *Web:* www.bachem.com

Baxter Corp 7125 Mississauga Rd .... Mississauga ON L5N0C2 905-369-6000
TF: 866-234-2345 ■ *Web:* www.baxter.ca

BD Diagnostics 7 Loveton Cir .... Sparks MD 21152 410-316-4000 316-4066
TF: 800-666-6433 ■ *Web:* www.bd.com

Bdf 91 Washington St .... Morristown NJ 07960 973-898-9800
Web: www.bdf.com

Phone | Fax

Beckman Coulter Genomics 36 Cherry Hill Dr. Danvers MA 01923 978-867-2600
Web: www.beckmangenomics.com

Becton Dickinson & Co 1 Becton Dr Franklin Lakes NJ 07417 201-847-6800
NYSE: BDX ■ *TF Cust Svc:* 888-237-2762 ■ *Web:* www.bd.com

Bee-alive Inc 7 New Lk Rd Valley Cottage NY 10989 845-268-0960
Web: www.beealive.com

Bexion Pharmaceuticals LLC 632 Russell St Covington KY 41011 859-757-1652
Web: www.bexionpharma.com

Bio-Pharm Inc 2091 Hartel St Levittown PA 19057 215-949-3711
Web: www.bio-pharminc.com

Bio-Rad Laboratories 1000 Alfred Nobel Dr Hercules CA 94547 510-724-7000 741-5824*
NYSE: BIO ■ **Fax:* Cust Svc ■ *TF:* 800-424-6723 ■ *Web:* www.bio-rad.com

Biocell Laboratories Inc
2001 University Dr Rancho Dominguez CA 90220 310-537-3300
TF: 800-222-8382 ■ *Web:* www.biocell.com

Biofilm Inc 3225 Executive Ridge Vista CA 92081 760-727-9030
Web: astroglide.com

BioGenex Laboratories Inc
4600 Norris Canyon Rd San Ramon CA 94583 925-275-0550
TF: 800-421-4149 ■ *Web:* www.biogenex.com

Biohelix Corp 500 Cummings Ste 5550 Beverly MA 01915 978-927-5056
TF: 866-800-5458 ■ *Web:* www.biohelix.com

Biomerica Inc 1533 Monrovia Ave Newport Beach CA 92663 949-645-2111
OTC: BMRA ■ *TF Cust Svc:* 800-854-3002 ■ *Web:* www.biomerica.com

BioMerieux Inc 595 Anglum Rd Hazelwood MO 63042 314-731-8500
TF: 800-634-7656 ■ *Web:* www.biomerieux.com

Bionostics Inc 7 Jackson Rd Devens MA 01434 978-772-7070 772-7072
TF General: 800-776-3856 ■ *Web:* www.bionostics.com

BiosPacific Inc 5980 Horton St Ste 225 Emeryville CA 94608 510-652-6155 652-4531
TF: 800-344-6686 ■ *Web:* www.biospacific.com

Biosynexus Inc 9298 Gaither Rd Gaithersburg MD 20877 301-330-5800

Boiron-Borneman Inc 6 Campus Blvd Newtown Square PA 19073 610-325-7464
Web: www.boironusa.com

Boreal Genomics Inc 5150 El Camino Real Los Altos CA 94022 604-822-8268
TF: 800-681-5644 ■ *Web:* www.borealgenomics.com

Burlington Drug Co Inc 91 Catamount Dr Milton VT 05468 802-893-5105
TF: 800-338-8703 ■ *Web:* www.burlingtondrug.com

Caldwell Consumer Health LLC 8 Elmer St Madison NJ 07940 973-360-1090
Web: bleedinggums.com

Calmoseptine Inc 16602 Burke Ln Huntington Beach CA 92647 714-840-3405
TF: 800-800-3405 ■ *Web:* www.calmoseptine.com

Calypte Biomedical Corp 15875 SW 72nd Ave Portland OR 97224 503-726-2227 601-6299
OTC: CBMC ■ *Web:* www.calypte.com

Cancap Pharmaceutical Ltd
13111 Vanier Pl Ste 180 Richmond BC V6V2J1 604-278-2188 278-2210
TF: 877-998-2378 ■ *Web:* www.cancappharma.com

Cancer Genetics Inc
Meadows Office Complex 201 Rt 17 N 2nd Fl Rutherford NJ 07070 201-528-9200
TF: 888-334-4988 ■ *Web:* www.cancergenetics.com

Cangene bioPharma Inc 1111 S Paca St Baltimore MD 21230 410-843-5000
TF: 800-441-4225 ■ *Web:* emergentcontractmanufacturing.com

Capricorn Products LLC 12 Rice St Portland ME 04103 207-321-0014
Web: www.capricornproducts.com

Carlsbad Technology Inc 5922 Farnsworth Ct Carlsbad CA 92008 760-431-8284
Web: carlsbadtech.com

Carma Laboratories Inc 5801 W Airways Ave Franklin WI 53132 414-421-7707
Web: www.mycarmex.com

Catalent Pharma Solutions Inc
14 Schoolhouse Rd Somerset NJ 08873 732-537-6200
Web: www.catalent.com

Cedarlane Laboratories Inc
4410 Paletta Ct Burlington ON L7L5R2 905-878-8891 288-0020*
**Fax Area Code:* 289 ■ *TF:* 800-268-5058 ■ *Web:* www.cedarlanelabs.com

Cellectar Inc 3301 Agriculture Dr Madison WI 53716 608-441-8120
Web: cellectarbiosciences.com

Centaur Pharmaceuticals Inc
1220 Memorex Dr Santa Clara CA 95050 408-822-1600
Web: www.centpharm.com

Centice Corp 215 Southport Dr Ste 1000 Morrisville NC 27560 919-653-0424
Web: www.centice.com

Centrix Pharmaceutical Inc
31 Inverness Ctr Pkwy Ste 270 Birmingham AL 35242 205-991-9870
Web: www.cenrx.com

Ceptaris Therapeutics Inc
101 Lindenwood Dr Ste 400 Malvern PA 19355 610-975-9290

Cetylite Industries 9051 River Rd Pennsauken NJ 08110 856-665-6111
Web: www.cetylite.com

Chematics Inc PO Box 293 North Webster IN 46555 574-834-2406 834-7427
TF: 800-348-5174 ■ *Web:* www.chematics.com

ChemGenes Corp 33 Industrial Way Wilmington MA 01887 978-694-4500
Web: www.chemgenes.com

Chiral Quest Inc
7 Deer Park Dr Ste C1 Monmouth Junction NJ 08852 732-274-0399
Web: www.chiralquest.com

ChiRhoClin Inc 4000 Blackburn Ln Ste 270 Burtonsville MD 20866 301-476-8388
Web: www.chirhoclin.com

Cholestech Corp 9975 Summers Ridge Rd San Diego CA 92121 510-732-7200
TF: 866-284-3684 ■ *Web:* www.alere.com

Chromaprobe Inc 378 Fee Fee Rd Maryland Heights MO 63043 314-738-0001 738-0001
TF: 888-964-1400 ■ *Web:* www.chromaprobe.com

Clarus Therapeutics Inc
555 Skokie Blvd Ste 340 Northbrook IL 60062 847-562-4300
Web: www.clarustherapeutics.com

Clinilabs Inc 423 W 55th St 4th Fl New York NY 10019 646-215-6400
Web: www.clinilabs.com

CLINIQA Corp 288 Distribution St San Marcos CA 92078 760-744-1900
Web: www.cliniqa.com

CNS Therapeutics Inc 332 Minnesota St W1750 St Paul MN 55101 651-207-6959
Web: www.gablofen.com

Cobalt Pharmaceuticals Inc
6500 Kitimat Rd Mississauga ON L5N2B8 905-814-1820
TF: 866-254-6111 ■ *Web:* actavis.ca

CoDa Therapeutics Inc
10505 Sorrento Vly Rd Ste 395 San Diego CA 92121 858-677-0474
Web: codatherapeutics.com

Cody Laboratories Inc 601 Yellowstone Ave Cody WY 82414 307-587-7099
Web: www.codylabs.com

Collegium Pharmaceutical Inc
400 Highland Corporate Dr Cumberland RI 02864 401-762-2000
Web: collegiumpharma.com

CoMentis Inc 280 Utah Ave Ste 275 South San Francisco CA 94080 650-869-7600
Web: www.athenagen.com

Cornerstone Pharmaceuticals Inc 1 Duncan Dr Cranbury NJ 08512 609-409-7050
Web: www.cornerstonepharma.com

CST Technologies Inc
55 Northern Blvd Ste 200 Great Neck NY 11021 516-482-9001 482-0186
Web: www.cstti.com

Daisy Blue Naturals
2610 Yh Hanson Ave Ste 108 Albert Lea MN 56007 507-373-0229
Web: daisybluenaturals.com

DakoCytomation 6392 Via Real Carpinteria CA 93013 805-566-6655 566-6688
TF Cust Svc: 800-400-3256 ■ *Web:* www.dako.com

DesigneRx Pharmaceuticals Inc
4941 Allison Pkwy Ste B Vacaville CA 95688 707-451-0441
Web: www.drxpharma.com

Diagnostics Biochem Canada Inc (DBC)
41 Byron Ave Dorchester ON N0L1G2 519-268-8872 268-7167
Web: www.dbc-labs.com

Diamond Drugs Inc 645 Kolter Dr Indiana PA 15701 724-349-1111
TF: 800-882-6337 ■ *Web:* www.diamondpharmacy.com

DiaSorin Inc 1951 NW Ave Stillwater MN 55082 651-439-9710 351-5669
TF: 855-677-0600 ■ *Web:* www.diasorin.com

Digestive Care Inc 1120 Win Dr Bethlehem PA 18017 610-882-0349
TF: 877-882-5950 ■ *Web:* www.digestivecare.com

Dik Drug Company LLC 160 Tower Dr Burr Ridge IL 60527 630-655-4000
Web: www.dikdrug.com

Dishman USA Inc 550 Union Ave Ste 9 Middlesex NJ 08846 732-560-4300
Web: www.wheelerjobin.com

DMS Pharmaceutical Group Inc
810 Busse Hwy Park Ridge IL 60068 847-518-1100
TF: 877-788-1100 ■ *Web:* www.dmspharma.com

DuPont Qualicon
Henry Clay Rd Bldg 400 Rt 141
PO Box 80400 Wilmington DE 19880 302-695-5300 351-6454
TF: 800-863-6842 ■ *Web:* dupont.com

Eco Lips 329 10th Ave SE Ste 213 Cedar Rapids IA 52401 319-364-2477
Web: www.ecolips.com

Edgemont Pharmaceuticals LLC
1250 Capital of Texas Hwy S Bldg 3 Ste 400 Austin TX 78746 512-550-8555
TF: 888-594-4332 ■ *Web:* www.edgemontpharma.com

Edimer Pharmaceuticals Inc
55 Cambridge Pkwy Ste 102W Cambridge MA 02142 617-758-4300
TF: 866-334-4240 ■ *Web:* www.edimerpharma.com

EDP Biotech Corp 6701 Baum Dr Ste 110 Knoxville TN 37919 865-246-0514
Web: www.edpbiotech.com

Emcure Pharmaceuticals USA INC
21/B Cotters Ln East Brunswick NJ 08816 732-238-7880
Web: www.emcureusa.com

Emmaus Medical Inc
20725 S Western Ave Ste 136 Torrance CA 90501 310-214-0065
Web: emmausmedical.com

Enzo Biochem Inc 527 Madison Ave New York NY 10022 212-583-0100 583-0150
NYSE: ENZ ■ *TF:* 800-522-5052 ■ *Web:* www.enzo.com

Enzo Life Sciences Inc 10 Executive Blvd Farmingdale NY 11735 631-694-7070
TF: 800-942-0430 ■ *Web:* www.enzolifesciences.com

Epiomed Therapeutics Inc 25 Mauchly Ste 316 Irvine CA 92618 949-398-7357
Web: www.epiomed.com

Euro-Pharm International Canada Inc
9400 Boul Langelier Montreal QC H1P3H8 514-323-8757 323-6325
TF: 888-929-0835 ■ *Web:* www.euro-pharm.com

Euthymics Bioscience 43 Thorndike St Cambridge MA 02141 617-758-0300
Web: www.euthymics.com

EXACT Sciences Corp 441 Charmany Dr Madison WI 53719 608-284-5700 284-5701
NASDAQ: EXAS ■ *Web:* www.exactsciences.com

Exalpha Biologicals Inc 2 Shaker Rd Unit B101 Shirley MA 01464 800-395-1137 461-0436*
**Fax Area Code:* 978 ■ *TF:* 800-395-1137 ■ *Web:* www.exalpha.com

Exoxemis Inc 6029 N 16th St Omaha NE 68110 402-884-2316

Face Stockholm Ltd 324 Joslen Blvd Hudson NY 12534 518-828-6600
TF: 888-334-3223 ■ *Web:* www.facestockholm.com

FibroGen Inc 409 Illinois St San Francisco CA 94158 415-978-1200
Web: www.fibrogen.com

Fitzgerald Industries International Inc
30 Sudbury Rd Ste 1A N Acton MA 01720 978-371-6446
Web: www.fitzgerald-fii.com

Galera Therapeutics Inc
2 W Liberty Blvd Ste 405 Malvern PA 19355 610-725-1500
Web: www.galeratx.com

Gen-Probe Inc 10210 Genetic Ctr Dr San Diego CA 92121 858-410-8000 288-3141*
**Fax Area Code:* 800 ■ *TF:* 800-523-5001 ■ *Web:* www.hologic.com

GenBio 15222 Ave of Science Ste A San Diego CA 92128 858-592-9300
TF Tech Supp: 800-288-4368 ■ *Web:* www.genbio.com

Genus Oncology LLC 650 Albany St Boston MA 02118 847-549-6500
Web: genusoncology.com

Gibson Laboratories Inc 1040 Manchester St Lexington KY 40508 859-254-9500 253-1476
TF: 800-477-4763 ■ *Web:* gibsonbioscience.com

Golden Bridge International Inc
9700 Harbour Pl Ste 129 Mukilteo WA 98275 425-493-1801
Web: www.gbi-inc.com

Golden State Medical Supply Inc
5187 Camino Ruiz Camarillo CA 93012 805-477-9866
TF: 800-284-8633 ■ *Web:* www.gsms.us

Goodwin Biotechnology Inc
1850 NW 69th Ave Plantation FL 33313 954-327-9656 587-6378
Web: www.goodwinbio.com

Graceway Pharmaceuticals LLC
340 Martin Luther King Junior Blvd Ste 500 Bristol TN 37620 423-274-2100

Company / Address	City	State	Zip	Phone	Fax
Green Pharmaceuticals Inc 591 Constitution Ave Ste A *Web:* snorestop.com	Camarillo	CA	93012	805-388-0600	
Guerbet LLC 120 W Seventh St Ste 108 *TF:* 877-729-6679 ■ *Web:* www.guerbet-us.com	Bloomington	IN	47404	812-333-0059	
Guy & O'Neill Inc 617 Tower Dr *Web:* www.guyandoneill.com	Fredonia	WI	53021	262-692-2469	
Haemotec Inc 383 Joseph Carrier	Vaudreuil-Dorion	QC	J7V5V5	450-424-3615	
HALO Pharmaceutical Inc 30 N Jefferson Rd *Web:* www.halopharma.com	Whippany	NJ	07981	973-428-4000	
Hanford Pharmaceuticals LLC 304 Oneida St *Web:* www.hanford.com	Syracuse	NY	13202	315-476-7418	
Healthy n Fit International 435 Yorktown Rd *Web:* behealthynfit.com	Croton On Hudson	NY	10520	914-271-6040	
Helena Laboratories Inc 1530 Lindbergh Dr *TF:* 800-231-5663 ■ *Web:* www.helena.com	Beaumont	TX	77704	409-842-3714	842-3094
Hemagen Diagnostics Inc 9033 Red Branch Rd *OTC:* HMGN ■ **Fax Area Code:* 410 ■ *TF:* 800-436-2436 ■ *Web:* www.hemagen.com	Columbia	MD	21045	443-367-5500	997-7812*
hermo Fisher Scientific Inc 8365 Valley Pike PO Box 307 *TF:* 800-528-0494 ■ *Web:* www.thermofisher.com	Middletown	VA	22645	800-556-2323	
Hitachi Chemical Diagnostics 630 Clyde Ct *TF:* 800-233-6278 ■ *Web:* www.hcdiagnostics.com	Mountain View	CA	94043	650-961-5501	969-2745
Honeys Place Inc 640 Glenoaks Blvd *TF:* 800-910-3246 ■ *Web:* www.honeysplace.com	San Fernando	CA	91340	818-256-1101	
Hospira Boulder Inc 4876 Sterling Dr *Web:* hospira.com	Boulder	CO	80301	303-938-1250	
Hovione LLC 40 Lake Dr *Web:* www.hovione.com	East Windsor	NJ	08520	609-918-2600	
HumanZyme Inc 2201 W Campbell Park Dr Ste 24 *Web:* www.humanzyme.com	Chicago	IL	60612	312-738-0127	
Huvepharma Inc 525 Wpark Dr Ste 230 *Web:* www.huvepharma.com	Peachtree City	GA	30269	495-958-5656	
Hycor Biomedical Inc 7272 Chapman Ave **Fax Area Code:* 714 ■ *TF Cust Svc:* 800-382-2527 ■ *Web:* www.hycorbiomedical.com	Garden Grove	CA	92841	800-382-2527	933-3222*
IDEXX Laboratories Inc 1 IDEXX Dr *NASDAQ:* IDXX ■ *TF:* 800-548-6733 ■ *Web:* www.idexx.com	Westbrook	ME	04092	207-556-0300	556-4346
ImmucorGamma Inc 3130 Gateway Dr PO Box 5625 *NASDAQ:* BLUD ■ *TF Cust Svc:* 800-829-2553 ■ *Web:* www.immucor.com	Norcross	GA	30091	770-441-2051	441-3807
Immuno-Mycologics Inc (IMMY) 2700 Technology Pl *TF:* 800-654-3639 ■ *Web:* www.immy.com	Norman	OK	73071	405-360-4669	
ImmunoDiagnostics Inc 1 Presidential Way Ste 104 *TF:* 800-573-1700 ■ *Web:* www.immunodx.com	Woburn	MA	01801	781-938-6300	938-7300
Immunovision Inc 1820 Ford Ave *TF:* 800-541-0960 ■ *Web:* www.immunovision.com	Springdale	AR	72764	479-751-7005	751-7002
InnoZen Inc 6429 Independence Ave	Woodland Hills	CA	91367	805-822-5091	
Inotek Pharmaceuticals Corp 91 Hartwell Ave 2nd Fl *Web:* inotekpharma.com	Lexington	MA	02421	978-232-9660	
Inova Diagnostics Inc 9900 Old Grove Rd *TF:* 800-545-9495 ■ *Web:* www.inovadx.com	San Diego	CA	92131	858-586-9900	586-9911
InSite Vision Inc 965 Atlantic Ave *OTC:* INSV ■ *Web:* www.insitevision.com	Alameda	CA	94501	510-865-8800	865-5700
Interleukin Genetics Inc 135 Beaver St *OTC:* ILIU ■ *TF Cust Svc:* 866-990-4363 ■ *Web:* www.ilgenetics.com	Waltham	MA	02452	781-398-0700	398-0720
Intermax Pharmaceuticals Inc 228 Sherwood Ave *Web:* synthopharmaceuticals.com	Farmingdale	NY	11735	631-777-3318	
International Immunology Corp 25549 Adams Ave *TF:* 800-843-2853 ■ *Web:* www.iicsera.com	Murrieta	CA	92562	951-677-5629	677-6752
International Isotopes Inc 4137 Commerce Cir *OTC:* INIS ■ *TF:* 800-699-3108 ■ *Web:* www.intisoid.com	Idaho Falls	ID	83401	208-524-5300	524-1411
InVitro International 330 E Orangethorpe Ave Ste D *TF:* 800-246-8487 ■ *Web:* www.invitrointl.com	Placentia	CA	92870	949-851-8356	851-4985
Invivis Pharmaceuticals Inc 547 Meadow Rd *Web:* www.invivis.com	Bridgewater	NJ	08807	908-818-9393	
Invivoscribe Technologies Inc 6330 Nancy Ridge Dr Ste 106 *TF:* 866-623-8105 ■ *Web:* www.invivoscribe.com	San Diego	CA	92121	858-224-6600	
Iso-Tex Diagnostics Inc PO Box 909 **Fax Area Code:* 281 ■ *TF:* 800-477-4839 ■ *Web:* www.isotexdiagnostics.com	Friendswood	TX	77549	800-477-4839	482-1070*
Jackson ImmunoResearch Laboratories Inc 872 W Baltimore Pk PO Box 9 *TF:* 800-367-5296 ■ *Web:* www.jacksonimmuno.com	West Grove	PA	19390	610-869-4024	869-0171
Jean Brown Assoc Inc 1045 East 3900 South Ste 100 *Web:* www.jeanbrownresearch.com	Salt Lake City	UT	84124	801-261-2000	
Jenken Biosciences Inc 2 Davis Dr Research Triangle Pk *Web:* www.jenkenbio.com	Research Triangle Park	NC	27709	919-765-0032	
Kalos Therapeutics Inc 4370 La Jolla Village Dr Ste 400 *Web:* www.kalostpx.com	San Diego	CA	92122	858-552-6890	
Kamiya Biomedical Co 12779 Gateway Dr *Web:* www.kamiyabiomedical.com	Seattle	WA	98168	206-575-8068	575-8094
Kc Pharmaceuticals Inc 3201 Producer Way *Web:* kc-ph.com	Pomona	CA	91768	909-598-9499	
Kern Health Systems 9700 Stockdale Hwy *TF:* 888-466-2219 ■ *Web:* www.kernfamilyhealthcare.com	Bakersfield	CA	93311	661-664-5000	
Keysource Medical Inc 7820 Palace Dr *Web:* www.keysourcemedical.com	Cincinnati	OH	45249	513-469-7881	
Kibow Biotech Inc 4781 W Chester Pike Newtown Business Ctr *TF:* 888-271-2560 ■ *Web:* www.kibowbiotech.com	Newtown Square	PA	19073	610-353-5130	
Kirkegaard & Perry Laboratories Inc 910 Clopper Rd *TF:* 800-638-3167 ■ *Web:* www.kpl.com	Gaithersburg	MD	20878	301-948-7755	948-0169
KMI Diagnostics Inc 8201 Central Ave NE Ste P *TF:* 888-564-3424 ■ *Web:* www.kmidiagnostics.com	Minneapolis	MN	55432	763-231-3313	780-2988
Kohl & Frisch Ltd 7622 Keele St *TF:* 800-265-2520 ■ *Web:* www.kohlandfrisch.com	Concord	ON	L4K2R5	800-265-2520	
Kolltan Pharmaceuticals Inc 300 George St Ste 530 *Web:* www.kolltan.com	New Haven	CT	06511	203-773-3000	
Kowa Pharmaceuticals America Inc 530 Industrial Park Blvd *Web:* www.kowapharma.com	Montgomery	AL	36117	334-288-1288	
KVK-TECH Inc 110 Terry Dr Ste 200 *Web:* www.kvktech.com	Newtown	PA	18940	215-579-1842	
Laboratoire Du-var Inc 1460 Rue Graham-Bell *Web:* www.du-var.com	Boucherville	QC	J4B6H5	450-641-4740	641-4743
Lantheus Medical Imaging Inc 331 Treble Cove Rd Bldg 200-2 *Web:* www.lantheus.com	North Billerica	MA	01862	978-667-9531	
Lawton's Drug Stores Ltd 236 Brownlow Ave Ste 270 *TF:* 866-990-1599 ■ *Web:* www.lawtons.ca	Dartmouth	NS	B3B1V5	902-468-1000	
LifeScan Inc 1000 Gibraltar Dr *TF:* 800-227-8862 ■ *Web:* www.lifescan.com	Milpitas	CA	95035	408-263-9789	946-6070
Lightning Powder Company Inc 13386 International Pkwy	Jacksonville	FL	32218	904-485-1836	741-5407
LNK International Inc 22 Arkay Dr *Web:* www.lnkintl.com	Hauppauge	NY	11788	631-435-3500	
MabVax Therapeutics Inc 11588 Sorrento Vly Rd Ste 20 *Web:* www.mabvax.com	San Diego	CA	92121	858-259-9405	
Maine Biotechnology Services Inc 1037 R Forest Ave *TF:* 800-925-9476 ■ *Web:* www.mainebiotechnology.com	Portland	ME	04103	207-797-5454	797-5595
Mallinckrodt Inc 675 McDonnell Blvd *TF:* 800-778-7898	Hazelwood	MO	63042	314-654-2000	654-6257
Marianna Industries Inc 11222 "I" St *TF:* 800-228-9060 ■ *Web:* www.mariannaind.com	Omaha	NE	68137	402-593-0211	
MCR American Pharmaceuticals Inc 16255 Aviation Loop *Web:* www.mcramerican.com	Brooksville	FL	34604	352-754-8587	
Medical Analysis Systems Inc 46360 Fremont Blvd *TF:* 800-232-3342 ■ *Web:* www.thermofisher.com	Fremont	CA	94538	510-979-5000	979-5002
Mediderm Laboratories 9840- 9842 Alburtis Ave *Web:* www.medidermstore.com	Santa Fe Springs	CA	90670	310-445-0600	
Medinox Inc 6120 Paseo Del Norte Ste B-2 *Web:* www.medinox.com	Carlsbad	CA	92009	760-603-8989	
MEDTOX Diagnostics Inc 1238 Anthony Rd **Fax Area Code:* 651 ■ *TF:* 800-334-1116 ■ *Web:* www.medtox.com	Burlington	NC	27215	336-226-6311	286-6222*
Memory Pharmaceuticals Corp 100 Philips Pkwy *Web:* www.memorypharma.com	Montvale	NJ	07645	201-802-7100	
Meridian Bioscience Inc 3471 River Hills Dr *NASDAQ:* VIVO ■ *TF Cust Svc:* 800-543-1980 ■ *Web:* www.meridianbioscience.com	Cincinnati	OH	45244	513-271-3700	272-5421
Miller Drug Inc 210 State St *Web:* www.millerdrug.com	Bangor	ME	04401	207-947-8369	
Miragen Therapeutics Inc 6200 Lookout Rd Ste 100 *Web:* www.miragentherapeutics.com	Boulder	CO	80301	303-531-5952	
Mirari Biosciences Inc 9610 Medical Ctr Dr Ste 240 *Web:* www.miraribiosciences.com	Rockville	MD	20850	240-447-6456	
Moderna Therapeutics Inc 320 Bent St *Web:* www.modernatx.com	Cambridge	MA	02141	617-714-6500	
Monobind Inc 100 N Pt Dr *Web:* www.monobind.com	Lake Forest	CA	92630	949-951-2665	951-3539
MonoSol Rx Inc 30 Technology Dr *Web:* www.monosolrx.com	Warren	NJ	07059	732-564-5000	
Mork Process Inc 4278 Hudson Dr *Web:* www.morkusa.com	Stow	OH	44224	330-928-3728	
Moss Inc PO Box 189 *TF:* 800-932-6677 ■ *Web:* www.mosssubstrates.com	Pasadena	MD	21123	410-768-3442	768-3971
Nanocopoeia Inc 1246 W University Ave Ste 463 *Web:* www.nanocopeia.com	St Paul	MN	55104	651-209-1184	
National Diagnostics Inc 305 Patton Dr *TF:* 800-526-3867 ■ *Web:* www.nationaldiagnostics.com	Atlanta	GA	30336	404-699-2121	699-2077
Neci 334 Hecla St *TF:* 888-648-7283 ■ *Web:* www.nitrate.com	Lake Linden	MI	49945	906-296-1000	
Neogen Corp 620 Lesher Pl *NASDAQ:* NEOG ■ *TF:* 800-234-5333 ■ *Web:* www.neogen.com	Lansing	MI	48912	517-372-9200	372-2006
NeuroGenetic Pharmaceuticals Inc 445 Marine View Ave Ste 101 *Web:* www.neurogeneticpharmaceuticals.com	Del Mar	CA	92014	858-461-4480	
New Century Pharmaceuticals Inc 895 Martin Rd *Web:* www.newcenturypharm.com	Huntsville	AL	35824	256-461-0024	
New Horizons Diagnostics Corp 9110 Red Branch Rd *TF:* 800-888-5015 ■ *Web:* www.nhdiag.com	Columbia	MD	21045	410-992-9357	992-0328
NexGenix Pharmaceuticals Holdings Inc 152 W 57th St Ste 11B *Web:* www.nexgenixpharm.com	New York	NY	10019	212-974-3006	
Noction Inc 1294 Lawrence Sta Rd *Web:* www.noction.com	Sunnyvale	CA	94089	650-618-9823	
Norgenix Pharmaceuticals LLC 101 W Saint John St Ste 307 *Web:* www.norgenixpharma.com	Spartanburg	SC	29306	864-580-2660	

Company	City	State	ZIP	Phone	Fax
Novartis Vaccines & Diagnostics 350 Massachusetts Ave *NYSE: NVS* ■ *Web:* www.novartis-vaccines.com	Cambridge	MA	02139	862-778-8300	
Novocol Pharmaceutical of Canada Inc 25 Wolseley Ct *Web:* www.septodont.ca	Cambridge	ON	N1R6X3	519-623-4800	623-4290
Nulab Inc 2180 Calumet St *Web:* www.nulabinc.com	Clearwater	FL	33765	727-446-1126	
Nuron Biotech Inc 1 E Uwchlan Ave Ste 302	Exton	PA	19341	610-968-6700	
NuTech Inc 1301 Clinic Dr *Web:* www.nutechrx.com	Tyler	TX	75701	903-592-8115	
Nutraceutics Corp 2900 Brannon Ave *Web:* www.nutraceutics.com	Saint Louis	MO	63139	314-664-6684	
Odan Laboratories Ltd 325 Stillview Ave *TF:* 800-387-9342 ■ *Web:* www.odanlab.com	Pointe-Claire	QC	H9R2Y6	514-428-1628	428-9783
Ohmx Corp 1801 Maple Ave Ste 6143 *Web:* www.ohmxbio.com	Evanston	IL	60201	847-491-8500	
Omega Biologicals Inc 910 Technology Blvd *Web:* omegabiologicals.com	Bozeman	MT	59718	406-586-3790	586-3792
Oncogenex Technologies Inc 1001 W Broadway Ste 400 *Web:* oncogenex.com	Vancouver	BC	V6H4B1	604-736-3678	
Ondine Biomedical Inc 1100 Melville St *TF:* 800-564-6253 ■ *Web:* www.ondinebio.com	Vancouver	BC	V6E4A6	604-669-0555	669-0533
OraSure Technologies Inc 220 E First St *NASDAQ: OSUR* ■ *TF:* 800-869-3538 ■ *Web:* www.orasure.com	Bethlehem	PA	18015	610-882-1820	882-1830
Oriel Therapeutics Inc 630 Davis Dr Ste 120	Morrisville	NC	27560	919-313-1290	
Orion Genomics LLC 4041 Forest Park Ave *Web:* www.oriongenomics.com	Saint Louis	MO	63108	314-615-6977	
Ortho-Clinical Diagnostics Inc 1001 US Rt 202 N PO Box 350 **Fax Area Code:* 585 ■ **Fax:* Cust Svc ■ *TF:* 800-828-6316 ■ *Web:* www.orthoclinical.com	Raritan	NJ	08869	800-828-6316	453-3660*
Oxford Biomedical Research Inc 2165 Avon Industrial Dr *TF:* 800-692-4633 ■ *Web:* www.oxfordbiomed.com	Rochester Hills	MI	48309	248-852-8815	852-4466
Pacific Biometrics Inc 645 Elliott Ave W Ste 300 *TF:* 800-767-9151 ■ *Web:* www.pacbio.com	Seattle	WA	98119	206-298-0068	
Pacific Nutritional Inc 6317 NE 131st Ave *Web:* www.pacnut.com	Vancouver	WA	98682	360-253-3197	
Paramount Beauty Distributing Assoc Inc 41 Mercedes Way Ste 34 *Web:* paramountbeauty.com	Edgewood	NY	11717	631-242-3737	
Parchem Trading Ltd 415 Huguenot St *TF:* 800-282-3982 ■ *Web:* www.parchem.com	New Rochelle	NY	10801	914-654-6800	
ParinGenix Inc 1792 Bell Tower Ln Ste 200	Weston	FL	33326	954-315-3660	
PBA Health 6300 Enterprise Rd *TF:* 800-333-8097 ■ *Web:* pbahealth.com	Kansas City	MO	64120	816-245-5700	
Pearl Therapeutics Inc 200 Saginaw Dr *Web:* www.pearltherapeutics.com	Redwood City	CA	94063	650-305-2600	
Peloton Therapeutics Inc 2330 Inwood Rd Ste 226 *Web:* www.pelotontherapeutics.com	Dallas	TX	75235	972-629-4100	
Peptides International Inc 11621 Electron Dr *TF:* 800-777-4779 ■ *Web:* www.pepnet.com	Louisville	KY	40299	502-266-8787	267-1329
PerkinElmer Inc 940 Winter St *NYSE: PKI* ■ *Web:* www.perkinelmer.com	Waltham	MA	02451	203-925-4602	944-4904
Permeon Biologics Inc 1 Kendall Sq Bldg 1400 W Ste 14203 **Fax Area Code:* 650 ■ *Web:* www.permeonbio.com	Cambridge	MA	02139	617-945-7780	595-5589*
Pfizer Centre Source 7000 Portage Rd *Web:* www.pfizercentreone.com	Kalamazoo	MI	49001	269-833-6164	
Phadia US Inc 4169 Commercial Ave *TF:* 800-346-4364 ■ *Web:* www.phadia.com	Portage	MI	49002	269-492-1940	
Phage Pharmaceuticals Inc 6868 Nancy Ridge Dr Ste 100	San Diego	CA	92121	858-427-9100	
Pharmaceutical Assoc Inc 1700 Perimeter Rd *TF:* 888-233-2334 ■ *Web:* www.paipharma.com	Greenville	SC	29605	864-277-7282	
Pharmaceutical Innovations Inc 897 Frelinghuysen Ave *Web:* www.pharminnovations.com	Newark	NJ	07114	973-242-2900	242-0578
Pharmaceutical Technologies Inc 14301 Fnb Pkwy	Omaha	NE	68154	402-964-9030	
Pharmaceutics International Inc 10819 Gilroy Rd *Web:* www.pharm-int.com	Hunt Valley	MD	21031	410-584-0001	
Pharmakon Compounding Inc 801 Congressional Blvd *Web:* pharmakonrx.net	Carmel	IN	46032	317-818-1059	
Pharmalucence Inc 29 Dunham Rd *TF:* 800-221-7554 ■ *Web:* www.pharmalucence.com	Billerica	MA	01821	781-275-7120	
Pharmametrics 220 Commerce Dr Ste 405 *Web:* pharmametricsinc.com	Ft Washington	PA	19034	215-274-1315	
Pharmasave Drugs (National) Ltd 8411 - 200th St Ste 201 *TF:* 800-661-6106 ■ *Web:* www.pharmasave.com	Langley	BC	V2Y0E7	604-455-2400	455-2493
Pharmascience Inc 6111 Royalmount Ave Ste 100 *TF:* 866-853-1178 ■ *Web:* www.pharmascience.com	Montreal	QC	H4P2T4	514-340-9800	342-7764
Pharmetics Inc 3695 AutoRt Des Laurentides *TF:* 877-472-4433 ■ *Web:* www.pharmetics.com	Laval	QC	H7L3H7	450-682-8580	
PhaseBio Pharmaceuticals Inc 1 Great Vly Pkwy Ste 30 *Web:* www.phasebio.com	Malvern	PA	19355	610-981-6500	
Pherin Pharmaceuticals Inc 4962 El Camino Real Ste 223 *Web:* www.pherin.com	Los Altos	CA	94022	650-961-2703	
Phoenix Pharmaceuticals Inc 330 Beach Rd *TF:* 800-988-1205 ■ *Web:* www.phoenixpeptide.com	Burlingame	CA	94010	650-558-8898	
Phylonix Pharmaceuticals Inc 100 Inman St Ste 300 *Web:* www.phylonix.com	Cambridge	MA	02139	617-441-6700	
Pierre Fabre Dermo Cosmetique 8 Campus Dr *Web:* www.pierre-fabre.com	Parsippany	NJ	07054	973-898-1042	
PlantForm Corp 1920 Yonge St Ste 200 *Web:* www.plantformcorp.com	Toronto	ON	M4S3E2	416-452-7242	
PLx Pharma Inc 8285 El Rio Ste 130 *Web:* www.plxpharma.com	Houston	TX	77054	713-842-1249	
Pointe Scientific Inc 5449 Research Dr PO Box 87188 *TF:* 800-445-9853 ■ *Web:* www.pointescientific.com	Canton	MI	48188	734-487-8300	483-1592
Polaris Pharmaceuticals Inc 9373 Towne Centre Dr Ste 150 *Web:* www.polarispharma.com	San Diego	CA	92121	858-452-6688	
Polymedco Inc 510 Furnace Dock Rd *TF:* 800-431-2123 ■ *Web:* www.polymedco.com	Cortlandt Manor	NY	10567	914-739-5400	739-5890
PolyPeptide Laboratories Inc 365 Maple Ave *TF:* 800-338-4965 ■ *Web:* www.polypeptide.com	Torrance	CA	90503	310-782-3569	
Polysciences Inc 400 Valley Rd *TF Cust Svc:* 800-523-2575 ■ *Web:* www.polysciences.com	Warrington	PA	18976	215-343-6484	343-0214
Prasco LLC 6125 Commerce Ct *TF:* 866-469-1414 ■ *Web:* www.prasco.com	Mason	OH	45040	513-618-3333	
Prescription Supply Inc 2233 Tracy Rd *Web:* www.prescriptionsupply.com	Northwood	OH	43619	419-661-6600	
Press Chemical & Pharmaceutical Laboratories Inc 4231 Donlyn Ct	Columbus	OH	43232	614-863-2802	
ProCertus BioPharm Inc 510 Charmany Dr Ste 175 B	Madison	WI	53719	608-277-7950	
Product Quest Mfg LLC 330 Carswell Ave *Web:* www.productquestmfg.com	Daytona Beach	FL	32117	386-239-8787	
Promega Corp 2800 Woods Hollow Rd *TF:* 800-356-9526 ■ *Web:* promega.com	Madison	WI	53711	608-274-4330	277-2516
Proteon Therapeutics Inc 200 W St *Web:* www.proteontherapeutics.com	Waltham	MA	02451	781-890-0102	
Proteos Inc 4717 Campus Dr *Web:* www.proteos.net	Kalamazoo	MI	49008	269-372-3480	
Prozyme Inc 3832 Bay Ctr Pl *TF:* 800-457-9444 ■ *Web:* www.prozyme.com	Hayward	CA	94545	510-638-6900	638-6919
Psyadon Pharmaceuticals Inc 20451 Seneca Meadows Pkwy *Web:* www.psyadonrx.com	Germantown	MD	20876	301-919-2020	
PTC Therapeutics Inc 100 Corporate Ct *Web:* www.ptcbio.com	South Plainfield	NJ	07080	908-222-7000	
Public Health Solutions 220 Church St Fl 5 *Web:* www.healthsolutions.org	New York	NY	10013	646-619-6400	
Purdue Pharma 575 Granite Ct *TF:* 800-387-5349 ■ *Web:* www.purdue.ca	Pickering	ON	L1W3W8	905-420-6400	420-4193
Qst Consultations Ltd 11275 Edgewater Dr *TF:* 866-757-4751 ■ *Web:* qstconsultations.com	Allendale	MI	49401	616-895-5461	
Quadris Medical 2030 Lookout Dr *Web:* quadrismedical.com	North Mankato	MN	56003	507-385-2709	
Quality Biological Inc 7581 Lindbergh Dr *Web:* www.qualitybiological.com	Gaithersburg	MD	20879	301-840-9331	
Quantimetrix Corp 2005 Manhattan Beach Blvd *TF:* 800-624-8380 ■ *Web:* quantimetrix.com	Redondo Beach	CA	90278	310-536-0006	536-9977
Quark Pharmaceuticals Inc 6501 Dumbarton Cir *Web:* quarkpharma.com	Fremont	CA	94555	510-402-4020	
Quidel Corp 10165 McKellar Ct *NASDAQ: QDEL* ■ *TF:* 800-874-1517 ■ *Web:* www.quidel.com	San Diego	CA	92121	858-552-1100	453-4338
R & D Systems Inc 614 McKinley Pl NE *TF:* 800-343-7475 ■ *Web:* www.rndsystems.com	Minneapolis	MN	55413	612-379-2956	656-4400
R X Canada 6711 Mississauga Rd *Web:* www.rxcanada.ca	Mississauga	ON	L5N2W3	905-821-2270	
Radient Pharmaceuticals Corp 2492 Walnut Ave Ste 100 *OTC: RXPC*	Tustin	CA	92780	714-505-4461	505-4464
Raritan Pharmaceuticals Inc 8 Joanna Ct *Web:* www.raritanpharm.com	East Brunswick	NJ	08816	732-432-8200	
Rasi Laboratories Inc 20 Roosevelt Ave *Web:* www.rasilaboratories.com	Somerset	NJ	08873	732-873-8500	
Research & Diagnostic Antibodies 2645 W Cheyenne Ave *TF:* 800-858-7322 ■ *Web:* www.rdabs.com	North Las Vegas	NV	89032	702-638-7800	638-7801
Reviva Pharmaceuticals Inc 3900 Freedom Circle Ste 101 *Web:* www.revivapharma.com	Santa Clara	CA	95054	408-960-2209	
RGR Pharma ltd 103 Crystal Harbour Dr *Web:* www.rgrpharma.com	Lasalle	ON	N9J3R6	519-734-6600	
Rhodes Technologies Inc 498 Washington St *Web:* www.rhodestec.com	Coventry	RI	02816	401-262-9200	
Rising Pharmaceuticals Inc 3 Pearl Ct Stes A/B *Web:* www.risingpharma.com	Allendale	NJ	07401	201-961-9000	
Roche Diagnostics Corp (RDC) 9115 Hague Rd PO Box 50457 *TF Cust Svc:* 800-428-5076 ■ *Web:* usdiagnostics.roche.com/en/corporate_information.html	Indianapolis	IN	46250	317-521-2000	521-2090
Rockland Immunochemicals Inc PO Box 326 *TF:* 800-656-7625 ■ *Web:* www.rockland-inc.com	Gilbertsville	PA	19525	610-369-1008	367-7825
RxMosaic Healthcare 711 Third Ave Fl 19 *Web:* rxmosaichealth.com	New York	NY	10017	212-336-7500	
SA Scientific Ltd 4919 Golden Quail *Web:* www.ntextechnologies.com	San Antonio	TX	78240	210-699-8800	699-6545
Saladax Biomedical Inc 116 Research Dr *Web:* www.saladax.com	Bethlehem	PA	18015	610-419-6731	
San-Mar Laboratories Inc 4 Warehouse Ln *Web:* processtechnologies.com	Elmsford	NY	10523	914-592-3130	

Company	City	State	Zip	Phone	Fax
Sanofi-Aventis US LLC 55 Corporate Dr *Web:* sanofi.us	Bridgewater	NJ	08807	908-981-5000	
Santen Inc 2100 Powell St 16th Fl *Web:* www.santeninc.com	Emeryville	CA	94608	415-268-9100	
Saskatchewan Health Research Foundation 253-111 Research Dr *TF:* 800-975-1699 ■ *Web:* www.shrf.ca	Saskatoon	SK	S7N3R2	306-975-1680	
Scantibodies Laboratory Inc 9336 Abraham Way *Web:* www.scantibodies.com	Santee	CA	92071	619-258-9300	258-9366
SCIMEDX Corp 100 Ford Rd *TF:* 800-221-5598 ■ *Web:* www.scimedx.com	Denville	NJ	07834	973-625-8822	625-8796
Scivolutions Inc 2260 Raeford Ct	Gastonia	NC	28052	704-853-0100	
Scripps Laboratories Inc 6838 Flanders Dr *Web:* www.scrippslabs.com	San Diego	CA	92121	858-546-5800	546-5812
Sigma-Aldrich Corp 3050 Spruce St *NASDAQ: SIAL* ■ **Fax Area Code:* 800 ■ *TF:* 800-325-3010 ■ *Web:* www.sigmaaldrich.com	Saint Louis	MO	63103	314-771-5765	325-5052*
Sinapis Pharma Inc 3610 Holly Grove Ave *Web:* www.sinapispharma.com	Jacksonville	FL	32217	904-619-0043	
Southern Biotechnology Assoc Inc 160A Oxmoor Blvd *TF:* 800-722-2255 ■ *Web:* www.southernbiotech.com	Birmingham	AL	35209	205-945-1774	945-8768
Specialty Medical Supplies 3882 NW 124th Ave *Web:* www.specialtymedicalsupplies.com	Coral Springs	FL	33065	954-752-5603	
St. Renatus LLC 1000 Centre Ave *TF:* 888-686-2314 ■ *Web:* www.st-renatus.com	Fort Collins	CO	80526	970-282-0156	
Stanbio Laboratory LP 1261 N Main St *TF:* 800-531-5535 ■ *Web:* www.stanbio.com	Boerne	TX	78006	830-249-0772	
Stason Pharmaceuticals Inc 11 Morgan *Web:* www.stason.com	Irvine	CA	92618	949-380-4327	
Stat Pharmaceuticals Inc 9545 Pathway St	Santee	CA	92071	619-956-4200	
Straight Arrow Products Inc 2020 Highland Ave *TF:* 800-827-9815 ■ *Web:* straightarrowinc.com	Bethlehem	PA	18020	610-882-9606	
Strategic Diagnostics Inc 111 Pencader Dr *NASDAQ: SDIX* ■ *TF:* 800-544-8881 ■ *Web:* www.sdix.com	Newark	DE	19702	302-456-6789	
Streck Inc 7002 S 109th St *TF:* 800-228-6090 ■ *Web:* www.streck.com	Omaha	NE	68128	402-333-1982	
Sun Pharmaceutical Industries Inc 270 Prospect Plains Rd *Web:* www.sunpharma.com	Cranbury	NJ	08512	609-495-2800	
Sunovion Pharmaceuticals Inc 84 Waterford Dr *TF:* 888-394-7377 ■ *Web:* www.sunovion.com	Marlborough	MA	01752	508-481-6700	
Super Thrifty Drugs Canada Ltd 381 Park Ave E *Web:* www.superthrifty.com	Brandon	MB	R7A7A5	204-728-1522	
SurModics Inc 9924 W 74th St *NASDAQ: SRDX* ■ *TF:* 866-787-6639 ■ *Web:* www.surmodics.com	Eden Prairie	MN	55344	952-829-2700	500-7001
Syndax Pharmaceuticals Inc 400 Totten Pond Rd Ste 110 *Web:* www.syndax.com	Waltham	MA	02451	781-419-1400	
Synergent Biochem Inc 12026 Centralia Rd Ste H *Web:* www.synergentbiochem.com	Hawaiian Gardens	CA	90716	562-809-3389	809-6191
Syntrix Biosystems Inc 215 Clay St NW Ste B-5 *Web:* www.syntrixbio.com	Auburn	WA	98001	253-833-8009	
Tec Laboratories Inc 7100 Tec Labs Way SW *TF:* 800-482-4464 ■ *Web:* www.teclabsinc.com	Albany	OR	97321	541-926-4577	
Techne Corp 614 McKinley Pl NE *NASDAQ: TECH* ■ *TF:* 800-343-7475 ■ *Web:* bio-techne.com	Minneapolis	MN	55413	612-379-8854	379-6580
Teco Diagnostics 1268 N Lakeview Ave *TF:* 800-222-9880 ■ *Web:* www.tecodiagnostics.com	Anaheim	CA	92807	714-463-1111	463-1169
Teikoku Pharma USA Inc 1718 Ringwood Ave *Web:* www.teikokuusa.com	San Jose	CA	95131	408-501-1800	
Ther-Rx Corp 1 Corporate Woods Dr *Web:* lumarahealth.com	Bridgeton	MO	63044	314-646-3700	
Theracrine Inc 1 Memorial Dr 7th Fl	Cambridge	MA	02142	617-218-1605	
Theragenics Corp 5203 Bristol Industrial Way *NYSE: TGX* ■ *Web:* www.theragenics.com	Buford	GA	30518	770-271-0233	831-5294
TheraVida Inc 177 Bovet Rd Ste 600 *Web:* www.theravida.com	San Mateo	CA	94402	650-638-2335	
Thermo Fisher Scientific Inc 3747 N Meridian Rd *TF:* 800-874-3723 ■ *Web:* www.piercenet.com	Rockford	IL	61101	815-968-0747	968-7316
Thermo Scientific 12076 Santa Fe Dr PO Box 14428 **Fax Area Code:* 800 ■ *TF:* 800-255-6730	Lenexa	KS	66215	913-888-0939	621-8251*
Theron Pharmaceuticals Inc 365 San Aleso Ave *Web:* www.theronpharma.com	Sunnyvale	CA	94085	408-792-7424	
Time-Cap Labs Inc 7 Michael Ave *Web:* www.timecaplabs.com	Farmingdale	NY	11735	631-753-9090	
Tocagen Inc 3030 Bunker Hill St Ste 230 *Web:* www.tocagen.com	San Diego	CA	92109	858-412-8400	
Tokai Pharmaceuticals Inc 255 State St 6th Fl *Web:* www.tokaipharmaceuticals.com	Boston	MA	02109	617-225-4305	
TOLMAR Holding Inc 701 Centre Ave *Web:* www.tolmar.com	Fort Collins	CO	80526	970-212-4500	
Torrent Pharma Inc 5380 Holiday Ter Ste 40 *Web:* ww2.torrentpharma.com	Kalamazoo	MI	49009	269-544-2299	
Townley Inc 389 Fifth Ave Rm 1100 *Web:* www.townleygirl.com	New York	NY	10016	212-779-0544	
Tragara Pharmaceuticals Inc 3152 Lionshead Ave *Web:* www.tragarapharma.com	Carlsbad	CA	92010	760-208-6900	
Trana Discovery Inc 2054-260 Kildare Farm Rd *Web:* www.tranadiscovery.com	Cary	NC	27518	919-342-6192	
Trevena Inc 1018 W Eighth Ave Ste A *Web:* www.trevenainc.com	King Of Prussia	PA	19406	610-354-8840	
Triad Isotopes Inc 4205 Vineland Rd Ste L1 *TF:* 866-310-0086 ■ *Web:* www.triadisotopes.com	Orlando	FL	32811	407-455-6700	

Company	City	State	Zip	Phone	Fax
Triarco Industries LLC 400 Hamburg Tpke *Web:* www.triarco.com	Wayne	NJ	07470	973-942-5100	
Triclinic Labs 1201 Cumberland Ave Ste S *Web:* www.tricliniclabs.com	West Lafayette	IN	47906	765-588-6200	
Trinity Biotech PLC 5919 Farnsworth Ct *NASDAQ: TRIB* ■ *TF:* 800-331-2291 ■ *Web:* www.trinitybiotech.com	Carlsbad	CA	92008	760-929-0500	929-0124
TVAX Biomedical Inc 8006 Reeder St *Web:* www.tvaxbiomedical.com	Lenexa	KS	66214	913-492-2221	
Tyger Scientific Inc 324 Stokes Ave *TF:* 888-329-8990 ■ *Web:* www.tygersci.com	Ewing	NJ	08638	609-434-0143	
Uman Pharma Inc 100 De L'Industrie Blvd *TF:* 877-444-9989 ■ *Web:* www.umanpharma.com	Candiac	QC	J5R1J1	450-444-9989	
Unique Pharmaceuticals Ltd 5920 S General Bruce Dr *Web:* www.upisolutions.com	Temple	TX	76502	254-933-0874	
Utak Laboratories Inc 25020 Ave Tibbitts *TF:* 800-235-3442 ■ *Web:* www.utak.com	Valencia	CA	91355	661-294-3935	294-9272
Valeo Pharma Inc 16667 Hymus Blvd Kirkland *TF:* 888-694-0865 ■ *Web:* www.valeopharma.com	Kirkland	QC	H9H4R9	514-694-0150	
Valley Wholesale Drug Company Inc 1401 W Fremont St PO Box 2065 *Web:* www.vwdco.com	Stockton	CA	95203	209-466-0131	
VersaPharm Inc 1775 W Oak Pkwy Ste 800 *Web:* www.versapharm.com	Marietta	GA	30062	770-499-8100	
Verus Pharmaceuticals Inc 12671 High Bluff Dr Ste 200 *Web:* www.veruspharm.com	San Diego	CA	92130	858-436-1600	
Viamet Pharmaceuticals Inc 2250 Perimeter Park Dr Ste 320 *Web:* www.viamet.com	Morrisville	NC	27560	919-467-8539	
Victus Inc 4918 SW 74th Ct *Web:* www.victus.com	Miami	FL	33155	305-663-2129	
VIRxSYS Corp 200 Perry Pkwy Ste 1A	Gaithersburg	MD	20877	301-987-0480	
VistaPharm Inc 630 Central Ave Ste B3 *Web:* www.vistapharm.com	New Providence	NJ	35242	205-981-1387	
Vitae Pharmaceuticals Inc 502 W Office Ctr Dr *Web:* www.vitaepharma.com	Fort Washington	PA	19034	215-461-2000	
Wako Chemicals USA Inc 1600 Bellwood Rd *TF:* 800-992-9256 ■ *Web:* www.wakousa.com	Richmond	VA	23237	804-271-7677	271-7791
Webco Hawaii Inc 2840 Mokumoa St *Web:* www.awdhi.com	Honolulu	HI	96819	808-839-4551	
World Wide Packaging LLC 15 Vreeland Rd Ste 4 *TF:* 800-950-0390 ■ *Web:* www.wwpinc.com	Florham Park	NJ	07932	973-805-6500	805-6510
Worthington Biochemical Corp 730 Vassar Ave *TF:* 800-445-9603 ■ *Web:* www.worthington-biochem.com	Lakewood	NJ	08701	732-942-1660	942-9270
Xeris Pharmaceuticals Inc 3208 Red River St Ste 300 *TF:* 888-570-4781 ■ *Web:* xerispharma.com	Austin	TX	78705	888-570-4781	
Xttrium Laboratories Inc 1200 E Business Ctr Dr *TF:* 800-587-3721 ■ *Web:* www.xttrium.com	Mt. Prospect	IL	60056	773-268-5800	
Zepto Metrix Corp 872 Main St *TF Cust Svc:* 800-274-5487 ■ *Web:* www.zeptometrix.com	Buffalo	NY	14202	716-882-0920	882-0959
ZLB Bioplasma Inc 801 N Brand Blvd Ste 1150	Glendale	CA	91203	818-244-2952	
Zymeworks Inc 540-1385 W 8th Ave *Web:* www.zymeworks.com	Vancouver	BC	V6H3V9	604-678-1388	737-7077

232 DISPLAYS - EXHIBIT & TRADE SHOW

Company	City	State	Zip	Phone	Fax
3D Exhibits Inc 2900 Lively Blvd *TF:* 800-471-9617 ■ *Web:* www.3dexhibits.com	Elk Grove Village	IL	60007	847-250-9000	860-8165
Agricenter International Inc 7777 Walnut Grove Rd Ste 9 *Web:* www.agricenter.org	Memphis	TN	38120	901-757-7777	
Benchmarc360? Inc 3220 Pointe Pkwy Ste 500 *Web:* www.benchmarc360.com	Atlanta	GA	30092	678-291-0011	
Cave City Convention Center 502 Mammoth Cave St *Web:* cavecity.com	Cave City	KY	42127	270-773-3131	
CB Displays International 5141 S Procyon *Web:* www.cbdisplays.com	Las Vegas	NV	89118	702-739-9301	
Condit Exhibits LLC 500 W Tennessee Ave *Web:* www.condit.com	Denver	CO	80223	303-744-7167	
David Monn LLC 135 W 27th St Ste 2 *Web:* davidmonn.com	New York City	NY	10001	212-242-2009	
Derse Exhibits Inc 3800 W Canal St *Web:* www.derse.com	Milwaukee	WI	53208	414-257-2000	
Design & Production Inc 7110 Rainwater Pl *Web:* www.d-and-p.com	Lorton	VA	22079	703-550-8640	339-0296
Downing Displays Inc 550 Techne Ctr Dr *TF:* 800-883-1800 ■ *Web:* www.downingdisplays.com	Milford	OH	45150	513-248-9800	248-2605
Dulles Expo & Conference Center 4320 Chantilly Shopping Ctr Dr *Web:* www.dullesexpo.com	Chantilly	VA	20151	703-378-0910	
Exhibits & More 7843 Goguen Dr *Web:* www.exhibitsandmore.com	Liverpool	NY	13090	315-652-0383	
Expon Exhibits 909 Fee Dr *TF:* 800-783-9766 ■ *Web:* www.exponexhibits.com	Sacramento	CA	95815	916-924-1600	
Frank Strategic Marketing Inc 8320 Main St *Web:* www.frankbiz.com	Ellicott City	MD	21043	410-203-1228	
Gilbert Displays Inc 110 Spagnoli Rd *TF:* 855-577-1100 ■ *Web:* www.gilbertdisplays.com	Melville	NY	11747	631-577-1100	577-1139
Group360 Inc 1227 Washington Ave *Web:* www.group360.com	Saint Louis	MO	63103	314-260-6360	
Hadley Exhibits Inc 1700 Elmwood Ave *Web:* hadleyexhibitsinc.com	Buffalo	NY	14207	716-874-3666	874-9994

Phone Fax

Hargrove Inc 1 Hargrove Dr .... Lanham MD 20706 301-306-9000
Web: www.caw.ca

HB Stubbs Co 27027 Mound Rd .... Warren MI 48092 586-574-9700 574-9741
Web: www.hbstubbs.com

Human Movement LLC 1111 S St .... Louisville CO 80027 855-464-6601
TF: 855-464-6601 ■ *Web:* www.humanmovement.me

Informex Holdings LLC
2nd Fl 212 Carnegie Ctr Ste 203 .... Princeton NJ 08540 609-759-4700
Web: www.informex.com

Launch Incentives Inc
224 Greenfield Ave Ste B .... San Anselmo CA 94960 415-457-1701
Web: www.launchincentives.com

Lynch Exhibits 7 Campus Dr...................... Burlington NJ 08016 609-387-1600 239-1669
Web: www.lynchexhibits.com

Marketechs Exhibit Design 3425 Woodbridge Cir.......... York PA 17406 717-764-2588
Web: www.marketechs.com

massAV 80 Cambridge St......................... Burlington MA 01803 800-423-7830
TF: 800-423-7830 ■ *Web:* www.massav.com

MG Design Assoc Corp 8778 100th St........... Pleasant Prairie WI 53158 262-947-8890 947-8898
Web: www.mgdesign.com

MJM Creative Services Inc 71 5th Ave. .... New York NY 10003 212-924-7070
Web: www.mjmcreative.com

Motor Trend Auto Shows Inc P.O. Box 4097......... Harrisburg PA 17111 717-566-6100
Web: www.motortrendautoshows.com

MyTicketIn com 2100 W Loop Ste 205 .... Houston TX 77027 713-429-1560
Web: www.myticketin.com

Northeern Kentucky Convention Center
1 W River Ctr Blvd .... Covington KY 41011 859-261-1500
Web: www.nkycc.com

Opts Ideas One Gate Six Rd Ste B203 .... Sausalito CA 94965 415-339-2020
Web: www.optsideas.com

Pamela Ferrari Productions
1625 Shirley Dr .... Pleasant Hill CA 94523 925-798-1284
Web: www.pamelaferrariproductions.com

Plan-it Interactive 150 W Industrial Way............... Benicia CA 94510 707-752-6010
Web: www.interactivegame.com

Quikey Manufacturing Co Inc 100 Thorpe Rd.......... Orlando FL 32824 407-859-7517
Web: m.quikey.com

R G Canning Companies 4525 E 59th Pl .... Maywood CA 90270 323-560-7469
Web: www.rgcshows.com

Rising Media Inc
211 E Victoria St Ste E .... Santa Barbara CA 93101 805-403-4075
Web: www.risingmedia.com

Siegel Display Products 300 Sixth Ave N.......... Minneapolis MN 55401 612-340-1493 230-5598*
**Fax Area Code:* 800 ■ *TF:* 800-626-0322 ■ *Web:* www.siegeldisplay.com

Sparks Exhibits & Environments
10232 Palm Dr.......................... Santa Fe Springs CA 90670 562-941-0101
Web: www.sparksonline.com

Zig Zibit Inc 6541 Meridian Dr Ste 143 .... Raleigh NC 27616 919-876-5828
Web: www.zigzibit.com

233 DISPLAYS - POINT-OF-PURCHASE

See Also Signs p. 3185

Phone Fax

Acrylic Design Assoc 6050 Nathan Ln N.............. Plymouth MN 55442 763-559-8395 559-2589
TF: 800-445-2167 ■ *Web:* www.acrylicdesign.com

AMD Industries Inc 4620 W 19th St.................... Cicero IL 60804 708-863-8900 863-2065
TF: 800-367-9999 ■ *Web:* www.amdpop.com

Apco Products Inc PO Box 236 .... Essex CT 06426 860-767-2108 767-7259
Web: www.apco-products.com

Archbold Container Corp
800 W Barre Rd PO Box 10.......................... Archbold OH 43502 419-445-8865 446-2529
TF: 800-446-2520 ■ *Web:* www.archboldcontainer.com

Arlington Display Industries
19303 W Davison St.............................. Detroit MI 48223 313-837-1212
Web: www.arlingtondisplay.com

Array Marketing 45 Progress Ave..................... Toronto ON M1P2Y6 416-299-4865 292-9759
TF: 800-295-4120 ■ *Web:* www.arraymarketing.com

Art-Phyl Creations 16250 NW 48th Ave............... Hialeah FL 33014 305-624-2333
TF: 800-327-8318 ■ *Web:* hookstoresales.com

Artkraft Strauss LLC 1776 Broadway Ste 1810 .... New York NY 10019 212-265-5155 265-5159
Web: www.artkraft.com

Cannon Equipment Co 15100 Business Pkwy .... Rosemount MN 55068 651-322-6300 322-1583
Web: www.cannonequipment.com

Chicago Display Marketing Corp 2021 W St........ River Grove IL 60171 708-842-0001 681-0010*
**Fax Area Code:* 800 ■ *TF:* 800-681-4340 ■ *Web:* www.chicagodisplay.com

Colony Inc 2500 Galvin Dr............................ Elgin IL 60123 847-426-5300
TF: 800-735-1300 ■ *Web:* www.colonydisplay.com

Concept Display & Packaging Corp
20 River Ter .... New York NY 10282 212-566-2359
Web: www.conceptdisplaycorp.com

Display Smart LLC 801 W 27th Terr .... Lawrence KS 66046 785-843-1869
TF: 888-843-1870 ■ *Web:* www.display-smart.com

Display Technologies LLC
1111 Marcus Ave Ste M68...................... Lake Success NY 11042 800-424-4220 321-1932*
**Fax Area Code:* 718 ■ *TF:* 800-424-4220 ■ *Web:* www.display-technologies.com

Felbro Inc 3666 E Olympic Blvd.................... Los Angeles CA 90023 323-263-8686 263-8874
TF: 800-733-5276 ■ *Web:* www.felbrodisplays.com

Frank Mayer & Assoc Inc 1975 Wisconsin Ave .... Grafton WI 53024 855-294-2875 377-3449*
**Fax Area Code:* 262 ■ *TF:* 855-294-2875 ■ *Web:* www.frankmayer.com

Harbor Industries Inc 14130 172nd Ave .... Grand Haven MI 49417 616-842-5330 842-1385
Web: www.harbor-ind.com

Hunter Display 14 Hewlett Ave .... East Patchogue NY 11772 631-475-5900 475-5950
TF: 800-767-2110 ■ *Web:* www.hunterdisplays.com

IDEAL 4800 S Austin Ave............................ Chicago IL 60638 708-594-3100 594-3109
Web: www.idealpop.com

Ideal Wire Works Inc 820 S Date Ave .... Alhambra CA 91803 626-282-0886

Kosakura & Assoc 3 Holland .... Irvine CA 92618 949-529-3400 529-3411
Web: www.kosakura.com

Phone Fax

Lakeshore Display Company Inc
2031 Washington Ave PO Box 983................ Sheboygan WI 53081 920-457-3695 457-5673
Web: www.lakeshoredisplay.com

Lingo Manufacturing Co 7400 Industrial Rd........... Florence KY 41042 859-371-2662 371-0283
TF Cust Svc: 800-354-9771 ■ *Web:* www.lingomfg.com

MDI Worldwide 38271 W 12-Mile Rd.......... Farmington Hills MI 48331 248-553-1900 488-5700*
**Fax:* Sales ■ *TF Sales:* 800-228-8925 ■ *Web:* www.mdiworldwide.com

Millrock
RiverRun Commercial 4660 Early Rd.......... Mt. Crawford VA 22841 540-437-3458
Web: www.riverruncommercial.com

Mpo Videotronics Inc 5069 Maureen Ln............. Moorpark CA 93021 805-499-8513 499-8206
Web: www.mpo-video.com

Nashville Display 306 Hartmann Dr .... Lebanon TN 37087 615-743-2900 743-2901
TF: 800-251-1150 ■ *Web:* www.nashvilledisplay.com

New Dimensions Research Corp
260 Spagnoli Rd................................ Melville NY 11747 631-694-1356 694-6097
TF: 800-637-8870 ■ *Web:* www.ndrc.com

Ovation Instore 57-13 49th Pl...................... Maspeth NY 11378 718-628-2600 386-8171
TF: 800-553-2202 ■ *Web:* www.ovationinstore.com

Rapid Displays 4300 W 47th St.................... Chicago IL 60632 773-927-1091 927-1091
TF: 800-356-5775 ■ *Web:* www.rapiddisplays.com

Service Products Inc 5900 W 51st St.............. Chicago IL 60638 773-767-2360 496-1818*
**Fax Area Code:* 708 ■ *Web:* www.serviceproductsinc.com

Thorco Industries Inc 1300 E 12th St .... Lamar MO 64759 417-682-3375 682-1326
TF: 800-445-3375 ■ *Web:* www.thorco.com

Trans World Marketing Corp
360 Murray Hill Pkwy....................... East Rutherford NJ 07073 201-935-5565 559-2011
Web: www.transworldmarketing.com

United Displaycraft 333 E Touhy Ave .... Des Plaines IL 60018 847-375-3800
TF General: 877-632-8767 ■ *Web:* www.uniteddisplaycraft.com

Universal Display & Fixtures Co
726 E Hwy 121 .... Lewisville TX 75057 972-221-5022 221-6624
TF: 800-235-0701

Visual Marketing Inc 154 W Erie St .... Chicago IL 60654 312-664-9177 664-9473
TF: 800-662-8640 ■ *Web:* www.vmichicago.com

Vulcan Industries Inc 300 Display Dr.................. Moody AL 35004 205-640-2400 640-2412
TF: 888-444-4417 ■ *Web:* www.vulcanind.com

DOOR & WINDOW GLASS

See Glass - Flat, Plate, Tempered p. 2353

234 DOORS & WINDOWS - METAL

See Also Shutters - Window (All Types) p. 3184

Phone Fax

AK Draft Seal Ltd 7470 Buller Ave .... Burnaby BC V5J4S5 604-451-1080
TF: 888-520-9009 ■ *Web:* www.draftseal.com

Allan Window Technologies Ltd 131 Caldari Rd....... Concord ON L4K3Z9 905-738-8600
TF: 800-760-5665 ■ *Web:* www.allanwindows.com

Allmetal Inc 1 Pierce Pl Ste 900 .... Itasca IL 60143 630-250-8090
Web: www.allmetalinc.com

Alweather Windows & Doors Ltd 27 Troop Ave ...... Dartmouth NS B3B2A7 902-468-2605
Web: www.awwd.ca

American Physical Security Group LLC
1030 Goodworth Dr .... Apex NC 27539 919-363-1894
Web: www.americanpsg.com

Amsco Windows Inc 1880 S 1045 W............. Salt Lake City UT 84104 801-978-5000 974-0498
TF: 800-748-4661 ■ *Web:* www.amscowindows.com

Anemostat 1220 Watsoncenter Rd PO Box 4938.......... Carson CA 90745 310-835-7500 835-0448
TF: 877-423-7426 ■ *Web:* www.anemostat.com

Asi Technologies Inc 5848 N 95th Ct .... Milwaukee WI 53225 414-464-6200 464-9863
TF: 800-558-7068 ■ *Web:* www.asidoors.com

ASSA ABLOY 110 Sargent Dr .... New Haven CT 06511 800-377-3948 777-9042*
**Fax Area Code:* 203 ■ **Fax:* Sales ■ *TF:* 800-377-3948 ■ *Web:* www.assaabloydss.com

Atkinson's Mirror and Glass 909 N Orchard St .... Boise ID 83706 208-375-3762 375-3774
Web: www.atkinsonsmirrorandglass.com

Atrium Cos Inc 3890 W NW Hwy Ste 500................ Dallas TX 75220 214-630-5757
Web: atrium.com

AWP Yale Ogron Mfg 8130 NW 74th Ave.............. Medley FL 33166 305-887-2646 883-1309
Web: www.awpwindowsanddoors.com

Babcock-Davis 9300 73rd Ave N .... Brooklyn Park MN 55428 763-488-9247 488-9248
TF: 888-412-3726 ■ *Web:* www.babcockdavis.com

Ceco Door 9159 Telecom Dr.......................... Milan TN 38358 731-686-8345 686-4211
Web: www.cecodoor.com

Champion Aluminum Corp 140 Eileen Way............ Syosset NY 11791 516-921-6200 921-6370
Web: www.championwindows.com

Clopay Bldg Products Inc 8585 Duke Blvd.............. Mason OH 45040 800-225-6729
TF: 800-225-6729 ■ *Web:* www.clopaydoor.com

Columbia Mfg Corp 14400 S San Pedro St .... Gardena CA 90248 310-327-9300 323-9862
TF: 800-729-3667 ■ *Web:* www.columbiamfg.com

Cook & Boardman Inc 9347 D Ducks Ln Ste A .... Charlotte NC 28273 704-334-8683 334-9366
Web: www.cookandboardman.com

Cookson Co 2417 S 50th Ave........................ Phoenix AZ 85043 602-272-4244 233-2132
TF: 800-294-4358 ■ *Web:* www.cooksondoor.com

Cornell Iron Works Inc 24 Elmwood Rd........... Mountain Top PA 18707 570-474-6773 474-9973
TF: 800-233-8366 ■ *Web:* www.cornelliron.com

Cornell Storefront Systems Inc
140 Maffet St .... Wilkes-barre PA 18705 570-706-2775
Web: www.cornellstorefronts.com

Curries Co 1502 12th St NW .... Mason City IA 50401 641-423-1334 424-8305
Web: www.curries.com

Dawson Metal Company Inc 825 Allen St .... Jamestown NY 14701 716-664-3815 664-3485
Web: www.dawsonmetal.com

Deansteel Manufacturing Co 111 Merchant .... San Antonio TX 78204 210-226-8271
TF: 800-825-8271 ■ *Web:* www.deansteel.com

Dominion Bldg Products
6949 Fairbanks N Houston Rd .... Houston TX 77040 800-826-2617 466-8177*
**Fax Area Code:* 713 ■ *TF:* 800-826-2617 ■ *Web:* www.dominionproducts.com

Door Components Inc 7980 Redwood Ave............ Fontana CA 92336 909-770-5700
TF: 866-989-3667 ■ *Web:* www.doorcomponents.com

				Phone	Fax
Drew Industries Inc 200 Mamaroneck Ave.	White Plains	NY	10601	914-428-9098	
NYSE: DW ■ *Web:* www.drewindustries.com					
Dunbarton Corp PO Box 8577	Dothan	AL	36304	800-633-7553	
TF: 800-633-7553 ■ *Web:* www.dunbarton.com					
Dynaflair Corp 8147 Eagle Palm Dr	Tampa	FL	33605	813-248-8100	
Web: www.dynaflair.com					
Eagle Window & Door Inc 2045 Kerper Blvd.	Dubuque	IA	52001	563-556-2270	
Web: www.eaglewindow.com					
EFCO Corp 1000 County Rd	Monett	MO	65708	417-235-3193	235-7313
TF: 800-221-4169 ■ *Web:* www.efcocorp.com					
Electric Power Door 522 W 27th St.	Hibbing	MN	55746	218-263-8366	
TF: 800-346-5760 ■ *Web:* www.electricpowerdoor.com					
Elixir Industries Inc 24800 Chrisanta Dr Ste 210	Mission Viejo	CA	92691	949-860-5000	860-5011
TF: 800-421-1942 ■ *Web:* www.elixirind.com					
Engineered Products Inc (EPI) 200 Jones St.	Verona	PA	15147	412-423-4000	423-4002
Web: www.epimetal.com					
Fimbel Architectural Door Specialties LLC PO Box 96	Whitehouse	NJ	08888	908-534-1732	
Web: www.fimbelads.com					
Fleming Door Products Ltd 101 Ashbridge Cir	Woodbridge	ON	L4L3R5	800-263-7515	427-1668*
**Fax Area Code:* 905 ■ *TF:* 800-263-7515 ■ *Web:* www.flemingdoor.com					
General Aluminum Company of Texas LLP 1001 W Crosby Rd	Carrollton	TX	75006	972-242-5271	242-7322
Web: www.miwd.com					
GlassCraft Door Co 2002 Brittmoore Rd.	Houston	TX	77043	713-690-8282	690-2919
TF: 800-766-2196 ■ *Web:* www.gcdoor.com					
Graham Architectural Products Corp 1551 Mt Rose Ave	York	PA	17403	717-849-8100	849-8148
TF: 800-755-6274 ■ *Web:* www.grahamwindows.com					
Habersham Metal Products Co 264 Stapleton Rd	Cornelia	GA	30531	706-778-2212	778-2769
Web: www.habershammetal.com					
Hehr International Inc 3333 Casitas Ave.	Los Angeles	CA	90039	323-663-1261	666-2372
Web: www.hehrintl.com					
Hope's Windows Inc 84 Hopkins Ave PO Box 580	Jamestown	NY	14702	716-665-5124	665-3365
Web: www.hopeswindows.com					
Hufcor Inc 2101 Kennedy Rd	Janesville	WI	53545	608-756-1241	756-1246
TF: 800-356-6968 ■ *Web:* www.hufcor.com					
Hygrade Metal Moulding Manufacturing Corp 1990 Highland Ave	Bethlehem	PA	18020	610-866-2441	866-3761
TF: 800-645-9475 ■ *Web:* www.hygrademetal.com					
International Revolving Door Co 2138 N Sixth Ave	Evansville	IN	47710	812-425-3311	426-2682
TF: 800-745-4726 ■ *Web:* www.intlentrance.com					
International Window Corp 5625 E Firestone Blvd.	South Gate	CA	90280	562-928-6411	928-3492
TF: 800-477-4032 ■ *Web:* www.intlwindow.com					
J T Walker Industries Inc 861 N Hercules Ave	Clearwater	FL	33765	727-461-0501	443-7167
Jamison Door Co 55 JV Jamison Dr	Hagerstown	MD	21740	301-733-3100	329-5155*
**Fax Area Code:* 240 ■ *TF:* 800-532-3667 ■ *Web:* www.jamisondoor.com					
Jantek Industries 230 Rt 70	Medford	NJ	08055	609-654-1030	654-1083
TF: 888-782-7937 ■ *Web:* jantekwindows.com					
Joyce Windows 1125 Berea Industrial Pkwy	Berea	OH	44017	440-239-9100	
TF: 800-824-7988 ■ *Web:* www.joycewindows.com					
Kane Manufacturing Corp 515 N Fraley St.	Kane	PA	16735	814-837-6464	
TF: 800-952-6399 ■ *Web:* www.kanesterling.com					
Kawneer Company Inc 555 Guthridge Ct.	Norcross	GA	30092	770-449-5555	734-1560
Web: www.kawneer.com					
Kinro Inc 2703 College Ave	Goshen	IN	46528	574-535-1125	
Web: www.kinro.com					
Krieger Specialty Products Co 4880 Gregg Rd	Pico Rivera	CA	90660	562-695-0645	692-0146
TF: 866-203-5060 ■ *Web:* www.kriegerproducts.com					
LaForce Inc 1060 W Mason St.	Green Bay	WI	54303	920-497-7100	497-4955
TF: 800-236-8858 ■ *Web:* www.laforceinc.com					
Liberty Glass & Metal Industries Inc 339 Riverside Dr.	North Grosvenordale	CT	06255	860-923-3623	
Web: www.libertywindowsystems.com					
Lockheed Window Corp Rt 100 PO Box 166	Pascoag	RI	02859	401-568-3061	568-2273
TF: 800-537-3061 ■ *Web:* www.lockheedwindow.com					
Logan Square Aluminum Supply Inc 2500 N Pulaski Rd	Chicago	IL	60639	773-235-2500	
Web: www.remodelerssupply.com					
Loxcreen Co Inc, The 1630 Old Dunbar Rd PO Box 4004	West Columbia	SC	29172	803-822-8200	822-8547
TF: 800-330-5699 ■ *Web:* www.loxcreen.com					
M-D Bldg Products Inc 4041 N Santa Fe Ave	Oklahoma City	OK	73118	405-528-4411	
TF Cust Svc: 800-654-8454 ■ *Web:* mdbuildingproducts.com					
Mannix Architectural Window Products 345 Crooked Hill Rd.	Brentwood	NY	11717	631-231-0800	231-0571
Web: mannixwindows.com					
McKeon Door Co 44 Sawgrass Dr	Bellport	NY	11713	631-803-3000	803-3030
TF: 800-266-9392 ■ *Web:* www.mckeondoor.com					
Megadoor Inc 611 Hwy 74 S Ste 100	Peachtree City	GA	30269	770-631-9086	
Web: www.megadoor.com					
MI Windows & Doors Inc 650 W Market St.	Gratz	PA	17030	717-365-3300	365-3780
Web: www.miwd.com					
Mid-America Precision Products LLC 1927 W Fourth St	Joplin	MO	64801	417-623-2285	
Web: www.midampp.com					
Milgo Industrial Inc 68 Lombardi St	Brooklyn	NY	11222	718-388-6476	963-0614
Web: www.milgo-bufkin.com					
MM Systems Corp 50 MM Way	Pendergrass	GA	30567	706-824-7500	824-7501
TF: 800-241-3460 ■ *Web:* www.mmsystemscorp.com					
Moss Supply Company Inc 5001 N Graham St.	Charlotte	NC	28269	704-596-8717	598-9012
TF: 800-438-0770 ■ *Web:* www.mosssupply.com					
Napoleon Spring Works 111 Weires Dr.	Archbold	OH	43502	419-445-1010	
Web: www.lynx-nsw.com					
National Guard Products Inc 4985 E Raines Rd.	Memphis	TN	38118	800-647-7874	255-7874
TF: 800-647-7874 ■ *Web:* www.ngpinc.com					
Northeast Bldg Products Corp 4280 Aramingo Ave	Philadelphia	PA	19124	215-535-7110	288-9880
Web: www.nbpcorporation.com					
Nystrom Inc 9300 73rd Ave N	Minneapolis	MN	55428	763-488-9200	317-8770*
**Fax Area Code:* 800 ■ *TF:* 800-547-2635 ■ *Web:* www.nystrom.com					
O'Keeffe's Inc 325 Newhall St.	San Francisco	CA	94124	415-822-4222	
TF: 888-653-3333 ■ *Web:* www.okeeffes.com					
Optimum Technologies Inc 570 Joe Frank Harris Pkwy PO Box 1537	Cartersville	GA	30120	770-386-3470	382-9047
Web: www.otitech.com					
Optimum Window Manufacturing 28 Canal St	Ellenville	NY	12428	845-647-1900	
Web: www.optimumwindow.com					
Overhead Door Corp 2501 S State Hwy 121 Bus Ste 200	Lewisville	TX	75067	469-549-7100	549-7281
TF: 800-275-3290 ■ *Web:* www.overheaddoor.com					
Overly Manufacturing Co 574 W Otterman St.	Greensburg	PA	15601	724-834-7300	830-2871
TF: 800-979-7300 ■ *Web:* www.overly.com					
Peelle Co 373 Nesconset Hwy Ste 311	Hauppauge	NY	11788	905-846-4545	846-2161
TF: 800-787-5020 ■ *Web:* www.peelledoor.com					
Peerless Products Inc 2403 S Main St	Fort Scott	KS	66701	620-223-4610	224-3107
TF: 800-279-9999 ■ *Web:* www.peerless-usa.com					
PGT Industries 1070 Technology Dr	Nokomis	FL	34275	941-480-1600	486-8369
TF: 800-282-6019 ■ *Web:* www.pgtindustries.com					
Phillips Manufacturing Co 4949 S 30th St.	Omaha	NE	68107	402-339-3800	
Web: www.phillipsmfg.com					
Pioneer Industries Inc 111 Kero Rd	Carlstadt	NJ	07072	201-933-1900	933-9580
Web: www.pioneerindustries.com					
Portal Inc 10 Tracy Dr	Avon	MA	02322	508-588-3030	
Web: www.portalincorporated.com					
Quaker Window Products Inc 504 S Hwy 63 PO Box 128	Freeburg	MO	65035	800-347-0438	744-5586*
**Fax Area Code:* 573 ■ *TF:* 800-347-0438 ■ *Web:* www.quakerwindows.com					
Raynor Garage Doors 1101 E River Rd.	Dixon	IL	61021	815-288-1431	
TF: 800-472-9667 ■ *Web:* www.raynor.com					
RC Aluminum Industries 2805 NW 75th Ave.	Miami	FL	33122	305-592-1515	392-2184
Rebco Inc 1171-1225 Madison Ave.	Paterson	NJ	07509	973-684-0200	684-0118
TF: 800-777-0787 ■ *Web:* www.rebcoinc.com					
Reese Enterprises Inc 16350 Asher Ave	Rosemount	MN	55068	651-423-1126	423-2662
TF: 800-328-0953 ■ *Web:* www.reeseusa.com					
Richards-Wilcox Inc 600 S Lake St	Aurora	IL	60506	800-253-5668	897-6994*
**Fax Area Code:* 630 ■ *TF:* 800-253-5668 ■ *Web:* www.richardswilcox.com					
Rochester Colonial Manufacturing Inc 1794 Lyell Ave	Rochester	NY	14606	585-254-8191	
Web: www.rochestercolonial.com					
Rytec Corp 1 Cedar Pkwy.	Jackson	WI	53037	262-677-9046	
Web: www.rytecdoors.com					
Seaway Manufacturing Corp 2250 E 33rd St.	Erie	PA	16510	814-898-2255	
Web: www.seawaymfg.com					
Sellmore Industries Inc 815 Smith St.	Buffalo	NY	14206	716-854-1600	856-4509
Web: www.sellmoreind.com					
Silver Line Bldg Products 1 Silver Line Dr.	North Brunswick	NJ	08902	732-247-2030	
Web: www.silverlinewindows.com					
Smith & DeShields Inc 165 NW 20th St.	Boca Raton	FL	33431	561-395-0808	
Web: www.smithanddeshields.com					
Southeastern Aluminum Products Inc 6701 Suemac Pl	Jacksonville	FL	32254	904-781-8200	224-8068
TF Sales: 800-243-8200 ■ *Web:* www.southeasternaluminum.com					
Southeastern Metals Mfg Company Inc 11801 Industry Dr.	Jacksonville	FL	32218	904-757-4200	
TF: 800-874-0335 ■ *Web:* www.semetals.com					
Special-Lite Inc PO Box 6	Decatur	MI	49045	269-423-7068	423-7610
TF: 800-821-6531 ■ *Web:* www.special-lite.com					
Stanley Access Technologies 65 Scott Swamp Rd	Farmington	CT	06032	860-677-2861	339-7923*
**Fax Area Code:* 877 ■ **Fax:* Cust Svc ■ *TF:* 800-722-2377 ■ *Web:* www.stanleyaccess.com					
Steelcraft Mfg Co 9017 Blue Ash Rd	Cincinnati	OH	45242	513-745-6400	451-7754*
**Fax Area Code:* 800 ■ *TF Cust Svc:* 877-613-8766 ■ *Web:* us.allegion.com					
Steves & Sons Inc 203 Humble Ave.	San Antonio	TX	78225	210-924-5111	924-0470*
**Fax:* Sales ■ *Web:* www.stevesdoors.com					
Sun Windows Inc 1515 E 18th St	Owensboro	KY	42303	270-684-0691	
Web: www.sunwindows.com					
Super Sky Products Inc 10301 N Enterprise Dr.	Mequon	WI	53092	262-242-2000	242-7409
TF: 800-558-0467 ■ *Web:* www.supersky.com					
Taylor Bldg Products 631 N First St	West Branch	MI	48661	989-345-5110	345-5116
TF: 800-248-3600 ■ *Web:* www.taylordoor.com					
Tempco Products Co 301 E Tempco Ave.	Robinson	IL	62454	618-544-3175	
Web: www.tempcoproducts.com					
Therma-Tru Corp 1750 Indian Wood Cir.	Maumee	OH	43537	419-891-7400	891-7411
TF: 800-537-8827 ■ *Web:* www.thermatru.com					
Thermo-Twin Industries Inc 1155 Allegheny Ave	Oakmont	PA	15139	412-826-1000	826-8188
TF: 800-641-2211 ■ *Web:* www.thermotwin.com					
TRACO 71 Progress Ave	Cranberry Township	PA	16066	724-776-7000	776-7014
TF: 800-992-4444 ■ *Web:* www.alcoa.com					
Traditional Door Design & Millwork Ltd 261 Regina Rd	Woodbridge	ON	L4L8M3	416-747-1992	
TF: 877-226-9930 ■ *Web:* www.traditionaldoor.com					
Tubelite Inc 4878 Mackinaw Trl	Reed City	MI	49677	800-866-2227	
TF: 800-866-2227 ■ *Web:* www.tubeliteinc.com					
Wayne-Dalton Corp 1 Door Dr PO Box 67	Mount Hope	OH	44660	330-674-7015	
TF: 800-827-3667 ■ *Web:* www.wayne-dalton.com					
West Window Corp 226 Industrial Pk Dr	Martinsville	VA	24112	276-638-2394	638-2300
TF: 800-446-4167 ■ *Web:* www.westwindow.com					
Western Window Systems 5621 S 25th St	Phoenix	AZ	85040	602-268-1300	
Web: westernwindowsystems.com					
Willo Products Company Inc 714 Willo Industrial Dr SE	Decatur	AL	35601	256-353-7161	350-8436
Web: www.willoproducts.com					
Won-Door Corp 1865 South 3480 West.	Salt Lake City	UT	84104	801-973-7500	974-5273
TF: 800-453-8494 ■ *Web:* www.wondoor.com					

Phone Fax

Young Windows Inc 680 Colwell Ln. . . . . Conshohocken PA 19428 610-828-5422 828-2144
Web: www.youngwindows.com

235 DOORS & WINDOWS - VINYL

Phone Fax

American Exteriors LLC
1169 W Littleton Blvd. . . . . Littleton CO 80120 303-794-6369
TF: 800-794-6369 ■ *Web:* www.amext.com

Amerimax Bldg Products Inc 5208 Tennyson Pkwy. . . . . Plano TX 75024 469-366-3200 448-8391*
**Fax Area Code:* 800 ■ *Web:* www.amerimaxbp.com

Associated Materials Inc Alside Div
PO Box 2010 . . . . Akron OH 44309 800-922-6009
TF Cust Svc: 800-922-6009 ■ *Web:* www.alside.com

CertainTeed Corp 750 E Swedesford Rd. . . . . Valley Forge PA 19482 610-341-7000 341-7777
TF Prod Info: 800-782-8777 ■ *Web:* www.certainteed.com

Champion Window Mfg Inc
12121 Champion Way . . . . Cincinnati OH 45241 513-346-4600 346-4614
TF: 877-424-2674 ■ *Web:* www.championwindow.com

Chelsea Bldg Products 565 Cedar Way. . . . . Oakmont PA 15139 800-424-3573 826-1598*
**Fax Area Code:* 412 ■ *TF:* 800-424-3573 ■ *Web:* www.chelseabuildingproducts.com

Fortune Brands Home & Hardware Inc
520 Lk Cook Rd . . . . Deerfield IL 60015 847-484-4400
Web: www.fbhs.com

Harry G Barr Co 6500 S Zero St. Fort Smith AR 72903 479-646-7891 646-8591
TF: 800-829-2277 ■ *Web:* www.weatherbarr.com

Larson Manufacturing Co 2333 Eastbrook Dr. . . . . Brookings SD 57006 605-692-6115
TF Cust Svc: 888-483-3768 ■ *Web:* www.larsondoors.com

Moss Supply Company Inc 5001 N Graham St . . . . Charlotte NC 28269 704-596-8717 598-9012
TF: 800-438-0770 ■ *Web:* www.mosssupply.com

PGT Industries 1070 Technology Dr . . . . Nokomis FL 34275 941-480-1600 486-8369
TF: 800-282-6019 ■ *Web:* www.pgtindustries.com

Ply Gem Windows 615 Carson St . . . . Bryan TX 77801 979-779-1051 822-3259

Provia Door Inc 2150 SR- 39 . . . . Sugarcreek OH 44681 330-852-4711 852-2107
TF General: 800-669-4711 ■ *Web:* www.provia.com

Quanex Building Products Corp
1900 W Loop S Ste 1500 . . . . Houston TX 77027 713-961-4600
TF Cust Svc: 888-475-0633 ■ *Web:* quanex.com

Rehau Inc 1501 EdwaRds Ferry Rd NE. . . . . Leesburg VA 20176 703-777-5255 777-3053
TF: 800-247-9445 ■ *Web:* www.rehau.com

Royal Group, The 71 Royal Group Crescent . . . . Woodbridge ON L4H1X9 905-264-0701 850-9184
TF: 800-263-2353 ■ *Web:* www.royalbuildingproducts.com

RubbAir Door Div Eckel Industries Inc
100 Groton Shirley Rd . . . . Ayer MA 01432 978-772-0480 772-7114
TF: 800-966-7822 ■ *Web:* www.rubbair.com

Soft-Lite LLC 10250 Philipp Pkwy . . . . Streetsboro OH 44241 330-528-3400 528-3501
TF: 800-551-1953 ■ *Web:* www.soft-lite.com

Statewide Remodeling Inc
2450 Esters Blvd Ste 200 . . . . DFW Airport TX 75261 214-677-9000
TF: 800-317-8283 ■ *Web:* www.statewideremodeling.com

Superseal Mfg Co Inc PO Box 795 . . . . South Plainfield NJ 07080 908-561-5910 561-7885
TF: 800-433-4873 ■ *Web:* www.supersealwindows.com

Thermal Industries Inc 3700 Haney C. . . . . Murrysville PA 15668 724-733-3880 733-3880
TF: 800-245-1540 ■ *Web:* www.thermalindustries.com

Veka Inc 100 Veka Dr. . . . . Fombell PA 16123 724-452-1000 452-1007
TF: 800-654-5589 ■ *Web:* www.vekainc.com

VINYLMAX LLC 2921 McBride Ct. . . . . Hamilton OH 45011 513-772-2247
Web: www.vinylmax.com

Weather Shield Manufacturing Inc
1 Weather Shield Plz PO Box 309. . . . . Medford WI 54451 715-748-2100 222-2146*
**Fax Area Code:* 800 ■ *TF:* 800-222-2995 ■ *Web:* www.weathershield.com

West Window Corp 226 Industrial Pk Dr . . . . Martinsville VA 24112 276-638-2394 638-2300
TF: 800-446-4167 ■ *Web:* www.westwindow.com

Windsor Windows & Doors
900 S 19th St . . . . West Des Moines IA 50265 515-223-6660 224-1938*
**Fax:* Cust Svc ■ *TF:* 800-218-6186 ■ *Web:* www.windsorwindows.com

236 DOORS & WINDOWS - WOOD

See Also Millwork p. 2771; Shutters - Window (All Types) p. 3184

Phone Fax

1st United Door Technologies Inc
7255 S Kyrene Ste 104. . . . . Tempe AZ 85283 480-705-6632
Web: www.firstudt.com

A B C Doors 5100 S Willow . . . . Houston TX 77035 713-729-9700
Web: www.abcdoors.com

Algoma Hardwoods Inc 1001 Perry St. . . . . Algoma WI 54201 920-487-5221 487-3636
TF: 800-678-8910 ■ *Web:* www.algomahardwoods.com

Allmar Inc 287 Riverton Ave. . . . . Winnipeg MB R2L0N2 204-668-1000 668-3029
TF: 800-230-5516 ■ *Web:* www.allmar.com

Andersen Corp 100 Fourth Ave N . . . . Bayport MN 55003 651-264-5150 264-5107*
**Fax:* Hum Res ■ *TF:* 888-888-7020 ■ *Web:* www.andersenwindows.com

Burton Lumber Corp 835 Wilson Rd. . . . . Chesapeake VA 23324 757-545-4613 545-8852
Web: burton-lumber.com

Combination Door Co 1000 Morris St . . . . Fond du Lac WI 54935 920-922-2050 922-2917
Web: www.combinationdoor.com

Construction Metals LLC 13169 B Slover Ave . . . . Fontana CA 92337 909-390-9880
TF: 800-576-9810 ■ *Web:* www.constructionmetals.com

DIRTT Environmental Solutions Ltd
7303 - 30th St SE. . . . . Calgary AB T2C1N6 403-723-5000
Web: www.dirtt.net

Endura Products Inc 8817 W Market St. . . . . Colfax NC 27235 336-668-2472
TF: 800-334-2006 ■ *Web:* www.enduraproducts.com

EverMark LLC 1050 Northbrook Pkwy . . . . Suwanee GA 30024 678-455-5188
Web: www.evermark-lnl.com

Fene-Tech Inc 264 St-Benoit E Blvd . . . . Amqui QC G5L2C5 418-629-4675 629-3982
Web: www.fene-tech.com

General Doors Corp 1 Monroe St PO Box 205 . . . . Bristol PA 19007 215-788-9277 788-9450
Web: www.general-doors.com

Phone Fax

Great Day Improvements LLC
700 E Highland Rd . . . . Macedonia OH 44056 330-468-0700
TF: 800-230-8301 ■ *Web:* www.greatdayimprovements.com

Haley Bros Inc 6291 Orangethorpe Ave. . . . . Buena Park CA 90620 714-670-2112 994-6971
TF: 800-854-5951 ■ *Web:* www.haleybros.com

Industrial Door Company Inc
360 Coon Rapids Blvd . . . . Minneapolis MN 55433 763-786-4730 786-9186
TF: 888-798-0199 ■ *Web:* www.idc-automatic.com

Jenkins Mfg Company Inc 1608 Frank Akers Rd . . . . Anniston AL 36207 256-831-7000 261-6116*
**Fax Area Code:* 800 ■ *TF:* 800-633-2323 ■ *Web:* www.monarchwindows.com

King Sash & Door Inc
2799 Hope Church Rd . . . . Winston-Salem NC 27127 336-774-3071
Web: www.kingsashanddoor.com

Larson Manufacturing Co 2333 Eastbrook Dr. . . . . Brookings SD 57006 605-692-6115
TF Cust Svc: 888-483-3768 ■ *Web:* www.larsondoors.com

Lincoln Wood Products Inc
1400 W Taylor St PO Box 375 . . . . Merrill WI 54452 800-967-2461 536-7090*
**Fax Area Code:* 715 ■ *TF:* 800-967-2461 ■ *Web:* www.lincolnwindows.com

Marvin Windows & Doors PO Box 100 . . . . Warroad MN 56763 218-386-1430
TF: 888-537-7828 ■ *Web:* www.marvin.com

Masonite International Corp
201 N Franklin St Ste 300. . . . . Tampa FL 33602 813-877-2726 739-0204
TF: 800-895-2723 ■ *Web:* www.masonite.com

Mathews Bros Co 22 Perkins Rd . . . . Belfast ME 04915 207-338-6490 338-6300
TF: 800-615-2004 ■ *Web:* www.mathewsbrothers.com

Mohawk Flush Doors Inc
980 Pt Township Dr PO Box 112 . . . . Northumberland PA 17857 570-473-3557 473-3737
Web: www.mohawkdoors.com

National Vinyl LLC 7 Coburn St . . . . Chicopee MA 01013 413-420-0548
TF: 800-424-5300 ■ *Web:* www.nvpwindows.com

Pella Corp 102 Main St . . . . Pella IA 50219 641-621-1000 621-6950
TF Cust Svc: 877-473-5527 ■ *Web:* www.pella.com

Quaker Window Products Inc
504 S Hwy 63 PO Box 128. . . . . Freeburg MO 65035 800-347-0438 744-5586*
**Fax Area Code:* 573 ■ *TF:* 800-347-0438 ■ *Web:* www.quakerwindows.com

RAM Industries Inc 13119 Mula Ct . . . . Stafford TX 77477 281-495-9056
Web: www.ramwindows.com

Semling-Menke Company Inc PO Box 378 . . . . Merrill WI 54452 715-536-9411 536-3067
TF: 800-333-2206 ■ *Web:* www.semcowindows.com

SNE Enterprises Inc 880 Southview Dr . . . . Mosinee WI 54455 715-693-7000 748-6508*
**Fax:* Hum Res ■ *TF:* 800-826-5509 ■ *Web:* crestlinewindows.com

Steves & Sons Inc 203 Humble Ave. . . . . San Antonio TX 78225 210-924-5111 924-0470*
**Fax:* Sales ■ *Web:* www.stevesdoors.com

Trustile Doors LLC 1780 E 66th Ave. . . . . Denver CO 80229 303-286-3931 288-6521
TF: 866-442-5302 ■ *Web:* www.trustile.com

Vancouver Door Company Inc 203 Fifth St NW . . . . Puyallup WA 98371 253-845-9581 845-3364
TF: 800-999-3667 ■ *Web:* www.vancouverdoorco.com

Weather Shield Manufacturing Inc
1 Weather Shield Plz PO Box 309. . . . . Medford WI 54451 715-748-2100 222-2146*
**Fax Area Code:* 800 ■ *TF:* 800-222-2995 ■ *Web:* www.weathershield.com

WIL-C-MEEK Corp PO Box 1746 . . . . Springfield MO 65804 417-521-2801
Web: meeks.com

Windsor Windows & Doors
900 S 19th St . . . . West Des Moines IA 50265 515-223-6660 224-1938*
**Fax:* Cust Svc ■ *TF:* 800-218-6186 ■ *Web:* www.windsorwindows.com

237 DRUG STORES

See Also Health Food Stores p. 2458

Phone Fax

4D Pharmacy Management Systems Inc
2520 Industrial Row Dr. . . . . Troy MI 48084 248-540-8066
Web: www.4dpharmacy.com

Advanced Lifeline Services Pharmacy Inc
9900 Shelbyville Rd Ste 2b. . . . . Louisville KY 40223 502-423-7525
Web: www.alspharmacy.com

Advanced Optical Systems Inc
6767 Old Madison Pike Ste 410. . . . . Huntsville AL 35806 256-971-0036
Web: www.aos-inc.com

Advanced Pharmacy Concepts Inc
6899 Post Rd . . . . North Kingstown RI 02852 401-295-7660
Web: www.apc-rx.com

Allergychoices Inc 2800 National Dr Ste 100 . . . . Onalaska WI 54650 608-793-1580
TF: 866-793-1680 ■ *Web:* allergychoices.com

Alpha Tech Pet Inc 119 Russell St Ste 21 . . . . Littleton MA 01460 781-861-7179
Web: www.alphatechpet.com

Alternatives for Industry Inc
2251 Whitfield Park Ave . . . . Sarasota FL 34243 941-739-6566
Web: www.afi-tools.com

American GNC Corp 888 E Easy St. . . . . Simi Valley CA 93065 805-582-0582
Web: www.americangnc.com

Apothecary Shoppe, The
1002 East South Temple. . . . . Salt Lake City UT 84102 801-521-6353
Web: www.mygnp.com

Apple Valley Medical Clinic Ltd
14655 Galaxie Ave . . . . Apple Valley MN 55124 952-432-6161
Web: www.applevalleymedicalcenter.com

Aquatrol Inc 237 N Euclid Way Ste H . . . . Anaheim CA 92801 714-533-3381
Web: aquatrol.com

Arbor Centers for Eyecare 2640 W 183rd St . . . . Homewood IL 60430 708-798-6633
TF: 866-798-6633 ■ *Web:* www.arboreyecare.com

Arizona Home Care LLC 1626 S Edward Dr . . . . Tempe AZ 85281 602-252-5000
Web: www.azhomecare.com

ARJ Infusion Services Inc 10049 Lakeview Ave . . . . Lenexa KS 66219 913-451-8804
Web: www.arjinfusion.com

ARW Optical Corp 2021 Capital Dr. . . . . Wilmington NC 28405 910-452-7373
Web: arwoptical.com

Assured Pharmacy Inc 11100 Ash St Ste 200. . . . . Leawood KS 66211 913-602-8344
OTC: APHYQ ■ *Web:* www.assuredrxservices.com

Balcones Dermatology Associates pa
7800 N Mopac Expy Ste 315 . . . . Austin TX 78759 512-459-4869
Web: www.balconesdermatology.com

Phone **Fax**

BCP Veterinary Pharmacy 1614 Webster St ... Houston TX 77003 713-771-1144
TF: 800-481-1729 ■ *Web:* www.bcpvetpharm.com

Bellevue Drug Co 254 Bellevue Ave ... Hammonton NJ 08037 609-561-0825
Web: bellevuedrug.com

Berr Pet Supply Inc 929 N Market Blvd ... Sacramento CA 95834 916-921-0145
Web: berrpet.com

Bi-Mart Corp 220 S Seneca Rd ... Eugene OR 97402 541-344-0681
Web: www.bimart.com

Blue Valley Public Safety Inc
509 James Rollo Dr ... Grain Valley MO 64029 816-847-7502
Web: www.bvpsonline.com

Borak Inc Dba Northfield Pharm
601 Water St S ... Northfield MN 55057 507-663-0344

Braswell Drugs Inc 1107 S Tyler St ... Covington LA 70433 985-892-0818

Brevard Eye Center Inc 665 S Apollo Blvd ... Melbourne FL 32901 321-984-3200
Web: www.brevardeye.com

Brite Pharmacy Inc Dba Vital Script
83 17/19 37th Ave ... Jackson Heights NY 11372 718-424-1101

Buffalo Pharmacies Inc 1479 Kensington Ave ... Buffalo NY 14215 716-832-0599
Web: www.buffalopharmacies.com

C Stuart Inc Dba Columbia Pharmacy
2840 Long Beach Blvd ... Long Beach CA 90806 562-426-0303

Cajahs Mountain Discount Drug Inc
2006 Connelly Springs Rd ... Lenoir NC 28645 828-726-8632

Calgary Co-Operative Association Ltd
110151 86th Ave SE Ste 110 ... Calgary AB T2H3A5 403-219-6025
Web: www.calgarycoop.com

Care Service Inc 34099 Melinz Pkwy Unit F ... Eastlake OH 44095 440-954-7709
Web: www.diabeticexpress.com

Carepoint Inc 215 E Bay St Ste 304 ... Charleston SC 29401 843-853-6999
TF: 800-296-1825 ■ *Web:* carepoint.com

Centric Health Resources Inc
17877 Chesterfield Airport Rd ... Chesterfield MO 63005 636-519-2400
Web: www.centrichealthresources.com

CHEM Rx 750 Park Pl ... Long Beach NY 11561 516-889-8770
Web: www.chemrx.net

Classic Care Pharmacy Corp 1320 Heine Ct ... Burlington ON L7L6L9 905-631-9027
Web: www.classiccare.ca

Classic Optical Laboratories Inc
3710 Belmont Ave ... Youngstown OH 44505 330-759-8245
Web: www.classicoptical.com

Cloneys Pharmacy Inc 525 Fifth St ... Eureka CA 95501 707-443-1614
Web: cloneys.com

Community Pharmacies LP 16 Commerce Dr Ste 1 ... Augusta ME 04332 800-730-4840
TF: 800-730-4840 ■ *Web:* www.communityrx.com

Complete Rx Ltd 3100 S Gessner Rd Ste 640 ... Houston TX 77063 713-355-1196 355-5404
Web: completerx.com

CVS Corp 1 CVS Dr ... Woonsocket RI 02895 401-765-1500 765-1500*
**Fax:* Cust Svc ■ *TF Cust Svc:* 888-607-4287 ■ *Web:* www.cvs.com

DailyMe Inc 4000 Hollywood Blvd Ste 745-S ... Hollywood FL 33021 954-922-2999
Web: www.dailyme.com

Data Rx Management 305 W Woodard St ... Denison TX 75020 903-465-0798
Web: www.data-rx.com

Davila Pharmacy Inc 1423 Guadalupe St ... San Antonio TX 78207 210-226-5293 224-9257
Web: www.davilapharmacy.com

Davis Ethical Pharmacy
124 N Long Beach Rd ... Rockville Centre NY 11570 516-764-3200

Discount Drug Mart Inc 211 Commerce Dr ... Medina OH 44256 330-725-2340 722-2990
TF: 800-833-6278 ■ *Web:* www.discount-drugmart.com

Doc's Drugs 230 Comet Dr ... Braidwood IL 60408 815-458-6104 458-6158
Web: www.docsdrugs.com

Dons Pharmacy 32 S Frederick Ave ... Oelwein IA 50662 319-283-5254

Dougherty's Holdings Inc
16250 Dallas Pkwy Ste 102 ... Dallas TX 75248 214-373-5300 860-0290*
**Fax Area Code:* 972 ■ *Web:* www.doughertys.com/corporate

Drugstore.com Inc 411 108th Ave NE Ste 1400 ... Bellevue WA 98004 800-378-4786 372-3800*
**Fax Area Code:* 425 ■ *TF:* 800-378-4786 ■ *Web:* www.drugstore.com

Empson Drug Co 212 N Main St ... Ashland City TN 37015 615-792-4644

Estates Pharmacy Inc 169-01 Hillside Ave ... Jamaica NY 11432 718-739-0311

Esther Pharmacy Inc 71 S Broadway ... Yonkers NY 10701 914-965-2661
Web: estherpharmacy.com

Eye Care for Animals 372 S Milwaukee Ave ... Wheeling IL 60090 847-215-3933
TF: 877-617-3937 ■ *Web:* www.eyecareforanimals.com

Eye Center Surgeons & Associates Ll
401 Meridian St N Ste 200 ... Huntsville AL 35801 256-705-3937
TF: 800-233-9083 ■ *Web:* www.eyecentersurgeons.com

Fagen Pharmacy 915 S Halleck St PO Box 662 ... Demotte IN 46310 219-987-6468 987-7226
Web: www.fagenpharmacy.com

Findleys Pharmacy Inc 136 W Main St ... Somerset PA 15501 814-445-7939
Web: findleyspharmacy.com

Flare Industries Inc
16310 Bratton Lnn Bldg 3 Ste 350 ... Austin TX 78728 512-836-9473
Web: www.flareindustries.com

Fraser Hearing & Optical Center
32925 Groesbeck Hwy ... Fraser MI 48026 586-293-8888
Web: www.fraseroptical.com

Fruth Pharmacy Inc 4016 Ohio River Rd ... Point Pleasant WV 25550 304-675-1612 675-7338
TF: 800-438-5390 ■ *Web:* www.fruthpharmacy.com

Gemmel Pharmacy Group Inc 143 N Euclid Ave ... Ontario CA 91762 909-988-0591
TF: 888-302-0229 ■ *Web:* www.gemmelrx.com

General Hearing Corp
175 Brookhollow Esplanade ... Harahan LA 70123 504-733-3767
TF: 800-824-3021 ■ *Web:* www.generalhearing.com

Geneva Woods Pharmacy Inc
501 W International Airport Rd Ste 1A ... Anchorage AK 99518 907-565-6100
Web: www.genevawoods.com

Gloyer'S Pharmacy Inc 1010 W Main St ... Tomball TX 77375 281-351-5454
Web: gloyersrx.com

Good Day Pharmacy 2033 Boise Ave ... Loveland CO 80538 970-669-7500
Web: www.gooddaypharmacy.com

Grandview Pharmacy Inc 2230 N Park Rd ... Connersville IN 47331 765-827-0847
Web: www.grandviewpharmacy.com

Phone **Fax**

Graymark Healthcare Inc
210 Pk Ave Ste 1350 ... Oklahoma City OK 73102 405-601-5300
NASDAQ: GRMH ■ *Web:* fdnh.com

GT Distributors Inc 100 McFarland Ave ... Rossville GA 30741 706-866-2764
Web: www.gtdist.com

Hallmark Pharmacy
1316 Sycamore School Rd Ste 130 ... Fort Worth TX 76134 817-293-2441

Harmon Stores Inc 650 Liberty Ave ... Union NJ 07083 866-427-6661 688-0376*
**Fax Area Code:* 908 ■ *TF:* 866-427-6661 ■ *Web:* www.harmondiscount.com

Hartig Drug Co 703 Main St ... Dubuque IA 52001 563-588-8700 588-8750
Web: www.hartigdrug.com

Health Care Unlimited Inc 1100 E Laurel Ave ... Mcallen TX 78501 956-994-9911
Web: www.hcuinc.com

Highlander Charter School, The
42 Lexington Ave ... Providence RI 02907 401-277-2600
Web: www.highlandercharter.org

Horton & Converse Pharmacy
120 Newport Ctr Dr Ste 250 ... Newport Beach CA 92660 949-640-1231
Web: www.hortonandconverse.com

In Focus Optical 202 Cherry St ... Milford CT 06460 203-882-7278
Web: www.infocussystems.com

International Eyecare Center Inc
2445 Broadway ... Quincy IL 62301 217-222-8800
Web: www.iec2020.com

Interstate Optical Co 680 Lindaire Ln ... Mansfield OH 44901 419-529-6800
Web: interstateoptical.com

Irsfeld Pharmacy PC 33 Ninth St W ... Dickinson ND 58601 701-483-4858
Web: irsfeldpharmacy.com

Janoka Inc Dba The Medicine Shoppe
542 S Eufaula Ave ... Eufaula AL 36027 334-687-0021

Jean Coutu Group (PJC) Inc
530 Rue Beriault ... Longueuil QC J4G1S8 450-646-9760
TSE: PJC.A ■ *TF:* 877-695-6175 ■ *Web:* www.jeancoutu.com

Katz Group
10104 103rd Ave Ste 1702 Bell Tower ... Edmonton AB T5J0H8 780-990-0505
TF: 866-323-9695 ■ *Web:* www.katzgroup.ca

Kinney Drugs Inc 520 E Main St ... Gouverneur NY 13642 315-287-3600
Web: www.kinneydrugs.com

Kizer Pharmacy LLC 1117 S Miles Ave Ste 1 ... Union City TN 38261 731-885-2226

KMC Exim Corp 1 Harbor Park Dr ... Port Washington NY 11050 516-621-6565

Kontos Inc Dba Alexander'S Pharmacy
505 Nashua Rd ... Dracut MA 01826 978-957-0330

Kopp Drug 1405 13th Ave ... Altoona PA 16601 814-949-9512

KPS Health Plans Inc
400 Warren Ave PO Box 339 ... Bremerton WA 98337 360-377-5576
Web: www.kpshealthplans.com

LA Central Pharmacy Inc
2221 Beverly Blvd ... Los Angeles CA 90057 213-483-3929
Web: mycentralpharmacy.com

Lacey Drug Company Inc 4797 S Main St ... Acworth GA 30101 770-974-3131
Web: laceydrug.com

Lachman Imports Inc 230 Fifth Ave Ste 900 ... New York NY 10001 212-532-1030
Web: www.guinotusa.com

Lee Silsby Compounding Pharmacy
3216 Silsby Rd ... Cleveland Heights OH 44118 216-321-4300 321-4303
TF: 800-918-8831 ■ *Web:* www.leesilsby.com

Lehan Drugs Inc 1407 S Fourth St ... Dekalb IL 60115 815-758-0911
Web: lehandrugs.com

Lewis Drug Inc 4409 E 26th St ... Sioux Falls SD 57103 605-367-2710 367-2876
Web: www.lewisdrug.com

Liberty Drug & Surgical Inc 195 Main St ... Chatham NJ 07928 973-635-6200 635-6208
TF: 877-816-0111 ■ *Web:* www.libertydrug.com

Love Stores 144 W 72nd St ... New York NY 10023 212-877-5351

Luzerne Optical Laboratories Ltd
180 N Wilkes Barre Blvd ... Wilkes-barre PA 18702 570-822-3183
Web: www.luzerneoptical.com

Mabiles Corner Pharmacy 100 Gulf St ... Coushatta LA 71019 318-932-5727

Majestic Drug Company Inc
4996 Main St Rt 42 ... South Fallsburg NY 12779 845-436-0011
Web: www.majesticdrug.com

Martin Avenue Pharmacy
10 W Martin Ave Ste 1 ... Naperville IL 60540 630-355-6400
Web: www.critterchronicle.com

Mast Drug Company Inc 1910 Ross Mill Rd ... Henderson NC 27537 252-438-3112
Web: www.mastdrug.com

Medical Center Pharmacy 2401 N Ocoee St ... Cleveland TN 37311 423-476-5548
TF: 877-753-9555 ■ *Web:* www.medicalcenterrx.com

Medical Park Pharmacy Inc 301 Penny Ln ... Morehead City NC 28557 252-726-0777
Web: www.medicalparkpharmacy.net

Medicap Pharmacies Inc
1 Rider Trail Plaza Dr ... Earth City MO 63045 314-993-6000
TF: 800-407-8055 ■ *Web:* www.medicap.com

MedMeme LLC 501 Seventh Ave Ste 508 ... New York NY 10018 212-725-5990
Web: www.medmeme.com

Mehron Inc
100 Red Schoolhouse Rd Ste C2 ... Spring Valley NY 10977 845-426-1700
Web: www.mehron.com

Mission Pharmacy Services LLC
201 N Jefferson St Ste 300 ... Kittanning PA 16201 877-758-2039
TF: 877-758-2039 ■ *Web:* www.missionpharmacy.com

Mission Road Pharmacy Inc
1155 N Mission Rd ... Los Angeles CA 90033 323-227-4646
Web: mrpscripts.com

Monitor Pharmacy Inc 2981 Midland Rd ... Bay City MI 48706 989-684-2343
Web: monitorpharmacy.com

Moreland Plaza Pharmacy Inc
827 W Moreland Blvd ... Waukesha WI 53188 262-542-4488

Moye's Pharmacy 4467 N Henry Blvd ... Stockbridge GA 30281 770-474-0704
Web: www.moyespharmacy.com

Navarro Discount Pharmacies 9400 ... Miami FL 33178 866-628-2776
TF: 866-628-2776 ■ *Web:* www.navarro.com

Neighborcare Health 2101 E Yesler Way ... Seattle WA 98122 206-461-7801
Web: www.neighborcare.org

Phone | Fax

New Era Optical Co 5575 N Lynch Ave. . . . . Chicago IL 60630 773-725-9600
Web: www.neweraopt.com

Nucara Pharmacy 209 E San Marnan Dr . . . . . Waterloo IA 50702 319-236-8891
TF: 800-359-2357 ■ *Web:* www.nucara.com

NuFACTOR Inc 41093 County Ctr Dr Ste B . . . . . Temecula CA 92591 951-296-2516
Web: www.nufactor.com

Nutri Pet Research Inc
227 State Rt 33 Ste 10 . . . . . Manalapan NJ 07726 732-786-8822
Web: www.nuprosupplements.com

Ocean Eyes Optical Inc 2907 Ocean Ave. . . . . Brooklyn NY 11235 718-332-1017
Web: coolframes.com

Ocu-ease Optical Products Inc
920 San Pablo Ave . . . . . Pinole CA 94564 510-724-0384
Web: www.ocuease.com

Oncology Plus Inc 1070 E Brandon Blvd . . . . . Brandon FL 33511 877-410-0779
TF: 877-410-0779 ■ *Web:* www.oncologyplus.com

Optical Physics Co 26610 Agoura Rd Ste 240 . . . . . Calabasas CA 91302 818-880-2907
Web: www.opci.com

Oronoque Pharmacy Inc 7365 Main St. . . . . Stratford CT 06614 203-378-1111

Owens Healthcare 2025 Court St Ste A . . . . . Redding CA 96001 530-339-7950
Web: www.owensmedicalsupply.com

Patient First Renal Solutions
11555 Heron Bay Blvd . . . . . Coral Springs FL 33076 954-473-4717
Web: pfrenal.com

PBM Plus Inc 300 Techne Ctr Dr Ste B . . . . . Milford OH 45150 513-248-3071
Web: www.pbmplus.com

Penobscot Community Health Center Inc
103 Maine Ave . . . . . Bangor ME 04401 207-992-9200
Web: pchc.com

Pet Health Pharmacy 12012 N 111th Ave. . . . . Youngtown AZ 85363 623-214-2791
TF: 800-742-0516 ■ *Web:* www.pethealthpharmacy.com

Pharma eMarket LLC 15 E Ridge Pk Ste 225. . . . . Conshohocken PA 19428 610-862-0909
Web: www.monitorforhire.com

Pharmaceutical Advisors LLC
316 Wall St 2nd Fl . . . . . Princeton NJ 08540 609-688-1330
Web: www.pharmadvisors.com

Pharmacy Outcomes Specialists LLC
41 E Main St Ste 200 . . . . . Lake Zurich IL 60047 847-540-9590
Web: www.pharmout.com

Pharmacy Providers of OK 3000 E Memorial Rd . . . . . Edmond OK 73013 405-557-5700

Phipps Pharmacy Inc 205 B Hospital Dr . . . . . Mckenzie TN 38201 731-352-0820
Web: phippspharmacy.com

Pilot Process Systems 306 Keystone Dr . . . . . Telford PA 18969 215-453-8010
Web: www.bioskids.com

Premium Rx National LLC 11736 Parklawn Dr . . . . . Rockville MD 20852 301-230-0908

Pro-tech Security Sales 1313 W Bagley Rd . . . . . Berea OH 44017 440-239-0100
TF: 800-888-4002 ■ *Web:* www.protechsales.com

Ragan & Massey Inc 100 Ponchatoula Pkwy. . . . . Ponchatoula LA 70454 985-386-6042
Web: raganandmassey.com

Ralston Drug & Discount Liquor
3147 Southmore Blvd. . . . . Houston TX 77004 713-524-3045 524-5981

Red Cross Pharmacy 425 Main St . . . . . Forest City PA 18421 570-785-5400
Web: www.rcrx.com

Red Cross Pharmacy Inc 52 E Arrow St . . . . . Marshall MO 65340 660-886-5535
Web: redcrosspharmacy.com

REM Optical Company Inc
10941 La Tuna Canyon Rd . . . . . Sun Valley CA 91352 818-504-3950
Web: www.remeyewear.com

Revolution Eyewear Inc
997 Flower Glen St . . . . . Simi Valley CA 93065 800-986-0010
TF: 800-986-0010 ■ *Web:* www.revolutioneyewear.com

Rite Aid Corp 30 Hunter Ln . . . . . Camp Hill PA 17011 717-761-2633
NYSE: RAD ■ *TF:* 800-748-3243 ■ *Web:* www.riteaid.com

Ritzman Pharmacies Inc 8614 Hartman Rd . . . . . Wadsworth OH 44281 330-335-2318 335-3222
Web: ritzmanrx.com

Rodman's Discount Food & Drugs
4301 Randolph Rd . . . . . Silver Spring MD 20906 301-946-3100
Web: www.rodmans.com

Rotz Pharmacy Inc 1338 Amherst St . . . . . Winchester VA 22601 540-662-8312
Web: rotzpharmacy.com

Rx Advantage Inc 7101 Hwy 90 Ste 300. . . . . Daphne AL 36526 251-625-6100
Web: www.rxadvantage-inc.com

Rx Inc Dba Lo Cost Pharmacy 612 E 69th St . . . . . Savannah GA 31405 912-352-0375

Rx.com 4710 Mercantile Dr . . . . . Fort Worth TX 76137 817-547-1000
Web: www.rx.com

RXD Pharmacies Inc 724 Haddon Ave. . . . . Collingswood NJ 08108 856-858-9292 854-1359

Rxusa Inc 81 Seaview Blvd. . . . . Port Washington NY 11050 516-467-2500 467-2539
TF: 800-764-3648 ■ *Web:* www.rxusa.com

Saar's Inc 32199 State Rt 20 . . . . . Oak Harbor WA 98277 360-675-3000
Web: www.saarsmarketplacefoods.com

Safeguard Products Inc 2710 Division Hwy . . . . . New Holland PA 17557 717-354-4586
Web: www.safeguardproducts.com

Sama Eye Wear 8460 Santa Monica Blvd . . . . . West Hollywood CA 90069 323-822-3955
Web: www.samaeyewear.net

Sav-Mor Drug Stores 43155 W Nine-Mile Rd . . . . . Novi MI 48376 248-348-1570 348-4316
Web: www.sav-mor.com

Select Rx 11414 E 51st St . . . . . Tulsa OK 74146 918-461-8103
Web: www.selectrx.com

Senior Care Pharmacy 4455 Morris Park Dr . . . . . Mint Hill NC 28227 704-545-8641
Web: www.seniorcarepharmacy.net

Setzer Pharmacy Inc 1685 Rice St. . . . . St Paul MN 55113 651-488-0251
Web: setzerrx.com

Shiraz Specialty Pharmacy
205 E Casino Rd Ste B17 . . . . . Everett WA 98208 425-356-3276
Web: www.shirazpharmacy.com

Shoppers Drug Mart Inc 243 Consumers Rd. . . . . Toronto ON M2J4W8 416-493-1220
TSE: SC ■ *Web:* www1.shoppersdrugmart.ca

Shore Drugs Inc 30 E Main St. . . . . Bay Shore NY 11706 631-665-3000

Skymed Pharmacy 1332 N Federal Hwy. . . . . Pompano Beach FL 33062 866-778-8255
TF: 866-778-8255 ■ *Web:* www.skymed.com

Slope Drugs & Surgical Supply Inc
406 Fifth Ave . . . . . Brooklyn NY 11215 718-788-8899

Phone | Fax

Smart Eye Care Center 255 Western Ave. . . . . Augusta ME 04330 207-622-5800
Web: www.smarteyecare.com

Stout'S Drug Store Inc 217 Chicago Ave. . . . . Savanna IL 61074 815-273-2713
Web: www.hartigdrug.com

Symons Capital Management Inc
650 Washington Rd Ste 800. . . . . Pittsburgh PA 15228 412-344-7690
TF: 888-344-7740 ■ *Web:* www.symonscapital.com

Theis Distributing Co 17984 Red Iron . . . . . Schertz TX 78154 210-651-4403
Web: www.theisco.com

Thrifty White Stores
6055 Nathan Lane N Ste 200 . . . . . Plymouth MN 55442 763-513-4300
TF: 800-642-3275 ■ *Web:* www.thriftywhite.com

Total Life Care Pharmacy
2731 Manhattan Blvd Ste B17 . . . . . Harvey LA 70058 504-355-4191
Web: www.tlcrxpharmacy.com

Transcript Pharmacy Inc
2506 Lakeland Dr Ste 201 . . . . . Jackson MS 39232 866-420-4041
TF: 866-420-4041 ■ *Web:* www.transcriptpharmacy.com

Upstate Pharmacy Ltd 40 N America Dr . . . . . West Seneca NY 14224 716-675-3784
Web: www.upstatepharmacy.com

US Script Inc 2425 W Shaw Ave . . . . . Fresno CA 93711 559-244-3700
Web: www.usscript.com

VirtuOx Inc 5850 Coral Ridge Dr Ste 304. . . . . Coral Springs FL 33076 954-344-7075
Web: www.virtuox.net

Vision Source LP 23824 Hwy 59 N Ste 101 . . . . . Kingwood TX 77339 281-312-1111
Web: www.visionsource.com

Vitacost.com Inc
5400 Broken Sound Blvd NW Ste 500 . . . . . Boca Raton FL 33487 800-381-0759
TF: 800-381-0759 ■ *Web:* www.vitacost.com

Vitamin Shoppe Inc 2101 91st St. . . . . North Bergen NJ 07047 201-868-5959 852-7153*
NYSE: VSI ■ **Fax Area Code:* 800 ■ *TF:* 800-223-1216 ■ *Web:* www.vitaminshoppe.com

Voss Pharmacy Inc 3303 S Halsted St. . . . . Chicago IL 60608 773-254-5221

Walgreen Co 200 Wilmot Rd . . . . . Deerfield IL 60015 847-940-2500 236-0862
TF Cust Svc: 800-925-4733 ■ *Web:* www.walgreens.com

West Coast Cosmetics Inc
21050 Superior St . . . . . Chatsworth CA 91311 818-349-8510
Web: www.westcoastcosmetics.com

White'S Pharmacy of Dalton LLC
2955B Cleveland Hwy. . . . . Dalton GA 30721 706-259-9707

Whitney Lab 1095 N Us Hwy 1 Ste 1 . . . . . Ormond Beach FL 32174 386-673-4770
Web: www.methadonehelp.com

Xerimis Inc 102 Executive Dr. . . . . Moorestown NJ 08057 856-727-9940
Web: www.xerimis.com

Zitomer Pharmacy Inc 969 Madison Ave Fl 1 . . . . . New York NY 10021 212-737-5560
Web: www.zitomer.com

DRUGS - MFR

See Biotechnology Companies p. 1859; Diagnostic Products p. 2192; Medicinal Chemicals & Botanical Products p. 2748; Pharmaceutical Companies p. 2934; Pharmaceutical Companies - Generic Drugs p. 2936; Vitamins & Nutritional Supplements p. 3296

238 DRUGS & PERSONAL CARE PRODUCTS - WHOL

Companies listed here distribute pharmaceuticals, over-the-counter (OTC) drugs, and/or personal care products typically found in drug stores.

Phone | Fax

Aaipharma Services Corp
2320 Scientific Park Dr. . . . . Wilmington NC 28405 910-254-7000
Web: www.alcaminow.com/redirect

Altamont Pharmacy Inc 12 N Third St . . . . . Altamont IL 62411 618-483-5614
Web: altamontpharmacy.com

Ambient Healthcare Inc 15851 SW 41st St Ste 600 . . . . . Davie FL 33331 954-796-3338
TF: 877-342-9352 ■ *Web:* www.ambienthealth.com

Ambrx Inc 10975 N Torrey Pines Rd. . . . . La Jolla CA 92037 858-875-2400
Web: www.ambrx.com

AmerisourceBergen Corp
1300 Morris Dr Ste 100 PO Box 959 . . . . . Chesterbrook PA 19087 610-727-7000 727-3600
NYSE: ABC ■ *TF:* 800-829-3132 ■ *Web:* www.amerisourcebergen.net

Aqua Pharmaceuticals LLC
158 W Gay St Ste 310. . . . . West Chester PA 19380 610-644-7000
Web: www.aquapharm.com

AquaCap Inc 4 Hillman Dr Ste 190 . . . . . Chadds Ford PA 19317 610-361-2800

Arctic Ease LLC 200 Shell Ln Ste 204. . . . . Phoenixville PA 19460 484-924-9186
Web: www.arcticease.com

Astrup Drug Inc 1305 First Ave SW. . . . . Austin MN 55912 507-433-4586
Web: www.astrupdrug.com

Auspex Pharmaceuticals Inc
3333 N Torrey Pines Court Ste 400 . . . . . La Jolla CA 92037 858-558-2400
TF: 800-487-7671 ■ *Web:* www.auspexpharma.com

Bach Pharma Inc 800 Turnpike St Ste 300. . . . . North Andover MA 01845 978-794-5510
Web: www.bachpharma.com

Bedford Road Pharmacy Inc
11306 Bedford Rd Ne . . . . . Cumberland MD 21502 301-777-1771 777-0119
TF: 800-788-6693 ■ *Web:* www.pharmacareofcumberland.com

BioMotiv LLC 3605 Warrensville Ctr Rd. . . . . Cleveland OH 44122 216-455-3200
TF: 800-477-6307 ■ *Web:* www.biomotiv.com

Buffalo Supply Inc 1650A Coal Creek Dr. . . . . Lafayette CO 80026 800-366-1812
TF: 800-366-1812 ■ *Web:* www.buffalosupply.com

Cadeau Express Inc 3494 E Sunset Rd . . . . . Las Vegas NV 89120 702-433-1333
TF: 800-240-0301 ■ *Web:* www.cadeauexpress.com

Camp Drugstore 600 Ferguson . . . . . Wood River IL 62095 618-254-6223

Camphor Technologies Inc
1584 Independence Blvd . . . . . Sarasota FL 34234 860-535-0241
Web: www.camphortech.com

Capellon Pharmaceuticals Ltd
7509 Flagstone St. . . . . Fort Worth TX 76118 817-595-5820
Web: www.capellon.com

Cardinal Health Distribution 7000 Cardinal Pl . . . . . Dublin OH 43017 614-757-5000 757-6000
Web: www.cardinalhealth.com/en.html

Phone | Fax

Cardinal Health Nuclear Pharmacy Services
7000 Cardinal Pl. Dublin OH 43017 614-757-5000 757-6000
TF: 800-326-6457 ■ *Web:* www.cardinalhealth.com

Carolina Medical Products Company Inc
8026 Us Hwy 264A. Farmville NC 27828 252-753-7111
Web: www.carolinamedical.com

Charles Bowman & Company Inc
3328 John F Donnelly Dr. Holland MI 49424 616-786-4000 786-2864
Web: www.charlesbowman.com

Complete Pharmacy Care Inc 4206 Dalrock Rd. Rowlett TX 75088 972-675-3300
TF: 866-804-6937 ■ *Web:* www.completepharmacycare.com

Connetics Corp 3160 Porter Dr. Palo Alto CA 94304 650-843-2800
Web: www.olux.com

Contract Pharmacy Services Inc
125 Titus Ave. Warrington PA 18976 267-487-9000 487-9050
Web: www.contractpharmacy.com

Correct Rx Pharmacy Services Inc
803-A Barkwood Ct. Linthicum MD 21090 410-636-9500
Web: www.correctrxpharmacy.com

CritiTech Inc 1849 E 1450 Rd. Lawrence KS 66044 785-841-7120
Web: www.crititech.com

Dakota Drug Inc 28 Main St N. Minot ND 58703 701-852-2141
TF: 800-437-2018 ■ *Web:* www.dakdrug.com

Danco Investors Group Lp 112 Second Ave N. Nashville TN 37201 615-251-9521

Drais Pharmaceuticals Inc
520 Us Hwy 22 Ste 201. Bridgewater NJ 08807 908-895-1200
Web: www.draispharma.com

DRAXIMAGE Inc 16751 Transcanada Hwy. Kirkland QC H9H4J4 514-630-7080
TF: 888-633-5343 ■ *Web:* www.draximage.com

Duchesnay Inc 950 Boul Mich'Le-Bohec. Blainville QC J7C5E2 450-433-7734 433-2211
Web: www.duchesnay.com

Eagle Vision Pharmaceutical Corp
175 Krauser Rd. Downingtown PA 19335 610-458-2346

Fabre-Kramer Pharmaceuticals Inc
5847 San Felipe Ste 2000. Houston TX 77057 713-975-6900
Web: www.fabrekramer.com

Familiprix Inc 6000 Rue Armand-Viau. Quebec QC G2C2C5 418-847-3311
TF: 800-463-5160 ■ *Web:* www.familiprix.com/en

Familymeds Inc 312 Farmington Ave. Farmington CT 06032 888-787-2800
TF: 888-787-2800 ■ *Web:* www.familymeds.com

Ferring Pharmaceuticals Inc
100 Interpace Pkwy. Parsippany NJ 07054 973-796-1600
TF: 888-337-7464 ■ *Web:* www.ferringusa.com

FoldRx Pharmaceuticals Inc
100 Acorn Park Dr 5th Fl. Cambridge MA 02140 617-252-5500
Web: www.foldrx.com

Forever Spring 2629 E Craig Rd Ste E. Las Vegas NV 89030 702-633-4283
TF: 800-523-4334 ■ *Web:* www.foreverspring.com

Forte Research Systems Inc
1200 John Q Hammons Dr Ste 300. Madison WI 53717 608-826-6000

Franck's Pharmacy Inc 7518 Soquel Dr. Aptos CA 95003 831-685-1100
Web: www.francks.com

Frank W Kerr Co 43155 W Nine Mile Rd. Novi MI 48376 248-349-5000
Web: www.fwkerr.com

Freedom Pharmaceuticals Inc
801 W New Orleans St. Broken Arrow OK 74011 918-615-6228
Web: freedomrxinc.com

Garden State Orthopaedic Center Inc
9 Post Rd. Oakland NJ 07436 201-337-5566
Web: gsortho.com/Garden_State_Orthopaedic/Main.html

Gavis Pharmaceuticals LLC 400 Campus Dr. Somerset NJ 08873 908-603-6080
Web: www.gavispharma.com

Gentell 3600 Boundbrook Ave. Feasterville Trevose PA 19053 215-788-2700
Web: www.gentell.com

Health Coalition Inc 8320 NW 30th Terr. Doral FL 33122 305-662-2988
TF: 800-456-7283 ■ *Web:* healthcoalition.com

Iden Cosmetics Inc 15500 Texaco St. Paramount CA 90723 562-630-2580
Web: www.idencosmetics.com

Iredale Mineral Cosmetics Ltd
28 Church St. Great Barrington MA 01230 413-528-1078
TF: 877-869-9420 ■ *Web:* www.janeiredale.com

J&B Medical Supply Co Inc
50496 W Pontiac Trail. Wixom MI 48393 248-896-6210
TF: 800-980-0047 ■ *Web:* www.jandbmedical.com

JM Smith Corp 101 W Saint John St Ste 305. Spartanburg SC 29306 864-582-1216
Web: www.jmsmithcorp.com

Kinray Inc 152-35 Tenth Ave. Whitestone NY 11357 718-767-1234 767-4706
TF: 800-854-6729 ■ *Web:* www.kinray.com

Kohll's Pharmacy & Homecare Inc 12759 Q St. Omaha NE 68137 402-895-6812
Web: www.kohlls.com

Lawrenceburg Medical Supply Inc
753 W Broadway. Lawrenceburg KY 40342 502-839-4557

Lil' Drug Store Products Inc
1201 Continental Pl Ne. Cedar Rapids IA 52402 800-553-5022
TF: 800-553-5022 ■ *Web:* www.lildrugstore.com

London Drugs Ltd 12251 Horseshoe Way. Richmond BC V7A4X5 604-272-7400
TF: 888-991-2299 ■ *Web:* www.londondrugs.com

Masters Pharmaceutical Inc
11930 Kemper Springs Dr. Cincinnati OH 45240 513-354-2690
Web: mastersrx.com

Mechanical Servants Inc 2755 Thomas St. Melrose Park IL 60160 708-615-9439 486-1501
TF: 800-351-2000 ■ *Web:* www.cvalet.com

Methapharm Inc 11772 W Sample Rd. Coral Springs FL 33065 954-341-0795
TF: 800-287-7686 ■ *Web:* www.methapharm.com

Miami-Luken Inc 265 S Pioneer Blvd. Springboro OH 45066 937-743-7775
Web: www.miamiluken.com

MorphoSys USA Inc
4350 Lassiter At N Hills Ave Ste 250. Raleigh NC 27609 919-878-7978

Morris & Dickson Co Ltd 410 Kay Ln. Shreveport LA 71115 318-797-7900 798-6007
TF: 800-388-3833 ■ *Web:* www.morrisdickson.com

Myoderm Inc 48 E Main St. Norristown PA 19401 610-233-3300
Web: www.myoderm.com

Neil Medical Group Inc 2545 Jetport Rd. Kinston NC 28504 800-735-9111
TF: 800-735-9111 ■ *Web:* www.neilmedical.com

North Carolina Mutual Wholesale Drug Co
816 Ellis Rd. Durham NC 27703 919-596-2151 596-1453
TF: 800-800-8551 ■ *Web:* www.mutualdrugcompany.com/?page_id=26

Omegachem Inc 480 rue Perreault. St-romuald QC G6W7V6 418-837-4444
TF: 800-661-6342 ■ *Web:* www.omegachem.com

Pamlab LLC 4099 Hwy 190 E Service Rd. Covington LA 70433 985-893-4097 893-6195
TF: 844-639-9725 ■ *Web:* pamlab.com

PanOptica Inc 150 Morristown Rd Ste 205. Bernardsville NJ 07924 908-766-2202
Web: panopticapharma.com

Park Compounding Pharmacy Inc
4333 Park Terrace Dr Ste 160. Westlake Village CA 91361 805-497-8258
Web: parkcompounding.com

Parmed Pharmaceuticals Inc
4220 Hyde Pk Blvd. Niagara Falls NY 14305 716-284-5666 727-6330*
**Fax Area Code:* 800 ■ *TF:* 800-727-6331 ■ *Web:* www.parmed.com

Pharmacommunications Group Inc
100 Renfrew Dr. Markham ON L3R9R6 905-477-3100
TF: 800-267-5409 ■ *Web:* www.pharmacommunications.com

PharmaForce Inc 960 Crupper Ave. Columbus OH 43229 614-436-2222
Web: www.pharmaforceinc.com

PharmaLogic Inc 1 S Ocean Blvd Ste 206. Boca Raton FL 33432 561-416-0085
Web: www.pharmalogic.info

Pharmgate LLC 161 N Franklin Tpke. Ramsey NJ 07446 201-327-3800 327-3802
Web: www.pharmgate.com

Phillips Drugstore Inc 123 E State St. Mauston WI 53948 608-847-5949
Web: www.phillipsrx.com

Plant Sciences Inc 342 Green Valley Rd. Watsonville CA 95076 831-728-7771 728-4967
Web: www.plantsciences.com

Plasma Services Group Inc
1840 County Line Rd Unit 100. Huntingdon Valley PA 19006 215-355-1288
Web: plasmaservicesgroup.com

PlasmaCare Inc 1128 Main St Ste 300. Cincinnati OH 45202 513-621-8728
Web: www.plasmacare.com

Procurity Inc 160 Eagle Dr. Winnipeg MB R2R1V5 204-632-5506

Putney Inc 1 Monument Sq Ste 400. Portland ME 04101 207-828-0880
TF: 866-683-0660 ■ *Web:* www.putneyvet.com

Quality King Distributors Inc
35 Sawgrass Drive Ste 3. Bellport NY 11713 631-737-5555 439-2202
Web: www.qkd.com

QVL Pharmacy Holdings Inc
4141 Blue Lk Cir Ste 124. Dallas TX 75244 972-788-2653
Web: www.qvlpharmacy.com

ReceptoPharm Inc 1537 NW 65th Ave. Plantation FL 33313 954-321-8988
Web: www.receptopharm.com

Reese Pharmaceutical Co 10617 Frank Ave. Cleveland OH 44106 800-321-7178 231-6444*
**Fax Area Code:* 216 ■ *TF:* 800-321-7178 ■ *Web:* www.reesechemical.com

RG Shakour Inc 254 Tpke Rd. Westborough MA 01581 800-661-2030
TF: 800-661-2030 ■ *Web:* interiorsbyrgshakour.com

Rx Scan 2478 Lackey Old State Rd. Delaware OH 43015 740-548-1725
TF: 800-572-2648 ■ *Web:* rxscan.com

SaveMart Pharmacy 241 W Roseville Rd. Lancaster PA 17601 717-569-7384
Web: www.savemartpa.com

Sheldon's Express Pharmacy Inc
843 Fairview Ave. Bowling Green KY 42101 270-842-4515
Web: www.sheldonsexpresspharmacy.com

Sigma Tau Pharmasource Inc
6925 Guion Rd. Indianapolis IN 46268 317-347-2800
Web: www.sigmataupharmasource.com

Silver Spur Corp 16010 Shoemaker Ave. Cerritos CA 90703 562-921-6880
Web: www.silverspurcorp.com

Sothys USA Inc 1500 NW 94th Ave. Miami FL 33172 305-594-4222 592-5785
TF: 800-325-0503 ■ *Web:* www.sothys-usa.com

Sova Pharmaceuticals Inc
11099 N Torrey Pines Rd Ste 290. La Jolla CA 92037 858-750-4700 750-4701
Web: www.sovapharma.com

Sprout Pharmaceuticals Inc 4208 Six Forks Rd. Raleigh NC 27609 844-746-5745
TF: 844-746-5745 ■ *Web:* www.addyi.com

SRS International Corp
Suite 208 7700 Leesburg Pk. Falls Church VA 22043 703-821-0157
Web: listen.dts.com

Strategic Pharmaceutical Solut
17014 NE Sandy Blvd. Portland OR 97230 503-802-7400
Web: vetsource.com

superDimension Inc
161 Cheshire Ln Ste 100. Minneapolis MN 55441 763-210-4000
Web: superdimension.com

SynDevRx Inc 1 Broadway 14th Fl. Cambridge MA 02142 617-401-3110
Web: www.syndevrx.com

Syndexa Pharmaceuticals Corp
480 Arsenal St Bldg 1. Watertown MA 02472 617-607-7283
Web: www.syndexa.com

Syreon Corp 260 - 1401 W Eighth Ave. Vancouver BC V6H1C9 604-676-5900
TF: 866-979-7366 ■ *Web:* www.syreon.com

Takeda Pharmaceuticals USAInc
1 Takeda Pkwy. Deerfield IL 60015 224-554-6500
Web: takedajobs.com

Tri-Med Pharmacy Services LLC
260 W Main St Ste 217. Hendersonville TN 37075 615-826-9393

UNFI Specialty Distribution Services
88 Huntoon Memorial Hwy. Leicester MA 01524 508-892-8171 892-4827
Web: unfi.com

US WorldMeds LLC 4010 Dupont Cir Ste L-07. Louisville KY 40207 502-815-8000
TF: 888-900-8796 ■ *Web:* www.usworldmeds.com

Value Drug Co 1 Golf View Dr. Altoona PA 16635 814-944-9316
Web: valuedrugco.com

Value Drug Mart Assoc Ltd 16504 - 121A Ave. Edmonton AB T5V1J9 780-453-1701
TF: 888-554-8258 ■ *Web:* www.valuedrugmart.com

Victory Pharma Inc 11682 El Camino Real. San Diego CA 92130 858-720-4500 720-4501
Web: www.victorypharma.com

Viroxis Corp 12621 Silicon Dr Ste 100. San Antonio TX 78249 210-558-8896
Web: www.viroxis.com

Zafgen Inc 175 Portland St 4th Fl. Boston MA 02114 617-622-4003
Web: www.zafgen.com

				Phone	Fax
Zeta Pharmaceuticals Inc 1 Paragon Dr ... Montvale *Web:* www.zetapharm.com	NJ	07645		201-930-4934	

239 DUDE RANCHES

See Also Resorts & Resort Companies p. 3068

			Phone	Fax
320 Guest Ranch Inc 205 Buffalo Horn Creek Rd ... Gallatin Gateway *TF:* 800-243-0320 ■ *Web:* www.320ranch.com	MT	59730	406-995-4283	
63 Ranch PO Box 979 ... Livingston *TF:* 888-395-5151 ■ *Web:* 63ranch.com	MT	59047	888-395-5151	
7 D Ranch 7D Ranch PO Box 100 ... Cody *TF:* 888-587-9885 ■ *Web:* www.7dranch.com	WY	82414	307-587-9885	587-9885
Absaroka Ranch PO Box 929 ... Dubois *Web:* www.absarokaranch.com	WY	82513	307-455-2275	455-2275
Air Ivanhoe Ltd Ivanhoe Lk Air Base ... Foleyet *Web:* www.air-ivanhoe.com	ON	P0M1T0	705-899-2155	
Alabama Wmu Camp 2001 E S Blvd ... Montgomery *Web:* alabamawmu.org	AL	36116	205-884-2425	
Aspen Canyon Ranch 13206 County Rd 3 ... Parshall *Web:* www.aspencanyon.com	CO	80468	970-725-3600	
Bar Lazy J Guest Ranch 447 County Rd 3 PO Box N ... Parshall *TF:* 800-396-6279 ■ *Web:* www.barlazyj.com	CO	80468	970-725-3437	725-0121
Black Mountain Ranch 4000 Conger Mesa Rd ... McCoy *TF:* 800-967-2401 ■ *Web:* www.blackmtnranch.com	CO	80463	970-653-4226	
Bonanza Creek Country Guest Ranch 523 Bonanza Creek Rd ... Martinsdale *TF:* 800-476-6045 ■ *Web:* www.bonanzacreekcountry.com	MT	59053	406-572-3366	572-3366
Brooks Lake Lodge & Guest Ranch 458 Brooks Lk Rd ... Dubois *TF:* 866-213-4022 ■ *Web:* www.brookslake.com	WY	82513	866-213-4022	
Brush Creek Ranch 66 Brush Creek Ranch Rd ... Saratoga *Web:* www.brushcreekranch.com	WY	82331	307-327-5284	327-5970
C Lazy U Ranch 3640 Colorado Hwy 125 PO Box 379 ... Granby *Web:* www.clazyu.com	CO	80446	970-887-3344	887-3917
Caliente Resorts LLC 21240 Gran Via Blvd ... Land O Lakes *Web:* www.calienteresort.com	FL	34637	813-996-3700	
Camp Arrowhead 20 Arrowhead Rd ... Pittsford *Web:* www.rochesterymca.org	NY	14534	585-383-4590	
Camp Chewonki 485 Chewonki Neck Rd ... Wiscasset *Web:* www.chewonki.org	ME	04578	207-882-7323	
CAMP Conferences Inc 540 W Frntage Rd Ste 2205 ... Northfield *Web:* www.campconferences.com	IL	60093	312-527-2800	
Camp Hilbert 5403 Monument Ave ... Richmond *Web:* www.weinsteinjcc.org	VA	23226	804-285-6500	
Camp Lebanon 1205 Acorn Rd ... Burtrum *TF:* 800-816-1502 ■ *Web:* camplebanon.org	MN	56318	320-573-2125	
Camp Ocean Pines Inc 1473 Randall Dr ... Cambria *Web:* campoceanpines.org	CA	93428	805-927-0254	
Camp Oty'okwa 24799 Purcell Rd ... South Bloomingville *Web:* campotyokwalodging.com	OH	43152	740-385-5279	
Camp Rocky Point 1586 Hanna Dr ... Denison *Web:* gsnetx.org	TX	75020	903-465-5270	
Camp Simcha 430 White Rd ... Glen Spey *Web:* campsimcha.org	NY	12737	845-856-1432	
Camp Sunshine 35 Acadia Rd ... Casco *Web:* campsunshine.org	ME	04015	207-655-3800	
Camp Tawonga 131 Steuart St Ste 460 ... San Francisco *Web:* tawonga.org	CA	94105	415-543-2267	
Cheley Colorado Camps Inc 601 Steele St ... Denver *Web:* www.cheley.com	CO	80206	303-377-3616	
Cherokee Park Ranch 436 Cherokee Hills Dr ... Livermore *TF:* 800-628-0949 ■ *Web:* www.cherokeeparkranch.com	CO	80536	970-493-6522	493-5802
Circle Z Ranch PO Box 194 ... Patagonia *TF:* 888-854-2525 ■ *Web:* www.circlez.com	AZ	85624	888-854-2525	
CM Ranch 167 Fish Hatchery Rd PO Box 217 ... Dubois *TF:* 800-455-0721 ■ *Web:* www.cmranch.com	WY	82513	307-455-2331	455-3984
Colorado Cattle Company & Guest Ranch 70008 County Rd 132 ... New Raymer *Web:* www.coloradocattlecompany.com	CO	80742	970-437-5345	
Colorado Trails Ranch 12161 County Rd 240 ... Durango *TF:* 800-323-3833 ■ *Web:* www.coloradotrails.com	CO	81301	970-247-5055	385-7372
Concordia Language Villages 8659 Thorsonveien Rd ... Bemidji *TF:* 800-450-2214 ■ *Web:* concordialanguagevillages.org	MN	56601	218-586-8600	
Coulter Lake Guest Ranch 80 County Rd 273 ... Rifle *TF:* 800-858-3046 ■ *Web:* www.coulterlake.com	CO	81650	970-625-1473	
Crossed Sabres Ranch 829 N Fork Hwy ... Cody *Web:* crossedsabresranch.com	WY	82414	307-587-3750	
Dedham Country Day School 90 Sandy Vly Rd ... Dedham *Web:* www.dedhamcountryday.org	MA	02026	781-329-0850	
Deer Valley Ranch 16825 County Rd 162 ... Nathrop *TF:* 877-897-1297 ■ *Web:* www.deervalleyranch.com	CO	81236	719-395-2353	
Drowsy Water Ranch PO Box 147 ... Granby *TF:* 800-845-2292 ■ *Web:* www.drowsywater.com	CO	80446	970-725-3456	
Dryhead Schively Ranch 1062 Rd 15 ... Lovell *Web:* www.dryheadranch.com	WY	82431	307-548-6688	
Eagle's Nest Foundation 942 W 4th St Ste 101 ... Winston Salem *Web:* www.enf.org	NC	27101	336-761-1040	
Eatons' Ranch 270 Eatons' Ranch Rd ... Wolf *TF:* 800-210-1049 ■ *Web:* eatonsranch.com	WY	82844	307-655-9285	
Echo Canyon Guest Ranch 12507 Echo Canyon Rd ... La Veta	CO	81055	719-742-5261	
Elk Mountain Ranch PO Box 910 ... Buena Vista *TF:* 800-432-8812 ■ *Web:* elkmtn.com	CO	81211	800-432-8812	
Elkhorn Ranch Montana 33133 Gallatin Rd ... Gallatin Gateway *Web:* www.elkhornranchmt.com	MT	59730	406-995-4291	
Flying E Ranch 2801 W Wickenburg Way ... Wickenburg *TF:* 888-684-2650 ■ *Web:* www.flyingeranch.com	AZ	85390	928-684-2690	684-5304
Fresh Air Fund 633 Third Ave 14th Fl ... New York *TF:* 800-367-0003 ■ *Web:* www.freshair.org	NY	10017	800-367-0003	
G Bar M Ranch PO Box 29 ... Clyde Park *Web:* www.gbarm.com	MT	59018	406-686-4423	
Greenhorn Creek Guest Ranch 2116 Greenhorn Ranch Rd ... Quincy *TF:* 800-334-6939 ■ *Web:* www.greenhornranch.com	CA	95971	530-283-0930	
Gros Ventre River Ranch PO Box 151 ... Moose *Web:* grosventreriverranch.com	WY	83012	307-733-4138	733-4272
Guided Discoveries Inc 27282 Calle Arroyo ... San Juan Capistrano *Web:* guideddiscoveries.org	CA	91711	909-625-6194	
Harbor Health Systems LLC 1 Venture Ste 130 ... Irvine *Web:* www.harborsys.com	CA	92618	949-273-7020	
Hawley Mountain Guest Ranch 4188 Main Boulder Rd ... McLeod *TF:* 877-496-7848 ■ *Web:* www.hawleymountain.com	MT	59052	406-932-5791	
Heart Six Ranch 16985 Buffalo Vly Rd PO Box 70 ... Moran **Fax Area Code:* 307 ■ *TF:* 888-543-2477 ■ *Web:* heartsix.com	WY	83013	888-543-2477	543-0918*
Hideout at Flitner Ranch Resort PO Box 206 ... Shell *TF:* 800-354-8637 ■ *Web:* www.thehideout.com	WY	82441	307-765-2080	765-2681
High Meadows Camp 1055 Willeo Rd ... Roswell *Web:* highmeadows.org	GA	30075	770-993-7975	
Home Ranch PO Box 822 ... Clark *TF:* 800-688-2982 ■ *Web:* www.homeranch.com	CO	80428	970-879-1780	879-1795
Homeplace Ranch RR 1 Site 2 ... Priddis *Web:* www.homeplaceranch.com	AB	T0L1W0	403-969-4444	
Horn Creek Conference Grounds Association 6758 County Rd 130 ... Westcliffe *Web:* www.horncreek.org	CO	81252	719-783-2205	
Horse Prairie Ranch 3300 Bachelor Mountain Rd ... Dillon *TF:* 888-726-2454 ■ *Web:* www.ranchlife.com	MT	59725	406-681-3166	
Horton Haven Christian Camp 3711 Reed Harris Rd ... Lewisburg *Web:* www.hortonhaven.org	TN	37091	931-364-7656	
Hume Lake Christian Camps Inc 5545 E Hedges Ave ... Fresno *Web:* www.humelake.org	CA	93727	559-305-7770	
Hunewill Cir H Ranch 1110 Hunewill Ranch Rd ... Bridgeport *Web:* www.hunewillranch.com	CA	93517	760-932-7710	
Kay El Bar Guest Ranch PO Box 2480 ... Wickenburg *TF:* 800-684-7583 ■ *Web:* www.kayelbar.com	AZ	85358	928-684-7593	684-4497
Kieve Camp 42 Kieve Rd ... Nobleboro *Web:* kieve.org	ME	04555	207-563-5172	
King Nummy Trail Camp Ground 205 Rt 47 S ... Cape May Court House *Web:* kingnummytrail.com	NJ	08210	609-465-4242	
Laramie River Dude Ranch 25777 County Rd 103 ... Jelm *TF:* 800-551-5731 ■ *Web:* www.lrranch.com	WY	82063	970-435-5716	
Latigo Ranch PO Box 237 ... Kremmling *TF:* 800-227-9655 ■ *Web:* www.latigotrails.com	CO	80459	970-724-9008	
Lazy K Bar Ranch PO Box 1550 ... Big Timber *Web:* lkbranch.com	MT	59011	406-537-9450	
Lazy L & B Ranch 1072 E Fork Rd ... Dubois *TF Cust Svc:* 800-453-9488 ■ *Web:* www.lazylb.com	WY	82513	307-455-2839	455-2849
Lone Mountain Ranch 750 Lone Mtn Ranch Rd PO Box 160069 ... Big Sky *TF:* 800-514-4644 ■ *Web:* www.lonemountainranch.com	MT	59716	406-995-4644	995-4670
Long Hollow Ranch 71105 Holmes Rd ... Sisters *TF:* 877-923-1901 ■ *Web:* www.lhranch.com	OR	97759	541-923-1901	
Lost Valley Ranch 29555 Goose Creek Rd ... Sedalia *Web:* ranchweb.com/dude-ranches/guest-ranches/lost-valley-ranch-co-usa	CO	80135	303-647-2311	
Lozier's Box R Ranch 552 Willow Creek Rd PO Box 100 ... Cora *TF:* 800-822-8466 ■ *Web:* www.boxr.com	WY	82925	307-367-4868	367-6260
Maranatha Bible Camp Inc 16800 E Maranatha Rd ... Maxwell *Web:* www.maranathacamp.org	NE	69151	308-582-4513	
McGinnis Meadows Cattle & Guest Ranch 6220 Mcginnis Meadows Rd ... Libby *Web:* www.mmgranch.net	MT	59923	406-293-5000	
Mountain Sky Guest Ranch PO Box 1219 ... Emigrant *Web:* www.mtnsky.com	MT	59027	406-333-4911	
Nantahala Outdoor Center Inc 13077 Hwy 19 W ... Bryson City *Web:* www.noc.com	NC	28713	828-488-2176	
New Life Camp 701 Mayhew Rd ... Rose City *Web:* newlifecamp.org	MI	48654	989-685-2949	
New York-New Jersey Trail Conference 156 Ramapo Vly Rd Rt 202 ... Mahwah *Web:* nynjtc.org	NJ	07430	201-512-9348	
Nine Quarter Cir Ranch 5000 Taylor Fork Rd ... Gallatin Gateway *Web:* www.ninequartercircle.com	MT	59730	406-995-4276	995-4276
North Fork Ranch (NFR) 55395 Hwy 285 PO Box B ... Shawnee *TF:* 800-843-7895 ■ *Web:* www.northforkranch.com	CO	80475	303-838-9873	838-1549
Ozark Interests Inc 155 Camp Ozark Dr ... Mount Ida *Web:* www.campozark.com	AR	71957	870-867-4131	
Pali Adventures Summer Camp 30778 Hwy 18 ... Running Springs *Web:* www.paliadventures.com	CA	92382	909-867-5743	
Paradise Guest Ranch PO Box 790 ... Buffalo **Fax Area Code:* 720 ■ *Web:* www.paradiseranch.com	WY	82834	307-684-7876	862-2126*
Peaceful Valley Ranch 475 Peaceful Vly Rd ... Lyons *TF:* 800-955-6343 ■ *Web:* www.peacefulvalley.com	CO	80540	303-747-2881	747-2167
Pine Butte Guest Ranch 351 S Fork Rd ... Choteau *TF:* 877-812-3698 ■ *Web:* www.nature.org	MT	59422	406-466-2158	

				Phone	Fax
Prescott Pines Camp 855 E Schoolhouse Gulch Rd *Web:* prescottpines.org	Prescott	AZ	86303	928-445-5225	
Price Canyon Ranch PO Box 39 *TF:* 800-727-0065 ■ *Web:* www.pricecanyon.com	Rodeo	NM	88056	520-558-2383	731-9453
ProCamps Inc 4600 McAuley Pl 4th Fl *Web:* www.procamps.com	Cincinnati	OH	45242	513-793-2267	
R Lazy S Ranch PO Box 308 *Web:* www.rlazys.com	Teton Village	WY	83025	307-733-2655	
Rainbow Trout Ranch (RTR) 1484 FDR 250 PO Box 458 *TF:* 800-633-3397 ■ *Web:* www.rainbowtroutranch.com	Antonito	CO	81120	719-376-5659	
Rancho de la Osa Guest Ranch PO Box 1 *TF:* 800-872-6240 ■ *Web:* www.ranchodelaosa.com	Sasabe	AZ	85633	520-240-3797	
Ranger Creek Ranch PO Box 47 *Web:* www.rangercreekranch.net	Shell	WY	82441	307-765-4636	
Rawah Ranch 11447 N County Rd 103 *TF:* 800-820-3152 ■ *Web:* www.rawahranch.com	Glendevey	CO	82063	800-820-3152	
Red Rock Ranch, The PO Box 38 *Web:* www.theredrockranch.com	Kelly	WY	83011	307-733-6288	733-6287
Rich Ranch 939 Cottonwood Lakes Rd *TF:* 800-532-4350 ■ *Web:* www.richranch.com	Seeley Lake	MT	59868	406-677-2317	
Rimrock Dude Ranch 2728 Northfork Rt *Web:* www.rimrockranch.com	Cody	WY	82414	307-587-3970	527-5014
Rock Springs Guest Ranch 64201 Tyler Rd *Web:* www.rocksprings.com	Bend	OR	97701	541-382-1957	
Seeds of Peace 183 Powhatan Rd *Web:* www.seedsofpeace.org	Otisfield	ME	04270	212-573-8040	
Seven Lazy P Guest Ranch PO Box 178 *Web:* www.sevenlazyp.com	Choteau	MT	59422	406-466-2044	
Skyhawks Sports Academy Inc 6311 E Mount Spokane Park Dr Ste B *Web:* www.skyhawks.com	Mead	WA	99021	509-466-6590	
Smith Fork Ranch 45362 Needle Rock Rd *TF:* 855-539-1492 ■ *Web:* www.smithforkranch.com	Crawford	CO	81415	970-921-3454	921-3475
Star Island Corp, The 30 Middle St *Web:* starisland.org	Portsmouth	NH	03801	603-430-6272	
Sundance Trail Guest Ranch 17931 Red Feather Lakes Rd *TF:* 800-357-4930 ■ *Web:* www.sundancetrail.com	Red Feather Lakes	CO	80545	970-224-1222	224-1222
Sweet Grass Ranch 460 Rein Ln *Web:* www.sweetgrassranch.com	Big Timber	MT	59011	406-537-4477	537-4477
Sylvan Dale Guest Ranch 2939 N County Rd 31 D *Web:* www.sylvandale.com	Loveland	CO	80538	970-667-3915	635-9336
T Cross Ranch LLC 82 Parque Creek Rd PO Box 638 *TF:* 877-827-6770 ■ *Web:* www.tcross.com	Dubois	WY	82513	307-455-2206	
Tadmor Camp 43943 Mcdowell Creek Dr *Web:* tadmor.org	Lebanon	OR	97355	541-451-4270	
Tanque Verde Ranch 14301 E Speedway *TF:* 800-234-3833 ■ *Web:* www.tanqueverderanch.com	Tucson	AZ	85748	520-296-6275	
Tarryall River Ranch 270015 County Rd 77 *TF:* 800-408-8407 ■ *Web:* tarryallranch.com	Lake George	CO	80827	719-748-1214	
Telenet Voip Inc 850 N Park View Dr *Web:* www.telenetvoip.com	El Segundo	CA	90245	310-253-9000	
Thousand Pines Christian Camp & Conference Center 359 Thousnd Pines Rd *TF:* 888-423-2267 ■ *Web:* www.thousandpines.com	Crestline	CA	92325	909-338-2705	
Three Bars Cattle & Guest Ranch 9500 Wycliffe Perry Creek Rd *TF:* 877-426-5230 ■ *Web:* www.threebarsranch.com	Cranbrook	BC	V1C7C7	250-426-5230	
Trail Creek Ranch 7100 W Trl Creek Rd *Web:* www.jacksonholetrailcreekranch.com	Wilson	WY	83014	307-733-2610	
Triangle C Dude Ranch 3737 Hwy 26 *TF:* 800-661-4928 ■ *Web:* www.trianglec.com	Dubois	WY	82513	307-455-2225	455-2031
Triangle X Ranch 2 Triangle X Ranch Rd	Moose	WY	83012	307-733-2183	733-8685
Triple J Wilderness Ranch 91 Mortimer Rd PO Box 310 *TF:* 800-826-1300 ■ *Web:* www.triplejranch.com	Augusta	MT	59410	406-562-3653	562-3836
Triple R Ranch PO Box 124 *Web:* www.rrrranch.com	Keystone	SD	57751	605-666-4605	
Tumbling River Ranch 3715 Pk County Rd 62 PO Box 30 *TF:* 800-654-8770 ■ *Web:* www.tumblingriver.com	Grant	CO	80448	303-838-5981	838-5133
UXU Ranch 1710 North Fork Highway *Web:* uxuranch.com	Cody	WY	82414	307-587-2143	
Vee Bar Guest Ranch 38 Vee Bar Ranch Rd *TF:* 800-483-3227 ■ *Web:* www.veebar.com	Laramie	WY	82070	307-745-7036	745-7433
Vista Verde Guest & Ski Ranch PO Box 770465 *TF:* 800-526-7433 ■ *Web:* www.vistaverde.com	Steamboat Springs	CO	80477	970-879-3858	879-6814
Wapiti Meadow Ranch 1667 Johnson Creek Rd *Web:* www.wapitimeadowranch.com	Cascade	ID	83611	208-633-3217	633-3219
Waunita Hot Springs Ranch 8007 County Rd 887 *Web:* www.waunita.com	Gunnison	CO	81230	970-641-1266	
Wesley Woods United Methodist Camp Clear Lake 1700 Clear Lk *Web:* www.wesleywoodscamp.com	Dowling	MI	49050	269-721-8291	
White Stallion Ranch 9251 W Twin Peaks Rd *TF:* 888-977-2624 ■ *Web:* www.wsranch.com	Tucson	AZ	85743	520-297-0252	744-2786
Whiteys Fish Camp 2032 County Rd 220 *Web:* www.whiteysfishcamp.com	Orange Park	FL	32003	904-269-4198	
Wilderness Trails Ranch 1766 County Rd 302 *TF:* 800-527-2624 ■ *Web:* www.wildernesstrails.com	Durango	CO	81303	970-247-0722	247-1006
Wind River Ranch PO Box 3410 *TF:* 800-523-4212 ■ *Web:* www.windriverranch.com	Estes Park	CO	80517	970-586-4212	586-2255
Wyman Center Inc 600 Kiwanis Dr *Web:* wymancenter.org	Eureka	MO	63025	636-938-5245	
Yellow Creek Falls Fish Camp 3595 Al Hwy 273 *Web:* yellowcreekfalls.com	Leesburg	AL	35983	256-526-8427	

240 DUPLICATION & REPLICATION SERVICES

				Phone	Fax
Andrew T Johnson Company Inc 15 Tremont Pl *Web:* www.andrewtjohnson.com	Boston	MA	02108	617-742-1610	523-0719
ARC 1981 N Broadway Ste 385 *NYSE: ARC* ■ *Web:* www.e-arc.com	Walnut Creek	CA	94596	925-949-5100	949-5101
ARC Global Document Management 1431 NW 17th Ave *Web:* www.e-arc.com	Portland	OR	97209	503-227-3424	223-4254
Avery Dennison Microreplication Div 207 Goode Ave *Web:* www.averydennison.com	Glendale	CA	91203	626-304-2000	
Campbell Blueprint & Supply Company Inc 3124 Broad Ave *Web:* memphisreprographics.com	Memphis	TN	38112	901-327-7385	
Corporate Disk Co 4610 Crime Pkwy *TF:* 800-634-3475 ■ *Web:* www.disk.com	McHenry	IL	60050	800-634-3475	
Dering Corp, The 1702 Hempstead Rd *Web:* www.echodatamedia.com	Lancaster	PA	17601	717-394-4200	
Digital Video Services 401 Hall ST SW *Web:* www.dvs.com	Grand Rapids	MI	49512	616-975-9911	
Illinois Blueprint Corp 800 SW Jefferson Ave *TF:* 800-747-7070 ■ *Web:* www.illinoisblue.com	Peoria	IL	61605	309-676-1300	676-1310
Online Copy Corp 48815 Kato Rd *TF:* 800-833-4460 ■ *Web:* onlinecopycorp.com	Fremont	CA	94539	800-833-4460	
Standard Digital Imaging 4426 S 108th St *TF:* 800-642-8062 ■ *Web:* www.standardsharev3.com	Omaha	NE	68137	402-592-1292	592-8003
Thomas Reprographics 600 N Central Expy *TF:* 800-877-3776 ■ *Web:* thomasprintworks.com	Richardson	TX	75080	972-231-7227	231-0623
Victory Studios 2247 15th Ave W *Web:* www.victorystudios.com	Seattle	WA	98119	206-282-1776	282-3535

241 DUTY-FREE SHOPS

See Also Gift Shops p. 2352

				Phone	Fax
Ambassador Duty Free Store 707 Patricia St *Web:* www.ambassadordutyfree.com	Windsor	ON	N9B0B5	519-977-9100	977-7811
Baja Duty Free (BDF) 4590 Border Village Rd *Web:* www.bajadutyfree.com	San Ysidro	CA	92173	619-428-6671	
Chezgal Merchandising Creations 8936 W 25th St *Web:* www.cmc-promotional-merchandising.com	Los Angeles	CA	90034	310-841-5893	
Duty Free Americas Inc 6100 Hollywood Blvd 7th Fl *Web:* www.dutyfreeamericas.com	Hollywood	FL	33024	954-986-7700	965-6800
Niagara Duty Free Shop 5726 Falls Ave *TF:* 877-642-4337 ■ *Web:* www.niagaradutyfree.com	Niagara Falls	ON	L2G7T5	905-374-3700	
OKK Trading Inc 5705 Union Pacific Ave *Web:* www.okktrading.com	Los Angeles	CA	90022	323-725-8800	
Peace Bridge Duty Free Inc 1 Peace Bridge Plz **Fax Area Code:* 905 ■ *TF:* 800-361-1302 ■ *Web:* www.dutyfree.ca	Buffalo	NY	14213	800-361-1302	871-6335*
Starboard Cruise Services Inc 8400 NW 36th St *TF:* 866-540-4785 ■ *Web:* www.starboardcruise.com	Miami	FL	33166	786-845-7300	845-1112
Tunnel Duty Free Shop Inc 465 Goyeau St *TF:* 800-669-2105 ■ *Web:* www.tunneldutyfree.com	Windsor	ON	N9A1H1	519-252-2713	

EDUCATIONAL INSTITUTIONS

See Children's Learning Centers p. 1937; Colleges - Tribal p. 1967; Colleges & Universities - Historically Black p. 1995; Preparatory Schools - Boarding p. 2970; Preparatory Schools - Non-boarding p. 2973

242 EDUCATIONAL INSTITUTION OPERATORS & MANAGERS

				Phone	Fax
Academic Approach LLC, The 342 W Armitage Ave *Web:* www.academicapproach.com	Chicago	IL	60614	773-348-8914	
Access College Foundation 7300 Newport Ave Ste 500 *Web:* www.accesscollege.org	Norfolk	VA	23505	757-962-6113	
AdvancePath Academics Inc 4125 Ironbound Rd Ste 201 *Web:* www.advancepath.com	Williamsburg	VA	23188	757-208-0900	
Aiesec Canada Inc 161 Eglinton Ave East Ste 402 *Web:* aiesec.ca	Toronto	ON	M4P1J5	416-368-1001	
Apollo Group Inc 4025 E Elwood St *NASDAQ: APOL* ■ *TF:* 800-990-2765 ■ *Web:* www.apollo.edu	Phoenix	AZ	85040	800-990-2765	
Aqua Data Inc 95 Fifth Ave *TF:* 800-567-9003 ■ *Web:* www.aquadata.com	Pincourt	QC	J7V5K8	514-425-1010	
Aqua Rehab Inc 2145 rue Michelin *Web:* www.aquarehab.com	Laval	QC	H7L5B8	450-687-3472	
Avenue100 Media Solutions Inc 1601 Trapelo Rd Ste 202 *Web:* avenue100.com	Waltham	MA	02451	781-683-3300	
Axonify Inc 460 Phillip St Ste 300 *TF:* 866-317-1992 ■ *Web:* www.axonify.com	Waterloo	ON	N2L5J2	519-585-1200	
Bridgepoint Education Inc 13500 Evening Creek Dr N Ste 600 *NYSE: BPI* ■ *TF:* 866-475-0317 ■ *Web:* www.bridgepointeducation.com	San Diego	CA	92128	858-486-1710	408-2903
Cambium Learning Group Inc 17855 Dallas Pkwy Ste 400 *Web:* www.cambiumlearning.com	Dallas	TX	75287	214-932-9500	

Phone Fax

Capella Education Co
225 S Sixth St 9th Fl. . . . . . Minneapolis MN 55402 612-339-8650
NASDAQ: CPLA ■ *TF Cust Svc:* 888-227-3552 ■ *Web:* www.capella.edu

Career Education Corp (CEC)
2895 Greenspoint Pkwy Ste 600. . . . . . Hoffman Estates IL 60196 847-781-3600 781-3610
NASDAQ: CECO ■ *TF:* 877-559-9222 ■ *Web:* www.careered.com

Carney, Sandoe & Associates, Limited Partnersh
44 Bromfield St. . . . . . Boston MA 02108 617-542-0260
TF: 800-225-7986 ■ *Web:* www.carneysandoe.com

Ccrc Community Link 1665 N Fourth St . . . . . . Breese IL 62230 618-651-9920
Web: www.community-links.net

Center of Vocational Alternative For Men
3770 N High St. . . . . . Columbus OH 43214 614-294-7117
TF: 877-521-2682 ■ *Web:* www.cova.org

Charter Schools USA
6245 N Federal Hwy 5th Fl . . . . . . Fort Lauderdale FL 33308 954-202-3500 202-3512
Web: www.charterschoolsusa.com

Chicago Lighthouse, The 1850 W Roosevelt Rd. . . . . . Chicago IL 60608 312-666-1331

Choice Solutions Inc 420 Lakeside Ave. . . . . . Marlborough MA 01752 508-229-0044

ClevrU Corp 1-564 Weber St N. . . . . . Waterloo ON N2L5C8 519-746-1898
Web: www.clevru.com

Connect-Colleges of Ontario 655 Bay St. . . . . . Toronto ON M5G2K4 416-351-0330
Web: www.collegesontario.org

Corinthian Colleges Inc
6 Hutton Centre Dr Ste 400. . . . . . Santa Ana CA 92707 916-431-6959
NASDAQ: COCO ■ *TF:* 888-370-7589 ■ *Web:* www.cci.edu

Custom Learning Designs Inc 375 Concord Ave . . . . . . Belmont MA 02478 617-489-1702
Web: www.cldinc.com

DeVRY Inc 3005 Highland Pkwy. . . . . . Downers Grove IL 60515 630-515-7700
NYSE: DV ■ *Web:* devryeducationgroup.com

Early Learning Coalition of Miami Dade & Monroe
2555 Ponce De Leon Blvd Ste 500 . . . . . . Coral Gables FL 33134 305-646-7220
Web: www.elcmdm.org

East Harlem Tutorial Program
2050 Second Ave . . . . . . New York NY 10029 212-831-0650
Web: ehtp.org

East Side House Inc 337 Alexander Ave. . . . . . Bronx NY 10454 718-665-5250
Web: www.eastsidehouse.org

eCornell 950 Danby Rd Ste 150 . . . . . . Ithaca NY 14850 607-330-3200
TF: 866-326-7635 ■ *Web:* www.ecornell.com

Ecra Group 5600 N River Rd 14th Fl . . . . . . Rosemont IL 60018 847-318-0072
Web: www.ecragroup.com

Education Management Corp (EDMC)
210 Sixth Ave 33rd Fl. . . . . . Pittsburgh PA 15222 412-562-0900 562-0598
NASDAQ: EDMC ■ *TF:* 800-275-2440 ■ *Web:* www.edmc.edu

Elenco Electronics Inc 150 W Carpenter Ave . . . . . . Wheeling IL 60090 847-541-3800
TF: 800-533-2441 ■ *Web:* www.elenco.com

Energy & Environmental Building Alliance, The
6520 Edenvale Blvd Ste 112. . . . . . Eden Prairie MN 55346 952-881-1098
Web: www.eeba.org

Engage Learning Systems 110 Spadina Ave. . . . . . Toronto ON M5V2K4 416-368-0188
Web: www.engagelearn.com

Fund for American Studies, The
1706 New Hampshire Ave NW . . . . . . Washington DC 20009 202-986-0384
Web: www.tfas.org

Goodwill Easter Seals of Gulf Coast
2448 Gordon Smith Dr . . . . . . Mobile AL 36617 251-471-1581
Web: gesgc.org

Higher Education Assistance Group Inc, The
60 Walnut St 4th Fl. . . . . . Wellesley Hills MA 02481 617-928-1975
Web: www.heag.us

Holy Family Institute
8235 Ohio River Blvd . . . . . . Pittsburgh PA 15202 412-766-4030
Web: www.hfi-pgh.org

Imagine Schools 1005 N Glebe Rd Ste 610 . . . . . . Arlington VA 22201 703-527-2600 527-0038
Web: www.imagineschools.org

Indiana Dunes Environmental Learning Center Inc
700 Howe Rd . . . . . . Chesterton IN 46304 219-395-9555
Web: www.duneslearningcenter.org

ITT Educational Services Inc
13000 N Meridian St . . . . . . Carmel IN 46032 317-706-9200
NYSE: ESI ■ *TF:* 800-388-3368 ■ *Web:* www.ittesi.com

Krm Information Services Inc
200 Spring St . . . . . . Eau Claire WI 54703 715-833-5207
Web: www.krm.com

Lake County Educational Service Ctr
382 Blackbrook Rd . . . . . . Painesville OH 44077 440-350-2563 350-2566

Lambda Solutions Inc 350 321 Water St . . . . . . Vancouver BC V6B1B8 604-687-2444
Web: www.lambdasolutions.net

Laureate Education Inc 650 S Exeter St . . . . . . Baltimore MD 21202 410-843-6100 843-8780
TF: 866-452-8732 ■ *Web:* www.laureate.net

Leona Group LLC 2125 University Pk Dr. . . . . . Okemos MI 48864 517-333-9030
TF: 800-656-6763 ■ *Web:* www.leonagroup.com

LifeLearn Inc 367 Woodlawn Rd W Unit 9. . . . . . Guelph ON N1H7K9 519-767-5043
TF: 888-770-2218 ■ *Web:* www.lifelearn.com

Lincoln Educational Services
200 Executive Dr. . . . . . West Orange NJ 07052 973-736-9340
NASDAQ: LINC ■ *TF:* 800-254-0547 ■ *Web:* www.lincolntech.edu

Lingo Media Corp 151 Bloor St W Ste 703. . . . . . Toronto ON M5S1S4 416-927-7000
TF: 866-927-7011 ■ *Web:* www.lingomedia.com

Literacy Council of Tyler
1530 Loop 323 SSW Rm 120. . . . . . Tyler TX 75711 903-533-0330
Web: www.lcotyler.org

Loyalist Group Ltd 1255 Bay St 8th Fl . . . . . . Toronto ON M5R2A9 416-969-9800
Web: www.loyalistgroup.com

MetaMetrics Inc 1000 Park Forty Plz Dr Ste 120. . . . . . Durham NC 27713 919-547-3400
Web: www.lexile.com

Metro Ecsu 3055 Old Hwy 8 Ste 302. . . . . . Minneapolis MN 55418 612-706-0811
Web: www.ecsu.k12.mn.us

Midtown Educational Foundation
718 S Loomis St. . . . . . Chicago IL 60607 312-738-8300
Web: midtown-metro.org

Mind Gym (USA) Inc 9 E 37th St. . . . . . New York NY 10016 646-649-4333
Web: us.themindgym.com

Phone Fax

N R S I 179 Lafayette Dr. . . . . . Syosset NY 11791 516-921-5500
TF: 800-331-3117 ■ *Web:* nrsi.com

NACCME-PrincetonCME
300 Rike Dr Ste A. . . . . . Millstone Township NJ 08535 609-371-1137
Web: www.naccme.com

National Equity Project 1720 Broadway 4th Fl. . . . . . Oakland CA 94612 510-208-0160
Web: www.nationalequityproject.org

National Heritage Academies
3850 Broadmoor Ave SE Ste 201. . . . . . Grand Rapids MI 49512 877-223-6402
TF General: 877-223-6402 ■ *Web:* www.nhaschools.com

Nebraska Student Loan Program Inc 1300 O St. . . . . . Lincoln NE 68508 402-475-8686
Web: nslp.org

New World Educational Center
5818 N 7th St Ste 200 . . . . . . Phoenix AZ 85014 602-238-9577
Web: www.nweccharter.com

Nobel Learning Communities Inc
1615 W Chester Pike Ste 200. . . . . . West Chester PA 19382 484-947-2000 947-2004
Web: www.nobellearning.com

Ohio Restaurant Association
1525 Bethel Rd Ste 201 . . . . . . Columbus OH 43220 614-442-3535
Web: www.ohiorestaurant.org

Orbis Education Services Inc
11595 N Meridian Ste 400 . . . . . . Carmel IN 46032 317-663-0260
Web: www.orbiseducation.com

Pacific Resources for Education & Learning
900 Ft St Mall Ste 1300 . . . . . . Honolulu HI 96813 808-441-1300
TF: 800-377-4773 ■ *Web:* www.prel.org

Precept Medical Communications Inc
3 Mtn View Rd 3rd Fl. . . . . . Warren NJ 07059 908-605-4801

Princeton Review Inc, The
111 Speen St Ste 550. . . . . . Framingham MA 01701 508-663-5050
Web: www.princetonreview.com

Project Adventure Conference Center
719 Cabot St. . . . . . Beverly MA 01915 978-524-4500
Web: www.project-adventure.org

Reach Out & Read 29 Mystic Ave. . . . . . Somerville MA 02145 617-629-8042
Web: www.reachoutandread.org

RM Educational Software Inc
310 Barnstable Rd Ste 101 A&B. . . . . . Hyannis MA 02601 508-862-0700
Web: www.rmeducation.com

Safe & Civil Schools 2451 Willamette St. . . . . . Eugene OR 97405 541-345-1442
TF: 800-323-8819 ■ *Web:* www.safeandcivilschools.com

Sales Performance International Inc
6201 Fairview Rd Ste 400. . . . . . Charlotte NC 28210 704-227-6500
Web: www.spisales.com

Scenarios Usa 80 Hanson Pl Ste 305 . . . . . . Brooklyn NY 11217 718-230-4381
Web: scenariosusa.org

Schoolwires Inc
330 Innovation Blvd Ste 301. . . . . . State College PA 16803 877-427-9413
TF: 877-427-9413 ■ *Web:* www.schoolwires.com

Sigmatech Inc 4901-C Corporate Dr. . . . . . Huntsville AL 35805 256-382-1188
Web: www.sigmatech.com

State Legislative Leaders Foundation
1645 Falmouth Rd Bldg D . . . . . . Centerville MA 02632 508-771-3821
Web: sllf.org

Strayer Education Inc 2303 Dulles Stn Blvd. . . . . . Herndon VA 20171 703-247-2500
NASDAQ: STRA ■ *Web:* www.strayereducation.com

Streambox Inc 1848 Westlake Ave N Ste 200. . . . . . Seattle WA 98109 206-956-0544
Web: www.streambox.com

Summer Search 500 Sansome St Ste 350. . . . . . San Francisco CA 94111 415-362-0500
Web: www.summersearch.org

Sylvan Learning Centers 1001 Fleet St. . . . . . Baltimore MD 21202 888-338-2283 843-8057*
**Fax Area Code:* 410 ■ *TF:* 888-338-2283 ■ *Web:* sylvanlearning.com

Symposia Medicus
399 Taylor Blvd Ste 201. . . . . . Pleasant Hill CA 94523 925-969-1789
Web: symposiamedicus.org

Take Charge America Inc 20620 N 19th Ave . . . . . . Phoenix AZ 85027 623-266-6100
Web: www.takechargeamerica.org

Tlg Technologies for Learning Group Inc
101-110 Princess St. . . . . . Winnipeg MB R3B1K7 204-940-4550
Web: tlg.ca

Turnaround for Children Inc
25 W 45th St 6th Fl. . . . . . New York NY 10036 646-786-6200
Web: turnaroundusa.org

United Bronx Parents Inc 773 Prospect Ave. . . . . . Bronx NY 10455 718-292-9808

Vertical Alliance Group Inc
1730 Galleria Oaks . . . . . . Texarkana TX 75503 903-792-3866
TF: 877-792-3866 ■ *Web:* www.verticalag.com

Work In Progress Coaching 102 Alta Verdi Dr . . . . . . Aptos CA 95003 831-685-1480
Web: www.wipcoaching.com

243 EDUCATIONAL MATERIALS & SUPPLIES

See Also Educational & Reference Software p. 2029; Office & School Supplies p. 2844

Phone Fax

American Educational Products Inc
401 Hickory St PO Box 2121 . . . . . . Fort Collins CO 80522 970-484-7445 484-1198
TF: 800-289-9299 ■ *Web:* www.amep.com

Carolina Biological Supply Co
2700 York Rd . . . . . . Burlington NC 27215 336-584-0381 584-7686
TF: 800-334-5551 ■ *Web:* www.carolina.com

Carson-Dellosa Publishing Company Inc
7027 Albert Pick Rd . . . . . . Greensboro NC 27409 336-632-0084 808-3271
TF: 800-321-0943 ■ *Web:* www.carsondellosa.com

Center Enterprises Inc 30 Shield St . . . . . . West Hartford CT 06110 860-953-4423 953-2948
TF Orders: 800-542-2214 ■ *Web:* www.centerenterprises.com

Claridge Products & Equipment Inc
601 Hwy 62 65 . . . . . . Harrison AR 72601 870-743-2200 743-1908
TF: 800-434-4610 ■ *Web:* www.claridgeproducts.com

Creative Teaching Press Inc 6262 Katella Ave . . . . . . Cypress CA 92649 714-895-5047 895-6547
TF: 800-444-4287 ■ *Web:* www.creativeteaching.com

Company	City	State	Zip	Phone	Fax
Delta Education LLC 80 NW Blvd. *TF:* 800-258-1302 ■ *Web:* www.deltaeducation.com	Nashua	NH	03063	603-889-8899	880-6520
Didax Inc 395 Main St *TF:* 800-458-0024 ■ *Web:* www.didax.com	Rowley	MA	01969	978-948-2340	948-2813
Education Ctr Inc 3515 W Market St Ste 200 *TF:* 800-714-7991 ■ *Web:* www.themailbox.com	Greensboro	NC	27403	336-854-0309	547-1587
Educational Insights Inc 380 N Fairway Dr *TF:* 800-995-4436 ■ *Web:* www.educationalinsights.com	Vernon Hills	IL	60061	800-995-4436	
Educational Supplies Inc 1506 S Salisbury Blvd *Web:* www.educationalsuppliesinc.com	Salisbury	MD	21801	410-543-2519	860-0584
Educators Resource Inc 2575 Schillingers Rd *Fax: Cust Svc ■ *TF Cust Svc:* 800-868-2368 ■ *Web:* www.erdealer.com	Semmes	AL	36575	800-868-2368	868-6212*
Evan-Moor Educational Publishers Inc 18 Lower Ragsdale Dr. *TF:* 800-777-4362 ■ *Web:* www.evan-moor.com	Monterey	CA	93940	831-649-5901	649-6256
Excelligence Learning Corp 2 Lower Ragsdale Dr Ste 125 *TF:* 800-627-2829 ■ *Web:* excelligence.com	Monterey	CA	93940	831-333-5572	333-5630
Fisher Science Education 4500 Turnberry Dr *TF:* 800-955-1177 ■ *Web:* www.fishersci.com	Hanover Park	IL	60133	800-766-7000	955-0740
Frog Street Press Inc 800 Industrial Blvd Ste 100 *TF:* 800-884-3764 ■ *Web:* www.frogstreet.com	Grapevine	TX	76051	800-884-3764	759-3828
Ghent Manufacturing Inc 2999 Henkle Dr *TF:* 800-543-0550 ■ *Web:* www.ghent.com	Lebanon	OH	45036	513-932-3445	932-9252
Great Source Education Group 181 Ballardvale St. *TF:* 800-289-4490 ■ *Web:* www.hmhco.com	Wilmington	MA	01887	800-289-4490	289-3994
Guidecraft USA 55508 Hwy 19 W *TF:* 800-524-3555 ■ *Web:* www.guidecraft.com	Winthrop	MN	55396	507-647-5030	647-3254
Hayes School Publishing Co Inc 321 Pennwood Ave. *Fax Area Code: 513 ■ *TF:* 800-926-0704 ■ *Web:* www.hayespub.com	Pittsburgh	PA	15221	412-371-2373	527-4526*
Incentive Publications Inc 2400 Crestmoor Dr. *TF Mktg:* 800-967-5325 ■ *Web:* www.incentivepublications.com	Nashville	TN	37215	615-385-2934	
Kaplan Early Learning Co 1310 Lewisville-Clemmons Rd. *Fax Area Code: 800 ■ *TF:* 800-334-2014 ■ *Web:* www.kaplanco.com	Lewisville	NC	27023	336-766-7374	452-7526*
Learning Resources 380 N Fairway Dr. *TF:* 800-222-3909 ■ *Web:* www.learningresources.com	Vernon Hills	IL	60061	847-573-8400	573-8425
Learning Works 181 Brackett St *Web:* www.learningworks.me	Portland	ME	04102	207-775-0105	780-1701
Learning Wrap-Ups Inc 1660 W Gordon Ave Ste 4 *TF:* 800-992-4966 ■ *Web:* www.learningwrapups.com	Layton	UT	84041	801-497-0050	497-0063
McDonald Publishing 567 Hanley Industrial Ct. *TF:* 800-722-8080 ■ *Web:* www.mcdonaldpublishing.com	Saint Louis	MO	63144	314-781-7400	781-7480
McGraw-Hill Education 8787 Orion Pl *TF:* 800-334-7344 ■ *Web:* www.mheducation.com/prek-12/segment/elementary.html	Columbus	OH	43240	800-334-7344	
National School Products 1523 Old Niles Ferry Rd *Fax Area Code: 800 ■ *TF:* 800-627-9393 ■ *Web:* www.nationalschoolproducts.com	Maryville	TN	37803	865-984-3960	289-3960*
Questar Assessment Inc 5550 Upper 147th St W *OTC: QUSA* ■ *TF Cust Svc:* 800-800-2598 ■ *Web:* www.questarai.com	Apple Valley	MN	55124	952-997-2700	
Rock 'N Learn Inc 105 Commercial Cir *TF:* 800-348-8445 ■ *Web:* www.rocknlearn.com	Conroe	TX	77304	936-539-2731	539-2659
Roylco Inc 3251 Abbeville Hwy PO Box 13409 *TF:* 800-362-8656 ■ *Web:* www.roylco.com	Anderson	SC	29624	864-296-0043	296-6736
School Specialty Inc PO Box 1579 *NASDAQ: SCHS* ■ *TF:* 888-388-3224 ■ *Web:* www.schoolspecialty.com	Appleton	WI	54912	920-734-5712	882-5603
Teacher Created Resources 6421 Industry Way *Fax Area Code: 800 ■ *TF:* 888-343-4335 ■ *Web:* www.teachercreated.com	Westminster	CA	92683	888-343-4335	525-1254*
Teaching & Learning Co 1204 Buchanan St *TF:* 800-444-1144 ■ *Web:* www.lorenzeducationalpress.com	Carthage	IL	62321	937-228-6118	223-2042
TREND Enterprises Inc 300 Ninth Ave SW *TF Cust Svc:* 800-860-6762 ■ *Web:* www.trendenterprises.com	New Brighton	MN	55112	651-631-2850	
World*Class Learning Materials PO Box 639 *TF:* 800-638-6470 ■ *Web:* www.wclm.com	Candler	NC	28715	800-638-6470	638-6499

244 EDUCATIONAL TESTING SERVICES - ASSESSMENT & PREPARATION

Company	City	State	Zip	Phone	Fax
ACT Inc 500 ACT Dr PO Box 168 *Web:* www.act.org	Iowa City	IA	52243	319-337-1000	337-1735
Alpine Testing Inc 51 W Ctr St. *TF:* 844-625-7463 ■ *Web:* www.alpinetesting.com	Orem	UT	84057	844-625-7463	
Anklesaria Group Inc 1172 Cuchara Dr *Web:* www.anklesaria.com	Del Mar	CA	92014	858-755-7119	
Applied Measurement Professionals Inc (AMP) 18000 W 105th St. *Web:* www.goamp.com	Olathe	KS	66061	913-895-4600	895-4650
Barron's Educational Series Inc 250 Wireless Blvd. *TF:* 800-645-3476 ■ *Web:* www.barronseduc.com	Hauppauge	NY	11788	631-434-3311	434-3723
Castle Worldwide Inc 900 Perimeter Pk Rd Ste G *TF:* 800-655-4845 ■ *Web:* www.castleworldwide.com	Morrisville	NC	27560	919-572-6880	361-2426
Clinton County Regional Educatonal Service Agency Resa 1013 S Us Hwy 27 *Web:* www.ccresa.org	Saint Johns	MI	48879	989-224-6831	
College Board 45 Columbus Ave. *Fax: PR ■ *TF:* 800-927-4302 ■ *Web:* www.collegeboard.org	New York	NY	10023	212-713-8000	713-8282*
Edcomm Inc 21 Penn Plz Ste 1010 *Web:* edcomm.com	New York	NY	10001	212-631-9400	
Educational Testing Service Rosedale Rd *Web:* www.ets.org	Princeton	NJ	08541	609-921-9000	734-5410
Fresh Air Educators Inc 203-1568 Carling Ave *TF:* 866-495-4868 ■ *Web:* www.freshaireducators.com	Ottawa	ON	K1Z7M4	866-495-4868	
General Educational Development Testing Service *American Council on Education* 1 Dupont Cir NW *TF:* 866-205-6267 ■ *Web:* www.acenet.edu	Washington	DC	20036	202-939-9300	
H & H Publishing Company Inc 1231 Kapp Dr *TF:* 800-366-4079 ■ *Web:* www.hhpublishing.com	Clearwater	FL	33765	727-442-7760	442-2195
Human Resources Research Organization (HumRRO) 66 Canal Ctr Plz Ste 400 *Web:* www.humrro.org	Alexandria	VA	22314	703-549-3611	549-9025
Kaplan Inc 6301 Kaplan University Ave *TF Cust Svc:* 800-258-2432 ■ *Web:* www.kaplan.com	Fort Lauderdale	FL	33309	954-515-3993	
Kentucky Science and Technology Corp 200 West Vine St Ste 420 *Web:* kstc.com	Lexington	KY	40507	859-233-3502	
McGraw-Hill Cos Inc CTB/McGraw-Hill Div 20 Ryan Ranch Rd *TF:* 800-538-9547 ■ *Web:* www.ctb.com	Monterey	CA	93940	831-393-0700	393-6528
National Summer Learning Association 575 S Charles St Ste 310 *Web:* www.summerlearning.org	Baltimore	MD	21201	410-856-1370	
NogginLabs Inc 4619 N Ravenswood Ave Ste 303 *Web:* www.nogginlabs.com	Chicago	IL	60640	773-878-9011	
Pearson Vue 5601 Green Vly Dr *Web:* www.pearsonvue.com	Bloomington	MN	55437	952-681-3000	681-3899
Praxis Series Online Educational Testing Service Teaching & Learning Div (ETS) PO Box 6051 *TF:* 800-772-9476 ■ *Web:* www.ets.org	Princeton	NJ	08541	609-771-7395	530-0581
Professional Examination Service 475 Riverside Dr Ste 600 *Web:* www.proexam.org	New York	NY	10115	212-367-4200	367-4266
Prometric 1501 S Clinton St *TF:* 866-776-6387 ■ *Web:* www.prometric.com	Baltimore	MD	21224	443-455-8000	
Red Stone Education Consulting Group 1105 11th St. *Web:* www.redstoneeducation.org	Rapid City	SD	57701	605-341-3585	
Silver Strong & Associates 227 1st St. *Web:* www.thoughtfulclassroom.com	Ho Ho Kus	NJ	07423	201-612-6605	
TestTakers 1 Plz Rd Ste 204 *Web:* www.ttprep.com	Greenvale	NY	11548	516-626-6100	

245 ELECTRIC COMPANIES - COOPERATIVES (RURAL)

See Also Utility Companies p. 3280

Companies listed here are members of the National Rural Electric Cooperative Association; most are consumer-owned, but some are public power districts. In addition, the companies listed are electricity distribution cooperatives. Companies that generate and/or transmit electricity, but do not distribute it, are not included.

Alabama

Company	City	State	Zip	Phone	Fax
Baldwin County Electric Membership Corp 19600 Hwy 59 *TF:* 800-837-3374 ■ *Web:* www.baldwinemc.org	Summerdale	AL	36580	251-989-6247	989-0148
Central Alabama Electric Co-op 1802 Hwy 31 N. *TF:* 800-545-5735 ■ *Web:* caec.coop	Prattville	AL	36067	334-365-6762	
Cherokee Electric Co-op 1550 Clarence Chestnut Bypass PO Box O. *TF:* 800-952-2667 ■ *Web:* www.cherokee.coop	Centre	AL	35960	256-927-5524	927-2278
Covington Electric Co-op Inc 18836 US Hwy 84 *TF:* 800-239-4121 ■ *Web:* www.cov-elect.com	Andalusia	AL	36421	334-222-4121	222-1546
Cullman Electric Co-op 1749 Eva Rd NE PO Box 1168 *TF:* 800-242-1806 ■ *Web:* www.cullmanec.com	Cullman	AL	35055	256-737-3201	
Dixie Electric Co-op 9100 Atlanta Hwy *TF:* 888-349-4332 ■ *Web:* www.dixie.coop	Montgomery	AL	36117	334-288-1163	
Franklin Electric Co-op Inc 225 Franklin St NW *TF:* 800-410-2732 ■ *Web:* areapower.coop	Russellville	AL	35653	256-332-2730	
Joe Wheeler Electric Membership Corp PO Box 460 *TF:* 800-239-6518 ■ *Web:* www.jwemc.org	Trinity	AL	35673	256-552-2300	355-0631
North Alabama Electric Co-op 41103 US Hwy 72. *TF:* 800-572-2900 ■ *Web:* www.naecoop.com	Stevenson	AL	35772	256-437-2281	437-2286
Pea River Electric Co-op 1311 W Roy Parker Rd PO Box 969 *TF:* 800-264-7732 ■ *Web:* www. peariver .com	Ozark	AL	36361	334-774-2545	774-2548
Pioneer Electric Co-op 300 Herbert St *TF:* 800-239-3092 ■ *Web:* www.pioneerelectric.com	Greenville	AL	36037	334-382-6636	382-8641
Sand Mountain Electric Co-op 402 Main St W *TF:* 877-843-2512 ■ *Web:* www.smec.coop	Rainsville	AL	35986	256-638-2153	638-4957
South Alabama Electric Co-op (SAEC) PO Box 449 *TF:* 800-556-2060 ■ *Web:* www.southaec.com	Troy	AL	36081	334-566-2060	566-8949
Southern Pine Electric Co-op 2134 S Blvd PO Box 528 *Web:* www.southernpine.org	Brewton	AL	36427	251-867-5415	867-5219
Tallapoosa River Electric Co-op 15163 US Hwy 431 S PO Box 675 *TF:* 800-332-8732 ■ *Web:* www.trec.coop	Lafayette	AL	36862	334-864-9331	864-0817
Tombigbee Electric Co-op Inc 7686 US Hwy PO Box 610 *TF:* 800-621-8069 ■ *Web:* www.tombigbee.net	Guin	AL	35563	205-468-3325	

Alaska

Name / Address	City	State	Zip	Phone	Fax
Alaska Village Electric Co-op Inc 4831 Eagle St — *Web:* www.avec.org	Anchorage	AK	99503	907-561-1818	562-4086
Barrow Utilities & Electric Co-op Inc (BUECI) 1295 Agvik St PO Box 449 — *Web:* www.bueci.org	Barrow	AK	99723	907-852-6166	852-6372
Chugach Electric Assn Inc 5601 Electron Dr — *TF:* 800-478-7494 ■ *Web:* www.chugachelectric.com	Anchorage	AK	99518	907-563-7494	562-0027
Copper Valley Electric Assn Inc (CVEA) Mile 187 Glenn Hwy PO Box 45 — *TF:* 866-835-2832 ■ *Web:* www.cvea.org	Glennallen	AK	99588	907-822-3211	822-5586
Cordova Electric Co-op Inc 705 Second St PO Box 20 — *Web:* www.cordovaelectric.com	Cordova	AK	99574	907-424-5555	
Golden Valley Electrical Assn Inc 758 Illinois St — *TF:* 800-770-4832 ■ *Web:* www.gvea.com	Fairbanks	AK	99701	907-452-1151	458-6365
Homer Electric Assn Inc 3977 Lake St — *TF:* 800-478-8551 ■ *Web:* www.homerelectric.com	Homer	AK	99603	907-235-8551	235-3313
Kodiak Electric Assn Inc 515 E Marine Way — *Web:* www.kodiakelectric.com	Kodiak	AK	99615	907-486-7700	
Kotzebue Electric Assn Inc PO Box 44 — *Web:* www.kea.coop	Kotzebue	AK	99752	907-442-3491	442-2482
Naknek Electric Assn Inc 1 School Rd	Naknek	AK	99633	907-246-4261	246-6242
Nushagak Electric & Telephone Co-op Inc 557 Kenny Wren Rd — *TF:* 800-478-5296 ■ *Web:* www.nushtel.com	Dillingham	AK	99576	907-842-5251	842-2799
Yakutat Power Inc Forrest Hwy	Yakutat	AK	99689	907-784-3248	784-3922

Arizona

Name / Address	City	State	Zip	Phone	Fax
Duncan Valley Electric Co-op Inc PO Box 440 — *TF:* 800-669-2503 ■ *Web:* www.dvec.org	Duncan	AZ	85534	928-359-2503	
Graham County Electric Inc 9 W Center St — *TF:* 800-577-9266 ■ *Web:* azgcec.coop	Pima	AZ	85543	928-485-2451	485-9491
Navopache Electric Co-op Inc 1878 W White Mtn Blvd — *TF:* 800-543-6324 ■ *Web:* www.navopache.org	Lakeside	AZ	85929	928-368-5118	368-6038
Sulphur Springs Valley Electric Co-op Inc 350 N Haskell Ave — *TF:* 877-877-6861	Willcox	AZ	85643	520-384-2221	384-5223
Tohono O'odham Utility Authority PO Box 816 — *Web:* www.toua.net	Sells	AZ	85634	520-383-2236	
Trico Electric Coop 8600 W Tangerine Rd — *Web:* www.trico.org	Marana	AZ	85653	520-744-2944	

Arkansas

Name / Address	City	State	Zip	Phone	Fax
Arkansas Valley Electric Co-op Corp 1811 W Commercial St PO Box 47 — *TF:* 800-468-2176 ■ *Web:* www.avecc.com	Ozark	AR	72949	479-667-2176	667-5238
Ashley-Chicot Electric Co-op Inc 307 E Jefferson St — *TF:* 800-281-5212 ■ *Web:* www.ashley-chicot.com	Hamburg	AR	71646	870-853-5212	853-2531
C & L Electric Co-op Corp 900 Church St PO Box 9 — *Web:* www.clelectric.com	Star City	AR	71667	870-628-4221	628-4676
Carroll Electric Co-op Corp 920 Hwy 62 Spur — *TF:* 800-432-9720 ■ *Web:* www.carrollecc.com	Berryville	AR	72616	870-423-2161	423-4815
Clay County Electric Co-op Corp 300 N Missouri Ave — *TF:* 800-521-2450 ■ *Web:* www.claycountyelectric.com	Corning	AR	72422	870-857-3521	857-3523
Craighead Electric Co-op Corp 4314 Stadium Blvd PO Box 7503 — *TF:* 800-794-5012 ■ *Web:* www.craigheadelectric.coop	Jonesboro	AR	72403	870-932-8301	972-5674
First Electric Co-op Corp 1000 S JP Wright Loop Rd — *TF:* 800-489-7405 ■ *Web:* www.firstelectric.coop	Jacksonville	AR	72076	501-982-4545	982-8450
Mississippi County Electric Co-op 510 N Broadway St — *TF:* 800-439-4563 ■ *Web:* www.mceci.com	Blytheville	AR	72315	870-763-4563	763-0513
North Arkansas Electric Co-op Inc 225 S Main St — *Web:* www.naeci.com	Salem	AR	72576	870-895-3221	895-6279
Ouachita Electric Co-op Corp 700 Bradley Ferry Rd PO Box 877 — *TF:* 877-252-4538 ■ *Web:* www.oecc.com	Camden	AR	71711	870-836-5791	
Ozarks Electric Co-op Corp 3641 W Wedington Dr — *TF:* 800-521-6144 ■ *Web:* www.ozarksecc.com	Fayetteville	AR	72704	479-521-2900	444-0943
Petit Jean Electric Co-op 270 Quality Dr PO Box 37 — *TF:* 800-786-7618 ■ *Web:* www.pjecc.com	Clinton	AR	72031	501-745-2493	745-4150
Rich Mountain Electric Co-op Inc 515 Janssen PO Box 897 — *TF:* 877-828-4074 ■ *Web:* www.rmec.com	Mena	AR	71953	479-394-4140	394-1211
South Central Arkansas Electric Co-op 4818 Highway 8 W PO Box 476 — *TF:* 800-814-2931 ■ *Web:* www.scaec.com	Arkadelphia	AR	71923	870-246-6701	
Southwest Arkansas Electric Co-op 2904 E Ninth St — *Web:* www.swrea.com	Texarkana	AR	71854	870-772-2743	773-2161
Woodruff Electric Co-op PO Box 1619 — *TF:* 888-559-6400 ■ *Web:* woodruffelectric.coop	Forrest City	AR	72336	870-633-2262	633-0629

California

Name / Address	City	State	Zip	Phone	Fax
Anza ElectricCo-op Inc 58470 Hwy 371 PO Box 391909 — *TF:* 844-311-7201 ■ *Web:* www.anzaelectric.org	Anza	CA	92539	951-763-4333	763-5297
Brightsource Energy Inc 1999 Harrison St Ste 2150 — *Web:* www.brightsourceenergy.com	Oakland	CA	94612	510-550-8161	550-8165
Plumas-Sierra Rural Electric Co-op 73233 SR 70 — *TF:* 800-555-2207 ■ *Web:* www.psrec.coop	Portola	CA	96122	530-832-4261	832-5761
Surprise Valley Electric Co-op 22595 US 395 — *TF:* 866-843-2667 ■ *Web:* www.surprisevalleyelectric.org	Alturas	CA	96101	530-233-3511	233-2190
Trinity County California 11 Court St Rm 230 PO Box 1613 — **Fax:* Admin ■ *Web:* www.trinitycounty.org	Weaverville	CA	96093	530-623-1382	623-8365*
Truckee Donner Public Utility District (TDPUD) 11570 Donner Pass Rd PO Box 309 — *Web:* www.tdpud.org	Truckee	CA	96160	530-587-3896	587-5056
Yuba County Water Agency 1220 F St — *Web:* www.ycwa.com	Marysville	CA	95901	530-741-6278	741-6541

Colorado

Name / Address	City	State	Zip	Phone	Fax
Delta-Montrose Electric Assn 11925 6300 Rd — *Web:* www.dmea.com	Montrose	CO	81401	970-249-4572	
Empire Electric Assn Inc 801 N Broadway — *TF:* 800-709-3726 ■ *Web:* www.eea.coop	Cortez	CO	81321	970-565-4444	
Grand Valley Rural Power Lines Inc 845 22 Rd PO Box 190 — *TF:* 877-760-7435 ■ *Web:* www.gvp.org	Grand Junction	CO	81505	970-242-0040	
Gunnison County Electric Assn Inc 37250 W Hwy 50 PO Box 180 — *TF:* 800-726-3523 ■ *Web:* www.gcea.coop	Gunnison	CO	81230	970-641-3520	641-5302
Highline Electric Assn 1300 S Interocean Ave — *TF:* 800-816-2236 ■ *Web:* www.hea.coop	Holyoke	CO	80734	970-854-2236	854-3652
Holy Cross Energy PO Box 2150 — *TF:* 877-833-2555 ■ *Web:* www.holycross.com	Glenwood Springs	CO	81602	970-945-5491	945-4081
Intermountain Rural Electric Assn 5496 Hwy 85 — **Fax Area Code: 720* ■ *TF:* 800-332-9540 ■ *Web:* www.irea.coop	Sedalia	CO	80135	303-688-3100	733-5872*
KC Electric Assn 422 Third Ave — *TF:* 800-700-3123 ■ *Web:* www.kcelectric.coop	Hugo	CO	80821	719-743-2431	743-2396
La Plata Electric Assn Inc 45 Stewart St — *TF:* 888-839-5732 ■ *Web:* www.lpea.com	Durango	CO	81303	970-247-5786	247-2674
Morgan County Rural Electric Assn 20169 US Hwy 34 — *TF:* 877-495-6487 ■ *Web:* www.mcrea.org	Fort Morgan	CO	80701	970-867-5688	867-3277
Mountain Parks Electric Inc 321 W Agate Ave — *TF:* 877-887-3378 ■ *Web:* www.mpei.com	Granby	CO	80446	970-887-3378	887-3996
Mountain View Electric Assn Inc 1655 Fifth St — *TF:* 800-388-9881 ■ *Web:* www.mvea.coop	Limon	CO	80828	719-775-2861	775-9513
Poudre Valley Rural Electric Assn Inc 7649 Rea Pkwy — *TF:* 800-432-1012 ■ *Web:* www.pvrea.com	Fort Collins	CO	80528	970-226-1234	
San Isabel Electric 893 E Enterprise Dr — *TF:* 800-279-7432 ■ *Web:* www.siea.com	Pueblo West	CO	81007	719-547-2160	547-2229
San Luis Valley Rural Electric Co-op 3625 US Hwy 160 W — *TF:* 800-332-7634 ■ *Web:* www.slvrec.com	Monte Vista	CO	81144	719-852-3538	
San Miguel Power Assn Inc 170 W Tenth Ave — *TF:* 800-864-7256 ■ *Web:* www.smpa.com	Nucla	CO	81424	970-864-7311	864-7257
Sangre de Cristo Electric Assn 29780 US Hwy 24 — *TF:* 800-933-3823 ■ *Web:* www.myelectric.coop	Buena Vista	CO	81211	719-395-2412	395-8742
Southeast Colorado Power Assn (SECPA) 901 W 3rd — *TF:* 800-332-8634 ■ *Web:* www.secpa.com	La Junta	CO	81050	719-384-2551	384-7320
United Power Inc 500 Co-op Way — *TF:* 800-468-8809 ■ *Web:* www.unitedpower.com	Brighton	CO	80603	303-659-0551	659-2172
White River Electric Assn (WREA) PO Box 958 — *TF:* 800-922-1987 ■ *Web:* wrea.org	Meeker	CO	81641	970-878-5041	878-5766
Y-W Electric Assn Inc 250 Main Ave PO Box Y — *TF:* 800-660-2291 ■ *Web:* ywelectric.coop	Akron	CO	80720	970-345-2291	345-2154
Yampa Valley Electric Assn Inc 435 Mack Ln Ste 203 — *TF:* 888-873-9832 ■ *Web:* www.yvea.com	Craig	CO	81626	970-879-1160	879-7270

Delaware

Name / Address	City	State	Zip	Phone	Fax
Delaware Electric Co-op Inc PO Box 600 — *TF:* 800-282-8595 ■ *Web:* www.delaware.coop	Greenwood	DE	19950	302-349-3147	349-3147

Florida

Name / Address	City	State	Zip	Phone	Fax
Central Florida Electric Co-op Inc 1124 N Young Blvd — *TF:* 800-227-1302 ■ *Web:* www.cfec.com	Chiefland	FL	32644	352-493-2511	493-4499
Choctawhatchee Electric Co-op Inc 1350 W Baldwin Ave — *TF:* 800-342-0990 ■ *Web:* www.chelco.com	DeFuniak Springs	FL	32435	850-892-2111	892-9243
Clay Electric Co-op Inc 7450 State Rd 100 — *TF:* 800-224-4917 ■ *Web:* www.clayelectric.com	Keystone Heights	FL	32656	352-473-8000	473-1403
Escambia River Electric Co-op Inc 3425 Florida 4 — *TF:* 800-235-3848 ■ *Web:* www.erec.net	Jay	FL	32565	850-675-4521	675-8415

					Phone	Fax
Florida Keys Electric Co-op Assn 91630 Overseas Hwy *TF:* 800-858-8845 ■ *Web:* www.fkec.com		Tavernier	FL	33070	305-852-2431	853-5381
Gulf Coast Electric Co-op Inc 722 W Hwy 22 PO Box 220 *TF:* 800-333-9392 ■ *Web:* www.gcec.com		Wewahitchka	FL	32465	850-639-2216	639-5061
Lee County Electric Co-op Inc 4980 Bayline Dr PO Box 3455 *TF:* 800-282-1643 ■ *Web:* www.lcec.net		North Fort Myers	FL	33917	239-995-2121	995-7904
Peace River Electric Co-op Inc 210 Metheny Rd PO Box 1310 **Fax Area Code:* 863 ■ *TF:* 800-282-3824 ■ *Web:* www.preco.coop		Wauchula	FL	33873	800-282-3824	773-3737*
Sumter Electric Co-op Inc PO Box 301 *TF:* 800-732-6141 ■ *Web:* www.secoenergy.com		Sumterville	FL	33585	352-793-3801	
Suwannee Valley Electric Co-op PO Box 160 *TF:* 800-752-0025 ■ *Web:* www.svec-coop.com		Live Oak	FL	32064	386-362-2226	364-5008
Talquin Electric Co-op Inc 1640 W Jefferson St *TF:* 888-271-8778 ■ *Web:* www.talquinelectric.com		Quincy	FL	32351	850-627-7651	627-2553
Tri-County Electric Co-op Inc 2862 W US Hwy 90 *TF:* 800-999-2285 ■ *Web:* www.tcec.com		Madison	FL	32340	850-973-2285	973-1209
West Florida Electric Co-op 5282 Peanut Rd *TF:* 800-342-7400 ■ *Web:* westflorida.coop		Graceville	FL	32440	850-263-3231	
Withlacoochee River Electric Co-op PO Box 278 *Web:* www.wrec.net		Dade City	FL	33526	352-567-5133	

Georgia

					Phone	Fax
Altamaha Electric Membership Corp 611 W Liberty Ave PO Box 346 *TF:* 800-822-4563 ■ *Web:* www.altamahaemc.com		Lyons	GA	30436	912-526-8181	526-4235
Amicalola Electric Membership Corp 544 Hwy 515 S *TF:* 800-282-7411 ■ *Web:* www.amicalolaemc.com		Jasper	GA	30143	706-253-5200	
Canoochee Electric Membership Corp 342 E Brazell St *TF:* 800-342-0134 ■ *Web:* www.canoocheeemc.com		Reidsville	GA	30453	800-342-0134	
Carroll Electric Membership Corp 155 N Hwy 113 *Web:* www.cemc.com		Carrollton	GA	30117	770-832-3552	832-0240
Central Georgia Electric Membership Corp 923 S Mulberry St **Fax:* Cust Svc ■ *TF:* 800-222-4877 ■ *Web:* www.cgemc.com		Jackson	GA	30233	770-775-7857	504-7877*
Coastal Electric Co-op 1265 S Coastal Hwy PO Box 109 *TF:* 800-421-2343		Midway	GA	31320	912-884-3311	884-2362
Cobb Electric Membership Corp 1000 EMC Pkwy PO Box 369 **Fax Area Code:* 678 ■ **Fax:* Hum Res ■ *Web:* www.cobbemc.com		Marietta	GA	30061	770-429-2100	355-3363*
Coweta-Fayette Electric Membership Corp 807 Collinsworth Rd *TF:* 877-746-4362 ■ *Web:* www.utility.org		Palmetto	GA	30268	770-502-0226	251-9788
Crisp County Power Commission Inc PO Box 1218 *Web:* www.crispcountypower.com		Cordele	GA	31010	229-273-3811	
Diverse Power Inc 1400 S Davis Rd *TF:* 800-845-8362 ■ *Web:* www.diversepower.com		LaGrange	GA	30241	706-845-2000	845-2020
Excelsior Electric Membership Corp 986 SE Broad St *Web:* www.excelsioremc.com		Metter	GA	30439	912-685-2115	685-5782
Flint Energies 3 S Macon St *TF:* 800-342-3616 ■ *Web:* www.flintenergies.com		Reynolds	GA	31076	478-847-3415	
Grady Electric Membership Corp (EMC) 1499 US Hwy 84 W *TF:* 877-757-6060 ■ *Web:* www.gradyemc.com		Cairo	GA	39828	229-377-4182	377-7176
Greystone Power Corp 4040 Bankhead Hwy *Web:* www.greystonepower.com		Douglasville	GA	30134	770-942-6576	489-0940
Habersham Electric Membership Corp 6135 Georgia 115 **Fax Area Code:* 800 ■ *TF:* 800-640-6812 ■ *Web:* www.habershamemc.com		Clarkesville	GA	30523	706-754-2114	640-6813*
Hart Electric Membership Corp 1071 Elberton Hwy **Fax Area Code:* 800 ■ *TF:* 800-241-4109 ■ *Web:* www.hartemc.com		Hartwell	GA	30643	706-376-4714	486-3277*
Irwin Electric Membership Corp 915 W Fourth St *TF:* 800-237-3745 ■ *Web:* www.irwinemc.com		Ocilla	GA	31774	229-468-7415	468-7009
Jackson Electric Membership Corp 850 Commerce Rd *TF:* 800-462-3691 ■ *Web:* www.jacksonemc.com		Jefferson	GA	30549	706-367-5281	
Jefferson Energy Co-op 3077 Hwy 17 PO Box 457 *TF:* 877-533-3377 ■ *Web:* www.jeffersonenergy.com		North Wrens	GA	30833	706-547-2167	
Little Ocmulgee Electric Membership Corp 26 W Railroad Ave *TF:* 800-342-1290 ■ *Web:* www.littleocmulgeeemc.com		Alamo	GA	30411	912-568-7171	
Middle Georgia Electric Membership Corp 600 Tippettville Rd *TF:* 800-342-0144 ■ *Web:* mgemc.com		Vienna	GA	31092	229-268-2671	268-7215
Mitchell Electric Membership Corp 475 Cairo Rd *TF:* 800-479-6034 ■ *Web:* www.mitchellemc.com		Camilla	GA	31730	229-336-5221	336-7088
North Georgia Electric Membership Corp 1850 Cleveland Hwy *Web:* www.ngemc.com		Dalton	GA	30721	706-259-9441	
Ocmulgee Electric Membership Corp 5722 Eastman St *TF:* 800-342-5509 ■ *Web:* www.ocmulgeeemc.com		Eastman	GA	31023	478-374-7001	
Oconee Electric Membership Corp 3445 US Hwy 80 W *TF:* 800-522-2930 ■ *Web:* www.oconeeemc.com		Dudley	GA	31022	478-676-3191	676-4200
Okefenoke Rural Electric Membership Corp (REMC) 14384 Cleveland St PO Box 602 *TF:* 800-262-5131 ■ *Web:* www.oremc.com		Nahunta	GA	31553	912-462-5131	462-6100
Pataula Electric Membership Corp 211 Barkley St		Cuthbert	GA	39840	229-732-3171	
Planters Electric Membership Corp 1740 Hwy 25 N PO Box 979 *TF:* 888-397-3742 ■ *Web:* www.plantersemc.com		Millen	GA	30442	478-982-4722	982-4798
Rayle Electric Membership Corp 616 Lexington Ave *Web:* www.rayleemc.com		Washington	GA	30673	706-678-2116	678-5381
Sawnee Electric Membership Corp 543 Atlantic Hwy *Web:* www.sawnee.com		Cumming	GA	30028	770-887-2363	
Slash Pine Electric Membership Corp 794 W Dame Ave *Web:* slashpineemc.com		Homerville	GA	31634	912-487-5201	487-2948
Snapping Shoals Electric Membership Corp 14750 Brown Bridge Rd *TF:* 888-999-1416 ■ *Web:* ssemc.com		Covington	GA	30016	770-786-3484	385-2720
Sumter Electric Membership Corp 1120 Felder St *TF:* 800-342-6978 ■ *Web:* www.sumteremc.com		Americus	GA	31709	229-924-8041	924-4982
Three Notch Electric Membership Corp PO Box 295 *TF:* 800-239-5377 ■ *Web:* www.threenotchemc.com		Donalsonville	GA	39845	229-524-5377	
Tri-County Electric Membership Corp PO Box 487 *TF:* 866-254-8100 ■ *Web:* www.tri-countyemc.com		Gray	GA	31032	478-986-8100	986-4733
Tri-State Electric Membership Corp (TSEMC) 2310 Blue Ridge Dr *TF:* 800-351-1111 ■ *Web:* www.tsemc.net		Blue Ridge	GA	30513	706-492-3251	492-7617
Upson County Electric Membership Corp 607 E Main St *Web:* www.upsonemc.com		Thomaston	GA	30286	706-647-5475	647-8545
Walton EMC 842 Hwy 78 NW PO Box 260 *Web:* www.waltonemc.com		Monroe	GA	30655	770-267-2505	267-1223
Washington Electric Membership Corp 258 N Harris St *TF:* 800-552-2577 ■ *Web:* www.washingtonemc.com		Sandersville	GA	31082	478-552-2577	

Idaho

					Phone	Fax
Clearwater Power Co 4230 Hatwai Rd PO Box 997 *TF:* 888-743-1501 ■ *Web:* www.clearwaterpower.com		Lewiston	ID	83501	208-743-1501	746-3902
Fall River Rural Electric Co-op Inc 1150 N 3400 E *TF:* 800-632-5726 ■ *Web:* www.fallriverelectric.com		Ashton	ID	83420	208-652-7431	652-7825
Idaho County Light & Power Co-op 1065 Hwy 13 *TF:* 877-212-0424 ■ *Web:* www.iclp.coop		Grangeville	ID	83530	208-983-1610	
Kootenai Electric Co-op Inc 2451 W Dakota Ave *TF:* 800-240-0459 ■ *Web:* www.kec.com		Hayden	ID	83835	208-765-1200	772-5858
Northern Lights Inc 421 Cherry St PO Box 269 *TF:* 800-326-9594 ■ *Web:* www.nli.coop		Sagle	ID	83860	208-263-5141	263-7412
Raft River Rural Electric Co-op Inc 155 N Main St PO Box 617 *TF:* 800-342-7732 ■ *Web:* www.rrelectric.com		Malta	ID	83342	208-645-2211	645-2300
Salmon River Electric Co-op Inc 1130 Main St PO Box 384 *TF:* 877-806-2283 ■ *Web:* www.srec.org		Challis	ID	83226	208-879-2283	879-2596
United Electric Co-op Inc 1330 21st St *Web:* www.unitedelectric.coop		Heyburn	ID	83336	208-679-2222	679-3333

Illinois

					Phone	Fax
Adams Electric Co-op 700 Eastwood St PO Box 247 *TF:* 800-232-4797 ■ *Web:* www.adamselectric.coop		Camp Point	IL	62320	217-593-7701	593-7120
Clinton County Electric Co-op Inc 475 N Main St PO Box 40 *TF:* 800-526-7282 ■ *Web:* cceci.com		Breese	IL	62230	618-526-7282	526-4561
Coles-Moultrie Electric Co-op 104 DeWitt Ave E PO Box 709 *Web:* www.cmec.coop		Mattoon	IL	61938	217-235-0341	
Corn Belt Energy Corp 1 Energy Way *TF:* 800-879-0339 ■ *Web:* www.cornbeltenergy.com		Bloomington	IL	61705	309-662-5330	663-4516
Eastern Illini Electric Co-op 330 W Ottawa PO Box 96 *TF:* 800-824-5102 ■ *Web:* eiec.org		Paxton	IL	60957	217-379-2131	379-2936
Egyptian Electric Co-op Assn PO Box 38 *TF:* 800-606-1505 ■ *Web:* www.eeca.coop		Steeleville	IL	62288	800-606-1505	
Illinois Rural Electric Co-op 2 S Main St *TF:* 800-468-4732 ■ *Web:* e-co-op.com		Winchester	IL	62694	217-742-3128	742-3831
Jo-Carroll Energy 793 US Hwy 20 W *TF:* 800-858-5522 ■ *Web:* www.jocarroll.com		Elizabeth	IL	61028	815-858-2207	858-3731
McDonough Power Co-op 1210 W Jackson St *Web:* mcdonoughpower.com		Macomb	IL	61455	309-833-2101	833-2104
Menard Electric Co-op 14300 State Hwy 97 PO Box 200 *TF:* 800-872-1203 ■ *Web:* www.menard.com		Petersburg	IL	62675	217-632-7746	632-2578
MJM Electric Co-op Inc (MJMEC) 264 NE St PO Box 80 *TF:* 800-648-4729 ■ *Web:* www.mjmec.coop		Carlinville	IL	62626	217-854-3137	854-3918
Rural Electric Convenience Co-op Co 3973 W SR 104 PO Box 19 *TF:* 800-245-7322 ■ *Web:* www.recc.coop		Auburn	IL	62615	217-438-6197	438-3212
Shelby Electric Co-op (SEC) 1355 IL-128 state PO Box 560 *TF:* 800-677-2612		Shelbyville	IL	62565	217-774-3986	774-3330

				Phone	Fax
SouthEastern Illinois Electric Co-op 585 Hwy 142 S PO Box 251	Eldorado	IL	62930	618-273-2611	273-3886
TF: 800-833-2611 ■ *Web:* www.seiec.com					
Southern Illinois Electric Co-op 7420 US Hwy 51 S	Dongola	IL	62926	618-827-3555	827-3585
TF: 800-762-1400 ■ *Web:* www.siec.coop					
Southwestern Electric Co-op Inc 525 US Rt 40 PO Box 549	Greenville	IL	62246	800-637-8667	664-4179*
**Fax Area Code:* 618 ■ *TF:* 800-637-8667 ■ *Web:* www.sweci.com					
Spoon River Electric Co-op Inc (SREC) 930 S Fifth Ave PO Box 340	Canton	IL	61520	309-647-2700	647-7354
TF: 877-404-2572 ■ *Web:* www.srecoop.org					
Tri-County Electric Co-op Inc 3906 Broadway St	Mount Vernon	IL	62864	618-244-5151	244-1496
TF: 800-244-5151 ■ *Web:* www.tricountycoop.com					
Wayne-White Counties Electric Co-op 1501 W Main St	Fairfield	IL	62837	618-842-2196	
TF: 888-871-7695 ■ *Web:* www.wwcec.com					
Western Illinois Electrical Co-op 524 N Madison St PO Box 338	Carthage	IL	62321	217-357-3125	357-3127
TF: 800-576-3125 ■ *Web:* www.wiec.net					

Indiana

				Phone	Fax
Bartholomew County Rural Electric Membership Corp 1697 W. Deaver Rd	Columbus	IN	47201	812-372-2546	
TF: 800-927-5672 ■ *Web:* www.bcremc.com					
Boone County Rural Electric Membership Corp 1207 Indianapolis Ave	Lebanon	IN	46052	765-482-2390	482-7869
TF: 800-897-7362 ■ *Web:* www.bremc.com					
Clark County REMC 7810 State Rd 60 PO Box 411	Sellersburg	IN	47172	812-246-3316	246-3947
TF: 800-462-6988 ■ *Web:* www.theremc.com					
Crawfordsville Electric Light & Power 808 Lafayette Ave	Crawfordsville	IN	47933	765-362-1900	
Web: metronetinc.com/crawfordsville					
Daviess-Martin County REMC 12628 E 75 N PO Box 430	Loogootee	IN	47553	812-295-4200	295-4216
TF: 800-762-7362 ■ *Web:* www.dmremc.com					
Decatur County Rural Electric Membership Corp 1430 W Main St PO Box 46	Greensburg	IN	47240	812-663-3391	663-8572
TF: 800-844-7362 ■ *Web:* www.dcremc.com					
Dubois Rural Electric Co-op Inc 1400 Energy Dr	Jasper	IN	47547	812-482-5454	
Web: www.duboisrec.com					
Fulton County Rural Electric Membership Corp 1448 W State Rd 14 PO Box 230	Rochester	IN	46975	574-223-3156	
Web: faqs.org					
Hendricks Power Co-op 86 N County Rd 500 E	Avon	IN	46123	317-745-5473	745-6865
TF: 800-876-5473 ■ *Web:* www.hendrickspower.com					
Jackson County Rural Electric Membership Corp 274 E Base Rd	Brownstown	IN	47220	812-358-4458	358-5719
TF: 800-288-4458 ■ *Web:* www.jacksonremc.com					
Jasper County Rural Electric Membership Corp 280 E 400 S	Rensselaer	IN	47978	219-866-4601	866-2199
TF: 888-866-7362 ■ *Web:* www.jasperremc.com					
Jay County Rural Electric Membership Corp 484 S 200 W PO Box 904	Portland	IN	47371	260-726-7121	726-6240
TF: 800-835-7362 ■ *Web:* www.jayremc.com					
Johnson County Rural Electric Membership Corp 750 International Dr	Franklin	IN	46131	317-736-6174	736-8185
TF: 800-382-5544 ■ *Web:* www.jcremc.com					
Kosciusko County Rural Electric Membership Corp 370 S 250 E	Warsaw	IN	46582	574-267-6331	267-7273
Web: kremc.com					
LaGrange County Rural Electric Membership Corp 1995 E US Hwy 20	LaGrange	IN	46761	260-463-7165	463-4329
TF: 877-463-7165 ■ *Web:* www.lagrangeremc.com					
Marshall County REMC 11299 12th Rd PO Box 250	Plymouth	IN	46563	574-936-3161	935-4162
Web: www.marshallremc.com					
Miami-Cass County Rural Electric Membership Corp 3086 W 100 N PO Box 168	Peru	IN	46970	765-473-6668	473-8770
TF General: 800-844-6668 ■ *Web:* mcremc.coop					
Noble REMC 300 Weber Rd PO Box 137	Albion	IN	46701	260-636-2113	636-3319
TF: 800-933-7362 ■ *Web:* www.nobleremc.com					
Northeastern REMC 4901 E Pk 30 Dr	Columbia City	IN	46725	260-244-6111	625-3407
Web: www.nremc.com					
Orange County Rural Electric Membership Corp 7133 N State Rd 337 PO Box 208	Orleans	IN	47452	812-865-2229	865-2061
TF: 888-337-5900 ■ *Web:* www.myremc.coop					
Parke County Rural Electric Membership Corp 119 W High St	Rockville	IN	47872	765-569-3133	569-3360
TF: 800-537-3913 ■ *Web:* www.parkecountyremc.com					
Rush Shelby Energy Inc 2777 S 840 W PO Box 55	Manilla	IN	46150	765-544-2600	544-2620
TF General: 800-706-7362 ■ *Web:* www.rse.coop					
South Central Indiana Rural Electric Membership Corp 300 Morton Ave	Martinsville	IN	46151	765-342-3344	
TF: 800-264-7362 ■ *Web:* www.sciremc.com					
Southeastern Indiana Rural Electric Membership Corp 712 S Buckeye St	Osgood	IN	47037	812-689-4111	689-6987
TF: 800-737-4111 ■ *Web:* www.seiremc.com					
Southern Indiana Rural Electric Co-op Inc 1776 Tenth St PO Box 219	Tell City	IN	47586	812-547-2316	547-6853
TF: 800-323-2316 ■ *Web:* www.sirec.com					
Steuben County Rural Electric Membership Corp 1212 S Wayne St	Angola	IN	46703	260-665-3563	665-7495
TF: 888-233-9088 ■ *Web:* www.remcsteuben.com					
Tipmont Rural Electric Membership Corp 403 S Main St	Linden	IN	47955	800-726-3953	
TF: 800-726-3953 ■ *Web:* www.tipmont.org					
Wabash County Rural Electric Membership Corp 350 Wedcor Ave	Wabash	IN	46992	260-563-2146	563-1523
TF: 800-563-2146 ■ *Web:* heartlandremc.com					
Wabash Valley Power Assn Inc 722 N High School Rd	Indianapolis	IN	46214	317-481-2800	243-6416
Web: www.wvpa.com					
Warren County Rural Electric Membership Corp 15 Midway St PO Box 37	Williamsport	IN	47993	765-762-6114	762-6117
TF: 800-872-7319 ■ *Web:* www.wcremc.com					
White County Rural Electric Membership Corp 302 N Sixth St	Monticello	IN	47960	574-583-7161	583-4156
TF: 800-844-7161 ■ *Web:* www.cwremc.com					
Whitewater Valley Rural Electric Membership Corp 101 Brownsville Ave	Liberty	IN	47353	765-458-5171	458-5938
TF: 800-529-5557 ■ *Web:* www.wwvremc.com					
WIN Energy Rural Electric Membership Corp 3981 S US Hwy 41	Vincennes	IN	47591	812-882-5140	886-0306
TF: 800-882-5140 ■ *Web:* www.winenergyremc.com					

Iowa

				Phone	Fax
Access Energy Co-op 1800 W Washington St	Mount Pleasant	IA	52641	319-385-1577	385-6873
TF: 866-242-4232 ■ *Web:* www.accessenergycoop.com					
Allamakee-Clayton Electric Co-op (ACEC) 229 Hwy 51 PO Box 715	Postville	IA	52162	563-864-7611	864-7820
TF: 888-788-1551 ■ *Web:* www.acrec.com					
Butler County Rural Electric Co-op 521 N Main PO Box 98	Allison	IA	50602	319-267-2726	267-2566
TF: 888-267-2726 ■ *Web:* www.butlerrec.coop					
Calhoun County Electric Co-op Assn 1015 Tonawanda St PO Box 312	Rockwell City	IA	50579	712-297-7112	297-7211
TF: 800-821-4879 ■ *Web:* www.calhounrec.coop					
Chariton Valley Electric Co-op 2090 Hwy 5 PO Box 486	Albia	IA	52531	641-932-7126	932-2534
TF: 800-475-1702 ■ *Web:* www.cvrec.com					
Consumers Energy 2074 242nd St	Marshalltown	IA	50158	641-752-1593	752-5738
TF: 800-696-6552 ■ *Web:* www.consumersenergy.net					
Corn Belt Power Co-op 1300 13th St N PO Box 508	Humboldt	IA	50548	515-332-2571	332-1375
Web: www.cbpower.coop					
East-Central Iowa Rural Electric Co-op 2400 Bing Miller Ln	Urbana	IA	52345	319-443-4343	443-4359
TF: 877-850-4343 ■ *Web:* www.ecirec.com					
Eastern Iowa Light & Power Co-op 600 E Fifth St PO Box 3003	Wilton	IA	52778	563-732-2211	732-2219
TF: 800-728-1242 ■ *Web:* www.easterniowa.com					
Farmers Electric Co-op Inc 1959 Yoder Ave SW	Kalona	IA	52247	319-683-2510	683-2506
Franklin Rural Electric Co-op 1560 Hwy 65 PO Box 437	Hampton	IA	50441	641-456-2557	456-5183
TF: 800-750-3557 ■ *Web:* www.franklinrec.coop					
Grundy County Rural Electric Co-op 102 E 'G' Ave	Grundy Center	IA	50638	319-824-5251	824-3118
TF: 800-390-7605 ■ *Web:* www.grundycountyrecia.com					
Harrison County Rural Electric Co-op 105 Enterprise Dr PO Box 2	Woodbine	IA	51579	712-647-2727	
Web: www.hcrec.coop					
Hawkeye REC 24049 Iowa 9	Cresco	IA	52136	563-547-3801	547-4033
TF: 800-658-2243 ■ *Web:* www.hawkeyerec.com					
Heartland Power Co-op 216 Jackson St PO Box 65	Thompson	IA	50478	641-584-2251	584-2253
TF: 888-584-9732 ■ *Web:* www.heartlandpower.com					
Humboldt County Rural Electric Co-op (HCREC) 1210 13th St N	Humboldt	IA	50548	515-332-1616	
TF: 800-452-1111 ■ *Web:* www.midlandpower.coop					
Iowa Lakes Electric Co-op 702 S First St	Estherville	IA	51334	712-362-7870	362-2819
TF: 800-225-4532 ■ *Web:* www.ilec.coop					
Linn County Rural Electric Co-op 5695 Rec Dr	Marion	IA	52302	319-377-1587	377-5875
Web: www.linncountyrec.com					
Lyon Rural Electric Co-op 116 S Marshall St	Rock Rapids	IA	51246	712-472-2506	472-3925
TF: 800-658-3976 ■ *Web:* www.lyonrec.coop					
Maquoketa Valley Rural Electric Co-op 109 N Huber St	Anamosa	IA	52205	319-462-3542	462-3217
TF: 800-927-6068 ■ *Web:* www.mvec.com					
Midland Power Co-op 1005 E Lincolnway PO Box 420	Jefferson	IA	50129	515-386-4111	386-2385
TF: 800-833-8876 ■ *Web:* www.midlandpower.coop					
Nishnabotna Valley Rural Electric Co-op 1317 Chatburn Ave	Harlan	IA	51537	712-755-2166	755-2351
TF: 800-234-5122 ■ *Web:* www.nvrec.com					
North West REC 1505 Albany Pl SE PO Box 435	Orange City	IA	51041	712-707-4935	707-4934
TF: 800-383-0476 ■ *Web:* www.nwrec.com					
Northwest Iowa Power Co-op (NIPCO) 31002 County Rd C38 PO Box 240	Le Mars	IA	51031	712-546-4141	546-8795
Web: www.nipco.coop					
Osceola Electric Co-op Inc 1102 Egret Dr PO Box 127	Sibley	IA	51249	712-754-2519	
TF: 888-754-2519 ■ *Web:* www.osceolaelectric.com					
Pella Co-op Electric Assn 2615 Washington St	Pella	IA	50219	641-628-1040	
TF: 800-619-1040 ■ *Web:* pella-cea.org					
Raccoon Valley Electric Co-op 28725 Hwy 30 PO Box 486	Glidden	IA	51443	712-659-3649	659-3716
TF: 800-253-6211 ■ *Web:* www.rvec.coop					
Southern Iowa Electric Co-op Inc 22458 Hwy 2 PO Box 70	Bloomfield	IA	52537	641-664-2277	664-3502
TF: 800-607-2027 ■ *Web:* www.sie.coop					
Southwest Iowa Rural Electric Co-op 1801 Grove Ave	Corning	IA	50841	641-322-3165	322-5274
TF: 888-591-1261 ■ *Web:* www.swiarec.coop					
TIP Rural Electric Co-op 612 W Des Moines St PO Box 534	Brooklyn	IA	52211	641-522-9221	522-9271
TF: 800-934-7976 ■ *Web:* www.tiprec.com					
Western Iowa Power Co-op 809 Iowa 39	Denison	IA	51442	712-263-2943	263-8655
TF: 800-253-5189 ■ *Web:* www.wipco.com					

Phone Fax

Woodbury County Rural Electric Co-op Assn
1495 Humboldt Ave .... Moville IA 51039 712-873-3125 873-5377
TF: 800-469-3125 ■ *Web:* woodburyrec.com

Kansas

Phone Fax

Ark Valley Electric Co-op Assn
10 E Tenth St .... South Hutchinson KS 67504 620-662-6661 665-0148
TF: 888-297-9212 ■ *Web:* www.arkvalley.com

Bluestem Electric Co-op Inc
614 E Hwy 24 PO Box 5 .... Wamego KS 66547 785-456-2212 456-2003
TF: 800-558-1580 ■ *Web:* www.bluestemelectric.com

Brown-Atchison Electric Co-op Assn Inc
1712 Central Ave PO Box 230 .... Horton KS 66439 785-486-2117 486-3910
Web: www.baelectric.com

Butler Rural Electric Co-op Assn Inc
216 S Vine St PO Box 1242 .... El Dorado KS 67042 316-321-9600 321-9980
TF: 800-464-0060 ■ *Web:* www.butler.coop

Caney Valley Electric Co-op Assn Inc, The
401 Lawrence St PO Box 308 .... Cedar Vale KS 67024 620-758-2262 758-2926
TF: 800-310-8911 ■ *Web:* www.caneyvalley.com

CMS Electric Co-op Inc 509 E Carthage St .... Meade KS 67864 620-873-2184
TF: 800-794-2353 ■ *Web:* www.cmselectric.com

Doniphan Electric Co-op Assn Inc
101 N Main PO Box 699 .... Troy KS 66087 785-985-3523
Web: www.donrec.org

DS&O Electric Cooperative Inc
129 W Main St PO Box 286 .... Solomon KS 67480 785-655-2011 655-2805
TF: 800-376-3533 ■ *Web:* www.dsoelectric.com

Flint Hills Rural Electric Co-op Assn Inc
1564 S 1000 Rd .... Council Grove KS 66846 620-767-5144
Web: www.flinthillsrec.com

Heartland Rural Electric Co-op
110 Enterprise St .... Girard KS 66743 620-724-8251 724-8253
TF: 888-835-9585 ■ *Web:* www.heartland-rec.com

Kaw Valley Electric Co-op Inc
1100 SW Auburn Rd .... Topeka KS 66615 785-478-3444 478-1088
TF: 800-794-2011 ■ *Web:* www.kawvalleyelectric.coop

Lane-Scott Electric Co-op Inc 410 S High .... Dighton KS 67839 620-397-5327
TF: 800-407-2217 ■ *Web:* www.lanescott.coop

Leavenworth-Jefferson Electric Co-op Inc
507 N Union St .... McLouth KS 66054 888-796-6111
TF: 888-796-6111 ■ *Web:* www.ljec.coop

Lyon-Coffey Electric Co-op Inc
1013 N 4th PO Box 229 .... Burlington KS 66839 620-364-2116 364-5122
TF: 800-748-7395 ■ *Web:* www.lyon-coffey.coop

Midwest Energy Inc 1330 Canterbury Dr .... Hays KS 67601 785-625-3437 625-1494
TF: 800-222-3121 ■ *Web:* www.mwenergy.com

Pioneer Electric Co-op Inc
1850 W Oklahoma St PO Box 368 .... Ulysses KS 67880 620-356-1211
TF: 800-794-9302 ■ *Web:* www.pioneerelectric.coop

Prairie Land Electric Co-op Inc
14935 US Hwy 36 .... Norton KS 67654 785-877-3323 877-3572
TF: 800-577-3323 ■ *Web:* www.prairielandelectric.com

Radiant Electric Co-op Inc PO Box 390 .... Fredonia KS 66736 620-378-2161 378-3164
TF: 800-821-0956 ■ *Web:* radiantec.coop

Rolling Hills Electric Co-op Inc
122 W Main St PO Box 307 .... Mankato KS 66956 785-378-3151 378-3219
TF: 877-906-5903 ■ *Web:* www.rollinghills.coop

Sedgwick County Electric Co-op
1355 S 383rd St W .... Cheney KS 67025 316-542-3131
Web: www.sedgwickcountyelectric.coop

Sumner-Cowley Electric Co-op Inc
2223 N A St PO Box 220 .... Wellington KS 67152 620-326-3356 326-6579
TF: 888-326-3356 ■ *Web:* www.sucocoop.com

Twin Valley Electric Co-op Inc
501 S Huston Ave .... Altamont KS 67330 620-784-5500
TF: 866-784-5500 ■ *Web:* www.twinvalleyelectric.coop

Victory Electric Co-op Assn Inc
3230 N 14th Ave .... Dodge City KS 67801 620-227-2139 227-8819
TF: 800-279-7915 ■ *Web:* www.victoryelectric.net

Western Co-op Electric Assn Inc
635 S 13th St .... WaKeeney KS 67672 785-743-5561 743-2717
TF: 800-456-6720 ■ *Web:* www.westerncoop.com

Wheatland Electric Co-op Inc
101 S Main St .... Scott City KS 67871 620-872-5885 872-7170
TF: 800-762-0436 ■ *Web:* www.weci.net

Kentucky

Phone Fax

Big Sandy Rural Electric Co-op Corp
504 11th St .... Paintsville KY 41240 606-789-4095 789-5454
TF: 888-789-7322 ■ *Web:* www.bigsandyrecc.com

Blue Grass Energy Co-op Corp
1201 Lexington Rd .... Nicholasville KY 40356 859-885-4191 885-2854
TF: 888-546-4243 ■ *Web:* www.bgenergy.com

Clark Energy Co-op Inc 2640 Ironworks Rd .... Winchester KY 40391 859-744-4251 744-4218
TF: 800-992-3269 ■ *Web:* www.clarkenergy.com

Cumberland Valley Electric Inc
6219 N US Hwy 25 E .... Gray KY 40734 800-513-2677 523-2698*
**Fax Area Code:* 606 ■ *TF:* 800-513-2677 ■ *Web:* www.cumberlandvalley.coop

Farmers Rural Electric Co-op Corp
504 S Broadway St .... Glasgow KY 42141 270-651-2191 651-7332
TF: 800-253-2191 ■ *Web:* www.farmersrecc.com

Fleming Mason Energy Co-op
1449 Elizaville Rd .... Flemingsburg KY 41041 606-845-2661 845-1008
Web: www.fmenergy.com

Grayson Rural Electric Co-op Corp
109 Bagby Pk .... Grayson KY 41143 606-474-5136 474-5862
TF: 800-562-3532 ■ *Web:* www.graysonrecc.com

Hickman-Fulton Counties Rural Electric Co-op Corp
1702 Moscow Ave .... Hickman KY 42050 270-236-2521 236-3028
TF: 800-633-1391

Inter-County Energy Co-op
1009 Hustonville Rd .... Danville KY 40422 859-236-4561 236-3627
TF: 888-266-7322 ■ *Web:* www.intercountyenergy.net

Jackson Energy Co-op 115 Jackson Energy Ln .... McKee KY 40447 606-364-1000 364-1007
TF: 800-262-7480 ■ *Web:* www.jacksonenergy.com

Jackson Purchase Energy Corp
2900 Irvin Cobb Dr .... Paducah KY 42002 270-442-7321 442-5337
TF: 800-633-4044 ■ *Web:* www.jpenergy.com

Kenergy Corp 6402 Old Corydon Rd .... Henderson KY 42419 270-826-3991 826-3999
TF: 800-844-4832 ■ *Web:* www.kenergycorp.com

Licking Valley Rural Electric Co-op Corp
271 Main St .... West Liberty KY 41472 606-743-3179 743-2415
TF: 800-596-6530 ■ *Web:* lvrecc.com

Meade County Rural Electric Co-op Corp
1351 Kentucky 79 .... Brandenburg KY 40108 270-422-2162 422-4705
Web: www.mcrecc.com

Nolin Rural Electric Co-op Corp
411 Ring Rd .... Elizabethtown KY 42701 270-765-6153 735-1053
TF: 888-637-4247 ■ *Web:* www.nolinrecc.com

Owen Electric Co-op Inc
8205 Hwy 127 N PO Box 400 .... Owenton KY 40359 502-484-3471
TF: 800-372-7612 ■ *Web:* www.owenelectric.com

Pennyrile Rural Electric Co-op Corp
2000 Harrison St PO Box 2900 .... Hopkinsville KY 42241 270-886-2555 885-6469
TF Cust Svc: 800-297-4710 ■ *Web:* www.precc.com

Salt River Electric Co-op Corp
111 W Brashear Ave .... Bardstown KY 40004 502-348-3931 348-1993
TF: 800-221-7465 ■ *Web:* www.srelectric.com

Shelby Energy Co-op Inc
620 Old Finchville Rd .... Shelbyville KY 40065 502-633-4420 633-2387
TF: 800-292-6585 ■ *Web:* www.shelbyenergy.com

South Kentucky Rural Electrical Co-op
925 N Main St PO Box 910 .... Somerset KY 42502 606-678-4121 679-8279
TF: 800-264-5112 ■ *Web:* www.skrecc.com

Taylor County RECC
625 W Main St PO Box 100 .... Campbellsville KY 42719 270-465-4101 789-3625
TF: 800-931-4551 ■ *Web:* www.tcrecc.com

Warren Rural Electric Co-op Corp
951 Fairview Ave .... Bowling Green KY 42101 270-842-6541 781-3299
TF: 866-319-3234 ■ *Web:* www.wrecc.com

West Kentucky Rural Electric Co-op Corp
PO Box 589 .... Mayfield KY 42066 270-247-1321
TF: 877-495-7322 ■ *Web:* www.wkrecc.com

Louisiana

Phone Fax

Beauregard Electric Co-op Inc
1010 E First St .... DeRidder LA 70634 337-463-6221 463-2809
TF: 800-367-0275 ■ *Web:* www.beci.org

Claiborne Electric Co-Op Inc
12525 Hwy 9 PO Box 719 .... Homer LA 71040 318-927-3504 927-6636

Concordia Electric Co-op Inc
1865 Hwy 84 W PO Box 98 .... Jonesville LA 71343 318-339-7969 339-7462
TF: 800-617-6282 ■ *Web:* www.concordiaelectric.com

Dixie Electric Membership Corp (DEMCO)
PO Box 15659 .... Baton Rouge LA 70895 225-261-1221
TF: 800-262-0221 ■ *Web:* www.demco.org

Jefferson Davis Electric Co-op
906 N Lk Arthur Ave PO Box 1229 .... Jennings LA 70546 337-824-4330 824-8936
TF: 800-256-5332 ■ *Web:* www.jdec.org

Northeast Louisiana Power Co-op Inc
1411 Landis St .... Winnsboro LA 71295 318-435-4523 435-3887
Web: nelpco.coop

Pointe Coupee Electric Membership Corp
2506 False River Dr PO Box 160 .... New Roads LA 70760 225-638-3751 638-8124
TF: 800-738-7232 ■ *Web:* www.pcemc.org

Southwest Louisiana Electric Membership Corp
3420 NE Evangeline Thruway .... Lafayette LA 70509 337-896-5384 896-2533
TF: 888-275-3626 ■ *Web:* www.slemco.com

Washington-Saint Tammany Electric Co-op
950 Pearl St PO Box N .... Franklinton LA 70438 985-839-3562 839-4315
TF: 866-672-9773 ■ *Web:* www.wste.coop

Maine

Phone Fax

Eastern Maine Electric Co-op Inc 21 Union St .... Calais ME 04619 207-454-7555
TF: 800-696-7444 ■ *Web:* www.emec.com

Maryland

Phone Fax

Choptank Electric Co-op Inc
24820 Meeting House Rd PO Box 430 .... Denton MD 21629 877-892-0001 479-3516*
**Fax Area Code:* 410 ■ *TF:* 877-892-0001 ■ *Web:* www.choptankelectric.com

Massachusetts

Phone Fax

Intergen 30 Corporate Dr .... Burlington MA 01803 781-993-3000 993-3005
Web: www.intergen.com

Taunton Municipal Lighting Plant PO Box 870 .... Taunton MA 02780 508-824-5844
Web: www.tmlp.com

Michigan

Phone Fax

Cherryland Electric Co-op
5930 US 31 S PO Box 298 .... Grawn MI 49637 231-486-9200 943-8204
TF: 800-442-8616 ■ *Web:* cherrylandelectric.coop

Phone Fax

Grand Haven Board of Lightand & Power (GHBLP)
1700 Eaton Dr. . . . . Grand Haven MI 49417 616-846-6250 846-3114
Web: www.ghblp.org

Great Lakes Energy Co-op 1323 Boyne Ave . . . . Boyne City MI 49712 888-485-2537 582-6213*
**Fax Area Code:* 231 ■ **Fax:* Cust Svc ■ *TF:* 888-485-2537 ■ *Web:* www.gtlakes.com

Midwest Energy Co-op 901 E State St. . . . . Cassopolis MI 49031 800-492-5989
TF: 800-492-5989 ■ *Web:* www.teammidwest.com

Ontonagon County Rural Assn
500 James K Paul St. . . . . Ontonagon MI 49953 906-884-4151
Web: countrylines.com

Presque Isle Electric & Gas Co-op PO Box 308 . . . . Onaway MI 49765 989-733-8515 733-2247
TF: 800-423-6634 ■ *Web:* www.pieg.com

Thumb Electric Co-op (TEC) 2231 Main St. . . . . Ubly MI 48475 989-658-8571

Minnesota

Phone Fax

Agralite Electric Co-op 320 Hwy 12 SE . . . . Benson MN 56215 320-843-4150 843-3738
TF: 800-950-8375 ■ *Web:* www.agralite.coop

Arrowhead Electric Co-op Inc
5401 W Hwy 61 PO Box 39 . . . . Lutsen MN 55612 218-663-7239 663-7850
TF: 800-864-3744 ■ *Web:* www.aecimn.com

Beltrami Electric Co-op Inc
4111 Technology Dr NW . . . . Bemidji MN 56601 218-444-2540 444-3676
TF: 800-955-6083 ■ *Web:* www.beltramielectric.com

Benco Electric Co-op 20946 549 Ave PO Box 8 . . . . Mankato MN 56002 507-387-7963 387-1269
TF: 888-792-3626 ■ *Web:* www.benco.org

Brown County Rural Electric Assn
24386 State Hwy 4 PO Box 529 . . . . Sleepy Eye MN 56085 507-794-3331 794-4282
TF: 800-658-2368 ■ *Web:* www.browncountyrea.coop

Clearwater-Polk Electric Co-op 315 Main Ave N . . . . Bagley MN 56621 218-694-6241 694-6245
TF: 888-694-3833 ■ *Web:* www.clearwater-polk.com

Connexus Energy Co-op 14601 Ramsey Blvd . . . . Ramsey MN 55303 763-323-2650 323-2603
TF: 877-382-4357 ■ *Web:* www.connexusenergy.com

Crow Wing Co-op Power & Light Co
Hwy 371 N PO Box 507 . . . . Brainerd MN 56401 218-829-2827 825-2209
TF: 800-648-9401 ■ *Web:* www.cwpower.com

Dakota Electric Assn 4300 220th St W . . . . Farmington MN 55024 651-463-6144 463-6144
TF: 800-874-3409 ■ *Web:* www.dakotaelectric.com

East Central Energy PO Box 39 . . . . Braham MN 55006 800-254-7944
TF: 800-254-7944 ■ *Web:* www.eastcentralenergy.com

Federated Rural Electric Assn
77100 US Hwy 71 PO Box 69 . . . . Jackson MN 56143 507-847-3520 728-8366
TF: 800-321-3520 ■ *Web:* www.federatedrea.com

Freeborn-Mower Co-op Services
2501 E Main St. . . . . Albert Lea MN 56007 507-373-6421 369-0259
TF: 800-734-6421 ■ *Web:* www.fmcs.coop

Goodhue County Co-op Electric Assn
1410 Northstar Dr. . . . . Zumbrota MN 55992 507-732-5117 732-5110
TF: 800-927-6864 ■ *Web:* www.gccea.com

Great River Energy 12300 Elm Creek Blvd . . . . Maple Grove MN 55369 763-445-5000 445-5050
TF: 888-521-0130 ■ *Web:* www.greatriverenergy.com

Itasca-Mantrap Co-op Electrical Assn
16930 County Rd 6. . . . . Park Rapids MN 56470 218-732-3377 732-5890
TF: 888-713-3377 ■ *Web:* www.itasca-mantrap.com

Lake Country Power 2810 Elida Dr . . . . Grand Rapids MN 55744 800-421-9959 326-8136*
**Fax Area Code:* 218 ■ *TF:* 800-421-9959 ■ *Web:* www.lakecountrypower.com

Lake Region Co-op Electrical Assn
1401 S Broadway PO Box 643 . . . . Pelican Rapids MN 56572 218-863-1171 863-1172
TF: 800-552-7658 ■ *Web:* www.lrec.coop

Lyon-Lincoln Electric Co-op Inc (LLEC)
205 W Hwy 14 PO Box 639 . . . . Tyler MN 56178 507-247-5505 247-5508
TF: 800-927-6276 ■ *Web:* www.llec.coop

McLeod Co-op Power Assn 1231 Ford Ave N. . . . . Glencoe MN 55336 320-864-3148 864-4850
TF: 800-494-6272 ■ *Web:* www.mcleodcoop.com

Meeker Co-op Light & Power Assn
1725 E US Hwy 12 PO Box 68 . . . . Litchfield MN 55355 320-693-3231 693-2980
TF: 800-232-6257 ■ *Web:* www.meeker.coop

Mille Lacs Electric Co-op PO Box 230. . . . . Aitkin MN 56431 218-927-2191 927-6822
TF: 800-450-2191 ■ *Web:* www.mlecmn.net

Minnesota Valley Co-op Light & Power Assn
501 S First St . . . . Montevideo MN 56265 320-269-2163 269-2302
TF: 800-247-5051 ■ *Web:* www.mnvalleyrec.com

Minnesota Valley Electric Co-op
125 Minnesota Vly Electric Dr PO Box 77024. . . . . Jordan MN 55352 952-492-2313 492-8281
TF: 800-282-6832 ■ *Web:* www.mvec.net

Nobles Co-op Electric
22636 US Hwy 59 PO Box 788. . . . . Worthington MN 56187 507-372-7331 372-5148
TF: 800-776-0517 ■ *Web:* www.noblesce.coop

North Itasca Electric Co-op Inc
301 Main Ave PO Box 227 . . . . Bigfork MN 56628 218-743-3131 743-3644
TF: 800-762-4048 ■ *Web:* www.northitascaelectric.com

North Star Electric Co-op
441 State Hwy 172 NW PO Box 719. . . . . Baudette MN 56623 218-634-2202 634-2203
TF: 888-634-2202 ■ *Web:* www.northstarelectric.coop

People's Energy Co-op 1775 Lk Shady Ave S . . . . Oronoco MN 55960 507-367-7000 367-7001
TF: 800-214-2694 ■ *Web:* www.peoplesrec.com

PKM Electric Co-op Inc 406 N Minnesota St . . . . Warren MN 56762 218-745-4711
TF: 800-552-7366 ■ *Web:* www.pkmcoop.com

Red Lake Electric Co-op Inc
412 International Dr PO Box 430 . . . . Red Lake Falls MN 56750 218-253-2168 253-2630
TF: 800-245-6068 ■ *Web:* www.redlakeelectric.com

Red River Valley Co-op Power Assn
109 Second Ave E. . . . . Halstad MN 56548 218-456-2139 456-2102
TF: 800-788-7784 ■ *Web:* www.rrvcoop.com

Redwood Electric Co-op 60 Pine St . . . . Clements MN 56224 507-692-2214
Web: www.greatriverenergy.com

Renville-Sibley Co-op Power Assn
103 Oak St PO Box 68 . . . . Danube MN 56230 320-826-2593 826-2679
TF: 800-826-2593 ■ *Web:* www.renville-sibley.coop

Roseau Electric Co-op Inc 1107 Third St NE. . . . . Roseau MN 56751 218-463-1543 463-3713
TF: 888-847-8840 ■ *Web:* roseauelectric.coop

South Central Electric Assn
71176 Tiell Dr PO Box 150. . . . . Saint James MN 56081 507-375-3164 375-3166
TF: 888-805-7232 ■ *Web:* www.southcentralelectric.com

Southern Minnesota Municipal Power Agency
500 First Ave SW . . . . Rochester MN 55902 507-285-0478 292-6414
Web: www.smmpa.com

Stearns ElectricAssn 900 E Kraft Dr . . . . Melrose MN 56352 320-256-4241 256-3618
TF: 800-962-0655 ■ *Web:* www.stearnselectric.org

Steele-Waseca Co-op Electric (SWCE)
2411 W Bridge St PO Box 485 . . . . Owatonna MN 55060 507-451-7340 446-4242
TF: 800-526-3514 ■ *Web:* www.swce.com

Todd-Wadena Electric Co-op
550 Ash Ave NE PO Box 431 . . . . Wadena MN 56482 218-631-3120 631-4188
TF: 800-321-8932 ■ *Web:* www.toddwadena.coop

Traverse Electric Co-op Inc
1618 Broadway PO Box 66. . . . . Wheaton MN 56296 320-563-8616 563-4863
TF: 800-927-5443 ■ *Web:* www.traverseelectric.com

Tri-County Electric Co-op
31110 Co-op Way PO Box 626. . . . . Rushford MN 55971 507-864-7783 864-2871
TF: 800-432-2285 ■ *Web:* www.tec.coop

Wild Rice Electric Co-op Inc
502 N Main PO Box 438. . . . . Mahnomen MN 56557 218-935-2517 935-2519
TF: 800-244-5709 ■ *Web:* www.wildriceelectric.com

Wright-Hennepin Co-op Electric Assn
6800 Electric Dr PO Box 330 . . . . Rockford MN 55373 763-477-3000 477-3054
TF: 800-943-2667 ■ *Web:* www.whe.org

Mississippi

Phone Fax

Alcorn County Electric Power Assn
1909 S Tate St . . . . Corinth MS 38834 662-287-4402 287-4088
TF: 866-448-3046 ■ *Web:* ace-power.com

Central Electric Power Assn 104 E Main St. . . . . Carthage MS 39051 601-267-5671
TF: 866-846-5671 ■ *Web:* www.centralepa.com

Coahoma Electric Power Assn 340 Hopson St . . . . Lyon MS 38645 662-624-8321 624-8327
Web: coahomaepa.com

Coast Electric Power Assn 18020 Hwy Ste 603. . . . . Kiln MS 39556 228-363-7000
TF Cust Svc: 800-624-3348 ■ *Web:* www.coastepa.com

Delta Electric Power Assn 1700 Hwy 82 W . . . . Greenwood MS 38930 662-453-6352
Web: deltaepa.com

Dixie Electric Power Assn PO Box 88 . . . . Laurel MS 39441 601-425-2535 425-2535
TF: 888-465-9209 ■ *Web:* www.dixieepa.com

East Mississippi Electric Power Assn (EMEPA)
2128 Hwy 39 N PO Box 5517. . . . . Meridian MS 39302 601-581-8600 482-0701
Web: www.emepa.com

Four County Electric Power Assn
5265 S Frontage Rd . . . . Columbus MS 39701 662-327-8900 327-8790
Web: www.4county.org

Magnolia Electric Power Assn PO Box 747 . . . . McComb MS 39649 601-684-4011 684-5535
Web: www.magnoliaepa.com

Monroe County Electric Power Assn
601 N Main St . . . . Amory MS 38821 662-256-2962
TF: 866-656-2962

North East MS EPA 10 PR 2050 PO Box 1037 . . . . Oxford MS 38655 662-234-6331 234-0046
TF: 877-234-6331 ■ *Web:* www.nemepa.org

Pearl River Valley Electric Power Assn
1422 Hwy 13 N PO Box 1217. . . . . Columbia MS 39429 601-736-2666
TF: 855-277-8372 ■ *Web:* www.prvepa.com

Pontotoc Electric Power Assn 12 S Main St. . . . . Pontotoc MS 38863 662-489-3211 489-5156
Web: pepa.com

Prentiss County Electric Power Assn
302 W Church St . . . . Booneville MS 38829 662-728-4433 728-4059
Web: www.pcepa.com

Singing River Electric Power Assn Inc
11187 Old Hwy 63 PO Box 767 . . . . Lucedale MS 39452 601-947-4211 947-6548
Web: www.singingriver.com

South Mississippi Electric Power Assn (SMEPA)
7037 US Hwy 49. . . . . Hattiesburg MS 39402 601-268-2083
Web: www.smepa.coop

Southern Pine Electric Power Assn
110 Risher St PO Box 60 . . . . Taylorsville MS 39168 601-785-6511 785-4980
TF: 800-231-5240 ■ *Web:* www.spepa.com

Southwest Mississippi Electric Power Assn
18671 Hwy 61 PO Box 5. . . . . Lorman MS 39096 800-287-8564
TF: 800-287-8564 ■ *Web:* www.southwestepa.com

Tallahatchie Valley Electric Power Assn
250 Power Dr . . . . Batesville MS 38606 662-563-4742 563-8615
Web: www.tvepa.com

Yazoo Valley Electric Power Assn
2255 Gordon Ave . . . . Yazoo City MS 39194 662-746-4251
TF: 800-281-5098 ■ *Web:* yazoovalley.com

Missouri

Phone Fax

Associated ElectricCo-op Inc
2814 S Golden PO Box 754 . . . . Springfield MO 65801 417-881-1204 885-9252
Web: www.aeci.org

Atchison-Holt Electric Co-op
18585 Industrial Rd PO Box 160 . . . . Rock Port MO 64482 660-744-5344
TF: 888-744-5366 ■ *Web:* www.ahec.coop

Barry Electric Co-op
4015 Main St PO Box 307 . . . . Cassville MO 65625 866-847-2333
TF: 866-847-2333

Barton County Electric Co-op 91 US-160 . . . . Lamar MO 64759 417-682-5636
TF: 800-286-5636 ■ *Web:* www.bartonelectric.com

Black River Electric Co-op
2600 Hwy 67 PO Box 31. . . . . Fredericktown MO 63645 573-783-3381 783-7343
TF: 800-392-4711 ■ *Web:* www.brec.coop

Boone Electric Co-op 1413 Rangeline St. . . . . Columbia MO 65201 573-449-4181
TF: 800-225-8143 ■ *Web:* www.booneelectric.coop

Phone *Fax*

Callaway Electric Co-op
1313 Co-op Dr PO Box 250 . . . Fulton MO 65251 573-642-3326
TF: 888-642-4840 ■ *Web:* www.callawayelectric.com

Central Missouri ElectricCo-op Inc
22702 Hwy 65 PO Box 939 . . . Sedalia MO 65302 660-826-2900
TF: 855-875-7165 ■ *Web:* www.cmecinc.com

Co-Mo Electric Co-op Inc
29868 Hwy 5 PO Box 220 . . . Tipton MO 65081 660-433-5521
TF: 800-781-0157 ■ *Web:* www.co-mo.coop

Consolidated Electric Co-op 3940 E Liberty St . . . Mexico MO 65265 573-581-3630 581-0990
TF: 800-621-0091 ■ *Web:* www.consolidatedelectric.com

Crawford Electric Co-op Inc
10301 N Service Rd PO Box 10 . . . Bourbon MO 65441 573-732-4415 732-5409
TF: 800-677-2667 ■ *Web:* www.crawfordelec.com

Cuivre River Electric Co-op 1112 E Cherry St . . . Troy MO 63379 636-528-8261 528-7696
TF: 800-392-3709 ■ *Web:* www.cuivre.com

Farmers' Electric Co-op
201 W Business 36 PO Box 680 . . . Chillicothe MO 64601 660-646-4281 646-3569
TF: 800-279-0496 ■ *Web:* www.fec-co.com

Gascosage Electric Co-op 803 S Hwy 28 PO Box G . . . Dixon MO 65459 573-759-7146 759-6020
TF: 866-568-8243 ■ *Web:* www.gascosage.com

Grundy Electric Co-op Inc 4100 Oklahoma Ave . . . Trenton MO 64683 660-359-3941 359-6030
TF: 800-279-2249 ■ *Web:* www.grundyec.com

Howard Electric Co-op
205 Hwy 5 & 240 N PO Box 391 . . . Fayette MO 65248 660-248-3311
TF: 877-352-0122 ■ *Web:* www.howardelectric.com

Howell-Oregon Electric Co-op Inc
6327 N US Hwy 63 PO Box 649 . . . West Plains MO 65775 417-256-2131 256-4571
TF: 855-385-9903 ■ *Web:* www.hoecoop.org

Intercounty Electric Co-op 102 Maple Ave . . . Licking MO 65542 573-674-2211
Web: www.ieca.coop

Laclede Electric Co-op 1400 E Rt 66 . . . Lebanon MO 65536 417-532-3164 532-8321
TF: 800-299-3164 ■ *Web:* www.lacledeelectric.com

Lewis County Rural Electric Co-op
18256 Hwy 16 PO Box 68 . . . Lewistown MO 63452 573-215-4000 215-4004
TF: 888-454-4485 ■ *Web:* www.lewiscountyrec.org

Macon Electric Co-op
31571 Bus Hwy 36 E PO Box 157 . . . Macon MO 63552 660-385-3157 385-3334
TF: 800-553-6901 ■ *Web:* www.maconelectric.com

N W Electric Power Co-op PO Box 565 . . . Cameron MO 64429 816-632-2121 632-3114
Web: www.nwepc.com

New-Mac Electric Co-op Inc 12105 E Hwy 86 . . . Neosho MO 64850 417-451-1515 451-9042
Web: www.newmac.com

Northeast Missouri Electric Power Co-op
3705 Business 61 PO Box 191 . . . Palmyra MO 63461 573-769-2107 769-4358
Web: www.northeast-power.coop

Osage Valley Electric Co-op Assn
1321 N Orange St . . . Butler MO 64730 660-679-3131 679-3142
TF: 800-889-6832 ■ *Web:* www.osagevalley.com

Ozark Border Electric Co-op
3281 S Westwood . . . Poplar Bluff MO 63901 573-785-4631
TF: 800-392-0567 ■ *Web:* www.ozarkborder.org

Pemiscot-Dunklin Electric Co-op
Hwy 412 W PO Box 509 . . . Hayti MO 63851 573-757-6641 757-6656
TF: 800-558-6641 ■ *Web:* www.pemdunk.com

Platte-Clay Electric Co-op Inc
1000 W Hwy 92 PO Box 100 . . . Kearney MO 64060 816-628-3121 628-3141
TF: 800-431-2131 ■ *Web:* www.pcec.coop

Ralls County Electric Co-op
17594 Hwy 19 PO Box 157 . . . New London MO 63459 573-985-8711 985-3658
TF: 877-985-8711 ■ *Web:* www.rallscountyelectric.com

Sac Osage Electric Co-op Inc
4815 E Hwy 54 PO Box 111 . . . El Dorado Springs MO 64744 417-876-2721 876-5368
TF: 800-876-2701 ■ *Web:* www.sacosage.com

Se-Ma-No Electric Co-op 601 N Business 60 . . . Mansfield MO 65704 417-924-3243
Web: semano.com

Three Rivers Electric Co-op
1324 E Main St PO Box 918 . . . Linn MO 65051 573-644-9000
TF: 800-892-2251 ■ *Web:* www.threeriverselectric.com

Tri-County Electric Co-op PO Box 159 . . . Lancaster MO 63548 660-457-3733 457-3736
TF: 888-457-3734 ■ *Web:* www.tricountyelectric.org

Webster Electric Co-op 1240 Spur Dr . . . Marshfield MO 65706 417-859-2216 859-4579
TF: 800-643-4305 ■ *Web:* www.websterec.com

White River Valley Electric Co-op Inc
2449 State Hwy 76 E . . . Branson MO 65616 417-335-9335 335-9250
TF: 800-879-4056 ■ *Web:* www.whiteriver.org

Montana

Phone *Fax*

Beartooth Electric Co-op Inc
1306 N Broadway St PO Box 1110 . . . Red Lodge MT 59068 406-446-2310 446-3934
TF: 800-472-9821 ■ *Web:* beartoothec.coopwebbuilder2.com

Big Flat Electric Co-op Inc 333 S Seventh St . . . Malta MT 59538 406-654-2040
TF: 800-242-2040 ■ *Web:* www.bigflatelectric.com

Fergus Electric Co-op Inc 84423 US Hwy 87 . . . Lewistown MT 59457 406-538-3465
Web: www.ferguselectric.coop

Flathead Electric Co-op Inc 2510 Hwy 2 E . . . Kalispell MT 59901 406-751-4483 752-4283
TF: 800-735-8489 ■ *Web:* www.flatheadelectric.com

Glacier Electric Co-op Inc 410 E Main St . . . Cut Bank MT 59427 406-873-5566 873-2071
TF: 800-347-6795 ■ *Web:* www.glacierelectric.com

Goldenwest Electric Co-op Inc 119 1 Ave SW . . . Wibaux MT 59353 406-796-2423

Hill County Electric Co-op Inc PO Box 2330 . . . Havre MT 59501 877-394-7804
TF: 877-394-7804 ■ *Web:* www.hcelectric.com

Lincoln Electric Co-op Inc (LEC)
500 Osloski Rd PO Box 628 . . . Eureka MT 59917 406-889-3301 889-3874
TF: 800-442-2994 ■ *Web:* www.lincolnelectric.coop

Lower Yellowstone Rural Electric Assn Inc
3200 W Holly St PO Box 1047 . . . Sidney MT 59270 406-488-1602 488-6524
TF: 844-441-5627 ■ *Web:* www.lyrec.com

Marias River Electric Co-op Inc PO Box 729 . . . Shelby MT 59474 406-434-5575 434-2531
Web: www.mariasriverec.com

McCone Electric Co-op Inc 110 Main St . . . Circle MT 59215 406-485-3430 485-3397
TF: 800-684-3605 ■ *Web:* www.mcconeelectric.coop

Phone *Fax*

Mid Yellowstone Elec Co-Op Inc
203 Elliott PO Box 386 . . . Hysham MT 59038 406-342-5521 342-5511

Missoula Electric Co-op Inc 1700 W Broadway . . . Missoula MT 59808 406-541-4433 541-6318
TF: 800-352-5200 ■ *Web:* www.missoulaelectric.com

Park Electric Co-op Inc
5706 US Hwy 89 S PO Box 1119 . . . Livingston MT 59047 406-222-3100 222-3418
TF: 888-298-0657 ■ *Web:* www.parkelectric.coop

Ravalli County Electric Co-op Inc
1051 Eastside Hwy . . . Corvallis MT 59828 406-961-3001 961-3230
Web: www.ravallielectric.com

Sheridan Electric Co-op Inc PO Box 227 . . . Medicine Lake MT 59247 406-789-2231 789-2234
TF: 888-472-1533 ■ *Web:* www.sheridanelectric.coop

Southeast Electric Co-op Inc (SECO)
110 S Main St . . . Ekalaka MT 59324 406-775-8762
TF: 888-485-8762 ■ *Web:* www.seecoop.com

Sun River Electric Co-op Inc
310 First Ave S PO Box 309 . . . Fairfield MT 59436 406-467-2527
TF: 800-452-7516 ■ *Web:* www.sunriverelectric.coop

Vigilante Electric Co-op Inc 225 E Bannack St . . . Dillon MT 59725 406-683-2327 683-4328
Web: www.vec.coop

Yellowstone Valley Electric Co-op
150 Co-op Way . . . Huntley MT 59037 406-348-3411 348-3414
TF: 800-736-5323 ■ *Web:* www.yvec.com

Nebraska

Phone *Fax*

Burt County Public Power District
613 N 13th St . . . Tekamah NE 68061 402-374-2631
TF: 888-835-1620 ■ *Web:* www.burtcoppd.com

Butler County Rural Public Power District
1331 N Fourth St . . . David City NE 68632 402-367-3081 367-6114
TF: 800-230-0569 ■ *Web:* www.butlerppd.com

Cedar-Knox Public Power District
56272 W Hwy 84 PO Box 947 . . . Hartington NE 68739 402-254-6291
Web: www.cedarknoxppd.com

Chimney Rock Public Power District
805 W Eigth St PO Box 608 . . . Bayard NE 69334 308-586-1824
TF: 877-773-6300 ■ *Web:* www.crppd.com

Cornhusker Public Power District
23169 235th Ave PO Box 9 . . . Columbus NE 68602 402-564-2821 564-9907
TF: 800-955-2773 ■ *Web:* www.cornhusker-power.com

Cuming County Public Power District
500 S Main St . . . West Point NE 68788 402-372-2463 372-5832
TF: 877-572-2463 ■ *Web:* www.ccppd.com

Custer Public Power District
625 E SE St PO Box 10 . . . Broken Bow NE 68822 308-872-2451 872-2378
TF: 888-749-2453 ■ *Web:* www.custerpower.com

Dawson Public Power District 75191 Rd 433 . . . Lexington NE 68850 308-324-2386
TF: 800-752-8305 ■ *Web:* www.dawsonpower.com

Elkhorn Rural Public Power District
206 N Fourth St . . . Battle Creek NE 68715 402-675-2185 675-6275
TF: 800-675-2185 ■ *Web:* www.erppd.com

Howard Greeley Rural Power
422 Howard Ave PO Box 105 . . . Saint Paul NE 68873 308-754-4457 754-4230
TF: 800-280-4962 ■ *Web:* www.howardgreeleyrppd.com

KBR Rural Public Power District
374 N Pine St PO Box 187 . . . Ainsworth NE 69210 402-387-1120
TF: 800-672-0009 ■ *Web:* kbrpower.com

Loup Public Power District (LPPD)
2404 15th St PO Box 988 . . . Columbus NE 68602 402-564-3171 564-0970
TF: 866-869-2087 ■ *Web:* www.loup.com

McCook Public Power District 1510 N Hwy 83 . . . McCook NE 69001 308-345-2500 345-4772
TF: 800-658-4285 ■ *Web:* www.mppdonline.com

Midwest Electric Co-op Corp 104 Washington Ave . . . Grant NE 69140 308-352-4356 352-4957
TF: 800-451-3691 ■ *Web:* www.midwestecc.com

Nebraska Public Power District
1414 15th St PO Box 499 . . . Columbus NE 68602 402-564-8561
TF: 877-275-6773 ■ *Web:* www.nppd.com

Niobrara Valley Electric Membership Corp
427 N Fourth St . . . O'Neill NE 68763 402-336-2803 336-4858
Web: www.nvemc.org

Norris Public Power District
606 Irving St PO Box 399 . . . Beatrice NE 68310 402-223-4038 228-2895
TF: 800-858-4707 ■ *Web:* www.norrisppd.com

North Central Public Power District
1409 Main St PO Box 90 . . . Creighton NE 68729 402-358-5112 358-5129
TF: 800-578-1060 ■ *Web:* www.ncppd.com

Northeast Nebraska Public Power District
1410 W Seventh St PO Box 350 . . . Wayne NE 68787 402-375-1360
TF: 800-750-9277 ■ *Web:* www.nnppd.com

Northwest Rural Public Power District
5613 State Hwy 87 PO Box 249 . . . Hay Springs NE 69347 308-638-4445 638-4448
TF: 800-847-0492 ■ *Web:* www.nrppd.com

Perennial Public Power District
2122 S Lincoln Ave . . . York NE 68467 402-362-3355 362-3623
TF: 800-289-0288 ■ *Web:* www.perennialpower.com

Polk County Rural Public Power District
115 W 3rd St PO Box 465 . . . Stromsburg NE 68666 402-764-4381 764-4382
TF: 888-242-5265 ■ *Web:* www.pcrppd.com

Seward County Rural Public Power District
3111 Progressive Rd PO Box 69 . . . Seward NE 68434 402-643-2951 646-4695
Web: www.sewardppd.com

South Central Public Power District (SCPPD)
275 S Main St PO Box 406 . . . Nelson NE 68961 402-225-2351
TF: 800-557-5254 ■ *Web:* www.southcentralppd.com

Southern Public Power District (SPPD)
4550 W Husker Hwy PO Box 1687 . . . Grand Island NE 68803 308-384-2350 384-5018
TF: 800-652-2013 ■ *Web:* www.southernpd.com

Southwest Public Power District
221 S Main St PO Box 289 . . . Palisade NE 69040 308-285-3295
TF: 800-379-7977 ■ *Web:* www.swppd.com

Stanton County Public Power District
807 Douglas St . . . Stanton NE 68779 402-439-2228 439-7000
TF: 877-439-2300 ■ *Web:* www.scppd.net

	City	State	Zip	Phone	Fax
Twin Valleys Public Power District 1145 Nasby St *TF:* 800-658-4266 ■ *Web:* www.twinvalleysppd.com	Cambridge	NE	69022	308-697-3315	697-4877
Wheat Belt Public Power District 2104 Illinois St *TF:* 800-261-7114 ■ *Web:* www.wheatbelt.com	Sidney	NE	69162	308-254-5871	254-2384

Nevada

	City	State	Zip	Phone	Fax
Overton Power District # 5 615 N Moapa Vly Blvd PO Box 395 *Web:* opd5.com	Overton	NV	89040	702-397-2512	
Valley Electric Assn Inc 800 E Hwy 372 PO Box 237 *TF:* 800-742-3330 ■ *Web:* www.vea.coop	Pahrump	NV	89048	775-727-5312	727-6320
Wells Rural Electric Co 1451 Humboldt Ave *Web:* www.wrec.coop	Wells	NV	89835	775-752-3328	752-3407

New Hampshire

	City	State	Zip	Phone	Fax
New Hampshire Electric Co-op 579 Tenney Mtn Hwy *TF:* 800-698-2007 ■ *Web:* www.nhec.com	Plymouth	NH	03264	603-536-1800	536-8682

New Jersey

	City	State	Zip	Phone	Fax
Sussex Rural Electric Co-op 64 County Rt 639 PO Box 346 *TF:* 877-504-6463 ■ *Web:* www.sussexrec.com	Sussex	NJ	07461	973-875-5101	875-4114

New Mexico

	City	State	Zip	Phone	Fax
Central Valley Electric Co-op Inc 1505 N 13th St PO Box 230 *Web:* www.cvecoop.org	Artesia	NM	88211	575-746-3571	
Columbus Electric Co-op Inc 900 N Gold St PO Box 631 *TF:* 800-950-2667 ■ *Web:* www.columbusco-op.org	Deming	NM	88031	505-546-8838	546-3128
Continental Divide ElectricCo-op Inc (CDEC) 200 E High St PO Box 1087 *Web:* www.cdec.coop	Grants	NM	87020	505-285-6656	287-2234
Farmers Electric Co-op Inc 3701 Thornton PO Box 550 *TF:* 800-445-8541 ■ *Web:* fecnm.org	Clovis	NM	88101	575-762-4466	
Jemez Mountains Electric Co-op PO Box 128 *TF:* 888-755-2105 ■ *Web:* www.jemezcoop.org	Espanola	NM	87532	505-753-2105	753-6958
Mora-San Miguel Electric Co-op PO Box 240 *TF:* 800-421-6773 ■ *Web:* www.moraelectric.org	Mora	NM	87732	575-387-2205	
Northern Rio Arriba Electric Co-op 1135 Camino Escondido PO Box 217 **Fax Area Code:* 505 ■ *Web:* www.noraelectric.org	Chama	NM	87520	575-756-2181	756-2200*
Otero County Electric Co-op Inc 202 Burro Ave PO Box 227 **Fax Area Code:* 505 ■ *TF:* 800-548-4660 ■ *Web:* www.ocec-inc.com	Cloudcroft	NM	88317	575-682-2521	682-3109*
Roosevelt County Electric Co-op Inc (RCEC) 121 N Main St PO Box 389 *Web:* www.rcec.org/content/office-location	Portales	NM	88130	575-356-4491	
Sierra Electric Co-op 610 Hwy 195 PO Box 290 **Fax Area Code:* 505 ■ *Web:* www.sierraelectric.org	Elephant Butte	NM	87935	575-744-5231	744-5819*
Socorro Electric Co-op Inc 215 Manzanares Ave PO Box H **Fax Area Code:* 505 ■ *TF:* 800-351-7575 ■ *Web:* www.socorroelectric.com	Socorro	NM	87801	575-835-0560	835-4449*
Springer Electric Co-op Inc 408 Maxwell Ave PO Box 698 *TF:* 800-288-1353 ■ *Web:* www.springercoop.com	Springer	NM	87747	575-483-2421	

New York

	City	State	Zip	Phone	Fax
Delaware County Electric Co-op (DCEC) 39 Elm St PO Box 471 *TF:* 866-436-1223 ■ *Web:* www.dce.coop	Delhi	NY	13753	607-746-2341	746-7548
Oneida-Madison Electric Co-op Inc 6630 State Rt 20 *Web:* www.oneida-madison.coop	Bouckville	NY	13310	315-893-1851	893-1857
Otsego Electric Co-op Inc (OEC) 3192 County Hwy 11 PO Box 128 *Web:* www.otsegoec.coop	Hartwick	NY	13348	607-293-6622	293-6624
Steuben Rural Electric Co-op Inc 9 Wilson Ave *TF:* 800-843-3414 ■ *Web:* www.steubenrec.coop	Bath	NY	14810	607-776-4161	776-2293

North Carolina

	City	State	Zip	Phone	Fax
Albemarle Electric Membership Corp PO Box 69 *TF:* 800-215-9915 ■ *Web:* www.aemc.coop	Hertford	NC	27944	252-426-5735	426-8270
Blue Ridge Electric Membership Corp 1216 Blowing Rock Blvd *TF:* 800-451-5474 ■ *Web:* blueridgeemc.com	Lenoir	NC	28645	828-758-2383	758-2699
Brunswick Electric Membership Corp 795 Ocean Hwy PO Box 826 *TF:* 800-842-5871 ■ *Web:* www.bemc.org	Shallotte	NC	28459	910-754-4391	755-4299
Cape Hatteras Electric Co-op 47109 Light Plant Rd PO Box 9 *TF:* 800-454-5616 ■ *Web:* www.chec.coop	Buxton	NC	27920	252-995-5616	995-4088
Carteret-Craven Electric Co-op (CCEC) 1300 Hwy 24 W PO Box 1490 *TF:* 800-682-2217 ■ *Web:* www.carteretcravenelectric.coop	Newport	NC	28570	252-247-3107	247-0235
Central Electric Membership Corp 128 Wilson Rd *TF:* 800-446-7752 ■ *Web:* www.centralelectriconline.com	Sanford	NC	27331	919-774-4900	774-1860
Cogentrix Energy Inc 9405 Arrowpoint Blvd *Web:* www.cogentrix.com	Charlotte	NC	28273	704-525-3800	529-5313
Edgecombe-Martin County Electric Membership Corp NC Hwy 33 E *TF:* 800-445-6486 ■ *Web:* www.ememc.com	Tarboro	NC	27886	252-823-2171	
EnergyUnited Electric Membership Corp PO Box 1831 *TF:* 800-522-3793 ■ *Web:* www.energyunited.com	Statesville	NC	28687	704-873-5241	878-0161
Four County Electric Membership Corp 1822 NC Hwy 53 W PO Box 667 *TF:* 888-368-7289 ■ *Web:* www.fourcty.org	Burgaw	NC	28425	910-259-2171	259-1860
French Broad Electric Membership Corp 3043 Nc 213 Hwy *Web:* www.frenchbroademc.com	Marshall	NC	28753	828-649-2051	649-2989
Halifax Electric Membership Corp 208 Whitfield St *TF:* 800-690-0522 ■ *Web:* www.halifaxemc.com	Enfield	NC	27823	252-445-5111	
Haywood Electric Membership Corp 376 Grindstone Rd *TF:* 800-951-6088 ■ *Web:* www.haywoodemc.com	Waynesville	NC	28785	828-452-2281	
Jones-Onslow Electric Membership Corp 259 Western Blvd *TF:* 800-682-1515 ■ *Web:* www.joemc.com	Jacksonville	NC	28546	910-353-1940	353-8000
Lumbee River Electric Membership Corp PO Box 830 *TF:* 800-683-5571 ■ *Web:* www.lumbeeriver.com	Red Springs	NC	28377	910-843-4131	843-6422
Pee Dee Electric Membership Corp (PDEMC) 575 US Hwy 52 S *TF:* 800-992-1626 ■ *Web:* www.pdemc.com	Wadesboro	NC	28170	704-694-2114	694-9636
Piedmont Electric Membership Corp 2500 Nc Hwy 86 S *Web:* www.pemc.coop	Hillsborough	NC	27278	919-732-2123	644-1030
Randolph Electric Membership Corp 879 McDowell Rd PO Box 40 *TF:* 800-672-8212 ■ *Web:* www.randolphemc.com	Asheboro	NC	27204	336-625-5177	626-1551
Roanoke Electric Co-op 518 NC 561 W *TF:* 800-433-2236 ■ *Web:* www.roanokeelectric.com	Aulander	NC	27805	252-539-4600	539-4612
Rutherford Electric Membership Corp 186 Hudlow Rd PO Box 1569 *TF:* 800-521-0920 ■ *Web:* www.remc.com	Forest City	NC	28043	828-245-1621	248-2319
South River Electric Membership Corp 17494 US 421 S PO Box 931 *TF:* 800-338-5530 ■ *Web:* www.sremc.com	Dunn	NC	28335	910-892-8071	230-2981
Surry-Yadkin Electric Membership Corp 510 S Main St *TF:* 800-682-5903 ■ *Web:* www.syemc.com	Dobson	NC	27017	336-356-8241	356-9744
Tideland Electric Membership Corp 25831 Hwy 264 E *TF:* 800-637-1079 ■ *Web:* www.tidelandemc.com	Pantego	Nc	27860	252-943-3046	943-3510
Union Power Co-op 1525 N Rocky River Rd *TF:* 800-922-6840 ■ *Web:* www.union-power.com	Monroe	NC	28110	704-289-3145	296-0408
Wake Electric 100 S Franklin St PO Box 1229 *TF:* 800-474-6300 ■ *Web:* www.wemc.com	Wake Forest	NC	27588	919-863-6300	

North Dakota

	City	State	Zip	Phone	Fax
Basin Electric Power Co-op 1717 E IH- Ave *Web:* www.basinelectric.com	Bismarck	ND	58501	701-223-0441	224-5336
Burke-Divide Electric Co-op Inc (BDEC) 9549 Hwy 5 W *TF:* 800-472-2983 ■ *Web:* www.bdec.coop	Columbus	ND	58727	701-939-6671	939-6666
Capital Electric Co-op Inc 4111 State St *TF:* 888-223-1513 ■ *Web:* www.capitalelec.com	Bismarck	ND	58503	701-223-1513	223-1557
Cass County Electric Co-op Inc 4100 32nd Ave SW *TF:* 800-248-3292 ■ *Web:* www.kwh.com	Fargo	ND	58104	701-356-4400	
Central Power Electric Co-op 525 20th Ave SW *Web:* www.centralpwr.com	Minot	ND	58701	701-852-4407	
Dakota Valley Electric Co-op 7296 Hwy 281 *TF:* 800-342-4671 ■ *Web:* www.dakotavalley.com	Edgeley	ND	58433	701-493-2281	493-2454
KEM Electric Co-op Inc 107 S Broadway *TF:* 800-472-2673 ■ *Web:* www.kemelectric.com	Linton	ND	58552	701-254-4666	254-4975
McKenzie Electric Co-op Inc 908 Fourth Ave NE *Web:* www.mckenzieelectric.com	Watford City	ND	58854	701-444-9288	444-3002
McLean Electric Co-op Inc 4031 Hwy 37 Bypass NW *TF:* 800-263-4922 ■ *Web:* www.mcleanelectric.com	Garrison	ND	58540	701-463-2291	
Mor-Gran-Sou Electric Co-op Inc 202 Sixth Ave W *TF:* 800-750-8212 ■ *Web:* www.morgransou.com	Flasher	ND	58535	701-597-3301	597-3915
Mountrail-Williams Electric Co-op 218 58th St W PO Box 1346 *TF:* 800-279-2667 ■ *Web:* www.mwec.com	Williston	ND	58802	701-577-3765	577-3777
Nodak Electric Co-op Inc 4000 32nd Ave S *TF:* 800-732-4373 ■ *Web:* www.nodakelectric.com	Grand Forks	ND	58201	701-746-4461	795-6701
North Central Electric Co-op Inc 538 11th St W *TF:* 800-247-1197 ■ *Web:* www.nceci.com	Bottineau	ND	58318	701-228-2202	228-2592
Northern Plains Electric Co-op 1515 W Main St *TF:* 800-882-2500 ■ *Web:* www.nplains.com	Carrington	ND	58421	701-652-3156	
Slope Electric Co-op Inc 116 E 12th St PO Box 338 *TF:* 800-559-4191 ■ *Web:* www.slopeelectric.coop	New England	ND	58647	701-579-4191	

			Phone	Fax
Verendrye Electric Co-op Inc 615 Hwy 52 ... Velva *TF:* 800-472-2141 ■ *Web:* www.verendrye.com	ND	58790	701-338-2855	624-0353

Ohio

			Phone	Fax
Adams Rural Electric Co-op Inc 4800 SR 125 ... West Union *TF:* 800-283-1846 ■ *Web:* www.adamsrec.com	OH	45693	937-544-2305	544-3877
Buckeye Rural Electric Co-op PO Box 200 ... Rio Grande *TF:* 800-231-2732 ■ *Web:* www.buckeyerec.coop	OH	45674	740-379-2025	379-2048
Butler Rural Electric Co-op Inc (BREC) 3888 Still-Beckett Rd ... Oxford *TF:* 800-255-2732 ■ *Web:* www.butlerrural.coop	OH	45056	513-867-4400	867-4422
Carroll Electric Co-op Inc 350 Canton Rd NW ... Carrollton *TF:* 800-232-7697 ■ *Web:* cecpower.coop	OH	44615	330-627-2116	627-7050
Darke Rural Electric Co-op Inc 1120 Fort Jefferson Rd ... Greenville *TF:* 866-692-6330 ■ *Web:* darkecountyohio.com	OH	45331	937-548-4114	
Denier Electric Co Inc 10891 SR- 128 ... Harrison *TF:* 800-676-3282 ■ *Web:* www.denier.com	OH	45030	513-738-2641	738-5855
Firelands Electric Co-op Inc 1 Energy Pl PO Box 32 ... New London *TF:* 800-533-8658 ■ *Web:* www.firelandsec.com	OH	44851	419-929-1571	929-8550
Frontier Power Co 770 S 2nd St PO Box 280 ... Coshocton *TF:* 800-624-8050 ■ *Web:* www.frontier-power.com	OH	43812	740-622-6755	622-0711
Guernsey-Muskingum Electric Co-op 17 S Liberty St ... New Concord *TF:* 800-521-9879 ■ *Web:* www.gmenergy.com	OH	43762	740-826-7661	826-7171
Hancock-Wood Electric Co-op Inc (HWEC) 1399 Business Pk Dr S PO Box 190 ... North Baltimore *TF:* 800-445-4840 ■ *Web:* www.hwe.coop	OH	45872	419-257-3241	257-3024
Holmes-Wayne Electric Co-op Inc 6060 Ohio 83 ... Millersburg *TF:* 866-674-1055 ■ *Web:* www.hwecoop.com	OH	44654	330-674-1055	674-1869
Logan County Co-op Power & Light Assn Inc 1587 County Rd 32 N ... Bellefontaine *Web:* www.loganrec.com	OH	43311	937-592-4781	592-5746
Lorain-Medina Rural Electric Co-op Inc 22898 W Rd ... Wellington *TF:* 800-222-5673 ■ *Web:* www.lmre.org	OH	44090	440-647-2133	647-4870
Mid Ohio Energy Co-op Inc 555 W Franklin St ... Kenton *TF:* 888-382-6732 ■ *Web:* www.midohioenergy.com	OH	43326	419-673-7289	673-8388
North Central Electric Co-op Inc 13978 E County Rd 56 ... Attica *TF:* 800-426-3072 ■ *Web:* www.ncelec.org	OH	44807	419-426-3072	426-1245
North Western Electric Co-op Inc 04125 State Rt 576 PO Box 391 ... Bryan *TF:* 800-647-6932 ■ *Web:* www.nwec.com	OH	43506	419-636-5051	636-0194
Paulding-Putman Electric Co-op 910 N Williams St ... Paulding *TF:* 800-686-2357 ■ *Web:* www.ppec.coop	OH	45879	419-399-5015	399-3026
Pioneer Electric Co-op 344 W US Rt 36 ... Piqua *TF:* 800-762-0997 ■ *Web:* www.pioneerec.com	OH	45356	937-773-2523	
South Central Power Company Inc 2780 Coon Path Rd ... Lancaster *TF:* 800-282-5064 ■ *Web:* www.southcentralpower.com	OH	43130	740-653-4422	681-4488
Union Rural Electric Co-op Inc 15461 US 36E ... Marysville *TF:* 800-642-1826 ■ *Web:* www.ure.com	OH	43040	937-642-1826	969-8442
Washington Electric Co-op Inc 406 Colegate Dr ... Marietta *TF:* 877-594-9324 ■ *Web:* www.weci.org	OH	45750	740-373-2141	373-2941

Oklahoma

			Phone	Fax
Alfalfa Electric Co-op Inc 121 E Main St ... Cherokee *TF:* 888-736-3837 ■ *Web:* www.alfalfaelectric.com	OK	73728	580-596-3333	596-2464
Caddo Electric Co-op PO Box 70 ... Binger *Web:* www.caddoelectric.com	OK	73009	405-656-2322	656-2327
Canadian Valley Electric Co-op 11277 S 356 PO Box 751 ... Seminole *TF:* 877-382-3680 ■ *Web:* www.canadianvalley.org	OK	74868	405-382-3680	382-8808
Central Rural Electric Co-op 3304 S Boomer Rd PO Box 1809 ... Stillwater *TF:* 800-375-2884 ■ *Web:* www.crec.coop	OK	74076	405-372-2884	372-8559
Choctaw Electric Co-op Inc 1033 N 4250 Rd ... Hugo *TF:* 800-780-6486 ■ *Web:* www.choctawelectric.coop	OK	74743	580-326-6486	326-2492
Cimarron Electric Co-op PO Box 299 ... Kingfisher *TF:* 800-375-4121 ■ *Web:* www.cimarronelectric.com	OK	73750	405-375-4121	375-4209
Cookson Hills Electric Co-op Inc 1002 E Main St ... Stigler *TF:* 800-328-2368 ■ *Web:* www.cooksonhills.com	OK	74462	918-967-4614	
Cotton Electric Co-op Inc 226 N Broadway ... Walters *TF:* 800-522-3520 ■ *Web:* www.cottonelectric.com	OK	73572	580-875-3351	875-3101
East Central Oklahoma Electric Co-op Inc 2001 S Wood Dr PO Box 1178 ... Okmulgee *Web:* www.ecoec.com	OK	74447	918-756-0833	756-6539
Harmon Electric Assn Inc (HEA) 114 N First St PO Box 393 ... Hollis *TF:* 800-643-7769 ■ *Web:* www.harmonelectric.com	OK	73550	580-688-3342	
Indian Electric Co-op Inc 2506 E Hwy 64 ... Cleveland *TF:* 800-482-2750 ■ *Web:* www.iecok.com	OK	74020	918-358-2514	
Kay Electric Co-op (KEC) 300 W Doolin Ave ... Blackwell *TF:* 800-535-1079 ■ *Web:* www.kayelectric.coop	OK	74631	580-363-1260	363-2308
Kiamichi Electric Co-op Inc (KEC) 966 SW Hwy 2 PO Box 340 ... Wilburton *TF:* 800-888-2731 ■ *Web:* www.kiamichielectric.org	OK	74578	918-465-2338	465-2405
Kiwash Electric Co-op Inc 120 W First St ... Cordell *TF:* 888-832-3362	OK	73632	580-832-3361	
Lake Region Electric Co-op Inc 516 S Lake Region Rd ... Hulbert *TF:* 800-364-5732 ■ *Web:* www.lrecok.coop	OK	74441	918-772-2526	
Northeast Oklahoma Electric Co-op Inc 443857 E Hwy 60 PO Box 948 ... Vinita *TF:* 800-256-6405 ■ *Web:* www.neelectric.com	OK	74301	918-256-6405	256-9380
Northfork Electric Co-op 311 E Madden St PO Box 400 ... Sayre *Web:* www.nfecoop.com	OK	73662	580-928-3366	928-3105
Northwestern Electric Co-op Inc 2925 William Ave ... Woodward *TF:* 800-375-7423 ■ *Web:* www.nwecok.coop	OK	73802	580-256-7425	254-2858
Oklahoma Electric Co-op 242 24th Ave NW ... Norman *Web:* www.okcoop.org	OK	73069	405-321-2024	217-6900
People's Electric Co-op 1600 N Country Club Rd ... Ada *Web:* www.peoplesec.com	OK	74820	580-332-3031	
Rural Electric Co-op Inc (REC) 801 N Industrial Heights PO Box 609 ... Lindsay *TF:* 800-259-3504 ■ *Web:* www.recok.coop	OK	73052	405-756-3104	756-8957
Southeastern Electric Co-op Inc 1514 E Hwy 70 PO Box 1370 ... Durant *TF:* 866-924-1315 ■ *Web:* www.se-coop.com	OK	74702	580-924-2170	924-6402
Southwest Rural Electric Assn 700 N Broadway PO Box 310 ... Tipton *TF:* 800-256-7973 ■ *Web:* www.swre.com	OK	73570	580-667-5281	667-5284
Stillwater Utilities Authority PO Box 1449 ... Stillwater *Web:* www.stillwater.org	OK	74076	405-372-0025	
Tri-County Electric 302 E Glaydas St PO Box 880 ... Hooker *TF:* 800-522-3315 ■ *Web:* www.tri-countyelectric.coop	OK	73945	580-652-2418	652-3151
Verdigris Valley Electric Co-op 8901 E 146th St N ... Collinsville *TF:* 800-870-5948 ■ *Web:* www.vvec.com	OK	74021	918-371-2584	371-9873
Western Farmers Electric Co-op 701 NE Seventh St ... Anadarko *Web:* www.wfec.com	OK	73005	405-247-3351	247-4451

Oregon

			Phone	Fax
Blachly-Lane Inc PO Box 70 ... Junction City *TF:* 800-446-8418 ■ *Web:* www.blachlylane.coop	OR	97448	541-688-8711	688-8958
Central Electric Co-op Inc (CEC) 2098 Hwy 97 N ... Redmond	OR	97756	541-548-2144	548-0366
Columbia Basin Electric Co-op 171 W Linden Way ... Heppner *Web:* cbec.cc	OR	97836	541-676-9146	
Columbia Power Co-op Assn 311 Wilson St PO Box 97 ... Monument	OR	97864	541-934-2311	934-2312
Consumers Power Inc (CPI) 6990 W Hills Rd PO Box 1180 ... Philomath *TF:* 800-872-9036 ■ *Web:* www.cpi.coop	OR	97370	541-929-3124	929-8673
Coos-Curry Electric Co-op Inc 43050 Hwy 101 PO Box 1268 ... Port Orford *Web:* www.ccec.coop	OR	97465	541-332-3931	332-3501
Harney Electric Co-op Inc 277 Lottery Ln PO Box 587 ... Hines *Web:* www.harneyelectric.org	OR	97738	541-573-2061	
Lane Electric Co-op 787 Bailey Hill Rd PO Box 21410 ... Eugene *Web:* www.laneelectric.com	OR	97402	541-484-1151	484-7316
Midstate Electric Co-op Inc 16755 Finley Butte Rd ... La Pine *TF:* 800-722-7219 ■ *Web:* www.midstateelectric.coop	OR	97739	541-536-2126	536-1423
Northern Wasco County People's Utility District 2345 River Rd ... The Dalles *Web:* nwasco.com	OR	97058	541-296-2226	298-3320
Oregon Trail Electric ConsumersCo-op Inc (OTEC) 4005 23rd St PO Box 226 ... Baker City *Web:* www.otecc.com	OR	97814	541-523-3616	
Salem Electric 633 Seventh St NW ... Salem *Web:* www.salemelectric.com	OR	97304	503-362-3601	371-2956
Tillamook People's Utility District 1115 Pacific Ave ... Tillamook *TF:* 800-422-2535 ■ *Web:* www.tpud.org	OR	97141	503-842-2535	842-4161
Umatilla Electric Co-op Assn 750 W Elm Ave ... Hermiston *Web:* www.umatillaelectric.com	OR	97838	541-567-6414	567-8142
Wasco Electric Co-op Inc 105 E Fourth St ... The Dalles *TF:* 800-341-8580 ■ *Web:* www.wascoelectric.com	OR	97058	541-296-2740	296-7781
West Oregon Electric Co-op Inc 652 Rose Ave PO Box 69 ... Vernonia *TF:* 800-777-1276 ■ *Web:* www.westoregon.org	OR	97064	503-429-3021	429-8440

Pennsylvania

			Phone	Fax
Adams Electric Co-op Inc 1338 Biglerville Rd PO Box 1055 ... Gettysburg *TF:* 888-232-6732 ■ *Web:* www.adamsec.coop	PA	17325	717-334-2171	334-3980
Bedford Rural Electric Co-op Inc 8846 Lincoln Hwy ... Bedford *TF:* 800-808-2732 ■ *Web:* www.bedfordrec.com	PA	15522	814-623-5101	623-7983
Citizens' Electric Co 1775 Industrial Blvd PO Box 551 ... Lewisburg *TF:* 877-487-9384 ■ *Web:* www.citizenselectric.com	PA	17837	570-524-2231	524-5887
Claverack Rural Electric Co-op Inc 32750 W US 6 ... Wysox *TF:* 800-326-9799 ■ *Web:* www.claverack.com	PA	18854	570-265-2167	265-6019
New Enterprise Rural Electric Co-op Inc 3596 Brumbaugh Rd ... New Enterprise *TF:* 800-270-3177 ■ *Web:* www.newenterpriserec.com	PA	16664	814-766-3221	766-3319
Northwestern Rural Electric Co-op Assn Inc 22534 State Rte Ste 86 ... Cambridge Springs **Fax Area Code:* 814 ■ *TF:* 800-352-0014 ■ *Web:* www.northwesternrec.com	PA	16403	800-472-7910	398-8064*

	City	State	ZIP	Phone	Fax
REA Energy Co-op Inc 75 Airport Rd *TF:* 800-211-5667 ■ *Web:* www.reaenergy.com	Indiana	PA	15701	724-349-4800	349-7151
Somerset Rural Electric Co-op 223 Industrial Pk Rd *TF:* 800-443-4255 ■ *Web:* www.somersetrec.com	Somerset	PA	15501	814-445-4106	
Sullivan County Rural Electric Co-op Inc (SCREC) 5675 Rt 87 PO Box 65 *TF:* 800-570-5081 ■ *Web:* www.screc.com	Forksville	PA	18616	570-924-3381	
Tri-County Rural Electric Co-op Inc 22 N Main St PO Box 526 *TF:* 800-343-2559 ■ *Web:* www.tri-countyrec.com	Mansfield	PA	16933	570-662-2175	662-2142
Tri-County Rural Electric Co-op Inc PO Box 526 *Web:* www.tri-countyrec.com	Mansfield	PA	16933	570-662-2175	
United Electric Co-op Inc 29 United Rd *TF:* 888-581-8969 ■ *Web:* www.prea.com	Du Bois	PA	15801	814-371-8570	
Valley Rural Electric Co-op Inc 10700 Fairgrounds Rd PO Box 477 *TF:* 800-432-0680 ■ *Web:* www.valleyrec.com	Huntingdon	PA	16652	814-643-2650	643-1678
Warren Electric Co-op Inc (WEC) 320 E Main St PO Box 208 *TF:* 800-364-8640 ■ *Web:* www.warrenec.coop	Youngsville	PA	16371	814-563-7548	563-7012

South Carolina

	City	State	ZIP	Phone	Fax
Aiken Electric Co-op Inc 2790 Wagener Rd *TF Tech Supp:* 877-264-5368 ■ *Web:* aikenco-op.org	Aiken	SC	29802	803-649-6245	641-8310
Berkeley Electric Co-op Inc 551 Rembert C Dennis Blvd *Web:* www.berkeleyelectric.coop	Moncks Corner	SC	29461	843-761-8200	572-1280
Black River Electric Co-op 1121 N Pike Rd W PO Box 130 *Web:* www.blackriver.coop	Sumter	SC	29151	803-469-8060	469-8320
Broad River Electric Co-op Inc 811 Hamrick St *TF:* 866-687-2667 ■ *Web:* www.broadriverelectric.com	Gaffney	SC	29342	864-489-5737	487-7808
Coastal Electric Co-op Inc 2269 Jefferies Hwy *TF:* 855-880-2743 ■ *Web:* www.coastal.coop	Walterboro	SC	29488	843-538-5700	538-5081
Edisto Electric Co-op Inc 896 Calhoun St *TF:* 800-433-3292 ■ *Web:* www.edistoelectric.com	Bamberg	SC	29003	803-245-5141	245-0188
Horry Electric Co-op Inc 2774 Cultra Rd *Web:* www.horryelectric.com	Conway	SC	29526	843-369-2211	
Laurens Electric Co-op Inc 2254 S Carolina 14 *TF:* 800-942-3141 ■ *Web:* laurenselectric.com	Laurens	SC	29360	800-942-3141	
Little River Electric Co-op Inc (LRECI) PO Box 220 *TF:* 800-459-2141 ■ *Web:* www.lreci.coop	Abbeville	SC	29620	864-366-2141	366-4524
Lynches River Electric Co-op Inc 1104 W McGregor St *TF:* 800-922-3486 ■ *Web:* www.lynchesriver.com	Pageland	SC	29728	843-672-6111	672-6118
Mid-Carolina Electric Co-op Inc PO Box 669 *TF Cust Svc:* 888-813-8000 ■ *Web:* www.mcecoop.com	Lexington	SC	29071	803-749-6555	
Newberry Electric Co-op Inc 882 Wilson Rd *TF:* 800-479-8838 ■ *Web:* www.nec.coop	Newberry	SC	29108	803-276-1121	276-4121
Pee Dee Electric Co-op Inc PO Box 491 *TF:* 866-747-0060 ■ *Web:* www.peedeeelectric.com	Darlington	SC	29540	843-665-4070	
Santee Electric Co-op Inc 424 Sumter Hwy *TF:* 800-922-1604 ■ *Web:* www.santee.org	Kingstree	SC	29556	843-355-6187	
Tri-County Electric Co-op 6473 Old State Rd *TF:* 877-874-1215 ■ *Web:* tri-countyelectric.net	Saint Matthews	SC	29135	803-874-1215	
York Electric Co-op Inc PO Box 150 *TF:* 800-582-8810 ■ *Web:* www.yorkelectric.net	York	SC	29745	803-684-4247	684-6306

South Dakota

	City	State	ZIP	Phone	Fax
Black Hills Electric Co-op 25191 Co-op Way PO Box 792 *TF:* 800-742-0085 ■ *Web:* www.bhec.com	Custer	SD	57730	605-673-4461	673-3147
Bon Homme Yankton Electric Assn 134 S Lidice St *TF:* 800-925-2929 ■ *Web:* www.byelectric.com	Tabor	SD	57063	605-463-2507	463-2419
Butte Electric Co-op 109 Dartmouth Ave *TF:* 800-928-8839 ■ *Web:* www.butteelectric.com	Newell	SD	57760	605-456-2494	
Cam-Wal Electric Co-op Inc 404 W Scranton St PO Box 135 **Fax Area Code:* 605 ■ *TF:* 800-269-7676 ■ *Web:* www.cam-walnet.com	Selby	SD	57472	800-269-7676	649-7031*
Charles Mix Electric Assn Inc 440 Lake St *TF:* 800-208-8587 ■ *Web:* www.cme.coop	Lake Andes	SD	57356	605-487-7321	487-7868
Cherry-Todd Electric Co-op Inc 625 W Second St *TF:* 800-856-4417 ■ *Web:* cherry-todd.com	Mission	SD	57555	605-856-4416	
Clay-Union Electric Corp 1410 E Cherry St PO Box 317 *TF:* 800-696-2832 ■ *Web:* www.clayunionelectric.coop	Vermillion	SD	57069	605-624-2673	
Codington-Clark Electric Co-op 3520 Ninth Ave SW PO Box 880 *TF:* 800-463-8938 ■ *Web:* www.codingtonclarkelectric.coop	Watertown	SD	57201	605-886-5848	886-5934
Dakota Energy Co-op Inc PO Box 830 *TF:* 800-353-8591 ■ *Web:* www.dakotaenergy.coop	Huron	SD	57350	605-352-8591	352-8578
Douglas Electric Co-op Inc 400 Main Ave	Armour	SD	57313	605-724-2323	724-2972
FEM Electric Assn Inc PO Box 468 *TF:* 800-587-5880 ■ *Web:* www.femelectric.coop	Ipswich	SD	57451	605-426-6891	426-6791
Grand Electric Co-op Inc 801 Coleman Ave PO Box 39 *TF:* 800-592-1803 ■ *Web:* www.grandelectric.coop	Bison	SD	57620	605-244-5211	244-7288
H-D Electric Co-op Inc 423 Third Ave S *TF:* 800-781-7474 ■ *Web:* h-delectric.coop	Clear Lake	SD	57226	605-874-2171	874-8173
Kingsbury Electric Co-op Inc 511 Us Hwy 14	De Smet	SD	57231	605-854-3522	854-3465
Lake Region Electric Assn Inc 1212 Main St *TF:* 800-657-5869 ■ *Web:* www.lakeregion.coop	Webster	SD	57274	605-345-3379	345-4442
Moreau-Grand Electric Co-op Inc 405 Ninth St *TF:* 800-952-3158 ■ *Web:* www.mge.coop	Timber Lake	SD	57656	605-865-3511	
Northern Electric Co-op Inc 39456 133nd St *TF:* 800-529-0310 ■ *Web:* www.northernelectric.coop	Bath	SD	57427	605-225-0310	225-1684
Oahe Electric Co-op Inc 102 S Cranford St PO Box 216 *TF:* 800-640-6243 ■ *Web:* www.oaheelectric.com	Blunt	SD	57522	605-962-6243	962-6306
Rosebud Electric Co-op Inc 512 Rosebud Ave PO Box 439 *TF:* 888-464-9304 ■ *Web:* www.rosebudelectric.com	Gregory	SD	57533	605-835-9624	835-9649
Sioux Valley-Southwestern Electric Co-op Inc 47092 SD Hwy 34 PO Box 216 *TF:* 800-234-1960 ■ *Web:* www.siouxvalleyenergy.com	Colman	SD	57017	605-534-3535	256-1693
Union County Electric Co-op Inc 122 W Main St *TF:* 888-356-3395 ■ *Web:* unioncounty.coop	Elk Point	SD	57025	605-356-3395	356-3397
West Central Electric Co-op Inc 204 Main St PO Box 17 *TF:* 800-242-9232 ■ *Web:* www.wce.coop	Murdo	SD	57559	605-669-2472	669-2358
West River Electric Assn Inc 1200 W Fourth Ave PO Box 412 **Fax Area Code:* 605 ■ *TF:* 888-279-2135 ■ *Web:* www.westriver.com	Wall	SD	57790	888-279-2135	279-2630*
Whetstone Valley Electric Co-op 1101 E Fourth Ave *TF:* 800-568-6631 ■ *Web:* whetstone.coop	Milbank	SD	57252	605-432-5331	432-5951

Tennessee

	City	State	ZIP	Phone	Fax
Appalachian Electric Co-op 1109 Hill Dr *Web:* aecoop.org	New Market	TN	37820	865-475-2032	475-0888
Caney Fork Electric Co-op Inc 920 Smithville Hwy PO Box 272 *TF:* 888-505-3030 ■ *Web:* www.caneyforkec.com	McMinnville	TN	37110	931-473-3116	473-4939
Chickasaw Electric Co-op 17970 US Hwy 64 E PO Box 459 *TF:* 866-465-3591 ■ *Web:* chickasaw.coop	Somerville	TN	38068	901-465-3591	465-5392
Cumberland Electric Membership Corp 1940 Madison St *Web:* www.cemc.org	Clarksville	TN	37043	931-645-2481	
Duck River Electric Membership Corp 305 Learning Way PO Box 89 *Web:* www.dremc.com	Shelbyville	TN	37160	931-684-4621	685-0013
Fayetteville Public Utilities 408 W College St *TF:* 800-379-2534 ■ *Web:* www.fayelectric.com	Fayetteville	TN	37334	931-433-1522	433-0646
Forked Deer Electric Co-op PO Box 67 *TF:* 844-333-2729 ■ *Web:* www.forkeddeer.com	Halls	TN	38040	731-836-7508	
Gibson Electric Membership Corp 1207 S College St PO Box 47 *Web:* www.gibsonemc.com	Trenton	TN	38382	731-855-4740	
Greeneville Light & Power System PO Box 1690 *TF:* 866-466-1438 ■ *Web:* www.glps.net	Greeneville	TN	37744	423-636-6200	636-6206
Holston Electric Co-op Inc 1200 W Main St *Web:* www.holstonelectric.com	Rogersville	TN	37857	423-272-8821	
La Follette Utilities Board 302 N Tennessee Ave PO Box 1411 *TF:* 800-352-1340 ■ *Web:* www.lub.org	La Follette	TN	37766	423-562-3316	566-0580
Middle Tennessee Electric Membership Corp 555 New Salem Rd *Web:* www.mtemc.com	Murfreesboro	TN	37129	615-890-9762	895-3594
Mountain Electric Co-op Inc PO Box 180 *TF Cust Svc:* 800-638-3788 ■ *Web:* www.mountainelectric.com	Mountain City	TN	37683	423-727-1800	727-1822
Newport Utilities PO Box 519 *TF:* 877-779-8581 ■ *Web:* www.newportutilities.com	Newport	TN	37822	423-625-2800	623-5767
Pickwick Electric Co-op 530 Mulberry Ave *TF:* 800-372-8258 ■ *Web:* www.pickwickec.com	Selmer	TN	38375	731-645-3411	645-7167
Plateau Electric Co-op 16200 Scott Hwy PO Box 4669 *Web:* www.plateauelectric.com	Oneida	TN	37841	423-569-8591	
Powell Valley Electric Co-op 325 Straight Creek Rd PO Box 1528 *Web:* billing.pve.coop	New Tazewell	TN	37825	423-626-5204	
Sequachee Valley Electric Co-op 512 Cedar Ave PO Box 31 *TF:* 800-923-2203 ■ *Web:* www.svalleyec.com	South Pittsburg	TN	37380	423-837-8605	837-9836
Southwest Tennessee Electric Membership Corp 1009 E Main St *TF:* 800-772-0472 ■ *Web:* www.stemc.com	Brownsville	TN	38012	731-772-1322	772-1037
Tennessee Valley Electric Co-op 590 Florence Rd *TF:* 866-925-4916 ■ *Web:* www.tvec.com	Savannah	TN	38372	731-925-4916	925-4919
Tri-County Electric Membership Corp 405 College St *TF:* 800-369-2111 ■ *Web:* www.tcemc.org	Lafayette	TN	37083	615-666-2111	688-2141
Upper Cumberland Electric Membership Corp 138 Gordonsville Hwy *TF:* 800-261-2940 ■ *Web:* www.ucemc.com	South Carthage	TN	37030	615-735-2940	735-2603
Volunteer Energy Co-op (VEC) PO Box 277 *Web:* www.vec.org	Decatur	TN	37322	423-334-5721	334-7003

Texas

	City	State	ZIP	Phone	Fax
Bandera Electric Co-op Inc 3172 State Hwy 16 N **Fax Area Code:* 830 ■ *TF:* 866-226-3372 ■ *Web:* banderaelectric.com	Bandera	TX	78003	866-226-3372	460-3030*
Bartlett Electric Co-op Inc 27492 Texas 95 *Web:* www.bartlettec.coop	Bartlett	TX	76511	254-527-3551	527-3221

Name / Address	City	State	Zip	Phone	Fax
Big Country Electric Co-op 1010 W S First St PO Box 518 *TF:* 888-662-2232 ■ *Web:* bigcountry.net	Roby	TX	79543	325-776-2244	
Bowie-Cass Electric Co-op Inc 117 N St. *TF:* 800-794-2919 ■ *Web:* www.bcec.com	Douglassville	TX	75560	903-846-2311	
Central Texas Electric Co-op Inc (CTEC) 386 Friendship Ln PO Box 553 *TF General:* 800-900-2832 ■ *Web:* www.ctec.coop	Fredericksburg	TX	78624	830-997-2126	
Coleman County Electric Co-op Inc 3300 N Hwy 84 PO Box 860 *TF:* 800-560-2128 ■ *Web:* www.colemanelectric.org	Coleman	TX	76834	325-625-2128	625-4600
Comanche Electric Co-op Assn 201 W Wrights Ave *TF:* 800-915-2533 ■ *Web:* www.ceca.coop	Comanche	TX	76442	325-356-2533	356-3038
Concho Valley Electric Co-op Inc 2530 Pulliam St PO Box 3388 *Web:* www.cvec.coop	San Angelo	TX	76902	325-655-6957	655-6950
Cooke County Electric Co-op 11799 W US Hwy 82 PO Box 530 **Fax:* Cust Svc ■ *TF:* 800-962-0296 ■ *Web:* www.cceca.com	Muenster	TX	76252	940-759-2211	759-4122*
CoServ Electric 7701 S Stemmons Fwy *TF:* 800-274-4014 ■ *Web:* coserv.com	Corinth	TX	76210	940-321-7800	270-6640
Deaf Smith Electric Co-op Inc 1501 E First St *TF:* 800-687-8189 ■ *Web:* Www.dsec.org	Hereford	TX	79045	806-364-1166	
Deep East Texas Electric Co-op Inc 880 Texas Hwy 21 E PO Box 736 *TF:* 800-392-5986 ■ *Web:* www.deepeast.com	San Augustine	TX	75972	936-275-2314	275-2135
Fannin County Electric Co-op Inc 1530 Silo Rd *Web:* www.fcec.coop	Bonham	TX	75418	903-583-2117	
Farmers Electric Co-op Inc 2000 E I-30 *TF:* 800-541-2662 ■ *Web:* www.fecelectric.com	Greenville	TX	75402	903-455-1715	455-8125
Fayette Electric Co-op Inc 357 N Washington St *TF:* 800-874-8290 ■ *Web:* www.fayette.coop	La Grange	TX	78945	979-968-3181	968-6752
Fort Belknap Electric Co-op Inc 1302 W Main PO Box 486 *Web:* www.fortbelknapec.com	Olney	TX	76374	940-564-2343	564-3247
Grayson-Collin Electric Co-op (GCEC) PO Box 548 *TF:* 800-967-5235 ■ *Web:* www.gcec.net	Van Alstyne	TX	75495	903-482-7100	
Greenbelt Electric Co-op Inc PO Box 948 *TF:* 800-527-3082 ■ *Web:* www.greenbeltelectric.coop	Wellington	TX	79095	806-447-2536	
Guadalupe Valley Electric Co-op Inc 825 E Sarah Dewitt Dr *TF:* 800-223-4832 ■ *Web:* www.gvec.org	Gonzales	TX	78629	830-857-1200	857-1205
Guadalupe-Blanco River Authority (GBRA) 933 E Ct St *Web:* www.gbra.org	Seguin	TX	78155	830-379-5822	379-9718
Hamilton County Electric Co-op Assn 420 N Rice St PO Box 753 *TF:* 800-595-3401 ■ *Web:* www.hamiltonelectric.coop	Hamilton	TX	76531	254-386-3123	386-8757
Hilco Electric Co-op Inc 115 E Main PO Box 127 *TF:* 800-338-6425 ■ *Web:* hilco.coop	Itasca	TX	76055	254-687-2331	687-2428
J-A-C Electric Co-op Inc 1784 FM 172 *Web:* www.jacelectric.com	Bluegrove	TX	76352	940-895-3311	
Jackson ElectricCo-op Inc 8925 State Hwy 111 S *Web:* www.jecec.com	Ganado	TX	77962	361-771-4400	771-4406
Jasper-Newton Electric Co-op Inc (JNEC) 812 S Margaret Ave *Web:* www.jnec.com	Kirbyville	TX	75956	409-423-2241	423-3648
Karnes Electric Co-op Inc 1007 N Hwy 123 *TF:* 888-807-3952 ■ *Web:* www.karnesec.org	Karnes City	TX	78118	830-780-3952	780-2347
Lamar County Electric Co-op Assn 1485 N Main St *TF:* 800-252-8080 ■ *Web:* www.lamarelectric.com	Paris	TX	75460	903-784-4303	
Lamb County Electric Co-op Inc 2415 S Phelps Ave *TF:* 800-365-9000 ■ *Web:* www.lcec.coop	Littlefield	TX	79339	806-385-5191	385-5197
Lighthouse Electric Co-op Inc PO Box 600 *Web:* www.lighthouse.coop	Floydada	TX	79235	806-983-2814	983-2804
Lyntegar Electric Co-op Inc PO Box 970 *TF:* 877-218-2308 ■ *Web:* lyntegar.coop	Tahoka	TX	79373	806-561-4588	561-4724
Magic Valley Electric Co-op Inc 1 3/4 Mile W Hwy 83 PO Box 267 *Web:* www.magval.com	Mercedes	TX	78570	956-903-3048	565-0457
McLennan County Electric Co-op 1111 Johnson Dr PO Box 357 *TF:* 800-840-2957 ■ *Web:* www.hotec.coop	McGregor	TX	76657	254-840-2871	840-4250
Medina Electric Co-op Inc PO Box 370 **Fax Area Code:* 830 ■ *TF:* 866-632-3532 ■ *Web:* www.medinaec.org	Hondo	TX	78861	866-632-3532	426-2796*
Navarro County Electric Co-op Inc 3800 Texas 22 PO Box 616 *TF:* 800-771-9095 ■ *Web:* navarroec.com	Corsicana	TX	75110	903-874-7411	874-8422
Navasota Valley Electric Co-op Inc 2281 E US Hwy 79 PO Box 848 *TF:* 800-443-9462 ■ *Web:* www.navasotavalley.com	Franklin	TX	77856	979-828-3232	828-5563
North Plains Electric Co-op Inc 14585 Hwy 83 N PO Box 1008 *TF:* 800-272-5482 ■ *Web:* www.npec.org	Perryton	TX	79070	806-435-5482	435-7225
Nueces Electric Co-op (NEC) 709 E Main St PO Box 260970 *TF:* 800-632-9288 ■ *Web:* www.nueceselectric.org	Robstown	TX	78380	361-387-2581	387-4139
Panola-Harrison Electric Co-op 410 E Houston St *TF:* 800-972-1093 ■ *Web:* www.phec.us	Marshall	TX	75670	903-935-7936	
Pedernales Electric Co-op Inc PO Box 1 *TF:* 888-554-4732 ■ *Web:* www.pec.coop	Johnson City	TX	78636	830-868-7155	868-4767
Rio Grande Electric Co-op Inc Hwy 90 & State Hwy 131 PO Box 1509 *TF:* 800-749-1509 ■ *Web:* www.riogrande.coop	Brackettville	TX	78832	830-563-2444	563-2450
Rusk County ElectricCo-op Inc 3162 State Hwy 43 E *Web:* www.rcelectric.org	Henderson	TX	75652	903-657-4571	657-5377
Sam Houston Electric Co-op Inc 1157 E Church St *TF:* 800-458-0381 ■ *Web:* www.samhouston.net	Livingston	TX	77351	936-327-5711	328-1244
San Bernard Electric Co-op Inc 309 W Main St *TF:* 800-364-3171 ■ *Web:* www.sbec.org	Bellville	TX	77418	979-865-3171	865-9706
San Patricio Electric Co-op Inc 402 E Sinton St *TF:* 888-740-2220 ■ *Web:* www.sanpatricioelectric.org	Sinton	TX	78387	361-364-2220	364-3467
South Plains Electric Co-op Inc PO Box 1830 *TF:* 800-658-2655 ■ *Web:* www.spec.coop	Lubbock	TX	79408	806-775-7766	775-7796
Southwest Texas Electric Co-op Inc 101 E Gillis St PO Box 677 *TF:* 800-643-3980 ■ *Web:* www.swtec.com	Eldorado	TX	76936	325-853-2544	853-3141
Swisher Electric Co-op Inc 401 SW Second St PO Box 67 *TF:* 800-530-4344 ■ *Web:* www.swisherelectric.org	Tulia	TX	79088	806-995-3567	995-2249
Taylor Electric Co-op Inc (TEC) 226 County Rd 287 Bldg A PO Box 250 *Web:* www.taylorelectric.com	Merkel	TX	79536	325-793-8500	793-1309
Texas Electric Co-ops Inc 1122 Colorado St 24th Fl *TF:* 800-301-2860 ■ *Web:* www.texas-ec.org	Austin	TX	78701	512-454-0311	
Tri-County Electric Co-op Inc 600 NW Pkwy. *TF:* 800-367-8232 ■ *Web:* www.tcectexas.com	Azle	TX	76020	817-444-3201	444-3542
Trinity Valley Electric Co-op Inc (TVEC) 1800 Hwy 243 E PO Box 888 *TF:* 800-766-9576 ■ *Web:* www.tvec.net	Kaufman	TX	75142	972-932-2214	932-6466
United Co-op Services 3309 N Main St PO Box 16 *Web:* www.united-cs.com	Cleburne	TX	76033	817-556-4000	556-4068
Victoria Electric Co-op Inc (VEC) 102 S Ben Jordan St *Web:* www.victoriaelectric.coop	Victoria	TX	77901	361-573-2428	573-5753
Wharton County Electric Co-op Inc (WCEC) 1815 E Jackson St *TF:* 800-460-6271 ■ *Web:* www.wcecnet.net	El Campo	TX	77437	979-543-6271	543-6259
Wise Electric Co-op Inc 1900 N Trinity St *TF:* 888-627-9326 ■ *Web:* www.wiseec.com	Decatur	TX	76234	940-627-2167	626-3060
Wood County Electric Co-op Inc 501 S Main St *TF:* 800-762-2203 ■ *Web:* www.wcec.org	Quitman	TX	75783	903-763-2203	763-5693

Utah

Name / Address	City	State	Zip	Phone	Fax
Dixie-Escalante Rural Electric Assn 71 E Hwy 56 *TF:* 800-874-0904 ■ *Web:* www.dixiepower.com	Beryl	UT	84714	435-439-5311	439-5352
Flowell Electric Assn Inc 495 North 3200 West	Fillmore	UT	84631	435-743-6214	743-5722
Garkane Energy Co-op Inc 120 West 300 South PO Box 465 *TF:* 800-747-5403 ■ *Web:* www.garkaneenergy.com	Loa	UT	84747	435-836-2795	836-2497
Moon Lake Electric Assn Inc 800 West Hwy 40 PO Box 278 *Web:* www.mleainc.com	Roosevelt	UT	84066	435-722-5400	

Vermont

Name / Address	City	State	Zip	Phone	Fax
Vermont Electric Co-op Inc 42 Wescom Rd *TF:* 800-832-2667 ■ *Web:* www.vermontelectric.coop	Johnson	VT	05656	802-635-2331	635-7645
Washington Electric Co-op 40 Church St *TF:* 800-932-5245 ■ *Web:* www.washingtonelectric.coop	East Montpelier	VT	05602	802-223-5245	

Virginia

Name / Address	City	State	Zip	Phone	Fax
BARC Electric Co-op 84 High St PO Box 264 **Fax Area Code:* 540 ■ *TF:* 800-846-2272 ■ *Web:* www.barcelectric.com	Millboro	VA	24460	800-846-2272	997-9011*
Central Virginia Electric Co-op 800 Co-op Way PO Box 247 *TF:* 800-367-2832 ■ *Web:* www.mycvec.com	Lovingston	VA	22949	434-263-8336	263-8339
Community Electric Co-op 52 W Windsor Blvd *TF:* 855-700-2667 ■ *Web:* www.comelec.coop	Windsor	VA	23487	757-242-6181	242-3923
Craig-Botetourt Electric Co-op State Rt 615	New Castle	VA	24127	540-864-5121	
Mecklenburg Electric Co-op 11633 Hwy Ninety Two *TF:* 800-989-4161 ■ *Web:* www.meckelec.org	Chase City	VA	23924	434-372-6100	372-6102
Northern Neck Electric Co-op Inc 85 St Johns St PO Box 288 *TF:* 800-243-2860 ■ *Web:* www.nnec.coop	Warsaw	VA	22572	804-333-3621	
Northern Virginia Electric Co-op PO Box 2710 *TF:* 888-335-0500 ■ *Web:* www.novec.com	Manassas	VA	20108	703-335-0500	
Old Dominion Electric Co-op (ODEC) 4201 Dominion Blvd. *Web:* odec.com	Glen Allen	VA	23060	804-747-0592	747-3742
Prince George Electric Co-op 7103 General Mahone Hwy PO Box 168 *Web:* www.pgec.coop	Waverly	VA	23890	804-834-2424	
Southside Electric Co-op Inc 2000 W Virgina Ave *TF:* 800-552-2118 ■ *Web:* www.sec.coop	Crewe	VA	23930	434-645-7721	645-1147

Washington

Name / Address	City	State	Zip	Phone	Fax
Benton Rural Electric Assn (BREA) 402 Seventh St PO Box 1150 *TF:* 800-221-6987 ■ *Web:* www.bentonrea.org	Prosser	WA	99350	509-786-2913	786-0291

				Phone	Fax
Big Bend Electric Co-op 1373 N Hwy 261 PO Box 348 *TF:* 866-844-2363 ■ *Web:* www.bbec.org	Ritzville	WA	99169	509-659-1700	659-1404
Columbia Rural Electric Assn Inc 115 E Main St *TF:* 800-642-1231 ■ *Web:* www.columbiarea.com	Dayton	WA	99328	509-382-2578	
Elmhurst Mutual Power & Light Co 120 132nd St S *TF:* 855-841-2178 ■ *Web:* www.elmhurstmutual.org	Tacoma	WA	98444	253-531-4646	531-8969
Energy Northwest 76 N Power Plant Loop *TF:* 800-468-6883 ■ *Web:* www.energy-northwest.com	Richland	WA	99354	509-372-5000	
Inland Power & Light Company Inc 10110 W Hallett Rd *TF:* 800-747-7151 ■ *Web:* www.inlandpower.com	Spokane	WA	99224	509-747-7151	747-7987
Nespelem Valley Electric Co-op Inc 1009 F St *TF:* 866-377-8642 ■ *Web:* www.nvec.org	Nespelem	WA	99155	509-634-4571	634-8138
OHOP Mutual Light Co 34014 Mountain Hwy E *Web:* ohop.coop	Eatonville	WA	98328	253-847-4363	847-2877
Okanogan County Electric Co-op 93 W Chewuch Rd *Web:* okanoganelectriccoop.com	Winthrop	WA	98862	509-996-2228	
Orcas Power & Light Co-op 183 Mt Baker Rd *Web:* www.opalco.com	Eastsound	WA	98245	360-376-3500	376-3505
Parkland Light & Water Co 12918 Pk Ave *Web:* www.plw.coop	Tacoma	WA	98444	253-531-5666	531-2684
Peninsula Light Co 13315 Goodnough Dr NW *TF:* 888-809-8021 ■ *Web:* www.penlight.org	Gig Harbor	WA	98332	253-857-5950	
Public Utility District #1 of Ferry County 686 S Clark Ave PO Box 1039 *Web:* www.fcpud.com	Republic	WA	99166	509-775-3325	775-3326
Tanner Electric Co 45710 SE North Bend Way *TF:* 800-472-0208 ■ *Web:* tannerelectric.coop	North Bend	WA	98045	425-888-0623	888-5688

Wisconsin

				Phone	Fax
Adams-Columbia Electric Co-op 401 E Lake St *TF:* 800-831-8629 ■ *Web:* acecwi.com	Friendship	WI	53934	608-339-3346	339-7756
Barron Electric Co-op 1434 State Hwy 25 N *TF:* 800-322-1008 ■ *Web:* www.barronelectric.com	Barron	WI	54812	715-537-3171	
Bayfield Electric Co-op Inc 68460 District St *TF:* 800-278-0166 ■ *Web:* www.bayfieldelectric.com	Iron River	WI	54847	715-372-4287	372-4318
Chippewa Valley Electric Co-op 317 S Eigth St *TF:* 800-300-6800 ■ *Web:* www.cvecoop.com	Cornell	WI	54732	715-239-6800	239-6160
Clark Electric Co-op 124 N Main St PO Box 190 *TF:* 800-272-6188 ■ *Web:* www.cecoop.com	Greenwood	WI	54437	715-267-6188	
Dairyland Power Co-op 3200 E Ave S *Web:* www.dairylandpower.com	La Crosse	WI	54601	608-788-4000	787-1420
Dunn Energy Co-op PO Box 220 *TF:* 800-924-0630 ■ *Web:* www.dunnenergy.com	Menomonie	WI	54751	715-232-6240	
Jackson Electric Co-op N6868 County Rd F PO Box 546 *TF:* 800-370-4607 ■ *Web:* www.jackelec.com	Black River Falls	WI	54615	715-284-5385	284-7143
Jump River Electric Co-op PO Box 99 *TF:* 866-273-5111 ■ *Web:* www.jrec.net	Ladysmith	WI	54848	715-532-5524	532-3065
Oakdale Electric Co-op PO Box 128 *TF:* 800-241-2468 ■ *Web:* www.oakdalerec.com	Oakdale	WI	54649	608-372-4131	372-5173
Oconto Electric Co-op PO Box 168 PO Box 168 *TF:* 800-472-8410 ■ *Web:* www.ocontoelectric.com	Oconto Falls	WI	54154	920-846-2816	
Pierce Pepin Co-op Services W7725 US Hwy 10 PO Box 420 *TF:* 800-924-2133 ■ *Web:* www.piercepepin.com	Ellsworth	WI	54011	715-273-4355	273-4476
Polk-Burnett Electric Co-op (PBEC) 1001 State Rd 35 *TF:* 800-421-0283 ■ *Web:* www.polkburnett.com	Centuria	WI	54824	715-646-2191	646-2404
Price Electric Co-op 508 N Lake Ave PO Box 110 *TF:* 800-884-0881 ■ *Web:* price-electric.com	Phillips	WI	54555	715-339-2155	339-2921
Richland Electric Co-op 1027 N Jefferson St *TF:* 800-242-8511 ■ *Web:* rec.coop	Richland Center	WI	53581	608-647-3173	647-4265
Riverland Energy Co-op N28988 State Rd 93 PO Box 277 *TF:* 800-411-9115 ■ *Web:* www.riverlandenergy.com	Arcadia	WI	54612	608-323-3381	323-3014
Saint Croix Electric Co-op 1925 Ridgeway St *TF:* 800-924-3407 ■ *Web:* www.scecnet.net	Hammond	WI	54015	715-796-7000	796-7070
Scenic Rivers Energy Co-op 231 N Sheridan St *TF:* 800-236-2141 ■ *Web:* www.sre.coop	Lancaster	WI	53813	608-723-2121	723-2688
Taylor Electric Co-op N1831 State Hwy 13 *TF:* 800-862-2407 ■ *Web:* www.taylorelectric.org	Medford	WI	54451	715-678-2411	678-2555
Vernon Electric Co-op 110 Saugstad Rd *TF:* 800-447-5051 ■ *Web:* www.vernonelectric.org	Westby	WI	54667	608-634-3121	634-7481

Wyoming

				Phone	Fax
Big Horn Rural Electric Co-op 208 S Fifth St PO Box 270 *TF:* 800-564-2419 ■ *Web:* www.bighornrea.com	Basin	WY	82410	307-568-2419	568-2402
Bridger Valley Extreme Access 40014 Business Loop 1-80 PO Box 399 *TF:* 800-276-3481 ■ *Web:* bvea.coop	Mountain View	WY	82939	307-786-2800	786-4362
Carbon Power & Light Inc 100 E Willow Ave PO Box 579 *TF:* 800-359-0249 ■ *Web:* www.carbonpower.com	Saratoga	WY	82331	307-326-5206	
Garland Light & Power Co 755 Hwy 14A *Web:* garlandpower.org	Powell	WY	82435	307-754-2881	754-5320
High Plains Power Inc 1775 E Monroe PO Box 713 *TF:* 800-445-0613 ■ *Web:* www.highplainspower.org	Riverton	WY	82501	307-856-9426	856-4207
High West Energy Inc (HWE) 6270 County Rd 212 *TF:* 888-834-1657 ■ *Web:* www.highwestenergy.com	Pine Bluffs	WY	82082	307-245-3261	245-9292
Lower Valley Energy 236 N Washington PO Box 188 *TF:* 800-882-5875 ■ *Web:* www.lvenergy.com	Afton	WY	83110	307-885-3175	885-5787
Powder River Energy Corp (PRE) 221 Main St PO Box 930 **Fax Area Code:* 307 ■ *TF:* 800-442-3630 ■ *Web:* www.precorp.coop	Sundance	WY	82729	800-442-3630	283-3527*
Wheatland Rural Electric Assn 2154 S St PO Box 1209 *TF:* 800-344-3351 ■ *Web:* www.wheatlandrea.com	Wheatland	WY	82201	307-322-2125	322-5340
Wyrulec Co 3978 US Hwy 26/85 *TF:* 800-628-5266 ■ *Web:* www.wyrulec.com	Torrington	WY	82240	307-837-2225	837-2115

246 ELECTRICAL & ELECTRONIC EQUIPMENT & PARTS - WHOL

				Phone	Fax
360 Systems Inc 3281 Grande Vista Dr *Web:* 360systems.com	Newbury Park	CA	91320	818-991-0360	
A1 Teletronics Inc 2550 118th Ave N 00 *Web:* www.a1teletronics.com	Saint Petersburg	FL	33716	727-576-5001	
ACF Components & Fasteners Inc 31012 Huntwood Ave *TF Cust Svc:* 800-227-2901 ■ *Web:* www.acfcom.com	Hayward	CA	94544	510-487-2100	471-7018
Actify LLC 7635 Interactive Way Ste 200 *TF:* 800-467-0830 ■ *Web:* www.actifywireless.com	Indianapolis	IN	46278	800-467-0830	
ADDvantage Technologies Group Inc 1221 E Houston *NASDAQ: AEY* ■ *Web:* www.addvantagetechnologies.com	Broken Arrow	OK	74012	918-251-9121	
Adi American Distributors Inc 2 Emery Ave *TF:* 800-877-0510 ■ *Web:* www.americandistr.com	Randolph	NJ	07869	973-328-1181	328-2302
Advance Electrical Supply Co 263 N Oakley Blvd *Web:* www.advanceelectrical.com	Chicago	IL	60612	312-421-2300	421-0926
Advanced MP Technology 1010 Calle Sombra *TF:* 800-492-3113 ■ *Web:* www.advancedmp.com	San Clemente	CA	92673	949-492-3113	492-9589
AE Petsche Company Inc 2112 W Div St *TF:* 844-237-7600 ■ *Web:* www.aepetsche.com	Arlington	TX	76012	817-461-9473	277-2887
Aesco Electronics Inc 2230 Picton Pkwy *TF:* 877-442-6987 ■ *Web:* www.aesco.com	Akron	OH	44312	330-245-2630	245-2631
Algo Communication Products Ltd 4500 Beedie St *TF:* 800-226-7722 ■ *Web:* www.algo.ca	Burnaby	BC	V5J5L2	604-438-3333	437-5726
Allan Crawford Associates Ltd 5805 Kennedy Rd *Web:* www.aca.ca	Mississauga	ON	L4Z2G3	905-890-2010	
Allied Electronics Inc 7151 Jack Newell Blvd S *TF:* 866-433-5722 ■ *Web:* www.alliedelec.com	Fort Worth	TX	76118	817-595-3500	595-6404
Allstar Magnetics LLC 6205 NE 63rd St *TF:* 800-356-5977 ■ *Web:* www.allstarmagnetics.com	Vancouver	WA	98661	360-693-0213	693-0639
Alltronics LLC 2761 Scoll Blvd *Web:* www.alltronics.com	Santa Clara	CA	95050	408-778-3868	
Altura Communication Solutions LLC 1335 S Acacia Ave *Web:* www.alturacs.com	Fullerton	CA	92831	714-948-8400	
America II Electronics Inc 2600 118th Ave N *TF:* 800-767-2637 ■ *Web:* www.americaii.com	Saint Petersburg	FL	33716	727-573-0900	572-9696
American Electric Supply Inc 1872 W Pomona Rd *Web:* www.amelect.com	Corona	CA	92880	951-734-7910	737-9906
Anadigm Inc 2036 N Gilbert Rd Ste 2-417 *Web:* www.anadigm.com	Mesa	AZ	85203	480-422-0191	
Anixter International Inc 2301 Patriot Blvd *NYSE: AXE* ■ **Fax Area Code:* 512 ■ *TF:* 800-492-1212 ■ *Web:* www.anixter.com	Glenview	IL	60025	224-521-8000	252-0003*
Ansett Aircraft Spares & Services Inc 12675 Encinitas Ave *Web:* www.ansettspares.com	Sylmar	CA	91342	818-362-1100	
Area 51 Esg Inc 51 Post *TF:* 877-476-8751 ■ *Web:* www.area51esg.com	Irvine	CA	92618	949-387-0051	
Argo International Corp 160 Chubb Ave *TF:* 877-274-6468 ■ *Web:* www.argointl.com	Lyndhurst	NJ	07071	201-561-7010	
Arizona Components Company Inc 2901 W McDowell Rd *Web:* www.azcompco.com	Phoenix	AZ	85009	602-269-5655	
Astrex Inc 205 Express St *TF:* 800-633-6360 ■ *Web:* www.astrex.net	Plainview	NY	11803	516-433-1700	433-1796
Audio Acoustics Inc 800 N Cedarbrook Ave *Web:* www.aaius.com	Springfield	MO	65802	417-869-0770	
Audio-technica Us Inc 1221 Commerce Dr *TF:* 800-667-3745 ■ *Web:* www.audio-technica.com	Stow	OH	44224	330-686-2600	688-3752
Austin Aerotech Repair Services Inc 2005 Windy Ter *Web:* www.austinaerotech.com	Cedar Park	TX	78613	512-335-6000	
Avnet Inc 2211 S 47th St *NYSE: AVT* ■ *TF:* 888-822-8638 ■ *Web:* www.avnet.com	Phoenix	AZ	85034	480-643-2000	
Axcesor Inc 2260 Dakota Dr *Web:* www.axcesor.com	Grafton	WI	53024	262-375-7530	
B&D Industries Inc 9720 Bell Ave Se *TF:* 866-315-8349 ■ *Web:* www.banddindustries.com	Albuquerque	NM	87123	505-299-4464	
Bach-Simpson Corp 109 Meg Dr PO Box 5484 *Web:* www.bach-simpson.com	London	ON	N6A4L6	519-452-3200	
Barnett Inc 801 W Bay St *TF:* 888-803-4467 ■ *Web:* www.e-barnett.com	Jacksonville	FL	32204	904-384-6530	
Bates Technologies Inc 9059 Technology Ln *Web:* www.batestech.com	Fishers	IN	46038	317-841-2400	

Phone / Fax

BaySpec Inc 1101 McKay Dr San Jose CA 95131 408-512-5928
Web: www.bayspec.com

Beacon Electric Supply 9630 Chesapeake Dr San Diego CA 92123 858-279-9770 279-9908
Web: www.beaconelectric.com

Bearcom Inc 4009 Distribution Dr Ste 200 Garland TX 75041 800-527-1670
TF Sales: 800-527-1670 ■ *Web:* www.bearcom.com

Becker Electric Supply Inc 1341 E Fourth St Dayton OH 45402 937-226-1341 226-1790
TF: 800-762-9515 ■ *Web:* www.beckerelectric.com

Belmont Trading Co Inc
3160 MacArthur Blvd Northbrook IL 60062 847-412-9690
Web: www.belmont-trading.com

Benfield Electric Supply Company Inc
25 Lafayette Ave North White Plains NY 10603 914-948-6660 993-0558
Web: www.benfieldelectric.com

Bertech-Kelex 640 Maple Ave Torrance CA 90503 310-787-0337
Web: www.bertech.com

Beyond Components 5 Carl Thompson Rd Westford MA 01886 800-971-4242 929-2302
TF: 800-971-4242 ■ *Web:* www.beyondcomponents.com

Billows Electric Supply Co
9100 State Rd Philadelphia PA 19136 215-332-9700 338-8320
TF: 877-519-7302 ■ *Web:* www.billows.com

Bisco Industries Inc 1500 N Lakeview Ave Anaheim CA 92807 800-323-1232
TF: 800-323-1232 ■ *Web:* www.biscoind.com

Border States Electric Supply 105 25th St N Fargo ND 58102 701-293-5834 237-9488
TF: 800-800-0199 ■ *Web:* www.borderstates.com

Brightstar Corp 9725 NW 117th Ave Ste 300 Miami FL 33178 305-421-6000 513-3959
Web: brightstar.com

Broadfield Distributing Inc
67A Glen Cove Ave Glen Cove NY 11542 516-676-2378 671-3092
TF: 800-634-5178 ■ *Web:* www.broadfield.com

Broken Arrow Electric Supply Inc
2350 W Vancouver Broken Arrow OK 74012 918-258-3581 251-3799
Web: www.baes.com

Buckles-Smith 801 Savaker Ave San Jose CA 95126 408-280-7777 280-0729
TF: 800-833-7362 ■ *Web:* www.buckles-smith.com

Burst Communication Inc
8200 S Akron St Ste 108 Centennial CO 80112 303-649-9600 649-9890
Web: www.burstvideo.com

Butler Supply Inc 965 Horan Dr Fenton MO 63026 636-349-9000 349-7877
TF: 800-850-9949 ■ *Web:* www.butlersupply.com

Byram Laboratories Inc 1 Columbia Rd Branchburg NJ 08876 800-766-1212
TF: 800-766-1212 ■ *Web:* www.byramlabs.com

C R International Inc
9105 Whiskey Bottom Rd Ste J Laurel MD 20723 301-210-1540
Web: www.cri-inc.net

Cadex Electronics Inc 22000 Fraserwood Way Richmond BC V6W1J6 604-231-7777 231-7755
TF: 800-565-5228 ■ *Web:* www.cadex.com

California Eastern Laboratories Inc (CEL)
4590 Patrick Henry Dr Santa Clara CA 95054 408-988-3500 988-0279
Web: www.cel.com

Capital Electric Supply Co
7310 W Roosevelt Ste 2 Phoenix AZ 85043 623-936-6789 936-6262
Web: www.capitalelectricsupplyco.com

Carlton Bates Co 3600 W 69th St Little Rock AR 72209 501-562-9100 562-9200
TF: 866-600-6040 ■ *Web:* www.carltonbates.com

Cell-Tel Government Systems Inc
8226-B Phillips Hwy Ste 290 Jacksonville FL 32256 904-363-1111 363-0032
TF: 800-737-7545 ■ *Web:* www.cell-tel.com

Central Wholesale Electrical Distributors Inc
6611 Preston Ave Livermore CA 94551 925-245-9310
Web: cwed.com

Centratel LLC 141 NW Greenwood Ave Ste 200 Bend OR 97701 541-383-8383
Web: www.centratel.com

Century Fasteners Corp 50-20 Ireland St Elmhurst NY 11373 718-446-5000 426-8119
TF: 800-221-0769 ■ *Web:* www.centuryfasteners.com

CK Technologies Inc 3629 Vista Mercado Camarillo CA 93012 805-987-4801
Web: www.ckt.com

Classic Components Corp 23605 Telo Ave Torrance CA 90505 310-539-5500
Web: www.class-ic.com

Clean Air Solutions Inc 826 Bayridge Pl Fairfield CA 94534 707-864-9499
Web: www.cleanroomspecialists.com

Cms Communications Inc 722 Goddard Ave Chesterfield MO 63005 800-755-9169
TF: 800-755-9169 ■ *Web:* www.cmsc.com

Codale Electric Supply Inc
5225 West 2400 South PO Box 702070 Salt Lake City UT 84120 801-975-7300 977-8833
TF: 800-300-6634 ■ *Web:* www.codale.com

Codan US Inc 8430 Kao Cir Manassas VA 20110 703-361-2721
Web: www.codan.com.au

Commodity Components International Inc
100 Summit St Peabody MA 01960 978-538-0020 538-3633
Web: www.cci-inc.com

Communications Supply Corp (CSC)
200 E Lies Rd Carol Stream IL 60188 630-221-6400 221-6420
TF: 800-468-2121 ■ *Web:* www.gocsc.com

Component InterTechnologies Inc
2426 Perry Hwy Hadley PA 16130 724-253-3161
Web: www.cit-hadley.com

Components Distributors Inc
2601 Blake St Ste 200 Denver CO 80205 800-777-7334 294-0998*
*Fax Area Code: 720 ■ *TF:* 800-777-7334 ■ *Web:* www.cdiweb.com

Computer Solutions Inc 4217 S 84th St Omaha NE 68127 402-339-7441
Web: www.csimicro.com

Comstock Telcom 5445 Equity Ave Reno NV 89502 775-856-2227
Web: www.comstocktel.com

Comtel Corp 39810 Grand River Ave Ste 180 Novi MI 48375 248-888-4730 888-4743
TF: 800-335-2505 ■ *Web:* www.comtel.com

Consolidated Electrical Distributors Inc (CED)
9201 J St Omaha NE 68127 402-592-7500
Web: www.ced-aec.com

Corporate Telephone Services 184 W Second St Boston MA 02127 617-625-1200
TF: 800-274-1211 ■ *Web:* corptelserv.com

Cortelco Inc 1703 Sawyer Rd Corinth MS 38834 662-287-5281 287-3889
TF: 800-288-3132 ■ *Web:* www.cortelco.com

Crescent Electric Supply Co
7750 Dunleith Dr East Dubuque IL 61025 815-747-3145 747-7720
Web: www.cesco.com

Cross Automation Inc 2001 Oak Pkwy Belmont NC 28012 704-523-2222 523-6500
TF General: 800-272-7537 ■ *Web:* www.cross-automation.com

Crum Electric Supply Co 1165 W English Ave Casper WY 82601 307-266-1278 577-1312
TF: 800-726-2239 ■ *Web:* www.crum.com

Dakota Supply Group (DSG) 2601 Third Ave N Fargo ND 58102 701-237-9440 237-6504
TF: 800-437-4702 ■ *Web:* www.dakotasupplygroup.com

Data Panel Sales 7313 Washington Ave S Minneapolis MN 55439 952-941-3511
Web: www.datapanel.com

Dee Electronics Inc 2500 16th Ave SW Cedar Rapids IA 52404 319-365-7551 365-8506
TF: 800-747-3331 ■ *Web:* www.dee-inc.com

Delta Controls Corp 585 Fortson St Shreveport LA 71107 318-424-8471
Web: www.deltacnt.com

Deltrol Corp 2740 S 20th St Milwaukee WI 53215 414-671-6800
Web: www.deltrol.com

Dependable Component Supply Corp
1003 E Newport Ctr Dr Deerfield Beach FL 33442 954-283-5800 283-5802
TF: 800-336-7100

Desco Inc 1205 Lincolnton Rd Salisbury NC 28147 704-633-6331 637-6966
Web: www.descoinc.com

Digi-Key Corp 701 Brooks Ave S Thief River Falls MN 56701 218-681-6674 681-3380
TF: 800-344-4539 ■ *Web:* www.digikey.com

Dii Computers Inc 2425 Blair Mill Rd Willow Grove PA 19090 215-657-5055
Web: www.d2computers.com

Diversified Electronics Co Inc
PO Box 566 Forest Park GA 30298 404-361-4840 361-6327
TF: 800-646-7278 ■ *Web:* www.diversifiedelectronics.com

Dolphin Technology Inc
2025 Gateway Pl Ste 270 San Jose CA 95110 408-392-0012
Web: www.dolphin-ic.com

Dominion Electric Supply Company Inc
5053 Lee Hwy Arlington VA 22207 703-536-4400 741-0423
TF: 800-525-5006 ■ *Web:* www.dominionelectric.com

Dow Electronics Inc 8603 E Adamo Dr Tampa FL 33619 813-626-5195 628-4990
TF: 800-627-2900 ■ *Web:* www.dowelectronics.com

Dowley Inc 40 N.E. 46th St Oklahoma City OK 73105 405-525-1656
Web: www.dowley.com

Duke Communications
1781 Jamestown Rd Ste 170 Williamsburg VA 23185 757-253-9000
Web: www.widomaker.com

E Sam Jones Distributor Inc 4898 S Atlanta Rd Smyrna GA 30080 404-351-3250 351-4140
TF: 800-624-9849 ■ *Web:* www.esamjones.com

Earl & Brown Co Inc 5825 SW Arctic Dr Beaverton OR 97005 503-670-1170 432-9237*
*Fax Area Code: 866 ■ *Web:* www.earlbrown.com

eASIC Corp 2585 Augustine Dr Ste 100 Santa Clara CA 95054 408-855-9200
Web: www.easic.com

Eck Supply Co 1405 W Main St Richmond VA 23220 804-359-5781 358-1353
Web: www.ecksupply.com

Elecraft Inc Po Box 69 Aptos CA 95001 831-763-4211
Web: www.elecraft.com

Electric Supply & Equipment Co
1812 E Wendover Ave Greensboro NC 27405 336-272-4123 274-4632
TF: 800-632-0268 ■ *Web:* www.ese-co.com

Electric Supply Inc 4407 N Manhattan Ave Tampa FL 33614 813-872-1894 874-1680
TF: 800-678-1894 ■ *Web:* www.electricsupplyinc.com

Electrical Wholesale Supply Company of Utah
158 East 4500 South Salt Lake City UT 84107 801-268-2555 268-2555
Web: www.borderstates.com

Electro Brand Inc
1127 S Mannheim Rd Ste 305 Westchester IL 60154 708-338-4400
TF: 800-982-3954 ■ *Web:* www.electrobrand-usa.com

Electro Dynamics Crystal Corp
9075 Cody St Overland Park KS 66214 913-888-1750
Web: www.electrodynamics.com

Electro-Matic Products Inc
23409 Industrial Pk Ct Farmington Hills MI 48335 248-478-1182 478-1472
TF: 888-879-1088 ■ *Web:* www.electro-matic.com

ElectroTech Inc 7101 Madison Ave W Minneapolis MN 55427 763-544-4288 542-8102
TF: 800-544-4288 ■ *Web:* www.electrotech-inc.com

Elliott Electric Supply Co
2526 N Stallings Dr PO Box 630610 Nacogdoches TX 75963 936-569-1184 569-1836
TF: 877-777-0242 ■ *Web:* www.elliottelectric.com

EM Microelectronic-US Inc
5475 Mark Dabling Blvd Ste 200 Colorado Springs CO 80918 719-593-2883
Web: www.emmicroelectronic.com

Enetics Inc 830 Canning Pkwy Victor NY 14564 585-924-5010
Web: www.enetics.com

EnGenius Technologies Inc 1580 Scenic Ave Costa Mesa CA 92626 714-432-8668
Web: www.engeniustech.com

Englewood Electrical Supply 716 Belvedere Dr Kokomo IN 46901 765-452-4087
TF: 800-417-7543 ■ *Web:* wesco.com

EPIR Technologies Inc
590 Territorial Dr Unit B Bolingbrook IL 60440 630-771-0203
Web: epirtech.com

Eric Electronics 2220 Lundy Ave San Jose CA 95131 408-432-1111 433-0570
TF General: 800-495-3742 ■ *Web:* www.ericnet.com

ESL ElectroScience Inc
416 E Church Rd King Of Prussia PA 19406 610-272-8000
Web: www.electroscience.com

Estech Systems Inc 3701 East Plano Pkwy Plano TX 75074 972-422-9700 422-9705
Web: www.esi-estech.com

Evans Enterprises Inc
1536 S Western Ave Oklahoma City OK 73109 405-631-1344 631-8948
TF: 800-423-8267 ■ *Web:* www.goevans.com

Ewing-Foley Inc 10061 Bubb Rd Ste 1000 Cupertino CA 95014 408-342-1200
Web: www.ewingfoley.com

Extrel CMS LLC 575 Epsilon Dr Pittsburgh PA 15238 412-963-7530
Web: www.extrel.com

Facility Solutions Group (FSG)
4401 Westgate Blvd Ste 310 Austin TX 78745 512-440-7985 440-0399
TF: 800-854-6465 ■ *Web:* www.fsgconnect.com

				Phone	Fax
Famous Enterprises Inc 109 N Union St. *Web:* www.famous-supply.com	Akron	OH	44304	330-762-9621	
FD Lawrence Electric Company Inc 3450 Beekman St *TF Cust Svc:* 800-582-4490 ■ *Web:* www.fdlawrence.com	Cincinnati	OH	45223	513-542-1100	542-2422
Feldman Bros Electrical Supply Co 26 Maryland Ave. *Web:* www.feldmanbros.com	Paterson	NJ	07503	973-742-7329	742-2220
Fiber Instruments Sales Inc 161 Clear Rd *TF Sales:* 800-500-0347 ■ *Web:* www.fiberinstrumentsales.com	Oriskany	NY	13424	315-736-2206	736-2285
Fiber Optic Center New Trust 23 Centre St *TF:* 800-473-4237 ■ *Web:* www.focenter.com	New Bedford	MA	02740	508-992-6464	
Fiber-Span LLC 3434 Rt 22West Ste 140 *Web:* www.fiber-span.com	Branchburg	NJ	08876	908-253-9080	
Fidelitone Inc 1260 Karl Ct *Web:* www.fidelitone.com	Wauconda	IL	60084	847-487-3300	469-6581
Flame Enterprises Inc 21500 Gledhill St. *TF:* 800-854-2255 ■ *Web:* www.flamecorp.com	Chatsworth	CA	91311	818-700-2905	700-9168
Floyd Bell Inc 720 Dearborn Park Ln. *TF:* 888-356-9323 ■ *Web:* www.floydbell.com	Columbus	OH	43085	614-294-4000	
Foxcom Inc 136 Main St Ste 300b *TF:* 866-663-7284 ■ *Web:* www.foxcom.com	Princeton	NJ	08540	609-514-1800	514-1881
Friedman Electric 1321 Wyoming Ave. *TF:* 800-545-5517 ■ *Web:* www.friedmanelectric.com	Exeter	PA	18643	570-654-3371	655-6194
Fromm Electric Supply Corp 2101 Centre Ave PO Box 15147 *TF:* 800-360-4441 ■ *Web:* www.frommelectric.com	Reading	PA	19605	610-374-4441	374-8756
FSG Lighting 4401 Westgate Blvd Ste 310 *TF:* 800-854-6465 ■ *Web:* www.fsgi.com	Austin	TX	78745	512-440-7985	440-0399
FTG Inc 725 Marshall Phelps Rd *TF:* 888-610-6020 ■ *Web:* www.farmstead.com	Windsor	CT	06095	860-610-6000	610-6001
Future Electronics 237 Hymus Blvd *TF Cust Svc:* 800-675-1619 ■ *Web:* www.futureelectronics.com	Pointe-Claire	QC	H9R5C7	514-694-7710	695-3707
Futurecom Systems Group Inc 3277 Langstaff Rd. *TF:* 800-701-9180 ■ *Web:* www.futurecom.com	Concord	ON	L4K5P8	905-660-5548	
Galco Industrial Electronics Inc 26010 Pinehurst Dr *TF:* 888-783-4611 ■ *Web:* www.galco.com	Madison Heights	MI	48071	248-542-9090	542-8031
GBH Communications Inc 1309 S Myrtle Ave. *TF:* 800-222-5424 ■ *Web:* www.gbh.com	Monrovia	CA	91016	800-222-5424	
George R Peters Assoc Inc PO Box 850 *TF:* 800-929-5972 ■ *Web:* www.grpeters.com	Troy	MI	48099	248-524-2211	524-1758
Graybar Electric Co Inc 34 N Meramec Ave *TF:* 800-472-9227 ■ *Web:* www.graybar.com	Saint Louis	MO	63105	314-573-9200	573-9455
Grayloc Products L L C 9342 Telge Rd *Web:* www.grayloc.com	Houston	TX	77095	713-466-8853	
Gross Electric Inc 2807 N Reynolds Rd *Web:* www.grosselectric.com	Toledo	OH	43615	419-537-1818	
Grove-Madsen Industries 390 E Sixth St *Web:* www.g-m-i.net	Reno	NV	89512	775-322-3400	322-3495
Gsolutionz Inc 625 E Santa Clara St Ste 100 *Web:* www.gsolutionz.com	Ventura	CA	93001	805-662-1500	
Halbrook & Miller Inc 2307 Springlake Rd Ste 110 *Web:* tmtel.com	Carrollton	TX	75006	972-243-4772	
Hamamatsu Corp 360 Foothill Rd *Web:* www.hamamatsu.com	Bridgewater	NJ	08807	908-231-0960	
Hammond Electronics Inc 1230 W Central Blvd *TF Sales:* 800-929-3672 ■ *Web:* www.hammondelec.com	Orlando	FL	32805	407-849-6060	872-0826
Hardware Specialty Company Inc 48-75 36th St *Web:* www.hardwarespecialty.com	Long Island	NY	11101	718-361-9393	706-0238
Harry Krantz Co 50 Heartland Blvd *Web:* www.harrykrantz.com	Edgewood	NY	11717	516-620-0111	
Hartford Electric Supply Co (HESCO) 30 Inwood Rd Ste 1 *TF:* 800-969-5444 ■ *Web:* www.hesconet.com	Rocky Hill	CT	06067	860-236-6363	236-0233
Hawking Technologies Inc 35 Hammond Ste 150 *Web:* www.hawkingtech.com	Irvine	CA	92618	949-206-6900	
Headsets Direct Inc 1454 W Gurley St Ste A *TF:* 800-914-7996 ■ *Web:* www.headsetsdirect.com	Prescott	AZ	86305	928-777-9100	
Heartland Label Printers Inc 1700 Stephen St **Fax Area Code:* 920 ■ *TF General:* 800-236-7914 ■ *Web:* www.hbs.net	Little Chute	WI	54140	800-236-7914	788-7739*
Heilind Electronics Inc 58 Jonspin Rd *TF:* 800-400-7041 ■ *Web:* www.heilind.com	Wilmington	MA	01887	978-657-4870	658-0278
Hi-Line Inc 2121 Vly View Ln *Web:* www.hi-line.com	Dallas	TX	75234	972-247-6200	
Hi-Techniques Inc 2515 Frazier Ave. *Web:* www.hi-techniques.com	Madison	WI	53713	608-221-7500	
HICO America Sales & Technology Inc 3 Penn Ctr W Ste 300 *Web:* www.hicoamerica.com	Pittsburg	PA	15276	412-787-1170	
Higgins Electric Inc. of Dothan 1350 Columbia Hwy *Web:* www.higginselectric.com	Dothan	AL	36301	334-793-4859	
Hite Co 3101 Beale Ave. *TF:* 800-252-3598 ■ *Web:* www.hiteco.com	Altoona	PA	16601	814-944-6121	944-3052
HITEC Group Ltd 1743 Quincy Ave Unit 155 *TF:* 800-288-8303 ■ *Web:* www.hitec.com	Naperville	IL	60540	800-288-8303	
HL Dalis Inc 35-35 24th St *TF:* 800-453-2547 ■ *Web:* www.hldalis.com	Long Island	NY	11106	718-361-1100	392-7654
Hotan Corp 751 N Canyons Pkwy *Web:* www.hotan.com	Livermore	CA	94551	925-290-1000	
Houston Wire & Cable Co (HWC) 10201 N Loop E *TF:* 800-468-9473 ■ *Web:* www.houwire.com	Houston	TX	77029	713-609-2100	609-2101
Hutton Communications Inc 2520 Marsh Ln *Web:* www.hol4g.com	Carrollton	TX	75006	972-417-0100	417-0180
IBS Electronics Inc 3506 W Lk Ctr Dr Ste D *TF:* 800-527-2888 ■ *Web:* www.ibselectronics.com	Santa Ana	CA	92704	714-751-6633	751-8159
ICX Global Inc 8206 E Park Meadows Dr.	Lone Tree	CO	80134	720-873-8400	

				Phone	Fax
IMS Inc 340 Progress Dr. *TF General:* 800-264-9837 ■ *Web:* www.imswire.com	Manchester	CT	06040	860-649-4415	649-0806
Independent Electric Supply Inc 1370 Bayport Ave *TF:* 855-437-4968 ■ *Web:* www.iesupply.com	San Carlos	CA	94070	650-594-9440	594-0484
Industrial Electric Wire & Cable Inc (IEWC) 5001 S Towne Dr *TF:* 800-344-2323 ■ *Web:* www.iewc.com	New Berlin	WI	53151	262-782-2323	957-1600
Informity Network LTD 731 N Sangamon St Ste 300 *Web:* www.informitynetwork.com	Chicago	IL	60622	312-361-6515	
Infosat Communications Inc 3130-114 Ave SE *Web:* www.infosat.com	Calgary	AB	T2Z3V6	403-543-8188	
InfoSonics Corp 4350 Executive Dr Ste 100 *NASDAQ: IFON* ■ *Web:* www.infosonics.com	San Diego	CA	92121	858-373-1600	373-1503
Insulectro 20362 Windrow Dr *Web:* www.insulectro.com	Lake Forest	CA	92630	949-587-3200	454-0066
Integrated Components Source (ICS) 3977 Camino Ranchero *Web:* www.yourdrive.com	Camarillo	CA	93012	805-822-5100	483-1300
Inter-Technical LLC PO Box 535 *Web:* www.inter-technical.com	Elmsford	NY	10523	914-347-2474	347-7230
International Electrical Sales Corp (IESCO) 7540 NW 66th St *Web:* www.iescomia.com	Miami	FL	33166	305-591-8390	591-3294
Interstate Connecting Components Inc 120 Mt Holly By Pass **Fax Area Code:* 856 ■ *TF:* 888-899-1990 ■ *Web:* www.connecticc.com	Lumberton	NJ	08048	800-422-3911	722-9425*
Interstate Electrical Supply Inc 2300 Second Ave *TF:* 800-903-4409 ■ *Web:* ieselc.com	Columbus	GA	31901	706-324-1000	576-5821
Jaco Electronics Inc 415 Oser Ave *OTC: JACO* ■ **Fax Area Code:* 631 ■ *TF:* 877-373-5226 ■ *Web:* www.jacoelect.com	Hauppauge	NY	11788	877-373-5226	231-1051*
Janesway Electronic Corp 404 N Terr Ave. *TF:* 800-431-1348 ■ *Web:* www.janesway.com	Mount Vernon	NY	10552	914-699-6710	699-6969
Jasco Products Inc 10 E Memorial Rd *TF:* 800-654-8483 ■ *Web:* byjasco.com	Oklahoma City	OK	73114	405-752-0710	752-1537
JH Larson Co 10200 51st Ave N. *TF:* 800-292-7970 ■ *Web:* www.jhlarson.com	Plymouth	MN	55442	763-545-1717	545-1144
Joliet Avionics Inc 43w730 Us Hwy 30 *Web:* www.jaair.com	Sugar Grove	IL	60554	630-584-3200	
JOWA USA Inc 59 Porter Rd. *Web:* www.consiliumus.com	Littleton	MA	01460	978-486-9800	
Justin Electronics Corp 400 Oser Ave Ste 800 *Web:* www.justinelectronics.com	Hauppauge	NY	11788	631-951-4900	951-4747
K G B Communictions L L C 3219 N Geronimo Ave *Web:* www.kgbcommunications.com	Tucson	AZ	85705	520-743-3300	
Kansas City Electrical Supply Co (KCES) 14851 W 99th St. *Web:* www.kcelectricalsupply.com	Lenexa	KS	66215	913-563-7000	563-7052
Kehoe Component Sales Inc 34 Foley Dr. *TF:* 800-228-7223 ■ *Web:* www.paceelectronics.com	Sodus	NY	14551	800-228-7223	
Kendall Electric Inc 131 Grand Trunk Ave *TF:* 800-632-5422 ■ *Web:* www.kendallelectric.com	Battle Creek	MI	49037	269-963-5585	
Kiddesigns Inc 1299 Main St *Web:* www.kiddesigns.com	Rahway	NJ	07065	732-574-9000	
Kikusui America Inc 1633 Bayshore Hwy Ste 331 *TF:* 877-876-2807 ■ *Web:* www.kikusuiamerica.com	Burlingame	CA	94010	650-259-5900	
Kirby Risk Corp 1815 Sagamore Pkwy N. *Web:* www.kirbyrisk.com	Lafayette	IN	47904	765-448-4567	
KJB Security Products Inc 841-B Fessiers Pkwy *Web:* www.kjbsecurity.com	Nashville	TN	37210	615-620-1370	
Kovalsky-Carr Electric Supply Company Inc 208 St Paul St. *Web:* www.kovalskycarr.com	Rochester	NY	14604	585-325-1950	546-6904
La Clef De Sol Inc 840 Bouvier *Web:* www.laclefdesol.com	Quebec	QC	G2J1A3	418-627-0840	
Laipac Technology Inc 20 Mural St Unit 5 *Web:* www.laipac.com	Richmond Hill	ON	L4B1K3	905-762-1228	763-1737
Lazo Technologies Inc 611 W Mockingbird Ln *Web:* www.lazotech.com	Dallas	TX	75247	214-652-9898	
Leff Electric 4700 Spring Rd. *TF:* 800-686-5333 ■ *Web:* www.leffelectric.com	Cleveland	OH	44131	216-432-3000	432-0051
Lester Sales Co Inc 4312 W Minnesota St *TF:* 800-544-6183 ■ *Web:* www.lestersalesco.com	Indianapolis	IN	46241	317-244-7811	248-2369
Lewis Electric Supply Company Inc 1306 Second St PO Box 2237 *TF:* 800-239-0681 ■ *Web:* www.lesupply.com	Muscle Shoals	AL	35662	256-383-0681	383-0834
LeWiz Communications Inc 1376 N Fourth St Ste 300 *Web:* www.lewiz.com	San Jose	CA	95112	408-452-9800	
Loeb Electric Co 1800 E Fifth Ave *Web:* www.loebelectric.com	Columbus	OH	43219	614-294-6351	294-7640
Lowe Electric Supply Co 1525 Forsyth St PO Box 4767 *TF:* 800-868-8661 ■ *Web:* www.loweelectric.com	Macon	GA	31208	478-743-8661	742-3374
Loyd's Electric Supply Inc (LES) 838 Stonetree Dr. *TF:* 800-492-4030 ■ *Web:* www.loydselectric.com	Branson	MO	65616	417-334-2171	334-6635
Ludeca Inc 1425 NW 88th Ave. *Web:* www.ludeca.com	Doral	FL	33172	305-591-8935	
Macnica Americas Inc 380 Stevens Ave Ste 206 *TF:* 888-399-4937 ■ *Web:* www.macnica.com/web/americas	Solana Beach	CA	92075	760-707-0120	
Madison Electric Co 31855 Van Dyke Ave. *Web:* www.madisonelectric.com	Warren	MI	48093	586-825-0200	825-0225
Main Electric Supply Co 6700 S Main St *Web:* www.mainelectricsupply.com	Los Angeles	CA	90003	323-753-5131	753-7750

Company	City	State	Zip	Phone	Fax
Maltby Electric Supply Company Inc 336 Seventh St *TF:* 800-339-0668 ■ *Web:* maltbyelectric.com	San Francisco	CA	94103	415-863-5000	863-5011
Mars Electric Co 38868 Mentor Ave. *TF:* 877-229-7227 ■ *Web:* www.mars-electric.com	Willoughby	OH	44094	440-946-2250	946-3214
Marsh Electronics Inc 1563 S 101st St. *TF Cust Svc:* 800-926-2774 ■ *Web:* www.marshelectronics.com	Milwaukee	WI	53214	414-475-6000	771-2847
Maurice Electrical Supply Co 500 Penn St NE *Web:* www.mauriceelectric.com	Washington	DC	20002	202-675-9400	
Mayer Electric Supply Co 3405 Fourth Ave S PO Box 1328 *TF:* 866-637-1255 ■ *Web:* www.mayerelectric.com	Birmingham	AL	35222	205-583-3500	322-2625
McNaughton-McKay Electric Company Inc 1357 E Lincoln Ave. *TF:* 888-626-2785 ■ *Web:* www.mc-mc.com	Madison Heights	MI	48071	248-399-7500	399-6828
Metro Wire & Cable Co 6636 Metropolitan Pkwy. *TF:* 800-633-1432 ■ *Web:* www.metrowire.net	Sterling Heights	MI	48312	586-264-3050	264-7390
Michigan Chandelier Company Inc 20855 Telegraph Rd *Web:* www.michand.com	Southfield	MI	48033	248-353-0510	353-0973
MicroRam Electronics Inc 222 Dunbar Ct *Web:* www.microram.com	Oldsmar	FL	34677	813-854-5500	
Mid-Coast Electric Supply Inc (MCESI) 1801 Stolz St PO Box 2505 *Web:* www.mcesi.com	Victoria	TX	77901	361-575-6311	575-5515
Mid-Island Electrical Supply 59 Mall Dr *TF:* 877-324-2636 ■ *Web:* www.mid-island.com	Commack	NY	11725	631-864-4242	864-6644
Midcom Data Technologies Inc 33493 W 14 Mile Rd Ste 150 *Web:* www.midcomdata.com	Farmington Hills	MI	48331	248-661-0100	
Midtown Electric Supply Corp 157 W 18th St *Web:* www.midtownelectric.com	New York	NY	10011	212-255-3388	255-3177
Mobile Communication of Gwinnett Inc 2241 Tucker Industrial Rd *Web:* www.callmc.com	Tucker	GA	30084	770-963-3748	
Mouser Electronics Corp 1000 N Main St *TF:* 800-346-6873 ■ *Web:* mouser.in	Mansfield	TX	76063	817-804-3888	804-3899
Murdock Industrial Supply 1111 E 1st *TF:* 800-362-2422 ■ *Web:* www.mcos.com	Wichita	KS	67202	316-262-4476	263-8100
Music People Inc 154 Woodlawn Rd Ste C **Fax Area Code:* 860 ■ *TF:* 800-289-8889 ■ *Web:* www.musicpeopleinc.com	Berlin	CT	06037	800-289-8889	828-1353*
NAC Group Inc 10001 16th St N Metropointe Commerce Park *Web:* www.newadvg.com	St. Petersburg	FL	33716	727-576-0550	
NACB Group Inc 10 Starwood Dr *TF:* 800-370-2737 ■ *Web:* www.ncabgroup.com	Hampstead	NH	03841	603-329-4551	
Nave Communications Co 8215 Dorsey Run Rd *Web:* www.ncctel.com	Jessup	MD	20794	301-725-6283	
Nedco Electronics 594 American Way **Fax Area Code:* 800 ■ *TF:* 800-605-2323 ■ *Web:* www.nedcoelectronics.com	Payson	UT	84651	801-465-1790	605-3836*
Nedco Supply Inc 4200 W Spring Mtn Rd *Web:* www.nedco.com	Las Vegas	NV	89102	702-367-0400	362-8365
Nelson Electric Supply Co Inc 926 State St *TF:* 800-806-3576 ■ *Web:* www.nelson-electric.com	Racine	WI	53404	262-635-5050	637-2465
NEP Electronics Inc 805 Mittel Dr *TF:* 800-284-7470 ■ *Web:* www.nepelectronics.com	Wood Dale	IL	60191	630-595-8500	595-8706
Netsource Technology Inc 30032 Aventura *Web:* www.nstechnology.com	Rancho Santa Margarita	CA	92688	949-713-0800	
Newton Instrument Company Inc 111 East A St *Web:* www.enewton.com	Butner	NC	27509	919-575-6426	
NF Smith & Assoc LP 5306 Hollister Rd *TF:* 800-468-7866 ■ *Web:* globalpurchasing.com	Houston	TX	77040	713-430-3000	430-3099
Nora Lighting Inc 6505 Gayhart St **Fax Area Code:* 800 ■ *TF:* 800-686-6672 ■ *Web:* www.noralighting.com	Commerce	CA	90040	323-767-2600	500-9955*
Northern Video Systems Inc 3625 Cincinnati Ave *TF:* 800-366-4472 ■ *Web:* www.tri-ed.com	Rocklin	CA	95765	916-543-4000	543-4020
Nsync Services Inc 850 Greenview Dr *TF:* 866-706-7962 ■ *Web:* www.nsyncservices.com	Grand Prairie	TX	75050	972-641-7426	641-8093
Nu Horizons Electronics Corp 70 Maxess Rd **Fax Area Code:* 256 ■ *TF:* 855-326-4757 ■ *Web:* www.arrow.com	Melville	NY	11747	631-396-5000	864-3349*
Nu-Lite Electrical Wholesalers 850 Edwards Ave *TF:* 800-256-1603 ■ *Web:* www.nulite.com	Harahan	LA	70123	504-733-3300	736-1617
Omni Cable Corp 2 Hagerty Blvd *TF:* 888-292-6664 ■ *Web:* www.omnicable.com	West Chester	PA	19382	610-701-0100	701-9870
One Link Wireless 7321 Broadway Ext *TF:* 800-259-2929 ■ *Web:* www.onelinkwireless.com	Oklahoma City	OK	73116	405-840-2345	
OneSource Distributors 3951 Oceanic Dr *Web:* www.1sourcedist.com	Oceanside	CA	92056	760-966-4500	966-4599
Orban Inc 8350 E Evans Rd Ste C-4 *Web:* www.orban.com	Scottsdale	AZ	85260	480-403-8300	
Orlando Diefenderfer Co 116 S Second St *Web:* www.diefenderfer.com	Allentown	PA	18105	610-434-9595	
Paige Electric Company LP 1160 Springfield Rd *TF:* 800-327-2443 ■ *Web:* www.paigeelectric.com	Union	NJ	07083	908-687-7810	687-2722
Parrish-Hare Electrical Supply LP 1211 Regal Row *Web:* www.parrish-hare.com	Dallas	TX	75247	214-905-1001	951-8101
Path Master Inc 1960 Midway Dr *TF:* 855-738-2722 ■ *Web:* www.pathmasterinc.com	Twinsburg	OH	44087	330-425-4994	425-9338
Pathcom Wireless Inc 315 First St East *Web:* www.pathcom.ca	Cochrane	AB	T4C1Z2	403-932-2559	932-2468
Peerless Electronics Inc 700 Hicksville Rd *TF:* 800-285-2121 ■ *Web:* www.peerlesselectronics.com	Bethpage	NY	11714	516-594-3500	593-2179
PEI-Genesis 2180 Hornig Rd *TF:* 800-675-1214 ■ *Web:* www.peigenesis.com	Philadelphia	PA	19116	215-673-0400	552-8022
Peter Parts Electronics Inc 6285 Dean Pkwy *Web:* www.peterparts.com	Ontario	NY	14519	585-265-2000	
PFT Alexander Inc 3250 E Grant St *Web:* www.pft-alexander.com	Signal Hill	CA	90755	562-595-1741	
Platt Electric Supply 10605 SW Allen Blvd *TF:* 800-257-5288 ■ *Web:* www.platt.com	Beaverton	OR	97005	503-641-6121	277-7497
Powell Electronics Inc 200 Commodore Dr *TF:* 800-235-7880 ■ *Web:* www.powell.com	Swedesboro	NJ	08085	856-241-8000	241-8630
Power & Telephone Supply Company Inc 2673 Yale Ave. *TF Cust Svc:* 800-238-7514 ■ *Web:* www.ptsupply.com	Memphis	TN	38112	901-866-3300	320-3082
Precise Tool & Gage Company Inc 30540 Se 84th St Unit 2 *Web:* www.precisetoolco.com	Preston	WA	98050	425-222-9567	
Priority Wire & Cable Inc PO Box 398 *TF General:* 800-945-5542 ■ *Web:* www.prioritywire.com	North Little Rock	AR	72115	501-372-5444	372-3988
Professional Electric Products Co (PEPCO) 33210 Lakeland Blvd *TF:* 800-872-7000 ■ *Web:* www.pepconet.com	Eastlake	OH	44095	440-946-3790	942-5883
Projections Unlimited Inc 15311 Varrenca Pkwy **Fax Area Code:* 949 ■ *TF Cust Svc:* 800-551-4405 ■ *Web:* www.gopui.com	Irvine	CA	92618	714-544-2700	789-0626*
QED Inc 1661 W Third Ave *TF:* 800-700-5011 ■ *Web:* www.qedelectric.com	Denver	CO	80223	303-825-5011	893-5019
Quebe Holdings Inc 1985 Founders Dr *Web:* www.quebe.com	Dayton	OH	45420	937-222-2290	
Queen City Electrical Supply Company Inc Third & Walnut St PO Box 1288 *Web:* www.queencityelec.com	Allentown	PA	18105	610-439-0525	439-8637
R O Whitesell & Associates Inc 3334 W Founders Rd *Web:* www.whitesell.com	Indianapolis	IN	46268	317-876-9000	
Radar Inc 22214 20TH Ave SE Ste 101 *Web:* www.radarinc.com	Bothell	WA	98021	425-424-2002	
Radiophone Engineering Inc 534 W Walnut St. *TF:* 800-369-2929 ■ *Web:* www.radiophonewireless.com	Springfield	MO	65806	417-862-6653	
Ralph Pill Electrical Supply Co 50 Von Hillern St *TF:* 800-897-1769 ■ *Web:* www.needco.com	Boston	MA	02125	617-265-8800	288-1776
Rawson Inc 2010 McAllister **Fax Area Code:* 713 ■ *TF:* 800-779-1414 ■ *Web:* www.rawsonlp.com	Houston	TX	77092	800-779-1414	684-1418*
Razoom Inc 545 Bryant St *Web:* www.razoom.com	Palo Alto	CA	94301	650-561-3037	
RCI Sound Systems 10721 Hanna St *Web:* www.rcisound.com	Beltsville	MD	20705	301-931-9001	
Reagan Wireless Corp 720 S Powerline Rd Ste D *TF:* 877-724-3266 ■ *Web:* www.reaganwireless.com	Deerfield Beach	FL	33442	954-596-2355	596-0070
Real Time Systems Inc 103 Industrial Loop Ste 1100 *Web:* www.real-time-sys.com	Fredericksburg	TX	78624	830-990-2340	
Red Peacock International Inc 1945 Gardena Ave *TF:* 877-774-0037 ■ *Web:* www.redpeacock.com	Glendale	CA	91204	818-265-7722	265-7750
Regency Lighting Co 9261 Jordan Ave **Fax Area Code:* 818 ■ *TF:* 800-284-2024 ■ *Web:* www.regencylighting.com	Chatsworth	CA	91311	800-284-2024	901-0118*
Renco Electronics Inc 595 International Pl *TF:* 800-645-5828 ■ *Web:* www.rencousa.com	Rockledge	FL	32955	321-637-1000	637-1600
Rexel Canada Inc 5600 Keaton Crescent *Web:* www.rexel.ca	Mississauga	ON	L5R3G3	905-712-4004	
Rexel Inc 14951 Dallas Pkwy PO Box 9085 *TF:* 888-739-3577 ■ *Web:* www.rexelusa.com	Dallas	TX	75254	972-387-3600	991-1831
Rexel Ryall Electrical Supplies 11775 E 45th Ave *TF:* 888-739-3577 ■ *Web:* www.rexelusa.com	Denver	CO	80239	303-629-7721	
Richardson Electronics Ltd 40 W 267 Keslinger Rd PO Box 393 *NASDAQ:* RELL ■ *TF Sales:* 800-348-5580 ■ *Web:* www.rell.com	LaFox	IL	60147	630-208-2200	208-2550
Rochester Electronics Inc 16 Malcolm Hoyt Dr *Web:* www.rocelec.com	Newburyport	MA	01950	978-462-9332	462-9512
Rochester Industrial Control Inc 6400 Furnace Rd *Web:* www.rochesterindustrial.com	Ontario	NY	14519	315-524-4555	
Rohde & Schwarz Inc 6821 Benjamin Franklin Dr *Web:* www.rohde-schwarz.com	Columbia	MD	21046	410-910-7800	
Rondout Electric Inc 33 Arlington Ave *Web:* rondoutelectric.net	Poughkeepsie	NY	12603	845-471-4810	471-1903
RS Electronics Inc 34443 Schoolcraft Rd **Fax Area Code:* 800 ■ *TF:* 866-600-6040 ■ *Web:* www.carltonbates.com/content/rs-electronics	Livonia	MI	48150	734-525-1155	544-2570*
Rumsey Electric Co 15 Colwell Ln *TF:* 800-462-2402 ■ *Web:* www.rumsey.com	Conshohocken	PA	19428	610-832-9000	941-8181
S K C Communication Products Inc 8320 Hedge Ln Terr **Fax Area Code:* 800 ■ *TF:* 800-882-7779 ■ *Web:* www.skccom.com	Shawnee Mission	KS	66227	913-422-4222	454-4752*
Sager Electronics Inc 19 Lorena Dr *TF:* 800-724-3780 ■ *Web:* www.sager.com	Middleboro	MA	02346	508-947-8888	947-0869
Sandusky Electric Inc 1513 Sycamore Line *TF:* 800-356-1243 ■ *Web:* www.sanduskyelectric.com	Sandusky	OH	44870	419-625-4915	625-9438
Santek Components LLC 1060 Holland Ave Ste A *Web:* www.santekcomp.com	Clovis	CA	93612	559-294-6015	
Schuster Electronics Inc 11320 Grooms Rd **Fax Area Code:* 330 ■ *TF:* 800-521-1358 ■ *Web:* www.schusterusa.com	Cincinnati	OH	45242	800-521-1358	425-1863*
Sciemetric Instruments Inc 359 Terry Fox Dr Ste 100 *TF:* 877-931-9200 ■ *Web:* www.sciemetric.com	Ottawa	ON	K2K2E7	613-254-7054	
Scott Electric 1000 S Main St PO Box S **Fax Area Code:* 800 ■ *TF:* 800-442-8045 ■ *Web:* www.scottelectricusa.com	Greensburg	PA	15601	724-834-4321	426-9598*
Secured Digital Applications Inc 230 Pk Ave 10th Fl *Web:* www.digitalapps.net	New York	NY	10169	212-551-1747	808-3020
SED International Inc 3505 Newpoint Pl Ste 450	Lawrenceville	GA	30043	770-243-1200	

Company	City	State	Zip	Phone	Fax
SED Systems 18 Innovation Blvd *Web:* www.sedsystems.ca	Saskatoon	SK	S7N3R1	306-931-3425	933-1486
Semi Dice Inc PO Box 3002 *Web:* www.semidice.com	Los Alamitos	CA	90720	562-594-4631	430-5942
SemiProbe Inc 276 E Allen St *Web:* www.semiprobe.com	Winooski	VT	05404	802-860-7000	
Sennheiser Electronics Corp 1 Enterprise Dr *TF:* 877-736-6434 ■ *Web:* en-us.sennheiser.com	Old Lyme	CT	06371	860-434-9190	434-1759
Sensorlink Corp 1360 Stonegate Way *Web:* www.sensorlink.com	Ferndale	WA	98248	360-595-1000	
Service Electric Supply Inc 15424 Oakwood Dr *Web:* www.servelectric.com	Romulus	MI	48174	734-229-9100	229-9101
Shanor Electric Supply Inc 1276 Military Rd *Web:* www.shanorelectric.com	Kenmore	NY	14217	716-876-0711	876-7375
Shealy Electrical Wholesalers Inc 422 Fairforest Way *TF:* 800-868-5980 ■ *Web:* www.shealyelectrical.com	Greenville	SC	29607	864-242-6880	235-6097
Shearer Equipment 7762 Cleveland Rd *Web:* www.shearerequipment.com	Wooster	OH	44691	330-345-9023	
Shepherd Electric Supply 7401 Pulaski Hwy *TF Sales:* 800-253-1777 ■ *Web:* www.shepherdelec.com	Baltimore	MD	21237	410-866-6000	866-6001
Sierra Electronics 690 E Glendale Ave Ste 9B *Web:* www.sierraelectronics.com	Sparks	NV	89432	775-359-1121	
Signalink Technologies Inc Units 13 & 14 2550 Acland Rd *TF:* 888-491-3883 ■ *Web:* www.signalink.com	Kelowna	BC	V1X7L4	250-491-3883	
Silego Technology Inc 1715 Wyatt Dr *Web:* www.silego.com	Santa Clara	CA	95054	408-327-8800	
Singing Machine Company Inc, The 6601 Lyons Rd Bldg A-7 *OTC: SMDM* ■ *TF:* 866-670-6888 ■ *Web:* www.singingmachine.com	Coconut Creek	FL	33073	954-596-1000	596-2000
Skywalker Communications Inc 9390 Veterans Memorial Pkwy *TF:* 800-844-9555 ■ *Web:* www.skywalker.com	O'Fallon	MO	63366	636-272-8025	272-8214
Skyway Towers LLC 20525 Amberfield Dr Ste 102 *Web:* www.skywaytowers.com	Land O Lakes	FL	34638	813-960-6200	
SMAR International Corp 6001 Stonington St Ste 100 *Web:* www.smar.com	Houston	TX	77040	713-849-2021	849-2022
Sommer Electric Corp 818 Third St NE *TF:* 800-766-6373 ■ *Web:* www.sommerelectric.com	Canton	OH	44704	330-455-9454	
Sonepar USA 510 Walnut St Ste 400 *Web:* www.sonepar-usa.com	Philadelphia	PA	19106	215-399-5900	
Sound Inc 1550 Shore Rd *Web:* www.soundinc.com	Naperville	IL	60563	630-369-2900	
SOURCE Inc 14060 Proton Rd *Web:* www.source.com	Dallas	TX	75244	972-371-2600	
Sousley Sound & Communications 1005 Tieton Dr *Web:* www.sousley.com	Yakima	WA	98902	509-248-4848	
South Dade Electrical Supply 13100 SW 87th Ave *Web:* www.south-dade.com	Miami	FL	33176	305-238-7131	251-5254
South Western Communications Inc 4871 Rosebud Ln *Web:* www.swc.net	Newburgh	IN	47630	812-477-6495	
Southern Controls Inc 3511 Wetumpka Hwy *TF:* 800-392-5770 ■ *Web:* www.southerncontrols.com	Montgomery	AL	36110	800-392-5770	
Spectra Integrated Systems Inc 8100 Arrowridge Blvd *TF:* 800-443-7561 ■ *Web:* www.sitechma.com	Charlotte	NC	28273	704-525-7099	523-8558
Spectra Merchandising International Inc 4230 N Normandy Ave *TF:* 800-777-5331 ■ *Web:* www.spectraintl.com	Chicago	IL	60634	773-202-8408	202-8409
Springfield Electric Supply Co 700 N Ninth St *TF:* 800-747-2101 ■ *Web:* www.springfieldelectric.com	Springfield	IL	62702	217-788-2100	788-2134
Standard Electric Co 2650 Trautner Dr *TF:* 800-322-0215 ■ *Web:* www.standardelectricco.com	Saginaw	MI	48603	989-497-2100	497-2101
Standard Electric Supply Co 222 N Emmber Ln PO Box 651 *TF:* 800-776-8222 ■ *Web:* www.standardelectricsupply.com	Milwaukee	WI	53233	414-272-8100	272-8111
Stanion Wholesale Electric Co 812 S Main St PO Box F *TF:* 866-782-6466 ■ *Web:* www.stanion.com	Pratt	KS	67124	620-672-5678	672-6220
State Electric Supply Company Inc 2010 Second Ave *TF Cust Svc:* 800-624-3417 ■ *Web:* www.stateelectric.com	Huntington	WV	25703	304-523-7491	525-8917
Steiner Electric Co 1250 Touhy Ave *TF:* 800-783-4637 ■ *Web:* www.steinerelectric.com/home	Elk Grove Village	IL	60007	847-228-0400	228-1352
Stereo Advantage Co 5110 Main St *Web:* www.theadvantage.com	Williamsville	NY	14221	716-626-3280	
Steven Engineering Inc 230 Ryan Way **Fax Area Code:* 888 ■ *TF:* 800-258-9200 ■ *Web:* www.stevenengineering.com	South San Francisco	CA	94080	650-588-9200	258-9200*
Stevens Communications Inc 11 S LaSalle St *Web:* www.stevenscom.com	Chicago	IL	60603	312-895-5200	
Stokes Electric Company Inc 1701 McCalla Ave *Web:* www.stokeselec.com	Knoxville	TN	37915	865-525-0351	971-4149
Stoneway Electric Supply Co 402 N Perry St *TF:* 800-841-1408 ■ *Web:* www.stoneway.com	Spokane	WA	99202	509-535-2933	534-4512
Storage Battery Systems Inc (SBS) N56 W16665 Ridgewood Dr *TF:* 800-554-2243 ■ *Web:* www.sbsbattery.com	Menomonee Falls	WI	53051	262-703-5800	703-3073
Stuart C Irby Co 815 Irby Dr *TF:* 866-687-4729 ■ *Web:* www.irby.com	Jackson	MS	39215	601-969-1811	422-1652
Summit Electric Supply Co 2900 Stanford NE *TF:* 800-824-4400 ■ *Web:* www.summit.com	Albuquerque	NM	87107	505-346-9000	346-1616
Surface Mount Distribution Inc (SMD) 1 Oldfield *TF:* 800-820-7634 ■ *Web:* www.smdinc.com	Irvine	CA	92618	949-470-7700	470-7777
SVT 7699 Lochlin Dr	Brighton	MI	48116	248-437-0041	
Swift Electrical Supply Co 100 Hollister Rd *Web:* www.swiftelectrical.com	Teterboro	NJ	07608	201-462-0900	
SYN-FAB Inc 7863 Schillinger Park Rd *Web:* www.synfab.com	Mobile	AL	36608	251-633-4942	
Syn-Tech Inc 3100 Ridgelake Dr Ste 101 *TF:* 800-535-7619 ■ *Web:* www.syntech-inc.com	Metairie	LA	70002	504-835-7825	835-7853
Tacoma Electric Supply Inc 1311 S Tacoma Way *TF:* 800-422-0540 ■ *Web:* www.tacomaelectric.com	Tacoma	WA	98409	253-475-0540	475-0707
Taitron Components Inc 28040 W Harrison Pkwy *NASDAQ: TAIT* ■ *TF:* 800-247-2232 ■ *Web:* www.taitroncomponents.com	Valencia	CA	91355	661-257-6060	257-6415
Talley Inc 12976 Sandoval St *Web:* www.talleycom.com	Santa Fe Springs	CA	90670	562-906-8000	
TCT Inc 11911 County Rd 125 W *Web:* www.tctinc.com	Odessa	TX	79765	432-561-8449	
TeL Systems 7235 Jackson Rd *TF:* 800-686-7235 ■ *Web:* www.telsystemsusa.com	Ann Arbor	MI	48103	734-761-4506	761-9776
Telcobuy com L L C 60 Weldon Pkwy *TF:* 877-350-0191 ■ *Web:* www.telcobuy.com	St. Louis	MO	63043	877-350-0191	
Tele-Communications Inc 5125 W 140th St **Fax Area Code:* 330 ■ *TF:* 877-841-8914	Brookpark	OH	44142	216-267-0800	869-8515*
Teleco Inc 430 Woodruff Rd Ste 300 *Web:* www.teleco.com	Greenville	SC	29607	864-297-4400	297-9983
Telephone Warehouse 1936 E McDowell Rd *Web:* www.telephonewarehouse.com	Phoenix	AZ	85006	602-254-5515	
Telesource Services LLC 1450 Highwood E *TF:* 800-525-4300 ■ *Web:* www.telesourcenet.com	Pontiac	MI	48340	248-335-3000	335-0470
Tempest Telecom Solutions LLC 136 W Canon Perdido Ste 100 *Web:* www.tempesttelecom.com	Santa Barbara	CA	93101	805-879-4800	
Terry-Durin Co 409 Seventh Ave SE *TF:* 800-332-8114 ■ *Web:* www.terrydurin.com	Cedar Rapids	IA	52401	319-364-4106	364-2562
Terrycomm 2700 Business Center Blvd *Web:* terrycomm.com	Melbourne	FL	32940	321-253-6067	
TESSCO Technologies Inc 11126 McCormick Rd *NASDAQ: TESS* ■ *TF:* 800-472-7373 ■ *Web:* www.tessco.com	Hunt Valley	MD	21031	410-229-1000	527-0005
Thorpe Electric Supply Co 27 Washington St *Web:* www.thorpeelectric.com	Rensselaer	NY	12144	518-462-5496	
Toa Canada Corp 6150 Kennedy Rd Unit 3 *Web:* www.toacanada.com	Mississauga	ON	L5T2J4	905-564-3570	
Tomba Communications LLC 718 Barataria Blvd *Web:* www.tomba.com	Marrero	LA	70072	504-340-2448	
Total Fire & Safety Inc 7909 Carr St *Web:* www.totalfire.com	Dallas	TX	75227	214-381-6116	381-4633
Transfer Devices Inc 45778 Northport Loop W *Web:* www.transferdevices.com	Fremont	CA	94538	510-445-1060	
Trebor International Inc 8100 South 1300 West *Web:* www.treborintl.com	West Jordan	UT	84088	801-561-0303	
Tredent Data Systems Inc 3241 Grande Vista Dr *Web:* www.tredent.com	Newbury Park	CA	91320	805-375-4911	
Trembly Assoc Inc 119 Quincy St NE *Web:* www.trembly.com	Albuquerque	NM	87108	505-266-8616	255-0635
Tri-Ed Distribution Inc 135 Crossways Pk Dr W *TF:* 888-874-3336 ■ *Web:* www.tri-ed.com	Woodbury	NY	11797	516-941-2800	
Tri-State Armature & Electrical Works Inc 330 GE Patterson PO Box 466 *TF:* 800-238-7654 ■ *Web:* www.tristatearmature.com	Memphis	TN	38126	901-527-8412	521-1065
Tri-State Utility Products Inc 1030 Atlanta Industrial Dr *TF:* 800-282-7985 ■ *Web:* tsup.com	Marietta	GA	30066	770-427-3119	427-3945
Trident Micro Systems 2 Trident Dr	Arden	NC	28704	828-684-7474	
TTI Inc 2441 NE Pkwy **Fax:* Hum Res ■ *TF Sales:* 800-225-5884 ■ *Web:* www.ttiinc.com	Fort Worth	TX	76106	817-740-9000	740-9898*
TURCK Chartwell Canada Inc 140 Duffield Dr *Web:* chartwell.ca	Markham	ON	L6G1B5	905-513-7100	
Turnkey Technologies Inc 2500 Main St Ext Ste 10 *Web:* www.turn-keytechnologies.com	Sayreville	NJ	08872	732-553-9100	
Turtle & Hughes Inc 1900 Lower Rd *Web:* turtle.com	Linden	NJ	07036	732-574-3600	574-3723
Tystar Corp 7050 Lampson Ave *Web:* www.tystar.com	Garden Grove	CA	92841	310-781-9219	
Unical Enterprises Inc 16960 Gale Ave *Web:* www.unical-usa.com	City Of Industry	CA	91745	626-965-5588	
Unique Communications Inc 3650 Coral Ridge Dr *TF:* 800-881-8182 ■ *Web:* www.uniquecommunications.com	Coral Springs	FL	33065	954-735-4002	735-2612
United Electrical Sales Ltd 4496 36th St *TF:* 800-432-5126 ■ *Web:* www.uesfl.com	Orlando	FL	32811	407-246-1992	246-1588
United Lighting & Supply Co 121 Chestnut Ave SE PO Box 307 *Web:* www.unitedlighting.com	Fort Walton Beach	FL	32548	850-244-8155	244-5629
United Utility Supply Co-op Inc 4515 Bishop Ln *TF:* 800-366-4887 ■ *Web:* www.uus.org	Louisville	KY	40218	502-957-2568	
Universal Remote Control Inc 500 Mamaroneck Ave *Web:* www.universalremote.com	Harrison	NY	10528	914-835-4484	
Upchurch Electrical Supply Co 2355 N Gregg St PO Box 8340 *Web:* www.upchurchelectrical.com	Fayetteville	AR	72703	479-521-2823	521-6673
Utility Lines Inc 206 W Walnut St *Web:* www.utilitylines.com	Davidson	NC	28036	704-896-8866	896-8868
Valex Corp 6080 Leland St *Web:* www.valex.com	Ventura	CA	93003	805-658-0944	

	City	State	ZIP	Phone	Fax
Valley Electric Supply Corp 1361 N State Rd PO Box 724 *TF:* 800-825-7877 ■ *Web:* www.vesupply.com	Vincennes	IN	47591	812-882-7860	882-7893
Van Meter Industrial Inc 850 32nd Ave SW *TF:* 800-247-1410 ■ *Web:* www.vanmeterinc.com	Cedar Rapids	IA	52404	319-366-5301	366-4709
Venkel Ltd 5900 Shepherd Mtn Cove *TF:* 800-950-8365 ■ *Web:* www.venkel.com	Austin	TX	78730	512-794-0081	794-0087
Versa Electronics 3943 Quebec Ave N *Web:* www.versaelectronics.com	Minneapolis	MN	55427	763-557-6737	557-8073
Viewsonics Inc 3103 N Andrews Ave *Web:* viewsonics.com	Pompano Beach	FL	33064	954-971-8439	
Viking Electric Supply Inc 451 Industrial Blvd W *TF:* 800-435-3345 ■ *Web:* www.vikingelectric.com	Minneapolis	MN	55413	612-627-1300	627-1313
Virginia West Electric Supply Co (WVES) 250 12-th St W *TF:* 800-624-3433 ■ *Web:* www.wvaelectric.com	Huntington	WV	25704	304-525-0361	525-2726
Voss Lighting PO Box 22159 *TF:* 866-292-0529 ■ *Web:* www.vosslighting.com	Lincoln	NE	68542	402-328-2281	
Vsa Inc 6929 Seward Ave *TF:* 800-888-2140 ■ *Web:* www.vsa1.com	Lincoln	NE	68507	402-467-3668	325-8033
Vyrian Inc 9894 Bissonnet St Ste 918 *Web:* www.vyrian.com	Houston	TX	77036	281-404-3420	
Wabash Electric Supply Inc 1400 S Wabash St *TF:* 800-552-7777 ■ *Web:* www.wabashelectric.com	Wabash	IN	46992	260-563-4146	563-4140
Walters Wholesale Electric Co 2825 Temple Ave *TF:* 800-700-5483 ■ *Web:* www.walterswholesale.com	Signal Hill	CA	90755	562-988-3100	988-3150
Warshauer Electric Supply Co 800 Shrewsbury Ave **Fax:* Sales ■ *Web:* www.warshauer.com	Tinton Falls	NJ	07724	732-741-6400	741-3866*
Weinstock Lamp Company Inc 34-30 Steinway St *Web:* www.weinstocklighting.com	Long Island	NY	11101	718-729-4848	729-4848
Weldylamont Assoc Inc 1040 W NW Hwy *Web:* www.weldy-lamont.com	Mount Prospect	IL	60056	847-398-4510	
Werner Electric Supply Co 2341 Industrial Dr *TF:* 800-236-5026 ■ *Web:* www.wernerelectric.com	Neenah	WI	54956	920-729-4500	729-4484
Wes-Garde Components Group Inc 190 Elliott St *TF:* 800-554-8866 ■ *Web:* www.wesgarde.com	Hartford	CT	06114	860-525-6907	527-6047
WESCO Distribution Inc 225 W Stn Sq Dr Ste 700 *Web:* www.wesco.com	Pittsburgh	PA	15219	412-454-2200	454-2505
West-Lite Supply Company Inc 12951 166th St **Fax Area Code:* 562 ■ *TF:* 800-660-6678 ■ *Web:* www.west-lite.com	Cerritos	CA	90703	800-660-6678	802-0154*
Western Electrical Sales Inc (WES) 521 Glide Ave Unit A *Web:* www.wesisales.com	West Sacramento	CA	95691	916-372-1001	372-1172
Western Extralite Co 1470 Liberty St *TF:* 800-279-8833 ■ *Web:* www.westernextralite.com	Kansas City	MO	64102	816-421-8404	421-6211
Wheatstone Corp 600 Industrial Dr *Web:* www.wheatstone.com	New Bern	NC	28562	252-638-7000	
White Radio LP 5228 Everest Dr *TF:* 877-386-1956 ■ *Web:* www.whiteradio.com	Mississauga	ON	L4W2R4	905-632-6894	
Whitlock Group 12820 W Creekk Pkwy *TF:* 800-726-9843 ■ *Web:* www.whitlock.com	Richmond	VA	23238	804-273-9100	273-9380
Wholesale Electric Supply Company LP 4040 Guls Fwy *Web:* www.wholesaleelectric.com	Houston	TX	77004	713-748-6100	749-8415
Wholesale Electric Supply Inc 1400 Waterall St *Web:* www.netwes.com	Texarkana	TX	75501	903-794-3404	794-3400
Wieland Electric Inc (WEI) 49 International Rd *TF:* 800-943-5263 ■ *Web:* www.wielandinc.com	Burgaw	NC	28425	910-259-5050	259-3691
Wild Woods Inc 3575 Cahuenga Blvd W Ste 400 *Web:* www.wwoods.com	Los Angeles	CA	90068	323-878-0400	
Williams Electronics Games Inc 3401 N California *Web:* www.pinball.com	Chicago	IL	60618	312-267-2240	
Williams Supply Inc 210 Seventh St *TF:* 800-533-6969 ■ *Web:* www.williams-supply.com	Roanoke	VA	24016	540-343-9333	342-3254
Willow Electrical Supply Inc 3828 River Rd *Web:* www.willowelectric.com	Schiller Park	IL	60176	847-801-5010	801-5020
Winncom Technologies Corp 30700 Carter St Ste A *Web:* www.winncom.com	Solon	OH	44139	440-498-9510	498-9511
Wiremasters Inc 1788 N Pt Rd *TF:* 800-635-5342 ■ *Web:* www.wiremasters.net	Columbia	TN	38401	615-791-0281	791-6182
Womack Electric Supply Co 518 Newton St *Web:* www.womackelectric.com	Danville	VA	24541	434-793-5134	792-8256
World Electric Supply Orlando Inc 4501 SW 34th St *Web:* www.worldelectricsupply.com	Orlando	FL	32811	407-447-2000	447-2008
World Micro Components Inc 205 Hembree Park Dr Ste 105 *Web:* www.worldmicro.com	Roswell	GA	30076	770-698-1900	
WorldViz LLC 614 Santa Barbara St *Web:* www.worldviz.com	Santa Barbara	CA	93101	805-966-0786	
WSA Distributing Inc 7222 Opportunity Rd *Web:* www.wsadistributing.com	San Diego	CA	92111	858-560-7800	
WW Grainger Inc 100 Grainger Pkwy *NYSE: GWW* ■ *TF:* 888-361-8649 ■ *Web:* www.grainger.com	Lake Forest	IL	60045	847-535-1000	
Xanga.Com Inc 555 Eigth Ave Ste 21F *Web:* www.xanga.com	New York	NY	10018	212-695-4940	
XP Power 990 Benicia Ave *TF:* 800-253-0490 ■ *Web:* www.xppower.com	Sunnyvale	CA	94085	408-732-7777	732-2002
Yucca Tele Communications Is The Subsidiary 201 W Second St *Web:* www.yucca.net	Portales	NM	88130	575-226-2255	
Zack Electronics Inc 1070 Hamilton Rd *TF:* 800-466-0449 ■ *Web:* www.zackelectronics.com	Duarte	CA	91010	626-303-0655	303-8694

247 ELECTRICAL EQUIPMENT FOR INTERNAL COMBUSTION ENGINES

See Also Automotive Parts & Supplies - Mfr p. 1830; Motors (Electric) & Generators p. 2787

	City	State	ZIP	Phone	Fax
Altronic Inc 712 Trumbull Ave *Web:* www.altronicinc.com	Girard	OH	44420	330-545-9768	545-9005
American Electronic Components 1101 Lafayette St *TF:* 888-847-6552 ■ *Web:* www.aecsensors.com	Elkhart	IN	46516	574-295-6330	293-8013
Andover Inc PO Box 4848 *Web:* www.andovercoils.com	Lafayette	IN	47903	765-447-1157	
CE Niehoff & Co 2021 Lee St *TF Tech Supp:* 800-643-4633 ■ *Web:* www.ceniehoff.com	Evanston	IL	60202	847-866-6030	492-1242
CPX Inc 410 Kent St *Web:* www.cpxinc.com	Kentland	IN	47951	812-718-5335	
Edge Products 1080 S Depot Dr *TF:* 888-360-3343 ■ *Web:* www.edgeproducts.com	Ogden	UT	84404	801-476-3343	476-3348
EMB Corp 1203 Hawkins Dr *Web:* www.embcorp.com	Elizabethtown	KY	42701	270-737-1996	737-1909
ETCO Inc Automotive Products Div 3004 62nd Ave E *TF:* 800-689-3826 ■ *Web:* www.etco.com	Bradenton	FL	34203	941-756-8426	758-7195
Fargo Assembly of Pennsylvania Inc 800 W Washington St PO Box 550 *Web:* www.fargopa.com	Norristown	PA	19404	610-272-6850	272-6858
Fisher Electric Technology 2801 72nd St N *Web:* www.fisherelectric.com	Saint Petersburg	FL	33710	727-345-9122	
Flight Systems Inc 505 Fishing Creek Rd *TF:* 800-403-3728 ■ *Web:* www.flightsystems.com	Lewisberry	PA	17339	717-932-9900	932-9925
Goodall Manufacturing Co 7558 Washington Ave S *TF:* 800-328-7730 ■ *Web:* www.goodallmfg.com	Eden Prairie	MN	55344	952-941-6666	941-2617
Hitachi Automotive Systems Americas Inc 955 Warwick Rd *Web:* www.hap.com	Harrodsburg	KY	40330	859-734-9451	734-5309
Ignition Systems & Controls LP 6300 W Hwy 80 *TF:* 800-777-5559 ■ *Web:* www.ignition-systems.com	Midland	TX	79706	432-697-6472	697-0563
Interconnect Wiring Harnesses Inc 5024 W Vickery Blvd *Web:* www.interconnect-wiring.com	Fort Worth	TX	76107	817-377-9473	732-8667
Kelly Aerospace 1404 E S Blvd *TF:* 888-461-6077 ■ *Web:* www.kellyaerospace.com	Montgomery	AL	36116	334-286-8551	227-8596
KRA International LLC 1810 Clover Rd *Web:* www.krainternational.com	Mishawaka	IN	46545	574-259-3550	255-1079
M & G Electronics Corp 889 Seahawk Cir	Virginia Beach	VA	23452	757-468-6000	468-5442
Mitsubishi Electric Automotive America Inc 4773 Bethany Rd *Web:* www.meaa-mea.com	Mason	OH	45040	513-398-2220	398-1121
Motorcar Parts & Accessories 2929 California St *TF:* 800-890-9988 ■ *Web:* www.motorcarparts.com	Torrance	CA	90503	310-212-7910	212-7581
NGK Spark Plugs Inc 46929 Magellan *TF:* 877-473-6767 ■ *Web:* www.ngksparkplugs.com	Wixom	MI	48393	248-926-6900	926-6910
Precision Parts & Remanufacturing Co 4411 SW 19th St *TF:* 800-654-3846 ■ *Web:* www.pprok.com	Oklahoma City	OK	73108	405-681-2592	681-2596
Prestolite Wire Corp 200 Galleria Officentre Ste 212 *TF:* 800-498-3132 ■ *Web:* www.prestolitewire.com	Southfield	MI	48034	248-355-4422	386-4462
Prettl Electric Corp 1721 White Horse Rd *Web:* www.prettl.com	Greenville	SC	29605	864-220-1010	220-1020
RE Phelon Company Inc 2063 University Pkwy *Web:* fenix-mfg.com	Aiken	SC	29801	803-649-1381	
Remy International Inc 600 Corp Dr *NYSE: REMY* ■ *TF:* 800-372-3555 ■ *Web:* www.remyinc.com	Pendleton	IN	46064	765-778-6499	
Standard Motor Products Inc 37-18 Northern Blvd *NYSE: SMP* ■ *Web:* www.smpcorp.com	Long Island	NY	11101	718-392-0200	729-4549
Syncro Corp PO Box 890 *Web:* www.syncrocorp.com	Arab	AL	35016	256-931-7800	931-7920
Transpo Electronics Inc 2150 Brengle Ave **Fax Area Code:* 407 ■ *TF:* 800-327-6903 ■ *Web:* www.waiglobal.com	Orlando	FL	32808	800-327-6903	298-4519*
Van Bergen & Greener Inc 1818 Madison St *TF:* 800-621-3889 ■ *Web:* www.starterdrives.com	Maywood	IL	60153	708-343-4700	343-9425

248 ELECTRICAL SIGNALS MEASURING & TESTING INSTRUMENTS

	City	State	ZIP	Phone	Fax
3M Telecommunications Div 6801 River Pl Blvd *TF:* 800-426-8688 ■ *Web:* 3m.com	Austin	TX	78726	800-426-8688	626-0329
Aeroflex 35 South Service Rd PO Box 6022 *TF:* 800-843-1553 ■ *Web:* www.aeroflex.com	Plainview	NY	11803	913-764-2452	
Allied Motion Technologies Inc 495 Commerce Dr Ste 3 *NASDAQ: AMOT* ■ *TF:* 888-392-5543 ■ *Web:* www.alliedmotion.com	Amherst	NY	14228	716-242-8634	
Analog Devices Inc 3 Technology Way *NASDAQ: ADI* ■ *TF:* 800-262-5643 ■ *Web:* www.analog.com	Norwood	MA	02062	781-329-4700	461-3113
Anritsu Co 490 Jarvis Dr *TF:* 800-267-4878 ■ *Web:* globalmap.anritsu.com	Morgan Hill	CA	95037	408-778-2000	776-1744
Associated Equipment Corp 5043 Farlan Ave *TF:* 800-949-1472 ■ *Web:* associatedequip.com	Saint Louis	MO	63115	314-385-5178	385-3254
Beede Electrical Instrument Co 88 Village St *Web:* www.beede.com	Penacook	NH	03303	603-753-6362	753-6201

Company	City	State	Zip	Phone	Fax
BEI Precision Systems & Space Company Inc 1100 Murphy Dr *Web:* www.beiprecision.com	Maumelle	AR	72113	501-851-4000	851-5452
BI Technologies Corp 4200 Bonita Pl *Web:* www.bitechnologies.com	Fullerton	CA	92835	714-447-2300	447-2745
Bird Electronic Corp 30303 Aurora Rd *TF:* 866-695-4569 ■ *Web:* birdrf.com	Solon	OH	44139	440-248-1200	248-5426
Bird Technologies Group Inc 30303 Aurora Rd *TF:* 866-695-4569 ■ *Web:* birdrf.com	Solon	OH	44139	440-248-1200	248-5426
Bruel & Kjaer Instruments Inc 2815 Colonnades Ct Ste A *TF:* 800-332-2040 ■ *Web:* www.bkhome.com	Norcross	GA	30071	770-209-6907	448-3246
Cascade Microtech Inc 2430 NW 206th Ave *NASDAQ: CSCD* ■ *TF:* 800-854-8400 ■ *Web:* www.cmicro.com	Beaverton	OR	97006	503-601-1000	601-1010
Chatsworth Data Corp 9735 Lurline Ave **Fax Area Code: 877* ■ *TF:* 877-380-6855 ■ *Web:* www.chatsworthdata.com	Chatsworth	CA	91311	818-350-5072	380-6855*
Cohu Inc 12367 Crosthwaite Cir *NASDAQ: COHU* ■ *TF:* 800-685-5050 ■ *Web:* www.cohu.com	Poway	CA	92064	858-848-8100	848-8185
Communications Manufacturing Co (CMC) 2234 Colby Ave *TF Orders:* 800-462-5532 ■ *Web:* www.gotocmc.com	Los Angeles	CA	90064	310-828-3200	
Curtis Instruments Inc 200 Kisco Ave *TF:* 800-777-3433 ■ *Web:* www.curtisinstruments.com	Mount Kisco	NY	10549	914-666-2971	666-2971
CXR Larus Corp 894 Faulstich Ct *Web:* www.cxr.com	San Jose	CA	95112	408-573-2700	
CyberOptics Corp 5900 Golden Hills Dr *NASDAQ: CYBE* ■ *TF Cust Svc:* 800-746-6315 ■ *Web:* www.cyberoptics.com	Minneapolis	MN	55416	763-542-5000	542-5100
Desco Industries Inc 3651 Walnut Ave *Web:* desco.descoindustries.com	Chino	CA	91710	909-627-8178	627-7449
DIT-MCO International Corp 5612 Brighton Terr *TF:* 800-821-3487 ■ *Web:* www.ditmco.com	Kansas City	MO	64130	816-444-9700	444-6843
Doble Engineering Co Inc 85 Walnut St *TF:* 888-443-6253 ■ *Web:* www.doble.com	Watertown	MA	02472	617-926-4900	926-0528
Dranetz-BMI 1000 New Durham Rd *TF:* 800-372-6832 ■ *Web:* www.dranetz.com	Edison	NJ	08818	732-287-3680	248-1834
DRS Test & Energy Management Inc 110 Wynn Dr *Web:* www.drs.com	Huntsville	AL	35805	256-895-2000	895-2356
EADS North American Defense Test & Services Inc 4 Goodyear *TF Cust Svc:* 800-722-2528	Irvine	CA	92618	949-859-8999	
EDAC Technologies Corp 1806 New Britain Ave *NASDAQ: EDAC* ■ *Web:* www.edactechnologies.com	Farmington	CT	06032	860-678-8140	674-2718
Electro-Metrics Corp 231 Enterprise Rd *Web:* www.electro-metrics.com	Johnstown	NY	12095	518-762-2600	762-2812
Everett Charles Technologies (ECT) 700 E Harrison Ave *Web:* www.ectinfo.com	Pomona	CA	91767	909-625-5551	624-9746
Everett Charles Technologies Inc Test Equipment Div 700 E Harrison Ave *Web:* www.ectinfo.com	Pomona	CA	91767	909-625-5551	624-9746
EXFO Inc 400 Godin Ave *NASDAQ: EXFO* ■ *TF:* 800-663-3936 ■ *Web:* www.exfo.com	Quebec	QC	G1M2K2	418-683-0211	683-2170
Fluke Biomedical 6920 Seaway Blvd *TF:* 800-443-5853 ■ *Web:* www.flukebiomedical.com	Everett	WA	98203	425-446-6945	446-5629
Fluke Corp 6920 Seaway Blvd *TF:* 877-355-3225 ■ *Web:* www.fluke.com	Everett	WA	98203	425-446-6100	446-5116
Fluke Networks Inc 6920 Seaway Blvd *TF:* 800-283-5853 ■ *Web:* www.flukenetworks.com	Everett	WA	98203	425-446-4519	446-5043
Frequency Electronics Inc 55 Charles Lindbergh Blvd *NASDAQ: FEIM* ■ *Web:* www.freqelec.com	Uniondale	NY	11553	516-794-4500	794-4340
Giga-Tronics Inc 4650 Norris Canyon Rd *NASDAQ: GIGA* ■ *TF:* 800-726-4442 ■ *Web:* www.gigatronics.com	San Ramon	CA	94583	925-328-4650	328-4700
Gleason M & M Precision Systems Corp 300 Progress Rd *TF:* 800-727-6333 ■ *Web:* www.gleason.com	Dayton	OH	45449	937-859-8273	859-4452
Gold Line Connector Inc PO Box 500 *Web:* www.gold-line.com	West Redding	CT	06896	203-938-2588	938-8740
Greenlee Textron 1390 Aspen Way *TF:* 800-642-2155 ■ *Web:* greenlee.com	Vista	CA	92081	760-598-8900	
Hickok Inc 10514 Dupont Ave *OTC: HICKA* ■ *TF:* 800-342-5080 ■ *Web:* www.hickok-inc.com	Cleveland	OH	44108	216-541-8060	761-9879
Hipotronics Inc 1650 Rt 22 PO Box 414 *Web:* www.hipotronics.com	Brewster	NY	10509	845-279-8091	279-2467
Hughes Corp Weschler Instruments Div 16900 Foltz Pkwy *TF:* 800-557-0064 ■ *Web:* www.weschler.com	Cleveland	OH	44149	440-238-2550	238-0660
ILX Lightwave Corp 31950 E Frontage Rd *TF:* 800-459-9459 ■ *Web:* www.newport.com	Bozeman	MT	59715	406-586-1244	586-9405
IMPulse NC Inc 100 IMPulse Way *Web:* www.impulsenc.com	Mount Olive	NC	28365	919-658-2200	658-2268
ISEC Inc 33 Inverness Dr *Web:* www.isecinc.com	Englewood	CO	80112	303-790-1444	
Itron Inc 2111 N Molter Rd *NASDAQ: ITRI* ■ *TF:* 800-635-5461 ■ *Web:* www.itron.com	Liberty Lake	WA	99019	509-924-9900	891-3355
Ixia 26601 W Agoura Rd *NASDAQ: XXIA* ■ *TF:* 877-367-4942 ■ *Web:* www.ixiacom.com	Calabasas	CA	91302	818-871-1800	871-1805
KLA-Tencor Corp 1 Technology Dr *NASDAQ: KLAC* ■ *TF:* 800-600-2829 ■ *Web:* www.kla-tencor.com	Milpitas	CA	95035	408-875-3000	875-4144
Knopp Inc 1307 66th St *TF:* 800-227-1848 ■ *Web:* www.knoppinc.com	Emeryville	CA	94608	510-653-1661	653-2202
Kuka Assembly & Test 5675 Dixie Hwy *Web:* www.kukaat.com	Saginaw	MI	48601	989-777-2111	777-5620
L-3 Electrodynamics Inc 3975 McMann Rd **Fax Area Code: 847* ■ *Web:* www.l-3com.com/edi	Cincinnati	OH	45245	513-943-2000	660-1751*
Landis Gyr Inc 2800 Duncan Rd *TF:* 888-390-5733 ■ *Web:* www.landisgyr.com	Lafayette	IN	47904	765-742-1001	742-0936
LeCroy Corp 700 Chestnut Ridge Rd *NASDAQ: LCRY* ■ *TF:* 800-553-2769 ■ *Web:* teledynelecroy.com	Chestnut Ridge	NY	10977	845-425-2000	425-8967
LTS Corp 7250 Woodmont Ave Ste 340	Bethesda	MD	20814	301-652-2121	
Megger 4271 Bronze Way *TF:* 800-723-2861 ■ *Web:* www.megger.com	Dallas	TX	75237	214-333-3201	331-7399
Micro Control Co 7956 Main St NE *TF:* 800-328-9923 ■ *Web:* www.microcontrol.com	Minneapolis	MN	55432	763-786-8750	786-6543
Monroe Electronics Inc 100 Housel Ave *TF:* 800-821-6001 ■ *Web:* www.monroe-electronics.com	Lyndonville	NY	14098	585-765-2254	765-9330
Nartron Corp 5000 N US 131 *Web:* www.nartron.com	Reed City	MI	49677	231-832-5525	832-3876
National Instruments Corp 11500 N Mopac Expy *NASDAQ: NATI* ■ *TF Cust Svc:* 800-433-3488 ■ *Web:* www.ni.com	Austin	TX	78759	512-794-0100	683-8411
Newport Electronics Inc 2229 S Yale St *TF Cust Svc:* 800-639-7678 ■ *Web:* www.newportinc.com	Santa Ana	CA	92704	714-540-4914	546-3022
NH Research Inc 16601 Hale Ave *Web:* www.nhresearch.com	Irvine	CA	92606	949-474-3900	474-7062
PerkinElmer Inc 940 Winter St *NYSE: PKI* ■ *Web:* www.perkinelmer.com	Waltham	MA	02451	203-925-4602	944-4904
Phase Matrix Inc 109 Bonaventura Dr *TF:* 877-447-2736 ■ *Web:* www.phasematrix.net	San Jose	CA	95134	408-428-1000	428-1500
Phenix Technologies Inc 75 Speicher Dr *Web:* www.phenixtech.com	Accident	MD	21520	301-746-8118	895-5570
Precision Flow Technologies Inc PO Box 149 *Web:* www.precisionflowtechnologies.com	Saugerties	NY	12477	845-247-0810	247-8764
Prime Technology LLC 344-352 Twin Lakes Rd PO Box 185 *Web:* www.primetechnology.com	North Branford	CT	06471	203-481-5721	481-8937
Prominent Fluid Controls Inc 136 Industry Dr *Web:* www.prominent.us	Pittsburgh	PA	15275	412-787-2484	787-0704
Radiodetection Corp 154 Portland Rd *TF:* 877-247-3797 ■ *Web:* spx.com/en/radiodetection	Bridgton	ME	04009	207-647-9495	647-9496
Rodale Electronics Inc 20 Oser Ave *Web:* www.rodaleelectronics.com	Hauppauge	NY	11788	631-231-0044	231-1345
Schlumberger Ltd 5599 San Felipe Ste 100 *NYSE: SLB* ■ *Web:* www.slb.com	Houston	TX	77056	713-513-2000	513-2006
Schweitzer E O Mfg Company Inc 450 Enterprise Pkwy *TF:* 888-870-7350 ■ *Web:* selinc.com//solutions/fault-indicators-and-sensors	Lake Zurich	IL	60047	847-362-8304	362-8396
Sencore Inc 3200 W Sencore Dr *Web:* www.sencore.com	Sioux Falls	SD	57107	605-339-0100	335-6379
Simpson Electric Co 520 Simpson Ave *Web:* www.simpsonelectric.com	Lac Du Flambeau	WI	54538	715-588-3311	588-1248
Snap-on Diagnostics 420 Barclay Blvd *TF:* 800-424-7226 ■ *Web:* www1.snapon.com	Lincolnshire	IL	60069	847-478-0700	
TEGAM Inc 10 Tegam Way *TF:* 800-666-1010 ■ *Web:* www.tegam.com	Geneva	OH	44041	440-466-6100	466-6110
Teradyne Inc 600 Riverpark Dr *NYSE: TER* ■ *Web:* www.teradyne.com	North Reading	MA	01864	978-370-2700	
Teradyne Inc Assembly Test Div 600 Riverpark Dr *TF:* 800-837-2396 ■ *Web:* teradyne.com	North Reading	MA	01864	978-370-2700	
Teradyne Inc Industrial/Consumer Div 600 Riverpark Dr *TF:* 800-837-2396 ■ *Web:* teradyne.com	North Reading	MA	01864	978-370-2700	
Teradyne Inc Semiconductor Test Div 600 Riverpark Dr *Web:* www.teradyne.com/std	North Reading	MA	01864	978-370-2700	
Test Electronics 821 Smith Rd *Web:* www.testelectronics.com	Watsonville	CA	95076	831-763-2000	763-2085
Trek Inc 11601 Maple Ridge Rd **Fax:* Sales ■ *TF:* 800-367-8735 ■ *Web:* www.trekinc.com	Medina	NY	14103	585-798-3140	798-3106*
Trilithic Inc 9710 Pk Davis Dr *TF:* 800-344-2412 ■ *Web:* www.trilithic.com	Indianapolis	IN	46235	317-895-3600	423-7604
Trio-Tech International 14731 Califa St *NYSE: TRT* ■ *Web:* www.triotech.com	Van Nuys	CA	91411	818-787-7000	787-9130
Tyco Electronics Corp Corcom Div 620 S Butterfield Rd *Web:* www.te.com/usa-en/products/emi-filters.html	Mundelein	IL	60060	847-680-7400	680-8169
Wems Electronics Inc 4650 W Rosecrans Ave *Web:* www.wems.com	Hawthorne	CA	90250	310-644-0251	644-5334
Wireless Telecom Group Inc 25 Eastmans Rd *NYSE: WTT* ■ *Web:* www.wirelesstelecomgroup.com	Parsippany	NJ	07054	973-386-9696	386-9191
Xcerra Corporation 1355 California Cir *NASDAQ: XCRA* ■ *Web:* www.ltxc.com	Milpitas	CA	95035	408-635-4300	635-4985
Yokogawa Corp of America 12530 W Airport Blvd *TF:* 800-888-6400 ■ *Web:* www.yokogawa.com/us	Sugar Land	TX	77478	281-340-3800	340-3838
Zetec Inc 8226 Bracken Pl SE Ste 100 *TF:* 800-643-1771 ■ *Web:* www.zetec.com	Snoqualmie	WA	98065	425-974-2700	974-2701

249 ELECTRICAL SUPPLIES - PORCELAIN

Company	City	State	Zip	Phone	Fax
American Technical Ceramics Corp 1 Norden Ln *Web:* www.atceramics.com	Huntington Station	NY	11746	631-622-4700	622-4748
Associated Ceramics & Technology Inc 400 N Pike Rd *Web:* www.associatedceramics.com	Sarver	PA	16055	724-353-1585	353-1050
CeramTec North America Corp Technology Pl *Web:* www.ceramtec.com	Laurens	SC	29360	864-682-3215	682-1140
CoorsTek Inc 600 Ninth St *TF:* 800-821-6110 ■ *Web:* www.coorstek.com	Golden	CO	80401	303-278-4000	271-7009
CPS Technologies Corp 111 S Worcester St *OTC: CPSH* ■ *Web:* www.alsic.com	Norton	MA	02766	508-222-0614	222-0220
Du-Co Ceramics Co 155 S Rebecca St PO Box 568 *Web:* www.du-co.com	Saxonburg	PA	16056	724-352-1511	352-1266
Electrical Distributors Co 1135 Auzerais Ave *Web:* www.electdist.com	San Jose	CA	95126	408-293-5818	287-1152

				Phone	Fax
Fair-Rite Products Corp 1 Commerical Row PO Box J TF: 888-324-7748 ■ Web: www.fair-rite.com	Wallkill	NY	12589	845-895-2055	895-2629
Ferronics Inc 45 O'Connor Rd. Web: www.ferronics.com	Fairport	NY	14450	585-388-1020	388-0036
Hadron Technologies Inc 4941 Allison St Ste 15 Web: www.hadrontechnologies.com	Arvada	CO	80002	303-431-7798	431-6168
International Ceramic Engineering 235 Brooks St. TF: 800-779-3321 ■ Web: www.intlceramics.com	Worcester	MA	01606	508-853-4700	852-4101
Kyocera Industrial Ceramics Corp 5713 E Fourth Plain Rd. TF: 800-826-0527 ■ Web: americas.kyocera.com	Vancouver	WA	98661	360-696-8950	696-9804
LAPP Insulator Co 130 Gilbert St *Fax: Cust Svc ■ Web: www.lappinsulators.com	Le Roy	NY	14482	585-768-6221	768-6219*
Maryland Ceramic & Steatite Company Inc PO Box 527 Web: www.marylandceramic.com	Bel Air	MD	21014	410-838-4114	457-4333
Medler Electric Company Inc 2155 Redman Dr *Fax Area Code: 989 ■ TF: 800-229-5740 ■ Web: www.medlerelectric.com	Alma	MI	48801	800-229-5740	463-4522*
Nu-Tec Tooling Company Inc 13115 State Rt 405 Web: www.nutectool.com	Watsontown	PA	17777	570-538-2571	
Paramont EO Inc 1000 Davey Rd Ste 100 Web: www.paramont-eo.com	Woodridge	IL	60517	708-345-0000	345-0816
Power & Composite Technologies LLC (PCT) 200 Wallins Corners Rd Web: www.pactinc.com	Amsterdam	NY	12010	518-843-6825	843-6723
Revere Electric Supply Co 2501 W Washington Blvd Web: www.revereelectric.com	Chicago	IL	60612	312-738-3636	
Saint-Gobain Advanced Ceramics Latrobe 4702 Rt 982 TF: 800-438-7237	Latrobe	PA	15650	724-539-6000	539-6070
Sunbelt Transfomer Ltd 1922 S Martin Luther King Jr Dr. TF: 800-433-3128 ■ Web: www.sunbeltusa.com	Temple	TX	76504	254-771-3777	771-5719
Superior Technical Ceramics Corp 600 Industrial Pk Rd Web: www.ceramics.net	Saint Albans	VT	05478	802-527-7726	527-1181
Trans-Tech Inc 5520 Adamstown Rd Web: www.trans-techinc.com	Adamstown	MD	21710	301-695-9400	695-7065
Victor Insulators Inc 280 Maple Ave Web: www.victorinsulators.com	Victor	NY	14564	585-924-2127	924-7906

250 ELECTROMEDICAL & ELECTROTHERAPEUTIC EQUIPMENT

See Also Medical Instruments & Apparatus - Mfr p. 2741

				Phone	Fax
ABIOMED Inc 22 Cherry Hill Dr NASDAQ: ABMD ■ TF: 800-422-8666 ■ Web: www.abiomed.com	Danvers	MA	01923	978-777-5410	777-8411
Adaptive Switch Laboratories Inc 125 Spur 191 Ste C Web: www.asl-inc.com	Spicewood	TX	78669	830-798-0005	
Affymetrix Inc 3420 Central Expy NASDAQ: AFFX ■ TF: 888-362-2447 ■ Web: www.affymetrix.com	Santa Clara	CA	95051	408-731-5000	731-5380
Alere Medical Inc 51 Sawyer Rd Ste 200 Web: www.alere.com	Waltham	MA	02453	781-647-3900	
ALR Technologies Inc 7400 Beaufont Springs Dr Ste 300 Web: www.alrt.com	Richmond	VA	23225	804-554-3500	
ALung Technologies Inc 2500 Jane St Ste 1 Web: www.alung.com	Pittsburgh	PA	15203	412-697-3370	
Amedica Corp 1885 West 2100 South TF: 855-839-3500 ■ Web: www.amedica.com	Salt Lake City	UT	84119	855-839-3500	
Arobella Medical LLC 5929 Baker Rd Ste 470 Web: www.advcircuit.com	Minnetonka	MN	55345	952-345-6840	
Arrhythmia Research Technology Inc 25 Sawyer Passway AMEX: HRT ■ Web: www.arthrt.com	Fitchburg	MA	01420	978-345-0181	342-0168
Artel 25 Bradley Dr TF: 888-406-3463 ■ Web: www.artel-usa.com	Westbrook	ME	04092	207-854-0860	
AutoMedx Inc 12321 Middlebrook Rd Ste 150 Web: www.automedx.biz	Germantown	MD	20874	301-916-9508	
Avancen MOD Corp 1156 Bowman Rd Ste 200 TF: 800-607-1230 ■ Web: www.avancen.com	Mount Pleasant	SC	29464	800-607-1230	
Axiobionics 6111 Jackson Rd Ste 200 TF: 800-552-3539 ■ Web: www.axiobionics.com	Ann Arbor	MI	48103	734-327-2946	
Beacon Medaes 1800 Overview Dr TF: 888-463-3427 ■ Web: www.beaconmedaes.com	Rock Hill	SC	29730	803-817-5600	817-5750
Bio Medical Innovations 814 Airport Way TF: 800-201-3958 ■ Web: www.leadlok.com	Sandpoint	ID	83864	800-201-3958	
BioForce Nanosciences 1615 Golden Aspen Dr Ste 101 *Fax Area Code: 540 ■ Web: www.bioforcenano.com	Ames	IA	50010	515-233-8333	231-5022*
Bovie Medical Corp 734 Walt Whitman Rd Ste 207 NYSE: BVX ■ TF: 800-888-4999 ■ Web: www.boviemedical.com	Melville	NY	11747	631-421-5452	
BSD Medical Corp (BSDM) 2188 West 2200 South NASDAQ: BSDM	Salt Lake City	UT	84119	801-972-5555	972-5930
BTE Technologies Inc 7455-L New Ridge Rd Web: www.btetech.com	Hanover	MD	21076	410-850-0333	
Camag Scientific Inc 515 Cornelius Harnett Dr Web: www.camagusa.com	Wilmington	NC	28401	910-343-1830	
Cardiac Science Corp 3303 Monte Villa Pkwy *Fax: Cust Svc ■ TF Cust Svc: 800-426-0337 ■ Web: www.cardiacscience.com	Bothell	WA	98021	425-402-2000	402-2001*
Cardiogenesis Corp 11 Musick Web: www.cryolife.com/products/cardiogenesis	Irvine	CA	92618	949-420-1800	
Care Fusion 1100 Bird Ctr Dr.	Palm Springs	CA	92262	760-778-7200	
CAS Medical Systems Inc 44 E Industrial Rd NASDAQ: CASM ■ TF: 800-227-4414 ■ Web: www.casmed.com	Branford	CT	06405	203-488-6056	488-9438
CNS Response Inc 85 Enterprise Ste 410 TF: 888-545-2677 ■ Web: www.cnsresponse.com	Aliso Viejo	CA	92656	949-420-4400	
Conmed Corp 525 French Rd NASDAQ: CNMD ■ *Fax Area Code: 800 ■ *Fax: Cust Svc ■ TF: 800-448-6506 ■ Web: www.conmed.com	Utica	NY	13502	315-797-8375	438-3051*
Cook Medical Inc 1186 Montgomery Ln TF General: 800-457-4500 ■ Web: www.cookmedical.com	Vandergrift	PA	15690	724-845-8621	845-2848
COSMED USA Inc 2211 N Elston Ave Ste 305 Web: www.cosmed.it	Chicago	IL	60614	773-645-8113	
CVAC Systems Inc 43397 Business Park Dr D2 Web: www.cvacsystems.com	Temecula	CA	92590	951-699-2086	
Cytosorbents Corp 7 Deer Park Dr Ste K Web: www.cytosorbents.com	Monmouth Junction	NJ	08852	732-329-8885	
Delsys Inc 23 Strathmore Rd Web: www.delsys.com	Natick	MA	01760	617-236-0599	
Draeger Medical Inc 3135 Quarry Rd *Fax Area Code: 215 ■ TF: 800-437-2437 ■ Web: www.draeger.com	Telford	PA	18969	800-437-2437	723-5935*
Dynatronics Corp 7030 Pk Centre Dr NASDAQ: DYNT ■ *Fax Area Code: 800 ■ TF: 800-874-6251 ■ Web: www.dynatronics.com	Salt Lake City	UT	84121	801-568-7000	221-1919*
EBR Systems Inc 686 W Maude Ave Ste 102 Web: www.ebrsystems.com	Sunnyvale	CA	94085	408-720-1906	
Eigen Video 13366 Grass Vly Ave Ste A TF: 888-924-2020 ■ Web: www.eigen.com	Grass Valley	CA	95945	530-274-1240	
Fisher & Paykel Healthcare Inc 173 Technology Dr Ste 100 TF: 800-446-3908 ■ Web: www.fphcare.co.nz	Irvine	CA	92618	949-453-4000	453-4001
Flowmetrics Inc 9201 Independence Ave Web: flowmetrics.com	Chatsworth	CA	91311	818-407-3420	
Futrex Inc 130 Western Maryland Pkwy Web: www.futrex.com	Hagerstown	MD	21740	301-733-9368	
Gambro Renal Products 14143 Denver W Pkwy TF: 800-525-2623 ■ Web: www.gambro.com	Lakewood	CO	80401	303-232-6800	222-6810
GE Healthcare Information Technologies 8200 W Tower Ave TF: 800-558-5102 ■ Web: gehealthcare.com	Milwaukee	WI	53223	414-355-5000	
GN ReSound North America 8001 E Bloomington Fwy TF: 888-735-4327 ■ Web: www.gnresound.com	Bloomington	MN	55420	888-735-4327	
Hansen Medical Inc 800 E Middlefield Rd Web: hansenmedical.com	Mountain View	CA	94043	650-404-5800	
HealthTronics Inc 9825 Spectrum Dr Bldg 3 TF: 888-252-6575 ■ Web: www.healthtronics.com	Austin	TX	78717	512-328-2892	439-8303
HeartWare Inc 4750 Wiley Post Way Ste 120 NASDAQ: WHRT ■ Web: heartware.com	Salt Lake City	UT	84116	801-355-6255	355-7622
Higgins Supply Company Inc 18-23 S St Web: www.higginssupply.com	Mcgraw	NY	13101	607-836-6474	836-6913
Hillenbrand Industries Inc 1 Batesville Blvd NYSE: HI ■ Web: www.hillenbrand.com	Batesville	IN	47006	812-934-7500	934-7613
Honeywell HomMed LLC 3400 Intertech Dr Ste 200 Web: www.honeywelllifecare.com	Brookfield	WI	53045	262-783-5440	
Impact Instrumentation Inc 27 Fairfield Pl Web: www.impactinstrumentation.com	West Caldwell	NJ	07006	973-882-1212	
Imperium Inc 5901-F Ammendale Rd Web: www.imperiuminc.com	Beltsville	MD	20705	301-431-2900	
Inovio Pharmaceuticals Inc 660 W Germantown Pk Ste 110 NASDAQ: INOVIO ■ TF: 877-446-6846 ■ Web: www.inovio.com	Plymouth	PA	19462	267-440-4200	
Invivo Therapeutics Holdings Corp 1 Kendall Sq Ste B14402 Web: www.invivotherapeutics.com	Cambridge	MA	02139	617-863-5500	
IVY Biomedical Systems Inc 11 Business Pk Dr TF: 800-247-4614 ■ Web: www.ivybiomedical.com	Branford	CT	06405	203-481-4183	481-8734
Kelyniam Global Inc 97 River Rd TF: 800-280-8192 ■ Web: www.kelyniam.com	Canton	CT	06019	800-280-8192	
Lifeline Scientific Inc 1 Pierce Pl Ste 475W Web: lifeline-scientific.com	Itasca	IL	60143	847-294-0300	
LiteCure LLC 250 Corporate Blvd Ste B Web: www.litecure.com	Newark	DE	19702	302-709-0408	
MAQUET Cardiac Assist 15 Law Dr TF: 800-777-4222 ■ Web: ca.maquet.com	Fairfield	NJ	07004	973-244-6100	
Masimo Corp 40 Parker TF: 800-326-4890 ■ Web: www.masimo.com	Irvine	CA	92618	949-297-7000	297-7001
Medical Education Technologies Inc (METI) 6300 Edgelake Dr TF: 866-462-7920 ■ Web: www.caehealthcare.com	Sarasota	FL	34240	941-377-5562	377-5590
Medical Graphics Corp 350 Oak Grove Pkwy NASDAQ: ANGN ■ TF: 800-950-5597 ■ Web: mgcdiagnostics.com	Saint Paul	MN	55127	651-484-4874	379-8227
Medtronic Inc 710 Medtronic Pkwy NE NYSE: MDT ■ TF Cust Svc: 800-328-2518 ■ Web: www.medtronic.com	Minneapolis	MN	55432	763-514-4000	514-4879
Medtronic of Canada Ltd 6733 Kitimat Rd TF: 800-268-5346 ■ Web: www.medtronic.com	Mississauga	ON	L5N1W3	905-826-6020	826-6620
Medtronic Perfusion Systems 7611 Northland Dr TF: 800-328-3320 ■ Web: www.medtronic.com	Brooklyn Park	MN	55428	763-391-9000	
MedX Health Corp 1495 Bonhill Rd Unit 1 Web: www.medxhealth.com	Mississauga	ON	L5T1M2	905-670-4428	
Mennen Medical Corp 950 Industrial Hwy Web: www.mennenmedical.com	SouthHampton	PA	18966	215-259-1020	675-6212
Meridian Medical Technologies Inc 6350 Stevens Forest Rd Ste 301 TF: 800-638-8093 ■ Web: www.meridianmeds.com	Columbia	MD	21046	443-259-7800	259-7801
MetaStat Inc 27 Drydock Ave 2nd fl Web: www.metastat.com	Boston	MA	02210	973-744-7618	

	City	State	Zip	Phone	Fax
Millennium Dental Technologies Inc 10945 S St Ste 104-A *Web:* www.lanap.com	Cerritos	CA	90703	562-860-2908	
Misonix Inc 1938 NEW Hwy *TF:* 800-694-9612 ■ *Web:* www.misonix.com	Farmingdale	NY	11735	631-694-9555	
Mortara Instrument Inc 7865 N 86th St *TF:* 800-231-7437 ■ *Web:* www.mortara.com	Milwaukee	WI	53224	414-354-1600	354-4760
National Magnetic Sensors Inc 141 Summer St *Web:* www.nationalmagnetic.com	Plantsville	CT	06479	860-621-6816	
Natus Medical Inc 1501 Industrial Rd *NASDAQ: BABY* ■ *TF:* 800-255-3901 ■ *Web:* www.natus.com	San Carlos	CA	94070	650-802-0400	802-0401
NeuroMetrix 62 Fourth Ave *NASDAQ: NURO* ■ *TF:* 888-786-7287 ■ *Web:* www.neurometrix.com	Waltham	MA	02451	781-890-9989	890-1556
Neuromonics Inc PO Box 351886 *TF:* 866-606-3876 ■ *Web:* www.neuromonics.com	Westminster	CO	80035	866-606-3876	
Newport Medical Instruments Inc 1620 Sunflower Ave *Web:* www.newportnmi.com	Costa Mesa	CA	92626	714-427-5811	
Non-Invasive Monitoring Systems Inc 4400 Biscayne Blvd *Web:* www.nims-inc.com	Miami	FL	33137	305-575-4200	
NovaTract Surgical Inc 170 Ft Path Rd Ste 13 *Web:* www.novatract.com	Madison	CT	06443	203-533-9710	
O-two Medical Technologies Inc 7575 Kimbel St *TF:* 800-387-3405 ■ *Web:* www.otwo.com	Mississauga	ON	L5S1C8	905-677-9410	677-2035
Oscor Inc 3816 DeSoto Blvd **Fax:* Cust Svc ■ *TF Cust Svc:* 800-726-7267 ■ *Web:* www.oscor.com	Palm Harbor	FL	34683	727-937-2511	934-9835*
OSI Systems Inc 12525 Chadron Ave *NASDAQ: OSIS* ■ *Web:* www.osi-systems.com	Hawthorne	CA	90250	310-978-0516	
Osprey Medical Inc 7600 Executive Dr *TF:* 855-860-7584 ■ *Web:* www.ospreymed.com	Eden Prairie	MN	55344	952-955-8230	
Pacific Biosciences Inc 1380 Willow Rd *Web:* www.pacb.com	Menlo Park	CA	94025	650-521-8000	
Paradigm Medical Industries Inc 4273 South 590 West *OTC: PDMI* ■ *TF:* 800-742-0671	Salt Lake City	UT	84123	801-977-8970	977-8973
Philips Respironics Georgia Inc 175 Chastain Meadows Ct *Web:* www.usa.philips.com/healthcare/country-selector.html	Kennesaw	GA	30144	770-499-1212	
Physio-Control Inc 11811 Willows Rd NE **Fax:* Acctg ■ *TF:* 800-442-1142 ■ *Web:* www.physio-control.com	Redmond	WA	98052	425-867-4000	881-2405*
Positron Corp 530 Oakmont Ln *TF:* 866-613-7587 ■ *Web:* www.positron.com	Westmont	IL	60559	317-576-0183	
PP Systems International Inc 110 Haverhill Rd Ste 301 *TF:* 866-211-9346 ■ *Web:* www.ppsystems.com	Amesbury	MA	01913	978-834-0505	
ProUroCare Medical Inc 6440 Flying Cloud Dr Ste 101 *Web:* www.prourocare.com	Eden Prairie	MN	55344	952-476-9093	
Pyng Medical Corp 210, 13480 Crestwood Pl *Web:* www.pyng.com	Richmond	BC	V6V2J9	604-303-7964	303-7987
Respironics Novametrix LLC 5 Technology Dr *TF:* 800-345-6443 ■ *Web:* www.respironics.com	Wallingford	CT	06492	724-387-4000	
Richard Wolf Medical Instruments Corp 353 Corporate Woods Pkwy *TF:* 800-323-9653 ■ *Web:* www.richardwolfusa.com	Vernon Hills	IL	60061	847-913-1113	913-1488
Rockwell Medical Inc 30142 Wixom Rd *NASDAQ: RMTI* ■ *TF:* 800-449-3353 ■ *Web:* www.rockwellmed.com	Wixom	MI	48393	248-960-9009	960-9119
SensorMedics Corp 22745 Savi Ranch Pkwy *TF:* 800-231-2466 ■ *Web:* www.carefusion.com	Yorba Linda	CA	92887	714-283-2228	
Siemens Medical Solutions Inc 51 Valley Stream Pkwy **Fax Area Code:* 610 ■ *TF:* 800-888-7436 ■ *Web:* healthcare.siemens.com	Malvern	PA	19355	888-826-9702	219-3124*
Solta Medical Inc 25881 Industrial Blvd *TF:* 877-782-2286 ■ *Web:* www.thermage.com	Hayward	CA	94545	877-782-2286	
SonarMed Inc 12220 N Meridian St Ste 150 *Web:* www.sonarmed.com	Carmel	IN	46032	317-489-3161	
Spacelabs Health Care 35301 SE Center St *TF:* 800-522-7025 ■ *Web:* www.spacelabshealthcare.com	Snoqualmie	WA	98065	425-396-3300	396-3301
SpectraScience Inc 11568 Sorrento Vly Rd Ste 11 *Web:* www.spectrascience.com	San Diego	CA	92121	858-847-0200	
SQI Diagnostics Inc 36 Meteor Dr *Web:* www.sqidiagnostics.com	Toronto	ON	M9W1A4	416-674-9500	
Starkey Labs-Canada Co 7310 Rapistan Ct *Web:* www.starkeycanada.ca	Mississauga	ON	L5N6L8	905-542-7555	
Sunshine Heart Inc 7651 ANAGRAM Dr *Web:* www.sunshineheart.com	Eden Prairie	MN	55344	952-345-4200	
TechniScan Inc 3216 S Highland Dr Ste 200 *Web:* www.techniscanmedicalsystems.com	Salt Lake City	UT	84106	801-521-0444	
Tensys Medical Inc 5825 Oberlin Dr Ste 100 *Web:* www.tensysmedical.com	San Diego	CA	92121	858-552-1941	
Theralase Technologies Inc 1945 Queen St E *Web:* www.theralase.com	Toronto	ON	M4L1H7	416-699-5273	
Thoratec Corp 6035 Stoneridge Dr *NASDAQ: THOR* ■ *TF:* 800-528-2577 ■ *Web:* www.thoratec.com	Pleasanton	CA	94588	925-847-8600	847-8574
Vasomedical Inc 180 Linden Ave *OTC: VASO* ■ *TF:* 800-455-3327 ■ *Web:* www.vasomedical.com	Westbury	NY	11590	516-997-4600	997-2299
VasSol Inc 348 Lathrop Ave *Web:* www.vassolinc.com	River Forest	IL	60305	708-366-7000	
Verisante Technology Inc 2309 W 41st Ave Ste 306 *Web:* www.verisante.com	Vancouver	BC	V6M2A3	604-605-0507	
Vicor Technologies Inc (NDA) 399 Autumn Dr	Bangor	PA	18013	570-897-5797	
VitaSound Audio Inc 2880 Zanker Rd Ste 203 *Web:* vitasound.com	San Jose	CA	95134	905-667-7205	
Watermark Medical LLC 1641 Worthington Rd Ste 320 *TF:* 877-710-6999 ■ *Web:* www.watermarkmedical.com	West Palm Beach	FL	33409	877-710-6999	
Welch Allyn Medical Products 4341 State St Rd *TF:* 800-289-2500 ■ *Web:* www.welchallyn.com	Skaneateles Falls	NY	13152	315-685-4100	685-4091
Welch Allyn Monitoring Inc 8500 SW Creekside Pl *TF Cust Svc:* 800-289-2500 ■ *Web:* welchallyn.com	Beaverton	OR	97008	503-530-7500	526-4200
Zecotek Photonics Inc 21331 Gordon Way Unit 1120 *Web:* www.zecotek.com	Richmond	BC	V6W1J9	604-233-0056	
Zeltiq Aesthetics Inc 4698 Willow Rd Ste 100 *Web:* www.zeltiq.com	Pleasanton	CA	94588	925-474-2500	
ZOLL Medical Corp 269 Mill Rd *TF:* 800-348-9011 ■ *Web:* www.zoll.com	Chelmsford	MA	01824	978-421-9655	421-0025
Zynex Inc 9990 PARK MEADOWS Dr *Web:* www.zynexmed.com	Lone Tree	CO	80124	303-703-4906	

251 ELECTRONIC BILL PRESENTMENT & PAYMENT SERVICES

See Also Application Service Providers (ASPs) p. 1738

	City	State	Zip	Phone	Fax
401 K Advisors LLC 1000 Skokie Blvd Ste 500 *Web:* 401kadvisorschicago.com	Wilmette	IL	60091	847-256-4300	
Acumen Business Connections Inc 1999 N Amidon Ave Ste 230 *Web:* acumenprocessing.com	Wichita	KS	67203	316-265-4477	
Adam's European Contracting Inc 589 Johnson Ave *Web:* www.adamseuro.com	Brooklyn	NY	11237	718-417-9000	
Alpha Card Services Inc 475 Veit Rd *TF:* 866-253-2227 ■ *Web:* www.alphacardservices.com	Huntingdon Valley	PA	19006	866-253-2227	
Arcus Capital Partners LLC 3060 Peachtree Rd NW Ste 1880 *Web:* www.arcuscp.com	Atlanta	GA	30305	404-949-2111	
Arthur Financial Services LLC 1205 Sam Bass Rd Ste 200 *Web:* www.arthurfinancial.com	Round Rock	TX	78681	512-218-6948	
Benefit Coordinators Corporation of California 2 Robinson Plz Ste 200 *Web:* www.benxcel.com	Pittsburgh	PA	15205	412-276-1111	
BGCantor Market Data LP 199 Water St One Seaport Plz *Web:* www.bgcmarketdata.com	New York	NY	10038	212-829-4840	
BlueWater Partners LLC 146 Monroe Ctr St NW Ste 701 *Web:* www.bluewaterpartners.com	Grand Rapids	MI	49503	616-988-9444	
Cameron Accounting & Financial Service 121 W 3rd St *Web:* www.cameron-mo.com	Cameron	MO	64429	816-632-3786	
Capital Merchant Solutions Inc 3005 Gill St Ste 2 *TF:* 877-495-2419 ■ *Web:* holyprocessing.com	Bloomington	IL	61704	877-495-2419	
Carbon Credit Capital LLC 561 Broadway Ste 6A *Web:* www.carboncreditcapital.com	New York	NY	10012	212-925-5697	
Check Cashing Place Inc, The 945 Fifth Ave *Web:* thecheckcashingplaceinc.com	San Diego	CA	92112	619-239-6151	
Chepenik Financial Services 1010 Orange Ave *Web:* www.chepenikfinancial.com	Winter Park	FL	32789	407-660-1010	
Corban Onesource 235 3rd St S Ste 300 *Web:* www.corbanone.com	St Petersburg	FL	33701	727-803-1800	
Crossbeam Capital LLC 7920 Norfolk Ave Ste 501 *Web:* www.crossbeamcapital.com	Bethesda	MD	20814	240-223-0821	
Financial Transmission Network Inc 13220 Birch Dr Ste 120 *Web:* www.ftni.com	Omaha	NE	68164	402-502-8777	
FIX Flyer LLC 225 Broadway Ste 1600 *TF:* 888-349-3593 ■ *Web:* www.fixflyer.com	New York	NY	10007	888-349-3593	
Flores Financial Services 314 Sage St Ste 100 *Web:* rflores.com	Lake Geneva	WI	53147	262-248-2771	
Freedman Financial Associates Inc 8 Essex Ctr Dr 3rd Fl *TF:* 800-588-8108 ■ *Web:* www.freedmanfinancial.com	Peabody	MA	01960	978-531-8108	
Gough Financial Group Inc 9415 E Harry St Ste 602 *Web:* www.gfgks.com	Wichita	KS	67207	316-683-8400	
Heartland Payment Systems Inc 90 Nassau St 2nd Fl *NYSE: HPY* ■ *TF:* 888-798-3131 ■ *Web:* www.heartlandpaymentsystems.com	Princeton	NJ	08542	609-683-3831	
Ifrah Financial Services Inc 17300 Chenal Pkwy Ste 150 *TF:* 800-954-3724 ■ *Web:* www.ifrahfinancial.com	Little Rock	AR	72223	501-821-7733	
Kaiser Financial Services 3087 Winch Rd *Web:* www.kaiserfinancial.com	Springfield	IL	62707	217-787-4845	
Konsultek 2230 Point Blvd Ste 800 *Web:* www.konsultek.com	Elgin	IL	60123	847-426-9355	
Landmark Financial Group LLC 181 Old Post Rd *TF:* 800-437-4214 ■ *Web:* landmark-mortgage.com	Southport	CT	06890	203-254-8422	
Lear Capital Inc 1990 S Bundy Dr Ste 600 *TF:* 800-576-9355 ■ *Web:* www.learcapital.com	Los Angeles	CA	90025	800-576-9355	
Local Investment Commission 3100 Broadway St Ste 1100 *Web:* www.kclinc.org	Kansas City	MO	64111	816-889-5050	
Loring, Wolcott & Coolidge Fiduciary Advisors LLP 230 Congress St *Web:* www.lwcotrust.com	Boston	MA	02110	617-523-6531	

Company	City	State	Zip	Phone	Fax
Mcnamara Financial Services Inc Marshfield Professional Ctr 1020 Plain St Ste 200 *Web:* www.mcnamarafinancial.com	Marshfield	MA	02050	781-834-2010	
Mdic Investment Advisory Service LLC 116 Kraft Ave Ste8 *Web:* www.mdicinc.com	Bronxville	NY	10708	914-793-4095	
Money Movers Inc PO Box 241 *TF:* 800-861-5029 ■ *Web:* moneymovers.com	Sebastopol	CA	95473	707-829-5557	
Netvantage Inc 6510 Hamilton Ave Ste1 *Web:* www.netvantageinc.com	Cincinnati	OH	45224	513-729-0207	
Orion Advisor Services LLC 17605 Wright St *Web:* www.orionadvisor.com	Omaha	NE	68130	402-496-3513	
PayPal Inc PO Box 45950 *Web:* www.paypal.com	Omaha	NE	68145	402-935-2050	
PSC Info Group 105 Montgomery Ave *Web:* www.pscinfogroup.com	Oaks	PA	19456	610-650-3900	
Riata Financial Services Inc 245 Landa St *Web:* riatafinancial.com	New Braunfels	TX	78130	830-606-5100	
Rtr Financial Services Inc 901 N Broadway Ste 3b *Web:* rtrfs.com	White Plains	NY	10603	914-644-1701	
Sather Financial Group Inc 120 E Constitution St *Web:* www.satherfinancial.com	Victoria	TX	77901	361-570-1800	
Scully Capital Services Inc 1730 M St Nw Ste 204 *Web:* www.scullycapital.com	Washington	DC	20036	202-775-3434	
Toussaint Capital Partners LLC 13 Broadway Ste 2 *Web:* www.toussaintcapital.com	Freehold	NJ	07728	212-328-1800	
U.S. Bankcard Services Inc 17171 E Gale Ave Ste 110 *TF:* 888-888-8872 ■ *Web:* www.usbsi.com	City Of Industry	CA	91745	888-888-8872	
USA Technologies Inc 100 Deerfield Ln Ste 140 *TF:* 800-633-0340 ■ *Web:* www.usatech.com	Malvern	PA	19355	800-633-0340	
Value Payment Systems LLC 2207 Crestmoor Rd Ste 200 *Web:* www.valuepaymentsystems.com	Nashville	TN	37215	615-730-6367	
Waldron Wealth Management LLC 1150 Old Pond Rd *Web:* www.waldronprivatewealth.com	Bridgeville	PA	15017	412-221-1005	
Wingate Financial Group Inc 450 Bedford St *Web:* www.wingatewealthadvisors.com	Lexington	MA	02420	781-862-7100	
Xetus Corp 100 View St Ste 106 *Web:* www.xetusone.com	Mountain View	CA	94041	650-237-1225	
ZETA Services Inc 651 Sherwood Pkwy *Web:* www.zetascore.com	Mountainside	NJ	07092	908-233-7200	

252 ELECTRONIC COMMUNICATIONS NETWORKS (ECNS)

See Also Securities Brokers & Dealers p. 3163; Securities & Commodities Exchanges p. 3170

ECNs are computerized trade-matching systems that unite best bid and offer prices and provide anonymity to investors.

Company	City	State	Zip	Phone	Fax
Archipelago Holdings LLC 100 S Wacker Dr Ste 1800 *Web:* www.tradearca.com	Chicago	IL	60606	312-960-1696	
Bluesocket Inc 1 Burlington Woods Dr Ste 210 *Web:* www.adtran.com	Burlington	MA	01803	781-328-0888	
Comm-Works Holdings LLC 1405 Xenium Ln N Ste 120 *TF:* 800-853-8090 ■ *Web:* www.comm-works.com	Minneapolis	MN	55441	763-258-5800	475-6656
Layer 3 Communications LLC 1555 Oakbrook Dr Ste 100 *TF:* 866-535-3924 ■ *Web:* www.layer3com.com	Norcross	GA	30093	770-225-5300	225-5298
Network Telephone Services Inc 21135 Erwin St *TF:* 800-742-5687 ■ *Web:* www.nts.net	Woodland Hills	CA	91367	818-992-4300	
NYFIX Inc 11 Wall St *Web:* www.nyse.com	New York	NY	10005	212-656-3000	
OTC Markets Group Inc 304 Hudson St 2nd Fl *OTC: OTCM* ■ *Web:* www.otcmarkets.com	New York	NY	10013	212-896-4400	868-3848
Vector Resources Inc 3530 Voyager St *Web:* www.vectorusa.com	Torrance	CA	90503	310-436-1000	436-1060

253 ELECTRONIC COMPONENTS & ACCESSORIES - MFR

See Also Printed Circuit Boards p. 2974; Semiconductors & Related Devices p. 3177

Company	City	State	Zip	Phone	Fax
10C Technologies Inc 14285 Midway Rd Ste 125 *Web:* www.10ctech.com	Addison	TX	75001	972-385-2486	
2D2C Inc 250 Pkwy Dr Ste 150 *Web:* www.safeplug.com	Lincolnshire	IL	60069	847-543-0980	
3M Electrical Products Div 6801 River Pl Blvd 3M Austin Ctr **Fax Area Code: 800* ■ *Web:* 3m.com	Austin	TX	78726	512-984-1800	245-0329*
3M Electronic Handling & Protection Div 6801 River Pl Blvd *TF:* 800-328-1368 ■ *Web:* 3m.com	Austin	TX	78726	800-328-1368	
3M Interconnect Solutions Div 6801 River Pl Blvd *TF:* 800-225-5373 ■ *Web:* www.3m.com	Austin	TX	78726	512-984-1800	
A.J. Antunes & Co 180 Kehoe Blvd *Web:* www.ajantunes.com	Carol Stream	IL	60188	630-784-1000	
Aavid Thermalloy LLC 70 Commercial St Ste 200 *TF:* 855-322-2843 ■ *Web:* www.aavid.com	Concord	NH	03301	603-224-9988	223-1790
AccuSpec Electronics LLC 8140 Hawthorne Dr *Web:* accuspecelectronic.com	Erie	PA	16509	814-464-2000	
Adco Circuits 2868 Bond St *Web:* www.adcocircuits.com	Rochester Hills	MI	48309	248-853-6620	853-6698
Advanced Bionics LLC 28515 Westinghouse Pl *TF:* 877-829-0026 ■ *Web:* www.advancedbionics.com	Valencia	CA	91355	661-362-1400	362-1503
AEM Inc 6610 Cobra Way *Web:* www.aem-usa.com	San Diego	CA	92121	858-481-0210	
Aeroflex Inc 35 S Service Rd PO Box 6022 *TSE: ARX* ■ *TF:* 800-843-1553 ■ *Web:* www.aeroflex.com	Plainview	NY	11803	516-694-6700	694-0658
Aerovox Inc 167 John Vertente Blvd *Web:* www.aerovox.com	New Bedford	MA	02745	508-994-9661	995-3000
AESP Inc 16295 NW 13th Ave *TF:* 800-446-2377 ■ *Web:* www.aesp.com	Miami	FL	33169	305-944-7710	949-4483
AJB Software Design Inc 5255 Solar Dr *Web:* www.ajbsoftware.com	Mississauga	ON	L4W5B8	905-282-1877	
Alacron Inc 71 Spit Brook Rd Ste 200 *Web:* www.alacron.com	Nashua	NH	03060	603-891-2750	
Aldelo LP 4641 Spyres Way Ste 4 *TF:* 800-801-6036 ■ *Web:* www.aldelo.com	Modesto	CA	95356	209-338-5488	
Alion Inc 870 Harbour Way S *Web:* www.alion.co	Richmond	CA	94804	510-965-0868	
Alliance Fiber Optic Products Inc 275 Gibralter Dr *NASDAQ: AFOP* ■ *Web:* www.afop.com	Sunnyvale	CA	94089	408-736-6900	736-2466
Alpha Group, The 3767 Alpha Way **Fax:* Sales ■ *TF:* 800-322-5742 ■ *Web:* www.alpha.com	Bellingham	WA	98226	360-647-2360	671-4936*
Alvesta 500 Oakmead Pkwy *Web:* www.alvesta.com	Sunnyvale	CA	94085	408-331-4800	
American Bright Optoelectronics Corp 13815-C Magnolia Ave *Web:* www.americanbrightled.com	Chino	CA	91710	909-628-5050	
American International Inc 1040 Avendia Acaso *TF:* 800-336-6500 ■ *Web:* www.aius.net	Camarillo	CA	93012	805-388-6800	388-7950
American Power Conversion Corp (APC) 132 Fairgrounds Rd *TF Cust Svc:* 800-788-2208 ■ *Web:* www.apc.com	West Kingston	RI	02892	401-789-5735	789-3710
AMETEK Automation & Process Technologies 1080 N Crooks *TF:* 800-635-0289 ■ *Web:* www.ametekapt.com	Clawson	MI	48017	248-435-0700	435-8120
Ametek HDR Power Systems Inc 3563 Interchange Rd *TF:* 888-797-2685 ■ *Web:* www.hdrpower.com	Columbus	OH	43204	614-308-5500	308-5506
AMETEK Solidstate Controls 875 Dearborn Dr *TF:* 800-635-7300 ■ *Web:* www.solidstatecontrolsinc.com	Columbus	OH	43085	614-846-7500	885-3990
Ametek TSE 108 Fifth Ave NW *Web:* ametekemc.com	Arlington	MN	55307	507-964-2237	
Amphenol Aerospace 40-60 Delaware Ave *TF:* 800-678-0141 ■ *Web:* www.amphenol-aerospace.com	Sidney	NY	13838	607-563-5011	563-5157
Amphenol Interconnect Products Corp (AIPC) 20 Valley St	Endicott	NY	13760	607-754-4444	786-4234*
Amphenol PCD 72 Cherry Hill Dr **Fax:* Sales ■ *Web:* www.amphenolpcd.com	Beverly	MA	01915	978-624-3400	927-1513*
Amphenol RF 4 Old Newtown Rd *TF:* 800-627-7100 ■ *Web:* www.amphenolrf.com	Danbury	CT	06810	203-743-9272	796-2032
Amphenol Sine Systems 44724 Morley Dr *Web:* www.amphenol-sine.com	Clinton Township	MI	48036	586-465-3131	
Amphenol Spectra-Strip 720 Sherman Ave *TF:* 800-846-6400 ■ *Web:* www.spectra-strip.com	Hamden	CT	06514	203-281-3200	281-5872
Amphenol-Tuchel Electronics 6900 Haggerty Rd Ste 200 *TF:* 800-380-8052 ■ *Web:* www.amphenol.info	Canton	MI	48187	734-451-6400	451-7197
AmRad Engineering Inc 32 Hargrove Grade *TF:* 800-445-6033 ■ *Web:* www.americanradionic.com	Palm Coast	FL	32137	386-445-6000	445-6871
Anaren Microwave Inc 6635 Kirkville Rd *NASDAQ: ANEN* ■ *TF:* 800-544-2414 ■ *Web:* www.anaren.com	East Syracuse	NY	13057	315-432-8909	432-9121
Antec Inc 47900 Fremont Blvd *TF:* 800-222-6832 ■ *Web:* www.antec.com	Fremont	CA	94538	510-770-1200	770-1288
API Delevan 270 Quaker Rd *Web:* www.delevan.com	East Aurora	NY	14052	716-652-3600	652-4814
Ardica Technologies Inc 2325 Third St Ste 424 *Web:* www.ardica.com	San Francisco	CA	94107	415-568-9270	
Aries Electronics Inc 2609 Bartram Rd PO Box 130 *Web:* www.arieselec.com	Bristol	PA	19007	908-996-6841	996-3891
Arradiance Inc 142 N Rd Ste F-150 *Web:* www.arradiance.com	Sudbury	MA	01776	978-369-8291	
ASC Capacitors 301 W O St *Web:* www.ascapacitor.com	Ogallala	NE	69153	308-284-3611	284-8324
Atotech USA Inc 1750 Overview Dr *Web:* www.atotech.com/en	Rock Hill	SC	29730	803-817-3500	817-3666
AudioQuest Inc 2621 White Rd *TF:* 800-747-2770 ■ *Web:* www.audioquest.com	Irvine	CA	92614	949-585-0111	
Auric Systems International 85 Grove St *Web:* www.auricsystems.com	Peterborough	NH	03458	603-924-6079	
AVG Automation 4140 Utica St *TF:* 877-774-3279 ■ *Web:* avg.net/index.htm	Bettendorf	IA	52722	877-774-3279	
Avionic Instruments Inc 1414 Randolph Ave *TF:* 800-468-3571 ■ *Web:* www.avionicinstruments.com	Avenel	NJ	07001	732-388-3500	382-4996
Avnet Electronics Marketing Inc 2211 S 47th St *TF:* 888-822-8638 ■ *Web:* avnetexpress.avnet.com	Phoenix	AZ	85034	480-643-2000	
AVX Corp 801 17th Ave S *NYSE: AVX* ■ *Web:* www.avx.com	Myrtle Beach	SC	29577	843-448-9411	
B & K Electric Wholesale 1225 S Johnson Dr *Web:* www.bk-electric.com	City Of Industry	CA	91745	626-965-5040	
Ballard Power Systems Inc 9000 Glenlyon Pkwy *NASDAQ: BLDP* ■ *Web:* www.ballard.com	Burnaby	BC	V5J5J8	604-454-0900	412-4700

Phone Fax

Banner Engineering Corp 9714 Tenth Ave N. Minneapolis MN 55441 763-544-3164 544-3213
TF: 888-373-6767 ■ *Web:* www.bannerengineering.com

Beacon Power Corp 65 Middlesex Rd Tyngsboro MA 01879 978-694-9121 649-7186

BEI Technologies Inc Industrial Encoder Div
7230 Hollister Ave Goleta CA 93117 805-968-0782 968-3154
TF Sales: 800-350-2727 ■ *Web:* www.beiied.com

Bel Stewart Connector
11118 Susquehanna Trl S Glen Rock PA 17327 717-235-7512 235-7954
Web: www.belfuse.com

Bergquist Co 18930 W 78th St Chanhassen MN 55317 952-835-2322 835-4156
TF: 800-347-4572 ■ *Web:* www.bergquistcompany.com

BH Electronics Inc 12219 Wood Lk Dr. Burnsville MN 55337 952-894-9590 894-9380
Web: www.bhelectronics.com

Bright View Technologies
5151 Mccrimmon Pkwy Ste 200 Morrisville NC 27560 919-228-4370
Web: www.brightviewtechnologies.com

C & D Technologies Inc
1400 Union Meeting Rd PO Box 3053 Blue Bell PA 19422 215-619-2700 619-7899
TF: 800-543-8630 ■ *Web:* www.cdtechno.com

C&D Technologies 11 Cabot Blvd Mansfield MA 02048 508-339-3000 339-6356
TF: 800-233-2765 ■ *Web:* www.murata-ps.com

Califone International Inc
9135 Alabama Ave Ste B. Chatsworth CA 91311 818-407-2400 407-2405
TF: 800-722-0500 ■ *Web:* www.califone.com

Camesa Inc 1615 Spur 529 Rosenberg TX 77471 281-342-4494
TF: 800-866-0001 ■ *Web:* www.camesainc.com

Campbell & George Co
1100 Industrial Rd Ste 12 San Carlos CA 94070 650-654-5000
Web: cgco.com

Canadian Solar Solutions Inc
545 Speedvale Ave W Guelph ON N1K1E6 519-954-2057
Web: canadiansolar.com

Canara Inc 181 Third St Ste 150 San Rafael CA 94901 415-839-7270
Web: www.canara.com

Car Charging Group Inc
1691 Michigan Ave Ste 425 Miami Beach FL 33139 305-521-0200
Web: www.carcharging.com

Celestica Inc 844 Don Mills Rd Toronto ON M3C1V7 416-448-5800 448-4810
NYSE: CLS ■ *TF:* 888-899-9998 ■ *Web:* www.celestica.com

CENTROSOLAR America Inc
8350 E Evans Rd Ste E-1 Scottsdale AZ 85260 480-348-2555
Web: www.centrosolaramerica.com

Chromasun Inc 1001 Bridgeway Ste 453 Sausalito CA 94965 650-521-6872
Web: www.chromasun.com

Circuit Assembly Corp 18 Thomas St Irvine CA 92618 949-855-7887 855-4298
Web: www.circuitassembly.com

City Electric Supply Inc 315 E Prentiss St Iowa City IA 52240 319-338-7561 338-8620
TF: 800-272-6111

Clary Corp 150 E Huntington Dr Monrovia CA 91016 626-359-4486 305-0254
TF: 800-551-6111 ■ *Web:* www.clary.com

Clinton Electronics Corp 6701 Clinton Rd Loves Park IL 61111 815-633-1444
TF: 800-549-6393 ■ *Web:* www.clintonelectronics.com

Cobra Wire & Cable Inc 2930 Turnpike Dr Hatboro PA 19040 215-674-8773
Web: www.cobrawire.com

Coilcraft Inc 1102 Silver Lk Rd Cary IL 60013 847-639-2361 639-1469
TF: 800-322-2645 ■ *Web:* www.coilcraft.com

Coils Inc 11716 Algonquin Rd PO Box 247 Huntley IL 60142 847-669-5115

Color Kinetics Distribution Inc
1247 Norwood Ave Itasca IL 60143 630-285-9772
Web: www.colorkinetics.com

Comdel Inc 11 Kondelin Rd Gloucester MA 01930 978-282-0620 282-4980
TF: 800-468-3144 ■ *Web:* www.comdel.com

Communications & Power Industries LLC
607 Hansen Way Palo Alto CA 94303 650-846-2900 846-3276*
**Fax: PR* ■ *TF:* 800-231-4818 ■ *Web:* www.cpii.com

Conelec of Florida LLC 3045 Tech Park Way Deland FL 32724 386-873-3800
Web: www.conelec.net

Conesys Inc 2280 208th St Torrance CA 90501 310-618-3737
Web: www.conesys.com

Cooper Industries 600 Travis St Ste 5400 Houston TX 77002 713-209-8400 209-8995
NYSE: ETN ■ *TF:* 866-853-4293 ■ *Web:* www.cooperindustries.com

Corning Gilbert Inc 5310 W Camelback Rd Glendale AZ 85301 623-245-1050 934-5160
Web: www.corning.com

Cornucopia Tool & Plastics Inc
448 Sherwood Rd PO Box 1915 Paso Robles CA 93447 805-369-0030 369-0033
TF: 800-235-4144 ■ *Web:* www.cornucopiaplastics.com

Creswell-Richardson Supply
900 Appling St Chattanooga TN 37406 423-894-4117
Web: www.creswellrichardson.com

Crystek Crystals Corp
12730 Commonwealth Dr Fort Myers FL 33913 239-561-3311 561-3311
TF: 800-237-3061 ■ *Web:* www.crystek.com

CTS Corp 905 W Blvd N Elkhart IN 46514 574-293-7511 293-6146
NYSE: CTS ■ *TF:* 800-757-6686 ■ *Web:* www.ctscorp.com

Cyber Power Systems Inc
4241 12th Ave E Ste 400 Shakopee MN 55379 952-403-9500 403-0009
TF: 877-297-6937 ■ *Web:* www.cyberpowersystems.com

Cyberex 5900 Eastport Blvd Richmond VA 23231 804-236-3300 236-3300
TF: 800-238-5000 ■ *Web:* www.tnbpowersolutions.com

Data Device Corp 105 Wilbur Pl. Bohemia NY 11716 631-567-5600 259-0246*
**Fax Area Code: 414* ■ *TF Cust Svc:* 800-332-5757 ■ *Web:* www.ddc-web.com

DataCan Services Corp
7485-45 Ave Close Ste 102 Red Deer AB T4P4C2 403-352-2245
Web: www.datacan.ca

Deep Imaging Technologies Inc
990 Village Sq Dr Tomball TX 77375 281-290-0492
Web: deepimaging.com

Delta Electronics Manufacturing Corp
416 Cabot St. Beverly MA 01915 978-927-1060 922-6430
Web: www.deltarf.com

Delta Group Inc 4801 Lincoln Rd NE Albuquerque NM 87109 505-883-7674 888-5460
Web: www.deltagroupinc.com

Delta Products Corp 4405 Cushing Pkwy Fremont CA 94538 510-668-5100 668-0680
Web: www.delta-americas.com

Phone Fax

Diamond Antenna & Microwave Corp
59 Porter Rd Littleton MA 01460 978-486-0039 486-0079
Web: www.diamondantenna.com

Dielectric Laboratories Inc 2777 US Rt 20 Cazenovia NY 13035 315-655-8710 655-0445

Digital Light Innovations
3201 Industrial Terr Ste 120 Austin TX 78758 512-617-4700
Web: www.dlinnovations.com

Digital Power Corp 41324 Christy St Fremont CA 94538 510-353-4023 657-2635
TF: 866-344-7697 ■ *Web:* www.digipwr.com

DigitalOptics Corp 3025 Orchard Pkwy San Jose CA 95134 408-473-2500
Web: www.doc.com

Dimation Inc 505 W Travelers Trl Burnsville MN 55337 952-746-3030
Web: www.dimation.com

DOW Kokam LLC 2125 Ridgewood Dr Midland MI 48642 989-698-3300

Dow-Key Microwave Corp 4822 McGrath St. Ventura CA 93003 805-650-0260 650-1734
TF: 800-266-3695 ■ *Web:* www.dowkey.com

DRS Laurel Technologies 246 Airport Rd Johnstown PA 15904 814-534-8900
Web: www.drs.com

DSA Encore LLC 50 Pocono Rd Brookfield CT 06804 203-740-4200
Web: www.dsaencore.com

Dynalloy Inc 14762 Bentley Cir Tustin CA 92780 714-436-1206 436-0511
Web: www.dynalloy.com

Dynamic Source Manufacturing Inc
Unit 117 2765 - 48th Ave NE Calgary AB T3J5M9 403-516-1888
Web: www.dynamicsourcemfg.com

e-Merchant Processing Inc 3125 Sterling Cir Boulder CO 80301 303-577-0330

Eby Co 4300 H St Philadelphia PA 19124 215-537-4700 537-4780
TF: 800-329-3430 ■ *Web:* www.ebycompany.com

Electrex Inc PO Box 948 Hutchinson KS 67504 800-319-3676 669-3740*
**Fax Area Code: 620* ■ *TF:* 800-319-3676 ■ *Web:* www.electrexinc.com

Electro-Mechanical Corp 1 Goodson St. Bristol VA 24201 276-669-4084 669-1869
Web: www.electro-mechanical.com

Electrocube Inc 3366 Pomona Blvd Pomona CA 91768 909-595-4037 357-8099*
**Fax Area Code: 626* ■ *TF:* 800-515-1112 ■ *Web:* www.electrocube.com

Electronic Instrumentation & Technology Inc (EIT)
108 Carpenter Dr Sterling VA 20164 703-478-0700 478-0291
Web: www.eit.com

Electroswitch Corp 180 King Ave Weymouth MA 02188 781-335-5200 335-4253
Web: www.electroswitch.com

Elma Electronic Inc 44350 Grimmer Blvd Fremont CA 94538 510-656-3400 656-3783
Web: www.elma.com

ELSAG North America LLC 7 Sutton Pl Brewster NY 10509 336-379-7135
Web: www.elsag.com

Emerging Power Inc 200 Holt St Hackensack NJ 07601 201-441-3590
Web: www.emergingpower.com

Emerson Network Power Connectivity Solutions
1050 Dearborn Dr. Columbus OH 43085 614-888-0246 841-6882
TF: 800-275-3500 ■ *Web:* www.emersonnetworkpower.com

EMF Corp 505 Pokagon Trl. Angola IN 46703 260-665-9541
TF: 800-847-2818 ■ *Web:* www.emfusa.com

Emrise Corp 2530 Meridian Pkwy Durham NC 27713 919-806-4722
Web: www.emrise.com

Emrise Electronics Corp
9485 Haven Ave Ste 100. Rancho Cucamonga CA 91730 909-987-9220
Web: www.emrise.com

Energy Conversion Devices Inc
2956 Waterview Dr. Rochester Hills MI 48309 248-293-0440
OTC: ENERQ

Enevate Corp 101 Theory Ste 200 Irvine CA 92617 949-243-0399
Web: www.enevate.com

ENrG Inc 155 Rano St Ste 300 Buffalo NY 14207 716-873-2939
Web: www.enrg.com

Eoff Electric Company Inc
3241 NW Industrial St Portland OR 97210 503-222-9411
TF: 800-285-3633 ■ *Web:* www.eoff.com

EPCOS Inc 485-B Rt 1 S Ste 200 Iselin NJ 08830 800-689-3717
TF: 800-689-3717 ■ *Web:* en.tdk.eu

eSilicon Corp 501 Macara Ave. Sunnyvale CA 94085 408-616-4600 991-9567
TF: 877-769-2447 ■ *Web:* www.esilicon.com

Espey Mfg & Electronics Corp
233 Ballston Ave. Saratoga Springs NY 12866 518-245-4400 245-4421
NYSE: ESP ■ *Web:* www.espey.com

Exatron Inc 2842 Aiello Dr. San Jose CA 95111 408-629-7600
Web: www.exatron.com

Fabrinet USA Inc 4104 24th St Ste 345 San Francisco CA 94114 408-888-4601
Web: www.fabrinet.com

Fawn Industries Inc
1920 Greenspring Dr Ste 140 Timonium MD 21093 410-308-9200 308-9202
Web: fawnplastics.com

Filnor Inc 227 N Freedom Ave PO Box 2328 Alliance OH 44601 330-821-7667 829-3175
Web: www.filnor.com

Forbes Snyder Tristate Cash
54 Northampton St Easthampton MA 01027 413-529-2950
TF: 800-222-4064 ■ *Web:* www.forbes-snyder.com

Foxlink International Inc 925 W Lambert Rd Ste C Brea CA 92821 714-256-1777 256-1700
Web: www.foxlink.com

Franklin Empire Inc 8421 Darnley Rd Montreal QC H4T2B2 514-341-9720 341-3907
TF: 800-361-5044 ■ *Web:* www.feinc.com

FRC Component Products Inc
1511 S Benjamin Ave Mason City IA 50401 641-424-0370
Web: frccorp.com

FuelCell Energy Inc 3 Great Pasture Rd Danbury CT 06810 203-825-6000
NASDAQ: FCEL ■ *Web:* www.fuelcellenergy.com

Fujitsu Components America Inc
250 E Caribbean Dr Sunnyvale CA 94089 408-745-4900 745-4970
Web: www.fujitsu.com

Full Swing Golf Inc 10890 Thornmint Rd San Diego CA 92127 858-675-1100
Web: www.fullswinggolf.com

General Microcircuits Inc
1133 N Main St PO Box 748 Mooresville NC 28115 704-663-5975 663-6569
Web: www.gmimfg.com

GoMotion Inc 10 Kendrick Rd Unit 3 Wareham MA 02571 508-322-7695
Web: www.gomotiongear.com

Company	City	State	ZIP	Phone	Fax
Greatbatch Inc 10000 Wehrle Dr *NYSE:* GB ■ *Web:* www.greatbatch.com	Clarence	NY	14031	716-759-5600	759-2562
Greenlee Textron 1390 Aspen Way *TF:* 800-642-2155 ■ *Web:* greenlee.com	Vista	CA	92081	760-598-8900	
Guestlogix Inc 111 Peter St Ste 302 *Web:* www.guestlogix.com	Toronto	ON	M5V2H1	416-642-0349	
GW Lisk Company Inc 2 S St *Web:* www.gwlisk.com	Clifton Springs	NY	14432	315-462-2611	462-7661
Harco Laboratories Inc 186 Cedar St *Web:* www.harcolabs.com	Branford	CT	06405	203-483-3700	
HCC Industries Inc 4232 Temple City Blvd. *Web:* www.hccindustries.com	Rosemead	CA	91770	626-443-8933	
Heliene Inc 520 Allen'S Side Rd *TF:* 855-363-2797 ■ *Web:* www.heliene.ca	Sault Sainte Marie	ON	P6A6K4	705-575-6556	
Heraeus Shin-Etsu America Inc 4600 NW Pacific Rim Blvd *Web:* sehamerica.com	Camas	WA	98607	360-834-4004	
Hirose Electric (USA) Inc 2688 Westhills Ct *Web:* www.hirose.com	Simi Valley	CA	93065	805-522-7958	522-3217
Hitachi Canada Ltd 5450 Explore Dr Ste 501 *TF:* 877-248-4237 ■ *Web:* www.hitachi.ca	Mississauga	ON	L4W5N1	905-629-9300	290-0141
Hitachi High Technologies America Inc 10 N Martingale Rd Ste 500 *Web:* www.hitachi-hightech.com/us	Schaumburg	IL	60173	847-273-4141	273-4407
Honeywell Electronic Materials 1349 Moffett Pk Dr *Web:* www.honeywell.com	Sunnyvale	CA	94089	408-962-2000	962-2257
Hubbell Power Systems Inc 210 N Allen St *TF:* 800-346-3062 ■ *Web:* www.hubbellpowersystems.com	Centralia	MO	65240	573-682-5521	682-8714
Hunting Innova 8383 N Sam Houston Pkwy W *Web:* www.hunting-intl.com	Houston	TX	77064	281-653-5500	653-5501
Hutchinson Technology Inc 40 W Highland Pk Dr *NASDAQ:* HTCH ■ *TF:* 800-419-1007 ■ *Web:* www.htch.com	Hutchinson	MN	55350	320-587-3797	
Illinois Capacitor Inc 3757 W Touhy Ave *Web:* www.illinoiscapacitor.com	Lincolnwood	IL	60712	847-675-1760	673-2850
IMP Holdings LLC 409 Growth Pkwy. *Web:* www.indianamarine.com	Angola	IN	46703	260-665-6112	
Innergy Power Corp Inc 9051 Siempre Viva Rd Bldg 6 Ste AB *Web:* www.innergypower.com	San Diego	CA	92154	619-710-0758	
Inrad Optics Inc 181 Legrand Ave. *Web:* www.inradoptics.com	Northvale	NJ	07647	201-767-1910	
Instantel Inc 309 Legget Dr. *TF:* 800-267-9111 ■ *Web:* www.instantel.com	Ottawa	ON	K2K3A3	613-592-4642	
Integrated Magnetics Inc 11248 Playa Ct *TF:* 800-421-6692 ■ *Web:* www.intemag.com	Culver City	CA	90230	310-391-7213	
Integrated Microwave Corp 11353 Sorrento Valley Rd. *Web:* www.imcsd.com	San Diego	CA	92121	858-259-2600	755-8679
International Resistive Company Inc (IRC) 736 Greenway Rd *Web:* www.irctt.com	Boone	NC	28607	828-264-8861	264-8865
Interpoint Corp PO Box 97005 *TF:* 800-822-8782 ■ *Web:* www.interpoint.com	Redmond	WA	98073	425-882-3100	882-1990
inTEST Corp 804 E Gate Dr Ste 200 *NYSE:* INTT ■ *Web:* www.intest.com	Mount Laurel	NJ	08054	856-505-8800	505-8801
InVue Security Products Inc 10715 Sikes Pl Ste 200 *TF:* 888-257-4272 ■ *Web:* www.alphaworld.com	Charlotte	NC	28277	704-206-7849	
ipDataTel LLC 13110 SW Fwy *TF:* 866-896-1818 ■ *Web:* www.ipdatatel.com	Sugar Land	TX	77478	713-452-2700	
Iterna 2600 Beverly Dr *Web:* iternacorp.com	Aurora	IL	60502	630-585-7400	
ITT Industries Inc 1133 Westchester Ave *NYSE:* ITT ■ *TF:* 800-254-2823 ■ *Web:* www.itt.com	White Plains	NY	10604	914-641-2000	696-2950
JAE Electronics Inc 142 Technology Dr Ste 100 *TF:* 800-523-7278 ■ *Web:* www.jae.com	Irvine	CA	92618	949-753-2600	753-2699
Jameson LLC 1451 Old N Main St *Web:* www.jamesonllc.com	Clover	SC	29710	803-222-6400	
Jenkins Electric Inc 5933 Brookshire Blvd *TF:* 800-438-3003 ■ *Web:* www.jenkins.com	Charlotte	NC	28216	800-438-3003	
Jewell Instruments LLC 850 Perimeter Rd *TF:* 800-227-5955 ■ *Web:* jewellinstruments.com	Manchester	NH	03103	603-669-6400	669-5962
Johanson Mfg Corp 301 Rockaway Valley Rd. **Fax:* Sales ■ *TF:* 800-477-1272 ■ *Web:* www.johansonmfg.com	Boonton	NJ	07005	973-334-2676	334-2954*
Joule Unlimited Inc 18 Crosby Dr *Web:* www.jouleunlimited.com	Bedford	MA	01730	781-533-9100	
K & L Microwave Inc 2250 Northwood Dr *Web:* www.klmicrowave.com	Salisbury	MD	21801	410-749-2424	749-1598
Kaiser Systems Inc (KSI) 126 Sohier Rd. *Web:* www.kaisersys.com	Beverly	MA	01915	978-922-9300	922-8374
Kathrein Inc Scala Div 555 Airport Rd. *Web:* www.kathrein.com	Medford	OR	97504	541-779-6500	
KEMET Corp PO Box 5928 *NYSE:* KEM ■ *Web:* www.kemet.com	Greenville	SC	29606	864-963-6300	
Kepco Inc 131-38 Sanford Ave. *TF:* 800-526-2324 ■ *Web:* www.kepcopower.com	Flushing	NY	11355	718-461-7000	767-1102
Key Tronic Corp 4424 N Sullivan Rd. *NASDAQ:* KTCC ■ *Web:* www.keytronic.com	Spokane	WA	99214	509-928-8000	927-5555
Knowles Corporation 1151 Maplewood Dr *Web:* www.knowlesinc.com	Itasca	IL	60143	630-250-5100	250-0575
KOA Speer Electronics Inc 199 Bolivar Dr *Web:* www.evalue-tech.com	Bradford	PA	16701	814-362-5536	
L-3 Communications Corp Display Systems Div 1355 Bluegrass Lakes Pkwy *Web:* www.l-3com.com	Alpharetta	GA	30004	770-752-7000	752-5525
L-Com Inc 45 Beechwood Dr *Web:* www.l-com.com	North Andover	MA	01845	978-682-6936	
La Marche Mfg Co 106 Bradrock Dr. *TF:* 888-232-9562 ■ *Web:* www.lamarchemfg.com	Des Plaines	IL	60018	847-299-1188	299-3061
Larco 210 NE Tenth Ave *TF Cust Svc:* 800-523-6996 ■ *Web:* larco.com	Brainerd	MN	56401	218-829-9797	829-0139
LeeMAH Electronics Inc 1088 Sansome St *Web:* www.leemah.com	San Francisco	CA	94111	415-394-1288	
Lenexpo Inc 1293 Mtn View Alviso Rd Ste A *TF:* 877-536-3976 ■ *Web:* www.atlona.com	Sunnyvale	CA	94089	408-962-0515	
Lexel Imaging Systems Inc 1501 Newtown Pike *TF:* 800-397-8121 ■ *Web:* www.lexelimaging.com	Lexington	KY	40511	859-243-5500	243-5555
LHV Power Corp 10221 Buena Vista Ave. *Web:* www.lhvpower.com	Santee	CA	92071	619-258-7700	
Light Engines LLC 29 Library Ln S	Sturbridge	MA	01566	508-347-0111	
LogiCan Technologies Inc 150 Karl Clark Rd *Web:* www.logican.com	Edmonton	AB	T6N1E2	780-450-4400	
Logitek Inc 110 Wilbur Pl *Web:* www.naii.com	Bohemia	NY	11716	631-567-1100	567-1823
Lorch Microwave Inc 1725 N Salisbury Blvd. *Web:* www.lorch.com	Salisbury	MD	21802	410-860-5100	
Lucix Corp 800 Avenida Acaso *Web:* www.lucix.com	Camarillo	CA	93012	805-987-3677	
Lumex Inc 290 E Helen Rd *TF:* 800-278-5666 ■ *Web:* www.lumex.com	Palatine	IL	60067	847-359-2790	359-8904
Luminit LLC 1850 W 205th St. *Web:* www.luminitco.com	Torrance	CA	90501	310-320-1066	
Lynn Electronics Corp 154 Railroad Dr *Web:* www.lynnelec.com	Ivyland	PA	18974	215-355-8200	
Magmotor Technologies Inc 10 Coppage Dr *Web:* www.inverpower.com	Worcester	MA	01603	508-459-5991	
MagneTek Inc N49 W13650 Campbell Dr. *NASDAQ:* MAG ■ *TF:* 800-288-8178 ■ *Web:* www.magnetek.com	Menomonee Falls	WI	53051	800-288-8178	298-3503
Magtech Industries Corp 5625-A S Arville St. *TF:* 888-954-4481 ■ *Web:* www.magtechind.com	Las Vegas	NV	89119	702-364-9998	
Maida Development Co 201 S Mallory St *Web:* www.maida.com	Hampton	VA	23663	757-723-0785	722-1194
Marlow Industries Inc 10451 Vista Pk Rd. *TF:* 877-627-5691 ■ *Web:* www.marlow.com	Dallas	TX	75238	214-340-4900	340-7728
Maxwell Technologies Inc 5271 Viewridge Ct Ste 100 *NASDAQ:* MXWL ■ *TF:* 877-511-4324 ■ *Web:* www.maxwell.com	San Diego	CA	92123	858-503-3300	503-3301
MC10 Inc 10 Maguire Rd Bldg 3 1st Fl. *Web:* www.mc10inc.com	Cambridge	MA	02421	617-234-4448	234-0093
McDonald Technologies International Inc 2310 McDaniel Dr *Web:* www.mcdonald-tech.com	Carrollton	TX	75006	972-421-4100	
Meggitt Safety Systems Inc 1915 Voyager Ave. *Web:* www.meggitt.com	Simi Valley	CA	93063	805-584-4100	578-3400
Merrimac Industries Inc 41 Fairfield Pl **Fax:* Sales ■ *Web:* www.craneae.com	West Caldwell	NJ	07006	973-575-1300	575-0531*
Methode Electronics Inc 7401 W Wilson Ave *NYSE:* MEI ■ *TF:* 877-316-7700 ■ *Web:* www.methode.com	Chicago	IL	60706	708-867-6777	867-6999
Micro-coax Inc 206 Jones Blvd *TF:* 800-223-2629 ■ *Web:* www.micro-coax.com	Pottstown	PA	19464	610-495-0110	495-6656
MicroPlanet Technology Corp 15530 Woodinville-Redmond Rd NE Ste B100 *Web:* www.microplanet.com	Woodinville	WA	98072	425-984-2740	
Microwave Engineering Corp 1551 Osgood St *Web:* www.microwaveeng.com	North Andover	MA	01845	978-685-2776	975-4363
Microwave Filter Company Inc 6743 Kinne St. *TF:* 800-448-1666 ■ *Web:* www.microwavefilter.com	East Syracuse	NY	13057	315-438-4700	
Miteq Inc 100 Davids Dr *Web:* www.miteq.com	Hauppauge	NY	11788	631-436-7400	436-7430
Molex Inc 2222 Wellington Ct *NASDAQ:* MOLX ■ *TF Cust Svc:* 800-786-6539 ■ *Web:* www.molex.com	Lisle	IL	60532	630-969-4550	969-1352
Morey Corp 100 Morey Dr *Web:* www.moreycorp.com	Woodridge	IL	60517	630-754-2300	754-2001
MS Kennedy Corp 4707 Dey Rd *Web:* www.mskennedy.com	Liverpool	NY	13088	315-701-6751	701-6752
MTI-Milliren Technologies Inc 2 New Pasture Rd *Web:* www.mti-milliren.com	Newburyport	MA	01950	978-465-6064	
MtronPTI 1703 E Hwy 50 *TF:* 800-762-8800 ■ *Web:* www.mtronpti.com	Yankton	SD	57078	605-665-9321	665-1709
Multi-Fineline Electronix Inc (Mflex) 3140 E Coronado St *NASDAQ:* MFLX ■ *Web:* www.mflex.com	Anaheim	CA	92806	714-238-1488	
Murata Electronics North America Inc 2200 Lake Pk Dr *TF:* 800-704-6079 ■ *Web:* www.murata.com	Smyrna	GA	30080	770-436-1300	436-3030
Netcom Inc 599 S Wheeling Rd *Web:* www.netcominc.com	Wheeling	IL	60090	847-537-6300	537-2700
NewComLink Inc 3900 N Capital Of Texas Hwy Ste 150 *TF:* 888-988-0603 ■ *Web:* vyze.com	Austin	TX	78746	888-988-0603	
Newport Corp 1791 Deere Ave. *NASDAQ:* NEWP ■ **Fax:* Sales ■ *TF Sales:* 800-222-6440 ■ *Web:* www.newport.com	Irvine	CA	92606	949-863-3144	253-1680*
Niles Audio Corp 1969 Kellog Ave *TF:* 800-289-4434 ■ *Web:* www.nilesaudio.com	Carlsbad	CA	92008	760-710-0992	
Nortech Systems Inc 7550 Meridian Cir N Ste 150 *NASDAQ:* NSYS ■ *TF:* 800-237-9576 ■ *Web:* www.nortechsys.com	Maple Grove	MN	55369	952-345-2244	
Nortek Security & Control LLC 1950 Camino Vida Roble Ste 150 *TF Cust Svc:* 800-421-1587 ■ *Web:* www.nortekcontrol.com	Carlsbad	CA	92008	760-438-7000	931-1340
Nova Research Inc 760 McMurray Rd 760 McMurray Rd *Web:* www.novasensors.com	Buellton	CA	93427	805-693-9600	
Novacap Inc 25111 Anza Dr. *Web:* knowlescapacitors.com/novacap	Valencia	CA	91355	661-295-5920	295-5928

				Phone	Fax
Novacentrix Corp 200-B Parker Dr Ste 580 . . . . Austin *Web:* www.novacentrix.com	TX	78728		512-491-9500	491-0002
NWL Transformers Inc 312 Rising Sun Rd . . . . Bordentown *TF:* 800-742-5695 ■ *Web:* www.nwl.com	NJ	08505		609-298-7300	298-1982
O M Jones Inc PO Box 4375 . . . . Sonora *Web:* www.micro-tronics.net	CA	95370		209-532-1008	532-1009
Oeco LLC 4607 SE International Way . . . . Milwaukie *Web:* www.oeco.com	OR	97222		503-659-5999	653-6310
Ohmite Manufacturing Co 1600 Golf Rd Ste 850 . . . . Rolling Meadows *TF:* 866-964-6483 ■ *Web:* www.ohmite.com	IL	60008		847-258-0300	
OK International 12151 Monarch St. . . . . Garden Grove *Web:* www.okinternational.com	CA	92841		714-799-9910	799-9533
Omron Corp 55 Commerce Dr . . . . Schaumburg *Web:* www.omron.com	IL	60173		224-520-7650	520-7680
On-Line Strategies Inc 7920 Belt Line Rd Ste 1150 . . . . Dallas *TF:* 866-237-4900 ■ *Web:* www.olsdallas.com	TX	75254		214-466-1000	
Onyx EMS LLC 2920 Kelly Ave . . . . Watertown *TF:* 800-772-7866 ■ *Web:* sparton.com	SD	57201		605-886-2519	886-5123
Oppenheimer Precision Products 173 Gibraltar Rd . . . . Horsham *Web:* www.oppiprecision.com	PA	19044		215-674-9100	
Oren Elliott Products Inc 128 W Vine St. . . . . Edgerton *Web:* www.orenelliottproducts.com	OH	43517		419-298-2306	298-3545
OSI Systems Inc 12525 Chadron Ave . . . . Hawthorne *NASDAQ: OSIS* ■ *Web:* www.osi-systems.com	CA	90250		310-978-0516	
OSRAM Sylvania Inc 100 Endicott St . . . . Danvers *Web:* www.sylvania.com	MA	01923		978-777-1900	750-2152
PACE Inc 255 Air Tool Dr . . . . Southern Pines *Web:* www.paceworldwide.com	NC	28387		910-695-7223	
Panamax Inc 1690 Corporate Cir. . . . . Petaluma *TF:* 800-472-5555 ■ *Web:* www.panamax.com	CA	94954		707-283-5900	283-5901
Para Systems Inc *Minuteman UPS* 1455 LeMay Dr . . . . Carrollton *TF:* 800-238-7272 ■ *Web:* www.minutemanups.com	TX	75007		972-446-7363	446-9011
PCB Group Inc 3425 Walden Ave. . . . . Depew *TF:* 800-828-8840 ■ *Web:* www.pcb.com	NY	14043		716-684-0001	684-0987
PerkinElmer Inc 940 Winter St . . . . Waltham *NYSE: PKI* ■ *Web:* www.perkinelmer.com	MA	02451		203-925-4602	944-4904
PG Life Link Inc 167 Gap Way. . . . . Erlanger *TF:* 800-287-4123 ■ *Web:* pglifelink.com	KY	41018		859-283-5900	372-6272
PhyleTec LLC 4150 Grange Hall Rd. . . . . Holly *Web:* www.phyletec.com	MI	48442		248-634-4000	
Piller Inc 45 Turner Rd. . . . . Middletown **Fax Area Code:* 845 ■ *TF:* 800-597-6937 ■ *Web:* www.piller.com	NY	10941		800-597-6937	692-0295*
Plastronics Socket Co Inc 2601 Texas Dr . . . . Irving *TF Cust Svc:* 800-582-5822 ■ *Web:* www.plastronics.com	TX	75062		972-258-2580	
Plug Power Inc 968 Albany-Shaker Rd . . . . Latham *NASDAQ: PLUG* ■ *TF:* 877-474-1993 ■ *Web:* www.plugpower.com	NY	12110		518-782-7700	782-9060
Polyflon Co 1 WillaRd Rd. . . . . Norwalk *Web:* www.polyflon.com	CT	06851		203-840-7555	840-7565
Positronic Industries Inc 423 N Campbell Ave PO Box 8247. . . . . Springfield *TF:* 800-641-4054 ■ *Web:* www.connectpositronic.com	MO	65801		417-866-2322	866-4115
Post Glover Resistors Inc 1369 Cox Rd . . . . Erlanger *TF Cust Svc:* 800-537-6144 ■ *Web:* www.postglover.com	KY	41018		859-283-0778	283-2978
Power-One Inc 740 Calle Plano. . . . . Camarillo *NASDAQ: PWER* ■ *Web:* www.power-one.com	CA	93012		805-987-8741	388-0476
Precision Cable Assemblies LLC 16830 Pheasant Dr. . . . . Brookfield *Web:* www.pca-llc.com	WI	53005		262-784-7887	784-0681
Precision Devices Inc 8840 N Greenview Dr. . . . . Middleton *Web:* www.pdixtal.com	WI	53562		608-831-4445	831-3343
Precision Interconnect Corp 10025 SW Freeman Ct . . . . Wilsonville *TF:* 800-522-6752 ■ *Web:* www.te.com	OR	97070		503-685-9300	685-9305
Progressive Dynamics Inc 507 Industrial Rd . . . . Marshall *Web:* www.progressivedyn.com	MI	49068		269-781-4241	781-7802
Proton Onsite 10 Technology Dr. . . . . Wallingford *Web:* www.protononsite.com	CT	06492		203-678-2000	949-8016
Pulse Engineering Inc 12220 World Trade Dr. . . . . San Diego *Web:* www.pulseelectronics.com	CA	92128		858-674-8100	674-8262
Q-tech Corp 10150 Jefferson Blvd. . . . . Culver City *Web:* www.q-tech.com	CA	90232		310-836-7900	836-2157
Q-tran Inc 304 Bishop Ave. . . . . Bridgeport *Web:* www.q-tran.com	CT	06610		203-367-8777	367-8771
Qual-Tron Inc (QTI) 9409 E 55th Pl. . . . . Tulsa *Web:* www.qual-tron.com	OK	74145		918-622-7052	664-8557
QualiTau Inc 830 Maude Ave. . . . . Mountain View *Web:* qualitau.com	CA	94043		408-522-9200	
Qualitel Corp 11831 Beverly Pk Rd . . . . Everett *Web:* www.qualitelcorp.com	WA	98204		425-423-8388	423-8398
Quartzdyne Inc 4334 W Links Dr. . . . . Salt Lake City *Web:* www.quartzdyne.com	UT	84120		801-266-6958	266-7985
Raritan Computer Inc 400 Cottontail Ln . . . . Somerset *TF:* 800-724-8090 ■ *Web:* www.raritan.com	NJ	08873		732-764-8886	764-8887
Record USA 4324 Phil Hargett Ct PO Box 3099. . . . . Monroe *TF Sales:* 800-438-1937 ■ *Web:* www.record-usa.com	NC	28111		704-289-9212	289-2024
Regal Research & Mfg Co Inc 1200 E Plano Pkwy . . . . Plano *Web:* www.regalresearch.com	TX	75074		972-494-0359	272-0220
Revionics Inc 2998 Douglas Blvd Ste 350 . . . . Roseville *Web:* www.revionics.com	CA	95661		916-797-6051	
RF Industries 7610 Miramar Rd Bldg 6000. . . . . San Diego *NASDAQ: RFIL* ■ *TF:* 800-233-1728 ■ *Web:* www.rfindustries.com	CA	92126		858-549-6340	549-6345
Ruhle Cos Inc 99 Wall St. . . . . Valhalla *Web:* www.ruhle.com	NY	10595		914-761-2600	761-0405
S & K Electronics Inc 56301 US Hwy 93. . . . . Ronan *Web:* www.skecorp.com	MT	59864		406-883-6241	883-6228
S V Microwave Inc 2400 Centre Pk W Dr . . . . West Palm Beach *Web:* www.svmicrowave.com	FL	33409		561-840-1800	842-6277
SAE Power Inc 1500 E Hamilton Ave Ste 118. . . . . Campbell *Web:* www.sae.com.hk	CA	95008		408-369-2200	
Samtec Inc 520 Parkeast Blvd . . . . New Albany *TF:* 800-726-8329 ■ *Web:* www.samtec.com	IN	47150		812-944-6733	948-5047
Schott Corp 1401 Air Wing Rd. . . . . San Diego *Web:* www.schottcorp.com	CA	92154		507-223-5572	223-5055
Schumacher Electric Corp 801 E Business Ctr Dr . . . . Mount Prospect **Fax Area Code:* 847 ■ *TF:* 800-621-5485 ■ *Web:* www.batterychargers.com	IL	60056		800-621-5485	298-1698*
Scosche Industries Inc PO Box 2901 . . . . Oxnard *TF:* 800-363-4490 ■ *Web:* www.scosche.com	CA	93034		805-486-4450	486-9996
Seiko Instruments USA Inc 21221 S Western Ave Ste 250 . . . . Torrance *TF Sales:* 800-688-0817 ■ *Web:* www.seikoinstruments.com	CA	90501		310-517-7700	517-7709
Semicon Assoc 695 Laco Dr. . . . . Lexington *Web:* www.semiconassociates.com	KY	40510		859-255-3664	255-6829
Semiconductor Circuits Inc 49 Range Rd . . . . Windham *Web:* www.dcdc.com	NH	03087		603-893-2330	893-6280
Sendec Corp 72 Perinton Pkwy . . . . Fairport *TF:* 800-295-8000 ■ *Web:* apitech.com	NY	14450		585-425-3390	425-3392
Sharp Microelectronics of the Americas 5700 NW Pacific Rim Blvd . . . . Camas *Web:* www.sharpsma.com	WA	98607		360-834-2500	834-8903
Shelly Assoc Inc 17171 Murphy Ave . . . . Irvine *Web:* www.shellyinc.com	CA	92614		949-417-8070	417-8075
Shogyo International Corp 6851 Jericho Tpke . . . . Syosset *Web:* www.shogyo.com	NY	11791		516-921-9111	921-3777
Sierra Nevada Corp (SNC) 444 Salomon Cir . . . . Sparks *Web:* www.sncorp.com	NV	89434		775-331-0222	331-0370
Sigma Electronics Inc 1027 Commercial Ave . . . . East Petersburg *TF:* 866-569-2681 ■ *Web:* www.sigmatechsys.com	PA	17520		717-569-2926	569-4056
Signal Transformer Company Inc 500 Bayview Ave. . . . . Inwood *TF:* 866-239-5777 ■ *Web:* www.signaltransformer.com	NY	11096		516-239-5777	239-7208
Silent Power Inc 8175 Industrial Park Rd Ste 100. . . . . Baxter *Web:* www.silentpwr.com	MN	56425		218-454-3030	
Simplex Inc 5300 Rising Moon Rd. . . . . Springfield *TF:* 800-637-8603 ■ *Web:* www.simplexdirect.com	IL	62711		217-483-1600	483-1616
SL Power Electronics Inc 6050 King Dr Bldg A . . . . Ventura **Fax Area Code:* 858 ■ *TF:* 800-235-5929 ■ *Web:* www.slpower.com	CA	93003		805-486-4565	712-2040*
Smart Electronics & Assembly Inc 2000 W Corporate Way. . . . . Anaheim *Web:* www.smartelec.com	CA	92801		714-991-6500	
Smart Power Systems Inc 1760 Stebbins Dr . . . . Houston *TF:* 800-882-8285 ■ *Web:* www.smartpowersystems.com	TX	77043		713-464-8000	984-0841
SMK Electronics Corp USA 1055 Tierra Del Rey . . . . Chula Vista *Web:* www.smk.co.jp	CA	91910		619-216-6400	216-6498
SMTC Corp 635 Hood Rd. . . . . Markham *NASDAQ: SMTX* ■ *Web:* www.smtc.com	ON	L3R4N6		905-479-1810	479-1877
SNC Mfg Company Inc 101 W Waukau Ave . . . . Oshkosh *TF:* 800-558-3325 ■ *Web:* www.sncmfg.com	WI	54902		920-231-7370	231-1090
Sorenson Communications Inc 4192 Riverboat Rd Ste 100. . . . . Salt Lake City *Web:* www.sorenson.com	UT	84123		801-287-9400	287-9401
Spang & Co 110 Delta Dr. . . . . Pittsburgh *Web:* www.spang.com	PA	15238		412-963-9363	696-0333
Spectrum Control Inc 8031 Avonia Rd . . . . Fairview *Web:* eis.apitech.com/	PA	16415		814-474-2207	474-2208
Spellman High Voltage Electronics Corp 475 Wireless Blvd. . . . . Hauppauge **Fax:* Sales ■ *Web:* www.spellmanhv.com	NY	11788		631-435-1600	435-1620*
Standex Electronics Inc 4538 Camberwell Rd . . . . Cincinnati *TF:* 866-782-6339 ■ *Web:* www.standexelectronics.com	OH	45209		513-871-3777	871-3779
STATS ChipPAC Test Services Inc 46429 Landing Pkwy . . . . Fremont *Web:* www.statschippac.com	CA	94538		408-586-0600	586-0601
Stevens Water Monitoring Systems 12067 NE Glenn Widing Dr Ste 106. . . . . Portland *TF:* 800-452-5272 ■ *Web:* www.stevenswater.com	OR	97220		503-469-8000	469-8100
Sumida America Inc 1251 N Plum Grove Rd Ste 150 . . . . Schaumburg *Web:* www.sumida.com	IL	60173		847-545-6700	
Superconductor Technologies Inc (STI) 460 Ward Dr. . . . . Santa Barbara *NASDAQ: SCON* ■ *TF:* 800-727-3648 ■ *Web:* www.suptech.com	CA	93111		805-690-4500	967-0342
Switchcraft Inc 5555 N Elston Ave. . . . . Chicago *Web:* www.switchcraft.com	IL	60630		773-792-2700	792-2129
SynQor Inc 155 Swanson Rd . . . . Boxborough *Web:* www.synqor.com	MA	01719		978-849-0600	849-0601
Sypris Electronics LLC 10901 N McKinley Dr . . . . Tampa *TF:* 800-937-9220 ■ *Web:* www.sypris.com	FL	33612		813-972-6000	972-6704
Sypris Solutions Inc 101 Bullitt Ln Ste 450. . . . . Louisville *NASDAQ: SYPR* ■ *TF:* 800-588-9119 ■ *Web:* www.sypris.com	KY	40222		502-329-2000	329-2050
System Sensor 3825 Ohio Ave . . . . Saint Charles *TF Tech Supp:* 800-736-7672 ■ *Web:* www.systemsensor.com	IL	60174		630-377-6580	377-6495
Systemes Pran Inc 399 Jacquard St Ste 100. . . . . Quebec *Web:* www.pransystems.com	QC	G1N4J6		418-688-7726	
Taiyo Yuden (USA) Inc 1930 N Thoreau Dr Ste 190 . . . . Schaumburg *TF:* 800-348-2496 ■ *Web:* www.t-yuden.com	IL	60173		847-925-0888	925-0899
TDI-Transistor Devices Inc 85 Horsehill Rd. . . . . Cedar Knolls *TF:* 800-488-6724 ■ *Web:* www.tdipower.com	NJ	07927		973-267-1900	267-2047
TDK Corp of America 475 Half Day Rd. . . . . Lincolnshire *Web:* www.tdk.com	IL	60069		847-699-2299	803-6296
TDK-Lambda Americas Inc 405 Essex Rd. . . . . Neptune *Web:* www.us.tdk-lambda.com/hp	NJ	07753		732-922-9300	922-1441

Phone | Fax

Teledyne Electronic Safety Products
19735 Dearborn St .... Chatsworth CA 91311 818-718-6640 998-3312
Web: www.teledynesafetyproducts.com

Telonic Berkeley Inc 1080 La Mirada Ct .... Vista CA 92081 760-744-8350 744-8360
TF Sales: 800-311-8805 ■ *Web:* www.telonicberkeley.com

Threshold Financial Technologies Inc
3269 American Dr .... Mississauga ON L4V1X5 905-678-7373
TF: 888-414-3733 ■ *Web:* www.threshold-fti.com

Times Microwave Systems Inc PO Box 5039 .... Wallingford CT 06492 203-949-8400 949-8423
TF: 800-867-2629 ■ *Web:* www.timesmicrowave.com

Toshiba America Inc
1251 Ave of the Americas Ste 4100 .... New York NY 10020 212-596-0600 593-3875
TF: 800-457-7777 ■ *Web:* www.toshiba.com

Total Technologies Ltd 9710 Research Dr .... Irvine CA 92618 949-465-0200 465-0212
TF: 800-669-4885 ■ *Web:* www.total-technologies.com

TRAK Microwave Corp 4726 Eisenhower Blvd .... Tampa FL 33634 813-901-7200 901-7491
TF: 888-283-8444 ■ *Web:* www.trak.com

Transcend Technologies Group Inc
3101 Zinfandel Dr Ste 200 .... Rancho Cordova CA 95670 916-421-4000
Web: www2.benefitsconnect.net

Tri Source Inc 84 Platt Rd .... Shelton CT 06484 203-926-9460 567-8181
Web: www.trisourceinc.com

Triton Systems Inc 21405 B St .... Long Beach MS 39560 228-575-3100
TF: 866-787-4866 ■ *Web:* www.tritonatm.com

TSI Power Corp 1103 W Pierce Ave .... Antigo WI 54409 715-623-0636 623-2426
TF: 800-874-3160 ■ *Web:* www.tsipower.com

Tyco Electronics Corp 1050 Westlakes Dr .... Berwyn PA 19312 610-893-9800
Web: www.te.com

United Chemi-Con Inc 9801 W Higgins Rd .... Rosemont IL 60018 847-696-2000 696-9278
TF: 800-344-4539 ■ *Web:* www.chemi-con.com

Usmilcom Inc 1952 E Mcfadden Ave .... Santa Ana CA 92705 714-835-3545
Web: www.usmilcom.com

V-TEK Inc 751 Summit Ave PO Box 3104 .... Mankato MN 56002 507-387-2039
Web: www.vtekusa.com

Viatran Corp 3829 Forest Pkwy Ste 500 .... Wheatfield NY 14120 716-629-3800 693-9162
TF: 800-688-0030 ■ *Web:* www.viatran.com

Vicor Corp 25 Frontage Rd .... Andover MA 01810 978-470-2900 475-6715
NASDAQ: VICR ■ *TF:* 800-869-5300 ■ *Web:* www.vicorpower.com

Vishay Intertechnology Inc 63 Lancaster Ave .... Malvern PA 19355 610-644-1300 296-0657
NYSE: VSH ■ *TF:* 800-567-6098 ■ *Web:* www.vishay.com

Wakefield Thermal Solutions Inc 33 Bridge St .... Pelham NH 03076 603-635-2800 635-1900
Web: www.wakefield-vette.com

Wellex Corp 551 Brown Rd .... Fremont CA 94539 510-743-1818 743-1899
Web: www.wellex.com

Western Electronics LLC 1550 S Tech Ln .... Meridian ID 83642 208-955-9700 465-9798*
**Fax Area Code:* 303 ■ *Web:* www.westernelectronics.com

Wilmore Electronics Company Inc
607 US 70-A E PO Box 1329 .... Hillsborough NC 27278 919-732-9351 732-9359
Web: www.wilmoreelectronics.com

Wireless Xcessories Group Inc
1840 County Line Rd Ste 301 .... Huntingdon Valley PA 19006 215-322-4600 233-0220*
OTC: WIRX ■ **Fax Area Code:* 888 ■ *TF:* 800-233-0013 ■ *Web:* www.wirexgroup.com

World Electronics Sales & Service Inc
3000 Kutztown Rd .... Reading PA 19605 610-939-9800 939-9895
TF: 800-523-0427 ■ *Web:* www.world-electronics.com

Xantrex Technology Inc 3700 Gilmore Way .... Burnaby BC V5G4M1 604-422-8595 420-1591
TF: 800-670-0707 ■ *Web:* www.xantrex.com

Yazaki North America Inc 6801 N Haggerty Rd .... Canton MI 48187 734-983-1000
Web: www.yazaki-na.com

Z Communications Inc 14118 Stowe Dr Ste B .... Poway CA 92064 858-621-2700 486-1927
TF: 877-808-1226 ■ *Web:* www.zcomm.com

Zentech Manufacturing Inc 6980 Tudsbury Rd .... Baltimore MD 21244 443-348-4500
Web: www.zentech.com/index.php

254 ELECTRONIC ENCLOSURES

Phone | Fax

A & J Mfg Co 14831 Franklin Ave .... Tustin CA 92780 714-544-9570 544-4215
Web: www.aj-racks.com

American Electric Technologies Inc (AETI)
1250 Wood Branch Park Dr Ste 600 .... Houston TX 77079 713-644-8182 838-1066*
NASDAQ: AETI ■ **Fax Area Code:* 409 ■ *Web:* www.aeti.com

APW Ltd PO Box 806 .... Pewaukee WI 53072 262-523-7600 523-7624

Buckeye ShapeForm 555 Marion Rd .... Columbus OH 43207 614-445-8433 445-8224
TF: 800-728-0776 ■ *Web:* www.buckeyeshapeform.com

Bud Industries Inc 4605 E 355th St .... Willoughby OH 44094 440-946-3200 951-4015
Web: www.budind.com

Crenlo LLC 1600 Fourth Ave NW .... Rochester MN 55901 507-289-3371 287-3405*
**Fax:* Sales ■ *Web:* www.crenlo.com

Dawson Metal Company Inc 825 Allen St .... Jamestown NY 14701 716-664-3815 664-3485
Web: www.dawsonmetal.com

Electrol Specialties Co 441 Clark St .... South Beloit IL 61080 815-389-2291 389-2294
Web: www.esc4cip.com

Emcor Enclosures 1600 Fourth Ave NW .... Rochester MN 55901 507-289-3371 287-3405*
**Fax:* Sales ■ *Web:* www.crenlo.com

Equipto Electronics Corp 351 Woodlawn Ave .... Aurora IL 60506 630-897-4691 897-5314
TF: 800-204-7225 ■ *Web:* www.equiptoelec.com

Gerome Mfg Co Inc 80 Laurel View Dr .... Smithfield PA 15478 724-438-8544 437-5608
Web: www.geromemfg.com

Global MetalForm LP 733 Davis St .... Scranton PA 18505 570-346-3871 346-1612
Web: www.markreuther.com/global401web

I-Bus Corp 3350 Scott Blvd Bldg 54 .... Santa Clara CA 95054 408-450-7880 450-7881
Web: www.ibus.com

JMR Electronics Inc 8968 Fullbridht Ave .... Chatsworth CA 91311 818-993-4801 993-9173*
**Fax:* Hum Res ■ *Web:* www.jmr.com

National Mfg Company Inc 12 River Rd .... Chatham NJ 07928 973-635-8846 635-7810
Web: www.natlmfg.com

Omega Tool 308 S Mtn View Ave .... San Bernardino CA 92408 909-888-0440 889-8740
Web: www.omegatool-usa.com

Optima Electronic Packaging Systems
1775 MacLeod Dr .... Lawrenceville GA 30043 770-496-4000 496-4041*
**Fax:* Sales ■ *Web:* optimastantron.com/en/optima-stantron

Pentair Inc 5500 Wayzata Blvd Ste 800 .... Minneapolis MN 55416 763-545-1730 656-5400
NYSE: PNR ■ *Web:* www.pentair.com

Stahlin Non-Metallic Enclosure
505 W Maple St .... Belding MI 48809 616-794-0700 794-3378
Web: www.stahlin.com

TRI MAP International Inc
111 Val Dervin Pkwy .... Stockton CA 95206 209-234-0100 234-5990
TF: 888-687-4627 ■ *Web:* www.trimapintl.com

Universal Enclosure Systems
1146 S Cedar Ridge Dr .... Duncanville TX 75137 972-298-0531 298-0614
Web: www.universalenclosures.com

Zero Manufacturing Inc
500 West 200 North .... North Salt Lake UT 84054 801-298-5900 292-9450
TF: 800-959-5050 ■ *Web:* www.zerocases.com

255 ELECTRONIC TRANSACTION PROCESSING

Phone | Fax

Alliance Data Systems Corp 7500 Dallas Pkwy .... Plano TX 75024 214-494-3000
NYSE: ADS ■ *Web:* www.alliancedata.com

Avid Payment Solutions
950 S Old Woodward Ste 220 .... Birmingham MI 48009 888-855-8644 671-9773*
**Fax Area Code:* 866 ■ *TF:* 888-855-8644 ■ *Web:* www.avidpays.com

Chase Paymentech Solutions LLC
14221 Dallas Pkwy .... Dallas TX 75254 800-708-3740 849-2148*
**Fax Area Code:* 214 ■ *TF Cust Svc:* 800-708-3740 ■ *Web:* www.chasepaymentech.com

Covera Solutions Inc
1021 Watervliet-Shaker Rd PO Box 13539 .... Albany NY 12205 866-526-8372 437-8286*
**Fax Area Code:* 518 ■ *TF:* 866-526-8372 ■ *Web:* www.coverasolutions.com

Elavon 2 Concourse Pkwy Ste 300 .... Atlanta GA 30328 678-731-5000 577-0661*
**Fax Area Code:* 865 ■ *TF:* 800-725-1243 ■ *Web:* www.elavon.com

Euronet Worldwide Inc 3500 College Blvd .... Leawood KS 66211 913-327-4200 327-1921
NASDAQ: EEFT ■ *Web:* www.euronetworldwide.com

Global Payments Inc 10 Glenlake Pkwy N Twr .... Atlanta GA 30328 770-829-8000
NYSE: GPN ■ *TF:* 800-560-2960 ■ *Web:* www.globalpaymentsinc.com

Litle & Co 900 Chelmsford St .... Lowell MA 01851 978-275-6500 937-7250
Web: www.litle.com

National Bankcard Systems
2600 Via Fortuna Ste 240 .... Austin TX 78746 512-494-9200
Web: enbs.com

National Processing Co
5100 Interchange Way .... Louisville KY 40229 800-683-2289
TF General: 877-300-7757 ■ *Web:* www.npc.net

Protegrity USA Inc 5 High Ridge Pk .... Stamford CT 06905 203-326-7200 348-1251
Web: www.protegrity.com

256 ELEVATORS, ESCALATORS, MOVING WALKWAYS

Phone | Fax

2H Offshore Inc
15990 N Barkers Landing Ste 200 .... Houston TX 77079 281-258-2000
Web: www.2hoffshore.com

2is Inc 75 W St .... Walpole MA 02081 508-850-7520
Web: www.2is-inc.com

3 U Technologies 11681 Leonidas Horton Rd .... Conroe TX 77304 936-441-3043
Web: www.3utech.com

4 Front 517 Seventh St .... Rapid City SD 57701 605-342-9470
Web: www.4front.biz

4g Unwired Inc 325 Fifth Ave Ste 100 .... Indialantic FL 32903 321-726-4183
Web: www.4gunwired.com

A-P-T Research Inc 4950 Research Dr NW .... Huntsville AL 35805 256-327-3373
Web: www.apt-research.com

Able Services 868 Folsom St .... San Francisco CA 94107 415-546-6534
TF: 800-461-9577 ■ *Web:* www.ableserve.com

Abna Engineering Inc 4140 Lindell Blvd .... Saint Louis MO 63108 314-454-0222
Web: abnacorp.com

Abonmarche Consultants Inc 361 First St .... Manistee MI 49660 231-723-1198
Web: www.abonmarche.com

ABOUT-Consulting LLC
330 Kennett Pike Ste 205 .... Chadds Ford PA 19317 610-388-9455
Web: www.about-consulting.com

Abx Engineering 880 Hinckley Rd .... Burlingame CA 94010 650-552-2322
TF: 800-366-4588 ■ *Web:* www.abxengineering.com

Accent Controls Inc 400 NW Platte Vly Dr .... Riverside MO 64150 816-483-6330
Web: www.accentcontrols.com

Accipiter Radar Technologies Inc
576 Hwy 20 W .... Fonthill ON L0S1C0 905-228-6888
Web: www.accipiterradar.com

Accutemp Engineering Inc 108 School St .... Watertown MA 02472 617-926-1221
Web: www.accutemp-eng.com

ACES Systems 10737 Lexington Dr .... Knoxville TN 37932 865-671-2003
Web: www.acessystems.com

Ackerman-practicon Inc 801 E Charleston Rd .... Palo Alto CA 94303 650-965-1000
Web: www.apcts.com

Acme Worldwide Enterprises Inc
1710 Randolph Ct SE .... Albuquerque NM 87106 505-243-0400
Web: www.acme-worldwide.com

Acoustics by Design Inc
124 Fulton St E Ste 200 .... Grand Rapids MI 49503 616-241-5810
Web: www.acousticsbydesign.com

Action Facilities Management Inc
115 Malone Dr .... Morgantown WV 26501 304-599-6850
Web: www.actionfacilities.com

Adams Communication & Engineering Technology Inc
11637 Terr Dr Ste 201 .... Waldorf MD 20602 301-861-5000
Web: www.adamscomm.com

Adaptive Flight Inc 885 Franklin Rd Ste 330 .... Marietta GA 30067 770-951-8755
Web: www.adaptiveflight.com

ADF Engineering Inc 228 Byers Rd Ste 202 .... Miamisburg OH 45342 937-847-2700
Web: www.adfengineering.com

Phone | Fax

Advanced Dynamics Corp Ltd
1700 Marie Victorin ... Saint-Bruno QC J3V6B9 450-653-7220
Web: www.advanceddynamics.com

Advanced Rotorcraft Technology Inc
1330 Charleston Rd ... Mountain View CA 94043 650-968-1464
Web: www.flightlab.com

Advanced Testing Technologies Inc
110 Ricefield Ln ... Hauppauge NY 11788 631-231-8777

Advantage Engineering LLC
910 Century Dr ... Mechanicsburg PA 17055 717-458-0800
Web: www.cmxengineering.com

Advantage Plastics & Engineering Inc
4524 Bishop Ln ... Louisville KY 40218 502-473-7331
Web: www.advantageplastics.net

AE Works Ltd 6587 Hamilton Ave ... Pittsburgh PA 15206 412-287-7333
Web: www.ae-works.com

AEC Engineering Inc 330 S 2nd Ave Ste 600 ... Minneapolis MN 55401 612-332-8905
Web: www.aecengineering.com

Aegir Systems 2151 Alessandro Dr Ste 211 ... Ventura CA 93001 805-648-2660
Web: www.aegir.com

Aegis Labs Inc 515 Great Cir Rd ... Nashville TN 37228 949-751-8089
Web: www.aegislabsinc.com

Aerocon Engineering Co 7716 Kester Ave ... Van Nuys CA 91405 818-785-2743
Web: www.aeroconengineering.com

Aerospec Inc 505 E Alamo Dr ... Chandler AZ 85225 480-892-7195
TF: 888-854-2376 ■ *Web:* www.aerospecinc.com

Afram Corp 1601 Olive St ... Saint Louis MO 63103 314-645-6299
Web: www.aframcorp.com

AGRA Foundations Ltd 7708 Wagner Rd ... Edmonton AB T6E5B2 780-468-3392
Web: www.agra.com

Air Liquide Group 2700 Post Oak Blvd ... Houston TX 77056 713-624-8000
Web: industry.airliquide.us

Alabama Goodwill Industries Inc
2350 Green Springs Hwy S ... Birmingham AL 35205 205-323-6331

Alabama Graphics & Engineering Supply Inc
2801 Fifth Ave S ... Birmingham AL 35233 205-252-8505
TF: 800-292-3806 ■ *Web:* www.algraphics.com

Albert A Webb Assoc 3788 Mccray St ... Riverside CA 92506 951-686-1070
Web: www.webbassociates.com

All Star Team Service LLC
2 Industrial Park Dr Ste B ... Waldorf MD 20602 240-607-6209

All-Points Technology Corp PC
3 Saddlebrook Dr ... Killingworth CT 06419 860-663-1697
Web: www.allpointstech.com

Allana Buick & Bers Inc 990 Commercial St ... Palo Alto CA 94303 650-543-5600
TF: 800-378-3405 ■ *Web:* www.abbae.com

Allied Corrosion Industries Inc
1550 Cobb Industrial Dr ... Marietta GA 30066 770-425-1355
TF: 800-241-0809 ■ *Web:* www.alliedcorrosion.com

Allied Resources Corp 106 Pitkin St ... East Hartford CT 06108 860-290-6665
Web: www.alliedr.com

Alloy Hardfacing & Engineering Company Inc
20425 Johnson Memorial Dr ... Jordan MN 55352 952-492-5569
Web: alloyhardfacing.com

Ally Plm Solutions Inc 9155 Governors Way ... Cincinnati OH 45249 513-984-0480
TF: 800-631-5961 ■ *Web:* www.allyplm.com

Alpha Consulting Engineers Inc
115 Limekiln Rd ... New Cumberland PA 17070 717-770-2500
Web: alphacei.com

Alpha Testing Inc 2209 Wisconsin St Ste 100 ... Dallas TX 75229 972-620-8911 620-1302
Web: alphatesting.com

Alphion Corp
196 Princeton Hightstown Rd Bldg 1A
... Princeton Junction NJ 08550 609-936-9001
Web: www.alphion.com

Alpine Building Maintenance Inc
3006 W Division St ... Arlington TX 76012 817-795-6470
Web: www.bksassociates.com

ALSTOM Power Inc 175 Addison Rd ... Windsor CT 06095 860-688-1911
Web: www.alstom.com

Alt & Witzig Engineering Inc 4105 W 99th St ... Carmel IN 46032 317-875-7000
Web: www.ascet.org

Alum-A-Lift Inc 7909 US Hwy 78 ... Winston GA 30187 770-489-0328
Web: www.alum-a-lift.com

Alvine Engineering Inc
1102 Douglas On The Mall ... Omaha NE 68102 402-346-7007
Web: www.alvine.com

American Aerospace Advisors Inc
1007 Ford St ... Bridgeport PA 19405 610-225-2604 225-3781
Web: americanaerospace.com

American Aerospace Controls Inc
570 Smith St ... Farmingdale NY 11735 631-694-5100
TF: 888-873-8559 ■ *Web:* www.a-a-c.com

American Combustion Industries Inc
7100 Holladay Tyler Rd Ste 233 ... Glenn Dale MD 20769 301-779-3400
Web: www.aci.com

American SensoRx Inc 31 N Monroe St ... Ridgewood NJ 07410 201-447-8999
Web: www.americansensorx.com

AMT Machine Systems Ltd 868 Fwy Dr N ... Columbus OH 43229 614-635-8050
TF: 866-204-0660 ■ *Web:* www.amtmachinesystems.com

Ana Properties 3630 N Josey Ln Ste 217 ... Carrollton TX 75007 972-939-0610

Analytical Design Service Corp
540 Avis Dr Ste E ... Ann Arbor MI 48108 734-761-2626
Web: www.adsc-usa.com

Anderson Cleaning 144 Garing Rd ... Chicora PA 16025 724-445-2849

Anderson Economic Group LLC
1555 Watertower Pl Ste 100 ... East Lansing MI 48823 517-333-6984
Web: aeg1.com

Anderson Pacific Engineering Construction Inc
1390 Norman Ave ... Santa Clara CA 95054 408-970-9900
Web: www.andpac.com

Anderson Perry & Assoc Inc 1901 N Fir St ... La Grande OR 97850 541-963-8309
Web: www.andersonperry.com

Phone | Fax

Andrews Hammock Powell Inc 250 Charter Ln ... Macon GA 31210 478-405-8301
Web: www.ahpengr.com

Antioch International Inc
410 Winding View ... New Braunfels TX 78132 402-289-2217
Web: www.antioch-intl.com

Apex Geoscience Inc 2120 Brandon Dr ... Tyler TX 75703 903-581-8080 581-8081
TF: 800-755-8461 ■ *Web:* www.apexgeo.com

Apogee Consulting Group PA
1151 Kildaire Farm Rd Ste 120 ... Cary NC 27511 919-858-7420
Web: www.acg-pa.com

Applied Mfg Technologies Inc
219 Kay Industrial Dr ... Orion MI 48359 248-409-2000
Web: www.robotprogrammers.com

Applied Physics Systems Inc 281 E Java Dr ... Sunnyvale CA 94089 650-965-0500
Web: www.appliedphysics.com

Applied Systems Engineering Inc
1480 Hickory St Ste 106 ... Niceville FL 32578 850-729-7550
Web: aseifl.com

AQUA TERRA Consultants Inc
2685 Marine Way Ste 1314 ... Mountain View CA 94043 650-962-1864
Web: www.aquaterra.com

Aquaveo LLC 3210 N Canyon Rd Ste 300 ... Provo UT 84604 801-691-5528
Web: www.aquaveo.com

Arcca Inc 2288 Second St Pk ... Penns Park PA 18943 215-598-9750
Web: www.arcca.com

Archibald Gray & McKay Ltd 553 Southdale Rd E ... London ON N6E1A2 519-685-5300
Web: www.agm.on.ca

Architectural Engineering Consultants Inc
40801 Hwy 6 24 Ste 214 ... Avon CO 81620 970-748-8520
Web: www.aec-vail.com

ARDL Inc 400 Aviation Dr ... Mount Vernon IL 62864 618-244-3235
Web: www.ardlinc.com

Areias Systems Inc
5900 Butler Ln Ste 280 ... Scotts Valley CA 95066 831-440-9800
Web: www.areiasys.com

Arizon Structures 11880 Dorsett Rd ... St. Louis MO 63043 314-739-0037
Web: www.arizoncompanies.com

Arkansas Power Electronics International Inc
535 W Research Ctr Blvd Ste 209 ... Fayetteville AR 72701 479-443-5759
Web: apei.net

Armstrong Consultants Inc
861 Rood Ave ... Grand Junction CO 81501 970-242-0101
Web: www.armstrongconsultants.com

Arnold & Assoc 14275 Midway Rd Ste 170 ... Addison TX 75001 972-991-1144
TF: 800-535-6329 ■ *Web:* www.elarnoldandassociates.com

Arnold Engineering Inc 345 Cessna Cir Ste 102 ... Corona CA 92880 951-898-0999
Web: www.arnoldeng.com

Arora & Assoc PC
1200 Lenox Dr Ste 200 ... Lawrence Township NJ 08648 609-844-1111
Web: www.arorapc.com

Arrayent Inc 2317 Broadway St ... Redwood City CA 94063 650-260-4520
Web: www.arrayent.com

Art Anderson Assoc Inc 202 Pacific Ave ... Bremerton WA 98337 360-479-5600
Web: www.artanderson.com

Artisan Industries Inc 73 Pond St ... Waltham MA 02451 781-893-6800
Web: www.artisanind.com

Arup North America Ltd
560 Mission St Ste 700 ... San Francisco CA 94105 415-957-9445
Web: www.arup.com

Ascendant Engineering Solutions
12303 Technology Blvd Ste 925 ... Austin TX 78727 512-371-5704
Web: aesaustin.com

Associated Engineering Group Ltd
9888 Jasper Ave Ste 500 ... Edmonton AB T5J5C6 780-451-7666 454-7698
Web: www.ae.ca

Astrodyne Corp 375 Forbes Blvd ... Mansfield MA 02048 508-964-6300
TF: 800-823-8082 ■ *Web:* www.astrodynetdi.com

Athavale Lystad & Assoc Inc
6720-B Rockledge Dr Ste 160 ... Bethesda MD 20817 301-816-3237
Web: www.alaengr.com

Atlantic Inertial Systems Inc
250 Knotter Dr ... Cheshire CT 06410 203-250-3676
Web: www.atlanticinertial.com

Aucoin & Assoc Inc 433 N C C Duson St ... Eunice LA 70535 337-457-7366

Audient Inc 20532 Crescent Bay Dr ... Lake Forest CA 92630 949-830-9412

Auto Comm Engineering Corp 109 Evergreen Dr ... Houma LA 70364 985-876-1855
Web: auto-comm.com

Availink Inc 20201 Century Blvd Ste 160 ... Germantown MD 20874 301-515-6716
Web: www.availink.com

Avatar Engineering Inc 14360 W 96th Ter ... Lenexa KS 66215 913-897-6757
Web: avatar-eng.com

Aviles Engineering Corp 5790 Windfern Rd ... Houston TX 77041 713-895-7645 895-7943
Web: www.avilesengineering.com

Avt Simulation Inc
2603 Challenger Tech Ct Ste 180 ... Orlando FL 32826 407-381-5311
Web: www.avtsim.com

Axens North America Inc
650 College Rd E Ste 1200 ... Princeton NJ 08540 609-243-8700
Web: www.axens.net

Aztec Communications Ltd 6830 Barney Rd ... Houston TX 77092 713-462-6707
Web: www.azteccom.com

Aztec Facility Services Inc
11000 S Wilcrest Dr Ste 125 ... Houston TX 77099 281-668-9000
Web: www.aztec1.com

Azure Green Consultants LLC 409 E Pioneer ... Puyallup WA 98372 253-770-3144
Web: www.azuregreenconsultants.com

B & W Fluid Dynamics Inc 901 Seaco Ave ... Deer Park TX 77536 281-534-9300

B G m Engineering Inc
14100 Simone Dr ... Shelby Township MI 48315 586-532-8670
Web: bgmengineering.net

B M Ross & Assoc Ltd 62 N St ... Goderich ON N7A2T4 519-524-2641
TF: 888-524-2641 ■ *Web:* www.bmross.net

Company	City	State	Zip	Phone	Fax
Babcock Power Services Inc 6 Kimball Ln Ste 210 *Web:* babcockpower.com	Lynnfield	MA	01940	508-852-7100	
Baird Hampton & Brown Inc 6300 Ridglea Pl Ste 700 *Web:* www.bhbinc.com	Fort Worth	TX	76116	817-338-1277	338-9245
Baisch Engineering Inc 809 Hyland Ave *Web:* www.baisch.com	Kaukauna	WI	54130	920-766-3521	
Bala Consulting Engineers Inc 443 S Gulph Rd *Web:* www.bala.com	King Of Prussia	PA	19406	610-649-8000	
Bancography Inc 2301 First Ave N Ste 103 *Web:* www.bancography.com	Birmingham	AL	35203	205-251-3227	
Barge Cauthen & Assoc Inc 6606 Charlotte Pk Ste 210 *Web:* bargecauthen.com	Nashville	TN	37209	615-356-9911	
Barnett Contracting Inc 7703 Bagby Ave *Web:* www.barnettcontracting.com	Waco	TX	76712	254-666-7117	666-7119
Barnett Tool & Engineering 2238 Palma Dr *Web:* www.barnettclutches.com	Ventura	CA	93003	805-642-9435	
Bartlett Holdings Inc 60 Industrial Park Rd *Web:* www.excelscaffold.com	Plymouth	MA	02360	508-746-6464	
Basin Holdings US LLC The Chrysler Bldg 405 Lexington Ave 71st Fl *Web:* www.basinholdings.com	New York	NY	10174	212-695-7376	
Bastion Technologies Inc 17625 El Camino Real Ste 330 *Web:* www.bastiontechnologies.com	Houston	TX	77058	281-283-9330	283-9333
Bat Assoc Inc 5151 Brook Hollow Pkwy Ste 250 *Web:* www.batassociates.com	Norcross	GA	30071	770-242-3908	
Bayside Engineering Inc 110 N 11th St Ste 100 *Web:* www.baysideng.com	Tampa	FL	33602	813-314-0314	
BBC Engineering Inc 8650 Business Park Dr *Web:* forteandtablada.com/company_history_bbce.asp	Shreveport	LA	71105	318-798-3344	
BCER Engineering Inc 5420 Ward Rd Ste 200 *Web:* www.bcer.com	Arvada	CO	80002	303-422-7400	
BDS Engineering Inc 6859 Federal Blvd *Web:* www.bdsengineering.com	Lemon Grove	CA	91945	619-582-4992	
Beardsley Design Assoc Architecture Engineering & Landscape Architecture PC 64 S St *Web:* www.beardsley.com	Auburn	NY	13021	315-253-7301	
BEARSCH COMPEAU KNUDSON Architects & Engineers PC 41 Chenango St *Web:* www.bckpc.com	Binghamton	NY	13901	607-772-0007	
Becht Engineering Company Inc 22 Church St PO Box 300 *Web:* www.becht.com	Liberty Corner	NJ	07938	908-580-1119	
Behnke Erdman & Whitaker Engineering Inc 2303 Camino Ramon Ste 220 *Web:* www.bewengineering.com	San Ramon	CA	94583	925-867-3330	
Benesyst Inc 800 Washington Ave N 8th Fl *TF:* 866-786-3366 ■ *Web:* www.benesyst.net	Minneapolis	MN	55401	800-422-4661	
Benton & Assoc Inc 1970 W Lafayette Ave *Web:* www.bentonassociates.com	Jacksonville	IL	62650	217-245-4146	
Best Maids 842 Lemay Ferry Rd	Saint Louis	MO	63125	314-544-6180	
BHE Environmental Inc 11733 Chesterdale Rd *Web:* www.powereng.com	Cincinnati	OH	45246	513-326-1500	326-1550
Big Enterprises Inc 105 Paul Mellon Ct Ste 15	Waldorf	MD	20602	301-843-7030	
Big Sky Engineering Inc 429 Venture Ct *Web:* www.bigskyeng.com	Verona	WI	53593	608-848-9898	
Bihrle Applied Research Inc 81 Research Dr *Web:* www.bihrle.com	Hampton	VA	23666	757-766-2416	
Binkley & Barfield Inc 1710 Seamist Dr *Web:* www.binkleybarfield.com	Houston	TX	77008	713-869-3433	
Biokinetics & Assoc Ltd 2470 Don Reid Dr *Web:* www.biokinetics.com	Ottawa	ON	K1H1E1	613-736-0384	
BioMimetic Systems Inc 810 Memorial Dr Ste 106 *Web:* www.biomimetic-systems.com	Cambridge	MA	02139	617-758-2505	
BL Harbert International LLC 820 Shades Creek Pkwy Ste 3000 *Web:* www.bharbert.com	Birmingham	AL	35209	404-841-4000	
Bleyl & Assoc 1715 S Capital Of Texas Hwy Ste 109 *Web:* bleylengineering.com	Austin	TX	78746	512-328-7878	328-7884
Blue Line Engineering Co 525 E Colorado Ave *Web:* www.bluelineengineering.com	Colorado Springs	CO	80903	719-447-1373	
Bluestone Engineering Inc 1990 N California Blvd Ste 830 *Web:* www.bergersongroup.com	Walnut Creek	CA	94596	925-932-7053	
Bms Communications Inc 4133 Guardian St	Simi Valley	CA	93063	805-526-1141	
Bocook Engineering Inc 312 10th St *Web:* bocook.com	Paintsville	KY	41240	606-789-5961	
Bohler Engineering PC 35 Technology Dr *Web:* www.atlantictraffic.com	Warren	NJ	07059	908-668-8300	
Bond Tool & Engineering 6190 N Riverview Dr *Web:* www.bondtool.com	Kalamazoo	MI	49004	269-344-5164	
Boomerang Management Enterprises LLC 1935 Samco Rd Ste 104 *Web:* boomerangme.com	Rapid City	SD	57702	605-718-2666	
Borghesi Building & Engineering Company Inc 2155 E Main St *Web:* www.borghesibuilding.com	Torrington	CT	06790	860-482-7613	
Bouthillette Parizeau 9825 Verville St *Web:* www.bpa.ca	Montreal	QC	H3L3E1	514-383-3747	383-8760
Bowne AE & T Group 235 E Jericho Tpke *Web:* www.bownegroup.com	Mineola	NY	11501	516-746-2350	
Boyle Energy Services & Technology Inc 28 Locke Rd *TF:* 800-428-8872 ■ *Web:* www.boyleenergy.com	Concord	NH	03301	603-227-5200	
Bragg's Electric Construction Company Inc 3000 Cantrell Rd *Web:* cdicon.com	Little Rock	AR	72202	501-666-6166	
Brandon Assocs Ltd 26 Sarah Dr *Web:* www.brandonassociates.com	Farmingdale	NY	11735	631-293-1414	
Breen Energy Solutions LLC 104 Broadway St *Web:* www.breenes.com	Carnegie	PA	15106	412-431-4499	
BRIC Engineered Systems Ltd 1101 Wentworth St W Ste D1 *TF:* 800-937-5135 ■ *Web:* www.briceng.com	Oshawa	ON	L1J8P7	905-436-8867	
Bridgers & Paxton Consulting Engineers Inc 4600-C Montgomery Blvd Ne *Web:* www.bpce.com	Albuquerque	NM	87109	505-883-4111	
Brittain Engineering 56 Third St NW *Web:* www.brittainengineering.com	Hickory	NC	28601	828-328-1813	
Brooks Borg Skiles Architecture Engineering 317 Sixth Ave Ste 400 *Web:* www.bbsae.com	Des Moines	IA	50309	515-244-7167	
Brooks Harbour & Assoc Inc 9342 Lindale Ave *Web:* www.arthursrestaurant.com	Baton Rouge	LA	70815	225-927-7430	
Brooks-ransom Assoc 7415 N Palm Ave Ste 100 *Web:* www.brooksransom.com	Fresno	CA	93711	559-449-8444	
Building Earth Sciences Inc 5545 Derby Dr *Web:* www.buildingandearth.com	Irondale	AL	35210	205-836-6300	
Burlington Engineering Inc 220 W Grove Ave *Web:* www.burlingtoneng.com	Orange	CA	92865	714-921-4045	
Burns Cooley Dennis Inc 551 Sunnybrook Rd *Web:* www.bcdgeo.com	Ridgeland	MS	39157	601-856-9911	
Burns Engineering Inc 10201 Bren Rd E *TF:* 800-328-3871 ■ *Web:* www.burnsengineering.com	Minnetonka	MN	55343	952-935-4400	
Burrell Consultng Group Inc 1001 Enterprise Way Ste 100 *Web:* www.burrellcg.com	Roseville	CA	95678	916-783-8898	
Butier Engineering Inc 17782 17th St Ste 107 *Web:* www.butier.com	Tustin	CA	92780	714-832-7222	
C & b Consulting Engineers 449 10th St *Web:* www.cbengineers.com	San Francisco	CA	94103	415-437-7330	
C & C Technologies Inc 730 E Kaliste Saloom Rd *Web:* www.cctechnol.com	Lafayette	LA	70508	337-210-0000	
C C Tatham & Assoc Ltd 115 Sandford Fleming Dr Ste 200 *Web:* www.cctatham.com	Collingwood	ON	L9Y5A6	705-444-2565	
Caen Engineering Inc 675 N Eckhoff St Ste G *Web:* www.caeneng.com	Orange	CA	92868	714-456-0800	
Caldera Engineering 695 South 320 West *Web:* www.calderaengineering.com	Provo	UT	84601	801-356-2862	
Cam Services Inc 5664 Selmaraine Dr *TF:* 800-576-3050 ■ *Web:* www.camservices.com	Culver City	CA	90230	310-390-3552	
Cameron Engineering & Assoc LLP 100 Sunnyside Blvd Ste 100 *Web:* www.cameronengineering.com	Woodbury	NY	11797	516-827-4900	
Campos Engineering Inc 7430 Greenville Ave *Web:* www.camposengineering.com	Dallas	TX	75231	214-696-6291	
Canard Aerospace Corp 250 Fuller St S Ste 201 *Web:* www.canardaero.com	Shakopee	MN	55379	952-944-7990	
Cannon Building Svc Inc 1640 Sierra Madre Cir *Web:* www.cannonbuilding.com	Placentia	CA	92870	714-630-9570	
Cape Design Engineering Co 191 Center St Ste 201 *Web:* www.cdeco.com	Cape Canaveral	FL	32920	321-799-2970	
Capital Engineering LLC 6933 Indianpolis Blvd *Web:* www.capital-eng.com	Hammond	IN	46324	219-844-1984	
Cardinal Building Maintenance 4952 W 128th Pl	Alsip	IL	60803	708-385-3575	
Carillion Canada Inc 7077 Keele St *Web:* www.carillion.ca	Concord	ON	L4K0B6	905-532-5200	
Carlile Macy Inc 15 Third St *Web:* www.carlilemacy.com	Santa Rosa	CA	95401	707-542-6451	
Carlson Group Inc 34 Executive Pk *Web:* www.carlson-dc.com	Irvine	CA	92614	949-251-0455	
Carnahan Proctor & Cross Inc 604 Courtland St Ste 101 *Web:* www.carnahan-proctor.com	Orlando	FL	32804	954-972-3959	
Carr Engineering Inc 12500 Castlebridge Dr *Web:* carrengineeringinc.com	Houston	TX	77065	281-894-8955	
Carroll & Blackman Inc 3120 Fannin St *Web:* www.cbieng.com	Beaumont	TX	77701	409-833-3363	833-0317
Carsan Engineering Inc 221 Corporate Cir Ste H	Golden	CO	80401	303-237-9608	
Caruso Turley Scott Inc 1215 W Rio Salado Pkwy Ste 200 *Web:* www.ctsaz.com	Tempe	AZ	85281	480-774-1700	
Cary Kopczynski & Company Inc PS Bellevue Pl 10500 Eighth St Ste 800 *Web:* www.ckcps.com	Bellevue	WA	98004	425-455-2144	
Cascadian Building Maintenance Ltd 7415 129th Ave SE *Web:* www.cascadian.org	Newcastle	WA	98056	425-264-0474	
Casne Engineering Inc 10604 NE 38th Pl Ste 205 *Web:* www.casne.com	Kirkland	WA	98033	425-522-1000	
Castle Breckenridge Management 5185 Comanche Dr Ste D *Web:* www.cbmgmt.com	La Mesa	CA	91942	619-697-3191	
Cator Ruma & Assoc Co 896 Tabor St *Web:* catorruma.com	Lakewood	CO	80401	303-232-6200	
CB Engineering Pacific Inc 909 Seventh Ave Ste 201 *Web:* www.cb-pacific.com	Kirkland	WA	98033	425-822-1702	
CBCL Ltd 1489 Hollis St *Web:* www.cbcl.ca	Halifax	NS	B3J2R7	902-421-7241	

	City	State	Zip	Phone	Fax
Cemcon Ltd 2280 White Oak Cir Ste 100 *Web:* www.cemcon.com	Aurora	IL	60502	630-862-2100	
CF Roark Welding & Engineering Company Inc 136 N Green St *Web:* www.roarkfab.com	Brownsburg	IN	46112	317-852-3163	
CFW Associated Engineers Inc 9200 Leesgate Rd Ste 200 *Web:* cfwengineers.com	Louisville	KY	40222	502-423-0805	
CGA Engineers Inc 8179 E 41st St *Web:* cgaengineers.com	Tulsa	OK	74145	918-749-5800	
CH Perez & Assoc Consulting Engineers in 9594 NW 41st St Ste 201 *Web:* p-a.cc	Doral	FL	33178	305-592-1070	
Chemi-Source Inc 2665 Vista Pacific Dr *Web:* www.mrm-usa.com	Oceanside	CA	92056	760-477-8177	
Chester Engineers Inc 1555 Coraopolis Heights Rd *Web:* www.chester-engineers.com	Moon Township	PA	15108	412-809-6600	
Chi Engineering Services Inc 430 W Rd *Web:* www.chiengineering.com	Portsmouth	NH	03801	603-433-5654	
Chisholm Fleming & Assoc 317 Renfrew Dr Ste 301 *TF:* 888-241-4149 ■ *Web:* www.chisholmfleming.com	Markham	ON	L3R9S8	905-474-1458	
Choice One Engineering Corp 440 E Hoewisher Rd *Web:* choiceoneengineering.com	Sidney	OH	45365	937-497-0200	
City of Clarksville 199 10th St *TF:* 800-342-1003 ■ *Web:* www.cityofclarksville.com	Clarksville	TN	37040	931-645-7464	
City of Vacaville Inc, The 650 Merchant St *Web:* www.ci.vacaville.ca.us	Vacaville	CA	95688	707-449-5100	
Clarion Technologies Inc 170 College Ave Ste 300 *Web:* www.clariontechnologies.com	Holland	MI	49423	616-698-7277	
Clarity Innovations Inc 1001 SE Water Ave Ste 400 *TF:* 877-683-3187 ■ *Web:* www.clarity-innovations.com	Portland	OR	97214	503-248-4300	
Clark Contractors Inc 19651 Descartes *Web:* www.clarkcontractors.com	Foothill Ranch	CA	92610	949-581-6577	
Clark Dietz Inc 125 W Church St *Web:* www.clark-dietz.com	Champaign	IL	61820	217-373-8900	
Clark Patterson Engineers Surveyor & Architects PC 205 St Paul St Ste 500 *Web:* www.clarkpattersonlee.com	Rochester	NY	14604	585-454-4570	
Clean Ones Corp PO Box 40008 *TF:* 800-367-4587 ■ *Web:* www.cleanones.com	Portland	OR	97204	503-224-5211	
Clear Align LLC 2550 Blvd Of The Generals Ste 280 *Web:* www.clearalign.com	Eagleville	PA	19403	484-956-0510	
Clearview Cleaning Service 1804 Windermere Ave	Wilmington	DE	19804	302-994-5215	
Clifton Assoc Ltd 340 Maxwell Cres *Web:* www.clifton.ca	Regina	SK	S4N5Y5	306-721-7611	
Clouse Engineering Inc 1642 E Orangewood Ave *Web:* clouseaz.com	Phoenix	AZ	85020	602-395-9300	
Cme Assoc Inc 32 Crabtree Ln *TF:* 888-291-3227 ■ *Web:* www.cmeengineering.com	Woodstock	CT	06281	860-928-7848	
CNC Engineering Inc 19 Bacon Rd *Web:* www.cnc1.com	Enfield	CT	06082	860-749-1780	
Coastal Planning & Engineering Inc 2481 NW Boca Raton Blvd *Web:* cbi.com/markets/infrastructure/maritime	Boca Raton	FL	33431	561-391-8102	
Cobb Architects LLC 67 Washtington St *Web:* www.cobbarchitecture.com	Charleston	SC	29403	843-856-7333	
Cobb Fendley & Assoc Inc 13430 Northwest Fwy Ste 1100 *Web:* www.cobfen.com	Houston	TX	77040	713-462-3242	462-3262
Cobra Engineering Inc 23801 La Palma Ave *Web:* www.cobrausa.com	Yorba Linda	CA	92887	714-692-8180	692-5019
Colorado Energy Management LLC 2575 Park Ln Ste 200 *Web:* www.coloradoenergy.com	Lafayette	CO	80026	303-442-5112	
Columbia Energy & Environmental Services Inc 1806 Terminal Dr *Web:* columbia-energy.com	Richland	WA	99354	509-946-7111	
Columbia Northwest Engineering 249 N Elder St *Web:* www.cnweng.com	Moses Lake	WA	98837	509-766-1226	
Colwill Engineering Mep & Fp 4750 E Adamo Dr *Web:* www.colwillengineering.com	Tampa	FL	33605	813-241-2525	
Comfort - Air Engineering Inc 11403 Jones Maltsberger Rd *Web:* www.comfort-air.com	San Antonio	TX	78216	210-494-1691	
Command Post Technologies Inc 1039 Champions Way *Web:* commandposttech.com	Suffolk	VA	23435	757-338-3039	
Common Sense Advisory Inc 100 Merrimack St *Web:* commonsenseadvisory.com	Lowell	MA	01852	978-275-0500	
Compton Engineering 156 Nixon St *Web:* www.comptonengineering.com	Biloxi	MS	39530	228-432-2133	
Computer Age Engineering Inc 867 E 38th St *Web:* www.caeweb.com	Marion	IN	46953	765-674-8551	
Concord Engineering Group 520 S Burnt Mill Rd *Web:* www.concord-engineering.com	Voorhees	NJ	08043	856-427-0200	
Consolidated Engineering Company Inc 1971 Mccollum Pkwy NW *Web:* www.cec-intl.com	Kennesaw	GA	30144	770-422-5100	
Continental Glass Systems Inc 325 W 74th Pl *Web:* www.cgsfl.com	Hialeah	FL	33014	305-231-1101	
Controlled Contamination Services LLC 4182 Sorrento Valley Blvd *TF:* 888-263-9886 ■ *Web:* www.cleanroomcleaning.com	San Diego	CA	92121	858-457-7598	
Conveyor Dynamics Inc 1111 W Holly St Ste A *Web:* www.conveyor-dynamics.com	Bellingham	WA	98225	360-671-2200	
Conway & Owen Inc 1455 Bluegrass Lakes Pkwy *Web:* www.conway-owen.com	Alpharetta	GA	30004	678-350-9000	
Cornerstone Commissioning Inc 11 Cold Spring Dr *Web:* www.cornerstonecx.com	Boxford	MA	01921	978-887-8177	
Corporate Image Maintenance 2116 S Wright St	Santa Ana	CA	92705	714-966-5325	
Corradino Group 200 s Fifth st *TF:* 800-880-8241 ■ *Web:* www.corradino.com	Louisville	KY	40202	502-587-7221	587-2636
Corrpro Canada Inc 10848 - 214 St *TF:* 800-661-8390 ■ *Web:* www.corrpro.ca	Edmonton	AB	T5S2A7	780-447-4565	
Corzo Castella Carballo Thompson Salman PA 901 Ponce De Leon Blvd Ste 900 *Web:* www.c3ts.com	Coral Gables	FL	33134	305-445-2900	
Cosentini Assoc Inc 2 Pennsylvania Plz 3rd Fl *Web:* www.cosentini.com	New York	NY	10121	212-615-3600	
County Engineers Assn of Ohio 6500 Busch Blvd Ste 100 *Web:* www.ceao.org	Columbus	OH	43229	614-221-0707	
Creative Engineering LLC 38 Milburn St *Web:* www.creativeengineering.com	Bronxville	NY	10708	914-771-5540	
Creative Engineers Inc 361 N E St *Web:* www.creativeengineers.com	York	PA	17403	443-807-1202	
CRL Technologies Inc 5247 Brawner Pl *Web:* www.crltechnologies.com	Alexandria	VA	22304	703-297-9900	
CRW Assoc 16980 Via Tazon Ste 320	San Diego	CA	92127	858-451-3030	
Crw Engineering Group LLC 3940 Arctic Blvd Ste 300 *Web:* www.crweng.com	Anchorage	AK	99503	907-562-3252	
Csw Stuber Stroeh Engineering Group Inc 1310 Redwood Way Ste 220	Petaluma	CA	94954	707-795-4764	
CTI & Assoc Inc 51331 W Pontiac Trl *Web:* cticompanies.com	Wixom	MI	48393	248-486-5100	
CTI Consultants Inc 13500 E Boundary Rd *Web:* www.cti-consultants.com	Midlothian	VA	23112	804-622-8630	
D & R International Ltd 1100 Wayne Ave Ste 700 *Web:* www.drintl.com	Silver Spring	MD	20910	301-588-9387	
Dacallc 2255 Button Gwinnett Dr *Web:* dacapainting.com	Atlanta	GA	30340	770-451-6433	
Dade Moeller & Assoc Inc 1835 Terminal Dr Ste 200 *Web:* www.dademoeller.com	Richland	WA	99354	509-946-0410	
Daimler Vans Mfg LLC 8501 Palmetto Commerce Pkwy *Web:* daimler.com	Ladson	SC	29456	843-695-5000	
Dalager Engineering Co 936 Railroad Ave	Bath	SD	57427	605-229-2412	
Danlaw Inc 41131 Vincenti Ct *Web:* www.danlawinc.com	Novi	MI	48375	248-476-5571	
Dare Enterprices Inc 700 River Ave Ste 215 *Web:* www.dareent.com	Pittsburgh	PA	15212	412-231-6100	
Dare Mighty Things Inc 1000 Market St Ste 102 *Web:* www.daremightythings.com	Portsmouth	NH	03801	603-431-4331	
Data Fusion Corp 10190 Bannock St *Web:* www.datafusion.com	Northglenn	CO	80260	720-872-2145	
Data Science Automation Inc 375 Valleybrook Rd Ste 106 *Web:* www.dsautomation.com	Mc Murray	PA	15317	724-942-6330	
David Mason & Assoc 800 S Vandeventer Ave *Web:* www.davidmason.com	Saint Louis	MO	63110	314-534-1030	
Day Automation Systems Inc 7931 Rae Blvd *Web:* dayautomation.com	Victor	NY	14564	585-924-4630	
Daylor Consulting Group Inc 10 Forbes Rd *Web:* www.daylor.com	Braintree	MA	02184	781-849-7070	
DBA Engineering Ltd 401 Hanlan Rd *TF:* 800-819-8833 ■ *Web:* www.dbaeng.com	Vaughan	ON	L4L3T1	905-851-0090	
Decimal Engineering Inc 2640 N Powerline Rd *Web:* www.decimal.net	Pompano Beach	FL	33069	954-975-7992	975-7994
Degree Controls Inc 18 Meadowbrook Dr *TF:* 877-334-7332 ■ *Web:* www.degreec.com	Milford	NH	03055	603-672-8900	
Delco Automation Inc 3735 Thatcher Ave *Web:* delcoautomation.com	Saskatoon	SK	S7R1B8	306-244-6449	665-7500
Delphi Engineering Group Inc 485 E 17th St Ste 400 *Web:* www.delphieng.com	Costa Mesa	CA	92627	949-515-1490	
Delta Engineers & Architects PC 184 Court St *Web:* www.deltaengineers.com	Binghamton	NY	13901	607-231-6600	
Denham-Blythe Company Inc 100 Trade St *Web:* www.denhamblythe.com	Lexington	KY	40511	859-255-7405	
Derector Robert Assoc 19 W 44th St Fl 10 *Web:* www.derector.com	New York	NY	10036	212-764-7272	
Diamond d General Engineering Inc 32500 State Hwy 16 *Web:* www.ddge.net	Woodland	CA	95695	530-662-2042	
Dickerson Engineering Inc 8101 N Milwaukee Ave *Web:* www.danaenterprises.com	Niles	IL	60714	847-966-0290	
Differentiation Strategies Inc 3349 Southgate Ct SW	Cedar Rapids	IA	52404	319-365-3489	
Digital Force Technologies LLC 9455 Waples St Ste 100 *Web:* www.digitalforcetech.com	San Diego	CA	92121	858-546-1244	
Dileo Engineering LLC 2241 W Larkspur Dr	Phoenix	AZ	85029	602-395-0756	
Dimension Energy Services 1 Fluor Daniel Dr Ste D1-7-50 *Web:* www.dimensionenergyservices.com	Sugar Land	TX	77478	832-564-4500	

Name / Address	City	State	Zip	Phone	Fax
Dimensional Control Systems Inc 580 Kirts Blvd Ste 309 — *Web:* 3dcs.com	Troy	MI	48084	248-269-9777	
DJ & A PC 3203 S Russell St — *TF:* 800-398-3522 ■ *Web:* www.djanda.com	Missoula	MT	59801	406-721-4320	
DJL Construction Inc 1550 Ampere St Ste 200 — *Web:* www.djl.ca	Boucherville	QC	J4B7L4	450-641-8000	655-1201
DLB Associates Consulting Engineers PC 265 Industrial Way W — *Web:* www.dlbassociates.com	Eatontown	NJ	07724	732-774-2000	
DNB Engineering Inc 5969 Robinson Ave — *Web:* www.dnbenginc.com	Riverside	CA	92503	951-637-2630	
Donohue & Assoc Inc 3311 Weeden Creek Rd — *Web:* www.donohue-associates.com	Sheboygan	WI	53081	920-208-0296	
Door Engineering Corp 1234 Ballentine Blvd — *Web:* www.dooreng.com	Norfolk	VA	23504	757-622-5355	
DoubleStar Inc 1161 Mcdermott Dr Ste 200 — *Web:* www.doublestarinc.com	West Chester	PA	19380	610-719-1900	
Dougherty Sprague Environmental Inc 3902 Industrial St Ste A — *Web:* www.dsei.com	Rowlett	TX	75088	972-412-8666	
Dungan Engineering pa 1574 Hwy 98 E — *TF:* 800-368-2573 ■ *Web:* dunganeng.com	Columbia	MS	39429	601-731-2600	
Dynamic Design Solutions Inc 3565 Centre Cir — *TF:* 866-337-2010 ■ *Web:* www.dynamicdesignsolutionsinc.com	Fort Mill	SC	29715	803-548-3609	
Dynamic Security Concepts Inc Hamilton Plz Ste 10 6090 Danenhauer Ln — *Web:* www.dscinc.net	Mays Landing	NJ	08330	609-625-3942	
Dynamic Test Solutions Inc 4360 W Chandler Blvd Ste 1 — *Web:* www.dynamic-test.com	Chandler	AZ	85226	480-632-0312	
E & a Consulting Group Inc 330 N 117th St — *Web:* www.eacg.com	Omaha	NE	68154	402-895-4700	
E C S 2741 S 21st Ave — *TF:* 800-621-0759 ■ *Web:* escalatorparts.com	Broadview	IL	60155	708-338-9700	
E I Team Inc 2060 Sheridan Dr — *Web:* www.eiteam.com	Buffalo	NY	14223	716-876-4669	
E Sciences Inc 34 E Pine St — *Web:* www.esciencesinc.com	Orlando	FL	32801	407-481-9006	
EBB Associates Inc 1064 W Ocean View Ave — *Web:* www.ebbweb.com	Norfolk	VA	23503	757-588-3939	
EC Source Services LLC 6644 E Thomas Rd — *Web:* ecsourceservices.com	Mesa	AZ	85215	480-245-7200	
ECM Consultants Inc 4409 Utica St Ste 200 — *Web:* ecmconsultants.com	Metairie	LA	70006	504-885-4080	
Ecom Engineering Inc 1796 Tribute Rd Ste 100 — *Web:* www.ecomeng.com	Sacramento	CA	95815	916-641-5600	
EDM International Inc 4001 Automation Way — *Web:* www.edmlink.com	Fort Collins	CO	80525	970-204-4001	
Edminster Hinshaw Russ & Assoc Inc 10555 Woffice Dr — *Web:* www.ehrainc.com	Houston	TX	77042	713-784-4500	
Elcon Assoc Inc 12670 NW Barnes Rd — *Web:* elconassociates.com	Portland	OR	97229	503-644-2490	
Electrical Consultants Inc 3521 Gabel Rd — *Web:* www.electricalconsultantsinc.com	Billings	MT	59102	406-259-9933	
Elevator Equipment Corp 4035 Goodwin Ave — *TF:* 888-577-3326 ■ *Web:* www.elevatorequipment.com	Los Angeles	CA	90039	323-245-0147	245-9771
Elevator Research & Manufacturing Corp 1417 Elwood St — *Web:* www.elevatorresearch.com	Los Angeles	CA	90021	213-746-1914	
Eleven Engineering Inc 10150 - 100 St Ste 900 — *Web:* elevenengineering.com	Edmonton	AB	T5J0P6	780-425-6511	
EM Research Inc 1301 Corporate Blvd — *Web:* www.emresearch.com	Reno	NV	89502	775-345-2411	
Emc2 3518 Riverside Dr Ste 202 — *Web:* www.emc-sq.com	Columbus	OH	43221	614-459-3200	
Ems-tech Inc 699 Dundas St W — *TF:* 844-450-8324 ■ *Web:* ems-tech.net	Belleville	ON	K8N4Z2	613-966-6611	
ENE Systems Inc 480 Neponset St Ste 11D — *Web:* enesystems.com	Canton	MA	02021	781-828-6770	
ENERActive Solutions LLC 700 Mattison Ave Ste A — *Web:* www.eneractivesolutions.com	Asbury Park	NJ	07712	732-988-8850	
Engineer Sales Co 2500 25th Ave N — *Web:* www.engineersales.com	Saint Petersburg	FL	33713	727-323-2100	
Engineering & Utility Contractors Assn 17 Crow Canyon Ct Ste 100	San Ramon	CA	94583	925-855-7900	
Engineering Data Design Corp 105 Daventry Ln Ste 100 — *TF:* 888-678-0683 ■ *Web:* ed2c.com	Louisville	KY	40223	502-412-4000	
Engineering Specialists Inc 21360 Gateway Ct — *Web:* www.engspec.com	Brookfield	WI	53045	262-783-8000	
Engineery System Solutions 4943 N 29th E Ste A — *Web:* www.es2eng.com	Idaho Falls	ID	83401	208-552-9874	
Enginetics Aerospace Corp 7700 New Carlisle Pk — *Web:* www.enginetics.com	Huber Heights	OH	45424	937-878-3800	
Enginuity Works Corp 2195 Defoor Hills Rd Nw — *Web:* www.enginuityworks.com	Atlanta	GA	30318	678-739-0001	
ENGStudios Inc 1931 Newport Blvd Ste B	Costa Mesa	CA	92627	949-642-2325	
Ensign Engineering p C 1111 Calhoun Ave — *Web:* www.ensignengineering.com	Bronx	NY	10465	718-863-5590	
Environment Control 3430 N First Ave — *Web:* www.environmentcontrol.com	Tucson	AZ	85719	520-292-3992	
Environmental Assessment & Remediation Management Inc 4097 Trl Creek Rd — *Web:* www.earmanagement.com	Riverside	CA	92505	951-735-5575	
Environmental Health & Engineering Inc 117 Fourth Ave — *TF:* 800-825-5343 ■ *Web:* www.eheinc.com	Needham	MA	02494	781-247-4300	
Equinox Engineering Ltd 909-5 Ave SW 10th Fl — *Web:* www.equinox-eng.com	Calgary	AB	T2P3G5	403-205-3833	
Equity Exploration Consultants Ltd 1-2075 Brigantine Dr	Coquitlam	BC	V3K7B8	604-522-9807	
Eran Engineering Inc 2672 Dow Ave	Tustin	CA	92780	714-543-2966	
ESE Inc 3600 DownWind Dr — *TF:* 800-236-4778 ■ *Web:* eseautomation.com	Marshfield	WI	54449	715-387-4778	
ESEA a California Corp 280 Second St Ste 270 — *Web:* esea.com	Los Altos	CA	94022	650-941-4175	
ESI FME Engineers 1800 E 16th St Ste B — *Web:* www.esifme.com	Santa Ana	CA	92701	714-835-2800	
Espo Engineering 855 Midway Dr — *Web:* www.espocorp.com	Willowbrook	IL	60527	630-789-2525	
Essig Research Inc 497 Cir Fwy — *Web:* www.essig.com	Cincinnati	OH	45246	513-942-7100	
Esys Corp 1670 N Opdyke Rd — *Web:* esysautomation.com	Auburn Hills	MI	48326	248-754-1900	
Etic Engineering 2285 Morello Ave — *Web:* www.eticeng.com	Pleasant Hill	CA	94523	925-602-4710	
Evans-Hamilton Inc 4608 Union Bay Pl N E — *Web:* www.evanshamilton.com	Seattle	WA	98105	206-526-5622	
Excalibur Engineering Services Inc 962 East 2100 North — *Web:* www.excalibur-engineering-services.com	North Logan	UT	84341	435-787-9599	
EXCEL Services Corp 11921 Rockville Pk Ste 100 — *Web:* www.excelservices.com	Rockville	MD	20852	301-984-4400	
exidacom LLC 64 N Main St — *Web:* www.exida.com	Sellersville	PA	18960	215-453-1720	
Expressworks International Inc 5619 Scotts Vly Dr — *Web:* www.expressworks.com	Scotts Valley	CA	95066	831-440-9300	
Facility Masters Inc 1604 Kerley Dr — *Web:* www.facilitymasters.com	San Jose	CA	95112	408-436-9090	
Fala Technologies Inc 430 Old Neighborhood Rd — *Web:* www.falatech.com	Kingston	NY	12401	845-336-4000	
Falcon Crest Aviation Supply Inc 8318 Braniff — *TF:* 800-833-8229 ■ *Web:* www.falconcrestaviation.com	Houston	TX	77061	713-644-2290	
Fard Engineers Inc 309 Lennon Ln Ste 200 — *Web:* www.fard.com	Walnut Creek	CA	94598	925-932-5505	
FCX Systems Inc 400 Fcx Ln — *Web:* www.fcxinc.com	Morgantown	WV	26501	304-983-0400	
Felsburg Holt & Ullevig Inc 6300 S Syracuse Way Ste 600 — *Web:* www.fhueng.com	Centennial	CO	80111	303-721-1440	
Fibertek Inc 13605 Dulles Technology Dr — *Web:* www.fibertek.com	Herndon	VA	20171	703-471-7671	
Fiberutilities Group LLC Armstrong Centre 222 Third Ave S E Ste 500 — *Web:* fiberutilities.com	Cedar Rapids	IA	52401	319-364-3200	
Figg Engineering Group 424 N Calhoun St — *Web:* www.figgbridge.com	Tallahassee	FL	32301	850-224-7400	
Finley Engineering Company Inc 104 E 11th St — *Web:* finleyusa.com	Lamar	MO	64759	417-682-5531	
Fitzgerald & Halliday Inc 72 Cedar St — *Web:* www.fhiplan.com	Hartford	CT	06106	860-247-7200	247-7206
Five Star Professional Maids 8714 N 52nd Ave	Omaha	NE	68152	402-502-3100	
Fluid Engineering Div 1432 Walnut St — *Web:* www.fluideng.com	Erie	PA	16502	814-453-5014	
Forster Electrical Engineering Inc 550 N Burr Oak Ave — *Web:* www.forstereng.com	Oregon	WI	53575	608-835-9009	
Fortemedia Inc 810 E Arques Ave — *Web:* www.fortemedia.com	Sunnyvale	CA	94085	408-861-8088	
Forza Silicon Corp 2947 Bradley St Ste 130 — *Web:* www.forzasilicon.com	Pasadena	CA	91107	626-796-1182	
Foster-Miller Inc 350 Second Ave — *Web:* www.qinetiq-na.com	Waltham	MA	02451	781-684-4000	
Frakes Engineering Inc 7950 Castleway Dr Ste 160 — *Web:* www.frakesengineering.com	Indianapolis	IN	46250	317-577-3000	
Fraser - A Weston & Sampson Co 22 High St — *Web:* www.jkfraser.com	Rensselaer	NY	12144	518-463-4400	
Fujitec America Inc 7258 Innovation Way — *Web:* www.fujitecamerica.com	Mason	OH	45040	513-932-8000	
Fuscoe Engineering Inc 16795 Von Karman Ave Ste 100 — *Web:* www.fuscoe.com	Irvine	CA	92606	949-474-1960	
Fusion Design 440 N Central Ave — *Web:* www.fusionnet.com	Campbell	CA	95008	408-378-9980	
FUTEK Advanced Sensor Technology Inc 10 Thomas — *TF:* 800-233-8835 ■ *Web:* www.futek.com	Irvine	CA	92618	949-465-0900	
Future Test Inc 1535 W Parkside Ln — *Web:* www.futuretest.com	Phoenix	AZ	85027	623-580-0162	
Futureguard Building Products Inc 101 Merrow Rd — *Web:* www.futureguard.net	Auburn	ME	04211	207-795-6536	
FVB Energy Inc 3901 Hwy 7 Ste 300 — *Web:* www.fvbenergy.com	Vaughan	ON	L4L8L5	905-265-9777	
Gamma Engineering Inc 601 Airport Dr — *Web:* www.gammaeng.com	Mansfield	TX	76063	817-477-2193	473-8198
Gartech Enterprises Inc 3037 W State Rd 256 — *Web:* gartechenterprises.com	Austin	IN	47102	812-794-4796	

	City	State	ZIP	Phone	Fax
Gas Unlimited 15999 City Walk Ste 200 *Web:* www.gasunlim.com	Sugar Land	TX	77479	281-295-5600	
Gausman & Moore Assoc 1700 Hwy 36 W *Web:* www.gausman.com	Roseville	MN	55113	651-639-9606	639-9618
Gayesco International LP 2859 Wside Dr *Web:* www.gayesco.com	Pasadena	TX	77502	713-941-8540	
GC Engineering Inc 10010 Indian School Rd Ne *Web:* www.occamconsultinggroup.com	Albuquerque	NM	87112	505-275-0022	
GCI Technologies Inc 1301 Precision Dr *Web:* gcitechnologies.com	Plano	TX	75074	972-423-8411	
GEC Inc 8282 Goodwood Blvd *Web:* www.gecinc.com	Baton Rouge	LA	70806	225-612-3000	
Gedeon Grc Consulting 6901 Jericho Tpke Ste 216 *Web:* gedeongrc.com	Syosset	NY	11791	516-873-7010	
GEL Group Inc, The 2040 Savage Rd *Web:* www.gel.com	Charleston	SC	29407	843-556-8171	
Gemma Power Systems LLC 769 Hebron Ave *Web:* www.gemmapower.com	Glastonbury	CT	06033	860-659-0509	
Geo Strata Environmental Consultants Inc 4718 College Pk	San Antonio	TX	78249	210-492-7282	
Geocal Inc 7290 S Fraser St *Web:* www.geocal.us	Centennial	CO	80112	303-337-0338	
Geotek Engineering & Testing Services Inc 909 E 50th St N *TF:* 800-354-5512 ■ *Web:* www.geotekeng.com	Sioux Falls	SD	57104	605-335-5512	
Gertsch-Baker Engineering & Design Inc 104 S Fourth St Ste 100 *Web:* www.gertschbaker.com	Laramie	WY	82070	307-742-6116	
Gibson Engineering Company Inc 90 Broadway *Web:* www.gibsonengineering.com	Norwood	MA	02062	781-769-3600	
Giffin Koerth Inc 40 University Ave Ste 800 *TF:* 800-564-5313 ■ *Web:* www.giffinkoerth.com	Toronto	ON	M5J1T1	416-368-1700	
Giles Engineering Assoc Inc N8 W22350 Johnson Dr *TF:* 800-782-0610 ■ *Web:* www.gilesengr.com	Waukesha	WI	53186	262-544-0118	
Ginn Group Inc, The 200 Westpark Dr Ste 100 *Web:* www.theginngroup.com	Peachtree City	GA	30269	404-669-9214	
gkkworks Construction Services Inc 2355 Main St Ste 220 *Web:* gkkworks.com	Irvine	CA	92614	949-250-1500	
Glen G Shaheen & Associates 1022 S Purpera Ave *Web:* www.gsaengineers.com	Gonzales	LA	70737	225-644-5523	
Global Performance Holdings Inc 30 Patewood Dr Patewood Plaza I Ste 200	Greenville	SC	29615	864-288-3009	404-2388
Global Systems Technologies Inc 109 Floral Vale Blvd *Web:* www.gstpa.com	Yardley	PA	19067	215-579-8200	
Globex Corp 3620 Stutz Dr *TF:* 800-533-8610 ■ *Web:* www.globexcorp.com	Canfield	OH	44406	330-533-0030	
Glumac Inc 150 California St *Web:* www.glumac.com	San Francisco	CA	94111	415-398-7667	
GMI Building Services Inc 8001 Vickers St *TF:* 866-803-4464 ■ *Web:* www.gmiweb.com	San Diego	CA	92111	866-803-4464	
Goetting & Assoc Inc 12042 Blanco Rd Ste 200 *Web:* www.goetting.com	San Antonio	TX	78216	210-530-7000	
Gompers Center Inc 6601 N 27th Ave *Web:* www.gomperscenter.org	Phoenix	AZ	85017	602-336-0061	
Goodwill of the East Bay 1301 30Th Ave *Web:* www.eastbaygoodwill.org	Oakland	CA	94601	510-698-7200	
Goodwin - Lasiter Inc 1609 S Chestnut St Ste 202 *Web:* glstexas.com	Lufkin	TX	75901	936-637-4900	
Gotech Inc 8383 Bluebonnet Blvd *Web:* www.gotech-inc.com	Baton Rouge	LA	70810	225-766-5358	
Govind Development LLC 9359 Ih 37 *Web:* www.govinddevelopment.com	Corpus Christi	TX	78409	361-241-2777	
GPA Technologies Inc 2368 Eastman Ave Ste 8 *Web:* www.gpatech.com	Ventura	CA	93003	805-643-7878	643-7474
Gray & Osborne Inc 701 Dexter Ave N Ste 200 *Web:* www.g-o.com	Seattle	WA	98109	206-284-0860	
Green Valley Consulting Engineers 335 Tesconi Cir *Web:* www.gvalley.com	Santa Rosa	CA	95401	707-579-0388	
Greenlancer Energy Inc 1150 Griswold St *Web:* www.greenlancer.com	Detroit	MI	48226	313-312-5101	
Greer Galloway Group Inc, The 973 Crawford Dr *Web:* www.greergalloway.com	Peterborough	ON	K9J3X1	705-743-5780	743-9592
Griffon Aerospace Inc 106 Commerce Cir *Web:* www.griffon-aerospace.com	Madison	AL	35758	256-258-0035	
Groom Energy Solutions LLC 96 Swampscott Rd *Web:* www.groomenergy.com	Salem	MA	01970	978-306-6052	
Group Delta Consultants 370 Amapola Ave Ste 212 *Web:* www.groupdelta.com	Torrance	CA	90501	310-320-5100	
Gryphon International Engineering Services Inc A CHA Co 80 King St Ste 404 *Web:* www.gryphoneng.com	Saint Catharines	ON	L2R7G1	905-984-8383	
GS Engineering Consultants Inc 2080 N Talbot Rd RR 1 *Web:* www.gsengineering.ca	Windsor	ON	N9A6J3	519-737-9162	
GT Technologies Inc 5859 Executive Dr *Web:* www.gttechnologies.com	Westland	MI	48185	734-467-8371	
Guy Engineering Services Inc 10759 E Admiral Pl *Web:* guyengr.com	Tulsa	OK	74116	918-437-0282	
H&S Constructors Inc 1616 Valero Way *TF:* 800-727-8602 ■ *Web:* www.hsconstructors.com	Corpus Christi	TX	78469	361-289-5272	
Hanover Engineering Assoc Inc 252 Brodhead Rd Ste 100 *Web:* www.hanovereng.com	Bethlehem	PA	18017	610-691-5644	
Hansen Thorp Pellinen Olson Inc 7510 Market Pl Dr *Web:* www.htpo.com	Eden Prairie	MN	55344	952-829-0700	
Hargis Engineers Inc 1201 Third Ave Ste 600 *Web:* www.hargis.biz	Seattle	WA	98101	206-448-3376	
Harper Houf Peterson Righ 205 SE Spokane St *Web:* www.hhpr.com	Portland	OR	97202	503-221-1131	
Harris & Sloan Consulting Group Inc 2295 Gateway Oaks Dr Ste 165 *Web:* www.hscgi.com	Sacramento	CA	95833	916-921-2800	
Hart Engineering Corp 800 Scenic View Dr *Web:* www.hartcompanies.com	Cumberland	RI	02864	401-658-4600	
Harwood Engineering Consultant 255 N 21st St *Web:* www.hecl.com	Milwaukee	WI	53233	414-475-5554	
Haulsey Engineering Inc 10755 Scripps Poway Pkwy Ste 466 *Web:* www.haulseyengr.com	San Diego	CA	92131	858-271-1780	
Haumiller Engineering 445 Renner Dr *Web:* www.haumiller.com	Elgin	IL	60123	847-695-9111	
Hermary Opto Electronics Inc 104-1500 Hartley Ave *Web:* www.hermarymachinevision.com	Coquitlam	BC	V3K7A1	604-517-4625	517-2195
HESS Construction + Engineering Services Inc 804 W Diamond Ave Ste 300 *TF:* 800-544-6056 ■ *Web:* www.hessedu.com	Gaithersburg	MD	20878	301-670-9000	
HH Angus & Assoc Ltd 1127 Leslie St *TF:* 866-955-8201 ■ *Web:* www.hhangus.com	Toronto	ON	M3C2J6	416-443-8200	
Highland Associates Ltd 102 Highland Ave *Web:* www.highlandassociates.com	Clarks Summit	PA	18411	570-586-4334	
Highland Engineering & Surveying Inc 1426 Memorial Dr *Web:* highland-engineering.com	Oakland	MD	21550	301-334-6185	
HighRes Biosolutions Inc 299 Washington St *Web:* www.highresbio.com	Woburn	MA	01801	781-932-1912	
Hollister-Whitney Elevator Corp 2603 N 24th St *Web:* www.hollisterwhitney.com	Quincy	IL	62305	217-222-0466	222-0493
Hope Amundson 1301 3rd Ave Ste 300 *Web:* hope-amundson.com	San Diego	CA	92101	619-232-4673	
Hopper Engineering Assoc Inc 300 Vista Del Mar *Web:* www.hopperengineering.com	Redondo Beach	CA	90277	310-373-5573	
Hoque & Assoc Inc 4325 S 34th St *Web:* www.hoqueandassociates.com	Phoenix	AZ	85040	480-921-1368	
Horner & Shifrin Inc 5200 Oakland Ave *Web:* www.hornershifrin.com	St Louis	MO	63110	314-531-4321	
Horrocks Engineers Inc 2162 Grove Pkwy Ste 400 *Web:* horrocksengineers.com	Pleasant Grove	UT	84062	801-763-5100	
Host Engineering Inc 593 Aa Deakins Rd *Web:* hosteng.com	Jonesborough	TN	37659	423-913-2587	
Howerton Engineering & Surveying 404 Main St *Web:* www.howertoneng.com	Greenup	KY	41144	606-473-5684	
Hunt Guillot & Assoc LLC 603 Reynolds Dr *TF:* 866-255-6825 ■ *Web:* www.hga-llc.com	Ruston	LA	71270	318-255-6825	
Hurst Rosche Engineers Inc 601 N Bruns Ln Ste B *Web:* hurst-rosche.com	Springfield	IL	62702	217-787-1199	
Hutchison Engineering Inc 1801 W Lafayette Ave *Web:* hutchisoneng.com	Jacksonville	IL	62650	217-245-7164	
Hy-capacity Engineering & Manufacturing Inc 1404 13th St S *Web:* www.hy-capacity.com	Humboldt	IA	50548	515-332-2125	
Hyatt Die Cast & Engineering Corp 4656 Lincoln Ave *Web:* www.hyattdiecast.com	Cypress	CA	90630	714-826-7550	
Hydroscience Engineers Inc 10569 Old Plrville Rd *Web:* hydroscience.com	Sacramento	CA	95827	916-364-1490	
Hyundai Repair by Rally Sport Engineering Inc 2136 Newport Blvd *Web:* hyundairepair.net	Costa Mesa	CA	92627	949-548-0978	
Idea Engineering Inc 32 E Sola St *Web:* www.ideaengineering.com	Santa Barbara	CA	93101	805-963-5399	
IJ Research Inc 2919 Tech Ctr Dr *Web:* www.ijresearch.com	Santa Ana	CA	92705	714-546-8522	
Imagize LLC 2855 Telegraph Ave Ste 510 *Web:* www.imagizellc.com	Berkeley	CA	94705	510-540-0260	
INCERTEC LLC 160 83rd Ave NE *Web:* www.incertec.com	Fridley	MN	55432	763-717-7016	
Inclinator Company of America 601 Gibson Blvd *Web:* www.inclinator.com	Harrisburg	PA	17104	717-939-8420	
Infinity Engineering Consultants L L C 2626 Canal St Ste 202 *Web:* www.infinityec.com	New Orleans	LA	70119	504-304-0548	
InfoTech Enterprises America Inc 330 Roberts St Ste 102 *TF:* 866-746-2133 ■ *Web:* cyient.com	East Hartford	CT	06108	860-528-5430	
Infrastructure & Energy Alternatives LLC 2 Westbrook Corporate Ctr Ste 200 *Web:* iea.net	Westchester	IL	60154	708-397-4200	
Infratech Corp 2036 Baker Ct *Web:* www.infratechcorp.com	Kennesaw	GA	30144	770-792-8700	
Ingenium Technologies Corp 4216 Maray Dr *Web:* www.ingeniumtech.com	Rockford	IL	61107	815-399-8803	
Innova Engineering Inc 2 Park Plz Ste 510 *Web:* www.innovaengineering.com	Irvine	CA	92614	949-975-9965	

Company	City	State	ZIP	Phone	Fax
Insight Product Development 4660 N Ravenswood Ave *Web:* www.insightpd.com	Chicago	IL	60640	773-907-9500	
Integrated Industrial Technologies 221 Seventh St Ste 200 *Web:* www.isquaredt.com	Pittsburgh	PA	15238	412-828-1200	
Integrated Management Services PA 126 E Amite St *Web:* www.imsengineers.com	Jackson	MS	39201	601-968-9194	
Integrated Solutions Inc 16602 N 23rd Ave Ste 109 *Web:* www.isiaz.com	Phoenix	AZ	85023	602-437-5209	
InterDesign Group Inc 141 E Ohio St *Web:* www.interdesign.com	Indianapolis	IN	46204	317-263-9655	
Interlink Network Systems Inc 495 Cranbury Rd *TF:* 877-872-6947 ■ *Web:* www.ilinknet.com	East Brunswick	NJ	08816	732-846-2226	
Intertek AIM 601 W California Ave	Sunnyvale	CA	94086	408-745-7000	
InTren Inc 18202 W Union Rd *Web:* www.intren.com	Union	IL	60180	815-923-2300	
Invotec Engineering Inc 10909 Industry Ln *Web:* www.invotec.com	Miamisburg	OH	45342	937-886-3232	
IOS Technologies Inc 3978 Sorrento Vly Blvd Ste 200 *Web:* www.ios3d.com	San Diego	CA	92121	858-202-3360	
Isaacson & Arfman Consulting Engineering Assoc pa 128 Monroe St Ne *Web:* iacivil.com	Albuquerque	NM	87108	505-268-8828	
ISC Engineering 1730 Evergreen St *Web:* www.iscengineering.com	Duarte	CA	91010	909-596-3315	
ISG Resources 11539 Park Woods Cir *Web:* www.isg-resources.com	Alpharetta	GA	30005	770-667-8830	
ITB Group Ltd 39555 Orchard Hill Pl Ste 157 *Web:* itbgroup.com	Novi	MI	48375	248-380-6310	
Itc Engineering Services Inc 9959 Calaveras Rd *Web:* www.itcemc.com	Sunol	CA	94586	925-862-2944	
J f Sato & Assoc Inc 5878 S Rapp St *Web:* www.jfsato.com	Littleton	CO	80120	303-797-1200	
J H I Engineering 3420 SW Macadam Ave *Web:* www.jhiengineering.com	Portland	OR	97239	503-223-7799	
J R Miller & Assoc 2700 Saturn St *Web:* www.jrma.com	Brea	CA	92821	714-524-1870	
J2 Engineering Inc 6921 Pistol Range Rd *Web:* www.j2-eng.com	Tampa	FL	33635	813-888-8861	
JA Woollam Company Inc 645 M St Ste 102 *Web:* www.jawoollam.com	Lincoln	NE	68508	402-477-7501	
Jackson & Tull Chartered Engineers 12201 Distribution Way *Web:* www.jnt.com	Beltsville	MD	20705	301-937-8255	
James Posey Assoc Inc 3112 Lord Baltimore Dr *Web:* www.jamesposey.com	Baltimore	MD	21244	410-265-6100	
James Tool Machine & Engineering Inc 130 Reep Dr *Web:* www.jamestool.com	Morganton	NC	28655	828-584-8722	
Jan-Pro Cleaning Systems Minneapolis 33 tenth Ave S Ste 200 *Web:* twincities.jan-pro.com	Hopkins	MN	55343	952-238-1005	
Janitronics Inc 1988 Central Ave *Web:* www.janitronicsinc.com	Albany	NY	12205	518-456-8484	
JC General Contractors Inc 8250 N Loop Dr Ste A *Web:* www.jc-general.com	El Paso	TX	79907	915-598-8008	
JCM Engineering Corp 2690 E Cedar St *Web:* www.jcmcorp.com	Ontario	CA	91761	909-923-3730	
Jedson Engineering 705 Central Ave *TF:* 866-729-3945 ■ *Web:* www.jedson.com	Cincinnati	OH	45202	513-965-5999	
Jeo Consulting Group Inc 142 W 11th St *Web:* www.pdiowa.com	Wahoo	NE	68066	402-443-4661	
JET Engineering Inc 1241 Park Pl Ne Ste E *Web:* www.jetinc.net	Cedar Rapids	IA	52402	319-294-6106	
Jet Parts Engineering Inc 4772 Ohio Ave S *Web:* www.jetpartsengineering.com	Seattle	WA	98134	206-281-0963	
JL Richards & Assoc Ltd 864 Lady Ellen Pl *Web:* www.jlrichards.ca	Ottawa	ON	K1Z5M2	613-728-3571	
JLR The Engineering Solutions Co 11611 Airport Rd Ste 201 *Web:* www.jlrcom.com	Everett	WA	98204	425-353-8089	
JM Turner Engineering Inc 1325 College Ave *TF:* 800-514-4220 ■ *Web:* www.jmteng.com	Santa Rosa	CA	95404	707-528-4503	
Johnson Engineering Inc 2122 Johnson St *TF:* 866-367-4400 ■ *Web:* www.johnsonengineering.com	Fort Myers	FL	33901	239-334-0046	334-3661
Joyner Keeny & Assoc 1051 N Winstead Ave *Web:* joynerkeeny.com	Rocky Mount	NC	27804	252-977-3124	
Js Dyer & Assoc Inc 8891 Research Dr	Irvine	CA	92618	949-296-8858	
JWS & Assoc Inc 10305 Latting Rd	Cordova	TN	38016	901-754-1239	
Kaback Enterprises Inc 45 W 25th St *Web:* www.kaback.com	New York	NY	10010	212-645-5100	
Kalsi Engineering Inc 745 Park Two Dr *Web:* www.kalsi.com	Sugar Land	TX	77478	281-240-6500	240-0255
Kapitan Engineering Inc 802 Franklin St *Web:* kapitan-eng.com	Sauk City	WI	53583	608-643-6477	
KASL Consulting Engineers Inc 7777 Greenback Ln Ste 104 *Web:* www.kasl.com	Citrus Heights	CA	95610	916-722-1800	
Keane Circuits Inc 341 Avondale Ave *Web:* www.keanecircuits.com	Haddonfield	NJ	08033	856-795-1181	
Keller Assoc Engineering Inc 131 SW Fifth Ave *Web:* www.kellerassociates.com	Meridian	ID	83642	208-288-1992	
Kelly Collins & Gentry Inc 1700 N Orange Ave Ste 400 *Web:* kcgcorp.com	Orlando	FL	32804	407-898-7858	
Kelly's Janitorial Service Inc 228 Hazel Ave *TF:* 800-227-0366 ■ *Web:* www.kellysjanitorial.com	Trenton	NJ	08638	609-771-0365	
KHAFRA Engineering Consultants Inc 225 Peachtree St NE Ste 1600 *Web:* www.khafra.com	Atlanta	GA	30303	404-525-2120	
Ki Ho Military Acquisition Consulting Inc 5501 Backlick Rd *Web:* www.kihomac.com	Springfield	VA	22151	703-960-5450	
Kiefner & Assoc Inc 585 Scherers Ct *Web:* www.kiefner.com	Worthington	OH	43085	614-888-8220	
Kim Engineering Inc 11127 New Hampshire Ave *Web:* www.kimengineering.com	Silver Spring	MD	20904	301-754-2882	
Kinetic Systems Inc 20 Arboretum Rd *Web:* www.kineticsystems.com	Boston	MA	02131	617-522-8700	
Kjeldsen Sinnock & Neudeck Inc 711 N Pershing Ave *Web:* www.ksninc.com	Stockton	CA	95203	209-946-0268	
klean image 13498 Pond Springs Rd *Web:* www.kleanimage.com	Austin	TX	78729	512-258-7003	250-1225
Kleen Polymers Inc 145 Rainbow St *Web:* www.kleenpolymers.com	Wadsworth	OH	44281	330-336-4212	
Klewin Construction Inc 444 Brickell Ave Ste 900	Miami	FL	33131	305-709-0700	
Knighthawk Engineering Inc 17625 El Camino Real Ste 412 *Web:* www.knighthawk.com	Houston	TX	77058	281-282-9200	
Knudsen-smith Engineering Inc 2525 W Greenway Rd Ste 302	Phoenix	AZ	85023	602-347-7447	
KPG PS 753 Ninth Ave N *Web:* www.kpg.com	Seattle	WA	98109	206-286-1640	
Krech Ojard & Assoc pa 227 W 1st St Ste 200 *Web:* www.krechojard.com	Duluth	MN	55802	218-727-3282	727-1216
KS Industries LP 6205 District Blvd *Web:* www.ksindustrieslp.com	Bakersfield	CA	93313	661-617-1700	
Kussmaul Electronics Company Inc 170 Cherry Ave *TF:* 800-346-0857 ■ *Web:* www.kussmaul.com	West Sayville	NY	11796	631-567-0314	
KZF Design Inc 700 Broadway St *Web:* www.kzf.com	Cincinnati	OH	45202	513-621-6211	
L & W Engineering Inc 107 Industrial Pkwy *Web:* www.lw-eng.com	Middlebury	IN	46540	574-825-5351	
L2 Consulting Services Inc 2100 E Hwy 290 *Web:* www.l2aviation.com	Dripping Springs	TX	78620	512-894-3414	
LA Fuess Partners Inc 3333 Lee Pkwy Ste 300 *Web:* www.lafp.com	Dallas	TX	75219	214-871-7010	
Lamb-Star Engineering LP 5700 W Plano Pkwy Ste 1000 *Web:* www.lamb-star.com	Plano	TX	75093	214-440-3600	
Lan Assoc Engineering Planning Architecture Surveying Inc 445 Godwin Ave Ste 9 *Web:* www.lan-nj.com	Midland Park	NJ	07432	201-447-6400	
Landa & Assoc Inc 5128 E Thomas Rd Ste 100 *Web:* www.landaandassociates.com	Phoenix	AZ	85018	602-443-5515	
Lanmark Engineering & Surveying Inc 9330 Vanguard Dr Ste 131	Anchorage	AK	99507	907-562-6050	
LARON Inc 4255 Santa Fe Dr *TF:* 800-248-3430 ■ *Web:* www.laron.com	Kingman	AZ	86401	928-757-8424	
LEA Group Holdings Inc 625 Cochrane Dr 9th Fl *Web:* www.lea.ca	Markham	ON	L3R9R9	905-470-0015	
Lifeport Inc 1610 Heritage St *Web:* www.lifeport.com	Woodland	WA	98674	360-225-1212	225-1214
Lilja Corp 229 Rickenbacker Cir *Web:* www.liljacorp.com	Livermore	CA	94551	925-455-2300	
Lin Engineering Inc 16245 Vineyard Blvd *Web:* www.linengineering.com	Morgan Hill	CA	95037	408-919-0200	
Loadmaster Universal Rigs Inc 6935 Brittmoore Rd *Web:* www.loadmastereng.com	Houston	TX	77041	281-598-7240	
Lochmueller Group 6200 Vogel Rd *TF:* 800-423-7411 ■ *Web:* www.blainc.com	Evansville	IN	47715	812-479-6200	
Los Gatos Research Inc 67 E Evelyn Ave Ste 3 *Web:* www.lgrinc.com	Mountain View	CA	94041	650-965-7772	
Lotek Wireless Inc 115 Pony Dr *Web:* www.lotek.com	Newmarket	ON	L3Y7B5	905-836-6680	836-6455
Mabbett & Associates Inc 5 Alfred Cir *Web:* www.mabbett.com	Bedford	MA	01730	781-275-6050	
MacLellan Services Inc 3120 Wall St Ste 100 *Web:* www.maclellan-usa.com	Lexington	KY	40513	859-219-5400	
MadgeTech Inc 6 Warner Rd *TF:* 877-671-2885 ■ *Web:* www.madgetech.com	Warner	NH	03278	603-456-2011	
Mainstream Engineering Corp 200 Yellow Pl *Web:* www.mainstream-engr.com	Rockledge	FL	32955	321-631-3550	
Makai Ocean Engineering Inc 41-305 Kalanianaole Hwy *Web:* www.makai.com	Waimanalo	HI	96795	808-259-8871	
ManTech Advanced Systems International Inc 12015 Lee Jackson Hwy *Web:* www.mantech.com	Fairfax	VA	22033	703-218-6000	
Martec Ltd 1888 Brunswick St Ste 400 *Web:* www.martec.com	Halifax	NS	B3J3J8	902-425-5101	
Matot Inc 2501 Van Buren St *TF:* 800-369-1070 ■ *Web:* www.matot.com	Bellwood	IL	60104	708-547-1888	547-1608
Matrix Composites Inc 275 Barnes Blvd *Web:* www.matrixcomp.com	Rockledge	FL	32955	321-633-4480	
Matrix Energy Services Inc 3221 Ramos Cir *TF:* 800-556-2123 ■ *Web:* www.matrixescorp.com	Sacramento	CA	95827	916-363-9283	
Matrix LLC 19 Ave D *TF:* 800-338-5603 ■ *Web:* www.cleanforhealth.com	Johnson City	NY	13790	607-766-0700	

Company / Address	City	State	ZIP	Phone	Fax
Maverick Construction Corp 1 Westinghouse Plz *Web:* www.maverickcorporation.com	Boston	MA	02136	617-361-6700	
McCall & Associates Inc 3308 Country Club Rd *Web:* www.mccallinc.com	Valdosta	GA	31605	229-242-2551	
McDowell & Assoc Inc 21355 Hatcher Ave *Web:* www.mcdowasc.com	Ferndale	MI	48220	248-399-2066	
McGiffert & Associates LLC 2814 Stillman Blvd *Web:* www.mcgiffert.com	Tuscaloosa	AL	35401	205-759-1521	
McGregor Metalworking Cos 2100 S Yellow Springs St *Web:* mcgregormetal.com	Springfield	OH	45506	937-325-5561	
McInnis Brothers Construction Inc 119 Pearl St *Web:* www.mcinnisbrothers.com	Minden	LA	71055	318-377-6134	
McQ Inc 1551 Forbes St *TF:* 866-373-2374 ■ *Web:* www.mcqinc.com	Fredericksburg	VA	22405	540-373-2374	
MDS Aero Support Corp 1220 Old Innes Rd Ste 200 *Web:* mdsaero.com	Ottawa	ON	K1B3V3	613-744-7257	
Meda Ltd 1575 Lauzon Rd *TF:* 888-518-6332 ■ *Web:* www.medagroup.com	Windsor	ON	N8S3N4	519-944-7221	944-6862
Metal Master Sales Corp 1159 N Main St *Web:* www.metalmaster.com	Glendale Heights	IL	60139	630-858-4750	
Metric Precision Machine & Engineering LLC 350 W Compton Blvd *Web:* metric-precision.com	Gardena	CA	90248	310-515-2584	
Metro-Clean Corp 936 W Greenfield Ave	Milwaukee	WI	53204	414-671-6660	
Mid-South Engineering Co 1658 Malvern Ave *Web:* www.mseco.com	Hot Springs	AR	71901	501-321-2276	
Minnesota Elevator Inc 19336 607th Ave *Web:* meielevatorsolutions.com	Mankato	MN	56001	507-245-3060	245-3956
MMI Engineering Ltd 475 14th St Ste 400 *Web:* www.mmiengineering.com	Oakland	CA	94612	510-836-3002	
Mobile Office Acquisition Corp 9155 Harrison Park Court - NEW *Web:* www.pacvan.com	Indianapolis	IN	46216	317-791-2020	
Moffitt Corp Inc 1351 13th Ave S Ste 130 *TF:* 800-474-3267 ■ *Web:* www.moffitthvac.com	Jacksonville Beach	FL	32250	904-241-9944	
Molding International & Engineering Inc 42136 Avenida Alvarado	Temecula	CA	92590	951-296-5010	
Monitor Elevator Products Inc 125 Ricefield Ln *TF:* 800-527-9156 ■ *Web:* www.mcontrols.com	Hauppauge	NY	11788	800-527-9156	
Motion Control Engineering Inc 11380 White Rock Rd *TF:* 800-444-7442 ■ *Web:* www.mceinc.com	Rancho Cordova	CA	95742	916-463-9200	
MVA Engineering Group Ltd 246 Waterloo St *Web:* www.mva.on.ca	London	ON	N6B2N4	519-668-4698	
Navmar Applied Sciences Corp 65 W St Rd Bldg C *Web:* www.nasc.com	Warminster	PA	18974	215-675-4900	
Neany Inc 44010 Commerce Ave Ste A *Web:* www.neanyinc.com	Hollywood	MD	20636	301-373-8700	
NELSON & Associates Interior Design & Space Planning Inc The NELSON Bldg 222-230 Walnut St *Web:* www.nelsononline.com	Philadelphia	PA	19106	215-925-6562	
Nexus Engineering Inc 1400 Lone Palm Ave *Web:* www.nexusengineering.net	Modesto	CA	95351	209-572-7399	
North American Cable Equipment Inc 1085 Andrew Dr Ste A *Web:* www.northamericancable.com	West Chester	PA	19380	610-429-1821	
Northstar Industries LLC 126 Merrimack St *Web:* www.northstarind.com	Methuen	MA	01844	978-975-5500	
Nth Consultants Ltd 41780 6 Mile Rd *Web:* www.nthconsultants.com	Northville	MI	48168	248-553-6300	
NuVision Engineering Inc River Park Commons 2403 Sidney St Ste 700 *Web:* www.nuvisioneng.com	Pittsburgh	PA	15203	412-586-1810	
Oblong Industries Inc 923 E Third St Ste 111 *Web:* oblong.com	Los Angeles	CA	90013	213-683-8863	
Omicron Architecture Engineering Construction Ltd 595 Burrard St Three Bentall Centre Fifth Fl PO Box 49369 *TF:* 877-632-3350 ■ *Web:* www.omicronaec.com	Vancouver	BC	V7X1L4	604-632-3350	
OMNI Engineering Services Inc 370 W Second St Ste 100 *Web:* omnimn.com	Winona	MN	55987	507-454-5293	
Optimum Engineering Solutions Inc Country Club View Dr Ste 1 *Web:* www.openso.com	Edwardsville	IL	62025	618-288-3131	
Opus International Consultants (Canada) Ltd 210-889 Harbourside Dr *Web:* www.opusinternational.ca	North Vancouver	BC	V6E4E6	604-990-4800	990-4805
Otis Elevator Co 10 Farm Springs Rd *Web:* www.otisworldwide.com	Farmington	CT	06032	860-676-6000	998-3910
P&R Enterprises Inc 5681 Columbia Pk Ste 101 *Web:* www.p-and-r.com	Falls Church	VA	22041	703-931-1000	
Parametric Solutions Inc 900 E Indiantown Rd *Web:* www.psnet.com	Jupiter	FL	33477	561-747-6107	
Paramount Building Solutions Inc 401 W Baseline Rd Ste 209 *Web:* www.paramountbldgsol.com	Tempe	AZ	85283	480-348-1177	
PCCI 300 N Lee St *Web:* www.pccii.com	Alexandria	VA	22314	703-684-2060	
Pensar Development Inc 900 E Pine St Ste 201 *Web:* www.pensardevelopment.com	Seattle	WA	98122	206-284-3134	
Piasecki Aircraft Corp 519 W Second St *Web:* www.piasecki.com	Essington	PA	19029	610-521-5700	
Piedmont Geotechnical 3000 Northfield Pl *Web:* www.ascomputer.com	Roswell	GA	30076	770-752-9205	
PIKA Technologies Inc 535 Legget Dr Ste 400 *Web:* www.pikatech.com	Ottawa	ON	K2K3B8	613-591-1555	591-9295
Pinnacle Asset Integrity Services 1 Pinnacle Way *Web:* www.pinnacleais.com	Pasadena	TX	77504	281-598-1330	
Planned Environments Inc 2219 Wlake Dr Ste 100	Austin	TX	78746	512-474-0806	
Potelco Inc 14103 Stewart Rd *Web:* www.potelco.net	Sumner	WA	98390	253-863-0484	
Power Quality Engineering Inc 3061 W Whitestone Blvd *Web:* www.pqeinc.com	Cedar Park	TX	78613	512-267-6656	
Process Plus LLC 135 Merchant St Ste 300 *Web:* www.processplus.com	Cincinnati	OH	45246	513-742-7590	
Protochips Inc 3800 Gateway Centre Blvd Ste 306 *Web:* www.protochips.com	Morrisville	NC	27560	919-341-2612	
Radiant Technologies Inc 2835 Pan American Fwy Ne *TF:* 800-289-7176 ■ *Web:* www.ferrodevices.com	Albuquerque	NM	87107	505-842-8007	
Radius Engineering Inc 1042 West 2780 South *Web:* www.radiuseng.com	Salt Lake City	UT	84119	801-886-2624	
Raisbeck Engineering Inc 4411 S Ryan Way *Web:* www.raisbeck.com	Seattle	WA	98178	206-723-2000	
Ralph S Inouye Company Ltd 2831 Awaawaloa St *Web:* www.rsinouye.com	Honolulu	HI	96819	808-839-9002	
Read Jones Christoffersen Ltd 1285 W Broadway Ste 300 *Web:* www.rjc.ca	Vancouver	BC	V6H3X8	604-738-0048	
Red Cedar Technology Inc 4572 S Hagadorn Rd Ste 3-A *Web:* www.redcedartech.com	East Lansing	MI	48823	517-664-1137	
Rescan Environmental Services Ltd 1111 W Hastings St 6th Fl *Web:* www.erm.com/en/locations/canada	Vancouver	BC	V6E2J3	604-689-9460	
RETEL Services Inc 5871 Glenridge Dr NE Ste 110 *Web:* www.retelservices.com	Atlanta	GA	30328	404-343-2375	
Rhinestahl Corp 7687 Innovation Way *Web:* www.rhinestahl.com	Mason	OH	45040	513-229-5300	
Ricon Corp 7900 Nelson Rd *TF:* 800-322-2884 ■ *Web:* www.riconcorp.com	Panorama City	CA	91402	818-267-3000	267-3001
Ripon Printers Inc 656 S Douglas St *Web:* www.riponprinters.com	Ripon	WI	54971	920-748-3136	
RJ Burnside & Assoc Ltd 15 Townline *Web:* www.rjburnside.com	Orangeville	ON	L9W3R4	519-941-5331	
RM Mechanical Inc 5998 W Gowen Rd *Web:* www.rmmechanical.net	Boise	ID	83709	208-362-0131	
Rutheford & Chekene 375 Beale St Ste 310 *Web:* www.ruthchek.com	San Francisco	CA	94105	415-568-4400	
S W Cole Engineering Inc 37 Liberty Dr *Web:* www.swcole.com	Bangor	ME	04401	207-848-5714	
S&ME Inc 6190 Enterprise Ct	Dublin	OH	43016	614-793-2226	
SAI Engineering Inc 13662 Office Pl Ste 101 *Web:* www.saimep.com	Woodbridge	VA	22192	703-590-8200	
Sauer Holdings Inc 30 51st St *Web:* sauerholdings.com	Pittsburgh	PA	15201	412-687-4100	
Schindler Elevator Corp 20 Whippany Rd **Fax:* Mail Rm ■ *TF:* 800-225-3123 ■ *Web:* www.schindler.com	Morristown	NJ	07960	973-397-6500	397-3619*
Schumacher Elevator Co 1 Schumacher Way PO Box 393 *TF:* 800-779-5438 ■ *Web:* www.schumacherelevator.com	Denver	IA	50622	319-984-5676	984-6316
Scientific Systems Company Inc 500 W Cummings Pk Ste 3000 *Web:* www.ssci.com	Woburn	MA	01801	781-933-5355	
Sematic USA 7852 Bavaria Rd *Web:* sematic.com	Twinsburg	OH	44087	216-524-0100	524-9710
Service Elements Inc 15029 N Thompson Peak Pkwy Ste B111-444 *Web:* www.serviceelements.com	Scottsdale	AZ	85260	480-538-0123	
Shenandoah Electronic Intelligence Inc 220 University Blvd	Harrisonburg	VA	22801	540-434-7075	
Sheppard T Powell Assoc LLC 1915 Aliceanna St *Web:* www.stpa.com	Baltimore	MD	21231	410-327-3500	
Sigma Space Corp 4600 Forbes Blvd *Web:* www.optotraffic.com	Lanham	MD	20706	301-552-6000	
Solid State Scientific Corp 27-2 Wright Rd *Web:* www.solidstatescientific.com	Hollis	NH	03049	603-465-5686	
Solusia Inc PO Box 11805 *Web:* www.solusia.com	Atlanta	GA	30355	404-601-1100	
SpaceAge Control Inc 38850 20th St E *Web:* www.spaceagecontrol.com	Palmdale	CA	93550	661-273-3000	
Stephenson Engineering Ltd 2550 Victoria Park Ave Ste 602 *Web:* www.stephenson-eng.com	Toronto	ON	M2J5A9	416-635-9970	
Suburban Motors Grafton Inc 139 N Main St *Web:* www.suburbanharley.com	Thiensville	WI	53092	262-242-2464	
Swenson Say Faget Inc 2124 Third Ave Ste 100 *Web:* ssfengineers.com	Seattle	WA	98121	206-443-6212	
Syscor Controls & Automation Inc 201 - 60 Bastion Sq *Web:* www.syscor.com	Victoria	BC	V8W1J2	250-361-1681	361-1682
Technical Systems Integration Inc 816 Greenbrier Cir Ste 208 *TF:* 800-566-8744 ■ *Web:* www.tecsysint.com	Chesapeake	VA	23320	757-424-5793	

	City	State	Zip	Phone	Fax
Technology for Energy Corp					
10737 Lexington Dr	Knoxville	TN	37932	865-966-5856	
Web: www.tec-usa.com					
Technosoft Engineering					
13400 Bishops Lnn Ste 30	Brookfield	WI	53005	262-317-8100	
Web: www.impactengsol.com					
Teleflex Turbine Services Corp					
12661 Challenger Pkwy Ste 250	Orlando	FL	32826	407-677-0813	
Web: www.turbinetech.com					
Telesto Solutions Inc					
2950 E Harmony Rd Ste 200	Fort Collins	CO	80528	970-484-7704	
Web: www.telesto-inc.com					
Thomas J Dyer Company Inc 5240 Lester Rd	Cincinnati	OH	45213	513-321-8100	
Web: www.groteenterprises.com					
Thompson Engineering Inc					
2970 Cottage Hill Rd Ste 190	Mobile	AL	36606	251-666-2443	
Web: www.tcocompanies.com					
ThyssenKrupp Access Inc 4001 E 138th St	Grandview	MO	64030	816-763-3100	763-4467
Ticom Geomatics Inc 9130 Jollyville Rd Ste 300	Austin	TX	78759	512-345-5006	
Web: www.ticom-geo.com					
Tidy Building Services Inc					
609 W William David Pkwy Ste 202	Metairie	LA	70005	504-838-9843	
Web: www.tidyusa.com					
Triumph Structures - Los Angeles Inc					
17055 E Gale Ave	City Of Industry	CA	91745	626-965-1630	
Web: www.triumphgroup.com					
TTL Inc 3516 Greensboro Ave	Tuscaloosa	AL	35401	205-345-0816	
Web: www.ttlinc.com					
Tulloch Engineering Inc 200 Main St	Thessalon	ON	P0R1L0	705-842-3372	
TF: 800-797-2997 ■ *Web:* www.tulloch.ca					
Tundra Engineering Associates Ltd					
1331 Macleod Trail SE	Calgary	AB	T2G1E1	403-777-2477	
Underground Imaging Technologies LLC					
308 Wolf Rd	Latham	NY	12110	518-783-9848	
Web: www.uit-systems.com					
United Consulting Group Ltd					
625 Holcomb Bridge Rd	Norcross	GA	30071	770-209-0029	
Web: www.unitedconsulting.com					
United Infrastructure Group Inc					
1691 Turnbull Ave	North Charleston	SC	29405	843-529-3010	
Web: uig.net					
United Services Inc 462 Forest St PO Box 1067	Kearny	NJ	07032	201-955-1300	
Web: www.unitedservicesinc.net					
Vaughn Coltrane Pharr & Associates Inc					
2060 E Exchange Pl	Tucker	GA	30084	678-567-4513	
TF: 877-230-5315 ■ *Web:* www.vcae.com					
Veneklasen Associates 1711 16Th St	Santa Monica	CA	90404	310-450-1733	
Web: www.veneklasen.com					
VersaTech Automation Services LLC					
11349 FM 529 Rd	Houston	TX	77041	713-939-6100	
Web: www.vtechas.com					
Vidaris Inc 360 Park Ave S	New York	NY	10010	212-689-5389	
Web: www.vidaris.com					
VPT Inc 1971 Kraft Dr	Blacksburg	VA	24060	540-552-5000	552-5003
Web: vptpower.com					
VTI Instruments Corp 2031 Main St	Irvine	CA	92614	949-955-1894	
Web: www.vtiinstruments.com					
Walker Engineering Inc 8451 Dunwoody Pl	Atlanta	GA	30350	770-641-7306	
Web: www.walkerengineer.com					
Ward Engineering Company Inc					
1353 S Seventh St PO Box 2498	Louisville	KY	40201	502-637-6521	
Web: www.wardengr.com					
Warren & Panzer Engineers PC 228 E 45th St	New York	NY	10017	212-922-0077	
Web: www.warrenpanzer.com					
Watson Industries Inc 3041 Melby Rd	Eau Claire	WI	54703	715-839-0628	
Web: www.watson-gyro.com					
Watthour Engineering Company Inc					
333 Crosspark Dr	Pearl	MS	39208	601-933-0900	
Web: www.watthour.com					
Waupaca Elevator Co Inc 1726 N BallaRd Rd	Appleton	WI	54911	920-991-9082	991-9087
TF: 800-238-8739 ■ *Web:* www.waupacaelevator.com					
Waveguide Consulting 1 W Court Sq	Decatur	GA	30030	404-815-1919	
Web: www.waveguide.com					
Weatherford Aerospace Inc					
1020 E Columbia St	Weatherford	TX	76086	817-594-5464	594-7450
Web: www.weatherfordaerospace.com					
Wells & Associates 1420 Spring Hill Rd Ste 610	Tysons	VA	22102	703-917-6620	
Web: www.wellsandassociates.com					
Western Commercial Services LLC					
2311 Industrial Rd	Las Vegas	NV	89102	702-384-7907	
Web: www.westerncommercial.net					
Westfield Engineering & Services Inc					
8310 McHard Rd	Houston	TX	77053	281-438-2047	
Wickham Glass Co 4747 N Webb Rd	Wichita	KS	67226	316-262-3403	
Web: www.wickhamglass.com					
Wiebe Forest Engineering Ltd					
3613 - 33rd St NW	Calgary	AB	T2L2A7	403-670-7300	
Web: www.wfe.ca					
Williams Engineering Canada Inc					
10065 Jasper Ave Ste 200	Edmonton	AB	T5J3B1	780-409-5300	
Web: www.williamsengineering.com					
Windermere Information Technology Systems LLC					
2000 Windermere Ct	Annapolis	MD	21401	410-266-1700	
Web: www.witsusa.com					
Wineman Technology Inc 1668 Champagne Dr N	Saginaw	MI	48604	989-771-3000	
Web: www.winemantech.com					
WorkingBuildings LLC					
1230 Peachtree St NE 300 Promenade	Atlanta	GA	30309	678-990-8001	
Web: www.workingbuildings.com					
WSB & Associates Inc					
701 Xenia Ave S Ste 300	Minneapolis	MN	55416	763-541-4800	
Web: www.wsbeng.com					
Wynston Hill Capital LLC					
488 Madison Ave 24th Fl	New York	NY	10022	212-521-1900	208-0978
Web: www.wynstonhill.com					
XCG Consultants Ltd 2620 Bristol Cir Ste 300	Oakville	ON	L6H6Z7	905-829-8880	
Web: www.xcg.com					
York Building Services Inc					
99 Grand St Ste 3	Moonachie	NJ	07074	855-443-9675	
TF: 855-443-9675 ■ *Web:* yorkbuildingservices.com					

257 EMBASSIES & CONSULATES - FOREIGN, IN THE US

See Also Travel & Tourism Information - Foreign Travel p. 3267

Foreign embassies in the U.S. generally include consular services among their functions. These embassy-based consulates are listed here only if their address differs from the embassy's.

	City	State	Zip	Phone	Fax
Afghanistan Embassy 2341 Wyoming Ave NW	Washington	DC	20008	202-483-6410	483-6488
TF: 866-323-8609 ■ *Web:* www.embassyofafghanistan.org					
Algeria Embassy 2118 Kalorama Rd NW	Washington	DC	20008	202-265-2800	986-5906
Web: www.algerianembassy.org					
Andorra Embassy 2 United Nations Plz 27th Fl	New York	NY	10017	212-750-8064	750-6630
Web: www.state.gov/r/pa/ei/bgn/3164.htm					
Angola Embassy 2108 16th St NW	Washington	DC	20009	202-785-1156	822-9049
Web: www.angola.org					
Antigua & Barbuda 305 E 47th St 6th Fl	New York	NY	10017	212-541-4117	
Web: antigua-barbuda.org					
Embassy 3216 New Mexico Ave NW	Washington	DC	20016	202-362-5122	362-5225
TF: 866-978-7299 ■ *Web:* www.antigua-barbuda.org					
Argentina					
Consulate General 2200 W Loop S Ste 1025	Houston	TX	77027	713-871-8935	
Web: www.chous.mrecic.gov.ar					
Consulate General					
5055 Wilshire Blvd Ste 210	Los Angeles	CA	90036	323-954-9155	934-9076
Web: clang.mrecic.gob.ar					
Consulate General 12 W 56th St	New York	NY	10019	212-603-0400	541-7746
Consulate General					
245 Peachtree Ctr Ave Ste 2101	Atlanta	GA	30303	404-880-0805	880-0806
Embassy 1600 New Hampshire Ave NW	Washington	DC	20009	202-238-6400	332-3171
Web: www.embassyofargentina.us					
Armenia Embassy 2225 R St NW	Washington	DC	20008	202-319-1976	
Web: www.armeniaemb.org					
Australia 150 E 42nd St 33rd Fl	New York	NY	10017	212-351-6600	351-6610
Web: unny.mission.gov.au					
Consulate General					
2029 Century Pk E Ste 3150	Los Angeles	CA	90067	310-229-2300	277-2258
Web: www.losangeles.consulate.gov.au					
Consulate General 150 E 42nd St 34th Fl	New York	NY	10017	212-351-6500	351-6501
Web: www.newyork.usa.embassy.gov.au					
Consulate General 1000 Bishop St PH	Honolulu	HI	96813	808-529-8100	529-8142
TF: 866-343-3086 ■ *Web:* www.usa.embassy.gov.au/whwh/hawaiicg.html					
Embassy 2005 Massachusetts Ave NW	Washington	DC	20036	202-558-2216	318-0771
TF: 800-345-6541 ■ *Web:* www.visahq.com					
Australian Consulate General					
Consulate General 123 N Wacker Dr Ste 1330	Chicago	IL	60606	312-419-1480	419-1499
Web: australia.visahq.com					
Austria 600 Third Ave 31st Fl	New York	NY	10016	917-542-8400	949-1840*
**Fax Area Code: 212* ■ *Web:* advantageaustria.org					
Consulate General 3524 International Ct NW	Washington	DC	20008	202-895-6700	
Web: www.austria.org					
Consulate General					
11859 Wilshire Blvd Ste 501	Los Angeles	CA	90025	310-444-9310	477-9897
TF: 800-255-2414 ■ *Web:* www.austria.org					
Consulate General 31 E 69th St	New York	NY	10021	212-933-5140	585-1992
Web: www.bmeia.gv.at/botschaft/gk-new-york.html					
Embassy 3524 International Ct NW	Washington	DC	20008	202-895-6700	895-6750
TF: 800-255-2414 ■ *Web:* www.austria.org					
Azerbaijan Embassy 2741 34th St NW	Washington	DC	20008	202-337-3500	
Web: www.azembassy.us					
Bahamas					
Consulate General 25 SE Second Ave	Miami	FL	33131	305-373-6295	373-6312
Web: bahamas.com					
Consulate General 231 E 46th St	New York	NY	10017	212-421-6420	688-5926
Web: www.bahamasny.net					
Embassy 2220 Massachusetts Ave NW	Washington	DC	20008	202-319-2660	319-2668
TF: 800-883-7421 ■ *Web:* nassau.usembassy.gov					
Bahrain 866 Second Ave 14th & 15th Fls	New York	NY	10017	212-223-6200	
Bangladesh Consulate General					
4201 Wilshire Blvd Ste 605	Los Angeles	CA	90010	323-932-0100	932-9703
Web: www.bangladeshconsulatela.com					
Barbados					
Consulate General					
2121 Poncedaleon Blvd Ste 1300	Coral Gables	FL	33134	305-442-1994	455-7975
Web: www.foreign.gov.bb					
Belarus Embassy 1619 New Hampshire Ave NW	Washington	DC	20009	202-986-1606	986-1805
Web: belarusfacts.by/belembassy					
Belgium 885 Second Ave 41st Fl	New York	NY	10017	212-378-6300	681-7618
Web: www.diplomatie.be/newyorkun					
Consulate General					
6100 Wilshire Blvd Ste 1200	Los Angeles	CA	90048	323-857-1244	
Web: www.diplomatie.be/losangeles					
Consulate General					
230 Peachtree St NW Ste 2710	Atlanta	GA	30303	404-659-2150	
Web: www.diplomatie.belgium.be/united_states					
Embassy 3330 Garfield St NW	Washington	DC	20008	202-333-6900	333-3079
Belize Embassy 2535 Massachusetts Ave NW	Washington	DC	20008	202-332-9636	332-6888
Web: www.embassyofbelize.gov.bz					
Benin Embassy 2124 Kalorama Rd NW	Washington	DC	20008	202-232-6656	265-1996
Web: www.beninembassy.us					
Bolivarian Republic of Venezuela					
Consulate General 545 Boylston St 3rd Fl	Boston	MA	02116	617-266-9368	
Web: newyork.embavenez-us.org					
Bolivia 801 Second Ave 4th Fl, Rm 42	New York	NY	10017	212-682-8132	
Consulate General 211 E 43rd St Ste 1004	New York	NY	10017	212-687-0530	687-0532

Phone Fax

Embassy 3014 Massachusetts Ave NW .... Washington DC 20008 202-483-4410 328-3712
Web: www.bolivia-usa.org

Bosnia & Herzegovina
Embassy 2109 E St NW .... Washington DC 20037 202-337-1500 337-1502
Web: www.bhembassy.org

Botswana Embassy
1531 New Hampshire Ave NW .... Washington DC 20036 202-244-4990 244-4164
Web: www.botswanaembassy.org

Brazil 747 Third Ave 9th Fl .... New York NY 10017 212-372-2600 371-5716
Web: www.un.int
Consulate General
300 Montgomery St Ste 300 .... San Francisco CA 94104 415-981-8170
Consulate General 175 Purchase St. .... Boston MA 02110 617-542-4000
Web: www.consulatebrazil.org
Consulate General 1233 W Loop S Ste 1150....... Houston TX 77027 713-961-3063 961-3070
TF: 800-326-2289 ■ *Web:* houston.itamaraty.gov.br
Consulate General
8484 Wilshire Blvd Ste 711 .... Beverly Hills CA 90211 323-651-2664 651-1274
TF: 877-782-5477 ■ *Web:* losangeles.itamaraty.gov.br
Consulate General 80 SW Eigth St 26th Fl........... Miami FL 33130 305-285-6200 285-6240
Web: miami.itamaraty.gov.br
Embassy 3006 Massachusetts Ave NW .... Washington DC 20008 202-238-2700
Web: washington.itamaraty.gov.br

Brunei Darussalam
Embassy 3520 International Ct NW .... Washington DC 20008 202-237-1838 885-0560
Web: www.bruneiembassy.org

Bulgaria 11 E 84th St .... New York NY 10028 212-737-4790 472-9865
Consulate General 121 E 62nd St .... New York NY 10021 212-935-4646 319-5955
Web: bulgaria-embassy.org
Embassy 1621 22nd St NW .... Washington DC 20008 202-387-0174 234-7973
TF: 800-961-6836 ■ *Web:* www.bulgaria-embassy.org

Burkina Faso Embassy
2005 Massachusetts Ave NW .... Washington DC 20008 202-332-5577 667-1882
TF: 800-345-6541 ■ *Web:* www.visahq.com

Burundi Embassy
2233 Wisconsin Ave NW Ste 212 .... Washington DC 20007 202-342-2574 342-2578
Web: www.burundiembassy-usa.org

Cambodia Embassy 4530 16th St NW .... Washington DC 20011 202-726-7742 726-8381
Web: www.embassyofcambodia.org

Cameroon Embassy 3400 International Dr NW........ Washington DC 20008 202-265-8790 387-3826
Web: www.cameroonembassyusa.org

Canada 885 Second Ave 14th Fl...................... New York NY 10017 212-848-1100 848-1195
TF: 800-267-8376 ■ *Web:* www.canadainternational.gc.ca
Consulate General 200 S Biscayne Blvd Ste 1600..... Miami FL 33131 305-579-1600 374-6774
Web: canadainternational.gc.ca
Consulate General 500 N Akard St Ste 2900 .... Dallas TX 75201 214-922-9806 922-9815
TF: 800-267-8376 ■ *Web:* www.canadainternational.gc.ca
Consulate General
1251 Ave of the Americas Concourse Level.......... New York NY 10020 212-596-1628 596-1790
TF: 800-267-8376 ■ *Web:* www.canadainternational.gc.ca
Consulate General 180 N Stetson Ave Ste 2400...... Chicago IL 60601 312-616-1860 616-1877
Web: www.can-am.gc.ca/chicago
Consulate General 701 Fourth Ave S 9th Fl..... Minneapolis MN 55415 612-333-4641 332-4061
Web: www.canadainternational.gc.ca
Consulate General
1175 Peachtree St NE 100 Colony Sq Ste 1700......... Atlanta GA 30361 404-532-2000 532-2050
Web: can-am.gc.ca
Consulate General 1251 Ave of the Americas...... New York NY 10020 212-596-1628
Web: can-am.gc.ca
Embassy 501 Pennsylvania Ave NW .... Washington DC 20001 202-682-1740 682-7726
TF: 800-567-6868 ■ *Web:* can-am.gc.ca

Cape Verde 27 E 69th St .... New York NY 10021 212-472-0333 794-1398
Embassy 3415 Massachusetts Ave NW .... Washington DC 20007 202-965-6820 965-1207
TF: 800-343-2347 ■ *Web:* www.virtualcapeverde.net

Chile
Consulate General 866 UN Plz Ste 601 .... New York NY 10017 212-980-3366 888-5288
Web: chile.gob.cl/es
Consulate General
870 Market St Ste 1058..................... San Francisco CA 94102 415-982-7662
Web: chile.gob.cl/san-francisco/en
Embassy 1732 Massachusetts Ave NW .... Washington DC 20036 202-785-1746 887-5579
TF: 855-310-8471 ■ *Web:* chilegobcl

Chile Mission 885 Second Ave 40th Fl .... New York NY 10017 917-322-6800 832-0236*
*Fax Area Code: 212

China 350 E 35th St......................................New York NY 10016 212-655-6100 634-7626
Web: www.china-un.org
Consulate General 1450 Laguna St .... San Francisco CA 94115 415-852-5941
Web: www.chinaconsulatesf.org
Consulate General 100 W Erie St................ Chicago IL 60654 312-803-0095 803-0110
Web: www.chinaconsulatechicago.org
Consulate General 3417 Montrose Blvd........... Houston TX 77006 713-520-1462 521-3064
Web: houston.china-consulate.org
Consulate General 443 Shatto Pl .... Los Angeles CA 90020 213-807-8088 807-1961
Web: losangeles.china-consulate.org
Embassy 2201 Wisconsin Ave NW Ste 110...... Washington DC 20007 202-337-1956 588-9760
Web: www.china-embassy.org

Colombia 140 E 57th St .... New York NY 10022 212-355-7776 355-7776
Web: www.colombiaun.org
Consulate General 500 N Michigan Ave Ste 2040... Chicago IL 60611 312-923-1196 923-1197
Web: nuevayork.consulado.gov.co
Consulate General 5851 San Felipe Ste 300 .... Houston TX 77057 713-527-8919 529-3395
Web: www.colhouston.org
Embassy 1724 Massachusetts Ave, NW.......... Washington DC 20036 202-387-8338 232-8643
Web: www.colombiaemb.org

Consulate General of Honduras
Consulate General 365 Canal St .... New Orleans LA 70130 504-522-3118

Consulate General of Liberia
866 UN Plz Ste 249 ....New York NY 10017 212-687-1033
Web: www.liberianconsulate-ny.com

Consulate General of Paraguay
801 Second Ave Ste 600..........................New York NY 10017 212-682-9441 682-9443
Web: www.consulparny.com

Phone Fax

Consulate General of Romania
Consulate General
11766 Wilshire Blvd Ste 560.................. Los Angeles CA 90025 310-444-0043
Web: www.consulateromania.org

Consulate General of Switzerland
633 Third Ave 30th Fl.............................New York NY 10017 212-599-5700 212-4266
Web: www.eda.admin.ch/newyork

Consulate General of the Republic of Suriname
6303 Blue Lagoon Dr Ste 325........................ Miami FL 33126 305-265-4655
Web: www.scgmia.com

Costa Rica 211 E 43rd St Rm 903 .... New York NY 10017 212-986-6373 986-6373
Consulate General
1605 W Olympic Blvd Ste 400.................. Los Angeles CA 90015 213-380-7915 380-5639
Web: www.costarica-embassy.org
Consulate General 2114 S St NW .... Washington DC 20008 202-480-2200 265-4795
Web: www.costarica-embassy.org
Consulate General 2730 SW Third Ave Ste 401....... Miami FL 33129 305-871-7485 522-0119*
*Fax Area Code: 786 ■ *Web:* www.costarica-embassy.org
Embassy 2114 S St NW..................... Washington DC 20008 202-499-2991 265-4795
Web: www.costarica-embassy.org

Croatia 820 Second Ave 19th Fl..................... New York NY 10017 212-986-1585 986-2011
Consulate General 369 Lexington Ave.......... New York NY 10017 212-599-3066 599-3106
Consulate General
11766 Wilshire Blvd Ste 1250................. Los Angeles CA 90025 310-477-1009
Web: www.croatiaemb.org
Consulate General 737 N Michigan Ave Ste 1030... Chicago IL 60611 312-482-9902
Web: www.croatiaemb.org
Embassy 2343 Massachusetts Ave NW .... Washington DC 20008 202-588-5899
Web: www.croatiaemb.org

Cyprus 13 E 40th St............................... New York NY 10016 212-481-6023 685-7316
Web: www.un.int
Consulate General 13 E 40th St .... New York NY 10016 212-686-6016 686-3660
Web: cyprusembassy.net
Embassy 2211 R St NW..................... Washington DC 20008 202-462-5772 483-6710
Web: www.cyprusembassy.net

Czech Republic 1109 Madison Ave.................. New York NY 10028 212-717-5643 717-5064
Web: www.mzv.cz/un.newyork
Consulate General
10990 Wilshire Blvd Ste 1100................. Los Angeles CA 90024 310-473-0889 473-9813
Web: www.mzv.cz/losangeles
Consulate General 321 E 73rd St.............. New York NY 10021 646-422-3344 422-3311
Web: www.mzv.cz/consulate.newyork
Embassy 3900 Spring of Freedom St NW .... Washington DC 20008 202-274-9100 966-8540
Web: www.mzv.cz

Democratic & Popular Republic of Algeria, The
Embassy - Consular Section
2118 Kalorama Rd NW......................... Washington DC 20008 202-265-2800
Web: www.embassy.org

Denmark
Consulate General 875 N Michigan Ave Ste 3950... Chicago IL 60611 800-345-6541 787-8744*
*Fax Area Code: 312 ■ *TF:* 800-345-6541 ■ *Web:* denmark.visahq.com
Embassy 3200 Whitehaven St NW............. Washington DC 20008 202-234-4300 328-1470
Web: usa.um.dk

Dominica
Embassy 3216 New Mexico Ave NW........... Washington DC 20016 202-364-6781 364-6791

Dominican Republic 144 E 44th St 4th Fl .... New York NY 10017 212-867-0833 297-2509
Web: www.un.int
Consulate General 1715 22nd St NW........... Washington DC 20008 773-714-4924
Web: www.domrep.org
Consulate General 1038 Brickell Ave............... Miami FL 33131 305-358-3220 358-2318
Web: www.domrep.org
Consulate General 1501 Broadway Ste 410....... New York NY 10036 212-768-2480 768-2677
Web: www.domrep.org
Consulate General 500 N Brand Blvd Ste 960 ...... Glendale CA 91203 818-504-6605 504-6617
Web: www.consulatedrwest.com
Consulate General 1715 22nd St NW........... Washington DC 20008 202-332-6280 387-2459
Web: www.domrep.org
Embassy 1715 22nd St NW.................. Washington DC 20008 202-332-6280 265-8057
Web: www.domrep.org

Ecuador 866 UN Plz Ste 516......................... New York NY 10017 212-935-1680 935-1835
Web: un.int
Consulate General
8484 Wilshire Blvd Ste 500................... Beverly Hills CA 90211 323-297-1150 297-1152
Web: cancilleria.gob.ec
Consulate General 400 Market St 4th Fl............ Newark NJ 07105 973-344-6900
Web: www.consuladoecuadornj.com
Consulate General 30 S Michigan Ave.......... Chicago IL 60603 312-338-1002 338-1004
Consulate General 4200 Westheimer Rd Ste 218.... Houston TX 77027 713-572-8731 572-8732
Web: www.cecunuevayork.com
Consulate General 1101 Brickell Ave Ste M102........ Miami FL 33131 305-373-8520 539-8313
Web: www.ecuador.org
Consulate General 800 Second Ave Ste 600 ...... New York NY 10017 212-808-0170 808-0188
Web: www.cecunuevayork.com
Embassy 2535 15th St NW .... Washington DC 20009 202-234-7200 234-3429
Web: www.ecuador.org

Egypt 304 E 44th St.................................. New York NY 10017 212-503-0300
Web: egyptembassy.net
Consulate General 500 N Michigan Ave Ste 1900... Chicago IL 60611 312-828-9162 828-9167
Web: egypt.embassy-online.net
Consulate General 1110 Second Ave Ste 201 ..... New York NY 10022 212-759-7120 308-7643
Web: www.egypt-nyc.com
Embassy 3521 International Ct NW .... Washington DC 20008 202-895-5400 244-4319
Web: www.egyptembassy.net

El Salvador 46 Pk Ave .... New York NY 10016 212-889-3608 725-3467
Consulate General
3450 Wilshire Blvd Ste 250................... Los Angeles CA 90010 213-383-6134 383-8599
Web: www.elsalvador.org
Consulate General 1400 16th St Ste 100........ Washington DC 20036 202-595-7500 270-9683*
*Fax Area Code: 713 ■ *Web:* www.elsalvador.org
Consulate General 1400 Sixth St Ste 100 .... Washington DC 20036 305-774-0840
Web: www.elsalvador.org
Embassy 1400 16th St NW Ste 100............ Washington DC 20036 202-595-7500 232-3763
Web: www.elsalvador.org

Name / Address	City	State	ZIP	Phone	Fax
Embassy of Bosnia & Herzegovina					
Consulate General 2109 E St NW	Washington	DC	20037	202-337-1500	337-2909
Web: www.bhembassy.org					
Embassy of Hungary 3910 Shoemaker St NW	Washington	DC	20008	202-362-6730	
Embassy of Israel					
Consulate General 3514 International Dr	Washington	DC	20008	202-364-5500	
Web: www.israelemb.org					
Embassy of Syria 2215 Wyoming Ave NW	Washington	DC	20008	202-232-6313	
Web: www.syrianembassy.us					
Embassy of the Kingdom of Bahrain					
Embassy 3502 International Dr NW	Washington	DC	20008	202-342-1111	362-2192
Web: www.bahrainembassy.org					
Estonia 305 E 47th St 6th Fl	New York	NY	10017	212-883-0640	514-0099*
*Fax Area Code: 646 ■ *Web:* www.un.estemb.org					
Consulate General 305 E 47th St 3 Dag Hammarskjold Pl Ste 6B	New York	NY	10016	212-883-0636	883-0648
Web: www.nyc.estemb.org					
Embassy 2131 Massachusetts Ave NW	Washington	DC	20008	202-588-0101	588-0108
Web: www.estemb.org					
Ethiopia Embassy 3506 International Dr NW	Washington	DC	20008	202-364-1200	587-0195
Web: www.ethiopianembassy.org					
Fiji Embassy 1707 L St NW Ste 200	Washington	DC	20036	202-337-8320	466-8325
TF: 800-932-3454 ■ *Web:* www.fijiembassydc.com					
Finland 866 UN Plz Ste 222	New York	NY	10017	212-355-2100	759-6156
Web: www.finlandun.org					
Consulate General 11900 W Olympic Blvd Ste 580	Los Angeles	CA	90064	310-203-9903	481-8981
Web: www.finland.org					
Consulate General 866 UN Plz Ste 250	New York	NY	10017	212-750-4400	750-4418
Web: www.finland.org					
Embassy 3301 Massachusetts Ave NW	Washington	DC	20008	202-298-5800	298-6030
Web: www.finland.org					
France 1 Dag Hammarskjold Plaza # 36	New York	NY	10017	212-371-0480	421-6889
Web: www.un.int					
Consulate General 1340 Poydras St Ste 1710	New Orleans	LA	70112	504-569-2870	569-2871
Web: www.consulfrance-nouvelleorleans.org					
Consulate General 1395 Brickell Ave Ste 1050	Miami	FL	33131	305-403-4185	403-4187
TF: 877-624-8737 ■ *Web:* www.consulfrance-miami.org					
Consulate General 205 N Michigan Ave Ste 3700	Chicago	IL	60601	312-327-5200	327-5201
TF: 866-858-4430 ■ *Web:* www.consulfrance-chicago.org					
Consulate General 777 Post Oak Blvd Ste 600	Houston	TX	77056	713-572-2799	572-2911
TF: 888-902-5322 ■ *Web:* www.consulfrance-houston.org					
Consulate General 10390 Santa Monica Blvd Ste 410	Los Angeles	CA	90025	310-235-3200	479-4813
Web: www.consulfrance-losangeles.org					
Consulate General 934 Fifth Ave	New York	NY	10021	212-606-3600	606-3614
TF: 800-772-1213 ■ *Web:* www.consulfrance-newyork.org					
Consulate General 540 Bush St	San Francisco	CA	94108	415-397-4330	433-8357
TF: 800-553-4133 ■ *Web:* www.consulfrance-sanfrancisco.org					
Consulate General 3475 Piedmont Rd NE Ste 1840	Atlanta	GA	30305	404-495-1660	495-1661
TF: 888-937-2623 ■ *Web:* www.consulfrance-atlanta.org					
Consulate General 31 St James Ave Ste 750	Boston	MA	02116	617-832-4400	
Web: www.consulfrance-boston.org					
Embassy 4101 Reservoir Rd NW	Washington	DC	20007	202-944-6000	944-6175
TF: 800-622-6232 ■ *Web:* www.ambafrance-us.org					
Gambia Embassy 2233 Wisconsin Ave NW Georgetown Plz Ste 240	Washington	DC	20007	202-785-1399	342-0240
Web: www.gambiaembassy.us					
Germany 871 UN Plz	New York	NY	10017	212-940-0400	940-0402
Web: www.new-york-un.diplo.de					
Consulate General 1330 Post Oak Blvd Ste 1850	Houston	TX	77056	713-627-7770	627-0506
Web: germany.info					
Consulate General 1960 Jackson St	San Francisco	CA	94109	415-775-1061	775-0187
Web: www.germany.info					
Consulate General 676 N Michigan Ave Ste 3200	Chicago	IL	60611	312-202-0480	202-0466
Web: germany.info					
Consulate General 285 Peachtree Ctr Ave NE Ste 901	Atlanta	GA	30303	404-659-4760	659-1280
TF: 866-687-8561 ■ *Web:* germany.info					
Consulate General 6222 Wilshire Blvd Ste 500	Los Angeles	CA	90048	323-930-2703	930-2805
Web: germany.info					
Consulate General 100 Biscayne Blvd Ste 2200	Miami	FL	33132	305-358-0290	358-0307
Web: germany.info					
Consulate General 871 UN Plz	New York	NY	10017	212-610-9700	610-9702
Web: germany.info					
Embassy 4645 Reservoir Rd NW	Washington	DC	20007	202-298-4000	
Web: www.germany.info					
Ghana 19 E 47th St	New York	NY	10017	212-832-1300	751-6743
Web: www.un.int/ghana					
Consulate General 19 E 47th St	New York	NY	10017	212-832-1300	751-6743
Web: ghanaconsulatenewyork.org					
Embassy 3512 International Dr NW	Washington	DC	20008	202-686-4520	686-4527
Web: www.ghanaembassy.org					
Greece 866 Second Ave 13th Fl	New York	NY	10017	212-888-6900	888-4440
Web: www.mfa.gr					
Consulate General 12424 Wilshire Blvd Ste 800	Los Angeles	CA	90025	310-826-5555	826-8670
Web: www.mfa.gr					
Consulate General 650 N St Clair St	Chicago	IL	60611	312-335-3915	335-3958
Web: www.mfa.gr					
Consulate General 86 Beacon St	Boston	MA	02108	617-523-0100	523-0511
Web: www.mfa.gr					
Consulate General 69 E 79th St	New York	NY	10075	212-988-5500	734-8492
Web: www.mfa.gr					
Consulate General 2441 Gough St	San Francisco	CA	94123	415-775-2102	776-6815
Web: www.mfa.gr					
Embassy 2217 Massachusetts Ave	Washington	DC	20008	202-939-1300	939-1324
Web: www.mfa.gr/usa/en/the-embassy					
Grenada 800 Second Ave Ste 400-K	New York	NY	10017	212-599-0301	
Embassy 1701 New Hampshire Ave NW	Washington	DC	20009	202-265-2561	265-2468
Web: www.grenadaembassyusa.org					
Guatemala 57 Pk Ave	New York	NY	10016	212-679-4760	685-8741
Web: www.un.int					
Consulate General 3013 Fountain View Dr Ste 210	Houston	TX	77057	713-953-9531	953-9383
Embassy 2220 R St NW	Washington	DC	20008	202-745-4953	
Web: www.consulateofguatemalaindenver.org					
Guinea Embassy 2112 Leroy Pl NW	Washington	DC	20008	202-986-4300	
Web: www.guineaembassyusa.com					
Guyana 801 Second Ave 5th Fl	New York	NY	10017	212-573-5828	573-6225
Web: www.guyana.org/govt/govt_offices.html					
Consulate General 308 W 38th St	New York	NY	10001	212-947-5110	947-5163
Web: www.guyana.org					
Embassy 2490 Tracy Pl NW	Washington	DC	20008	202-265-6900	232-1297
Web: guyana.org					
Haiti 801 Second Ave Ste 600	New York	NY	10017	212-370-4840	661-8698
Consulate General 815 2nd Ave 6th Fl	New York	NY	10017	212-697-9767	
Web: www.embassypages.com/missions/embassy21725					
Consulate General 220 S State St Ste 2110	Chicago	IL	60604	312-922-4004	922-7122
Web: www.haitianconsulate.org					
Consulate General 259 SW 13th St	Miami	FL	33130	305-859-2003	854-7441
Web: haiti.org					
Consulate General 545 Boylston St Rm 201	Boston	MA	02116	617-266-3660	778-6898
Embassy 2311 Massachusetts Ave NW	Washington	DC	20008	202-332-4090	745-7215
Web: www.haiti.org					
Holy See 25 E 39th St	New York	NY	10016	212-370-7885	370-9622
Web: www.holyseemission.org					
Apostolic Nunciature 3339 Massachusetts Ave NW	Washington	DC	20008	202-333-7121	337-4036
Web: www.holyseemission.org					
Honduras 866 UN Plz Ste 417	New York	NY	10017	212-752-3370	223-0498
Web: www.un.int					
Consulate General 4439 W Fullerton Ave	Chicago	IL	60639	773-342-8281	
Web: hondurasemb.org					
Consulate General 7400 Harwin Dr Ste 200	Houston	TX	77036	281-377-5127	785-5931*
*Fax Area Code: 713 ■ *Web:* www.consuladohondurashouston.org					
Consulate General 3550 Wilshire Blvd Ste 410	Los Angeles	CA	90010	213-383-9244	383-9306
Web: www.consulate-los-angeles.com/honduras.html					
Consulate General 870 Market St Ste 875	San Francisco	CA	94102	415-392-0076	
Web: www.hondurasemb.org					
Embassy 3007 Tilden St NW	Washington	DC	20008	202-966-7702	966-9751
TF: 800-375-5283 ■ *Web:* www.hondurasemb.org					
Hungary Consulate General 223 E 52nd St	New York	NY	10022	212-752-0669	755-5986
Iceland 800 Third Ave 36th Fl	New York	NY	10022	212-593-2700	593-6269
Web: www.iceland.is					
Consulate General 800 Third Ave 36th Fl	New York	NY	10022	646-282-9360	282-9369
Web: www.iceland.is/iceland-abroad					
Embassy House of Sweden 2900 K St NW Ste 509	Washington	DC	20007	202-265-6653	265-6656
Web: www.iceland.is/iceland-abroad/us					
India 235 E 43rd St	New York	NY	10017	212-490-9660	490-9656
Web: www.un.int					
Consulate General 540 Arguello Blvd	San Francisco	CA	94118	415-668-0662	668-9764
TF: 866-978-0055 ■ *Web:* www.cgisf.org					
Consulate General 455 N Cityfront Plz Dr Ste 850	Chicago	IL	60611	312-595-0405	595-0417
Web: www.indianconsulate.com					
Embassy 2107 Massachusetts Ave NW	Washington	DC	20008	202-939-7000	265-4351
Web: www.indianembassy.org					
Embassy - Consular Wing 2536 Massachusetts Ave NW	Washington	DC	20008	202-939-9806	
Web: www.indianembassy.org					
Indonesia 325 E 38th St	New York	NY	10016	212-972-8333	972-9780
Web: www.indonesiamission-ny.org					
Consulate General 211 W Wacker Dr 8th Fl	Chicago	IL	60606	312-920-1880	920-1881
Web: www.indonesiachicago.org					
Consulate General 5 E 68th St	New York	NY	10021	212-879-0600	570-6206
Web: www.kemlu.go.id					
Embassy 2020 Massachusetts Ave NW	Washington	DC	20036	202-775-5200	775-5365
Web: www.embassyofindonesia.org					
Ireland 1 Dag Hammarskjold Plz # 885	New York	NY	10017	212-421-6934	752-4726
Web: www.un.int					
Consulate General 100 Pine St Ste 3350	San Francisco	CA	94111	415-392-4214	392-0885
Web: www.dfa.ie/irish-consulate/sanfrancisco					
Embassy 2234 Massachusetts Ave NW	Washington	DC	20008	202-462-3939	232-5993
TF: 866-560-1050 ■ *Web:* www.dfa.ie/irish-embassy/usa					
Israel 800 Second Ave	New York	NY	10017	212-499-5000	499-5515
Web: embassies.gov.il					
Consulate General 1100 Spring St NW Ste 440	Atlanta	GA	30309	404-487-6500	
Web: www.israelemb.org					
Consulate General 456 Montgomery St Ste 2100	San Francisco	CA	94104	415-844-7500	844-7555
Web: www.israelemb.org					
Consulate General 100 Biscayne Blvd Ste 1800	Miami	FL	33132	305-925-9400	
Web: www.israelemb.org					
Embassy 3514 International Dr NW	Washington	DC	20008	202-364-5500	
Web: www.israelemb.org					
Italy 885 Second Ave 49th Fl	New York	NY	10017	212-486-9191	486-1036
Web: www.italyun.esteri.it					
Consulate General 2590 Webster St	San Francisco	CA	94115	415-292-9200	931-7205
Web: www.conssanfrancisco.esteri.it					
Consulate General 4000 Ponce de Leon Ste 590	Coral Gables	FL	33146	305-374-6322	374-7945
Web: www.consmiami.esteri.it					
Consulate General 150 S Independence Mall W Public Ledger Bldg Ste 1026	Philadelphia	PA	19106	215-592-7329	592-9808
TF: 800-531-0840 ■ *Web:* www.consfiladelfia.esteri.it					
Consulate General 1300 Post Oak Blvd Ste 660	Houston	TX	77056	713-850-7520	850-9113
TF: 800-637-9314 ■ *Web:* www.conshouston.esteri.it					

Phone Fax

Consulate General 690 Pk Ave New York NY 10021 212-737-9100 249-4945
Web: www.consnewyork.esteri.it
Consulate General 600 Atlantic Ave 17th Fl Boston MA 02210 617-722-9201 722-9407
TF: 888-225-5427 ■ *Web:* www.consboston.esteri.it
Embassy 3000 Whitehaven St NW Washington DC 20008 202-612-4400 518-2154
TF: 800-222-1222 ■ *Web:* www.ambwashingtondc.esteri.it

Jamaica Embassy 1520 New Hampshire Ave NW Washington DC 20036 202-452-0660 452-0036
Web: www.embassyofjamaica.org

Japan 866 UN Plz 2nd Fl New York NY 10017 212-223-4300 751-1966
Web: www.un.int
Consulate General 3601 C St Ste 1300 Anchorage AK 99503 907-562-8424 562-8434
Web: www.anchorage.us.emb-japan.go.jp
Consulate General
3438 Peachtree Rd Phipps Tower Ste 850 Atlanta GA 30326 404-240-4300 240-4311
Web: www.atlanta.us.emb-japan.go.jp
Consulate General 1742 Nuuanu Ave Honolulu HI 96817 808-543-3111 543-3170
Web: www.honolulu.us.emb-japan.go.jp
Consulate General 737 N Michigan Ave Ste 1100 Chicago IL 60611 312-280-0400 280-9568
Web: www.chicago.us.emb-japan.go.jp
Consulate General
50 Fremont St Ste 2300 San Francisco CA 94105 415-777-3533 974-3660
Web: www.sf.us.emb-japan.go.jp
Consulate General 1801 W End Ave Ste 900 Nashville TN 37203 615-340-4300 340-4311
Web: www.nashville.us.emb-japan.go.jp
Consulate General
400 Renaissance Ctr Ste 1600 Detroit MI 48243 313-567-0120 567-0274
Web: www.detroit.us.emb-japan.go.jp
Consulate General
Wells Fargo Ctr 1300 SW Fifth Ave Ste 2700 Portland OR 97201 503-221-1811 224-8936
Web: www.portland.us.emb-japan.go.jp
Consulate General 1225 17th St Ste 3000 Denver CO 80202 303-534-1151 534-3393
Web: www.denver.us.emb-japan.go.jp
Consulate General
350 S Grand Ave Ste 1700 Los Angeles CA 90071 213-617-6700 617-6727
Web: www.la.us.emb-japan.go.jp
Consulate General 299 Pk Ave 18th Fl New York NY 10171 212-371-8222 371-1294
Web: www.ny.us.emb-japan.go.jp
Consulate General 601 Union St Ste 500 Seattle WA 98101 206-682-9107 624-9097
Web: www.seattle.us.emb-japan.go.jp
Consulate General
80 SW Eigth St Brickell Bay View Ctr Ste 3200 Miami FL 33130 305-530-9090 530-0950
Web: www.miami.us.emb-japan.go.jp
Consulate General
600 Atlantic Ave Federal Reserve Plz 14th Fl Boston MA 02210 617-973-9772 542-1329
Web: www.boston.us.emb-japan.go.jp
Embassy 2520 Massachusetts Ave NW Washington DC 20008 202-238-6700 328-2187
Web: us.emb-japan.go.jp

Jordan
Embassy 3504 International Dr NW Washington DC 20008 202-966-2664 966-3110
Web: www.jordanembassyus.org

Kazakhstan
Consulate 305 E 47th St 3rd Fl New York NY 10017 212-888-3024 888-3025
Web: www.kazconsulny.org
Embassy 1401 16th St NW Washington DC 20036 202-232-5488 232-5845
Web: www.kazakhembus.com

Kenya Embassy 2249 R St NW Washington DC 20008 202-387-6101 462-3829
Web: www.kenyaembassy.com

Korea Republic of 335 E 45th St New York NY 10017 212-439-4000 986-1083
Web: www.un.int
Consulate General
455 N City Front Plz Dr NBC Tower Ste 2700 Chicago IL 60611 312-822-9485 822-9849
Web: usa-chicago.mofat.go.kr
Consulate General 3243 Wilshire Blvd Los Angeles CA 90010 213-385-9300 385-1849
Web: south-korea.embassy-online.net
Consulate General 460 Pk Ave New York NY 10022 646-674-6000
Consulate General 2033 Sixth Ave Ste 1125 Seattle WA 98121 206-441-1011
TF: 800-375-5283
Consulate General 2756 Pali Hwy Honolulu HI 96817 808-595-6109 595-3046
Web: usa-honolulu.mofat.go.kr

Kuwait Embassy 2940 Tilden St NW Washington DC 20008 202-966-0702 966-0517
TF: 800-688-9889 ■ *Web:* www.kuwaitembassy.us

Lao People's Democratic Republic Embassy
2222 S St NW Washington DC 20008 202-332-6416 332-4923
Web: www.laoembassy.com

Latvia Embassy 2306 Massachusetts Ave NW Washington DC 20008 202-328-2840 328-2860
Web: www.mfa.gov.lv

Lebanon 866 UN Plz Rm 531-533 New York NY 10017 212-355-5460 838-2819
Consulate General 9 E 76th St New York NY 10021 212-744-7905
Web: nylebcons.org
Embassy 2560 28th St NW Washington DC 20008 202-939-6300 939-6324
Web: www.lebanonembassyus.org

Lesotho Embassy 2511 Massachusetts Ave NW Washington DC 20008 202-797-5533 234-6815
Web: lesothoemb-usa.gov.ls

Liberia
Consulate General
866 United Nations Plaza Ste 249 New York NY 10017 212-687-1025 599-3189
Web: liberianconsulate-ny.com
Embassy 5201 16th St NW Washington DC 20011 202-723-0437 723-0436
Web: www.liberianembassyus.org

Liechtenstein Embassy
2900 K St NW Ste 602B Washington DC 20007 202-331-0590
Web: www.liechtensteinusa.org

Lithuania
Consulate General
420 Fifth Ave Ste 304 3rd Fl New York NY 10018 212-354-7840 354-7911
Web: usa.mfa.lt
Embassy 2622 16th St NW Washington DC 20009 202-234-5860 328-0466
Web: www.usa.mfa.lt

Luxembourg
Consulate General 17 Beekman Pl New York NY 10022 212-888-6664 888-6116
Web: newyork-cg.mae.lu/en
Consulate General 1 Sansome St Ste 830 San Francisco CA 94104 415-788-0816 788-0985
Web: sanfrancisco.mae.lu
Embassy 2200 Massachusetts Ave NW Washington DC 20008 202-265-4171 328-8270
Web: washington.mae.lu

Madagascar Embassy
2374 Massachusetts Ave NW Washington DC 20008 202-265-5525
Web: www.madagascar-embassy.org

Malaysia 313 E 43rd St New York NY 10017 212-986-6310 490-8576
Web: www.un.int/malaysia
Consulate General 550 S Hope St Ste 400 Los Angeles CA 90071 213-892-1238
Web: www.malaysianconsulatela.com
Embassy 3516 International Ct NW Washington DC 20008 202-572-9700 572-9882
Web: www.kln.gov.my/web/usa_washington/home

Mali Embassy 2130 R St NW Washington DC 20008 202-332-2249 332-6603
Web: www.maliembassy.us

Malta Embassy 2017 Connecticut Ave NW Washington DC 20008 202-462-3611
Web: www.malta-citizenship.info

Marshall Islands Embassy
2433 Massachusetts Ave NW Washington DC 20008 202-234-5414 232-3236
Web: www.rmiembassyus.org

Mauritania Embassy 2129 Leroy Pl NW Washington DC 20008 202-232-5700
Web: www.mauritaniaembassy.com

Mauritius Embassies 1709 N St NW Washington DC 20036 202-244-1491 966-0983
Web: www.maurinet.com/embasydc.html

Mexico 3810 Ventor Ave Atlantic City NJ 08401 609-344-0366
Web: mexicorestaurantbar.com
Consulate General 571 N Grand Ave Nogales AZ 85621 520-287-2521 287-3175
Web: www.sre.gob.mx
Consulate General 800 Brazos St Ste 330 Austin TX 78701 512-478-2866 478-8008
Web: www.sre.gob.mx
Consulate General 1010 Eigth St Sacramento CA 95814 916-441-3287
Web: www.mexico.us/consulate.htm
Consulate General 910 E San Antonio St El Paso TX 79901 915-533-3644 532-7163
Web: www.sre.gob.mx
Consulate General 127 Navarro St San Antonio TX 78205 210-227-9145
Consulate General 1612 Farragut St Laredo TX 78040 956-723-0990 723-1741
Web: www.sre.gob.mx
Consulate General 5350 Leesdale Dr Ste 100 Denver CO 80246 303-331-1110 331-0169
Web: consulmex.sre.gob.mx/denver
Consulate General 204 S Ashland Ave Chicago IL 60607 312-738-2383
Consulate General 27 E 39th St New York NY 10016 212-217-6400
Consulate General 4506 Carolinas St Houston TX 77004 713-271-6800 271-3201
TF: 877-639-4835 ■ *Web:* www.sre.gob.mx
Consulate General 1911 Pennsylvania Ave Washington DC 20006 202-728-1600 728-1698
Web: embamex2.sre.gob.mx/eua/index.php/es
Consulate General 532 Folsom St San Francisco CA 94105 415-354-1700
Web: www.consulmexsf.com
Embassy 1911 Pennsylvania Ave NW Washington DC 20006 202-728-1600 728-1766
Web: embamex.sre.gob.mx

Micronesia 300 E 42nd St Ste 1600 New York NY 10017 212-697-8370 697-8295
TF: 800-469-4828 ■ *Web:* www.fsmgov.org/fsmun
Consulate 1725 N St NW Ste 910 Washington DC 20036 202-223-4383 223-4391
TF: 877-730-9753 ■ *Web:* www.fsmembassydc.org

Moldova Embassy 2101 S St NW Washington DC 20008 202-667-1130 667-2624
Web: www.embassy.org

Mongolia Embassy 2833 M St NW Washington DC 20007 202-333-7117 298-9227
Web: www.mongolianembassy.us

Morocco
Consulate General 10 E 40th St 24th Fl New York NY 10016 212-758-2625 779-7441
Web: www.moroccanconsulate.com
Embassy 1601 21st St NW Washington DC 20009 202-462-7979
Web: embassywashingtondc.com

Mozambique Embassy
1525 New Hampshire Ave NW Washington DC 20036 202-293-7146 835-0245
Web: www.embamoc-usa.org

Myanmar Embassy 2300 S St NW Washington DC 20008 202-332-3344 332-4351
Web: www.mewashingtondc.com

Nepal 820 Second Ave Ste 17B New York NY 10017 212-370-3988 953-2038
Embassy 2131 Leroy Pl NW Washington DC 20008 202-667-4550 667-5534
Web: www.nepalembassyusa.org

Netherlands
Consulate General 303 E Wacker Dr Ste 2600 Chicago IL 60601 312-780-1314 856-9218
Web: www.the-netherlands.org/organization/consulate-general-chicago/consulate-general-in-chicago.html
Consulate General 666 Third Ave 19th Fl New York NY 10017 877-388-2443 246-9679*
**Fax Area Code: 212* ■ *TF:* 877-388-2443 ■ *Web:* www.the-netherlands.org
Embassy 4200 Linnean Ave NW Washington DC 20008 877-388-2443 362-3430*
**Fax Area Code: 202* ■ *TF:* 877-388-2443 ■ *Web:* www.the-netherlands.org

New Zealand
Consulate General
2425 Olympic Blvd Ste 600-E Santa Monica CA 90404 310-566-6555
Web: www.nzcgla.com
Embassy 37 Observatory Cir NW Washington DC 20008 202-328-4800 667-5227
TF: 855-844-2835 ■ *Web:* www.mfat.govt.nz/en/embassies

Nicaragua 820 Second Ave Ste 801 New York NY 10017 212-490-7997 286-0815
Web: www.un.int
Consulate General 8989 Westheimer St Houston TX 77063 713-789-2762
Web: www.consuladodenicaragua.com
Consulate General 820 Second Ave Ste 802 New York NY 10017 212-986-6562
Web: consuladonicamiami.com
Embassy 1627 New Hampshire Ave NW Washington DC 20009 202-939-6570
Web: consuladodenicaragua.com

Niger Embassy 2204 R St NW Washington DC 20008 202-483-4224 483-3169
Web: www.embassyofniger.org

Nigeria
Consulate General 828 Second Ave New York NY 10017 212-850-2200 687-1476
Web: www.nigeriahouse.com
Embassy 3519 International Ct NW Washington DC 20008 202-986-8400
Web: www.nigeriaembassyusa.org

Norway 825 Third Ave 39th Fl New York NY 10022 646-430-7510
Web: www.norway-un.org
Consulate General 3410 W Dallas St Houston TX 77019 713-620-4200 620-4290
Web: www.norway.org/Embassy
Consulate General 924 E 21st St Minneapolis MN 55404 612-332-3338 332-1386
Web: www.norway.org

	City	State	Zip	Phone	Fax
Consulate General 825 Third Ave 38th Fl.	New York	NY	10022	646-430-7599	
Web: www.norway.org/embassy					
Embassy 2720 34th St NW	Washington	DC	20008	202-333-6000	337-0870
Web: www.norway.org					
Oman Embassy 2535 Belmont Rd NW	Washington	DC	20008	202-387-1980	
Web: www.omani.info					
Pakistan 8 E 65th St	New York	NY	10065	212-879-8600	744-7348
Web: www.pakun.org					
Consulate General 12 E 65th St	New York	NY	10065	212-879-5800	517-6987
Web: www.pakistanconsulateny.org					
Consulate General 10850 Wilshire Blvd Ste 1250	Los Angeles	CA	90024	310-441-5114	441-9256
Web: www.pakconsulatela.org					
Embassy 3517 International Ct NW	Washington	DC	20008	202-243-6500	686-1534
Web: www.embassyofpakistanusa.org					
Palau					
Embassy 1701 Pennsylvania Ave NW Ste 300	Washington	DC	20006	202-349-8598	
Web: palauembassy.com					
Panama 866 UN Plz Ste 4030	New York	NY	10017	212-421-5420	421-2694
Web: www.panama-un.org/en.html					
Consulate General 1100 Poydras St Ste 2615	New Orleans	LA	70163	504-525-3458	524-8960
Web: www.consulateofpanama.com					
Consulate General 2862 McGill Terrace NW	Washington	DC	20008	305-447-3700	447-4142
Web: embassyofpanama.org					
Embassy 2862 McGill Terr NW	Washington	DC	20008	202-483-1407	
Web: embassyofpanama.org					
Papua New Guinea Embassy 1779 Massachusetts Ave NW Ste 805	Washington	DC	20036	202-745-3680	745-3679
Web: www.pngembassy.org					
Paraguay 801 Second Ave Ste 702	New York	NY	10017	212-687-3490	818-1282
Consulate General 25 SE Second Ave Ste 705	Miami	FL	33131	305-374-9090	374-5522
Web: www.consulparmiami.org					
Embassy 2400 Massachusetts Ave NW	Washington	DC	20008	202-483-6960	234-4508
Permenent Mission of Argentina 1 UN Plz	New York	NY	10017	212-688-6300	980-8395
Permenent Mission of Turkey 821 UN Plz 10th Fl	New York	NY	10017	212-682-8717	949-0086
Peru 820 Second Ave Ste 1600	New York	NY	10017	212-687-3336	972-6975
Consulate General 870 Market St Ste 1067	San Francisco	CA	94102	415-362-7136	362-2836
TF: 877-714-7378 ■ *Web:* www.consuladoperu.com					
Consulate General 100 Hamilton Plaza	Paterson	NJ	07505	973-278-3324	278-0254
TF: 877-714-7378 ■ *Web:* www.consuladoperu.com					
Consulate General 1001 S Monaco Pkwy Ste 210	Denver	CO	80224	303-355-8555	355-8555
Web: www.consuladoperu.com					
Consulate General 5177 Richmond Ave Ste 695	Houston	TX	77056	713-355-9517	355-9377
TF: 877-714-7378 ■ *Web:* www.consuladoperu.com					
Consulate General 3450 Wilshire Blvd Ste 800	Los Angeles	CA	90010	213-252-5910	252-8130
TF: 877-714-7378 ■ *Web:* www.consuladoperu.com					
Consulate General 444 Brickell Ave Ste M135	Miami	FL	33131	877-714-7378	381-6027*
*Fax Area Code: 305 ■ *TF:* 877-714-7378 ■ *Web:* www.consuladoperu.com					
Consulate General 180 N Michigan Ave Ste 1830	Chicago	IL	60601	312-782-1599	704-6969
TF: 877-714-7378 ■ *Web:* www.consuladoperu.com					
Consulate General 241 E 49th St	New York	NY	10017	646-735-3828	735-3866
Web: www.consuladoperu.com					
Philippines 556 Fifth Ave 5th Fl	New York	NY	10036	212-764-1300	840-8602
Web: www.un.int					
Consulate General 447 Sutter St 6th Fl Philippine Ctr Bldg	San Francisco	CA	94108	415-433-6666	421-2641
TF: 877-700-0669 ■ *Web:* www.philippinessanfrancisco.org					
Consulate General 30 N Michigan Ave Ste 2100	Chicago	IL	60602	312-332-6458	332-3657
TF: 888-259-7838 ■ *Web:* www.chicagopcg.com					
Consulate General 3435 Wilshire Blvd Ste 550	Los Angeles	CA	90010	213-639-0980	639-0990
Web: www.philippineconsulatela.org					
Consulate General 556 Fifth Ave	New York	NY	10036	212-764-1330	764-6010
TF: 866-589-1878 ■ *Web:* www.newyorkpcg.org					
Embassy 1600 Massachusetts Ave NW	Washington	DC	20036	202-467-9300	467-9417
TF: 800-527-2820 ■ *Web:* www.philippineembassy-usa.org					
Poland 9 E 66th St	New York	NY	10065	212-744-2506	517-6771
Web: nowyjorkonz.msz.gov.pl					
Embassy 2640 16th St NW	Washington	DC	20009	202-234-3800	
Web: www.polandembassy.org					
Qatar 809 UN Plz 4th Fl	New York	NY	10017	212-486-9335	758-4952
Web: www.un.org					
Consulate General 1990 Post Oak Blvd Ste 900	Houston	TX	77056	713-355-8221	355-8184
Embassy 2555 M St NW	Washington	DC	20037	202-274-1600	
Web: www.qatarembassy.net					
Romania 573-577 Third Ave	New York	NY	10016	212-682-3273	
Web: www.un.int					
Consulate General 200 E 38th St	New York	NY	10016	212-682-9123	
Web: newyork.mae.ro/en					
Royal Thai Consulate General					
Consulate General 351 E 52nd St	New York	NY	10022	212-754-1770	754-1907
Web: www.thaiconsulnewyork.com					
Russia 136 E 67th St	New York	NY	10065	212-861-4900	628-0252
Web: russiaun.ru					
Consulate General 600 University St Ste 2510	Seattle	WA	98121	206-728-0232	
Web: seattle.mid.ru/web/seattle-en/main					
Consulate General 2790 Green St	San Francisco	CA	94123	415-928-6878	929-0306
Web: www.consulrussia.org					
Consulate General 9 E 91st St	New York	NY	10128	212-534-3782	
Web: ruscon.org					
Embassy 2650 Wisconsin Ave NW	Washington	DC	20007	202-298-5700	298-5735
Web: www.russianembassy.org					
Rwanda Embassy 1875 Connecticut Ave N W	Washington	DC	20009	202-232-2882	232-4544
Web: www.rwandaembassy.org					
Saint Kitts & Nevis Embassy 414 E 75th St 5th Fl	New York	NY	10021	202-686-2636	686-5740
Web: www.stkittsnevis.org					
Saint Lucia 800 Second Ave Fl 5	New York	NY	10017	212-697-9360	697-4993
Web: saintluciamissionun.org					
Consulate General 800 Second Ave 9th Fl	New York	NY	10017	212-697-9360	697-4993
Web: saintluciaconsulateny.org					
Embassy 3216 New Mexico Ave NW	Washington	DC	20016	202-364-6792	
TF: 800-456-3984 ■ *Web:* www.state.gov/r/pa/ei/bgn/2344.htm					
Saint Vincent & the Grenadines					
Consulate General 801 Second Ave 21st Fl	New York	NY	10017	212-687-4490	949-5946
Web: www.ny.consulate.gov.vc					
Embassy 3216 New Mexico Ave NW	Washington	DC	20016	202-364-6730	364-6736
Web: www.embsvg.com					
Saudi Arabia					
Consulate General 5718 Westheimer Rd Ste 1500	Houston	TX	77057	713-785-5577	273-6937
Web: www.saudiembassy.net					
Consulate General 866 Second Ave 5th Fl	New York	NY	10017	212-752-2740	688-2719
Web: www.saudiembassy.net					
Embassy 601 New Hampshire Ave NW	Washington	DC	20037	202-342-3800	944-5983
Web: www.saudiembassy.net					
Serbia 854 Fifth Ave	New York	NY	10021	212-879-8700	879-8705
Web: www.un.int					
Consulate General 201 E Ohio St Ste 200	Chicago	IL	60611	312-670-6707	670-6787
Web: www.scgchicago.org					
Embassy 2134 Kalorama Rd NW	Washington	DC	20008	202-332-0333	332-3933
Web: www.serbiaembusa.org					
Seychelles					
Embassy 800 Second Ave Ste 400C	New York	NY	10017	212-972-1785	
Singapore 318 E 48th St	New York	NY	10022	212-223-3331	826-5028
Web: www.mfa.gov.sg/newyork					
Consulate General 595 Market St Ste 2450	San Francisco	CA	94105	415-543-4775	543-4788
Web: www.mfa.gov.sg					
Embassy 3501 International Pl NW	Washington	DC	20008	202-537-3100	537-0876
Web: www.mfa.gov.sg					
Slovakia Embassy 3523 International Ct NW	Washington	DC	20008	202-237-1054	237-6438
Web: www.mzv.sk/washington					
Slovenia					
Consulate General 120 E 56th St Ste 320	New York	NY	10022	212-370-3006	
Web: www.culture.si/en/Depot:Consulate_General_of_the_Republic_of_Slovenia_New_York					
Embassy 2410 California St NW	Washington	DC	20036	202-386-6601	386-6633
Web: washington.embassy.si					
South Africa 333 E 38th St 9th Fl	New York	NY	10016	212-213-5583	692-2498
Web: www.southafrica-newyork.net					
Consulate General 200 S Michigan Ave Ste 600	Chicago	IL	60604	312-939-7929	939-2588
Web: www.sachicago.pwpsystems.com					
Consulate General 333 E 38th St 9th Fl	New York	NY	10016	212-213-4880	213-0102
Web: www.southafrica-newyork.net					
Embassy 3051 Massachusetts Ave NW	Washington	DC	20008	202-232-4400	265-1607
Web: www.saembassy.org					
South African Consulate-General 6300 Wilshire Blvd Ste 600	Los Angeles	CA	90048	323-651-0902	323-5969
Web: www.dirco.gov.za					
Spain 245 E 47th St 36th Fl	New York	NY	10017	212-661-1050	949-7247
Web: www.spainun.org					
Consulate General 1405 Sutter St	San Francisco	CA	94109	415-922-2995	931-9706
Consulate General 150 E 58th St 30th Fl	New York	NY	10155	212-355-4080	644-3751
Web: spainculturenewyork.org					
Embassy 2375 Pennsylvania Ave NW	Washington	DC	20037	202-452-0100	833-5670
Sri Lanka					
Consulate General 3250 Wilshire Blvd Ste 1405	Los Angeles	CA	90010	213-387-0210	387-0216
Web: www.srilankaconsulatela.com					
Embassy 2148 Wyoming Ave NW	Washington	DC	20008	202-483-4025	232-7181
Web: www.slembassyusa.org					
Sudan Embassy 2210 Massachusetts Ave NW	Washington	DC	20008	202-338-8565	667-2406
Web: www.sudanembassy.org					
Suriname Embassy 4301 Connecticut Ave NW Ste 460	Washington	DC	20008	202-244-7488	244-5878
Web: www.surinameembassy.org					
Sweden					
Consulate General 445 Pk Ave 19th Fl	New York	NY	10022	212-888-3000	888-3125
Web: www.swedenabroad.com					
Consulate General 505 Sansome St Ste 1010	San Francisco	CA	94111	415-788-2631	788-6841
Web: www.swedenabroad.com/en-gb/embassies/san-francisco					
Embassy 2900 K St NW	Washington	DC	20007	202-467-2600	467-2699
Web: www.swedenabroad.com					
Switzerland 633 Third Ave 29th Fl	New York	NY	10011	212-286-1540	599-4266
Web: www.eda.admin.ch					
Consulate General 456 Montgomery St Ste 1500	San Francisco	CA	94104	415-788-2272	788-1402
Web: www.eda.admin.ch/sanfrancisco					
Consulate General 11859 Wilshire Blvd Ste 501	Los Angeles	CA	90025	310-575-1145	575-1982
Web: www.eda.admin.ch/losangeles					
Embassy 2900 Cathedral Ave NW	Washington	DC	20008	202-745-7900	387-2564
Web: www.swissemb.org					
Tajikistan					
Embassy 1005 New Hampshire Ave	Washington	DC	20037	202-223-6090	223-6091
Web: www.tajemb.us					
Tanzania 307 E 53rd St 4th Floor	New York	NY	10022	212-697-3612	697-3618
Embassy 1232 22nd St NW	Washington	DC	20037	202-939-6125	797-7408
Web: www.tanzaniaembassy-us.org					
Thailand 351 E 52nd St	New York	NY	10022	212-754-1770	688-3029
Web: www.thaicgny.com					
Consulate General 611 N Larchmont Blvd 2nd Fl	Los Angeles	CA	90004	323-962-9574	962-2128
Web: www.thaiconsulatela.org					
Embassy 1024 Wisconsin Ave NW	Washington	DC	20007	202-944-3600	944-3611
Web: www.thaiembdc.org					
Tonga					
Consulate General 360 Post St Ste 604	San Francisco	CA	94108	415-781-0365	781-3964
Web: www.tongaconsul.com					

				Phone	Fax
Trinidad & Tobago Embassy					
1708 Massachusetts Ave NW	Washington	DC	20036	202-467-6490	785-3130
Web: www.ttembassy.com					
Turkey					
Consulate General					
455 N Cityfront Plz Dr Ste 2900	Chicago	IL	60611	312-263-0644	263-1449
Web: www.chicago.cg.mfa.gov.tr					
Consulate General 1990 Post Oak Blvd Ste 1300	Houston	TX	77056	713-622-5849	623-6639
TF: 888-566-7656 ■ *Web:* www.houston.cg.mfa.gov.tr					
Consulate General					
6300 Wilshire Blvd Ste 2010	Los Angeles	CA	90048	323-655-8832	655-8681
TF: 800-874-8875 ■ *Web:* www.losangeles.cg.mfa.gov.tr					
Consulate General 825 Third Ave 28th Fl	New York	NY	10022	646-430-6560	983-1293*
**Fax Area Code:* 212 ■ *Web:* www.newyork.cg.mfa.gov.tr					
Embassy 2525 Massachusetts Ave NW	Washington	DC	20008	202-612-6700	319-1639
TF: 877-367-8875 ■ *Web:* www.washington.emb.mfa.gov.tr/default.aspx					
Turkmenistan					
Embassy 2207 Massachusetts Ave NW	Washington	DC	20008	202-588-1500	280-1003
Uganda Embassy 5911 16th St NW	Washington	DC	20011	202-726-7100	726-1727
Web: washington.mofa.go.ug					
Ukraine 220 E 51st St	New York	NY	10022	212-355-9455	355-9455
Consulate General 10 E Huron St	Chicago	IL	60611	312-642-4388	
Web: www.ukrchicago.com					
United Arab Emirates Embassy					
3522 International Ct NW	Washington	DC	20008	202-243-2400	243-2432
Web: www.uae-embassy.org					
United Kingdom 1 Dag Hammarskjold Plz	New York	NY	10017	212-745-9200	745-9316
Web: www.gov.uk					
Consulate General 1 Broadway	Cambridge	MA	02142	617-245-4500	
Web: www.gov.uk					
Consulate General 625 N Michigan Ave Ste 2200	Chicago	IL	60611	312-970-3800	
Web: www.gov.uk					
Consulate General 133 Peachtree St NE	Atlanta	GA	30303	404-954-7700	
Web: www.gov.uk					
Consulate General 1301 Fannin S Ste 2400	Houston	TX	77002	713-659-6270	
Web: www.gov.uk					
Consulate General 845 Third Ave	New York	NY	10022	212-745-0200	
Web: www.gov.uk					
Consulate General 1 Sansome St Ste 850	San Francisco	CA	94104	415-617-1300	
Web: www.gov.uk					
Embassy 3100 Massachusetts Ave NW	Washington	DC	20008	202-588-6500	
Web: www.gov.uk					
Uruguay 866 UN Plz Ste 322	New York	NY	10017	212-752-8240	593-0935
Web: www.un.int/uruguay					
Consulate General					
429 Santa Monica Blvd Ste 400	Santa Monica	CA	90401	310-394-5777	394-5140
Web: www.conurula.org					
Embassy 1913 'I' St NW	Washington	DC	20006	202-331-1313	331-8142
Web: mrree.gub.uy					
Uzbekistan					
Consulate General 801 Second Ave 20th Fl	New York	NY	10017	212-754-7403	
Web: www.uzbekconsulny.org					
Embassy 1746 Massachusetts Ave NW	Washington	DC	20036	202-887-5300	293-6804
Web: www.uzbekistan.org					
Venezuela 335 E 46th St	New York	NY	10017	212-557-2055	557-3528
Web: www.un.int					
Consulate General					
2401 Fountain View Dr Ste 220	Houston	TX	77057	713-974-0028	974-1413
Web: venezuela-us.org/houston					
Vietnam 866 UN Plaza Ste 428	New York	NY	10017	212-644-0594	644-5732
Web: www.un.int					
Consulate General					
1700 California St Ste 580	San Francisco	CA	94109	415-922-1707	922-1848
Web: www.vietnamconsulate-sf.org					
Embassy 1233 20th St NW Ste 400	Washington	DC	20036	202-861-0737	861-0917
Web: vietnamembassy-usa.org					
Zambia Embassy 2419 Massachusetts Ave NW	Washington	DC	20008	202-265-9717	332-0826
Web: www.zambiaembassy.org					
Zimbabwe Embassy					
1608 New Hampshire Ave NW	Washington	DC	20009	202-332-7100	483-9326

258 EMBROIDERY & OTHER DECORATIVE STITCHING

				Phone	Fax
BMG Conveyor Services of Florida Inc					
5010 16th Ave South	Tampa	FL	33619	813-247-3620	
Web: www.bmgtampa.com					
Branded Emblem Co Inc 7920 Foster St	Overland Park	KS	66204	913-648-0573	648-7444
TF: 800-448-2267 ■ *Web:* www.campdavid.com					
Carolace Embroidery Company Inc					
2147 Hudson Terrace Unit 3	Fort Lee	NJ	07024	201-945-2151	
Web: www.trimplace.com					
Chemtex Print Usa Inc					
3061 E Maria St	Rancho Dominguez	CA	90221	310-900-1818	
Web: chemtexprint.com					
Clothworks Textiles Inc 6250 Stanley Ave S	Seattle	WA	98108	206-762-7886	
Web: www.clothworks.com					
CR Daniels Inc 3451 Ellicott Ctr Dr	Ellicott City	MD	21043	410-461-2100	461-2987
TF: 800-933-2638 ■ *Web:* www.crdaniels.com					
David Textiles Inc 1920 S Tubeway Ave	Commerce	CA	90040	323-728-3231	
Web: www.davidtextiles.com					
Duck River Textile Inc					
1000 New County Rd Ste 2	Secaucus	NJ	07094	201-533-1000	
Web: duckrivertextile.com					
EmbroidMe Inc 2121 Vista Pkwy	West Palm Beach	FL	33411	561-640-7367	640-6062
TF: 877-877-0234 ■ *Web:* www.embroidme.com					
Fabri-Quilt Inc 901 E 14th Ave	North Kansas City	MO	64116	816-421-2000	471-2853
TF: 800-279-0622 ■ *Web:* www.fabri-quilt.com					
FlagZone LLC 105A Industrial Dr	Gilbertsville	PA	19525	800-976-4201	
TF: 800-976-4201 ■ *Web:* www.theflagzone.com					
G&G Outfitters Inc 4901 Forbes Blvd	Lanham	MD	20706	301-731-2099	
Web: www.ggoutfitters.com					
Gensco Equipment (1990) Inc 53 Carlaw Ave	Toronto	ON	M4M2R6	416-465-7521	
TF: 800-268-6797 ■ *Web:* www.genscoequip.com					
Herrschners Inc 2800 Hoover Rd	Stevens Point	WI	54481	715-341-8686	341-2250
TF: 800-713-1239 ■ *Web:* www.herrschners.com					
Jubilee Embroidery Company Inc 411 Hwy 601	Lugoff	SC	29078	803-438-2934	
Kasbar National Industries Inc					
370 Reed Rd Ste 200	Broomall	PA	19008	610-544-7117	544-9799
Web: milliken.com					
Lion Bros Company Inc					
300 Red Brook Blvd	Owings Mills	MD	21117	800-365-6543	
TF Cust Svc: 800-365-6543					
Luv N' Care Ltd 3030 Aurora Ave	Monroe	LA	71201	800-588-6227	
TF: 800-588-6227 ■ *Web:* www.nuby.com					
Monarch Textile Rental Services Inc					
2810 Foundation Dr	South Bend	IN	46628	574-233-9433	
TF: 800-589-9434 ■ *Web:* www.monarchlinen.com					
Moritz Embroidery Works Inc					
Pocono Mtn Business Park 405 Industrial Park Dr					
PO Box 187	Mount Pocono	PA	18344	570-839-9600	839-9430
TF: 800-533-4183 ■ *Web:* www.moritzembroidery.com					
MP Global Products Inc 2500 Old Hadar Rd	Norfolk	NE	68701	402-379-9695	
TF: 888-379-9695 ■ *Web:* www.mpglobalproducts.com					
Natco 346 W Cerritos Ave	Glendale	CA	91204	818-409-0019	
Web: www.natcoglobal.com					
National Emblem Inc 17036 S Avalon Blvd	Carson	CA	90746	310-515-5055	515-5966
TF: 800-877-6185 ■ *Web:* www.nationalemblem.com					
Osgood Textile Company Inc					
333 Park St	West Springfield	MA	01089	413-737-6488	
TF: 888-674-6638 ■ *Web:* www.osgoodtextile.com					
Penn Emblem Co 10909 Dutton Rd	Philadelphia	PA	19154	800-793-7366	632-6166*
**Fax Area Code:* 215 ■ *TF:* 800-793-7366 ■ *Web:* www.pennemblem.com					
Saint Louis Embroidery					
1759 Scherer Pkwy	Saint Charles	MO	63303	636-724-2200	
TF: 800-457-6676 ■ *Web:* patch.com/stcharles					
Schweizer Emblem Co 1022 Busse Hwy	Park Ridge	IL	60068	847-292-1022	292-1028
TF Cust Svc: 800-942-5215 ■ *Web:* www.schweizer-emblem.com					
Silkscreening by Classic Graphix					
12152 Woodruff Ave	Downey	CA	90241	562-940-0806	
Web: www.classicgraphix.com					
SK Textile Inc 2938 E 54th St	Vernon	CA	90058	323-581-8986	
Web: www.sktextile.com					
Stahls' Inc 20600 Stephens St	St. Clair Shores	MI	48080	586-772-5551	
Web: www.stahls.com					
Stitchmaster LLC 309-B S Regional Rd	Greensboro	NC	27409	336-852-6448	
Web: www.stitchmaster.com					
Superior Pleating & Stitching					
3671 E Olympic Blvd	Los Angeles	CA	90023	323-261-3964	261-0122
Taylor Stitch 3 Bailey Dr Sw	Lilburn	GA	30047	770-381-9370	
Web: taylorstitch.com					
Textile Management Systems Inc					
10 TimberLn Dr	Hammond	LA	70403	985-345-9590	
Web: www.rmaster.com					
Thread Logic 16775 Greystone Ln	Jordan	MN	55352	800-347-1612	
TF: 800-347-1612 ■ *Web:* www.threadlogic.com					
Todd Rutkin Inc 5801 S Alameda St	Los Angeles	CA	90001	323-584-9225	
Web: toddrutkin.com					
Wold Oil Properties Inc					
139 W Second St Ste 200	Casper	WY	82601	307-265-7252	
Web: www.woldoil.com					

259 EMPLOYMENT OFFICES - GOVERNMENT

				Phone	Fax
Employment & Training Administration					
200 Constitution Ave NW	Washington	DC	20210	866-487-2365	
TF: 866-487-2365 ■ *Web:* www.doleta.gov					
US Dept of Labor 200 Constitution Ave NW	Washington	DC	20210	202-693-4700	693-4754
Web: www.dol.gov/vets					
Alaska Employment Security Div PO Box 115509	Juneau	AK	99811	907-465-2712	465-4537
Web: www.labor.state.ak.us/esd/home.htm					
Arizona Employment Administration					
PO Box 6123	Phoenix	AZ	85005	602-542-3957	542-2491
Web: www.azdes.gov					
Arkansas Dept of Workforce Services					
2 Capitol Mall	North Little Rock	AR	72201	501-682-2121	682-2273
Web: www.arkansas.gov					
California Employment Development Dept					
800 Capitol Mall MIC 83	Sacramento	CA	95814	916-654-8210	657-5294
Web: www.edd.ca.gov					
Colorado Labor & Employment Dept					
633 17th St Ste 201	Denver	CO	80203	303-318-8000	
TF: 800-390-7936 ■ *Web:* www.coworkforce.com					
Connecticut Labor Dept					
200 Folly Brook Blvd	Wethersfield	CT	06109	860-263-6000	263-6699
Web: www.ctdol.state.ct.us					
Delaware Employment & Training Div					
4425 N Market St	Wilmington	DE	19802	302-761-8085	
Web: www.delawareworks.com					
District of Columbia (PSC)					
Aging Office 441 Fourth St NW Ste 900 S	Washington	DC	20001	202-724-5622	724-4979
Web: www.dcoa.dc.gov					
Georgia Employment Services Div					
148 Andrew Young International Blvd NE	Atlanta	GA	30303	404-232-3515	
Web: www.dol.state.ga.us					
Hawaii Workforce Development Div					
201 Merchant St Ste 1805	Honolulu	HI	96813	808-695-4620	695-4618
Web: www.hawaii.gov					
Idaho Labor Dept 317 W Main St	Boise	ID	83735	208-332-3570	334-6300
Web: labor.idaho.gov/dnn/idl					
Indiana Workforce Development Dept					
10 N Senate Ave	Indianapolis	IN	46204	317-232-7670	233-4793
TF: 800-891-6499 ■ *Web:* www.in.gov					

Phone Fax

Iowa Workforce Development
1000 E Grand Ave — Des Moines IA 50319 515-281-5387 281-4698
TF: 800-562-4692 ■ *Web:* www.iowaworkforce.org

Louisiana Workforce Commission
1001 N 23rd St — Baton Rouge LA 70802 225-342-3111 342-7960
TF: 877-529-6757 ■ *Web:* www.laworks.net

Maine Employment Services Bureau
55 State House Station — Augusta ME 04330 207-623-7981 287-5933
Web: www.mainecareercenter.com

Maryland Workforce Development Div
1100 N Eutaw St Rm 616 — Baltimore MD 21201 410-767-2400 767-2986
Web: www.dllr.state.md.us/employment

Massachusetts Workforce Development Dept
1 Ashburton Pl Rm 1301 — Boston MA 02108 617-626-7100 727-1090
Web: www.mass.gov

Michigan Career Education & Workforce Programs
201 N Washington Sq Victor Office Center — Lansing MI 48913 517-335-5858 373-0314
TF: 888-253-6855 ■ *Web:* www.michigan.gov/mdcd

Mississippi Employment Security Commission
1235 Echelon Pkwy PO Box 1699 — Jackson MS 39215 601-321-6000 321-6004
TF: 888-844-3577 ■ *Web:* www.mdes.ms.gov

Montana Workforce Services Div PO Box 1728 — Helena MT 59624 406-444-4100 444-3037
Web: wsd.dli.mt.gov

Nebraska Workforce Development - Dept of Labor
550 S 16th St PO Box 94600 — Lincoln NE 68509 402-471-2600 471-9867
Web: dol.nebraska.gov

Nevada Dept of Employment Training & Rehabilitation
500 E Third St — Carson City NV 89713 775-684-3911 684-3908
Web: www.nvdetr.org

New Hampshire Employment Security (NHES)
32 S Main St — Concord NH 03301 603-224-3311 228-4145
TF: 800-852-3400 ■ *Web:* www.nh.gov

New Jersey Workforce New Jersey
1 John Fitch Plz Fl 3 — Trenton NJ 08611 609-292-2305 695-1174
Web: lwd.dol.state.nj.us

New Mexico Dept of Workforce Solutions
301 W DeVargas — Santa Fe NM 87501 505-827-7434 827-7346
Web: www.dws.state.nm.us

New York Labor Dept WA Harriman Campus Bldg 12 — Albany NY 12240 518-457-9000 457-6908
TF: 888-469-7365 ■ *Web:* www.labor.ny.gov

North Carolina Employment Security Commission
700 Wade Ave PO Box 25903 — Raleigh NC 27605 919-707-1010 733-9420
Web: desncc.com/deshome

Ohio Workforce Developement Office
4020 E Fifth Ave PO Box 1618 — Columbus OH 43219 888-296-7541 644-7102*
**Fax Area Code:* 614 ■ *TF:* 888-296-7541 ■ *Web:* www.jfs.ohio.gov/owd

Oklahoma Employment Security Commission
PO Box 52003 — Oklahoma City OK 73152 405-557-5400 557-5355
Web: www.ok.gov

Oregon Employment Dept 875 Union St NE — Salem OR 97311 503-451-2400 947-1472
TF: 877-345-3484 ■ *Web:* www.oregon.gov

Pennsylvania Workforce Investment Board
901 N Seventh St Ste 103 — Harrisburg PA 17120 717-772-4966
Web: www.paworkforce.state.pa.us

Rhode Island Labor & Training Dept
1511 Pontiac Ave — Cranston RI 02920 401-462-8000 462-8872
Web: www.dlt.state.ri.us

South Dakota Career Ctr Div
116 W Missouri Ave — Pierre SD 57501 605-773-3372 773-6680
Web: www.sdjobs.org

Tennessee Labor & Workforce Development Dept
220 French Landing Dr — Nashville TN 37243 615-741-6642 741-5078
Web: www.state.tn.us

Texas Workforce Commission 101 E 15th St — Austin TX 78778 512-463-2222
Web: twc.state.tx.us

Utah
Administrative Office of the Courts
PO Box 140241 — Salt Lake City UT 84114 801-578-3800 578-3843
Web: www.utcourts.gov

Virginia Employment Commission
703 E Main St — Richmond VA 23219 804-786-1485 225-3923
Web: www.vec.virginia.gov

Washington Employment Security Dept
212 Maple Pk Ave SE — Olympia WA 98504 360-902-9500
Web: www.esd.wa.gov

Wisconsin Workforce Development Dept
201 E Washington Ave — Madison WI 53702 608-266-3131 266-1784
Web: dwd.wisconsin.gov

260 EMPLOYMENT SERVICES - ONLINE

Phone Fax

3C Consulting Corp 850 W Jackson Blvd — Chicago IL 60607 312-226-8118
Web: www.3ccomp.com

680 Partners LLC 680 5th Ave 9th Fl — New York NY 10019 212-931-5311
Web: www.680partners.com

A One Staffing LLC 3639 New Getwell Rd Ste 1 — Memphis TN 38118 901-367-5757
Web: www.aonestaffing.com

A Pavillion Agency Inc 15 E 40 St Ste 400 — New York NY 10016 212-889-6609
Web: pavillionagency.com

A-Check America Inc 1501 Research Park Dr — Riverside CA 91204 951-750-1501
Web: www.acheckglobal.com

A-Star Staffing Inc
2835 Camino Del Rio S Ste 220 — San Diego CA 92108 619-574-7600
Web: www.astarstaffing.com

A.B. Data Ltd 600 A B Data Dr — Milwaukee WI 53217 414-961-6400
Web: abdata.com

A.D. Susman & Associates Inc
3033 Chimney Rock Rd Ste 690 — Houston TX 77056 713-668-7998
Web: www.adsusman.com

A.J. O'Neal & Associates Inc
109 Falkenburg Rd N — Tampa FL 33619 813-654-4199
Web: www.ajoneal.com

Phone Fax

A1 Staffing & Recruiting Agency Inc
7407 NW 23rd St — Bethany OK 73008 405-787-7600
Web: www.a1staffingok.com

Abba Staffing & Consulting Services
2350 Airport Fwy Ste 130 — Bedford TX 76022 817-354-2800
Web: www.abbastaffing.com

Abbott Smith 11697 W Grand Ave — Northlake IL 60164 708-223-1194

Abeln, Magy, Underberg & Associates Inc
800 E Wayzata Blvd Ste 200 — Wayzata MN 55391 952-476-4938
Web: www.abelnmagy.com

Abl Employment 777 Guelph Line Ste 212 — Burlington ON L7R3N2 905-631-7050
Web: www.ablemployment.com

About Face Productions Inc
956 s bartlett rd — Bartlett IL 60103 630-540-2444
Web: www.aboutfaceproductions.biz

Abraham & London Ltd 7 Old Sherman Tpke — Danbury CT 68104 203-798-7537
Web: www.abrahamlondon.com

Absolute Consulting Inc
7552 Navarre Pkwy Unit 63 — Navarre FL 32566 850-939-8965
Web: www.absoluteconsulting.com

Accu Personnel Inc 911 Kings Hwy N — Cherry Hill NJ 08034 856-482-2222
Web: www.accustaffing.com

Accufacts Pre-Employment Screening Inc
2180 State Rd 434 W Ste 4150 — Longwood FL 32779 407-682-5051
Web: www.accufacts.com

Accurate Staffing Consultants Inc
804 1st Ave S — Conover NC 28613 828-466-1018
Web: www.accuratestaffing.com

Acsys Inc 111 Anza Blvd Ste 400 — Burlingame CA 94010 650-579-1111
Web: www.acsysinc.com

Active Staffing Services 41 W 33rd St Fl 3 — New York NY 10001 212-244-6444
Web: www.activestaffing.com

Ad-Vance Talent Solutions Inc
3911 Gulf Park Loop Ste 103 — Bradenton FL 34203 941-739-8883
Web: ad-vance.com

Adams & Garth Staffing
2119 Berkmar Dr — Charlottesville VA 22901 434-974-7878
Web: adamsandgarth.com

Add Staff Inc 2118 Hollow Brook Dr — Colorado Springs CO 80918 719-528-8888
Web: www.addstaffinc.com

Adguide Publications Inc
3109 W 50 St Ste 121 — Minneapolis MN 55410 952-848-2211
Web: www.collegerecruiter.com

ADP National Account Services
4125 Hopyard Rd — Pleasanton CA 94588 925-737-3500

ADP Screening & Selection Services Inc
301 Remington St — Fort Collins CO 80524 970-484-7722
Web: www.adpselect.com

Advance Employment Services 416 Elmwood Rd — Lansing MI 48917 517-887-0377

Advance Search Technical Staffing
950 Lee St Ste 205 — Des Plaines IL 60016 847-375-8100
Web: www.advancesearch.com

Advantage RN LLC 8892 Beckett Rd — West Chester OH 45069 513-874-8717
TF: 866-301-4045 ■ *Web:* www.advantagern.com

Aes, an Employment Source Inc
1335 N Main St — Meridian ID 83642 208-887-7740
Web: www.anemploymentsource.com

agriCAREERS Inc 613 Main St PO Box 140 — Massena IA 50853 800-633-8387 779-3366*
**Fax Area Code:* 712 ■ *TF:* 800-633-8387 ■ *Web:* www.agricareersinc.com

Aim Personnel Service 183 Whiting St 13 — Hingham MA 02043 781-740-8808
Web: aimpersonnel.com

Airetel Staffing Inc
415 Montgomery Rd Ste 125 — Altamonte Springs FL 32714 407-788-2015
Web: www.airetel.com

Alar Staffing Corp 1901 E Fourth St Ste 150 — Santa Ana CA 92705 714-667-3100
Web: www.alarstaffing.com

Alaska Executive Search Inc
821 N St Ste 201 — Anchorage AK 99501 907-276-5707
Web: www.akexec.com

Albertini Group Inc 5550 LBJ Fwy Ste 700 — Dallas TX 75240 972-726-5550
Web: www.kingsleygate.com

All-Star Recruiting LLC 6119 Lyons Rd — Coconut Creek FL 33073 800-928-0229
TF: 800-928-0229 ■ *Web:* www.allstarrecruiting.com

Allegiant International LLC 1710 N Main St — Auburn IN 46706 866-841-3671
TF: 866-841-3671 ■ *Web:* www.allegiantworks.com

Allen Partners Inc 14900 Intrurbn Ave S — Seattle WA 98168 206-812-1440
Web: www.allen-partners.com

Alliance Legal Staffing Solutions
2909 Cole Ave Ste 230 — Dallas TX 75204 214-954-1250
Web: www.alliancelegal.com

Allied Personnel Services Inc
11821 Queens Blvd Ste 310 — New York NY 11375 718-261-7979
Web: www.alliedpersonnel.com

Allied Staffing Inc
556 n diamond bar blvd — Diamond bar CA 91765 909-861-5200
Web: www.alliedstaffinginc.com

Alluvion Staffing Inc
4190 BelFt Rd Enterprise Park Bldg 4th Fl
Ste 420 — Jacksonville FL 32216 904-296-0626
Web: www.alluvionstaffing.com

Alpha Rae Personnel Inc
347 W Berry St Ste 700 — Fort Wayne IN 46802 260-426-8227
TF: 800-837-8940 ■ *Web:* www.alpha-rae.com

Alpha Search Advisory Partners LLC
14 Tower Pl 1st Fl — Roslyn NY 11576 516-626-7896
Web: www.alphasearchadvisory.com

Andcor Companies Inc 825 Wayzata Blvd E — Wayzata MN 55391 952-404-8060
Web: www.andcor.com

Andela Inc 147 Lexington Ave, PH — New York NY 10016 212-848-9800
Web: www.andela.co

Andiamo Partners 17 State St 8th Fl — New York NY 10004 212-488-1595
Web: www.andiamogo.com

APA Search Inc 1 Byram Brook Pl Ste 103 — Armonk NY 10504 914-273-6000
Web: www.apasearch.com

	City	State	ZIP	Phone	Fax
Apple & Assoc Inc					
395 Saint Thomas Ch Rd PO Box 996	Chapin	SC	29036	803-932-2000	
Web: www.appleassoc.com					
Arbor Associates Inc 15 Court Sq Ste 1050	Boston	MA	02108	617-227-8829	
Web: www.arbor-associates.com					
Arc San Joaquin Inc 41 W Yokuts Ave	Stockton	CA	95207	209-955-1625	
Web: www.arc-sj.org					
Arcadia Resources Inc					
9320 Priority Way W Dr	Indianapolis	IN	46240	317-569-8234	
Web: www.arcadiaresourcesinc.com					
Arctern Inc 10332 Main St Ste 150	Fairfax	VA	22030	703-738-6669	
Web: www.arctern.com					
Arrow Staffing Services 499 W State St	Redlands	CA	92373	909-792-1252	
Web: www.arrowstaffing.com					
Artists for Humanity Inc 100 W 2nd St	Boston	MA	02127	617-268-7620	
Web: www.afhboston.org					
Artizen Inc 200 Main St Ste #21A	Redwood City	CA	94063	650-261-9400	
Web: www.artizen.com					
Arvon Inc 5544 Greenwich Rd Ste 102	Virginia Beach	VA	23462	757-499-9900	
Web: www.arvon.com					
Asap Personnel Services Inc					
10301 N Rodney Parham Rd	Little Rock	AR	72227	501-537-2727	
Web: m.asapworksforme.com					
Ascot Staffing 1939 Harrison St Ste 150	Oakland	CA	94612	510-839-9520	
Web: www.ascotstaffing.com					
Asereth Medical Services Inc					
257 Fair Oaks Ave Ste 100	Pasadena	CA	91105	626-449-0099	
Web: www.asereth.com					
Ashton Staffing Inc 3590 Cherokee St Ste 303	Kennesaw	GA	30144	770-419-1776	
Web: www.ashtonstaffing.com					
Asset Staffing Inc 14 NE 1st Ave Ste 1209	Miami	FL	33132	305-371-5969	
Web: www.assetstaffing.com					
Astyra Corp 411 E Franklin St Ste 105	Richmond	VA	23219	804-433-1100	
Web: www.astyra.com					
Atrium Staffing Services Ltd					
71 Fifth Ave 3rd Fl	New York	NY	10003	212-292-0550	
Web: www.atriumstaff.com					
Avenue Staffing 7000 57th Ave N Ste 120	Crystal	MN	55428	763-537-6104	
Web: www.avenuestaffing.com					
Avjobs Inc PO Box 260830	Littleton	CO	80163	303-683-2322	624-8691*
**Fax Area Code:* 888 ■ *TF:* 888-624-8691 ■ *Web:* www.avjobs.com					
B2B Staffing Services Inc 4141 Ball Rd #150	Cypress	CA	90630	714-243-4104	
Web: www.b2bstaffingservices.com					
Babich & Associates 6030 E Mockingbird Ln	Dallas	TX	75206	214-823-9999	
Web: www.babich.com					
Backtrack Inc 8850 Tyler Blvd	Mentor	OH	44060	440-205-8280	
TF: 800-991-9694 ■ *Web:* backtracker.com					
BAJobs com 652 Bair Is Rd Ste 301	Redwood City	CA	94063	650-298-8100	
Web: www.bajobs.com					
Baltimore Teachers Union					
5800 Metro Dr Ste 200	Baltimore	MD	21215	410-358-6600	
Web: www.baltimoreteachers.org					
BANK W Holdings LLC					
5 Bedford Farms Dr Ste 304	Bedford	NH	03110	603-792-2345	
Web: www.bankwholdings.com					
Banner Personnel Service Inc					
1701 Woodfield Rd Ste 600	Schaumburg	IL	60173	847-706-9180	
Web: www.bannerpersonnel.com					
Barrett Group Llc, The					
100 Jefferson Blvd Ste 310	Warwick	RI	02888	401-921-5443	
Web: www.careerchange.com					
Barton Staffing Solutions Inc 723 Aurora Ave	Aurora	IL	60505	630-897-3591	
Web: bartonstaffing.com					
Bayforce Technology Solutions Inc					
5100 W Kennedy Blvd Ste 425	Tampa	FL	33609	813-386-0663	
Web: www.bayforce.com					
Bayside Solutions Inc					
6160 Stoneridge Mall Rd Ste 320	Pleasanton	CA	94588	800-220-0074	
TF: 800-220-0074 ■ *Web:* www.baysidesolutions.com					
Bcg Attorney Search 175 S Lk Ave Unit 200	Pasadena	CA	91101	800-298-6440	
TF: 800-298-6440 ■ *Web:* www.bcgsearch.com					
Bear Staffing Services Inc 47 S Broad St	Woodbury	NJ	08096	866-580-2327	
TF: 866-580-2327 ■ *Web:* www.bearstaff.com					
BECO Inc 200 S Prospect	Park Ridge	IL	60068	847-825-8000	
Web: www.becogroup.com					
BelFlex Staffing Network 127 E Fourth St	Cincinnati	OH	45202	513-241-8367	
Web: www.belflex.com					
Bergen Briller Group LLC, The					
1787 Wrightstown Rd	Newtown	PA	18940	215-369-4190	
Web: www.bbgsearch.com					
Berman & Larson Associates					
38 E. Ridgewood Ave Ste 209	Ridgewood	NJ	07450	201-909-0906	
Web: jobsbl.com					
Beyond 1060 First Ave Ste 100	King of Prussia	PA	19406	610-878-2800	878-2801
Web: www.beyond.com					
Beyond.com Inc 1060 First Ave Ste 100	King of Prussia	PA	19406	610-878-2800	
Web: www.beyond.com					
BH Solutions Group Inc					
1000 S Cleveland Massillon Rd Ste 2	Akron	OH	44333	330-666-6970	
Web: www.bhsolutionsgroup.com					
BlueAlly LLC 1919 Gallows Rd Ste 600	Tysons Corner	VA	22182	703-259-8484	
Web: www.blueally.com					
Bolt Staffing Service Inc					
3427 Broadway St Ste F4	American Canyon	CA	94503	707-552-7800	
Web: www.boltstaffing.com					
Bowen Workforce Solutions Inc					
602 12 Ave Sw Ste 700	Calgary	AB	T2R1J3	403-262-1156	
TF: 866-692-6936 ■ *Web:* www.bowenworks.ca					
Boyle Ogata Bregman 17461 Derian Ave Ste 202	Irvine	CA	92614	949-474-0115	
Web: www.bobsearch.com					
Brickforce Staffing Inc 2 Ethel Rd Ste 204-B	Edison	NJ	08817	732-819-7770	
Web: www.brickforce.com					
Bridge Personnel Services					
2800 W Higgins Rd Ste 680	Hoffman Estates	IL	60195	847-885-9696	
Web: www.bridgepersonnel.com					
Bridge Technical Talent LLC					
2730 S County Trail	East Greenwich	RI	02818	401-398-1900	
Web: www.bridge-talent.com					
BRIDGES USA Inc 477 N 5th St	Memphis	TN	38105	901-452-5600	
Web: www.bridgesusa.org					
Brine Group Staffing Solutions Inc					
800 District Ave Ste 120	Burlington	MA	01803	781-272-3400	
Web: brinegroup.com					
Broadband Express LLC 374 Westdale Ave	Westerville	OH	43082	614-823-6464	
Web: www.broadbandexpress.com					
Brockton Area Workforce Investment Board Inc					
34 School St 2nd Fl	Brockton	MA	02301	508-584-3234	
Web: bawib.org					
Brokers Group LLC, The 512 Executive Dr	Princeton	NJ	08540	609-924-8900	
Web: www.talonpro.com					
Broome Employment Center 171 Frnt St	Binghamton	NY	13905	607-778-2136	
Web: www.broometiogaworks.com					
Bryant Bureau 18600 Florence St Ste C6a	Roseville	MI	48066	586-772-6452	
Web: bryantbureau.net					
Bryant Staffing 377 Hoes Ln Ste 200	Piscataway	NJ	08854	732-981-0440	
Web: www.bryantstaffing.com					
BSG Team Ventures Inc 224 Clarendon St Ste 41	Boston	MA	02116	617-266-4333	
Web: www.bostonsearchgroup.com					
Buckman Enochs Coss & Associates					
590 Enterprise Dr	Lewis Center	OH	43035	614-825-6215	
Web: becsearch.com					
Burnetts Staffing Inc 2710 Ave E E	Arlington	TX	76011	817-385-8880	
Web: www.burnetts.com					
Burning Glass International Inc 1 Lewis Wharf	Boston	MA	02110	617-227-4800	
Web: www.burning-glass.com					
Buzz Co, The 62 W Huron St Ste 2W	Chicago	IL	60654	312-255-0808	
Web: www.buzzco.com					
Bwbacon Group 621 kalamath st	Denver	CO	80204	303-593-1425	
Web: www.bwbacon.com					
Caler Group Inc, The 23337 Lago Mar Cir	Boca Raton	FL	33433	561-394-8045	
Web: www.calergroup.com					
Callos & Associates					
1375 S Main St Ste 101	North Canton	OH	44720	614-575-4900	
Web: www.callos.com					
CalSAE 717 13th St Lwr Level	Sacramento	CA	95814	916-443-8980	
Web: www.calsae.org					
Cameo Personnel Systems Inc 440 S Main St	Milltown	NJ	08850	732-613-0088	
Web: www.crsco.com					
Cameron Smith & Associates Inc					
3350 S Pinnacle Hills Pkwy Ste 101	Rogers	AR	72758	479-271-6042	
Web: www.csarecruiters.com					
Cameron Tucker Consulting					
425 Soledad St Ste 450	San Antonio	TX	78205	210-348-7333	
Web: www.cameronmatch.com					
Campus2careers Inc 4700 Guadalupe St Ste A342	Austin	TX	78751	512-354-7690	
Web: www.campus2careers.com					
CampusCareerCenter Inc					
2464 Massachusetts Ave Ste 210	Cambridge	MA	02140	617-661-2613	
Web: www.campuscareercenter.com					
Canon Recruiting Group LLC					
26531 Summit Cir	Santa Clarita	CA	91350	661-252-7400	
Web: www.canonrecruiting.com					
Capital Workforce Partners					
1 Union Pl 3rd Fl	Hartford	CT	06103	860-522-1111	
Web: www.capitalworkforce.org					
CapitolWorks Inc 2000 P St NW	Washington	DC	20036	202-785-2020	
Web: www.capitolworks.com					
Cardinal Services Inc 1721 Indian Wood Cir A	Maumee	OH	43537	419-893-5400	
Web: www.cardinalstaffing.com					
Care Finders Inc 191 Main St	Hackensack	NJ	07601	201-342-5122	
Web: carefinders.org					
Care Resources Inc 1026 Cromwell Bridge Rd	Baltimore	MD	21286	410-583-1515	
Web: www.careresourcesinc.com					
Career Alliance Inc 711 N Saginaw St Ste 300	Flint	MI	48503	810-233-5974	
Web: www.careeralliance.org					
Career Exposure inc 805 SW Broadway	Portland	OR	97205	503-221-7779	
Career Exposure Inc 805 SW Bdwy Ste 2260	Portland	OR	97205	503-221-7779	
Web: www.mbacareers.com					
Career Foundations Inc					
4011 Westchase Blvd Ste 200	Raleigh	NC	27607	919-828-1000	
Web: www.careerfoundations.com					
Career Solutions International Inc					
400 Lexington Green Ln	Sanford	FL	32771	407-688-6727	
Web: www.csigroup.net					
CareerBoard LLC 23245 Mercantile Rd	Beachwood	OH	44122	216-595-1632	
Web: www.careerboard.com					
CareerPlanners Inc 19037 Raines Dr	Rockville	MD	20855	301-216-9597	
Web: www.careerplanners.com					
careerSMITH Inc					
537 Newport Ctr Dr Ste 364	Newport Beach	CA	92660	949-760-8666	
Web: www.careersmith.com					
CareSource Home Health & Hospice LLC					
1624 East 4500 South	Salt Lake City	UT	84117	801-266-7200	
Web: caresourcehealthcare.com					
Carney Group, The 925 Harvest Dr Ste 240	Blue Bell	PA	19422	215-646-6200	
Web: www.carneyjobs.com					
Carolinas Constructions Solutions Inc					
6712 Old Pineville Rd	Charlotte	NC	28217	704-578-1567	
TF: 866-521-5624 ■ *Web:* www.staffccs.com					
Carroll Technology Services Inc					
6400 Ridge Rd Ste 9	Eldersburg	MD	21784	410-552-0422	
Web: www.carrolltech.net					
Carter Group LLC, The					
1621 University Blvd South	Mobile	AL	36609	251-342-0999	
Web: www.thecartergroup.com					

	City	State	Zip	Phone	Fax
CASCO International Inc 4205 E Dixon Blvd *Web:* www.cashort.com	Shelby	NC	28152	704-482-9591	
Catalyst Awareness Inc 355 Elmira Rd N Ste 127 *TF:* 866-749-3697 ■ *Web:* catalystawareness.com	Guelph	ON	N1K1S5	866-749-3697	
Celerity Staffing Solutions 6273 University Ave *Web:* www.celeritystaffing.com	Middleton	WI	53562	608-238-3410	
CFO Selections LLC 14432 SE Eastgate Way Lincoln Executive Ctr II Ste 400 *Web:* www.cfoselections.com	Bellevue	WA	98007	206-686-4480	
Chameleon Technologies Inc 520 Kirkland Way Ste 101 *Web:* www.chameleontechinc.com	Kirkland	WA	98033	425-827-1173	
Chandler Group Executive Search Inc 4165 Shoreline Dr Ste 220 *Web:* www.chandgroup.com	Spring Park	MN	55384	952-471-3000	
Charm City Concierge Inc 1437 E Ft Ave *Web:* www.charmcityconcierge.com	Baltimore	MD	21230	410-727-4569	
ChaseSource LP 3311 W Alabama *Web:* www.chasesource.com	Houston	TX	77098	713-874-3000	
Chatham Search International Inc 3 Lion Gardiner *Web:* www.chathamct.com	Cromwell	CT	06416	860-635-5538	
Chicago Nannies Inc 101 N Marion St Ste 300 *TF:* 866-900-9605 ■ *Web:* www.chicagonanniesinc.com	Oak Park	IL	60301	708-524-2101	
Children First Home Healthcare Service 4448 Edgewater Dr *TF:* 800-207-0802 ■ *Web:* www.childrenfirsthomecare.com	Orlando	FL	32804	407-513-3000	
Choctaw Management Services Enterprise 2101 W Arkansas St *Web:* www.cmse.net	Durant	OK	74701	580-924-8280	
ClaimReturn LLC 3004 Irving Blvd *Web:* claimreturn.com	Dallas	TX	75247	817-953-2424	
Clark Personnel Service 1180 Montlimar Dr *Web:* www.clarkpersonnel.com	Mobile	AL	36609	251-471-6777	
Clearbridge Technology Group 6 Fortune Dr *TF:* 877-808-2284 ■ *Web:* www.clearbridgetech.com	Billerica	MA	01821	781-916-2284	
ClearStaff Inc 251 N Bolingbrook Dr *Web:* www.stanfordproducts.com	Woodridge	IL	60517	630-985-0100	
Cn Staffing Inc 1201 Richardson Dr Ste 150 *Web:* www.cnstaffing.com	Richardson	TX	75080	972-484-3922	
Coast Personnel 2295 De La Cruz Blvd *Web:* www.coastjobs.com	Santa Clara	CA	95050	408-653-2100	
Coastal Administrative Services Inc 103 E Holly Ste 214 *TF:* 800-870-1831 ■ *Web:* www.coastaladmin.com	Bellingham	WA	98225	800-870-1831	
Coddington Group LLC, The 115 W St Ste 300 *Web:* www.coddingtongroup.com	Annapolis	MD	21401	410-263-6200	
College Nannies & Tutors Inc 1415 Wayzata Blvd E *Web:* www.collegenanniesandtutors.com/nanny	Wayzata	MN	55391	952-476-0613	
Completech Inc 5960 Stoneridge Dr Ste 204 *Web:* www.completech.com	Pleasanton	CA	94588	925-462-9600	
ComputerJobs.com Inc 1995 N Pk Pl SE *TF:* 800-850-0045 ■ *Web:* www.computerjobs.com	Atlanta	GA	30339	770-850-0045	850-0369
Condustrial Inc 105 East N St *TF:* 888-794-7798 ■ *Web:* www.condustrial.com	Greenville	SC	29601	864-235-3619	
Conexess Group LLC 4336 Kenilwood Dr *Web:* www.conexess.com	Nashville	TN	37204	615-242-1014	
Controllers Group Inc 1818 The Alameda *Web:* www.controllersgroup.net	San Jose	CA	95126	408-294-0004	
Conway & Greenwood Inc 1122 Oberlin Rd Ste 310 *Web:* www.conwaygreenwood.com	Raleigh	NC	27605	919-833-4800	
CoWorx Staffing Services LLC 1375 Plainfield Ave *Web:* www.coworxstaffing.com	Watchung	NJ	07069	908-757-5300	
CPI Group Inc, The 112 5th St N *Web:* www.cpi-group.com	Columbus	MS	39703	662-328-1042	
CPM Ltd Inc 2225 Camino del Rio S Ste E *Web:* cpm-ltd.com	San Diego	CA	92108	619-293-3606	
CPSI Consulting Inc 720-A Maiden Choice Ln *Web:* www.cpsiconsulting.com	Baltimore	MD	21228	410-455-0005	
Crandall Associates Inc 6 Litchfield Rd Ste 316 *Web:* www.crandallassociates.com	Port Washington	NY	11050	516-767-6800	
Crist|Kolder Associates LLC 3250 Lacey Rd Ste 450 *Web:* www.cristkolder.com	Downers Grove	IL	60515	630-321-1110	
Crowe-Innes & Associates 1120 Mar W Ste D *Web:* www.croweinnes.com	Tiburon	CA	94920	415-789-1422	
CSH Consulting Inc 18325 N Allied Way Ste 210 *Web:* go-impact.com	Phoenix	AZ	85054	480-307-9000	
Csi Recruiting 1905 Sherman St Ste 245 *Web:* www.csirecruiting.com	Denver	CO	80203	303-996-0400	
CSS International Inc 115 River Landing Dr Daniel Island *Web:* www.cssus.com	Charleston	SC	29492	843-849-8712	
Culinary Services of America Inc 6363 Wilshire Blvd Ste 305 *Web:* www.culinarystaffing.com	Los Angeles	CA	90048	323-965-7582	
CVCertify Inc 1282 Auburn Grove Ln *Web:* www.cvcertify.com	Reston	VA	20194	703-662-1485	
D N Schwartz & Co 160 W 71st St Ste 12H *Web:* www.dnschwartz.com	New York	NY	10023	212-787-5017	
Dako Services Inc 2966 Industrial Row *Web:* www.dakogroup.com	Troy	MI	48084	248-655-0100	
Darrell Walker Personnel Systems 11 W Oxmoor Rd Ste G *Web:* www.darrellwalker.com	Birmingham	AL	35209	205-942-1133	
DataStarUSA Inc 5904 Stonecreek Dr., Ste 120 *Web:* www.datastarusa.com	The Colony	TX	75056	214-291-2000	
David Aplin & Associates Ltd 2300 Oxford Tower 10235-101 St *Web:* www.aplin.com	Edmonton	AB	T5J3G1	780-428-6663	
Dax Safety & Staffing Solutions LLC 307 Nw 110th Ter *Web:* daxsafety.com	Kansas City	MO	64155	816-935-9137	
Delta Dallas Protech LP 15950 N Dallas Pkwy Ste 500 *Web:* www.deltadallas.com	Dallas	TX	75248	972-788-2300	
Delta Staffing LLC 6100 Dixie Hwy Ste B *Web:* www.delta-staffing.com	Clarkston	MI	48346	248-394-3940	
Denham Corp 567 W Shaw Ave Ste C1 *Web:* www.denham.net	Fresno	CA	93704	559-222-5284	
Depaul Industries 4950 NE Martin Luther King Junior Blvd *Web:* www.depaulindustries.com	Portland	OR	97211	503-281-1289	
Detering Consulting Inc 306 Ferne Ave *Web:* www.deteringconsulting.com	Palo Alto	CA	94306	650-493-4977	
Diamond Personnel LLC 352 Seventh Ave 3rd Fl *Web:* www.diamondjob.com	New York	NY	10001	212-631-7520	
Dice Inc 4101 NW Urbandale Dr *TF:* 877-386-3323 ■ *Web:* www.dice.com	Urbandale	IA	50322	515-280-1144	280-1452
Diedre Moire Corporation Inc 510 Horizon Center *Web:* www.diedremoire.com	Robbinsville	NJ	08691	609-584-9000	
DISCO International Inc 15 W 44th St 5th Fl *Web:* discointer.com	New York	NY	10036	212-382-0025	
Diversity Advertising Inc 11271 Ventura Blvd Ste 151 *Web:* www.hispanic-jobs.com	Studio City	CA	91604	818-530-4852	
Docusoft America Corp 246 W Woods Creek Rd *Web:* www.docusoft.com	Morgan	UT	84050	801-845-1040	
Doherty Staffing Solutions Inc 7645 Metro Blvd Ste 1 *Web:* www.dohertystaffing.com	Edina	MN	55439	952-832-8885	
Domari & Associates Inc 135 Triple Diamond Blvd Unit 100 *Web:* www.domarijobs.com	North Venice	FL	34275	941-488-4440	
Doostang Inc 129 W 29th St, 500s *Web:* www.doostang.com	New York	NY	10001	650-561-3226	
Dployit Inc 14673 Midway Rd Ste 108 *Web:* www.dployit.com	Addison	TX	75001	214-550-6124	
DreamJobs 6545 W Central Ave Ste 102 *Web:* www.dreamjobsna.com	Toledo	OH	43617	567-455-5500	
Drivestaff 114 N Hale St Ste 208 *Web:* www.drivestaff.com	Wheaton	IL	60187	630-941-3748	
E-ventexe 8775 Sierra College Blvd Ste 300 *Web:* www.e-ventexe.com	Roseville	CA	95661	916-458-5820	
Eastern Design Services PO Box 17606 *Web:* easterndesign.com	Greenville	SC	29606	864-271-1228	
Economic Technology Solutions Inc 3242 Players Club Cir Ste 10 *Web:* www.economictechnology.com	Memphis	TN	38125	901-748-3610	
ECU Staffing Multi Services Inc 3837 N High School Rd Ste 3 *Web:* www.ecustaffing.com	Indianapolis	IN	46254	317-918-7585	
eIT Professionals Corp 42180 Ford Rd Ste 275 *Web:* www.eitprofessionals.com	Canton	MI	48187	734-416-0059	
Elastic Inc 1955 Landings Dr *Web:* elasticsales.com	Mountain View	CA	94043	650-618-3100	
Eliassen Group LLC 30 Audubon Rd *Web:* www.eliassen.com	Wakefield	MA	01880	781-246-1600	
Emerge Financial Wellness Inc 530 Church St Ste 301 *TF:* 800-791-1725 ■ *Web:* www.emergebenefit.com	Nashville	TN	37219	800-791-1725	
EmpireWorks Inc 1940 Olivera Rd *TF:* 888-278-8200 ■ *Web:* www.empireworks.com	Concord	CA	94520	888-278-8200	
EmplawyerNet 2331 Westwood Blvd *TF:* 800-270-2688 ■ *Web:* www.emplawyernet.com	Los Angeles	CA	90064	800-270-2688	
Emplicity 9851 Irvine Ctr Dr *Web:* www.emplicity.com	Irvine	CA	92618	714-668-1388	
Employco USA Inc 350 E Ogden Ave *Web:* www.employco.com	Westmont	IL	60559	630-920-0000	
EmploymentGuide.com 150 Granby St *TF:* 877-876-4039 ■ *Web:* www.employmentguide.com	Norfolk	VA	23510	877-876-4039	
EnterTech LLC 6625 Fincher Rd *Web:* www.etpeople.com	Waleska	GA	30183	678-388-9221	
Escamilla & Sons Inc 23820 Potter Rd *Web:* www.esons.com	Salinas	CA	93908	831-771-5400	
Esquire Inc 21241 Bentura Blvd Ste 293 *Web:* www.esquiresearch.com	Los Angeles	CA	91364	818-712-9700	
Ethan Allen Personnel Group Inc 59 Academy St *Web:* www.eaworkforce.com	Poughkeepsie	NY	12601	845-471-9700	
ettain group Inc 127 W Worthington Ave Ste 100 *Web:* www.ettaingroup.com	Charlotte	NC	28203	704-525-5499	
EverStaff LLC 6500 Rockside Rd Ste. 385 Ste *Web:* www.everstaff.com	Cleveland	OH	44131	216-369-2566	
Evins Personnel Consultants Inc 2013 W Anderson Ln *Web:* www.evinspersonnelconsultants.com	Austin	TX	78757	512-454-9561	
Evolve Digital Labs 7374 Elm St *Web:* evolvedigitallabs.com	Maplewood	MO	63143	314-260-7455	
Excel Partners Inc 1177 Summer St *Web:* www.excel-partners.com	Stamford	CT	06905	203-978-6200	
Excel Personnel Inc 10111 Inverness Main St Ste 419 *Web:* www.excelpersonnel.com	Englewood	CO	80112	303-427-4600	
ExecUNet Inc 295 Westport Ave *TF:* 800-637-3126 ■ *Web:* www.execunet.com	Norwalk	CT	06851	203-750-1030	840-8320
Executrade 9917 112 St Nw *Web:* www.executrade.com	Edmonton	AB	T5K1L6	780-944-1122	

Company	City	State	ZIP	Phone	Fax
Expanxion 860 Hampshire Rd Ste I *Web:* expanxion.com	Westlake Village	CA	91361	650-261-0211	
Expert Recruiters 883 Helmcken St *TF:* 888-407-7799 ■ *Web:* www.expertrecruiters.com	Vancouver	BC	V6Z1B1	604-689-3600	
Fahrenheit Group LLC, The 1700 Bayberry Court Ste 201 *Web:* thefahrenheitgroup.com	Richmond	VA	23226	804-955-4440	
Federal Staffing Resources LLC 2200 Somerville Rd Ste 300 *TF:* 866-886-2300 ■ *Web:* fsrpeople.com	Annapolis	MD	21401	410-990-0795	
Fetch Recruiting Inc 21143 Hawthorne Blvd Ste 322 *Web:* fetchrecruiting.com	Torrance	CA	90503	310-375-4384	
Filter Talent 1425 4th Ave Ste 1000 *TF:* 800-336-0809 ■ *Web:* www.filtertalent.com	Seattle	WA	98101	800-336-0809	
First Associates Ltd 55 E Jackson Blvd Ste 2150 *Web:* www.firstassoc.com	Chicago	IL	60604	312-253-4000	
First Call Nursing Services Inc 1313 N Milpitas Blvd Ste 210 *Web:* www.firstcallnursingservices.com	Milpitas	CA	95035	408-262-1533	
First Rate Staffing Corp 2775 W Thomas Rd Ste 107 *Web:* www.first-ratestaffing.com	Phoenix	AZ	85018	602-442-5277	
Firstoption Staffing 3708 NW Loop 410 *Web:* www.firstoptionstaffing.com	San Antonio	TX	78229	210-733-3700	
Flesher & Associates Inc 445 S San Antonio Rd Ste 103 *Web:* www.flesher.com	Los Altos	CA	94022	650-917-9900	
Flexible Resources Inc 304 Main Ave Ste 299 *Web:* www.flexibleresources.com	Norwalk	CT	06902	203-351-1180	
Focus Industrial Workforces 8651 Hauser Ct *Web:* www.workatfocus.com	Lenexa	KS	66215	913-268-1222	
Forward Edge LLC 3428 Hauck Rd Ste K *Web:* www.forward-edge.net	Cincinnati	OH	45241	513-761-3343	
FSO Onsite Outsourcing 19 W 44th St 9th Fl. *Web:* www.fso.co	New York	NY	10036	212-204-1193	
Full Employment Council Inc 1740 Paseo Blvd. *Web:* www.feckc.org	Kansas City	MO	64108	816-471-2330	
Fusion Recruitment Group Ltd 900 Howa St Ste 330 *Web:* www.fusion-recruitment.com	Vancouver	BC	V6Z2M4	604-678-5627	
Future Force Inc 15800 NW 57th Ave *Web:* www.futureforcepersonnel.com	Miami Lakes	FL	33014	305-557-4900	
G-Force Protective Services & Training Academy Inc 14331 SW 120 St Ste 103 *Web:* www.gforcemiami.com	Miami	FL	33186	305-380-1212	
Galaxy Software Solutions Inc 5820 N Lilley Rd Ste 8 *TF:* 877-269-4774 ■ *Web:* www.galaxy-soft.com	Canton	MI	48187	734-983-9030	
Garms Group, The 553 N Ave Ste 250 *Web:* garms.com	Barrington	IL	60010	847-382-7200	
Generate Content LLC 1545 26th St Ste 200 *Web:* www.defymedia.com	Santa Monica	CA	90404	310-255-0460	
Getintegrated Inc 616 Water St Ste 329 *Web:* www.getintegrated.com	Baltimore	MD	21202	410-685-6100	
Global HR Research LLC 24201 Walden Ctr Dr Ste 206 *TF:* 800-790-1205 ■ *Web:* www.ghrr.com	Bonita Springs	FL	34134	239-274-0048	
Global LT Inc 1871 Woodslee Dr *Web:* www.global-lt.com	Troy	MI	48083	248-786-0999	
Good Jobs Inc, The 2120 E Jarvis St *Web:* www.thegoodjobs.com	Milwaukee	WI	53211	414-949-5627	
GOOD SEARCH LLC, The 4 Valley Rd *Web:* tgsus.com	Westport	CT	06880	203-539-0847	
Goodwill Keystone Area Inc 1150 Goodwill Dr *Web:* www.yourgoodwill.org	Harrisburg	PA	17101	717-232-1831	
Grahall LLC 50 Fairlee Rd *Web:* www.grahall.com	Waban	MA	02468	917-453-4341	
Graham Personnel Services 2100 w cornwallis dr *Web:* www.grahamjobs.com	Greensboro	NC	27408	336-288-9330	
Grapevine Executive Recruiters Inc 269 Richmond St W *Web:* www.grapevinerecruiters.com	Toronto	ON	M5V1X1	416-581-1445	
Greene Resources Inc 400 Spring Forest Rd *Web:* www.greeneresources.com	Raleigh	NC	27609	919-862-8602	
Greenridge Business Systems Corp 2701 - 83 Garry St *Web:* www.greenridge.ca	Winnipeg	MB	R3C4J9	204-775-3500	
Greer Management Group Inc 3109 Charles B Root Wynd *Web:* www.thegreergroup.com	Raleigh	NC	27612	919-571-0051	
Grimes Legal 8264 Louisville Rd *Web:* www.grimeslegal.com	Bowling Green	KY	42101	270-782-3820	
Gromwell LLC 15 W 39th St 11th Fl *Web:* www.gromwell.com	New York	NY	10018	212-972-9300	
GRUS Inc 109 N Brush St Unit 160 *Web:* www.gruspersonnel.com	Tampa	FL	33602	727-791-6205	
Gsp International Inc 90 Woodbridge Ctr Dr Ste 110 *Web:* gspintl.com	Woodbridge	NJ	07095	732-602-0100	
Gunther Douglas Inc 3400 Mariposa St *Web:* www.guntherdouglas.com	Denver	CO	80211	303-534-4441	
Guru.com 5001 Baum Blvd Ste 760 *TF:* 888-678-0136 ■ *Web:* www.guru.com	Pittsburgh	PA	15213	412-687-1316	687-4466
H Ka Staffing Services 800 Waukegan Rd Ste 200 *Web:* www.hkastaffing.com	Glenview	IL	60025	847-998-9300	
Hansell Tierney Inc 2955 80th Ave SE Ste 102 *Web:* hanselltierney.com	Mercer Island	WA	98040	206-232-3080	
Happy Faces Personnel Group Inc 4333 Lynburn Dr *Web:* www.happyfaces.net	Tucker	GA	30084	770-414-9071	
Harvard Student Agencies Inc 67 Mt Auburn St *Web:* www.hsa.net	Cambridge	MA	02138	617-495-3030	
Harvest Technical Service Inc 1839 Ygnacio Valley Rd Ste 390 *Web:* www.harvtech.com	Walnut Creek	CA	94598	925-937-4874	
Haskel Thompson & Associates LLC 12734 Kenwood Ln Ste 74 *Web:* haskelthompson.com	Fort Myers	FL	33907	239-437-4600	
Hawthorne Executive Search 6303 Oleander Dr Ste 104b *Web:* hawthornesearch.com	Wilmington	NC	28403	910-798-1800	
HCTec LLC 7105 S Springs Dr Ste 208 *Web:* www.hctec.com	Franklin	TN	37067	615-577-4030	
Headquist International 230 Florence St Ste 1 *Web:* hedquistintl.com	Crystal Lake	IL	60014	815-479-1700	
HealthCareSource Inc 100 Sylvan Rd Ste 100 *TF:* 800-869-5200 ■ *Web:* www.healthcaresource.com	Woburn	MA	01801	800-869-5200	829-6600
HealthForce Ontario Marketing & Recruitment Agency 163 Queen St E *TF:* 800-596-4046 ■ *Web:* www.healthforceontario.ca	Toronto	ON	M5A1S1	416-862-2200	
Hedy Co Inc 3031 W March Ln *Web:* www.hedyholmesstaffing.com	Stockton	CA	95219	209-957-9630	
Helping Hand Nursing Service Inc 8305 S Saginaw St *Web:* www.helpinghandhealthcare.com	Grand Blanc	MI	48439	810-606-8400	
Herring Impact Group LLC, The 12977 N Outer 40 Dr Ste 300 *Web:* www.impactgrouphr.com	St. Louis	MO	63141	314-453-9002	
HigherMe inc 27 Parsons St. *Web:* www.higherme.com	Boston	MA	02135	617-784-1052	
HighPoint Technology Solutions Inc 10642 SW Gingermill Dr *Web:* www.mhighpoint.com	Port Saint Lucie	FL	34987	305-338-3761	
Hire Demand 106 Pinehurst Dr *Web:* hiredemand.com	Cranberry Township	PA	16066	724-538-3434	
Hire Quest LLC 4560 Great Oak Dr. *Web:* hirequestllc.com	North Charleston	SC	29418	843-723-7400	
Hire Source Inc, The 24 Wooster Ave Ste 1 *Web:* thehiresource.com	Waterbury	CT	06708	203-757-4000	
Hired 1200 Plymouth Ave N *Web:* www.hired.org	Minneapolis	MN	55411	612-529-3342	
Hired Inc 1455 Market St Fl 19 *Web:* hired.com	San Francisco	CA	94103	415-813-4987	
Hodges-Mace Benefits Group Inc 5775-D Glenridge Dr Ste 350 *Web:* www.hodgesmace.com	Atlanta	GA	30328	404-574-6110	
Hospital Employee Labor Pool 5400 Orange Ave *Web:* www.helpstaffs.com	Cypress	CA	90630	714-243-3510	
Hotel Pro Staffing LLC 1950 N Park Pl Ste 330 *Web:* www.gohotelpro.com	Atlanta	GA	30339	770-937-9007	
Hotline to HR Inc 110 Confederation Pkwy	Concord	ON	L4K4T8	416-619-7867	
Howard E. Nyhart Company Inc, The 8415 Allison Pointe Blvd Ste 300 *Web:* www.nyhart.com	Indianapolis	IN	46250	317-845-3500	
HR Advisors Inc 25411 Cabot Rd Ste 212 *Web:* www.hradvisors.com	Laguna Hills	CA	92653	949-497-7329	
HR Works Inc 200 WillowBrook Ofc Park. *TF:* 877-219-9062 ■ *Web:* www.hrworks-inc.com	Fairport	NY	14450	585-381-8340	
HR1 Services Inc 2030 Powers Ferry Rd Nw #120 *Web:* www.hr1.com	Atlanta	GA	30339	770-541-7823	
HRCG Inc 1202 E Dover Dr *Web:* ezpublishtest.hrconsultinggroup.com	Provo	UT	84604	801-765-4417	
HRO Partners LLC 1237 Yorkshire Cove *Web:* www.hro-partners.com	Memphis	TN	38119	901-737-0123	
Hughes Agency, The 700 E 13th St *Web:* www.hughesstaffingagency.com	North Little Rock	AR	72114	501-791-3303	
Human Dynamics Inc 11863 W 112th St Ste 110 *Web:* www.hdynamics.com	Overland Park	KS	66210	913-663-2088	
i-Hire Inc 307 Sonora Dr *Web:* www.i-hire.com	San Mateo	CA	94402	650-678-2808	
I-Tech Solutions Inc 10 New England Business Ctr Ste 302 *Web:* www.i-techsolutions.com	Andover	MA	01810	978-794-8333	
i-Vantage Inc 400 Talcott Ave *Web:* www.i-vantage.com	Watertown	MA	02472	617-393-2338	
Idea Foundry 4551 Forbes Ave Ste 200 *Web:* ideafoundry.org	Pittsburgh	PA	15213	412-682-3067	
IFG Project Resourcing LLC Research Triangle Park 2530 Meridian Pkwy Ste 300 *Web:* www.ifgpr.com	Raleigh	NC	27713	919-806-4458	
iforce LLC 1110 Morse Rd Ste 200 *Web:* www.iforceservices.com	Columbus	OH	43229	614-436-5627	
Ignite Technical Resources Ltd 1295 - 355 Burrard St. *Web:* www.ignitetechnical.com	Vancouver	BC	V6C2G8	604-687-6795	
iMatch LLC 1417 Fourth Ave Ste 810 *Web:* www.imatch.com	Seattle	WA	98101	206-262-1661	
Imko Enterprises Inc 900 N Belt Hwy *Web:* www.imko.com	Saint Joseph	MO	64506	816-233-4040	
Impact Benefit Management Services LLC 10930 Crabapple Rd Ste 102 *Web:* www.impactbms.com	Roswell	GA	30075	770-709-6000	

Company / Address	City	State	Zip	Phone	Fax
Incepture Inc 8381 Dix Ellis Trail Ste 105 — *TF:* 877-347-7151 ■ *Web:* www.incepture.com	Jacksonville	FL	32225	877-347-7151	
Industry Specific Solutions LLC 24901 Northwestern Hwy Ste 400 — *TF:* 877-356-3450 ■ *Web:* industryspecificstaffing.com	Southfield	MI	48075	877-356-3450	
InjuryFree Inc 20250 144Th Ave NE Ste 305 — *Web:* www.ergostat.com	Woodinville	WA	98072	206-363-7676	
InnoSource Inc 6085 Emerald Pkwy — *Web:* www.innosourceinc.com	Dublin	OH	43016	614-775-1400	
Intellect Resources Inc 3824 N Elm St Ste 102 — *TF:* 877-554-8911 ■ *Web:* www.intellectresources.com	Greensboro	NC	27455	877-554-8911	
International Foundation of Employee Benefit Plans (IFEBP) 18700 W Bluemound Rd — *TF:* 888-334-3327 ■ *Web:* www.ifebp.org	Brookfield	WI	53045	262-786-6700	786-8670
Ish Entertainment LLC 1950 Sawtelle Blvd — *Web:* ish.tv	Los Angeles	CA	90025	310-500-1095	
Island Staffing 4263 Oceanside Blvd Ste 106-160 — *Web:* www.islandstaffing.us	Oceanside	CA	92056	760-547-5018	
Istaff Inc 1325 Satellite Blvd Nw Ste 1305 — *Web:* www.istaff.com	Suwanee	GA	30024	770-962-9604	
ITP Worldwide Inc 20 N Main St Ste 300 — *Web:* www.itpww.com	Sherborn	MA	01770	508-650-1031	
Its Technologies Inc 7060 Spring Meadows Dr W Ste D — *Web:* www.itstechnologies.com	Holland	OH	43528	419-842-2100	
J. s Firm LLC 8205 Camp Bowie W Blvd Ste 214	Fort Worth	TX	76116	817-560-0300	
Jaci Carroll Staffing Services Inc 751 Straits TurnPk Ste 3000 — *Web:* www.jacicarroll.com	Middlebury	CT	06762	203-574-4838	
Jack of All Trades Personnel Services 2701 Franklin Ave — *Web:* www.joatwaco.com	Waco	TX	76710	254-754-7997	
Jackie Matchett Personnel Inc 519 Heritage Rd Ste 2B — *Web:* www.jackiematchett.com	Southbury	CT	06488	203-405-6111	
Jacob Group, The 6190 Virginia Pkwy One Jacob Pl Ste 100 — *Web:* www.jacobgroup.com	Mckinney	TX	75071	214-544-9030	
Jacobs Management Group Inc 1420 Walnut St — *Web:* www.jacobsmgt.com	Philadelphia	PA	19102	215-732-6400	
James Farris Associates Ltd 909 NW 63rd St — *Web:* www.jamesfarris.com	Oklahoma City	OK	73116	405-525-5061	
JBCConnect 3621 Hayden Ave — *Web:* www.jbcconnect.com	Culver City	CA	90232	310-601-7231	
JCSI Corporate Staffing 2 South St — *TF:* 888-527-4462 ■ *Web:* www.jcsi.net	Grafton	MA	01519	774-760-1800	
JDA Professional Services Inc 701 N Post Oak Rd Ste 610 — *Web:* www.jdapsi.com	Houston	TX	77024	713-548-5400	
Jeepnee Inc 511 Chabot Rd Ste 123 — *Web:* www.jeepnee.com	Pleasanton	CA	12345	925-264-1213	
Jes Search Firm Inc One Atlanta Plz 950 E Paces Ferry Rd Ste 2245 — *Web:* www.jessearch.com	Atlanta	GA	30326	404-812-0622	
Jet Professionals LLC 114 Charles A Lindbergh Dr Teterboro Airport — *Web:* www.jet-professionals.com	Teterboro	NJ	07608	201-393-6900	
Job Finders Employment Service Co 1729 W Bdwy Ste 4 — *Web:* www.jobfindersusa.com	Columbia	MO	65203	573-446-4250	
Jobboom Inc 800 rue du Sq Victoria Mezzanine - Bureau 5 — *Web:* www.jobboom.com	Montreal	QC	H4Z0A3	514-504-2539	
JobDig Inc 5051 Hwy 7 Ste 240 — *Web:* www.jobdig.com	Saint Louis Park	MN	55416	952-929-5627	
JobHive Inc 701 E Bridger Ave Ste 400 — *TF:* 855-562-4483 ■ *Web:* jobhive.com	Las Vegas	NV	89101	855-562-4483	
JobMonkey Inc PO Box 3956 — *TF:* 800-230-1095 ■ *Web:* www.jobmonkey.com	Seattle	WA	98124	800-230-1095	
JobSync Inc 430 Colorado Ave Ste 302 — *Web:* www.jobsync.com	Santa Monica	CA	90401	617-548-8306	
JobTarget LLC 225 State St Ste 300 — *Web:* www.jobtarget.com	New London	CT	06320	860-440-0635	
Josephine's Personnel Services Inc 2158 Ringwood Ave — *Web:* www.jps-inc.com	San Jose	CA	95131	408-943-0111	
JSMN International Inc 591 Summit Ave Ste 522 — *Web:* www.jsmninc.com	Jersey City	NJ	07306	201-792-6800	
Judys Staffing Services Inc 3070 Harrodsburg Rd — *Web:* www.judysstaffing.com	Lexington	KY	40503	859-223-5005	
Juju Inc 151 First Ave Ste 19 — *Web:* www.juju.com	New York	NY	10003	212-537-3898	
JUNO Healthcare Staffing System Inc 411 Fifth Ave Ste 1006 — *Web:* www.junohealthcare.com	New York	NY	10016	212-685-5866	
Justworks Inc 29 E 19th St 7th Fl — *Web:* www.justworks.com	New York	NY	10003	646-663-1347	
K A Hamilton & Assoc 159 Perry Hwy Ste 100 — *TF:* 800-746-4726 ■ *Web:* rcn.com	Pittsburgh	PA	15229	412-459-0122	
Kane Partners LLC 1816 W Point Pike Ste 221 — *Web:* www.kanepartners.net	Lansdale	PA	19446	215-699-5500	
Katalyst Group Inc 6464 W Sunset Blvd — *Web:* www.katalystgroup.com	Los Angeles	CA	90028	323-327-5366	
Kavaliro Staffing Services 12001 Research Pkwy Ste 344 — *Web:* www.kavaliro.com	Orlando	FL	32826	407-243-6006	
Kaye Personnel Inc 1868 Marlton Pike E — *Web:* kayepersonnel.com	Cherry Hill	NJ	08003	856-489-1200	
Kazan International Inc 1430 US Hwy 206 Ste 220 — *Web:* www.kazansearch.com	Bedminster Township	NJ	07921	908-901-0900	
Keller Augusta Partners LLC 45 Newbury St Ste 204 — *Web:* www.kelleraugusta.com	Boston	MA	02116	617-247-0505	
Kendall & Davis Company Inc 3668 S Geyer Rd Ste 100 — *TF:* 866-675-3755 ■ *Web:* www.kendallanddavis.com	St. Louis	MO	63127	866-675-3755	
Key Corporate Services LLC 9746 Olympia Dr — *Web:* kcsllc.net	Fishers	IN	46037	317-598-1950	
Kipe Technology Resources 14725 SW Millikan Way — *Web:* www.kipetech.com	Beaverton	OR	97006	503-590-7000	
Koren Rogers 4 W Red Oak Ln Ste 312 — *Web:* www.korenrogers.com	White Plains	NY	10604	914-686-5800	
Kovasys Inc 500 Pl d'Armes Ste 1800 — *TF:* 888-568-2747 ■ *Web:* www.kovasys.com	Montreal	QC	H2X2T7	888-568-2747	
KPM VIPER Consulting LLC South Shore Executive Park 10 Forbes Rd — *Web:* www.kpm-us.com	Braintree	MA	02184	781-380-3520	
Kreuzberger & Associates 1000 Fourth St — *Web:* www.kreuzberger.com	San Rafael	CA	94901	415-459-2300	
KWCG Inc 12255 Pkwy Centre Dr — *TF:* 877-464-5924 ■ *Web:* www.kwcg.us	San Diego	CA	92064	877-464-5924	
Landmark Staffing Resources Inc 2901 E Enterprise Ave Ste 600 — *Web:* www.landmarkstaffing.com	Appleton	WI	54913	920-731-3130	
Lawton Group, The 4747 Viewridge Ave Ste 210 — *Web:* www.tlcstaffing.com	San Diego	CA	92123	858-569-6260	
Legal Resources Inc 127 Peachtree St Ste 1005 — *Web:* www.legalresources.com	Atlanta	GA	30303	404-584-9000	
Legal Search 510 E 85th St Apt 9f — *Web:* www.legalsearchusa.com	New York	NY	10028	212-472-3000	
Levert Personnel Resources Inc 17 Frood Rd — *Web:* www.levert.ca	Sudbury	ON	P3C4Y9	705-525-8367	
Liaison Creative Services 3003 S Kearney St — *Web:* www.liaisonresources.com	Denver	CO	80222	303-446-8550	
Liberty Staffing LLC 28 Mallard Cove Rd — *Web:* www.libertystaffing.com	Barrington	RI	02806	267-256-2301	
Life Advantages LLC 600 First Ave N Ste 307 — *Web:* www.lifeadvantages.com	St. Petersburg	FL	33701	727-381-9446	
Life Style Staffing 6765 W Greenfield Ave — *Web:* www.lifestylestaffing.com	Milwaukee	WI	53214	414-475-0090	
Lindsey & Company Inc 484 Boston Post Rd — *Web:* www.lindseycompany.com	Darien	CT	06820	203-655-1590	
Linium Staffing LLC 124 Hebron Ave Eric Town Sq — *Web:* www.liniumstaffing.com	Glastonbury	CT	06033	860-659-1900	
Link Executive Search Inc 730 Second Ave S US Trust Bldg Ste 400 — *Web:* link-us.net	Minneapolis	MN	55402	612-884-7000	
Ll Roberts Group 7475 Skillman St Ste 102c — *TF:* 877-878-6463 ■ *Web:* www.llroberts.com	Dallas	TX	75231	214-221-6463	
Longs Human Resource Services 19 midtown park w — *Web:* www.longshrs.com	Mobile	AL	36606	251-476-4080	
Lorelei Personnel Inc 1 Auer Ct — *Web:* www.loreleipersonnel.com	East Brunswick	NJ	08816	732-390-1170	
LyonsHR 1941 Florence Blvd — *Web:* www.lyonshr.com	Florence	AL	35630	256-767-5900	
Madison & Associates Inc 4108 Holly Rd — *Web:* www.tdmadison.com	Virginia Beach	VA	23451	757-425-9950	
Maglio & Company Whlse Fruits 4287 N Port Washington Rd — *Web:* www.maglioproduce.com	Milwaukee	WI	53212	414-906-8800	
Majesty Hospitality Staffing 1720 Regal Row Ste 115 — *Web:* www.majestyhospitalitystaffing.com	Dallas	TX	75235	713-682-1828	
Mancino Burfield Edgerton 12 Roszel Rd Ste C-101 — *Web:* www.mbels.com	Princeton	NJ	08540	609-520-8400	
Manning Search Group Llc 1101 Saint Peters Howell Rd — *Web:* manningsearchgroup.com	Saint Peters	MO	63376	636-447-4900	
MarketPro Inc 53 Perimeter Ctr E Ste 200 — *Web:* marketproinc.com	Atlanta	GA	30346	404-222-9992	
Mason & Blair LLC 1762 Technology Dr Ste 206 — *Web:* www.masonblair.com	San Jose	CA	95110	408-436-6300	
Mastertech Services Inc 691 Corporate Cir — *Web:* www.mastertechservices.com	Golden	CO	80401	303-278-7300	
Mathys Potestio LLC 917 SW Oak St N Pacific Bldg Ste 313 — *Web:* www.mathys-potestio.com	Portland	OR	97205	503-781-2872	
Maven Group LLC, The 320 N Salem St Ste 204 — *Web:* www.themavengroup.com	Apex	NC	27502	919-386-1010	
Maxcomm Inc 5671 S Redwood Rd Ste 20 — *Web:* www.maxcomminc.com	Salt Lake City	UT	84123	801-631-0890	
Maxsys 173 Dalhousie St — *TF:* 800-429-5177 ■ *Web:* maxsys.ca	Ottawa	ON	K1N7C7	613-562-9943	
Maxum Services Inc 941 S Lewis St Ste A — *Web:* www.maxumllc.com	New Iberia	LA	70560	337-364-9526	
Maxus Group Inc 345 Seventh Ave Fl 4 — *Web:* maxusgroup.com	New York	NY	10001	212-823-2010	

Phone Fax

Mcdermott & Bull Executive Search
2 Venture Ste 100 ... Irvine CA 92618 949-753-1700
Web: mbsearch.com

Mcintyre Associates 5 Essex Ct ... Farmington CT 06032 860-284-1000
Web: www.mcassoc.com

MDT Labor LLC 2325 Paxton Church Rd Ste B ... Harrisburg PA 17110 888-454-9202
TF: 888-454-9202 ■ *Web:* www.mdttechnical.com

Meador Staffing Services Inc
722 Fairmont Pkwy Ste A ... Pasadena TX 77504 713-941-0616
Web: www.meador.com

Medix Staffing Solutions Inc
477 E Butterfield Rd Ste 400 ... Lombard IL 60148 630-725-9041
Web: medixteam.com

Medpoint Search 4011 Garrott St ... Houston TX 77006 713-524-4443
Web: www.medpointsearch.com

Medrec Inc 85 NE Loop 410 Ste 610 ... San Antonio TX 78216 210-494-2343
Web: www.medrec-pt.com

Mega Force Staffing Services Inc
1001 Hay St ... Fayetteville NC 28305 910-484-0133
Web: www.megaforce.com

Melwood Horticultural Training Center In
5606 Dower House Rd ... Upper Marlboro MD 20772 301-599-8000
Web: www.melwood.org

Mercer Morgan 8350 E Raintree Dr ... Scottsdale AZ 85260 480-281-1833
Web: mercermorgan.com

Metasys Technologies Inc
3460 Summit Ridge Pkwy Ste 401 ... Duluth GA 30096 678-218-1600
Web: www.metasysinc.com

Mike Ferry Organization, The
7220 S Cimarron Rd Ste 300 ... Las Vegas NV 89113 702-982-6260
Web: www.mikeferry.com

Miller Jones Recruiting Inc
235 W Giaconda Way Ste 215 ... Tucson AZ 85704 520-206-9300
Web: millerjonesrecruiting.com

Miller Resources International Inc
83 Stultz Rd ... Dayton NJ 08810 609-395-1800
Web: www.millerjobs.com

Milliner & Associates LLC
4181 E 96th St Ste 120 ... Indianapolis IN 46240 317-218-1195
Web: www.millinerandassoc.com

Mind Your Business Inc (myb)
305 Eighth Ave E ... Hendersonville NC 28792 888-869-2462
TF: 888-869-2462

Mindseeker 20130 Lakeview Ctr Plz ... Ashburn VA 20147 571-313-5950
Web: www.mindseeker.com

Miracles Can Happen Inc 1600 Church Ave ... Brooklyn NY 11226 718-693-3400
Web: miraclescanhappeninc.com

MISource Inc 11940 Sheldon Rd ... Tampa FL 33626 813-286-9888
Web: www.misource.net

Mmc Systems Inc 44632 Guilford St, Ste 101 ... Ashburn VA 20147 201-484-7966
Web: www.mmcsystems.com

MonsterTRAK 11845 W Olympic Blvd Ste 500 ... Los Angeles CA 90064 800-999-8725
TF: 800-999-8725 ■ *Web:* college.monster.com

Moore Temporaries Inc 184 Pleasant Vly St ... Methuen MA 01844 978-682-4994
Web: www.moorestaffing.com

Morales Group Inc 5628 W 74th St ... Indianapolis IN 46278 317-472-7600
Web: moralesgroup.net

Morgan Hunter Companies
7600 W 110th St ... Overland Park KS 66210 913-491-3434
Web: www.morganhunter.com

Mosaic Company Inc, The
555 S Renton Village Pl ... Renton WA 98057 425-254-1724
Web: www.themosaiccompany.com

Mosse & Mosse Insurance Associates LLC
50 Salem St Bldg B ... Lynnfield MA 01940 781-224-1709
Web: www.mosseandmosse.com

Mundy Contract Maintenance Inc
11150 S Wilcrest ... Houston TX 77099 281-530-8711
Web: www.mundycos.com

MyOpenJobs LLC 203 Main St Ste 100 ... Lake Dallas TX 75065 800-396-4822
TF: 800-396-4822 ■ *Web:* www.myopenjobs.com

Myra Binstock Legal Search
121 Squire Hill Rd ... Upper Montclair NJ 07043 973-783-6006
Web: www.myrabinstock.com

N-Tier Solutions Inc 2596 Landmark Dr ... Winston-Salem NC 27103 336-765-3500
Web: www.n-tiersolutions.com

National Able Network Inc 180 N Wabash Ave ... Chicago IL 60601 312-782-3335
Web: www.nationalable.org

National Diversity Newspaper Job Bank
c/o Morris Communications 725 Broad St ... Augusta GA 30901 706-724-0851
TF: 800-622-6358 ■ *Web:* www.morris.com

National Older Worker Career Center
3811 N Fairfax Dr Ste 900 ... Arlington VA 22203 703-558-4200
Web: www.nowcc.org

NationJob Inc 920 Morgan St Ste T ... Des Moines IA 50309 800-292-7731 243-5384*
**Fax Area Code: 515* ■ *TF:* 800-292-7731 ■ *Web:* www.nationjob.com

Net-Temps Inc
55 Middlesex St Ste 220 ... North Chelmsford MA 01863 978-251-7272 251-7250
TF: 800-307-0062 ■ *Web:* www.net-temps.com

Netchex 1100 N Causeway Blvd Ste 1 ... Mandeville LA 70471 985-220-1410
Web: www.netchexonline.com

Newport Strategic Search Inc
175 Calle Magdalena ... Encinitas CA 92024 760-274-0100
Web: www.newportsearch.com

nGroup Inc 1184 Springmaid Ave Ste 104 ... Fort Mill SC 29708 704-719-2210
Web: www.ngroupworkforce.com

Nine Star Enterprises Inc 730 I St ... Anchorage AK 99501 907-279-7827
Web: www.ninestar.com

Northwest Software Inc
1800 Nw 169th Pl Ste B150 ... Beaverton OR 97006 503-629-5947
Web: www.nwsi.com

Nova Management Inc 659 Abrego St Ste 5 ... Monterey CA 93940 831-373-4544
Web: www.novamanagement.com

Phone Fax

Nowhirecom 21220 Kelly Rd ... Eastpointe MI 48021 586-778-8491
TF: 800-724-8546 ■ *Web:* www.nowhire.com

NSTAR Global Services Inc 120 Partlo St ... Garner NC 27529 877-678-2766
TF: 877-678-2766 ■ *Web:* www.nstarglobalservices.com

Olesky Associates Inc
865 Washington St Ste 3 ... Newtonville MA 02460 781-235-4330
TF: 800-486-4330 ■ *Web:* www.olesky.com

Oliver Staffing Inc
350 Lexington Ave Ste 401 ... New York NY 10016 212-634-1234
Web: www.oliverstaffing.com

Olympic Staffing Services 588 S Grand Ave ... Covina CA 91724 626-447-3558
Web: www.olystaffing.com

ON Search Partners LLC 6240 SOM Ctr Rd Ste 230 ... Solon OH 44139 440-318-1006
Web: www.onpartners.com

On Target Staffing LLC 398 Comstock St ... New Brunswick NJ 08901 732-249-8344
Web: www.ontargetstaffingllc.com

On Time Staffing LLC
2 Aquarium Dr Ferry Terminal Bldg Ste 150 ... Camden NJ 08103 866-333-3007
TF: 866-333-3007 ■ *Web:* www.ontimestaffing.com

One Stop Career Center
359 Bill France Blvd ... Daytona Beach FL 32114 386-323-7001
Web: www.careersourcefv.com

OneSource Inc 1124 Hwy 315 ... Wilkes-barre PA 18702 570-825-3411
Web: www.onesourcehrsolutions.com

Ongig Inc 708 Montgomery St ... San Francisco CA 94111 415-857-2304
Web: www.ongig.com

Onug Communications Inc 3315 Atlantic Ave ... Raleigh NC 27604 919-876-5455
Web: onugsolutions.com

OperationsInc LLC 992 High Ridge Rd 2nd Fl ... Stamford CT 06905 203-322-0538
Web: www.operationsinc.com

Opti Staffing Group 3601 C St Ste 1220 ... Anchorage AK 99503 907-677-9675
Web: optistaffing.com

Optimal Care Health Service
221 W 7th St Apt 3 ... Wilmington DE 19801 302-425-0900
Web: research.hsj.co.uk

Outsource Staffing Inc 2611 Laurel St ... Beaumont TX 77702 409-813-2900
Web: outsourcestaffinginc.com

Pace Staffing Network Inc
2275-116th Ave NE Ste 200 ... Bellevue WA 98004 425-454-1075
Web: www.pacestaffing.com

Paladin Partners 838 Kirkland Ave ... Kirkland WA 98033 425-260-5354
Web: www.paladinpartners.com

Paladin Registry LLC
69 Lincoln Blvd Ste A 275 ... Lincoln CA 95648 916-253-3334
Web: paladinregistry.com

Palo Alto Staffing Services
2471 E Bayshore Rd Ste 525 ... Palo Alto CA 94303 650-493-0223
Web: www.paloaltostaffing.com

Parallel Partners Inc
1212 S Naper Blvd Ste 119-307 ... Naperville IL 60540 630-428-0600
Web: www.parallelpartners.com

Parallon Workforce Management Solutions
1000 Sawgrass Corporate Pkwy 6th Fl ... Sunrise FL 33323 954-858-1833
Web: www.allaboutstaffing.com

Partnersolve Llc 4520 Overbrook Way ... Cumming GA 30041 770-888-0440
Web: partnersolve.com

PCI Group LLC
10801 W Charleston Blvd Ste 650 ... Las Vegas NV 89135 702-515-7490
Web: www.hillpci.com

Penda Aiken Inc 330 Livingston St ... Brooklyn NY 11217 718-643-4880
Web: www.pendaaiken.com

Penmac Staffing Services Inc
447 South Ave ... Springfield MO 65806 417-831-9100
Web: www.penmac.com

Penski Inc 50 Market St ... Potsdam NY 13676 315-265-8860
Web: www.penski.com

People Plus Industrial Inc 1095 Nebo Rd ... Madisonville KY 42431 270-825-8939
TF: 888-825-1500 ■ *Web:* www.peopleplusinc.com

Peoplecomm Inc 148 Woodbine Ave ... Northport NY 11768 800-735-1629
TF: 800-735-1629

Peoplelink Staffing Solutions LLC
431 E Colfax Ave Ste 200 ... South Bend IN 46617 574-232-5400
Web: www.peoplelinkstaffing.com

Perfect Fit Placement Inc 1263 Berlin Tpke ... Berlin CT 06037 860-828-3127
Web: www.perfectfitplacement.com

Perkins Group Inc, The
10701 McMullen Creek Pkwy Ste D ... Charlotte NC 28226 704-543-1111
Web: www.perkinsgroup.com

Peterson's Nelnet LLC 121 S 13th St Ste 201 ... Lincoln NE 68508 609-896-8669
TF: 877-338-7772 ■ *Web:* www.essayedge.com

PHC Northwest Inc 5312 Ne 148th Ave ... Portland OR 97230 503-261-1266
Web: www.phcnw.com

Pinnacle Group International 130 Water St ... New York NY 10005 212-968-1200
Web: www.pinnaclegroup.com

Placement Strategies Inc
6965 El Camino Real Ste 105-200 ... Carlsbad CA 92009 909-597-0668
TF: 866-445-0710 ■ *Web:* www.placementstrategies.com

Planet Forward LLC
800 Hillgrove Ave Ste 105 ... Western Springs IL 60558 708-505-4036
Web: theplanetforward.com

Platinum HR Management LLC 4512 Farragut Rd ... Brooklyn NY 11203 718-859-1600
Web: www.platinumhrm.com

Platinum Personnel 1475 Ellis St ... Kelowna BC V1Y2A3 250-979-7200
TF: 800-652-1511 ■ *Web:* www.platinumpersonnel.ca

Polk Works One-stop Centers
500 E Lk Howard Dr ... Winter Haven FL 33881 863-508-1100
Web: www.careersourcepolk.com

Preference Personnel Inc 2600 Ninth Ave S ... Fargo ND 58103 701-293-6905
Web: www.preferencepersonnel.com

Premier Nursing Services Inc
444 W Ocean Blvd Ste 1050 ... Long Beach CA 90802 562-437-4313
Web: www.premiernursing.com

	City	State	Zip	Phone	Fax
Prescreen America Inc 505 W Abram St Ste 100 *Web:* www.prescreenamerica.com	Arlington	TX	76010	817-861-6666	
PRIMUS Global Services Inc 1300 W Walnut Hill Ln Ste 160 *Web:* primusglobal.com	Irving	TX	75038	972-753-6500	
Priority Business Services Inc 27 Brookline *Web:* www.prioritystaffing.biz	Aliso Viejo	CA	92656	949-222-1122	
Priority Staffing Solutions Inc 42 W 38th St Rm 503 *Web:* www.prioritystaff.com	New York	NY	10018	212-213-2277	
PRN Health Services Inc 4321 W College Ave Ste 200 *TF:* 888-830-8811 ■ *Web:* www.prnhealthservices.com	Appleton	WI	54914	888-830-8811	
Pro Staff Sales Inc 6080 Wellington Ave *Web:* www.prostaffsales.com	Gainesville	GA	30506	678-407-0382	
ProCare One Nurses LLC 4041 MacArthur Blvd Ste 150 *Web:* www.procareone.com	Newport Beach	CA	92660	949-251-1950	
Procel Temporary Services 2447 Pacific Coast Hwy Ste 207 *TF:* 800-338-9905 ■ *Web:* www.procelnurses.com	Hermosa Beach	CA	90254	310-372-0560	
Profiles Placement 20 S Charles St *Web:* careerprofiles.com	Baltimore	MD	21201	410-244-6400	
Project Connect 1025 W Johnson St 141 Educational Science Bldg *Web:* careers.education.wisc.edu	Madison	WI	53706	608-262-1755	262-9074
ProPeople Staffing Services Inc 10369 W Emerald St *Web:* www.propeoplestaffing.com	Boise	ID	83704	208-345-5747	
Protocall Group, The 1 Mall Dr Ste 100 *Web:* protocallgroup.com	Cherry Hill	NJ	08002	856-667-7500	
Psi Personnel LLC 252 W Swamp Rd Ste 29 *Web:* www.psipersonnel.com	Doylestown	PA	18901	215-345-6778	
PsiNapse Technology Ltd 5820 Stoneridge Mall Rd Ste 212 *Web:* www.psinapse.com	Pleasanton	CA	94588	925-225-0400	
Psr Associates Inc 6629 thornton palms dr *Web:* www.psrassociates.com	Tampa	FL	33647	813-412-5246	
Psychiatrists Only LLC 2970 Clairmont Rd Ste 650	Atlanta	GA	30329	404-315-7889	
Quad656 LLC 656 E Swedesford Rd *Web:* www.quad656.com	Wayne	PA	19087	610-687-6441	
Qualified Staffing Services 5361 Gateway Centre Ste D *Web:* www.q-staffing.com	Flint	MI	48507	810-230-0368	
Qualitek Services Inc 700 N Wickham Rd Ste 101 *Web:* www.qualitek.biz	Melbourne	FL	32935	321-259-2400	
Quik Travel Staffing Inc 175 E Olive Ave Ste 101 *Web:* www.qtstaffing.com	Burbank	CA	91502	818-569-3500	
Quorum Associates LLC 1005 Chapman St *Web:* www.quorumassociates.com	Yorktown Heights	NY	10598	914-320-6251	
R E Sutton & Associates LLC 67 E Garner Rd *Web:* www.resutton.com	Brownsburg	IN	46112	317-852-1937	
Randstad US L P 2015 S Park Pl *TF:* 800-382-7297 ■ *Web:* www.randstadusa.com	Atlanta	GA	30339	800-382-7297	
RCS Corp 955 Colony Pkwy *Web:* www.rcscorporation.com	Aiken	SC	29803	803-641-0100	
Readyforce Inc 1010 Doyle St Ste 200 *Web:* www.readyforce.com	Menlo Park	CA	94025	650-543-1400	
Reardon Associates Inc 450 Washington St Ste LL5 *Web:* www.reardonassociates.com	Dedham	MA	02026	781-329-2660	
Recruiters of Minnesota Inc 10500 E Bren Rd Bren Rd Business Ct Ste 110 *Web:* www.recruitersofmn.com	Minnetonka	MN	55343	952-767-0089	
Recruiting Source Inc, The 7487 Nw 4th St *Web:* the-recruiting-source-inc.hub.biz	Plantation	FL	33317	954-585-0266	
Recruitmilitary LLC 422 W Loveland Ave *Web:* recruitmilitary.com	Loveland	OH	45140	513-683-5020	
RecruitWise 704 S Illinois Ave Ste C-202 *Web:* www.recruitwise.jobs	Oak Ridge	TN	37830	865-425-0405	
Reeder & Associates Ltd 1095 Old Roswell Rd Ste F *Web:* www.reederassoc.com	Roswell	GA	30076	770-649-7523	
Reel Group Inc 16420 Park Ten Pl Ste 100 *Web:* www.reelgroup.com	Houston	TX	77084	832-358-2663	
Regional Personnel Services Inc 502 Us Hwy 22 Ste 1 *Web:* www.regionalpersonnel.com	Lebanon	NJ	08833	908-534-8113	
Rehabilities Inc 8655 Haven Ave Ste 200 *Web:* www.rehabilities.com	Rancho Cucamonga	CA	91730	909-989-5699	
Reliance One Inc 8031 Ortonville Rd Ste 130 *Web:* www.reliance-one.com	Clarkston	MI	48348	248-922-4500	
RemX Financial Staffing 2730 E Camelback Rd Ste 210 *Web:* www.remxfinancial.com	Phoenix	AZ	85016	602-954-8468	
Renhill Staffing Services of Texas Inc 102 Rilla Vista Dr *Web:* www.renhillmgmt.com	San Antonio	TX	78216	210-828-0508	
Renoir Staffing Services Inc 1301 Marina Vlg Pkwy Ste 350 *TF:* 866-672-3709 ■ *Web:* www.renoirstaffing.com	Alameda	CA	94501	866-672-3709	
Resource Mfg 7033 Commonwealth Ave Ste 4 *Web:* www.resourcemfg.com	Jacksonville	FL	32220	904-693-3686	
Response Staffing Solutions Inc 56 W 45th St 2nd Fl *Web:* www.responseco.com	New York	NY	10036	212-983-8870	
Reveal Global Intelligence 10800 Sikes Place Ste 205 *Web:* www.revealglobal.com	Charlotte	NC	28277	704-844-6000	
Richmar Associates Inc 283 Brokaw Rd *Web:* www.richmarstaffing.com	Santa Clara	CA	95050	408-727-6070	
RightStaff Inc 4919 McKinney Ave *Web:* www.rightstaffinc.com	Dallas	TX	75205	214-953-0900	
Riverside Staffing Services Inc 2322 E Kimberly Rd Paul Revere Sq Ste 20S *Web:* www.riversidestaffing.com	Davenport	IA	52807	563-355-5212	
Rockit Science Solutions Inc 4 Airline Dr Ste 101 *Web:* rockitscienceinc.com	Albany	NY	12205	518-785-6617	
Rolinc Staffing 333 W Hampden Ave Ste 545 *Web:* rolinc.com	Englewood	CO	80110	303-781-0055	
Royall & Company Inc 1920 E Parham Rd *Web:* www.royall.com	Richmond	VA	23228	804-741-8965	
Rubicon Programs 2500 Bissell Ave *Web:* www.rubiconprograms.org	Richmond	CA	94804	510-235-1516	
Rumpf Corp, The 701 Jefferson Ave *Web:* www.job1usa.com	Toledo	OH	43604	419-255-5005	
Run Consultants LLC 925 N Point Pkwy Ste 160 *TF:* 866-457-2193 ■ *Web:* www.runconsultants.com	Alpharetta	GA	30005	866-457-2193	
Ryan Alternative Staffing Inc 6936 Market St *Web:* www.ryanstaffing.com	Boardman	OH	44512	330-781-1172	
Ryan Miller & Assoc 400 N Brand Blvd Ste 930 *Web:* www.ryan-miller.com	Glendale	CA	91203	818-638-5080	
S I Systems Ltd 335 8th Ave SW Ste 1210 *Web:* www.sisystems.com	Calgary	AB	T2P1C9	403-450-5174	
S2Verify LLC Box 2597 *Web:* www.s2verify.com	Roswell	GA	30077	770-649-8282	
Sally Silver Companies 470 Totten Pond Rd *Web:* www.sallysilver.com	Waltham	MA	02451	781-890-7272	
Salus Group Benefits Inc 37525 Mound Rd *TF:* 866-991-9907 ■ *Web:* www.salusgroupbenefits.com	Sterling Heights	MI	48310	866-991-9907	
Sanford Rose Associates International Inc 19111 N Dallas Pkwy Ste 201 *Web:* sanfordrose.net	Dallas	TX	75287	972-616-7870	
Savela & Associates Inc 3595 Grandview PkwySte 450 *Web:* www.savela.com	Birmingham	AL	35243	205-444-0080	
Search Guru Inc, The 21887 Lorain Rd Ste 71 *Web:* www.thesearchguru.com	Cleveland	OH	44126	440-306-2418	
Search Wizards Inc 15 Paradise Plz Ste 261 *Web:* www.searchwizards.net	Sarasota	FL	34239	404-846-9500	
Searchlight Group Inc 1 W St Apt 3602 *Web:* www.searchlightjobs.com	New York	NY	10004	212-425-4800	
Searchpros Staffing 6363 Auburn Blvd *Web:* spstaffing.com	Citrus Heights	CA	95621	916-721-6000	
Searchwright Inc 101 2nd St Ste 2200 *Web:* searchwright.com	San Francisco	CA	94105	415-538-1500	
Select Group LLC, The 5420 Wade Park Blvd Ste 100 *Web:* www.selectgroup.com	Raleigh	NC	27607	919-459-1400	
Select Technical Staffing Inc 1025 S 108th St Ste 205 *Web:* selecttechnicalstaffing.com	Milwaukee	WI	53214	414-476-9331	
Seraaj Family Homes Inc 400 Cotton Gin Rd *Web:* www.seraajfh.com	Montgomery	AL	36117	334-271-2402	
Serviko Inc 2670 Rue Duchesne *Web:* www.serviko.com	Saint-laurent	QC	H4R1J3	514-332-2600	
Sesame Software Inc File 74625 P.O. Box 60000 *TF:* 866-474-7575 ■ *Web:* www.sesamesoftware.com	San Francisco	CA	94160	866-474-7575	
Set & Service Resources LLC 8303 Six Forks Rd Ste 207 *Web:* www.sasrlink.com	Raleigh	NC	27615	919-787-5571	
SetFocus LLC 4 Century Dr *Web:* www.setfocus.com	Parsippany	NJ	07054	973-889-0211	
Seven Step RPO 3 Ctr Plz *Web:* www.sevenstepprpo.com	Boston	MA	02108	773-639-3333	
Sharf Woodward & Associates Inc 5900 Sepulveda Blvd *TF:* 877-482-6687 ■ *Web:* www.swjobs.com	Sherman Oaks	CA	91411	818-989-2200	
Sill Associates 21 Edgewood Dr *Web:* www.sillandassociates.com	Mechanicsburg	PA	17055	717-691-6730	
Silverman McGovern Staffing & Recruiting 284 W Exchange St *Web:* www.silvermanmcgovern.com	Providence	RI	02903	401-632-0580	
Sirius Technical Services Inc 6215 Rangeline Rd Ste 102 *Web:* www.siriustechnical.com	Theodore	AL	36582	251-443-1166	
Skillforce Inc 405 Williams Court Ste 100 *TF:* 866-581-8989 ■ *Web:* www.skillforce.com	Baltimore	MD	21220	866-581-8989	
Skills International LLC 11 Falcon Lks Dr *Web:* www.skillsinternational.com	South Barrington	IL	60010	647-725-3360	
SkillStorm Commercial Services LLC 6414 NW Fifth Way *Web:* www.skillstorm.com	Ft Lauderdale	FL	33309	954-566-4647	
Smart Staffing Service Inc 132 Central St Ste 210 *Web:* www.smart-tek.net	Foxboro	MA	02035	508-698-9988	
SmartIT Staffing Inc 6500 Technology Ctr Dr Ste 300 *Web:* getsmarterit.com	Indianapolis	IN	46278	317-634-0211	

Name / Address	City	State	Zip	Phone	Fax
Snapdragon Associates Llc 8 Commerce Dr Ste 102A *Web:* www.snapdragonassociates.com	Bedford	NH	03110	603-621-9037	
Social Work p.r.n. Inc 10680 Barkley Ste 100 *Web:* www.socialworkprn.com	Overland Park	KS	66212	913-648-2984	
Sockwell Partners Inc 800 E Blvd Ste 200 *Web:* www.sockwell.com	Charlotte	NC	28203	704-372-1865	
Solv Staffing LLC 333 W Hampden Ave Ste 830 *Web:* www.solvnetwork.com	Englewood	CO	80110	303-590-1640	
Solvate com Inc 405 Greenwich St Ste 2A *Web:* www.solvate.com	New York	NY	10013	646-720-7110	
Sonic Sales & Service 2101 W Kansas St *Web:* sonicequipment.com	Liberty	MO	64068	816-407-9183	
SophLogic Global LLC 8374 Market St Ste 133 *Web:* www.sophlogic.com	Bradenton	FL	34202	941-932-8570	
Source One Personnel Inc 2 Carnegie Rd *Web:* www.source1-financial.com	Lawrenceville	NJ	08648	609-895-9700	
Source2 Inc 1245 W Fairbanks Ave Ste 400 *Web:* www.source2.com	Winter Park	FL	32803	407-893-3711	
SourcePoint Staffing LLC 12745 W Capitol Dr *Web:* www.sourcepointstaffing.com	Brookfield	WI	53005	414-755-8600	
SOURCERY Recruiting Services Inc, The 604 Mission St Ste 502 *Web:* www.thesourcery.com	San Francisco	CA	94105	415-418-7156	
Southern Healthcare Agency Inc PO Box 320999 *TF:* 800-880-2772 ■ *Web:* www.southernhealthcare.com	Flowood	MS	39232	601-933-0037	
Sparks IT Solutions 1775 Greensboro Sta Pl Tower II Ste 300 *Web:* www.sparksitsolutions.com	Mclean	VA	22102	703-821-2650	
Spence Associates International Inc 530 Bufflehead Dr *Web:* www.spenceassociates.com	Kiawah Island	SC	29455	843-768-6706	
Spencer Gray LLC 1565 Hotel Circle S Ste 300 *Web:* spencergray.com	San Diego	CA	92108	619-281-3900	
Spherion Canada 1 Queen St E Ste 901	Toronto	ON	M5C2W5	604-273-1440	
Sprocket Staffing Services 35 Colby Ave *TF:* 800-269-1441 ■ *Web:* sprocketstaffing.com	Manasquan	NJ	08736	800-269-1441	
Staff Right Inc 10825 Plano Rd Ste 3 *Web:* www.staff-rightinc.com	Dallas	TX	75238	214-221-9000	
Staffing 360 Solutions Inc Ste 1526 641 Lexington Ave *Web:* www.staffing360solutions.com	New York	NY	10022	212-634-6462	
Staffing Options & Solutions Inc 6249 S E St Ste E *TF:* 800-554-7823 ■ *Web:* www.staffingoptionsandsolutions.com	Indianapolis	IN	46227	317-791-2456	
Staffing Resource Group Inc, The 3505 E Frntage Rd Ste 320 *TF:* 877-774-7742 ■ *Web:* www.srg-us.com	Tampa	FL	33607	877-774-7742	
Staffworks Group 20505 W 12 Mile Rd **Fax Area Code:* 248 ■ *TF:* 877-304-9690 ■ *Web:* staffworksgroup.com	Southfield	MI	48076	877-304-9690	416-1103*
StartDate Labs Inc 197 Main St *Web:* www.startdatelabs.com	Meridian	NH	03770	603-442-6782	
StartUpHire LLC 415 Church St Ste 203 *Web:* www.startuphire.com	Vienna	VA	22180	703-865-6350	
StayTop Systems Inc 4340 Almaden Expy Ste 204 *Web:* www.staytop.com	San Jose	CA	95118	408-266-4477	
Steno Employment Services Inc 8560 Vineyard Ave Ste 208 *Web:* stenoinc.com	Rancho Cucamonga	CA	91730	909-476-1404	
Sterling Global Human Resource Consulting 2415 E Camelback Esplanade Bldg III Ste 1090 *Web:* www.sterlinghrconsulting.com	Phoenix	AZ	85016	602-470-8012	
StraussGroup Inc 8203 Main St Ste 2 *Web:* straussgroup.com	Williamsville	NY	14221	716-631-3200	
Suh'dutsing Technologies LLC 600 North 100 East *Web:* cedarbandcorp.com/suhdutsingtech	Cedar City	UT	84721	435-867-0604	
Synergy Employment Group. Inc 14 Greenfield Rd *Web:* www.synergyempgroup.com	Lancaster	PA	17602	717-824-4005	
Synergy Legal Staffing 500 E Morehead St Ste 101 *Web:* www.synergylegalstaffing.com	Charlotte	NC	28202	704-366-4540	
Synergy PEO LLC 180 N Michigan Ave 11th Fl *Web:* www.mysynergy.com	Chicago	IL	60601	312-899-1024	
Synnefo Technology Solutions Inc A Forsythe Co 821 Walden Office Sq 4th Fl *Web:* www.synnefo.com	Schaumburg	IL	60173	847-241-4901	
Tacoma Goodwill Industries 714 S 27th St *Web:* tacomagoodwill.org	Tacoma	WA	98409	253-573-6500	
Talent Connections LLC 4805 W Village Way Ste 2401 *Web:* www.talentconnections.net	Smyrna	GA	30080	770-552-1550	
Talent Strategy Group LLC 201 W 72nd St *Web:* www.talentstrategygroup.com	New York	NY	10023	203-482-8103	
Talent Zoo Inc 1736 Defoor Pl Nw *Web:* www.talentzoo.com	Atlanta	GA	30318	404-607-1955	
TalentFusion Inc 343 Huntington Rd *Web:* www.talentfusion.com	Worthington	MA	01098	413-238-0138	
TalentLens Inc 19500 Bulverde Rd *TF:* 888-298-6227 ■ *Web:* talentlens.com	San Antonio	TX	78259	888-298-6227	
TalentSoup LLC 1900 Hosea L Williams Dr NE *Web:* www.talentsoup.com	Atlanta	GA	30317	678-528-7407	
Targeted Job Fairs Inc 4441 Glenway Ave *TF:* 800-695-1939 ■ *Web:* www.targetedjobfairs.com	Cincinnati	OH	45205	800-695-1939	
Taylor & Hill Inc 9941 Rowlett Rd *TF:* 800-318-0231 ■ *Web:* www.taylorandhill.com	Houston	TX	77075	713-941-2671	
Taylor Hodson Inc 133 W 19th St *Web:* www.taylorhodson.com	New York	NY	10011	212-924-8300	
TDB Communications Inc 10901 W 84 Ter Ste 105 *Web:* www.tdbcommunications.com	Lenexa	KS	66214	913-327-7400	
Teach Away Inc 147 Liberty St *TF:* 855-483-2242 ■ *Web:* www.teachaway.com	Toronto	ON	M6K3G3	416-628-1386	
Teachers on Reserve LLC 604 Sonora Ave *TF:* 800-457-1899 ■ *Web:* teachersonreserve.com	Glendale	CA	91201	818-502-5800	
Tech-ed Services Inc 6121 Sebring Dr *Web:* www.teservices.com	Columbia	MD	21044	410-772-5840	
Temps Plus Inc 268 N Lincoln Ave Ste 12 *Web:* www.tempsplus.com	Corona	CA	92882	951-549-8309	
Terry Neese Personnel Services 2709 W I 44 Service Rd *Web:* tneesepersonnel.com	Oklahoma City	OK	73112	405-942-8551	
ThinkBRQ LLC 20 Hicksville Rd Ste 7 *Web:* www.thinkbrq.com	Massapequa	NY	11758	516-541-3100	
Thomas Employment 8320 Tyler Blvd *Web:* thomasemployment.com	Mentor	OH	44060	440-974-2010	
Thomas Wood Professionals 202 S St Ste 13 *Web:* www.thomaswoodpros.com	Sausalito	CA	94965	415-944-8754	
Tiffany Stuart Solutions Inc 390 Diablo Rd Ste 220 *Web:* www.go2dynamic.com	Danville	CA	94526	925-855-3600	
Time Services Inc 6422 Lima Rd *Web:* www.timeservices.com	Fort Wayne	IN	46818	260-489-2020	
Titan Recruitment Solutions Ltd 355 Burrard St *Web:* titanrecruitment.com	Vancouver	BC	V6C2G8	604-687-6785	
TNS Employee Insights 65 Oakwood Rd *Web:* www.foresightint.com	Lake Zurich	IL	60047	847-726-4677	
Topaz International Inc 3 Regent St Ste 305 *Web:* topattorneys.com	Livingston	NJ	07039	973-597-0500	
Total Hr 2626 Foothill Blvd Ste 200 *Web:* www.totalhrmanagement.com	La Crescenta	CA	91214	818-248-0049	
Tpi Staffing Inc 21840 Northwest Fwy Ste E *Web:* www.tpistaffing.com	Cypress	TX	77429	281-890-2220	
Tradesmen International Inc 9760 Shepard Rd *Web:* www.tradesmeninternational.com	Macedonia	OH	44056	440-349-3432	
TransTech IT Staffing 248 Spring Lk Dr *Web:* www.trans-tech.com	Itasca	IL	60143	630-250-8880	
Tri Starr Services of Pennsylvania Inc 2201 Oregon Pk *Web:* www.tristarrjobs.com	Lancaster	PA	17601	717-560-2111	
Tricom Technical Services 11115 Ash St *Web:* www.tricomts.com	Leawood	KS	66212	913-652-0600	
Trillium Talent Resources Group 99 Sheppard Ave W *Web:* www.trilliumhr.com	Toronto	ON	M2N1M4	416-497-2624	
TriMech Services LLC 4461 Cox Rd Ste 302 *Web:* www.trimech.com	Glen Allen	VA	23060	804-257-9965	
TS Consulting International 20300 S Vermont Ave Ste 265 *Web:* www.tsconsult.com	Torrance	CA	90502	310-965-9810	
Tula International Inc PO Box 550628 *Web:* www.tulainternational.com	Atlanta	GA	30355	404-543-2835	
Turnkey Sports & Entertainment Inc 9 Tanner St *Web:* turnkeyse.com	Haddonfield	NJ	08033	856-685-1450	
Ultimate Placements LLC 1 Park Centre Ste 305A *Web:* www.ultimateplacements.com	Wadsworth	OH	44281	330-334-0285	
Ultracare of Manhattan Ltd 800 2nd Ave Rm 905 *Web:* www.ultracareofmanhattan.com	New York	NY	10017	212-883-8877	
Unique Employment Services Inc 4646 Corona Dr Ste 100 *Web:* www.uniquehr.com	Corpus Christi	TX	78411	361-852-6392	
UniQue Personnel Consultants Inc 2501 Chatham Rd Ste 310 *Web:* www.uniquepers.com	Springfield	IL	62704	217-787-9400	
United Information Technologies Corp 2818 Corporate Pkwy *Web:* www.uitonline.com	Algonquin	IL	60102	847-658-1222	
United Personnel Services Inc 289 Bridge St *TF:* 800-363-8200 ■ *Web:* www.unitedpersonnel.com	Springfield	MA	01103	413-736-0800	
United Screening Services Corp 4343 W Flagler St Ste 350 *Web:* www.unitedscreening.com	Coral Gables	FL	33134	305-774-1711	
United Staffing Systems Inc 130 William St 5th Fl	New York	NY	10038	212-743-0200	
United Talent LLC 500 Leon Sullivan Way *Web:* www.unitedtalentwv.com	Charleston	WV	25301	304-556-1190	
Urban Interns LLC 24 Mayhew Ave *Web:* www.urbaninterns.com	Larchmont	NY	10538	917-854-5559	
Urpan Technologies Inc 341 Cobalt Way Ste 208 *Web:* www.urpantech.com	Sunnyvale	CA	94085	408-245-0006	
USA Staffing Inc 2010 Philadelphia St Ste #8 *Web:* www.usastaffing.com	Ames	IA	50010	515-292-5775	
USAFact Inc 6240 Box Springs Blvd *Web:* www.usafactinc.com	Riverside	CA	92507	951-656-7800	
VanderHouwen & Associates Inc 6342 SW Macadam Ave *Web:* www.vanderhouwen.com	Portland	OR	97239	503-299-6811	
Vault Inc 132 W 31st St 17th Fl *Web:* www.vault.com	New York	NY	10001	212-366-4212	366-6117
Vector Technical Inc 38033 Euclid Ave Ste T-9 *Web:* www.vectortechnicalinc.com	Willoughby	OH	44094	440-946-8800	
VerisVisalign 920 S Broad St *Web:* www.verisvisalign.com	Lansdale	PA	19446	215-393-5001	

Phone Fax

Versalign Inc 1719 Delaware Ave. . . . . Wilmington DE 19806 302-225-7800
Web: www.versalign.com

VetJobs Inc PO Box 71445 . . . . . Marietta GA 30007 770-993-5117
TF: 877-838-5627 ■ *Web:* www.vetjobs.com

Victory Search Group
20701 N Scottsdale Rd Ste 107-300. . . . . Scottsdale AZ 85255 480-585-0073
Web: www.victorysearchgroup.com

Vincent Benjamin Group Llc
2415 E Camelback Rd Ste 1000 . . . . . Phoenix AZ 85016 602-595-9900
Web: www.vincentbenjamin.com

Vision Enterprises Inc 602 W 5th Ave Ste B . . . . . Naperville IL 60563 630-596-4000
Web: www.visionsds.com

Visiont 2650 106th St Ste 215 . . . . . Urbandale IA 50322 515-331-0010
Web: www.visiont-solutions.com

VISTA Staffing Solutions Inc
275 East 200 South . . . . . Salt Lake City UT 84111 801-487-8190
Web: www.vistastaff.com

Walker Elliott 11200 Westheimer Ste 365 . . . . . Houston TX 77042 713-482-3750
Web: www.walker-elliott.com

Wareforce Inc 19 Morgan . . . . . Irvine CA 92618 949-472-9000
Web: www.wareforce.com

Waterstone Group Inc, The
1145 W Main Ave Ste 209 . . . . . De Pere WI 54115 920-964-0333
TF: 800-291-3836 ■ *Web:* www.waterstonegroup.net

Wavestaff Inc 783 Rio Del Mar Blvd Ste 67 . . . . . Aptos CA 95003 831-689-9800
Web: www.wavestaff.com

WCG International Consultants Ltd
5 - 915 Ft St . . . . . Victoria BC V8V3K3 250-389-0699
Web: www.wcgservices.com

Wellness Coaches USA LLC
725 Skippack Pk Ste 300 . . . . . Blue Bell PA 19422 215-628-4454
Web: www.wellnesscoachesusa.com

Wentworth Company Inc, The 479 W Sixth St. . . . . San Pedro CA 90731 310-519-0113
Web: www.wentco.com/

Westaff (USA) Inc 298 N Wiget Ln. . . . . Walnut Creek CA 94598 925-930-5300
Web: www.westaff.com

Westways Staffing Services Inc
500 City Pkwy W Ste 130 . . . . . Orange CA 92868 714-712-4150
Web: www.westwaysstaffing.com

Wfa Staffing 9001 N 76th St Ste 201 . . . . . Milwaukee WI 53223 414-365-3651
Web: wfastaffing.com

Wood Personnel Services
1139 Nw Broad St Ste 107 . . . . . Murfreesboro TN 37129 615-890-8400
Web: wpscareers.com

Woodmoor Group 755 Hwy 105 Ste 2A. . . . . Palmer Lake CO 80133 719-488-8589
Web: www.woodmoor.com

Workforce Alliance Inc
1951 N Military Trl Ste D . . . . . West Palm Beach FL 33409 561-340-1060
Web: www.careersourcepbc.com

Workincom Inc 343 Church St . . . . . Santa Cruz CA 95060 775-336-3366
Web: www.workin.com

Workplace Benefit Solutions LLC
1667 Elm St Ste 3. . . . . Manchester NH 03101 603-668-0400
Web: www.workplacebenefitsolutions.com

Workplace Group Inc, The
10 Ridgedale Ave . . . . . Florham Park NJ 07932 973-377-4665
Web: ww.workplacegroup.com

Workplace Staffing Services
2923 Smith Rd Ste 201. . . . . Akron OH 44333 330-926-1880
Web: www.workplacestaff.com

Xcel HR Corp 7361 Calhoun Pl Ste 600. . . . . Rockville MD 20855 978-562-3312
Web: www.xcelhr.com

York Employment Services Inc
990 N Ontario Mills Dr Ste C . . . . . Ontario CA 91764 909-581-0181
Web: www.yorkemployment.com

Your HR Group Inc 12871 Research Blvd Ste 200 . . . . . Austin TX 78750 512-794-9639
Web: austinhr.com

Zachary Piper LLC 1410 Spring Hill Rd Ste 300. . . . . Mclean VA 22012 703-649-4001
TF: 888-487-8812 ■ *Web:* www.zacharypiper.com

261 ENGINEERING & DESIGN

See Also Surveying, Mapping, Related Services p. 3212

Phone Fax

219 Design 67 E Evelyn Ave Ste 11 . . . . . Mountain View CA 94041 650-969-4219
Web: www.219design.com

3D Research Corp 360D Quality Cir Ste 450 . . . . . Huntsville AL 35806 256-705-5410
Web: www.3drc.com

7 Layers Inc 15 Musick . . . . . Irvine CA 92618 949-716-6512
Web: www.7layers.com

804 Technology LLC 5381 Hwy N Ste 201 . . . . . Cottleville MO 63004 636-928-0330
Web: 804technology.com

89 North Inc 1 Mill St Unit 285 . . . . . Burlington VT 05401 802-881-0302
Web: www.89north.com

A & N Associates Inc
6716 Alexander Bell Dr Ste 118 . . . . . Columbia MD 21046 410-872-0050
Web: www.anassoc.com

A Epstein & Sons International Inc
600 W Fulton St . . . . . Chicago IL 60661 312-454-9100 454-9100
Web: www.epsteinglobal.com

A H Lundberg Associates Inc
13201 Bel Red Rd. . . . . Bellevue WA 98005 425-283-5070
Web: www.lundbergassociates.com

A&S Engineers Inc
Main Link Business Park 10377 Stella Link . . . . . Houston TX 77025 713-942-2700
Web: www.ainsworth-sherwood.com

A.C. Coy Co 395 Vly Brook Rd. . . . . Canonsburg PA 15317 724-820-1820
Web: www.accoy.com

Aavispro LLC 113 Amberwood Ct. . . . . Bethel Park PA 15102 412-833-5444
Web: www.aavispro.com

Abha Architects Inc 1621 N Lincoln St. . . . . Wilmington DE 19806 302-658-6426
Web: abha.com

Phone Fax

Abraxas Energy Consulting LLC
811 Palm St . . . . . San Luis Obispo CA 93401 805-547-2050
Web: www.abraxasenergy.com

Academy Solutions Group LLC
6700 Alexander Bell Dr Ste 195 . . . . . Columbia MD 21046 410-290-0871
Web: www.asg-llc.com

Acoustical Design Group Inc
5799 Broadmoor St . . . . . Shawnee Mission KS 66202 913-384-1261
Web: www.adgkc.com

Acrion Technologies Inc
7777 Exchange St Ste 5 . . . . . Cleveland OH 44125 216-659-5566
Web: www.acrion.com

Acta Inc 2790 Skypark Dr Ste 310 . . . . . Torrance CA 90505 310-530-1008
Web: www.actainc.com

Acumen Enterprises Inc 1504 Falcon. . . . . Desoto TX 75115 972-572-0701
Web: acumen-enterprises.com

Adams Rehmann & Heggan Assoc
850 S White Horse Pk. . . . . Hammonton NJ 08037 609-561-0482
Web: arh-us.com

ADAPT Corp 1733 Woodside Rd Ste 220 . . . . . Redwood City CA 94061 650-306-2400
Web: www.adaptsoft.com

ADD Inc 311 Summer St . . . . . Boston MA 02210 617-234-3100 661-7118
Web: www.addinc.com

ADEX Machining Technologies LLC
260 Feaster Rd . . . . . Greenville SC 29615 864-416-3100
Web: adexmachining.com

Adjeleian Allen Rubeli Ltd
75 Albert St Ste 1005 . . . . . Ottawa ON K1P5E7 613-232-5786
Web: www.aar.on.ca

Adobe Associates Inc 1220 N Dutton Ave. . . . . Santa Rosa CA 95401 707-541-2300
Web: www.adobeinc.com

Advanced Design Corp 9447B Lorton Market St . . . . . Lorton VA 22079 703-550-5510
Web: www.advdesign.com

Advanced Engineering & Environmental Services Inc
2016 S Washington St . . . . . Grand Forks ND 58201 701-746-8087
Web: www.ae2s.com

Advanced Government Solutions Inc
2138 Priest Bridge CT Ste 4 . . . . . Crofton MD 21114 240-260-4040
Web: www.usgcinc.com

Advanced Sciences & Technologies LLC
20 E Taunton . . . . . Berlin NJ 08009 856-719-9001
Web: adv-sci-tech.com

Advanced Technology & Research Corp
6650 Eli Whitney Dr . . . . . Columbia MD 21046 443-766-7888
Web: www.atrcorp.com

AECOM Technology Corp
555 S Flower St 37th Fl . . . . . Los Angeles CA 90071 213-593-8000 593-8730
Web: www.aecom.com

Aecometric Corp 374 Ohio Rd . . . . . Richmond Hill ON L4C2Z9 905-883-9555
Web: aecometric.com

Aegis Technologies Group Inc, The
410 Jan Davis Dr . . . . . Huntsville AL 35806 256-922-0802
Web: aegistg.com

Aegis Technology Inc
12630 G Westminster Ave . . . . . Santa Ana CA 92706 714-265-1238
Web: www.aegistech.net

Aeplog Inc 12800 Middle Brook Rd. . . . . Germantown MD 20874 301-528-2800

Affiliated Engineers Inc (AEI)
5802 Research Pk Blvd. . . . . Madison WI 53719 608-238-2616 238-2614
Web: www.aeieng.com

Agi Goldratt Institute
440 Wheelers Farms Rd Ste 304. . . . . Milford CT 06461 203-624-9026
Web: www.goldratt.com

Aging Aircraft Consulting LLC
64 Green St. . . . . Warner Robins GA 31093 478-923-8786
Web: www.agingaircraftconsulting.com

Agnew Associates Inc 13033 Quaker Ave Ste A . . . . . Lubbock TX 79423 806-799-0753
Web: www.agnewassociates.com

AGRA Industries Inc 1211 W Water St . . . . . Merrill WI 54452 715-536-9584
Web: www.agraind.com

AGUIRRE Corp 10670 N Central Expwy 6th Fl . . . . . Dallas TX 75231 972-788-1508 788-1583
Web: www.aguirreroden.com

AHA Consulting Engineers Inc
24 Hartwell Ave 3rd Fl . . . . . Lexington MA 02421 781-372-3000
Web: www.aha-engineers.com

AHJ Engineers PC 5418 N Eagle Rd Ste 140. . . . . Boise ID 83713 208-323-0199
Web: ahjengineers.com

Ahtna Engineering Services LLC
110 W 38th Ave Ste 100. . . . . Anchorage AK 99503 907-646-2969
Web: www.ahtnaes.com

AI Signal Research Inc
3411 Triana Blvd SW . . . . . Huntsville AL 35805 256-551-0008 551-0099
Web: www.aisignal.com

AIA Engineers Ltd 15310 Park Row . . . . . Houston TX 77084 281-493-4140
Web: aiainc.wix.com/aia-engineers

Aillet/Fenner/Jolly/Mcclelland Inc
3003 Knight St Ste 120. . . . . Shreveport LA 71105 318-425-7452
Web: afjmc.com

Aim Engineering & Surveying Inc
5300 Lee Blvd. . . . . Lehigh Acres FL 33971 239-332-4569
TF: 800-226-4569 ■ *Web:* aimengineering.com

Ainley & Associates Ltd
280 Pretty River Pkwy. . . . . Collingwood ON L9Y4J5 705-445-3451
Web: www.ainleygroup.com

Air Diffusion Systems 3964 Grove Ave . . . . . Gurnee IL 60031 847-782-0044
Web: airdiffusion.com

Aircon Engineering Inc 7 Williams St. . . . . Cumberland MD 21502 301-722-7269
Web: www.airconeng.com

Airflow Sciences Corp 12190 Hubbard St. . . . . Livonia MI 48150 734-525-0300
Web: www.airflowsciences.com

AirPol Inc 1000A Lake St . . . . . Ramsey NJ 07446 973-599-4400 428-6048
Web: www.airpol.com

AKRF Inc 440 Pk Ave S. . . . . New York NY 10016 212-696-0670 779-9721
TF: 800-899-2573 ■ *Web:* www.akrf.com

Company / Address	City	State	Zip	Phone	Fax
Alan Plummer & Assoc Inc 1320 S University Dr	Fort Worth	TX	76107	817-806-1700	870-2536
Web: www.apaienv.com					
Albert Kahn Assoc Inc 7430 Second Ave Albert Kahn Bldg	Detroit	MI	48202	313-202-7000	202-7001
Web: www.albertkahn.com					
Alberta Boilers Safety Association 9410 20 Av Nw	Edmonton	AB	T6N0A4	780-437-9100	
Web: www.absa.ca					
Alion Science & Technology 1750 Tysons Blvd Ste 1300	McLean	VA	22102	703-918-4480	250-0810*
**Fax Area Code:* 913 ■ *TF:* 877-439-9227 ■ *Web:* www.alionscience.com					
Alisto Engineering Group Inc 2737 N Main St Ste 200	Walnut Creek	CA	94597	925-279-5000	
Web: www.alisto.com					
Allen & Hoshall Inc 1661 International Dr Ste 100	Memphis	TN	38120	901-820-0820	683-1001
Web: www.allenhoshall.com					
Alliance Support Partners Inc 5036 Commercial Cir Ste C	Concord	CA	94520	925-363-5382	
Web: asp-support.com					
Alliance Water Resources Inc 206 S Keene St	Columbia	MO	65251	573-874-8080	
Web: alliancewater.com					
Allied Power Group LLC 10131 Mills Rd	Houston	TX	77070	281-444-3535	
TF: 888-830-3535 ■ *Web:* www.alliedpg.com					
Allnorth Consultants Limited 2001 Pg Paulpmill Rd PO Box 968	Prince George	BC	V2L4V1	250-614-7291	
Web: allnorth.com					
Alpine Engineering & Design Inc 111 W Canyon Crest Rd	Alpine	UT	84004	801-763-8484	
Web: www.alpineeng.com					
AM Kinney 150 E Fourth St	Cincinnati	OH	45202	513-421-2265	
TF: 800-265-3682 ■ *Web:* www.amkinney.com					
Ambrose Engineering Inc W66n215 Commerce Ct	Cedarburg	WI	53012	262-377-7602	
Web: ambeng.com					
AMCS Corp 135 US Hwy 202-206 Ste 12	Bedminster	NJ	07921	908-719-6560	
Web: www.amcscorp.com					
American Consulting Inc 7260 Shadeland Stn	Indianapolis	IN	46256	317-547-5580	543-0270
Web: www.structurepoint.com					
American Engineering Testing Inc 550 Cleveland Ave N	Saint Paul	MN	55114	651-659-9001	659-1379
TF: 800-972-6364 ■ *Web:* www.amengtest.com					
Amico Group 2199 Blackacre Dr RR #1	Oldcastle	ON	N0R1L0	519-737-1577	
Web: www.amicoaffiliates.com					
Ammann & Whitney Inc 96 Morton St	New York	NY	10014	212-462-8500	929-5356
Web: www.ammann-whitney.com					
Amory Engineers PC PO Box 1768 25 Depot St	Duxbury	MA	02332	781-934-0178	
Web: amoryengineers.com					
Ams Mechanical Systems Inc 140 E Tower Dr	Burr Ridge	IL	60527	630-887-7700	887-0770
TF: 800-794-5033 ■ *Web:* www.amsmechanicalsystems.com					
Amset Technical Consulting 1864 S Elmhurst Rd	Mount Prospect	IL	60056	847-229-1155	
TF: 888-982-6783 ■ *Web:* www.amsetusa.com					
Ana Consultants LLC 5000 Thompson Terr	Colleyville	TX	76034	817-335-9900	
Anamet Inc 26102 Eden Landing Rd	Hayward	CA	94545	510-887-8811	
Web: anametinc.com					
Anderson Engineering of New Prague Inc 20526 330th St	New Prague	MN	56071	507-364-7373	
Web: aenpi.com					
Anderson, Eckstein & Westrick Inc 51301 Schoenherr Rd	Shelby Township	MI	48315	586-726-1234	
Web: www.aewinc.com					
Antonucci & Assoc Arch & Engrs 50 Fifth Ave	Pelham	NY	10803	914-636-4000	
Web: www.aa-ae.com					
Antron Engineering & Machine Co Inc 170 Mechanic St	Bellingham	MA	02019	508-966-2803	
Web: www.antroneng.com					
Anvil Corp 1675 W Bakerview Rd	Bellingham	WA	98226	360-671-1450	
Web: www.anvilcorp.com					
Apex Companies LLC 15850 Crabbs Branch Way Ste 200	Rockville	MD	20855	301-417-0200	975-0169
Web: www.apexcos.com					
Apollo Professional Svc 29 Stiles Rd Ste 302	Salem	NH	03079	866-277-3343	
TF: 866-277-3343 ■ *Web:* www.apollopros.com					
Applied Analysis Inc 515 Groton Rd Ste 101	Westford	MA	01821	978-392-4500	
Web: www.discover-aai.com					
Applied Control Engineering Inc 700 Creek View Rd	Newark	DE	19711	302-738-8800	
Web: ace-net.com					
Applied Flow Technology Corp 2955 Professional Pl Ste 301	Colorado Springs	CO	80904	719-686-1000	
Web: www.aft.com					
Applied Math Modeling Inc 75 S Main St Ste 7 PO Box 144	Concord	NH	03301	603-369-3793	
Web: www.coolsimsoftware.com					
Applied Technology & Management Inc 5550 NW 111th Blvd	Gainesville	FL	32653	800-275-6488	
TF: 800-275-6488 ■ *Web:* www.appliedtm.com					
APS Technology Inc 7 Laser Ln	Wallingford	CT	06492	860-613-4450	284-7428*
**Fax Area Code:* 203 ■ *Web:* www.aps-tech.com					
Aqua Science Engineers Inc 55 Oak Ct Ste 220	Danville	CA	94526	925-820-9391	
Aquafor Beech Ltd 2600 Skymark Ave Bldg 6 Ste 202	Mississauga	ON	L4W5B2	905-629-0099	
Web: www.aquaforbeech.com					
Aqualified LLC 525 Webb Industrial Dr Ste 211	Marietta	GA	30062	770-422-1349	
Web: www.aqualified.com					
Aquatech Consultancy Inc 1 Commercial Blvd Ste 201	Novato	CA	94949	415-884-2121	
Web: www.noleak.com					
Aqwest 8276 Eagle Rd	Larkspur	CO	80118	303-681-0456	
Web: www.aqwest.com					
Arcadis 630 Plz Dr Ste 200	Highlands Ranch	CO	80129	720-344-3500	344-3535
Web: www.arcadis.com//en/united-states/cookie-wall					
Arcata Assoc Inc 2588 Fire Mesa St	Las Vegas	NV	89128	702-642-9500	968-2237
Web: www.arcataassoc.com					
Arcsine Engineering 950 Executive Way	Redding	CA	96002	530-222-7204	
Web: www.arc-sine.com					
Arctic Engineering Company Inc 8410 Minnesota St	Merrillville	IN	46410	219-947-4999	
Web: arcticengineering.com					
Ardmore Associates LLC 33 N Dearborn St Ste 1720	Chicago	IL	60602	312-795-1400	
Web: www.ardmoreassociates.com					
ARGO Systems LLC 1362 Mellon Rd Ste 100	Hanover	MD	21076	410-768-2444	
TF: 877-994-2746 ■ *Web:* www.argo-sys.com					
Argon Technologies Inc 4612 Wesley St	Greenville	TX	75401	903-455-5036	
Web: www.argontech.com					
Aria Group Inc 17395 Daimler St	Irvine	CA	92614	949-475-2915	
Web: www.aria-group.com					
Arias & Associates Inc 142 Chula Vista Dr	San Antonio	TX	78232	210-308-5884	
Web: www.ariasinc.com					
Arion Systems Inc 15040 Conference Ctr Dr Ste 200	Chantilly	VA	20151	703-815-1130	
Web: arionsys.com					
Arkel International Inc 1048 Florida Blvd	Baton Rouge	LA	70802	225-343-0525	336-1849
Web: www.arkel.com					
Arnold Sanders Consulting Engineers Inc 12651 Mcgregor Blvd Ste 103	Fort Myers	FL	33919	239-267-3666	
Web: arnoldsanders.com					
Arquitectonica International Corp 2900 Oak Ave	Miami	FL	33133	305-372-1812	372-1175
Web: arquitectonica.com					
Array Healthcare Facilities Solutions 2520 Renaissance Blvd Ste 110	King of Prussia	PA	19406	610-270-0599	270-0995
Web: www.array-architects.com					
Arro Consulting Inc 108 W Airport Rd	Lititz	PA	17543	717-569-7021	
Web: www.thearrogroup.com					
Arsee Engineers Inc 9715 Kincaid Dr	Fishers	IN	46037	317-594-5152	
Web: arsee-engineers.com					
Arthur Dyson & Assoc 1295 N Wishon Ave	Fresno	CA	93728	559-486-3582	486-3582
Web: www.arthurdyson.com					
Arw Engineers Inc 1594 West Park Cir Ste 100	Ogden	UT	84404	801-782-6008	
Web: www.arwengineers.com					
ASCG Inc 300 W 31st Ave	Anchorage	AK	99503	907-339-6500	339-5327
Web: www.whpacific.com					
ASG Renaissance 22226 Garrison St	Dearborn	MI	48124	313-565-4700	565-4701
TF: 800-238-0890 ■ *Web:* www.asgren.com					
ASI Automation LLC 475 Applejack Ct	Sparta	MI	49345	616-887-8201	
Ata Engineering Inc 11995 El Camino Real Ste 200	San Diego	CA	92130	858-480-2000	
Web: ata-e.com					
Athena Automation Ltd 372 New Enterprise Way	Vaughan	ON	L4H0S8	905-265-0277	
Web: www.athenaautomation.com					
Atlantic Testing Laboratories Ltd 6431 US Highway 11	Canton	NY	13617	315-386-4578	386-1012
Web: www.atlantictesting.com					
AtlasPower Inc 10 Futurity Pl	Tijeras	NM	87059	505-286-9625	
Web: www.atlaspower.com					
ATSI Inc 415 Commerce Dr	Amherst	NY	14228	716-691-9200	
Web: atsi.com					
Atsim Inc 1825 George Ave Ste 1F	Annapolis	MD	21401	410-990-1711	
Austin Co 6095 Parkland Blvd	Cleveland	OH	44124	440-544-2600	544-2661
Web: www.theaustin.com					
Austrian & Assoc Inc 2530 Superior Ave Ste 202	Cleveland	OH	44114	216-621-6631	
Automatan Inc 2911 Apache Dr	Plover	WI	54467	715-341-6501	
Web: www.automatan.com					
Automation Services & Controls Inc 16765 Park Cir Dr	Chagrin Falls	OH	44023	440-543-8146	
Web: www.ascdrives.com					
Avail Technologies Inc 2026 Sandy Dr	State College	PA	16803	814-234-3394	
Web: www.availtec.com					
Avion Solutions Inc 4905 Research Dr NW	Huntsville	AL	35805	256-721-7006	
Web: avionsolutions.com					
Avionics Test & Analysis Corp 4540 E Hwy 20 Ste 6	Niceville	FL	32578	850-897-4553	897-4331
Web: avtest.com					
Axion BioSystems Inc 1819 Peachtree Rd NE Ste 350	Atlanta	GA	30309	404-477-2557	
Web: www.axionbiosystems.com					
Axis Inc 3008 W Willow Knolls Dr	Peoria	IL	61614	309-691-3988	
Web: axis-inc.com					
Ayres Assoc Inc 3433 Oakwood Hills Pkwy	Eau Claire	WI	54701	715-834-3161	831-7500
Web: www.ayresassociates.com					
Azimuth Inc 3741 Morgantown Industrial Park	Morgantown	WV	26501	304-292-3700	
Web: www.azimuthinc.com					
Aztec Engineering Group Inc 4561 E Mcdowell Rd	Phoenix	AZ	85008	602-454-0402	
Web: aztec.us					
Aztech Innovations Inc 805 Bayridge Dr	Kingston	ON	K7P1T5	613-384-9400	
Web: www.aztechinc.com					
B & W Engineering Corp 3303 Harbor Blvd	Costa Mesa	CA	92626	714-540-9975	
Web: b-w-engineering.com					
B G Consultants Inc 4806 Vue Du Lac Pl	Manhattan	KS	66503	785-537-7448	537-8793
Web: www.bgcons.com					
B Jcc Inspections 1000 Banks Draw	Rexford	MT	59930	406-882-4825	
TF: 877-248-6006 ■ *Web:* www.bjccinspections.com					
B W Smith Structural Engineers 12435 Ventura Ct	Studio City	CA	91604	818-505-9409	
B.R. Fries & Associates Inc 34 W 32nd St	New York	NY	10001	212-563-3300	
Web: www.brfries.com					

Company	City	State	Zip	Phone	Fax
BA Consulting Group Ltd 45 St Clair Ave W Ste 300 *Web:* www.bagroup.com	Toronto	ON	M4V1K9	416-961-7110	
Bachelor Controls Inc 123 N Washington Ave *Web:* bachelorcontrols.com	Sabetha	KS	66534	785-284-3482	
Ballard Group Inc, The 2525 S Wadsworth Blvd Ste 200 *Web:* www.theballardgroup.com	Lakewood	CO	80227	303-988-4514	
Ballinger 833 Chestnut St Ste 1400 *Web:* www.ballinger.com	Philadelphia	PA	19107	215-446-0900	446-0901
Bantrel Inc 700 6th Ave SW Ste 1400 *Web:* www.bantrel.com	Calgary	AB	T2P0T8	403-290-5000	
Bantu Inc 8133 Lessburg Pk Ste 250 **Fax Area Code:* 888 ■ *Web:* www.bantu.com	Vienna	VA	22182	703-766-4577	828-1726*
Bar Engineering Company Ltd 5237 70th Ave *Web:* www.bareng.ca	Lloydminster	AB	T9V3N6	780-875-1683	
Bard Rao + Athanas Consulting Engineers Inc 10 Guest St 4th Fl *Web:* www.brplusa.com	Boston	MA	02135	617-254-0016	924-9339
Barge Waggoner Sumner & Cannon 211 Commerce St Ste 600 *Web:* www.bargewaggoner.com	Nashville	TN	37201	615-254-1500	255-6572
Barnett Engineering Ltd 7710 5 St Se Ste 215 *Web:* barnett-engg.com	Calgary	AB	T2H2L9	403-255-9544	
Barr Engineering Co 4700 W 77th St *TF:* 800-632-2277 ■ *Web:* www.barr.com	Minneapolis	MN	55435	952-832-2600	832-2601
Bartlett & West Engineers Inc 1200 SW Executive Dr *TF:* 888-200-6464 ■ *Web:* www.bartwest.com	Topeka	KS	66615	785-272-2252	
Barton & Loguidice PC 290 Elwood Davis Rd *Web:* bartonandloguidice.com	Liverpool	NY	13088	315-457-5200	
Basic Commerce & Industries 304 Harper Dr Ste 203 *Web:* www.bcisse.com	Moorestown	NJ	08057	856-778-1660	
Baskerville-Donovan Inc 449 W Main St *Web:* baskervilledonovan.com	Pensacola	FL	32502	850-438-9661	
Bass, Nixon & Kennedy Inc 6310 Chapel Hill Rd 250 *Web:* www.bnkinc.com	Raleigh	NC	27607	919-851-4422	
Batta Environmental Associates Inc Delaware Industrial Park 6 Garfield Way *Web:* www.battaenv.com	Newark	DE	19713	302-737-3376	
Bax Engineering Co 221 Point W Blvd *Web:* www.baxengineering.com	Saint Charles	MO	63301	636-928-5552	
Baxter & Woodman Inc 8678 Ridgefield Rd *Web:* baxterwoodman.com	Crystal Lake	IL	60012	815-459-1260	455-0450
Bayer-Risse Engineering Inc 78 Rt 173 W *Web:* bayer-risse.com	Hampton	NJ	08827	908-735-2255	
BBG-BBGM 1825 K St NW Ste 300 *Web:* www.bbg-bbgm.com	Washington	DC	20006	202-452-1644	452-1647
Bcc Engineering Inc 6401 SW 87th Ave Ste 200 *Web:* www.bcceng.com	Miami	FL	33173	305-670-2350	
Bcg Engineering & Consulting Inc 3012 26th St *Web:* www.bcgengineers.com	Metairie	LA	70002	504-454-3866	
Beacon Energy Services Inc 2685 Temple Ave *Web:* www.beaconenergyservices.com	Signal Hill	CA	90755	562-997-3087	
Beam Engineering For Advanced 809 S Orlando Ave *Web:* www.beamco.com	Winter Park	FL	32789	407-629-1282	
Beam, Longest & Neff LLC 8126 Castleton Rd *Web:* www.b-l-n.com	Indianapolis	IN	46250	317-849-5832	
Becher-Hoppe Associates Inc 330 Fourth St *Web:* www.becherhoppe.com	Wausau	WI	54403	715-845-8000	
Bechtel Corp 50 Beale St *Web:* www.bechtel.com	San Francisco	CA	94105	415-768-1234	768-9038
Bechtel North America 3000 Post Oak Blvd *Web:* www.bechtel.com	Houston	TX	77056	713-235-2000	960-9031
Beck Paul Associates pa 12 Kulick Rd *Web:* www.pbanj.com	Fairfield	NJ	07004	973-276-1700	
Beckart Environmental Inc 6900 46th St *Web:* beckart.com	Kenosha	WI	53144	262-656-7680	
BEI Engineering Group Inc Dba Banks Engineering 10511 Six Mile Cypress Pkwy	Fort Myers	FL	33966	239-939-5490	
Belcan Corp 10200 Anderson Way *TF:* 800-423-5226 ■ *Web:* belcancorporation.com	Cincinnati	OH	45242	513-891-0972	
Bellamy Management Services LLC 901 D St Sw Ste 1009 *Web:* www.bms-llc.com	Washington	DC	20024	202-863-2270	
Bellevue Mechanical Inc 1331 120th Ave NE *Web:* www.bmimech.com	Bellevue	WA	98005	425-453-2140	
Belstar Inc 8408 Arlington Blvd Ste 200 *Web:* www.belstar.com	Fairfax	VA	22031	703-645-0280	
Belt Collins 2153 N King St Ste 200 *Web:* www.beltcollins.com	Honolulu	HI	96819	808-521-5361	538-7819
Ben Dyer Associates Inc 11721 Woodmore Rd Ste 200 *Web:* www.bendyer.com	Mitchellville	MD	20721	301-430-2000	
Bender Engineering Inc 10037 E River St *TF:* 800-255-5675 ■ *Web:* www.maintstar.com	Irvine	CA	92618	949-458-7560	
Benesch 205 N Michigan Ave Ste 2400 *Web:* web.benesch.com	Chicago	IL	60601	312-565-0450	565-2947
Bennett & Pless Inc 47 Perimeter Ctr E Ste 110 *Web:* www.bennett-pless.com	Atlanta	GA	30346	678-990-8700	
Berg-Oliver Associates Inc 14701 St Mary's Ln Ste 400 *Web:* www.bergoliver.com	Houston	TX	77079	281-589-0898	
Berger/ABAM Engineers Inc 33301 Ninth Ave S Ste 300 *Web:* www.abam.com	Federal Way	WA	98003	206-431-2300	431-2250
Bergmann Assoc Inc 28 E Main St 200 1st Federal Plaza *TF:* 800-724-1168 ■ *Web:* www.bergmannpc.com	Rochester	NY	14614	585-232-5135	325-8303
Bermello Ajamil & Partners 2601 S Bayshore Dr *Web:* www.bermelloajamil.com/	Miami	FL	33133	305-859-2050	859-9638
Bertsche Engineering Corp 711 Dartmouth Ln *Web:* www.bertsche.com	Buffalo Grove	IL	60089	847-537-8757	
Best Richard N 15 Trail Rd *Web:* rnbest.com	Levittown	PA	19056	215-949-9240	
Beyer Blinder Belle Architects & Planners LLC 41 E 11th St 20th Fl *Web:* www.beyerblinderbelle.com	New York	NY	10271	212-777-7800	475-7424
Bezek-Durst-Seiser Inc 3330 C St Ste 200 *Web:* bdsak.com	Anchorage	AK	99503	907-562-6076	
Bfa Systems Inc 3325 Triana Blvd PO Box 1527 *Web:* bfasystems.com	Huntsville	AL	35805	256-922-8791	
Bgl Asset Services Llc 1611 S Isabella Rd *Web:* www.bglas.com	Mt Pleasant	MI	48858	989-772-8888	
BHE Consulting 276 Libbey Industrial Pkwy *Web:* www.bheconsulting.com	Weymouth	MA	02189	781-340-5871	
Biff Duncan Associates Inc 450 Shrewsbury Plz *TF:* 866-335-2433 ■ *Web:* www.biffduncan.com	Shrewsbury	NJ	07702	732-876-0263	
Biggs Cardosa Assoc Inc 865 The Alameda *Web:* biggscardosa.com	San Jose	CA	95126	408-296-5515	
Bills Engineering Inc 1124 Ft St Mall Ste 200 *Web:* billsengineering.com	Honolulu	HI	96813	808-792-2022	
Bionetics Corp, The 101 Production Dr Ste 100 *TF:* 800-868-0330 ■ *Web:* www.bionetics.com	Yorktown	VA	23693	757-873-0900	
Bionomic Industries Inc 777 Corporate Dr *Web:* bionomicind.com	Mahwah	NJ	07430	201-529-1094	
Biopass Medical Systems Inc 7401 Wiles Rd Ste 222 *Web:* www.biopass.com	Coral Springs	FL	33067	954-575-1588	
Birket Engineering Inc 162 W Plant St *Web:* www.birket.com	Winter Garden	FL	34787	407-290-2000	
Bissell Professional Group Inc 3512 N Croatan Hwy *Web:* www.bissellprofessionalgroup.com	Kitty Hawk	NC	27949	252-261-3266	
Bissett Resource Consultants Ltd 250 839 - 5 Ave SW *Web:* www.bissettres.com	Calgary	AB	T2P3C8	403-294-1888	
BKF Engineers 255 Shoreline Dr Ste 200 *Web:* www.bkf.com	Redwood City	CA	94065	650-482-6300	482-6399
BL Cos 355 Research Pkwy *TF:* 800-301-3077 ■ *Web:* www.blcompanies.com	Meriden	CT	06450	203-630-1406	630-2615
Blackwell Engineering 566 E Market St *Web:* www.blackwellengineering.com	Harrisonburg	VA	22801	540-432-9555	
Blair, Church & Flynn Consulting Engineers 451 Clovis Ave Ste 200 *Web:* www.bcf-engr.com	Clovis	CA	93612	559-326-1400	
Blank Wesselink Cook & Associates Inc 2623 E Pershing Rd *Web:* www.bwcinc.com	Decatur	IL	62526	217-428-0973	
Bliss & Nyitray Inc 800 Douglas Rd Ste 300 *Web:* www.bnienginers.com	Coral Gables	FL	33134	305-442-7086	
BMC Group Inc 600 First Ave Ste 300 *Web:* www.bmcgroup.com	Seattle	WA	98104	206-516-3300	
Bme Assocs 10 Liftbridge Ln E *Web:* www.bmepc.com	Fairport	NY	14450	585-377-7360	
Bmt Fleet Technology Ltd 311 Legget Dr *Web:* www.fleetech.com	Kanata	ON	K2K1Z8	613-592-2830	
Bmt Syntek Technologies Inc 877 Baltimore Annapolis Blvd Ste 110 *Web:* www.bmtsyntek.com	Severna Park	MD	21146	703-525-3403	
BNA Consulting Inc 635 S State St *Web:* www.bnaconsulting.com	Salt Lake City	UT	84111	801-532-2196	
BNP Associates Inc 101 E Ridge Office Park Ste 103 *Web:* www.bnpassociates.com	Danbury	CT	06810	203-792-3000	
Bojo Engineering 473 Sapena Ct Ste 19 *Web:* www.bojoinc.com	Santa Clara	CA	95054	408-844-8211	
Bokam Engineering Inc 2720 S Shannon St *Web:* www.bokam.com	Santa Ana	CA	92704	714-513-2200	
Boksa Marine Design 16132 Churchview Dr Ste 205 *Web:* boksamarinedesign.com	Lithia	FL	33547	813-654-9800	
Bollinger, Lach & Associates Inc 333 Pierce Rd Ste 200 *Web:* www.bollingerlach.com	Itasca	IL	60143	630-438-6400	
Bolton & Menk Inc 1960 Premier Dr *Web:* www.bolton-menk.com	Mankato	MN	56001	507-625-4171	625-4177
Bombard Electric LLC 3570 W Post Rd *Web:* www.bombardelectric.com	Las Vegas	NV	89118	702-263-3570	
BOS Solutions Ltd 635-8th Ave SW Ste 1200 *Web:* www.bos-solutions.com	Calgary	AB	T2P3M3	403-234-8103	
Boston Engineering Corp 300 Bear Hill Rd *Web:* www.boston-engineering.com	Waltham	MA	02451	781-466-8010	
Boston Industrial Consulting 89 Newbury St *Web:* bicinc.com	Danvers	MA	01923	978-739-0399	
Boston Jetsearch Inc 200 Hanscom Dr Ste 207 *Web:* www.bostonjetsearch.com	Bedford	MA	01730	781-274-0074	
Boswell Engineering 330 Phillips Ave *Web:* www.boswellengineering.com	South Hackensack	NJ	07606	201-641-0770	641-1831
Boucher & James Inc 1456 Ferry Rd Bldg Ste 500 *Web:* bjengineers.com	Doylestown	PA	18901	215-345-9400	

Phone | Fax

Boudreau-Espley-Pitre Corp
1040 Lorne St Unit 3 .... Sudbury ON P3C4R9 705-675-7720
TF: 877-675-7720 ■ Web: www.bestech.com

Bow Engineering & Development Inc
1953 S Beretania St Ph A .... Honolulu HI 96826 808-941-8853
Web: www.bowengineering.com

Bowman Barrett & Associates Inc
130 E Randolph St Ste 2650 .... Chicago IL 60601 312-228-0100
Web: bbandainc.com

Bowman Foster & Associates P C
4 Interstate Corporate Ctr .... Norfolk VA 23502 757-466-7400
Web: www.bfa-eng.com

Bowser Morner Inc 1419 Miami St .... Toledo OH 43605 419-691-4800
Web: www.bowser-morner.com

Bracewell Engineering Inc
PO Box 21 .... San Juan Bautista CA 95045 831-623-2526
Web: bracewellengineering.com

Brander Construction Technology Inc
2357 W Mason St .... Green Bay WI 54303 920-499-0260
Web: branderct i.com

Braun Intertec Corp
11001 Hampshire Ave S .... Bloomington MN 55438 952-995-2000 995-2020
TF: 800-279-6100 ■ Web: www.braunintertec.com

Brayton Energy Llc 75 Lafayette Rd # B .... Hampton NH 03842 603-601-0450
Web: www.braytonenergy.com

Breault Research Organization Inc
6400 E Grant Rd Ste 350 .... Tucson AZ 85715 520-721-0500
Web: www.breault.com

Breen Engineering Inc 1983 W 190th St .... Torrance CA 90504 310-464-8404
Web: www.breeneng.com

Bresslergroup 1216 Arch St 7th Fl .... Philadelphia PA 19107 215-561-5100
Web: www.bresslergroup.com

Brevium Inc 11602 S Redwood Rd Ste B205 .... Riverton UT 84095 801-302-2299
Web: brevium.com

Bricmont Inc
500 Technology Dr
Southpointe Industrial Pk .... Canonsburg PA 15317 724-746-2300 746-9420
Web: www.andritz.com

Bridge Diagnostics Inc 5398 Manhattan Cir .... Boulder CO 80303 303-494-3230
Web: www.bridgetest.com

Brierley Associates LLC 990 S Broadway Ste 222 .... Denver CO 80209 303-703-1405
Web: brierleyassociates.com

Brinjac Engineering Inc 114 N Second St .... Harrisburg PA 17101 717-233-4502 233-0833
TF: 877-274-6526 ■ Web: www.brinjac.com

Bristol Harbor Group Inc
99 Poppasquash Rd Unit H .... Bristol RI 02809 401-253-4318
Web: www.bristolharborgroup.com

Broaddus & Associates Inc
1301 S Capital of Texas Hwy Ste A 302 .... Austin TX 78746 512-329-8822
Web: www.broaddusassociates.com

Brock Solutions Inc 86 Ardelt Ave .... Kitchener ON N2C2C9 519-571-1522 571-1721
TF: 877-702-7625 ■ Web: www.brocksolutions.com

Brooke Ocean Technology Ltd
461 Windmill Rd .... Dartmouth NS B3A1J9 902-468-2928
Web: www.brooke-ocean.com

Brooks & Sparks Inc 21020 Park Row Dr .... Katy TX 77449 281-578-9595
Web: www.brooksandsparks.com

Brown & Caldwell Consulting Engineers
201 N Civic Dr Ste 115 .... Walnut Creek CA 94596 925-937-9010 937-9026
Web: www.brownandcaldwell.com

Brown & Gay Engineers Inc
10777 Westheimer Rd Ste 400 .... Houston TX 77042 281-558-8700 558-9701
Web: www.browngay.com

Bruce E Brooks & Associates Inc
2209 Chestnut St .... Philadelphia PA 19103 215-569-0400
Web: www.brucebrooks.com

BRUNS-PAK Corp 999 New Durham Rd .... Edison NJ 08817 732-248-4455
Web: bruns-pak.com

BSA Life Structures 9365 Counselors Row .... Indianapolis IN 46240 317-819-7878 819-7288
Web: www.bsalifestructures.com

BSK & Assoc 550 W Locust Ave .... Fresno CA 93650 559-497-2880
Web: www.bskinc.com

Bsm Consulting Engineers Inc
801 Commercial St .... Astoria OR 97103 503-325-8065
Web: bsmengineering.com

Buffalo Engineering PC 4245 Union Rd .... Cheektowaga NY 14225 716-633-5300
Web: buffaloengineering.com

Buford Goff & Assoc Inc 1331 Elmwood Ave .... Columbia SC 29201 803-254-6302
Web: bgainc.com

Building Leaders Inc PO Box 408263 Ste 200b .... Chicago IL 60640 773-769-4409
Web: www.buildingleaders.com

Bulldog Automation 653 Riverside St .... Portland ME 04103 207-772-9561
Web: bulldogautomation.com

Bulldog Marine
1740 Hudson Bridge Rd Ste 1012 .... Stockbridge GA 30281 251-650-1195
Web: www.bulldogmarine.biz

Burgess & Niple Inc 5085 Reed Rd .... Columbus OH 43220 614-459-2050 451-1385
Web: www.burgessniple.com

Burk-Kleinpeter Inc (BKI) 4176 Canal St .... New Orleans LA 70119 504-486-5901 483-6298
Web: www.bkiusa.com

Burkett & Wong Engineers Inc
3434 Fourth Ave .... San Diego CA 92103 619-299-5550
Web: www.bwesd.com

Burkett Engineering Inc
105 E Robinson St Ste 501 .... Orlando FL 32801 407-246-1260
Web: burkettengineering.com

Burns & McDonnell 9400 Ward Pkwy .... Kansas City MO 64114 816-333-9400
Web: www.burnsmcd.com

Burns, Delatte & Mccoy Inc
320 Westcott St Ste 100 .... Houston TX 77007 713-861-3016
Web: www.bdmi-ce.com

Bursich Associates Inc 2129 E High St .... Pottstown PA 19464 610-323-4040
Web: www.bursich.com

Burtech Pipeline 102 Second St .... Encinitas CA 92024 760-634-2822
Web: www.burtechpipeline.com

Butler Fairman & Seufert Inc
8450 Wfield Blvd Ste 300 .... Indianapolis IN 46240 317-713-4615
Web: bfsengr.com

Byce & Associates Inc 487 Portage St .... Kalamazoo MI 49007 269-381-6170
Web: www.byce.com

Byers Engineering Co 6285 Barfield Rd .... Atlanta GA 30328 404-843-1000 843-2000
Web: www.byers.com

C & S Companies (CSCOS)
499 Col Eileen Collins Blvd .... Syracuse NY 13212 315-455-2000 455-9667
TF: 877-277-6583 ■ Web: www.cscos.com

C R Hipp Construction Inc
4981 Dorchester Rd Ste .... North Charleston SC 29418 843-744-4477
Web: www.crhippconstruction.com

C S Davidson Inc 38 N Duke St .... York PA 17401 717-846-4805
Web: csdavidson.com

C. P. Richards Construction Company Inc
2680 ABCO Ct .... Lithonia GA 30058 678-244-1450
Web: www.cprichardsconstruction.com

C14 Consulting Group LLC 1307 Summerhill Dr .... Malvern PA 19355 610-291-2726
Web: www.c14consultinggroup.com

C2AE 725 Prudden St .... Lansing MI 48906 517-371-1200
Web: www.c2ae.com

C3 Corp 3300 E Venture Dr .... Appleton WI 54911 920-749-9944
Web: www.c3ingenuity.com

Cabem Technologies LLC
90 Oak St Ste 302 PO Box 260 .... Newton Upper Falls MA 02464 508-541-3123
Web: www.cabem.com

Cable Aml Inc 2271 W 205th St Ste 101 .... Torrance CA 90501 310-222-5599
Web: cableaml.com

Calder Richards Consulting Engineers
634 South 400 West Ste 100 .... Salt Lake City UT 84101 801-466-1699
Web: crceng.com

Caldwell Associates Architects Inc
116 N Tarragona St .... Pensacola FL 32502 850-432-9500
Web: www.caldwell-assoc.com

Caldwell Richards Sorensen Inc
2060 East 2100 South .... Salt Lake City UT 84109 801-359-5565
Web: crsengineers.com

Caloris Engineering LLC 8649 Commerce Dr .... Easton MD 21601 410-822-6900
Web: caloris.com

Calvin Giordano & Assoc Inc
1800 Eller Dr Ste 600 .... Fort Lauderdale FL 33316 954-921-7781
Web: cgasolutions.com

Cameron & Company Inc
573 West 3560 South Ste 1 .... Salt Lake City UT 84115 801-268-3584
Web: www.cameronconst.com

Campbell Grinder Co 1226 Pontaluna Rd .... Spring Lake MI 49456 231-798-6464 798-6466
Web: www.campbellgrinder.com

Cannon Design 2170 Whitehaven Rd .... Grand Island NY 14072 716-773-6800 773-5909
Web: www.cannondesign.com

Capital Excavation Co 2967 Business Park Dr .... Buda TX 78610 512-440-1717
Web: capitalexcavation.com

Captec Engineering Inc 300 SW St Lucie Ave .... Stuart FL 34994 772-692-4344
Web: gocaptec.com

Caribou Road Services Ltd 5110 52nd Ave .... Pouce Coupe BC V0C2C0 250-786-5440
Web: www.cariburoads.com

Carl Walker Inc 5136 Lovers Ln .... Portage MI 49002 269-381-2222
Web: www.carlwalker.com

Carlo Gavazzi Inc 750 Hastings Ln .... Buffalo Grove IL 60089 847-465-6100
TF: 800-222-2659 ■ Web: www.gavazzionline.com

Carlson, Brigance & Doering Inc
5501 W William Cannon Dr .... Austin TX 78749 512-280-5160
Web: cbdeng.com

Carman-Dunne PC 2 Lakeview Ave .... Lynbrook NY 11563 516-599-5563

Carollo Engineers
2700 Ygnacio Vly Rd Ste 300 .... Walnut Creek CA 94598 925-932-1710 930-0208
TF: 800-523-5826 ■ Web: www.carollo.com

Carroll Engineering Corp 949 Easton Rd .... Warrington PA 18976 215-343-5700 343-0875
Web: www.carrollengineering.com

Carter & Sloope Inc 6310 Peake Rd .... Macon GA 31210 478-477-3923
Web: cartersloope.com

CAS Inc PO Box 11190 .... Huntsville AL 35814 256-971-6126 922-4207
TF: 800-729-8686 ■ Web: cascares.cas-inc.com

Casco Bay Engineering Inc 424 Fore St .... Portland ME 04101 207-842-2800
Web: cascobayengineering.com

Cashin Assoc PC
1200 Veterans Memorial Hwy Ste 200 .... Hauppauge NY 11788 631-348-7600
Web: cashinassociates.com

Cass Construction Inc 1100 Wagner Dr .... El Cajon CA 92020 619-590-0929
Web: www.cassconstruction.com

Cates Engineering Ltd
7500 Iron Bar Ln Ste 209 .... Gainesville VA 20155 571-261-9280
Web: www.cateseng.com

Cavadeas Engineering Corp
10045 N State Rd 27 Ste 200 .... Hayward WI 54843 715-634-4176
Web: cavadeasengineering.com

Caviness Lambert Engineering LLC
508 E N St Ste 202 .... Greenville SC 29601 864-242-5844
Web: www.cl-e.com

CDH Energy Corp 2695 Bingley Rd PO Box 641 .... Cazenovia NY 13035 315-655-1063
Web: www.cdhenergy.com

CDI Corporation 1717 Arch St 35th Fl .... Philadelphia PA 19103 215-569-2200
TF: 866-472-2203 ■ Web: www.cdicorp.com

CDM Smith Inc 50 Hampshire St .... Cambridge MA 02139 617-452-6000
Web: cdmsmith.com

CDR Maguire 8669 NW 36 St Ste 340 .... Doral FL 33166 786-235-8534
Web: www.cdrmaguire.com

Cell Point Systems Inc
51 Federal St Ste 303 .... San Francisco CA 94107 415-397-4400
Web: www.cellpointsystems.com

Company	City	State	Zip	Phone	Fax
Centra Technology Inc 25 Burlington Mall Rd *Web:* www.centratechnology.com	Burlington	MA	01803	781-272-7887	272-7836
Century Engineering Inc 10710 Gilroy Rd *Web:* www.centuryeng.com	Hunt Valley	MD	21031	443-589-2400	
Cerami & Associates Inc 404 Fifth Ave *Web:* www.ceramiassociates.com	New York	NY	10018	212-370-1776	
Ces Network Services Inc 920 County Rd 376 *Web:* www.cesnetser.com	Barksdale	TX	78828	972-241-3683	
Cesare Joseph a & Associates Geotechnical Engineeering Consu 7108 S Alton Way Bldg B *Web:* cesareinc.com	Centennial	CO	80112	303-220-0300	
Ceso Inc 8534 Yankee St Ste 2B *Web:* cesoinc.com	Dayton	OH	45458	937-435-8584	
CET Engineering Services 1240 N Mountain Rd *Web:* ghd.com	Harrisburg	PA	17112	717-541-0622	
CH Guernsey & Co 5555 N Grand Blvd *Web:* www.guernsey.us	Oklahoma City	OK	73112	405-416-8100	416-8111
Chamlin & Assoc Inc 3017 Fifth St *Web:* chamlin.com	Peru	IL	61354	815-223-3344	
Charles Gojer & Associates Inc 11615 Forest Central Dr *Web:* www.cgojer.com	Dallas	TX	75243	214-340-1199	
Charlie Bravo Aviation Llc 160 Terminal Rd Ste 100 *Web:* www.wepushtin.com	Georgetown	TX	78628	512-868-9000	
Chastain-Skillman Inc 4705 Old Rd 37 *Web:* www.chastainskillman.com	Lakeland	FL	33813	863-646-1402	647-3806
Chaudhary & Assoc Inc 211 Gateway Rd W Ste 204 *Web:* chaudhary.com	Napa	CA	94558	707-255-2729	
Chavez Grieves Consulting Engrs Inc 4700 Lincoln Rd NE *Web:* www.cg-engrs.com	Albuquerque	NM	87109	505-344-4080	
Chehayeb & Assoc Inc 3702 W Azeele St *Web:* chehayeb.com	Tampa	FL	33609	813-876-1415	
Chemic Engineers & Constructors Inc 4820 Fm 2004 Rd *Web:* chemic.com	Hitchcock	TX	77563	409-986-6504	
Chemical & Industrial Engineering Inc 1930 Bishop Ln Ste 800 *Web:* www.cieng.com	Louisville	KY	40218	502-451-4977	451-9574
Chemstress Consultant Co 39 S Main St *Web:* www.chemstress.com	Akron	OH	44308	330-535-5591	535-1431
ChemTech Consultants Inc 1370 Washington Pk *Web:* www.chemtech88.com	Bridgeville	PA	15017	412-221-1360	221-5685
Chemtex International Inc 1979 Eastwood Rd *Web:* www.chemtex.com	Wilmington	NC	28403	910-509-4400	509-4567
Chester Valley Engineers Inc 83 Chestnut Rd *Web:* www.chesterv.com	Paoli	PA	19301	610-644-4623	
Chiang Patel & Yerby 1820 Regal Row Ste 200 *Web:* www.cpyi.com	Dallas	TX	75235	214-638-0500	638-3723
CHL Systems 476 Meetinghouse Rd *Web:* www.chlsystems.com	Souderton	PA	18964	215-723-7284	723-9115
Chs Engineers Inc 12507 Bel Red Rd Ste 101 *Web:* www.chsengineers.com	Bellevue	WA	98005	425-637-3693	
CIMA Technologies 1035 Eastside Rd *Web:* cima-technologies.com	El Paso	TX	79915	915-775-1919	
Ciorba Group Inc 5507 N Cumberland Ave Ste 402 *Web:* www.ciorba.com	Chicago	IL	60656	773-775-4009	
Cirtec Medical Systems LLC 55 Deer Park Dr *Web:* cirtecmed.com	East Longmeadow	MA	01028	413-525-5700	
Citygate GIS LLC 125 Cathedral St *Web:* www.citygategis.com	Annapolis	MD	21401	410-295-3333	
Civil & Environmental Consultants Inc 333 Baldwin Rd *TF:* 800-365-2324 ■ *Web:* www.cecinc.com	Pittsburgh	PA	15205	412-429-2324	429-2114
Civil Consulting Group Pllc 1515 Heritage Dr *Web:* civilgroup.net	Mckinney	TX	75069	972-569-9193	
Civil Dynamics Inc 109a Route 515 *Web:* www.civildynamics.com	Stockholm	NJ	07460	973-697-3496	
Civil Site Design Group PLLC 630 Southgate Ave Ste A *Web:* www.civil-site.com	Nashville	TN	37203	615-248-9999	
Civil Works Engineers Inc 3151 Airway Ave *Web:* civilworksengineers.com	Costa Mesa	CA	92626	714-966-9060	
Civiltec Engineering Inc 118 W Lime Ave *Web:* www.civiltec.com	Monrovia	CA	91016	626-357-0588	
Civiltech Engineering Inc 450 E Devon Ave Ste 300 *Web:* civiltechinc.com	Itasca	IL	60143	630-773-3900	
Civtech Designs Inc 11012 Rhodenda Pl *Web:* civtechdesigns.com	Upper Marlboro	MD	20772	240-244-5517	
CJL Engineering Inc 1550 Coraopolis Heights Rd Ste 340 *Web:* www.cjlengineering.com	Moon Township	PA	15108	412-262-1220	
Ckgp/Pw & Assoc Inc 989 Chicago Rd *Web:* ckgppw.com	Troy	MI	48083	248-577-0400	
Clark Builders Ltd 4703 - 52 Ave *Web:* www.clarkbuilders.com	Edmonton	AB	T6B3R6	780-395-3300	
Clark Engineering Corp 621 Lilac Dr N *TF:* 877-246-9196 ■ *Web:* www.clark-eng.com	Minneapolis	MN	55422	763-545-9196	
Class 1 Controls Inc 1720 Elmview Dr *Web:* www.class1controls.com	Houston	TX	77080	713-467-8397	
Classic Industrial Services Inc 6748 Complex Dr *Web:* www.classicindustrial.com	Baton Rouge	LA	70809	225-756-4450	
Cleary Zimmermann Engineers Inc 1344 S Flores St *Web:* www.clearyzimmermann.com	San Antonio	TX	78204	210-447-6100	
Cleland Site Prep Inc PO Box 3822 *Web:* www.clelandsiteprep.com	Bluffton	SC	29910	843-987-0500	
Close Jensen & Miller PC 1137 Silas Deane Hwy	Wethersfield	CT	06109	860-563-9375	
Cloward H2o 2696 N University Ave *Web:* www.clowardh2o.com	Provo	UT	84604	801-375-1223	
Clyde Bergemann Bachmann Inc 416 Lewiston Junction Rd *Web:* www.cbpg.com	Auburn	ME	04210	207-784-1903	
Cma Engineers 35 Bow St *Web:* cmaengineers.com	Portsmouth	NH	03801	603-431-6196	
CMG Environmental 67 Hall Rd	Sturbridge	MA	01566	774-241-0901	
Cmj Engineering & Testing Inc 7636 Pebble Dr *Web:* www.cmjengr.com	Fort Worth	TX	76118	817-284-9400	
Cng Engineering PLLC 1917 N New Braunfels Ave Ste 201 *Web:* cngengineering.com	San Antonio	TX	78208	210-224-8841	
COACT Inc 9140 Guilford Rd Ste N *Web:* www.coact.com	Columbia	MD	21046	301-498-0150	
Code Environmental Services Inc 400 Middlesex Ave *Web:* www.codeenvironmental.com	Carteret	NJ	07008	732-969-2700	
Coe & Van Loo Consultants Inc 4550 N 12th St *Web:* www.cvlci.com	Phoenix	AZ	85014	602-264-6831	
Cogent Industrial Technologies 13091 Vanier Pl Ste 180 *Web:* www.cogentind.com	Richmond	BC	V6V2J1	604-207-8878	
Cohesionforce Inc 360C Quality Cir *Web:* cohesionforce.com	Huntsville	AL	35806	256-562-0600	
Colbert, Matz, Rosenfelt Inc 2835 Smith Ave Ste G *Web:* www.cmrengineers.com	Baltimore	MD	21209	410-653-3838	
Coler & Colantonio Inc 101 Accord Pk Dr *Web:* www.col-col.com	Norwell	MA	02061	781-982-5400	
Columbia Telecommunications Corp 10613 Concord St *Web:* www.ctcnet.us	Kensington	MD	20895	301-933-1488	
Columbus Engineering Consultants Ltd 840 Michigan Ave *Web:* ceceng.net	Columbus	OH	43215	614-228-3500	
Colvin Engineering Assoc Inc 244 West 300 North *Web:* cea-ut.com	Salt Lake City	UT	84103	801-322-2400	
Commonwealth Assoc Inc PO Box 1124 *Web:* www.cai-engr.com	Jackson	MI	49204	517-788-3000	788-3003
Compass Systems Inc 21471 Great Mills Rd *Web:* www.compass-sys-inc.com	Lexington Park	MD	20653	301-737-4640	
Composite Technology Development Inc 2600 Campus Dr *Web:* www.ctd-materials.com	Lafayette	CO	80026	303-664-0394	
Composites Innovation Centre 158 Commerce Dr *Web:* www.compositesinnovation.ca	Winnipeg	MB	R3P0Z6	204-262-3400	
Compumation Inc 205 W Grand Ave *Web:* www.compumation.com	Bensenville	IL	60106	630-860-1921	
Comsearch 19700 Janelia Farm Blvd *Web:* www.comsearch.com	Ashburn	VA	20147	703-726-5500	726-5600
Comtrac Services Inc 1669 Litton Dr *Web:* comtracinc.com	Stone Mountain	GA	30083	770-934-9595	
Con-Tech Carpentry LLC 366 W Fourth St *Web:* www.contechcarpentry.com	Eureka	MO	63025	636-938-4748	
Concept Systems Inc 1957 Fescue St Se *Web:* conceptsystemsinc.com	Albany	OR	97322	541-791-8140	
Concepts NREC 217 Billings Farm Rd *TF:* 888-299-8057 ■ *Web:* www.conceptsnrec.com	White River Junction	VT	05001	802-296-2321	296-2325
Conco-west Inc 322 E Wetmore St *Web:* www.concowestinc.com	Manteca	CA	95337	209-239-2110	
Coneco Engineers & Scientists Inc 4 First St *Web:* www.coneco.com	Bridgewater	MA	02324	508-697-3191	
Conewago Enterprises Inc 660 Edgegrove Rd *Web:* www.conewago.com	Hanover	PA	17331	717-632-7722	
Configure One Inc 900 Jorie Blvd Ste 190 *Web:* www.configureone.com	Oak Brook	IL	60523	630-368-9950	
Connexsys Engineering Inc 3075 Research Dr	Richmond	CA	94806	510-243-2050	
Consultant Engineering Service Inc 811 W 5th St 101 *Web:* www.ceseng.net	Winston Salem	NC	27101	336-724-0139	
Control Point Corp 110 Castilian Dr Ste 200 *Web:* control-pt.com	Goleta	CA	93117	805-882-1884	
Converse Consultants 717 S Myrtle Ave *Web:* www.converseconsultants.com	Monrovia	CA	91016	626-930-1200	930-1212
Cook Coggin Engineers Inc 703 Crossover Rd *Web:* cookcoggin.com	Tupelo	MS	38802	662-842-7381	
Cook Flatt & Strobel Engineers 9229 Ward Pkwy *Web:* cfse.com	Kansas City	MO	64114	816-333-4477	
Coon Engineering Inc (CEI) 2832 W Wilshire Blvd *Web:* www.coonengineering.com	Oklahoma City	OK	73116	405-842-0363	842-0364
Cooper Carry Inc 191 Peachtree St NE Ste 2400 *Web:* www.coopercarry.com	Atlanta	GA	30303	404-237-2000	237-0276
Cooper Engineering Co Inc 2600 College Dr *Web:* www.cooperengineering.net	Rice Lake	WI	54868	715-234-7008	
Cooper Zietz Engineers Inc 620 S W Fifth Ave Ste 1225	Portland	OR	97204	503-253-5429	
Corestates Inc 4191 Pleasant Hill Rd *Web:* www.core-eng.com	Duluth	GA	30096	770-242-9550	

Phone | Fax

Corgan Assoc Inc 401 N Houston St Dallas TX 75202 214-748-2000
Web: www.corgan.com
Corrosion Probe Inc
12 Industrial Park Rd Centerbrook CT 06409 860-767-4402
Web: www.cpiengineering.com
Corrpro Cos Inc 1055 W Smith Rd Medina OH 44256 330-723-5082 722-7654
TF: 800-443-3516 ■ *Web:* www.corrpro.com
Costello Inc 9990 Richmond Ave Ste 450 Houston TX 77042 713-783-7788
Web: www.costelloinc.com
Costich Engineering & Land Surveying PC
217 Lake Ave Rochester NY 14608 585-458-3020
Web: costich.com
Cox & Dinkins Inc 724 Beltline Blvd Columbia SC 29205 803-254-0518
Web: coxanddinkins.com
CPH Engineers 500 W Fulton St Sanford FL 32771 866-609-0688 330-0639*
*Fax Area Code: 407 ■ *TF:* 866-609-0688 ■ *Web:* www.cphengineers.com
Craig Test Boring Company Inc
5435 Harding Hwy PO Box 427 Mays Landing NJ 08330 800-584-2277
TF: 800-584-2277 ■ *Web:* craigtestboring.com
Craven Thompson & Associates Inc
3563 NW 53rd St Fort Lauderdale FL 33309 954-739-6400
Web: www.craventhompson.com
Crawford Consulting Services Inc
239 Highland Ave East Pittsburgh PA 15112 412-823-0400
Web: www.crawfordconsultingservices.com
Crawford Murphy & Tilly Inc
2750 W Washington St Springfield IL 62702 217-787-8050
Web: www.cmtengr.com
Crenshaw Consulting Engineers Inc
3516 Bush St Ste 200 Raleigh NC 27609 919-871-1070
Web: www.crenshawconsulting.com
Crew Engineers Inc 1250 Rt 23 N Butler NJ 07405 973-492-3300
Web: crewengineers.com
Crist Engineers Inc 1405 N Pierce St Little Rock AR 72207 501-664-1552
Web: cristengineers.com
Cromwell Architect Engineers Inc
101 S Spring St Little Rock AR 72201 501-372-2900
Web: www.cromwell.com
Crossey Engineering Ltd
2255 Sheppard Ave E Ste E-331 Toronto ON M2J4Y1 416-497-3111
Web: www.cel.ca
Crossroad Engineers 3417 Sherman Dr Beech Grove IN 46107 317-780-1555
Web: www.crossroadengineers.com
Crystal Engineering Solutions Inc
645 Executive Dr Troy MI 48083 248-588-1390
Web: www.crystaleng.com
CSA Engineering Inc 2565 Leghorn St Mountain View CA 94043 650-210-9000
Web: www.csaengineering.com
CSI Technologies LLC 2202 Oil Ctr Ct Houston TX 77073 281-784-7990
Web: www.csi-tech.net
CSS-Dynamac Corp 10301 Democracy Ln Ste 300 Fairfax VA 22030 703-691-4612 691-4615
TF: 800-888-4612 ■ *Web:* www.css-dynamac.com
CT Consultants Inc 8150 Sterling Ct Mentor OH 44060 440-951-9000 951-7487
TF: 800-925-0988 ■ *Web:* www.ctconsultants.com
CTA Architects Engineers 13 N 23rd St Billings MT 59101 406-248-7455 248-3779
Web: www.ctagroup.com
Ctl Engineering Inc PO Box 44548 Columbus OH 43204 614-276-8123 276-6377
Web: www.ctleng.com
CTL/Thompson Inc 1971 W 12th Ave Denver CO 80204 303-825-0777 825-4252
Web: www.ctlthompson.com
Cubex Inc 9794 Charlotte Hwy Fort Mill SC 29707 803-547-0748
Web: cubexinc.com
Curtain Wall Design & Consulting Inc
8070 Park Ln Ste 400 Dallas TX 75231 972-437-4200
Web: cdc-usa.com
Custom Engineering Inc
12760 E Us Hwy 40 Independence MO 64055 816-350-1473
Web: www.customengr.com
CYMRI L L C 11011 Richmond Ave Ste 525 Houston TX 77042 713-479-7070
Web: caprockoil.com
Cyril J Demeyere Limited 261 Broadway Tillsonburg ON N4G4H8 519-688-1000
Web: www.cjdleng.com
D & S Engineering Inc 70 Spring St Millinocket ME 04462 207-723-6871
Web: dsenginc.com
D. Crupi & Sons Ltd
85 Passmore Ave Agincourt Toronto ON M1V4S9 416-291-1986
Web: www.crupigroup.com
D3 Technical Services LLC
4600 W Kearney Ste 100 Springfield MO 65803 417-831-7171
Web: www.d3tech.net
Daniel Consultants Inc
8950 State Rt 108 229 Columbia MD 21045 410-995-0090
Web: www.danielconsultants.com
Dannenbaum Engineering Corp 3100 W Alabama Houston TX 77098 713-520-9570
Web: www.dannenbaum.com
Darr & Collins LLC 1425 NW 150th St Edmond OK 73013 405-285-2400
Web: darrcollins.com
Dataline LLC 6703 Albunda Dr PO Box 50816 Knoxville TN 37950 865-588-7740 847-7419*
*Fax Area Code: 703 ■ *TF:* 800-666-9858 ■ *Web:* www.datalinellc.com
Datasyst Engineering & Testing Services Inc
S14W33511 Hwy 18 Delafield WI 53018 262-968-4003
TF: 800-969-4050 ■ *Web:* www.datasysttest.com
Datum Engineers Inc 6516 Forest Park Rd Dallas TX 75235 214-358-0174
Web: datumengineers.com
Datum Inspection Services Inc
21442 N 20th Ave Phoenix AZ 85027 602-997-1340
Web: datum-inspection.com
David Evans & Assoc Inc (DEA)
2100 SW River Pkwy Portland OR 97201 503-223-6663 223-2701
TF: 800-721-1916 ■ *Web:* www.deainc.com
David L Adams Assoc Inc 1536 Ogden St Denver CO 80218 303-455-1900
David Stires Assoc LLC
678 Us Hwy 202/206 N Bridgewater NJ 08807 908-252-7000
Web: dastires.com

Davis & Floyd Inc 1319 Hwy 72 221 E Greenwood SC 29649 864-229-5211 229-7844
Web: www.davisfloyd.com
Davroc & Associates Ltd
2051 Williams Pkwy Units 20 and 21 Brampton ON L6S5T4 905-792-7792
Web: www.davroc.com
Dayton T Brown Inc 1175 Church St Bohemia NY 11716 631-589-6300 589-0046
TF: 800-232-6300 ■ *Web:* www.dtb.com
DC Engineering PC 440 E Corporate Dr Ste 103 Meridian ID 83642 208-288-2181
Web: www.dcengineering.net
DCS Corp 6909 Metro Park Dr Ste 500 Alexandria VA 22310 571-227-6000
Web: dcscorp.com
Degenkolb Engineers 235 Montgomery San Francisco CA 94104 415-392-6952 981-3157
Web: www.degenkolb.com
Deighton Associates Ltd 223 Brock St N Unit 7 Whitby ON L1N4H6 905-665-6605
TF: 888-219-6605 ■ *Web:* www.deighton.com
Delco Electric Inc 1 Nw 132Nd St Oklahoma City OK 73114 405-302-0099
Web: www.delcoelectric.com
Delex Systems Inc 1953 Gallows Rd Ste 700 Vienna VA 22182 703-734-8300 893-5338
Web: www.delex.com
Delixus Inc 1160 Ridgemont Pl Concord CA 94521 925-672-2623
Web: www.delixus.com
Delon Hampton & Assoc Chartered
900 Seventh St NW Ste 800 Washington DC 20001 202-898-1999 371-2073
Web: www.delonhampton.com
Delphinus Engineering Inc
650 Baldwin Tower Eddystone PA 19022 610-874-9160
Web: www.delphinus.com
Deltawrx 21700 Oxnard St Ste 530 Woodland Hills CA 91367 818-227-9300
Web: www.deltawrx.com
Depotstar Inc 6180 140th Ave NW Ramsey MN 55303 763-506-9990
Web: www.depotstar.com
Derek Engineering Inc
2800 Constant Comment Pl Louisville KY 40299 502-266-0041
Web: www.derekengineering.com
Desai Nasr Consulting Engineers Inc
6765 Daly Rd West Bloomfield MI 48322 248-932-2010
Web: www.desainasr.com
Design 3 Engineering Inc
1211 24th St W Ste 7 Billings MT 59102 406-245-5599
Design Concepts Inc 5301 Buttonwood Dr Madison WI 53718 608-316-8400
Web: www.design-concepts.com
Design Integrity Inc
1155 W Fulton Market 2nd Fl Chicago IL 60607 312-942-0602
Web: www.designintegrity.com
Design Systems Inc
38799 W 12 Mile Rd Farmington Hills MI 48331 248-489-4300
Designers Midwest
9563 Montgomery Rd Ste 104 Cincinnati OH 45242 513-793-6670
Web: www.designeers.com
DesignworksUSA Inc
2201 Corporate Ctr Dr Newbury Park CA 91320 805-499-9590
Web: designworksusa.com
Deteq Services 1771 Westborough Dr Katy TX 77449 281-828-3030
Web: www.deteqservices.com
Device Engineering Inc 385 E Alamo Dr Chandler AZ 85225 480-303-0822
Web: www.deiaz.com
Dewalt Corp 1930 22nd St Bakersfield CA 93301 661-323-4600
Web: dewaltcorp.com
Dewberry & Davis 8401 Arlington Blvd Fairfax VA 22031 703-849-0100 849-0100
Web: www.dewberry.com
Dexter Wilson Engineering 2234 Faraday Ave Carlsbad CA 92008 760-438-4422
Web: www.dwilsoneng.com
DfR Solutions LLC
5110 Roanoke Pl Ste 101 College Park MD 20740 301-474-0607
Web: www.dfrsolutions.com
Dfw Consulting Group Inc 1616 Corporate Ct Irving TX 75038 972-929-1199
Web: dfwcgi.com
Diamond Z Engineering Inc 5670 State Rd Cleveland OH 44134 440-842-6501
Web: diamondzengineering.com
Dias, Clifford Pe PC 7 Dey St New York NY 10007 212-608-4811
Web: www.diaseng.com
Dibble & Associates Consulting
7500 N Dreamy Draw Dr Ste 200 Phoenix AZ 85020 602-957-1155
Web: www.dibblecorp.com
Dileonardo International Inc 2348 Post Rd Warwick RI 02886 401-732-2900
Web: dileonardo.com
Dimension Engineering LLC 5171 Hudson Dr Hudson OH 44236 330-634-1430
Web: dimensionengineering.com
Dimension Group I LP, The 10755 Sandhill Rd Dallas TX 75238 214-343-9400
Web: www.dimensiongrp.com
Dimitri J Ververelli Inc 211 N 13th St Philadelphia PA 19107 215-496-0000
Web: djvinc.com
Diversified Technology Consultants Inc (DTC)
2321 Whitney Ave Ste 301 Hamden CT 06518 203-239-4200
Web: www.teamdtc.com
Dixon Assoc Engineering LLC
313 E Jimmie Leeds Rd 2nd Fl Galloway NJ 08205 609-652-7131
Web: dixonassociates.com
DLR Group Inc 6457 Frances Ste 200 Omaha NE 68106 402-393-4100 393-8747
Web: www.dlrgroup.com
DLZ Corp 6121 Huntley Rd Columbus OH 43229 614-888-0040 436-0161
TF: 800-336-5352 ■ *Web:* dlz.com
DMK Assoc Inc 435 Commercial Ct Venice FL 34292 941-412-1293
Dobil Laboratories Inc 727 Butler St Pittsburgh PA 15223 412-782-3399
Web: dobil.com
Doerfer Engineering Corp PO Box 816 Waverly IA 50677 877-483-4700
TF: 877-483-4700 ■ *Web:* www.doerfer.com
DOF Subsea USA Inc
5365 W Sam Houston Pkwy N Ste 390 Houston TX 77041 713-896-2500
Web: www.dofsubsea.com
Dominion Engineering Associates Inc
8511 Indian Hills Ct Ste 202 Fredericksburg VA 22407 540-710-9339
Web: www.dea-inc.net

Company	City	State	ZIP	Phone	Fax
Don Ray George & Assoc Inc 1604 Rio Grande St *Web:* drgainc.com	Austin	TX	78701	512-476-1245	476-6025
Donald W Mcintosh Associates 2200 N Park Ave *Web:* dwma.com	Winter Park	FL	32789	407-644-4068	
Donofrio Kottke & Assoc Inc 7530 Wward Way *Web:* donofrio.cc	Madison	WI	53717	608-833-7530	
Doucet & Associates Inc 7401B Hwy 71 W Ste 160 *Web:* www.doucetengineers.com	Austin	TX	78735	512-583-2600	
Dowl LLC 4041 B St *Web:* www.dowl.com	Anchorage	AK	99503	907-562-2000	
Downes Associates Inc 2129 Northwood Dr *Web:* www.downesassociates.com	Salisbury	MD	21801	410-546-4422	
DPIS Engineering LLC 1600 E Hufsmith Rd *Web:* www.dpis.ws	Tomball	TX	77375	281-351-0048	
Dubois & King Inc 28 N Main St *Web:* www.dubois-king.com	Randolph	VT	05060	802-728-3376	
Dudek 605 Third St *Web:* dudek.com	Encinitas	CA	92024	760-942-5147	
Duffner Engineering 50 W Summit Dr *Web:* duffnerengineering.com	Emerald Hills	CA	94062	650-701-1055	
Dyer Riddle Mills & Precourt Inc (DRMP) 941 Lk Baldwin Ln *TF:* 800-375-3767 ■ *Web:* www.drmp.com	Orlando	FL	32814	407-896-0594	896-4836
Dynamic Civil Solutions Inc 2210 Second Ave N *Web:* dcseng.com	Birmingham	AL	35203	205-358-7256	
Dynamic Research Inc 355 Van Ness Ave Ste 200 *Web:* www.dynres.com	Torrance	CA	90501	310-212-5211	
Dynamix Engineering Ltd 855 Grandview Ave *Web:* dynamix-ltd.com	Columbus	OH	43215	614-443-1178	
DynaTen Corp 4375 Diplomacy Rd *Web:* www.dynaten.com	Fort Worth	TX	76155	817-616-2200	
E. L. Robinson Engineering Co 5088 Washington St W *Web:* www.elrobinson.com	Charleston	WV	25313	304-776-7473	
E.S. Fox Ltd 9127 Montrose Rd *TF:* 866-233-8933 ■ *Web:* www.esfox.com	Niagara Falls	ON	L2E7J9	905-354-3700	
E2 Consulting Engineers Inc 450 E 17th Ave Ste 200 *TF:* 888-835-9400 ■ *Web:* www.e2.com	Denver	CO	80203	303-232-9800	238-8972
E3 Consulting LLC 3333 S Bannock St Ste 740 *Web:* www.e3co.com	Englewood	CO	80110	303-762-7060	
EADS Group 1126 Eigth Ave *TF:* 800-626-0904 ■ *Web:* www.eadsgroup.com	Altoona	PA	16602	814-944-5035	944-4862
Eagle Engineering Inc 2013 Van Bruen Ave *Web:* www.eagleonline.net	Indian Trail	NC	28079	704-882-4222	
EarthRes Group Inc 6912 Old Easton Rd PO Box 468 *TF:* 800-264-4553 ■ *Web:* www.earthres.com	Pipersville	PA	18947	215-766-1211	
EBA Engineering Inc 4813 Seton Dr *Web:* ebaengineering.com	Baltimore	MD	21215	410-358-7171	
Ecm International 404 Executive Ctr Blvd *Web:* ecmintl.com	El Paso	TX	79902	915-351-1900	351-1908
Eco Engineering LLC 11815 Hwy Dr Ste 600 *Web:* www.ecoengineering.com	Cincinnati	OH	45241	513-985-8300	
ECS Corporate Services LLC 14026 Thunderbolt Pl Ste 300 **Fax Area Code:* 541 ■ *Web:* www.ecslimited.com	Chantilly	VA	20151	571-299-6000	474-2479*
Edm Services Inc 4100 Guardian St *Web:* edmsvc.com	Simi Valley	CA	93063	805-527-3300	
Edmond Scientific Co 4100 Monument Creek Dr Ste 540 *Web:* www.edmondsci.com	Fairfax	VA	22030	703-766-3871	
Ehvert Mission Critical 200 Adelaide St W Ste 201 *Web:* www.ehvert.com	Toronto	ON	M5H1W7	416-868-1933	
Eichleay Engineers Inc of California 1390 Willow Pass Rd Ste 600 *Web:* www.eichleay.com	Concord	CA	94520	925-689-7000	689-7006
Einhorn Yaffee Prescott Architecture & Engineering PC NanoFab E 257 Fuller Rd 1st Fl *Web:* www.eypaedesign.com	Albany	NY	12203	518-795-3800	
Eisman & Russo Inc 6455 Powers Ave *Web:* eismanandrusso.com	Jacksonville	FL	32217	904-733-1478	636-8828
EJM Engineering Inc 411 S Wells St Ste 1000 *Web:* www.ejmengineering.com	Chicago	IL	60607	312-922-1700	
El Dorado Engineering Inc 2964 West 4700 South *Web:* www.eldoradoengineering.com	Salt Lake City	UT	84118	801-966-8288	
Electric Power Systems Inc 3305 Arctic Blvd Ste 201 *Web:* www.epsinc.com	Anchorage	AK	99503	907-522-1953	
Elite Electronic Engineering Inc 1516 Centre Cir *Web:* www.elitetest.com	Downers Grove	IL	60515	630-495-9770	
Ellicom Inc 905 Rue De Nemours *Web:* ellicom.com	Quebec	QC	G1H6Z5	418-623-8804	
ELM Engineering Inc 900 Center Pk Dr *Web:* elmengr.com	Charlotte	NC	28217	704-335-0396	
Elwer Engineering Services 2202 Wolf Wy Ste 1110 *Web:* www.eescompanies.com	West Des Moines	IA	50265	515-276-2588	
Emats Inc 480 Claypool Hill Mall Rd *Web:* www.emats-inc.com	Cedar Bluff	VA	24609	276-963-8888	
EMC-Tempest Technical Support Services 2190 E Winston Rd *Web:* www.emctempest.com	Anaheim	CA	92806	714-778-1726	
EMCOR Services Betlem 704 Clinton Ave South *TF:* 800-423-8536 ■ *Web:* www.emcorbetlem.com	Rochester	NY	14620	585-271-5500	
Emjay Engineering & Construction Company Inc 1706 Whitehead Rd *Web:* emjaycons.com	Baltimore	MD	21207	410-298-2000	
EMK Consultants of Florida Inc 7815 N Dale Mabry Hwy *TF:* 800-347-2607 ■ *Web:* www.emkfla.com	Tampa	FL	33614	813-931-8900	
Emprise Corp 3900 Kennesaw 75 Pkwy N W Ste 125 *Web:* www.emprise-usa.com	Kennesaw	GA	30144	770-425-1420	
Emtec Consultants, Professional Engineers PLLC 3555 Veterans Memorial Hw *Web:* www.emtec-engineers.com	Ronkonkoma	NY	11779	631-981-3990	
EN Engineering 28100 Torch Pkwy Ste 400 *Web:* www.enengineering.com	Warrenville	IL	60517	630-353-4000	353-7777
Encon International 7307 Remcon Cir 101 *Web:* www.enconinternational.com	El Paso	TX	79912	915-833-3740	
Encotech Engineering Cnsltnts 8500 Bluffstone Cv *Web:* www.encotechengineering.com	Austin	TX	78759	512-338-1101	
Encur Inc 200 Division St *Web:* encur.com	Keyport	NJ	07735	732-264-2098	
EnerCom Inc 800 18th St Ste 200 *Web:* www.enercominc.com	Denver	CO	80264	303-296-8834	
Enercon Services Inc 5100 E Skelly Dr Ste 450 *Web:* www.enercon.com	Tulsa	OK	74135	918-665-7693	665-7232
Energy Engineering Assoc Inc 6615 Vaught Ranch Rd Ste 200	Austin	TX	78730	512-744-4400	
Energy Initiatives Group LLC 176 Worcester-Providence TurnPk Ste 102 *Web:* www.eig-llc.com	Sutton	MA	01590	508-865-8021	
ENERGYneering Solutions Inc 15820 Barclay Dr *Web:* energyneeringsolutions.com	Sisters	OR	97759	541-549-8766	
Enertech Consultants Inc 494 Salmar Ave 200 *Web:* enertech.net	Campbell	CA	95008	408-866-7266	
Engeo Inc 2010 Crow Canyon Pl Ste 250 *Web:* engeo.com	San Ramon	CA	94583	925-866-9000	
Engineering & Environmental Consultants Inc 4625 E Ft Lowell Rd *TF:* 800-887-2103 ■ *Web:* www.eec-info.com	Tucson	AZ	85712	520-321-4625	321-0333
Engineering Planning & Management Inc 959 Concord St *Web:* www.epm-inc.com	Framingham	MA	01701	508-875-2121	879-3291
Ennead Architects 320 W 13 St *Web:* www.ennead.com	New York	NY	10014	212-807-7171	
Enovity Inc 100 Montgomery St *Web:* enovity.com	San Francisco	CA	94104	415-974-0390	
Enroute Computer Solutions Inc 2511 Fire Rd Ste A4 *Web:* enroute-computer.com	Egg Harbor Township	NJ	08234	609-569-9255	
ENSCO Inc 3110 Fairview Pk Dr Ste 300 *TF:* 800-367-2682 ■ *Web:* www.ensco.com	Falls Church	VA	22042	703-321-9000	321-7863
Envar Services Inc 505 Milltown Rd *Web:* www.envarservices.com	North Brunswick	NJ	08902	732-296-9601	
Envieta LLC 7175 Columbia Gateway Dr Ste T *Web:* envieta.com	Columbia	MD	21046	410-290-1136	
Enviro-Sciences Inc 111 Howard Blvd Ste 108 *Web:* www.enviro-sciences.com	Mount Arlington	NJ	07856	973-398-8183	
Envirocon Inc 101 International Dr *Web:* www.envirocon.com	Missoula	MT	59808	406-523-1150	
Envirosearch Operations Inc 4166-15 Side Rd *Web:* www.envirosearchoperations.ca	Rockwood	ON	N0B2K0	905-854-4441	
Envisioneering Inc 5904 Richmond Hwy Ste 300 **Fax Area Code:* 703 ■ *Web:* www.envisioneeringinc.com	Alexandria	VA	22303	571-483-4100	317-1970*
Eoa Inc 1410 Jackson St *TF:* 800-794-2482 ■ *Web:* eoainc.com	Oakland	CA	94612	510-832-2852	
Epiphany Productions Inc 104 Hume Ave *Web:* www.epiphanyproductions.com	Alexandria	VA	22301	703-683-7500	
Eps Group, Inc Engineers, Planners & Surveyors 2045 S Vineyard Ste 101 *Web:* www.epsgroupinc.com	Mesa	AZ	85210	480-503-2250	
Erdman Anthony 145 Culver Rd Ste 200 *Web:* erdmananthony.com	Rochester	NY	14620	585-427-8888	
Erica Lane Enterprises Inc 3226 Bob Wallace Ave SW Ste 114 *Web:* eleinc.com	Huntsville	AL	35805	256-536-7117	536-7133
eSentio Technologies 700 12Th St NW Ste 700 *Web:* www.esentio.com	Washington	DC	20005	202-628-6010	
ESI Inc of Tennessee 1250 Roberts Blvd *Web:* esitenn.com	Kennesaw	GA	30144	770-427-6200	
Espa Corp Inc 7120 Grand Blvd Ste 100 *Web:* kci.com	Houston	TX	77054	713-680-0080	
Estes Mcclure & Assoc Inc 3608 Wway St *Web:* estesmcclure.com	Tyler	TX	75703	903-581-2677	
Etalex Inc 8501 Jarry St E *Web:* www.etalex.ca	Montreal	QC	H1J1H7	514-351-2000	
Etc Group Inc 1997 South 1100 East *Web:* www.etcgrp.com	Salt Lake City	UT	84106	801-278-1927	
Etegent Technologies Ltd 1775 Mentor Ave *TF:* 800-860-4867 ■ *Web:* www.sdltd.com	Cincinnati	OH	45212	513-631-0579	
Evans Mechwart Hambleton & Tilton Inc (EMHT) 5500 New Albany Rd *Web:* www.emht.com	Columbus	OH	43054	614-775-4500	775-4800
Ewing Cole 100 N Sixth St *Web:* ewingcole.com	Philadelphia	PA	19106	215-923-2020	574-9163
Exceletech Coating & Applications LLC 221 N Hwy 27 Ste I *Web:* www.excelcoatings.com	Clermont	FL	34711	352-394-2155	
Exodyne Inc 8433 N Black Canyon Hwy *Web:* www.exodyne.com	Phoenix	AZ	85021	602-995-3700	995-4091
Experts-conseils Cep Inc 1345 Boul Louis-xiv *Web:* www.expcep.com	Quebec	QC	G2L1M4	418-622-4480	

				Phone	Fax
Exponential Engineering Co					
2950 East Harmony Rd Ste 265	Fort Collins	CO	80528	970-207-9648	
Web: www.exponentialengineering.com					
Extech LLC 455 Main St Bldg 1 Ste A-B	Deep River	CT	06417	860-526-2610	
Web: www.extechllc.com					
Extreme Engineering Solutions Inc					
3225 Deming Way Ste 120	Middleton	WI	53562	608-833-1155	
Web: xes-inc.com					
F & ME Consultants 3112 Devine St	Columbia	SC	29205	803-254-4540	
Web: fandme.com					
Fabre Engineering Inc 119 Gregory Sq	Pensacola	FL	32502	850-433-6438	
Web: www.fabreinc.com					
Facility Dynamics Engineering					
6760 Alexander Bell Dr	Columbia	MD	21046	410-290-0900	
Web: facilitydynamics.com					
Facility Group Inc 2233 Lake Pk Dr	Smyrna	GA	30080	770-437-2700	437-3900
Web: fdgatlanta.com					
Fairwinds International Inc					
128 Northpark Blvd	Covington	LA	70433	985-809-3808	
Web: www.fairwindsintl.com					
Fakouri Electrical Engineering Inc					
30001 Comercio	Rancho Santa Margarita	CA	92688	800-669-8862	
TF: 800-669-8862 ■ *Web:* www.fee-ups.com					
Fanning/Howey Assoc Inc 1200 Irmscher Blvd	Celina	OH	45822	419-586-2292	586-3393
TF: 800-452-3573 ■ *Web:* www.fhai.com					
Farner, Barley & Associates Inc					
4450 NE 83rd Rd	Wildwood	FL	34785	352-748-3126	
Web: www.farnerbarley.com					
Farnsworth Group Inc 2709 McGraw Dr	Bloomington	IL	61704	309-663-8435	
Web: www.f-w.com					
Farwest Corrosion Control Co					
1480 W Artesia Blvd	Gardena	CA	90248	310-532-9524	532-3934
TF: 888-532-7937 ■ *Web:* www.farwestcorrosion.com					
Fastek International Ltd					
1425 60th St Ne	Cedar Rapids	IA	52402	319-294-6664	
Web: www.fastekintl.com					
FATA Hunter Inc 1040 Iowa Ave Ste 100	Riverside	CA	92507	951-328-0200	
Web: www.fatahunter.com					
Fay Spofford & Thorndike LLC					
5 Burlington Woods	Burlington	MA	01803	781-221-1000	229-1115
TF: 800-835-8666 ■ *Web:* www.fstinc.com					
FDH Inc 1033 Skokie Blvd Ste 320	Northbrook	IL	60062	224-757-0001	
Web: www.fdh-inc.com					
Feed Forward Inc 1834 W Oak Pkwy	Marietta	GA	30062	770-426-4422	
Web: feedforward.com					
Fehr-Graham & Assoc LLC					
221 E Main St Ste 200	Freeport	IL	61032	815-235-7643	
Web: fehr-graham.com					
Fentress Bradburn Architects Ltd 421 Broadway	Denver	CO	80203	303-722-5000	722-5080
Web: www.fentressarchitects.com					
FEV Inc 4554 Glenmeade Ln	Auburn Hills	MI	48326	248-373-6000	
Web: fev.com					
Fiore Industries Inc					
8601 Washington St NE Ste B	Albuquerque	NM	87113	505-255-9797	
Web: fiore-ind.com					
Firepoint Technologies Inc					
27-180 Wilkinson Rd	Brampton	ON	L6T4W8	905-874-9400	
Web: www.firepoint.ca					
Fishbeck Thompson Carr & Huber Inc					
1515 Arboretum Dr SE	Grand Rapids	MI	49546	616-575-3824	464-3993
Web: www.ftch.com					
Fitzpatrick Engineering Group PLLC					
19520 W Catawba Ave Ste 311	Cornelius	NC	28031	704-987-9114	
Web: www.fegstructural.com					
Flad & Assoc 644 Science Dr	Madison	WI	53711	608-238-2661	238-6727
Web: www.flad.com					
Flatter & Associates Inc					
805 Princess Anne St Ste 201	Fredericksburg	VA	22401	540-658-1922	
Web: www.flatterassociates.com					
Fleet-Fisher Engineering Inc					
4250 E Camelback Rd Ste 410K	Phoenix	AZ	85018	602-264-3335	
Web: www.ffeng.com					
Fleetway Inc 155 Chain Lk Dr Ste 200	Halifax	NS	B3S1B3	902-494-5700	
Web: www.fleetway.ca					
Fletcher-Thompson Inc 3 Corporate Dr Ste 500	Shelton	CT	06484	203-225-6500	
Web: www.fletcherthompson.com					
Flexicell Inc 10463 Wilden Dr	Ashland	VA	23005	804-550-7300	
Web: flexicell.com					
Flint Surveying & Engineering Company Inc					
5370 Miller Rd	Swartz Creek	MI	48473	810-230-1333	
TF: 800-624-6089 ■ *Web:* fse.us					
Florida Turbine Technologies Inc					
1701 Military Trl Ste 110	Jupiter	FL	33458	561-427-6400	
Web: www.fttinc.com					
Fluor Daniel Inc 3 Polaris Way	Aliso Viejo	CA	92698	949-349-2000	349-2585
Web: www.fluor.com					
Fluoresco Lighting & Sign Corp					
5505 S Nogales Hwy PO Box 27042	Tucson	AZ	85726	520-623-7953	884-0161
Web: www.fluoresco.com					
Foit-Albert Associates 763 Main St	Buffalo	NY	14203	716-856-3933	
Web: www.foit-albert.com					
Food Perspectives Inc					
13755 First Ave N Ste 500	Plymouth	MN	55441	763-553-7787	
Web: foodperspectives.com					
Ford Bacon & Davis					
12021 Lakeland Pk Blvd	Baton Rouge	LA	70809	225-292-0050	257-3752
Web: www.fbd.com					
Forell-Elsesser Engineers Inc					
160 Pine St Ste 600	San Francisco	CA	94111	415-837-0700	
Web: www.forell.com					
Foresite Group Inc					
5185 Peachtree Pkwy Ste 240	Norcross	GA	30092	770-368-1399	
Web: fg-inc.net					
Forsythe & Long Engineering 4560 Helton Dr	Florence	AL	35630	256-760-0000	

				Phone	Fax
Forte & Tablada Inc 9107 Interline Ave	Baton Rouge	LA	70809	225-927-9321	
Web: forteandtablada.com					
Fortis Construction Inc					
1705 SW Taylor St Ste 200	Portland	OR	97205	503-459-4477	
Web: fortisconstruction.com					
Fosdick & Hilmer Inc 525 Vine St	Cincinnati	OH	45202	513-241-5640	
Web: www.fosdickandhilmer.com					
Foth & Van Dyke & Assoc Inc					
2121 Innovation Ct PO Box 5095	Green Bay	WI	54115	920-497-2500	497-8516
Web: www.foth.com					
FOX Engineering Associates Inc					
414 S 17th St Ste 107	Ames	IA	50010	515-233-0000	
Web: www.foxeng.com					
Fpm Group Ltd 909 Marconi Ave	Ronkonkoma	NY	11779	631-737-6200	
Web: www.fpm-group.com					
Fralinger Engineering PA 629 Shiloh Pk	Bridgeton	NJ	08302	856-451-2990	
Web: fralinger.com					
Fred Porter & Assoc Inc Dba Porter & Assoc Inc					
1200 21st St	Bakersfield	CA	93301	661-327-0362	
Fred Wilson & Associates Inc					
3970 Hendricks Ave	Jacksonville	FL	32207	904-398-8636	
Web: www.fredwilson.com					
Fredrick, Fredrick & Heller Engineers Inc					
672 E Royalton Rd	Broadview Heights	OH	44147	440-546-9696	
Web: www.ffhengineers.com					
Freese & Nichols Inc					
4055 International Plz Ste 200	Fort Worth	TX	76109	817-735-7300	735-7491
Web: www.freese.com					
French-Reneker Assoc Inc					
1501 S Main St PO Box 135	Fairfield	IA	52556	641-472-5145	
Web: frenchrenekerassociates.com					
Freyer & Laureta Inc 144 N San Mateo Dr	San Mateo	CA	94401	650-344-9901	344-9920
Web: freyerlaureta.com					
Freyssinet Inc 44880 Falcon Pl Ste 100	Sterling	VA	20166	703-378-2500	
Web: www.freyssinetusa.com					
Frymire Engineering Company Inc					
2818 Satsuma Dr	Dallas	TX	75229	972-620-3500	
Web: www.frymire.com					
FTF Engineering Inc 1916 Mcallister St	San Francisco	CA	94115	415-931-8460	
Web: ftfengineering.com					
Fugro Consultants LP 6100 Hillcroft Ave	Houston	TX	77081	713-369-5400	369-5518
Web: www.fugro.com/about-fugro/locations/fugro-consultants-inc					
Fulghum Macindoe & Associates Inc					
10330 Hardin Vly Rd Ste 201	Knoxville	TN	37932	865-690-6419	
Web: www.fulghummacindoe.com					
Function Engineering Inc 163 Everett Ave	Palo Alto	CA	94301	650-326-8834	
Web: function.com					
Fuss & O'Neill Consulting Engineers Inc					
146 Hartford Rd	Manchester	CT	06040	860-646-2469	533-5143
TF: 800-286-2469 ■ *Web:* www.fando.com					
Future Research Corp					
675 Discovery Dr Bldg 2 Ste 102	Huntsville	AL	35806	256-430-4304	
Web: www.future-research.com					
Future Technologies Inc					
3877 Fairfax Ridge Rd	Fairfax	VA	22030	703-278-0199	385-0886
Web: www.ftechi.com					
G & m Compliance Inc 154 S Cypress St	Orange	CA	92866	714-628-1020	
Web: www.gmcompliance.com					
G & W Engineering Corp					
138 Weldon Pkwy	Maryland Heights	MO	63043	314-469-3737	
Web: gandwengineering.com					
G Systems LP 1240 Campbell Rd Ste 100	Richardson	TX	75081	972-234-6000	
Web: www.gsystems.com					
G3 Technologies Inc					
10280 Old Columbia Rd Ste 260	Columbia	MD	21046	410-290-8110	
Web: www.g3ti.net					
Gables Search Group Inc					
37721 Vine St Ste 1	Willoughby	OH	44094	440-951-9990	
GAI Consultants Inc 385 E Waterfront Dr	Homestead	PA	15120	412-476-2000	
Web: www.gaiconsultants.com					
GaN Corp 11247 S Memorial Pkwy	Huntsville	AL	35803	256-489-2471	
Web: www.gancorp.com					
Gannett Fleming Inc 207 Senate Ave	Camp Hill	PA	17011	717-763-7211	763-8150
TF: 800-233-1055 ■ *Web:* www.gannettfleming.com					
Gap Engineering Inc 802 Dominion Dr	Katy	TX	77450	281-578-0500	
Web: www.gap-eng.com					
Garcia Galuska & De Sousa Inc					
370 Faunce Corner Rd	North Dartmouth	MA	02747	508-998-5700	
Web: www.g-g-d.com					
Garing Taylor & Assoc Inc 141 S Elm St	Arroyo Grande	CA	93420	805-489-1321	
Garver Engineers					
4701 Northshore Dr	North Little Rock	AR	72118	501-376-3633	
Web: www.garverusa.com					
Gaskins Surveying Company Inc					
1266 Powder Springs Rd	Marietta	GA	30064	770-424-7168	
Web: www.gscsurvey.com					
Gaussian Inc 340 Quinnipiac St Bldg 40	Wallingford	CT	06492	203-284-2501	
Web: www.gaussian.com					
GDS Associates Inc 1850 Pkwy Pl Ste 800	Marietta	GA	30067	770-425-8100	
Web: www.gdsassociates.com					
GEI Consultants Inc 400 Unicorn Pk Dr	Woburn	MA	01801	781-721-4000	721-4073
TF: 888-434-9679 ■ *Web:* www.geiconsultants.com					
Gekko Engineering Inc 1210 E 223rd St	Carson	CA	90745	310-513-0000	
Web: gekkoeng.com					
Gem Engineering Inc 1762 Watterson Trl	Louisville	KY	40299	502-493-7100	
Web: www.gemeng.com					
Gemini Engineering Inc					
5940 Macleod Trail S.W. Ste 700	Calgary	AB	T2H2G4	403-255-2006	
Web: www.geminieng.ab.ca					
Genesis Engineers Inc					
1850 Gravers Rd	Plymouth Meeting	PA	19462	610-592-0280	
Web: www.geieng.com					
Gensler 2 Harrison St Ste 400	San Francisco	CA	94105	415-433-3700	836-4599
Web: gensler.com					

Company	City	State	ZIP	Phone	Fax
Geo-Marine Inc 6850 Versar Ctr *Web:* www.geo-marine.com	Springfield	VA	22151	972-423-5480	
Geo-slope International Ltd 633 6 Ave Sw Ste 1400 *Web:* www.geo-slope.com	Calgary	AB	T2P2Y5	403-269-2002	
Geoconcepts Engineering 19955 Highland Vista Dr *Web:* geoconcepts-eng.com	Ashburn	VA	20147	703-726-8030	
GeoEngineers Inc 8410 154th Ave NE *TF:* 888-624-8373 ■ *Web:* www.geoengineers.com	Redmond	WA	98052	425-861-6000	861-6050
Geometric Americas Inc 50 Kirts Blvd Ste A *Web:* geometricglobal.com	Troy	MI	48084	248-404-3500	
Geopentech 525 N Cabrillo Park Dr *Web:* geopentech.com	Santa Ana	CA	92701	714-796-9100	
George Butler Assoc Inc 9801 Renner Blvd *Web:* www.gbateam.com	Lenexa	KS	66219	913-492-0400	577-8200
George G Sharp Inc 22 Cortlandt St Ste 10 *Web:* www.georgesharp.com	New York	NY	10007	212-732-2800	732-2809
George Reed Inc 140 Empire Ave *Web:* www.georgereed.com	Modesto	CA	95354	209-523-0734	
George, Miles & Buhr LLC 206 W Main St *Web:* www.gmbnet.com	Salisbury	MD	21801	410-742-3115	
Geosol Inc 5795 Nw 151st St	Hialeah	FL	34683	727-786-7955	
GeoSyntec Consultants Inc 5901 Broken Sound Pkwy NW Ste 300 *TF:* 866-676-1101 ■ *Web:* www.geosyntec.com	Boca Raton	FL	33487	561-995-0900	995-0925
Geotechnical Services Inc 9312 G Ct *Web:* gsinetwork.com	Omaha	NE	68127	402-339-6104	
Geotechnologies Inc 3200 Wellington Court Ste G *Web:* www.geotechpa.com	Raleigh	NC	27615	919-954-1514	
Geotest Engineering Inc 5600 Bintliff Dr *Web:* geotesteng.com	Houston	TX	77036	713-266-0588	266-2977
GGC Engineers Inc 148 N High St	Gahanna	OH	43230	614-471-7310	
Ghafari Assoc Inc 17101 Michigan Ave **Fax:* Hum Res ■ *TF:* 800-289-7822 ■ *Web:* www.ghafari.com	Dearborn	MI	48126	313-441-3000	441-1545*
GHD Inc 2235 Mercury Way Ste 150 *Web:* www.ghd.com	Santa Rosa	CA	95407	707-523-1010	
GHR Engineers & Assoc Inc 1615 S Neil St *Web:* ghrinc.com	Champaign	IL	61820	217-356-0536	
Gibson-Thomas Engineering Company Inc 1004 Ligonier St *Web:* www.gibson-thomas.com	Latrobe	PA	15650	724-539-8562	
Giffels-Webster Engineers Inc 28 W Adams Ste 1200 *Web:* giffelswebster.com	Detroit	MI	48226	313-962-4442	
Gillespie, Prudhon & Associates Inc 16111 Se 106th Ave Ste 100 *TF:* 800-595-2145 ■ *Web:* www.gpatelecom.com	Clackamas	OR	97015	503-657-0424	
Gilsanz, Murray, Steficek LLP 129 W 27th St Fl 5 *Web:* www.gmsllp.com	New York	NY	10001	212-254-0030	
Gipe Assoc Inc 8719 Brooks Dr *Web:* gipe.net	Easton	MD	21601	410-822-8688	
Glacier Technologies LLC 1200 Golden Key Cir Ste 400 *Web:* www.glacier-tech.com	El Paso	TX	79925	915-751-6014	
Glassfab Tempering Services Inc 1448 Mariani Ct *Web:* www.glassfabtempering.com	Tracy	CA	95376	209-229-1060	
Gleason Research Associates Inc 5030 Bradford Dr NW Bldg One Ste 220 *Web:* www.grainc.net	Huntsville	AL	35805	256-883-7000	
Glenmount Global Solutions 5960 Southport Rd *Web:* www.glenmountglobal.com	Portage	IN	46368	219-762-0700	762-1636
Glex Inc 12900 Fm 529 Rd *Web:* www.glexinc.com	Houston	TX	77041	713-849-4985	
Glhn Architects & Engineers Inc 2939 E Broadway Blvd *Web:* glhn.com	Tucson	AZ	85716	520-881-4546	
Global Design Alliance Inc (GDA) 26 Grammercy Pk S 4B *Web:* www.globalda.com	New York	NY	10003	917-887-3860	
Globetrotters Engineering Corp 300 S Wacker Dr Ste 400 *Web:* www.gec-group.com	Chicago	IL	60606	312-922-6400	
Golder Assoc Inc 3730 Chamblee Tucker Rd *Web:* www.golder.com	Atlanta	GA	30341	770-496-1893	934-9476
Gomez & Sullivan PC 288 Genesee St *Web:* gomezandsullivan.com	Utica	NY	13502	315-724-4860	
Gonzalez Design Group 29401 Stevenson Hwy *Web:* www.gonzalez-group.com	Madison Heights	MI	48071	248-548-6010	548-3160
Gonzalez Strength & Assoc 2176 Pkwy Lk Dr *Web:* www.gonzalez-strength.com	Hoover	AL	35244	205-942-2486	
Goodgame Company Inc 2311 Third Ave South *Web:* www.goodgamecompany.com	Pell City	AL	35128	205-338-2551	
Gould Evans International 4041 Mill St *Web:* www.gouldevans.com	Kansas City	MO	64111	816-931-6655	931-9640
GPD Group 520 S Main St Ste 2531 *Web:* www.gpdgroup.com	Akron	OH	44311	330-572-2100	
GRAEF-USA Inc 1 H1y Creek Corporate Ctr 125 S 84th St Ste 401 *Web:* graef-usa.com	Milwaukee	WI	53214	414-259-1500	259-0037
Gravitec Systems Inc 9453 Coppertop Loop NE *Web:* www.gravitec.com	Bainbridge Island	WA	98110	206-780-2898	
Greeley & Hansen 100 S Wacker Dr Ste 1400 *TF:* 800-837-9779 ■ *Web:* www.greeley-hansen.com	Chicago	IL	60606	312-558-9000	558-1006
Greenberg Farrow 44 W 28th St *Web:* www.greenbergfarrow.com	New York	NY	10001	212-725-9530	
Greenman-Pedersen Inc 325 W Main St *Web:* www.gpinet.com	Babylon	NY	11702	631-587-5060	587-5029
Gresham Smith & Partners 511 Union St 1400 Nashville City Ctr *Web:* www.greshamsmith.com	Nashville	TN	37219	615-770-8100	227-4013
Grossman & Keith Engineering Co 10408 Greenbriar Pl *Web:* grossman-keith.com	Oklahoma City	OK	73159	405-691-3213	
Groupe Stavibel Inc 532 7e Rue Ouest bureau 101 *Web:* www.stavibel.qc.ca	Amos	QC	J9T3W7	819-732-8355	
Gruzen Samton LLC 320 W 13th St 9th Fl *Web:* www.gruzensamton.com	New York	NY	10014	212-477-0900	477-1257
GRW Engineers Inc 801 Corporate Dr *Web:* www.grwinc.com	Lexington	KY	40503	859-223-3999	223-8917
GS Engineering Inc 47500 Us Hwy 41	Houghton	MI	49931	906-482-1235	482-1236
Gstek Inc 911 Cedar Rd Ste A *Web:* www.gstekinc.com	Chesapeake	VA	23322	757-548-1597	
Gts Technologies Inc 441 Friendship Rd *Web:* gtstech.com	Harrisburg	PA	17111	717-236-3006	
Guerin & Vreeland Engineering Inc 272 Rt 206	Flanders	NJ	07836	973-252-9340	
Guido Perla & Associates Inc 701 Fifth Ave Ste 1200 *Web:* www.gpai.com	Seattle	WA	98104	206-768-1515	
Gulf Interstate Engineering Co 16010 Barkers Pt Ln Ste 600 *Web:* www.gie.com	Houston	TX	77079	713-850-3400	850-3579
Gulf Regional Planning Commission 1232 Pass Rd *Web:* grpc.com	Gulfport	MS	39501	228-864-1167	
Gwa Electrical Engineers Inc 168 Laurelhurst Ave *Web:* www.gwainc.net	Columbia	SC	29210	803-252-6919	
Gwin Dobson & Foreman Inc 3121 Fairway Dr *Web:* www.gdfengineers.com	Altoona	PA	16602	814-943-5214	
H E Bergeron Engineers Inc 2605 White Mtn Hwy *Web:* hebengineers.com	North Conway	NH	03860	603-356-6936	
H. T. Lyons Inc 7165 Ambassador Dr *Web:* m.htlyons.com	Allentown	PA	18106	610-530-2600	
Haag Engineering Co 4949 W Royal Ln *TF:* 800-527-0168 ■ *Web:* haagengineering.com	Irving	TX	75063	214-614-6500	
Hahn Engineering Inc 3060 S Dale Mabry Hwy *Web:* www.hahneng.com	Tampa	FL	33629	813-831-8599	
Hakanson Anderson Assoc Inc 3601 Thurston Ave *Web:* www.haa-inc.com	Anoka	MN	55303	763-427-5860	
HAKS Engineers PC 40 Wall St *Web:* www.haks.net	New York	NY	10005	212-747-1997	
Halcrow Yolles 207 Queens Quay W Ste 550 PO Box 132 *Web:* ch2m.com/corporate/about_us/halcrow.asp	Toronto	ON	M5J1A7	416-363-8123	
Haley & Aldrich Inc 465 Medford St Ste 2200 *Web:* www.haleyaldrich.com	Boston	MA	02129	617-886-7400	886-7600
Halff Assoc Inc 1201 N Bowser Rd *Web:* www.halff.com	Richardson	TX	75081	214-346-6200	739-0095
Hall & Foreman Inc 17782 E 17th St Ste 200 *Web:* www.hfinc.com	Tustin	CA	92780	714-665-4500	
Hamilton Engineering & Surveyi 3409 W Lemon St *Web:* www.hamiltonengineering.us	Tampa	FL	33609	813-250-3535	
Hammel Green & Abrahamson Inc 701 Washington Ave N *TF:* 888-442-8255 ■ *Web:* www.hga.com	Minneapolis	MN	55401	612-758-4000	758-4199
Hampton, Lenzini & Renwick Inc 380 Shepard Dr *Web:* www.hlrengineering.com	Elgin	IL	60123	847-697-6700	
Hanson Professional Services Inc 1525 S Sixth St *Web:* www.hanson-inc.com	Springfield	IL	62703	217-788-2450	788-2503
Hardesty & Havover LLP 1501 Broadway Ste 310 *Web:* www.hardesty-hanover.com	New York	NY	10036	212-944-1150	391-0297
Harris & Assoc Inc 1401 Willow Pass Rd **Fax Area Code:* 866 ■ *Web:* www.weareharris.com	Concord	CA	94520	925-827-4900	356-0998*
Harris Civil Engineers LLC 1200 Hillcrest St Ste 200 *Web:* www.harriscivilengineers.com	Orlando	FL	32803	407-629-4777	
Harris Group Inc 300 Elliott Ave W *Web:* www.harrisgroup.com	Seattle	WA	98119	206-494-9400	494-9500
Harris Smariga & Assoc Inc 125 S Carroll St Ste 100	Frederick	MD	21701	301-662-4488	
Hart Crowser Inc 1700 Westlake Ave N Ste 200 *Web:* www.hartcrowser.com	Seattle	WA	98109	206-324-9530	328-5581
Hatch Mott Macdonald Group 27 Bleeker St *Web:* www.hatchmott.com	Millburn	NJ	07041	973-379-3400	376-1072
Hatfield & Dawson 9500 Greenwood Ave N *Web:* hatdaw.com	Seattle	WA	98103	206-783-9151	
Hawk Technology Ltd 8080 Centennial Expy *Web:* www.hawktechnology.com	Rock Island	IL	61201	309-787-6200	
Hawkins & Associates Engineering Inc 436 Mitchell Rd *Web:* www.hawkins-eng.com	Modesto	CA	95354	209-575-4295	
Hayden Consulting Engineers In 12480 SW 68th Ave *Web:* hayden-engineers.com	Tigard	OR	97223	503-968-9994	
Hayes James & Associates Inc 3005 Breckinridge Blvd *Web:* www.hayesjames.com	Duluth	GA	30096	770-923-1600	
Hazen & Sawyer PC 498 Seventh Ave 11th Fl *TF:* 800-858-9876 ■ *Web:* www.hazenandsawyer.com	New York	NY	10018	212-777-8400	614-9049
HC Nutting Co *Terracon Co* 611 Lunken Pk Dr *Web:* www.terracon.com	Cincinnati	OH	45226	513-321-5816	321-0294
Hcs Group Inc 1030 First St E PO Box 873 *Web:* hcsgroup.com	Humble	TX	77338	281-540-4838	
HDR Engineering Inc 8404 Indian Hills Dr **Fax:* Hum Res ■ *TF:* 800-366-4411 ■ *Web:* www.hdrinc.com	Omaha	NE	68114	402-399-1000	548-5015*
Heapy Engineering Inc 1400 W Dorothy Ln *Web:* heapy.com	Dayton	OH	45409	937-224-0861	

Phone Fax

Heatwave Labs Inc
195 Aviation Way Ste 100 Watsonville CA 95076 831-722-9081
Web: www.cathode.com
Heberly & Associates 615 First W Havre MT 59501 406-265-6741
Web: www.heberlyeng.com
Hedges Engineering & Consulting Inc
913 Kincaid Ave Sumner WA 98390 253-891-9365
Heery International Inc 999 Peachtree St NE Atlanta GA 30309 404-881-9880 875-1283
TF: 866-840-3940 ■ *Web:* www.heery.com
Hef Usa Corp 2015 Progress Rd Springfield OH 45505 937-323-2556
Web: www.hefusa.net
Hegemony Inc 520 W Roosevelt Rd Wheaton IL 60187 630-690-5200
Web: hegemony.com
Henderson Paddon & Associates Ltd
945 Third Ave E Ste 212 Owen Sound ON N4K2K8 519-376-7612
Henman Engineering & Machine Inc
3301 W Mt Pleasant Blvd Muncie IN 47302 765-288-8098
Web: henmaneng.com
Henneman Engineering 1605 S State St Champaign IL 61820 217-359-1514
TF: 888-616-0216 ■ *Web:* henneman.com
Herbert Rowland & Grubic Inc (HRG)
369 E Pk Dr Harrisburg PA 17111 717-564-1121 564-1158
Web: www.hrg-inc.com
Hethcoat & Davis Inc
278 Franklin Rd Ste 200 Brentwood TN 37027 615-577-4300
Web: www.hdengr.com
HF Lenz Co 1407 Scalp Ave Johnstown PA 15904 814-269-9300 269-9301
Web: www.hflenz.com
HGM Associates Inc 640 Fifth Ave Council Bluffs IA 51501 712-323-0530
Web: www.hgmonline.com
HGS Engineering Inc 1121 Noble St Anniston AL 36201 256-236-1848
Web: hgsengineeringinc.com
Hi-Tec Industries Inc
1000 Sixth Ave NE Portage La Prairie MB R1N3C5 204-239-4270
Web: www.hitecindustries.ca
Hi-tech Machining & Engineering LLC
1075 E Wieding Rd Tucson AZ 85706 520-889-8325
Web: www.hi-techmachining.net
Hi-Tech Systems Engineering Co
2700 Old Centre Rd Portage MI 49024 269-488-7788
TF: 866-312-1893 ■ *Web:* www.htse.com
Hi-Test Laboratories Inc 1104 Arvon Rd Arvonia VA 23004 434-581-3204
Web: hitestlabs.com
High Mesa Consulting Group Inc
6010 Midway Park Blvd Ne Ste B Albuquerque NM 87109 505-345-4250
Web: highmesacg.com
Hill International Inc 303 Lippincott Ctr Marlton NJ 08053 856-810-6200 810-1309
NYSE: HIL ■ *Web:* www.hillintl.com
HJ Foundation Inc 8275 N W 80 St Miami FL 33166 305-592-8181
Web: www.hjfoundation.com
HKS Inc 1919 McKinney Ave Dallas TX 75201 214-969-5599 969-3397
Web: www.hksinc.com
HL Turner Group Inc, The 27 Locke Rd Concord NH 03301 603-228-1122
TF: 800-305-2289 ■ *Web:* hlturner.com
Hla Engineers Inc 7267 Envoy Ct Dallas TX 75247 214-267-0930 267-0970
Web: hlaengineers.com
HLW International 115 Fifth Ave 5th Fl New York NY 10003 212-353-4600 353-4666
Web: www.hlw.com
HMC Archtiect 3546 Councours St Ontario CA 91764 909-989-9979 483-1400
TF: 800-350-9979 ■ *Web:* www.hmcarchitects.com
Hn Burns Engineering Corp
3275 Progress Dr Ste A Orlando FL 32826 407-273-3770
Web: www.hnbec.com
HNTB Corp 715 Kirk Dr Kansas City MO 64105 816-472-1201 472-4060
Web: www.hntb.com
Hodge Engineering Inc
2615 Jahn Ave Nw Ste E5 Gig Harbor WA 98335 253-857-7055
Web: hodgeengineering.squarespace.com
Hodges Harbin Newberry & Tribble
3920 Arkwright Rd Macon GA 31210 478-743-7175
Web: hhnt.com
Hoffmann & Feige Inc 3 Fallsview Ln Brewster NY 10509 845-277-4401
Web: hoffmann-feige.com
Hogle-Ireland Inc 2860 Michelle Dr Ste 100 Irvine CA 92606 949-553-1427
Holdrege & Kull Consulting Engineers & Geologists
792 Searls Ave Nevada City CA 95959 530-478-1305
Web: holdregeandkull.com
Horizon Environmental Corp
4771 50th St Se Grand Rapids MI 49512 616-554-3210
Web: horizonenv.com
Houle Chevrier Engineering Ltd
32 Steacie Dr Ste Kanata ON K2K2A9 613-836-1422
Web: hceng.ca
Howard R Green Co 8710 Earhart Ln SW Cedar Rapids IA 52404 319-841-4000 841-4012
Web: www.hrgreen.com
HPD, LLC 23563 W Main St Plainfield IL 60544 815-609-2000
TF: 866-362-0993 ■ *Web:* veoliawatertechnologies.com
Hrl Laboratories LLC 3011 Malibu Canyon Rd Malibu CA 90265 310-317-5000 317-5483
Web: www.hrl.com
HRP Associates Inc 197 Scott Swamp Rd Farmington CT 06032 800-246-9021
TF: 800-246-9021 ■ *Web:* www.hrpassociates.com
HSA Engineering Consulting Services Inc
5701 Euper Ln Ste A Fort Smith AR 72903 479-452-8922
Web: hsaconsultants.com
Hubbell Roth & Clark Inc
555 Hulet Dr PO Box 824 Bloomfield Hills MI 48303 248-454-6300 338-2592
Web: www.hrc-engr.com
Huitt-Zollars Inc 1717 McKinney Ave Ste 1400 Dallas TX 75202 214-871-3311 871-0757
TF: 866-667-6572 ■ *Web:* www.huitt-zollars.com
Hull & Assoc Inc 6397 Emerald Pkwy Ste 200 Dublin OH 43016 614-793-8777
Web: hullinc.com
Humantech Inc 1161 Oak Vly Dr Ann Arbor MI 48108 734-663-6707
Web: www.humantech.com

Hunsaker & Assoc Irvine Inc 3 Hughes Irvine CA 92618 949-583-1010 583-0759
Web: www.hunsaker.com
Hussey Gay Bell (HGBD)
329 Commercial Dr Ste 200 Savannah GA 31406 912-354-4626
Web: www.husseygaybell.com
Hydromantis Environmental Software Solutions Inc
407 King St W Hamilton ON L8P1B5 905-522-0012
Web: www.hydromantis.com
Hygun Group Inc 4180 Providence Rd Ste 109 Marietta GA 30062 770-973-0838
Web: www.hygun.com
I E T Inc 3539 Glendale Ave Toledo OH 43614 419-385-1233
Web: www.ieteng.com
I&S Group Inc 115 E Hickory St Ste 300 Mankato MN 56001 507-387-6651
Web: is-grp.com
IC Thomasson Assoc Inc
2950 Kraft Dr Ste 500 Nashville TN 37204 615-346-3400
Web: icthomasson.com
ICF International Inc 9300 Lee Hwy Fairfax VA 22031 703-934-3000 934-3740
NASDAQ: ICFI ■ *Web:* www.icfi.com
iCyt Visionary Bioscience Inc
2100 S Oak St Champaign IL 61820 217-328-9396
IDD Process & Packaging 5450 Tech Cir Moorpark CA 93021 805-529-9890
TF: 800-621-4144 ■ *Web:* www.iddeas.com
IDEO 100 Forest Ave Palo Alto CA 94301 650-289-3400 289-3707
TF: 866-369-9888 ■ *Web:* www.ideo.com
IDS Group Inc 1 Peters Canyon Rd Irvine CA 92606 949-387-8500
Web: idsgi.com
IHI Southwest Technologies Inc
6766 Culebra Rd San Antonio TX 78238 210-256-4100
Web: www.ihiswt.com
Image Custom Engineering 5011 E 5th St Ste 170A Katy TX 77493 281-829-4000
Web: www.image-ces.com
Image Engineering Group Ltd
635 Westport Pkwy Grapevine TX 76051 817-410-2858
Web: www.iegltd.com
Imagine One Technology & Management Ltd
416 Colonial Ave Colonial Beach VA 22443 804-224-1555
Web: www.imagine-one.com
Imata & Assoc Inc 171 Kapiolani St Hilo HI 96720 808-935-6827
Impelsys Inc Broad St 16th Fl Ste 55 New York NY 10004 212-239-4138
Web: www.impelsys.com
Imperial Electronic Assembly Inc
1000 Federal Rd Brookfield CT 06804 203-740-8425 740-8450
Web: www.impea.com
Indus Technology Inc 2243 San Diego Ave San Diego CA 92110 619-299-2555 299-2444
Web: www.industechnology.com
Infomagnetics Technologies Corp
330 Saint Mary Ave Winnipeg MB R3C3Z5 204-989-4630
Web: www.imt.ca
InForm Product Development Inc
1869 Haynes Dr Sun Prairie WI 53590 608-825-4700
Web: www.in-form.com
Infrastructure Alternatives
7888 Childsdale Ne Rockford MI 49341 616-866-1600
Web: infralt.com
Inhand Electronics 30 W Gude Dr Rockville MD 20850 240-558-2014
Web: inhand.com
Innova Technologies Inc 1432 S Jones Blvd Las Vegas NV 89146 702-220-6640
Web: www.innovanv.com
Innovation Genesis LLC 75 Arlington St Ste 500 Boston MA 02116 617-234-0070
Web: www.productgenesis.com
Insitu Inc 118 E Columbia River Way Bingen WA 98605 509-493-8600
Web: insitu.com
INSTRUMAR Limited 39 Pippy Pl 3rd Fl St. John's NL A1B3X2 709-726-8460
Web: www.instrumar.com
Intech Inc 2802 Belle Arbor Ave Chattanooga TN 37406 423-622-3700
Web: www.intech-intl.com
Integral Group Inc 427 13th St Oakland CA 94612 510-663-2070
Web: www.rumseyengineers.com
Integrity Applications Inc (IAI)
15020 Conference Ctr Dr Ste 100 Chantilly VA 20151 703-378-8672 378-8978
Web: www.integrity-apps.com
Intelitech Group Inc, The
12009 Ne 99th St Ste 1480 Vancouver WA 98682 360-260-9780
Web: www.intelitechgroup.com
Intelligent Automation Inc
15400 Calhoun Dr Ste 400 Rockville MD 20855 301-294-5200 294-5201
Web: www.i-a-i.com
INTERA Inc 1812 Centre Creek Dr Ste 300 Austin TX 78754 512-425-2000
Web: www.intera.com
International Electronic Machines Corp (IEM)
850 River St Troy NY 12180 518-268-1636 268-1639
Web: www.iem.net
Intertek Group PLC 801 Travis St Ste 1500 Houston TX 77002 713-407-3500 407-3697
TF: 800-967-5352 ■ *Web:* www.intertek.com
Intrinsix Corp 100 Campus Dr Marlborough MA 01752 508-658-7600
TF: 800-783-0330 ■ *Web:* www.intrinsix.com
Invodane Engineering Ltd 30 Lesmill Rd Unit 2 Toronto ON M3B2T6 416-443-8049
Web: www.invodane.com
Isani Consultants 3143 Yellowstone Blvd Houston TX 77054 713-747-2399
Web: www.isaniconsultants.com
iSense Acquisition LLC 27700 SW 95th Ave Wilsonville OR 97070 503-783-5050
Isine Inc 4155 Veterans Memorial Hwy Ronkonkoma NY 11779 631-913-4400
Web: isine.com
J r d Systems Inc
42450 Hayes Rd Ste 3 Clinton Township MI 48038 586-416-1500
Web: www.jrdsi.com
J-U-B Engineers Inc 250 S Beechwood Ave Ste 201 Boise ID 83709 208-376-7330
Web: jub.com
J.V. Driver Installations Ltd 212- 3601 82 Ave Leduc AB T9E0H7 780-980-5837
Web: www.jvdriver.com
Jacobs Engineering Group Inc
155 N Lake Ave PO Box 7084 Pasadena CA 91101 626-578-3500
NYSE: JEC ■ *Web:* www.jacobs.com

	City	State	Zip	Phone	Fax
Jacobs Technology Inc 600 William Northern Blvd *Web:* www.jacobstechnology.com	Tullahoma	TN	37388	931-455-6400	
James C Hailey & Co 7518 Hwy 70 S Ste 100 *Web:* jchengr.com	Nashville	TN	37221	615-883-4933	883-4937
James Machine Works LLC 1521 Adams St *TF:* 800-259-6104 ■ *Web:* www.jmwinc.net	Monroe	LA	71201	318-322-6104	388-4245
Javan Engineering Inc 465 Maryland Dr Ste 100 *Web:* javanengineering.com	Ft Washington	PA	19034	215-654-7890	
Jenike & Johanson Inc 400 Business Park Dr. *Web:* jenike.com	Tyngsboro	MA	01879	978-649-3300	
Jerry Pittman & Associates Inc 12504 Hwy 57 *Web:* www.jerrypittman.com	Vancleave	MS	39565	228-826-9255	
Jeter Cook & Jepson Architects Inc (JCJ) 120 Huyshope Ave Ste 400 *Web:* www.jcj.com	Hartford	CT	06106	860-247-9226	
Jewell Assoc Engineers Inc 560 Sunrise Dr *Web:* jewellassoc.com	Spring Green	WI	53588	608-588-7484	
JF Taylor Inc 21610 S Essex Dr. *Web:* jfti.com	Lexington Park	MD	20653	301-862-3939	
JMP Engineering Inc 4026 Meadowbrook Dr Unit 143 *TF:* 855-228-8668 ■ *Web:* www.jmpeng.com	London	ON	N6L1C9	519-652-2741	
John A Martin & Association Inc 950 S Grand Ave 4th Fl. *Web:* www.johnmartin.com	Los Angeles	CA	90015	213-483-6490	483-3084
John M. Campbell & Co 1215 Crossroads Blvd *TF:* 800-821-5933 ■ *Web:* www.jmcampbell.com	Norman	OK	73072	405-321-1383	321-4533
Johnson & Pace Inc 1201 W Loop 281 Ste 100 *Web:* www.johnsonpace.com	Longview	TX	75604	903-753-0663	
Johnson Fain 1201 N Broadway *Web:* www.johnsonfain.com	Los Angeles	CA	90012	323-224-6000	224-6030
Johnson Mirmiran & Thompson (JMT) 72 Loveton Cir. *TF:* 800-472-2310 ■ *Web:* www.jmt.com	Sparks	MD	21152	410-329-3100	472-2200
Johnson Spellman & Assoc Inc 6991 Peachtree Industrial Blvd *Web:* jsace.com	Norcross	GA	30092	770-447-4555	
Jones & Henry Engineers Ltd 3103 Executive Pkwy *Web:* jheng.com	Toledo	OH	43606	419-473-9611	
Jones Edmunds & Assoc Inc 730 NE Waldo Rd *Web:* www.jonesedmunds.com	Gainesville	FL	32641	352-377-5821	377-3166
Jp Harvey Engineering Solutions 29 Kings Way *Web:* www.jphes.com	Hampton	VA	23669	757-722-7074	
Jr Gales & Assoc Inc 2704 Brownsville Rd	Pittsburgh	PA	15227	412-885-8885	
Juneau Assoc Inc PC 2100 State St. *Web:* jaipc.com	Granite City	IL	62040	618-877-1400	
JVA Inc 1319 Spruce St *Web:* www.jvajva.com	Boulder	CO	80302	303-444-1951	
Jviation Inc 35 S 400 W Ste 200 *Web:* jviation.com	St George	UT	84770	435-673-4677	
K&M Technology Group LLC 10077 Grogan's Mill Rd Ste 300 *Web:* www.kmtechnology.com	The Woodlands	TX	77380	281-298-6900	
K2 Engineering Services Inc 85 Rangeway Rd *Web:* k2-eng.com	North Billerica	MA	01862	978-600-1333	600-1331
Kanata Energy Group Ltd 1900 112 - Fourth Ave SW Sun Life Plz III - E Twr *Web:* www.kanataenergy.com	Calgary	AB	T2P0H3	587-774-7000	
Kanawha Stone Company Inc 409 Jacobson Dr *Web:* www.kanawhastone.com	Poca	WV	25159	304-755-8271	755-8274
Kap Medical 1395 Pico St *Web:* www.kapmedical.com	Corona	CA	92881	951-340-4360	
Kaplan McLaughlin Diaz 222 Vallejo St *Web:* www.kmdarchitects.com	San Francisco	CA	94111	415-398-5191	394-7158
Kappes, Cassiday & Associates Inc 7950 Security Cir *Web:* kcareno.com	Reno	NV	89506	775-972-7575	
Karges-Faulconbridge Inc 670 County Rd B W *Web:* www.kaa-eng.com	Saint Paul	MN	55113	651-771-0880	
Kavanagh Associates 10585 Rookwood Dr. *Web:* kavassoc.com	San Diego	CA	92131	858-549-6744	
KBA Inc 11201 SE Eighth St Ste 160 *Web:* kbacm.com	Bellevue	WA	98004	425-455-9720	
KBR Inc 601 Jefferson St. *TF:* 888-203-1112 ■ *Web:* www.kbr.com	Houston	TX	77002	713-753-2000	
KCF Technologies Inc 336 S Fraser St *Web:* www.kcftech.com	State College	PA	16801	814-867-4097	
KCI Technologies Inc 936 Ridgebrook Rd *TF:* 800-572-7496 ■ *Web:* kci.com	Sparks	MD	21152	410-316-7800	316-7817
Kebs Inc 2116 Haslett Rd *Web:* www.kebs.com	Haslett	MI	48840	517-339-1014	
Kec Engineering 200 N Sherman Ave. *Web:* www.kecengineering.com	Corona	CA	92882	951-734-3010	
Keith & Schnars PA 6500 N Andrews Ave *TF:* 800-488-1255 ■ *Web:* www.keithandschnars.com	Fort Lauderdale	FL	33309	954-776-1616	771-7690
Kellam Berg Engineering & Surveys Ltd 5800 1a St Sw *Web:* www.kellamberg.com	Calgary	AB	T2H0G1	403-640-0900	
Ken Garner Manufacturing - Rho Inc 1201 E 28th St # B *TF:* 888-454-7207 ■ *Web:* www.kgarnermfg.com	Chattanooga	TN	37404	423-698-6200	
Kennedy Consulting Ltd 205 E University Ave. *Web:* kci-ltd.com	Georgetown	TX	78626	512-864-2833	
Kennedy/Jenks Consultants 303 Second St Ste 300 S *Web:* www.kennedyjenks.com	San Francisco	CA	94107	415-243-2150	896-0999
Kenvirons Inc 452 Versailles Rd *Web:* www.kenvirons.com	Frankfort	KY	40601	502-695-4357	695-4363
Ketchmark & Assoc Inc 145 Tower Dr *Web:* ketchmark.com	Burr Ridge	IL	60527	630-850-7774	
Kier & Wright Civil Engineers 2850 Collier Canyon Rd *Web:* kierwright.com	Livermore	CA	94551	925-245-8788	
Kinectrics Inc 800 Kipling Ave *Web:* www.kinectrics.com	Toronto	ON	M8Z6C4	416-207-6000	
King Engineering Assoc Inc 4921 Memorial Hwy Ste 300 *Web:* www.kingengineering.com	Tampa	FL	33634	813-880-8881	
Kirkham Michael Inc 12700 W Dodge Rd *Web:* www.kirkham.com	Omaha	NE	68154	402-393-5630	255-3850
Kirksey 6909 Portwest Dr *Web:* www.kirksey.com	Houston	TX	77024	713-850-9600	850-7308
Kisinger Campo & Assoc Corp 201 N Franklin St Ste 400 *Web:* kisingercampo.com	Tampa	FL	33602	813-871-5331	871-5135
Kittelson & Associates Inc 610 SW Alder Ste 700 *Web:* www.kittelson.com	Portland	OR	97205	503-228-5230	
KJWW Engineering Consultants PC 623 26th Ave *Web:* www.kjww.com	Rock Island	IL	61201	309-788-0673	786-5967
KKE Architects Inc 300 First Ave N	Minneapolis	MN	55401	612-339-4200	
Klein & Hoffman Inc 150 S Wacker Dr. *Web:* kleinandhoffman.com	Chicago	IL	60606	312-251-1900	
Kleingers Group Inc, The 6305 Centre Park Dr *Web:* kleingers.com	West Chester	OH	45069	513-779-7851	
Klotz Assoc Inc 1160 Dairy Ashford St *Web:* www.klotz.com	Houston	TX	77079	281-589-7257	
KM Ng Assoc Inc 6243 Ih 10 W	San Antonio	TX	78201	210-736-6623	
Kmj Consulting Inc 120 E Lancaster Ave Ste 105 *Web:* www.kmjinc.com	Ardmore	PA	19003	610-896-1996	
Kmm Technologies Inc 2525 Emerson Dr Ste 101 *Web:* kmmtechnologies.com	Frederick	MD	21702	240-286-2321	
Kmn Structural Engineering Inc 321 N Rampart St Ste 145	Orange	CA	92868	714-937-9060	
KMS Solutions LLC 205 S Whiting St Ste 400 *Web:* www.kmssol.com	Alexandria	VA	22304	703-823-8405	
Kna Consulting Engineers Inc 9931 Muirlands Blvd *Web:* www.knaconsulting.com	Irvine	CA	92618	949-462-3200	
Knott Laboratory LLC 7185 S Tucson Way *Web:* www.knottlab.com	Englewood	CO	80112	303-925-1900	
Kohli & Kaliher Assoc Inc 2244 Baton Rouge Ave *Web:* kohlikaliher.com	Lima	OH	45805	419-227-1135	
Kohn Pedersen Fox Assoc PC 11 W 42nd St *Web:* www.kpf.com	New York	NY	10036	212-977-6500	956-2526
Kohrs Lonnemann Heil Engineers Psc 1538 Alexandria Pk.	Ft Thomas	KY	41075	859-442-8050	
Kolar Corp 412 S Washington Ste 200 *Web:* kolarcorp.com	Royal Oak	MI	48067	248-543-0500	
Koops Inc 987 Productions Ct *Web:* koops.com	Holland	MI	49423	616-395-0230	
KPFF Consulting Engineers Inc 1601 Fifth Ave Ste 1600 *Web:* www.kpff.com	Seattle	WA	98101	206-622-5822	622-8130
Kramer Gehlen & Associates Inc 400 Columbia St Ste 240 *Web:* kramer-gehlen.com	Vancouver	WA	98660	360-693-1621	
Kratos Defense & Security Solutions Inc 4820 Eastgate Mall Ste 200 *TF:* 877-548-7911 ■ *Web:* www.kratosdefense.com	San Diego	CA	92121	858-332-3700	812-7301
Krazan & Assoc Inc 215 W Dakota Ave *Web:* www.krazan.com	Clovis	CA	93612	559-348-2200	348-2201
Kroeschell Inc 3222 N Kennicott Ave *Web:* www.kroeschell.com	Arlington Heights	IL	60004	312-649-7980	649-3654
KS Energy Services LLC 19705 W Lincoln Ave *Web:* www.ksenergyservices.com	New Berlin	WI	53146	262-574-5100	
KSA Engineers Inc 140 E Tyler St Ste 600 Ste 600 *TF:* 877-572-3647 ■ *Web:* www.ksaeng.com	Longview	TX	75601	903-236-7700	236-7779
Kta-Tator Inc 115 Technology Dr *TF:* 800-582-4243 ■ *Web:* ktagage.com	Pittsburgh	PA	15275	412-788-1300	788-1306
Kuhlmann Design Group Inc (KDGI) 66 Progress Pkwy *Web:* www.kdginc.com	Maryland Heights	MO	63043	314-434-8898	434-8280
Kuljian Corp 1880 JF Kennedy Blvd. *Web:* www.kuljian.com	Philadelphia	PA	19103	215-243-1900	243-1942
Kumar & Assoc Inc 2390 S Lipan St *Web:* kumarusa.com	Denver	CO	80223	303-742-9700	
L m Engineering Inc 2720 Intertech Dr. *Web:* cybozone.com	Youngstown	OH	44509	206-441-6068	
La Jolla Bioengineering Institute 505 Coast Blvd S Ste 411 *Web:* www.ljbi.org	La Jolla	CA	92037	858-456-7500	
LaBella Associates PC 300 State St Ste 201 *Web:* www.labellapc.com	Rochester	NY	14614	585-454-6110	
Lacasse & Weston Inc 203 Anderson St Ste 201 *Web:* lacasseandweston.com	Portland	ME	04101	207-839-3650	
Land Design Consultants Inc 2700 E Foothill Blvd *Web:* ldcla.com	Pasadena	CA	91107	626-578-7000	

Phone Fax

Land Development Consultants Inc
14201 NE 200th St Ste 100 .... Woodinville WA 98072 425-806-1869
Web: ldccorp.com

Landis Corp 6446 Fairway Ave Se .... Salem OR 97306 503-584-1576
Web: landisconsulting.com

Landmark Consultants Inc
141 Ninth St .... Steamboat Springs CO 80477 970-871-9494
Web: www.landmark-co.com

Landmark Testing & Engineering
795 E Factory Dr .... St George UT 84790 435-986-0566
Web: landmarktesting.com

Lane Engineering LLC 117 Bay St .... Easton MD 21601 410-822-8003
Web: www.leinc.com

Langan Engineering & Environmental Services Inc
619 River Dr Ctr 1 .... Elmwood Park NJ 07407 201-794-6900 794-7501
Web: www.langan.com

Langdon Wilson Architecture Planning Interiors
1055 Wilshire Blvd Ste 1500 .... Los Angeles CA 90017 213-250-1186 482-4654
Web: www.langdonwilson.com

Lanier & Assoc Consulting Engi Neers Inc
4101 Magazine St .... New Orleans LA 70115 504-895-0368
Web: lanier-engineers.com

LaPrairie Crane 235 Front St Ste 209 .... Tumbler Ridge BC V0C2W0 250-242-5561
Web: www.laprairiegroup.com

Larry M Jacobs & Assoc Inc 328 E Gadsden .... Pensacola FL 32501 850-434-0846
Web: lmj-a.com

Larry Snyder & Company Inc
4820 N Towne Centre Dr .... Ozark MO 65721 417-887-6897
Web: lscinc.com

Larson Design Group Inc
1000 Commerce Pk Dr Ste 201 PO Box 487 .... Williamsport PA 17701 570-323-6603 323-9902
TF: 877-323-6603 ■ *Web:* www.larsondesigngroup.com

Larson Engineering Inc
3524 Labore Rd .... White Bear Lake MN 55110 651-481-9120
Web: larsonengr.com

Lathrop Engineering Inc
1101 S Winchester Blvd .... San Jose CA 95128 408-260-2111
Web: www.lathropeng.com

Lauren Engineers & Constructors Inc
901 S First St .... Abilene TX 79602 325-670-9660
TF: 800-433-7300 ■ *Web:* www.laurenec.com

Lawson-Fisher Associates PC
525 W Washington Ave Ste 200 .... South Bend IN 46601 574-234-3167
Web: lawson-fisher.com

LBA Group Inc 3400 Tupper Dr .... Greenville NC 27834 252-757-0279 752-9155
TF: 800-522-4464 ■ *Web:* www.lbagroup.com

Lc Engineers Inc 1471 Pinewood St Bldg 3 .... Rahway NJ 07065 732-340-9190
Web: www.lcengineers.com

Lee Burkhart Liu Inc
13335 Maxella Ave .... Marina del Rey CA 90292 310-829-2249 829-1736

Leedy & Petzold Assoc LLC
12970 W Bluemound Rd .... Elm Grove WI 53122 262-860-1544

Lefler Engineering Inc 1651 Second St .... San Rafael CA 94901 415-456-4220
Web: leflerengineering.com

Leighton Group Inc 17781 Cowan St .... Irvine CA 92614 949-250-1421 250-1114
Web: leightongeo.com

LeMessurier Consultants
1380 Soldiers Field Rd .... Boston MA 02135 617-868-1200
Web: www.lemessurier.com

Leo A Daly 8600 Indian Hills Dr .... Omaha NE 68114 402-391-8111 391-8111
Web: www.leoadaly.com

Lerch Bates Inc 8089 S Lincoln St Ste 300 .... Littleton CO 80122 303-795-7956
Web: www.lerchbates.com

Lesco Design & Mfg Company Inc
1120 Ft Pickens Rd .... Lagrange KY 40031 502-222-7101
Web: lescodesign.com

Lewis Innovative Technologies Inc
110 Johnston St SE .... Decatur AL 35601 256-905-0775
Web: lewisinnovative.com

Lexington Technologies in 99 Rome St .... Farmingdale NY 11735 631-755-8660
Web: lexingtontech.net

LHB Inc 21 W Superior St Ste 500 .... Duluth MN 55802 218-727-8446
Web: www.lhbcorp.com

Life Cycle Engineering Inc
4360 Corporate Rd .... N Charleston SC 29405 843-744-7110
Web: lce.com

Lilker Associates Consulting Engineers PC
1001 Ave of the Americas Fl 9 .... New York NY 10018 212-695-1000
Web: www.lilker.com

Lincus Inc 8727 S Priest Dr .... Tempe AZ 85284 480-598-8431
Web: lincusenergy.com

Linebach - Funkhouser Inc 114 Fairfax Ave .... Louisville KY 40207 502-895-5009
Web: linebachfunkhouser.com

Linfield Hunter & Junius 3608 18th St 200 .... Metairie LA 70002 504-833-5300
Web: www.lhjunius.com

Link Technologies 9500 Hillwood Dr Ste 112 .... Las Vegas NV 89134 702-233-8703
Web: www.linktechconsulting.com

Lionakis Beaumont Design Group Inc
1919 19th St .... Sacramento CA 95811 916-558-1900 558-1919
Web: lionakis.com

LiRo Group 3 Aerial Way .... Syosset NY 11791 516-938-5476 937-5421
Web: www.liro.com

LJB Inc 2500 Newmark Dr .... Miamisburg OH 45342 937-259-5000 259-5100
TF: 866-552-3536 ■ *Web:* www.ljbinc.com

Ljm Engineering Group Inc 439 Rte Hwy E 46 .... Rockaway NJ 07866 973-586-3004
Web: www.ljmengineering.com

LMN Architects 801 Second Ave Ste 501 .... Seattle WA 98104 206-682-3460 343-9388
Web: www.lmnarchitects.com

Lmw Engineering Group LLC 2539 Brunswick Ave .... Linden NJ 07036 908-862-7600
Web: www.ftcny.com

Locating Inc 2575 Westside Pkwy Ste 100 .... Alpharetta GA 30004 678-461-3900
Web: www.locatinginc.com

Phone Fax

Lochsa Engineering Inc
6345 S Jones Blvd Ste 100 .... Las Vegas NV 89118 702-365-9312
TF: 866-606-9784 ■ *Web:* www.lochsa.com

Lockwood Andrews & Newnam Inc
2925 Briar Pk Dr .... Houston TX 77042 713-266-6900 266-2089
Web: www.lan-inc.com

Lockwood Kessler & Bartlett Inc 1 Aerial Way .... Syosset NY 11791 516-938-0600 931-6344
Web: www.lkbinc.com

Logistics Value Integrations Inc
3828 Farr Oak Cir .... Fairfax VA 22030 703-934-4218
Web: www.logvalu.com

Lohan Caprile Goettsch Architects
Goettsch Partners 224 S Michigan Ave 17th Fl .... Chicago IL 60604 312-356-0600 356-0601
Web: www.gpchicago.com

Long Engineering Inc
2550 Heritage Court Ste 100 .... Atlanta GA 30339 770-951-2495
Web: www.longeng.com

Looney Ricks Kiss Architects
175 Toyota Plz Ste 600 .... Memphis TN 38103 901-521-1440
Web: www.lrk.com

LORE Product Design Engineering & Development Inc
36 Eglinton Ave W Ste 707 .... Toronto ON M4R1A1 416-489-9008
Web: www.designlore.com

Louis Berger Group Inc 412 Mt Kemble Ave .... Morristown NJ 07960 973-407-1000
Web: www.louisberger.com

Loyola Enterprises Inc
2984 S Lynnhaven Rd Ste 101 .... Virginia Beach VA 23452 757-498-6118
Web: www.loyola.com

LPA Inc 5161 California Ave Ste 100 .... Irvine CA 92617 949-261-1001 260-1190
Web: www.lpainc.com

Lps Integration Inc
230 Great Cir Rd Ste 218 .... Nashville TN 37228 615-254-0581
Web: www.lpsintegration.com

LRL Associates Ltd 5430 Canotek Rd .... Ottawa ON K1J9G2 613-842-3434
Web: www.lrl.ca

LS3P Assoc Ltd 205 1/2 King St .... Charleston SC 29401 843-577-4444 722-4789
Web: www.ls3p.com

LTL Consultants Ltd 1 Town Ctr Dr .... Oley PA 19547 610-987-9290
Web: www.ltlconsultants.com

Lumos & Assoc Inc 800 E College Pkwy .... Carson City NV 89706 775-883-7077 883-7114
TF: 800-621-7155 ■ *Web:* www.lumosinc.com

Lutz, Daily & Brain LLC
6400 Glenwood St .... Shawnee Mission KS 66202 913-831-0833
Web: www.ldbeng.com

LVM-JEGEL 1821 Albion Rd Unit 7 .... Toronto ON M9W5W8 416-213-1060

M & H Enterprises Inc 19450 Hwy 249 Ste 600 .... Houston TX 77070 281-664-7222
Web: mhes.com

M Gingerich Gereaux & Assoc
240 N Industrial Dr .... Bradley IL 60915 815-939-4921

M Neils Engineering Inc 100 Howe Ave .... Sacramento CA 95825 916-923-4400
Web: mneilsengineering.com

M S Benbow & Associates Professional Engineering Corp
2450 Severn Ave .... Metairie LA 70001 504-832-2000
Web: www.msbenbow.com

M Squared Engineering LLC
W62n215 Washington Ave .... Cedarburg WI 53012 262-376-4246
Web: msquaredengineering.com

M W Consulting Engineers LLC
222 Wall St Ste 200 .... Spokane WA 99201 509-838-9020
Web: www.mwengineers.com

M-E Engineers Inc 10055 W 43rd Ave .... Wheat Ridge CO 80033 303-421-6655 421-0331
Web: www.me-engineers.com

M/E Engineering PC 150 N Chestnut St .... Rochester NY 14604 585-288-5590 288-0233
Web: www.meengineering.com

M3 Engineering & Technology Corp
2051 W Sunset Rd .... Tucson AZ 85704 520-293-1488
Web: m3eng.com

Ma Engineers Inc
5160 Carroll Canyon Rd Ste 200 .... San Diego CA 92121 858-200-0030
Web: www.ma-engr.com

Macarthur Associated Consultants LLC
25 NW 146th St Ste 250E .... Oklahoma City OK 73013 405-848-2471
Web: www.macokc.com

Macaulay-Brown Inc 4021 Executive Dr .... Dayton OH 45430 937-426-3421 426-5364
TF: 800-669-4000 ■ *Web:* www.macb.com

Macina Bose Copeland & Assoc Inc
1035 Central Pkwy N .... San Antonio TX 78232 210-545-1122

Macintosh Engineering 2 Mill Rd Ste 100 .... Wilmington DE 19806 302-252-9200
Web: macintosheng.com

MacKay & Somps (MSCE) 5142 Franklin Dr Ste B .... Pleasanton CA 94588 925-225-0690 225-0698
Web: www.msce.com

Macritchie Engineering Inc 197 Quincy Ave .... Braintree MA 02184 781-848-4464
Web: macritchie.net

Madsen Kneppers & Assoc Inc
100 Pringle Ave Ste 340 .... Walnut Creek CA 94596 925-934-3235
Web: mkainc.com

Magnusson Klemencic Assoc Inc
1301 Fifth Ave Ste 3200 .... Seattle WA 98101 206-292-1200 292-1201
Web: www.mka.com

Mahlum Architects Inc 71 Columbia St 4Fl .... Seattle WA 98104 206-441-4151 441-0478
Web: www.mahlum.com

Mainelli Wagner & Associates Inc
6920 Van Dorn St Ste A .... Lincoln NE 68506 402-421-1717
Web: www.mwaeng.com

Malouf Engineering International Inc
17950 Preston Rd Ste 720 .... Dallas TX 75252 972-783-2578 783-2583
Web: www.maloufengineering.com

Management Consulting Inc
1961 Diamond Springs Rd .... Virginia Beach VA 23455 757-460-0879 457-9337
TF: 888-892-0787 ■ *Web:* www.manconinc.com

Manders Merighi Portadin Farrell Architects LLC
1138 E Chestnut Ave Bldg 4 .... Vineland NJ 08360 856-696-9155

Mannik & Smith Group Inc 1800 Indian Wood Cir .... Maumee OH 43537 419-891-2222
TF: 888-891-6321 ■ *Web:* manniksmithgroup.com

Phone Fax

Map Assoc Inc Dba North Star Engineering
111 Mission Ranch Blvd. Chico CA 95926 530-893-1600
MAR Inc 1803 Research Blvd Ste 204. Rockville MD 20850 301-231-0100 453-9871*
*Fax Area Code: 240 ■ Web: www.marinc.com
March Consulting Associates Inc
200 201 21st St E. Saskatoon SK S7K0B8 306-651-6330
Web: www.marchconsulting.com
Maren Engineering 111 W Taft Dr South Holland IL 60473 708-333-6250
TF: 800-875-1038 ■ Web: marenengineering.com
Marine Systems Corp 70 Fargo St Seaport Ctr Boston MA 02210 617-542-3345 542-2461
Web: www.mscorp.net
Mark Thomas & Company Inc
2290 N First St Ste 304 San Jose CA 95131 408-453-5373 453-5390
Web: www.markthomas.com
MarketCounsel LLC 61 W Palisade Ave Englewood NJ 07631 201-705-1200
Web: www.marketcounsel.com
Marshall Miller & Assoc
5415 SW Westgate Dr Ste 100 Portland VA 97221 503-419-2500 419-2600
Web: cardno.com
Martenson & Eisele Inc 1377 Midway Rd. Menasha WI 54952 920-731-0381
Web: www.martenson-eisele.com
Martin Mechanical Design Inc
702 28th Ave N Ste 200 Fargo ND 58102 701-293-7957
Martronic Engineering Inc
80 W Cochran St Ste B Simi Valley CA 93065 805-583-0808
TF: 800-960-0808 ■ Web: meilaser.com
Marx | Okubo Associates Inc
455 Sherman St Ste 200 Denver CO 80203 303-861-0300
Web: www.marxokubo.com
Maschoff Design Engineering Inc
1325 Kenilworth Dr. Woodbury MN 55125 651-578-3565
Web: www.mdeeng.com
Maser Consulting PA
331 Newman Springs Rd Ste203 Red Bank NJ 07701 732-383-1950 383-1984
Web: www.maserconsulting.com
Materials and Electrochemical Research Corp
7960 S Kolb Rd Tucson AZ 85706 520-574-1980
Web: www.merholdings.com
Matis Warfield Inc 10540 York Rd Ste M. Cockeysville MD 21030 410-683-7004
Web: matiswarfield.com
Matrix Computer Solutions Inc
3001 Bridgeway Ste K314. Sausalito CA 94965 415-331-3600
Web: www.matrixcomp.net
Matrix Design Group Inc 1601 Blake St Ste 200 Denver CO 80202 303-572-0200
Web: www.matrixdesigngroup.com
Matrix Engineering Pllc
112 Walter Jetton Blvd Paducah KY 42001 270-442-5600
Web: matrixengineer.com
Mattern & Craig Inc 701 First St SW. Roanoke VA 24016 540-345-9342
Web: matternandcraig.com
MBH Architects 2470 Mariner Sq Loop Alameda CA 94501 510-865-8663 865-1611
Web: www.mbharch.com
MBS Assoc Inc 7800 E Kemper Rd Ste 160. Cincinnati OH 45249 513-645-1600 680-4587
TF: 888-469-9301 ■ Web: www.mbsassociates.com
Mc Donough Engineering Corp
5625 Schumacher Ln Houston TX 77057 713-975-9990
Web: www.mectx.com
MC Squared Inc 17 Harbourton Ridge Dr Pennington NJ 08534 609-474-8100
Web: www.mcsqd.com
McClure Engineering Associates Inc
4700 Kennedy Dr East Moline IL 61244 309-792-9305
Web: www.mcclureengineering.com
Mccool Carlson Green Inc
421 W First Ave Ste 300 Anchorage AK 99501 907-563-8474
Web: mcgalaska.com
McCormick Taylor & Assoc Inc
2 Commerce Sq 10th Fl Philadelphia PA 19103 215-592-4200 592-0682
Web: www.mccormicktaylor.com
McCrone Inc 20 Ridgely Ave Annapolis MD 21401 410-267-8621
Web: mccrone-engineering.com
Mcdaniel Tech Services Inc
2005 N Yellowood Ave Broken Arrow OK 74012 918-294-1628
Web: www.mcdanieltsi.com
McDonough Bolyard Peck Inc (MBP)
3040 Williams Dr Williams Plz 1 Ste 300 Fairfax VA 22031 703-641-9088 641-8965
TF: 800-898-9088 ■ Web: www.mbpce.com
MCG Architecture 111 Pacifica Ste 280 Irvine CA 92618 949-553-1117
Web: www.mcgarchitecture.com
McGill Smith Punshon Inc
3700 Park 42 Dr Ste 190B Cincinnati OH 45241 513-759-0004
TF: 800-759-8065 ■ Web: www.mcgillsmithpunshon.com
Mcgoodwin Williams & Yates Inc (MWY)
302 E Millsap Rd Fayetteville AR 72703 479-443-3404 443-4340
Web: www.mwyusa.com
McKim & Creed PA 243 N Front St. Wilmington NC 28401 910-343-1048 251-8282
Web: www.mckimcreed.com
Mckinney & Company Inc 100 S Railroad Ave Ashland VA 23005 804-798-1451
Web: mckinney-usa.com
McLaren Performance Technologies Inc
32233 W Eight Mile Rd. Livonia MI 48152 248-477-6240 477-3349
Web: www.linamar.com
McLaughlin Research Corp
132 Johnnycake Hill Rd Middletown RI 02842 401-849-4010
TF: 800-556-7154 ■ Web: www.mrcds.com
Mcmahon Assoc Inc
425 Commerce Dr Ste 200 Fort Washington PA 19034 215-283-9444
Web: mcmahonassociates.com
McMahon Group 1445 McMahon Dr. Neenah WI 54956 920-751-4200 751-4284
Web: www.mcmgrp.com
Mcmillen Engineering Inc
115 Wayland Smith Dr Uniontown PA 15401 724-439-8110
Web: mcmilleng.com
MCR LLC 2010 Corporate Ridge Ste 350. McLean VA 22102 703-506-4600 506-8601
Web: www.mcri.com

Phone Fax

Mcs Advertising 4110 Progress Blvd Ste 1c. Peru IL 61354 815-224-3011
Web: www.mcsadv.com
Mctish Kunkel & Assoc 3500 Winchester Rd Allentown PA 18104 610-841-2700
Web: mctish.com
Mcveigh & Mangum Engineering Inc
9133 Rg Skinner Pkwy Jacksonville FL 32256 904-483-5200
Web: mcveighmangum.com
MDA Engineering Inc 1415 Holland Rd Maumee OH 43537 419-893-3141
MDA Information Systems Inc
6011 Executive Blvd Rockville MD 20852 240-833-8200 833-8201
TF: 800-642-1687 ■ Web: www.mdafederal.com
Mead & Hunt Inc 6501 Watts Rd. Madison WI 53719 608-273-6380 273-6391
Web: www.meadhunt.com
Mecanica Solutions Inc
6300 Cote-de-Liesse Ste 200 Montreal QC H4T1E3 514-340-1818
Web: www.mecanicasolutions.com
Meers Engineering Inc
209 S Danville Dr Ste B 200 Abilene TX 79605 325-691-1200 691-1206
Web: www.meersengineering.com
MEI Technologies Inc 18050 Saturn Ln Ste 300 Houston TX 77058 281-283-6200
Web: www.meitechinc.com
Meier Enterprises Inc 12 W. Kennewick Ave. Kennewick WA 99336 509-735-1589
TF: 800-239-7589 ■ Web: meierinc.com
Melick-Tully & Assoc PC
117 Canal Rd South Bound Brook NJ 08880 732-356-3400
Web: melick-tully.com
Mellor Engineering Inc 887 North 100 East Ste 1 Lehi UT 84043 801-768-0658
Web: mellorengineering.com
Mendoza Ribas Farinas & Assoc
6265 Executive Blvd Rockville MD 20852 301-468-8882
Meridian West Consultants LLC 7603 S Main St Midvale UT 84047 801-542-7082
Web: www.meridian-west.com
Merrick & Co 2450 S Peoria St Aurora CO 80014 303-751-0741 751-2581
TF: 800-544-1714 ■ Web: www.merrick.com
Merritt Environmental Consulting Corp
77 Arkay Dr. Hauppauge NY 11788 631-617-6200
Web: merrittec.com
Mesa Assoc Inc PO Box 196. Madison AL 35758 256-258-2100 258-2103
Web: www.mesainc.com
Met-Chem Canada Inc
555, Blvd Rene-Levesque Ouest 3e etage Montreal QC H2Z1B1 514-288-5211
Web: www.met-chem.com
Met-scan Canada Ltd 30 Kern Rd Ste 104. Toronto ON M3B1T1 416-391-2200
Web: www.met-scan.com
Meta Environmental Inc 49 Clarendon St. Watertown MA 02472 617-923-4662
Web: metaenv.com
Methane Specialists 621 Via Alondra Ste 611 Camarillo CA 93012 805-987-5356
Web: methanespecialists.com
Metro-Can Construction Ltd
10470 152 St Ste 520. Surrey BC V3R0Y3 604-583-1174
Web: www.metrocan.com
Mge Engineering Inc 7415 Greenhaven Dr Sacramento CA 95831 916-421-1000
Web: www.mgeeng.com
MHC Engineers Inc 150 Eighth St San Francisco CA 94103 415-512-7141
Web: mhcengr.com
Michael Baker Corp
100 Airsite Dr Airsite Business Pk Moon Township PA 15108 412-269-6300 463-0503*
NYSE: BKR ■ *Fax Area Code: 757 ■ TF: 800-553-1153 ■ Web: www.mbakercorp.com
Michaud Cooley Erickson & Assoc Inc
1200 Metropolitan Ctr Ste 1200 Minneapolis MN 55402 612-339-4941 339-8354
Web: www.michaudcooley.com
Mickle Wagner Coleman Inc
3434 Country Club Ave Fort Smith AR 72903 479-649-8484
Web: www.mwc-engr.com
Microlynx Systems Ltd 1925 18 Ave Ne Ste 107 Calgary AB T2E7T8 403-275-7346
TF: 866-835-4332 ■ Web: www.microlynxsystems.com
Middough Assoc Inc 1901 E 13th St Cleveland OH 44114 216-367-6000 367-6020*
*Fax: Hum Res ■ Web: www.middough.com
Mide Technology Corp 200 Boston Ave Medford MA 02155 781-306-0609
Web: mide.com
Midrex Technologies
2725 Water Ridge Pkwy Ste 100 Charlotte NC 28217 704-373-1600 373-1611
Web: www.midrex.com
Mikro Systems Inc
1180 Seminole Trl Ste 220 Charlottesville VA 22901 434-244-6480
Web: www.mikrosystems.com
Mikros Engineering Inc
8755 Wyoming Ave N. Brooklyn Park MN 55445 763-424-4642
TF: 800-394-5499 ■ Web: www.mikros.com
Milhouse Engineering & Construction Inc
60 E Van Buren St Ste 1501 Chicago IL 60605 312-987-0061
Web: milhouseinc.com
Milian & Swain Associates Inc 2025 SW 32nd Ave Miami FL 33145 305-441-0123
Web: www.milianswain.com
Miller Engineers & Scientists
5308 S 12th St Sheboygan WI 53081 920-458-6164
TF: 800-969-7013 ■ Web: www.startwithmiller.com
Miller Pacific Engineering Group
504 Redwood Blvd Ste 220 Novato CA 94947 415-382-3444
Web: www.millerpac.com
Millogic Ltd 89 Cambridge St Burlington MA 01803 339-234-5700
Web: millogic.com
Mills & Assoc Inc 3242 Henderson Blvd Tampa FL 33609 813-876-5869
Mine Development Assoc 210 S Rock Blvd Reno NV 89502 775-856-5700
Web: www.mda.com
Minnetronix Inc 1635 Energy Park Dr. St Paul MN 55108 651-917-4060
Web: minnetronix.com
Missman Inc 1011 27th Ave PO Box 6040 Rock Island IL 61201 309-788-7644 788-7691
TF: 800-969-3029 ■ Web: missman.com
Mkec Engineering Consultants Inc
411 N Webb Rd Wichita KS 67206 316-684-9600
Web: mkec.com

Company / Address	City	State	Zip	Phone	Fax
Modern Process Equipment Inc 3125 S Kolin Ave *Web:* mpechicago.com	Chicago	IL	60623	773-254-3929	
Modern Technology Solutions Inc (MTSI) 5285 Shawnee Rd Ste 400 *Web:* www.mtsi-va.com	Alexandria	VA	22312	703-564-3800	
Modjeski & Masters Inc 100 Sterling Pkwy Ste 302 *TF:* 888-663-5375 ■ *Web:* www.modjeski.com	Mechanicsburg	PA	17050	717-790-9565	790-9564
Moffatt & Nichol Engineers 3780 Kilroy Airport Way # 750 *TF:* 888-399-6609 ■ *Web:* www.moffattnichol.com	Long Beach	CA	90806	562-590-6500	590-6512
Mohr & Assoc Inc 1324 N Hearne Ave Ste 301 *Web:* www.mohrandassoc.com	Shreveport	LA	71107	318-686-7190	
Monte R Lee & Co 100 NW 63rd St Ste 100 *Web:* www.mrleng.com	Oklahoma City	OK	73116	405-842-2405	
Moody Nolan Inc 300 Spruce St Ste 300 *Web:* www.moodynolan.com	Columbus	OH	43215	614-461-4664	280-8881
Moon-matz Ltd 1435 Hurontario St *Web:* moon-matz.com	Mississauga	ON	L5G3H5	905-274-7556	
Moore Bass Consulting Inc 805 N Gadsden St *Web:* moorebass.com	Tallahassee	FL	32303	850-222-5678	
Moreland & Altobelli Assoc Inc 2211 Beaver Ruin Rd Ste 190 *Web:* www.maai.net	Norcross	GA	30071	770-263-5945	263-0166
Morell Engineering & Development LLC 112 N Marion St *Web:* www.morellengineering.com	Athens	AL	35611	256-867-4957	
Morgan-Keller Inc 70 Thomas Johnson Dr Ste 200 *TF:* 800-725-5051 ■ *Web:* www.morgankeller.com	Frederick	MD	21702	301-663-0626	
Morley & Assoc Inc 4800 Rosebud Ln *Web:* www.morleyandassociates.com	Newburgh	IN	47630	812-464-9585	464-2514
Morris Architects 1001 Fannin St Ste 300 *Web:* www.morrisarchitects.com	Houston	TX	77002	713-622-1180	
Morrison Hershfield Group Inc 125 Commerce Valley Dr W Ste 300 *TF:* 888-649-4730 ■ *Web:* www.morrisonhershfield.com	Markham	ON	L3T7W4	416-499-3110	
Morrison-Maierle Inc 1 Engineering Pl *Web:* www.m-m.net	Helena	MT	59604	406-442-3050	
Moseley Technical Services Inc 7500 S Memorial Pkwy Ste 215-R *Web:* www.moseleytechnical.com	Huntsville	AL	35802	256-880-0446	
Mpe Engineering Ltd Ste 260 E Atrium 2635 37 Ave NE *Web:* www.mpe.ab.ca	Calgary	AB	T1Y5Z6	403-329-3442	
MS Consultants Inc 333 E Federal St *Web:* www.msconsultants.com	Youngstown	OH	44503	330-744-5321	744-5256
MS Technology Inc 137 Union Vly Rd *Web:* mstechnology.com	Oak Ridge	TN	37830	865-483-0895	
MSA Consulting Inc 34200 Bob Hope Dr *Web:* www.msaconsultinginc.com	Rancho Mirage	CA	92270	760-320-9811	
MSA Professional Services Inc 1230 South Blvd *Web:* msa-ps.com	Baraboo	WI	53913	608-356-2771	
MSE Power Systems Inc 403 New Karner Rd *Web:* www.msepower.com	Albany	NY	12205	518-452-7718	452-7716
Muermann Engineering LLC 116 Fremont St *Web:* www.me-pe.com	Kiel	WI	53042	920-894-7800	
Mueser Rutledge Consulting Engineers (MRCE) 14 Penn Plaza 225 W 34th St 6th Fl *Web:* www.mrce.com	New York	NY	10122	917-339-9300	339-9400
Muller Engineering Company Inc 777 S Wadsworth Blvd *Web:* www.mullereng.com	Lakewood	CO	80226	303-988-4939	
Multax Systems Inc 505 N Sepulveda Blvd Ste 7 *TF:* 800-888-0199 ■ *Web:* www.multax.net	Manhattan Beach	CA	90266	310-379-8398	379-1142
Municipal Infrastructure Group Ltd, The 2300 Steeles Ave W Ste 120 *Web:* www.tmig.ca	Vaughan	ON	L4K5X6	905-738-5700	
Mustang Engineering LP 16001 Pk Ten Pl *Web:* www.mustangeng.com	Houston	TX	77084	713-215-8000	215-8506
Mustang Technology Group Lp 6900 K Ave *Web:* mustangtechnology.com	Plano	TX	75074	972-747-0707	
Mw Davis Dumas & Associates Inc 2720 Third Ave S *Web:* www.mwdda.com	Birmingham	AL	35233	205-252-0246	
MWH Americas Inc 370 Interlocken Blvd *Web:* mwhglobal.com	Broomfield	CO	80021	303-410-4000	
Mwl Engineering Corp 6825 Sw 81st St *Web:* mwleng.com	Miami	FL	33143	305-661-3357	
N K Bhandari, Consulting Engineers PC 1005 W Fayette St Ste 4A *Web:* nkbpc.com	Syracuse	NY	13204	315-428-1177	
Nadel Architects 1990 S Bundy Dr Ste 400 *Web:* www.nadelarc.com	Los Angeles	CA	90025	310-826-2100	826-0182
Nadine International Inc 2570 Matheson Blvd E Ste 110 *Web:* www.nadineintl.on.ca	Mississauga	ON	L4W4Z3	905-602-1850	
Naik Consulting Group p C 200 Metroplex Dr Ste 403 *Web:* www.naikgroup.com	Edison	NJ	08817	732-777-0030	
Nalpro Business Solutions LLC Brier Hill Ct Bldg C *TF:* 888-868-6360 ■ *Web:* www.nalpro.com	East Brunswick	NJ	08816	732-390-1400	
Nanohmics Inc 6201 E Oltorf St *Web:* nanohmics.com	Austin	TX	78741	512-389-9990	
Nasland Engineering 4740 Rufner St *Web:* www.nasland.com	San Diego	CA	92111	858-292-7770	
Nathan D. Maier Consulting Engineers Inc 8080 Park Ln Two NorthPark Ste 600 *Web:* www.ndmce.com	Dallas	TX	75231	214-739-4741	
National Security Technologies LLC 2621 Losee Rd *Web:* www.nstec.com	Las Vegas	NV	89030	702-295-1000	295-2448
NBBJ 223 Yale Ave N *Web:* www.nbbj.com	Seattle	WA	98109	206-223-5555	621-2300
NCA Architects PA 1306 Rio Grande Blvd NW	Albuquerque	NM	87104	505-255-6400	
Neel-Schaffer Inc 125 S Congress St Ste 1100 *Web:* www.neel-schaffer.com	Jackson	MS	39201	601-948-3178	948-3071
Neff Engineering Co 7114 Innovation Blvd	Fort Wayne	IN	46818	260-489-6007	489-6204
Neil O. Anderson & Associates Inc 902 Industrial Way *Web:* noanderson.com	Lodi	CA	95240	209-367-3701	
Nesbitt Engineering Inc (NEI) 227 N Upper St *Web:* www.nei-ky.com	Lexington	KY	40507	859-233-3111	259-2717
Netxar Technologies Inc 17 Calle Ponce *Web:* www.netxar.com	San Juan	PR	00917	787-765-0058	
Neundorfer Inc 4590 Hamann Pkwy *Web:* www.neundorfer.com	Willoughby	OH	44094	440-942-8990	
New England Construction Company Inc 293 Bourne Ave *Web:* www.neconstruction.com	Rumford	RI	02916	401-434-0112	
New Holland Engineering 43 E Front St *Web:* gutterhangers.net	New Holland	OH	43145	740-495-5200	
New Tech Global (NTG) 1030 Regional Pk Dr *Web:* www.ntglobal.com	Houston	TX	77060	281-951-4330	951-8719
Newcomb & Boyd 303 Peachtree Ctr Ave NE Ste 525 *Web:* www.newcomb-boyd.com	Atlanta	GA	30303	404-730-8400	730-8401
Nextgen Networks Inc 200 Katonah Ave Ste A *TF:* 866-639-8436 ■ *Web:* www.nninet.com	Katonah	NY	10536	866-639-8436	
Nexus Technologies Inc 11 National Ave *Web:* www.nexus-tech.net	Fletcher	NC	28732	828-681-2844	
Nfra Inc 77 E Thomas Rd Ste 200 *Web:* www.nfrainc.us	Phoenix	AZ	85012	602-277-0967	
Niles Bolton Assoc Inc (NBA) 3060 Peachtree Rd NW Ste 600 *Web:* www.nilesbolton.com	Atlanta	GA	30305	404-365-7600	365-7610
Ninyo & Moore 5710 Ruffin Rd *TF:* 800-427-0401 ■ *Web:* www.ninyoandmoore.com	San Diego	CA	92123	858-576-1000	576-9600
Nobis Engineering Inc 18 Chenell Dr *Web:* nobiseng.com	Concord	NH	03301	603-224-4182	
Noble Technologies Corp 2020 Noble Dr *Web:* www.nobletek.com	Wooster	OH	44691	330-287-1500	
Nomerel L l c 7107 S Yale Ave Ste 306 *Web:* www.nomerel.com	Tulsa	OK	74136	918-770-4099	
NORAM Engineering & Constructors Ltd 200 Granville St Ste 1800 *Web:* www.noram-eng.com	Vancouver	BC	V6C1S4	604-681-2030	
Nordmin Engineering Ltd 160 Logan Ave *Web:* nordmin.com	Thunder Bay	ON	P7A6R1	807-683-1730	
Northern Digital 5555 Business Pk *Web:* ndi.us	Bakersfield	CA	93309	661-322-6044	
Northwest Hydraulic Consultants 16300 Christensen Rd Ste 350 *Web:* nhcweb.com	Seattle	WA	98188	206-241-6000	
Northwestern Engineering Co PO Box 2624 *Web:* www.nwemanagement.com	Rapid City	SD	57709	605-394-3310	341-2558
Notkin Hawaii Inc 738 Kaheka St Ste 301 *Web:* www.notkinhi.com	Honolulu	HI	96814	808-941-6600	
Nova Group Inc 185 Devlin Rd *Web:* www.novagrp.com	Napa	CA	94558	707-257-3200	
Nova Pole International Inc 19433 96th Ave Ste 102 *TF:* 866-874-8889 ■ *Web:* www.novapole.com	Surrey	BC	V4N4C4	604-881-0090	
Novariant Inc 45700 Northport Loop E *Web:* www.novariant.com	Fremont	CA	94538	510-933-4800	933-4801
NTB Assoc Inc 525 Louisiana Ave *Web:* ntbainc.com	Shreveport	LA	71101	318-226-9199	
Nuezra 2620 Augustine Dr Ste 101	Santa Clara	CA	95054	408-492-9856	
Nussbaumer & Clarke Inc 3556 Lk Shore Rd Ste 500 *Web:* www.nussclarke.com	Buffalo	NY	14219	716-827-8000	
NV5 2525 Natomas Pk Dr Ste 300 *TF:* 877-941-2068 ■ *Web:* www.nv5.com	Sacramento	CA	95833	916-641-9100	641-9222
O'Brien & Gere Engineers Inc 333 W Washington St *Web:* www.obg.com	East Syracuse	NY	13202	315-956-6100	463-7554
O'Connell Robertson & Associates Inc 811 Barton Springs Rd Ste 900 *Web:* www.oconnellrobertson.com	Austin	TX	78704	512-478-7286	
O'day Consultants Inc 2710 Loker Ave W Ste 100 *Web:* www.odayconsultants.com	Carlsbad	CA	92010	760-931-7700	
O'kane Consultants Inc 112 Research Dr *Web:* www.okc-sk.com	Saskatoon	SK	S7N3R3	306-955-0702	
O'Neal Inc 10 Falcon Crest Dr *Web:* www.onealinc.com	Greenville	SC	29607	864-298-2000	298-2200
O'Reilly Talbot & Okun Assoc Inc 293 Bridge St *Web:* oto-env.com	Springfield	MA	01103	413-788-6222	
OASIS Alignment Services Inc 255 Pickering Rd *Web:* www.oasisalignment.com	Rochester	NH	03867	603-332-9641	
Ocean Tug & Barge Engineering Corp 258 E Main St Ste 401 *Web:* www.oceantugbarge.com	Milford	MA	01757	508-473-0545	
Odell Assoc Inc 800 W Hill St 3rd Fl *Web:* www.odell.com	Charlotte	NC	28208	704-414-1000	414-1111
Offshore Process Services Inc 1206 Park Dr *Web:* www.opsincusa.com	Mandeville	LA	70471	985-727-2900	

Phone | Fax

Oil Field Development Engineering LLC
12121 Wickchester Ln ....Houston TX 77079 281-679-9060
Web: ofdeng.com

Olson Engineering Inc
365 W Round Bunch Rd ....Bridge City TX 77611 409-697-3333
Web: www.o-engr.com/contactus.php

Olsson Assoc 1111 Lincoln Mall Ste 111 ....Lincoln NE 68508 402-474-6311 474-5160
TF: 877-831-6389 ■ *Web:* olssonassociates.com

Omni Link Corp 1750 Valley View Ln Ste 320 ....Dallas TX 75234 972-620-9000
Web: www.omnilinkcorp.com

Omni-Means Ltd 943 Reserve Dr Ste 100 ....Roseville CA 95678 916-782-8688 782-8689
Web: www.omnimeans.com

Omnni Associates Inc 1 Systems Dr ....Appleton WI 54914 920-735-6900
TF: 800-571-6677 ■ *Web:* omnni.com

Ontario Society of Professional Engineers
4950 Yonge St Ste 2200....North York ON M2N6K1 416-223-9961
Web: www.students.ospe.on.ca

Operational Technologies Corp
4100 NW Loop 410 Ste 230....San Antonio TX 78229 210-731-0000 731-0008
TF: 855-276-6136 ■ *Web:* www.otcorp.com

Optimized Process Designs Inc 25610 Clay Rd....Katy TX 77493 281-371-7500
Web: www.opd-inc.com

Orbital Engineering Inc 1344 Fifth Ave....Pittsburgh PA 15219 412-261-9100 261-2308
Web: www.orbitalengr.com

Orchard Hiltz & McCliment Inc (OHM)
34000 Plymouth Rd ....Livonia MI 48150 734-522-6711 522-6427
TF: 888-522-6711 ■ *Web:* www.ohm-advisors.com

ORI Services Corp 4565 Ruffner St Ste 201 ....San Diego CA 92111 858-576-4422
Web: www.oriservices.com

Ortloff Engineers Ltd 415 W Wall Ave Ste 2000 ....Midland TX 79701 432-685-0277 685-0258
Web: www.ortloff.com

Overlook Systems Technologies Inc
1950 Old Gallows Rd Ste 400....Vienna VA 22182 703-893-1411 356-9029
Web: www.overlooksys.com

Owen Group Inc 220 Technology Dr Ste 100....Irvine CA 92618 949-860-4800 860-4810
Web: www.owengroup.com

P K Electrical 681 Sierra Rose Dr Ste B ....Reno NV 89511 775-826-9010
Web: pkelectrical.com

P T Systems Inc 1980 Olivera Rd Ste A....Concord CA 94520 925-676-0709
Web: www.ptsystemsinc.com

P2S Engineering Inc
5000 E Spring St 8th Fl ....Long Beach CA 90815 562-497-2999
Web: www.p2seng.com

Pacific Surveying & Engineering Services Inc
1812 Cornwall Ave....Bellingham WA 98225 360-671-7387
Web: www.psesurvey.com

Pacifica Engineering Inc
21520 30th Dr SE Ste 210 ....Bothell WA 98021 425-984-2700
Web: www.pacifica-engineering.com

Pacifica Services Inc
106 S Mentor Ave Ste 200....Pasadena CA 91106 626-405-0131 405-0059
Web: www.pacificaservices.com

Packer Engineering Inc
1950 N Washington St....Naperville IL 60563 630-505-5722
Web: www.packereng.com

Padre Associates Inc 1861 Knoll Dr....Ventura CA 93003 805-644-2220
Web: www.padreinc.com

Pageau Morel et Associes Inc
210 Cr,mazie Blvd. W Ste 110 ....Montreal QC H2P1C6 819-776-4665
Web: www.pageaumorel.com

PageSoutherlandPage (PSPAEC)
1100 Louisiana St Ste 1 ....Houston TX 77002 713-871-8484 871-8440
Web: pagethink.com

PAL General Engineering Inc
5374 Eastgate Mall....San Diego CA 92121 858-638-7100
Web: www.palsd.com

Pape-Dawson Engineers Inc 555 E Ramsey....San Antonio TX 78216 210-375-9000 375-9010
Web: www.pape-dawson.com

Paragon Engineering Services Inc
2201 S Queen St....York PA 17402 717-854-7374 854-5533
Web: www.peservices.org

Parametrix Inc 1002 15th St SW....Auburn WA 98001 253-269-1330
Web: www.parametrix.com

Pare Corp 8 Blackstone Vly Pl ....Lincoln RI 02865 401-334-4100
Web: parecorp.com

Parker Development Company Inc
4525 Serrano Pkwy....El Dorado Hills CA 95762 916-939-4060
Web: www.parkerdevco.com

Parkhill Smith & Cooper Inc 4222 85th St....Lubbock TX 79423 806-473-2200 473-3500
TF: 800-400-6646 ■ *Web:* www.team-psc.com

Parsons Brinckerhoff Inc 1 Penn Plz 2nd Fl....New York NY 10119 212-465-5000 465-5096

Parsons Corp 100 W Walnut St....Pasadena CA 91124 626-440-2000 440-2630
Web: www.parsons.com

Parsons Infrastructure & Technology
100 W Walnut St....Pasadena CA 91124 626-440-4000 830-0287*
**Fax Area Code:* 256 ■ *Web:* www.parsons.com

Passero Associates 242 W Main St Ste 100....Rochester NY 14614 585-325-1000
TF: 800-836-0365 ■ *Web:* www.passero.com

Patel Burica & Assoc Inc 9283 Research Dr ....Irvine CA 92618 949-943-8080 352-2209*
**Fax Area Code:* 714 ■ *Web:* www.pbastructural.com

Patrick Engineering Inc 4970 Varsity Dr ....Lisle IL 60532 630-795-7200
TF: 800-799-7050 ■ *Web:* www.patrickengineering.com

Patriot Engineering & Environmental Inc
6330 E 75th St Ste 216....Indianapolis IN 46250 317-576-8058
Web: patrioteng.com

Patti Engineering Inc
2110 E Walton Blvd Ste A....Auburn Hills MI 48326 248-364-3200
Web: pattiengineering.com

Paul C Rizzo Assoc Inc 500 Penn Ctr Blvd ....Pittsburgh PA 15235 412-856-9700
Web: www.rizzoassoc.com

Paulus Engineering Inc 2871 E Coronado St ....Anaheim CA 92806 714-632-3975
Web: www.paulusengineering.com

Paulus Sokolowski & Sartor LLC
67 Mountain Blvd Ste B ....Warren NJ 07059 732-560-9700
Web: www.psands.com

Payette Assoc Inc 290 Congress St 5th Fl....Boston MA 02210 617-895-1000
Web: www.payette.com

Payne-huber Engineering Inc
8211 E Regal Pl Ste 104....Tulsa OK 74133 918-492-0975
Web: payne-huber.com

PBS Engineering & Environmenal Inc
4412 SW Corbett Ave....Portland OR 97239 503-248-1939
Web: pbsenv.com

PC Krause & Associates Inc
3016 Covington St....West Lafayette IN 47906 765-464-8997
Web: pcka.com

PCA Engineering Inc
57 Cannonball Rd PO Box 196....Pompton Lakes NJ 07442 973-616-4501 616-4451
TF: 800-666-7221 ■ *Web:* pcaengineering.com/default.asp

Pearl Engineering Corp
110 E Grand Ave PO Box 425....Wisconsin Rapids WI 54494 715-424-4008
Web: www.pearlengineering.com

Pearson Engineering Associates Inc
8825 N 23rd Ave Ste 11....Phoenix AZ 85021 602-264-0807
TF: 866-747-9754 ■ *Web:* www.peaeng.com

PEDCo E & A Services Inc
11499 Chester Rd Ste 301 ....Cincinnati OH 45246 513-782-4920
Web: www.pedcoea.com

Pegasus Engineering Inc
301 W State Rd 434 Ste 309....Winter Springs FL 32708 407-992-9160
Web: www.pegasusengineering.net

PegasusTSI Inc 5310 Cypress Ctr Dr Ste 200....Tampa FL 33609 813-876-2424
Web: www.pegasustsi.com

Pei Cobb Freed & Partners Architects LLP
88 Pine St....New York NY 10005 212-751-3122 872-5443
Web: www.pcfandp.com

Penn Pro Inc 4000 State Rd 60 E PO Box 89....Mulberry FL 33860 863-648-9990
Web: www.pennpro.net

Pennterra Engineering Inc
3075 Enterprise Dr Ste 100....State College PA 16801 814-231-8285
Web: www.pennterra.com

Penta Engineering PA 13835 S Lakes Dr ....Charlotte NC 28273 704-588-8877
Web: pentaengr.com

PeopleTec Inc 4901-I Corporate Dr NW ....Huntsville AL 35805 256-319-3800
Web: www.peopletec.com

Pepg LLC 9270 S Sandy Pkwy ....Sandy UT 84070 801-562-2521 562-2551
Web: pepg.net

Perkins & Will 410 N Michigan Ave Ste 1600....Chicago IL 60611 312-755-0770 755-0775
Web: www.perkinswill.com

Perkowitz + Ruth Architects
111 W Ocean Blvd 21st Fl ....Long Beach CA 90802 562-628-8000 628-8001
Web: www.prarchitects.com

Perry & Associates LLC
221 N La Salle St Ste 3100....Chicago IL 60601 312-364-9112
Web: www.perryllc.com

Perteet Inc 2707 Colby Ave Ste 900 Ste900 ....Everett WA 98201 425-252-7700 339-6018
TF: 800-615-9900 ■ *Web:* www.perteet.com

Pes Environmental Inc 1682 Novato Blvd Ste 100 ....Novato CA 94947 415-899-1600
Web: www.pesenv.com

Peter Basso Associates Inc
5145 Livernois Ste 100....Troy MI 48098 248-879-5666
Web: www.peterbassoassociates.com

Peterson Structural Engineers Inc
5319 Sw Westgate Dr Ste 215 ....Portland OR 97221 503-292-1635
Web: psengineers.com

Petitt Barraza LLC
1651 N Glenville Dr Ste 208....Richardson TX 75081 214-221-9955
Web: www.petittbarraza.com

Peto MacCallum Ltd 165 Cartwright Ave....Toronto ON M6A1V5 416-785-5110
Web: www.petomaccallum.com

Pettigrew & Assoc PA 100 E Navajo ....Hobbs NM 88240 575-393-9827
Web: pettigrew.us

Pfeiler & Assoc Engineers Inc 14181 Fern Ave....Chino CA 91710 909-993-5800
Web: pfeilerassociates.com

Phoenix Analysis & Design Inc
7755 S Research Dr Ste 110....Tempe AZ 85284 480-813-4884
Web: padtinc.com

Physical Resource Engineering Inc
4655 N Flowing Wells Rd....Tucson AZ 85705 520-690-1669
Web: www.prengr.com

Picco Engineering 350 Caldari Rd....Concord ON L4K4J4 905-760-9688
TF: 888-772-0773 ■ *Web:* www.picco-engineering.com

Pie Consulting & Engineering Inc
6275 Joyce Dr Ste 200....Arvada CO 80403 303-552-0177
Web: www.pieglobal.com

Pieper O'Brien Herr Architects Ltd
3000 Royal Blvd South....Alpharetta GA 30022 770-569-1706
Web: www.poharchitects.com

Piercon Solutions LLC
63 Beaverbrook Rd Ste 201 ....Lincoln Park NJ 07035 973-628-9330
Web: piercon.net

Pincock Allen & Holt A Div of Runge Inc
165 S Union Blvd Ste 950 ....Lakewood CO 80228 303-986-6950 987-8907
Web: www.rpmglobal.com

PINNACLE Converting Equipment 1720 Toal St....Charlotte NC 28206 704-376-3855
Web: www.pinnacleconverting.com

Pinnacle Engineering Inc
7660 Woodway Dr Ste 350....Houston TX 77063 713-784-1005
Web: www.pinnacleengr.com

Piping Systems Engineering 1905 S Lindsay Rd....Mesa AZ 85201 480-345-0052
Web: piping-systems.com

Pittsburgh Design Services Inc PO Box 469....Carnegie PA 15106 412-276-3000
Web: www.pittsdesign.com

Plateau Excavation Inc
375 Lee Industrial Blvd....Austell GA 30168 770-948-2600
Web: plateauexcavation.com

				Phone	Fax
Pliteq Inc 1370 Don Mills Rd Unit 300 ... Toronto *Web:* pliteq.com	ON	M3B3N7	416-449-0049	
Poggemeyer Design Group Inc 1168 N Main St ... Bowling Green *Web:* www.poggemeyer.com	OH	43402	419-352-7537	353-0187
Polaris Consulting Engineers 214 W Main St 208 ... Moorestown *Web:* www.polarisce.com	NJ	08057	856-778-5400	
Polarity Inc 11294 Sunrise Park Dr ... Rancho Cordova *Web:* www.polarity.net	CA	95742	916-635-3050	
Poly Plant Project Inc 3099 N Lima St ... Burbank *Web:* www.polyplantproject.com	CA	91504	818-848-2111	
Polyengineering Inc 1935 Headland Ave ... Dothan *TF:* 888-793-4700 ■ *Web:* www.polyengineering.com	AL	36303	334-793-4700	
Pond & Co 3500 Pkwy Ln Ste 600 ... Norcross *Web:* pondco.com	GA	30092	678-336-7740	
Porter Consulting Engineers PC 552 State St ... Meadville *TF:* 800-541-5941 ■ *Web:* www.pceengineers.com	PA	16335	814-337-4447	
Portfolio Defense 7 Mount Lassen Dr Ste D150 ... San Rafael *Web:* portfoliodefense.com	CA	94903	415-492-8262	
Power & Control Engineering Solutions LLC 12611 East 60th St Ste 200 ... Tulsa *Web:* www.pcescorp.com	OK	74146	918-627-7237	
Power Engineering Corp PO Box 766 ... Wilkes-Barre *TF:* 800-626-0903 ■ *Web:* www.powerengineeringcorp.com	PA	18703	570-823-8822	823-8143
Power Engineers Inc 3940 Glenbrook Dr PO Box 1066 ... Hailey *Web:* www.powereng.com	ID	83333	208-788-3456	788-2082
Powercast Corp 566 Alpha Dr ... Pittsburgh *Web:* www.powercastco.com	PA	15238	724-238-3700	
PPM Consultants Inc 2508 Ticheli Rd ... Monroe *TF:* 800-761-8675 ■ *Web:* www.ppmco.com	LA	71202	318-323-7270	323-6593
Prefix Corp 1300 W Hamlin Rd ... Rochester Hills *Web:* www.prefix.com	MI	48309	248-650-1330	
Prein & Newhof Inc 3355 Evergreen Dr NE ... Grand Rapids *Web:* www.preinnewhof.com	MI	49525	616-364-8491	364-6955
Premier Civil Engineering LLC 1302 Calle Del Norte Ste 2 ... Laredo *Web:* premier-ce.com	TX	78041	956-717-1199	
Prestige Technicall Services 7908 Cincinnati Dayton Rd Ste T ... West Chester *Web:* www.prestigetechnical.com	OH	45069	513-779-6800	
Preston Partnership 115 Perimeter Ctr Pl Ste 950 ... Atlanta *Web:* www.theprestonpartnership.com	GA	30346	770-396-7248	396-2945
Pribuss Engineering Inc 523 Mayfair Ave ... South San Francisco *Web:* www.pribuss.com	CA	94080	650-588-0447	
Pride Signs Ltd 255 Pinebush Rd ... Cambridge *Web:* www.pridesigns.com	ON	N1T1B9	519-622-4040	
Prima-Temp Inc 2820 Wilderness Pl Ste C ... Boulder *Web:* prima-temp.com	CO	80301	303-443-6611	
Principle Engineering Group Inc 833 E Plaza Cir Ste 100 ... Yuma	AZ	85365	928-782-5700	
Priority Designs Inc 100 S Hamilton Rd ... Columbus *Web:* www.prioritydesigns.com	OH	43213	614-337-9979	337-9499
Prism Maritime LLC 1416 Kelland Dr Ste B ... Chesapeake *Web:* prismmaritime.com	VA	23320	757-460-8800	
Pro Star Aviation LLC 5 Industrial Dr ... Londonderry *Web:* www.prostaraviation.com	NH	03053	603-627-7827	
Proctor Engineering Group Ltd 418 Mission Ave ... San Rafael *Web:* www.proctoreng.com	CA	94901	415-451-2480	
Product Development Technologies Inc 1 Corporate Dr ... Lake Zurich *Web:* www.pdt.com	IL	60047	847-821-3000	821-3020
Professional Engineering Consultants PA 303 S Topeka St ... Wichita *Web:* www.pec1.com	KS	67202	316-262-2691	262-3003
Professional Service Industries Inc (PSI) 1901 S Meyers Rd Ste 400 ... Oakbrook Terrace *TF:* 800-548-7901 ■ *Web:* www.psiusa.com	IL	60181	630-691-1490	691-1587
Project Resources Inc 3760 Convoy St Ste 230 ... San Diego *Web:* www.priworld.com	CA	92111	858-505-1000	505-1010
ProjectDesign Consultants 701 B St Ste 800 ... San Diego *Web:* www.projectdesign.com	CA	92101	619-235-6471	234-0349
PROJECTXYZ Inc 1500 Perimeter Pkwy Ste 426 ... Huntsville *Web:* projectxyz.com	AL	35806	256-721-9001	
Prolitec Inc 1235 W Canal St ... Milwaukee *Web:* www.prolitec.com	WI	53233	414-615-4630	
Promation Engineering Inc 16138 Flight Path Dr ... Brooksville *Web:* promationei.com	FL	34604	352-544-8436	
Propak Systems Ltd 440 East Lk Rd NE ... Airdrie *TF:* 800-408-4434 ■ *Web:* www.propaksystems.com	AB	T4A2J8	403-912-7000	
Protean Design Group Inc 100 E Pine St Ste 600 ... Orlando *Web:* www.proteandg.com	FL	32801	407-246-0044	
Protection Engineering Consultants LLC 14144 Trautwein Rd ... Austin *Web:* www.protection-consultants.com	TX	78737	512-380-1988	
Protostatix Engineering Consultants 10117 Jasper Ave NW Ste 1100 ... Edmonton *Web:* protostatix.com	AB	T5J1W8	780-423-5855	
Provenance Consulting 301 W Sixth St Ste 200 ... Borger *Web:* www.provenanceconsulting.com	TX	79007	806-273-5100	
Proz com 235 Harrison St ... Syracuse *Web:* www.proz.com	NY	13202	315-463-7323	
Pruitt Eberly & Stone Inc 1852 Century Pl Ne ... Atlanta *Web:* www.pesengineers.com	GA	30345	770-457-5923	
PSARA Technologies Inc 10925 Reed Hartman Hwy Ste 220 ... Cincinnati *Web:* psara.com	OH	45242	513-791-4418	
Psomas 555 S Flower St Ste 4300 ... Los Angeles *Web:* www.psomas.com	CA	90071	213-223-1400	
PTI Engineered Plastics Inc 50900 Corporate Dr ... Macomb *Web:* www.teampti.com	MI	48044	586-263-5100	263-6680
Purdy-McGuire Inc 17300 Dallas Pkwy Ste 3000 ... Dallas *Web:* www.purdy-mcguire.com	TX	75248	972-239-5357	
Q. Grady Minor & Associates PA 3800 Via Del Rey ... Bonita Springs *Web:* www.gradyminor.com	FL	34134	239-947-1144	
QCA Systems Ltd #16 7355 72 St ... Delta *Web:* www.qcasystems.com	BC	V4G1L5	604-940-0868	
Quad Three Group Inc 37 N Washington St ... Wilkes-Barre *Web:* www.quad3.com	PA	18701	570-829-4200	
Qualis Corp 689 Discovery Dr NW Ste 400 ... Huntsville *Web:* www.qualis-corp.com	AL	35806	256-971-1707	
Quality Solutions Inc 128 N First St ... Colwich *TF:* 888-328-2454 ■ *Web:* www.qsifacilities.com	KS	67030	316-721-3656	
Qualortran Inc 236 Carpenter Rd Ne ... Calhoun *Web:* qualortran.com	GA	30701	706-295-4510	
Quantum Marine Engineering of Florida Inc 3790 Sw 30th Ave ... Fort Lauderdale *Web:* www.quantumhydraulic.com	FL	33312	954-587-4205	
Quantum Signal LLC 200 N Ann Arbor St ... Saline *Web:* quantumsignal.com	MI	48176	734-429-9100	
Quantum Technology Sciences Inc 1980 N Atlantic Ave Ste 201 ... Cocoa Beach *Web:* www.qtsi.com	FL	32931	321-868-0288	
Quest Convergence Systems Inc 43 Metcalf Dr ... Belleville *TF:* 877-933-8776 ■ *Web:* questai.com	IL	62223	618-398-3311	
Quorum Consulting Inc 180 Sansome St 10th Fl ... San Francisco *Web:* quorumconsulting.com	CA	94104	415-835-0190	
R & A Tool & Engineering Co 39127 Ford Rd ... Westland *Web:* www.randatool.com	MI	48185	734-981-2000	
R e Dimond & Associates Inc 732 N Capitol Ave ... Indianapolis *Web:* www.redimond.com	IN	46204	317-634-4672	
R G Engineering Inc 505 London Bridge Rd Unit 101 ... Virginia Beach *Web:* www.rgengineering.com	VA	23454	757-463-3045	
R J Behar & Company Inc 6861 SW 196th Ave Ste 302 ... Fort Lauderdale *Web:* www.rjbehar.com	FL	33332	954-680-7771	
R J Wood & Co 652 Arlington Pl ... Macon	GA	31201	478-741-7044	
R T Patterson Company Inc 230 Third Ave 2nd Fl ... Pittsburgh *Web:* www.rtpatterson.com	PA	15222	412-227-6600	227-6672
R-S-H Engineering Inc 909 N 18th St Ste 200 ... Monroe *TF:* 888-340-4884 ■ *Web:* www.rsh.com	LA	71201	318-323-4009	
R.M.Thornton Inc 120 Westhampton Ave ... Capitol Heights *Web:* www.rmthornton.com	MD	20743	301-350-5000	
R.O. Anderson Engineering Inc 1603 Esmeralda ... Minden *Web:* www.roanderson.com	NV	89423	775-782-2322	
R2t Inc 580 W Crssvlle Rd ... Roswell *Web:* www.r2tinc.com	GA	30075	770-569-7038	
Rae Engineering & Inspection Ltd 4810 93 St Nw ... Edmonton *Web:* www.raeengineering.ca	AB	T6E5M4	780-469-2401	
Rahmberg Stover & Associates LLC 789 Vinewood Ave ... Birmingham *Web:* rahmbergstover.com	MI	48009	248-203-7710	
Railplan International Inc 1200 Bernard Dr ... Baltimore *Web:* www.railplan.com	MD	21223	410-947-5900	
Ramaker & Assoc Inc 1120 Dallas St ... Sauk City *Web:* ramaker.com	WI	53583	608-643-4100	
Ramey Kemp & Assoc Inc 5808 Faringdon Pl Ste 100 ... Raleigh *Web:* rameykemp.com	NC	27609	919-872-5115	
Ranal Inc 2851 High Meadow Cir Ste 120 ... Auburn Hills *Web:* www.ranalgroup.com	MI	48326	248-852-5955	
Rangaswamy & Assoc Inc 304 W Liberty St ... Louisville *Web:* rangaswamy.com	KY	40202	502-589-2212	
Rapid Global Business Solutions Inc 1200 Stephenson Hwy ... Troy *Web:* www.rgbsi.com	MI	48083	248-589-1135	
Rathgeber Goss Associates PC 15871 Crabbs Branch Way ... Rockville *Web:* www.rath-goss.com	MD	20855	301-590-0071	
Ravi Engineering & Land Surveying PC 2110 S Clinton Ave Ste 1 ... Rochester *Web:* www.ravieng.com	NY	14618	585-223-3660	
Raymond L Goodson Jr Inc 5445 La Sierra Ste 300 LB 17 ... Dallas *Web:* rlginc.com	TX	75231	214-739-8100	739-6354
Raytheon Polar Services Co 7400 S Tucson Way ... Centennial *Web:* rpsc.raytheon.com	CO	80112	303-790-8606	
RBA Group Inc, The 7 Campus Dr Ste 300 ... Parsippany *Web:* www.rbagroup.com	NJ	07054	973-946-5600	984-5421
RBC Inc 100 N Pitt St Ste 300 ... Alexandria *Web:* www.rbcinc.com	VA	22314	703-549-6921	549-6926
RCM Technologies Inc 2500 McClellan Ave Ste 350 ... Pennsauken *NASDAQ: RCMT* ■ *TF:* 800-322-2885 ■ *Web:* www.rcmt.com	NJ	08109	856-356-4500	356-4600
Rcr Technology Corp 251 N Illinois St ... Indianapolis *Web:* www.rcrtechnology.com	IN	46204	317-624-9500	
Reaction Engineering International Inc 77 West 200 South Ste 210 ... Salt Lake City *Web:* www.reaction-eng.com	UT	84101	801-364-6925	

Company / Address	City	State	ZIP	Phone	Fax
Ready Technologies Inc 101 Capitol Way N Ste 301	Olympia	WA	98501	360-413-9800	
TF: 877-892-9104 ■ Web: www.readyengineering.com					
Realtime Technologies Inc 1523 N Main St	Royal Oak	MI	48067	248-548-4876	
Web: www.simcreator.com					
Rec Consulting Inc 2442 Second Ave	San Diego	CA	92101	619-232-9200	
Web: rec-consultants.com					
Reese Engineering Inc 2021 Pine Hall Rd	State College	PA	16801	814-234-2548	
Web: www.reeseinc.com					
Rega Engineering 1620 S 70th St Ste 103	Lincoln	NE	68506	402-484-7342	
Web: regaengineering.com					
Regulus 238 N Main St	Woodstock	VA	22664	540-459-2142	
Web: regulus-group.com					
Reid Middleton Inc 728 134th St SW Ste 200	Everett	WA	98204	425-741-3800	
Web: www.reidmiddleton.com					
Reigstad & Associates Inc 192 Ninth St W Ste 200	Saint Paul	MN	55102	651-292-1123	
Web: www.reigstad.com					
Reliability Center 501 Westover Ave	Hopewell	VA	23860	804-458-0645	
TF: 800-457-0645 ■ Web: www.reliability.com					
Remington & Vernick Engineers Inc 232 Kings Hwy E	Haddonfield	NJ	08033	856-795-9595	795-1882
Web: www.rve.com					
Research & Development Solutions Inc 7921 Jones Branch Dr	Mclean	VA	22102	703-893-9533	
Web: rdsi.com					
Research Management Consultants Inc 816 Camarillo Springs Rd Ste J	Camarillo	CA	93012	805-987-5538	987-2868
Web: www.rmci.com					
Resources Applications Designs & Controls Inc 3220 E 59th St	Long Beach	CA	90805	562-272-7231	
Respec Inc 3824 Jet Dr	Rapid City	SD	57703	605-394-6400	394-6456
Web: www.respec.com					
Retrocom Energy Strategies Inc 2378 Maritime Dr Ste 110	Elk Grove	CA	95758	916-226-6415	
Web: www.retrostrategies.com					
Rettew Assoc Inc 3020 Columbia Ave	Lancaster	PA	17603	717-394-3721	394-1063
TF: 800-738-8395 ■ Web: www.rettew.com					
Revolutionary Engineering Inc 36865 Schoolcraft Rd	Livonia	MI	48150	734-432-9334	
Web: www.revoleng.com					
Reynolds Smith & Hills Inc 10748 Deerwood Pk Blvd	Jacksonville	FL	32256	904-256-2500	256-2501
TF: 800-741-2014 ■ Web: www.rsandh.com					
RGA Environmental Inc 1466 66th St	Emeryville	CA	94608	510-547-7771	
Web: www.rgaenv.com					
RHP Mechanical Systems Inc 1008 E Fourth St	Reno	NV	89512	775-322-9434	
Web: www.rhpinc.net					
Ribbeck Engineering Inc 14335 Sw 120th St Ste 205	Miami	FL	33186	305-383-5909	
Web: ribbeck.co					
Richard Brady & Associates 3710 Ruffin Rd	San Diego	CA	92123	858-496-0500	
Web: www.richardbrady.com					
Richardson Smith Gardner & Associates 14 N Boylan Ave	Raleigh	NC	27603	919-828-0577	
Web: www.smithgardnerinc.com					
Ricker, Atkinson, Mcbee & Associates Inc 2105 S Hardy Dr Ste 13	Tempe	AZ	85282	480-921-8100	
Web: www.rammeng.com					
Ridgetop Group Inc 3580 W Ina Rd	Tuscan	AZ	85741	520-742-3300	
Web: www.ridgetop-group.com					
Rindt-McDuff Associates Inc 334 Cherokee St NE	Marietta	GA	30060	770-427-8123	
Web: www.rindt-mcduff.com					
Rio Technical Services LLC 4200 S Hulen	Fort Worth	TX	76109	817-735-8264	
Ripa Engineering Corp 9555 Owensmouth Ave Nbr 8	Chatsworth	CA	91311	818-773-8722	
Web: ripaeng.com					
Risk Integrated LLC 37 Main St	Cold Spring	NY	10516	845-598-1620	
Web: www.riskintegrated.com					
Rist-Frost-Shumway Engineering PC 71 Water St	Laconia	NH	03246	603-524-4647	
Web: www.rfsengineering.com					
Rivermoor Engineering LLC 146 Front St	Scituate	MA	02066	781-545-2848	
Web: rivermoorengineering.com					
RK Engineering Group Inc 4000 Werly Pl Ste 280	Newport Beach	CA	92660	949-474-0809	
Web: rkengineer.com					
RK&K 81 Mosher St	Baltimore	MD	21217	410-728-2900	
Web: www.rkk.com					
RKR Hess Assoc Inc 112 N Courtland St	East Stroudsburg	PA	18301	570-421-1550	
Web: rkrhess.com					
RM Towill Corp 2024 N King St Ste 200	Honolulu	HI	96819	808-842-1133	842-1937
Web: www.rmtowill.com					
RMA Group Inc 12130 Santa Margarita Ct	Rancho Cucamonga	CA	91730	909-989-1751	
Web: www.rmacompanies.com					
RMC Water & Environment Inc 2175 N California Blvd Ste 315	Walnut Creek	CA	94596	925-627-4100	
Web: www.rmcwater.com					
RMF Engineering Inc 5520 Research Pk Dr Ste 300	Baltimore	MD	21228	410-576-0505	385-0327
TF: 800-938-5760 ■ Web: www.rmf.com					
RNL Design 1050 17th St Ste A200	Denver	CO	80265	303-295-1717	292-0845
Web: www.rnldesign.com					
Roake & Assoc Inc 1684 Quincy Ave	Naperville	IL	60540	630-355-3232	
Web: roake.com					
Robert Allan Ltd 1639 Second Ave W Ste 230	Vancouver	BC	V6J1H3	604-736-9466	
Web: www.ral.ca					
Robert E. Lee & Associates Inc 1250 Centennial Centre Blvd	Hobart	WI	54155	920-662-9641	
Web: www.releeinc.com					
Roberts & Schaefer Co 222 S Riverside Plz Ste 1800	Chicago	IL	60606	312-236-7292	726-2872
Robson Technologies Inc 135 E Main Ave	Morgan Hill	CA	95037	408-779-8008	
Web: www.testfixtures.com					
Rocscience 31 Balsam Ave	Toronto	ON	M4E3B5	416-698-8217	
Web: www.rocscience.com					
Roddey Engineering Services Inc 10100 Woolworth Rd	Keithville	LA	71047	318-221-1996	
Web: www.themartincompanies.com/roddey-engineering-services-inc					
Rodeberg & Berryman Inc 119 S First St	Montevideo	MN	56265	320-269-7695	
Rogers Engineering & Manufacturing Inc 112 S Center St	Cambridge City	IN	47327	765-478-5444	
Web: rogersengineering.net					
Rolls Anderson & Rolls 115 Yellowstone Dr	Chico	CA	95973	530-895-1422	
Web: rarcivil.com					
Roma Design Group 1527 Stockton St	San Francisco	CA	94133	415-616-9900	
Web: roma.com					
Ronald T Jepson & Assoc Ps 222 Grand Ave	Bellingham	WA	98225	360-733-5760	
Web: jepsonengineering.com					
Rosenwasser Grossman Consulting 519 8h Ave 20th Fl	New York	NY	10018	212-564-2424	
Web: www.rosenwassergrossman.com					
Roshanian & Associates Inc 6404 Wilshire Blvd	Los Angeles	CA	90048	323-933-5252	
Web: www.roshanian.com					
Ross & Baruzzini 6 S Old Orchard	Saint Louis	MO	63119	314-918-8383	918-1766
Web: www.rossbar.com					
Rotating Machinery Services Inc 2760 Baglyos Cir	Bethlehem	PA	18020	484-821-0702	
Web: www.rotatingmachinery.com					
Rothenbuhler Engineering 524 Rhodes Rd PO Box 708	Sedro Woolley	WA	98284	360-856-0836	856-2183
Web: www.rothenbuhlereng.com					
Rowan Williams Davies & Irwin Inc 650 Woodlawn Rd W	Guelph	ON	N1K1B8	519-823-1311	
Web: www.rwdi.com					
Royal Engineering Inc 34450 Commerce Rd	Fraser	MI	48026	586-294-9400	
Web: royalinc.com					
RSA Engineering Inc 2522 Arctic Blvd Ste 200	Anchorage	AK	99503	907-276-0521	
RSP Architects 1220 Marshall St NE	Minneapolis	MN	55413	612-677-7100	677-7499
Web: www.rsparch.com					
RT Tanaka Engineers Inc 871 Kolu St Ste 201	Wailuku	HI	96793	808-242-6861	
RTKL Assoc Inc 901 S Bond St	Baltimore	MD	21231	410-537-6000	276-2136
Web: www.rtkl.com					
Ruekert & Mielke Inc W233 N2080 Ridgeview Pkwy	Waukesha	WI	53188	262-542-5733	542-5631
Web: www.ruekert-mielke.com					
Runtime Design Automation 2560 Mission College Blvd Ste 130	Santa Clara	CA	95054	408-492-0940	
Web: rtda.com					
RW Engineering & Surveying Inc 6225 N 89th Cir	Omaha	NE	68134	402-573-2205	
Web: rwomaha.com					
Ryan-Biggs Assoc PC 257 Ushers Rd	Clifton Park	NY	12065	518-406-5506	
Web: ryanbiggs.com					
S & B Engineers & Constructors Ltd 7825 Pk Pl Blvd	Houston	TX	77087	713-645-4141	643-8029
Web: www.sbec.com					
S Systems Corp 5777 W Century Blvd Ste 520	Los Angeles	CA	90045	310-215-0248	642-3738
Web: www.s-sc.com					
S.S. Mechanical Corp 17631 Metzler Ln	Huntington Beach	CA	92647	714-847-1317	
Web: www.ssmechanical.biz					
S/L/A/M Collaborative 80 Glastonbury Blvd	Glastonbury	CT	06033	860-657-8077	657-3141
Web: www.slamcoll.com					
S2L Inc 531 Versailles Dr Ste 202	Maitland	FL	32751	407-475-9163	
Web: s2li.com					
SA Healy Co 901 N Green Valley Pkwy Ste 260	Henderson	NV	89074	702-754-6400	754-6450
Web: www.sahealy.com					
Sabre Industries Inc 8653 E Hwy 67	Alvarado	TX	76009	817-852-1700	852-1703
TF: 866-254-3707 ■ Web: www.sabreindustriesinc.com					
Sadat Associates Inc 1545 Lamberton Rd	Trenton	NJ	08611	609-826-9600	
Web: www.sadat.com					
Sage Consulting Group 1623 Blake St Ste 400	Denver	CO	80202	303-571-0237	
Web: www.sageconsulting.com					
SAI Consulting Engineers Inc 1350 Penn Ave Ste 300	Pittsburgh	PA	15222	412-392-8750	392-8785
Web: www.saiengr.com					
Sam Zax Assoc 14 Wood Rd	Braintree	MA	02184	781-303-1700	
Samuel Engineering Inc 8450 E Crescent Pkwy	Greenwood Village	CO	80111	303-714-4840	
Web: www.samuelengineering.com					
San Jose Redevelopment Agency 200 E Santa Clara St 14th Fl	San Jose	CA	95113	408-535-8500	
Web: www.sjredevelopment.org					
Sanborn Head & Assoc Inc 20 Foundry St	Concord	NH	03301	603-229-1900	
Web: sanbornhead.com					
Sarafinchin Associates Ltd 238 Galaxy Blvd	Toronto	ON	M9W5R8	416-674-1770	
Web: www.sarafinchin.com					
Sargent & Lundy LLC 55 E Monroe St	Chicago	IL	60603	312-269-2000	269-3454
Web: www.sargentlundy.com					
Sasaki Assoc Inc 64 Pleasant St	Watertown	MA	02472	617-926-3300	924-2748
Web: www.sasaki.com					
Sathre Bergquist Inc 150 Broadway Ave S	Wayzata	MN	55391	952-476-6000	
Web: sathre.com					
Savin Engineers PC 3 Campus Dr	Pleasantville	NY	10570	914-769-3200	747-6686
Web: www.savinengineers.com					
SC Engineers Inc 17075 Via Del Campo 1st Fl	San Diego	CA	92127	858-946-0333	
Web: scengineers.net					
Scale Models Unlimited 400 S Front St Ste 300	Memphis	TN	38103	901-577-5155	
Web: www.smu.com					

Name / Address	City	State	Zip	Phone	Fax
Schaeffer & Associates Ltd 6 Ronrose Dr *Web:* www.schaeffers.com	Concord	ON	L4K4R3	905-738-6100	
Schaeffer Nassar Schneidegg Consulting Engineers LLC 1425 Cantillon Blvd *Web:* www.snsce.com	Mays Landing	NJ	08330	609-625-7400	
Schafer Corp 321 Billerica Rd *Web:* www.schafercorp.com	Chelmsford	MA	01824	703-516-6000	
Scheeser Buckley Mayfield Inc 1540 Corporate Woods Pkwy *Web:* www.sbmce.com	Uniontown	OH	44685	330-896-4664	
Schemmer Assoc Inc, The 1044 N 115th St	Omaha	NE	68154	402-493-4800	
SchenkelShultz Architects 200 E Robinson St Ste 300 *Web:* www.schenkelshultz.com	Orlando	FL	32801	407-872-3322	872-3303
Schnabel Engineering Inc 9800 JEB Stuart Pkwy Ste 200 *Web:* www.schnabel-eng.com	Glen Allen	VA	23059	804-264-3222	264-3244
Schneider Corp 8901 Otis Ave *TF:* 866-973-7100 ■ *Web:* schneidercorp.com	Indianapolis	IN	46216	317-826-7100	826-7200
Schofield Brothers of New England Inc 1071 Worcester Rd *TF:* 800-696-2874 ■ *Web:* www.schofieldbros.com	Framingham	MA	01701	508-879-0030	
SCS Engineers 3900 Kilroy Airport Way Ste 100 *TF:* 800-326-9544 ■ *Web:* www.scsengineers.com	Long Beach	CA	90806	562-426-9544	427-0805
SE Technologies LLC 98 Vanadium Rd Bldg D *Web:* www.se-env.com	Bridgeville	PA	15017	412-221-1100	257-6103
Sea Engineering Inc 863 N Nimitz *Web:* seaengineering.com	Honolulu	HI	96817	808-536-3603	
Sea-Land Chemical Co 821 Wpoint Pkwy *Web:* sealandchem.com	Westlake	OH	44145	440-871-7887	
Seacon Engineering Associates Inc 716B Lakeside Dr W *Web:* www.seaconeng.com	Mobile	AL	36693	251-662-0300	
Sebago Technics Inc 75 John Roberts Rd Ste 1A *Web:* sebago-technics.com	South Portland	ME	04106	207-200-2100	
Sebesta Blomberg & Assoc Inc 1450 Energy Park Dr Ste 300 *TF:* 877-706-6858 ■ *Web:* www.sebesta.com	St Paul	MN	55108	651-634-0775	
SEI Group Inc 689 Discovery Dr Ste 310 *Web:* www.seigroupinc.com	Huntsville	AL	35806	256-533-0500	
Seismic LLC 7550 Teague Rd Ste 404 *Web:* www.seismicllc.com	Hanover	MD	21076	410-799-7700	
Senga Engineering 1525 E Warner Ave *TF:* 877-878-8159 ■ *Web:* senga-eng.com	Santa Ana	CA	92705	714-549-8011	
Sensorwise Inc 2908 Rogerdale Rd *Web:* www.sensorwise.com	Houston	TX	77042	713-952-3350	
SENTEL Corp 1101 King St Ste 550 *Web:* www.sentel.com	Alexandria	VA	22314	703-739-0084	739-6028
SGS Architects Engineers Inc 1 Tyler Ct *Web:* www.sgsarchitects.com	Carlisle	PA	17015	717-249-4569	
Shah & Associates Inc 416 N Frederick Ave *Web:* www.shahpe.com	Gaithersburg	MD	20877	301-926-2797	
Shah Smith & Assoc Inc 2825 Wilcrest Ste 350 *Web:* shahsmith.com	Houston	TX	77042	713-780-7563	
Sheladia Assoc Inc 15825 Shady Grove Rd Ste 100 *Web:* www.sheladia.com	Rockville	MD	20850	301-590-3939	948-7174
Shelby Engineering Ltd 9632 54 Ave Nw *Web:* www.shelbyengineering.ca	Edmonton	AB	T6E5V1	780-438-2540	
Shepley Bulfinch 2 Seaport Ln *Web:* shepleybulfinch.com	Boston	MA	02210	617-423-1700	451-2420
Shermco Industries Inc 2425 E Pioneer Dr *Web:* www.shermco.com	Irving	TX	75061	972-793-5523	
Sherwood Design Engineers 58 Maiden Ln 3rd Fl *Web:* www.sherwoodengineers.com	San Francisco	CA	94108	415-677-7300	
Sherwood-Logan & Assoc Inc 2140 Renard Ct *Web:* sherwoodlogan.com	Annapolis	MD	21401	410-841-6810	
Shield Engineering Inc 4301 Taggart Creek Rd *Web:* www.shieldengineering.com	Charlotte	NC	28208	704-394-6913	
Shive-Hattery Inc (SH) 316 Second St SE Ste 500 PO Box 1599 *TF:* 800-798-0227 ■ *Web:* www.shive-hattery.com	Cedar Rapids	IA	52406	319-362-0313	362-2883
SHN Consulting Engineers & Geologists Inc 812 W Wabash *Web:* www.shn-engr.com	Eureka	CA	95501	707-441-8855	
Short-Elliott-Hendrickson Inc 3535 Vadnais Ctr Dr *TF:* 800-325-2055 ■ *Web:* www.sehinc.com	Saint Paul	MN	55110	651-490-2000	490-2150
Shumaker Consulting Engineer PC 143 Court St *Web:* www.shumakerengineering.com	Binghamton	NY	13901	607-798-8081	
Shutler Consulting Engineers Inc 12503 Bel Red Rd *Web:* shutler.com	Bellevue	WA	98005	425-450-4075	
SI Organization Inc, The 15052 Conference Ctr Dr *Web:* www.vencore.com	Chantilly	VA	20151	571-313-6000	
Sid Goldstien - Civil Engineer 650 Alamo Pintado Rd Ste 302 *Web:* sjgce.com	Solvang	CA	93463	805-688-1526	
Sierra Pacific West 2125 La Mirada Dr *Web:* sierrapacificwest.com	Vista	CA	92081	760-599-0755	
Sigit Automation Inc 840 Seventh Ave SW Ste 1710 *Web:* www.sigit.com	Calgary	AB	T2P3G2	403-723-4256	
Signa Engineering Corp 2 Northpoint Dr Ste 700 *Web:* www.signaengineering.com	Houston	TX	77060	281-774-1000	
Silver Engineering Inc 255 E Dr Ste A *Web:* silvereng.com	Melbourne	FL	32904	321-676-7596	
Silverman & Light Inc 1201 Park Ave Ste 100 *Web:* www.silvermanlight.com	Emeryville	CA	94608	510-655-1200	
Simbex LLC 10 Water St Ste 410 *Web:* www.simbex.com	Lebanon	NH	03766	603-448-2367	
Simmons Engineering Corp 400 Regency Dr *TF:* 800-252-3381 ■ *Web:* simcut.com	Glendale Heights	IL	60139	630-912-2880	
Simon & Assoc Inc 3200 Commerce St *TF:* 800-763-4234 ■ *Web:* simonassoc.com	Blacksburg	VA	24060	540-951-4234	
SimPhonics Inc 3226 N Falkenburg Rd *Web:* www.simphonics.com	Tampa	FL	33619	813-623-9917	
Simpson Gumpertz & Heger Inc 41 Seyon St Bldg 1 Ste 500 *TF:* 800-729-7429 ■ *Web:* www.sgh.com	Waltham	MA	02453	781-907-9000	907-9009
Simulent Inc 203 College St Ste 302 *Web:* www.simulent.com	Toronto	ON	M5T1P9	416-979-5544	
Sinclair Pratt Cameron PC 1630 Donna Dr Ste 103 *Web:* spc-eng.com	Virginia Beach	VA	23451	757-417-0565	
Site Design Concepts Inc 127 W Market St Ste 200 *Web:* sitedc.com	York	PA	17401	717-757-9414	
SJB Group Inc 5745 Essen Ln Ste 200 *Web:* www.sjbgroup.com	Baton Rouge	LA	70810	225-769-3400	769-3596
SKA Consulting Engineers Inc 300 Pomona Dr *Web:* skaeng.com	Greensboro	NC	27407	336-855-0993	
Skelton, Brumwell & Associates Inc 93 Bell Farm Rd Ste 107 *TF:* 877-726-1141 ■ *Web:* www.skeltonbrumwell.ca	Barrie	ON	L4M5G1	705-726-1141	
Skidmore Owings & Merrill 224 S Michigan Ave Ste 1000 *Web:* www.som.com	Chicago	IL	60604	312-554-9090	360-4545
SM Engineering Co 9 Ninth Ave N *Web:* www.smeng.com	Hopkins	MN	55343	952-938-7407	
Smallwood Reynolds Stewart Stewart & Assoc Inc (SRSSA) 1 Piedmont Ctr 3565 Piedmont Rd Ste 303 *Web:* www.srssa.com	Atlanta	GA	30305	404-233-5453	264-0929
Smith Engineering Co 2201 San Pedro Dr NE 4-200 *Web:* www.smithengineering.pro	Albuquerque	NM	87110	505-884-0700	
Smith Seckman Reid Inc 2995 Sidco Dr *Web:* ssr-inc.com	Nashville	TN	37204	615-383-1113	
SmithGroup Inc 500 Griswold St Ste 1700 *Web:* www.smithgroupjjr.com	Detroit	MI	48226	313-983-3600	983-3636
SMS Concast America Inc 100 Sandusky St *Web:* www.sms-concast.ch	Pittsburgh	PA	15212	412-237-8950	237-8951
SMS Demag Inc 100 Sandusky St *Web:* sms-millcraft.us	Pittsburgh	PA	15212	412-231-1200	231-3995
SNC Lavalin Group Inc 455 Rene-Levesque Blvd W *TSE:* SNC ■ *Web:* www.snclavalin.com	Montreal	QC	H2Z1Z3	514-393-1000	866-0795
Snowline Engineering 4261 Business Dr *TF:* 800-361-6083 ■ *Web:* www.snowlineengineering.com	Cameron Park	CA	95682	530-677-2675	
Snyder & Assoc Inc PO Box 1159 *TF General:* 888-964-2020 ■ *Web:* www.snyder-associates.com	Ankeny	IA	50023	515-964-2020	964-7938
Sofec Inc 14741 Yorktown Plaza *Web:* www.sofec.com	Houston	TX	77040	713-510-6600	510-6601
Software Synergy Inc 151 Hwy 33 E *Web:* ssi-corp.com	Manalapan	NJ	07726	732-617-9300	
Soil & Materials Engineers Inc 43980 Plymouth Oaks Blvd *Web:* sme-usa.com	Plymouth	MI	48170	734-454-9900	454-0629
Soil Consusltant Engineering (SCE) 9303 Ctr St *Web:* www.soilconsultants.net	Manassas	VA	20110	703-366-3000	366-3400
Solekai Systems Corp 3398 Carmel Mtn Rd *Web:* www.solekai.com	San Diego	CA	92121	858-436-2040	436-2041
Somat Engineering Inc 660 Woodward Ave Ste 2430 *Web:* www.somateng.com	Detroit	MI	48226	313-963-2721	
Sonalysts Inc 215 Waterford Pkwy N *TF:* 800-526-8091 ■ *Web:* www.sonalysts.com	Waterford	CT	06385	860-442-4355	447-8883
Sonometrics Corp 500 Nottinghill Rd *Web:* www.sonometrics.com	London	ON	N6K3P1	519-474-6464	
Sound Vision 432 Boston Post Rd *Web:* www.soundvisioninc.com	Wayland	MA	01778	508-358-9000	
Soutex Inc 357 Rue Jackson *Web:* www.soutex.ca	Quebec	QC	G1N4C4	418-871-2455	
Southern Company Services Inc 42 Inverness Ctr Pkwy *Web:* www.southerncompany.com	Birmingham	AL	35242	205-992-6011	
SPACECO Inc 9575 W Higgins Rd Ste 700 *Web:* www.spacecoinc.com	Rosemont	IL	60018	847-696-4060	696-4065
Spagnuolo & Assoc LLC 3057 W Market St Ste 201 *Web:* spagnuoloassoc.com	Fairlawn	OH	44333	330-836-6661	
Spalding Dedecker Assoc Inc 905 S Blvd E *Web:* sda-eng.com	Rochester Hills	MI	48307	248-844-5400	
Spears-Votta & Assoc Inc 7526 Harford Rd *Web:* www.spearsvotta.com	Baltimore	MD	21234	410-254-5800	
Spec Ops Inc 319 Business Ln *TF:* 800-774-3854 ■ *Web:* www.specopsinc.com	Ashland	VA	23005	804-752-4790	
SPEC Services Inc 10540 Talbert Ave *Web:* www.specservices.com	Fountain Valley	CA	92708	714-963-8077	963-0364
Spectrum Solutions Inc 114 Castle Dr *Web:* spectrumsi.com	Madison	AL	35758	256-830-9759	
SPI/Mobile Pulley Works Inc 905 S Ann St *TF:* 866-334-6325 ■ *Web:* www.spimpw.com	Mobile	AL	36605	251-653-0606	653-0668
Spitzer Engineering LLC 730 Fifth Ave Ste 2202	New York	NY	10019	212-765-5170	

Company	City	State	Zip	Phone	Fax
Sponseller Group Inc 1600 Timber Wolf Dr *TF:* 800-776-1625 ■ *Web:* www.sponsellergroup.com	Holland	OH	43528	419-861-3000	
Spr Inc 789 N Water St Ste 100 *Web:* www.sprcompanies.com	Milwaukee	WI	53202	414-224-7961	
Sproule Associates Ltd 900 N Tower Sun Life Plz 140 Fourth Ave SW *TF:* 877-777-6135 ■ *Web:* www.sproule.com	Calgary	AB	T2P3N3	403-294-5500	
SRF Consulting Group Inc 1 Carlson Pkwy N Ste 150 *Web:* www.srfconsulting.com	Minneapolis	MN	55447	763-475-0010	475-2429
SRK Consulting Inc 7175 W Jefferson Ave Ste 3000 *Web:* www.na.srk.com	Lakewood	CO	80235	303-985-1333	985-9947
SSOE Inc 1001 Madison Ave *Web:* www.ssoe.com	Toledo	OH	43624	419-255-3830	255-6101
Staggs & Fisher Consulting Engineers Inc 3264 Lochness Dr *Web:* sfengineering.com	Lexington	KY	40517	859-271-3246	
Stanley Consultants Inc 225 Iowa Ave *TF:* 800-553-9694 ■ *Web:* www.stanleyconsultants.com	Muscatine	IA	52761	563-264-6600	264-6658
Stantec 3200 Bailey Ln Ste 200 *Web:* www.stantec.com	Naples	FL	34105	239-649-4040	
Stantec Inc 400 E Vine St Ste 300 *NYSE: STN* ■ **Fax Area Code:* 803 ■ *TF:* 866-782-6832 ■ *Web:* www.stantec.com	Lexington	KY	40507	859-233-2100	929-0510*
Stantec Inc 10160-112 St *NYSE: STN* ■ *Web:* www.stantec.com	Edmonton	AB	T5K2L6	780-917-7000	917-7330
Steger & Bizzell Engineering Inc 1978 S Austin Ave *Web:* stegerbizzell.com	Georgetown	TX	78626	512-930-9412	
Stellar Engineering Inc 2899 E Coronado St Unit E	Anaheim	CA	92806	714-632-0040	
Stellar Solutions Inc 250 Cambridge Ave Ste 204 *Web:* stellarsolutions.com	Palo Alto	CA	94306	650-473-9866	
Stem Engineering Group 875 Queen St E *Web:* stemeng.ca	Sault Sainte Marie	ON	P6A2B3	705-942-6628	
Steven Schaefer Associates Inc 10411 Medallion Dr *TF:* 800-542-3302 ■ *Web:* schaefer-inc.com	Cincinnati	OH	45241	513-542-3300	
Stimmel Associates PA 601 N Trade St Ste 200 *Web:* www.stimmelpa.com	Winston-Salem	NC	27101	336-723-1067	
Strand Assoc Inc 910 W Wingra Dr *Web:* www.strand.com	Madison	WI	53715	608-251-4843	251-8655
Strata Inc 8653 W Hackamore Dr *Web:* stratageotech.com	Boise	ID	83709	208-376-8200	
Stratasys Inc 7665 Commerce Way *NASDAQ: SSYS* ■ *TF:* 800-937-3010 ■ *Web:* www.stratasys.com	Eden Prairie	MN	55344	952-937-3000	937-0070
Stray Light Optical Technologies Inc 821 S Lk Rd South	Scottsburg	IN	47170	812-752-9104	
STRONE Inc 2717 Coventry Rd *Web:* www.strone.ca	Oakville	ON	L6H5V9	905-829-5707	
Studio Red Inc 115 Independence Dr *Web:* www.studiored.com	Menlo Park	CA	94025	650-324-2244	
STV Group Inc 205 W Welsh Dr *Web:* www.stvinc.com	Douglassville	PA	19518	610-385-8200	385-8500
STV Inc 225 Pk Ave S 5th Fl *Web:* www.stvinc.com	New York	NY	10003	212-777-4400	529-5237
Subcoe 117 Pembina Rd *Web:* www.subcoe.com	Sherwood Park	AB	T8H0J4	780-467-3477	
SUBNET Solutions Inc 4639 Manhattan Rd SE Ste 100 *Web:* www.subnet.com	Calgary	AB	T2G4B3	403-270-8885	
Subsea 7 (Us) LLC 10787 Clay Rd *Web:* subsea7.com	Houston	TX	77041	713-430-1100	
Suburban Electrical Engineers/ Contractors Inc 709 Hickory Farm Ln *Web:* suburbanelectric.com	Appleton	WI	54914	920-739-5156	
Sun Engineering Services Inc 5405 Garden Grove Blvd *TF:* 888-604-5888 ■ *Web:* www.sunengr.net	Westminster	CA	92683	714-379-2300	
Sunland Group Inc 1033 La Posada Dr Ste 370 *TF:* 866-732-8500 ■ *Web:* www.sunlandgrp.com	Austin	TX	78752	512-494-0208	
Sunrise Engineering Inc 25 East 500 North *Web:* sunrise-eng.com	Fillmore	UT	84631	435-743-6151	
Support Systems Assoc Inc (SSAI) 709 S Harbor City Blvd Ste 350 *Web:* www.ssai.org	Melbourne	FL	32901	321-724-5566	724-6673
Sur-Flo Plastics & Engineering Inc 24358 Groesbeck Hwy *Web:* www.sur-flo.com	Warren	MI	48089	586-773-0400	773-8946
Swanson Rink Inc 1120 Lincoln St 1200 *Web:* www.swansonrink.com	Denver	CO	80203	303-832-2666	
Swat Energy Inc 3220 Blume Dr Ste 118	Richmond	CA	94806	510-758-1568	
Symmes Maini & McKee Assoc (SMMA) 1000 Massachusetts Ave **Fax Area Code:* 800 ■ *Web:* www.smma.com	Cambridge	MA	02138	617-547-5400	648-4920*
Synchrony Inc 4655 Technology Dr *Web:* www.synchrony.com	Salem	VA	24153	540-444-4200	444-4201
Syndesi Solutions Inc 611 E Hobbs St *Web:* www.syndesisolutions.com	Athens	AL	35611	256-867-4135	
Synerlution Inc Po Box 4336 *Web:* www.synerlution.com	Aguadilla	PR	00605	787-493-0864	
Synesis International Inc 30 Creekview Ct *Web:* www.synesisintl.com	Greenville	SC	29615	864-288-1550	
SYNEXXUS Inc 2425 Wilson Blvd Ste 400 *Web:* www.synexxus.com	Arlington	VA	22201	401-855-9600	
Syska & Hennessy Group 11 W 42nd St *TF:* 800-328-1600 ■ *Web:* www.syska.com	New York	NY	10036	212-921-2300	556-3333
System Dynamics International Inc (SDI) 560 Discovery Dr NW *Web:* www.sdi-inc.com	Huntsville	AL	35806	256-895-9000	895-9443
Systems & Processes Engineering Corp (SPEC) 6800 Burleson Rd Ste 320 *Web:* www.spec.com	Austin	TX	78744	512-479-7732	494-0756
Systems Planning & Analysis Inc (SPA) 2001 N Beauregard St *Web:* www.spa.com	Alexandria	VA	22311	703-399-7550	
Systems Technologies Inc 185 Rt 36 *Web:* www.systek.com	West Long Branch	NJ	07764	732-571-6400	571-6401
T Bailey Inc 12441 Bartholomew Rd *Web:* www.tbailey.com	Anacortes	WA	98221	360-293-0682	
T-solutions Inc 860 Greenbrier Cir Ste 405 *Web:* www.tsoln-inc.com	Chesapeake	VA	23320	757-410-9450	
TABCON Engineering 494 McNicoll Ave Ste 201 *Web:* www.tabcon.com	Toronto	ON	M2H2E1	416-491-7006	
Taber Consultants 3911 W Capitol Ave *TF:* 888-423-0573 ■ *Web:* www.taberconsultants.com	West Sacramento	CA	95691	916-371-1690	
Tait & Assoc Inc 701 N Parkcenter Dr *Web:* tait.com	Santa Ana	CA	92705	714-560-8200	
Talascend LLC 5700 Crooks Rd Ste 450 *Web:* talascend.com	Troy	MI	48098	248-537-1300	
Talbert & Bright Inc 4810 Shelley Dr *Web:* talbertandbright.com	Wilmington	NC	28405	910-763-5350	
Talon Energy Services Inc 215 Water St Atlantic Pl Ste 301 *Web:* talonenergyservices.ca	St. John's	NL	A1C6C9	709-739-8450	
Tanco Engineering Inc 1400 Taurus Ct *Web:* tancoeng.com	Loveland	CO	80537	970-776-4200	
Tandel Systems Inc 3982 Tampa Rd *Web:* www.tandelsystems.com	Oldsmar	FL	34677	727-530-1110	
Tangent Design Engineering 2719 7 Ave Ne *Web:* www.tangentservices.com	Calgary	AB	T2A2L9	403-274-4647	
Tank Industry Consultants Inc 7740 W New York St *Web:* tankindustry.com	Indianapolis	IN	46214	317-271-3100	
TASS Inc 12016 115th Ave NE Ste 100 *Web:* www.tassinc.com	Kirkland	WA	98034	425-821-2200	
Taylor & Syfan Consulting Engineers Inc 684 Clarion Ct *TF:* 800-579-3881 ■ *Web:* www.taylorsyfan.com	San Luis Obispo	CA	93401	805-547-2000	
Taylor Wiseman & Taylor (TWT) 124 Gaither Dr Ste 150 *Web:* www.taylorwiseman.com	Mount Laurel	NJ	08054	856-235-7200	722-9250
Tdm Technical Services 3924 Chesswood Dr *Web:* www.tdm.ca	Toronto	ON	M3J2W6	416-777-0007	
TeamLogic IT Inc 25909 Plz *Web:* www.teamlogicit.com	Mission Viejo	CA	92691	949-582-6300	
Tech 4 3547 French Rd *Web:* tech4.com	De Pere	WI	54115	920-532-0480	
Tech Conveyor Inc 195 Strykers Rd *Web:* www.techconveyor.com	Phillipsburg	NJ	08865	908-454-1515	
Tech-Marine Business Inc 9253 Old Keene Mill Rd *Web:* www.tmbhq.com	Burke	VA	22015	703-455-0887	
Techni Core Professionals Inc 4681 Research Park Blvd *Web:* www.techni-core.com	Huntsville	AL	35806	256-704-0234	
Technical Field Engineering Inc 1114 Ridgecrest Ave	North Augusta	SC	29841	803-279-0331	
Tectonic Engineering & Surveying Consultants PC 70 Pleasant Hill Rd *TF:* 800-829-6531 ■ *Web:* tectonicengineering.com	Mountainville	NY	10953	845-534-5959	
TEECOM Design Group 1333 Broadway Ste 601 *Web:* teecom.com	Oakland	CA	94612	510-337-2800	
Tejas Research & Engineering LP 9185 Six Pines Dr *Web:* www.tejasre.com	The Woodlands	TX	77380	281-466-8700	
Telamon Engineering Consultant 855 Folsom St *Web:* www.telamoninc.com	San Francisco	CA	94107	415-837-1336	
Teledyne Brown Engineering Inc 300 Sparkman Dr **Fax:* Hum Res ■ *TF:* 800-933-2091 ■ *Web:* www.tbe.com	Huntsville	AL	35807	256-726-1000	726-5556*
Telics 652 Bush River Rd Ste 220 *Web:* www.telics.com	Columbia	SC	29210	803-798-6642	
Tempress Technologies Inc 18858 72nd Ave S *Web:* tempresstech.com	Kent	WA	98032	425-251-8120	
Tepa LLC 5045 List Dr *Web:* tepa.com	Colorado Springs	CO	80919	719-596-8114	
Terracon 18001 W 106th St *TF:* 800-593-7777 ■ *Web:* www.terracon.com	Olathe	KS	66061	913-599-6886	599-0574
Terracon Geotechnique Ltd 800 734 - Seventh Ave SW *Web:* www.terracon.ca	Calgary	AB	T2P3P8	403-266-1150	
Terragon Environmental Technologies Inc 651 rue Bridge *Web:* terragon.net	Montreal	QC	H3K2C8	514-938-3772	
Test Connection Inc, The 11400 Cronridge Dr Ste H *Web:* www.ttci.info	Owings Mills	MD	21117	410-526-2800	
Testing Engineers & Consultants Inc 1343 Rochester Rd *Web:* www.tectest.com	Troy	MI	48083	248-588-6200	
Testwell Laboratories Inc 47 Hudson St	Ossining	NY	10562	914-762-9004	
Tetra Tech EC Inc 1000 the American Rd **Fax Area Code:* 303 ■ *Web:* www.tteci.com	Morris Plains	NJ	07950	973-630-8000	980-3539*
Tetra Tech Inc 3475 E Foothill Blvd *NASDAQ: TTEK* ■ *Web:* www.tetratech.com	Pasadena	CA	91107	626-351-4664	351-5291
Tetra Tech WEI Inc 330 Bay St Ste 900 *Web:* www.wardrop.com	Toronto	ON	M5H2S8	416-368-9080	
Tetra Tech/KCM 3475 E Foothill Blvd *NASDAQ: TTEK* ■ *Web:* www.tetratech.com	Pasadena	CA	91107	626-351-4664	351-5291
Texas Design Interests LLC 6001 W William Cannon Dr Ste 203C *Web:* tdi-llc.net	Austin	TX	78749	512-301-3389	

Company	City	State	Zip	Phone	Fax
Thelen Assoc Inc 1398 Cox Ave. *Web:* www.thelenassoc.com	Erlanger	KY	41018	859-746-9400	746-9408
Thermal Tech 5141 Forsyth Commerce Rd Unit 1 *Web:* tti-fl.com	Orlando	FL	32807	407-373-0042	
Thermasource LLC 3883 Airway Dr Ste 340 *Web:* thermasource.com	Santa Rosa	CA	95403	707-523-2960	
Thermo Design Engineering Ltd 1424 - 70th Ave *Web:* www.thermodesign.com	Edmonton	AB	T6P1P5	780-440-6064	
Thielsch Engineering Inc 195 Frances Ave. *Web:* thielsch.com	Cranston	RI	02910	401-467-6454	
Think-A-Move Ltd 23307 Commerce Park *Web:* www.think-a-move.com	Beachwood	OH	44122	216-765-8875	
Thomas F Moran Inc 48 Constitution Dr	Bedford	NH	03110	603-472-4488	
Thomas Russell LLC 7050 S Yale Ave Ste 210 *Web:* www.thomasrussellco.com	Tulsa	OK	74136	918-481-5682	
Thompson & Litton Inc 103 E Main St. *Web:* t-l.com	Wise	VA	24293	276-328-2161	
Thorburn Assoc Inc 20880 Baker Rd *Web:* ta-inc.com	Castro Valley	CA	94546	510-886-7826	
Thornton-Tomasetti Group Inc (TTINC) 2000 L St NW Ste 600 *Web:* www.thorntontomasetti.com	Washington	DC	20036	202-580-6300	580-6301
Three Streams Engineering Ltd Ste 401 1925-18th Ave NE *Web:* www.threestreams.com	Calgary	AB	T2E7T8	403-536-5000	
Tighe & Bond Inc 53 Southampton Rd *Web:* www.tighebond.com	Westfield	MA	01085	413-562-1600	562-5317
Timmons Group Inc 1001 Boulders Pkwy Ste 300 *Web:* www.timmons.com	Richmond	VA	23225	804-200-6500	
Tindale Oliver & Associates Inc 1000 N Ashley Dr *Web:* www.tindaleoliver.com	Tampa	FL	33602	813-224-8862	
Tipping Mar & Assoc 1906 Shattuck Ave. *Web:* tippingmar.com	Berkeley	CA	94704	510-549-1906	
TL Industries Inc 2541 Tracy Rd. *Web:* www.tlindustries.com	Northwood	OH	43619	419-666-8144	666-6534
TLC Engineering for Architecture 255 S Orange Ave # 1600 *Web:* www.tlc-engineers.com	Orlando	FL	32801	407-841-9050	317-7182
TLM Associates Inc 117 E Lafayette St *Web:* www.tlmassociates.com	Jackson	TN	38301	731-988-9840	
TMAD Taylor & Gaines (TTG) 300 N Lake Ave 14th Fl. *Web:* www.tmadengineers.com	Pasadena	CA	91101	626-463-2711	
TMP Architecture 1191 W Sq Lk Rd *Web:* www.tmp-architecture.com	Bloomfield Hills	MI	48302	248-338-4561	338-0223
TMP Consulting Engineers Inc 52 Temple Pl *Web:* www.tmpeng.com	Boston	MA	02111	617-357-6060	
Toledo Engineering Company Inc 3400 Executive Pkwy PO Box 2927 *Web:* www.teco.com	Toledo	OH	43606	419-537-9711	537-1369
Tolunay-Wong Engineers Inc 10710 S Sam Houston Pkwy W *Web:* tweinc.com	Houston	TX	77031	713-722-7064	722-0319
Traffic Engineering Consultants Inc 6000 S Western Ste 300 *Web:* tecok.com	Oklahoma City	OK	73139	405-720-7721	
Traffic Planning & Design Inc 2500 E High St Ste 650 *Web:* www.trafficpd.com	Pottstown	PA	19464	610-326-3100	
Trandes Corp 4601 Presidents Dr Ste 360 *Web:* www.trandes.com	Lanham	MD	20706	301-459-0200	459-1069
TransCore Holdings Inc 8158 Adams Dr. *TF:* 800-923-4824 ■ *Web:* www.transcore.com	Hummelstown	PA	17036	717-561-2400	564-8439
Transmission Engineering Company Inc 1851 N Penn Rd *Web:* www.tecoinc.com	Hatfield	PA	19440	215-822-6737	
Transnuclear Inc 7135 Minstrel Way Ste 300 *Web:* www.transnuclear.com	Columbia	MD	21045	410-910-6900	
TranSystems Corp 2400 Pershing Rd Ste 400 *Web:* www.transystems.com	Kansas City	MO	64108	816-329-8700	329-8703
Trayer Engineering Corp 898 Pennsylvania Ave. *TF:* 800-377-1774 ■ *Web:* trayer.com	San Francisco	CA	94107	415-285-7770	
TRC Worldwide Engineering Inc (TRCWW) 217 Ward Cir *Web:* www.trcww.com	Brentwood	TN	37027	615-661-7979	661-0644
Trenton Engineering Company Inc 2193 Spruce St. *Web:* trentoneng.com	Trenton	NJ	08638	609-882-0616	
Tri Star Engineering Inc 3000 16th St. *Web:* www.star3.com	Bedford	IN	47421	812-277-0208	277-0219
Tri Tech Surveying Company LP 10401 Westoffice Dr. *Web:* www.surveyingcompany.com	Houston	TX	77042	713-667-0800	
Triad Consulting Engineers Inc 2740 State Rt 10 Ste 2 *Web:* www.triadcei.com	Morris Plains	NJ	07950	973-984-1919	
Triaxis Engineering Inc 1600 Sw Western Blvd *Web:* www.triaxiseng.com	Corvallis	OR	97333	541-766-4600	
Trident Environmental & Engineeri 110 L St Ste 1 *Web:* tridenteng.com	Antioch	CA	94509	925-706-6931	
Trideum Corp 555 Discovery Dr Ste 150 *Web:* trideum.com	Huntsville	AL	35806	256-704-6100	
Trihydro Corp 1252 Commerce Dr. *Web:* trihydro.com	Laramie	WY	82070	307-745-7474	
TriLeaf Inc 10845 Olive Blvd Ste 310 *TF:* 800-652-5552 ■ *Web:* www.trileaf.com	Saint Louis	MO	63141	314-997-6111	997-8066
Triodyne Inc 666 Dundee Rd Ste 103 *Web:* www.triodyne.com	Northbrook	IL	60062	847-677-4730	647-2047
TriTeq Lock and Security LLC 701 Gullo *Web:* www.triteqlock.com	Elk Grove Village	IL	60007	847-640-7002	
Truevance Management Inc 7666 Blanding Blvd *TF:* 800-285-2028 ■ *Web:* www.truenetcommunications.com	Jacksonville	FL	32244	904-777-9052	
Trussell Technologies Inc 232 N Lk Ave Ste 300 *Web:* www.trusselltech.com	Pasadena	CA	91101	626-486-0560	
TS Civil Engineering Inc 1776 Technology Dr. *Web:* tscivil.com	San Jose	CA	95110	408-452-9300	
TSM Corp 7622 Bartlett Corporate Dr *Web:* tsmcorporation.com	Bartlett	TN	38133	901-373-0300	
Tsoi/Kobus & Assoc Inc (TKA) 1 Brattle Sq PO Box 9114 *Web:* www.tka-architects.com	Cambridge	MA	02238	617-475-4000	475-4445
Turner EnviroLogic Inc 1140 SW 34 Ave. *Web:* www.tenviro.com	Deerfield Beach	FL	33442	954-422-9787	
Tysinger Hampton & Partners Inc 3428 Bristol Hwy *Web:* tysinger-engineering.com	Johnson City	TN	37601	423-282-2687	
UELS LLC 85 South 200 East *Web:* www.uintahgroup.com	Vernal	UT	84078	435-789-1017	
Ulteig Engineers Inc 3350 38th Ave S *TF:* 888-858-3441 ■ *Web:* www.ulteig.com	Fargo	ND	58104	701-280-8500	237-3191
UNI Engineering Inc 156 Stockton St. *Web:* uni-engineering.com	Hightstown	NJ	08520	609-448-4633	
Unicon Inc 1760 E Pecos Rd Ste 432 *Web:* www.unicon.net	Gilbert	AZ	85295	480-558-2400	
Unified Industries Inc 6551 Loisdale Ct Ste 400 *TF:* 800-666-1642 ■ *Web:* www.uii.com	Springfield	VA	22150	703-922-9800	971-5892
Unified Theory Inc 1811 Weir Dr Ste 365 *Web:* www.unifiedtheory.net	Saint Paul	MN	55125	651-578-8100	
United States Steel Corp 600 Grant St *NYSE:* X ■ *TF:* 866-433-4801 ■ *Web:* www.ussteel.com	Pittsburgh	PA	15219	412-433-1121	
Universal Technical Resource Services Inc (UERS) 950 Kings Hwy N Ste 208 *Web:* www.utrs.com	Cherry Hill	NJ	08034	856-667-6770	667-7586
Universal Technology Corp (UTC) 1270 N Fairfield Rd. *Web:* www.utcdayton.com	Dayton	OH	45432	937-426-2808	426-0839
UniversalPegasus International Inc 4848 Loop Central Dr *TF General:* 800-966-1811 ■ *Web:* www.universalpegasus.com	Houston	TX	77081	713-977-7770	977-1047
Urbahn Architects 49 W 37th St 6th Fl *Web:* www.urbahn.com	New York	NY	10018	212-239-0220	
Urban Engineers Inc 530 Walnut St 14th Fl. *Web:* www.urbanengineers.com	Philadelphia	PA	19106	215-922-8080	922-8082
Ursa Navigation Solutions Inc 616 Innovation Dr. *Web:* ursanav.com	Chesapeake	VA	23320	757-312-0790	
Urwiler & Walter Inc 3126 Main St *Web:* urwilerwalter.com	Sumneytown	PA	18084	215-234-4562	
US Infrastructure Group Inc 774 Second St.	Helena	AL	35080	205-358-3070	
US Trackworks LLC 1165 142nd Ave *Web:* ustrackworks.com	Wayland	MI	49348	616-877-4284	
USM Business Systems Inc 14175 Sullyfield Cir *Web:* usmsystems.com	Chantilly	VA	20151	703-263-0855	
Utility Engineering 1515 Arapahoe St Tower 1 Ste 700	Denver	CO	80202	303-928-4400	928-4368
UTSI International Corp 1560 W Bay Area Blvd Ste 300 *Web:* www.utsi.com	Friendswood	TX	77546	281-480-8786	
V. B. Cook Company Ltd 740 S Syndicate Ave. *Web:* www.cookeng.com	Thunder Bay	ON	P7E1E9	807-625-6700	
V3 Cos Ltd 7325 Janes Ave *Web:* v3co.com	Woodridge	IL	60517	630-724-9200	
Vadum Inc 601 Hutton St Ste 109 *Web:* www.vaduminc.com	Raleigh	NC	27606	919-341-8241	
Valcom Consulting Group Inc 85 Albert St. *TF:* 866-561-5580 ■ *Web:* www.valcom.ca	Ottawa	ON	K1P6A4	613-594-5200	
Valsamis Inc 5814 Northdale St *Web:* valsamis.com	Houston	TX	77087	713-640-1500	
Van Dijk Westlake Reed Leskosky (WRL) 1422 Euclid Ave Ste 300 *Web:* www.wrldesign.com	Cleveland	OH	44115	216-522-1350	
Vanadium Group Corp 134 Three Degree Rd *TF:* 800-685-0354 ■ *Web:* zoominfo.com	Pittsburgh	PA	15237	412-367-6060	630-8430
Vanasse Hangen Brustlin Inc (VHB) 101 Walnut St PO Box 9151 *Web:* www.vhb.com	Watertown	MA	02472	617-924-1770	924-2286
VanDemark & Lynch Inc 4305 Miller Rd *Web:* www.vandemarklynch.com	Wilmington	DE	19802	302-764-7635	
Vanderweil Engineers 274 Summer St *Web:* www.vanderweil.com	Boston	MA	02210	617-423-7423	423-7401
Vanteon Corp 250 Cross Keys Office Pk Bldg 250 *TF:* 888-506-5677 ■ *Web:* www.vanteon.com	Fairport	NY	14450	585-419-9555	248-0537
Vaughn Coast & Vaughn Inc 154 S Marietta St *Web:* vaughncoastvaughn.com	St Clairsville	OH	43950	740-695-7256	
Vectech Pharmaceutical Consultants Inc 12501 E Grand River Ave *TF:* 800-966-8832 ■ *Web:* www.vectech.com	Brighton	MI	48116	248-478-5820	
Veenstra & Kimm Inc 3000 Westown Pkwy. *TF:* 800-241-8000 ■ *Web:* www.v-k.net	West Des Moines	IA	50266	515-225-8000	
Vektrel LLC 9988 Hibert St Ste 104 *Web:* www.vektrel.com	San Diego	CA	92131	858-564-0301	

Phone Fax

Veloxiti Inc 3650 Brookside Pkwy Ste 500 ... Alpharetta GA 30022 770-518-4228
Web: www.asinc.com

Verdant Power LLC
888 Main St The Octagon Ste 1 ... New York NY 10044 212-888-8887
Web: www.verdantpower.com

Verifact Corp 11220 W Loop 1604 N ... San Antonio TX 78254 210-523-5696
Web: verifactcorp.com

Versar Inc 6850 Versar Ctr ... Springfield VA 22151 703-750-3000 642-6825
NYSE: VSR ■ *TF Cust Svc:* 800-283-7727 ■ *Web:* www.versar.com

Vigen Construction Inc PO Box 6109 ... Grand Forks ND 58206 218-773-1159 773-3454
Web: www.vigenconstruction.com

Villaverd Inc 1218 E Yandell Dr Ste 201 ... El Paso TX 79902 915-351-8822
Web: villaverdeinc.com

Virent Energy Systems Inc 3571 Anderson St ... Madison WI 53704 608-663-0228
Web: www.virent.com

Vista Engineering Corp
1030 Pleasantview Terr ... Ridgefield NJ 07657 201-945-9434
Web: vistaengineeringcorp.com

Visual Engineering Inc 164 Main St 2nd Fl ... Los Altos CA 94022 650-949-5410
Web: www.ve.com

Vitetta 2 International Pl ... Philadelphia PA 19113 215-218-4747 405-2729
Web: www.vitetta.com

Vizient Ii LLC 3129 State St Unit 2 ... Bettendorf IA 52722 563-355-4812
Web: vizient.com

VOA Assoc Inc 224 S Michigan Ave Ste 1400 ... Chicago IL 60604 312-554-1400 554-1412
Web: www.voa.com

Volkert & Assoc Inc 3809 Moffett Rd ... Mobile AL 36618 251-342-1070 342-7962
Web: www.volkert.com

Vollmer Inc 3822 Sandwich St ... Windsor ON N9C1C1 519-966-6100
Web: www.vollmer.ca

VSE Corp 2550 Huntington Ave ... Alexandria VA 22303 703-960-4600 329-4623
NASDAQ: VSEC ■ *TF:* 800-455-4873 ■ *Web:* www.vsecorp.com

W & H Pacific 12100 NE 195th St Ste 300 ... Bothell WA 98011 425-951-4800 951-4808
Web: www.whpacific.com

W R Chesnut Engineering Inc 14 Spielman Rd ... Fairfield NJ 07004 973-227-6995
Web: chesnuteng.com

W R Systems Ltd 11351 Random Hills Rd Ste 400 ... Fairfax VA 22030 703-934-0200
Web: wrsystems.com

Wade-Trim Group Inc 500 Griswold Ave Ste 2500 ... Detroit MI 48226 313-961-3650 961-0898
TF: 800-482-2864 ■ *Web:* www.wadetrim.com

Waldemar S Nelson & Company Inc
1200 St Charles Ave ... New Orleans LA 70130 504-523-5281 523-4587
Web: www.wsnelson.com

Waldron Engineering & Construction Inc
37 Industrial Dr ... Exeter NH 03833 603-772-7153
Web: www.waldron.com

Walker Martin & Hatch LLC 321 D St Ne ... Washington DC 20002 202-543-9004
Web: walkermartinhatch.com

Walker Parking Consultants/Restoration Engineers Inc
2121 Hudson Ave ... Kalamazoo MI 49008 269-381-6080 343-5811
Web: www.walkerparking.com

Wallace Engineering Structural Consultants Inc
200 E Brady ... Tulsa OK 74103 918-584-5858
Web: www.wallacesc.com

Wallace Roberts & Todd LLC
1700 Market St 28th Fl ... Philadelphia PA 19103 215-732-5215 732-2551
TF: 800-978-4450 ■ *Web:* www.wrtdesign.com

Walter P Moore 1301 Mckinney St Ste 1100 ... Houston TX 77010 713-630-7300 630-7396
TF: 800-364-7300 ■ *Web:* www.walterpmoore.com

Ware Malcomb 10 Edelman ... Irvine CA 92618 949-660-9128 863-1581
Web: www.waremalcomb.com

Warren Group Inc, The 7805 Saint Andrews Rd ... Irmo SC 29063 803-732-6600
Web: www.warrenforensics.com

Washington Corp PO Box 16630 ... Missoula MT 59808 406-523-1300 523-1399
Web: www.washcorp.com

Wastech Controls & Engineering Inc
21201 Itasca St ... Chatsworth CA 91311 818-998-3500
Web: www.wastechengineering.com

Watek Engineering Corp
12122B Heritage Park Cir ... Silver Spring MD 20906 301-933-9690
Web: www.watek.com

Water Technology Inc 100 Park Ave ... Beaver Dam WI 53916 920-887-7375
Web: www.watertechnologyinc.com

Watermark Environmental Inc 175 Cabot St ... Lowell MA 01854 978-452-9696
Web: www.watermarkenv.com

Watkins Hamilton Ross Architects Inc
1111 Louisiana St Fl 26 ... Houston TX 77002 713-665-5665 665-6213
Web: www.whrarchitects.com

Watson Engineering Inc 16445 Racho Rd ... Taylor MI 48180 734-285-2200
Web: watsoneng.com

Wavetronix LLC 78 East 1700 South ... Provo UT 84606 801-734-7200
Web: www.wavetronix.com

WC Cammett Engineering Inc 297 Elm St ... Amesbury MA 01913 978-388-2157
Web: www.cammett.com

WD Partners 7007 Discovery Blvd ... Dublin OH 43017 614-634-7000
Web: www.wdpartners.com

Weidlinger Assoc 40 Wall St ... New York NY 10005 212-367-3000 367-3030
Web: www.wai.com

Weir International Inc
1431 Opus Pl Executive Towers W I
Ste 210 ... Downers Grove IL 60515 630-968-5400
Web: www.weirintl.com

Welkin Sciences LLC
102 S Tejon St Ste 200 ... Colorado Springs CO 80903 719-520-5115
Web: www.welkinsciences.com

Wenck Assoc Inc PO Box 249 ... Maple Plain MN 55359 763-479-4200 479-4242
Web: www.wenck.com

West Consultants Pllc 405 S Sterling St ... Morganton NC 28655 828-433-5661
Web: west-consultants.com

Westech International Inc
2500 Louisiana Blvd NE Ste 325 ... Albuquerque NM 87110 505-888-6666 837-9424
Web: www.westech-intl.com

Phone Fax

Westermeyer Industries Inc 1441 State Rt 100 ... Bluffs IL 62621 217-754-3277
Web: www.westermeyerind.com

Western Engineering Contractors Inc
3171 Rippey Rd ... Loomis CA 95650 916-652-3990 652-3995
Web: www.westeng.com

Westfall Engineers Inc 14583 Big Basin Way ... Saratoga CA 95070 408-867-0244
Web: westf.com

Westinghouse Electric Co
1000 Westinghouse Dr Ste 572A ... Cranberry Township PA 16066 412-374-4111
Web: www.westinghousenuclear.com

Weston & Sampson Inc 5 Centennial Dr ... Peabody MA 01960 978-532-1900 977-0100
TF: 800-726-7766 ■ *Web:* www.westonandsampson.com

Weston Solutions Inc
1400 Weston Way PO Box 2653 ... West Chester PA 19380 610-701-3000 701-3186
Web: www.westonsolutions.com

Wetland Studies & Solutions Inc
5300 Wellington Branch Dr ... Gainesville VA 20155 703-679-5600
Web: www.wetlandstudies.com

Wheaton & Sprague Engineering Inc
1100 Campus Dr Ste 200 ... Stow OH 44224 330-923-5560
Web: www.wheatonsprague.com

Whipsaw Inc 434 S First St ... San Jose CA 95113 408-297-9771
Web: www.whipsaw.com

Whitlock & Weinberger
490 Mendocino Ave Ste 201 ... Santa Rosa CA 95401 707-542-9500
Web: w-trans.com

Whitman Requardt & Assoc 801 S Caroline St ... Baltimore MD 21231 410-235-3450 243-5716
Web: www.wrallp.com

Whitney Bailey Cox & Magnani LLC
849 Fairmount Ave Ste 100 ... Baltimore MD 21286 410-512-4500 324-4100
Web: www.wbcm.com

Wight & Co 2500 N Frontage Rd ... Darien IL 60561 630-969-7000 969-7979
Web: wightco75.com

Wiley & Wilson Inc 127 Nationwide Dr ... Lynchburg VA 24502 434-947-1901
Web: wileywilson.com

Willbros Downstream LLC
4400 Post Oak Pkwy Ste 1000 ... Houston TX 77027 918-556-3600
TF: 888-310-7712 ■ *Web:* www.willbros.com

Willbros Engineers Inc 2087 E 71st St ... Tulsa OK 74136 918-496-0400 491-9436
Web: www.willbros.com

Willdan 2401 E Katella Ave Ste 300 ... Anaheim CA 92806 714-940-6300 940-4920
TF: 800-424-9144 ■ *Web:* www.willdan.com

Willdan Energy Solutions Inc
6120 Stoneridge Mall Rd Ste 250 ... Pleasanton CA 94588 925-416-4200
Web: www.willdangroup.com

Williams & Works Inc 549 Ottawa NW ... Grand Rapids MI 49503 616-224-1500
Web: williams-works.com

Williams Notaro & Assoc LLC
3928 Pender Dr Ste 220 ... Fairfax VA 22030 703-563-0381
Web: wnainc.com

Wilson & Company Engineers & Arch
4900 Lang Ave Ne ... Albuquerque NM 87109 505-348-4000
Web: wilsonco.com

Wilson T Ballard Co 17 Gwynns Mill Ct ... Owings Mills MD 21117 410-363-0150
Web: www.wtbco.com

Wimberly Allison Tong & Goo
700 Bishop St Ste 1800 ... Honolulu HI 96813 808-521-8888 521-3888
Web: www.watg.com

Wink Inc 8641 United Plaza Blvd ... Baton Rouge LA 70809 225-932-6000 932-9035
Web: www.willbros.com

Wiss Janney Elstner Assoc Inc
330 Pfingsten Rd ... Northbrook IL 60062 847-272-7400 291-9599
Web: www.wje.com

Wke Inc 400 N Tustin Ave Ste 275 ... Santa Ana CA 92705 714-953-2665
Web: www.wke-inc.com

WMA Consulting Engineers Ltd
815 S Wabash Ave ... Chicago IL 60605 312-786-4310
Web: www.wmace.com

Wolfberg Alvarez & Partners
3225 Aviation Ave Ste 400 ... Miami FL 33133 305-666-5474 666-4994
Web: www.wolfbergalvarez.com

Wong Engineers Inc
4578 Feather River Dr Ste A ... Stockton CA 95219 209-476-0011

Wood Consulting Services Inc
8161 Maple Lawn Blvd Ste 375 ... Fulton MD 20759 301-377-5300
Web: woodcons.com

Wood Patel & Assoc Inc
2051 W Northern Ave Ste 100 ... Phoenix AZ 85021 602-335-8500 335-8580
Web: www.woodpatel.com

Woodard & Curran 41 Hutchins Dr ... Portland ME 04102 207-774-2112
TF: 800-426-4262 ■ *Web:* www.woodardcurran.com

Woolpert Inc 4454 Idea Ctr Blvd ... Dayton OH 45430 937-461-5660 461-0743
Web: www.woolpert.com

Workforce Insight Inc 1600 Wynkoop Ste 5B ... Denver CO 80202 303-309-4006
Web: www.workforceinsight.com

Wright Water Engineers Inc
2490 W 26th Ave Ste 100a ... Denver CO 80211 303-480-1700 480-1020
Web: www.wrightwater.com

Wright-Pierce 99 Main St ... Topsham ME 04086 207-725-8721
Web: www.wright-pierce.com

Wunderlich-Malec Engineering Inc
5501 Feltl Rd ... Minnetonka MN 55343 952-933-3222
Web: www.wmeng.com

Zapata Inc 6302 Fairview Rd Ste 600 ... Charlotte NC 28210 704-358-8240
Web: zapatainc.com

Zephyr Environmental Corp
2600 Via Fortuna Ste 450 ... Austin TX 78746 512-329-5544 329-8253
TF: 800-452-5558 ■ *Web:* www.zephyrenv.com

ZETA-TECH Associates Inc
900 Kings Hwy N Ste 208 ... Cherry Hill NJ 08034 856-779-7795
Web: www.zetatech.com

Zeton Inc 740 Oval Ct ... Burlington ON L7L6A9 905-632-3123
TF: 877-299-3866 ■ *Web:* www.zeton.com

				Phone	Fax
ZFA Structural Engineers 1212 Fourth St Ste Z. Web: www.zfa.com	Santa Rosa	CA	95404	707-526-0992	

262 ENGINES & TURBINES

See Also Aircraft Engines & Engine Parts p. 1724; Automotive Parts & Supplies - Mfr p. 1830; Motors (Electric) & Generators p. 2787

				Phone	Fax
Alturdyne Inc 660 Steele St. Web: www.alturdyne.com	El Cajon	CA	92020	619-440-5531	442-0481
Anatech Electronics Inc 70 Outwater Ln. Web: www.anatechelectronics.com	Garfield	NJ	07026	973-772-4242	
Arrow Engine Co 2301 E Independence St. TF: 800-331-3662 ■ Web: www.arrowengines.com	Tulsa	OK	74110	918-583-5711	592-1481
Briggs & Stratton Corp 12301 W Wirth St. NYSE: BGG ■ TF: 800-444-7774 ■ Web: www.briggsandstratton.com	Milwaukee	WI	53222	414-259-5333	
Brunswick Corp 1 N Field Ct. NYSE: BC ■ Web: www.brunswick.com	Lake Forest	IL	60045	847-735-4700	735-4765
Brunswick Corp Mercury Marine Div W 6250 Pioneer Rd. TF: 866-408-6372 ■ Web: www.mercurymarine.com	Fond du Lac	WI	54935	920-929-5040	
Capstone Turbine Corp 21211 Nordhoff St. NASDAQ: CPST ■ TF: 866-422-7786 ■ Web: www.capstoneturbine.com	Chatsworth	CA	91311	818-734-5300	734-5320
Caterpillar Inc 100 NE Adams St. NYSE: CAT ■ Web: www.cat.com	Peoria	IL	61629	309-675-1000	
Caterpillar Remanufacturing 751 International Dr	Franklin	IN	46131	317-738-2117	738-4614
Chromium Corp 14911 Quorum Dr Ste 600. TF: 888-346-4747 ■ Web: www.chromcorp.com	Dallas	TX	75254	216-271-4910	
Clayton Industries 17477 Hurley St. TF: 800-423-4585 ■ Web: www.claytonindustries.com	City of Industry	CA	91744	626-435-1200	435-0180
Cummins Inc 500 Jackson St PO Box 3005. NYSE: CMI ■ TF: 800-343-7357 ■ Web: www.cummins.com	Columbus	IN	47201	812-377-5000	377-3334
Delaware Mfg Industries Corp 3776 Commerce Ct. TF: 800-248-3642 ■ Web: www.dmic.com	Wheatfield	NY	14120	716-743-4360	743-4370
Detroit Diesel Corp 13400 Outer Dr. Web: www.demanddetroit.com	Detroit	MI	48239	313-592-5000	592-7288
Dresser-Rand Control Systems 1202 W Sam Houston Pkwy N. Web: www.dresser-rand.com/products/controls	Houston	TX	77043	713-365-2630	
Dresser-Rand Steam Turbines 10205 Westheimer Rd. Web: www.dresser-rand.com	Houston	TX	77042	713-354-6100	354-6110
Electro Steam Generator Corp 50 Indel Ave PO Box 438. TF: 866-617-0764 ■ Web: www.electrosteam.com	Rancocas	NJ	08073	609-288-9071	288-9078
EnPro Industries Inc 5605 Carnegie Blvd Ste 500. NYSE: NPO	Charlotte	NC	28209	704-731-1500	
EnPro Industries Inc Fairbanks Morse Engine 701 White Ave. TF: 800-356-6955 ■ Web: www.fairbanksmorse.com	Beloit	WI	53511	800-356-6955	
Exergonix Inc 101 SE 30th St. Web: www.exergonix.com	Lees Summit	MO	64082	816-875-4790	
GE Aviation 1 Neumann Way. Web: www.geaviation.com	Cincinnati	OH	45215	513-243-2000	
Globe Turbocharger Specialties Inc 201 Edison Way. Web: www.globeturbocharger.com	Reno	NV	89502	775-856-7337	
H & H Mfg Company Inc 2 Horne Dr.	Folcroft	PA	19032	610-532-8100	461-4620
Hatch & Kirk Inc 5111 Leary Ave NW. TF: 800-426-2818 ■ Web: www.hatchkirk.com	Seattle	WA	98107	206-783-2766	782-6482
HDM Hydraulics LLC 125 Fire Tower Dr. Web: www.hdmhydraulics.com	Tonawanda	NY	14150	716-694-8004	694-4164
Hercules Engine Components Co 2770 S Erie St. TF: 800-345-0662	Massillon	OH	44646	330-830-2498	830-4081
Industrial Parts Depot LLC 23231 Normandie Ave. Web: www.ipdparts.com	Torrance	CA	90501	310-530-1900	
INI Power Systems Inc 175 Southport Dr Ste 100. Web: inipowersystems.com	Morrisville	NC	27560	919-677-7112	
JASPER Engines & Transmissions 815 Wernsing Rd PO Box 650. TF: 800-827-7455 ■ Web: www.jasperengines.com	Jasper	IN	47547	812-482-1041	634-1820
John Deere Power Systems 3801 W Ridgeway Ave PO Box 5100. *Fax Area Code: 319 ■ TF: 800-533-6446 ■ Web: www.deere.com	Waterloo	IA	50704	800-533-6446	292-5075*
KMS Ventures Inc 1301 W 25th St Ste 300. TF: 844-282-7433	Austin	TX	78705	512-474-6312	
Kohler Engines 444 Highland Dr. *Fax: Sales ■ TF: 800-544-2444 ■ Web: www.kohlerengines.com	Kohler	WI	53044	920-457-4441	459-1570*
Marine Power Holding LLC 17506 Marine Power Industrial Pk. Web: www.marinepowerusa.com	Ponchatoula	LA	70454	985-386-2081	386-4010
Northern Lights Inc 4420 14th Ave NW. TF: 800-762-0165 ■ Web: www.northern-lights.com	Seattle	WA	98107	206-789-3880	782-5455
NREC Power Systems 5222 Hwy 311. TF: 800-851-6732 ■ Web: www.nrecps.com	Houma	LA	70360	985-872-5480	872-0611
Pratt & Whitney Canada Inc 1000 Marie-Victorin Blvd. TF: 800-268-8000 ■ Web: www.pwc.ca	Longueuil	QC	J4G1A1	450-677-9411	647-3620
Solar Turbines Inc 2200 Pacific Hwy. *Fax: Sales ■ Web: mysolar.cat.com	San Diego	CA	92101	619-544-5000	544-5825*
Springfield ReManufacturing Corp 650 N Broadview Pl. TF: 800-772-7733 ■ Web: www.srcreman.com	Springfield	MO	65802	417-862-3501	
SRC Holdings Corp 531 S Union Ave. Web: www.srcholdings.com	Springfield	MO	65802	417-862-2337	
Voith Siemens Hydro Power 760 E Berlin Rd. Web: www.voith.com	York	PA	17408	717-792-7000	792-7263
Volvo Penta of the Americas Inc 1300 Volvo Penta Dr. TF: 800-522-1959 ■ Web: www.volvopenta.com	Chesapeake	VA	23320	757-436-2800	436-5150
Wartsila North America Inc 16330 Air Ctr Blvd. TF: 877-927-8745 ■ Web: www.wartsila.com	Houston	TX	77032	281-233-6200	233-6233
Westerbeke Corp 150 John Hancock Rd Miles Standish Industrial Pk. TF: 800-582-7846 ■ Web: www.westerbeke.com	Taunton	MA	02780	508-823-7677	884-9688
Western Diesel Services Inc 1100 Research Blvd. TF: 855-257-6937	Saint Louis	MO	63132	314-868-8620	868-9314

263 ENVELOPES

				Phone	Fax
ADM Corp 100 Lincoln Blvd. TF: 800-327-0718 ■ Web: www.admcorporation.com	Middlesex	NJ	08846	732-469-0900	469-0785
Alvah Bushnell Co 519 E Chelten Ave. TF: 800-255-7434 ■ Web: www.bushnellco.com	Philadelphia	PA	19144	215-842-9520	843-7725
AmericanChurch Inc 525 McClurg Rd PO Box 3120. TF: 800-446-3035 ■ Web: www.americanchurch.com	Youngstown	OH	44513	330-758-4545	
B & W Press Inc 401 E Main St. TF: 877-246-3467 ■ Web: www.bwpress.com	Georgetown	MA	01833	978-352-6100	352-5955
Bowers Envelope Co 5331 N Tacoma Ave. TF: 800-333-4321 ■ Web: www.bowersenvelope.com	Indianapolis	IN	46220	317-253-4321	254-2239
Cenveo Inc 201 Broad St 1 Canterberry Green. NYSE: CVO ■ Web: www.cenveo.com	Stamford	CT	06901	203-595-3000	
Curtis 1000 Inc 1725 Breckinridge Pkwy Ste 500. *Fax Area Code: 800 ■ TF: 877-287-8715 ■ Web: www.curtis1000.com	Duluth	GA	30096	678-380-9095	944-8817*
Federal Envelope Co 608 Country Club Dr. Web: www.federalenvelope.com	Bensenville	IL	60106	630-595-2000	595-1212
Heinrich Envelope Corp 925 Zane Ave N. TF: 800-346-7957 ■ Web: www.heinrichenvelope.com	Minneapolis	MN	55422	763-544-3571	544-6287
Love Envelopes Inc 10733 E Ute St. TF: 800-532-9747 ■ Web: www.loveenvelopes.com	Tulsa	OK	74116	918-836-3535	832-9978
Mackay Envelope Corp 2100 Elm St SE. TF: 800-622-5299 ■ Web: mackaymitchell.com	Minneapolis	MN	55414	800-622-5299	
Motion Envelope Inc 1455 Terre Colony Ct. Web: i3plasticcards.com	Dallas	TX	75212	214-634-2131	634-2132
National Church Supply Co, The PO Box 269. TF: 800-627-9900 ■ Web: www.ncssolutions.org	Chester	WV	26034	304-387-5200	387-5266
Papercone Corp 3200 Fern Vly Rd. TF: 800-626-5308 ■ Web: papercone.com	Louisville	KY	40213	502-961-9493	961-9346
Poly-Pak Industries Inc 125 Spagnoli Rd. *Fax Area Code: 631 ■ TF: 800-969-1993 ■ Web: www.poly-pak.com	Melville	NY	11747	800-969-1993	454-6366*
Response Envelope Inc 1340 S Baker Ave. TF: 800-750-0046 ■ Web: www.response-envelope.com	Ontario	CA	91761	909-923-5855	923-3639
Royal Envelope Co 4114 S Peoria St. Web: royalenv.com	Chicago	IL	60609	773-376-1212	376-0011
Tension Envelope Corp 819 E 19th St. *Fax Area Code: 816 ■ TF: 800-388-5122 ■ Web: tensionenvelope.com	Kansas City	MO	64108	800-388-5122	283-1498*
Top Flight Inc 1300 Central Ave. TF: 800-777-3740 ■ Web: www.topflightpaper.com	Chattanooga	TN	37408	423-266-8171	266-6857
Western States Envelope & Label Co 4480 N 132nd St. TF: 800-558-0514 ■ Web: www.wsel.com	Butler	WI	53007	262-781-5540	781-5791
Worcester Envelope Co 22 Millbury St. *Fax: Sales ■ TF: 800-343-1398 ■ Web: www.worcesterenvelope.com	Auburn	MA	01501	508-832-5394	832-3796*

264 EQUIPMENT RENTAL & LEASING

See Also Credit & Financing - Commercial p. 2171; Credit & Financing - Consumer p. 2172; Fleet Leasing & Management p. 2287

264-1 Computer Equipment Leasing

				Phone	Fax
Data Sales Company Inc 3450 W Burnsville Pkwy. TF: 800-328-2730 ■ Web: www.datasales.com	Burnsville	MN	55337	952-890-8838	895-3369
Electro Rent Corp 6060 Sepulveda Blvd. NASDAQ: ELRC ■ TF Sales: 800-688-1111 ■ Web: www.electrorent.com	Van Nuys	CA	91411	818-787-2100	786-4354
First Equipment Co PO Box 2129. TF: 888-780-8631 ■ Web: www.firstequipment.com	Addison	TX	75001	972-380-2300	380-8350
Hitachi Credit America Ltd 800 Connecticut Ave. Web: hitachicapitalamerica.com	Norwalk	CT	06854	203-275-5685	
LaSalle Systems Leasing Inc 6111 N River Rd. Web: www.elasalle.com	Rosemont	IL	60018	847-823-9600	823-1646
Leasing Technologies International Inc 221 Danbury Rd. Web: www.ltileasing.com	Wilton	CT	06897	203-563-1100	563-1112
Manufacturers' Lease Plans Inc 818 E Osborn Rd Ste 200. Web: www.leaseplans.com	Phoenix	AZ	85014	602-944-4411	944-4417
Newport Leasing Inc 4750 Von Karman Ave. TF Cust Svc: 800-274-0042 ■ Web: www.newportleasing.com	Newport Beach	CA	92660	949-476-8476	
Rent-A-PC Inc 265 Oser Ave. TF: 800-800-8686 ■ Web: www.smartsourcerentals.com	Hauppauge	NY	11788	631-273-8888	
Summit Funding Group Inc 4680 Parkway Dr Ste 300. TF: 866-489-1222 ■ Web: www.summit-funding.com	Mason	OH	45040	513-489-1222	
Vicom Computer Services Inc 400 Broadhollow Rd. Web: www.vicomnet.com	Farmingdale	NY	11735	631-694-3900	694-2640

264-2 Home & Office Equipment Rental (General)

Company	City	State	Zip	Phone	Fax
Bakercorp 3020 Old Ranch Pkwy Ste 220 *Web:* www.bakercorp.com	Seal Beach	CA	90740	562-430-6262	430-4865
Bestway Inc 12400 Coit Rd Ste 950 *TF:* 800-316-4567 ■ *Web:* www.bestwayrto.com	Dallas	TX	75251	214-630-6655	630-8404
Brook Furniture Rental Inc 100 N Field Dr Ste 220 *TF:* 877-285-7368 ■ *Web:* www.bfr.com	Lake Forest	IL	60045	847-810-4000	283-0478
Buddy's Home Furnishings 6608 E Adamo Dr **Fax Area Code:* 813 ■ *TF:* 866-779-5085 ■ *Web:* www.buddyrents.com	Tampa	FL	33619	866-779-5085	626-8195*
Celtic Commercial Finance 4 Pk Plz Ste 300 *Web:* www.celticfinance.com	Irvine	CA	92614	949-263-3880	263-1331
Classic Party Rentals 901 W. Hillcrest Blvd *TF:* 800-678-3854 ■ *Web:* www.classicpartyrentals.com	Inglewood	CA	90301	310-535-3660	
Exhibitors Carpet Service Inc 6112 W 73rd St	Bedford Park	IL	60638	773-247-0604	
GFC Leasing Co 2675 Research Pk Dr **Fax Area Code:* 608 ■ *TF:* 800-333-5905 ■ *Web:* gfcleasing.com	Madison	WI	53711	800-677-7877	271-9703*
Independent Rental Inc 2020 S Cushman St **Fax Area Code:* 907 ■ *TF:* 888-456-6595 ■ *Web:* www.independentrentalinc.com	Fairbanks	AK	99701	888-456-6595	456-2927*
LMG Inc PO Box 770429 *TF:* 888-226-3100 ■ *Web:* www.lmg.net	Orlando	FL	32877	407-850-0505	438-8422
Marlin Business Services Inc 300 Fellowship Rd *NASDAQ: MRLN* ■ *TF:* 888-479-9111 ■ *Web:* www.marlinfinance.com	Mount Laurel	NJ	08054	888-479-9111	479-1100
Party Rental Ltd 275 N St *Web:* www.partyrentalltd.com	Teterboro	NJ	07608	201-727-4700	727-4701
Projection Presentation Technology 5803 Rolling Rd *TF:* 800-377-7650 ■ *Web:* projection.com	Springfield	VA	22152	703-912-1334	912-1350
Rent Rite 1260 E Higgins Rd *Web:* www.rentriteequipment.com	Elk Grove Village	IL	60007	847-640-8860	437-4402
Rent-A-Center Inc 5501 Headquarters Dr *NASDAQ: RCII* ■ **Fax Area Code:* 972 ■ **Fax:* Cust Svc ■ *TF:* 800-422-8186 ■ *Web:* www.rentacenter.com/rent-a-center-home	Plano	TX	75024	800-422-8186	943-0113*
Rug Doctor LP 4701 Old Shepard Pl **Fax Area Code:* 888 ■ *TF:* 800-784-3628 ■ *Web:* www.rugdoctor.com	Plano	TX	75093	972-673-1400	261-6602*
Somerset Capital Group Ltd 612 Wheelers Farms Rd *TF:* 877-282-9922 ■ *Web:* www.somersetcapital.com	Milford	CT	06461	203-701-5100	301-3253

264-3 Industrial & Heavy Equipment Rental

Company	City	State	Zip	Phone	Fax
Aggreko 4607 W Admiral Doyle Dr *Web:* www.aggreko.com	New Iberia	LA	70560	337-367-7884	
AH Harris & Son Inc 367 Alumni Rd *TF:* 800-382-6555 ■ *Web:* www.ahharris.com	Newington	CT	06111	860-665-9494	665-9444
Ahern Rentals Inc 4241 Arville St *TF:* 800-589-6797 ■ *Web:* www.ahern.com	Las Vegas	NV	89103	702-362-0623	362-9316
Allied Steel Construction Co Inc 2211 NW First Terr *TF:* 800-522-4658 ■ *Web:* www.alliedsteelerectors.com	Oklahoma City	OK	73107	405-232-7531	236-3705
American Equipment Co 2106 Anderson Rd *Web:* www.ameco.com	Greenville	SC	29611	864-295-7800	295-7843
APi Supply Inc 624 Arthur St NE *Web:* www.apisupplyinc.com	Minneapolis	MN	55413	612-379-8000	379-8038
Beco Equipment Co 5555 Dahlia St *Web:* www.becoequipment.com	Commerce	CO	80022	303-288-2613	288-5776
Broussard Bros Inc 25817 Louisiana Hwy 333 *Web:* www.broussardbrothers.com	Abbeville	LA	70510	337-893-5303	
Buck & Knobby Equipment Co 6220 Sterns Rd *TF:* 855-213-2825 ■ *Web:* www.buckandknobby.com	Ottawa Lake	MI	49267	734-856-2811	856-2709
Cloverdale Equipment Co 13133 Cloverdale St *TF:* 888-388-9182 ■ *Web:* www.cloverdale-equip.com	Oak Park	MI	48237	248-399-6600	399-7730
Cornell & Co Inc 224 Cornell Ln *Web:* www.cornellcraneandsteel.com	Westville	NJ	08093	856-742-1900	742-8186
D & D Equipment Rental Inc 10936 Shoemaker Ave *Web:* www.ddrental.com	Santa Fe Springs	CA	90670	562-595-4555	903-8881
Equipment Technology LLC 341 NW 122nd St **Fax Area Code:* 405 ■ *TF:* 888-748-3841 ■ *Web:* etiequipment.com	Oklahoma City	OK	73114	888-748-3841	755-6829*
Ervin Leasing Co 3893 Research Pk Dr *TF:* 800-748-0015 ■ *Web:* www.ervinleasing.com	Ann Arbor	MI	48108	800-748-0015	968-2808
Essex Crane Rental Corp 1110 Lake Cook Rd Ste 220 *TF:* 888-991-4100 ■ *Web:* www.essexcrane.com	Buffalo Grove	IL	60089	847-215-6500	215-6535
Force Construction Company Inc 990 N National Rd *Web:* www.forceco.com	Columbus	IN	47201	812-372-8441	372-5424
G & C Equipment Corp 1875 W Redondo Beach Blvd Ste 102 *Web:* www.gandccorp.com	Gardena	CA	90247	310-515-6715	515-5046
H & E Equipment Services Inc 11100 Mead Rd *NASDAQ: HEES* ■ *TF:* 866-467-3682 ■ *Web:* www.he-equipment.com	Baton Rouge	LA	70809	225-298-5200	
Hawthorne Machinery Co 16945 Camino San Bernardo *TF:* 800-437-4228 ■ *Web:* www.hawthornecat.com	San Diego	CA	92127	858-674-7000	674-7155
HB Rentals LC 5813 Hwy 90 E *TF:* 800-262-6790 ■ *Web:* hbrentals.com	Broussard	LA	70518	337-839-1641	839-1628
Hertz equipment rental 5500 Commerce Blvd *Web:* www.hertzequip.com	Rohnert Park	CA	94928	707-586-4444	
Hertz Equipment Rental Corp 225 Brae Blvd **Fax Area Code:* 888 ■ *TF:* 800-654-3131 ■ *Web:* www.hertzequip.com	Park Ridge	NJ	07656	201-307-2000	817-7694*
Independent Rental Inc 2020 S Cushman St **Fax Area Code:* 907 ■ *TF:* 888-456-6595 ■ *Web:* www.independentrentalinc.com	Fairbanks	AK	99701	888-456-6595	456-2927*
Klochko Equipment Rental Company Inc 2782 Corbin Ave *TF:* 800-783-7368 ■ *Web:* www.klochko.com	Melvindale	MI	48122	313-386-7220	386-2530
Leppo Inc PO Box 154 *TF:* 800-453-7762 ■ *Web:* www.leppos.com	Tallmadge	OH	44278	330-633-3999	630-1599
Marco Crane & Rigging Co 221 S 35th Ave *TF:* 800-668-2671 ■ *Web:* www.marcocrane.com	Phoenix	AZ	85009	602-272-2671	352-0413
Maxim Crane Works 1225 Washington Pk *TF:* 877-629-5438 ■ *Web:* www.maximcrane.com	Bridgeville	PA	15017	412-504-0200	504-0126
Medico Industries Inc 1500 Hwy 315 *TF:* 800-633-0027 ■ *Web:* medicoind.com	Wilkes-Barre	PA	18711	570-825-7711	824-1169
Mitcham Industries Inc (MII) 8141 Hwy 75 S PO Box 1175 *NASDAQ: MIND* ■ **Fax:* Sales ■ *Web:* www.mitchamindustries.com	Huntsville	TX	77340	936-291-2277	295-1922*
Morrow Equipment Company LLC 3218 Pringle Rd SE PO Box 3306 *Web:* www.morrow.com	Salem	OR	97302	503-585-5721	363-1172
Mustang Rental Services Inc 15907 E Fwy *Web:* www.mustangcat.com	Channelview	TX	77530	281-452-7368	
National Construction Rentals Inc 15319 Chatsworth St **Fax Area Code:* 800 ■ *TF:* 800-352-5675 ■ *Web:* www.rentnational.com	Mission Hills	CA	91345	818-221-6000	896-8411*
Norcal Rental Group LLC 318 Stealth Ct *TF:* 800-649-6629 ■ *Web:* www.crescorent.com	Livermore	CA	94551	925-961-0130	456-9760
Quantum Analytics 3400 East Third Ave *TF:* 800-992-4199 ■ *Web:* www.lqa.com	Foster City	CA	94404	650-312-0900	
Raymond Handling Concepts Corp 41400 Boyce Rd *TF:* 800-675-2500 ■ *Web:* www.raymondhandling.com	Fremont	CA	94538	510-745-7500	745-7686
Rush Enterprises Inc 555 IH 35 S Ste 500 *NASDAQ: RUSHA* ■ *TF:* 800-973-7874 ■ *Web:* www.rushenterprises.com	New Braunfels	TX	78130	830-626-5200	626-5310
Safway Services Inc N 19 W 24200 Riverwood Dr *TF:* 800-558-4772 ■ *Web:* www.safway.com	Waukesha	WI	53188	262-523-6500	523-9808
Skyworks LLC 100 Thielman Dr *TF:* 877-601-5438 ■ *Web:* www.skyworksllc.com	Buffalo	NY	14206	716-822-5438	
Stanley W Bowles Corp 3375 Joseph Martin Hwy PO Box 4706 *Web:* www.bowlesproperties.com	Martinsville	VA	24115	276-956-3442	956-7038
Star Rentals Inc 1919 Fourth Ave S *TF:* 800-825-7880 ■ *Web:* www.starrentals.com	Seattle	WA	98134	206-622-7880	
Stephenson Equipment Inc (SEI) 7201 Paxton St *TF:* 800-325-6455 ■ *Web:* www.stephensonequipment.com	Harrisburg	PA	17111	717-564-3434	564-7580
Sunbelt Rentals Inc 2341 Deerfield Dr *TF General:* 800-667-9328 ■ *Web:* www.sunbeltrentals.com	Fort Mill	SC	29715	704-348-2676	
T & T Truck & Crane Service Inc 1375 N Olive St *Web:* www.truckandcrane.com	Ventura	CA	93001	805-648-3348	
Tetra Corporate Services LLC 6995 Union Park Ctr Ste 360 *TF:* 800-417-0548 ■ *Web:* www.tetracsi.com	Salt Lake City	UT	84047	801-566-2600	365-6263
Thomas Instrument & Machine Company Inc 3440 First St *Web:* www.thomasinstrument.com	Brookshire	TX	77423	281-375-6300	375-5264
Timco Services Inc 1724 E Milton Rd	Lafayette	LA	70508	337-233-5185	856-8158
Traffic Control Service Inc 2435 Lemon Ave **Fax Area Code:* 562 ■ *TF:* 800-763-3999 ■ *Web:* www.trafficmanagement.com	Signal Hill	CA	90755	800-763-3999	424-0266*
United Crane Rentals Inc 111 N Michigan Ave	Kenilworth	NJ	07033	908-245-6260	245-1708
United Rentals 3266 E Washington St *TF:* 844-873-4948 ■ *Web:* www.unitedrentals.com	Phoenix	AZ	85233	602-267-3898	
United Rentals Inc 224 Selleck St *NYSE: URI* ■ *TF:* 800-877-3687 ■ *Web:* www.unitedrentals.com	Stamford	CT	06902	203-622-3131	622-6080
Western Oilfields Supply Co 3404 State Rd **Fax:* Acctg ■ *TF:* 800-742-7246 ■ *Web:* www.rainforrent.com	Bakersfield	CA	93308	661-399-9124	392-9427*

264-4 Medical Equipment Rental

Company	City	State	Zip	Phone	Fax
American Shared Hospital Services 4 Embarcadero Ctr Ste 3700 *NYSE: AMS* ■ *TF:* 800-735-0641 ■ *Web:* www.ashs.com	San Francisco	CA	94111	415-788-5300	788-5660
Dynasplint Systems Inc 770 Ritchie Hwy Ste W21 **Fax Area Code:* 800 ■ *TF:* 800-638-6771 ■ *Web:* www.dynasplint.com	Severna Park	MD	21146	410-544-9530	380-3784*
First Lease Inc 1 Walnut Grove Dr Ste 300 **Fax Area Code:* 215 ■ *TF:* 866-493-4778 ■ *Web:* www.firstleaseonline.com	Horsham	PA	19044	866-493-4778	283-9870*
Freedom Medical Inc 219 Welsh Pool Rd *TF:* 800-784-8849 ■ *Web:* www.freedommedical.com	Exton	PA	19341	610-903-0200	903-0180
King's Medical Co 1894 Georgetown Rd *Web:* www.kingsmedical.com	Hudson	OH	44236	330-653-3968	656-0600
Modern Medical Modalities Corp 439 Chestnut St *NYSE: MODM*	Union	NJ	07083	908-933-0216	
Universal Hospital Services Inc 7700 France Ave S Ste 275 *TF:* 800-847-7368 ■ *Web:* www.uhs.com	Minneapolis	MN	55435	952-893-3200	893-0704

264-5 Transport Equipment Rental

Company	City	State	Zip	Phone	Fax
Eurotainer Inc 5810 Wilson Rd Ste 200 *Web:* www.eurotainer.com	Humble	TX	77396	832-300-5001	300-5050

	City	State	ZIP	Phone	Fax
EXSIF Worldwide Inc 2700 Westchester Ave Ste 400 *Web:* www.exsif.com	Purchase	NY	10577	914-848-4200	848-4201
Flexi-Van Leasing Inc 251 Monroe Ave. *TF:* 866-965-9288 ■ *Web:* www.flexi-van.com	Kenilworth	NJ	07033	908-276-8000	276-7666
GATX Rail Canada 1801 Magill College Ave. *Web:* www.cgtx.com	Montreal	QC	H3A2N4	514-931-7343	931-5534
GE Rail Car Services 161 N Clark St 7th Fl *TF:* 800-626-2000	Chicago	IL	60601	312-853-5000	
GLNX Corp 10077 Grogan's Mill Rd Ste 450 *Web:* www.glnx.com	The Woodlands	TX	77380	281-363-7053	363-7060
Greenbrier Co 1 Centerpointe Dr Ste 200 *NYSE:* GBX ■ *TF:* 800-343-7188 ■ *Web:* www.gbrx.com	Lake Oswego	OR	97035	503-684-7000	684-7553
Procor Ltd 2001 Speers Rd *TF:* 888-977-6267 ■ *Web:* www.procor.com	Oakville	ON	L6L2X9	905-827-4111	
Railserve Inc 1691 Phoenix Blvd Ste 110 *TF:* 800-345-7245 ■ *Web:* www.railserveinc.com	Atlanta	GA	30349	770-996-6838	996-6830
TAL International Group Inc 100 Manhattanville Rd *NYSE:* TAL ■ *Web:* www.talinternational.com	Purchase	NY	10577	914-251-9000	697-2549
TTX Co 101 N Wacker Dr. *TF:* 800-889-4357 ■ *Web:* www.ttx.com	Chicago	IL	60606	312-853-3223	984-3790

265 ETHICS COMMISSIONS

	City	State	ZIP	Phone	Fax
Federal Election Commission 999 E St NW. *TF:* 800-424-9530 ■ *Web:* www.fec.gov	Washington	DC	20463	202-694-1100	
US Office of Government Ethics 1201 New York Ave NW Ste 500 *Web:* www.oge.gov	Washington	DC	20005	202-482-9300	482-9237
Alabama Ethics Commission 100 N Union St Ste 104 *Web:* www.ethics.alabama.gov	Montgomery	AL	36104	334-242-2997	242-0248
Alaska Legislative Ethics Committee 716 W 4th Ave Ste 230 *Web:* anchorage.akleg.gov	Anchorage	AK	99501	907-269-0111	269-0229
Arakansas Ethics Commission PO Box 1917 *TF:* 800-422-7773 ■ *Web:* www.arkansasethics.com	Little Rock	AR	72203	501-324-9600	324-9606
California Fair Political Practices Commission 428 J St Ste 620 *TF:* 866-275-3772 ■ *Web:* www.fppc.ca.gov	Sacramento	CA	95814	916-322-5660	322-0886
Connecticut Ethics Commission 18-20 Trinity St Ste 205 *Web:* www.ct.gov/ethics/site/default.asp	Hartford	CT	06106	860-263-2400	263-2402
Delaware Public Integrity Commission 410 Federal St Margaret O'Neill Bldg Ste 3 *Web:* www.depic.delaware.gov	Dover	DE	19901	302-739-2399	739-2398
Florida Ethics Commission 3600 Maclay Blvd S Ste 201 *Web:* www.ethics.state.fl.us	Tallahassee	FL	32312	850-488-7864	488-3077
Georgia Transparency & Campaign Finance Commission 200 Piedmont Ave SE Ste 1402 *TF:* 866-589-7327 ■ *Web:* www.ethics.state.ga.us	Atlanta	GA	30334	404-463-1980	
Indiana State Ethics Commission (OIG) 315 W Ohio St Rm 104 *Web:* www.in.gov/ig	Indianapolis	IN	46202	317-232-3850	232-0707
Iowa Ethics & Campaign Disclosure Board 510 E 12th St Ste 1-A *Web:* www.state.ia.us	Des Moines	IA	50319	515-281-4028	281-3701
Kansas Governmental Ethics Commission 109 W Ninth St Ste 504 *Web:* www.kansas.gov	Topeka	KS	66612	785-296-4219	296-2548
Kentucky Legislative Ethics Commission 22 Mill Creek Pk. *Web:* www.klec.ky.gov	Frankfort	KY	40601	502-573-2863	573-2929
Louisiana Ethics Board 617 N Third St LaSalle Bldg Ste 10-36 *TF:* 800-842-6630 ■ *Web:* www.ethics.state.la.us	Baton Rouge	LA	70802	225-219-5600	381-7271
Maine Governmental Ethics & Election Practices Commission 45 Memorial Cir *Web:* www.maine.gov	Augusta	ME	04330	207-287-4179	287-6775
Maryland Ethics Commission 45 Calvert St 3rd Fl. *TF:* 877-669-6085 ■ *Web:* ethics.maryland.gov	Annapolis	MD	21401	410-260-7770	260-7746
Massachusetts State Ethics Commission 1 Ashburton Pl Rm 619 *Web:* www.mass.gov/ethics	Boston	MA	02108	617-371-9500	723-5851
Minnesota Campaign Finance & Public Disclosure Board 658 Cedar St Ste 190 *TF:* 800-657-3889 ■ *Web:* www.cfboard.state.mn.us	Saint Paul	MN	55155	651-296-5148	296-1722
Mississippi Ethics Commission 146 E Amite St Ste 103 *Web:* www.ethics.state.ms.us	Jackson	MS	39201	601-359-1285	354-6253
Montana Commissioner of Political Practices 1205 Eigth Ave PO Box 202401 *Web:* www.politicalpractices.mt.gov	Helena	MT	59620	406-444-2942	444-1643
Nebraska Accountability & Disclosure Commission PO Box 95086 *Web:* nadc.nebraska.gov	Lincoln	NE	68509	402-471-2522	471-6599
Nevada Commission on Ethics 704 W Nye Ln Ste 204 *Web:* www.ethics.nv.gov	Carson City	NV	89703	775-687-5469	687-1279
New Jersey Ethical Standards Commission 28 W State St Rm 1407 PO Box 082 *Web:* www.state.nj.us/lps/ethics	Trenton	NJ	08625	609-292-1892	633-9252
New Mexico Ethics Administration 325 Don Gaspar St Ste 300 *TF:* 800-477-3632 ■ *Web:* www.sos.state.nm.us	Santa Fe	NM	87501	505-827-3600	
North Carolina Ethics Board 424 N Blount St *Web:* www.ethicscommission.nc.gov	Raleigh	NC	27601	919-715-2071	715-1644
Ohio Ethics Commission 30 W Spring St L3 *Web:* www.ethics.ohio.gov	Columbus	OH	43215	614-466-7090	466-8368
Oklahoma Ethics Commission 2300 N Lincoln Blvd Rm B5 *Web:* www.ok.gov	Oklahoma City	OK	73105	405-521-3451	521-4905
Oregon Government Standards & Practices Commission 3218 Pringle Rd SE Ste 220 *Web:* www.oregon.gov	Salem	OR	97302	503-378-5105	373-1456
Pennsylvania State Ethics Commission 309 Finance Bldg PO Box 11470 *TF:* 800-932-0936 ■ *Web:* www.ethics.state.pa.us	Harrisburg	PA	17108	717-783-1610	787-0806
Rhode Island Ethics Commission 40 Fountain St *Web:* www.ethics.ri.gov	Providence	RI	02903	401-222-3790	222-3382
South Carolina Ethics Commission 5000 Thurmond Mall Ste 250 *Web:* www.state.sc.us	Columbia	SC	29201	803-253-4192	253-7539
Texas Ethics Commission 201 E 14th St 10th Fl *Web:* www.ethics.state.tx.us	Austin	TX	78701	512-463-5800	463-5777
Washington Public Disclosure Commission PO Box 40908 *Web:* www.pdc.wa.gov	Olympia	WA	98504	360-753-1111	753-1112
West Virginia Ethics Commission 210 Brooks St Ste 300 *TF:* 866-558-0664 ■ *Web:* www.ethics.wv.gov	Charleston	WV	25301	304-558-0664	558-2169
Wisconsin Ethics Board 212 E Washington Ave 3rd Fl *Web:* www.gab.wi.gov	Madison	WI	53703	608-266-8123	264-9319

266 EXECUTIVE RECRUITING FIRMS

	City	State	ZIP	Phone	Fax
Accretive Solutions Inc 1 S Wacker Dr Ste 950 *Web:* www.accretivesolutions.com	Chicago	IL	60606	312-994-4600	994-4638
Barton Assoc Inc 701 Richmond Ave *Web:* www.bartona.com	Houston	TX	77006	713-961-9111	
Battalia Winston International 555 Madison Ave 19th Fl *Web:* www.battaliawinston.com	New York	NY	10022	212-308-8080	308-1309
Bishop Partners Ltd 28 W 44th St #1120 *Web:* www.bishoppartners.com	New York	NY	10036	212-986-3419	575-1050
Boyden World Corp 50 Broadway *TF:* 877-226-9336 ■ *Web:* www.boyden.com	Hawthorne	NY	10532	914-747-0093	747-0108
Canny Bowen Inc 400 Madison Ave Ste 11-D *Web:* www.cannybowen.com	New York	NY	10017	212-949-6611	949-5191
Chadick Ellig Inc 300 Pk Ave *Web:* www.chadickellig.com	New York	NY	10022	212-688-8671	308-4510
Chicago Legal Search Ltd 180 N LaSalle St *Web:* www.chicagolegalsearch.com	Chicago	IL	60601	312-251-2580	251-0223
Choi & Burns LLC 156 W 56th St 18th Fl *Web:* www.choiburns.com	New York	NY	10019	212-755-7051	355-2610
Christian & Timbers 25825 Science Pk Dr. *TF:* 800-299-9630 ■ *Web:* www.ctnet.com	Cleveland	OH	44122	216-464-8710	
Cole Warren & Long Inc 2 Penn Ctr Ste 312	Philadelphia	PA	19102	215-563-0701	563-2907
Compass Group Ltd 401 S Old Woodward Ave Ste 460	Birmingham	MI	48009	248-540-9110	647-8288
Cook Assoc Inc 212 W Kinzie St *Web:* www.cookassociates.com	Chicago	IL	60654	312-329-0900	
Dahl Morrow International 11260 Roger Bacon St Ste 204 *Web:* www.dahl-morrowintl.com	Reston	VA	20190	703-787-8117	
Daniel & Yeager (D&Y) 6767 Old Madison Pk Ste 690 *Fax Area Code: 256 ■ *TF:* 800-955-1919 ■ *Web:* www.dystaffing.com	Huntsville	AL	35806	800-955-1919	551-1075*
DHR International 71 South Wacker Dr Ste 2700 *Web:* www.dhrinternational.com	Chicago	IL	60606	312-782-1581	782-2096
Dieckmann & Assoc 500 N Michigan Ave	Chicago	IL	60611	312-819-5900	
Diversified Search Cos 2005 Market St 33rd Fl. *TF:* 800-423-3932 ■ *Web:* www.divsearch.com	Philadelphia	PA	19103	215-732-6666	568-8399
Early Cochran & Olson LLC 1 E Upper Wacker Dr Ste 2510 *Web:* www.ecollc.com	Chicago	IL	60601	312-595-4200	595-4209
Eastman & Beaudine Inc 7201 Bishop Rd Ste 220 *Web:* www.eastman-beaudine.com	Plano	TX	75024	972-312-1012	
Egon Zehnder International Inc 1 N Wacker Dr Ste 2300 *Web:* www.egonzehnder.com	Chicago	IL	60606	312-260-8800	782-2846
Fergus Partnership Consulting Inc 14 Wall St # 3C *Web:* www.ferguslex.com	New York	NY	10005	212-767-1775	315-0351
Halbrecht Lieberman Assoc Inc 32 Surf Rd *Web:* www.hlassoc.com	Westport	CT	06880	203-222-4890	222-4895
Heath/Norton Assoc 301 Crocus Ct Ste L-7	Dayton	NJ	08810	732-329-4663	
Heidrick & Struggles International Inc 233 S Wacker Dr Ste 4900 *NASDAQ:* HSII ■ *Web:* www.heidrick.com	Chicago	IL	60606	312-496-1000	496-1048
Herbert Mines Assoc Inc 375 Pk Ave *Web:* www.herbertmines.com	New York	NY	10152	212-355-0909	
Horton International LLC 29 S Main St *Web:* www.hortoninternational.com	West Hartford	CT	06107	860-521-0101	521-0140
Howard Fischer Assoc International 1800 Kennedy Blvd Ste 700 *Web:* www.hfischer.com	Philadelphia	PA	19103	215-568-8363	568-4815
Hughes & Sloan Inc 1360 Peachtree St NE *Web:* hughesandsloan.com	Atlanta	GA	30309	404-873-3421	
IMC Group of Cos 120 White Plains Rd Ste 405 *Web:* www.the-imc.com	Tarrytown	NY	10591	914-468-7050	468-7051
Kenzer Group LLC 1 Penn Plz *Web:* www.kenzer.com	New York	NY	10119	212-308-4300	
Korn/Ferry International 1900 Ave of the Stars Ste 2600 *NYSE:* KFY ■ *TF:* 877-345-3610 ■ *Web:* www.kornferry.com	Los Angeles	CA	90067	310-552-1834	553-6452

				Phone	Fax
Kovensky Daniels 1250 Connecticut Ave NW Ste 200	Washington	DC	20036	202-261-3555	832-1838*
*Fax Area Code: 413 ■ Web: www.kovdan.com					
Major Lindsey & Africa 555 Montgomery St Ste 1500	San Francisco	CA	94111	415-956-1010	398-2425
Web: www.mlaglobal.com					
Management Recruiters International Worldwide Inc 1717 Arch St 36th Fl	Philadelphia	PA	19103	800-875-4000	
TF: 800-875-4000 ■ Web: www.mrinetwork.com					
Mestel & Company Inc 575 Madison Ave Ste 3000	New York	NY	10022	646-356-0500	356-0545
Web: www.mestel.com					
MSI International Inc 650 Pk Ave	King of Prussia	PA	19406	610-265-2000	265-2213
Web: www.msimsi.com					
National Search Assoc 2035 Corte del Nogal Ste 100	Carlsbad	CA	92011	760-431-1115	683-3044
Web: www.nsasearch.com					
Nordeman Grimm 65 E 55th St 33rd Fl	New York	NY	10022	212-935-1000	
Web: www.nordemangrimm.com					
Pittleman & Assoc 336 E 43rd St	New York	NY	10017	212-370-9600	370-9608
Web: www.pittlemanassociates.com					
Rice Cohen International 301 Oxford Vly Rd Ste 1506A	Yardley	PA	19067	215-321-4100	
Web: ricecoheninternational.com					
Rusher Loscavio & LoPresto 369 Pine St Ste 221	San Francisco	CA	94104	415-765-6583	
Web: www.rll.com					
Russell Reynolds Assoc Inc 200 Pk Ave 23rd Fl	New York	NY	10166	212-351-2000	370-0896
TF: 800-259-0470 ■ Web: www.russellreynolds.com					
Spencer Reed Group Inc 6900 College Blvd Ste 1	Overland Park	KS	66211	913-663-4400	663-4464
TF: 800-477-5035 ■ Web: www.spencerreed.com					
Stanton Chase International 400 E Pratt St Ste 420	Baltimore	MD	21202	410-528-8400	528-8409
Web: www.stantonchase.com					
Swan Legal Search 11400 Olympic Blvd Ste 200	Los Angeles	CA	90064	310-201-2500	
Web: www.swanlegal.com					
Tyler & Co 400 Northridge Rd Ste 1250	Atlanta	GA	30350	770-396-3939	396-6693
TF: 800-989-6789 ■ Web: www.tylerandco.com					
Whitney Partners 747 Third Ave 17th Fl	New York	NY	10017	212-508-3500	508-3540
Web: www.whitneypartners.net					
Witt/Kieffer Ford Hadelman & Lloyd 2015 Spring Rd Ste 510	Oak Brook	IL	60523	630-990-1370	990-1382
TF: 888-281-1370 ■ Web: www.wittkieffer.com					
Wyatt & Jaffe 2751 Hennepin Ave S Ste 286	Minneapolis	MN	55408	612-285-2858	285-2786
Web: www.wyattjaffe.com					
XEC Solutions Inc 5655 Lindero Canyon Rd Ste 521	Westlake Village	CA	91362	818-991-1400	575-8099
Web: xecsolutions.com					

267 EXERCISE & FITNESS EQUIPMENT

See Also Sporting Goods p. 3193

				Phone	Fax
Body-Solid Inc 1900 Des Plaines Ave	Forest Park	IL	60130	708-427-3500	427-3556
TF: 800-833-1227 ■ Web: www.bodysolid.com					
Cybex International Inc 10 Trotter Dr	Medway	MA	02053	508-533-4300	533-5500
NASDAQ: CYBI ■ TF: 888-462-9239 ■ Web: www.cybexintl.com					
Heartline Fitness Products Inc 8041 Cessna Ave Ste 200	Gaithersburg	MD	20879	301-921-0661	330-5479
TF: 800-262-3348 ■ Web: www.heartlinefitness.com					
Hoggan Health Industries Inc 8020 South 1300 West	West Jordan	UT	84088	801-572-6500	
TF: 800-678-7888 ■ Web: hogganhealth.net					
Hoist Fitness Systems Inc 9990 Empire St Ste 130	San Diego	CA	92126	858-578-7676	578-9558
TF: 800-548-5438 ■ Web: www.hoistfitness.com					
HYDRO-FIT Inc 160 Madison St	Eugene	OR	97402	541-484-4361	484-1443
TF Cust Svc: 800-346-7295 ■ Web: www.hydrofit.com					
ICON Health & Fitness Inc 1500 South 1000 West	Logan	UT	84321	435-750-5000	
TF: 800-999-3756 ■ Web: www.iconfitness.com					
IronMaster LLC 14562 167th Ave SE	Monroe	WA	98272	360-217-7780	217-8415
TF: 800-533-3339 ■ Web: www.ironmaster.com					
Nautilus Inc 16400 SE Nautilus Dr	Vancouver	WA	98684	360-694-7722	694-7755
NYSE: NLS ■ TF: 800-628-8458 ■ Web: nautilusinc.com					
New York Barbells 160 Home St	Elmira	NY	14904	607-733-8038	733-1010
TF: 800-446-1833 ■ Web: www.newyorkbarbells.com					
Precor Inc 20031 142nd Ave NE	Woodinville	WA	98072	425-486-9292	486-3856
TF: 800-786-8404 ■ Web: www.precor.com					
Pro Star Sports Inc 1133 Winchester Ave	Kansas City	MO	64126	816-241-9737	241-2459
TF: 800-821-8482 ■ Web: www.prostarsports.com					
Soloflex Inc 22590 NW Badertscher Rd	Hillsboro	OR	97124	800-547-8802	
TF: 800-547-8802 ■ Web: www.soloflex.com					
Spirit Manufacturing Inc 3000 Nestle Rd	Jonesboro	AR	72401	870-935-1107	935-7611
TF: 800-258-4555 ■ Web: www.spiritfitness.com					
Star Trac by Unisen Inc 14410 Myford Rd	Irvine	CA	92606	714-669-1660	838-6286
TF: 800-228-6635 ■ Web: www.startrac.com					
True Fitness Technology Inc 865 Hoff Rd	O'Fallon	MO	63366	636-272-7100	272-7148
TF: 800-426-6570 ■ Web: www.truefitness.com					
Vectra Fitness Inc 7901 S 190th St	Kent	WA	98032	425-291-9550	291-9650
TF: 800-283-2872 ■ Web: www.vectrafitness.com					
Woodway USA W229 N591 Foster Ct	Waukesha	WI	53186	262-548-6235	522-6235
TF: 800-966-3929 ■ Web: www.woodway.com					
York Barbell Co Inc 3300 BoaRd Rd	York	PA	17406	717-767-6481	764-0044
TF Cust Svc: 800-358-9675 ■ Web: www.yorkbarbell.com					

268 EXPLOSIVES

				Phone	Fax
Accurate Energetics Systems LLC 5891 Hwy 230 W	McEwen	TN	37101	931-729-4207	729-4214
Web: www.aesys.biz					
Action Manufacturing Co 100 E Erie Ave	Philadelphia	PA	19134	215-739-6400	
Web: www.action-mfg.com					
Alliant Powder 2299 Snake River Ave	Lewiston	ID	83501	800-379-1732	
TF: 800-276-9337 ■ Web: www.alliantpowder.com					
Austin Powder Co 25800 Science Pk Dr Ste 300	Cleveland	OH	44122	216-464-2400	464-4418
TF: 800-321-0752 ■ Web: www.austinpowder.com					
Buckley Powder Co 42 Inverness Dr E	Englewood	CO	80112	303-790-7007	790-7033
TF: 800-333-2266 ■ Web: www.buckleypowder.com					
Can-Blast Inc 755 Wallace Rd Unit 3	North Bay	ON	P1B8K4	705-474-3431	476-7643
Web: www.can-blast.com					
Cartridge Actuated Devices Inc (CAD) 51 Dwight Pl	Fairfield	NJ	07004	973-575-1312	575-6039
Web: cartactdev.com					
Combined Systems Inc 388 Kinsman Rd	Jamestown	PA	16134	724-932-2177	
Web: www.combinedsystems.com					
Dyno Nobel Inc 2795 E Cottonwood Pkwy Ste 500	Salt Lake City	UT	84121	801-364-4800	328-6452
TF: 800-473-2675 ■ Web: www.dynonobel.com					
Ensign-Bickford Aerospace & Defense Co 640 Hopmeadow St PO Box 429	Simsbury	CT	06070	860-843-2289	
Web: www.ebaerospaceanddefense.com					
General Dynamics Ordnance & Tactical Systems Inc 11399 16th Court N Ste 200	Saint Petersburg	FL	33716	727-578-8100	
Web: www.gd-ots.com					
Hanley Industries Inc 3640 Seminary Rd PO Box 1058	Alton	IL	62002	618-465-8892	
Web: www.hanleyindustries.com					
Hodgdon Powder Company Inc 6231 Robinson St	Shawnee Mission	KS	66202	913-362-9455	362-1307
Web: www.hodgdon.com					
Nammo Inc 2000 N 14th St Ste 250	Arlington	VA	22201	703-524-6100	
Web: www.nammoinc.com					
Orica USA Inc 33101 E Quincy Ave	Watkins	CO	80137	303-268-5000	268-5250
Web: www.oricaminingservices.com					
Pyrotechnic Specialties Inc 1661 Juniper Creek Rd	Byron	GA	31008	478-956-5400	
Web: www.pyrotechonline.com					
Schaefer Pyrotechnics Inc 376 Hartman Bridge Rd	Ronks	PA	17572	717-687-0647	
Senex Explosives Inc 710 Millers Run Rd	Cuddy	PA	15031	412-221-3218	221-6032
Special Devices Inc 14370 White Sage Rd	Moorpark	CA	93021	805-553-1200	387-1001
Web: www.specialdevices.com					
Stresau Laboratory Inc N8265 Medley Rd	Spooner	WI	54801	715-635-2777	635-7979
Web: www.stresau.com					
Teledyne Reynolds Inc 5005 McConnell Ave	Los Angeles	CA	90066	310-823-5491	822-8046
Web: www.teledynereynolds.com					

269 EYE BANKS

See Also Organ & Tissue Banks p. 2861; Transplant Centers - Blood Stem Cell p. 3261

Eye banks listed here are members of the Eye Bank Association of America (EBAA), an accrediting body for eye banks. The EBAA medical standards for member eye banks are endorsed by the American Academy of Ophthalmology.

				Phone	Fax
Alabama Eye Bank 500 Robert Jemison Rd	Birmingham	AL	35209	800-423-7811	
TF: 800-423-7811 ■ Web: www.alabamaeyebank.org					
Alcon Laboratories Inc 6201 S Fwy	Fort Worth	TX	76134	817-293-0450	568-7128
TF: 800-862-5266 ■ Web: www.alcon.com					
Arkansas Lions Eye Bank & Laboratory 4301 W Markham St Slot 523-1	Little Rock	AR	72205	501-686-5822	686-7037
Web: eye.uams.edu					
Baton Rouge Regional Eye Bank 7777 Hennessy Blvd Ste 1005	Baton Rouge	LA	70808	225-766-8996	765-4366
Web: www.eyebankbr.org					
Center for Organ Recovery & Education (CORE) 204 Sigma Dr RIDC Pk	Pittsburgh	PA	15238	412-963-3550	
TF: 800-366-6777 ■ Web: www.core.org					
Central Ohio Lions Eye Bank 262 Neil Ave Ste 140	Columbus	OH	43215	614-545-2057	
Web: www.coleb.org					
Cincinnati Eye Bank for Sight Restoration Inc 4015 Executive Pk Dr Ste 330	Cincinnati	OH	45241	513-861-3716	483-3984
Web: www.cintieb.org					
Dakota Lions Sight & Health 4501 W 61st St Ste 201	Sioux Falls	SD	57107	701-250-9390	250-1880
TF: 800-372-3751 ■ Web: www.dakotasight.org					
Donor Network of Arizona 201 W Coolidge St	Phoenix	AZ	85013	602-222-2200	222-2202
TF: 800-447-9477 ■ Web: www.dnaz.org					
Donor Network West 12667 Alcosta Blvd Ste 600	Oakland	CA	94607	925-480-3101	
TF: 888-570-9400 ■ Web: www.donornetworkwest.org					
Eye Bank Assn of America (EBAA) 1015 18th St NW Ste 1010	Washington	DC	20036	202-775-4999	429-6036
TF: 888-491-8833 ■ Web: www.restoresight.org					
Eye Bank for Sight Restoration Inc 120 Wall St 3rd Fl	New York	NY	10005	212-742-9000	269-3139
TF: 866-287-3937 ■ Web: www.eyedonation.org					
Eye Bank of British Columbia 2550 Willow St Eye Care Ctr 3rd Fl	Vancouver	BC	V5Z3N9	604-875-4567	875-5316
TF: 800-667-2060 ■ Web: www.eyebankofbc.ca					
Eye Bank of Canada Ontario Div 1929 Bayview Ave	Toronto	ON	M5T3A9	416-978-7355	978-1522
Web: www.eyebank.utoronto.ca					

Phone Fax

Great Plains Lions Eye Bank
Texas Tech University Health Sciences Ctr
3601 Fourth St Ste BAB104-HSC ... Lubbock TX 79430 806-743-2242 743-1431
Web: www.ttuhsc.edu/eye

Hawaii Lions Eye Bank & Makana Foundation
405 N Kuakini St Ste 801 ... Honolulu HI 96817 808-536-7416
Web: www.hlebmf.org

Heartland Lions Eye Bank
10100 N Ambassador Dr Ste 200 ... Kansas City MO 64153 816-454-5454 727-3843*
**Fax Area Code:* 410 ■ *TF:* 800-756-4824

Heartland Lions Eye Bank
10801 Pear Tree Ln Ste 170 ... Saint Ann MO 63074 314-428-4373

Idaho Lions Eye Bank 1090 N Cole Rd ... Boise ID 83704 208-338-5466 338-6543
TF: 800-546-6889 ■ *Web:* www.idaholions.org

International Cornea Project
9246 Lightwave Ave Ste 120 ... San Diego CA 92123 858-694-0400 565-7368
TF: 800-393-2265 ■ *Web:* www.sdeb.org

International Sight Restoration Inc
3808 Gunn Hwy Ste B ... Tampa FL 33618 813-264-6003 264-6007
TF: 877-477-3210 ■ *Web:* www.internationalsight.com

LABS Inc 6933 S Revere Pkwy ... Centennial CO 80112 720-528-4750 528-4786
TF: 866-393-2244 ■ *Web:* www.labs-inc.org

LifePoint Inc 3950 Faber Pl Dr ... Charleston SC 29405 843-763-7755 763-6393
TF: 800-462-0755 ■ *Web:* www.lifepoint-sc.org

LifePoint Inc 164 Lott Ct Ste B ... West Columbia SC 29169 843-763-7755 794-1831*
**Fax Area Code:* 803 ■ *TF:* 800-462-0755 ■ *Web:* lifepoint-sc.org

LifeShare of the Carolinas
1200 Ridgefield Blvd Ste 150 ... Asheville NC 28806 828-665-0107 665-4729
TF: 800-932-4483 ■ *Web:* www.lifesharecarolinas.org

Lions Eye Bank Alberta Society
7007 14th St SW ... Calgary AB T2V1P9 403-943-3406
Web: www.act4sight.com

Lions Eye Bank for Long Island
North Shore University Hospital
350 Community Dr ... Manhasset NY 11030 516-465-8430 465-8434
Web: www.northwell.edu

Lions Eye Bank of Lexington
3290 Blazer Pkwy Ste 201 ... Lexington KY 40509 859-323-6740 323-5927
Web: www.mc.uky.edu

Lions Eye Bank of Manitoba & Northwest Ontario Inc
691 Wolseley Ave ... Winnipeg MB R3G1C3 204-788-8507
TF: 800-552-6820 ■ *Web:* www.eyebankmanitoba.com

Lions Eye Bank of Nebraska Inc
University of Nebraska Medical Ctr
985541 Nebraska Medical Ctr ... Omaha NE 68198 402-559-4039
TF: 800-225-7244 ■ *Web:* www.eyebanknebraska.org

Lions Eye Bank of Northwest Pennsylvania Inc
5105 Richmond St ... Erie PA 16509 814-866-3545 864-1875

Lions Eye Bank of Texas at Baylor College of Medicine
Dept of Opthalmology 6565 Fannin St NC-205 ... Houston TX 77030 713-798-4714 798-4645
Web: www.bcm.edu

Lions Eye Bank of Wisconsin 2401 American Ln ... Madison WI 53704 608-233-2354 233-2895
TF: 877-233-2354 ■ *Web:* lebw.org

Lions Medical Eye Bank & Research Ctr of Eastern Virginia Inc
600 Gresham Dr ... Norfolk VA 23507 800-453-6059 388-3744*
**Fax Area Code:* 757 ■ *TF:* 800-453-6059 ■ *Web:* www.lionseyebank.org

Lone Star Lions Eye Bank
102 E Wheeler St PO Box 347 ... Manor TX 78653 512-457-0638 457-0658
TF: 800-977-3937 ■ *Web:* www.lsleb.org

Medical Eye Bank of Florida
2902 N Orange Ave ... Orlando FL 32804 407-422-2020

Medical Eye Bank of Maryland 815 Pk Ave ... Baltimore MD 21201 410-752-2020 783-0183
TF: 800-756-4824 ■ *Web:* www.tbionline.org

Medical Eye Bank of West Virginia
3 Courtney Dr ... Charleston WV 25304 304-926-9200 926-6779

Midwest Eye Banks 4889 Venture Dr ... Ann Arbor MI 48108 734-780-2100 780-2143
TF: 800-247-7250 ■ *Web:* www.midwesteyebanks.org

Minnesota Lions Eye Bank
1000 Westgate Dr Ste 260 ... Saint paul MN 55114 612-625-5159 626-1192
TF Cust Svc: 866-887-4448 ■ *Web:* www.mnlionseyebank.org

Mississippi Lions Eye Bank 431 Katherine Dr ... Flowood MS 39232 601-420-5739
Web: www.mslionseyebank.org

National Disease Research Interchange (NDRI)
1628 John F Kennedy Blvd
8 Penn Ctr 8th Fl ... Philadelphia PA 19103 215-557-7361 557-7154
TF: 800-222-6374 ■ *Web:* www.ndriresource.org

New Mexico Lions Eye Bank
2501 Yale Blvd SE Ste 100 ... Albuquerque NM 87106 505-266-3937
TF: 888-616-3937 ■ *Web:* www.nmleb.org

North Carolina Eye Bank Inc
3900 Westpoint Blvd Ste F ... Winston-Salem NC 27103 336-765-0932 765-8803
TF: 800-552-9956 ■ *Web:* miraclesinsight.org

Northeast Pennsylvania Lions Eye Bank Inc
Lehigh Valley Hospital
2346 Jacksonville Rd ... Bethlehem PA 18017 610-625-3800
TF: 800-637-2393 ■ *Web:* www.paeyebank.org

Northwest La Lions Eye Bank 721 Blvd St ... Shreveport LA 71104 318-222-7999 222-8779

Oklahoma Lions Eye Bank
3840 N Lincoln Blvd ... Oklahoma City OK 73105 405-557-1393

Old Dominion Eye Bank (ODEF)
9200 Arboretum Pkwy Ste 104 ... Richmond VA 23236 804-560-7540 560-4752
TF: 800-832-0728 ■ *Web:* www.odef.org

Oregon Lions Sight & Hearing Foundation
1010 NW 22nd Ave Ste 144 ... Portland OR 97210 503-413-7399
TF: 800-635-4667 ■ *Web:* www.olshf.org

Regional Tissue Bank QEII Health Sciences Centre
5788 University Ave Rm 431 MacKenzie Bldg ... Halifax NS B3H1V7 902-473-4171 473-2170
TF: 800-314-6515 ■ *Web:* www.cdha.nshealth.ca/regional-tissue-bank

Rochester Eye & Tissue Bank
524 White Spruce Blvd ... Rochester NY 14623 585-272-7890 272-7897
TF: 800-568-4321 ■ *Web:* www.rehpb.org

Rocky Mountain Lions Eye Bank (RMLEB)
1675 Aurora Crt Ste El2049 PO Box 6026 ... Aurora CO 80045 720-848-3937 848-3938
TF: 800-444-7479 ■ *Web:* www.corneas.org

Phone Fax

San Antonio Eye Bank
9150 Huebner Rd Ste 105 ... San Antonio TX 78240 210-614-1209 614-1422
Web: www.saeyebank.org

San Diego Eye Bank (SDEB)
9246 Lightwave Ave Ste 120 ... San Diego CA 92123 858-694-0400 565-7368
TF: 800-393-2265 ■ *Web:* www.sdeb.org

Sight Society of Northeastern New York Inc
Lions Eye Bank at Albany 6 Executive Pk Dr ... Albany NY 12203 518-489-7606 489-7607
Web: www.lionseyebankalbany.org

SightLife 221 Yale Ave N Ste 450 ... Seattle WA 98109 206-682-8500 682-4666
TF: 800-847-5786 ■ *Web:* www.sightlife.org

South Dakota Lions Eye Bank
4501 W 61st St N ... Sioux Falls SD 57107 605-373-1008 373-1261
TF: 800-245-7846 ■ *Web:* www.dakotasight.org

Southern Eye Bank 2701 Kingman St Ste 200 ... Metairie LA 70006 504-891-3937 891-2401
Web: www.southerneyebank.com

Tennessee District 12-O Lions Eye Bank
979 E Third St Ste A250 ... Chattanooga TN 37403 423-778-4000
Web: www.tennesseelions.com

University of Louisville Lions Eye Bank
301 E Muhammad Ali Blvd ... Louisville KY 40202 502-852-5457
Web: www.ulleb.org

Upstate New York Transplant Services Inc
110 Broadway ... Buffalo NY 14203 716-853-6667 853-6674
TF: 800-227-4771 ■ *Web:* www.unyts.org

Utah Lions Eye Bank
John A Moran Eye Ctr
65 Mario Capecchi Dr ... Salt Lake City UT 84132 801-581-2039 585-5703
Web: www.utaheyebank.org

Western Texas Lions Eye Bank Alliance
2030 Pullman St Ste 4 ... San Angelo TX 76902 325-653-8666 655-2847
TF: 866-226-7632 ■ *Web:* www.wtleb.org

270 FABRIC STORES

See Also Patterns - Sewing p. 2911

Phone Fax

Britex Fabrics LLC 146 Geary St ... San Francisco CA 94108 415-392-2910 392-3906
Web: www.britexfabrics.com

Everfast Inc 203 Gale Ln ... Kennett Square PA 19348 610-444-9700 444-1221
TF Cust Svc: 800-213-6366 ■ *Web:* www.calicocorners.com

Fishman's Fabrics Inc 1101 S Des Plaines St ... Chicago IL 60607 312-922-7250 922-7402
Web: www.fishmansfabrics.com

Hancock Fabrics Inc 1 Fashion Way ... Baldwyn MS 38824 662-365-6000
Web: hancockfabrics.com

Jo-Ann Fabrics & Crafts 5555 Darrow Rd ... Hudson OH 44236 330-656-2600 463-6760
TF: 888-739-4120 ■ *Web:* www.joann.com

Jo-Ann Stores Inc (JAS) 5555 Darrow Rd ... Hudson OH 44236 330-656-2600 463-6760
TF: 888-739-4120 ■ *Web:* www.joann.com

Mary Maxim Inc
2001 Holland Ave PO Box 5019 ... Port Huron MI 48061 810-987-2000 987-5056
TF: 800-962-9504 ■ *Web:* www.marymaxim.com

Scrapbook Factory Inc 2004 W Hwy 50 Ste D ... Ofallon IL 62269 618-628-8877
Web: www.scrapbookfactorystore.com

Vogue Fabrics 718 Main St ... Evanston IL 60202 847-864-9600
Web: www.voguefabricsstore.com

271 FACILITIES MANAGEMENT SERVICES

See Also Correctional & Detention Management (Privatized) p. 2162

Phone Fax

ABM Industries Inc 8020 W Doe Ste C ... Visalia SC 93291 559-651-1612
Web: www.abm.com

Agracel Inc 2201 Willenborg Ave ... Effingham IL 62401 217-342-4443
TF: 800-600-8085 ■ *Web:* agracel.com

Alexander Company Inc, The
145 E Badger Rd Ste 200 ... Madison WI 53713 608-258-5580 258-5599
Web: www.alexandercompany.com

American Pool Enterprises Inc
11515 Cronridge Dr # Q ... Owings Mills MD 21117 443-471-1190 471-1189
Web: www.americanpool.com

Apparatus Inc 1401 N Meridian St ... Indianapolis IN 46202 317-254-8488
Web: apparatus.net

ARAMARK Uniform & Career Apparel LLC
2860 Rudder Rd ... Memphis TN 38118 800-272-6275
TF: 800-272-6275 ■ *Web:* www.aramarkuniform.com

Bechta Group Ltd 1780 S Bellaire St Ste 100 ... Denver CO 80222 303-860-0990
Web: bechtagroup.com

Big Horn Energy 376 33rd St ... Cody WY 82414 307-587-5613

Brookfield Global Integrated Solutions
7400 Birchmount Rd ... Markham ON L3R4E6 905-943-4100
Web: www.brookfieldgis.com

Creative Dining Services 1 Royal Pk Dr Ste 3 ... Zeeland MI 49464 616-748-1700 748-1900
Web: www.creativedining.com

Elite Show Services Inc
2878 Camino Del Rio S Ste 260 ... San Diego CA 92108 619-574-1589 574-1588
Web: www.eliteservicesusa.com

Financial & Realty Services LLC
1110 Bonifant St Ste 301 ... Silver Spring MD 20910 301-650-9112
TF: 800-650-9714 ■ *Web:* frsllc.com

FLIK Hotels & Conference Centers
3 International Dr 2nd Fl ... Rye Brook NY 10573 914-935-5394
Web: www.flikccm.compass-usa.com

Harrison Senior Living Inc
300 Strode Ave ... East Fallowfield PA 19320 610-384-6310 383-3945
Web: harrisonseniorliving.com

IAP Worldwide Services Inc
7315 N Atlantic Ave ... Cape Canaveral FL 32920 321-784-7100
TF: 877-296-8010 ■ *Web:* www.iapws.com

Kansas Turnpike Authority (KTA) 9401 E Kellogg ... Wichita KS 67207 316-682-4537
Web: www.ksturnpike.com

Phone Fax

L & M Technologies Inc
4209 Balloon Pk Rd NE .... Albuquerque NM 87109 505-343-0200 343-0300
Web: www.lmtechnologies.com

Lasalle Management Company LLC
192 Bastille Ln .... Ruston LA 71270 318-232-1500
Web: lasallecorrections.com

Logistics Applications
2760 Eisenhower Ave .... Alexandria VA 22314 703-317-9800
Web: logapp.com

Mainthia Technologies Inc
7055 Engle Rd Ste 502 .... Cleveland OH 44130 440-816-0202 816-1121
Web: www.mainthia.com

Marenzana Group Inc 780 Third Ave .... New York NY 10017 212-735-0011

New York State Bridge Authority PO Box 1010 .... Highland NY 12528 845-691-7245 691-3560
TF: 800-333-8655 ■ *Web:* www.nysba.state.ny.us

Olympia Entertainment Inc 2211 Woodward Ave .... Detroit MI 48201 313-471-3200 471-3595
Web: www.olympiaentertainment.com

OMNIPLEX World Services Corp
14151 Pk Meadow Dr Ste 300 .... Chantilly VA 20151 703-652-3100 652-3101
TF: 800-356-3406 ■ *Web:* www.omniplex.com

Penguin Logistics LLC 4500 Brooktree Rd .... Wexford PA 15090 724-772-9800
Web: mhfservices.com

Philotechnics Ltd 201 Renovare Blvd .... Oak Ridge TN 37830 865-483-1551
TF: 888-723-9278 ■ *Web:* www.philotechnics.com

Phoenix Park 'n Swap 3801 E Washington St .... Phoenix AZ 85034 602-273-1250
TF: 800-772-0852 ■ *Web:* www.americanparknswap.com

Sarakem Corp 15 Buell St .... Hanover NH 03755 603-643-5720
Web: sarakem.com

Serco Group Inc 1818 Library St Ste 1000 .... Reston VA 20190 703-939-6000 939-6001
Web: www.serco.com

Summit Aerospace 1260 NW 57th Ave .... Miami FL 33126 305-267-6400
Web: summitmro.com

Terranear PMC LLC 5005 W Royal Ln Ste 216 .... Irving TX 75063 972-929-1095
Web: www.terranear.com

United Space Alliance (USA) 600 Gemini Ave .... Houston TX 77058 281-212-6200 212-6177
TF: 800-367-5690 ■ *Web:* unitedspacealliance.com

Vinnell Corp 12150 E Monument Dr .... Fairfax VA 22033 703-385-4544

Viox Services Inc 15 W Voorhees St .... Cincinnati OH 45215 513-948-8469
TF: 888-846-9462 ■ *Web:* www.viox-services.com

Wastren Advantage Inc 1571 Shyville Rd .... Piketon OH 45661 740-443-7924
Web: www.wastrenadvantage.com

Xanterra Parks & Resorts
6312 S Fiddlers Green Cir
Ste 600-N .... Greenwood Village CO 80111 303-600-3400 600-3600
TF: 800-236-7916 ■ *Web:* www.xanterra.com

272 FACTORS

Factors are companies that buy accounts receivable (invoices) from other businesses at a discount.

Phone Fax

Action Capital Corp 230 Peachtree St Ste 910 .... Atlanta GA 30343 404-524-3181 577-4880
TF: 800-525-7767 ■ *Web:* www.actioncapital.com

Advantage Funding Corp 1000 Parkwood Cir SE .... Atlanta GA 30339 770-955-2274
TF: 800-241-2274 ■ *Web:* www.advantagefunding.com

AmeriFactors 215 Celebration Pl Ste 340 .... Celebration FL 34747 407-566-1150 566-1250
TF: 800-884-3863 ■ *Web:* www.amerifactors.com

Applied Capital Inc
3700 Rio Grande Blvd NW Ste 4 .... Albuquerque NM 87107 505-342-1840 342-2246
Web: www.appliedcapital.net

Asta Funding Inc 210 Sylvan Ave .... Englewood Cliffs NJ 07632 201-567-5648
NASDAQ: ASFI ■ *TF:* 866-389-7627 ■ *Web:* www.astafunding.com

Bibby Financial Services
600 TownPark Ln Ste 450 .... Kennesaw GA 30144 877-882-4229
TF: 877-882-4229 ■ *Web:* www.bibbyusa.com

Capital-Plus Inc (CPI)
3250 W Henderson Rd Ste 201 .... Columbus OH 43220 614-848-7620
Web: www.capitalplusfactoring.com

Crestmark Bank 5480 Corporate Dr Ste 350 .... Troy MI 48098 888-999-8050 641-5101*
**Fax Area Code:* 248 ■ *TF:* 888-999-8050 ■ *Web:* www.crestmark.com

Diversified Funding Services Inc
125 Habersham Dr Ste C .... Fayetteville GA 30214 770-603-0055
TF: 888-603-0055 ■ *Web:* www.divfunding.com

DSA Factors 3126 N Lincoln Ave PO Box 577520 .... Chicago IL 60657 773-248-9000 248-9005
Web: www.dsafactors.com

Goodman Factors 3010 LBJ Fwy Ste 140 .... Dallas TX 75234 972-241-3297 243-6285
TF: 877-446-6362 ■ *Web:* www.goodmanfactors.com

Hamilton Group 100 Elwood Davis Rd .... North Syracuse NY 13212 315-413-0086 413-0087
TF: 800-351-3066 ■ *Web:* www.hamiltongroup.net

LSQ Funding Group LC 2600 Lucien Way Ste 100 .... Maitland FL 32751 800-474-7606
TF: 800-474-7606 ■ *Web:* www.lsqgroup.com

Magnolia Financial Inc 187 W Broad St .... Spartanburg SC 29306 864-573-9900 573-9912
TF: 866-573-0611 ■ *Web:* www.magfinancial.com

Mazon Assoc Inc 800 W Airport Fwy Ste 900 .... Irving TX 75062 972-554-6967 554-0951
TF: 800-442-2740 ■ *Web:* mazonfactoring.com

Merchant Factors Corp 1441 Broadway 22nd Fl .... New York NY 10018 212-840-7575 869-1752
Web: www.merchantfactors.com

Performance Funding 11022 N 28th Dr .... Phoenix AZ 85029 602-912-0200
Web: www.performancefunding.com

Porter Capital Corp 2112 First Ave N .... Birmingham AL 35203 205-322-5442 322-7719
TF: 800-737-7344 ■ *Web:* www.portercap.net

Prestige Capital Corp 400 Kelby St 14th Fl .... Fort Lee NJ 07024 201-944-4455 944-9477
Web: www.pcc-cash.com

Quantum Corporate Funding Ltd
1140 Ave of the Americas 16th Fl .... New York NY 10036 212-768-1200 944-8216
TF: 800-352-2535 ■ *Web:* www.quantumfunding.com

Riviera Finance 220 Ave I .... Redondo Beach CA 90277 800-872-7484 454-8122*
**Fax Area Code:* 651 ■ *TF:* 800-872-7484 ■ *Web:* www.rivierafinance.com

Rosenthal & Rosenthal Inc 1370 Broadway .... New York NY 10018 212-356-1400 356-0910
Web: www.rosenthalinc.com

Phone Fax

RTS Financial Service
9300 Metcalf Ste 301 .... Overland Park KS 66212 877-242-4390
TF: 877-242-4390 ■ *Web:* www.rtsfinancial.com

Seven Oaks Capital Assoc LLC
7854 Anselmo Ln PO Box 82360 .... Baton Rouge LA 70810 225-757-1919 757-1916
TF: 800-511-4588 ■ *Web:* www.sevenoakscapital.com

TCE Capital Corp 505 Consumers Rd Ste 707 .... Toronto ON M2J4V8 416-497-7400 497-3139
TF: 800-465-0400 ■ *Web:* www.tcecapital.com

Transport Clearings East Inc
210 E Woodlawn Rd .... Charlotte NC 28217 704-527-1820 527-1851
Web: www.tceast.com

United Capital Funding Corp
146 Second St N Ste 200 .... Saint Petersburg FL 33701 727-894-8232 898-4205
Web: www.ucfunding.com

273 FARM MACHINERY & EQUIPMENT - MFR

See Also Lawn & Garden Equipment p. 2645

Phone Fax

ADM Alliance Nutrition Inc 1000 N 30th St .... Quincy IL 62301 217-222-7100
TF: 800-292-3333 ■ *Web:* www.admani.com

AGCO Corp (AGCO) 4205 River Green Pkwy .... Duluth GA 30096 770-813-9200
NYSE: AGCO ■ *TF:* 877-525-4384 ■ *Web:* www.agcocorp.com

Agile Manufacturing Inc
720 Industrial Pk Rd .... Anderson MO 64831 417-845-6065 845-6069

Alamo Group Inc 1627 E Walnut .... Seguin TX 78155 830-379-1480 372-9683
NYSE: ALG ■ *TF Cust Svc:* 800-788-6066 ■ *Web:* www.alamo-group.com

All-American Co-op PO Box 125 .... Stewartville MN 55976 507-533-4222 280-0066
TF: 888-354-4058 ■ *Web:* www.allamericancoop.com

Allied Systems Co 21433 SW Oregon St .... Sherwood OR 97140 503-625-2560 625-7269
TF: 800-285-7000 ■ *Web:* www.alliedsystems.com

Amadas Industries Inc 1100 Holland Rd .... Suffolk VA 23434 757-539-0231 934-3264
Web: www.amadas.com

Amarillo Wind Machine Co 20513 Ave 256 .... Exeter CA 93221 559-592-4256 592-4194
TF: 800-311-4498 ■ *Web:* www.amarillowind.com

Amerequip Corp 1015 Calumet Ave .... Kiel WI 53042 920-894-2000 894-3799
Web: www.amerequip.com

Anholt Technologies Inc 440 Church Rd .... Avondale PA 19311 610-268-2758
Web: anholt.com

Applegate Livestock Equipment Inc
902 S State Rd 32 .... Union City IN 47390 765-964-4631
Web: www.applegatelivestock.com

Arts-Way Mfg Co Inc 5556 Hwy 9 PO Box 288 .... Armstrong IA 50514 712-864-3131 864-3154
NASDAQ: ARTW ■ *TF:* 800-535-4517 ■ *Web:* www.artsway-mfg.com

Atom-Jet Industries Ltd 2110 Park Ave .... Brandon MB R7B0R9 204-728-8590 726-5734
TF: 800-573-5048 ■ *Web:* atomjet.com

B & H Manufacturing Inc 141 County Rd 34 E .... Jackson MN 56143 507-847-2802
TF: 800-240-3288 ■ *Web:* www.bhmfg.com

Berg Equipment Co 2700 W Veterans Pkwy .... Marshfield WI 54449 715-384-2151 387-6777
TF: 800-494-1738 ■ *Web:* www.bergequipment.com

Big Dutchman Inc 3900 John F Donnelly Dr .... Holland MI 49424 616-392-5981 392-6188
Web: www.bigdutchmanusa.com

Bigham Brothers Inc 705 E Slaton Rd .... Lubbock TX 79452 806-745-0384
Web: www.bighambrothers.com

Bou-Matic PO Box 8050 .... Madison WI 53708 608-222-3484
Web: www.boumatic.com

Bourgault Industries Ltd
1 mile NE side Hwy 368 .... St. Brieux SK S0K3V0 306-275-2300
Web: www.bourgault.com

Bowie Industries Inc 1004 E Wise St .... Bowie TX 76230 940-872-1106 872-4792
TF: 800-433-0934 ■ *Web:* www.bowieindustries.com

Brillion Iron Works Inc 200 Pk Ave .... Brillion WI 54110 920-756-2121 756-3062
TF: 855-320-0373 ■
Web: landoll.com/content/index.php/products/farm_equipment

Brock Grain Systems
611 N Higbee St PO Box 2000 .... Milford IN 46542 574-658-4191 658-4133
Web: www.brockgrain.com

Brown Mfg Corp 6001 E Hwy 27 .... Ozark AL 36360 800-633-8909 795-3029*
**Fax Area Code:* 334 ■ *TF:* 800-633-8909 ■ *Web:* www.brownmfgcorp.com

Broyhill Co 1 N Market Sq .... Dakota City NE 68731 402-987-3412 987-3601
TF: 800-228-1003 ■ *Web:* www.broyhill.com

Bucklin Tractor & Implement Co
115 W Railroad PO Box 127 .... Bucklin KS 67834 620-826-3271 826-3760
TF: 800-334-4823 ■ *Web:* www.btiequip.com

Buhler Versatile Inc 1260 Clarence Ave .... Winnipeg MB R3T1T2 204-661-8711 654-2503
TF: 888-524-1003 ■ *Web:* www.buhlerindustries.com

Bushnell Illinois Tank Co 650 W Davis St .... Bushnell IL 61422 309-772-3106 772-2045
Web: www.schuldbushnell.com

Cal-Coast Dairy Systems Inc 424 S Tegner Rd .... Turlock CA 95380 209-634-9026 634-3458
TF Cust Svc: 800-732-6826 ■ *Web:* www.calcoastinc.com

Carter Day International Inc
500 73rd Ave NE .... Minneapolis MN 55432 763-571-1000 571-3012
Web: www.carterday.com

Chick Master Incubator Co
945 Lafayette Rd PO Box 704 .... Medina OH 44258 330-722-5591 723-0233
TF: 800-727-8726 ■ *Web:* www.chickmaster.com

CLAAS of America Inc 8401 S 132nd St .... Omaha NE 68145 402-861-1000
Web: www.claasofamerica.com

Conrad-American Inc PO Box 2000 .... Houghton IA 52631 800-553-1791 469-4402*
**Fax Area Code:* 319 ■ *TF General:* 800-553-1791 ■ *Web:* www.conradamerican.com

Covington Planter Co 410 Hodges Ave .... Albany GA 31701 229-888-2032 888-0448
Web: www.covingtonplanter.com

CTAQ 1000 rue Raoul-Charette .... Joliette QC J6E8S6 450-755-4122
Web: www.intelia.com

CTB Inc 611 N Higbee St PO Box 2000 .... Milford IN 46542 574-658-4191 658-3471
TF: 800-261-8651 ■ *Web:* www.ctbinc.com

Custom Products of Litchfield Inc
1715 S Sibley Ave .... Litchfield MN 55355 320-693-3221 693-7252
TF: 800-222-5463 ■ *Web:* www.cpcabs.com

Daco Inc 609 Airport Rd .... North Aurora IL 60542 630-897-8797 897-4076

Danuser Machine Co 500 E Third St .... Fulton MO 65251 573-642-2246 642-2240
Web: www.danuser.com

Phone Fax

Dig Corp 1210 Activity Dr ... Vista CA 92081 760-727-0914
TF: 800-322-9146 ■ *Web:* www.digcorp.com

Driptech Inc 2580 Wyandotte St Ste B ... Mountain View CA 94043 415-793-6735
Web: www.driptech.com

DuraTech Industries International Inc
PO Box 1940 ... Jamestown ND 58401 701-252-4601 252-0502
TF: 800-243-4601 ■ *Web:* www.duratechindustries.net

Egging Co, The 12145 Rd 38 ... Gurley NE 69141 308-884-2233
Web: www.egging.com

EGM LLC 3748 Industrial Park Dr ... Mobile AL 36693 251-662-1250
Web: www.egm-llc.com

Empire Plow Company Inc 3140 E 65th St ... Cleveland OH 44127 216-641-2290 441-4709
Web: www.mckayempire.com

EVH Mfg Company LLC 4895 Red Bluff Rd ... Loris SC 29569 843-756-2555 756-4436
TF: 888-990-2555 ■ *Web:* hardeebyevh.com

EZ Trail Inc 1050 E Columbia St PO Box 168 ... Arthur IL 61911 217-543-3471 543-3473
TF: 800-677-2802 ■ *Web:* www.e-ztrail.com

Fabrication JR Tardif Inc
62 Blvd Cartier ... Rivi Re-Du-Loup QC G5R6B2 418-862-7273
TF: 877-962-7273 ■ *Web:* www.jrtardif.com

Finn Corp 9281 Le St Dr ... Fairfield OH 45014 513-874-2818 874-2914
TF: 800-543-7166 ■ *Web:* www.finncorp.com

Flint Cliffs Manufacturing Co
1600 Bluff Rd ... Burlington IA 52601 319-752-2781 752-5538

Forsbergs Inc
1210 Pennington Ave PO Box 510 ... Thief River Falls MN 56701 218-681-1927 681-2037
TF Cust Svc: 800-654-1927 ■ *Web:* www.forsbergs.com

Gandy Co 528 Gandrud Rd ... Owatonna MN 55060 507-451-5430 451-2857
TF: 800-443-2476 ■ *Web:* www.gandy.net

GMP Metal Products Inc 3883 Delor St ... Saint Louis MO 63116 314-481-0300 481-1379
TF: 800-325-9808 ■ *Web:* www.gmpmetal.com

GSI Group Inc 1004 E Illinois St ... Assumption IL 62510 217-226-4421
Web: www.grainsystems.com

Hagie Manufacturing Co PO Box 273 ... Clarion IA 50525 515-532-2861 532-3553
TF: 800-247-4885 ■ *Web:* www.hagie.com

Hanson Silo Co 11587 County Rd 8 SE ... Lake Lillian MN 56253 320-664-4171 664-4140
Web: www.hansonsilo.com

Hardi Inc 1500 W 76th St ... Davenport IA 52806 563-386-1730 386-1280
TF: 866-770-7063 ■ *Web:* www.hardi-us.com

Harsh International Inc 600 Oak Ave ... Eaton CO 80615 970-454-2291
Web: www.harshenviro.com

Hastings Equity Grain Bin Mfg Co
1900 Summit Ave ... Hastings NE 68901 402-462-2189 462-2900
TF: 888-883-2189 ■ *Web:* www.hastingstanks.com

HCC Inc 1501 First Ave ... Mendota IL 61342 815-539-9371 539-3135
TF: 800-548-6633 ■ *Web:* www.hccincorporated.com

HD Hudson Manufacturing Co
500 N Michigan Ave ... Chicago IL 60611 312-644-2830 644-7989
TF: 800-977-7293 ■ *Web:* www.hdhudson.com

Heartland Equipment Inc 2100 N Falls Blvd ... Wynne AR 72396 800-530-7617 238-8545*
**Fax Area Code:* 870 ■ *TF:* 800-530-7617 ■ *Web:* www.tractorscraper.com

Henderson Manufacturing Inc
1085 S Third St ... Manchester IA 52057 563-927-2828 927-2521
TF: 800-359-4970 ■ *Web:* www.henderson-mfg.com

Herschel-Adams Inc 1301 N 14th St ... Indianola IA 50125 800-247-2167
TF: 800-247-2167 ■ *Web:* www.alamo-group.com

Hiniker Co 58766 240th St ... Mankato MN 56002 507-625-6621 625-5883*
**Fax:* Sales ■ *TF:* 800-433-5620 ■ *Web:* www.hiniker.com

Honiron Corp 400 Canal St ... Jeanerette LA 70544 337-276-6314
Web: www.honiron.com

Howse Implement Company Inc
2013 Hwy 184 E PO Box 86 ... Laurel MS 39441 601-428-0841 425-4900
Web: howseimplement.com

Hutchinson/Mayrath/TerraTrack Industries
514 W Crawford PO Box 629 ... Clay Center KS 67432 785-632-2161 632-5964
TF: 800-523-6993 ■ *Web:* www.hutchinson-mayrath.com

Irridelco International Corp
440 Sylvan Ave ... Englewood Cliffs NJ 07632 201-569-3030

ISS LLC 820 E 20th St ... Cookeville TN 38501 931-526-1106
Web: www.sproutnet.com

Jamesway Incubator Co Inc 30 High Ridge Ct ... Cambridge ON N1R7L3 519-624-4646
TF: 800-438-8077 ■ *Web:* www.jamesway.com

Johnson Farm Machinery Company Inc
152 W Kentucky Ave ... Woodland CA 95695 530-662-1788 666-5585
Web: www.jfmco.com

KBH Corp, The 395 Anderson Blvd ... Clarksdale MS 38614 662-624-5471
TF: 800-843-5241 ■ *Web:* www.kbhequipment.com

Kelley Manufacturing Co
80 Vernon Dr PO Box 1467 ... Tifton GA 31793 229-382-9393 382-5259
TF: 800-444-5449 ■ *Web:* www.kelleymfg.com

Kelly Ryan Equipment Co 900 Kelly Ryan Dr ... Blair NE 68008 402-426-2151 426-2186
TF: 800-640-6967 ■ *Web:* www.kryan.com

Kinze Manufacturing Inc 2172 M Ave ... Williamsburg IA 52361 319-668-1300
Web: kinze.com

Kirby Mfg Inc 484 S Hwy 59 ... Merced CA 95341 209-723-0778 723-3941
Web: www.kirbymfg.com

KMW Ltd PO Box 327 ... Sterling KS 67579 620-278-3641 278-2388
TF: 800-445-7388 ■ *Web:* www.kmwloaders.com

Krone North America 3363 Miac Cove ... Memphis TN 38118 901-842-6011
Web: www.krone-northamerica.com

Kubota Tractor Corp 3401 Del Amo Blvd ... Torrance CA 90503 310-370-3370 370-3166
TF: 888-458-2682 ■ *Web:* www.kubota.com

Kuhn Knight Inc
1501 W Seventh Ave PO Box 0167 ... Brodhead WI 53520 608-897-2131 897-2561
Web: www.kuhnnorthamerica.com

Lindsay Corp 2222 N 111th St ... Omaha NE 68164 402-829-6800 829-6834
NYSE: LNN ■ *TF:* 866-404-5049 ■ *Web:* www.lindsay.com

Loftness Specialized Farm Equipment Inc
650 S Main St PO Box 337 ... Hector MN 55342 320-848-6266 848-6269
TF: 800-828-7624 ■ *Web:* www.loftness.com

LS Tractor USA LLC 6900 Corporation Pkwy ... Battleboro NC 27809 252-984-0700
Web: www.lstractorusa.com

Lund Industrial Group
400 E Industrial Pk Rd ... Holly Springs MS 38635 662-252-2340 252-3352
Web: www.lundonline.com

MacDon Industries Ltd 680 Moray St ... Winnipeg MB R3J3S3 204-885-5590 832-7749
Web: www.macdon.com

Mathews Co 500 Industrial Ave ... Crystal Lake IL 60012 815-459-2210 459-5889
TF: 800-323-7045 ■ *Web:* www.mathewscompany.com

Mertz Mfg LLC 1701 N Waverly St ... Ponca City OK 74601 580-762-5646 767-8411
TF: 800-654-6433 ■ *Web:* www.mertzok.com

Meyer Manufacturing Corp
County Hwy A W 574 W Ctr Ave PO Box 405 ... Dorchester WI 54425 715-654-5132
Web: www.meyermfg.com

Miller Saint Nazianz Inc 511 E Main St ... Saint Nazianz WI 54232 920-773-2121 773-1200
TF: 800-247-5557 ■ *Web:* www.millerstn.com

Modern Group Ltd 1655 Louisiana St ... Beaumont TX 77701 409-833-2665
TF Cust Svc: 800-231-8198 ■ *Web:* www.modernusa.com

Montgomery Industries International Inc
2017 Thelma St ... Jacksonville FL 32206 904-355-4055 355-0401
Web: www.montgomeryindustries.com

Moorfeed Corp 1445 Brookville Way Ste R ... Indianapolis IN 46239 317-545-7171 542-7317
Web: www.moorfeed.com

Orchard Machinery Corp 2700 Colusa Hwy ... Yuba City CA 95993 530-673-2822 673-0296
Web: www.shakermaker.com

Orthman Manufacturing Inc
75765 Rd 435 PO Box B ... Lexington NE 68850 308-324-4654 324-5001
TF: 800-658-3270 ■ *Web:* www.orthman.com

Osborne Industries Inc 120 N Industrial Ave ... Osborne KS 67473 785-346-2192 346-2194
TF: 800-255-0316 ■ *Web:* www.osborneindustries.com

Oxbo International Corp 7275 Batavia Byron Rd ... Byron NY 14422 585-548-2665 548-2599
Web: www.oxbocorp.com

P & H Manufacturing Co 604 S Lodge St ... Shelbyville IL 62565 217-774-2123 774-5341
Web: www.phmfg.com

Peerless Manufacturing Co US Hwy 82 E ... Shellman GA 39886 229-679-5353 679-5542
TF: 800-225-4617 ■ *Web:* www.peerlessmfg.cc

Performance Feeders Inc 251 Dunbar ... Oldsmar FL 34677 813-855-2685 855-4296
Web: www.performancefeeders.com

Precision Tank & Equipment Company Inc
3503 Conover Rd ... Virginia IL 62691 217-452-7228 452-3956
TF: 800-258-4197 ■ *Web:* www.precisiontank.com

Rainbow Manufacturing Co PO Box 70 ... Fitzgerald GA 31750 229-423-4341 423-4645*
**Fax:* Cust Svc ■ *Web:* www.rainbowirrigation.com

Rayne Plane Inc 9107 Grand Prairie Hwy ... Church Point LA 70525 337-334-2101 634-2813*
**Fax Area Code:* 713 ■ *Web:* www.rayneplane.com

Reinke Mfg Co Inc 5325 Reinke Rd ... Deshler NE 68340 402-365-7251 365-4370
TF: 866-365-7381 ■ *Web:* www.reinke.com

Root-Lowell Manufacturing Co
1000 Foreman Rd PO Box 289 ... Lowell MI 49331 616-897-9211 897-8223
TF: 800-748-0098 ■ *Web:* www.rlflomaster.com

Schlagel Inc 491 N Emerson ... Cambridge MN 55008 763-689-5991
Web: www.schlagel.com

Schuette Mfg & Steel Sales Inc 5028 Hwy 42 ... Manitowoc WI 54220 920-758-2491 758-2599
Web: www.schuettemfg.com

Scranton Mfg Company Inc
101 State St PO Box 336 ... Scranton IA 51462 712-652-3396 652-3399
TF: 800-831-1858 ■ *Web:* www.scrantonmfg.com

Seed Hawk Inc Hwy 9 PO Box 123 ... Langbank SK S0G2X0 306-538-2221
Web: www.seedhawk.com

Shivvers Inc 614 W English St ... Corydon IA 50060 641-872-1005 872-1593
TF: 800-245-9093 ■ *Web:* www.shivvers.com

Simonsen Industries Inc 500 Iowa 31 ... Quimby IA 51049 712-445-2211 445-2626
TF: 800-831-4860 ■ *Web:* www.simonsen-industries.com

Sioux Steel Co 196 1/2 E Sixth St ... Sioux Falls SD 57104 605-336-1750 336-2528
TF: 800-557-4689 ■ *Web:* www.siouxsteel.com

Spudnik Equipment Co 584 W 100 N Rd ... Blackfoot ID 83221 208-785-0480 785-1497
Web: www.spudnik.com

Star Forge Inc 1801 S Ihm Blvd ... Freeport IL 61032 815-235-7750 235-4813
Web: www.starmfg.com

Stock Equipment Co
16490 Chillicothe Rd ... Chagrin Falls OH 44023 440-543-6000 543-5944
TF: 888-742-1249 ■ *Web:* www.schenckprocess.com/stockequipment

Sudenga Industries Inc 2002 Kingbird Ave ... George IA 51237 712-475-3301 475-3320
TF: 888-783-3642 ■ *Web:* www.sudenga.com

Sukup Manufacturing Co
1555 255th St PO Box 677 ... Sheffield IA 50475 641-892-4222 892-4629
Web: www.sukup.com

Sun Circle Inc 286 S G St ... Arcata CA 95521 707-822-5777
TF: 800-458-6543 ■ *Web:* americanhydroponics.com

T-l Irrigation Co
151 E Hwy 6 AB Rd PO Box 1047 ... Hastings NE 68902 402-462-4128 330-4268*
**Fax Area Code:* 800 ■ *TF:* 800-330-4264 ■ *Web:* www.tlirr.com

Taylor Pittsburgh Mfg 7 Rocky Mt Rd ... Athens TN 37303 423-745-3110
Web: taylorpittsburgh.com

Tigercat Industries Inc 54 Morton Ave E ... Brantford ON N3R7J7 519-753-2000
Web: www.tigercat.com

Top Air Sprayers 601 S Broad St ... Kalida OH 45853 419-532-3121 532-2468
TF: 800-322-6301 ■ *Web:* www.topairequip.com

Toro Co Irrigation Div 5825 Jasmine St ... Riverside CA 92504 800-654-1882 451-1390
TF: 800-654-1882 ■ *Web:* www.toro.com

Unverferth Mfg Company Inc 601 S Broad St ... Kalida OH 45853 419-532-3121 532-2468
TF: 800-322-6301 ■ *Web:* www.unverferth.com

Valmont Industries Inc 1 Valmont Plz ... Omaha NE 68154 402-963-1000
NYSE: VMI ■ *TF:* 800-825-6668 ■ *Web:* www.valmont.com

Vermeer Corp 1210 Vermeer Rd E PO Box 200 ... Pella IA 50219 641-628-3141 621-7773
TF: 800-829-0051 ■ *Web:* www2.vermeer.com

Westfield Industries Ltd 74 Hwy 205 E ... Rosenort MB R0G1W0 204-746-2396
TF: 866-467-7207 ■ *Web:* www.grainaugers.com

Wiese Industries Inc 1501 Fifth St PO Box 39 ... Perry IA 50220 515-465-9854 465-9858
TF: 800-568-4391 ■ *Web:* www.wiesecorp.com

Woods Equipment Co 1000 W Cherokee St ... Sioux Falls SD 57104 605-336-3860
Web: woodsequipment.com

Woods Equipment Co
2606 S Illinois Rt 2 PO Box 1000 ... Oregon IL 61061 815-732-2141 732-7580*
**Fax:* Sales ■ *TF:* 800-319-6637 ■ *Web:* www.woodsequipment.com

				Phone	Fax
Worksaver Inc 9 Worksaver Trl PO Box 100 *Web:* www.worksaver.com	Litchfield	IL	62056	217-324-5973	
Wylie Spray Center 702 E 40th St *TF:* 888-249-5162 ■ *Web:* www.wyliesprayers.com	Lubbock	TX	79404	806-763-1335	763-1092
Yargus Manufacturing Inc PO Box 238 *Web:* yargus.com	Marshall	IL	62441	217-826-6352	
Yetter Manufacturing Inc 109 S McDonough St PO Box 358 *TF:* 800-447-5777 ■ *Web:* yetterco.com	Colchester	IL	62326	309-776-4111	776-3222

274 FARM MACHINERY & EQUIPMENT - WHOL

				Phone	Fax
Abilene Machine Inc PO Box 129 *TF:* 800-255-0337 ■ *Web:* www.abilenemachine.com	Abilene	KS	67410	785-655-9455	655-3838
Ag West Supply Inc 9055 Rickreall Rd *TF:* 800-842-2224 ■ *Web:* www.agwestsupply.com	Rickreall	OR	97371	503-363-2332	363-5662
Ag-Land Implement Inc Hwy 63 N PO Box 31 *Web:* www.aglandimplement.com	New Hampton	IA	50659	641-394-4226	394-3936
Ag-Pro Companies US 84 *Web:* www.agprocompanies.com/en/boston.html	Dixie	GA	31629	229-263-4133	
Agri-Service 300 Agri-Service Way *TF:* 800-388-3599 ■ *Web:* www.agri-service.com	Kimberly	ID	83341	208-734-7772	734-7775
Apple Farm Service Inc 10120 W Versailles Rd *Web:* www.applefarmservice.com	Covington	OH	45318	937-526-4851	
Arends & Sons Inc 715 S Sangamon Ave *TF:* 800-637-6052 ■ *Web:* www.arends-sons.com	Gibson City	IL	60936	217-784-4241	784-8749
Arends Bros Inc 1190 E 1200N Rd *TF:* 800-356-6811 ■ *Web:* www.arendshoganwalker.com	Melvin	IL	60952	217-388-7717	388-2882
Baker Implement Co 421 E Main St *Web:* www.bakerimplement.com	Portageville	MO	63873	573-379-5455	379-5313
BE Implement Co 1645 FM 403 PO Box 752 *TF:* 800-725-5435 ■ *Web:* www.beimplement.com	Brownfield	TX	79316	806-637-3594	637-8992
Beard Implement Co 216 Frederick St *Web:* www.beardimplement.com	Arenzville	IL	62611	217-997-5514	
Belarus Tractor International Inc 7842 N Faulkner Rd *TF:* 800-356-2336 ■ *Web:* www.belarus.com	Milwaukee	WI	53224	800-356-2336	
Bell Equipment Inc 511 Fourth St *TF:* 800-343-2355 ■ *Web:* belleq.com	Nezperce	ID	83543	208-937-2402	937-2118
Berchtold Equipment Co Inc 330 E 19th St *TF:* 800-691-7817 ■ *Web:* www.berchtold.com	Bakersfield	CA	93305	661-323-7817	325-4059
Big W Sales 1040 W Charter Way *Web:* www.bigwsales.com	Stockton	CA	95206	209-464-9493	
Blain Supply Inc 3507 E Racine St *Web:* www.farmandfleet.com	Janesville	WI	53547	608-754-2821	
Blanchard Compact Equipment 1410 Ashville Hwy *TF:* 888-799-3606 ■ *Web:* www.blanchardmachinery.com	Spartanburg	SC	29303	864-582-1245	
Browning Equipment Inc 800 E Main St *Web:* www.browningequipment.com	Purcellville	VA	20132	540-338-7123	338-5835
Burks Tractor Co Inc 3140 Kimberly Rd *TF:* 800-247-7419 ■ *Web:* www.burkstractor.com	Twin Falls	ID	83301	208-733-5543	734-9852
Carco International Inc 2721 Midland Blvd *TF:* 800-824-3215 ■ *Web:* www.carcoint.com	Fort Smith	AR	72904	479-441-3270	441-3273
Carrico Implement Company Inc 3160 US 24 Hwy *TF:* 877-542-4099 ■ *Web:* www.carricoimplement.com	Beloit	KS	67420	785-738-5744	738-2648
Coleman Equipment Inc 24000 W 43rd St *Web:* www.colemanequip.com	Bonner Springs	KS	66012	913-422-3040	422-3044
Delta Ridge Implement Inc 1150 US Hwy 425 *Web:* stihldealer.net	Rayville	LA	71269	318-728-6423	728-6426
Ernie Williams Ltd 2613 Hwy 18 E *TF:* 888-535-4096 ■ *Web:* www.erniewilliamsltd.com	Algona	IA	50511	515-295-3561	
Farm Implement & Supply Company Inc 1200 S Washington Hwy 183 *TF:* 888-589-6029 ■ *Web:* www.farmimp.com	Plainville	KS	67663	785-434-4824	434-7390
Farmer Boy Ag Systems Inc PO Box 435 **Fax Area Code:* 717 ■ *TF:* 800-845-3374 ■ *Web:* www.farmerboyag.com	Myerstown	PA	17067	800-845-3374	866-6233*
Farmers Supply Sales Inc 1409 E Ave *TF:* 800-493-4917 ■ *Web:* www.farmers.com	Kalona	IA	52247	319-656-2291	
Fruit Growers Supply Company Inc 14130 Riverside Dr *Web:* www.fruitgrowers.com	Sherman Oaks	CA	91423	818-986-6480	783-1941
Gardner Inc 3641 Interchange Rd *TF:* 800-848-8946 ■ *Web:* www.gardnerinc.com	Columbus	OH	43204	614-456-4000	456-4001
Garton Tractor Inc 2400 N Golden State Blvd *TF:* 877-872-2767 ■ *Web:* gartontractor.com	Turlock	CA	95382	209-632-3931	632-8006
Giles & Ransome Inc Ransome Engine Power Div 2975 Galloway Rd *TF:* 877-726-7663 ■ *Web:* www.ransome.com	Bensalem	PA	19020	215-639-4300	245-2830
Glade & Grove Supply Inc 305 CR 17 W PO Box 760 *TF:* 800-433-4451 ■ *Web:* www.gladeandgrove.com	Avon Park	FL	33826	561-996-3095	996-2048
Golden Spike Equipment Co 1352 W Main St PO Box 70 *TF:* 800-821-4474 ■ *Web:* www.gspike.com	Tremonton	UT	84337	435-257-5346	257-5719
Greenline Equipment 14750 S Pony Express Rd *TF:* 888-201-5500 ■ *Web:* stotzequipment.com	Bluffdale	UT	84065	801-966-4231	966-4313
Grossenburg Implement Inc 31341 US Hwy 18 *TF:* 800-658-3440 ■ *Web:* www.grossenburg.com	Winner	SD	57580	605-842-2040	842-3485
Hamilton Equipment Inc 567 S Reading Rd PO Box 478 *Web:* www.haminc.com	Ephrata	PA	17522	717-733-7951	733-1783
Harcourt Equipment 313 Hwy 169 & 175 E *TF:* 800-445-5646 ■ *Web:* www.kcnielsen.com	Harcourt	IA	50544	515-354-5332	
Harry J Whelchel Co 1332 Stuart St	Chattanooga	TN	37406	423-698-4415	
HB Duvall Inc 901 E Patrick St PO Box 70 *Web:* www.hbduvall.com	Frederick	MD	21701	301-662-1125	695-0265
HH Halferty & Sons Inc 1300 S US Hwy 169 *Web:* www.halfertyandsons.com	Smithville	MO	64089	816-532-0221	
Hillsboro Equipment Inc E18898 Hwy 33 *TF:* 800-521-5133 ■ *Web:* www.hillsboroequipment.com	Hillsboro	WI	54634	608-489-2275	489-2717
HOLT Texas Ltd 3302 S WW White Rd *TF:* 800-275-4658 ■ *Web:* www.holtcat.com	San Antonio	TX	78222	210-648-1111	648-0079
Honey Bee Manufacturing Ltd Friggstad Rd 4km S PO Box 120 *Web:* www.honeybee.ca	Frontier	SK	S0N0W0	306-296-2297	
Hoober Inc 3452 Old Philadelphia Pk PO Box 518 *TF:* 800-732-0017 ■ *Web:* www.hoober.com	Intercourse	PA	17534	717-768-8231	768-3005
Horizon Equipment 402 Sixth St *Web:* horizonequip.com	Manning	IA	51455	712-653-2574	
Hoxie Implement Co Inc 933 Oak Ave Hwy 23&24 *Web:* www.hoxieimplement.com	Hoxie	KS	67740	785-675-3201	675-3438
Hultgren Implements Inc 5698 State Hwy 175 *TF:* 800-827-1650 ■ *Web:* hultgrenimplement.com	Ida Grove	IA	51445	712-364-3105	
Hurst Farm Supply Inc 105 Ave D *TF:* 800-535-8903 ■ *Web:* www.hurstfs.com	Abernathy	TX	79311	806-298-2541	298-2936
Implement Sales Company LLC 1574 Stone Ridge Dr *TF:* 800-955-9592 ■ *Web:* implementsalesga.com	Stone Mountain	GA	30083	770-908-9439	908-8123
Jacobi Sales Inc 425 Main St NE PO Box 67 *Web:* www.jacobisales.com	Palmyra	IN	47164	812-364-6141	364-6157
James River Equipment 11047 Leadbetter Rd *Web:* jamesriverequipment.com	Ashland	VA	23005	804-798-6001	
JD Equipment Inc 1660 US 42 NE *TF:* 800-659-5646 ■ *Web:* www.jdequipment.com	London	OH	43140	614-879-6620	879-5767
Jerry Pate Turf & Irrigation Inc 301 Schubert Dr *TF:* 800-700-7004 ■ *Web:* www.jerrypate.com	Pensacola	FL	32504	850-479-4653	484-8596
JJ Nichting Co Inc 1342 Pilot Grove Rd *Web:* jjnichting.com	Pilot Grove	IA	52648	319-469-4461	469-4703
John Day Co 6263 Abbott Dr *TF:* 800-767-2273 ■ *Web:* www.johnday.com	Omaha	NE	68110	402-455-8000	457-3812
JS Woodhouse Company Inc 1314 Union St *Web:* www.jswoodhouse.com	West Springfield	MA	01090	413-736-5462	732-3786
Kelly Sauder Rupiper Equipment LLC 805 E Howard St *Web:* www.ksrequipment.com	Pontiac	IL	61764	815-842-1149	
Lansdowne-Moody Company LP 8445 E Fwy *Web:* www.lmtractor.com	Houston	TX	77029	713-672-8366	
Larchmont Engineering & Irrigation Co 11 Larchmont Ln PO Box 66 *TF:* 877-862-2550 ■ *Web:* www.larchmont-eng.com	Lexington	MA	02420	781-862-2550	862-0173
Lawrence Tractor Company Inc 2530 E Main St *Web:* www.lawrencetractor.com	Visalia	CA	93292	559-734-7406	734-8325
Lazar Equipment Ltd 520 9th St W *Web:* www.lazarequipment.com	Meadow Lake	SK	S9X1S8	306-236-5222	
Liechty Farm Equipment Inc 1701 S Defiance St *TF:* 800-272-5898 ■ *Web:* www.kennfeldgroup.com	Archbold	OH	43502	419-445-1565	445-1779
Linder Equipment Co 311 E Kern St *Web:* www.linderequipment.com	Tulare	CA	93274	559-685-5000	685-0452
Littau Harvester Inc 855 Rogue Ave *TF:* 866-262-2495 ■ *Web:* www.littauharvester.com	Stayton	OR	97383	503-769-5953	
Luber Bros Inc 5224 Bear Creek Ct *Web:* www.luber.com	Irving	TX	75061	972-313-2020	
Maine Potato Growers Inc 56 Parsons St *Web:* www.mpgco-op.com	Presque Isle	ME	04769	207-764-2471	764-8450
MDMA Equipment Dealers Inc N6291 State Hwy 25 *TF:* 888-672-8864 ■ *Web:* tractorcentral.com	Durand	WI	54736	715-672-8915	672-4112
Mid-State Equipment Inc W 1115 Bristol Rd *TF:* 877-677-4020 ■ *Web:* www.midstateequipment.com	Columbus	WI	53925	920-623-4020	623-4500
Miller Machinery & Supply Co 127 NE 27th St	Miami	FL	33137	413-618-8474	
Monroe Tractor & Implement Company Inc 1001 Lehigh Stn Rd *TF:* 866-683-5338 ■ *Web:* www.monroetractor.com	Henrietta	NY	14467	585-334-3867	334-0001
N & S Tractor Co 600 S Hwy 59 *Web:* www.nstractor.com	Merced	CA	95341	209-383-5888	
Nueces Farm Center Inc 4587 US-77 Business *Web:* www.nuecesfarmcenter.net	Robstown	TX	78380	361-289-0066	
Peterson Tractor Co 955 Marina Blvd *TF:* 800-590-5945 ■ *Web:* www.petersoncat.com	San Leandro	CA	94577	510-357-6200	352-4570
Pioneer Equipment Co 21276 Lassen Ave *Web:* www.pioneercvcsouth.com	Five Points	CA	93624	559-884-2431	884-2805
Premier Equipment LLC 2025 US Hwy 14 W *TF:* 800-627-5469 ■ *Web:* www.premiereqhuron.com	Huron	SD	57350	605-352-7100	
Price Bros Equipment Co 619 S Washington St *Web:* www.pricebroseq.com	Wichita	KS	67211	316-265-9577	265-1062
RDO Equipment Co 3401 38th St S *TF:* 800-342-4643 ■ *Web:* www.rdoequipment.com	Fargo	ND	58104	701-282-5400	282-8220
Revels Tractor Company Inc 2217 N Main St *TF:* 800-849-5469 ■ *Web:* www.revelstractor.com	Fuquay Varina	NC	27526	919-552-5697	
Riesterer & Schnell Inc N2909 Hwy 32 *Web:* www.rands.com	Pulaski	WI	54162	920-822-3077	
RN Johnson Inc (RNJ) 269 Main St PO Box 448 *Web:* www.rnjohnsoninc.com	Walpole	NH	03608	603-756-3321	756-3452
Rockingham New Holland Inc 600 W Market St *Web:* rockinghamnh.com	Harrisonburg	VA	22802	540-434-6791	434-6780
Roeder Implement Inc 2550 Rockdale Rd *TF:* 800-557-1184 ■ *Web:* www.roederimplement.com	Dubuque	IA	52003	563-557-1184	583-1821
Rose Bros Inc 302 Main St *Web:* rosebrosinc.com	Lingle	WY	82223	307-837-2261	
Ryan Lawn & Tree Inc 9120 Barton St *Web:* ryanlawn.com	Overland Park	KS	66214	913-381-1505	
Schilling Bros Inc 705 N Rt 49 PO Box 96 *Web:* www.schillingbros.com	Casey	IL	62420	217-932-5941	
Schilling Bros Inc 5400 US Hwy 45 *Web:* www.schillingbros.com	Mattoon	IL	61938	217-234-6478	

	City	State	ZIP	Phone	Fax
Schmidt Machine Co 7013 Ohio 199	Upper Sandusky	OH	43351	419-294-3814	294-2607
TF: 866-368-3814 ■ *Web:* www.schmidtmachine.com					
SEMA Equipment Inc 11555 Hwy 60 Blvd	Wanamingo	MN	55983	507-824-2256	824-2668
TF: 800-569-1377 ■ *Web:* www.semaequip.com					
Simpson Norton Corp 4144 S Bullard Ave	Goodyear	AZ	85338	623-932-5116	932-5299
TF: 877-859-8676 ■ *Web:* www.simpsonnorton.com					
Sioux Automation Ctr Inc 877 First Ave NW	Sioux Center	IA	51250	712-722-1488	722-1487
TF: 866-722-1488 ■ *Web:* www.siouxautomation.com					
Sloan Implement Co 120 N Business 51	Assumption	IL	62510	217-226-4411	226-3351
TF: 800-745-4020 ■ *Web:* www.sloans.com					
Spartan Distributors Inc 487 W Div St	Sparta	MI	49345	616-887-7301	
TF: 800-822-2216 ■ *Web:* www.spartandistributors.com					
Stoller International Inc 15521 E 1830 N Rd	Pontiac	IL	61764	815-844-6197	842-3213
Web: www.stollerih.com					
Straub International Inc 214 SW 40th Ave	Great Bend	KS	67530	620-792-5256	793-5167
TF: 800-658-1706 ■ *Web:* www.straubint.com					
Studer Super Service Inc 1703-6th St	Monroe	WI	53566	608-328-8331	
Teeter Irrigation Inc 2729 W Oklahoma	Ulysses	KS	67880	620-353-1111	
TF: 800-524-5497 ■ *Web:* www.teeterirrigation.com					
Texas Timberjack Inc 6004 S First St	Lufkin	TX	75901	936-634-3365	639-3673
Web: www.texastimberjack.com					
Thomas Equipment Inc 204 Upper Kent Rd	Upper Kent	NB	E7J2E4	506-278-5695	
Web: www.thomasloaders.com					
Titan Machinery Inc 7955 179th Ave SE	Wahpeton	ND	58075	701-642-8424	
NASDAQ: TITN ■ *TF:* 800-654-4313 ■ *Web:* www.titanmachinery.com					
Tom Hassenfritz Equipment Co 1300 W Washington St	Mount Pleasant	IA	52641	319-385-3114	385-3731
TF: 800-634-4885 ■ *Web:* www.the-co.com					
Torrence's Farm Implement Inc 190 E Hwy 86 PO Box C	Heber	CA	92249	760-352-5355	352-8707
Web: www.torrencesfarmimplements.com					
Tractor Supply Co 5401 Virginia Way	Brentwood	TN	37027	877-718-6750	
NASDAQ: TSCO ■ *TF:* 877-718-6750 ■ *Web:* www.tractorsupply.com					
Valley Truck & Tractor Company Inc 793 N First St	Dixon	CA	95620	707-678-2395	
Web: www.valleytruckandtractor.com					
Wade Inc 1505 Hwy 82 W	Greenwood	MS	38930	662-453-6312	455-3287
Web: www.wadeincorporated.com					
Washington County Tractor Inc PO Box 1619	Brenham	TX	77834	979-836-4591	836-7446
TF: 800-256-5655 ■ *Web:* www.wctractor.com					
West Central Coop 406 First St	Ralston	IA	51459	712-667-3200	
Web: www.west-central.com					
Western Equipment Distributors Inc 20224 80th Ave S	Kent	WA	98032	253-872-8858	
Web: www.western-equip.com					
Western Implement Co Inc 2919 N Ave	Grand Junction	CO	81504	970-242-7960	242-5241
TF: 800-338-6639 ■ *Web:* www.westernimplement.com					
WG Leffelman & Sons Inc 340 N Metcalf Ave	Amboy	IL	61310	815-857-2513	857-3105
White's Inc 4614 Navigation Blvd PO Box 2344	Houston	TX	77011	713-928-2632	944-8373*
**Fax Area Code:* 888 ■ *TF:* 800-231-9559 ■ *Web:* www.whitesinc.com					
Witmer's Inc 39821 SR 14	Salem	OH	44460	330-427-2147	427-2611
TF: 888-427-6025 ■ *Web:* www.witmersinc.com					
Wyandot Tractor & Implement Co 10264 County Hwy 121	Upper Sandusky	OH	43351	419-294-2349	
Web: www.findlay-imp.com/wyandot/default.asp					
Wyatt-Quarles Seed Co 730 US Hwy 70 W	Garner	NC	27529	919-772-4243	772-4278
TF: 800-662-7591 ■ *Web:* www.wqseeds.com					

275 FARM PRODUCT RAW MATERIALS

	City	State	ZIP	Phone	Fax
ADM Corn Processing 4666 Faries Pkwy	Decatur	IL	62526	217-424-5200	
TF: 866-574-9690 ■ *Web:* www.adm.com					
ADM Grain Co 4666 E Faries Pkwy	Decatur	IL	62526	217-424-5200	
Web: www.adm.com/en-us/pages/default.aspx					
Agri Co-op 310 Logan St	Holdrege	NE	68949	308-995-8626	
Web: www.agrico-op.com					
Allenberg Cotton Co 7255 Goodlett Farms Pkwy	Cordova	TN	38016	901-383-5000	383-5010
Web: www.ldcom.com					
Alliance Grain Co 1306 W Eigth St	Gibson City	IL	60936	217-784-4284	784-8949
TF: 800-222-2451 ■ *Web:* www.alliance-grain.com					
Apache Farmers Co-op 230 W Floyd PO Box 332	Apache	OK	73006	580-588-3110	588-9277
Web: www.apachecoop.com					
Aurora Co-op Elevator Co 605 12th St PO Box 209	Aurora	NE	68818	402-694-2106	694-6943
TF: 800-642-6795 ■ *Web:* www.auroracoop.com					
Birdsong Corp 612 Madison Ave	Suffolk	VA	23434	757-539-3456	
Web: www.birdsong-peanuts.com					
Bunge Ltd 50 Main St	White Plains	NY	10606	914-684-2800	
NYSE: BG ■ *Web:* www.bunge.com					
C & F Foods Inc 15620 E Valley Blvd	City of Industry	CA	91744	626-723-1000	723-1212
Web: www.cnf-foods.com					
Calcot Ltd 1900 E Brundage Ln	Bakersfield	CA	93307	661-327-5961	
Web: www.calcot.net					
Cargill Inc 15407 McGinty Rd W	Wayzata	MN	55391	952-742-7575	
TF: 800-227-4455 ■ *Web:* www.cargill.com					
Cargill Ltd 300-240 Graham Ave PO Box 5900	Winnipeg	MB	R3C4C5	204-947-0141	947-6444
TF: 888-855-8558 ■ *Web:* www.cargill.ca					
Central Connecticut Co-op Farmers Assn 10 Apel Pl PO Box 8500	Manchester	CT	06042	860-649-4523	643-5305
TF: 800-640-4523 ■ *Web:* www.cccfeeds.com					
Central Iowa Co-op 2829 Westown Pkwy Ste 350	West Des Moines	IA	50266	515-225-1334	225-8511
TF: 800-513-3938 ■ *Web:* www.heartlandcoop.com					
Ceres Solutions LLP 2112 Indianapolis Rd PO Box 432	Crawfordsville	IN	47933	765-362-6700	362-7010
TF General: 800-878-0952 ■ *Web:* ceresllp.com					
Co-Alliance LLP 5250 E US Hwy 36 Bldg 1000	Avon	IN	46123	317-745-4491	718-1850
TF: 800-525-0272 ■ *Web:* www.co-alliance.com					
Co-op Elevator Co 7211 E Michigan Ave	Pigeon	MI	48755	989-453-4500	453-3942
TF: 800-968-0601 ■ *Web:* www.coopelev.com					
Effingham Equity Inc 201 W Roadway Ave	Effingham	IL	62401	217-342-4101	347-7601
TF: 800-223-1337 ■ *Web:* theequity.com					
Farmers Co-op 208 W Depot	Dorchester	NE	68343	402-946-2211	946-2062
TF: 800-642-6439 ■ *Web:* www.farmersco-operative.com					
Farmers Co-op Co 2321 N Loop Dr Ste 220	Ames	IA	50010	515-817-2100	
Web: www.fccoop.com					
Federated Co-operatives Ltd 401 22nd St E PO Box 1050	Saskatoon	SK	S7K0H2	306-244-3311	244-3403
Web: www.coopconnection.ca					
Frick Services Inc 570 E Boundary Rd	Portage	IN	46368	219-787-8548	787-8101
Web: www.frickservices.com					
Frontier Co-op 211 S Lincoln PO Box 37	Brainard	NE	68626	402-545-2811	545-2821
TF: 800-869-0379 ■ *Web:* www.frontiercooperative.com					
Heartland Co-op 2829 Westown Pkwy Ste 350	West Des Moines	IA	50266	515-225-1334	225-8511
TF: 800-513-3938 ■ *Web:* www.heartlandcoop.com					
Italgrani USA Inc 7900 Van Buren St	Saint Louis	MO	63111	314-638-1447	752-7621
TF: 800-274-1274 ■ *Web:* italgraniusa.com					
James Richardson International (JRI) 2800 One Lombard Pl	Winnipeg	MB	R3B0X8	204-934-5961	947-2647
Web: www.richardson.ca					
Joy Dog Food PO Box 305	Pinckneyville	IL	62274	800-245-4125	357-3651*
**Fax Area Code:* 618 ■ *TF:* 800-245-4125 ■ *Web:* www.joypetfood.com					
Kelley Bean Company Inc 2407 Cir Dr	Scottsbluff	NE	69361	308-635-6438	635-7345
Web: www.kelleybean.com					
MaxYield Co-op 313 Third Ave NE PO Box 49	West Bend	IA	50597	515-887-7211	887-7291
TF: 800-383-0003 ■ *Web:* www.maxyieldcooperative.com					
Mont Eagle Mills Inc 804 W Main St	Oblong	IL	62449	618-592-4211	
Web: monteaglemills.com					
NEW Co-op Inc 2626 First Ave S	Fort Dodge	IA	50501	515-955-2040	955-5565
TF: 800-362-2233 ■ *Web:* www.newcoop.com					
NF Davis Drier & Elevator Inc 9421 N Dos Palos Ave	Firebaugh	CA	93622	559-659-3035	659-2275
Northwest Grain Growers Inc 850 N Fourth Ave	Walla Walla	WA	99362	509-525-6510	529-6050
TF: 800-994-4290 ■ *Web:* www.nwgrgr.com					
Parrish & Heimbecker Ltd (P&H) 201 Portage Ave Ste 1400	Winnipeg	MB	R3B3K6	204-956-2030	943-8233
TF: 800-665-8937 ■ *Web:* www.parrishandheimbecker.com					
Pendleton Grain Growers Inc 1000 SW Dorian St PO Box 1248	Pendleton	OR	97801	541-278-5035	276-4839
TF: 800-422-7611 ■ *Web:* www.pggcountry.com					
Plains Cotton Co-op Assn 3301 E 50th St PO Box 2827	Lubbock	TX	79408	806-763-8011	
TF: 800-333-8011 ■ *Web:* www.pcca.com					
PremierCo-op Inc 2104 W Pk Ct	Champaign	IL	61821	217-355-1983	355-3478
Web: www.grandprairiecoop.com					
Rockingham Co-Operative 101 W Grace St	Harrisonburg	VA	22801	540-434-3856	434-6890
Web: www.rockinghamcoop.com					
Scoular Co 2027 Dodge St	Omaha	NE	68102	402-342-3500	342-5568
TF: 800-488-3500 ■ *Web:* www.scoular.com					
South Dakota Wheat Growers Assn 908 Lamont St SE	Aberdeen	SD	57401	605-225-5500	225-0859
TF: 888-429-4902 ■ *Web:* www.wheatgrowers.com					
Staplcotn Co-op Assn Inc 214 W Market St	Greenwood	MS	38930	662-453-6231	453-6274
TF: 800-293-6231 ■ *Web:* www.staplcotn.com					
Stratton Equity Co-op Co Inc 98 Colorado Ave PO Box 25	Stratton	CO	80836	719-348-5326	
TF: 800-438-7070 ■ *Web:* www.strattoncoop.com					
Virginia Diner Inc, The 322 W Main St	Wakefield	VA	23888	757-899-6213	
Web: www.vadiner.com					
Western Iowa Co-op 3330 Moville St PO Box 106	Hornick	IA	51026	712-874-3211	874-3230
TF: 800-488-3201					

276 FARM SUPPLIES

	City	State	ZIP	Phone	Fax
Abilene Ag Service & Supply Inc 303 S 14th St	Abilene	TX	79602	325-677-4371	
Ag-Land FS Inc 1505 Valle Vista Blvd	Pekin	IL	61554	309-346-4145	
Web: www.aglandfs.com					
Agfinity 260 Factory Rd	Eaton	CO	80615	970-454-4000	
TF: 800-433-4688 ■ *Web:* www.aglandinc.com					
Agri Producers Inc 205 Main St	Tampa	KS	67483	785-965-2221	965-2263
Web: www.api.coop					
AgVantage FS Inc 1600 Eigth St SW	Waverly	IA	50677	319-483-4900	483-4992
TF: 800-346-0058 ■ *Web:* www.agvantagefs.com					
Alforex Seeds 38001 County Rd 27	Woodland	CA	95695	530-666-3331	666-5317
TF: 877-560-5181 ■ *Web:* www.alforexseeds.com					
Allied Seed LLC 9311 Hwy 45	Nampa	ID	83686	208-466-6700	466-9074
Web: www.alliedseed.com					
BFG Supply Co LLC PO Box 479	Burton	OH	44021	440-834-1883	834-1885
TF: 800-883-0234 ■ *Web:* www.bfgsupply.com					
BinghamCo-op Inc PO Box 887	Blackfoot	ID	83221	208-785-3440	785-3444
Web: www.binghamcoop.com					
Bleyhl Farm Service Inc 940 E Wine Country Rd	Grandview	WA	98930	509-882-2248	882-4208
TF Cust Svc: 800-862-6806 ■ *Web:* www.bleyhl.com					
Bradley Caldwell Inc 200 Kiwanis Blvd	Hazleton	PA	18202	570-455-7511	455-0385*
**Fax:* Cust Svc ■ *TF Cust Svc:* 800-257-9100 ■ *Web:* www.bradleycaldwell.com					
Carroll Service Co 505 W Illinois Rt 64	Lanark	IL	61046	815-493-2181	493-6173
Web: carrollsvc.com					
Central Valley Co-op 900 30th Pl NW	Owatonna	MN	55060	507-451-1230	451-7579
TF: 800-270-2339 ■ *Web:* centralvalleycoop.com					
Chem Nut Inc 800 Business Pk Dr	Leesburg	GA	31763	229-883-7050	439-0842
CHS Inc 5500 Cenex Dr	Inver Grove Heights	MN	55077	651-355-6000	
NASDAQ: CHSCP ■ *TF:* 800-232-3639 ■ *Web:* www.chsinc.com					
Co-op Feed Dealers Inc 380 Broome Corporate Pkwy PO Box 670	Conklin	NY	13748	607-651-9078	651-9078
TF Cust Svc: 800-333-0895 ■ *Web:* www.cfd.coop					
Countryside Co-op 514 E Main St	Durand	WI	54736	715-672-8947	672-5131
TF: 800-236-7585 ■ *Web:* www.countrysidecoop.com					

Company	City	State	Zip	Phone	Fax
CropKing Inc 134 W Dr TF: 800-321-5656 ■ Web: www.cropking.com	Lodi	OH	44254	330-302-4203	302-4204
Crystal Valley Coop 721 W Humphrey PO Box 210 TF: 800-622-2910 ■ Web: www.crystalvalley.coop	Lake Crystal	MN	56055	507-726-6455	726-6901
Dragon Claw USA Inc 16033 Arrow Hwy TF: 800-238-5296 ■ Web: www.dcamerica.net	Irwindale	CA	91706	626-480-0068	480-0018
Edon Farmers Co-op Assn Inc 205 S Michigan PO Box 308 TF: 800-878-4093 ■ Web: www.edonfarmerscoop.com	Edon	OH	43518	419-272-2121	485-4509
Evergreen FS Inc 402 N Hershey Rd. TF: 877-963-2392 ■ Web: www.evergreen-fs.com	Bloomington	IL	61704	309-663-2392	663-0494
Farm Service Co-op 2308 Pine St TF: 800-452-4372 ■ Web: www.fscoop.com	Harlan	IA	51537	712-755-3185	755-7098
Farmers Co-op Assn 105 Jackson St TF: 800-864-3847 ■ Web: www.fcajackson.com	Jackson	MN	56143	507-847-4160	847-2521
Farmers Feed & Grain Company Inc 306 Birch St PO Box 291 Web: www.ffgcoinc.com	Riceville	IA	50466	641-985-2147	985-4000
Farmway Inc 204 E Ct St PO Box 568 Web: www.farmwaycoop.com	Beloit	KS	67420	785-738-2241	738-9659
Federation Co-op 108 N Water St. TF: 800-944-1784 ■ Web: www.fedcoop.com	Black River Falls	WI	54615	715-284-5354	284-9672
Fifield Land Co 4307 Fifield Rd. TF: 800-536-6395 ■ Web: www.kfseeds.com	Brawley	CA	92227	760-344-6391	344-6394
Florida Fertilizer Company Inc PO Box 1087 Web: www.floridafertilizer.com	Wauchula	FL	33873	863-773-4159	
Frenchman Valley Farmers Co-op Exchange 202 Broadway TF: 800-538-2667 ■ Web: www.fvcoop.com	Imperial	NE	69033	308-882-3200	882-3242
Gold Star FS Inc 101 NE St TF: 800-443-8497 ■ Web: www.goldstarfs.com	Cambridge	IL	61238	309-937-3369	937-5465
Gowan Company LLC PO Box 5569 TF: 800-883-1844 ■ Web: www.gowanco.com	Yuma	AZ	85366	928-783-8844	
Grangetto's Farm & Garden Supply Co 1105 W Mission Ave TF: 800-536-4671 ■ Web: www.grangettos.com	Escondido	CA	92025	760-745-4671	
GROWMARK Inc 1701 Towanda Ave Web: www.growmark.com	Bloomington	IL	61701	309-557-6000	
Growth Products Ltd 80 Lafayette Ave TF: 800-648-7626 ■ Web: www.growthproducts.com	White Plains	NY	10603	914-428-1316	
Hummert International Inc 4500 Earth City Expy TF: 800-325-3055 ■ Web: www.hummert.com	Earth City	MO	63045	314-506-4500	506-4510
Hutchinson Co-Op PO Box 158 TF: 800-795-1299 ■ Web: www.hutchcoop.com	Hutchinson	MN	55350	320-587-4647	
Intermountain Farmers Assn 1147 West 2100 South Web: www.ifa-coop.com	Salt Lake City	UT	84119	801-972-2122	972-2186
Keller Grain & Feed Inc 7977 Main St Web: www.kellergrain.com	Greenville	OH	45331	937-448-2284	448-2102
Kreamer Feed Inc PO Box 38 TF: 800-767-4537 ■ Web: www.kreamerfeed.com	Kreamer	PA	17833	570-374-8148	374-2007
Kugler Co 209 W Third St PO Box 1748 TF: 800-445-9116 ■ Web: www.kuglercompany.com	McCook	NE	69001	308-345-2280	345-7756
Lakes Area Co-op 459 Third Ave SE PO Box 247 Web: lakesareacoop.com	Perham	MN	56573	218-346-6240	346-6241
Legend Seeds Inc PO Box 241 TF: 800-678-3346 ■ Web: www.legendseeds.net	De Smet	SD	57231	605-854-3346	854-3135
Luckey Farmers Inc 1200 W Main St PO Box 217 Web: www.luckeyfarmers.com	Woodville	OH	43469	419-849-2711	849-2720
Martrex Inc 1107 Hazeltine Blvd Ste 535 TF: 800-328-3627 ■ Web: www.martrexinc.com	Minnetonka	MN	55345	952-933-5000	933-1889
McFarlane Mfg Company Inc 1259 Water St PO Box 100 TF: 800-627-8569 ■ Web: www.mcfarlanes.net	Sauk City	WI	53583	608-643-3321	643-2309
Meherrin Agricultural & Chemical Co Inc 413 Main St TF: 800-775-0333 ■ Web: fda.gov	Severn	NC	27877	252-585-1744	585-1718
MFA Inc 201 Ray Young Dr. Web: www.mfaincorporated.com	Columbia	MO	65201	573-874-5111	876-5505
New Alliance FS Inc 802 W N St Web: agrilandfs.com	Moravia	IA	52571	641-724-3233	
NEW Co-op Inc 2626 First Ave S TF: 800-362-2233 ■ Web: www.newcoop.com	Fort Dodge	IA	50501	515-955-2040	955-5565
Northwest Wholesale Inc 1567 N Wenatchee Ave TF: 800-874-6607 ■ Web: www.nwwinc.com	Wenatchee	WA	98801	509-662-2141	663-4540
Nu Way Co-op Inc PO Box Q TF: 800-445-4118 ■ Web: www.nuwaycoop.com	Trimont	MN	56176	507-639-2311	639-4006
Orange Belt Supply Co 25244 Rd 204	Lindsay	CA	93221	559-562-2574	732-7029
Orangeburg Pecan Company Inc 761 Russell St TF: 800-845-6970 ■ Web: www.uspecans.com	Orangeburg	SC	29115	803-534-4277	
Orscheln Farm & Home LLC 1800 Overcenter Dr PO Box 698 TF: 800-498-5090 ■ Web: www.orscheln.com	Moberly	MO	65270	660-263-4377	269-3500
Pacific Coast Chemical Co 2424 Fourth St Web: www.pcchem.com	Berkeley	CA	94710	510-549-3535	549-0890
Panhandle Co-op Assn 401 S Beltline Hwy W TF Cust Svc: 800-732-4546 ■ Web: www.panhandlecoop.com	Scottsbluff	NE	69361	308-632-5301	632-5375
Paris Farmers' Union PO Box D TF: 800-639-3603 ■ Web: www.parisfarmersunion.net	South Paris	ME	04281	207-743-8976	743-8564
Pickseed West Disc Inc 33149 Hwy 99 E Web: www.pickseed.com	Tangent	OR	97389	541-926-8886	926-1599
ProVision Partners Coop PO Box 14 Web: provisionpartners.coop	Stratford	WI	54484	715-687-4443	
Quality Liquid Feeds Inc PO Box 240 TF: 800-236-2345 ■ Web: www.qlf.com	Dodgeville	WI	53533	608-935-2345	
Red River Specialties Inc 1324 N Hearne Ave Ste 120 TF: 800-256-3344 ■ Web: www.rrsi.com	Shreveport	LA	71107	318-425-5944	424-6562
Reedsville Co-op Assn Inc PO Box 460 TF: 800-236-4047 ■ Web: www.countryvisionscoop.com	Reedsville	WI	54230	920-754-4321	754-4536
Richardson Seeds Inc PO Box 60 Web: www.richardsonseeds.com	Vega	TX	79092	806-267-2379	267-2820
S R C Corp PO Box 30676 TF: 800-888-4545 ■ Web: www.steveregan.com	Salt Lake City	UT	84130	801-268-4500	268-4596
Siegers Seed Co 13031 Reflections Dr TF: 800-962-4999 ■ Web: www.siegers.com	Holland	MI	49424	616-786-4999	994-0333
Silver Edge Co-op 39999 Hilton Rd TF: 800-632-5953 ■ Web: www.silveredgecoop.com	Edgewood	IA	52042	563-928-6419	
Southern FS Inc 2002 E Main St PO Box 728 TF: 800-492-7684 ■ Web: southernfs.com	Marion	IL	62959	618-993-2833	997-2526
Southern States Co-op Inc 6606 W Broad St TF: 866-372-8272 ■ Web: www.southernstates.com	Richmond	VA	23230	804-281-1000	281-1141
Southern States Frederick Co-op Inc 500 E South St TF: 866-633-5747 ■ Web: www.southernstates.com	Frederick	MD	21701	301-663-6164	663-8173
Stanislaus Farm Supply Co 624 E Service Rd. TF: 800-323-0725 ■ Web: www.farmsupply.coop	Modesto	CA	95358	209-538-7070	541-3191
Tennessee Farmers Co-op 180 Old Nashville Hwy TF: 800-366-2667 ■ Web: www.ourcoop.com	La Vergne	TN	37086	615-793-8011	
TriOak Foods Inc 103 W Railroad St PO Box 68 Web: www.trioak.com	Oakville	IA	52646	319-766-2230	
United Suppliers Inc 30473 260th St PO Box 538 TF: 800-782-5123 ■ Web: www.unitedsuppliers.com	Eldora	IA	50627	641-858-2341	858-5493
Universal Co-ops Inc (UCOOP) 1300 Corporate Ctr Curve Web: www.ucoop.com	Eagan	MN	55121	651-239-1000	
Van Horn Inc PO Box 380 TF: 800-252-1615 ■ Web: www.vanhorninc.com	Cerro Gordo	IL	61818	217-677-2131	677-2134
Virginia Fork Produce Company Inc 719 Virginia Rd.	Edenton	NC	27932	252-482-2165	
Wabash Valley Service Company Inc 909 N Ct St TF: 888-869-8127 ■ Web: www.wabashvalleyfs.com	Grayville	IL	62844	618-375-2311	375-5351
West Agro Inc 11100 N Congress Ave Web: www.delavalcleaningsolutions.com	Kansas City	MO	64153	816-891-1600	891-1595
Western Consolidated Co-op 520 Co Rd 9 PO Box 78 TF: 800-368-3310 ■ Web: www.west-con.com	Holloway	MN	56249	320-394-2171	394-2180
Western Reserve Farm Co-op Inc 14961 S State Ave PO Box 339 TF: 888-427-6672 ■ Web: www.wrfc.com	Middlefield	OH	44062	440-632-1192	632-1258
Wilbur-Ellis Co 345 California St 27th Fl. Web: www.wilburellis.com/pages/home.aspx	San Francisco	CA	94104	415-772-4000	772-4011
Wilco Farmers 200 Industrial Way TF: 800-382-5339 ■ Web: www.wilco.coop	Mount Angel	OR	97362	503-845-6122	845-9310
Yankton Ag Service 114 Mulberry St. TF: 800-456-5528 ■ Web: yanktonag.com	Yankton	SD	57078	605-665-3691	

277 FASHION DESIGN HOUSES

See Also Clothing & Accessories - Mfr p. 1941

Company	City	State	Zip	Phone	Fax
Armani Exchange 568 Broadway TF: 800-717-2929 ■ Web: www.armaniexchange.com	New York	NY	10012	212-431-6000	
BCBG Max Azria 2761 Fruitland Ave Web: www.bcbg.com	Vernon	CA	90058	323-589-2224	277-5461
Carolina Herrera Ltd 501 Seventh Ave 17th Fl. Web: www.carolinaherrera.com	New York	NY	10018	212-944-5757	944-7996
Christian Dior 712 Fifth Ave 37th Fl TF: 800-929-3467 ■ Web: dior.com	New York	NY	10019	212-582-0500	582-1063
Cynthia Rowley 376 Bleecker St Web: www.cynthiarowley.com	New York	NY	10014	212-242-3803	
Diane Von Furstenberg 440 W 14th St TF: 888-472-2383 ■ Web: world.dvf.com	New York	NY	10014	212-741-6607	753-1180
Donna Karan International Inc 550 Seventh Ave TF General: 877-316-0975 ■ Web: www.donnakaran.com	New York	NY	10018	212-789-1500	789-1820
Evy of California Inc 810A S Flower St Web: www.evy.com	Los Angeles	CA	90017	213-746-4647	746-9788
Kay Green Design Inc 859 Outer Rd. TF: 800-226-5186 ■ Web: www.kaygreendesign.com	Orlando	FL	32814	407-246-7155	426-7873
Marc Bouwer 141 Fulton St 2nd Fl	New York	NY	10038	212-242-7510	
Marc Jacobs International 72 Spring St *Fax Area Code: 212 ■ TF: 877-707-6272 ■ Web: www.marcjacobs.com	New York	NY	10012	877-707-6272	965-5510*
Max Mara USA Inc 530 Seventh Ave.	New York	NY	10018	212-536-6200	302-1134
Michael Kors 11 W 42nd St Web: www.michaelkors.com	New York	NY	10036	212-201-8100	
Norma Kamali 11 W 56th St Web: www.normakamali.com	New York	NY	10019	212-957-9797	956-1060
Oscar De La Renta Ltd 11 W. 42nd St Web: www.oscardelarenta.com	New York	NY	10036	212-282-0500	768-9110
Prada 610 W 52nd St Web: www.prada.com	New York	NY	10019	212-974-2555	246-3653
Vivienne Tam 40 Mercer St At Grand Web: viviennetam.com	New York	NY	10013	212-966-2398	

278 FASTENERS & FASTENING SYSTEMS

See Also Hardware - Mfr p. 2449; Precision Machined Products p. 2968

Company	City	State	Zip	Phone	Fax
Air Industries Corp 12570 Knott St Web: www.air-industries.com	Garden Grove	CA	92841	714-892-5571	892-7904
Allfast Fastening Systems Inc 15200 Don Julian Rd Web: www.allfastinc.com	City of Industry	CA	91745	626-968-9388	968-9393

Company	City	State	ZIP	Phone	Fax
Atlas Bolt & Screw Co 1628 Troy Rd. *TF:* 800-321-6977 ■ *Web:* www.atlasfasteners.com	Ashland	OH	44805	419-289-6171	289-2564
Avibank Manufacturing Inc 11500 Sherman Way *Web:* www.avibank.com	North Hollywood	CA	91605	818-392-2100	255-2094
B & G Mfg Company Inc 3067 Unionville Pk. **Fax:* Sales ■ *TF:* 800-366-3067 ■ *Web:* www.bgmfg.com	Hatfield	PA	19440	215-822-1925	822-1006*
Bristol Industries 630 E Lambert Rd. **Fax:* Sales ■ *Web:* www.bristol-ind.com	Brea	CA	92821	714-990-4121	529-6726*
Captive Fastener Corp 19 Thornton Rd. *TF:* 800-526-4430 ■ *Web:* www.captive-fastener.com	Oakland	NJ	07436	201-337-6800	337-1012
Chicago Rivet & Machine Co 901 Frontenac Rd *AMEX:* CVR ■ *Web:* www.chicagorivet.com	Naperville	IL	60563	630-357-8500	983-9314
Cold Heading Co 21777 Hoover Rd. *Web:* www.coldheading.com	Warren	MI	48089	586-497-7000	497-7007
CONTMID Group 24000 Western Ave. *Web:* www.contmid.com	Park Forest	IL	60466	708-747-1200	747-9373
Decker Manufacturing Corp 703 N Clark St *Web:* www.deckernut.com	Albion	MI	49224	517-629-3955	629-3535
ELF Fastening Systems Inc 29019 Solon Rd *TF:* 800-248-2376 ■ *Web:* www.etf-fastening.com	Solon	OH	44139	440-248-8655	248-0423
Elgin Fastener Group 4 S Pk Ave ste203 *Web:* www.elginfasteners.com	Batesville	IN	47006	812-689-8917	689-6635
Fastco Industries Inc PO Box 141427 *Web:* fastcoindustries.com	Grand Rapids	MI	49514	616-453-5428	453-2490
Ford Fasteners Inc 110 S Newman St *TF:* 800-272-3673 ■ *Web:* www.fordfasteners.com	Hackensack	NJ	07601	201-487-3151	487-1919
Hohmann & Barnard Inc 30 Rasons Ct *TF:* 800-645-0616 ■ *Web:* www.h-b.com	Hauppauge	NY	11788	631-234-0600	234-0683
Indiana Automotive Fasteners Inc 1300 Anderson Blvd *Web:* www.iafi.com	Greenfield	IN	46140	317-467-0100	467-2782
ITW Brands 955 National Pkwy Ste 95500 *TF:* 877-489-2726 ■ *Web:* www.itwbrands.com	Schaumburg	IL	60173	847-944-2260	619-8344
ITW Buildex 1349 W Bryn Mawr *TF:* 800-284-5339 ■ *Web:* www.itwbuildex.com	Itasca	IL	60143	630-595-3500	595-3549
Lawrence Screw Products Inc 7230 W Wilson Ave *Web:* www.lawrencescrew.com	Harwood Heights	IL	60706	708-867-5150	867-7052
Mid-States Bolt & Screw Co 4126 Somers Dr *TF:* 800-482-0867 ■ *Web:* www.midstatesbolt.com	Burton	MI	48529	810-744-0123	744-3798
Mid-States Screw Corp 1817 18th Ave *TF:* 888-354-6772 ■ *Web:* www.midstatesscrew.com	Rockford	IL	61104	815-397-2440	398-1047
Monogram Aerospace Fasteners 3423 S Garfield Ave *Web:* www.monogramaerospace.com	Los Angeles	CA	90040	323-722-4760	721-1851
Ms Aerospace Inc 13928 Balboa Blvd *TF:* 866-487-2365 ■ *Web:* www.msaerospace.com	Sylmar	CA	91342	818-833-9095	833-9525
National Rivet & Manufacturing Co 21 E Jefferson St *TF:* 888-324-5511 ■ *Web:* www.nationalrivet.com	Waupun	WI	53963	920-324-5511	324-3388
Ohio Nut & Bolt Co 5250 W 164th St *TF:* 800-362-0291 ■ *Web:* www.on-b.com	Brook Park	OH	44142	216-267-2240	267-3228
Pan American Screw Inc 630 Reese Dr SW *TF Cust Svc:* 800-951-2222 ■ *Web:* www.panamericanscrew.com	Conover	NC	28613	828-466-0060	466-0070
PennEngineering & Manufacturing Corp 5190 Old Easton Rd *TF:* 800-237-4736 ■ *Web:* www.pemnet.com	Danboro	PA	18916	215-766-8853	766-3680
Robertson Inc 97 Bronte St N *TF:* 800-268-5090 ■ *Web:* www.robertsonscrew.com	Milton	ON	L9T2N8	905-878-2861	878-2867
Scovill Fasteners Inc 1802 Scovill Dr **Fax:* Cust Svc ■ *TF Cust Svc:* 888-726-8455 ■ *Web:* www.scovill.com	Clarkesville	GA	30523	706-754-1000	754-4000*
SPS Technologies Inc 301 Highland Ave *Web:* www.spstech.com	Jenkintown	PA	19046	215-572-3000	572-3790
Stafast Products Inc 505 Lk Shore Blvd *TF:* 800-782-3278 ■ *Web:* shop.stafast.com	Painesville	OH	44077	440-357-5546	357-7137
TriMas Corp 39400 Woodward Ave Ste 130 *Web:* www.trimascorp.com	Bloomfield Hills	MI	48304	248-631-5450	631-5455
Vertex Distribution 523 Pleasant St Bldg 10 *Web:* www.vertexdistribution.com	Attleboro	MA	02703	508-431-1120	431-1114

279 FENCES - MFR

See Also Recycled Plastics Products p. 3057

Company	City	State	ZIP	Phone	Fax
Acorn Wire & Iron Works Inc 2035 S Racine Ave *TF:* 800-552-2676 ■ *Web:* www.acornwire.com	Chicago	IL	60608	773-585-0600	585-2403
Boulanger, Roland & Cie Ltd 235 rue St-Louis *Web:* www.boulanger.qc.ca	Warwick	QC	J0A1M0	819-358-4100	
Carris Reels Inc 46 Ripley Rd *Web:* www.carris.com	Rutland	VT	05701	802-773-9111	
Cherry Tree Design 320 Pronghorn Trl *TF:* 800-634-3268 ■ *Web:* www.cherrytreedesign.com	Bozeman	MT	59718	406-582-8800	
Conifex Timber Inc 980 700 W Georgia St PO Box 10070 *TF:* 866-301-2949 ■ *Web:* www.conifex.com	Vancouver	BC	V7Y1B6	604-216-2949	
Dare Products Inc 860 Betterly Rd PO Box 157 *TF:* 800-922-3273 ■ *Web:* www.dareproducts.com	Battle Creek	MI	49015	269-965-2307	965-3261
Easy Drive Stake Inc 4111 Todd Ln.	Austin	TX	78744	512-447-9879	
Epicurean Cutting Surfaces Inc 1325 N 59th Ave W *Web:* www.epicureancs.com	Duluth	MN	55807	218-740-3500	
Federal Program Integrators LLC 12 Wabanaki Way *Web:* www.fedintegrators.com	Indian Island	ME	04468	207-817-7334	
Gizmo Art Production Inc 1315 Egbert Ave *Web:* www.gizmosf.com	San Francisco	CA	94124	415-222-6181	
Holland Bowl Mill 120 James St. *TF:* 800-774-1230 ■ *Web:* www.hollandbowlmill.com	Holland	MI	49424	616-396-6513	
Kalinich Fence Company Inc 12223 Prospect Rd *Web:* www.kalinichfenceco.com	Strongsville	OH	44149	440-238-6127	238-2178
Lafitte Cork & Capsule Inc 45 Executive Ct *Web:* www.lafitte-usa.com	Napa	CA	94558	707-258-2675	
Master Halco Inc 1321 Greenway Dr **Fax Area Code:* 800 ■ **Fax:* Cust Svc ■ *TF:* 800-883-8384 ■ *Web:* www.masterhalco.com	Irving	TX	75038	972-714-7300	542-8488*
Matelski Lumber Co 2617 M 75 S *Web:* www.matelskilumbercompany.com	Boyne Falls	MI	49713	231-549-2780	
Merchants Metals Inc 900 Ashwood Pkwy Ste 600 *TF:* 800-272-6171 ■ *Web:* www.merchantsmetals.com	Atlanta	GA	30338	770-960-2880	
Paddle Tramps Manufacturing Co 1317 University Ave *Web:* www.paddletramps.com	Lubbock	TX	79401	806-765-9901	
Peavey Performance Systems 10749 W 84th Ter *Web:* www.safetyjackpot.com	Lenexa	KS	66214	913-888-0600	
Riverdale Mills Corp 130 Riverdale St *TF:* 800-762-6374 ■ *Web:* www.riverdale.com	Northbridge	MA	01534	508-234-8715	234-9593
Sauk Technologies 300 N Dekora Woods Blvd	Saukville	WI	53080	262-268-3800	
Taiga Building Products Ltd 4710 Kingsway Ste 800 *TF:* 800-663-1470 ■ *Web:* www.taigabuilding.com	Burnaby	BC	V5H4M2	604-438-1471	
Tru-Link Fence Co 5440 Touhy Ave *TF:* 800-568-9300 ■ *Web:* www.tru-link.com	Skokie	IL	60077	847-568-9300	
Viridis Energy Inc Suite 520, 700 W. Pender St. *Web:* www.viridisenergy.ca	Vancouver	BC	V6C1G8	604-669-7831	
Walnut Hollow Farm Inc 1409 State Rd 23 *TF:* 800-395-5995 ■ *Web:* www.walnuthollow.com	Dodgeville	WI	53533	608-935-2341	
Western Bee Supplies Inc 5 Ninth Ave E *Web:* www.westernbee.com	Polson	MT	59860	406-883-2918	

280 FERTILIZERS & PESTICIDES

See Also Farm Supplies p. 2281

Company	City	State	ZIP	Phone	Fax
Abell Corp 2500 Sterlington Rd *TF:* 800-325-7204 ■ *Web:* www.ouachitafertilizer.com	Monroe	LA	71203	800-325-7204	
Agricultural Commodities Inc 2224 Oxford Rd	New Oxford	PA	17350	717-624-8249	
Agrium Inc 13131 Lk Fraser Dr SE *NYSE:* AGU ■ **Fax:* PR ■ *TF:* 877-247-4861 ■ *Web:* www.agrium.com	Calgary	AB	T2J7E8	403-225-7000	225-7609*
Airgas Specialty Products 2530 Sever Rd Ste 300 **Fax Area Code:* 770 ■ *TF:* 800-295-2225 ■ *Web:* www.airgasspecialtyproducts.com	Lawrenceville	GA	30043	800-295-2225	717-2222*
Alabama Farmers Co-op Inc PO Box 2227 *TF:* 888-255-2667 ■ *Web:* www.alafarm.com	Decatur	AL	35601	256-353-6843	350-1770
Alco Industries Inc 820 Adams Ave Ste 130 *Web:* www.alcoind.com	Norristown	PA	19403	610-666-0930	666-0752
Amvac Chemical Corp 4100 E Washington Blvd *TF:* 800-424-9300 ■ *Web:* www.amvac-chemical.com	Los Angeles	CA	90023	323-264-3910	268-1028
Apache Nitrogen Products Inc 1436 S Apache Powder Rd PO Box 700 *Web:* apachenitrogen.com	Benson	AZ	85602	520-720-2217	720-4158
Brandt Consolidated Inc 211 IL-125 *Web:* www.brandt.co	Pleasant Plains	IL	62677	217-476-3438	
California Ammonia Co (CALAMCO) 1776 W March Ln Ste 420 *TF:* 800-624-4200 ■ *Web:* www.calamco.com	Stockton	CA	95207	209-982-1000	983-0822
Certis USA LLC 9145 Guilford Rd Ste 175 **Fax Area Code:* 301 ■ *TF:* 800-250-5024 ■ *Web:* www.certisusa.com	Columbia	MD	21046	800-250-5024	604-7015*
CF Industries Inc 4 Pkwy N Ste 400 *Web:* www.cfindustries.com	Deerfield	IL	60015	847-405-2400	405-2711
CFC Farm & Home Ctr 15172 Brandy Rd PO Box 2002 *TF:* 800-284-2667 ■ *Web:* www.cfcfarmhome.net	Culpeper	VA	22701	540-825-2200	825-2200
Coastal Agrobusiness Inc 3702 Evans St PO Box 856 *TF:* 800-758-1828 ■ *Web:* www.coastalagro.com	Greenville	NC	27835	252-756-1126	756-3282
Degesch America Inc PO Box 116 *TF:* 800-330-2525 ■ *Web:* www.degeschamerica.com	Weyers Cave	VA	24486	540-234-9281	234-8225
Dow AgroSciences LLC 9330 Zionsville Rd **Fax Area Code:* 800 ■ *TF:* 800-331-6451 ■ *Web:* www.dowagro.com	Indianapolis	IN	46268	317-337-3000	905-7326*
Dow Chemical Co, The 100 Independence Mall W *Web:* www.dow.com	Philadelphia	PA	19106	215-592-3000	
Drexel Chemical Co 1700 Ch Ave PO Box 13327 *Web:* www.drexchem.com	Memphis	TN	38113	901-774-4370	774-4666
DuPont Crop Protection PO Box 80705 *TF:* 888-638-7668 ■ *Web:* www.dupont.com	Wilmington	DE	19880	302-774-1000	999-4399
Enforcer Products Inc PO Box 1060 *TF:* 888-805-4357 ■ *Web:* www.enforcer.com	Cartersville	GA	30120	888-805-4357	
FMC Corp 2929 Walnut St *NYSE:* FMC ■ *TF:* 888-548-4486 ■ *Web:* www.fmc.com	Philadelphia	PA	19104	215-299-6000	299-5998
Frit Industries Inc 1792 Jodie Parker Rd *TF:* 800-633-7685 ■ *Web:* www.fritind.com	Ozark	AL	36360	334-774-2515	774-9306
Good Earth Inc PO Box 290 *Web:* www.goodearth.org	Lancaster	NY	14086	716-684-8111	684-3722
Helena Chemical Co 225 Schilling Blvd Ste 300 *Web:* www.helenachemical.com	Collierville	TN	38017	901-761-0050	821-5455
Hillshire Brands 2200 W Don Tyson Pkwy *TF:* 800-323-7117 ■ *Web:* www.tysonfoods.com/hillshire-brands.aspx	Springdale	AR	72762	479-290-6397	
Hintzsche Fertilizer Inc 2 S 181 County Line Rd	Maple Park	IL	60151	630-557-2406	557-2557
HJ Baker & Bros Inc 2 Corporate Dr Ste 545 *Web:* hjbaker.com	Shelton	CT	06484	203-682-9200	227-8351
Ibe Trade Corp 950 Third Ave 3rd Fl *Web:* www.ibetrade.com	New York	NY	10022	212-593-3255	308-3642

				Phone	Fax
Intrepid Potash Inc 700 17th St Ste 1700 *NYSE: IPI* ■ *TF:* 800-451-2888 ■ *Web:* www.intrepidpotash.com	Denver	CO	80202	303-296-3006	298-7502
JR Simplot Co 999 W Main St Ste 1300 *TF:* 800-832-8893 ■ *Web:* www.simplot.com	Boise	ID	83702	208-336-2110	389-7515
Kellogg Garden Products 350 W Sepulveda Blvd *TF:* 800-232-2322 ■ *Web:* www.kellogggarden.com	Carson	CA	90745	800-232-2322	
Kirby Agri Inc 500 Running Pump Rd PO Box 6277 *TF:* 800-745-7524 ■ *Web:* www.kirbyagri.com	Lancaster	PA	17607	717-299-2541	293-9306
Koch Nitrogen Co 4111 E 37th St N *Web:* www.kochind.com	Wichita	KS	67220	316-828-4382	
Kronos Micronutrients 213 W Moxee Ave PO Box 1167 *TF:* 800-541-4086 ■ *Web:* www.kronoslp.com	Moxee	WA	98936	509-248-4911	248-4916
Landec Ag LLC 201 N Michigan St *TF:* 800-241-7252 ■ *Web:* incotec.com	Oxford	IN	47971	765-385-1000	
Lebanon Seaboard Corp 1600 E Cumberland St *TF:* 800-233-0628 ■ *Web:* www.lebsea.com	Lebanon	PA	17042	717-273-1685	
Living Earth Technology Co 1901 California Crossing *Web:* www.livingearth.net	Dallas	TX	75220	972-506-8575	
MFA Inc 201 Ray Young Dr *Web:* www.mfaincorporated.com	Columbia	MO	65201	573-874-5111	876-5505
Miller Chemical & Fertilizer Corp 120 Radio Rd PO Box 333 *TF:* 800-233-2040 ■ *Web:* www.millerchemical.com	Hanover	PA	17331	717-632-8921	632-4581
Na-Churs/Alpine Solutions 421 Leader St *TF:* 800-622-4877 ■ *Web:* www.nachurs.com	Marion	OH	43302	740-382-5701	383-2615
PBI/Gordon Corp 1217 W 12th St PO Box 014090 *TF:* 800-821-7925 ■ *Web:* www.pbigordon.com	Kansas City	MO	64101	816-421-4070	474-0462
Potash Corp 1101 Skokie Blvd *TF:* 800-667-0403 ■ *Web:* www.potashcorp.com	Northbrook	IL	60062	847-849-4200	849-4695
Potash Corp of Saskatchewan Inc 122 First Ave S Ste 500 *NYSE: POT* ■ *TF:* 800-667-3930 ■ *Web:* www.potashcorp.com	Saskatoon	SK	S7K7G3	306-933-8500	652-2699
Safeguard Chemical Corp 411 Wales Ave *TF:* 800-536-3170 ■ *Web:* www.safeguardchemical.com	Bronx	NY	10454	718-585-3170	585-3657
SC Johnson & Son Inc 1525 Howe St *Web:* www.scjohnson.com	Racine	WI	53403	262-260-2154	260-6004
Scotts Miracle Gro Products Inc 14111 Scottslawn Rd *TF:* 888-270-3714 ■ *Web:* www.scotts.com/smg	Marysville	OH	43041	937-644-0011	
Scotts Miracle-Gro Co 14111 Scottslawn Rd *NYSE: SMG* ■ *TF Cust Svc:* 800-543-8873 ■ *Web:* www.scotts.com	Marysville	OH	43041	937-644-0011	
Share Corp 7821 N Faulkner Rd *TF:* 800-776-7192 ■ *Web:* www.sharecorp.com	Milwaukee	WI	53224	414-355-4000	355-0516
Southern States Chemical Co 1600 E President St *TF:* 888-337-8922 ■ *Web:* www.sschemical.com	Savannah	GA	31404	912-232-1101	232-1103
Spectrum Brands 3001 Deming Way *TF:* 800-566-7899 ■ *Web:* www.spectrumbrands.com	Middleton	WI	53711	608-275-3340	
Stoller USA 4001 W Sam Houston Pkwy N Ste 100 *TF:* 800-539-5283 ■ *Web:* www.stollerusa.com	Houston	TX	77043	713-461-1493	461-4467
Summit Chemical Co 235 S Kresson St *TF:* 800-227-8664 ■ *Web:* www.summitchemical.com	Baltimore	MD	21224	410-522-0661	522-0833
Syngenta Corp 3411 Silverside Rd Ste 100 *TF:* 800-555-2470 ■ *Web:* www.syngenta.com	Wilmington	DE	19810	302-425-2000	425-2001
Syngenta Crop Protection Inc 410 Swing Rd PO Box 18300 **Fax:* Sales ■ *TF:* 800-797-5040 ■ *Web:* www.syngenta.com	Greensboro	NC	27409	336-632-6000	632-7353*
Tender Corp 106 Burndy Rd *TF:* 800-258-4696 ■ *Web:* www.tendercorp.com	Littleton	NH	03561	603-444-5464	444-6735
Trans-Resources Inc 200 W 57th St	New York	NY	10019	212-515-4100	515-4111
Valley Fertilizer & Chemical Company Inc 201 Valley Rd PO Box 816	Mount Jackson	VA	22842	540-477-3121	477-3123
Van Diest Supply Co 1434 220th St PO Box 610 *TF:* 800-779-2424 ■ *Web:* www.vdsc.com	Webster City	IA	50595	515-832-2366	832-2955
Woodstream Corp 69 N Locust St *TF All:* 800-800-1819 ■ *Web:* www.woodstream.com/index.cfm	Lititz	PA	17543	717-626-2125	626-1912
Y-Tex Corp 1825 Big Horn Ave PO Box 1450 *TF:* 800-443-6401 ■ *Web:* www.y-tex.com	Cody	WY	82414	307-587-5515	527-6433

281 FESTIVALS - BOOK

				Phone	Fax
Amelia Island Book Festival PO Box 15286 *Web:* www.ameliaislandbookfestival.org	Fernandina Beach	FL	32035	904-624-1665	
Baltimore Book Festival 10 E Baltimore St 10th Fl *Web:* baltimorebookfestival.com	Baltimore	MD	21202	410-752-8632	385-0361
Banff Mountain Book Festival 107 Tunnel Mountain Dr PO Box 1020 Stn 38 *Web:* www.banffcentre.ca	Banff	AB	T1L1H5	403-762-6100	762-6277
Boston Globe Book Festival PO Box 55819 PO Box 2378 *TF:* 888-694-5623 ■ *Web:* www.bostonglobe.com	Boston	MA	02205	888-694-5623	
Buckeye Book Fair 205 W Liberty St *Web:* www.buckeyebookfair.com	Wooster	OH	44691	330-262-3244	
Great Salt Lake Book Festival Utah Humanities Council 202 W 300 N *TF:* 877-786-7598 ■ *Web:* www.utahhumanities.org	Salt Lake City	UT	84103	801-359-9670	531-7869
Latino Book & Family Festival (LBFF) 3445 Catalina Dr	Carlsbad	CA	92010	858-603-8680	
Los Angeles Times Festival of Books Los Angeles Times 202 W First St *TF:* 800-528-4637 ■ *Web:* events.latimes.com	Los Angeles	CA	90012	213-237-2335	237-2335
Miami Book Fair International (MBFI) 300 NE Second Ave Freedom Twr, 7th Fl *Web:* www.miamibookfair.com	Miami	FL	33132	305-237-3258	
National Book Festival Library of Congress 101 Independence Ave SE *TF:* 888-714-4696 ■ *Web:* www.loc.gov/bookfest	Washington	DC	20540	202-707-2777	707-9199
NOVELLO Festival of Reading Public Library of Charlotte & Mecklenburg County 310 N Tryon St *Web:* www.cmlibrary.org	Charlotte	NC	28202	704-416-0100	
South Carolina Book Festival PO Box 5287 *Web:* www.schumanities.org	Columbia	SC	29250	803-771-2477	771-2487
Southern Festival of Books Humanities Tennessee 306 Gay St Ste 306 *Web:* www.humanitiestennessee.org	Nashville	TN	37201	615-770-0006	770-0007
Southern Kentucky Book Fest Western Kentucky University Libraries & Museum Cravens Library Rm 106 *Web:* www.sokybookfest.org	Bowling Green	KY	42101	270-745-5016	745-6422
Texas Book Festival 610 Brazos St Ste 200 *TF:* 800-222-8733 ■ *Web:* www.texasbookfestival.org	Austin	TX	78701	512-477-4055	322-0722
Virginia Festival of the Book Virginia Foundation for the Humanities 145 Ednam Dr *TF:* 877-451-5098 ■ *Web:* virginiahumanities.org	Charlottesville	VA	22903	434-924-3296	296-4714

282 FESTIVALS - FILM

				Phone	Fax
AFI Fest 2021 N Western Ave *TF:* 866-234-3378 ■ *Web:* www.afi.com	Los Angeles	CA	90027	323-856-7600	467-4578
Anchorage Film Festival 1231 W Northern Lights Blvd Ste 844 *TF:* 800-544-0786 ■ *Web:* www.anchoragefilmfestival.org	Anchorage	AK	99503	907-338-3761	
Ann Arbor Film Festival 217 N First St *Web:* www.aafilmfest.org	Ann Arbor	MI	48104	734-995-5356	995-5396
Arpa International Film Festival 2919 Maxwell St *Web:* www.affma.org	Los Angeles	CA	90027	323-663-1882	663-1882
Austin Film Festival 1801 Salina St Ste 210 *TF:* 800-310-3378 ■ *Web:* www.austinfilmfestival.com	Austin	TX	78702	512-478-4795	478-6205
Beverly Hills Film Festival 9663 Santa Monica Blvd Ste 777 *Web:* www.beverlyhillsfilmfestival.com	Beverly Hills	CA	90210	310-779-1206	
Boston Film Festival 126 S St *Web:* www.bostonfilmfestival.org	Rockport	MA	01966	617-523-8388	
Brooklyn International Film Festival 180 S Fourth St Ste 2S *Web:* www.brooklynfilmfestival.org	Brooklyn	NY	11211	718-486-8181	599-5039
Chicago International Film Festival Cinema Chicago 30 E Adams St Ste 800 *TF:* 800-982-2787 ■ *Web:* www.chicagofilmfestival.com	Chicago	IL	60603	312-683-0121	683-0122
Cleveland International Film Festival 2510 Market Ave *Web:* www.clevelandfilm.org	Cleveland	OH	44113	216-623-3456	623-0103
DC Independent Film Festival (DCIFF) 701 Pennsylvania Ave NW *Web:* dciff-indie.org	Washington	DC	20004	202-737-2300	
Denver International Film Festival 1510 York 3rd Fl *TF:* 866-293-1566 ■ *Web:* www.denverfilm.org	Denver	CO	80206	303-595-3456	595-0956
Fort Lauderdale International Film Festival 503 SE Sixth St *Web:* www.fliff.com	Fort Lauderdale	FL	33301	954-760-9898	760-9099
Full Frame Documentary Film Festival 320 Blackwell St Ste 101 *Web:* www.fullframefest.org	Durham	NC	27701	919-687-4100	
Heartland Film Festival 1043 Virginia Ave Ste 2 *Web:* heartlandfilm.org	Indianapolis	IN	46203	317-464-9405	464-9409
High Falls Film Festival 45 E Ave Ste 400 *Web:* www.highfallsfilmfestival.com	Rochester	NY	14604	585-279-8312	
Hot Springs Documentary Film Festival (HSDFF) 659 Ouachita Ave PO Box 6450 *Web:* www.hsdfi.org	Hot Springs	AR	71901	501-538-0452	321-0211
Los Angeles International Short Film Festival 1610 Argyle Ave Ste 113 *Web:* www.lashortsfest.com	Hollywood	CA	90028	323-461-4400	
Maryland Film Festival 34 E 25th St *Web:* www.mdfilmfest.com	Baltimore	MD	21218	410-752-8083	
Miami International Film Festival 300 NE 2nd Ave Bldg 5 Rm 5501 *Web:* www.miamifilmfestival.com	Miami	FL	33132	305-237-3456	
Mill Valley Film Festival (MVFF) 1001 Lootens Pl Ste 220 *Web:* www.mvff.com	San Rafael	CA	94901	415-383-5256	383-8606
Minneapolis/St Paul International Film Festival 125 SE Main St Ste 341 *Web:* www.mnfilmarts.org	Minneapolis	MN	55414	612-331-7563	
Montreal World Film Festival 1432 Rue de Bleury *Web:* www.ffm-montreal.org	Montreal	QC	H3A2J1	514-848-3883	848-3886
Nashville Film Festival 161 Rains Ave *Web:* www.nashvillefilmfestival.org	Nashville	TN	37203	615-742-2500	
New Hampshire Film Festival 28 Chestnut St *Web:* www.nhfilmfestival.com	Portsmouth	NH	03801	603-436-2400	
New Orleans Film Festival 900 Camp St *Web:* neworleansfilmsociety.org	New Orleans	LA	70130	504-309-6633	309-0923
New York Film Festival 70 Lincoln Ctr Plaza *Web:* www.filmlinc.org	New York	NY	10023	212-875-5610	875-5636
Outfest-Los Angeles Gay & Lesbian Film Festival 3470 Wilshire Blvd Ste 935 *Web:* www.outfest.org	Los Angeles	CA	90010	213-480-7088	480-7099

Phone | Fax

Phoenix Film Festival
7000 E Mayo Blvd Ste 1059 .... Phoenix AZ 85054 602-955-6444
Web: www.phoenixfilmfestival.com

Portland International Film Festival
1219 SW Pk Ave .... Portland OR 97205 503-221-1156 294-0874
Web: www.nwfilm.org

Riverrun International Film Festival
305 W Fourth St Ste 1A .... Winston-Salem NC 27101 336-724-1502 724-1112
Web: www.riverrunfilm.com

Rochester International Film Festival
PO Box 17746 .... Rochester NY 14617 585-234-7411
Web: www.rochesterfilmfest.org

San Diego Film Festival
2683 Via de la Valle Ste G210 .... Del Mar CA 92014 619-818-2221
Web: www.sdfilmfest.com

San Francisco Film Society
39 Mesa St Ste 110 .... San Francisco CA 94129 415-561-5000 440-1760
Web: www.sfiff.org

San Jose Film Festival - CineQuest
PO Box 720040 .... San Jose CA 95172 408-995-5033 995-5713
Web: www.cinequest.org

Santa Barbara International Film Festival
1528 Chapala St Ste 203 .... Santa Barbara CA 93101 805-963-0023 962-2524
Web: sbiff.org

Sarasota Film Festival 332 Cocoanut Ave .... Sarasota FL 34236 941-364-9514 364-8411
TF: 800-435-7352 ■ *Web:* www.sarasotafilmfestival.com

Seattle International Film Festival
305 Harrison St .... Seattle WA 98109 206-464-5830 264-7919
Web: www.siff.net

Sidewalk Moving Picture Festival
310 18th St N .... Birmingham AL 35203 205-324-0888
Web: www.sidewalkfest.com

Sonoma Valley Film Festival 103A E Napa St .... Sonoma CA 95476 707-933-2600 933-2602
Web: www.sonomafilmfest.org

South by Southwest Film Festival
500 E Cesar Chavez St .... Austin TX 78701 512-467-7979 451-0754
Web: www.sxsw.com

Sundance Film Festival 1895 Sidewinder Dr .... Park City UT 84060 801-328-3456
Web: www.sundance.org/festival

Telluride Film Festival 800 Jones St .... Berkeley CA 94710 510-665-9494 665-9589
Web: www.telluridefilmfestival.org

Toronto International Film Festival Inc
Reitman Sq 350 King St W .... Toronto ON M5V3X5 888-599-8433
TF: 888-599-8433 ■ *Web:* www.tiff.net

Worldfest Houston International Film Festival
PO Box 56566 .... Houston TX 77240 713-629-3700
TF: 866-965-9955 ■ *Web:* www.houstontheatre.com

283 FIRE PROTECTION SYSTEMS

See Also Personal Protective Equipment & Clothing p. 2926; Safety Equipment - Mfr p. 3142; Security Products & Services p. 3171

Phone | Fax

BRK Brands Inc 3901 Liberty St Rd .... Aurora IL 60504 630-851-7330 851-7452
TF: 800-323-9005 ■ *Web:* www.firstalert.com

Fike Corp 704 SW Tenth St .... Blue Springs MO 64015 816-229-3405 228-9277
TF: 877-342-3453 ■ *Web:* www.fike.com

Fire & Life Safety America 3017 Vernon Rd .... Richmond VA 23228 804-222-1381 222-4393
TF: 800-252-5069 ■ *Web:* flsamerica.com

Fire Systems West Inc 206 Frontage Rd N Ste C .... Pacific WA 98047 253-833-1248 735-0113
Web: www.firesystemswest.com

Firecom Inc 39-27 59th St .... Woodside NY 11377 718-899-6100 899-1932
TF: 888-347-3269 ■ *Web:* firecominc.com

First Alert Inc 3901 Liberty St Rd .... Aurora IL 60504 630-851-7330 851-9254
TF: 800-323-9005 ■ *Web:* www.firstalert.com

Gamewell FCI 12 Clintonville Rd .... Northford CT 06472 203-484-7161 484-7118
TF: 800-606-1983 ■ *Web:* www.gamewell-fci.com

Harrington Signal Co 2519 Fourth Ave .... Moline IL 61265 309-762-0731 762-8215
Web: www.harringtonsignal.com

Honeywell Fire Solutions 1 Fire-Lite Pl .... Northford CT 06472 203-484-7161 484-7118
TF: 800-627-3473 ■ *Web:* www.firelite.com

Kidde Aerospace 4200 Airport Dr NW .... Wilson NC 27896 252-237-7004 246-7181*
**Fax:* Hum Res ■ *Web:* utcaerospacesystems.com

Meggitt Safety Systems Inc
1915 Voyager Ave .... Simi Valley CA 93063 805-584-4100 578-3400
Web: www.meggitt.com

Potter Electric Signal Company Inc
5757 Phantom Dr Ste 125 .... Hazelwood MO 63042 314-878-4321 595-6999
TF: 800-325-3936 ■ *Web:* www.pottersignal.com

Siemens Bldg Technologies Inc Fire Safety Div
8 Fernwood Rd .... Florham Park NJ 07932 973-593-2600 593-6670
TF: 888-303-3353 ■ *Web:* usa.siemens.com/infrastructure-cities/us/en

Silent Knight 7550 Meridian Cir Ste 100 .... Maple Grove MN 55369 763-493-6400 493-6475
TF: 800-328-0103 ■ *Web:* www.silentknight.com

Smeal Fire Apparatus Co
610 W Fourth St PO Box 8 .... Snyder NE 68664 402-568-2224 568-2346
Web: www.smeal.com

Task Force Tips Inc 3701 Innovation Way .... Valparaiso IN 46383 219-462-6161 464-7155
TF: 800-348-2686 ■ *Web:* www.tft.com

Tyco SimplexGrinnell 50 Technology Dr .... Westminster MA 01441 978-731-2500
TF: 800-746-7539 ■ *Web:* www.simplexgrinnell.com

Viking Corp 210 N Industrial Pk Dr .... Hastings MI 49058 269-945-9501 945-9599
TF: 800-968-9501 ■ *Web:* www.vikingcorp.com

284 FIREARMS & AMMUNITION (NON-MILITARY)

See Also Sporting Goods p. 3193; Weapons & Ordnance (Military) p. 3305

Phone | Fax

American Derringer Corp 127 N Lacy Dr .... Waco TX 76705 254-799-9111 799-7935
Web: www.amderringer.com

Beretta USA Corp 17601 Beretta Dr .... Accokeek MD 20607 301-283-2191 283-0189
TF: 800-237-3882 ■ *Web:* www.berettausa.com

Connecticut Valley Arms (CVA)
1685 Boggs Rd Ste 300 .... Duluth GA 30096 770-449-4687 242-8546
TF: 800-320-8767 ■ *Web:* www.cva.com

Crosman Corp 7629 Rt 5 & 20 .... Bloomfield NY 14469 585-657-6161 657-5405
TF: 800-724-7486 ■ *Web:* www.crosman.com

Defense Technology/Federal Laboratories
1855 S Loop PO Box 248 .... Casper WY 82601 307-235-2136 473-2713
TF: 877-248-3835 ■
Web: www.safariland.com/our-brands/defense-technology

Federal Cartridge Co 900 Ehlen Dr .... Anoka MN 55303 800-379-1732 323-2506*
**Fax Area Code:* 763 ■ **Fax:* Hum Res ■ *TF:* 800-379-1732 ■ *Web:* www.federalpremium.com

Freedom Arms Inc 314 Wyoming 239 .... Freedom WY 83120 307-883-2468 883-2005
Web: www.freedomarms.com

Glock Inc 6000 Highlands Pkwy .... Smyrna GA 30082 770-432-1202 433-8719
Web: www.glock.com

Green Mountain Rifle Barrel Co
153 W Main St PO Box 2670 .... Conway NH 03818 603-447-1095 447-1099
Web: www.gmriflebarrel.com

Gun Parts Corp 226 Williams Ln .... Kingston NY 12401 845-679-4867 486-7278*
**Fax Area Code:* 877 ■ *TF:* 866-686-7424 ■ *Web:* www.gunpartscorp.com

H & R 1871 60 Industrial Rowe .... Gardner MA 01440 866-776-9292 548-7801*
**Fax Area Code:* 336 ■ *TF:* 866-776-9292 ■ *Web:* www.hr1871.com

Heckler & Koch Inc 5675 Transport Blvd .... Columbus GA 31907 706-568-1906 568-9151
Web: www.hk-usa.com

Heritage Mfg Inc 16175 NW 49th Ave .... Miami Lakes FL 33014 305-685-5966 687-6721
Web: www.heritagemfg.com

Hornady Manufacturing Co
3625 W Old Potash Hwy .... Grand Island NE 68803 308-382-1390 382-5761
TF: 800-338-3220 ■ *Web:* www.hornady.com

Knight Rifles 213 Dennis st Athens .... Athens TN 37303 866-518-4181
TF: 866-518-4181 ■ *Web:* www.knightrifles.com

Lyman Products Corp 475 Smith St .... Middletown CT 06457 860-632-2020 632-1699
TF: 800-225-9626 ■ *Web:* www.lymanproducts.com

Marlin Firearms Co PO Box 1871 .... Madison NC 27025 800-544-8892 548-7801*
**Fax Area Code:* 336 ■ *TF Cust Svc:* 800-544-8892 ■ *Web:* www.marlinfirearms.com

OF Mossberg & Sons Inc 7 Grasso Ave .... North Haven CT 06473 203-230-5300 230-5420*
**Fax:* Mktg ■ *TF:* 800-363-3555 ■ *Web:* www.mossberg.com

Olin Corp Winchester Div
427 N Shamrock St .... East Alton IL 62024 618-258-2000
TF: 800-356-2666 ■ *Web:* www.winchester.com

Remington Arms Company Inc
870 Remington Dr PO Box 700 .... Madison NC 27025 336-548-8700 548-7801
TF: 800-243-9700 ■ *Web:* www.remington.com

Savage Arms Inc 100 Springdale Rd .... Westfield MA 01085 413-568-7001 378-4688*
**Fax Area Code:* 714 ■ *TF:* 800-243-3220 ■ *Web:* www.savagearms.com

SIG SAUER Inc 18 Industrial Dr .... Exeter NH 03833 603-772-2302 772-9082
TF: 866-345-6744 ■ *Web:* www.sigsauer.com

Smith & Wesson Corp 2100 Roosevelt Ave .... Springfield MA 01104 413-781-8300 747-3317
TF Cust Svc: 800-331-0852 ■ *Web:* www.smith-wesson.com

Smith & Wesson Holding Corp
2100 Roosevelt Ave .... Springfield MA 01104 413-781-8300 747-3317
NASDAQ: SWHC ■ *TF:* 800-372-6454 ■ *Web:* www.smith-wesson.com

Springfield Armory 420 W Main St .... Geneseo IL 61254 309-944-5631 944-3676
TF: 800-680-6866 ■ *Web:* www.springfield-armory.com

Taurus International Mfg Inc 16175 NW 49th Ave .... Miami FL 33014 305-624-1115 624-1126
TF: 800-327-3776 ■ *Web:* www.taurususa.com

Weatherby Inc 1605 Commerce Way .... Paso Robles CA 93446 805-227-2600 237-0427
TF: 800-227-2016 ■ *Web:* www.weatherby.com

Williams Gun Sight Co 7389 Lapeer Rd .... Davison MI 48423 810-653-2131 658-2140
TF: 800-530-9028 ■ *Web:* www.williamsgunsight.com

285 FISHING - COMMERCIAL

Phone | Fax

American Seafoods Holdings LLC
2025 First Ave Ste 900 .... Seattle WA 98121 206-374-1515 374-1516
Web: www.americanseafoods.com

Arctic Storm Management Group LLC
2727 Alaskan Way Pier 69 .... Seattle WA 98121 206-547-6557 547-3165
TF: 800-929-0908 ■ *Web:* www.arcticstorm.com

Blue North Fisheries Inc 2930 Westlake Ave N .... Seattle WA 98109 206-352-9252 352-9380
Web: bluenorth.com

Bon Secour Fisheries Inc
17449 County Rd 49 S .... Bon Secour AL 36511 251-949-7411 949-6478
Web: www.bonsecourfisheries.com

Canadian Fishing Co Foot of Gore Ave .... Vancouver BC V6A2Y7 604-681-0211 681-3277
Web: www.canfisco.com

JH Miles & Co Inc 902 S Hampton Ave .... Norfolk VA 23510 757-622-9264 622-9261

Lund's Fisheries Inc 997 Ocean Dr .... Cape May NJ 08204 609-884-7600 884-0664
Web: www.lundsfish.com

North Pacific Corp
5612 Lake Washington Blvd NE .... Kirkland WA 98033 425-822-1001 822-1004
Web: www.npc-usa.com

Nova Fisheries 2532 Yale Ave E .... Seattle WA 98102 206-781-2000 781-9011
TF: 888-458-6682 ■ *Web:* www.novafish.com

Ocean Beauty Seafoods Inc 1100 W Ewing St .... Seattle WA 98119 206-285-6800
TF: 800-365-8950 ■ *Web:* www.oceanbeauty.com

Raffield Fisheries Inc
1624 Grouper Ave PO Box 309 .... Port Saint Joe FL 32456 850-229-8229 229-8782
Web: www.raffieldfisheries.com

Sahlman Seafoods Inc
1601 Sahlman Dr PO Box 5009 .... Tampa FL 33605 813-248-5726 247-5787
Web: www.sahlmanseafood.com

Trident Seafood Corp 5303 Shilshole Ave NW .... Seattle WA 98107 206-783-3818 782-7195
Web: www.tridentseafoods.com

Wanchese Fish Co
2000 Northgate Commerce Pkwy .... Suffolk VA 23435 757-673-4500
Web: www.wanchese.com

286 FIXTURES - OFFICE & STORE

See Also Commercial & Industrial Furniture *p. 2339*

Phone | Fax

Able Steel Equipment Co Inc
50-02 23rd St .... Long Island NY 11101 718-361-9240 937-5742
TF: 800-428-8722 ■ *Web:* www.ablesteelequipment.com

Advanced Equipment Corp
2401 W Commonwealth Ave .... Fullerton CA 92833 714-635-5350 525-6083
Web: www.advancedequipment.com

American Sanitary Partition Corp
300 Enterprise St PO Box 99 .... Ocoee FL 34761 407-656-0611 656-8189
Web: www.am-sanitary-partition.com

Ampco Products Inc 11400 NW 36th Ave .... Miami FL 33167 305-821-5700 642-5300*
**Fax Area Code:* 866 ■ *Web:* www.ampco.com

Angola Wire Products Inc 803 Wohlert St .... Angola IN 46703 260-665-9447 665-6182
TF: 800-800-7225 ■ *Web:* www.angolawire.com

Architectural Bronze Aluminum Corp
655 Deerfield Rd Ste 100 .... Deerfield IL 60015 800-339-6581 266-7301*
**Fax Area Code:* 847 ■ *TF:* 800-339-6581 ■ *Web:* www.architecturalbronze.com

Aspects Inc 9441 Opal Ave .... Mentone CA 92359 909-794-7722 794-6996

Bel-Mar Wire Products Inc 2343 N Damen Ave .... Chicago IL 60647 773-342-3800 342-0038
Web: www.belmarwire.net

Benner-Nawman Inc 3450 Sabin Brown Rd .... Wickenburg AZ 85390 928-684-2813 684-7041
TF: 800-992-3833 ■ *Web:* www.bnproducts.com

Bennett Mfg Company Inc 13315 Railroad St .... Alden NY 14004 716-937-9161 937-3137
Web: www.bennettmfg.com

Best-Rite Mfg 2885 Lorraine Ave .... Temple TX 76501 800-749-2258 697-6258
TF: 800-749-2258 ■ *Web:* www.moorecoinc.com

Big Timberworks Inc 1 Rabel Ln .... Gallatin Gateway MT 59730 406-763-4639
Web: bigtimberworks.com

Bob-Leon Plastics Inc 5151 Franklin Blvd .... Sacramento CA 95820 916-452-4063 452-3759
Web: www.bob-leon.com

Borroughs Corp 3002 N Burdick St .... Kalamazoo MI 49004 269-342-0161 342-4161
TF: 800-748-0227 ■ *Web:* www.borroughs.com

Boston Group 400 Riverside Ave .... Medford MA 02155 800-225-1633
TF: 800-225-1633 ■ *Web:* www.bostonretail.com

Cal-Partitions Inc 23814 President Ave .... Harbor City CA 90710 310-539-1911
Web: www.calpartitions.com

Cano Corp 225 Industrial Rd .... Fitchburg MA 01420 978-342-0953
Web: www.canocorp.com

Carolina Cabinet Co 3363 Hwy 301 N .... Wilson NC 27893 252-291-5181 291-8039
Web: www.3c-inc.net

Century Kitchen Inc
Rt 309 And Railroad Crossing .... Colmar PA 18915 215-822-1300
Web: www.centurykitchens.com

Churchill Cabinet Co 4616 W 19th St .... Cicero IL 60804 708-780-0070 780-9762
TF Sales: 800-379-9776 ■ *Web:* www.chicago-gaming.com

Consolidated Storage Cos 225 Main St .... Tatamy PA 18085 610-253-2775 859-2121*
**Fax Area Code:* 888 ■ *TF Cust Svc:* 800-323-0801 ■ *Web:* www.equipto.com

Cres-Cor 5925 Heisley Rd .... Mentor OH 44060 440-350-1100 350-7267
TF: 877-273-7267 ■ *Web:* www.crescor.com

Crown Metal Manufacturing Co 765 S SR 83 .... Elmhurst IL 60126 630-279-9800 279-9807
Web: www.crownmetal.com

Datum Filing Systems Inc 89 Church Rd .... Emigsville PA 17318 717-764-6350 764-6656
TF: 800-828-8018 ■ *Web:* datumstorage.com

DeBourgh Manufacturing Co
27505 Otero Ave PO Box 981 .... La Junta CO 81050 800-328-8829 384-8161*
**Fax Area Code:* 719 ■ *TF:* 800-328-8829 ■ *Web:* www.debourgh.com

Design Workshops 486 Lesser St .... Oakland CA 94601 510-434-0727 434-0727
Web: www.design-workshops.com

Dixie Store Fixtures & Sales Company Inc
2425 First Ave N .... Birmingham AL 35203 205-322-2442 322-2445
TF: 800-323-4943 ■ *Web:* www.dixiestorefixtures.com

Durham Manufacturing Co 201 Main St .... Durham CT 06422 860-349-3427 349-8235
TF: 800-243-3774 ■ *Web:* www.durhammfg.com

Econoco Corp 300 Karin Ln .... Hicksville NY 11801 516-935-7700 505-8300*
**Fax Area Code:* 800 ■ *TF:* 800-645-7032 ■ *Web:* www.econoco.com

Edsal Mfg Company Inc 4400 S Packers Ave .... Chicago IL 60609 773-254-0600
Web: www.edsal.com

EQUIPTO 225 Main St .... Tatamy PA 18085 610-253-2775 859-2121*
**Fax Area Code:* 888 ■ *TF:* 800-323-0801 ■ *Web:* www.equipto.com

Ex-Cell Metal Products Inc
11240 Melrose St .... Franklin Park IL 60131 847-451-0451 261-9448
TF: 800-392-3557 ■ *Web:* www.ex-cell.com

Eyelematic Mfg Company Inc 1 Seemar Rd .... Watertown CT 06795 860-274-6791 274-8464

Farmington Displays Inc 21 Hyde Rd .... Farmington CT 06032 860-677-2497 677-1418
Web: www.fdi-group.com

Ferrante Manufacturing Co 6626 Gratiot Ave .... Detroit MI 48207 313-571-1111
Web: ferrantemfg.com

Frazier Industrial Co 91 Fairview Ave .... Long Valley NJ 07853 908-876-3001 876-3615
TF: 800-859-1342 ■ *Web:* www.frazier.com

General Partitions Manufacturing Corp
1702 Peninsula Dr PO Box 8370 .... Erie PA 16505 814-833-1154 838-3473
Web: generalpartitions.com

Giannelli Cabinets 19443 Londelius St .... Northridge CA 91324 818-882-9787

Giffin Interior & Fixture Inc
500 Scotti Dr .... Bridgeville PA 15017 412-221-1166 221-3745
Web: giffininterior.com

Goebel Fixture Co 528 Dale St .... Hutchinson MN 55350 320-587-2112 587-2378
Web: www.gf.com

Hamilton Sorter Co Inc 3158 Production Dr .... Fairfield OH 45014 513-870-4400 503-9963*
**Fax Area Code:* 800 ■ *TF:* 800-503-9966 ■ *Web:* www.hamiltonsorter.com

Handy Store Fixtures Inc 337 Sherman Ave .... Newark NJ 07114 973-242-1600 642-6222
TF: 800-631-4280 ■ *Web:* www.handystorefixtures.com

Harbor Industries Inc 14130 172nd Ave .... Grand Haven MI 49417 616-842-5330 842-1385
Web: www.harbor-ind.com

Holcomb & Hoke Mfg Company Inc
1545 Van Buren St .... Indianapolis IN 46203 317-784-2448 781-9164
Web: www.foldoor.com

Phone | Fax

Hoosier Co 5421 W 86th St PO Box 681064 .... Indianapolis IN 46268 317-872-8125 872-7183
TF: 800-521-4184 ■ *Web:* www.hoosierco.com

Hufcor Inc 2101 Kennedy Rd .... Janesville WI 53545 608-756-1241 756-1246
TF: 800-356-6968 ■ *Web:* www.hufcor.com

Hurco Design & Mfg 200 W 33rd St .... Ogden UT 84401 905-567-2600 394-8218*
**Fax Area Code:* 801

IDX Corp 1 Rider Trail Plaza Dr Ste 400 .... Earth City MO 63045 314-739-4120 739-4129
Web: www.idxcorporation.com

Imperial Counters Inc 725 Spiral Blvd .... Hastings MN 55033 651-437-3903 438-3855
Web: www.imperialcounters.com

InterMetro Industries Corp
651 N Washington St .... Wilkes-Barre PA 18705 570-825-2741 823-2852*
**Fax:* Hum Res ■ *TF Cust Svc:* 800-992-1776 ■ *Web:* www.metro.com

International Visual Corp (IVC)
11500 Blvd Armand Bombardier .... Montreal QC H1E2W9 514-643-0570 643-4867
TF: 866-643-0570 ■ *Web:* www.ivcweb.com

Jaken Company Inc 14420 My ford rf .... Irvine CA 90623 714-522-1700
TF: 800-401-7225 ■ *Web:* www.jaken.com

Jesco-Wipco Industries Inc
950 Anderson Rd PO Box 388 .... Litchfield MI 49252 517-542-2903 542-2501
TF: 800-455-0019 ■ *Web:* www.jescoonline.com

JL Industries Inc 4450 W 78th St Cir .... Bloomington MN 55435 952-835-6850 835-2218
TF: 800-554-6077 ■ *Web:* www.activarcpg.com

John Boos & Co 3601 S Banker St PO Box 609 .... Effingham IL 62401 217-347-7701 347-7705
TF: 888-431-2667 ■ *Web:* www.johnboos.com

JR Jones Fixture Co 3216 Winnetka Ave N .... Minneapolis MN 55427 763-544-4239 544-3106
Web: jonesfixture.com

Kardex Systems Inc 114 Westview Ave .... Marietta OH 45750 740-374-9300 374-9953*
**Fax:* Mktg ■ *TF:* 800-639-5805 ■ *Web:* www.kardex.com

Karges Furniture Company Inc
1501 W Maryland St .... Evansville IN 47710 812-425-2291 425-4016
TF: 800-252-7437 ■ *Web:* www.karges.com

Kawneer Company Inc 555 Guthridge Ct .... Norcross GA 30092 770-449-5555 734-1560
Web: www.kawneer.com

Kent Corp 4446 Pinson Valley Pkwy .... Birmingham AL 35215 205-853-3420 856-3622
Web: www.kentcorp.com

Killion Industries Inc 1380 Poinsettia Ave .... Vista CA 92081 760-727-5102 727-5108
TF: 800-421-5352 ■ *Web:* www.killionindustries.com

Knickerbocker Partition Corp
193 Hanse Ave PO Box 690 .... Freeport NY 11520 516-546-0550 546-0549
Web: www.knickerbockerpartition.com

Kwik-Wall Co 1010 E Edwards St .... Springfield IL 62703 217-522-5553 522-1170
TF: 800-280-5945 ■ *Web:* www.kwik-wall.com

LA Darling Co 1401 Hwy 49B .... Paragould AR 72450 870-239-9564
TF: 800-643-3499 ■ *Web:* www.ladarling.com

Lista International Corp 106 Lowland St .... Holliston MA 01746 508-429-1350 429-0711
TF Cust Svc: 800-722-3020 ■ *Web:* www.listaintl.com

Lozier Corp 6336 John J Pershing Dr .... Omaha NE 68110 402-457-8000 457-8297*
**Fax:* Cust Svc ■ *TF:* 800-228-9882 ■ *Web:* www.lozier.com

Lyon Work Space Products 420 N Main St .... Montgomery IL 60538 630-892-8941 892-8966
TF: 800-433-8488 ■ *Web:* www.lyonworkspace.com

M.E.G. LLC 502 S Green St PO Box 240 .... Cambridge City IN 47327 800-645-3315 478-4439*
**Fax Area Code:* 765 ■ *TF Cust Svc:* 800-645-3315 ■ *Web:* www.megfixtures.com

Metpar Corp 95 State St .... Westbury NY 11590 516-333-2600 333-2618
Web: www.metpar.com

Miller/Zell Inc 4715 Frederick Dr SW .... Atlanta GA 30336 404-691-7400 699-2189
Web: www.millerzell.com

Millrock
RiverRun Commercial 4660 Early Rd .... Mt. Crawford VA 22841 540-437-3458
Web: www.riverruncommercial.com

Modern Woodcrafts LLC
72 NW Dr Farmington Industrial Pk .... Plainville CT 06062 860-677-7371 676-8381
Web: www.modernwoodcrafts.com

Modernfold Inc 215 W New Rd .... Greenfield IN 46140 800-869-9685 410-5016*
**Fax Area Code:* 866 ■ *TF:* 800-869-9685 ■ *Web:* www.modernfold.com

Modular Systems Inc 169 Pk St .... Fruitport MI 49415 231-865-3167 865-6101
Web: www.mod-eez.com

Monarch Industries Inc 99 Main St .... Warren RI 02885 401-247-5200
Web: www.monarchinc.com

National Partitions 10300 Goldenfern Ln .... Knoxville TN 37931 865-670-2100
TF: 888-818-5749 ■ *Web:* www.nationalpartitions.com

NNM Peterson Manufacturing Co
24133 W 143rd St .... Plainfield IL 60544 815-436-9201 436-2863
TF: 800-826-9086 ■ *Web:* www.peterson-mfg.com

Northway Industries Inc
434 Paxtonville Rd PO Box 277 .... Middleburg PA 17842 570-837-1564 837-1575
Web: www.northwayind.com

Oak & More Ltd 4949 SE 25th Ave .... Portland OR 97202 503-245-4522 245-4503

Pacific Fixture Company Inc
12860 San Fernando Rd Unit B .... Sylmar CA 91342 818-362-2130 367-8968
TF: 800-272-2349 ■ *Web:* www.pacificfixture.com

Packard Industries Inc 1515 US 31 N .... Niles MI 49120 269-684-2550 684-2422
TF: 800-253-0866

Pan-Osten Co 6944 Louisville Rd .... Bowling Green KY 42101 270-783-3900 783-3911
TF: 800-472-6678 ■ *Web:* www.panoston.com

Panelfold Inc 10700 NW 36th Ave .... Miami FL 33167 305-688-3501 688-0185
TF: 800-433-3222 ■ *Web:* www.panelfold.com

Pentwater Wire Products Inc (PWP)
474 Carroll St PO Box 947 .... Pentwater MI 49449 231-869-6911 869-4020
TF: 877-869-6911 ■ *Web:* www.pentwaterwire.com

Plasticrest Products Inc 4519 W Harrison St .... Chicago IL 60624 773-826-2163 826-4227
TF: 800-828-2163 ■ *Web:* signaturejewelrypackaging.com

Racks Inc PO Box 530840 .... San Diego CA 92153 619-661-0987
TF: 877-920-7225 ■ *Web:* www.racksinc.com

RC Smith Co 14200 Southcross Dr W .... Burnsville MN 55306 952-854-0711 854-8160
TF: 800-747-7648 ■ *Web:* www.rcsmith.com

Reeve Store Equipment Co
9131 Bermudez St PO Box 276 .... Pico Rivera CA 90660 562-949-2535 949-3862
TF: 800-927-3383 ■ *Web:* www.reeveco.com

Republic Storage Systems LLC
1038 Belden Ave NE .... Canton OH 44705 330-438-5800 454-7772
TF Sales: 800-477-1255 ■ *Web:* www.republicstorage.com

Phone Fax

Ridg-U-Rak Inc 120 S Lake St. . . . North East PA 16428 814-725-8751 725-5659
TF: 866-479-7225 ■ *Web:* www.ridgurak.com

Russ Bassett Co 8189 Byron Rd. . . . Whittier CA 90606 562-945-2445 698-8972
TF: 800-350-2445 ■ *Web:* www.russbassett.com

Salsbury Industries Inc 1010 E 62nd St. . . . Los Angeles CA 90001 323-846-6700 846-6800
TF: 800-624-5299 ■ *Web:* www.mailboxes.com

Sandusky Cabinets Inc
16125 Widmere Rd PO Box 517. . . . Arvin CA 93203 661-854-5551 854-2003
TF Cust Svc: 800-886-8688 ■ *Web:* www.sanduskycabinets.com

Semasys Inc 702 Ashland St. . . . Houston TX 77007 713-869-8331 869-5077
TF Cust Svc: 800-231-1425 ■ *Web:* www.semasys.com

Showbest Fixture Corp 4112 Sarellen Rd . . . . Henrico VA 23231 804-222-5535 222-7220
Web: www.showbest.com

Southern Imperial Inc 1400 Eddy Ave. . . . Rockford IL 61103 815-877-7041
TF Cust Svc: 800-747-4665 ■ *Web:* www.southernimperial.com

SpaceGuard Products Inc 711 S Commerce Dr . . . . Seymour IN 47274 812-523-3044 428-5758*
**Fax Area Code:* 800 ■ *TF:* 800-841-0680 ■ *Web:* www.spaceguardproducts.com

Spacesaver Corp 1450 Janesville Ave . . . . Fort Atkinson WI 53538 800-255-8170 563-2702*
**Fax Area Code:* 920 ■ *TF:* 800-492-3434 ■ *Web:* www.spacesaver.com

Sparks Marketing Group Inc
2828 Charter Rd. . . . Philadelphia PA 19154 215-676-1100
TF: 800-925-7727 ■ *Web:* www.sparksonline.com

Spectrum Industries Inc 925 First Ave . . . . Chippewa Falls WI 54729 715-723-6750 335-0473*
**Fax Area Code:* 800 ■ *TF:* 800-235-1262 ■ *Web:* www.spectrumfurniture.com

SPG International 11230 Harland Dr . . . . Covington GA 30014 877-503-4774 577-2210*
**Fax Area Code:* 800 ■ *TF:* 877-503-4774 ■ *Web:* www.spgusa.com

Stanley Vidmar Storage Technologies
11 Grammes Rd . . . . Allentown PA 18103 800-523-9462 523-9934
TF: 800-523-9462 ■ *Web:* www.stanleyvidmar.com

Stanly Fixtures Company Inc
11635 NC 138 Hwy PO Box 616. . . . Norwood NC 28128 704-474-3184 474-3011
Web: www.stanlyfixtures.com

Stevens Industries Inc 704 W Main St . . . . Teutopolis IL 62467 217-540-3100 857-7101
Web: www.stevensind.com

Stevens Wire Products Inc 351 NW 'F' St . . . . Richmond IN 47374 765-966-5534 962-3586
Web: www.stevenswire.com

Store Kraft Mfg Co 500 Irving St . . . . Beatrice NE 68310 402-223-2348 223-1268
Web: www.storekraft.com

Streater Inc 411 S First Ave. . . . Albert Lea MN 56007 800-527-4197 373-7630*
**Fax Area Code:* 507 ■ *TF:* 800-527-4197 ■ *Web:* www.streater.com

Structural Concepts Corp 888 Porter Rd . . . . Muskegon MI 49441 231-798-8888 798-4960
TF: 800-433-9489 ■ *Web:* www.structuralconcepts.com

Stylmark Inc PO Box 32008. . . . Minneapolis MN 55432 763-574-7474 574-1415
TF: 800-328-2495 ■ *Web:* www.stylmark.com

Sumner Group Inc 6717 Waldemar Ave . . . . Saint Louis MO 63139 314-633-8000 633-8002
Web: www.sumner-group.com

Tarrant Interiors Inc 5000 S Fwy. . . . Fort Worth TX 76115 817-922-5000 922-5015

Tesko Welding & Manufacturing Co
7350 W Montrose Ave . . . . Norridge IL 60706 708-452-0045 452-0112
TF: 800-621-4514 ■ *Web:* teskoenterprises.com

Timely Inc 10241 Norris Ave . . . . Pacoima CA 91331 818-492-3500 899-2677
TF: 800-247-6242 ■ *Web:* www.timelyframes.com

TJ Hale Co W 139 N 9499 Hwy 145. . . . Menomonee Falls WI 53051 262-255-5555 255-5678
TF: 800-236-4253 ■ *Web:* www.tjhale.com

Trendway Corp 13467 Quincy St PO Box 9016. . . . Holland MI 49422 616-399-3900
TF: 800-968-5344 ■ *Web:* www.trendway.com

Trion Industries Inc 297 Laird St. . . . Wilkes-Barre PA 18702 570-824-1000 824-0802
TF: 800-444-4665 ■ *Web:* www.trioninline.com

Unarco Material Handling Inc
701 16th Ave E . . . . Springfield TN 37172 800-862-7261 382-2777*
**Fax Area Code:* 615 ■ *TF:* 800-862-7261 ■ *Web:* www.unarcorack.com

Viking Metal Cabinet Co
24047 W Lockport St Ste 209. . . . Plainfield IL 60544 800-776-7767 863-7065*
**Fax Area Code:* 630 ■ *TF:* 800-776-7767 ■ *Web:* www.vikingmetal.com

VIRA Insight LLC 1 Buckingham Ave. . . . Perth Amboy NJ 08861 732-442-8472 442-8464
Web: www.virainsight.com/welcome

W/M Display Group 1040 W 40th St. . . . Chicago IL 60609 773-254-3700 254-3188
TF: 800-443-2000 ■ *Web:* www.wmdisplay.com

Weis/Robart Partitions Inc
3501 E La Palma Ave . . . . Anaheim CA 92806 714-666-0108 666-0110
Web: www.weisrobart.com

Western Pacific Storage Systems Inc
300 E Arrow Hwy . . . . San Dimas CA 91773 800-732-9777 451-0311*
**Fax Area Code:* 909 ■ *TF:* 800-732-9777 ■ *Web:* www.wpss.com

WJ Egli Company Inc 205 E Columbia St. . . . Alliance OH 44601 330-823-3666 823-0011

287 FLAGS, BANNERS, PENNANTS

Phone Fax

Aaa Flag & Banner Manufacturing Co
8955 National Blvd. . . . Los Angeles CA 90034 800-266-4222 836-7253*
**Fax Area Code:* 310 ■ *TF:* 800-266-4222 ■ *Web:* www.aaaflag.com

Annin & Co 105 Eisenhower Pkwy . . . . Roseland NJ 07068 973-228-9400 228-4905
TF: 888-252-4569 ■ *Web:* www.annin.com

Eder Flag Mfg Company Inc
1000 W Rawson Ave. . . . Oak Creek WI 53154 414-764-3522
TF: 800-558-6044 ■ *Web:* www.ederflagnews.com

Metro Flag 353 Richard Mine Rd Ste 100 . . . . Wharton NJ 07885 973-366-1776 366-0956
Web: nationalflag.com

National Banner Co 11938 Harry Hines Blvd . . . . Dallas TX 75234 972-241-2131 468-0700*
**Fax Area Code:* 800 ■ *TF:* 800-527-0860

Olympus Flag & Banner 9000 W Heather Ave . . . . Milwaukee WI 53224 414-355-2010 355-1931
TF: 800-558-9620 ■ *Web:* olympusgrp.com

288 FLASH MEMORY DEVICES

Phone Fax

Advanced Micro Devices Inc (AMD)
1 AMD Pl PO Box 3453 . . . . Sunnyvale CA 94088 408-749-4000
NYSE: AMD ■ *TF:* 800-538-8450 ■ *Web:* www.amd.com

Kingston Technology Co
17600 Newhope St. . . . Fountain Valley CA 92708 714-435-2600 435-2699
TF: 800-835-6575 ■ *Web:* www.kingston.com

Lexar Media Inc 47300 Bayside Pkwy . . . . Fremont CA 94538 510-413-1200
TF: 877-747-4031 ■ *Web:* www.lexar.com

Micron Technology Inc 8000 S Federal Way. . . . Boise ID 83707 208-368-4000 368-4617
NASDAQ: MU ■ *TF:* 888-363-2589 ■ *Web:* www.micron.com

PNY Technologies Inc 299 Webro Rd . . . . Parsippany NJ 07054 973-515-9700 560-5590*
**Fax:* Sales ■ *TF:* 800-769-7079 ■ *Web:* www3.pny.com

SanDisk Corp 601 McCarthy Blvd . . . . Milpitas CA 95035 408-801-1000 801-8657
NASDAQ: SNDK ■ *TF:* 866-726-3475 ■ *Web:* www.sandisk.com

Sharp Microelectronics of the Americas
5700 NW Pacific Rim Blvd . . . . Camas WA 98607 360-834-2500 834-8903
Web: www.sharpsma.com

Sony Electronics Inc 1 Sony Dr. . . . Park Ridge NJ 07656 201-930-1000
TF Cust Svc: 800-222-7669 ■ *Web:* www.sony.com

Spansion Inc 915 DeGuigne Dr. . . . Sunnyvale CA 94085 408-962-2500
NYSE: CODE ■ *TF:* 866-772-6746 ■ *Web:* www.spansion.com

289 FLEET LEASING & MANAGEMENT

Phone Fax

Allstate Leasing Inc 1 Olympic Pl. . . . Towson MD 21204 800-223-4885
TF: 800-223-4885 ■ *Web:* www.allstateleasing.com

Automotive Resources International
4001 Leadenhall Rd . . . . Mount Laurel NJ 08054 856-778-1500
Web: www.arifleet.com

Donlen Corp 2315 Sanders Rd. . . . Northbrook IL 60062 847-714-1400
TF: 800-323-1483 ■ *Web:* www.donlen.com

Emkay Inc 805 W Thorndale Ave . . . . Itasca IL 60143 630-250-7400 250-7400
TF: 800-621-2001 ■ *Web:* www.emkay.com

Executive Car Leasing Inc
7807 Santa Monica Blvd. . . . Los Angeles CA 90046 323-654-5000 848-9015
TF: 800-994-2277 ■ *Web:* www.executivecarleasing.com

GE Equipment Services 120 Long Ridge Rd . . . . Stamford CT 06902 203-357-4000

Lease Plan USA 1165 Sanctuary Pkwy . . . . Alpharetta GA 30004 770-933-9090 202-8700*
**Fax Area Code:* 678 ■ *TF:* 800-457-8721 ■ *Web:* www.leaseplan.com

Leasing Assoc Inc
12600 N Featherwood Dr Ste 400. . . . Houston TX 77034 832-300-1300 300-1317
TF: 800-449-4807 ■ *Web:* www.theleasingcompany.com

Lily Transportation Corp 145 Rosemary St. . . . Needham MA 02494 781-449-8811 449-7128
Web: www.lily.com

Motorlease Corp 1506 New Britain Ave . . . . Farmington CT 06032 860-677-9711 674-8677
TF: 800-243-0182 ■ *Web:* motorlease.com

Park Avenue Auto Group 250 W Passaic St . . . . Maywood NJ 07607 201-843-7900 843-4941
Web: www.parkavemotors.com

RUAN Transportation Management Systems
666 Grand Ave 3200 Ruan Ctr . . . . Des Moines IA 50309 515-245-2500 245-2611
TF: 866-782-6669 ■ *Web:* www.ruan.com

Wheels Inc 666 Garland Pl. . . . Des Plaines IL 60016 847-699-7000 699-4047*
**Fax:* Mail Rm ■ *Web:* www.wheels.com

FLOOR COVERINGS - MFR

See Carpets & Rugs p. 1893; Flooring - Resilient p. 2288; Tile - Ceramic (Wall & Floor) p. 3247

290 FLOOR COVERINGS STORES

Phone Fax

Action Floor Systems LLC 4781 N US Hwy 51 . . . . Mercer WI 54547 715-476-3512
Web: www.actionfloors.com

Allied Property Services LLC Dba Cmq Floor Covering
2524 Ford Rd . . . . Bristol PA 19007 215-785-5900

Architectural Surfaces Inc
5801 Midway Park NE . . . . Albuquerque NM 87109 505-889-0124
Web: www.architectstudio.com

Augusta Flooring Inc 202 Bobby Jones Expy . . . . Martinez GA 30907 706-650-0400
Web: augustafloor.com

Award Hardwood Floors LLP 401 N 72nd Ave . . . . Wausau WI 54401 715-849-8080 849-8181

Big d Floor Covering Supplies
7412 Anaconda Ave . . . . Garden Grove CA 92841 714-894-2443
Web: bigdsupply.com

Blue Ridge Builders Supply Inc
5221 Rockfish Gap Tpke. . . . Charlottesville VA 22903 434-823-1387
Web: www.brbs.net

Boa-Franc Inc 1255-98th St . . . . Saint-georges QC G5Y8J5 418-227-1181
TF: 800-463-1303 ■ *Web:* www.boa-franc.com

Bois BSL Energie Inc
1081 Rue Industrielle CP4 . . . . Mont-joli QC G5H3T9 418-775-5360
Web: www.smartlog.ca

Butler Carpet Mart Inc Dba Bob'S Carpet Mart
10815 Us Hwy 19 N . . . . Clearwater FL 33764 727-571-9998

Carol'S Carpet Inc 1640 NE Blvd . . . . Montgomery AL 36117 334-603-8713
Web: carolscarpetmontgomery.com

Carpet House 1320 Woodlawn . . . . Lincoln IL 62656 217-735-2531

Carpet King Inc 1815 W River Rd N . . . . Minneapolis MN 55411 612-588-7600
Web: www.carpet-king.com

Carpet Tech 6613 19th St . . . . Lubbock TX 79407 806-795-5142
Web: www.callcarpettech.com

Carpetile Co 8 W Main St . . . . Plano IL 60545 630-552-3400

Century Tile Supply Co 747 E Roosevelt Rd . . . . Lombard IL 60148 630-495-2300 237-8257*
**Fax Area Code:* 773 ■ *TF:* 888-845-3968 ■ *Web:* www.century-tile.com

Circle Floors Inc 1911 Revere Beach Pkwy. . . . Everett MA 02149 617-381-6600
Web: jzaino.powweb.com/circlefloors

Clark-Dunbar Flooring Superstore
3232 Empire Dr . . . . Alexandria LA 71301 318-445-0262
TF: 800-256-1467 ■ *Web:* www.clarkdunbarsuperstore.com

Clayton Tile Distributing Company Inc
535 Woodruff Rd . . . . Greenville SC 29607 864-288-6290
Web: claytontileco.com

Name / Address	City	State	Zip	Phone	Fax
Coleman Floor Company Inc 1930 N Thoreau Dr Ste 100	Schaumburg	IL	60173	847-259-6100	
Web: www.colemanfloor.com					
Commercial Contractors Inc 4900 Fairbanks St.	Anchorage	AK	99503	907-563-1911	
Web: www.aphome.com					
Commercial Interior Resources Inc 1761 Reynolds Ave.	Irvine	CA	92614	949-752-1470	
Web: www.cir-resource.com					
Contract Furnishings Mart 22230 84th Ave S Ste 110	Kent	WA	98032	503-542-8900	
Web: www.cfmfloors.com					
Coyle Carpet One Inc 250 W Beltline Hwy	Madison	WI	53713	608-257-0291	
Web: www.coylecarpet.com					
Dean Hardwoods Inc 9244 Industrial Blvd	Leland	NC	28451	910-763-5409	
Web: www.deanwood.com					
Designer Floors of Texas 3841 Ranch Rd 620 S.	Austin	TX	78738	512-263-3333	
Web: austin.abbeycarpet.com					
Dolphin Carpet & Tile 3550 NW 77th Ct	Miami	FL	33122	305-591-4141	378-1700
TF: 800-639-3566 ■ *Web:* www.dolphincarpet.com					
Eckards Home Improvement 2402 N Belt Hwy	Saint Joseph	MO	64506	816-279-4522	
TF: 800-264-2794 ■ *Web:* eckardsflooring.com					
EG Penner Building Centres 200 Park Rd W	Steinbach	MB	R5G1A1	204-326-1325	
TF: 800-353-8733 ■ *Web:* www.egpenner.com					
Elias Wilf Corp 10234 S Dolfield Rd	Owings Mills	MD	21117	410-363-2400	
Web: www.flooryou.com					
Elkton Supply Company Inc 202 W Main St.	Elkton	MD	21921	410-398-1900	
Web: www.elktonsupply.com					
Elte 80 Ronald Ave	Toronto	ON	M6E5A2	416-785-7885	
TF: 888-276-3583 ■ *Web:* www.elte.com					
Essis & Sons Inc 6220 Carlisle Pk	Mechanicsburg	PA	17050	717-697-9423	
Web: carpetmechanicsburg.com					
Everett Carpet Co 318 Ashman St	Midland	MI	48640	989-835-7191	
Web: everettcarpet.com					
Farrell Distributing 19 Delaware Ave	Endicott	NY	13760	607-754-0707	
Web: www.farrelldistributing.com					
Feizy Import & Export Co Ltd 1949 Stemmons Fwy	Dallas	TX	75207	214-747-6000	760-0521
TF: 800-779-0877 ■ *Web:* feizy.com					
Floor Coverings International 5250 Triangle Pwy Ste 100	Norcross	GA	30092	770-874-7600	
TF Sales: 800-955-4324 ■ *Web:* www.floorcoveringsinternational.com					
Floor King Inc 10961 Research Blvd	Austin	TX	78759	512-346-7034	
Web: flooring.net					
Flooring Sales Group 1251 First Ave S	Seattle	WA	98134	206-624-7800	622-8407
TF: 877-478-3577 ■ *Web:* www.greatfloors.com					
Furniture Outlets USA Inc 140 E Hinks Ln	Sioux Falls	SD	57104	605-336-5000	336-5010
TF: 877-395-8998 ■ *Web:* www.thefurnituremart.com					
G & W Commercial Flooring Inc 6407 S 211th St.	Kent	WA	98032	253-479-1760	
Web: gwcfloor.com					
Great Floors LLC 524 E Sherman Ave	Coeur d'Alene	ID	83814	208-664-5405	
Web: greatfloors.com					
Hagopian & Sons Inc 14000 W 8 Mile Rd.	Oak Park	MI	48237	248-399-2323	
Web: www.originalhagopian.com					
Harry L Murphy Inc 42 Bonaventura Dr.	San Jose	CA	95134	408-955-1100	955-1111
Web: harrylmurphyinc.com					
Hi Tech Data Floors Inc 1885 Swarthmore Ave.	Lakewood	NJ	08701	732-905-1799	
TF: 800-544-8321 ■ *Web:* hitechdatafloors.com					
Holmes Tile & Marble Company Inc 1202 Falls St	Jonesboro	AR	72401	870-932-8011	
Web: holmestile.com					
JJJ Floor Covering Inc 4831 Passons Blvd Ste A	Pico Rivera	CA	90660	562-692-9008	
Web: www.jjjfloorcovering.com					
Landers Premier Flooring Inc 2601 Mchale Ct Ste 140	Austin	TX	78758	512-873-9470	
Web: landerspremierflooring.com					
Lumber Liquidators Inc 1455 VFW Pkwy	West Roxbury	MA	02132	617-327-1222	750-7802*
**Fax Area Code:* 978 ■ *TF:* 800-227-0332 ■ *Web:* www.lumberliquidators.com					
Mccabes Quality Carpet & Linoleum Inc 101 Genesee St.	Marquette	MI	49855	906-228-8821	
Web: mccabesflooring.com					
MCI Inc 26 First Ave N	Waite Park	MN	56387	320-227-4061	
Web: www.mcicarpetonewaitepark.com					
Mill Creek Carpet & Tile Co 6845 E 41st St.	Tulsa	OK	74145	918-621-4000	
Web: www.millcreekcarpet.com					
Miller's Carpet One 15615 Hwy 99	Lynnwood	WA	98087	425-312-6259	
Web: www.carpetone.com					
Narita Trading Company Inc 24 Park Ave.	Clifton	NJ	07014	718-628-4382	
Web: www.naritatrading.com					
Pyramid Floor Covering Inc 38 Harbor Park Dr.	Port Washington	NY	11050	516-932-7200	
Web: www.pyramidfloors.com					
Quality Craft Ltd 17750-65A Ave Ste 301	Surrey	BC	V3S5N4	604-575-5550	
TF: 800-663-2252 ■ *Web:* www.qualitycraft.com					
Redi-Carpet Inc 10225 Mula Rd Ste 120	Stafford	TX	77477	832-310-2000	310-2001
Web: www.redicarpet.com					
Roysons Corp 40 Vanderhoof Ave	Rockaway	NJ	07866	973-625-7923	625-5917
TF: 888-769-7667 ■ *Web:* www.roysons.com					
Saint Paul Linoleum & Carpet Co 2956 Ctr Ct	Eagan	MN	55121	651-686-7770	686-6660
Web: www.stpaullinocpt.com					
Sergenian's Residential Flooring 2805 W Beltline Hwy	Madison	WI	53713	608-271-1111	
Web: sergenians.com					
Spraggins Flooring Inc 3815 Silver Star Rd	Orlando	FL	32808	407-295-4150	
Web: www.spragginsflooring.com					
Starline Associates Inc 3901 Sw 47th Ave Ste 410	Davie	FL	33314	954-792-1965	
TF: 866-752-6548 ■ *Web:* www.starlineusa.com					
Teragren Fine Bamboo Flooring Panels & Veneer 12715 Miller Rd Ne Ste 301	Bainbridge Island	WA	98110	206-842-9477	
TF: 800-929-6333 ■ *Web:* www.teragren.com					
Third Floor Inc, The 5410 Wilshire Blvd Ste 1000	Los Angeles	CA	90036	323-931-6633	
Web: www.thethirdfloorinc.com					
Tom Duffy Co 5200 Watt Ct Ste B	Fairfield	CA	94534	800-479-5671	
TF: 800-479-5671 ■ *Web:* www.tomduffy.com					
Total Kitchen & Bath Inc 155 S Rohlwing Rd.	Addison	IL	60101	630-495-2010	
Web: www.totalstonesolutions.com					
Weisshouse 324 S Highland Ave	Pittsburgh	PA	15206	412-441-8888	
Web: weisshouse.com					

291 FLOORING - RESILIENT

See Also Recycled Plastics Products p. 3057

Name / Address	City	State	Zip	Phone	Fax
American Biltrite Inc 57 River St.	Wellesley Hills	MA	02481	781-237-6655	237-6880
OTC: ABLT ■ *Web:* www.ambilt.com					
American Floor Products Company Inc 7977 Cessna Ave	Gaithersburg	MD	20879	800-342-0424	987-0422*
**Fax Area Code:* 301 ■ *TF:* 800-342-0424 ■ *Web:* www.afco-usa.com					
Ari Products Inc 102 Gaither Dr Ste 3	Mount Laurel	NJ	08054	856-234-0757	
Web: www.ariproducts.com					
Armstrong World Industries Inc 2500 Columbia Ave	Lancaster	PA	17603	717-397-0611	396-6133*
NYSE: AWI ■ **Fax:* Hum Res ■ *TF Cust Svc:* 800-233-3823 ■ *Web:* www.armstrong.com					
Buchanan Hardwoods Inc 600 Baptist Line Rd	Aliceville	AL	35442	205-373-8710	
Web: www.buchananhardwoods.com					
Chiro Inc 2260 S Vista Ave	Bloomington	CA	92316	909-879-1160	
Web: www.mrcleansystems.com					
Classic Floors Inc 13725 S Mur Len Rd.	Olathe	KS	66062	913-780-2171	
Web: www.classicfloors.com					
Congoleum Corp 3500 Quakerridge Rd PO Box 3127	Mercerville	NJ	08619	609-584-3000	584-3521
TF: 800-274-3266 ■ *Web:* www.congoleum.com					
Country Floors Inc 15 E 16th St	New York	NY	10003	212-627-8300	242-1604
Web: www.countryfloors.com					
De Ruijter int Usa 120 Harvest Dr.	Coldwater	OH	45828	419-678-3909	
Web: www.deruijterusa.com					
DFS Flooring Inc 15651 Saticoy St	Van Nuys	CA	91406	818-374-5200	
Web: www.dfsflooring.com					
Expanko Inc 180 Gordon Dr Ste 113	Exton	PA	19341	800-345-6202	363-0735*
**Fax Area Code:* 610 ■ *TF:* 800-345-6202 ■ *Web:* www.expanko.com					
Floor Seal Technology Inc 1005 Ames Ave	Milpitas	CA	95035	408-436-8181	
Web: floorsealadmin.wpengine.com					
Florida Brick & Clay Company Inc (FBC) 1708 Turkey Creek Rd	Plant City	FL	33567	813-754-1521	754-5469
Web: www.floridabrickandclay.com					
Forbo Flooring Systems 8 Maplewood Dr Humboldt Industrial Pk	Hazleton	PA	18202	800-842-7839	450-0258*
**Fax Area Code:* 570 ■ **Fax:* Cust Svc ■ *TF Cust Svc:* 800-842-7839 ■ *Web:* www.forbo.com/flooring/en-us					
Formica Corp 10155 Reading Rd.	Cincinnati	OH	45241	513-786-3400	
TF: 800-367-6422 ■ *Web:* www.formica.com					
Fryer-Knowles Inc 205 S Dawson St	Seattle	WA	98108	206-767-7710	
TF: 800-544-6052 ■ *Web:* www.fryerk.com					
Hambro Forest Products Inc 445 Elk Valley Rd	Crescent City	CA	95531	707-464-6131	464-9375
Interior Specialists Inc 1630 Faraday Ave	Carlsbad	CA	92008	760-929-6700	
Web: www.isidc.com					
JTJ Commercial Interiors Inc 200 Shady Grove Rd.	Nashville	TN	37214	615-872-9363	
Web: jtjcommercialinteriors.com					
Leewens Corp 630 Seventh Ave PO Box 2549	Kirkland	WA	98033	425-827-7667	
Web: www.leewens.com					
Mannington Mills Inc 75 Mannington Mills Rd.	Salem	NJ	08079	856-935-3000	339-6124
TF Cust Svc: 800-356-6787 ■ *Web:* www.mannington.com					
Natco Products Corp 155 Brookside Ave.	West Warwick	RI	02893	401-828-0300	823-7670
Pergo Inc 3128 Highwoods Blvd Ste 100	Raleigh	NC	27604	800-337-3746	
TF: 800-337-3746 ■ *Web:* na.pergo.com					
Pionite Decorative Surfaces 1 Pionite Rd	Auburn	ME	04210	207-784-9111	
Web: www.pionite.com					
RCA Rubber Co 1833 E Market St	Akron	OH	44305	330-784-1291	794-6446
TF: 800-321-2340 ■ *Web:* www.rcarubber.com					
Regupol America 33 Keystone Dr.	Lebanon	PA	17042	800-537-8737	675-2199*
**Fax Area Code:* 717 ■ *TF:* 800-537-8737 ■ *Web:* www.regupol.com					
Roppe Corp 1602 N Union St.	Fostoria	OH	44830	419-435-8546	435-1056
TF: 800-537-9527 ■ *Web:* www.roppe.com					
Stonhard Inc 1000 E Pk Ave	Maple Shade	NJ	08052	856-779-7500	
TF Cust Svc: 800-854-0310 ■ *Web:* www.stonhard.com					
Sun Interiors Ltd 2329 Severn Ave	Metairie	LA	70001	504-833-8104	
Web: suninteriors.com					
Superior Mfg Group 5655 W 73rd St	Chicago	IL	60638	708-458-4600	458-4730
TF: 800-621-2802 ■ *Web:* www.notrax.com					
Surface Shields Inc 10457 163rd Pl	Orland Park	IL	60467	708-226-9810	226-9817
TF: 800-754-9685 ■ *Web:* www.surfaceshields.com					
Synthetic Turf Resources 809 Kenner St	Dalton	GA	30721	706-272-4200	
Web: syntheticturfresources.com					
Tarkett Inc 1001 Yamaska St E	Farnham	QC	J2N1J7	450-293-3173	293-8489
TF: 800-363-9276 ■ *Web:* www.tarkettna.com					
Vintage Design Inc 22895 Eastpark Dr	Yorba Linda	CA	92887	714-974-4822	
Web: www.vintagedesigninc.com					

292 FLORISTS

See Also Flowers-by-Wire Services p. 2291; Garden Centers p. 2349

Name / Address	City	State	Zip	Phone	Fax
1-800-Flowers.com Inc 1 Old Country Rd Ste 500	Carle Place	NY	11514	516-237-6000	
NASDAQ: FLWS ■ *TF:* 800-356-9377 ■ *Web:* ww30.1800flowers.com					

	City	State	Zip	Phone	Fax
A Few of My Favorite Things 108 N Sixth St *Web:* afewofmyfavoritethingsflowershop.com	Wyoming	IL	61491	309-695-9966	
Abbey Party Rents 411 Allan St *Web:* www.abbeyrentssf.com	Daly City	CA	94014	415-715-6900	
Alaska Experience Theater & Gift Shop 333 W Fourth Ave *Web:* alaskaexperiencetheatre.com	Anchorage	AK	99501	907-272-9076	
Angel Plants Inc 560 W Deer Park Ave *Web:* www.angelplants.com	Dix Hills	NY	11746	631-242-7788	
Arrow Florist & Park Avenue Greenhouses Inc 757 Pk Ave *TF:* 800-556-7097 ■ *Web:* www.arrowflorist.net	Cranston	RI	02910	401-785-1900	785-4120
Artistic Ribbon & Novelty Company Inc 22 W 21st St Fl 3 *Web:* www.artisticribbon.com	New York	NY	10010	212-255-4224	
Ashland Addison Florist Co 1640 W Fulton St *Web:* www.ashaddflorist.com	Chicago	IL	60612	312-432-1800	
Astoria-Pacific Inc 15130 SE 82nd Dr *TF:* 800-536-3111 ■ *Web:* www.astoria-pacific.com	Clackamas	OR	97015	503-657-3010	
Avila Retail Development & Management LLC 5001 Ellison St NE *Web:* www.avilaretail.com	Albuquerque	NM	87109	505-341-3753	
Bachman's Inc 6010 Lyndale Ave S *TF:* 888-222-4626 ■ *Web:* www.bachmans.com	Minneapolis	MN	55419	612-861-7311	861-7748
Baisch & Skinner Inc 2721 Lasalle St *TF:* 800-523-0013 ■ *Web:* www.baischandskinner.com	Saint Louis	MO	63104	314-664-1212	
Barry-owen Co Inc 5625 Smithway St *TF:* 800-682-6682 ■ *Web:* www.barryowen.com	Los Angeles	CA	90040	323-724-4800	724-4996
Bert R Hybels Inc 3322 Grand Prairie Rd *Web:* www.hybels.com	Kalamazoo	MI	49006	269-382-4921	
Billy Heroman's Flowerland 10812 N Harrell'S Ferry Rd *Web:* www.billyheromans.com	Baton Rouge	LA	70816	225-272-7673	
Birthday Direct 120 Commerce St *TF:* 888-491-9185 ■ *Web:* www.birthdaydirect.com	Muscle Shoals	AL	35661	256-381-0310	
BloomNation LLC 8889 W Olympic Blvd *TF:* 877-702-5666 ■ *Web:* www.bloomnation.com	Beverly Hills	CA	90211	877-702-5666	
Blossom Bucket, The 13305 Wooster St NW	North Lawrence	OH	44666	330-834-2551	
Boesen the Florist 3422 Beaver Ave *TF:* 800-274-4761 ■ *Web:* www.boesen.com	Des Moines	IA	50310	515-274-4761	
Boite a Fleur De Laval Inc La 3266 Boul Sainte-Rose *TF:* 800-784-3495 ■ *Web:* alaboiteafleurs.com	Laval	QC	H7P4K8	450-622-0341	
Bonnett Wholesale Florists 119 Eigth St E *Web:* www.bonnettwholesale.com	Milan	IL	61264	309-787-4401	
Booman Floral 2302 Bautista Ave *Web:* www.boomanfloral.com	Vista	CA	92084	760-630-4170	
Brian's Toys W730 State Rd 35 *Web:* www.brianstoys.com	Fountain City	WI	54629	608-687-7572	
Bunches 14 1/2 N Santa Cruz Ave *Web:* buncheslosgatos.com	Los Gatos	CA	95030	408-395-5451	
Burchell Nursery Inc, The 12000 Hwy 120 *TF:* 800-828-8733 ■ *Web:* www.burchellnursery.com	Oakdale	CA	95361	209-845-8733	847-0284
Cactus Flower Florists 10822 N Scottsdale Rd **Fax:* Sales ■ *TF:* 800-922-2887 ■ *Web:* www.cactusflower.com	Scottsdale	AZ	85254	480-483-9200	483-9200*
Calendarscom LLC 6411 Burleson Rd *Web:* www.calendars.com	Austin	TX	78744	512-386-7220	
Callaway Partners LLC 600 Galleria Pkwy SE Ste 1400 *Web:* www.warbirdconsulting.com	Atlanta	GA	30339	404-496-5230	
Calyx Flowers 6655 Shelburne Rd *Web:* www.calyxflowers.com	Shelburne	VT	05482	802-985-3001	985-1304
Canada Flowers 4073 Longhurst Ave *TF:* 888-705-9999 ■ *Web:* www.canadaflowers.ca	Niagara Falls	ON	L2E6G5	905-354-2713	
Cathy's Concepts Inc 6900 E 30th St *Web:* www.cathysconcepts.com	Indianapolis	IN	46219	317-860-1700	
Century City Flower Mart 9551 W Pico Blvd *Web:* www.centurycityflowermarket.com	Los Angeles	CA	90035	310-277-6737	
City Florist of Redlands 122 Cajon St *Web:* cityfloristofredlands.com	Redlands	CA	92373	909-793-4141	
Collectors Alliance Inc 1942 Swarthmore Ave *Web:* www.collectorsalliance.com	Lakewood	NJ	08701	732-730-3580	
Colwell Flower Shop & Wedding Boutique 2448 Brightwood Rd Se *Web:* www.colwellflowershop.com	New Philadelphia	OH	44663	330-339-1661	
Connell's Map Lee Flowers & Gifts 2408 E Main St *TF:* 800-790-8980 ■ *Web:* www.cmlflowers.com	Bexley	OH	43209	614-237-8653	
Continental Flowers Inc 8101 NW 21 St *Web:* www.continentalflowers.com	Miami	FL	33122	305-594-4214	
Country Lane Flower Shop 729 S Michigan Ave *TF:* 800-764-7673 ■ *Web:* www.countrylaneflowers.com	Howell	MI	48843	517-546-1111	
Danson Decor Inc 3425 Douglas B Floreani *TF:* 800-363-1865 ■ *Web:* www.dansondecor.com	St Laurent	QC	H4S1Y6	514-335-2435	
Dead Ringer Putter Co 228 W Baltimore Ave	Clifton Heights	PA	19018	610-284-4653	
Dejuan Stroud Inc 348 W 36th St *Web:* www.dejuanstroud.com	New York	NJ	10018	732-224-8333	
DeLoache Flowers 2927 Millwood Ave *Web:* deloacheflowershop.com	Columbia	SC	29205	803-256-1681	
Dr Delphinium Designs & Events 5806 W Lovers Ln & Tollway *TF:* 800-783-8790 ■ *Web:* www.drdelphinium.com	Dallas	TX	75225	214-522-9911	525-1240
Eastern Floral & Gift Shop 818 Butterworth St SW *TF:* 800-494-2202 ■ *Web:* www.easternfloral.com	Grand Rapids	MI	49504	616-949-2200	
Eufloria Flowers 885 Mesa Rd *Web:* www.eufloriaflowers.com	Nipomo	CA	93444	805-929-4683	
Everbloom Growers Inc 20450 SW 248th St	Homestead	FL	33031	305-248-1478	
Felly's Flowers Inc PO Box 6620 *TF:* 800-993-7673 ■ *Web:* www.fellys.net	Madison	WI	53716	800-993-7673	
Flower City Communications LLC 1848 Lyell Ave *Web:* flowercitycommunications.com	Rochester	NY	14606	585-458-5350	
Flower Factory Inc 5655 Whipple Ave NW *Web:* www.flowerfactory.com	North Canton	OH	44720	330-494-0010	
Flower Patch Inc 4370 S 300 W *TF General:* 888-865-6858 ■ *Web:* www.flowerpatch.com	Murray	UT	84107	801-747-2824	263-7896
Flower Pot Florists 2314 N Broadway St *TF:* 800-824-7792 ■ *Web:* www.knoxvilleflowerpot.com	Knoxville	TN	37917	865-523-5121	
Flowerbud.com PO Box 761 *Web:* www.flowerbud.com	Lake Oswego	OR	97034	503-697-1790	
Flowers & Fancies-greenlea 11404 Cronridge Dr *Web:* www.flowersandfancies.com	Owings Mills	MD	21117	410-653-0600	
Flowers by Anthony Inc 3300 SW Ninth St Ste 1 *Web:* flowersbyanthony.com	Des Moines	IA	50315	515-288-6789	
Flowers By Burton Inc 426 Old Walt Whitman Rd *Web:* flowersbyburton.com	Melville	NY	11747	631-424-3377	
Flowers by Sleeman for All Seasons & Reasons Ltd 1201 Memorial Rd *TF:* 800-400-4023 ■ *Web:* flowersbysleeman.com	Houghton	MI	49931	906-482-4023	
Flowers Chemical Laboratories Inc 481 Newburyport Ave *Web:* www.flowerslabs.com	Altamonte Springs	FL	32701	407-339-5984	
Formaggio Kitchen on Line LLC 244 Huron Ave *TF:* 888-212-3224 ■ *Web:* www.formaggiokitchen.com	Cambridge	MA	02138	617-354-4750	
Fossil Creek Nursery Inc 7029 S College Ave *Web:* www.fossilcreek.com	Fort Collins	CO	80525	970-226-4924	
Foster City Flowers & Gifts 1160 Chess Dr Ste 1 *TF:* 800-970-7673 ■ *Web:* www.fostercity-flowers.com	Foster City	CA	94404	650-573-6607	578-6756
Frantz Wholesale Nursery LLC 12161 Delaware Rd *Web:* frantznursery.com	Hickman	CA	95323	209-874-1459	
Freeman's Flowers & Event Consultants 2934 Duniven Cir *TF:* 800-846-3104 ■ *Web:* www.freemansflowers.com	Amarillo	TX	79109	806-355-4451	
Fruit Co, The 2900 Van Horn Dr *TF:* 800-387-3100 ■ *Web:* www.thefruitcompany.com	Hood River	OR	97031	541-387-3100	
FTD Inc 3113 Woodcreek Dr **Fax Area Code:* 630 ■ *TF Cust Svc:* 800-736-3383 ■ *Web:* www.ftd.com	Downers Grove	IL	60515	800-736-3383	719-6170*
Gainans Flowers 1211 24th St W Ste 3 *Web:* www.gainans.com	Billings	MT	59102	406-652-1650	
Galaxy Glass 208 N W Blvd	Newfield	NJ	08344	856-697-3934	
Gift of Life Foundation 3861 Research Park Dr *TF:* 866-500-5801 ■ *Web:* giftoflifemichigan.org	Ann Arbor	MI	48108	734-973-1577	
Gifts for You LLC 2425 Curtiss St *TF:* 866-443-8748 ■ *Web:* www.giftsforyounow.com	Downers Grove	IL	60515	630-771-0095	
Giftwares Co 436 First Ave *Web:* www.giftwaresco.com	Royersford	PA	19468	610-792-8177	
Golden Flowers 2600 NW 79th Ave *Web:* terrafloristvancouver.com	Doral	FL	33122	305-599-0193	
Goldin & Company Ltd 263 Stanley St	Winnipeg	MB	R3A0W8	204-982-1188	
Greeters of Hawaii Ltd 300 Rodgers Blvd Ste 266 *TF:* 800-366-8559 ■ *Web:* www.greetersofhawaii.com	Honolulu	HI	96819	808-836-0161	833-7756
Grower Direct Fresh Cut Flowers 6303 Wagner Rd *TF:* 877-277-4787 ■ *Web:* www.growerdirect.com	Edmonton	AB	T6E4N4	780-436-7774	436-3336
Guggisberg Cheese Inc 5060 SR- 557 *Web:* www.babyswiss.com	Millersburg	OH	44654	330-893-2500	
H & P Sales Inc 2022 Victory Dr *Web:* www.handpsalesinc.com	Vista	CA	92084	760-727-2614	
Hardin's Florist Supply 329 W Bowman Ave *TF:* 800-672-8226 ■ *Web:* www.hardins.com	Liberty	NC	27298	336-622-3035	
Higdon Florist 201 E 32nd St *TF:* 800-641-4726 ■ *Web:* www.higdonflorist.com	Joplin	MO	64804	417-624-7171	
Hillcrest Garden 95 W Century Rd *TF:* 800-437-7000 ■ *Web:* hillcrestgarden.com	Paramus	NJ	07652	201-599-3030	
Howard Bros Florists 8700 S Pennsylvania Ave *TF:* 800-648-0524 ■ *Web:* www.howardbrothersflorist.com	Oklahoma City	OK	73159	405-632-4747	632-1672
Jacobson Floral Supply Inc 500 Albany St *Web:* www.jacobsonfloral.com	Boston	MA	02118	617-426-4287	
John Wolf Florist 6228 Waters Ave *TF:* 800-944-6435 ■ *Web:* www.johnwolfflorist.com	Savannah	GA	31406	912-352-9843	
Johns Greenhouse & Florist Shop 517 Copeland St *Web:* johnsgreenhouses-florist.com	Brockton	MA	02301	508-588-0955	
Johnston the Florist Inc 14179 Lincoln Way *TF:* 800-356-9371 ■ *Web:* www.johnstontheflorist.com	North Huntingdon	PA	15642	412-751-2821	
Jon's Nursery Inc 24546 Nursery Way *TF:* 800-322-4289 ■ *Web:* jonsnursery.com	Eustis	FL	32736	352-357-4289	
Jonathan Club Charitable Fund 545 S Figueroa St *Web:* www.jc.org	Los Angeles	CA	90071	213-624-0881	
Joyce Florist 2729 S Hampton Rd *TF:* 800-527-1520 ■ *Web:* www.joyceflorist.com	Dallas	TX	75224	214-942-1776	
KaBloomcom Ltd 305 Harvard St *Web:* www.kabloom.com	Brookline	MA	02446	617-730-9966	
Ken's Flower Shop 140 W S Boundary St *TF:* 800-253-0100 ■ *Web:* www.kensflowers.com	Perrysburg	OH	43551	419-874-1333	
KITSON 115 S Robertson Blvd	Los Angeles	CA	90048	310-859-2652	
Krueger Wholesale Florist Inc 10706 Tesch Ln *Web:* kruegerwholesale.com	Rothschild	WI	54474	715-359-7202	

Phone Fax

Kuhn Flowers Inc 3802 Beach Blvd ....Jacksonville FL 32207 904-398-8601
TF: 800-458-5846 ■ *Web:* kuhnflowers.com

La Canada Flowers
5971 University Ave Ste 312......................San Diego CA 92115 619-582-5021
Web: www.lacanadaflowers.com

Las Vegas Floral & Plant Wholesale 2404 We ...... Las Vegas NV 89102 702-221-1220
Web: floracouture.com

Lester's Florist Inc 2100 Bull St ....Savannah GA 31401 912-233-6066
TF: 800-841-1103 ■ *Web:* www.lestersflorist.com

Lewistown Florist Store
129 S Main St Ste 200..........................Lewistown PA 17044 717-248-9683
Web: www.lewistownflorist.com

Lloyd's Florist 9216 Preston Hwy...................Louisville KY 40229 502-968-5428 964-5696
TF: 800-264-1825 ■ *Web:* www.lloydsflorist.net

Locker's Florist 1640 S 83rd St................... West Allis WI 53214 414-276-7673
Web: www.lockersflorist.com

Luurtsema Sales Inc 6672 Ctr Industrial Dr............ Jenison MI 49428 616-669-9301
Web: luurtsema.com

Martina's Flowers & Gifts 3830 Washington Rd .... Augusta GA 30907 706-863-7172
TF: 800-927-1204 ■ *Web:* www.martinas.com

Mayesh Wholesale Florist Inc
5401 W 104th St..............................Los Angeles CA 90045 310-348-4921
TF: 888-462-9374 ■ *Web:* www.mayesh.com

Mellano & Co 766 Wall St........................Los Angeles CA 90014 213-622-0796
TF: 888-635-5266 ■ *Web:* www.mellano.com

Metropolitan Plant & Flower Exchange
2125 Fletcher Ave.................................Fort Lee NJ 07024 201-944-1050
TF: 800-638-7613 ■ *Web:* www.metroplantexchange.com

Midwest Trading Horticultural Supplies Inc
48w805 Il Rt 64 .... Maple Park IL 60151 630-365-1990
TF: 800-546-9522 ■ *Web:* www.midwest-trading.com

Milgro Nursery LLC 1085 Victoria Ave ....Oxnard CA 93030 805-985-0855

Misco Home and Garden 100 S Washington Ave .... Dunellen NJ 08812 732-752-7500 752-6305
Web: www.miscohomeandgarden.com

Missouri Office Systems & Supplies
941 W 141st Terrace Ste B.......................Kansas City MO 64145 816-761-5152 761-5170

Nakase Bros Wholesale Nursery
9441 Krepp Dr ....Huntington Beach CA 92646 714-962-6604
TF: 800-747-4388 ■ *Web:* www.nakasebros.com

Nanz & Kraft Florists Inc
141 Breckenridge Ln.............................Louisville KY 40207 502-897-6551 897-2082
TF: 800-897-6551 ■ *Web:* www.nanzandkraft.com

National Floral Supply Inc
3825 LeonaRdtown Rd Ste 4.........................Waldorf MD 20601 301-932-7600
TF: 800-932-2772 ■ *Web:* www.flowersonbase.com

Niagara Helicopters Ltd
3731 Victoria Ave..............................Niagara Falls ON L2E6V5 905-357-5672
TF: 800-281-8034 ■ *Web:* www.niagarahelicopters.com

Norton's Flowers & Gifts
2900 Washtenaw Ave .... Ypsilanti MI 48197 734-434-2700
TF: 800-682-8667 ■ *Web:* www.nortonsflowers.com

Nottawaseppi Huron Band of Potawatomi's FireKeepers Development Authority
11177 E Michigan Ave ....Battle Creek MI 49014 877-353-8777
TF: 877-353-8777 ■ *Web:* www.firekeeperscasino.com

Office Playground Inc
715 Southpoint Blvd Ste 100 .... Petaluma CA 94954 415-483-1196
TF: 800-458-1948

Performance Plants Inc 700 Gardiners Rd .... Kingston ON K7M3X9 613-545-0390
Web: www.performanceplants.com

Phillip's Flower Shops Inc 524 N Cass Ave.......... Westmont IL 60559 630-719-5200 719-2292
TF: 800-356-7257 ■ *Web:* www.800florals.com

Phoenix Flower Shops
5733 E Thomas Rd Ste 4 ....Scottsdale AZ 85251 480-289-4000
TF: 888-311-0404 ■ *Web:* www.phoenixflowershops.com

Plant Interscapes Inc 6436 Babcock Rd...............San Antonio TX 78249 281-304-7190
Web: www.plantinterscapes.com

Platon Craft & Floral Inc
1327 N Carolan Ave ....Burlingame CA 94010 650-373-7888

Pleasant Nursery Inc 4234 W Wabash ....Springfield IL 62711 217-522-2222
Web: pleasant-nursery.com

Pope Scientific Inc
351 N Dekora Woods Blvd ....Saukville WI 53080 262-268-9300
Web: www.popeinc.com

Primitives by Kathy Inc
1817 William Penn Way...........................Lancaster PA 17601 866-295-2849
TF: 866-295-2849 ■ *Web:* www.primitivesbykathy.com

Proflowers.com 4840 Eastgate Mall..................San Diego CA 92121 800-580-2913
TF: 800-580-2913 ■ *Web:* www.proflowers.com

Provide Commerce Inc 4840 Eastgate Mall...........San Diego CA 92121 858-729-2800 909-4201
TF Cust Svc: 800-776-3569

Royal Expressions Flowers & Gifts
131 S Ln St.......................................Blissfield MI 49228 517-486-4351

Royer's Flowers Inc 201 Rohrerstown Rd ....Lancaster PA 17603 717-397-0376
Web: www.royers.com

Russell Florist Inc 5001 Gravois Ave............... Saint Louis MO 63116 314-351-4676 351-6842
Web: russellfloriststlouis.net

Sawyer Nursery Inc 5401 Port Sheldon St...........Hudsonville MI 49426 616-669-9094
TF: 888-378-7800 ■ *Web:* www.sawyernursery.com

Schroeder's Flowerland Inc
1530 S Webster Ave .... Green Bay WI 54301 920-436-6363
TF: 800-236-4769 ■ *Web:* www.schroederflowers.com

Schubert Nursery Inc 7715 Gorman Dr ....Browns Summit NC 27214 336-656-1981

Shibata Floral Company Supplies
620 Brannan St..............................San Francisco CA 94107 415-495-8611
Web: www.shibatafc.com

Shirl K Floral Designs 2701 Pontoon Rd............Granite City IL 62040 618-797-6210
Web: www.shirlkfloral.com

Smith Southwestern Inc 1850 N Rosemont ....Mesa AZ 85205 480-854-9545
TF: 800-783-3909 ■ *Web:* www.smith-southwestern.com

Strange's Florist Inc
3313 Mechanicsville Pk ....Richmond VA 23223 804-321-2200
TF: 800-421-4070 ■ *Web:* stranges.com

Success Promotions 14304 S Outer 40 Rd ....Chesterfield MO 63017 314-878-1999
Web: www.successpromotions.com

Phone Fax

Sunwest Silver Company Inc
324 Lomas Blvd NW.......................... Albuquerque NM 87102 505-243-3781
TF: 800-771-3781 ■ *Web:* www.sunwestsilver.com

Swenson & Silacci Flowers 110 John St .... Salinas CA 93901 831-424-2725
Web: www.onlineflowers.com

Technical Glass Products Inc
881 Callendar Blvd.............................Painesville OH 44077 440-639-6399
Web: www.technicalglass.com

Thirstystone Resources Inc
1304 Corporate Dr ....Gainesville TX 76240 940-668-6793 668-6207
TF: 800-829-6888 ■ *Web:* www.thirstystone.com

Thurbers of Richmond Inc
7324 Port Side Dr..............................Midlothian VA 23112 804-639-5770

Tipton & Hurst Inc 1801 N Grant St................Little Rock AR 72207 501-666-3333
TF: 800-666-3333 ■ *Web:* www.tiptonhurst.com

Triple Oaks Nursery & Herb Garden
2359 Delsea Dr................................Franklinville NJ 08322 856-694-4272
Web: www.tripleoaks.com

United Nations Assoc Information & Un Icef Center
1403B Addison St...............................Berkeley CA 94704 510-849-1752
Web: unausaeastbay.org

US Retail Flowers Inc
810 S 12th St PO Box 330 .... Lebanon PA 17042 717-273-4090
Web: royers.com

USA Bouquet Company Inc, The 1500 NW 95 Ave .... Miami FL 33172 786-437-6500
Web: www.usabq.com

Valley Flowers Inc 3675 Foothill Rd ....Carpinteria CA 93013 805-684-6651
Web: valleyflowers.com

Van Belle Nursery Inc 34825 Hallert Rd ....Abbotsford BC V3G1R3 604-853-3415
Web: www.vanbelle.com

Veldkamp's Flowers 9501 W Colfax Ave............ Lakewood CO 80215 303-232-2673
TF: 800-247-3730 ■ *Web:* www.veldkampsflowers.com

Villere's Florist 750 Martin Behrman Ave...............Metairie LA 70005 504-833-3716
TF: 800-845-5373 ■ *Web:* www.villeresflowers.com

Viviano Flower Shop
32050 Harper Ave........................Saint Clair Shores MI 48082 586-293-0227
TF: 800-848-4266 ■ *Web:* viviano.com

Vogue Flowers & Gifts Ltd 1114 N Blvd............ Richmond VA 23230 804-353-9600
Web: www.vogueflowers.com

Warners Florist 179 S Montgomery St........... Hollidaysburg PA 16648 814-695-9431

Washington Floral Service Inc 2701 S 35th St......... Tacoma WA 98409 253-472-8343
TF: 800-351-5515 ■ *Web:* www.washingtonfloral.com

Watanabe Floral Inc 1607 Hart St.................Honolulu HI 96817 808-832-9360
TF: 888-832-9360 ■ *Web:* www.watanabefloral.com

Westbrook Floral Ltd 109 Av Lindsay .... Dorval QC H9P2S6 514-636-1255
Web: westbrookfloral.com

Winston Bros Inc 131 Newbury St ....Boston MA 02116 617-541-1100
TF: 800-457-4901 ■ *Web:* www.winstonflowers.com

Winward International Inc 3089 Whipple Rd.........Union City CA 94587 510-487-8686
TF: 800-888-8898 ■ *Web:* www.winwardsilks.com

Wondertreats Inc 2200 Lapham Dr .... Modesto CA 95354 209-521-8881
Web: www.wondertreats.com

Worrell Corp 305 S Post Rd.......................Indianapolis IN 46219 317-895-9708
TF: 800-297-9599 ■ *Web:* worrellcorp.com

293 FLOWERS & NURSERY STOCK - WHOL

See Also Horticultural Products Growers p. 2482

Phone Fax

Allstate Floral & Craft Inc 14038 Park Pl ....Cerritos CA 90703 562-926-2302 926-8613
TF: 800-433-4056 ■ *Web:* allstatefloral.com

Arazoza Brothers Corp 15901 SW 242nd St .... Homestead FL 33031 305-246-3223
Web: www.arazozabrothers.com

Atwoods Distributing Inc 5400 Owen K Garriott............Enid OK 73703 580-233-3702
Web: www.atwoods.com

Ball Horticultural Co 622 Town Rd .... West Chicago IL 60185 630-231-3600 231-3605
TF: 800-879-2255 ■ *Web:* www.ballhort.com

Blumen Gardens Inc 403 Edward St................ Sycamore IL 60178 815-895-3737
Web: blumengardens.com

Central Garden & Pet Co
1340 Treat Blvd Ste 600.........................Walnut Creek CA 94597 925-948-4000
NASDAQ: CENT ■ *Web:* www.central.com

Claymore C Sieck Wholesale Florist
311 E Chase St....................................Baltimore MD 21202 410-685-4660 685-1547
TF: 800-624-7134 ■ *Web:* www.sieck.com

Cleveland Plant & Flower Co
12920 Corporate Dr .... Cleveland OH 44130 216-898-3500
TF: 888-231-7569 ■ *Web:* www.cpfco.com

Country Silk Inc 100 S Washington Ave............... Dunellen NJ 08812 732-752-5556 752-7550
Web: www.countrysilk.com

Cut Flower Wholesale Inc 2122 Faulkner Rd NE ....Atlanta GA 30324 404-320-1619 634-7922
Web: www.cutflower.com

Delaware Valley Wholesale Florist Inc (DVWF)
520 Mantua Blvd N................................Sewell NJ 08080 856-468-7000 464-2772
TF: 800-676-1212 ■ *Web:* www.dvwf.com

Denver Wholesale Florists Co 4800 Dahlia St...........Denver CO 80216 303-399-0970 376-3123
TF: 800-829-8280 ■ *Web:* www.dwfwholesale.com

Distinctive Designs International Inc
120 Sibley Dr .... Russellville AL 35654 256-332-7390
TF: 800-243-4787 ■ *Web:* www.distinctivedesigns.com

Dodds & Eder Inc 221 S St.........................Oyster Bay NY 11771 516-922-4412
Web: doddsandeder.com

Esprit Miami 3043 NW 107th Ave .... Miami FL 33172 305-591-2244 591-2603
TF: 800-327-2320 ■ *Web:* www.espritmiami.com

Florist Distributing Inc 2403 Bell Ave..............Des Moines IA 50321 515-243-5228 282-9241
TF: 800-373-3741 ■ *Web:* www.fdionline.net

Holmberg Farms Inc 13430 Hobson Simmons Rd.........Lithia FL 33547 800-282-3562
TF: 800-282-3562 ■ *Web:* www.holmbergfarms.com

Johnson Nursery Corp 985 Johnson Nursery Rd..........Willard NC 28478 910-285-7861
Web: www.johnson-nursery.com

	City	State	Zip	Phone	Fax
Karthauser & Sons Inc W 147 N 11100 Fond du Lac Ave *TF:* 800-338-8620 ■ *Web:* www.karthauser.net	Germantown	WI	53022	262-255-7815	255-6920
Kennicott Bros 452 N Ashland Ave *TF:* 866-346-2826 ■ *Web:* www.kennicott.com	Chicago	IL	60622	312-492-8200	492-8202
L & L Nursery Supply Co Inc 2552 Shenandoah Way *TF:* 800-624-2517 ■ *Web:* www.llsupply.net	San Bernardino	CA	92407	909-591-0461	
Magnetecs Corp 10524 La Cienega Blvd *Web:* www.magnetecs.com	Inglewood	CA	90304	310-670-7700	
Monterey Bay Nursery Inc 748 San Miguel Canyon Rd *Web:* www.montereybaynsy.com	Watsonville	CA	95077	831-724-6361	
Norben Import Corp 99 S Newman St *Web:* www.larksilk.com	Hackensack	NJ	07601	201-487-0855	487-0787
Oklahoma Flower Market Inc, The 36 N Broadway Cir	Oklahoma City	OK	73103	405-232-3143	
Pennock Co 7135 Colonial Ln *Web:* www.pennock.com	Pennsauken	NJ	08109	215-492-7900	951-6498
Pittsburgh Cut Flower Co 1901 Liberty Ave *TF:* 800-837-2837 ■ *Web:* www.pittsburghcutflower.com	Pittsburgh	PA	15222	412-355-7000	391-0649
Rexius Forest By-Products Inc 1275 Bailey Hill Rd *Web:* www.rexius.com	Eugene	OR	97402	541-342-1835	343-4802
Roman J Claprood Co 242 N Grant Ave *Web:* rjclaprood.com	Columbus	OH	43215	614-221-5515	
Roy Houff Co, The 6200 S Oak Pk Ave *Web:* royhouff.com	Chicago	IL	60638	773-586-8666	586-8790
Sylvan Nursery Inc 1028 Horseneck Rd *Web:* sylvannursery.com	Westport	MA	02790	508-636-4573	
Tapscott's 1403 E 18th St *TF:* 800-626-1922 ■ *Web:* www.tapfloral.com	Owensboro	KY	42303	270-684-2308	683-3702
Teters Floral Products Inc 1425 S Lillian Ave *TF:* 800-999-5996 ■ *Web:* www.teters.com	Bolivar	MO	65613	417-326-7654	326-8061
Teufel Nursery Inc 3431 NW John Olsen Pl *Web:* www.teufellandscape.com	Hillsboro	OR	97124	503-646-1111	646-1112
Van Well Nursery 2821 Grant Rd *TF:* 800-572-1553 ■ *Web:* www.vanwell.net	East Wenatchee	WA	98802	509-886-8189	886-0294
Van Zyverden Inc 8079 Van Zyverden Rd *TF:* 800-332-2852 ■ *Web:* www.vanzyverden.com	Meridian	MS	39305	601-679-8274	679-8039
W & E Radtke Inc W168 N12276 Century Ln *Web:* weradtke.com	Germantown	WI	53022	262-253-1412	
Zieger & Sons Inc 6215 Ardleigh St *TF:* 800-752-2003 ■ *Web:* www.zieger.com	Philadelphia	PA	19138	215-438-7060	

294 FLOWERS-BY-WIRE SERVICES

	City	State	Zip	Phone	Fax
Teleflora Inc 11444 Olympic Blvd *Web:* www.teleflora.com	Los Angeles	CA	90064	310-966-5700	966-3612

295 FOIL & LEAF - METAL

	City	State	Zip	Phone	Fax
Accurate Metal Fabricating 1657 N Kostner Ave *Web:* www.accuratemetalfab.com	Chicago	IL	60639	773-235-0400	
Action SuperAbrasive Products Inc 945 Greenbriar Pkwy *Web:* www.actionsuper.com	Brimfield	OH	44240	330-673-7333	
Ad-vance Magnetics Inc 625 Monroe St *Web:* www.advancemag.com	Rochester	IN	46975	574-223-3158	
Adamson Industries Corp 45 Research Dr *Web:* www.adamsonindustries.com	Haverhill	MA	01832	978-681-0370	
Advex Corp 121 Floyd Thompson Dr *Web:* www.advex.net	Hampton	VA	23666	757-865-0920	
AFC Finishing Systems Inc 250 Airport Pkwy *Web:* www.afc-ca.com	Oroville	CA	95965	530-533-8907	
Air Cycle Corp 2200 Ogden Ave Ste 100 *TF:* 800-909-9709 ■ *Web:* www.aircycle.com	Lisle	IL	60532	800-909-9709	
Alamo Industrial Inc 1502 East Walnut St **Fax Area Code:* 830 ■ *TF:* 800-356-6286 ■ *Web:* www.alamo-industrial.com	Seguin	TX	78155	800-356-6286	379-0864*
Alphi Manufacturing Inc 576 Beck St *Web:* www.alphimfg.com	Jonesville	MI	49250	517-849-9945	
American Alloy Fabrication Inc 2842 Jordan Ln Nw *Web:* www.americanalloy.com	Huntsville	AL	35816	256-837-6369	
American Products Inc (API) 13909 Lynmar Blvd *Web:* www.americanprod.com	Tampa	FL	33626	813-925-0144	
American Ramp Sales Co 601 S Mckinley Ave *Web:* www.americanrampcompany.com	Joplin	MO	64801	417-206-6816	
Analytical Industries Inc 2855 Metropolitan Pl *Web:* www.aii1.com	Pomona	CA	91767	909-392-6900	
API Foils Inc 329 New Brunswick Ave *Web:* www.apigroup.com	Rahway	NJ	07065	732-382-6800	
ARC Technology Solutions LLC 165 Ledge St Ste 4 *Web:* www.arcserv.com	Nashua	NH	03060	603-883-3027	
Architectural Brass Co 1130 Donald Lee Hollowell Pkwy Nw *Web:* www.architecturalbrass.com	Atlanta	GA	30318	404-351-0594	
Astro Manufacturing & Design Corp 34459 Curtis Blvd *Web:* www.astromfg.com	Eastlake	OH	44095	440-946-8171	
Automated Precision Inc 15000 Johns Hopkins Dr *Web:* www.apisensor.com	Rockville	MD	20850	240-268-0400	
Automotive Resources Inc 12775 Randolph Ridge Ln *TF:* 800-562-3250 ■ *Web:* www.ari-hetra.com	Manassas	VA	20109	703-359-6265	
Axton Inc 441 Derwent Pl Annacis Business Park *Web:* www.axton.ca	Delta	BC	V3M5Y9	604-522-2731	
B&G Equipment Company Inc 135 Region S Dr *TF:* 800-544-8811 ■ *Web:* www.bgequip.com	Jackson	GA	30233	678-688-5601	
Begneaud Manufacturing Inc 306 E Amedee Dr *Web:* www.begno.com	Lafayette	LA	70583	337-237-5069	
Ben O'neal Company Inc 3003 Tenth Ave *Web:* www.benonealcompany.com/home.html	Chattanooga	TN	37407	423-624-3359	
Binder Metal Products Inc 14909 S Broadway *Web:* www.bindermetal.com	Gardena	CA	90248	323-321-4835	
Bob's Barricades Inc 921 Shotgun Rd *Web:* www.bobsbarricades.com	Sunrise	FL	33326	954-423-2627	
Boston Barricade Company Inc 1151 19th St *Web:* www.bostonbarricade.com	Vero Beach	FL	32960	772-569-7202	
Brinkman International Group Inc 167 Ames St *Web:* www.brinkmanig.com	Rochester	NY	14611	585-235-4545	
Bromma Inc 2285 Durham Rd *Web:* www.bromma.com	Roxboro	NC	27573	919-471-4000	
Brudi Bolzoni Auramo Inc 17635 Hoffman Way *Web:* www.bolzoni-auramo.com	Homewood	IL	60430	708-957-8809	
Buff & Shine Manufacturing Inc 2139 E Del Amo Blvd *TF:* 800-659-2833 ■ *Web:* www.buffandshine.com	Compton	CA	90220	310-886-5111	
Buffalo Abrasives Inc 960 Erie Ave *Web:* www.buffaloabrasives.com	North Tonawanda	NY	14120	716-693-3856	
Busche Enterprise Division Inc 1563 E State Rd 8 *Web:* www.busche-cnc.com	Albion	IN	46701	260-636-7030	
BW Rogers Co 195 S Main St Ste 400 *Web:* www.bwrogers.com	Akron	OH	44308	330-315-3100	
C&C Metal Products Corp 456 Nordhoff Pl *Web:* www.ccmetal.com	Englewood	NJ	07631	201-569-7300	
CAM Innovation Inc 215 Philadelphia St *Web:* www.caminnovation.com	Hanover	PA	17331	717-637-5988	
Carter Enterprises Inc 119 W Main St *Web:* www.carterent.com	Arcadia	IN	46030	317-984-1497	
Catlow Inc 2750 US Rt 40 *Web:* catlow.com	Tipp City	OH	45371	937-898-3236	
CBR Laser Inc 340 Rt 116 W *Web:* www.cbrlaser.com	Plessisville	QC	G6L2Y2	819-362-9339	
Century 3-Plus LLC 2410 W Aero Park Ct *Web:* www.centinc.com	Traverse City	MI	49686	231-946-7500	
Chem-pak Inc 242 Corning Way *TF:* 800-336-9828 ■ *Web:* www.chem-pak.com	Martinsburg	WV	25405	304-262-1880	
Chemetal 39 O'Neil St *TF:* 800-807-7341 ■ *Web:* www.chmetal.com	EastHampton	MA	01027	413-529-0718	529-9898
Chicago Powdered Metal Products Co 9700 Waveland Ave *Web:* www.chipm.com	Franklin Park	IL	60131	847-678-2836	
Clark Technology Systems Inc 159 Harveys Ln *Web:* www.clarkts.com	Milton	PA	17847	570-742-1819	
Colliflower Inc 9320 Pulaski Hwy *Web:* www.colliflower.com	Baltimore	MD	21220	410-686-1200	
Columbiana Hi Tech LLC 1802 Fairfax Rd *Web:* www.chtnuclear.com	Greensboro	NC	27407	336-497-3600	
Compx Security Products Inc 200 Old Mill Rd *Web:* www.compxnet.com	Mauldin	SC	29662	864-297-6655	
Comtec Manufacturing Inc 1012 Delaum Rd *Web:* www.comtecmfg.com	Saint Marys	PA	15857	814-834-9300	
Concast Metal Products Co 131 Myoma Rd PO Box 816 *Web:* www.concast.com	Mars	PA	16046	724-538-4000	
Concord Steel Centre Ltd 147 Ashbridge Cir *Web:* www.concordsteel.com	Woodbridge	ON	L4L3R5	905-856-1717	
Creamer Metal Products Inc 77 S Madison Rd *Web:* creamermetal.com	London	OH	43140	740-852-1752	
Crown Roll Leaf Inc 91 Illinois Ave *TF:* 800-631-3831 ■ *Web:* www.crownrollleaf.com	Paterson	NJ	07503	973-742-4000	742-0219
Cryomagnetics Inc 1006 Alvin Weinberg Dr *Web:* www.cryomagnetics.com	Oak Ridge	TN	37830	865-482-9551	
Curtiss-Wright Flow Control Corp 13925 Ballantyne Corporate Pl Ste 400 *Web:* www.cwfc.com	Charlotte	NC	28277	704-869-4602	
Dalco Metals Inc 857 Walworth St *Web:* www.dalcometals.com	Walworth	WI	53184	262-275-6175	
Dalmec Inc 469 Fox Ct *Web:* www.dalmec.com	Bloomingdale	IL	60108	630-307-8426	
Detroit Tool Metal Products Inc 949 Bethel Rd *Web:* www.ironform.com	Lebanon	MO	65536	312-374-4829	
Dexmet Corp 22 Barnes Industrial Rd S *Web:* www.dexmet.com	Wallingford	CT	06492	203-294-4440	
Diamond Z Manufacturing 11299 Bass Ln *TF:* 800-949-2383 ■ *Web:* www.diamondz.com	Caldwell	ID	83605	208-585-2929	
DiSanto Technology Inc 10 Constitution Blvd S *Web:* www.disanto.com	Shelton	CT	06484	203-712-1030	
Diversified Metal Products Inc 3710 N Yellowstone Hwy *Web:* www.diversifiedmetal.com	Idaho Falls	ID	83401	208-529-9655	
Dixie Metal Products Inc 442 Sw 54th Ct *Web:* www.dixiemetals.com	Ocala	FL	34474	352-873-2554	
Durable Packaging International Inc 750 Northgate Pkwy *Web:* www.durablepackaging.com	Wheeling	IL	60090	847-541-4400	
Edmonton Exchanger Group of Cos 5545-89 St *Web:* www.edmontonexchanger.com	Edmonton	AB	T6E5W9	780-468-6722	

Company / Address	City	State	Zip	Phone	Fax
Electro Prime Group LLC 4510 Lint Ave Ste B. Web: www.electroprime.com	Toledo	OH	43612	419-476-0100	
FBN Metal Products 5020 S Nathaniel Lyon St. Web: fbnmetal.com	Battlefield	MO	65619	417-882-2830	
Ferragon Corp 11103 Memphis Ave. Web: www.ferragon.com	Cleveland	OH	44144	216-671-6161	
Ferrell-Ross Roll Manufacturing Inc 102 FM 2856 (Holly Sugar Rd). Web: www.ferrellross.com	Hereford	TX	79045	806-364-9051	
Ferrousouth 38 County Rd 370. Web: www.ferrousmetalprocessing.com	Iuka	MS	38852	662-424-0115	
Formco Metal Products Inc 556 Clayton Ct. Web: www.formcometal.com	Wood Dale	IL	60191	630-766-4441	
Fort Wayne Metals Inc 9609 Ardmore Ave. Web: www.fwmetals.com	Fort Wayne	IN	46809	260-747-4154	
Freeman Metal Products Inc 2124 US Hwy 13 S. Web: www.freemanmetal.com	Ahoskie	NC	27910	252-332-5390	
Fulton Bellows LLC 2801 Red Dog Ln. Web: www.fultonbellows.com	Knoxville	TN	37914	865-546-0550	
Gamber-Johnson Inc 3001 Borham Ave. Web: www.gamberjohnson.com	Stevens Point	WI	54481	715-344-3482	
GH Metal Solutions Inc 2890 Airport Rd NW. Web: www.ghmetalsolutions.com	Fort Payne	AL	35968	256-845-5411	
Glendo Corp PO Box 1153. Web: www.glendo.com	Emporia	KS	66801	620-343-1084	
Global Gear & Machining LLC 2500 Curtiss St. Web: www.globalgearllc.com	Downers Grove	IL	60515	630-969-9400	
Golberg Companies Inc 4179 County Rd 40 Nw. Web: www.gcilift.com	Garfield	MN	56332	320-834-2211	
Gould Electronics Inc 2929 W Chandler Blvd	Chandler	AZ	85224	480-899-0343	
Grace Manufacturing Inc 614 Sr 247. Web: www.gracemfg.com	Russellville	AR	72802	479-968-5455	
Gray Metal Products Inc 495 Rochester St. Web: www.graymetal.com	Avon	NY	14414	585-226-8660	
Handi-Foil Corp 135 E Hintz Rd. Web: www.handi-foil.com	Wheeling	IL	60090	847-520-1000	
Harbor Manufacturing Inc 8300 W 185th St. Web: www.harbormfg.com	Tinley Park	IL	60487	708-614-6400	
Herr-Voss Corp 130 Main St. Web: www.herr-voss.com	Callery	PA	16024	724-538-3180	
Hodge Products Inc PO Box 1326. TF: 800-778-2217 ■ Web: www.hpionline.com	El Cajon	CA	92020	800-778-2217	
Hoover Materials Handling Group Inc 2135 Hwy Six S. Web: www.hooversolutions.com	Houston	TX	77077	281-870-8402	
HW Metal Products Inc 19480 SW 118th Ave. Web: www.hwmetals.com	Tualatin	OR	97062	503-692-1690	
HyPro Inc 600 S Jefferson St PO Box 370. Web: www.hypro.com	Waterford	WI	53185	262-534-5141	
Ideal Shield LLC 2525 Clark St. TF: 866-825-8659 ■ Web: www.idealshield.com	Detroit	MI	48209	313-842-7290	
J L Manufacturing Inc 12310 WA-99	Everett	WA	98204	425-355-3330	
Jireh Metal Inc 3635 Nardin St. Web: www.jirehmetal.com	Grandville	MI	49418	616-531-7581	
John R Wald Company Inc 10576 Fairgrounds Rd. Web: www.jrwald.com	Huntingdon	PA	16652	814-643-3908	
Johnson Screens Inc 1950 Old Hwy 8 NW. Web: www.water.bilfinger.com	New Brighton	MN	55112	651-636-3900	
JW Winco Inc 2815 S Calhoun Rd. Web: www.jwwinco.com	New Berlin	WI	53151	262-786-8227	
King Machine & Tool Co 1237 Sanders Ave Sw. Web: www.kmtco.com	Massillon	OH	44647	330-833-7217	
KrisDee & Associates Inc 755 Schneider Dr. Web: www.krisdee.com	South Elgin	IL	60177	847-608-8300	
Lisega Inc 375 Lisega Blvd. Web: www.lisega.de	Newport	TN	37821	423-625-2000	
Mancor Industries Inc 2485 Speers Rd. Web: www.mancor.com	Oakville	ON	L6L2X9	905-827-3737	844-0999
Manncorp Inc 1610 Republic Rd. Web: www.manncorp.com	Huntingdon Valley	PA	19006	215-830-1200	
Master Magnetics Inc 747 S Gilbert St. Web: www.magnetsource.com	Castle Rock	CO	80104	303-688-3966	
Matandy Steel & Metal Products LLC 1200 Central Ave. Web: www.matandy.com	Hamilton	OH	45011	513-844-2277	
Meridian Lightweight Technologies Inc 25 MacNab Ave. Web: www.meridian-mag.com	Strathroy	ON	N7G4H6	519-246-9600	245-6605
Metal Culverts Inc 2107 Rear Missouri Blvd. Web: www.metalculverts.com	Jefferson City	MO	65109	573-636-7312	
Microflex Inc 1800 N US Hwy 1. Web: www.microflexinc.com	Ormond Beach	FL	32174	386-677-8100	
Mid-State Machine & Fabricating Corp 2730 Mine and Mill Rd. Web: www.midstatefl.com	Lakeland	FL	33801	863-665-6233	
MPI Group LLC, The 319 N Hills Rd. Web: www.metalproductsinc.com	Corbin	KY	40701	606-523-0461	
Newman Brothers Inc 5609 Ctr Hill Ave. Web: www.newmanbrothers.com	Cincinnati	OH	45216	513-242-0011	
Northshore Manufacturing Inc 530 Recycle Ctr Dr. Web: www.builtritehandlers.com	Two Harbors	MN	55616	218-834-5555	
Oak-Mitsui Inc 80 First St. TF: 800-424-8802 ■ Web: www.oakmitsui.com	Hoosick Falls	NY	12090	518-686-4961	686-8080
October Company Inc 51 Ferry St. TF: 800-628-9346 ■ Web: octobercompany.com	EastHampton	MA	01027	413-527-9380	527-0091
Pasco 2600 S Hanley Rd Ste 450. Web: pascosystems.com	Saint Louis	MO	63144	314-781-2212	
Pauli Systems Inc 1820 Walters Ct. Web: www.paulisystems.com	Fairfield	CA	94533	707-429-2434	
Pearlman Industries Inc 6210 S Garfield Ave. Web: www.pearlabrasive.com	Commerce	CA	90040	562-927-5561	
Penn Engineering Components 29045 Ave Penn. Web: www.pennengineering.com	Valencia	CA	91355	661-295-2080	
Perfection Metal Products Inc 3393 De La Cruz Blvd.	Santa Clara	CA	95054	408-496-2950	
Precision Hose 2200 Centre Park Ct. TF: 877-850-2662 ■ Web: www.precisionhose.com	Stone Mountain	GA	30087	770-413-5680	
Precision Manufacturing Group LLC 501 Little Falls Rd. Web: www.servometer.com	Cedar Grove	NJ	07009	973-785-4630	
Prentex Alloy Fabricators Inc 3108 Sylvan Ave. *Fax Area Code: 972 ■ TF: 877-773-6839 ■ Web: www.prentex.com	Dallas	TX	75212	214-748-7837	748-7850*
ProSteel Security Products Inc 1400 S State St. Web: www.prosteel.us	Provo	UT	84603	801-373-2385	
PSM Industries Inc 14000 Avalon Blvd. Web: www.psmindustries.com	Los Angeles	CA	90061	310-715-9800	
Reel-Neat Systems Inc 6408 S Eastern Ave. Web: www.reelomatic.com	Oklahoma City	OK	73149	405-672-0000	
Regal Metal Products Co 3615 Union Ave Se. Web: www.regalmetalproducts.com	Minerva	OH	44657	330-868-6343	
Reo Hydraulics & Manufacturing 18475 Sherwood St. Web: www.regroup.com	Detroit	MI	48234	313-891-2244	
River City Metal Products Inc 655 Godfrey Ave SW. Web: www.rcmpinc.com	Grand Rapids	MI	49510	616-235-3746	
Riverhawk Company LP 215 Clinton Rd. Web: www.riverhawk.com	New Hartford	NY	13413	315-768-4855	
Rivers Metal Products Inc 3100 N 38th St. Web: www.riversmetal.com	Lincoln	NE	68504	402-466-2329	
Robinson Fin Machines Inc 13670 Us Hwy 68. Web: www.robfin.com	Kenton	OH	43326	419-674-4152	
Rochester Metal Products Corp 616 Indiana Ave PO Box 488. Web: www.rochestermetals.com	Rochester	IN	46975	574-223-3164	
Sandbox Industries Inc 1000 W Fulton Market Ste 213. Web: www.sandboxindustries.com	Chicago	IL	60607	312-243-4100	
Screen Tech Inc 470 Needles Dr. Web: www.screentechinc.com	San Jose	CA	95112	408-885-8750	
Selig Group Inc 342 E Wabash Ave. Web: www.seligsealing.com	Forrest	IL	61741	815-785-2100	
Shade Systems Inc 4150 Sw 19th St. TF: 800-609-6066 ■ Web: www.shadesystemsinc.com	Ocala	FL	34474	352-237-0135	
Smart Machine Technologies Inc 650 Frith Dr. Web: www.smartmachine.com	Ridgeway	VA	24148	276-632-9853	
Spartan Light Metal Products Inc 3668 S Geyer Rd Ste 210. Web: www.spartanlmp.com	St. Louis	MO	63127	314-620-2500	
Spinco Metal Products Inc 1 Country Club Dr. Web: www.spincometal.com	Newark	NY	14513	315-331-6285	
Steel Craft Technologies Inc 8057 Graphic Dr NE. Web: www.steelcrafttech.com	Belmont	MI	49306	616-866-4400	
Suhm Spring Works Inc 2710 McKinney. Web: www.suhm.net	Houston	TX	77003	713-224-9293	
Superior Metal Products Inc 2463 Hwy 107. Web: www.superiormetal.com	Chuckey	TN	37641	423-257-2154	257-3617
Superior Metal Technologies LLC 9850 E 30th St. Web: www.superiormetals.us	Indianapolis	IN	46229	317-897-9850	
Tam Metal Products Inc 55 Whitney Rd. Web: www.tam-ind.com	Mahwah	NJ	07430	201-848-7800	
Topcraft Metal Products Inc 5112 40th Ave. Web: www.topcraftmetal.com	Hudsonville	MI	49426	616-669-1790	
TrafFix Devices Inc 160 Avenida La Pata. Web: www.traffixdevices.com	San Clemente	CA	92673	949-361-5663	
Tricor Metals Inc 3225 W Old Lincoln Way. Web: www.tricormetals.com	Wooster	OH	44691	330-264-3299	
Trulock Tool Co 113 Drayton St. Web: trulockchokes.com	Whigham	GA	39897	229-762-4678	
Turbotec Products Inc 651 Day Hill Rd. Web: turbotecproducts.com	Windsor	CT	06095	860-731-4200	
United Metal Products Inc 1920 E Encanto Dr. Web: www.unitedmetal.com	Tempe	AZ	85281	480-968-9550	
USM Aerostructures Corp 74 W Sixth St. Web: www.usmaero.com	Wyoming	PA	18644	570-613-1234	
Utica Metal Products Inc 1526 Lincoln Ave. Web: www.uticametals.com	Utica	NY	13502	315-732-6163	
V&M Precision Machining & Grinding 1130 Columbia St. Web: www.vm-machining.com	Brea	CA	92821	714-257-4850	
Valco Manufacturing Company Inc 925 Boren Rd. Web: www.valcomfg.com	Duncan	OK	73533	580-255-4300	
Vooner Flogard Corp 4729 Stockholm Ct. TF: 800-345-7879 ■ Web: www.vooner.com	Charlotte	NC	28273	704-552-9314	
Wagman Metal Products Inc 400 S Albemarle St. Web: www.wagmanmetal.com	York	PA	17403	717-854-2120	
Warren Co, The 2201 Loveland Ave. TF: 800-562-0357 ■ Web: www.thewarrencompany.com	Erie	PA	16506	800-562-0357	
Wayne Metal Products Inc 5461 Benchmark Ln. Web: www.waynemetalproductsinc.com	Sanford	FL	32773	407-321-7168	
Weiser Metal Products 34311 E M72 PO Box 370. Web: www.weisermetal.com	Lincoln	MI	48742	989-736-6055	736-6717
Welded Ring Products Company Inc 2180 W 114th St. Web: www.weldedring.com	Cleveland	OH	44102	216-961-3800	

				Phone	Fax
Weldship Corp 225 W Second St. Web: www.weldship.com	Bethlehem	PA	18015	610-861-7330	

296 FOOD PRODUCTS - MFR

See Also Agricultural Products p. 1715; Bakeries p. 1838; Beverages - Mfr p. 1855; Ice - Manufactured p. 2555; Livestock & Poultry Feeds - Prepared p. 2680; Meat Packing Plants p. 2735; Pet Products p. 2928; Poultry Processing p. 2967; Salt p. 3143

				Phone	Fax
AlturnaMATS Inc 701 E Spring St Mailbox #9 TF: 800-438-9336 ■ Web: www.alturnamats.com	Titusville	PA	16354	814-827-8884	
Broaster Company LLC, The 2855 Cranston Rd Web: www.broaster.com	Beloit	WI	53511	608-365-0193	
Brown International Corporation LLC 333 Ave M NW Web: www.brown-intl.com	Winter Haven	FL	33881	863-299-2111	
Cantrell Machine Company Inc 1400 S Bradford St Web: www.cantrell.com	Gainesville	GA	30503	770-536-3611	
Computerway Food Systems 635 Southwest St Web: www.mycfs.com	High Point	NC	27260	336-841-7289	
Conchita Foods Inc 10051 NW 99th Ave Ste 3 Web: www.conchita-foods.com	Miami	FL	33178	305-888-9703	888-1020
Contemar Silo Systems Inc 30 Pennsylvania Ave Unit 8 TF: 800-567-2741 ■ Web: www.contemar.com	Concord	ON	L4K4A5	905-669-3604	
Fetco 600 Rose Rd Web: www.fetco.com	Lake Zurich	IL	60047	847-821-1177	
Flatout Inc 1422 Woodland Dr. TF: 866-944-5445 ■ Web: www.flatoutbread.com	Saline	MI	48176	734-944-4262	
Graybill Machines Inc 221 W Lexington Rd Web: www.graybillmachines.com	Lititz	PA	17543	717-626-5221	
John Bean Technologies Corp 70 W Madison Ste 4400 Web: www.jbtcorporation.com	Chicago	IL	60602	312-861-5900	
Koss Industrial Inc 1943 Commercial Way TF: 800-844-6261 ■ Web: www.kossindustrial.com	Green Bay	WI	54311	920-469-5300	
Microthermics Inc 3216 Wellington Ct Ste 101 Web: www.microthermics.com	Raleigh	NC	27615	919-878-8045	
Nemco Food Equipment Ltd 301 Meuse Argonne Web: www.nemcofoodequip.com	Hicksville	OH	43526	419-542-7751	
NuTEC Manufacturing 908 Garnet Ct. Web: nutecmfg.com	New Lenox	IL	60451	815-722-2800	
Prime Equipment Group Inc 2000 E Fulton St Web: www.primeequipmentgroup.com	Columbus	OH	43205	614-253-8590	
Qualtech Inc 1880 Leon-Harmel St Web: www.qualtech.ca	Quebec	QC	G1N4K3	418-686-3802	
Remco Products Corp 4735 W 106th St TF: 800-585-8619 ■ Web: remcoproducts.com	Zionsville	IN	46077	317-876-9856	
Revent Inc 100 Ethel Rd W. TF: 800-822-9642 ■ Web: www.revent.com	Piscataway	NJ	08854	732-777-9433	
Rhee Bros Inc 7461 Coca Cola Dr. Web: www.rheebros.com	Hanover	MD	21076	410-381-9000	381-4989
Starflex Corp 204 Turner Rd	Jonesboro	GA	30236	770-471-2111	
Sunny Dell Foods Inc 135 N Fifth St Web: www.sunnydell.com	Oxford	PA	19363	610-932-5164	932-9479
Thomsen Group LLC 1303 43rd St TF: 800-558-4018 ■ Web: www.lcthomsen.com	Kenosha	WI	53140	800-558-4018	
US Beverage Net Inc 499 S Warren St 2nd Fl Web: www.usbeveragenet.com	Syracuse	NY	13202	315-579-2025	
Wixon Inc 1390 E Bolivar Ave. TF: 800-841-5304 ■ Web: www.wixon.com	Saint Francis	WI	53235	414-769-3000	769-3024
Wolf-tec Inc 20 Kieffer Ln Web: www.wolf-tec.com	Kingston	NY	12401	845-340-9727	

296-1 Bakery Products - Fresh

				Phone	Fax
Alessi Bakeries Inc 2909 W Cypress St. Web: www.alessibakeries.com	Tampa	FL	33609	813-879-4544	
Alfred Nickles Bakery Inc 26 N Main St. TF: 800-597-9096 ■ Web: www.nicklesbakery.com	Navarre	OH	44662	330-879-5635	879-5896
Amoroso's Baking Co 845 S 55th St Web: www.amorosobaking.com	Philadelphia	PA	19143	215-471-4710	471-5323
Arnie's Inc 722 Leonard St NW Web: www.arniesrestaurants.com	Grand Rapids	MI	49503	616-454-3098	
Bakewise Brands Inc 1688 N Wayneport Rd	Macedon	NY	14502	315-986-9999	986-7200
Bama Pie Ltd 5377 E 66th St N Web: www.bama.com	Tulsa	OK	74117	918-592-0778	
Barker Specialty Products LLC 27 Realty Dr PO Box 478 Web: www.barkercompany.com	Cheshire	CT	06410	319-293-3777	
Bays Corp PO Box 1455 TF: 800-367-2297 ■ Web: www.bays.com	Chicago	IL	60690	800-367-2297	
Better Baked Foods Inc 56 Smedley St. Web: www.betterbaked.com	North East	PA	16428	814-725-8778	725-8785
Bimbo Bakeries USA PO Box 976 *Fax Area Code: 610 ■ TF: 800-984-0989 ■ Web: www.bimbobakeriesusa.com	Horsham	PA	19044	800-984-0989	320-9286*
Brown's Bakery 1226 Versailles Rd Web: www.brownbakery.com	Lexington	KY	40508	859-225-8400	
Byrnes & Kiefer Coompany 131 Kline Ave Web: www.bkcompany.com	Callery	PA	16024	724-538-5200	538-9292
Calise & Sons Bakery Inc 2 Quality Dr TF: 800-225-4737 ■ Web: www.calisebakery.com	Lincoln	RI	02865	401-334-3444	334-0938
Carolina Foods Inc 1807 S Tryon St Web: carolinafoodsinc.com	Charlotte	NC	28203	704-333-9812	
Cloverhill Bakery Inc 2035 N Narragansett Ave Web: www.cloverhill.com	Chicago	IL	60639	773-745-9800	745-1647
Country Oven Bakery Inc 2840 Pioneer Dr	Bowling Green	KY	42101	270-782-3200	782-7170
Dakota Brands International Inc 2121 13th St NE Web: www.dakotabrands.com	Jamestown	ND	58401	701-252-5073	
De Wafelbakkers LLC 10000 Crystal Hill Rd. TF: 800-924-3391 ■ Web: www.dewafelbakkers.com	North Little Rock	AR	72113	501-791-3320	791-0309
Delight Grecian Foods Inc 1201 Tonne Rd TF: 800-621-4387 ■ Web: www.greciandelight.com	Elk Grove Village	IL	60007	847-364-1010	364-1077
Dinkel's Bakery 3329 N Lincoln Ave. TF Orders: 800-822-8817 ■ Web: www.dinkels.com	Chicago	IL	60657	773-281-7300	281-6169
Ellison Bakery 4108 W Ferguson Rd. Web: www.ebakery.com	Fort Wayne	IN	46809	260-747-6136	747-1954
Fantini Baking Company Inc 375 Washington St TF: 800-223-9037 ■ Web: www.fantinibakery.com	Haverhill	MA	01832	978-373-1273	373-6250
Flowers Foods Inc 1919 Flowers Cir NYSE: FLO ■ *Fax: Mktg ■ Web: www.flowersfoods.com	Thomasville	GA	31757	229-226-9110	226-1318*
Franz Family Bakeries 2901 6th Ave S Web: franzbakery.com	Seattle	WA	98134	206-726-7535	
Franz Family Bakeries William's Div 340 NE 11th St Web: franzbakery.com	portland	OR	97232	541-772-5816	
Fresh Start Bakeries 145 S State College Blvd Ste 200 Web: www.freshstartbakeries.com	Brea	CA	92821	714-256-8900	256-8916
Greyston Bakery Inc 104 Alexander St. TF: 800-289-2253 ■ Web: greyston.com	Yonkers	NY	10701	914-375-1510	375-1514
H & S Bakery Inc 601 S Caroline St TF: 800-959-7655 ■ Web: www.hsbakery.com	Baltimore	MD	21231	410-276-7254	558-3096
Heinemann's Bakeries LLC PO Box 558265 Web: www.heinemanns.com	Chicago	IL	60655	616-885-9094	885-9031
Heiners Bakery Inc 1300 Adams Ave. TF: 800-776-8411 ■ Web: heinersbakery.com	Huntington	WV	25704	304-523-8411	
Herman Seekamp Inc 1120 W Fullerton Ave Web: www.clydesdonuts.com	Addison	IL	60101	630-628-6555	628-6838
JTM Foods Inc 2126 E 33rd St Web: www.jjsbakery.net	Erie	PA	16510	814-899-0886	899-9862
Klosterman Baking Company Inc 4760 Paddock Rd TF: 877-301-1004 ■ Web: www.klostermanbakery.com	Cincinnati	OH	45229	513-242-1004	242-8257
Lawler Foods Ltd Inc PO Box 2558 TF: 800-541-8285 ■ Web: www.lawlers.com	Humble	TX	77347	281-446-0059	446-3806
Leidenheimer Baking Co 1501 Simon Bolivar Ave TF: 800-259-9099 ■ Web: www.leidenheimer.com	New Orleans	LA	70113	504-525-1575	525-1596
Lepage Bakeries Inc 1919 Flowers Cir Web: www.flowersfoods.com	Thomasville	GA	31757	229-226-9110	
Lewis Bakeries Inc 500 N Fulton Ave Web: lewisbakeries.net	Evansville	IN	47710	812-425-4642	425-7609
Little Dutch Boy Bakery Inc 12349 South 970 East	Draper	UT	84020	801-571-3800	571-3802
Martin's Famous Pastry Shoppe Inc 1000 Potato Roll Ln TF Cust Svc: 800-548-1200 ■ Web: potatorolls.com	Chambersburg	PA	17201	717-263-9580	263-6687
Mary Ann's Baking Co 8371 Carbide Ct Web: maryannsbaking.com	Sacramento	CA	95828	916-681-7444	681-7470
McKee Foods Corp PO Box 750 TF Cust Svc: 800-522-4499 ■ Web: www.mckeefoods.com	Collegedale	TN	37315	423-238-7111	
Morabito Baking Company Inc 757 Kohn St TF: 800-525-7747 ■ Web: www.morabito.com	Norristown	PA	19401	610-275-5419	275-0358
Oak State Products Inc PO Box 549 Web: www.oakstate.com	Wenona	IL	61377	815-853-4348	
Omni Baking Co 2621 Freddy Ln. Web: www.omnibaking.com	Vineland	NJ	08360	856-205-1485	
Orlando Baking Company Inc 7777 Grand Ave TF: 800-362-5504 ■ Web: www.orlandobaking.com	Cleveland	OH	44104	216-361-1872	391-3469
Pan-O-Gold Baking Co 444 E St Germain TF: 800-444-7005 ■ Web: www.panogold.com	Saint Cloud	MN	56304	320-251-9361	
Pechters Baking 840 Jersey St. Web: pechters.com	Harrison	NJ	07029	973-483-3374	
Pepperidge Farm Inc 595 Westport Ave TF PR: 888-737-7374 ■ Web: www.pepperidgefarm.com	Norwalk	CT	06851	203-846-7000	846-7145
Piantedosi Baking Company Inc 240 Commercial St TF: 800-339-0080 ■ Web: www.piantedosi.com	Malden	MA	02148	781-321-3400	324-5647
Ralcorp Frozen Bakery Products 3250 Lacey Rd Ste 600 Web: www.ralcorpfrozen.com	Downers Grove	IL	60515	630-455-5200	920-8945
Richmond Baking Co 520 N Sixth St Web: www.richmondbaking.com	Richmond	IN	47374	765-962-8535	962-2253
Rockland Bakery Inc 94 Demarest Mill Rd W Web: www.rocklandbakery.com	Nanuet	NY	10954	845-623-5800	623-6921
Rothbury Farms PO Box 202 TF: 877-684-2879 ■ Web: rothburyfarms.com	Grand Rapids	MI	49501	877-684-2879	
Schmidt Baking Company Inc 7801 Fitch Ln Web: www.schmidtbaking.com	Baltimore	MD	21236	410-668-8200	882-2051
Schwebel Baking Co PO Box 6018 TF: 800-860-2867 ■ Web: www.schwebels.com	Youngstown	OH	44501	330-783-2860	782-1774
Signature Breads Inc 100 Justin Dr. TF: 888-602-6533 ■ Web: www.signaturebreads.com	Chelsea	MA	02150	888-602-6533	
Sokol & Co 5315 Dansher Rd. TF Cust Svc: 800-328-7656 ■ Web: www.solofoods.com	Countryside	IL	60525	708-482-8250	
Specialty Bakers Inc 450 S State Rd Web: www.sbiladyfingers.com	Marysville	PA	17053	717-957-2131	
Svenhard's Swedish Bakery Inc 335 Adeline St Web: www.svenhards.com	Oakland	CA	94607	510-834-5035	839-6797

				Phone	Fax
Table Talk Pies Inc 120 Washington St	Worcester	MA	01610	508-798-8811	798-0848
Web: www.tabletalkpie.com					
Tasty Baking Co 4300 S 26th St	Philadelphia	PA	19112	215-221-8500	
TF: 800-248-2789 ■ *Web:* www.tastykake.com					
Turano Baking Co 6501 Roosevelt Rd	Berwyn	IL	60402	708-788-9220	788-3075
Web: www.turano.com					
Wenner Bread Products Inc 33 Rajon Rd	Bayport	NY	11705	631-563-6262	
TF: 800-869-6262 ■ *Web:* www.wennerbakery.com					
Wolferman's 2500 S Pacific Hwy PO Box 9100	Medford	OR	97501	800-999-0169	999-7548
TF: 800-999-0169 ■ *Web:* www.wolfermans.com					

296-2 Bakery Products - Frozen

				Phone	Fax
Athens Pastries & Frozen Foods Inc					
13600 Snow Rd	Brookpark	OH	44142	216-676-8500	324-1875*
**Fax Area Code:* 210 ■ *TF:* 800-837-5683 ■ *Web:* www.athens.com					
Bridgford Foods Corp 1308 N Patt St	Anaheim	CA	92801	714-526-5533	526-4360
NASDAQ: BRID ■ *TF:* 800-854-3255 ■ *Web:* www.bridgford.com					
Country Oven Bakery Inc					
2840 Pioneer Dr	Bowling Green	KY	42101	270-782-3200	782-7170
Dessert Innovations Inc 25-B Enterprise Blvd	Atlanta	GA	30336	404-691-5000	691-5001
TF: 800-359-7351 ■ *Web:* www.dessertinnovations.com					
Don Lee Farms 200 E Beach Ave	Inglewood	CA	90302	310-674-3180	673-7008
Web: donleefarms.com					
Eli's Cheesecake Co					
6701 W Forest Preserve Dr	Chicago	IL	60634	773-736-3417	205-3801
TF: 800-999-8300 ■ *Web:* www.elicheesecake.com					
Guttenplans Frozen Dough 100 Hwy 36	Middletown	NJ	07748	732-495-9480	
TF General: 888-422-4357 ■ *Web:* www.guttenplan.com					
James Skinner Baking Co 4657 G St	Omaha	NE	68117	402-734-1672	734-0516
TF: 800-358-7428 ■ *Web:* www.skinnerbaking.com					
Main Street Gourmet Inc 170 Muffin Ln	Cuyahoga Falls	OH	44223	330-929-0000	
TF: 800-678-6246 ■ *Web:* www.mainstreetgourmet.com					
Maplehurst Inc 50 Maplehurst Dr	Brownsburg	IN	46112	317-858-9000	
TF: 800-344-4235 ■ *Web:* www.maplehurstbakeries.com					
Rhino Foods Inc 79 Industrial Pkwy	Burlington	VT	05401	802-862-0252	865-4145
TF: 800-639-3350 ■ *Web:* www.rhinofoods.com					
Vie de France Yamazaki Inc					
2070 Chain Bridge Rd Ste 500	Vienna	VA	22182	703-442-9205	821-2695
TF General: 800-446-4404 ■ *Web:* www.vdfy.com					

296-3 Butter (Creamery)

				Phone	Fax
AMPI 315 N Broadway	New Ulm	MN	56073	507-354-8295	
TF: 800-533-3580 ■ *Web:* www.ampi.com					
Cabot Creamery 193 Home Farm Way	Waitsfield	VT	05673	802-229-9361	
TF: 888-792-2268 ■ *Web:* www.cabotcheese.coop					
California Dairies Inc 2000 N Plz Dr	Visalia	CA	93291	559-625-2200	625-5433
Web: www.californiadairies.com					
Challenge Dairy Products Inc					
11875 Dublin Blvd Ste B230	Dublin	CA	94568	925-828-6160	551-7591
Web: www.challengedairy.com					
Farmers Co-op Creamery Inc (FCC)					
700 N Hwy 99 W	McMinnville	OR	97128	503-472-2157	472-3821
Web: www.farmerscoop.org					
Grassland Dairy Products Company Inc					
N 8790 Fairgrounds Ave PO Box 160	Greenwood	WI	54437	715-267-6182	267-6044
TF: 800-428-8837 ■ *Web:* www.grassland.com					
O-AT-KA Milk Products Co-op Inc					
700 Ellicott St	Batavia	NY	14020	585-343-0536	343-4473
TF: 800-828-8152 ■ *Web:* www.oatkamilk.com					
Plainview Milk Products Co-Op					
130 Second St SW	Plainview	MN	55964	507-534-3872	534-3992
TF: 800-356-5606 ■ *Web:* www.plainviewmilk.com					
Schreiber Foods Inc PO Box 19010	Green Bay	WI	54307	920-437-7601	
Web: www.schreiberfoods.com					
Sommermaid Creamery Inc PO Box 350	Doylestown	PA	18901	215-345-6160	345-4945
Web: www.sommermaid.com					

296-4 Cereals (Breakfast)

				Phone	Fax
Big G Cereals PO Box 9452 PO Box 9452	Minneapolis	MN	55440	800-248-7310	764-8330*
**Fax Area Code:* 763 ■ **Fax:* PR ■ *TF:* 800-248-7310 ■ *Web:* www.generalmills.com					
Bob's Red Mill Natural Foods Inc					
13521 SE Pheasant Ct	Milwaukie	OR	97222	503-654-3215	653-1339
TF: 800-553-2258 ■ *Web:* www.bobsredmill.com					
Gilster-Mary Lee Corp					
1037 State St PO Box 227	Chester	IL	62233	618-826-2361	826-2973
Web: gilstermarylee.com					
Homestead Mills 221 N River St PO Box 1115	Cook	MN	55723	218-666-5233	666-5236
TF: 800-652-5233 ■ *Web:* www.homesteadmills.com					
Honeyville Grain Inc					
11600 Dayton Dr	Rancho Cucamonga	CA	91730	909-980-9500	980-6503
TF: 888-810-3212 ■ *Web:* www.honeyville.com					
Hyde & Hyde Inc 300 El Sobrante Rd	Corona	CA	92879	951-817-2300	270-3526
Web: www.hydeandhyde.com					
Kellogg Co 1 Kellogg Sq PO Box 3599	Battle Creek	MI	49016	269-961-2000	961-2871
NYSE: K ■ *TF Cust Svc:* 800-962-1413 ■ *Web:* www.kelloggs.com					
Lundberg Family Farms					
5370 Church St PO Box 369	Richvale	CA	95974	530-882-4551	882-4500
Web: www.lundberg.com					
New England Natural Bakers					
74 Fairview St E	Greenfield	MA	01301	413-772-2239	772-2936
TF: 800-910-2884 ■ *Web:* www.newenglandnaturalbakers.com					
Organic Milling Co 505 W Allen Ave	San Dimas	CA	91773	909-599-0961	599-5180
TF: 800-638-8686 ■ *Web:* www.organicmilling.com/contact.html					
Quaker Oats Co 555 W Monroe St	Chicago	IL	60661	312-821-1000	
TF: 800-367-6287 ■ *Web:* www.quakeroats.com					
Weetabix Co Inc 300 Nickerson Rd	Marlborough	MA	01752	978-368-0991	
TF: 800-343-0590 ■ *Web:* www.weetabixusa.com					

296-5 Cheeses - Natural, Processed, Imitation

				Phone	Fax
AMPI 315 N Broadway	New Ulm	MN	56073	507-354-8295	
TF: 800-533-3580 ■ *Web:* www.ampi.com					
Barker Specialty Products LLC					
27 Realty Dr PO Box 478	Cheshire	CT	06410	319-293-3777	
Web: www.barkercompany.com					
Bel/Kaukauna USA 1500 E N Ave	Little Chute	WI	54140	920-788-3524	
Web: www.kaukaunacheese.com					
Berner Foods Inc 2034 E Factory Rd	Dakota	IL	61018	815-563-4222	563-4017
TF: 800-819-8199 ■ *Web:* www.bernerfoods.com					
Biery Cheese Co 6544 Paris Ave	Louisville	OH	44641	330-875-3381	875-5896
Web: www.bierycheese.com					
Boar's Head Provisions Co Inc					
1819 Main St Ste 800	Sarasota	FL	34236	941-955-0994	366-0354
Web: www.boarshead.com					
Bongards' Creameries 13200 County Rd 51	Norwood	MN	55368	952-466-5521	466-5556
Web: www.bongards.com					
Burnett Dairy Co-op 11631 SR- 70	Grantsburg	WI	54840	715-689-2468	689-2135
TF: 800-854-2716 ■ *Web:* www.burnettdairy.com					
Cabot Creamery 193 Home Farm Way	Waitsfield	VT	05673	802-229-9361	
TF: 888-792-2268 ■ *Web:* www.cabotcheese.coop					
Cacique Inc 14923 Procter Ave	La Puente	CA	91746	626-961-3399	369-8083*
**Fax:* Sales ■ *TF:* 800-521-6987 ■ *Web:* caciqueinc.com					
Calabro Cheese Corp					
580 Coe Ave PO Box 120186	East Haven	CT	06512	203-469-1311	469-6929
Web: www.calabrocheese.com					
California Dairies Inc 2000 N Plz Dr	Visalia	CA	93291	559-625-2200	625-5433
Web: www.californiadairies.com					
Colonna Bros Inc PO Box 808	North Bergen	NJ	07047	201-864-1115	
Web: www.colonnabrothers.com					
ConAgra Foods Retail Products Co Deli Foods Group					
215 W Field Rd	Naperville	IL	60563	630-857-1000	
TF: 877-266-2472 ■ *Web:* www.conagrafoods.com					
Dairiconcepts LP 3253 E Chestnut Expy	Springfield	MO	65802	417-829-3400	829-3401
TF: 877-596-4374 ■ *Web:* www.dairiconcepts.com					
Dairy Farmers of America Inc					
10220 N Ambassador Dr	Kansas City	MO	64153	816-801-6455	801-6456
TF: 888-332-6455 ■ *Web:* www.dfamilk.com					
Dairy Food USA Inc 2819 County Rd F	Blue Mounds	WI	53517	608-437-5598	437-8850
Web: www.dairyfoodusa.com					
Ellsworth Co-op Creamery Inc					
232 N Wallace St	Ellsworth	WI	54011	715-273-4311	273-5318
Web: www.ellsworthcheese.com					
Empire Cheese Inc 4520 County Rd 6	Cuba	NY	14727	585-968-1552	968-2660
Web: greatlakescheese.com					
F & A Dairy Products Inc 212 State Rd 35 S	Dresser	WI	54009	715-755-3485	755-3480
Web: www.fadairy.com					
Farmdale Creamery Inc					
1049 W Baseline St	San Bernardino	CA	92411	909-889-3002	888-2541
TF: 800-346-7306 ■ *Web:* farmdale.net					
First District Assn (FDA) 101 S Swift Ave	Litchfield	MN	55355	320-693-3236	693-6243
Web: www.firstdistrict.com					
Fleur De Lait Foods Inc 400 S Custer Ave	New Holland	PA	17557	717-355-8580	355-8546
Galaxy Nutritional Foods Inc					
66 Whitecap Dr	North Kingstown	RI	02852	401-667-5000	
TF: 800-441-9419 ■ *Web:* goveggiefoods.com					
Golden Cheese Company of California					
1138 W Rincon St	Corona	CA	92880	951-493-4700	
Web: waterboards.ca.gov					
Gossner Foods Inc 1051 N 1000 W	Logan	UT	84321	435-713-6100	713-6200
TF: 800-944-0454 ■ *Web:* www.gossner.com					
Grande Cheese Co 301 E Main St	Lomira	WI	53048	800-772-3210	269-1445*
**Fax Area Code:* 920 ■ *TF:* 800-772-3210 ■ *Web:* www.grandecig.com					
Great Lakes Cheese Company Inc					
17825 Great Lakes Pkwy	Hiram	OH	44234	440-834-2500	834-1002
Web: www.greatlakescheese.com					
Hilmar Cheese Company Inc PO Box 910	Hilmar	CA	95324	209-667-6076	634-1408
TF: 888-300-4465 ■ *Web:* www.hilmarcheese.com					
Holmes Cheese Co 9444 SR-39	Millersburg	OH	44654	330-674-6451	674-6673
Jerome Cheese Co 547 W Nez Perce	Jerome	ID	83338	208-324-8806	324-8892
TF: 800-757-7611 ■ *Web:* daviscofoods.com					
Klondike Cheese Co W7839 Hwy 81	Monroe	WI	53566	608-325-3021	325-3027
Web: www.klondikecheese.com					
Kraft Foods North America Inc 3 Lakes Dr	Northfield	IL	60093	847-646-2000	
NASDAQ: KHC ■ *Web:* www.kraftheinzcompany.com					
Le Sueur Cheese Company Inc 719 N Main St	Le Sueur	MN	56058	507-665-3353	665-2820
TF: 800-247-0871 ■ *Web:* daviscofoods.com					
Leprino Foods Co 1830 W 38th Ave	Denver	CO	80211	303-480-2600	480-2605
Web: www.leprinofoods.com					
Los Altos Food Products Inc					
15130 Nelson Ave	City of Industry	CA	91744	626-330-6555	330-6755
Web: www.losaltosfoods.com					
Mancuso Cheese Co 612 Mills Rd	Joliet	IL	60433	815-722-2475	722-1302
Web: mancusocheese.com					
Marathon Cheese Corp 304 E St PO Box 185	Marathon	WI	54448	715-443-2211	443-3843
Web: www.mcheese.com					
Miceli Dairy Products 2721 E 90th St	Cleveland	OH	44104	216-791-6222	
Web: www.miceli-dairy.com					
Pace Dairy Foods Co 2700 Vly High Dr NW	Rochester	MN	55901	507-288-6315	
Saputo Inc 6869 boul Metropolitain	Saint-Leonard	QC	H1P1X8	514-328-6662	328-3364
NYSE: SAP ■ *Web:* www.saputo.com					
Sargento Foods Inc 1 Persnickety Pl	Plymouth	WI	53073	920-893-8484	892-5390
TF: 800-243-3737 ■ *Web:* www.sargento.com					
Sartori Food Corp 107 Pleasant View Rd	Plymouth	WI	53073	920-893-6061	892-2732
TF Cust Svc: 800-558-5888 ■ *Web:* www.sartoricheese.com					

Company	City	State	Zip	Phone	Fax
Schreiber Foods Inc PO Box 19010 — *Web:* www.schreiberfoods.com	Green Bay	WI	54307	920-437-7601	
Sun-Re Cheese Corp 178 Lenker Ave	Sunbury	PA	17801	570-286-1511	286-5123
Swiss Valley Farms 247 Research Pkwy PO Box 4493 — *TF:* 800-747-6113 ■ *Web:* www.swissvalley.com	Davenport	IA	52808	563-468-6600	468-6613
Tillamook County Creamery Assn Inc 4185 Hwy 101 N — *Web:* www.tillamook.com	Tillamook	OR	97141	503-815-1300	
Tropical Cheese Industries Inc 450 Fayette St PO Box 1357 — *TF:* 888-874-4928 ■ *Web:* www.tropicalcheese.com	Perth Amboy	NJ	08861	732-442-4898	442-8227
Valley Queen Cheese Factory Inc 200 E Railway Ave — *Web:* www.vqcheese.com	Milbank	SD	57252	605-432-4563	432-9383
Wapsie Valley Creamery Inc 300 Tenth St NE	Independence	IA	50644	319-334-7193	

296-6 Chewing Gum

Company	City	State	Zip	Phone	Fax
Concord Confections Ltd 345 Courtland Ave — *TF:* 800-267-0037 ■ *Web:* ic.gc.ca/eic/site/icgc.nsf/eng/home	Concord	ON	L4K5A6	905-660-8989	660-8979
Ford Gum & Machine Company Inc 18 Newton Ave — *Web:* www.fordgum.com	Akron	NY	14001	716-542-4561	542-4610
Lotte USA Inc 5243 Wayne Rd — *Web:* koalasmarch-usa.com	Battle Creek	MI	49037	269-963-6664	963-6695
Topps Company Inc 1 Whitehall St — *TF:* 800-489-9149 ■ *Web:* www.topps.com	New York	NY	10004	212-376-0300	376-0573
Wrigley Co, The 410 N Michigan Ave — *TF:* 888-985-2064 ■ *Web:* www.wrigley.com	Chicago	IL	60611	312-644-2121	

296-7 Coffee - Roasted (Ground, Instant, Freeze-Dried)

Company	City	State	Zip	Phone	Fax
Allegro Coffee Co 12799 Claude Ct — *TF:* 800-530-3995 ■ *Web:* www.allegro-coffee.com	Thornton	CO	80241	303-444-4844	920-5468
ARCO Coffee Company 2206 Winter St — *TF:* 800-283-2726 ■ *Web:* www.arcocoffee.com	Superior	WI	54880	715-392-4771	392-4776
Autocrat Coffee Inc 10 Blackstone Vly Pl — *TF:* 800-288-6272 ■ *Web:* www.autocrat.com	Lincoln	RI	02865	401-333-3300	333-3719
Bargreen Coffee Co 2821 Rucker Ave — *Web:* bargreenscoffee.com	Everett	WA	98201	425-252-3161	
Boyd Coffee Co 19730 NE Sandy Blvd — *TF Cust Svc:* 800-545-4077 ■ *Web:* www.boyds.com	Portland	OR	97230	503-666-4545	669-2223
Cadillac Coffee Co 194 E Maple Rd — *TF:* 800-438-6900 ■ *Web:* www.cadillaccoffee.com	Troy	MI	48083	248-545-2266	
Coffee Holding Company Inc 3475 Victory Blvd — *NASDAQ: JVA* ■ *TF:* 800-458-2233 ■ *Web:* www.coffeeholding.com	Staten Island	NY	10314	718-832-0800	832-0892
Community Coffee Co PO Box 2311 — *TF:* 800-688-0990 ■ *Web:* www.communitycoffee.com	Baton Rouge	LA	70821	800-884-5282	643-8199
DeCoty Coffee Company Inc 1920 Austin St — **Fax Area Code:* 325 ■ *TF:* 800-588-8001 ■ *Web:* www.decoty.com	San Angelo	TX	76903	800-588-8001	655-6837*
Excellent Coffee Company Inc 259 E Ave — *Web:* excellentcoffee.com	Pawtucket	RI	02860	401-724-6393	724-0560
Farmer Bros Co 20333 S Normandie Ave — *NASDAQ: FARM* ■ *TF:* 800-735-2878 ■ *Web:* www.farmerbros.com	Torrance	CA	90502	310-787-5200	
Frontier Natural Products Co-op 3021 78th St PO Box 299 — *TF:* 800-669-3275 ■ *Web:* www.frontiercoop.com	Norway	IA	52318	319-227-7996	227-7966
Hawaiian Isles Kona Coffee Co 2839 Mokumoa St — *TF Orders:* 800-657-7716 ■ *Web:* www.hawaiianisles.com	Honolulu	HI	96819	808-839-3255	
Keurig Green Mountain Inc 33 Coffee Ln — *NASDAQ: GMCR* ■ *Web:* www.greenmountaincoffee.com	Waterbury	VT	05676	802-244-5621	
McCullagh Coffee 245 Swan St — *TF:* 800-753-3473 ■ *Web:* www.mccullaghcoffee.com	Buffalo	NY	14204	800-753-3473	
Melitta Canada Inc 50 Ronson Dr Unit 150 — *TF:* 800-565-4882 ■ *Web:* www.melitta.ca	Toronto	ON	M9W1B3	800-565-4882	
Nestle USA Inc 800 N Brand Blvd — **Fax:* Sales ■ *Web:* www.nestle.com	Glendale	CA	91203	818-549-6000	553-3547*
New England Coffee Co 100 Charles St — **Fax Area Code:* 781 ■ *TF:* 800-225-3537 ■ *Web:* www.newenglandcoffee.com	Malden	MA	02148	800-225-3537	388-2838*
Old Mansion Foods 3811 Corporate Rd PO Box 1838 — *TF:* 800-476-1877 ■ *Web:* www.oldmansionfoods.com	Petersburg	VA	23805	804-862-9889	861-8816
Paul deLima Co Inc 7546 Morgan Rd — *TF:* 800-962-8864 ■ *Web:* www.delimacoffee.com	Liverpool	NY	13090	315-457-3725	457-3730
Port City Java Inc 101 Portwatch Way — *Web:* www.portcityjava.com	Wilmington	NC	28412	910-796-6646	
Red Diamond Inc 400 Park Ave — *TF:* 800-292-4651 ■ *Web:* www.reddiamond.com	Moody	AL	35004	205-577-4000	
Reily Foods Co 640 Magazine St — *TF:* 800-535-1961 ■ *Web:* www.frenchmarketcoffee.com	New Orleans	LA	70130	504-524-6131	539-5427
Royal Cup Coffee 160 Cleage Dr — **Fax Area Code:* 205 ■ *TF Cust Svc:* 800-366-5836 ■ *Web:* www.royalcupcoffee.com	Birmingham	AL	35217	800-366-5836	271-6071*
S & D Coffee Inc 300 Concord Pkwy PO Box 1628 — *TF Cust Svc:* 800-933-2210 ■ *Web:* www.sdcoffeetea.com	Concord	NC	28026	704-782-3121	721-5792
Stewarts Private Blend Food Inc 4110 W Wrightwood Ave — *Web:* www.stewarts.com	Chicago	IL	60639	773-489-2500	
Texas Coffee Co Inc 3297 S M L King Jr Pkwy — *TF:* 800-259-3400 ■ *Web:* www.texjoy.com	Beaumont	TX	77705	409-835-3434	
Torke Coffee Roasting Company Inc 3455 Paine Ave — *TF:* 800-242-7671 ■ *Web:* www.torkecoffee.com	Sheboygan	WI	53081	920-458-4114	458-0488
Van Roy Coffee Co, The 4569 Spring Rd — *TF:* 877-826-7669 ■ *Web:* www.vanroycoffee.com	Cleveland	OH	44131	216-749-7069	
White Coffee Corp 18-35 Steinway Pl — *TF:* 800-221-0140 ■ *Web:* www.whitecoffee.com	Astoria	NY	11105	718-204-7900	956-8504

296-8 Confectionery Products

Company	City	State	Zip	Phone	Fax
Adams & Brooks Inc 1915 S Hoover St — *Web:* www.adams-brooks.com	Los Angeles	CA	90007	213-749-3226	746-7614
ADM Cocoa Div 77 W Wacker Dr — *TF:* 800-637-5843 ■ *Web:* www.adm.com	Chicago	IL	60601	217-424-5200	
Andes Candies Inc 1400 E Wisconsin St	Delavan	WI	53115	262-728-9121	728-6794
Anthony-Thomas Candy Co 1777 Arlingate Ln — *TF:* 877-226-3921 ■ *Web:* www.anthony-thomas.com	Columbus	OH	43228	614-274-8405	
Asher's Chocolates 80 Wambold Rd — *TF:* 800-223-4420 ■ *Web:* www.ashers.com	Souderton	PA	18964	215-721-3000	721-3265
Atkinson Candy Co 1608 W Frank Ave — *TF:* 800-231-1203 ■ *Web:* www.atkinsoncandy.com	Lufkin	TX	75904	936-639-2333	639-2337
Barry Callebaut USA LLC 400 Industrial Pk Rd — *TF:* 866-443-0460 ■ *Web:* www.barry-callebaut.com	Saint Albans	VT	05478	802-524-9711	524-5148
Best Sweet Inc 288 Mazeppa Rd — *TF:* 888-211-5530 ■ *Web:* www.bestco.com	Mooresville	NC	28115	704-664-4300	
Blommer Chocolate Co 600 W Kinzie St — *TF:* 800-621-1606 ■ *Web:* www.blommer.com	Chicago	IL	60610	312-226-7700	
Boyer Candy Inc 821 17th St — *Web:* www.boyercandies.com	Altoona	PA	16602	814-944-9401	943-2354
Brown & Haley PO Box 1596 — *TF:* 800-426-8400 ■ *Web:* www.brown-haley.com	Tacoma	WA	98401	800-426-8400	
Ce De Candy Inc 1091 Lousons Rd — *Web:* www.smarties.com	Union	NJ	07083	908-964-0660	
Charms Co 7401 S Cicero Ave — **Fax Area Code:* 415 ■ *TF:* 800-267-0037 ■ *Web:* tootsie.com	Chicago	IL	60629	773-838-3400	401-0087*
Cherrydale Farms Fundraising 707 N Vly Forge Rd — *TF:* 877-619-4822 ■ *Web:* www.cherrydale.com	Lansdale	PA	19446	877-619-4822	
Chocolates a la Carte Inc 28455 Livingston Ave — **Fax Area Code:* 661 ■ **Fax:* Sales ■ *TF Cust Svc:* 800-818-2462 ■ *Web:* www.chocolatesalacarte.com	Valencia	CA	91355	800-818-2462	257-4999*
Decko Products Inc 2105 Superior St — *Web:* www.decko.com	Sandusky	OH	44870	419-626-5757	626-3135
Eaton Farm Confectioners Inc 30 Burbank Rd — *TF:* 800-343-9300 ■ *Web:* www.eatonfarmcandies.com	Sutton	MA	01590	508-865-5235	865-7087
Elmer Candy Corp 401 N Fifth St — *Web:* elmerchocolate.com	Ponchatoula	LA	70454	985-386-6166	
Esther Price Candies Inc 1709 Wayne Ave — *TF:* 800-782-0326 ■ *Web:* www.estherprice.com	Dayton	OH	45410	937-253-2121	
Farley's & Sathers Candy Company Inc 1 Sather Plz — *Web:* www.ferrarausa.com	Round Lake	MN	56167	507-945-8181	
FB Washburn Candy Corp 137 Perkins Ave — *Web:* www.fbwashburncandy.com	Brockton	MA	02302	508-588-0820	588-2205
Ferrara Pan Candy Co 7301 Harrison St — *Web:* www.ferrarausa.com	Forest Park	IL	60130	708-366-0500	
Ferrero USA Inc 600 Cottontail Ln — *Web:* www.ferrerousa.com	Somerset	NJ	08873	732-764-9300	764-9300
Fowler's Chocolate Co 100 River Rock Dr Ste 102 — *TF:* 800-824-2263 ■ *Web:* www.fowlerschocolates.com	Buffalo	NY	14207	716-877-9983	877-9959
Frankford Candy & Chocolate Co Inc 9300 Ashton Rd — *Web:* www.frankfordcandy.com	Philadelphia	PA	19114	215-735-5200	735-0721
Ganong Bros Ltd 1 Chocolate Dr — *Web:* www.ganong.com	Saint Stephen	NB	E3L2X5	506-465-5600	465-5610
Gayle's Chocolates 417 S Washington Ave — *Web:* www.gayleschocolates.com	Royal Oak	MI	48067	248-398-0001	
Gertrude Hawk Chocolates Inc 9 Keystone Pk — **Fax Area Code:* 570 ■ *TF:* 866-932-4295 ■ *Web:* www.gertrudehawkchocolates.com	Dunmore	PA	18512	800-822-2032	338-0947*
Ghirardelli Chocolate Co 1111 139th Ave — *TF:* 800-877-9338 ■ *Web:* www.ghirardelli.com	San Leandro	CA	94578	800-877-9338	
Goetze's Candy Company Inc 3900 E Monument St — *TF Orders:* 800-295-8058 ■ *Web:* www.goetzecandy.com	Baltimore	MD	21205	410-342-2010	522-7681
Guittard Chocolate Co 10 GuittaRd Rd — *TF:* 800-468-2462 ■ *Web:* www.guittard.com	Burlingame	CA	94010	650-697-4427	692-2761
Harry London Candies Inc 5353 Lauby Rd — *TF Cust Svc:* 800-333-3629 ■ *Web:* www.fanniemay.com	North Canton	OH	44720	330-494-0833	499-6902
Hershey Co 100 Crystal A Dr — *NYSE: HSY* ■ *TF Cust Svc:* 800-468-1714 ■ *Web:* www.thehersheycompany.com	Hershey	PA	17033	800-468-1714	
Hillside Candy Co 35 Hillside Ave — *TF:* 800-524-1304 ■ *Web:* www.hillsidecandy.com	Hillside	NJ	07205	973-926-2300	926-4440
James Candy Co 1519 Boardwalk — *TF Orders:* 800-441-1404 ■ *Web:* www.jamescandy.com	Atlantic City	NJ	08401	609-344-1519	344-0246
Jelly Belly Candy Co 1 Jelly Belly Ln — **Fax:* Cust Svc ■ *TF:* 800-323-9380 ■ *Web:* www.jellybelly.com	Fairfield	CA	94533	707-428-2800	423-4436*
Joyva Corp 53 Varick Ave — *Web:* www.joyva.com	Brooklyn	NY	11237	718-497-0170	366-8504
Just Born Inc 1300 Stefko Blvd — *TF:* 800-445-5787 ■ *Web:* www.justborn.com	Bethlehem	PA	18017	610-867-7568	867-3983
Katharine Beecher Candies 1250 Slate Hill Rd — *TF:* 800-233-7082 ■ *Web:* www.padutchcandies.com	Camp Hill	PA	17011	717-761-5440	761-5702
Koeze Co PO Box 9470 — **Fax Area Code:* 866 ■ *TF:* 800-555-9688 ■ *Web:* www.koeze.com	Grand Rapids	MI	49509	800-555-9688	817-0147*
Lammes Candies Since 1885 Inc PO Box 1885 — *TF:* 800-252-1885 ■ *Web:* www.lammes.com	Austin	TX	78767	512-310-2223	238-2019
Lincoln Snacks Co 5020 S 19th St	Lincoln	NE	68512	402-328-9345	
Lindt & Sprungli USA 1 Fine Chocolate Pl — *TF:* 877-695-4638 ■ *Web:* www.lindtusa.com	Stratham	NH	03885	603-778-8100	778-3102
Lucks Co, The 3003 S Pine St — **Fax:* Orders ■ *TF:* 800-426-9778 ■ *Web:* www.lucks.com	Tacoma	WA	98409	253-383-4815	383-0071*

	City	State	Zip	Phone	Fax
Madelaine Chocolate Novelties Inc 9603 Beach Ch Dr *TF:* 800-322-1505 ■ *Web:* www.madelainechocolate.com	Rockaway Beach	NY	11693	718-945-1500	318-4607
Malleys Chocolates 13400 Brookpark Rd **Fax Area Code:* 800 ■ *TF:* 800-835-5684 ■ *Web:* www.malleys.com	Cleveland	OH	44135	216-362-8700	211-0567*
Mars Snack Food 800 High St *Web:* www.mars.com	Hackettstown	NJ	07840	908-852-1000	850-2734
Masterson Company Inc 4023 W National Ave *Web:* www.mastersoncompany.com	Milwaukee	WI	53215	414-647-1132	647-1170
Moonstruck Chocolate Co 6600 N Baltimore Ave *TF:* 800-557-6666 ■ *Web:* www.moonstruckchocolate.com	Portland	OR	97203	503-247-3448	247-3450
Morley Candy Makers Inc 23770 Hall Rd *TF:* 800-651-7263 ■ *Web:* www.sanderscandy.com	Clinton Township	MI	48036	586-468-4300	
Munson's Candy Kitchen Inc 174 Hop River Rd *TF:* 888-686-7667 ■ *Web:* www.munsonschocolates.com	Bolton	CT	06043	860-649-4332	649-7209
Nestle USA Inc 800 N Brand Blvd **Fax:* Sales ■ *Web:* www.nestle.com	Glendale	CA	91203	818-549-6000	553-3547*
Palmer Candy Co 2600 Hwy 75 N PO Box 326 *Web:* www.palmercandy.com	Sioux City	IA	51102	712-258-5543	258-3224
Paradise Inc 1200 W MLK Jr Blvd *OTC:* PARF ■ **Fax Area Code:* 813 ■ *TF:* 800-330-8952 ■ *Web:* www.paradisefruitco.com	Plant City	FL	33563	800-330-8952	754-3168*
Pearson's Candy Co 2140 W Seventh St *TF Cust Svc:* 800-328-6507 ■ *Web:* www.pearsoncandy.com	Saint Paul	MN	55116	651-698-0356	696-2222
Pennsylvania Dutch Candies 1250 Slate Hill Rd *TF:* 800-233-7082 ■ *Web:* www.padutchcandies.com	Camp Hill	PA	17011	717-761-5440	761-5702
Pez Candy Inc 35 Prindle Hill Rd *Web:* www.pez.com	Orange	CT	06477	203-795-0531	799-1679
PLB Sports Inc Penn Ctr W Bldg 3 Ste 411 *Web:* www.plbsports.com	Pittsburgh	PA	15276	412-787-8800	
Primrose Candy Co 4111 W Parker Ave *Web:* www.primrosecandy.com	Chicago	IL	60639	773-276-9522	
RM Palmer Co 77 S Second Ave *Web:* www.rmpalmer.com	West Reading	PA	19611	610-372-8971	378-5208
Russell Stover Candies Inc 4900 Oak St *TF:* 800-477-8683 ■ *Web:* www.russellstover.com	Kansas City	MO	64112	816-842-9240	
Santa Cruz Nutritionals 2200 Delaware Ave **Fax:* Sales ■ *Web:* www.santacruznutritionals.com	Santa Cruz	CA	95060	831-457-3200	454-0915*
Sconza Candy Co 1 Sconza Candy Ln *Web:* www.sconzacandy.com	Oakdale	CA	95361	209-845-3700	845-3737
See's Candies Inc 210 El Camino Real *TF Cust Svc:* 800-877-7337 ■ *Web:* www.sees.com	South San Francisco	CA	94080	650-761-2490	
Sorbee International Ltd 9990 Global Rd *TF:* 800-654-3997 ■ *Web:* www.sorbee.com	Philadelphia	PA	19115	215-645-1111	677-7736
Spangler Candy Co 400 N Portland St PO Box 71 *TF Sales:* 888-636-4221 ■ *Web:* www.spanglercandy.com	Bryan	OH	43506	419-636-4221	636-3695
Standard Candy Company Inc 715 Massman Dr *Web:* www.googoo.com	Nashville	TN	37210	615-889-6360	889-7775
Storck USA LP 325 N LaSalle St Ste 400 *TF:* 800-852-5542 ■ *Web:* www.storck.com	Chicago	IL	60654	312-467-5700	467-9722
Supreme Chocolatier LLC 1150 S Ave *Web:* www.supremechocolatier.com	Staten Island	NY	10314	718-761-9600	
Sweet Candy Co Inc 3780 W Directors Row *TF:* 800-669-8669 ■ *Web:* www.sweetcandy.com	Salt Lake City	UT	84104	801-886-1444	886-1404
T R Toppers Inc 320 Fairchild *TF:* 800-748-4635 ■ *Web:* www.trtoppers.com	Pueblo	CO	81001	719-948-4902	948-4908
Tootsie Roll Industries Inc 7401 S Cicero Ave *NYSE:* TR ■ *TF:* 866-972-6879 ■ *Web:* www.tootsie.com	Chicago	IL	60629	773-838-3400	838-3534
Vitasoy USA Inc 1 New England Way *TF:* 800-848-2769 ■ *Web:* www.vitasoy-usa.com	Ayer	MA	01432	978-772-6880	
Waymouth Farms Inc 5300 Boone Ave *TF:* 800-527-0094 ■ *Web:* www.goodsensesnacks.com	New Hope	MN	55428	763-533-5300	533-9890
Wolfgang Candy Co 50 E Fourth Ave *TF:* 800-248-4273 ■ *Web:* www.wolfgangcandy.com	York	PA	17404	717-843-5536	845-2881
World's Finest Chocolate Inc 4801 S Lawndale **Fax Area Code:* 877 ■ *TF:* 888-821-8452 ■ *Web:* www.worldsfinestchocolate.com	Chicago	IL	60632	888-821-8452	256-2685*
Y & S Candies 400 Running Pump Rd	Lancaster	PA	17603	717-299-1261	394-9109
Zachary Confections Inc 2130 IN-28 **Fax Area Code:* 765 ■ *TF Cust Svc:* 800-445-4222 ■ *Web:* www.zacharyconfections.com	Frankfort	IN	46041	800-445-4222	659-1491*

296-9 Cookies & Crackers

	City	State	Zip	Phone	Fax
Benzel's Pretzel Bakery Inc 5200 Sixth Ave *TF:* 800-344-4438 ■ *Web:* www.benzels.com	Altoona	PA	16602	814-942-5062	942-4133
Bremner Biscuit Co 4600 Joliet St *TF:* 866-972-6879 ■ *Web:* www.bremnerbiscuitco.com	Denver	CO	80239	303-371-8180	371-8185
Buckeye Snack Food Co 11677 Chesterdale Rd	Cincinnati	OH	45246	513-458-6200	
Christie Cookie Co 1205 Third Ave N *TF:* 800-458-2447 ■ *Web:* www.christiecookies.com	Nashville	TN	37208	615-242-3817	242-5572
Deep Foods Inc 1090 Springfield Rd *Web:* www.deepfoods.com	Union	NJ	07083	908-810-7500	810-8482
Delyse Inc 505 Reactor Way *TF:* 800-441-6887 ■ *Web:* www.delyse.com	Reno	NV	89502	775-857-1811	
Ellison Bakery 4108 W Ferguson Rd *Web:* www.ebakery.com	Fort Wayne	IN	46809	260-747-6136	747-1954
Fehr Foods Inc 5425 N First St *Web:* www.fehrfoods.com	Abilene	TX	79603	325-691-5425	
Gurley's Foods 1118 E Hwy 12 *Web:* www.gurleysfoods.com	Willmar	MN	56201	320-235-0600	
J & J Snack Foods Corp 6000 Central Hwy *NASDAQ:* JJSF ■ *TF:* 800-486-9533 ■ *Web:* www.jjsnack.com	Pennsauken	NJ	08109	856-665-9533	665-6718
Joy Cone Co 3435 Lamor Rd *TF:* 800-242-2663 ■ *Web:* www.joycone.com	Hermitage	PA	16148	724-962-5747	962-3470
Keystone Pretzels 124 W Airport Rd **Fax Area Code:* 717 ■ *TF:* 888-572-4500 ■ *Web:* www.keystonepretzels.com	Lititz	PA	17543	888-572-4500	560-2241*
Little Dutch Boy Bakery Inc 12349 South 970 East	Draper	UT	84020	801-571-3800	571-3802
Norse Dairy Systems 1740 Joyce Ave *TF:* 800-637-2663 ■ *Web:* www.norse.com	Columbus	OH	43219	614-294-4931	
Pretzels Inc 123 Harvest Rd PO Box 503 *TF:* 800-456-4838 ■ *Web:* www.pretzels-inc.com	Bluffton	IN	46714	260-824-4838	824-0895
Richmond Baking Co 520 N Sixth St *Web:* www.richmondbaking.com	Richmond	IN	47374	765-962-8535	962-2253
Rudolph Foods Company Inc 6575 Bellefontaine Rd *TF:* 800-241-7675 ■ *Web:* www.rudolphfoods.com	Lima	OH	45804	419-648-3611	648-4087
Silver Lake Cookie Company Inc 141 Freeman Ave *TF:* 800-645-9048 ■ *Web:* www.silverlakecookie.com	Islip	NY	11751	631-581-4000	581-4510
Snyder's of Hanover 1250 York St PO Box 6917 *TF:* 800-233-7125 ■ *Web:* snyderslance.com	Hanover	PA	17331	717-632-4477	632-7207
T. Marzetti Company. PO Box 29163 *TF:* 800-999-1835 ■ *Web:* www.marzetti.com	Columbus	OH	43229	800-999-1835	
Tom Sturgis Pretzels Inc 2267 Lancaster Pk *TF:* 800-817-3834 ■ *Web:* www.tomsturgispretzels.com	Reading	PA	19607	610-775-0335	
Venus Wafers Inc 100 Research Rd *Web:* www.venuswafers.com	Hingham	MA	02043	781-740-1002	740-0791
Wege Pretzel Co PO Box 334 *TF:* 800-888-4646 ■ *Web:* www.wege.com	Hanover	PA	17331	800-888-4646	

296-10 Dairy Products - Dry, Condensed, Evaporated

	City	State	Zip	Phone	Fax
Abbott Laboratories Ross Products Div 625 Cleveland Ave *TF PR:* 800-227-5767 ■ *Web:* abbottnutrition.com	Columbus	OH	43215	614-624-7485	
AMPI 315 N Broadway *TF:* 800-533-3580 ■ *Web:* www.ampi.com	New Ulm	MN	56073	507-354-8295	
California Dairies Inc 2000 N Plz Dr *Web:* www.californiadairies.com	Visalia	CA	93291	559-625-2200	625-5433
Dairy Farmers of America Inc 10220 N Ambassador Dr *TF:* 888-332-6455 ■ *Web:* www.dfamilk.com	Kansas City	MO	64153	816-801-6455	801-6456
Davisco International Inc 719 N Main St *TF:* 800-757-7611 ■ *Web:* www.daviscofoods.com	Le Sueur	MN	56058	507-665-8811	665-3701
Erie Foods International Inc 401 Seventh Ave PO Box 648 *TF:* 800-447-1887 ■ *Web:* www.eriefoods.com	Erie	IL	61250	309-659-2233	659-2822
Farmers Co-op Creamery Inc (FCC) 700 N Hwy 99 W *Web:* www.farmerscoop.org	McMinnville	OR	97128	503-472-2157	472-3821
Foremost Farms USA E10889A Penny Ln *TF:* 800-362-9196 ■ *Web:* www.foremostfarms.com	Baraboo	WI	53913	608-355-8700	355-8699
Galloway Company Inc 601 S Commercial St *Web:* www.gallowaycompany.com	Neenah	WI	54956	920-722-7741	722-1927
Gehl's Guernsey Farms Inc N116 W15970 Main St *TF:* 800-521-2873 ■ *Web:* www.gehls.com	Germantown	WI	53022	262-251-8572	251-8744
Instantwhip Foods Inc 2200 Cardigan Ave **Fax:* Sales ■ *TF Cust Svc:* 800-544-9447 ■ *Web:* www.instantwhip.com	Columbus	OH	43215	614-488-2536	488-0307*
Jackson-Mitchell Inc PO Box 934 *Web:* meyenberg.com	Turlock	CA	95381	209-667-0786	
John Volpi & Company Inc 5263 Northrup Ave *TF:* 800-288-3439 ■ *Web:* www.volpifoods.com	St Louis	MO	63110	314-772-8550	
Maple Island Inc 2497 Seventh Ave E Ste 105 *TF:* 800-369-1022 ■ *Web:* www.maple-island.com	St Paul	MN	55109	651-773-1000	773-2155
Mead Johnson Nutritionals 2701 Patriot Blvd 4th Fl *Web:* www.meadjohnson.com	Glenview	IL	60026	847-832-2420	
Milk Products LLC PO Box 150 *TF:* 800-657-0793 ■ *Web:* www.milkproductsinc.com	Chilton	WI	53014	920-849-2348	849-9014
Nestle USA Inc 800 N Brand Blvd **Fax:* Sales ■ *Web:* www.nestle.com	Glendale	CA	91203	818-549-6000	553-3547*
O-AT-KA Milk Products Co-op Inc 700 Ellicott St *TF:* 800-828-8152 ■ *Web:* www.oatkamilk.com	Batavia	NY	14020	585-343-0536	343-4473
Ohio Processors Inc 244 E First St *Web:* www.instantwhip.com/home.html	London	OH	43140	740-852-9243	
Penn Maid Foods Inc 10975 Dutton Rd *Web:* www.pennmaid.com	Philadelphia	PA	19154	215-824-2800	
Sinton Dairy Foods Co LLC 3801 Sinton Rd *TF:* 800-388-4970	Colorado Springs	CO	80907	719-633-3821	667-7470
Valentine Enterprises Inc 1291 Progress Ctr Ave *Web:* www.veiusa.com	Lawrenceville	GA	30043	770-995-0661	995-0725
Vern Dale Products Inc 8445 Lyndon St *Web:* www.verndaleproducts.com	Detroit	MI	48238	313-834-4190	834-6280

296-11 Diet & Health Foods

	City	State	Zip	Phone	Fax
Alle Processing Corp 56-20 59th St *Web:* alleprocessing.com	Maspeth	NY	11378	718-894-2000	326-4642
AMS Health Sciences Inc 4000 N Lindsay *TF:* 800-426-4267 ■ *Web:* www.amsonline.com	Oklahoma City	OK	73105	405-842-0131	843-4935
BAZI Inc 1730 Blake St Ste 305 *Web:* www.drinkbazi.com	Denver	CO	80202	303-316-8577	
Eden Foods Inc 701 Tecumseh Rd *TF Cust Svc:* 800-248-0320 ■ *Web:* www.edenfoods.com	Clinton	MI	49236	517-456-7424	456-6075
Grow Company Inc 55 Railroad Ave *Web:* www.growco.us	Ridgefield	NJ	07657	201-941-8777	941-1881
Health Hut 1512 First Ave NE *Web:* healthhutcr.com	Cedar Rapids	IA	52402	319-362-7345	369-0440

				Phone	Fax
Isagenix International LLC 2225 S Price Rd. Chandler	AZ	85286	480-889-5747	636-5386
TF: 877-877-8111 ■ *Web:* isagenix.com				
Medifast Inc 11445 Cronhill Dr. Owings Mills	MD	21117	800-209-0878	
NYSE: MED ■ *TF:* 800-209-0878 ■ *Web:* www.medifast1.com				
Nutrition 21 Inc 3 Manhattanville Rd Purchase	NY	10577	914-701-4500	696-0860
Web: www.nutrition21.com				
RC Fine Foods PO Box 236 Belle Mead	NJ	08502	908-359-5500	359-6957
TF: 800-526-3953 ■ *Web:* www.rcfinefoods.com				
Seasons' Enterprises Ltd 1790 W Cortland Ct Ste B PO Box 965 Addison	IL	60101	630-628-0211	
Web: www.seasonssnacks.com				
Tahitian Noni International 333 W Riverpark Dr Provo	UT	84604	801-234-1000	234-1001
TF Cust Svc: 800-445-2969 ■ *Web:* morinda.com				
TreeHouse Foods Inc 2021 Spring Rd Ste 600 Oak Brook	IL	60523	708-483-1300	
NYSE: THS ■ *Web:* www.treehousefoods.com				
Vitaminerals Inc 1815 Flower St Glendale	CA	91201	800-432-1856	
TF: 800-432-1856 ■ *Web:* www.cryogel.tv				

296-12 Fats & Oils - Animal or Marine

			Phone	Fax
Baker Commodities Inc 4020 Bandini Blvd. Vernon	CA	90058	323-268-2801	
Web: www.bakercommodities.com				
Coast Packing Co 3275 E Vernon Ave Vernon	CA	90058	323-277-7700	277-7712
Darling International Inc 251 O'Connor Ridge Blvd Ste 300 Irving	TX	75038	972-717-0300	
NYSE: DAR ■ *TF:* 855-327-7761 ■ *Web:* www.darlingii.com				
GA Wintzer & Son Co 204 W Auglaize St Wapakoneta	OH	45895	419-739-4900	738-9058
TF: 800-331-1801 ■ *Web:* www.gawintzer.com				
Griffin Industries Inc 4413 Tanner Church Rd Ellenwood	GA	30294	404-363-1320	
Web: griffinind.com				
Harbinger Group Inc 450 Pk Ave 27th Fl New York	NY	10022	212-906-8555	
NYSE: HRG ■ *Web:* www.harbingergroupinc.com				
Jacob Stern & Sons Inc 1464 E Valley Rd Santa Barbara	CA	93108	805-565-1411	565-1415
TF Cust Svc: 800-223-7054 ■ *Web:* www.jacobstern.com				
Kaluzny Bros Inc 1528 Mound Rd Rockdale	IL	60436	815-744-1453	729-5069
Omega Protein Corp 2105 City W Blvd Ste 500 Houston	TX	77042	713-623-0060	940-6122
Web: www.omegaprotein.com				
San Luis Tallow Co 445 Prado Rd San Luis Obispo	CA	93401	805-543-8660	
Werner G Smith Inc 1730 Train Ave Cleveland	OH	44113	216-861-3676	861-3680
TF General: 800-535-8343 ■ *Web:* www.wernergsmithinc.com				

296-13 Fish & Seafood - Canned

			Phone	Fax
Acme Smoked Fish Corp 30 Gem St Brooklyn	NY	11222	718-383-8585	
Web: www.acmesmokedfish.com				
Beaver Street Fisheries Inc 1741 W Beaver St Jacksonville	FL	32209	904-354-8533	
TF: 800-874-6426 ■ *Web:* beaverstreetfisheries.com				
Bumble Bee Seafoods Inc PO Box 85362 San Diego	CA	92186	858-715-4000	
TF: 800-800-8572 ■ *Web:* www.bumblebee.com				
High Liner Foods Inc (HLF) 1 Highliner Ave Portsmouth	NH	03801	603-431-6865	
NYSE: HLF ■ *Web:* www.highlinerfoods.com				
Icicle Seafoods Inc 4019 21st Ave W Seattle	WA	98199	206-282-0988	282-7222
Web: www.icicleseafoods.com				
Inlet Fish Producers Inc PO Box 114 Kenai	AK	99611	907-283-9275	
Web: www.inletfish.com				
Los Angeles Smoking & Curing Co (LASCCO) 1100 W Ewing St Seattle	WA	98119	206-285-6800	
TF: 800-365-8950 ■ *Web:* www.oceanbeauty.com				
Nelson Crab Inc 3088 Kindred Ave Tokeland	WA	98590	800-262-0069	
TF: 800-262-0069 ■ *Web:* seatreats.stores.yahoo.net				
Noon Hour Food Products Inc 215 N Des Plaines Chicago	IL	60661	312-382-1177	
TF Cust Svc: 888-463-6332				
Overwaitea Food Group 19855 92A Ave Langley	BC	V1M3B6	604-888-1213	
TF: 800-242-9229 ■ *Web:* www.owfg.com				
Pacific Choice Seafoods Co 16797 SE 130th Ave Clackamas	OR	97015	707-442-2981	
Web: www.pacseafood.com				
Peter Pan Seafoods Inc 2200 Sixth Ave Ste 1000 Seattle	WA	98121	206-728-6000	441-9090
TF: 800-331-3522 ■ *Web:* www.ppsf.com				
Petersburg Fisheries PO Box 1147 Petersburg	AK	99833	907-772-4294	772-4472
TF: 877-772-4294 ■ *Web:* www.hookedonfish.com				
RJ Peacock Canning Co 72 Water St. Lubec	ME	04652	207-733-5556	733-0936
Snow's/Doxsee Inc 994 Ocean Dr. Cape May	NJ	08204	609-884-0440	898-2409
Vita Food Products Inc 2222 W Lake St Chicago	IL	60612	312-738-4500	
TF: 800-989-8482 ■ *Web:* www.vitafoodproducts.com				
Westward Seafoods 2101 Fourth Ave Ste 1700 Seattle	WA	98121	206-682-5949	682-1825
Web: www.westwardseafoods.com				

296-14 Fish & Seafood - Fresh or Frozen

			Phone	Fax
Bama Sea Products 756 28th St S Saint Petersburg	FL	33712	727-327-3474	322-0580
Web: www.bamasea.com				
Blount Seafood Corp 630 Currant Rd. Fall River	MA	02720	774-888-1300	888-1399
TF Hotline: 800-274-2526 ■ *Web:* www.blountseafood.com				
Bon Secour Fisheries Inc 17449 County Rd 49 S Bon Secour	AL	36511	251-949-7411	949-6478
Web: www.bonsecourfisheries.com				
Chef John Folse & Company Inc 2517 S Philippe Ave Gonzales	LA	70737	225-644-6000	
Web: www.jfolse.com				
Chesapeake Bay Packing LLC 800 Terminal Ave Newport News	VA	23607	757-244-8440	244-8500
Web: www.chesapeakebaypacking.com				
Coast Seafoods Co 14711 NE 29th Pl Ste 111 Bellevue	WA	98007	425-702-8800	
Web: coastseafoods.com				
Consolidated Catfish Cos LLC 299 S St PO Box 271 Isola	MS	38754	662-962-3101	962-0114
TF: 800-228-3474 ■ *Web:* countryselect.com				
Crocker & Winsor Seafoods Inc PO Box 51905 Boston	MA	02205	617-269-3100	269-3376
TF: 800-225-1597 ■ *Web:* www.crockerwinsor.com				
Eastern Fisheries Inc 14 Hervey Tichon Ave New Bedford	MA	02740	508-993-5300	991-2226
Web: easternfisheries.com				
Eastern Shore Foods LLC 13249 Lankford Hwy Mappsville	VA	23407	757-824-5651	
Fishermen's Pride Processors 4510 S Alameda St Vernon	CA	90058	323-232-8300	232-8833
Web: www.neptunefoods.com				
Freshwater Farm Products LLC 4554 State Hwy 12 E PO Box 850 Belzoni	MS	39038	662-247-4205	247-4442
TF: 800-748-9338 ■ *Web:* www.freshwatercatfish.com				
Gorton's Inc 128 Rogers St Gloucester	MA	01930	978-283-3000	281-8295
TF: 800-222-6846 ■ *Web:* www.gortons.com				
Great Northern Products Ltd 2700 Plainfield Pk Cranston	RI	02921	401-490-4590	490-5595
Web: northernproducts.com				
King & Prince Seafood Corp 1 King & Prince Blvd Brunswick	GA	31520	912-265-5155	
TF: 800-841-0205 ■ *Web:* www.kpseafood.com				
Metompkin Bay Oyster Co 101 N 11th St Ste 105 Crisfield	MD	21817	410-968-0660	968-0670
Web: www.metompkinseafood.com				
Morey's Seafood International LLC 1218 Hwy 10 S Motley	MN	56466	218-352-6345	
TF: 800-808-3474 ■ *Web:* www.moreys.com				
Netuno USA Inc 18501 Pines Blvd Ste 206 Pembroke Pines	FL	33029	305-513-0904	513-3904
Web: www.netunousa.com				
Ocean Beauty Seafoods Inc 1100 W Ewing St Seattle	WA	98119	206-285-6800	
TF: 800-365-8950 ■ *Web:* www.oceanbeauty.com				
Orca Bay Seafoods Inc 900 Powell Ave SW Renton	WA	98057	425-204-9100	
Web: orcabayseafoods.com				
Overwaitea Food Group 19855 92A Ave Langley	BC	V1M3B6	604-888-1213	
TF: 800-242-9229 ■ *Web:* www.owfg.com				
Pinnacle Foods Corp 399 Jefferson Rd Parsippany	NJ	07054	973-541-6620	
TF: 866-266-7596 ■ *Web:* www.pinnaclefoodscorp.com				
Riverside Foods Inc 2520 Wilson St Two Rivers	WI	54241	920-793-4511	794-7332
TF: 800-678-4511 ■ *Web:* riversidefoods.com				
Sea Fresh USA Inc 45 All American Way North Kingstown	RI	02852	401-583-0200	
Web: seafreshusa.com				
Sea Harvest Packing Co PO Box 818 Brunswick	GA	31521	912-264-3212	264-2749
TF: 800-627-4300 ■ *Web:* www.seaharvest.com				
Sea Watch International Ltd 8978 Glebe Pk Dr Easton	MD	21601	410-822-7500	822-1266
Web: www.seawatch.com				
Seafood Producers Co-op 2875 Roeder Ave Bellingham	WA	98225	360-733-0120	733-0513
Web: www.spcsales.com				
Simmons Farm Raised Catfish Inc 2628 Erickson Rd Yazoo City	MS	39194	662-746-5687	746-8625
Web: www.simmonscatfish.com				
Stoller Fisheries 1301 18th St PO Box B Spirit Lake	IA	51360	712-336-1750	336-4681
TF: 800-831-5174 ■ *Web:* www.stollerfisheries.com				
Sugiyo USA Inc PO Box 468 Anacortes	WA	98221	360-293-0180	293-6964
Web: www.sugiyo.com				
Tampa Bay Fisheries Inc 3060 Gallagher Rd Dover	FL	33527	813-752-8883	
TF: 800-732-3663 ■ *Web:* www.tbfish.com				
Texas Pack Inc 508 Port Rd Port Isabel	TX	78578	956-943-5461	943-6630
Thomas Seafood of Carteret Inc 421 Merrimon Rd Beaufort	NC	28516	252-728-2391	
Tichon Seafood Corp 7 Conway St New Bedford	MA	02740	508-999-5607	990-8271
Web: tichonseafood.com				
Trident Seafood Corp 5303 Shilshole Ave NW Seattle	WA	98107	206-783-3818	782-7195
Web: www.tridentseafoods.com				
UniSea Inc 15400 NE 90th St PO Box 97019 Redmond	WA	98073	425-881-8181	
TF: 800-535-8509 ■ *Web:* www.unisea.com				
Wanchese Fish Co 2000 Northgate Commerce Pkwy Suffolk	VA	23435	757-673-4500	
Web: www.wanchese.com				

296-15 Flavoring Extracts & Syrups

			Phone	Fax
Brady Enterprises Inc 167 Moore Rd East Weymouth	MA	02189	781-337-5000	337-9338
David Michael & Co Inc 10801 Decatur Rd. Philadelphia	PA	19154	215-632-3100	887-3339*
**Fax Area Code:* 909 ■ *TF:* 800-363-5286 ■ *Web:* www.dmflavors.com				
DD Williamson & Company Inc 100 S Spring St Louisville	KY	40206	502-895-2438	
TF: 800-227-2635 ■ *Web:* www.ddwcolor.com				
Emerald Kalama Chemical LLC 1296 Third St NW Kalama	WA	98625	360-673-2550	673-3564
TF: 877-300-9545 ■ *Web:* www.emeraldmaterials.com				
Firmenich Inc 250 Plainsvoro Plainsboro	NJ	08536	609-452-1000	452-6077
Web: www.firmenich.com				
Frutarom Corp 9500 Railroad Ave North Bergen	NJ	07047	201-861-9500	861-9267*
**Fax:* Cust Svc ■ *TF:* 866-229-7198 ■ *Web:* www.frutarom.com				
Givaudan Flavors Corp 1199 Edison Dr. Cincinnati	OH	45216	513-948-8000	
Web: www.givaudan.com				
I Rice & Company Inc 11500 Roosevelt Blvd Bldg D Philadelphia	PA	19116	215-673-7423	673-2616
TF: 800-232-6022 ■ *Web:* www.iriceco.com				
Jel Sert Co Rt 59 & Conde St West Chicago	IL	60185	630-876-4838	
TF: 800-323-2592 ■ *Web:* www.jelsert.com				

Company / Address	City	State	Zip	Phone	Fax
Kalsec Inc 3713 W Main St	Kalamazoo	MI	49006	269-349-9711	382-3060
TF: 800-323-9320 ■ *Web:* www.kalsec.com					
Limpert Bros Inc 202 NW Blvd PO Box 1480	Vineland	NJ	08362	856-691-1353	794-8968
TF: 800-691-1353 ■ *Web:* www.limpertbrothers.com					
Lyons Magnus Inc 3158 E Hamilton Ave	Fresno	CA	93702	800-344-7130	233-8249*
**Fax Area Code:* 559 ■ *TF:* 800-344-7130 ■ *Web:* www.lyonsmagnus.com					
M & F Worldwide Corp 35 E 62nd St	New York	NY	10065	212-572-8600	
NYSE: MFW ■ *Web:* www.mandfworldwide.com					
Mother Murphy's Labs Inc 2826 S Elm St PO Box 16846	Greensboro	NC	27416	336-273-1737	273-2615
TF: 800-849-1277 ■ *Web:* www.mothermurphys.com					
Nielsen-Massey Vanillas Inc 1550 S Shields Dr	Waukegan	IL	60085	847-578-1550	578-1570
TF: 800-525-7873 ■ *Web:* www.nielsenmassey.com					
Northwestern Flavors Inc 120 N Aurora St	West Chicago	IL	60185	630-231-0489	
Phillips Syrup Corp 28025 Ranney Pkwy	Westlake	OH	44145	440-835-8001	835-1148
TF: 800-350-8443 ■ *Web:* www.phillipssyrup.com					
Sea Breeze Inc 441 Rt 202	Towaco	NJ	07082	973-334-7777	334-2617
TF: 800-732-2733 ■ *Web:* www.seabreezesyrups.com					
Sensient Technologies Corp 777 E Wisconsin Ave	Milwaukee	WI	53202	414-271-6755	347-3785
NYSE: SXT ■ *TF:* 800-558-9892 ■ *Web:* www.sensient.com					
Sethness Products Co 3422 W Touhy Ave	Lincolnwood	IL	60712	847-329-2080	329-2090
TF: 888-772-1880 ■ *Web:* www.sethness.com					
Symrise Inc 300 N St	Teterboro	NJ	07608	201-288-3200	462-2200
Web: www.symrise.com					
T Hasegawa USA Inc 14017 183rd St	Cerritos	CA	90703	714-522-1900	522-6800
Web: www.thasegawa.com					
Virginia Dare Extract Company Inc 882 Third Ave	Brooklyn	NY	11232	718-788-1776	768-3978
Web: www.virginiadare.com					
Western Syrup Co 13766 Milroy Pl	Santa Fe Springs	CA	90670	562-921-4485	
TF: 800-521-3888 ■ *Web:* www.jogue.com					
Wild Flavors Inc 1261 Pacific Ave	Erlanger	KY	41018	859-342-3600	342-3610*
**Fax:* Sales ■ *TF:* 800-263-5286 ■ *Web:* www.wildflavors.com					
Zink & Triest Company Inc 200 Highpoint Dr	Chalfont	PA	18914	215-469-1950	

296-16 Flour Mixes & Doughs

Company / Address	City	State	Zip	Phone	Fax
Abitec Corp Inc PO Box 569	Columbus	OH	43215	614-429-6464	299-8279
TF Sales: 800-555-1255 ■ *Web:* www.abiteccorp.com					
Bake'n Joy Foods Inc 351 Willow St	North Andover	MA	01845	978-683-1414	683-1713
TF: 800-666-4937 ■ *Web:* www.bakenjoy.com					
Cereal Food Processors Inc 2001 Shawnee Mission Pkwy	Mission Woods	KS	66205	913-890-6300	
Web: www.cerealfood.com					
Dawn Food Products Inc 3333 Sargent Rd	Jackson	MI	49201	517-789-4400	789-4465
TF Cust Svc: 800-292-1362 ■ *Web:* www.dawnfoods.com					
Gilster-Mary Lee Corp 1037 State St PO Box 227	Chester	IL	62233	618-826-2361	826-2973
Web: gilstermarylee.com					
Langlois Co 10810 San Sevaine Way	Mira Loma	CA	91752	951-360-3900	
TF: 800-962-5993 ■ *Web:* www.langloiscompany.com					
Pinnacle Foods Corp 399 Jefferson Rd	Parsippany	NJ	07054	973-541-6620	
TF: 866-266-7596 ■ *Web:* www.pinnaclefoodscorp.com					
Puratos Corp 1941 Old Cuthbert Rd	Cherry Hill	NJ	08034	856-428-4300	428-2939
Web: www.puratos.com					
Rhodes International Inc PO Box 25487	Salt Lake City	UT	84125	801-972-0122	
TF Cust Svc: 800-876-7333 ■ *Web:* www.rhodesbread.com					
Southern Maid Donut Flour Co 3615 Cavalier Dr	Garland	TX	75042	972-272-6425	276-3549
Web: www.southernmaiddonuts.com					
Subco Foods Inc 4350 S Taylor Dr	Sheboygan	WI	53081	920-457-7761	457-3899
TF: 800-473-0757 ■ *Web:* www.subcofoods.com					
Watson Foods Company Inc 301 Heffernan Dr	West Haven	CT	06516	203-932-3000	932-8266
TF: 800-388-3481 ■ *Web:* www.watson-inc.com					

296-17 Food Emulsifiers

Company / Address	City	State	Zip	Phone	Fax
ADM Specialty Food Ingredients Div 4666 E Faries Pkwy	Decatur	IL	62526	217-424-5200	
TF: 800-637-5843 ■ *Web:* www.adm.com					
American Lecithin Company Inc 115 Hurley Rd Unit 2B	Oxford	CT	06478	203-262-7100	262-7101
TF: 800-364-4416 ■ *Web:* www.americanlecithin.com					
Bunge Ltd 50 Main St	White Plains	NY	10606	914-684-2800	
NYSE: BG ■ *Web:* www.bunge.com					
Crest Foods Company Inc 905 Main St	Ashton	IL	61006	815-453-7411	453-7744
TF: 877-273-7893 ■ *Web:* www.crestfoods.com					
Frutarom Corp 9500 Railroad Ave	North Bergen	NJ	07047	201-861-9500	861-9267*
**Fax:* Cust Svc ■ *TF:* 866-229-7198 ■ *Web:* www.frutarom.com					

296-18 Fruits & Vegetables - Dried or Dehydrated

Company / Address	City	State	Zip	Phone	Fax
Basic American Foods 2185 N California Blvd Ste 215	Walnut Creek	CA	94596	925-472-4000	472-4314
Web: www.baf.com					
Bernard Food Industries Inc 1125 Hartrey Ave	Evanston	IL	60204	847-869-5222	869-5315
TF: 800-323-3663 ■ *Web:* www.bernardfoods.com					
Concord Foods Inc 10 Minuteman Way	Brockton	MA	02301	508-580-1700	584-9425
Web: www.concordfoods.com					
Custom Culinary 2505 S Finley Rd	Lombard	IL	60148	630-928-4898	
Web: www.customculinary.com					
Del Monte Foods Co 1 Maritime Plaza	San Francisco	CA	94111	415-247-3000	247-3311
TF Cust Svc: 800-543-3090 ■ *Web:* www.delmonte.com					
Derco Foods 2670 W Shaw Ln	Fresno	CA	93711	559-435-2664	435-8520
Web: www.dercofoods.com					
Freskeeto Frozen Foods Inc 8019 Rt 209	Ellenville	NY	12428	845-647-5111	
TF: 800-356-3663					
Garry Packing Inc 11272 E Central Ave	Del Rey	CA	93616	559-888-2126	888-2848
TF: 800-248-2126 ■ *Web:* www.garryscs.com					
Graceland Fruit Inc 1123 Main St	Frankfort	MI	49635	231-352-7181	352-4711
TF: 800-352-7181 ■ *Web:* www.gracelandfruit.com					
Idaho Supreme Potatoes Inc 614 E 800 N PO Box 246	Firth	ID	83236	208-346-6841	346-4104
Web: idahosupreme.com					
Idaho-Pacific Corp 4723 E 100 N PO Box 478	Ririe	ID	83443	208-538-6971	538-5082
TF Sales: 800-238-5503 ■ *Web:* www.idahopacific.com					
Larsen Farms 2650 N 2375 E	Hamer	ID	83425	208-662-5501	662-5568
TF Sales: 800-767-6104 ■ *Web:* www.larsenfarms.com					
Meridian Foods 201 E Babb Rd	Eaton	IN	47338	765-396-3344	396-3430
National Raisin Co PO Box 219	Fowler	CA	93625	559-834-5981	834-1055
Web: www.nationalraisin.com					
Nonpareil Corp 40 N 400 W	Blackfoot	ID	83221	208-785-5880	785-3656
Web: nonpareilfarms.com					
Northwest Pea & Bean Company Inc 6109 E Desmet Ave	Spokane	WA	99212	509-534-3821	534-4350
Web: co-ag.com					
Oregon Freeze Dry Inc 525 25th Ave SW	Albany	OR	97322	541-926-6001	
Web: www.ofd.com					
Oregon Potato Co PO Box 3110	Pasco	WA	99302	509-545-4545	
TF: 800-336-6311 ■ *Web:* www.oregonpotato.com					
Small Planet Foods Inc 106 Woodworth St	Sedro Woolley	WA	98284	360-855-0100	
TF: 800-624-4123 ■ *Web:* www.smallplanetfoods.com					
Stapleton-Spence Packing Co 1530 The Alameda Ste 320	San Jose	CA	95126	408-297-8815	297-0611
TF: 800-297-8815 ■ *Web:* www.stapleton-spence.com					
Sun-Maid Growers of California 13525 S Bethel Ave	Kingsburg	CA	93631	559-896-8000	897-6209
Web: sunmaid.com					
Sunsweet Growers Inc 901 N Walton Ave	Yuba City	CA	95993	530-674-5010	751-5238
TF: 800-417-2253 ■ *Web:* www.sunsweet.com					
Tree Top Inc 220 E Second Ave	Selah	WA	98942	509-697-7251	698-1421
Web: www.treetop.com					
Tule River Co-op Dryer Inc 16548 Rd 168 PO Box 4477	Porterville	CA	93257	559-686-4685	

296-19 Fruits & Vegetables - Pickled

Company / Address	City	State	Zip	Phone	Fax
B & G Foods Inc 4 Gatehall Dr Ste 110	Parsippany	NJ	07054	973-401-6500	
NYSE: BGS ■ *Web:* www.bgfoods.com					
Bay View Food Products Inc 2606 N Huron Rd	Pinconning	MI	48650	989-879-3555	879-2659
Web: www.bayviewfoods.com					
Beaverton Foods Inc 7100 NW Century Blvd	Hillsboro	OR	97124	503-646-8138	644-9204
TF: 800-223-8076 ■ *Web:* www.beavertonfoods.com					
Best Maid Products Inc PO Box 1809	Fort Worth	TX	76101	817-335-5494	
TF: 800-447-3581 ■ *Web:* www.bestmaidproducts.com					
Cain's Foods Inc 114 E Main St	Ayer	MA	01432	978-772-0300	772-0200
TF: 800-225-0601 ■ *Web:* www.cainsfoods.com					
Cajun Chef Products Inc 519 Joseph Rd	Saint Martinville	LA	70582	337-394-7112	394-7115
Clorox Co 1221 Broadway	Oakland	CA	94612	510-271-7000	832-1463
NYSE: CLX ■ *TF Cust Svc:* 800-424-9300 ■ *Web:* www.thecloroxcompany.com					
Conway Import Co Inc 11051 W Addison St	Franklin Park	IL	60131	847-455-5600	304-4021*
**Fax Area Code:* 800 ■ *TF:* 800-323-8801 ■ *Web:* conwaydressings.com					
Eastern Foods Inc 1000 Naturally Fresh Blvd	Atlanta	GA	30349	800-765-1950	
TF: 800-765-1950 ■ *Web:* www.naturallyfresh.com					
GLK Foods LLC 11 Clark St	Shortsville	NY	14548	855-572-8800	
TF: 855-572-8800 ■ *Web:* www.glkfoods.com					
Gold Pure Food Products Inc 1 Brooklyn Rd	Hempstead	NY	11550	516-483-5600	483-5798
Web: www.goldshorseradish.com					
Henri's Food Products Company Inc 8622 N 87th St	Milwaukee	WI	53224	414-365-5720	
HV Food Products Co 1221 Broadway	Oakland	CA	94612	510-271-7000	832-1463
Web: www.hiddenvalley.com					
JG Van Holten & Son Inc 703 W Madison St PO Box 66	Waterloo	WI	53594	920-478-2144	478-2316
Web: www.vanholtenpickles.com					
Kaplan & Zubrin Inc 146 Kaighns Ave	Camden	NJ	08103	856-964-1083	
TF: 800-248-1736					
Ken's Foods Inc 1 D'Angelo Dr	Marlborough	MA	01752	508-229-1100	229-1146
Web: www.kensfoods.com					
Kikkoman Foods Inc N 1365 Six Corners Rd	Walworth	WI	53184	262-275-6181	275-9452
Web: www.kikkoman.com					
KT's Kitchens Inc 1065 E Walnut St Ste C	Carson	CA	90746	310-764-0850	764-0855
Web: www.ktskitchens.com					
Langlois Co 10810 San Sevaine Way	Mira Loma	CA	91752	951-360-3900	
TF: 800-962-5993 ■ *Web:* www.langloiscompany.com					
Lee Kum Kee Inc 14841 Don Julian Rd	City of Industry	CA	91746	626-709-1888	709-1899
TF Orders: 800-654-5082 ■ *Web:* lkk.com					
Litehouse Inc 1109 N Ella Ave	Sandpoint	ID	83864	208-265-3700	
TF: 800-669-3169 ■ *Web:* www.litehousefoods.com					
MA Gedney Co 2100 Stoughton Ave	Chaska	MN	55318	952-448-2612	448-1790
TF: 888-244-0653 ■ *Web:* www.gedneyfoods.com					
Maurice's Gourmet Barbeque PO Box 6847	West Columbia	SC	29171	803-791-5887	791-8707
TF: 800-628-7423 ■ *Web:* www.piggiepark.com					
McIlhenny Co Hwy 329	Avery Island	LA	70513	337-365-8173	
TF Orders: 800-634-9599 ■ *Web:* www.tabasco.com					
Meduri Farms Inc PO Box 636	Dallas	OR	97338	503-623-0308	
Web: www.medurifarms.com					

				Phone	Fax
Moody Dunbar Inc 2000 Waters Edge Dr Ste 21 *TF:* 800-251-8202 ■ *Web:* moodydunbar.com	Johnson City	TN	37604	423-952-0100	952-0289
Morehouse Foods Inc 760 Epperson Dr *Web:* www.morehousefoods.com	City of Industry	CA	91748	626-854-1655	854-1656
Mullins Food Products Inc 2200 S 25th Ave *Web:* www.mullinsfood.com	Broadview	IL	60155	708-344-3224	344-0153
Newman's Own Inc 246 Post Rd E *Web:* www.newmansown.com	Westport	CT	06880	203-222-0136	227-5630
NewStar Fresh Foods LLC 900 Work St *TF:* 888-782-7220 ■ *Web:* www.newstarfresh.com	Salinas	CA	93901	831-758-7800	758-7869
Old Dutch Mustard Co 98 Cutter Mill Rd *Web:* pilgrimfoods.net	Great Neck	NY	11021	516-466-0522	466-0762
Olds Products Co 10700 88th Ave *TF:* 800-233-8064 ■ *Web:* www.oldsproducts.com	Pleasant Prairie	WI	53158	262-947-3500	947-3517
Pacific Choice Brands Inc 4667 E Date Ave	Fresno	CA	93725	559-237-5583	237-2078
Plochman Inc 1333 N Boudreau Rd *Web:* www.plochman.com	Manteno	IL	60950	815-468-3434	468-8755
Spring Glen Fresh Foods Inc 314 Spring Glen Dr PO Box 518 *TF:* 800-641-2853 ■ *Web:* www.springglen.com	Ephrata	PA	17522	717-733-2201	721-6720
Swanson Pickle Company Inc 11561 Heights Ravenna Rd	Ravenna	MI	49451	231-853-2289	853-6281
T Marzetti Co 1105 Schrock Rd *TF:* 800-999-1835 ■ *Web:* www.marzetti.com	Columbus	OH	43229	614-846-2232	848-8330
Walden Farms 1209 W St Georges Ave **Fax Area Code:* 908 ■ *TF:* 800-229-1706 ■ *Web:* www.waldenfarms.com	Linden	NJ	07036	800-229-1706	925-9537*
Yamasa Corp USA 3500 Fairview Industrial Dr SE *Web:* www.yamasausa.com	Salem	OR	97302	503-363-8550	363-8710

296-20 Fruits, Vegetables, Juices - Canned or Preserved

				Phone	Fax
American Spoon Foods Inc 1668 Clarion Ave *TF:* 800-222-5886 ■ *Web:* www.spoon.com	Petoskey	MI	49770	231-347-9030	
Apple & Eve Inc 2 Seaview Blvd *TF:* 866-487-2365 ■ *Web:* www.appleandeve.com	Port Washington	NY	11050	516-621-1122	621-2164
Ardmore Farms Inc 1915 N Woodland Blvd *Web:* www.juice4u.com	DeLand	FL	32724	330-753-2293	848-4287
B & G Foods Inc 4 Gatehall Dr Ste 110 *NYSE: BGS* ■ *Web:* www.bgfoods.com	Parsippany	NJ	07054	973-401-6500	
Baumer Foods Inc 2424 Edenborn Ave Ste 510 *Web:* www.baumerfoods.com	Metairie	LA	70001	504-482-5761	483-2425
Beckman & Gast Company Inc 282 W Kremer-Hoying Rd PO Box 307 *Web:* www.beckmangast.com	Saint Henry	OH	45883	419-678-4195	
Braswell Food Co 226 N Zetterower Ave *TF:* 800-673-9388 ■ *Web:* www.braswells.com	Statesboro	GA	30458	912-764-6191	489-1572
Brooklyn Bottling Co 643 S Rd **Fax Area Code:* 718	Milton	NY	12547	845-795-2171	649-2596*
Bruce Foods Corp PO Box 1030 *TF:* 800-299-9082 ■ *Web:* www.brucefoods.com	New Iberia	LA	70561	337-365-8101	369-9026
Burnette Foods Inc 701 US Hwy 31 *Web:* www.burnettefoods.com	Elk Rapids	MI	49629	231-264-8116	264-9597
Bush Bros & Co 1016 E Weisgarber Rd *Web:* www.bushbeans.com	Knoxville	TN	37909	865-588-7685	
Campbell Soup Co 1 Campbell Pl *NYSE: CPB* ■ *TF:* 800-257-8443 ■ *Web:* www.campbellsoupcompany.com	Camden	NJ	08103	856-342-4800	342-3878
Carriage House Cos Inc, The 196 Newton St **Fax:* Sales ■ *TF:* 800-828-8915	Fredonia	NY	14063	716-673-1000	673-8443*
Cherry Growers Inc 6331 US Hwy 31 *Web:* www.cherrygrowers.net	Grawn	MI	49637	231-276-9241	276-7075
Cincinnati Preserving Company Inc 3015 E Kemper Rd *TF Cust Svc:* 800-222-9966 ■ *Web:* www.clearbrookfarms.com	Cincinnati	OH	45241	513-771-2000	771-8381
Citrus Systems Inc 125 Jackson Ave N *Web:* www.citrussystems.com	Hopkins	MN	55343	952-935-0410	
Cornelius Seed Corn Co 14760 317th Ave *TF:* 800-218-1862 ■ *Web:* www.corneliusseed.com	Bellevue	IA	52031	563-672-3463	672-3521
Country Pure Foods Inc 681 W Waterloo Rd *Web:* www.countrypurefoods.com	Akron	OH	44314	330-753-2293	848-4287
Crookham Company Inc PO Box 520 *Web:* www.crookham.com	Caldwell	ID	83606	208-459-7451	454-2108
Daily Juice Products 1 Daily Way *Web:* www.dailyscocktails.com	Verona	PA	15147	412-828-9020	
Del Monte Foods Co 1 Maritime Plaza *TF Cust Svc:* 800-543-3090 ■ *Web:* www.delmonte.com	San Francisco	CA	94111	415-247-3000	247-3311
Del Monte Fresh Produce Co 241 Sevilla Ave *TF Cust Svc:* 800-950-3683 ■ *Web:* www.freshdelmonte.com	Coral Gables	FL	33134	305-520-8400	567-0320
Diana Fruit Company Inc 651 Mathew St *Web:* www.dianafruit.com	Santa Clara	CA	95050	408-727-9631	727-9890
Dole Packaged Foods Co 1 Dole Dr *Web:* dole.com	Westlake Village	CA	91362	818-874-4000	874-4893
Don Pepino Sales Co 123 Railroad Ave *TF:* 888-281-6400 ■ *Web:* www.donpepino.com	Williamstown	NJ	08094	856-629-7429	629-6340
Escalon Premier Brands 1905 McHenry Ave *TF:* 800-255-5750 ■ *Web:* www.escalon.net	Escalon	CA	95320	209-838-7341	
Faribault Foods Inc 222 S Ninth St Ste 3380 *Web:* www.faribaultfoods.com	Minneapolis	MN	55402	612-333-6461	
Fremont Co 802 N Front St	Fremont	OH	43420	419-334-8995	334-8120
Furmano Foods Inc 770 Cannery Rd PO Box 500 *TF:* 877-877-6032 ■ *Web:* www.furmanos.com	Northumberland	PA	17857	570-473-3516	473-7367
Giorgio Foods Inc PO Box 96 *TF:* 800-220-2139 ■ *Web:* www.giorgiofoods.com	Temple	PA	19560	610-926-2139	926-7012
Gray & Co 3325 W Polk Rd Ste 230 *Web:* www.cherryman.com	Hart	MI	49420	503-248-4729	248-4729
Growers Co-op Grape Juice Company Inc 112 N Portage St *Web:* www.concordgrapejuice.com	Westfield	NY	14787	716-326-3161	326-6566
Hanover Foods Corp 1550 York St PO Box 334 *OTC: HNFSA* ■ *TF:* 800-888-4646 ■ *Web:* www.hanoverfoods.com	Hanover	PA	17331	717-632-6000	
Hawaiian Sun Products Inc 259 Sand Island Access Rd *Web:* www.hawaiiansunproducts.com	Honolulu	HI	96819	808-845-3211	842-0532
Hirzel Canning Company & Farms 411 Lemoyne Rd *TF:* 800-837-1631 ■ *Web:* www.deifratelli.com	Northwood	OH	43619	419-693-0531	693-4859
HJ Heinz Co 1 PPG Pl Ste 3100 *TF:* 800-255-5750 ■ *Web:* www.kraftheinzcompany.com	Pittsburgh	PA	15230	412-456-5700	
House Foods America Corp 7351 Orangewood Ave *TF:* 877-333-7077 ■ *Web:* www.house-foods.com	Garden Grove	CA	92841	714-901-4350	901-4235
Indian Summer Co-op 3958 W Chauvez Rd	Ludington	MI	49431	231-845-6248	843-9453*
Ingomar Packing Co 9950 S Ingomar Grade PO Box 1448 *Web:* www.ingomarpacking.com	Los Banos	CA	93635	209-826-9494	854-6292
J. Lieb Foods Inc PO Box 389 *Web:* www.jliebfoods.com	Forest Grove	OR	97116	503-359-9279	
Jasper Wyman & Son PO Box 100 *TF Sales:* 800-341-1758 ■ *Web:* www.wymans.com	Milbridge	ME	04658	800-341-1758	
JM Smucker Co 1 Strawberry Ln *NYSE: SJM* ■ *TF:* 888-550-9555 ■ *Web:* www.smuckers.com	Orrville	OH	44667	330-682-3000	
JM Smucker Pennsylvania Inc 300 Keck Ave	New Bethlehem	PA	16242	814-275-1323	275-1340
Johanna Foods Inc 20 Johanna Farm Rd PO Box 272 *TF:* 800-727-6700 ■ *Web:* www.johannafoods.com	Flemington	NJ	08822	908-788-2200	
Knouse Foods Co-op Inc 800 Peach Glen-Idaville Rd *Web:* www.knouse.com	Peach Glen	PA	17375	717-677-8181	677-7069
Lakeside Foods Inc 808 Hamilton St *TF:* 800-466-3834 ■ *Web:* www.lakesidefoods.com	Manitowoc	WI	54220	920-684-3356	686-4033
Langers Juice Company Inc 16195 Stephens St *Web:* www.langers.com	City of Industry	CA	91745	626-336-1666	961-2021
Lassonde Pappas 1 Colons Dr Ste 200 *TF:* 800-257-7019 ■ *Web:* www.clementpappas.com	Carneys Point	NJ	08069	856-455-1000	455-8746
Lawrence Foods Inc 2200 Lunt Ave *Web:* www.lawrencefoods.com	Elk Grove Village	IL	60007	847-437-2400	437-2567
Leelanau Fruit Co 2900 SW Bay Shore Dr *TF:* 800-431-0718 ■ *Web:* www.leelanaufruit.com	Suttons Bay	MI	49682	231-271-3514	271-4367
LiDestri Foods Inc 815 Whitney Rd W *Web:* www.lidestrifoods.com	Fairport	NY	14450	585-377-7700	377-8150
Louis Maull Co, The 219 N Market St *Web:* www.maull.com	Saint Louis	MO	63102	314-241-8410	
Lyons Magnus Inc 3158 E Hamilton Ave **Fax Area Code:* 559 ■ *TF:* 800-344-7130 ■ *Web:* www.lyonsmagnus.com	Fresno	CA	93702	800-344-7130	233-8249*
Maui Land & Pineapple Company Inc 120 Kane St PO Box 187 *Web:* www.mauiland.com	Kahului	HI	96733	808-877-3351	
Mayer Bros Apple Products Inc 3300 Transit Rd *Web:* www.mayerbrothers.com	West Seneca	NY	14224	716-668-1787	668-2437
Moody Dunbar Inc 2000 Waters Edge Dr Ste 21 *TF:* 800-251-8202 ■ *Web:* moodydunbar.com	Johnson City	TN	37604	423-952-0100	952-0289
Morgan Foods Inc 90 W Morgan St *TF:* 888-430-1780 ■ *Web:* www.morganfoods.com	Austin	IN	47102	812-794-1170	794-1211
Mott's LLP PO Box 869077 *TF Consumer Info:* 800-426-4891 ■ *Web:* www.motts.com	Plano	TX	75086	800-426-4891	
Mrs Clark's Foods 740 SE Dalbey Dr *TF:* 800-736-5674 ■ *Web:* www.mrsclarks.com	Ankeny	IA	50021	515-299-6400	
Muir Glen Organic Tomato Products PO Box 9452 *TF:* 800-624-4123 ■ *Web:* www.muirglen.com	Minneapolis	MN	55440	800-248-7310	
Mullins Food Products Inc 2200 S 25th Ave *Web:* www.mullinsfood.com	Broadview	IL	60155	708-344-3224	344-0153
Mushroom Co, The 902 Woods Rd *Web:* www.themushroomcompany.com	Cambridge	MD	21613	410-221-8971	221-8952
National Fruit Product Co Inc 701 Fairmont Ave **Fax:* Sales ■ *TF:* 800-655-4022 ■ *Web:* www.whitehousefoods.com	Winchester	VA	22601	540-723-9614	665-4671*
Ocean Spray Cranberries Inc 1 Ocean Spray Dr *TF:* 800-662-3263 ■ *Web:* www.oceanspray.com	Lakeville-Middleboro	MA	02349	508-946-1000	946-4594
Odwalla Inc 1625 North Market Blvd *TF:* 800-952-5210 ■ *Web:* www.odwalla.com	Sacramento	CA	95834	800-952-5210	
Pacific Coast Producers 631 N Cluff Ave *TF:* 877-618-4776 ■ *Web:* canned-fresh.com	Lodi	CA	95240	209-367-8800	367-1084
Pastorelli Food Products Inc 162 N Sangamon St *TF:* 800-767-2829 ■ *Web:* www.pastorelli.com	Chicago	IL	60607	312-666-2041	666-2415
President Global Corp 6965 Aragon Cir	Buena Park	CA	90620	714-994-2990	523-3142
Ray Bros & Noble Canning Company Inc 3720 E 150 S PO Box 314 *Web:* www.tiptonguide.com	Hobbs	IN	46047	765-675-7451	675-7400
Red Gold Inc 120 E Oak St *Web:* www.redgold.com	Orestes	IN	46063	765-754-7527	
Ryan Trading Corp 2500 Westchester Ave Ste 102 *Web:* www.ryantrading.com	Purchase	NY	10577	914-253-6767	253-6722
Seneca Foods Corp 3736 S Main St *NASDAQ: SENEA* ■ *Web:* www.senecafoods.com	Marion	NY	14505	315-926-8100	926-8300
Simply Orange Juice Co 2659 Orange Ave *TF:* 800-871-2653 ■ *Web:* www.simplyorangejuice.com	Apopka	FL	32703	800-871-2653	
Southern Gardens Citrus 1820 Country Rd 833 *Web:* www.ussugar.com/citrus	Clewiston	FL	33440	863-983-3030	983-3060
Stanislaus Food Products Co 1202 D St **Fax Area Code:* 209 ■ *TF:* 800-327-7201 ■ *Web:* www.stanislausfoodproducts.com	Modesto	CA	95354	800-327-7201	521-4014*

				Phone	Fax
Stapleton-Spence Packing Co 1530 The Alameda Ste 320 TF: 800-297-8815 ■ Web: www.stapleton-spence.com	San Jose	CA	95126	408-297-8815	297-0611
Sun Orchard Inc 1198 W Fairmont Dr TF: 800-505-8423 ■ Web: www.sunorchard.com	Tempe	AZ	85282	800-505-8423	
Talk O'Texas Brands Inc 1610 Roosevelt St TF: 800-749-6572 ■ Web: www.talkotexas.com	San Angelo	TX	76905	325-655-6077	
Tip Top Canning Co 505 S Second St PO Box 126 TF: 800-352-2635 ■ Web: www.tiptopcanning.com	Tipp City	OH	45371	937-667-3713	667-3802
Tree Top Inc 220 E Second Ave Web: www.treetop.com	Selah	WA	98942	509-697-7251	698-1421
Truitt Bros Inc 1105 Front St NE *Fax: Sales ■ TF: 800-547-8712 ■ Web: www.truittbros.com	Salem	OR	97301	503-362-3674	588-2868*
TW Garner Food Co 4045 Indiana Ave Web: www.texaspete.com	Winston-Salem	NC	27105	336-661-1550	661-1901
Valley Processing Inc 108 E Blaine Ave PO Box 246 Web: valleyprocessing.com	Sunnyside	WA	98944	509-837-8084	837-3481
Vegetable Juices Inc 7400 S Narragansett Ave TF General: 888-776-9752 ■ Web: www.vegetablejuices.com	Chicago	IL	60638	708-924-9500	924-9510
Vita-Pakt Citrus Products 707 N Barranca Ave Web: www.vita-pakt.com	Covina	CA	91723	626-332-1101	966-8196
Welch's Inc 300 Baker Ave Ste 101 Web: www.welchs.com	Concord	MA	01742	978-371-1000	
Whitlock Packaging Corp 1701 S Lee St Web: whitlockpkg.com	Fort Gibson	OK	74434	918-478-4300	
Zeigler Beverage Co 1513 N Broad St TF Sales: 800-854-6123 ■ Web: www.zeiglers.com	Lansdale	PA	19446	215-855-5161	855-4548

296-21 Fruits, Vegetables, Juices - Frozen

				Phone	Fax
Apio Inc PO Box 727 TF Sales: 800-454-1355 ■ Web: www.apioinc.com	Guadalupe	CA	93434	805-343-2835	
Ardmore Farms Inc 1915 N Woodland Blvd Web: www.juice4u.com	DeLand	FL	32724	330-753-2293	848-4287
Bernatello's PO Box 729 TF: 800-622-6935 ■ Web: www.bernatellos.com	Maple Lake	MN	55358	952-831-6622	831-6606
Capitol City Produce 16550 Commercial Ave TF: 800-349-1583 ■ Web: www.capitolcityproduce.com	Baton Rouge	LA	70816	225-272-8153	272-8152
Cherry Growers Inc 6331 US Hwy 31 Web: www.cherrygrowers.net	Grawn	MI	49637	231-276-9241	276-7075
Coloma Frozen Foods Inc 4145 Coloma Rd TF: 800-642-2723 ■ Web: www.colomafrozen.com	Coloma	MI	49038	269-849-0500	849-0886
Del Mar Food Products Corp 1720 Beach Rd Web: delmarfoods.com	Watsonville	CA	95076	831-722-3516	722-7690
Dole Food Company Inc 1 Dole Dr NYSE: DOLE ■ TF: 800-232-8888 ■ Web: www.dole.com	Westlake Village	CA	91362	818-879-6600	
Fresh Frozen Foods LLC 643 N 98th St Ste 133	Omaha	NE	68114	706-367-9851	
Frozsun Inc 701 W Kimberly Ave Ste 210 Web: sunrisegrowers.com	Placentia	CA	92870	714-630-6292	
Giorgio Foods Inc PO Box 96 TF: 800-220-2139 ■ Web: www.giorgiofoods.com	Temple	PA	19560	610-926-2139	926-7012
Graceland Fruit Inc 1123 Main St TF: 800-352-7181 ■ Web: www.gracelandfruit.com	Frankfort	MI	49635	231-352-7181	352-4711
HJ Heinz Co 1 PPG Pl Ste 3100 TF: 800-255-5750 ■ Web: www.kraftheinzcompany.com	Pittsburgh	PA	15230	412-456-5700	
HPC Foods Ltd 288 Libby St TF: 877-370-0919 ■ Web: hpcfoods.com	Honolulu	HI	96819	808-848-2431	841-4398
JR Simplot Co 999 W Main St Ste 1300 TF: 800-832-8893 ■ Web: www.simplot.com	Boise	ID	83702	208-336-2110	389-7515
Lakeside Foods Inc 808 Hamilton St TF: 800-466-3834 ■ Web: www.lakesidefoods.com	Manitowoc	WI	54220	920-684-3356	686-4033
Lamb Weston Inc 8701 W Gage Blvd *Fax: Sales ■ Web: www.lambweston.com	Kennewick	WA	99336	509-735-4651	736-0395*
Leelanau Fruit Co 2900 SW Bay Shore Dr TF: 800-431-0718 ■ Web: www.leelanaufruit.com	Suttons Bay	MI	49682	231-271-3514	271-4367
Lewis Dreyfus Citrus Inc (LDCI) 355 S Ninth St	Winter Garden	FL	34787	407-656-1000	656-1229
McCain Foods Ltd 181 Bay St Ste 3600 TF: 800-938-7799 ■ Web: www.mccain.com	Toronto	ON	M5J2T3	416-955-1700	
McCain Foods USA Inc 2275 Cabot Dr TF: 800-938-7799 ■ Web: www.mccainusa.com	Lisle	IL	60532	800-938-7799	
Milne Fruit Products Inc 804 Bennett Ave Web: www.milnefruit.com	Prosser	WA	99350	509-786-2611	786-4915
Mrs Clark's Foods 740 SE Dalbey Dr TF: 800-736-5674 ■ Web: www.mrsclarks.com	Ankeny	IA	50021	515-299-6400	
National Frozen Foods Corp 1600 Fairview Ave E Ste 200 Web: www.nffc.com	Seattle	WA	98102	206-322-8900	322-4458
NORPAC Foods Inc 930 W Washington St TF: 800-733-9311 ■ Web: www.norpac.com	Stayton	OR	97383	503-769-2101	
Patterson Frozen Foods Inc 100 W Las Palmas Ave Web: www.pattersonfrozenfoods.com	Patterson	CA	95363	209-892-2611	
Penobscot McCrum LLC 28 Pierce St TF: 800-435-4456 ■ Web: www.penobscotmccrum.com	Belfast	ME	04915	207-338-4360	338-5742
Peterson Farms Inc 3104 W Baseline Rd PO Box 115 Web: www.petersonfarmsinc.com	Shelby	MI	49455	231-861-7101	
Pictsweet Co, The 10 Pictsweet Dr *Fax Area Code: 888 ■ Web: www.pictsweet.com	Bells	TN	38006	731-663-7600	662-7651*
Seabrook Bros & Sons Inc 85 Finley Rd Web: www.seabrookfarms.com	Bridgeton	NJ	08302	856-455-8080	455-9282
Seneca Foods Corp 3736 S Main St NASDAQ: SENEA ■ Web: www.senecafoods.com	Marion	NY	14505	315-926-8100	926-8300
Smith Frozen Foods Inc 101 Depot St Web: www.smithfrozenfoods.com	Weston	OR	97886	541-566-3515	566-3772
Sweet Ovations 1741 Tomlinson Rd Web: www.sweetovations.com	Philadelphia	PA	19116	215-676-3900	613-2115
Sysco Seattle Inc 22820 54th Ave S Web: seattle.sysco.com	Kent	WA	98032	206-622-2261	721-2787
Townsend Farms Inc 23400 NE Townsend Way Web: www.townsendfarms.com	Fairview	OR	97024	503-666-1780	
Tree Top Inc 220 E Second Ave Web: www.treetop.com	Selah	WA	98942	509-697-7251	698-1421
Twin City Foods Inc 10120 269th Pl NW Web: twincityfoods.com	Stanwood	WA	98292	206-515-2400	515-2499
Vita-Pakt Citrus Products 707 N Barranca Ave Web: www.vita-pakt.com	Covina	CA	91723	626-332-1101	966-8196
Wawona Frozen Foods Inc 100 W Alluvial Ave Web: www.wawona.com	Clovis	CA	93611	559-299-2901	299-1921

296-22 Gelatin

				Phone	Fax
Gelita USA Inc PO Box 927 TF: 800-223-9244 ■ Web: www.gelita.com	Sioux City	IA	51102	712-943-5516	943-3372
Langlois Co 10810 San Sevaine Way TF: 800-962-5993 ■ Web: www.langloiscompany.com	Mira Loma	CA	91752	951-360-3900	
Milligan & Higgins Maple Ave PO Box 506 Web: www.milligan1868.com	Johnstown	NY	12095	518-762-4638	762-7039
Nitta Gelatin Inc 598 Airport Blvd Ste 900 TF: 888-648-8287 ■ Web: www.nitta-gelatin.com	Morrisville	NC	27560	919-238-3300	238-3222
Subco Foods Inc 4350 S Taylor Dr TF: 800-473-0757 ■ Web: www.subcofoods.com	Sheboygan	WI	53081	920-457-7761	457-3899
Swagger Foods Corp 900 Corporate Woods Pkwy Web: www.swaggerfoods.com	Vernon Hills	IL	60061	847-913-1200	

296-23 Grain Mill Products

				Phone	Fax
ACH Food Cos Inc 7171 Goodlet Farms Pkwy TF: 800-691-1106 ■ Web: www.achfood.com	Cordova	TN	38016	901-381-3000	381-2968
ADM Corn Processing Div 4666 E Faries Pkwy TF: 800-637-5843 ■ Web: www.adm.com	Decatur	IL	62526	217-424-5200	424-5978
ADM Milling Co (ADM) 8000 W 110th St TF: 800-422-1688 ■ Web: www.adm.com	Overland Park	KS	66210	913-491-9400	
Ag Processing Inc 12700 W Dodge Rd PO Box 2047 TF: 800-247-1345 ■ Web: www.agp.com	Omaha	NE	68103	402-496-7809	
American Rice Inc 10700 N Fwy Ste 800 Web: www.amrice.com	Houston	TX	77037	281-272-8800	272-8782
Bartlett & Co 4900 Main St Ste 12 TF: 800-888-6300 ■ Web: www.bartlettandco.com	Kansas City	MO	64112	816-753-6300	
Bay State Milling Co 100 Congress St *Fax Area Code: 617 ■ TF: 800-553-5687 ■ Web: www.baystatemilling.com	Quincy	MA	02169	800-553-5687	479-8910*
Beaumont Rice Mills Inc 1800 Pecos St Web: bmtricemills.com	Beaumont	TX	77701	409-832-2521	832-6927
Blendex Company Inc 11208 Electron Dr TF: 800-626-6325 ■ Web: www.blendex.com	Louisville	KY	40299	502-267-1003	267-1024
Cereal Food Processors Inc 2001 Shawnee Mission Pkwy Web: www.cerealfood.com	Mission Woods	KS	66205	913-890-6300	
Chelsea Milling Co 201 W N St PO Box 460 TF: 800-727-2460 ■ Web: www.jiffymix.com	Chelsea	MI	48118	734-475-1361	475-4630
Cormier Rice Milling Co Inc 501 W Third St	De Witt	AR	72042	870-946-1479	
Farmers Rice Co-op PO Box 15223 TF: 800-326-2799 ■ Web: www.farmersrice.com	Sacramento	CA	95851	916-923-5100	920-3321
Farmers Rice Milling Co 3211 Hwy 397 S Web: www.frmco.com	Lake Charles	LA	70615	337-433-5205	433-1735
Florida Crystals Corp 1 N Clematis St Ste 200 Web: www.floridacrystals.com	West Palm Beach	FL	33401	561-366-5100	366-5158
Gold Medal PO Box 9452 *Fax Area Code: 763 ■ TF: 800-248-7310 ■ Web: www.generalmills.com	Minneapolis	MN	55440	800-248-7310	764-8330*
Grain Processing Corp 1600 Oregon St Web: www.grainprocessing.com	Muscatine	IA	52761	563-264-4265	264-4289
Hodgson Mill Inc 1100 Stevens Ave TF: 800-347-0105 ■ Web: www.hodgsonmill.com	Effingham	IL	62401	217-347-0105	347-0198
Hopkinsville Milling Co PO Box 669 Web: sunflourflour.com	Hopkinsville	KY	42241	270-886-1231	886-6407
House-Autry Mills Inc 7000 US Hwy 301 S TF: 800-849-0802 ■ Web: www.house-autry.com	Four Oaks	NC	27524	800-849-0802	
HR Wentzel Sons Inc 5521 Waggoners Gap Rd PO Box 125	Landisburg	PA	17040	717-789-3306	789-0128
Indian Harvest Specialtifoods Inc 1012 Paul Bunyan Dr SE *Fax Area Code: 218 ■ TF Orders: 800-346-7032 ■ Web: inharvest.com	Bemidji	MN	56601	800-346-7032	751-8519*
King Milling Co 115 S Broadway St Web: www.kingmilling.com	Lowell	MI	49331	616-897-9264	897-4350
Knappen Milling Co 110 S Water St TF: 800-562-7736 ■ Web: www.knappen.com	Augusta	MI	49012	269-731-4141	
Lacey Milling Co 217 W Fifth St	Hanford	CA	93230	559-584-6634	
Mallet & Company Inc 51 Arch St Ext TF: 800-245-2757 ■ Web: www.malletoil.com	Carnegie	PA	15106	412-276-9000	276-9002
Manildra Group USA 4210 Shawnee Mission Pkwy Ste 312A TF: 800-323-8435 ■ Web: manildrausa.com	Shawnee Mission	KS	66205	913-362-0777	362-0052
Mars Snack Food 800 High St Web: www.mars.com	Hackettstown	NJ	07840	908-852-1000	850-2734
Mennel Milling Co 128 W Crocker St TF: 800-688-8151 ■ Web: www.mennel.com	Fostoria	OH	44830	419-435-8151	436-5150
MGP Ingredients Inc 100 Commercial St PO Box 130 NASDAQ: MGPI ■ TF: 800-255-0302 ■ Web: www.mgpingredients.com	Atchison	KS	66002	913-367-1480	367-0192

Company	City	State	Zip	Phone	Fax
Minn-Dak Growers Ltd 4034 40th Ave N *Web:* www.minndak.com	Grand Forks	ND	58203	701-746-7453	780-9050
Morrison Milling Co 319 E Prairie St *TF:* 800-531-7912 ■ *Web:* morrisonmilling.com	Denton	TX	76201	940-387-6111	566-5992
North Dakota Mill & Elevator 1823 Mill Rd. *TF:* 800-538-7721 ■ *Web:* www.ndmill.com	Grand Forks	ND	58203	701-795-7000	795-7272
Pacific Grain Products International Inc 351 Hanson Way PO Box 2060 *TF Cust Svc:* 800-333-0110	Woodland	CA	95776	530-662-5056	662-6074
Pacific International Rice Mills Inc 845 Kentucky Ave *TF:* 800-747-4764 ■ *Web:* www.pirmirice.com	Woodland	CA	95695	530-661-6028	661-6028
Producers Rice Mill Inc PO Box 1248 *TF:* 800-369-7675 ■ *Web:* www.producersrice.com	Stuttgart	AR	72160	870-673-4444	
Riceland Foods Inc PO Box 927 *Web:* www.riceland.com	Stuttgart	AR	72160	870-673-5500	
RiceTec Inc 1925 FM 2917 PO Box 1305 *TF:* 877-580-7423 ■ *Web:* www.ricetec.com	Alvin	TX	77511	281-393-3532	393-3532
Riviana Foods Inc PO Box 2636 *Web:* www.riviana.com	Houston	TX	77252	713-529-3251	
Rock River Lumber & Grain Co 5502 Lyndon Rd PO Box 68 *TF:* 800-605-4333 ■ *Web:* www.rockriverag.com	Prophetstown	IL	61277	815-537-5131	
Roquette America 1417 Exchange St PO Box 6647 *Web:* www.roquette.com	Keokuk	IA	52632	319-524-5757	
Shawnee Milling Company Inc 201 S Broadway PO Box 1567 *TF:* 800-654-2600 ■ *Web:* www.shawneemilling.com	Shawnee	OK	74802	405-273-7000	273-7333
Siemer Milling Co 111 W Main St PO Box 670 *TF:* 800-826-1065 ■ *Web:* www.siemermilling.com	Teutopolis	IL	62467	217-857-3131	857-3092
SunOpta Inc 2838 Bovaird Dr W *TSE: SOY* ■ *Web:* www.sunopta.com	Brampton	ON	L7A0H2	905-455-2528	455-2529
Wilkins-Rogers Inc 27 Frederick Rd. *TF Cust Svc:* 877-438-4338 ■ *Web:* wrmills.com	Ellicott City	MD	21043	410-465-5800	

296-24 Honey

Company	City	State	Zip	Phone	Fax
Barkman Honey 120 Santa Fe St *TF:* 800-364-6623 ■ *Web:* barkmanhoney.com	Hillsboro	KS	67063	800-364-6623	
Dutch Gold Honey Inc 2220 Dutch Gold Dr *TF:* 800-846-2753 ■ *Web:* www.dutchgoldhoney.com	Lancaster	PA	17601	717-393-1716	393-8687
Fisher Honey Co 1 Belle Ave Bldg 21 *Web:* www.fisherhoney.com	Lewistown	PA	17044	717-242-4373	
Glorybee Foods Inc 120 N Seneca Rd *TF:* 800-456-7923 ■ *Web:* www.glorybee.com	Eugene	OR	97402	541-689-0913	689-9692
Honey Acres 1557 Hwy 67 N **Fax Area Code:* 920 ■ *TF:* 800-558-7745 ■ *Web:* www.honeyacres.com	Ashippun	WI	53003	800-558-7745	474-4018*
Honeytree Inc 8570 M 50 *TF:* 800-968-1889 ■ *Web:* honeytreehoney.com	Onsted	MI	49265	517-467-2482	
Miller's Honey Co Inc 3000 SW Temple *Web:* www.millerhoney.com	Salt Lake City	UT	84115	801-486-8479	486-8494
Pure Sweet Honey Farm Inc 514 Commerce Pkwy. *Web:* puresweethoney.com	Verona	WI	53593	608-845-9601	
Silverbow Honey Company Inc 1120 E Wheeler Rd *TF:* 866-444-6639 ■ *Web:* www.silverbowhoney.com	Moses Lake	WA	98837	509-765-6616	765-6549
Sioux Honey Assn Co-op 301 Lewis Blvd *Web:* www.suebee.com	Sioux City	IA	51101	712-258-0638	258-1332
TW Burleson & Son Inc 301 Peters St *Web:* www.burlesons-honey.com	Waxahachie	TX	75165	972-937-4810	937-8711
Wixson Honey Inc 4937 Lakemont-Himrod Rd *Web:* wixsonhoney.com	Dundee	NY	14837	607-243-7301	

296-25 Ice Cream & Frozen Desserts

Company	City	State	Zip	Phone	Fax
Anderson Erickson Dairy Co 2420 E University Ave *TF:* 800-234-7257 ■ *Web:* www.aedairy.com	Des Moines	IA	50317	515-265-2521	263-6301
Arista Industries Inc 557 Danbury Rd *Web:* www.aristaindustries.com	Wilton	CT	06897	203-761-1009	
Attune Foods Inc 900 Kearny St Ste 600 *Web:* www.attunefoods.com	San Francisco	CA	94133	415-486-2101	
Aurora Organic Dairy Corp 1919 14th St Ste 300 *Web:* www.auroraorganic.com	Boulder	CO	80302	720-564-6296	
Baldwin Richardson Foods Company Inc 20201 S La Grange Rd Ste 200 *TF Cust Svc:* 866-644-2732 ■ *Web:* www.brfoods.com	Frankfort	IL	60423	815-464-9994	464-9995
Barber Dairies Inc 36 Barber Ct *Web:* www.barbersdairy.com	Birmingham	AL	35209	205-942-2351	
Ben & Jerry's Homemade Inc 30 Community Dr *Web:* www.benjerry.com	South Burlington	VT	05403	802-846-1500	846-1538
Berkeley Farms Inc 25500 Clawiter Rd **Fax:* Sales ■ *Web:* www.berkeleyfarms.com	Hayward	CA	94545	510-265-8600	265-8754*
Blue Bell Creameries Inc PO Box 1807 *Web:* www.bluebell.com	Brenham	TX	77834	979-836-7977	
Borden Dairy Co 8750 N Central Expy Ste 400 *Web:* www.lalafoods.com	Dallas	TX	75231	214-459-1100	
Broughton Foods Co 1701 Green St *TF:* 800-283-2479 ■ *Web:* www.broughtonfoods.com	Marietta	OH	45750	740-373-4121	
Butterball Farms Inc 1435 Buchanan Ave SW *Web:* www.butterballfarms.com	Grand Rapids	MI	49507	616-243-0105	
Cedar Crest Specialties Inc 7269 Hwy 60 PO Box 260 *TF Hotline:* 800-877-8341 ■ *Web:* www.cedarcresticecream.com	Cedarburg	WI	53012	262-377-7252	377-5554
Cento Fine Foods Inc 100 Cento Blvd *Web:* www.cento.com	West Deptford	NJ	08086	856-853-5445	
Coleman Dairy Inc 6901 I-30 *TF:* 800-365-1551 ■ *Web:* hilanddairy.com	Little Rock	AR	72209	501-748-1700	748-1710
Creamland Dairies Inc PO Box 961447 *TF:* 800-395-7004 ■ *Web:* www.creamland.com	Albuquerque	NM	87105	505-247-0721	246-9696
Crossroad Farms Dairy 400 S Shortridge Rd	Indianapolis	IN	46219	317-229-7600	229-7676
Dean Foods 400 S Chamber Dr	Decatur	IN	46733	260-724-2136	724-2136
Dreyer's Grand Ice Cream Inc 5929 College Ave *Web:* dreyers.com	Oakland	CA	94618	510-652-8187	
Farrs Better Foods 2575 South 300 West *TF:* 877-553-2777 ■ *Web:* www.farrsicecream.com	South Salt lake City	UT	84115	801-484-8724	484-8768
Galliker Dairy Company Inc 143 Donald Ln *TF:* 800-477-6455 ■ *Web:* www.gallikers.com	Johnstown	PA	15907	814-266-8702	
Gandy's Dairies Inc 201 University Blvd *TF:* 877-382-4357 ■ *Web:* search.lubbockonline.com	Lubbock	TX	79415	806-762-8844	
Graeter's Inc 2145 Reading Rd *TF:* 800-721-3323 ■ *Web:* www.graeters.com	Cincinnati	OH	45202	513-721-3323	
Green Foods Corp 2220 Camino Del Sol *TF:* 800-777-4430 ■ *Web:* www.greenfoods.com	Oxnard	CA	93030	805-983-7470	
Heisler's Cloverleaf Dairy 743 Catawissa Rd *Web:* www.heislersdairy.com	Tamaqua	PA	18252	570-668-3399	668-3041
Hershey Creamery Co 301 S Cameron St *TF:* 888-240-1905 ■ *Web:* www.hersheyicecream.com	Harrisburg	PA	17101	717-238-8134	233-7195
High Road Craft Ice Cream Inc 1730 W Oak Commons Ct *Web:* www.highroadcraft.com	Marietta	GA	30062	678-701-7623	
Hiland Dairy Co PO Box 2270 *TF:* 800-641-4022 ■ *Web:* www.hilanddairy.com	Springfield	MO	65801	417-862-9311	
Ice Cream Specialties 8419 Hanley Industrial Ct *Web:* www.northstarfrozentreats.com	Saint Louis	MO	63144	314-962-2550	
J & J Snack Foods Corp 6000 Central Hwy *NASDAQ: JJSF* ■ *TF:* 800-486-9533 ■ *Web:* www.jjsnack.com	Pennsauken	NJ	08109	856-665-9533	665-6718
Klinke Bros Ice Cream Co 2450 Scaper Cove	Memphis	TN	38114	901-743-8250	743-8254
Newport Creamery Inc 35 Stockanosset Cross Rd PO Box 8819 *Web:* www.newportcreamery.com	Cranston	RI	02920	401-946-4000	
Perry's Ice Cream Company Inc 1 Ice Cream Plz *TF:* 800-873-7797 ■ *Web:* www.perrysicecream.com	Akron	NY	14001	716-542-5492	542-2544
Pet Dairy 2900 Bristol Hwy *Web:* petdairy.com	Johnson City	TN	37601	423-283-5700	
Royal Ice Cream Co 6200 Euclid Ave *Web:* www.pierres.com	Cleveland	OH	44103	216-432-1144	432-0433
Schwan Food Co 115 W College Dr *TF:* 800-533-5290 ■ *Web:* www.theschwanfoodcompany.com	Marshall	MN	56258	507-532-3274	
Southwest Cheese Company LLC 1141 Curry County Rd Ste 4 *Web:* www.southwestcheese.com	Clovis	NM	88101	575-742-9200	
Stonyfield Farm Inc 10 Burton Dr *Web:* www.stonyfield.com	Londonderry	NH	03053	603-437-4040	
Sugar Creek Foods International 301 N El Paso St *TF:* 800-445-2715 ■ *Web:* getsugarcreek.com	Russellville	AR	72801	800-445-2715	
Tofutti Brands Inc 50 Jackson Dr *NYSE: TOF* ■ *Web:* www.tofutti.com	Cranford	NJ	07016	908-272-2400	272-9492
Turkey Hill Dairy Inc 2601 River Rd *TF:* 800-693-2479 ■ *Web:* www.turkeyhill.com	Conestoga	PA	17516	717-872-5461	872-0602
Turner Dairy Farms Inc 1049 Jefferson Rd *TF:* 800-892-1039 ■ *Web:* www.turnerdairy.net	Pittsburgh	PA	15235	412-372-2211	
Umpqua Dairy Products Co 1686 Se N St PO Box 1306 *TF:* 800-222-6455 ■ *Web:* www.umpquadairy.com	Grants Pass	OR	97526	541-672-2638	673-0256
Wells Enterprises Inc 1 Blue Bunny Dr *TF All:* 888-309-1742 ■ *Web:* www.wellsenterprisesinc.com	Le Mars	IA	51031	712-546-4000	548-3008
Yarnell Ice Cream Co 205 S Spring St *Web:* www.yarnells.com	Searcy	AR	72143	501-268-6355	
YoCream International Inc 5858 NE 87th Ave *TF:* 800-962-7326 ■ *Web:* www.yocream.com	Portland	OR	97220	503-256-3754	256-3976

296-26 Meat Products - Prepared

Company	City	State	Zip	Phone	Fax
Advance Brands LLC 3540 S Blvd Ste 225 *Web:* www.advancedbrands.com	Edmond	OK	73013	405-562-1500	
Aidells Sausage Co 1625 Alvarado St *TF:* 877-243-3557 ■ *Web:* www.aidells.com	San Leandro	CA	94577	510-614-5450	614-2287
Albertville Quality Foods Inc 130 Quality Dr *TF:* 800-353-2806 ■ *Web:* www.albertvillequalityfoods.com	Albertville	AL	35950	256-840-9923	840-9906
Alderfer Inc 382 Main St PO Box 2 *TF Sales:* 800-222-2319 ■ *Web:* www.alderfermeats.com	Harleysville	PA	19438	800-222-2319	
Aliments Asta Inc 511 Ave De La Gare *TF:* 800-463-1355 ■ *Web:* alimentsasta.com	St Alexandre-De-Kamouraska	QC	G0L2G0	418-495-2728	495-2879
American Foods Group Inc 544 Acme St *TF:* 800-345-0293 ■ *Web:* www.americanfoodsgroup.com	Green Bay	WI	54302	920-437-6330	
Ballard's Farm Sausage Inc 7275 Right Fork Wilson Creek *TF General:* 800-346-7675 ■ *Web:* www.ballardsfarm.com/main.htm	Wayne	WV	25570	304-272-5147	272-5336
Bar-S Foods Co PO Box 29049 *TF:* 800-699-4115 ■ *Web:* www.bar-s.com	Phoenix	AZ	85038	800-699-4115	
Beef Products Inc 891 Two Rivers Dr *Web:* www.beefproducts.com	Dakota Dunes	SD	57049	605-217-8000	217-8001
Berks Packing Company Inc 307-323 Bingaman St PO Box 5919 **Fax Area Code:* 610 ■ *TF:* 800-882-3757 ■ *Web:* www.berksfoods.com	Reading	PA	19610	800-882-3757	378-1210*
Best Provision Company Inc 144 Avon Ave *TF:* 800-631-4466 ■ *Web:* www.bestprovision.com	Newark	NJ	07108	973-242-5000	648-0041

Company	City	State	ZIP	Phone	Fax
Bi-County Scale & Equipment Co 75 Kean St *Web:* www.bicountyscale.com	West Babylon	NY	11704	631-643-2300	
Blue Grass Quality Meats 2645 Commerce Dr *Web:* www.bluegrassqualitymeats.com	Crescent Springs	KY	41017	859-331-7100	331-4273
Blue Ribbon Meats Inc 3316 W 67th Pl *Web:* blueribbonmeats.com	Cleveland	OH	44102	216-631-8850	
Boar's Head Provisions Co Inc 1819 Main St Ste 800 *Web:* www.boarshead.com	Sarasota	FL	34236	941-955-0994	366-0354
Bobak Sausage Co 5275 S Archer Ave *Web:* www.bobak.com	Chicago	IL	60632	773-735-5334	
Bridgford Foods Corp 1308 N Patt St *NASDAQ: BRID* ■ *TF:* 800-854-3255 ■ *Web:* www.bridgford.com	Anaheim	CA	92801	714-526-5533	526-4360
Brown Packing Company Inc 116 Willis St	Gaffney	SC	29341	864-489-5723	
Burger's Ozark Country Cured Hams Inc 32819 hwy 87 *TF:* 800-203-4424 ■ *Web:* www.smokehouse.com	California	MO	65018	573-796-3134	796-3137
Busseto Foods Inc 1351 N Crystal Ave *Web:* www.busseto.com	Fresno	CA	93728	559-485-9882	
Carando Inc 20 Carando Dr *Web:* carando.com	Springfield	MA	01104	413-781-5620	
Caribbean Products Ltd 3624 Falls Rd *TF:* 888-689-5068	Baltimore	MD	21211	888-689-5068	
Carl Buddig & Co 950 175th St *TF:* 888-633-5684 ■ *Web:* www.buddig.com	Homewood	IL	60430	708-798-0900	798-1284
Carlton Foods Corp 880 Texas 46 *TF:* 800-628-9849 ■ *Web:* www.carltonfoods.com	New Braunfels	TX	78130	830-625-7583	
Carolina Pride Foods Inc 1 Packer Ave *Web:* carolinapride.publishpath.com	Greenwood	SC	29646	864-229-5611	
Cattaneo Bros Inc 769 Caudill St *TF:* 800-243-8537 ■ *Web:* www.cattaneobros.com	San Luis Obispo	CA	93401	805-543-7188	543-4698
Cher-Make Sausage Co 2915 Calumet Ave *TF:* 800-242-7679 ■ *Web:* www.cher-make.com	Manitowoc	WI	54220	920-683-5980	682-2588
Chicago Meat Authority Inc (CMA) 1120 W 47th Pl *TF:* 800-383-3811 ■ *Web:* www.chicagomeat.com	Chicago	IL	60609	773-254-3811	254-5851
Chicopee Provision Co Inc 19 Sitarz St *TF:* 800-924-6328 ■ *Web:* www.bluesealkielbasa.com	Chicopee	MA	01013	413-594-4765	
Citterio USA Corp 2008 SR 940 *TF:* 800-435-8888 ■ *Web:* www.citteriousa.com	Freeland	PA	18224	570-636-3171	636-5340
Cloverdale Foods Co 3015 34th St NW **Fax Area Code:* 701 ■ *TF:* 800-669-9511 ■ *Web:* www.cloverdalefoods.com	Mandan	ND	58554	800-669-9511	663-0690*
Continental-Capri Inc 250 Jackson St	Englewood	NJ	07631	201-568-7100	568-7180
Cook's Ham Inc 200 S Second St *TF:* 800-332-8400 ■ *Web:* www.mycooksham.com	Lincoln	NE	68508	402-475-6700	
Counts Sausage Company Inc 222 Church St	Prosperity	SC	29127	803-364-2392	
D'Artagnan Inc 280 Wilson Ave Ste 1 *Web:* www.dartagnan.com	Newark	NJ	07105	973-344-0565	
Daniele Inc PO Box 106 *TF:* 800-451-2535 ■ *Web:* www.danielefoods.com	Pascoag	RI	02859	401-568-6228	568-4788
Dean Sausage Company Inc 3750 Pleasant Vly Rd PO Box 750 *Web:* www.deansausage.com	Attalla	AL	35954	256-538-6082	538-2584
Dearborn Sausage Co Inc 2450 Wyoming Ave *Web:* www.dearbornsausage.com	Dearborn	MI	48120	313-842-2375	842-2640
Dewied International Inc 5010 IH- 10 E *TF:* 800-992-5600 ■ *Web:* www.dewied.com	San Antonio	TX	78219	210-661-6161	662-6112
Dietz & Watson Inc 5701 Tacony St *TF:* 800-333-1974 ■ *Web:* www.dietzandwatson.com	Philadelphia	PA	19135	215-831-9000	831-1044
Fabbri Sausage Manufacturing Co 166 N Aberdeen St *Web:* www.fabbrisausage.com	Chicago	IL	60607	312-829-6363	
Family Brands International LLC 1001 Elm Hill Rd PO Box 429 **Fax Area Code:* 865 ■ *TF:* 800-356-4455 ■ *Web:* www.fbico.com	Lenoir City	TN	37771	800-356-4455	986-7171*
Fargo Packing & Sausage Co 307 E Main Ave *Web:* qualitymeats.com	West Fargo	ND	58078	701-282-3211	
Farmington Foods Inc 7419 W Franklin St *Web:* www.farmingtonfoods.com	Forest Park	IL	60130	708-771-3600	
Fisher Meats Inc 85 Front St N *Web:* fischermeatsnw.com	Issaquah	WA	98027	425-392-3131	392-0168
Frank Wardynski & Sons Inc 336 Peckham St *Web:* www.wardynski.com	Buffalo	NY	14206	716-854-6083	
Fred Usinger Inc 1030 N Old World Third St *TF:* 800-558-9998 ■ *Web:* www.usinger.com	Milwaukee	WI	53203	414-276-9100	291-5277
Freedom Sausage Inc 4155 E 1650th Rd	Earlville	IL	60518	815-792-8276	792-8283
Fremont Beef Co 960 S Schneider St *Web:* www.fremontbeef.com	Fremont	NE	68025	402-727-7200	
G & G Supermarket Inc 1211 W College Ave *Web:* www.gandgmarket.com	Santa Rosa	CA	95401	707-546-6877	
Gallo Salame 2411 Baumann Ave *TF:* 800-988-6464 ■ *Web:* gallosalame.com	San Lorenzo	CA	94580	800-988-6464	
Garcia Foods Inc PO Box 13280 *Web:* www.garciafoods.com	San Antonio	TX	78213	210-349-6262	
Gaytan Foods 15430 Proctor Ave *TF:* 800-242-9826 ■ *Web:* www.gaytanfoods.com	City Of Industry	CA	91745	626-330-4553	
Gold Star Sausage Co 2800 Walnut St *Web:* ww.goldstarsausage.com	Denver	CO	80205	303-295-6400	294-0495
Golden State Foods 18301 Von Karman Ave Ste 1100 *Web:* www.goldenstatefoods.com	Irvine	CA	92612	949-252-2000	252-2080
Great Lakes Packing Co 1535 W 43rd St *Web:* glpacking.com	Chicago	IL	60609	773-927-6660	927-8587
Green Tree Packing Co 65 Central Ave *Web:* www.greentreepacking.com	Passaic	NJ	07055	973-473-1305	473-7975
Grote & Weigel Inc 76 Granby St *Web:* www.groteandweigel.com	Bloomfield	CT	06002	860-242-8528	242-4162
Habbersett Scrapple Inc 103 S Railroad Ave *TF:* 800-338-4727 ■ *Web:* www.habbersettscrapple.com	Bridgeville	DE	19933	800-338-4727	
Hatfield Quality Meats Inc 2700 Clemens Rd *TF:* 800-743-1191 ■ *Web:* www.hatfieldqualitymeats.com	Hatfield	PA	19440	215-368-2500	

Company	City	State	ZIP	Phone	Fax
Hazle Park Packing Co 260 Washington Ave Hazle Pk *TF:* 800-238-4331 ■ *Web:* hazlepark.com	Hazletownship	PA	18202	570-455-7571	455-6030
Hormel Foods Corp 1 Hormel Pl *NYSE: HRL* ■ *TF:* 800-523-4635 ■ *Web:* www.hormel.com	Austin	MN	55912	507-437-5611	
Hummel Bros Inc 180 Sargent Dr *Web:* hummelbros.3dcartstores.com	New Haven	CT	06511	203-787-4113	
Interstate Meat Distributors Inc 9550 SE Last Rd	Clackamas	OR	97015	503-656-0633	
John Hofmeister & Son Inc 2386 S Blue Island Ave *Web:* www.hofhaus.com	Chicago	IL	60608	773-847-0700	847-6624
John Morrell & Co 805 E Kemper Rd **Fax Area Code:* 408 ■ **Fax:* Cust Svc ■ *TF:* 800-722-1127 ■ *Web:* www.johnmorrell.com	Cincinnati	OH	45246	513-346-3540	220-9679*
Johnsonville Sausage LLC PO Box 906 *TF:* 888-556-2728 ■ *Web:* www.johnsonville.com	Sheboygan Falls	WI	53085	888-556-2728	
Jones Dairy Farm 800 Jones Ave *TF:* 800-635-6637 ■ *Web:* www.jonesdairyfarm.com	Fort Atkinson	WI	53538	920-563-2431	563-6801
Karl Ehmer Inc 48 S Ocean Ave *Web:* www.karlehmer.com	Patchogue	NY	11772	631-289-3448	
Kayem Foods Inc 75 Arlington St *TF:* 800-426-6100 ■ *Web:* www.kayem.com	Chelsea	MA	02150	617-889-1600	889-5478
Kent Quality Foods Inc 703 Leonard St NW *TF:* 800-748-0141 ■ *Web:* www.kqf.com	Grand Rapids	MI	49504	800-748-0141	
Kessler's Inc 1201 Hummel Ave *TF:* 800-382-1328 ■ *Web:* www.kesslerfoods.com	Lemoyne	PA	17043	717-763-7162	763-4982
Keystone Foods LLC 300 Bar Harbor Dr Ste 600 5 Tower Bridge *Web:* www.keystonefoods.com	West Conshohocken	PA	19428	610-668-6700	
King's Command Foods Inc 7622 S 188th St *Web:* www.kingscommand.com	Kent	WA	98032	425-251-6788	251-0523
Kiolbassa Provision Co 1325 S Brazos St *TF:* 800-456-5465 ■ *Web:* www.kiolbassa.com	San Antonio	TX	78207	713-747-7383	
Klement Sausage Co Inc 207 E Lincoln Ave *Web:* www.klements.com	Milwaukee	WI	53207	414-744-2330	744-2438
Koegel Meats Inc 3400 W Bristol Rd *Web:* www.koegelmeats.com	Flint	MI	48507	810-238-3685	238-2467
Kowalski Sausage Company Inc 2270 Holbrook Ave *Web:* www.kowality.com	Hamtramck	MI	48212	313-873-8200	873-4220
Kronos Products Inc 1 Kronos Dr *TF:* 800-621-0099 ■ *Web:* www.kronosproducts.com	Glendale Heights	IL	60139	800-621-0099	
Land O'Frost Inc 16850 Chicago Ave *Web:* www.landofrost.com	Lansing	IL	60438	708-474-7100	
Les Trois Petits Cochons Inc 4223 First Ave 2nd Fl *Web:* www.3pigs.com	Brooklyn	NY	11232	212-219-1230	941-9726
Lopez Foods Inc 6016 NW 120th Ct *Web:* www.lopezfoods.com	Oklahoma City	OK	73162	405-603-7500	
Louie's Finer Meats Inc Hwy 63 N 2025 Superior Ave *Web:* www.louiesfinermeats.com	Cumberland	WI	54829	715-822-4728	822-3150
Maid-Rite Steak Company Inc 105 Keystone Industrial Pk *TF:* 800-233-4259 ■ *Web:* maidritesteak.com	Dunmore	PA	18512	570-343-4748	969-2878
Makowski's Real Sausage Co 2710 S Poplar Ave *Web:* realsausage.com	Chicago	IL	60608	312-842-5330	
Maple Leaf Foods Inc 30 St Clair Ave W Ste 1500 *TSE: MFI* ■ *Web:* www.mapleleaf.ca	Toronto	ON	M4V3A1	416-926-2000	
Marathon Enterprises Inc 9 Smith St *TF:* 800-722-7388 ■ *Web:* sabrett.com	Englewood	NJ	07631	201-935-3330	935-5693
Marfood USA Inc 21655 Trolley Industrial Dr *Web:* marfoodusa.com	Taylor	MI	48180	313-292-4100	
Martin Rosol Inc 45 Grove St *Web:* martinrosolsinc.com	New Britain	CT	06053	860-223-2707	
Martin`s Abattoir & Wholesale Meats Inc 1600 Martin Rd *Web:* www.martinmeats.com	Godwin	NC	28344	910-567-6102	
Meadow Farms Sausage Co 6215 S Western Ave *Web:* meadowfarmssausage.com	Los Angeles	CA	90047	323-752-2300	
Milan Salami Company Inc 1155 67th St	Oakland	CA	94608	510-654-7055	
Miller Packing Co 1122 Industrial Way PO Box 1390 *TF:* 800-624-2328 ■ *Web:* www.millerhotdogs.com	Lodi	CA	95241	209-339-2310	
Mims Meat Company Inc 12634 E Farway	Houston	TX	77015	713-453-0151	
Mongolia Casing Corp 4706 Grand Ave	Maspeth	NY	11378	718-628-3800	
Mrs Ressler's Food Products Co 5501 Tabor Ave *Web:* www.ressler.com	Philadelphia	PA	19120	215-744-4700	744-4750
National Steak Processors Inc 301 E Fifth Ave *Web:* www.nationalsteak.com	Owasso	OK	74055	918-274-8787	
Natural Casing Co 410 E Railroad St PO Box A **Fax Area Code:* 715 ■ *TF:* 877-515-0270 ■ *Web:* www.naturalcasingco.com	Peshtigo	WI	54157	877-515-0270	582-3931*
Neto Sausage Co Inc 288 Brokaw Rd *TF:* 888-482-6386 ■ *Web:* www.netosausage.com	Santa Clara	CA	95050	408-296-0818	296-0538
Nossack Fine Meats Ltd 7240 Johnstone Dr Ste 100 *Web:* www.nossack.com	Red Deer	AB	T4P3Y6	403-346-5006	
Oberto Sausage Co 7060 S 238th St *TF:* 877-453-7591 ■ *Web:* www.oberto.com	Kent	WA	98032	253-854-7056	437-6151
Odom's Tennessee Pride Sausage Inc 1201 Neelys Bend Rd *TF:* 866-484-8641 ■ *Web:* www.tnpride.com	Madison	TN	37115	615-868-1360	860-4703
Old Wisconsin Sausage Co 5030 PlaybiRd Rd **Fax Area Code:* 708 ■ *TF:* 877-451-7988 ■ *Web:* www.oldwisconsin.com	Sheboygan	WI	53083	877-451-7988	798-1284*
Omni Custom Meats Inc 151 Vanderbilt Ct *Web:* omnimeats.com	Bowling Green	KY	42103	270-796-6664	
OSI Industries LLC 1225 Corporate Blvd *Web:* www.osigroup.com	Aurora	IL	60505	630-851-6600	692-2340

Phone Fax

Palama Meat Company Inc 2029 Lauwiliwili St . . . Kapolei HI 96707 808-682-8305 834-8895
Web: sbcontract.com

Palmyra Bologna Company Inc 230 N College St . . . Palmyra PA 17078 717-838-6336
TF: 800-282-6336 ■ *Web:* www.seltzerslebanon.com

Park 100 Foods Inc 326 E Adams St . . . Tipton IN 46072 765-675-3480 675-3474
TF: 800-854-6504 ■ *Web:* www.park100foods.com

Peer Foods Group Inc 1200 W 35th St 3rd Fl . . . Chicago IL 60609 773-927-1440 927-9859
TF: 800-365-5644 ■ *Web:* www.peerfoods.com

Pine Ridge Farms 1800 SE Maury St . . . Des Moines IA 50317 515-266-4100
Web: www.pineridgefarmspork.com

Plumrose USA Inc
1901 Butterfield Rd Ste 305 . . . Downers Grove IL 60515 732-624-4040
TF: 800-526-4909 ■ *Web:* www.plumroseusa.com

Pocino Foods Co 14250 Lomitas Ave . . . City of Industry CA 91746 626-968-8000 968-0196
TF: 800-345-0150 ■ *Web:* www.pocinofoods.com

Premio Foods Inc 50 Utter Ave . . . Hawthorne NJ 07506 973-427-1106
Web: www.premiofoods.com

Quality Sausage Company Ltd 1925 Lone Star Dr . . . Dallas TX 75212 214-634-3400 634-2296
Web: www.qualitysausage.com

Quantum Foods LLC 750 S Schmidt Rd . . . Bolingbrook IL 60440 630-679-2300

R Torre & Company Inc
233 E Harris Ave . . . South San Francisco CA 94080 650-875-1200
Web: www.perfectpalate.com

Randolph Packing Co 275 Roma Jean Pkwy . . . Streamwood IL 60107 630-830-3100
TF: 800-451-1607 ■ *Web:* www.randolphpacking.com

Reser's Fine Foods Inc 15570 SW Jenkins Rd . . . Beaverton OR 97006 503-643-6431
TF: 800-333-6431 ■ *Web:* www.resers.com

Richwood Meat Company Inc 2751 N Santa Fe Ave . . . Merced CA 95348 209-722-8171
Web: www.richwoodmeat.com

Rosina Food Products Inc 170 French Rd . . . Buffalo NY 14227 716-668-0123
Web: www.rosina.com

Ruprecht Co 1301 Allanson Rd . . . Mundelein IL 60060 312-829-4100
Web: www.ruprechtcompany.com

Saags Products Inc 1799 Factor Ave . . . San Leandro CA 94577 510-352-8000
Web: www.saags.com

Sadler's Smokehouse Ltd PO Box 1088 . . . Henderson TX 75653 903-655-7265
TF: 800-777-5581 ■ *Web:* www.sadlerssmokehouse.com

Sahlen Packing Company Inc 318 Howard St . . . Buffalo NY 14206 716-852-8677
TF: 800-466-8165 ■ *Web:* www.sahlen.com

Schaller & Weber Inc 22-35 46th St . . . Astoria NY 11105 718-721-5480 956-9157
TF Orders: 800-847-4115 ■ *Web:* www.schallerweber.com

Silver Star Meats Inc
1720 Middletown Rd PO Box 393 . . . McKees Rocks PA 15136 412-771-5539
TF: 800-548-1321 ■ *Web:* www.silverstarmeats.com

Smith Packing Company Inc
105-125 Washington St . . . Utica NY 13503 315-732-5125 732-5129
Web: www.smithpacking.com

Smithfield Foods Inc 200 Commerce St . . . Smithfield VA 23430 757-365-3000
NYSE: SFD ■ *Web:* www.smithfieldfoods.com

Specialty Foods Group Inc
21 Enterprise Pkwy Ste 400 . . . Hampton VA 23666 757-952-1200
Web: www.specialtyfoodsgroup.com

Stampede Meat Inc 7351 S 78th Ave . . . Bridgeview IL 60455 800-353-0933
TF: 800-353-0933 ■ *Web:* www.stampedemeat.com

Standard Casing Company Inc, The
165 Chubb Ave . . . Lyndhurst NJ 07071 201-434-6300
Web: www.standardcasing.com

Standard Meat Company LP 5105 Investment Dr . . . Dallas TX 75236 214-561-0561 561-0560
TF: 866-859-6313 ■ *Web:* www.standardmeat.com

Stevison Ham Co 125 Stevison Ham Rd . . . Portland TN 37148 615-325-4161 325-5914
Web: www.tennesseetraditions.com

Stock Yards Packing Co Inc
2457 W North Ave . . . Melrose Park IL 60160 877-785-9273
TF: 877-785-9273 ■ *Web:* www.stockyards.com

Storer Meats Company Inc 3700 Clark Ave . . . Cleveland OH 44109 216-621-7538 361-0622
Web: fivestarbrandmeats.com

Sugar Creek Packing Co
2101 Kenskill Ave . . . Washington Court House OH 43160 740-335-7440 551-5263*
**Fax Area Code:* 513 ■ *TF:* 800-848-8205 ■ *Web:* www.sugarcreek.com

Suzanna's Kitchen Inc 4025 Buford Hwy . . . Duluth GA 30096 770-476-9900 476-8899
Web: www.suzannaskitchen.com

Sysco Kansas City Inc 1915 E Kansas City Rd . . . Olathe KS 66061 913-829-5555 780-8625
TF: 800-735-3341 ■ *Web:* www.kc.sysco.com

Sysco Newport Meat Company Inc 16691 Hale Ave . . . Irvine CA 92606 949-474-4040
Web: www.newportmeat.com

TF Kinnealey & Company Inc 1100 Pearl St . . . Brockton MA 02301 508-638-7700
TF: 800-225-4950 ■ *Web:* www.kinnealey.com

Tyson Prepared Foods Inc 5701 McNutt Rd . . . Santa Teresa NM 88008 575-589-0100
TF: 888-301-7304 ■ *Web:* www.tyson.com

US Premium Beef LLC (USPB)
12200 N Ambassador Dr PO Box 20103 . . . Kansas City MO 64163 816-713-8800 713-8810
TF: 866-877-2525 ■ *Web:* www.uspremiumbeef.com

Vienna Sausage Manufacturing Co
2501 N Damen Ave . . . Chicago IL 60647 773-278-7800
TF: 800-366-3647 ■ *Web:* www.viennabeef.com

Vincent Giordano Corp
2600 Washington Ave . . . Philadelphia PA 19146 215-467-6629 467-6339
Web: www.vgiordano.com

Vista International Packaging LLC
1126 88th Pl . . . Kenosha WI 53143 262-694-2276 694-4824

Vollwerth & Co 200 Hancock St PO Box 239 . . . Hancock MI 49930 906-482-1550
TF: 800-562-7620 ■ *Web:* www.vollwerth.com

Wimmer's Meat Products Inc 126 W Grant St . . . West Point NE 68788 402-372-2437 372-5659
TF Cust Svc: 800-762-9865 ■ *Web:* www.wimmersmeats.com

Zweigles Inc 651 Plymouth Ave N . . . Rochester NY 14608 585-546-1740 546-8721
Web: www.zweigles.com

296-27 Milk & Cream Products

Phone Fax

Agri-Mark Inc PO Box 5800 . . . Lawrence MA 01842 978-689-4442 794-8304
Web: agrimark.coop

Phone Fax

Alta Dena Dairy 17851 E Railrd . . . City of Industry CA 91748 800-535-1369
TF Orders: 800-535-1369 ■ *Web:* www.altadenadairy.com

AMPI 315 N Broadway . . . New Ulm MN 56073 507-354-8295
TF: 800-533-3580 ■ *Web:* www.ampi.com

Anderson Dairy Inc 801 Searles Ave . . . Las Vegas NV 89101 702-642-7507 642-3480
Web: www.andersondairy.com

Anderson Erickson Dairy Co
2420 E University Ave . . . Des Moines IA 50317 515-265-2521 263-6301
TF: 800-234-7257 ■ *Web:* www.aedairy.com

Barber Dairies Inc 36 Barber Ct . . . Birmingham AL 35209 205-942-2351
Web: www.barbersdairy.com

Bartlett Dairy Inc 105-03 150th St . . . Jamaica NY 11435 718-658-2299 725-2527
Web: www.bartlettny.com

Berkeley Farms Inc 25500 Clawiter Rd . . . Hayward CA 94545 510-265-8600 265-8754*
**Fax:* Sales ■ *Web:* www.berkeleyfarms.com

Broughton Foods Co 1701 Green St . . . Marietta OH 45750 740-373-4121
TF: 800-283-2479 ■ *Web:* www.broughtonfoods.com

California Dairies Inc 2000 N Plz Dr . . . Visalia CA 93291 559-625-2200 625-5433
Web: www.californiadairies.com

Century Foods International 400 Century Ct . . . Sparta WI 54656 608-269-1900 269-1910
Web: www.centuryfoods.com

Clover Farms Dairy PO Box 14627 . . . Reading PA 19612 610-921-9111
TF: 800-323-0123 ■ *Web:* www.cloverfarms.com

Cloverland Green Spring Dairy Inc
2701 Loch Raven Rd . . . Baltimore MD 21218 410-235-4477
TF Orders: 800-492-0094 ■ *Web:* www.cloverlanddairy.com

Coleman Dairy Inc 6901 I-30 . . . Little Rock AR 72209 501-748-1700 748-1710
TF: 800-365-1551 ■ *Web:* hilanddairy.com

Crossroad Farms Dairy
400 S Shortridge Rd . . . Indianapolis IN 46219 317-229-7600 229-7676

Dannon Co 100 Hillside Ave . . . White Plains NY 10603 914-872-8400 872-1565*
**Fax:* Hum Res ■ *Web:* www.dannon.com

Darigold Inc 1130 Rainier Ave S . . . Seattle WA 98144 206-284-7220
Web: darigold.com

Dean Foods Co 2711 N Haskell Ave Ste 3400 . . . Dallas TX 75204 214-303-3400 303-3499
NYSE: DF ■ *TF:* 800-395-7004 ■ *Web:* www.deanfoods.com

Eagle Family Foods Inc 1 Strawberry Ln . . . Orrville OH 44667 888-656-3245 684-6410*
**Fax Area Code:* 330 ■ *TF:* 888-656-3245 ■ *Web:* www.eaglebrand.com

Farmers Select LLC 7321 N Loop Rd . . . El Paso TX 79915 915-772-2736 772-0907

Farmland Dairies LLC 520 Main Ave . . . Wallington NJ 07057 973-777-2500 249-3849*
**Fax:* Sales ■ *Web:* www.skimplus.com

Galliker Dairy Company Inc 143 Donald Ln . . . Johnstown PA 15907 814-266-8702
TF: 800-477-6455 ■ *Web:* www.gallikers.com

Guida-Seibert Dairy Co 433 Pk St . . . New Britain CT 06051 860-224-2404 225-0035
TF: 800-832-8929 ■ *Web:* www.supercow.com

Harrisburg Dairies Inc 2001 Herr St . . . Harrisburg PA 17105 717-233-8701 231-4584
TF: 800-692-7429 ■ *Web:* www.harrisburgdairies.com

Heritage Foods LLC 4002 Westminster Ave . . . Santa Ana CA 92703 714-775-5000 775-7677
TF Orders: 800-321-5960 ■ *Web:* stremicksheritagefoods.com

Hiland Dairy Co PO Box 2270 . . . Springfield MO 65801 417-862-9311
TF: 800-641-4022 ■ *Web:* www.hilanddairy.com

Kemps LLC 1270 Energy Ln . . . Saint Paul MN 55108 651-379-6500
TF: 800-322-9566 ■ *Web:* kemps.com

Kleinpeter Farms Dairy LLC
14444 Airline Hwy . . . Baton Rouge LA 70817 225-753-2121
Web: www.kleinpeterdairy.com

Land O'Lakes Inc Dairyman's Div 400 S 'M' St . . . Tulare CA 93274 559-687-8287
TF: 800-328-4155 ■ *Web:* landolakesinc.com

Lehigh Valley Dairies Inc 880 Allentown Rd . . . Lansdale PA 19446 215-855-8205
Web: www.lehighvalleydairyfarms.com

Lifeway Foods Inc 6431 W Oakton St . . . Morton Grove IL 60053 847-967-1010 967-6558
NASDAQ: LWAY ■ *TF:* 877-281-3874 ■ *Web:* lifewaykefir.com

Maple Hill Farms Inc 12 Burr Rd PO Box 767 . . . Bloomfield CT 06002 860-242-9689 243-2490
Web: mhfct.com

Marcus Dairy Inc 4 Eagle Rd . . . Danbury CT 06810 203-748-5611 791-2759
TF: 800-243-2511 ■ *Web:* www.marcusdairy.com

Meadow Brook Dairy 2365 Buffalo Rd . . . Erie PA 16510 814-899-3191 464-9152
Web: www.meadowbrookdairy.com

Michigan Milk Producers Assn 41310 Bridge St . . . Novi MI 48375 248-474-6672 474-0924
Web: www.mimilk.com

Milkco Inc 220 Deaverview Rd . . . Asheville NC 28806 828-254-9560
TF: 800-842-8021 ■ *Web:* www.milkco.com

Oakhurst Dairy 364 Forest Ave . . . Portland ME 04101 207-772-7468 874-0714
TF: 800-482-0718 ■ *Web:* www.oakhurstdairy.com

Parmalat Canada Ltd 405 the W Mall 10th Fl . . . Toronto ON M9C5J1 800-563-1515
TF: 800-563-1515 ■ *Web:* www.parmalat.ca

Penn Maid Foods Inc 10975 Dutton Rd . . . Philadelphia PA 19154 215-824-2800
Web: www.pennmaid.com

Prairie Farms Dairy Inc
1100 N Broadway St . . . Carlinville IL 62626 217-854-2547 854-6426
TF: 800-654-2547 ■ *Web:* www.prairiefarms.com

Pride of Main Street Dairy 214 Main St S . . . Sauk Centre MN 56378 320-351-8300 351-8500

Producers Dairy Foods Inc 250 E Belmont Ave . . . Fresno CA 93701 559-264-6583
TF: 800-660-1171 ■ *Web:* www.producersdairy.com

Purity Dairies Inc 360 Murfreesboro Rd . . . Nashville TN 37210 615-244-1970 242-8547
Web: www.puritydairies.com

Readington Farms Inc 12 Mill Rd . . . Whitehouse Station NJ 08889 908-534-2121 534-5235

Royal Crest Dairy Inc 350 S Pearl St . . . Denver CO 80209 303-777-2227 744-9173
TF: 888-226-6455 ■ *Web:* www.royalcrestdairy.com

Rutter Dairy Inc 2100 N George St . . . York PA 17404 717-848-9827 845-8751
Web: www.rutters.com

Schneider Valley Farms Dairy
1860 E Third St . . . State College PA 17701 814-237-3426
Web: schneidersdairypgh.com

Schneider's Dairy Inc 726 Frank St . . . Pittsburgh PA 15227 412-881-3525 881-7722
Web: www.schneidersdairypgh.com

Shamrock Foods 3900 E Camelback Rd Ste 300 . . . Phoenix AZ 85018 602-477-2500
TF: 800-289-3663 ■ *Web:* www.shamrockfoods.com

Smith Dairy 1381 Dairy Ln . . . Orrville OH 44667 330-683-8710 684-6728
TF: 800-776-7076 ■ *Web:* www.smithsbrand.com

Southeast Milk Inc
1950 SE Hwy 484 PO Box 3790 . . . Belleview FL 34420 800-598-7866 245-9434*
**Fax Area Code:* 352 ■ *TF:* 800-598-7866 ■ *Web:* www.southeastmilk.org

Company	City	State	ZIP	Phone	Fax
Springfield Creamery Inc 29440 Airport Rd *Web:* www.nancysyogurt.com	Eugene	OR	97402	541-689-2911	689-2915
Stonyfield Farm Inc 10 Burton Dr *Web:* www.stonyfield.com	Londonderry	NH	03053	603-437-4040	
Superior Dairy Inc 4719 Navarre Rd SW *TF:* 800-597-5460 ■ *Web:* reliableplant.com	Canton	OH	44706	330-477-4515	
T Marzetti Company Allen Milk Div 1709 Frank Rd *Web:* marzetti.com	Columbus	OH	43223	614-279-8673	
Umpqua Dairy Products Co 1686 Se N St PO Box 1306 *TF:* 800-222-6455 ■ *Web:* www.umpquadairy.com	Grants Pass	OR	97526	541-672-2638	673-0256
United Dairy Farmers 3955 Montgomery Rd *TF General:* 866-837-4833 ■ *Web:* www.uniteddairy.com	Cincinnati	OH	45212	513-396-8700	396-8736
United Dairy Inc 300 N Fifth St *TF:* 800-252-1542 ■ *Web:* www.uniteddairy.com	Martins Ferry	OH	43935	740-633-1451	633-6759
WhiteWave Foods Co 12002 Airport Way *TF:* 888-820-9283 ■ *Web:* www.whitewave.com	Broomfield	CO	80021	303-635-4000	
Whittier Farms Inc 90 Douglas Rd PO Box 455 *Web:* www.whittierfarms.com	Sutton	MA	01590	508-865-0640	865-1096
Wilcox Farms Inc 40400 Harts Lake Valley Rd *Web:* www.wilcoxfarms.com	Roy	WA	98580	360-458-7774	458-3995

296-28 Nuts - Edible

Company	City	State	ZIP	Phone	Fax
Azar Nut Co 1800 NW Dr *TF:* 800-351-8178	El Paso	TX	79912	915-877-4079	877-1198
Beer Nuts Inc 103 N Robinson St *Web:* www.beernuts.com	Bloomington	IL	61701	309-827-8580	827-0914
Dahlgren & Co Inc 1220 Sunflower St *Web:* www.sunflowerseed.com	Crookston	MN	56716	218-281-2985	281-7350
Diamond Foods Inc 1050 S Diamond St *NASDAQ: DMND* ■ *Web:* www.diamondfoods.com	Stockton	CA	95205	209-467-6000	461-7309
Gurley's Foods 1118 E Hwy 12 *Web:* www.gurleysfoods.com	Willmar	MN	56201	320-235-0600	
Hines Nut Co Inc 990 S St Paul St *TF:* 800-561-6374 ■ *Web:* www.hinesnut.com	Dallas	TX	75201	214-939-0253	
John B Sanfilippo & Son Inc 1703 N Randall Rd *NASDAQ: JBSS* ■ *TF:* 800-874-8734 ■ *Web:* www.jbssinc.com	Elgin	IL	60123	847-289-1800	289-1843
Kar's Nuts 1200 E 14 Mile Rd *TF:* 800-527-6887 ■ *Web:* www.karsnuts.com	Madison Heights	MI	48071	248-588-1903	588-1902
King Nut Co 31900 Solon Rd *TF:* 800-860-5464 ■ *Web:* www.kingnut.com	Solon	OH	44139	440-248-8484	248-0153
Leavitt Corp 100 Santilli Hwy *Web:* teddie.com	Everett	MA	02149	617-389-2600	387-9085
Pippin Snack Pecan Co 1332 Old Pretoria Rd *Web:* georgiapecan.org	Albany	GA	31721	229-432-9316	
Priester Pecan Company Inc PO Box 381 *TF:* 800-277-3226 ■ *Web:* www.priesters.com	Fort Deposit	AL	36032	334-227-4301	227-4294
South Georgia Pecan Co 309 S Lee St *TF:* 800-627-6630 ■ *Web:* georgiapecan.com	Valdosta	GA	31601	229-244-1321	247-6361
Superior Nut Co Inc 225 Monsignor O'Brien Hwy *Web:* www.superiornut.com	Cambridge	MA	02141	617-876-3808	876-8225
Trophy Nut Company Inc 320 N Second St *TF:* 800-729-6887 ■ *Web:* www.trophynut.com	Tipp City	OH	45371	937-667-8478	667-4656
Wricley Nut Products Co 480 Pattison Ave *Web:* wricleynutproductsco.com	Philadelphia	PA	19148	215-467-1106	
Young Pecan Co 1831 W Evans St Ste 200 *TF All:* 800-829-6864	Florence	SC	29501	843-662-8591	664-2344

296-29 Oil Mills - Cottonseed, Soybean, Other Vegetable Oils

Company	City	State	ZIP	Phone	Fax
Abitec Corp Inc PO Box 569 *TF Sales:* 800-555-1255 ■ *Web:* www.abiteccorp.com	Columbus	OH	43215	614-429-6464	299-8279
Ag Processing Inc 12700 W Dodge Rd PO Box 2047 *TF:* 800-247-1345 ■ *Web:* www.agp.com	Omaha	NE	68103	402-496-7809	
American Lecithin Company Inc 115 Hurley Rd Unit 2B *TF:* 800-364-4416 ■ *Web:* www.americanlecithin.com	Oxford	CT	06478	203-262-7100	262-7101
Bunge Ltd 50 Main St *NYSE: BG* ■ *Web:* www.bunge.com	White Plains	NY	10606	914-684-2800	
Cargill Inc 15407 McGinty Rd W *TF:* 800-227-4455 ■ *Web:* www.cargill.com	Wayzata	MN	55391	952-742-7575	
Hartsville Oil Mill 311 Washington St	Darlington	SC	29532	843-393-2855	395-5598
Owensboro Grain Co 822 E Second St *TF:* 800-874-0305 ■ *Web:* www.owensborograin.com	Owensboro	KY	42303	270-926-2032	686-6509
Planters Cotton Oil Mill Inc 2901 Planters Dr *TF:* 800-264-7070 ■ *Web:* www.plantersoil.com	Pine Bluff	AR	71601	870-534-3631	534-1421
Producers Co-op Oil Mill 6 SE Fourth St *Web:* www.producerscoop.net	Oklahoma City	OK	73129	405-232-7555	236-4887
Pyco Industries Inc PO Box 841 *Web:* www.pycoindustriesinc.com	Lubbock	TX	79404	806-747-3434	
Valley Co-op Oil Mill 1910 N Expwy 77 PO Box 533609 *Web:* valleycoopoilmill.com	Harlingen	TX	78553	956-425-4545	425-4264

296-30 Oils - Edible (Margarine, Shortening, Table Oils, etc)

Company	City	State	ZIP	Phone	Fax
Aarhuskarlshamn USA Inc 131 Marsh St *Web:* www.aak.com	Newark	NJ	07114	973-741-5049	344-6638
ACH Food Cos Inc 7171 Goodlet Farms Pkwy *TF:* 800-691-1106 ■ *Web:* www.achfood.com	Cordova	TN	38016	901-381-3000	381-2968
Fuji Vegetable Oil Inc 1 Barker Ave *Web:* www.fujioilusa.com	White Plains	NY	10601	914-761-7900	
Golden Foods/Golden Brands LLC 2520 Seventh St Rd *TF:* 800-622-3055 ■ *Web:* www.gfgb.com	Louisville	KY	40208	502-636-3712	636-3904
Kagome Creative Foods LLC 710 N Pearl St *Web:* www.kagomeusa.com	Osceola	AR	72370	870-563-2601	563-3824
Par-Way Tryson Co 107 Bolte Ln *TF:* 800-844-4554 ■ *Web:* www.parwaytryson.com	Saint Clair	MO	63077	636-629-4545	629-1330
Star Fine Foods 2680 W Shaw Ln *Web:* www.starfinefoods.com	Fresno	CA	93711	559-498-2900	
Ventura Foods LLC 40 Pt Dr *TF:* 800-421-6257 ■ *Web:* www.venturafoods.com	Brea	CA	92821	714-257-3700	257-3702
Veronica Foods Co 1991 Dennison St *Web:* www.evoliveoil.com	Oakland	CA	94606	510-535-6833	532-2837

296-31 Pasta

Company	City	State	ZIP	Phone	Fax
A Zerega's Sons Inc PO Box 241 *Web:* www.zerega.com	Fair Lawn	NJ	07410	201-797-1400	797-0148
American Italian Pasta Co (AIPC) 1251 NW Briarcliff Pkwy Ste 500 *Web:* makesameal.com	Kansas City	MO	64116	816-584-5000	
Carla's Pasta Inc 50 Talbot Ln *Web:* www.carlaspasta.com	South Windsor	CT	06074	860-436-4042	
Dakota Growers Pasta Company Inc 1 Pasta Ave *TF:* 866-569-4411 ■ *Web:* www.viterra.com	Carrington	ND	58421	701-652-2855	652-3552
Everfresh Food Corp 501 Huron Blvd SE	Minneapolis	MN	55414	612-331-6393	331-1172
Foulds Inc 520 E Church St *Web:* fouldspasta.com	Libertyville	IL	60048	847-362-3062	
Gilster-Mary Lee Corp 1037 State St PO Box 227 *Web:* gilstermarylee.com	Chester	IL	62233	618-826-2361	826-2973
Monterey Pasta Co 2315 Moore Ave *TF:* 800-588-7782 ■ *Web:* www.montereygourmetfoods.com	Fullerton	CA	92833	800-588-7782	
Nanka Seimen Co 3030 Leonis Blvd	Vernon	CA	90058	323-585-9967	
New World Pasta Co 85 Shannon Rd **Fax:* Sales ■ *TF Sales:* 800-730-5957 ■ *Web:* www.newworldpasta.com	Harrisburg	PA	17112	717-526-2200	526-2468*
Nissin Foods USA Company Inc 2001 W Rosecrans Ave **Fax Area Code:* 310 ■ **Fax:* Sales ■ *Web:* www.nissinfoods.com	Gardena	CA	90249	323-321-6453	515-3751*
OB Macaroni Co PO Box 53 *TF Orders:* 800-553-4336 ■ *Web:* www.obmacaroni.com	Fort Worth	TX	76101	817-335-4629	335-4726
Peking Noodle Co Inc 1514 N San Fernando Rd *TF:* 877-735-4648 ■ *Web:* www.pekingnoodle.com	Los Angeles	CA	90065	323-223-2023	
Philadelphia Macaroni Co 760 S 11th St *Web:* www.philamacaroni.com	Philadelphia	PA	19147	215-923-3141	925-4298

296-32 Peanut Butter

Company	City	State	ZIP	Phone	Fax
Algood Food Co 7401 Trade Port Dr *Web:* www.algoodfood.com	Louisville	KY	40258	502-637-3631	637-1502
Carriage House Cos Inc, The 196 Newton St **Fax:* Sales ■ *TF:* 800-828-8915	Fredonia	NY	14063	716-673-1000	673-8443*
Edwards-Freeman Inc 441 E Hector St	Conshohocken	PA	19428	610-828-7440	
Jimbo's Jumbos Inc 185 Peanut Dr PO Box 465 *TF General:* 800-334-4771 ■ *Web:* www.jimbosjumbos.com	Edenton	NC	27932	800-334-4771	
JM Smucker Co 1 Strawberry Ln *NYSE: SJM* ■ *TF:* 888-550-9555 ■ *Web:* www.smuckers.com	Orrville	OH	44667	330-682-3000	
John B Sanfilippo & Son Inc 1703 N Randall Rd *NASDAQ: JBSS* ■ *TF:* 800-874-8734 ■ *Web:* www.jbssinc.com	Elgin	IL	60123	847-289-1800	289-1843
Leavitt Corp 100 Santilli Hwy *Web:* teddie.com	Everett	MA	02149	617-389-2600	387-9085
Producers Peanut Company Inc PO Box 250 *TF:* 800-847-5491 ■ *Web:* www.producerspeanut.com	Suffolk	VA	23434	757-539-7496	934-7730

296-33 Salads - Prepared

Company	City	State	ZIP	Phone	Fax
Chelten House Products Inc 607 Heron Dr *Web:* www.cheltenhouse.com	Bridgeport	NJ	08014	856-467-1600	467-4769
D'Arrigo Bros Company of California Inc PO Box 850 *TF Cust Svc:* 800-995-5939 ■ *Web:* www.andyboy.com	Salinas	CA	93902	831-455-4500	455-4445
Earth Island 9201 Owensmouth Ave *TF:* 888-394-3949 ■ *Web:* followyourheart.com	Chatsworth	CA	91311	818-725-2820	725-2812
Herold's Salads Inc 17512 Miles Ave *TF:* 800-427-2523 ■ *Web:* www.heroldssalads.com	Cleveland	OH	44128	216-991-7500	
Home Made Brand Foods Inc 2 Opportunity Way	Newburyport	MA	01950	978-462-3663	462-7117
Kayem Foods Inc 75 Arlington St *TF:* 800-426-6100 ■ *Web:* www.kayem.com	Chelsea	MA	02150	617-889-1600	889-5478
Ready Pac Produce Inc 4401 Foxdale Ave **Fax Area Code:* 626 ■ *TF:* 800-800-7822 ■ *Web:* www.readypac.com	Irwindale	CA	91706	800-800-7822	856-0088*
Reser's Fine Foods Inc 15570 SW Jenkins Rd *TF:* 800-333-6431 ■ *Web:* www.resers.com	Beaverton	OR	97006	503-643-6431	
Sandridge Food Corp (SFC) 133 Commerce Dr *TF:* 800-672-2523 ■ *Web:* www.sandridge.com	Medina	OH	44256	330-725-2348	722-3998
Suter Company Inc 258 May St *TF:* 800-435-6942 ■ *Web:* www.suterco.com	Sycamore	IL	60178	815-895-9186	895-4814

296-34 Sandwiches - Prepared

Company	City	State	ZIP	Phone	Fax
Bridgford Foods Corp 1308 N Patt St. NASDAQ: BRID ■ TF: 800-854-3255 ■ Web: www.bridgford.com	Anaheim	CA	92801	714-526-5533	526-4360
Cloverdale Foods Co 3015 34th St NW *Fax Area Code: 701 ■ TF: 800-669-9511 ■ Web: www.cloverdalefoods.com	Mandan	ND	58554	800-669-9511	663-0690*
Hormel Foods Corp 1 Hormel Pl. NYSE: HRL ■ TF: 800-523-4635 ■ Web: www.hormel.com	Austin	MN	55912	507-437-5611	
Konop Cos 1725 Industrial Dr. TF: 800-770-0477 ■ Web: www.konopcompanies.com	Green Bay	WI	54302	920-468-8517	468-1190
Landshire Inc 12 Tucker Dr TF: 800-969-2747 ■ Web: www.landshire.com	Caseyville	IL	62232	618-293-6525	
Lloyd's Barbecue Co 1455 Mendota Heights Rd Web: hormel.com/brands/hormel-lloyds	Mendota Heights	MN	55120	651-688-6000	681-1430
Sunburst Foods Inc 1002 Sunburst Dr Web: www.sunburstfoods.net	Goldsboro	NC	27534	919-778-2151	778-9203

296-35 Snack Foods

Company	City	State	ZIP	Phone	Fax
Azteca Foods Inc PO Box 427 Web: www.aztecafoods.com	Summit-Argo	IL	60501	708-563-6600	
Better Made Snack Foods Inc 10148 Gratiot Ave. TF: 800-332-2394 ■ Web: www.bmchips.com	Detroit	MI	48213	313-925-4774	925-6028
Bickel's Snack Foods 1120 Zinns Quarry Rd *Fax: Cust Svc ■ TF: 800-233-1933 ■ Web: www.bickelssnacks.com	York	PA	17404	717-843-0738	843-4569*
Cape Cod Potato Chip Co 100 Breed's Hill Rd TF: 888-881-2447 ■ Web: www.capecodchips.com	Hyannis	MA	02601	508-775-3358	775-2808
Chester Inc 555 Eastport Ctr Dr. Web: chesterinc.com	Valparaiso	IN	46383	219-465-7555	
CJ Vitner & Co 4202 W 45th St. Web: www.vitners.com	Chicago	IL	60632	773-523-7900	523-9143
Evans Food Group Ltd 4118 S Halsted St. TF: 888-643-8267 ■ Web: www.evansfood.com	Chicago	IL	60609	773-254-7400	254-7791
Frito-Lay North America 7701 Legacy Dr TF: 800-352-4477 ■ Web: www.fritolay.com	Plano	TX	75024	972-334-7000	334-2019
Golden Flake Snack Foods Inc 1 Golden Flake Dr. TF: 800-239-2447 ■ Web: www.goldenflake.com	Birmingham	AL	35205	205-323-6161	458-7121
Herr Foods Inc 20 Herr Dr PO Box 300 TF: 800-344-3777 ■ Web: www.herrs.com	Nottingham	PA	19362	610-932-9330	932-1190
Ideal Snacks Corp 89 Mill St Web: www.idealsnacks.com	Liberty	NY	12754	845-292-7000	292-7000
Keystone Food Products Inc PO Box 326 Web: www.keystonesnacks.com	Easton	PA	18044	610-258-0888	250-0721
Martin's Potato Chips Inc 5847 Lincoln Hwy W PO Box 28. Web: www.martinschips.com	Thomasville	PA	17364	717-792-3565	792-4906
Mike-Sell's Potato Chip Co 333 Leo St PO Box 115 TF: 800-257-4742 ■ Web: www.mike-sells.com	Dayton	OH	45404	937-228-9400	461-5707
Mission Foods 1159 Cottonwood Ln Ste 200 TF: 800-443-7994 ■ Web: www.missionfoodservice.com	Irving	TX	75038	972-232-5000	
Old Dutch Foods Inc 2375 Terminal Rd Web: www.olddutchfoods.com	Roseville	MN	55113	651-633-8810	633-8894
Smith Bros Co 3501 W 48th Pl TF: 800-621-0225 ■ Web: www.thesmithbrothers.com	Chicago	IL	60632	773-927-3737	
Snacks Unlimited 1 General Mills Blvd TF: 800-248-7310 ■ Web: www.generalmills.com	Minneapolis	MN	55426	763-764-7600	
Snyder of Berlin 1313 Stadium Dr TF: 800-374-7949 ■ Web: www.snyderofberlin.com	Berlin	PA	15530	814-267-4641	
Tim's Cascade Snacks 1150 Industry Dr N. Web: www.timschips.com	Algona	WA	98001	253-833-0255	
Uncle Ray's LLC 14245 Birwood St. TF: 800-800-3286 ■ Web: www.unclerays.com	Detroit	MI	48238	313-834-0800	834-0443
UTZ Quality Foods Co 900 High St. TF: 800-367-7629 ■ Web: www.utzsnacks.com	Hanover	PA	17331	717-637-6644	633-5102
Wise Foods Inc 228 Rasely St Ste 75 TF: 888-759-4401 ■ Web: www.wisesnacks.com	Berwick	PA	18603	770-426-5821	
Wyandot Inc 135 Wyandot Ave *Fax: Cust Svc ■ TF: 800-992-6368 ■ Web: www.wyandotsnacks.com	Marion	OH	43302	740-383-4031	382-0115*

296-36 Specialty Foods

Company	City	State	ZIP	Phone	Fax
AFP Advanced Food Products LLC 402 S Custer Ave Web: www.afpllc.com	New Holland	PA	17557	717-355-8667	355-8848
Alphin Bros Inc 2302 US 301 S Web: alphinbrothers.com	Dunn	NC	28334	910-892-8751	892-2709
Ameriqual Group LLC 18200 Hwy 41 N Web: ameriqualgroup.com	Evansville	IN	47725	812-867-1444	867-0278
Amy's Kitchen Inc PO Box 449 Web: www.amys.com	Petaluma	CA	94953	707-781-6600	
Armanino Foods of Distinction Inc 30588 San Antonio St. OTC: AMNF ■ TF: 800-255-5855 ■ Web: www.armaninofoods.com	Hayward	CA	94544	510-441-9300	441-0101
Avanti Foods 109 Depot St TF: 800-243-3739 ■ Web: www.avantifoods.com	Walnut	IL	61376	815-379-2155	379-9357
Beech-Nut Nutrition Corp 1 Nutritious Pl TF: 800-233-2468 ■ Web: www.beechnut.com	Amsterdam	NY	12010	800-233-2468	
Bellisio Foods Inc 1201 Harman Pl Ste 302 Web: www.bellisiofoods.com	Minneapolis	MN	55403	612-371-8222	337-8427
Border Foods Inc 4065 J St SE TF: 800-323-4358 ■ Web: www.borderfoodsinc.com	Deming	NM	88030	800-323-4358	
Bruce Foods Corp PO Box 1030 TF: 800-299-9082 ■ Web: www.brucefoods.com	New Iberia	LA	70561	337-365-8101	369-9026
Buddy's Kitchen Inc 12105 Nicollet Ave Web: www.buddyskitchen.com	Burnsville	MN	55337	952-894-2540	895-1664
Camino Real Foods Inc 2638 E Vernon Ave TF: 800-421-6201 ■ Web: www.caminorealkitchens.com	Vernon	CA	90058	323-585-6599	585-5420
Campbell Soup Co 1 Campbell Pl. NYSE: CPB ■ TF: 800-257-8443 ■ Web: www.campbellsoupcompany.com	Camden	NJ	08103	856-342-4800	342-3878
Champion Foods LLC 23900 Bell Rd Web: www.championfoods.com	New Boston	MI	48164	734-753-3663	753-5366
Chungs Gourmet Foods 3907 Dennis St Web: www.chungsfoods.com	Houston	TX	77004	713-741-2118	741-2330
Cromers Inc 1700 Huger St TF: 800-322-7688 ■ Web: www.cromers.com	Columbia	SC	29201	800-322-7688	
Cuisine Solutions Inc 1501 Moran Rd Unit 100 OTC: CUSI ■ TF: 888-285-4679 ■ Web: www.cuisinesolutions.com	Sterling	VA	20166	703-270-2900	270-2994
D & D Foods Inc 9425 N 48th St TF: 800-208-0364 ■ Web: hy-vee.com	Omaha	NE	68152	402-571-4113	
Del Monte Foods Co 1 Maritime Plaza TF Cust Svc: 800-543-3090 ■ Web: www.delmonte.com	San Francisco	CA	94111	415-247-3000	247-3311
Deli Express 16101 W 78th St TF: 800-328-8184 ■ Web: www.deliexpress.com	Eden Prairie	MN	55344	800-328-8184	
Durrset Amigos Ltd 4669 Hwy 90 W TF: 800-580-3477 ■ Web: www.amigosfoods.com	San Antonio	TX	78237	210-798-5360	798-5365
Ebro Foods Inc 1330 W 43rd St Web: www.ebrofoods.com	Chicago	IL	60609	773-696-0150	696-0151
Eden Foods Inc 701 Tecumseh Rd TF Cust Svc: 800-248-0320 ■ Web: www.edenfoods.com	Clinton	MI	49236	517-456-7424	456-6075
El Encanto Inc 2001 Fourth St SW PO Box 293 TF: 800-888-7336 ■ Web: www.buenofoods.com	Albuquerque	NM	87103	505-243-2722	242-1680
Ener-G Foods Inc 5960 First Ave S PO Box 84487 TF: 800-331-5222 ■ Web: www.ener-g.com	Seattle	WA	98124	206-767-3928	764-3398
Fairmont Foods of Minnesota 905 E Fourth St Web: www.fairmontfoods.com	Fairmont	MN	56031	507-238-9001	238-9560
Fiesta Canning Co Inc 1480 E Bethany Home Ste 110 Web: www.fiestacan.com	Phoenix	AZ	85014	602-212-2424	274-7233
Frozen Specialties Inc 8600 S Wilkinson Wy Ste G Web: www.frozenspecialties.com	Perrysburg	OH	43551	419-867-2005	
Gerber Products Co 445 State St TF: 800-284-9488 ■ Web: www.gerber.com	Fremont	MI	49412	800-284-9488	
Grandma Brown's Beans Inc 5837 Scenic Ave.	Mexico	NY	13114	315-963-7221	963-4072
Hain Celestial Group Inc 4600 Sleepytime Dr. NASDAQ: HAIN ■ TF: 800-434-4246 ■ Web: www.hain-celestial.com	Boulder	CO	80301	800-434-4246	
Hanover Foods Corp 1550 York St PO Box 334 OTC: HNFSA ■ TF: 800-888-4646 ■ Web: www.hanoverfoods.com	Hanover	PA	17331	717-632-6000	
HJ Heinz Co 1 PPG Pl Ste 3100 TF: 800-255-5750 ■ Web: www.kraftheinzcompany.com	Pittsburgh	PA	15230	412-456-5700	
Home Market Foods Inc 140 Morgan Dr. TF: 800-367-8325 ■ Web: www.homemarketfoods.com	Norwood	MA	02062	781-948-1500	702-6171
Home Run Inn Frozen Foods Corp 1300 International Pkwy Web: www.homeruninnpizza.com	Woodridge	IL	60517	630-783-9696	783-0069
Homestead Pasta Co 315 S Maple Ave Bldg 106 Web: www.homesteadpasta.com	South San Francisco	CA	94080	650-615-0750	615-0764
Hormel Foods Corp 1 Hormel Pl. NYSE: HRL ■ TF: 800-523-4635 ■ Web: www.hormel.com	Austin	MN	55912	507-437-5611	
J & B Sausage Company Inc 100 Main St Web: www.jbfoods.com	Waelder	TX	78959	830-788-7511	788-7279
JM Smucker Co 1 Strawberry Ln. NYSE: SJM ■ TF: 888-550-9555 ■ Web: www.smuckers.com	Orrville	OH	44667	330-682-3000	
Juanita's Foods Inc PO Box 847 PO Box 847 TF: 800-303-2965 ■ Web: www.juanitasfoods.com	Wilmington	CA	90748	800-303-2965	
Kahiki Foods Inc 1100 Morrison Rd. TF: 855-524-4540 ■ Web: www.kahiki.com	Columbus	OH	43230	614-322-3180	751-0039
La Reina Inc 316 N Ford Blvd TF: 800-367-7522 ■ Web: www.lareinainc.com	Los Angeles	CA	90022	323-268-2791	
La Tapatia Tortilleria Inc 104 E Belmont Ave. Web: www.tortillas4u.com	Fresno	CA	93701	559-441-1030	441-1712
Lamb Weston Inc 8701 W Gage Blvd *Fax: Sales ■ Web: www.lambweston.com	Kennewick	WA	99336	509-735-4651	736-0395*
Leon's Texas Cuisine Co 2100 Redbud Blvd. Web: www.texascuisine.com	McKinney	TX	75069	972-529-5050	
Little Lady Foods Inc 2323 Pratt Blvd. Web: www.littleladyfoods.com	Elk Grove Village	IL	60007	847-631-3500	
Mancini Foods PO Box 157 *Fax Area Code: 863 ■ TF: 800-741-1778 ■ Web: www.mancinifoods.com	Zolfo Springs	FL	33890	800-741-1778	735-1172*
Manischewitz Company, The 80 Ave K Web: www.rabfoodgroup.com	Newark	NJ	07105	201-553-1100	
McCain Foods Ltd 181 Bay St Ste 3600 TF: 800-938-7799 ■ Web: www.mccain.com	Toronto	ON	M5J2T3	416-955-1700	
McCain Foods USA Inc 2275 Cabot Dr TF: 800-938-7799 ■ Web: www.mccainusa.com	Lisle	IL	60532	800-938-7799	
Michael Angelo's Gourmet Foods Inc 200 Michael Angelo Way TF: 877-482-5426 ■ Web: www.michaelangelos.com	Austin	TX	78728	512-218-3500	
Morgan Foods Inc 90 W Morgan St TF: 888-430-1780 ■ Web: www.morganfoods.com	Austin	IN	47102	812-794-1170	794-1211
Mott's LLP PO Box 869077 TF Consumer Info: 800-426-4891 ■ Web: www.motts.com	Plano	TX	75086	800-426-4891	
Nardone Bros Baking Company Inc 420 New Commerce Blvd TF: 800-822-5320 ■ Web: www.nardonebros.com	Wilkes-Barre	PA	18706	570-823-0141	823-2581
Ole Mexican Foods Inc 6585 Crescent Dr. Web: olemex.com	Norcross	GA	30071	770-582-9200	582-9400

Phone Fax

Overhill Farms Inc 2727 E Vernon Ave.................Vernon CA 90058 323-582-9977 582-6122
NYSE: OFI ■ *TF:* 800-859-6406 ■ *Web:* www.overhillfarms.com

Panhandle Foods Inc
1980 Smith Township SR.......................Burgettstown PA 15021 724-947-2216
Web: panhandlefoodsales.com

Papa John's International Inc
PO Box 99900...Louisville KY 40269 877-547-7272
NASDAQ: PZZA ■ *TF:* 877-547-7272 ■ *Web:* www.papajohns.com

Pastorelli Food Products Inc
162 N Sangamon St.....................................Chicago IL 60607 312-666-2041 666-2415
TF: 800-767-2829 ■ *Web:* www.pastorelli.com

Pinnacle Foods Corp 399 Jefferson Rd.............Parsippany NJ 07054 973-541-6620
TF: 866-266-7596 ■ *Web:* www.pinnaclefoodscorp.com

Preferred Meal Systems Inc
5240 St Charles Rd.....................................Berkeley IL 60163 708-318-2500 493-2690
TF Cust Svc: 800-886-6325 ■ *Web:* preferredmeals.com

Quaker Oats Co 555 W Monroe St ....Chicago IL 60661 312-821-1000
TF: 800-367-6287 ■ *Web:* www.quakeroats.com

Request Foods Inc PO Box 2577.....................Holland MI 49422 616-786-0900 786-9180
Web: www.requestfoods.com

Ruiz Foods Inc PO Box 37...........................Dinuba CA 93618 559-591-5510
TF: 800-477-6474 ■ *Web:* www.elmonterey.com

Schwan Food Co 115 W College Dr ....Marshall MN 56258 507-532-3274
TF: 800-533-5290 ■ *Web:* www.theschwanfoodcompany.com

Seviroli Foods 601 Brook St.......................Garden City NY 11530 516-222-6220 222-0534
Web: www.seviroli.com

Small Planet Foods Inc
106 Woodworth St...........................Sedro Woolley WA 98284 360-855-0100
TF: 800-624-4123 ■ *Web:* www.smallplanetfoods.com

Suter Company Inc 258 May St....................Sycamore IL 60178 815-895-9186 895-4814
TF: 800-435-6942 ■ *Web:* www.suterco.com

Tastefully Simple Inc
1920 Turning Leaf Ln SW.........................Alexandria MN 55318 320-763-0695 763-2458
Web: www.tastefullysimple.com

Vanee Foods Company Inc 5418 McDermott Dr.........Berkeley IL 60163 708-449-7300 449-2558
Web: vaneefoodservice.com

Windsor Foods 3355 W Alabama St Ste 730............Houston TX 77098 713-843-5200 960-9709
TF: 800-458-4054 ■ *Web:* www.windsorfoods.com

Winter Gardens Quality Foods Inc
304 Commerce St PO Box 339....................New Oxford PA 17350 717-624-4911 624-7729
TF: 800-242-7637 ■ *Web:* www.wintergardens.com

296-37 Spices, Seasonings, Herbs

Phone Fax

Abco Laboratories Inc 2450 S Watney Way ....Fairfield CA 94533 707-432-2200 432-2240
TF: 800-678-2226 ■ *Web:* www.abcolabs.com

Ajinomoto Food Ingredients LLC
8430 W Bryn Mawr Ave Ste 635.....................Chicago IL 60631 773-714-1436
Web: www.ajiusafood.com

Aliments Ouimet-Cordon Bleu Inc
8383 Rue J-Ren Ouimet ....Anjou QC H1J2P8 514-352-3000
Web: www.cordonbleu.ca

All American Seasonings 10600 E 54th Ave.............Denver CO 80239 303-623-2320 623-1920
Web: www.allamericanseasonings.com

American Outdoor Products Inc
6350 Gunpark Dr ....Boulder CO 80301 303-581-0518
TF: 800-641-0500 ■ *Web:* www.backpackerspantry.com

Basic American Foods
2185 N California Blvd Ste 215 ....Walnut Creek CA 94596 925-472-4000 472-4314
Web: www.baf.com

Benson's Gourmet Seasonings PO Box 638 ....Azusa CA 91702 626-969-4443 969-2912
TF: 800-325-5619 ■ *Web:* www.bensonsgourmetseasonings.com

Blendex Company Inc 11208 Electron Dr ....Louisville KY 40299 502-267-1003 267-1024
TF: 800-626-6325 ■ *Web:* www.blendex.com

Cedarome Canada Inc 3650 Matte Blvd Ste E-22.......Brossard QC J4Y2Z2 450-659-8000 659-8010
Web: www.cedarome.com

Celtrade Canada Inc 7566 Bath Rd ....Mississauga ON L4T1L2 905-678-1322
Web: www.celtradecanada.ca

Circle Foods LLC 8411 Siempre Viva Rd.............San Diego CA 92154 619-671-3900
Web: www.circlefoods.com

Flavurence Corp 1916 Tubeway Ave Commerce........Commerce CA 90040 323-727-1957

Frontier Natural Products Co-op
3021 78th St PO Box 299................................Norway IA 52318 319-227-7996 227-7966
TF: 800-669-3275 ■ *Web:* www.frontiercoop.com

Fuchs North America
9740 Reisterstown Rd.........................Owings Mills MD 21117 410-363-1700 363-6619
TF: 800-365-3229 ■ *Web:* www.fuchsna.com

Golden Specialty Foods LLC 14605 Best Ave...........Norwalk CA 90650 562-802-2537
Web: www.goldenspecialtyfoods.com

Griffith Laboratories Worldwide Inc
1 Griffith Ctr..Alsip IL 60803 708-371-0900 371-4783
Web: www.griffithfoods.com/pages/default.aspx

Harris Freeman & Company LP
3110 E Miraloma Ave ....Anaheim CA 92806 714-765-1190
Web: www.harrisfreeman.com

Johnny's Fine Foods Inc 319 E 25th St................Tacoma WA 98421 253-383-4597
TF General: 800-962-1462 ■ *Web:* www.johnnysfinefoods.com

Lucile's Famous Creole Seasonings
2124 14th St..Boulder CO 80302 303-442-4743 939-9848
Web: www.luciles.com

McCormick & Co Inc 18 Loveton Cir ....Sparks MD 21152 410-771-7244
NYSE: MKC ■ *Web:* www.mccormickcorporation.com

McCormick & Company Inc McCormick Flavor Div
226 Schilling Cir ....Hunt Valley MD 21031 410-771-7500
TF: 800-322-7742 ■ *Web:* www.mccormickforchefs.com

McCormick & Company Inc US Consumer Products Div
211 Schilling Cir ....Hunt Valley MD 21031 410-527-6000
Web: www.mccormick.com

McCormick Ingredients 18 Loveton Cir ....Sparks MD 21152 410-771-7301
TF: 800-632-5847 ■ *Web:* www.mccormick.com

Phone Fax

Newly Weds Foods Inc 4140 W Fullerton Ave...........Chicago IL 60639 773-489-7000 292-3809
TF: 800-621-7521 ■ *Web:* www.newlywedsfoods.com

Pepsi Bottling Ventures LLC
4141 Parklake Ave Ste 600..........................Raleigh NC 27612 919-865-2300
TF: 800-662-8792 ■ *Web:* www.pepsibottlingventures.com

Precision Foods Inc
11457 Olde Cabin Rd Ste 100 ....Saint Louis MO 63141 314-567-7400 567-5402
TF: 800-442-5242 ■ *Web:* www.precisionfoods.com

Produits Alimentaires Berthelet Inc
1805 Berlier St ....Laval QC H7L3S4 514-334-5503 334-3584
Web: www.berthelet.com

Pyure Brands 2277 Trade Ctr Way......................Naples FL 34109 305-509-5096
Web: www.pyuresweet.com

Rex Fine Foods Inc 1536 River Oaks Rd W ....Harahan LA 70123 504-602-9487
Web: www.rexfoods.com

Royal Food Products LLC
2322 E Minnesota St ....Indianapolis IN 46203 317-782-2660
Web: www.royalfp.com

Sabra Dipping Co LLC 2420 49th St....................Astoria NY 11103 888-957-2272
TF: 888-957-2272 ■ *Web:* www.sabra.com

SensoryEffects Flavor Co
231 Rock Industrial Park Dr ....Bridgeton MO 63044 314-291-5444
TF: 800-422-5444 ■ *Web:* www.sensoryeffects.com

Soy Vay Enterprises Inc 5969 Hillside Dr...............Felton CA 95018 831-335-3824
Web: www.soyvay.com

Specialty Commodities Inc 1530 47th St NW ....Fargo ND 58102 701-282-8222
Web: www.scifargo.com

Spice Hunter Inc
184 Suburban Rd PO Box 8110 ....San Luis Obispo CA 93403 800-444-3061 544-9046*
**Fax Area Code:* 805 ■ **Fax:* Cust Svc ■ *TF:* 800-444-3061 ■ *Web:* www.spicehunter.com

Spice World Inc 8101 Presidents Dr....................Orlando FL 32809 800-433-4979 857-7171*
**Fax Area Code:* 407 ■ *TF:* 800-433-4979 ■ *Web:* www.spiceworldinc.com

Tampico Spice Company Inc
5941 S Central Ave..................................Los Angeles CA 90001 323-235-3154 232-8686
Web: www.tampicospice.com

Tulocay & Company Inc 388 Devlin Rd Napa Valley........Napa CA 94558 707-253-7655
Web: www.madeinnapavalley.com

Wizard's Cauldron Inc 878 Firetower Rd...........Yanceyville NC 27379 336-694-5665
Web: www.wizardscauldron.com

World Spice Inc 223 E Highland Pkwy ....Roselle NJ 07203 908-245-0600 245-0696
TF: 800-234-1060 ■ *Web:* www.wsispice.com

Zatarain's Inc 82 First St...............................Gretna LA 70053 504-367-2950 362-2004
Web: mccormick.com/zatarains

296-38 Sugar & Sweeteners

Phone Fax

Alma Plantation Ltd 4612 Alma Rd ....Lakeland LA 70752 225-627-6632

Amalgamated Sugar Co LLC
1951 S Saturn Way Ste 100...............................Boise ID 83709 208-383-6500 383-6688

American Crystal Sugar Co 101 Third St N ....Moorhead MN 56560 218-236-4400
Web: www.crystalsugar.com

C & H Sugar Co Inc
2300 Contra Costa Blvd Ste 600.................Pleasant Hill CA 94523 800-773-1803
TF: 800-773-1803 ■ *Web:* www.chsugar.com

Cajun Sugar Co-op Inc 2711 Northside Rd ....New Iberia LA 70563 337-365-3401 365-7820
Web: amscl.org

Cora-Texas Mfg Company Inc
32505 Louisiana 1 PO Box 280 ....White Castle LA 70788 225-545-3679 545-8360
Web: www.coratexas.com

Cumberland Packing Corp 2 Cumberland St ....Brooklyn NY 11205 718-858-4200 260-9017
Web: www.sweetnlow.com

Florida Crystals Corp
1 N Clematis St Ste 200.....................West Palm Beach FL 33401 561-366-5100 366-5158
Web: www.floridacrystals.com

Hawaiian Commercial & Sugar Co 1 Hansen St....... Puunene HI 96784 808-877-0081 871-7663
Web: www.hcsugar.com

Lafourche Sugars Corp
141 Lk Leighton Quarters Rd ....Thibodaux LA 70301 985-447-3210 447-8728

Lula Westfield LLC
451 Hwy 1005 PO Box 10.......................Paincourtville LA 70391 985-369-6450 369-6139

MA Patout & Son Ltd
3512 J Patout Burns Rd ....Jeanerette LA 70544 337-276-4592 276-4247
Web: www.mapatout.com

Merisant Worldwide Inc
125 S Wacker Dr Ste 3150...........................Chicago IL 60606 312-840-6000 840-5146
Web: www.merisant.com

Michigan Sugar Company Inc
2600 S Euclid Ave ....Bay City MI 48706 989-686-0161 671-3695
Web: www.michigansugar.com

Minn-Dak Farmers Co-op 7525 Red River Rd.........Wahpeton ND 58075 701-642-8411 642-6814
Web: www.mdfarmerscoop.com

Rio Grande Valley Sugar Growers
PO Box 459 ....Santa Rosa TX 78593 956-636-1411 636-1046
Web: www.rgvsugar.com

Southern Minnesota Beet Sugar Co-op
83550 CR 21 PO Box 500.............................Renville MN 56284 320-329-8305 329-3252
Web: www.smbsc.com

Sterling Sugars Inc 611 Irish Bend Rd.................Franklin LA 70538 337-828-0620 828-1757
Web: amscl.org

Sugar Cane Growers Co-op of Florida
1500 W Sugar House Rd ....Belle Glade FL 33430 561-996-5556
Web: www.scgc.org

US Sugar Corp 111 Ponce de Leon Ave ....Clewiston FL 33440 863-983-8121
Web: www.ussugar.com

Western Sugar Co-op 7555 E Hampden Ave Ste 600.......Denver CO 80231 303-830-3939 830-3941
TF: 800-523-7497 ■ *Web:* www.westernsugar.com

296-39 Syrup - Maple

Phone Fax

Carriage House Cos Inc, The 196 Newton St..........Fredonia NY 14063 716-673-1000 673-8443*
**Fax:* Sales ■ *TF:* 800-828-8915

				Phone	Fax
Golden Eagle Syrup Company Inc 205 First Ave SE *Web:* www.goldeneaglesyrup.com	Fayette	AL	35555	205-932-5294	
H Fox & Company Inc 416 Thatford Ave. *Web:* www.foxs-syrups.com	Brooklyn	NY	11212	718-385-4600	345-4283
Maple Grove Farms of Vermont 1052 Portland St. *TF:* 800-525-2540 ■ *Web:* www.maplegrove.com	Saint Johnsbury	VT	05819	802-748-5141	748-9647
Pinnacle Foods Corp 399 Jefferson Rd *TF:* 866-266-7596 ■ *Web:* www.pinnaclefoodscorp.com	Parsippany	NJ	07054	973-541-6620	
Richards Maple Products Inc 545 Water St. *TF:* 800-352-4052 ■ *Web:* www.richardsmapleproducts.com	Chardon	OH	44024	800-352-4052	
Sea Breeze Inc 441 Rt 202 *TF:* 800-732-2733 ■ *Web:* www.seabreezesyrups.com	Towaco	NJ	07082	973-334-7777	334-2617

296-40 Tea

				Phone	Fax
4C Foods Corp 580 Fountain Ave *Web:* www.4c.com	Brooklyn	NY	11208	718-272-4242	272-2899
Bigelow Tea 201 Black Rock Tpke *TF:* 888-244-3569 ■ *Web:* www.bigelowtea.com	Fairfield	CT	06825	888-244-3569	
Celestial Seasonings Inc 4600 Sleepytime Dr *Fax: Cust Svc ■ *TF:* 800-351-8175 ■ *Web:* www.celestialseasonings.com	Boulder	CO	80301	303-530-5300	581-1332*
Eastern Tea Corp 1 Engelhard Dr *Web:* www.easterntea.com	Monroe Township	NJ	08831	609-860-1100	
Fee Bros Inc 453 Portland Ave *Web:* www.feebrothers.com	Rochester	NY	14605	585-544-9530	
Redco Foods Inc 1 Hansen Island *TF:* 800-556-6674 ■ *Web:* www.redrosetea.com	Little Falls	NY	13365	315-823-1300	
S & D Coffee Inc 300 Concord Pkwy PO Box 1628 *TF Cust Svc:* 800-933-2210 ■ *Web:* www.sdcoffeetea.com	Concord	NC	28026	704-782-3121	721-5792

296-41 Vinegar & Cider

				Phone	Fax
Boyajian Inc 144 Will Dr *TF General:* 800-965-0665 ■ *Web:* www.boyajianinc.com	Canton	MA	02021	781-828-9966	
Consumers Vinegar & Spice Company Inc 4723 S Washtenaw Ave *Web:* cvsco.com	Chicago	IL	60632	773-376-4100	376-6224
Creole Fermentation Industries Inc 7331 Den Frederick Rd	Abbeville	LA	70510	337-898-9377	898-9376
Gold Pure Food Products Inc 1 Brooklyn Rd *Web:* www.goldshorseradish.com	Hempstead	NY	11550	516-483-5600	483-5798
Heintz & Weber Co Inc 150 Reading Ave. *TF:* 800-438-6878 ■ *Web:* www.webersmustard.com	Buffalo	NY	14220	716-852-7171	852-7173
Knouse Foods Co-op Inc 800 Peach Glen-Idaville Rd *Web:* www.knouse.com	Peach Glen	PA	17375	717-677-8181	677-7069
MA Gedney Co 2100 Stoughton Ave *TF:* 888-244-0653 ■ *Web:* www.gedneyfoods.com	Chaska	MN	55318	952-448-2612	448-1790
Mizkan Americas Inc 1661 Feehanville Dr Ste 300 *TF:* 800-323-4358 ■ *Web:* www.mizkan.com	Mount Prospect	IL	60056	847-590-0059	590-0405
National Fruit Product Co Inc 701 Fairmont Ave *Fax: Sales ■ *TF:* 800-655-4022 ■ *Web:* www.whitehousefoods.com	Winchester	VA	22601	540-723-9614	665-4671*
Pastorelli Food Products Inc 162 N Sangamon St *TF:* 800-767-2829 ■ *Web:* www.pastorelli.com	Chicago	IL	60607	312-666-2041	666-2415
Rex Wine Vinegar Co 828-30 Raymond Blvd.	Newark	NJ	07105	973-589-6911	
Silver Palate 211 Knickerbocker Rd *Web:* silverpalate.com	Dumont	NJ	07628	201-568-0110	

296-42 Yeast

				Phone	Fax
Brolite Products Inc 1900 S Pk Ave *TF:* 888-276-5483 ■ *Web:* www.bakewithbrolite.com	Streamwood	IL	60107	630-830-0340	830-0356
DSM Food Specialties Inc 45 Waterview Blvd *TF:* 800-526-0189 ■ *Web:* www.dsm.com	Parsippany	NJ	07054	973-257-1063	257-8420
Lesaffre Yeast Corp 7475 W Main St *TF Cust Svc:* 877-677-7000 ■ *Web:* www.lesaffreyeastcorp.com	Milwaukee	WI	53214	877-677-7000	
Minn-Dak Yeast Company Inc 18175 Red River Rd W *TF:* 800-348-0991 ■ *Web:* www.dakotayeast.com/home.html	Wahpeton	ND	58075	701-642-3300	642-1908
Ohly Americas 3388 Bacon St. *TF:* 800-321-2689 ■ *Web:* www.ohly.com	Rhinelander	WI	54501	320-587-2481	587-8617

297 FOOD PRODUCTS - WHOL

See Also Beverages - Whol p. 1857

				Phone	Fax
Carlsen & Associates 1439 Grove St *Web:* carlsenassociates.com	Healdsburg	CA	95448	707-431-2000	
Chocolate Factory Theater 549 49th Ave *Web:* chocolatefactorytheater.org	Long Island	NY	11101	718-482-7069	
Lassen's Health Food 2150 Thousand Oaks Blvd. *Web:* www.lassens.com	Thousand Oaks	CA	91362	805-495-2609	
Mayway Corp 1338 Mandela Pkwy *Web:* mayway.com	Oakland	CA	94607	510-208-3113	
Optimus Inc 1000 NW 159 Dr. *Web:* www.markys.com	Miami Gardens	FL	33169	305-628-4650	
Quantum Inc PO Box 2791 *TF:* 800-448-1448 ■ *Web:* www.quantumhealth.com	Eugene	OR	97402	541-345-5556	
Saladino's Inc 3325 W Figarden Dr. *Web:* www.saladinos.com	Fresno	CA	93711	559-271-3700	271-3701

297-1 Baked Goods - Whol

				Phone	Fax
Fresh Start Bakeries 145 S State College Blvd Ste 200 *Web:* www.freshstartbakeries.com	Brea	CA	92821	714-256-8900	256-8916
Tri-State Baking Co 6800 S Washington St. *Web:* afiama.com	Amarillo	TX	79118	806-373-6696	
Turano Baking Co 6501 Roosevelt Rd *Web:* www.turano.com	Berwyn	IL	60402	708-788-9220	788-3075
Wheat Montana Farms Inc 10778 US Hwy 287 *TF:* 800-535-2798 ■ *Web:* www.wheatmontana.com	Three Forks	MT	59752	406-285-3614	285-3749

297-2 Coffee & Tea - Whol

				Phone	Fax
Barrie House Coffee Company Inc 4 Warehouse ln. *TF:* 800-876-2233 ■ *Web:* www.barriehouse.com	Elmsford	NY	10523	800-876-2233	
Becharas Bros Coffee Co Inc 14501 Hamilton Ave *TF:* 800-944-9675 ■ *Web:* www.becharas.com	Highland Park	MI	48203	313-869-4700	869-7940
Capricorn Coffees Inc 353 Tenth St *TF:* 800-541-0758 ■ *Web:* www.capricorncoffees.com	San Francisco	CA	94103	415-621-8500	621-9875
Coffee Bean International 9120 NE Alderwood Rd. *TF:* 800-877-0474 ■ *Web:* www.coffeebeanintl.com	Portland	OR	97220	503-227-4490	225-9604
Coffee Masters Inc 7606 Industrial Ct. *TF:* 800-334-6485 ■ *Web:* www.coffeemasters.com	Spring Grove	IL	60081	815-675-0088	675-3166
Red Diamond Inc 400 Park Ave. *TF:* 800-292-4651 ■ *Web:* www.reddiamond.com	Moody	AL	35004	205-577-4000	
Royal Cup Coffee 160 Cleage Dr *Fax Area Code: 205 ■ *TF Cust Svc:* 800-366-5836 ■ *Web:* www.royalcupcoffee.com	Birmingham	AL	35217	800-366-5836	271-6071*

297-3 Confectionery & Snack Foods - Whol

				Phone	Fax
AMCON Distributing Co 7405 Irvington Rd *NYSE:* DIT ■ *TF:* 888-201-5997 ■ *Web:* www.amcon.com	Omaha	NE	68122	402-331-3727	331-4834
Annabelle Candy Company Inc 27211 Industrial Blvd *Web:* annabellecandy.com	Hayward	CA	94545	510-783-2900	785-7675
Brown & Haley PO Box 1596. *TF:* 800-426-8400 ■ *Web:* www.brown-haley.com	Tacoma	WA	98401	800-426-8400	
Burklund Distributors Inc 2500 N Main St Ste 3 *TF:* 800-322-2876 ■ *Web:* www.burklund.com	East Peoria	IL	61611	309-694-1900	694-6788
Continental Concession Supplies Inc 575 Jericho Turnpike Ste 300 *TF:* 800-516-0090 ■ *Web:* www.ccsicandy.com	Jericho	NY	11753	516-739-8777	739-8750
Diamond Bakery Co 756 Moowaa St *Web:* www.diamondbakery.com	Honolulu	HI	96817	808-847-3551	847-7482
Eby-Brown Co 280 W Shuman Blvd Ste 280 *TF:* 800-553-8249 ■ *Web:* www.eby-brown.com	Naperville	IL	60563	630-778-2800	778-2830
Edward A. Berg & Sons Inc (EAB) 75 W Century Rd *Web:* www.eaberg.com	Paramus	NJ	07652	201-845-8200	845-8201
Foreign Candy Company Inc 1 Foreign Candy Dr *TF:* 800-831-8541 ■ *Web:* www.foreigncandy.com	Hull	IA	51239	712-439-1496	439-3207
Frito-Lay North America 7701 Legacy Dr *TF:* 800-352-4477 ■ *Web:* www.fritolay.com	Plano	TX	75024	972-334-7000	334-2019
Harold Levinson Assoc (HLA) 21 Banfi Plz *TF:* 800-325-2512 ■ *Web:* www.hlacigars.com	Farmingdale	NY	11735	631-962-2400	962-9000
Hines Nut Co Inc 990 S St Paul St *TF:* 800-561-6374 ■ *Web:* www.hinesnut.com	Dallas	TX	75201	214-939-0253	
Keilson-Dayton Co 107 Commerce Pk Dr. *TF:* 800-759-3174 ■ *Web:* keilsondayton.com	Dayton	OH	45404	937-236-1070	236-2124
Kennedy Wholesale Inc 16014 Adelante St. *TF:* 877-292-2639 ■ *Web:* www.kennedywholesale.com	Irwindale	CA	91706	818-241-9977	241-3046
McDonald Wholesale Co 2350 W Broadway St. *TF:* 877-722-5503 ■ *Web:* www.mcdonaldwhsl.com	Eugene	OR	97402	541-345-8421	345-7146
Old Dutch Foods Inc 2375 Terminal Rd *Web:* www.olddutchfoods.com	Roseville	MN	55113	651-633-8810	633-8894
Showtime Concession Supply Inc 200 SE 19th St *Web:* www.showplacemarket.com/showtimeconcessionsupply	Moore	OK	73160	405-895-9902	
Sultana Distribution Services Inc 600 Food Ctr Dr *TF:* 877-617-5500 ■ *Web:* www.sultanadist.com	Bronx	NY	10474	718-617-5500	617-5225
Superior Nut & Candy Company Inc 1111 W 40th St. *Web:* www.superiornutandcandy.com	Chicago	IL	60609	773-254-7900	254-9171
Superior Nut Co Inc 225 Monsignor O'Brien Hwy. *Web:* www.superiornut.com	Cambridge	MA	02141	617-876-3808	876-8225
Taste of Nature Inc 2828 Donald Douglas Loop N Ste A *Web:* www.candyasap.com	Santa Monica	CA	90405	310-396-4433	396-4432
Thayer Distribution Inc 333 Swedesboro Ave. *Web:* www.thayerdist.com	Gibbstown	NJ	08027	856-687-0000	224-7129
Torn & Glasser Inc 1622 E Olympic Blvd PO Box 21823 *Web:* www.tornandglasser.com	Los Angeles	CA	90021	213-627-6496	688-0941
Trophy Nut Company Inc 320 N Second St. *TF:* 800-729-6887 ■ *Web:* www.trophynut.com	Tipp City	OH	45371	937-667-8478	667-4656

297-4 Dairy Products - Whol

Company / Address	City	State	ZIP	Phone	Fax
Ambriola Company Inc 7 Patton Dr	West Caldwell	NJ	07006	800-962-8224	
TF: 800-962-8224 ■ *Web:* www.ambriola.com					
AMPI 315 N Broadway	New Ulm	MN	56073	507-354-8295	
TF: 800-533-3580 ■ *Web:* www.ampi.com					
Broughton Foods Co 1701 Green St	Marietta	OH	45750	740-373-4121	
TF: 800-283-2479 ■ *Web:* www.broughtonfoods.com					
Clofine Dairy Products Inc 1407 New Rd	Linwood	NJ	08221	609-653-1000	653-0127
TF: 800-441-1001 ■ *Web:* www.clofinedairy.com					
Clover-Stornetta Farms Inc PO Box 750369	Petaluma	CA	94975	707-769-3235	778-9166
TF: 800-237-3315 ■ *Web:* www.cloverpetaluma.com					
Cream-O-Land Dairy Inc 529 Cedar Ln	Florence	NJ	08518	609-499-3601	499-3896
TF: 800-220-6455 ■ *Web:* www.creamoland.com					
Erie Foods International Inc 401 Seventh Ave PO Box 648	Erie	IL	61250	309-659-2233	659-2822
TF: 800-447-1887 ■ *Web:* www.eriefoods.com					
Hautly Cheese Company Inc 251 Axminister Dr	Fenton	MO	63026	636-533-4400	533-4401
Web: www.hautly.com					
Hillcrest Foods 2695 E 40th St	Cleveland	OH	44115	216-361-4625	
TF: 800-952-4344 ■ *Web:* www.hillcrestfoods.com					
Lowville Producers Dairy Co-op 7396 Utica Blvd	Lowville	NY	13367	315-376-3921	376-3442
Web: www.gotgoodcheese.com					
Luberski Inc 310 N Harbor Blvd Ste 205	Fullerton	CA	92832	714-680-3447	680-3380
TF: 800-326-3220 ■ *Web:* www.hiddenvilla.com					
Maryland & Virginia Milk Producers Co-op Assn Inc 1985 Isaac Newton Sq W	Reston	VA	20190	703-742-6800	742-7459
TF: 800-552-1976 ■ *Web:* www.mdvamilk.com					
Masters Gallery Foods Inc 328 County Hwy PP PO Box 170	Plymouth	WI	53073	920-893-8431	
TF General: 800-236-8431 ■ *Web:* www.mastersgalleryfoods.com					
Plains Dairy Products 300 N Taylor St	Amarillo	TX	79107	806-374-0385	
TF: 800-365-5608 ■ *Web:* www.plainsdairy.com					
Prairie Farms Dairy Inc 1100 N Broadway St	Carlinville	IL	62626	217-854-2547	854-6426
TF: 800-654-2547 ■ *Web:* www.prairiefarms.com					
Purity Dairies Inc 360 Murfreesboro Rd	Nashville	TN	37210	615-244-1970	242-8547
Web: www.puritydairies.com					
Queensboro Farm Products Inc 156-02 Liberty Ave Ste 1	Jamaica	NY	11433	718-658-5000	
Roberts Dairy Co 2901 Cuming St	Omaha	NE	68131	402-344-4321	346-0277
TF: 800-779-4321 ■ *Web:* hilanddairy.com					
Rockview Dairies Inc 7011 Stewart & Gray Rd	Downey	CA	90241	562-927-5511	928-9866
TF: 800-423-2479 ■ *Web:* www.rockviewfarms.com					
Schenkel's All-Star Dairy LLC 1019 Flax Mill Rd	Huntington	IN	46750	260-356-4225	
Schneider's Dairy Inc 726 Frank St	Pittsburgh	PA	15227	412-881-3525	881-7722
Web: www.schneidersdairypgh.com					
Simco Sales Service of Pennsylvania Inc 101 Commerce Dr	Moorestown	NJ	08057	856-813-2300	
Web: www.jackjillicecream.com					
Sunshine Dairy Foods Inc 801 NE 21st Ave	Portland	OR	97232	503-234-7526	
Web: www.sunshinedairyfoods.com					
Sure Winner Foods Inc 2 Lehner Rd	Saco	ME	04072	207-282-1258	286-1410
TF: 800-640-6447 ■ *Web:* www.swfoods.com					
Umpqua Dairy Products Co 1686 Se N St PO Box 1306	Grants Pass	OR	97526	541-672-2638	673-0256
TF: 800-222-6455 ■ *Web:* www.umpquadairy.com					

297-5 Fish & Seafood - Whol

Company / Address	City	State	ZIP	Phone	Fax
Arrowac Fisheries Inc 4039 21st Ave W Ste 200 Fisherman's Commerce Bldg	Seattle	WA	98199	206-282-5655	282-9329
Web: www.arrowac-merco.com					
Beaver Street Fisheries Inc 1741 W Beaver St	Jacksonville	FL	32209	904-354-8533	
TF: 800-874-6426 ■ *Web:* beaverstreetfisheries.com					
Blount Seafood Corp 630 Currant Rd	Fall River	MA	02720	774-888-1300	888-1399
TF Hotline: 800-274-2526 ■ *Web:* www.blountseafood.com					
Bon Secour Fisheries Inc 17449 County Rd 49 S	Bon Secour	AL	36511	251-949-7411	949-6478
Web: www.bonsecourfisheries.com					
California Shellfish Co 505 Beach St Ste 200	San Francisco	CA	94133	415-923-7400	
Cassidy Fine Foods 3657 Old Getwell Rd	Memphis	TN	38118	901-542-5100	542-5150
ConAgra Foods Foodservice Co 5 ConAgra Dr	Omaha	NE	68102	800-357-6543	
TF: 800-357-6543 ■ *Web:* www.conagrafoodservice.com					
Del Mar Seafoods Inc 331 Ford St	Watsonville	CA	95076	831-763-3000	763-2444
Web: www.delmarseafoods.com					
Golden-Tech International Inc 2461 152nd Ave NE	Redmond	WA	98052	425-869-1461	867-1368
TF: 800-311-8090 ■ *Web:* www.gtiinc.com					
Inland Seafood Corp 1651 Montreal Cir	Tucker	GA	30084	404-350-5850	350-5871
TF: 800-883-3474 ■ *Web:* www.inlandseafood.com					
Interamerican Trading & Products Corp 1800 Purdy Ave	Miami Beach	FL	33139	305-885-9666	
Ipswich Shellfish Co Inc 8 Hayward St	Ipswich	MA	01938	978-356-4371	356-9235
TF: 800-477-9424 ■ *Web:* www.ipswichshellfish.com					
LD Amory & Co Inc 101 S King St	Hampton	VA	23669	757-722-1915	723-1184
Web: virginiaseafood.org					
Maine Lobster Direct 48 Union Wharf	Portland	ME	04101	800-556-2783	772-0169*
**Fax Area Code:* 207 ■ *TF:* 800-556-2783 ■ *Web:* www.mainelobsterdirect.com					
Mazzetta Co 1990 St Johns Ave	Highland Park	IL	60035	847-433-1150	433-8973
Web: www.mazzetta.com					
Metropolitan Poultry & Seafood Co 1920 Stanford Ct	Landover	MD	20785	301-772-0060	772-1013
TF: 800-522-0060 ■ *Web:* www.metropoultry.com					
Morey's Seafood International LLC 1218 Hwy 10 S	Motley	MN	56466	218-352-6345	
TF: 800-808-3474 ■ *Web:* www.moreys.com					
Morley Sales Company Inc 119 N Second St	Geneva	IL	60134	630-845-8750	845-8749
Web: www.morleysales.com					
Oceanpro Industries Ltd 1900 Fenwick St NE	Washington	DC	20002	202-529-3003	
Web: www.profish.com					
Pacific Giant Inc 4625 District Blvd	Vernon	CA	90058	323-587-5000	
Web: www.pacificgiant.com					
Premier Pacific Seafoods Inc 111 W Harrison St	Seattle	WA	98119	206-286-8584	286-8810
Web: prempac.com					
Quirch Foods Co 7600 NW 82nd Pl	Miami	FL	33166	305-691-3535	593-0272
TF: 800-458-5252 ■ *Web:* www.quirchfoods.com					
Red Chamber Co 1912 E Vernon Ave	Vernon	CA	90058	323-234-9000	231-8888
Web: www.redchamber.com					
Sager's Seafood Plus Inc 4802 Bridal Wreath Dr	Richmond	TX	77406	281-342-8833	
TF: 800-929-3474 ■ *Web:* sagersseafoodplus.com					
Slade Gorton Company Inc 225 Southampton St	Boston	MA	02118	617-442-5800	442-9090
TF: 800-225-1573 ■ *Web:* www.sladegorton.com					
Southern Foods Inc 3500 Old Battleground Rd	Greensboro	NC	27410	336-545-3800	545-5281
Web: www.southernfoods.com					
Stavis Seafoods Inc 212 Northern Ave Ste 305	Boston	MA	02210	617-482-6349	
TF: 800-390-5103 ■ *Web:* www.stavis.com					
Tri Marine Fish Co 220 Cannery St	San Pedro	CA	90731	310-547-1144	
Web: www.trimarinegroup.com					
Troyer Foods Inc 17141 State Rd 4	Goshen	IN	46528	574-533-0302	533-3851
TF: 800-876-9377 ■ *Web:* www.troyers.com					
Val's Distributing Co 6124 E 30th St N PO Box 581583	Tulsa	OK	74115	918-835-9987	835-3808

297-6 Frozen Foods (Packaged) - Whol

Company / Address	City	State	ZIP	Phone	Fax
Baja Foods LLC 636 W Root St	Chicago	IL	60609	773-376-9030	
Web: www.bajafoodsllc.com					
Cedar Farms 2100 Hornig Rd	Philadelphia	PA	19116	215-934-7100	934-5851
TF: 800-220-2217 ■ *Web:* www.cedarfarms.com					
ConAgra Foods Foodservice Co 5 ConAgra Dr	Omaha	NE	68102	800-357-6543	
TF: 800-357-6543 ■ *Web:* www.conagrafoodservice.com					
Dot Foods Inc 1 Dot Way PO Box 192	Mount Sterling	IL	62353	217-773-4411	773-3321
TF: 800-366-3687 ■ *Web:* www.dotfoods.com					
Happy & Healthy Products Inc 1600 S Dixie Hwy Ste 200	Boca Raton	FL	33432	561-367-0739	368-5267
Web: www.fruitfull.com					
Paris Foods Corp 3965 Ocean Gateway PO Box 121	Trappe	MD	21673	410-200-9595	
Web: www.parisfoods.com					
Quality Frozen Foods Inc 1663 62nd St	Brooklyn	NY	11204	718-256-9100	234-3755
Web: www.qualityfrozenfoods.com					
Sun Belt Food Company Inc 4755 Technology Way Ste 209	Boca Raton	FL	33431	561-995-9100	997-5664
Web: www.sunbeltfoods.com					
Trudeau Distributing Co 25 Cliff Rd W Ste 115	Burnsville	MN	55337	952-882-8295	
Web: www.trudeaudistributing.com					
Wilcox Frozen Foods Inc 2200 Oakdale Ave	San Francisco	CA	94124	415-282-4116	282-3044

297-7 Fruits & Vegetables - Fresh - Whol

Company / Address	City	State	ZIP	Phone	Fax
Albert's Organics Inc 3268 E Vernon Ave	Vernon	CA	90058	800-899-5944	
TF: 800-899-5944 ■ *Web:* www.albertsorganics.com					
Alpine Fresh Inc 9300 NW 58th St Ste 201	Miami	FL	33178	305-594-9117	594-8506
TF: 800-292-8777 ■ *Web:* www.alpinefresh.com					
Anthony Marano Company Inc 3000 S Ashland Ave	Chicago	IL	60608	773-321-7500	
Web: www.anthonymarano.com					
Banacol Marketing Corp 355 Alhambra Cir Ste 1510	Coral Gables	FL	33134	305-441-9036	446-4291
TF: 877-324-7619 ■ *Web:* www.banacol.com					
Belair Produce Company Inc 7226 Pkwy Dr	Hanover	MD	21076	410-782-8000	782-8009
TF: 888-782-8008 ■ *Web:* www.belairproduce.com					
Bernard Zell Anshe Emet Day School 3751 N Broadway St	Chicago	IL	60613	773-281-1858	281-4709
Web: www.bernardzell.org					
Bix Produce Co 1415 L'Orient St	Saint Paul	MN	55117	651-487-8000	487-1314
TF: 800-642-9514 ■ *Web:* www.bixproduce.com					
Bland Farms Inc 1126 Raymond Bland Rd	Glennville	GA	30427	912-654-1330	654-3532
Web: www.blandfarms.com					
Bouten Construction Co 627 N Napa St	Spokane	WA	99202	509-535-3531	535-6047
Web: www.boutenconstruction.com					
Brothers Produce Inc 3173 Produce Row	Houston	TX	77023	713-924-4196	921-3060
Web: www.brothersproduce.com					
Calavo Growers Inc 1141-A Cummings Rd	Santa Paula	CA	93060	805-525-1245	921-3287
NASDAQ: CVGW ■ *TF:* 800-654-8758 ■ *Web:* www.calavo.com					
Caro Foods Inc 2324 Bayou Blue Rd	Houma	LA	70364	985-872-1483	876-0825
TF: 800-395-2276 ■ *Web:* www.performancefoodservice.com/Caro					
Community Suffolk Inc 304 Second St	Everett	MA	02149	617-389-5200	389-6680
Web: community-suffolk.com					
Consumers Produce Co 1 21st St	Pittsburgh	PA	15222	412-281-0722	281-6541
Web: www.consumersproduce.com					
Costa Fruit & Produce 18 Bunker Hill Industrial Pk PO Box 290754	Boston	MA	02129	617-241-8007	241-8007
TF: 800-322-1374 ■ *Web:* www.freshideas.com					

Phone Fax

Country Fresh Mushroom Co
289 Chambers Rd PO Box 490 Toughkenamon PA 19374 610-268-3043 268-0479
Web: www.countryfreshmushrooms.com
Crosset Company Inc 10295 Toebben Dr Independence KY 41051 859-283-5830 817-7634
TF: 800-347-4902 ■ *Web:* crosset.com
D'Arrigo Bros Company of New York Inc
315 Hunts Pt Terminal Market Bronx NY 10474 718-991-5900 960-0544
Web: www.darrigony.com
Del Monte Fresh Produce Co
241 Sevilla Ave Coral Gables FL 33134 305-520-8400 567-0320
TF Cust Svc: 800-950-3683 ■ *Web:* www.freshdelmonte.com
DiMare Bros/New England Farms Packing Co
84 New England Produce Ctr Chelsea MA 02150 617-889-3800
Web: dimarefresh.com
DiMare Fresh Inc 4629 Diplomacy Rd Fort Worth TX 76155 817-385-3000
Web: www.dimarefresh.com
Dole Food Company Hawaii 802 Mapunapuna St Honolulu HI 96819 808-861-8015 861-8020
TF: 800-697-9100 ■ *Web:* www.dolefruithawaii.com
Egan Bernard & Co 1900 Old Dixie Hwy Fort Pierce FL 34946 800-327-6676 465-1181*
**Fax Area Code:* 772 ■ *TF:* 800-327-6676 ■ *Web:* www.dneworld.com
Federal Fruit & Produce Co 1890 E 58th Ave Denver CO 80216 303-292-1303
Web: www.fedfruit.com
FreshPoint Inc 1390 Enclave Pkwy Houston TX 77077 281-899-4242
Web: www.freshpoint.com
Freshway Foods 601 Stolle Ave Sidney OH 45365 937-498-4664 498-4124
Web: www.freshwayfoods.com
Frieda's Inc 4465 Corporate Ctr Dr Los Alamitos CA 90720 714-826-6100 816-0273*
**Fax:* Sales ■ *TF:* 800-241-1771 ■ *Web:* www.friedas.com
General Produce Co 1330 N 'B' St Sacramento CA 95814 916-441-6431 441-2483
TF: 800-366-4991 ■ *Web:* www.generalproduce.com
Gold Harbor Commodities Inc
9750 Third Ave NE Seattle WA 98115 206-527-3494
Web: www.goldharbor.com
Graves Menu Maker Foods Inc
913 Big Horn Dr Jefferson City MO 65109 573-893-3000 893-2172
Web: www.menumakerfoods.com
H Smith Packing Corp 99 Ft Fairfield Rd Presque Isle ME 04769 207-764-4540 764-2816
TF: 800-393-9898 ■ *Web:* www.smithsfarm.com
Hearn Kirkwood 7251 Standard Dr Hanover MD 21076 410-712-6000 712-0020
TF General: 800-777-9489 ■ *Web:* www.hearnkirkwood.com
Heeren Bros Inc 1060 Hall St SW Grand Rapids MI 49503 616-452-8641 243-7070
Web: www.heerenbros.com
Hollar & Greene Produce Co Inc
230 Cabbage Rd PO Box 3500 Boone NC 28607 828-264-2177 264-4413
TF: 800-222-1077 ■ *Web:* www.hollarandgreene.com
Indianapolis Fruit Company Inc
4501 Massachusetts Ave Indianapolis IN 46218 317-546-2425 543-0521
TF: 800-377-2425 ■ *Web:* www.indyfruit.com
Kegel's Produce Inc 2851 Old Tree Dr Lancaster PA 17603 717-392-6612
TF: 800-535-3435 ■ *Web:* kegels.com
Melissa's/World Variety Produce Inc
5325 S Soto St Vernon CA 90058 800-588-0151
TF: 800-588-0151 ■ *Web:* www.melissas.com
Mission Produce Inc 2500 Vineyard Ave Ste 300 Oxnard CA 93036 805-981-3650 981-3660
Web: www.worldsfinestavocados.com
Moore Food Distributors Co 9910 Page Ave Saint Louis MO 63132 314-426-1300
TF: 800-467-7878 ■ *Web:* www.moorefooddist.com
Muir Enterprises Inc
3575 West 900 South PO Box 26775 Salt Lake City UT 84104 801-363-7695 322-1640*
**Fax:* Sales ■ *TF:* 877-268-2002 ■ *Web:* www.coppercanyonfarms.com
North Bay Produce Inc PO Box 988 Traverse City MI 49685 800-678-1941 946-1902*
**Fax Area Code:* 231 ■ *TF:* 800-678-1941 ■ *Web:* www.northbayproduce.com
Oneonta Trading Corp 1 Oneonta Way Wenatchee WA 98801 509-663-2191 663-6333
Web: www.oneonta.com
Organic Valley Family of Farms 1 Organic Way LaFarge WI 54639 888-444-6455
TF: 888-444-6455 ■ *Web:* www.organicvalley.coop
Pacific Coast Fruit Co
201 NE Second Ave Ste 100 Portland OR 97232 503-234-6411 963-5435
TF: 800-423-4945 ■ *Web:* www.pcfruit.com
Pandol Bros Inc 401 Rd 192 Delano CA 93215 661-725-3755 725-4741
Web: www.pandol.com
Paramount Export Co 175 Filbert St Ste 201 Oakland CA 94607 510-839-0150 839-1002
Web: www.paramountexport.net
Peak of the Market 1200 King Edward St Winnipeg MB R3H0R5 204-632-7325
Web: www.peakmarket.com
Peirone Produce Co 9818 W Hallett Rd Spokane WA 99224 509-838-3515 838-3916
Procacci Bros Sales Corp
3333 S Front St Philadelphia PA 19148 215-463-8000 467-1144
Web: www.procaccibrothers.com
Produce Source Partners 13167 Telcourt Rd Ashland VA 23005 804-262-8300 264-2313
TF: 800-344-4728 ■ *Web:* www.producesourcepartners.com
Progressive Produce Co 5790 Peachtree St Los Angeles CA 90040 323-890-8100 890-8113
TF: 800-900-0757 ■ *Web:* www.progressiveproduce.com
ProPacificfresh 70 Pepsi Way PO Box 1069 Durham CA 95938 530-893-0596 893-5973
TF: 888-232-0908 ■ *Web:* www.propacificfresh.com
Sambazon Inc 1160 Calle Cordillera San Clemente CA 92673 949-498-8618 498-8619
TF: 877-726-2296 ■ *Web:* www.sambazon.com
Sandridge Food Corp (SFC) 133 Commerce Dr Medina OH 44256 330-725-2348 722-3998
TF: 800-672-2523 ■ *Web:* www.sandridge.com
Simonian Fruit Co 511 N Seventh St PO Box 340 Fowler CA 93625 559-834-5921 834-2363
Web: www.simonianfruit.com
Strobe Celery & Vegetable Co
2404 S Wolcott Ave Chicago IL 60608 773-446-4000 226-7644*
**Fax Area Code:* 312 ■ *Web:* www.strube.com
Sunkist Growers Inc 27770 Entertainment Dr Valencia CA 91355 818-986-4800
Sunnyridge Farm Inc
1900 Fifth St NW PO Box 3036 Winter Haven FL 33881 863-294-8856 595-4095
Web: www.sunnyridge.com
Superior Foods Inc 275 Westgate Dr Watsonville CA 95076 831-728-3691 722-0926
Web: www.superiorfoods.com
Taylor Farms Inc PO Box 1649 Salinas CA 93902 831-676-9765
TF: 866-675-6120 ■ *Web:* www.taylorfarms.com

Phone Fax

W. R. Vernon Produce Co PO Box 4054 Winston-Salem NC 27101 336-725-9741 761-1841
TF: 800-222-6406 ■ *Web:* www.vernonproduce.com

297-8 Groceries - General Line

Phone Fax

ACE Bakery Ltd 1 Hafis Rd Toronto ON M6M2V6 416-241-3600
Web: www.acebakery.com
Acme Food Sales Inc 5940 1st Ave S Seattle WA 98108 206-762-5150
TF: 800-777-2263 ■ *Web:* www.acmefood.com
Active Organics Inc 1097 Yates St Lewisville TX 75057 972-221-7500
TF: 800-541-1478 ■ *Web:* www.activeorganics.com
Adams Extract & Spice LLC 3217 Johnston Rd Gonzales TX 78629 830-672-1850 672-8100
Web: www.adamsextract.com
ADM Agri-Industries Co 5550 Maplewood Dr Windsor ON N9C0B9 519-972-8100
Web: adm.com
Affiliated Foods Inc 1401 W Farmers Ave Amarillo TX 79118 806-372-3851
TF: 800-234-3661 ■ *Web:* www.afiama.com
Affiliated Foods Midwest 1301 W Omaha Ave Norfolk NE 68701 402-371-0555 371-1884
Web: www.afmidwest.com
AJC International 5188 Roswell Rd NW Atlanta GA 30342 404-252-6750 252-9340
Web: www.ajcfood.com
Aladdin Bakers Inc 240 25th St Brooklyn NY 11232 718-499-1818
Web: www.aladdinbakersinc.com
Albert Guarnieri Co 1133 E Market St Warren OH 44483 330-394-5636 394-4982
TF: 800-686-2639 ■ *Web:* www.albertguarnieri.com
Albertsons LLC 250 E Parkcenter Boise ID 83706 208-395-6200
Web: www.albertsons.com
Ale-8-one Bottling Co 25 Carol Rd Winchester KY 40391 859-744-3484
Web: ale8one.com
Aliments Novali Foods Inc
3080 Rue St-Prosper Saint-Hyacinthe QC J2S2A4 450-773-9944
Allann Bros Coffee Co 1852 Fescue St SE Albany OR 97322 541-812-8000
Web: www.allannbrothers.com
Allen Flavors Inc 23 Progress St Edison NJ 08820 908-561-5995
Web: www.allenflavors.com
Aloft Charlotte Uptown at the EpiCentre
210 E Trade St Charlotte NC 28202 704-333-1999
Web: www.aloftcharlotteuptown.com
AMCON Distributing Co 7405 Irvington Rd Omaha NE 68122 402-331-3727 331-4834
NYSE: DIT ■ *TF:* 888-201-5997 ■ *Web:* www.amcon.com
American Seaway Foods Inc
5300 Richmond Rd Bedford Heights OH 44146 216-292-7000 968-1618*
**Fax Area Code:* 412
Amster-Kirtz Co 2830 Cleveland Ave NW Canton OH 44709 330-535-6021
TF: 800-257-9338 ■ *Web:* www.amsterkirtz.com
Anderson-DuBose Co 5300 Tod Ave SW Lordstown OH 44481 440-248-8800 824-2256*
**Fax Area Code:* 330 ■ *Web:* anderson-dubose.com
Animal Supply Company LLC
32001 32nd Ave S Ste 420 Federal Way WA 98001 253-237-0400
TF: 800-323-2963 ■ *Web:* www.animalsupplycompany.com
Apetito Canada Ltd 12 Indell Ln Brampton ON L6T3Y3 905-799-1022
TF: 800-268-8199 ■ *Web:* apetito.ca
Arcobasso Foods Inc 8850 Pershall Rd Hazelwood MO 63042 314-381-8083
Web: www.arcobasso.com
Armelle Supermarket
140 W Boynton Beach Blvd Boynton Beach FL 33435 561-739-6543
Asiana Cuisine Enterprises Inc
1447 W 178th St Gardena CA 90248 310-327-2233
Web: acesushi.com
Associated Food Stores Inc
1850 West 2100 South Salt Lake City UT 84119 801-973-4400 978-8551
TF Cust Svc: 888-574-7100 ■ *Web:* www.afstores.com
Associated Grocers Inc 8600 Anselmo Ln Baton Rouge LA 70810 225-444-1000 763-6194
TF: 800-637-2021 ■ *Web:* www.agbr.com
Associated Grocers of Florida Inc
1141 SW 12th Ave Pompano Beach FL 33069 954-876-3000 876-3003
Web: www.agfla.com
Associated Grocers of New England Inc
11 Co-op Way Pembroke NH 03275 603-223-6710 223-5672
TF: 800-242-2248 ■ *Web:* www.agne.com
Associated Grocers of the South
3600 Vanderbilt Rd Birmingham AL 35217 205-841-6781
TF: 800-695-6051 ■ *Web:* www.agsouth.com
Associated Wholesale Grocers Inc
5000 Kansas Ave Kansas City KS 66106 913-288-1000 288-1587
Web: www.awginc.com
Associated Wholesalers Inc PO Box 67 Robesonia PA 19551 610-693-3161 693-3171*
**Fax:* Orders ■ *TF:* 800-927-7771 ■ *Web:* www.awiweb.com
Astra Foods Inc 6430 Market St Upper Darby PA 19082 610-352-4400
Web: www.astrafoods.com
Atalanta Corp 1 Atalanta Plaza Elizabeth NJ 07206 908-351-8000 351-1693
Web: www.atalantacorp.com
Au Ptit Marche De Notre Dame
552 Rue Notre Dame Bon-Conseil QC J0C1A0 819-336-2686
Bakery Barn Inc 111 Terence Dr Pittsburgh PA 15236 412-655-1113
Web: bakery-barn.net
Barbara Timken Ccna 304 Timberwood Cir Lafayette LA 70508 337-989-2653
Baron Spices Inc 1440 Kentucky Ave Saint Louis MO 63110 314-535-9020
Web: www.baronspices.com
Bartush-Schnitzius Foods Co
1137 N Kealy St Lewisville TX 75057 972-219-1270
Web: www.bartushfoods.com
Bassham Wholesale Egg Company Inc
5409 Hemphill St Fort Worth TX 76115 817-921-1600
Web: www.basshamfoods.com
Bay Bread LLC 2325 Pine St San Francisco CA 94115 415-440-0356
Berry Coffee Co 14825 Martin Dr Eden Prairie MN 55344 952-937-8697
Web: www.berrycoffee.com
Bill & Ralphs Inc 118 B & R Dr Sarepta LA 71071 318-539-2071
Bill's Distributing Ltd 5900 Packer Dr Ne Menomonie WI 54751 715-235-5820

Company	City	State	Zip	Phone	Fax
Boston Organics 50 Terminal St *Web:* bostonorganics.com	Charlestown	MA	02129	617-242-1700	
Bozzuto's Inc 275 School House Rd *OTC: BOZZ* ■ **Fax:* Sales ■ *Web:* www.bozzutos.com	Cheshire	CT	06410	203-272-3511	250-2880*
Bragg Live Food Products Inc PO Box 7 *Web:* bragg.com	Santa Barbara	CA	93102	805-968-1020	
Brenham Wholesale Grocery Co 602 W First St *TF:* 800-392-4869 ■ *Web:* www.bwgroc.com	Brenham	TX	77833	979-836-7925	830-0346
Bridge City Food Mktg Inc 110 SE Second Ave	Portland	OR	97214	503-239-8024	
Brim's Snack Foods 3045 Bartlett Corporate Dr Ste 101 *Web:* www.brimsnacks.com	Bartlett	TN	38133	901-377-9016	
Brownie Baker, The 4870 W Jacquelyn Ave *Web:* www.browniebaker.com	Fresno	CA	93722	559-277-7070	
Browns Corner Short Stop 5550 Auburn Way S *Web:* 76.com	Auburn	WA	98092	253-833-7185	
Bruceton Farm Service Inc 1768 Mileground Rd *Web:* www.bfscompanies.com	Morgantown	WV	26505	304-291-6980	
Bryant Convenience Inc 510 Bryant St	Denver	CO	80204	303-534-1379	
Bud's Best Cookies Inc 2070 Pkwy Office Cir *Web:* www.budsbestcookies.com	Hoover	AL	35244	205-987-4840	
Buona Vita Inc 1 S Industrial Blvd *Web:* www.buonavitainc.com	Bridgeton	NJ	08302	856-453-7972	
C & S Wholesale Grocers Inc 47 Old Ferry Rd PO Box 821 *Web:* www.cswg.com	Brattleboro	VT	05301	802-464-6333	
Camp Olympia 723 Olympia Dr *TF:* 800-735-6190 ■ *Web:* www.campolympia.com	Trinity	TX	75862	936-594-2541	594-8143
Canton Food Co 750 S Alameda St *Web:* www.cantonfoodco.com	Los Angeles	CA	90021	213-688-7707	
Canyon Specialty Foods Inc 11035 Switzer Ave	Dallas	TX	75238	214-352-1771	
Captain Kens Foods Inc 344 Robert St S *Web:* www.captainkens.com	Saint Paul	MN	55107	651-298-0071	
Carlie C's IGA Inc 10 Carlie C'S Dr *Web:* www.carliecs.com	Dunn	NC	28334	910-892-4124	
Carnicerias Jimenez 4204 W N Ave *Web:* www.carniceriasjimenez.com	Chicago	IL	60639	773-486-5805	
Carrington Foods Company Inc 200 Jacintoport Blvd # D *Web:* www.carringtonfoods.com	Saraland	AL	36571	251-675-9700	
Caruthers Raisin Packing Company Inc 12797 S Elm Ave	Caruthers	CA	93609	559-864-9448	
Cash-Wa Distributing Co 401 W Fourth St *TF:* 800-652-0010 ■ *Web:* www.cashwa.com	Kearney	NE	68845	308-237-3151	234-6018
Catania-Spagna Corp 1 Nemco Way *Web:* www.cataniausa.com	Ayer	MA	01432	978-772-7900	
CB Ragland Co 2720 Eugenia Ave **Fax:* Hum Res ■ *Web:* www.cbragland.com	Nashville	TN	37211	615-254-2841	254-2842*
CD Hartnett Co 302 N Main St *Web:* esite.cd-hartnett.com	Weatherford	TX	76086	817-594-3813	594-9714
Central Grocers Co-op Inc 2600 W Haven Ave **Fax Area Code:* 847 ■ *Web:* www.central-grocers.com	Joliet	IL	60433	815-553-8800	288-8710*
Chef's Requested Foods Inc 2600 Exchange Ave *Web:* www.chefsrequested.com	Oklahoma City	OK	73108	405-239-2610	
Ciranda Inc 221 Vine St *Web:* www.ciranda.com	Hudson	WI	54016	715-386-1737	
Citarella 2135 Broadway *Web:* www.citarella.com	New York	NY	10023	212-874-0383	
Clean Foods Inc 760 E Santa Maria St *Web:* cafealtura.com	Santa Paula	CA	93060	805-933-3027	
Coastal Foods Inc 14212 Interdr W	Houston	TX	77032	281-987-8985	987-8988
Coastal Pacific Food Distributors Inc (CPFD) 1015 Performance Dr **Fax:* Cust Svc ■ *TF:* 800-500-2611 ■ *Web:* www.cpfd.com	Stockton	CA	95206	209-983-2454	983-8009*
Convenience Retailers LLC 80980 Us Hwy 111	Indio	CA	92201	760-347-2900	
County Beverage Company Inc 1290 SE Hamblen Rd *Web:* www.countybev.com	Lees Summit	MO	64081	816-525-4550	
Cracker Box, The 6682 Hwy 7	Bismarck	AR	71929	501-865-2249	
Create a Pack Foods Inc W1344 Industrial Dr *Web:* create-a-pack.com	Ixonia	WI	53066	262-567-6069	
Creme Curls Bakery Inc 5292 Lawndale Ave *Web:* www.cremecurls.com	Hudsonville	MI	49426	616-669-2468	
Dallo Enterprises 5075 Federal Blvd *Web:* www.harvestranchmarkets.com	San Diego	CA	92102	619-527-3385	
Dara's Fast Lane Store 1709 Ft Riley Blvd *Web:* darascornermarket.com	Saint George	KS	66502	785-537-2150	
Deb-El Food Products LLC 2 Papetti Plaza *TF:* 800-421-0330 ■ *Web:* www.debelfoods.com	Elizabeth	NJ	07206	908-351-0330	
Devault Foods 1 Devault Ln *TF:* 800-426-2874 ■ *Web:* www.devaultfoods.com	Devault	PA	19432	610-644-2536	
DiCarlo Distributors Inc 1630 N Ocean Ave *TF:* 800-342-2756 ■ *Web:* www.dicarlofood.com	Holtsville	NY	11742	631-758-6000	758-6096
Dinovite Inc 101 Miller Dr *Web:* www.dinovite.com	Crittenden	KY	41030	859-428-1000	
Dipasa USA Inc 6600 Fm 802 Ste B *Web:* dipasausa.com	Brownsville	TX	78526	956-831-4072	831-5893
Dismex Food Inc 12255 SW 133rd Ct *Web:* www.dismexfood.com	Miami	FL	33186	305-238-6146	238-4032
Divvies LLC 700 Oakridge Common *Web:* www.divvies.com	South Salem	NY	10590	914-533-0333	
Dolce Europa 7520 Fullerton Rd	Springfield	VA	22153	703-451-9501	
Doublebees 111 Bill Foster Memorial Hwy *Web:* www.doublebees.com	Cabot	AR	72023	501-605-8989	
Dutch Maid Bakery Inc 50 Park St *Web:* www.dutchmaidbakery.com	Dorchester	MA	02122	617-265-5417	
Dutch Valley Bulk Food Distributors Inc 7615 Lancaster Ave *TF:* 800-733-4191 ■ *Web:* www.dutchvalleyfoods.com	Myerstown	PA	17067	717-933-4191	933-5466
E. G. Ayers Distributing Inc 5819 S Broadway St *Web:* www.ayersdistributing.com	Eureka	CA	95503	707-445-2077	445-5719
Eagle Beverage Corp 1043 County Rt 25 *Web:* www.eaglebev.com	Oswego	NY	13126	315-343-5221	
Eastland Food Corp 8305 Stayton Dr *Web:* www.eastlandfood.com	Jessup	MD	20794	301-621-8140	
El Rancho Supermercado 22291 Redwood Rd	Castro Valley	CA	94546	510-728-1945	
El Tapatio Markets Inc 13635 Fwy Dr *Web:* www.eltapatiomarkets.com	Santa Fe Springs	CA	90670	562-293-4200	
Ellwood Thompson 10 S Thompson St *Web:* www.ellwoodthompsons.com	Richmond	VA	23221	804-359-7525	
Empire Food Brokers of Ohio Inc 11243 Cornell Pk Dr *Web:* www.empirefoods.com	Cincinnati	OH	45242	513-793-6241	
Ettline Foods Corp 525 N State St *Web:* www.ettline.com	York	PA	17403	717-848-1564	
Europa Market Company Inc, The 8100 Water St *Web:* www.europa-market.com	Saint Louis	MO	63111	314-631-7288	
F Mcconnell & Sons Inc 11102 Lincoln Hwy E *TF:* 800-552-0835 ■ *Web:* www.fmcconnell.com	New Haven	IN	46774	260-493-6607	749-6116
Farm Stores Corp 16777 Old Cutler Rd *Web:* www.farmstores.com	Palmetto Bay	FL	33157	305-677-0645	
Farner-Bocken Co 1751 US Hwy 30 E PO Box 368 *TF:* 800-274-8692 ■ *Web:* farner-bocken.com	Carroll	IA	51401	712-792-3503	792-3503
Feesers Inc 5561 Grayson Rd *TF:* 800-326-2828 ■ *Web:* www.feesers.com	Harrisburg	PA	17111	717-564-4636	558-7445
Felbro Food Products Inc 5700 W Adams Blvd *Web:* www.employeepraise.com	Los Angeles	CA	90016	323-936-5266	
Field Trip Factory 2211 N Elston Ave Ste 304 *TF:* 800-987-6409 ■ *Web:* www.fieldtripfactory.com	Chicago	IL	60614	800-987-6409	
Fill in Foods 10554 Scott Hwy	Helenwood	TN	37755	423-663-2749	
Fiorucci Foods Inc 1800 Ruffin Mill Rd *Web:* www.fioruccifoods.com	Colonial Heights	VA	23834	804-520-7775	
Fisher Foods Mktg Inc 5215 Fulton Dr NW *Web:* www.fishersfoods.com	Canton	OH	44718	330-497-3000	
Flash Foods Inc 215 Pendleton St *Web:* www.flashfoods.com	Waycross	GA	31501	912-285-4011	
Flavor Dynamics Inc 640 Montrose Ave *TF:* 888-271-8424 ■ *Web:* www.flavordynamics.com	South Plainfield	NJ	07080	908-822-8855	
Flavorchem Corp 1525 Brook Dr *Web:* www.flavorchem.com	Downers Grove	IL	60515	630-932-8100	
Flavour Tech International LLC 66 Industrial Ave	Little Ferry	NJ	07643	201-440-3281	
Food 4 Less 255 E March Ln *Web:* food-4-less.com	Stockton	CA	95207	209-957-4917	
Food Services of America Inc 16100 N 71st St Ste 400 *TF:* 800-528-9346 ■ *Web:* www.fsafood.com	Scottsdale	AZ	85254	480-927-4000	927-4299
Franklin Supply Inc 75 Lee St *Web:* franklinsupplyinc.com	Franklin	LA	70538	337-828-3208	
Fresh Food Concepts Inc 6535 Caballero Blvd Bldg C *Web:* www.ffci.us	Buena Park	CA	90620	714-562-5000	562-5002
Fresh Foods Corp of America 1528 S Hayford Rd *Web:* www.cyruspies.com	Airway Heights	WA	99001	509-624-5000	
Fresh Grocer at Chester Avenue, The 5406 Chester Ave *Web:* thefreshgrocer.com	Philadelphia	PA	19143	215-730-0881	
Fuji Health Science Inc 3 Terri Ln Ste 12 *TF:* 877-385-4777 ■ *Web:* www.fujihealthscience.com	Burlington	NJ	08016	609-386-3030	
G r Manufacturing Inc 4800 Commerce Dr *TF:* 800-841-8001 ■ *Web:* www.grtractors.com	Trussville	AL	35173	205-655-8001	
George E DeLallo Co Inc 6390 Rt 30 *TF:* 877-335-2556 ■ *Web:* www.delallo.com	Jeannette	PA	15644	724-523-6577	523-0981
Get & Go Market 10950 Beech Daly Rd	Taylor	MI	48180	313-295-3434	
Giardoni Foods Inc 44 W Jefryn Blvd Ste R *Web:* giardonifoods.com	Deer Park	NY	11729	631-586-2331	
Glory Foods Inc 901 Oak St *Web:* www.gloryfoods.com	Columbus	OH	43205	614-252-2042	
Glover Foods Inc 119 Old Anderson Ville Rd	Americus	GA	31719	229-924-2974	
Gold Coast Ingredients Inc 2429 Yates Ave *TF:* 800-352-8673 ■ *Web:* www.goldcoastinc.com	Commerce	CA	90040	323-724-8935	
Golden Platter Foods Inc 37 Tompkins Point Rd *Web:* goldenplatter.com	Newark	NJ	07114	973-242-0290	
Granite Falls Energy LLC 15045 Hwy 23 SE *TF:* 877-485-8595 ■ *Web:* www.granitefallsenergy.com	Granite Falls	MN	56241	320-564-3100	
Grocers Supply International Inc 3131 E Holcombe Blvd PO Box 14200 *Web:* www.grocerssupply.com	Houston	TX	77021	713-747-5000	
Grocery People Ltd, The 14505 Yellowhead Trl *TF:* 800-461-9401 ■ *Web:* www.tgp.ca	Edmonton	AB	T5L3C4	780-447-5700	
Grocery Supply Co 130 Hillcrest Dr *TF:* 800-231-1938 ■ *Web:* www.grocerysupply.com	Sulphur Springs	TX	75482	903-885-7621	439-3249
Hannaford Bros Co 145 Pleasant Hill Rd *TF:* 800-213-9040 ■ *Web:* www.hannaford.com	Scarborough	ME	04074	800-213-9040	
Hansen Beverage Co 2661 Green River Rd *TF:* 877-265-3632 ■ *Web:* www.hansens.com	Corona	CA	92879	800-426-7367	
Hardings Market-West Inc 211 Bannister *Web:* www.hardings.com	Plainwell	MI	49080	269-685-9807	
Harold L King & Company Inc 1420 Stafford St *Web:* king-coffee.com	Redwood City	CA	94063	650-368-2233	
Harris Soup Co, The 17711 NE Riverside Pkwy *TF:* 800-307-7687 ■ *Web:* www.harrysfresh.com	Portland	OR	97230	503-257-7687	

				Phone	Fax

Harvest Health Foods
1944 Eastern Ave SE . . . Grand Rapids MI 49507 616-245-6268
Web: www.harvesthealthfoods.com

Harvey Alpert & Company Inc
2014 S Sepulveda Blvd Ste 200 . . . Los Angeles CA 90025 310-689-6000

Henry's Foods Inc 104 Mckay Ave N . . . Alexandria MN 56308 320-763-3194
Web: www.henrysfoods.com

High Country Beverage Corp 5706 Wright Dr. . . . Loveland CO 80538 970-622-8444
Web: www.highcountrybeverage.com

Highway 11 Food Mart 322 Chesnee Hwy. . . . Gaffney SC 29341 864-489-4958

Holsum of Fort Wayne Inc 136 Murray St. . . . Fort Wayne IN 46803 260-456-2130
Web: www.holsum.com

Honey Farms Inc 505 Pleasant St . . . Worcester MA 01609 508-753-7678
Web: www.myhoneyfarms.com

Honor Foods 1801 N Fifth St . . . Philadelphia PA 19122 215-236-1700
TF: 800-462-2890 ■ *Web:* honorfoods.com

Huy Fong Foods Inc 5001 Earle Ave. . . . Rosemead CA 91770 626-286-8328
Web: www.huyfong.com

Imperial Trading Co Inc 701 Edwards Ave . . . Elmwood LA 70123 504-733-1400 855-1416*
**Fax Area Code:* 877 ■ *TF Cust Svc:* 800-775-4504 ■ *Web:* www.imperialtrading.com

Inderbitzin Distributors Inc
901 Valley Ave NW. . . . Puyallup WA 98371 253-922-2592
Web: www.inderbitzin.com

J&J Foods Inc 1075 Jesse Jewell Pkwy SW . . . Gainesville GA 30501 770-287-7217
Web: www.jandjfoods.com

Jace Holdings Ltd 6649 Butler Crescent. . . . Saanichton BC V8M1Z7 250-483-1715
TF: 800-667-8280 ■ *Web:* www.thriftyfoods.com

Jana Foods LLC 100 Wood Ave S Ste 206. . . . Iselin NJ 08830 201-866-5001
Web: www.janafoods.com

JM Swank Co 395 Herky St . . . North Liberty IA 52317 319-626-3683
TF: 800-593-6333 ■ *Web:* www.jmswank.com

Johnny's Stop n Shop 505 S Commercial St . . . Emporia KS 66801 620-343-3803

Johnson Bros Bakery Supply
10731 N Interstate 35 . . . San Antonio TX 78233 800-590-2575 599-3102*
**Fax Area Code:* 210 ■ *TF:* 877-446-2767 ■ *Web:* www.jbrosbakerysupply.com

Johnson O'hare Company Inc 1 Progress Rd. . . . Billerica MA 01821 978-663-9000 262-2200
Web: www.johare.com

Jonathan Lord Corp 87 Carlough Rd . . . Bohemia NY 11716 631-563-4445
TF: 800-814-7517 ■ *Web:* jonathanlord.com

Jordano's Inc 550 S Patterson Ave . . . Santa Barbara CA 93111 805-964-0611 964-3821
TF: 800-325-2278 ■ *Web:* www.jordanos.com

JTM Provisions Company Inc 200 Sales Dr. . . . Harrison OH 45030 513-367-4900
Web: www.jtmfoodgroup.com

Just Bagels Manufacturing Inc 527 Casanova St. . . . Bronx NY 10474 718-328-9700 328-9997
Web: www.justbagels.com

Kelley Foods of Alabama Inc
1697 Lower Curtis Rd. . . . Elba AL 36323 334-897-5761
Web: www.kelleyfoods.com

Key Food Stores Co-op Inc 1200 S Ave . . . Staten Island NY 10314 718-370-4200
Web: keyfood.com

King's County Market 13735 Roundlake Blvd. . . . Andover MN 55304 763-422-1768
Web: kingscountymarket.com

Kings Super Markets Inc 700 Lanidex Plaza. . . . Parsippany NJ 07054 800-325-4647
TF: 800-325-4647 ■ *Web:* kingsfoodmarkets.com

Koa Trading Co 2975 Aukele St. . . . Lihue HI 96766 808-245-6961 245-8036

L & W Group Inc 30845 Huntwood Ave. . . . Hayward CA 94544 510-475-0111

La Petite Bretonne Inc
1210 Boul Mich Le-Bohec . . . Blainville QC J7C5S4 450-435-3381 435-0944
TF: 800-361-3381 ■ *Web:* www.petitebretonne.com

La Preferida Inc 3400 W 35th St . . . Chicago IL 60632 773-254-7200
Web: www.lapreferida.com

Labatt Food Service 4500 Industry Pk Dr . . . San Antonio TX 78218 210-661-4216 661-0973
Web: www.labattfood.com

Lang Naturals Inc 20 Silva Ln . . . Middletown RI 02842 401-848-7700
Web: www.langnaturals.com

Larue Coffee 2631 S 156th Cir . . . Omaha NE 68130 402-333-9099
TF: 800-658-4498 ■ *Web:* www.laruecoffee.com

Lasco Foods Inc 4553 Gustine Ave. . . . St Louis MO 63116 314-832-1906
Web: www.lascofoods.com

Laurel Grocery Co Inc 129 Barbourville Rd . . . London KY 40744 800-467-6601 878-9361*
**Fax Area Code:* 606 ■ *TF:* 800-467-6601 ■ *Web:* laurelgrocery.com

Lee's Marketplace Inc 555 East 1400 North. . . . Logan UT 84341 435-755-5100
Web: www.leesmarketplace.com

LFI Inc 271 Us Hwy 46 Ste C101 . . . Fairfield NJ 07004 973-882-0550
Web: lfiincorporated.com

Liberty Vegetable Oil Co
15306 S Carmenita Rd . . . Santa Fe Springs CA 90670 562-921-3567
Web: www.libertyvegetableoil.com

Lifetech Resources LLC 9540 Cozycroft Ave. . . . Chatsworth CA 91311 818-885-1199
Web: www.lifetechresources.com

Limra Trading 30 Mall Dr W . . . Jersey City NJ 07310 201-792-7003

Long Wholesale Distributors Inc
5173 Pioneer Rd. . . . Meridian MS 39301 601-482-3144
Web: www.longwholesale.com

Longo Bros Fruit Markets Inc
8800 Huntington Rd . . . Vaughan ON L4H3M6 905-264-4100
Web: www.longos.com

Lowes Wilshire Market 301 N Richman Ave. . . . Fullerton CA 92832 714-870-7310

Luke Soules Acosta 2003 Rickety Ln Ste D . . . Tyler TX 75703 903-561-4241

Magnetic Springs Water Co 1917 Joyce Ave. . . . Columbus OH 43219 614-421-1780
TF: 800-572-2990 ■ *Web:* www.magneticsprings.com

Maines Paper & Food Service Co
101 Broome Corporate Pkwy . . . Conklin NY 13748 607-779-1200 723-3245*
**Fax:* Cust Svc ■ *TF:* 800-366-3669 ■ *Web:* www.maines.net

Maple Ridge Farms Inc 975 S Park View Cir . . . Mosinee WI 54455 715-693-4346
Web: www.mapleridge.com

Marche Akhavan 6170 Rue Sherbrooke O . . . Montreal QC H4B1L8 514-485-4744
Web: akhavanfood.com

Market of Choice 1475 Siskiyou Blvd . . . Ashland OR 97520 541-488-2773
Web: www.marketofchoice.com

Market Semiotics PO Box 1457. . . . Castleton VT 05735 802-273-3800
Web: www.marketsemiotics.com

Marquez Bros International Inc
5801 Rue Ferrari. . . . San Jose CA 95138 408-960-2700
Web: www.marquezbrothers.com

Maverick Enterprises Inc 751 E Gobbi St . . . Ukiah CA 95482 707-463-5591
Web: www.maverickcaps.com

Maxi Foods LLC 8616 California Ave. . . . Riverside CA 92504 951-688-0538
Web: www.maxifoods.com

Maya Overseas Foods Inc 48-85 Maspeth Ave. . . . Maspeth NY 11378 718-894-5145 894-5178
Web: www.mayafoods.com

McLane Company Inc 4747 McLane Pkwy . . . Temple TX 76504 254-771-7500 771-7244
TF: 800-299-1401 ■ *Web:* www.mclaneco.com

McLane Foodservice Inc 2085 Midway Rd. . . . Carrollton TX 75006 972-364-2000 771-7244*
**Fax Area Code:* 254 ■ *TF:* 800-299-1401 ■ *Web:* www.mclaneco.com

Merchants Co 1100 Edwards St . . . Hattiesburg MS 39401 601-583-4351 582-5333
TF: 800-451-8346 ■ *Web:* www.themerchantscompany.com

Metro Supermarkets 156 Main St S . . . Brampton ON L6W2C9 905-459-6212
Web: metro.ca

Metropolis Coffee Company LLC
1039 W Granville Ave Ste 1041 . . . Chicago IL 60660 773-764-0400
Web: metropoliscoffee.com

Mineral Resources International 1990 W 3300 S . . . Ogden UT 84401 801-731-7040 731-7985
TF: 800-731-7866 ■ *Web:* www.mineralresourcesint.com

Mockler Beverage Co 11811 Reiger Rd. . . . Baton Rouge LA 70809 225-408-4283
Web: mocklerbeverage.com

Monin Inc 2100 Range Rd . . . Clearwater FL 33765 727-461-3033
Web: www.monin.com

Mrs Stratton's Salads Inc
380 Industrial Ln . . . Birmingham AL 35211 205-940-9640
Web: www.mrsstrattons.com

MWS Enterprises Inc 5701 Transit Rd. . . . East Amherst NY 14051 716-689-0600
Web: www.arrowmart.com

Nash Finch Co 7600 France Ave S. . . . Minneapolis MN 55440 952-832-0534 844-1237
NASDAQ: NAFC ■ *Web:* spartannash.com

National Flavors Inc 1206 E Crosstown. . . . Kalamazoo MI 49001 269-344-3640
Web: www.nationalflavors.com

New Century Snacks 5560 E Slauson Ave . . . Commerce CA 90040 323-278-9578
Web: www.newcenturysnacks.com

Nice N Easy Grocery Shoppes Inc
7840 Oxbow Rd . . . Canastota NY 13032 315-697-2287
Web: www.niceneasy.com

North Coast Co-op Inc 811 I St . . . Arcata CA 95521 707-822-5000

Northern Eagle Beverage Co 600 16th St. . . . Carlstadt NJ 07072 201-531-7100
Web: www.northerneaglebeverage.com

Nuherbs co 3820 Penniman Ave . . . Oakland CA 94619 510-534-4372
TF: 800-233-4307 ■ *Web:* www.nuherbs.com

Olean Wholesale Grocery Co-op Inc
1587 Haskell Rd PO Box 1070 . . . Olean NY 14760 716-372-2020
TF: 888-835-3026 ■ *Web:* www.oleanwholesale.com

Omega Alpha Pharmaceuticals Inc
795 Pharmacy Ave . . . Scarborough ON M1L3K2 416-297-6900
Web: omegaalpha.ca

Oppenheimer Cos Inc 877 W Main Ste 700. . . . Boise ID 83702 208-343-4883
TF: 800-727-9939 ■ *Web:* www.oppcos.com

P J Noyes Company Inc 89 Bridge St . . . Lancaster NH 03584 603-788-4952
TF: 800-522-2469 ■ *Web:* www.pjnoyes.com

Paint Sundries Solutions Inc
930 Seventh Ave. . . . Kirkland WA 98033 425-827-9200
Web: www.paintsundries.com

Par Mar Stores 114 A Westview Ave. . . . Marietta OH 45750 304-572-3500
Web: www.parmarstores.com

Paris Gourmet of New York Inc 145 Grand St. . . . Carlstadt NJ 07072 800-727-8791 939-5613*
**Fax Area Code:* 201 ■ *TF:* 800-727-8791 ■ *Web:* www.parisgourmet.com

Pasco Corp of America 6500 N Marine Dr . . . Portland OR 97203 503-289-6500
Web: www.pascoamerica.com

Patty Palace Ltd 595 Middlefield Rd . . . Scarborough ON M1V3S2 416-297-0510
Web: pattypalace.net

Pearson Foods Corp
1024 Ken O Sha Ind Park Dr SE . . . Grand Rapids MI 49508 616-245-5053
Web: www.pearsonfoods.com

Peppers Unlimited of Louisiana Inc
602 W Bridge St . . . St Martinville LA 70582 337-394-8035
Web: www.peppersunlimitedofla.com

Performance Food Group Co
12500 W Creek Pkwy . . . Richmond VA 23238 804-484-7700
Web: www.pfgc.com

Performance Foodservice 12500 W Creek Pkwy . . . Richmond VA 23238 804-484-7700
TF: 800-535-5053 ■ *Web:* performancefoodservice.com

Perishable Distributors of Iowa Ltd
2741 SE PDI Pl. . . . Ankeny IA 50021 515-965-6300 965-1105
Web: www.contactpdi.com

Peter Gillhams Natural Vitality
4879 Fountain Ave . . . Los Angeles CA 90029 888-324-9904
TF: 888-324-9904 ■ *Web:* www.vites.com

Pharmore Ingredients Inc
12569 South 2700 West Ste 201 . . . Riverton UT 84065 801-446-8188
Web: pharmore.com

Piggly Wiggly 2400 J Terrell Wooten Dr . . . Bessemer AL 35020 205-481-2300
Web: www.pwadc.com

Piggly Wiggly Carolina Company Inc
PO Box 118047 . . . Charleston SC 29423 843-554-9880 745-2730
TF: 800-243-9880 ■ *Web:* thepig.net

Pittsville Pdq Inc 549 NW SR- 131 . . . Holden MO 64040 816-850-6915
Web: shell.com

Power Buying Dealers Exxonmobil Convenience Stores
2459 W 208th St Ste 100 . . . Torrance CA 90501 310-212-9999
Web: www.vitalife.com

Pure Express Mart 4002 Knight Arnold Rd. . . . Memphis TN 38118 901-794-3100

Purity Wholesale Grocers Inc
5400 Broken Sound Blvd NW. . . . Boca Raton FL 33487 561-994-9360
TF: 800-323-6838 ■ *Web:* www.pwg-inc.com

Red Lodge Beverages 7 Pepsi Dr . . . Red Lodge MT 59068 406-446-2040

Riba Foods Inc 3735 Arc St. . . . Houston TX 77063 713-975-7001 975-7036
Web: www.ribafoods.com

				Phone	Fax
Ricker Oil Company Inc 30 W 11th St. Web: rickersrewards.com	Anderson	IN	46016	765-643-3016	
Rigsby Food Mart 5602 Us Hwy 87 E. Web: texaco.com	San Antonio	TX	78222	210-648-0093	
Rishi Tea LLC 185 S 33rd Ct. TF: 866-747-4483 ■ Web: rishi-tea.com	Milwaukee	WI	53208	414-747-4001	
Ritt-beyer & Weir Inc 9900 S Franklin Dr. Web: www.rbwinc.com	Franklin	WI	53132	414-421-9505	
RL Jordan Oil Co 1451 Fernwood Glendale Rd. Web: www.hotspotcstore.com	Spartanburg	SC	29307	864-585-2784	
Roman Meal Company Inc 2101 S Tacoma Way. Web: www.romanmeal.com	Tacoma	WA	98411	253-475-0964	
Rutan Poly Industries Inc 39 Siding Pl. TF: 800-872-1474 ■ Web: www.rutanpoly.com	Mahwah	NJ	07430	201-529-1474	
S Abraham & Sons Inc PO Box 1768. TF General: 866-248-3163 ■ Web: www.sasinc.com	Grand Rapids	MI	49501	616-453-6358	453-9259
Sac n Pac 1405 United Dr. Web: www.sacnpac.com	San Marcos	TX	78666	512-392-6484	
Safeway Foods Inc MS 10501 PO Box 29093. Web: safeway.com	Phoenix	AZ	85038	317-547-8528	
Sahadi Fine Foods Inc 4215 First Ave. Web: www.sahadifinefoods.com	Brooklyn	NY	11232	718-369-0100	
Sams Discount Food Mart 5703 Timuquana Rd.	Jacksonville	FL	32210	904-573-8899	
Santini Foods Inc 16505 Worthley Dr. Web: www.santinifoods.com	San Lorenzo	CA	94580	510-317-8888	
Satin Fine Foods Inc 32 Leone Ln Ste 1. Web: satinice.com	Chester	NY	10918	845-469-1034	
Saver Systems Inc PO Box 1058. Web: www.savergroup.com	Campbellsville	KY	42719	270-465-8675	
Schiff's Restaurant Service Inc 3410 N Main Ave. Web: www.myschiffs.com	Scranton	PA	18508	570-343-1294	969-6255
Schuette Stores Inc 17919 Saint Rose Rd. Web: www.onlinegrocer.com	Breese	IL	62230	618-526-7203	
Shah Distributors Inc 540 Patrice Pl. Web: shahdistributors.com	Gardena	CA	90248	310-719-1011	
Shaheen Bros Inc PO Box 897. Web: www.shaheenbros.com	Amesbury	MA	01913	978-388-6776	388-6617
Shamrock Foods 3900 E Camelback Rd Ste 300. TF: 800-289-3663 ■ Web: www.shamrockfoods.com	Phoenix	AZ	85018	602-477-2500	
Shanks Extracts Inc 350 Richardson Dr. TF: 800-346-3135 ■ Web: www.shanks.com	Lancaster	PA	17603	717-393-4441	
Soderholm Wholesale Foods 1100 Wilburn Rd.	Sun Prairie	WI	53590	608-834-9850	
Southco Distributing Co 2201 S John St. TF: 800-969-3172 ■ Web: www.southcodistributing.com	Goldsboro	NC	27530	919-735-8012	735-0097
Spartan Stores Inc 850 76th St SW PO Box 8700. NASDAQ: SPTN ■ Web: spartannash.com	Grand Rapids	MI	49518	616-878-2000	
Specialty Brands Of America Inc 1400 Old Country Rd. TF: 877-795-3599 ■ Web: bgfoods.com	Westbury	NY	11590	516-997-6969	
Speedee Mart Inc 3670 Paradise Rd.	Las Vegas	NV	89169	702-733-7950	
St. Clair Foods Inc 3100 Bellbrook Dr. Web: www.stclair.com	Memphis	TN	38116	901-396-8680	
St. Joe Petroleum Co 2520 S Second St. Web: www.stjoepetroleum.com	Saint Joseph	MO	64501	816-279-0770	
Star Market Inc 702 Pratt Ave NW. Web: www.huntsvillestarmarket.com	Huntsville	AL	35801	256-534-4509	
Steins Thriftway Foods Inc 135 Central Ave N.	Watkins	MN	55389	320-764-2980	
Sukhi's Gourmet Indian Foods 23682 Clawiter Rd. Web: sukhis.com	Hayward	CA	94545	510-264-9265	
Sunny Morning 5330 NW 35th Ave. Web: www.sunnymorning.com	Fort Lauderdale	FL	33309	954-735-3447	
Sunshine Foods Partners 1115 Main St. Web: www.sunshinefoodstores.com	Saint Helena	CA	94574	707-963-7070	
Super Store Industries 16888 McKinley Ave PO Box 549. TF: 888-292-8004 ■ Web: ssica.com	Lathrop	CA	95330	209-858-2010	
SUPERVALU Inc 7075 Flying Cloud Dr. NYSE: SVU ■ TF Cust Svc: 877-322-8228 ■ Web: www.supervalu.com	Eden Prairie	MN	55344	952-828-4000	
SUPERVALU International 495 E 19th St. Web: www.supervaluinternational.com	Tacoma	WA	98421	253-593-3198	
SYGMA Network Inc 5550 Blazer Pkwy Ste 300. *Fax Area Code: 614 ■ TF: 877-441-1144 ■ Web: www.sygmanetwork.com	Dublin	OH	43017	877-441-1144	734-2550*
Sysco Central Ohio Inc 2400 Harrison Rd. *Fax Area Code: 907 ■ TF: 800-735-3341 ■ Web: sysco.com	Columbus	OH	43204	614-272-0655	565-5627*
SYSCO Corp 1390 Enclave Pkwy. NYSE: SYY ■ Web: www.sysco.com	Houston	TX	77077	281-584-1390	
Sysco Denver Inc 5000 Beeler St. TF: 800-366-6696 ■ Web: www.syscodenver.com	Denver	CO	80238	303-585-2000	
Sysco Food Services of Idaho Inc 5710 Pan Am Ave. TF: 800-747-9726 ■ Web: www.syscoidaho.com	Boise	ID	83716	208-345-9500	387-2598
Sysco Grand Rapids 3700 Sysco Ct SE. TF: 800-669-6967 ■ Web: www.syscogr.com	Grand Rapids	MI	49512	616-949-3700	977-4510
Sysco Hampton Roads Inc 7000 Harbour View Blvd. TF: 800-234-2451 ■ Web: www.sysco.com	Suffolk	VA	23435	757-673-4000	673-4148
Tarrier Foods Corp 3915 Zane Trace Dr. Web: www.tarrierfoods.com	Columbus	OH	43228	614-876-8595	
Taste Maker Foods LLC 1415 E Mclemore Ave # 1425. Web: www.tomlinsonassociates.com	Memphis	TN	38106	901-274-4407	
Thomas & Howard Wholesale Grocers Inc 209 Flintlake Rd PO Box 23659.	Columbia	SC	29223	803-788-5520	699-9097
Thoms Proestler Co 8001 TPC Rd. TF: 800-747-1234 ■ Web: www.performancefoodservice.com	Rock Island	IL	61204	309-787-1234	787-1254
Thor Inc 1280 W 2550 S St. Web: www.thor.com	Ogden	UT	84401	801-393-3312	621-3298
Tom Cat Bakery Inc 43-05 Tenth St. Web: www.tomcatbakery.com	Long Island	NY	11101	718-786-7659	
Tony's Meats & Specialty Foods 874 W Happy Canyon Rd. Web: tonysmarket.com	Castle Rock	CO	80108	303-814-3888	
Topco Assoc LLC 7711 Gross Pt Rd. TF: 888-423-0139 ■ Web: www.topco.com	Skokie	IL	60077	847-676-3030	676-4949
Tower Isles Frozen Foods Ltd 2025 Atlantic Ave. Web: www.towerislespatties.com	Brooklyn	NY	11233	718-495-2626	
Treatt USA Inc 4900 Lakeland Commerce Pkwy. Web: www.treattusa.com	Lakeland	FL	33805	863-668-9500	
Tri Venture Mktg Inc 2525 Drane Field Rd Ste 1.	Lakeland	FL	33811	863-648-1881	
Tri-Cities Beverage Corp 612 Industrial Park Dr. Web: tricitiesbeverage.com	Newport News	VA	23608	757-874-6600	
Tripifoods Inc 1427 William St. Web: www.tripifoods.com	Buffalo	NY	14206	716-853-7400	852-7400
Truco Enterprises LP 10515 King William Dr. Web: ontheborderproducts.com	Dallas	TX	75367	972-869-4600	869-8050
Uncle Giuseppe's of Smithtown 95 Rt 111. Web: www.uncleg.com	Smithtown	NY	11787	631-863-0900	
UNFI Specialty Distribution Services 88 Huntoon Memorial Hwy. Web: unfi.com	Leicester	MA	01524	508-892-8171	892-4827
Unified Grocers Inc 5200 Sheila St. TF: 800-724-7762 ■ Web: www.unifiedgrocers.com	Commerce	CA	90040	323-264-5200	729-6610
UniPro Foodservice Inc 2500 Cumberland Pkwy Ste 600. Web: www.uniprofoodservice.com	Atlanta	GA	30339	770-952-0871	
United Natural Foods Inc (UNFI) 313 Iron Horse Way. NASDAQ: UNFI ■ Web: www.unfi.com	Providence	RI	02908	401-528-8634	
Valley Fine Foods Company Inc 3909 Park Rd Ste H. Web: www.cafferata.com	Benicia	CA	94510	707-746-6888	
Valley Natural Foods 13750 County Rd 11. Web: www.valleynaturalfoods.com	Burnsville	MN	55337	952-891-1212	
Vantage General Store 551 Main St.	Vantage	WA	98950	509-856-2803	
Vend Mart Inc 1950 Williams St. Web: www.vendmart.com	San Leandro	CA	94577	510-297-5132	352-8363
Venda Ravioli Inc 265 Atwells Ave. Web: www.vendaravioli.com	Providence	RI	02903	401-421-9105	
Vistar/VSA Corp 12650 E Arapahoe Rd. TF: 800-880-9900 ■ Web: www.vistar.com	Centennial	CO	80112	303-662-7100	662-7565
W L Halsey Grocery Company Inc PO Box 6485. TF: 800-621-0240 ■ Web: www.halseyfoodservice.com	Huntsville	AL	35824	256-772-9691	461-8386
Wakefern Food Corp 600 York St. TF: 800-746-7748 ■ Web: www.shoprite.com	Elizabeth	NJ	07207	908-527-3300	
Wellington Foods Inc 1930 California Ave. Web: www.wellingtonfoods.com	Corona	CA	92881	951-547-7000	
White Rose Inc 380 Middlesex Ave. Web: www.whiterose.com	Carteret	NJ	07008	732-541-5555	541-3730
Williamson Street Grocery Company Op 1221 Williamson St. Web: www.willystreet.coop	Madison	WI	53703	608-251-0884	
Wind River Petroleum Inc 2046 E Murray Holladay Rd Ste 200.	Salt Lake City	UT	84117	801-272-9229	
Wing's Food Products 50 Torlake Cres. Web: www.wings.ca	Toronto	ON	M8Z1B8	416-259-2662	259-3414
Winkler Inc 535 E Medcalf St. TF: 800-621-3843 ■ Web: www.winklerinc.com	Dale	IN	47523	812-937-4421	937-2044
Woeber Mustard Mfg Company Inc 1966 Commerce Cir PO Box 388. Web: www.woebermustard.com	Springfield	OH	45501	937-323-6281	
Wood-Fruitticher Grocery Company Inc 2900 Alton Rd. TF: 800-328-0026 ■ Web: www.woodfruitticher.com	Birmingham	AL	35210	205-836-9663	836-9681
Woolco Foods Inc 135 Amity St. Web: woolcofoods.net	Jersey City	NJ	07304	201-716-2700	
World Nutrition Inc 9449 N 90th St Ste 116. Web: www.bodylabs.net	Scottsdale	AZ	85258	480-921-1188	
Wynn Starr Foods of Kentucky Inc 4820 Allmond Ave.	Louisville	KY	40214	502-368-6345	
Zausner Foods Corp 400 S Custer Ave.	New Holland	PA	17557	717-355-8505	

297-9 Meats & Meat Products - Whol

				Phone	Fax
Allied Specialty Foods Inc 313 Hickory Pl. Web: www.alliedsteaks.com	Vineland	NJ	08360	856-507-1100	
Amigos Meat Distributors-East LP 611 Crosstimber. Web: www.amigosfoods.biz	Houston	TX	77022	713-928-3111	
Aurora Packing Company Inc 125 S Grant St. Web: aurorabeef.com	North Aurora	IL	60542	630-897-0551	897-0647
Ava Pork Products Inc 383 W John St Hicksville. Web: www.avapork.com	Hicksville	NY	11802	516-750-1500	750-1501
Bruss Co 3548 N Kostner Ave. TF: 800-621-3882 ■ Web: bruss.com	Chicago	IL	60641	773-282-2900	282-6966
Buckhead Beef of Florida 355 Progress Rd. Web: buckheadbeef.com	Auburndale	FL	33823	863-508-1050	
Calumet Diversified Meats Inc 10000 80th Ave. TF: 800-752-7427 ■ Web: www.porkchops.com	Pleasant Prairie	WI	53158	262-947-7200	947-7209
Cambridge Packing Co Inc 41-43 Foodmart Rd. *Fax Area Code: 800 ■ TF: 800-722-6726 ■ Web: www.cambridgepacking.com	Boston	MA	02118	617-269-6700	889-9898*

Phone | Fax

Cardinal Meat Specialists Ltd
155 Hedgedale Rd .... Brampton ON L6T5P3 905-459-4436
TF: 800-363-1439 ■ Web: www.cardinalmeats.com
Cell Response Formulation LLC 4115 S Pub Pl. .... Jackson WY 83002 307-734-7839
TF: 888-364-7839 ■ Web: www.mulliganstewpetfood.com
Colorado Boxed Beef Co 302 Progress Rd .... Auburndale FL 33823 863-967-0636
Web: www.coloradoboxedbeef.com
ConAgra Foods Foodservice Co 5 ConAgra Dr .... Omaha NE 68102 800-357-6543
TF: 800-357-6543 ■ Web: www.conagrafoodservice.com
Cusack Wholesale Meat Inc
301 SW 12th St .... Oklahoma City OK 73109 405-232-2114 232-2127
TF: 800-241-6328 ■ Web: www.cusackmeats.com
Cypress Food Distributors Inc
3111 N University Dr Ste 612 .... Coral Springs FL 33065 954-344-2900 344-3607
Web: www.cypressfood.com
Dairyland Corp 1300 Viele Ave .... Bronx NY 10474 718-842-8700 378-2234
Day-Lee Foods Inc 13055 Molette St .... Santa Fe Springs CA 90670 562-903-3020
Web: www.day-lee.com
Deen Meats PO Box 4155 PO Box 4155 .... Fort Worth TX 76164 817-335-2257 338-9256
TF: 800-333-3953 ■ Web: www.deenmeat.com
Ditta Meat Co PO Box 5623 .... Pasadena TX 77508 281-487-2010
Web: www.dittameat.com
Flanders Provision Company LLC
1104 Gilmore St .... Waycross GA 31501 912-283-5191
Web: www.flandersprovision.com
Freshwater Fish Mktg Corp 1199 Plessis Rd .... Winnipeg MB R2C3L4 204-983-6601
Web: www.freshwaterfish.com
Green Tree Packing Co 65 Central Ave .... Passaic NJ 07055 973-473-1305 473-7975
Web: www.greentreepacking.com
Heartland Meat Company Inc 3461 Main St .... Chula Vista CA 91911 619-407-3668 407-3678
TF: 888-407-3668 ■ Web: www.heartlandmeat.com
Jensen Meat Company Inc 2525 Birch St. .... Vista CA 92081 760-727-6700 727-8598
Web: www.jensenmeat.com
Keystone Foods LLC
300 Bar Harbor Dr
Ste 600 5 Tower Bridge .... West Conshohocken PA 19428 610-668-6700
Web: www.keystonefoods.com
Manda Fine Meats 2445 Sorrel Ave. .... Baton Rouge LA 70802 225-344-7636 344-7647
TF: 800-343-2642 ■ Web: www.mandafinemeats.com
Michael's Finer Meats & Seafoods
3775 Zane Trace Dr .... Columbus OH 43228 614-527-4900 527-4520
TF: 800-282-0518 ■ Web: www.michaelsmeats.com
Midamar Corp PO Box 218 .... Cedar Rapids IA 52406 319-362-3711 362-4111
TF: 800-362-3711 ■ Web: www.midamar.com
Northwestern Meat Inc 2100 NW 23rd St. .... Miami FL 33142 305-633-8112 633-6907
Web: www.numeat.com
Orrell's Food Service 9827 S NC Hwy 150 .... Linwood NC 27299 336-752-2114 752-2060
Web: www.orrellsfoodservice.com
Paper Pak Industries (PPI) 1941 N White Ave .... La Verne CA 91750 909-392-1750 392-1760
TF: 888-293-6529 ■ Web: www.paperpakindustries.com
Porky Products Corp 400 Port Carteret Dr. .... Carteret NJ 07008 732-541-0200 969-6110
TF General: 800-952-0265
Pucci Foods 25447 Industrial Blvd .... Hayward CA 94545 510-300-6800
Web: www.puccifoods.com
Quality Meats & Seafoods 700 Ctr St. .... West Fargo ND 58078 701-282-0202
TF: 800-342-4250 ■ Web: www.qualitymeats.com
Quirch Foods Co 7600 NW 82nd Pl .... Miami FL 33166 305-691-3535 593-0272
TF: 800-458-5252 ■ Web: www.quirchfoods.com
Sampco Inc 651 W Washington Blvd Ste 300 .... Chicago IL 60661 312-346-1506 346-8302
TF: 800-767-0689 ■ Web: www.sampcoinc.com
Southern Foods Inc
3500 Old Battleground Rd .... Greensboro NC 27410 336-545-3800 545-5281
Web: www.southernfoods.com
Tapia Bros Co 6067 District Blvd. .... Maywood CA 90270 323-560-7415 560-8924
Web: www.tapiabrothers.com
Thumann Inc 670 Dell Rd .... Carlstadt NJ 07072 201-935-3636 935-2226
Web: www.thumanns.com
Trim-Rite Food Corp
801 Commerce Pkwy .... Carpentersville IL 60110 847-649-3400 649-3420
TF: 800-626-9442 ■ Web: www.trim-rite.com
Troyer Foods Inc 17141 State Rd 4 .... Goshen IN 46528 574-533-0302 533-3851
TF: 800-876-9377 ■ Web: www.troyers.com
U W Provision Company Inc PO Box 620038 .... Middleton WI 53562 608-836-7421 836-6328
TF: 800-832-0517 ■ Web: www.uwprovision.com
Williams Sausage Company Inc
5132 Old Troy Hickman Rd. .... Union City TN 38261 731-885-5841 885-5884
TF: 866-626-4282 ■ Web: www.williams-sausage.com

297-10 Poultry, Eggs, Poultry Products - Whol

Phone | Fax

Acme Farms Inc 1024 S King St .... Seattle WA 98104 206-323-4300
Butts Foods Inc 2596 Bransford Ave. .... Nashville TN 37204 731-423-3456 423-4566
TF: 800-962-8570 ■ Web: www.buttsfoods.com
Chino Valley Ranchers 5611 Peck Rd .... Arcadia CA 91006 800-354-4503
TF: 800-354-4503 ■ Web: www.chinovalleyranchers.com
Dutt & Wagner of Virginia Inc
1142 W Main St .... Abingdon VA 24210 276-628-2116 628-4619
TF: 800-688-2116 ■ Web: duttandwagner.com
Harker's Distribution Inc 801 Sixth St SW .... Le Mars IA 51031 712-546-8171
Web: lemarssentinel.com
Hemmelgarn & Sons Inc 3763 Philothea Rd .... Coldwater OH 45828 419-678-2351 678-4922
House of Raeford Farms Inc 520 E Central Ave .... Raeford NC 28376 910-875-5161
TF: 800-888-7539 ■ Web: www.houseofraeford.com
Metropolitan Poultry & Seafood Co
1920 Stanford Ct .... Landover MD 20785 301-772-0060 772-1013
TF: 800-522-0060 ■ Web: www.metropoultry.com
Norbest Inc PO Box 890. .... Moroni UT 84646 800-453-5327 597-5416*
*Fax Area Code: 888 ■ TF: 800-453-5327 ■ Web: www.norbest.com
Nulaid Foods Inc 200 W Fifth St .... Ripon CA 95366 209-599-2121 599-5220
Web: www.nulaid.com

Phone | Fax

Quirch Foods Co 7600 NW 82nd Pl .... Miami FL 33166 305-691-3535 593-0272
TF: 800-458-5252 ■ Web: www.quirchfoods.com
RW Sauder Inc 570 Furnace Hills Pk. .... Lititz PA 17543 717-626-2074 626-0493
Web: www.saudereggs.com
Troyer Foods Inc 17141 State Rd 4 .... Goshen IN 46528 574-533-0302 533-3851
TF: 800-876-9377 ■ Web: www.troyers.com
Zacky Farms
13200 Crossroads Pkwy N Ste 250 .... City of Industry CA 91746 562-641-2020 641-2040
TF: 800-888-0235 ■ Web: www.zacky.com

297-11 Specialty Foods - Whol

Phone | Fax

Camerican International Inc 45 Eisenhower Dr. .... Paramus NJ 07652 201-587-0101 587-2040*
*Fax: Hum Res ■ Web: camerican.com
Charles C. Parks Co 500 Belvedere Dr. .... Gallatin TN 37066 615-452-2406 451-4212
TF: 800-873-2406 ■ Web: www.charlescparks.com
ConAgra Foods Foodservice Co 5 ConAgra Dr .... Omaha NE 68102 800-357-6543
TF: 800-357-6543 ■ Web: www.conagrafoodservice.com
Condal Distributors 531 Dupont St .... Bronx NY 10474 718-589-1100 589-9200
Conway Import Co Inc
11051 W Addison St. .... Franklin Park IL 60131 847-455-5600 304-4021*
*Fax Area Code: 800 ■ TF: 800-323-8801 ■ Web: conwaydressings.com
CRS Onesource 2803 Tamarack Rd PO Box 1984 .... Owensboro KY 42302 270-684-1469 685-5696
TF: 800-264-0710 ■ Web: www.crsonesource.com
Diaz Wholesale & Mfg Co Inc
5501 Fulton Industrial Blvd .... Atlanta GA 30336 404-344-5421 344-3003
Web: www.diazfoods.com
Ellis Coffee Co 2835 Bridge St .... Philadelphia PA 19137 215-537-9500 535-5311
TF: 800-822-3984 ■ Web: www.elliscoffee.com
Essex Grain Products 9 Lee Blvd. .... Frazer PA 19355 610-647-3800 647-4990
TF: 800-441-1017 ■ Web: www.essexgrain.com
Garden Spot Distributors Inc
191 Commerce Dr .... New Holland PA 17557 717-354-4936
Web: www.gardenspotdist.com
Ginsburg Bakery Inc
300 N Tennessee Ave .... Atlantic City NJ 08401 609-345-2265 345-2268
Web: www.ginsburgbakery.com
Gregory's Foods Inc 1301 Trapp Rd. .... Eagan MN 55121 651-454-0277 454-2254
Web: www.gregorysfoods.com
Hain Celestial Group Inc 4600 Sleepytime Dr. .... Boulder CO 80301 800-434-4246
NASDAQ: HAIN ■ TF: 800-434-4246 ■ Web: www.hain-celestial.com
Harlan Bakeries-Avon LLC 7597 E US Hwy 36 .... Avon IN 46123 317-272-3600 272-1110
Web: www.harlanbakeries.com
Indiana Sugars Inc 911 Virginia St. .... Gary IN 46402 219-886-9151 886-5124
Web: www.sugars.com
Industrial Commodities Inc PO Box 4380 .... Glen Allen VA 23060 800-523-7902
TF: 800-523-7902 ■ Web: www.industrialcommodities.com
J Sosnick & Sons Inc
258 Littlefield Ave. .... South San Francisco CA 94080 650-952-2226
TF: 800-223-2194 ■ Web: www.sosnick.com
JFC International Inc 7101 E Slauson Ave .... Los Angeles CA 90040 323-721-6100 721-6133
Web: www.jfc.com
Joffrey's Coffee & Tea Co 3803 Corporex Pk Dr .... Tampa FL 33619 813-250-0404
TF: 800-458-5282 ■ Web: www.joffreys.com
John E Koerner & Company Inc
4820 Jefferson Hwy .... New Orleans LA 70121 800-333-1913 734-0630*
*Fax Area Code: 504 ■ TF: 800-333-1913 ■ Web: www.koerner-co.com
King Milling Co 115 S Broadway St .... Lowell MI 49331 616-897-9264 897-4350
Web: www.kingmilling.com
Lecoq Cuisine Corp 35 Union Ave .... Bridgeport CT 06607 203-334-1010 334-1800
Web: www.lecoqcuisine.com
Lipari Foods LLC 26661 Bunert Rd .... Warren MI 48089 586-447-3500 447-3524
Web: liparifoods.com
Lomar Distributing 2500 Dixon St .... Des Moines IA 50316 515-244-3105 244-0515
Losurdo Foods Inc 20 Owens Rd .... Hackensack NJ 07601 201-343-6680 343-8078
Web: www.losurdofoods.com
Love & Quiches Desserts 178 Hanse Ave .... Freeport NY 11520 516-623-8800 623-8817
TF: 800-525-5251 ■ Web: www.loveandquiches.com
Mitsui Foods International 35 Maple St .... Norwood NJ 07648 201-750-0500 750-0150
Web: www.mitsuifoods.com
Morris J Golombeck Inc 960 Franklin Ave .... Brooklyn NY 11225 718-284-3505 693-1941
Web: www.golombeckspice.com
Mutual Trading Company Ltd
431 Crocker St .... Los Angeles CA 90013 213-626-9458 626-5130
Web: www.lamtc.com
Nantze Springs Inc 156 W Carroll St .... Dothan AL 36301 334-794-4218
Web: www.nantzesprings.com
Neiman Bros Company Inc 3322 W Newport Ave .... Chicago IL 60618 773-463-3000 463-3181
Web: www.neimanbrothers.com
O S F Flavors Inc 40 Baker Hollow Rd. .... Windsor CT 06095 860-298-8350 298-8363
TF: 800-466-6015 ■ Web: www.osfflavors.com
Otis McAllister Inc 160 Pine St Ste 350. .... San Francisco CA 94111 415-421-6010 421-6016
Web: www.otismac.com
Otto Brehm Inc PO Box 249 .... Yonkers NY 10710 914-968-6100 968-8926
TF: 800-272-6886 ■ Web: www.ottobrehm.com
Producers Rice Mill Inc PO Box 1248 .... Stuttgart AR 72160 870-673-4444
TF: 800-369-7675 ■ Web: www.producersrice.com
Rain Creek Baking Co, The 2401 W Almond Ave. .... Madera CA 93637 559-674-4445 674-4466
TF: 800-530-0505 ■ Web: www.raincreekbaking.com
ReNew Life Formulas Inc
2076 Sunnydale Blvd .... Clearwater FL 33765 727-450-1061 594-5468*
*Fax Area Code: 866 ■ TF: 800-830-1800 ■ Web: www.renewlife.com
Riceland Foods Inc PO Box 927 .... Stuttgart AR 72160 870-673-5500
Web: www.riceland.com
Ron-Son Foods Inc PO Box 38 .... Swedesboro NJ 08085 856-241-7333 241-7338
Web: www.ronsonfoods.com
Roxy Trading Inc 389 Humane Way .... Pomona CA 91768 626-610-1388 610-1339
Web: www.roxytrading.com
Royal Pacific Tea Company Inc, The
PO Box 6277 .... Scottsdale AZ 85261 480-951-8251 951-0092
Web: www.royalpacificintl.com

				Phone	Fax
Schreiber Foods International Inc 600 E Crescent Ave Ste 103 *TF:* 800-631-7070 ■ *Web:* www.ambrosia-foods.com	Upper Saddle River	NJ	07458	201-327-3535	327-2812
Setton Pistachio of Terra Bella Inc 9370 Rd 234 PO Box 11089 *Web:* www.settonfarms.com	Terra Bella	CA	93270	559-535-6050	535-6089
Silver Springs Bottled Water Company Inc PO Box 926 **Fax Area Code:* 352 ■ *TF:* 800-556-0334 ■ *Web:* www.ssbwc.com	Silver Springs	FL	34489	800-556-0334	368-2374*
SK Food International Inc 4666 Amber Vly Pkwy *Web:* www.skfood.com	Fargo	ND	58104	701-356-4106	356-4102
Sturm Foods Inc PO Box 287 *TF:* 800-347-8876 ■ *Web:* www.sturmfoods.com	Manawa	WI	54949	920-596-2511	596-3040
Sugar Foods Corp 950 Third Ave 21st Fl *TF:* 800-732-8963 ■ *Web:* www.sugarfoods.com	New York	NY	10022	212-753-6900	753-6988
Sunsweet Growers Inc 901 N Walton Ave *TF:* 800-417-2253 ■ *Web:* www.sunsweet.com	Yuba City	CA	95993	530-674-5010	751-5238
Sysco Indianapolis LLC 4000 W 62nd St **Fax Area Code:* 877 ■ *TF:* 800-347-3920 ■ *Web:* www.syscoindy.com	Indianapolis	IN	46268	317-291-2020	717-4561*
SYSCO Philadelphia LLC 600 Packer Ave *Web:* www.syscophilly.com/ordereze/1000/Page.aspx	Philadelphia	PA	19148	215-463-8200	218-1618
T. J. Harkins Co 279 Beaudin Blvd	Bolingbrook	IL	60440	630-427-3400	783-1806
United Sugars Corp 7803 Glenroy Rd Ste 300 *TF:* 800-984-3585 ■ *Web:* www.unitedsugars.com	Bloomington	MN	55439	952-896-0131	896-0400
Westway Trading Corp 365 Canal St Ste 2929 *Web:* www.westwaytrading.com	New Orleans	LA	70130	504-581-1620	522-1638
Wildflower Bread Co 7755 E Gray Rd *Web:* www.wildflowerbread.com	Scottsdale	AZ	85260	480-951-9453	951-9464
William George Co Inc 1002 Mize Ave *Web:* www.williamgeorgeinc.com	Lufkin	TX	75904	936-634-7738	634-7794
Woodland Foods Inc 3751 Sunset Ave *Web:* www.woodlandfoods.com	Waukegan	IL	60087	847-625-8600	625-5050
Yamamoto of Orient Inc 122 Voyager St *Web:* www.yamamotoyama.com	Pomona	CA	91768	909-594-7356	595-5849

298 FOOD PRODUCTS MACHINERY

See Also Food Service Equipment & Supplies p. 2315

				Phone	Fax
Abec Inc 3998 Schelden Cir *Web:* www.abec.com	Bethlehem	PA	18017	610-861-4666	861-2636
Acme Pizza & Bakery Equipment Inc 7039 E Slauson Blvd *Web:* www.acmepbe.com	Commerce	CA	90040	323-722-7900	726-4700
Adamatic Equipment Corp 607 Industrial Way W *Web:* www.belshaw-adamatic.com	Eatontown	NJ	07724	732-544-8400	544-0735
Alto-Shaam Inc W 164 N 9221 Water St PO Box 450 *TF:* 800-329-8744 ■ *Web:* www.alto-shaam.com	Menomonee Falls	WI	53052	262-251-3800	251-7067
American Permanent Ware Inc 729 Third Ave *TF:* 800-527-2100 ■ *Web:* www.apwwyott.com	Dallas	TX	75226	214-421-7366	565-0976
Anderson International Corp 6200 Harvard Ave *TF:* 800-336-4730 ■ *Web:* www.andersonintl.net	Cleveland	OH	44105	216-641-1112	641-0709
Atlas Metal Industries 1135 NW 159th Dr *TF Cust Svc:* 800-762-7565 ■ *Web:* www.atlasfoodserv.com	Miami	FL	33169	305-625-2451	623-0475
Atlas Pacific Engineering Co 1 Atlas Ave *TF:* 800-588-5438 ■ *Web:* www.atlaspacific.com	Pueblo	CO	81001	719-948-3040	948-3058
Baader-Johnson 2955 Fairfax Trafficway *Web:* www.baader.com	Kansas City	KS	66115	913-621-3366	
Baker Perkins Inc 3223 Kraft Ave SE *Web:* bakerperkins.com	Grand Rapids	MI	49512	616-784-3111	784-0973
Belshaw Bros Inc 1750 22nd Ave S *TF:* 800-578-2547 ■ *Web:* www.belshaw-adamatic.com	Seattle	WA	98144	206-322-5474	322-5425
Bepex International LLC 333 Taft St NE *Web:* www.bepex.com	Minneapolis	MN	55413	612-331-4370	627-1444
Bettcher Industries Inc PO Box 336 *TF:* 800-321-8763 ■ *Web:* www.bettcher.com	Vermilion	OH	44089	440-965-4422	
BIRO Mfg Co 1114 W Main St *Web:* www.birosaw.com	Marblehead	OH	43440	419-798-4451	798-9106
Brewmatic Co 20333 S Normandie Ave PO Box 2959 *TF:* 800-421-6860 ■ *Web:* www.brewmatic.com	Torrance	CA	90509	310-787-5444	787-5412
C Cretors & Co 3243 N California Ave *TF:* 800-228-1885 ■ *Web:* www.cretors.com	Chicago	IL	60618	773-588-1690	588-7141
Carlisle Cos Inc 13925 Ballantyne Corporate Pl Ste 400 *NYSE: CSL* ■ *TF:* 800-248-5995 ■ *Web:* www.carlisle.com	Charlotte	NC	28277	704-501-1100	501-1190
Casa Herrerra Inc 2655 N Pine St *TF:* 800-624-3916 ■ *Web:* www.casaherrera.com	Pomona	CA	91767	909-392-3930	392-0231
CE Rogers Co 1895 Frontage Rd *TF:* 800-279-8081 ■ *Web:* www.cerogers.com	Mora	MN	55051	320-679-2172	679-2180
Chester-Jensen Company Inc PO Box 908 *TF:* 800-685-3750 ■ *Web:* www.chester-jensen.com	Chester	PA	19016	610-876-6276	876-0485
Cleveland Range Co 1333 E 179th St *TF:* 800-338-2204 ■ *Web:* www.clevelandrange.com	Cleveland	OH	44110	216-481-4900	481-3782
Colborne Corp 28495 N Ballard Dr *Web:* www.colbornefoodbotics.com	Lake Forest	IL	60045	847-371-0101	371-0101
CPM Wolverine Proctor LLC 251 Gibraltar Rd *TF:* 800-428-0846 ■ *Web:* www.cpm.net	Horsham	PA	19044	215-443-5200	443-5206
Delfield Co 980 S Isabella Rd *TF:* 800-733-8821 ■ *Web:* www.delfield.com	Mount Pleasant	MI	48858	989-773-7981	773-3210
Duke Manufacturing Co 2305 N Broadway *TF:* 800-735-3853 ■ *Web:* www.dukemfg.com	Saint Louis	MO	63102	314-231-1130	231-5074
Dunkley International Inc 1910 Lake St *TF:* 800-666-1264 ■ *Web:* www.dunkleyinternational.com	Kalamazoo	MI	49001	269-343-5583	343-5614
Dupps Co 548 N Cherry St *Web:* www.dupps.com	Germantown	OH	45327	937-855-6555	855-6554
Edlund Company Inc 159 Industrial Pkwy *TF:* 800-772-2126 ■ *Web:* www.edlundco.com	Burlington	VT	05401	802-862-9661	862-4822
Feldmeier Equipment Inc 6800 Townline Rd *TF:* 800-258-0118 ■ *Web:* www.feldmeier.com	Syracuse	NY	13211	315-454-8608	454-3701
Fish Oven & Equipment Corp 120 W Kent Ave *TF:* 877-526-8720 ■ *Web:* www.fishoven.com	Wauconda	IL	60084	847-526-8686	
Fitzpatrick Co 832 Industrial Dr *Web:* www.fitzmill.com	Elmhurst	IL	60126	630-530-3333	530-0832
Food Warming Equipment Company Inc 7900 S Rt 31 *TF Sales:* 800-222-4393 ■ *Web:* www.fwe.com	Crystal Lake	IL	60014	815-459-7500	459-7989
Frymaster LLC 8700 Line Ave *TF Cust Svc:* 800-221-4583 ■ *Web:* www.frymaster.com	Shreveport	LA	71106	318-865-1711	868-5987
Fulton Iron & Mfg LLC 3844 Walsh St *Web:* www.fultoniron.net	Saint Louis	MO	63116	314-752-2400	
Garland Commercial Industries 185 S St **Fax Area Code:* 800 ■ *TF:* 800-424-2411 ■ *Web:* www.garland-group.com	Freeland	PA	18224	570-636-1000	624-0218*
Gem Equipment of Oregon Inc PO Box 359 *Web:* www.gemequipment.com	Woodburn	OR	97071	503-982-9902	981-6316
Globe Food Equipment Co 2153 Dryden Rd *TF:* 800-347-5423 ■ *Web:* www.globefoodequip.com	Dayton	OH	45439	937-299-5493	299-8623
Great Western Mfg Co Inc 2017 S Fourth St PO Box 149 *TF:* 800-682-3121 ■ *Web:* www.gwmfg.com	Leavenworth	KS	66048	913-682-2291	682-1431
Grindmaster Crathco Systems Inc 4003 Collins Ln *TF:* 800-695-4500 ■ *Web:* www.grindmaster.com	Louisville	KY	40245	502-425-4776	425-4664
GS Blodgett Corp 44 Lakeside Ave *TF:* 800-331-5842 ■ *Web:* www.blodgett.com	Burlington	VT	05401	802-658-6600	864-0183
Hayes & Stolz Industrial Manufacturing Co 3521 Hemphill St PO Box 11217 *TF:* 800-725-7272 ■ *Web:* www.hayes-stolz.com	Fort Worth	TX	76110	817-926-3391	926-4133
Heat & Control Inc 21121 Cabot Blvd *TF:* 800-227-5980 ■ *Web:* www.heatandcontrol.com	Hayward	CA	94545	510-259-0500	259-0600
Henny Penny Corp 1219 US 35 W PO Box 60 **Fax Area Code:* 800 ■ *TF:* 800-417-8417 ■ *Web:* www.hennypenny.com	Eaton	OH	45320	937-456-8400	417-8402*
Hobart Corp 701 S Ridge Ave *TF Cust Svc:* 800-333-7447 ■ *Web:* www.hobartcorp.com	Troy	OH	45374	937-332-3000	332-2852
Hollymatic Corp 600 E Plainfield Rd *Web:* www.hollymatic.com	Countryside	IL	60525	708-579-3700	579-1057
Horix Manufacturing Co 1384 Island Ave	McKees Rocks	PA	15136	412-771-1111	331-8599
Idaho Steel Products Co 255 E Anderson St *Web:* www.idahosteel.com	Idaho Falls	ID	83401	208-522-1275	522-6041
Insinger Machine Co 6245 State Rd *Web:* insingermachine.com	Philadelphia	PA	19135	215-624-4800	624-6966
ITW Food Equipment Group 701 S Ridge Ave *Web:* www.hobartcorp.com	Troy	OH	45374	937-332-3000	332-2852
Jarvis Products Corp 33 Anderson Rd *Web:* www.jarvisproducts.com	Middletown	CT	06457	860-347-7271	347-6978
Key Technology Inc 150 Avery St *NASDAQ: KTEC* ■ *TF:* 877-341-5668 ■ *Web:* www.key.net	Walla Walla	WA	99362	509-529-2161	527-1331
Kuhl Corp 39 Kuhl Rd PO Box 26 *Web:* www.kuhlcorp.com	Flemington	NJ	08822	908-782-5696	782-2751
Kwik Lok Corp 2712 S 16th Ave PO Box 9548 *TF:* 800-688-5945 ■ *Web:* www.kwiklok.com	Yakima	WA	98909	509-248-4770	457-6531
Lawrence Equipment Inc 2034 Peck Rd *TF:* 800-423-4500 ■ *Web:* www.lawrenceequipment.com	El Monte	CA	91733	626-442-2894	350-5181
Lewis M Carter Mfg Co PO Box 428 *TF:* 800-332-8232 ■ *Web:* www.lmcarter.com	Donalsonville	GA	39845	229-524-2197	524-2531
LK Industries 1357 W Beaver St *TF:* 800-531-4975 ■ *Web:* www.loadking.com	Jacksonville	FL	32209	904-354-8882	
Lucks Co, The 3003 S Pine St **Fax:* Orders ■ *TF:* 800-426-9778 ■ *Web:* www.lucks.com	Tacoma	WA	98409	253-383-4815	383-0071*
Luthi Machinery Co Inc 1 Atlas Ave *Web:* www.luthi.com	Pueblo	CO	81001	719-948-1110	948-4273
M-E-C Co 1400 W Main St *Web:* www.m-e-c.com	Neodesha	KS	66757	620-325-2673	325-2678
Manitowoc Beverage Equipment 2100 Future Dr *TF:* 800-367-4233 ■ *Web:* www.manitowocbeverage.com	Sellersburg	IN	47172	812-246-7000	246-9922
Manitowoc Company Inc 2400 S 44th St *NYSE: MTW* ■ *Web:* www.manitowoc.com	Manitowoc	WI	54220	920-684-4410	
Market Forge Industries Inc 35 Garvey St **Fax Area Code:* 800 ■ *TF:* 866-698-3188 ■ *Web:* www.mfii.com	Everett	MA	02149	617-387-4100	227-2659*
Marlen International Inc 4780 NW 41st St Ste 100 **Fax Area Code:* 913 ■ *TF:* 800-862-7536 ■ *Web:* www.marlen.com	Riverside	MO	64150	800-862-7536	888-6440*
Merco-Savory Inc 1111 N Hadley Rd *TF Cust Svc:* 800-547-2513 ■ *Web:* www.mercoproducts.com	Fort Wayne	IN	46804	260-459-8200	436-0735
Meyer Machine Company Inc 3528 Fredericksburg Rd PO Box 5460 *Web:* www.meyer-industries.com	San Antonio	TX	78201	210-736-1811	
Microfluidics International Corp 90 Glacier Dr Ste 1000 *TF:* 800-370-5452 ■ *Web:* www.microfluidicscorp.com	Westwood	MA	02090	617-969-5452	965-1213
Middleby Corp 1400 Toastmaster Dr *NASDAQ: MIDD* ■ *TF:* 800-331-5842 ■ *Web:* www.middleby.com	Elgin	IL	60120	847-741-3300	741-0015
Myers Engineering Inc 8376 Salt Lk Ave *Web:* www.myersmixer.com	Bell	CA	90201	323-560-4723	771-7789
Nitta Casings Inc 141 Southside Ave *TF Cust Svc:* 800-526-3970 ■ *Web:* www.nittacasings.com	Bridgewater	NJ	08807	908-218-4400	725-2835
Oliver Products Co 445 Sixth St NW *TF:* 800-253-3893 ■ *Web:* www.oliverproducts.com	Grand Rapids	MI	49504	616-456-7711	456-5820
Peerless Food Equipment 500 S Vandemark Rd *TF:* 800-999-3327 ■ *Web:* www.peerlessfood.com	Sidney	OH	45365	937-492-4158	492-3688
Peerless Machinery Corp 500 S Vandemark Rd PO Box 769 *TF:* 877-795-7377 ■ *Web:* www.peerlessfood.com	Sidney	OH	45365	937-492-4158	492-3688
Philadelphia Mixing Solutions, Ltd 1221 E Main St *Web:* www.philamixers.com	Palmyra	PA	17078	717-832-2800	832-1740

Phone | Fax

Piper Products Inc 300 S 84th Ave .... Wausau WI 54401 715-842-2724 842-3125
TF: 800-544-3057 ■ *Web:* www.piperonline.net

Pitco Frialator Inc PO Box 501 .... Concord NH 03302 603-225-6684 225-8472
TF: 800-258-3708 ■ *Web:* pitco.com

Planet Products Corp 4200 Malsbary Rd .... Cincinnati OH 45242 513-984-5544 984-5580
Web: www.planet-products.com

Prince Castle Inc 355 E Kehoe Blvd.............. Carol Stream IL 60188 630-462-8800 462-1460
TF: 800-722-7853 ■ *Web:* www.princecastle.com

Resina West Inc 27455 Bostik Ct.................. Temecula CA 92590 951-296-6585 296-5018
Web: www.resina.com

RMF Steel Products Co 4417 E 119th St............ Grandview MO 64030 816-765-4101 765-0067
Web: rmfworks.com

Ross Industries Inc 5321 Midland Rd .... Midland VA 22728 540-439-3271 439-2740
TF: 800-336-6010 ■ *Web:* www.rossindinc.com

S Howes Company Inc 25 Howard St............. Silver Creek NY 14136 716-934-2611
TF: 888-255-2611 ■ *Web:* www.showes.com

SaniServ Inc 451 E County Line Rd................ Mooresville IN 46158 317-831-7030 831-7036
TF: 800-733-8073 ■ *Web:* www.saniserv.com

Schlueter Co 310 N Main St .... Janesville WI 53545 608-755-5444 755-5440
TF: 800-359-1700 ■ *Web:* www.schlueterco.com

Server Products Inc
3601 Pleasant Hill Rd PO Box 98 .... Richfield WI 53076 262-628-5600 628-5110
TF: 800-558-8722 ■ *Web:* www.server-products.com

Sonic Corp 1 Research Dr.......................... Stratford CT 06615 203-375-0063 378-4079
TF: 866-493-1378 ■ *Web:* www.sonicmixing.com

Southbend Inc 1100 Old Honeycutt Rd .... Fuquay Varina NC 27526 919-762-1000 762-1121
TF: 800-755-4777 ■ *Web:* www.southbendnc.com

Stoelting LLC 502 Hwy 67 .... Kiel WI 53042 920-894-2293 894-7029
TF: 800-558-5807 ■ *Web:* www.stoelting.com

Stolle Machinery Co LLC 6949 S Potomac St........ Centennial CO 80112 303-708-9044 708-9045
Web: www.stollemachinery.com

Taylor 750 N Blackhawk Blvd .... Rockton IL 61072 815-624-8333 624-8000
TF: 800-255-0626 ■ *Web:* www.taylor-company.com

Tomlinson Industries 13700 Broadway Ave........... Cleveland OH 44125 216-587-3400 939-7598*
**Fax Area Code:* 604 ■ *Web:* www.tomlinsonind.com

Town Food Service Equipment Co 72 Beadel St....... Brooklyn NY 11222 718-388-5650 388-5860
TF: 800-221-5032 ■ *Web:* www.townfood.com

Ultrafryer Systems Inc 302 Spencer Ln............ San Antonio TX 78201 210-731-5000 731-5099
Web: www.ultrafryer.com

Union Standard Equipment Co 801 E 141st St........... Bronx NY 10454 718-585-0200 993-2650
TF: 877-282-7333 ■ *Web:* www.unionmachinery.com

United Bakery Equipment Co Inc
15815 W 110th St.................................. Lenexa KS 66219 913-541-8700 541-0781
TF: 888-823-2253 ■ *Web:* www.ubeusa.com

Univex Corp 3 Old Rockingham Rd .... Salem NH 03079 603-893-6191 893-1249
TF: 800-258-6358 ■ *Web:* www.univexcorp.com

Urschel Laboratories Inc
2503 Calumet Ave PO Box 2200.................... Valparaiso IN 46384 219-464-4811 462-3879
TF: 844-877-2435 ■ *Web:* www.urschel.com

Van Doren Sales Inc 10 NE Cascade Ave........... East Wenatchee WA 98802 509-886-1837 886-2837
TF: 866-886-1837 ■ *Web:* www.vandorensales.com

Vendome Copper & Brass Works Inc
729 Franklin St.................................... Louisville KY 40202 502-587-1930 589-0639
Web: www.vendomecopper.com

Viking Range Corp 111 Front St.................. Greenwood MS 38930 662-455-1200 455-3127
TF: 888-845-4641 ■ *Web:* www.vikingrange.com

Volckening Inc 6700 Third Ave..................... Brooklyn NY 11220 718-836-4000 748-2811
Web: www.volckening.com

Walker Stainless Equipment Co LLC
625 W State St .... New Lisbon WI 53950 608-562-7500

Wells Bloomfield Industries 10 Sunnen Dr .... Saint Louis MO 63143 888-356-5362 264-6666*
**Fax Area Code:* 800 ■ *TF:* 888-356-5362 ■ *Web:* www.wellsbloomfield.com

Wenger Manufacturing Inc 714 Main St .... Sabetha KS 66534 785-284-2133 284-3771
Web: www.wenger.com

Wilbur Curtis Company Inc 6913 Acco St........... Montebello CA 90640 323-837-2300 837-2406
TF: 800-421-6150 ■ *Web:* www.wilburcurtis.com

Winston Industries LLC 2345 Carton Dr .... Louisville KY 40299 502-495-5400 495-5458
TF: 800-234-5286 ■ *Web:* www.winstonind.com

Witte Company Inc 507 Rt 31 S PO Box 47.......... Washington NJ 07882 908-689-6500 537-6806
Web: www.witte.com

299 FOOD SERVICE

See Also Restaurant Companies p. 3078

Phone | Fax

A'viands LLC 1751 County Rd B W Ste 300............ Roseville MN 55113 651-631-0940
TF: 888-872-3788 ■ *Web:* www.aviands.com

Advance Food Company Inc
9987 Carver Rd Ste 500 .... Cincinnati OH 45242 800-969-2747
TF: 800-969-2747 ■ *Web:* www.advancepierre.com

Aircraft Service International Group
201 S Orange Ave Ste 1100 .... Orlando FL 32801 407-648-7373 206-5391
Web: www.asig.com

American Food & Vending Corp
124 Metropolitan Pk Dr .... Syracuse NY 13088 315-457-9950 457-9103
TF: 800-466-9261 ■ *Web:* www.afvusa.com

Bon Appetit Management Co
100 Hamilton Ave Ste 400 .... Palo Alto CA 94301 650-798-8000 798-8090
Web: www.bamco.com

Bran-Zan Holdings Inc
1548 Barclay Blvd............................ Buffalo Grove IL 60089 866-266-9670
TF: 866-266-9670 ■ *Web:* www.branzan.com

Canteen Service Co 712 Industrial Dr .... Owensboro KY 42301 270-683-2471
TF: 800-467-2471 ■ *Web:* www.canteenatyourservice.com

Canteen Vending Services
Compass Group 2400 Yorkmont Rd .... Charlotte NC 28217 704-328-4000
TF: 800-357-0012 ■ *Web:* www.compass-usa.com

Cara Operations Ltd 199 Four Valley Dr .... Vaughan ON L4K0B8 905-760-2244
TF: 800-860-4082 ■ *Web:* www.cara.com

Centerplate 2187 Atlantic St .... Stamford CT 06902 203-975-5900
TF: 800-698-6992 ■ *Web:* www.centerplate.com

Phone | Fax

Chefs' Warehouse Holdings LLC
100 E Ridge Rd.................................. Ridgefield CT 06877 718-842-8700
Web: www.chefswarehouse.com

CL Swanson Corp 4501 Femrite Dr.................. Madison WI 53716 608-221-7640 221-7648
Web: www.swansons.net

Compass Group North American Div (CGNAD)
2400 Yorkmont Rd .... Charlotte NC 28217 704-328-4000
TF: 800-357-0012 ■ *Web:* www.compass-usa.com

Culinaire International 2100 Ross Ave Ste 3100 .... Dallas TX 75201 214-754-1880 754-1891
Web: www.culinaireintl.com

Edsung Foodservice 1337 Mookaula St.............. Honolulu HI 96817 808-845-3931
Web: edsung.com

Excelsior Grand 2380 Hylan Blvd .... Staten Island NY 10306 718-987-4800 987-4803
Web: www.excelsiorgrand.com

Five Star Food Service Inc
6005 Century Oaks Dr Ste 100.................. Chattanooga TN 37416 423-643-2600
TF: 800-327-0043 ■ *Web:* www.fivestar-food.com

Flying Food Group 5370 S Cicero Ave .... Chicago IL 60638 312-243-2122 264-2490
Web: www.flyingfood.com

Food Bank For New York City
39 Broadway 10th Fl.............................. New York NY 10006 212-566-7855 566-1463
TF: 866-692-3663 ■ *Web:* www.foodbanknyc.org

Garb-ko Inc 3925 Fortune Blvd .... Saginaw MI 48603 989-799-6937
Web: 7-eleven.com

GC Partners Inc 3816 Forrestgate Dr .... Winston-Salem NC 27103 336-767-1600
Web: www.gcpartners.com

General Mills Inc 1 General Mills Blvd............. Minneapolis MN 55426 800-248-7310 764-8330*
NYSE: GIS ■ **Fax Area Code:* 763 ■ **Fax:* PR ■ *TF:* 800-248-7310 ■ *Web:* www.generalmills.com

Guest Services Inc 3055 Prosperity Ave .... Fairfax VA 22031 703-849-9300 641-4690
TF: 800-345-7534 ■ *Web:* www.guestservices.com

HMSHost Corp 6905 Rockledge Dr # 1 .... Bethesda MD 20817 240-694-4100 694-4790
Web: www.hmshost.com

Host America Corporate Dining Inc
1 Leonardo Dr.................................. North Haven CT 06473 203-239-4678 234-1503

Institutional Wholesale Co 535 Dry Vly Rd .... Cookeville TN 38506 931-537-4000 537-4017*
**Fax:* Cust Svc ■ *TF:* 800-239-9588 ■ *Web:* goiwc.com

Island Oasis 141 Norfolk St PO Box 769............... Walpole MA 02081 508-660-1176
TF: 800-777-4752 ■ *Web:* www.islandoasis.com

Lackmann Culinary Services
303 Crossways Pk Dr........................... Woodbury NY 11797 516-364-2300 364-9788

Lee Bros Foodservice Inc 660 E Gish Rd .... San Jose CA 95112 408-275-0700 275-0416
Web: www.leebros.com

Love & Quiches Desserts 178 Hanse Ave............. Freeport NY 11520 516-623-8800 623-8817
TF: 800-525-5251 ■ *Web:* www.loveandquiches.com

Maximum Quality Foods Inc 3351 Tremley Pt Rd.......... Linden NJ 07036 908-474-0003 474-1320
Web: www.maximumqualityfoods.com

Morrison Management Specialists Inc
5801 Peachtree Dunwoody Rd .... Atlanta GA 30342 800-225-4368 845-3333*
**Fax Area Code:* 404 ■ *TF General:* 800-225-4368 ■ *Web:* www.iammorrison.com

Nantze Springs Inc 156 W Carroll St .... Dothan AL 36301 334-794-4218
Web: www.nantzesprings.com

Nutrition Management Services Co
2071 Kimberton Rd, Chester Ste................... Kimberton PA 19442 610-935-2050
Web: www.nmsc.com

Open Kitchen Inc 1161 W 21st St..................... Chicago IL 60608 312-666-5335 666-9242
TF: 800-339-5334 ■ *Web:* www.openkitchens.com

Port City Java Inc 101 Portwatch Way .... Wilmington NC 28412 910-796-6646
Web: www.portcityjava.com

Rodrigo's Online Store 1320 N Manzanita............... Orange CA 92867 714-633-7844
Web: www.rodrigos-shop.com

Romeo & Sons Inc 100 Romeo Ln .... Uniontown PA 15401 724-438-5561 438-1149
Web: www.romeofoods.com

Sanese Services Inc 6465 Busch Blvd.............. Columbus OH 43229 614-436-1234
Web: avifoodsystems.com

SeamlessWeb Professional Solutions LLC
232 Madison Ave Ste 1409........................ New York NY 10016 212-944-7755

Signature Services Corp 2705 Hawes Ave .... Dallas TX 75235 214-353-2661
TF: 800-929-5519 ■ *Web:* www.signatureservices.com

Sodexo Inc 9801 Washingtonian Blvd .... Gaithersburg MD 20878 800-763-3946 987-4438*
**Fax Area Code:* 301 ■ *TF:* 800-763-3946 ■ *Web:* www.sodexousa.com

Spartan Foods of America Inc
4250 Orchard Park Blvd .... Spartanburg SC 29303 864-595-6262
Web: www.mamamarys.com

Sportservice Corp 40 Fountain Plz.................... Buffalo NY 14202 716-858-5000
TF: 800-828-7240 ■ *Web:* delawarenorth.com

Summit Food Service Distributors Inc
580 Industrial Rd .... London ON N5V1V1 519-453-3410 453-5148
TF: 800-265-9267 ■ *Web:* summit.colabor.com

SYSCO Philadelphia LLC 600 Packer Ave .... Philadelphia PA 19148 215-463-8200 218-1618
Web: www.syscophilly.com/ordereze/1000/Page.aspx

Sysco Portland Inc 26250 SW Pkwy Ctr Dr .... Wilsonville OR 97070 503-682-8700 682-6699
Web: www.syscoportland.com

Taher Inc 5570 Smetana Dr .... Minnetonka MN 55343 952-945-0505 945-0444
Web: www.taher.com

Trujillo & Sons Inc 3325 NW 62nd ST.................... Miami FL 33147 305-696-8701 696-4510
Web: www.trujilloandsons.com

Universal Sodexho
9801 Washingtonian Blvd..................... Gaithersburg MD 20878 301-987-4000
TF: 888-763-3967 ■ *Web:* sodexousa.com/usen/default.aspx

Value Creation Partners Inc
445 Hutchinson Ave .... Columbus OH 43235 614-515-5515

Zaugs Inc 4100 W Wisconsin Ave .... Appleton WI 54913 920-734-9881 734-4322

300 FOOD SERVICE EQUIPMENT & SUPPLIES

See Also Food Products Machinery p. 2314

Phone | Fax

Adams-Burch Inc 1901 Stanford Ct .... Landover MD 20785 301-276-2000 341-5114
TF Cust Svc: 800-347-8093 ■ *Web:* www.adams-burch.com

Advance Tabco 200 Heartland Blvd .... Edgewood NY 11717 631-242-4800 242-6900
TF: 800-645-3166 ■ *Web:* www.advancetabco.com

Company / Address	City	State	Zip	Phone	Fax
Anderson-DuBose Co 5300 Tod Ave SW *Fax Area Code:* 330 ■ *Web:* anderson-dubose.com	Lordstown	OH	44481	440-248-8800	824-2256*
Atlanta Fixture & Sales Co 3185 NE Expy *TF:* 800-282-1977 ■ *Web:* www.atlantafixture.com	Atlanta	GA	30341	770-455-8844	986-9202
Bargreen Ellingson Inc 2925 70th Ave E *TF:* 866-722-2665 ■ *Web:* www.bargreen.com	Fife	WA	98424	253-722-2600	896-3620
Boelter Cos Inc N22W23685 Ridgeview Pkwy W *TF:* 800-263-5837 ■ *Web:* www.boelter.com	West Waukesha	WI	53188	262-523-6200	523-6003
Bolton & Hay Inc 2701 Delaware Ave *TF:* 800-362-1861 ■ *Web:* www.boltonhay.com	Des Moines	IA	50317	515-265-2554	
Browne & Co 100 Esna Pk Dr *TF:* 866-306-3672 ■ *Web:* www.browneco.com	Markham	ON	L3R1E3	905-475-6104	475-5843
Browne-Halco Inc 788 Morris Turnpike Ste 202 *Fax Area Code:* 908 ■ *TF:* 888-289-1005 ■ *Web:* www.halco.com	Short Hills	NJ	07078	973-232-1065	964-6677*
Cambro Manufacturing Co 5801 Skylab Rd *Fax:* Cust Svc ■ *TF:* 800-833-3003 ■ *Web:* www.cambro.com	Huntington Beach	CA	92647	714-848-1555	842-3430*
Carlisle FoodService Products Inc 4711 E Hefner Rd *TF:* 800-654-8210 ■ *Web:* www.carlislefsp.com	Oklahoma City	OK	73131	405-475-5600	475-5607
CHUDNOW Mfg Company Inc 3055 New St PO Box 10 *Web:* www.chudnowmfg.com	Oceanside	NY	11572	516-593-4222	593-4156
Curtis Restaurant Supply & Equipment Co 6577 E 40th St *TF:* 800-766-2878 ■ *Web:* www.curtisequipment.com	Tulsa	OK	74145	918-622-7390	665-0990
Eagle Group Inc 100 Industrial Blvd *TF:* 800-441-8440 ■ *Web:* www.eaglegrp.com	Clayton	DE	19938	302-653-3000	653-2065
Edsung Foodservice 1337 Mookaula St *Web:* edsung.com	Honolulu	HI	96817	808-845-3931	
Edward Don & Co 2500 S Harlem Ave *TF Cust Svc:* 800-777-4366 ■ *Web:* www.don.com	North Riverside	IL	60546	800-777-4366	
Genpak Carthage 505 E Cotton St *TF:* 800-626-6695 ■ *Web:* www.genpak.com	Carthage	TX	75633	903-693-7151	
HB Hunter Co 1512 Brown Ave PO Box 1599	Norfolk	VA	23504	757-664-5200	664-2372
Hotel & Restaurant Supply Inc 5020 Arundel Rd PO Box 6 *TF:* 800-782-6651 ■ *Web:* www.hnrsupply.com	Meridian	MS	39302	601-482-7127	482-7170
Intedge Mfg 1875 Chumley Rd *TF:* 866-969-9605 ■ *Web:* www.intedge.com	Woodruff	SC	29388	864-969-9601	969-9604
InterMetro Industries Corp 651 N Washington St *Fax:* Hum Res ■ *TF Cust Svc:* 800-992-1776 ■ *Web:* www.metro.com	Wilkes-Barre	PA	18705	570-825-2741	823-2852*
Kittredge Equipment Co Inc 100 Bowles Rd *TF:* 800-423-7082 ■ *Web:* www.kittredgeequipment.com	Agawam	MA	01001	413-304-4100	786-7086
Lakeside Manufacturing Inc 4900 W Electric Ave *TF:* 800-558-8565 ■ *Web:* www.elakeside.com	West Milwaukee	WI	53219	414-902-6400	902-6446
Lancaster Colony Commercial Products Inc 3902 Indianola Ave *TF:* 800-292-7260 ■ *Web:* www.lccpinc.com	Columbus	OH	43214	614-263-2850	263-2857
Maines Paper & Food Service Co 101 Broome Corporate Pkwy *Fax:* Cust Svc ■ *TF:* 800-366-3669 ■ *Web:* www.maines.net	Conklin	NY	13748	607-779-1200	723-3245*
Manitowoc Foodservice 2227 Welbilt Blvd *Web:* www.manitowocfoodservice.com	New Port Richey	FL	34655	727-375-7010	
McLane Foodservice Inc 2085 Midway Rd *Fax Area Code:* 254 ■ *TF:* 800-299-1401 ■ *Web:* www.mclaneco.com	Carrollton	TX	75006	972-364-2000	771-7244*
N Wasserstrom & Sons Inc 2300 Lockbourne Rd *TF:* 800-444-4697 ■ *Web:* www.wasserstrom.com	Columbus	OH	43207	614-228-5550	737-8501
PBI Market Equipment Inc 2667 Gundry Ave *TF:* 800-421-3753 ■ *Web:* www.pbimarketing.com	Signal Hill	CA	90755	562-595-4785	426-2262
Perkins Equipment Div 630 John Hancock Rd *TF:* 800-733-5708 ■ *Web:* www.perkins1.com	Taunton	MA	02780	508-824-2800	821-2670
RAPIDS Wholesale Equipment Co 6201 S Gateway Dr *TF:* 800-472-7431 ■ *Web:* rapidswholesale.com	Marion	IA	52302	319-447-1670	447-1680
Regal Ware Inc 1675 Reigle Dr *Web:* www.regalware.com	Kewaskum	WI	53040	262-626-2121	626-8565
Reinhart Food Service 7735 Westside Industrial Dr *Web:* www.rfsdelivers.com	Jacksonville	FL	32219	904-781-9888	
Restaurant & Stores Equipment Co 230 West 700 South *Web:* rescoslc.com	Salt Lake City	UT	84101	801-364-1981	
Restaurant Technologies Inc 2250 Pilot Knob Rd Ste 100 *TF:* 888-796-4997 ■ *Web:* www.rti-inc.com	Mendota Heights	MN	55120	651-796-1600	379-4082
Ricos Products Company Inc 830 S Presa St *Web:* www.ricos.com	San Antonio	TX	78210	210-222-1415	226-6453
Service Ideas Inc 2354 Ventura Dr *TF:* 800-328-4493 ■ *Web:* www.serviceideas.com	Woodbury	MN	55125	651-730-8800	730-8880
Smith & Greene Co 19015 66th Ave S *TF:* 800-232-8050 ■ *Web:* www.smithandgreene.com	Kent	WA	98032	425-656-8000	
Southern Foods Inc 3500 Old Battleground Rd *Web:* www.southernfoods.com	Greensboro	NC	27410	336-545-3800	545-5281
Standex International Corp Food Service Equipment Group 11 Keewaydin Dr *NYSE: SXI* ■ *TF:* 800-647-1284 ■ *Web:* www.standex.com	Salem	NH	03079	603-893-9701	893-7324
SYSCO Corp 1390 Enclave Pkwy *NYSE: SYY* ■ *Web:* www.sysco.com	Houston	TX	77077	281-584-1390	
TriMark USA Inc 505 Collins St *TF:* 800-755-5580 ■ *Web:* www.trimarkusa.com	South Attleboro	MA	02703	508-399-2400	761-3605
United Restaurant Equipment Company Inc 1 Executive Park Dr *Web:* www.unitedrestaurant.com	North Billerica	MA	01862	978-439-5500	262-9999
US Foods Culinary Equipment & Supplies 2621 Fairview Ave N Ste 2 *TF:* 866-636-2338 ■ *Web:* www.usfoodsculinaryequipmentandsupplies.com	Roseville	MN	55113	651-638-8993	
Vollrath Co LLC, The 1236 N 18th St *TF:* 800-624-2051 ■ *Web:* vollrath.com	Sheboygan	WI	53081	920-457-4851	459-6570
Wasserstrom Co 477 S Front St *TF:* 866-634-8927 ■ *Web:* www.wasserstrom.com	Columbus	OH	43215	614-228-6525	737-8911
Western Pioneer Sales Co 406 E Colorado St *Web:* westernpioneersales.com	Glendale	CA	91205	818-244-1466	

301 FOOTWEAR

Company / Address	City	State	Zip	Phone	Fax
Acor Orthopaedic Inc 18530 S Miles Pkwy *TF:* 800-237-2267 ■ *Web:* www.acor.com	Cleveland	OH	44128	216-662-4500	662-4547
Acushnet Co 333 Bridge St *Fax:* Hum Res ■ *TF:* 800-225-8500 ■ *Web:* www.acushnetcompany.com	Fairhaven	MA	02719	508-979-2000	979-3927*
Aerosoles Inc 201 Meadow Rd *TF:* 800-798-9478 ■ *Web:* www.aerosoles.com	Edison	NJ	08817	732-985-6900	
Aldo Shoes 2300 Emile Belanger *TF:* 888-818-2536 ■ *Web:* www.aldoshoes.com	Montreal	QC	H4R3J4	514-747-2536	
Allen-Edmonds Shoe Corp 201 E Seven Hills Rd *TF Cust Svc:* 800-235-2348 ■ *Web:* www.allenedmonds.com	Port Washington	WI	53074	262-235-6512	
Ariat International Inc 3242 Whipple Rd *Web:* ariat.com	Union City	CA	94587	510-477-7000	
Asics America Corp 29 Parker Ste 100 *TF:* 800-333-8404 ■ *Web:* www.asics.com/us/en-us	Irvine	CA	92618	949-453-8888	453-0292
ATP-USA Mfg LLC 600 Putnam Pike Ste 8	Greenville	RI	02858	401-767-3100	766-5327
Badorf Shoe Co Inc 1958 Auction Rd *TF:* 800-325-1545 ■ *Web:* www.badorfshoe.com	Manheim	PA	17545	717-653-0155	
Barbour Welting Company Div Barbour Corp 1001 N Montello St *TF:* 800-955-9649 ■ *Web:* www.barbourcorp.com	Brockton	MA	02301	508-583-8200	583-4113
Belleville Shoe Manufacturing Co 100 Premier Dr *Web:* www.bellevilleboot.com	Belleville	IL	62220	618-233-5600	257-1112
Benchmark Brands Inc 5250 Triangle Pkwy Ste 200 *Web:* www.benchmarkbrands.com	Norcross	GA	30092	770-242-1254	
Brooks Sports Inc 19910 N Creek Pkwy Ste 200 *TF:* 800-227-6657 ■ *Web:* www.brooksrunning.com	Bothell	WA	98011	800-227-6657	
Capezio/Ballet Makers Inc 1 Campus Rd *TF Acctg:* 800-533-1887 ■ *Web:* www.capezio.com	Totowa	NJ	07512	973-595-9000	595-9120
Cardinal Shoe Corp 468 Canal St *Web:* cardinalshoe.com	Lawrence	MA	01840	978-686-9706	
Cels Enterprises Inc 3485 S La Cienega Blvd *Web:* www.chineselaundry.com	Los Angeles	CA	90016	310-838-2103	838-8732
Charles David of California 5731 Buckingham Pkwy	Culver City	CA	90230	310-348-5050	348-5041
Cherokee Inc 5990 Sepulveda Blvd Ste 600 *NASDAQ: CHKE* ■ *Web:* www.thecherokeegroup.com	Sherman Oaks	CA	91411	818-908-9868	
Chinese Laundry Shoes 3485 S La Cienega Blvd *TF:* 888-935-8825 ■ *Web:* www.chineselaundry.com	Los Angeles	CA	90016	310-838-2103	
Clark Cos NA 156 Oak St *TF Cust Svc:* 800-211-5461 ■ *Web:* www.clarksusa.com	Newton Upper Falls	MA	02464	617-964-1222	
Cole-Haan 8701 Keystone Crossing *TF:* 800-695-8945 ■ *Web:* www.colehaan.com	Indianapolis	IN	46240	317-810-0160	
Connors Footwear 20 Whitcher St	Lisbon	NH	03585	603-838-6694	838-2278
Consolidated Shoe Company Inc 22290 Timberlake Rd *Fax:* Sales ■ *TF:* 800-368-7463 ■ *Web:* www.consolidatedshoe.com	Lynchburg	VA	24502	434-239-0391	582-5631*
Cowtown Boots 11401 Gateway Blvd W *TF:* 800-580-2698 ■ *Web:* store.cowtownboots.com	El Paso	TX	79936	915-593-2929	593-2249
Crocs Inc 6328 Monarch Pk Pl *NASDAQ: CROX* ■ *TF:* 866-306-3179 ■ *Web:* www.crocs.com	Niwot	CO	80503	303-848-7000	
Dan Post Boot Co 1751 Alpine Dr *Web:* www.danpostboots.com	Clarksville	TN	37040	931-645-1626	
Danner Shoe Manufacturing Co 17634 NE Airport *TF Cust Svc:* 800-345-0430 ■ *Web:* www.danner.com	Portland	OR	97230	503-251-1100	251-1119
Deckers Outdoor Corp 495-A S Fairview Ave *NYSE: DECK* ■ *TF:* 877-337-8333 ■ *Web:* www.deckers.com	Goleta	CA	93117	805-967-7611	967-9722
Drew Shoe Corp 252 Quarry Rd *TF:* 800-837-3739 ■ *Web:* www.drewshoe.com	Lancaster	OH	43130	740-653-4271	
East Lion Corp 318 Brea Canyon Rd *TF:* 877-939-1818 ■ *Web:* www.eastlioncorp.com	City of Industry	CA	91789	626-912-1818	935-5858
Eastland Shoe Mfg Corp 4 Meeting House Rd *TF:* 888-988-1998 ■ *Web:* www.eastlandshoe.com	Freeport	ME	04032	207-865-6314	865-9261
ES Originals Inc 440 9th Ave 7th Fl *TF General:* 800-677-6577 ■ *Web:* www.esoriginals.com	New York	NY	10001	212-736-8124	736-8366
Famous Footwear 247 Junction Rd *TF Cust Svc:* 800-888-7198 ■ *Web:* www.famousfootwear.com	Madison	WI	53717	608-833-3340	
Fancy Feet Inc 26650 Harding St	Oak Park	MI	48237	248-398-8460	398-5650
Finish Line Inc, The 3308 N Mitthoeffer Rd *NASDAQ: FINL* ■ *TF:* 888-777-3949 ■ *Web:* www.finishline.com	Indianapolis	IN	46235	317-899-1022	
Florsheim Inc 333 W Estabrook Blvd *Fax Area Code:* 414 ■ *TF:* 866-454-0449 ■ *Web:* www.florsheim.com	Glendale	WI	53212	866-454-0449	908-1601*
Foot Locker Inc 112 W 34th St *NYSE: FL* ■ *TF:* 800-952-5210 ■ *Web:* www.footlocker-inc.com	New York	NY	10120	212-720-3700	
Foot Solutions Inc 4101 Roswell Rd Ste 800 *Web:* footsolutions.com	Marietta	GA	30062	770-984-0844	
Foot-So-Port Shoe Corp 405 E Forest St *Web:* www.footsoport.com	Oconomowoc	WI	53066	262-567-4416	
Footaction Inc 112 W 34th St *Web:* www.footaction.com	New York	NY	10120	715-261-9588	
Footstar Inc 933 MacArthur Blvd *TF:* 800-322-2885 ■ *Web:* www.footstar.com	Mahwah	NJ	07430	201-934-2000	
Gateway Shoe Co 910 Kehro Mill Rd Ste 112 *TF:* 800-539-6063 ■ *Web:* www.gatewayshoes.com	Ballwin	MO	63011	636-256-7050	527-3797
Genesco Inc 1415 Murfreesboro Rd *NYSE: GCO* ■ *Web:* www.genesco.com	Nashville	TN	37217	615-367-7000	

Phone Fax

Georgia Boot Inc 39 E Canal St ... Nelsonville OH 45764 740-753-1951
TF: 877-795-2410 ■ *Web:* www.georgiaboot.com

HH Brown Shoe Company Inc 124 W Putnam Ave ... Greenwich CT 06830 203-661-2424 661-1818
TF: 888-444-2769 ■ *Web:* www.hhbrown.com

Hush Puppies Co 9341 Courtland Dr NE ... Rockford MI 49351 616-866-5500 866-5625*
**Fax:* Acctg ■ *TF:* 866-699-7365 ■ *Web:* www.hushpuppies.com

Ilani Shoes Ltd 1350 Broadway ... New York NY 10018 212-947-5830

Impo International Inc PO Box 639 ... Santa Maria CA 93456 800-367-4676
TF: 800-367-4676 ■ *Web:* www.impo.com

Inter-Pacific Corp 2257 Colby Ave ... Los Angeles CA 90064 310-473-7591 479-8701
TF: 877-605-8414

International Marketing Assn (IMA)
3509 Virginia Beach Blvd ... Virginia Beach VA 23452 757-490-9860 490-0716
Web: www.imacorporate.com

Jack Schwartz Shoes Inc
155 Ave of the Americas ... New York NY 10013 212-691-4700
Web: www.lugz.com

John Reyer Shoe Store 40 S Water Ave ... Sharon PA 16146 800-245-1550
TF Cust Svc: 800-245-1550 ■ *Web:* www.reyers.com

Johnston & Murphy Inc 1415 Murfreesboro Rd ... Nashville TN 37217 615-367-7168
TF: 800-424-2854 ■ *Web:* www.johnstonmurphy.com

Justin Boot Co Inc 610 W Daggett St ... Fort Worth TX 76104 817-332-7797 521-9801*
**Fax Area Code:* 405 ■ **Fax:* Cust Svc ■ *TF Cust Svc:* 800-548-1021 ■ *Web:* www.justinboots.com

K-Swiss Inc 31248 Oak Crest Dr ... Westlake Village CA 91361 818-706-5100 706-5390
NASDAQ: KSWS ■ *TF:* 800-938-8000 ■ *Web:* www.kswiss.com

Kaepa USA Inc 9050 Autobahn Dr Ste 500 ... Dallas TX 75237 800-880-9200
TF: 800-880-9200 ■ *Web:* www.kaepa.com

Keds Corp 1400 Industries Rd ... Richmond IN 47374 800-680-0966 446-1339
TF: 800-680-0966 ■ *Web:* www.keds.com

Kenneth Cole Productions Inc 603 W 50th St ... New York NY 10019 212-265-1500 315-8279*
NYSE: KCP ■ **Fax:* Cust Svc ■ *TF:* 800-536-2653 ■ *Web:* www.kennethcole.com

L A Gear Inc 844 Moraga Dr ... Los Angeles CA 90049 310-889-3499
Web: www.lagear.com

La Sportiva North America Inc
3850 Frontier Ave Ste 100 ... Boulder CO 80301 303-443-8710
Web: www.sportiva.com

LaCrosse Footwear Inc 17634 NE Airport ... Portland OR 97230 800-323-2668
TF Cust Svc: 800-323-2668 ■ *Web:* lacrossefootwear.com

Lady Foot Locker (LFL) 112 W 34th St ... New York NY 10120 212-720-3700
TF: 800-991-6686 ■ *Web:* www.footlocker-inc.com

Lake Catherine Footwear
3770 Malvern Rd PO Box 6048 ... Hot Springs AR 71901 800-819-1901
TF: 800-819-1901 ■ *Web:* munroshoes.com

Lamey-Wellehan Inc 940 Turner St ... Auburn ME 04210 207-784-6595 784-9650
TF: 800-370-6900 ■ *Web:* www.lwshoes.com

Lucchese Boot Co 20 ZANE GREY ... El Paso TX 79906 888-582-1883
TF: 800-637-6888 ■ *Web:* www.lucchese.com

Lyn-Flex West Inc
405 Red Oak Rd PO Box 570 ... Owensville MO 65066 573-437-4125 437-2350
Web: www.lynflex.com

Marty's Shoe Outlet Inc 121 Carver Ave ... Westwood NJ 07675 201-497-6637
TF General: 888-662-7897 ■ *Web:* www.martyshoes.com

Meramec Group Inc 338 Ramsey St ... Sullivan MO 63080 573-468-3101 860-3101
Web: www.meramec.com

Mercury International
20 Alice Agnew Dr ... North Attleboro MA 02763 508-699-9000
Web: mercuryfootwear.com

Merrell Footwear 9341 Courtland Dr NE ... Rockford MI 49351 616-866-5500 866-5625
TF Cust Svc: 800-288-3124 ■ *Web:* www.merrell.com/us/en

Mizuno USA 4925 Avalon Ridge Pkwy ... Norcross GA 30071 770-441-5553 448-3234
TF: 800-966-1211 ■ *Web:* www.mizunousa.com

Montello Heel Mfg Inc 13 Emerson Ave ... Brockton MA 02301 508-586-0603
Web: www.montelloheel.com

Munro & Co Inc
3770 Malvern Rd 71901 PO Box 6048 ... Hot Springs AR 71902 501-262-6000 262-6165
TF: 800-819-1901 ■ *Web:* munroshoes.com

New Balance Athletic Shoe Inc
20 Guest St Brighton Landing ... Brighton MA 02135 617-783-4000 787-9355
TF: 800-595-9138 ■ *Web:* www.newbalance.com

Nike Inc 1 Bowerman Dr ... Beaverton OR 97005 503-671-6453 646-6926
NYSE: NKE ■ *TF Cust Svc:* 800-344-6453 ■ *Web:* www.nike.com

Novus Inc 655 Calle Cubitas ... Guaynabo PR 00969 787-272-4546 272-4500
TF: 888-530-4546 ■ *Web:* www.novushoes.com

Nunn-Bush Shoe Co Inc 333 W Estabrook Blvd ... Glendale WI 53212 414-908-1600
Web: nunnbush.com

ONGUARD Industries 1850 Clark Rd ... Havre de Grace MD 21078 410-272-2000 272-3346
TF: 800-365-2282 ■ *Web:* www.onguardindustries.com

Otomix Inc 747 Glasgow Ave ... Inglewood CA 90301 310-215-6100
TF: 800-701-7867 ■ *Web:* www.otomix.com

Payless ShoeSource Inc 3231 SE Sixth Ave ... Topeka KS 66607 785-233-5171 368-7519
TF: 877-452-7500 ■ *Web:* www.collectivebrands.com

Pentland USA Inc
3333 New Hyde Pk Rd Ste 200 ... New Hyde Park NY 11042 516-365-1333 365-2333
Web: www.pentland.com

Phoenix Footwear Group Inc
5937 Darwin Ct Ste 109 ... Carlsbad CA 92008 760-602-9688
OTC: PXFG ■ *TF:* 888-218-7275 ■ *Web:* www.phoenixfootwear.com

Propet USA Inc 2415 W Valley Hwy N ... Auburn WA 98001 253-854-7600 854-7607
TF: 800-877-6738 ■ *Web:* www.propetusa.com

Puma North America Inc 10 Lyberty Way ... Westford MA 01886 978-698-1000 968-1150
TF General: 888-565-7862 ■ *Web:* www.puma.com

PW Minor & Son Inc 3 Tread Easy Ave ... Batavia NY 14020 585-343-1500 343-1514
TF: 800-333-4067 ■ *Web:* www.pwminor.com

Quabaug Corp 18 School St ... North Brookfield MA 01535 508-867-7731
Web: www.vibram.com

Rack Room Shoes 8310 Technology Dr ... Charlotte NC 28262 704-501-4674 547-8153
Web: www.rackroomshoes.com

Red Wing Shoe Company Inc 314 Main St ... Red Wing MN 55066 651-388-8211
TF Cust Svc: 800-733-9464 ■ *Web:* www.redwingshoes.com

Reebok International Ltd 1895 JW Foster Blvd ... Canton MA 02021 781-401-5000 401-7402*
**Fax:* Cust Svc ■ *TF:* 866-870-1743 ■ *Web:* www.reebok.com

RG Barry Corp 13405 Yarmouth Dr NW ... Pickerington OH 43147 614-864-6400 866-9787
NASDAQ: DFZ ■ *TF:* 800-848-7560 ■ *Web:* www.rgbarry.com

Phone Fax

Rockport Company Inc 1895 JW Foster Blvd ... Canton MA 02021 781-401-5000
TF: 800-828-0545 ■ *Web:* www.rockport.com

Rocky Shoes & Boots Inc 39 E Canal St ... Nelsonville OH 45764 740-753-3130
NASDAQ: RCKY ■ *TF:* 877-795-2410 ■ *Web:* www.rockyboots.com

Romika USA LLC 3405 Del Webb Ave NE ... Salem OR 97301 503-588-8117
TF: 888-777-4174 ■ *Web:* www.romikausa.com

Safety Shoe Distributors of Oki
10156 Reading Rd ... Cincinnati OH 45241 513-563-4220
Web: safetyshoedistributors.com

SAS Shoemakers 1717 SAS Dr ... San Antonio TX 78224 877-782-7463
TF: 877-782-7463 ■ *Web:* www.sasshoes.com

Saucony Inc 191 Spring St ... Lexington MA 02420 800-282-6575
TF: 800-282-6575 ■ *Web:* www.saucony.com

Saxon Shoes Inc 11800 W Broad St Ste 2750 ... Richmond VA 23233 804-285-3473 285-8526
TF General: 800-686-5616 ■ *Web:* shop.saxonshoes.com

Schwartz & Benjamin Inc 20 W 57th St 4th Fl ... New York NY 10019 212-541-9092 974-0609

Sebago Inc 9341 Courtland Dr ... Rockford MI 49351 616-866-5500 866-5625
TF: 866-699-7367 ■ *Web:* www.sebago.com

SG Footwear Inc 3 University Plaza Ste 400 ... Hackensack NJ 07601 201-342-1200 342-4405
Web: www.sgfootwear.com

Shoe Carnival Inc 7500 E Columbia St ... Evansville IN 47715 812-867-6471
NASDAQ: SCVL ■ *TF Cust Svc:* 800-430-7463 ■ *Web:* www.shoecarnival.com

Shoe Sensation Inc 253 America Pl ... Jeffersonville IN 47130 812-288-7659 288-7747
Web: www.shoesensation.com

Shoe Show of Rocky Mountain Inc
2201 Trinity Church Rd ... Concord NC 28027 704-782-4143 782-3411
TF Cust Svc: 888-557-4637 ■ *Web:* www.shoeshow.com

Shtofman Co 1905 W Gentry Pkwy ... Tyler TX 75702 903-592-0861 592-8380

Skechers USA Inc
228 Manhattan Beach Blvd ... Manhattan Beach CA 90266 310-318-3100
NYSE: SKX ■ *TF Cust Svc:* 800-746-3411 ■ *Web:* www.skechers.com

Spalding PO Box 90015 ... Bowling Green KY 42103 855-253-4533 729-4800*
**Fax Area Code:* 877 ■ *TF:* 855-253-4533 ■ *Web:* www.spalding.com

Stanbee Company Inc 70 Broad St ... Carlstadt NJ 07072 201-933-9666 933-7985
Web: www.stanbee.com

Stride Rite Corp 191 Spring St ... Lexington MA 02420 617-824-6000 824-6969
TF Cust Svc: 800-299-6575 ■ *Web:* www.striderite.com

Super Shoe Stores Inc 601 Dual Hwy ... Hagerstown MD 21740 866-842-7510
TF: 866-842-7510 ■ *Web:* www.supershoes.com

Teva Sport Sandals 123 N Leroux St ... Flagstaff AZ 86001 928-779-5938
TF General: 800-367-8382 ■ *Web:* www.teva.com

Timberland Co, The 200 Domain Dr ... Stratham NH 03885 603-772-9500
NYSE: VFC ■ *TF:* 800-258-0855 ■ *Web:* www.timberland.com

Tony Lama Boot Company Inc 1137 Tony Lama St ... El Paso TX 79915 915-778-8311
Web: www.tonylama.com

Topline Corp 13150 SE 32nd St ... Bellevue WA 98005 425-643-3003 643-3846
Web: www.toplinecorp.com

Trimfoot Co LLC 115 Trimfoot Terr ... Farmington MO 63640 800-325-6116 756-8482*
**Fax Area Code:* 573 ■ *TF:* 800-325-6116 ■ *Web:* www.trimfootco.com

TT Group Inc 702 Carnation Dr ... Aurora MO 65605 417-678-2181
Web: www.tt-group.com

Vans Inc 15700 Shoemaker Ave ... Santa Fe Springs CA 90670 855-909-8267
TF: 855-909-8267 ■ *Web:* www.vans.com

Weinbrenner Shoe Co Inc 108 S Polk St ... Merrill WI 54452 715-536-5521 536-1172
TF General: 800-569-6817 ■ *Web:* www.weinbrennerusa.com

West Coast Shoe Co
52828 NW Shoe Factory Ln PO Box 607 ... Scappoose OR 97056 503-543-7114 543-7110
TF: 800-326-2711 ■ *Web:* www.wescoboots.com/builder/default.aspx

Weyco Group Inc 333 W Estabrook Blvd ... Glendale WI 53212 414-908-1880 908-1603
NASDAQ: WEYS ■ *TF:* 866-454-0449 ■ *Web:* www.weycogroup.com

Wolverine World Wide Inc
9341 Courtland Dr NE ... Rockford MI 49351 616-866-5500
Web: wolverineworldwide.com

302 FORESTRY SERVICES

See Also Timber Tracts p. 3247

Phone Fax

American Forest Management Inc
407 N Pike Rd E PO Box 1919 ... Sumter SC 29151 803-773-5461 773-4248
Web: www.americanforestmanagement.com

Baldwin Aviation Safety & Compliance
11 Palmetto Pkwy ... Hilton Head Island SC 29926 843-342-5434
Web: www.baldwinaviation.com

Bioforest Technologies Inc
59 Industrial Park Crescent ... Sault Sainte Marie ON P6B5P3 705-942-5824 942-8829
Web: bioforest.ca

Boundary County School District
6577 Main St Ste 101 ... Bonners Ferry ID 83805 208-267-3146
Web: bcsd101.com

Cascade Timber Consulting Inc 3210 Hwy 20 ... Sweet Home OR 97386 541-367-2111 367-2117
Web: cascadetimber.com

Central Yavapai Fire District
8555 E Yavapai Rd ... Prescott Valley AZ 86314 928-772-7711
Web: centralyavapaifire.org

CH Fenstermaker & Associates LLC
135 Regency Sq ... Lafayette LA 70508 337-237-2200
Web: www.fenstermaker.com

Columbia River Log Scaling & Grading Bureau
260 Oakway Ctr ... Eugene OR 97401 541-342-6007
Web: www.crls.com

Continental Design & Engineering Inc
1524 Jackson St ... Anderson IN 46016 765-778-9999
Web: continental-design.com

Cooperative Forestiere Des Hautes-Laurentides
395 Boul Des Ruisseaux ... Des Ruisseaux QC J9L1R6 819-623-4422
Web: www.cfhl.qc.ca

Curtis Contracting Inc 7481 Theron Rd ... West Point VA 23181 804-843-4633
Web: www.curtiscontracting.net

Environmental Consultants Inc
295 Buck Rd Ste 203 ... SouthHampton PA 18966 215-322-4040
Web: www.eci-consulting.com

	City	State	ZIP	Phone	Fax
F & W Forestry Services Inc 1310 W Oakridge Dr *Web:* www.fwforestry.com	Albany	GA	31707	229-883-0505	
Faller Davis & Assoc in 5525 W Cypress St *Web:* www.fallerdavis.com	Tampa	FL	33607	813-261-5136	
Firezat 5173 Waring Rd Ste 158 *Web:* www.firezat.com	San Diego	CA	92120	619-955-6788	
Fountains America Inc 175 Barnstead Rd Ste 4 *Web:* www.fountainsamerica.com	Pittsfield	NH	03263	603-435-8234	
Fountains Forestry Inc 175 Barnstead Rd *Web:* www.fountainforestry.com	Pittsfield	NH	03263	603-435-8234	435-7274
Georgia Timberlands Inc 3250 Waterville Rd *Web:* gatimberlands.com	Macon	GA	31206	478-788-4660	
Green Diamond Resource Co 1301 Fifth Ave Ste 2700 *Web:* www.greendiamond.com	Seattle	WA	98101	206-224-5800	
Hal Hays Construction Inc 4181 Latham St *Web:* www.halhays.com	Riverside	CA	92501	951-788-0703	275-0752
International Air Response Inc 6250 S Taxiway Cir *Web:* www.internationalairresponse.com	Mesa	AZ	85212	480-840-9860	840-9866
Lake County Forest Preserve District 2000 N Milwaukee Ave *Web:* www.lcfpd.org	Libertyville	IL	60048	847-367-6640	367-6649
Pro-west & Associates Inc 8239 State 371 Nw *Web:* www.prowestgis.com	Walker	MN	56484	218-547-3374	
Resource Management Service LLC 31 Inverness Ctr Pkwy Ste 360 **Fax Area Code:* 205 ■ *TF:* 800-995-9516 ■ *Web:* www.resourcemgt.com	Birmingham	AL	35242	800-995-9516	991-2807*
Sealaska Corp 1 Sealaska Plz Ste 400 *Web:* www.sealaska.com	Juneau	AK	99801	907-586-1512	586-2304
Southwest Conservation Corps 701 Camino Del Rio Ste 101 *Web:* sccorps.org	Durango	CO	81301	970-259-8607	
Summit Engineering Inc 131 Summit Dr *Web:* www.summit-engr.com	Pikeville	KY	41501	606-432-1447	
US Underwater Services LP 123 Sentry Dr *Web:* www.neptunems.com	Mansfield	TX	76063	817-447-7321	
Vestra Resources Inc 5300 Aviation Dr *TF:* 877-983-7872 ■ *Web:* www.vestra.com	Redding	CA	96002	530-223-2585	

303 FOUNDATIONS - COMMUNITY

See Also Charitable & Humanitarian Organizations p. 1754

	City	State	ZIP	Phone	Fax
Adelphoi Village Inc 1119 Village Way *Web:* www.adelphoivillage.org	Latrobe	PA	15650	724-520-1111	520-1878
Arcus Foundation 402 E Michigan Ave *Web:* www.arcusfoundation.org	Kalamazoo	MI	49007	269-373-4373	
Arizona Community Foundation 2201 E Camelback Rd Ste 405B *TF:* 800-222-8221 ■ *Web:* www.azfoundation.org	Phoenix	AZ	85016	602-381-1400	381-1575
Boston Foundation 75 Arlington St 10th Fl *Web:* www.tbf.org	Boston	MA	02116	617-338-1700	338-1604
California Community Foundation 445 S Figueroa St Ste 3400 *Web:* www.calfund.org	Los Angeles	CA	90071	213-413-4130	383-2046
California Wellness Foundation (CWF) 6320 Canoga Ave Ste 1700 *Web:* www.calwellness.org	Woodland Hills	CA	91367	818-702-1900	702-1999
Canadian Breast Cancer Foundation 375 University Ave Ste 301 *Web:* www.cbcf.org	Toronto	ON	M5G2J5	416-815-1313	
Chicago Community Trust & Affiliates 111 E Wacker Dr Ste 1400 *Web:* www.cct.org	Chicago	IL	60601	312-616-8000	616-7955
Cleveland Foundation 1422 Euclid Ave Ste 1300 *TF:* 877-554-5054 ■ *Web:* www.clevelandfoundation.org	Cleveland	OH	44115	216-861-3810	
Colorado Trust 1600 Sherman St *TF:* 888-847-9140 ■ *Web:* www.coloradotrust.org	Denver	CO	80203	303-837-1200	839-9034
Columbus Foundation, The 1234 E Broad St *Web:* www.columbusfoundation.org	Columbus	OH	43205	614-251-4000	251-4009
Communities Foundation of Texas Inc 5500 Caruth Haven Ln *Web:* www.cftexas.org	Dallas	TX	75225	214-750-4222	750-4210
Community Foundation for Greater Atlanta Inc 191 Peachtree St NE Ste 1000, 10th Fl *Web:* www.cfgreateratlanta.org	Atlanta	GA	30303	404-688-5525	688-3060
Community Foundation for Greater New Haven 70 Audubon St *TF:* 877-829-5500 ■ *Web:* www.cfgnh.org	New Haven	CT	06510	203-777-2386	787-6584
Community Foundation for the National Capital Region 1201 15th St NW Ste 420 *Web:* www.thecommunityfoundation.org	Washington	DC	20005	202-955-5890	955-8084
Community Foundation of Greater Memphis 1900 Union Ave *Web:* www.cfgm.org	Memphis	TN	38104	901-728-4600	722-0010
Community Foundation Serving Richmond & Central Virginia, The 7501 Boulders View Dr Ste 110 *Web:* www.tcfrichmond.org	Richmond	VA	23225	804-330-7400	330-5992
Community Foundation Silicon Valley 60 S Market St Ste 1000 *Web:* www.siliconvalleycf.org	San Jose	CA	95113	408-278-2200	
Dayton Foundation 40 N Main St Ste 500 *TF:* 877-222-0410 ■ *Web:* www.daytonfoundation.org	Dayton	OH	45423	937-222-0410	222-0636
Eclipse Foundation 102 Centrepointe Dr *Web:* www.eclipse.org	Nepean	ON	K2G6B1	613-224-9461	
Eye Foundation of Kansas City 2300 Holmes St *Web:* vrf-kc.org	Kansas City	MO	64108	816-404-1750	
Family Service Foundation Inc 5301 76th Ave *Web:* www.fsfinc.org	Landover Hills	MD	20784	301-459-2121	
Foundation for the Carolinas 217 S Tryon St *TF:* 800-973-7244 ■ *Web:* www.fftc.org	Charlotte	NC	28202	704-973-4500	973-4599
Gill Foundation Inc 2215 market st *Web:* gillfoundation.org	Denver	CO	80205	303-292-4455	
Global Endowment Management LP 550 S Tryon St Ste 3500 *Web:* www.globalendowment.com	Charlotte	NC	28202	704-333-8282	
Greater Cincinnati Foundation 200 W Fourth St *Web:* www.gcfdn.org	Cincinnati	OH	45202	513-241-2880	852-6886
Greater Kansas City Community Foundation & Affiliated Trusts (GKCCF) 1055 Broadway Ste 130 *Web:* www.growyourgiving.org	Kansas City	MO	64105	816-842-0944	842-8079
Greater Milwaukee Foundation 101 W Pleasant St Ste 210 *Web:* www.greatermilwaukeefoundation.org	Milwaukee	WI	53212	414-272-5805	272-6235
Hartford Foundation for Public Giving 10 Columbus Blvd 8th Fl *Web:* www.hfpg.org	Hartford	CT	06106	860-548-1888	524-8346
Hawaii Community Foundation 65-1279 Kawaihae Rd *TF:* 888-731-3863 ■ *Web:* www.hawaiicommunityfoundation.org	Kamuela	HI	96743	808-537-6333	521-6286
Houston Endowment Inc 600 Travis St Ste 6400 *Web:* www.houstonendowment.org	Houston	TX	77002	713-238-8100	238-8101
Jack Kent Cooke Foundation 44325 woodridge pkwy *Web:* www.jkcf.org	Landsdowne	VA	20176	703-723-8000	
Jay and Rose Phillips Family Foundation The 615 First Ave NE Ste 330 *Web:* phillipsfamilymn.org	Minneapolis	MN	55413	612-623-1654	
Kenneth Rainin Foundation 155 Grand Ave Ste 1000 *Web:* www.krfoundation.org	Oakland	CA	94612	510-625-5200	
Lcms Foundation 361 Beaumont Hwy *Web:* www.lfnd.org	Lebanon	CT	06249	860-450-0943	
Longwood Foundation Inc 100 West 10th St Ste 1109 *Web:* longwoodfoundation.com	Wilmington	DE	19801	302-654-2477	
Marin Community Foundation 5 Hamilton Landing Ste 200 *Web:* www.marincf.org	Novato	CA	94949	415-464-2500	464-2555
Minneapolis Foundation 80 S Eigth St 800 IDS Ctr *TF:* 866-305-0543 ■ *Web:* www.minneapolisfoundation.org	Minneapolis	MN	55402	612-672-3878	672-3846
Nebraska Christian College Foundation 12550 S 114th St *Web:* nechristian.edu	Papillion	NE	68046	402-935-9400	
Nelda C and H J Lutcher Stark Foundation The 601 W Green PO Box 909 *Web:* www.starkfoundation.org	Orange	TX	77631	409-883-3513	
New York Community Trust 909 Third Ave 22nd Fl *TF:* 877-829-5500 ■ *Web:* www.nycommunitytrust.org	New York	NY	10022	212-686-0010	532-8528
Northwest Area Foundation 60 Plato Blvd E Ste 400 *Web:* www.nwaf.org	Saint Paul	MN	55107	651-224-9635	225-7701
Oakland Schools Foundation 3700 Coolidge Ave *Web:* www.oaklandschoolsfoundation.org	Oakland	CA	94602	510-842-3461	
Omaha Community Foundation (OCF) 302 S 36th St Ste 100 *TF:* 800-794-3458 ■ *Web:* www.omahafoundation.org	Omaha	NE	68131	402-342-3458	342-3582
Oregon Community Foundation, The 1221 SW Yamhill St Ste 100 *Web:* www.oregoncf.org	Portland	OR	97205	503-227-6846	274-7771
Pacific Salmon Foundation 1682 7th Ave W Ste 300 *Web:* www.psf.ca	Vancouver	BC	V6J4S6	604-664-7664	
Peninsula Community Foundation 19101 Peninsula Club Dr *Web:* www.thepeninsulacommunityfoundation.org	Cornelius	NC	28031	704-237-0630	
Pittsburgh Foundation 5 PPG Pl Ste 250 *Web:* www.pittsburghfoundation.org	Pittsburgh	PA	15222	412-391-5122	391-7259
Prostate Cancer Foundation 1250 Fourth St *Web:* www.prostatecancerfoundation.org	Santa Monica	CA	90401	310-570-4700	
Purple Heart Service Foundation 7008 Little River Tpke *Web:* www.purpleheartcars.org	Annandale	VA	22003	703-256-6139	
Quality Texas Foundation 1402 Corinth St Ste 143 *Web:* www.texas-quality.org	Dallas	TX	75215	214-565-8550	
RCMP 73 Leikin Dr *Web:* www.rcmp-grc.gc.ca	Ottawa	ON	K1A0R2	613-993-2999	
Rhode Island Foundation 1 Union Stn *Web:* www.rifoundation.org	Providence	RI	02903	401-274-4564	331-8085
Robert Sterling Clark Foundation Inc 135 E 64th St *Web:* www.rsclark.org	New York	NY	10065	212-288-8900	
Saint Paul Foundation, The 101 Fifth St E Ste 2400 *TF:* 800-875-6167 ■ *Web:* www.saintpaulfoundation.org	Saint Paul	MN	55101	651-224-5463	224-8123
San Diego Foundation, The 2508 Historic Decatur Rd Ste 200 *Web:* www.sdfoundation.org	San Diego	CA	92106	619-235-2300	239-1710
San Diego Futures Foundation 4283 El Cajon Blvd Ste 220 *Web:* www.sdfutures.org	San Diego	CA	92105	619-269-1684	
San Francisco Foundation 1 Embarcadero Ctr Ste 1400 *Web:* www.sff.org	San Francisco	CA	94104	415-733-8500	477-2783

Phone *Fax*

Seattle Foundation 1200 Fifth Ave Ste 1300............ Seattle WA 98101 206-622-2294 622-7673
Web: www.seattlefoundation.org

St. Anns School Endowment 45 Water St............ Brooklyn NY 11201 718-834-8794
Web: www.stannswarehouse.org

Sycuan Band of Kumeyaay Nation
5459 Sycuan Rd.................................El Cajon CA 92019 619-445-2613
Web: www.sycuantribe.com

Vancouver Foundation
475 W Georgia St Ste 200 ....Vancouver BC V6B4M9 604-688-2204
Web: www.vancouverfoundation.ca

304 FOUNDATIONS - CORPORATE

See Also Charitable & Humanitarian Organizations p. 1754

Phone *Fax*

Abbott Laboratories Fund
100 Abbott Pk Rd.............................Abbott Park IL 60064 224-667-6100
NYSE: ABT ■ *Web:* abbott.com

Aetna Foundation Inc 151 Farmington Ave............Hartford CT 06156 860-273-6382
Web: www.aetna.com

Allstate Insurance Co 2775 Sanders Rd........... Northbrook IL 60062 847-402-5000 326-7517
NYSE: ALL ■ *Web:* www.allstate.com

Burroughs Wellcome Fund
21 TW Alexander Dr
PO Box 13901 ....Research Triangle Park NC 27709 919-991-5100 991-5160
Web: www.bwfund.org

Cargill Foundation 15407 McGinty Rd W Ste 46.........Wayzata MN 55391 877-765-8867 742-1087*
**Fax Area Code:* 952 ■ *TF:* 800-227-4455 ■ *Web:* www.cargill.com

CIGNA Foundation 900 Cottage Grove Rd............Bloomfield CT 06002 866-438-2446
NYSE: CI ■ *TF:* 866-438-2446 ■ *Web:* cigna.com/index.html

Coca-Cola Foundation Inc PO Box 1734..............Atlanta GA 30301 800-438-2653
TF: 800-438-2653 ■ *Web:* www.coca-colacompany.com

Dow Chemical Company Foundation 2030 Dow Ctr.....Midland MI 48674 989-636-1000 636-4460
TF: 800-331-6451 ■ *Web:* www.dow.com/about/corp/social/social.htm

ExxonMobil Foundation Inc
5959 Las Colinas Blvd..............................Irving TX 75039 972-444-1000 444-1405
Web: exxonmobil.com

GE Foundation 3135 Easton Tpke....................Fairfield CT 06828 203-373-3216 373-3029
Web: www.ge.com

General Mills Foundation PO Box 9452.........Minneapolis MN 55440 800-248-7310 764-8330*
**Fax Area Code:* 763 ■ *TF:* 800-248-7310 ■ *Web:* www.generalmills.com

General Motors Foundation Inc PO Box 33170.........Detroit MI 48232 800-222-1020
TF: 800-222-1020 ■ *Web:* www.gm.com

Georgia Power Foundation Inc 96 Annex..............Atlanta GA 30396 404-506-5000
Web: www.southerncompany.com

Hallmark Corp Foundation 2501 McGee St.........Kansas City MO 64108 800-425-5627 274-5061*
**Fax Area Code:* 816 ■ *TF:* 800-425-5627 ■ *Web:* corporate.hallmark.com

Hess Corp 1185 Ave of the Americas.................New York NY 10036 212-997-8500
Web: www.hess.com

HJ Heinz Company Foundation 600 Grant St.........Pittsburgh PA 15219 651-450-4064 442-3227*
**Fax Area Code:* 412 ■ *Web:* www.kraftheinzcompany.com

Humana Foundation Inc
500 W Main St Ste 208............................Louisville KY 40202 502-580-4140 580-1256
TF: 888-431-4748 ■ *Web:* www.humanafoundation.org

IBM International Foundation 1 New OrchaRd Rd.......Armonk NY 10504 914-499-1900
Web: www.ibm.com

Koch Foundation Inc
4421 NW 39th Ave Bldg 1 Ste 1....................Gainesville FL 32606 352-373-7491
Web: www.thekochfoundation.org

Lutheran Community Foundation
625 Fourth Ave S Ste 200.......................Minneapolis MN 55415 612-340-4110 340-4109
TF: 800-365-4172 ■ *Web:* infaithfound.org

Mead Westvaco Office Products Group
4751 Hempstead Station Dr..........................Dayton OH 45429 937-495-6323

MetLife Foundation
2701 Queens Plz N 1 MetLife Plz..................Long Island NY 11101 212-578-2555
Web: www.metlife.com

Motorola Foundation 1303 E Algonquin Rd ....Schaumburg IL 60196 847-576-5000
Web: motorola.com

New York Life Foundation 51 Madison Ave...........New York NY 10010 212-576-7341
Web: www.newyorklife.com

New York Times Co Foundation Inc
229 W 43rd St ....New York NY 10036 212-210-0100
Web: crainsnewyork.com

Pfizer Foundation Inc 235 E 42nd St.................New York NY 10017 212-733-2323
Web: www.pfizer.com

Principal Financial Group Foundation Inc
711 High St ....Des Moines IA 50392 502-855-3673 246-5475*
**Fax Area Code:* 515 ■ *TF:* 800-986-3343 ■ *Web:* www.principal.com/about/giving

Revlon Foundation Inc 237 Pk Ave...................New York NY 10017 800-473-8566
TF Cust Svc: 800-473-8566 ■ *Web:* www.revlon.com

SBC Foundation 130 E Travis St Ste 350 ....San Antonio TX 78205 800-591-9663
TF: 800-591-9663 ■ *Web:* www.att.com

Scripps Howard Foundation
312 Walnut St PO Box 5380.......................Cincinnati OH 45201 513-977-3035 977-3800
TF: 800-888-3000 ■ *Web:* www.scripps.com/foundation

Union Pacific Foundation 1400 Douglas St............Omaha NE 68179 402-544-5600
Web: up.com/aboutup/community/foundation/index.htm

UPS Foundation 55 Glenlake Pkwy NE ....Atlanta GA 30328 404-828-7123
Web: sustainability.ups.com

Wal-Mart Foundation 702 SW Eigth St.............Bentonville AR 72716 479-273-4000 273-6850
NYSE: WMT ■ *TF:* 800-438-6278 ■ *Web:* giving.walmart.com

Whirlpool Foundation 2000 N M-63............Benton Harbor MI 49022 269-923-5000
TF: 800-952-9245 ■ *Web:* www.whirlpoolcorp.com

Xerox Foundation 45 Glover Ave......................Norwalk CT 06856 800-275-9376
TF: 800-275-9376 ■ *Web:* www.xerox.com

305 FOUNDATIONS - PRIVATE

See Also Charitable & Humanitarian Organizations p. 1754

Phone *Fax*

A Glimmer of Hope Foundation
3600 N Capital of Texas Hwy Bldg B Ste 330............Austin TX 78746 512-328-9944
Web: www.aglimmerofhope.org

Adolph Coors Foundation
215 Saint Paul St Ste 300..........................Denver CO 80206 303-388-1636 388-1684

Ahmanson Foundation 9215 Wilshire Blvd.........Beverly Hills CA 90210 310-278-0770
Web: www.theahmansonfoundation.org

Aid Matrix Foundation, The 11701 Luna Rd...........Dallas TX 75234 469-357-6209
Web: www.aidmatrix.org

AIDS Foundation of Chicago
200 W Jackson Blvd Ste 2200 ....Chicago IL 60606 312-922-2322
TF: 866-895-2437 ■ *Web:* www.aidschicago.org

AIDS Healthcare Foundation
6255 W Sunset Blvd 21st Fl.....................Los Angeles CA 90028 323-860-5200
Web: www.aidshealth.org

Akron Community Foundation 345 W Cedar St..........Akron OH 44307 330-376-8522
Web: www.akroncf.org

Alberta Cancer Foundation 1331 29 St Nw...........Calgary AB T2N4N2 403-521-3433
Web: www.donate.albertacancer.ca

Alfred P Sloan Foundation
630 Fifth Ave Ste 2550..........................New York NY 10111 212-649-1649 757-5117
Web: www.sloan.org

Amity Foundation of California 2260 Watson Way........Vista CA 92083 888-508-9269
TF: 888-508-9269

Amon G Carter Foundation
201 Main St Ste 1945...........................Fort Worth TX 76102 817-332-2783 332-2787
Web: www.agcf.org

Andrew W Mellon Foundation 140 E 62nd St.........New York NY 10065 212-838-8400 888-4172
Web: www.mellon.org

Andy Warhol Foundation For The Visual Arts Inc
65 Bleecker St 7th Fl...........................New York NY 10012 212-242-2524
Web: www.warholfoundation.org

Animal Protection of New Mexico Inc Foundation
Po Box 11395.............................Albuquerque NM 87192 505-265-2322
Web: apnm.org

Annenberg Foundation
101 W Elm St Ste 640.......................Conshohocken PA 19428 610-341-9066 964-8688
Web: www.annenbergfoundation.org

Annie E Casey Foundation 701 St Paul St............Baltimore MD 21202 410-547-6600 547-6624
TF: 800-222-1099 ■ *Web:* www.aecf.org

Anschutz Family foundation, The
555 Seventeenth St Ste 2400 ....Denver CO 80202 303-293-2338
Web: www.anschutzfamilyfoundation.org

Archibald Bush Foundation
332 Minnesota St Ste E-900......................Saint Paul MN 55101 651-227-0891 297-6485
Web: www.bushfoundation.org

Arizona Scholarship Fund
4850 E Baseline Rd Ste 112...........................Mesa AZ 85206 480-497-4564
Web: www.azscholarships.org

Arnold & Mabel Beckman Foundation
100 Academy Dr.......................................Irvine CA 92617 949-721-2222
Web: www.beckman-foundation.org

Art Gallery of Ontario 317 Dundas St W..............Toronto ON M5T1G4 416-979-6660
TF: 877-225-4246 ■ *Web:* www.ago.net

Arthur Vining Davis Foundations
225 Water St..................................Jacksonville FL 32202 904-359-0670 359-0675
TF: 888-427-4313 ■ *Web:* www.avdf.org

Arts Foundation of Cape Cod, The
232 Main St Ste B.................................Hyannis MA 02601 508-362-0066
Web: www.artsfoundation.org

Ayn Rand Institute, Endowment
2121 Alton Pkwy Ste 250............................Irvine CA 92606 949-222-6550
Web: www.aynrand.org

Barr Foundation 136 NE Olive Way................Boca Raton FL 33432 561-394-6514 391-7601
Web: www.oandp.com

Benton Foundation 1625 K St NW 11th Fl..........Washington DC 20006 202-638-5770 638-5771
Web: www.benton.org

Bill & Melinda Gates Foundation PO Box 23350........Seattle WA 98102 206-709-3100 709-3180
TF: 800-728-3843 ■ *Web:* www.gatesfoundation.org

Bluebonnet Trail Elementary
11316 Farmhaven Rd ....Austin TX 78754 512-278-4125
Web: www.manorisd.net

Breakeven Inc 355 Apple Creek Blvd Ste 200..........Markham ON L3R9X7 905-752-1500
Web: www.causeview.com

Brown Foundation Inc 2217 Welch St................Houston TX 77019 713-523-6867 523-2917
Web: www.brownfoundation.org

Canada-Israel Industrial Research & Development Foundation
371A Richmond Rd.................................Ottawa ON K2A0E7 613-724-1284
Web: www.ciirdf.ca

Careers The Next Generation Foundation
10470 176 St Nw...............................Edmonton AB T5S1L3 780-426-3414
TF: 888-757-7172 ■ *Web:* nextgen.org

Carnegie Corp of New York 437 Madison Ave.........New York NY 10022 212-371-3200 754-4073
TF: 800-336-7323 ■ *Web:* www.carnegie.org

Center Township Trustee of Marion Company Indiana
863 Massachusetts Ave ....Indianapolis IN 46204 317-633-3610
Web: www.centergov.org

Centre for Addiction & Mental Health Foundation
901 King St W Ste 502..............................Toronto ON M5V3H5 416-979-6909
TF: 800-414-0471 ■ *Web:* www.supportcamh.ca

Challenged Athletes Foundation
9591 Waples St ....San Diego CA 92121 858-866-0959
Web: www.challengedathletes.org

Champlin Foundations, The
2000 Chapel View Blvd.............................Cranston RI 02920 212-620-4230
Web: foundationcenter.org

Organization	City	State	ZIP	Phone	Fax
Charles & Helen Schwab Foundation 1650 S Amphlett Blvd Ste 300 *Web:* www.schwabfoundation.org	San Mateo	CA	94402	650-655-2410	655-2411
Charles Hayden Foundation 140 Broadway *Web:* foundationcenter.org	New York	NY	10005	212-785-3677	
Charles Stewart Mott Foundation 503 S Saginaw St Ste 1200 *Web:* www.mott.org	Flint	MI	48502	810-238-5651	766-1753
Chatlos Foundation PO Box 915048 *Web:* www.chatlos.org	Longwood	FL	32791	407-862-5077	
Chautauqua Region Community Foundation Inc 418 Spring St *Web:* crcfonline.org	Jamestown	NY	14701	716-661-3390	
Cicatelli Associates Inc-ccd 100 Edgewood Ave Ne Ste 900	Atlanta	GA	30303	404-521-2151	
Colonial Williamsburg Foundation PO Box 1776 *TF:* 800-447-8679 ■ *Web:* www.history.org	Williamsburg	VA	23187	757-229-1000	
Colorado School of Mines Foundation Inc, The 1812 Illinois St *Web:* giving.mines.edu	Golden	CO	80401	303-273-3275	
Columbus Jewish Foundation 1175 College Ave *Web:* www.jewishcolumbus.org	Columbus	OH	43209	614-338-2365	
Commonwealth Fund 1 E 75th St *Web:* www.commonwealthfund.org	New York	NY	10021	212-606-3800	606-3500
Community College Foundation, The 1901 Royal Oaks Dr Ste 100 *Web:* www.communitycollege.org	Sacramento	CA	95815	916-418-5115	
ConnectEd 2150 Shattuck Ste 1200 *Web:* www.connectedcalifornia.org	Berkeley	CA	94704	510-849-4945	
Conrad N Hilton Foundation 100 W Liberty St Ste 840 *Web:* www.hiltonfoundation.org	Reno	NV	89501	775-323-4221	
Corporation for Public Broadcasting (CPB) 401 Ninth St NW *TF:* 800-272-2190 ■ *Web:* www.cpb.org	Washington	DC	20004	202-879-9600	879-9700
Dave Thomas Foundation for Adoption 716 Mt Airyshire Blvd Ste 100 *TF:* 800-275-3832 ■ *Web:* www.davethomasfoundation.org	Columbus	OH	43235	800-275-3832	
David Bohnett Foundation 245 S Beverly Dr *Web:* www.bohnettfoundation.org	Beverly Hills	CA	90212	310-276-0001	
David Suzuki Foundation 2211 Fourth Ave W *TF:* 800-453-1533 ■ *Web:* www.davidsuzuki.org	Vancouver	BC	V6K4S2	604-732-4228	
Donald W Reynolds Foundation 1701 Village Ctr Cir *Web:* www.dwreynolds.org	Las Vegas	NV	89134	702-804-6000	
Doris Duke Charitable Foundation (DDCF) 650 Fifth Ave 19th Fl *Web:* www.ddcf.org	New York	NY	10019	212-974-7000	974-7590
Duke Endowment 100 N Tryon St Ste 3500 *Web:* www.dukeendowment.org	Charlotte	NC	28202	704-376-0291	376-9336
Edna McConnell Clark Foundation 415 Madison Ave 10th Fl *Web:* www.emcf.org	New York	NY	10017	212-551-9100	421-9325
Elfenworks Foundation 20 park rd *Web:* elfenworks.org	Burlingame	CA	94010	650-347-9700	
Ellison Medical Foundation 104 E Ridgeville Blvd *Web:* www.ellisonfoundation.org	Mount Airy	MD	21771	301-829-6410	657-1828
Energy Foundation, The Fifth Fl 301 Battery St *Web:* www.ef.org	San Francisco	CA	94111	415-561-6700	
Evangelical Lutheran Good Samaritan Foundation, The 4800 W 57th St *Web:* www.good-sam.com	Sioux Falls	SD	57108	605-362-3100	
Evelyn & Walter Haas Jr Fund 114 Sansome St Ste 600 *Web:* www.haasjr.org	San Francisco	CA	94104	415-856-1400	856-1500
Ewing Marion Kauffman Foundation (EMKF) 4801 Rockhill Rd *TF:* 800-385-1607 ■ *Web:* www.kauffman.org	Kansas City	MO	64110	816-932-1000	932-1484
Facey Medical Group & Foundation 11211 Sepulveda Blvd *Web:* www.facey.com	Mission Hills	CA	91345	818-365-9531	
Fannie & John Hertz Foundation 2300 First St Ste 250 *Web:* www.hertzfoundation.org	Livermore	CA	94550	925-373-1642	
FJC 520 Eighth Ave 20th Fl *TF:* 888-448-3352 ■ *Web:* www.fjc.org	New York	NY	10018	212-714-0001	
Flinn Foundation, The 1802 N Central Ave *Web:* www.flinn.org	Phoenix	AZ	85004	602-744-6800	
Flintridge Operating Foundation 236 W Mountain St Ste 106 *Web:* www.flintridge.org	Pasadena	CA	91103	626-449-0839	
Flora Family Foundation, The 2121 Sand Hill Rd Ste 123 *Web:* www.florafamily.org	Menlo Park	CA	94025	650-233-1335	
Florida School Choice Fund Inc PO Box 1670 *TF:* 877-735-7837 ■ *Web:* www.stepupforstudents.org	Jacksonville	FL	33601	877-735-7837	
Food & Water Watch 1616 P St Nw Ste 300 *Web:* www.foodandwaterwatch.org	Washington	DC	20036	202-683-2500	
Food Corps 281 Park Ave South *Web:* foodcorps.org	New York	NY	10010	212-596-7045	
Ford Family Foundation 1600 NW Stewart Pkwy *Web:* www.tfff.org	Roseburg	OR	97471	541-957-5574	957-5720
Ford Foundation 320 E 43rd St *Web:* www.fordfoundation.org	New York	NY	10017	212-573-5000	351-3677
Free Methodist Foundation, The 8050 Spring Arbor Rd *TF:* 800-325-8975 ■ *Web:* fmfoundation.org	Spring Arbor	MI	49283	517-750-2727	
Fremont Area Community Foundation 4424 W 48th St *Web:* facommunityfoundation.org	Fremont	MI	49412	231-924-5350	
GAR Foundation Andrew Jackson House 277 E Mill St *Web:* www.garfdn.org	Akron	OH	44308	330-576-2926	
Gates Family Foundation 1390 Lawrence St *TF:* 866-590-4377 ■ *Web:* www.gatesfamilyfoundation.org	Denver	CO	80204	303-722-1881	316-3038
George Kaiser Family Foundation 7030 S Yale Ave Ste 600 *Web:* www.gkff.org	Tulsa	OK	74136	918-392-1612	
George S & Dolores Dore Eccles Foundation 79 S Main St 14th Fl *Web:* www.gsecclesfoundation.org	Salt Lake City	UT	84111	801-246-5340	350-3510
Georgia Northwestern Technical College Foundation Inc 1 Maurice Culberson Dr Sw *TF:* 866-983-4682 ■ *Web:* www.coosavalleytech.edu	Rome	GA	30161	706-295-6842	
Geraldine R Dodge Foundation 14 Maple Ave *Web:* www.grdodge.org	Morristown	NJ	07962	973-540-8442	540-1211
Gleaner's Food Bank of Indianapolis 3737 Waldemere Ave *Web:* www.gleaners.org	Indianapolis	IN	46241	317-925-0191	
Global Citizen Year Inc 1625 Clay St Ste 400 *Web:* globalcitizenyear.org	Oakland	CA	94612	415-963-9293	
GlobalGiving Foundation Inc 1816 12th St N W 3rd Fl *Web:* www.globalgiving.org	Washington	DC	20009	202-232-6212	
Goizueta Foundation 4401 Northside Pkwy Ste 520 *Web:* www.goizuetafoundation.org	Atlanta	GA	30327	404-239-0390	239-0018
Goodcity 5049 W Harrison St *Web:* www.goodcitychicago.org	Chicago	IL	60644	773-473-4790	
Gordon & Betty Moore Foundation PO Box 29910 *Web:* www.moore.org	San Francisco	CA	94129	415-561-7700	
Granite State Independent Living Foundation 21 Chenell Dr *TF:* 800-826-3700 ■ *Web:* www.gsil.org	Concord	NH	03301	603-228-9680	
Greater Texas Foundation 6100 Foundation Pl Dr *Web:* greatertexasfoundation.org	Bryan	TX	77807	979-779-6100	
Hall Family Foundation PO Box 419580 MD 323 *Web:* www.hallfamilyfoundation.org	Kansas City	MO	64141	816-274-8516	274-8547
Harry & Jeanette Weinberg Foundation Inc, The 7 Park Ctr Ct *Web:* hjweinbergfoundation.org	Owings Mills	MD	21117	410-654-8500	
Hearst Foundation, The 300 W 57th St 26th Fl *TF:* 800-841-7048 ■ *Web:* hearstfdn.org	New York	NY	10019	212-649-3750	586-1917
Help Foundation Inc 3622 Prospect Ave E *Web:* www.helpfoundationinc.org	Cleveland	OH	44115	216-432-4810	
Henry J Kaiser Family Foundation 2400 Sand Hill Rd *Web:* www.kff.org	Menlo Park	CA	94025	650-854-9400	854-4800
Henry Luce Foundation Inc 51 Madison Ave 30th Fl *Web:* www.hluce.org	New York	NY	10010	212-489-7700	581-9541
Henry M. Jackson Foundation For the Advancement of Military Medicine Inc 6720-A Rockledge Dr Ste 100 *Web:* www.hjf.org	Bethesda	MD	20817	240-694-2000	
Herbert H & Grace A Dow Foundation 1018 W Main St *Web:* www.hhdowfoundation.org	Midland	MI	48640	989-631-3699	631-0675
Hispanics in Philanthropy 414 13th St Ste 200 *Web:* www.hiponline.org	Oakland	CA	94612	415-837-0427	
Horace W Goldsmith Foundation 375 Pk Ave Rm 1602 *Web:* akfengyo.com.tr	New York	NY	10152	212-319-8700	319-2881
Hudson-Webber Foundation 333 W Ft St Ste 1310 *Web:* www.hudson-webber.org	Detroit	MI	48226	313-963-7777	
Human Development Foundation 1350 Remington Rd Ste W *Web:* www.hdf.com	Schaumburg	IL	60173	847-490-0100	
Idaho Community Foundation Inc 210 W State St *TF:* 800-657-5357 ■ *Web:* www.idcomfdn.org	Boise	ID	83702	208-342-3535	
Incentive Research Foundation 100 Chesterfield Business Pkwy Ste 200 *Web:* theirf.org	St. Louis	MO	63005	314-473-5601	
IU School of Medicine - Office of Gift Development 1110 W Michigan St Lo 506 *Web:* medgifts.medicine.iu.edu	Indianapolis	IN	46202	317-274-3270	
J Bulow Campbell Foundation 3050 Peachtree Rd NW Ste 270 *Web:* www.jbcf.org	Atlanta	GA	30305	404-658-9066	
JA & Kathryn Albertson Foundation 501 Baybrook Ct *Web:* www.jkaf.org	Boise	ID	83706	208-424-2600	
James Irvine Foundation 1 Bush St Ste 800 *Web:* www.irvine.org	San Francisco	CA	94104	415-777-2244	777-0869
JE & LE Mabee Foundation Inc 401 S Boston Ave Ste 3001 *Web:* www.mabeefoundation.com	Tulsa	OK	74103	918-584-4286	
John D & Catherine T MacArthur Foundation 140 S Dearborn St *Web:* www.macfound.org	Chicago	IL	60603	312-726-8000	920-6258
John S & James L Knight Foundation 200 S Biscayne Blvd Ste 3300 *Web:* www.knightfoundation.org	Miami	FL	33131	305-908-2600	908-2698
John Simon Guggenheim Memorial Foundation 90 Pk Ave *Web:* www.gf.org	New York	NY	10016	212-687-4470	697-3248
John Templeton Foundation 300 Conshohocken State Rd Ste 500 *Web:* www.templeton.org	West Conshohocken	PA	19428	610-941-2828	825-1730
Jones Family Foundation 31021 Lakeview Ave *Web:* www.jonesfamilyfoundation.org	Red Wing	MN	55066	651-388-7941	
Joyce Foundation 70 W Madison St Ste 2750 *Web:* www.joycefdn.org	Chicago	IL	60602	312-782-2464	782-4160

Phone | Fax

Joyce Theatre Foundation 175 Eighth Ave. New York NY 10011 212-691-9740
Web: www.joyce.org

Kakkis Everylife Foundation
77 Digital Dr Ste 210 Novato CA 94949 415-884-0223
Web: everylifefoundation.org

Kansas Health Foundation 309 E Douglas Wichita KS 67202 316-262-7676
TF: 800-373-7681 ■ *Web:* www.kansashealth.org

Kate B Reynolds Charitable Trust
128 Reynolda Village Winston-Salem NC 27106 336-397-5500 723-7765
TF: 800-485-9080 ■ *Web:* www.kbr.org

Kidango Inc 44000 Old Warm Springs Blvd. Fremont CA 94538 408-258-3710
TF: 800-262-4252 ■ *Web:* www.kidango.org

Kids Cancer Care Foundation of Alberta
609 14 St Nw Calgary AB T2N2A1 403-216-9210
Web: www.kidscancercare.ab.ca

Kiwanis International Foundation
3636 Woodview Trace Indianapolis IN 46268 317-875-8755 879-0204
TF: 800-549-2647 ■ *Web:* www.kiwanis.org

Kresge Foundation 3215 W Big Beaver Rd. Troy MI 48084 248-643-9630
Web: www.kresge.org

Krishnamurti Foundation of America
134 Besant Rd Ojai CA 93023 805-646-2726
Web: kfa.org

Krochet Kids International
1630 Superior Ave Unit C Costa Mesa CA 92627 949-791-2560
Web: www.krochetkids.org

Lake Avenue Community Foundation Inc
712 E Villa St Pasadena CA 91101 626-449-4960
Web: www.lakeavefoundation.org

Landesa 1424 Fourth Ave Ste 300 Seattle WA 98101 206-528-5880
Web: www.landesa.org

Lasalle College High School Endowment
8605 Cheltenham Ave. Wyndmoor PA 19038 215-233-2911
Web: www.lschs.org

Liberty Fund Inc
8335 Allison Pt Trial Ste 300 Indianapolis IN 46250 317-842-0880 579-6060
TF: 800-955-8335 ■ *Web:* www.libertyfund.org

Liliuokalani Trust 1300 Halona St Honolulu HI 96817 808-847-1302
Web: www.onipaa.org

Lilly Endowment Inc 2801 N Meridian St. Indianapolis IN 46208 317-924-5471 926-4431
Web: www.lillyendowment.org

Lois Pope LIFE Foundation
6274 Linton Blvd Ste 103 Delray Beach FL 33484 561-865-0955
Web: www.life-edu.org

Los Altos Community Foundation
183 Hillview Ave Los Altos CA 94022 650-949-5908
Web: www.losaltoscf.org

Lown Cardiovascular Research Foundation
21 Longwood Ave Brookline MA 02446 617-992-9322
Web: lowninstitute.org

Lumina Foundation for Education
30 S Meridian St Ste 700 Indianapolis IN 46204 317-951-5300
TF: 800-834-5756 ■ *Web:* www.luminafoundation.org

Lyndhurst Foundation 517 E Fifth St Chattanooga TN 37403 423-756-0767
Web: www.lyndhurstfoundation.org

Magic Johnson Foundation Inc
9100 Wilshire Blvd Beverly Hills CA 90212 310-247-2033 786-8796
Web: magicjohnson.org

Maravilla Foundation 5723 Union Pacific Ave Commerce CA 90022 323-721-4162

Marbridge Foundation Inc
2310 Bliss Spillar Rd Manchaca TX 78652 512-282-1144
Web: marbridge.org

McCune Foundation 6 PPG Pl Ste 750 Pittsburgh PA 15222 412-644-8779 644-8059
Web: www.mccune.org

McKnight Foundation
710 Second St S Ste 400 Minneapolis MN 55401 612-333-4220 332-3833
Web: www.mcknight.org

Meadows Foundation Inc 3003 Swiss Ave. Dallas TX 75204 214-826-9431 827-7042
TF: 800-826-9431 ■ *Web:* www.mfi.org

Meals on Wheels Inc of Tarrant County Endowment Fund
320 S Fwy. Fort Worth TX 76104 817-336-0912
Web: mealsonwheels.org

Meyer Memorial Trust
425 NW Tenth Ave Ste 400 Portland OR 97209 503-228-5512
Web: www.mmt.org

Michael J Fox Foundation for Parkinson's Research
Grand Central Stn PO Box 4777 New York NY 10163 800-708-7644
TF: 800-708-7644 ■ *Web:* www.michaeljfox.org

Midland Area Community Foundation
76 Ashman Cir Midland MI 48640 989-839-9661
Web: www.midlandfoundation.org

Milken Family Foundation 1250 Fourth St. Santa Monica CA 90401 310-570-4800 570-4801
Web: www.mff.org

MJ Murdock Charitable Trust
703 Broadway St Ste 710 Vancouver WA 98660 360-694-8415 694-1819
Web: www.murdock-trust.org

Mobile Area Education Foundation
605 Bel Air Blvd Ste 400 Mobile AL 36606 251-476-0002
Web: maef.net

Moody Foundation
2302 Post Office St Ste 704 Galveston TX 77550 409-797-1500
Web: www.moodyf.org

Morris & Gwendolyn Cafritz Foundation
1825 K St NW Ste 1400 Washington DC 20006 202-223-3100 296-7567
Web: www.cafritzfoundation.org

Narrow Gate Foundation 242 Dry Prong Rd Williamsport TN 38487 931-583-0633
Web: narrowgate.org

Nathan Cummings Foundation
475 Tenth Ave 14th Fl. New York NY 10018 212-787-7300
Web: www.nathancummings.org

National Foundation for Cancer Research (NFCR)
4600 E W Hwy Ste 525 Bethesda MD 20814 301-654-1250 654-5824
TF: 800-321-2873 ■ *Web:* www.nfcr.org

National PTA 1250 N Pitt St. Alexandria VA 22314 703-518-1200
TF: 800-307-4782 ■ *Web:* pta.org

Nebraska Humane Society Foundation 8929 Ft St Omaha NE 68134 402-444-7800
Web: www.nehumanesociety.org

Nellie Mae Education Foundation
1250 Hancock St Ste 205N Quincy MA 02169 781-348-4200 348-4299
TF: 877-635-5436 ■ *Web:* www.nmefoundation.org

New Leaders for New Schools
30 W 26th St 2nd Fl New York NY 10010 646-792-1070
Web: www.newleaders.org

New York Road Runners Club 9 E 89th St New York NY 10128 212-860-4455
Web: www.nyrr.org

Noyce Foundation
419 S San Antonio Rd Ste 213 Los Altos CA 94022 650-856-2600
Web: www.noycefdn.org

NYU Alumni Association 25 W Fourth St 4th Fl New York NY 10012 212-998-6912
Web: www.alumni.nyu.edu

Ogden-Weber Applied Technology College Foundation
200 N Washington Blvd Ogden UT 84404 801-627-8300
Web: www.owatc.edu

Olmsted Center for Sight 1170 Main St Buffalo NY 14209 716-882-1025
Web: www.olmstedcenter.org

Open Society Institute 400 W 59th St. New York NY 10019 212-548-0600 548-4679
Web: www.opensocietyfoundations.org

Orfalea Family Foundation
1283 Coast Village Cir Ste 2 Santa Barbara CA 93108 805-565-7550
Web: www.orfaleafoundation.org

Ottawa Regional Cancer Foundation The
1500 Alta Vista Dr. Ottawa ON K1G3Y9 613-247-3527
TF: 855-247-3527 ■ *Web:* www.ottawacancer.ca

Otto Bremer Foundation
30 E Seventh St Ste 2900 Saint Paul MN 55101 651-227-8036
Web: www.ottobremer.org

Pacific Legal Foundation 930 G St. Sacramento CA 95814 916-419-7111
Web: www.pacificlegal.org

Packard Humanities Institute, The (PHI)
300 Second St Los Altos CA 94022 650-948-0150
Web: www.packhum.org

Padre Pio Foundation of America Inc
463 Main St Cromwell CT 06416 860-635-4996
Web: padrepio.com

Pangaea Global AIDS Foundation
436 14th St Ste 920 Oakland CA 94612 510-379-4003
Web: pangaeaglobal.org

Patient Advocate Foundation Inc
700 Thimble Shoals Blvd Ste 200 Newport News VA 23606 800-532-5274
TF: 800-532-5274 ■ *Web:* www.patientadvocate.org

Paul G Allen Family Foundation
505 Fifth Ave S Ste 900 Seattle WA 98104 206-342-2030 342-3000
Web: www.pgafamilyfoundation.org

Pew Charitable Trusts
2005 Market St 1 Commerce Sq Ste 1700 Philadelphia PA 19103 215-575-9050 575-4939
TF: 800-351-6801 ■ *Web:* www.pewtrusts.org

Phi Kappa Phi Foundation
7576 Goodwood Blvd Baton Rouge LA 70806 225-388-4917
TF: 800-804-9880 ■ *Web:* www.phikappaphi.org

Phillips Brooks School Endowment
2245 Avy Ave Menlo Park CA 94025 650-854-4545
Web: www.phillipsbrooks.org

Princeton Public Library 65 Witherspoon St Princeton NJ 08542 609-924-9529
Web: www.princeton.lib.nj.us

Public Interest Network 1543 Wazee St Ste 400 Denver CO 80202 303-573-5995
Web: www.publicinterestnetwork.org

Public Welfare Foundation 1200 U St NW. Washington DC 20009 202-965-1800
TF: 800-275-7934 ■ *Web:* www.publicwelfare.org

Research Corp 4703 E Camp Lowell Dr Ste 201 Tucson AZ 85712 520-571-1111 571-1119
Web: www.rescorp.org

Retirement Research Foundation
8765 W Higgins Rd Ste 430 Chicago IL 60631 773-714-8080 714-8089
Web: www.rrf.org

Richard King Mellon Foundation
500 Grant St Ste 4106 Pittsburgh PA 15219 412-392-2800
TF: 800-424-9836 ■ *Web:* foundationcenter.org

Robert A Welch Foundation
5555 San Felipe St Ste 1900 Houston TX 77056 713-961-9884
Web: www.welch1.org

Robert R McCormick Tribune Foundation
205 N Michigan Ave Ste 4300 Chicago IL 60611 312-445-5000 445-5001
TF: 800-435-7352 ■ *Web:* www.mccormickfoundation.org

Robert W Woodruff Foundation Inc
191 Peachtree St NE Ste 3540 Atlanta GA 30303 404-522-6755 522-7026
Web: www.woodruff.org

Robert Wood Johnson Foundation PO Box 2316 Princeton NJ 08543 877-843-7953
TF: 877-843-7953 ■ *Web:* www.rwjf.org

Rockefeller Bros Fund
475 Riverside Dr Ste 900 New York NY 10115 212-812-4200 812-4299
Web: www.rbf.org

Rockefeller Foundation 420 Fifth Ave New York NY 10018 212-869-8500 764-3468*
*Fax: Mail Rm ■ *Web:* www.rockefellerfoundation.org

Rose & Sherle Wagner Foundation
224 W 29th St Fl 12 New York NY 10001 212-239-0022
Web: yayanetwork.org

Roy J Carver Charitable Trust 202 Iowa Ave Muscatine IA 52761 563-263-4010 263-1547
Web: www.carvertrust.org

Saint Luke Institute Foundation Inc
8901 New Hampshire Ave. Silver Spring MD 20903 301-445-7970
Web: sli.org

Salesforce.Com Foundation
The Landmark @ One Market Ste 300 San Francisco CA 94105 800-667-6389
TF: 800-667-6389 ■ *Web:* www.salesforce.org

San Diego Yacht Club Sailing Foundation
1011 Anchorage Ln San Diego CA 92106 619-221-8400
Web: sdycsf.org

Sarcoma Foundation of America Inc, The
9899 Main St Ste 204 Damascus MD 20872 301-253-8687
Web: www.curesarcoma.org

				Phone	Fax
Scholarship Foundation of Santa Barbara 2253 Las Positas Rd *Web:* www.sbscholarship.org	Santa Barbara	CA	93105	805-687-6065	
Sen. George J Mitchell Scholarship Resea 75 Washington Ave Ste 2E *Web:* mitchellinstitute.org	Portland	ME	04101	207-773-7700	
Seniors First Foundation Inc 5395 L B Mcleod Rd *Web:* www.seniorsfirstinc.org	Orlando	FL	32811	407-292-0177	
Seva Foundation 1786 Fifth St *TF:* 877-764-7382 ■ *Web:* www.seva.org	Berkeley	CA	94710	510-845-7382	
Shubert Foundation Inc, The 234 W 44th St *Web:* www.shubertfoundation.org	New York	NY	10036	212-944-3777	
Sierra Health Foundation 1321 Garden Hwy *Web:* www.sierrahealth.org	Sacramento	CA	95833	916-922-4755	
Smith Richardson Foundation Inc 60 Jesup Rd *Web:* www.srf.org	Westport	CT	06880	203-222-6222	
Spencer Foundation 625 N Michigan Ave Ste 1600 *Web:* www.spencer.org	Chicago	IL	60611	312-337-7000	337-0282
St. Croix Valley Foundation 516 Second St Ste 214 *Web:* www.scvfoundation.org	Hudson	WI	54016	715-386-9490	
St. Hope Foundation 6800 W Loop S Ste 560 *Web:* www.offeringhope.org	Bellaire	TX	77401	713-839-7111	
Starr Foundation 399 Pk Ave 17th Fl *Web:* www.starrfoundation.org	New York	NY	10022	212-909-3600	
StayClassy Productions Inc 533 F St Ste 300 *Web:* www.classy.org	San Diego	CA	92101	619-961-1892	
Stowers Institute For Medical Research 1000 E 50th St *Web:* www.stowers.org	Kansas City	MO	64110	816-926-4000	926-2000
Student Agencies Foundation Inc 409 College Ave *Web:* www.studentagencies.com	Ithaca	NY	14850	607-272-2000	
Student Veterans of America PO Box 77673 *TF:* 866-320-3826 ■ *Web:* www.studentveterans.org	Washington	DC	20013	202-223-4710	
Sunlight Foundation 1818 N St NW Ste 300 *Web:* www.sunlightfoundation.com	Washington	DC	20036	202-742-1520	
Sunrise Children Foundation 2795 E Desert Inn Rd Ste 100 *Web:* www.sunrisechildren.org	Las Vegas	NV	89121	702-731-8373	
Sunrise House Foundation Inc 37 Sunset Inn Rd PO Box 600 *Web:* www.sunrisehouse.com	Lafayette	NJ	07848	973-383-6300	
Surdna Foundation Inc 330 Madison Ave 30th Fl *Web:* www.surdna.org	New York	NY	10017	212-557-0010	557-0003
Sutter East Bay Medical Foundation 3687 Mt Diablo Blvd Ste 200 *Web:* www.sebmf.org	Lafayette	CA	94549	925-962-6600	
T Buck Suzuki Environmental Foundation 326 12th St Ste 100 *Web:* www.bucksuzuki.org	New Westminster	BC	V3M4H6	604-519-3635	
T4 Global Inc PO Box 130266 *Web:* t4global.org	Dallas	TX	75313	214-205-4245	
Temple Kol Ami Emanu-el Foundation Inc 8200 Peters Rd *Web:* tkae.org	Plantation	FL	33324	954-472-1988	
Terra Foundation for American Art 120 E Erie St *Web:* terraamericanart.org	Chicago	IL	60611	312-664-3939	664-2052
Texas Methodist Foundation 11709 Boulder Ln Ste 100 *TF:* 800-933-5502 ■ *Web:* www.tmf-fdn.org	Austin	TX	78726	512-331-9971	
Thomas Jefferson Foundation PO Box 316 *Web:* www.monticello.org	Charlottesville	VA	22902	434-984-9808	977-7757
Tides Canada Foundation 400-163 W Hastings St *TF:* 866-843-3722 ■ *Web:* tidescanada.org	Vancouver	BC	V6B1H5	604-647-6611	
Tides Foundation Po Box 29903 *Web:* www.tides.org	San Francisco	CA	94129	415-561-6400	
Toledo Community Foundation 300 Madison Ave Ste 1300 *Web:* www.toledocf.org	Toledo	OH	43604	419-241-5049	
Tuality Healthcare Foundation Inc 335 SE Eighth Ave *Web:* www.tuality.org/foundation	Hillsboro	OR	97123	503-681-1170	
Turner Foundation Inc 133 Luckie St 2nd Fl *Web:* www.turnerfoundation.org	Atlanta	GA	30303	404-681-9900	681-0172
UCF Foundation Inc 12424 Research Pkwy Ste 250 *Web:* ucffoundation.org	Orlando	FL	32826	407-882-1220	
UCLA Foundation, The 10920 Wilshire Blvd Ste 900 *Web:* www.uclafoundation.org	Los Angeles	CA	90024	310-794-3193	
Universitas Foundation of Canada 3005 Ave Maricourt *TF:* 877-710-7377 ■ *Web:* www.universitas.ca	Quebec	QC	G1W4T8	418-651-8975	
Utility Notification Center of Colorado 16361 Table Mtn Pkwy *Web:* colorado811.org	Golden	CO	80403	303-232-1991	
Van Andel Institute 333 Bostwick Ave NE *Web:* www.vai.org	Grand Rapids	MI	49503	616-234-5000	234-5001
Verland Foundation Inc, The 212 Iris Rd *Web:* verland.org	Sewickley	PA	15143	412-741-2375	
Vira I Heinz Endowment 625 Liberty Ave 30 Dominion Twr *Web:* www.heinz.org	Pittsburgh	PA	15222	412-281-5777	281-5788
Wallace Foundation, The 5 Penn Plz 7th Fl *Web:* www.wallacefoundation.org/pages/default.aspx	New York	NY	10001	212-251-9700	679-6990
Walter & Elise Haas Fund 1 Lombard St Ste 305	San Francisco	CA	94111	415-398-4474	
Walton Family Foundation Inc (WFF) PO Box 2030 *Web:* www.waltonfamilyfoundation.org	Bentonville	AR	72712	479-464-1570	464-1580
Way to Happiness Foundation International, The 201 E Broadway *Web:* www.thewaytohappiness.org	Glendale	CA	91205	818-254-0600	
Wayne & Gladys Valley Foundation 1939 Harrison St Ste 510 *Web:* foundationcenter.org	Oakland	CA	94612	510-466-6060	
Weingart Foundation 1055 W Seventh St Ste 3050 *Web:* www.weingartfnd.org	Los Angeles	CA	90017	213-688-7799	688-1515
Wesley Foundation-msu 3625 Midland Ave	Memphis	TN	38111	901-458-5808	
Whitehall Foundation Inc 125 Worth Ave. *Web:* www.whitehall.org	Palm Beach	FL	33480	561-655-4474	
William & Flora Hewlett Foundation 2121 Sand Hill Rd *Web:* www.hewlett.org	Menlo Park	CA	94025	650-234-4500	234-4501
William Penn Foundation 100 N 18th St 2 Logan Sq 11th Fl *Web:* www.wpennfdn.org	Philadelphia	PA	19103	215-988-1830	988-1823
Wisconsin Alumni Research Foundation 614 Walnut St 13th Fl. *Web:* www.warf.org	Madison	WI	53726	608-263-2500	
WK Kellogg Foundation 1 Michigan Ave E *Web:* www.wkkf.org	Battle Creek	MI	49017	269-968-1611	968-0413
WM Keck Foundation 550 S Hope St Ste 2500 *Web:* www.wmkeck.org	Los Angeles	CA	90071	213-680-3833	
Women's Foundation of Colorado, The The Chambers Ctr 1901 E Asbury Ave *Web:* www.wfco.org	Denver	CO	80208	303-285-2960	
Women's Independence Scholarship Program Inc (WISP) 4900 Randall Pkwy Ste H *TF:* 866-255-7742 ■ *Web:* www.wispinc.org	Wilmington	NC	28403	910-397-7742	397-0023
XanGo Goodness 2889 Ashton Blvd *TF:* 877-469-2646 ■ *Web:* www.xango.com	Lehi	UT	84043	801-816-8000	

306 FOUNDRIES - INVESTMENT

				Phone	Fax
Aero Metals Inc 1201 E Lincoln Way *Web:* www.aerometals.com	La Porte	IN	46350	219-326-1976	326-1972
Bescast Inc 4600 E 355th St *Web:* www.bescast.com	Willoughby	OH	44094	440-946-5300	946-8437
Bimac Corp 3034 Dryden Rd *Web:* www.bimac.com	Dayton	OH	45439	937-299-7333	299-7367
Consolidated Casting Corp 1501 S I-45 *TF:* 800-649-5289 ■ *Web:* www.consolicast.com	Hutchins	TX	75141	972-225-7305	225-2970
Dolphin Inc 740 S 59th Ave *Web:* www.dolphincasting.com	Phoenix	AZ	85043	602-272-6747	233-9570
Engineered Precision Casting Company Inc 952 Palmer Ave *Web:* www.epcast.com	Middletown	NJ	07748	732-671-2424	671-8615
FS Precision Tech Co LLC 3025 E Victoria St *Web:* www.fs-precision.com	Rancho Dominguez	CA	90221	310-638-0595	631-1664
Hitchiner Mfg Company Inc 594 Elm St *Web:* www.hitchiner.com	Milford	NH	03055	603-673-1100	673-7960
Houser & Plessl Wealth Management Group 5100 W Tilghman St Ste 240 *Web:* houserplessl.com	Allentown	PA	18104	610-530-0700	
PCC Structurals Inc 4600 SE Harney Dr *Web:* www.pccstructurals.com	Portland	OR	97206	503-777-3881	
Pennsylvania Precision Cast Parts Inc 521 N Third Ave PO Box 1429 *Web:* www.ppcpinc.com	Lebanon	PA	17042	717-273-3338	273-2662
Post Precision Castings Inc 21 Walnut St *Web:* www.postprecision.com	Strausstown	PA	19559	610-488-1011	488-6928
Precision Metalsmiths Inc 15583 Brookpark Rd *Web:* avalon-castings.com	Cleveland	OH	44142	216-481-8900	
Remet Corp 210 Commons Rd *TF:* 877-939-0171 ■ *Web:* www.remet.com	Utica	NY	13502	315-797-8700	787-4848
Stainless Foundry & Engineering Inc 5110 N 35th St *Web:* www.stainlessfoundry.com	Milwaukee	WI	53209	414-462-7400	462-7303
Waltek Inc 14310 Sunfish Lk Blvd *TF:* 800-937-9496 ■ *Web:* www.waltekinc.com	Ramsey	MN	55303	763-427-3181	427-3216

307 FOUNDRIES - IRON & STEEL

See Also Foundries - Nonferrous (Castings) p. 2324

				Phone	Fax
Aarrowcast Inc 2900 E Richmond St *Web:* www.aarrowcast.com	Shawano	WI	54166	715-526-3600	526-9758
Allegheny Technologies Inc 1000 Six PPG Pl *NYSE:* ATI ■ *TF Sales:* 800-258-3586 ■ *Web:* www.atimetals.com	Pittsburgh	PA	15222	412-394-2800	
Alloy Engineering & Casting Co 1700 W Washington St **Fax Area Code:* 260 ■ *TF:* 800-348-2880 ■ *Web:* www.wirco.com	Champaign	IL	61821	217-398-3200	897-2525*
American Cast Iron Pipe Co (ACIPCO) 1501 31st Ave N *TF:* 800-442-2347 ■ *Web:* www.american-usa.com	Birmingham	AL	35207	205-325-7701	
AMSTED Industries Inc 180 N Stetson St Ste 1800 *Web:* www.amsted.com	Chicago	IL	60601	312-645-1700	
Atlas Foundry Company Inc 601 N Henderson Ave *Web:* www.atlasfdry.com	Marion	IN	46952	765-662-2525	662-2902
Badger Foundry Co 1058 E Mark St *Web:* www.badgerfoundry.com	Winona	MN	55987	507-452-5760	452-6469

Company	City	State	Zip	Phone	Fax
Bailey Metal Products Ltd 1 Caldari Rd *Web:* www.bmp-group.com	Concord	ON	L4K3Z9	905-738-6738	
Bay Cast Inc 2611 Ctr Ave *Web:* www.baycast.com	Bay City	MI	48708	989-892-0511	892-0599
Benton Foundry Inc 5297 SR 487 *Web:* www.bentonfoundry.com	Benton	PA	17814	570-925-6711	925-6929
Bremen Castings Inc 500 N Baltimore St **Fax Area Code:* 574 ■ *TF:* 800-837-2411 ■ *Web:* www.bremencastings.com	Bremen	IN	46506	800-837-2411	546-5016*
Buck Company Inc 897 Lancaster Pk *Web:* www.buckcompany.com	Quarryville	PA	17566	717-284-4114	284-3737
Campbell Foundry Co 800 Bergen St *Web:* www.campbellfoundry.com	Harrison	NJ	07029	973-483-5480	483-1843
Canada Alloy Casting Co 529 Manitou Dr *Web:* www.cac.ca	Kitchener	ON	N2C1S2	519-895-1161	895-1169
Cast-Fab Technologies Inc 3040 Forrer St *Web:* www.cast-fab.com	Cincinnati	OH	45209	513-758-1000	758-1002
Castalloy Inc 1701 Industrial Ln PO Box 827 *TF:* 800-211-0900 ■ *Web:* www.castalloycorp.com	Waukesha	WI	53189	262-547-0070	547-2215
Casting Solutions LLC 2345 Licking Rd *Web:* www.burnhamfoundry.com	Zanesville	OH	43701	740-452-9371	
Charter Dura-Bar 2100 W Lake Shore Dr *Web:* charterdura-bar.com	Woodstock	IL	60098	815-338-3900	
Columbia Steel Casting Co Inc 10425 N Bloss Ave *TF:* 800-547-9471 ■ *Web:* www.columbiasteel.com	Portland	OR	97203	503-286-0685	286-1743
Columbus Castings 2211 Parsons Ave *Web:* www.columbuscastings.com	Columbus	OH	43207	614-444-2121	
Complex Steel & Wire Corp 36254 Annapolis St *TF:* 800-521-0666 ■ *Web:* www.complexsteel.com	Wayne	MI	48184	734-326-1600	326-7421
Delta Centrifugal Corp PO Box 1043 *TF Sales:* 888-433-3100 ■ *Web:* www.deltacentrifugal.com	Temple	TX	76503	254-773-9055	
Dixie Southern Industrial Inc 1060 N Commonwealth Ave *Web:* www.dsisteel.com	Polk City	FL	33868	863-984-1900	984-1825
Donsco Inc 124 N Front St *Web:* www.donsco.com	Wrightsville	PA	17368	717-252-1561	252-4530
Dotson Company Inc 200 W Rock St *Web:* www.dotson.com	Mankato	MN	56001	507-345-5018	345-1270
Douglas Steel Fabricating Corp 1312 S Waverly Rd *Web:* www.douglassteel.com	Lansing	MI	48917	517-322-2050	322-0050
Duraloy Technologies Inc 120 Bridge St **Fax:* Sales ■ *Web:* www.duraloy.com	Scottdale	PA	15683	724-887-5100	887-5224*
Eagle Foundry Co Inc PO Box 250 *Web:* www.eaglefoundryco.com	Eagle Creek	OR	97022	503-637-3048	637-3091
EJ Group Inc 301 Spring St *TF:* 800-874-4100 ■ *Web:* americas.ejco.com	East Jordan	MI	49727	231-536-2261	536-4458
Elyria Foundry Co 120 Filbert St *Web:* www.elyriafoundry.com	Elyria	OH	44036	440-322-4657	323-1101
Eureka Foundry Co 1601 Reggie White Blvd *Web:* www.eurekafoundryco.com	Chattanooga	TN	37402	423-267-3328	756-2607
Farrar Corp 142 W Burns St *TF:* 800-536-2215 ■ *Web:* www.farrarusa.com	Norwich	KS	67118	620-478-2212	478-2200
Frazier & Frazier Industries Inc 817 S First St PO Box 279 *Web:* www.ffcastings.com	Coolidge	TX	76635	254-786-2293	786-2284
Frog Switch & Mfg Co 600 E High St *TF:* 800-233-7194 ■ *Web:* www.frogswitch.com	Carlisle	PA	17013	717-243-2454	243-7768
Gartland Foundry Company Inc 330 Grant St *Web:* www.gartlandfoundry.com	Terre Haute	IN	47802	812-232-0226	232-7569
Goldens' Foundry & Machine Co (GFMCO) 600 12th St *Web:* www.gfmco.com	Columbus	GA	31902	706-323-0471	596-2850
Great Lakes Castings LLC 800 N Washington Ave *Web:* www.greatlakescastings.com	Ludington	MI	49431	231-843-2501	845-1534
Grede Holdings LLC 4000 Town Ctr Ste 500 *Web:* www.grede.com	Southfield	MI	48075	248-440-9500	440-9577
Harrison Steel Castings Co Inc 900 S Mound St *TF:* 800-659-4722 ■ *Web:* www.hscast.com	Attica	IN	47918	765-762-2481	762-2487
Hensley Industries Inc 2108 Joe Field Rd PO Box 29779 **Fax:* Cust Svc ■ *TF:* 888-406-6262 ■ *Web:* www.hensleyind.com	Dallas	TX	75229	972-241-2321	241-0915*
Hitachi Metals America Ltd 2 Manhattanville Rd Ste 301 *TF:* 800-777-5757 ■ *Web:* www.hitachimetals.com	Purchase	NY	10577	914-694-9200	694-9279
Howco Metals Management 9611 Telge Rd *TF:* 800-392-7720 ■ *Web:* www.howcogroup.com	Houston	TX	77095	281-649-8800	649-8900
Huron Casting Inc 7050 Hartley St PO Box 679 *Web:* www.huroncasting.com	Pigeon	MI	48755	989-453-3933	453-3319
Intat Precision Inc 2148 N State Rd 3 PO Box 488 *Web:* www.intat.com	Rushville	IN	46173	765-932-5323	932-3032
Interstate Castings Co 3823 Massachusetts Ave *Web:* www.interstatecastings.com	Indianapolis	IN	46218	317-546-2427	546-4004
Jencast PO Box 1509 *TF:* 800-331-2662 ■ *Web:* www.jencast.com	Coffeyville	KS	67337	620-251-5700	251-3622
Johnson Brass & Machine Foundry Inc 270 N Mill St PO Box 219 *Web:* www.johnsoncentrifugal.com	Saukville	WI	53080	262-377-9440	284-7066
Johnstown Specialty Castings Inc 545 Central Ave **Fax:* Sales ■ *Web:* whemco.com	Johnstown	PA	15902	814-535-9000	536-0868*
Maddox Foundry & Machine Works Inc 13370 SW 170th St *Web:* www.maddoxfoundry.com	Archer	FL	32618	352-495-2121	495-3962
Maynard Steel Casting Co 2856 S 27th St *Web:* www.maynardsteel.com	Milwaukee	WI	53215	414-645-0440	645-7378
McWane Inc 2900 Hwy 280 Ste 300 *Web:* www.mcwane.com	Birmingham	AL	35223	205-414-3100	414-3170
Milwaukee Malleable & Grey Iron Works 2773 S 29th St *Web:* milwtool.com	Milwaukee	WI	53201	414-645-0200	
Minnotte Corp Minnotte Sq *Web:* www.minnotte.com	Pittsburgh	PA	15220	412-922-1633	922-5051
Motor Castings Co 1323 S 65th St *Web:* www.motorcastings.com	Milwaukee	WI	53214	414-476-1434	476-2845
Neenah Foundry Co 2121 Brooks Ave *TF:* 800-558-5075 ■ *Web:* www.nfco.com	Neenah	WI	54956	920-725-7000	729-3661
Northern Iron & Machine 867 Forest St *Web:* www.northernim.com	Saint Paul	MN	55106	651-778-3300	778-1321
Omaha Steel Castings Co 921 E 12th St *Web:* www.omahasteel.com/contact-us.html	Wahoo	NE	68066	402-558-6000	558-0327
Osco Industries Inc PO Box 1388 *Web:* www.oscoind.com	Portsmouth	OH	45662	740-354-3183	353-1504
Pacific States Cast Iron Pipe Co 1401 East 2000 South PO Box 1219 *Web:* mcwaneductile.com	Provo	UT	84603	801-373-6910	377-0338
Pacific Steel Casting Company Inc 1333 Second St *Web:* www.pacificsteel.com	Berkeley	CA	94710	510-525-9200	524-4673
Paxton-Mitchell Co 108 S 12th St *Web:* www.paxton-mitchell.com	Blair	NE	68008	402-426-3131	345-6772
Prospect Foundry LLC 1225 Winter St NE *Web:* www.prospectfdry.com	Minneapolis	MN	55413	612-331-9282	331-4122
Quaker City Castings Inc 310 E Euclid Ave *Web:* www.qccast.com	Salem	OH	44460	330-332-1566	332-1159
Quality Castings Co 1200 N Main St *Web:* www.qcfoundry.com	Orrville	OH	44667	330-682-6010	683-3153
Richmond Foundry 126 Collins Rd *Web:* www.matrixmetalsllc.com	Richmond	TX	77469	281-342-5511	
Rodney Hunt Co 46 Mill St *TF:* 800-448-8860 ■ *Web:* www.rodneyhunt.com	Orange	MA	01364	978-544-2511	544-7204
Samuel Steel Pickling Co 1400 Enterprise Pkwy *Web:* www.samuelsteel.com	Twinsburg	OH	44087	330-963-3777	963-0770
Sawbrook Steel Castings Co 425 Shepherd Ave *Web:* www.sawbrooksteel.com	Cincinnati	OH	45215	513-554-1700	554-0092
Sentinel Bldg Systems Inc 237 S Fourth St PO Box 348 *TF:* 800-327-0790 ■ *Web:* www.sentinelbuildings.com	Albion	NE	68620	402-395-5076	395-6369
Sharon Coating LLC 277 Sharpsville Ave *TF:* 800-456-1794 ■ *Web:* www.us.nlmk.com	Sharon	PA	16146	724-983-6464	981-3009
Sioux City Foundry Co 801 Div St *TF:* 800-831-0874 ■ *Web:* www.siouxcityfoundry.com	Sioux City	IA	51102	712-252-4181	252-4197
Sivyer Steel Corp 225 S 33rd St *Web:* www.sivyersteel.com	Bettendorf	IA	52722	563-355-1811	355-3946
Smith Foundry Co 1855 E 28th St *Web:* www.smithfoundry.com	Minneapolis	MN	55407	612-729-9395	729-2519
Spokane Steel Foundry Co 3808 N Sullivan Rd Bldg 1 *Web:* spokaneindustries.com	Spokane	WA	99216	509-924-0440	924-9448
Standard Alloys & Mfg PO Box 969 *TF:* 800-231-8240 ■ *Web:* www.ksb.com/standard_alloys	Port Arthur	TX	77640	409-983-3201	983-7837
Steel Service Corp 2260 Flowood Dr PO Box 321425 *TF:* 800-844-9222 ■ *Web:* www.steelservicecorp.com	Jackson	MS	39232	601-939-9222	939-9359
T & B Foundry Co 2469 E 71st St	Cleveland	OH	44104	216-391-4200	
Talladega Castings & Machine Co Inc 228 N Ct St *TF:* 800-766-6708 ■ *Web:* www.tmsco.com	Talladega	AL	35160	256-362-5550	362-1321
Talladega Machinery & Supply Co Inc 301 N Johnson Ave PO Box 736 *TF Cust Svc:* 800-289-8672 ■ *Web:* www.tmsco.com	Talladega	AL	35161	256-362-4124	761-2579
Taylor & Fenn Co 22 Deerfield Rd *Web:* www.taylorfenn.com	Windsor	CT	06095	860-249-7531	525-2961
Tyler Pipe Co 11910 CR 492 **Fax Area Code:* 800 ■ *TF:* 800-527-8478 ■ *Web:* www.tylerpipe.com	Tyler	TX	75706	903-882-5511	248-9537*
Unicast Co 241 N Washington St *Web:* www.unicastco.com	Boyertown	PA	19512	610-367-0155	367-2787
Union Electric Steel Corp 726 Bell Ave *Web:* www.uniones.com	Carnegie	PA	15106	412-429-7655	276-1711
Urick Foundry Co 1501 Cherry St *Web:* www.urick.net	Erie	PA	16502	814-454-2461	454-1397
US Pipe & Foundry Co 2 Chase Corporate Drive Ste 200 **Fax Area Code:* 205 ■ *TF:* 866-347-7473 ■ *Web:* www.uspipe.com	Birmingham	AL	35244	866-347-7473	417-8411*
Walker Machine & Foundry Corp PO Box 4587 *Web:* www.walkerfoundry.com	Roanoke	VA	24015	540-344-6265	342-2278
Waukesha Foundry Company Inc 1300 Lincoln Ave **Fax:* Sales ■ *TF:* 800-727-0741 ■ *Web:* www.waukeshafoundry.com	Waukesha	WI	53186	262-542-0741	549-8440*
Waupaca Foundry 1955 Brunner Dr PO Box 249 *TF:* 800-669-6820 ■ *Web:* www.waupacafoundry.com	Waupaca	WI	54981	715-258-6611	258-9268
Wheeling-Nisshin Inc 400 Penn St *Web:* www.wheeling-nisshin.com	Follansbee	WV	26037	304-527-2800	527-0985
Willman Industries Inc 338 S Main St *Web:* www.willmanind.com	Cedar Grove	WI	53013	920-668-8526	668-8998
Winsert Inc 2645 Industrial Pkwy S PO Box 0198 *Web:* www.winsert.com	Marinette	WI	54143	715-732-1703	732-2824
Wollaston Alloys Inc 205 Wood Rd *Web:* www.wollastonalloys.com	Braintree	MA	02184	781-848-3333	848-3993

308 FOUNDRIES - NONFERROUS (CASTINGS)

See Also Foundries - Iron & Steel p. 2322

Company	City	State	ZIP	Phone	Fax
Advance Die Casting Co 3760 N Holton St *Web:* www.advancediecasting.com	Milwaukee	WI	53212	414-964-0284	964-8092
Ahresty Wilmington Corp 2627 S South St *Web:* www.ahresty.com	Wilmington	OH	45177	937-382-6112	382-5871
Akron Foundry Co 2728 Wingate Ave *Web:* www.akronfoundry.com	Akron	OH	44314	330-745-3101	745-7999
Alloy Die Casting Co 6550 Caballero Blvd **Fax:* Sales ■ *Web:* alloydie.com	Buena Park	CA	90620	714-521-9800	521-5510*
Aurora Metals Divison LLC 1995 Greenfield Ave *Web:* www.aurorametals.com	Montgomery	IL	60538	630-844-4900	844-6839
Bardane Mfg PO Box 70 *Web:* www.bardane.com	Jermyn	PA	18433	570-876-4844	876-1938
Basic Aluminum Castings Co 1325 E 168th St *Web:* www.basicaluminum.com	Cleveland	OH	44110	216-481-5606	481-7031
Blaser Die Casting Co 5700 Third Ave S	Seattle	WA	98108	206-767-7800	767-7055
Brillcast Inc 3400 Wentworth Dr SW *Web:* www.brillcast.com	Grand Rapids	MI	49519	616-534-4977	534-0880
Buck Company Inc 897 Lancaster Pk *Web:* www.buckcompany.com	Quarryville	PA	17566	717-284-4114	284-3737
Bunting Bearings Corp 1001 Holland Pk Blvd *TF:* 888-286-8464 ■ *Web:* www.buntingbearings.com	Holland	OH	43528	419-866-7000	866-0653
Cast Technologies Inc 1100 SW Washington St *Web:* casttechnologies.net	Peoria	IL	61602	309-676-2157	676-2167
Cast-Rite Corp 515 E Airline Way *Web:* www.cast-rite.com	Gardena	CA	90248	310-532-2080	532-0605
Chicago White Metal Casting Inc 649 N Rt 83 *Web:* www.cwmdiecast.com	Bensenville	IL	60106	630-595-4424	595-4474
Consolidated Metco Inc 13940 N Rivergate Blvd **Fax Area Code:* 503 ■ **Fax:* Sales ■ *TF Sales:* 800-547-9473 ■ *Web:* www.conmet.com	Portland	OR	97203	800-547-9473	240-5488*
Consolidated Precision Products 8333 Wilcox Ave *Web:* cppcorp.com	Cudahy	CA	90201	323-773-2363	562-3174
Deco Products Co 506 Sanford St *TF:* 800-327-9751 ■ *Web:* www.decoprod.com	Decorah	IA	52101	563-382-4264	382-9845
Del Mar Die Casting Co 12901 S Western Ave **Fax Area Code:* 310 ■ *TF:* 800-624-7468	Gardena	CA	90249	323-321-0600	327-1951*
Denison Industries (DI) 22 Fielder Dr *Web:* www.denisonindustries.com	Denison	TX	75020	903-786-6500	786-6575
Dynacast Inc 14045 Ballantyne Corporate Pl *Web:* www.dynacast.com	Charlotte	NC	28277	704-927-2790	927-2791
Eck Industries Inc 1602 N Eigth St PO Box 967 *Web:* www.eckindustries.com	Manitowoc	WI	54221	920-682-4618	682-9298
Electric Materials Co 50 S Washington St *TF:* 800-356-2211 ■ *Web:* www.elecmat.com	North East	PA	16428	814-725-9621	725-3620
Empire Die Casting Co Inc 635 Highland Rd E *Web:* www.empiredie.com	Macedonia	OH	44056	330-467-0750	467-9118
Falcon Foundry Co 96 Sixth St *Web:* www.falconfoundry.com	Lowellville	OH	44436	330-536-6221	
Fall River Group 670 S Main *Web:* www.fallrivergroup.com	Fall River	WI	53932	920-484-3311	
General Die Casters Inc 2150 Highland Rd *TF:* 800-332-2278 ■ *Web:* www.generaldie.com	Twinsburg	OH	44087	330-657-2300	657-2192
Gibbs Die Casting Corp 369 Community Dr *Web:* www.gibbsdc.com	Henderson	KY	42420	270-827-1801	827-7840
Globalfoundries Inc 2600 Great America Way *Web:* www.globalfoundries.com	Santa Clara	CA	95054	408-462-3900	
H-J Enterprises Inc 3010 High Ridge Blvd *Web:* www.h-j.com	High Ridge	MO	63049	636-677-3421	376-1915
Halex Co 23901 Aurora Rd **Fax Area Code:* 440 ■ *TF:* 800-749-3261 ■ *Web:* www.halexco.com	Bedford Heights	OH	44146	800-749-3261	439-1792*
Harmony Castings LLC 251 Perry Hwy *Web:* www.harmonycastings.com	Harmony	PA	16037	724-452-5811	452-0118
Hoffmann Die Cast Corp 229 Kerth St *Web:* www.hoffmanndc.com	Saint Joseph	MI	49085	269-983-1102	983-2928
Howmet Castings 1 Misco Dr *Web:* www.alcoa.com	Whitehall	MI	49461	231-894-5686	894-7607
ICG Castings Inc 9864 Church St	Bridgman	MI	49106	269-782-2108	783-3104
Imperial Die Casting Co 2249 Old Liberty Rd *Web:* www.rcmindustries.com	Liberty	SC	29657	864-859-0202	855-1597
Johnson Brass & Machine Foundry Inc 270 N Mill St PO Box 219 *Web:* www.johnsoncentrifugal.com	Saukville	WI	53080	262-377-9440	284-7066
Kitchen-Quip Inc 405 E Marion St *Web:* www.kqcasting.com	Waterloo	IN	46793	260-837-8311	837-7919
Lee Brass Co 1800 Golden Springs Rd *TF General:* 800-876-1811 ■ *Web:* www.leebrass.com	Anniston	AL	36207	800-876-1811	876-1800
Littlestown Foundry Inc 150 Charles St PO Box 69 *TF:* 800-471-0844 ■ *Web:* www.littlestownfoundry.com	Littlestown	PA	17340	717-359-4141	359-5010
Madison Precision Products Inc 94 E 400 N *Web:* www.madisonprecision.com	Madison	IN	47250	812-273-4702	273-2451
Madison-Kipp Corp 201 Waubesa St *TF:* 800-356-6148 ■ *Web:* www.madison-kipp.com	Madison	WI	53704	800-356-6148	
Magnolia Metal Corp 10675 Bedford Ave Ste 200 *TF:* 800-228-4043 ■ *Web:* www.magnoliabronze.com	Omaha	NE	68134	402-455-8760	455-8762
New Products Corp 448 N Shore Dr	Benton Harbor	MI	49022	269-925-2161	934-6180
NGK Metals Corp 917 Hwy 11 S **Fax Area Code:* 877 ■ *TF:* 800-523-8268 ■ *Web:* www.ngkmetals.com	Sweetwater	TN	37874	423-337-5500	645-2328*
Ohio Decorative Products Inc 220 S Elizabeth St *Web:* www.ohiodec.com	Spencerville	OH	45887	419-647-4191	647-4202
Pacific Die Casting Corp 6155 S Eastern Ave *Web:* www.pacdiecast.com	Commerce	CA	90040	323-725-1332	728-1115
Park-Ohio Holdings Corp (PKOH) 6065 Parkland Blvd *NASDAQ: PKOH* ■ *Web:* www.pkoh.com	Cleveland	OH	44124	440-947-2000	947-2099
PHB Inc 7900 W Ridge Rd *Web:* www.phbcorp.com	Fairview	PA	16415	814-474-5511	474-3091
Piad Precision Casting Corp 112 Industrial Pk Rd *TF:* 800-441-9858 ■ *Web:* www.piad.com	Greensburg	PA	15601	724-838-5500	838-5520
Premier Die Casting Co 1177 Rahway Ave *TF:* 800-394-3006 ■ *Web:* www.diecasting.com	Avenel	NJ	07001	732-634-3000	634-0590
Premier Tool & Die Cast Corp 9886 N Tudor Rd *TF:* 800-417-8717 ■ *Web:* www.premierdiecast.com	Berrien Springs	MI	49103	269-471-7715	471-3855
Reliable Castings Corp 3530 Spring Grove Ave *TF:* 866-722-2278 ■ *Web:* www.reliablecastings.com	Cincinnati	OH	45223	513-541-2627	541-5696
Ridco Casting Co 6 Beverage Hill Ave *Web:* www.ridco.com	Pawtucket	RI	02860	401-724-0400	724-6320
Selmet Inc 33992 SE 7 Mile Ln PO Box 689 *Web:* www.selmetinc.com	Albany	OR	97322	541-926-7731	928-9346
Stahl Specialty Co 111 E Pacific PO Box 6 *TF:* 800-821-7852 ■ *Web:* www.stahlspecialty.com	Kingsville	MO	64061	816-597-3322	597-3485
Talladega Castings & Machine Co Inc 228 N Ct St *TF:* 800-766-6708 ■ *Web:* www.tmsco.com	Talladega	AL	35160	256-362-5550	362-1321
Tampa Brass & Aluminum 8511 Florida Mining Blvd *Web:* www.tampabrass.com	Tampa	FL	33634	813-885-6064	882-3271
Techni-Cast Corp 11220 Garfield Ave **Fax:* Sales ■ *TF:* 800-923-4585 ■ *Web:* www.techni-cast.com	South Gate	CA	90280	562-923-4585	861-4259*
Texas Die Casting Inc 600 S Loop 485 *Web:* www.texasdiecasting.com	Gladewater	TX	75647	903-845-2224	845-6155
Top Die Casting Co 13910 Dearborn Ave *Web:* www.topdie.com	South Beloit	IL	61080	815-389-2599	389-3057
Travis Pattern & Foundry Inc 1413 E Hawthorne Rd *Web:* www.pduinc.com	Spokane	WA	99218	509-466-3545	467-6465
Twin City Die Castings Co 1070 33rd Ave SE *Web:* www.tcdcinc.com	Minneapolis	MN	55414	651-645-3611	645-0724
United Titanium Inc 3450 Old Airport Rd *TF:* 800-321-4938 ■ *Web:* www.unitedtitanium.com	Wooster	OH	44691	330-264-2111	263-1336
Walker Die Casting Inc 1125 Higgs Rd PO Box 1189 *Web:* www.walkerdiecasting.com	Lewisburg	TN	37091	931-359-6206	359-8030
Ward Aluminum Casting Co 642 Growth Ave *Web:* www.wardcorp.com	Fort Wayne	IN	46808	260-426-8700	420-1919
Watry Industries Inc 3312 Lakeshore Dr *Web:* www.watry.com	Sheboygan	WI	53081	920-457-4886	457-5241
Wisconsin Aluminum Foundry Company Inc 838 S 16th St *Web:* www.wafco.com	Manitowoc	WI	54220	920-682-8286	682-7285
Wollaston Alloys Inc 205 Wood Rd *Web:* www.wollastonalloys.com	Braintree	MA	02184	781-848-3333	848-3993
Wolverine Bronze Co 28178 Hayes Rd **Fax:* Sales ■ *Web:* www.wolverinebronze.com	Roseville	MI	48066	586-776-8180	776-4510*
Yoder Industries Inc 2520 Needmore Rd *Web:* www.yoderindustries.com	Dayton	OH	45414	937-278-5769	278-6321

309 FRAMES & MOULDINGS

Company	City	State	ZIP	Phone	Fax
Alexander Moulding Mill Co 250 US 281	Hamilton	TX	76531	254-386-3187	
Alexandria Moulding 20352 Powerdam Rd **Fax Area Code:* 800 ■ *TF:* 866-377-2539 ■ *Web:* www.alexmo.com	Alexandria	ON	K0C1A0	613-525-2784	265-8746*
ELSAL Inc 800 A St *Web:* www2.elsal.com	San Rafael	CA	94901	415-472-8388	472-8389
Groovfold Inc 1050 W State St *TF:* 800-367-1133 ■ *Web:* www.groovfold.com	Newcomerstown	OH	43832	740-498-8363	498-8782
Larson-Juhl 3900 Steve Reynolds Blvd **Fax Area Code:* 770 ■ **Fax:* Hum Res ■ *TF:* 800-221-4123 ■ *Web:* www.larsonjuhl.com	Norcross	GA	30093	800-221-4123	279-5297*
Monarch Industries Inc 99 Main St *Web:* www.monarchinc.com	Warren	RI	02885	401-247-5200	
North American Enclosures Inc 65 Jetson Ln *TF:* 800-645-9209 ■ *Web:* www.naeframes.com	Central Islip	NY	11722	631-234-9500	234-9504
Peterson Picture Frame Company Inc 2720 W Belmont Ave *Web:* www.peterson-picture.com	Chicago	IL	60618	773-463-8888	463-4603
Quanex Building Products 2270 Woodale Dr *TF:* 800-233-4383 ■ *Web:* www.quanex.com	Mounds View	MN	55112	763-231-4000	
Royal Mouldings Ltd 135 Bearcreek Rd PO Box 610 *TF:* 800-368-3117 ■ *Web:* www.royalbuildingproducts.com	Marion	VA	24354	276-783-8161	782-3285
Sunset Moulding Company Inc 2231 Paseo Ave *Web:* www.sunsetmoulding.com	Live Oak	CA	95953	530-695-1000	695-2560
Uniek Inc 805 Uniek Dr **Fax:* Mktg ■ *Web:* www.uniekinc.com	Waunakee	WI	53597	608-849-9999	849-9799*
Woodgrain Distribution 80 Shelby St *TF:* 800-756-0199 ■ *Web:* www.woodgraindistribution.com	Montevallo	AL	35115	205-665-2546	665-3432

FRAMES & MOULDINGS - METAL

See Doors & Windows - Metal p. 2197

310 FRANCHISES

See Also Auto Supply Stores p. 1818; Automotive Services p. 1834; Bakeries p. 1838; Beauty Salons p. 1851; Business Service Centers p. 1884; Candles p. 1890; Car Rental Agencies p. 1891; Children's Learning Centers p. 1937; Cleaning Services p. 1940; Remodeling, Refinishing, Resurfacing Contractors p. 2090; Convenience Stores p. 2148; Health Food Stores p. 2458; Home Inspection Services p. 2480; Hotels & Hotel Companies p. 2536; Ice Cream & Dairy Stores p. 2555; Laundry & Drycleaning Services p. 2627; Optical Goods Stores p. 2859; Pest Control Services p. 2927; Printing Companies - Commercial Printers p. 2976; Real Estate Agents & Brokers p. 3041; Restaurant Companies p. 3078; Staffing Services p. 3206; Travel Agency Networks p. 3265; Weight Loss Centers & Services p. 3311
Please see the category on Hotel & Resort Operation & Management for listings of hotel franchises.

Phone *Fax*

1-800-Got-Junk 887 Great Northern Way .... Vancouver BC V5T4T5 800-468-5865
TF: 800-468-5865 ■ *Web:* www.1800gotjunk.com

1-800-Water Damage 1167 Mercer St.................. Seattle WA 98109 206-381-3041
TF: 800-928-3732 ■ *Web:* www.1800waterdamage.com

A-Ok Rentals Inc 950 Bloomfield Ave............ West Caldwell NJ 07006 973-575-7900 575-7847
Web: www.affiliatedcarrental.com

ABC Seamless 3001 Fiechtner Dr .... Fargo ND 58103 701-293-5952
TF: 800-732-6577 ■ *Web:* www.abcseamless.com

Abrakadoodle Inc 46030 Manekin Pl Ste 110 .... Sterling VA 20166 703-860-6570
Web: www.abrakadoodle.com

ActionCOACH 5781 S Ft Apache Rd................. Las Vegas NV 89148 702-795-3188 795-3183
TF: 888-483-2828 ■ *Web:* www.actioncoach.com

Aire Serv Heating & Air Conditioning Inc
1020 N University Parks Dr Ste 101........................Waco TX 76707 254-523-3600
TF: 855-259-2280 ■ *Web:* www.aireserv.com

Aire-Master of America Inc 1821 N State Hwy Cc..........Nixa MO 65714 417-725-2691 725-5737
TF: 800-525-0957 ■ *Web:* www.airemaster.com

All Tune & Lube Brakes & More Inc
8334 Veteran's Hwy .... Millersville MD 21108 410-987-1011
TF: 877-978-1758 ■ *Web:* www.alltuneandlube.com

AmeriSpec Inc 3839 Forest Hill Irene Rd..............Memphis TN 38125 901-820-8500
TF: 877-769-5217 ■ *Web:* www.amerispec.com

Arby's Restaurant Group Inc
1155 Perimeter Ctr W...............................Atlanta GA 30338 678-514-4100
Web: arbys.com

Archadeck 2924 Emerywood Pkwy Ste 101............ Richmond VA 23294 804-353-6999
TF: 800-722-4668 ■ *Web:* www.archadeck.com

Bad Ass Coffee Co of Hawaii Inc
155 W Malvern Ave .... Salt Lake City UT 84115 239-213-0527 463-2606*
**Fax Area Code:* 801 ■ *Web:* badasscoffeestore.com

Baskin-Robbins Inc 130 Royall St.....................Canton MA 02021 781-737-3000
TF: 800-859-5339 ■ *Web:* www.baskinrobbins.com

Beef O'Bradys Inc 5660 W Cypress St Ste A ....Tampa FL 33607 813-226-2333
TF: 800-728-8878 ■ *Web:* www.beefobradys.com

Ben & Jerry's Homemade Inc
30 Community Dr......................... South Burlington VT 05403 802-846-1500 846-1538
Web: www.benjerry.com

Benjamin Franklin Plumbing
50 Central Ave Ste 920........................... Sarasota FL 34236 941-366-9692 951-0942
TF: 800-471-0809 ■ *Web:* www.benjaminfranklinplumbing.com

Big Apple Bagels 500 Lk Cook Rd Ste 475............ Deerfield IL 60015 847-948-7520 405-8140
TF: 800-251-6101 ■ *Web:* www.babcorp.com

Big Boy Restaurants International LLC
4199 Marcy St ....Warren MI 48091 586-759-6000
Web: www.bigboy.com

Bojangles' Restaurants Inc
9432 Southern Pine Blvd .... Charlotte NC 28273 704-335-1804
TF: 800-366-9921 ■ *Web:* www.bojangles.com

Boston Pizza Restaurants LP
1501 LBJ Fwy Ste 450 .... Dallas TX 75234 972-484-9022 484-7630
TF: 866-277-8721 ■ *Web:* www.bostons.com

BrickKicker Inc 849 N Ellsworth St.................. Naperville IL 60563 800-821-1820 420-2270*
**Fax Area Code:* 630 ■ *TF:* 800-821-1820 ■ *Web:* www.brickkicker.com

Bruegger's Enterprises 159 Bank St................ Burlington VT 05401 802-660-4020
Web: www.brueggers.com

BuildingStars Inc
33 Worthington Access Dr .... Maryland Heights MO 63043 314-991-3356
Web: www.buildingstars.com

Candy Bouquet International Inc
510 Mclean St ....Little Rock AR 72202 501-375-9990 375-9998
TF: 877-226-3901 ■ *Web:* www.candybouquet.com

Captain D's LLC
624 Grassmere Park Dr Ste 30 ....Nashville TN 37211 615-391-5461
TF: 800-314-4819 ■ *Web:* www.captainds.com

Car-X Assoc Corp
1375 E Woodfield Rd Ste 500................... Schaumburg IL 60173 847-273-8920 619-3310
Web: www.carx.com

CardSmart Retail Corp 11 Executive Ave................Edison NJ 08817 888-782-7050 726-2384*
**Fax Area Code:* 401 ■ *TF:* 888-782-7050 ■ *Web:* www.cardsmart.com

Carlson Wagonlit Travel Inc
701 Carlson Pkwy.............................. Minnetonka MN 55305 800-213-7295 212-2409*
**Fax Area Code:* 763 ■ *TF:* 800-213-7295 ■ *Web:* www.carlsonwagonlit.com

Carvel Express 200 Glenridge Pt Pkwy Ste 200 ....Atlanta GA 30342 800-322-4848
TF: 800-322-4848 ■ *Web:* www.carvel.com

CertaPro Painters Ltd 150 Green Tree Rd Ste 1003 .... Oaks PA 19456 800-689-7271 650-9997*
**Fax Area Code:* 610 ■ *TF:* 800-689-7271 ■ *Web:* www.certapro.com

Phone *Fax*

Certified Restoration DryCleaning Network LLC
2060 Coolidge Hwy .... Berkley MI 48072 800-963-2736 246-7868*
**Fax Area Code:* 248 ■ *TF:* 800-963-2736 ■ *Web:* www.restorationdrycleaning.com

Charley's Grilled Subs
2500 Farmers Dr Ste 140 .... Columbus OH 43235 614-923-4700 923-4701
TF: 800-437-8325 ■ *Web:* www.charleys.com

Checkers Drive-In Restaurants Inc
4300 W Cypress St Ste 600 ....Tampa FL 33607 813-283-7000 283-7208
TF: 800-800-8072 ■ *Web:* www.checkers.com

Chester's International LLC
3500 Colonnade Pkwy Ste 325...................Birmingham AL 35243 205-949-4690 298-0332
TF: 800-554-4537 ■ *Web:* www.chestersinternational.com

Christmas Decor Inc 709 E 44th St .... Lubbock TX 79404 806-722-1225
Web: www.christmasdecor.net

CiCi Enterprises LP 1080 W Bethel Rd................. Coppell TX 75019 972-745-4200 745-4203

Cleaning Authority 7230 Lee DeForest Dr ....Columbia MD 21046 410-740-1900 740-1906
TF: 888-658-0659 ■ *Web:* www.thecleaningauthority.com

Closet Factory 12800 S Broadway ....Los Angeles CA 90061 310-516-7000 516-8065
TF: 800-838-7995 ■ *Web:* www.closetfactory.com

Coffee Beanery Ltd, The 3429 Pierson Pl............. Flushing MI 48433 800-441-2255 733-1536*
**Fax Area Code:* 810 ■ *TF:* 800-441-2255 ■ *Web:* www.coffeebeanery.com

Cold Stone Creamery Inc
9311 E Via De Ventura .... Scottsdale AZ 85258 480-362-4800 362-4812
TF Cust Svc: 866-452-4252 ■ *Web:* www.coldstonecreamery.com

Color Me Mine Enterprises Inc
3722 San Fernando Rd .... Glendale CA 91204 818-291-5900 312-5501*
**Fax Area Code:* 858 ■ *Web:* www.colormemine.com

Color-Glo International 7111 Ohms Ln............ Minneapolis MN 55439 952-835-1338
TF: 800-333-8523 ■ *Web:* colorglo.com

ComForcare Senior Services Inc
2520 Telegraph Rd Ste 100 ....Bloomfield Hills MI 48302 248-745-9700 745-9763
TF: 800-886-4044 ■ *Web:* www.comforcare.com

Computer Explorers 12715 Telge Rd..................Cypress TX 77429 800-531-5053
TF: 800-531-5053 ■ *Web:* www.computerexplorers.com

Computer Troubleshooters USA
755 Commerce Dr Ste 605 .... Decatur GA 30030 800-877-0020
TF: 877-704-1702 ■ *Web:* www.dentsply.com

Contours Express Inc 156 Imperial Way .... Nicholasville KY 40356 855-589-9662 241-2234*
**Fax Area Code:* 859 ■ *TF:* 855-589-9662 ■ *Web:* www.contoursexpress.com

Cookies By Design Inc 1865 Summit Ave Ste 605 ....Plano TX 75074 972-398-9536 398-9542
TF: 800-945-2665 ■ *Web:* www.cookiesbydesign.com

Coverall Cleaning Concepts
5201 Congress Ave Ste 275...................... Boca Raton FL 33487 866-296-8944 922-2423*
**Fax Area Code:* 561 ■ *TF:* 800-537-3371 ■ *Web:* www.coverall.com

Craters & Freighters 331 Corporate Cir Ste J............Golden CO 80401 800-736-3335 399-9964*
**Fax Area Code:* 303 ■ *TF:* 800-736-3335 ■ *Web:* www.cratersandfreighters.com

Creative Colors International Inc
19015 S Jodi Rd Ste E ....Mokena IL 60448 708-478-1437 478-1636
TF: 800-933-2656 ■ *Web:* www.wecanfixthat.com

Crest Foods Inc 101 W Renner Rd Ste 240........... Richardson TX 75082 214-495-9533 853-5347
Web: www.nestlecafe.com

Crestcom International Ltd
6900 E Belleview Ave .... Greenwood Village CO 80111 303-267-8200
Web: www.crestcomleadership.com

Critter Control Inc
9435 E Cherry Bend Rd ....Traverse City MI 49684 231-947-2400 947-9440
TF: 800-451-6544 ■ *Web:* www.crittercontrol.com

Crown Trophy 529 N State Rd ....Briarcliff Manor NY 10510 914-941-0020 941-3039
Web: www.crowntrophy.com

CruiseOne Inc
1201 W Cypress Creek Rd Ste 100.............Fort Lauderdale FL 33309 800-278-4731
TF: 800-278-4731 ■ *Web:* www.cruiseone.com

Culver Franchising System Inc
1240 Water St.............................. Prairie du Sac WI 53578 608-643-7980 643-7982
Web: www.culvers.com

D'Angelo Sandwich Shops 600 Providence Hwy..........Dedham MA 02026 781-461-1200 461-1896
TF: 800-727-2446 ■ *Web:* www.dangelos.com

Dairy Queen 7505 Metro Blvd .... Minneapolis MN 55439 952-830-0200 830-0227
TF: 800-883-4279 ■ *Web:* www.dairyqueen.com

Decor & You Inc 900 Main St S .... Southbury CT 06488 203-264-3500
TF: 800-477-3326 ■ *Web:* www.decorandyou.com

Decorating Den Systems Inc 8659 Commerce Dr .... Easton MD 21601 410-822-9001
TF: 800-332-3367 ■ *Web:* www.decoratingden.com

Denny's Inc 203 E Main St.......................Spartanburg SC 29319 864-597-8000 597-7708*
**Fax:* Mktg ■ *Web:* www.dennys.com

DirectBuy Inc 8450 Broadway.......................Merrillville IN 46410 219-736-1100 755-6279
TF: 800-320-3462 ■ *Web:* www.directbuy.com

Domino's Pizza Inc
30 Frank Lloyd Wright Dr .... Ann Arbor MI 48106 734-930-3030
NYSE: DPZ ■ *TF:* 800-253-8182 ■ *Web:* dominos.com

Dr Vinyl & Assoc Ltd 1350 SE Hamblen Rd .... Lees Summit MO 64081 816-525-6060
TF General: 800-531-6600 ■ *Web:* www.drvinyl.com

DreamMaker Bath & Kitchen by Worldwide
510 N Valley Mills Dr Ste 304 ....Waco TX 76710 800-583-2133
TF: 800-583-2133 ■ *Web:* www.dreammaker-remodel.com

Dunkin' Donuts 130 Royall St.........................Canton MA 02021 781-737-3000 737-4000
TF Cust Svc: 800-859-5339 ■ *Web:* www.dunkindonuts.com

Duraclean International Inc
220 W Campus Dr .... Arlington Heights IL 60004 847-704-7100 704-7101
TF: 800-862-5326 ■ *Web:* www.duraclean.com

Edible Arrangements LLC 95 Barnes Rd........... Wallingford CT 06492 304-894-8901 774-0531*
**Fax Area Code:* 203 ■ *TF Cust Svc:* 877-363-7848 ■ *Web:* www.ediblearrangements.com

EmbroidMe Inc 2121 Vista Pkwy..............West Palm Beach FL 33411 561-640-7367 640-6062
TF: 877-877-0234 ■ *Web:* www.embroidme.com

Emerging Vision Inc 520 Eigth Ave Ste 2300..........New York NY 10018 646-737-1500
Web: www.emergingvision.com

Express Employment Professionals
8516 NW Expy ....Oklahoma City OK 73162 405-840-5000
TF: 800-222-4057 ■ *Web:* www.expresspros.com

Express Oil Change 1880 S Pk Dr ....Hoover AL 35244 205-945-1771 413-8732
TF: 888-945-1771 ■ *Web:* www.expressoil.com

Extreme Pita 2187 Dunwin Dr.................... Mississauga ON L5L1X2 905-820-7887
TF: 800-563-6688 ■ *Web:* www.extremepita.com

	Phone	Fax
Famous Dave's of America Inc 12701 Whitewater Dr Ste 200 ... Minnetonka MN 55343 *NASDAQ: DAVE* ■ *TF:* 800-929-4040 ■ *Web:* www.famousdaves.com	952-294-1300	
Fantastic Sams Inc 500 Cummings Ctr Ste 1100 ... Beverly MA 01915 *Web:* www.fantasticsams.com	651-770-1449	
Fast-Fix Jewelry & Watch Repairs 451 Altamonte Ave ... Altamonte Springs FL 32701 *TF:* 800-359-0407 ■ *Web:* www.fastfix.com	407-261-1595	261-1595
FasTracKids International Ltd 6900 E Belleview Ave Ste 100 ... Greenwood Village CO 80111 *TF:* 888-576-6888 ■ *Web:* fastrackids.com	303-224-0200	224-0222
Figaro's Italian Pizza Inc 1500 Liberty St SE Ste 160 ... Salem OR 97302 *TF:* 888-344-2767 ■ *Web:* www.figaros.com	503-371-9318	363-5364
Firehouse Restaurant Group Inc 3400 Kori Rd Ste 8 ... Jacksonville FL 32257 *Web:* www.firehousesubs.com	904-886-8300	886-2111
Fish Window Cleaning Services Inc 200 Enchanted Pkwy ... Manchester MO 63021 *TF:* 877-707-3474 ■ *Web:* www.fishwindowcleaning.com	636-779-1500	530-7856
Floor Coverings International 5250 Triangle Pwy Ste 100 ... Norcross GA 30092 *TF Sales:* 800-955-4324 ■ *Web:* www.floorcoveringsinternational.com	770-874-7600	
Foot Solutions Inc 4101 Roswell Rd Ste 800 ... Marietta GA 30062 *Web:* footsolutions.com	770-984-0844	
Fox's Pizza Den Inc 4425 Willaim Penn Hwy ... Murrysville PA 15668 *TF:* 800-899-3697 ■ *Web:* www.foxspizza.com	724-733-7888	
Furniture Medic 3839 S Forest Hill Irene Rd ... Memphis TN 38125 *TF:* 800-877-9933 ■ *Web:* www.furnituremedic.com	800-877-9933	
GNC Inc 300 Sixth Ave 14th Fl ... Pittsburgh PA 15222 *NYSE: GNC* ■ *TF:* 877-462-4700 ■ *Web:* www.gnc.com	877-462-4700	
Goddard Systems Inc 1016 W Ninth Ave ... King of Prussia PA 19406 *TF:* 800-463-3273 ■ *Web:* www.goddardschool.com	610-265-8510	
Golden Chick 1131 Rockingham Dr ... Richardson TX 75080 *Web:* www.goldenchick.com	972-831-0911	831-0401
Golden Corral Corp 5151 Glenwood Ave ... Raleigh NC 27612 *Web:* goldencorral.com	919-781-9310	881-4654
Golden Krust Carribean Bakery & Grill 3958 Pk Ave ... Bronx NY 10457 *Web:* www.goldenkrustbakery.com	718-655-7878	583-1883
Grease Monkey International 7450 E Progress Pl ... Greenwood Village CO 80111 *TF:* 800-822-7706 ■ *Web:* www.greasemonkeyintl.com	303-308-1660	308-5908
Great American Cookie Company Inc 3300 Chambers Rd Ste 170 ... Horseheads NY 14845 *TF:* 877-639-2361 ■ *Web:* www.greatamericancookies.com	877-639-2361	
Great Clips Inc 7700 France Ave S Ste 425 ... Minneapolis MN 55435 *TF:* 800-999-5959 ■ *Web:* www.greatclips.com	952-893-9088	844-3444
Great Harvest Bread Co 28 S Montana St ... Dillon MT 59725 *TF:* 800-442-0424 ■ *Web:* www.greatharvest.com	406-683-6842	683-5537
Great Steak & Potato Co 9311 E Via de Ventura ... Scottsdale AZ 85258 *TF:* 866-452-4252 ■ *Web:* www.thegreatsteak.com	480-362-4800	362-4812
Griswold Special Care Inc 717 Bethlehem Pike Ste 300 ... Erdenheim PA 19038 **Fax Area Code:* 469 ■ *TF:* 855-303-9470 ■ *Web:* www.griswoldhomecare.com	215-402-0200	277-3820*
Growth Coach, The 10700 Montgomery Rd Ste 300 ... Cincinnati OH 45242 *TF:* 888-292-7992 ■ *Web:* www.thegrowthcoach.com	888-292-7992	
Gymboree Corp 500 Howard St ... San Francisco CA 94105 *NASDAQ: GYMB* ■ *TF:* 877-449-6932 ■ *Web:* www.gymboree.com	415-278-7000	278-7100
Handyman Matters Inc 12567 W Cedar Dr ... Lakewood CO 80228 *TF:* 866-349-6946 ■ *Web:* www.handymanmatters.com	303-984-0177	984-0133
Happy & Healthy Products Inc 1600 S Dixie Hwy Ste 200 ... Boca Raton FL 33432 *Web:* www.fruitfull.com	561-367-0739	368-5267
Hayes Handpiece Franchises Inc 5375 Avenida Encinas Ste C ... Carlsbad CA 92008 *TF:* 800-228-0521 ■ *Web:* www.hayeshandpiece.com	760-602-0521	
Hobbytown USA 1233 Libra Dr ... Lincoln NE 68512 *Web:* www.hobbytown.com	402-434-5050	
Hollywood Tans 11 Enterprise Crt ... Sewell NJ 08080 *Web:* www.hollywoodtans.com	609-698-6400	
Homes & Land Magazine Affiliates LLC 1830 E Pk Ave ... Tallahassee FL 32301 *TF:* 800-277-7800 ■ *Web:* www.homesandland.com	850-575-0189	574-2525
HomeTeam Inspection Service Inc 575 Chamber Dr ... Milford OH 45150 **Fax Area Code:* 513 ■ *TF:* 800-598-5297 ■ *Web:* www.hometeam.com	800-598-5297	831-6010*
HomeVestors of America Inc 6500 Greenville Ave Ste 400 ... Dallas TX 75206 *TF:* 866-200-6475 ■ *Web:* www.homevestors.com	972-761-0046	761-9022
HouseMaster 92 E Main St Ste 301 ... Somerville NJ 08876 *TF:* 800-526-3939 ■ *Web:* www.housemaster.com	732-469-6565	469-7405
Hungry Howie's Pizza & Subs Inc 30300 Stephenson Hwy Ste 200 ... Madison Heights MI 48071 *Web:* www.hungryhowies.com	248-414-3300	414-3301
Ident-A-Kid Services of America 1780 102nd Ave N Ste 100 ... Saint Petersburg FL 33716 *TF:* 800-890-1000 ■ *Web:* www.identakid.com	727-577-4646	576-8258
IHOP Corp 450 N Brand Blvd ... Glendale CA 91203 *TF:* 866-444-5144 ■ *Web:* www.ihop.com	818-240-6055	637-4730
Inspiring Wellness LLC 665 S Orange Ave Ste 7 ... Sarasota FL 34236 *Web:* www.babybootcamp.com	941-953-5000	
Instant Imprints 5897 Oberlin Dr Ste 200 ... San Diego CA 92121 *TF:* 800-542-3437 ■ *Web:* www.instantimprints.com	858-642-4848	453-6513
Interim HealthCare Inc 1601 Sawgrass Corporate Pkwy ... Sunrise FL 33323 *TF:* 800-338-7786 ■ *Web:* www.interimhealthcare.com	954-858-6000	858-2720
iSold It 1106 E Colorado Ave ... Pasadena CA 91106 *Web:* www.i-soldit.com	626-584-0844	
Jackson Hewitt Inc 3 Sylvan Way Ste 301 ... Parsippany NJ 07054 *OTC: JHTXQ* ■ *TF:* 800-234-1040 ■ *Web:* www.jacksonhewitt.com	800-234-1040	
Jazzercise Inc 2460 Impala Dr ... Carlsbad CA 92010 *TF Cust Svc:* 800-348-4748 ■ *Web:* www.jazzercise.com	760-476-1750	602-7180
Jenny Craig International Inc 5770 Fleet St ... Carlsbad CA 92008 *TF:* 800-443-2331 ■ *Web:* www.jennycraig.com	760-696-4000	696-4506
Jet's America Inc 37501 Mound Rd ... Sterling Heights MI 48310 *Web:* www.jetspizza.com	586-268-5870	268-6762
Juice It Up! Franchise Corp 17915 Sky Pk Cir Ste J ... Irvine CA 92614 *TF:* 888-705-8423 ■ *Web:* www.juiceitup.com	949-475-0146	475-0137
Keller Williams Realty Inc 807 Las Cimas Pkwy Ste 200 ... Austin TX 78746 *Web:* www.kw.com	512-327-3070	328-1433
KFC Corp 1441 Gardiner Ln ... Louisville KY 40213 *TF:* 800-225-5532 ■ *Web:* www.kfc.com	920-923-2321	
Kid to Kid 1244 Township Line Rd ... Drexel Hill PA 19026 *Web:* www.kidtokid.com	610-446-2544	
Kinderdance International Inc 5238 Valleypointe Pkwy ... Roanoke VA 24019 *TF:* 800-554-2334 ■ *Web:* www.kinderdance.com	321-984-4448	984-4490
Kitchen Tune-Up Inc 813 Cir Dr ... Aberdeen SD 57401 *TF:* 800-333-6385 ■ *Web:* www.kitchentuneup.com	605-225-4049	
Lady of America Franchise Corp 500 E Broward Blvd Ste 1650 ... Fort Lauderdale FL 33394 *Web:* www.ladyofamerica.com	954-217-8660	
Lawn Doctor Inc 142 SR 34 ... Holmdel NJ 07733 *TF:* 800-845-0580 ■ *Web:* www.lawndoctor.com	800-631-5660	
Learning Express Inc 29 Buena Vista St ... Devens MA 01434 *TF:* 888-725-8697 ■ *Web:* www.learningexpress.com	978-889-1000	889-1010
Liberty Tax Service Inc 1716 Corporate Landing Pkwy ... Virginia Beach VA 23454 *TF Cust Svc:* 800-790-3863 ■ *Web:* www.libertytax.com	757-493-8855	493-0169
Lil' Angels Photography 6831 Crumpler Blvd Ste 101 ... Olive Branch MS 38654 *Web:* lilangelsphoto.com	662-890-9103	890-9104
Little Caesars Inc 2211 Woodward Ave ... Detroit MI 48201 *TF:* 800-722-3727 ■ *Web:* www.littlecaesars.com	313-983-6409	
Little Gym International Inc 7001 N Scottsdale Rd ... Paradise Valley AZ 85253 *TF General:* 888-228-2878 ■ *Web:* www.thelittlegym.com	888-228-2878	
Living Assistance Services Inc 937 Haverford Rd Ste 200 ... Bryn Mawr PA 19010 *TF:* 800-365-4189 ■ *Web:* www.livingassistance.com	800-365-4189	
Long John Silver's Restaurants Inc 9505 Williamsburg Plaza ... Louisville KY 40222 *Web:* www.ljsilvers.com	502-815-6100	
Mad Science Group 8360 Bougainville St Ste 201 ... Montreal QC H4P2G1 *TF:* 800-586-5231 ■ *Web:* www.madscience.org	514-344-4181	344-6695
Magnetsigns Adv Inc 4225 38th St ... Camrose AB T4V3Z3 *TF:* 800-219-8977 ■ *Web:* www.magnetsigns.com	780-672-8720	672-8716
Maid Brigade USA/Minimaid Canada 4 Concourse Pkwy Ste 200 ... Atlanta GA 30328 *TF:* 866-800-7470 ■ *Web:* www.maidbrigade.com	770-551-9630	391-9092
MaidPro Corp 180 Canal St ... Boston MA 02114 *TF:* 888-624-3776 ■ *Web:* www.maidpro.com	617-742-8787	720-0700
Manhattan Bagel Co Inc 555 Zang St Ste 300 ... Lakewood CO 80228 *TF:* 800-224-3563 ■ *Web:* www.manhattanbagel.com	303-568-8000	
Martinizing Dry Cleaning 8944 Columbia Rd Ste J ... Loveland OH 45140 *TF:* 800-827-0207 ■ *Web:* www.martinizing.com	800-827-0207	
Mathnasium LLC 5120 W Goldleaf Cir Ste 300 ... Los Angeles CA 90056 **Fax Area Code:* 310 ■ *TF:* 877-601-6284 ■ *Web:* www.mathnasium.com	323-421-8000	943-2111*
Maui Wowi Inc 9311 E Via de Ventura Ste 300 ... Scottsdale AZ 85258 *Web:* www.mauiwowi.com	303-781-7800	
McDonald's Corp 1 McDonald's Plz ... Oak Brook IL 60523 *NYSE: MCD* ■ *TF:* 800-244-6227 ■ *Web:* www.mcdonalds.com	630-623-3000	
Medicap Pharmacies Inc 1 Rider Trail Plaza Dr ... Earth City MO 63045 *TF:* 800-407-8055 ■ *Web:* www.medicap.com	314-993-6000	
Merle Norman Cosmetics Inc 9130 Bellanca Ave ... Los Angeles CA 90045 *TF:* 800-421-6648 ■ *Web:* www.merlenorman.com	310-641-3000	641-7144
Merlin Corp 3815 E Main St ... Saint Charles IL 60174 *TF:* 800-652-9910 ■ *Web:* www.merlins.com	630-513-8200	513-1388
Midas International Corp 1300 Arlington Heights Rd ... Itasca IL 60143 *TF:* 800-621-8545 ■ *Web:* www.midas.com	630-438-3000	438-3700
Minuteman Press International Inc 61 Executive Blvd ... Farmingdale NY 11735 *TF:* 800-645-3006 ■ *Web:* www.minutemanpress.com	631-249-1370	249-5618
Money Mailer LLC 12131 Western Ave ... Garden Grove CA 92841 **Fax Area Code:* 847 ■ *TF:* 800-468-5865 ■ *Web:* www.moneymailer.com	714-889-3800	265-7624*
Mr Appliance Corp 304 E Church Ave ... Killeen TX 76541 **Fax Area Code:* 254 ■ *TF:* 888-998-2011 ■ *Web:* www.mrappliance.com	888-998-2011	537-0745*
Mr Handyman International LLC 3948 Ranchero Dr Ste 1C ... Ann Arbor MI 48108 *TF Cust Svc:* 855-632-2126 ■ *Web:* www.mrhandyman.com	800-289-4600	
Mr Hero Restaurants 7010 Engle Rd Ste 100 ... Middleburg Heights OH 44130 *TF:* 888-860-5082 ■ *Web:* www.mrhero.com	440-625-3080	625-3081
My Favorite Muffin 500 Lk Cook Rd Ste 475 ... Deerfield IL 60015 *TF:* 800-251-6101 ■ *Web:* www.babcorp.com	847-948-7520	405-8140
Nathan's Famous Inc 1 Jericho Plz 2nd Fl ... Jericho NY 11753 *NASDAQ: NATH* ■ *Web:* www.nathansfamous.com	516-338-8500	338-7220
National Property Inspections Inc (NPI) 9375 Burt St Ste 201 ... Omaha NE 68114 **Fax Area Code:* 800 ■ *TF:* 800-333-9807	402-333-9807	933-2508*
Navis Pack & Ship Centers 6551 S Revere Pkwy Ste 250 ... Centennial CO 80111 **Fax Area Code:* 303 ■ *TF:* 800-344-3528 ■ *Web:* www.gonavis.com	800-344-3528	741-6653*

	City	State	Zip	Phone	Fax
Nutrilawn Inc 25-1040 Martin Grove Rd *Web:* www.nutrilawn.com	Toronto	ON	M9W4W1	416-620-7100	
OctoClean Franchising Systems 3357 Chicago Ave *Web:* www.octoclean.com	Riverside	CA	92507	951-683-5859	
OpenWorks 4742 N 24th St Ste 450 *TF:* 800-777-6736 ■ *Web:* www.openworksweb.com	Phoenix	AZ	85016	602-224-0440	468-3788
Orange Julius of America 7505 Metro Blvd *TF:* 866-793-7582 ■ *Web:* www.dairyqueen.com	Minneapolis	MN	55439	952-830-0200	
Outdoor Connection Inc 424 Neosho *Web:* www.outdoor-connection.com	Burlington	KS	66839	620-364-5500	364-5563
Padgett Business Services 160 Hawthorne Pk **Fax Area Code:* 706 ■ *TF:* 800-723-4388 ■ *Web:* www.padgettbusinessservices.com	Athens	GA	30606	800-723-4388	543-8537*
Pak Mail Centers of America Inc 7173 S Havana St Ste 600 *TF Cust Svc:* 800-778-6665 ■ *Web:* www.pakmail.com	Centennial	CO	80112	303-957-1000	957-1015
Palm Beach Tan Inc 633 E State Hwy 121 Ste 500 *Web:* www.palmbeachtan.com	Coppell	TX	75019	972-966-5300	406-2508
Papa John's International Inc 2002 Papa John's Blvd *NASDAQ: PZZA* ■ *TF:* 877-547-7272 ■ *Web:* www.papajohns.com	Louisville	KY	40299	502-261-7272	
Papa Murphy's International Inc 8000 NE Pkwy Dr Ste 350 *Web:* www.papamurphys.com	Vancouver	WA	98662	360-260-7272	260-0500
Party City Corp 25 Green Pond Rd Ste 1 *TF:* 800-727-8924 ■ *Web:* www.partycity.com	Rockaway	NJ	07866	973-453-8600	
Pearle Vision Inc 4000 Luxottica Pl *Web:* www.pearlevision.com	Mason	OH	45040	513-765-4321	765-6388
Perkins Restaurant & Bakery 6075 Poplar Ave Ste 800 *TF:* 800-877-7375 ■ *Web:* www.perkinsrestaurants.com	Memphis	TN	38119	901-766-6400	
Perma-Glaze Inc 1638 Research Loop Rd Ste 160 *TF:* 800-332-7397 ■ *Web:* www.permaglaze.com	Tucson	AZ	85710	520-722-9718	296-4393
Pet Supplies "Plus" Inc 17197 N Laurel Prk Dre Ste 402 *Web:* www.petsuppliesplus.com	Livonia	MI	48152	734-793-6600	
Petland Inc 250 Riverside St *TF:* 800-221-5935 ■ *Web:* petland.com	Chillicothe	OH	45601	740-775-2464	775-2575
Physicians Weight Loss Centers of America Inc 395 Springside Dr *TF:* 800-205-7887 ■ *Web:* www.pwlc.com	Akron	OH	44333	330-666-7952	666-2197
PIP Printing & Document Services Inc 26722 Plaza Dr Ste 200 *Web:* www.pip.com	Mission Viejo	CA	92691	949-348-5000	348-5066
Pizza Inn Inc 3551 Plano Pkwy *NASDAQ: RAVE* ■ *TF:* 877-574-9924 ■ *Web:* www.pizzainn.com	The Colony	TX	75056	877-574-9924	
Pizza Ranch Inc 204 19th St SE *TF:* 800-321-3401 ■ *Web:* www.pizzaranch.com	Orange City	IA	51041	800-321-3401	
Plato's Closet 23021 Outer Dr *TF:* 800-592-8049 ■ *Web:* www.platoscloset.com	Allen Park	MI	48101	313-278-2300	
Postal Connections of America 6136 Frisco Sq Blvd Ste 400 *TF:* 800-767-8257 ■ *Web:* www.postalconnections.com	Frisco	TX	75034	800-767-8257	
PostalAnnex+ Inc 7580 Metropolitan Dr Ste 200 *TF:* 800-456-1525 ■ *Web:* www.postalannex.com	San Diego	CA	92108	619-563-4800	563-9850
PostNet International Franchise Corp 1819 Wazee St *TF:* 800-841-7171 ■ *Web:* www.postnet.com	Denver	CO	80202	303-771-7100	771-7133
Powerhouse Gym International 355 S Old Woodward Ste 150 **Fax Area Code:* 249 ■ *Web:* www.powerhousegym.com	Birmingham	MI	48009	248-476-2888	530-9816*
Precision Auto Care Inc 748 Miller Dr SE *OTC: PACI* ■ **Fax Area Code:* 703 ■ *TF:* 866-944-8863 ■ *Web:* www.precisiontune.com	Leesburg	VA	20175	866-944-8863	771-7108*
PremierGarage Systems LLC 21405 N 15th Ln *TF:* 866-590-9411 ■ *Web:* www.premiergarage.com	Phoenix	AZ	85027	480-483-3030	
Pressed4Time Inc 8 Clock Tower Pl Ste 110 **Fax Area Code:* 978 ■ *TF:* 800-423-8711 ■ *Web:* www.pressed4time.com	Maynard	MA	01754	800-423-8711	823-8301*
Primrose School Franchising Co 3660 Cedarcrest Rd *TF:* 800-745-0677 ■ *Web:* www.primroseschools.com	Acworth	GA	30101	770-529-4100	529-1551
Priority Management Systems Inc 11160 Silversmith Pl *TF:* 800-437-1032 ■ *Web:* www.prioritymanagement.com	Richmond	BC	V7A5E4	604-214-7772	
Pro Image Sports 233 N 1250 W Ste 200 *Web:* www.proimagesports.com	Centerville	UT	84014	801-296-9999	296-1319
ProForma 8800 E Pleasant Vly Rd *TF:* 800-825-1525 ■ *Web:* www.proforma.com	Independence	OH	44131	216-520-8400	
Property Damage Appraisers Inc (PDA) 6100 SW Blvd Ste 200 *TF:* 800-749-7324 ■ *Web:* www.pdacorporation.com	Fort Worth	TX	76109	800-749-7324	866-4732
Qdoba Restaurant Corp 4865 WaRd Rd Ste 500 *Web:* www.qdoba.com	Wheat Ridge	CO	80033	720-898-2300	898-2396
RadioShack Corp 300 RadioShack Cir *NYSE: RSH* ■ *TF:* 800-843-7422 ■ *Web:* www.radioshack.com	Fort Worth	TX	76102	817-882-9380	
Rainbow International 1010 N University Pk Dr *TF:* 855-724-6269 ■ *Web:* www.rainbowintl.com	Waco	TX	76707	254-756-5463	745-2592
Re-Bath LLC 16879 N 75th Ave Ste 101 *TF:* 800-426-4573 ■ *Web:* rebath.com	Peoria	AZ	85382	800-426-4573	
RE/MAX International Inc 5075 S Syracuse St *TF Cust Svc:* 800-525-7452 ■ *Web:* www.remax.com	Denver	CO	80237	303-770-5531	796-3599
Real Living Inc 77 E Nationwide Blvd *Web:* www.realliving.com	Columbus	OH	43215	614-459-7400	
Realty Executives International Inc 7600 N 16th St Ste 100 *TF:* 800-252-3366 ■ *Web:* www.realtyexecutives.com	Phoenix	AZ	85020	602-957-0747	224-5542
Red Robin Gourmet Burgers Inc 6312 S Fiddlers Green Cir Ste 200-N *NASDAQ: RRGB* ■ *Web:* www.redrobin.com	Greenwood Village	CO	80111	303-846-6000	846-6013
Rescuecom Corp 2560 Burnet Ave **Fax Area Code:* 315 ■ *TF:* 800-737-2837 ■ *Web:* www.rescuecom.com	Syracuse	NY	13206	800-737-2837	433-5228*

	City	State	Zip	Phone	Fax
Results Travel 701 Carlson Pkwy *TF:* 800-456-4000 ■ *Web:* www.carlson.com	Minnetonka	MN	55305	763-212-5000	
Right at Home Inc 6464 Crt St Ste 150 *TF:* 877-697-7537 ■ *Web:* www.rightathome.net	Omaha	NE	68106	402-697-7537	697-0289
Rita's Water Ice Franchise Co LLC 1401 Bridgetown Pike *Web:* www.ritasice.com	Feasterville	PA	19053	215-322-8774	
RSVP Publications 6730 W Linebaugh Ave Ste 201 *TF:* 800-360-7787 ■ *Web:* www.rsvppublications.com	Tampa	FL	33625	813-960-7787	549-3306
Ruby Tuesday Inc 150 W Church Ave *NYSE: RT* ■ *Web:* www.rubytuesday.com	Maryville	TN	37801	865-379-5700	
Sandler Sales Institute 10411 Stevenson Rd *Web:* www.sandler.com	Stevenson	MD	21153	410-653-1993	358-7858
Screenmobile 72-050A Corporate Way *Web:* www.screenmobile.com	Thousand Palms	CA	92276	760-343-3500	
Sea Tow Services International Inc 1560 Youngs Ave PO Box 1178 *TF:* 800-473-2869 ■ *Web:* www.seatow.com	Southold	NY	11971	631-765-3660	
Second Cup Ltd 6303 Airport Rd *TF:* 877-212-1818 ■ *Web:* www.secondcup.com	Mississauga	ON	L4V1R8	877-212-1818	
Shefield Group 2265 W Railway St *Web:* www.shefield.com	Abbotsford	BC	V2S2E3	604-859-1014	859-1711
Signs by Tomorrow USA Inc 8681 Robert Fulton Dr *TF:* 800-765-7446 ■ *Web:* www.signsbytomorrow.com	Columbia	MD	21046	410-312-3600	312-3520
Sir Speedy Inc 26722 Plaza Dr *TF:* 800-854-8297 ■ *Web:* www.sirspeedy.com	Mission Viejo	CA	92691	949-348-5000	348-5066
Snap-on Inc 2801 80th St *NYSE: SNA* ■ *TF:* 877-762-7664 ■ *Web:* www.snapon.com	Kenosha	WI	53143	262-656-5200	656-5577
Sonny's Franchise Co 2605 Maitland Ctr Pkwy Ste C *Web:* www.sonnysbbq.com	Maitland	FL	32751	407-660-8888	
Sport Clips Inc 110 Briarwood Dr *TF:* 800-872-4247 ■ *Web:* www.sportclips.com	Georgetown	TX	78628	512-869-1201	
Spring-Green Lawn Care Corp 11909 Spaulding School Dr *TF:* 800-435-4051 ■ *Web:* www.spring-green.com	Plainfield	IL	60585	815-436-8777	436-9056
Stork News of America Inc 1305 Hope Mills Rd Ste A *TF:* 800-633-6395 ■ *Web:* www.storknews.com	Fayetteville	NC	28304	910-429-2229	426-2473
Stretch-N-Grow International Inc PO Box 7599 *TF:* 800-348-0166 ■ *Web:* www.stretch-n-grow.com	Seminole	FL	33775	800-348-0166	
Successories Inc 1040 Holland Dr **Fax Area Code:* 561 ■ *TF:* 800-535-2773 ■ *Web:* www.successories.com	Boca Raton	FL	33487	800-535-2773	952-4097*
Super Wash Inc 707 W Lincolnway PO Box 188 *Web:* www.superwash.com	Morrison	IL	61270	815-772-2111	772-7160
SuperCoups 350 Revolutionary Dr *TF:* 800-626-2620 ■ *Web:* www.supercoups.com	East Taunton	MA	02718	508-977-2000	
Supercuts 7201 Metro Blvd **Fax Area Code:* 952 ■ *TF:* 877-857-2070 ■ *Web:* www.supercuts.com	Minneapolis	MN	55439	877-857-2070	947-7300*
SuperShuttle International Inc 14500 N Northsight Blvd Ste 329 *Web:* www.supershuttle.com	Scottsdale	AZ	85260	480-609-3000	
Terminix International Company LP 860 Ridge Lk Blvd **Fax Area Code:* 901 ■ **Fax:* Mktg ■ *TF:* 855-212-6399 ■ *Web:* www.terminix.com	Memphis	TN	38120	866-399-0453	363-8541*
Treats International Franchise Corp 238 Queen St S 2nd Fl *TF:* 800-461-4003 ■ *Web:* www.treats.com	Mississauga	ON	L5M1L5	613-563-4073	563-1982
Truly Nolen of America Inc 3636 E Speedway Blvd **Fax Area Code:* 520 ■ *TF:* 800-468-7859 ■ *Web:* www.trulynolen.com	Tucson	AZ	85716	800-528-3442	322-4002*
Tuffy Assoc Corp 7150 Granite Cir *TF:* 800-228-8339 ■ *Web:* www.tuffy.com	Toledo	OH	43617	419-865-6900	865-7343
United Financial Services Group 325 Chestnut St Ste 3000 *Web:* www.unitedfsg.com	Philadelphia	PA	19106	215-238-0300	238-9056
United Shipping Solutions 6985 Union Pk Ctr Ste 565 *Web:* www.usshipit.com	Midvale	UT	84047	801-352-0012	352-0339
UPS Store, The 6060 Cornerstone Ct W *TF:* 800-789-4623 ■ *Web:* www.theupsstore.com	San Diego	CA	92121	858-455-8800	
Valpak Direct Marketing Systems Inc 8605 Largo Lakes Dr *TF:* 800-237-6266 ■ *Web:* www.valpak.com	Largo	FL	33773	800-237-6266	
Weed Man 2399 Royal Windsor Dr *Web:* www.weedmancanada.com	Mississauga	ON	L5J1K9	905-823-8300	
Wetzel's Pretzels LLC 35 Hugus Alley Ste 300 *Web:* www.wetzels.com	Pasadena	CA	91103	626-432-6900	432-6904
Wild Birds Unlimited Inc 11711 N College Ave Ste 146 *TF:* 800-326-4928 ■ *Web:* www.wbu.com	Carmel	IN	46032	317-571-7100	571-7110
WineStyles Inc 5515 Mills Civic Pkwy Ste 110 *TF:* 866-424-9463 ■ *Web:* www.winestyles.com	West Des Moines	IA	50266	866-424-9463	
Wing Zone Franchise Corp 900 Cir 75 Pkwy Ste 930 *TF:* 877-946-4966 ■ *Web:* wingzonefranchise.com	Atlanta	GA	30339	404-875-5045	875-6631
Wingstop Restaurants Inc 1101 E Arapaho Rd Ste 150 *Web:* www.wingstop.com	Richardson	TX	75081	972-686-6500	
Wireless Toyz Ltd 29155 NW Hwy *TF:* 866-237-2624 ■ *Web:* www.wirelesstoyz.com	Southfield	MI	48034	248-426-8200	
Wireless Zone 34 Industrial Pk Pl **Fax Area Code:* 989 ■ *TF:* 888-881-2622 ■ *Web:* www.wirelesszone.com	Middletown	CT	06457	860-632-9494	652-0520*
Woodcraft Supply LLC 1177 Rosemar Rd **Fax Area Code:* 304 ■ *TF:* 800-535-4482 ■ *Web:* www.woodcraft.com	Parkersburg	WV	26105	800-535-4482	428-8271*
World Inspection Network International Inc 12345 Lk City Way NE Ste 365 *TF:* 800-309-6753 ■ *Web:* www.wini.com	Seattle	WA	98125	800-309-6753	
Worldwide Express 2602 McKinney Ave Ste 400 *TF:* 800-758-7447 ■ *Web:* www.wwex.com	Dallas	TX	75204	214-720-2400	720-2446

Phone Fax

WSI Internet 5580 Explorer Dr Ste 600 .... Mississauga ON L4W4Y1 905-678-7588 678-7242
TF: 888-678-7588 ■ *Web:* www.wsicorporate.com
Yogen Fruz 210 Shields Ct. .... Markham ON L3R8V2 905-479-8762 479-5235
Web: www.yogenfruz.com
Young Rembrandts 23 N Union St .... Elgin IL 60123 847-742-6966 742-7197
Web: www.youngrembrandts.com
Ziebart International Corp 1290 E Maple Rd .... Troy MI 48083 248-588-4100 588-0431*
**Fax:* Orders ■ *TF:* 800-877-1312 ■ *Web:* www.ziebart.com

311 FREIGHT FORWARDERS

See Also Logistics Services (Transportation & Warehousing) p. 2681

Phone Fax

A & S Services Group LLC 310 N Zarfoss Dr .... York PA 17404 717-759-3017 235-2456
TF: 800-227-6782 ■ *Web:* askinard.com
A Pm Systems Inc 1440 21st St Ste 101 .... Rockford IL 61108 215-295-1097
Web: apmsystems.com
Advance Transportation Systems Inc
1125 Glendale Milford Rd. .... Cincinnati OH 45215 513-771-4848
TF: 800-878-4849 ■ *Web:* www.atslogistics.com
Aeropost International Services Inc
6703 NW Seventh St Ste 4567 .... Miami FL 33126 305-592-5534
Web: www.aeropost.com
Air Courier Dispatch 12333 S Van Ness Ave .... Hawthorne CA 90250 607-748-9507
Web: www.aics.com
Airways Freight Corp
3849 W Wedington Dr .... Fayetteville AR 72704 479-442-6301 442-6522
TF: 800-643-3525 ■ *Web:* www.airwaysfreight.com
AIT Worldwide Logistics 701 N Rohlwing Rd .... Itasca IL 60143 630-766-8300
Web: aitworldwide.com
Alaska Tanker Company LLC
15400 NW Greenbrier Pkwy Parkside Bldg
Ste A400 .... Beaverton OR 97006 503-207-0046
Web: www.aktanker.com
Alba Wheels Up International Inc
525 Washington Blvd .... Jersey City NJ 07310 201-435-7050 435-5650
Web: www.albawheelsup.com
Allen Lund Company Inc
4529 Angeles Crest Hwy Ste 300 .... La Canada CA 91011 800-777-6142
TF: 800-777-6142 ■ *Web:* www.allenlund.com
Alliance International Forwarders Inc
7155 Old Katy Rd .... Houston TX 77024 713-428-3100 428-3101
Alliance Shippers Inc
516 Sylvan Ave .... Englewood Cliffs NJ 07632 201-227-0400
Web: alliance.com
Aloha Freight Forwarders Inc
1800 S Anderson Ave .... Compton CA 90220 310-631-6116
Web: www.alohafreight.com
Apex Maritime Ord 1900 E Golf Rd .... Schaumburg IL 60173 630-227-9818
Web: apexshipping.com
Arrow Freight Management Inc
1001 Berryville st .... El Paso TX 79928 888-598-9891
TF: 888-598-9891 ■ *Web:* www.arrowelp.com
Autobahn Freight Lines Ltd 27 Automatic Rd. .... Brampton ON L6S5N8 416-741-5454
TF: 877-989-9994 ■ *Web:* www.autobahnfreight.com
Axsun Inc 4900 Armand Frappier .... Saint-Hubert QC J3Z1G5 450-445-3003
TF: 888-992-9786 ■ *Web:* www.axsungroup.com
Barthco International Inc
5101 S Broad St .... Philadelphia PA 19112 215-238-8600 592-1254
TF General: 877-401-6400 ■ *Web:* www.ohl.com
Bassler Energy Services Inc 8050 Hwy 21 W .... Caldwell TX 77836 979-535-4593
Web: www.basslerenergyservices.com
Big Daddy Drayage Inc 575 Ave P .... Newark NJ 07105 973-522-1717
Web: www.bigdaddydrayage.com
Big Freight Systems Inc 360 Hwy 12 N. .... Steinbach MB R5G1A6 204-326-3434
Web: www.bigfreight.com
Blue-Grace Logistics LLC
2846 S Falkenburg Rd .... Riverview FL 33578 813-641-0357
TF: 800-697-4477 ■ *Web:* www.mybluegrace.com
BNX Shipping Inc 910 E 236th St .... Carson CA 90745 310-764-0999
TF: 844-221-3091 ■ *Web:* bnxlogistics.bkihost.net
Bolanos & Company Inc 8708 Killam Indus Blvd .... Laredo TX 78045 956-722-0976
Web: www.bolanos.com
Bulk Connection Inc 15 Allen St .... Mystic CT 06355 860-572-9111
Web: www.bulkconnection.com
Buscemi Co, International LLC
PO Box 88065 Ste 201 .... Los Angeles CA 90301 310-568-1011
Web: buscemico.com
Capital Transportation Solutions LLC
1915 Vaughn Rd. .... Kennesaw GA 30144 770-690-8684
Web: shipwithcts.com
Carbon Resources of Florida Inc
11023 Gatewood Dr Ste 103 .... Bradenton FL 34211 941-747-2630
Web: www.carbonresourcesofflorida.com
CBSL Transportation Services Inc
4750 S Merrimac Ave .... Chicago IL 60638 708-496-1100
Web: www.cbsltrans.com
CDA 8500 S Tryon St .... Charlotte NC 28273 704-504-1877
Web: cdausa.01.cycrosuite.com/itool3/frontend/en/site__2
CDS Logistics Management Inc
1225 Bengies Rd Ste A .... Baltimore MD 21220 410-314-8000
TF: 866-649-9559 ■ *Web:* www.cdslogistics.net
Certified Freight Logistics Inc
1344 White Ct. .... Santa Maria CA 93458 805-925-9900
Web: www.cflrecruiting.com
CEVA Ground US LP 15390 Vickery Dr .... Houston TX 77032 281-227-5000
Web: www.selectscg.com
Ceva Logistics US Holdings Inc
10751 Deerwood Park Blvd 201 .... Jacksonville FL 32256 904-928-1400 928-1550
Web: cevalogistics.com
CH Powell Co 75 Shawmut Rd .... Canton MA 02021 781-302-7300
Web: chpowell.com

Phone Fax

Cold Star Freight Systems Inc
1015 Henry Eng Pl .... Victoria BC V9B6B2 250-381-3399
TF: 800-201-1277 ■ *Web:* www.coldstarfreight.com
Coldiron Companies Inc 200 N Sooner Rd .... Edmond OK 73034 405-562-2910
Web: www.coldironcompanies.com
Combined Express Inc 3685 Marshall Ln .... Bensalem PA 19020 215-633-1535
TF: 800-777-0458 ■ *Web:* www.combinedexpress.com
Concordia International Forwarding Inc
70 E Sunrise Hwy Ste 605 .... Valley Stream NY 11581 516-561-1100 561-1323
Web: www.concordiafreight.com
ContainerWorld Forwarding Services Inc
16133 Blundell Rd .... Richmond BC V6W0A3 604-276-1300
TF: 877-838-8880 ■ *Web:* www.containerworld.com
Continental Traffic Service Inc (CTSI)
5100 Poplar Ave 15th Fl .... Memphis TN 38137 901-766-1500 766-1520
TF: 888-836-5135 ■ *Web:* www.ctsi-global.com
Corporate Traffic Inc
2002 Southside Blvd .... Jacksonville FL 32216 904-727-0051 727-6804
Web: www.corporate-traffic.com
D & B Logistics 720 Washington St .... Hanover MA 02339 781-829-4500
Web: www.dblinc.net
D J Powers Company Inc
5000 Business Ctr Dr Ste 1000 .... Savannah GA 31405 912-234-7241
Web: www.djpowers.com
Daybreak Express Inc 500 Ave P .... Newark NJ 07105 973-589-5931
Web: www.daybreakexpress.com
DHL Global Forwarding (Canada) Inc
6200 Edwards Blvd .... Mississauga ON L5T2V7 954-626-2419 405-9301*
**Fax Area Code:* 905
Dimerco Express (USA) Corp 955 Dillon Dr .... Wood Dale IL 60191 630-595-7310
Web: dimerco.com
DJS International Services Inc
4215 Gateway Dr Ste 100 .... Colleyville TX 76034 972-929-8433
Web: www.djsintl.com
Dupre' Transport LLC 201 Energy Pkwy .... Lafayette LA 70508 337-237-8471
Web: www.duprelogistics.com
Evans Delivery Company Inc PO Box 268 .... Pottsville PA 17901 570-385-9048 385-9058
TF: 800-666-7885 ■ *Web:* www.evansdelivery.com
Excel Transportation Inc 333 Ongman Rd .... Prince George BC V2K4K9 250-563-7356
Web: exceltransportation.ca
Faye Stewart Transportation Service LLC
3056 N 33rd Ave. .... Phoenix AZ 85017 602-233-3500
Web: www.fayestewarttrans.com
FESCO Agencies NA Inc
1000 Second Ave Ste 1310 .... Seattle WA 98104 206-583-0860 583-0889
TF: 800-275-3372 ■ *Web:* www.fesco-na.com
Fetch Logistics Inc
25 Northpointe Pkwy Ste 200 .... Amherst NY 14228 716-689-4556 689-9676
TF: 800-964-4940 ■ *Web:* www.fetchlogistics.com
First Coast Logistics Services Inc
11460 Boote Blvd Ste 1 .... Jacksonville FL 32218 904-757-6008
Web: www.firstcoast.net
Fleetgistics Holdings Inc 2251 Lynx Ln Ste 7 .... Orlando FL 32804 407-843-6505
Web: www.fleetgistics.com
Foreign Trade Export Packing Co
1350 Lathrop St .... Houston TX 77020 713-672-8211
Web: www.ftep.com
FPA Customs Brokers Inc 152-31 134th Ave .... Jamaica NY 11434 718-527-2280
Web: www.fpajfk.com
Freight Logistics Inc PO Box 1712 .... Medford OR 97501 541-734-5617
TF: 800-866-7882 ■ *Web:* www.shipfli.com
Frontier Logistics LP 1806 S 16th St. .... La Porte TX 77571 800-610-6808 307-2399*
**Fax Area Code:* 281 ■ *TF:* 800-610-6808 ■ *Web:* www.frontierlogistics.com
FTS International Express Inc
400 Country Club Dr .... Bensenville IL 60106 630-694-0644 694-0778
Web: www.fts.com
Garcia Express LLC 639 S 54th Ave .... Phoenix AZ 85043 602-352-0150
Web: www.garciaexpress.com
Gateway Logistics Group Inc, The
18201 Viscount Rd .... Houston TX 77032 281-443-7447
Web: www.gateway-group.com
Gazelle Transportation Inc
34915 Gazelle Ct .... Bakersfield CA 93308 661-322-8868
Web: www.gazelletrans.com
Geodis Wilson Canada Ltd 3061 Orlando Dr .... Mississauga ON L4V1R4 905-677-5266
Web: www.geodis.com/freight-forwarding-@/en/view-1852-category.html/1850
Gif Services Inc 2525 Brunswick Ave Ste 204 .... Linden NJ 07036 908-474-1270
Web: www.gifservices.com
Gold Coast Freightways Inc 12250 NW 28th Ave. .... Miami FL 33167 305-687-3560 685-8056
TF: 877-465-3585 ■ *Web:* www.gcfreight.com
GoodShip International Inc
699 Lively Blvd .... Elk Grove Village IL 60007 847-621-1444
Web: www.goodship.com
Graulich International Inc 6411 NW 35th Ave .... Miami FL 33147 305-836-1700 836-1763
Web: www.graulichinternational.com
Gravy Train Express LLC 65 Gravy Train Ln. .... Lewistown PA 17044 717-242-8515
Web: gravytrainllc.com
Group Transportation Services Inc
5876 Darrow Rd .... Hudson OH 44236 330-342-8700
GTO 2000 Inc PO Box 2819 .... Gainesville GA 30503 770-287-9233
Web: www.gto2000.com
HA Logistics Inc 5175 Johnson Dr .... Pleasanton CA 94588 925-251-9300 251-9333
TF: 800-449-5778 ■ *Web:* www.halogistics.com
Hancock International Corp 351 Main Pl .... Carol Stream IL 60188 630-510-7697
Web: hancock-international.com
Harbor Freight Transport Corp 301 Craneway St. .... Newark NJ 07114 973-589-6700 589-6677
Web: www.harborusa.com
Hassett Air Express 877 S Rt 83 .... Elmhurst IL 60126 630-530-6524
Web: hassettexpress.com
Hawaiian Express Service Inc
3623 Munster Ave .... Hayward CA 94545 510-783-6100 782-5794
Web: www.hawaiianexpressinc.com

Company	City	State	Zip	Phone	Fax
Holland Transportation Management Inc 305 N Center St *Web:* www.hollandtms.com	Statesville	NC	28677	704-872-4269	
Hubtrucker Inc 315 Freeport St Ste B *Web:* hubtrucker.com	Houston	TX	77015	713-547-5482	
I. C. S. Customs Service Inc 1099 Morse Ave *Web:* www.icscustoms.com	Elk Grove Village	IL	60007	847-718-9998	
ICAT Logistics Inc 6805 Douglas Legum Dr 3rd Fl *Web:* www.icatlogistics.com	Elkridge	MD	21075	443-459-8070	
Incopro Corp 17200 SH 249 Ste 210 *Web:* www.incopro.com	Houston	TX	77064	281-227-9880	
IntegraCore LLC 6077 W Wells Park Rd *Web:* www.integracore.com	West Jordan	UT	84081	801-975-9411	
Interdom LLC 11800 S 75th Ave Ste 2N *TF:* 800-935-0851 ■ *Web:* www.interdompartners.com	Palos Heights	IL	60463	800-935-0851	
J & A Freight Systems Inc 4704 Irving Park Rd Ste 8 **Fax Area Code:* 773 ■ *TF:* 877-668-3378 ■ *Web:* jandafreight.com	Chicago	IL	60641	877-668-3378	205-7725*
Jan Packaging Inc 100 Harrison St *Web:* www.janpackaging.com	Dover	NJ	07801	973-361-7200	
Jas Forwarding USA Inc 6165 Barfield Rd *Web:* jas.com	Atlanta	GA	30328	770-688-1206	
JD & Billy Hines Trucking Inc 407 Hines Blvd *Web:* www.hinestrucking.com	Prescott	AZ	71857	870-887-9400	
Jefferson Forwarding 2222 Jefferson St *Web:* casaduana.com	Laredo	TX	78040	956-723-0111	
JHOC Inc 323 Cash Memorial Blvd	Forest Park	GA	30297	404-675-1950	
Johanson Transportation Service Inc 5583 E Olive Ave *Web:* www.johansontrans.com	Fresno	CA	93727	559-458-2200	
JW Hampton Jr & Company Inc 161-15 Rockaway Blvd *Web:* jwhampton.com	Jamaica	NY	11434	718-276-0301	
K&L Freight Management Inc 745 S Rohlwing Rd *Web:* www.kandlfreight.com	Addison	IL	60101	630-607-1500	
KCC Transport Systems Inc 311 W Artesia Blvd *Web:* www.kccusa.com	Compton	CA	90220	310-764-5933	
Kem Krest Corp 2040 Toledo Rd *Web:* www.kemkrest.com	Elkhart	IN	46516	574-389-2650	
Knichel Logistics LP 5347 William Flynn Hwy 2nd Fl *Web:* www.knichellogistics.com	Gibsonia	PA	15044	724-449-3300	
Knitney Lines Inc PO Box 350 *TF General:* 866-564-8639 ■ *Web:* www.knitneylines.com	Scranton	PA	18505	570-457-5060	457-6725
KW International Inc 18655 S Bishop Ave *Web:* www.kwinternational.com	Carson	CA	90746	310-354-6944	
Kyfi Inc 4300 Fern Vly Rd *Web:* www.kyfi.com	Louisville	KY	40219	502-810-9800	
L E Coppersmith Inc 525 S Douglas St *TF:* 888-827-4388 ■ *Web:* www.coppersmith.com	El Segundo	CA	90245	310-607-8000	607-8001
L. H. P. Transportation Services Inc 2032 E Kearney Ste 213 *Web:* www.lhp-transport.com	Springfield	MO	65803	417-865-7577	
L. J. Rogers Inc 421 Currant Rd *Web:* www.ljrogers.com	Fall River	MA	02720	508-636-6658	
LeanLogistics Inc 1351 S Waverly Rd *TF:* 866-584-7280 ■ *Web:* www.leanlogistics.com	Holland	MI	49423	616-738-6400	738-6462
Leman USA Inc 1860 Renaissance Blvd *Web:* us.leman.com	Sturtevant	WI	53177	262-884-4700	884-4690
Linkex Inc 2230 Lyndon B Johnson Fwy Ste 300 *Web:* www.linkex.us	Dallas	TX	75234	972-481-9900	
Logfret Inc 6801 W Side Ave *Web:* www.logfret.com	North Bergen	NJ	07047	201-817-1140	656-7876
Logistics Plus Inc 1406 Peach St *TF:* 866-564-7587 ■ *Web:* www.logisticsplus.net	Erie	PA	16501	814-461-7600	461-7635
Longhorn Imports Inc 2202 E Union Bower *TF:* 800-641-8348 ■ *Web:* longhornimports.com	Irving	TX	75061	972-721-9102	579-4890
Lynden Inc 18000 International Blvd Ste 800 *TF:* 888-596-3361 ■ *Web:* www.lynden.com	Seattle	WA	98188	206-241-8778	243-8415
M&M Transport Services Inc 21 Mcgrath Hwy Ste 204 *Web:* www.mmtransport.com	Quincy	MA	02169	617-769-9370	
Marinsa Miami Corp 12250 SW 133 Ct *Web:* marinsa.com	Miami	FL	33186	305-252-0118	
Maritime Company For Navigation, The 249 Shipyard Blvd *Web:* themaritimecompany.com	Wilmington	NC	28412	910-343-8900	
Masterpiece International Ltd 39 Broadway 14th Fl *Web:* www.masterpieceintl.com	New York	NY	10006	212-825-4800	825-7010
Metro Express Transportation Services Inc 875 Fee Fee Rd *TF:* 800-805-0073 ■ *Web:* www.metroexpressinc.com	St. Louis	MO	63043	314-993-1511	
MHF Inc 2328 Evans City Rd *Web:* mhftrans.com	Zelienople	PA	16063	724-452-3900	
Mihlfeld & Assoc Inc 2841 E Division St *Web:* www.mihlfeld.com	Springfield	MO	65803	417-831-6727	
MLS Freight Logistics (MLS) 1802 S Expy 281 *Web:* mlsfreight.com	Edinburg	TX	78542	956-292-2700	
Modaexpress of USA Inc 900 Secaucus Rd Unit A *Web:* www.modaexpress.com	Secaucus	NJ	07094	201-325-8808	
Morrison Express Corp USA 2000 S Hughes Way *Web:* www.morrisonexpress.com	El Segundo	CA	90245	310-322-8999	322-6688
MSE Express America Inc 2700 Delta Ln *Web:* www.tasexpress.com	Elk Grove Village	IL	60007	847-238-2600	
MSM Transportation Inc 124 Commercial Rd *TF:* 800-667-4175 ■ *Web:* wheelsgroup.com	Bolton	ON	L7E1K4	905-951-6800	
MVP Global Logistics LLC 580 Chelsea St Ste 212 *Web:* mvpgloballogistics.com	East Boston	MA	02128	617-569-6300	
N2it Containers LP 6012 Murphy St	Houston	TX	77033	713-644-5055	
Nippon Express USA Inc 590 Madison Ave Ste 2401 *Web:* www.nipponexpressusa.com	New York	NY	10022	212-405-1650	758-2595
Noble Logistic Services Inc 5390 Greens Rd *Web:* www.ndlilogistics.com	Houston	TX	77032	713-690-0200	
Norvanco International Inc 4301 W Vly Hwy Ste 100 *Web:* www.norvanco.com	Sumner	WA	98390	253-987-4031	987-4015
NVC Logistics Group Inc 1 Pond Rd *Web:* www.nvclogistics.com	Rockleigh	NJ	07647	201-767-0911	
OCEANAIR Inc 186A Lee Burbank Hwy *Web:* www.oceanair.net	Revere	MA	02151	781-286-2700	
Oceane Marine Shipping Inc 407 E Maple St *TF:* 888-262-3263 ■ *Web:* oceanems.com	Cumming	GA	30040	770-888-5941	
Oceanex Income Fund 630 Rene-Levesque Blvd W Ste 2550 *Web:* www.oceanex.com	Montreal	QC	H3B1S6	514-875-9595	
OIA Global Logistics Inc 2100 SW River Parkway *Web:* oiaglobal.com	Portland	OR	97201	503-736-5900	
Ontario Northland Transportation Commission 555 Oak St E *Web:* www.ontarionorthland.ca	North Bay	ON	P1B8L3	705-472-4500	
OTS Astracon LLC 3115 Beam Rd PO Box 19413 *Web:* otsusa.org	Charlotte	NC	28217	704-424-5522	424-5622
Pac Marine Express Inc 19401 S Main St Ste 102 *Web:* www.gopacmarine.com	Gardena	CA	90248	310-329-2478	
Page & Jones Inc 52 N Jackson St 36602 PO Box 2167 *Web:* www.pageandjones.com	Mobile	AL	36652	251-432-1646	
Pan Pacific Express Corp 19481 Harborgate Way *Web:* www.panpacificusa.com	Torrance	CA	90501	310-638-3888	
Pan Star Express Corp 1134 Tower Ln *Web:* www.panstarexpress.com	Bensenville	IL	60106	630-787-1672	
Phoenix International Freight Services Ltd 14701 Charlson Rd **Fax Area Code:* 630 ■ *TF:* 855-229-6128 ■ *Web:* www.chrobinson.com	Eden Prairie	MN	55347	952-937-6761	766-6395*
Pioneer Transfer LLC 2034 S St Aubin St PO Box 2567 **Fax Area Code:* 712 ■ *TF:* 800-325-4650 ■ *Web:* www.pioneertransfer.com	Sioux City	IA	51106	800-325-4650	274-2946*
Poten & Partners Inc 805 Third Ave *Web:* www.poten.com	New York	NY	10022	212-230-2000	355-0295
Priefert Manufacturing Company Inc 2630 S Jefferson Ave PO box 1540 *Web:* www.priefert.com	Mount Pleasant	TX	75456	903-572-1741	
Primary Freight Services Inc 6545 Caballero Blvd *TF:* 800-635-0013 ■ *Web:* www.primaryfreight.com	Buena Park	CA	90620	310-635-3000	
Priority Distribution Inc 330 Milltown Rd Ste W31 *Web:* www.pdi3pl.com	East Brunswick	NJ	08816	732-234-1919	
ProTrans International Inc 8311 N Perimeter Rd *Web:* www.protrans.com	Indianapolis	IN	46241	317-240-4100	
Pulau Electronics Corp 12633 Challenger Pkwy *Web:* www.pulau.com	Orlando	FL	32826	407-380-9191	380-9786
Quality Customs Broker Inc 4464 S Whitnall Ave *TF:* 888-813-4647 ■ *Web:* www.qualitybrokers.com	Saint Francis	WI	53235	414-482-9447	482-9448
Quality Transportation 36-40 37th St Ste 201 *TF:* 800-677-2838 ■ *Web:* www.qualitytca.com	Long Island	NY	11101	212-308-6333	308-6595
R & D Transportation Services Inc 4036 Adolfo Rd *TF:* 800-966-7114 ■ *Web:* rdtsi.com	Camarillo	CA	93012	805-529-7511	
Raymond Express International (REI) 320 Harbor Way *Web:* www.reiexpress.com	South San Francisco	CA	94080	650-871-8560	952-3288
Ready Auto Transport LLC 1030 N Colorado St Ste 109 *Web:* www.readyautotransport.com	Gilbert	AZ	85233	480-558-3200	
Recon Logistics LLC 10205 Queens Way Ste 5 *TF:* 866-424-7153 ■ *Web:* reconlogistics.com	Chagrin Falls	OH	44023	440-708-2306	
Riege Software International u s a 73 Redding Rd *Web:* www.riege.com	Georgetown	CT	06829	203-544-9475	
Rmx Global Logistics 35715 US Hwy 40 Bldg B **Fax Area Code:* 303 ■ *TF:* 888-824-7365 ■ *Web:* www.rmxglobal.com	Evergreen	CO	80439	888-824-7365	674-3803*
Rock-It Cargo USA Inc 5432 W 104th St *TF:* 800-973-1727 ■ *Web:* www.rockitcargo.com	Los Angeles	CA	90045	310-410-0935	410-0628
Rogers & Brown Custom Brokers Inc 2 Cumberland St *TF:* 866-738-8197 ■ *Web:* www.rogers-brown.com	Charleston	SC	29401	843-577-3630	
Romar Transportation Systems Inc 3500 S Kedzie Ave *TF:* 800-621-5416 ■ *Web:* www.romartrans.com	Chicago	IL	60632	773-376-8800	650-1644
Rpl Associates Inc 21650 W 11 Mile Rd *Web:* www.rplassociates.com	Southfield	MI	48076	248-353-0011	
RTL Robinson Enterprises Ltd 350 Old Airport Rd *Web:* westcanbulk.ca/rtl	Yellowknife	NT	X1A2P4	867-873-6271	
Ryder CRSA Logistics 1275 Kingsway Ave *Web:* www.crsalog.com	Port Coquitlam	BC	V3C1S2	604-941-8228	
Samuel Shapiro & Company Inc 100 N Charles St One Charles Ctr Ste 1200 *Web:* www.shapiro.com	Baltimore	MD	21201	410-539-0540	

Phone | Fax

Satellite Logistics Group Inc
12621 Featherwood Ste 390........ Houston TX 77034 281-902-5500 902-5501
TF: 877-795-7540 ■ *Web:* www.slg.com

Saturn Freight Systems Inc PO Box 680308........ Marietta GA 30067 770-952-3490
Web: www.saturnfreight.com

Scarbrough International Ltd
10841 Ambassador Dr........ Kansas City MO 64153 816-891-2400
Web: www.scarbrough-intl.com

Schenker Inc 150 Albany Ave........ Freeport NY 11520 516-377-3000
Web: www.dbschenkerusa.com

Schenker of Canada Ltd
5935 Airport Rd 10th Fl........ Mississauga ON L4V1W5 905-676-0676
TF: 800-461-3686 ■ *Web:* www.dbschenker.ca

Scott Logistics Corp PO Box 391........ Rome GA 30162 706-234-1184 234-1184
TF: 800-893-6689 ■ *Web:* www.scottlogistics.com

Senderex Cargo Inc 17022 Montanero Ave Ste 6........ Carson CA 90746 310-342-2900 642-0427
Web: www.senderex.com

Senvoy LLC 115 SE Yamhill St........ Portland OR 97214 503-234-7722
TF: 866-373-6869 ■ *Web:* www.senvoy.com

Serra International Inc
75 Montgomery St Ste 300........ Jersey City NJ 07302 201-860-9600
Web: www.serraintl.com

Seven R Transportation Inc
2818 Queen City Dr Ste G........ Charlotte NC 28266 704-391-0694
Web: www.sevenr.com

Sho-Air International
5401 Argosy Ave........ Huntington Beach CA 92649 949-476-9111 476-9991
TF: 800-227-9111 ■ *Web:* www.shoair.com

Simcoe Parts Service Inc
6795 Industrial Pkwy........ Alliston ON L9R1W1 705-435-7814
Web: www.simcoeparts.com

Smith Systems Transportation Inc
417 Ninth Ave........ Scottsbluff NE 69361 800-897-5571
TF: 800-897-5571 ■ *Web:* smithsystemsus.weebly.com

Sos Global Express Inc 2803 Trent Rd........ New Bern NC 28562 252-635-1400
Web: sosglobal.com

Sotech Nitram Inc 1695 Boul Laval........ Laval QC H7S2M2 450-975-2100
TF: 877-664-8726 ■ *Web:* www.sotechnitram.com

Sound Brokerage International LLC
3600 Port Of Tacoma Rd Ste 301........ Tacoma WA 98424 253-922-7718
Web: www.soundbrokerage.com

Star Asia International Inc 208 Church St........ Decatur GA 30030 404-761-6900
Web: www.star-asia.com

Stone Transport Inc 3495 Hack Rd........ Saginaw MI 48601 989-754-4788
Web: www.stonetransport.com

Sunset Transportation Inc
11325 Concord Village Ave........ St Louis MO 63123 800-849-6540
TF: 800-849-6540 ■ *Web:* www.sunsettrans.com

Suntrans International Inc
1550 W Glenlake Ave........ Itasca IL 60143 630-285-9900
Web: www.suntrans.com

Superior Freight Services Inc
1230 Trapp Rd........ Saint Paul MN 55121 952-854-5053
Web: www.supfrt.com

Team Drive-Away Inc 23712 W 83rd Ter........ Shawnee KS 66227 913-825-4776
Web: www.teamdriveaway.com

Tech Transport Inc PO Box 431........ Milford NH 03055 603-673-0898
Web: www.techtransport.com

Technical Traffic Consultants Corp
30 Hemlock Dr........ Congers NY 10920 845-623-6144
Web: www.technicaltraffic.com

Terminal Corp, The 2001 E McComas St Ste A........ Baltimore MD 21224 800-560-7207
TF: 800-560-7207 ■ *Web:* www.termcorp.com

Thill Logistics Inc 355 Byrd Ave........ Neenah WI 54956 920-967-8000
Web: www.thilllogistics.com

Thompson, Ahern & Company Ltd
6299 Airport Rd Ste 506........ Mississauga ON L4V1N3 905-677-3471
TF: 877-262-8226 ■ *Web:* www.taco.ca

Time Definite Services Inc
1360 Madeline Ln Ste 300........ Elgin IL 60124 800-466-8040
TF: 800-466-8040 ■ *Web:* timedefinite.com

Total Quality Logistics Inc (TQL)
4289 Ivy Pointe Blvd........ Cincinnati OH 45245 513-831-2600 965-7630
TF: 800-580-3101 ■ *Web:* www.tql.com

Total Transportation Concept
8728 Avaition Blvd........ Inglewood CA 90301 310-337-0515
Web: www.totaltrans.com

Towne Air Freight 24805 US 20 W........ South Bend IN 46628 423-636-3380
TF: 800-726-6654 ■ *Web:* www.towneair.com

Trademark Transportation Inc
739 Vandalia St........ Saint Paul MN 55114 651-646-2500
TF: 800-646-2550 ■ *Web:* www.trademarktrans.com

Trancy Logistics America Corp
1670 Dolwick Rd Ste 8........ Erlanger KY 41018 859-282-7780
Web: trancyamerica.com

Trans-Border Global Freight Systems Inc
2103 Route 9........ Round Lake NY 12151 518-785-6000 785-6239
TF: 800-493-9444 ■ *Web:* www.tbgfs.com

Transaver LLC 116 Fayette St........ Manlius NY 13104 315-682-1666
Web: www.transaver.com

TransCore Link Logistics Corp
6660 Kennedy Rd Ste 205........ Mississauga ON L5T2M9 800-263-6149
TF: 800-263-6149 ■ *Web:* www.transcore.ca

TransGroup Express Inc
18850 Eighth Ave S Ste 100........ Seattle WA 98148 206-244-0330
Web: www.transgroup.com

TransGuardian Inc
International Jewelry Ctr 550 S Hill St Lobby 103
.... Los Angeles CA 90013 213-622-5877
Web: www.transguardian.com

TRANSInternational System Inc
130 E Wilson Bridge Rd Ste 150 Ste 150........ Worthington OH 43085 614-891-4942 891-4929
TF: 800-340-7540 ■ *Web:* www.trnj.com

Transit Systems Inc
999 Old Eagle School Rd Ste 114........ Wayne PA 19087 800-626-1257
TF: 800-626-1257 ■ *Web:* www.transitsystems.com

Transmaritime Central Inc
14213 Transportation Ave........ Laredo TX 78045 956-724-8417
Web: www.transmaritime.com/httpdocs/dynamicdata/default.asp

Transmodal Corp 48 S Franklin Tpke........ Ramsey NJ 07446 201-316-1600
Web: www.transmodal.net

Transportation Management Assoc Inc
344 Oak Grove Church Rd........ Mocksville NC 27028 800-745-8292
TF: 800-745-8292 ■ *Web:* www.tmaco.com

TransportGistics Inc
4170 Veterans Memorial Hwy Ste 202........ Bohemia NY 11716 631-567-4100
Web: www.transportgistics.com

TransX Group of Cos 2595 Inkster Blvd........ Winnipeg MB R3C2E6 204-632-6694
TF: 877-558-9444 ■ *Web:* www.transx.com

TranzAct Technologies Inc
360 W Butterfield Rd 4th Fl........ Elmhurst IL 60126 630-833-0890 833-8538
Web: www.tranzact.com

Travelers Transportation Services Inc
195 Heart Lk Rd South........ Brampton ON L6W3N6 905-457-8789
TF: 800-265-8789 ■ *Web:* www.travelers.ca

Tricor America Inc
717 Airport Blvd........ South San Francisco CA 94080 650-877-3650 583-3197
Web: www.tricor.com

Triple B Forwarders Inc 1511 Glen Curtis St........ Carson CA 90746 310-604-5840
TF: 800-228-8465 ■ *Web:* www.tripleb.com

Tucker Company Worldwide Inc
900 Dudley Ave........ Cherry Hill NJ 08002 856-317-9600
TF: 800-229-7780 ■ *Web:* tuckerco.com

U-Freight America Inc
320 Corey Way........ South San Francisco CA 94080 650-583-6527 583-8122

Updike Distribution Logistics LLC
4411 W Roosevelt St........ Phoenix AZ 85043 602-682-1800
Web: www.updikedl.com

UTXL Inc 10771 NW Ambassador Dr........ Kansas City MO 64153 816-891-7770
Web: www.utxl.com

Valley Express Llc 6003 State Rd 76........ Oshkosh WI 54904 920-231-1677
Web: www.valleyexpress.net

Vascor Ltd 100 Farmers Bank Dr Ste 300........ Georgetown KY 40324 502-570-2020
Web: www.vascorlogistics.com

Veeco Holdings LLC 6801 W Side Ave........ North Bergen NJ 07047 201-865-6200
Web: www.veeco1.com

Victory Transportation Systems Inc
9009 N Loop E Ste 165........ Houston TX 77029 713-682-8900
Web: www.victorytrucks.com

Ware Pak Inc 2427 Bond St........ University Park IL 60484 708-534-2600
Web: www.ware-pak.com

Wellcorp Express Inc
8616 La Tijera Blvd Ste 310........ Los Angeles CA 90045 310-645-6410
Web: welltonexpress.com.hk

Wider Consolidated Inc 175-35 148th Rd 2nd Fl........ Jamica NY 11434 718-244-8800
Web: widerlogistics.com

Wilk Forwarding Company Inc
2900 Emerson Expy........ Jacksonville FL 32207 904-346-3550

Worldtrans Services Inc
7130 Miramar Rd Ste 100a........ San Diego CA 92121 858-536-7900
TF: 800-736-3769 ■ *Web:* www.worldtransinc.com

WR Zanes & Company of Louisiana Inc
223 Tchoupitoulas St........ New Orleans LA 70130 504-524-1301 524-1309
Web: www.wrzanes.com

Yusen Logistics (Americas) Inc
300 Lighting Way........ Secaucus NJ 07094 201-553-3800
Web: www.us.yusen-logistics.com

312 FREIGHT TRANSPORT - DEEP SEA (DOMESTIC PORTS)

Phone | Fax

Alaska Marine Lines Inc
5615 W Marginal Way SW........ Seattle WA 98106 206-763-4244 764-5782
TF Cust Svc: 800-326-8346 ■ *Web:* www.lynden.com

Algoma Central Corp
63 Church St Ste 600........ St. Catharines ON L2R3C4 905-687-7888
Web: www.algonet.com

Berman Moving & Storage Inc
23800 Corbin Dr........ Cleveland OH 44128 216-663-8816
TF: 800-333-0582 ■ *Web:* www.bermanmovers.com

Coastal Transportation Inc 4025 13th Ave W........ Seattle WA 98119 206-282-9979 283-9121
TF: 800-544-2580 ■ *Web:* www.coastaltransportation.com

Crowley Maritime Corp
9487 Regency Square Blvd........ Jacksonville FL 32225 904-727-2200 727-2501
TF: 800-276-9539 ■ *Web:* www.crowley.com

CSL Group Inc, The 759 Sq Victoria 6th Fl........ Montreal QC H2Y2K3 514-982-3800
Web: www.csl.ca

Express Marine Inc PO Box 329........ Pennsauken NJ 08110 856-541-4600 541-0338
Web: www.expressmarine.com

Freightquote.com Inc 16025 W 113th St........ Lenexa KS 66219 800-323-5441
TF: 800-323-5441 ■ *Web:* www.freightquote.com

Hapag-Lloyd America Inc 401 E Jackson St........ Tampa FL 33602 813-276-4600
TF: 800-282-8977 ■ *Web:* www.hapag-lloyd.com/en

Inchcape Shipping Services Inc
11 N Water St Ste 9290........ Mobile AL 36602 251-461-2747
Web: www.iss-shipping.com

Intermarine LLC
365 Canal St One Canal Pl Ste 2400........ New Orleans LA 70130 504-529-2100
Web: www.intelifuse.com

International Shipholding Corp
11 N Water Ste 18290........ Mobile AL 36602 251-243-9100
NYSE: ISH ■ *TF:* 800-826-3513 ■ *Web:* www.intship.com

Keystone Shipping Co 1 Bala Plz E Ste 600........ Bala Cynwyd PA 19004 610-617-6800 617-6899
Web: www.keyship.com

Loveland SC & Co 127 W Supawna Rd........ Pennsville NJ 08070 856-935-8100

Phone Fax

Matson Navigation Co 555 12th St ... Oakland CA 94607 510-628-4000 628-7380
TF Cust Svc: 800-462-8766 ■ *Web:* www.matson.com

Mormac Marine Group Inc
1 Landmark Sq Ste 710 ... Stamford CT 06901 203-977-8900 977-8933

Northland Services Inc
6700 W Marginal Way SW ... Seattle WA 98106 206-763-3000 767-5579
TF: 800-426-3113 ■ *Web:* www.northlandservices.com

Overseas Shipholding Group Inc
666 Third Ave ... New York NY 10017 212-953-4100 578-1832
TF: 800-851-9677 ■ *Web:* www.osg.com

Seaboard Marine 8001 NW 79th Ave ... Miami FL 33166 305-863-4444 863-4400
TF: 866-676-8886 ■ *Web:* www.seaboardmarine.com

Totem Ocean Trailer Express Inc
32001 32nd Ave S Ste 200 ... Federal Way WA 98001 253-449-8100 449-8225
TF: 800-426-0074 ■ *Web:* www.totemaritime.com

Trailer Bridge Inc
10405 New Berlin Rd E ... Jacksonville FL 32226 904-751-7100 751-7444
OTC: TRBRQ ■ *TF:* 800-554-1589 ■ *Web:* www.trailerbridge.com

US Shipping Corp 399 Thornall St 8th Fl ... Edison NJ 08837 732-635-1500 635-1918
TF: 866-942-6592 ■ *Web:* www.usslp.com

Western Pioneer Inc 4601 Shilshole Ave NW ... Seattle WA 98107 206-789-1930 781-2486
TF: 800-426-6783 ■ *Web:* www.wpioneer.com

Young Bros Ltd PO Box 3288 ... Honolulu HI 96801 808-543-9311
TF: 800-572-2743 ■ *Web:* www.htbyb.com

313 FREIGHT TRANSPORT - DEEP SEA (FOREIGN PORTS)

Phone Fax

Alter Barge Line Inc 2117 State St ... Bettendorf IA 52722 563-344-5100
Web: www.alterlogistics.com

American Overseas Marine Corp
100 Newport Ave Ext ... Quincy MA 02171 617-786-8300 472-4925
Web: gdamsea.com

Antillean Marine Shipping Corp
3038 NW N River Dr ... Miami FL 33142 305-633-6361
TF: 888-633-6361 ■ *Web:* www.antillean.com

Artemus Group
317 Office Square Lane Ste 202B ... Virginia Beach VA 23462 757-201-6811
Web: www.artemus.us

Atlantic Container Line (ACL) 50 Cardinal Dr ... Westfield NJ 07090 908-518-5300 518-7321
TF: 800-225-1235 ■ *Web:* www.aclcargo.com

Bisso Marine Company Inc 11311 Neeshaw Dr ... Houston TX 77065 281-897-1500
Web: www.bissomarine.com

Ceres Consulting LLC
3808 Cookson Rd E St Louis ... St Louis IL 62201 618-271-7903
Web: www.ceresbarge.com

CSL International Inc 152 Conant St ... Beverly MA 01915 978-922-1300 922-1772
Web: www.cslships.com

Dura Freight Inc 20405 E Business Pkwy ... Walnut CA 91789 909-595-8100
Web: www.durafreight.com

Eagle Bulk Shipping Inc
300 First Stamford Pl ... Stamford CT 06902 212-785-2500
Web: www.eagleships.com

Eagle Maritime Consultants Inc
1600 Space Park Dr ... Houston TX 77058 281-333-9880 333-9885
Web: www.eaglemaritime.com

Eagle Van Lines Inc 5041 Beech Pl ... Temple Hills MD 20748 301-899-2022
Web: www.eaglevanlines.com

Fednav Ltd
1000 Rue de la GauchetiFre O Bureau 3500 ... Montreal QC H3B4W5 514-878-6500 878-6642
TF General: 800-678-4842 ■ *Web:* www.fednav.com

GDB International Inc 1 Home News Row ... New Brunswick NJ 08901 732-246-3001 246-3004
Web: www.gdbinternational.com

Genco Shipping & Trading Ltd
299 Pk Ave 12th Fl ... New York NY 10171 646-443-8550
NYSE: GNK ■ *Web:* www.gencoshipping.com

General Maritime Corp 299 Pk Ave Ste 2 ... New York NY 10171 212-763-5600
Web: www.generalmaritimecorp.com

Grand Power Logistics Group Inc
Ste 2806 505 - Sixth St SW Ste 2806 ... Calgary AB T2P1X5 403-237-8211
Web: www.grandpowerlogistics.com

Groupe Desgagnes Inc 21 March-Champlain St ... Quebec QC G1K8Z8 418-692-1000
Web: www.groupedesgagnes.com

Hamburg Sud North America Inc 465 S St ... Morristown NJ 07960 973-775-5300 916-5901*
**Fax Area Code:* 770 ■ *TF:* 888-228-8241 ■ *Web:* www.hamburgsud.com

Hapag-Lloyd America Inc 401 E Jackson St ... Tampa FL 33602 813-276-4600
TF: 800-282-8977 ■ *Web:* www.hapag-lloyd.com/en

Inchcape Shipping Services Inc
11 N Water St Ste 9290 ... Mobile AL 36602 251-461-2747
Web: www.iss-shipping.com

Interlake Steamship Co, The
7300 Engle Rd ... Middleburg Heights OH 44130 440-260-6900
Web: www.interlake-steamship.com

Interlog USA Inc 2818A Anthony Ln S ... Minneapolis MN 55418 612-789-3456 789-2118
TF: 800-603-6030 ■ *Web:* www.interlogusa.com

International Shipholding Corp
11 N Water Ste 18290 ... Mobile AL 36602 251-243-9100
NYSE: ISH ■ *TF:* 800-826-3513 ■ *Web:* www.intship.com

K Line America Inc
8730 Stony Pt Pkwy Ste 400 ... Richmond VA 23235 804-560-3600
TF: 800-609-3221 ■ *Web:* www.k-line.com

Liberty Maritime Corp
1979 Marcus Ave Ste 200 ... Lake Success NY 11042 516-488-8800 488-8806
Web: libertygl.com

Maersk Inc 9300 Arrowpoint Blvd ... Charlotte NC 28273 973-514-5000
Web: maerskline.com

Maersk Line Ltd 1 Commercial Pl 20th Fl ... Norfolk VA 23510 757-857-4800
Web: www.maersklinelimited.com

Main Industries Inc 107 E St ... Hampton VA 23661 757-380-0180
Web: www.mainindustries.com

Maritime Helicopters 3520 Faa Rd ... Homer AK 99603 907-235-7771
Web: www.maritimehelicopters.com

Phone Fax

Mckeil Marine Ltd 208 Hillyard St ... Hamilton ON L8L6B6 905-528-4780
TF: 800-454-4780 ■ *Web:* www.mckeil.com

North America Cosco Inc
100 Lighting Way Ste 1 ... Secaucus NJ 07094 201-422-0500
Web: www.coscoamericas.com

Northern Transportation Co Ltd
42003 Mackenzie Hwy ... Hay River NT X0E0R9 867-587-2442
TF: 866-935-6825 ■ *Web:* www.ntcl.com

Ocean Flow International LLC
2100 W Loop S Ste 500 ... Houston TX 77027 713-328-6700
Web: www.ocean-flow.com

Overseas Shipholding Group Inc
666 Third Ave ... New York NY 10017 212-953-4100 578-1832
TF: 800-851-9677 ■ *Web:* www.osg.com

Pasha Group Inc
5725 Paradise Dr Ste 1000 ... Corte Madera CA 94925 415-927-6400 924-5672
Web: www.pashagroup.com

Rand Logistics Inc
333 Washington St Ste 201 ... Jersey City NJ 07302 212-644-3450
Web: www.randlogisticsinc.com

Seaboard Marine 8001 NW 79th Ave ... Miami FL 33166 305-863-4444 863-4400
TF: 866-676-8886 ■ *Web:* www.seaboardmarine.com

Sealift Inc 68 W Main St ... Oyster Bay NY 11771 516-922-1000
Web: www.sealiftinc.com

Stevens Towing Company Inc
4170 Hwy 165 ... Yonges Island SC 29449 843-889-2254
Web: www.stevens-towing.com

Stolt-Nielsen Transportation Group
800 Connecticut Ave 4th Fl E ... Norwalk CT 06854 203-838-7100 299-0067
Web: www.stolt-nielsen.com

Teras Cargo Transport (America) LLC
5358 33rd Ave NW Ste 302 ... Gig Harbor WA 98335 253-857-9209
Web: www.terasamerica.com

Tidewater Inc 601 Poydras St Ste 1900 ... New Orleans LA 70130 504-568-1010
NYSE: TDW ■ *TF:* 800-678-8433 ■ *Web:* www.tdw.com

Tropical Shipping 5 E 11th St ... Riviera Beach FL 33404 561-881-3900
TF: 800-367-6200 ■ *Web:* tropical.com

UTC Overseas Inc
370 W Passaic St Ste 3000 ... Rochelle Park NJ 07662 201-270-4600
Web: www.utcoverseas.com

Wallenius Wilhelmsen Lines Americas
188 Broadway PO Box 1232 ... Woodcliff Lake NJ 07677 201-307-0069
Web: www.2wglobal.com

Wallenius Wilhelmsen Logistics
PO Box 1232 ... Woodcliff Lake NJ 07677 201-307-1300
Web: www.2wglobal.com

314 FREIGHT TRANSPORT - INLAND WATERWAYS

Phone Fax

A & B Freight Line Inc 4805 Sandy Hollow Rd ... Rockford IL 61125 815-874-4700
TF: 800-231-2235 ■ *Web:* www.aandbfreight.com

American Commercial Barge Lines Inc
1701 E Market St ... Jeffersonville IN 47130 800-457-6377 288-1664*
**Fax Area Code:* 812 ■ *TF:* 800-457-6377 ■ *Web:* www.bargeacbl.com

American Steamship Co
500 Essjay Rd
Centerpointe Corporate Pk ... Williamsville NY 14221 716-635-0222 635-0220
Web: www.americansteamship.com

AMJ Campbell International
1445 Courtneypark Dr E ... Mississauga ON L5T2E3 905-670-6683
TF: 800-363-6683 ■ *Web:* www.amj-international.com

Andrie Inc 561 E Western Ave ... Muskegon MI 49442 231-728-2226 726-6747
TF: 800-722-2421 ■ *Web:* www.andrietg.com

Bear Cartage & Intermodal Inc 8600 Joliet Rd ... Mccook IL 60525 708-924-9093
Web: www.bearcartage.com

Becker Transportation Inc
1501 S Bulington Ave ... Hastings NE 68901 402-461-4454
Web: www.beckertrans.com

Best Way Logistics 14004 Century Ln ... Grandview MO 64030 816-767-8008
TF: 877-923-7892 ■ *Web:* bestwaylogistics.com

Big Apple Car Inc 169 Bay 17th St ... Brooklyn NY 11214 718-331-9500
Web: www.bigapplecar.com

Big Dog Logistics LLP 1235 N Loop W ... Houston TX 77008 713-996-8171

Bouchard Transportation Company Inc
58 S Service Rd Ste 150 ... Melville NY 11747 631-390-4900 390-4905
Web: www.bouchardtransport.com

Braden-Burry Expediting Ltd
18 Yellowknife Airport 100 McMillan St ... Yellowknife NT X1A3T2 867-766-8666
Web: www.bbex.com

Brighton Cromwell LLC
111 Canfield Ave Bldg C 1-10 ... Randolph NJ 07869 973-252-4100
Web: www.brightoncromwell.com

Budway Enterprises Inc 13600 Napa St ... Fontana CA 92335 909-463-0500
Web: www.budway.net

Calyx Transportation Group Inc
107 Alfred Kuehne Blvd ... Brampton ON L6T4K3 905-494-4747
Web: www.calyxinc.com

Canal Barge Company Inc 835 Union St ... New Orleans LA 70112 504-581-2424 584-1505
Web: www.canalbarge.com

CareGo Holdings Inc 400 Longwood Rd South ... Hamilton ON L8P4Z3 905-592-4900
Web: carego.com

Cargo Pacific Logistics
800 Mark St ... Elk Grove Village IL 60007 847-750-1230
Web: www.cargopacificlogistics.com

Celtic Marine Corp
3888 S Sherwood Forest Blvd
Celtic Ctr Bldg 1 ... Baton Rouge LA 70816 225-752-2490 752-2582
Web: www.celticmarine.com

Clark Freight Lines Inc 5129 Pine Ave ... Pasadena TX 77503 281-487-3160
Web: www.clarkfreight.com

	City	State	Zip	Phone	Fax
Cline Design Assoc of Wilmington Pllc 125 N Harrington St *Web:* www.clinedesignassoc.com	Raleigh	NC	27603	919-833-6413	
Cole International Inc 3033 - 34th Ave NE *Web:* www.coleintl.com	Calgary	AB	T1Y6X2	403-262-2771	
Crounse Corp 400 Marine Way *Web:* www.crounse.com	Paducah	KY	42003	270-444-9611	444-9615
Crowley Maritime Corp 9487 Regency Square Blvd *TF:* 800-276-9539 ■ *Web:* www.crowley.com	Jacksonville	FL	32225	904-727-2200	727-2501
Custom Global Logistics LLC 317 W Lk St *TF:* 800-446-8336 ■ *Web:* www.customgl.com	Northlake	IL	60164	800-446-8336	
Dayton Freight Lines Inc 6450 Poe Ave *Web:* www.daytonfreight.com	Dayton	OH	45414	937-264-4060	
De Well Container Shipping Corp 1 Cross Island Plz Ste 302 *Web:* de-well.com	Rosedale	NY	11422	718-528-1888	
Delmar International Inc 10636 Cote de Liesse *TF:* 888-433-5627 ■ *Web:* www.delmarcargo.com	Montreal	QC	H8T1A5	514-636-8800	
Falcon Express Transportation Inc 6804 Virginia Manor Rd *TF:* 800-296-9696 ■ *Web:* www.fxtran.com	Beltsville	MD	20705	240-264-1215	
FastAsset Inc 170 W Rd Ste 15 *Web:* www.fastasset.com	Portsmouth	NH	03801	603-559-9900	
FDSI Logistics Inc 5703 Corsa Ave *Web:* www.fdsi.com	Westlake Village	CA	91362	818-971-3300	
Fednav Ltd 1000 Rue de la GauchetiFre O Bureau 3500 *TF General:* 800-678-4842 ■ *Web:* www.fednav.com	Montreal	QC	H3B4W5	514-878-6500	878-6642
Focus Logistics Inc 1311 Howard Dr *TF:* 877-924-3600 ■ *Web:* focuslogisticsinc.com	West Chicago	IL	60185	630-231-8200	
Fraser Direct Distribution Services Ltd 8300 Lawson Rd *Web:* www.fraserdirect.ca	Milton	ON	L9T0A4	905-877-4411	
Freight Handlers Inc 310 N Judd Pkwy NE *Web:* fhiworks.com	Fuquay Varina	NC	27526	919-552-3157	
Frontline Logistics Inc 10315 Grand River Ste 300 *Web:* www.frontlinelogistics.com	Brighton	MI	48116	734-449-9474	
Hackbarth Delivery Service Inc 3504 Brookdale Dr N *TF:* 800-277-3322 ■ *Web:* www.hackbarthdelivery.com	Mobile	AL	36618	251-478-1401	
Horizon Freight Lines Inc 6579 S Us Hwy 31 *Web:* www.horizonfreightlines.com	Edinburgh	IN	46124	812-526-3380	
Hunter Marine Transport Inc 6615 Robertson Ave *Web:* www.huntermarine.net	Nashville	TN	37209	615-352-6935	
I C C Logistics Services Inc 960 S Broadway Ste 110 *Web:* www.icclogistics.com	Hicksville	NY	11801	516-822-1183	
ICECORP Logistics Inc 1600 Courtneypark Dr E *Web:* icecorp.ca	Mississauga	ON	L5T2W8	905-672-7400	
Ingram Barge Co 4400 HaRding Rd *Web:* www.ingrambarge.com	Nashville	TN	37205	615-298-8200	298-8213
Integral Transportation Networks Corp 6975 D Pacific Cir *Web:* www.itn-logistics.com	Mississauga	ON	L5T2H3	905-362-1111	
Itochu Logistics (USA) Corp 1830 W 205th St *Web:* www.ilogi.co.jp	Torrance	CA	90501	310-787-6500	
ITS Logistics LLC 620 Spice Island Dr *Web:* www.its4logistics.com	Sparks	NV	89431	775-358-5300	
J S Logistics 4550 Gustine Ave *TF:* 800-814-2634 ■ *Web:* www.jslogistics.com	Saint Louis	MO	63116	314-832-6008	
J.M. Rodgers Company Inc 1975 Linden Blvd *Web:* www.jmrodgers.com	Elmont	NY	11003	516-872-5570	
Keltic Transportation Inc 90 MacNaughton Ave Caledonia Industrial Park *TF:* 888-854-1233 ■ *Web:* www.keltictransportation.com	Moncton	NB	E1H3L9	506-854-1233	
Kreative Carriers Transportation & Logistic Services Inc 61 Bluewater Rd *TF:* 888-274-2444 ■ *Web:* www.kreativecarriers.com	Bedford	NS	B4B1G8	888-274-2444	
L & M Botruc Rental Inc 18692 W Main St *Web:* www.botruc.com	Galliano	LA	70354	985-475-5733	475-5669
La Corporation D'urgences-Sant, 3232 Rue Belanger *Web:* www.urgences-sante.qc.ca	Montreal	QC	H1Y3H5	514-723-5600	
Laidlaw Carriers Bulk LP 240 Universal Rd *Web:* www.laidlaw.ca	Woodstock	ON	N4S0A9	519-539-0471	
Lawndale Logistics 1239 12th Ave *Web:* www.lawndalelogistics.com	Grafton	WI	53024	262-375-3684	
Lipsey Logistics Worldwide LLC 1701 Oakbrook Dr Ste D	Norcross	GA	30093	678-336-1180	
Logistic Dynamics Inc 1140 Wehrle Dr *Web:* www.logisticdynamics.com	Amherst	NY	14221	716-250-3477	
Logistics Store, The 26 Westwoods Dr *Web:* www.thelogisticsstore.com	Liberty	MO	64068	816-781-0450	
LTI Trucking Services Inc 411 N 10th St Ste 500 *TF:* 800-642-7222 ■ *Web:* www.ltitrucking.com	St. Louis	MO	63101	800-642-7222	
Lykes Cartage Company Inc 8606 Wall St Bldg 19 *Web:* www.lykescartage.com	Austin	TX	78754	512-933-9060	
Lynnco Supply Chain Solutions Inc 2448 E 81St St Ste 2600 *Web:* lynnco-scs.com	Tulsa	OK	74137	918-664-5540	
Mackie Group 933 Bloor St W *TF:* 800-565-4646 ■ *Web:* www.mackiegroup.com	Oshawa	ON	L1J5Y7	905-728-2400	
Magellan Transport Logistics 2511 St Johns Bluff Rd Ste 107 *Web:* www.magellantransportlogistics.com	Jacksonville	FL	32246	904-620-0311	
Mammoet USA Inc 20525 Farm-to-Market Rd 521 *Web:* www.mammoet.com	Rosharon	TX	77583	281-369-2200	
Marquette Transportation Company LLC 150 Ballard Cir **Fax Area Code: 270* ■ *TF:* 800-456-9404 ■ *Web:* www.marquettetrans.com	Paducah	KY	42001	800-456-9404	441-7544*
MG Maher & Company Inc 365 Canal St Ste 1600 *Web:* www.mgmaher.com	New Orleans	LA	70130	504-581-3320	
Midwest Energy Resources Co 2400 W Winter St PO Box 787 *Web:* www.midwestenergy.com	Superior	WI	54880	715-392-9807	392-9137
Milgram & Company Ltd 400 - 645 Wellington *TF:* 800-879-6144 ■ *Web:* www.milgram.com	Montreal	QC	H3C0L1	514-288-2161	
Mobile One Courier Services Inc 1457 Miller Store Rd Ste 101 *Web:* www.mobileonecourier.com	Virginia Beach	VA	23455	757-622-9500	
Navcor Inc 700 W Georgia St Ste 980 *Web:* www.navcor.com	Vancouver	BC	V7Y1B6	604-688-9090	
NEPW Logistics Inc 55 Logistics Dr *Web:* www.nepw.com	Auburn	ME	04210	207-333-3345	
Nex Transport Inc 13900 SR- 287 *Web:* nextransportinc.com	East Liberty	OH	43319	937-645-3761	642-3032
Oak Harbor Freight Lines Inc 1339 W Valley Hwy N PO Box 1469 *Web:* www.oakh.com	Auburn	WA	98071	253-288-8300	
OATS Inc 2501 Maguire Blvd Ste 101 *Web:* www.oatstransit.org	Columbia	MO	65201	573-443-4516	
Overseas Express Consolidators (Canada) Inc 725 Montee De Liesse *Web:* www.oecgroup.ca	Saint Laurent	QC	H4T1P5	514-905-1246	
Ozark Trucking Inc 4916 Dudley Blvd *Web:* www.ozarktruckinginc.com	Mcclellan	CA	95652	916-561-5400	
Paul's Hauling Ltd 250 Oak Point Hwy *Web:* www.paulshauling.com	Winnipeg	MB	R2R1V1	204-633-4330	
Primco Dene Ltd PO Box 2070 *Web:* www.primcodene.com	Cold Lake	AB	T9M1P5	780-594-4034	
R d s Delivery Service Company Inc 436 E 11th St Frnt A *Web:* www.rdsdelivery.com	New York	NY	10009	212-260-5800	
RBS Bulk Systems Inc 610 Moraine Rd NE *Web:* www.rbsbulk.com	Calgary	AB	T2A2P3	403-248-1530	
Rigel Shipping Canada Inc 3521 Rt 134 *Web:* www.rigelcanada.com	Shediac Cape	NB	E4P3G6	506-533-9000	
Rockpoint Logistics LLC 901 Bilter Rd *Web:* www.rockpointlogistics.com	Aurora	IL	60502	630-801-2900	
Rowland Transportation Inc 40824 Messick Rd *Web:* www.rowlandtransportation.com	Dade City	FL	33525	352-567-2002	
Roy Miller Freight Lines LLC 3165 E Coronado St *TF:* 800-336-5673 ■ *Web:* www.roymiller.com	Anaheim	CA	92806	714-632-5511	
Scanwell Logistics (NYC) Inc 1995 Linden Blvd *Web:* www.scanwell.com	Elmont	NY	11003	516-285-8100	
SCI Logistics Ltd 180 Attwell Dr Ste 600 *TF:* 866-773-7735 ■ *Web:* www.scilogistics.com	Toronto	ON	M9W6A9	416-401-3011	
St. Lawrence Seaway Management Corp 202 Pitt St *Web:* www.seaway.ca	Cornwall	ON	K6J3P7	613-932-5170	
Stone Belt Freight Lines Inc 101 W Dillman Rd *TF:* 800-264-2340 ■ *Web:* www.stonebeltfreight.com	Bloomington	IN	47403	812-824-6741	
Summit Travel Group 830 Menlo Ave Ste 110 *TF:* 877-232-4465 ■ *Web:* www.summittravelgroup.com	Menlo Park	CA	94025	650-373-4400	
Tidewater Barge Lines Inc 6305 NW Old Lower River Rd *TF:* 800-562-1607 ■ *Web:* www.tidewater.com	Vancouver	WA	98660	360-693-1491	694-8981
Transports J.M. Bernier Inc 75 rue des Erables *Web:* www.jmbernier.qc.ca	Metabetchouan-lac-a-la-croix	QC	G8G1P9	418-349-3496	
Tri-line Carriers L.p 235185 Ryan Rd *TF:* 800-661-9191 ■ *Web:* www.triline.ca	Rocky View	AB	T1X0K1	800-661-9191	
TST Solutions Inc 5200 Maingate Dr *Web:* www.tstoverland.com	Mississauga	ON	L4W1G5	905-625-7500	
Van-Kam Freightways Ltd 10155 Grace Rd *TF:* 800-663-2161 ■ *Web:* www.vankam.com	Surrey	BC	V3V3V7	604-582-7451	
Vedder Transportation Group, The 400 Riverside Rd *TF:* 866-857-1375 ■ *Web:* www.vtlg.com	Abbotsford	BC	V2S4P4	866-857-1375	
Versacold International Corp 2115 Commissioner St *TF:* 800-563-2653 ■ *Web:* www.versacold.com	Vancouver	BC	V5L1A6	604-255-4656	
Warrior & Gulf Navigation LLC (WGN) 50 Viaduct Rd *Web:* www.tstarinc.com	Mobile	AL	36611	251-452-6000	
Westcan Bulk Transport Ltd 12110 - 17th St NE *Web:* www.westcanbulk.ca	Edmonton	AB	T6S1A5	780-472-6633	
Wheels Group Inc 5090 Orbitor Dr *Web:* www.wheelsgroup.com	Mississauga	ON	L4W5B5	905-602-2700	
Zenith Freight Lines LLC 210 Dehart Motor Terminal Rd SW *Web:* www.zenithcompanies.com	Conover	NC	28613	828-465-7036	

315 FRUIT GROWERS

See Also Crop Preparation Services p. 1718; Wines - Mfr p. 1856

315-1 Berry Growers

	City	State	Zip	Phone	Fax
AD Makepeace Company Inc 158 Tihonet Rd *Web:* www.admakepeace.com	Wareham	MA	02571	508-295-1000	291-7453

	City	State	ZIP	Phone	Fax
Atlantic Blueberry Co 7201 Weymouth Rd *Web:* www.atlanticblueberry.com	Hammonton	NJ	08037	609-561-8600	561-5033
Brady Farms Inc 14786 Winans St	West Olive	MI	49460	616-842-3916	842-8357
California Giant Inc 75 Sakata Ln *Web:* www.calgiant.com	Watsonville	CA	95076	831-728-1773	728-0613
Cherryfield Foods Inc 320 Ridge Rd PO Box 128 *Web:* www.oxfordfrozenfoods.com	Cherryfield	ME	04622	207-546-7573	546-2713
Driscoll Strawberry Assoc Inc 345 Westridge Dr *TF:* 800-871-3333 ■ *Web:* www.driscolls.com	Watsonville	CA	95077	800-871-3333	
Fujii Farms Inc 2511 S Troutdale Rd PO Box 188 *Web:* fujiifarms.com	Troutdale	OR	97060	503-665-6659	661-2799
Habelman Bros Co Inc 10688 Estate Rd *Web:* www.habelmancranberries.com	Tomah	WI	54660	608-372-2444	
Jasper Wyman & Son PO Box 100 *TF Sales:* 800-341-1758 ■ *Web:* www.wymans.com	Milbridge	ME	04658	800-341-1758	
Michigan Blueberry Growers Assn 4726 County Rd 215 *Web:* www.blueberries.com	Grand Junction	MI	49056	269-434-6791	
Naturipe Berry Growers 1611 Bunker Hill way *Web:* www.naturipeberrygrowers.com	Salinas	CA	93906	831-722-2430	
Reenders Blueberries Farms 14079 168th Ave *Web:* www.reendersblueberryfarms.com	Grand Haven	MI	49417	616-842-5238	
Reiter Affiliated Cos 1767 San Juan Rd *Web:* berry.net	Aromas	CA	93030	805-483-1000	
Sandy Farms 34500 SE Hwy 211	Boring	OR	97009	503-668-4525	668-8813
Sunrise Growers 701 W Kimberly St Ste 210 *Web:* www.sunrisegrowers.com	Placentia	CA	92870	714-630-2050	630-0215

315-2 Citrus Growers

	City	State	ZIP	Phone	Fax
A Duda & Sons Inc 1200 Duda Trail *Web:* www.duda.com	Oviedo	FL	32765	407-365-2111	365-2147
Alico Inc (ALCO) 10070 Daniels Interstate Ct Ste 100 *NASDAQ: ALCO* ■ *Web:* www.alicoinc.com	Fort Myers	FL	33913	863-675-2966	
Ben Hill Griffin Inc 700 S SR 17 PO Box 127	Frostproof	FL	33843	863-635-2251	635-7333
Blue Banner Company Inc 2601 Third St *Web:* pe.com	Riverside	CA	92502	951-686-2422	
Corona College Heights Orange & Lemon Assn 8000 Lincoln Ave *Web:* www.cchcitrus.com	Riverside	CA	92504	951-688-1811	689-5115
ECA Edinburg Citrus Association 401 W Chapin St	Edinburg	TX	78541	956-383-2743	
Egan Bernard & Co 1900 Old Dixie Hwy **Fax Area Code: 772* ■ *TF:* 800-327-6676 ■ *Web:* www.dneworld.com	Fort Pierce	FL	34946	800-327-6676	465-1181*
G & S Packing 16600 Florida 25	Weirsdale	FL	32195	352-821-2251	
Graves Bros Co 2770 Indian River Blvd Ste 201 *Web:* www.gravesbrotherscompany.com	Vero Beach	FL	32960	772-562-3886	562-3565
Highland Exchange Service Co-op 5916 Waverly Rd	Waverly	FL	33877	863-439-3661	439-5383
Leroy E Smith's Sons Inc 4776 Old Dixie Hwy *Web:* leroysmith.com	Vero Beach	FL	32967	772-567-3421	
Limoneira Co 1141 Cummings Rd *NASDAQ: LMNR* ■ *TF:* 866-321-8953 ■ *Web:* www.limoneira.com	Santa Paula	CA	93060	805-525-5541	525-8211
Nelson & Co Inc 110 E Broadway	Oviedo	FL	32765	407-365-6631	
Saticoy Lemon Assn 7560 E Bristol Rd *Web:* www.saticoylemon.com	Ventura	CA	93003	805-654-6500	
Silver Springs Citrus Inc 25411 N Mare Ave *Web:* silverspringscitrus.com	Howey in the Hills	FL	34737	352-324-2101	324-2033
Southern Gardens Citrus 1820 Country Rd 833 *Web:* www.ussugar.com/citrus	Clewiston	FL	33440	863-983-3030	983-3060
Sunkist Growers Inc 27770 Entertainment Dr	Valencia	CA	91355	818-986-4800	
Villa Park Orchards Assn 960 Third St *Web:* vpoa.net	Fillmore	CA	93016	805-524-0411	

315-3 Deciduous Tree Fruit Growers

	City	State	ZIP	Phone	Fax
Auvil Fruit Co Inc 21902 SR 97 *Web:* www.auvilfruit.com	Orondo	WA	98843	509-784-1033	784-1712
Bertuccio Farms 2410 Airline Hwy *Web:* www.thefarmbertuccios.com	Hollister	CA	95023	831-636-0821	
Big Six Farms 5575 Zenith Mill Rd	Fort Valley	GA	31030	478-825-7504	825-1194
Blue Bird Inc 10135 Mill Rd *Web:* bluebirdpears.net	Peshastin	WA	98847	509-548-1700	548-0288
Blue Mountain Growers Inc 231 E Broadway Ave	Milton-Freewater	OR	97862	541-938-3391	938-5304
Blue Star Growers Inc 200 Blue Star Rd	Cashmere	WA	98815	509-782-2922	
Borton & Sons Inc 2550 Borton Rd *Web:* www.bortonfruit.com	Yakima	WA	98903	509-966-3905	966-5131
Broetje Orchards 1111 Fishhook Pk Rd *Web:* www.firstfruits.com	Prescott	WA	99348	509-749-2217	749-2354
Capital Agricultural Property Services Inc 801 Warrenville Rd Ste 150 *TF:* 800-243-2060 ■ *Web:* www.capitalag.com	Lisle	IL	60532	630-434-9150	434-9343
Chappell Farms Inc 166 Boiling Springs Rd *Web:* www.chappellfarms.com	Barnwell	SC	29812	803-584-2565	584-3676
Chelan Fruit Marketing 5 Howser Rd *Web:* www.chelanfresh.com	Chelan	WA	98816	509-682-4252	682-2651
Cowiche Growers Inc 251 Cowiche City Rd *Web:* www.cowichegrowers.com	Cowiche	WA	98923	509-678-4168	678-5678
Evans Fruit Farm 200 Cowiche City Rd PO Box 70 *Web:* www.evansfruitco.com	Cowiche	WA	98923	509-678-4127	678-5450
EW Brandt & Sons Inc (EWB) 561 Ragan Rd *Web:* rembrandtfruit.com	Wapato	WA	98951	509-877-3193	
Fagundes Agribusiness 8700 Fargo Ave *Web:* fagundes.net	Hanford	CA	93230	559-582-2000	582-0683
Fowler Packing Company Inc 8570 S Cedar Ave *Web:* fowlerpacking.com	Fresno	CA	93725	559-834-5911	834-5272
Henggeler Packing Company Inc 6730 Elmore Rd PO Box 313	Fruitland	ID	83619	208-452-4212	452-5416
Highland Fruit Growers Inc 8304 Wide Hollow Rd	Yakima	WA	98908	509-966-3990	966-3992
Hudson River Fruit Distributors 65 Old Indian Rd *TF:* 800-640-2774 ■ *Web:* hudsonriverfruit.com	Milton	NY	12547	800-640-2774	
Ito Packing Company Inc 707 W S Ave PO Box 707 *Web:* itopack.com	Reedley	CA	93654	559-638-2531	
McDougal & Sons 305 Olds Stn Rd	Wenatchee	WA	98801	509-662-2136	
Mt Konocti Growers Inc 2550 Big Vly Rd PO Box 365 *Web:* mtkonoctiwines.com	Kelseyville	CA	95451	707-279-4213	
National Fruit Product Co Inc 701 Fairmont Ave **Fax:* Sales ■ *TF:* 800-655-4022 ■ *Web:* www.whitehousefoods.com	Winchester	VA	22601	540-723-9614	665-4671*
Orchard View Farms Inc 4055 Skyline Rd *Web:* www.orchardviewfarms.com	The Dalles	OR	97058	541-298-4496	298-1808
Oregon Cherry Growers Inc 1520 Woodrow NE *TF:* 800-367-2536 ■ *Web:* oregoncherry.com	Salem	OR	97301	503-364-8421	362-2647
P-R Farms Inc 2917 E Shepherd Ave *Web:* www.prfarms.com	Clovis	CA	93619	559-299-0201	299-7292
Rice Fruit Co 2760 Carlisle Rd *TF:* 800-627-3359 ■ *Web:* www.ricefruit.com	Gardners	PA	17324	717-677-8131	
Stadelman Fruit LLC 111 Meade St PO BOX 445 *Web:* www.stadelmanfruit.com	Zillah	WA	98953	509-829-5145	
Stemilt Growers Inc PO Box 2779 *Web:* www.stemilt.com	Wenatchee	WA	98807	509-663-1451	
Sun Valley Packing Co 7381 Ave 432	Reedley	CA	93654	559-591-1515	591-1616
Sun World International Inc 16350 Drive Rd *Web:* www.sun-world.com	Bakersfield	CA	93308	661-392-5000	
Symms Fruit Ranch Inc 14068 Sunny Slope Rd *Web:* symmsfruit.com	Caldwell	ID	83607	208-459-4821	459-6932
Thiara Bros Orchards 1205 Kibby Rd	Merced	CA	95340	209-383-6126	383-1012
Titan Farms 5 RW Du Bose Rd *Web:* www.titanfarms.com	Ridge Spring	SC	29129	803-685-5381	685-5885
Twin Hill Ranch 1689 Pleasant Hill Rd	Sebastopol	CA	95472	707-823-2815	
Valley View Packing Company Inc 7547 Sawtelle Ave *Web:* www.valleyviewpacking.com	Yuba City	CA	95991	530-673-7356	673-9432

315-4 Fruit Growers (Misc)

	City	State	ZIP	Phone	Fax
Brooks Tropicals Inc 18400 SW 256th St PO Box 900160 **Fax:* Sales ■ *TF:* 800-327-4833 ■ *Web:* www.brookstropicals.com	Homestead	FL	33090	305-247-3544	246-5827*
Calavo Growers Inc 1141-A Cummings Rd *NASDAQ: CVGW* ■ *TF:* 800-654-8758 ■ *Web:* www.calavo.com	Santa Paula	CA	93060	805-525-1245	921-3287
Chiquita Brands International Inc 250 E Fifth St *NYSE: CQB* ■ *Web:* chiquita.com	Cincinnati	OH	45202	513-784-8000	
Del Monte Fresh Produce Co 241 Sevilla Ave *TF Cust Svc:* 800-950-3683 ■ *Web:* www.freshdelmonte.com	Coral Gables	FL	33134	305-520-8400	567-0320
Dole Food Company Inc 1 Dole Dr *NYSE: DOLE* ■ *TF:* 800-232-8888 ■ *Web:* www.dole.com	Westlake Village	CA	91362	818-879-6600	
Growers Express LLC 1219 Abbott St PO Box 948 **Fax:* Sales ■ *Web:* www.growersexpress.com	Salinas	CA	93901	831-757-9700	422-4246*
Jewel Date Co 84675 60th Ave *Web:* www.shieldsdategarden.com	Thermal	CA	92274	760-399-4474	399-4476
Martori Farms 7332 E Butherus Dr *Web:* www.martorifarms.com	Scottsdale	AZ	85260	480-998-1444	
Maui Land & Pineapple Company Inc 120 Kane St PO Box 187 *Web:* www.mauiland.com	Kahului	HI	96733	808-877-3351	
Mission Produce Inc 2500 Vineyard Ave Ste 300 *Web:* www.worldsfinestavocados.com	Oxnard	CA	93036	805-981-3650	981-3660
Mount Dora Farms 16398 Jacinto Ft Blvd *Web:* www.mountdorafarms.com	Houston	TX	77015	713-821-7439	
Valley Fig Growers 2028 S Third St *Web:* www.valleyfig.com	Fresno	CA	93702	559-237-3893	237-3898
Van Drunen Farms 300 W Sixth St *Web:* www.vandrunenfarms.com	Momence	IL	60954	815-472-3100	472-3850

315-5 Grape Vineyards

	City	State	ZIP	Phone	Fax
Del Rey Packing 5287 S Del Rey Ave *Web:* delreypacking.com	Del Rey	CA	93616	559-888-2031	888-2715
John Kautz Farms 5490 E Bear Oak Rd	Lodi	CA	95240	209-334-4786	339-1689
Lion Raisins 9500 S De Wols Ave PO Box 1350 *Web:* www.lionraisins.com	Selma	CA	93662	559-834-6677	834-6622
National Grape Co-op Assn Inc 2 S Portage St	Westfield	NY	14787	716-326-5200	326-5494
National Raisin Co PO Box 219 *Web:* www.nationalraisin.com	Fowler	CA	93625	559-834-5981	834-1055

Company	City	State	Zip	Phone	Fax
Niven Family Wine Estates 4915 Orcutt Rd *Web:* www.baileyana.com	San Luis Obispo	CA	93401	805-597-8200	
Pacific Agri Lands Inc 5206 Hammett Rd	Modesto	CA	95358	209-545-1623	
Scheid Vineyards Inc 305 Hilltown Rd *Web:* www.scheidvineyards.com	Salinas	CA	93908	831-455-9990	455-9998
Spring Mountain Vineyards 2805 Spring Mtn Rd *TF:* 877-769-4637 ■ *Web:* www.springmtn.com	Saint Helena	CA	94574	707-967-4188	963-2753
Sun Valley Packing Co 7381 Ave 432	Reedley	CA	93654	559-591-1515	591-1616
Sun World International Inc 16350 Drive Rd *Web:* www.sun-world.com	Bakersfield	CA	93308	661-392-5000	
Symms Fruit Ranch Inc 14068 Sunny Slope Rd *Web:* symmsfruit.com	Caldwell	ID	83607	208-459-4821	459-6932
Vino Farms Inc 1377 E Lodi Ave	Lodi	CA	95240	209-334-6975	369-8765
Windsor Vineyards 205 Concourse Blvd *TF:* 800-289-9463 ■ *Web:* www.windsorvineyards.com	Santa Rosa	CA	95403	800-289-9463	

316 FUEL DEALERS

Company	City	State	Zip	Phone	Fax
AC & T Company Inc 11535 Hopewell Rd *TF:* 800-458-3835 ■ *Web:* www.acandt.com	Hagerstown	MD	21740	301-582-2700	
Aero ALL-GAS Company Inc, The 3150 Main St *TF:* 800-255-4277 ■ *Web:* www.allgas.com	Hartford	CT	06120	860-278-2376	
Alaska Aerofuel Inc 5859 Aerofuel Pl *Web:* www.alaskaaerofuel.com	Fairbanks	AK	99709	907-474-0062	
Alexander Oil Company Inc Intersection of 1-10 and 123 N Bypass P.O. Box 469 *Web:* alexander-oil.com	Seguin	TX	78155	830-379-1736	
Alvin Hollis & Co 1 Hollis St *TF:* 800-649-5090 ■ *Web:* www.alvinhollis.com	South Weymouth	MA	02190	781-335-2100	335-6134
AmeriGas Inc 460 N Gulph Rd *Web:* www.amerigas.com	King of Prussia	PA	19406	610-337-7000	768-7647
AmeriGas Partners LP 460 N Gulph Rd *NYSE: APU* ■ *TF:* 800-427-4968 ■ *Web:* www.amerigas.com	King of Prussia	PA	19406	610-337-7000	992-3259
AOC Holding Company Inc 4506 State 359 and Loop 20 *Web:* www.argpetro.com	Laredo	TX	78042	956-722-5251	
Apollo Oil LLC 1175 Early Dr *TF:* 800-473-5823 ■ *Web:* www.apollooil.com	Winchester	KY	40391	859-744-5444	745-5823
Atlanta Fuel Co 2324 Donald Lee Hollowell Pkwy *Web:* atlantafuel.com	Atlanta	GA	30318	404-792-9888	
Automotive Service Inc 910 Mtn Home Rd PO Box 2157 *TF:* 800-383-3421 ■ *Web:* berkspottstownheatingoil.com	Sinking Spring	PA	19608	610-678-3421	678-3515
Axmen 7655 Us Hwy 10 W *Web:* www.axmen.com	Missoula	MT	59808	406-728-7020	
Barrett Oil Inc 2126 W Bay St *Web:* www.barrettoil.com	Savannah	GA	31415	912-234-7231	
Baytec Service LLC 4761 Hwy 146 200 *Web:* www.bayteccontainers.com	Bacliff	TX	77518	281-559-2334	
Berico Fuels Inc 2200 E Bessemer Ave *Web:* berico.com	Greensboro	NC	27405	336-273-8663	
Best Aire LLC 3648 Rockland Cir *Web:* www.best-aire.com	Millbury	OH	43447	419-726-0055	
Blossman Gas Inc 809 Washington Ave *TF:* 800-256-7762 ■ *Web:* www.blossmangas.com	Ocean Springs	MS	39564	888-256-7762	
Bottini Fuel Oil Co 157 W Main St *Web:* www.bottinifuel.com	Wappingers Falls	NY	12590	845-297-5580	
Bowden Oil Company Inc PO Box 145 *TF:* 800-280-0393 ■ *Web:* www.bowdenoil.com	Sylacauga	AL	35150	256-245-5611	249-2975
Bowers & Burrows Oil Co 213 Young St *Web:* bbfuels.net	Henderson	NC	27536	252-492-0181	
Buckley Energy Group Ltd 154 Admiral St *Web:* www.santaenergy.com	Bridgeport	CT	06605	203-336-3541	
Burns & McBride Inc 240 S DuPont Hwy *TF:* 800-756-5110 ■ *Web:* www.burnsandmcbride.com	New Castle	DE	19720	302-656-5110	
Campora Inc 2525 E Mariposa Rd *Web:* www.campora.com	Stockton	CA	95205	209-466-8611	
Carroll Independent Fuel Co 2700 Loch Raven Rd *Web:* www.carrollhomeservices.com	Baltimore	MD	21218	410-235-1070	235-3842
Cheshire Oil Company Inc 678 Marlborough St PO Box 586 *Web:* www.cheshireoil.com	Keene	NH	03431	603-352-0001	
Columbia Utilities Heating Corp 1350 60 St *Web:* www.columbiautilities.com	Brooklyn	NY	11219	718-851-6655	
Consumer Oil & Supply Co 100 Railroad St	Braymer	MO	64624	660-645-2721	
Coop Gas Inc 4395 Hwy 56 *Web:* ballooncountry.com	Pauline	SC	29374	864-583-6546	
Cota & Cota Inc 4 Green St *Web:* www.cotaoil.com	Bellows Falls	VT	05101	802-463-0000	
Crus Oil Inc 2260 SW Temple *Web:* crusoil.com	Salt Lake City	UT	84115	801-466-8783	
D F Richard Inc 124 Broadway *TF:* 800-649-6457 ■ *Web:* www.dfrichard.com	Dover	NH	03821	603-742-2020	
Davis Oil Co 904 Jernigan St *Web:* www.davis-company.com	Perry	GA	31069	478-987-2443	
DDLC Energy 410 Bank St *Web:* ddlcenergy.com	New London	CT	06320	860-271-2020	271-2050
Delta Western Inc 420 L St Ste 101 *Web:* www.deltawestern.com	Anchorage	AK	99501	907-276-2688	
District Petroleum Products Inc 1814 River Rd Ste 100 *Web:* hymiler.com	Huron	OH	44839	419-433-8373	433-9646
E E Wine Inc 9108 Centreville Rd *Web:* www.eewine.com	Manassas	VA	20110	703-368-6568	
Ed Staub & Sons Petroleum Inc 1301 Esplanade Ave *TF:* 800-435-3835 ■ *Web:* www.edstaub.com	Klamath Falls	OR	97601	800-435-3835	
Energy Petroleum Co 2130 Kienlen Ave *Web:* www.energypetroleum.com	St. Louis	MO	63121	314-383-3700	
Energy Transfer Equity LP 3738 Oak Lawn Ave *NYSE: ETE* ■ *Web:* www.energytransfer.com	Dallas	TX	75219	214-981-0700	981-0703
Energy Transfer Partners LP 3738 Oak Lawn Ave *NYSE: ETP* ■ *Web:* www.energytransfer.com	Dallas	TX	75219	214-981-0700	981-0703
Essex Oil Co 2174 Springfield Ave *Web:* essexoil.com	Vauxhall	NJ	07088	973-372-7700	
Factor Gas Liquids Inc 240 Vidal St N *Web:* www.factorgas.com	Sarnia	ON	N7T5Y3	519-332-8978	
Farm & Home Oil Co 3115 State Rd *TF:* 800-776-7263 ■ *Web:* www.suburbanpropane.com	Telford	PA	18969	800-776-7263	
Farmers Union Oil Co of Southern Valley (FUOSV) 204 S Front St *Web:* www.fuosv.com	Fairmount	ND	58030	701-474-5440	474-5445
FC Haab Company Inc 2314 Market St *TF:* 800-486-5663 ■ *Web:* www.fchaab.com	Philadelphia	PA	19103	215-563-0800	563-9448
Felicia Oil Company Inc R78 Commercial St	Gloucester	MA	01930	978-283-3808	
Ferrellgas Partners LP 1 Liberty Plaza *NYSE: FGP* ■ *TF:* 888-337-7355 ■ *Web:* www.ferrellgas.com	Liberty	MO	64068	816-792-1600	
First Corporate Sedans Inc 60 E 42nd St Ste 2424 *TF:* 800-473-8876 ■ *Web:* www.fcsny.com	New York	NY	10165	212-972-2282	286-9130
Fred M Schildwachter & Sons Inc 1400 Ferris Pl *TF:* 800-642-3646 ■ *Web:* www.schildwachteroil.com	Bronx	NY	10461	718-828-2500	828-3661
G. A. Bove & Sons Inc 76 Railroad St *Web:* www.bovefuels.com	Mechanicville	NY	12118	518-664-5111	
Gary Jet Center Inc 5401 Industrial Hwy *Web:* www.garyjetcenter.com	Gary	IN	46406	219-944-1210	
Gas Inc 77 Jefferson Pkwy *Web:* www.gasinc.net	Newnan	GA	30263	770-502-8800	
Gateway Energy Services Corp 400 Rella Blvd Ste 300 *Web:* www.gesc.com	Montebello	NY	10901	845-503-5100	
Glassmere Fuel Service Inc 1967 Saxonburg Blvd *TF:* 800-235-9054 ■ *Web:* www.glassmerefuel.com	Tarentum	PA	15084	724-265-4646	
Great Eastern Energy LLC 3044 Coney Is Ave *Web:* greateasterngas.com	Brooklyn	NY	11235	718-648-0900	
Heritagenergy Inc 625 Sawkill Rd *Web:* www.heritagenergy.com	Kingston	NY	12401	845-336-2000	
Kingston Oil Supply Corp 2926 Rt 32 N *TF:* 800-755-6726 ■ *Web:* www.koscocomfort.com	Saugerties	NY	12477	845-247-2200	246-0207
Kolkhorst Petroleum Co 1685 E Washington *TF:* 800-548-6671 ■ *Web:* www.kolkhorst.com	Navasota	TX	77868	936-825-6868	870-3355
Lakes Gas Co 655 S Lk St *Web:* www.lakesgasco.com	Forest Lake	MN	55025	651-464-3345	
Landmark Industries Ltd 11111 Wilcrest Green Dr Ste 100 PO Box 42374 *Web:* www.landmarkindustries.com	Houston	TX	77042	713-789-0310	789-2907
Lansing Ice & Fuel Co 911 Ctr St *Web:* propanefuellansing.com	Lansing	MI	48906	517-372-3850	
Lawes Coal Company Inc Sycamore Ave PO Box 258 *Web:* www.lawescompany.com	Shrewsbury	NJ	07702	732-741-6300	
Lazzari Fuel Company LLC 11 Industrial Way *TF:* 800-242-7265 ■ *Web:* www.lazzari.com	Brisbane	CA	94005	415-467-2970	
Lewis & Raulerson Inc 1759 State St *Web:* www.lewisandraulerson.com	Waycross	GA	31501	912-283-5951	283-8281
Lincoln Land Oil Co PO Box 4307 *TF:* 800-238-4912 ■ *Web:* www.lincolnlandoil.com	Springfield	IL	62708	217-523-5050	523-5001
Lynch Oil Company Inc 1244 E Carroll St *Web:* www.lynchoilco.com	Kissimmee	FL	34744	407-847-4161	
Manitoba Agricultural Services Corp Unit 100 - 1525 First St S *Web:* www.masc.mb.ca	Brandon	MB	R7A7A1	204-726-6850	
Martin Resource Management Corp (MRMC) PO Box 191 *TF:* 888-334-7473 ■ *Web:* www.martinmidstream.com	Kilgore	TX	75663	903-983-6200	983-6271
Mazzo Oil Co Inc 139 Van Winkle Ave *Web:* mazzoenergy.com	Garfield	NJ	07026	973-473-5181	
McMullen Oil Co Inc 11965 49th St N *Web:* www.mcmullenoil.com	Clearwater	FL	33762	727-573-0016	
Metro Energy Group 1011 Hudson Ave *TF:* 800-951-2941 ■ *Web:* www.metroenergynj.com	Ridgefield	NJ	07657	201-941-3470	941-6854
Mirabito Fuel Group Inc 49 Ct St PO Box 5306 *TF:* 800-934-9480 ■ *Web:* mirabito.com	Binghamton	NY	13902	607-352-2800	584-5130
Mitchell Fuel Company Inc 1209 Sullivan Ave *Web:* www.mitchellfuel.com	South Windsor	CT	06074	860-644-2561	
Mitchell Supreme Fuel Co 532 Freeman St *TF:* 800-832-7090 ■ *Web:* www.supremeenergyinc.com	Orange	NJ	07050	973-678-1800	672-0148
Mutual Liquid Gas & Equipment Co Inc 17117 S Broadway St **Fax Area Code:* 310 ■ *TF:* 800-633-3574	Gardena	CA	90248	323-321-3771	515-2633*
Nebraska Iowa Supply Company Inc 1160 Lincoln St PO Box 368 *Web:* www.neiasupply.com	Blair	NJ	68008	402-426-2171	
Noonan Energy Corp 86 Robbins Rd *Web:* www.noonanenergy.com	Springfield	MA	01104	413-734-7396	
O'Rourke Petroleum Inc 223 McCarty Dr *Web:* www.orpp.com	Houston	TX	77029	713-672-4500	
Osage Exploration & Development Inc 2445 Fifth Ave Ste 310	San Diego	CA	92101	619-677-3956	
PAFCO LLC 201 S Orange Ave Ste 1575 *Web:* www.pafcollc.com	Orlando	FL	32801	407-206-5287	
Palmer Gas Company Inc 13 Hall Farm Rd *Web:* palmergas.com	Atkinson	NH	03811	603-898-7986	

Company / Address	City	State	Zip	Phone	Fax
Parman Energy Corp 7101 Cockrill Bend Blvd *Web:* www.parmanenergy.com	Nashville	TN	37209	615-350-7920	
Payne Oil Company Inc 209 Graham Rd *Web:* payneoil.com	Graham	NC	27253	336-578-0404	
Petroleum Heat and Power Co Inc 9 W Broad St 3rd Fl *Web:* www.petro.com	Stamford	CT	06902	203-325-5400	
Petroleum Marketers Inc 3000 Ogden Rd	Roanoke	VA	24018	540-772-4900	772-6900
Phelps Sungas Inc 224 Cross Rd *TF:* 800-458-1085 ■ *Web:* sungas.com	Geneva	NY	14456	315-789-3285	
Planters Oil Inc 217 S Main St	Fitzgerald	GA	31750	229-423-2231	
Polsinello Fuels Inc 241 Riverside Ave Drawer 211 *Web:* www.polsinello.com	Rensselaer	NY	12144	518-463-0084	463-4086
Prairie Pride Co-op 1100 E Main St *Web:* www.prairiepridecoop.com	Marshall	MN	56258	507-532-9686	
Quick Fuel Fleet Services Inc 11815 W Bradley Rd *Web:* www.quickfuel.com	Milwaukee	WI	53224	414-359-0700	
Range LP Gas 1613 E Camp St *Web:* rangelp.com	Ely	MN	55731	218-365-8888	
Rawhide Chemoil Inc 2650 N Rawhide Dr *Web:* www.rawhidechemoil.com	Fremont	NE	68025	402-721-7601	
Reinhardt Corp 3919 State Hwy 23 *Web:* www.reinhardthomeheating.com	West Oneonta	NY	13861	607-432-6633	
Ricochet Fuel Distributors Inc 1201 Royal Pkwy *Web:* www.ricochetfuel.com	Euless	TX	76040	817-268-5910	
Riggins Inc 3938 S Main Rd *Web:* www.rigginsoil.com	Vineland	NJ	08360	856-825-7600	
River Bend Business Products 304 Downtown Plz *Web:* www.riverbendbusiness.com	Fairmont	MN	56031	507-235-3800	
Robison Oil Corp 500 Executive Blvd *Web:* www.robisonoil.com	Elmsford	NY	10523	914-345-5700	
Santoro Oil Company Inc 101 Corliss St *Web:* www.santorooil.com	Providence	RI	02904	401-942-5000	
Sharp Energy Inc 648 Ocean Hwy *TF:* 888-742-7740 ■ *Web:* www.sharpenergy.com	Pocomoke City	MD	21851	888-742-7740	
Shipley Energy 415 Norway St **Fax Area Code:* 800 ■ *TF:* 800-839-1849 ■ *Web:* www.shipleyenergy.com	York	PA	17403	717-848-4100	839-1849*
Southeast Fuels Inc 604 Green Vly Rd Ste 207 *Web:* www.southeastfuels.com	Greensboro	NC	27408	336-854-1106	547-8720
Spencer Oil Company Inc 16410 Common Rd *Web:* spenceroilcompany.com	Roseville	MI	48066	586-775-5022	776-8264
Standard Oil Of Connecticut Inc 299 Bishop Ave *Web:* www.standardsecurity.com	Bridgeport	CT	06610	203-334-5532	
Star Gas Partners LP 2187 Atlantic St *NYSE:* SGU ■ *TF:* 800-960-7546 ■ *Web:* www.Star-Gas.com	Stamford	CT	06902	203-328-7310	328-7470
Stripes Convenience Stores 4525 Ayers St *NYSE:* SUSS ■ *TF:* 800-569-3585 ■ *Web:* stripesstores.com/index.cms	Corpus Christi	TX	78415	361-884-2464	884-2494
Suburban Propane LP 1 Suburban Plz 240 Rt 10 W PO Box 206 *TF:* 800-776-7263 ■ *Web:* www.suburbanpropane.com	Whippany	NJ	07981	973-887-5300	
Super Save Group 19395 Langley By-pass *TF:* 800-665-2800 ■ *Web:* www.supersave.ca	Surrey	BC	V3S6K1	604-533-4423	
Superior Plus Energy Services Inc 1870 S Winton Rd Ste 200 *Web:* www.griffithenergy.com	Rochester	NY	14618	585-328-3930	
Tiger Fuel Company Inc 200 Carlton Rd PO Box 1607 *Web:* www.tigerfuel.com	Charlottesville	VA	22902	434-293-6157	
Tropigas De Puerto Rico Inc Urb Industrial Luchetti Calle C Lote 30 *Web:* tropigaspr.com	Bayamon	PR	00961	787-641-8002	
United Propane Gas Companies Inc 4200 Cairo Rd PO Box 2450 *Web:* www.upgas.com	Paducah	KY	42002	270-442-5557	
Western Natural Gas Co 2960 Strickland St *Web:* www.westernnaturalgas.com	Jacksonville	FL	32254	904-387-3511	387-6034
Wever Petroleum Inc 100 S Hudson St *Web:* www.weverpetroleum.com	Mechanicville	NY	12118	518-664-7331	
WH Riley & Son Inc 35 Chestnut St *Web:* www.whriley.com	North Attleboro	MA	02760	508-699-4651	699-7712
William G. Satterlee & Sons Inc 12475 Route 119 Hwy N *Web:* www.satterleefuel.com	Rochester Mills	PA	15771	724-397-2400	
William R Peterson Oil Co 12 W Rd	Marlborough	CT	06480	860-295-9200	
Wilson of Wallingford Inc 221 Rogers Ln PO Box 185 *TF:* 888-607-2621 ■ *Web:* www.wilsonoilandpropane.com	Wallingford	PA	19086	610-566-7600	566-7608
Wo Stinson & Son Ltd 4726 Bank St *TF:* 800-267-9714 ■ *Web:* www.wostinson.com	Ottawa	ON	K1T3W7	613-822-7400	
Woodford Oil Company Inc 13th St PO Box 567 *Web:* www.woodfordoil.com	Elkins	WV	26241	304-636-2688	
Woodruff Energy 73 Water St PO Box 777 *TF:* 800-557-1121 ■ *Web:* www.woodruffenergy.com	Bridgeton	NJ	08302	856-455-1111	455-4085
Worley & Obetz Inc 85 White Oak Rd PO Box 429 *TF:* 800-697-6891 ■ *Web:* www.worleyobetz.com	Manheim	PA	17545	717-665-6891	665-2867

317 FUND-RAISING SERVICES

Company / Address	City	State	Zip	Phone	Fax
1-Stop Translation USA LLC 3700 Wilshire Blvd Ste 630 *Web:* www.1stopasia.com	Los Angeles	CA	90010	213-480-0011	
A All Languages Ltd 421 Bloor St E Ste 306 *TF:* 800-567-8100 ■ *Web:* www.alllanguages.com	Toronto	ON	M4W3T1	416-975-5000	
ABS Direct Inc 4724 Enterprise Way *Web:* www.absdirectinc.com	Modesto	CA	95356	209-545-6090	
ACCU Translations 3 Mays Crescent *Web:* www.accutranslation.com	Waterdown	ON	L0R2H4	905-639-0323	
AccuConference 6300 Ridglea Pl Ste 318 *TF:* 800-977-4607 ■ *Web:* www.accuconference.com	Ft Worth	TX	76116	800-977-4607	
Accuimage LLC 2807 Biloxi Ave *Web:* www.accuimagellc.com	Nashville	TN	37204	615-242-7226	
Ackroo Inc 62 Steacie Dr Ste 201 *Web:* ackroo.com	Ottawa	ON	K2K2A9	613-599-2396	
Acsion Industries Inc P.O. Box 429 *Web:* www.acsion.com	Pinawa	MB	R0E1L0	204-753-2255	
Active Concepts Inc 389 Fifth Ave Ste 506 *Web:* www.activeconceptsinc.com	New York	NY	10016	212-679-4994	
Advantage Fund Raising Consulting Inc 208 Passaic Ave *Web:* sos.wa.gov	Fairfield	NJ	07004	973-575-9196	575-5614
Air Compressor Solutions 3001 Kermit Hwy *TF:* 800-527-4137 ■ *Web:* acsir.com	Odessa	TX	79764	432-335-5900	
Alqimi Technology Solutions Inc 9210 Corporate Blvd Ste 150 *Web:* www.alqimi.com	Rockville	MD	20850	301-337-0100	
Amerilist Inc 978 Route 45 Ste L2 *TF:* 800-457-2899 ■ *Web:* www.amerilist.com	Pomona	NY	10970	845-362-6737	
APC Integrated Services Inc 770 SPIRIT OF SAINT LOUIS Blvd *TF:* 888-294-7886 ■ *Web:* www.apcisg.com	CHESTERFIELD	MO	63005	888-294-7886	
Apelles LLC 3700 Corporate Dr Ste 240 *Web:* www.apellesnow.com	Columbus	OH	43231	614-899-7322	
Apollo Health Street Inc 2 Brighton Rd Ste 300 *Web:* www.apollohealthstreet.com	Clifton	NJ	07012	973-405-5002	
Aq Technologies 60 E Van Buren *Web:* www.aqtechnologies.com	Chicago	IL	60605	312-867-5400	
Arctic Information Technology Inc 3500 Eide St Ste 300 *Web:* www.arcticit.com	Anchorage	AK	99503	907-261-9500	
Artex Risk Solutions Inc 2 Pierce Pl *Web:* www.artexrisk.com	Itasca	IL	60143	630-694-5050	
Assured Document Destruction Inc 8050 Arville St Ste 105 *Web:* shreddinglv.com	Las Vegas	NV	89139	702-614-0001	
Avantpage Translations 1138 Villaverde Ln *TF:* 877-269-5264 ■ *Web:* www.avantpage.com	Davis	CA	95618	530-750-2040	
Barchart.com Inc 330 S Wells Ste 618 *TF:* 800-238-5814 ■ *Web:* www.barchart.com	Chicago	IL	60606	312-554-8122	
Barkley Kalpak Associates Inc 315 W 39th St Rm 608 Studio 607 *Web:* www.bka.net	New York	NY	10018	212-947-1502	
Barnet Associates LLC 2 Round Lake Rd *TF:* 888-827-7070 ■ *Web:* www.barnetassociates.com	Ridgefield	CT	06877	888-827-7070	
Barrent Group, The 3056 104th Sreet *Web:* www.barrentgroup.com	Urbandale	IA	50322	515-276-2527	
Barton Cotton Inc 3030 Waterview Ave **Fax Area Code:* 410 ■ *TF:* 800-638-4652 ■ *Web:* www.bartoncotton.com	Baltimore	MD	21230	800-348-1102	536-0491*
Bayaud Industries Inc 333 W Bayaud Ave *Web:* www.bayaudenterprises.org	Denver	CO	80223	303-830-6885	
BBH Consulting Inc 80 E Antelope Dr Ste 110 *Web:* www.bbhconsulting.com	Layton	UT	84015	801-779-4405	
BCF Solutions Inc 2300 9th St S Ste 200 *Web:* bcfsolutions.com	Arlington	VA	22204	703-717-9912	
Be Media 655 Hawaii St *Web:* bemedia.com	El Segundo	CA	90245	310-725-8500	
BeenVerified Inc 307 Fifth Ave 16th Fl *TF:* 888-579-5910 ■ *Web:* www.beenverified.com	New York	NY	10016	888-579-5910	
Bentz Whaley Flessner 7251 Ohms Ln *TF:* 800-921-0111 ■ *Web:* www.bwf.com	Minneapolis	MN	55439	952-921-0111	921-0109
Big Mountain Imaging 4725 Copper Sage St *Web:* bigmountain.com	Las Vegas	NV	89115	702-739-7318	
Blue Lan Group Inc 79 Sandwich Rd *Web:* www.bluelangroup.com	Plymouth	MA	02360	508-747-0433	
Bold Ideas 645 N Michigan Ave Ste 800	Chicago	IL	60611	312-280-0440	
Bounce Ideas Inc 102 Conference Blvd *Web:* www.bounceideas.ca	Toronto	ON	M1C2E7	416-286-6656	
Brakeley Briscoe Inc 322 W Bellevue Ave Ste 204 *TF:* 800-416-3086 ■ *Web:* www.brakeleybriscoe.com	San Mateo	CA	94402	650-344-8883	
Britestar Business Solutions Inc 1305 Governors Ct Ste B *Web:* britestarbusiness.com	Abingdon	MD	21009	410-679-0441	
Builder Fusion Inc 424 West 800 North Ste 202 *Web:* www.builderfusion.com	Orem	UT	84057	801-765-0191	
C12 Group LLC, The 4101 Piedmont Pkwy *Web:* www.c12group.com	Greensboro	NC	27410	336-841-7100	
Cargill Assoc Inc 4701 Altamesa Blvd *TF:* 800-433-2233 ■ *Web:* www.cargillassociates.com	Fort Worth	TX	76133	817-292-9374	
Carver & Associates Inc 4177 Northeast Expy *Web:* www.carverassoc.com	Atlanta	GA	30340	770-446-2677	
Casnet 947 W Waterloo Rd *Web:* gotocasnet.com	Akron	OH	44314	330-848-8800	
Cdh 15 Ionia Ave Sw *Web:* www.cdh.com	Grand Rapids	MI	49503	616-776-1117	
Center Partners Inc 4401 Innovation Dr *Web:* www.qualfon.com	Fort Collins	CO	80525	970-206-9000	
Central Ontario Healthcare Procurement Alliance 95 Mural St *TF:* 866-897-8812 ■ *Web:* www.cohpa.ca	Richmond Hill	ON	L4B3G2	905-886-5319	
Changing Our World Inc 220 E 42nd St 5th Fl *Web:* www.changingourworld.com	New York	NY	10017	212-499-0866	
Chapman Cubine Adams + Hussey 2000 15th St N Ste 550 *Web:* www.ccah.com	Arlington	VA	22201	703-248-0025	248-0029

Company / Address	City	State	Zip	Phone	Fax
Chapter IV Investors 301 S Tryon St Ste 1850 *Web:* www.chapterivinvestors.com	Charlotte	NC	28202	704-644-4070	
Clayton Capital Partners 8112 Maryland Ave Ste 250 *Web:* claytoncapitalpartners.com	St. Louis	MO	63105	314-725-9939	
Cohen Group, The 500 Eighth St. NW Ste 200 *Web:* www.cohengroup.net	Washington	DC	20004	202-863-7200	
Compass iTech LLC 6501 Congress Ave Ste 100 *Web:* www.compassprofusion.com	Boca Raton	FL	33487	561-756-8285	
Concord Servicing Corp 4150 N Drinkwater Blvd *TF:* 866-493-6393 ■ *Web:* www.concordservicing.com	Scottsdale	AZ	85251	866-493-6393	
ConsultKAP Inc 3115 Woodchuck Way SW Dept 101 *Web:* www.consultkap.com	Conyers	GA	30094	770-918-9390	
Content Solutions 1413 E Mckinney St *Web:* www.yourcontentsolutions.com	Denton	TX	76209	940-384-9407	
Cox North America Inc 8181 Coleman Rd *TF:* 800-822-8114 ■ *Web:* www.cox-applicators.com	Haslett	MI	48840	517-339-3330	
Cpi Human Resources Solutions Inc 5203 Maverick Dr *Web:* www.cpipartners.com	Austin	TX	78727	512-335-9347	
Cramer & Assoc *Hodge Cramer & Assoc* 555 Metro Pl N Ste 500 *Web:* www.cramerfundraising.com	Dublin	OH	43017	614-766-4483	
Creative Sign Designs 12801 Commodity Pl Ste 200 *TF:* 800-804-4809 ■ *Web:* www.creativesigndesigns.com	Tampa	FL	33626	813-818-7100	
Crosbie & Company Inc 150 King St W Sun Life Financial Tower 15th Fl *TF:* 866-873-7002 ■ *Web:* www.crosbieco.com	Toronto	ON	M5H1J9	416-362-7726	
CrowdFlower Inc 2111 Mission St Ste 302 *Web:* www.crowdflower.com	San Francisco	CA	94110	415-471-1920	
Crown Consulting Inc 1400 Key Blvd Ste 1100 *Web:* www.crownci.com	Arlington	VA	22209	703-650-0663	
CSA Group 178 Rexdale Blvd *TF:* 800-463-6727 ■ *Web:* www.csagroup.org	Toronto	ON	M9W1R3	416-747-4000	
Cull Martin & Assoc Inc 320 N Jensen Rd *Web:* www.cullmartin.com	Vestal	NY	13850	607-722-3884	722-4264
Cummings Co Inc 3500 Fairmount St Ste 504	Dallas	TX	75219	214-526-1772	665-9590
Customer Value Partners Inc 3701 Pender Dr Ste 200 *Web:* www.cvpcorp.com	Fairfax	VA	22030	703-345-9100	
Data Guardian 9136 Portage Industrial Dr *Web:* www.kalamazooxray.com	Portage	MI	49024	269-327-6296	
Detail Planners Llc 1452 Distant Oaks Dr *Web:* www.detailplanners.com	Wesley Chapel	FL	33543	813-991-1348	
Dialogue Marketing Inc 300 E Big Beaver Rd 4th Fl Ste 400 *Web:* www.dialogue-marketing.com	Troy	MI	48083	248-836-2600	
Diamond Energy Services Inc 1521 N Service Rd W *Web:* www.diamondenergy.ca	Swift Current	SK	S9H3S9	306-778-6682	
Diversitec LLC 14321 Sommerville Ct *Web:* www.diversitec.com	Midlothian	VA	23113	804-379-6772	
DM Contact Management 100-645 Tyee Rd *Web:* www.dmcontact.com	Victoria	BC	V9A6X5	250-383-8267	
Dynamic Direct Courier 57 Newkirk Rd *Web:* dynamicdirectcourier.com	Richmond Hill	ON	L4E1A4	905-884-4801	
eCoast Marketing Services 35E Industrial Way Ste 201 *Web:* www.ecoastmarketing.com	Rochester	NH	03867	603-516-7450	
Economic Opportunity Board Of Clark County 330 W Washington Ave Ste 7 *Web:* www.eobccnv.org	Las Vegas	NV	89106	702-647-3307	647-3125
Eggleston Services 6431 Tidewater Dr *Web:* egglestonservices.org	Norfolk	VA	23509	757-625-2311	
Eichelbergers Inc 107 Texaco Rd *Web:* www.eichelbergers.com	Mechanicsburg	PA	17050	717-766-4800	
eLawMarketing 25 Robert Pitt Dr Ste 209G *TF:* 866-833-6245 ■ *Web:* www.elawmarketing.com	Monsey	NY	10952	866-833-6245	
EMI Network Inc 312 Elm St Ste 1150 *Web:* www.eminetwork.com	Cincinnati	OH	45202	513-579-1950	
Employers Association, The 3020 W Arrowood Rd *Web:* www.employersassoc.com	Charlotte	NC	28273	704-522-8011	
Encoll Corp. Inc 4576 Enterprise St *Web:* www.encoll.com	Fremont	CA	94538	510-795-8581	
Endeavor IP Inc 46TH Fl, 140 BROADWAY *Web:* www.enip.com	New York	NY	10005	212-858-7514	
Endurant Business Solutions 12100 Singletree Ln Ste 163 *Web:* www.endurant.com	Eden Prairie	MN	55344	952-746-1373	
Engine Control & Monitoring PO Box 40 *Web:* www.ecm-co.com	Los Altos	CA	94023	408-734-3433	
Enviro-Shred LLC 1045 2nd Ave Northwest *Web:* envirosrhedllc.com	Hickory	NC	28601	828-328-9333	
Equi Tax Inc 17111 Rolling Creek Dr Ste 200 *Web:* www.equitaxinc.com	Houston	TX	77090	281-444-4866	
Extended Presence 3570 E 12th Ave Ste 200 *TF:* 800-398-8957 ■ *Web:* www.extendedpresence.com	Denver	CO	80206	303-325-8600	
Fam Funds 384 N Grand St PO Box 310 *TF:* 800-721-5391 ■ *Web:* www.famfunds.com	Cobleskill	NY	12043	518-234-4393	234-4473
Fearless Records 11783 Cardinal Cir *Web:* www.fearlessrecords.com	Garden Grove	CA	92843	714-638-7090	
Field Nation LLC 310 Fourth Ave S Ste 8100 *TF:* 877-573-4353 ■ *Web:* www.fieldnation.com	Minneapolis	MN	55415	877-573-4353	
FilterBoxx Water & Environmental Corp 5716 Burbank Rd SE *TF:* 877-868-4747 ■ *Web:* filterboxx.com	Calgary	AB	T2H1Z4	403-203-4747	
FinTrack Systems 194 Calyer St *Web:* www.fintrack.com	Brooklyn	NY	11222	212-742-1800	
Florida Coast Equipment Co 9775 Boynton Beach Blvd *Web:* www.floridacoasteq.com	Boynton Beach	FL	33437	561-369-0414	
Format International Inc 10715 Kahlmeyer Dr *Web:* www.format-international.com	Saint Louis	MO	63132	314-428-2671	
Fort Docs 533 Pacific Ave *Web:* www.rmscd.com	Santa Rosa	CA	95407	707-571-8313	
Freeman Enterprises Inc 20 E 46th St Ste 800 *Web:* www.freemanent.com	New York	NY	10017	212-490-6565	
Fulco Fulfillment Inc 26 Richboynton Rd *Web:* www.fulcofulfillment.com	Dover	NJ	07801	973-361-1700	
Gale Force Petroleum Inc 100 King St W Ste 5700 *TF:* 888-440-3411 ■ *Web:* www.galeforcepetroleum.com	Toronto	ON	M5X1C7	888-440-3411	
Galveston Central Appraisal District 9850 Emmett F Lowry Expy Ste A *TF:* 866-277-4725 ■ *Web:* www.galvestoncad.org	Texas City	TX	77591	409-935-1980	
GAP Solutions Inc 205 Van Buren St Ste 205 *Web:* www.gapsi.com	Herndon	VA	20170	703-707-2090	
Georgia Duplicating Products Inc 1180 Eisenhower Pkwy *Web:* www.gadup.com	Macon	GA	31206	478-781-8991	
Gift Planning Assoc 4417 11th St NW *Web:* www.giftplanner1.com	Albuquerque	NM	87107	415-970-2380	
Gilligan & Ferneman LLC 1754 Business Ctr Ln *TF:* 800-720-4152 ■ *Web:* gilliganandferneman.com	Kissimmee	FL	34758	800-720-4152	
Gis Assocs Inc 806a Nw 16th Ave *Web:* gis-associates.com	Gainesville	FL	32601	352-384-1465	
Global Corporate College 6001 Cochran Rd Ste 305 *Web:* globalcorporatecollege.com	Solon	OH	44139	440-793-0202	
Global Pacific Financial Services Ltd 10430 144 St *TF:* 800-561-1177 ■ *Web:* www.globalpacific.com	Surrey	BC	V3T4V5	800-561-1177	
Gonser Gerber 1776 Legacy Cir Ste 100 *Web:* www.gonsergerber.com	Naperville	IL	60563	630-505-1433	
Greater Giving Inc 1920 N W Amberglen Pkwy Ste 140 *TF:* 800-276-5992 ■ *Web:* greatergiving.com	Beaverton	OR	97006	800-276-5992	
Grenzebach Glier & Assoc Inc 401 N Michigan Ave Ste 2800 *Web:* www.grenzebachglier.com	Chicago	IL	60611	312-372-4040	589-6358
GroveWare Technologies Ltd 90 Eglinton Ave E Ste 411 *TF:* 877-701-9378 ■ *Web:* www.groveware.com	Toronto	ON	M4P2Y3	877-701-9378	
GTS Consultants 2 Monmouth Ave *Web:* gtsconsultants.com	Freehold	NJ	07728	732-409-0900	
Hamdard Center for Health & Human Services 228 E Lk St Ste 300 *Web:* www.hamdardcenter.org	Addison	IL	60101	630-835-1430	
Hanwha L&C Canada Inc 2860 Innovation Dr *Web:* www.hanwhasurfaces.com	London	ON	N6M065	519-433-0486	
Hardline Installation Inc 1759 Green Cove Rd St B *Web:* www.hardlineinstallation.com	Brasstown	NC	28902	828-835-8209	
Health Revenue Assurance Holdings Inc Ste 304 8551 W Sunrise Blvd	Plantation	FL	33322	954-472-2340	
High Tech Design Safety LLC 15304 Rainbow One St Ste 101 *Web:* hightechdesignsafety.com	Austin	TX	78734	512-266-0222	
Ho-Chunk Inc 1 Mission Dr *Web:* www.hochunkinc.com	Winnebago	NE	68071	402-878-2809	
hrQ Inc 2859 Umatilla St *Web:* www.hrqinc.com	Denver	CO	80211	303-455-1118	
ICX Group Inc SunTrust Tower 76 S Laura St Ste 1300 *Web:* www.icxgroup.com	Jacksonville	FL	32202	904-208-2200	
IFS Financial Services Inc 250 Brownlow Ave Ste 1 *TF:* 800-565-1153 ■ *Web:* www.ifs-finance.com	Dartmouth	NS	B3B1W9	902-481-6106	
Iknow LLC 100 Overlook Ctr 2nd Fl *Web:* www.iknow.us	Princeton	NJ	08540	609-419-0500	
Info Cubic LLC 9250 E Costilla Ave Ste 525 *TF:* 877-360-4636 ■ *Web:* www.infocubic.net	Greenwood Village	CO	80112	303-220-0170	
Infoshred LLC 3 Craftsman Rd *Web:* www.infoshred.com	East Windsor	CT	06088	860-627-5800	
Inline Packaging LLC 1205 18th Ave S *Web:* www.inlinepkg.com	Princeton	MN	55371	763-631-1555	
Insight Resource Group 3 Altarinda Rd Ste 301 *Web:* www.insightresourcegroup.com	Orinda	CA	94563	925-254-4114	
Institutional Advancement Programs Inc 65 Main St Ste 208	Tuckahoe	NY	10707	914-779-4092	961-3114
Intellimeter Canada Inc 1125 Squires Beach Rd *Web:* intellimeter.on.ca	Pickering	ON	L1W3T9	905-839-9199	
Interuniversity Services Inc 1550 Bedford Hwy *Web:* www.interuniversity.ns.ca	Bedford	NS	B4A1E6	902-453-2470	
Intronix Technologies Inc 26 McEwan Dr West Unit 15 *TF:* 800-819-9996 ■ *Web:* www.intronixtech.com	Bolton	ON	L7E1E6	905-951-3361	
ISK Biosciences Corp 7474 Auburn Rd Ste 2 *Web:* www.iskbc.com	Painesville	OH	44077	440-357-4640	
Issuer Direct Corp 500 Perimeter Park Dr Ste D *TF:* 877-481-4014 ■ *Web:* www.issuerdirect.com	Morrisville	NC	27560	877-481-4014	

				Phone	Fax
Itco Solutions Inc 1003 Whitehall Ln *Web:* www.itcosolutions.com	Redwood City	CA	94061	650-367-0514	
Itgroove Professional Services Ltd 1035 Nakini Pl *Web:* itgroove.net	Brentwood Bay	BC	V8M1A3	250-220-4575	
ITR of Georgia Inc 3346 Montreal *Web:* www.itrofgeorgia.com	Tucker	GA	30084	770-496-0366	
J M Field Marketing Inc 3570 NW 53rd Ct *Web:* www.jmfieldmarketing.com	Fort Lauderdale	FL	33309	954-523-1957	
John Brown Ltd Inc 46 Grove St PO Box 296 *Web:* www.johnbrownlimited.com	Peterborough	NH	03458	603-924-3834	924-7998
Jopari Solutions Inc 1855 Gateway Blvd Ste 500 *Web:* www.jopari.com	Concord	CA	94520	925-459-5200	
Joseph C. Sansone Co 18040 Edison Ave *Web:* www.jcsco.com	Chesterfield	MO	63005	636-537-2700	
Jrm & Associates Inc 160 Cupped Oak Dr Ste A *Web:* www.jrmassociates.com	Stallings	NC	28104	704-882-2044	
Jumpstart Automotive Group 550 Kearny St Ste 500 *Web:* www.jumpstartautomotivegroup.com	San Francisco	CA	94108	415-844-6300	
K3 Enterprises Inc 504 Cumberland St Ste 300 *Web:* www.k3-enterprises.com	Fayetteville	NC	28301	910-307-3017	
KCI Aviation 2100 Aviation Way *Web:* www.kciaviation.com	Bridgeport	WV	26330	304-842-3591	
King Business Interiors Inc 6155 Huntley Rd Ste D *Web:* www.kbiinc.com	Columbus	OH	43229	614-430-0020	
Las Vegas Events 770 E Warm Springs Rd Ste 140 *Web:* lasvegasevents.com	Las Vegas	NV	89119	702-260-8605	
Las Vegas Presort LLC 3655 E Patrick Ln Ste 300 *Web:* lasvegaspresort.net	Las Vegas	NV	89120	702-320-0450	
Lathrop & Clark LLP 740 Regent St Ste 400 *Web:* www.boardmanclark.com	Madison	WI	53715	608-257-7766	
LeadSwell PO Box 170432 *Web:* www.leadswell.com	San Francisco	CA	94117	415-518-6701	
Leap Group Llc, The 11 Waverly Rd *Web:* www.leapgroup.com	San Anselmo	CA	94960	415-456-7404	
Leigh Bureau Inc 92 E Main St Ste 200 *Web:* www.leighbureau.com	Somerville	NJ	08876	908-253-8600	
Levy Diamond Bello & Associates LLC 497 Bic Dr *Web:* www.ldbassociates.com	Milford	CT	06461	203-876-1000	
Lipman Hearne Inc 200 S Michigan Ave Ste 1600 *Web:* www.lipmanhearne.com	Chicago	IL	60604	312-356-8000	356-4005
Live Auctioneers LLC 220 12th Ave 2nd Fl *Web:* www.liveauctioneers.com	New York	NY	10001	212-947-4428	
Lockard David 15 W Highland Ave *Web:* davidlockard.com	Philadelphia	PA	19118	215-753-0661	
Locordia Inc 16600 Sherman Way Ste 170 *Web:* www.locordia.com	Van Nuys	CA	91406	818-827-1328	
London Economics International LLC 717 Atlantic Ave Ste 1A *Web:* www.londoneconomics.com	Boston	MA	02111	617-933-7200	
LW Robbins Assoc 201 Summer St *TF:* 800-229-5972 ■ *Web:* www.robbinskersten.com	Holliston	MA	01746	800-229-5972	
MacIntyre Assoc Inc 106 W State St *Web:* www.macintyreassociates.com	Kennett Square	PA	19348	610-925-5925	
Mail Dispatch LLC 9710 Distribution Ave *TF:* 800-275-0450 ■ *Web:* www.maildispatch.com	San Diego	CA	92121	800-275-0450	
Manus Group, The 3168 Hwy 17, Ste D *Web:* www.themanusgroup.com	Fleming Island	FL	32003	904-264-5406	
Mcc Planners Inc 290 N Queen St Ste 208 *Web:* mccplanners.com	Toronto	ON	M9C5L2	416-621-6622	
MCMC LLC 300 Crown Colony Dr Ste 203 *Web:* www.mcmcllc.com	Quincy	MA	02169	617-375-7700	
MD&E Inc 5805 State Bridge Rd Ste G-371 *Web:* www.mdeclarity.com	Johns Creek	GA	30097	678-291-9690	
Medbuy Corp 4056 Meadowbrook Dr Unit 135 *Web:* www.medbuy.ca	London	ON	N6L1E4	519-652-1688	
Miami Direct Inc 8200 NW 41 St Ste 225 *Web:* www.gbm.net	Miami	FL	33166	305-597-3998	
Michael Quinlan Inc 3752 N Lowell *Web:* www.michaeljquinlan.com	Chicago	IL	60641	773-286-6237	
Milieu Design Corp 48 E Hintz Rd *Web:* www.milieu-design.com	Wheeling	IL	60090	847-465-1160	
Minnesuing Acres 8084 E Minnesuing Acres Dr *Web:* www.minnesuingacres.com	Lake Nebagamon	WI	54849	715-374-2262	
Mopals Com Inc 109 Atlantic Ave *Web:* www.mopals.com	Toronto	ON	M6K1X4	416-362-4888	
MSDSonline Inc 350 N Orleans Ste 950 *Web:* www.msdsonline.com	Chicago	IL	60654	312-881-2000	
MyUSACorporation.com Inc 1 Radisson Plz Ste 800 *TF:* 877-330-2677 ■ *Web:* myusacorporation.com	New Rochelle	NY	10801	877-330-2677	
National Franchise Sales 1601 Dove St Ste 150 *Web:* www.nationalfranchisesales.com	Newport Beach	CA	92660	949-428-0480	
NetTel Partners 125 N 8th St, *Web:* www.nettelpartners.com	Philadelphia	PA	19106	267-908-7890	
Netzel Grigsby Assoc Inc 9696 Culver Blvd Ste 105 *Web:* www.netzelgrigsby.com	Culver City	CA	90232	310-836-7624	836-9357
New Age Industrial Corporation Inc 16788 E Hwy 36 PO Box 520 *Web:* www.newageindustrial.com	Norton	KS	67654	785-877-5121	
Nomadic Display Capitol Inc 5617 Industrial Dr *TF:* 800-336-5019 ■ *Web:* www.nomadicdisplay.com	Springfield	VA	22151	703-912-4700	
NorAm Capital Holdings Inc 15303 N Dallas Pkwy Ste 1030 *TF:* 888-886-6726 ■ *Web:* noramcapitalholdings.com	Addison	TX	75001	888-886-6726	
Nova Corp Inc 74 W Sheffield Ave *Web:* nova-corp.com	Englewood	NJ	07631	201-567-4404	
Nova Express Millennium Inc 105 - 14271 Knox Way *TF:* 877-566-6839 ■ *Web:* www.novex.ca	Richmond	BC	V6V2Z4	604-278-8044	
oberoSPM 7560 Airport Rd Unit 12 *TF:* 888-815-2996 ■ *Web:* oberosolutions.com	Mississauga	ON	L4T4H4	888-815-2996	
Odesia Group Inc 1 Pl Ville-Marie Ste 560 *Web:* www.odesia.com	Montreal	QC	H3B2C4	514-876-1155	
Office Liquidators Inc 11111 W Sixth Ave Unit A *Web:* m.officeliquidators.com	Denver	CO	80215	303-759-3375	
OM Records 665 3rd St Ste 425 *Web:* www.om-records.com	San Francisco	CA	94107	415-904-1800	
Omni Workspace Co 1300 N Washington Ave Ste 200 *Web:* www.omniworkspace.com	Minneapolis	MN	55411	612-627-1700	
Omnilingua Worldwide LLC 306 Sixth Ave SE *Web:* www.omnilingua.com	Cedar Rapids	IA	52401	319-365-8565	
On 3 Promotional Partners 1543 Sheridan Rd *Web:* www.on3promopartners.com	Kenosha	WI	53140	262-551-8715	
OnCorp Direct Inc 1033 Bay St Ste 313 *TF:* 800-461-7772 ■ *Web:* www.oncorp.com	Toronto	ON	M5S3A5	416-964-2677	
Operon Systems L L C W6416 Greenville Dr *Web:* www.operonsystems.com	Greenville	WI	54942	920-882-8720	
Optimum Card Solution LLC 855 S Fiene Dr *Web:* optimumcard.com	Addison	IL	60101	630-458-0077	
Ounce of Prevention Fund of Florida Inc, The 111 N Gadsden St Ste 200 *Web:* www.ounce.org	Tallahassee	FL	32301	850-921-4494	
Parallon Business Solutions LLC 6640 Carothers Pkwy *Web:* parallon.com	Franklin	TN	37067	615-807-8000	
Parenty Reitmeier Inc 605 Des Meurons St *TF:* 877-445-3737 ■ *Web:* www.parentyreitmeier.com	Winnipeg	MB	R2H2R1	204-237-3737	
Parsec Inc 1100 Gest St *Web:* www.parsecinc.com	Cincinnati	OH	45203	513-621-6111	
parts com Inc 121 E First St *Web:* www.parts.com	Sanford	FL	32771	407-302-1314	
Patented Acquisition Corp 2490 CrossPointe Dr *Web:* thinkpatented.com	Miamisburg	OH	45342	937-353-2299	
Payment Services Corp Inc 360 Albert St Ste 1220 *TF:* 866-972-0616 ■ *Web:* www.paymentservicescorp.com	Ottawa	ON	K1R7X7	866-972-0616	
PEP Direct Inc 19 Stoney Brook Dr	Wilton	NH	03086	603-654-6141	654-2159
Periodical Publishers' Service Bureau 1 N Superior St *Web:* www.ppsb.com	Sandusky	OH	44870	419-626-0623	
Phillips & Assoc PO Box 241040 *Web:* www.phillipsontheweb.com	Los Angeles	CA	90024	310-247-0963	247-0966
Phone Ware Inc 8902 Activity Rd *TF:* 800-243-8329 ■ *Web:* www.phonewareinc.com	San Diego	CA	92126	858-459-3000	
Planit Measuring Co, The 94 Lkshore Rd E Unit C *Web:* www.planitmeasuring.com	Mississauga	ON	L5G1E3	905-271-7010	
Pmj Solutions Inc 604 Park Pl *Web:* www.pmjsolutions.com	Rivervale	NJ	07675	201-664-8920	
Polymer Solutions Inc 2903-C Commerce St *Web:* www.polymersolutions.com	Blacksburg	VA	24060	540-961-4300	
Practice Concepts 2706 Harbor Blvd *TF:* 877-778-2020 ■ *Web:* www.practiceconcepts.com	Costa Mesa	CA	92626	714-545-5110	
Premier Courier Service Inc 410 Eighth Ave *Web:* www.premier-nyc.com	New York	NY	10001	212-684-0901	
Product Support Solutions Inc 7172 Regional St Ste 431 *Web:* www.psshelp.com	Dublin	CA	94568	925-208-2450	
ProKarma Inc 14780 Sw Osprey Dr *Web:* www.prokarma.com	Beaverton	OR	97007	971-317-0700	
Provista LLC 220 E Las Colinas Blvd *Web:* www.provistaco.com	Irving	TX	75039	972-830-0000	
Pursuant 5151 Belt Line Rd Ste 900 *Web:* www.pursuant.com	Dallas	TX	75254	214-866-7700	
QCSS Inc 21925 Field Pkwy Ste 210 *TF:* 888-229-7046 ■ *Web:* www.qcssinc.com	Deer Park	IL	60010	847-229-7046	
R d d Associates LLC 930 Riverview Dr Ste 400 *Web:* www.rddassociates.com	Totowa	NJ	07512	973-812-8070	
R G S Financial Corp 1700 Jay Ell Drÿ Ste 150 *Web:* www.rgsfinancial.com	Carrollton	TX	75006	469-791-4700	
Radish Tools 12 Mckendree Ave *Web:* www.radishtools.com	Annapolis	MD	21401	443-321-2732	
Rdr Group Inc 48 Tamarack Ln *Web:* rdrgroup.com	Pomona	NY	10970	845-354-3897	
Redeye Distribution Inc 449a Trollingwood Rd *Web:* redeyeusa.com	Haw River	NC	27258	336-578-5202	
Reed Brennan Media Associates Inc 628 Virginia Dr *TF:* 800-708-7311 ■ *Web:* www.rbma.com	Orlando	FL	32803	407-894-7300	
Reliant Inventory Services Inc 11050 Fancher Rd Lot 110 *Web:* www.reliant-inv.com	Westerville	OH	43082	614-855-2960	
Rethink Innovations 118 Burrs Rd Ste C1 *Web:* www.myrethink.com	Westampton	NJ	08060	609-784-8427	
RGIS LLC 2000 E Taylor Rd *Web:* www.rgis.com	Auburn Hills	MI	48326	248-651-2511	

	City	State	ZIP	Phone	Fax
Rite-solutions Inc 1 Corporate Pl 2nd Fl *Web:* www.rite-solutions.com	Middletown	RI	02842	860-599-1969	
Rival Capital Management Inc 160 - 99 Scurfield Bvld. *Web:* rivalcapital.ca	Winnipeg	MB	R3Y1Y1	204-992-6210	
Robbinex Inc 41 Stuart St *Web:* www.robbinex.com	Hamilton	ON	L8L1B5	905-523-7510	
Roger Black Studio Inc 245 Fifth Ave Rm 2345 *Web:* rogerblack.com	New York	NY	10016	212-481-9800	
Romeo Entertainment Group Inc 5247 N 129th St. *Web:* www.romeoent.com	Omaha	NE	68164	402-359-1010	
Round Sky Inc 848 N Rainbow Blvd Ste 326 *TF:* 855-450-3618 ■ *Web:* www.roundsky.com	Las Vegas	NV	89107	855-450-3618	
Ruotolo Assoc Inc (RA) 29 Broadway Ste 210 *TF:* 800-786-8656 ■ *Web:* www.ruotoloassociates.com	Cresskill	NJ	07626	201-568-3898	568-8783
Sageworks Inc 5565 Centerview Dr. *Web:* www.sageworks.com	Raleigh	NC	27606	919-851-7474	
Sandi Gornati Inc 250 A Lyon Ln *Web:* www.sgi-solutions.com	Birmingham	AL	35211	205-941-2575	
Sanky Perlowin Assoc Inc *Sanky Communications Inc* 599 11th Ave 6th Fl *Web:* www.sankyinc.com	New York	NY	10036	212-868-4300	
Scanning America Inc 1440 N 3rd St. *Web:* www.scanningamerica.com	Lawrence	KS	66044	785-749-7471	
SDG Corp 55 N Water St *Web:* www.sdgc.com	Norwalk	CT	06854	203-866-8886	
Shareintel 151 Rowayton Ave *Web:* www.shareintel.com	Rowayton	CT	06853	203-838-5471	
Ship-Right Solutions LLC 165 Pleasant Ave *Web:* www.shiprightsolutions.com	South Portland	ME	04106	207-321-3500	
Show Management Services Inc 1963 University Ln *Web:* www.rocexhibitions.com	Lisle	IL	60532	630-271-8210	
Shred Works Inc 1601 Bayshore Hwy Ste 211 *Web:* www.shredworks.com	Burlingame	CA	94010	510-729-7110	
Skystone Ryan *Skystone Partners LLC* 635 W Seventh St Ste 107 *Web:* www.skystonepartners.com	Cincinnati	OH	45203	513-241-6778	
SMARTLogix Inc 10306 Barberville Rd *Web:* www.smartlogixinc.com	Ft. Mill	SC	29707	803-547-8265	
Smarttech Enterprises 1300 Chisolm Trl *Web:* www.smarttechreport.com	Dayton	OH	45458	937-885-7144	
SMI Companies Inc 1456 Hwy 317 South *Web:* www.smicompanies.com	Franklin	LA	70538	337-836-9894	
SNtial Technologies Inc 125 Ainslie Ct. *Web:* www.sntialtech.com	Westmont	IL	60559	630-452-4735	
South Atlantic Packaging Corp 3932 Westpoint Blvd *Web:* southatlanticpackaging.com	Winston-Salem	NC	27103	336-774-3122	
Special Journeys LLC 422 S 153rd Cir *Web:* www.specialjourneys.org	Omaha	NE	68154	402-991-5520	
Spectrum Llc 717 King St Ste 350 *Web:* www.spectrumbrokers.com	Alexandria	VA	22314	703-836-7170	
Stirling Mercantile Corp 450 - 400 Burrard St. *Web:* www.stirlingmercantile.com	Vancouver	BC	V6C3A6	604-484-0070	
Stoneacre Inc 3135 Springbank Ln, Ste 100 *Web:* www.stoneacreinc.com	Charlotte	NC	28226	704-719-5800	
Sun Energy Solutions 2101 S Yale St *Web:* www.sunindustriesinc.com	Santa Ana	CA	92704	714-210-5141	
Superior Exhibits and Design Inc 777 Lunt Ave *Web:* www.superiorexhibits.com	Elk Grove Village	IL	60007	847-364-9380	
Sureshred Security 3166 Diablo Ave *TF:* 888-606-0008 ■ *Web:* www.sureshred.com	Hayward	CA	94545	510-784-1150	
Swim Across America Inc 5 Stanley Rd *Web:* www.swimacrossamerica.org	Darien	CT	06820	980-237-9127	
SWOT Management Group Inc 105 Raider Blvd Ste 201 *Web:* www.swotmg.com	Hillsborough	NJ	08844	908-359-7968	
Synergent 2 Ledgeview Dr *TF:* 800-341-0180 ■ *Web:* www.synergentcorp.com	Westbrook	ME	04092	207-773-5671	
TeamBonding 298 Tosca Dr *TF:* 888-398-8326 ■ *Web:* www.teambonding.com	Stoughton	MA	02072	888-398-8326	
TechTrans International Inc 2200 Space Park Ste 410 *Web:* www.tti-corp.com	Houston	TX	77058	281-335-8000	
TechXpress Inc 3450 Broad St Ste 108 *Web:* www.techxpress.net	San Luis Obispo	CA	93401	805-541-4400	
Telematic Controls Inc 3364 114 Ave Se *Web:* www.telematic.com	Calgary	AB	T2Z3V6	403-253-7939	
Telenet Marketing Solutions Llc 1915 New Jimmy Daniel Rd *Web:* www.telenetmarketing.com	Athens	GA	30622	706-353-1940	
Ter Molen Watkins & Brandt LLC 2 N Riverside Plz Ste 1030 *Web:* www.twbfundraising.com	Chicago	IL	60606	312-222-0560	222-0565
Texenergy 2611 E Pioneer Dr. *Web:* www.tempoair.com	Irving	TX	75061	972-579-2000	
TharpeRobbins Company Inc, The 149 Crawford Rd. *Web:* www.tharperobbins.com	Statesville	NC	28625	704-872-5231	
Thermosoft International Corp 701 corporate Woods Pkwy *TF:* 800-308-8057 ■ *Web:* www.thermosoft.com	Vernon Hills	IL	60061	847-279-3800	
Thetubestore Inc 120 Lancing Dr. *TF:* 877-570-0979 ■ *Web:* www.thetubestore.com	Hamilton	ON	L8W3A1	905-570-0979	
Ti Squared Technologies Inc 1305 Clark Mill Rd *Web:* tisquaredtech.com	Sweet Home	OR	97386	541-367-2929	
TIS Group 100 Village Ctr Dr Ste 260 *Web:* theinstitutionalstrategist.com	North Oaks	MN	55127	651-379-5070	
Total Parts Plus Inc 70 Ready Ave NW *Web:* www.totalpartsplus.com	Fort Walton Beach	FL	32548	850-244-7293	
Townsend Oil Company Inc 27 Cherry St PO Box 90 *TF:* 800-888-2888 ■ *Web:* www.townsendtotalenergy.com	Danvers	MA	01923	800-888-2888	
Trade Technologies Inc 3939 Bee Cave Rd Ste B-22 *Web:* www.tradetechnologies.com	Austin	TX	78746	512-327-9996	
Trademark Co, The 344 Maple Ave W Ste 151 *TF:* 800-906-8626 ■ *Web:* www.thetrademarkcompany.com	Vienna	VA	22180	800-906-8626	
Transcepta LLC 135 Columbia Ste 202 *Web:* www.trancascapital.com	Aliso Viejo	CA	92656	949-382-2840	
Travelink Inc 404 BNA Dr #650 *Web:* www.travelink.com	Nashville	TN	37217	615-367-4900	
Trendl Associates 941 W Winona St Ste 1w *Web:* www.trendl.net	Chicago	IL	60640	773-728-6973	
Trifecta Marketing Group Inc 10124 Hanover Glen Rd *Web:* www.trifectamg.com	Charlotte	NC	28210	704-543-8292	
TRSB Inc 276 Saint-Jacques St Ste 900 *Web:* www.trsb.com	Montreal	QC	H2Y1N3	514-844-4682	
Ultraex Inc 2633 Barrington Ct *Web:* www.ultraex.com	Hayward	CA	94545	510-786-3490	
United Document Destruction & Storage 1110 Commons Blvd *Web:* uniteddocument.com	Reading	PA	19605	610-557-1799	
US Market Access Center 10 S Third St 3rd Fl *Web:* usmarketaccess.com	San Jose	CA	95113	408-351-3300	
Van Groesbeck & Co 2124 Hanovar Ave *Web:* www.vangroesbeckco.com	Richmond	VA	23220	804-285-3176	359-7271
Vantage Sourcing LLC 328 Ross Clark Cir *TF:* 866-580-4562 ■ *Web:* www.vantagesourcing.com	Dothan	AL	36303	866-580-4562	
Vertex Business Services LLC 250 E Arapaho Rd *Web:* www.vertexgroup.com	Richardson	TX	75081	214-576-1000	
Vision Offices Executive Suites Lp 14362 N Frank Lloyd Wright Blvd Ste 1000 *Web:* visionoffices.com	Scottsdale	AZ	85260	480-477-7777	
Vitech Business Group Inc 4164 Meridian St Ste 200 *Web:* www.vitechgroup.com	Bellingham	WA	98229	360-647-1622	
Vokle Inc 2006 Montana Ave *Web:* www.vokle.com	Santa Monica	CA	90403	818-723-2083	
VXI Global Solutions Inc 220 W 1st St 3rd Fl. *Web:* www.vxiusa.com	Los Angeles	CA	90012	213-637-1300	
W Squared.com 5500 Maryland Way Ste 200 *Web:* www.wsquared.com	Brentwood	TN	37027	615-577-4927	
Whitney Jones Inc 119 Brookstown Ave Ste PH2 *Web:* www.whitneyjonesinc.com	Winston-Salem	NC	27101	336-722-2371	
WineDirect Inc 1190 Airport Blvd Ste 200 *Web:* www.winedirect.com	Napa	CA	94558	707-603-4000	
World Services LLC 1954 Airport Rd Ste 201 *Web:* worldservicesusa.com	Chamblee	GA	30341	404-486-5986	
Xerox Mortgage Services Inc 9040 Roswell Rd Ste 700 *Web:* www.xerox-xms.com	Sandy Springs	GA	30350	678-460-2460	
Youth Consultation Service (Inc) 284 Broadway *Web:* www.ycs.org	Newark	NJ	07104	973-482-8411	
Zerion Group LLC 235 S Maitland Ave Ste 100 *Web:* www.zeriongroup.com	Maitland	FL	32751	321-229-1089	

318 FURNACES & OVENS - INDUSTRIAL PROCESS

	City	State	ZIP	Phone	Fax
AFC Holcroft LLC 49630 Pontiac Trl *Web:* www.afc-holcroft.com	Wixom	MI	48393	248-624-8191	624-3710
AGF Burner Inc 814 Asbury Ave *Web:* www.agfburner.com	Asbury Park	NJ	07712	732-730-8090	730-8060
AJAX Electric Co 60 Tomlinson Rd *Web:* www.ajaxelectric.com	Huntingdon Valley	PA	19006	215-947-8500	947-6757
Ajax Tocco Magnethermic Corp 1745 Overland Ave NE *TF:* 800-547-1527 ■ *Web:* www.ajaxtocco.com	Warren	OH	44483	330-372-8511	372-8608
Alabama Specialty Products Inc 152 Metal Samples Rd PO Box 8 *TF:* 888-388-1006 ■ *Web:* www.alspi.com	Munford	AL	36268	256-358-5200	358-4515
Alpha 1 Induction Service Ctr Inc 1525 Old Alum Creek Dr. *TF:* 800-991-2599 ■ *Web:* www.alpha1induction.com	Columbus	OH	43209	614-253-8900	253-8981
Armor Group Inc, The 4600 N Mason-Montgomery Rd *TF:* 800-255-0393 ■ *Web:* www.thearmorgroup.com	Mason	OH	45040	800-255-0393	
AVS Inc 60 Fitchburg Rd *TF:* 800-772-0710 ■ *Web:* www.avsinc.com	Ayer	MA	01432	978-772-0710	772-6462
Belco Industries Inc 9138 W Belding Rd *Web:* www.belcoind.com	Belding	MI	48809	616-794-0410	
Bloom Engineering Co Inc 5460 Curry Rd *Web:* www.bloomeng.com	Pittsburgh	PA	15236	412-653-3500	653-2253
BriskHeat Corp 1055 Gibbard Ave. *TF:* 800-848-7673 ■ *Web:* www.briskheat.com	Columbus	OH	43201	614-294-3376	294-3807
Callidus Technologies Inc 7130 S Lewis St Ste 335 *Web:* www.callidus.com	Tulsa	OK	74136	918-496-7599	488-9450
Cambridge Engineering Inc PO Box 1010 *TF:* 800-899-1989 ■ *Web:* www.cambridge-eng.com	Chesterfield	MO	63006	636-532-2233	530-6133
CCI Thermal Technologies Inc 5918 Roper Rd *TF Cust Svc:* 800-661-8529 ■ *Web:* www.ccithermal.com	Edmonton	AB	T6B3E1	780-466-3178	468-5904

Company	City	State	Zip	Phone	Fax
Cl Hayes 33 Fwy Dr. *Web:* www.cihayes.com	Cranston	RI	02920	401-467-5200	467-2108
CMI EFCO Inc 435 W Wilson St *TF:* 877-225-2674 ■ *Web:* www.cmigroupe.com	Salem	OH	44460	330-332-4661	332-4661
Consarc Corp 100 Indel Ave **Fax:* Sales ■ *Web:* www.consarc.com	Rancocas	NJ	08073	609-267-8000	267-1366*
Consutech Systems LLC PO Box 15119 *Web:* www.consutech.com	Richmond	VA	23227	804-746-4120	730-9056
Despatch Industries Inc 8860 207th St W *TF:* 800-726-0110 ■ *Web:* www.despatch.com	Lakeville	MN	55044	952-469-5424	469-4513
Detroit Radiant Product Co 21400 Hoover Rd *TF:* 800-222-1100 ■ *Web:* www.reverberray.com	Warren	MI	48089	586-756-0950	756-2626
Detroit Stoker Co 1510 E First St *TF:* 800-786-5374 ■ *Web:* www.detroitstoker.com	Monroe	MI	48161	734-241-9500	241-7126
Eclipse Inc 1665 Elmwood Rd **Fax:* Cust Svc ■ *TF:* 888-826-3473 ■ *Web:* www.eclipsenet.com	Rockford	IL	61103	815-877-3031	877-3336*
Eisenmann Corp 150 E Dartmoor Dr *Web:* www.eisenmann.com	Crystal Lake	IL	60014	815-455-4100	455-1018
Electric Heating Equipment Co 1240 Oronoque Rd	Milford	CT	06461	203-882-0199	
Fast Heat Inc 776 Oaklawn Ave *TF:* 877-747-8575 ■ *Web:* www.fastheat.com	Elmhurst	IL	60126	630-833-5400	833-2040
Gas-Fired Products Inc 305 Doggett St *TF:* 800-830-3983 ■ *Web:* www.gasfiredproducts.com	Charlotte	NC	28203	704-372-3485	332-5843
GC Broach Co 7667 E 46th Pl *Web:* www.broach.com	Tulsa	OK	74145	918-664-7420	627-4083
Glenro Inc 39 McBride Ave *TF:* 888-453-6761 ■ *Web:* www.glenro.com	Paterson	NJ	07501	973-279-5900	279-9103
Glo-Quartz Electric Heater Company Inc 7084 Maple St *TF Sales:* 800-321-3574 ■ *Web:* www.gloquartz.com	Mentor	OH	44060	440-255-9701	255-7852
Hauck Manufacturing Co 100 N Harris St *Web:* www.hauckburner.com	Cleona	PA	17042	717-272-3051	273-9882
Heatrex Inc PO Box 515 *TF:* 800-394-6589 ■ *Web:* www.heatrex.com	Meadville	PA	16335	814-724-1800	333-6580
Henry F Teichmann Inc 3009 Washington Rd *Web:* www.hft.com	McMurray	PA	15317	724-941-9550	941-3479
Hotwatt Inc 128 Maple St **Fax:* Sales ■ *Web:* www.hotwatt.com	Danvers	MA	01923	978-777-0070	774-2409*
Huppert Industries Inc 16808 S Lathrop Ave *Web:* www.huppert.com	Harvey	IL	60426	708-339-2020	339-2225
Inductoheat Inc 32251 N Avis Dr *TF:* 800-624-6297 ■ *Web:* www.inductoheat.com	Madison Heights	MI	48071	248-585-9393	589-1062
Inductotherm Group 10 Indel Ave PO Box 157 *TF:* 800-257-9527 ■ *Web:* www.inductotherm.com	Rancocas	NJ	08073	609-267-9000	
Industrial Combustion Inc 351 21st St *Web:* www.ind-comb.com	Monroe	WI	53566	608-325-3141	325-4379
Industrial Heater Corp 30 Knotter Dr *Web:* www.industrialheater.com	Cheshire	CT	06410	203-250-0500	250-0599
Industronics Service Co 489 Sullivan Ave *TF:* 800-878-1551 ■ *Web:* www.industronics.com	South Windsor	CT	06074	860-289-1551	289-3526
International Thermal Systems LLC (ITS) 4697 W Greenfield Ave *Web:* internationalthermalsystems.com	Milwaukee	WI	53214	414-672-7700	672-8800
IntriCon Corp 1260 Red Fox Rd *NASDAQ:* IIN ■ *Web:* www.intricon.com	Arden Hills	MN	55112	651-636-9770	636-9503
Ipsen Inc PO Box 6266 *TF:* 800-727-7625 ■ *Web:* www.ipsenusa.com	Rockford	IL	61125	815-332-4941	332-4995
John Zink Company LLC 11920 E Apache St *TF:* 800-421-9242 ■ *Web:* www.johnzink.com	Tulsa	OK	74116	918-234-1800	234-2700
Johnson Gas Appliance Co 520 E Ave NW *TF:* 800-553-5422 ■ *Web:* www.johnsongas.com	Cedar Rapids	IA	52405	319-365-5267	365-6282
JT Thorpe & Son Inc 1060 Hensley St *Web:* www.jtthorpe.com	Richmond	CA	94801	510-233-2500	233-2901
Koch Chemical Technology Group LLC 4111 E 37th St N *Web:* www.kochind.com/IndustryAreas/process.aspx	Wichita	KS	67220	316-828-5500	
Lanly Co, The 26201 Tungsten Rd *Web:* www.lanly.com	Cleveland	OH	44132	216-731-1115	731-7900
Lepel Corp 200-G Executive Dr *Web:* lepel.com	Edgewood	NY	11717	631-586-3300	586-3232
Novatec Inc 222 Thomas Ave *TF:* 800-237-8379 ■ *Web:* www.novatec.com	Baltimore	MD	21225	410-789-4811	789-4638
Paragon Industries Inc 2011 S Town E Blvd *TF:* 800-876-4328 ■ *Web:* www.paragonweb.com	Mesquite	TX	75149	972-288-7557	222-0646
Phoenix Solutions Co 5480 Nathan Ln N Ste 110 *Web:* www.phoenixsolutionsco.com	Plymouth	MN	55442	763-544-2721	546-5617
Pillar Induction Co 21905 Gateway Rd *TF:* 800-558-7733 ■ *Web:* www.pillar.com	Brookfield	WI	53045	262-317-5300	317-5353
Procedyne Corp 11 Industrial Dr *Web:* www.procedyne.com	New Brunswick	NJ	08901	732-249-8347	249-7220
Process Combustion Corp 5460 Curry Rd *Web:* www.pcc-sterling.com	Pittsburgh	PA	15236	412-655-0955	650-5569
Pyronics Inc 17700 Miles Rd *TF:* 800-883-9218 ■ *Web:* www.selas.com	Cleveland	OH	44128	216-662-8800	663-8954
Radio Frequency Company Inc 150 Dover Rd *Web:* www.radiofrequency.com	Millis	MA	02054	508-376-9555	376-9944
Radyne Corp 211 W Boden St *TF:* 800-236-8360 ■ *Web:* www.radyne.com	Milwaukee	WI	53207	414-481-8360	481-8303
Rapid Engineering Inc 1100 7-Mile Rd NW *TF:* 800-536-3461 ■ *Web:* www.rapidengineering.com	Comstock Park	MI	49321	616-784-0500	784-1910
Red-Ray Mfg Co Inc 10-22 County Line Rd *TF:* 800-883-9218 ■ *Web:* www.selas.com	Branchburg	NJ	08876	908-722-0040	722-2535
SECO/Warwick Corp 180 Mercer St *Web:* www.secowarwick.com	Meadville	PA	16335	814-332-8400	724-1407
Selas Heat Technology Company LLC 130 Keystone Dr *TF:* 800-523-6500 ■ *Web:* www.selas.com	Montgomeryville	PA	18936	215-646-6600	646-3536
St. Johnson Co 925 Stanford Ave *TF:* 800-225-1348 ■ *Web:* www.stjohnson.com	Oakland	CA	94608	510-652-6000	652-4302
Steelman Industries Inc 2800 Hwy 135 N *TF:* 800-287-6633 ■ *Web:* www.steelman.com	Kilgore	TX	75662	903-984-3061	984-1384
StrikoDynarad 501 E Roosevelt Ave *TF:* 855-787-4561 ■ *Web:* www.strikodynarad.com	Zeeland	MI	49464	616-772-3705	772-5271
Surface Combustion Inc 1700 Indian Wood Cir *TF:* 800-537-8980 ■ *Web:* www.surfacecombustion.com	Maumee	OH	43537	419-891-7150	891-7151
Swindell Dressler International Co 5100 Casteel Dr *Web:* www.swindelldressler.com	Coraopolis	PA	15108	412-788-7100	
T-M Vacuum Products Inc 630 S Warrington Ave *Web:* www.tmvacuum.com	Cinnaminson	NJ	08077	856-829-2000	829-0990
Tempco Electric Heater Corp 607 N Central Ave *TF:* 888-268-6396 ■ *Web:* www.tempco.com	Wood Dale	IL	60191	630-350-2252	350-0232
Tenova Core 100 Corporate Ctr Dr *Web:* www.tenovacore.com	Coraopolis	PA	15108	412-262-2240	262-2055
Thermal Circuits Inc 1 Technology Way *TF:* 800-808-4328 ■ *Web:* www.thermalcircuits.com	Salem	MA	01970	978-745-1162	741-3420
Thermal Engineering Corp 2741 The Blvd *TF:* 800-331-0097 ■ *Web:* www.tecinfrared.com	Columbia	SC	29209	803-783-0750	783-0756
Thermal Equipment Corp 2030 E University Dr *Web:* www.thermalequipment.com	Rancho Dominguez	CA	90220	310-328-6600	603-9625
Thermal Product Solutions 3827 Riverside Rd *TF:* 800-873-4468 ■ *Web:* www.thermalproductsolutions.com	Riverside	MI	49084	269-849-2700	849-3021
Thermcraft Inc 3950 Overdale Rd *Web:* www.thermcraftinc.com	Winston-Salem	NC	27107	336-784-4800	784-0634
Trent Inc 201 Leverington Ave *TF:* 800-544-8736 ■ *Web:* www.trentheat.com	Philadelphia	PA	19127	215-482-5000	482-9389
Truheat Inc 700 Grand St *TF:* 800-879-6199 ■ *Web:* www.ddrheating.com	Allegan	MI	49010	269-673-2145	673-7219
Webster Engineering & Mfg Company LLC 619 Industrial Rd *Web:* www.webster-engineering.com	Winfield	KS	67156	620-221-7464	221-9447
Wisconsin Oven Corp 2675 Main St *Web:* www.wisoven.com	East Troy	WI	53120	262-642-3938	363-4018

319 FURNITURE - MFR

See Also Baby Products p. 1836; Cabinets - Wood p. 1886; Fixtures - Office & Store p. 2286; Mattresses & Adjustable Beds p. 2734; Recycled Plastics Products p. 3057

Company	City	State	Zip	Phone	Fax
Unisource Solutions Inc 8350 Rex Rd *Web:* www.unisourceit.com	Pico Rivera	CA	90660	562-949-1111	949-7110

319-1 Commercial & Industrial Furniture

Company	City	State	Zip	Phone	Fax
Abco Office Furniture 4121 Rushton St *TF:* 800-336-0070 ■ *Web:* www.abcofurniture.com	Florence	AL	35630	256-767-4100	760-1247
Adelphia Steel Equipment Co 7372 State Rd *TF:* 800-865-8211 ■ *Web:* www.adelphiafurniture.com	Philadelphia	PA	19136	215-333-6300	331-6090
Allied Plastics Company Inc 2001 Walnut St *TF Cust Svc:* 800-999-0386 ■ *Web:* www.alliedplasticsco.com	Jacksonville	FL	32206	904-359-0386	353-4746
Allsteel Inc 2210 Second Ave *TF Cust Svc:* 888-255-7833 ■ *Web:* www.allsteeloffice.com	Muscatine	IA	52761	563-272-4800	272-4887
Anthro Corp 10450 SW Manhasset Dr **Fax Area Code:* 800 ■ *TF:* 800-325-3841 ■ *Web:* www.anthro.com	Tualatin	OR	97062	503-691-2556	325-0045*
Artistic Frame Corp 979 Third Ave 17th Fl *Web:* www.artisticframe.com	New York	NY	10022	212-289-2100	289-2101
Bernhardt Furniture Company Inc 1839 Morganton Blvd *Web:* www.bernhardt.com	Lenoir	NC	28645	828-758-9811	
Bestar Inc 4220 Villeneuve St *TF:* 888-823-7827 ■ *Web:* www.bestar.ca	Lac-Megantic	QC	G6B2C3	819-583-1017	
Bevco Precision Manufacturing Co 21320 Doral Rd *TF:* 800-864-2991 ■ *Web:* www.bevco.com	Waukesha	WI	53186	262-798-9200	
BGD Cos Inc 5323 Lakeland Ave N *TF:* 800-699-3537 ■ *Web:* www.bgdcompanies.com	Minneapolis	MN	55429	612-338-6804	338-4942
Biofit Engineered Products 15500 Biofit Way *TF:* 800-597-0246 ■ *Web:* www.biofit.com	Bowling Green	OH	43402	419-823-1089	823-1342
Boling Furniture Co 311 NE Church Rd *Web:* bolingfurniture.com	Mount Olive	NC	28365	919-635-2400	635-4845
Borroughs Corp 3002 N Burdick St *TF:* 800-748-0227 ■ *Web:* www.borroughs.com	Kalamazoo	MI	49004	269-342-0161	342-4161
Bright Chair Co 51 Railroad Ave *TF:* 888-524-5997 ■ *Web:* www.brightchair.com	Middletown	NY	10940	845-343-2196	
CabotWrenn 405 Rink Dam Rd PO Box 1767 *Web:* www.cabotwrenn.com	Hickory	NC	28603	828-495-4607	495-1294
Carolina Business Furniture LLC 535 Archdale Blvd *TF:* 800-763-0212 ■ *Web:* www.carolinabusinessfurniture.com	Archdale	NC	27263	336-431-9400	431-9511
Carson's Inc PO Box 14186 *Web:* www.carsonsofhp.com	Archdale	NC	27263	336-397-4339	
Cramer Inc 1222 Quebec St **Fax Area Code:* 816 ■ *TF:* 800-366-6700 ■ *Web:* www.cramerinc.com	North Kansas City	MO	64116	800-366-6700	471-7188*
CTB Corp 26327 Fallbrook Ave *Web:* www.ctbcorp.com	Wyoming	MN	55092	651-462-3550	
Danver 1 Grand St *TF:* 888-441-0537 ■ *Web:* www.danver.com	Wallingford	CT	06492	203-269-2300	265-6190
Dar-Ran Furniture Industries 2402 Shore St *TF:* 800-334-7891 ■ *Web:* www.darran.com	High Point	NC	27263	336-861-2400	861-6485

Phone | Fax

Dauphin North America 300 Myrtle Ave ... Boonton NJ 07005 973-263-1100 220-3844*
*Fax Area Code: 800 ■ TF Cust Svc: 800-631-1186 ■ Web: www.dauphin.com

Davis Furniture Industries Inc
2401 S College Dr ... High Point NC 27261 336-889-2009 889-0031
Web: www.davis-furniture.com

Delco Office Systems Div Delco Assoc Inc
55 Old Field Pt Rd ... Greenwich CT 06830 203-661-5101
Web: radarfrog.gatehousemedia.com

Emeco 805 W Elm Ave ... Hanover PA 17331 717-637-5951 633-6018
TF: 800-366-5951 ■ Web: www.emeco.net

Ergotron Inc 1181 Trapp Rd ... Saint Paul MN 55121 651-681-7600 681-7710
TF Sales: 800-888-8458 ■ Web: www.ergotron.com

Executive Office Concepts Inc
1705 S Anderson Ave ... Compton CA 90220 310-537-1657
Web: www.eoccorp.com

Fillip Metal Cabinet Co 4500 W 47th St ... Chicago IL 60632 773-733-7527 376-7507
TF: 800-535-0733 ■ Web: www.fillipmetal.com

First Office 1204 E Sixth St ... Huntingburg IN 47542 800-983-4415 683-7155*
*Fax Area Code: 812 ■ *Fax: Cust Svc ■ TF: 800-983-4415 ■ Web: www.firstoffice.com

Flex-Y-Plan Industries Inc 6960 W Ridge Rd ... Fairview PA 16415 814-474-1565 474-2129
TF Cust Svc: 800-458-0552 ■ Web: www.fyp.com

Flexible-Montisa 323 Acorn St ... Plainwell MI 49080 269-924-0730 685-9195
TF Cust Svc: 800-875-6836 ■ Web: www.montisawork.com

Flexsteel Industries Inc 385 Bell St ... Dubuque IA 52001 563-556-7730
NASDAQ: FLXS ■ Web: www.flexsteel.com

Furniture Values International LLC
601 N 75 Th Ave ... Phoenix AZ 85043 602-442-5600 278-0103
Web: www.aspenhome.net

Geiger International Inc
6095 Fulton Industrial Blvd SW ... Atlanta GA 30336 404-344-1100 836-7519
TF: 800-456-6452 ■ Web: www.geigerfurniture.com

Global Industries Inc 17 W Stow Rd ... Marlton NJ 08053 856-596-3390 596-5684
TF: 800-220-1900 ■ Web: www.globalfurnituregroup.com/us

Groupe Lacasse LLC 99 St-Pierre St ... Sainte-Pie QC J0H1W0 450-772-2495 248-1865*
*Fax Area Code: 888 ■ *Fax: Cust Svc ■ TF: 888-522-2773 ■ Web: www.groupelacasse.com

Gunlocke Company LLC 1 Gunlocke Dr ... Wayland NY 14572 585-728-5111 728-8334*
*Fax: Hum Res ■ TF Cust Svc: 800-828-6300 ■ Web: www.gunlocke.com

H Wilson Co 2245 Delany Rd ... Waukegan IL 60087 800-245-7224 327-1698
TF: 800-245-7224 ■ Web: www.luxorfurn.com

Hausmann Industries Inc 130 Union St ... Northvale NJ 07647 201-767-0255 767-1369
TF: 888-428-7626 ■ Web: www.hausmann.com

Haworth Inc 1 Haworth Ctr ... Holland MI 49423 616-393-3000 393-1570
TF: 800-344-2600 ■ Web: www.haworth.com

Herman Miller Inc 855 E Main Ave ... Zeeland MI 49464 616-654-3000
NASDAQ: MLHR ■ TF: 888-443-4357 ■ Web: www.hermanmiller.com

High Point Furniture Industries Inc
1104 Bedford St PO Box 2063 ... High Point NC 27261 336-431-7101 434-1964
TF: 800-447-3462 ■ Web: www.hpfi.com

Hirsh Industries Inc
3636 Westown Pkwy Ste 100 ... West Des Moines IA 50266 515-299-3200 299-3300
TF: 800-383-7414 ■ Web: www.hirshindustries.com

HON Co 200 Oak St ... Muscatine IA 52761 563-272-7100 328-7257*
*Fax Area Code: 800 ■ TF: 800-553-8230 ■ Web: www.hon.com

Huot Manufacturing Co 550 Wheeler St N ... Saint Paul MN 55104 651-646-1869 646-0457
TF: 800-832-3838 ■ Web: www.huot.com

IAC Industries 895 Beacon St ... Brea CA 92821 714-990-8997 990-0557
TF: 800-989-1422 ■ Web: www.iacindustries.com

Indiana Furniture 1224 Mill St ... Jasper IN 47546 812-482-5727 482-9035
TF: 800-422-5727 ■ Web: www.indianafurniture.com

Interior Crafts Inc 2513 W Cullerton Ave ... Chicago IL 60608 773-376-8160 376-9578
Web: interiorcraftsinc.com

Invincible Office Furniture Co
842 S 26th St PO Box 1117 ... Manitowoc WI 54220 920-682-4601 683-2970
TF: 877-682-4601 ■ Web: www.invinciblefurniture.com

Izzydesign 17237 Van Wagoner Rd ... Spring Lake MI 49456 616-916-9369
TF: 800-543-5449 ■ Web: www.izzyplus.com

Jasper Desk Co 415 E Sixth St ... Jasper IN 47546 812-482-4132 482-9552
TF Cust Svc: 800-365-7994 ■ Web: www.jasperdesk.com

Jasper Seating Company Inc
Jasper Group 225 Clay St ... Jasper IN 47546 812-482-3204 482-1548
TF: 800-622-5661 ■ Web: www.jaspergroup.us.com

JSJ Corp 700 Robbins Rd ... Grand Haven MI 49417 616-842-6350 847-3112
Web: www.jsjcorp.com

Khoury Inc 1129 Webster Ave PO Box 1746 ... Waco TX 76703 254-754-5481 754-1606
TF: 800-725-6765 ■ Web: www.khouryinc.com

KI 1330 Bellevue St ... Green Bay WI 54302 920-468-8100 468-0280
TF: 800-424-2432 ■ Web: ki.com

Kimball Hospitality 1180 E 16th St ... Jasper IN 47549 276-666-8933 634-4324*
*Fax Area Code: 812 ■ TF: 800-634-9510 ■ Web: www.kimballhospitality.com

Kimball Office Furniture Co 1600 Royal St ... Jasper IN 47549 800-482-1818 482-8300*
*Fax Area Code: 812 ■ TF: 800-482-1818 ■ Web: www.kimballoffice.com

Knoll Inc 1235 Water St ... East Greenville PA 18041 215-679-7991
NYSE: KNL ■ TF Cust Svc: 800-343-5665 ■ Web: www.knoll.com

Lakeside Manufacturing Inc
4900 W Electric Ave ... West Milwaukee WI 53219 414-902-6400 902-6446
TF: 800-558-8565 ■ Web: www.elakeside.com

LB Furniture Industries LLC 99 S Third St ... Hudson NY 12534 518-828-1501
TF: 800-221-8752 ■ Web: www.lbempire.com

Liberty Furniture Industries
6195 Purdue Dr SW ... Atlanta GA 30336 404-629-1003 629-0717*
*Fax: Cust Svc ■ Web: www.mylibertyfurniture.com

Luxor Div EBSCO Industries Inc
2245 Delany Rd ... Waukegan IL 60087 847-244-1800 327-1698*
*Fax Area Code: 800 ■ TF: 800-323-4656 ■ Web: www.luxorfurn.com

Magna Design Inc 26246 Twelve Trees Ln NW ... Poulsbo WA 98370 360-394-1300
TF: 800-426-1202 ■ Web: www.magnadesign.com

Martin Furniture 2345 Britannia Blvd ... San Diego CA 92154 800-268-5669 671-5199*
*Fax Area Code: 619 ■ TF Cust Svc: 800-268-5669 ■ Web: www.martinfurniture.com

Marvel Group Inc 3843 W 43rd St ... Chicago IL 60632 800-621-8846 237-0358*
*Fax: Cust Svc ■ TF Cust Svc: 800-621-8846 ■ Web: www.marvelgroup.com

Maxon Furniture Inc 660 SW 39th St Ste 150 ... Renton WA 98057 800-876-4274 257-2635
TF Cust Svc: 800-876-4274 ■ Web: www.maxonfurniture.com

Phone | Fax

Mayline Group 619 N Commerce St PO Box 728 ... Sheboygan WI 53082 920-457-5537 457-7388
TF: 800-822-8037 ■ Web: www.mayline.com

McDowell-Craig Office Furniture
13146 Firestone Blvd ... Norwalk CA 90650 562-921-4441
Web: www.mcdowellcraig.com

Midwest Commercial Interiors
987 SW Temple ... Salt Lake City UT 84101 801-505-4288
Web: www.midwestcommercialinteriors.com

MLP Seating Corp 950 Pratt Blvd ... Elk Grove Village IL 60007 847-956-1700 956-1776
TF: 800-723-3030 ■ Web: www.mlpseating.com

MTS Seating Inc 7100 Industrial Dr ... Temperance MI 48182 734-847-3875 329-0687*
*Fax Area Code: 800 ■ Web: www.mtsseating.com

National Business Services 1601 Magoffin Ave ... El Paso TX 79901 915-544-1271
Web: www.nbsinc.com

National Office Furniture 1205 Kimball Blvd ... Jasper IN 47549 800-482-1717 482-8800*
*Fax Area Code: 812 ■ TF: 800-482-1717 ■ Web: www.nationalofficefurniture.com

NER Data Products Inc 307 S Delsea Dr ... Glassboro NJ 08028 888-637-3282 881-5524*
*Fax Area Code: 856 ■ TF: 888-637-3282 ■ Web: www.nerdata.com

Neutral Posture Inc 3904 N Texas Ave ... Bryan TX 77803 979-778-0502 778-0408
TF: 800-446-3746 ■ Web: neutralposture.com

Nomanco Inc 501 Nmc Dr ... Zebulon NC 27597 919-269-6500 269-7936
TF: 800-345-7279 ■ Web: www.nomaco.com

Nova Solutions Inc 421 Industrial Ave ... Effingham IL 62401 217-342-7070 940-6682*
*Fax Area Code: 800 ■ TF: 800-730-6682 ■ Web: www.novadesk.com

Office Chairs Inc 14815 Radburn Ave ... Santa Fe Springs CA 90670 562-802-0464 926-5561
TF: 866-624-4968 ■ Web: ocicontract.com

Omni International Inc
435 12th St SW PO Box 1409 ... Vernon AL 35592 205-695-9173 695-6465

Open Plan Systems Inc
4700 Deepwater Terminal Rd ... Richmond VA 23234 804-275-2468 275-2329
TF: 844-677-6771 ■ Web: www.openplan.com

Paoli Inc 201 E Martin St ... Orleans IN 47452 800-472-8669 865-1516*
*Fax Area Code: 812 ■ TF: 800-472-8669 ■ Web: www.paoli.com

Penco Products Inc 1820 Stonehenge Dr ... Oaks PA 19456 800-562-1000 666-7561*
*Fax Area Code: 610 ■ TF: 800-562-1000 ■ Web: www.pencoproducts.com

Plymold 615 Centennial Dr ... Kenyon MN 55946 800-759-6653
TF: 800-759-6653 ■ Web: www.plymold.com

Reconditioned Systems Inc (RSI)
2636 S Wilson St Ste 105 ... Tempe AZ 85282 480-968-1772 894-1907
TF: 800-280-5000 ■ Web: www.rsisystemsfurniture.com

Robertson Furniture Company Inc
890 Elberton St ... Toccoa GA 30577 706-886-1494 886-8998
TF: 800-241-0713 ■ Web: www.robertson-furniture.com

Rush Industries Inc 118 N Wrenn St ... High Point NC 27260 336-886-7700 886-2227
TF: 800-524-0258 ■ Web: www.rushfurniture.com

Safco Products Co 9300 W Research Ctr Rd ... New Hope MN 55428 763-536-6700 536-6784
TF Cust Svc: 800-328-3020 ■ Web: www.safcoproducts.com

Sedgewick Industries 667 W Ward Ave ... High Point NC 27260 336-885-9300 885-9174
Web: www.sedgewick.com

Shafer Commercial Seating 4101 E 48th Ave ... Denver CO 80216 303-322-7792 393-1836
Web: www.shafer.com

Shure Manufacturing Corp 1901 W Main St ... Washington MO 63090 636-390-7100 390-7171
TF: 800-227-4873 ■ Web: www.shureusa.com

Southwood Furniture Corp 2860 Nathan St ... Hickory NC 28602 828-465-1776 465-0858
Web: www.southwoodfurn.com

Spectrum Industries Inc 925 First Ave ... Chippewa Falls WI 54729 715-723-6750 335-0473*
*Fax Area Code: 800 ■ TF: 800-235-1262 ■ Web: www.spectrumfurniture.com

Statton Furniture Mfg Company Inc
504 E First St ... Hagerstown MD 21740 301-739-0360 739-8421
Web: www.statton.com

Steelcase Inc 801 44th St SE PO Box 1967 ... Grand Rapids MI 49501 616-247-2710 247-2256*
NYSE: SCS ■ *Fax: Mail Rm ■ TF: 888-783-3522 ■ Web: www.steelcase.com/asia-en

Stevens Industries Inc 704 W Main St ... Teutopolis IL 62467 217-540-3100 857-7101
Web: www.stevensind.com

Stylex PO Box 5038 ... Delanco NJ 08075 800-257-5742 461-5574*
*Fax Area Code: 856 ■ TF: 800-257-5742 ■ Web: www.stylexseating.com

TAB Products Co 605 Fourth St ... Mayville WI 53050 888-466-8228 304-4947*
*Fax Area Code: 800 ■ TF: 888-466-8228 ■ Web: www.tab.com

Techline USA LLC 500 S Div St ... Waunakee WI 53597 608-849-4181 850-2379
TF: 800-356-8400

Teknion Corp 1150 Flint Rd ... Toronto ON M3J2J5 416-661-3370 661-4586
Web: www.teknion.com

Tennsco Corp 201 Tennsco Dr PO Box 1888 ... Dickson TN 37056 615-446-8000 722-0134*
*Fax Area Code: 800 ■ TF Cust Svc: 866-446-8686 ■ Web: www.tennsco.com

Trendway Corp 13467 Quincy St PO Box 9016 ... Holland MI 49422 616-399-3900
TF: 800-968-5344 ■ Web: www.trendway.com

Tuohy Furniture Corp 42 St Albans Pl ... Chatfield MN 55923 507-867-4280 867-3374
TF Cust Svc: 800-533-1696 ■ Web: www.tuohyfurniture.com

Ulrich Planfiling Equipment Corp
2120 Fourth Ave PO Box 135 ... Lakewood NY 14750 716-763-1815 763-1818
Web: www.ulrichcorp.com

Viking Acoustical Corp 21480 Heath Ave ... Lakeville MN 55044 952-469-3405 469-4503
TF: 800-328-8385 ■ Web: www.vikingusa.com

Vitro Seating Products Inc
201 Madison St ... Saint Louis MO 63102 314-241-2265 241-8723
TF Cust Svc: 800-325-7093 ■ Web: www.vitroseating.com

Watson Furniture Group Inc
26246 Twelve Trees Ln NW ... Poulsbo WA 98370 360-394-1300 394-1322
TF: 800-426-1202 ■ Web: www.watsonfurniture.com

West Coast Industries Inc
10 Jackson St ... San Francisco CA 94111 415-621-6656 552-5368
TF: 800-243-3150 ■ Web: www.westcoastindustries.com

Workplace Systems Inc 562 Mammoth Rd ... Londonderry NH 03053 603-622-3727 622-0174
TF: 800-258-9700 ■ Web: www.workplacesystemsinc.com

Wright Line LLC 160 Gold Star Blvd ... Worcester MA 01606 508-852-4300 853-8904
TF: 800-225-7348 ■ Web: www.wrightline.com

319-2 Household Furniture

Phone | Fax

Acacia Home & Garden Inc
101 McLin Creek Rd N PO Box 426 ... Conover NC 28613 828-465-1700 465-4205
Web: www.acaciahomeandgarden.com

Alan White Co 506 Thomas St. ... Stamps AR 71860 870-533-4471
Web: www.alanwhiteco.com

Albany Industries Inc 504 N Glenfield Rd ... New Albany MS 38652 662-534-9800 534-9805
TF: 877-534-9804 ■ *Web:* www.albanyindustries.com

Ameriwood Industries Inc
410 E S First St. ... Wright City MO 63390 636-745-3351
TF General: 800-489-3351 ■ *Web:* www.ameriwood.com

Ashley Furniture Industries Inc 1 Ashley Way ... Arcadia WI 54612 608-323-6225 323-6008
TF: 800-477-2222 ■ *Web:* www.ashleyfurniture.com

Baby's Dream Furniture Inc
411 Industrial Blvd ... Buena Vista GA 31803 229-649-4404 649-2007
TF: 800-835-2742 ■ *Web:* www.babysdream.com

Bassett Furniture Industries Inc
3525 Fairystone Pk Hwy PO Box 626 ... Bassett VA 24055 714-222-1010
NASDAQ: BSET ■ *TF:* 877-525-7070 ■ *Web:* www.bassettfurniture.com

Bauhaus USA Inc 1 Bauhaus Dr ... Saltillo MS 38866 662-869-2664 869-5910
Web: www.bauhaususa.com

Bellini 495 Central Ave ... Scarsdale NY 10583 914-472-7336
Web: www.bellini.com

Berg Furniture 120 E Gloucester Pike ... Barrington NJ 08007 856-310-0511 310-0512
Web: www.bergfurniture.com

Bielecky Bros Inc 979 Third Ave ... New York NY 10022 212-753-2355 751-9369
Web: www.bieleckybrothers.com

Bradington-Young 1340 14th Ave Ct SW ... Hickory NC 28602 704-435-5881 435-4276
Web: www.bradington-young.com

Broyhill Furniture Industries Inc
3483 Hickory Blvd ... Hudson NC 28638 800-225-0265
TF Cust Svc: 800-225-0265 ■ *Web:* www.broyhillfurniture.com

Brueton Industries Inc 146 Hanse Ave ... Freeport NY 11520 516-379-3400 543-4520
TF Cust Svc: 800-221-6783 ■ *Web:* www.brueton.com

Bush Industries Inc 1 Mason Dr ... Jamestown NY 14701 716-665-2000 665-2074
TF: 800-950-4782 ■ *Web:* www.bushfurniture.com

Bushline Inc 707 Industrial Pk Rd ... New Tazewell TN 37825 423-626-5246
Web: bushline.com

Canadel Furniture Inc 700 Canadel Ave ... Louiseville QC J5V2L6 819-228-8471 228-8389
Web: www.canadel.com

Capris Furniture Industries Inc
1401 NW 27th Ave ... Ocala FL 34475 352-629-8889 732-7310
Web: www.caprisfurniture.com

Carrom 218 E Dowland St. ... Ludington MI 49431 231-845-1263 843-9276
TF: 800-223-6047 ■ *Web:* www.carrom.com

Carson's Inc PO Box 14186 ... Archdale NC 27263 336-397-4339
Web: www.carsonsofhp.com

Century Furniture LLC 401 11th St NW ... Hickory NC 28601 828-328-1851 328-2176
TF: 800-852-5552 ■ *Web:* www.centuryfurniture.com

Chromcraft Revington Inc
1330 Win Hentschel Blvd ... West Lafayette IN 47906 765-807-2640
OTC: CRCV ■ *Web:* www.chromcraft-revington.com

Classic Leather Inc PO Box 2404 ... Hickory NC 28603 828-328-2046 324-6212
Web: www.classic-leather.com

Craftmaster Furniture Corp
221 Craftmaster Rd. ... Hiddenite NC 28636 828-632-9786 632-0301
Web: www.cmfurniture.com

Cresent Fine Furniture PO Box 1438 ... Gallatin TN 37066 615-452-1671
Web: www.cresent.com

DeFehr Furniture Ltd 125 Furniture Pk ... Winnipeg MB R2G1B9 204-988-5630 663-4458
TF: 877-333-3471 ■ *Web:* www.defehr.com

DMI Furniture Inc
9780 Ormsby Stn Rd Ste 2000 ... Louisville KY 40223 502-426-4351
Web: www.dmifurniture.com

Dorel Industries Inc 1255 Greene Ave Ste 300 ... Montreal QC H3Z2A4 514-934-3034 934-9379
TSE: DII.B ■ *Web:* www.dorel.com

Durham Furniture Inc 450 Lambton St W ... Durham ON N0G1R0 519-369-2345 369-6515
Web: durhamfurniture.com

Dutailier Group Inc 299 Rue Chaput ... Sainte-Pie QC J0H1W0 450-772-2403 772-5055
TF: 800-363-9817 ■ *Web:* www.dutailier.com

El Ran Furniture Ltd
2751 Transcanada Hwy ... Pointe-Claire QC H9R1B4 514-630-5656
TF: 800-361-6546 ■ *Web:* www.elran.com

Ethan Allen Interiors Inc Ethan Allen Dr. ... Danbury CT 06811 888-324-3571 743-8298*
NYSE: ETH ■ **Fax Area Code:* 203 ■ *TF:* 888-324-3571 ■ *Web:* www.ethanallen.com

Evenflo Company Inc 1801 Commerce Dr ... Piqua OH 45356 800-233-5921
TF: 800-233-5921 ■ *Web:* www.evenflo.com

Fairfield Chair Co PO Box 1710 ... Lenoir NC 28645 828-758-5571 758-0211
Web: www.fairfieldchair.com

Finnleo Sauna 575 Cokato St E ... Cokato MN 55321 800-346-6536 286-2224*
**Fax Area Code:* 320 ■ *TF:* 800-346-6536 ■ *Web:* www.finnleo.com

Flexsteel Industries Inc 385 Bell St ... Dubuque IA 52001 563-556-7730
NASDAQ: FLXS ■ *Web:* www.flexsteel.com

Franklin Corp 600 Franklin Dr ... Houston MS 38851 662-456-4286 456-0008
Web: franklincorp.com

Furniture Values International LLC
601 N 75 Th Ave ... Phoenix AZ 85043 602-442-5600 278-0103
Web: www.aspenhome.net

Hancock & Moore PO Box 3444 ... Hickory NC 28603 828-495-8235 495-3021
Web: www.hancockandmoore.com

Harden Furniture Inc
8550 Mill Pond Way ... McConnellsville NY 13401 315-245-1000 245-2884
Web: www.hardenfurniture.com

Hekman 860 E Main Ave ... Zeeland MI 49464 616-748-2660 748-2645
Web: www.hekman.com

Henkel Harris Company Inc
2983 S Pleasant Vly Rd ... Winchester VA 22601 540-667-4900 667-8261
Web: www.henkelharris.com

Hooker Furniture Corp
440 E Commonwealth Blvd ... Martinsville VA 24112 276-632-0459 388-2289*
NASDAQ: HOFT ■ **Fax Area Code:* 800 ■ **Fax:* Cust Svc ■ *TF Cust Svc:* 800-422-1511 ■ *Web:* www.hookerfurniture.com

Hughes Furniture Industries Inc
952 S Stout Rd ... Randleman NC 27317 336-498-8700 498-8750
Web: www.hughesfurniture.com

Human Touch 3030 Walnut Ave ... Long Beach CA 90807 562-426-8700 426-9690
TF: 800-742-5493 ■ *Web:* www.humantouch.com

Interior Crafts Inc 2513 W Cullerton Ave ... Chicago IL 60608 773-376-8160 376-9578
Web: interiorcraftsinc.com

J-Art Iron Co 9435 Jefferson Blvd ... Culver City CA 90232 310-202-1126 202-1642
Web: www.jartiron.com

Kessler Industries 8600 Gateway Blvd E ... El Paso TX 79907 915-591-8161 598-7353
Web: www.kesslerind.com

King Hickory Furniture Co 1820 Main Ave SE ... Hickory NC 28602 828-322-6025 328-2159
Web: www.kinghickory.com

Klaussner Home Furnishings 405 Lewallen Rd ... Asheboro NC 27205 336-625-6174 625-5584
Web: www.klaussner.com

La-Z-Boy Inc 1284 N Telegraph Rd ... Monroe MI 48162 734-242-1444 457-2005*
NYSE: LZB ■ **Fax:* Sales ■ *TF:* 800-375-6890 ■ *Web:* www.la-z-boy.com

Lamont Ltd 1530 Bluff Rd ... Burlington IA 52601 319-753-5131 753-0946
TF: 800-553-5621 ■ *Web:* www.lamontlimited.com

Leathercraft PO Box 639 ... Conover NC 28613 800-627-1561 627-1562
TF: 800-627-1561 ■ *Web:* www.leathercraft-furniture.com

Lexington Home Brands 1300 National Hwy ... Thomasville NC 27360 336-474-5300
Web: www.lexington.com

Little Tikes Co, The 2180 Barlow Rd ... Hudson OH 44236 800-321-0183
TF Cust Svc: 800-321-0183 ■ *Web:* www.littletikes.com

Mantua Mfg Co 7900 Northfield Rd ... Walton Hills OH 44146 800-333-8333 929-8014
TF Orders: 800-333-8333 ■ *Web:* www.bedframes.com

Marge Carson Inc 9056 Garvey Ave ... Rosemead CA 91770 626-571-1111
Web: margecarson.com

McGuire Furniture Co 1201 Bryant St ... San Francisco CA 94103 415-626-1414 864-8593
TF: 800-662-4847 ■ *Web:* www.mcguirefurniture.com

Michael Thomas Furniture Inc
100 E Newberry Ave ... Liberty NC 27298 336-622-3075
Web: themtcompany.com

Million Dollar Baby 841 Washington Blvd ... Montebello CA 90640 323-728-9988
Web: www.milliondollarbaby.com

Mitchell Gold & Bob Williams Co (MGBW)
135 One Comfortable Pl ... Taylorsville NC 28681 828-632-9200 632-2693
TF: 800-789-5401 ■ *Web:* www.mgbwhome.com

New England Woodcraft Inc PO Box 165 ... Forest Dale VT 05745 802-247-8211 247-8042
Web: www.newoodcraft.com

Nichols & Stone 1 Stickley Dr PO Box 480 ... Manlius NY 13104 315-682-1554
Web: www.nichols-stone.com

Norwalk Furniture Corp 100 Furniture Pkwy ... Norwalk OH 44857 419-744-3200
Web: www.norwalkfurniture.com

Pearson Co 1420 Progress Ave ... High Point NC 27260 336-882-8135
TF: 800-225-0265 ■ *Web:* www.pearsonco.com

Perdue Woodworks Inc 2415 Creek Dr ... Rapid City SD 57703 605-341-2101 341-1565
Web: www.perduesinc.com

Progressive Furniture Inc PO Box 308 ... Archbold OH 43502 828-459-2151 459-9702
Web: www.progressivefurniture.com

Riverside Furniture Corp 1400 S Sixth St ... Fort Smith AR 72901 479-785-8100 785-6009
Web: www.riverside-furniture.com

Robern Inc 701 N Wilson Ave ... Bristol PA 19007 215-826-9800
TF: 800-877-2376 ■ *Web:* www.robern.com

Room & Board Inc
4600 Olson Memorial Hwy ... Golden Valley MN 55422 763-521-4431 520-0811
TF: 800-301-9720 ■ *Web:* www.roomandboard.com

Rumble Tuff Inc 865 North 1430 West ... Orem UT 84057 801-609-8168 796-2688
TF: 855-228-8388 ■ *Web:* www.rumbletuff.com

Rush Industries Inc 118 N Wrenn St ... High Point NC 27260 336-886-7700 886-2227
TF: 800-524-0258 ■ *Web:* www.rushfurniture.com

Sam Moore Furniture Industries 1556 Dawn Dr ... Bedford VA 24523 540-586-8253 586-8497
Web: www.sammoore.com

Sauder Woodworking Co
502 Middle St PO Box 156 ... Archbold OH 43502 419-446-2711 446-3692
TF Cust Svc: 800-523-3987 ■ *Web:* www.sauder.com

Schnadig International Corp 4200 Tudor Ln ... Greensboro NC 27410 800-468-8730
TF: 800-468-8730 ■ *Web:* www.schnadig.com

Shermag Inc 3035 Boul Industriel ... Sherbrooke QC J1L2T9 819-566-1515 566-7323
Web: www.shermag.com

Sherrill Furniture Co 2405 Highland Ave NE ... Hickory NC 28601 828-322-2640
Web: www.sherrillfurniture.com

Sico North America Inc 7525 Cahill Rd ... Minneapolis MN 55439 952-941-1700 941-6737
TF: 800-328-6138 ■ *Web:* www.sicoinc.com

Southern Motion Inc 161 Prestige Dr ... Pontotoc MS 38863 662-488-9301
Web: www.southernmotion.com

Southwood Furniture Corp 2860 Nathan St ... Hickory NC 28602 828-465-1776 465-0858
Web: www.southwoodfurn.com

Standard Furniture Mfg Company Inc
801 Hwy 31 S ... Bay Minette AL 36507 251-937-6741 937-1178*
**Fax:* Cust Svc ■ *TF General:* 877-788-1899 ■ *Web:* www.standard-furniture.com

Stanley Furniture Co Inc
200 North Hamilton St ... High Point NC 27260 877-772-4858
NASDAQ: STLY ■ *TF:* 877-772-4858 ■ *Web:* www.stanleyfurniture.com

Statton Furniture Mfg Company Inc
504 E First St ... Hagerstown MD 21740 301-739-0360 739-8421
Web: www.statton.com

Storkcraft Baby 7433 Nelson Rd ... Richmond BC V6W1G3 604-274-5121 274-9727
TF: 877-274-0277 ■ *Web:* www.storkcraftdirect.com

Style Line Furniture Inc 116 Godfrey Rd ... Verona MS 38879 662-566-1113 566-7657
Web: styleline.us

Suncast Corp 701 N Kirk Rd ... Batavia IL 60510 630-879-2050 879-6112
TF: 800-444-3310 ■ *Web:* suncast.com

Swaim Inc 1801 S College Dr ... High Point NC 27260 336-885-6131 885-6227
Web: www.swaim-inc.com

Techline USA LLC 500 S Div St ... Waunakee WI 53597 608-849-4181 850-2379
TF: 800-356-8400

Phone | Fax

Thomasville Furniture Industries Inc
401 E Main St PO Box 339 .... Thomasville NC 27361 336-472-4000
Web: www.thomasville.com

Vanguard Furniture Co Inc 109 Simpson St .... Conover NC 28613 828-328-5601
Web: www.vanguardfurniture.com

Walter E Smithe Furniture Inc
1251 W Thorndale Ave .... Itasca IL 60143 630-285-8000 620-1552
TF: 800-948-4263 ■ *Web:* www.smithe.com

Whittier Wood Products
3787 W First Ave PO Box 2827 .... Eugene OR 97402 541-687-0213 687-2060
TF: 800-653-3336 ■ *Web:* www.whittierwood.com

Winners Only Inc 1365 Pk Ctr Dr .... Vista CA 92081 760-599-0300
Web: www.winnersonly.com

Woodland Furniture 4475 S 15th W .... Idaho Falls ID 83402 208-523-9006
Web: www.woodlandfurniture.com

Zenith Products Corp 400 Lukens Dr .... New Castle DE 19720 800-892-3986 326-8400*
**Fax Area Code:* 302 ■ **Fax:* Cust Svc ■ *TF:* 800-892-3986 ■ *Web:* zenith-products.com

319-3 Institutional & Other Public Buildings Furniture

Phone | Fax

Achieva Inc 197 Funder Dr PO Box 729 .... Mocksville NC 27028 336-751-7104
TF: 800-788-7213 ■ *Web:* www.achievaweb.com

Adden Furniture Inc 710 Chelmsford St .... Lowell MA 01851 978-454-7848 453-1449
TF: 800-625-3876 ■ *Web:* www.addenfurniture.com

American Desk 1302 Industrial Blvd .... Temple TX 76504 800-433-3142 773-7370*
**Fax Area Code:* 254 ■ *TF:* 800-433-3142 ■ *Web:* americandesk.com

American Seating Co
401 American Seating Ctr NW .... Grand Rapids MI 49504 616-732-6600 732-6401
TF Cust Svc: 800-748-0268 ■ *Web:* www.americanseating.com

Artco-Bell Corp 1302 Industrial Blvd .... Temple TX 76504 254-778-1811 771-0827
TF: 877-778-1811 ■ *Web:* www.artcobell.com

Bay Concepts Inc (BCI) 1036-47th Ave PO Box 7229 ..... Oakland CA 94601 510-534-4511 534-4515

Bretford Manufacturing Inc
11000 Seymour Ave .... Franklin Park IL 60131 847-678-2545 343-1779*
**Fax Area Code:* 800 ■ *TF:* 800-521-9614 ■ *Web:* www.bretford.com

Brodart Co 500 Arch St .... Williamsport PA 17701 570-326-2461
TF: 800-233-8467 ■ *Web:* www.brodart.com

Columbia Mfg Inc 1 Cycle St .... Westfield MA 01085 413-562-3664 568-5345
Web: www.columbiamfginc.com

ENOCHS Examining Room Furniture
PO Box 50559 .... Indianapolis IN 46250 800-428-2305 580-2944*
**Fax Area Code:* 317 ■ **Fax:* Cust Svc ■ *TF Cust Svc:* 800-428-2305 ■ *Web:* www.enochsmed.com

ErgoGenesis LLC 1 BodyBilt Pl .... Navasota TX 77868 936-825-1700 825-1725
TF: 800-364-5299 ■ *Web:* www.ergogenesis.com

Fleetwood Group Inc 11832 James St .... Holland MI 49424 616-396-1142
TF: 800-257-6390 ■ *Web:* www.fleetwoodgroup.com

Fordham Equipment Co
1204 Village Market Place Ste 262 .... Morrisville NC 27560 919-467-0708
TF: 866-467-0708 ■ *Web:* www.fordhamplastics.com

Furniture by Thurston 12250 Charles Dr .... Grass Valley CA 95945 530-272-4331 272-4962
Web: thurstonmfg.net

Gaylord Bros 7282 William Barry Blvd .... Syracuse NY 13212 315-457-5070 453-5030
TF: 800-345-5330 ■ *Web:* www.gaylord.com

Gunlocke Company LLC 1 Gunlocke Dr .... Wayland NY 14572 585-728-5111 728-8334*
**Fax:* Hum Res ■ *TF Cust Svc:* 800-828-6300 ■ *Web:* www.gunlocke.com

HAECO Americas 10262 Norris Ave .... Pacoima CA 91331 818-896-2938
Web: www.haeco.aero

Hard Mfg Company Inc 230 Grider St .... Buffalo NY 14215 800-873-4273
TF: 800-873-4273 ■ *Web:* www.hardmfg.com

Herman Miller for Health Care
855 E Main Ave PO Box 302 .... Zeeland MI 49464 616-654-3000
TF: 888-443-4357 ■ *Web:* www.hermanmiller.com/healthcare

Hill-Rom Services Inc 1069 SR 46 E .... Batesville IN 47006 812-934-7777 934-8189
TF: 800-267-2337 ■ *Web:* www.hill-rom.com

Hussey Seating Co 38 Dyer St Ext .... North Berwick ME 03906 207-676-2271 676-2222*
**Fax:* Sales ■ *TF:* 800-341-0401 ■ *Web:* www.husseyseating.com

Imperial Woodworks Inc PO Box 7835 PO Box 7835 .... Waco TX 76714 800-234-6624 741-0736*
**Fax Area Code:* 254 ■ *TF:* 800-234-6624 ■ *Web:* www.pews.com

Interkal Inc 5981 E Cork St .... Kalamazoo MI 49048 269-349-1521 349-6530
Web: www.interkal.com

Irwin Seating Company Inc
3251 Fruit Ridge NW .... Grand Rapids MI 49544 616-574-7400 574-7411
TF: 866-464-7946 ■ *Web:* www.irwinseating.com

Joerns Healthcare 5001 Joerns Dr .... Stevens Point WI 54481 715-341-3600 457-8827*
**Fax Area Code:* 800 ■ *TF:* 800-826-0270

Kimball Hospitality 1180 E 16th St .... Jasper IN 47549 276-666-8933 634-4324*
**Fax Area Code:* 812 ■ *TF:* 800-634-9510 ■ *Web:* www.kimballhospitality.com

KLN Steel Products Co 2 Winnco Dr .... San Antonio TX 78218 210-227-4747 227-4047
TF: 800-624-9101 ■ *Web:* www.kln.com

LB Furniture Industries LLC 99 S Third St .... Hudson NY 12534 518-828-1501
TF: 800-221-8752 ■ *Web:* www.lbempire.com

List Industries Inc
401 Jim Moran Blvd .... Deerfield Beach FL 33442 954-429-9155 428-3843
TF: 800-776-1342 ■ *Web:* www.listindustries.com

Luxor Div EBSCO Industries Inc
2245 Delany Rd .... Waukegan IL 60087 847-244-1800 327-1698*
**Fax Area Code:* 800 ■ *TF:* 800-323-4656 ■ *Web:* www.luxorfurn.com

Meadows Office Furniture Co 71 W 23rd St .... New York NY 10010 212-741-0333 741-0303
Web: meadowsofficeinteriors.com

Meco Corp 1500 Industrial Rd .... Greeneville TN 37745 800-251-7558 639-1055*
**Fax Area Code:* 423 ■ *TF:* 800-251-7558 ■ *Web:* www.meco.net

Midwest Folding Products Inc
1414 S Western Ave .... Chicago IL 60608 312-666-3366 666-2606
TF: 800-621-4716 ■ *Web:* www.midwestfolding.com

Mitchell Furniture Systems Inc
1700 W St Paul Ave .... Milwaukee WI 53233 414-342-3111 342-4239
TF: 800-290-5960 ■ *Web:* www.mitchell-tables.com

Mity-Lite Inc 1301 West 400 North .... Orem UT 84057 801-224-0589 224-6191
TF: 800-909-8034 ■ *Web:* www.mitylite.com

MLP Seating Corp 950 Pratt Blvd .... Elk Grove Village IL 60007 847-956-1700 956-1776
TF: 800-723-3030 ■ *Web:* www.mlpseating.com

Phone | Fax

Monroe Table Co 316 N Walnut St .... Colfax IA 50054 515-674-3511 674-3513

Nemschoff Healthcare Furniture and Clinic Furniture
909 N Eigth St .... Sheboygan WI 53081 800-203-8916 459-1234*
**Fax Area Code:* 920 ■ *TF Cust Svc:* 800-203-8916 ■ *Web:* www.nemschoff.com

New Holland Church Furniture
313 Prospect St PO Box 217 .... New Holland PA 17557 800-648-9663 354-2481*
**Fax Area Code:* 717 ■ *TF:* 800-648-9663 ■ *Web:* www.newhollandwood.com

Omni International Inc
435 12th St SW PO Box 1409 .... Vernon AL 35592 205-695-9173 695-6465

Parisi Royal Inc 305 Pheasant Run .... Newtown PA 18940 215-968-6677 968-3580

Scholarcraft Inc PO Box 170748 .... Birmingham AL 35217 205-841-1922
Web: www.scholarcraft.com

Shelby Williams Industries Inc
810 W Hwy 25/70 .... Newport TN 37821 423-623-0031 319-9371*
**Fax Area Code:* 866 ■ *TF General:* 800-873-3252 ■ *Web:* shelbywilliams.com

Sico North America Inc 7525 Cahill Rd .... Minneapolis MN 55439 952-941-1700 941-6737
TF: 800-328-6138 ■ *Web:* www.sicoinc.com

Spectrum Industries Inc 925 First Ave .... Chippewa Falls WI 54729 715-723-6750 335-0473*
**Fax Area Code:* 800 ■ *TF:* 800-235-1262 ■ *Web:* www.spectrumfurniture.com

Sturdisteel Co PO Box 2655 .... Waco TX 76702 800-433-3116
TF: 800-433-3116 ■ *Web:* www.sturdisteel.com

Tesco Industries LP 1035 E Hacienda .... Bellville TX 77418 800-699-5824 865-9074*
**Fax Area Code:* 979 ■ *TF:* 800-699-5824 ■ *Web:* www.tesco-ind.com

TMI Systems Design Corp 50 S Third Ave W .... Dickinson ND 58601 701-456-6716 456-6700
TF: 800-456-6716 ■ *Web:* www.tmisystems.com

UMF Medical 1316 Eisenhower Blvd .... Johnstown PA 15904 814-266-8726 266-1870
TF: 800-638-5322 ■ *Web:* www.umfmedical.com

Valley City Mfg Co Ltd, The 64 Hatt St .... Dundas ON L9H2G3 905-628-2253 628-0753
Web: www.valleycity.com

Virco Manufacturing Corp 2027 Harpers Way .... Torrance CA 90501 310-533-0474 258-7367*
NASDAQ: VIRC ■ **Fax Area Code:* 800 ■ *TF Cust Svc:* 800-448-4726 ■ *Web:* www.virco.com

Wieland 13737 Main St PO Box 1000 .... Grabill IN 46741 260-627-3686 627-6496
TF: 888-943-5263 ■ *Web:* www.wielandhealthcare.com

Winco Inc 5516 SW First Ln .... Ocala FL 34474 352-854-2929 854-9544
TF: 800-237-3377 ■ *Web:* www.wincomfg.com

Worden Company Inc 199 E 17th St .... Holland MI 49423 616-392-1848 392-2542
TF: 800-748-0561 ■ *Web:* www.wordencompany.com

319-4 Outdoor Furniture

Phone | Fax

A Homecrest Outdoor Living LLC
1250 Homecrest Ave .... Wadena MN 56482 218-631-1000
Web: www.homecrest.com

Belson Outdoors Inc 111 N River Rd .... North Aurora IL 60542 630-897-8489 897-0573
TF: 800-323-5664 ■ *Web:* www.belson.com

Bemis Manufacturing Co 300 Mill St .... Sheboygan Falls WI 53085 920-467-4621 467-8573
TF: 800-558-7651 ■ *Web:* www.bemismfg.com

Brown Jordan Co 9860 Gidley St .... El Monte CA 91731 800-743-4252
TF: 800-743-4252 ■ *Web:* www.brownjordan.com

CFI Manufacturing Inc 2150 Whitfield Ave .... Sarasota FL 34243 941-751-1000

Cox Industries Inc
860 Cannon Bridge Rd PO Box 1124 .... Orangeburg SC 29116 803-534-7467 534-1410
TF: 800-476-4401 ■ *Web:* www.coxwood.com

DuMor Inc PO Box 142 .... Mifflintown PA 17059 717-436-2106 436-9839
TF: 800-598-4018 ■ *Web:* www.dumor.com

Gardenside Ltd 808 Anthony St Ste 140 .... Berkeley CA 94710 415-455-4500 455-4505
TF: 888-999-8325 ■ *Web:* www.gardenside.com

Hatteras Hammocks Inc 305 Industrial Blvd .... Greenville NC 27834 252-758-0641 758-0375
TF: 800-643-3522 ■ *Web:* www.hatterashammocks.com

Hill Co 8040 Germantown Ave .... Philadelphia PA 19118 215-247-7600 247-7603
Web: www.hill-company.com

J Robert Scott Inc 500 N Oak St .... Inglewood CA 90302 310-680-4300
TF: 877-207-5130 ■ *Web:* www.jrobertscott.com

Kay Park Recreation Corp 1301 Pine St .... Janesville IA 50647 800-553-2476 987-2900*
**Fax Area Code:* 319 ■ **Fax:* Cust Svc ■ *TF Cust Svc:* 800-553-2476 ■ *Web:* www.kaypark.com

Kessler Industries 8600 Gateway Blvd E .... El Paso TX 79907 915-591-8161 598-7353
Web: www.kesslerind.com

Kingsley-Bate Ltd 7200 Gateway Ct .... Manassas VA 20109 703-361-7000 361-7001
Web: www.kingsleybate.com

Mallin Casual Furniture 1 Minson Way .... Montebello CA 90640 800-251-6537 513-1047*
**Fax Area Code:* 323 ■ *TF:* 800-251-6537 ■ *Web:* minson.com/mallin

Minson Corp 1 Minson Way .... Montebello CA 90640 323-513-1041 513-1047
TF: 800-251-6537 ■ *Web:* www.minson.com

OW Lee Company Inc 1822 E Francis St .... Ontario CA 91761 909-947-3771 947-6614
TF: 800-776-9533 ■ *Web:* www.owlee.com

RIO Brands 10981 Decatur Rd .... Philadelphia PA 19154 215-632-2800 824-1172
Web: riobrands.com

RJ Thomas Mfg Company Inc PO Box 946 .... Cherokee IA 51012 712-225-5115 225-5796
TF: 800-762-5002 ■ *Web:* www.pilotrock.com

Telescope Casual Furniture Inc
82 Church St .... Granville NY 12832 518-642-1100 642-2536
Web: telescopecasual.com

Tropitone Furniture Co Inc 5 Marconi .... Irvine CA 92618 949-951-2010 972-5714*
**Fax Area Code:* 800 ■ **Fax:* Cust Svc ■ *Web:* www.tropitone.com

Twin Oaks Hammocks 138 Twin Oaks Rd .... Louisa VA 23093 540-894-5125 894-4112
TF: 800-688-8946 ■ *Web:* www.twinoakshammocks.com

Wabash Valley Manufacturing Inc
505 E Main St .... Silver Lake IN 46982 260-352-2102 352-2160
TF: 800-253-8619 ■ *Web:* www.wabashvalley.com

Walpole Woodworkers Inc 767 E St Rt 7 .... Walpole MA 02081 508-668-2800 668-7301
TF Cust Svc: 800-343-6948 ■ *Web:* www.walpolewoodworkers.com

Winston Furniture 540 Dolphin Rd .... Haleyville AL 35565 205-486-9211
Web: www.winstonfurniture.com

320 FURNITURE - WHOL

Phone | Fax

A Lava & Son Co 4800 S Kilbourn Ave .... Chicago IL 60632 773-254-2800
Web: www.alavason.com

Company / Address	City	State	Zip	Phone	Fax
Adirondack Direct 3040 48th Ave *TF:* 800-221-2444 ■ *Web:* www.adirondack.com	Long Island	NY	11101	718-204-4500	
AFD Contract Furniture Inc 810 Seventh Ave # 2 *Web:* www.afd-inc.com	New York	NY	10019	212-721-7100	721-7175
All Purpose Manufacturing Inc 614 Airport Rd *Web:* www.apmfg.net	Oceanside	CA	92058	760-967-8464	
Amini Innovation Corp 8725 Rex Rd *Web:* www.amini.com	Pico Rivera	CA	90660	562-222-2500	222-2525
ATD-American Co 135 Greenwood Ave **Fax Area Code:* 800 ■ *TF:* 866-283-9327 ■ *Web:* www.atdamerican.com	Wyncote	PA	19095	215-576-1380	523-2300*
BCinteriors 3550 Frontier Ave Ste C2 *Web:* www.bcinteriors.com	Boulder	CO	80301	303-443-3666	
Bellia Office Furniture Inc 1047 N Broad St *Web:* www.bellia.net	Woodbury	NJ	08096	856-845-2234	
Benjamin West 2655 Crescent Dr *Web:* www.benjaminwest.com	Lafayette	CO	80026	303-530-3885	
Berco Inc 1120 Montrose Ave *Web:* www.bercoinc.com	Saint Louis	MO	63104	314-772-4700	
BIF New York Inc 465 Barell Ave *Web:* www.bifnewyork.com	Carlstadt	NJ	07072	201-933-7777	
Borden Office Equipment Co 141 N Fifth St *Web:* www.bordenofficeequipment.com	Steubenville	OH	43952	740-283-3321	
Brondell Inc 2183 Sutter St *Web:* brondell.com	San Francisco	CA	94115	415-315-9000	
Brown & Saenger 711 W Russell St PO Box 84040 *TF:* 800-952-3509 ■ *Web:* www.brown-saenger.com	Sioux Falls	SD	57118	605-336-1960	332-0963
Business Furniture Corp 6102 Victory Way *TF:* 800-774-5544 ■ *Web:* businessfurniture.net	Indianapolis	IN	46278	317-216-1600	216-1602
Business Furniture Inc 10 Lanidex Ctr W *Web:* www.bfionline.com	Parsippany	NJ	07054	973-503-0730	503-1565
California Office Furniture 1724 Tenth St *TF:* 877-442-6959 ■ *Web:* caloffice.com	Sacramento	CA	95811	916-442-6959	442-3480
Carithers Wallace Courtenay Co 4343 NE Expy *TF:* 800-292-8220 ■ *Web:* www.c-w-c.com	Atlanta	GA	30340	770-493-8200	491-6374
Carolina Wholesale Office Machine Company Inc 425 E Arrowhead Dr *Web:* www.cwholesale.com	Charlotte	NC	28213	704-598-8101	
Carroll Seating Company Inc 10 Lincoln St *TF:* 800-972-3779 ■ *Web:* www.carrollseating.com	Kansas City	KS	66103	816-471-2929	471-3001
Champion Industries Inc PO Box 2968 PO Box 2968 *OTC: CHMP* ■ *TF:* 800-624-3431 ■ *Web:* champion-industries.com	Huntington	WV	25728	304-528-2791	528-2746
COECO Office Systems Co 2521 N Church St *TF:* 800-682-6844 ■ *Web:* www.coeco.com	Rocky Mount	NC	27804	252-977-1121	985-1566
Commercial Furniture Interiors Inc 1154 Rt 22 W *Web:* www.cfioffice.com	Mountainside	NJ	07092	908-518-1670	654-8436
Conklin Office Furniture 56 N Canal St *Web:* www.conklinoffice.com	Holyoke	MA	01040	413-315-6777	
Corporate Environments 1636 NE Expwy *Web:* www.corporateenvironments.com	Atlanta	GA	30329	404-492-8775	679-8950
Corry Contract Inc 21 Maple Ave *Web:* www.corrycontract.com	Corry	PA	16407	814-665-8221	
Cubicles Office Environments Inc 2560 Fortune Way *Web:* www.sandiegocubicles.com	Vista	CA	92081	760-560-5800	
Culver-Newlin Inc Schl Furn 840 S Wanamaker Ave *Web:* www.culver-newlin.com	Ontario	CA	91761	909-390-3715	
Dancker Sellew & Douglas 291 Evans Way	Somerville	NJ	08876	908-231-1600	231-0469
Ebel Inc 8270 Arlington Expy *Web:* www.ebelinc.com	Jacksonville	FL	32211	904-399-2777	
Egan Visual Inc 300 Hanlan Rd *TF:* 888-609-8886 ■ *Web:* www.egan.com	Woodbridge	ON	L4L3P6	905-851-2826	851-3426
Elrod's Cost Plus #2 2025 Ft Worth Ave *Web:* www.elrodscostplus.com	Dallas	TX	75208	214-942-1104	
Empire Office Inc 105 Madison Ave Ste 15 *Web:* www.empireoffice.com	New York	NY	10016	212-607-5500	607-5650
Enriching Spaces 1360 Kemper Meadow Dr *Web:* www.enrichingspaces.com	Cincinnati	OH	45240	513-851-0933	742-6415
Evergreen Enterprises Inc 5915 Midlothian Trnpk *TF:* 800-774-3837 ■ *Web:* www.myevergreen.com	Richmond	VA	23225	804-231-1800	231-2888
EVS Ltd 3702 W Sample St *TF:* 800-364-3218 ■ *Web:* www.evsltd.com	South Bend	IN	46619	574-233-5707	
Facilitec Inc 4501 E McDowell Rd	Phoenix	AZ	85008	602-275-0101	
Facilitech Inc 1111 Vly View Ln *Web:* www.businessinteriors.com	Irving	TX	75061	817-858-2000	
Fournitures De Bureau Denis Inc 2990 boul Le Corbusier *Web:* www.denis.ca	Laval	QC	H7L3M2	450-687-3110	
Furniture Consultants Inc 1 Penn Plz 55th Fl *Web:* www.fcifurnitureconsultants.com	New York	NY	10119	212-229-4500	807-0036
General Office Products Co 4521 Hwy 7 *Web:* www.gopco.com	Minneapolis	MN	55416	952-925-7500	925-7531
GL Seaman & Co 4201 International Pkwy *Web:* glsc.com	Carrollton	TX	75007	214-764-6400	764-6420
Glover Sales Group LLC 221 Cockeysville Rd *TF:* 800-966-9016	Cockeysville	MD	21030	410-771-8000	771-8010
GT Grandstands Inc 2810 Sydney Rd *Web:* www.gtgrandstands.com	Plant City	FL	33566	813-305-1415	
Haldeman-Homme Inc 430 Industrial Blvd NE	Minneapolis	MN	55413	612-331-4880	
Hangman Products Inc 6400 Variel Ave *Web:* www.hangmanproducts.com	Woodland Hills	CA	91367	818-610-0487	
Hart Furniture Company Inc 12 Harold Hart Rd *Web:* www.hartfurnitureco.com	Siler City	NC	27344	919-742-4141	663-2925
Henricksen & Co 1101 W River Pkwy Ste 100 *Web:* www.henricksen.com	Minneapolis	MN	55415	612-455-2200	877-3300
Heritage Office Furnishings 1588 Rand Ave *TF:* 888-775-4555 ■ *Web:* www.heritageoffice.com	Vancouver	BC	V6P3G2	604-688-2381	
Hummels Office Equipment Co 25 Canal St *Web:* www.hummelsop.com	Mohawk	NY	13407	315-866-3860	
Intereum 845 Berkshire Ln N *Web:* www.intereum.com	Plymouth	MN	55441	763-417-3300	417-3309
Interiors Inc 1325 N Dutton Ave *Web:* interiorsincorporated.com	Santa Rosa	CA	95401	707-544-4770	544-0722
J L Business Interiors Inc 515 Schoenhaar Dr PO Box 303 *TF:* 866-338-5524 ■ *Web:* www.jlbusinessinteriors.com	West Bend	WI	53090	262-338-2221	338-2269
Jules Seltzer Assoc 9020 W Olympic Blvd *Web:* www.julesseltzer.com	Beverly Hills	CA	90211	310-274-7243	274-7243
Kayhan International Ltd 1475 E Woodfield Rd Ste 104 *Web:* www.kayhan.com	Schaumburg	IL	60173	847-843-5060	
KBM Workspace 160 w santa clara st Ste 102 *Web:* www.kbmworkspace.com	San Jose	CA	95113	408-351-7100	938-0699
Kentwood Office Furniture Inc 3063 Breton Rd SE *TF:* 877-698-6250 ■ *Web:* www.kentwoodoffice.com	Grand Rapids	MI	49512	616-957-2320	957-2361
Lee Company Inc 27 S 12th St *Web:* leecompanyinc.com	Terre Haute	IN	47807	812-235-8155	235-3587
Lenoir Empire Furniture 1625 Cherokee Rd *Web:* lenoirempirefurniture.com	Johnson City	TN	37604	423-929-7283	929-7040
Loth Inc 3574 E Kemper Rd *Web:* www.lothexperts.com	Cincinnati	OH	45241	513-554-4900	554-8700
Magnussen Home Furnishings Ltd 66 Hincks St *Web:* www.magnussen.com	New Hamburg	ON	N3A2A3	519-662-3040	662-3733
Mazany Office Interiors 428 Livingston Ave *Web:* www.mazanyoffice.com	Jamestown	NY	14701	716-487-1617	
MISSCO Contract Sales 2510 Lakeland Terr Ste 100 *Web:* www.missco.com	Jackson	MS	39216	601-987-8600	
Najarian Furniture Company Inc 17560 Rowland St *TF:* 888-781-3088 ■ *Web:* www.najarianfurniture.com	City of Industry	CA	91748	626-839-8700	839-8707
National Business Furniture Inc 735 N Water St Ste 440 *TF Sales:* 800-558-1010 ■ *Web:* www.nationalbusinessfurniture.com	Milwaukee	WI	53202	414-276-8511	276-8371
Nevers Industries Inc 14125 21st Ave N *TF:* 800-258-5591 ■ *Web:* www.nevers.com	Minneapolis	MN	55447	763-210-4206	
Nickerson Corp PO Box 5751 *Web:* www.nickersoncorp.com	Bay Shore	NY	11706	631-666-0200	
North Country Business Products Inc 1112 S Railroad St SE *TF:* 800-937-4140 ■ *Web:* www.ncbpinc.com	Bemidji	MN	56601	218-751-4140	755-6039
Office Environments Inc 11407 Granite St *TF:* 888-861-2525 ■ *Web:* www.office-environments.com	Charlotte	NC	28273	704-714-7200	714-7400
Office Furniture Team 4204 Lindbergh Dr *Web:* www.oftoffice.com	Addison	TX	75001	972-503-8326	
Office Pavilion 10030 Bent Oak Dr *Web:* www.ophouston.com	Houston	TX	77040	713-803-0000	803-0001
Office Plus of Lake County 1428 Glen Flora Ave *Web:* www.getofficeplus.com	Waukegan	IL	60085	847-662-5393	662-8761
Office Star Products 1901 S Archibald PO Box 3520 *TF:* 800-950-7262 ■ *Web:* www.officestar.net	Ontario	CA	91761	909-930-2000	930-5419
Ohio Desk Co 1122 Prospect Ave E *Web:* www.ohiodesk.com	Cleveland	OH	44115	216-623-0600	623-0611
OMED of Nevada LLC 800 Stillwell Rd	Reno	NV	89512	775-857-3008	
OneWorkplace 475 Brannan St Ste 210 *Web:* oneworkplace.com	San Francisco	CA	94107	415-357-2200	
Pacific Design Ctr 8687 Melrose Ave *Web:* www.pacificdesigncenter.com	West Hollywood	CA	90069	310-657-0800	652-8576
Paragon Furniture Management Inc 2224 E Randol Mill Rd *TF:* 800-451-8546 ■ *Web:* www.paragoninc.com	Arlington	TX	76011	817-633-3242	
Patton Sales Corp 1095 E California St *Web:* www.pattonscorp.com	Ontario	CA	91761	909-988-0661	
Peabody Office Furniture Corp 234 Congress St *Web:* www.peabodyoffice.com	Boston	MA	02110	617-542-1902	
Pear Commercial Interiors Inc 1515 Arapahoe St Ste 100 *Web:* www.pearcom.com	Denver	CO	80202	303-824-2000	824-2001
Pigott Inc 3815 Ingersoll Ave *Web:* www.pigottnet.com	Des Moines	IA	50312	515-279-8879	279-7338
Pivot Interiors 2740 Zanker Rd Ste 100 *Web:* www.pivotinteriors.com	San Jose	CA	95134	408-432-5600	432-5601
Planned Furniture Promotions Inc 9 Moody Rd Bldg D Ste 18 *Web:* www.pfpnow.com	Enfield	CT	06082	860-749-1472	
Quality Enclosures Inc 2025 Porter Lk Dr *Web:* www.qualityenclosures.com	Sarasota	FL	34240	941-378-0051	
R & M Office Furniture 9615 Oates Dr *TF:* 800-660-1756 ■ *Web:* www.randmoffice.com	Sacramento	CA	95827	916-362-1756	362-1086
Red Thread 300 E River Dr *Web:* www.red-thread.com	East Hartford	CT	06108	860-528-9981	528-1843
RH Kyle Furniture Co 1352 Hansford St	Charleston	WV	25301	304-346-0671	
Rieke Office Interiors 2000 Fox Ln *Web:* www.rieke.com	Elgin	IL	60123	847-622-9711	
Sarreid Ltd 3905 Airport Dr NW *Web:* www.sarreid.com	Wilson	NC	27896	252-291-1414	237-1592

Phone Fax

Saxton Inc Design Group
600 Third St Se Ste 300 .... Cedar Rapids IA 52401 319-365-6967
Web: www.saxtoninc.com

Southern Office Furniture Distributors Inc
7820 Thorndike Rd .... Greensboro NC 27409 336-668-4192 668-2076

Sterling Collection Inc, The
1730 First St .... San Fernando CA 91340 818-837-4680 361-2250
Web: www.sterling-collection.com

Superior Medical Supply Inc
11005 Dover St Unit 1100 .... Broomfield CO 80021 303-460-1411
TF: 877-460-1411

Systechs Inc 249 W Baywood Ave Ste B .... Orange CA 92865 714-283-2890
Web: www.systechs.com

Tangram Interiors Inc
9200 Sorensen Ave .... Santa Fe Springs CA 90670 562-365-5000 365-5399
Web: www.tangraminteriors.com

Teammates Commercial Interiors
320 S Teller St Ste 250 .... Lakewood CO 80226 303-639-5885
Web: www.team-mates.com

Tolar Manufacturing Company Inc
258 Mariah Cir .... Corona CA 92879 951-808-0081
Web: www.tolarmfg.com

Trade Products Corp 12124 Popes Head Rd .... Fairfax VA 22030 703-502-9000 502-9399
TF: 888-352-3580 ■ *Web:* www.tradeproductscorp.com

Treasure Garden Inc
13401 Brooks Dr Ste A .... Baldwin Park CA 91706 626-814-0168
Web: treasuregarden.com

Trinity Hardwood Distributors Inc
110 East Oregon .... Dallas TX 75203 214-948-3001 946-1219
TF: 800-492-9856 ■ *Web:* www.trinityhardwood.net

UCC Totalhome 8450 Broadway .... Merrillville IN 46411 219-736-1100
Web: www.ucctops.com

Waldner's Business Environment
125 Rt 110 .... Farmingdale NY 11735 631-844-9300
Web: www.waldners.com

Wasserstrom Co 477 S Front St .... Columbus OH 43215 614-228-6525 737-8911
TF: 866-634-8927 ■ *Web:* www.wasserstrom.com

Wholesale Interiors Inc 794 Golf Ln .... Bensenville IL 60106 630-238-8877
Web: www.interiorexpressoutlet.com

Winners Only Inc 1365 Pk Ctr Dr .... Vista CA 92081 760-599-0300
Web: www.winnersonly.com

Workplace Solutions
30800 Telegraph Rd Ste 2985 .... Bingham Farms MI 48025 248-430-2500
Web: www.myworkplacesolutions.com

Workscapes Inc 1173 N Orange Ave .... Orlando FL 32804 407-599-6770
Web: www.workscapes.com

321 FURNITURE STORES

See Also Department Stores p. 2191

Phone Fax

A A Office Equipment & Furniture
2140 American Ave .... Hayward CA 94545 510-782-6110
Web: www.aaoffice.com

A D Wynne Co Inc 710 Baronne St .... New Orleans LA 70113 504-585-0800 522-7070
Web: www.adwynne.com

A Diamond Production Inc
2150 Cesar Chavez St .... San Francisco CA 94124 415-920-6800
Web: www.thefutonshop.com

Activeforevercom 10799 N 90th St .... Scottsdale AZ 85260 480-459-3202
TF: 800-377-8033 ■ *Web:* www.activeforever.com

Addison House Interiors Inc
5201 Nw 77th Ave Ste 400 .... Doral FL 33166 305-640-2400
TF: 800-426-2988 ■ *Web:* www.addisonhouse.com

Afinety Inc 1956 Cotner Ave .... Los Angeles CA 90025 310-996-2700
TF: 877-423-4638 ■ *Web:* www.afinety.com

Agati Inc 1219 W Lake St .... Chicago IL 60607 312-829-1977
TF: 866-418-8710 ■ *Web:* www.agati.com

Albany Bedding LLC 3900 Pecan Grove Ct .... Albany GA 31701 229-420-7399

All Makes Office Equipment Co 2558 Farnam St .... Omaha NE 68131 402-341-2413
TF: 800-341-2413 ■ *Web:* www.allmakes.com

Allen Furniture City Inc 7808 L St .... Omaha NE 68127 402-331-8480
Web: allenshome.com

Ambella Home Collection Corporate Office
4910 Lakawana St .... Dallas TX 75247 214-631-8901

AMC Industries LLC 1120 N 28th St .... Tampa FL 33605 813-989-9663
Web: www.amcind.com

America The Beautiful Dreamer Inc
9700 Ne 126th Ave .... Vancouver WA 98682 360-816-0167
Web: www.atbd.com

American Factory Direct Furniture Outlets Inc
210 New Camellia Blvd .... Covington LA 70433 985-845-2465
Web: www.afd-furniture.com

American Freight Ohio Inc
2770 Lexington Ave .... Mansfield OH 44904 419-884-2224
Web: www.americanfreight.us

American Furniture Warehouse Co
8501 Grant St .... Thornton CO 80229 303-289-3300
TF: 888-615-9415 ■ *Web:* www.afwonline.com

American Home Furnishings
3535 Menaul Blvd NE .... Albuquerque NM 87107 505-883-2211 816-6521
TF: 800-854-6755 ■ *Web:* www.americanhome.com

American Office Equipment Company Inc
309 N Calvert St .... Baltimore MD 21202 410-539-7529
Web: www.americanoffice.com

American Surplus Inc 1 Noyes Ave Bldg B .... Rumford RI 02916 401-434-4355
TF: 800-876-3736 ■ *Web:* www.americansurplus.com

Ameublements Tanguay Inc
7200 Rue Armand-Viau .... Ville de Quebec QC G2C2A7 418-847-4411 847-4848
Web: www.tanguay.ca

Andreas Furniture Company Inc
114 Dover Rd Ne .... Sugarcreek OH 44681 330-852-2494
TF: 800-846-7448 ■ *Web:* www.andreasfurniture.com

Phone Fax

APG Office Furnishings Inc
12075 Northwest Blvd Ste 100 .... Cincinnati OH 45246 513-621-9111
Web: www.apgof.com

Applied Knowledge Group Inc
2100 Reston Pkwy Ste 400 .... Reston VA 20191 703-860-1145
Web: www.akgroup.com

Arcadia Chair Co 5692 Fresca Dr .... La Palma CA 90623 714-562-8200
Web: www.encoreseating.com

Arenson Office Furnishings Inc
1115 Broadway 6th Fl .... New York NY 10010 646-395-3563
Web: www.aof.com

Arenson Office Furniture
8185 Camino Santa Fe .... San Diego CA 92121 858-453-2411
Web: www.arensonof.com

Arizona Leather Company Inc 4235 Schaefer Ave .... Chino CA 91710 909-993-5101
TF: 888-669-5328 ■ *Web:* www.arizonaleather.com

ART Furniture Inc 1165 Auto Ctr Dr .... Ontario CA 91761 909-390-1039
Web: www.arthomefurnishings.com

Atlantic Corporate Interiors Inc (ACI)
7001 Muirkirk Meadows Dr Ste A .... Beltsville MD 20705 301-931-3600 931-3601
Web: www.aciinc.com

August Inc 354 Congress Park Dr .... Centerville OH 45459 937-434-2520
TF: 800-318-5242 ■ *Web:* www.augustinc.com

Avis Furniture Co 1410 Union Ave .... Kansas City MO 64101 816-421-5939
Web: www.avisfurniture.com

Back To Bed Inc 700 Hill Top Dr .... Itasca IL 60143 630-931-4602
Web: www.backtobed.com

Bad Boy Furniture Warehouse Ltd 500 Fenmar Dr .... Weston ON M9L2V5 416-667-7546
Web: www.badboy.ca

Badcock's Economy Furniture Store Inc
3931 RCA Blvd .... Palm Beach Gardens FL 33410 561-694-8588
Web: badcocksfl.com

Baer's Furniture Co Inc
1589 Northwest 12th Ave .... Pompano Beach FL 33069 954-582-4200
Web: baers.com

Baileys Furniture Outlet Inc
350 W Intl Airport Rd Ste 100 .... Anchorage AK 99518 907-563-4083
Web: www.baileysfurniture.com

Bar Productscom Inc 1990 Lake Ave SE .... Largo FL 33771 727-584-2093
TF: 800-256-6396 ■ *Web:* www.barproducts.com

Barn Furniture Mart Inc
6206 N Sepulveda Blvd .... Van Nuys CA 91411 818-780-4070
TF: 888-302-2276 ■ *Web:* www.barnfurnituremart.com

Bay View Plaza Furniture Inc 2181 E Pass Rd .... Gulfport MS 39507 228-896-4400
Web: bayviewfurniture.com

Beaufurn LLC 5269 US Hwy 158 .... Advance NC 27006 888-766-7706
TF: 888-766-7706 ■ *Web:* www.beaufurn.com

Becks Furniture Inc 11840 Folsom Blvd .... Rancho Cordova CA 95742 916-353-5000
Web: www.becksfurniture.com

Bedroom Store Inc 2440 Adie Rd .... Maryland Heights MO 63043 314-822-2617
Web: www.thebedroomstore.com

Beiter's Inc 560 Montgomery Pk .... South Williamsport PA 17702 570-326-2073
Web: www.beiters.com

Belfort Furniture Inc 22250 and 22267 Shaw Rd .... Dulles VA 20166 703-406-7600
Web: www.belfortfurniture.com

Bernie & Phyl's Furniture 308 E Main St .... Norton MA 02766 508-286-4000
Web: www.bernieandphyls.com

Best Material Handling Inc
4754 N Chestnut St .... Colorado Springs CO 80907 719-599-9191
TF: 800-933-5270 ■ *Web:* www.best-materials.com

bkm Officeworks
9201 Spectrum Ctr Blvd Ste 100 .... San Diego CA 92123 858-569-4700
Web: www.bkmofficeworks.com

Blackledge Furniture 233 Sw Second St .... Corvallis OR 97333 541-753-4851
TF: 800-782-4851 ■ *Web:* www.blackledgefurniture.com

Blacklion International Inc 10605 Park Rd .... Charlotte NC 28210 704-541-1148
Web: www.blacklion.com

Bmea Enterprises Inc 13370 Kirkham Way .... Poway CA 92064 858-513-6584

Bob Mills Furniture Company LLC
3600 W Reno Ave .... Oklahoma City OK 73107 405-947-6500
Web: bobmillsfurniture.com

Bob's Discount Furniture Inc
428 Tolland Tpke .... Manchester CT 06042 860-645-3208
Web: www.mybobs.com

Boss Chair Inc 5353 Jillson St .... Commerce CA 90040 323-262-1919 262-2300
TF: 800-593-1888 ■ *Web:* www.bosschair.com

Boston Bed Company Inc, The
1113 Commonwealth Ave .... Boston MA 02215 617-782-3830

Boston Inc 2917 Business Park Dr .... Stevens Point WI 54482 715-344-7700
Web: www.furnitureappliancemart.com

Bratt Decor Inc 5 N Haven St .... Baltimore MD 21224 703-448-6833
Web: www.brattdecor.com

Bridgeport Inc 1432 Old W Main St .... Red Wing MN 55066 651-388-1264
Web: www.bridgeport.com

Brownstone Furniture 3435 Regatta Blvd .... Richmond CA 94804 510-236-0762
Web: brownstonefurniture.com

Bunch/Shoemaker Inc 7026 Old Katy Rd No 152 .... Houston TX 77024 713-426-2850
Web: bunchshoemaker.com

Cabinet Discounters Inc 9500 Berger Rd .... Columbia MD 21046 410-793-1265
Web: www.cabinetdiscounters.com

Cabot House Inc 10 Industrial Way .... Amesbury MA 01913 978-834-9280 373-8058
Web: www.cabothouse.com

Capital Office Systems 3201 Industrial Ave .... Fairbanks AK 99701 907-777-1500
Web: www.capital-office.com

Cardi's Furniture 1 Furniture Way .... Swansea MA 02777 508-379-7510
TF: 866-419-4096 ■ *Web:* www.cardis.com

Carol House Furniture Co
2332 Millpark Dr .... Maryland Heights MO 63043 314-427-4200
Web: www.carolhouse.com

Carolina Mattress Guild Inc
385 N Dr # Business .... Thomasville NC 27360 336-476-1333

Carr & Co 2556 Piney Rd .... Morganton NC 28655 828-433-5200
Web: www.carr.com

	City	State	Zip	Phone	Fax
Casa Linda Furniture Inc 4815 Whittier Blvd *Web:* www.furniturecasalinda.com	Los Angeles	CA	90022	323-263-3851	
Caseys Furniture Inc 11 S Second St	Temple	TX	76501	254-773-5555	
Casual Designs Furniture Inc 36523 Lighthouse Rd *TF:* 888-629-1717 ■ *Web:* www.casualdesignsfurniture.com	Selbyville	DE	19975	302-436-8224	
Cemco Partitions Inc 5340 Us Hwy 220 N *Web:* www.cemcopartitions.com	Summerfield	NC	27358	336-643-6316	
CG Sparks World Furniture LLC 454 South 500 West *Web:* www.cgsparks.com	Salt Lake City	UT	84101	801-519-6900	
Chair King Inc, The 5405 W Sam Houston Pkwy N *Web:* www.chairking.com	Houston	TX	77041	713-690-1919	
Chairish 1657 Defoor Ave NW	Atlanta	GA	30318	404-351-5717	
Charles Eisen & Assoc Inc 595 S Broadway Ste 110E *Web:* www.egg-and-dart.com	Denver	CO	80209	303-744-3200	
Charlotte Appliances Inc 3200 Lake Ave *TF:* 800-244-0405 ■ *Web:* www.charlotteappliance.com	Rochester	NY	14612	585-663-5050	
Cherryman Industries 5690 Lindbergh Ln *Web:* cherrymanindustries.com	Bell	CA	90201	323-780-0859	
Cholla Custom Cabinets Inc 1727 E Deer Vly Rd	Phoenix	AZ	85024	623-322-9949	
Circle Furniture Inc 19 Craig Rd *Web:* outlet.circlefurniture.com	Acton	MA	01720	978-263-4509	
City Furniture Inc 6701 N Hiatus Rd *TF:* 888-882-5436 ■ *Web:* www.cityfurniture.com	Tamarac	FL	33321	954-597-2200	718-3360
City Mattress Inc 12660 Bonita Beach Rd *Web:* www.citymattress.com	Bonita Springs	FL	34135	239-908-2700	
CJ & Associates Inc 16915 W Victor Rd *Web:* www.cjassociatesinc.com	New Berlin	WI	53151	262-786-1772	
CoCaLo Inc 2920 Red Hill Ave *Web:* www.cocalo.com	Costa Mesa	CA	92626	714-434-7200	
Colder's Inc 333 S 108th St *Web:* www.colders.com	West Allis	WI	53214	414-476-1574	
Compass Office Solutions LLC 3320 Enterprise Way *Web:* www.compass-office.com	Miramar	FL	33025	954-430-4590	
Conlin's Furniture Inc 739 S 20th St W *Web:* www.conlins.com	Billings	MT	59102	406-656-4900	
Container Mktg Inc 110 Matthews Dr *Web:* www.iwantcmi.com	Americus	GA	31709	229-924-5622	
Contract Office Group Inc 1731 Technology Dr *Web:* www.cog.com	San Jose	CA	95110	408-213-1790	
Contract Resource Group LLC 7108 Old Katy Rd Ste 150 *Web:* www.crgoffice.com	Houston	TX	77024	713-803-0100	
Cook Brothers Inc 1740 N Kostner Ave *Web:* www.cookbrothers.com	Chicago	IL	60639	773-770-1200	
Copenhagen 1701 E Camelback Rd *Web:* www.copenhagenliving.com	Phoenix	AZ	85016	602-266-8060	
Copper Creek Canyon 3953 E 82nd St *Web:* www.coppercreekcanyon.com	Indianapolis	IN	46240	317-577-2990	
Corporate Facilities Inc 2129 Chestnut St *Web:* www.cfi-knoll.com	Philadelphia	PA	19103	215-279-9999	
Corporate Interior Systems 3311 E Broadway Rd *Web:* www.cisinphx.com	Phoenix	AZ	85040	602-304-0100	
Coulter's Furniture 1324 Windsor Ave *Web:* www.coulters.com	Windsor	ON	N8X3L9	519-253-7422	253-3744
Country Home Furniture LLC 1352 Main St *Web:* www.chfs1.com	East Earl	PA	17519	717-354-2329	
CS Wo & Sons Ltd 702 S Beretenia St *Web:* www.cswo.com	Honolulu	HI	96813	808-543-5388	
Cumberland Furniture 321 Terminal St Sw *TF:* 800-401-7877 ■ *Web:* www.cumberlandfurniture.com	Grand Rapids	MI	49548	800-401-7877	
Dallas Desk Inc 15207 Midway Rd *Web:* dallasdesk.com	Addison	TX	75001	972-788-1802	
Daniels Home Center 255 S Euclid St *Web:* www.danielshomecenter.com	Anaheim	CA	92802	714-999-1285	
Darvin Furniture 15400 S La Grange Rd *Web:* darvin.com	Orland Park	IL	60462	708-460-4100	
Dates Weiser Furniture Corp 1700 Broadway St *TF:* 800-466-7037 ■ *Web:* www.datesweiser.com	Buffalo	NY	14212	716-891-1700	
Dearden's Furniture Co 700 S Main St *Web:* www.deardens.com	Los Angeles	CA	90014	213-362-9600	
Deco Designs Systems Furniture Inc 1435 Koll Cir Ste 106 *Web:* www.decodesigns.com	San Jose	CA	95112	408-919-0234	
Decor Rest Furniture Ltd 208 Jacobs Pl	High Point	NC	27260	336-884-3420	
Designed Business Interiors of Topeka Inc 107 W Sixth St *Web:* dbi-topeka.com	Topeka	KS	66603	785-233-2078	
Desks Inc Business Furniture 445 Bryant St Unit 8 *Web:* www.desks-incorporated.com	Denver	CO	80204	303-777-7778	
DFW Furniture Warehouse 2500 Fairmont Ave	Fairmont	WV	26554	304-367-8980	
Dillmeier Enterprises Inc 2903 Industrial Park Rd *Web:* www.dillmeierglass.com	Van Buren	AR	72956	479-474-7733	
Dixie Furniture Co 282 Richmond Hill	West Helena	AR	72390	870-572-3493	
Docuforce 8343 E 32nd St N *Web:* www.docuforce.biz	Wichita	KS	67226	316-636-5400	
Dufresne Furniture Ltd 116 Nature Pk Way *Web:* www.dufresne.ca	Winnipeg	MB	R3P0X8	204-989-9898	989-9885
E S Kluft & Company LLC 11096 Jersey Blvd Ste 101 *Web:* www.kluftmattress.com	Rancho Cucamonga	CA	91730	909-373-4211	
Easylife Furniture Inc 6101 Knott Ave	Buena Park	CA	90620	714-367-1640	
Eaton Clothing & Furniture Center 116 E Lovett St *Web:* www.eatoncounty.org	Charlotte	MI	48813	517-543-4334	
EC Power International Inc 5120 Woodway Ste 5005 *Web:* www.ec-power.com	Houston	TX	77056	713-626-8700	
El Dorado Furniture Corp 4200 NW 167th St *TF:* 888-451-7800 ■ *Web:* www.eldoradofurniture.com	Miami	FL	33054	305-624-2400	
Empresas Berrios Inc PO Box 674	Cidra	PR	00739	787-653-9393	
Epoch Design 17617 Ne 65th St Ste 2 *TF:* 800-589-7990 ■ *Web:* www.epochbydesign.com	Redmond	WA	98052	425-284-0880	
Ethan Allen Interiors Inc Ethan Allen Dr *NYSE: ETH* ■ **Fax Area Code:* 203 ■ *TF:* 888-324-3571 ■ *Web:* www.ethanallen.com	Danbury	CT	06811	888-324-3571	743-8298*
Expression Home Gallery 2273 S La Crosse Ave Ste 105	Colton	CA	92324	909-433-3990	
Factory Direct Furniture & Mattress 2330 Freedom Dr	Charlotte	NC	28208	704-393-2750	
Family Furniture Centers Inc 7870 Central Ave *Web:* www.familyfurniture.com	Landover	MD	20785	301-499-4300	
Famous Tate Electric Co 8317 N Armenia Ave *Web:* www.famoustate.com	Tampa	FL	33604	813-935-3151	
Fastfurnishings.com 340 S Lemon Ave Ste 6043 *Web:* www.fastfurnishings.com	Walnut	CA	91789	443-371-3278	
FCC Commercial Furniture Inc 8452 Old Hwy 99 N *Web:* www.fccfurn.com	Roseburg	OR	97470	541-673-3351	
Fisher Home Furnishings 2175 N Main St *Web:* www.fisherhf.com	Logan	UT	84341	435-753-1018	
Flegels Home Furnishings 870 Santa Cruz Ave *Web:* www.flegels.com	Menlo Park	CA	94025	650-326-9661	
Florida Business Interiors 767 Stirling Ctr Pl *Web:* www.4fbi.com	Lake Mary	FL	32746	407-805-9911	
Forum Manufacturing Inc 77 Brown St *Web:* www.forummfg.com	Milford Center	OH	43045	937-349-8685	
Franklin Interiors Inc 2740 Smallman St Ste 600 *Web:* franklininteriors.com	Pittsburgh	PA	15222	412-261-2525	255-4089
Fredrick Furniture Inc 703 G Ave *Web:* frederickfurnitureinc.com	Grundy Center	IA	50638	319-824-5235	
Freed's Fine Furnishings Inc 3645 Sturgis Rd *Web:* freedsfurniture.com	Rapid City	SD	57702	605-343-2538	343-3662
Fulkerson Services Inc 111 Parce Rd *Web:* fulkersonservices.com	Fairport	NY	14450	585-223-2541	
Furniture Buy Consignment Inc 1348 W Main St *Web:* furniturebuyconsignment.com	Lewisville	TX	75067	972-436-4389	
Furniture Factory Outlet LLC 901 Industrial Park Rd	Muldrow	OK	74948	918-427-0241	
Furniture Fair 7200 Dixie Hwy *Web:* www.furniturefair.com	Fairfield	OH	45014	513-874-5553	
Furniture Mall of Kansas 1901 SW Wanamaker Rd *Web:* www.furnituremallofkansas.com	Topeka	KS	66604	785-271-0684	
Gabberts Inc 3501 Galleria *Web:* www.gabberts.com	Minneapolis	MN	55435	952-927-1500	
Gallery Model Homes Inc 6006 N Fwy *Web:* www.galleryfurniture.com	Houston	TX	77076	713-694-5570	
Gardner Mattress Corp 254 Canal St *Web:* www.gardnermattress.com	Salem	MA	01970	978-341-4780	
Gardner White Furniture Company Inc 21001 Groesbeck Hwy *Web:* www.gardner-white.com	Warren	MI	48089	586-774-8853	
GCI Outdoor Inc 66 Killingworth Rd *Web:* www.gcioutdoor.com	Higganum	CT	06441	860-345-9595	
Gibraltar Steel Furniture Inc 9976 Westwanda Dr *TF:* 800-416-3635 ■ *Web:* www.gibraltarfurniture.com	Beverly Hills	CA	90210	310-276-8889	
Globe Business Interiors 6454 Centre Park Dr *Web:* www.g-b-i.com	West Chester	OH	45069	513-771-5550	
Golden Chair Inc 958 Washington Rd *Web:* www.goldenchair.com	Houlka	MS	38850	662-568-7830	
Gorman's 29145 Telegraph Rd *Web:* www.gormans.com	Southfield	MI	48034	248-353-9880	
Gothic Cabinet Craft Inc 5877 57th St *Web:* www.gothiccabinetcraft.com	Maspeth	NY	11378	347-881-1458	
Gracious Living Corp 7200 Martin Grove Rd *TF:* 800-465-5660 ■ *Web:* www.graciousliving.com	Woodbridge	ON	L4L9J3	905-264-5660	
Grand Furniture Discount Store 836 E Little Creek Rd *Web:* www.grandfurniture.com	Norfolk	VA	23518	757-588-1331	
Grand Home Furnishings 4235 Electric Rd SW *Web:* www.grandhomefurnishings.com	Roanoke	VA	24018	540-776-7000	776-5528
Great American Home Store 5295 Pepper Chase Dr *Web:* www.greatamericanhomestore.com	Southaven	MS	38671	662-996-1000	
Gressco Ltd 328 Moravian Vly Rd *TF:* 800-345-3480 ■ *Web:* gresscoltd.com	Waunakee	WI	53597	608-849-6300	
Groupe Ameublement Focus Inc 1310 Rue Nobel *Web:* www.groupefocus.com	Boucherville	QC	J4B5H3	514-644-5551	644-5555
Hampton Office Products Inc 248 Donohoe Rd *Web:* www.hamptonoffice.com	Greensburg	PA	15601	724-836-6430	
Harden House, The 626 Grand Central St	Clearwater	FL	33756	727-442-7546	
Hart Furniture Company Inc 12 Harold Hart Rd *Web:* www.hartfurnitureco.com	Siler City	NC	27344	919-742-4141	663-2925

Company	City	State	ZIP	Phone	Fax
Haverty Furniture Cos Inc 780 Johnson Ferry Rd NE Ste 800 *NYSE: HVT* ■ *TF:* 888-428-3789 ■ *Web:* www.havertys.com	Atlanta	GA	30342	404-443-2900	443-4169
Haynes Furniture Company Inc 5324 Virginia Beach Blvd *Web:* www.haynesfurniture.com	Virginia Beach	VA	23462	757-497-9681	552-1545
Healthy Back Store LLC 11714 Baltimore Ave *Web:* www.healthyback.com	Beltsville	MD	20705	703-339-7100	
Heliodyne Corp 4910 Seaport Ave *TF:* 888-878-8750 ■ *Web:* www.heliodyne.com	Richmond	CA	94804	510-237-9614	
Heliotrope 248 W Ponce De Leon Ave	Decatur	GA	30030	404-371-0100	
Hernandez Office Supply 119 N 17th St *Web:* www.hernandezsupply.com	Nederland	TX	77627	409-724-0135	
Heuristic Workshop Inc 203 W Jackson Ave *Web:* www.heuristicworkshop.com	Knoxville	TN	37902	865-523-9867	
Hill Country Furniture Partners Ltd 1431 Fm 1101 *Web:* www.hillcountryholdings.com	New Braunfels	TX	78130	830-515-1400	
Hill Home Furnishings Inc 116 N Fifth St *Web:* hillhomefurnishings.com	Beatrice	NE	68310	402-228-4085	
HM Richards Inc 414 Rd 2790 *Web:* www.hmrichards.com	Guntown	MS	38849	662-365-9485	
Hollywood Bed & Spring Manufacturing Co 5959 Corvette St *Web:* www.hollywoodbed.com	Commerce	CA	90040	323-887-9500	
Home & Hearth 2090 E Main St *Web:* www.homeandhearth-mainst.com	Cortlandt Manor	NY	10567	914-734-9773	
Home Comfort Furniture & Mattress Center Inc 7016 Glenwood Ave *Web:* www.homecomfortfurniture.com	Raleigh	NC	27612	919-781-3900	
Homelegance Inc 3129 Corp Pl *Web:* www.homelegance.com	Hayward	CA	94545	510-783-8010	
Howell Furniture Galleries Inc 6095 Folsom Dr *Web:* howellfurniture.com	Beaumont	TX	77706	409-832-2544	
Hudson's Furniture Showroom Inc 3290 W State Rd 46 *Web:* www.hudsonsfurniture.com	Sanford	FL	32771	407-708-5635	
Huggy Bear's Cupboards Inc 2731 N Hayden Island Dr *Web:* www.huggybear.com	Portland	OR	97217	503-289-5541	
Hurwitz-Mintz Furniture Co 1751 Airline Dr *TF:* 888-957-9555 ■ *Web:* www.hurwitzmintz.com	Metairie	LA	70001	504-378-1000	523-7273
IcwUSACom Inc 1487 Kingsley Dr *TF:* 800-558-4435 ■ *Web:* icwusa.com	Medford	OR	97504	541-608-2824	
IKEA 420 Alan Wood Rd *TF:* 800-434-4532 ■ *Web:* www.ikea.com	Conshohocken	PA	19428	610-834-0180	
Imperial Hardware Company Inc 355 W Olive Ave *Web:* www.imperialstores.com	El Centro	CA	92243	760-353-5280	
Innovative Mattress Solutions LLC 2982 Winfield Rd *Web:* www.innovativemattresssolutions.com	Winfield	WV	25213	304-586-2863	
Inside Source Inc 985 Industrial Rd Ste 101 *Web:* www.insidesource.com	San Carlos	CA	94070	650-508-9101	
Intelligent Interiors Inc 16837 Addison Rd Ste 500 *Web:* www.intelligentinteriors.net	Addison	TX	75001	972-716-9979	
Interior Design Services Inc 209 Powell Pl *TF:* 800-433-7446 ■ *Web:* www.ids-tn.com	Brentwood	TN	37027	615-376-1200	
Interior Office Solutions Inc 17800 Mitchell N *Web:* www.interiorofficesolutions.com	Irvine	CA	92614	949-724-9444	
International Contract Furnishings Inc (ICF) 19 Ohio Ave **Fax Area Code:* 888 ■ *TF:* 800-237-1625 ■ *Web:* www.icfsource.com	Norwich	CT	06360	860-886-1700	784-8209*
International Market Centers 209 S Main St *Web:* www.imchighpointmarket.com	High Point	NC	27260	336-888-3700	
Inviting Home.com 4700 SW 51st St Unit 219 **Fax Area Code:* 954 ■ *TF:* 866-751-6606 ■ *Web:* www.invitinghome.com	Davie	FL	33314	781-444-8001	616-8037*
Irpinia Kitchens 278 Newkirk Rd *Web:* www.irpinia.com	Richmond Hill	ON	L4C3G7	905-780-7722	
J P Kane's Town & Country Furniture 641 Missouri Ave N *Web:* jpkfurniture.com	Largo	FL	33770	727-584-2121	
Jayson Home & Garden 1885 N Clybourn Ave *TF:* 800-472-1885 ■ *Web:* jaysonhome.com	Chicago	IL	60614	773-248-8180	
Jerome's Furniture Warehouse 16960 Mesamint St **Fax Area Code:* 858 ■ *TF:* 866-633-4094 ■ *Web:* www.jeromes.com	San Diego	CA	92127	866-633-4094	753-0826*
Joe Tahan's Furniture Liquidation Centers Inc 131 Henry St *Web:* www.tahans.com	Rome	NY	13440	315-339-2330	
John Portman & Assoc Inc 303 Peachtree Ctr Ave Ste 575 *Web:* www.portmanusa.com	Atlanta	GA	30303	404-614-5555	
Johnny Janosik Inc 11151 Trussum Pond Rd *Web:* www.johnnyjanosik.com	Laurel	DE	19956	302-875-5955	
Jonathan Louis International Ltd 544 W 130th St *Web:* www.jonathanlouis.net	Gardena	CA	90248	323-770-3330	
Jordan'S Furniture Company Inc 450 Revolutionary Dr *Web:* jordans.com	E Taunton	MA	02718	508-828-4000	
K B L Design Center 6710 N Big Hollow Rd *Web:* www.kbldesign.com	Peoria	IL	61615	309-692-8700	
Kane Furniture Corp 5700 70th Ave N *Web:* www.kanesfurniture.com	Pinellas Park	FL	33781	727-545-9555	541-6960
Kegworkscom 1460 Military Rd *Web:* www.kegworks.com	Buffalo	NY	14217	716-856-9675	
Kehoe Custom Wood Designs Inc 1320 N Miller St Ste D *Web:* kehoecustomwood.com	Anaheim	CA	92806	714-993-0444	
Ken Ton Fabricators Inc 2505 Main St *Web:* www.kentonfab.com	Buffalo	NY	14214	716-832-1200	
Kensington Furniture & Mattress 200 Tilton Rd *Web:* www.kensingtonfurniture.com	Northfield	NJ	08225	609-241-9102	
Kittle's Home Furnishings Center Inc 8600 Allisonville Rd *Web:* www.kittles.com	Indianapolis	IN	46250	317-849-5300	
Knoxville Wholesale Furniture Co Inc 410 North Peters Rd *Web:* www.knoxvillewholesalefurniture.com	Knoxville	TN	37922	865-671-5300	
Kookoo Bear Baby & Kids 12060 Etris Rd *Web:* www.kookoobearkids.com	Roswell	GA	30075	770-771-5665	
Kravet Fabrics Inc 8687 Melrose Ave Ste B624 *Web:* www.kravetcanada.com	West Hollywood	CA	90069	310-659-7100	
L & M Office Furniture Inc 4444 S 91st E Ave *Web:* www.l-mofficefurn.com	Tulsa	OK	74145	918-664-1010	
Lack's Valley Stores Ltd 1300 San Patricia St *TF:* 800-870-6999 ■ *Web:* www.lacksvalley.com	Pharr	TX	78577	956-702-3361	782-5740
Lastick Furniture Inc 269 E High St *Web:* www.lastickfurniture.com	Pottstown	PA	19464	610-323-4000	
Leaders Casual Furniture 6303 126th Ave *Web:* www.leadersfurniture.com	Largo	FL	33773	727-538-5577	
Leath Furniture LLC 4370 Peachtree Rd *Web:* www.leathfurniture.com	Atlanta	GA	30319	404-848-0880	
Leather Creations Inc 2692 Peachtree Sq *Web:* leathercreationsfurniture.com	Atlanta	GA	30360	678-584-1000	
Legacy Classic Furniture Inc 2575 Penny Rd *Web:* www.legacyclassic.com	High Point	NC	27265	336-449-4600	
Legends Furniture Inc 10300 W Buckeye Rd *Web:* legendsfurniture.com	Tolleson	AZ	85353	623-931-6500	
Leick Furniture Inc 2219 S 19th St	Sheboygan	WI	53081	920-451-4060	
Levin Furniture Co 5280 Rt 30 *Web:* www.levinfurniture.com	Greensburg	PA	15601	724-834-3550	
Lexington Furniture Company Inc, The 3024 Blake James Dr	Lexington	KY	40509	859-254-4412	
Lifestyle Enterprises Inc 529 Townsend Ave *Web:* www.lifestyle-datong.com	High Point	NC	27263	336-882-7900	882-9122
Lindsey Office Furnishings 2223 First Ave N *Web:* www.lindseyof.com	Birmingham	AL	35203	205-251-9088	
Living Spaces Furniture LLC 14501 Artesia Blvd *TF:* 877-266-7300 ■ *Web:* www.livingspaces.com	La Mirada	CA	90638	877-266-7300	
Logo Inc 117 SE Pkwy *Web:* www.logobrands.com	Franklin	TN	37064	615-261-2100	
London Luxury Bedding Inc 271 N Ave Ste 412 *Web:* www.londonlux.com	New Rochelle	NY	10801	914-636-2100	
Louis Shanks of Texas 2930 W Anderson Ln *Web:* www.louisshanksfurniture.com	Austin	TX	78757	512-451-6501	451-6520
Lozano Caseworks Inc 242 W Hanna St	Colton	CA	92324	909-783-7530	
Luminaire (Miami) Inc 8950 NW 33rd St *Web:* www.luminaire.com	Miami	FL	33172	305-437-7975	
MacKenzie-Childs LLC 3260 SR- 90 *TF:* 888-665-1999 ■ *Web:* www.mackenzie-childs.com	Aurora	NY	13152	315-364-7123	
Macy's 111 N State St *Web:* www.macys.com	Chicago	IL	60602	312-781-1000	
Marlo Furniture Company Inc 3300 Marlo Ln *Web:* www.marlofurniture.com	Forestville	MD	20747	301-735-2000	
Marmol Radziner & Associates AIA 12210 Nebraska Ave *Web:* www.marmol-radziner.com	Los Angeles	CA	90025	310-826-6222	
Marshall Furniture Inc 999 Anita Ave *Web:* www.marshallfurniture.com	Antioch	IL	60002	847-395-9350	
Mash Studios Inc 12705 Venice Blvd *Web:* mashstudios.com	Los Angeles	CA	90066	310-313-4700	
Massoud Furniture Manufacturing Inc 8351 Moberly Ln *TF:* 800-762-2797 ■ *Web:* www.massoudfurniture.com	Dallas	TX	75227	214-388-8655	
Mathis Bros Furniture Inc 6611 S 101 St E Ave *TF Cust Svc:* 800-329-3434 ■ *Web:* www.mathisbrothers.com	Tulsa	OK	74133	918-461-7785	
Maurice Vaughan Furniture Co 610 E Stuart Dr *Web:* www.mauricevaughaninc.com	Galax	VA	24333	276-236-9781	
Maynard Furniture Company Inc 725 Anderson St *TF:* 866-420-5249 ■ *Web:* www.maynardshomefurnishings.com	Belton	SC	29627	864-338-7751	
Mayo Manufacturing Corp 4101 Terry St *Web:* www.mayofurniture.com	Texarkana	TX	75501	903-838-0518	838-4531
Mcneills Furniture & Appliance of Denton Inc 104 W Oak *Web:* mcneillsappliance.com	Denton	TX	76201	940-382-6932	
Mealey's Furniture Inc 908 W St Rd *Web:* www.mealeysfurniture.com	Warminster	PA	18974	215-672-1333	
Meredith O'Donnell Inc 1751 Post Oak Blvd *Web:* www.meredithodonnell.com	Houston	TX	77056	713-526-7332	
Michael Taylor Designs Inc 155 Rhode Island St *Web:* www.michaeltaylordesigns.com	San Francisco	CA	94103	415-558-9940	
Miskelly Furniture 101 Airport Rd *TF:* 888-939-6288 ■ *Web:* www.miskellys.com	Jackson	MS	39208	601-939-6288	933-5950
Morris Furniture Co Inc 2377 Commerce Ctr Dr *TF:* 800-243-0000 ■ *Web:* morrisathome.com	Fairborn	OH	45324	937-874-7100	
Moser Corp 601 N 13th St *TF:* 800-632-4564 ■ *Web:* www.mosercorporation.com	Rogers	AR	72756	479-636-3481	
N o a Medical Industries Inc 801 Terry Ln *TF:* 800-633-6068 ■ *Web:* www.noamedical.com	Washington	MO	63090	636-239-7600	

Phone | Fax

N Tepperman Ltd 2595 Ouellette Ave Windsor ON N8X4V8 519-969-9700
TF: 800-265-5062 ■ *Web:* www.teppermans.com

Nashville Office Interiors 1621 Church St Nashville TN 37203 615-329-1811
TF: 877-342-0294 ■ *Web:* www.noifurniture.com

National Furniture Liquidators I LLC
2870 Plant Atkinson Rd Se Smyrna GA 30080 404-603-9714
Web: www.nflinc.com

NB Liebman & Company Inc
4705 Carlisle Pk Mechanicsburg PA 17050 717-761-4550
Web: www.nbliebman.com

Near North Business Machines 86 W Rd Huntsville ON P1H1M1 705-787-0517
Web: nearnorthbusiness.com

Nebraska Furniture Mart Inc 700 S 72nd St Omaha NE 68114 402-397-6100
TF: 800-336-9136 ■ *Web:* www.nfm.com

Niche Modern Home 1901 Hwy 190 Mandeville LA 70448 985-624-4045
Web: nichemodernhome.biz

Nickerson Business Supplies 876A Lebanon St Monroe OH 45050 513-539-6600
TF: 888-385-9922 ■ *Web:* nickbiz.com

Norco Products Furniture Mfrs
4985 Blue Mtn Rd Missoula MT 59804 406-251-3800
Web: www.norcoproducts.com

Norcon Industries Inc 5412 E Calle Cerrito Guadalupe AZ 85283 480-839-2324
Web: www.norconindustries.net

Northland Furniture Co 681 Se Glenwood Dr Bend OR 97702 541-389-3600
Web: www.northlandfurniture.com

Norwood Furniture 216 N Gilbert Rd Gilbert AZ 85234 480-892-0174
Web: www.norwoodfurniture.com

Nucraft Furniture Co 5151 W River Dr Comstock Park MI 49321 616-784-6016
TF: 877-682-7238 ■ *Web:* www.nucraft.com

Office Express Supply Inc 8005 W 20th Ave Hialeah FL 33014 305-557-1667
Web: www.xpressbuy.com

Office Furniture Installers Inc
3167 Spaulding St Omaha NE 68111 402-451-8009
Web: www.ofi-usa.com

Office Furniture Partnership Inc, The
67 E Pk Pl Morristown NJ 07960 973-267-6966
Web: www.officefurniturepartnership.com

OFIS LP, The 7110 Old Katy Rd Houston TX 77024 713-629-5599
Web: theofis.com

Olinde's Furniture 9536 Airline Hwy Baton Rouge LA 70815 225-926-3380
Web: www.olindes.com

Olum's of Binghamton Inc 3701 Vestal Pkwy E Vestal NY 13850 607-729-5775 729-6166
TF Cust Svc: 855-264-8674 ■ *Web:* www.olums.com

Osborne Wood Products Inc 4618 Hwy 123 Toccoa GA 30577 706-886-1065
Web: www.osbornewood.com

Ostermancron Inc 10830 Millington Ct Cincinnati OH 45242 513-771-3377
Web: www.ostermancron.com

Otterbine Barebo Inc 3840 Main Rd E Emmaus PA 18049 610-965-6018
TF: 800-237-8837 ■ *Web:* www.otterbine.com

Paris Kitchens 245 W Beaver Creek Rd Richmond Hill ON L4B1L1 905-886-5751
Web: pariskitchens.com

Parker Furniture
10375 SW Beaverton-Hillsdale Hwy Beaverton OR 97005 503-644-0155 275-1087*
*Fax Area Code: 971 ■ *TF:* 866-515-9673 ■ *Web:* www.parker-furniture.com

Patioshoppers Inc 41188 Sandalwood Cir Murrieta CA 92562 951-696-1700
TF: 800-940-6123 ■ *Web:* www.patioshoppers.com

Pier 1 Kids 100 Pier 1 Pl Fort Worth TX 76102 817-252-8000 252-8995
TF: 800-433-4035 ■ *Web:* www.pier1.com

Porters of Racine 301 Sixth St Racine WI 53403 262-633-6363
TF: 800-558-3245 ■ *Web:* www.portersofracine.com

Preservation Technologies LP
111 Thomson Park Dr Cranberry Township PA 16066 724-779-2111
TF: 800-416-2665 ■ *Web:* www.ptlp.com

Privilege International Inc
2419 Firestone Blvd South Gate CA 90280 323-585-0777
Web: www.privilegeinc.com

R C Furniture Inc 1111 S Jellick Ave Industry CA 91748 626-964-4100
Web: www.rcfurniture.com

Ravensberg Inc 1338 Strassner Dr Saint Louis MO 63144 314-968-4020
Web: www.ravensberg.com

Raymour & Flanigan Furniture PO Box 220 Liverpool NY 13088 315-453-2500
Web: www.raymourflanigan.com

Reborn Cabinets 2981 E La Palma Ave Anaheim CA 92806 714-630-2220
TF: 888-273-2676 ■ *Web:* www.reborncabinets.com

Refurbished Office Furniture
1212 N 39th St Ste 200 Tampa FL 33605 813-241-4515
Web: www.rofinc.net

Regency Furniture Inc 7900 Cedarville Rd Brandywine MD 20613 301-782-3800
Web: www.regencyfurniture.com

Regency Seating Inc 2375 Romig Rd Akron OH 44320 330-848-3700
TF: 866-816-9822 ■ *Web:* regencyof.com

Robb & Stucky International
13170 S Cleveland Ave Fort Myers FL 33907 239-415-2800
Web: robbstuckyintl.com

Roche Bobios 200 Madison St New York NY 10016 212-889-0700
Web: www.roche-bobois.com

Rocky Top Furniture Inc 8957 Lexington Rd Lancaster KY 40444 859-548-2828
TF: 800-332-1143 ■ *Web:* www.rockytoplogfurniture.com

Romar Cabinet & Top Company Inc
23949 S Northern Illinois Dr Channahon IL 60410 815-467-9900
Web: www.romarcabinet.com

Roomplace, The 1000-46 Rohlwing Rd Lombard IL 60148 630-261-3900
Web: www.theroomplace.com

Roomstores of Phoenix LLC, The
3011 E Broadway Rd Ste 100 Phoenix AZ 85040 602-268-1111
Web: arizonaroomstore.com

Roost Home Furnishings
200 Gate Five Rd Number 116 Sausalito CA 94965 415-339-9500
Web: www.roostco.com

Rosewood Industries Inc 1203 E Central Ter Stigler OK 74462 800-228-3306
TF: 800-228-3306 ■ *Web:* www.rosewood.net

Phone | Fax

Rothman Furniture Stores Inc
2101 E Terra Ln O'Fallon MO 63366 636-978-3500 696-4300
Web: www.rothmanfurniture.com

Rotmans Furniture & Carpet
725 Southbridge St Worcester MA 01610 508-755-5276
TF: 800-768-6267 ■ *Web:* www.rotmans.com

Royal Discount Furniture Company Inc
122 S Main St Memphis TN 38103 901-527-6407
Web: www.royalfurniture.com

Royals Inc 324 SW 16th St Belle Glade FL 33430 561-996-7646 996-4480
Web: royalsfurnitureinc.com

RTA Furniture Corporation
5500 Linglestown Rd Harrisburg PA 17112 717-540-5500
Web: www.justcabinets.com

S Rose Inc 1213 Prospect Ave E Cleveland OH 44115 216-781-8200

Sam Clar Office Furniture Inc
1221 Diamond Way Concord CA 94520 925-602-3900
TF: 800-726-2527 ■ *Web:* www.samclar.com

Sam Levitz Furniture 3430 E 36th St Tucson AZ 85713 520-624-7443
Web: www.samlevitz.com

Sam's Appliance & Television Rental Inc
5050 E Belknap St Fort Worth TX 76117 817-665-5050
Web: www.samsfurniture.com

San Francisco Design Ctr
2 Henry Adams St Ste 450 San Francisco CA 94103 415-490-5800 490-5885
Web: www.sfdesigncenter.com

Sawbridge Studios 1015 Tower Ct Winnetka IL 60093 847-441-2441
Web: sawbridge.com

Schewel Furniture Company Inc 1031 Main St Lynchburg VA 24504 434-522-0200 522-0207
Web: schewels.com

Schmidt-Goodman Office Products
1920 N Broadway Rochester MN 55906 507-282-3870
TF: 800-247-0663 ■ *Web:* www.schmidtgoodman.com

Scott Rice Office Works 14720 W 105th St Lenexa KS 66215 913-888-7600
Web: www.scottrice.com

Sedlak Interiors Inc 34300 Solon Rd Solon OH 44139 440-248-2424
TF: 800-260-2949 ■ *Web:* www.sedlakinteriors.com

Sei/Aarons Inc 3108 Piedmont Rd Ne Ste 160 Atlanta GA 30305 404-495-9707
Web: seiaarons.com

Selden's Home Furnishings 1802 62nd Ave E Tacoma WA 98424 253-922-5700
TF: 800-870-7880 ■ *Web:* seldens.com

Senator International Inc 1630 Holland Rd Maumee OH 43537 419-887-5805
Web: www.thesenatorgroup.com/americas/allermuir

Sheely's Furniture & Appliance Company Inc
11450 S Ave North Lima OH 44452 330-549-3901
TF: 877-549-9144 ■ *Web:* www.sheelys.com

Shenandoah Furniture Inc
225 Beaver Creek Dr Martinsville VA 24112 276-632-0502
Web: www.shenandoahfurniture.com

Sheridan Group Inc, The 2045 Pontius Ave Los Angeles CA 90025 310-575-0664
Web: www.sheridaninc.com

Shofer'S Furniture Company LLC
930 S Charles St Baltimore MD 21230 410-752-4212
Web: shofers.com

Shops at Carolina Furniture of Williamsburg
5425 Richmond Rd Williamsburg VA 23188 757-565-3000 565-4476
TF: 800-582-8916 ■ *Web:* www.carolina-furniture.com

Sit 'n Sleep 14300 S Main St Gardena CA 90248 310-604-8903 604-8903
TF: 877-262-4006 ■ *Web:* www.sitnsleep.com

Sitonit Seating 6415 Katella Ave Cypress CA 90630 714-995-4800
Web: www.sitonit.net

Sleep America Inc 1202 N 54th Ave Ste 111 Phoenix AZ 85043 602-269-7000

Slumberland Inc 3060 Centerville Rd Little Canada MN 55117 651-482-7500
TF: 888-957-7586 ■ *Web:* www.slumberland.com

Smart Furniture Inc 430 Market St Chattanooga TN 37402 423-267-7007
TF: 888-467-6278 ■ *Web:* www.smartfurniture.com

Smith Village Home Furnishings 34 N Main St Jacobus PA 17407 717-428-1921
TF: 800-242-1921 ■ *Web:* smithvillage.com

Snuggle Bugz 3245 Fairview St Burlington ON L7N3L1 905-631-0005
Web: snugglebugz.ca

Southern Finishing 801 E Church St Martinsville VA 24112 276-632-4901
Web: www.southernfinishing.com

Southern Furniture Company of Conover Inc
1099 Second Ave Pl SE Conover NC 28613 828-464-0311
Web: www.southernfurniture.net

Spears Furniture Co 7004 Salem Ave Lubbock TX 79424 806-747-3401
Web: spearsfurniture.com

Specified Woodworking Corp
9327 Washington Blvd N Ste A Laurel MD 20723 301-598-8200
Web: www.specifiedwoodworking.com

Spiller Furniture 5605 Mcfarland Blvd Northport AL 35476 205-333-2030
Web: www.spillerfurniture.com

Spine Align Inc 741 Chicago Dr Holland MI 49423 616-392-4565
Web: www.chirobed.com

Sprintz Furniture Showroom Inc
6205 Cockrill Bend Cir Nashville TN 37209 615-234-3200
Web: sprintz.com

Stacy Furniture 1900 S Main St Ste 200 Grapevine TX 76051 817-424-8800
Web: www.stacyfurniture.com

Stageright Corp 495 Pioneer Pkwy Clare MI 48617 989-386-7393
TF: 800-438-4499 ■ *Web:* www.stageright.com

Standard Office Supply 35 Sheridan St Nw Washington DC 20011 202-829-4820
TF: 888-829-4820 ■ *Web:* www.standardofficesupply.com

Star Furniture Company Inc
16666 Barker Springs Rd Houston TX 77084 281-492-6661
TF: 800-364-6661 ■ *Web:* www.starfurniture.com

Stein World Inc 5321 E Shelby Dr Memphis TN 38118 901-261-3050
Web: www.steinworld.com

Steinhafels W 231 N 1013 County Hwy F Waukesha WI 53186 262-436-4600 436-4601
TF Cust Svc: 866-351-4600 ■ *Web:* www.steinhafels.com

Sterling Furniture Co
2051 South 1100 East Salt Lake City UT 84106 801-467-1579

				Phone	Fax
Stone County Ironworks 408 Ironworks Dr. Web: stonecountyironworks.com	Mountain View	AR	72560	870-269-8108	
Sunnyland Outdoor & Casual Furniture 7879 Spring Vly Rd Ste 125. TF: 877-239-3716 ■ Web: www.sunnylandfurniture.com	Dallas	TX	75254	972-239-3716	
Superior Woodcraft Inc 160 N Hamilton St. Web: www.superiorwoodcraft.com	Doylestown	PA	18901	215-348-9942	
Swartz Kitchens & Baths 5550 Allentown Blvd (Route 22). Web: swartzkitchens.com	Harrisburg	PA	17112	717-652-7111	
SWC Office Furniture Outlet 375 Fairfield Ave. Web: swcoffice.com	Stamford	CT	06902	203-967-8367	
Symar Installations Inc 1960 Foxridge Dr. Web: symarinstallations.com	Kansas City	KS	66106	913-236-4441	
TC Mill Work Inc 3433 Marshall Ln. Web: www.tcmillwork.com	Bensalem	PA	19020	215-245-4210	
Techline Bozeman-mcphie Cabinetry 435 E Main St. Web: www.mcphiecabinetry.com	Bozeman	MT	59715	406-586-1708	
Terra Furniture Inc 14819 Salt Lk Ave. Web: www.terrafurniture.com	City Of Industry	CA	91746	626-912-8523	
Thomas-Hines Co 3027 W Cary St	Richmond	VA	23221	804-355-2782	
Thrifty Office Furniture 1023 S Miami Blvd. Web: www.thriftyofficefurniture.com	Durham	NC	27703	919-598-8454	
Toms-Price Co 303 E Front St. Web: www.tomsprice.com	Wheaton	IL	60187	630-668-7878	
Town & Country Furniture 6545 Airline Hwy. Web: www.tcfurniture.com	Baton Rouge	LA	70805	225-355-6666	355-7459
trade associates group Ltd 1730 W Wrightwood Ave. Web: www.tagltd.com	Chicago	IL	60614	773-871-1300	
Tri-boro Shelving & Partition Corp 300 Dominion Dr. TF: 800-633-3070 ■ Web: www.triboroshelving.com	Farmville	VA	23901	434-315-5600	
Trinity Business Furniture 6089 Kennedy Rd. TF: 855-311-6660 ■ Web: www.trinityfurniture.com	Trinity	NC	27370	336-472-6660	
Trivest Partners LP 550 S Dixie Hwy Ste 300. Web: www.trivest.com	Coral Gables	FL	33146	305-858-2200	
Troy Wesnidge Inc 2024 S Main St. Web: www.wesnidge.com	Newcastle	OK	73065	405-387-4720	
True North America Inc 2052 Alton Pkwy. Web: trueinnovations.com	Irvine	CA	92606	714-368-7464	
TUFF SHED Inc 1777 S Harrison St Ste 600. Web: www.tuffshed.com	Denver	CO	80210	303-753-8833	
Tupelo Furniture Market Inc 1879 N Coley Rd. Web: www.tupelofurnituremarket.com	Tupelo	MS	38801	662-842-4442	
Turners Fine Furniture Co 707 Second St W. Web: turnerfurniture.com	Tifton	GA	31794	229-382-3266	
Twentieth Modern 7470 Beverly Blvd. Web: www.twentieth.net	Los Angeles	CA	90036	323-904-1200	
U.S. Quality Furniture Services Inc 8920 Winkler Dr Ste 100. Web: www.usqfs.com	Houston	TX	77017	713-943-7016	
Unger Furniture Company of Sauk Centre Inc 516 Sinclair Lewis Ave	Sauk Centre	MN	56378	320-352-2247	
United Corporate Furnishings Inc 1780 N Market Blvd	Sacramento	CA	95834	916-553-5900	
Urban Barn Ltd 4085 Marine Way Ste 1. TF: 844-456-2200 ■ Web: www.urbanbarn.com	Burnaby	BC	V5J5E2	604-456-2200	
USA Baby 793 Springer Dr. TF: 800-767-9464 ■ Web: www.usababy.com	Lombard	IL	60148	630-652-0600	
Usine Rotec Inc 125 Rue De L'eglise Rr 1. Web: www.rotecbeds.com	Baie-du-febvre	QC	J0G1A0	450-783-6444	783-6446
Value City Furniture 40 East 53rd St. Web: www.valuecitynj.com	Bayonne	NJ	07002	201-436-2000	
Value City Furniture 4300 E Fifth Ave. TF: 888-751-8552 ■ Web: www.valuecityfurniture.com	Columbus	OH	43219	888-672-2411	
Victory Furniture 9040 W Pico Blvd. TF: 800-953-2000 ■ Web: www.victoryfurniture.com	Los Angeles	CA	90035	800-953-2000	
W H Cress Company Inc 9966 Sw Katherine St. Web: www.whcress.com	Tigard	OR	97223	503-620-1664	
Walker Furniture 301 S Martin L King Blvd. Web: www.walkerfurniture.com	Las Vegas	NV	89106	702-384-9300	
Walker's Furniture Inc 3808 N Sullivan Rd Bldg 22-C. TF: 866-667-6655 ■ Web: www.walkersfurniture.com	Spokane Valley	WA	99216	509-535-1995	
Warehouse Home Furnishings Distributors Inc 1851 Telfair St PO Box 1140. *Fax Area Code: 478 ■ TF: 800-456-0424 ■ Web: farmershomefurniture.com	Dublin	GA	31021	800-456-0424	275-6276*
Waterbeds n Stuff Inc 3933 Brookham Dr. Web: www.bedsnstuff.com	Grove City	OH	43123	614-871-1171	
Wayneco Inc 800 Hanover Rd. Web: www.waynecoinc.com	York	PA	17408	717-225-4413	
Wayside Furniture Inc 1367 Canton Rd. TF: 877-499-3968 ■ Web: www.wayside-furniture.com	Akron	OH	44312	330-733-6221	
WB Mason Company Inc 59 Centre St. Web: www.wbmason.com	Brockton	MA	02303	508-586-3434	
Weekends Only Inc 349 Marshall Ave 3rd Fl. TF: 855-803-5888 ■ Web: www.weekendsonly.com	Saint Louis	MO	63119	314-447-1500	447-1591
Weir's Furniture Village Inc 3219 Knox St. Web: www.weirsfurniture.com	Dallas	TX	75205	214-528-0321	
Wells Home Furnishings 101 Bowers Rd. TF: 800-249-7753 ■ Web: www.wellshome.com	Charleston	WV	25314	304-343-3600	
Wenger Furniture Appliance & Electronics 4552 Whittier Blvd. Web: www.wengerfurniture.com	Los Angeles	CA	90022	323-261-1136	261-0968
Westco Home Furnishings Inc 400 NW Veterans Blvd. Web: www.westcohomefurnishings.com	Miami	OK	74354	918-540-2464	540-1186
Western Contract 11455 Folsom Blvd. Web: www.westerncontract.com	Rancho Cordova	CA	95742	916-638-3338	638-2698
WG&R Furniture Co 900 Challenger Dr. TF: 888-947-7782 ■ Web: www.wgrfurniture.com	Green Bay	WI	54311	920-469-4880	
Whalen Furniture Manufacturing Inc 1578 Air Wing Rd. Web: www.whalenfurniture.com	San Diego	CA	92154	619-423-9948	
Wieser & Cawley Furniture 1301 Colegate Dr. TF: 800-339-0094 ■ Web: wieserandcawleyfurniture.com	Marietta	OH	45750	740-373-1676	
William M Bloomfield Inc 170 Barnard Ave	San Jose	CA	95125	408-998-2995	
Willis Furniture Company Inc 4220 Virginia Beach Blvd. Web: willisfurniture.com	Virginia Beach	VA	23452	757-340-2112	
Wine Appreciation Guild 450 Taraval Str Ste 201. Web: wineappreciation.com	South San Francisco	CA	94080	650-866-3020	
Wittigs Office Interiors Ltd 2013 Broadway St. Web: www.wittigs.com	San Antonio	TX	78215	210-270-0100	
WL Rubottom Company Inc 320 W Lewis St. Web: wlrubottom.com	Ventura	CA	93001	805-648-6943	
Wolf Furniture Inc 1620 N Tuckahoe St. Web: www.wolffurniture.com	Bellwood	PA	16617	814-742-4380	
Wood You Furniture 11700 San Jose Blvd. Web: www.woodyou.com	Jacksonville	FL	32223	904-370-1333	
Woodley'S Fine Furniture Inc 320 S Sunset St. Web: woodleys.com	Longmont	CO	80501	303-443-5692	
Woodstock Furniture Outlet 100 Robin Rd Ext. Web: www.woodstockoutlet.com	Acworth	GA	30102	678-255-1000	
Workplace Resource LLC 4400 NE Loop 410 Ste 130. TF: 800-580-3000 ■ Web: www.hmwrasa.com	San Antonio	TX	78218	512-472-7300	
WS Badcock Corp (WSBC) PO Box 497. TF: 800-223-2625 ■ Web: www.badcock.com	Mulberry	FL	33860	800-223-2625	
Yamada Enterprises 16552 Burke Ln. Web: www.yamadaenterprises.com	Huntington Beach	CA	92647	714-843-9882	
Zuri Furniture 4880 Alpha Rd. Web: zurifurniture.com	Dallas	TX	75244	972-716-9874	

322 GAMES & GAMING

See Also Casino Companies p. 1893; Casinos p. 1894; Lotteries, Games, Sweepstakes p. 2687; Toys, Games, Hobbies p. 3256

				Phone	Fax
Ac Coin & Slot 201 W Decatur Ave. TF: 800-284-7568	Pleasantville	NJ	08232	609-641-7811	383-2758
American Gaming & Electronics 9500 W 55th St Ste A. TF: 800-336-6630 ■ Web: www.agegaming.com	Countryside	IL	60525	708-290-2100	290-2200
Amtote International Inc 11200 Pepper Rd. *Fax: Acctg ■ TF: 800-345-1566 ■ Web: www.amtote.com	Hunt Valley	MD	21031	410-771-8700	785-5299*
Arachnid Inc 6212 Material Ave. TF: 800-435-8319 ■ Web: www.bullshooter.com	Loves Park	IL	61111	815-654-0212	654-0447
Aristocrat Technologies 7230 Amigo St. TF: 800-748-4156 ■ Web: www.aristocratgaming.com	Las Vegas	NV	89119	702-270-1000	270-1001
Bmi Gaming Inc 3500 NW Boca Raton Blvd Ste 721. Web: www.bmigaming.com	Boca Raton	FL	33431	561-391-7200	892-2268
Douglas Press Inc 2810 Madison St. TF: 800-323-0705 ■ Web: www.douglaspress.com	Bellwood	IL	60104	708-547-8400	
eLottery Inc 46 Southfield Ave 3 Stamford Landing Ste 370. Web: www.elottery.com	Stamford	CT	06902	203-388-1808	388-1808
FortuNet Inc 3901 Graphic Center Dr Ste C. Web: www.fortunet.com	Las Vegas	NV	89118	702-796-9090	
Gaming Partners International Corp 1700 Industrial Rd. NASDAQ: GPIC ■ TF: 800-728-5766 ■ Web: gpigaming.com	Las Vegas	NV	89102	702-384-2425	
International Game Technology (IGT) 9295 Prototype Dr. NYSE: IGT ■ TF: 800-522-4700 ■ Web: www.igt.com	Reno	NV	89521	775-448-7777	
Jacobs Entertainment Inc 17301 W Colfax Ave Ste 250. Web: jacobsentertainmentinc.com	Golden	CO	80401	303-215-5200	
Konami Gaming Inc 585 Trade Ctr Dr. TF: 866-544-7568 ■ Web: www.gaming.konami.com/corporate/home.aspx	Las Vegas	NV	89119	702-616-1400	367-0007
Littlefield Corp 2501 N Lamar Blvd. OTC: LTFD ■ Web: www.littlefield.com	Austin	TX	78705	512-476-5141	
Mondial International Corp 101 Secor Ln PO Box 8369. Web: mondialgroup.com	Pelham Manor	NY	10803	914-738-7411	738-7521
Monolith Productions Inc 12131 113th Ave NE Ste 300. Web: www.lith.com	Kirkland	WA	98034	425-739-1500	
Newport Diversified Inc 2301 Dupont Dr Ste 500. Web: www.nd-inc.com	Irvine	CA	92612	949-851-1355	
Nickels & Dimes Inc 1844 N Preston Rd. Web: www.tilt.com	Celina	TX	75009	847-856-1064	
PokerTek Inc 1150 Crews Rd Ste F. NASDAQ: PTEK ■ Web: www.pokertek.com	Matthews	NC	28105	704-849-0860	
Scientific Games Corp 750 Lexington Ave 25th Fl. NASDAQ: SGMS ■ TF: 800-827-2946 ■ Web: www.scientificgames.com	New York	NY	10022	212-754-2233	
Skee-Ball Amusement Games 121 Liberty Ln. Web: www.skeeball.com	Chalfont	PA	18914	215-997-8900	997-8982
Smart Industries Corp 1626 Delaware Ave. TF: 800-553-2442 ■ Web: www.smartind.com	Des Moines	IA	50317	515-265-9900	265-3148

Phone | Fax

Valley-Dynamo 7224 Burns Rd Richland Hills TX 76118 972-595-5365 595-5380
TF: 800-826-7856 ■ *Web:* www.vdlp.net

Video King Gaming Systems (VKGS LLC)
2717 N 118 Cir Ste 210 Omaha NE 68164 402-951-2970 951-2990
TF: 800-635-9912 ■ *Web:* www.videokingnetwork.com

Western Regional Off-Track Betting Corp
8315 Park Rd Batavia NY 14020 585-343-1423 343-6873
Web: www.westernotb.com

WMS Gaming Inc 800 S Northpoint Blvd Waukegan IL 60085 847-785-3000 785-3058
TF: 800-522-4700 ■ *Web:* www.wms.com

323 GARDEN CENTERS

See Also Horticultural Products Growers p. 2482; Seed Companies p. 3176

Phone | Fax

Armstrong Garden Centers Inc (AGC)
2200 E Rt 66 Ste 200 Glendora CA 91740 626-914-1091 335-0257
Web: www.armstronggarden.com

Baron Brothers Nursery Inc
7568 Santa Rosa Rd Camarillo CA 93012 805-484-0085
Web: www.baronbrothers.com

Behnke Nurseries Co 11300 Baltimore Ave Beltsville MD 20705 301-937-1100 937-8034
Web: www.behnkes.com

Breck's PO Box 65 Guilford IN 47022 513-354-1511 354-1505
Web: www.brecks.com

Cal Herbold Nursery 9403 E Ave Hesperia CA 92345 760-244-6125

Calloway's Nursery Inc
4200 Airport Fwy Ste 200 Fort Worth TX 76117 817-222-1122
OTC: CLWY ■ *Web:* www.calloways.com

Champlain Valley Equipment Inc
453 Exchange St Middlebury VT 05753 802-388-4967
Web: www.champlainvalleyequipment.com

Corbitt Manufacturing Co Inc
854 NW Guerdon St Lake City FL 32055 386-755-2555
Web: www.cypress-mulch.com

DA Hoerr & Sons Inc 8020 N Shadetree Dr Peoria IL 61615 309-691-4561
Web: www.hoerrnursery.com

Earl May Seed & Nursery 208 N Elm St Shenandoah IA 51603 712-246-1020 246-2210
TF: 877-800-5556 ■ *Web:* www.earlmay.com

Farmers Market Garden Ctr Inc
4110 N Elston Ave Chicago IL 60618 773-539-1200
Web: www.gardenchicago.com

Flowerwood Garden Ctr 7625 Us Hwy 14 Crystal Lake IL 60012 815-459-6200
Web: www.flowerwoodgardencenter.net

Fruit Basket Flowerland 765 28th St SW Wyoming MI 49509 616-532-7404 531-7858
Web: www.myflowerland.com

Gardener's Supply Co 128 Intervale Rd Burlington VT 05401 802-660-3500
TF: 800-863-1700 ■ *Web:* www.gardeners.com

Greenbrier Farms Inc 225 Sign Pine Rd Chesapeake VA 23322 757-421-2141
TF: 800-829-2141 ■ *Web:* www.historicgreenbrierfarms.com

Home & Garden Showplace 8600 W Bryn Mawr Chicago IL 60631 773-695-5000
TF: 877-502-4641 ■ *Web:* truevaluecompany.com/gardencenters

Home Depot Inc 2455 Paces Ferry Rd NW Atlanta GA 30339 770-433-8211
NYSE: HD ■ *TF Cust Svc:* 800-553-3199 ■ *Web:* www.homedepot.com

Johnson's Garden Centers 2707 W 13th St Wichita KS 67203 316-942-1443
TF: 888-542-8463 ■ *Web:* www.johnsonsgarden.com

Johnson's Nursery Inc
W180 N 6275 Marcy Rd Menomonee Falls WI 53051 262-252-4988 252-4495
Web: www.johnsonsnursery.com

JW Jung Seed Co 335 S High St Randolph WI 53956 800-297-3123 692-5864
TF: 800-297-3123 ■ *Web:* www.jungseed.com

L. J. Thalmann Co 3132 Lake Ave Wilmette IL 60091 847-256-0561 256-4978
Web: www.chaletnursery.com

Lowe's Cos Inc 1000 Lowe's Blvd Mooresville NC 28117 704-758-1000
NYSE: LOW ■ *TF:* 800-445-6937 ■ *Web:* www.lowes.com

Mahoney's Garden Ctr 242 Cambridge St Winchester MA 01890 781-729-5900
Web: www.mahoneysgarden.com

McKay Nursery Company Inc
750 S Monroe St PO Box 185 Waterloo WI 53594 920-478-2121 478-3615
TF: 800-236-4242 ■ *Web:* www.mckaynursery.com

Meadows Farms Inc 43054 John Mosby Hwy Chantilly VA 20152 703-327-3940
Web: www.meadowsfarms.com

Michigan Bulb Co PO Box 4180 Lawrenceburg IN 47025 513-354-1498 354-1499
Web: www.michiganbulb.com

Milaeger's Inc 4838 Douglas Ave Racine WI 53402 262-639-2040 681-6192
TF: 800-669-1229 ■ *Web:* www.milaegers.com

North Haven Gardens Inc 7700 Northaven Rd Dallas TX 75230 214-363-5316
Web: www.nhg.com

Oakland Nursery Inc 1156 Oakland Pk Ave Columbus OH 43224 614-268-3511
Web: www.oaklandnursery.com

Panhandle Co-op Assn
401 S Beltline Hwy W Scottsbluff NE 69361 308-632-5301 632-5375
TF Cust Svc: 800-732-4546 ■ *Web:* www.panhandlecoop.com

Pike Nurseries Holding LLC
3555 Koger Blvd Ste 360 Duluth GA 30096 770-921-1022
Web: www.pikenursery.com

Plant Delights Nursery Inc 9241 Sauls Rd Raleigh NC 27603 919-772-4794 662-0370
Web: www.plantdelights.com

Plants of the Southwest 3095 Agua Fria Rd Santa Fe NM 87507 505-438-8888 438-8800
TF: 800-788-7333 ■ *Web:* www.plantsofthesouthwest.com

Pleasant View Gardens Inc 7316 Pleasant St Loudon NH 03307 603-435-8361 435-6849
TF: 866-862-2974 ■ *Web:* www.pvg.com

Por La Mar Nursery Inc
905 S Patterson Ave Santa Barbara CA 93160 805-699-4500
Web: www.porlamarnursery.com

Ritchie Tractor 1746 W Lmar Alxander Pkwy Maryville TN 37801 865-981-3199
TF: 888-319-0282 ■ *Web:* www.ritchietractor.com

Round Butte Seed Growers Inc 505 C St Culver OR 97734 541-546-5222
TF: 866-385-7001 ■ *Web:* helenaculver.com

Phone | Fax

San Gabriel Nursery & Florist
632 S San Gabriel Blvd San Gabriel CA 91776 626-286-3782
Web: www.sgnurserynews.com/site

Shanti Bithi Nursery 3047 High Ridge Rd Stamford CT 06903 203-329-0768
Web: www.shantibithi.com

Siebenthaler Co 3001 Catalpa Dr Dayton OH 45405 937-274-1154
Web: www.siebenthaler.com

Sloat Garden Ctr Inc 420 Coloma St Sausalito CA 94965 415-332-0657
Web: www.sloatgardens.com

Stein Garden & Gift Centers Inc
5400 S 27th St Milwaukee WI 53221 414-761-5400 761-8812
Web: www.shopsteins.com

Summerwinds Nursery 17826 N Tatum Blvd Phoenix AZ 85032 602-867-1822
Web: www.summerwindsnursery.com

TLC Florist & Greenhouse Inc
105 W Memorial Rd Oklahoma City OK 73114 405-751-0630
Web: www.tlcgarden.com

Treelands Inc 1000 Huntington Tpke Bridgeport CT 06610 203-372-3511 371-6023
Web: treelandgardencenter.com

Twombly Nursery 163 Barn Hill Rd Monroe CT 06468 203-261-2133 261-9230
Web: www.twomblynursery.com

Village Nurseries 1589 N Main St Orange CA 92867 800-542-0209 279-3199*
**Fax Area Code:* 714 ■ *TF:* 800-542-0209 ■ *Web:* www.villagenurseries.com

Wal-Mart Stores Inc 702 SW Eigth St Bentonville AR 72716 479-273-4000
NYSE: WMT ■ *TF Cust Svc:* 800-925-6278 ■ *Web:* corporate.walmart.com

Walker Nursery Co 3809 Manchester Hwy Mcminnville TN 37110 931-668-4622
Web: walkernurseryco.com

Waterloo Gardens Inc 200 N Whitford Rd Exton PA 19341 610-363-0800
Web: www.waterloogardens.com

Weingartz Supply Co 46061 Van Dyke Ave Utica MI 48317 586-731-7240
TF: 855-669-7278 ■ *Web:* weingartz.com

White Flower Farm Inc 30 Irene St Torrington CT 06790 860-496-9624 496-1418
TF Cust Svc: 800-411-6159 ■ *Web:* www.whiteflowerfarm.com

Zamzows Inc 1201 N Franklin Blvd Nampa ID 83687 208-465-3630
Web: www.zamzows.com

324 GAS STATIONS

See Also Convenience Stores p. 2148

Phone | Fax

Addington Oil Corp
2154 US Hwy 23 N Ste 102 Weber City VA 24290 276-386-3961
Web: www.addingtonoil.com

Alpena Oil Co Inc 235 Water St Alpena MI 49707 989-356-1098 356-9486
TF: 800-968-1098 ■ *Web:* www.alpenaoil.net

AMBEST Inc 5115 Maryland Way Brentwood TN 37027 615-371-5187 371-5186
TF: 800-910-7220 ■ *Web:* www.am-best.com

Arfa Enterprises Inc 4300 Haddonfield Rd Pennsauken NJ 08109 856-486-0550

Autotronics U S A LLC 700 N Benton Ave Springfield MO 65802 417-864-4400
Web: www.autotronics.net

B&t Service Station Contractors
630 S Frontage Rd Nipomo CA 93444 805-929-8944
TF: 888-862-2552 ■ *Web:* btssc.com

Beck Oil Co 3345 Main St Keokuk IA 52632 319-524-9237
Web: www.beckoilco.com

Berne Cooperative Association Inc 158 W Main St Ute IA 51060 712-885-2249
Web: www.bernecoopassoc.com

Bi-Mor Stations Inc 1890 S Pacific Hwy Medford OR 97501 541-772-2061 779-2602

Blossman Oil Company Inc PO Box 89 Covington LA 70434 985-898-2663
Web: www.blossmanoil.com

BP PLC 28100 Torch Pkwy Warrenville IL 60555 800-333-3991
NYSE: BP ■ *TF:* 800-333-3991 ■ *Web:* www.bp.com

Busler Enterprises Inc
2601 N St Joseph Ave Evansville IN 47720 812-424-7511
TF: 800-457-3232 ■ *Web:* buslerlubricants.com

Chevron Corp 6001 Bollinger Canyon Rd San Ramon CA 94583 925-842-1000
NYSE: CVX ■ *TF Cust Svc:* 800-368-8357 ■ *Web:* www.chevron.com

Colonial Group Inc 101 N Lathrop Ave Savannah GA 31415 912-236-1331 235-3881
Web: colonialgroupinc.com

Cone Solvents, Inc. 6185 Cockrill Bend Cir Nashville TN 37209 615-350-6166
Web: conesolvents.com

Dakota Plains Co-op 151 Ninth Ave NW Valley City ND 58072 701-845-0812 845-2680
TF: 800-288-7922 ■ *Web:* www.chsdakotaplainsag.com

Dunlap Oil Company Inc 759 S Haskell Ave Willcox AZ 85643 520-384-2248 384-5159
TF: 800-854-1646 ■ *Web:* www.dunlapoil.com

Englefield Oil Co 447 James Pkwy Heath OH 43056 740-928-8215 928-1531
TF Cust Svc: 800-837-4458 ■ *Web:* www.englefieldoil.com

Erickson Oil Products Inc 1231 Industrial St Hudson WI 54016 715-386-8241 386-2022
Web: www.freedomvalu.com

Exxon Mobil Corp 5959 Las Colinas Blvd Irving TX 75039 972-444-1000 444-1433
NYSE: XOM ■ *TF:* 800-252-1800 ■ *Web:* www.exxonmobil.com

Fabian Oil Inc 20 Oak St PO Box 99 Oakland ME 04963 207-465-2000
Web: www.fabianoil.com

FL Roberts & Company Inc 93 W Broad St Springfield MA 01105 413-781-7444 781-4328
Web: www.flroberts.com

Forward Corp 219 N Front St Standish MI 48658 989-846-4501
TF: 800-664-4501 ■ *Web:* www.forwardcorp.com

Freedom Oil Co 814 W Chestnut St Bloomington IL 61701 309-828-7750
Web: www.freedomoil.com

Gas 'n' Shop Inc 701 Marina Bay Pl Lincoln NE 68528 402-475-1101 475-0976
Web: gitnsplit.com

Gas Depot Oil Company Inc
8700 N Waukegan Rd Ste 200 Morton Grove IL 60053 847-581-0303
Web: www.gasdepot.com

GasAmerica Services Inc 2700 W Main St Greenfield IN 46140 317-468-2515 864-3091*
**Fax Area Code:* 937 ■ *TF:* 800-643-1948 ■ *Web:* www.speedway.com

Gate Petroleum Co
9540 San Jose Blvd PO Box 23627 Jacksonville FL 32241 904-737-7220 732-7660
TF: 866-571-1982 ■ *Web:* www.gatepetro.com

Gawfco Enterprises Inc
587 Ygnacio Vly Rd Walnut Creek CA 94596 925-979-0560
Web: www.gawfco.com

Company	City	State	Zip	Phone	Fax
Getty Realty Corp 2 Jericho Plaza Ste 110 — *NYSE:* GTY ■ *Web:* www.gettyrealty.com	Jericho	NY	11753	516-478-5400	
Graham Enterprise Inc 446 Morris Ave — *Web:* www.grahamei.com	Mundelein	IL	60060	847-837-0777	837-0778
Greystone Oil & Gas LLP 1616 S Voss Rd Ste 400 — *Web:* www.greystone.biz	Houston	TX	77057	832-333-4000	
Holly Refining & Marketing Co 1700 S Union Ave — *Web:* www.hollyfrontier.com	Tulsa	OK	74107	918-594-6600	
Houston Food Bank, The 535 Portwall St — *TF:* 866-384-4277 ■ *Web:* www.houstonfoodbank.org	Houston	TX	77029	713-223-3700	
Hunt & Sons Inc 5750 S Watt Ave — *TF:* 800-734-2999 ■ *Web:* www.huntnsons.com	Sacramento	CA	95829	916-383-4868	383-1005
Imperial Oil Resources Ltd 237 Fourth Ave SW PO Box 2480 Stn M — *TF:* 800-567-3776 ■ *Web:* www.imperialoil.ca	Calgary	AB	T2P3M9	800-567-3776	
Interfuel Llc 7102 Fullerton Rd — *Web:* www.interfuel.com	Springfield	VA	22150	703-455-1900	
Iowa 80 Group Inc 515 Sterling Dr PO Box 639 — *Web:* www.iowa80group.com	Walcott	IA	52773	563-284-6965	
J & H Oil Co 2696 Chicago Dr SW — *Web:* www.jhoil.com	Wyoming	MI	49519	616-534-2181	245-0618
Jubitz Corp 33 NE Middlefield Rd — *TF:* 800-523-0600 ■ *Web:* www.jubitz.com	Portland	OR	97211	503-283-1111	240-5834
Lassus Bros Oil Inc 1800 Magnavox Way — *Web:* lassus.com	Fort Wayne	IN	46804	260-436-1415	436-0340
Mcclure Truck Stop 530 Friend Way — *Web:* www.mcclureoilcorp.com	Lebanon	IN	46052	765-482-0005	
Mid-Atlantic Convenience Stores LLC 1011 Boulder Springs Dr Ste 100	Richmond	VA	23225	804-706-4702	
Midtex Oil LP 3455 IH 35 South — *Web:* midtexoil.com	New Braunfels	TX	78132	830-625-4214	
MM Fowler Inc 4220 Neal Rd — *Web:* familyfareconveniencestores.com	Durham	NC	27705	919-309-2925	309-9924
Monroe Oil Co 519 E Franklin St — *TF General:* 800-452-2717 ■ *Web:* www.monroeoilco.com	Monroe	NC	28112	704-289-5438	
Moto Mart 3301 hiawatha ave — *Web:* www.mymotomart.com	Minneapolis	MN	55406	612-722-9665	
Native Pride 11359 Rt 20 — *Web:* nativepride.com	Irving	NY	14081	716-934-5130	
NELLA Oil Co 2360 Lindbergh St — *TF:* 800-995-0401 ■ *Web:* nellaoil.com	Auburn	CA	95602	530-885-0401	885-5851
Ney Oil Company Inc 145 S Water St — *TF:* 800-962-9839 ■ *Web:* www.neyoil.com	Ney	OH	43549	419-658-2324	658-2723
O'Connell Oil Assoc Inc 545 Merrill Rd — *TF:* 800-464-4894 ■ *Web:* www.oconnelloil.com	Pittsfield	MA	01201	413-499-4800	499-6072
Olds-olympic Inc PO Box 186 — *Web:* www.olds-olympic.com	Lynnwood	WA	98046	425-778-1000	771-4346
PDQ Food Stores Inc 2002 Parmenter St — *Web:* www.pdqstores.com	Middleton	WI	53562	608-831-6600	
Peak Energy Inc 2707 Asheville Rd — *Web:* www.haywoodoil.com	Waynesville	NC	28786	828-456-9035	
Pilot Travel Centers LLC 5508 Lonas Dr — *TF:* 800-562-6210 ■ *Web:* www.pilotflyingj.com	Knoxville	TN	37939	865-938-1439	
Ports Petroleum Company Inc 1337 Blachleyville Rd — *Web:* www.portspetroleum.com	Wooster	OH	44691	330-264-1885	
Quality Oil Company LLC 1540 Silas Creek Pkwy — *Web:* www.qualityoilnc.com	Winston-Salem	NC	27127	336-722-3441	721-9520
RaceTrac Petroleum Inc 3225 Cumberland Blvd Ste 100 — *TF:* 888-636-5589 ■ *Web:* www.racetrac.com	Atlanta	GA	30339	770-431-7600	319-7944
Riiser Energy 709 S 20th Ave — *Web:* www.riiser.com	Wausau	WI	54401	715-845-7272	
Rip Griffin Truck Travel Ctr Inc 4710 Fourth St — *TF:* 800-333-9330 ■ *Web:* www.ripgriffin.com	Lubbock	TX	79416	806-795-8785	795-6574
Sampson-Bladen Oil Co Inc 510 Commerce St PO Box 469 — *TF:* 800-849-4177 ■ *Web:* www.sboil.com	Clinton	NC	28329	910-592-4177	
Sapp Bros Truck Stops Inc 9915 S 148th St — *Web:* sappbros.net/travel-centers	Omaha	NE	68138	402-895-7038	895-1957
Sayle Oil Company Inc 410 W Main — *Web:* www.sayleoil.com	Charleston	MS	38921	662-647-5802	
Schmuckal Oil Co 1516 Barlow St — *Web:* www.schmuckaloil.com	Traverse City	MI	49686	231-946-2800	941-7435
Scott-Gross Company Inc 664 Magnolia Ave — **Fax Area Code:* 859 ■ *TF:* 800-967-6874 ■ *Web:* www.scottgross.com	Lexington	KY	40505	800-967-6874	737-5452*
Service Oil Inc 1718 E Main Ave — *Web:* www.stamart.com	West Fargo	ND	58078	701-277-1050	277-1723
Shepherd Oil Company LP 1831 S Main — *Web:* www.shepherdoil.com	Blackwell	OK	74631	580-363-4280	
Shirtcliff Oil Co PO Box 6003 — *TF:* 800-422-0536 ■ *Web:* www.shirtcliffoil.com	Myrtle Creek	OR	97457	541-863-5268	863-5144
Speedway LLC 500 Speedway Dr — *TF Cust Svc:* 800-643-1948 ■ *Web:* www.speedway.com	Enon	OH	45323	937-864-3001	
Spencer Cos Inc 120 Woodson St — *TF:* 800-633-2910 ■ *Web:* www.spencercos.com	Huntsville	AL	35801	256-533-1150	535-2910
Super Quik Inc 2000 Ashland Dr Ste 105 — *Web:* www.superquik.net	Ashland	KY	41101	606-836-9641	
Swifty Oil Company Inc 1515 W Tipton St	Seymour	IN	47274	812-522-1640	
Thornton Oil Corp 10101 Linn Stn Rd Ste 200 — *TF:* 800-928-8022 ■ *Web:* www.thorntonsinc.com	Louisville	KY	40223	502-425-8022	327-9026
Town Pump Inc 600 S Main St — *TF:* 800-823-4931 ■ *Web:* www.townpump.com	Butte	MT	59701	406-497-6700	497-6060
TravelCenters of America 24601 Ctr Ridge Rd Ste 200 — **Fax:* Mktg ■ *TF:* 800-632-9240 ■ *Web:* www.ta-petro.com	Westlake	OH	44145	440-808-9100	808-3301*
Triple A Oil 12342 Inwood Rd	Dallas	TX	75244	972-503-3333	392-7502
True North Energy LLC 5565 Airport Hwy — *TF:* 888-245-9336 ■ *Web:* www.truenorth.org	Toledo	OH	43615	419-868-6800	868-1458
UPI Energy LP 105 Silvercreek Pkwy N Ste 200 — *TF:* 800-396-2667 ■ *Web:* www.upienergylp.com	Guelph	ON	N1H8M1	519-821-2667	
Van De Pol Enterprises Inc 4895 S Airport Way — *Web:* www.vandepol.us	Stockton	CA	95206	209-465-3421	
Vermont Gas Systems Inc 85 Swift St — *TF:* 800-639-8081 ■ *Web:* www.vermontgas.com	South Burlington	VT	05403	802-863-4511	863-8872
W & H Co-op Oil Co 407 13th St N — *TF:* 800-392-3816 ■ *Web:* whcoop.com	Humboldt	IA	50548	515-332-2782	332-1559
Wallace Oil Co-Voco 5370 Oakdale Rd	Smyrna	GA	30082	404-799-9400	799-0322
Wallis Oil Co 106 E Washington St — *TF:* 800-467-6652 ■ *Web:* www.wallisco.com	Cuba	MO	65453	573-885-2277	885-4760
Wesco Inc 1460 Whitehall Rd — **Fax Area Code:* 231 ■ *TF:* 800-968-0200 ■ *Web:* www.gowesco.com	Muskegon	MI	49445	800-968-0200	719-4301*
Wills Group Inc, The 6355 Crain Hwy — *Web:* www.willsgroup.com	La Plata	MD	20646	301-932-3600	
Wilson Oil Inc 95 Panel Way — *Web:* www.wilcoxandflegel.com	Longview	WA	98632	360-575-9222	

325 GAS TRANSMISSION - NATURAL GAS

Companies that transmit or store natural gas but do not distribute it.

Company	City	State	Zip	Phone	Fax
Aka Energy Group LLC 65 Mercado St Ste 250 — *Web:* www.akaenergy.com	Durango	CO	81301	970-764-6650	375-2216
ANR Pipeline Co 717 Texas St — *TF:* 800-827-5267 ■ *Web:* www.anrpl.com/company_info	Houston	TX	77002	832-320-5230	
Boardwalk Pipeline Partners LP 3800 Frederica St — *NYSE:* BWP ■ *TF:* 866-913-2122 ■ *Web:* bwpmlp.com	Owensboro	KY	42301	270-686-3620	688-5872
British Gas Services Inc (BG) 811 Main St — *Web:* www.bg-group.com	Houston	TX	77002	713-622-7100	
Cheniere Energy Inc 700 Milam St Ste 800 — *NYSE:* LNG ■ *TF:* 877-375-5002 ■ *Web:* www.cheniere.com	Houston	TX	77002	713-375-5000	375-6000
Colorado Interstate Gas Co PO Box 1087 — *Web:* www.cigco.com	Colorado Springs	CO	80944	719-520-4245	
ConocoPhillips Alaska Inc 700 G St PO Box 100360	Anchorage	AK	99501	907-276-1215	263-4731
DCP Midstream Partners LP 370 17th St Ste 2775 — *NYSE:* DPM ■ *Web:* dcppartners.com	Denver	CO	80202	303-633-2900	605-2225
Duke Energy Corp 550 S Tryon St Mail Drop WP 890 — *TF:* 800-521-2232 ■ *Web:* m.duke-energy.com	Charlotte	NC	28202	713-627-5400	
Enterprise Products Partners LP 1100 Louisiana St 10th Fl — *NYSE:* EPD ■ *Web:* www.enterpriseproducts.com	Houston	TX	77002	713-381-6500	
Gas Transmission-Northwest 1400 SW Fifth Ave Ste 900 — *TF:* 888-750-6275 ■ *Web:* www.gastransmissionnw.com	Portland	OR	97201	888-750-6275	
Iroquois Gas Transmission System LP 1 Corporate Dr Ste 600 — *TF:* 800-888-3982 ■ *Web:* www.iroquois.com	Shelton	CT	06484	203-925-7200	929-9501
Kern River Gas Transmission Co 2755 E Cottonwood Pkwy Ste 300 — *TF:* 800-420-7500 ■ *Web:* www.kernrivergas.com	Salt Lake City	UT	84121	801-937-6000	
Kinder Morgan 1001 Louisiana St Ste 1000 — *NYSE:* KMI ■ *TF:* 800-247-4122 ■ *Web:* www.kindermorgan.com	Houston	TX	77002	713-369-9000	230-5675
Kinder Morgan Energy Partners LP 500 Dallas St Ste 1000 — *NYSE:* KMI ■ **Fax Area Code:* 403 ■ **Fax:* Hum Res ■ *TF:* 866-208-3372 ■ *Web:* www.kindermorgan.com	Houston	TX	77002	713-369-9000	514-6401*
Kinder Morgan Inc 1001 Louisiana St Ste 1000 — *NYSE:* KMI ■ *Web:* www.kindermorgan.com	Houston	TX	77002	713-369-9000	
Kinder Morgan Management LLC 500 Dallas St 1 Allen Ctr Ste 1000 — *NYSE:* KMI ■ *TF:* 800-781-4152 ■ *Web:* www.kindermorgan.com	Houston	TX	77002	713-369-9000	
NiSource 1700 MacCorkle Ave SE	Charleston	WV	25314	304-357-2000	357-2000
Northern Natural Gas Co 1111 S 103rd St — *TF:* 877-654-0646 ■ *Web:* northernnaturalgas.com	Omaha	NE	68124	402-398-7000	398-7006
Northwest Pipeline LLC 295 Chipeta Way — *Web:* www.northwest.williams.com	Salt Lake City	UT	84108	801-583-8800	
Paiute Pipeline Co 5241 W Spring Mtn Rd — *Web:* www.paiutepipeline.com	Las Vegas	NV	89146	702-876-7178	873-3820
Questar Gas Management Co PO Box 45360 — *TF:* 800-323-5517 ■ *Web:* questargas.com	Salt Lake City	UT	84145	801-324-5111	
Questar Pipeline Co PO Box 45360 — *Web:* www.questarpipeline.com	Salt Lake City	UT	84145	801-324-5604	
Regency Energy Partners LP 2001 Bryan St Ste 3700 — *NASDAQ:* RGNC ■ *Web:* regencygasservices.com	Dallas	TX	75201	214-750-1771	750-1749
SemGroup LP 6120 S Yale Ave Ste 700 — *Web:* www.semgroupcorp.com	Tulsa	OK	74136	918-524-8100	
Seminole Energy Services LLC 1323 E 71st St Ste 300 — *Web:* www.seminoleenergy.com	Tulsa	OK	74136	918-492-2840	492-3075
Spark Energy Gas LP 2105 Citywest Blvd — *TF:* 877-547-7275 ■ *Web:* www.sparkenergy.com	Houston	TX	77042	877-547-7275	374-8007
Trailblazer Pipeline Co 2442 P Rd	Heartwell	NE	68945	308-563-3221	
TransCanada Pipelines Ltd 450 First St SW — *TF:* 800-661-3805 ■ *Web:* www.transcanada.com	Calgary	AB	T2P5H1	403-920-2000	920-2200
Tri-Gas & Oil Company Inc 3941 Federalsburg Hwy PO Box 465 — *TF:* 800-638-7802 ■ *Web:* www.trigas-oil.com	Federalsburg	MD	21632	410-754-8184	754-9158
Veresen Inc 222 Third Ave SW — *TSE:* VSN ■ *Web:* www.veresen.com	Calgary	AB	T2P0B4	403-296-0140	213-3648
WBI Energy 1250 W Century Ave — *TF:* 877-924-4677 ■ *Web:* www.wbienergy.com	Bismarck	ND	58503	701-530-1064	
WBI Holdings Inc 1250 W Century Ave — *TF General:* 877-924-4677 ■ *Web:* www.wbienergy.com	Bismarck	ND	58503	877-924-4677	

Phone Fax

Williams Gas Pipeline Gulfstream
1905 Intermodal Cir Ste 310 Palmetto FL 34221 800-440-8475
TF: 800-440-8475 ■ *Web:* co.williams.com

Williams Partners LP 1 Williams Ctr Tulsa OK 74172 918-573-2000 573-8805
NYSE: WPZ ■ *TF:* 800-600-3782 ■ *Web:* investor.williams.com

326 GASKETS, PACKING, SEALING DEVICES

See Also Automotive Parts & Supplies - Mfr p. 1830

Phone Fax

A F A Industries 140 E Pond Dr Romeo MI 48065 586-752-2900
Web: www.afaindustries.com

Abric (North America) Inc
220 Barren Springs Dr Ste 1 Houston TX 77090 281-569-7100
Web: www.abric.com

Accratronics Seals Corp 2211 Kenmere Ave Burbank CA 91504 818-843-1500 841-2117
Web: www.accratronics.com

Accro Gasket Inc 511 Princeland Ct Corona CA 92879 951-340-1562 340-1604

Aesseal Inc 355 Dunavant Dr Rockford TN 37853 865-531-0192
Web: www.aesseal.com

AGIS LLC 16 Poplar St Ambler PA 19002 215-646-8010
Web: www.agismfg.com

Akron Gasket & Packing Enterprises Inc
445 NE Ave Tallmadge OH 44278 330-633-3742
TF: 800-888-2088 ■ *Web:* www.akrongasket.com

All Custom Gasket & Materials
355 Watline Ave Mississauga ON L4Z1P3 905-507-4580 507-4589
Web: www.allcustomgasket.com

American Casting & Manufacturing Corp
51 Commercial St Plainview NY 11803 516-349-7010 349-8389
TF: 800-342-0333 ■ *Web:* www.americancasting.com

American Gasket & Rubber Co
119 E Commerce Dr Schaumburg IL 60173 847-882-8333 882-9333
Web: agr.tekni-plex.com

American Packing & Gasket Co (APG)
6039 Armour Dr PO Box 213 Houston TX 77020 713-675-5271 675-2730
TF: 800-888-5223 ■ *Web:* callapg.com

Amesbury Group Inc 57 S Hunt Rd Amesbury MA 01913 978-834-3262 289-6699*
**Fax Area Code:* 800 ■ *Web:* www.amesbury.com

APM Hexseal Corp 44 Honeck St Englewood NJ 07631 201-569-5700 569-4106
TF: 800-498-9034 ■ *Web:* www.apmhexseal.com

Apple Rubber Products Inc 310 Erie St Lancaster NY 14086 716-684-6560 684-8302
TF Cust Svc: 800-828-7745 ■ *Web:* www.applerubber.com

AR Thomson Group 7930 130th St Surrey BC V3W0H7 604-507-6050 507-6098
TF: 800-410-9116 ■ *Web:* www.arthomson.com

Archer Advanced Rubber Components Inc
2860 Lowery St Winston-Salem NC 27101 336-996-7776
Web: www.archerseal.com

Artus Corp PO Box 511 Englewood NJ 07631 201-568-1000 568-8865
Web: www.artuscorp.com

Atlantic Gasket Corp 3908 Frankford Ave Philadelphia PA 19124 215-533-6400 533-4130
TF: 800-229-8881 ■ *Web:* www.atlanticgasket.com

Auburn Manufacturing Co 29 Stack St Middletown CT 06457 860-346-6677 346-1334
TF: 800-427-5387 ■ *Web:* www.auburn-mfg.com

AW Chesterton Co 500 Unicorn Pk Dr Woburn MA 01801 781-438-7000 438-8971
TF: 888-400-4872 ■ *Web:* www.chesterton.com

Bal Seal Engineering Company Inc
19650 Pauling Foothill Ranch CA 92610 949-460-2100 460-2300
TF: 800-366-1006 ■ *Web:* www.balseal.com

Basic Rubber & Plastics Co
8700 Boulder Ct Walled Lake MI 48390 248-360-7400 360-7101
Web: www.basicrubber.com

Bentley Mfg Company Inc
520 Pk Industrial Dr La Habra CA 90631 562-501-2955 697-5319
TF: 800-424-2425 ■ *Web:* www.gasketsonline.com

California Gasket & Rubber Corp
533 W Collins Ave Orange CA 92867 310-323-4250
TF: 800-635-7084 ■ *Web:* www.calgasket.com

Calpico Inc 1387 San Mateo Ave South San Francisco CA 94080 650-588-2241
TF: 800-998-9115 ■ *Web:* www.calpicoinc.com

Cascade Rubber Products Inc
1828 Nw Quimby St Portland OR 97209 503-248-1992
Web: cascaderubber.com

CE Conover & Company Inc 4106 Blanche Rd Bensalem PA 19020 215-639-6666 639-1799
TF: 800-266-6837 ■ *Web:* conoverseals.com

CGR Products Inc 4655 US Hwy 29 N Greensboro NC 27405 336-621-4568 375-5324
TF: 877-313-6785 ■ *Web:* www.cgrproducts.com

Chambers Gasket & Manufacturing Co
4701 W Rice St Chicago IL 60651 773-626-8800 626-1430
Web: www.chambersgasket.com

Chicago Gasket Co 1285 W N Ave Chicago IL 60622 773-486-3060 486-3784
TF: 800-833-5666 ■ *Web:* www.chicagogasket.com

Chicago-Wilcox Mfg Co
16928 State St PO Box 126 South Holland IL 60473 800-323-5282 339-9876*
**Fax Area Code:* 708 ■ *TF:* 800-323-5282 ■ *Web:* www.chicagowilcox.com

Cinchseal Associates Inc 731 Hylton Rd Pennsauken NJ 08110 856-662-5162
Web: www.cinchseal.com

Cincinnati Gasket Packing & Manufacturing Inc
40 Illinois Ave Cincinnati OH 45215 513-761-3458 761-2994
Web: www.cgindustrialglass.com

Cometic Gasket Inc 8090 Auburn Rd Concord OH 44077 440-354-0777 354-0350
TF: 800-752-9850 ■ *Web:* www.cometic.com

Conservco Water Conservation Products LLC
550 W Plumb Ln Ste B-147 Reno NV 89509 775-747-3333
Web: www.dripstop.com

Corpus Christi Gasket & Fastener Inc
PO Box 4074 Corpus Christi TX 78469 361-884-6366 884-0695
TF: 800-460-6366 ■ *Web:* www.ccgasket.com

Ct Gasket & Polymer Company Inc
12308 Cutten Rd Houston TX 77066 800-299-1685
TF: 800-299-1685 ■ *Web:* www.ctgasket.com

Phone Fax

DAR Industrial Products Inc
2 Union Hill Bldg 1 West Conshohocken PA 19428 610-825-4900 825-4901
Web: www.darindustrial.com

Delta Rubber Co 39 Wauregan Rd PO Box 300 Danielson CT 06239 860-779-0300 774-0402
Web: nninc.com

Eagle Burgmann Industries LP
10035 Brookriver Dr Houston TX 77040 800-303-7735
TF General: 800-303-7735 ■ *Web:* www.eagleburgmann.com

EnPro Industries Inc
5605 Carnegie Blvd Ste 500 Charlotte NC 28209 704-731-1500
NYSE: NPO

Eriks Seals & Plastics Inc
15600 Trinity Blvd Ste 100 Fort Worth TX 76155 682-292-5060
Web: www.eriksusa.com

Fast Group Houston Inc 8103 Rankin Rd Humble TX 77396 281-446-6662
Web: www.fast-houston.com

FB Wright Company Inc
9999 Mercier Ave PO Box 770 Dearborn MI 48121 313-843-8250
Web: www.fbwright.com

Fibreflex Packing & Manufacturing Company Inc
5101 Umbria St Philadelphia PA 19128 215-482-1490
Web: www.fibreflex.com

Flexitallic Ltd 6915 Hwy 225 Deer Park TX 77536 281-604-2400
Web: www.flexitallic.com

Flow Dry Technology Inc
379 Albert Rd PO Box 190 Brookville OH 45309 937-833-2161 833-3208
TF: 800-533-0077 ■ *Web:* flowdry.com

Flowserve Corp 5215 N O'Connor Blvd Ste 2300 Irving TX 75039 972-443-6500 443-6800
NYSE: FLS ■ *TF:* 800-350-1082 ■ *Web:* www.flowserve.com

Forest City Technologies Inc 299 Clay St Wellington OH 44090 440-647-2115 647-2644
Web: www.forestcitytech.com

Freudenberg-NOK General Partnership
47690 E Anchor Ct Plymouth MI 48170 734-451-0020 451-0043
Web: www.fst.com

Gasket & Seal Fabricators Inc
1640 Sauget Industrial Pkwy East Saint Louis IL 62206 618-332-0425
Web: www.gasketandseal.com

Gasket Engineering Company Inc
4500 E 75th Terr Kansas City MO 64132 816-363-8333 363-3558
Web: www.gasketeng.com

Gasket Manufacturing Co 18001 Main St Gardena CA 90248 310-217-5600 217-5608
TF: 800-442-7538 ■ *Web:* www.gasketmfg.com

Gaskets Inc 301 W Hwy 16 Rio WI 53960 920-992-3137 992-3124
TF: 800-558-1833 ■ *Web:* www.gasketsinc.com

Greene Tweed & Co 2075 Detwiler Rd Kulpsville PA 19443 215-256-9521 256-0189
Web: www.gtweed.com

Higbee Inc 6741 Thompson Rd Syracuse NY 13211 315-432-8021 432-0227
Web: higbee.sealanddesign.com

Hoosier Gasket Corp
2400 Enterprise Pk Pl Indianapolis IN 46218 317-545-2000 545-5500
Web: www.hoosiergasket.com

Houston Mfg Specialty Company Inc
9909 Wallisville Rd Houston TX 77013 713-675-7400
TF: 800-231-6030 ■ *Web:* www.houmfg.com

IG Inc 720 S Sara Rd Mustang OK 73064 405-376-9393 376-3933
TF: 800-654-8433 ■ *Web:* www.igok.com

Ilene Industries Inc 301 Stanley Blvd Shelbyville TN 37160 931-684-8731 684-8735
TF: 800-251-1602 ■ *Web:* www.ileneindustries.com

Indian Springs Mfg Company Inc
2095 W Genesee Rd Baldwinsville NY 13027 315-635-6101
Web: www.indiansprings.com

Industrial Custom Products Inc
2801 37th Ave NE Minneapolis MN 55421 612-781-2255 781-1144
TF: 800-654-0886 ■ *Web:* www.industrialcustom.com

Industrial Gasket & Shim Company Inc (IGS)
200 Country Club Rd Meadow Lands PA 15347 724-222-5800
TF: 800-229-1447 ■ *Web:* www.igsind.com

Inertech Supply Inc
641 Monterey Pass Rd Monterey Park CA 91754 626-282-2000
Web: inertech.com

Intek Plastic Inc 1000 Spiral Blvd Hastings MN 55033 888-468-3531 437-3805*
**Fax Area Code:* 651 ■ *TF:* 888-468-3531 ■ *Web:* www.intekplastics.com

Interface Solutions Inc 216 Wohlsen Way Lancaster PA 17603 800-942-7538 207-6080*
**Fax Area Code:* 717 ■ *TF:* 800-942-7538 ■ *Web:* www.interfacematerials.com

Jade Engineered Plastic Inc
121 Broadcommon Rd Bristol RI 02809 401-253-4440 253-1605
TF: 800-557-9155 ■ *Web:* www.jadeplastics.com

James Walker Manufacturing Co
511 W 195th St Glenwood IL 60425 708-754-4020
Web: www.jameswalker.biz

John Crane Canada Inc 423 Green Rd N Stoney Creek ON L8E3A1 905-662-6191 662-1564
Web: www.johncrane.com

John Crane Inc 6400 W Oakton St Morton Grove IL 60053 847-967-2400 967-2400
Web: www.johncrane.com

Kaydon Ring & Seal Inc 1600 Wicomico St Baltimore MD 21230 410-547-7700 576-9059
Web: www.kaydonringandseal.com

Kimber Manufacturing Inc
555 Taxter Rd Ste 235 Elmsford NY 10523 406-758-2222
TF: 888-243-4522 ■ *Web:* www.kimberamerica.com

Lamons Gasket Co 7300 Airport Blvd Houston TX 77061 713-222-0284 547-9502
TF: 800-231-6906 ■ *Web:* www.lamonsgasket.com

Leader Global Technologies Inc
905 W 13th St Deer Park TX 77536 281-542-0600
Web: www.leadergt.com

LGS Technologies LP 2950 W Wintergreen Rd Lancaster TX 75134 972-224-9201
Web: www.lgstechnologies.com

Marco Rubber 35 Woodworkers Way Seabrook NH 03874 603-468-3600
TF: 800-775-6525 ■ *Web:* www.marcorubber.com

Marsh Industries Inc 49680 Leona Dr Chesterfield MI 48051 586-949-9300 949-1290
Web: www.marshindustries.com

Melrath Gasket
1500 John F Kennedy Blvd Ste 200 Philadelphia PA 19102 215-223-6000

Mesa Industries Inc 1726 S Magnolia Ave Monrovia CA 91016 626-359-9361 359-7985
Web: www.mesaetp.com

Phone *Fax*

Netherland Rubber Co 2931 Exon Ave. Cincinnati OH 45241 513-733-0883 733-1096
TF: 800-582-1877 ■ *Web:* www.netherlandrubber.com

Novagard Solutions Inc 5109 Hamilton Ave Cleveland OH 44114 216-881-8111 881-6977
TF: 800-380-0138 ■ *Web:* www.novagard.com

Ohio Gasket & Shim Company Inc 976 Evans Ave Akron OH 44305 330-630-2030 630-2075
TF: 800-321-2438 ■ *Web:* www.ogsindustries.com

Omega Shielding Products Inc
1384 Pompton Ave. Cedar Grove NJ 07009 973-890-7455
TF: 800-828-5784 ■ *Web:* www.omegashielding.com

Pacific States Felt & Mfg Company Inc
23850 Clawiter Rd Hayward CA 94545 510-783-0277 783-4725
TF: 800-566-8866 ■ *Web:* www.pacificstatesfelt.net

Parco Inc 1801 S Archibald Ave. Ontario CA 91761 909-947-2200 923-0288
Web: www.parcoinc.com

Parker Hannifin Corp TechSeal Div
3025 W Croft Cir Spartanburg SC 29302 864-573-7332 583-4299
Web: www.parker.com

Peck B G Company Inc 50 Shepard St. Lawrence MA 01843 978-686-4181
Web: www.bgpeck.com

Pemko Mfg Company Inc 4226 Transport St. Ventura CA 93003 805-642-2600 642-4109
TF: 800-283-9988 ■ *Web:* www.pemko.com

Performance Polymer Technologies Co
8801 Washington Blvd Ste 109 Roseville CA 95678 916-677-1414 677-1474
Web: www.pptech.com

PPC Mechanical Seals 2769 Mission Dr Baton Rouge LA 70805 225-356-4333 355-2126
TF: 800-731-7325 ■ *Web:* www.ppcmechanicalseals.com

Precision Gasket Co (PGC) 5732 Lincoln Dr. Edina MN 55436 952-942-6711
Web: www.pgc-solutions.com

Presray Corp 32 Nelson Hill Rd PO Box 200 Wassaic NY 12592 845-373-9300 855-8034
Web: www.presray.com

Press-Seal Gasket Corp 2424 W State Blvd Fort Wayne IN 46808 260-436-0521 436-1908
TF: 800-348-7325 ■ *Web:* www.press-seal.com

Presscut Industries Inc
1730 Briercroft Ct. Carrollton TX 75006 972-389-0615 245-2488
TF: 800-442-4924 ■ *Web:* www.presscut.com

Pureflex Inc 4855 Broadmoor Ave. Kentwood MI 49512 616-554-1100 554-3633
Web: www.pureflex.com

Rotor Clip Company Inc 187 Davidson Ave. Somerset NJ 08873 732-469-7333 469-7898
TF Cust Svc: 800-557-6867 ■ *Web:* www.rotorclip.com

Rubbercraft Corp of California
3701 Conant St. Long Beach CA 90808 310-328-5402 618-1832
Web: www.rubbercraft.com

Santa Fe Rubber Products Inc
12306 E Washington Blvd Whittier CA 90606 562-693-2776 693-4936
Web: www.santaferubber.com

Schlegel Systems Inc 1555 Jefferson Rd. Rochester NY 14623 585-427-7200
TF: 888-924-7694 ■ *Web:* www.amesbury.com

Seal Methods Inc
11915 Shoemaker Ave Santa Fe Springs CA 90670 562-944-0291 946-9439
TF: 800-423-4777 ■ *Web:* www.sealmethodsinc.com

Sealing Devices Inc 4400 Walden Ave. Lancaster NY 14086 716-684-7600 684-0760
TF Cust Svc: 800-727-3257 ■ *Web:* www.sealingdevices.com

Sealing Equipment Products Co Inc
123 Airpark Industrial Rd Alabaster AL 35007 800-633-4770
TF Cust Svc: 800-633-4770 ■ *Web:* www.sepcousa.com

Seals-Eastern Inc 134 Pearl St. Red Bank NJ 07701 732-747-9200
Web: www.sealseastern.com

Secon Rubber & Plastics Inc 240 Kaskaskia Dr. Red Bud IL 62278 618-282-7700
Web: www.seconrubber.com

Sorbothane Inc 2144 State Rt 59. Kent OH 44240 330-678-9444
TF: 800-838-3906 ■ *Web:* www.sorbothane.com

Southern Rubber Company Inc
2209 Patterson St. Greensboro NC 27407 336-299-2456
Web: southernrubber.com

Specification Rubber Products Inc
1568 First St N Alabaster AL 35007 205-663-2521 663-1875
TF: 800-633-3415 ■ *Web:* www.specrubber.com

Stein Seal Company Inc
1500 Industrial Blvd Kulpsville PA 19443 215-256-0201 256-4818
Web: www.steinseal.com

Sur-Seal Gasket & Packing Inc
6156 Wesselman Rd. Cincinnati OH 45248 800-345-8966 574-2220*
**Fax Area Code:* 513 ■ *TF:* 800-345-8966 ■ *Web:* www.sur-seal.com

T & E Industries Inc 215 Watchung Ave. Orange NJ 07050 973-672-5454 672-0180
TF Sales: 800-245-7080 ■ *Web:* www.teindustries.com

Thermoseal 2350 Campbell Rd Sidney OH 45365 937-498-2222
Web: www.thermosealinc.com

Trelleborg Sealing Solutions
5503 Distribution Dr. Fort Wayne IN 46825 260-749-2709
Web: www.tss.trelleborg.com/global/en/company/manufacturingcapabilities/engineeredplastics/oringenergizedptfeseals/tssfortwayneusa/tss-fortwayne-usa.html

Triseal Corp 11920 Price Rd Hebron IL 60034 815-648-2473
TF: 800-910-7325 ■ *Web:* www.triseal.com

Trostel Ltd 901 Maxwell St Lake Geneva WI 53147 262-248-4481 248-6406
Web: www.trostel.com

United Gasket Corp 1633 55th Ave Cicero IL 60804 708-656-3700 656-6292
Web: www.unitedgasket.com

UTEX Industries Inc 10810 Katy Fwy Ste 100 Houston TX 77043 713-467-1000 467-3602
TF: 800-359-9230 ■ *Web:* www.utexind.com

Vellumoid Inc 54 Rockdale St. Worcester MA 01606 508-853-2500 852-0741
TF: 800-609-5558 ■ *Web:* www.vellumoid.com

William H Harvey 4334 S 67th St Omaha NE 68117 402-331-1175 321-9532*
**Fax Area Code:* 800 ■ *TF:* 800-321-9532 ■ *Web:* www.oatey.com

Zero International Inc 415 Concord Ave. Bronx NY 10455 718-585-3230 292-2243
TF: 800-635-5335 ■ *Web:* www.zerointernational.com

327 GIFT SHOPS

See Also Card Shops p. 1892; Duty-Free Shops p. 2204; Home Furnishings Stores p. 2474

Phone *Fax*

Arribas Bros Inc 1500 Live Oak Ln Orlando FL 32830 407-828-4840 828-8019
Web: www.arribas.com

Atkinson Trading Co 3911 W Saragosa St. Chandler AZ 85226 480-899-9597

Atlantic Center For The Arts Inc
1414 Art Ctr Ave New Smyrna Beach FL 32168 386-427-6975
TF: 800-393-6975 ■ *Web:* atlanticcenterforthearts.org

Brookstone Inc 1 Innovation Way Merrimack NH 03054 603-880-9500 577-8004
TF Cust Svc: 800-846-3000 ■ *Web:* www.brookstone.com

CM Paula Co 6049 Hi-Tek Ct. Mason OH 45040 800-543-4464 293-8471
TF: 800-543-4464 ■ *Web:* www.cmpaula.com

Colors of The West LLC 201 W Rt 66 Williams AZ 86046 928-635-9559
Web: colorsofthewestusa.com

Disney Consumer Products
500 S Buena Vista St Burbank CA 91521 818-560-1000 553-5402*
**Fax Area Code:* 215 ■ **Fax:* Cust Svc ■ *TF PR:* 855-553-4763 ■ *Web:* thewaltdisneycompany.com

Evelyn Hill Inc 1 Liberty Island New York NY 10004 212-363-3180
Web: www.thestatueofliberty.com

Friendly Gift Shop Inc 1812 Marsh Rd Wilmington DE 19810 302-475-6560
Web: facebook.com

GiftCertificates.com 11510 Blondo St Omaha NE 68164 800-773-7368 445-0075*
**Fax Area Code:* 402 ■ *TF:* 800-773-7368 ■ *Web:* www.giftcertificates.com

Hazelwood Enterprises Inc 402 N 32nd St. Phoenix AZ 85008 602-275-7709
Web: hazelwoods.com

Historical Research Ctr Inc
2107 Corporate Dr Boynton Beach FL 33426 800-985-9956
TF: 800-985-9956 ■ *Web:* www.names.com

Hummel Gift Shop 1656 Garfield Rd. New Springfield OH 44443 330-549-3728

Kirlins Inc 532 Maine St. Quincy IL 62301 217-222-0813 224-9400
Web: www.kirlins.com

Mathews Jewelers 126 Strickland Dr. Orange TX 77630 409-886-7233
Web: mathewsjewelers.com

Mole Hollow Candles Ltd
208 Charlton Rd Rt 20 PO Box 223 Sturbridge MA 01566 800-445-6653 998-9292*
**Fax Area Code:* 888 ■ *TF Cust Svc:* 800-445-6653 ■ *Web:* www.moleholl owcandles.com

New Seasons Market 7300 SW Beaverton Hwy. Portland OR 97225 503-292-6838
Web: www.newseasonsmarket.com

Olympia Promotions & Distribution
226 E Jericho Tpke Mineola NY 11501 516-775-4500
TF: 800-846-7874 ■ *Web:* olympiapromo.com

Only in San Francisco
Pier 39 Dock D11 Pier 39 Concourse San Francisco CA 94107 415-397-0143 956-8124
Web: www.onlyinsanfrancisco.net

Oregon Connection 1125 S First St Coos Bay OR 97420 541-267-7804
TF: 800-255-5318 ■ *Web:* www.oregonconnection.com

Pacific Trade International Inc
5515 Security Ln Ste 1100 Rockville MD 20852 301-816-4200 816-4220
Web: chesapeakebaycandle.com

Paradies Shops 2849 Paces Ferry Rd Atlanta GA 30339 404-344-7905 349-3226
Web: paradieslagardere.com

PM Parties Inc
701 Matthews Mint Hill Rd Ste C Matthews NC 28105 704-841-1370

Red Rocket Fireworks Company Inc
1166 Porter Rd Rock Hill SC 29730 803-329-2577
Web: blackcatfireworks.com

Rockstar Industries LLP 6012 12th Ave S. Seattle WA 98108 206-297-8330

San Francisco Music Box Co
5370 W 95th St. Prairie Village KS 66207 800-227-2190 481-4677*
**Fax Area Code:* 888 ■ *TF:* 800-227-2190 ■ *Web:* www.sanfranciscomusicbox.com

Sanrio Inc 570 Eccles Ave South San Francisco CA 94080 650-952-2880 872-1077
TF: 800-759-6454 ■ *Web:* www.sanrio.com

Silver Towne LP
120 E Union City Pike PO Box 424 Winchester IN 47394 765-584-7481 584-1246
TF: 800-788-7481 ■ *Web:* www.silvertowne.com

Soap Plant 4633 Hollywood Blvd. Los Angeles CA 90027 323-663-0122
Web: www.soapplant.com

Spencer Gifts LLC
6826 Black Horse Pk Egg Harbor Township NJ 08234 609-645-3300
Web: spencersonline.com

Tuesday Morning Corp 6250 LBJ Fwy. Dallas TX 75240 972-387-3562 387-2344
NASDAQ: TUES ■ *TF:* 800-457-0099 ■ *Web:* www.tuesdaymorning.com

Wall Drug Store Inc PO Box 401 Wall SD 57790 605-279-2175 279-2699
Web: www.walldrug.com

Wendell August Forge Inc
2074 Leesburg-Grove City Rd Mercer PA 16137 724-748-9501
TF: 866-354-5192 ■ *Web:* www.wendellaugust.com

Yankee Candle Company Inc PO Box 110 South Deerfield MA 01373 413-665-8306 665-4815
TF: 877-803-6890 ■ *Web:* www.yankeecandle.com

328 GIFTS & NOVELTIES - WHOL

Phone *Fax*

Accoutrements 10915 47th Ave W Mukilteo WA 98275 425-349-3838 349-5188
TF: 800-886-2221 ■ *Web:* www.accoutrements.com

Admiral Exchange Company Inc 1443 Union St San Diego CA 92101 619-239-2165

Aerial Photography Services Inc (APS)
2511 S Tryon St Charlotte NC 28203 704-333-5143 333-4911
Web: www.aps-1.com

Angel Sales Inc 4147 N Ravenswood Ave. Chicago IL 60613 773-883-8858 883-8889
Web: www.angelsales.com

Blair Cedar & Novelty Works Inc
680 W US Hwy 54 Camdenton MO 65020 573-346-2235 346-5534
TF: 800-325-3943 ■ *Web:* www.blaircedar.com

Bright Ideas in Broad Ripple Inc
7425 Westfield Blvd Indianapolis IN 46240 317-257-4111 257-4174
Web: www.bright-ideas.org

Company	City	State	ZIP	Phone	Fax
Drysdales Inc 3220 S Memorial Dr *TF:* 800-444-6481 ■ *Web:* www.drysdales.com	Tulsa	OK	74145	918-664-6481	832-8900
Fridgedoor.com 65 School St *TF:* 800-955-3741 ■ *Web:* www.fridgedoor.com	Quincy	MA	02169	617-770-7913	801-8026
Hayes Specialties Corp 1761 E Genesee *TF:* 800-248-3603 ■ *Web:* www.ehayes.com	Saginaw	MI	48601	989-755-6541	755-2341
Hornung's Golf Products Inc 815 Morris St *TF:* 800-323-3569 ■ *Web:* www.hornungs.com	Fond du Lac	WI	54935	920-922-2640	922-4986
Kurt S Adler Inc 7 W 34th St *Web:* www.kurtadler.com	New York	NY	10001	212-924-0900	807-0575
Morrow Enterprises 350 130th Ave *Web:* morrowent.com	Vero Beach	FL	32968	772-257-3300	
Northwestern Products Inc 721 Industrial Pk Rd	Ashland	WI	54806	715-685-9500	
Sanrio Inc 570 Eccles Ave *TF:* 800-759-6454 ■ *Web:* www.sanrio.com	South San Francisco	CA	94080	650-952-2880	872-1077
Service Systems Assoc Inc 4699 Marion St *Web:* www.kmssa.com	Denver	CO	80216	303-322-3031	815-1698
Star Sales Company Inc 1803 N Central St **Fax Area Code:* 865 ■ *TF:* 800-347-9494 ■ *Web:* www.starsalescompany.com	Knoxville	TN	37917	781-933-2145	524-4889*
Trends International LLC 5188 W 74th St *TF:* 866-406-7771 ■ *Web:* www.trendsinternational.com	Indianapolis	IN	46268	317-388-1212	388-1414
Unique Industries Inc 4750 League Island Blvd **Fax Area Code:* 800 ■ *TF:* 800-888-0559 ■ *Web:* www.favors.com	Philadelphia	PA	19112	215-336-4300	888-1490*
US Balloon Mfg Company Inc 140 58th St **Fax Area Code:* 800 ■ *TF:* 800-285-4000	Brooklyn	NY	11220	718-492-9700	832-9872*
Variety Distributors Inc 609 Seventh St *TF:* 800-274-1095 ■ *Web:* www.varietydistributors.com	Harlan	IA	51537	712-755-2184	755-5041
WinCraft Inc 1124 W Fifth St *TF:* 800-533-8006 ■ *Web:* www.wincraft.com	Winona	MN	55987	507-454-5510	453-0690

329 GLASS - FLAT, PLATE, TEMPERED

Company	City	State	ZIP	Phone	Fax
ABC Window Company Inc 621 S Bon View Ave	Ontario	CA	91761	909-391-6491	
Abrisa Industrial Glass Inc 200 S Hallock Dr *Web:* abrisatechnologies.com	Santa Paula	CA	93060	805-525-4902	
AGC Flat Galss North America Inc 11175 Cicero Dr Ste 400 *TF:* 800-251-0441 ■ *Web:* us.agc.com	Alpharetta	GA	30022	404-446-4200	446-4221
Anthony International 12391 Montera Ave *TF:* 800-772-0900 ■ *Web:* www.anthonyintl.com	Sylmar	CA	91342	818-365-9451	361-9611
Apogee Enterprises Inc 4400 W 78th St Ste 520 *NASDAQ: APOG* ■ *TF:* 877-752-3432 ■ *Web:* www.apog.com	Minneapolis	MN	55435	952-835-1874	
Basco Shower Enclosures 7201 Snider Rd *TF:* 800-543-1938 ■ *Web:* www.bascoshowerdoor.com	Mason	OH	45040	513-573-1900	
Binswanger Glass 965 Ridge Lk Blvd Ste 305 *TF:* 800-365-9922 ■ *Web:* www.binswangerglass.com	Memphis	TN	38120	800-365-9922	
Bullseye Glass Co 3722 SE 21st Ave *TF:* 888-220-3002 ■ *Web:* www.bullseyeglass.com	Portland	OR	97202	503-232-8887	238-9963
Cameron Glass Inc 3550 W Tacoma St *Web:* www.camglass.com	Broken Arrow	OK	74012	918-254-6000	252-4665
Cardinal Glass Industries 775 Prairie Center Dr *Web:* www.cardinalcorp.com	Eden Prairie	MN	55344	952-229-2600	935-5538
City Glass Co 8037 H St *Web:* www.cityglasscompany.com	Omaha	NE	68127	402-593-1242	
Core Six Precision Glass 1737 Endeavor Dr *Web:* www.coresix.com	Williamsburg	VA	23185	757-888-1361	
D & W Inc 941 Oak St *TF:* 800-255-0829 ■ *Web:* www.dwincorp.com	Elkhart	IN	46514	574-264-9674	264-9859
Gentex Corp 600 N Centennial St *NASDAQ: GNTX* ■ *Web:* www.gentex.com	Zeeland	MI	49464	616-772-1800	772-7348
Glaz-Tech Industries Inc 2207 E Elvira Rd *TF:* 800-755-8062 ■ *Web:* www.glaztech.com	Tucson	AZ	85756	520-629-0268	629-8811
Gray Glass Co 217-44 98th Ave *TF:* 800-523-3320 ■ *Web:* www.grayglass.net	Queens Village	NY	11429	718-217-2943	217-0280
Guardian Industries Corp 2300 Harmon Rd *TF:* 800-822-5599 ■ *Web:* www.guardian.com	Auburn Hills	MI	48326	248-340-1800	340-9988
Hartung Agalite Glass Co 17830 W Valley Hwy *TF:* 800-552-2227 ■ *Web:* www.hartung-glass.com	Seattle	WA	98188	425-656-2626	656-2601
Hartung Glass Industries 10450 SW Ridder Rd *TF:* 800-552-2227 ■ *Web:* hartung-glass.com	Wilsonville	OR	97070	503-682-3846	
Hehr International Inc 3333 Casitas Ave *Web:* www.hehrintl.com	Los Angeles	CA	90039	323-663-1261	666-2372
JNL Glass Inc 618 E Gutierrez St Ste B1 *Web:* jnlglass.com	Santa Barbara	CA	93103	805-957-1685	
Kokomo Opalescent Glass Co 1310 S Market St *TF:* 877-475-6329 ■ *Web:* www.kog.com	Kokomo	IN	46902	765-457-8136	459-5177
Northwestern Industries Inc 2500 W Jameson St *TF:* 800-426-2771 ■ *Web:* www.nwiglass.com	Seattle	WA	98199	206-285-3140	285-3603
Obrien Glass Co 4916 W SR- 97	Springfield	IL	62707	217-522-5660	
ODL Inc 215 E Roosevelt Ave **Fax:* Cust Svc ■ *TF:* 800-253-3900 ■ *Web:* www.odl.com	Zeeland	MI	49464	616-772-9111	772-9110*
Oldcastle BuildingEnvelope 5005 Lyndon B Johnson Fwy Ste 1050 *TF:* 866-653-2278 ■ *Web:* www.obe.com	Dallas	TX	75244	866-653-2278	
Oran Safety Glass Inc 48 Industrial Pkwy	Emporia	VA	23847	434-336-1620	
Paul Wissmach Glass Company Inc 420 Stephen St PO Box 228 *Web:* www.wissmachglass.com	Paden City	WV	26159	304-337-2253	337-8800
Pilkington Holdings Inc 811 Madison Ave *Web:* www.pilkington.com	Toledo	OH	43697	419-247-3731	247-3821
PPG Industries Inc 1 PPG Pl *NYSE: PPG* ■ **Fax:* Hum Res ■ *Web:* www.ppg.com	Pittsburgh	PA	15272	412-434-3131	434-4291*
Prelco Inc 94 Blvd Cartier *TF:* 800-463-1325 ■ *Web:* www.prelco.ca	Rivi Re-Du-Loup	QC	G5R2M9	418-862-2274	
Rainbow Art Glass Inc 1761 Rt 34 S *TF:* 800-526-2356 ■ *Web:* www.rainbowartglass.com	Farmingdale	NJ	07727	732-681-6003	681-4984
Rambusch Decorating Co 160 Cornelison Ave *Web:* www.rambusch.com	Jersey City	NJ	07304	201-333-2525	433-3355
Royal Glass Company Inc 3200 De La Cruz Blvd	Santa Clara	CA	95054	408-969-0444	
Saint-Gobain Corp 20 Moores Rd	Valley Forge	PA	19087	610-893-6000	341-7777
SCHOTT North America, Inc. 615 Hwy 68 *Web:* www.us.schott.com/flatglass/english	Sweetwater	TN	37874	423-337-3522	337-7979
Spectrum Glass Co PO Box 646 *TF:* 800-426-3120 ■ *Web:* www.spectrumglass.com	Woodinville	WA	98072	425-483-6699	483-9007
Thermoseal Glass Corp 400 Water St *Web:* www.thermoseal.com	Gloucester City	NJ	08030	856-456-3109	456-0989
Torstenson Glass Co 3233 N Sheffield Ave *Web:* www.tglass.com	Chicago	IL	60657	773-525-0435	525-0009
Tru Vue Inc 9400 W 55th St *TF:* 800-621-8339 ■ *Web:* www.tru-vue.com	McCook	IL	60525	708-485-5080	485-5980
Viracon Inc 800 Pk Dr *TF:* 800-533-2080 ■ *Web:* www.viracon.com	Owatonna	MN	55060	507-451-9555	444-3555
Virginia Mirror Co Inc 300 Moss St S *TF:* 800-368-3011 ■ *Web:* va-glass.com	Martinsville	VA	24112	276-632-9816	956-3020
Wasco Products Inc 85 Spencer Dr Unit A *TF:* 800-388-0293 ■ *Web:* www.wascoskylights.com	Wells	ME	04073	207-324-8060	

330 GLASS FIBERS

Company	City	State	ZIP	Phone	Fax
Advanced Glazings Ltd 870 King's Rd *Web:* www.advancedglazings.com	Sydney	NS	B1P6R7	902-794-2899	
Anchor Glass Container Corp 401 E Jackson St Ste 1100 *Web:* www.anchorglass.com	Tampa	FL	33602	813-884-0000	
Armour Group Inc 350 E Las Olas Blvd Ste 800 *Web:* www.thearmourgroup.com	Fort Lauderdale	FL	33301	954-767-2030	
Capitol Aluminum & Glass Corp 1276 W Main St *TF:* 800-331-8268 ■ *Web:* www.capitol-windows.com	Bellevue	OH	44811	419-483-7050	
Carlex Glass Co 77 Excellence Way *Web:* www.carlex.com	Vonore	TN	37885	423-884-1105	
City Glass Company of Colorado Springs 414 W Colorado Ave *Web:* www.cityglasscompany.net	Colorado Springs	CO	80905	719-634-2891	
Corning Inc 1 Riverfront Plz *NYSE: GLW* ■ *Web:* www.corning.com	Corning	NY	14831	607-974-9000	
Culver Glass Co 2619 Nw Industrial St *Web:* www.culver-glass.com	Portland	OR	97210	503-226-2520	
Evanite Fiber Corp 1115 SE Crystal Lake Dr *Web:* hollingsworth-vose.com	Corvallis	OR	97333	541-753-1211	753-0388
Fiberoptics Technology Inc 1 Quassett Rd *TF Cust Svc:* 800-433-5248 ■ *Web:* www.fiberopticstech.com	Pomfret	CT	06258	860-928-0443	928-7664
Giant Glass Company Inc 1000 Osgood St *Web:* www.safelite.com/giant-glass?utm_source=referral&utm_medium=redirect&utm_campaign=giantglass	North Andover	MA	01845	978-688-8211	
Gordon Glass Co 5116 Warrensville Center Rd *Web:* www.technologylk.com	Maple Heights	OH	44137	216-663-9830	
Ibis Tek LLC 220 S Noah Dr *Web:* www.ibistek.com	Saxonburg	PA	16056	724-586-6005	
Incom USA Inc 294 Southbridge Rd *Web:* www.incomusa.com	Charlton	MA	01507	508-765-9151	765-0041
JN Phillips Glass Company Inc 11 Wheeling Ave *Web:* www.jnphillips.com	Woburn	MA	01801	781-939-3400	
Magnatex Inc 2520 Ridgemar Ct	Louisville	KY	40207	502-493-0558	
Mesko Glass & Mirror Company Inc 801 Wyoming Ave *Web:* www.mesko.com	Scranton	PA	18509	570-346-0777	
Moderne Glass Company Inc 1000 Industrial Blvd *Web:* www.glassamerica.com	Aliquippa	PA	15001	724-857-5700	
Nashville Tempered Glass Corp 1860 Air Ln Dr *Web:* www.egpglass.com	Nashville	TN	37210	615-889-6350	
Novatech Group Inc 160 Murano St *TF:* 844-986-8001 ■ *Web:* www.novatechgroup.com	Sainte-julie	QC	J3E0C6	844-986-8001	
Sentinel Process 3265 Sunset Ln *TF:* 800-345-3569 ■ *Web:* www.sentinelprocess.com	Hatboro	PA	19040	919-462-7108	
Shaw Glass Company Inc 55 Bristol Dr *Web:* www.solarseal.com	South Easton	MA	02375	508-238-0112	
Syracuse Glass Company Inc 1 General Motors Dr PO Box 381 *Web:* www.syracuseglass.com	Syracuse	NY	13206	315-437-9971	
Tec5USA Inc 80 Skyline Dr *Web:* www.tec5usa.com	Plainview	NY	11803	516-653-2000	
Vitrum Industries Ltd 9739 201 St	Langley	BC	V1M3E7	604-882-3513	
Western States Glass Corp 43443 Osgood Rd PO Box 6058 *Web:* www.westernstatesglass.com	Fremont	CA	94538	510-623-5000	

331 GLASS JARS & BOTTLES

Company	City	State	ZIP	Phone	Fax
Leone Industries Co 443 SE Ave	Bridgeton	NJ	08302	856-455-2000	
New High Glass Inc 12713 SW 125th Ave *Web:* www.newhighglass.net	Miami	FL	33186	305-232-0840	251-7622
Owens-Illinois Inc 1 Michael Owens Way *NYSE: OI* ■ *Web:* www.o-i.com	Perrysburg	OH	43551	567-336-5000	

332 GLASS PRODUCTS - INDUSTRIAL (CUSTOM)

				Phone	Fax
Abrisa Technologies 200 S Hallock Dr .... *Fax Area Code: 805 ■ TF: 877-622-7472 ■ Web: www.abrisatechnologies.com	Santa Paula	CA	93060	877-622-7472	525-8604*
Bassett Mirror Company Inc PO Box 627 .... Web: www.bassettmirror.com	Bassett	VA	24055	276-629-3341	
Elan Technology 169 Elan Ct .... Web: www.elantechnology.com	Midway	GA	31320	912-880-3526	
Flex-O-Lite Inc 50 Crestwood Executive Ctr Ste 522 .... TF: 800-325-9525 ■ Web: www.flexolite.com	Saint Louis	MO	63126	800-325-9525	541-3193
Fredericks Co, The 2400 Philmont Ave .... Web: www.fredrickscompany.com	Huntingdon Valley	PA	19006	215-947-2500	947-7464
Headwest Inc 15650 S Avalon Blvd .... Web: www.headwestinc.com	Compton	CA	90220	310-532-5420	532-5920
Henderson Glass Inc 715 S Blvd E .... *Fax Area Code: 248 ■ TF: 800-694-0672 ■ Web: www.hendersonglass.com	Rochester Hills	MI	48307	800-694-0672	829-4799*
King Precision Glass Inc 177 S Indian Hill Blvd .... TF: 866-554-2773 ■ Web: www.kingprecisionglass.com	Claremont	CA	91711	909-626-3526	625-0173
Lang-Mekra North America LLC 101 Tillessen Blvd .... TF: 888-635-7248 ■ Web: www.lang-mekra.com	Ridgeway	SC	29130	803-337-5264	337-5265
Lenoir Mirror Company Inc 401 Kincaid St .... TF: 800-438-8204 ■ Web: www.lenoirmirror.com	Lenoir	NC	28645	828-728-3271	728-5010
North American Specialty Glass 2175 Kumry Rd PO Box 70 .... TF: 888-785-5962 ■ Web: www.naspecialtyglass.com	Trumbauersville	PA	18970	215-536-0333	536-6872
Precision Electronic Glass Inc 1013 Hendee Rd .... TF: 800-982-4734 ■ Web: www.pegglass.com	Vineland	NJ	08360	856-691-2234	691-3090
Richland Glass Company Inc 1640 SW Blvd .... TF: 800-959-0312 ■ Web: www.richlandglass.com	Vineland	NJ	08360	856-691-1697	
Swift Glass Company Inc 131 W 22nd St .... TF: 800-537-9438 ■ Web: www.swiftglass.com	Elmira Heights	NY	14903	607-733-7166	732-5829

333 GLASSWARE - LABORATORY & SCIENTIFIC

				Phone	Fax
Ace Glass Inc 1430 NW Blvd PO Box 688 .... *Fax Area Code: 800 ■ TF: 800-223-4524 ■ Web: www.aceglass.com	Vineland	NJ	08360	856-692-3333	543-6752*
Altira Inc 3225 NW 112th St .... Web: www.altira.com	Miami	FL	33167	305-687-8074	
Bellco Glass Inc 340 Edrudo Rd .... TF: 800-257-7043 ■ Web: www.bellcoglass.com	Vineland	NJ	08360	856-691-1075	691-3247
Bioscreen Testing Services Inc 3904 Del AMO Blvd Ste 801 .... Web: www.bioscreen.com	Torrance	CA	90503	310-214-0043	370-3642
Bottlemate Inc 2095 Leo Ave .... Web: www.bottlemate.com	Commerce	CA	90040	323-887-9009	
Container Manufacturing Inc 50 Baekeland Ave .... Web: www.containermanufacturing.com	Middlesex	NJ	08846	732-563-0100	
Corning Inc 1 Riverfront Plz .... NYSE: GLW ■ Web: www.corning.com	Corning	NY	14831	607-974-9000	
Eden Labs LLC 1601 W Fifth St Ste 240 .... Web: edenlabs.com	Columbus	OH	43212	614-374-2455	
Gerresheimer Glass Inc 537 Crystal Ave .... Web: www.gerresheimer.com	Vineland	NJ	08360	856-692-3600	
Industrial Container & Supply Company Inc 1845 South 5200 West .... Web: www.industrialcontainer.com	Salt Lake City	UT	84104	801-972-1561	
Quadrex Corp PO Box 3881 .... TF Sales: 800-275-7033 ■ Web: www.quadrexcorp.com	Woodbridge	CT	06525	203-393-3112	393-0391
Wale Apparatus Co Inc 400 Front St .... TF: 800-334-9253 ■ Web: www.waleapparatus.com	Hellertown	PA	18055	610-838-7047	838-7440
WB Bottle Supply Company Inc 3400 S Clement Ave .... TF: 800-738-3931 ■ Web: www.wbbottle.com	Milwaukee	WI	53207	414-482-4300	

334 GLASSWARE & POTTERY - HOUSEHOLD

See Also Table & Kitchen Supplies - China & Earthenware p. 3214

				Phone	Fax
Anchor Hocking Co 519 Pierce Ave .... *Fax Area Code: 800 ■ TF: 800-562-7511 ■ Web: www.anchorhocking.com	Lancaster	OH	43130	740-681-6478	848-0082*
Berney-Karp Inc 3350 E 26th St .... TF: 800-237-6395 ■ Web: www.ceramic-source.com	Los Angeles	CA	90058	323-260-7122	260-7245
Blenko Glass Co PO Box 67 .... TF: 877-425-3656 ■ Web: www.blenko.com	Milton	WV	25541	304-743-9081	
Ceramo Company Inc 681 Kasten Dr .... TF: 800-325-8303 ■ Web: www.ceramousa.com	Jackson	MO	63755	573-243-3138	243-3130
Enesco LLC 225 Windsor Dr .... TF: 800-436-3726 ■ Web: www.enesco.com	Itasca	IL	60143	630-875-5300	875-5350
Fenton Art Glass Co 700 Elizabeth St .... TF Cust Svc: 800-933-6766 ■ Web: www.fentonartglass.com	Williamstown	WV	26187	304-375-6122	375-6459
Friedman Bros Decorative Arts 9015 NW 105th Way .... TF: 800-327-1065 ■ Web: www.friedmanmirrors.com	Medley	FL	33178	305-887-3170	885-5331
Gardner Glass Products Inc 301 Elkin Hwy PO Box 1570 .... TF: 800-334-7267 ■ Web: www.gardnerglass.com	North Wilkesboro	NC	28659	800-334-7267	
Haeger Industries Inc 7 Maiden Ln .... TF Cust Svc: 800-288-2529 ■ Web: www.haegerpotteries.com	Dundee	IL	60118	847-426-3441	
Haggerty Enterprises Inc 370 Kimberly Dr .... TF: 800-336-5282 ■ Web: www.lavalamp.com	Carol Stream	IL	60188	630-315-3300	
Libbey Inc 300 Madison Ave PO Box 10060 .... NYSE: LBY ■ TF: 888-794-8469 ■ Web: www.libbey.com	Toledo	OH	43699	419-325-2100	
Marshall Pottery 4901 Elysian Fields Rd .... TF: 888-768-8721 ■ Web: marshallpotterystore.com	Marshall	TX	75672	903-927-5400	938-8222
Pfaltzgraff Co PO Box 21769 .... *Fax: Cust Svc ■ TF: 800-999-2811 ■ Web: www.pfaltzgraff.com	York	PA	17402	800-999-2811	717-2481*
Rauch Industries Inc 2408 Forbes Rd	Gastonia	NC	28056	704-867-5333	864-2081
Swarovski North America Ltd 1 Kenney Dr .... *Fax Area Code: 800 ■ TF: 800-289-4900 ■ Web: www.swarovski.com	Cranston	RI	02920	401-463-6400	870-5660*
Waterford Wedgwood USA Inc 1330 Campus Pkwy .... Web: wedgwood.com	Wall	NJ	07753	732-938-5800	

335 GLOBAL DISTRIBUTION SYSTEMS (GDSS)

A global distribution system (GDS) is a computer reservations system that includes reservations databases of air travel suppliers in many countries. GDSs typically are owned jointly by airlines operating in different countries.

				Phone	Fax
Amadeus North America Inc 3470 NW 82nd Ave Ste 1000 .... TF: 888-262-3387 ■ Web: www.amadeus.com	Miami	FL	33122	305-499-6000	499-6889
American Sales Company Inc 4201 Walden Ave .... Web: www.americansalescompany.net	Lancaster	NY	14086	716-686-7000	685-6144
Century Distributors Inc 15710 Crabbs Branch Way .... Web: www.centurydist.com	Rockville	MD	20855	301-212-9100	212-9681
Pegasus Solutions Inc 5430 LBJ Fwy Ste 1100 .... TF: 800-843-4343 ■ Web: www.pegs.com	Dallas	TX	75240	214-234-4000	234-4040
Sabre Inc 3150 Sabre Dr .... Web: www.sabre.com	Southlake	TX	76092	682-605-1000	

336 GOURMET SPECIALTY SHOPS

				Phone	Fax
Graber Olive House Inc 315 E Fourth St .... *Fax Area Code: 909 ■ TF: 800-996-5483 ■ Web: www.graberolives.com	Ontario	CA	91764	800-996-5483	984-2180*
Harry & David Holdings Inc 2500 S Pacific Hwy .... TF Cust Svc: 877-322-1200 ■ Web: www.harryanddavid.com	Medford	OR	97501	877-322-1200	233-2300
Hickory Farms Inc 811 Madison Ave .... *Fax Area Code: 419 ■ TF: 800-753-8558 ■ Web: www.hickoryfarms.com	Toledo	OH	43604	800-753-8558	893-0164*
Logan Farms Honey Glazed Hams 10560 Westheimer Rd .... TF: 800-833-4267 ■ Web: www.loganfarmsinc.com	Houston	TX	77042	713-781-4335	977-0532
M&M Meat Shops 640 Trillium Dr PO Box 2488 .... Web: www.mmfoodmarket.com	Kitchener	ON	N2H6M3	519-895-1075	895-0762
Stew Leonard's 100 Westport Ave .... Web: stewleonards.com	Norwalk	CT	06851	203-847-7214	

337 GOVERNMENT - CITY

				Phone	Fax
Abilene City Hall 555 Walnut St .... Web: www.abilenetx.com	Abilene	TX	79601	325-676-6200	676-6229
Akron City Hall 146 S High St Rm 211 .... Web: www.akronohio.gov	Akron	OH	44308	330-375-2133	375-2468
Albany City Hall 24 Eagle St .... Web: www.albanyny.org	Albany	NY	12207	518-434-5100	434-5013
Alexandria City Hall 301 King St .... Web: www.alexandriava.gov	Alexandria	VA	22314	703-838-4000	838-6433
Allentown City Hall 435 Hamilton St .... Web: www.allentownpa.gov	Allentown	PA	18101	610-437-7539	437-7554
Amarillo City Hall 509 E Seventh Ave .... Web: www.ci.amarillo.tx.us	Amarillo	TX	79101	806-378-3000	378-9394
Anaheim City Hall 200 S Anaheim Blvd .... Web: www.anaheim.net	Anaheim	CA	92805	714-765-5162	765-5164
Anchorage City Hall 632 Sixth Ave Second Fl Ste 250 PO Box 196650 .... Web: www.muni.org	Anchorage	AK	99519	907-343-4431	
Ann Arbor City Hall 301 E Huron St .... Web: www.a2gov.org	Ann Arbor	MI	48104	734-794-6000	994-1765
Annapolis City Hall 160 Duke of Gloucester St .... Web: www.ci.annapolis.md.us	Annapolis	MD	21401	410-263-7997	216-9284
Arlington (TX) City Hall 101 W Abram St .... Web: www.arlington-tx.gov/government/city-hall	Arlington	TX	76010	817-275-3271	459-6116
Asheville City Hall 70 Ct Plaza PO Box 7148 .... Web: www.ashevillenc.gov	Asheville	NC	28802	828-259-5600	259-5499
Atlanta City Hall 55 Trinity Ave SW Ste 2500 .... Web: www.atlantaga.gov	Atlanta	GA	30303	404-330-6004	658-6893
Atlantic City City Hall 1301 Bacharach Blvd .... Web: www.cityofatlanticcity.org	Atlantic City	NJ	08401	609-347-5300	347-6408
Augusta (GA) Municipal Hall 535 Telfair St .... Web: www.augustaga.gov	Augusta	GA	30901	706-821-2300	826-4790
Aurora City Hall 15151 E Alameda Pkwy .... Web: www.auroragov.org	Aurora	CO	80012	303-739-7015	739-7594
Austin City Hall PO Box 1088 .... Web: www.austintexas.gov	Austin	TX	78767	512-974-2000	
Bakersfield City Hall 1600 Truxtun Ave # 300 .... Web: bakersfieldcity.us	Bakersfield	CA	93301	661-326-3751	324-1850
Bangor City Hall 73 Harlow St .... Web: www.bangormaine.gov	Bangor	ME	04401	207-992-4200	945-4449
Bar Harbor Town Hall 93 Cottage St .... Web: www.barharbormaine.gov	Bar Harbor	ME	04609	207-288-4098	288-4461

	City	State	ZIP	Phone	Fax
Baton Rouge City Hall 222 St Louis St Ste 301 *Web:* www.brgov.com	Baton Rouge	LA	70802	225-389-3100	389-5203
Billings City Hall 210 N 27th St *Web:* www.ci.billings.mt.us	Billings	MT	59101	406-657-8210	657-8390
Biloxi City Hall PO Box 429 *Web:* www.biloxi.ms.us	Biloxi	MS	39533	228-435-6254	435-6129
Birmingham City Hall 710 N 20th St *Web:* www.birminghamal.gov	Birmingham	AL	35203	205-254-2000	254-2926
Bismarck City Hall 500 E Front St *Web:* www.bismarcknd.gov	Bismarck	ND	58504	701-355-1540	221-6883
Bloomington City Hall 401 N Morton St *Web:* www.bloomington.in.gov	Bloomington	IN	47404	812-339-2261	349-3570
Boise City Hall 150 N Capitol Blvd *Web:* www.cityofboise.org	Boise	ID	83702	208-384-4422	384-4420
Boston City Hall 1 City Hall Plaza *Web:* www.cityofboston.gov	Boston	MA	02201	617-635-4601	248-1937
Boulder City Hall PO Box 791 *Web:* bouldercolorado.gov	Boulder	CO	80306	303-441-3388	441-4478
Branson City Hall 110 W Maddux St Ste 205 *Web:* www.cityofbranson.org	Branson	MO	65616	417-334-3345	335-4354
Bridgeport City Hall 999 Broad St *TF:* 800-978-2828 ■ *Web:* bridgeportct.gov	Bridgeport	CT	06604	203-576-7201	576-3913
Brownsville City Hall 1001 E Elizabeth St *Web:* www.cob.us	Brownsville	TX	78520	956-548-6000	546-4021
Buffalo City Hall 65 Niagara Sq *Web:* www.ci.buffalo.ny.us	Buffalo	NY	14202	716-851-4200	851-4360
Burlington City Hall 149 Church St *Web:* www.burlingtonvt.gov	Burlington	VT	05401	802-865-7000	865-7014
Calgary City Hall 800 Macleod Trail SE PO Box 2100 *Web:* www.calgary.ca	Calgary	AB	T2P2M5	403-268-2489	538-6111
Carson City City Hall 201 N Carson St *Web:* carson.org	Carson City	NV	89701	775-887-2100	887-2139
Casper City Hall 200 N David St *Web:* www.casperwy.gov	Casper	WY	82601	307-235-8400	235-7575
Cedar Rapids City Hall 3851 River Ridge Dr NE *Web:* www.cedar-rapids.org	Cedar Rapids	IA	52402	319-286-5670	286-5130
Champaign City Hall 102 N Neil St *Web:* www.ci.champaign.il.us	Champaign	IL	61820	217-403-8700	403-8980
Charleston (SC) City Hall 50 Broad St *Web:* www.charleston-sc.gov	Charleston	SC	29401	843-577-6970	720-3959
Charleston (WV) City Hall 200 Civic Ctr Dr *Web:* www.cityofcharleston.org	Charleston	WV	25301	304-348-8000	348-8157
Charlotte City Hall Charlotte-Mecklenburg Government Ctr 600 E 4th St *Web:* charmeck.org	Charlotte	NC	28202	704-336-2241	336-6644
Chattanooga City Hall 101 E 11th St Ste 100 *Web:* www.chattanooga.gov	Chattanooga	TN	37402	423-757-5152	
Cheyenne City Hall 2101 O'Neil Ave *TF:* 855-491-1859 ■ *Web:* www.cheyennecity.org	Cheyenne	WY	82001	307-637-6200	637-6454
Chicago City Hall 121 N La Salle St *Web:* cityofchicago.org	Chicago	IL	60602	312-744-4000	
Chula Vista City Hall 276 Fourth Ave *Web:* www.ci.chula-vista.ca.us	Chula Vista	CA	91910	619-691-5044	476-5379
Cincinnati City Hall 801 Plum St *Web:* www.cincinnati-oh.gov	Cincinnati	OH	45202	513-352-3000	
Cleveland City Hall 601 Lakeside Ave *Web:* www.cleveland-oh.gov	Cleveland	OH	44114	216-664-2000	
Colorado Springs City Hall 107 N Nevada Ave Ste 205 *Web:* www.springsgov.com	Colorado Springs	CO	80903	719-385-5900	385-5488
Columbia (MO) City Hall 701 E Broadway PO Box 6015 *Web:* www.como.gov	Columbia	MO	65205	573-874-7111	
Columbus Consolidated Government Ctr 100 Tenth St *Web:* www.columbusga.org	Columbus	GA	31901	706-653-4000	
Concord City Hall 41 Green St *Web:* www.concordnh.gov	Concord	NH	03301	603-225-8500	225-8592
Corpus Christi City Hall 1201 Leopard St PO Box 9277 *Web:* www.cctexas.com	Corpus Christi	TX	78469	361-826-2489	
Dallas City Hall 1500 Marilla St *Web:* www.dallascityhall.com	Dallas	TX	75201	214-670-4538	670-3946
Dayton City Hall 101 W Third St PO Box 22 *Web:* www.daytonohio.gov	Dayton	OH	45401	937-333-3636	333-4297
Daytona Beach City Hall 301 S Ridgewood Ave Rm 210 PO Box 2451 *Web:* www.codb.us	Daytona Beach	FL	32114	386-671-8100	671-8115
Des Moines City Hall 400 Robert D Ray Dr *Web:* www.dmgov.org	Des Moines	IA	50309	515-283-4500	237-1645
Detroit City Hall 2 Woodward Ave Ste 200 *Web:* detroitmi.gov	Detroit	MI	48226	313-224-3270	224-1466
Dover City Hall 15 ELoockerman St *Web:* www.cityofdover.com	Dover	DE	19901	302-736-7008	736-7177
Dubuque City Hall 50 W 13th St *Web:* www.cityofdubuque.org	Dubuque	IA	52001	563-589-4100	589-0890
Duluth City Hall 411 W First St *Web:* www.duluthmn.gov	Duluth	MN	55802	218-730-5500	730-5923
Durham City Hall 101 City Hall Plaza *Web:* www.durhamnc.gov	Durham	NC	27701	919-560-1200	560-4835
Edmonton City Hall 1 Sir Winston Churchill Sq 3rd Fl *Web:* www.edmonton.ca	Edmonton	AB	T5J2R7	780-442-5311	496-8210
El Paso City Hall 2 Civic Ctr Plaza *Web:* www.elpasotexas.gov	El Paso	TX	79901	915-541-4000	541-4501
Erie City Hall 626 State St *Web:* www.erie.pa.us	Erie	PA	16501	814-870-1234	870-1296
Eugene City Hall 125 E 8th Ave 2nd Fl *Web:* www.eugene-or.gov	Eugene	OR	97401	541-682-5010	682-5414
Evansville City Hall 1 NW ML King Jr Blvd *Web:* www.evansvillegov.net	Evansville	IN	47708	812-436-4992	436-4999
Fairbanks City Hall 800 Cushman St *Web:* www.fairbanksalaska.us	Fairbanks	AK	99701	907-459-6771	452-5913
Fargo City Hall 200 N Third St *Web:* www.cityoffargo.com	Fargo	ND	58102	701-241-1310	476-4136
Flagstaff City Hall 211 W Aspen Ave *Web:* www.flagstaff.az.gov	Flagstaff	AZ	86001	928-774-5281	779-7696
Fort Collins City Hall 300 Laporte Ave *Web:* www.fcgov.com	Fort Collins	CO	80521	970-221-6505	224-6107
Fort Lauderdale City Hall 100 N Andrews Ave *Web:* www.fortlauderdale.gov	Fort Lauderdale	FL	33301	954-828-5000	828-5017
Fort Wayne City Hall 1 Main St *Web:* www.cityoffortwayne.org	Fort Wayne	IN	46802	260-427-1221	427-1371
Fort Worth City Hall 1000 Throckmorton St *Web:* fortworthtexas.gov	Fort Worth	TX	76102	817-392-2255	392-6187
Frankfort City Hall PO Box 697 *Web:* frankfort.ky.gov	Frankfort	KY	40602	502-875-8523	
Fremont City Hall PO Box 5006 *Web:* www.fremont.gov	Fremont	CA	94537	510-284-4000	284-4001
Fresno City Hall 2600 Fresno St Rm 2064 *Web:* www.fresno.gov	Fresno	CA	93721	559-621-7770	621-7776
Garden Grove City Hall 11222 Acacia Pkwy *Web:* www.ci.garden-grove.ca.us	Garden Grove	CA	92840	714-741-5000	741-5044
Garland City Hall 200 N Fifth St *Web:* www.ci.garland.tx.us	Garland	TX	75040	972-205-2000	205-2504
Gettysburg Borough Hall 59 E High St *Web:* www.gettysburg-pa.gov	Gettysburg	PA	17325	717-334-1160	334-7258
Glendale (AZ) City Hall 5850 W Glendale Ave *Web:* www.glendaleaz.com	Glendale	AZ	85301	623-930-2000	930-2690
Glendale (CA) City Hall 613 E Broadway Rm 110 *Web:* glendaleca.gov	Glendale	CA	91206	818-548-2090	241-5386
Grand Forks City Hall 255 N Fourth St *Web:* www.grandforksgov.com	Grand Forks	ND	58203	701-746-2626	787-3740
Grand Rapids City Hall 300 Monroe Ave NW *Web:* grcity.us	Grand Rapids	MI	49503	616-456-3010	456-4607
Green Bay City Hall 100 N Jefferson St Rm 106 *Web:* www.ci.green-bay.wi.us	Green Bay	WI	54301	920-448-3010	448-3016
Greensboro City Hall 300 W Washington St PO Box 3136 *Web:* www.greensboro-nc.gov	Greensboro	NC	27401	336-373-2489	373-2117
Greenville City Hall 206 S Main St *TF:* 800-829-4477 ■ *Web:* www.greenvillesc.gov	Greenville	SC	29601	864-232-2273	
Gulfport City Hall 2309 15th St *Web:* gulfport-ms.gov	Gulfport	MS	39501	228-868-5700	868-5800
Harrisburg City Hall 10 N Second St *Web:* www.harrisburgpa.gov	Harrisburg	PA	17101	717-255-3060	255-3081
Hartford City Hall 550 Main St *Web:* www.hartford.gov	Hartford	CT	06103	860-522-4888	
Hattiesburg City Hall PO Box 1898 PO Box 1898	Hattiesburg	MS	39403	601-545-4500	
Helena City Hall 316 N Pk Ave *Web:* www.helenamt.gov	Helena	MT	59623	406-447-8410	447-8434
Hialeah City Hall 501 Palm Ave *Web:* hialeahfl.gov	Hialeah	FL	33010	305-883-5820	883-5814
Hilton Head Island Town Hall 1 Town Ctr Ct *Web:* www.hiltonheadislandsc.gov	Hilton Head Island	SC	29928	843-341-4600	842-7728
Honolulu City Hall 530 S King St *Web:* www.honolulu.gov	Honolulu	HI	96813	808-768-4141	768-5552
Hot Springs City Hall 133 Convention Blvd *Web:* www.cityhs.net	Hot Springs	AR	71901	501-321-6843	321-6809
Houston City Hall 901 Bagby St *Web:* www.houstontx.gov	Houston	TX	77002	713-247-1000	247-2355
Huntington Beach City Hall 2000 Main St *Web:* www.ci.huntington-beach.ca.us	Huntington Beach	CA	92648	714-536-5511	374-1557
Huntsville City Hall PO Box 308 *Web:* www.hsvcity.com	Huntsville	AL	35804	256-427-5240	427-5257
Independence City Hall 111 E Maple Ave *Web:* www.ci.independence.mo.us	Independence	MO	64050	816-325-7000	325-7012
Indianapolis City Hall 200 E Washington St Ste 2501 *Web:* www.indy.gov	Indianapolis	IN	46204	317-327-3601	327-3980
Irving City Hall 825 W Irving Blvd *Web:* www.ci.irving.tx.us	Irving	TX	75060	972-721-2600	721-2420
Jackson (MS) City Hall 219 S President St *Web:* www.jacksonms.gov	Jackson	MS	39201	601-960-1084	960-2193
Jackson (WY) Town Hall 150 E Pearl Ave *Web:* townofjackson.com	Jackson	WY	83001	307-733-3932	739-0919
Jacksonville City Hall 117 W Duval St Ste 400 *Web:* www.coj.net	Jacksonville	FL	32202	904-630-1776	630-2391
Jefferson City City Hall 320 E McCarty St *Web:* www.jeffersoncitymo.gov	Jefferson City	MO	65101	573-634-6304	634-6329
Jersey City City Hall 280 Grove St *Web:* www.cityofjerseycity.com	Jersey City	NJ	07302	201-547-5000	547-5461
Johnson City City Hall 601 E Main St *Web:* www.johnsoncitytn.com	Johnson City	TN	37601	423-434-6000	434-6295
Kansas City (KS) City Hall 701 N Seventh St *Web:* www.wycokck.org	Kansas City	KS	66101	913-573-5000	573-5210

				Phone	Fax
Kansas City (MO) City Hall 414 E 12th St *Web:* www.kcmo.gov	Kansas City	MO	64106	816-513-3360	513-3353
Key West City Hall 3132 Flagler Ave *Web:* www.cityofkeywest-fl.gov	Key West	FL	33040	305-809-3700	809-3833
Knoxville City Hall 400 W Main St *Web:* www.knoxvilletn.gov	Knoxville	TN	37902	865-215-2000	215-2085
Lansing City Hall 124 W Michigan Ave 9th Fl *Web:* www.lansingmi.gov	Lansing	MI	48933	517-483-4131	377-0068
Las Cruces City Hall 200 N Church St *Web:* www.las-cruces.org	Las Cruces	NM	88001	575-541-2000	541-2117
Las Vegas City Hall 495 S. Main St *Web:* www.lasvegasnevada.gov	Las Vegas	NV	89101	702-229-6011	386-9108
Lincoln City Hall 555 S Tenth St *Web:* www.lincoln.ne.gov	Lincoln	NE	68508	402-441-7515	441-6533
Little Rock City Hall 500 W Markham St *Web:* www.littlerock.org	Little Rock	AR	72201	501-371-4500	371-4498
Long Beach City Hall 333 W Ocean Blvd *Web:* www.longbeach.gov	Long Beach	CA	90802	562-570-6101	570-6789
Los Angeles City Hall 200 N Spring St Rm 360 *Web:* www.lacity.org	Los Angeles	CA	90012	213-473-3231	978-1027
Louisville City Hall 601 W Jefferson St *Web:* www.louisvilleky.gov	Louisville	KY	40202	502-574-1100	574-4420
Lubbock City Hall 1625 13th St *Web:* www.ci.lubbock.tx.us	Lubbock	TX	79401	806-775-3000	775-3002
Macon City Hall 700 Poplar St *Web:* www.maconbibb.us	Macon	GA	31201	478-751-7400	
Madison City Hall 210 Martin Luther King Jr Blvd Rm 403 *Web:* www.cityofmadison.com	Madison	WI	53703	608-266-4611	267-8671
Manchester City Hall 1 City Hall Plaza W wing *Web:* www.manchesternh.gov	Manchester	NH	03101	603-624-6455	624-6481
Memphis City Hall 125 N Main St *Web:* www.cityofmemphis.org	Memphis	TN	38103	901-576-6500	
Mesa City Hall PO Box 1466 *Web:* www.mesaaz.gov	Mesa	AZ	85211	480-644-2221	644-2821
Miami City Hall 3500 Pan American Dr *Web:* www.ci.miami.fl.us	Miami	FL	33133	305-250-5400	250-5410
Milwaukee City Hall 200 E Wells St *Web:* www.city.milwaukee.gov	Milwaukee	WI	53202	414-286-2200	286-3191
Minneapolis City Hall 350 S Fifth St *Web:* www.ci.minneapolis.mn.us	Minneapolis	MN	55415	612-673-3000	673-3812
Mobile City Hall 205 Government St *Web:* www.cityofmobile.org	Mobile	AL	36602	251-208-7411	208-7576
Modesto City Hall PO Box 642 *Web:* www.modestogov.com	Modesto	CA	95353	209-577-5200	571-5152
Monterey City Hall 580 Pacific St *Web:* www.monterey.org	Monterey	CA	93940	831-646-3935	646-3702
Montgomery City Hall 103 N Perry St *Web:* www.montgomeryal.gov	Montgomery	AL	36104	334-241-4400	
Montpelier City Hall 39 Main St *Web:* montpelier-vt.org	Montpelier	VT	05602	802-223-9502	223-9519
Morgantown City Hall 389 Spruce St *Web:* www.morgantownwv.gov	Morgantown	WV	26505	304-284-7439	
Myrtle Beach City Hall 937 Broadway St *Web:* www.cityofmyrtlebeach.com	Myrtle Beach	SC	29577	843-918-1000	918-1028
Naples City Hall 735 Eigth St S *Web:* www.naplesgov.com	Naples	FL	34102	239-213-1015	213-1025
Nashville & Davidson County Metropolitan City Hall 100 Metropolitan Courthouse *Web:* www.nashville.gov	Nashville	TN	37201	615-862-6000	862-6040
New Haven City Hall 165 Church St *Web:* www.cityofnewhaven.com	New Haven	CT	06510	203-946-8200	946-7683
New Orleans City Hall 1300 Perdido St *Web:* www.nola.gov	New Orleans	LA	70112	504-658-4000	658-4938
New York City Hall Broadway & Murray Sts *Web:* www.nyc.gov	New York	NY	10007	212-788-2656	
Newark City Hall 920 Broad St *Web:* www.ci.newark.nj.us	Newark	NJ	07102	973-733-8004	733-5352
Newport City Hall 43 Broadway *Web:* www.cityofnewport.com	Newport	RI	02840	401-846-9600	845-2510
Newport News City Hall 2400 Washington Ave *Web:* www.nnva.gov	Newport News	VA	23607	757-926-8634	926-3503
Norfolk City Hall 810 Union St *Web:* www.norfolk.gov	Norfolk	VA	23510	757-664-4000	664-4226
Oakland City Hall 1 Frank H Ogawa Plaza *Web:* www.oaklandnet.com	Oakland	CA	94612	510-444-2489	
Ocean City City Hall 301 Baltimore Ave *TF:* 800-626-2326 ■ *Web:* www.oceancitymd.gov	Ocean City	MD	21842	410-289-8931	289-7385
Ogden City Hall 2549 Washington Blvd *Web:* www.ogdencity.com	Ogden	UT	84401	801-629-8150	629-8154
Oklahoma City City Hall 200 N Walker Ave *Web:* www.okc.gov	Oklahoma City	OK	73102	405-297-2578	297-3124
Olympia City Hall PO Box 1967 *Web:* olympiawa.gov	Olympia	WA	98507	360-753-8447	709-2791
Omaha City Hall 1819 Farnam St Ste LC1 *Web:* www.ci.omaha.ne.us	Omaha	NE	68183	402-444-5550	444-5263
Orlando City Hall 400 S Orange Ave *Web:* www.cityoforlando.net	Orlando	FL	32801	407-246-2221	246-2842
Ottawa City Hall 110 Laurier Ave W *TF:* 866-261-9799 ■ *Web:* www.ottawa.ca/city_hall/index_en.html	Ottawa	ON	K1P1J1	613-580-2400	
Oxnard City Hall 300 W 3rd St *Web:* www.oxnard.org	Oxnard	CA	93030	805-385-7803	
Palm Springs City Hall 3200 E Tahquitz Canyon Way *Web:* www.ci.palm-springs.ca.us	Palm Springs	CA	92262	760-323-8299	322-8332
Paterson City Hall 155 Market St *Web:* www.patersonnj.gov	Paterson	NJ	07505	973-321-1500	
Pensacola City Hall 180 Governmental Ctr *Web:* www.cityofpensacola.com	Pensacola	FL	32521	850-435-1626	
Peoria City Hall 419 Fulton St Ste 401 *Web:* www.peoriagov.org	Peoria	IL	61602	309-494-8565	494-8574
Philadelphia City Hall 1234 Market St 17th Fl *Web:* philafound.org	Philadelphia	PA	19107	215-563-6417	
Phoenix City Hall 200 W Washington St 11th Fl *Web:* www.phoenix.gov	Phoenix	AZ	85003	602-262-7111	495-5583
Pierre City Hall 222 E Dakota Ave *Web:* ci.pierre.sd.us	Pierre	SD	57501	605-773-7407	773-7406
Pittsburgh City Hall 414 Grant St City-County Bldg *Web:* pittsburghpa.gov	Pittsburgh	PA	15219	412-255-2883	255-2821
Plano City Hall 1520 Ave K *Web:* www.plano.gov	Plano	TX	75074	972-941-7000	423-9587
Pocatello City Hall 911 N Seventh Ave *Web:* www.pocatello.us	Pocatello	ID	83201	208-234-6163	234-6297
Portland (ME) City Hall 389 Congress St *Web:* www.portlandmaine.gov	Portland	ME	04101	207-874-8610	874-8612
Portland (OR) City Hall 1221 SW Fourth Ave Rm 110 *Web:* portlandoregon.gov	Portland	OR	97204	503-823-4000	823-3588
Providence City Hall 25 Dorrance St *Web:* providenceri.com	Providence	RI	02903	401-421-7740	
Provo City Hall 351 W Ctr St *Web:* provo.org	Provo	UT	84601	801-852-6100	852-6107
Quebec City Hall 2 Rue des Jardins *Web:* www.ville.quebec.qc.ca	Quebec	QC	G1R4S9	418-641-6651	
Rapid City City Hall 300 Sixth St *Web:* www.rcgov.org	Rapid City	SD	57701	605-394-4110	394-6793
Rehoboth Beach City Hall 229 Rehoboth Ave *Web:* www.cityofrehoboth.com	Rehoboth Beach	DE	19971	302-227-6181	227-4643
Reno City Hall PO Box 1900 *Web:* www.reno.gov	Reno	NV	89505	775-334-2030	334-2432
Richmond City Hall 6911 Rd No 3 *Web:* www.richmondgov.com	Richmond	VA	23219	804-646-7000	
Riverside City Hall 3900 Main St *Web:* www.riversideca.gov	Riverside	CA	92522	951-826-5312	826-5470
Rochester Mayor's 201 Fourth St SE *Web:* rochestermn.gov	Rochester	MN	55904	507-328-2700	287-7979
Rochester (NY) City Hall 30 Church St *Web:* cityofrochester.gov	Rochester	NY	14614	585-428-7045	428-6059
Rockford City Hall 425 E State St *Web:* www.ci.rockford.il.us	Rockford	IL	61104	815-987-5590	967-6952
Sacramento City Hall 915 'I' St *Web:* www.cityofsacramento.org	Sacramento	CA	95814	916-808-7200	808-7672
Saint Augustine City Hall PO Box 210 *Web:* www.staugustinegovernment.com	Saint Augustine	FL	32085	904-825-1040	209-4286
Saint Louis City Hall 1200 Market St *Web:* stlouis-mo.gov	Saint Louis	MO	63103	314-622-3201	622-4061
Saint Paul City Hall 15 W Kellogg Blvd 390 City Hall *Web:* www.stpaul.gov	Saint Paul	MN	55102	651-266-8510	266-8521
Saint Petersburg City Hall PO Box 2842 *Web:* www.stpete.org	Saint Petersburg	FL	33731	727-893-7111	892-5102
Salem City Hall 555 Liberty St SE Rm 220 *Web:* www.cityofsalem.net	Salem	OR	97301	503-588-6255	588-6354
Salt Lake City City Hall 451 S State St *Web:* www.slcgov.com	Salt Lake City	UT	84111	801-535-7704	535-6331
San Antonio City Hall PO Box 839966 *Web:* www.sanantonio.gov	San Antonio	TX	78283	210-207-7040	207-7027
San Bernardino City Hall 300 N 'D' St *Web:* www.ci.san-bernardino.ca.us	San Bernardino	CA	92418	909-384-5211	384-5158
San Diego City Hall 202 C St *TF:* 866-470-1308 ■ *Web:* www.sandiego.gov	San Diego	CA	92101	619-533-4000	533-4045
San Jose City Hall 200 Santa Clara St *Web:* www.sanjoseca.gov	San Jose	CA	95113	408-535-3500	292-6731
Santa Ana City Hall 20 Civic Ctr Plaza *Web:* www.ci.santa-ana.ca.us	Santa Ana	CA	92701	714-647-6900	647-6954
Santa Fe City Hall 200 Lincoln Ave *Web:* www.santafenm.gov	Santa Fe	NM	87501	505-955-6520	
Savannah City Hall PO Box 1027 *Web:* savannahga.gov	Savannah	GA	31402	912-651-6441	651-4260
Scottsdale City Hall 7447 E Indian School Rd *Web:* www.scottsdaleaz.gov	Scottsdale	AZ	85251	480-312-3111	312-2888
Scranton City Hall 340 N Washington Ave *Web:* www.scrantonpa.gov	Scranton	PA	18503	570-348-4100	348-4207
Seattle City Hall 600 Fourth Ave 2nd Fl *Web:* www.seattle.gov	Seattle	WA	98104	206-684-8888	684-8587
Shreveport City Hall PO Box 31109 *Web:* www.shreveportla.gov	Shreveport	LA	71130	318-673-5370	673-5099
Sioux Falls City Hall 224 W 9th St *Web:* siouxfalls.org	Sioux Falls	SD	57104	605-367-8000	367-7801
South Bend City Hall 227 W Jefferson Blvd Ste 1300 S *Web:* www.southbendin.gov/government/content/departments	South Bend	IN	46601	574-235-9221	235-9173
Spokane City Hall 808 W Spokane Falls Blvd *Web:* www.spokanecity.org	Spokane	WA	99201	509-625-6250	
Springfield (IL) City Hall 800 E Monroe St Rm 300 *Web:* www.springfield.il.us	Springfield	IL	62701	217-789-2200	789-2109
Springfield (MA) City Hall 36 Ct St *Web:* www.springfield-ma.gov/cos	Springfield	MA	01103	413-787-6000	
Springfield (MO) City Hall 840 Boonville Ave *Web:* www.springfieldmo.gov/home	Springfield	MO	65802	417-864-1000	864-1649
Stamford City Hall 888 Washington Blvd 10th Fl *Web:* www.stamfordct.gov	Stamford	CT	06901	203-977-4150	977-5845

				Phone	Fax
Stockton City Hall 425 N El Dorado St *Web:* www.stocktongov.com	Stockton	CA	95202	209-937-8212	937-7149
Tacoma City Hall 747 Market St *Web:* www.cityoftacoma.org	Tacoma	WA	98402	253-591-5000	591-5300
Tallahassee City Hall 300 S Adams St *Web:* talgov.com	Tallahassee	FL	32301	850-891-0000	
Tampa City Hall 306 E Jackson St *Web:* www.tampagov.net	Tampa	FL	33602	813-274-8251	274-7050
Tempe City Hall 31 E Fifth St *Web:* www.tempe.gov	Tempe	AZ	85281	480-350-8221	350-8930
Toledo City Hall 1 Government Ctr Ste 2120 *Web:* toledo.oh.gov	Toledo	OH	43604	419-245-1050	245-1072
Topeka City Hall 215 SE 7th St *Web:* www.topeka.org	Topeka	KS	66603	785-368-3754	368-3966
Toronto City Hall 100 Queen St W *Web:* www.toronto.ca	Toronto	ON	M5H2N2	416-392-8016	392-2980
Trenton City Hall 319 E State St *Web:* www.trentonnj.org	Trenton	NJ	08608	609-989-3185	989-3190
Tucson City Hall 255 W Alameda St *Web:* tucsonaz.gov	Tucson	AZ	85701	520-791-4204	791-5198
Tulsa City Hall 175 E 2nd St Fl 14 *Web:* www.cityoftulsa.org	Tulsa	OK	74103	918-596-2100	596-9010
Tupelo City Hall 71 E Troy St *Web:* www.tupeloms.gov	Tupelo	MS	38804	662-841-6513	840-2075
Tuscaloosa City Hall 2201 University Blvd *Web:* www.ci.tuscaloosa.al.us	Tuscaloosa	AL	35401	205-248-5311	349-0147
Vancouver (BC) City Hall 453 W 12th Ave PO Box 7747 *Web:* vancouver.ca	Vancouver	BC	V5Y1V4	604-873-7000	873-7051
Vancouver (WA) City Hall PO Box 1995 *Web:* www.cityofvancouver.us	Vancouver	WA	98668	360-487-8000	274-8049
Virginia Beach City Hall 2401 Courthouse Dr Municipal Ctr Bldg 1 *Web:* www.vbgov.com	Virginia Beach	VA	23456	757-385-3111	
Washington (DC) City Hall 1350 Pennsylvania Ave NW *Web:* www.dc.gov	Washington	DC	20004	202-727-1000	727-0505
West Palm Beach City Hall 200 Second St *Web:* wpb.org	West Palm Beach	FL	33401	561-822-1200	822-1424
Wheeling City Council Chambers 1500 Chapline St *Web:* www.wheelingchamber.com	Wheeling	WV	26003	304-234-3694	
Wichita City Hall 455 N Main St 1st Fl *Web:* www.wichita.gov	Wichita	KS	67202	316-268-4331	
Winston-Salem City Hall 101 N Main St PO Box 2511 *Web:* www.cityofws.org	Winston-Salem	NC	27101	336-727-8000	748-3060
Yonkers City Hall 40 S Broadway *Web:* www.yonkersny.gov	Yonkers	NY	10701	914-377-6000	
Youngstown City Hall 26 S Phelps St *Web:* youngstownmuniclerk.com	Youngstown	OH	44503	330-742-8859	

338 GOVERNMENT - COUNTY

				Phone	Fax
Abbeville County 21 Old Calhoun Falls Rd *Web:* www.abbevillecountysc.com/sheriff.aspx	Abbeville	SC	29620	864-366-5312	
Accomack County 23296 Courthouse Ave Ste 203 *Web:* www.co.accomack.va.us	Accomac	VA	23301	757-787-5700	787-2468
Adair County 424 Public Sq *Web:* www.columbia-adaircounty.com	Columbia	KY	42728	270-384-2801	
Adair County 400 Public Sq *Web:* www.adaircountyiowa.org/contact-us	Greenfield	IA	50849	641-743-2546	743-2565
Adair County 106 W Washington St *Web:* adaircountymissouri.com	Kirksville	MO	63501	660-665-3350	
Adair County PO Box 31 *Web:* adair.oklahoma.usassessor.com	Stilwell	OK	74960	918-696-2012	696-6729
Adams County 450 S Fourth Ave *Web:* www.co.adams.co.us	Brighton	CO	80601	303-654-6100	
Adams County 500 Ninth St *Web:* www.adamscountyia.com	Corning	IA	50841	641-322-3240	322-4647
Adams County 201 Industrial Ave PO Box 48 *Web:* www.co.adams.id.us	Council	ID	83612	208-253-6125	253-6127
Adams County 313 W Jefferson St *Web:* www.co.adams.in.us	Decatur	IN	46733	260-724-5300	724-5313
Adams County PO Box 95 *Web:* www.adamscounty.org	Hastings	NE	68901	402-461-7107	461-7185
Adams County PO Box 1008 *Web:* www.adamscountyms.net	Natchez	MS	39121	601-442-2431	
Adams County 507 Vermont St *Web:* www.co.adams.il.us	Quincy	IL	62301	217-277-2150	277-2155
Adams County 210 W Broadway *Web:* www.co.adams.wa.us	Ritzville	WA	99169	509-659-3257	659-0118
Adams County 110 W Main St *Web:* adamscountyoh.gov	West Union	OH	45693	937-544-2011	
Addison County 7 Mahady Ct *Web:* www.addisoncounty.com	Middlebury	VT	05753	802-388-7741	388-8066
Aiken County 828 Richland Ave W *TF:* 866-876-7074 ■ *Web:* www.aikencountysc.gov	Aiken	SC	29801	803-642-2012	
Alachua County 12 SE First St *Web:* www.alachuacounty.us	Gainesville	FL	32601	352-374-5204	
Alamance County 124 W Elm St *Web:* www.alamance-nc.com	Graham	NC	27253	336-228-1312	570-6788
Alameda County 1221 Oak St Ste 555 *Web:* www.acgov.org	Oakland	CA	94612	510-272-6984	272-3784
Alamosa County 8900 Independence Way *Web:* www.alamosacounty.org	Alamosa	CO	81101	719-589-4848	589-1900
Albany County 112 State St Rm 1100 *Web:* www.albanycounty.com	Albany	NY	12207	518-447-7040	447-5589
Albemarle County 401 McIntire Rd *Web:* www.albemarle.org	Charlottesville	VA	22902	434-296-5841	296-5800
Alcorn County 600 Waldron St PO Box 179 *Web:* www.alcorncounty.org	Corinth	MS	38834	662-286-7733	286-2548
Aleutians East Borough 3380 C St Ste 205 *TF:* 888-383-2699 ■ *Web:* www.aleutianseast.org	Anchorage	AK	99503	907-274-7555	276-7569
Alexander County 2000 Washington Ave *Web:* www.alexandercountyil.com	Cairo	IL	62914	618-734-0107	
Alexander County 621 Liledoun Rd *Web:* alexandercountync.gov	Taylorsville	NC	28681	828-632-9332	632-0059
Alexandria (Independent City) 301 King St Ste 2300 *Web:* alexandriava.gov	Alexandria	VA	22314	703-838-4500	
Alfalfa County 300 S Grand Ave **Fax Area Code:* 405	Cherokee	OK	73728	580-596-3269	596-2254*
Alger County 101 Ct St *Web:* algercourthouse.com	Munising	MI	49862	906-387-2076	387-2156
Allamakee County 110 Allamakee St *Web:* www.allamakeecounty.com	Waukon	IA	52172	563-864-7454	
Allegany County 7 Ct St County Courthouse *Web:* www.alleganyco.com	Belmont	NY	14813	585-268-9270	268-5881
Allen County 715 S Calhoun St County Courthouse Rm 201 *Web:* www.allencounty.us	Fort Wayne	IN	46802	260-449-7245	
Allen County 1 N Washington St *TF:* 866-444-1407 ■ *Web:* www.allencounty.org	Iola	KS	66749	620-365-1407	365-1441
Allen County 301 N Main St *Web:* www.allencountyohio.com	Lima	OH	45801	419-228-3700	222-8427
Allen County PO Box 115 *Web:* www.allencountykentucky.com	Scottsville	KY	42164	270-237-4782	
Allen Parish PO Box 1280 *TF:* 888-639-4868 ■ *Web:* www.allenparish.com	Oberlin	LA	70655	337-639-4868	639-4911
Allendale County 526 Memorial Ave *Web:* www.allendalecounty.com	Allendale	SC	29810	803-584-3438	584-7042
Alpena County 720 W Chisholm St *Web:* www.alpenacounty.org	Alpena	MI	49707	989-354-9500	354-9648
Alpine County 99 Waters St PO Box 158 *Web:* www.alpinecountyca.gov	Markleeville	CA	96120	530-694-2281	694-2491
Amador County 810 Ct St *Web:* www.co.amador.ca.us	Jackson	CA	95642	209-223-6470	257-0619
Amelia County 16360 Dunn St Ste 101 *Web:* www.ameliacova.com	Amelia Courthouse	VA	23002	804-561-3039	561-6039
Amherst County 153 Washington St *Web:* www.countyofamherst.com	Amherst	VA	24521	434-946-9400	946-9370
Amite County PO Box 680 *Web:* www.amitecounty.ms	Liberty	MS	39645	601-657-8022	657-8288
Anaconda-Deer Lodge County 800 S Main *Web:* adlc.us	Anaconda	MT	59711	406-563-4000	563-4001
Anchorage Municipality 632 W Sixth Ave # 250 *Web:* www.muni.org	Anchorage	AK	99501	907-343-4311	343-4313
Anderson County PO Box 8002 PO Box 8002 *Web:* www.andersoncountysc.org	Anderson	SC	29624	864-260-4000	
Anderson County 100 N Main St Rm 111 *Web:* www.andersoncountychamber.org	Clinton	TN	37716	865-457-5400	
Anderson County 100 E 4th Ave *Web:* andersoncountyks.org	Garnett	KS	66032	785-448-6841	
Anderson County 151 S Main St *Web:* andersoncountyclerk.ky.gov	Lawrenceburg	KY	40342	502-839-3041	839-3043
Anderson County 500 N Church St *Web:* www.co.anderson.tx.us	Palestine	TX	75801	903-723-7432	723-4625
Andrew County PO Box 206 *Web:* www.andrewcounty.org	Savannah	MO	64485	816-324-3624	324-6154
Andrews County 215 NW First St Annex Bldg *Web:* www.co.andrews.tx.us	Andrews	TX	79714	432-524-1426	
Anne Arundel County 44 Calvert St	Annapolis	MD	21401	410-222-7000	
Anoka County 325 E Main St *Web:* anokacounty.us	Anoka	MN	55303	763-422-7350	422-6919
Anson County 101 S Greene St *Web:* www.co.anson.nc.us	Wadesboro	NC	28170	704-994-3201	
Antelope County 501 Main St *Web:* antelopecounty.nebraska.gov	Neligh	NE	68756	402-887-4410	887-4719
Antrim County 203 E Cayuga St *Web:* www.antrimcounty.org	Bellaire	MI	49615	231-533-6353	533-6935
Apache County 75 W Cleveland St *Web:* www.co.apache.az.us	Saint Johns	AZ	85936	928-337-4364	337-2771
Appling County 69 Tippins St *Web:* www.baxley.org	Baxley	GA	31513	912-367-8100	367-8161
Aransas County 301 N Live Oak St *Web:* www.aransascounty.org	Rockport	TX	78382	361-790-0122	790-0119
Arenac County PO Box 747 *Web:* www.arenaccountygov.com	Standish	MI	48658	989-846-4626	
Arkansas County 302 S College St	Stuttgart	AR	72160	870-673-2418	
Arlington County 2100 Clarendon Blvd Ste 300 *Web:* www.arlingtonva.us	Arlington	VA	22201	703-228-3130	228-7430
Armstrong County 100 Trice St PO Box 189	Claude	TX	79019	806-226-3221	
Armstrong County 450 E Market St *Web:* www.co.armstrong.pa.us	Kittanning	PA	16201	724-543-2500	
Arthur County 205 Fir St *Web:* arthurcounty.nebraska.gov	Arthur	NE	69121	308-764-2201	
Ascension Parish 208 E Railroad St *Web:* www.ascensionparish.net	Gonzales	LA	70737	225-621-5709	621-5704
Ashe County Chamber of Commerce 1 N Jefferson Ave Ste C PO Box 31 *TF:* 888-343-2743 ■ *Web:* ashechamber.com	West Jefferson	NC	28694	336-846-9550	
Ashland County 142 W Second St *Web:* www.ashlandcounty.org	Ashland	OH	44805	419-282-4242	
Ashland County 201 W Main St Ste 202 *Web:* www.co.ashland.wi.us	Ashland	WI	54806	715-682-7000	

Name / Address	City	State	Zip	Phone	Fax
Ashley County 215 E Jefferson St	Hamburg	AR	71646	870-853-2000	
Web: local.arkansas.gov/local.php?agency=Ashley%20County					
Asotin County 135 Second St	Asotin	WA	99402	509-243-2016	243-4978
Web: www.co.asotin.wa.us					
Assumption Parish 4813 Hwy 1 PO Box 520	Napoleonville	LA	70390	985-369-7435	369-2972
TF: 800-315-9513 ■ *Web:* www.assumptionla.com					
Atascosa County 1 Courthouse Cir Dr Ste 102	Jourdanton	TX	78026	830-767-2511	769-1021
Web: www.co.atascosa.tx.us					
Atchison County 423 N Fifth St	Atchison	KS	66002	913-367-1653	367-0227
Web: www.atchisoncountyks.org					
Atchison County 405 S Main St PO Box 243	Rock Port	MO	64482	660-744-6562	744-6564
TF: 800-989-4115 ■ *Web:* www.atchisoncounty.org					
Athens County Board of Developmental Disabilities 801 W Union St	Athens	OH	45701	740-594-3539	
Web: athenscbdd.org					
Athens-Clarke County 325 E Washington St Rm 200 PO Box 1868	Athens	GA	30601	706-613-3031	613-3033
Web: www.athensclarkecounty.com					
Atkinson County PO Box 518	Pearson	GA	31642	912-422-3391	422-3429
Web: www.atkinsoncounty.org					
Atlantic County 5901 E Main St	Mays Landing	NJ	08330	609-641-7867	625-4738
Web: www.aclink.org					
Atoka County PO Box 900	Atoka	OK	74525	580-889-3341	889-7584
Web: atokaok.org					
Attala County 230 W Washington St	Kosciusko	MS	39090	662-289-2921	289-7662
Web: attalacounty.net					
Audrain County 101 N Jefferson St Rm 101	Mexico	MO	65265	573-473-5820	581-2380
Web: www.audraincounty.org					
Audubon County 318 Leroy St Ste 6	Audubon	IA	50025	712-563-4275	
Web: www.auduboncounty.org					
Auglaize County 209 S Blackhoof St Ste 201	Wapakoneta	OH	45895	419-739-6710	
TF: 877-836-3206 ■ *Web:* www.auglaizecounty.org					
Augusta County 18 Government Ctr Ln	Verona	VA	24482	540-245-5600	245-5621
Web: www.co.augusta.va.us					
Augusta-Richmond County 535 Telfair St	Augusta	GA	30901	706-821-2300	826-4790
Web: www.augustaga.gov					
Aurora County 401 N Main St PO Box 366	Plankinton	SD	57368	605-942-7165	942-7170
Web: ujs.sd.gov					
Austin County 1 E Main St	Bellville	TX	77418	979-865-5911	865-8786
Web: www.austincounty.com					
Avery County PO Box 115	Newland	NC	28657	828-733-2910	
Web: www.averycounty.com					
Avoyelles Parish 675 Government St	Marksville	LA	71351	318-253-8085	
Web: avoyellesso.org					
Baca County 741 Main St	Springfield	CO	81073	719-523-4372	
Web: www.springfieldcolorado.com					
Bacon County 504 N Pierce St PO Box 450	Alma	GA	31510	912-632-5859	632-7710
Web: www.almaone.com					
Bailey County 300 S First St	Muleshoe	TX	79347	806-272-3044	272-3538
Web: www.co.bailey.tx.us					
Baker County 1995 Third St Ste 150	Baker City	OR	97814	541-523-8207	523-8240
Web: www.bakercounty.org					
Baker County 339 E Macclenny Ave	Macclenny	FL	32063	904-259-8113	
Web: www.bakercountyfl.org					
Baldwin County 322 Courthouse Sq	Bay Minette	AL	36507	251-937-9561	580-2500
Web: www.baldwincountyal.gov					
Baldwin County 121 N Wilkinson St Ste 314	Milledgeville	GA	31061	478-445-4791	445-6320
Web: www.baldwincountyga.com					
Baltimore County 401 Bosley Ave	Towson	MD	21204	410-887-2139	
Web: baltimorecountymd.gov					
Bamberg County 2340 Main Hwy	Bamberg	SC	29003	803-245-5128	245-5156
Web: www.bambergsc.com					
Banner County 206 State St	Harrisburg	NE	69345	308-436-5265	
Bannock County PO Box 4016	Pocatello	ID	83205	208-236-7211	236-7363
Web: www.bannockcounty.us					
Baraga County 16 N Third St	L'Anse	MI	49946	906-524-6183	
Web: www.baragacounty.org/contactlocation					
Barbour County 8 N Main St	Philippi	WV	26416	304-457-3454	457-5983
Web: barbourcounty.wv.gov					
Barnes County 230 Fourth St NW Rm 202	Valley City	ND	58072	701-845-8500	
Web: www.co.barnes.nd.us					
Barnstable County PO Box 427	Barnstable	MA	02630	508-362-2511	
Web: www.barnstablecounty.org					
Barnwell County 141 Main St	Barnwell	SC	29812	803-541-1020	
Barren County 117-1A N Public Sq	Glasgow	KY	42141	270-651-3783	651-1083
Barron County 330 E LaSalle Ave	Barron	WI	54812	715-537-6200	537-6277
Web: www.co.barron.wi.us					
Barrow County 233 E Broad St	Winder	GA	30680	770-307-3005	307-3141
Web: www.barrowga.org					
Barry County 220 W State St	Hastings	MI	49058	269-945-1290	945-0209
Web: barrycounty.org					
Barry County Clerk 700 Main St Ste 2	Cassville	MO	65625	417-847-2561	
Web: barrycountycollector.com					
Bartholomew County 234 Washington St	Columbus	IN	47201	812-379-1600	
Web: www.bartholomewco.com					
Barton County 1400 Main St Ste 202	Great Bend	KS	67530	620-793-1835	793-1990
Web: www.bartoncounty.org					
Barton County 1004 Gulf St	Lamar	MO	64759	417-682-3529	682-4100
Web: www.bartoncounty.com					
Bartow County 135 W Cherokee Ave Ste 251	Cartersville	GA	30120	770-387-5030	387-5023
Web: www.bartowga.org					
Bastrop County 804 Pecan St	Bastrop	TX	78602	512-581-4000	
Web: www.co.bastrop.tx.us					
Bates County 1 N Delaware St	Butler	MO	64730	660-679-3371	679-9922
Web: www.batescounty.net					
Bath County 17 W Main St	Owingsville	KY	40360	606-674-2613	674-9526
Web: bathcounty.ky.gov/pages/default.aspx					
Bath County PO Box 309	Warm Springs	VA	24484	540-839-7221	839-7222
TF: 888-823-1710 ■ *Web:* www.bathcountyva.org					
Baxter County 1 E Seventh St Fl 1 Baxter County Courthouse	Mountain Home	AR	72653	870-425-3475	
Web: www.baxtercounty.org					
Bay County 515 Ctr Ave Ste 101	Bay City	MI	48708	989-895-4280	895-4284
TF: 877-229-9960 ■ *Web:* www.baycounty-mi.gov					
Bay County 300 E Fourth St	Panama City	FL	32401	850-763-9061	
Web: www.co.bay.fl.us					
Bayfield County PO Box 878	Washburn	WI	54891	715-373-6100	373-6153
Web: www.bayfieldcounty.org					
Baylor County 301 N Washington PO Box 31	Seymour	TX	76380	940-889-3148	889-8882
Web: www.cityofseymour.org					
Beadle County 450 3rd St SW	Huron	SD	57350	605-353-7161	
Web: beadle.sdcounties.org					
Bear Lake County 7 E Ctr St PO Box 190	Paris	ID	83261	208-945-2212	
Web: www.bearlakecounty.info					
Beaufort County 102 Ribaut Rd	Beaufort	SC	29902	843-255-5050	
Web: www.co.beaufort.sc.us					
Beaufort County 121 W Third St	Washington	NC	27889	252-946-0079	946-7722
Web: www.co.beaufort.nc.us					
Beauregard Parish PO Box 100	DeRidder	LA	70634	337-463-8595	462-3916
Web: beauregardclerk.org					
Beaver County PO Box 338	Beaver	OK	73932	580-625-3151	
Web: www.okcounties.org					
Beaver County 810 Third St Courthouse	Beaver	PA	15009	724-728-5700	
Web: www.beavercountypa.gov					
Beaver County 105 E Ctr St PO Box 789	Beaver	UT	84713	435-438-6490	438-6462
Web: beaver.utah.gov					
Beaverhead County 2 S Pacific St Ste 16	Dillon	MT	59725	406-683-3700	683-3728
Web: www.beaverheadcounty.org					
Becker County 915 Lake Ave	Detroit Lakes	MN	56501	218-846-7311	846-7257*
**Fax:* Acctg ■ *Web:* www.co.becker.mn.us					
Beckham County PO Box 67	Sayre	OK	73662	580-928-2457	928-2467
Web: beckham.okcounties.org					
Bedford County 200 S Juliana St	Bedford	PA	15522	814-949-6500	623-4831
Web: www.bedford.sapdc.org					
Bedford County 122 E Main St Ste 202	Bedford	VA	24523	540-586-7601	586-0406
Web: www.co.bedford.va.us					
Bedford County 104 Public Sq N	Shelbyville	TN	37160	931-684-9695	
Web: www.shelbyvilletn.com					
Bedford (Independent City) 215 E Main St	Bedford	VA	24523	540-587-6001	
Web: www.bedfordva.gov/reversion.shtml					
Bee County 105 W Corpus Christi St Rm 103	Beeville	TX	78102	361-362-3245	362-3247
Web: www.co.bee.tx.us					
Belknap County 34 County Dr	Laconia	NH	03246	603-527-5400	527-5409
Web: www.belknapcounty.org					
Bell County 101 E Central Ave PO Box 480	Belton	TX	76513	254-933-5160	933-5176
TF: 800-460-2355 ■ *Web:* www.bellcountytx.com					
Bell County PO Box 157	Pineville	KY	40977	606-337-6143	337-5415
Web: www.bellcountyclerk.ky.gov					
Belmont County 101 W Main St Courthouse	Saint Clairsville	OH	43950	740-695-2121	
Web: www.belmontcountyohio.org/county-departments					
Beltrami County 619 Beltrami Ave NW Courthouse	Bemidji	MN	56601	218-333-4120	333-4209
Web: www.co.beltrami.mn.us					
Ben Hill County 402A E Pine St	Fitzgerald	GA	31750	229-426-5100	426-5630
Web: www.benhillcounty.com					
Benewah County 701 College Ave	Saint Maries	ID	83861	208-245-3212	245-9152
Web: www.idaho.gov					
Bennett County 201 State St	Martin	SD	57551	605-685-6516	685-2255
Web: www.bennettcosheriff.org/deputies.html					
Bennington County 100 Veterans Memorial Dr	Bennington	VT	05201	802-447-3311	447-1163
TF: 800-229-0252 ■ *Web:* www.bennington.com					
Benson County PO Box 213	Minnewaukan	ND	58351	701-473-5345	473-5571
Web: www.bensoncountynd.com/contact.htm					
Bent County 725 Bent Ave	Las Animas	CO	81054	719-456-1600	456-0375
Web: www.bentcounty.org					
Benton County 215 E Central St Ste 217	Bentonville	AR	72712	479-271-1013	271-1019
Web: www.bentoncountyar.gov					
Benton County 408 SW Monroe Ave Ste 111	Corvallis	OR	97339	541-766-6800	766-6893
Web: www.co.benton.or.us					
Benton County 615 Hwy 23 PO Box 189	Foley	MN	56329	320-968-5205	968-5353
Web: www.co.benton.mn.us					
Benton County 7122 W Okanogan Pl Bldg A	Kennewick	WA	99336	509-735-3591	736-3066
Web: www.co.benton.wa.us					
Benton County 111 E Fourth St	Vinton	IA	52349	319-472-2766	
Web: pocahontas.countycriminal.com/court-records-search/WV					
Benton County 1231 Hirsch Pkwy PO Box 852	Warsaw	MO	65355	660-438-8412	438-8413
Web: www.bentoncomo.com					
Benzie County 448 Ct Pl	Beulah	MI	49617	231-882-9671	882-5941
TF: 800-315-3593 ■ *Web:* www.benzieco.net					
Bergen County 1 Bergen County Plaza Rm 580	Hackensack	NJ	07601	201-336-7300	336-7304
Web: www.co.bergen.nj.us					
Berkeley County 1003 Hwy 52 PO Box 6122	Moncks Corner	SC	29461	843-719-4234	
Web: www.berkeleycountysc.gov					
Berkeley County Council 400 W Stephen St Ste 201	Martinsburg	WV	25401	304-264-1923	267-1794
Web: www.berkeleycountycomm.org					
Berks County *Law Library* 633 Ct St 4th Fl	Reading	PA	19601	610-478-3370	478-6375
Web: www.co.berks.pa.us					
Berkshire County 66 Allen St	Pittsfield	MA	01201	413-499-4000	447-9641
Web: 1berkshire.com					
Bernalillo County 1 Civic Plaza NW 10th Fl	Albuquerque	NM	87102	505-468-7000	768-4329
Web: www.bernco.gov					
Berrien County 201 N Davis St Ste 105	Nashville	GA	31639	229-686-7461	686-7819
Web: www.berriencountygeorgia.com					
Berrien County 701 Main St	Saint Joseph	MI	49085	269-983-7111	982-8642
Web: www.berriencounty.org					

				Phone	Fax
Bertie County 106 Dundee St PO Box 530 *Web:* www.co.bertie.nc.us	Windsor	NC	27983	252-794-5300	794-5327
Bexar County 100 Dolorosa St. *Web:* www.bexar.org	San Antonio	TX	78205	210-335-2011	335-2252
Bibb County 157 SW Davidson Dr *Web:* www.bibbal.com	Centreville	AL	35042	205-926-3114	
Bibb County 700 Poplar St. *Web:* maconbibb.us	Macon	GA	31201	478-751-7400	
Bienville Parish 100 Courthouse Dr Rm 100 *Web:* www.bienvilleparish.org	Arcadia	LA	71001	318-263-2123	
Big Horn County 420 W C St. *Web:* www.bighorncountywy.gov	Basin	WY	82410	307-568-2357	568-9375
Big Horn County 121 W Third St. *Web:* www.bighorncountymt.gov/departments/treasurer	Hardin	MT	59034	406-665-9735	665-9706
Big Stone County 20 SE Second St. *Web:* www.bigstonecounty.org	Ortonville	MN	56278	320-839-6376	
Billings County 495 Fourth St PO Box 168 *Web:* www.billingscountynd.gov	Medora	ND	58645	701-623-4377	623-4761
Bingham County 501 N Maple St Ste 205 *Web:* www.co.bingham.id.us	Blackfoot	ID	83221	208-782-3013	
Black Hawk County 316 E Fifth St *Web:* www.co.black-hawk.ia.us	Waterloo	IA	50703	319-833-3012	
Blackford County 110 W Washington St *Web:* gov.blackfordcounty.org	Hartford City	IN	47348	765-348-1620	348-7222
Bladen County 166 E Broad St Rm 105 *Web:* www.bladennc.govoffice3.com	Elizabethtown	NC	28337	910-862-6700	862-6767
Blaine County 145 Lincoln Ave *Web:* www.blainecounty.ne.gov	Brewster	NE	68821	308-547-2222	547-2228
Blaine County 420 Ohio St *TF:* 800-666-6124 ■ *Web:* blainecounty-mt.gov	Chinook	MT	59523	406-442-9830	357-2199
Blaine County 206 First Ave S Ste 200 *Web:* www.co.blaine.id.us	Hailey	ID	83333	208-788-5505	788-5501
Blaine County 212 N Weigle *Web:* www.watonga.com	Watonga	OK	73772	580-623-5890	
Blair County 423 Allegheny St. *Web:* www.blairco.org	Hollidaysburg	PA	16648	814-693-3000	693-3033
Blanco County 101 E Pecan Dr PO Box 65 *Web:* www.co.blanco.tx.us	Johnson City	TX	78636	830-868-0973	868-2084
Bland County 612 Main St Ste 104 *Web:* www.blandcountyva.gov	Bland	VA	24315	276-688-4622	688-9758
Bleckley County 112 N. Second St. *Web:* www.bleckley.org	Cochran	GA	31014	478-934-3200	
Bledsoe County PO Box 205 *Web:* www.pikeville-bledsoe.com	Pikeville	TN	37367	423-447-2791	
Blount County 341 Ct St *Web:* www.blounttn.org	Maryville	TN	37804	865-273-5700	273-5705
Blount County 220 Second Ave E Rm 106 *Web:* www.co.blount.al.us	Oneonta	AL	35121	205-625-4160	625-5961
Blue Earth County 204 S Fifth St *Web:* www.co.blue-earth.mn.us	Mankato	MN	56001	507-304-4000	
Board of Supervisors 201 State St.	Boone	IA	50036	515-433-0500	432-8102
Boise County 420 Main St PO Box 1300 *Web:* www.boisecounty.us	Idaho City	ID	83631	208-392-4431	392-4473
Bolivar County 200 S Ct St *Web:* www.co.bolivar.ms.us	Cleveland	MS	38732	662-846-5877	846-5880
Bollinger County 207 Mayfield Dr. *Web:* bcmnh.org	Marble Hill	MO	63764	573-238-1174	
Bon Homme County 300 W 18th Ave PO Box 6 *Web:* ujs.sd.gov	Tyndall	SD	57066	605-589-4215	589-4245
Bond County 203 W College Ave *Web:* www.bondcountyil.com/circuitclerk/circuitclerk.html	Greenville	IL	62246	618-664-3208	664-2257
Bonner County 215 S First Ave *Web:* bonnercounty.us	Sandpoint	ID	83864	208-265-1432	
Bonneville County 605 N Capital Ave. *Web:* www.co.bonneville.id.us	Idaho Falls	ID	83402	208-529-1350	
Boone County 222 S Fourth St *Web:* www.co.boone.ne.us	Albion	NE	68620	402-395-2055	
Boone County 601 N Main St *TF:* 877-225-7077 ■ *Web:* www.boonecountyil.org	Belvidere	IL	61008	815-547-4770	547-3579
Boone County 2950 E Washington St *Web:* www.boonecountyky.org	Burlington	KY	41005	859-334-2242	334-2193
Boone County 801 E Walnut St *Web:* www.showmeboone.com	Columbia	MO	65201	573-886-4270	886-4254
Boone County 100 N Main St Ste 201 *Web:* boonecountyar.com	Harrison	AR	72601	870-741-8428	741-9724
Boone County 116 W Washington St. *Web:* boonecounty.in.gov	Lebanon	IN	46052	765-483-4458	483-5243
Boone County 200 State St *Web:* www.boonecountywv.org	Madison	WV	25130	304-369-3925	
Bosque County PO Box 617 *Web:* www.bosquecounty.us	Meridian	TX	76665	254-435-2382	435-2152
Botetourt County 1 W Main St 1st Fl *Web:* www.co.botetourt.va.us	Fincastle	VA	24090	540-473-8220	
Bottineau County 314 W 5th St *Web:* www.bottineau.com	Bottineau	ND	58318	701-228-3983	
Boulder County 1750 33rd St Ste 201 *Web:* www.bouldercounty.org	Boulder	CO	80301	303-413-7770	413-7775
Boundary County PO Box 419 *Web:* www.boundarycountyid.org	Bonners Ferry	ID	83805	208-267-5504	267-7814
Bourbon County 210 S National Ave *Web:* bourboncountyks.org	Fort Scott	KS	66701	620-223-3800	223-5832
Bowie County 710 James Bowie Dr *Web:* www.co.bowie.tx.us	New Boston	TX	75570	903-628-2571	628-6729
Bowman County 104 First St NW Ste 3 *Web:* www.bowmannd.com	Bowman	ND	58623	701-523-3450	523-5443
Box Butte County 7006 Otoe Rd	Alliance	NE	69301	308-762-4607	762-2867
Box Elder County 01 S Main St. *TF:* 877-390-2326 ■ *Web:* www.boxeldercounty.org	Brigham City	UT	84302	435-734-3300	723-7562
Boyd County PO Box 26 *Web:* boydcounty.ne.gov	Butte	NE	68722	402-775-2391	775-2146
Boyle County 321 W Main St. *Web:* www.boyleky.com	Danville	KY	40422	859-238-1110	238-1108
Bracken County 116 W Miami St PO Box 264 *Web:* www.brackencounty.ky.gov	Brooksville	KY	41004	606-735-2300	735-2615
Bradford County 945 N Temple Ave PO Box B *Web:* www.bradford-co-fla.org	Starke	FL	32091	904-966-6280	964-4454
Bradford County 301 Main St Courthouse *Web:* www.bradfordcountypa.org	Towanda	PA	18848	570-265-1727	265-1729
Bradley County 155 N Ocoee St *Web:* www.bradleyco.net	Cleveland	TN	37311	423-728-7226	478-8845
Bradley County 101 E Cedar St *Web:* www.countycriminal.com/court-records	Warren	AR	71671	870-226-3464	
Branch County 31 Div St *Web:* www.countyofbranch.com	Coldwater	MI	49036	517-279-4301	278-4130
Brantley County 33 Allen Rd *Fax Area Code: 916	Nahunta	GA	31553	912-462-5256	462-5648*
Braxton County 300 Main St PO Box 486 *Web:* www.braxtoncounty.wv.gov	Sutton	WV	26601	304-765-2833	765-2947
Brazoria County 111 E Locust St. *Web:* brazoriacountytx.gov	Angleton	TX	77515	979-849-5711	
Brazos County 300 E 26th St Ste 120 *Web:* www.brazoscountytx.gov	Bryan	TX	77803	979-361-4135	
Breathitt County PO Box 227 *Web:* www.breathittcounty.com	Jackson	KY	41339	606-666-5060	666-7018
Breckinridge County PO Box 227 *Web:* www.breckinridgecountyky.com	Hardinsburg	KY	40143	270-756-2269	756-2364
Bremer County 415 E Bremer Ave *Web:* www.co.bremer.ia.us	Waverly	IA	50677	319-352-0130	
Brevard County 400 S St Ste 1-A *Web:* www.brevardcounty.us	Titusville	FL	32780	321-264-6750	264-6751
Brewster County 201 W Ave E *Web:* brewstercountytx.com	Alpine	TX	79830	432-837-3366	837-6217
Briscoe County PO Box 555 *Web:* www.co.briscoe.tx.us	Silverton	TX	79257	806-823-2134	823-2359
Bristol Bay Borough PO Box 189 *Web:* www.bristolbayboroughak.us	Naknek	AK	99633	907-246-4224	246-6633
Bristol County 9 Ct St	Taunton	MA	02780	508-824-9681	821-3101
Bristol County 10 Ct St *Web:* www.bristolri.us	Bristol	RI	02809	401-253-7000	253-3080
Bristol (Independent City) 497 Cumberland St Rm 210 *Web:* www.bristolva.org	Bristol	VA	24201	276-645-7321	821-6097
Bronx County 851 Grand Concourse Ste 301 *Web:* www.nyc.gov	Bronx	NY	10451	718-590-3500	590-3537
Brooke County 632 Main St *Web:* www.brookewv.org	Wellsburg	WV	26070	304-737-3661	
Brookings County 314 Sixth Ave *Web:* www.brookingscountysd.gov	Brookings	SD	57006	605-696-8205	696-8211
Brooks County 100 E Miller St *Web:* co.brooks.tx.us	Falfurrias	TX	78355	361-325-5604	325-4944
Broome County 44 Hawley St *Web:* www.gobroomecounty.com	Binghamton	NY	13901	607-778-2451	778-2243
Broomfield City & County 1 DesCombes Dr *Web:* www.ci.broomfield.co.us	Broomfield	CO	80020	303-469-3301	438-6296
Broward County 115 S Andrews Ave Rm 409 *Web:* www.broward.org	Fort Lauderdale	FL	33301	954-357-7000	
Brown County 25 Market St Ste 1 *Web:* www.brown.sd.us	Aberdeen	SD	57401	605-626-7105	626-4010
Brown County 148 W Fourth St *Web:* supremecourt.nebraska.gov	Ainsworth	NE	69210	402-387-2864	382-3374
Brown County 800 Mt Orab Pike Ste 101 *Web:* www.county.brown.oh.us	Georgetown	OH	45121	937-378-3956	378-6324
Brown County 305 E Walnut Ste 120 *Web:* www.co.brown.wi.us	Green Bay	WI	54301	920-448-4016	448-4498
Brown County 601 Oregon St *Web:* ks-brown.manatron.com	Hiawatha	KS	66434	785-742-2581	742-7705
Brown County 200 Ct St Rm 4 *Web:* www.illinoiscourts.gov/circuitcourt/CircuitCourtJudges/CCC_County.asp#Brown	Mount Sterling	IL	62353	217-773-2713	773-3648
Brown County PO Box 85 *Web:* thebrowncountychamber.org	Nashville	IN	47448	812-988-0234	988-7334
Brown County 14 S State St PO Box 248 *Web:* www.co.brown.mn.us	New Ulm	MN	56073	507-233-6600	359-1430
Brule County 300 S Courtland St Ste 111 *Web:* brulecounty.org	Chamberlain	SD	57325	605-734-4580	
Brunswick County 250 Grey Water Rd *Web:* www.brunswickcountync.gov	Bolivia	NC	28422	910-253-2657	253-2022
Brunswick County 216 N Main St. *Web:* www.brunswickco.com	Lawrenceville	VA	23868	434-848-2215	848-4307
Bryan County PO Box 1789 *Web:* www.ok.gov	Durant	OK	74702	580-924-2202	
Bryan County 51 N Courthouse St. *Web:* www.bryancountyga.org	Pembroke	GA	31321	912-653-3819	653-4691
Buchanan County 1012 Walnut St PO Box 950 *Web:* www.buchanancountyonline.com	Grundy	VA	24614	276-935-6503	935-4479
Buchanan County 210 Fifth Ave NE *Web:* www.co.buchanan.ia.us	Independence	IA	50644	319-334-2196	332-0959
Buchanan County 411 Jules St. *Web:* www.co.buchanan.mo.us	Saint Joseph	MO	64501	816-271-1437	271-1535
Buckingham County 13360 W James Anderson Hwy *Web:* buckinghamcountyva.org	Buckingham	VA	23921	434-969-4242	969-1638
Bucks County 55 E Ct St *TF:* 888-942-8257 ■ *Web:* www.buckscounty.org	Doylestown	PA	18901	215-348-6000	
Buena Vista County 215 E Fifth St *Web:* www.co.buena-vista.ia.us	Storm Lake	IA	50588	712-749-2545	749-2703
Buffalo County 407 S Second St. *Web:* www.buffalocounty.com	Alma	WI	54610	608-685-6209	685-6213
Buffalo County PO Box 1270 *Web:* buffalocounty.ne.gov	Kearney	NE	68848	308-236-1226	233-3649
Bullitt County 300 S Buckman St *Web:* www.bullittcounty.org	Shepherdsville	KY	40165	502-543-2262	
Bulloch County 115 N Main St *Web:* www.bullochcounty.net	Statesboro	GA	30458	912-764-6245	764-8634

Name / Address	City	State	ZIP	Phone	Fax
Bullock County					
106 Conecuh Ave PO Box 87	Union Springs	AL	36089	334-738-5411	
Web: www.bullockcountyal.com					
Buncombe County 205 College St Ste 300	Asheville	NC	28801	828-250-4100	250-6077
Web: www.buncombecounty.org					
Bureau County 700 S Main St	Princeton	IL	61356	815-866-3606	
Web: www.bureaucounty-il.com					
Burke County PO Box 310	Bowbells	ND	58721	701-377-2718	
Web: www.burkecountynd.com					
Burke County PO Box 89	Waynesboro	GA	30830	706-554-2324	554-0350
Web: www.burkecounty-ga.gov					
Burleigh County 514 E Thayer Ave PO Box 1055	Bismarck	ND	58502	701-222-6690	222-6758
TF: 877-222-6682 ■ *Web:* www.ndcourts.gov					
Burleson County 100 W Buck St Ste 203	Caldwell	TX	77836	979-567-2329	567-2376
Web: www.co.burleson.tx.us					
Burlington County 49 Rancocas Rd	Mount Holly	NJ	08060	609-265-5122	265-0696
Web: www.co.burlington.nj.us					
Burnet County 220 S Pierce St	Burnet	TX	78611	512-756-5420	756-5410
Web: www.burnetcountytexas.org					
Burnett County 7410 County Rd K	Siren	WI	54872	715-349-2181	349-2830
Web: www.burnettcounty.com/gov					
Burt County 111 N 13th St Ste 12	Tekamah	NE	68061	402-374-2955	374-2956
Web: www.burtcounty.ne.gov					
Butler County 428 Sixth St	Allison	IA	50602	319-267-2487	267-2488
Web: www.butlercoiowa.org					
Butler County 290 S Main St PO Box 1208	Butler	PA	16003	724-284-5233	284-5244
Web: www.co.butler.pa.us					
Butler County 451 N Fifth St	David City	NE	68632	402-367-7430	367-3329
Web: www.co.butler.ne.us					
Butler County 205 W Central Ave	El Dorado	KS	67042	316-322-4300	322-4387
TF: 800-822-6104 ■ *Web:* www.bucoks.com					
Butler County 315 High St	Hamilton	OH	45011	513-887-3278	887-3966
TF: 800-582-4267 ■ *Web:* www.butlercountyohio.org					
Butler County PO Box 449	Morgantown	KY	42261	270-526-5676	526-2658
Web: www.revenue.ky.gov					
Butler County 100 N Main St Rm 202	Poplar Bluff	MO	63901	573-686-8050	686-8066
Web: butler.countyportal.net					
Butler County Revenue Commission					
700 Ct Sq	Greenville	AL	36037	334-382-3221	382-0385
Web: butlercountyal.com					
Butte County 248 W Grand	Arco	ID	83213	208-527-8288	
Butte County 25 County Ctr Dr	Oroville	CA	95965	530-538-7691	538-7975
Web: www.buttecounty.net					
Butte County Extension Office					
849 Fifth Ave	Belle Fourche	SD	57717	605-892-3371	892-9064
Web: butte.sdcounties.org					
Butte-Silver Bow County 155 W Granite St	Butte	MT	59703	406-497-6200	497-6328
Web: www.co.silverbow.mt.us					
Butts County 625 W 3rd St # 4 Ste 4	Jackson	GA	30233	770-775-8200	775-8211
Web: buttscountyga.com					
Cabarrus County 65 Church St S	Concord	NC	28025	704-920-2100	920-2820
Web: www.cabarruscounty.us					
Cabell County 750 Fifth Ave Ste 300	Huntington	WV	25701	304-526-8625	526-8632
Web: www.cabellcounty.org					
Caddo County PO Box 68	Anadarko	OK	73005	405-247-6609	
Web: www.ok.gov					
Caddo Parish 505 Travis St 8th Fl	Shreveport	LA	71101	318-226-6900	429-7630
Web: www.caddo.org					
Calaveras County 891 Mountain Ranch Rd	San Andreas	CA	95249	209-754-6370	754-6733
Web: calaverasgov.us					
Calcasieu Parish 1000 Ryan St	Lake Charles	LA	70601	337-437-3550	
Web: www.cppj.net					
Caldwell County 49 E Main St	Kingston	MO	64650	816-586-2571	
Web: caldwellcountymo.org					
Caldwell County 905 W Ave NW	Lenoir	NC	28645	828-757-1300	757-1295
Web: www.co.caldwell.nc.us					
Caldwell County 110 S Main St	Lockhart	TX	78644	512-398-1824	398-1816
Web: www.co.caldwell.tx.us					
Caldwell Parish PO Box 1737	Columbia	LA	71418	318-649-2681	649-5930
Web: lpgov.org					
Caledonia County 1126 Main St Ste 1	Saint Johnsbury	VT	05819	802-748-6600	748-1972
Calhoun County PO Box 230	Grantsville	WV	26147	304-354-6725	354-6725
Web: calhouncounty.wv.gov					
Sheriff's Office 178 S Murphree St	Pittsboro	MS	38951	662-412-3149	
Callahan County 100 W 4th St	Baird	TX	79504	325-854-1155	854-1227
Web: www.co.callahan.tx.us					
Callaway County 10 E Fifth St	Fulton	MO	65251	573-642-0730	642-7181
Web: callawaycountyclerk.com					
Calloway County 101 S Fifth St Ste 5	Murray	KY	42071	270-753-3923	759-9611
Web: calloway.clerkinfo.net					
Calumet County 206 Ct St	Chilton	WI	53014	920-849-2361	849-1469
Web: www.co.calumet.wi.us					
Calvert County 175 Main St	Prince Frederick	MD	20678	410-535-1600	
Web: www.co.cal.md.us					
Camas County 501 Soldier Rd	Fairfield	ID	83327	208-764-2242	764-2349
Web: www.idaho.gov/aboutidaho/county/camas.html					
Cambria County 200 S Ctr St	Ebensburg	PA	15931	814-472-1540	472-0761
Web: www.cambriacountypa.gov					
Camden County 117 N NC 343 PO Box 190	Camden	NC	27921	252-338-1919	333-1603
Web: camdencountync.gov					
Camden County 520 Market St Rm 102	Camden	NJ	08102	856-225-5300	
TF: 866-226-3362 ■ *Web:* www.camdencounty.com					
Camden County 1 Court Circle, Ste 3	Camdenton	MO	65020	573-346-4440	
Web: www.camdenmo.org					
Camden County PO Box 99	Woodbine	GA	31569	912-576-7395	576-5647
Web: www.co.camden.ga.us					
Cameron County 964 E Harrison St	Brownsville	TX	78520	956-544-0815	544-0813
Web: www.co.cameron.tx.us					
Cameron County 20 E Fifth St	Emporium	PA	15834	814-486-2315	
Web: www.pacourts.us					
Cameron Parish 148 Smith Cir PO Box 1280	Cameron	LA	70631	337-775-5718	775-5567
Web: www.parishofcameron.net					

Name / Address	City	State	ZIP	Phone	Fax
Camp County 126 Church St	Pittsburg	TX	75686	903-856-2731	856-2309
Web: www.co.camp.tx.us					
Campbell County 1635 Reata Dr	Gillette	WY	82718	307-682-0552	682-8418
Web: www.ccgov.net					
Campbell County 570 Main St Ste A21	Jacksboro	TN	37757	423-562-4985	566-3852
Web: campbellcountytn.gov					
Campbell County 1098 Monmouth St Ste 204	Newport	KY	41071	859-292-3845	
Web: www.campbellcountyky.org					
Campbell County 732 Village Hwy	Rustburg	VA	24588	434-332-9517	332-9518
Web: www.co.campbell.va.us					
Canadian County 201 N Choctaw St	El Reno	OK	73036	405-262-1070	422-2411
Web: www.canadiancounty.org					
Candler County 705 N Lewis St	Metter	GA	30439	912-685-2835	685-4823
Candler County 500 Ave K PO Box 1527	Moore Haven	FL	33471	863-946-6000	946-2860
Web: www.myglades.com					
Cannon County 200 W Main St	Woodbury	TN	37190	615-563-4278	
Web: www.cannontn.com					
Canyon County 1115 Albany St	Caldwell	ID	83605	208-454-7300	454-7525
Web: www.canyoncounty.org					
Cape Girardeau County 1 Barton Sq Ste 301	Jackson	MO	63755	573-243-3547	204-2418
Web: www.capecounty.us					
Cape May County					
7 N Main St PO Box 5000	Cape May Court House	NJ	08210	609-465-1010	465-8625
Web: capemaycountynj.gov					
Carbon County 2 Hazard Sq PO Box 129	Jim Thorpe	PA	18229	570-325-3611	325-3622
Web: www.carboncounty.com					
Carbon County 120 E Main St	Price	UT	84501	435-636-3200	
Web: carbon.utah.gov					
Carbon County PO Box 1017	Rawlins	WY	82301	800-228-3547	
TF: 800-228-3547 ■ *Web:* www.wyomingcarboncounty.com					
Carbon County 17 W 11th St PO Box 887	Red Lodge	MT	59068	406-446-1220	446-2640
Web: www.co.carbon.mt.us					
Caribou County 159 S Main	Soda Springs	ID	83276	208-547-4324	547-4759
TF: 800-972-7660 ■ *Web:* www.cariboucounty.us					
Carlisle County PO Box 176	Bardwell	KY	42023	270-628-3233	628-0191
Web: carlislecountyclerk.com/printable-forms					
Carlton County PO Box 130	Carlton	MN	55718	218-384-9166	384-9182
Web: www.co.carlton.mn.us					
Caroline County 117 Ennis St	Bowling Green	VA	22427	804-633-5380	633-4970
Web: www.co.caroline.va.us					
Caroline County 109 Market St	Denton	MD	21629	410-479-0660	479-4060
Web: www.carolinemd.org					
Carroll County 114 E Sixth St	Carroll	IA	51401	712-792-4923	
Web: www.co.carroll.ia.us					
Carroll County					
423 College St Rm 408 PO Box 338	Carrollton	GA	30112	770-830-5800	830-5992
Web: www.carrollcountyga.com					
Carroll County 440 Main St Courthouse	Carrollton	KY	41008	502-732-7005	
Web: www.carrollcountyky.com					
Carroll County 8 S Main Ste 6	Carrollton	MO	64633	660-542-0615	542-1444
Carroll County					
105 B E Washington St PO Box 59	Carrollton	MS	38917	662-237-4413	237-6959
Web: carrollcountyms.org					
Carroll County 119 S Lisbon St Ste 201	Carrollton	OH	44615	330-627-4869	627-6656
Web: www.carrollcountyohio.net					
Carroll County 101 W Main St	Delphi	IN	46923	765-564-4485	
Web: www.carrollnet.org					
Carroll County 605-1 Pine St	Hillsville	VA	24343	276-730-3070	730-3071
Web: carrollcountyva.org					
Carroll County 625 High St Ste 103	Huntingdon	TN	38344	731-986-1936	986-1935
Web: www.carrollcounty-tn-chamber.com					
Carroll County 8215 Black Oak Rd	Mount Carroll	IL	61053	815-244-2035	
TF: 800-485-0145 ■ *Web:* www.gocarrollcounty.com					
Carroll County 225 N Ctr St	Westminster	MD	21157	410-386-2011	840-8932
Web: www.ccgovernment.carr.org					
Carroll County Sheriff's Office					
95 Water Village Rd PO Box 190	Ossipee	NH	03864	603-539-2284	
Web: carrollcountynh.net					
Carroll CountyClerk 210 W Church St	Berryville	AR	72616	870-423-2022	
Carson City (Independent City)					
201 N Carson St	Carson City	NV	89701	775-887-2100	887-2286
Web: carson.org					
Carson County PO Box 487	Panhandle	TX	79068	806-537-3873	537-3623
Web: www.co.carson.tx.us					
Carter County 101 1St Ave SW	Ardmore	OK	73401	580-223-8162	
TF: 800-231-8668 ■ *Web:* cartercountyok.us					
Carter County 214 Pk St PO Box 315	Ekalaka	MT	59324	406-775-8749	775-8750
Web: www.cartercountymt.info					
Carter County 500 Veterans Pkwy	Elizabethton	TN	37643	423-547-3859	
Web: tourcartercounty.com					
Carter County 300 W Main St Rm 232	Grayson	KY	41143	606-474-5188	
Web: www.cartercountyclerksoffice.com					
Carter County 105 Main St	Van Buren	MO	63965	573-323-4513	
Carteret County Courthouse Sq	Beaufort	NC	28516	252-728-8450	728-2092
Web: carteretcountync.gov					
Carver County 606 E Fourth St	Chaska	MN	55318	952-361-1500	361-1491
Web: www.co.carver.mn.us					
Cascade County 325 Second Ave N # 100	Great Falls	MT	59401	406-454-6800	454-6703
Web: www.co.cascade.mt.us					
Cass County 5 W Seventh St	Atlantic	IA	50022	712-243-5503	
Web: www.atlanticiowa.com/county					
Cass County PO Box 132	Cassopolis	MI	49031	269-445-3701	445-5018
Web: casscountymi.org					
Cass County 211 Ninth St S	Fargo	ND	58103	701-241-5600	241-5728
Web: www.casscountynd.gov					
Cass County PO Box 449	Linden	TX	75563	903-756-5071	756-8057
Web: www.co.cass.tx.us					
Cass County 200 Ct Pk	Logansport	IN	46947	574-753-7740	722-1556
Web: co.cass.in.us					
Cass County 346 Main St	Plattsmouth	NE	68048	402-296-9300	296-9332
Web: www.cassne.org					

Phone Fax

Cass County 100 E Springfield St PO Box 203 . . . . Virginia IL 62691 217-452-7225 452-7219
Web: www.illinoiscourts.gov/circuitcourt/CircuitCourtJudges/CCC_County.asp#Cass

Cassia County 1459 Overland Ave. . . . . Burley ID 83318 208-878-7302 878-9109
Web: www.cassiacounty.org

Castro County 100 E Bedford St . . . . Dimmitt TX 79027 806-647-3338 647-5438
Web: www.co.castro.tx.us

Catahoula Parish
301 Bushley St PO Box 654 . . . . Harrisonburg LA 71340 318-744-5497 744-5488
Web: www.laclerksofcourt.org

Catawba County PO Box 389 . . . . Newton NC 28658 828-465-8201 465-8392
Web: www.co.catawba.nc.us

Catoosa County 875 Lafayette St. Ringgold GA 30736 706-965-2500
Web: www.catoosa.com

Cattaraugus County 303 Ct St . . . . Little Valley NY 14755 716-938-9111
Web: www.cattco.org

Cavalier County 901 Third St Ste 11. . . . . Langdon ND 58249 701-256-3475 256-3536
Web: www.ccjda.org

Cayuga County 160 Genesee St. . . . . Auburn NY 13021 315-253-1271
Web: www.cayugacounty.us

Cecil County 129 E Main St Rm 108 . . . . Elkton MD 21921 410-996-5375
Web: www.ccgov.org

Cedar County 101 S Broadway . . . . Hartington NE 68739 402-254-7411 254-7410
Web: www.co.cedar.ne.us

Cedar County 400 Cedar St . . . . Tipton IA 52772 563-886-2101 886-3594
Web: www.cedarcounty.org

Centre County
420 Holmes St Willowbank Office Bldg . . . . Bellefonte PA 16823 814-355-6700 355-6980
Web: centrecountypa.gov

Cerro Gordo County 220 N Washington Ave. . . . . Mason City IA 50401 641-421-3065 421-3072
Web: co.cerro-gordo.ia.us

Chaffee County 104 Crestone Ave . . . . Salida CO 81201 719-539-4004 539-8588
Web: www.chaffeecounty.org

Chambers County 404 Washington Ave . . . . Anahuac TX 77514 409-267-8309 267-8315
Web: www.co.chambers.tx.us

Champaign County 1776 E Washington St. . . . . Urbana IL 61802 217-384-3776 384-3896
Web: www.co.champaign.il.us

Champaign County 1512 S US Hwy 68 Ste A100. . . . . Urbana OH 43078 937-484-1611 484-1609
Web: www.co.champaign.oh.us

Chariton County 306 S Cherry St . . . . Keytesville MO 65261 660-288-3273
Web: www.rootsweb.ancestry.com

Charles County 200 Baltimore St . . . . La Plata MD 20646 301-645-0600 645-0560
Web: www.charlescountymd.gov

Charles Mix County PO Box 490 . . . . Lake Andes SD 57356 605-487-7131 487-7221
Web: charlesmix.sdcounties.org

Charleston County 4045 Bridge View. . . . . Charleston SC 29405 843-958-4030 958-4035
Web: www.charlestoncounty.org

Charlevoix County 203 Antrim St. . . . . Charlevoix MI 49720 231-547-7200 547-7217
TF: 800-548-9157 ■ *Web:* www.charlevoixcounty.org

Charlotte County
250 LeGrande Ave Ste A
PO Box 608 . . . . Charlotte Court House VA 23923 434-542-5117 542-5248
Web: www.charlotteva.com

Charlotte County 18500 Murdoch Cir . . . . Port Charlotte FL 33948 941-743-1300
Web: www.charlottecountyfl.gov

Charlottesville (Independent City)
605 E Main St. . . . . Charlottesville VA 22902 434-970-3101 970-3890
Web: www.charlottesville.org

Charlton County 68 Kingsland Ste B. . . . . Folkston GA 31537 912-496-2549
Web: georgia.gov/cities-counties/charlton-county

Chase County 300 Pearl St . . . . Cottonwood Falls KS 66845 620-273-6423
Web: chasecountychamber.org/county-government

Chase County PO Box 1299. . . . . Imperial NE 69033 308-882-7510 882-7552
Web: www.co.chase.ne.us

Chatham County 124 Bull St. . . . . Savannah GA 31401 912-652-7869 652-7874
Web: www.chathamcounty.org

Chattooga County 10102 Commerce St. . . . . Summerville GA 30747 706-857-0700 857-0742
Web: www.chattoogacountyga.org

Chautauqua County 3 N Erie St . . . . Mayville NY 14757 716-753-4211 753-4756
Web: www.co.chautauqua.ny.us

Chautauqua County 215 N Chautauqua St. . . . . Sedan KS 67361 620-725-5800 725-5801
Web: chautauquacountyks.com

Cheatham County 100 Public Sq . . . . Ashland City TN 37015 615-792-4316
Web: www.cheathamcountytn.gov

Cheboygan County 870 S Main St . . . . Cheboygan MI 49721 231-627-8808
Web: www.cheboygancounty.net

Chelan County 350 Orondo Ave . . . . Wenatchee WA 98801 509-667-6380 667-6611
Web: www.co.chelan.wa.us

Chemung County 210 Lake St PO Box 588. . . . . Elmira NY 14902 607-737-2920
Web: www.chemungcounty.com

Chenango County 5 Ct St. . . . . Norwich NY 13815 607-337-1700 337-1455
Web: www.co.chenango.ny.us

Cherokee County 90 N St Ste 310 . . . . Canton GA 30114 678-493-6511 493-6013
Web: www.cherokeega.com

Cherokee County 260 Cedar Bluff Rd Ste 103 . . . . Centre AL 35960 256-927-3668
Web: www.cherokee-chamber.org

Cherokee County 520 W Main St . . . . Cherokee IA 51012 712-225-6744 225-6749
Web: www.cherokeecountyiowa.com

Cherokee County 110 W Maple . . . . Columbus KS 66725 620-429-2042
Web: cherokeecountyks.gov

Cherokee County 210 N Limestone St . . . . Gaffney SC 29340 864-487-2560

Cherokee County 75 Peachtree St. . . . . Murphy NC 28906 828-837-5527 837-9684
Web: cherokeecounty-nc.gov

Cherokee County 165 E Sixth St Ste 203 Ste 203. . . . . Rusk TX 75785 903-683-6540 683-5953
TF: 800-541-2524 ■ *Web:* www.co.cherokee.tx.us

Cherokee County 213 W Delaware St. . . . . Tahlequah OK 74464 918-456-3171
Web: oklahomacounty.org

Cherry County PO Box 120 . . . . Valentine NE 69201 402-376-2771 376-3095
Web: www.co.cherry.ne.us

Chesapeake City Hall 306 Cedar Rd . . . . Chesapeake VA 23322 757-382-6151 382-6678
Web: cityofchesapeake.net

Cheshire County 12 Ct St. . . . . Keene NH 03431 603-352-6902
Web: www.co.cheshire.nh.us

Phone Fax

Chester County 140 Main St PO Box 580. . . . . Chester SC 29706 803-385-2605
Web: www.chestercounty.org

Chester County
313 W Market St Ste 6202 PO Box 2748 . . . . West Chester PA 19380 610-344-6100 344-5995
TF: 800-692-1100 ■ *Web:* www.chesco.org

Chesterfield County 200 W Main St Ste K. . . . . Chesterfield SC 29709 843-792-2536 623-6944
Web: www.chesterfield.k12.sc.us

Chesterfield County PO Box 70. . . . . Chesterfield VA 23832 804-748-1201 751-4993
Web: www.chesterfield.gov

Cheyenne County PO Box 567 . . . . Cheyenne Wells CO 80810 719-767-5685 767-8730
Web: www.co.cheyenne.co.us

Cheyenne County 212 E Washington . . . . Saint Francis KS 67756 785-332-8850
Web: www.cheyennecounty.org

Cheyenne County 1000 Tenth Ave PO Box 217 . . . . Sidney NE 69162 308-254-2141 254-5049*
**Fax:* Hum Res ■ *Web:* www.co.cheyenne.ne.us

Chickasaw County 1 Pinson Sq. . . . . Houston MS 38851 662-456-2513
Web: chickasaw.msghn.org

Chickasaw Voting Information
8 E Prospect St . . . . New Hampton IA 50659 641-394-2100 394-5541
Web: www.chickasawcoia.org

Chicot County
108 Main St County Courthouse . . . . Lake Village AR 71653 870-265-8040 265-8018
Web: chicotcounty.arkansas.gov

Childress County 1710 Ave F NW PO Box 1. . . . . Childress TX 79201 940-937-6062 937-3386
Web: www.childresscad.org

Chilton County PO Box 1948. . . . . Clanton AL 35046 205-755-1551 280-7204
Web: www.chiltoncounty.org

Chippewa County 711 N Bridge St . . . . Chippewa Falls WI 54729 715-726-7980 726-7987
Web: www.co.chippewa.wi.us

Chippewa County 629 N 11th St. . . . . Montevideo MN 56265 320-269-7447 269-7412*
**Fax:* Acctg ■ *Web:* www.co.chippewa.mn.us

Chippewa County 319 Ct St . . . . Sault Sainte Marie MI 49783 715-726-4597 635-6385*
**Fax Area Code:* 906 ■ *Web:* www.co.chippewa.wi.us

Chisago County 313 N Main St. . . . . Center City MN 55012 651-257-1300 213-8876
TF: 888-234-1246 ■ *Web:* www.co.chisago.mn.us

Chittenden County 175 Main St. . . . . Burlington VT 05401 802-863-3467
Web: www.ccrpcvt.org

Choctaw County 55 E Quinn St PO Box 737. . . . . Ackerman MS 39735 662-285-3778 285-2440
Web: choctawcountyms.com

Choctaw County 117 S Mulberry St Ste 9. . . . . Butler AL 36904 205-459-2155
Web: Www.alabama.gov

Chouteau County 1308 Franklin St. . . . . Fort Benton MT 59442 406-622-5151 622-3012
Web: www.co.chouteau.mt.us

Chowan County 113 E King St. . . . . Edenton NC 27932 252-482-8431
Web: www.chowancounty-nc.gov

Christian County 511 S Main St. . . . . Hopkinsville KY 42240 270-887-4105
Web: www.christiancounty.org

Christian County 100 W Church St Rm 206. . . . . Ozark MO 65721 417-581-6360 581-8331
Web: www.christiancountymo.gov

Christian County 101 S Main St PO Box 647 . . . . Taylorville IL 62568 217-824-4969 824-5105
Web: christiancountyil.com

Churchill County 155 N Taylor St Ste 110 . . . . Fallon NV 89406 775-423-6028
Web: nv-churchillcounty.civicplus.com

Cibola County 515 W High Ave . . . . Grants NM 87020 505-285-2510
Web: www.co.cibola.nm.us

Cimarron County PO Box 145. . . . . Boise City OK 73933 580-544-2251
Web: www.ok.gov/tax

Citrus County 110 N Apopka Ave. Inverness FL 34450 352-341-6400 341-6491
Web: www.clerk.citrus.fl.us

City of Buena Vista 2039 Sycamore Ave . . . . Buena Vista VA 24416 540-261-6121
Web: www.bvcity.org

City of Clinton Sheriff Department
184 Detention Dr PO Box 451. . . . . Clinton AR 72031 501-745-2112
Web: www.vbcso.com

Clackamas County 2051 Kaen Rd . . . . Oregon City OR 97045 503-655-8551 650-5688
Web: www.clackamas.us

Claiborne County 404 Market St. . . . . Port Gibson MS 39150 601-437-4232 437-4409
Web: www.claiborne.k12.ms.us

Claiborne County 1740 Main St . . . . Tazewell TN 37879 423-626-9270
Web: www.claibornepartnership.com

Claiborne Parish 512 E Main St . . . . Homer LA 71040 318-927-9601
Web: www.claiborneone.org

Clallam County 223 E Fourth St Ste 2. . . . . Port Angeles WA 98362 360-417-2318 417-2493
Web: www.clallam.net

Clare County 225 W Main PO Box 438 . . . . Harrison MI 48625 989-539-2510 539-6616
Web: www.clareco.net

Clarendon County 19 N Brooks St . . . . Manning SC 29102 803-435-4405
Web: www.clarendoncounty.com

Clarion County 421 Main St Courthouse. . . . . Clarion PA 16214 814-226-4000 227-2501
Web: www.co.clarion.pa.us

Clark County 401 Clay St. . . . . Arkadelphia AR 71923 870-246-4491 246-6505
Web: www.clarkcountyarkansas.com

Clark County 913 Highland St. . . . . Ashland KS 67831 620-635-2813 635-2051
Web: www.clarkcountyks.com

Clark County 320 W Main St. . . . . Grangeville ID 83530 208-983-2751 983-1428
Web: www.idaho.gov

Clark County 501 E Ct Ave. . . . . Jeffersonville IN 47130 812-285-6275 285-6366
Web: www.co.clark.in.us

Clark County 252 N Morgan St . . . . Kahoka MO 63445 660-727-1072
Web: www.mogenclark.com

Clark County 500 S Grand Central Pkwy . . . . Las Vegas NV 89155 702-455-0000
Web: www.clarkcountynv.gov

Clark County
501 Archer Ave County Courthouse . . . . Marshall IL 62441 217-826-8311
Web: www.clarkcountyil.org

Clark County 517 Ct St . . . . Neillsville WI 54456 715-743-5148 743-5154
Web: www.co.clark.wi.us

Clark County 101 N Limestone St Ste 112. . . . . Springfield OH 45502 937-521-1680 328-2436
Web: www.clarkcountyohio.gov

Clark County PO Box 5000 . . . . Vancouver WA 98666 360-397-2000 397-6099
Web: www.co.clark.wa.us

Clark County 34 S Main St . . . . Winchester KY 40391 859-745-0200 737-5678
Web: www.clarkcoky.com

Name / Address	City	State	ZIP	Phone	Fax
Clarke County 101 N Church Ct Ste B	Berryville	VA	22611	540-955-5100	
Web: www.clarkecounty.gov					
Clarke County PO Box 548	Grove Hill	AL	36451	251-275-3507	275-8517
Web: clarkecountyal.com					
Clarke County 100 S Main	Osceola	IA	50213	641-342-6096	
Web: www.clarkecountyia.org					
Clarke County 100 Church St PO Box 689	Quitman	MS	39355	601-776-5701	
TF: 877-462-3222 ■ *Web:* www.visitclarkecounty.com					
Clatsop County 820 Exchange St 2nd Fl	Astoria	OR	97103	503-325-8511	325-9307
Web: www.co.clatsop.or.us					
Clay County 25 Ct Sq	Ashland	AL	36251	256-354-2198	354-4778
Web: claycountyprobate.com					
Clay County 609 E National Ave Rm 213	Brazil	IN	47834	812-448-9036	
Clay County 424 Brown St	Celina	TN	38551	931-243-3338	243-6809
Web: www.dalehollowlake.org					
Clay County 712 Fifth St	Clay Center	KS	67432	785-632-2552	632-5856
Web: claycountykansas.org					
Clay County 111 W Fairfield St PO Box 67	Clay Center	NE	68933	402-762-3463	762-3506
Web: www.claycounty.ne.gov					
Clay County 155 Wilson St	Fort Gaines	GA	39851	229-768-3155	768-3672
Clay County 477 Houston St	Green Cove Springs	FL	32043	904-284-6376	284-9780
Web: www.claycountygov.com					
Clay County 33 Main St	Hayesville	NC	28904	828-389-0089	389-9749
Web: www.clayconc.com					
Clay County PO Box 548	Henrietta	TX	76365	940-538-4631	538-5597
Web: www.co.clay.tx.us					
Clay County 1 Courthouse Sq	Liberty	MO	64068	816-407-3600	
Web: claycoelections.com					
Clay County PO Box 160	Louisville	IL	62858	618-665-3626	665-3607
Web: www.claycountyillinois.org					
Clay County 807 11th St N	Moorhead	MN	56560	218-299-5012	299-5195
Web: claycountymn.gov					
Clay County 215 W Fourth St	Spencer	IA	51301	712-262-9438	
Web: www.co.clay.ia.us					
Clay County 211 W Main St Ste 200	Vermillion	SD	57069	605-677-7120	677-7104
Web: www.claycountysd.org					
Clay County PO Box 815	West Point	MS	39773	662-494-3124	492-4059
Web: www.claycountyms.com					
Clayton County 111 High St NE	Elkader	IA	52043	563-245-2204	245-1175
Web: www.claytoncountyiowa.net					
Clayton County 112 Smith St	Jonesboro	GA	30236	770-477-3211	477-3217
Web: www.co.clayton.ga.us					
Clear Creek County PO Box 2000	Georgetown	CO	80444	303-679-2312	679-2440
Web: www.co.clear-creek.co.us					
Clearfield County 230 E Market St	Clearfield	PA	16830	814-765-2641	765-2640
Web: www.clearfieldco.org					
Clearwater County 213 Main Ave N	Bagley	MN	56621	218-694-6520	694-6244*
**Fax:* Acctg ■ *Web:* www.co.clearwater.mn.us					
Clearwater County 150 Michigan Ave	Orofino	ID	83544	208-476-3615	
Web: www.clearwatercounty.org					
Cleburne County 300 W Main St	Heber Springs	AR	72543	501-362-8402	362-4605
Web: www.cleburnecountyar.com					
Cleburne County 120 Vickery St Rm 202	Heflin	AL	36264	256-463-2651	
Web: cleburnecounty.us					
Clermont County 101 E Main St Rm 322	Batavia	OH	45103	513-732-7300	732-7826
Web: www.clermontcountyohio.gov					
Cleveland County 2550 W Franklin Rd	Norman	OK	73069	405-701-8888	
Web: www.clevelandcountyok.com					
Cleveland County PO Box 368	Rison	AR	71665	870-325-6214	
Web: www.argenweb.net/cleveland					
Cleveland County 311 E Marion St	Shelby	NC	28150	704-484-4800	484-4930
Web: www.clevelandcounty.com					
Clinch County 46 S College St	Homerville	GA	31634	912-487-5321	487-5068
Web: www.clinchcounty.com					
Clinton County 46 S S St 2nd Fl Courthouse	Wilmington	OH	45177	937-382-2316	383-3455
Web: www.co.clinton.oh.us					
Fiscal Court 100 S Cross St	Albany	KY	42602	606-387-5234	387-7651
Web: clintoncounty.ky.gov					
Cloud County 811 Washington St	Concordia	KS	66901	785-243-8110	
Web: www.cloudcountyks.org					
Coahoma County PO Box 98	Clarksdale	MS	38614	662-624-3000	624-3040
Web: www.coahomacounty.net					
Coal County 4 N Main St	Coalgate	OK	74538	580-927-2103	927-4003
Cobb County 100 Cherokee St Ste 300	Marietta	GA	30090	770-528-1000	528-2606
Web: www.cobbcounty.org					
Cochise County 1415 W Melody Ln Bldg G	Bisbee	AZ	85603	520-432-9200	432-5016
Web: cochise.az.gov					
Cochran County 100 N Main St	Morton	TX	79346	806-266-5508	266-9027
Web: www.co.cochran.tx.us					
Cocke County Tourism 433 B Prospect Ave	Newport	TN	37821	423-625-9675	
Web: www.cockecounty.com					
Coconino County 219 E Cherry Ave	Flagstaff	AZ	86001	928-774-5011	
TF: 800-559-9289 ■ *Web:* www.coconino.az.gov					
Codington County 14 First Ave SE	Watertown	SD	57201	605-882-6288	
Web: www.codington.org					
Coffee County 101 S Peterson Ave	Douglas	GA	31533	912-384-4799	384-0291
Web: www.coffeecountygov.com					
Coffee County 2 County Complex	New Brockton	AL	36351	334-894-5556	
Web: www.coffeecounty.us					
Coffee County 1329 McArthur Dr	Manchester	TN	37355	931-723-5106	723-8248
Web: www.coffeecountytn.org					
Coffey County 110 S Sixth St	Burlington	KS	66839	620-364-2191	364-8975
Web: www.coffeycountyks.org					
Coke County PO Box 150	Robert Lee	TX	76945	325-453-2631	453-2650
Web: co.coke.tx.us					
Colbert County 201 N Main St	Tuscumbia	AL	35674	256-386-8500	386-8510
Web: www.colbertcounty.org					
Cole County 301 E High St Ste 100	Jefferson City	MO	65101	573-634-9100	634-8031
Web: www.colecounty.org					
Coleman County 100 W Live Oak	Coleman	TX	76834	325-625-2889	
Web: www.co.coleman.tx.us					
Coles County 651 Jackson Ave Rm 122	Charleston	IL	61920	217-348-0501	348-7337
Web: www.co.coles.il.us					
Colfax County 230 N Third St PO Box 1498	Raton	NM	87740	575-445-9661	445-2902
Web: www.co.colfax.nm.us					
Colfax County 411 E 11th St	Schuyler	NE	68661	402-352-8504	
Web: www.colfaxne.com					
Colleton County 31 Klein St	Walterboro	SC	29488	843-549-1725	549-7215
Web: www.colletoncounty.org					
Collin County 200 S McDonald St Ste 120	McKinney	TX	75069	972-548-4100	547-5731
TF: 800-336-5996 ■ *Web:* www.collincountytx.gov/pages/default.aspx					
Collingsworth County 800 W Ave 2nd Fl Rm 1	Wellington	TX	79095	806-447-5408	447-5418
Web: co.collingsworth.tx.us					
Colonial Heights (Independent City) 201 James Ave PO Box 3401	Colonial Heights	VA	23834	804-520-9265	520-9207
Web: www.colonialheightsva.gov					
Colorado County 318 Springs St Ste 103	Columbus	TX	78934	979-732-2155	732-8852
Web: www.co.colorado.tx.us					
Colquitt County PO Box 517	Moultrie	GA	31776	229-616-7056	616-7498
Web: www.ccboc.com					
Columbia County 35 W Main St	Bloomsburg	PA	17815	570-389-5600	784-0257
Web: www.columbiapa.org					
Columbia County 341 E Main St	Dayton	WA	99328	509-382-4542	382-2490
Web: www.columbiaco.com					
Columbia County PO Box 498	Evans	GA	30809	706-868-3379	868-3348
Web: www.columbiacountyga.gov					
Columbia County 560 Warren St	Hudson	NY	12534	518-828-3339	
Web: columbiacountyny.com					
Columbia County 135 NE Hernando Ave # 203	Lake City	FL	32055	386-755-4100	
Web: www.columbiacountyfla.com					
Columbia County PO Box 177	Portage	WI	53901	608-742-9654	742-9602
Web: www.co.columbia.wi.us					
Columbia County 230 Strand St	Saint Helens	OR	97051	503-397-3796	397-7266
Web: www.co.columbia.or.us					
Columbiana County 105 S Market St	Lisbon	OH	44432	330-424-7777	
Web: www.columbianacounty.org					
Columbus County PO Box 1587	Whiteville	NC	28472	910-641-3000	
Web: www.columbusco.org					
Columbus-Muscogee County PO Box 1340	Columbus	GA	31902	706-653-4000	
Web: www.columbusga.com					
Colusa County 546 Jay St	Colusa	CA	95932	530-458-0500	458-0512
Web: countyofcolusa.org					
Comal County 199 Main Plaza	New Braunfels	TX	78130	830-221-1100	620-5506
TF: 877-724-9475 ■ *Web:* www.co.comal.tx.us					
Comanche County 304 S Austin St	Comanche	TX	76442	325-356-3233	
Comanche County 315 SW Fifth St Ste 304	Lawton	OK	73501	580-355-5214	
Web: www.comanchecounty.us					
Concho County PO Box 98	Paint Rock	TX	76866	325-732-4322	732-2040
Web: www.co.concho.tx.us					
Concordia Parish PO Box 790	Vidalia	LA	71373	318-336-4204	336-8777
Web: www.concordiaclerk.org					
Conecuh County PO Box 347	Evergreen	AL	36401	251-578-2095	
Web: www.alabama.gov					
Conejos County 6683 County Rd 13	Conejos	CO	81129	719-376-2014	
Web: www.conejoscounty.org					
Contra Costa County 651 Pine St 3rd Fl	Martinez	CA	94553	925-335-1080	335-1098
Web: www.co.contra-costa.ca.us					
Converse County 107 N Fifth St Ste 114	Douglas	WY	82633	307-358-2244	770-3590*
**Fax Area Code:* 866 ■ *Web:* www.conversecounty.org					
Conway County 117 S Moose St	Morrilton	AR	72110	501-354-9621	
Web: prsearch.com					
Cook County 69 W Washington Ste 500	Chicago	IL	60602	312-603-5656	603-0902
Web: www.co.cook.il.us					
Cook County 411 W Second St	Grand Marais	MN	55604	218-387-3647	387-3007
Web: www.co.cook.mn.us					
Cooke County 101S Dixon	Gainesville	TX	76240	940-668-5420	668-5522
Web: www.co.cooke.tx.us					
Cooper County 200 Main St	Boonville	MO	65233	660-882-2114	882-5645
Web: coopercountymo.org					
Coos County 250 N Baxter St	Coquille	OR	97423	541-396-3121	396-4861
Web: www.co.coos.or.us					
Coos County PO Box 10	West Stewartstown	NH	03597	603-246-3321	246-8117
Web: www.cooscountynh.us					
Coosa County PO Box 10	Rockford	AL	35136	256-377-1350	377-2524
Web: www.coosacountyal.com					
Copiah County 122 S Lowe St PO Box 507	Hazlehurst	MS	39083	601-894-1858	
Web: www.copiahcounty.org					
Corson County 242 Second Ave E PO Box 317	McIntosh	SD	57641	605-273-4481	273-4481
Web: corson.sdcounties.org					
Cortland County 46 Greenbush St Ste 101	Cortland	NY	13045	607-753-5021	753-5378
Web: www.cortland-co.org					
Coryell County 620 E Main St PO Box 237	Gatesville	TX	76528	254-865-5911	865-8631
Web: www.co.coryell.tx.us					
Coshocton County 401 1/2 Main St	Coshocton	OH	43812	740-622-1753	622-4917
Web: coshoctoncounty.net					
Costilla County 233 Main St Ste C PO Box 99	San Luis	CO	81152	719-672-3681	672-3856
Web: www.colorado.gov					
Cottle County PO Box 717	Paducah	TX	79248	806-492-3823	492-2625
Web: www.co.cottle.tx.us					
Cotton County 301 N Broadway	Walters	OK	73572	580-875-3029	
Cottonwood County 900 Third Ave	Windom	MN	56101	507-831-1905	831-4553
Web: www.co.cottonwood.mn.us					
County & Circuit Clerk 206 W 3rd St	Fordyce	AR	71742	870-352-2307	
County of Greene 93 E High St	Waynesburg	PA	15370	724-852-5210	852-5327
TF: 888-852-5399 ■ *Web:* www.co.greene.pa.us					
Covington County 260 Hillcrest Dr PO Box 188	Andalusia	AL	36420	334-428-2540	428-2606
Web: www.covcounty.com					
Covington County PO Box 1679	Collins	MS	39428	601-765-4242	
Web: www.msgw.org					
Covington (Independent City) 333 W Locust St	Covington	VA	24426	540-965-6300	965-6303
Web: www.covington.va.us					

Phone Fax

Coweta County 22 E Broad St ... Newnan GA 30263 770-254-2601 254-2606
Web: www.coweta.ga.us

Cowley County 311 E Ninth Ave ... Winfield KS 67156 620-221-5400 221-5498
Web: www.cowleycounty.org

Cowlitz County 312 SW First Ave ... Kelso WA 98626 360-577-3016
Web: www.co.cowlitz.wa.us

Craig County PO Box 308 ... New Castle VA 24127 540-864-5010 864-5590
Web: www.craigcountyva.gov

Craig County 301 W Canadian Ave Ste 2 ... Vinita OK 74301 918-256-2507
Web: www.okgenweb.org/~okcraig

Craighead County 511 S Main St ... Jonesboro AR 72401 870-933-4520 933-4514
Web: www.craigheadcounty.org

Crane County 201 W Sixth St ... Crane TX 79731 432-558-3581 558-1185
Web: www.co.crane.tx.us

Craven County 406 Craven St ... New Bern NC 28560 252-636-6600 637-0526
Web: www.cravencountync.gov

Crawford County 112 E Mansfield St ... Bucyrus OH 44820 419-562-5876 562-3491
Web: www.crawford-co.org

Crawford County 1202 Broadway Ste 5 ... Denison IA 51442 712-263-3045 263-8382
Web: www.crawfordcounty.org

Crawford County
715 Judicial Plaza Dr PO Box 375 ... English IN 47118 812-338-2565 338-2507
Web: www.in.gov/judiciary/2958.htm

Crawford County 111 E Forest Ave ... Girard KS 66743 620-724-6115 724-6007
Web: www.crawfordcountykansas.org

Crawford County 200 W Michigan Ave ... Grayling MI 49738 989-344-3206 344-3223
Web: www.crawfordco.org

Crawford County 1011 Hwy 341 N PO Box 1059 ... Roberta GA 31078 478-836-3782 836-5818
Web: crawfordcountyga.org

Crawford County 903 Diamond Pk ... Meadville PA 16335 814-333-7400 337-0457
Web: crawfordcountyfairpa.com

Crawford County 225 N Beaumont Rd ... Prairie du Chien WI 53821 608-326-0200
TF: 877-794-2372 ■ *Web:* www.crawfordcountywi.org

Crawford County 100 Douglas St ... Robinson IL 62454 618-546-1212 546-0140
Web: www.crawfordcountycentral.com

Crawford County 302 Main St PO Box AS ... Steelville MO 65565 573-775-2376 775-3066
TF: 866-566-8267 ■ *Web:* crawfordcountymo.net

Crawford County
300 Main St County Courthouse Rm 7 ... Van Buren AR 72956 479-474-1312 471-3236
Web: crawford-county.org

Creek County 317 E Lee St Rm 100 ... Sapulpa OK 74066 918-224-4084
Web: www.okcountyrecords.com

Crenshaw County PO Box 167 ... Luverne AL 36049 334-335-6575
Web: www.sos.alabama.gov

Crisp County 210 S Seventh St ... Cordele GA 31015 229-276-2672 276-2675
Web: www.crispcounty.com

Crittenden County 100 Ct St County Courthouse ... Marion AR 72364 870-739-3200
Web: crittendencounty.arkansas.gov

Crittenden County 107 S Main St ... Marion KY 42064 270-965-3403
Web: www.crittenden.clerkinfo.net

Crockett County PO Box C ... Ozona TX 76943 325-392-2022 392-3742
Web: www.co.crockett.tx.us

Crook County 300 NE Third St Rm 23 ... Prineville OR 97754 541-447-6553 416-2145
Web: www.co.crook.or.us

Crook County 309 Cleveland St PO Box 37 ... Sundance WY 82729 307-283-1323 283-3038
Web: www.crookcounty.wy.gov

Crosby County 201 W Aspen St Ste 102 ... Crosbyton TX 79322 806-675-2334
Web: www.co.crosby.tx.us

Cross County 705 E Union St Rm 8 ... Wynne AR 72396 870-238-5735 238-5739
Web: crosscountyar.org

Crow Wing County 326 Laurel St ... Brainerd MN 56401 218-824-1067 824-1054
TF: 888-829-6680 ■ *Web:* crowwing.us

Crowley County 631 Main St Ste 102 ... Ordway CO 81063 719-267-5225 267-4608
Web: www.colorado.gov

Culberson County PO Box 158 ... Van Horn TX 79855 432-283-2058 283-9234
Web: www.co.culberson.tx.us

Cullman County 500 Second Ave SW ... Cullman AL 35055 256-739-3530
Web: www.co.cullman.al.us

Culpeper County 151 N Main St # 201 ... Culpeper VA 22701 540-727-3427 727-3460
Web: web.culpepercounty.gov

Cumberland County 27 Fayette St ... Bridgeton NJ 08302 856-451-8000 455-1410
Web: www.co.cumberland.nj.us

Cumberland County 212 N Main St ... Burkesville KY 42717 270-864-3726 864-5884
Web: cumberlandcountyclerk.com

Cumberland County 34 South Main St Ste 206 ... Crossville TN 38555 931-484-8444 484-7511
Web: www.crossville-chamber.com

Cumberland County PO Box 1829 ... Fayetteville NC 28302 910-437-1921 678-7717
Web: www.co.cumberland.nc.us

Cumberland County 142 Federal St Rm 102 ... Portland ME 04101 207-871-8380 871-8292
Web: www.cumberlandcounty.org

Cumberland County 140 Courthouse Sq PO Box 146 ... Toledo IL 62468 217-849-2631 849-2968
Web: cumberlandco.org

Cuming County 200 S Lincoln St Rm 202 ... West Point NE 68788 402-372-6002
Web: extension.unl.edu/statewide/cuming

Currituck County
153 Courthouse Rd Ste 204 PO Box 39 ... Currituck NC 27929 252-232-2075 232-3551
Web: www.co.currituck.nc.us

Curry County 700 N Main St Ste 7 ... Clovis NM 88101 575-763-6016
Web: currycounty.org

Curry County
29821 Ellensburg Ave PO Box 746 ... Gold Beach OR 97444 541-247-3296 247-6440
Web: www.co.curry.or.us

Cusseta-Chattahoochee County
Courthouse Annex 377 Broad St PO Box 299 ... Cusseta GA 31805 706-989-3602 989-2005
Web: www.ugoccc.us

Custer County PO Box 300 ... Arapaho OK 73620 405-522-0018 331-1131*
**Fax Area Code:* 580 ■ *Web:* custer.okcounties.org

Custer County 431 S Tenth St ... Broken Bow NE 68822 308-872-5701
Web: www.co.custer.ne.us

Custer County 801 E Main Ave ... Challis ID 83226 208-879-2360 879-5246
Web: www.co.custer.id.us

Custer County 420 Mt Rushmore Rd Ste 6 ... Custer SD 57730 605-673-4816
Web: ujs.sd.gov

Phone Fax

Custer County 205 S Sixth St ... Westcliffe CO 81252 719-783-2441 783-2885
Web: www.custercountygov.com

Cuyahoga County 1219 Ontario St ... Cleveland OH 44113 216-443-7010 443-5091
Web: www.cuyahogacounty.us

Dade County 71 Case Ave ... Trenton GA 30752 706-657-4625 657-8284
Web: www.dadecounty-ga.gov

Daggett County 95 N First W ... Manila UT 84046 435-784-3154 784-3335
Web: www.daggettcounty.org

Dakota County 1601 Broadway ... Dakota City NE 68731 402-987-2126 987-2186
Web: www.dakotacountyne.org

Dakota County 1560 Hwy 55 ... Hastings MN 55033 651-438-8100 438-4405
Web: www.co.dakota.mn.us

Dale County 202 Hwy 123 S Ste C ... Ozark AL 36360 334-774-6025 774-1841
Web: dalecountyal.org

Dallam County PO Box 1352 ... Dalhart TX 79022 806-244-4751
Web: www.dallam.org

Dallas County 801 Ct St ... Adel IA 50003 515-993-5814
Web: www.co.dallas.ia.us

Dallas County PO Box 3404 ... Buffalo MO 65622 417-238-4011
Web: buffalococ.com

Dallas County 411 Elm St ... Dallas TX 75202 214-653-7361 653-7057
Web: www.dallascounty.org

Dallas County 105 Lauderdale ... Selma AL 36702 334-874-2553 874-2587
Web: www.dallascounty-al.org

Dane County 210 ML King Jr Blvd Rm 106A ... Madison WI 53703 608-266-4121
Web: www.countyofdane.com

Daniels County 120 Main St PO Box 91 ... Scobey MT 59263 406-487-2061
Web: scobeymt.com

Danville (Independent City)
401 Patton St PO Box 3300 ... Danville VA 24543 434-799-5168 799-6502
Web: www.danville-va.gov

Dare County 954 Marshall Collins Dr ... Manteo NC 27954 252-475-5800 473-1817
Web: www.co.dare.nc.us

Darke County 520 S Broadway St ... Greenville OH 45331 937-547-7300 547-7367
Web: www.co.darke.oh.us

Darlington County 1 Public Sq ... Darlington SC 29532 843-398-4100 393-8539
Web: www.darcosc.com

Dauphin County 2 S Second St 3rd Fl ... Harrisburg PA 17101 717-780-6636 780-6468
TF: 800-328-0058 ■ *Web:* www.dauphincounty.org

Davidson County
913 Greensboro St PO Box 1067 ... Lexington NC 27293 336-242-2000 248-8440
Web: www.co.davidson.nc.us

Davidson County 205 Metro Courthouse ... Nashville TN 37201 615-862-6770 862-6774
Web: www.nashville.gov

Davie County 123 S Main St ... Mocksville NC 27028 336-753-6040 751-7408
Web: www.daviecountync.gov

Daviess County 212 St Ann St ... Owensboro KY 42303 270-685-8434
Web: www.daviessky.org

Daviess County 200 E Walnut St ... Washington IN 47501 812-254-8664
Web: www.daviesscounty.org

Daviess County Clerk 102 N Main St ... Gallatin MO 64640 660-663-2641
Web: daviesscountysheriff.com

Davis County 28 E State St PO Box 618 ... Farmington UT 84025 801-451-3324 451-3421
Web: www.co.davis.ut.us

Davis County Clerk of Courts
100 Courthouse Sq ... Bloomfield IA 52537 641-664-2011 664-2041
Web: www.daviscountyiowa.org

Davison County Auditor 200 E Fourth Ave ... Mitchell SD 57301 605-995-8608 995-8618
Web: www.davisoncounty.org

Dawes County 451 Main St ... Chadron NE 69337 308-432-0100 432-5179
Web: dawes-county.com

Dawson County 25 Justice Way Ste 2214 ... Dawsonville GA 30534 706-344-3501 344-3504
Web: www.dawsoncounty.org

Dawson County 207 W Bell St ... Glendive MT 59330 406-377-3058 687-3563
Web: www.dawsoncountymontana.com

Dawson County PO Box 1268 ... Lamesa TX 79331 806-872-3778 872-2473
Web: www.co.dawson.tx.us

Dawson County 700 N Washington ... Lexington NE 68850 308-324-2127 324-9832
Web: dawsoncountyne.org

Day County 711 W First St ... Webster SD 57274 605-345-3771 345-3818
Web: ujs.sd.gov

Deaf Smith County 140 E Third St ... Hereford TX 79045 806-364-0625 364-6895
Web: deafsmithcad.org

Dearborn County 215 W High St ... Lawrenceburg IN 47025 812-537-8877 532-2021
Web: dearborncounty.org

Decatur County PO Box 726 ... Bainbridge GA 39818 229-248-3030 246-2062
Web: decaturcountyga.org

Decatur County 22 W Main St ... Decaturville TN 38329 731-852-2131
Web: www.decaturcountytn.org

Decatur County 150 Courthouse Sq Ste 244 ... Greensburg IN 47240 812-663-8223 662-6627
Web: www.decaturcounty.in.gov

Decatur County 207 N Main St ... Leon IA 50144 641-446-4322 446-3616
Web: www.decaturcountyiowa.org

Defiance County 500 Ct St ... Defiance OH 43512 419-782-4761 782-8449
Web: www.defiance-county.com

DeKalb County 109 W Main St PO Box 248 ... Maysville MO 64469 816-449-5402 449-2440
Web: dekalbcountymo.com

DeKalb County 556 N McDonough St ... Decatur GA 30030 404-371-2000
Web: www.co.dekalb.ga.us

DeKalb County 111 Grand Ave SW Ste 200 ... Fort Payne AL 35967 256-845-8500 845-8502
Web: www.dekalbcountyal.us

DeKalb County 732 S Congress Blvd ... Smithville TN 37166 615-597-5176
Web: www.dekalbtennessee.com

DeKalb County 110 E Sycamore St ... Sycamore IL 60178 815-895-7149 895-7148
Web: www.dekalbcounty.org

Del Norte County 981 H St Ste 200 ... Crescent City CA 95531 707-464-7204 464-1165
Web: www.co.del-norte.ca.us

Delaware County 101 N Sandusky St ... Delaware OH 43015 740-833-2100 833-2099
Web: www.co.delaware.oh.us

Delaware County PO Box 426 ... Delhi NY 13753 607-746-2123 746-6924
Web: www.co.delaware.ny.us

Name / Address	City	State	Zip	Phone	Fax
Delaware County 301 E Main St *Web:* www.co.delaware.ia.us	Manchester	IA	52057	563-927-4942	927-3074
Delaware County 100 W Main St *Web:* www.co.delaware.in.us	Muncie	IN	47305	765-747-7730	747-7768
Delta County 200 W. Bonham St *Web:* www.deltacountytx.com/sheriff.html	Cooper	TX	75432	903-395-4118	395-4455
Delta County 501 Palmer St Ste 211 *Web:* www.deltacounty.com	Delta	CO	81416	970-874-2150	874-2161
Delta County 310 Ludington St *Web:* www.deltami.org	Escanaba	MI	49829	906-789-5105	789-5196
Denali Borough PO Box 480 *Web:* www.denaliborough.govoffice.com	Healy	AK	99743	907-683-1330	683-1340
Dent County 400 N Main St *Web:* salemmo.com	Salem	MO	65560	573-729-4144	
Denton County 1450 E McKinney *Web:* dentoncounty.com	Denton	TX	76209	940-349-2012	349-2019
Denver City & County 201 W Colfax Ave 1st Fl *Web:* www.denvergov.org	Denver	CO	80202	720-865-8400	
Des Moines County 513 N Main St *Web:* www.dmcounty.com	Burlington	IA	52601	319-753-8232	
Deschutes County 1300 NW Wall St Ste 200 *Web:* www.deschutes.org	Bend	OR	97701	541-330-4631	385-3202
Desha County 608 Robert S Moore Ave PO Box 188 *Web:* deshacounty.arkansas.gov	Arkansas City	AR	71630	870-877-2426	
DeSoto County 201 E Oak St *Web:* desotobocc.com	Arcadia	FL	34266	863-993-4800	993-4809
DeSoto County 365 Losher St *Web:* www.desotocountyms.gov	Hernando	MS	38632	662-429-1460	
DeSoto Parish 101 Texas St PO Box 1206 *Web:* desotoparishclerk.org	Mansfield	LA	71052	318-872-3110	872-4202
Deuel County 718 Third St PO Box 327 *Web:* www.co.deuel.ne.us	Chappell	NE	69129	308-874-3308	874-3472
Deuel County 408 Fourth St W *Web:* www.deuelcountysd.com	Clear Lake	SD	57226	605-874-2312	874-1306
Dewey County PO Box 368 *Web:* www.okgenweb.org/~okdewey	Taloga	OK	73667	580-328-5521	
Dewey County Clerk of Courts PO Box 96 *Web:* ujs.sd.gov	Timber Lake	SD	57656	605-865-3566	865-3641
DeWitt County 201 W Washington St PO Box 439 *Web:* www.dewittcountyill.com	Clinton	IL	61727	217-935-7780	
Dickens County 512 Montgomery St PO Box 120 *Web:* co.dickens.tx.us	Dickens	TX	79229	806-623-5531	623-5240
Dickenson County 293 Main St PO Box 1098 *Web:* www.dickensonva.org	Clintwood	VA	24228	276-926-1676	926-1649
Dickey County 205 15th St N PO Box 238 *Web:* www.dickeynd.com	Ellendale	ND	58436	701-349-4348	349-3277
Dickinson County PO Box 248 *Web:* www.dkcoks.org	Abilene	KS	67410	785-263-3774	263-2045
Dickinson County 705 S Stephenson Ave PO Box 609 *Web:* www.dickinsoncountymi.gov	Iron Mountain	MI	49801	906-774-0988	774-4660
Dickinson County 1802 Hill Ave *Web:* dickinsoncountyiowa.org	Spirit Lake	IA	51360	712-336-3356	
Dickson County PO Box 267 *Web:* www.dicksoncountytn.gov	Charlotte	TN	37036	615-789-7003	789-6075
Dillon County 109 S Third Ave PO Box 449 *Web:* dilloncounty.sc.gov	Dillon	SC	29536	843-774-1400	774-1443
Dimmit County 103 N Fifth St *Web:* www.dimmitcounty.org	Carrizo Springs	TX	78834	830-876-2323	
Dinwiddie County 14016 Boydton Plank Rd *Web:* www.dinwiddieva.us	Dinwiddie	VA	23841	804-469-4500	469-4503
Divide County 300 N Main *Web:* www.ndaco.org	Crosby	ND	58730	701-328-7300	
Dixie County 214 NE 351 Hwy PO Box 2600 *Web:* dixie.fl.gov	Cross City	FL	32628	352-498-1206	498-1207
Dixon County PO Box 395 *Web:* www.co.dixon.ne.us	Ponca	NE	68770	402-755-5604	755-5651
Doddridge County 118 E Ct St Rm 102 *Web:* doddridgecounty.wv.gov	West Union	WV	26456	304-873-2631	873-1840
Dodge County PO Box 818 *Web:* www.dodgecountyga.com	Eastman	GA	31023	478-374-4361	374-8121
Dodge County 435 N Pk *Web:* www.dodgecounty.ne.gov	Fremont	NE	68025	402-727-2767	727-2764
Dodge County 127 E Oak St *Web:* www.co.dodge.wi.us	Juneau	WI	53039	920-386-3602	386-3928
Dodge County 22 Sixth St E *Web:* www.co.dodge.mn.us	Mantorville	MN	55955	507-635-6239	635-6265
Dolores County 409 N Main St *Web:* www.dolorescounty.org	Dove Creek	CO	81324	970-677-2383	677-2815
Dona Ana County 845 N Motel Blvd *Web:* donaanacounty.org	Las Cruces	NM	88007	575-647-7200	585-5538
Doniphan County PO Box 278 *Web:* www.dpcountyks.com	Troy	KS	66087	785-985-3513	985-3723
Donley County 300 S Sully St PO Box 909 *Web:* www.co.donley.tx.us	Clarendon	TX	79226	806-874-3625	874-1181
Dooly County 110 E Union St PO Box 308 *Web:* www.doolychamber.com	Vienna	GA	31092	229-268-8275	268-8200
Door County 421 Nebraska St *Web:* www.co.door.wi.gov	Sturgeon Bay	WI	54235	920-746-2200	746-2330
Dorchester County 501 Ct Ln *TF:* 800-272-9829 ■ *Web:* www.docogonet.com	Cambridge	MD	21613	410-228-1700	228-9641
Dorchester County 101 Ridge St *Web:* www.dorchestercounty.net	Saint George	SC	29477	843-563-0260	563-0288
Dougherty County 222 Pine Ave *Web:* www.albany.ga.us	Albany	GA	31701	229-431-2121	438-3967
Douglas County 305 Eigth Ave W *Web:* www.co.douglas.mn.us	Alexandria	MN	56308	320-762-3877	762-2389
Douglas County 706 Braddock St PO Box 36 *Web:* ujs.sd.gov	Armour	SD	57313	605-724-2585	724-2508
Douglas County 203 SE Second Ave	Ava	MO	65608	417-683-4713	
Douglas County 100 Third St *Web:* www.douglas.co.us	Castle Rock	CO	80104	303-660-7401	688-1293
Douglas County 8700 Hospital Dr *Web:* www.celebratedouglascounty.com	Douglasville	GA	30134	770-949-2000	
Douglas County 1100 Massachusetts St First Level *Web:* www.douglascountyks.org	Lawrence	KS	66044	785-832-5167	
Douglas County 1616 8th St PO Box 218 *Web:* cltr.douglasnv.us	Minden	NV	89423	775-782-9020	782-9016
Douglas County 1819 Farnam St *Web:* www.douglascounty-ne.gov	Omaha	NE	68183	402-444-7025	444-6559
Douglas County 1036 SE Douglas St *Web:* www.co.douglas.or.us	Roseburg	OR	97470	541-672-3311	440-4408
Douglas County 1313 Belknap St *Web:* www.douglascountywi.org	Superior	WI	54880	715-395-1341	395-1421
Douglas County 401 S Ctr St PO Box 467 *Web:* www.douglascountyil.com	Tuscola	IL	61953	217-253-2411	253-2233
Douglas County 213 Rainer St *Web:* www.douglascountywa.net	Waterville	WA	98858	509-745-8537	745-9045
Drew County 210 S Main St	Monticello	AR	71655	870-460-6260	
Dubuque County 720 Central Ave *Web:* www.dubuquecounty.org	Dubuque	IA	52001	563-589-4432	
Duchesne County 734 N Ctr St *Web:* www.duchesne.utah.gov	Duchesne	UT	84021	435-738-1100	738-5522
Dukes County PO Box 190 *Web:* www.dukescounty.org	Edgartown	MA	02539	508-696-3840	696-3841
Dundy County PO Box 506 *Web:* www.co.dundy.ne.us	Benkelman	NE	69021	308-423-2058	
Dunklin County PO Box 567 *Web:* www.courts.mo.gov	Kennett	MO	63857	573-888-2456	888-0319
Dunn County PO Box 105 *Web:* dunncountynd.org	Manning	ND	58642	701-573-4448	573-4323
Dunn County 800 Wilson Ave *Web:* co.dunn.wi.us	Menomonie	WI	54751	715-232-1677	232-2534
DuPage County 421 N County Farm Rd *Web:* www.dupageco.org	Wheaton	IL	60187	630-407-5500	407-5501
Duplin County 112 Duplin St Ste 101 *Web:* www.duplincountync.com	Kenansville	NC	28349	910-296-2150	296-2156
Durham County 200 E Main St *Web:* dconc.gov	Durham	NC	27701	919-560-0000	560-0020
Dutchess County 22 Market St *Web:* www.co.dutchess.ny.us	Poughkeepsie	NY	12601	845-486-2120	
Duval County 117 W Duval St *Web:* www.coj.net	Jacksonville	FL	32202	904-630-2489	630-2906
Dyer County 115 Market St PO Box 1360 *Web:* tn.gov	Dyersburg	TN	38025	731-286-7814	288-7719
Eagle County PO Box 850 *Web:* www.eaglecounty.us	Eagle	CO	81631	970-328-8600	328-8716
Early County PO Box 693 *Web:* georgia.gov/cities-counties/early-county	Blakely	GA	39823	229-723-4304	723-8684
East Baton Rouge Parish 1755 Florida St *Web:* www.brgov.com	Baton Rouge	LA	70802	225-389-3129	
East Carroll Parish 400 First St PO Box 246 *Web:* www.ecsheriff.com	Lake Providence	LA	71254	318-559-2800	559-2567
East Feliciana Parish PO Box 427 PO Box 599 *Web:* www.felicianatourism.org	Clinton	LA	70722	225-683-5145	
Eastland County 100 W Main PO Box 110 *Web:* www.eastlandcountytexas.com	Eastland	TX	76448	254-629-1583	629-8125
Eaton County 1045 Independence Blvd *Web:* eatoncounty.org	Charlotte	MI	48813	517-543-7500	541-0666
Eau Claire County 721 Oxford Ave *Web:* co.eau-claire.wi.us	Eau Claire	WI	54703	715-839-4801	839-4854
Echols County 110 General Beloach St *Web:* echolscountyga.com	Statenville	GA	31648	229-559-6538	
Ector County 300 N Grant Ave Rm 111 *Web:* www.co.ector.tx.us	Odessa	TX	79761	432-498-4130	498-4177
Eddy County 101 W Greene St Ste 110 *Fax Area Code: 575 ■ *Web:* www.co.eddy.nm.us	Carlsbad	NM	88220	505-887-9511	234-1835*
Eddy County 524 Central Ave *Web:* www.cityofnewrockford.com	New Rockford	ND	58356	701-947-2434	947-2279
Edgar County 115 W Ct St *Web:* edgarcountyillinois.com	Paris	IL	61944	217-466-7433	466-7430
Edgecombe County 201 St Andrew St PO Box 10 *Web:* www.edgecombecountync.gov	Tarboro	NC	27886	252-641-7852	641-0456
Edgefield County 129 Courthouse Sq PO Box 34 *Web:* www.edgefieldcounty.sc.gov	Edgefield	SC	29824	803-637-4080	
Edmonson County PO Box 830 *Web:* edmonsoncountyclerk.com	Brownsville	KY	42210	270-597-2624	597-9714
Edmunds County PO Box 384 *Web:* www.edmunds.sdcounties.org	Ipswich	SD	57451	605-426-6671	426-6323
Edwards County 50 E Main St *Web:* www.sos.state.il.us/departments/archives/irad/edwards.html	Albion	IL	62806	618-445-2115	
Edwards County 721 Marsh Ave *Web:* www.edwardscounty.org	Kinsley	KS	67547	620-659-2711	659-3613
Edwards County PO Box 348 *Web:* www.edwardscountytexas.us	Rocksprings	TX	78880	830-683-6122	
Effingham County 101 N Fourth St PO Box 628 *Web:* www.co.effingham.il.us	Effingham	IL	62401	217-342-6535	342-3577
Effingham County 601 N Laurel St *Web:* www.effinghamcounty.org	Springfield	GA	31329	912-754-2123	754-4157
El Dorado County 360 Fair Ln Bldg B *Web:* edcgov.us	Placerville	CA	95667	530-621-5490	621-2147
El Paso County 200 S Cascade Ave *Web:* www.elpasoco.com	Colorado Springs	CO	80903	719-520-6200	520-6212
El Paso County 500 E San Antonio Ave *Web:* www.co.el-paso.tx.us	El Paso	TX	79901	915-546-2000	546-2012
Elbert County 215 Comanche St PO Box 7 *Web:* www.elbertcounty-co.gov	Kiowa	CO	80117	303-621-2131	621-2343

Phone | Fax

Elbert County Chamber Of Commerce
104 Heard St. ... Elberton GA 30635 706-283-5651 283-5722
Web: www.elbertga.com

Elk County PO Box 606 ... Howard KS 67349 620-374-2490 374-2771
TF: 877-504-2490 ■ *Web:* elkcountyks.org

Elk County 250 Main St ... Ridgway PA 15853 814-776-1161 776-5379
Web: www.co.elk.pa.us

Elkhart County 117 N Second St. ... Goshen IN 46526 574-535-6743
Web: www.elkhartcountyindiana.com

Elko County 569 Ct St ... Elko NV 89801 775-738-5398 753-8535
Web: www.elkocountynv.net

Elliott County PO Box 710 ... Sandy Hook KY 41171 606-738-5826 738-5627
Web: www.elliottcounty.ky.gov

Ellis County PO Box 176 ... Arnett OK 73832 580-885-7975 885-7258
Web: www.ellis.oklahoma.usassessor.com

Ellis County 2700 Vine St ... Hays KS 67601 785-628-3102
Web: www.ellisco.org

Ellis County 1201 N Hwy 77 Ste B ... Waxahachie TX 75165 972-825-5000
Web: www.co.ellis.tx.us

Ellsworth County 210 N Kansas St ... Ellsworth KS 67439 785-472-4161 472-3818
Web: www.ellsworthcounty.org

Elmore County 150 S Fourth E St Ste 5 ... Mountain Home ID 83647 208-587-2129 587-2134
Web: www.elmorecounty.org

Elmore County 100 E Commerce St. ... Wetumpka AL 36092 334-567-1156
Web: www.elmoreco.org

Emanuel County 101 N Main St ... Swainsboro GA 30401 478-237-3881
Web: emanuelchamber.org

Emery County 75 E Main PO Box 907 ... Castle Dale UT 84513 435-381-5106 381-5183
Web: www.emerycounty.com

Emmet County 609 First Ave N ... Estherville IA 51334 712-362-4261 362-7454
Web: www.emmetcountyia.com

Emmet County 200 Div St Ste 130 ... Petoskey MI 49770 231-348-1702 348-0602
TF: 866-731-1204 ■ *Web:* www.emmetcounty.org

Emmons County 100 NW Fourth St PO Box 272 ... Linton ND 58552 701-254-5410
Web: emmonscounty.tripod.com

Emporia (Independent City) 201 S Main St ... Emporia VA 23847 434-634-3332 634-0003
Web: www.ci.emporia.va.us

Erath County 100 W Washington ... Stephenville TX 76401 254-965-1452 965-5732
Web: www.co.erath.tx.us

Erie County 92 Franklin St ... Buffalo NY 14202 716-858-8785 858-6550
Web: www.erie.gov

Erie County 140 W Sixth St ... Erie PA 16501 814-451-6344 451-6334
Web: www.eriecountypa.gov

Erie County 323 Columbus Ave ... Sandusky OH 44870 419-627-7705
Web: www.erie-county-ohio.net

Escambia County 314 Belleville Ave ... Brewton AL 36426 251-867-0300
Web: www.co.escambia.al.us

Esmeralda County PO Box 547 ... Goldfield NV 89013 775-485-6309 485-6376
TF: 800-884-4072 ■ *Web:* www.accessesmeralda.com

Essex County 7559 Ct St PO Box 247 ... Elizabethtown NY 12932 518-873-3320 451-8738

Essex County
465 Dr Martin Luther King Jr Blvd Rm 558 ... Newark NJ 07102 973-621-4921 621-5695
Web: essexcountynj.org

Essex County 32 Federal St ... Salem MA 01970 978-741-0200
Web: essexcountyma.net

Essex County 305 Prince St ... Tappahannock VA 22560 804-443-4611 445-1216
Web: www.essex-virginia.org

Estill County 130 Main St Ste 102 ... Irvine KY 40336 606-723-5156 723-5108
Web: www.estillky.com

Etowah County 800 Forrest Ave ... Gadsden AL 35901 256-549-5300 549-5400
Web: www.etowahcounty.org

Eureka County 10 S Main St ... Eureka NV 89316 775-237-5262 237-6015
Web: www.co.eureka.nv.us

Evangeline Parish 200 Ct St Ste 104 ... Ville Platte LA 70586 337-363-5671 363-5780
Web: evangelineparishclerkofcourt.com/contact.aspx

Evans County 3 Freeman St ... Claxton GA 30417 912-739-1141
Web: www.claxtonevanschamber.com

Fairbanks North Star Borough
809 Pioneer Rd ... Fairbanks AK 99701 907-459-1000 459-1224
Web: www.co.fairbanks.ak.us

Fairfax County 12000 Government Ctr Pkwy ... Fairfax VA 22035 703-324-2531 324-3956
Web: fairfaxcounty.gov

Fairfax (Independent City)
10455 Armstrong St ... Fairfax VA 22030 703-324-7329 385-7811
Web: fairfaxcounty.gov

Fairfield County 210 E Main St ... Lancaster OH 43130 740-652-7075 687-6048
Web: www.co.fairfield.oh.us

Fairfield County 150 Danbury Rd ... Ridgefield CT 06877 803-712-6526 712-1506
Web: www.fairfieldsc.com

Fairfield County 1061 Main St ... Bridgeport CT 06604 203-579-6527
Web: www.jud.state.ct.us/directory/directory/directions/25.htm

Fall River County 906 N River St ... Hot Springs SD 57747 605-745-5131 745-6835
Web: ujs.sd.gov

Fallon County 10 W Fallon St PO Box 1061 ... Baker MT 59313 406-778-3152
Web: www.falloncounty.net

Falls Church (Independent City)
300 Pk Ave ... Falls Church VA 22046 703-248-5001 248-5146
Web: www.fallschurchva.gov

Falls County 520 Lawrence St ... Corpus Christi TX 78401 254-883-1408
Web: www.texasfile.com/texas-deed-records-directory/falls-county-clerk

Fannin County 400 W Main St Ste 100 ... Blue Ridge GA 30513 706-632-2203 632-2507
Web: fannincountyga.org

Fannin County
101 Sam Rayburn Dr County Courthouse Ste 102 ... Bonham TX 75418 903-583-7486 640-4241
Web: www.co.fannin.tx.us

Faribault County 415 N Main St ... Blue Earth MN 56013 507-526-6221
Web: faribaultcountyrecorder.com

Faulkner County 801 Locust St ... Conway AR 72034 501-450-4909 450-4938
Web: www.faulknercounty.org

Fauquier County 10 Hotel St Ste 204 ... Warrenton VA 20186 540-422-8001 422-8022
Web: www.fauquiercounty.gov

Fayette County 401 N Central Ave # 6 ... Connersville IN 47331 765-825-1013 827-4902

Phone | Fax

Fayette County
103 First Ave NW Courthouse Annex Ste 2 ... Fayette AL 35555 205-932-4510 932-2902
Web: fayettecountyal.org

Fayette County 140 Stonewall Ave W ... Fayetteville GA 30214 770-460-5730
Web: www.fayettecountyga.gov

Fayette County 310 Oyler Ave. ... Oak Hill WV 25901 304-465-5617
Web: www.fayettecounty.com

Fayette County 246 W Colorado St. ... La Grange TX 78945 979-968-3251 968-8531
Web: www.co.fayette.tx.us

Fayette County
133 S Main St Ste 401 ... Washington Court House OH 43160 740-335-0720 333-3530
Web: www.fayette-co-oh.com

Fayette County 114 N Vine St ... West Union IA 52175 563-422-5694 422-3137
Web: fayettecountyiowa.org

Fayette County Goverment
221 S Seventh St Ste 106 ... Vandalia IL 62471 618-283-5000 283-5004
Web: www.fayettecountyillinois.org

Fentress County 101 S Main St ... Jamestown TN 38556 931-879-9948
Web: www.jamestowntn.org

Fergus County 712 W Main St ... Lewistown MT 59457 406-535-5026 535-6076
Web: www.co.fergus.mt.us

Ferry County 290 E Tessie Ave ... Republic WA 99166 509-775-5229 775-5230
Web: www.ferry-county.com

Fillmore County 900 G St ... Geneva NE 68361 402-759-4931 759-4307
Web: www.fillmorecounty.org

Fillmore County 101 Fillmore St ... Preston MN 55965 507-765-3356 765-4571
Web: www.co.fillmore.mn.us

Finney County 311 N Ninth St PO Box M ... Garden City KS 67846 620-272-3542 272-3599
Web: www.finneycounty.org

Fisher County PO Box 368 ... Roby TX 79543 325-776-2401 776-3274
Web: www.co.fisher.tx.us

Flagler County 1769 E Moody Blvd Bldg 2 ... Bunnell FL 32110 386-313-4000
Web: www.flaglercounty.org

Flathead County 800 S Main St ... Kalispell MT 59901 406-758-5503 758-5861
Web: flathead.mt.gov

Florence County 180 N Irby St ... Florence SC 29501 843-665-3035 665-3070
Web: www.florenceco.org

Florence County 501 Lake Ave ... Florence WI 54121 715-528-3201 528-4762
Web: www.florencecountywi.com

Floyd County 101 S Main St ... Charles City IA 50616 641-228-7777 228-7772
Web: www.floydcoia.org

Floyd County PO Box 218 ... Floyd VA 24091 540-745-9300 745-9305
Web: www.floydcova.org

Floyd County PO Box 455 ... New Albany IN 47151 812-949-2551 981-0352
Web: www.floydcounty.in.gov

Floyd County 313 Westminster St Ste 210 ... Prestonsburg KY 41653 606-886-0364
Web: www.floydcountykentucky.com

Floyd County 12 E Fourth Ave Ste 209 ... Rome GA 30162 706-291-5110 291-5248
Web: www.romefloyd.com

Fluvanna County 132 Main St ... Palmyra VA 22963 434-591-1910 591-1911
Web: www.fluvannacounty.org

Foard County 101 S Main St ... Crowell TX 79227 940-684-1919

Fond du Lac County PO Box 1557 ... Fond du Lac WI 54936 920-929-3000 929-3293
Web: www.fdlco.wi.gov

Ford County 100 Gunsmoke St 4th Fl ... Dodge City KS 67801 620-227-4670 227-4699
Web: www.fordcounty.net

Forest County 200 E Madison St ... Crandon WI 54520 715-478-2422
Web: www.forestcountywi.com

Forest County 526 Elm St Ste 3 ... Tionesta PA 16353 814-755-3537 755-8837
Web: www.co.forest.pa.us

Forrest County 641 Main St ... Hattiesburg MS 39401 601-545-6000
Web: www.co.forrest.ms.us

Forsyth County 110 E Main St Ste 010 ... Cumming GA 30040 770-781-2120
Web: forsythco.com

Forsyth County 200 N Main St ... Winston-Salem NC 27101 336-761-2250 761-2018
Web: www.co.forsyth.nc.us

Fort Bend County 301 Jackson St Ste 101 ... Richmond TX 77469 281-342-3411 341-8669
Web: www.fortbendcountytx.gov

Foster County PO Box 257 ... Carrington ND 58421 701-652-1001 652-2173
Web: www.fostercounty.com

Fountain County
301 4th St County Courthouse ... Covington IN 47932 765-793-2411
Web: www.in.gov/judiciary/2948.htm

Franklin County 33 Market St Ste 203 ... Apalachicola FL 32320 850-653-8861
Web: www.franklincountyflorida.com

Franklin County PO Box 607 ... Benton IL 62812 618-438-3221 435-3405
Web: franklincountyil.gov

Franklin County 459 Main St ... Brookville IN 47012 765-647-5111 647-3224
Web: franklincounty.in.gov

Franklin County 211 Athens St PO Box 313 ... Carnesville GA 30521 706-384-4390 384-3506
Web: franklincountyga.gov

Franklin County 14 N MAIN ST ... Chambersburg PA 17201 717-264-4125 267-3438
Web: www.franklincountypa.gov

Franklin County 369 S High St 3rd Fl ... Columbus OH 43215 614-462-3650
Web: www.franklincountyohio.gov

Franklin County 615 Wilton Rd ... Farmington ME 04938 207-778-4215 778-2438
Web: www.franklincountymaine.org

Franklin County 315 W Main St ... Frankfort KY 40602 502-875-8702 875-8718
Web: franklincounty.ky.gov

Franklin County 405 15th Ave ... Franklin NE 68939 308-425-6202 425-6093
Web: co.franklin.ne.us

Franklin County 12 First Ave NW PO Box 28 ... Hampton IA 50441 641-456-5626 456-5628
Web: www.co.franklin.ia.us/pages/clerk

Franklin County 113 Market St ... Louisburg NC 27549 919-496-5994 496-2683
Web: www.franklincountync.us

Franklin County 355 W Main St ... Malone NY 12953 518-483-6770 483-0141
TF: 800-397-8686 ■ *Web:* franklincony.org

Franklin County PO Box 267 ... Meadville MS 39653 601-384-2320
Web: franklin.msghn.org

Franklin County 200 N Kaufman St ... Mount Vernon TX 75457 903-537-2342 537-2962
Web: www.co.franklin.tx.us

Phone Fax

Franklin County 315 S Main St — Ottawa KS 66067 785-229-3410 229-3419
Web: www.franklincoks.org
Franklin County 211 W Commercial St — Ozark AR 72949 479-667-3818
Franklin County 1016 N Fourth Ave — Pasco WA 99301 509-545-3535 545-3573
Web: www.co.franklin.wa.us
Franklin County 39 W Oneida St — Preston ID 83263 208-852-1090 852-1094
Web: www.franklincountyidaho.org
Franklin County 1255 Franklin St — Rocky Mount VA 24151 540-483-3030
Web: www.franklincountyva.org
Franklin County
405 N Jackson Ave PO Box 1028 — Russellville AL 35653 256-332-8850
Web: www.franklincountyal.org
Franklin County 17 Church St — Saint Albans VT 05478 802-524-2444
Web: www.visitfranklincountyvt.com
Franklin County 400 E Locust — Union MO 63084 636-583-6355 583-7320
Web: www.franklinmo.org
Franklin County 855 Dinah Shore Blvd Ste 3 — Winchester TN 37398 931-967-2905
Web: www.franklincotn.us
Franklin (Independent City) 1020 Pretlow St — Franklin VA 23851 757-562-8550 562-1156
Web: www.courts.state.va.us
Franklin Parish 6550 Main St — Winnsboro LA 71295 318-435-5133
Web: laclerksofcourt.org
Frederick County 107 N Kent St — Winchester VA 22601 540-665-5600 667-0370
Web: www.co.frederick.va.us
Fredericksburg (Independent City)
715 Princess Ann St — Fredericksburg VA 22401 540-372-1010 372-1201
Web: www.fredericksburgva.gov
Freeborn County 411 S Broadway — Albert Lea MN 56007 507-377-5116 377-5109
Web: www.co.freeborn.mn.us
Freestone County 103 E Main PO Box 1010 — Fairfield TX 75840 903-389-2635
Web: www.co.freestone.tx.us
Fremont County 615 Macon Ave Rm 102 — Canon City CO 81212 719-276-7330 276-7338
Web: www.fremontco.com
Fremont County 450 N Second St — Lander WY 82520 307-332-2405 857-3682
TF: 800-967-2297 ■ *Web:* fremontcountywy.org
Fremont County 151 W First N St — Saint Anthony ID 83445 208-624-7332 624-7335
Web: www.co.fremont.id.us
Fremont County 506 Filmore St PO Box 299 — Sidney IA 51652 712-374-2122 374-6202
Web: www.co.fremont.ia.us
Fresno County 1100 Van Ness Ave — Fresno CA 93721 559-488-1710 488-1830
Web: www.co.fresno.ca.us
Frio County 500 E San Antonio St PO Box 9 — Pearsall TX 78061 830-334-3668
Web: www.co.frio.tx.us
Frontier County PO Box 40 — Stockville NE 69042 308-367-8641 367-8730
Web: www.co.frontier.ne.us
Fulton County 141 Pryor St — Atlanta GA 30303 404-612-4000
Web: www.co.fulton.ga.us
Fulton County 2216 Myron Cory Dr Ste 1 — Hickman KY 42050 270-236-2594 236-7904
Web: www.fultoncounty.ky.gov
Fulton County 2 N Main St — Gloversville NY 12078 518-725-0641 725-0643
Web: fultonmontgomeryny.org
Fulton County 100 N Main St — Lewistown IL 61542 309-547-3041 547-3326
Web: www.fultonco.org
Fulton County 116 W Market St Ste 203 — McConnellsburg PA 17233 717-485-3691 485-9411
Web: www.co.fulton.pa.us
Fulton County 815 Main St — Rochester IN 46975 574-223-4824 223-8304
Web: www.co.fulton.in.us
Fulton County 123 S Main St Courthouse Sq — Salem AR 72576 870-895-3310
Web: www.argenweb.net/fulton
Fulton County 152 S Fulton St Ste 270 — Wauseon OH 43567 419-337-9255 337-9285
Web: www.fultoncountyoh.com
Furnas County PO Box 387 — Beaver City NE 68926 308-268-4145 268-3205
Web: furnascounty.ne.gov
Gadsden County 10 E Jefferson St — Quincy FL 32351 850-875-8601 875-8612
Web: www.gadsdengov.net
Gage County 612 Grant St Rm 21 — Beatrice NE 68310 402-223-1344 223-1380
Web: www.gagecountynebraska.us
Gaines County 101 S Main St PO Box 847 — Seminole TX 79360 432-758-5411 758-4031
Web: co.gaines.tx.us
Galax (Independent City) 111 E Grayson St — Galax VA 24333 276-236-5773 236-2889
Web: www.galaxva.com
Gallatin County 311 W Main St — Bozeman MT 59715 406-582-3050 582-3068
Web: gallatincomt.virtualtownhall.net
Gallatin County 102 W High St — Warsaw KY 41095 859-567-5411 567-5444
Web: gallatincounty.ky.gov
Gallia County 18 Locust St — Gallipolis OH 45631 740-446-4612 446-4804
Web: galliacountychamber.org
Galveston County
600 59th St Second Fl Ste 2001
PO Box 17253 — Galveston TX 77550 409-766-2200
Web: www.galvestoncountytx.gov
Garden County 611 Main St — Oshkosh NE 69154 308-772-3924 772-0124
Web: www.co.garden.ne.us
Garfield County 250 S 8th PO Box 218 — Burwell NE 68823 308-346-4161
Web: www.garfieldcounty.ne.gov
Garfield County 114 W Broadway Rm 106 — Enid OK 73701 580-237-0220 249-5989
Web: www.qpublic.net
Garfield County 108 Eigth St — Glenwood Springs CO 81601 970-945-2377 947-1078
Web: www.garfield-county.com
Garfield County PO Box 370 — Jordan MT 59337 406-557-6178
Web: www.garfieldcounty.com
Garfield County 375 North 700 West — Panguitch UT 84759 435-676-2678
Web: gcutsheriff.com
Garfield County 789 Main St PO Box 915 — Pomeroy WA 99347 509-843-3731
Web: www.co.garfield.wa.us
Garland County 501 Ouachita Ave — Hot Springs AR 71901 501-622-3610 624-0665
Web: www.garlandcounty.org
Garrard County 15 Public Sq Ste 3 — Lancaster KY 40444 859-792-3531 792-2010
Web: www.garrardcounty.ky.gov
Garrett County 203 S Fourth St Rm 207 — Oakland MD 21550 301-334-8970 334-5000
Web: www.garrettcounty.org

Phone Fax

Garvin County 201 W Grant St — Pauls Valley OK 73075 405-238-2772
Web: okcountyrecords.com
Garza County PO Box 366 — Post TX 79356 806-495-4430 495-4431
Web: www.garzacounty.net
Gasconade County 119 E First St Rm 23 — Hermann MO 65041 573-486-3100 486-3693
Web: www.gasconadecountyassessor.com
Gaston County 128 W Main Ave PO Box 1578 — Gastonia NC 28053 704-866-3111 866-3147
Web: www.gastongov.com
Gates County 200 Ct St — Gatesville NC 27938 252-357-2411 357-0073*
**Fax:* Financial ■ *TF:* 800-272-9829 ■ *Web:* www.gatescounty.govoffice2.com
Geary County 200 E 8th — Junction City KS 66441 785-238-3912 238-5419
Web: ks-geary.manatron.com
Geauga County 470 Ctr St Bldg 4 — Chardon OH 44024 440-285-2222
Web: www.co.geauga.oh.us
Gem County 415 E Main St — Emmett ID 83617 208-365-4561 365-7795
Web: www.co.gem.id.us
Genesee County 15 Main St Ste 1 — Batavia NY 14020 585-344-2550 344-8582
Web: www.co.genesee.ny.us
Genesee County 900 S Saginaw St — Flint MI 48502 810-257-3550 257-3464
Web: www.co.genesee.mi.us
Geneva County 123 Main St — Geneva AL 36340 334-393-4769
Web: www.genevacounty.us
Gentry County 200 W Clay St — Albany MO 64402 660-726-3618 726-4102
Web: www.gentrycounty.net
Georgetown County
129 Screven St PO Box 421270 — Georgetown SC 29442 843-545-3063 545-3292
Web: www.georgetowncountysc.org
Gibson County 101 N Main — Princeton IN 47670 812-385-4885 385-3089
Web: gibsoncounty-in.gov
Gila County 1400 E Ash St — Globe AZ 85501 928-425-3231
TF: 800-304-4452 ■ *Web:* co.gila.az.us
Gilchrist County 112 S Main St — Trenton FL 32693 352-463-3170 463-3166
Web: gilchrist.fl.us
Giles County 315 North Main St — Pearisburg VA 24134 540-921-1722 921-3825
Web: www.gilescounty.org
Giles County 1 Public Sq — Pulaski TN 38478 931-363-1509 424-4795
Web: www.gilescounty-tn.us
Gillespie County 101 W Main St Unit 13 — Fredericksburg TX 78624 830-997-6515 997-9958
Web: www.gillespiecounty.org
Gilmer County 368 Craig St PO Box 505 — Ellijay GA 30540 706-635-7400 635-7410
Web: www.gilmerchamber.com
Gilmer County 10 Howard St — Glenville WV 26351 304-462-7641
Web: courtswv.gov
Gilpin County 203 Eureka St — Central City CO 80427 303-582-5321 582-3086
Web: www.co.gilpin.co.us
Glacier County 512 E Main St — Cut Bank MT 59427 406-873-2711 873-4218
Web: www.glaciercountygov.com
Gladwin County 401 W Cedar Ave — Gladwin MI 48624 989-426-7351 426-6917
Web: www.gladwinco.com
Glascock County PO Box 66 — Gibson GA 30810 706-598-2671 598-0124
Web: www.glascockcountyga.com
Glasscock County 117 E Currie St — Garden City TX 79739 432-354-2371
Web: www.co.glasscock.tx.us
Glenn County 526 W Sycamore St Ste B1 — Willows CA 95988 530-934-6400 934-6419
Web: www.countyofglenn.net
Gloucester County 6467 Main St — Gloucester VA 23061 804-693-4042 693-6004
Web: gloucesterva.info/mainwebsitedomainaddress/tabid/1448/default.aspx
Gloucester County 2 S Broad St PO Box 337 — Woodbury NJ 08096 856-853-3237 853-3327
Web: gloucestercountynj.gov
Glynn County 701 G St — Brunswick GA 31520 912-554-7400 554-7596
Web: www.glynncounty.org
Gogebic County 200 N Moore St — Bessemer MI 49911 906-663-4518 663-4660
Web: www.gogebic.org
Golden Valley County 150 First Ave SE — Beach ND 58621 701-872-3713
Web: www.beachnd.com
Golden Valley County 107 Kemp St PO Box 10 — Ryegate MT 59074 406-568-2231 568-2428
Web: www.co.golden-valley.mt.us
Goliad County 127 N Courthouse Sq PO Box 50 — Goliad TX 77963 361-645-3294 645-3858
Web: www.co.goliad.tx.us
Gonzales County 1709 Sarah Dewitt Dr — Gonzales TX 78629 830-672-2801 672-2636
Web: co.gonzales.tx.us
Goochland County 1800 Sandy Hook Rd — Goochland VA 23063 804-556-5800 556-4617
Web: www.goochlandva.us
Goodhue County 454 W Sixth St — Red Wing MN 55066 651-267-4800
Web: www.co.goodhue.mn.us
Gooding County 145 Seventh Ave E PO Box 417 — Gooding ID 83330 208-934-4841 934-5085
Gordon County 201 N Wall St — Calhoun GA 30701 706-629-3795 629-9516
Web: www.gordoncounty.org
Goshen County 2125 E 'A' St PO Box 160 — Torrington WY 82240 307-532-4051 532-7375
Web: www.goshencounty.org
Gosper County 507 Smith Ave PO Box 136 — Elwood NE 68937 308-785-2611 785-2300
Web: www.co.gosper.ne.us
Gove County 520 Washington St Ste 105 PO Box 128 — Gove KS 67736 785-938-2300 938-4486
Web: www.govecountyks.com/county-clerk
Grady County 250 N Broad St — Cairo GA 39828 229-377-1512 377-1039
Web: www.gradycountyga.gov
Grady County 326 Choctaw St — Chickasha OK 73018 405-224-7388 222-4506
Web: www.gradycountyok.com
Grafton County
3855 Dartmouth College Hwy PO Box 4 — North Haverhill NH 03774 603-787-6800
Web: www.nhdeeds.com/grafton/GrHome.html
Graham County 34 Wall St Ste 407 — Asheville NC 28801 828-255-0182 254-2286
TF: 866-962-6246 ■ *Web:* www.main.nc.us
Graham County 921 W Thatcher Blvd — Safford AZ 85546 928-428-3250 428-5951
Web: www.graham.az.gov
Grainger County PO Box 101 — Rutledge TN 37861 865-828-4222
Web: www.graingertn.com
Grand County 308 W Byers Ave — Hot Sulphur Springs CO 80451 970-725-3347 725-0100
Web: www.co.grand.co.us
Grand County 125 E Ctr St — Moab UT 84532 435-259-1321 259-2959
Web: www.grandcountyutah.net

Phone Fax

Grand Forks County 124 S Fourth St ... Grand Forks ND 58206 701-787-2733
Web: www.gfcounty.nd.gov
Grand Isle County 9 Hyde Rd PO Box 49 ... Grand Isle VT 05458 802-372-8830 372-8815
Web: www.grandislevt.org
Grand Traverse County 400 Boardman Ave ... Traverse City MI 49684 231-922-4760 922-4658
Web: www.co.grand-traverse.mi.us
Granite County
220 N Sansome St PO Box 925 ... Philipsburg MT 59858 406-859-3771 859-3817
Web: www.co.granite.mt.us
Grant County 301 W Main St ... John Day OR 97845 541-575-0547
TF: 800-769-5664 ■ *Web:* www.gcoregonlive.com
Grant County 106 Second Ave PO Box 164 ... Carson ND 58529 701-622-3615 622-3717
Web: grantcountynd.com
Grant County 10 Second St NE ... Elbow Lake MN 56531 218-685-4825 685-5349
Web: www.co.grant.mn.us
Grant County 35 C St NW PO Box 37 ... Ephrata WA 98823 509-754-2011 765-2160
TF: 800-572-0119 ■ *Web:* www.grantcountywa.gov
Grant County 105 E Harrison St ... Hyannis NE 69350 308-458-2422 471-4020*
**Fax Area Code: 402 ■ *Web:* local.dmv.org
Grant County 111 S Jefferson St ... Lancaster WI 53813 608-723-2675 723-4048
Web: www.grantcounty.org
Grant County 101 E Fourth St ... Marion IN 46952 765-668-8121 668-6541
Web: www.grantcounty.net
Grant County 112 E Guthrie St Rm 105 ... Medford OK 73759 580-395-2284
Web: grantcountyok.com
Grant County 210 E 5th Ave ... Milbank SD 57252 605-432-6711 432-9004*
**Fax: Acctg ■ *Web:* grantcounty.sd.gov
Grant County PO Box 114 ... Petersburg WV 26847 304-257-2168 257-5454
Web: www.grantcounty-wv.com
Grant County 101 W Ctr St ... Sheridan AR 72150 870-942-2631 942-3564
Web: grantcountyar.com
Grant County 1400 Hwy 180 ... Silver City NM 88061 575-574-0000 574-0073
Web: www.grantcountynm.com
Grant County 108 S Glenn St ... Ulysses KS 67880 620-356-1335 356-3081
Web: www.grantcoks.org
Grant County 107 N Main St ... Williamstown KY 41097 859-824-3321 824-3367
Web: grantcounty.ky.gov
Grant Parish 512 Main St PO Box 208 ... Colfax LA 71417 318-627-3274 627-5931
Web: www.gpsb.org
Granville County
141 Williamsboro St PO Box 1286 ... Oxford NC 27565 919-693-4761
Web: www.granvillecounty.org
Gratiot County
County Courthouse 214 E Ctr St PO Box 437 ... Ithaca MI 48847 989-875-5215 875-5254
Web: www.gratiotmi.com
Graves County 101 E S St ... Mayfield KY 42066 270-247-3626 247-1274
Web: gravescounty.ky.gov
Gray County PO Box 487 ... Cimarron KS 67835 620-855-3618 855-3107
Web: www.grayco.org
Gray County PO Box 1902 ... Pampa TX 79066 806-669-8004 669-8054
Web: www.co.gray.tx.us
Grays Harbor County 100 W Bdwy ... Montesano WA 98563 360-249-3842 249-6381
Web: www.co.grays-harbor.wa.us
Grayson County 129 Davis St PO Box 130 ... Independence VA 24348 276-773-2231 773-3338
Web: www.courts.state.va.us
Grayson County 100 W Houston St ... Sherman TX 75090 903-813-4207 868-9691
Web: www.co.grayson.tx.us
Grayson County Chamber of Commerce
425 S Main St ... Leitchfield KY 42754 270-259-5587
Web: www.graysoncountychamber.com
Greeley County PO Box 287 ... Greeley NE 68842 308-428-3625 428-3022
Web: greeleycounty.ne.gov
Greeley County 510 Broadway PO Box 656 ... Tribune KS 67879 620-376-2548 376-2549
TF: 888-204-1781 ■ *Web:* www.greeleycounty.org
Green County 203 W Ct St ... Greensburg KY 42743 270-932-4024 932-3635
Web: www.greencounty.ky.gov
Green County 1016 16th Ave ... Monroe WI 53566 608-328-9430 328-2835
TF: 800-947-3529 ■ *Web:* www.co.green.wi.gov
Green Lake County 492 Hill St ... Green Lake WI 54941 920-294-4005 294-4009
Web: www.co.green-lake.wi.us
Greenbrier County 200 W Washington St ... Lewisburg WV 24901 304-647-6602
TF: 800-833-2068 ■ *Web:* www.greenbrierwv.com
Greene County 411 Main St ... Catskill NY 12414 518-719-3270 719-3793
Web: www.greenegovernment.com
Greene County 400 Morrow Ave ... Eutaw AL 35462 205-372-3349
Web: www.greenecountyalabama.com
Greene County 204 N Cutler St ... Greeneville TN 37745 423-798-1708
Web: www.greenecountytngov.com
Greene County 1034 Silver Dr ... Greensboro GA 30642 706-453-7716 453-9555
Web: www.greenecountyga.gov
Greene County 114 N Chestnut St ... Jefferson IA 50129 515-386-2516 386-2321
Web: www.co.greene.ia.us
Greene County 450 High St ... Jackson MS 39201 601-359-3694 359-2407
Web: mssc.state.ms.us
Greene County 301 N Greene St ... Snow Hill NC 28580 252-747-4700
Web: www.co.greene.nc.us
Greene County 940 N Boonville Ave ... Springfield MO 65802 417-868-4055 868-4170
Web: www.greenecountymo.org
Greene County 22 Ct St ... Stanardsville VA 22973 434-985-5208 985-6723
Web: www.greenecountyva.gov
Greene County 35 Green St ... Xenia OH 45385 937-562-5006 562-5331
Web: www.co.greene.oh.us
Greenlee County 223 Fifth St ... Clifton AZ 85533 928-865-2072 865-4417
Web: www.co.greenlee.az.us
Greensville County 337 S Main St ... Emporia VA 23847 434-348-4215 348-4020
Web: www.greensvillecountyva.gov
Greenup County 301 Main St ... Greenup KY 41144 606-473-7394 473-5354
Web: greenupcountyclerk.com
Greenville County 305 E N St ... Greenville SC 29601 864-467-8551 467-8540
Web: www.greenvillecounty.org
Greenwood County 311 N Main St ... Eureka KS 67045 620-583-8121 583-8124
Web: www.greenwoodcounty.org

Phone Fax

Greenwood County
600 Monument St Park Plaza Ste 102
PO Box P-103 ... Greenwood SC 29646 864-942-8502 942-8566
Web: www.greenwoodsc.gov
Greer County 119 E Jefferson St ... Mangum OK 73554 580-782-2444 782-2229
Web: www.greercountychamber.com
Gregg County 101 E Methvin Ste 200 ... Longview TX 75601 903-236-8430 237-2574
Web: www.co.gregg.tx.us
Grenada County 59 Green St Ste 8 ... Grenada MS 38902 662-226-1941 227-2865
Web: www.grenadamississippi.com
Griggs County 808 Rollin Ave SW ... Cooperstown ND 58425 701-797-3613
Web: www.cooperstownnd.com
Grundy County 68 Cumberland St PO Box 177 ... Altamont TN 37301 931-692-3721 692-3718
Web: www.grundycountytn.net
Grundy County 706 G Ave ... Grundy Center IA 50638 319-824-5229
Web: www.grundycounty.org
Grundy County PO Box 675 ... Morris IL 60450 815-941-3222 942-2222
Web: www.grundyco.org
Grundy County 700 Main St ... Trenton MO 64683 660-359-4040 359-6786
Web: grundycountymo.com
Guadalupe County 211 W Ct St ... Seguin TX 78155 830-303-4188 401-0300
Web: www.co.guadalupe.tx.us
Guernsey County 627 Wheeling Ave Ste 300 ... Cambridge OH 43725 740-432-9200 432-9359
Web: www.guernseycounty.org
Guilford County PO Box 3427 ... Greensboro NC 27402 336-641-7556
Web: www.co.guilford.nc.us
Gulf County
1000 Cecil Costin Sr Blvd Rm 148 ... Port Saint Joe FL 32456 850-229-6112 229-6174
Web: www.gulfcounty-fl.gov
Gunnison County 221 N Wisconsin St Ste C ... Gunnison CO 81230 970-641-1516 641-7956
Web: gunnisoncounty.org
Guthrie County 200 N Fifth St ... Guthrie Center IA 50115 641-747-3415
Web: guthriecounty.org
Gwinnett County
75 Langley Dr
Gwinnett Justice & Administration Ctr ... Lawrenceville GA 30045 770-822-8000 822-7097
Web: www.gwinnettcounty.com
Haakon County 140 Howard Ave PO Box 70 ... Philip SD 57567 605-859-2627 859-2257
Web: ujs.sd.gov/County_Information/haakon.aspx
Habersham County 555 Monroe St Ste 20 ... Clarkesville GA 30523 706-839-0200 839-0219
Web: www.habershamga.com
Haines Borough 103 Third Ave S PO Box 1209 ... Haines AK 99827 907-766-2231 766-2716
Web: www.hainesalaska.gov
Hale County
Hale County Sheriff's office PO Box 160 ... Greensboro AL 36744 334-624-7719
Hale County 500 Broadway Rm 140 ... Plainview TX 79072 806-291-5261
Web: whc.net
Halifax County 33 S Granville St ... Halifax NC 27839 252-583-1131 583-9921
Web: www.halifaxnc.com
Halifax County 134 S Main St ... Halifax VA 24558 434-476-3300 476-3384
Web: www.halifaxcountyva.gov
Hall County 225 Green St SE ... Gainesville GA 30501 770-531-7025 531-7070
Web: www.hallcounty.org
County Courthouse 512 Main St Ste 1 ... Memphis TX 79245 806-259-2627 259-5078
Web: www.texasfile.com
Hamblen County
2415 N Davy Crockett Pkwy (Hwy 25E) ... Morristown TN 37814 423-586-1993 318-2508
Web: www.hamblencountytn.gov
Hamilton County 1111 13th St Ste 1 ... Aurora NE 68818 402-694-3443
Web: www.co.hamilton.ne.us
Hamilton County 625 Georgia Ave Rm 201 ... Chattanooga TN 37402 423-209-6500 209-6501
Web: www.hamiltontn.gov
Hamilton County 138 E Ct St Rm 603 ... Cincinnati OH 45202 513-946-4400 946-4444
Web: www.hamilton-co.org
Hamilton County
County Courthouse 102 N Rice Ste 107 ... Hamilton TX 76531 254-386-3518 386-8727
Web: www.hamiltoncountytx.org
Hamilton County 207 NE First St Rm 106 ... Jasper FL 32052 386-792-1288 792-3524
Web: www.hamiltoncountyflorida.com
Hamilton County 102 County View Dr ... Lake Pleasant NY 12108 518-548-7111 548-9740
Web: www.hamiltoncounty.com
Hamilton County
1 Hamilton County Sq Ste 106 ... Noblesville IN 46060 317-776-9629 776-9664
Web: hamiltoncounty.in.gov
Hamilton County PO Box 1167 ... Syracuse KS 67878 620-384-5629 384-5853
Web: www.syracuseks.gov
Hamilton County 2300 Superior St ... Webster City IA 50595 515-832-9535 832-9514
Web: www.hamiltoncounty.org
Hamlin County 300 Fourth St PO Box 208 ... Hayti SD 57241 605-783-3232 783-1330
Web: hamlincountysheriff.com
Hampden County 50 State St ... Springfield MA 01102 413-748-8600
Web: hcbar.org
Hampshire County 99 Main St ... NorthHampton MA 01060 413-584-1300 584-1465
Web: www.hampshirecog.org
Hampshire County 66 N High St ... Romney WV 26757 304-822-5112 822-4039
Web: hampshirecountyclerk.weebly.com
Hampton County
201 Jackson Ave W
B T Deloach Administrative Bldg ... Hampton SC 29924 803-914-2103 914-2107
Web: www.hamptoncountysc.org
Hampton (Independent City) 22 Lincoln St ... Hampton VA 23669 757-727-8311
Web: hampton.gov
Hancock County 854 Highway 90 Ste A ... Bay Saint Louis MS 39520 228-467-2100 467-2503
Web: www.hancockcounty.ms.gov
Hancock County PO Box 39 ... Carthage IL 62321 217-357-3911
Hancock County 50 State St Ste 7 ... Ellsworth ME 04605 207-667-9542 667-1412
Web: www.co.hancock.me.us
Hancock County 300 S Main St ... Findlay OH 45840 419-424-7037 424-7801
Web: www.co.hancock.oh.us
Hancock County PO Box 70 ... Garner IA 50438 641-923-2532
Web: www.hancockcountyia.org
Hancock County 9 E Main St ... Greenfield IN 46140 317-477-1135
Web: www.hancockcoingov.org

Name / Address	City	State	Zip	Phone	Fax
Hancock County 225 Main Cross St *Web:* www.hancockky.us	Hawesville	KY	42348	270-927-6117	
Hancock County PO Box 367 *Web:* www.hancockcountywv.org	New Cumberland	WV	26047	304-564-3311	564-5941
Hancock County 418 Harrison St PO Box 575 *Web:* www.hancockcountytn.com	Sneedville	TN	37869	423-733-2519	733-4509
Hancock County 12630 Broad St *TF:* 800-255-0135 ■ *Web:* hancockcountyga.gov	Sparta	GA	31087	706-444-5746	444-6221
Hand County 415 W First Ave *Web:* ujs.sd.gov	Miller	SD	57362	605-853-3337	853-3779
Hanover County 7497 County Complex Rd *Web:* hanovercounty.gov	Hanover	VA	23069	804-365-6000	365-6234
Hansford County 15 NW Ct *Web:* www.co.hansford.tx.us	Spearman	TX	79081	806-659-4110	659-4168
Hanson County 720 5th St PO Box 127 *Web:* ujs.sd.gov	Alexandria	SD	57311	605-239-4446	239-9446
Haralson County 70 Murphy Campus Blvd *Web:* www.haralson.org	Waco	GA	30182	770-537-5594	537-5873
Hardee County 412 W Orange St Rm A-203 *Web:* www.hardeecounty.net	Wauchula	FL	33873	863-773-6952	773-0958
Hardeman County 100 N Main St *Web:* hardemancountytn.com	Bolivar	TN	38008	731-658-3541	
Hardeman County PO Box 30 *Web:* hardemantx.com	Quanah	TX	79252	940-663-2911	663-6302
Hardin County 1215 Edgington Ave County Courthouse *Web:* www.co.hardin.ia.us	Eldora	IA	50627	641-939-8109	939-8245
Hardin County PO Box 124 *Web:* www.hardincountyil.org	Elizabethtown	IL	62931	618-287-4333	
Hardin County 14 Public Sq *Web:* www.hccoky.org	Elizabethtown	KY	42701	270-765-2171	765-6193
Hardin County 1 Courthouse Sq Ste 100 *Web:* www.co.hardin.oh.us	Kenton	OH	43326	419-674-2205	
Hardin County 495 Main St *TF:* 800-552-3866 ■ *Web:* www.tourhardincounty.org	Savannah	TN	38372	731-925-3921	925-6987
Harding County 410 Ramsland St PO Box 534 *Web:* ujs.sd.gov	Buffalo	SD	57720	605-375-3351	375-3432
Hardy County 204 Washington St Rm 111 *TF:* 800-222-1222 ■ *Web:* hardycounty.com	Moorefield	WV	26836	304-530-0250	530-0251
Harlan County 311 Main St *TF:* 800-762-5498 ■ *Web:* www.harlantourism.org	Alma	NE	68920	800-762-5498	
Harlan County 201 S Main St *Web:* www.harlancountytrails.com	Harlan	KY	40831	606-573-4495	573-9485
Harnett County PO Box 759 *Web:* www.harnett.org	Lillington	NC	27546	910-893-7555	814-2662
Harney County 450 N Buena Vista Ste 14 *Web:* www.co.harney.or.us	Burns	OR	97720	541-573-6641	573-8370
Harper County 201 N Jennings Ave *TF:* 877-537-2110 ■ *Web:* www.harpercountyks.gov	Anthony	KS	67003	620-842-5555	842-3455
Harper County 311 SE 1st	Buffalo	OK	73834	580-735-2010	
Harris County 112 S College St PO Box 426 *TF:* 888-478-0010 ■ *Web:* www.harriscountychamber.org	Hamilton	GA	31811	706-628-0010	628-4429
Harris County 201 Caroline St 4th Fl *Web:* harriscountytx.gov	Houston	TX	77002	713-755-5000	
Harrison County 1501 Main St PO Box 169 *Web:* harrisoncountysheriffmo.org	Bethany	MO	64424	660-425-3199	
Harrison County 100 W Market St *Web:* www.harrisoncountyohio.org	Cadiz	OH	43907	740-942-8510	
Harrison County 301 W Main St County Courthouse *Web:* www.harrisoncountywv.com	Clarksburg	WV	26301	304-624-8500	624-8673
Harrison County 300 N Capitol Ave Rm 203 *Web:* harrisoncounty.in.gov	Corydon	IN	47112	812-738-4289	738-3126
Harrison County 313 Oddville Ave *Web:* www.harrisoncountyfiscalcourt.com	Cynthiana	KY	41031	859-234-7130	234-8049
Harrison County 1801 23rd Ave *Web:* www.co.harrison.ms.us	Gulfport	MS	39501	228-865-4036	868-1480
Harrison County 111 N Second Ave *Web:* www.harrisoncountyia.org	Logan	IA	51546	712-644-3123	644-2643
Harrison County Clerk 200 W Houston PO Box 1365 Ste 143	Marshall	TX	75671	903-935-8403	
Harrisonburg (Independent City) 345 S Main St *Web:* www.harrisonburgva.gov	Harrisonburg	VA	22801	540-432-7701	432-7778
Hart County 800 Chandler St *Web:* www.hartcountyga.org	Hartwell	GA	30643	706-376-2024	376-9477
Hart County 200 Main St *Web:* www.hartcounty.ky.gov	Munfordville	KY	42765	270-524-2751	524-0458
Hartley County 900 Main St *Web:* www.co.hartley.tx.us	Channing	TX	79018	806-235-3582	235-2316
Harvey County 800 N Main PO Box 687 *Web:* www.harveycounty.com	Newton	KS	67114	316-284-6840	284-6856
Haskell County 1 Ave D *Web:* www.co.haskell.tx.us	Haskell	TX	79521	940-864-3448	
Haskell County 202 E Main St *Web:* haskell.oklahoma.usassessor.com	Stigler	OK	74462	918-967-2611	967-4640
Haskell County PO Box 518 *Web:* www.haskellcounty.org	Sublette	KS	67877	620-675-2263	675-2681
Hawaii County 1055 Kinoole St Ste 101 *Web:* www.hawaiicounty.gov	Hilo	HI	96720	808-961-8255	961-8603
Hawkins County 110 E Main St *Web:* www.hawkinscountytn.gov	Rogersville	TN	37857	423-272-7002	
Hayes County 505 Troth St PO Box 370 *Web:* www.hayescounty.ne.gov	Hayes Center	NE	69032	308-286-3413	286-3208
Hays County 110 E Martin Luther King St *Web:* www.co.hays.tx.us	San Marcos	TX	78666	512-393-7738	393-7735
Haywood County 1 N Washington St *Web:* www.haywoodcountybrownsville.com	Brownsville	TN	38012	731-772-1432	772-3864
Haywood County 1233 N Main St Annex II *Web:* www.haywoodnc.net	Waynesville	NC	28786	828-452-6633	452-6750
Heard County PO Box 40 *Web:* www.heardcountyga.com	Franklin	GA	30217	706-675-3821	675-2493
Hemphill County 400 Main St Ste 200 *Web:* co.hemphill.tx.us	Canadian	TX	79014	806-323-6521	323-5260
Hempstead County 400 S Washington Hope *Web:* www.hempsteadcountyar.com	Hope	AR	71801	870-777-6164	
Henderson County 125 N Prairieville St Rm 101 PO Box 632 *Web:* henderson-county.com	Athens	TX	75751	903-675-6140	675-6105
Henderson County 145 N Main St Ste 500	Henderson	KY	42420	270-826-7505	
Henderson County 1 Historic Courthouse Sq *Web:* www.hendersoncountync.org	Hendersonville	NC	28792	828-697-4808	692-9855
Henderson County 17 Monroe Ave Ste 2 *Web:* hendersoncountytn.gov	Lexington	TN	38351	731-968-2856	968-6644
Henderson County PO Box 308 *Web:* www.cyberdriveillinois.com	Oquawka	IL	61469	309-867-2911	
Hendricks County 1 Courthouse Sq *Web:* www.co.hendricks.in.us	Danville	IN	46122	317-745-9231	745-9306
Hendry County PO Box 1760 *Web:* www.hendryfla.net	LaBelle	FL	33975	863-675-5217	
Hennepin County 300 S Sixth St *Web:* hennepin.us	Minneapolis	MN	55487	612-348-3081	348-8701
Henrico County 4301 E Parham Rd *Web:* henrico.us	Henrico	VA	23228	804-501-4000	501-5214
Henry County 101 Ct Sq Ste H	Abbeville	AL	36310	334-585-2753	
Henry County 307 W Ctr St *Web:* www.henrycty.com	Cambridge	IL	61238	309-937-3578	
Henry County 100 W Franklin St *Web:* henrycomo.com	Clinton	MO	64735	660-885-7204	
Henry County PO Box 7 *Web:* www.henrycountyva.gov/Collinsville-District.html	Collinsville	VA	24078	276-634-4601	634-4781
Henry County 140 Henry Pkwy *Web:* www.co.henry.ga.us	McDonough	GA	30253	770-954-2400	288-7616
Henry County 100 E Washington St *Web:* www.henrycountyiowa.us	Mount Pleasant	IA	52641	319-385-2632	385-4144
Henry County 1853 Oakwood Ave *Web:* www.henrycountyohio.com	Napoleon	OH	43545	419-592-4876	
Henry County 1215 Race St PO Box B *Web:* www.henryco.net	New Castle	IN	47362	765-529-6401	521-7046
Henry County PO Box 202 *Web:* www.henryweb.com	New Castle	KY	40050	502-845-5707	
Henry County 101 W Washington St *Web:* henrycountytn.org	Paris	TN	38242	731-642-5212	642-6531
Herkimer County 109 Mary St Ste 1111 *Web:* www.herkimercounty.org	Herkimer	NY	13350	315-867-1129	867-1349
Hernando County 16110 Aviation Loop Dr *Web:* www.co.hernando.fl.us	Brooksville	FL	34604	352-754-4000	754-4477
Hettinger County 336 Pacific Ave *Web:* www.hettingercounty.net	Mott	ND	58646	701-824-4227	
Hickman County 114 N Central Ave # 202 *Web:* www.hickmancountytn.com	Centerville	TN	37033	931-729-2621	729-9951
Hickman County 110 E Clay St County Courthouse *Web:* hickmancountyclerkky.com	Clinton	KY	42031	270-653-2131	
Hickory County 100 New Hermitage Dr *Web:* www.hickorylibrary.org	Hermitage	MO	65668	417-745-6939	745-2132
Hidalgo County 100 N Closner *TF:* 888-318-2811 ■ *Web:* tx-hidalgocounty.civicplus.com	Edinburg	TX	78539	956-318-2100	318-2105
Highland County 119 Governor Foraker Pl *Web:* www.co.highland.oh.us	Hillsboro	OH	45133	937-393-1911	393-5850
Highland County Main St *Web:* www.highlandcova.org	Monterey	VA	24465	540-468-2347	468-3447
Highlands County 430 S Commerce Ave *Web:* www.hcbcc.net	Sebring	FL	33870	863-402-6500	402-6507
Hill County 315 Fourth St *Web:* www.hillcounty.us	Havre	MT	59501	406-265-5481	265-3693
Hill County PO Box 398 *Web:* www.co.hill.tx.us	Hillsboro	TX	76645	254-582-4030	582-4003
Hillsborough County 329 Mast Rd *Web:* www.hillsboroughcountynh.org	Goffstown	NH	03045	603-627-5600	627-5603
Hillsborough County 800 E Twigg St *Web:* www.hillsboroughcounty.org	Tampa	FL	33602	813-276-8100	
Hillsdale County 29 N Howell St *Web:* www.co.hillsdale.mi.us	Hillsdale	MI	49242	517-437-3391	437-3392
Hinds County 316 S President St *Web:* www.co.hinds.ms.us	Jackson	MS	39205	601-968-6501	968-6794
Hinsdale County 311 N Henson St *TF:* 877-944-7575 ■ *Web:* www.hinsdalecountycolorado.us	Lake City	CO	81235	970-944-2225	944-2630
Hitchcock County 229 E D St *Web:* hitchcockcounty.ne.gov	Trenton	NE	69044	308-334-5646	334-5398
Hocking County 1 E Main St *Web:* www.co.hocking.oh.us	Logan	OH	43138	740-385-3000	385-7413
Hockley County 802 Houston St Ste 213 *Web:* www.co.hockley.tx.us	Levelland	TX	79336	806-894-4404	
Hodgeman County PO Box 247 *Web:* www.hodgemancountyks.com	Jetmore	KS	67854	620-357-6421	357-6313
Hoke County 227 N Main St *Web:* www.hoke-raeford.com	Raeford	NC	28376	910-875-8751	
Holmes County 106 E Byrd Ave *Web:* www.holmescountyonline.com	Bonifay	FL	32425	850-547-6153	
Holmes County 6 W Jackson St *Web:* holmescountychamber.com	Millersburg	OH	44654	330-674-3975	
Holmes County Chamber of Commerce 104 W China St *Web:* www.holmescountymississippi.com	Lexington	MS	39095	662-834-3372	834-4544
Holt County 204 N Fourth St PO Box 329 *Web:* www.co.holt.ne.us	O'Neill	NE	68763	402-336-1762	336-1762
Holt County 102 W Nodaway St PO Box 437 *Web:* holtcounty.org	Oregon	MO	64473	660-446-3303	446-3353
Honolulu City & County 530 S King St Rm 100 *Web:* www.honolulu.gov	Honolulu	HI	96813	808-768-3810	768-3835
Hood County 100 E Pearl St Ste 5 *Web:* www.co.hood.tx.us	Granbury	TX	76048	817-579-3222	579-3227

	City	State	Zip	Phone	Fax
Hood River County 601 State St *Web:* www.co.hood-river.or.us	Hood River	OR	97031	541-386-3970	386-9392
Hooker County PO Box 184 *Web:* www.co.hooker.ne.us	Mullen	NE	69152	308-546-2244	546-2490
Hopewell (Independent City) 300 N Main St Rm 217 *Web:* www.hopewellva.gov	Hopewell	VA	23860	804-541-2243	541-2248
Hopkins County 24 Union St *Web:* www.hopkinscountykentucky.org	Madisonville	KY	42431	270-821-7361	
Hopkins County 118 Church St *Web:* www.hopkinscountytx.org	Sulphur Springs	TX	75482	903-438-4074	
Horry County 1301 Second Ave *Web:* www.horrycounty.org	Conway	SC	29526	843-915-5080	915-6081
Hot Spring County 210 Locust St	Malvern	AR	72104	501-332-2291	
Hot Springs County 415 Arapahoe St *Web:* www.hscounty.com	Thermopolis	WY	82443	307-864-3515	864-3333
Houghton County 401 E Houghton Ave *Web:* www.houghtoncounty.net	Houghton	MI	49931	906-482-1150	483-0364
Houston County PO Box 370 *Web:* www.co.houston.tx.us	Crockett	TX	75835	936-544-3255	544-8061
Houston County 68 S Spring St PO Box 603 *Web:* www.houstoncochamber.com	Erin	TN	37061	931-289-5100	
Houston County 200 Carl Vinson Pkwy *Web:* www.houstoncountyga.com	Warner Robins	GA	31088	478-542-2115	923-5697
Howard County 300 Main St *Web:* www.co.howard.tx.us	Big Spring	TX	79720	432-264-2213	264-2215
Howard County 3430 Courthouse Dr *Web:* www.co.ho.md.us	Ellicott City	MD	21043	410-313-2022	313-3051
Howard County 1 Courthouse Sq *Web:* www.courts.mo.gov	Fayette	MO	65248	660-248-2194	
Howard County 104 N Buckeye St Ste 114 *Web:* www.howardcountyin.gov	Kokomo	IN	46901	765-456-2204	456-2267
Howard County 421 N Main St Rm 10 *Web:* howardcountytaxcollection.com	Nashville	AR	71852	870-845-7508	845-7505
Howard County PO Box 25 *Web:* www.howardcounty.ne.gov	Saint Paul	NE	68873	308-754-4343	754-4266
Howell County 35 Court Sq *Web:* www.howellcounty.net	West Plains	MO	65775	417-256-2591	
Hubbard County 301 Ct Ave County Courthouse *Fax: Acctg ■ *Web:* www.co.hubbard.mn.us	Park Rapids	MN	56470	218-732-2300	732-3645*
Hudson County 257 Cornelison Ave 4th Fl *Web:* www.hudsoncountyclerk.org	Jersey City	NJ	07302	201-369-3470	369-3478
Hudspeth County 109 Brown St *TF:* 888-368-4689 ■ *Web:* www.txdmv.gov	Sierra Blanca	TX	79851	915-369-2331	369-3005
Huerfano County 401 Main St Ste 201 *Web:* www.huerfano.us	Walsenburg	CO	81089	719-738-2370	738-3996
Hughes County 104 East Capitol Ave PO Box 1238	Pierre	SD	57501	405-379-2746	
Hughes County 104 E Capitol Ave PO Box 1238 *Web:* ujs.sd.gov	Pierre	SD	57501	605-773-3713	773-3875
Humboldt County 203 Main St *Web:* www.humboldtcountyia.org	Dakota City	IA	50529	515-332-1571	
Humboldt County 825 5th St *Web:* www.humboldtgov.org	Eureka	CA	95501	707-445-7256	445-7041
Humboldt County 50 W Fifth St *Web:* www.hcnv.us	Winnemucca	NV	89445	775-623-6300	623-6302
Humphreys County PO Box 547y PO Box 547 *Web:* humphreys.msghn.org	Belzoni	MS	39038	662-247-1740	
Humphreys County 102 Thompson St *Web:* www.humphreystn.com	Waverly	TN	37185	931-296-7795	
Hunt County PO Box 1316 *Web:* www.huntcounty.net	Greenville	TX	75403	903-408-4130	
Hunterdon County 71 Main St *Web:* www.co.hunterdon.nj.us	Flemington	NJ	08822	908-788-1221	782-4068
Huntingdon County 223 Penn St County Courthouse *Web:* www.huntingdoncounty.net	Huntingdon	PA	16652	814-643-3091	643-8152
Huntington County 201 N Jefferson St County Courthouse Rm 103 *Web:* www.huntington.in.us	Huntington	IN	46750	260-358-4804	358-4823
Huron County 250 E Huron Ave Rm 305 *Web:* www.huroncounty.com	Bad Axe	MI	48413	989-269-6431	269-6152
Huron County County Courthouse 2 E Main St 2nd Fl *Web:* www.hccommissioners.com	Norwalk	OH	44857	419-668-5113	
Hutchinson County PO Box 1186 *Web:* www.co.hutchinson.tx.us	Stinnett	TX	79083	806-878-4002	
Hyde County 30 Oyster Creek Rd *Web:* hydecountync.gov	Swanquarter	NC	27885	252-926-4178	926-3701
Iberia Parish 300 Iberia St Ste 400 *Web:* www.iberiaparishgovernment.com	New Iberia	LA	70560	337-365-8246	369-4470
Iberville Parish 58050 Meriam St *Web:* www.ibervilleparish.com	Plaquemine	LA	70764	225-687-5160	
Ida County 401 Moorehead St *Web:* idacounty.org	Ida Grove	IA	51445	712-364-2626	
Idaho County 320 W Main St Rm 5 *Web:* www.idahocounty.org	Grangeville	ID	83530	208-983-2751	
Imperial County 940 W Main St Rm 202 *Web:* www.co.imperial.ca.us	El Centro	CA	92243	760-482-4427	482-4271
Independence County 192 E Main St *Web:* www.independencecounty.com	Batesville	AR	72501	870-793-8800	793-8803
Indian River County 1801 27th St *Web:* www.ircgov.com	Vero Beach	FL	32960	772-567-8000	978-1822
Indiana County 350 N Fourth St *TF:* 888-559-6355 ■ *Web:* www.countyofindiana.org	Indiana	PA	15701	724-465-3805	465-3179
Ingham County 315 S Jefferson St PO Box 179 *Web:* www.ingham.org	Mason	MI	48854	517-676-7201	676-7254
Inyo County PO Box N *Web:* www.inyocounty.us	Independence	CA	93526	760-878-0292	878-2241
Ionia County 100 W Main St *Web:* www.ioniacounty.org	Ionia	MI	48846	616-527-5322	527-8201
Iosco County 422 W Lake St *Web:* www.iosco.net	Tawas City	MI	48763	989-362-3485	
Iowa County 222 N Iowa St Ste 102 *Web:* www.iowacounty.org	Dodgeville	WI	53533	608-935-0318	935-3024
Iowa County PO Box 266 *Web:* www.co.iowa.ia.us	Marengo	IA	52301	319-642-3914	
Iredell County 200 S Ctr St PO Box 788 *Web:* www.co.iredell.nc.us	Statesville	NC	28687	704-878-3000	878-5355
Irion County PO Box 736 *Web:* www.co.irion.tx.us	Mertzon	TX	76941	325-835-2421	835-2008
Iron County 2 S Sixth St	Crystal Falls	MI	49920	906-875-3221	875-6775
Iron County 300 Taconite St Ste 101 *Web:* www.co.iron.wi.gov	Hurley	WI	54534	715-561-3375	561-2928
Iron County 220 S Shepherd St *Web:* icsomo.org	Ironton	MO	63650	573-546-7051	
Iron County 68 S 100 E *Web:* www.ironcounty.net	Parowan	UT	84761	435-477-8360	477-8847
Iroquois County 1001 E Grant St Rm 106 *Web:* www.co.iroquois.il.us	Watseka	IL	60970	815-432-6978	432-6999
Irwin County 301 E 1st St *Web:* irwincountyrealty.com	Ocilla	GA	31774	229-468-0050	
Isabella County 200 N Main St *Web:* www.isabellacounty.org	Mount Pleasant	MI	48858	989-772-0911	773-7431
Isanti County 555 18th Ave SW *Web:* www.co.isanti.mn.us	Cambridge	MN	55008	763-689-3859	689-8226
Island County 1 NE Seventh St *Web:* www.islandcountywa.gov/pages/home.aspx	Coupeville	WA	98239	360-679-7354	679-7381
Isle of Wight County 17090 Monument Cir # 123 *Web:* www.co.isle-of-wight.va.us	Isle of Wight	VA	23397	757-365-6204	357-9171
Itasca County 123 NE Fourth St *Web:* www.co.itasca.mn.us	Grand Rapids	MN	55744	218-327-2847	327-2848
Itawamba County 107 W Wiygul St *Web:* itawambams.com	Fulton	MS	38843	662-862-2159	862-3421
Izard County 400 Ct St *Web:* izardcountyar.org	Melbourne	AR	72556	870-368-4316	
Jack County 100 Main St *Web:* jackcounty.org	Jacksboro	TX	76458	940-567-2111	
Jackson County 307 Main St *Web:* www.co.jackson.wi.us	Black River Falls	WI	54615	715-284-0208	284-0270
Jackson County PO Box 318 *Web:* www.jacksoncounty.in.gov	Brownstown	IN	47220	812-358-6116	358-6187
Jackson County 115 W Main St Rm 101 *Web:* www.co.jackson.tx.us	Edna	TX	77957	361-782-3563	
Jackson County 101 E Hull Ave *Web:* www.jacksoncotn.com	Gainesboro	TN	38562	931-268-9888	
Jackson County 400 New York Ave Rm 202 *Web:* ks-jackson.manatron.com	Holton	KS	66436	785-364-2358	364-5257
Jackson County 405 Fourth St Ste 5 *Web:* www.co.jackson.mn.us	Jackson	MN	56143	507-847-2763	847-4718
Jackson County 275 Portsmouth St *Web:* www.jacksoncountyohio.us	Jackson	OH	45640	740-286-3301	286-4754
Jackson County 67 Athens St *Web:* www.jacksoncountygov.com	Jefferson	GA	30549	706-367-6312	367-9083
Jackson County 700 S Main *Web:* ujs.sd.gov/County_Information/jackson.aspx	Kadoka	SD	57543	605-837-2122	837-2120
Jackson County 415 E 12th St *Web:* 16thcircuit.org	Kansas City	MO	64106	816-881-3000	
Jackson County 201 W Platt St *Web:* www.co.jackson.ia.us	Maquoketa	IA	52060	563-652-3144	652-4738
Jackson County 5000 General Jackson Pkwy *Web:* www.jacksoncounty.com	Jefferson	GA	30549	850-482-8060	
Jackson County PO Box 175 *Web:* www.jacksoncounty.ky.gov	McKee	KY	40447	606-287-8562	287-7190
Jackson County 10 S Oakdale Ave Rm 214 Courthouse *Web:* www.co.jackson.or.us	Medford	OR	97501	541-774-6035	774-6455
Jackson County 1001 Walnut St County Courthouse *Web:* www.co.jackson.il.us	Murphysboro	IL	62966	618-687-7360	687-7359
Jackson County 3405 S Main St PO Box 155 *TF:* 800-234-1040 ■ *Web:* jacksoncountyema.us	Newport	AR	72043	870-523-6011	
Jackson County PO Box 998 *Web:* www.co.jackson.ms.us	Pascagoula	MS	39568	228-769-3040	769-3348
Jackson County 100 Ct St N *Web:* jacksoncounty.wv.gov	Ripley	WV	25271	304-373-2250	
Jackson County 102 E Laurel St *Web:* jacksoncountyal.com	Scottsboro	AL	35768	256-574-9280	574-9321
Jackson County 401 Grindstaff Cove Rd *Web:* www.jacksonnc.org	Sylva	NC	28779	828-586-4055	
Jackson County 404 Fourth St *Web:* www.jacksoncountyco.com	Walden	CO	80480	970-723-4660	
Jackson County Courthouse, The 101 N Main St *Web:* jackson.okcounties.org	Altus	OK	73521	580-482-2370	
Jackson Parish 500 E Ct St Ste 103 *Web:* www.jacksonparishpolicejury.org	Jonesboro	LA	71251	318-259-2424	
James City County PO Box 8784 *Web:* www.jamescitycountyva.gov	Williamsburg	VA	23187	757-253-6728	253-6833
Jasper County PO Box 611 *Web:* www.co.jasper.ms.us	Bay Springs	MS	39422	601-764-2700	764-3999
Jasper County 302 S Main St Rm 102 *Web:* www.jaspercounty.org	Carthage	MO	64836	417-358-0416	358-0415
Jasper County 121 N Austin *Web:* www.co.jasper.tx.us	Jasper	TX	75951	409-384-6226	384-7198
Jasper County 126 W Greene St Ste 18 *Web:* jaspercountyga.org	Monticello	GA	31064	706-468-4900	468-4942
Jasper County 101 First St N *Web:* www.co.jasper.ia.us	Newton	IA	50208	641-792-7016	792-1053
Jasper County 204 W Washington St Ste 2 *Web:* www.jaspercountyillinois.org/localgovernment.php	Newton	IL	62448	618-783-3124	
Jasper County 115 W Washington St Ste 204 *Web:* www.jaspercountyin.com	Rensselaer	IN	47978	219-866-4926	

	City	State	Zip	Phone	Fax
Jasper County PO Box 248	Ridgeland	SC	29936	843-726-7710	
Web: www.jaspercountychamber.com					
Jay County 504 W Arch St	Portland	IN	47371	260-726-8080	726-2220
Web: www.co.jay.in.us					
Jeff Davis County 100 Ct Ave	Fort Davis	TX	79734	432-426-3251	
Web: www.co.jeff-davis.tx.us					
Jefferson County 114 Pearl St	Beaumont	TX	77701	409-835-8475	839-2394
Web: www.co.jefferson.tx.us					
Jefferson County 716 Richard Arrington Jr Blvd N Ste 210	Birmingham	AL	35203	205-325-5555	325-4860
Web: jeffconline.jccal.org					
Jefferson County 210 W Centennial Ave	Boulder	MT	59632	406-225-4020	225-4149
Web: www.jeffersoncounty-mt.gov					
Jefferson County 155 Main St 2nd Fl	Brookville	PA	15825	814-849-3696	849-4084
Web: jeffersoncountypa.com					
Jefferson County PO Box 208	Charles Town	WV	25414	304-728-3215	
Web: www.jeffersoncountywv.org					
Jefferson County PO Box 890	Dandridge	TN	37725	865-397-9642	397-0164
TF: 877-237-3847 ■ *Web:* www.jefferson-tn-chamber.org					
Jefferson County 411 Fourth St	Fairbury	NE	68352	402-793-5585	
Web: www.co.jefferson.ne.us					
Jefferson County 51 W Briggs Ave	Fairfield	IA	52556	641-472-3235	
Web: www.jeffersoncountyiowa.com/court.htm					
Jefferson County 1483 Main St PO Box 145	Fayette	MS	39069	601-786-3021	786-6009
Web: jeffersoncountyms.gov					
Jefferson County 100 Jefferson County Pkwy	Golden	CO	80419	303-279-6511	271-8197
Web: www.jeffco.us					
Jefferson County 729 Maple St	Hillsboro	MO	63050	636-797-5466	797-5360
Web: www.jeffcomo.org					
Jefferson County 320 S Main St Rm 109	Jefferson	WI	53549	920-674-7140	674-7368
Web: www.wisconline.com/counties/jefferson					
Jefferson County 217 E Broad St	Louisville	GA	30434	478-625-3332	625-4007
Web: www.jeffersoncounty.org					
Jefferson County 300 E Main St	Madison	IN	47250	812-265-8900	
Web: jeffersoncounty.in.gov					
Jefferson County 66 SE 'D' St Ste C	Madras	OR	97741	541-475-4451	325-5018
Web: co.jefferson.or.us					
Jefferson County 300 Jefferson St PO Box 321	Oskaloosa	KS	66066	785-863-2461	863-3135
Web: www.jfcountyks.com					
Jefferson County 1820 Jefferson St	Port Townsend	WA	98368	360-385-9100	385-9382
Web: www.co.jefferson.wa.us					
Jefferson County 210 Courthouse Way Ste 100	Rigby	ID	83442	208-745-7756	745-9397
Web: www.co.jefferson.id.us					
Jefferson County 301 Market St Courthouse	Steubenville	OH	43952	740-283-8500	283-8599
Web: www.jeffersoncountyoh.com					
Jefferson County 175 Arsenal St	Watertown	NY	13601	315-785-3081	785-5145
Web: www.co.jefferson.ny.us					
Jefferson County 220 N Main St Rm 103	Waurika	OK	73573	580-228-2029	
Web: prsearch.com					
Jefferson Davis County 1025 Third St PO Box 342	Prentiss	MS	39474	601-792-5903	792-0291
Web: www.jeffdavisms.com					
Jefferson Parish 200 Derbigny St Ste 3100	Gretna	LA	70053	504-364-2600	
Web: www.jeffparish.net					
Jenkins County 548 Cotton Ave	Millen	GA	30442	478-982-5595	
Web: www.jenkinscountyga.com					
Jennings County 25 N Pike St	Vernon	IN	47282	812-352-3070	
Web: jenningscounty-in.gov					
Jerauld County 205 S Wallace	Wessington Springs	SD	57382	605-539-1202	539-1203
Web: ujs.sd.gov/County_Information/jerauld.aspx					
Jerome County 300 N Lincoln Ave	Jerome	ID	83338	208-644-2715	
Web: jeromecountyid.us					
Jersey County 209 N State St	Jerseyville	IL	62052	618-498-5571	
Web: www.jerseycounty.org					
Jessamine County 101 N Main St	Nicholasville	KY	40356	859-885-4161	
Web: www.jessamineco.com					
Jim Hogg County 102 E Tilley St	Hebbronville	TX	78361	361-527-4031	
Jim Wells County PO Box 1459	Alice	TX	78333	361-668-5702	
Web: www.co.jim-wells.tx.us					
Jo Daviess County 330 N Bench St	Galena	IL	61036	815-777-0161	777-3688
Web: www.jodaviess.org					
Johnson County 76 N Main St	Buffalo	WY	82834	307-684-7272	684-2708
Web: www.johnsoncountywyoming.org					
Johnson County 215 Main St	Clarksville	AR	72830	479-754-2175	
Web: local.arkansas.gov					
Johnson County 204 S Buffalo Ave	Cleburne	TX	76033	817-556-6323	
Web: www.johnsoncountytx.org					
Johnson County 5 E Jefferson St 1st Fl	Franklin	IN	46131	317-346-4700	736-3749
Web: co.johnson.in.us					
Johnson County 913 S Dubuque St	Iowa City	IA	52240	319-356-6093	337-0495
Web: www.johnson-county.com					
Johnson County 222 W Main St	Mountain City	TN	37683	423-727-9633	727-7047
Web: www.tn.gov					
Johnson County 111 S Cherry St Ste 1200	Olathe	KS	66061	913-715-0775	715-0800
TF: 800-766-3777 ■ *Web:* jocogov.org					
Johnson County 351 Broadway	Tecumseh	NE	68450	402-335-6300	335-6311
Web: www.co.johnson.ne.us					
Johnson County PO Box 96	Vienna	IL	62995	618-658-3611	658-9665
Web: theviennatimes.com					
Johnson County 300 N Holden St	Warrensburg	MO	64093	660-747-6161	
Johnson County 2557 E Elm St	Wrightsville	GA	31096	478-864-3484	864-1343
Web: www.johnsonco.org					
Johnson County Clerk 230 Ct St	Paintsville	KY	41240	606-789-2557	
Web: johnsoncountyclerkky.com					
Johnston County 207 E Johnston St PO Box 1049	Smithfield	NC	27577	919-989-5100	989-5179
Web: www.johnstonnc.com					
Johnston County 403 W Main St	Tishomingo	OK	73460	405-379-5280	
Web: oklahoma.usassessor.com					
Jones County 500 W Main St	Anamosa	IA	52205	319-462-2282	
Web: www.jonescountyiowa.org					
Jones County PO Box 552	Anson	TX	79501	325-823-3762	823-4223
Web: www.co.jones.tx.us					
Jones County PO Box 1359	Gray	GA	31032	478-986-6405	986-6462
Web: www.jonescountyga.org					
Jones County PO Box 527	Laurel	MS	39441	601-649-3031	428-2047
Web: www.jonescounty.com					
Jones County 310 Main St PO Box 448	Murdo	SD	57559	605-669-2361	669-2641
Web: ujs.sd.gov/County_Information/jones.aspx					
Jones County 101 Market St	Trenton	NC	28585	252-448-7351	
Web: www.jonescountync.gov					
Josephine County 500 NW Sixth St	Grants Pass	OR	97526	541-474-5240	474-5246
Web: www.co.josephine.or.us					
Juab County 160 N Main St	Nephi	UT	84648	435-623-3410	
Web: www.co.juab.ut.us					
Judith Basin County 91 Third St N PO Box 339	Stanford	MT	59479	406-566-2277	
Web: co.judith-basin.mt.us					
Juneau City & Borough 155 S Seward St	Juneau	AK	99801	907-586-5278	586-5385
Web: www.juneau.org					
Juneau County 220 Wisconsin 82 Trunk	Mauston	WI	53948	608-847-9300	
Web: www.juneaucounty.com					
Juniata County 498 Jefferson St	Mifflintown	PA	17059	717-436-5152	436-7734
Web: www.co.juniata.pa.us					
Kalamazoo County 201 W Kalamazoo Ave	Kalamazoo	MI	49007	269-383-8840	384-8143
Web: www.kalcounty.com					
Kalkaska County 605 N Birch St	Kalkaska	MI	49646	231-258-3336	
Web: www.tcchamber.org					
Kanabec County 18 N Vine St	Mora	MN	55051	320-679-6466	679-6431
Web: www.kanabeccounty.org					
Kanawha County 409 Virginia St E	Charleston	WV	25301	304-357-0130	357-0585
Web: www.kanawha.us					
Kandiyohi County PO Box 936	Willmar	MN	56201	320-231-6202	231-6263
Web: www.co.kandiyohi.mn.us					
Kane County 719 Batavia Ave Bldg A	Geneva	IL	60134	630-232-5930	232-9188
Web: www.countyofkane.org					
Kane County 78 S 100 E	Kanab	UT	84741	435-644-5033	
TF: 800-733-5263 ■ *Web:* www.visitsouthernutah.com					
Kankakee County 189 E Ct St	Kankakee	IL	60901	815-937-2990	939-8831
Web: www.co.kankakee.il.us					
Karnes County 101 N Panna Maria Ave Ste 9	Karnes City	TX	78118	830-780-3938	780-4576
Web: www.co.karnes.tx.us					
Kauai County 4386 Rice St Ste 101	Lihue	HI	96766	808-241-4800	241-6207
Web: www.kauai.gov					
Kaufman County 100 W Mulberry St	Kaufman	TX	75142	972-932-4331	
Web: www.kaufmancounty.net					
Kay County 201 S Main St	Newkirk	OK	74647	580-362-2565	362-3668
Web: www.courthouse.kay.ok.us					
Kearney County 424 N Colorado Ave	Minden	NE	68959	308-832-2723	832-2729
Web: www.kearneycounty.ne.gov					
Kearny County PO Box 86	Lakin	KS	67860	620-355-6422	355-7382
Web: www.kearnycountykansas.com					
Keith County 511 N Spruce St Ste 102	Ogallala	NE	69153	308-284-4726	284-6277
Web: www.co.keith.ne.us					
Kemper County PO Box 188	De Kalb	MS	39328	601-743-2754	
Web: countycriminal.com/court-records					
Kenai Peninsula Borough 144 N Binkley St	Soldotna	AK	99669	907-262-4441	262-8615
Web: www.kpb.us					
Kendall County 201 E San Antonio St	Boerne	TX	78006	830-249-9343	249-1763
Web: www.co.kendall.tx.us					
Kendall County 111 W Fox St	Yorkville	IL	60560	630-553-4104	553-4119
Web: www.co.kendall.il.us					
Kenedy County 139 N Main	Sarita	TX	78385	361-294-5785	294-5788
Web: www.co.kenedy.tx.us					
Kennebec County 125 State St	Augusta	ME	04330	207-622-0971	623-4083
Web: www.kennebeccounty.org					
Kenosha County 1010 56th St	Kenosha	WI	53140	262-653-2552	653-2564
Web: www.co.kenosha.wi.us					
Kent County 400 High St	Chestertown	MD	21620	410-778-7435	778-7482
Web: www.kentcounty.com					
Kent County 555 S Bay Rd	Dover	DE	19901	302-744-2305	736-2279
Web: www.co.kent.de.us					
Kent County 300 Monroe Ave NW	Grand Rapids	MI	49503	616-632-7640	632-7645
Web: www.accesskent.com					
Kent County PO Box 9	Jayton	TX	79528	806-237-3801	
Web: kentcountysherifftx.com					
Kenton County 303 Ct St	Covington	KY	41011	859-392-1600	
Web: www.kentoncounty.org					
Keokuk County 101 S Main St	Sigourney	IA	52591	641-622-2210	622-2171
Web: www.keokukcountyia.com					
Kern County 1115 Truxtun Ave 5th Fl	Bakersfield	CA	93301	661-868-3198	868-3190
Web: www.co.kern.ca.us					
Kerr County 700 Main St Rm 122	Kerrville	TX	78028	830-792-2255	895-1861
Web: www.co.kerr.tx.us					
Kershaw County 1121 Broad St Rm 202	Camden	SC	29020	803-425-7226	425-6044
Web: www.kershaw.sc.gov					
Ketchikan Gateway Borough 1900 First Ave Ste 115	Ketchikan	AK	99901	907-228-6604	247-8439
Web: www.borough.ketchikan.ak.us					
Kewaunee County 613 Dodge St	Kewaunee	WI	54216	920-388-7144	
Web: www.kewauneeco.org					
Keweenaw County 902 College Ave	Houghton	MI	49931	906-482-5240	
Web: www.keweenaw.org					
Keya Paha County PO Box 349	Springview	NE	68778	402-497-3791	497-3799
Web: www.co.keya-paha.ne.us					
Kidder County 120 E Broadway Kidder County Courthouse	Steele	ND	58482	701-475-2632	475-2202
Web: ndcourts.gov					
Kimball County 114 E Third St	Kimball	NE	69145	308-235-2241	235-3654
Web: www.co.kimball.ne.us					
Kimble County 501 Main St Courthouse	Junction	TX	76849	325-446-3353	446-2986
Web: www.co.kimble.tx.us					

County	City	State	Zip	Phone	Fax
King & Queen County 242 Allens Cir Ste L PO Box 177 *Web:* www.kingandqueenco.net	King & Queen Court House	VA	23085	804-785-5975	785-5999
King County PO Box 66 *Web:* www.tdcj.state.tx.us	Guthrie	TX	79236	806-596-4470	
King County 401 5th Ave Ste 800 *TF:* 800-325-6165 ■ *Web:* www.kingcounty.gov	Seattle	WA	98104	206-296-1586	296-0194
King George County 9483 Kings Hwy Ste 3 *Web:* www.king-george.va.us	King George	VA	22485	540-775-3322	775-5466
King William County 351 Courthouse Ln PO Box 215 *Web:* www.kingwilliamcounty.us	King William	VA	23086	804-769-4938	
Kingfisher County 101 S Main St	Kingfisher	OK	73750	405-375-3887	
Kingman County 130 N Spruce St *Web:* kingmancoks.com	Kingman	KS	67068	620-532-2521	
Kings County 360 Adams St Rm 189 *Web:* www.nycourts.gov/courts/2jd/kingsclerk	Brooklyn	NY	11201	347-404-9772	
Kings County 680 Campus Dr *Web:* www.countyofkings.com	Hanford	CA	93230	559-582-3211	582-6639
Kingsbury County 202 2nd St SE *Web:* ujs.sd.gov	De Smet	SD	57231	605-854-3811	854-9080
Kinney County 501 S Ann St *Web:* www.co.kinney.tx.us	Brackettville	TX	78832	830-563-2521	563-2644
Kiowa County 1305 Goff *Web:* onlinedmv.com	Eads	CO	81036	719-438-5421	
Kiowa County 211 E Florida Ave *Web:* kiowacountyks.org	Greensburg	KS	67054	620-723-3366	723-3234
Kiowa County 302 N. Lincoln	Hobart	OK	73651	580-726-5286	
Kit Carson County 251 16th St # 103 *Web:* www.kitcarsoncounty.org	Burlington	CO	80807	719-346-8638	346-7242
Kitsap County 614 Div St MS 4 *Web:* www.kitsapgov.com	Port Orchard	WA	98366	360-337-7146	337-4632
Kittitas County 205 W Fifth Ave Ste 108 *Web:* www.co.kittitas.wa.us	Ellensburg	WA	98926	509-962-7508	962-7679
Kittson County 410 Fifth St SE Ste 214 *Web:* www.visitnwminnesota.com	Hallock	MN	56728	218-843-2655	
Klamath County 305 Main St *TF:* 800-377-6094 ■ *Web:* www.klamathcounty.org	Klamath Falls	OR	97601	541-883-5134	883-5165
Kleberg County PO Box 1327 *Web:* www.co.kleberg.tx.us	Kingsville	TX	78364	361-595-8548	593-1355
Klickitat County 205 S Columbus Ave Rm 204 MS CH 10 *Web:* www.klickitatcounty.org	Goldendale	WA	98620	509-773-5744	773-4559
Knox County PO Box 196 *Web:* www.knoxcountytexas.org	Benjamin	TX	79505	940-459-2441	459-2005
Knox County 206 Main St *Web:* www.co.knox.ne.us	Center	NE	68724	402-288-5604	288-5605
Knox County 200 S Cherry St *Web:* www.knoxcountyil.com	Galesburg	IL	61401	309-343-3121	
Knox County 400 W Main St Ste 603 *Web:* www.knoxcounty.org	Knoxville	TN	37902	865-215-2534	215-2038
Knox County 117 E High St Ste 161 *Web:* www.co.knox.oh.us	Mount Vernon	OH	43050	740-393-6703	393-6705
Knox County 62 Union St *Web:* knoxcountymaine.gov	Rockland	ME	04841	207-594-0420	594-0443
Knox County 316 Main St *Web:* www.knoxcountychamber.com	Vincennes	IN	47591	812-882-6440	
Kodiak Island Borough 710 Mill Bay Rd *Web:* www.kodiakak.us	Kodiak	AK	99615	907-486-9300	
Koochiching County 715 Fourth St *Web:* www.co.koochiching.mn.us	International Falls	MN	56649	218-283-1152	283-1151
Kootenai County 451 N Government Way *Web:* www.co.kootenai.id.us	Coeur d'Alene	ID	83814	208-446-1000	446-1188
Kosciusko County 121 N Lake St *Web:* www.kcgov.com	Warsaw	IN	46580	574-372-2331	
Kossuth County 114 W State St *Web:* www.co.kossuth.ia.us	Algona	IA	50511	515-295-2718	295-3071
La Crosse County 400 N Fourth St Rm 1210 *Web:* www.co.la-crosse.wi.us	La Crosse	WI	54601	608-785-9581	785-9741
La Paz County 1108 S Joshua Ave *Web:* www.co.la-paz.az.us	Parker	AZ	85344	928-669-6115	669-9709
La Plata County 1060 E Second Ave Ste 134 *Web:* www.co.laplata.co.us	Durango	CO	81301	970-382-6280	382-6285
La Porte County 813 Lincolnway *TF:* 800-654-3441 ■ *Web:* www.laportecounty.org	La Porte	IN	46350	219-326-6808	
La Salle County 101 Courthouse Sq Ste 107 *Web:* www.co.la-salle.tx.us	Cotulla	TX	78014	830-879-4432	483-5101
Labette County 501 Merchant St *Web:* www.labettecounty.com	Oswego	KS	67356	620-795-2138	795-2928
Lac qui Parle County (LQP) 600 Sixth St *Web:* www.lqpco.com	Madison	MN	56256	320-598-7444	598-3125
Lackawanna County 436 Spruce St *Web:* www.lackawannacounty.org	Scranton	PA	18503	570-963-6723	963-6387
Laclede County 200 N Adams Ave *Web:* www.lacledecountymissouri.org	Lebanon	MO	65536	417-532-5471	588-9288
Lafayette Consolidated Government 705 W University Ave PO Box 4017-C *Web:* www.lafayettegov.org	Lafayette	LA	70506	337-291-8200	
Lafayette County 626 Main St PO Box 40 *Web:* www.co.lafayette.wi.gov	Darlington	WI	53530	608-776-4850	776-8893
Lafayette County 1 Courthouse Sq *Web:* lafayettecounty.arkansas.gov	Lewisville	AR	71845	870-921-4858	921-4505
Lafayette County 1001 Main St *Web:* www.lafayettecountymo.com	Lexington	MO	64067	660-259-4315	259-6109
Lafayette County 300 N Lamar Blvd *Web:* www.lafayettecoms.com	Oxford	MS	38655	662-236-2717	234-5402
Lafourche Parish 402 Green St PO Box 5548 *TF:* 800-834-8832 ■ *Web:* www.lafourchegov.org	Thibodaux	LA	70302	985-446-8427	446-8459
LaGrange County 114 W Michigan St *Web:* lagrangecounty.org	LaGrange	IN	46761	260-499-6300	

County	City	State	Zip	Phone	Fax
Lake County 895 Michigan Ave PO Box 130 *TF:* 800-245-3240 ■ *Web:* www.lakecountymichigan.com	Baldwin	MI	49304	231-745-4331	
Lake County 2293 N Main St *Web:* www.lakecountyin.org	Crown Point	IN	46307	219-755-3535	
Lake County 255 N Forbes St *Web:* www.co.lake.ca.us	Lakeport	CA	95453	707-263-2371	263-2207
Lake County 513 Ctr St *Web:* www.lakecountyor.org	Lakeview	OR	97630	541-947-6006	947-6015
Lake County PO Box 917 *Web:* www.lakecountyco.com	Leadville	CO	80461	719-486-1410	486-3972
Lake County 200 E Ctr St *Web:* ujs.sd.gov/County_Information/lake.aspx	Madison	SD	57042	605-256-5644	256-5080
Lake County 25 N Pk Pl *Web:* www.lakecountyohio.org	Painesville	OH	44077	440-350-2500	
Lake County 106 Fourth Ave E *Web:* lakemt.gov	Polson	MT	59860	406-883-7208	883-7283
Lake County 550 W Main St *Web:* lakecountyfl.gov	Tavares	FL	32778	352-742-4102	
Lake County 601 Third Ave *Web:* www.co.lake.mn.us	Two Harbors	MN	55616	218-834-8300	834-8360
Lake County 18 N County St *Web:* www.lakecountyil.gov	Waukegan	IL	60085	847-377-2000	
Lake of the Woods County 206 Eigth Ave SE *Web:* www.co.lake-of-the-woods.mn.us	Baudette	MN	56623	218-634-2836	634-2509
Lamar County 408 Thomaston St Ste E *Web:* www.lamarcountyga.com	Barnesville	GA	30204	770-358-5146	358-5149
Lamar County 119 N Main St Rm 109 *Web:* www.co.lamar.tx.us	Paris	TX	75460	903-737-2420	782-1100
Lamar County 403 Main St **Fax:* Administration ■ *Web:* www.lamarcounty.com	Purvis	MS	39475	601-794-3406	794-1049*
Lamb County 100 6th St	Littlefield	TX	79339	806-385-4222	385-6485
Lamoille County PO Box 455 *Web:* www.lamoilleeconomy.org	Morrisville	VT	05661	802-888-5640	851-1136
LaMoure County PO Box 217 *Web:* www.lamourend.com	La Moure	ND	58458	701-883-5987	
Lampasas County 409 Pecan St PO Box 347 *Web:* www.co.lampasas.tx.us	Lampasas	TX	76550	512-556-8271	556-8270
Lancaster County 50 N Duke St *Web:* www.co.lancaster.pa.us	Lancaster	PA	17602	717-299-8000	293-7208
Lancaster County PO Box 1809 *Web:* mylancastersc.org	Lancaster	SC	29721	803-285-1581	
Lancaster County 8265 Mary Ball Rd *Web:* www.courts.state.va.us	Lancaster	VA	22503	804-462-5611	462-9978
Lancaster County 555 S Tenth St Rm 108 *Web:* www.lancaster.ne.gov	Lincoln	NE	68508	402-441-7481	441-8728
Lander County 315 S Humboldt St *Web:* landercountynv.org	Battle Mountain	NV	89820	775-635-5738	
Lane County PO Box 290 *Web:* www.kansastreasurers.org	Dighton	KS	67839	620-397-2802	397-2802
Lane County 125 E Eigth Ave *Web:* www.lanecounty.org	Eugene	OR	97401	541-682-4203	682-4616
Langlade County 800 Clermont St *Web:* www.co.langlade.wi.us	Antigo	WI	54409	715-627-6200	627-6303
Lanier County 56 W Main St Ste 9 *Web:* www.laniercountyboc.com	Lakeland	GA	31635	229-482-2088	
Lapeer County 255 Clay St *Web:* lapeercountyweb.org	Lapeer	MI	48446	810-667-0356	
Laramie County 309 W 20th St *Web:* laramiecountyclerk.com	Cheyenne	WY	82001	307-633-4264	633-4240
Larimer County 1 Old Town Sq *Web:* www.larimer.org	Fort Collins	CO	80524	970-498-7860	498-7906
LaRue County 209 W High St *Web:* www.laruecounty.org	Hodgenville	KY	42748	270-358-3544	358-4528
Las Animas County 200 E First St Rm 204 *Web:* lasanimascounty.org	Trinidad	CO	81082	719-846-2981	845-2591
LaSalle County 707 E Etna Rd *TF:* 800-247-5243 ■ *Web:* www.lasallecounty.org	Ottawa	IL	61350	815-433-3366	433-9522
LaSalle Parish PO Box 1288 *Web:* www.lpgov.org	Jena	LA	71342	318-992-2101	992-2103
Lassen County 220 S Lassen St Ste 5 *Web:* www.lassencounty.org	Susanville	CA	96130	530-251-8217	257-3480
Latah County 522 S Adams St PO Box 8068 *Web:* www.latah.id.us	Moscow	ID	83843	208-882-8580	883-7203
Latimer County 109 N Central St Rm 109 *Web:* www.latimer.okcountytreasurers.com	Wilburton	OK	74578	918-465-3450	465-4005
Lauderdale County PO Box 1059 *Web:* www.lauderdalecountyonline.com	Florence	AL	35631	256-760-5750	
Lauderdale County 410 Constitution Ave 11th Fl *Web:* www.lauderdalecounty.org	Meridian	MS	39301	601-482-9746	
Lauderdale County 123 S Jefferson St *Web:* www.lauderdalecountytn.org	Ripley	TN	38063	731-635-9541	
Laurel County 101 S Main St Rm 203 *Web:* laurelcountyclerk.com	London	KY	40741	606-864-5158	
Laurens County 117 E Jackson St *Web:* www.laurenscoga.org	Dublin	GA	31040	478-272-4755	272-3895
Laurens County 100 Hillcrest Sq # B *Web:* www.laurenscountysc.org	Laurens	SC	29360	864-984-3538	984-3726
Lavaca County 412 N Texana *Web:* www.co.lavaca.tx.us	Hallettsville	TX	77964	361-798-3612	798-1610
Lawrence County 916 15th St Ste 31 *Web:* www.bedfordonline.com	Bedford	IN	47421	812-275-7543	278-8845
Lawrence County 90 Sherman St **Fax:* Acctg ■ *Web:* www.lawrence.sd.us	Deadwood	SD	57732	605-578-1941	578-1065*
Lawrence County 111 S Fourth St Ste 11 *Web:* www.lawrencecountyohio.org	Ironton	OH	45638	740-533-4355	
Lawrence County 240 W Gaines St *Web:* lawcotn.org	Lawrenceburg	TN	38464	931-762-7700	
Lawrence County 12521 Hwy 157 Ste L *Web:* www.lawrencealabama.com	Moulton	AL	35650	256-974-1658	974-2400

	City	State	Zip	Phone	Fax
Lawrence County 1 Courthouse Sq PO Box 188 *Web:* lawrencecountymoassessor.com	Mount Vernon	MO	65712	417-466-2831	466-3931
Lawrence County County Courthouse 430 Court St *TF:* 855-564-6116 ■ *Web:* www.co.lawrence.pa.us	New Castle	PA	16101	724-658-2541	652-9646
Lawrence County 315 W Main *Web:* www.lawrencecountysheriffsoffice.com	Walnut Ridge	AR	72476	870-886-2525	
Le Sueur County 88 S Pk Ave *Web:* www.co.le-sueur.mn.us	Le Center	MN	56057	507-357-2251	357-6433
Lea County 100 N Main St Ste 11 *Web:* www.leacounty.net	Lovington	NM	88260	575-396-8619	396-3293
Leake County 103 N Pearl St *Web:* www.leakems.com	Carthage	MS	39051	601-267-9231	
Leavenworth County 300 Walnut St *TF:* 855-893-9533 ■ *Web:* www.leavenworthcounty.org	Leavenworth	KS	66048	913-684-0421	
Lebanon County 400 S Eigth St Rms 102 Municipal Bldg *Web:* www.lebcounty.org	Lebanon	PA	17042	717-228-4419	
Lee County PO Box G *Web:* www.leecounty.ky.gov	Beattyville	KY	41311	606-464-4100	464-4145
Lee County 112 E Second St PO Box 329 *Web:* leecountyil.com	Dixon	IL	61021	815-288-3309	288-6492
Lee County 933 Ave H *Web:* www.leecounty.org	Fort Madison	IA	52627	319-372-6557	372-8200
Lee County PO Box 398 *Web:* www.leegov.com	Fort Myers	FL	33902	239-533-2259	
Lee County PO Box 419 *Web:* www.co.lee.tx.us	Giddings	TX	78942	979-542-3684	542-2623
Lee County 110 Starksville Avenue North *Web:* www.lee.ga.us	Leesburg	GA	31763	229-759-6000	
Lee County 15 E Chestnut St *Web:* lee.ark.org	Marianna	AR	72360	870-295-7715	
Lee County 7992 Villanow Dr *Web:* www.leecountync.gov	Sanford	NC	27332	919-718-4605	
Lee County 510 N Commerce St *Web:* www.leecosheriff.com	Tupelo	MS	38804	662-841-9040	
Leelanau County 8527 E Government Ctr Dr *TF:* 866-256-9711 ■ *Web:* www.leelanau.cc	Suttons Bay	MI	49682	231-256-9824	256-0174
LeFlore County 100 S Broadway PO Box 100 *Web:* leflore.okcountytreasurers.com	Poteau	OK	74953	918-647-3525	647-7122
Leflore County PO Box 848 *Web:* www.greenwoodms.com	Greenwood	MS	38935	662-453-4152	
Lehigh County 455 W Hamilton St Rm 132 *Web:* www.lehighcounty.org	Allentown	PA	18101	610-782-3148	
Lemhi County 206 Courthouse Dr *Web:* www.lemhicountyidaho.org	Salmon	ID	83467	208-756-2815	756-8424
Lenawee County 425 N Main St Third Fl Judicial Bldg *Web:* www.lenawee.mi.us	Adrian	MI	49221	517-264-4599	264-4790
Lenoir County 130 S Queen St PO Box 3289 *Web:* www.co.lenoir.nc.us	Kinston	NC	28502	252-559-6450	559-6454
Leon County PO Box 98 *Web:* www.co.leon.tx.us	Centerville	TX	75833	903-536-2352	
Leslie County PO Box 619 *Web:* www.lesliecounty.ky.gov	Hyden	KY	41749	606-672-3200	672-7373
Letcher County 156 Main St Ste 102 *Web:* letchercounty.ky.gov	Whitesburg	KY	41858	606-633-2129	633-7105
Levy County 355 S Ct St PO Box 310 *Web:* www.levycounty.org	Bronson	FL	32621	352-486-5218	486-5167
Lewis & Clark County 316 N Pk Ave *Web:* www.lccountymt.gov	Helena	MT	59623	406-447-8200	447-8370
Lewis County 7660 N State St *Web:* www.lewiscountyny.org	Lowville	NY	13367	315-376-5333	376-3768
Economic Development 106 N Ct St PO Box 10	Hohenwald	TN	38462	931-796-6012	796-6020
Lexington (Independent City) 300 E Washington St *Web:* lexingtonva.gov	Lexington	VA	24450	540-462-3700	463-5310
Lexington-Fayette County 162 E Main St *Web:* local.dmv.org	Lexington	KY	40507	859-253-3344	231-9619
Liberty County PO Box 523 *Web:* www.libertycountyflorida.com	Bristol	FL	32321	850-643-2359	
Liberty County 112 N Main St *Web:* www.libertycounty.org	Hinesville	GA	31310	912-876-2164	
Liberty County 1923 Sam Houston St *Web:* www.co.liberty.tx.us	Liberty	TX	77575	936-336-4600	336-4640
Licking County 20 S Second St *Web:* www.lcounty.com	Newark	OH	43055	740-670-5110	670-5119
Limestone County 310 W Washington St *Web:* limestonelicense.com	Athens	AL	35611	256-233-6430	
Lincoln County PO Box 978 *TF:* 800-613-4667 ■ *Web:* brookhavenchamber.org	Brookhaven	MS	39602	601-833-1411	
Lincoln County 104 N Main St **Fax:* Acctg ■ *Web:* www.lincolncountysd.org	Canton	SD	57013	605-764-2581	764-0134*
Lincoln County 300 Central Ave	Carrizozo	NM	88301	575-648-2385	
Lincoln County 800 Manvel Ave	Chandler	OK	74834	405-258-1264	
Lincoln County 450 Logan St *Web:* www.co.lincoln.wa.us	Davenport	WA	99122	509-725-1401	725-1150
Lincoln County 112 Main St S *Web:* www.lincolncountytngov.com	Fayetteville	TN	37334	931-433-3045	433-9304
Lincoln County PO Box 497 *Web:* www.lincolncountywv.org	Hamlin	WV	25523	304-824-7990	824-2444
Lincoln County 103 Third Ave *Web:* www.lincolncountyco.us	Hugo	CO	80821	719-743-2444	743-2524
Lincoln County 319 N Rebecca St **Fax:* Acctg ■ *Web:* www.co.lincoln.mn.us	Ivanhoe	MN	56142	507-694-1529	694-1198*
Lincoln County 925 Sage Ave *TF:* 800-442-9001 ■ *Web:* www.lcwy.org	Kemmerer	WY	83101	307-877-9056	877-3101
Lincoln County 512 California Ave *Web:* www.lincolncountymt.us	Libby	MT	59923	406-293-7781	293-8577
Lincoln County 216 E Lincoln Ave *Web:* www.lincolncoks.com	Lincoln	KS	67455	785-524-4757	524-5008
Lincoln County 210 Humphrey St *Web:* www.lcgagov.org	Lincolnton	GA	30817	706-359-4444	359-4729
Lincoln County 115 W Main St *Web:* www.co.lincoln.nc.us	Lincolnton	NC	28092	704-736-8471	736-8718
Lincoln County 1110 E Main St *Web:* www.co.lincoln.wi.us	Merrill	WI	54452	715-536-6200	536-6528
Lincoln County 225 W Olive St Rm 201 *Web:* www.co.lincoln.or.us	Newport	OR	97365	541-265-4131	265-4950
Lincoln County 301 N Jeffers St *Web:* www.co.lincoln.ne.us	North Platte	NE	69101	308-534-4350	535-3527
Lincoln County PO Box 90 *Web:* www.co.lincoln.nv.us	Pioche	NV	89043	775-962-5390	962-5180
Lincoln County 111 W 'B' St Ste C *Web:* www.lincolncountyid.us	Shoshone	ID	83352	208-886-7641	886-2798
Lincoln County 102 E Main St County Courthouse *Web:* www.lincolnky.com	Stanford	KY	40484	606-365-2534	365-4514
Lincoln County 201 Main St *Web:* lincolncountycollector.com/office-information	Troy	MO	63379	636-528-6300	
Lincoln County PO Box 249 *Web:* www.lincolncountymaine.me	Wiscasset	ME	04578	207-882-6311	882-4320
Lincoln Parish 100 W Texas Ave *Web:* www.lincolnparish.org	Ruston	LA	71270	318-251-5150	
Linn County 300 Fourth Ave SW *Web:* www.co.linn.or.us	Albany	OR	97321	541-967-3831	926-5109
Linn County 123 Fifth St SE *Web:* www.linncounty.org	Cedar Rapids	IA	52401	319-892-5005	892-5009
Linn County 108 N High St *Web:* marcelinemo.us	Linneus	MO	64653	660-895-5417	895-5527
Linn County PO Box 350 *Web:* www.linncountyks.com	Mound City	KS	66056	913-795-2660	795-2004
Lipscomb County PO Box 70 *Web:* www.co.lipscomb.tx.us	Lipscomb	TX	79056	806-862-3091	862-3004
Litchfield County 6 Titus Rd PO Box 396 *Web:* www.litchfieldcty.com	Litchfield	CT	06759	860-567-5060	
Live Oak County PO Box 280 *Web:* www.co.live-oak.tx.us	George West	TX	78022	361-449-2733	
Livingston County 6 Ct St *Web:* www.co.livingston.state.ny.us	Geneseo	NY	14454	585-243-7010	
Livingston County 200 E Grand River Ave *Web:* www.livgov.com	Howell	MI	48843	517-546-0500	546-4354
Livingston County 112 W Madison St *Web:* livingstoncountyil.gov	Pontiac	IL	61764	815-844-2006	842-1844
Livingston County 335 Ct St *Web:* www.livingstonco.ky.gov	Smithland	KY	42081	270-928-2162	928-2162
Livingston Parish 20399 Government Blvd *Web:* www.livingstonparishla.gov	Livingston	LA	70754	225-686-4400	
Llano County PO Box 40 *Web:* www.co.llano.tx.us	Llano	TX	78643	325-247-4455	247-2406
Logan County 117 E Columbus St *Web:* www.co.logan.oh.us	Bellefontaine	OH	43311	937-599-7283	599-7268
Logan County Courthouse Sq	Booneville	AR	72855	501-963-2618	
Logan County 601 Broadway St PO Box 278 *Web:* www.co.logan.il.us	Lincoln	IL	62656	217-732-4148	732-6064
Logan County 300 Stratton St *Web:* www.logancounty.wv.gov	Logan	WV	25601	304-792-8626	792-8511
Logan County 710 W 2nd St *Web:* kansastreasurers.org	Oakley	KS	67748	785-671-3216	671-0065
Logan County 116 S Main St PO Box 358 *Web:* www.loganchamber.com	Russellville	KY	42276	270-726-2206	
Logan County 317 Main St PO Box 8 *Web:* www.stapleton-ne.com	Stapleton	NE	69163	308-636-2441	636-2678
Logan County 315 Main St Ste 3 *Web:* www.colorado.gov	Sterling	CO	80751	970-522-1544	522-2063
Logan County Oklahoma 301 E Harrison Ste 102 *Web:* logancountyok.com	Guthrie	OK	73044	405-282-0266	282-0267
Long County 459 S McDonald St *Web:* longcountyboc.com	Ludowici	GA	31316	912-545-2143	545-2150
Lonoke County 301 N Ctr St *Web:* www.lonokecircuitclerk.com	Lonoke	AR	72086	501-676-2368	
Lorain County 225 Ct St *Web:* www.loraincounty.us	Elyria	OH	44035	440-329-5536	329-5404
Los Angeles County 500 W Temple St *Web:* www.lacounty.gov	Los Angeles	CA	90012	213-974-1311	680-1122
Loudon County 100 River Rd *Web:* www.loudoncounty.org	Loudon	TN	37774	865-458-5411	
Loudoun County 1 Harrison St SE PO Box 7000 *Web:* www.loudoun.gov	Leesburg	VA	20177	703-777-0200	777-0325
Louisa County 1 Woolfolk Ave *Web:* www.louisacounty.com	Louisa	VA	23093	540-967-0401	967-3411
Louisa County 117 S Main St *Web:* www.louisacountyiowa.org	Wapello	IA	52653	319-523-4541	523-4542
Louisville-Jefferson County 527 W Jefferson St *Web:* www.louisvilleky.gov	Louisville	KY	40202	502-574-3427	
Loup County 408 Fourth St PO Box 187 *Web:* www.co.loup.ne.us	Taylor	NE	68879	308-942-6146	942-3103
Love County 405 W Main St Ste 203 *Web:* love.okcounties.org	Marietta	OK	73448	580-276-3059	
Loving County 100 Bell St PO Box 194	Mentone	TX	79754	806-775-1338	
Lowndes County 505 Second Ave N	North Columbus	MS	39701	662-329-5884	
Lowndes County 325 W Savannah Ave *Web:* www.lowndescounty.com	Valdosta	GA	31601	229-671-2400	245-5222
Lubbock County 904 Broadway St Rm 207 *Web:* www.co.lubbock.tx.us	Lubbock	TX	79401	806-775-1000	775-7950
Lucas County 916 Braden St *Web:* lucas.iowaassessors.com	Chariton	IA	50049	641-774-4411	774-1615
Lucas County 1 Government Ctr Ste 800 *Web:* www.co.lucas.oh.us	Toledo	OH	43604	419-213-4500	213-4532
Luce County 407 W Harrie St *Web:* www.lucecountymi.com/#!92nd-district-court/c1j6s	Newberry	MI	49868	906-293-5521	

	City	State	Zip	Phone	Fax
Lumpkin County 99 Courthouse Hill Ste A	Dahlonega	GA	30533	706-864-3742	864-4760
Web: www.lumpkincounty.gov					
Lunenburg County 11413 Courthouse Rd.	Lunenburg	VA	23952	434-696-2142	
Web: www.lunenburgva.org					
Luzerne County 200 N River St	Wilkes-Barre	PA	18711	570-825-1500	825-9343
Web: www.luzernecounty.org					
Lyman County PO Box 38	Kennebec	SD	57544	605-869-2247	
Web: www.lymancounty.org					
Lynchburg (Independent City) 900 Church St	Lynchburg	VA	24504	434-856-2489	847-1536
Web: www.lynchburgva.gov					
Lynn County PO Box 937	Tahoka	TX	79373	806-561-4750	561-4988
Web: www.co.lynn.tx.us					
Lyon County PO Box 310	Eddyville	KY	42038	270-388-2331	388-0634
Web: www.lyoncounty.ky.gov					
Lyon County 430 Commercial St	Emporia	KS	66801	620-341-3243	341-3415
Web: www.lyoncounty.org					
Lyon County 607 W Main St.	Marshall	MN	56258	507-537-6722	537-6091*
**Fax:* Acctg ■ *Web:* www.lyonco.org					
Lyon County 206 S Second Ave	Rock Rapids	IA	51246	712-472-8530	
Web: www.lyoncountyiowa.com					
Lyon County 27 S Main St	Yerington	NV	89447	775-463-6501	463-5305
Web: www.lyon-county.org					
Mackinac County 100 S Marley St	Saint Ignace	MI	49781	906-643-7300	643-7302
Web: www.mackinaccounty.net					
Macomb County 40 N Main St 1st Fl	Mount Clemens	MI	48043	586-469-5120	
Web: macombgov.org					
Macon County 141 S Main St Rm 104	Decatur	IL	62523	217-424-1305	423-0922
Web: co.macon.il.us					
Macon County 5 W Main St.	Franklin	NC	28734	828-349-2025	349-2400
Web: www.maconnc.org					
Macon County 201 County Courthouse	Lafayette	TN	37083	615-666-2363	
Web: www.maconcountytn.com					
Macon County 410 N Missouri St Ste D	Macon	MO	63552	660-385-5627	
Web: www.maconcounty.org					
Macon County 109 N Dooly St	Montezuma	GA	31063	478-472-2391	
Web: www.maconcountyga.org					
Macon County 101 E Northside St Courthouse	Tuskegee	AL	36083	334-727-5120	
Web: alabama.travel					
Macoupin County 201 E Main	Carlinville	IL	62626	217-854-3214	854-7361
Web: www.macoupincountyil.gov					
Madera County 200 W Fourth St.	Madera	CA	93637	559-675-7703	673-3302
Web: www.madera-county.com					
Madison County 16 E Ninth St	Anderson	IN	46016	765-641-9419	648-1375
Web: www.madisoncty.com					
Madison County 146 W Ctr St.	Canton	MS	39046	601-859-1177	859-5875
Web: www.madison-co.com					
Madison County 91 Albany Ave	Danielsville	GA	30633	706-795-6355	795-5715
Web: www.qpublic.net					
Madison County 157 N Main St Ste 109	Edwardsville	IL	62025	618-692-6290	692-8903
Web: www.co.madison.il.us					
Madison County 1 Courthouse Sq	Fredericktown	MO	63645	573-783-6544	
Web: madisoncountymo.us					
Madison County 100 Northside Sq	Huntsville	AL	35801	256-532-3492	532-6994
Web: madisoncountyal.gov					
Madison County 201 Main St	Huntsville	AR	72740	479-738-2747	
Web: madisoncogov.com					
Madison County 100 E Main St Ste 105	Jackson	TN	38301	731-423-6022	
Web: www.co.madison.tn.us					
Madison County PO Box 618	London	OH	43140	740-852-2972	845-1660
Web: www.co.madison.oh.us					
Madison County 248 SW Range Ave PO Box 237	Madison	FL	32340	850-973-2788	973-8864
TF: 877-272-3642 ■ *Web:* www.madisonfl.org					
Madison County 1313 N Main St	Madison	NE	68748	402-454-3311	
Web: www.madisoncountyne.com					
Madison County 110 N Main St	Madison	VA	22727	540-948-4455	
Web: www.madison-va.com					
Madison County PO Box 142	Marshall	NC	28753	828-649-2531	649-0187
Web: www.madisoncountync.org					
Madison County PO Box 389	Rexburg	ID	83440	208-359-6200	356-8396
Web: www.co.madison.id.us					
Madison County 100 Wallace St PO Box 185	Virginia City	MT	59755	406-843-4230	843-5207
Web: madisoncountymt.gov					
Madison County 138 N Ct St Bldg 4 PO Box 668	Wampsville	NY	13163	315-366-2261	
Web: madisoncounty.ny.gov					
Madison County 73 Jefferson St.	Winterset	IA	50273	515-462-1185	
Web: www.madisoncounty.com					
Magoffin County 249 Mountain Pkwy Dr PO Box 430	Salyersville	KY	41465	606-349-2313	
Web: magoffincounty.ky.gov					
Mahaska County 106 S First St Mahaska Courthouse 2nd Fl	Oskaloosa	IA	52577	641-673-7786	
Web: www.mahaskacounty.org					
Mahoning County 120 Market St	Youngstown	OH	44503	330-740-2104	740-2105
Web: www.mahoningcountyoh.gov					
Major County 500 E Broadway	Fairview	OK	73737	580-227-4665	227-3243
Malheur County 251 B St W	Vale	OR	97918	541-473-5151	473-5523
Web: www.malheurco.org					
Manassas (Independent City) 9027 Ctr St.	Manassas	VA	20110	703-257-8200	335-0042
Web: www.manassascity.org					
Manassas Park (Independent City) 1 Pk Ctr Ct	Manassas Park	VA	20111	703-335-8800	335-0053
Web: www.cityofmanassaspark.us					
Manatee County 1112 Manatee Ave W.	Bradenton	FL	34205	941-748-4501	
Web: www.mymanatee.org					
Manitowoc County PO Box 2000	Manitowoc	WI	54221	920-683-4030	683-2733
Web: www.co.manitowoc.wi.us					
Marathon County 500 Forest St	Wausau	WI	54403	715-261-1500	261-1515
Web: www.co.marathon.wi.us					
Marengo County 101 E Coats Ave.	Linden	AL	36748	334-295-2200	
Web: www.marengocountyal.com					

	City	State	Zip	Phone	Fax
Maricopa County 301 W Jefferson St 10th Fl.	Phoenix	AZ	85003	602-506-3415	506-6402
Web: www.maricopa.gov					
Maries County 211 Fourth St	Vienna	MO	65582	573-422-3388	
Web: mariesco.org					
Marin County 3501 Civic Ctr Dr	San Rafael	CA	94903	415-499-6450	
Web: www.marincounty.org					
Marinette County 1926 Hall Ave	Marinette	WI	54143	715-732-7406	732-7532
Web: www.marinettecounty.com					
Marion County 250 Broad St	Columbia	MS	39429	601-736-2691	
Web: www.marioncounty-ms.us					
Marion County 200 Jackson St	Fairmont	WV	26554	304-367-5410	366-6532
Web: www.marioncountywv.com					
Marion County PO Box 1168	Hamilton	AL	35570	205-921-3561	
Web: marioncountyalabama.org					
Marion County 200 E Washington St Ste W122	Indianapolis	IN	46204	317-327-4740	
Web: www.indy.gov					
Marion County 1 Courthouse Sq	Jasper	TN	37347	423-942-2552	
Web: www.marioncountychamber.com					
Marion County 102 W Austin St	Jefferson	TX	75657	903-665-3971	
Web: www.co.marion.tx.us					
Marion County 214 E Main St Ste 10	Knoxville	IA	50138	641-828-2257	
Web: www.redrockarea.com					
Marion County 223 N Spalding Ave Ste 201	Lebanon	KY	40033	270-692-2651	692-9487
Web: www.marioncounty.ky.gov					
Marion County 200 S Third St Ste 104	Marion	KS	66861	620-382-2185	382-3420
TF: 800-305-8851 ■ *Web:* www.marioncoks.net					
Marion County 100 N Main St	Marion	OH	43302	740-223-4270	223-4279
Web: www.co.marion.oh.us					
Marion County 103 W Ct St	Marion	SC	29571	843-423-8225	423-8306
Web: www.marionsc.org					
Marion County 100 S Main St	Palmyra	MO	63461	573-769-2549	769-4312
TF: 888-870-5943 ■ *Web:* courts.mo.gov					
Marion County 118 Cross Creek Blvd	Salem	IL	62881	618-548-3878	548-3866
Web: www.marioncountyhealthdept.org					
Marion County PO Box 14500	Salem	OR	97309	503-588-5225	373-4408
Web: www.co.marion.or.us					
Mariposa County 5100 Bullion St PO Box 784	Mariposa	CA	95338	209-966-3222	966-5147
Web: www.mariposacounty.org					
Marlboro County PO Box 419	Bennettsville	SC	29512	843-479-5600	479-5639
Web: www.marlborocounty.sc.gov					
Marquette County 234 W Baraga Ave	Marquette	MI	49855	906-225-8151	225-8155
Web: www.co.marquette.mi.us					
Marquette County PO Box 186	Montello	WI	53949	608-297-9136	
Web: www.co.marquette.wi.us					
Marshall County 1101 Main St	Benton	KY	42025	270-527-4750	
Web: www.marshallcounty.net					
Marshall County 911 Vander Horck PO Box 130	Britton	SD	57430	605-448-5213	448-5201
Web: ujs.sd.gov/County_Information/marshall.aspx					
Marshall County 424 Blount Ave	Guntersville	AL	35976	256-571-7701	
Web: www.marshallco.org					
Marshall County 520 J M Ash Dr	Holly Springs	MS	38635	662-252-3916	252-7168
Web: marshallcoms.com					
Marshall County 122 N Prairie St PO Box 328	Lacon	IL	61540	309-246-6325	246-3667
Web: www.marshallcountyillinois.com					
Marshall County 1 E Main St 3rd Fl	Marshalltown	IA	50158	641-754-6355	754-6349
Web: www.co.marshall.ia.us					
Marshall County 1201 Broadway	Marysville	KS	66508	785-562-5361	562-5262
Web: ks-marshall.manatron.com					
Marshall County PO Box 459	Moundsville	WV	26041	304-845-1220	845-5891
Web: www.marshallcountywv.org					
Marshall County 211 W Madison St	Plymouth	IN	46563	574-936-8922	936-8893
Web: www.co.marshall.in.us					
Marshall County 208 E Colvin Ave	Warren	MN	56762	218-745-4851	
Web: www.visitnwminnesota.com					
Martin County 201 Lake Ave Ste 201	Fairmont	MN	56031	507-238-3211	238-3259*
**Fax:* Acctg ■ *Web:* co.martin.mn.us					
Martin County PO Box 460	Inez	KY	41224	606-298-2810	298-0143
Web: peoplesmart.com					
Martin County 129 Main St	Shoals	IN	47581	812-247-3652	
Martin County 301 N St Peter St	Stanton	TX	79782	432-756-3336	607-2992
Web: www.martincountytexas.us					
Martin County PO Box 9016	Stuart	FL	34995	772-288-5576	288-5548
Web: www.martin.fl.us					
Martin County 305 E Main St PO Box 308	Williamston	NC	27892	252-792-2515	
Web: www.martincountyncgov.com					
Martinsville (Independent City) PO Box 1112	Martinsville	VA	24114	276-403-5106	403-5280
Web: www.martinsville-va.gov					
Mason County 125 N Plum PO Box 77	Havana	IL	62644	309-543-6661	543-2085
Web: www.masoncountyil.org					
Mason County 304 E Ludington Ave	Ludington	MI	49431	231-843-8202	843-1972
Web: www.masoncounty.net					
Mason County PO Box 702	Mason	TX	76856	325-347-5253	347-6868
Web: www.co.mason.tx.us					
Mason County 221 Stanley Reed Ct St	Maysville	KY	41056	606-564-6706	564-7315
Web: www.masoncountykentucky.com					
Mason County 200 Sixth St.	Point Pleasant	WV	25550	304-675-1110	675-4982
Web: www.masoncounty.wv.gov					
Mason County PO Box 340	Shelton	WA	98584	360-427-9670	
Web: www.co.mason.wa.us					
Massac County 1 Superman Sq	Metropolis	IL	62960	618-524-5213	
Web: www.illinoiscourts.gov/circuitcourt/circuitmap/1st.asp#massac					
Matagorda County 1700 Seventh St Rm 202	Bay City	TX	77414	979-244-7680	244-7688
Web: www.co.matagorda.tx.us					
Matanuska-Susitna Borough 350 E Dahlia Ave	Palmer	AK	99645	907-745-4801	745-9845
Web: matsugov.us					
Mathews County PO Box 463	Mathews	VA	23109	804-725-2550	725-7456
Web: co.mathews.va.us					
Maui County 200 S High St	Wailuku	HI	96793	808-270-7748	270-7171
Web: www.co.maui.hi.us					

				Phone	Fax
Maury County 106 W 6th St PO Box 1076	Columbia	TN	38402	931-388-2155	
Web: www.mauryalliance.com					
Maverick County Rt 3 US Hwy 57 N PO Box 1033	Eagle Pass	TX	78852	830-773-2321	
Web: co.maverick.tx.us					
Mayes County 1 Ct Pl Ste 120	Pryor	OK	74361	918-825-2426	
Web: mayes.okcounties.org					
McClain County 121 N Second St PO Box 629	Purcell	OK	73080	405-527-3360	
Web: www.mcclain-co-ok.us					
McCone County 1004 C Ave PO Box 199	Circle	MT	59215	406-485-3505	485-2689
Web: mcconecountymt.com					
McCook County 130 W Essex PO Box 504	Salem	SD	57058	605-425-2781	425-3144
Web: www.mccookcountysd.com					
McCormick County 133 S Mine St Rm 102	McCormick	SC	29835	864-852-2231	
Web: www.mccormickcountysc.org					
McCracken County 2705 Olivet Church Rd	Paducah	KY	42001	270-554-9520	444-4704
McCreary County Tourist Commission PO Box 699	Whitley City	KY	42653	606-376-3008	
TF: 877-209-1012 ■ *Web:* www.mccrearycounty.com					
McCulloch County 199 Courthouse Sq Rm 103	Brady	TX	76825	325-597-0733	597-0606
Web: co.mcculloch.tx.us					
McCurtain County 108 N Central St	Idabel	OK	74745	580-286-2370	
Web: okcountyrecords.com					
McDonald County 602 Main St PO Box 606	Pineville	MO	64856	417-223-7523	223-2881
Web: www.mcdonaldcountygov.com					
McDowell County 60 E Court St	Marion	NC	28752	828-652-7121	
Web: www.mcdowellgov.com					
McDowell County 90 Wyoming St Ste 201	Welch	WV	24801	304-436-8548	436-8572
Web: www.mcdowellcounty.wv.gov					
McDuffie County PO Box 158	Thomson	GA	30824	404-679-4940	
Web: www.dca.state.ga.us					
McHenry County 407 Main St S Rm 201	Towner	ND	58788	701-537-5724	
Web: www.mchenrycountynd.com					
McHenry County 2200 N Seminary Ave	Woodstock	IL	60098	815-334-4000	334-8727
Web: www.co.mchenry.il.us					
McIntosh County 112 1st St NE PO Box 200	Ashley	ND	58413	701-288-3450	288-3671
McIntosh County PO Box 584	Darien	GA	31305	912-437-6671	437-6416
Web: georgia.gov					
McIntosh County 1st & Foley PO Box 107	Eufaula	OK	74432	918-689-2611	689-2611
Web: oklahoma.usassessor.com					
McKean County 500 W Main St	Smethport	PA	16749	814-887-5571	887-2242
TF: 800-482-1280 ■ *Web:* www.mckeancountypa.org					
McKenzie County PO Box 699	Watford City	ND	58854	701-444-2804	444-3916
TF: 800-701-2804 ■ *Web:* county.mckenziecounty.net					
McKinley County 207 W Hill Ave	Gallup	NM	87301	505-863-6866	863-1419
Web: www.co.mckinley.nm.us					
McLean County 115 E Washington St Rm 102	Bloomington	IL	61701	309-888-5190	888-5932
Web: www.co.mclean.il.us					
McLean County 210 Main St PO Box 127	Calhoun	KY	42327	270-273-3213	273-9965
Web: www.mcleancounty.ky.gov					
McLean County 712 Fifth Ave	Washburn	ND	58577	701-462-8541	462-8212
Web: www.mcleancountynd.gov					
McLennan County 501 Washington Ave	Waco	TX	76701	254-757-5078	757-5146
Web: www.co.mclennan.tx.us					
McLeod County 830 11th St	Glencoe	MN	55336	320-864-5551	
Web: www.co.mcleod.mn.us					
McMinn County 5 S Hill St Ste A	Athens	TN	37303	423-745-4440	744-1657
Web: mcminncountytn.gov					
McNairy County County Courthouse 170 W Ct Ave Rm 104	Selmer	TN	38375	731-645-3511	646-1414
Web: www.mcnairycountytn.com					
McPherson County 706 Main St PO Box 248	Leola	SD	57456	605-439-3361	439-3297
Web: ujs.sd.gov/County_Information/mcpherson.aspx					
McPherson County 117 N Maple Courthouse PO Box 425	McPherson	KS	67460	620-241-3656	241-1168
Web: www.mcphersoncountyks.us					
Meade County 516 Hillcrest Dr PO Box 614	Brandenburg	KY	40108	270-422-2152	
Web: countyclerk.meadecounty.ky.gov					
Meade County PO Box 278	Meade	KS	67864	620-873-8700	873-8713
Web: www.meadeco.org					
Meade County 1425 Sherman St PO Box 939	Sturgis	SD	57785	605-347-2356	347-3526
Web: www.meadecounty.org					
Meagher County 15 W Main St	White Sulphur Springs	MT	59645	406-547-3612	547-3388
Web: meaghercounty.mt.gov					
Mecklenburg County 393 Washington St PO Box 307	Boydton	VA	23917	434-738-6191	738-6861
Web: www.mecklenburgva.com					
Mecklenburg County 600 E Fourth St 11th Fl Charlotte-Mecklenburg Government Ctr	Charlotte	NC	28202	704-336-2472	336-5887
Web: charmeck.org					
Mecosta County 400 Elm St	Big Rapids	MI	49307	231-796-2505	592-0121
Web: www.co.mecosta.mi.us					
Medina County 1100 16th St	Hondo	TX	78861	830-741-6000	741-6015
Web: www.medinacountytexas.org					
Meeker County 325 N Sibley Ave	Litchfield	MN	55355	320-693-5200	
Web: www.co.meeker.mn.us					
Meigs County					
Economic Development Office 238 W Main St	Pomeroy	OH	45769	740-992-3034	992-7942
Web: www.meigscountyohio.com					
Mellette County S First & McKinley St PO Box 257	White River	SD	57579	605-259-3230	259-3030
Web: ujs.sd.gov/County_Information/mellette.aspx					
Menard County 102 S Seventh St PO Box 465	Petersburg	IL	62675	217-632-2415	
Web: www.menardcountyil.com					
Menard County Texas PO Box 1038	Menard	TX	76859	325-396-4682	396-2047
Web: www.menardtexas.com					
Mendocino County 501 Low Gap Rd Rm 1020	Ukiah	CA	95482	707-463-4376	463-4257
Web: www.co.mendocino.ca.us					
Menifee County Clerk PO Box 123	Frenchburg	KY	40322	606-768-3512	768-6738
Web: www.menifeecountyclerk.com					
Menominee County PO Box 279	Keshena	WI	54135	715-799-3311	
Web: www.wisconline.com/counties/menominee					
Menominee County 839 Tenth Ave	Menominee	MI	49858	906-863-9968	863-8839
Web: www.menomineecounty.com					
Merced County 2222 M St	Merced	CA	95340	209-385-7637	385-7375
Web: www.co.merced.ca.us					
Mercer County PO Box 66	Aledo	IL	61231	309-582-7021	582-7022
Web: www.mercercountyil.org					
Mercer County 220 W Livingston St Rm A201	Celina	OH	45822	419-586-3178	586-1699
Web: www.mercercountyohio.org					
Mercer County 124A S Main St	Harrodsburg	KY	40330	859-734-2365	
Web: www.merceronline.com					
Mercer County 109 Courthouse	Mercer	PA	16137	724-662-7548	
Web: www.mcc.co.mercer.pa.us					
Mercer County 621 Commerce St PO Box 4088	Bluefield	WV	24701	304-325-8438	324-8483
TF: 800-221-3206 ■ *Web:* www.visitmercercounty.com					
Mercer County PO Box 39	Stanton	ND	58571	800-441-2649	
TF: 800-441-2649 ■ *Web:* www.mercercountynd.com					
Mercer County PO Box 8068	Trenton	NJ	08650	609-585-6200	989-1111
Web: www.nj.gov/counties/mercer					
Meriwether County PO Box 428	Greenville	GA	30222	706-672-1314	
Web: meriwethercountyga.gov					
Merrick County PO Box 27	Central City	NE	68826	308-946-2881	946-2332
Web: www.merrickcounty.ne.gov					
Mesa County PO Box 20000	Grand Junction	CO	81502	970-244-1800	256-1588
Web: www.mesacounty.us					
Metcalfe County 100 E Stockton Ste 1	Edmonton	KY	42129	270-432-4821	
Web: www.metcalfecountyclerk.com					
Miami County 201 S Pearl St Ste 102	Paola	KS	66071	913-294-3976	294-9544
Web: www.miamicountyks.org					
Miami County PO Box 184	Peru	IN	46970	765-472-3901	472-1778
Web: miamicountyin.gov					
Miami County 201 W Main St	Troy	OH	45373	937-335-1920	
Web: www.co.miami.oh.us					
Miami-Dade County 111 NW First St Ste 220	Miami	FL	33128	305-375-5218	
Web: www.miamidade.gov					
Middlesex County 56 Paterson St	New Brunswick	NJ	08901	732-519-3200	
Web: www.judiciary.state.nj.us					
Judicial Department Small Claims 1 Ct St	Middletown	CT	06457	860-756-7800	343-6423
Web: www.jud.ct.gov					
Midland County 220 W Ellsworth St	Midland	MI	48640	989-832-6739	832-6680
Web: www.co.midland.mi.us					
Midland County 500 N Loraine St Fourth Fl PO Box 1350	Midland	TX	79702	432-688-4401	688-4926
Web: www.co.midland.tx.us					
Mifflin County 20 N Wayne St	Lewistown	PA	17044	717-248-6733	248-3695
Web: www.co.mifflin.pa.us					
Milam County 107 W Main St	Cameron	TX	76520	254-697-7049	697-7055
Web: www.milamcounty.net					
Millard County 765 S Hwy 99 Ste 6	Fillmore	UT	84631	435-743-5227	
Web: www.millardcounty.com					
Mille Lacs County 635 Second St SE	Milaca	MN	56353	320-983-8313	983-8384
Web: www.co.mille-lacs.mn.us					
Miller County 400 Laurel St Rm 105	Texarkana	AR	71854	870-774-1501	
Web: www.millercountyar.org					
Miller County 2001 Missouri 52	Tuscumbia	MO	65082	573-369-1900	
Web: millercountymissouri.org					
Mills County 418 Sharp St County Courthouse	Glenwood	IA	51534	712-527-4880	
Web: www.millscoia.us					
Mills County PO Box 646	Goldthwaite	TX	76844	325-648-2711	648-3251
Web: www.co.mills.tx.us					
Milwaukee County 901 N Ninth St	Milwaukee	WI	53233	414-278-4067	223-1379
Web: county.milwaukee.gov					
Miner County 217 S Main St PO Box 129	Howard	SD	57349	605-772-4561	
Web: www.minercountybank.com					
Mineral County 1201 N Main St PO Box 70	Creede	CO	81130	719-658-2575	658-2764
Web: www.mineralcountycolorado.com					
Mineral County 150 Armstrong St	Keyser	WV	26726	304-788-3924	788-4109
Web: www.mineralcountywv.com					
Mineral County 300 River St PO Box 396	Superior	MT	59872	406-822-3577	822-3579
Web: www.co.mineral.mt.us					
Mingo County 75 E 2nd Ave	Williamson	WV	25661	304-235-0378	
Web: mingocountywv.com					
Minidoka County 715 G St PO Box 368	Rupert	ID	83350	208-436-7111	436-0737
Web: www.minidoka.id.us					
Minnehaha County 415 N Dakota Ave	Sioux Falls	SD	57104	605-367-4206	367-8314
Web: www.minnehahacounty.org					
Missaukee County 111 S Canal PO Box 800	Lake City	MI	49651	231-839-4967	839-3684
Web: www.missaukee.org					
Mississippi County 200 W Walnut St Rm 204	Blytheville	AR	72315	870-763-3212	838-7784
Web: www.mcagov.com					
Mississippi County 200 N Main St	Charleston	MO	63834	573-683-2146	683-6071
Web: www.misscomo.net					
Missoula County 200 W Broadway St	Missoula	MT	59802	406-721-5700	258-4899
Web: www.missoulacounty.us					
Mitchell County 26 Crimson Laurel Cir # 5	Bakersville	NC	28705	828-688-2139	688-4443
Web: www.mitchellcounty.org					
Mitchell County PO Box 190	Beloit	KS	67420	785-738-3652	738-5524
Web: www.mcks.org					
Mitchell County 26 N Ct St PO Box 187	Camilla	GA	31730	229-336-2000	336-2003
Web: www.mitchellcountyga.net					
Mitchell County 26 Crimson Laurel Cir Ste 2	Bakersville	NC	28705	325-728-3481	
Web: www.mitchellcountytexas.us					
Mitchell County 508 State St	Osage	IA	50461	641-732-3726	732-3728
Mobile County 205 Government St	Mobile	AL	36644	251-574-5077	
Web: www.mobilecountyal.gov					
Modoc County 204 S Ct St STE 100	Alturas	CA	96101	530-233-7663	233-2434
Web: www.co.modoc.ca.us					
Moffat County 221 W Victory Way	Craig	CO	81625	970-824-9104	824-0351
Web: colorado.gov/cs/satellite/cnty-moffat/cbon/1251574649345					
Mohave County PO Box 7000	Kingman	AZ	86402	928-753-0729	753-5103
Web: www.mohavecounty.us					

Phone | Fax

Moniteau County 200 E Main St. . . . . California MO 65018 573-796-4521
Monmouth County 1 E Main St. . . . . Freehold NJ 07728 732-431-7324 409-7566
Web: co.monmouth.nj.us/index.aspx
Mono County PO Box 237 . . . . . Bridgeport CA 93517 760-932-5530 932-5531
Web: www.monocounty.ca.gov
Monona County 610 Iowa Ave. . . . . Onawa IA 51040 712-423-2491
Web: www.mononacounty.org
Monongalia County 243 High St Rm 123. . . . . Morgantown WV 26505 304-291-7230
Web: www.co.monongalia.wv.us
Monroe County 124 W Commerce St . . . . . Aberdeen MS 39730 662-369-6488 369-6489
Web: www.gomonroe.org
Monroe County 10 Benton Ave E. . . . . Albia IA 52531 641-932-5212 932-5905
Web: www.monroecoia.us
Monroe County 301 N College Ave Rm 201 . . . . . Bloomington IN 47404 812-349-2600 349-2610
Web: www.co.monroe.in.us
Monroe County 123 Madison St . . . . . Clarendon AR 72029 870-747-3632 747-5961
Web: monroecounty.arkansas.gov
Monroe County 38 W Main St PO Box 189. . . . . Forsyth GA 31029 478-994-7000 994-7294
Web: www.monroecountygeorgia.com
Monroe County 1100 SimontonSt. . . . . Key West FL 33040 305-294-4641
Web: www.monroecounty-fl.gov
Monroe County 103 College St Ste 1 . . . . . Madisonville TN 37354 423-442-2220 442-9542
Web: www.monroegovernment.org
Monroe County 106 E First St. . . . . Monroe MI 48161 734-240-7020 240-7045
Web: www.co.monroe.mi.us
Monroe County PO Box 8 . . . . . Monroeville AL 36461 251-743-4107 575-7934
Web: www.monroecountyal.com
Monroe County 300 N Main Rm 101. . . . . Paris MO 65275 660-327-4320 327-5063
Web: www.monroecountycollector.com
Monroe County 202 S K St Rm 1 . . . . . Sparta WI 54656 608-269-8705 269-8747
Web: www.co.monroe.wi.us
Monroe County 610 Monroe St. . . . . Stroudsburg PA 18360 570-420-3400
Web: www.pacourts.us
Monroe County 200 N Main St Ste D . . . . . Tompkinsville KY 42167 270-487-5471 487-8821
Web: monroecountyclerkky.com
Monroe County 216 Main St PO Box 350 . . . . . Union WV 24983 304-772-3096 772-4191
Web: www.monroecountywv.net
Monroe County 100 S Main St . . . . . Waterloo IL 62298 618-939-8681 939-8639
Web: monroecountyil.org
Monroe County 101 N Main St Rm 12 . . . . . Woodsfield OH 43793 740-472-5181 472-2526
Web: www.monroecountyohio.net
Montague County PO Box 77 . . . . . Montague TX 76251 940-894-2461 894-3110
Web: www.co.montague.tx.us
Montcalm County PO Box 368. . . . . Stanton MI 48888 989-831-7339 831-7474
Web: montcalm.org
Monterey County 168 W Alisal St. . . . . Salinas CA 93901 831-755-5115 757-5792
Web: www.co.monterey.ca.us
Montezuma County 601 N Mildred Rd . . . . . Cortez CO 81321 970-565-7580 565-3420
Montgomery County
755 Roanoke St Ste 2E. . . . . Christiansburg VA 24073 540-382-6954 382-6943
Web: www.montva.com
Montgomery County 1 Millennium Plaza . . . . . Clarksville TN 37040 931-648-8482 553-5160
Web: www.mcgtn.org
Montgomery County PO Box 1500. . . . . Fonda NY 12068 518-853-3834 853-8220
Web: www.co.montgomery.ny.us
Montgomery County
1 Courthouse Sq PO Box 595. . . . . Hillsboro IL 62049 217-532-9530 532-9581
Web: www.montgomeryco.com
Montgomery County PO Box 1667. . . . . Montgomery AL 36102 334-832-1210 832-2533
Web: www.mc-ala.org
Montgomery County 723 N Sturgeon St. . . . . Montgomery City MO 63361 573-564-3160 564-3802
Web: www.montgomerycitymo.org
Montgomery County 1 George St. . . . . Mount Ida AR 71957 870-887-3521
Montgomery County
44 W Main St Fiscal Ct. . . . . Mount Sterling KY 40353 859-498-8707 498-1040
Web: www.montgomerycounty.ky.gov
Montgomery County 310 W Broad St. . . . . Mount Vernon GA 30445 912-583-2363 583-2026
Web: www.montgomerycountyga.gov
Montgomery County PO Box 311. . . . . Norristown PA 19404 610-278-3346 278-5188
Web: www.montcopa.org
Montgomery County 105 Coolbaugh St. . . . . Red Oak IA 51566 712-623-3180 623-6540
Web: www.montgomerycountyiowa.com
Montgomery County 101 Monroe St . . . . . Rockville MD 20850 240-777-2500 777-2517
Web: www.montgomerycountymd.gov
Montgomery County 203 W Main St . . . . . Troy NC 27371 910-576-6011 576-2635
Web: montgomery.ces.ncsu.edu
Montgomery County PO Box 71. . . . . Winona MS 38967 662-283-2333
Web: montgomery.msghn.org/addresses.html
Montmorency County PO Box 789. . . . . Atlanta MI 49709 989-785-8013 785-8014
Web: montmorencycountymichigan.us
Montour County 29 Mill St . . . . . Danville PA 17821 570-271-3010 271-3089
Web: www.montourco.org
Montrose County 161 S Townsend. . . . . Montrose CO 81401 970-249-3362 249-7761
Web: www.co.montrose.co.us
Moody County 101 E Pipestone Ave . . . . . Flandreau SD 57028 605-997-3181
Web: moodycounty.net
Moore County PO Box 905 . . . . . Carthage NC 28327 910-947-6363 947-1874
Web: www.co.moore.nc.us
Moore County 715 S Dumas Ave Rm 304 . . . . . Dumas TX 79029 806-935-5654 935-9004
Web: co.moore.tx.us
Moore County 196 Main St PO Box 206 . . . . . Lynchburg TN 37352 931-759-7346
Web: www.lynchburgtn.com
Morehouse Parish 100 E Madison Ave. . . . . Bastrop LA 71220 318-281-3343 281-3775*
**Fax:* Morehouse Clerk of Court ■ *Web:* 4jdc.com
Morgan County 77 Fairfax St Ste 102 . . . . . Berkeley Springs WV 25411 304-258-8547 258-8545
Web: www.morgancountywv.gov
Morgan County PO Box 668 . . . . . Decatur AL 35602 256-351-4730 351-4738
Web: www.co.morgan.al.us
Morgan County PO Box 1399 . . . . . Fort Morgan CO 80701 970-542-3521 542-3520
Web: www.co.morgan.co.us
Morgan County 300 West State St. . . . . Jacksonville IL 62651 217-243-8581 243-8368
Web: www.morgancounty-il.com
Morgan County 150 E Washington St . . . . . Madison GA 30650 706-342-0725 343-6450
Web: www.morganga.org
Morgan County 180 S Main St . . . . . Martinsville IN 46151 765-342-1007 342-1111
Web: www.morgancounty.in.gov
Morgan County 358 E Main St . . . . . McConnelsville OH 43756 740-962-2533 962-3316
Web: www.morgan.lib.oh.us
Morgan County PO Box 886 . . . . . Morgan UT 84050 801-845-4011 829-6176
Web: www.morgan-county.net
Morgan County 100 E Newton St. . . . . Versailles MO 65084 573-378-5436 378-5991
Web: morgan-county.org
Morgan County 1226 Knoxville Hwy . . . . . Wartburg TN 37887 888-205-5017
TF: 888-205-5017 ■ *Web:* sextonfordofmorgancounty.com
Morgan County 450 Prestonsburg St . . . . . West Liberty KY 41472 606-743-3949 743-2111
Web: www.morgancounty.ky.gov
Morrill County 606 L St. . . . . Bridgeport NE 69336 308-262-0860 262-1469
Web: www.co.morrill.ne.us
Morris County 10 Ct St . . . . . Morristow KS 07960 620-767-5518
Morris County 500 Broadnax St. . . . . Daingerfield TX 75638 903-645-3911 645-5729
Web: www.co.morris.tx.us
Morris County PO Box 315 . . . . . Morristown NJ 07963 973-285-6120
Web: morriscountynj.gov
Morrison County 213 SE First Ave . . . . . Little Falls MN 56345 320-632-2941
TF: 866-401-1111 ■ *Web:* www.co.morrison.mn.us
Morrow County 100 Ct St PO Box 788 . . . . . Heppner OR 97836 541-676-9061 676-9876
Web: morrowcountyoregon.com
Morrow County 48 E High St. . . . . Mount Gilead OH 43338 419-947-4085
Web: morrowcounty.info
Morton County PO Box 1116. . . . . Elkhart KS 67950 620-697-2157 697-2159
Web: www.mtcoks.com
Morton County 210 Second Ave NW. . . . . Mandan ND 58554 701-667-3300 667-3453
Web: www.co.morton.nd.us
Motley County
Judges Office 701 Dundee Ave . . . . . Matador TX 79244 806-347-2234 347-2072
Moultrie County
County Courthouse 10 S Main St, Ste 6. . . . . Sullivan IL 61951 217-728-4389 728-8178
Web: moultriecountyil.com
Mountrail County 101 N Main St . . . . . Stanley ND 58784 701-627-4835
Web: www.co.mountrail.nd.us
Mower County 201 First St NE . . . . . Austin MN 55912 507-437-9535 437-9471
Web: www.co.mower.mn.us
Muhlenberg County PO Box 137 . . . . . Greenville KY 42345 270-338-2520 338-6116
Web: www.muhlenbergcounty.ky.gov
Multnomah County 1221 SW Fourth Ave . . . . . Portland OR 97204 503-823-4000
Web: multco.us
Murray County PO Box 1129. . . . . Chatsworth GA 30705 706-695-2413 695-8721
Web: www.murraycountyga.org
Murray County 2500 28th St. . . . . Slayton MN 56172 507-836-6148 836-8904
Web: www.murray-countymn.com
Murray County 10th Wyandotte St PO Box 442. . . . . Sulphur OK 73086 580-622-5106
Muscatine County 401 E Third St. . . . . Muscatine IA 52761 563-263-5821 263-7248
Web: www.co.muscatine.ia.us
Muskegon County 990 Terrace St. . . . . Muskegon MI 49442 231-724-6520 724-6673
Web: www.co.muskegon.mi.us
Muskingum County 401 Main St . . . . . Zanesville OH 43701 740-455-7104
Web: www.muskingumcounty.org
Muskogee County 229 W Okmulgee Ave . . . . . Muskogee OK 74401 918-682-6602
Web: www.cityofmuskogee.com
Musselshell County 506 Main St. . . . . Roundup MT 59072 406-323-1104
Web: musselshellcounty.org
Nacogdoches County 101 W Main St Rm 205. . . . . Nacogdoches TX 75961 936-560-7733 559-5926
Web: co.nacogdoches.tx.us
Nance County 209 Esther St PO Box 338 . . . . . Fullerton NE 68638 308-536-2331 536-2742
Web: www.co.nance.ne.us
Nantucket County 16 Broad St. . . . . Nantucket MA 02554 508-228-7216 325-5313
Web: www.nantucket-ma.gov
Napa County 1195 Third St Ste 310. . . . . Napa CA 94559 707-253-4421 253-4176
TF: 877-279-2976 ■ *Web:* www.countyofnapa.org
Nash County 120 W Washington St Ste 3072 . . . . . Nashville NC 27856 252-459-9800 459-9817
Web: www.co.nash.nc.us
Nassau County PO Box 870. . . . . Fernandina Beach FL 32035 904-491-7300 491-3629
TF: 888-615-4398 ■ *Web:* www.nassauflpa.com
Nassau County 240 Old Country Rd . . . . . Mineola NY 11501 516-571-2664 742-4099
Web: www.nassaucountyny.gov
Natchitoches Parish
200 Church St Ste 210. . . . . Natchitoches LA 71457 318-352-2714
Web: www.nppj.org
Natrona County 200 N Ctr St. . . . . Casper WY 82601 307-235-9200
Web: www.natronacounty-wy.gov
Navajo County
100 E Code Talkers Dr PO Box 668 . . . . . Holbrook AZ 86025 928-524-4000 524-4261
Web: www.navajocountyaz.gov
Navarro County PO Box 423 . . . . . Corsicana TX 75151 903-654-3040 654-3097
Web: www.co.navarro.tx.us
Nelson County 113 E Steven Foster St. . . . . Bardstown KY 40004 502-348-1820 348-1822
Web: nelsoncountyclerk.com
Nelson County 210 B Ave W Ste 203. . . . . Lakota ND 58344 701-247-2462
TF: 800-472-2286 ■ *Web:* nelsonco.org
Nelson County 84 Courthouse Sq PO Box 336 . . . . . Lovingston VA 22949 434-263-7000 263-7004
Web: www.nelsoncounty-va.gov
Nemaha County 1824 N St . . . . . Auburn NE 68305 402-274-4213 274-4389
Web: www.nemahacounty.ne.gov
Nemaha County 607 Nemaha . . . . . Seneca KS 66538 785-336-2106 336-6450
Web: ks-nemaha.manatron.com
Neosho County 100S Main St Rm 104 PO Box 138 . . . . . Erie KS 66733 620-244-3858 244-3860
Web: www.neoshocountyks.org
Neshoba County 401 Beacon St Ste 201. . . . . Philadelphia MS 39350 601-656-3581
Web: www.neshoba.org
Ness County 102 W Main PO Box 262. . . . . Ness City KS 67560 785-798-2413
Web: www.nesscountychamber.com
Nevada County 950 Maidu Ave . . . . . Nevada City CA 95959 530-265-1218
Web: www.mynevadacounty.com

Name / Address	City	State	Zip	Phone	Fax
Nevada County Depot & Museum 403 W First St S PO Box 592	Prescott	AR	71857	870-887-5821	
Web: www.depotmuseum.org					
New Kent County 12001 Courthouse Cir PO Box 98	New Kent	VA	23124	804-966-9520	966-9528
Web: www.co.new-kent.va.us					
New York County 60 Centre St	New York	NY	10007	646-386-5955	374-5790*
**Fax Area Code:* 212 ■ *Web:* www.nyc.gov					
Newaygo County 1087 Newell St	White Cloud	MI	49349	231-689-7200	689-7205
Web: www.countyofnewaygo.com					
Newberry County 1226 College St PO Box 10	Newberry	SC	29108	803-321-2110	321-2111
Web: www.newberrycounty.net					
Newport County 45 Washington Sq	Newport	RI	02840	401-841-8330	846-1673
Web: www.courts.ri.gov					
Newport News (Independent City) 2400 Washington Ave	Newport News	VA	23607	757-926-8411	926-3503
Web: www.nnva.gov					
Newton County 1124 Clark St	Covington	GA	30014	678-625-1202	
Web: www.co.newton.ga.us					
Newton County PO Box 68	Decatur	MS	39327	601-635-2368	
Web: newton.msgen.info					
Newton County PO Box 312	Jasper	AR	72641	870-446-5124	
Web: www.newtoncountysheriff.org					
Newton County 201 N 3rd St	Kentland	IN	47951	219-474-6081	474-5749
TF: 888-663-9866 ■ *Web:* www.newtoncounty.in.gov					
Newton County 4117 S 240 W	Morocco	IN	47963	417-451-8220	
Newton County 115 Ct St PO Box 484	Newton	TX	75966	409-379-5341	379-9049
Web: www.co.newton.tx.us					
Nez Perce County 1230 Main St PO Box 896	Lewiston	ID	83501	208-799-3020	799-3070
Web: www.co.nezperce.id.us					
Niagara County PO Box 461	Lockport	NY	14095	716-439-7022	439-7066
Web: www.niagaracounty.com					
Nicholas County PO Box 227	Carlisle	KY	40311	859-289-3730	
Web: www.carlisle-nicholascounty.org					
Commission 700 Main St Ste 1	Summersville	WV	26651	304-872-7830	872-7863
Web: www.nicholascountywv.org					
Nicollet County 501 S Minnesota Ave	Saint Peter	MN	56082	507-931-6800	931-9220
Web: www.co.nicollet.mn.us					
Niobrara County PO Box 420	Lusk	WY	82225	307-334-2211	
Web: www.county-clerk.net/countyclerk.asp?state=Wyoming&county=Niobrara					
Noble County 101 N Orange St	Albion	IN	46701	260-636-2736	636-4000
Web: www.nobleco.org					
Noble County 15708 McConnelsville Rd	Caldwell	OH	43724	740-732-5188	732-2651
Web: www.drc.ohio.gov					
Noble County 300 Courthouse Dr Ste 1	Perry	OK	73077	580-336-5187	336-2481
Nobles County 1530 Airport Rd	Worthington	MN	56187	507-372-8263	372-4994
Web: www.co.nobles.mn.us					
Nodaway County 403 N Market	Maryville	MO	64468	660-582-2251	582-5282
Web: www.nodawaycountymo.us					
Nolan County 100 E Third St Ste 108	Sweetwater	TX	79556	325-235-2462	236-9416
Web: www.co.nolan.tx.us					
Norfolk County 614 High St	Dedham	MA	02026	781-461-6105	326-6480
Web: www.norfolkcounty.org					
Norfolk (Independent City) 810 Union St Rm 1101	Norfolk	VA	23510	757-664-4242	664-4239
Web: www.norfolk.gov					
Norman County 16 Third Ave E PO Box 146	Ada	MN	56510	218-784-5473	784-4531
Web: www.co.norman.mn.us					
North Slope Borough PO Box 69	Barrow	AK	99723	907-852-2611	852-0229
Web: www.north-slope.org					
Northampton County 669 Washington St	Easton	PA	18042	610-559-6700	
Web: www.northamptoncounty.org					
Northampton County PO Box 36	Eastville	VA	23347	757-678-0465	678-5410
Web: www.co.northampton.va.us					
Northampton County PO Box 808	Jackson	NC	27845	252-534-2501	534-1166
Web: www.northamptonnc.com					
Northumberland County PO Box 217	Heathsville	VA	22473	804-580-3700	580-2261
Web: www.co.northumberland.va.us					
Northumberland County 201 Market St 2nd Fl	Sunbury	PA	17801	570-988-4167	988-4497
TF: 800-692-4332 ■ *Web:* www.northumberlandco.org					
Northwest Arctic Borough PO Box 1110	Kotzebue	AK	99752	907-442-2500	442-2930
TF: 800-478-1110 ■ *Web:* www.nwabor.org					
Norton County 105 S Kansas PO Box 70	Norton	KS	67654	785-877-5700	
Web: www.nortoncounty.net					
Norton (Independent City) 618 Virginia Ave PO Box 618	Norton	VA	24273	276-679-1160	679-3510
Web: www.nortonva.org					
Nottoway County 344 W Ct House Rd PO Box 92	Nottoway	VA	23955	434-645-8696	645-8667
Web: www.nottoway.org					
Nowata County 229 N Maple St	Nowata	OK	74048	918-273-0808	273-1936
Noxubee County 503 S Washington St PO Box 308	Macon	MS	39341	800-487-0165	
TF: 800-487-0165 ■ *Web:* noxubeecountyms.com					
Nuckolls County PO Box 366	Nelson	NE	68961	402-225-4361	225-4301
Web: www.nuckollscounty.ne.gov					
Nueces County 901 Leopard St Ste 201	Corpus Christi	TX	78401	361-888-0459	888-0329
Web: www.co.nueces.tx.us					
Nye County PO Box 1031	Tonopah	NV	89049	775-482-8127	482-8133
Web: www.co.nye.nv.us					
O'Brien County PO Box 340	Primghar	IA	51245	712-957-3045	957-3046
Web: www.obriencounty.com					
Obion County 1604B W Reelfoot Ave	Union City	TN	38261	731-884-2133	884-2719
Web: www.tn.gov					
Ocean County 118 Washington St	Toms River	NJ	08753	732-929-2018	349-4336
Web: www.co.ocean.nj.us					
Oceana County 100 State St Ste 1	Hart	MI	49420	231-873-4328	873-1391
Web: www.oceana.mi.us					
Ochiltree County 511 S Main St	Perryton	TX	79070	806-435-8039	435-2081
Web: www.co.ochiltree.tx.us					
Oconee County 415 S Pine St PO Box 678	Walhalla	SC	29691	864-638-4280	638-4280
Web: www.oconeesc.com					
Oconto County 301 Washington St	Oconto	WI	54153	920-834-6800	834-6867
Web: www.co.oconto.wi.us					
Ogemaw County 806 W Houghton Ave	West Branch	MI	48661	989-345-0215	345-7223
Web: www.ogemawcountymi.gov/hours.php					
Ogle County 105 S 5th St	Oregon	IL	61061	815-732-3201	732-6273
Web: www.oglecounty.org					
Oglethorpe County 341 W Main St	Lexington	GA	30648	706-743-5270	743-8371
Web: onlineoglethorpe.com					
Ohio County 413 Main St PO Box 185	Rising Sun	IN	47040	812-438-3264	438-1215
Ohio County 1500 Chapline St Rm 205	Wheeling	WV	26003	304-234-3656	234-3829
Web: www.ohiocounty.wv.gov/countygovernmentagencies/Pages/countyclerk.aspx					
Okaloosa County 101 E James Lee Blvd	Crestview	FL	32536	850-689-5000	689-5818
Web: www.co.okaloosa.fl.us					
Okanogan County 149 N Third Ave PO Box 980	Okanogan	WA	98840	509-422-7170	422-7174
Web: www.okanogancounty.org					
Okeechobee County 304 NW Second St	Okeechobee	FL	34972	863-763-6441	763-9529
Web: www.co.okeechobee.fl.us					
Oklahoma County 320 Robert S Kerr Ave	Oklahoma City	OK	73102	405-270-0082	
Web: www.oklahomacounty.org					
Okmulgee County 314 W Seventh St	Okmulgee	OK	74447	918-756-3042	
Web: www.okgenweb.org/~okokmulg					
Oktibbeha County 101 E Main St	Starkville	MS	39759	662-323-5834	
Web: www.gtpdd.com/counties/oktibbeha					
Oldham County 100 W Jefferson St	LaGrange	KY	40031	502-222-1476	222-3210
Web: www.oldhamcounty.net					
Oldham County PO Box 360	Vega	TX	79092	806-267-2667	267-2671
Web: www.co.oldham.tx.us					
Oliver County 115 W Main	Center	ND	58530	701-794-8777	794-3476
Web: ndcourts.gov					
Oneida County 10 Ct St	Malad City	ID	83252	208-766-4116	
Web: oneidasheriff.net					
Oneida County 1 S Oneida Ave PO Box 400	Rhinelander	WI	54501	715-369-6144	369-6230
Web: www.co.oneida.wi.gov					
Oneida County 800 Pk Ave	Utica	NY	13501	315-792-9039	
Web: kidsoneida.org					
Onondaga County 401 Montgomery St	Syracuse	NY	13202	315-435-2226	435-3455
Web: www.ongov.net					
Onslow County 4024 Richland Hwy	Jacksonville	NC	28540	910-347-4717	455-7878
Web: onslowcountync.gov					
Ontario County 20 Ontario St	Canandaigua	NY	14424	585-396-4200	393-2951
Web: www.co.ontario.ny.us					
Ontonagon County 725 Greenland Rd	Ontonagon	MI	49953	906-884-4699	884-2916
Orange County 109 State St	Montpeiler	VT	05609	802-685-4610	685-3246
Web: www.vermontjudiciary.org/gtc/criminal/default.aspx					
Orange County 255 Main St	Goshen	NY	10924	845-291-2700	291-2724
Web: www.co.orange.ny.us					
Orange County 106 E Margaret Ln	Hillsborough	NC	27278	919-732-8181	
Web: www.co.orange.nc.us					
Orange County 801 W Div	Orange	TX	77631	409-882-7055	882-7012
Web: www.co.orange.tx.us					
Orange County 200 Dailey Dr	Orange	VA	22960	540-661-4550	661-4599
TF: 866-803-8641 ■ *Web:* www.ocss-va.org					
Orange County 201 S Rosalind Ave 5th Fl	Orlando	FL	32802	407-836-7350	836-5879
Web: www.orangecountyfl.net					
Orange County 1 Ct St	Paoli	IN	47454	812-723-2649	723-0239
Web: www.co.orange.in.us					
Orange County 12 Civic Ctr Plaza	Santa Ana	CA	92702	714-834-2500	834-2675
Web: ocgov.com					
Orangeburg County 1406 Amelia St	Orangeburg	SC	29118	803-533-6263	534-3848
Web: www.orangeburgcounty.org					
Oregon County PO Box 324	Alton	MO	65606	417-778-7475	
Orleans County 3 S Main St Ste 2	Albion	NY	14411	585-589-5334	589-0181
Web: www.orleansny.com					
Orleans County 247 Main St	Newport	VT	05855	802-334-3344	334-3385
Web: bgs.vermont.gov/facilities/east/orleanscourt					
Orleans Parish 839 St Charles Ave Ste 305	New Orleans	LA	70130	504-309-1004	
Web: www.neworleans.com					
Osage County 205 E Main St	Linn	MO	65051	573-897-2139	
Web: www.osagecountyhd.org					
Osage County PO Box 226	Lyndon	KS	66451	785-828-4812	828-4749
Web: www.osageco.org					
Osage County 900 S St Paul Ave	Pawhuska	OK	74056	918-287-3535	287-6011
Web: ocso.net					
Osborne County PO Box 160	Osborne	KS	67473	785-346-2431	346-5252
Web: www.osbornecounty.org					
Osceola County 1 Courthouse Sq	Kissimmee	FL	34741	407-343-3500	
Web: www.osceola.org					
Osceola County 301 W Upton Ave	Reed City	MI	49677	231-832-3261	832-6149
Web: www.osceola-county.org					
Osceola County 300 Seventh St	Sibley	IA	51249	712-754-2523	
Web: www.osceolacountyia.com					
Oscoda County PO Box 399	Mio	MI	48647	989-826-1109	826-1136
Web: www.oscodacountymi.com					
Oswego County 46 E Bridge St	Oswego	NY	13126	315-349-8235	349-8237
Web: www.co.oswego.ny.us					
Otero County 1000 New York Ave Ste 109	Alamogordo	NM	88310	575-434-8849	443-2941
Web: www.co.otero.nm.us					
Otero County 13 W Third St Rm 210	La Junta	CO	81050	719-383-3020	383-3026
Web: www.oterogov.com					
Otoe County PO Box 726	Nebraska City	NE	68410	402-873-9500	
Web: www.co.otoe.ne.us					
Otsego County 197 Main St	Cooperstown	NY	13326	607-547-4202	547-4260
Web: www.otsegocounty.com					
Otsego County 225 W Main St	Gaylord	MI	49735	989-731-7504	
Web: www.otsegocountymi.gov					
Ottawa County 414 Washington St	Grand Haven	MI	49417	616-846-8320	846-8179
Web: www.co.ottawa.mi.us					
Ottawa County 123 East Central Ste 101	Miami	OK	74354	918-542-9408	
Ottawa County 307 N Concord St Ste 130	Minneapolis	KS	67467	785-392-2279	392-2011
Web: www.ottawacounty.org					
Ottawa County 315 Madison St	Port Clinton	OH	43452	419-734-6710	734-6898
Web: www.co.ottawa.oh.us					
Otter Tail County 520 Fir Ave W	Fergus Falls	MN	56537	218-998-8000	998-8438
Web: www.co.ottertail.mn.us					

	City	State	ZIP	Phone	Fax
Ouachita County 109 Goodgame St *Web:* www.ouachitacountysheriff.org	Camden	AR	71701	870-231-5300	231-4329
Ouachita Parish 301 South Grand St Ste 104 *Web:* www.opclerkofcourt.com	Monroe	LA	71201	318-327-1444	327-1462
Ouray County 541 Fourth St PO Box C *Web:* www.ouraycountyco.gov	Ouray	CO	81427	970-325-4961	325-0452
Outagamie County 410 S Walnut St *Web:* www.outagamie.org	Appleton	WI	54911	920-832-5077	832-2200
Overton County 317 E University St Rm 22 *Web:* www.overtoncountytn.com	Livingston	TN	38570	931-823-2631	823-2696
Owen County 100 N Thomas St *Web:* owencounty.ky.gov	Owenton	KY	40359	502-484-3405	484-1004
Owen County 60 S Main St County Courthouse Fl 1 Rm 100 *Web:* www.owencounty.in.gov	Spencer	IN	47460	812-829-5030	
Owsley County PO Box 500 *Web:* elect.ky.gov/contactcountyclerks/pages/n-o.aspx	Booneville	KY	41314	606-593-5735	593-5737
Owyhee County PO Box 128 *Web:* www.owyheecounty.net	Murphy	ID	83650	208-495-2421	495-1173
Oxford County 26 Western Ave PO Box 179 *Web:* www.oxfordcounty.org	South Paris	ME	04281	207-743-6359	743-1545
Ozark County 361 Main St PO Box 605 *Web:* www.ozarkcounty.net	Gainesville	MO	65655	417-679-4913	
Ozaukee County PO Box 994 *Web:* www.co.ozaukee.wi.us	Port Washington	WI	53074	262-284-8110	284-8100
Pacific County PO Box 67 *Web:* www.co.pacific.wa.us	South Bend	WA	98586	360-875-9300	
Page County 112 E Main St *Web:* www.co.page.ia.us	Clarinda	IA	51632	712-542-2516	542-6005
Page County 117 S Ct St *Web:* www.pagecounty.virginia.gov	Luray	VA	22835	540-743-4142	
Palm Beach County 301 N Olive Ave *Web:* www.co.palm-beach.fl.us	West Palm Beach	FL	33401	561-355-2001	355-3990
Palo Pinto County PO Box 219 *Web:* www.co.palo-pinto.tx.us	Palo Pinto	TX	76484	940-659-1277	
Pamlico County PO Box 776 *Web:* www.co.pamlico.nc.us	Bayboro	NC	28515	252-745-3133	745-5514
Panola County 110 Sycamore St Rm 201 *Web:* www.co.panola.tx.us	Carthage	TX	75633	903-693-0302	
Park County 1002 Sheridan Ave *TF:* 800-786-2844 ■ *Web:* www.parkcounty.us	Cody	WY	82414	307-527-8510	527-8515
Park County 501 Main St PO Box 1373 *Web:* www.parkco.us	Fairplay	CO	80440	719-836-2771	836-3273
Park County 414 E Callender St *Web:* www.parkcounty.org	Livingston	MT	59047	406-222-4110	
Parke County 116 W High St Rm 204 *Web:* www.parkecounty-in.gov	Rockville	IN	47872	765-569-5132	
Parker County 1112 Santa Fe Dr *Web:* parkercountytx.com	Weatherford	TX	76086	817-594-7461	
Parmer County 401 Third St *Web:* www.co.parmer.tx.us	Farwell	TX	79325	806-481-3691	481-9548
Pasco County 7530 Little Rd *Web:* www.pascocountyfl.net	New Port Richey	FL	34654	727-847-2411	847-8969
Pasquotank County PO Box 39 *Web:* www.co.pasquotank.nc.us	Elizabeth City	NC	27907	252-335-0865	335-0866
Passaic County 401 Grand St *Web:* www.passaiccountynj.org	Paterson	NJ	07505	973-225-3632	754-1920
Patrick County 106 Rucker St PO Box 466 *Web:* www.co.patrick.va.us	Stuart	VA	24171	276-694-6094	694-2160
Paulding County 240 Constitution Blvd *Web:* www.paulding.gov	Dallas	GA	30132	770-443-7550	443-7537
Paulding County 115 N Williams St Ste 101 *Web:* www.pauldingcountyauditor.com	Paulding	OH	45879	419-399-8205	399-5713
Pawnee County 715 Broadway *Web:* www.pawneecountykansas.com	Larned	KS	67550	620-285-3721	285-2559
Pawnee County 500 Harrison St Rm 203 *Web:* www.cityofpawnee.com	Pawnee	OK	74058	918-762-3741	
Pawnee County 625 Sixth St PO Box 431 *Web:* www.co.pawnee.ne.us	Pawnee City	NE	68420	402-852-2963	852-2963
Payette County 1130 Third Ave N Rm 104 *Web:* www.payettecounty.org	Payette	ID	83661	208-642-6000	642-6011
Payne County 315 W Sixth St Ste 202 *Web:* www.paynecounty.org	Stillwater	OK	74074	405-747-8310	747-8304
Peach County 205 W Church St *Web:* www.peachcounty.net	Fort Valley	GA	31030	478-825-2535	825-2678
Pearl River County 200 S Main St PO Box 431 *Web:* www.pearlrivercounty.net	Poplarville	MS	39470	601-403-2300	
Pecos County 103 W Callaghan St *Web:* www.co.pecos.tx.us	Fort Stockton	TX	79735	432-336-7555	336-7557
Pembina County 301 Dakota St W Ste 1 *Web:* www.pembinacountynd.gov	Cavalier	ND	58220	701-265-4231	265-4876
Pemiscot County 610 Ward Ave *Web:* www.courts.mo.gov	Caruthersville	MO	63830	573-333-0187	333-4157
Pend Oreille County 229 S Garden Ave *Web:* www.pendoreilleco.org	Newport	WA	99156	509-447-2435	447-2734
Pender County PO Box 5 *Web:* www.pendercountync.gov	Burgaw	NC	28425	910-259-1200	259-1402
Pendleton County 233 Main St *Web:* pendletoncounty.ky.gov	Falmouth	KY	41040	859-654-4321	654-5047
Pendleton County 100 S Main St PO Box 187 *Web:* www.pendletoncounty.wv.gov	Franklin	WV	26807	304-358-7573	358-2473
Pennington County 315 St Joseph St *Web:* pennco.org	Rapid City	SD	57701	605-394-2171	
Pennington County 101 Main Ave N PO Box 616 *Web:* co.pennington.mn.us	Thief River Falls	MN	56701	218-745-6733	683-7026
Penobscot County 97 Hammond St *Web:* www.penobscot-county.net	Bangor	ME	04401	207-942-8535	
Peoria County 324 Main St Rm 101 *Web:* www.co.peoria.il.us	Peoria	IL	61602	309-672-6059	672-6054

	City	State	ZIP	Phone	Fax
Pepin County 740 Seventh Ave W *Web:* www.co.pepin.wi.us	Durand	WI	54736	715-672-8857	672-8677
Perkins County 100 E Main St PO Box 426 *Web:* ujs.sd.gov/County_Information/perkins.aspx	Bison	SD	57620	605-244-5626	244-7110
Perkins County PO Box 156 *Web:* www.co.perkins.ne.us	Grant	NE	69140	308-352-7560	352-7562
Perquimans County PO Box 45 *Web:* www.co.perquimans.nc.us	Hertford	NC	27944	252-426-8484	426-4034
Perry County 333 7th St *TF:* 888-343-6262 ■ *Web:* www.perrycountyindiana.org	Tell City	IN	47586	812-547-7933	547-8378
Perry County PO Box 210 *Web:* www.perrycounty.ky.gov	Hazard	KY	41701	606-439-1816	439-1686
Perry County PO Box 16 *Web:* www.perrycountytennessee.com/government/perry-county-government	Linden	TN	37096	931-589-2216	589-2215
Perry County 1293 Washington St *Web:* www.perrycountyalabamachamber.com	Marion	AL	36756	334-683-9622	
Perry County 103 S Main St *Web:* chancery10.com	New Augusta	MS	39462	601-964-8398	
Perry County 25 W Main St PO Box 37 *Web:* www.perryco.org	New Bloomfield	PA	17068	717-582-2131	582-5162
Perry County 105 N Main St PO Box 207 *Web:* www.perrycountycourt.com	New Lexington	OH	43764	740-342-3156	342-2188
Perry County 310 W Main St Ste 101 *Web:* perrycoarkansas.org	Perryville	AR	72126	501-889-5128	889-2574
Perry County 3764 State Rts 13-127 Rm 110 PO Box 438 *Web:* perrycountyclerk.com	Pinckneyville	IL	62274	618-357-5116	357-3365
Pershing County PO Box 736 PO Box 820 *Web:* www.pershingcounty.net	Lovelock	NV	89419	775-273-2208	273-3015
Person County 304 S Morgan St Rm 212 *Web:* www.personcounty.net	Roxboro	NC	27573	336-597-1720	599-1609
Petersburg (Independent City) 135 N Union St Ste 202 *Web:* www.petersburg-va.org	Petersburg	VA	23803	804-733-2301	
Petroleum County 302 E Main PO Box 226	Winnett	MT	59087	406-429-5311	
Pettis County 415 S Ohio *Web:* www.pettiscomo.com	Sedalia	MO	65301	660-826-5000	
Phelps County PO Box 404 *Web:* www.phelpsgov.org	Holdrege	NE	68949	308-995-4469	995-4368
Phelps County 200 N Main St *Web:* www.phelpscounty.org	Rolla	MO	65401	573-458-6000	458-6119
Philadelphia County City Hall Broad & Market St *Web:* phila.gov	Philadelphia	PA	19107	215-686-1776	567-7380
Phillips County 620 Cherry St Ste 100 *Web:* phillipscounty.arkansas.gov	Helena	AR	72342	870-338-5505	338-5509
Phillips County PO Box 484 *Web:* phillipscofair.com	Holyoke	CO	80734	970-854-3616	
Phillips County PO Box 1420 PO Box 1637 *Web:* www.maltachamber.com	Malta	MT	59538	406-654-1776	654-1776
Phillips County 301 State St *Web:* phillipscounty.org	Phillipsburg	KS	67661	785-543-6825	
Piatt County 101 W Washington St *Web:* www.piattcounty.org	Monticello	IL	61856	217-762-9487	762-7563
Pickaway County 139 W Franklin St *Web:* www.pickaway.org	Circleville	OH	43113	740-474-6093	474-8988
Pickens County 1266 E Church St *Web:* pickenscountyga.gov	Jasper	GA	30143	706-253-8809	
Pickett County 1 Courthouse Sq Ste 200 *TF:* 888-406-4704 ■ *Web:* dalehollow.com/info-resources/government	Byrdstown	TN	38549	931-864-3798	864-6615
Pierce County PO Box 679 *Web:* pc.pcgeorgia.com	Blackshear	GA	31516	912-449-2022	449-2024
Pierce County 414 W Main St PO Box 119 *Web:* www.co.pierce.wi.us	Ellsworth	WI	54011	715-273-6851	273-6853
Pierce County 111 W Ct St Rm 1 *Web:* www.co.pierce.ne.us	Pierce	NE	68767	402-329-4225	329-6439
Pierce County 240 SE Second St Ste 8 *Web:* www.piercecountynd.gov	Rugby	ND	58368	701-776-6161	776-5707
Pierce County 930 Tacoma Ave S Rm 110 *Web:* www.co.pierce.wa.us	Tacoma	WA	98402	253-798-7455	798-3428
Pike County 115 W Main St	Bowling Green	MO	63334	573-324-2412	
Pike County PO Box 309 *Web:* www.co.pike.ms.us	Magnolia	MS	39652	601-783-3362	
Pike County 506 Broad St *TF:* 866-681-4947 ■ *Web:* www.pikepa.org	Milford	PA	18337	570-296-7613	296-6055
Pike County PO Box 219	Murfreesboro	AR	71958	870-285-2231	
Pike County 801 E Main St	Petersburg	IN	47567	812-354-6025	
Pike County 146 Main St PO Box 631 *Web:* www.revenue.ky.gov	Pikeville	KY	41502	606-432-6211	432-6222
Pike County 100 E Washington St Courthouse *Web:* www.pikeil.org	Pittsfield	IL	62363	217-285-6812	
Pike County 120 W Church St PO Box 1147 *Web:* Www.alabama.gov	Troy	AL	36081	334-566-6374	
Pike County 126 W 2nd St PO Box 134 *Web:* www.piketravel.com	Waverly	OH	45690	740-947-9650	941-0255
Pima County 130 W Congress St 10th Fl *Web:* webcms.pima.gov	Tucson	AZ	85701	520-740-8661	740-8171
Pinal County 31 N Pinal St *Web:* pinalcountyaz.gov	Florence	AZ	85232	520-866-6000	866-6512
Pine County 635 Northridge Dr NW *TF:* 800-450-7463 ■ *Web:* www.co.pine.mn.us	Pine City	MN	55063	320-591-1400	
Pinellas County 315 Ct St Rm 601 *Web:* www.pinellascounty.org	Clearwater	FL	33756	727-464-3485	464-4384
Pipestone County 416 S Hiawatha Ave *Web:* www.mncounties.org	Pipestone	MN	56164	507-825-6740	
Piscataquis County 50 Mayo St *Web:* www.pcedc.org	Dover-Foxcroft	ME	04426	207-564-3638	
Pitkin County 530 E Main St Ste 101 *Web:* pitkinclerk.org	Aspen	CO	81611	970-920-5180	
Pitt County 1717 W Fifth St *Web:* www.pittcountync.gov	Greenville	NC	27834	252-902-1000	830-6311

Phone | Fax

Pittsburg County 115 E Carl Albert Pkwy McAlester OK 74501 918-423-6895 423-7379
Web: pittsburg.okcountytreasurers.com
Pittsylvania County 1 Center St PO Box 426 Chatham VA 24531 434-432-7700
Web: pittsylvaniacountyva.gov
Piute County 550 N Main Junction UT 84740 435-577-2840 577-2433
Web: www.piute.org
Placer County 2954 Richardson Dr Auburn CA 95603 530-886-5600 886-5687
Web: www.placer.ca.gov
Plaquemines Parish 301 Main St Belle Chasse LA 70037 504-297-5536
Web: www.plaqueminesparish.com
Platte County 2610 14th St Columbus NE 68601 402-563-4902 564-4164
Platte County 415 Third St Platte City MO 64079 816-858-2232 858-3363
Web: www.co.platte.mo.us
Platte County PO Box 728 Wheatland WY 82201 307-322-2315 322-2245
Web: www.plattecountywyoming.com
Pleasants County 301 Ct Ln Saint Marys WV 26170 304-684-7882
Plumas County 520 Main St Rm 104 Quincy CA 95971 530-283-6155 283-6415
Web: www.countyofplumas.com
Plymouth County 215 Fourth Ave SE Le Mars IA 51031 712-546-6100 546-5784*
**Fax:* Acctg ■ *Web:* www.co.plymouth.ia.us
Plymouth County 134 Ct St Plymouth MA 02360 508-747-7533
Web: www.seeplymouth.com
Pocahontas County PO Box 275 Marlinton WV 24954 800-336-7009
TF: 800-336-7009 ■ *Web:* www.pocahontascountywv.com
Pocahontas County
99 Ct Sq County Courthouse Pocahontas IA 50574 712-335-4208
Web: countycriminal.com/court-records
Poinsett County 1500 Justice Dr Harrisburg AR 72432 870-578-5411 578-4417
Web: www.poinsettcountysheriff.org
Pointe Coupee Parish 201 E Main St New Roads LA 70760 225-638-9596
Web: laclerksofcourt.org
Polk County 100 Polk County Plaza Ste 110 Balsam Lake WI 54810 715-485-9226 485-9104
Web: www.co.polk.wi.us
Polk County 330 W Church St Bartow FL 33830 863-534-6000 534-7655
Web: www.polk-county.net
Polk County 6239 Hwy 411 PO Box 128 Benton TN 37307 423-338-4527 338-4558
Web: www.polkgovernment.com
Polk County 102 E Broadway Ste 6 Bolivar MO 65613 417-326-4032 777-8693
Polk County 40 Courthouse Sq PO Box 308 Columbus NC 28722 828-894-3301 894-2263
Web: www.co.polk.nc.us
Polk County 816 Marion Ave Ste 210 Crookston MN 56716 218-281-2332 281-2204
Web: www.co.polk.mn.us
Polk County 850 Main St Dallas OR 97338 503-623-9217 623-0717
Web: co.polk.or.us
Polk County 111 Ct Ave Des Moines IA 50309 515-286-3000 323-5225
Web: www.polkcountyiowa.gov
Polk County 101 W Church St Livingston TX 77351 936-327-6804 327-6874
Web: www.co.polk.tx.us
Polk County 507 Church Ave Mena AR 71953 479-394-8145
Polk County PO Box 276 Osceola NE 68651 402-747-5431 747-2656
Web: polkcounty.nebraska.gov
Pondera County 20 Fourth Ave SW Conrad MT 59425 406-271-4000
Web: www.ponderacountymontana.org
Pontotoc County 301 S Broadway Ave Ada OK 74820 580-332-1425
Pontotoc County PO Box 209 Pontotoc MS 38863 662-489-3900
Pope County 130 E Minnesota Ave Glenwood MN 56334 320-634-5727
Web: www.mncounties.org
Pope County 125 State Hwy 146 W Golconda IL 62938 618-683-4011 683-6022
Web: es.popek12.org
Pope County
102 W Main St County Courthouse, Ste 6 Russellville AR 72801 479-968-6064 967-2291
Web: www.popecountyar.com
Poquoson (Independent City)
500 City Hall Ave Poquoson VA 23662 757-868-3000 868-3101
Web: www.ci.poquoson.va.us
Portage County 449 S Meridian St 7th Fl Ravenna OH 44266 330-297-3600 297-3610
TF: 800-772-3799 ■ *Web:* www.co.portage.oh.us
Portage County 1516 Church St Stevens Point WI 54481 715-346-1351 346-1486
Web: www.co.portage.wi.us/countyclerk
Porter County 155 Indiana Ave Valparaiso IN 46383 219-465-3445
Web: porterco.org
Posey County 126 E Third St Rm 132 Mount Vernon IN 47620 812-838-1300 838-1344
Web: www.poseycountyin.gov
Pottawatomie County 325 N Broadway Shawnee OK 74801 405-273-1727
Web: www.pottcoso.com
Pottawatomie County PO Box 187 Westmoreland KS 66549 785-457-3314 457-3507
Web: www.pottcounty.org
Potter County 900 S Polk St Ste 500 Amarillo TX 79101 806-379-2275 379-2296
Web: www.co.potter.tx.us
Potter County 1 North Main St Coudersport PA 16915 814-274-8290 274-8284
Web: www.pottercountypa.net
Potter County 201 S Exene PO Box 67 Gettysburg SD 57442 605-765-9472 765-9670
Web: ujs.sd.gov/County_Information/potter.aspx
Powder River County PO Box 270 Broadus MT 59317 406-436-2361 436-2151
Web: prco.mt.gov
Powell County 409 Missouri Ave Deer Lodge MT 59722 406-846-3680
Web: www.powellcountymontana.com
Powell County PO Box 506 Stanton KY 40380 606-663-2834 663-2905
Web: www.powellcounty.ky.gov
Power County 543 Bannock Ave American Falls ID 83211 208-226-7610
Web: www.co.power.id.us
Poweshiek County PO Box 218 Montezuma IA 50171 641-623-5644
Web: www.poweshiekcounty.org
Powhatan County
3880 Old Buckingham Rd Ste C PO Box 37 Powhatan VA 23139 804-598-5660 598-5608
Web: www.powhatanva.com
Prairie County
200 Ct House Sq Ste 101 Ste 101 Des Arc AR 72040 870-256-4137
Web: prairiecountysheriff.org
Prairie County 217 W Pk St Terry MT 59349 406-635-5575 635-5576
Web: visitterrymt.com

Pratt County
Pratt County Court House 300 S Ninnescah Pratt KS 67124 620-672-4112 672-9541
Web: www.prattcounty.org
Preble County 101 E Main St Eaton OH 45320 937-456-8143 456-8114
Web: www.prebco.org
Prentiss County 1901-B E Chambers Booneville MS 38829 662-728-6232
Web: prentisscountysheriff.com
Presidio County PO Box 879 Marfa TX 79843 432-729-4081 729-4920
Web: www.txdmv.gov
Presque Isle County PO Box 110 Rogers City MI 49779 989-734-3810 734-7635
Web: www.presqueislecounty.org
Price County 126 Cherry St Phillips WI 54555 715-339-3325 339-3089
Web: www.co.price.wi.us
Prince Edward County
111 S St Second Fl PO Box 304 Farmville VA 23901 434-392-5145 392-3913
Web: www.co.prince-edward.va.us
Prince George County
6602 Courts Dr PO Box 68 Prince George VA 23875 804-722-8669 732-1967
Web: www.princegeorgeva.org
Prince George's County
14741 Governor Oden Bowie Dr Upper Marlboro MD 20772 301-952-3600
Web: www.princegeorgescountymd.gov
Prince William County 1 County Complex Ct Woodbridge VA 22192 703-792-6000
Providence County 1 Dorrance Plaza Providence RI 02903 401-458-5400
Web: www.courts.ri.gov
Pueblo County 215 W Tenth St Pueblo CO 81003 719-583-6000 583-4894
Web: pueblo.org
Pulaski County 401 W Markham St Ste 100 Little Rock AR 72201 501-340-8500 340-8340
Web: pulaskicounty.net
Pulaski County 143 Third St NW Ste 1 Pulaski VA 24301 540-980-7705 980-7717
Web: www.pulaskicounty.org
Pulaski County 100 N Main St Ste 202 Somerset KY 42501 606-678-4853 679-8642
TF: 877-655-7154 ■ *Web:* www.pcgovt.com
Pulaski County 101 Dublin Park Rd Dublin VA 24084 573-774-4701
Web: www.visitpulaskicounty.org
Pulaski County 28 Parkway Dr. PO Box 720 Somerset KY 42502 606-679-6361
Web: www.pulaskionline.org
Pushmataha County 302 SW B St Antlers OK 74523 580-298-2512
Web: www.usgennet.org
Putnam County 40 Gleneida Ave Rm 100 Carmel NY 10512 845-225-3641 228-0231
Web: www.putnamcountyny.com
Putnam County 121 S Dixie Ave Cookeville TN 38501 931-526-7106 372-8201
Web: www.putnamcountytn.gov
Putnam County 117 Putnam Dr Ste A Eatonton GA 31024 706-485-5826 923-2345
Web: www.putnamcountyga.us
Putnam County 1 Courthouse Sq St Greencastle IN 46135 765-653-2648
Web: www.co.putnam.in.us
Putnam County 120 N Fourth St PO Box 236 Hennepin IL 61327 815-925-7129 925-7549
Web: www.co.putnam.il.us
Putnam County
130 Orie Griffin Blvd PO Box 1578 Palatka FL 32177 386-329-0800
TF: 800-426-9975 ■ *Web:* www.pcso.us
Putnam County 3389 Winfield Rd Winfield WV 25213 304-586-0202
Web: www.putnamcounty.org
Putnam County Commissioners
245 E Main St Ste 101 Ottawa OH 45875 419-523-3656
Web: www.putnamcountyohio.com
Quay County PO Box 1246 Tucumcari NM 88401 575-461-2112 461-6208*
**Fax Area Code:* 505 ■ *Web:* www.quaycounty-nm.gov
Queen Anne's County 107 N Liberty St Centreville MD 21617 410-758-4098 758-1170
Web: qac.org/410/qactv---website
Queens County 120-55 Queens Blvd Kew Gardens NY 11415 718-286-6000
Web: www.queensda.org
Quitman County PO Box 582 Georgetown GA 39854 229-334-2159 334-2158
Web: www.qpublic.net
Quitman County 220 Chestnut St Ste 1 Marks MS 38646 662-326-2661
Rabun County 25 Courthouse Sq Ste 201 Clayton GA 30525 706-782-5271
Web: www.gamountains.com
Racine County 730 Wisconsin Ave Racine WI 53403 262-636-3333 636-3491
Web: www.racineco.com
Radford (Independent City) 619 Second St Radford VA 24141 540-731-3610 731-3699
Web: www.courts.state.va.u
Raleigh County 215 Main St Beckley WV 25801 304-255-9178 255-9111
TF: 800-509-6568 ■ *Web:* raleighcountyassessor.com
Ralls County 311 S Main St PO Box 466 New London MO 63459 573-985-5633 985-3446
Web: www.courts.mo.gov
Ramsey County 524 Fourth Ave NE Devils Lake ND 58301 701-662-7001
Web: www.co.ramsey.nd.us
Ramsey County 15 W Kellogg Blvd Saint Paul MN 55102 651-266-8000 266-8039
TF: 866-520-7225 ■ *Web:* www.ramseycounty.us
Randall County PO Box 660 Canyon TX 79015 806-468-5505
Web: www.randallcounty.org
Randolph County 725 McDowell Rd 2nd Fl Asheboro NC 27205 336-318-6300 318-6853
Web: www.co.randolph.nc.us
Randolph County 1 Taylor St Chester IL 62233 618-826-5000 826-3761
Web: randolphcountyclerk.com
Randolph County 1302 N Randolph Ave Elkins WV 26241 304-636-2780
TF: 800-422-3304 ■ *Web:* www.randolphcountywv.com
Randolph County 110 S Main St Huntsville MO 65259 660-277-5822
TF: 844-277-6555 ■ *Web:* www.randolphcounty-mo.com
Randolph County 3355 US Hwy 431 Ste 11 Roanoke AL 36274 334-863-7280 863-7280
Web: www.randolphcountyal.com
Randolph County 100 S Main St PO Box 230 Winchester IN 47394 765-584-7207
Web: www.randolphcounty.us
Rankin County 211 E Government St Ste A Brandon MS 39042 601-825-1475 825-9600
Web: www.rankinchamber.com
Ransom County 204 5th Ave W Lisbon ND 58054 701-683-6128 683-5826
Web: www.ag.ndsu.edu/ndsuag
Rapides Parish PO Box 952 Alexandria LA 71309 318-473-8153 473-4667
Web: rapidesclerk.org
Rappahannock County 290 Gay St PO Box 519 Washington VA 22747 540-675-5330 675-5331
Web: www.rappahannockcountyva.gov

Name / Address	City	State	Zip	Phone	Fax
Ravalli County 215 S Fourth St Ste C	Hamilton	MT	59840	406-375-6212	375-6595
Web: ravalli.us					
Rawlins County 607 Main St.	Atwood	KS	67730	785-626-3351	
Web: www.rawlinscounty.info					
Ray County 100 W Main St County Courthouse.	Richmond	MO	64085	816-776-3377	
Web: raycountycourthouse.com					
Reagan County 3rd St	Big Lake	TX	76932	325-884-2090	
Real County PO Box 750	Leakey	TX	78873	830-232-5202	232-6888
Web: www.co.real.tx.us					
Red Lake County 124 Langevin Ave	Red Lake Falls	MN	56750	218-253-2996	
Web: www.redlakecounty.org					
Red River County 200 N Walnut St	Clarksville	TX	75426	903-427-2401	427-5510
Web: www.co.red-river.tx.us					
Red River Parish Clerk of Court's Office					
PO Box 485	Coushatta	LA	71019	318-932-6741	932-3126
Web: www.redriverclerk.com					
Red Willow County 502 Norris Ave	McCook	NE	69001	308-345-1552	345-4460
Web: www.co.red-willow.ne.us					
Redwood County 403 S Mill St PO Box 130	Redwood Falls	MN	56283	507-637-4016	637-4017
Web: www.co.redwood.mn.us					
Reeves County 100 E Fourth St.	Pecos	TX	79772	432-445-5467	445-3997
Web: reevescountytexas.net					
Refugio County 808 Commerce St PO Box 704	Refugio	TX	78377	361-526-2233	526-1325
Web: www.co.refugio.tx.us					
Reno County 206 W First St.	Hutchinson	KS	67501	620-694-2934	694-2534
Web: renogov.org					
Rensselaer County 1600 Seventh Ave	Troy	NY	12180	518-270-2900	270-2961
Web: www.rensco.com					
Renville County PO Box 68	Mohall	ND	58761	701-756-6398	756-6494
Web: www.ndcourts.gov					
Renville County 500 E DePue Ave 3rd Fl	Olivia	MN	56277	320-523-3680	523-3689
Web: www.renvillecountymn.com					
Republic County 1815 M St	Belleville	KS	66935	785-527-7231	
Web: www.republiccounty.org					
Reynolds County 2323 Green St	Centerville	MO	63633	573-648-2491	
Web: reynoldsso.org					
Rhea County 444 2nd Ave	Dayton	TN	37321	423-775-7832	
Web: www.rheacountytn.gov					
Rice County 320 NW Third St	Faribault	MN	55021	507-332-6101	332-5999
Web: www.co.rice.mn.us					
Rice County 101 W Commercial St	Lyons	KS	67554	620-257-2232	257-3039
Web: www.ricecounty.us					
Rich County 20 S Main St	Randolph	UT	84064	435-793-2415	
Web: www.utahreach.org					
Richardson County 1700 Stone St	Falls City	NE	68355	402-245-2911	245-2946
Web: www.co.richardson.ne.us					
Richland County 2020 Hampton St.	Columbia	SC	29204	803-576-2050	576-2137
Web: www.richlandonline.com					
Richland County 50 Pk Ave E	Mansfield	OH	44902	419-774-5550	774-5862
Web: www.richlandcountyoh.us					
Richland County 103 W Main St.	Olney	IL	62450	618-392-3111	393-4005
Web: ci.olney.il.us					
Richland County					
181 W Seminary St PO Box 310	Richland Center	WI	53581	608-647-2197	647-6134
Web: www.co.richland.wi.us					
Richland County 201 W Main St.	Sidney	MT	59270	406-433-1708	433-3731
Web: www.richland.org					
Richland County 418 Second Ave N	Wahpeton	ND	58075	701-642-7700	642-7701
Web: www.co.richland.nd.us					
Richland Parish 708 Julia St.	Rayville	LA	71269	318-728-2061	728-7004
Web: lpgov.org					
Richmond County 125 S Hancock St	Rockingham	NC	28379	910-997-8211	997-8208
Web: richmondnc.com					
Richmond County 130 Stuyvesant Pl	Staten Island	NY	10301	718-556-7240	390-5269
Web: www.nyc.gov					
Richmond County 101 Ct Cir PO Box 1000	Warsaw	VA	22572	804-333-3781	333-5396
Web: www.co.richmond.va.us					
Riley County 110 Courthouse Plaza.	Manhattan	KS	66502	785-537-6300	537-6394
Web: rileycountyks.gov					
Ringgold County 109 W Madison St.	Mount Ayr	IA	50854	641-464-3231	
Rio Blanco County 555 Main St PO Box 1067	Meeker	CO	81641	970-878-9460	878-3587
Web: www.co.rio-blanco.co.us					
Rio Grande County 965 Sixth St.	Del Norte	CO	81132	719-657-3334	657-2621
Web: www.riograndecounty.org					
Ripley County 209 W Highway St	Doniphan	MO	63935	573-996-2212	
Web: www.ripleycountymissouri.org					
Ripley County 115 N Main St	Versailles	IN	47042	812-689-6115	689-6000
Web: www.ripleycounty.com					
Ritchie County 115 E Main St.	Harrisville	WV	26362	304-643-2164	643-2906
Web: www.ritchiecounty.wv.gov					
Roane County 1209 N Kentucky St	Kingston	TN	37763	865-376-5556	
TF: 888-483-1377 ■ *Web:* www.roanealliance.org					
Roane County 200 Main St	Spencer	WV	25276	304-927-2860	927-2489
Web: roanecounty.wv.gov					
Roanoke County 5204 Bernard Dr.	Roanoke	VA	24018	540-772-2004	561-2884
Web: roanokecountyva.gov					
Roanoke (Independent City)					
210 Reserve Ave SW.	Roanoke	VA	24016	540-853-2000	853-1138
Web: www.roanokeva.gov					
Roberts County 122 E Water St PO Box 458	Miami	TX	79059	806-868-2341	868-3381
Web: www.uccsource.com					
Roberts County 411 2nd Ave E	Sisseton	SD	57262	605-698-7336	698-4277*
**Fax:* Acctg ■ *Web:* roberts.sdcounties.org					
Robertson County PO Box 1029	Franklin	TX	77856	979-828-4130	828-1260
Web: www.co.robertson.tx.us					
Robertson County 26 Ct St	Mount Olivet	KY	41064	606-724-5212	724-5022
Web: www.robertsoncounty.ky.gov					
Robertson County 511 S Brown St	Springfield	TN	37172	615-384-5895	384-2218
Web: www.robertsoncountytn.org					
Robeson County 701 N Elm St	Lumberton	NC	28358	910-671-3000	671-3010
Web: www.co.robeson.nc.us					
Rock County 400 State St	Bassett	NE	68714	402-684-3933	
Web: www.rockcounty.ne.gov					
Rock County 51 S Main St.	Janesville	WI	53545	608-757-5660	757-5662
Web: www.co.rock.wi.us					
Rock County 204 E Brown St.	Luverne	MN	56156	507-283-5020	
Web: www.co.rock.mn.us					
Rock Island County 1504 Third Ave.	Rock Island	IL	61201	309-786-4451	
Web: www.rockislandcounty.org					
Rockbridge County 150 S Main St.	Lexington	VA	24450	540-463-4361	463-5981
Web: www.co.rockbridge.va.us					
Rockcastle County 205 E Main St Rm 102	Mount Vernon	KY	40456	606-256-2831	
Web: www.rockcastlecountyky.com					
Rockdale County 922 Ct St.	Conyers	GA	30012	770-278-7900	278-7921
Web: rockdaleclerk.com					
Rockingham County 10 Rt 125.	Brentwood	NH	03833	603-642-5526	642-5930
Web: www.nhdeeds.com					
Rockingham County 20 E Gay St	Harrisonburg	VA	22802	540-564-3000	
Web: www.rockinghamcountyva.gov					
Rockingham County 371 US Hwy 65 PO Box 101	Wentworth	NC	27375	336-342-8101	342-8105
Web: www.co.rockingham.nc.us					
Rockland County 11 New Hempstead Rd	New City	NY	10956	845-638-5100	638-5675
Web: rocklandgov.com					
Roger Mills County 500 E Broadway PO Box 708	Cheyenne	OK	73628	580-497-3350	
Web: www.rogermills.org					
Rogers County 219 S Missouri St	Claremore	OK	74017	918-923-4400	
Web: www.rogerscounty.org					
Rolette County PO Box 276	Rolla	ND	58367	701-477-3816	
Web: www.rolettecounty.com					
Rooks County 115 N Walnut St	Stockton	KS	67669	785-425-6391	425-6015
Web: www.rookscounty.net					
Roosevelt County 400 2nd Ave S	Wolf Point	MT	59201	575-356-4990	356-8307
Web: www.rooseveltcounty.com					
Roosevelt County 400 Second Ave S	Wolf Point	MT	59201	406-653-6250	653-6289
Web: rooseveltcounty.org					
Roscommon County 500 Lake St	Roscommon	MI	48653	989-275-5923	275-8640
Web: www.roscommoncounty.net					
Roseau County 606 Fifth Ave SW	Roseau	MN	56751	218-463-2541	
Web: www.visitnwminnesota.com/Roseau.htm					
Rosebud County 1200 Main St	Forsyth	MT	59327	406-346-7661	
Web: www.rosebudmontana.com					
Ross County 2 N Paint St Ste B	Chillicothe	OH	45601	740-702-3010	702-3018
Web: www.co.ross.oh.us					
Routt County					
136 Sixth St PO Box 775227	Steamboat Springs	CO	80477	970-870-5405	871-8140
Web: www.co.routt.co.us					
Rowan County 130 W Innes St	Salisbury	NC	28144	704-636-0361	638-3092
Web: rowancountync.gov					
Court house 627 E Main St 2nd Fl.	Morehead	KY	40351	606-784-5212	784-2923
Web: rowancountyclerk.com					
Runnels County 613 Hutchings Ave Rm 303.	Ballinger	TX	76821	325-365-2137	365-4823
Web: www.co.runnels.tx.us					
Rush County					
101 E Second St County Courthouse	Rushville	IN	46173	765-932-2077	938-1163*
**Fax:* Acctg ■ *Web:* www.rushcounty.in.gov					
Rusk County 115 N Main St Ste 206	Henderson	TX	75652	903-657-0330	657-0062
Web: www.co.rusk.tx.us					
Rusk County 311 Miner Ave E	Ladysmith	WI	54848	715-532-2100	532-2237
Web: www.ruskcounty.org					
Russell County 410 Monument Sq PO Box 397	Jamestown	KY	42629	270-343-2112	343-2134
Web: www.rcfcky.com					
Russell County 137 Highland Dr PO Box 1208	Lebanon	VA	24266	276-889-8000	889-8011
Web: www.russellcountyva.us					
Russell County 1000 Broad St.	Phenix City	AL	36867	334-298-7979	
Web: russellcountyprobate.us					
Russell County 401 N Main St PO Box 113	Russell	KS	67665	785-483-4641	483-5725
Web: ks-russellco.manatron.com					
Rutherford County 319 N Maple St Ste 121	Murfreesboro	TN	37130	615-898-7800	898-7830
Web: rutherfordcountytn.gov					
Rutherford County 289 N Main St	Rutherfordton	NC	28139	828-287-6060	287-6210*
**Fax:* 15 ■ *Web:* www.rutherfordcountync.gov					
Rutland Region Chamber of Commerce					
50 Merchants Row	Rutland	VT	05701	802-773-2747	773-2772
TF: 800-756-8880 ■ *Web:* www.rutlandvermont.com					
Sabine County 1555 Worth St PO Box 717	Hemphill	TX	75948	409-787-2732	787-2158
Web: www.sabinecountytexas.com					
Sabine Parish 400 S Capitol St PO Box 419	Many	LA	71449	318-256-6223	
Web: www.sabineparishclerk.com					
Sac County 100 NW State St	Sac City	IA	50583	712-662-4492	662-7358
Web: www.saccounty.org					
Sacramento County 700 H St Rm 7650	Sacramento	CA	95814	916-874-5833	874-5885
Web: www.saccounty.net					
Sagadahoc County 752 High St	Bath	ME	04530	207-443-8200	443-8213
Web: www.sagcounty.com					
Saginaw County 111 S Michigan Ave	Saginaw	MI	48602	989-790-5200	
Web: www.saginawcounty.com					
Saguache County 501 Fourth St PO Box 176	Saguache	CO	81149	719-655-2512	655-2730
Web: www.saguachecounty.net					
Saint Charles County 201 N 2nd St	St. Charles	MO	63301	636-949-7470	822-4012*
**Fax Area Code: 800*					
Saint Charles Parish					
15045 River Rd PO Box 302	Hahnville	LA	70057	985-783-5000	783-2067
Web: www.stcharlesgov.net					
Saint Clair County 165 Fifth Ave Ste 100	Ashville	AL	35953	205-594-2100	594-2110
Web: www.stclairco.com					
Saint Clair County 10 Public Sq.	Belleville	IL	62220	618-277-6600	277-8783
Saint Clair County					
201 McMorran Blvd Rm 2900	Port Huron	MI	48060	810-985-2200	985-4796
Web: www.stclaircounty.org					
Saint Croix County 1101 Carmichael Rd	Hudson	WI	54016	715-386-4600	381-4400
Web: www.co.saint-croix.wi.us					
Saint Francis County					
313 S Izard St Ste 10 PO Box 1817	Forrest City	AR	72335	870-261-1700	
Web: stfranciscountyar.org					

Phone | Fax

Saint Francois County 1 W Liberty St ... Farmington MO 63640 573-756-3623 431-6967
Web: www.sfcgov.org
Saint James Parish 5800 Hwy 44 PO Box 106 ... Convent LA 70723 225-562-2286 562-2279
Web: www.stjamesla.com
Saint John the Baptist Parish
1801 W Airline Hwy ... LaPlace LA 70068 985-652-9569 652-4131
Web: www.sjbparish.com
Saint Johns County
4010 Lewis Speedway ... Saint Augustine FL 32084 904-819-3600 819-3661
Web: www.co.st-johns.fl.us
Saint Joseph County
125 W Main St PO Box 189 ... Centreville MI 49032 269-467-5500 467-5628
Web: www.stjosephcountymi.org
Saint Joseph County 101 S Main St ... South Bend IN 46601 574-235-9635 235-9838
Web: www.stjosephcountyindiana.com
Saint Landry Parish 118 S Ct St PO Box 750 ... Opelousas LA 70571 337-942-5606
Web: www.stlandry.org
Saint Lawrence County 48 Ct St ... Canton NY 13617 315-379-2237 379-2302
Web: www.co.st-lawrence.ny.us
Saint Louis County 41 S Central Ave ... Clayton MO 63105 314-615-5000 615-7890
Web: www.stlouisco.com
Saint Mary's County
41770 Baldridge St PO Box 653 ... Leonardtown MD 20650 301-475-4200 475-4935
Web: www.co.saint-marys.md.us
Sainte Genevieve County 55 S 3rd St ... Sainte Genevieve MO 63670 573-883-5589 883-5312
Salem County 94 Market St ... Salem NJ 08079 856-935-7510 935-6725
TF: 877-222-3737 ■ *Web:* www.salemcountynj.gov/cmssite
Salem (Independent City)
114 N Broad St PO Box 869 ... Salem VA 24153 540-375-3000
Web: salemva.gov
Saline County 200 N Main St Ste 117 ... Benton AR 72015 501-303-5630
Web: www.salinecounty.org
Saline County 10 E Poplar St ... Harrisburg IL 62946 618-253-8197 252-3073
Web: salinecounty.illinois.gov
Saline County 19 E Arrow St ... Marshall MO 65340 660-886-7777 886-2603
Web: www.salinecountymo.org
Saline County 300 W Ash Rm 215 ... Salina KS 67402 785-309-5820 309-5826
Web: www.saline.org
Saline County 215 S Ct St ... Wilber NE 68465 402-821-2374 821-3381
Web: www.co.saline.ne.us
Salt Lake County
2001 S State St Ste S2200 ... Salt Lake City UT 84190 801-468-3000 468-3440
Web: slco.org
Sampson County 435 Rowan Rd ... Clinton NC 28328 910-592-6308 592-1945
Web: www.sampsonnc.com
San Augustine County 223 N Harrison ... San Augustine TX 75972 936-275-2452 275-2263
Web: www.co.san-augustine.tx.us
San Benito County 440 Fifth St Rm 206 ... Hollister CA 95023 831-636-4029 636-2939
Web: www.cosb.us
San Bernardino County
385 N Arrowhead Ave ... San Bernardino CA 92415 909-387-8306
TF: 888-818-8988 ■ *Web:* sbcounty.gov
San Diego County 1600 Pacific Hwy Rm 166 ... San Diego CA 92101 619-531-5413 531-5219
Web: www.sandiegocounty.gov
San Francisco City & County
1 Dr Carlton B Goodlett Pl
City Hall Rm 168 ... San Francisco CA 94102 415-554-4950 554-4951
Web: sfgsa.org
San Jacinto County 1 State Hwy 150 Rm 2 ... Coldspring TX 77331 936-653-2324 653-5604
Web: www.co.san-jacinto.tx.us
San Joaquin County
222 E Weber Ave Second Fl Rm 202 PO Box 990 ... Stockton CA 95201 209-468-2400 468-0371
Web: www.sjgov.org
San Juan County 100 S Oliver Dr ... Aztec NM 87410 505-334-9481 334-3168
Web: www.sjcounty.net
San Juan County 350 Ct St Number 5 ... Friday Harbor WA 98250 360-378-2163 378-3967
Web: www.sanjuanco.com
San Juan County PO Box 338 ... Monticello UT 84535 435-587-3223 587-2425
Web: www.sanjuancounty.org
San Juan County 1557 Greene St ... Silverton CO 81433 970-387-5671
Web: sanjuancountycolorado.us
San Luis Obispo County
1055 Monterey St ... San Luis Obispo CA 93408 805-781-5000 834-4636*
**Fax Area Code:* 800 ■ *Web:* www.slocounty.ca.gov
San Mateo County 455 County Ctr 4th Fl ... Redwood City CA 94063 650-599-1388
Web: www.smcgov.org
San Miguel County 500 W National St Ste 200 ... Las Vegas NM 87701 505-425-9333 425-7019
Web: www.smcounty.net
San Miguel County PO Box 548 ... Telluride CO 81435 970-728-3954 728-4808
Web: www.sanmiguelcounty.org
San Saba County
500 E Wallace St County Courthouse ... San Saba TX 76877 325-372-3614 372-6484
Web: www.co.san-saba.tx.us
Sanborn County 604 W Sixth St ... Woonsocket SD 57385 605-796-4515
Web: ujs.sd.gov
Sanders County 111 Main St PO Box 519 ... Thompson Falls MT 59873 406-827-6942 827-4388
Web: co.sanders.mt.us
Sandoval County 1500 Idalia Rd Bldg D ... Bernalillo NM 87004 505-867-7500
Web: www.sandovalcounty.com
Sandusky County 622 Croghan St ... Fremont OH 43420 419-334-6100 334-6104
Web: www.sandusky-county.com
Sangamon County 200 S Ninth St Rm 204 ... Springfield IL 62701 217-753-6700
Web: www.co.sangamon.il.us
Sanilac County 60 W Sanilac Ave Rm 203 ... Sandusky MI 48471 810-648-3212 648-5466
Web: www.sanilaccounty.net
Santa Barbara County PO Box 159 ... Santa Barbara CA 93102 805-568-2550 568-3247
Web: www.countyofsb.org
Santa Clara County
70 W Hedding St 11th Fl E Wing ... San Jose CA 95110 408-299-5105 295-2192
Web: www.sccgov.org
Santa Cruz County 2150 N Congress Dr ... Nogales AZ 85621 520-761-7800
Web: www.co.santa-cruz.az.us
Santa Cruz County 701 Ocean St Rm 230 ... Santa Cruz CA 95060 831-454-2800
Web: www.co.santa-cruz.ca.us
Santa Fe County 102 Grant Ave ... Santa Fe NM 87504 505-986-6200 995-2740
TF: 877-607-0741 ■ *Web:* www.co.santa-fe.nm.us
Santa Rosa County 6495 Caroline St Ste F ... Milton FL 32570 850-983-1900
Web: www.santarosa.fl.gov
Saratoga County 40 McMaster St ... Ballston Spa NY 12020 518-885-5381 884-4726
Web: www.saratogacountyny.gov
Sargent County 355 Main St ... Forman ND 58032 701-724-6241 724-6244
TF: 866-634-8387 ■ *Web:* sargentnd.com
Sarpy County 1210 Golden Gate Dr Ste 1118 ... Papillion NE 68046 402-593-2100 593-4360
Web: www.co.sarpy.ne.us
Sauk County 505 S Broadway St ... Baraboo WI 53913 608-355-3286 355-3522
Web: www.co.sauk.wi.us
Saunders County PO Box 61 ... Wahoo NE 68066 402-443-8101 443-8174
Web: www.saunderscounty.ne.gov
Sawyer County 10610 Main St Ste 10 ... Hayward WI 54843 715-634-4866 634-3666
TF: 877-699-4110 ■ *Web:* www.sawyercountygov.org
Schenectady County 620 State St ... Schenectady NY 12305 518-285-8435 388-4224
Web: www.schenectadycounty.com
Schleicher County 164 US 190 ... Eldorado TX 76936 325-853-2593
Schley County 49 Pecan St ... Ellaville GA 31806 229-937-2609
Schoharie County 284 Main St PO Box 429 ... Schoharie NY 12157 518-295-8347 295-8482
Web: www.schohariecounty-ny.gov
Schoolcraft County 300 Walnut St Rm 169 ... Manistique MI 49854 906-341-3630
Web: www.schoolcraftcounty.net
Schuyler County Hwy 136 E ... Lancaster MO 63548 660-457-3784 457-3016
Web: www.courts.mo.gov
Schuyler County PO Box 200 ... Rushville IL 62681 217-322-4734 322-6164
Web: www.schuylercountyillinois.com
Schuyler County 105 Ninth St ... Watkins Glen NY 14891 607-535-8133 535-8130
Web: www.schuylercounty.us
Schuylkill County 401 N Second St ... Pottsville PA 17901 570-622-5570 628-1210
Web: www.co.schuylkill.pa.us
Scioto County 602 Seventh St Rm 103 ... Portsmouth OH 45662 740-355-8259 354-2057
Scotland County PO Box 489 ... Laurinburg NC 28353 910-277-2406 277-2411
Web: www.scotlandcounty.org
Scotland County 117 S Market St ... Memphis MO 63555 660-465-7705
Scott County 131 S Winchester St PO Box 188 ... Benton MO 63736 573-545-3549 545-3540
Web: www.scottcountymo.com
Scott County 416 W Fourth St ... Davenport IA 52801 563-326-8647 326-8298
Web: www.scottcountyiowa.com
Scott County 100 E Main St ... Forest MS 39074 601-469-1922 469-5180
Scott County 336 Water St ... Gate City VA 24251 276-386-6521 386-9198
Web: www.scottcountyva.com
Scott County 101 E Main St ... Georgetown KY 40324 502-863-7850 863-7852
Web: www.scottky.com
Scott County 282 Ct St ... Huntsville TN 37756 423-663-2588
Web: www.scottcounty.com
Scott County 210 W 4th St ... Scott City KS 67871 620-872-2640
Web: ks-scott.manatron.com
Scott County 200 Fourth Ave W ... Shakopee MN 55379 952-445-7750 496-8257
Web: www.co.scott.mn.us
Scott County 100 W 1 St Ste 1 ... Waldron AR 72958 479-637-2666 637-0124
Scott County 35 E Market St ... Winchester IL 62694 217-742-5217 742-5853
Web: www.illinoiscourts.gov/circuitcourt/circuitcourtjudges/ccc_county.asp
Scotts Bluff County 1825 Tenth St ... Gering NE 69341 308-436-6600 436-3178
Web: www.scottsbluffcounty.org
Screven County 101 S Main St ... Sylvania GA 30467 912-564-7878
Web: www.screvencounty.com
Scurry County 1806 25th St Ste 300 ... Snyder TX 79549 325-573-5332 573-7396
Web: www.co.scurry.tx.us
Searcy County PO Box 1385 ... Marshall AR 72650 870-448-2557
Web: searcycountyarkansas.org
Sebastian County 35 S Sixth St Rm 105 ... Fort Smith AR 72901 479-782-5065 784-1567
Web: sebastiancountyar.gov
Sedgwick County 315 Cedar St Ste 200 ... Julesburg CO 80737 970-474-2531 474-3507
Web: sedgwickcountygov.net
Sedgwick County 525 N Main St Rm 211 ... Wichita KS 67203 316-660-9222 383-7961
Web: sedgwickcounty.org
Seminole County 200 S Knox Ave ... Donalsonville GA 39845 229-524-2878
Web: www.seminolecountyga.com
Seminole County 1101 E First St ... Sanford FL 32771 407-665-7945 665-7939*
**Fax:* Hum Res ■ *Web:* www.seminolecountyfl.gov
Seminole County 126 S Wewoka Ave PO Box 779 ... Wewoka OK 74884 405-257-6465 257-6262
Web: seminole.oklahoma.usassessor.com
Seneca County 111 Madison St ... Tiffin OH 44883 419-447-4550
Web: www.seneca-county.com
Seneca County 1 DiPronio Dr ... Waterloo NY 13165 315-539-1945 539-3789
Web: www.co.seneca.ny.us
Sequatchie County 22 Cherry St PO Box 595 ... Dunlap TN 37327 423-949-2522
Web: www.sequatchiecounty-tn.gov
Sequoyah County 120 E Chickasaw Ave ... Sallisaw OK 74955 918-775-9321 775-7861
Sevier County 115 N 3rd St Ste 102 ... De Queen AR 71832 870-642-2852 642-3896
Web: www.seviercountyar.com
Sevier County 125 Ct Ave Ste 202 E ... Sevierville TN 37862 865-453-5502 453-6830
Web: www.seviercountytn.org
Seward County 515 N Washington ... Liberal KS 67901 620-626-3212
Web: www.sewardcountyks.org
Seward County PO Box 190 ... Seward NE 68434 402-643-2883
Web: www.connectseward.org
Shackelford County 225 S Main St ... Albany TX 76430 325-762-2232 762-2830
Web: shackelfordcounty.org
Shannon County 18529 Main St ... Eminence MO 65466 573-226-3315 226-5321
Sharkey County PO Box 218 ... Rolling Fork MS 39159 662-873-2755
Web: sharkey.msghn.org/addresses.html
Sharp County 718 Ash Flat Dr ... Ash Flat AR 72513 870-994-7334
Web: www.ark.org/propertytax/sharp/index.php
Shasta County 1643 Market St ... Redding CA 96099 530-225-5730 225-5454
Web: www.co.shasta.ca.us
Shawano County 311 N Main St ... Shawano WI 54166 715-526-9150 524-5157
Web: www.co.shawano.wi.us

				Phone	Fax
Shawnee County 200 SE Seventh St *Web:* www.snco.us	Topeka	KS	66603	785-233-8200	291-4912
Sheboygan County 615 N 6th St *Web:* www.co.sheboygan.wi.us	Sheboygan	WI	53081	920-459-3003	459-0304
Shelby County 100 Hurst St *Web:* www.co.shelby.tx.us	Center	TX	75935	936-598-5600	598-3701
Shelby County Main St *Web:* www.shelbyal.com	Columbiana	AL	35051	205-669-3760	
Shelby County 612 Ct St *TF:* 800-735-3942 ■ *Web:* www.shco.org	Harlan	IA	51537	712-755-3831	755-3200
Shelby County 301 E Main St Rm 8	Shelbyville	IL	62565	217-774-4421	
Shelby County 25 W Polk St *Web:* www.co.shelby.in.us	Shelbyville	IN	46176	317-392-6330	392-6393
Shelby County 1000 Detention Rd *Web:* shelbycounty.ky.gov/pages/default.aspx	Shelbyville	KY	40065	502-633-2343	647-1457
Shelby County 203 SE Service Rd	Ste B	MO	63469	573-633-2181	822-9651
Shelby County 129 E Ct St Ste 100 *Web:* www.co.shelby.oh.us	Sidney	OH	45365	937-498-7226	498-1293
Shenandoah County 600 N Main St Ste 102 *Web:* shenandoahcountyva.us	Woodstock	VA	22664	540-459-6167	459-6192
Sheridan County 215 E Second St *Web:* www.co.sheridan.nd.us	McClusky	ND	58463	701-363-2207	
Sheridan County 100 W Laurel Ave *Web:* www.co.sheridan.mt.us	Plentywood	MT	59254	406-765-1660	765-2609
Sheridan County PO Box 39 PO Box 39 *Web:* sheridancountyne.com	Rushville	NE	69360	308-327-5650	
Sheridan County 224 S Main St Ste B-2 *Web:* www.sheridancounty.com	Sheridan	WY	82801	307-674-2500	
Sherman County 813 Broadway Ste 302 *Web:* ks-sherman.manatron.com	Goodland	KS	67735	785-890-4825	
Sherman County PO Box 456 *Web:* www.co.sherman.ne.us	Loup City	NE	68853	308-745-1513	745-1820
Sherman County PO Box 270 *Web:* www.co.sherman.tx.us	Stratford	TX	79084	806-366-2371	366-5670
Shiawassee County 208 N Shiawassee St *Web:* www.shiawassee.net	Corunna	MI	48817	989-743-2242	743-2241
Shoshone County 700 Bank St *Web:* www.shoshonecounty.org	Wallace	ID	83873	208-752-3331	752-4304
Sibley County 400 Ct St *Web:* www.co.sibley.mn.us	Gaylord	MN	55334	507-237-4051	237-4062
Sierra County 100 Courthouse Sq Ste 11 PO Box D *Web:* www.sierracounty.ca.gov	Downieville	CA	95936	530-289-3295	289-2830
Simpson County 103 W Cedar St *Web:* www.simpsoncountyclerk.ky.gov	Franklin	KY	42134	270-586-8161	586-6464
Simpson County PO Box 459 *Web:* www.simpsontax.com	Mendenhall	MS	39114	601-847-1744	847-2119
Sioux County PO Box 158 *Web:* www.co.sioux.ne.us	Harrison	NE	69346	308-668-2443	668-2443
Siskiyou County 201 Fourth St *Web:* www.co.siskiyou.ca.us	Yreka	CA	96097	530-842-8005	842-8013
Sitka City & Borough 100 Lincoln St *Web:* www.cityofsitka.com	Sitka	AK	99835	907-747-3294	747-7403
Skagit County 205 W Kincaid St Rm 103 *Web:* www.skagitcounty.net	Mount Vernon	WA	98273	360-336-9440	
Skamania County 240 Vancouver Ave PO Box 790 *Web:* www.skamaniacounty.org	Stevenson	WA	98648	509-427-3770	427-3777
Slope County 206 S Main St	Amidon	ND	58620	701-879-6272	879-4392
Smith County 122 Turner High Cir *Web:* www.smithcountychamber.org	Carthage	TN	37030	615-735-9833	
Smith County PO Box 517 *Web:* www.smithcounty.ms.gov	Raleigh	MS	39153	601-782-4751	782-4007
Smith County 218 S Grant St *Web:* www.smithcoks.com	Smith Center	KS	66967	785-282-5110	686-4014
Smyth County 109 W Main St Rm 144 *Web:* www.smythcounty.org	Marion	VA	24354	276-782-4044	782-4045
Snohomish County 3000 Rockefeller Ave *Web:* snohomishcountywa.gov	Everett	WA	98201	425-388-3411	
Snyder County 9 W Market St *Web:* www.snydercounty.org	Middleburg	PA	17842	570-837-4207	837-4282
Socorro County 101 Plaza St *Web:* www.socorrochamber.org	Socorro	NM	87801	575-835-0424	
Solano County 675 Texas St Ste 1900	Fairfield	CA	94533	707-784-7485	784-6311
Somerset County 11916 Somerset Ave Rm 111 *Web:* www.visitsomerset.com	Princess Anne	MD	21853	410-651-0320	
Somerset County 41 Ct St *Web:* www.somersetcounty-me.org	Skowhegan	ME	04976	207-474-9861	474-7405
Somerset County 300 N Ctr Ave *Web:* www.co.somerset.pa.us	Somerset	PA	15501	814-445-1400	445-1447
Somerset County 20 Grove St *Web:* www.co.somerset.nj.us	Somerville	NJ	08876	908-231-7006	253-8853
Sonoma County 575 Admin Dr Ste 104A *Web:* sonomacounty.ca.gov	Santa Rosa	CA	95403	707-565-2431	565-3778
Southampton County 22350 Main St *Web:* www.southamptoncounty.org	Courtland	VA	23837	757-653-2200	653-2547
Spalding County PO Box 1087 *Web:* www.spaldingcounty.com	Griffin	GA	30224	770-467-4200	
Spartanburg County 180 Magnolia St *Web:* www.spartanburgcounty.org	Spartanburg	SC	29306	864-596-2591	
Spencer County 200 Main St PO Box 12 *Web:* spencercounty.in.gov	Rockport	IN	47635	812-649-6028	649-6030
Spencer County 2 W Main St PO Box 397 *Web:* www.spencercountyky.gov	Taylorsville	KY	40071	502-477-3215	
Spokane County 1116 W Broadway Ave *Web:* www.spokanecounty.org	Spokane	WA	99260	509-477-2265	477-2274
Spotsylvania County 1905 Courthouse Rd PO Box 99 *Web:* www.spotsylvania.va.us	Spotsylvania	VA	22553	540-507-7010	507-7019
St.Louis County 100 N 5th Ave W *Fax: Acctg ■ *Web:* www.stlouiscountymn.gov	Duluth	MN	55802	218-726-2450	726-2469*

				Phone	Fax
Stafford County 209 N Broadway St *Web:* www.staffordcounty.org	Saint John	KS	67576	620-549-3295	549-3298
Stafford County 1300 Ct House Rd *Web:* staffordcountyva.gov	Stafford	VA	22554	540-658-8600	
Stanislaus County 1021 I St Ste 101 *Web:* www.stancounty.com	Modesto	CA	95354	209-525-5250	525-5804
Stanley County Auditor 8 E Second Ave *Web:* stanleycounty.org	Fort Pierre	SD	57532	605-223-7780	223-7791
Stanly County 201 S Second St 1000 N First St *Web:* www.co.stanly.nc.us	Albemarle	NC	28001	704-986-3600	
Stanton County PO Box 190 *Web:* stantoncountyks.com	Johnson	KS	67855	620-492-2140	492-2688
Stanton County PO Box 347 *Web:* www.co.stanton.ne.us	Stanton	NE	68779	402-439-2222	439-2200
Stark County 225 Fourth St NE *Web:* starkcountyohio.gov	Canton	OH	44702	330-451-7432	451-7190
Stark County PO Box 130 *Fax: Acctg ■ *Web:* starkcountynd.gov	Dickinson	ND	58602	701-456-7630	456-7634*
Stark County 130 W Main St PO Box 426 *Web:* www.starkcountyillinois.com/Circuit_Clerk.html	Toulon	IL	61483	309-286-5911	
Starke County 53 E Washington St County Courthouse *Web:* co.starke.in.us	Knox	IN	46534	574-772-9128	772-9169
Staunton (Independent City) 113 E Beverley St *Web:* www.staunton.va.us	Staunton	VA	24401	540-332-3874	332-3970
Stearns County 705 Courthouse Sq Rm 121 *Web:* www.co.stearns.mn.us	Saint Cloud	MN	56303	320-656-3601	656-6393
Steele County PO Box 296 *Web:* www.co.steele.nd.us	Finley	ND	58230	701-524-2152	
Steele County 111 E Main St *Web:* www.co.steele.mn.us	Owatonna	MN	55060	507-444-7700	444-7491
Stephens County 200 W Walker St *Web:* www.co.stephens.tx.us	Breckenridge	TX	76424	254-559-3700	559-9645
Stephens County 101 S 11th St *Web:* okcountytreasurers.com	Duncan	OK	73533	580-255-4193	
Stephens County 37 W Tugalo St PO Box 386 *Web:* www.stephenscountyga.com	Toccoa	GA	30577	706-886-9491	886-2185
Stephenson County 50 W Douglas St Ste 500 *Web:* www.co.stephenson.il.us	Freeport	IL	61032	815-235-8289	235-8378
Steuben County 206 E Gale St *Web:* www.co.steuben.in.us	Angola	IN	46703	260-668-1000	668-3702
Steuben County 3 E Pulteny Sq *Web:* www.steubencony.org	Bath	NY	14810	607-664-2563	
Stevens County 215 S Oak St *Web:* www.co.stevens.wa.us	Colville	WA	99114	509-684-3751	684-8310
Stevens County 200 E Sixth St *Web:* www.stevenscoks.org	Hugoton	KS	67951	620-544-2541	544-4094
Stevens County 400 Colorado Ave PO Box 530 *Web:* www.co.stevens.mn.us	Morris	MN	56267	320-208-6600	589-7288
Stewart County 225 Donelson Pkwy PO Box 67 *Web:* www.stewartcogov.com	Dover	TN	37058	931-232-7616	232-4934
Stewart County Commissioner 552 Martin Luther King Junior Dr *Web:* www.stewartcountyga.gov	Lumpkin	GA	31815	229-838-6769	
Stillwater County 400 Third Ave N *Web:* stillwatercountymt.gov	Columbus	MT	59019	406-322-8000	322-8007
Stoddard County 106 S Prairie St *Web:* idasc.org	Bloomfield	MO	63825	573-568-4400	
Stokes County 1012 Main St PO Box 250 *Web:* www.co.stokes.nc.us	Danbury	NC	27016	336-593-4400	593-4401
Stone County 108 E Fourth St *Web:* www.stoneco-mo.us	Galena	MO	65656	417-357-6127	357-6861
Stone County HC 71 Box 1427 *Web:* www.arkansasties.com	Mountain View	AR	72560	870-269-5550	
Stone County 323 E Cavers Ave PO Box 7 *Web:* www.stonecountygov.com	Wiggins	MS	39577	601-928-5246	928-6464
Stonewall County PO Box P *Web:* www.stonewallcountytexas.us	Aspermont	TX	79502	940-989-2272	989-2715
Storey County 26 S B St *Web:* storeycounty.org	Virginia City	NV	89440	775-847-0968	847-0949
Story County 1315 S B Ave *Web:* www.storycountyiowa.gov	Nevada	IA	50201	515-382-7410	
Strafford County 259 County Farm Rd *Web:* www.co.strafford.nh.us	Dover	NH	03820	603-742-1458	743-4407
Stutsman County 511 Second Ave SE *Web:* www.co.stutsman.nd.us	Jamestown	ND	58401	701-252-9035	251-6325
Sublette County PO Box 250 *Web:* www.sublettewyo.com	Pinedale	WY	82941	307-367-4372	367-6396
Suffolk County County Rd 51 *Web:* www.suffolkcountyny.gov	Riverhead	NY	11901	631-852-1400	
Suffolk (Independent City) 441 Market St *Web:* www.suffolkva.us	Suffolk	VA	23434	757-514-4000	
Sullivan County 3411 Hwy 126 *Web:* www.sullivancountytn.gov	Blountville	TN	37617	423-323-6428	279-2725
County Clerk 109 N Main St Ste 5	Milan	MO	63556	660-265-3786	
Sully County PO Box 265 *Web:* www.sullycounty.net	Onida	SD	57564	605-258-2541	258-2884
Summers County 120 Ballengee St *Web:* www.summerscountywv.org	Hinton	WV	25951	304-466-7104	
Summit County 175 S Main St *Web:* co.summitoh.net	Akron	OH	44308	330-643-2500	643-2507
Summit County PO Box 1538 *Web:* www.co.summit.co.us	Breckenridge	CO	80424	970-453-2561	453-3540
Summit County 60 N Main St *Web:* www.co.summit.ut.us	Coalville	UT	84017	435-336-3203	336-3030
Sumner County 101 Public Sq PO Box 549 *Web:* www.sumnertn.org	Gallatin	TN	37066	615-452-4367	451-6027
Sumner County 501 N Washington Ave *Web:* www.co.sumner.ks.us	Wellington	KS	67152	620-326-3395	326-2116

	City	State	ZIP	Phone	Fax
Sumter County 500 W Lamar St PO Box 295	Americus	GA	31709	229-928-4500	928-4503
Web: sumtercountyga.us					
Sumter County 502 Lafayette St PO Box 1619	Livingston	AL	35470	205-652-1580	652-1580
Web: www.sumteralchamber.com					
Sumter County 141 N Main St	Sumter	SC	29150	803-436-2227	436-2223
Web: www.sumtercountysc.org					
Sunflower County 200 Main St	Indianola	MS	38751	662-887-1252	
Superior Court Clerk Office 4800 Tower Hill Rd	Wakefield	RI	02879	401-782-4121	782-4190
Web: www.courts.ri.gov					
Surry County 118 Hamby Rd	Dobson	NC	27017	336-386-3700	
Web: www.co.surry.nc.us					
Surry County 45 School St	Surry	VA	23883	757-294-5271	294-5204
Web: www.surrycountyva.gov					
Susquehanna County 75 Public Ave	Montrose	PA	18801	570-278-4600	278-9268
TF: 800-932-0313 ■ *Web:* www.susqco.com					
Sussex County 2 The Cr PO Box 589	Georgetown	DE	19947	302-855-7700	855-7749
Web: www.sussexcountyde.gov					
Sussex County 15080 Courthouse Rd PO Box 1397	Sussex	VA	23884	434-246-1000	246-6013
Web: www.sussexcountyva.gov					
Sutter County 433 Second St	Yuba City	CA	95991	530-822-7134	822-7214
Web: www.co.sutter.ca.us					
Sutton County 300 E Oak St	Sonora	TX	76950	325-387-3815	
Web: co.sutton.tx.us					
Suwannee County 212 N Ohio Ave	Live Oak	FL	32064	386-362-3071	362-4758
Web: www.suwanneechamber.com					
Swain County 101 Mitchell St PO Box 2321	Bryson City	NC	28713	828-488-9273	
Web: www.swaincountync.gov					
Sweet Grass County 115 W Fifth Ave PO Box 888	Big Timber	MT	59011	406-932-5152	932-3026
Web: sweetgrasscountygov.com					
Sweetwater County 80 W Flaming Gorge Way	Green River	WY	82935	307-872-3732	
Web: www.sweet.wy.us					
Swift County PO Box 288	Benson	MN	56215	320-843-2744	
Web: www.swiftcounty.com					
Swisher County 119 S Maxwell St	Tulia	TX	79088	806-995-3294	995-4121
Web: www.co.swisher.tx.us					
Switzerland County 212 W Main St County Courthouse	Vevay	IN	47043	812-427-3302	427-3179
Web: switzerland-county.com					
Talbot County 11 N Washington St County Courthouse	Easton	MD	21601	410-770-8010	770-8007
Web: talbotcountymd.gov					
Talbot County 74 West Monroe St PO Box 155	Talbotton	GA	31827	706-665-3220	665-8199
Web: talbotcountyga.org					
Taliaferro County PO Box 114	Crawfordville	GA	30631	706-456-2229	456-2904
Web: taliaferrocountyga.org					
Talladega County PO Box 6170	Talladega	AL	35161	256-362-1357	761-2147
Web: www.talladegacountyal.org					
Tallapoosa County 125 N Broadnax St Rm 131	Dadeville	AL	36853	256-825-4268	
Web: tallaco.com					
Tama County 104 W State St PO Box 61	Toledo	IA	52342	641-484-3980	484-5127
Web: www.tamacounty.org					
Taney County 132 David St PO Box 156	Forsyth	MO	65653	417-546-7200	546-2519
Web: www.taneycounty.org					
Tangipahoa Parish 206 E Mulberry St	Amite	LA	70422	985-748-3211	
Web: www.tangipahoa.org					
Taos County 105 Albright St Ste A	Taos	NM	87571	575-737-6300	737-6314
Web: www.taoscounty.org					
Tarrant County 100 E Weatherford St	Fort Worth	TX	76196	817-884-1195	884-3295
Web: www.tarrantcounty.com					
Tattnall County PO Box 759	Reidsville	GA	30453	912-557-6323	557-3046
Web: www.tattnall.com					
Taylor County 300 Oak St	Abilene	TX	79602	325-674-1231	674-1279
Web: www.taylorcountytexas.org					
Taylor County 405 Jefferson St County Courthouse	Bedford	IA	50833	712-523-2095	
Web: taylorcountyiowa.org					
Taylor County 203 N Ct St Ste 5	Campbellsville	KY	42718	270-628-3922	
Web: www.kactfo.com					
Taylor County 214 W Main St	Grafton	WV	26354	304-265-1401	265-3016
Web: taylorcounty.wv.gov					
Taylor County 224 S Second St	Medford	WI	54451	715-748-1460	748-1415
Web: www.co.taylor.wi.us					
Taylor County PO Box 620	Perry	FL	32348	850-838-3506	838-3549
Web: taylorclerk.com					
Tazewell County 11 S Fourth St Fl 2 Ste 203	Pekin	IL	61554	309-477-2264	477-2244
Web: www.tazewell.com					
Tazewell County 101 E Main St	Tazewell	VA	24651	276-385-1235	
Web: courts.state.va.us					
Tehama County 633 Washington St Rm 11	Red Bluff	CA	96080	530-527-3350	527-1745
Web: www.co.tehama.ca.us					
Telfair County 91 Telfair Ave	McRae	GA	31055	229-868-5688	868-7950
Web: georgia.gov/cities-counties/telfair-county					
Teller County PO Box 959	Cripple Creek	CO	80813	719-689-2988	686-7900
Web: www.co.teller.co.us					
Tensas Parish 201 Hancock St	Saint Joseph	LA	71366	318-766-3921	766-3926
Web: www.laclerksofcourt.org					
Terrebonne Parish PO Box 1569	Houma	LA	70361	985-868-5660	868-5143
Web: terrebonneclerk.org					
Terrell County 105 E Hackberry	Sanderson	TX	79848	432-345-2391	345-2740
Web: www.co.terrell.tx.us					
Terry County 500 W Main St Rm 105	Brownfield	TX	79316	806-637-8551	637-4874
Web: www.co.terry.tx.us					
Teton County PO Box 610	Choteau	MT	59422	406-466-2151	466-2151
Web: www.tetoncomt.org					
Teton County 89 N Main St Ste 1	Driggs	ID	83422	208-354-8770	354-8776
Web: tetoncountyidaho.gov					
Teton County PO Box 1727	Jackson	WY	83001	307-733-4430	739-8681
Web: www.tetonwyo.org					
Texas County PO Box 197	Guymon	OK	73942	580-338-3141	338-4311
Web: www.txcountyok.com					
Texas County 210 N Grand Ave Ste 201	Houston	MO	65483	417-967-4709	967-2091
Web: www.texascountymissouri.gov					
Thayer County 225 N Fourth St Rm 201 PO Box 208	Hebron	NE	68370	402-768-6126	768-2129
Web: www.thayercounty.ne.gov					
Thomas County 300 N Ct	Colby	KS	67701	785-460-4500	460-4503
Web: www.thomascountyks.com					
Thomas County 110 N Crawford St PO Box 920	Thomasville	GA	31799	229-225-4100	226-3430
Web: www.thomascountyboc.org					
Thomas County Clerk 503 Main St	Thedford	NE	69166	308-645-2261	645-2623
Web: thomascountynebraska.us					
Throckmorton County 105 N Minter	Throckmorton	TX	76483	940-849-2501	849-3032
Thurston County 2000 Lakeridge Dr SW Bldg 2	Olympia	WA	98502	360-786-5430	753-4033
Web: www.co.thurston.wa.us					
Thurston County PO Box 159	Pender	NE	68047	402-385-2343	385-3544
Web: www.thurstoncountynebraska.us					
Tift County 225 N Tift Ave	Tifton	GA	31794	229-386-7850	
Web: www.tiftcounty.org					
Tillamook County 201 Laurel Ave	Tillamook	OR	97141	503-842-3403	842-1384
Web: www.co.tillamook.or.us					
Tioga County Clerk 16 Ct St PO Box 307	Owego	NY	13827	607-687-8660	687-8686
Web: www.tiogacountyny.com					
Tippah County 212 E Jefferson St	Ripley	MS	38663	662-837-3353	837-3006
Web: www.tippahcounty.ripley.ms					
Tippecanoe County 20 N Third St	Lafayette	IN	47901	765-463-2306	423-9196
Web: www.tippecanoe.in.gov					
Tipton County 220 Highway 51 N Ste 2	Covington	TN	38019	901-476-0207	476-0297
Web: www.tiptonco.com					
Tipton County 101 E Jefferson St	Tipton	IN	46072	765-675-2794	
Web: www.tiptonpl.lib.in.us					
Titus County 100 W 1st Ste 204	Mount Pleasant	TX	75455	903-577-6796	572-5078
Web: www.co.titus.tx.us					
Todd County 221 First Ave S Ste 200	Long Prairie	MN	56347	320-732-6447	732-4001*
**Fax:* Acctg ■ *Web:* www.co.todd.mn.us					
Tolland County 69 Brooklyn St	Rockville	CT	06066	860-875-6294	
Web: www.jud.state.ct.us/directory/directory/directions/38.htm					
Tom Green County 122 W Harris Ave	San Angelo	TX	76903	325-659-6444	659-6459
Web: www.co.tom-green.tx.us					
Tompkins County 320 N Tioga St	Ithaca	NY	14850	607-274-5431	
Web: www.nycourts.gov					
Tooele County 47 S Main St	Tooele	UT	84074	435-843-3140	882-7317
Web: www.co.tooele.ut.us					
Toole County 226 First St S	Shelby	MT	59474	406-424-8310	424-8301
Web: toolecountymt.gov					
Toombs County 100 Courthouse Sq PO Box 112	Lyons	GA	30436	912-526-3311	526-1004
Web: www.toombscountyga.gov					
Torrance County 205 Ninth St PO Box 48	Estancia	NM	87016	505-246-4725	384-5294
Web: www.torrancecountynm.org					
Towns County 1411 Jack Dayton Cir	Young Harris	GA	30582	706-896-4966	
TF: 800-984-1543 ■ *Web:* www.mountaintopga.com					
Travis County PO Box 1748	Austin	TX	78767	512-854-9020	854-4464
Treasure County PO Box 392	Hysham	MT	59038	406-342-5547	
Trego County 18001 283 Hwy	WaKeeney	KS	67672	785-743-6385	
TF: 877-962-7248 ■ *Web:* www.wakeeney.org					
Trempealeau County 36245 Main St	Whitehall	WI	54773	715-538-2311	538-4210
TF: 877-538-2311 ■ *Web:* www.tremplocounty.com					
Treutlen County PO Box 229	Soperton	GA	30457	912-529-6173	529-6996
Web: soperton-treutlen.org					
Trigg County PO Box 672	Cadiz	KY	42211	270-522-8459	522-9489
Web: www.triggcounty.ky.gov					
Trimble County 4874 Hwy 421 N PO Box 312	Bedford	KY	40006	502-255-0062	255-0063
Web: www.trimblecounty.com					
Trinity County PO Box 456	Groveton	TX	75845	936-642-1208	642-3004
Web: www.co.trinity.tx.us					
Tripp County Historical Society 200 E Third St	Winner	SD	57580	605-842-2266	842-2267
Web: ujs.sd.gov					
Troup County PO Box 866	LaGrange	GA	30241	706-883-1740	883-1724
Web: www.troupcountyga.org					
Trousdale County 240 Broadway	Hartsville	TN	37074	615-374-9243	374-9243
Web: hartsvilletrousdale.com					
Trumbull County 160 High St NW	Warren	OH	44481	330-675-2451	675-2462
Tucker County 215 First St Ste 201	Parsons	WV	26287	304-478-2414	478-2217
Web: www.tuckercounty.wv.gov					
Tulare County 2800 W Burrel Ave	Visalia	CA	93291	559-636-5005	733-6318
Web: www.tularecounty.ca.gov					
Tulsa County 500 S Denver Ave Ste 120	Tulsa	OK	74103	918-596-5801	596-5819
Web: www.tulsacounty.org					
Tunica County Admnistrators Department 1058 S Ct St	Tunica	MS	38676	662-363-1465	
Web: www.tunicacounty.com					
Tuolumne County 2 S Green St	Sonora	CA	95370	209-533-5511	533-5510
Web: www.co.tuolumne.ca.us					
Turner County PO Box 191	Ashburn	GA	31714	229-567-2334	567-4794
TF: 800-436-7442 ■ *Web:* georgia.gov					
Turner County 400 S Main St	Parker	SD	57053	605-297-3115	
Web: turner.sdcounties.org					
Tuscaloosa County 714 Greensboro Ave	Tuscaloosa	AL	35401	205-349-3870	
Web: www.tuscco.com					
Tuscarawas County 125 E High Ave	New Philadelphia	OH	44663	330-365-3243	343-4682
Web: www.co.tuscarawas.oh.us					
Twiggs County Commissioners 425 N Railroad St	Jeffersonville	GA	31044	478-945-3629	
Web: www.twiggscounty.us					
Twin Falls County 630 Addison Ave W 2nd Fl	Twin Falls	ID	83301	208-736-4004	736-4155
Web: www.twinfallscounty.org					
Tyler County 100 Bluff St Rm 110	Woodville	TX	75979	409-283-2281	283-6305
Web: www.co.tyler.tx.us					
Tyler County Assessor 121 Main St	Middlebourne	WV	26149	304-758-4781	758-2126
Web: www.tylercountywv.com					

Phone Fax

Tyrrell County 108 S Water St . . . Columbia NC 27925 252-796-1371
Web: www.visittyrrellcounty.com

Uinta County 225 Ninth St PO Box 810 . . . Evanston WY 82931 307-783-0306 783-0376
Web: www.uintacounty.com

Uintah County 147 E Main St . . . Vernal UT 84078 435-781-0770 781-6701
TF: 800-966-4680 ■ *Web:* www.co.uintah.ut.us

Ulster County 240 Fair St . . . Kingston NY 12401 845-340-3288 340-3299
Web: ulstercountyny.gov

Umatilla County 216 SE Fourth St . . . Pendleton OR 97801 541-278-6236 278-6345
Web: www.co.umatilla.or.us

Unicoi County 100 Main St PO Box 713 . . . Erwin TN 37650 423-743-3000
Web: www.unicoicounty.org

Unified Government of Wyandotte County/Kansas City
701 N Seventh St Ste 323 . . . Kansas City KS 66101 913-573-5260 573-5005
Web: www.wycokck.org

Union County 65 Courthouse St PO Box 1 . . . Blairsville GA 30512 706-439-6000 439-6004
Web: unioncountyga.gov

Union County 1103 S First St . . . Clayton NM 88415 575-374-9253
TF: 800-390-7858 ■ *Web:* claytonnm.org

Union County 300 N Pine St Ste 6 . . . Creston IA 50801 641-782-7315 782-8241
Web: www.unioncountyiowa.org

Union County
101 N Washington Rm 102 County Courthouse . . . El Dorado AR 71730 870-864-1910 864-1927
Web: unioncountyar.com

Union County 209 E Main St Ste 230 . . . Elk Point SD 57025 605-356-2132
Web: unioncountysd.org

Union County 301 S Main St Ste 1 . . . Anna IL 62906 618-833-5711 833-5496
Web: www.shawneeheartland.com/government.html

Union County 1106 K Ave . . . La Grande OR 97850 541-963-1001 963-1079
TF: 800-735-1232 ■ *Web:* www.union-county.org

Union County 103 S Second St . . . Lewisburg PA 17837 570-524-8781 524-8785
Web: www.unioncountypa.org

Union County 26 W Union St . . . Liberty IN 47353 765-458-6121 458-5263

Union County 1001 Main St PO Box 848 . . . Maynardville TN 37807 865-992-2811 992-2812
Web: www.comeherecomehome.com

Union County 100 W Main St . . . Morganfield KY 42437 270-389-1334
Web: www.unioncounty.ky.gov

Union County 210 W Main St . . . Union SC 29379 864-429-1600 429-1603
Web: www.countyofunion.org

Union County Clerk 215 W 6th St . . . Marysville OH 43040 937-645-3006
Web: co.union.oh.us

Union Parish 100 E Bayou St Ste 105 . . . Farmerville LA 71241 318-368-3055 368-3861
Web: upclerk.com

Upshur County 40 W Main St Rm 101 . . . Buckhannon WV 26201 304-472-1068
Web: www.buchamber.com

Upshur County PO Box 730 . . . Gilmer TX 75644 903-843-4015 843-4504
Web: www.countyofupshur.com

Upson County 106 E Lee St Ste 110 . . . Thomaston GA 30286 706-647-3293 647-7030
Web: upsoncountyga.org

Upton County 205 E 10th St . . . Rankin TX 79778 432-693-2861 693-2129
Web: co.upton.tx.us

Utah County 100 E Ctr St Ste 2200 . . . Provo UT 84606 801-851-8000
Web: www.co.utah.ut.us

Uvalde County PO Box 284 . . . Uvalde TX 78802 830-278-6614 278-8692
Web: www.uvaldecounty.com

Val Verde County PO Box 1267 . . . Del Rio TX 78841 830-774-7564 774-7608
Web: valverdecounty.texas.gov

Valencia County 444 Luna Ave . . . Los Lunas NM 87031 505-866-2014 866-2023
Web: www.co.valencia.nm.us

Valley County 219 N Main St . . . Cascade ID 83611 208-382-7150 382-7107
Web: www.co.valley.id.us

Valley County 125 S 15th St . . . Ord NE 68862 308-728-3700 728-7725
Web: www.co.valley.ne.us

Van Buren County PO Box 475 . . . Keosauqua IA 52565 319-293-3129 293-6404
Web: vanburencoia.org

Van Buren County 212 E Paw Paw St Ste 101 . . . Paw Paw MI 49079 269-657-8218 657-8298
Web: www.vbco.org

Van Wert County 114 E Main St . . . Van Wert OH 45891 419-238-6159 238-4528
Web: www.vanwertcounty.org

Van Zandt County 121 E Dallas St Rm 202 . . . Canton TX 75103 903-567-6503 567-6722
Web: www.vanzandtcounty.org

Vance County 122 Young St Ste E . . . Henderson NC 27536 252-738-2040
Web: www.vancecounty.org

Vanderburgh County 1 NW ML King Jr Blvd . . . Evansville IN 47708 812-435-5241 435-5963
Web: www.vanderburghgov.org

Venango County Courthouse Annex 1174 Elk St . . . Franklin PA 16323 814-432-9500 432-3149
Web: www.co.venango.pa.us

Ventura County 800 S Victoria Ave . . . Ventura CA 93009 805-654-5000
Web: www.countyofventura.org

Vermilion County
6 N Vermilion St Fl 1 Courthouse Annex . . . Danville IL 61832 217-554-1900 554-1914
Web: www.co.vermilion.il.us

Vermilion Parish 100 N State St Ste 101 . . . Abbeville LA 70510 337-898-1992 898-9803
Web: www.vermilionparishclerkofcourt.com

Vermillion County 255 S Main St . . . Newport IN 47966 765-492-5345
TF: 800-340-8155 ■ *Web:* www.vermilliongov.us

Vernon County 100 W Cherry St . . . Nevada MO 64772 417-448-2500 667-6035
Web: www.vernoncountymo.org

Vernon County Courthouse Annex Rm 108 . . . Viroqua WI 54665 608-637-5380
Web: www.wisconline.com/counties/vernon

Victoria County 115 N Bridge St Ste 103 . . . Victoria TX 77901 361-575-1478 575-6276
Web: www.victoriacountytx.org

Vigo County 121 Oak St . . . Terre Haute IN 47807 812-462-3367
Web: www.vigocounty.in.gov

Vilas County 330 Ct St . . . Eagle River WI 54521 715-479-3600 479-3605
Web: www.co.vilas.wi.us

Vinton County
100 E Main St County Courthouse . . . McArthur OH 45651 740-596-4571 596-4571
Web: www.vintoncounty.com

Virginia Beach (Independent City)
2401 Courthouse Dr
Municipal Ctr Bldg 1 . . . Virginia Beach VA 23456 757-385-4242 427-5626
Web: www.vbgov.com

Phone Fax

Volusia County 123 W Indiana Ave . . . DeLand FL 32720 386-736-5920 822-5707
Web: volusia.org

Wabash County 710 NE St . . . Wabash IN 46992 260-563-7171
Web: www.wabashcountycvb.com

Wabash County Clerk 401 N Market St . . . Mount Carmel IL 62863 618-262-4561
Web: state.il.us

Wabasha County 625 Jefferson Ave . . . Wabasha MN 55981 651-565-4410 565-3159*

Wabaunsee County 215 Kansas Ave PO Box 278 . . . Alma KS 66401 785-765-3508 765-3704
Web: ks-wabaunsee.manatron.com

Wadena County 415 S Jefferson St . . . Wadena MN 56482 218-631-7650 631-7635
Web: www.co.wadena.mn.us

Wagoner County 307 E Cherokee St . . . Wagoner OK 74467 918-485-2367 485-8033
Web: www.ok.gov/wagonercounty

Wahkiakum County 64 Main St . . . Cathlamet WA 98612 360-795-3558 795-8813
Web: www.co.wahkiakum.wa.us

Wake County 336 Fayetteville St . . . Raleigh NC 27601 919-856-6160 856-6168
Web: www.wakegov.com

Wakulla County 3056 Crawfordville Hwy . . . Crawfordville FL 32327 850-926-0905 926-0938
Web: www.wakullaclerk.com

Waldo County PO Box D . . . Belfast ME 04915 207-338-1710 338-6360
Web: www.waldocountyme.gov

Walker County PO Box 1207 . . . Huntsville TX 77342 936-436-4933 436-4920
Web: www.co.walker.tx.us

Walker County 1801 Third Ave S PO Box 1447 . . . Jasper AL 35502 205-384-7230 384-7003
Web: www.walkercounty.com

Walker County 101 S Duke St PO Box 445 . . . La Fayette GA 30728 706-638-1437 638-1453
Web: www.walkerga.us

Walla Walla County 315 W Main St . . . Walla Walla WA 99362 509-527-3200 527-3235
Web: www.co.walla-walla.wa.us

Wallace County PO Box 508 . . . Sharon Springs KS 67758 785-852-4935
Web: www.wallacecounty.net/government/localgov.php

Waller County 836 Austin St . . . Hempstead TX 77445 979-826-3357
TF: 800-901-4412 ■ *Web:* www.wallercounty.org

Wallowa County 101 S River St Rm 100 . . . Enterprise OR 97828 541-426-4543 426-5901
Web: www.co.wallowa.or.us

Walsh County 600 Cooper Ave . . . Grafton ND 58237 701-352-1300 352-1104
Web: www.co.walsh.nd.us

Walthall County PO Box 227 . . . Tylertown MS 39667 601-876-2680
Web: www.co.walthall.ms.us

Walton County PO Box 1260 . . . DeFuniak Springs FL 32435 850-892-8115
Web: www.co.walton.fl.us

Walton County Board-Commissioner
303 S Hammond Dr Ste 330 . . . Monroe GA 30655 770-267-1301
Web: www.waltoncountyga.org

Walworth County 100 W Walworth St PO Box 1001 . . . Elkhorn WI 53121 262-741-4241 741-4287
Web: www.co.walworth.wi.us

Walworth County PO Box 292 . . . Selby SD 57472 605-649-7602 649-7867
Web: walworthco.org

Wapello County 101 W Fourth St . . . Ottumwa IA 52501 641-652-3352 683-0053
Web: www.wapellocounty.org

Ward County PO Box 5005 . . . Minot ND 58702 701-857-6600 857-6454
Web: co.ward.nd.us

Ward County
County Courthouse 400 S Allen St Ste 101 . . . Monahans TX 79756 432-943-3294 943-6054
Web: www.co.ward.tx.us

Ware County 800 Church St . . . Waycross GA 31501 912-287-4300 287-4301
Web: www.warecounty.com

Warren County 413 Second St . . . Belvidere NJ 07823 908-475-6211 475-6208
Web: www.co.warren.nj.us

Warren County
429 E Tenth St Ste 100 Courthouse . . . Bowling Green KY 42102 270-842-9416 843-5319
Web: warrencountyclerkky.com

Warren County 220 N Commerce Ave Ste 100 . . . Front Royal VA 22630 540-636-4600 636-6066
Web: www.warrencountyva.net

Warren County 115 N Howard St . . . Indianola IA 50125 515-961-1033 961-1071
Web: www.co.warren.ia.us

Warren County 1340 State Rt 9 . . . Lake George NY 12845 518-761-6429 761-6551
Web: www.warrencountyny.gov

Warren County 406 Justice Dr . . . Lebanon OH 45036 513-695-1358
Web: www.co.warren.oh.us

Warren County 110 S Ct Sq PO Box 574 . . . McMinnville TN 37111 931-473-6611 473-4741
Web: www.warrentn.com

Warren County 100 W Broadway . . . Monmouth IL 61462 309-734-8592 734-7406
Web: www.warrencountyil.com

Warren County 1009 Cherry St . . . Vicksburg MS 39183 601-636-4415
Web: www.co.warren.ms.us

Warren County 204 Fourth Ave . . . Warren PA 16365 814-728-3412
Web: www.warren-county.net

Warren County 46 S Norwood St PO Box 27 . . . Warrenton GA 30828 706-465-9604
Web: www.warrencountyga.com

Warren County 104 W Main St . . . Warrenton MO 63383 636-456-3331
Web: warrencountymo.org

Warren County 602 W Ridgeway St PO Box 619 . . . Warrenton NC 27589 252-257-3115 257-5971
Web: www.warrencountync.com

Warren County 125 N Monroe St Ste 11 . . . Williamsport IN 47993 765-762-3510 762-7251
Web: www.in.gov

Warrick County 107 W Locust St Ste 301 . . . Boonville IN 47601 812-897-6120 897-6189
Web: www.warrickcounty.gov

Wasatch County 25 N Main St . . . Heber City UT 84032 435-657-3221 654-5048
Web: www.wasatch.utah.gov

Wasco County 511 Washington St . . . The Dalles OR 97058 541-506-2530 298-3607
Web: www.co.wasco.or.us

Waseca County 307 N State St . . . Waseca MN 56093 507-835-0610 835-0633*
**Fax:* Acctg ■ *Web:* www.co.waseca.mn.us

Washakie County PO Box 260 . . . Worland WY 82401 307-347-3131 347-9366
Web: www.washakiecounty.net

Washburn County PO Box 639 . . . Shell Lake WI 54871 715-468-4600 468-4725
Web: www.co.washburn.wi.us

Washington County 1 Government Ctr Pl Ste A . . . Abingdon VA 24210 276-525-1300 525-1309
Web: www.washcova.com

Washington County 150 Ash Ave . . . Akron CO 80720 970-345-2701 345-2702
Web: co.washington.co.us

Name / Address	City	State	Zip	Phone	Fax
Washington County 400 S Johnstone Ave *Web:* countycourthouse.org	Bartlesville	OK	74003	918-337-2840	
Washington County PO Box 466 *Web:* www.co.washington.ne.us	Blair	NE	68008	402-426-6822	426-6825
Washington County 100 E Main St Ste 102 *Web:* www.co.washington.tx.us	Brenham	TX	77833	979-277-6200	277-6278
Washington County PO Box 531 *Web:* www.washingtoncountyal.com	Chatom	AL	36518	251-847-2214	
Washington County 280 N College Ave Ste 300 *Web:* www.co.washington.ar.us	Fayetteville	AR	72701	479-444-1711	444-1894
Washington County 383 Broadway Bldg A *Web:* www.co.washington.ny.us	Fort Edward	NY	12828	518-746-2170	746-2177
Washington County 900 Washington Ave PO Box 309 *Web:* www.washingtoncountyms.us	Greenville	MS	38701	662-378-8355	332-4452
Washington County 100 W Washington St *Web:* www.washco-md.net	Hagerstown	MD	21740	240-313-2200	313-2201
Washington County 155 N First Ave *Web:* www.co.washington.or.us	Hillsboro	OR	97124	503-846-8611	
Washington County PO Box 297 *Web:* www.washingtoncountymaine.com	Machias	ME	04654	207-255-3127	255-3313
Washington County 205 Putnam *Web:* www.washingtongov.org	Marietta	OH	45750	740-373-6623	373-5713
Washington County 65 State St	Montpelier	VT	05602	802-828-2091	
Washington County 116 Adams St PO Box 1007 *Web:* www.washconc.org	Plymouth	NC	27962	252-793-5823	793-1183
Washington County 102 N Missouri St *Web:* www.washingtoncountymo.us	Potosi	MO	63664	573-438-6111	438-2009
Washington County 197 E Tabernacle St *Web:* washco.utah.gov	Saint George	UT	84770	435-634-5700	
Washington County 99 Public Sq Ste 102 *Web:* www.washingtoncounty.in.gov	Salem	IN	47167	812-883-5748	
Washington County 119 Jones St *Web:* washingtoncountyga.gov	Sandersville	GA	31082	478-552-3288	
Washington County 117 Cross Main St *Web:* washingtoncountyky.com	Springfield	KY	40069	859-336-5410	336-5407
Washington County 14949 62nd St N *Web:* www.co.washington.mn.us	Stillwater	MN	55082	651-430-6001	430-6017
Washington County 224 W Main St *Web:* co.washington.ia.us	Washington	IA	52353	319-653-7741	653-7787
Washington County 214 C St Ste 3 *Web:* www.washingtoncountyks.gov/county-departments/clerk	Washington	KS	66968	785-325-2461	
Washington County 1 S Main St Ste 1005 *Web:* www.co.washington.pa.us	Washington	PA	15301	724-228-6787	
Washington County 256 East Ct *Web:* www.co.washington.id.us	Weiser	ID	83672	208-414-2092	414-3925
Washington County 432 E Washington St Ste 2027 PO Box 1986 *Web:* www.co.washington.wi.us	West Bend	WI	53095	262-335-4400	306-2208
Washington Parish 909 Pearl St *Web:* www.washingtonparishalerts.org	Franklinton	LA	70438	985-839-7825	839-7827
Washita County 111 E Main Ste 3 *Web:* washita.oklahoma.usassessor.com	Cordell	OK	73632	580-832-2468	832-4110
Washoe County 1001 E. Ninth St *Web:* www.washoecounty.us	Reno	NV	89512	775-328-2000	
Washtenaw County PO Box 8645 *Web:* www.ewashtenaw.org	Ann Arbor	MI	48107	734-222-6850	222-6715
Watauga County 842 W King St Courthouse *Web:* www.wataugacounty.org	Boone	NC	28607	828-265-8000	264-3230
Watonwan County 710 Seventh Ave S PO Box 518 *Web:* www.co.watonwan.mn.us	Saint James	MN	56081	507-375-1236	375-5010
Waukesha County 515 W Moreland Blvd Rm 120 *Web:* www.waukeshacounty.gov	Waukesha	WI	53188	262-548-7010	548-7722
Waupaca County 811 Harding St *Web:* www.co.waupaca.wi.us	Waupaca	WI	54981	715-258-6200	258-6212
Waushara County 209 S St Marie St PO Box 300 *Web:* www.co.waushara.wi.us	Wautoma	WI	54982	920-787-0431	
Wayne County PO Box 435 *Web:* www.waynecountyiowa.com	Corydon	IA	50060	641-872-1536	872-2843
Wayne County Coleman A Young Municipal Ctr 2 Woodward Ave 2nd Fl *Web:* waynecounty.com	Detroit	MI	48226	313-224-6262	
Wayne County 224 E Walnut St Ste 466 *Web:* www.waynegov.com	Goldsboro	NC	27530	919-731-1435	731-1446
Wayne County 3019 fair st	Poplar Bluff	MO	63901	573-785-6402	686-5467
Wayne County 925 Ct St *Web:* waynecountypa.gov	Honesdale	PA	18431	570-253-5970	253-5432
Wayne County 341 E Walnut St *Web:* www.waynecountyga.us	Jesup	GA	31546	912-427-5900	427-5906
Wayne County 18 S Main St PO Box 189 *Web:* www.waynecountyutah.org	Loa	UT	84747	435-836-2765	836-2479
Wayne County 26 Church St *Web:* www.co.wayne.ny.us	Lyons	NY	14489	315-946-5400	946-5407
Wayne County 55 N Main St Ste 106 *Web:* www.waynecounty.ky.gov	Monticello	KY	42633	606-348-5721	
Wayne County 401 E Main St *Web:* www.co.wayne.in.us	Richmond	IN	47374	765-973-9237	973-9321
Wayne County 510 Pearl St PO Box 248 *Web:* www.waynecountyne.org	Wayne	NE	68787	402-375-2288	375-4137
Wayne County 610 Azalea Dr County Courthouse *Web:* waynecounty.ms	Waynesboro	MS	39367	601-735-6056	735-6246
Wayne County PO Box 848 *Web:* www.waynecountytn.org	Waynesboro	TN	38485	931-722-3653	722-5994
Wayne County 428 W Liberty St *Web:* www.wayneohio.org	Wooster	OH	44691	330-287-5400	287-5407
Wayne County Clerk 700 Hendricks St *Web:* waynecountywv.org	Wayne	WV	25570	304-272-6352	
Waynesboro (Independent City) 503 W Main St *Web:* www.waynesboro.va.us	Waynesboro	VA	22980	540-942-6600	942-6671
Weakley County 116 W Main St Rm 104 Room G01 *Web:* www.weakleycountytn.gov	Dresden	TN	38225	731-364-3643	364-9577
Webb County 1110 Washington St *Web:* www.webbcounty.com	Laredo	TX	78040	956-523-4143	523-5012
Weber County 2380 Washington Blvd Ste 350 *Web:* www.webercountyutah.gov	Ogden	UT	84401	801-399-8454	399-8314
Webster County 25 Us Hwy 41A S PO Box 19 *Web:* webstercountyclerk.ky.gov	Dixon	KY	42409	270-639-7006	639-7029
Webster County 701 Central Ave *Web:* webstercountyia.org	Fort Dodge	IA	50501	515-573-1452	
Webster County 101 S Crittenden St *Web:* www.webstercountymo.gov	Marshfield	MO	65706	417-468-2222	859-3614
Webster County PO Box 29	Preston	GA	31824	229-828-3525	
Webster County 621 N Cedar St Ste 2 *Web:* www.co.webster.ne.us	Red Cloud	NE	68970	402-746-2716	746-2710
Webster County Webster County Courthouse 2 Ct Sq *Web:* www.webstercounty.wv.gov	Webster Springs	WV	26288	304-847-5780	847-5780
Weld County PO Box 758 *Web:* www.co.weld.co.us	Greeley	CO	80632	970-336-7204	352-0242
Wells County 102 W Market St Ste 201 *Web:* www.wellscounty.org	Bluffton	IN	46714	260-824-6479	824-6559
Wells County 700 Railway St N *Web:* www.wellscountynd.com	Fessenden	ND	58438	701-547-3122	
West Baton Rouge Parish PO Box 757 *Web:* www.wbrcouncil.org	Port Allen	LA	70767	225-383-4755	387-0218
West Carroll Parish PO Box 1078 *Web:* www.laclerksofcourt.org	Oak Grove	LA	71263	318-428-3281	428-9896
West Feliciana Parish PO Box 1921 *Web:* www.lpgov.org	Saint Francisville	LA	70775	225-635-3864	635-3705
Westchester County 110 Dr Martin Luther King Jr Blvd 3rd Fl *Web:* www.westchesterclerk.com	White Plains	NY	10601	914-995-3080	995-4030
Westmoreland County 2 N Main St Courthouse Sq Ste 101 *Web:* www.co.westmoreland.pa.us	Greensburg	PA	15601	724-830-3100	830-3029
Westmoreland County PO Box 1000 *Web:* www.westmoreland-county.org	Montross	VA	22520	804-493-0130	493-0134
Weston County 400 Stampede St PO Box 130 *Web:* www.westongov.com	Newcastle	WY	82701	307-746-4775	
Wetzel County PO Box 156 *Web:* www.wetzelcounty.wv.gov	New Martinsville	WV	26155	304-455-8217	455-5256
Wexford County 437 E Div St *Web:* www.wexfordcounty.org	Cadillac	MI	49601	231-779-9453	779-9745
Wharton County PO Box 69 *Web:* www.co.wharton.tx.us	Wharton	TX	77488	979-532-2381	532-8426
Whatcom County 311 Grand Ave *Web:* www.co.whatcom.wa.us	Bellingham	WA	98225	360-676-6777	676-6693
Wheatland County 201 A Ave NW *Web:* mbcc.mt.gov	Harlowton	MT	59036	406-632-4891	632-4880
Wheeler County PO Box 654 *Web:* www.wheelercounty.org	Alamo	GA	30411	912-568-7808	568-7808
Wheeler County PO Box 127 *Web:* wheelercounty.ne.gov	Bartlett	NE	68622	308-654-3235	654-3470
Wheeler County 701 Adams St PO Box 447 *Web:* wheelercounty-oregon.com	Fossil	OR	97830	541-763-2911	
Wheeler County PO Box 465 *Web:* www.co.wheeler.tx.us	Wheeler	TX	79096	806-826-5544	826-3282
White County 301 E Main St PO Box 339 *Web:* www.whitecounty-il.gov	Carmi	IL	62821	618-382-7211	382-2322
White County 1235 Helen Hwy *Web:* www.whitecounty.net	Cleveland	GA	30528	706-865-2235	865-1324
White County 110 N Main St *Web:* whitecountyin.us	Monticello	IN	47960	574-583-7032	583-1532
White County 300 N Spruce St *Web:* www.whitecountyar.org	Searcy	AR	72143	501-279-6200	279-6233
White County County Courthouse Rm 205 *Web:* spartatnchamber.com	Sparta	TN	38583	931-836-3203	836-3204
White Pine County 801 Clark St Ste 4 *Web:* www.whitepinecounty.net	Ely	NV	89301	775-289-2341	289-2544
Whiteside County 200 E Knox St *Web:* www.whiteside.org	Morrison	IL	61270	815-772-5100	
Whitfield County PO Box 248 *Web:* www.whitfieldcountyga.com	Dalton	GA	30722	706-876-2559	275-7540
Whitley County 101 W Van Buren St *Web:* whitleygov.com	Columbia City	IN	46725	260-248-3102	248-3137
Whitley County Court Clerk 200 Main St Ste 2 *Web:* whitleycountyfiscalcourt.com	Williamsburg	KY	40769	606-549-6002	549-2790
Whitman County 400 N Main St *Web:* www.co.whitman.wa.us	Colfax	WA	99111	509-397-6240	397-3546
Wibaux County PO Box 199 *Web:* wibauxco.com	Wibaux	MT	59353	406-796-2481	
Wichita County 206 S Fourth St *Web:* www.wichita.k-state.edu	Leoti	KS	67861	785-532-6011	
Wichita County 900 Seventh St Ste 250 *Web:* www.co.wichita.tx.us	Wichita Falls	TX	76301	940-766-8100	716-8554
Wicomico County 125 N Div St *Web:* www.wicomicocounty.org	Salisbury	MD	21803	410-548-4801	548-4803
Wilbarger County 1700 Wilbarger St County Courthouse Rm 15 *Web:* www.co.wilbarger.tx.us	Vernon	TX	76384	940-552-5486	553-1202
Wilcox County 103 N Broad St *TF:* 866-694-5824 ■ *Web:* wilcoxcountygeorgia.com	Abbeville	GA	31001	229-467-2737	467-2000
Wilkes County 22 W Robert Toombs Ave PO Box 661 *Web:* www.washingtonwilkes.org	Washington	GA	30673	706-678-2511	
Wilkes County 110 N St *Web:* www.wilkescounty.net	Wilkesboro	NC	28697	336-651-7346	651-7546

				Phone	Fax
Wilkin County PO Box 219 Web: www.co.wilkin.mn.us	Breckenridge	MN	56520	218-643-7172	643-7167
Wilkinson County 100 Bacon St Web: wilkinsoncounty.net	Irwinton	GA	31042	478-946-2236	946-3767
Wilkinson County PO Box 40	Woodville	MS	39669	601-888-3538	888-6776
Will County 302 N Chicago St Web: www.willcountyillinois.com	Joliet	IL	60432	815-740-4615	
Willacy County 576 W Main St 1st Fl Web: co.willacy.tx.us	Raymondville	TX	78580	956-689-2710	689-9849
Williams County 1 Courthouse Sq Web: www.co.williams.oh.us	Bryan	OH	43506	419-636-2059	636-0643
Williams County PO Box 2047 Web: www.williamsnd.com	Williston	ND	58802	701-577-4540	577-4535
Williamsburg County 201 W Main St Web: www.williamsburgcounty.sc.gov	Kingstree	SC	29556	843-355-9321	355-1587
Williamsburg (Independent City) 401 Lafayette St Web: www.williamsburgva.gov	Williamsburg	VA	23185	757-220-6100	220-6107
Williamson County 1320 W Main St PO Box 624 Web: www.williamsoncounty-tn.gov	Franklin	TN	37064	615-790-5712	790-5610
Williamson County 710 Main St Web: www.wilco.org	Georgetown	TX	78626	512-943-1100	943-1616
Williamson County 201 W Main St Web: www.williamsoncountyil.gov	Marion	IL	62959	618-993-1314	998-0922
Wilson County 1103 Fourth St Ste 2 Web: co.wilson.tx.us	Floresville	TX	78114	830-393-7346	393-7345
Register of Deeds 101 N Goldsboro St PO Box 1728 Web: www.wilson-co.com	Wilson	NC	27894	252-399-2935	237-4341
Winchester (Independent City) 5 N Kent St Web: www.winchesterva.gov	Winchester	VA	22601	540-667-5770	
Windham County 11 Jail St Web: www.windhamcountyvt.gov	Newfane	VT	05345	802-365-4942	365-4945
Windham County 155 Church St Web: jud.ct.gov	Putnam	CT	06260	860-928-7749	
Winkler County 100 E Winkler St Web: www.co.winkler.tx.us	Kermit	TX	79745	432-586-3161	586-3535
Winn Parish Police Jury 119 W Main St Ste 102	Winnfield	LA	71483	318-628-5824	
Winnebago County PO Box 2808 Web: www.co.winnebago.wi.us	Oshkosh	WI	54903	920-236-4800	303-3025
Winneshiek County 201 W Main St TF: 866-227-9874 ■ Web: winneshiekcounty.org	Decorah	IA	52101	563-382-9219	
Winona County 177 Main St Web: www.co.winona.mn.us	Winona	MN	55987	507-457-6350	454-9365
Winston County PO Box 309 Web: winstoncountycircuitclerk.org	Double Springs	AL	35553	205-489-5533	
Winston County 311 W Park St Web: www.winstoncountyms.com	Louisville	MS	39339	662-773-8719	773-8909
Wirt County PO Box 53 Web: www.wirtcounty.wv.gov	Elizabeth	WV	26143	304-275-4271	275-3418
Wise County 200 N Trinity St Web: www.co.wise.tx.us	Decatur	TX	76234	940-627-3351	627-2138
Wise County 206 E Main St Ste 223 PO Box 570 Web: www.wisecounty.org	Wise	VA	24293	276-328-2321	328-9780
Wolfe County 10 Ct St Web: kentuckycountyclerks.com	Campton	KY	41301	606-668-3515	
Wood County 1 Courthouse Sq TF: 866-860-4140 ■ Web: www.co.wood.oh.us	Bowling Green	OH	43402	419-354-9000	
Wood County 1 Ct Sq PO Box 1474 Web: www.woodcountywv.com	Parkersburg	WV	26102	304-424-1850	
Wood County PO Box 1796 Web: www.mywoodcounty.com	Quitman	TX	75783	903-763-2711	763-5641
Wood County PO Box 8095 Web: www.co.wood.wi.us	Wisconsin Rapids	WI	54495	715-421-8460	421-8808
Woodbury County 620 Douglas St Web: www.woodburycountyiowa.gov	Sioux City	IA	51101	712-279-6611	
Woodford County 190 N Main St County Courthouse *Fax Area Code: 877 ■ Web: kwib.ky.gov	Versailles	KY	40383	859-873-5122	817-6585*
Woodruff County 500 N Third St Web: www.prsearch.com/arkansas	Augusta	AR	72006	870-347-2391	
Woods County 407 Government St PO Box 431 Web: woods.oklahoma.usassessor.com	Alva	OK	73717	580-327-3118	327-6230
Woodson County 105 W Rutledge St Rm 226 Web: www.woodsoncounty.net	Yates Center	KS	66783	620-625-8605	625-8670
Woodward County 1600 Main St Ste 9 Web: woodwardcounty.org	Woodward	OK	73801	580-256-8097	254-6840
Worcester County 1 W Market St Rm 1103 Web: www.co.worcester.md.us	Snow Hill	MD	21863	410-632-1194	632-3131
Worcester District Registry of Deeds 90 Front St	Worcester	MA	01608	508-798-7717	
Worth County PO Box 450 Web: worthcounty.us	Grant City	MO	64456	660-564-2219	564-2432
Worth County 1000 Central Ave Web: www.worthcounty.org	Northwood	IA	50459	641-324-2840	324-2360
Worth County 201 N Main St Web: worthcountyboc.com	Sylvester	GA	31791	229-776-8200	776-8232
Wright County 10 Second St NW Rm 201 Web: www.co.wright.mn.us	Buffalo	MN	55313	763-682-7539	682-7300
Wright County 115 N Main St Web: www.wrightcounty.org	Clarion	IA	50525	515-532-2771	532-2669
Wright County 200 N Main St PO Box 862 Web: www.wcida.com	Mountain Grove	MO	65711	417-547-7060	547-7061
Wyandot County 109 S Sandusky Ave County Courthouse Web: www.co.wyandot.oh.us	Upper Sandusky	OH	43351	419-294-1432	294-6414
Wyoming County PO Box 309 Web: wyomingcounty.com	Pineville	WV	24874	304-732-8000	732-9659
Wyoming County 1 Courthouse Sq Web: wyocopa.org	Tunkhannock	PA	18657	570-836-3200	
Wyoming County 143 N Main St Ste 104 Web: www.wyomingco.net	Warsaw	NY	14569	585-786-8810	786-3703
Wythe County 340 S Sixth St Web: www.wytheco.org	Wytheville	VA	24382	276-223-6020	223-6030
Yadkin County 217 E Willow St Web: yadkincountync.gov	Yadkinville	NC	27055	336-679-4200	679-6005
Yakima County 128 N Second St Rm 323 Web: www.yakimacounty.us	Yakima	WA	98901	509-574-1430	
Yamhill County 414 NE Evans St Web: co.yamhill.or.us	McMinnville	OR	97128	503-434-7518	434-7520
Yancey County PO Box 6 Web: www.yanceycountync.gov	Burnsville	NC	28714	828-682-3819	682-4301
Yankton County 410 Walnut St Ste 205 Web: ujs.sd.gov	Yankton	SD	57078	605-668-3080	668-5411
Yates County 417 Liberty St TF: 866-212-5160 ■ Web: www.yatescounty.org	Penn Yan	NY	14527	315-536-5120	536-5545
Yavapai County 1015 Fair St Web: www.yavapai.us	Prescott	AZ	86305	928-771-3200	771-3257
Yazoo County PO Box 186 TF: 800-381-0662 ■ Web: visityazoo.org	Yazoo City	MS	39194	662-746-1815	746-1816
Yell County PO Box 219	Danville	AR	72833	479-495-4850	229-5634
Yellow Medicine County 415 9th Ave Web: mncourts.gov	Granite Falls	MN	56241	320-564-3325	564-4435
Yellowstone County 217 N 27th St Web: co.yellowstone.mt.gov	Billings	MT	59101	406-256-2720	
Yoakum County PO Box 309 Web: www.co.yoakum.tx.us	Plains	TX	79355	806-456-7491	456-2258
Yolo County 625 Ct St Ste 202 Web: yolocounty.org	Woodland	CA	95695	530-666-8150	668-4029
York County 45 Kennebunk Rd PO Box 399 Web: www.yorkcountyme.gov	Alfred	ME	04002	207-324-1577	
York County 510 N Lincoln Ave Web: www.yorkcounty.ne.gov	York	NE	68467	402-362-7759	362-7558
York County 45 N George St Web: yorkcountypa.gov	York	PA	17401	717-771-9612	771-9096
York County 6 S Congress St Web: www.yorkcountygov.com	York	SC	29745	803-684-8507	684-8575
York County 300 Ballard St PO Box 316 Web: courts.state.va.us	Yorktown	VA	23690	757-890-3450	890-3459
Young County 516 Fourth St Rm 104 Web: co.young.tx.us	Graham	TX	76450	940-549-8432	521-0305
Yuba County 915 Eigth St Ste 115 Web: www.co.yuba.ca.us	Marysville	CA	95901	530-749-7575	749-7312
Yuma County 310 Ash St Ste F Web: www.yumacounty.net	Wray	CO	80758	970-332-5809	
Yuma County 198 S Main St Web: www.yumacountyaz.gov	Yuma	AZ	85364	928-373-1010	373-1120
Zapata County 200 E Seventh St Ste 115 Web: www.co.zapata.tx.us	Zapata	TX	78076	956-765-9920	765-9926
Zavala County 200 E Uvalde St County Courthouse Web: www.co.zavala.tx.us	Crystal City	TX	78839	830-374-2331	374-5955

339 GOVERNMENT - STATE

See Also Correctional Facilities - State p. 2163; Employment Offices - Government p. 2243; Ethics Commissions p. 2275; Governors - State p. 2441; Legislation Hotlines p. 2646; Lotteries, Games, Sweepstakes p. 2687; Parks - State p. 2878; Sports Commissions & Regulatory Agencies - State p. 3200; Student Assistance Programs p. 3210; Veterans Nursing Homes - State p. 3292

339-1 Alabama

				Phone	Fax
Administrative Office of Alabama Courts 300 Dexter Ave TF: 866-954-9411 ■ Web: www.alacourt.gov	Montgomery	AL	36104	334-954-5000	
Agriculture & Industries Dept 1445 Federal Dr PO Box 3336 Web: agi.alabama.gov	Montgomery	AL	36109	334-240-7171	240-7190
Alabama Commission on Higher Education 100 N Union St PO Box 302000 Web: ache.alabama.gov	Montgomery	AL	36104	334-242-1998	242-0268
Alabama Ethics Commission 100 N Union St Ste 104 Web: www.ethics.alabama.gov	Montgomery	AL	36104	334-242-2997	242-0248
Alabama Higher Education Commission 100 N Union St PO Box 302000 Web: www.ache.state.al.us	Montgomery	AL	36130	334-242-1998	242-0268
Alabama Prepaid Affordable College Tuition (PACT) Program 100 N Union St Ste 660 TF: 800-252-7228 ■ Web: www.treasury.state.al.us	Montgomery	AL	36130	334-242-7514	
Alabama State Legislature State House 11 S Union St TF: 800-499-3051 ■ Web: www.legislature.state.al.us/senate/senate.html	Montgomery	AL	36130	334-242-7600	
Alabama State Port Authority PO Box 1588 Web: www.asdd.com	Mobile	AL	36633	251-441-7234	441-7216
Archives & History Dept 624 Washington Ave Web: www.archives.state.al.us	Montgomery	AL	36130	334-242-4435	240-3433
Arts Council 201 Monroe St Ste 110 Web: www.arts.alabama.gov	Montgomery	AL	36130	334-242-4076	240-3269
Attorney General 501 Washington Ave	Montgomery	AL	36130	334-242-7300	
Banking Dept 401 Adams Ave Ste 680 Web: www.bank.state.al.us	Montgomery	AL	36130	334-242-3452	242-3500
Child Support Enforcement Div 50 N Ripley St Web: www.dhr.state.al.us	Montgomery	AL	36130	334-242-1310	

				Phone	Fax
Conservation & Natural Resources Dept 64 N Union St PO Box 301450 *TF:* 800-262-3151 ■ *Web:* www.outdooralabama.com	Montgomery	AL	36130	334-242-3486	
Consumer Affairs Office 11 S Union St *Web:* www.aldoi.gov	Montgomery	AL	36130	334-242-7334	
Corrections Dept 301 S Ripley St *Web:* www.doc.state.al.us	Montgomery	AL	36104	334-353-3883	353-3891
Crime Victims Compensation Commission 5845 Carmichael Rd *TF:* 800-541-9388 ■ *Web:* acvcc.alabama.gov	Montgomery	AL	36117	334-290-4420	290-4455
Dept of Industrial Relations 649 Monroe St *Web:* labor.alabama.gov	Montgomery	AL	36131	334-242-8005	242-3960
Dept of Transportation 1409 Coliseum Blvd *Web:* www.dot.state.al.us	Montgomery	AL	36130	334-242-6207	353-6530
Economic & Community Affairs Dept PO Box 5690 *Web:* adeca.alabama.gov	Montgomery	AL	36103	334-242-5100	242-5099
Education Dept 50 N Ripley St PO Box 302101 *Web:* www.alsde.edu	Montgomery	AL	36104	334-242-9700	242-9708
Emergency Management Agency 5898 County Rd 41 PO Box 2160 *TF:* 800-843-0699 ■ *Web:* www.ema.alabama.gov	Clanton	AL	35046	205-280-2200	280-2410
Environmental Management Dept 1400 Coliseum Blvd *Web:* www.adem.state.al.us	Montgomery	AL	36110	334-271-7700	271-7950
Finance Dept 600 Dexter Ave Ste N-105 *Web:* www.finance.state.al.us	Montgomery	AL	36130	334-242-7160	353-3300
Forensic Sciences Dept 525 Carter Hill Rd *Web:* www.adfs.alabama.gov	Montgomery	AL	36106	334-242-2938	240-3284
Highway Patrol Div 301 S Ripley St PO Box 1511 *Web:* www.dps.alabama.gov	Montgomery	AL	36102	334-242-4395	277-3285
Historical Commission 468 S Perry St *Web:* www.preserveala.org	Montgomery	AL	36104	334-242-3184	240-3477
Homeland Security Dept PO Box 304115	Montgomery	AL	36130	334-956-7250	223-1120
Housing Finance Authority PO Box 242967 *Web:* www.ahfa.com	Montgomery	AL	36124	334-244-9200	244-9214
Human Resources Dept Gordon Persons Bldg 50 N Ripley St Ste 2104 *Web:* www.dhr.state.al.us	Montgomery	AL	36130	334-242-1310	353-1115
Information Services Div 64 N Union St Ste 200 *Web:* www.isd.state.al.us	Montgomery	AL	36130	334-242-8600	
Insurance Dept 201 Monroe St Ste 502 PO Box 303351 *Web:* www.aldoi.gov	Montgomery	AL	36104	334-269-3550	241-4192
Labor Dept 649 Monroe St *Web:* www.labor.alabama.gov	Montgomery	AL	36131	334-242-8620	242-0539
Legislature 11 S Union St *Web:* www.legislature.state.al.us	Montgomery	AL	36130	334-242-7560	
Lieutenant Governor 11 S Union St Ste 725 *Web:* www.ltgov.state.al.us	Montgomery	AL	36130	334-242-7900	242-4661
Mental Health & Mental Retardation Dept 100 N Union St PO Box 301410 *TF:* 800-367-0955 ■ *Web:* mh.alabama.gov	Montgomery	AL	36130	334-242-3454	
Motor Vehicle Div 50 N Ripley St *Web:* revenue.alabama.gov	Montgomery	AL	36104	334-242-9000	
National Guard PO Box 3711 *Web:* www.alguard.state.al.us	Montgomery	AL	36109	334-271-7200	
Pardons & Paroles Board 301 S Ripley St PO Box 302405 *Web:* www.pardons.state.al.us	Montgomery	AL	36130	334-353-7771	242-1809
Public Health Dept 201 Monroe St *TF:* 800-252-1818 ■ *Web:* www.adph.org	Montgomery	AL	36104	334-206-5300	206-5534
Public Safety Dept 502 Washington Ave *Web:* dps.alabama.gov	Montgomery	AL	36104	334-242-4259	
Public Service Commission 100 N Union St RSA Union PO Box 304260 *TF:* 800-392-8050 ■ *Web:* www.psc.state.al.us	Montgomery	AL	36130	334-242-5218	242-0509
Rehabilitation Services Dept 602 S Lawrence St *TF:* 800-441-7607 ■ *Web:* www.rehab.alabama.gov	Montgomery	AL	36104	334-293-7500	293-7383
Revenue Dept 50 N Ripley St *Web:* www.revenue.alabama.gov	Montgomery	AL	36132	334-242-1170	
Robert Bentley Governor 600 Dexter Ave *Web:* www.governor.alabama.gov	Montgomery	AL	36130	334-242-7100	353-0004
Secretary of State PO Box 5616 *Web:* www.sos.state.al.us	Montgomery	AL	36103	334-242-7200	242-4993
Securities Commission 770 Washington Ave Ste 570 *TF:* 800-222-1253 ■ *Web:* www.asc.state.al.us	Montgomery	AL	36130	334-242-2984	242-0240
Senior Services Dept 201 Monroe Ste 350 *Web:* alabamaageline.gov	Montgomery	AL	36104	334-242-5743	
State Parks Div 64 N Union St *TF:* 800-252-7275 ■ *Web:* www.alapark.com	Montgomery	AL	36130	800-252-7275	
Tourism Department 401 Adams Ave PO Box 4927 *TF:* 800-252-2262 ■ *Web:* www.tourism.alabama.gov	Montgomery	AL	36104	334-242-4169	242-4554
Treasury Dept 600 Dexter Ave Ste S-106 *Web:* www.treasury.state.al.us	Montgomery	AL	36104	334-242-7500	242-7592
Veterans Affairs Dept 770 Washington Ave # 530 *Web:* www.va.state.al.us	Montgomery	AL	36104	334-242-5077	242-5102
Vital Records PO Box 5625 *Web:* www.adph.org	Montgomery	AL	36103	334-206-5418	
Weights & Measures Div 1445 Federal Dr	Montgomery	AL	36107	334-240-7133	
Workers'' Compensation Div 649 Monroe St *Web:* labor.alabama.gov/wc	Montgomery	AL	36131	334-353-0990	353-8262

339-2 Alaska

				Phone	Fax
Aging Commission 150 Third St PO Box 116093 *Web:* dhss.alaska.gov	Juneau	AK	99801	907-465-3250	465-1398
Alaska Commission on Postsecondary Education PO Box 110510 *TF:* 800-441-2962 ■ *Web:* acpe.alaska.gov	Juneau	AK	99811	907-465-2962	465-5316
Alaska Employment Security Div PO Box 115509 *Web:* www.labor.state.ak.us/esd/home.htm	Juneau	AK	99811	907-465-2712	465-4537
Alaska Legislative Ethics Committee 716 W 4th Ave Ste 230 *Web:* anchorage.akleg.gov	Anchorage	AK	99501	907-269-0111	269-0229
Arts Council 411 W Fourth Ave Ste 1E *Web:* www.eed.state.ak.us	Anchorage	AK	99501	907-269-6610	269-6601
Attorney General PO Box 110300 *Web:* www.law.state.ak.us	Juneau	AK	99811	907-465-3600	465-2075
Banking Securities & Corporations Div 333 Willoughby Ave Fl 9 PO Box 110807 *TF:* 888-925-2521 ■ *Web:* www.commerce.alaska.gov	Juneau	AK	99801	907-465-2521	465-1230
Behavioral Health Div PO Box 110620 *Web:* www.hss.state.ak.us/dbh	Juneau	AK	99811	907-465-3370	465-2668
Child Support Enforcement Div 550 W Seventh Ave Ste 310 *Web:* www.csed.state.ak.us	Anchorage	AK	99501	907-269-6900	269-6650
Children's Services Office PO Box 110630 *Web:* www.hss.state.ak.us/ocs	Juneau	AK	99811	907-465-3191	465-3397
Commerce Community & Economic Development Dept 333 Willoughby Ave PO Box 11080 *Web:* www.commerce.state.ak.us	Juneau	AK	99811	907-465-2500	465-5442
Corrections Dept PO Box 112000 *Web:* www.correct.state.ak.us	Juneau	AK	99811	907-465-3399	465-3390
Court System 303 K St *Web:* www.courts.alaska.gov	Anchorage	AK	99501	907-264-0547	264-0585
Dept of Administration,Personnel Div and Labor relations 10th Fl State Office Bldg PO Box 110201 *Web:* opd.doa.alaska.gov	Juneau	AK	99811	907-465-4430	465-2576
Education & Early Development Dept 801 W Tenth St Ste 200 PO Box 110500 *Web:* www.eed.state.ak.us	Juneau	AK	99811	907-465-2800	465-4156
Enterprise Technology Services Div PO Box 110206 **Fax Area Code: 907 ■ *TF:* 888-565-8680 ■ *Web:* www.alaska.gov	Juneau	AK	99811	888-565-8680	465-3450*
Environmental Conservation Dept 410 Willoughby Ave Ste 303 *Web:* www.alaska.gov	Juneau	AK	99801	907-465-5066	465-5070
Fish & Game Dept 1255 W Eigth St PO Box 25526 *Web:* www.adfg.alaska.gov	Juneau	AK	99802	907-465-4100	465-2332
Health & Social Services Dept PO Box 110601 *Web:* www.hss.state.ak.us	Juneau	AK	99811	907-465-3030	465-3068
History & Archeology Office 550 W Seventh Ave Ste 1310 *Web:* dnr.alaska.gov/parks/oha	Anchorage	AK	99501	907-269-8721	269-8908
Homeland Security & Emergency Services Div PO Box 5750 *Web:* www.ak-prepared.com	Fort Richardson	AK	99505	907-428-7000	428-7009
Housing Finance Corp 4300 Boniface Pkwy 99504 PO Box 101020 *TF:* 800-478-2432 ■ *Web:* www.ahfc.us	Anchorage	AK	99504	907-338-6100	338-9218
Insurance Div PO Box 110805 *Web:* www.commerce.alaska.gov	Juneau	AK	99811	907-465-2515	465-3422
Labor & Workforce Development Dept 111 W Eigth St PO Box 21149 *Web:* www.labor.state.ak.us	Juneau	AK	99802	907-465-2700	465-2784
Lieutenant Governor PO Box 110001 *Web:* www.gov.state.ak.us	Juneau	AK	99811	907-465-3500	465-3532
Measurement Standards Div 12050 Industry Way Bldg O Ste 6 *Web:* www.dot.state.ak.us	Anchorage	AK	99515	907-222-0900	222-1011
Military & Veterans Affairs Dept (DMVA) PO Box 5800 *TF:* 888-248-3682 ■ *Web:* dmva.alaska.gov	Fort Richardson	AK	99505	907-428-6896	
Motor Vehicles Div 3300 B Fairbanks St *Web:* www.alaska.gov	Anchorage	AK	99503	907-269-5559	269-6084
Natural Resources Dept 550 W. 7th Ave Ste 1100 *Web:* dnr.alaska.gov	Anchorage	AK	99501	907-269-8667	269-8917
Occupational Licensing Div 333 Willoughby Ave # 9 *Web:* www.commerce.state.ak.us	Juneau	AK	99801	907-465-2534	465-2974
Parks & Outdoor Recreation Div 550 W Seventh Ave Ste 1260 *Web:* dnr.alaska.gov/parks	Anchorage	AK	99501	907-269-8400	269-8901
Parole Board 550 W Seventh Ave Ste 601 *Web:* www.correct.state.ak.us/parole-board	Anchorage	AK	99501	907-269-4642	269-4697
Permanent Fund Dividend Div 333 Willoughby Ave 11th Fl *Web:* www.pfd.alaska.gov	Juneau	AK	99811	907-465-2326	465-3470
Postsecondary Education Commission 3030 Vintage Blvd PO Box 110510 *TF:* 800-441-2962 ■ *Web:* acpe.alaska.gov	Juneau	AK	99801	907-465-2962	465-5316
Public Assistance Div 350 Main St Rm 304 PO Box 110640 *Web:* dhss.alaska.gov	Juneau	AK	99811	907-465-3347	465-5154
Real Estate Commission 550 W Seventh Ave Ste 1500 *Web:* www.commerce.alaska.gov	Anchorage	AK	99501	907-269-8162	269-8156
Regulatory Commission 550 W Eigth Ave Ste 300 *Web:* www.alaska.gov	Anchorage	AK	99501	907-276-6222	276-0160

				Phone	Fax
Revenue Dept PO Box 110400 Ste 1820 PO Box 110400 *Web:* www.revenue.state.ak.us	Juneau	AK	99811	907-465-2300	465-2389
State Legislature State Capitol *Web:* w3.legis.state.ak.us	Juneau	AK	99801	907-465-4648	465-2864
State Libraries Archives & Museums Div 333 Willoughby Ave PO Box 110571 *Web:* www.eed.state.ak.us/lam	Juneau	AK	99811	907-465-2910	465-2151
State Medical Examiner 5455 Dr Martin Luther King Jr Ave *Web:* www.hss.state.ak.us/dph/sme	Anchorage	AK	99507	907-334-2200	334-2216
State Troopers Div 5700 E Tudor Rd *Web:* www.dps.state.ak.us	Anchorage	AK	99507	907-269-5511	337-2059
Supreme Court 303 K St *Web:* courts.alaska.gov/ctinfo.htm	Anchorage	AK	99501	907-264-0612	264-0878
Tourism Development Office PO Box 118004 *Web:* www.commerce.alaska.gov	Juneau	AK	99811	907-465-2510	465-3767
Transportation & Public Facilities Dept 3132 Ch Dr *Web:* www.dot.state.ak.us	Juneau	AK	99811	907-465-3900	586-8365
Violent Crimes Compensation Board 333 Willoughby Ave State Office Bldg Fl 10 *Web:* doa.alaska.gov	Juneau	AK	99801	907-465-3040	465-2379
Vital Statistics Bureau 5441 Commercial Blvd *Web:* dhss.alaska.gov/dph/vitalstats/pages/default.aspx	Juneau	AK	99801	907-465-3391	465-3618
Vocational Rehabilitation Div 801 W Tenth St Ste 200 *TF:* 800-478-2815 ■ *Web:* www.labor.state.ak.us	Juneau	AK	99801	907-465-2814	465-2856
Workers' Compensation Div 1111 W Eigth St Rm 305 PO Box 115512 *Web:* www.labor.state.ak.us/wc	Juneau	AK	99801	907-465-2790	465-2797

339-3 Arizona

				Phone	Fax
Administrative Office of the Cts 1501 W Washington St *Web:* www.azcourts.gov	Phoenix	AZ	85007	602-542-9301	542-9484
Agriculture Dept 1688 W Adams St *Web:* agriculture.az.gov	Phoenix	AZ	85007	602-542-4373	542-5420
Arizona Employment Administration PO Box 6123 *Web:* www.azdes.gov	Phoenix	AZ	85005	602-542-3957	542-2491
Arizona Lottery 4740 E University Dr *Web:* arizonalottery.com	Phoenix	AZ	85034	480-921-4400	
Arizona Racing Dept 1110 W Washington St Ste 260 *Web:* racing.az.gov	Phoenix	AZ	85007	602-364-1700	364-1703
Arts Commission 417 W Roosevelt St *Web:* azarts.gov	Phoenix	AZ	85003	602-255-5882	256-0282
Attorney General 1275 W Washington St *TF:* 888-377-6108 ■ *Web:* www.azag.gov	Phoenix	AZ	85007	602-542-5025	542-4085
Boxing Commission 1110 W Washington St Ste 260 *Web:* azboxingandmma.gov	Phoenix	AZ	85007	602-364-1700	364-1703
Children Youth & Families Div 1789 W Jefferson St *TF:* 866-229-5553 ■ *Web:* www.azdes.gov	Phoenix	AZ	85007	602-542-0419	542-3330
Commerce Dept 1700 W Washington St Ste 600 *Web:* www.azcommerce.com	Phoenix	AZ	85007	602-771-1100	771-1200
Consumer Protection & Antitrust Unit 1275 W Washington St *Web:* www.azag.gov	Phoenix	AZ	85007	602-542-5763	542-4579
Corrections Dept 1601 W Jefferson St *Web:* corrections.az.gov	Phoenix	AZ	85007	602-542-5497	542-2859
Criminal Justice Commission 1110 W Washington St Ste 230 *Web:* www.azcjc.gov	Phoenix	AZ	85007	602-364-1146	364-1175
Education Dept 1535 W Jefferson St *Web:* www.azed.gov	Phoenix	AZ	85007	602-542-4361	542-5440
Emergency & Military Affairs Dept 5636 E McDowell Rd *Web:* www.azdema.gov	Phoenix	AZ	85008	602-267-2700	267-2954
Executive Clemency Board 1645 W Jefferson St Rm 101 *Web:* boec.az.gov	Phoenix	AZ	85007	602-542-5656	542-5680
Financial Institutions 2910 N 44th St Ste 310 *Web:* www.azdfi.gov	Phoenix	AZ	85018	602-771-2800	381-1225
Game & Fish Dept 5000 W Carefree Hwy *Web:* www.azgfd.com	Phoenix	AZ	85086	602-942-3000	
Government Information Technology Agency 100 N 15th Ave Ste 440 *Web:* www.azdfi.gov	Phoenix	AZ	85007	602-364-4482	364-4799
Health Services Dept 150 N 18th Ave *Web:* www.azdhs.gov	Phoenix	AZ	85007	602-364-3150	542-1062
Highway Patrol Div PO Box 6638 *Web:* www.azdps.gov	Phoenix	AZ	85005	602-223-2000	223-2928
Historic Preservation Office 1300 W Washington St *TF:* 800-285-3703 ■ *Web:* www.azstateparks.com	Phoenix	AZ	85007	602-542-4174	542-4180
Housing Dept 1110 W Washington St Ste 310 *Web:* azhousing.gov	Phoenix	AZ	85007	602-771-1000	771-1002
Industrial Commission 800 W Washington St *Web:* www.ica.state.az.us	Phoenix	AZ	85007	602-542-4411	542-3373
Insurance Dept 2910 N 44th St 2nd Fl *Web:* azinsurance.gov	Phoenix	AZ	85018	602-912-8400	912-8452
Land Dept 1616 W Adams St *Web:* land.az.gov	Phoenix	AZ	85007	602-542-4602	
Legislature Capitol Complex 1700 W Washington St *TF:* 800-352-8404 ■ *Web:* www.azleg.state.az.us	Phoenix	AZ	85007	602-926-3559	926-3429
Medical Board 9545 Doubletree Ranch Rd *Web:* www.azmd.gov	Scottsdale	AZ	85258	480-551-2700	551-2704
Motor Vehicle Div PO Box 2100 *TF:* 800-251-5866 ■ *Web:* www.azdot.gov/mvd	Phoenix	AZ	85001	602-255-0072	
Nursing Board 4747 N Seventh St Ste 200 *Web:* www.azbn.gov	Phoenix	AZ	85014	602-771-7800	771-7888
Office of the Governor 1700 W Washington St *Web:* www.governor.state.az.us	Phoenix	AZ	85007	602-542-4331	542-7601
Postsecondary Education Commission 2020 N Central Ave Ste 550 *Web:* highered.az.gov	Phoenix	AZ	85004	602-258-2435	258-2483
Real Estate Dept 2910 N 44th St Ste 100 *Web:* www.re.state.az.us	Phoenix	AZ	85018	602-771-7799	468-0562
Rehabilitation Services Admin 1789 W Jefferson St 2nd Fl NW *TF:* 800-563-1221 ■ *Web:* www.azdes.gov	Phoenix	AZ	85007	602-542-3332	542-3778
Revenue Dept 1600 W Monroe St *Web:* www.azdor.gov	Phoenix	AZ	85007	602-716-6090	542-4772
Secretary of State 1700 W Washington St W Wing 7th Fl *Web:* www.azsos.gov	Phoenix	AZ	85007	602-542-4285	542-1575
Securities Div 1300 W Washington St 3rd Fl *Web:* www.azinvestor.gov	Phoenix	AZ	85007	602-542-4242	594-7470
State Boards Office 1400 W Washington St Ste 230 *Web:* ppse.az.gov	Phoenix	AZ	85007	602-542-5709	542-1253
State Compensation Fund 3030 N Third St *Web:* www.nvfc.org	Phoenix	AZ	85012	602-631-2000	631-2213
State Parks 1300 W Washington St *Web:* www.azstateparks.com	Phoenix	AZ	85007	602-542-4174	542-4188
Supreme Court 1501 W Washington St *Web:* azcourts.gov	Phoenix	AZ	85007	602-542-9300	542-9480
Tourism Office 1110 W Washington St Ste 155 *TF:* 888-520-3434 ■ *Web:* visitarizona.com	Phoenix	AZ	85007	602-364-3700	364-3701
Treasurer 1700 W Washington St 1st Fl *TF:* 877-365-8310 ■ *Web:* www.aztreasury.gov	Phoenix	AZ	85007	602-542-7800	542-7176
Veterans'' Service Dept 3839 N Third St Ste 200 *Web:* www.azdvs.gov	Phoenix	AZ	85012	602-255-3373	255-1038
Vital Records Office 1818 W Adams St *Web:* www.azdhs.gov	Phoenix	AZ	85007	602-364-1300	364-1257
Weights & Measures Dept 4425 W Olive Ave Ste 134 **Fax Area Code: 623* ■ *TF:* 800-277-6675 ■ *Web:* www.azdwm.gov	Glendale	AZ	85302	602-771-4920	939-8586*

339-4 Arkansas

				Phone	Fax
Administrative Office of the Cts 625 Marshall St *Web:* courts.arkansas.gov	Little Rock	AR	72201	501-682-9400	682-9410
Aging & Adult Services Div PO Box 1437 *Web:* www.daas.ar.gov	Little Rock	AR	72203	501-682-2441	682-8155
Arakansas Ethics Commission PO Box 1917 *TF:* 800-422-7773 ■ *Web:* www.arkansasethics.com	Little Rock	AR	72203	501-324-9600	324-9606
Arakansas Higher Education Dept 423 Main St Ste 400 *Web:* www.adhe.edu	Little Rock	AR	72201	501-371-2000	371-2001
Arkansas Bill Status-Senate State Capitol Rm 320 *Web:* www.arkleg.state.ar.us	Little Rock	AR	72201	501-682-5951	
Arkansas Dept of Workforce Services 2 Capitol Mall *Web:* www.arkansas.gov	North Little Rock	AR	72201	501-682-2121	682-2273
Arkansas Financial Aid Office 114 Silas Hunt Hall *TF:* 800-547-8839 ■ *Web:* finaid.uark.edu	Fayetteville	AR	72701	479-575-3806	575-7790
Arkansas Racing Commission 1509 W Seventh St Rm 505 *Web:* www.dfa.arkansas.gov	Little Rock	AR	72201	501-682-1467	682-5273
Arts Council 323 Ctr St Ste 1500 *Web:* www.arkansasarts.org	Little Rock	AR	72201	501-324-9766	324-9207
Attorney General 323 Ctr St Ste 200 *TF Consumer Info:* 800-482-8982 ■ *Web:* www.ag.state.ar.us	Little Rock	AR	72201	501-682-2007	682-8084
Bank Dept 400 HaRdin Rd Ste 100	Little Rock	AR	72211	501-324-9019	324-9028
Bureau of Standards 4608 W 61st St *Web:* plantboard.arkansas.gov/Standards	Little Rock	AR	72209	501-570-1159	562-7605
Child Support Enforcement Office 1509 W Seventh St *TF:* 800-264-2445 ■ *Web:* dfa.arkansas.gov	Little Rock	AR	72201	501-682-8398	
Children & Family Services Div Slot S560 PO Box 1437 *Web:* humanservices.arkansas.gov	Little Rock	AR	72203	501-682-8772	682-6968
Consumer Protection Div 323 Ctr St Ste 200 *Web:* arkansasag.gov	Little Rock	AR	72201	501-682-2007	
Contractors Licensing Board 4100 RichaRds Rd *Web:* aclb.arkansas.gov	North Little Rock	AR	72117	501-372-4661	372-2247
Correction Dept PO Box 8707 *Web:* www.ark.org	Pine Bluff	AR	71611	870-267-6999	
Cosmetology Board 101 E Capitol Ave Ste 108 *Web:* www.accessarkansas.org	Little Rock	AR	72201	501-682-2168	682-5640
Crime Victims Reparations Board 323 Ctr St Ste 200 *TF:* 800-448-3014 ■ *Web:* arkansasag.gov	Little Rock	AR	72201	501-682-1020	
Development Finance Authority 423 Main St Ste 500 *Web:* www.arkansas.gov	Little Rock	AR	72201	501-682-5900	682-5859
Education Dept 4 Capitol Mall *Web:* arkansased.org	Little Rock	AR	72201	501-682-4475	682-1079
Environmental Quality Dept 5301 Northshore Dr *Web:* www.adeq.state.ar.us	Little Rock	AR	72118	501-682-0744	682-0798

Agency / Address	City	State	ZIP	Phone	Fax
Finance & Administration Dept 1509 W Seventh St *Web:* dfa.arkansas.gov	Little Rock	AR	72201	501-682-2242	682-1029
Game & Fish Commission 2 Natural Resource Dr. *TF:* 800-364-4263 ■ *Web:* www.agfc.com	Little Rock	AR	72205	501-223-6300	
General Assembly State Capitol Bldg *Web:* www.arkleg.state.ar.us	Little Rock	AR	72201	501-682-6107	682-2917
Governor State Capitol Bldg *Web:* www.arkansas.gov	Little Rock	AR	72201	501-682-2345	682-1382
Health & Human Services Dept 4815 W Markham St *Web:* www.healthy.arkansas.gov	Little Rock	AR	72205	501-661-2000	671-1450
Heritage Dept 323 Ctr St Ste 1500 *Web:* www.arkansasheritage.com	Little Rock	AR	72201	501-324-9150	324-9154
Highway & Transportation Dept 10324 I- 30 *TF:* 800-245-1672 ■ *Web:* www.arkansashighways.com	Little Rock	AR	72209	501-569-2000	569-2400
Human Services Dept PO Box 1437 *Web:* humanservices.arkansas.gov	Little Rock	AR	72203	501-682-1001	
Information Systems Dept (DIS) 1 Capitol Mall PO Box 3155 *Web:* www.dis.arkansas.gov	Little Rock	AR	72201	501-682-9990	682-4310
Insurance Dept 1200 W Third St *TF:* 800-282-9134 ■ *Web:* insurance.arkansas.gov	Little Rock	AR	72201	501-371-2600	371-2618
Labor Dept 10421 W Markham St *Web:* www.labor.ar.gov	Little Rock	AR	72205	501-682-4500	682-4506
Lieutenant Governor 500 Woodlane St Ste 270 State Capitol *Web:* www.ltgovernor.arkansas.gov	Little Rock	AR	72201	501-682-2144	
Motor Vehicle Office 1900 W Seventh St Rm 2030 *Web:* www.dfa.arkansas.gov	Little Rock	AR	72203	501-682-4630	682-1116
Natural Resources Commission 101 E Capitol Ste 350 *Web:* www.anrc.arkansas.gov	Little Rock	AR	72201	501-682-1611	682-3991
Parks & Tourism Dept 1 Capitol Mall *TF:* 800-628-8725 ■ *Web:* www.arkansas.com	Little Rock	AR	72201	501-682-7777	682-1364
Public Accountancy Board 101 E Capitol Ave Ste 450 *Web:* www.arkansas.gov	Little Rock	AR	72201	501-682-1520	682-5538
Public Service Commission 1000 Ctr St (PSC Bldg) *Web:* www.arkansas.gov	Little Rock	AR	72201	501-682-2051	682-1717
Real Estate Commission 612 S Summit St *Web:* arec.arkansas.gov	Little Rock	AR	72201	501-683-8010	683-8020
Rehabilitation Services 525 W Capitol Ave *TF:* 800-330-0632 ■ *Web:* ace.arkansas.gov	Little Rock	AR	72201	501-296-1600	296-1655
Revenue Div PO Box 1272 *Web:* www.dfa.arkansas.gov	Little Rock	AR	72203	501-682-7089	682-7900
Secretary of State 500 Woodlane Ave Ste 256 *Web:* www.sos.arkansas.gov	Little Rock	AR	72201	501-682-1010	682-3510
Securities Dept 201 E Markham St Rm 300 *TF:* 800-981-4429 ■ *Web:* securities.arkansas.gov	Little Rock	AR	72201	501-324-9260	324-9268
State Medical Board 1401 West Capitol Ave *Web:* www.armedicalboard.org	Little Rock	AR	72202	501-296-1802	296-1805
State Police 1 State Police Plaza Dr *Web:* www.asp.state.ar.us	Little Rock	AR	72209	501-618-8000	
Supreme Court 625 Marshall St 1320 Justice Bldg *Web:* courts.arkansas.gov/cotc	Little Rock	AR	72201	501-682-6849	682-6877
Treasurer 500 Woodlane State Capitol Ste 220 *Web:* www.artreasury.gov	Little Rock	AR	72201	501-682-5888	682-9692
Veterans Affairs Dept 2200 Fort Roots Dr Bldg 65 Rm 119 *Web:* www.veterans.arkansas.gov	North Little Rock	AR	72114	501-370-3820	370-3829
Vital Records Div 4815 W Markham St Slot 44 *TF:* 800-637-9314 ■ *Web:* www.healthy.arkansas.gov	Little Rock	AR	72205	501-661-2336	
Worker's Compensation Commission 324 S Spring St *TF:* 800-622-4472 ■ *Web:* www.awcc.state.ar.us	Little Rock	AR	72203	501-682-3930	682-2777

339-5 California

Agency / Address	City	State	ZIP	Phone	Fax
Administrative Office of the Cts 455 Golden Gate Ave 3rd Fl *Web:* www.courtinfo.ca.gov	San Francisco	CA	94102	415-865-4200	865-4205
Aging Dept 1300 National Dr Ste 200 *Web:* www.aging.ca.gov	Sacramento	CA	95834	916-419-7500	928-2267
Arts Council 1300 'I' St Ste 930 *TF:* 800-201-6201 ■ *Web:* www.cac.ca.gov	Sacramento	CA	95814	916-322-6555	322-6575
Attorney General PO Box 944255 *Web:* oag.ca.gov	Sacramento	CA	94244	916-445-9555	324-5341
Bureau of Real Estate 2201 Broadway PO Box 187000 *Web:* www.dre.ca.gov	Sacramento	CA	95818	916-227-0782	227-0777
California Athletic Commission 1430 Howe Ave *Web:* www.dca.ca.gov	Sacramento	CA	95825	916-263-2195	263-2197
California Bill Status-Assembly State Capitol Rm 3196 *Web:* www.leginfo.ca.gov/bilinfo.html	Sacramento	CA	95814	916-445-2323	
California Employment Development Dept 800 Capitol Mall MIC 83 *Web:* www.edd.ca.gov	Sacramento	CA	95814	916-654-8210	657-5294
California Fair Political Practices Commission 428 J St Ste 620 *TF:* 866-275-3772 ■ *Web:* www.fppc.ca.gov	Sacramento	CA	95814	916-322-5660	322-0886
California Horse Racing Board 1010 Hurley Way Rm 300 *Web:* www.chrb.ca.gov	Sacramento	CA	95825	916-263-6000	263-6042
California Student Aid Commission PO Box 419027 *TF:* 888-224-7268 ■ *Web:* www.csac.ca.gov	Rancho Cordova	CA	95741	916-526-8999	526-8002
Child Support Services Dept PO Box 419064 *TF:* 866-901-3212 ■ *Web:* www.childsup.ca.gov	Sacramento	CA	95741	916-464-5000	464-5211
Conservation Dept 801 K St MS 24-01 *Web:* www.conservation.ca.gov	Sacramento	CA	95814	916-322-1080	445-0732
Consumer Affairs Dept 400 R St *Web:* www.dca.ca.gov	Sacramento	CA	95814	916-445-1254	445-3755
Corporations Dept 1515 K St Ste 200 *TF:* 866-275-2677	Sacramento	CA	95814	916-445-7205	
Corrections Dept PO Box 942883 *TF:* 877-256-6877 ■ *Web:* www.cdcr.ca.gov	Sacramento	CA	94283	877-256-6877	
Economic Development Dept 915 I St 3rd Fl *Web:* portal.cityofsacramento.org	Sacramento	CA	95814	916-808-7223	
Education Dept 1430 N St Ste 5602 *Web:* www.cde.ca.gov	Sacramento	CA	95812	916-319-0800	319-0100
Emergency Services Office 3650 Schriever Ave *Web:* www.caloes.ca.gov	Mather	CA	95655	916-845-8510	
Energy Commission 1516 Ninth St *Web:* www.energy.ca.gov	Sacramento	CA	95814	916-654-4287	
Environmental Protection Agency 555 Capitol Mall *Web:* www.calepa.ca.gov	Sacramento	CA	95814	916-445-3846	445-6401
Finance Dept State Capitol Rm 1145 *Web:* www.dof.ca.gov	Sacramento	CA	95814	916-445-3878	
Fish & Game Dept 1416 Ninth St 12th Fl *TF:* 888-334-2258 ■ *Web:* www.dfg.ca.gov	Sacramento	CA	95814	916-445-0411	653-7387
Food & Agriculture Dept 1220 N St *Web:* www.cdfa.ca.gov	Sacramento	CA	95814	916-654-0433	654-0403
Health Care Services Dept PO Box 997413 MS 8502 *TF:* 800-735-2929 ■ *Web:* www.dhcs.ca.gov	Sacramento	CA	95899	800-735-2929	
Historic Preservation Office PO Box 942896 *Web:* www.ohp.parks.ca.gov	Sacramento	CA	94296	916-653-6624	653-9824
Housing Finance Agency 500 Capitol Mall Ste 1400 *TF:* 877-922-5432 ■ *Web:* www.calhfa.ca.gov	Sacramento	CA	95814	916-322-3991	
Industrial Relations Dept 455 Golden Gate Ave *Web:* www.dir.ca.gov	San Francisco	CA	94102	415-703-5050	703-5058
Insurance Dept 300 Capitol Mall Ste 1700 *Web:* www.insurance.ca.gov	Sacramento	CA	95814	916-492-3500	445-5280
Lieutenant Governor State Capitol Rm 1114 *Web:* www.ltg.ca.gov	Sacramento	CA	95814	916-445-8994	323-4998
Medical Board 2005 Evergreen St Ste 1200 *Web:* www.mbc.ca.gov	Sacramento	CA	95815	916-263-2382	263-2944
Mental Health Dept 1600 Ninth St PO Box 944202 *Web:* www.dds.ca.gov	Sacramento	CA	94244	916-654-1690	
Military Dept 9800 Goethe Rd *Web:* www.calguard.ca.gov	Sacramento	CA	95827	916-854-3000	
Motor Vehicles Dept PO Box 942869 *Web:* www.dmv.ca.gov	Sacramento	CA	95818	916-657-6437	657-5716
Office of the Governor State Capitol Ste 1173 *Web:* www.gov.ca.gov	Sacramento	CA	95814	916-445-2841	558-3160
Office of Vital Records PO Box 997410 **Fax Area Code:* 800 ■	Sacramento	CA	95899	916-445-2684	858-5553*
Parks & Recreation Dept PO Box 942896 *TF:* 800-777-0369 ■ *Web:* www.parks.ca.gov	Sacramento	CA	94296	916-653-6995	657-3903
Postsecondary Education Commission 1303 J St Ste 500 *Web:* www.cpec.ca.gov	Sacramento	CA	95814	916-445-7933	327-4417
Prison Terms Board 1515 K St Ste 600 *Web:* www.cold.ca.gov	Sacramento	CA	95814	916-445-4071	
Public Utilities Commission 505 Van Ness Ave *TF:* 800-848-5580 ■ *Web:* www.cpuc.ca.gov	San Francisco	CA	94102	415-703-2782	703-1758
Rehabilitation Dept 721 Capitol Mall *Web:* www.rehab.cahwnet.gov	Sacramento	CA	95814	916-324-1313	
Secretary of State 1500 11th St *Web:* www.sos.ca.gov	Sacramento	CA	95814	916-653-6814	653-4620
State Legislature State Capitol *Web:* www.leginfo.ca.gov	Sacramento	CA	95814	916-324-4676	445-1830
Supreme Court 333 W Santa Clara St Ste 1060 *Web:* www.courts.ca.gov	San Jose	CA	95113	408-277-1004	
Teacher Credentialing Commission 1900 Capitol Ave *TF:* 888-921-2682 ■ *Web:* www.ctc.ca.gov	Sacramento	CA	95814	916-445-7254	
Transportation Dept 1120 N St *Web:* www.dot.ca.gov	Sacramento	CA	95814	916-654-5266	654-6608
Treasurer PO Box 942809 *Web:* www.treasurer.ca.gov	Sacramento	CA	94209	916-653-2995	653-3125
Veterans Affairs Dept 1227 'O' St *TF:* 800-221-8998 ■ *Web:* www.calvet.ca.gov	Sacramento	CA	95814	916-653-2158	653-2456
Victim Compensation Program PO Box 3036 **Fax Area Code:* 866 ■ *TF:* 800-777-9229 ■ *Web:* www.vcgcb.ca.gov/victims	Sacramento	CA	95812	800-777-9229	902-8669*
Workers' Compensation Div PO Box 420603 *Web:* www.dir.ca.gov/dwc	San Francisco	CA	94142	415-703-4600	703-4664

339-6 Colorado

				Phone	Fax
State Government Information 1525 Sherman St *Web:* www.colorado.gov	Denver	CO	80203	303-866-5000	
Aging & Adult Services Div 1575 Sherman St Ground Fl *TF:* 800-773-1366 ■ *Web:* www.colorado.gov	Denver	CO	80203	303-866-2636	866-2696
Agriculture Dept 700 Kipling St Ste 4000 *Web:* www.colorado.gov/ag	Lakewood	CO	80215	303-239-4100	239-4125
Arts Council 1625 Broadway Ste 2700 *Web:* www.coloradocreativeindustries.org	Denver	CO	80202	303-892-3840	892-3848
Attorney General 1525 Sherman St 5th Fl *Web:* www.coloradoattorneygeneral.gov	Denver	CO	80203	303-866-4494	866-5691
Banking Div 1560 Broadway St Ste 975 *Web:* colorado.gov/cs	Denver	CO	80202	303-894-7575	894-7570
Child Support Enforcement Div 1575 Sherman St 5th Fl *Web:* www.childsupport.state.co.us	Denver	CO	80203	303-866-4300	866-4360
Children Youth & Families Office 1575 Sherman St *Web:* www.colorado.gov	Denver	CO	80203	303-866-5700	866-2214
Colorado CollegeInvest 1560 Broadway Ste 1700 *TF:* 800-448-2424 ■ *Web:* collegeinvest.org	Denver	CO	80202	303-376-8800	296-4811
Colorado Labor & Employment Dept 633 17th St Ste 201 *TF:* 800-390-7936 ■ *Web:* www.coworkforce.com	Denver	CO	80203	303-318-8000	
Colorado Lottery 212 W Third St Ste 210 *TF:* 800-999-2959 ■ *Web:* www.coloradolottery.com	Pueblo	CO	81003	719-546-2400	546-5208
Corrections Dept 2862 S Cir Dr *Web:* www.doc.state.co.us	Colorado Springs	CO	80906	719-579-9580	
Economic Development Commission 1625 Broadway Ste 2700 *Web:* www.advancecolorado.com	Denver	CO	80202	303-892-3840	892-3848
Education Dept 201 E Colfax Ave *Web:* www.cde.state.co.us	Denver	CO	80203	303-866-6600	830-0793
Educator Licensing Unit 201 E Colfax Ave *Web:* www.cde.state.co.us	Denver	CO	80203	303-866-6628	866-6866
Emergency Management Office 9195 E Mineral Ave Ste 200 *Web:* www.colorado.gov	Centennial	CO	80112	720-852-6600	852-6750
General Assembly 200 E Colfax Ave. *Web:* www.leg.state.co.us	Denver	CO	80203	303-866-3521	
Governor 136 State Capitol Bldg. *Web:* www.colorado.gov/governor	Denver	CO	30203	303-866-2471	866-2003
Higher Education Commission 1380 Lawrence St Ste 1200 *Web:* www.state.co.us	Denver	CO	80203	303-866-2723	866-4266
Historical Society 1300 Broadway *Web:* www.historycolorado.org	Denver	CO	80203	303-866-3682	
Housing & Finance Authority 1981 Blake St *TF:* 800-877-2432 ■ *Web:* www.chfainfo.com	Denver	CO	80202	303-297-2432	297-2615
Human Services Dept 1200 Federal Blvd **Fax Area Code: 720* ■ *Web:* www.colorado.gov	Denver	CO	80204	303-866-5700	944-3019*
Insurance Div 1560 Broadway Ste 850 *Web:* www.colorado.gov	Denver	CO	80202	303-894-7499	894-7455
Lieutenant Governor 130 State Capitol Bldg *Web:* colorado.gov	Denver	CO	80203	303-866-2087	866-5469
Measurements Standards Section 3125 Wyandot St *Web:* www.colorado.gov/ag	Denver	CO	80211	303-867-9217	477-4248
Medical Examiners Board 1560 Broadway Ste 1350 *Web:* colorado.gov/cs	Denver	CO	80202	303-894-7690	894-7692
Motor Vehicle Div 1881 Pierce St *Web:* www.colorado.gov/revenue/dmv	Lakewood	CO	80214	303-205-5600	205-5940
Natural Resources Dept 1313 Sherman St Rm 718 *TF:* 800-536-5308 ■ *Web:* www.dnr.state.co.us	Denver	CO	80203	303-866-3311	866-2115
Office of Information Technology 601 E 18th Ave Ste 250	Denver	CO	80203	303-764-7700	764-7725
Parks & Outdoor Recreation Div 1313 Sherman St Rm 618 *TF Campground Resv:* 800-678-2267 ■ *Web:* cpw.state.co.us	Denver	CO	80203	303-866-3437	866-3206
Parole Board 1600 W 24th St Bldg 54 *Web:* www.ccjrc.org/resources.shtml	Pueblo	CO	81003	719-583-5800	583-5805
Public Health & Environment Dept (CDPHE) 4300 Cherry Creek Dr S *TF:* 800-886-7689 ■ *Web:* www.colorado.gov	Denver	CO	80246	303-692-2000	782-0095
Public Utilities Commission 1560 Broadway Ste 250 *TF:* 800-888-0170 ■ *Web:* advancecolorado.com	Denver	CO	80203	303-894-2000	894-2071
Real Estate Commission 1560 Bdwy Ste 925 *Web:* www.dora.state.co.us/real-estate	Denver	CO	80202	303-894-2166	894-2683
Regulatory Agencies Dept 1560 Broadway Ste 1550 *TF:* 800-886-7675 ■ *Web:* cdn.colorado.gov	Denver	CO	80202	303-894-7855	894-7885
Secretary of State 1700 Broadway 2nd Fl *Web:* www.sos.state.co.us	Denver	CO	80290	303-894-2200	869-4860
Securities Div 1560 Broadway Ste 900 *Web:* cdn.colorado.gov	Denver	CO	80202	303-894-2320	
State Court Administrator 1301 Pennsylvania St Ste 300 *TF:* 800-888-0001 ■ *Web:* www.courts.state.co.us	Denver	CO	80203	303-837-3668	837-2340
State Patrol 700 Kipling St *Web:* www.colorado.gov	Lakewood	CO	80215	303-239-4500	239-4485
Supreme Court 1560 Broadway Ste 1800 *TF:* 877-888-1370 ■ *Web:* www.coloradosupremecourt.com	Denver	CO	80202	303-866-6400	
Tourism Office 1625 Broadway Ste 2700 *Web:* www.colorado.com	Denver	CO	80202	303-892-3840	892-3848
Transportation Dept 4201 E Arkansas Ave. *Web:* www.coloradodot.info	Denver	CO	80222	303-757-9228	757-9153
Treasurer 200 E Colfax Ave State Capitol Ste 140 *Web:* www.colorado.gov	Denver	CO	80203	303-866-2441	866-2123
Victims Programs Office 700 Kipling St Ste 1000 *TF:* 888-282-1080 ■ *Web:* dcj.state.co.us/ovp	Lakewood	CO	80215	303-239-5719	239-4491
Vital Records Section 4300 Cherry Creek Dr S *Web:* www.cdc.gov/nchs/w2w.htm	Denver	CO	80246	303-692-2200	
Vocational Rehabilitation Div 1575 Sherman St 4th Fl *TF:* 866-870-4595 ■ *Web:* www.dvrcolorado.com	Denver	CO	80203	303-866-4150	866-4905
Wildlife Div 6060 Broadway *Web:* cpw.state.co.us	Denver	CO	80216	303-297-1192	
Workers Compensation Div 633 17th St Ste 400 *TF:* 888-390-7936 ■ *Web:* www.colorado.gov	Denver	CO	80202	303-318-8700	318-8710

339-7 Connecticut

				Phone	Fax
State Government Information 101 E River Dr *Web:* www.ct.gov	East Hartford	CT	06108	860-622-2200	
Accountancy Board 30 Trinity St *Web:* www.sots.ct.gov	Hartford	CT	06106	860-509-6179	509-6247
Administrative Services Dept 165 Capitol Ave 4th Fl *Web:* www.das.state.ct.us	Hartford	CT	06106	860-713-5100	713-7459
Aging Commission 210 Capitol Ave Ste 508 *Web:* www.cga.ct.gov	Hartford	CT	06106	860-240-5200	240-5204
Agriculture Dept 165 Capitol Ave *Web:* www.ct.gov/doag	Hartford	CT	06106	860-713-2500	713-2515
Attorney General 55 Elm St *Web:* www.ct.gov	Hartford	CT	06106	860-808-5318	808-5387
Banking Dept 260 Constitution Plaza *TF:* 800-831-7225 ■ *Web:* www.ct.gov	Hartford	CT	06103	860-240-8299	240-8178
Chief Medical Examiner 11 Shuttle Rd *TF:* 800-842-1508 ■ *Web:* www.ct.gov	Farmington	CT	06032	860-679-3980	679-1257
Child Support Assistance 55 Elm St *Web:* www.ct.gov	Hartford	CT	06106	860-808-5150	
Commission on Culture & Tourism 1 Constitution Plaza *Web:* www.cultureandtourism.org	Hartford	CT	06103	860-256-2800	256-2811
Connecticut Ethics Commission 18-20 Trinity St Ste 205 *Web:* www.ct.gov/ethics/site/default.asp	Hartford	CT	06106	860-263-2400	263-2402
Connecticut Labor Dept 200 Folly Brook Blvd *Web:* www.ctdol.state.ct.us	Wethersfield	CT	06109	860-263-6000	263-6699
Consumer Protection Dept 165 Capitol Ave *TF:* 800-842-2649 ■ *Web:* www.ct.gov	Hartford	CT	06106	860-713-6100	707-1966
Correction Dept 24 Wolcott Hill Rd. *Web:* www.ct.gov/doc	Wethersfield	CT	06109	860-692-7780	692-7783
Department of Education PO Box 150471 *Web:* www.ct.gov	Hartford	CT	06115	860-713-6969	713-7017
Dept of Consumer Protection 165 Capitol Ave *TF:* 800-842-2649 ■ *Web:* www.ct.gov	Hartford	CT	06106	860-713-6100	713-7239
Dept of Consumer Protection 165 Capitol Ave *TF:* 800-842-2649 ■ *Web:* www.ct.gov	Hartford	CT	06106	860-713-6100	713-7239
Economic & Community Development Dept 505 Hudson St *Web:* www.ct.gov	Hartford	CT	06106	860-270-8000	270-8188
Emergency Management and Homeland Security Div 25 Sigourney St 6th Fl *TF:* 800-397-8876 ■ *Web:* www.ct.gov/hls	Hartford	CT	06106	860-256-0800	256-0815
Environmental and Energy Protection Dept 79 Elm St *Web:* www.ct.gov	Hartford	CT	06106	860-424-3000	424-4051
General Assembly 300 Capitol Ave Rm 5100 *Web:* www.cga.ct.gov	Hartford	CT	06106	860-240-0100	240-0122
Governor 210 Capitol Ave *Web:* www.ct.gov	Hartford	CT	06106	860-566-4840	524-7395
Higher Education Dept 61 Woodland St *TF:* 800-842-0229 ■ *Web:* www.ctdhe.org	Hartford	CT	06105	860-947-1800	947-1310
Housing Finance Authority 999 W St *Web:* www.chfa.org	Rocky Hill	CT	06067	860-721-9501	571-4367
Information Technology Dept 101 E River Dr *Web:* www.ct.gov	East Hartford	CT	06108	860-622-2200	610-0672
Insurance Dept 153 Market St Ste 7 *Web:* www.ct.gov	Hartford	CT	06103	860-297-3800	566-7410
Judicial Branch 231 Capitol Ave *Web:* www.jud.state.ct.us	Hartford	CT	06106	860-757-2100	757-2130
Lieutenant Governor 210 Capitol Ave Rm 304 *Web:* www.ct.gov	Hartford	CT	06106	860-524-7384	524-7304
Motor Vehicles Dept 60 State St *Web:* www.ct.gov	Wethersfield	CT	06161	860-263-5700	524-4898
Parole Board 55 W Main St Ste 520 *Web:* www.ct.gov	Waterbury	CT	06702	203-805-6605	805-6652
Public Health Dept 410 Capitol Ave *Web:* www.ct.gov	Hartford	CT	06134	860-509-8000	509-7111
Public Utility Control Dept 10 Franklin Sq *TF:* 800-382-4586 ■ *Web:* www.ct.gov	New Britain	CT	06051	860-827-2935	
Rehabilitation Services Bureau 25 Sigourney St 11th Fl *TF:* 800-537-2549 ■ *Web:* www.ct.gov	Hartford	CT	06106	860-424-4844	424-4850
Secretary of State 30 Trinity St *Web:* www.sots.ct.gov	Hartford	CT	06106	860-509-6200	509-6209
State Parks Div 79 Elm St *TF:* 866-287-2757 ■ *Web:* www.ct.gov	Hartford	CT	06106	860-424-3000	424-4070
State Police Div 1111 Country Club Rd *Web:* ct.gov	Middletown	CT	06457	860-685-8000	685-8354

Phone | Fax

Supreme Court 231 Capitol Ave Hartford CT 06106 860-757-2200 757-2217
Web: www.jud.state.ct.us/external/supapp

Transportation Dept 2800 Berlin Tpke. Newington CT 06111 860-594-2000 594-3008
Web: www.ct.gov

Treasurer 55 Elm St Hartford CT 06106 860-702-3000
Web: www.ct.gov

Veterans Affairs Dept 287 W St Rocky Hill CT 06067 860-721-5891 721-5904
TF: 800-447-0961 ■ *Web:* www.ct.gov/ctva

Victim Services Office
225 Spring St 4th Fl Wethersfield CT 06109 800-822-8428
TF: 800-822-8428 ■ *Web:* www.jud.state.ct.us

Workers' Compensation Commission
21 Oak St 4th Fl Hartford CT 06106 860-493-1500 247-1361
TF: 800-223-9675 ■ *Web:* www.wcc.state.ct.us

339-8 Delaware

Phone | Fax

Administrative Office of the Cts
500 N King St 11th Fl Wilmington DE 19801 302-255-0090 255-2217
Web: www.courts.delaware.gov

Aging & Adults with Physical Disabilites Services Div
1901 N DuPont Hwy New Castle DE 19720 302-255-9390
Web: www.dhss.delaware.gov

Agriculture Dept 2320 S DuPont Hwy Dover DE 19901 302-739-4811
TF: 800-282-8685 ■ *Web:* dda.delaware.gov

Arts Div 820 N French St 4th Fl Wilmington DE 19801 302-577-8278 577-6561
Web: www.artsdel.org

Attorney General 820 N French St Wilmington DE 19801 302-577-8400 577-6630
Web: attorneygeneral.delaware.gov

Bank Commissioner 555 E Loockerman St Ste 210 Dover DE 19901 302-739-4235 739-3609
Web: banking.delaware.gov

Chief Medical Examiner 200 S Adam St Wilmington DE 19801 302-577-3420 577-3416
Web: dhss.delaware.gov/dhss/ocme

Child Support Enforcement Div (DCSE)
84A Christiana Rd New Castle DE 19720 302-577-7171 395-6734
TF: 800-464-4357 ■ *Web:* www.dhss.delaware.gov/dhss/dcse

Consumer Protection Unit
820 N French St 5th Fl Wilmington DE 19801 302-577-8600 577-6499
Web: attorneygeneral.delaware.gov

Correction Dept 245 McKee Rd Dover DE 19904 302-739-5601 739-8220*
**Fax:* Mail Rm ■ *Web:* doc.delaware.gov

Delaware Harness Racing Commission
2320 S Dupont Hwy Dover DE 19901 302-698-4599 697-6287
Web: dda.delaware.gov

Delaware Higher Education Commission
401 Federal St Ste 2 Dover DE 19901 302-735-4000
Web: www.doe.state.de.us

Delaware Public Integrity Commission
410 Federal St Margaret O'Neill Bldg Ste 3 Dover DE 19901 302-739-2399 739-2398
Web: www.depic.delaware.gov

Delaware Thoroughbred Racing Commission
2320 S DuPont Hwy Dover DE 19901 302-698-4599
Web: dda.delaware.gov

Div of Motor Vehicles
303 Transportation Cir PO Box 698 Dover DE 19903 302-744-2500
Web: www.dmv.de.gov

Economic Development Office 99 Kings Hwy Dover DE 19901 302-739-4271 739-5749
Web: dedo.delaware.gov

Education Dept 401 Federal St Ste 2 Dover DE 19901 302-735-4035 739-4654
Web: www.doe.state.de.us

Emergency Management Agency
165 Brick Store Landing Rd Smyrna DE 19977 302-659-3362 659-6855
TF: 877-729-3362 ■ *Web:* dema.delaware.gov

Finance Dept 820 N French St 8th Fl Wilmington DE 19801 302-577-8979 577-8982
Web: finance.delaware.gov

Fish & Wildlife Div 89 Kings Hwy Dover DE 19901 302-739-9921 739-6157
Web: www.dnrec.state.de.us/fw

General Assembly Legislative Hall PO Box 1401 Dover DE 19903 302-744-4162 739-6890
Web: www.legis.delaware.gov

Governor 150 William Penn St 2nd Fl Dover DE 19901 302-577-3210 739-2775
Web: governor.delaware.gov

Health & Social Services Dept
1901 N DuPont Hwy New Castle DE 19720 302-255-9675 255-4429
Web: www.dhss.delaware.gov/dhss

Historical & Cultural Affairs Div 21 The Green Dover DE 19901 302-736-7400 739-5660
Web: www.history.delaware.gov/aboutagency.shtml

Housing Authority 18 The Green Dover DE 19901 302-739-4263 739-6122
Web: www.delaware.gov

Lieutenant Governor 150 William Penn St 3rd Fl Dover DE 19901 302-744-4333
Web: ltgov.delaware.gov

Natural Resources & Environmental Control Dept
89 Kings Hwy Dover DE 19901 302-739-9902 739-6242
Web: www.dnrec.state.de.us

Parks & Recreation Div 89 Kings Hwy Dover DE 19901 302-739-9200 739-3817
TF Campground Resv: 877-987-2757 ■ *Web:* www.destateparks.com

Parole Board 820 N French St 5th Fl Wilmington DE 19801 302-577-5233 577-3501
Web: delaware.gov

Professional Regulation Div
861 Silver Lake Blvd Ste 203 Dover DE 19904 302-744-4500 739-2711
Web: www.dpr.delaware.gov

Professional Standards Board 401 Federal St Dover DE 19901 302-735-4000 739-4654
Web: www.doe.k12.de.us/csa/profstds/default.shtml

Revenue Div 820 N French St 1st Fl Wilmington DE 19801 302-577-8200 577-8202
Web: revenue.delaware.gov

Secretary of State 401 Federal St Ste 3 Dover DE 19901 302-739-4111 739-3811
Web: sos.delaware.gov

Securities Div 820 N French St 5th Fl Wilmington DE 19801 302-577-8424 577-6987
Web: attorneygeneral.delaware.gov

Services for Children Youth & Their Families Dept
1825 Faulkland Rd Wilmington DE 19805 302-633-2500 995-8290
Web: www.delaware.gov

State Police Div PO Box 430 Dover DE 19903 302-739-5901 739-5966
Web: dsp.delaware.gov

Supreme Court 820 N French St Wilmington DE 19801 302-577-8425 577-3702
Web: www.courts.delaware.gov

Technology & Information Dept
801 Silver Lake Blvd Dover DE 19904 302-739-9500 739-6251
Web: dti.delaware.gov

Tourism Office 99 Kings Hwy Dover DE 19901 302-739-4271 739-5749
TF: 866-284-7483 ■ *Web:* www.visitdelaware.com

Treasurer 820 Silver Lake Blvd Ste 100 Dover DE 19904 302-672-6700 739-5635
Web: www.treasury.delaware.gov

Unemployment Insurance Div
4425 N Market St Wilmington DE 19802 302-761-8446
Web: uicc.delawareworks.com

Veterans Affairs Commission
802 Silverlake Blvd Ste 100 Dover DE 19904 302-739-2792 739-2794
Web: veteransaffairs.delaware.gov

Violent Crimes Compensation Board
240 N James St Ste 203 Newport DE 19804 302-995-8383
Web: regulations.delaware.gov

Vital Statistics Office PO Box 637 Dover DE 19903 302-283-7130 283-7131
Web: www.dhss.delaware.gov

Vocational Rehabilitation Div (DVR)
4425 N Market St Wilmington DE 19802 302-761-8275
Web: dvr.delawareworks.com

Weights & Measures Office 2320 S DuPont Hwy Dover DE 19901 302-739-4811 697-6287
TF: 800-282-8685 ■ *Web:* dda.delaware.gov

339-9 District of Columbia

Phone | Fax

Government Information 920 Varnum St NE Washington DC 20017 202-727-1000
Web: dc.gov

Aging Office 441 Fourth St NW Ste 900 S Washington DC 20001 202-724-5622 724-4979
Web: www.dcoa.dc.gov

Banking Bureau PO Box 96378 Washington DC 20090 202-727-8000 535-1197
Web: disb.dc.gov

Commission on the Arts & Humanities
200 I St SE Washington DC 20003 202-724-5613 727-4135
Web: www.dcarts.dc.gov/dcarts

Consumer & Regulatory Affairs Dept
1100 4th St SW Washington DC 20024 202-442-4400 442-9445

Convention & Tourism Corp
901 7th St NW 4th Fl Washington DC 20001 202-789-7000 789-7037
TF: 800-422-8644 ■ *Web:* washington.org

Crime Victims Compensation Program
515 Fifth St NW Rm 109 Court Bldg A Washington DC 20001 202-879-4216 879-4230
Web: www.dccourts.gov

DC Tuition Assistance Grant Program
810 First St NE Washington DC 20001 202-727-2824 727-2834
TF: 877-485-6751 ■ *Web:* www.osse.dc.gov

Dept of Insurance Securities & Banking
810 First St NE Ste 701 Washington DC 20002 202-727-8000
Web: disb.dc.gov

District of Columbia Bill Status
1350 Pennsylvania Ave NW Washington DC 20004 202-724-8080 347-3070
Web: dccouncil.us

District of Columbia Lottery & Charitable Games Control Board
2101 ML King Jr Ave SE Washington DC 20020 202-645-8000
Web: www.dclottery.com

Economic Development
1350 Pennsylvania Ave NW Ste 317 Washington DC 20004 202-727-6365 727-6703
Web: dmped.dc.gov

Historic Preservation Office (HPO)
1100 Fourth St SW Ste E650 Washington DC 20024 202-442-7600 442-7638
Web: planning.dc.gov

Homeland Security & Emergency Management Agency
2720 Martin Luther King Jr Ave SE 8th Fl Washington DC 20032 202-727-6161
Web: hsema.dc.gov

Housing Finance Agency 815 Florida Ave NW Washington DC 20001 202-777-1600
Web: www.dchfa.org

Human Services Dept
64 New York Ave NE 6th Fl Washington DC 20002 202-671-4200
Web: www.dhs.dc.gov

Paternity & Child Support Enforcement Office
441 Fourth St NW Ste 550N Washington DC 20001 202-442-9900
Web: cssd.dc.gov

Public Service Commission
1333 H St Ste 200 W Tower Washington DC 20005 202-626-5100
Web: www.dcpsc.org

Rehabilitation Services Administration (RSA)
1125 15th St NW Washington DC 20005 202-730-1700
Web: dds.dc.gov

Securities Bureau 810 First St NE Ste 701 Washington DC 20002 202-727-8000 535-1196
Web: disb.dc.gov

Vital Records Division
825 N Capitol St NE 1st Fl Washington DC 20002 202-671-5000
Web: doh.dc.gov

Weights & Measures Office
1110 Fourth St SW Washington DC 20020 202-442-4400 442-9445
Web: dcra.dc.gov

339-10 Florida

Phone | Fax

Agriculture & Consumer Services Dept
State Capitol PL-10 Tallahassee FL 32399 850-488-3022
Web: www.freshfromflorida.com

Attorney General State Capitol PL-01 Tallahassee FL 32399 850-487-1963 487-2564
TF: 866-966-7226 ■ *Web:* myfloridalegal.com

	City	State	ZIP	Phone	Fax
Business & Professional Regulation Dept 1940 N Monroe St *TF:* 866-532-1440 ■ *Web:* www.myfloridalicense.com/dbpr	Tallahassee	FL	32399	850-487-1395	
Chief Financial Officer 200 E Gaines St *Web:* www.myfloridacfo.com	Tallahassee	FL	32399	850-413-3089	
Citrus Dept 605 E Main St PO Box 9010 *Web:* www.floridacitrus.org	Bartow	FL	33830	863-272-8180	
Colleges & Universities Div 325 W Gaines St *Web:* www.fldoe.org	Tallahassee	FL	32399	850-245-0505	245-9667
Consumer Services Div 2005 Apalachee Pkwy *TF:* 800-435-7352 ■ *Web:* www.freshfromflorida.com	Tallahassee	FL	32399	800-435-7352	
Corrections Dept 501 S Calhoun St *Web:* www.dc.state.fl.us	Tallahassee	FL	32399	850-488-5021	
Cultural Affairs Div 329 N Meridian St *Web:* florida-arts.org	Tallahassee	FL	32301	850-254-6470	245-6454
Education Dept 325 W Gaines St Ste 1514 *TF:* 800-445-6739 ■ *Web:* www.fldoe.org	Tallahassee	FL	32399	850-245-0505	245-9667
Elder Affairs Dept 4040 Esplanade Way *Web:* www.elderaffairs.state.fl.us	Tallahassee	FL	32399	850-414-2000	414-2004
Emergency Management Div 2555 Shumard Oak Blvd *Web:* www.floridadisaster.org	Tallahassee	FL	32399	850-413-9900	488-7841
Environmental Protection Dept 3900 Commonwealth Blvd MS 10 *Web:* www.dep.state.fl.us	Tallahassee	FL	32399	850-245-2118	245-2128
Financial Services Dept 200 E Gaines St *TF:* 800-342-2762 ■ *Web:* www.myfloridacfo.com	Tallahassee	FL	32399	850-413-3100	
Fish & Wildlife Conservation Commission 620 S Meridian St *Web:* myfwc.com	Tallahassee	FL	32399	850-488-4676	
Florida Bill Status 111 W Madison St Rm 704 *TF:* 800-342-1827 ■ *Web:* www.leg.state.fl.us	Tallahassee	FL	32399	850-488-4371	
Florida Ethics Commission 3600 Maclay Blvd S Ste 201 *Web:* www.ethics.state.fl.us	Tallahassee	FL	32312	850-488-7864	488-3077
Florida Lottery Dept 250 Marriott Dr **Fax:* Hum Res ■ *Web:* www.flalottery.com	Tallahassee	FL	32301	850-487-7777	*
Florida Prepaid College Board PO Box 6567 **Fax Area Code:* 850 ■ **Fax:* Cust Svc ■ *TF:* 800-552-4723 ■ *Web:* www.myfloridaprepaid.com	Tallahassee	FL	32314	800-552-4723	309-1766*
Florida Student Financial Assistance Office 1940 N Monroe St Ste 70 *TF:* 888-827-2004 ■ *Web:* www.floridastudentfinancialaid.org	Tallahassee	FL	32303	850-410-5200	488-3612
Historical Resources Div 500 S Bronough St Ste 305 *Web:* www.flheritage.com	Tallahassee	FL	32399	850-245-6300	245-6435
Housing Finance Corp 227 N Bronough St Ste 5000 *Web:* www.floridahousing.org	Tallahassee	FL	32301	850-488-4197	488-9809
Information Technology Services 644 W Call St *Web:* www.its.fsu.edu	Tallahassee	FL	32306	850-644-4357	644-4554
Insurance Regulation Office 200 E Gaines St *TF:* 800-342-2762 ■ *Web:* floir.com	Tallahassee	FL	32301	850-413-3140	
Law Enforcement Dept 2331 Phillips Rd PO Box 1489 *Web:* www.fdle.state.fl.us	Tallahassee	FL	32302	850-410-7000	
Legislature 111 W Madison St *Web:* www.leg.state.fl.us	Tallahassee	FL	32399	850-488-4371	
Lieutenant Governor State Capitol 400 S Monroe St *Web:* www.flgov.com	Tallahassee	FL	32399	850-488-7146	921-6114
Medical Quality Assurance Div 4052 Bald Cypress Way *Web:* www.floridahealth.gov	Tallahassee	FL	32399	850-488-0595	
Military Affairs Dept 82 Marine St *Web:* dma.myflorida.com	St. Augustine	FL	32084	904-823-0364	
Office of the Governor State Capitol *Web:* www.myflorida.com	Tallahassee	FL	32399	850-488-7146	487-0801
Parole Commission 4070 Esplanade Way *Web:* www.fcor.state.fl.us	Tallahassee	FL	32399	850-488-3417	414-1915
Public Service Commission 2540 Shumard Oak Blvd *Web:* www.floridapsc.com	Tallahassee	FL	32399	850-413-6042	487-1716
Recreation & Parks Div 3900 Commonwealth Blvd MS 500 *TF Campground Resv:* 800-326-3521 ■ *Web:* www.dep.state.fl.us	Tallahassee	FL	32399	850-245-2157	
Secretary of State RA Gray Bldg 500 S Bronough St *TF:* 800-955-8771 ■ *Web:* dos.myflorida.com	Tallahassee	FL	32399	850-245-6500	245-6125
State Cts Administrator Office 500 S Duval St *Web:* www.flcourts.org	Tallahassee	FL	32399	850-922-5081	488-0156
Supreme Court 500 S Duval St *Web:* www.flcourts.org	Tallahassee	FL	32399	850-488-0125	
Transportation Dept 605 Suwannee St *Web:* www.dot.state.fl.us	Tallahassee	FL	32399	850-414-5200	414-5201
Veterans' Affairs Dept 11351 Ulmerton Rd Rm 311-K *Web:* www.floridavets.org	Largo	FL	33778	727-518-3202	
Vital Records Bureau PO Box 210 *Web:* www.floridahealth.gov	Jacksonville	FL	32231	904-359-6900	
Vocational Rehabilitation Services Div 2002 Old St Augustine Rd Bldg A *TF:* 800-451-4327 ■ *Web:* www.rehabworks.org	Tallahassee	FL	32301	850-245-3399	
Workers' Compensation Div 200 E Gaines St *Web:* www.myfloridacfo.com	Tallahassee	FL	32399	850-413-3089	

339-11 Georgia

	City	State	ZIP	Phone	Fax
State Government Information 7 Martin Luther King JrDr Ste 643 *TF:* 800-436-7442 ■ *Web:* www.georgia.gov	Atlanta	GA	30303	678-436-7442	
Administrative Office of the Cts 244 Washington St SW Ste 300 *Web:* www.georgiacourts.org	Atlanta	GA	30334	404-656-5171	651-6449
Aging Services Div 2 Peachtree St NW Fl 33 *Web:* aging.dhs.georgia.gov	Atlanta	GA	30303	404-657-5258	657-5285
Agriculture Dept 19 ML King Jr Dr SW *Web:* www.agr.state.ga.us	Atlanta	GA	30334	404-656-3627	656-9380
Arts Council 260 14th St NW Ste 401 *TF:* 800-222-6006 ■ *Web:* www.gpb.org/education	Atlanta	GA	30318	404-685-2400	
Attorney General 40 Capitol Sq SW *Web:* georgia.gov	Atlanta	GA	30334	404-656-3300	657-8733
Banking & Finance Dept 2990 Brandywine Rd Ste 200 *Web:* www.ganet.org	Atlanta	GA	30341	770-986-1633	
Child Support Enforcement Office 2 Peachtree St NW *Web:* dcss.dhs.georgia.gov	Atlanta	GA	30303	404-657-3865	
Community Affairs Dept 60 Executive Pk S NE *Web:* www.dca.state.ga.us	Atlanta	GA	30329	404-679-4940	679-0589
Composite Medical Board 2 Peachtree St NW 36th Fl *Web:* medicalboard.georgia.gov	Atlanta	GA	30303	404-656-3913	656-9723
Corrections Dept 300 Patrol Rd Forsyth *TF:* 888-343-5627 ■ *Web:* www.dcor.state.ga.us	Atlanta	GA	31029	404-656-4661	
Department of Behavioral Health & Developmental Disabilities 2 Peachtree St NW Ste 22-224 *Web:* dbhdd.georgia.gov	Atlanta	GA	30303	404-657-2252	
Department of Driver Services 2206 E View Pkwy *Web:* www.dds.ga.gov	Conyers	GA	30013	678-413-8400	
Economic Development Dept 75 Fifth St NW Ste 1200 *Web:* www.georgia.org	Atlanta	GA	30308	404-962-4000	
Education Dept 205 Jesse Hill Jr Dr SE Ste 2066E *Web:* www.gadoe.org	Atlanta	GA	30334	404-656-2800	651-8737
Emergency Management Agency (GEMA) 935 E Confederate Ave SE PO Box 18055 *TF:* 800-879-4362 ■ *Web:* www.gema.ga.gov	Atlanta	GA	30316	404-635-7000	635-7205
Environmental Protection Div 2 Martin Luther King Jr Dr Ste 1152 E Tower *TF:* 888-373-5947 ■ *Web:* www.georgiaepd.org	Atlanta	GA	30334	404-657-5947	
Family & Children Services Div 2 Peachtree St NW Ste 19-400 *Web:* dfcs.dhs.georgia.gov	Atlanta	GA	30303	404-651-9361	657-5105
General Assembly State Capitol *Web:* www.legis.ga.gov	Atlanta	GA	30334	404-656-5020	651-8086
Georgia Bill Status-House 309 State Capitol *Web:* www.house.ga.gov	Atlanta	GA	30334	404-656-5015	
Georgia Employment Services Div 148 Andrew Young International Blvd NE *Web:* www.dol.state.ga.us	Atlanta	GA	30303	404-232-3515	
Georgia Ports Authority PO Box 2406 *TF:* 800-342-8012 ■ *Web:* www.gaports.com	Savannah	GA	31402	912-964-3811	964-3921
Georgia Student Finance Commission 2082 E Exchange Pl Ste 200 *TF:* 800-505-4732 ■ *Web:* www.gsfc.org	Tucker	GA	30084	770-724-9000	724-9089
Georgia Transparency & Campaign Finance Commission 200 Piedmont Ave SE Ste 1402 *TF:* 866-589-7327 ■ *Web:* www.ethics.state.ga.us	Atlanta	GA	30334	404-463-1980	
Governor 203 State Capitol *Web:* www.gov.georgia.gov	Atlanta	GA	30334	404-656-1776	657-7332
Governor's Office of Consumer Protection 2 ML King Jr Dr Ste 356 **Fax Area Code:* 404 ■ *TF:* 800-869-1123 ■ *Web:* consumer.georgia.gov	Atlanta	GA	30334	800-869-1123	651-9018*
Historic Preservation Div 254 Washington St SW *Web:* www.georgiashpo.org	Atlanta	GA	30334	404-656-2840	
Housing Finance Div 60 Executive Pk S NE *Web:* www.dca.state.ga.us	Atlanta	GA	30329	404-679-0607	679-4837
Human Resources Dept 2 Peachtree St NW Ste 29-250 *Web:* dhs.georgia.gov	Atlanta	GA	30303	404-656-5680	651-8669
Information Technology Office 258 Fourth St NW Rich Bldg *Web:* www.oit.gatech.edu	Atlanta	GA	30332	404-894-7173	
Insurance Commissioner 2 Martin Luther King, Jr. Drive W Tower, Ste 704 *Web:* www.gainsurance.org	Atlanta	GA	30334	404-656-2070	656-4030
Labor Dept 148 Andrew Young International Blvd NE *Web:* www.dol.state.ga.us	Atlanta	GA	30303	404-232-7300	
Lieutenant Governor 240 State Capitol *Web:* ltgov.georgia.gov	Atlanta	GA	30334	404-656-5030	656-6739
Natural Resources Dept 2 ML King Jr Dr SE Ste 1252E *Web:* www.gadnr.org	Atlanta	GA	30334	404-656-3500	656-0770
Professional Licensing Boards Div 237 Coliseum Dr	Macon	GA	31217	478-207-2440	207-1660
Public Health Div 2 Peachtree St NW Ste 15-470 *Web:* dph.georgia.gov	Atlanta	GA	30303	404-657-2700	657-2715
Public Service Commission 244 Washington St SW Ste 126 *Web:* www.psc.state.ga.us	Atlanta	GA	30334	404-656-4501	656-2341

Phone | Fax

Rehabilitation Services Div
148 Andrew Young International Blvd NE ..... Atlanta GA 30303 404-232-7300
Web: georgia.gov/agencies/georgia-department-labor
Revenue Dept 1800 Century Ctr Blvd NE ..... Atlanta GA 30345 404-417-4477 417-2101
Web: www.etax.dor.ga.gov
Secretary of State 214 State Capitol ..... Atlanta GA 30334 404-656-2881
Web: georgia.gov
Securities & Business Regulation Div
2 Martin Luther King Jr Dr W Tower Ste 802 ..... Atlanta GA 30334 478-207-2440 657-8410*
**Fax Area Code:* 404 ■ *TF:* 844-753-7825 ■ *Web:* sos.ga.gov/index.php/?section=securities
State Patrol PO Box 1456 ..... Atlanta GA 30371 404-624-7000
Web: www.dps.georgia.gov
Supreme Court
244 Washington St SW
Rm 572 State Office Annex Bldg ..... Atlanta GA 30334 404-656-3470 656-2253
Web: www.gasupreme.us
Tourism Div 75 Fifth St NW Ste 1200 ..... Atlanta GA 30308 404-962-4000
TF Resv: 800-255-0056 ■ *Web:* georgia.org/georgia_slide/tourism
University System Board of Regents
270 Washington St SW ..... Atlanta GA 30334 404-656-2250 651-9301
Web: www.usg.edu
Veterans Service Dept
Floyd Veterans Memorial Bldg Ste 970E ..... Atlanta GA 30334 404-656-2300 656-7006
Web: veterans.georgia.gov
Vital Records Office 2600 Skyland Dr NE ..... Atlanta GA 30319 404-679-4701
Web: dph.georgia.gov
Wildlife Resources Div
2070 US Hwy 278 SE ..... Social Circle GA 30025 770-918-6400 557-3030*
**Fax Area Code:* 706 ■ *Web:* georgiawildlife.org
Workers' Compensation Board
270 Peachtree St NW ..... Atlanta GA 30303 404-656-2048 651-9467
Web: www.sbwc.georgia.gov

339-12 Hawaii

Phone | Fax

State Government Information
201 Merchant St Ste 1805 ..... Honolulu HI 96813 808-695-4620 695-4618
Web: portal.ehawaii.gov
Administrative Office of the Cts
417 S King St Rm 206 ..... Honolulu HI 96813 808-539-4900 539-4855
Web: www.courts.state.hi.us
Aging Office (HCOA) 250 S Hotel St Rm 406 ..... Honolulu HI 96813 808-586-0100
Web: www.hcoahawaii.org
Agriculture Dept 1428 S King St ..... Honolulu HI 96814 808-973-9560
Web: hdoa.hawaii.gov
Attorney General 425 Queen St ..... Honolulu HI 96813 808-586-1500 586-1239
Web: ag.hawaii.gov
Budget & Finance Dept
201 Merchant St Ste 1805 ..... Honolulu HI 96813 808-695-4620 586-1976
Web: portal.ehawaii.gov
Business Economic Development & Tourism Dept
PO Box 2359 ..... Honolulu HI 96804 808-586-2355 586-2377
Web: www.hawaii.gov
Child Support Enforcement Agency
601 Kamokila Blvd Ste 251 ..... Kapolei HI 96707 888-317-9081
TF: 888-317-9081 ■ *Web:* ag.hawaii.gov
Civil Defense Div 3949 Diamond Head Rd ..... Honolulu HI 96816 808-733-4300 733-4287
Web: scd.hawaii.gov
Commerce & Consumer Affairs Dept
335 Merchant St ..... Honolulu HI 96813 808-586-2727
Web: cca.hawaii.gov
Consumer Protection Office
235 S Beretania St Ste 801 ..... Honolulu HI 96813 808-586-2630 586-2640
Web: cca.hawaii.gov
Department of Accounting & General Services
1151 Punchbowl St ..... Honolulu HI 96813 808-586-1920 586-1922
Web: www.hawaii.gov
Education Dept 1390 Miller St ..... Honolulu HI 96813 808-586-3230 586-3234
Web: www.hawaiipublicschools.org
Forestry & Wildlife Div
1151 Punchbowl St Rm 325 ..... Honolulu HI 96813 808-587-0166 587-0160
Web: hawaii.gov
Governor 415 S Beretania St State Capitol ..... Honolulu HI 96813 808-586-0034 586-0006
Web: governor.hawaii.gov
Hawaii Bill Status 415 S Beretania St Rm 401 ..... Honolulu HI 96813 808-587-0478 587-0793
Web: www.capitol.hawaii.gov
Hawaii Postsecondary Education Commission
2444 Dole St Bachman Hall Rm 209 ..... Honolulu HI 96822 808-956-8213 956-5156
TF: 877-531-2333 ■ *Web:* hawaii.edu
Hawaii Workforce Development Div
201 Merchant St Ste 1805 ..... Honolulu HI 96813 808-695-4620 695-4618
Web: www.hawaii.gov
Historic Preservation Div
601 Kamokila Blvd Rm 555 ..... Kapolei HI 96707 808-692-8015 692-8020
Web: dlnr.hawaii.gov
Human Resources Development Dept
235 S Beretania St Rm 1400 ..... Honolulu HI 96813 808-587-1100 587-1106
Web: dhrd.hawaii.gov
Human Services Dept PO Box 339 ..... Honolulu HI 96809 808-586-4997 586-4890
Web: humanservices.hawaii.gov
Information Consortium
1136 Union Mall Rm 600 ..... Honolulu HI 96813 808-587-1143 587-1146
Web: www.hawaii.gov
Insurance Div 201 Merchant St Ste 1805 ..... Honolulu HI 96813 808-695-4620 695-4618
Web: www.hawaii.gov
Labor & Industrial Relations Dept
830 Punchbowl St ..... Honolulu HI 96813 808-586-8842 586-9099
Web: www.dlir.state.hi.us
Land & Natural Resources Dept
1151 Punchbowl St ..... Honolulu HI 96813 808-587-0400 587-0390
Web: dlnr.hawaii.gov

Phone | Fax

Legislature 415 S Beretania St ..... Honolulu HI 96813 808-587-0478 587-0681
Web: www.capitol.hawaii.gov
Lieutenant Governor
415 S Beretania St 5th Fl ..... Honolulu HI 96813 808-586-0255 586-0231
Web: ltgov.hawaii.gov
Measurement Standards Branch 1851 Auiki St ..... Honolulu HI 96819 808-832-0690 832-0683
Web: hdoa.hawaii.gov/qad/measurement-standards-branch
Motor Vehicle Safety Office
601 Kamokila Blvd Rm 511 ..... Kapolei HI 96707 808-692-7650 692-7665
Web: hidot.hawaii.gov
Paroling Authority 1177 Alakea St Ground Fl ..... Honolulu HI 96813 808-587-1300
Web: www.hawaii.gov
Professional & Vocational Licensing Div
PO Box 3469 ..... Honolulu HI 96801 808-586-2708
Web: www.hawaii.gov
Public Safety Dept 919 Ala Moana Blvd Fl 4 ..... Honolulu HI 96814 808-587-1288 587-1282
Web: dps.hawaii.gov
Public Utilities Commission
465 S King St Rm 103 ..... Honolulu HI 96813 808-586-2020
Web: www.state.hi.us
Securities Compliance Div 335 Merchant St ..... Honolulu HI 96813 808-586-2744 586-3977
Web: www.hawaii.gov
Sheriffs Div Pier 20 ..... Honolulu HI 96817 808-587-3621
Web: dps.hawaii.gov
Social Services Div 810 Richards St Ste 400 ..... Honolulu HI 96813 808-586-5675 586-5700
Web: www.hawaii.gov
State Foundation for Culture & the Arts
250 S Hotel St 2nd Fl ..... Honolulu HI 96813 808-586-0300 586-0308
Web: sfca.hawaii.gov
State Parks Div PO Box 621 ..... Honolulu HI 96809 808-587-0300 587-0311
Web: www.state.hi.us
Supreme Court 417 S King St ..... Honolulu HI 96813 808-539-4919 539-4928
Web: www.courts.state.hi.us
Taxation Dept 830 Punchbowl St Rm 221 ..... Honolulu HI 96813 808-587-4242 587-1488
TF: 800-222-3229 ■ *Web:* tax.hawaii.gov
Teacher Standards Board
650 Iwilei Rd Ste 201 ..... Honolulu HI 96817 808-586-2600 586-2606
Web: www.htsb.org
Tourism Authority 1801 Kalakaua Ave 1st Fl ..... Honolulu HI 96815 808-973-2255 973-2253
Web: www.hawaiitourismauthority.org
Transportation Dept 869 Punchbowl St ..... Honolulu HI 96813 808-587-2160 587-2313
Web: www.hawaii.gov
Veterans Services Office
459 Patterson Rd E-Wing Rm 1-A103 ..... Honolulu HI 96819 808-433-0420 433-0385
Web: dod.hawaii.gov
Vocational Rehabilitation Div
1901 Bachelot St ..... Honolulu HI 96817 808-586-9744 586-9755
TF: 800-316-8005 ■ *Web:* humanservices.hawaii.gov/vocationalrehab

339-13 Idaho

Phone | Fax

Accountancy Board 3101 W Main St Ste 210 ..... Boise ID 83702 208-334-2490 334-2615
Web: www.isba.idaho.gov
Administrative Director of the Courts
PO Box 83720 ..... Boise ID 83720 208-334-2246 947-7590
Web: www.isc.idaho.gov
Aging Commission (ICOA)
341 W Washington Fl 3 PO Box 83720 ..... Boise ID 83702 208-334-3833 334-3033
TF: 800-926-2588 ■ *Web:* www.idahoaging.com
Agriculture Dept 2270 Old Penitentiary Rd ..... Boise ID 83712 208-332-8500 334-2170
Web: www.agri.state.id.us
Arts Commission 2410 Old Penitentiary Rd ..... Boise ID 83712 208-334-2119 334-2488
TF: 800-278-3863 ■ *Web:* www.arts.idaho.gov
Attorney General PO Box 83720 ..... Boise ID 83720 208-334-2520
Web: www.state.id.us
Board of Medicine
1755 N Westgate Dr Ste 140 PO Box 83720 ..... Boise ID 83704 208-327-7000 327-7005
TF: 800-333-0073 ■ *Web:* www.bom.idaho.gov
Child Support Services Bureau PO Box 83720 ..... Boise ID 83720 208-334-2479 334-0666
Web: www.healthandwelfare.idaho.gov
Consumer Protection Unit PO Box 83720 ..... Boise ID 83720 208-332-0102
Web: www.state.id.us
Correction Board 1299 N Orchard St Ste 110 ..... Boise ID 83706 208-658-2000 327-7404
Web: www.idoc.idaho.gov
Crime Victims Compensation Program
PO Box 83720 ..... Boise ID 83720 208-334-6000 334-2321
TF: 800-950-2110 ■ *Web:* www.iic.idaho.gov
Department of Commerce
700 W State St PO Box 83720 ..... Boise ID 83720 208-334-2470 334-2631
TF: 800-842-5858 ■ *Web:* commerce.idaho.gov
Education Dept 650 W State St PO Box 83720 ..... Boise ID 83720 208-332-6800 334-2228
Web: www.sde.idaho.gov
Finance Dept 800 Pk Blvd Ste 200 PO Box 83720 ..... Boise ID 83712 208-332-8000 332-8096
Web: www.finance.idaho.gov
Fish & Game Dept 600 S Walnut St ..... Boise ID 83712 208-334-3700 334-2114
Web: www.fishandgame.idaho.gov
Health & Welfare Dept
450 W State St Tenth Fl PO Box 83720 ..... Boise ID 83720 208-334-5500 334-5926*
**Fax:* PR ■ *Web:* www.healthandwelfare.idaho.gov
Historical Society 2205 Old Penitentiary Rd ..... Boise ID 83712 208-334-2682 334-2774
Web: history.idaho.gov
Homeland Security Bureau
4040 W Guard St Bldg 600 ..... Boise ID 83705 208-422-3040 422-3044
TF: 800-344-0984 ■ *Web:* www.bhs.idaho.gov
Housing & Finance Assn 565 W Myrtle Ave ..... Boise ID 83702 208-331-4882 331-4804
TF: 800-526-7145 ■ *Web:* www.idahohousing.com
Idaho Bill Status PO Box 83720 ..... Boise ID 83720 208-334-2475 334-2125
Web: www.legislature.idaho.gov
Idaho Lottery 1199 Shoreline Ln Ste 100 ..... Boise ID 83702 208-334-2600 334-2610
TF: 800-432-5688 ■ *Web:* www.idaholottery.com

Phone Fax

Idaho Racing Commission 700 S Stratford Dr . . . . Meridian ID 83642 208-884-7080 884-7098
Web: isp.idaho.gov

Insurance Dept 700 W State St PO Box 83720 . . . . Boise ID 83720 208-334-4250 334-4398
Web: www.doi.idaho.gov

Lands Dept 300 N Sixth St Ste 103 PO Box 83720 . . . . Boise ID 83720 208-334-0200 334-5342
Web: www.idl.idaho.gov

Legislature PO Box 83720 . . . . Boise ID 83720 208-334-2475 334-2125
Web: www.legislature.idaho.gov

Lieutenant Governor State Capitol . . . . Boise ID 83720 208-334-2200 334-3259
Web: www.lgo.idaho.gov

Motor Vehicles Div 3311 W State St PO Box 7129 . . . . Boise ID 83707 208-334-8000 334-8739
Web: itd.idaho.gov

National Board For Professional Teaching Standards
PO Box 83720 . . . . Boise ID 83720 208-332-6882 334-4664
Web: www.sde.idaho.gov

Occupational Licenses Bureau 700 W State St . . . . Boise ID 83702 208-334-3233 334-3945
Web: www.ibol.idaho.gov

Office of the Governor PO Box 83720 Ste 228 . . . . Boise ID 83720 208-334-2100 334-3454
Web: www.gov.idaho.gov

Pardon & Parole Commission PO Box 83720 . . . . Boise ID 83720 208-334-2520
Web: www.state.id.us

Parks & Recreation Dept 5657 Warm Springs Ave . . . . Boise ID 83716 855-514-2429
TF: 855-514-2429 ■ *Web:* www.parksandrecreation.idaho.gov

Public Utilities Commission PO Box 83720 . . . . Boise ID 83720 208-334-0300 334-3762
TF: 800-432-0369 ■ *Web:* www.puc.idaho.gov

Real Estate Commission
575 E Parkcenter Blvd Ste 180 . . . . Boise ID 83706 208-334-3285 334-2050
TF: 866-447-5411 ■ *Web:* www.irec.idaho.gov

Secretary of State 700 W Jefferson St Rm 205 . . . . Boise ID 83720 208-334-2100
Web: sos.idaho.gov

Supreme Court PO Box 83720 . . . . Boise ID 83720 208-334-2210 334-2616
Web: www.isc.idaho.gov

Tax Commission 800 E Pk Blvd . . . . Boise ID 83712 208-334-7660 334-7844
TF: 800-972-7660 ■ *Web:* www.tax.idaho.gov

Tourism Development Div
700 W State St PO Box 83720 . . . . Boise ID 83720 208-334-2470 334-2631
TF General: 800-847-4843 ■ *Web:* www.visitidaho.org

Transportation Dept PO Box 7129 . . . . Boise ID 83707 208-334-8000 334-3858
Web: www.itd.idaho.gov

Treasurer
700 W Jefferson St Ste 126 PO Box 83720 . . . . Boise ID 83720 208-334-3200 332-2959
Web: sto.idaho.gov

Veterans Services Div 351 Collins Rd . . . . Boise ID 83702 208-577-2310
Web: www.veterans.idaho.gov

Vital Records & Health Statistics Bureau
PO Box 83720 . . . . Boise ID 83720 208-334-5988
Web: www.healthandwelfare.idaho.gov

Vocational Rehabilitation Div
650 W State St Rm 150 . . . . Boise ID 83720 208-334-3390 334-5305
Web: www.vr.idaho.gov

Weights & Measures Bureau 2216 Kellogg Ln . . . . Boise ID 83712 208-332-8690 334-2378
Web: www.agri.state.id.us

339-14 Illinois

Phone Fax

Administrative Office of the Illinois Courts
3101 Old Jacksonville Rd . . . . Springfield IL 62704 217-558-4490
Web: www.state.il.us/court

Aging Dept 421 E Capitol Ave Ste 100 . . . . Springfield IL 62701 217-785-3356 785-4477
Web: illinois.gov/aging

Agriculture Dept PO Box 19281 . . . . Springfield IL 62794 217-782-2172 785-4505
Web: www.agr.state.il.us

Attorney General 100 W Randolph St 12th Fl . . . . Chicago IL 60601 312-814-3000
Web: www.illinoisattorneygeneral.gov

Attorney General 500 S Second St . . . . Springfield IL 62706 217-782-1090
Web: www.illinoisattorneygeneral.gov

Banks & Real Estate Div
500 E Monroe St 3rd Fl . . . . Springfield IL 62701 217-782-3000
Web: www.idfpr.com

Child Support Enforcement Div
509 S Sixth St . . . . Springfield IL 62701 800-447-4278
TF: 800-447-4278 ■ *Web:* www.childsupportillinois.com

Children & Family Services Dept
406 E Monroe St . . . . Springfield IL 62701 217-785-2509 524-0014
Web: www.state.il.us/dcfs

Commerce & Economic Opportunity Dept
620 E Adams St . . . . Springfield IL 62701 217-782-7500 524-0864
Web: illinois.gov/dceo

Commerce Commission 527 E Capitol Ave . . . . Springfield IL 62701 217-785-1407
Web: www.state.il.us/icc

Community College Board
401 E Capitol Ave . . . . Springfield IL 62701 217-785-0123 524-4981
Web: www.iccb.state.il.us

Crime Victims Services Div
100 W Randolf Rd 13th Fl . . . . Chicago IL 60601 312-814-2581 814-7105
TF: 800-228-3368 ■ *Web:* www.illinoisattorneygeneral.gov

Driver Services Office
2701 S Dirksen Pkwy . . . . Springfield IL 62723 217-782-6212
Web: www.cyberdriveillinois.com/departments/drivers

Emergency Management Agency
2200 S Dirksen Pkwy . . . . Springfield IL 62703 217-782-7860
Web: www.state.il.us/iema

Environmental Protection Agency
1021 N Grand Ave E . . . . Springfield IL 62794 217-782-3397 782-9039
Web: www.epa.state.il.us

General Assembly 705 Stratton Bldg . . . . Springfield IL 62706 217-782-2000
Web: www.ilga.gov

Governor State Capitol Bldg Rm 207 . . . . Springfield IL 62706 217-782-6830 524-4049
Web: www.illinois.gov/gov

Phone Fax

Healthcare & Family Services Dept
201 S Grand Ave E 3rd Fl . . . . Springfield IL 62763 217-782-1200 524-7979
Web: www.hfs.illinois.gov

Historic Preservation Agency
1 Old State Capitol Plaza . . . . Springfield IL 62701 217-785-7930 785-7937
Web: www.state.il.us

Housing Development Authority
401 N Michigan Ave Ste 900 . . . . Chicago IL 60611 312-836-5200
Web: www.ihda.org

Human Services Dept
100 S Grand Ave E 3rd Fl . . . . Springfield IL 62762 217-557-1601
TF: 800-843-6154 ■ *Web:* www.dhs.state.il.us

Illinois Bill Status 705 Stratton Bldg . . . . Springfield IL 62706 217-782-3944 524-6059
Web: www.ilga.gov/legislation

Illinois Higher Education Board
431 E Adams St 2nd Fl . . . . Springfield IL 62701 217-782-2551 782-8548
Web: www.ibhe.org

Illinois Lottery 101 W Jefferson St . . . . Springfield IL 62702 217-524-6435 877-0436*
*Fax Area Code: 866 ■ *TF:* 800-252-1775 ■ *Web:* www.illinoislottery.com

Illinois Racing Board
100 W Randolph St Ste 5-700 . . . . Chicago IL 60601 312-814-2600 323-0273*
*Fax Area Code: 866 ■ *Web:* www2.illinois.gov

Illinois Student Assistance Commission
1755 Lake Cook Rd . . . . Deerfield IL 60015 847-948-8500 831-8549*
*Fax: Cust Svc ■ *TF:* 800-899-4722 ■ *Web:* collegeillinois.org

Insurance Div 320 W Washington St 4th Fl . . . . Springfield IL 62767 217-782-4515 782-5020
Web: insurance.illinois.gov

Labor Dept 160 N LaSalle St Ste C-1300 . . . . Chicago IL 60601 312-793-2800 793-5257
Web: www.illinois.gov

Mental Health Div 100 W Randolf St Ste 3-400 . . . . Chicago IL 60601 312-814-2811
TF: 800-252-2923 ■ *Web:* illinois.gov/dceo

Military Affairs Dept
1301 N MacArthur Blvd . . . . Springfield IL 62702 217-761-3569 761-3527
Web: www.il.ngb.army.mil

Natural Resources Dept
1 Natural Resources Way . . . . Springfield IL 62702 217-782-6302
Web: dnr.state.il.us

Professional Regulation Div
320 W Washington St 3rd Fl . . . . Springfield IL 62786 217-785-0820 782-7645
Web: www.ildpr.com

Public Health Dept 535 W Jefferson St . . . . Springfield IL 62761 217-782-4977 782-3987
Web: www.idph.state.il.us

Revenue Dept 101 W Jefferson St . . . . Springfield IL 62702 217-782-3336
TF: 800-732-8866 ■ *Web:* www.revenue.state.il.us

Secretary of State 213 State Capitol . . . . Springfield IL 62756 217-782-2201
TF: 800-252-8980 ■ *Web:* www.cyberdriveillinois.com

Securities Dept
300 W Jefferson St Ste 300-A . . . . Springfield IL 62702 217-782-2256 782-8876
Web: www.cyberdriveillinois.com

State Board of Education 100 N First St . . . . Springfield IL 62777 217-782-4321 524-4928
Web: www.isbe.state.il.us

State Police
801 S Seventh St PO Box 19461 . . . . Springfield IL 62794 217-782-7263 785-2821
Web: www.isp.state.il.us

Supreme Court 200 E Capitol Ave . . . . Springfield IL 62701 217-782-2035
Web: www.state.il.us/court

Tourism Bureau 100 W Randolph St Ste 3-400 . . . . Chicago IL 60601 312-814-4732 814-6175
TF: 800-226-6632 ■ *Web:* www.enjoyillinois.com

Treasurer Capitol Bldg 219 Statehouse . . . . Springfield IL 62701 217-782-2211 785-2777
Web: www.treasurer.il.gov/contact-us.aspx

Veterans Affairs Dept
James R. Thompson Ctr 100 W Randolph
Ste 5-570 . . . . Chicago IL 60601 312-814-5391 524-0344*
*Fax Area Code: 217 ■ *TF:* 800-437-9824 ■ *Web:* www2.illinois.gov

Vital Records Div 605 W Jefferson St . . . . Springfield IL 62702 217-782-6553
Web: www.idph.state.il.us/vitalrecords

Wildlife Resources Div
1 Natural Resources Way . . . . Springfield IL 62702 217-782-6384
Web: www.dnr.state.il.us

Workers' Compensation Commission
100 W Randolph St 8th Fl . . . . Chicago IL 60601 312-814-6611 814-6523
TF: 866-352-3033 ■ *Web:* www.iwcc.il.gov

339-15 Indiana

Phone Fax

State Government Information
402 W Washington St Rm W160A . . . . Indianapolis IN 46204 317-233-0800
TF: 800-457-8283 ■ *Web:* www.in.gov

Agriculture Dept 101 W Ohio St Ste 1200 . . . . Indianapolis IN 46204 317-232-8770 232-1362
Web: www.in.gov/isda

Arts Commission 150 W Market St Ste 618 . . . . Indianapolis IN 46204 317-232-1268 232-5595
Web: www.in.gov/arts

Attorney General
302 W Washington St 5th Fl . . . . Indianapolis IN 46204 317-232-6201 232-7979
Web: www.in.gov/attorneygeneral

Child Support Bureau
402 W Washington St . . . . Indianapolis IN 46204 317-232-2350
TF: 800-840-8757 ■ *Web:* www.in.gov/dcs/support

Consumer Protection Div
402 W Washington St 5th Fl . . . . Indianapolis IN 46204 317-232-6330 233-4393
TF: 800-382-5516 ■ *Web:* www.in.gov

Correction Dept
302 W Washington St Rm E334 . . . . Indianapolis IN 46204 317-232-5715 232-6798
Web: in.gov/idoc

Disability Aging & Rehabilitative Services Div
402 W Washington St Rm W451 . . . . Indianapolis IN 46204 317-232-1147 232-1240
TF: 800-545-7763 ■ *Web:* www.in.gov

Economic Development Corp
1 N Capitol Ave Ste 700 . . . . Indianapolis IN 46204 317-232-8800 232-4146
Web: www.iedc.in.gov

Education Dept
115 W Washington St Rm 229 . . . . Indianapolis IN 46204 317-232-6610 232-9121

Phone | Fax

Environmental Management Dept
100 N Senate Ave Rm 1301 ... Indianapolis IN 46204 317-232-8611 233-6647
TF: 800-451-6027 ■ *Web:* www.in.gov/idem

Family & Social Services Admin
402 W Washington St Rm W461 PO Box 7083 ... Indianapolis IN 46207 800-545-7763 232-6478*
**Fax Area Code:* 317 ■ *TF:* 800-545-7763 ■ *Web:* www.in.gov/fssa

Finance Authority
1 N Capitol Ave Ste 900 ... Indianapolis IN 46204 317-233-4332 232-6786
Web: www.in.gov

Financial Institutions Dept
402 W Washington St ... Indianapolis IN 46204 317-232-3955 232-7655
Web: www.in.gov

Fish & Wildlife Div
402 W Washington St Rm W273 ... Indianapolis IN 46204 317-232-4080 232-8150
Web: www.in.gov/dnr/fishwild

General Assembly
State House 200 W Washington St ... Indianapolis IN 46204 317-232-9600 232-2554
TF: 800-382-9842 ■ *Web:* www.in.gov/legislative

Governor
State House 200 W Washington St Rm 206 ... Indianapolis IN 46204 317-232-4567 232-3443
Web: www.in.gov

Health Dept 2 N Meridian St ... Indianapolis IN 46204 317-233-1325
Web: www.in.gov

Higher Education Commission
101 W Ohio St Ste 550 ... Indianapolis IN 46204 317-464-4400 464-4410
Web: www.in.gov

Historical Bureau
140 N Senate Ave Rm 130 ... Indianapolis IN 46204 317-232-2537 232-3728
Web: www.in.gov/history

Homeland Security Dept
302 W Washington St Rm E208 ... Indianapolis IN 46204 317-232-3980 232-3895
Web: www.in.gov/dhs

Housing Finance Authority
30 S Meridian St Ste 1000 ... Indianapolis IN 46204 317-232-7777 232-7778
Web: www.in.gov

Indiana Bill Status
State House 200 W Washington St Ste 220 ... Indianapolis IN 46204 317-233-5293
Web: www.in.gov/apps/lsa/session/billwatch

Indiana Horse Racing Commission
150 W Market St Ste 530 ... Indianapolis IN 46204 317-233-3119 233-4470
Web: www.in.gov

Indiana Lottery
201 S Capitol Ave Ste 1100 ... Indianapolis IN 46225 317-264-4800
TF: 800-955-6886 ■ *Web:* www.in.gov

Indiana Port Commission
150 W Market St Ste 100 ... Indianapolis IN 46204 317-232-9200 232-0137
TF: 800-232-7678 ■ *Web:* www.portsofindiana.com

Indiana State Ethics Commission
315 W Ohio St Rm 104 ... Indianapolis IN 46202 317-232-3850 232-0707
Web: www.in.gov/ig

Indiana Students Assistance Commission
150 W Market St Ste 500 ... Indianapolis IN 46204 317-232-2350 232-3260
TF: 888-528-4719 ■ *Web:* www.in.gov

Indiana Workforce Development Dept
10 N Senate Ave ... Indianapolis IN 46204 317-232-7670 233-4793
TF: 800-891-6499 ■ *Web:* www.in.gov

Insurance Dept
311 W Washington St Ste 300 ... Indianapolis IN 46204 317-232-2385 232-5251
TF Cust Svc: 800-622-4461 ■ *Web:* www.in.gov

Labor Dept 402 W Washington St Rm W195 ... Indianapolis IN 46204 317-232-2655
Web: www.in.gov/labor

Lieutenant Governor
200 W Washington St Ste 230 ... Indianapolis IN 46204 317-232-9856
Web: in.gov/lg

Motor Vehicles Bureau
100 N Senate Ave Rm N440 ... Indianapolis IN 46204 317-233-6000 233-3135
Web: www.in.gov

Natural Resources Dept
402 W Washington St ... Indianapolis IN 46204 317-232-4200 233-6811
Web: www.in.gov/dnr

Parole Services Div
302 W Washington St Rm E-334 ... Indianapolis IN 46204 317-232-5757
Web: in.gov/ai/errors/idoc_404.html

Professional Licensing Agency
302 W Washington St Rm E034 ... Indianapolis IN 46204 317-232-2980 232-2312
Web: www.in.gov/pla

Professional Standards Div
101 W Ohio St Ste 300 ... Indianapolis IN 46204 317-232-9010 232-9023

Revenue Dept 100 N Senate Ave Rm N128 ... Indianapolis IN 46204 317-232-2240 245-4877*
**Fax Area Code:* 574 ■ *Web:* www.in.gov/dor

Secretary of State
200 W Washington St Rm 201 ... Indianapolis IN 46204 317-232-6531 233-3283
Web: www.in.gov

Securities Div
302 W Washington St Rm E111 ... Indianapolis IN 46204 317-232-6681 233-3675
Web: www.in.gov

State Court Administration Div
30 S Meridian St Ste 500 ... Indianapolis IN 46204 317-232-2542 233-6586
Web: www.in.gov

State Parks & Reservoirs Div
402 W Washington St Rm W298 ... Indianapolis IN 46204 317-232-4124 232-4132
TF: 800-622-4931 ■ *Web:* www.in.gov

State Police 100 N Senate Ave 3rd Fl ... Indianapolis IN 46204 317-232-8248 232-0652
Web: www.in.gov/isp

Supreme Court
State House 200 W Washington St Rm 315 ... Indianapolis IN 46204 317-232-2540 232-8372
Web: www.in.gov/judiciary/supreme

Technology Office
100 N Senate Ave Ste N-551 ... Indianapolis IN 46204 317-232-3172 232-0748
Web: www.in.gov

Tourism Development Office
1 N Capitol Ave Ste 100 ... Indianapolis IN 46204 317-232-8860 233-6887
TF: 800-457-8283 ■ *Web:* www.in.gov

Transportation Dept
100 N Senate Ave Rm N755 ... Indianapolis IN 46204 317-232-5533 232-0238
Web: www.in.gov

Treasurer
State House 200 W Washington St Rm 242 ... Indianapolis IN 46204 317-232-6386 233-1780
Web: www.in.gov/tos

Utility Regulatory Commission
302 W Washington St Rm E306 ... Indianapolis IN 46204 317-232-2701 232-6758
Web: www.in.gov/iurc

Veterans' Affairs Dept
302 W Washington St Rm E120 ... Indianapolis IN 46204 317-232-3910 232-7721
Web: www.in.gov

Victims Services Div
101 W Washington St Ste 1170 ... East Tower Indianapolis IN 46204 317-232-1233 233-3912
TF: 800-353-1484 ■ *Web:* www.in.gov

Vital Records Office PO Box 7125 ... Indianapolis IN 46206 317-233-2700
Web: www.cdc.gov/nchs/w2w/indiana.htm

Weights & Measures Div
2525 Shadeland Ave Unit D3 ... Indianapolis IN 46219 317-356-7078 351-2877
Web: www.in.gov/isdh/23288.htm

Worker's Compensation Board
402 W Washington St Rm W196 ... Indianapolis IN 46204 317-232-3808
Web: in.gov/wcb

339-16 Iowa

Phone | Fax

State Government Information
1305 E Walnut St ... Des Moines IA 50319 515-281-5011
Web: www.iowa.gov

Adult Children & Family Services Div
1305 E Walnut St ... Des Moines IA 50319 515-281-8746 564-4044
TF: 800-735-2942 ■ *Web:* www.dhs.state.ia.us

Agriculture & Land Stewardship Dept
502 E Ninth St ... Des Moines IA 50319 515-281-5321 281-6236
Web: www.iowaagriculture.gov

Arts Council 600 E Locust ... Des Moines IA 50319 515-242-6194 242-6498
Web: www.iowaartscouncil.org

Attorney General 1305 E Walnut St 2nd Fl ... Des Moines IA 50319 515-281-5164 281-4209
Web: www.state.ia.us/government/ag

Banking Div 200 E Grand Ave Ste 300 ... Des Moines IA 50309 515-725-0505

Child Support Recovery Unit PO Box 9125 ... Des Moines IA 50306 888-229-9223
TF: 888-229-9223 ■ *Web:* secureapp.dhs.state.ia.us/childsupport

Commerce Dept 1918 SE Hulsizer Rd ... Ankeny IA 50021 515-281-7400 281-5329
Web: commerce.iowa.gov

Community Development Div 200 E Grand Ave ... Des Moines IA 50309 515-725-3000 725-3010
Web: www.iowaeconomicdevelopment.com/community

Consumer Protection Div
1305 E Walnut St 2nd Fl ... Des Moines IA 50319 515-281-5926 281-6771
TF: 888-777-4590 ■ *Web:* www.iowaattorneygeneral.org

Corrections Dept 420 Watson Powell Jr Way ... Des Moines IA 50309 515-242-5702
Web: www.doc.state.ia.us

Economic Development Dept 200 E Grand Ave ... Des Moines IA 50309 515-242-4700
Web: www.state.ia.us/government/ided

Education Dept 400 E 14th St ... Des Moines IA 50319 515-281-3436 242-5988
Web: www.iowa.gov

Elder Affairs Dept 510 E 12th St Ste 2 ... Des Moines IA 50309 515-242-3333
TF: 800-532-3213 ■ *Web:* www.iowaaging.gov

Emergency Management Div
7105 NW 70th Ave Camp Dodge Bldg W-4 ... Des Moines IA 50131 515-281-3231 725-3260
Web: homelandsecurity.iowa.gov

Environmental Services Div
11101 Aurora Ave ... Urbandale IA 50322 515-279-8042 279-1853
Web: www.iesiowa.com

General Assembly
State Capitol 1007 E Grand Ave ... Des Moines IA 50319 515-281-5129
Web: www.legis.iowa.gov

Governor 1007 East Grand Ave State Capitol ... Des Moines IA 50319 515-281-5211
Web: governor.iowa.gov

Human Services Dept
1305 E Walnut St Fl 5 SE ... Des Moines IA 50319 515-669-8002 242-6036
Web: www.dhs.state.ia.us

Information Technology Dept
1305 E Walnut St Level B ... Des Moines IA 50319 515-281-5503
Web: www.state.ia.us

Insurance Div 330 Maple St ... Des Moines IA 50319 515-281-5705 281-3059
Web: www.iid.state.ia.us

Iowa Ethics & Campaign Disclosure Board
510 E 12th St Ste 1-A ... Des Moines IA 50319 515-281-4028 281-3701
Web: www.state.ia.us

Iowa Lottery 2323 Grand Ave ... Des Moines IA 50312 515-323-4633 *
**Fax:* Hum Res ■ *Web:* www.ialottery.com

Iowa Workforce Development
1000 E Grand Ave ... Des Moines IA 50319 515-281-5387 281-4698
TF: 800-562-4692 ■ *Web:* www.iowaworkforce.org

Medical Examiners Board
400 SW Eigth St Ste C ... Des Moines IA 50309 515-281-5171 242-5908
Web: medicalboard.iowa.gov

Motor Vehicle Div
100 Euclid Ave PO Box 9204 ... Des Moines IA 50306 515-244-9124
TF: 800-532-1121 ■ *Web:* www.dmvusa.com

Natural Resource Dept 502 E Ninth St ... Des Moines IA 50319 515-281-5918 281-6794
Web: www.iowadnr.gov

Natural Resources Dept 502 E Ninth St ... Des Moines IA 50319 515-281-5918 281-6794
Web: www.iowadnr.gov

Office of Governor 1007 E Grand Ave ... Des Moines IA 50319 515-281-5211
Web: www.ltgovernor.iowa.gov

Parks & Preserves Bureau 502 E Ninth St ... Des Moines IA 50319 515-281-5918
Web: iowadnr.gov

Parole Board 510 E 12th St Ste 3 ... Des Moines IA 50319 515-725-5757 725-5762
Web: www.bop.state.ia.us

Professional Licensing & Regulation Div
200 E Grand Ave Ste 390 ... Des Moines IA 50309 515-243-4723 281-4862
Web: www.state.ia.us/government/com/prof

Public Health Dept 321 E 12th St ... Des Moines IA 50319 515-281-5787 281-4958
Web: www.idph.state.ia.us

				Phone	Fax
Regents Board 11260 Aurora Ave *Web:* regents.iowa.gov	Urbandale	IA	50322	515-281-3934	281-6420
Revenue & Finance Dept 1305 E Walnut *TF:* 800-367-3388 ■ *Web:* www.iowa.gov	Des Moines	IA	50319	515-281-3204	
Secretary of State 321 E 12th St 1st Fl *Web:* sos.iowa.gov	Des Moines	IA	50319	515-281-5204	242-5953
Securities Bureau 340 Maple St *Web:* www.iid.state.ia.us/securities_complaint	Des Moines	IA	50319	515-281-5705	281-3059
State Court Administration 1111 E Ct Ave *Web:* www.iowacourts.gov	Des Moines	IA	50319	515-281-5241	
State Historical Society 600 E Locust St *Web:* www.iowahistory.org	Des Moines	IA	50319	515-281-5111	242-6498
State Patrol Div 215 E Seventh St *Web:* www.dps.state.ia.us/isp	Des Moines	IA	50319	515-725-6090	
Supreme Court 1111 E Ct Ave Iowa Judicial Branch Bldg *Web:* iowautility.org	Des Moines	IA	50319	515-281-5911	
Transportation Dept 800 Lincoln Way *Web:* iowadot.gov	Ames	IA	50010	515-239-1101	
Treasurer State Treasurer's Office Capitol Bldg *Web:* www.treasurer.state.ia.us	Des Moines	IA	50319	515-281-5368	281-7562
Utilities Board 1375 E Ct Ave Rm 69 *TF:* 877-565-4450 ■ *Web:* www.state.ia.us/government/com/util	Des Moines	IA	50319	515-725-7300	
Veterans Affairs Dept 7105 NW 70th Ave Camp Dodge Bldg A6A *Web:* va.iowa.gov	Johnston	IA	50131	515-242-5331	242-5659
Vital Records Bureau 321 E 12th St Lucas State Office Bldg 1st Fl *Web:* www.idph.state.ia.us	Des Moines	IA	50319	515-281-4944	281-0479
Vocational Rehabilitation Services Div 510 E 12th St *Web:* www.ivrs.iowa.gov	Des Moines	IA	50319	515-281-4311	281-7645
Weights & Measures Bureau 502 E Ninth St *Web:* www.iowaagriculture.gov/weightsandmeasures.asp	Des Moines	IA	50319	515-725-1492	

339-17 Kansas

				Phone	Fax
Accountancy Board 900 SW Jackson St Ste 556 *Web:* www.ksboa.org	Topeka	KS	66612	785-296-2162	291-3501
Aging Dept 503 S Kansas Ave *Web:* www.kdads.ks.gov	Topeka	KS	66603	785-296-4986	296-0256
Agriculture Dept 109 SW Ninth St *Web:* agriculture.ks.gov	Topeka	KS	66612	785-296-3556	296-8389
Attorney General 120 SW Tenth Ave 2nd Fl *Web:* ag.ks.gov	Topeka	KS	66612	785-296-2215	296-6296
Banking Commissioner 700 SW Jackson St Ste 300 *Web:* www.osbckansas.org	Topeka	KS	66603	785-296-2266	296-0168
Chief Legal Governor's Office 2nd Fl Capitol Bldg *Web:* www.kansas.gov	Topeka	KS	66612	785-368-8767	
Commerce Dept 1000 SW Jackson St Ste 100 *Web:* www.kansascommerce.com	Topeka	KS	66612	785-296-3481	296-5055
Conservation Commission 109 SW Ninth St Ste 500 *Web:* agriculture.ks.gov	Topeka	KS	66612	785-296-3600	296-6172
Consumer Protection Div 534 S Kansas Ave Ste 1210 *TF:* 800-452-6727 ■ *Web:* www.kansas.gov	Topeka	KS	66603	785-296-5059	296-5563
Corp Commission 1500 SW Arrowhead Rd *Web:* www.kcc.state.ks.us	Topeka	KS	66604	785-271-3220	271-3354
Corrections Dept 900 SW Jackson St Ste 400 *Web:* www.dc.state.ks.us	Topeka	KS	66612	785-296-3317	296-0014
Cosmetology Board 714 SW Jackson St Ste 100 *Web:* www.kansas.gov/kboc	Topeka	KS	66603	785-296-3155	296-3002
Crime Victims Compensation Board 120 SW 10th Ave 2nd Fl *Web:* ag.ks.gov/victim-services/victim-compensation	Topeka	KS	66612	785-296-2359	296-0652
Emergency Management Div 2800 SW Topeka Blvd *Web:* www.kansas.gov	Topeka	KS	66611	785-296-5059	
Healing Arts Board 800 SW Jackson Lower Level Ste A *TF:* 888-886-7205 ■ *Web:* www.ksbha.org	Topeka	KS	66612	785-296-7413	296-0852
Health & Environment Dept 1000 SW Jackson St *Web:* www.kdheks.gov	Topeka	KS	66612	785-296-1500	
Highway Patrol 122 SW Seventh St *Web:* www.kansashighwaypatrol.org	Topeka	KS	66603	785-296-6800	
Historical Society 6425 SW Sixth Ave *Web:* www.kshs.org	Topeka	KS	66615	785-272-8681	272-8682
Housing Resources Corp 611 S Kansas Ave Ste 300 *Web:* www.kshousingcorp.org	Topeka	KS	66603	785-296-5865	296-8985
Information Systems & Communications Div 900 SW Jackson *Web:* da.ks.gov	Topeka	KS	66612	785-296-3343	296-1168
Insurance Dept 420 SW Ninth St *TF:* 800-432-2484 ■ *Web:* www.ksinsurance.org	Topeka	KS	66612	785-296-3071	296-2283
Judicial Administrator 301 W Tenth St Kansas Judicial Ctr *Web:* www.kscourts.org	Topeka	KS	66612	785-296-2256	296-7076
Kansas Bill Status 300 SW Tenth Ave State Capitol Bldg Rm 343N *Web:* www.kslegislature.org	Topeka	KS	66612	785-296-2391	296-1153
Kansas Governmental Ethics Commission 109 W Ninth St Ste 504 *Web:* www.kansas.gov	Topeka	KS	66612	785-296-4219	296-2548
Kansas Lottery 128 N Kansas Ave *TF:* 800-544-9467 ■ *Web:* kslottery.com	Topeka	KS	66603	785-296-5700	
Legislature 300 SW Tenth Ave State Capitol Bldg *Web:* www.kslegislature.org	Topeka	KS	66612	785-296-2391	296-1153
Lieutenant Governor 300 SW Tenth Ave State Capitol Bldg Rm 222 *Web:* kansashighwaypatrol.org	Topeka	KS	66612	785-296-2213	
Motor Vehicles Div 915 SW Harrison St Rm 159 *Web:* www.ksrevenue.org	Topeka	KS	66626	785-296-3621	296-3852
Real Estate Commission 120 SE Sixth Ave Ste 200 *Web:* www.accesskansas.org/krec	Topeka	KS	66603	785-296-3411	296-1771
Regents Board 1000 SW Jackson St Ste 520 *Web:* www.kansasregents.org	Topeka	KS	66612	785-296-3421	296-0983
Rehabilitation Services Div 915 SW Harrison Docking State Office Bldg 9th Fl N *Web:* www.dcf.ks.gov	Topeka	KS	66612	785-368-7471	368-7467
Revenue Dept 915 SW Harrison St *Web:* www.ksrevenue.org	Topeka	KS	66612	785-296-3041	368-8392
Secretary of State 120 SW Tenth Ave 1st Fl *Web:* www.kssos.org	Topeka	KS	66612	785-296-4564	296-4570
Securities Commission 618 S Kansas Ave 2nd Fl *Web:* www.securities.state.ks.us	Topeka	KS	66603	785-296-3307	296-6872
Social & Rehabilitation Services Dept 915 SW Harrison St 6th Fl *Web:* dcf.ks.gov	Topeka	KS	66612	785-296-3959	296-2173
Supreme Court 301 SW 10th Ave Rm 374 **Fax Area Code:* 620 ■ *Web:* kansas.gov	Topeka	KS	66612	785-296-3229	378-4531*
Technical Professions Board 900 SW Jackson St Ste 507 *Web:* www.ksbtp.ks.gov	Topeka	KS	66612	785-296-3053	
Travel & Tourism Development Div 1020 S Kansas Ave Ste 200 *TF:* 800-252-6727 ■ *Web:* www.travelks.com	Topeka	KS	66612	785-296-2009	296-6988
Treasurer 900 SW Jackson St Ste 201 *TF:* 800-432-0386 ■ *Web:* www.kansasstatetreasurer.com	Topeka	KS	66612	785-296-3171	296-7950
Veterans Affairs Commission 700 SW Jackson St Ste 701 *Web:* kcva.ks.gov	Topeka	KS	66603	785-296-3976	296-1462
Vital Statistics Div 1000 SW Jackson *Web:* www.kdheks.gov/vital	Topeka	KS	66612	785-296-1400	
Weights & Measures Div Forbes Field Bldg 282 PO Box 19282 *Web:* www.kansas.gov	Topeka	KS	66619	785-862-2415	
Wildlife & Parks Dept 1020 S Kansas Ave Ste 200 *Web:* www.kdwpt.state.ks.us	Topeka	KS	66612	785-296-2281	296-6953
Workers' Compensation Div 401 SW Topeka Blvd Ste 2 *TF:* 800-332-0353 ■ *Web:* www.dol.ks.gov	Topeka	KS	66603	785-296-4000	

339-18 Kentucky

				Phone	Fax
State Government Information 229 W Main St Ste 400 *TF:* 877-855-3573 ■ *Web:* kentucky.gov	Frankfort	KY	40601	502-875-3733	875-3722
Accountancy Board 332 W Broadway Ste 310 *Web:* www.cpa.ky.gov	Louisville	KY	40202	502-595-3037	595-4500
Aging Services Office 275 E Main St Ste 3E-E *Web:* www.chfs.ky.gov/dail	Frankfort	KY	40621	502-564-6930	564-4595
Arts Council 500 Mero St 21st Fl Capital Plaza Tower *TF:* 888-833-2787 ■ *Web:* www.artscouncil.ky.gov	Frankfort	KY	40601	502-564-3757	564-2839
Attorney General State Capitol Bldg 700 Capitol Ave Ste 120 *Web:* www.e-archives.ky.gov	Frankfort	KY	40601	502-696-5614	564-2894
Child Support Div 730 Schenkel Ln *TF:* 800-248-1163 ■ *Web:* www.chfs.ky.gov	Frankfort	KY	40601	502-564-2285	564-5988
Consumer Protection Div 1024 Capital Ctr Dr Ste 200 *TF:* 888-432-9257 ■ *Web:* www.ag.ky.gov	Frankfort	KY	40601	502-696-5389	573-8317
Corrections Dept 275 E Main St Rm G-41 PO Box 2400 *Web:* www.corrections.ky.gov	Frankfort	KY	40602	502-564-4726	564-5037
Crime Victims Compensation Board 130 Brighton Pk Blvd *TF:* 800-469-2120 ■ *Web:* www. cvcb.ky.gov	Frankfort	KY	40601	502-573-2290	573-4817
Department of Revenue 501 High St PO Box 68 *Web:* www.revenue.ky.gov	Frankfort	KY	40601	502-564-4581	564-3875
Economic Development Cabinet 500 Mero St *Web:* www.thinkkentucky.com	Frankfort	KY	40601	502-564-7670	564-3256
Education Dept 500 Mero St *Web:* www.education.ky.gov/KDE	Frankfort	KY	40601	502-564-4770	564-5680
Education Professional Standards Board 100 Airport Dr 3rd Fl *TF:* 888-598-7667 ■ *Web:* www.kyepsb.net	Frankfort	KY	40601	502-564-4606	564-7080
Emergency Management Div 100 Minuteman Pkwy *Web:* www.kyem.ky.gov	Frankfort	KY	40601	502-607-5721	607-1614
Energy and Environment Cabinet 500 Mero St Ste 5 *Web:* www.eec.ky.gov	Frankfort	KY	40601	502-564-3350	564-3969
Environmental Protection Dept 200 Fair Oaks Ln *Web:* www.dep.ky.gov	Frankfort	KY	40601	502-564-2150	564-4245
Finance & Administration Cabinet Capitol Annex Rm 383 *Web:* www.finance.ky.gov	Frankfort	KY	40601	502-564-4240	564-6785
Financial Institutions Dept 1025 Capital Ctr Dr Ste 200 *TF:* 800-223-2579 ■ *Web:* www.kfi.ky.gov	Frankfort	KY	40601	502-573-3390	573-2182

				Phone	Fax
Fish & Wildlife Resources Dept 1 Game Farm Rd. *TF:* 800-858-1549 ■ *Web:* fw.ky.gov	Frankfort	KY	40601	502-564-3400	564-6508
General Assembly 700 Capitol Ave State Capitol Bldg. *TF:* 800-372-7181 ■ *Web:* www.lrc.state.ky.us	Frankfort	KY	40601	502-564-8100	564-6543
Governor State Capitol Bldg 700 Capitol Ave Rm 100 *Web:* www.governor.ky.gov	Frankfort	KY	40601	502-564-2611	564-2517
Governor's Office for Technology 101 Cold Harbor Dr *Web:* www.got.state.ky.us	Frankfort	KY	40601	502-564-1201	
Hairdressers & Cosmetologists Board 111 St James Ct Ste A	Frankfort	KY	40601	502-564-4262	564-0481
Health & Family Services Cabinet 275 E Main St 5th Fl W. *Web:* www.chfs.ky.gov	Frankfort	KY	40621	502-564-7042	564-7091
Historical Society 100 W Broadway *TF:* 877-444-7867 ■ *Web:* www.history.ky.gov	Frankfort	KY	40601	502-564-1792	
Housing Corp 1231 Louisville Rd. *TF:* 800-633-8896 ■ *Web:* www.kyhousing.org	Frankfort	KY	40601	502-564-7630	564-5708
Insurance Dept 215 W Main St. *TF:* 800-595-6053	Frankfort	KY	40602	502-564-3630	
Kentucky Bill Status 702 Capitol Ave Rm 424F. *Web:* kentuckyhouserepublicans.org	Frankfort	KY	40601	502-564-8100	
Kentucky Higher Education Assistance Authority 100 Airport Rd *TF:* 800-928-8926 ■ *Web:* www.kheaa.com	Frankfort	KY	40602	800-928-8926	
Kentucky Horse Racing Authority 4063 Iron Works Pkwy Bldg B *Web:* khrc.ky.gov	Lexington	KY	40511	859-246-2040	246-2039
Kentucky Legislative Ethics Commission 22 Mill Creek Pk. *Web:* www.klec.ky.gov	Frankfort	KY	40601	502-573-2863	573-2929
Kentucky Lottery Corp 1011 W Main St *TF:* 800-937-8946 ■ *Web:* www.kylottery.com	Louisville	KY	40202	502-560-1500	560-1532
Labor Cabinet 1047 US Hwy 127 S Ste 4 *Web:* www.labor.ky.gov	Frankfort	KY	40601	502-564-3070	564-5387
Lieutenant Governor State Capitol Bldg 700 Capitol Ave Ste 142 *Web:* www.ltgovernor.ky.gov	Frankfort	KY	40601	502-564-2611	564-2849
Medical Licensure Board 310 Whittington Pkwy Ste 1B *Web:* www.kbml.ky.gov	Louisville	KY	40222	502-429-7150	429-7158
Natural Resources Dept 2 Hudson Hollow *Web:* www.dnr.ky.gov	Frankfort	KY	40601	502-564-6940	564-5698
Parks Dept 500 Mero St. *Web:* kentuckytourism.com	Frankfort	KY	40601	502-564-2172	
Parole Board PO Box 2400 *Web:* justice.ky.gov	Frankfort	KY	40602	502-564-3620	564-8995
Postsecondary Education Council 1024 Capital Ctr Dr Ste 320 *Web:* www.cpe.ky.gov	Frankfort	KY	40601	502-573-1555	573-1535
Public Service Commission PO Box 615 *TF:* 800-772-4636 ■ *Web:* www.psc.state.ky.us	Frankfort	KY	40602	502-564-3940	564-3460
Real Estate Commission (KREC) 10200 Linn Stn Rd Ste 201. *TF General:* 888-373-3300 ■ *Web:* www.krec.ky.gov	Louisville	KY	40223	502-429-7250	429-7246
Secretary of State The Capitol Bldg 700 Capital Ave Ste 152 *Web:* www.sos.ky.gov	Frankfort	KY	40601	502-564-3490	564-5687
Supreme Court 700 Capitol Ave Rm 235. *Web:* apps.courts.ky.gov	Frankfort	KY	40601	502-564-5444	564-2665
Travel and Tourism Dept 500 Mero St Ste 2200. *TF:* 800-225-8747 ■ *Web:* www.kentuckytourism.com	Frankfort	KY	40601	502-564-4930	564-5695
Treasury 1050 US Hwy 127 S Ste 100 *Web:* www.kytreasury.com	Frankfort	KY	40601	502-564-4722	564-6545
Vehicle Regulation Div 200 Mero St 3rd Fl.	Frankfort	KY	40601	502-564-7000	564-6403
Veterans Affairs Dept (KDVA) 1111B Louisville Rd *TF:* 800-572-6245 ■ *Web:* www.veterans.ky.gov	Frankfort	KY	40601	502-564-9203	564-9240
Vital Statistics Div 275 E Main St Ste 1EA *Web:* www.chfs.ky.gov	Frankfort	KY	40621	502-564-4212	227-9849
Vocational Rehabilitation Dept 275 E Main St MS 2E-K *TF:* 800-372-7172 ■ *Web:* ovr.ky.gov	Frankfort	KY	40601	502-564-4440	564-6745
Workers Claims Dept (DWC) 657 Chamberlin Ave. *TF:* 800-554-8601 ■ *Web:* www.labor.ky.gov/workersclaims	Frankfort	KY	40601	502-564-5550	564-5732

339-19 Louisiana

				Phone	Fax
Agriculture & Forestry Dept 5825 Florida Blvd *Web:* www.ldaf.state.la.us	Baton Rouge	LA	70806	225-922-1234	922-1253
Arts Div PO Box 44247 *Web:* www.crt.state.la.us	Baton Rouge	LA	70804	225-342-8180	342-8173
Attorney General PO Box 94005. *Web:* www.ag.state.la.us	Baton Rouge	LA	70804	225-326-6705	326-6793
Board of Regents PO Box 3677 *Web:* www.regents.state.la.us	Baton Rouge	LA	70821	225-342-4253	342-6926
Certified Public Accountants Board 601 Poydras St Ste 1770 *Web:* www.cpaboard.state.la.us	New Orleans	LA	70130	504-566-1244	566-1252
Community Services Office 627 N 4th St. **Fax Area Code:* 225 ■ *TF:* 888-524-3578 ■ *Web:* www.dss.state.la.us	Baton Rouge	LA	70802	888-524-3578	342-2268*
Consumer Protection Office PO Box 94095. **Fax Area Code:* 225 ■ *TF:* 800-351-4889 ■ *Web:* www.ag.state.la.us	Baton Rouge	LA	70804	800-351-4889	326-6499*
Contractors Licensing Board 2525 Quail Dr *Web:* www.lslbc.louisiana.gov	Baton Rouge	LA	70808	225-765-2301	765-2431
Crime Victims Reparations Board 1885 Wooddale Blvd Rm 1230 *Web:* www.lcle.state.la.us	Baton Rouge	LA	70806	225-925-4842	
Culture Recreation & Tourism Dept PO Box 94361 *Web:* www.crt.state.la.us	Baton Rouge	LA	70804	225-342-8115	342-3207
Education Dept PO Box 94064 **Fax Area Code:* 225 ■ *TF:* 877-453-2721 ■ *Web:* www.louisianabelieves.com	Baton Rouge	LA	70804	877-453-2721	342-0193*
Environmental Quality Dept 602 N Fifth St *TF:* 866-896-5337 ■ *Web:* www.deq.louisiana.gov	Baton Rouge	LA	70802	225-219-5337	
Financial Institutions Office PO Box 94095 *Web:* www.ofi.state.la.us	Baton Rouge	LA	70804	225-925-4660	925-4548
Health & Hospitals Dept PO Box 629 *Web:* www.dhh.state.la.us	Baton Rouge	LA	70821	225-342-9500	342-5568
Historic Preservation Div Capitol Annex Bldg 1051 N Third St PO Box 44247 *Web:* doa.louisiana.gov	Baton Rouge	LA	70802	225-342-8160	219-9772
Homeland Security & Emergency Preparedness Office 7667 Independence Blvd *Web:* lerc.dps.louisiana.gov	Baton Rouge	LA	70806	225-925-7500	925-7501
Housing Finance Agency 2415 Quail Dr. *TF:* 888-454-2001 ■ *Web:* www.lhfa.state.la.us	Baton Rouge	LA	70808	225-763-8700	763-8710
Information Services Office 1201 N Third St *Web:* louisiana.gov	Baton Rouge	LA	70802	225-342-0900	342-0902
Insurance Dept PO Box 94214 *TF:* 800-259-5300 ■ *Web:* www.ldi.state.la.us	Baton Rouge	LA	70804	225-342-5900	
Judicial Administrators Office 400 Royal St Ste 1190 *Web:* www.lasc.org	New Orleans	LA	70130	504-310-2550	
Legislature PO Box 94062. *TF:* 800-256-3793 ■ *Web:* www.legis.state.la.us	Baton Rouge	LA	70804	225-342-2456	
Lieutenant Governor 1051 N Third St *Web:* www.crt.state.la.us	Baton Rouge	LA	70802	225-342-7009	342-1949
Louisiana Ethics Board 617 N Third St LaSalle Bldg Ste 10-36. *TF:* 800-842-6630 ■ *Web:* www.ethics.state.la.us	Baton Rouge	LA	70802	225-219-5600	381-7271
Louisiana Lottery Corp 555 Laurel St *Web:* louisianalottery.com	Baton Rouge	LA	70801	225-297-2000	297-2005
Louisiana Office of Student Financial Assistance 602 N Fifth St PO Box 91202 *TF:* 800-259-5626 ■ *Web:* www.osfa.la.gov	Baton Rouge	LA	70802	225-219-1012	208-1496
Louisiana Racing Commission 320 N Carrollton Ave Ste 2-B *Web:* horseracing.louisiana.gov	New Orleans	LA	70119	504-483-4000	483-4898
Louisiana Workforce Commission 1001 N 23rd St. *TF:* 877-529-6757 ■ *Web:* www.laworks.net	Baton Rouge	LA	70802	225-342-3111	342-7960
Medical Examiners Board (LSBME) 630 Camp St PO Box 30250. *Web:* www.lsbme.louisiana.gov	New Orleans	LA	70130	504-568-6820	568-8893
Natural Resources Dept PO Box 94396 *Web:* dnr.louisiana.gov	Baton Rouge	LA	70804	225-342-4500	342-5861
Office of the Governor PO Box 94004. *TF:* 866-366-1121 ■ *Web:* www.gov.state.la.us	Baton Rouge	LA	70804	225-342-7015	342-7099
Public Safety & Corrections Dept 504 Mayflower St PO Box 94304 *Web:* www.doc.louisiana.gov	Baton Rouge	LA	70804	225-342-6633	342-3095
Public Service Commission PO Box 91154 *TF:* 800-256-2397 ■ *Web:* www.lpsc.org	Baton Rouge	LA	70821	225-342-4404	342-2831
Real Estate Commission PO Box 14785. *TF:* 800-821-4529 ■ *Web:* www.lrec.state.la.us	Baton Rouge	LA	70898	225-765-0191	765-0637
Rehabilitation Services 627 N Fourth St *Web:* www.dss.louisiana.gov	Baton Rouge	LA	70802	225-686-7257	
Revenue Dept 617 N Third St PO Box 201 *TF:* 855-307-3893 ■ *Web:* www.rev.state.la.us	Baton Rouge	LA	70801	855-307-3893	
Secretary of State PO Box 94125 *Web:* www.sos.la.gov	Baton Rouge	LA	70804	225-922-2880	922-2003
Securities Commission 8660 United Plaza Blvd Ste 200 *Web:* gov.louisiana.gov	Baton Rouge	LA	70809	225-925-4660	925-4524
State Parks Office PO Box 44426 *TF:* 888-677-1400 ■ *Web:* www.crt.state.la.us	Baton Rouge	LA	70804	225-342-8111	342-8107
State Police PO Box 66614. *Web:* www.lsp.org	Baton Rouge	LA	70896	225-925-6006	
Supreme Court 400 Royal St. *Web:* www.lasc.org	New Orleans	LA	70112	504-310-2300	
Tourism Office 1051 N Third Stt PO Box 94291 *Web:* www.crt.state.la.us	Baton Rouge	LA	70802	225-342-8100	342-1051
Treasurer 900 N Third St Fl 3 PO Box 44154 *Web:* www.treasury.state.la.us/default.aspx	Baton Rouge	LA	70802	225-342-0010	342-0046
Veterans Affairs Dept PO Box 94095 *TF:* 877-432-8982 ■ *Web:* www.vetaffairs.la.gov	Baton Rouge	LA	70804	225-219-5000	219-5590
Weights & Measures Div PO Box 3098. *Web:* vwwwprd.doa.louisiana.gov	Baton Rouge	LA	70821	225-922-1341	923-4877
Wildlife & Fisheries Dept PO Box 98000 *TF:* 800-442-2511 ■ *Web:* www.wlf.louisiana.gov	Baton Rouge	LA	70898	225-765-2800	765-2892
Workers' Compensation Office PO Box 94040 *Web:* www.laworks.net/WorkersComp/OWC_MainMenu.asp	Baton Rouge	LA	70804	225-342-8980	342-5665

339-20 Maine

Phone | Fax

State Government Information 26 Edison Dr . . . Augusta ME 04330 207-624-9494
TF: 888-577-6690 ■ *Web:* www.maine.gov

Administrative Office of the Cts
PO Box 4820 . . . Portland ME 04112 207-822-0792
Web: courts.maine.gov

Agriculture Dept 28 State House Stn . . . Augusta ME 04333 207-287-3871 287-7548
Web: www.maine.gov

Arts Commission 193 State St. . . . Augusta ME 04330 207-287-2724 287-2725
Web: mainearts.maine.gov

Attorney General 6 State House Stn . . . Augusta ME 04333 207-626-8800
Web: www.maine.gov

Chief Medical Examiner 37 State House Stn . . . Augusta ME 04333 207-624-7180 624-7178
Web: www.maine.gov

Child & Family Services Office 221 State St . . . Augusta ME 04333 207-287-5060 287-5031
Web: maine.gov/dhhs/ocfs

Conservation Dept 22 State House Stn. . . . Augusta ME 04333 207-287-2211 287-2400
Web: maine.gov/dacf

Consumer Protection Unit 6 State House Stn. . . . Augusta ME 04333 207-626-8849
TF: 800-436-2131 ■ *Web:* www.maine.gov

Corrections Dept
25 Tyson Dr Third Fl 111 State House Stn . . . Augusta ME 04333 207-287-2711 287-4370
Web: www.maine.gov

Economic & Community Development Dept
59 State House Stn . . . Augusta ME 04333 207-624-9800
TF: 800-541-5872 ■ *Web:* www.maine.gov

Education Dept 23 State House Stn . . . Augusta ME 04333 207-624-6600 624-6700
Web: www.maine.gov/education

Elder Services Office 11 Statehouse Stn . . . Augusta ME 04333 800-624-8404
TF: 800-624-8404 ■ *Web:* maine.gov/dhhs/oes

Environmental Protection Dept
17 State House Stn . . . Augusta ME 04333 207-287-7688 287-7814
TF: 800-452-1942 ■ *Web:* www.maine.gov

Financial Institutions Bureau
35 Anthony Ave 11 State House Stn . . . Augusta ME 04333 207-624-8090 624-8124
TF: 800-452-1926 ■ *Web:* www.maine.gov

Governor 1 State House Stn . . . Augusta ME 04333 207-287-3531 287-1034
TF: 888-577-6690 ■ *Web:* www.maine.gov/governor

Health Bureau 11 State House Stn . . . Augusta ME 04333 207-287-8016 287-9058
Web: www.maine.gov

Historic Preservation Commission
65 State House Stn . . . Augusta ME 04333 207-287-2132 287-2335
Web: www.maine.gov

Housing Authority 353 Water St . . . Augusta ME 04330 207-626-4600 626-4678
Web: www.mainehousing.org

Human Services Dept 221 State St . . . Augusta ME 04333 207-287-3707
Web: www.maine.gov

Information Services Bureau
145 State House Stn . . . Augusta ME 04333 207-624-8800 287-4563
Web: www.maine.gov

Inland Fisheries & Wildlife Dept
41 State House Stn . . . Augusta ME 04333 207-287-8000 287-6395
Web: www.maine.gov

Insurance Bureau 34 State House Stn . . . Augusta ME 04333 207-624-8475 624-8599
TF: 800-300-5000 ■ *Web:* www.maine.gov/pfr/insurance

Labor Dept PO Box 259 . . . Augusta ME 04332 207-623-7900
Web: www.state.me.us/labor

Legislature 115 State House Stn . . . Augusta ME 04333 207-287-1615 287-1621
Web: maine.gov/legis

Licensure in Medicine Board 161 Capitol St. . . . Augusta ME 04330 207-287-3601 287-6590
Web: www.docboard.org

Maine Employment Services Bureau
55 State House Station . . . Augusta ME 04330 207-623-7981 287-5933
Web: www.mainecareercenter.com

Maine Finance Authority of Maine
5 Community Dr PO Box 949 . . . Augusta ME 04332 207-623-3263 623-0095
TF: 800-228-3734 ■ *Web:* www.famemaine.com

Maine Governmental Ethics & Election Practices Commission
45 Memorial Cir . . . Augusta ME 04330 207-287-4179 287-6775
Web: www.maine.gov

Motor Vehicles Bureau 29 State House Stn . . . Augusta ME 04333 207-624-9000 624-9013
Web: www.maine.gov/sos/bmv

Parks & Land Bureau 22 State House Stn . . . Augusta ME 04333 207-287-3821 287-6170
Web: www.maine.gov

Parole Board 111 State House Stn. . . . Augusta ME 04333 207-287-2711 287-4370
Web: www.maine.gov

Public Utilities Commission
18 State House Stn . . . Augusta ME 04333 207-287-3831 287-1039
Web: www.maine.gov

Quality Assurance & Regulations Div
22 State House Station 18 Elkins Lane . . . Augusta ME 04333 207-287-3841
Web: www.maine.gov

Rehabilitation Services Bureau
150 State House Stn . . . Augusta ME 04333 800-698-4440 287-5292*
**Fax Area Code:* 207 ■ *TF:* 800-698-4440 ■ *Web:* www.maine.gov/rehab

Revenue Services 24 State House Stn . . . Augusta ME 04333 207-287-2076 287-3618
Web: www.maine.gov

Secretary of State 148 State House Stn . . . Augusta ME 04333 207-626-8400 287-8598
Web: www.maine.gov/sos

Securities Div 76 Northern Ave . . . Gardiner ME 04345 207-624-8551 624-8590
Web: www.maine.gov

State Police 45 Commerce Dr . . . Augusta ME 04333 207-624-7200 624-7088
Web: www.maine.gov/dps/msp

Supreme Court 205 Newbury St Rm 139 . . . Portland ME 04101 207-822-4146
Web: courts.maine.gov/maine_courts/supreme

Tourism Office 59 State House Stn . . . Augusta ME 04333 888-624-6345 624-6331*
**Fax Area Code:* 877 ■ *TF:* 888-624-6345 ■ *Web:* www.visitmaine.com

Transportation Dept 16 State House Stn . . . Augusta ME 04333 207-624-3000 624-3001
Web: www.maine.gov/mdot

University of Maine System Board of Trustees
16 Central St . . . Bangor ME 04401 207-973-3211 973-3296
Web: www.maine.edu

Veterans' Services Bureau
117 State House Stn . . . Augusta ME 04333 207-430-6035 626-4509
Web: www.maine.gov

Victims' Compensation Program
6 State House Sta . . . Augusta ME 04333 207-624-7882 624-7730
Web: www.maine.gov

Vital Records Office 11 State House Stn . . . Augusta ME 04333 207-287-3181 287-1093
Web: www.maine.gov/dhhs

Workers' Compensation Board
27 State House Stn . . . Augusta ME 04333 207-287-3751 287-7198
Web: www.maine.gov

339-21 Maryland

Phone | Fax

State Government Information State House . . . Annapolis MD 21401 410-974-3901
TF: 800-811-8336 ■ *Web:* www.maryland.gov

Administrative Office of the Cts
580 Taylor Ave . . . Annapolis MD 21401 410-260-1400 974-2169
Web: www.courts.state.md.us

Aging Dept 301 W Preston St Rm 1007 . . . Baltimore MD 21201 410-767-1100 333-7943
Web: www.aging.maryland.gov

Agriculture Dept 50 Harry S Truman Pkwy . . . Annapolis MD 21401 410-841-5700 841-5914
Web: mda.maryland.gov

Assessments & Taxation Dept
301 W Preston St 8th Fl . . . Baltimore MD 21201 410-767-1184
TF: 888-246-5941 ■ *Web:* www.dat.state.md.us

Attorney General 200 St Paul Pl 16th Fl. . . . Baltimore MD 21202 410-576-6300 576-7040
Web: www.oag.state.md.us

Business & Economic Development Dept
217 E Redwood St . . . Baltimore MD 21202 410-767-6300 333-6911
Web: business.maryland.gov

Chief Medical Examiner 111 Penn St . . . Baltimore MD 21201 410-333-3250 333-3063
Web: dhmh.maryland.gov

Court of Appeals 361 Rowe Blvd 4th Fl . . . Annapolis MD 21401 410-260-1500
TF: 800-926-2583 ■ *Web:* www.courts.state.md.us/coappeals

Criminal Injuries Compensation Board
6776 Reisterstown Rd Ste 206 . . . Baltimore MD 21215 410-585-3010 764-3815
TF: 888-679-9347 ■ *Web:* msa.maryland.gov

Department of Budget & Management
45 Calvert St . . . Annapolis MD 21401 800-705-3493
TF: 800-705-3493 ■ *Web:* dbm.maryland.gov

Education Dept 200 W Baltimore St . . . Baltimore MD 21201 410-767-0100 333-2226
TF: 888-246-0016 ■ *Web:* www.marylandpublicschools.org

Emergency Management Agency
5401 Rue St Lo Dr . . . Reisterstown MD 21136 410-517-3600 517-3610
TF: 877-636-2872 ■ *Web:* mema.state.md.us

Environment Dept 1800 Washington Blvd . . . Baltimore MD 21230 410-537-3000 537-3888
TF: 800-633-6101 ■ *Web:* www.mde.state.md.us

Financial Regulation Div
500 N Calvert St Rm 402 . . . Baltimore MD 21202 410-230-6097
Web: www.dllr.state.md.us

Fisheries Service 580 Taylor Ave . . . Annapolis MD 21401 410-260-8281 260-8279
Web: www.dnr.state.md.us/fisheries

General Assembly 90 State Cir . . . Annapolis MD 21401 410-841-3000 841-3850
Web: www.mlis.state.md.us

Governor State House 100 State Cir . . . Annapolis MD 21401 410-974-3901
Web: www.gov.state.md.us

Health & Mental Hygiene Dept
201 W Preston St 5th Fl . . . Baltimore MD 21201 410-767-6500 767-6489
Web: dhmh.maryland.gov

Higher Education Commision
839 Bestgate Rd Ste 400 . . . Annapolis MD 21401 410-260-4500 260-3200
TF: 800-974-0203 ■ *Web:* www.mhec.state.md.us

Historical & Cultural Programs Div
100 Community Pl 3rd Fl . . . Crownsville MD 21032 410-514-7600 514-7678
Web: www.marylandhistoricaltrust.net

Housing & Community Development Dept
100 Community Pl . . . Crownsville MD 21032 800-756-0119 987-4070*
**Fax Area Code:* 410 ■ *TF:* 800-756-0119 ■ *Web:* www.dhcd.state.md.us

Insurance Administration 525 St Paul Pl . . . Baltimore MD 21202 410-468-2000 468-2020
TF: 800-492-6116 ■ *Web:* www.mdinsurance.state.md.us

Labor & Industry Div 1100 N Eutaw St Rm 606 . . . Baltimore MD 21201 410-767-2241 767-2986
Web: www.dllr.state.md.us

Maryland Dept of Legislative Services
90 State Cir . . . Annapolis MD 21401 410-946-5400 946-5405
TF: 800-492-7122 ■ *Web:* www.mlis.state.md.us

Maryland Ethics Commission
45 Calvert St 3rd Fl . . . Annapolis MD 21401 410-260-7770 260-7746
TF: 877-669-6085 ■ *Web:* ethics.maryland.gov

Maryland Racing Commission
500 N Calvert St Rm 201 . . . Baltimore MD 21202 410-230-6320
Web: www.dllr.state.md.us

Maryland State Athletic Commission
500 N Calvert St Rm 304 . . . Baltimore MD 21202 410-230-6223 333-6314
Web: www.dllr.state.md.us/license/occprof/athlet.html

Maryland State Lottery
1800 Washington Blvd Ste 330 . . . Baltimore MD 21230 410-230-8790 230-8728
Web: www.mdlottery.com

Maryland Workforce Development Div
1100 N Eutaw St Rm 616 . . . Baltimore MD 21201 410-767-2400 767-2986
Web: www.dllr.state.md.us/employment

Motor Vehicle Administration
6601 Ritchie Hwy NE . . . Glen Burnie MD 21062 410-768-7000 768-7506
Web: www.mva.maryland.gov

Natural Resources Dept 580 Taylor Ave . . . Annapolis MD 21401 410-260-8021 260-8024
TF: 877-620-8367 ■ *Web:* dnr2.maryland.gov

Parole & Probation Div
6776 Reisterstown Rd . . . Baltimore MD 21215 410-585-3500
TF: 877-227-8031 ■ *Web:* msa.maryland.gov

Phone | Fax

Physician Quality Assurance Board
4201 Patterson Ave. Baltimore MD 21215 410-764-4777 358-2252
TF: 800-492-6836

Public Service Commission
6 St Paul St 16th Fl. Baltimore MD 21202 410-767-8000 333-6495
TF: 800-492-0474 ■ *Web:* www.psc.state.md.us

Secretary of State
16 Francis St Jeffery Bldg 1st Fl. Annapolis MD 21401 410-974-5521 974-5190
Web: www.sos.state.md.us

Securities Div 200 St Paul Pl 20th Fl Baltimore MD 21202 410-576-6360 576-6532
Web: www.oag.state.md.us/Securities

Social Services Administration
311 W Saratoga St Baltimore MD 21201 410-767-7216 333-0127
Web: www.dhr.state.md.us

State Arts Council 175 W Ostend St Ste E Baltimore MD 21230 410-767-6555 333-1062
Web: www.msac.org

State Forest & Park Service
580 Taylor Ave Rm E-3 Annapolis MD 21401 410-260-8186 260-8191
TF Campground Resv: 877-620-8367 ■ *Web:* dnr2.maryland.gov

State Police 1201 Reisterstown Rd Pikesville MD 21208 410-653-4200
TF: 800-525-5555 ■ *Web:* www.mdsp.org

Teacher Certification & Accreditation Div
200 W Baltimore St. Baltimore MD 21201 410-767-0412
TF: 866-772-8922 ■ *Web:* www.marylandpublicschools.org

Tourism Development Office
217 E Redwood St 9th Fl Baltimore MD 21202 410-767-3400 333-6643
TF: 800-543-1036 ■ *Web:* visitmaryland.org

Treasurer 80 Calvert St Rm 109 Annapolis MD 21401 410-260-7533 974-3530
TF: 800-974-0468 ■ *Web:* www.treasurer.state.md.us

Veterans Affairs Dept
31 Hopkins Plaza Rm 1231 Baltimore MD 21201 410-230-4444 230-4445
TF: 800-446-4926 ■ *Web:* veterans.maryland.gov

Vital Records Div 6550 Reisterstown Rd Baltimore MD 21215 410-764-3038
TF: 800-832-3277 ■ *Web:* www.dhmh.maryland.gov

Weights & Measures Section
50 Harry S Truman Pkwy Rm 410 Annapolis MD 21401 410-841-5700 841-2765
Web: mda.maryland.gov

Workers' Compensation Commission
10 E Baltimore St Baltimore MD 21202 410-864-5100
Web: www.wcc.state.md.us

339-22 Massachusetts

Phone | Fax

Agricultural Resources Dept
251 Cswy St Ste 500 Boston MA 02114 617-626-1700 626-1850
Web: www.mass.gov

Attorney General 1 Ashburton Pl Boston MA 02108 617-727-2200
Web: www.mass.gov

Banks Div 1000 Washington St Ste 710 Boston MA 02118 617-956-1501 956-1599
TF: 800-495-2265 ■ *Web:* www.mass.gov

Business Development Office
10 Pk Plaza Ste 5220 Boston MA 02116 617-973-8600 973-8554
Web: www.mass.gov

Child Support Enforcement Div
51 Sleeper St 4th Fl Boston MA 02205 617-660-1234 626-3894
TF: 800-332-2733 ■ *Web:* www.mass.gov

Correction Dept 50 Maple St Milford MA 01757 508-422-3300 422-3386
Web: www.mass.gov

Cultural Council 10 St James Ave 3rd Fl Boston MA 02116 617-727-3668 727-0044
Web: www.massculturalcouncil.org

Department of Elementary and Secondary Education
350 Main St Malden MA 02148 781-388-3300 338-3399
Web: www.doe.mass.edu

Emergency Management Agency
400 Worcester Rd Framingham MA 01702 508-820-2000 820-2030
Web: www.mass.gov

Environmental Protection Dept 1 Winter St Boston MA 02108 617-292-5500 556-1049
Web: mass.gov/eea/agencies/massdep

Executive Office of Transportation
10 Pk Plaza Ste 3170 Boston MA 02116 617-973-7000 973-8031
TF: 800-219-9936 ■ *Web:* www.massdot.state.ma.us

Fish & Game Dept 251 Cswy St Ste 400 Boston MA 02114 617-626-1500 626-1505
Web: mass.gov/eea/pagenotfound.html

General Court State House Boston MA 02133 617-722-2000
Web: malegislature.gov

Governor State House Executive Office Rm 360 Boston MA 02133 617-725-4000 727-9725
Web: www.mass.gov

Historical Commission
220 William T Morrissey Blvd Boston MA 02125 617-727-8470 727-5128
Web: www.sec.state.ma.us

Housing & Community Development Dept
100 Cambridge St Ste 300 Boston MA 02114 617-573-1100 573-1120
Web: mass.gov/hed/economic/eohed/dhcd

Housing Finance Agency 1 Beacon St Boston MA 02108 617-854-1000 854-1029
Web: www.masshousing.com

Information Technology Div
1 Ashburton Pl Rm 804 Boston MA 02108 617-727-2040 727-2779
Web: www.mass.gov

Insurance Div 1000 Washington St Ste 810 Boston MA 02118 617-521-7794 521-7490
TF: 877-563-4467 ■ *Web:* mass.gov/ocabr/government/oca-agencies/doi-lp

Massachusetts Bill Status
1 Ashburton Pl Rm 1611 Boston MA 02108 617-727-7030 742-4528
TF: 800-392-6090 ■ *Web:* malegislature.gov

Massachusetts Higher Education Board
1 Ashburton Pl Rm 1401 Boston MA 02108 617-994-6950 727-6397
Web: www.mass.edu

Massachusetts State Boxing Commission
1 Ashburton Pl Rm 1301 Boston MA 02108 617-727-3200 727-5732
Web: www.mass.gov/mbc

Massachusetts State Ethics Commission
1 Ashburton Pl Rm 619 Boston MA 02108 617-371-9500 723-5851
Web: www.mass.gov/ethics

Massachusetts State Lottery Commission
60 Columbian St. Braintree MA 02184 781-849-5555 849-5546
Web: www.masslottery.com

Massachusetts State Racing Commission
1 Ashurton Pl 11th Fl Boston MA 02108 617-727-2581
Web: www.mass.gov

Massachusetts Workforce Development Dept
1 Ashburton Pl Rm 1301 Boston MA 02108 617-626-7100 727-1090
Web: www.mass.gov

Medical Examiner 720 Albany St Boston MA 02118 617-267-6767 266-6763
Web: www.mass.gov

Mental Health Dept 25 Staniford St Boston MA 02214 617-626-8000
Web: www.mass.gov/eohhs/gov/departments/dmh

Parole Board 12 Mercer Rd Natick MA 01760 508-650-4500 650-4599
TF: 888-298-6272 ■ *Web:* mass.gov/eopss/agencies/parole-board

Professional Licensure Div
1000 Washington St Ste 710 Boston MA 02118 617-727-3074 727-2197
Web: mass.gov/ocabr/government/oca-agencies/dpl-lp

Public Health Dept 250 Washington St Boston MA 02108 617-624-6000 624-5206
Web: mass.gov/eohhs/gov/departments/dph

Public Protection & Advocacy Bureau
100 Cambridge St. Boston MA 02114 617-727-2200
Web: www.sec.state.ma.us

Public Utilities Dept 1 S Stn Boston MA 02110 617-305-3500 345-9101
Web: www.mass.gov/eea

Registry of Motor Vehicles PO Box 55891 Boston MA 02205 617-351-4500
Web: www.massrmv.com

Rehabilitation Commission
27 Wormwood St Ste 600 Boston MA 02210 617-204-3600
Web: www.mass.gov

Revenue Dept PO Box 7010 Boston MA 02204 617-626-2201
TF: 800-392-6089 ■ *Web:* www.mass.gov/dor

Secretary of the Commonwealth
State House Rm 337 Boston MA 02133 617-727-9180 742-4722
Web: www.sec.state.ma.us

Securities Div 1 Ashburton Pl Rm 1710 Boston MA 02108 617-878-3152 248-0177
Web: www.sec.state.ma.us/sct

Standards Div 1 Ashburton Pl Rm 1301 Boston MA 02108 617-727-3480 727-5705
Web: www.mass.gov

State Parks & Recreation Div
251 Cswy St Ste 900 Boston MA 02114 617-626-1250 626-1351
Web: mass.gov

State Police Dept 470 Worcester Rd Framingham MA 01702 508-820-2300 820-2211
Web: www.mass.gov

Supreme Judicial Ct 1 Pemberton Sq Ste 2500 Boston MA 02108 617-557-1000 723-3577
Web: www.mass.gov/courts

Transitional Assistance Dept
600 Washington St Boston MA 02111 617-348-8500
Web: www.mass.gov

Travel & Tourism Office 10 Pk Plaza Ste 4510 Boston MA 02116 617-973-8500 973-8525
TF: 800-227-6277 ■ *Web:* www.massvacation.com

Treasurer State House Rm 227 Boston MA 02133 617-367-6900 248-0372
Web: mass.gov/treasury

Veterans' Services Dept
600 Washington St Ste 1100 Boston MA 02111 617-727-3578 727-5903
Web: www.mass.gov/veterans

Victim Compensation & Assistance Div
1 Ashburton Pl 19th Fl Boston MA 02108 617-727-2200
Web: www.mass.gov

Vital Records & Statistics Registry
150 Mt Vernon St 1st Fl Dorchester MA 02125 617-740-2600
Web: www.mass.gov

339-23 Michigan

Phone | Fax

Aging Services Office
201 N Washington Sq Ste 920 Lansing MI 48933 517-323-3687
Web: leadingagemi.org

Arts & Cultural Affairs Council
300 N Washington Sq. Lansing MI 48913 517-241-3972 241-3979
Web: www.michigan.gov

Attorney General 525 W Ottawa St Lansing MI 48933 517-373-1110 373-3042
TF: 877-765-8388 ■ *Web:* www.michigan.gov

Child Support Office
235 S Grand Ave PO Box 30037 Lansing MI 48933 866-661-0005
TF: 866-661-0005 ■ *Web:* www.michigan.gov/dhs

Civil Rights Dept
110 W Michigan Ave Ste 800
Capitol Tower Bldg Lansing MI 48933 517-335-3165 241-0546
Web: www.michigan.gov/mdcr

Civil Service Dept
Capitol Commons Ctr 400 S Pine St Lansing MI 48913 517-373-3030 373-7690
TF: 800-788-1766 ■ *Web:* www.michigan.gov

Community Health Dept
Capitol View Bldg 201 Townsend St Lansing MI 48913 517-373-3740
TF: 800-649-3777 ■ *Web:* www.michigan.gov/mdch

Consumer Protection Div PO Box 30213 Lansing MI 48909 517-373-1140 241-3771
Web: www.michigan.gov/ag

Corrections Dept
206 E Michigan Ave Grandview Plaza
PO Box 30003 Lansing MI 48909 517-335-1426 373-6883
Web: www.michigan.gov/corrections

Crime Victims Services Commission
320 S Walnut St Garden Level Lewis Cass Bldg Lansing MI 48913 877-251-7373 373-2439*
**Fax Area Code:* 517 ■ *TF:* 877-251-7373 ■ *Web:* www.michigan.gov

Driver & Vehicle Bureau 7064 Crowner Dr Lansing MI 48918 517-322-1460 322-5458
Web: www.michigan.gov/sos

Drug Control Policy Office
320 S Walnut St Lewis Cass Bldg 5th Fl. Lansing MI 48913 517-373-4700 241-2199
Web: www.michigan.gov/mdch

				Phone	Fax
Economic Development Corp (MEDC) 300 N Washington Sq *TF:* 888-522-0103 ■ *Web:* www.michiganbusiness.org	Lansing	MI	48913	517-373-9808	241-3683
Education Dept 608 W Allegan St PO Box 30008 *Web:* www.michigan.gov	Lansing	MI	48909	517-373-3324	
eLibrary Information 702 W Kalamazoo St PO Box 30007 *TF:* 877-479-0021 ■ *Web:* www.michigan.gov	Lansing	MI	48909	517-373-4331	373-5700
Emergency Management & Homeland Security Div PO Box 30636 *Web:* michigan.gov	Lansing	MI	48909	517-336-6198	333-4987
Environmental Quality Dept 3423 N Logan St *Web:* www.michigan.gov	Lansing	MI	48906	517-373-7917	
Financial & Insurance Regulation PO Box 30220 *TF:* 877-999-6442 ■ *Web:* www.michigan.gov	Lansing	MI	48909	517-373-0220	335-4978
Gaming Control Board 3062 West Grand Blvd Ste L-700 **Fax Area Code:* 517 ■ *Web:* www.michigan.gov/mgcb	Detroit	MI	48202	313-456-4100	241-0510*
Governor PO Box 30013 *Web:* www.michigan.gov/gov	Lansing	MI	48909	517-373-3400	335-6863
Human Services Dept 235 S Grand Ave PO Box 30037 *Web:* www.michigan.gov/dhs	Lansing	MI	48909	517-373-2035	335-6101
Labor & Economic Growth Dept 611 W Ottawa St *Web:* www.michigan.gov	Lansing	MI	48933	517-373-1820	373-2129
Lieutenant Governor PO Box 30013 *Web:* www.michigan.gov/ltgov	Lansing	MI	48909	517-373-3400	
Management & Budget Dept PO Box 30026 *Web:* www.michigan.gov/dmb	Lansing	MI	48909	517-373-1004	373-7268
Michigan Career Education & Workforce Programs 201 N Washington Sq Victor Office Center *TF:* 888-253-6855 ■ *Web:* www.michigan.gov/mdcd	Lansing	MI	48913	517-335-5858	373-0314
Michigan Education Trust PO Box 30198 *TF General:* 800-638-4543 ■ *Web:* www.setwithmet.com	Lansing	MI	48909	517-335-4767	373-6967
Michigan Racing Commissioners Office 525 W Allegan St PO Box 30773 *Web:* www.michigan.gov	Lansing	MI	48909	517-335-1420	241-3018
Michigan State Lottery 101 E Hillsdale St PO Box 30023 *Web:* www.michigan.gov/lottery	Lansing	MI	48909	517-335-5600	335-5644
Michigan Student Financial Services Bureau Austin Bldg 430 W Allegan **Fax Area Code:* 517 ■ *TF General:* 800-642-5626 ■ *Web:* www.michigan.gov/mistudentaid	Lansing	MI	48922	888-447-2687	335-6792*
Military & Veterans Affairs Dept 3411 N ML King Blvd *Web:* www.michigan.gov/dmva	Lansing	MI	48906	517-481-8000	
Parks & Recreation Div PO Box 30257 *TF Campground Resv:* 800-447-2757 ■ *Web:* www.michigan.gov/dnr	Lansing	MI	48909	517-373-9900	373-4625
Public Service Commission PO Box 30221 *Web:* www.michigan.gov/mpsc	Lansing	MI	48909	517-241-6180	241-6181
Rehabilitation Services 201 N Washington Sq 4th Fl *Web:* www.michigan.gov	Lansing	MI	48933	517-373-3390	335-7277
Secretary of State 430 W Allegan St 4th Fl *Web:* www.michigan.gov	Lansing	MI	48918	517-373-2510	
State Court Administrator 925 W Ottawa St *Web:* courts.mi.gov	Lansing	MI	48913	517-373-0130	373-7517
State Historic Preservation Office 702 W Kalamazoo St PO Box 30740 *Web:* www.michigan.gov	Lansing	MI	48909	517-373-1630	335-0348
State Housing Development Authority PO Box 30044 *Web:* www.michigan.gov/mshda	Lansing	MI	48909	517-373-8370	335-4797
State Police Dept 714 S Harrison Rd *Web:* www.michigan.gov/msp	East Lansing	MI	48823	517-332-2521	336-6255
Supreme Court PO Box 30052 *Web:* courts.mi.gov	Lansing	MI	48909	517-373-0120	
Transportation Dept PO Box 30050 *Web:* www.michigan.gov/mdot	Lansing	MI	48909	517-373-2090	373-0167
Travel Michigan 300 N Washington Sq *TF:* 888-784-7328 ■ *Web:* www.michigan.org	Lansing	MI	48913	517-373-0670	373-0059
Treasurer 430 W Allegan St *Web:* www.michigan.gov/treasury	Lansing	MI	48922	517-373-3200	373-4968
Unemployment Insurance Agency Cadillac Pl Ste 11-500 *Web:* www.michigan.gov/uia	Detroit	MI	48202	313-456-2400	456-2424
Vital Records Div 201 Townsend St Capitol View Bldg 3rd Fl *Web:* www.michigan.gov/mdch	Lansing	MI	48913	517-335-8656	
Wildlife Div PO Box 30444 *Web:* www.michigan.gov/dnr	Lansing	MI	48909	517-373-1263	373-6705
Workers Compensation Agency PO Box 30016 *Web:* www.michigan.gov/wca	Lansing	MI	48909	517-322-1106	322-6689

339-24 Minnesota

				Phone	Fax
Aging Board 540 Cedar St *TF:* 800-882-6262 ■ *Web:* www.mnaging.org	Saint Paul	MN	55155	651-431-2500	
Arts Board 400 Sibley St Ste 200 *TF:* 800-866-2787 ■ *Web:* www.arts.state.mn.us	Saint Paul	MN	55101	651-215-1600	215-1602
Attorney General 1400 Bremer Tower 445 Minnesota St *TF:* 800-657-3787 ■ *Web:* www.ag.state.mn.us	Saint Paul	MN	55101	651-296-3353	297-4193
Attorney General's Office 445 Minnesota St Ste 1400 *TF:* 800-657-3787 ■ *Web:* www.ag.state.mn.us	Saint Paul	MN	55101	651-296-3353	
Child Support Enforcement Div 444 Lafayette Rd *Web:* mn.gov	Saint Paul	MN	55155	651-431-2000	431-7517
Commerce Dept 85 Seventh Pl E Ste 500 *Web:* mmd.admin.state.mn.us	Saint Paul	MN	55101	651-539-1500	539-1547
Corrections Dept 1450 Energy Pk Dr Ste 200 *Web:* www.corr.state.mn.us	Saint Paul	MN	55108	651-361-7200	642-0223
Department of Education 1500 Hwy 36 W *Web:* education.state.mn.us	Roseville	MN	55113	651-582-8200	582-8202
Department of Public Safety 444 Minnesota St *Web:* www.dps.mn.gov	Saint Paul	MN	55101	651-201-7100	296-5937
Driver & Vehicle Services Div 445 Minnesota St Ste 190 Town Sq Bldg *Web:* dps.mn.gov/divisions/dvs/Pages/default.aspx	Saint Paul	MN	55101	651-297-3298	296-3141
Employment & Economic Development Dept (DEED) 1st National Bank Bldg 332 Minnesota St Ste E200 *TF:* 800-657-3858 ■ *Web:* mn.gov/deed	Saint Paul	MN	55101	651-259-7114	
Enterprise Technology Office 658 Cedar St *Web:* www.mmb.state.mn.us	Saint Paul	MN	55155	651-201-8000	
Finance Dept 658 Cedar St Ste 400 *TF:* 800-627-3529 ■ *Web:* www.mmb.state.mn.us	Saint Paul	MN	55155	651-201-8000	296-8685
Fish & Wildlife Div 500 Lafayette Rd *Web:* www.dnr.state.mn.us	Saint Paul	MN	55155	651-259-5180	297-7272
Governor 130 State Capitol 75 Rev Dr Martin Luther King Jr Blvd *TF:* 800-657-3717 ■ *Web:* mn.gov	Saint Paul	MN	55155	651-201-3400	296-2089
Health Dept PO Box 64975 *TF:* 888-345-0823 ■ *Web:* www.health.state.mn.us	Saint Paul	MN	55164	651-201-5000	
Historical Society 345 Kellogg Blvd W *TF:* 800-657-3773 ■ *Web:* www.mnhs.org	Saint Paul	MN	55102	651-259-3000	
Homeland Security & Emergency Management Div 445 Minnesota St Ste 223 *Web:* dps.mn.gov/divisions/hsem	Saint Paul	MN	55101	651-201-7400	296-0459
Housing Finance Authority 400 Sibley St Ste 300 *TF:* 800-657-3769 ■ *Web:* www.mnhousing.gov	Saint Paul	MN	55101	651-296-7608	296-8139
Human Services Dept 444 Lafayette Rd *Web:* mn.gov	Saint Paul	MN	55155	651-431-2000	296-6244
Labor & Industry Dept 443 Lafayette Rd N *TF:* 800-342-5354 ■ *Web:* www.doli.state.mn.us	Saint Paul	MN	55155	651-284-5005	284-5727
Legislature 75 Constitution Ave State Capitol *TF:* 800-657-3550 ■ *Web:* www.leg.state.mn.us	Saint Paul	MN	55155	651-296-2146	
Medical Practice Board 2829 University Ave SE Ste 500 *TF:* 800-657-3709 ■ *Web:* mn.gov	Minneapolis	MN	55414	612-617-2130	617-2166
Minnesota Bill Status-Senate 100 Rev Dr Martin Luther King Junior Blvd *Web:* www.house.leg.state.mn.us	Saint Paul	MN	55155	651-296-2146	
Minnesota Campaign Finance & Public Disclosure Board 658 Cedar St Ste 190 *TF:* 800-657-3889 ■ *Web:* www.cfboard.state.mn.us	Saint Paul	MN	55155	651-296-5148	296-1722
Minnesota Office of Higher Education 1450 Energy Pk Dr Ste 350 *TF:* 800-657-3866 ■ *Web:* www.ohe.state.mn.us	Saint Paul	MN	55108	651-642-0567	642-0675
Minnesota State Lottery 2645 Long Lake Rd *Web:* www.mnlottery.com	Saint Paul	MN	55113	651-635-8273	
Natural Resources Dept 500 Lafayette Rd *TF:* 888-646-6367 ■ *Web:* www.dnr.state.mn.us	Saint Paul	MN	55155	651-296-6157	
Office of State Registrar 85 E Seventh Pl Third Fl PO Box 64882 *Web:* www.health.state.mn.us/divs/chs/osr	Saint Paul	MN	55164	651-201-5970	
Parks & Recreation Div 500 Lafayette Rd *TF:* 888-646-6367 ■ *Web:* dnr.state.mn.us/contact/index.html	Saint Paul	MN	55155	651-296-6157	
Public Utilities Commission 121 Seventh Pl E Ste 350 *TF:* 800-657-3782 ■ *Web:* mn.gov/puc	Saint Paul	MN	55101	651-296-7124	297-7073
Revenue Dept 600 N Roberts St *TF:* 800-652-9094 ■ *Web:* www.revenue.state.mn.us	Saint Paul	MN	55101	651-296-3403	
Secretary of State 60 Empire Dr Ste 100 *Web:* www.sos.state.mn.us	Saint Paul	MN	55103	651-296-2803	215-0682
State Court Administrator 25 Rev Dr Martin Luther King Jr Blvd Rm 135 *Web:* www.mncourts.gov	Saint Paul	MN	55155	651-296-2474	297-5636
Supreme Court 25 Rev Dr Martin Luther King Jr Blvd *Web:* www.mncourts.gov	Saint Paul	MN	55155	651-297-7650	
Transportation Dept 395 John Ireland Blvd *TF:* 800-657-3774 ■ *Web:* www.dot.state.mn.us	Saint Paul	MN	55155	651-296-3000	
Veterans Affairs Dept 20 W 12th St Room 206 *Web:* mn.gov	Saint Paul	MN	55155	651-296-2562	296-3954
Weights & Measures Div 14305 Southcross Dr W Ste 150 **Fax Area Code:* 952	Burnsville	MN	55306	651-539-1555	435-4040*
Workers'' Compensation Div 443 Lafayette Rd *TF:* 800-342-5354 ■ *Web:* www.dli.mn.gov	Saint Paul	MN	55155	651-284-5005	

339-25 Mississippi

	City	State	ZIP	Phone	Fax
State Government Information 200 S Lamar Ste 800 *TF:* 877-290-9487 ■ *Web:* www.ms.gov	Jackson	MS	39201	601-351-5023	
Administrative Office of the Courts 450 High St PO Box 117 *Web:* courts.ms.gov	Jackson	MS	39205	601-576-4630	576-4630
Archives & History Dept 200 N St PO Box 571 *Web:* www.mdah.state.ms.us	Jackson	MS	39201	601-576-6850	576-6975
Arts Commission 501 NW St Ste 1101-A *Web:* www.arts.state.ms.us	Jackson	MS	39201	601-359-6030	359-6008
Attorney General PO Box 220 *Web:* www.ago.state.ms.us	Jackson	MS	39205	601-359-3680	
Banking & Consumer Finance Dept PO Box 23729 *TF:* 800-844-2499 ■ *Web:* www.dbcf.state.ms.us	Jackson	MS	39225	601-359-1031	359-3557
Child Support Enforcement Div 750 N State St *TF:* 800-345-6347	Jackson	MS	39202	601-359-4929	
Consumer Protection Div PO Box 22947 *TF:* 800-281-4418 ■	Jackson	MS	39225	601-359-4230	359-4231
Contractors Board 215 Woodline Dr Ste B *TF:* 800-880-6161 ■ *Web:* msboc.us	Jackson	MS	39232	601-354-6161	354-6715
Corrections Dept 723 N President St *Web:* www.mdoc.state.ms.us	Jackson	MS	39202	601-359-5600	359-5624
Development Authority 501 NW St *Web:* www.mississippi.org	Jackson	MS	39201	601-359-3449	359-2832
Education Dept 359 N West St Ste 270	Jackson	MS	39201	601-359-3768	
Emergency Management Agency PO Box 5644 *TF:* 800-222-6362 ■ *Web:* www.msema.org	Pearl	MS	39288	601-933-6362	933-6800
Enviromental Quality Dept PO Box 20305 *Web:* www.deq.state.ms.us	Jackson	MS	39289	601-961-5611	354-6356
Family & Children Services Div 750 N State St *TF:* 800-345-6347	Jackson	MS	39202	601-359-4570	
Finance & Administration Dept 1301 Wolfolk Bldg Ste B *Web:* www.dfa.state.ms.us	Jackson	MS	39201	601-359-3402	359-2405
Governor PO Box 139 *Web:* mississippi.gov	Jackson	MS	39205	601-359-3150	359-3741
Health Dept PO Box 1700 *Web:* www.msdh.state.ms.us	Jackson	MS	39215	601-576-7400	
Higher Learning Institutions Board of Trustees 3825 Ridgewood Rd Ste 915 *TF:* 800-327-2980 ■ *Web:* www.ihl.state.ms.us	Jackson	MS	39211	601-432-6198	432-6972
Historic Preservation Div PO Box 571 *Web:* www.mdah.state.ms.us/hpres	Jackson	MS	39205	601-576-6940	576-6955
Home Corp 735 Riverside Dr *Web:* www.mshomecorp.com	Jackson	MS	39202	601-718-4642	718-4643
Human Services Dept 750 N State St *Web:* www.mdhs.state.ms.us	Jackson	MS	39205	601-359-4500	
Information Technology Services Dept 301 N Lamar St Ste 508 *Web:* www.its.ms.gov	Jackson	MS	39201	601-359-1395	354-6016
Insurance Dept 1001 Woolfolk State Office Bldg 501 NW St PO Box 79 *TF:* 800-562-2957 ■ *Web:* www.mid.ms.gov	Jackson	MS	39201	601-359-3569	
Legislature New Capitol PO Box 1018 *Web:* billstatus.ls.state.ms.us	Jackson	MS	39215	601-359-3770	359-3935
Medical Licensure Board 1867 Crane Ridge Dr Ste 200-B *Web:* www.msbml.ms.gov	Jackson	MS	39216	601-987-3079	987-4159
Mississippi Bill Status PO Box 2611 *Web:* billstatus.ls.state.ms.us	Jackson	MS	39215	601-359-2420	
Mississippi Employment Security Commission 1235 Echelon Pkwy PO Box 1699 *TF:* 888-844-3577 ■ *Web:* www.mdes.ms.gov	Jackson	MS	39215	601-321-6000	321-6004
Mississippi Ethics Commission 146 E Amite St Ste 103 *Web:* www.ethics.state.ms.us	Jackson	MS	39201	601-359-1285	354-6253
Mississippi Student Financial Aid Office 3825 Ridgewood Rd *TF:* 800-327-2980 ■ *Web:* www.ihl.state.ms.us/financialaid	Jackson	MS	39211	601-432-6997	432-6527
Motor Vehicle Commission 1755 Lelia Dr *Web:* www.mmvc.state.ms.us	Jackson	MS	39236	601-987-3995	987-3997
Parole Board 660 N St Ste 100 A *Web:* www.mpb.state.ms.us	Jackson	MS	39202	601-576-3520	576-3528
Public Accountancy Board (MSBPA) 5 Old River Pl Ste 104 *Web:* www.msbpa.ms.gov	Jackson	MS	39202	601-354-7320	354-7290
Public Health Statistics Bureau 571 Stadium Dr PO Box 1700 *Web:* www.msdh.state.ms.us/phs	Jackson	MS	39215	601-576-7960	
Public Service Commission PO Box 1174 *Web:* www.psc.state.ms.us	Jackson	MS	39215	601-961-5434	961-5469
Real Estate Commission 2506 Lakeland Dr Ste 300 *Web:* www.mrec.state.ms.us	Flowood	MS	39232	601-932-6770	932-2990
Rehabilitation Services Dept 1281 Highway 51 PO Box 1698 *TF:* 800-443-1000 ■ *Web:* www.mdrs.ms.gov	Madison	MS	39110	800-443-1000	
Securities Div 401 Mississippi St *Web:* www.sos.ms.gov	Jackson	MS	39201	601-359-1350	359-1499
State Medical Examiner PO BOX 958 *Web:* www.dps.state.ms.us	Jackson	MS	39205	601-987-1212	
Supreme Court PO Box 117 *Web:* courts.ms.gov	Jackson	MS	39205	601-359-3694	359-2407
Tax Commission PO Box 22828 *Web:* www.dor.ms.gov	Jackson	MS	39225	601-923-7000	
Treasury Dept 501 N West St Ste 1101	Jackson	MS	39205	601-359-3600	
Veterans Affairs Board (MSVAB) PO Box 5947 *Web:* www.vab.ms.gov	Pearl	MS	39288	601-576-4850	576-4868
Weights & Measures Div 121 N Jefferson St	Jackson	MS	39201	601-359-1100	
Wildlife Fisheries & Parks Dept 1505 Eastover Dr *Web:* www.mdwfp.com	Jackson	MS	39211	601-432-2400	
Worker's Compensation Commission PO Box 5300 *Web:* www.mwcc.state.ms.us	Jackson	MS	39296	601-987-4200	

339-26 Missouri

	City	State	ZIP	Phone	Fax
Revenue Dept 301 W High St *Web:* dor.mo.gov	Jefferson City	MO	65101	573-526-3669	
Agriculture Dept 1616 Missouri Blvd PO Box 630 *Web:* mda.mo.gov	Jefferson City	MO	65102	573-751-4211	751-1784
Arts Council 815 Olive St Ste 16 *Web:* www.missouriartscouncil.org	Saint Louis	MO	63101	314-340-6845	340-7215
Attorney General 207 W High St PO Box 899 *Web:* www.ago.mo.gov	Jefferson City	MO	65102	573-751-3321	751-0774
Child Support Enforcement Div PO Box 109002 *TF:* 800-859-7999 ■ *Web:* www.dss.mo.gov/cse	Jefferson City	MO	65102	800-859-7999	
Conservation Dept 2901 W Truman Blvd *Web:* www.mdc.mo.gov	Jefferson City	MO	65109	573-751-4115	751-4467
Consumer Protection Div 207 W High St PO Box 899 *TF:* 800-392-8222 ■ *Web:* ago.mo.gov/divisions/consumerprotection.htm	Jefferson City	MO	65102	573-751-3321	751-0774
Corrections Dept PO Box 236 *Web:* www.doc.mo.gov	Jefferson City	MO	65102	573-522-1118	
Crime Victims' Compensation Unit PO Box 1589 *Web:* www.dps.mo.gov	Jefferson City	MO	65102	573-526-6006	
Economic Development Dept 301 W High St PO Box 1157 *Web:* www.ded.mo.gov/Ded	Jefferson City	MO	65102	573-751-4962	526-7700
Elementary & Secondary Education Dept 205 Jefferson St PO Box 480 *TF:* 800-735-2966 ■ *Web:* www.dese.mo.gov	Jefferson City	MO	65101	573-751-4212	751-8613
Emergency Management Agency 2302 Militia Dr PO Box 116 *Web:* www.sema.dps.mo.gov	Jefferson City	MO	65102	573-526-9100	634-7966
Family Services Div PO Box 2320 *Web:* www.dss.mo.gov/fsd	Jefferson City	MO	65102	573-751-3221	
Finance Div PO Box 716 *TF:* 888-246-7225 ■ *Web:* www.finance.mo.gov	Jefferson City	MO	65102	573-751-3242	751-9192
General Assembly State Capitol *Web:* www.moga.mo.gov	Jefferson City	MO	65101	573-751-4633	
Governor PO Box 720 *Web:* www.governor.mo.gov	Jefferson City	MO	65102	573-751-3222	
Healing Arts Board 3605 Missouri Blvd PO Box 4 *Web:* www.pr.mo.gov	Jefferson City	MO	65102	573-751-0098	751-3166
Health & Senior Services Dept 912 Wildwood PO Box 570 *Web:* www.health.mo.gov	Jefferson City	MO	65102	573-751-6400	751-6010
Higher Education Dept 3515 Amazonas Dr *TF:* 800-473-6757 ■ *Web:* www.dhe.mo.gov	Jefferson City	MO	65109	573-751-2361	751-6635
Historical Preservation Office 1101 Riverside Dr *Web:* www.dnr.mo.gov	Jefferson City	MO	65101	573-751-7858	522-6262
Housing Development Commission 3435 Broadway *Web:* www.mhdc.com	Kansas City	MO	64111	816-759-6600	759-6828
Insurance Dept 301 W High St Ste 530 *Web:* insurance.mo.gov	Jefferson City	MO	65101	573-751-4126	751-1165
Labor & Industrial Relations Dept 3315 W Truman Blvd Rm 214 PO Box 599 *Web:* www.labor.mo.gov/lirc	Jefferson City	MO	65102	573-751-2461	751-7806
Lieutenant Governor State Capitol Bldg Rm 224 *Web:* ltgov.mo.gov	Jefferson City	MO	65101	573-751-4727	751-9422
Missouri Lottery 1823 Southridge Dr PO Box 1603 *Web:* www.molottery.com	Jefferson City	MO	65109	573-751-4050	751-5188
Motor Vehicles & Drivers Licensing Div PO Box 500 *Web:* dor.mo.gov/drivers	Jefferson City	MO	65106	573-751-3505	751-2195
Natural Resources Dept PO Box 176 *TF Cust Svc:* 800-361-4827 ■ *Web:* www.dnr.mo.gov	Jefferson City	MO	65102	573-751-3443	751-7627
Professional Registration Div 3605 Missouri Blvd PO Box 1335 **Fax Area Code:* 800 ■ *TF:* 800-735-2966 ■ *Web:* www.pr.mo.gov	Jefferson City	MO	65102	573-751-0293	735-2966*
Public Service Commission 200 Madison St PO Box 360 *TF:* 800-819-3180 ■ *Web:* www.psc.mo.gov	Jefferson City	MO	65102	573-751-3234	
Real Estate Commission 3605 Missouri Blvd PO Box 1339 *Web:* www.pr.mo.gov/realestate.asp	Jefferson City	MO	65102	573-751-2628	751-2777
Secretary of State PO Box 778 *Web:* www.sos.mo.gov	Jefferson City	MO	65102	573-751-4936	526-4903
Securities Div 600 W Main St PO Box 1276 *TF:* 800-721-7996 ■ *Web:* s1.sos.mo.gov	Jefferson City	MO	65102	573-751-4704	
Social Services Dept PO Box 1527 *Web:* www.dss.mo.gov	Jefferson City	MO	65102	573-751-4815	751-3203
State Courts Administrator PO Box 104480 *TF:* 888-541-4894 ■ *Web:* www.courts.mo.gov	Jefferson City	MO	65110	888-541-4894	

	City	State	Zip	Phone	Fax
State Highway Patrol 1510 E Elm St *Web:* www.mshp.dps.missouri.gov	Jefferson City	MO	65102	573-751-3313	751-9419
State Parks Div PO Box 176 *TF:* 800-334-6946 ■ *Web:* www.mostateparks.com	Jefferson City	MO	65102	573-751-2479	
Supreme Court 207 W High St *TF:* 888-541-4894 ■ *Web:* www.courts.mo.gov/page.jsp?id=27	Jefferson City	MO	65101	573-751-4144	
Tourism Div PO Box 1055 *TF:* 800-519-2100 ■ *Web:* www.visitmo.com	Jefferson City	MO	65102	573-751-4133	751-5160
Transportation Dept 105 W Capitol Ave *TF:* 888-275-6636 ■ *Web:* www.modot.org	Jefferson City	MO	65102	573-751-2551	751-6555
Treasurer PO Box 210 *Web:* www.treasurer.mo.gov	Jefferson City	MO	65102	573-751-8533	751-0343
Veterans Commission 205 Jefferson St Fl 12 *Web:* mvc.dps.mo.gov	Jefferson City	MO	65102	573-751-3779	
Vital Records Bureau 930 Wildwood PO Box 570 *Web:* www.sos.mo.gov	Jefferson City	MO	65102	573-751-6400	
Vocational & Adult Education Div 3024 Dupont Cir PO Box 480 *TF:* 877-222-8963 ■ *Web:* dese.mo.gov/college-career-readiness	Jefferson City	MO	65109	573-751-3251	751-1441
Weights & Measures Div 1616 Missouri Blvd PO Box 630 *Web:* agriculture.mo.gov/weights	Jefferson City	MO	65102	573-751-4316	
Workers Compensation Div PO Box 58 *TF:* 800-775-2667 ■ *Web:* www.labor.mo.gov/DWC	Jefferson City	MO	65102	573-751-4231	751-2012

339-27 Montana

	City	State	Zip	Phone	Fax
State Government Information PO Box 200113 *Web:* www.mt.gov	Helena	MT	59620	406-444-2511	444-2701
Arts Council PO Box 202201 *TF:* 800-282-3092 ■ *Web:* www.art.mt.gov	Helena	MT	59620	406-444-6430	444-6548
Attorney General 215 N Sanders St *Web:* dojmt.gov	Helena	MT	59601	406-444-2026	444-3549
Banking & Financial Institutions Div Rm 155 Mitchell Bldg 125 N Roberts St PO Box 200101 *TF:* 800-914-8423 ■ *Web:* www.banking.mt.gov	Helena	MT	59620	406-841-2920	841-2930
Child & Family Services Div PO Box 8005 *TF:* 866-820-5437 ■ *Web:* dphhs.mt.gov	Helena	MT	59604	406-841-2400	841-2487
Commerce Dept 301 S Pk Ave PO Box 200501 *Web:* www.commerce.mt.gov	Helena	MT	59601	406-841-2700	841-2701
Community Development Div 301 S Pk Ave PO Box 200523 *Web:* www.comdev.mt.gov	Helena	MT	59601	406-841-2770	841-2771
Consumer Protection Office PO Box 200151 *TF:* 800-481-6896 ■ *Web:* dojmt.gov	Helena	MT	59620	406-444-4500	442-2174
Corrections Dept 5 S Last Chance Gulch PO Box 201301 *Web:* www.cor.mt.gov	Helena	MT	59620	406-444-3930	444-4920
Court Administration 215 N Sanders St Rm 315 *Web:* www.montanacourts.org	Helena	MT	59620	406-444-5490	
Department of Labor & Industry - Business Standards 301 S Pk Rm 430 PO Box 200513 *Web:* www.bsd.dli.mt.gov	Helena	MT	59620	406-841-2300	
Disability Services Div 111 N Sanders St Ste 305	Helena	MT	59601	406-444-2995	
Environmental Quality Dept PO Box 200901 *Web:* montanatu.org	Helena	MT	59620	406-444-2544	
Forensic Science Div 2679 Palmer St *Web:* dojmt.gov/crime	Missoula	MT	59808	406-728-4970	549-1067
Healthcare Licensing Bureau 301 S Pk Ave Rm 430 *Web:* mt.gov	Helena	MT	59620	406-841-2303	841-2305
Highway Patrol Div 2550 Prospect Ave PO Box 201419 *Web:* dojmt.gov/highwaypatrol	Helena	MT	59620	406-444-3780	444-4169
Historical Society 225 N Roberts St *Web:* helenamt.com	Helena	MT	59601	406-442-4120	
Housing Div PO Box 200528 *Web:* www.housing.mt.gov	Helena	MT	59620	406-841-2840	841-2841
Information Technology Services Div 125 N Roberts St *TF:* 800-628-4917 ■ *Web:* www.itsd.mt.gov	Helena	MT	59601	406-444-2700	444-2701
Insurance Div 1315 E Lockey *Web:* uid.dli.mt.gov	Helena	MT	59604	406-444-3783	
Labor & Industry Dept PO Box 1728 *Web:* www.dli.mt.gov	Helena	MT	59624	406-444-2840	444-1394
Lieutenant Governor PO Box 200801 *Web:* www.governor.mt.gov	Helena	MT	59620	406-444-3111	444-5529
Montana Commissioner of Political Practices 1205 Eigth Ave PO Box 202401 *Web:* www.politicalpractices.mt.gov	Helena	MT	59620	406-444-2942	444-1643
Montana Higher Education Board of Regents 2500 Broadway St PO Box 203201 *TF:* 877-501-1722 ■ *Web:* www.mus.edu	Helena	MT	59620	406-444-6570	444-1469
Montana Legislative Services 1301 E Sixth Ave PO Box 201706 *Web:* leg.mt.gov	Helena	MT	59620	406-444-3064	444-3036
Motor Vehicle Div 302 N Roberts St, PO Box 201430 *Web:* dojmt.gov/driving	Helena	MT	59620	406-444-3933	
Natural Resources & Conservation Dept 1625 11th Ave *Web:* www.dnrc.mt.gov	Helena	MT	59620	406-444-2074	444-2684
Office of Governor PO Box 200801 *Web:* www.governor.mt.gov	Helena	MT	59620	406-444-3111	444-5529
Public Education Board 46 N Last Chance Gulch PO Box 200601 *Web:* bpe.mt.gov	Helena	MT	59620	406-444-6576	444-0847
Public Health & Human Services Dept 111 N Sanders *Web:* mt.gov	Helena	MT	59604	406-444-5622	444-1970
Public Service Commission 1701 Prospect Ave	Helena	MT	59601	406-444-6199	444-7618
Revenue Dept PO Box 5805 *TF:* 866-859-2254 ■ *Web:* revenue.mt.gov	Helena	MT	59604	406-444-6900	444-3696
Secretary of State 1301 E Sixth Ave PO Box 202801 *Web:* www.sos.mt.gov	Helena	MT	59601	406-444-2034	444-3976
Securities Dept 840 Helena Ave *TF:* 800-332-6148 ■ *Web:* www.sao.mt.gov	Helena	MT	59601	406-444-2040	444-3497
State Auditor Office 840 Helena Ave *Web:* www.sao.mt.gov	Helena	MT	59601	406-444-2040	444-3497
State Legislature 1301 E Sixth Ave *Web:* www.leg.mt.gov	Helena	MT	59620	406-444-3060	444-3036
Supreme Court 215 N Sanders St Rm 323 *Web:* courts.mt.gov	Helena	MT	59620	406-444-3858	444-5705
Transportation Dept 2701 Prospect Ave PO Box 201001 *Web:* www.mdt.mt.gov	Helena	MT	59620	406-444-6200	444-7643
Victim Services Office 2225 11th Ave PO Box 201410 *TF:* 800-498-6455 ■ *Web:* dojmt.gov/victims	Helena	MT	59620	406-444-1907	444-9680
Vital Records Bureau 111 N Sanders St *TF:* 888-877-1946 ■ *Web:* montanagenealogy.com	Helena	MT	59604	406-444-4228	444-1803
Weights & Measures Program 301 South Park, Room 430 PO Box 200513 *Web:* www.bsd.dli.mt.gov/bc/ms_index.asp	Helena	MT	59620	406-443-8065	443-8163
Wildlife And Parks 1420 E Sixth Ave PO Box 200701 *Web:* www.fwp.mt.gov	Helena	MT	59620	406-444-2535	444-4952
Worker's Compensation Ct 1625 11th Avenue PO Box 537 *Web:* www.wcc.dli.mt.gov	Helena	MT	59624	406-444-7794	444-7798

339-28 Nebraska

	City	State	Zip	Phone	Fax
State Electrical Division 521 S 14th St Ste 300 *Web:* www.electrical.nebraska.gov	Lincoln	NE	68508	402-471-3550	471-4297
Aging Div PO Box 95026 *Web:* dhhs.ne.gov	Lincoln	NE	68509	402-471-2307	
Agriculture Dept 301 Centennial Mall S *Web:* www.nda.nebraska.gov	Lincoln	NE	68509	402-471-2341	471-2759
Arts Council 1004 Farnam St *TF:* 800-341-4067 ■ *Web:* www.nebraskaartscouncil.org	Omaha	NE	68131	402-595-2122	
Attorney General 2115 State Capitol *Web:* www.ago.ne.gov	Lincoln	NE	68509	402-471-2683	471-3297
Banking & Finance Dept (NDBF) 1230 'O' St Ste 400 PO Box 95006 *Web:* www.ndbf.ne.gov	Lincoln	NE	68508	402-471-2171	471-3062
Child Support Enforcement Div PO Box 95026 *TF:* 877-631-9973 ■ *Web:* dhhs.ne.gov	Lincoln	NE	68509	402-471-3121	471-7311
Correctional Services Dept PO Box 94661 *Web:* www.corrections.state.ne.us	Lincoln	NE	68509	402-471-2654	
Crime Victim Reparations Programs 301 Centennial Mall S PO Box 94946 *Web:* www.ncc.state.ne.us	Lincoln	NE	68509	402-471-2194	471-2837
Economic Development Dept 301 Centennial Mall S PO Box 94666 *TF:* 800-426-6505 ■ *Web:* www.neded.org	Lincoln	NE	68509	402-471-3747	471-3778
Education Dept 301 Centennial Mall S *Web:* www2.ed.gov	Lincoln	NE	68509	402-471-2295	471-4433
Emergency Management Agency 1300 Military Rd *TF:* 877-297-2368 ■ *Web:* www.nema.ne.gov	Lincoln	NE	68508	402-471-7421	471-7433
Environmental Quality Dept 1200 N St Ste 400 *TF:* 877-253-2603 ■ *Web:* www.deq.state.ne.us	Lincoln	NE	68508	402-471-2186	471-2909
Game & Parks Commission PO Box 30370 *Web:* outdoornebraska.ne.gov	Lincoln	NE	68503	402-471-0641	471-5528
Governor PO Box 94848 *Web:* www.governor.nebraska.gov	Lincoln	NE	68509	402-471-2244	471-6031
Health & Human Services Dept 301 Centennial Mall S *TF:* 800-430-3244 ■ *Web:* dhhs.ne.gov	Lincoln	NE	68508	402-471-3121	471-9449
Historical Society 1500 R St *TF:* 800-833-6747 ■ *Web:* www.nebraskahistory.org	Lincoln	NE	68501	402-471-3270	471-3100
Insurance Dept 941 O St Ste 400 *TF:* 877-564-7323 ■ *Web:* www.doi.nebraska.gov	Lincoln	NE	68508	402-471-2201	471-4610
Investment Finance Authority 1230 'O' St Ste 200 *TF:* 800-204-6432 ■ *Web:* www.nifa.org	Lincoln	NE	68508	402-434-3900	434-3921
Lieutenant Governor 1445 K St Ste 2315 *Web:* governor.nebraska.gov	Lincoln	NE	68508	402-471-2256	471-6031
Motor Vehicles Dept PO Box 94789 *Web:* www.dmv.state.ne.us	Lincoln	NE	68509	402-471-3918	
Natural Resources Dept 301 Centennial Mall S 4th Fl *Web:* nebraska.gov	Lincoln	NE	68509	402-471-2363	471-2900
Nebraska Accountability & Disclosure Commission PO Box 95086 *Web:* nadc.nebraska.gov	Lincoln	NE	68509	402-471-2522	471-6599
Nebraska Coordinating Commission for Postsecondary Educatio 140 N Eigth St Ste 300 PO Box 95005 *Web:* www.ccpe.state.ne.us	Lincoln	NE	68509	402-471-2847	471-2886
Nebraska State Racing Commission 5903 Walker Ave *Web:* nebraskaracingcommission.com	Lincoln	NE	68507	402-471-4155	
Nebraska Workforce Development - Dept of Labor 550 S 16th St PO Box 94600 *Web:* dol.nebraska.gov	Lincoln	NE	68509	402-471-2600	471-9867

Agency / Address	City	State	Zip	Phone	Fax
Parks Div 2200 N 33rd St Web: outdoornebraska.ne.gov	Lincoln	NE	68503	402-471-0641	471-5528
Parole Board PO Box 94754 Web: www.parole.state.ne.us	Lincoln	NE	68509	402-471-2156	471-2453
Power Review Board 301 Centennial Mall S Web: powerreviewboard.nebraska.gov	Lincoln	NE	68508	402-471-2301	471-3715
Public Accountancy Board 140 N Eigth St Ste 290 Web: www.nbpa.ne.gov	Lincoln	NE	68508	402-471-3595	471-4484
Public Service Commission 1200 N St Ste 300 TF: 800-526-0017 ■ Web: psc.nebraska.gov	Lincoln	NE	68508	402-471-3101	471-0254
Real Estate Commission 1200 N St Ste 402 PO Box 94667 Web: www.nrec.ne.gov	Lincoln	NE	68509	402-471-2004	471-4492
Revenue Dept 301 Centennial Mall S Second Fl PO Box 94818 Web: revenue.nebraska.gov	Lincoln	NE	68509	402-471-5729	471-5608
Secretary of State 1445 K St Ste 2300 Web: sos.ne.gov	Lincoln	NE	68508	402-471-2554	471-3237
Securities Bureau 1230 'O' St Ste 400 PO Box 95006 Web: www.ndbf.ne.gov	Lincoln	NE	68508	402-471-3445	
State Court Administrator 1213 State Capitol PO Box 98910 Web: supremecourt.nebraska.gov	Lincoln	NE	68509	402-471-3730	471-2197
State Patrol PO Box 94907 Web: statepatrol.nebraska.gov	Lincoln	NE	68509	402-471-4545	
Supreme Court State Capitol Bldg Web: court.nol.org	Lincoln	NE	68509	402-471-3730	471-3480
Teacher Certification Office PO Box 94987 Web: www.teaching-certification.com	Lincoln	NE	68509	402-471-2295	
Travel & Tourism Div PO Box 98907 TF: 877-632-7275 ■ Web: www.visitnebraska.com	Lincoln	NE	68509	402-471-3796	471-3026
Treasurer PO Box 94788 State Capitol Rm 2005 Web: www.treasurer.org/up	Lincoln	NE	68508	402-471-2455	471-4390
Veterans' Affairs Dept 301 Centennial Mall S Fl 1 PO Box 95083 Web: www.vets.state.ne.us	Lincoln	NE	68509	402-471-2458	471-2491
Vital Statistics Div 1033 "O" St Ste 130 PO Box 95065 Web: dhhs.ne.gov	Lincoln	NE	68509	402-471-2871	
Vocational Rehabilitation Services Div 3901 N 27th St Ste 6 TF: 800-472-3382	Lincoln	NE	68521	402-471-3231	471-6309
Weights & Measures Div 301 Centennial Mall S Web: www.nda.nebraska.gov	Lincoln	NE	68508	402-471-4292	471-2759
Workers' Compensation Court 1010 Lincoln Mall Ste 100 TF: 800-599-5155 ■ Web: allworkerscomp.com	Lincoln	NE	68508	402-471-6468	471-2700

339-29 Nevada

Agency / Address	City	State	Zip	Phone	Fax
Accountancy Board 1325 Airmotive Way Ste 220 Web: www.nvaccountancy.com	Reno	NV	89502	775-786-0231	786-0234
Administrative Office of the Courts 201 S Carson St Ste 250 Web: nevadajudiciary.us	Carson City	NV	89701	775-684-1700	684-1723
Aging Services Div 1860 E Sahara Ave Web: adsd.nv.gov	Las Vegas	NV	89104	702-486-3545	486-3572
Arts Council 716 N Carson St Ste A Web: nac.nevadaculture.org	Carson City	NV	89701	775-687-6680	687-6688
Attorney General 100 N Carson St Web: ag.nv.gov	Carson City	NV	89701	775-684-1100	684-1108
Business & Industry Dept 555 E Washington Ave Ste 4900 Web: www.business.nv.gov	Las Vegas	NV	89101	702-486-2750	486-2758
Child & Family Services Div 4126 Technology Way 3rd Fl Web: www.dcfs.state.nv.us	Carson City	NV	89706	775-684-4400	684-4455
Child Support Enforcement Office 1470 College Pkwy TF: 800-992-0900 ■ Web: dwss.nv.gov	Carson City	NV	89706	775-684-0500	684-0646
Conservation & Natural Resources Dept 901 S Stewart St Ste 1003 Web: www.dcnr.nv.gov	Carson City	NV	89701	775-684-2700	684-2715
Consumer Affairs Div 555 E Washington Ave Ste 4900 Web: www.fightfraud.nv.gov	Las Vegas	NV	89101	702-486-7355	
Corrections Dept PO Box 7011 *Fax Area Code: 702 ■ Web: www.doc.nv.gov	Carson City	NV	89702	775-887-3285	486-9908*
Economic Development Commission 808 W Nye Ln TF: 800-336-1600 ■ Web: www.diversifynevada.com	Carson City	NV	89703	775-687-9900	687-9924
Education Dept 700 E Fifth St Web: www.doe.nv.gov	Carson City	NV	89701	775-687-9200	687-9101
Emergency Management Div 2478 Fairview Dr Web: dem.nv.gov	Carson City	NV	89701	775-687-0400	687-0322
Environmental Protection Div 901 S Stewart St Ste 4001 Web: www.ndep.nv.gov	Carson City	NV	89701	775-687-4670	687-5856
Gaming Commission 1919 College Pkwy PO Box 8003 Web: gaming.nv.gov	Carson City	NV	89706	775-684-7750	687-5817
Governor 101 N Carson St Web: nevadatreasurer.gov	Carson City	NV	89701	775-684-5670	684-5683
Health Div 4150 Technology Way Web: www.health.nv.gov	Carson City	NV	89706	775-684-4200	684-4211
Highway Patrol Div 555 Wright Way Web: nevadadot.com	Carson City	NV	89711	775-687-5300	
Historic Preservation Office 901 S Stewart St Ste 5004 Web: www.nvshpo.org	Carson City	NV	89701	775-684-3448	684-3442
Human Resources Dept 4126 Technology Way Rm 100 Web: dhhs.nv.gov	Carson City	NV	89706	775-684-4000	
Information Technology Dept 100 N Stewart St Ste 100 Web: it.nv.gov	Carson City	NV	89701	775-684-5800	
Insurance Div 1818 E College Pkwy Ste 103 Web: doi.nv.gov	Carson City	NV	89706	775-687-0700	687-0787
Legislature 401 S Carson St Web: www.leg.state.nv.us	Carson City	NV	89701	775-684-6800	
Lieutenant Governor 101 N Carson St Ste 2 Web: www.ltgov.nv.gov	Carson City	NV	89701	775-684-7111	684-7110
Medical Examiners Board 1105 Terminal Way Ste 301 Web: www.medboard.nv.gov	Reno	NV	89502	775-688-2559	688-2321
Motor Vehicles Dept 555 Wright Way TF: 877-368-7828 ■ Web: www.dmvnv.com	Carson City	NV	89711	775-684-4368	
Nevada Bill Status 401 S Carson St TF: 800-978-2878 ■ Web: www.leg.state.nv.us	Carson City	NV	89701	775-684-3360	684-3330
Nevada Commission on Ethics 704 W Nye Ln Ste 204 Web: www.ethics.nv.gov	Carson City	NV	89703	775-687-5469	687-1279
Nevada Dept of Employment Training & Rehabilitation 500 E Third St Web: www.nvdetr.org	Carson City	NV	89713	775-684-3911	684-3908
Nevada State Athletic Commission 555 E Washington Ave Ste 3300 Web: www.boxing.nv.gov	Las Vegas	NV	89101	702-486-2575	486-2577
Parole & Probation Div 1445 Old Hot Springs Rd Ste 104 Web: www.dps.nv.gov	Carson City	NV	89706	775-684-2600	
Postsecondary Education Commission 3663 E Sunset Rd Ste 202 Web: www.cpe.state.nv.us	Las Vegas	NV	89120	702-486-7330	486-7340
Public Safety Dept 555 Wright Way Web: www.nhp.nv.gov	Carson City	NV	89711	775-684-4650	
Public Utilities Commission 1150 E William St Web: puc.nv.gov	Carson City	NV	89701	775-684-6101	684-6110
Real Estate Div 2501 E Sahara Ave Ste 102 Web: www.red.state.nv.us	Las Vegas	NV	89104	702-486-4033	486-4275
Rehabilitation Div 1370 S Curry St Web: detr.state.nv.us	Carson City	NV	89703	775-684-4040	684-4184
Secretary of State 101 N Carson St Ste 3 TF: 800-450-8594 ■ Web: www.nvsos.gov	Carson City	NV	89701	775-684-5708	684-5725
State Parks Div 901 S Stewart St 5th Fl Web: www.parks.nv.gov	Carson City	NV	89701	775-684-2770	684-2777
Supreme Court 201 S Carson St Ste 250 Web: www.nevadajudiciary.us	Carson City	NV	89701	775-684-1600	
System of Higher Education 2601 Enterprise Rd Web: www.nevada.edu	Reno	NV	89512	775-784-4901	784-1127
Taxation Dept 1550 E College Pkwy Ste 115 Web: tax.nv.gov	Carson City	NV	89706	775-684-2000	684-2020
Teacher Licensure Office 700 E Fifth St Web: www.doe.nv.gov	Carson City	NV	89701	775-687-9115	687-9101
Tourism & Cultural Affairs Dept 716 N Carson St Ste A Web: www.nevadaculture.org	Carson City	NV	89701	775-687-8393	684-5446
Tourism Commission 401 N Carson St TF: 800-237-0774 ■ Web: www.travelnevada.com	Carson City	NV	89701	775-687-4322	
Transportation Dept 1263 S Stewart St Web: www.nevadadot.com	Carson City	NV	89712	775-888-7000	888-7115
Treasurer 101 N Carson St Ste 4 Web: nevadatreasurer.gov	Carson City	NV	89701	775-684-5600	684-5781
Veterans Services Office 5460 Reno Corporate Dr Web: www.veterans.nv.gov	Reno	NV	89511	775-688-1653	688-1656
Vital Statistics Office 4150 Technology Way Ste 104	Carson City	NV	89706	775-684-4242	684-4156
Weights & Measures Bureau 2150 Frazier Ave Web: agri.nv.gov	Sparks	NV	89431	775-353-3782	688-2533
Welfare Div 1470 College Pkwy TF: 800-992-0900 ■ Web: carson.org	Carson City	NV	89706	775-684-0500	

339-30 New Hampshire

Agency / Address	City	State	Zip	Phone	Fax
State Government Information 64 S St Web: www.nh.gov	Concord	NH	03301	603-271-1110	
Accountancy Board 78 Regional Dr Bldg 2 Web: www.nh.gov	Concord	NH	03301	603-271-3286	271-8702
Administrative Office of the Courts 2 Charles Doe Dr Web: www.courts.state.nh.us/aoc	Concord	NH	03301	603-271-2521	513-5454
Agriculture Markets & Food Dept PO Box 2042 Web: agriculture.nh.gov	Concord	NH	03302	603-271-3551	271-1109
Arts Council 2 1/2 Beacon St 2nd Fl Web: www.nh.gov/nharts	Concord	NH	03301	603-271-2789	271-3584
Attorney General 33 Capitol St Web: www.nh.gov	Concord	NH	03301	603-271-3658	271-2110
Banking Dept 53 Regional Dr Ste 200 TF: 800-437-5991 ■ Web: www.nh.gov	Concord	NH	03301	603-271-3561	271-1090
Board of Medicine 2 Industrial Pk Dr Ste 8 Web: www.nh.gov	Concord	NH	03301	603-271-1203	271-6702
Bureau of Elderly & Adult Services (BEAS) 129 Pleasant St Web: www.dhhs.nh.gov	Concord	NH	03301	603-271-4680	271-4643
Chief Medical Examiner 246 Pleasant St Ste 218 Web: doj.nh.gov/medical-examiner	Concord	NH	03301	603-271-1235	271-6308

	City	State	Zip	Phone	Fax
Child Support Services 129 Pleasant St *TF:* 800-852-3345 ■ *Web:* www.dhhs.nh.gov/dcss	Concord	NH	03301	603-271-4427	271-4787
Children Youth & Families Div 129 Pleasant St 4th Fl. *Web:* www.dhhs.state.nh.us	Concord	NH	03301	603-271-4451	271-4729
Consumer Protection and Antitrust Bureau 33 Capitol St. *Web:* www.doj.nh.gov	Concord	NH	03301	603-271-3641	271-2110
Corrections Dept PO Box 1806. *Web:* www.nh.gov	Concord	NH	03302	603-271-5600	271-5643
Division of Vital Records Administration 71 S Fruit St *TF:* 800-735-2964 ■ *Web:* www.sos.nh.gov/vitalrecords	Concord	NH	03301	603-271-4650	271-3447
Education Dept 101 Pleasant St *Web:* www.education.nh.gov	Concord	NH	03301	603-271-3494	271-1953
Emergency Management Office 33 Hazen Dr *Web:* www.nh.gov	Concord	NH	03305	603-271-2231	225-7341
Environmental Services Dept 29 Hazen Dr PO Box 95 *TF:* 800-735-2964 ■ *Web:* des.nh.gov	Concord	NH	03301	603-271-3503	271-2867
Fish & Game Dept 11 Hazen Dr *Web:* www.wildlife.state.nh.us	Concord	NH	03301	603-271-3511	271-1438
General Court 107 N Main St *Web:* gencourt.state.nh.us	Concord	NH	03301	603-271-2154	
Governor State House 107 N Main St Rm 208 *Web:* www.nh.gov	Concord	NH	03301	603-271-2121	271-7680
Historical Resources Div 19 Pillsbury St *Web:* www.nh.gov/nhdhr	Concord	NH	03301	603-271-3483	271-3433
Housing Finance Authority PO Box 5087. *TF:* 800-439-7247 ■ *Web:* www.nhhfa.org	Manchester	NH	03108	603-472-8623	472-8501
Insurance Dept 21 S Fruit St Ste 14 *Web:* www.nh.gov	Concord	NH	03301	603-271-2261	271-1406
Joint Board of Licensure & Certification 57 Regional Dr *Web:* www.nh.gov	Concord	NH	03301	603-271-2219	271-6990
Motor Vehicles Div 23 Hazen Dr *Web:* nh.gov/safety/divisions/dmv	Concord	NH	03305	603-227-4000	
New Hampshire Employment Security 32 S Main St. *TF:* 800-852-3400 ■ *Web:* www.nh.gov	Concord	NH	03301	603-224-3311	228-4145
New Hampshire Lottery Commission 14 Integra Dr. *TF:* 800-852-3324 ■ *Web:* www.nhlottery.com	Concord	NH	03301	603-271-3391	271-1160
New Hampshire Postsecondary Education Commission 64 South St Ste 300 *TF:* 800-735-2964 ■ *Web:* www.nh.gov	Concord	NH	03301	603-271-2555	271-2696
Parks & Recreation Div 172 Pembroke Rd *Web:* www.nhstateparks.org	Concord	NH	03301	603-271-3556	271-3553
Public Utilities Commission 21 S Fruit St Ste 10 *TF Consumer Assistance:* 800-852-3793 ■ *Web:* www.puc.state.nh.us	Concord	NH	03301	603-271-2431	271-3878
Real Estate Commission 25 Capitol St Rm 434 *Web:* www.nh.gov/nhrec	Concord	NH	03301	603-271-2701	271-1039
Resources & Economic Development Dept PO Box 1856 *Web:* www.dred.state.nh.us	Concord	NH	03302	603-271-2411	271-2629
Revenue Administration Dept 45 Chenell Dr. *Web:* www.revenue.nh.gov	Concord	NH	03301	603-271-2191	
Secretary of State 107 N Main St State House Rm 204 *Web:* www.sos.nh.gov	Concord	NH	03301	603-271-3242	271-6316
State Office of Veterans Services 275 Chestnut St Rm 517. *Web:* www.nh.gov	Manchester	NH	03101	603-624-9230	624-9236
State Police Div 33 Hazen Dr *Web:* nh.gov/safety/divisions/nhsp	Concord	NH	03305	603-223-8813	271-6497
Supreme Court 1 Charles Doe Dr *Web:* www.courts.state.nh.us	Concord	NH	03301	603-271-2646	
Teacher Credentialing Bureau 101 Pleasant St. *Web:* www.education.nh.gov	Concord	NH	03301	603-271-3494	
Transportation Dept PO Box 483. *Web:* www.nh.gov/dot	Concord	NH	03301	603-271-3734	271-3914
Travel & Tourism Development Office PO Box 1856 *TF:* 800-262-6660 ■ *Web:* www.visitnh.gov	Concord	NH	03302	603-271-2665	271-6870
Treasury Dept 25 Capitol St Rm 121. *Web:* www.nh.gov/treasury	Concord	NH	03301	603-271-2621	271-3922
Victims' Assistance Commission 33 Capitol St *TF:* 800-300-4500 ■ *Web:* www.nh.gov	Concord	NH	03301	603-271-1284	223-6291
Vocational Rehabilitation Office 21 S Fruit St Ste 20 *TF:* 800-299-1647 ■ *Web:* www.education.nh.gov	Concord	NH	03301	603-271-3471	271-7095
Weights & Measures Bureau PO Box 2042. *Web:* agriculture.nh.gov	Concord	NH	03302	603-271-3685	271-1109

339-31 New Jersey

	City	State	Zip	Phone	Fax
Administrative Office of the Cts 25 Market St PO Box 037 *Web:* www.judiciary.state.nj.us	Trenton	NJ	08625	609-984-0275	984-6968
Agriculture Dept PO Box 330. *Web:* www.state.nj.us/agriculture	Trenton	NJ	08625	609-292-3976	292-3978
Arts Council 225 W State St PO Box 306. *Web:* nj.gov	Trenton	NJ	08625	609-292-6130	989-1440
Attorney General 25 Market St PO Box 080 *Web:* www.state.nj.us	Trenton	NJ	08625	609-292-4925	292-3508
Banking & Insurance Dept 20 W State St PO Box 325 *TF:* 800-446-7467 ■ *Web:* www.state.nj.us/dobi	Trenton	NJ	08625	609-292-7272	984-5273
Board of Public Utilities 2 Gateway Ctr *Web:* www.state.nj.us/bpu	Newark	NJ	07102	973-648-2013	648-4195
Child Support Office 175 S Broad St PO Box 8068 *TF:* 877-655-4371 ■ *Web:* www.njchildsupport.org	Trenton	NJ	08650	877-655-4371	
Commerce Economic Growth & Tourism Commission 20 W State St PO Box 820 *Web:* www.state.nj.us/commerce	Trenton	NJ	08625	609-777-0885	777-4097
Community Affairs Dept 101 S Broad St PO Box 204 *Web:* www.nj.gov/dca	Trenton	NJ	08625	609-777-3474	292-3292
Consumer Affairs Div 124 Halsey St *Web:* www.state.nj.us	Newark	NJ	07102	973-504-6200	648-3538
Corrections Dept PO Box 863. *Web:* www.state.nj.us	Trenton	NJ	08625	609-292-4036	292-9083
Economic Development Authority PO Box 990 **Fax:* PR ■ *Web:* www.njeda.com	Trenton	NJ	08625	609-292-1800	292-5722*
Education Dept PO Box 500 *Web:* www.state.nj.us/education	Trenton	NJ	08625	609-292-4450	777-4099
Emergency Management Office PO Box 7068 *Web:* www.njsp.org/feedback.html	West Trenton	NJ	08628	609-882-2000	
Environmental Protection Dept 401 E State St PO Box 402 *Web:* www.state.nj.us/dep	Trenton	NJ	08625	609-292-2885	292-1921
Fish Game & Wildlife Div PO Box 400 *Web:* www.state.nj.us/dep/fgw	Trenton	NJ	08625	609-292-9410	984-1414
Governor 125 W State St PO Box 001. *Web:* www.state.nj.us/governor	Trenton	NJ	08625	609-292-6000	292-3454
Health & Senior Services Dept PO Box 360 *Web:* www.state.nj.us/health	Trenton	NJ	08625	609-292-7837	984-5474
Historical Commission 225 W State St PO Box 305 *Web:* www.state.nj.us	Trenton	NJ	08625	609-292-6062	633-8168
Housing & Mortgage Finance Agency 637 S Clinton Ave PO Box 18550. *Web:* www.state.nj.us/dca/hmfa	Trenton	NJ	08650	609-278-7400	278-1754
Human Services Dept 240 W State St PO Box 700 *Web:* www.state.nj.us/humanservices	Trenton	NJ	08625	609-292-3717	292-3824
Information Technology Office PO Box 212 *Web:* www.nj.gov/it/oit	Trenton	NJ	08625	609-633-8975	633-8888
Labor & Workforce Development Dept PO Box 110 *Web:* lwd.state.nj.us	Trenton	NJ	08625	609-659-9045	633-9271
Mental Health Services Div PO Box 272 *TF:* 800-382-6717 ■ *Web:* www.state.nj.us/humanservices/dmhs	Trenton	NJ	08625	609-777-0700	777-0662
Military & Veterans' Affairs Dept 101 Eggert Crossing Rd *TF:* 800-624-0508 ■ *Web:* www.state.nj.us	Lawrenceville	NJ	08648	609-530-4600	530-7100
Motor Vehicle Commission 225 E State St PO Box 160 *TF:* 888-486-3339 ■ *Web:* www.state.nj.us/mvc	Trenton	NJ	08666	609-292-6500	
New Jersey Bill Status State House Annex PO Box 068 *TF:* 800-792-8630 ■ *Web:* www.njleg.state.nj.us	Trenton	NJ	08625	609-292-4840	777-2440
New Jersey Ethical Standards Commission 28 W State St Rm 1407 PO Box 082. *Web:* www.state.nj.us/lps/ethics	Trenton	NJ	08625	609-292-1892	633-9252
New Jersey Higher Education Commission 20 W State St PO Box 542 *Web:* www.state.nj.us	Trenton	NJ	08625	609-292-4310	292-7225
New Jersey Higher Education Student Assistance Authority 4 Quakerbridge Plaza PO Box 540 *TF:* 800-792-8670 ■ *Web:* www.hesaa.org	Trenton	NJ	08625	609-584-4480	588-7389
New Jersey Lottery PO Box 041. *Web:* www.state.nj.us	Trenton	NJ	08625	609-599-5800	599-5935
New Jersey Racing Commission 140 E Front St *Web:* www.njpublicsafety.org	Trenton	NJ	08625	609-292-0613	599-1785
New Jersey State Athletic Control Board 25 Market St 1st Fl W Wing *Web:* www.state.nj.us/lps/sacb	Trenton	NJ	08625	609-292-0317	292-3756
New Jersey Workforce New Jersey 1 John Fitch Plz Fl 3. *Web:* lwd.dol.state.nj.us	Trenton	NJ	08611	609-292-2305	695-1174
Parks & Forestry Div PO Box 404 *Web:* www.state.nj.us/dep/parksandforests	Trenton	NJ	08625	609-292-2733	984-0503
Parole Board PO Box 862 *Web:* www.state.nj.us/parole	Trenton	NJ	08625	609-292-4257	943-4769
Personnel Dept 44 S Clinton Ave PO Box 317 *Web:* www.nj.gov	Trenton	NJ	08625	609-292-4145	984-1064
Secretary of State 125 W State St PO Box 300 *Web:* www.state.nj.us	Trenton	NJ	08625	609-984-1900	292-7665
Securities Bureau 153 Halsey St Sixth Fl PO Box 47029. *TF:* 866-446-8378 ■ *Web:* www.state.nj.us/lps/ca/bos	Newark	NJ	07101	973-504-3600	
State Legislature State House Annex PO Box 068 *Web:* www.njleg.state.nj.us	Trenton	NJ	08625	609-292-4840	777-2440
State Medical Examiner PO Box 360 *Web:* www.nj.gov	Trenton	NJ	08608	609-826-7100	
State Police PO Box 7068. *Web:* www.state.nj.us/lps/njsp	West Trenton	NJ	08628	609-882-2000	882-6920
Supreme Court PO Box 970. *Web:* www.judiciary.state.nj.us/supreme	Trenton	NJ	08625	609-292-4837	396-9056
Transportation Dept 1035 PkwyAve PO Box 600. *Web:* www.state.nj.us/transportation	Trenton	NJ	08625	609-530-2000	
Travel & Tourism Div 225 W State St PO Box 460 *TF:* 800-847-4865 ■ *Web:* www.visitnj.org	Trenton	NJ	08625	609-599-6540	
Treasurer PO Box 002 *Web:* www.state.nj.us/treasury	Trenton	NJ	08625	609-292-6748	984-3888
Victims of Crime Compensation Board 50 Pk Pl. *TF:* 877-658-2221 ■ *Web:* www.nj.gov/oag/njvictims	Newark	NJ	07102	973-648-2107	648-3937
Vital Statistics Bureau 140 E Front St *Web:* www.state.nj.us	Trenton	NJ	08608	609-292-4087	

Name / Address	City	State	ZIP	Phone	Fax
Vocational Rehabilitation Services Div (DVRS) 1 John Fitch Way PO Box 110 *Web:* jobs4jersey.com	Trenton	NJ	08625	609-292-5987	292-8347
Weights & Measures Office 1261 US Hwy 1 Ste 9 *Web:* www.state.nj.us	Avenel	NJ	07001	732-815-4840	382-5298
Workers' Compensation Div PO Box 381 *Web:* lwd.dol.state.nj.us/labor/wc	Trenton	NJ	08625	609-292-2515	984-2515

339-32 New Mexico

Name / Address	City	State	ZIP	Phone	Fax
Administrative Office of the Cts 237 Don Gaspar St Rm 25 *Web:* www.nmcourts.com	Santa Fe	NM	87501	505-827-4800	
Adult Parole Board 4337 NM 14 PO Box 27116 *Web:* www.corrections.state.nm.us	Santa Fe	NM	87502	505-827-8645	827-8533
Aging Agency 2550 Cerrillos Rd *Web:* www.nmaging.state.nm.us	Santa Fe	NM	87505	505-476-4799	476-4836
Agriculture Dept 3190 S Espina PO Box 30005 *Web:* www.nmda.nmsu.edu	Las Cruces	NM	88003	575-646-3007	
Arts Div 407 Galisteo St Ste 270 *Web:* www.nmarts.org	Santa Fe	NM	87501	505-827-6490	827-6043
Attorney General PO Box 1508 *Web:* www.nmag.gov	Santa Fe	NM	87504	505-827-6000	827-5826
Child Support Enforcement Div PO Box 25110 *Web:* www.hsd.state.nm.us/csed	Santa Fe	NM	87504	505-476-7207	476-7045
Children Youth & Families Dept PO Box 5160 **Fax Area Code:* 505 ■ *TF:* 800-610-7610 ■ *Web:* www.cyfd.org	Santa Fe	NM	87502	800-432-2075	827-9978*
Consumer Protection Div 408 Galisteo St Villagra Bldg PO Box 1508 *Web:* www.nmag.gov/consumer	Santa Fe	NM	87501	505-827-6000	827-5826
Corrections Dept (NMCD) 4337 NM 14 PO Box 27116 *Web:* www.corrections.state.nm.us	Santa Fe	NM	87502	505-827-8645	827-8533
Crime Victims Reparation Commission 8100 Mountain Rd NE Ste 106 *TF:* 800-306-6262 ■ *Web:* www.cvrc.state.nm.us	Albuquerque	NM	87110	505-841-9432	841-9437
Department of Information Technology 715 Alta Vista St PO Box 22550 *Web:* www.doit.state.nm.us	Santa Fe	NM	87505	505-827-0000	
Department of Veterans Services 490 Old SF Trail *TF:* 866-433-8387 ■ *Web:* www.dvs.state.nm.us	Santa Fe	NM	87504	505-827-6300	827-6372
Dept of Workforce Solutions 401 Broadway NE PO Box 1928 *Web:* www.dws.state.nm.us	Albuquerque	NM	87103	505-841-8576	841-8491
Economic Development Dept PO Box 20003 *TF:* 800-374-3061 ■ *Web:* www.gonm.biz	Santa Fe	NM	87504	505-827-0300	827-0328
Education Dept 300 Don Gaspar St *Web:* www.sde.state.nm.us	Santa Fe	NM	87501	505-827-5800	827-6696
Energy Minerals & Natural Resources Dept 1220 S St Francis Dr	Santa Fe	NM	87505	505-476-3200	476-3220
Environment Dept 1190 St Francis Dr Ste 4050 *TF:* 800-219-6157 ■ *Web:* www.nmenv.state.nm.us	Santa Fe	NM	87502	505-827-2855	827-2836
Finance & Administration Dept 407 Galisteo St Ste 166 *Web:* www.newmexico.gov	Santa Fe	NM	87501	505-827-4985	827-4984
Financial Institutions Div 2550 Cerrillos Rd *Web:* www.rld.state.nm.us	Santa Fe	NM	87505	505-476-4885	476-4670
Game & Fish Dept 1 Wildlife Way *Web:* www.wildlife.state.nm.us	Santa Fe	NM	87507	505-476-8000	476-8116
Governor State Capitol Bldg 490 Santa Fe Trail Rm 400 *Web:* www.governor.state.nm.us	Santa Fe	NM	87501	505-827-3000	476-2226
Health Dept 1190 S St Francis Dr Ste N-4100 *Web:* nmhealth.org	Santa Fe	NM	87505	505-827-2613	827-2530
Highway & Transportation Dept (NMDOT) 1120 Cerrillos Rd PO Box 1149 *TF General:* 800-432-4269 ■ *Web:* www.dot.state.nm.us	Santa Fe	NM	87504	505-827-5100	
Historic Preservation Div 407 Galisteo St Ste 236 *Web:* www.nmhistoricpreservation.org	Santa Fe	NM	87501	505-827-6320	827-6338
Human Services Dept (NMHSD) PO Box 2348 *Web:* www.hsd.state.nm.us	Santa Fe	NM	87504	505-827-7750	827-6286
Lieutenant Governor 490 Old Santa Fe Trail Rm 417 *TF:* 800-432-4406 ■ *Web:* www.ltgov.state.nm.us	Santa Fe	NM	87501	505-476-2250	476-2257
Lottery 4511 Osuna Rd NE PO Box 93190 *Web:* www.nmlottery.com	Albuquerque	NM	87199	505-342-7600	342-7511
Medical Board 2055 S Pacheco Bldg 400 *Web:* www.nmmb.state.nm.us	Santa Fe	NM	87505	505-476-7220	476-7237
Mortgage Finance Authority 344 Fourth St SW *TF:* 800-444-6880 ■ *Web:* www.nmmfa.org	Albuquerque	NM	87102	505-843-6880	243-3289
New Mexico Dept of Workforce Solutions 301 W DeVargas *Web:* www.dws.state.nm.us	Santa Fe	NM	87501	505-827-7434	827-7346
New Mexico Ethics Administration 325 Don Gaspar St Ste 300 *TF:* 800-477-3632 ■ *Web:* www.sos.state.nm.us	Santa Fe	NM	87501	505-827-3600	
New Mexico Higher Education Dept 2048 Galisteo St *TF:* 800-279-9777 ■ *Web:* www.hed.state.nm.us	Santa Fe	NM	87505	505-476-8400	476-8453
New Mexico Legislative Council Services 625 Don Gaspar Ave *Web:* www.nmlegis.gov	Santa Fe	NM	87501	505-986-4600	
New Mexico Racing Commission 4900 Alameda NE *Web:* www.nmrc.state.nm.us	Albuquerque	NM	87113	505-222-0700	222-0713
Professional (Educator) Licensure Unit 300 Don Gaspar St *Web:* www.ped.state.nm.us	Santa Fe	NM	87501	505-827-6581	827-4148
Public Accountancy Board 5200 Oakland Ave NE # C *Web:* www.rld.state.nm.us	Albuquerque	NM	87113	505-222-9800	
Public Regulation Commission PO Box 1269 *Web:* www.nmprc.state.nm.us	Santa Fe	NM	87504	505-827-4500	827-4747
Public Safety Dept PO Box 1628 *Web:* www.dps.nm.org	Santa Fe	NM	87504	505-827-9000	
Regulation & Licensing Dept 2550 Cerrillos Rd *Web:* www.rld.state.nm.us	Santa Fe	NM	87505	505-476-4500	476-4511
Secretary of State 325 Don Gaspar Ave Ste 300 *TF:* 800-477-3632 ■ *Web:* www.sos.state.nm.us	Santa Fe	NM	87503	505-827-3600	827-8081
Securities Div 2550 Cerrillos Rd *Web:* www.rld.state.nm.us/Securities	Santa Fe	NM	87505	505-476-4580	984-0617
Standards & Consumers Services Div MSC 3170 PO Box 30005 *Web:* www.nmda.nmsu.edu	Las Cruces	NM	88003	575-646-1616	646-2361
State Legislature State Capitol Rm 100 *Web:* www.nmlegis.gov	Santa Fe	NM	87501	505-986-4751	986-4680
State Parks Div 1220 S St Francis Dr	Santa Fe	NM	87505	505-476-3355	
State Police Div 4491 Cerrillos Rd PO Box 1628 *Web:* www.nmsp.dps.state.nm.us	Santa Fe	NM	87507	505-827-9300	827-3394
Supreme Court 237 Don Gaspar Ave *Web:* nmsupremecourt.nmcourts.gov	Santa Fe	NM	87501	505-827-4860	827-4837
Taxation & Revenue Dept 1100 S St Francis Dr *Web:* www.tax.newmexico.gov	Santa Fe	NM	87504	505-827-0700	
Tourism Dept 491 Old Santa Fe Trail *TF:* 800-545-2070 ■ *Web:* www.newmexico.org	Santa Fe	NM	87503	800-545-2070	
Treasurer 2055 S Pacheco St *Web:* www.nmsto.gov	Santa Fe	NM	87505	505-995-1120	995-1195
Vital Records & Health Statistics Bureau 1105 S St Francis Dr *TF:* 866-534-0051 ■ *Web:* nmhealth.org/about/erd/bvrhs/vrp	Santa Fe	NM	87502	505-827-0121	
Vocational Rehabilitation Div 435 St Michaels Dr Bldg D *TF:* 800-224-7005 ■ *Web:* www.dvrgetsjobs.com	Santa Fe	NM	87505	505-954-8500	954-8562
Workers' Compensation Admin 2410 Ctr Ave SE PO Box 27198 *TF:* 800-255-7965 ■ *Web:* www.workerscomp.state.nm.us	Albuquerque	NM	87125	505-841-6000	

339-33 New York

Name / Address	City	State	ZIP	Phone	Fax
State Government Information NYS State Capitol Bldg *Web:* www.ny.gov	Albany	NY	12224	518-474-8390	
Aging Office 2 Empire State Plaza *TF:* 800-342-9871 ■ *Web:* www.aging.ny.gov	Albany	NY	12223	800-342-9871	
Arts Council 175 Varick St 3rd Fl *Web:* www.nysca.org	New York	NY	10014	212-627-4455	
Attorney General State Capitol *Web:* www.oag.state.ny.us	Albany	NY	12224	518-474-7330	474-5481
Banking Dept 1 State St **Fax Area Code:* 212 ■ **Fax:* Hum Res ■ *TF:* 877-226-5697 ■ *Web:* www.dfs.ny.gov	New York	NY	10004	800-342-3736	709-3582*
Child Support Enforcement Div 40 N Pearl St *Web:* www.childsupport.ny.gov	Albany	NY	12243	518-474-9081	
Children & Family Services Office 52 Washington St *Web:* ocfs.ny.gov/main	Rensselaer	NY	12144	518-473-7793	486-7550
Correctional Services Dept 1220 Washington Ave Bldg 2 *Web:* www.doccs.ny.gov	Albany	NY	12226	518-457-8126	457-7070
Court of Appeals 20 Eagle St *Web:* www.nycourts.gov	Albany	NY	12207	518-455-7700	
Crime Victims Board 845 Central Ave *Web:* www.ovs.ny.gov	Albany	NY	12206	518-457-8727	457-8658
Division of Consumer Protection 5 Empire State Plaza Ste 2101 *TF:* 800-697-1220 ■ *Web:* www.dos.ny.gov	Albany	NY	12223	518-474-3514	474-2474
Education Dept 89 Washington Ave **Fax:* Hum Res ■ *Web:* www.nysed.gov	Albany	NY	12234	518-474-3852	*
Emergency Management Office (OEM) 1220 Washington Ave Bldg 22 Ste 101 *Web:* www.dhses.ny.gov/oem	Albany	NY	12226	518-292-2200	322-4985
Empire State Development 30 S Pearl St *TF:* 800-782-8369 ■ *Web:* www.empire.state.ny.us	Albany	NY	12245	518-292-5100	292-5812
Environmental Conservation Dept 625 Broadway 14th Fl *Web:* www.dec.ny.gov	Albany	NY	12233	518-891-0235	402-9016
Fish Wildlife & Marine Resources Div 50 Wolf Rd Rm 290 *Web:* www.dec.ny.gov	Albany	NY	12233	518-457-3682	
Governor State Capitol Executive Chamber *Web:* www.ny.gov	Albany	NY	12224	518-474-8390	474-1513
Health Dept Empire State Plaza Corning II Tower **Fax Area Code:* 518 ■ *TF:* 866-881-2809 ■ *Web:* www.health.ny.gov	Albany	NY	12237	866-881-2809	473-7071*
Historic Preservation Div PO Box 189 *TF:* 800-456-2267 ■ *Web:* www.nysparks.com	Waterford	NY	12188	518-237-8643	
Housing Finance Agency 641 Lexington Ave *Web:* www.nyshcr.org	New York	NY	10022	212-688-4000	872-0789
Insurance Dept 1 Commerce Plaza *Web:* www.dfs.ny.gov	Albany	NY	12260	518-474-6600	
Investor Protection & Securities Bureau 120 Broadway 23rd Fl *Web:* www.ag.ny.gov	New York	NY	10271	212-416-8200	416-8816

				Phone	Fax
Lieutenant Governor NYS State Capitol Bldg *Web:* www.governor.ny.gov	Albany	NY	12224	518-474-8390	
Lower Manhattan Development Corp 1 Liberty Plaza 20th Fl *Web:* www.renewnyc.com	New York	NY	10006	212-962-2300	962-2431
Mental Health Office 44 Holland Ave *TF:* 800-597-8481 ■ *Web:* www.omh.ny.gov	Albany	NY	12229	518-474-4403	474-2149
Military & Naval Affairs Div 330 Old Niskayuna Rd *Web:* dmna.ny.gov	Latham	NY	12110	518-786-4786	786-4785
Motor Vehicles Dept 6 Empire State Plaza *TF:* 800-368-1186 ■ *Web:* www.dmv.ny.gov	Albany	NY	12228	518-473-5595	
New York Athletic Commission 123 William St 20th Fl *TF:* 866-269-3769 ■ *Web:* www.dos.ny.gov	New York	NY	10038	212-417-5700	417-4987
New York Bill Status 202 Legislative Office Bldg *TF:* 800-342-9860 ■ *Web:* www.assembly.state.ny.us	Albany	NY	12248	518-455-4218	
New York Higher Education Services Corp 99 Washington Ave *TF:* 888-697-4372 ■ *Web:* www.hesc.ny.gov	Albany	NY	12255	518-473-1574	473-3749
New York Labor Dept WA Harriman Campus Bldg 12 *TF:* 888-469-7365 ■ *Web:* www.labor.ny.gov	Albany	NY	12240	518-457-9000	457-6908
New York State Education Dept 89 Washington Ave 5N EB *Web:* www.highered.nysed.gov	Albany	NY	12234	518-474-3901	
Office of Court Admin 25 Beaver St Rm 852 *TF:* 800-268-7869 ■ *Web:* www.courts.state.ny.us/admin	New York	NY	10004	212-428-2100	428-2188
Office of the Professions 89 Washington Ave 2nd Fl *Web:* www.op.nysed.gov	Albany	NY	12234	518-474-3817	474-1449
Parks Recreation & Historic Preservation Office 1 Empire State Plaza *TF Campground Resv:* 800-456-2267 ■ *Web:* www.nysparks.com	Albany	NY	12238	518-474-0456	486-2924
Parole Div 97 Central Ave *Web:* www.parole.ny.gov	Albany	NY	12206	518-473-9400	473-6037
Power Authority 30 S Pearl St 10th Fl *Web:* www.nypa.gov	Albany	NY	12207	518-433-6700	
Public Service Commission 90 Church St *Web:* www.dps.ny.gov	New York	NY	12223	518-474-7080	473-2838
Secretary of State 41 State St *Web:* www.dos.ny.gov	Albany	NY	12231	518-473-2492	474-4765
State Comptroller 110 State St 15th Fl *Web:* www.osc.state.ny.us	Albany	NY	12236	518-474-4044	473-3004
State Legislature Nys Senate Ste 321 *Web:* www.nysenate.gov	Albany	NY	12247	518-455-2800	
State Police Div 1220 Washington Ave Bldg 22 *Web:* nytrooper.com	Albany	NY	12226	518-457-6811	
Taxation & Finance Dept WA Harriman Campus Bldg 9 *TF:* 800-225-5829 ■ *Web:* www.tax.ny.gov	Albany	NY	12227	518-457-5149	
Technology Office 255 Greenwich Fl 9 *Web:* www.nyc.gov	Albany	NY	12220	212-788-5889	
Temporary & Disability Assistance Office 40 N Pearl St 16th Fl *TF:* 800-342-3009 ■ *Web:* www.otda.ny.gov	Albany	NY	12243	518-473-1090	
Tourism Div PO Box 2603 *TF:* 800-225-5697 ■ *Web:* www.iloveny.com	Albany	NY	12223	518-473-1064	
Transportation Dept 50 Wolf Rd *Web:* www.dot.ny.gov	Albany	NY	12205	518-457-7082	485-5217
Veterans' Affairs Div 333 E Washington St Ste 430 *TF:* 888-838-7697 ■ *Web:* www.veterans.ny.gov	Albany	NY	12223	315-428-4046	
Vital Records Office PO Box 2602 *TF:* 877-854-4481 ■ *Web:* www.health.ny.gov	Albany	NY	12220	518-474-3077	474-9168
Vocational & Educational Services for Individuals 1 Commerce Plaza Rm 1606 *Web:* www.acces.nysed.gov	Albany	NY	12234	518-474-2714	474-8802
Workers' Compensation Board 328 State St *TF:* 877-632-4996 ■ *Web:* www.wcb.ny.gov	Schenectady	NY	12305	518-462-8880	

339-34 North Carolina

				Phone	Fax
Administrative Office of the Cts PO Box 2448 *Web:* www.nccourts.org	Raleigh	NC	27602	919-733-7107	715-5779
Aging & Adult Service Div 693 Palmer Dr *Web:* www.ncdhhs.gov	Raleigh	NC	27603	919-733-3983	733-0443
Agriculture Dept 2 W Edenton St 1001 MSC *Web:* www.ncagr.gov	Raleigh	NC	27699	919-733-7125	733-1141
Arts Council MSC 4632 Dept of Cultural Resources *Web:* www.ncarts.org	Raleigh	NC	27699	919-807-6500	807-6532
Attorney General 114 W Edenton St *Web:* www.ncdoj.com	Raleigh	NC	27603	919-716-6400	716-6750
Banking Commission 316 W Edenton St *Web:* www.nccob.org	Raleigh	NC	27603	919-733-3016	733-6918
Child Support Enforcement Section PO Box 20800 *Web:* www.ncdhhs.gov	Raleigh	NC	27619	252-789-5225	
Commerce Dept 301 N Wilmington St *Web:* www.nccommerce.com	Raleigh	NC	27699	919-733-4151	733-9299
Consumer Protection Division 114 W Edenton St *Web:* www.ncdoj.com	Raleigh	NC	27603	919-716-6000	716-6050
Correction Dept 214 W Jones St 4201 MSC *Web:* www.doc.state.nc.us	Raleigh	NC	27699	919-716-3700	716-3794
Cultural Resources Dept 109 E Jones St *Web:* www.ncdcr.gov	Raleigh	NC	27601	919-807-7385	733-1620
Emergency Management Div 4201 Mail Service Ctr *Web:* www.ncem.org	Raleigh	NC	27699	919-716-3100	733-5406
General Assembly 16 W Jones St *Web:* www.ncleg.net	Raleigh	NC	27601	919-733-7928	715-2880
Governor 116 W Jones St *Web:* www.governor.state.nc.us	Raleigh	NC	27603	919-733-5811	733-2120
Health & Human Services Dept 2001 MSC *Web:* www.ncdhhs.gov	Raleigh	NC	27699	919-733-4534	715-4645
Housing Finance Agency 3508 Bush St *Web:* www.nchfa.com	Raleigh	NC	27609	919-877-5700	877-5701
Information Technology Services Office (ITS) PO Box 17209 *Web:* www.its.nc.gov	Raleigh	NC	27619	919-981-5555	
Insurance Dept 1201 MSC *Web:* www.ncdoi.com	Raleigh	NC	27699	919-807-6750	733-0085
Labor Dept 4 W Edenton St *Web:* www.nclabor.com	Raleigh	NC	27601	919-733-7166	733-6197
Lieutenant Governor 310 N Blount St *Web:* ltgov.nc.gov	Raleigh	NC	27601	919-733-7350	733-6595
Marine Fisheries Div PO Box 769 *TF:* 800-682-2632 ■ *Web:* www.ncfisheries.net	Morehead City	NC	28557	252-726-7021	
Mental Health Developmental Disabilities & Substance 2001 Mail Service Center *Web:* www.ncdhhs.gov/mhddsas	Raleigh	NC	27699	919-855-4800	733-4962
Motor Vehicles Div 1100 New Bern Ave *Web:* local.dmv.org	Raleigh	NC	27699	919-715-7000	
North Carolina Bill Status 16 W Jones St *Web:* www.ncleg.net	Raleigh	NC	27601	919-733-4111	
North Carolina Community College System 200 W Jones St *Web:* nccommunitycolleges.edu	Raleigh	NC	27603	919-807-7100	807-7164
North Carolina Employment Security Commission 700 Wade Ave PO Box 25903 *Web:* desncc.com/deshome	Raleigh	NC	27605	919-707-1010	733-9420
North Carolina Ethics Board 424 N Blount St *Web:* www.ethicscommission.nc.gov	Raleigh	NC	27601	919-715-2071	715-1644
North Carolina State Ports Authority 2202 Burnett Blvd PO Box 9002 *TF:* 800-334-0682 ■ *Web:* www.ncports.com	Wilmington	NC	28402	910-763-1621	
Parks & Recreation Div 217 W Jones St 1615 MSC *TF:* 877-722-6762 ■ *Web:* www.ncparks.gov	Raleigh	NC	27604	919-707-9300	
Parole Commission 4222 MSC *Web:* www.ncdps.gov	Raleigh	NC	27699	919-716-3010	716-3987
Public Instruction Dept 301 N Wilmington St *Web:* www.ncpublicschools.org	Raleigh	NC	27601	919-807-3300	807-3445
Real Estate Commission 1313 Navajo Dr *Web:* ncrec.gov	Raleigh	NC	27609	919-875-3700	877-4221
Revenue Dept 4701 Atlantic Ave Ste 118 *Web:* www.dor.state.nc.us	Raleigh	NC	27604	919-707-0880	
Secretary of State PO Box 29622 *Web:* www.secstate.state.nc.us	Raleigh	NC	27699	919-807-2005	807-2010
Securities Div PO Box 29622 *Web:* www.secretary.state.nc.us	Raleigh	NC	27626	919-733-3924	821-0818
Social Services Div 2401 MSC *Web:* www.ncdhhs.gov	Raleigh	NC	27699	919-733-3055	733-9386
Standards Div 2 W Edenton St 1050 MSC *Web:* www.ncagr.gov	Raleigh	NC	27699	919-733-3313	715-0524
State Highway Patrol 512 N Salisbury St *Web:* www.nccrimecontrol.org	Raleigh	NC	27699	919-716-4080	716-3923
State Personnel Office 116 W Jones St *Web:* www.oshr.nc.gov	Raleigh	NC	27603	919-807-4800	733-0653
State Treasurer 325 N Salisbury St *Web:* www.nctreasurer.com	Raleigh	NC	27603	919-508-5176	508-5167
Supreme Court 2 E Morgan St PO Box 2170 *Web:* www.nccourts.org	Raleigh	NC	27602	919-831-5700	
Tourism Div 301 N Wilmington St *TF:* 800-847-4862 ■ *Web:* www.visitnc.com	Raleigh	NC	27601	919-733-4171	733-8582
Transportation Dept 1 S Wilmington St *TF:* 877-368-4968 ■ *Web:* www.ncdot.gov	Raleigh	NC	27611	877-368-4968	
Utilities Commission 4325 Mail Service Ctr *TF:* 866-380-9816 ■ *Web:* www.ncuc.commerce.state.nc.us	Raleigh	NC	27699	919-733-7328	733-7300
Veterans Affairs Div 1315 Mail Service Ctr *Web:* www.doa.nc.gov	Raleigh	NC	27699	919-733-3851	
Victims Compensation Services Div 4232 Mail Service Ctr *TF:* 800-826-6200 ■ *Web:* www.nccrimecontrol.org	Raleigh	NC	27699	919-733-7974	
Vital Records Unit 225 N McDowell St *Web:* www.vitalrecords.nc.gov	Raleigh	NC	27601	919-733-3000	733-1511
Vocational Rehabilitation Services Div 2801 MSC *Web:* www.ncdhhs.gov	Raleigh	NC	27699	919-855-3500	733-7968

339-35 North Dakota

				Phone	Fax
State Government Information 600 E Blvd Ave Dept 130 *Web:* www.nd.gov	Bismarck	ND	58505	701-328-2471	328-3230
Accountancy Board 2701 S Columbia Rd *TF:* 800-532-5904 ■ *Web:* www.nd.gov	Grand Forks	ND	58201	701-775-7100	775-7430
Aging Services Div 1237 W Divide Ave Ste 6 *Web:* www.nd.gov	Bismarck	ND	58501	701-328-4601	328-8744
Agriculture Dept 600 E Blvd Ave Dept 602 *TF:* 800-242-7535 ■ *Web:* www.nd.gov	Bismarck	ND	58505	701-328-2231	328-4567
Attorney General 600 E Blvd Ave Dept 125 *TF:* 800-366-6888 ■ *Web:* www.ag.nd.gov	Bismarck	ND	58505	701-328-2210	
Child Support Enforcement Div 1600 E Century Ave Ste 7 *TF:* 800-231-4255 ■ *Web:* www.nd.gov/dhs/services/childsupport	Bismarck	ND	58501	701-328-3582	328-6575
Children & Family Services Div 600 E Blvd Ave *Web:* www.nd.gov	Bismarck	ND	58505	701-328-2316	328-3538

				Phone	Fax
Consumer Protection Div 1050 E Interstate Ave Ste 200 *TF:* 800-472-2600 ■ *Web:* www.ag.state.nd.us	Bismarck	ND	58503	701-328-3404	
Corrections & Rehabilitation Dept 3100 Railroad Ave *Web:* www.nd.gov	Bismarck	ND	58501	701-328-6390	328-6651
Court Administrator Office 600 E Blvd Ave Dept 180 *Web:* www.ndcourts.gov	Bismarck	ND	58505	701-328-4216	328-2092
Crime Victims Compensation Program PO Box 5521 *TF:* 800-445-2322 ■ *Web:* www.ndcrimevictims.org	Bismarck	ND	58506	701-328-6195	
Drivers License & Traffic Safety Div 608 E Blvd Ave *Web:* www.dot.nd.gov/public/divdist/dlts.htm	Bismarck	ND	58505	701-328-2600	328-2435
Economic Development & Finance Div 1600 E Century Ave Ste 200-B *TF:* 866-432-5682 ■ *Web:* www.business.nd.gov	Bismarck	ND	58503	701-328-5300	328-5320
Education Standards & Practices Board 2718 Gateway Ave Dept 303 *Web:* www.nd.gov	Bismarck	ND	58503	701-328-9641	328-9647
Emergency Management Div PO Box 5511 *Web:* www.nd.gov/des	Bismarck	ND	58506	701-328-8100	328-8181
Financial Institutions Dept 2000 Schafer St Ste G *TF:* 800-366-6888 ■ *Web:* www.nd.gov/dfi	Bismarck	ND	58501	701-328-9933	328-0290
Game & Fish Dept 100 N Bismarck Expy *Web:* www.gf.nd.gov	Bismarck	ND	58501	701-328-6300	328-6352
Governor 600 E Blvd Ave Dept 101 *Web:* www.governor.nd.gov	Bismarck	ND	58505	701-328-2200	328-2205
Health Dept 600 E Blvd Ave Dept 301 *Web:* www.ndhealth.gov	Bismarck	ND	58505	701-328-2372	328-4727
Highway Patrol 600 E Blvd Ave Dept 504 *Web:* www.nd.gov	Bismarck	ND	58505	701-328-2455	328-1717
Historical Society 612 E Blvd Ave *Web:* www.nd.gov	Bismarck	ND	58505	701-328-2666	328-3710
Housing Finance Agency PO Box 1535 *TF:* 800-292-8621 ■ *Web:* www.ndhfa.org	Bismarck	ND	58502	701-328-8080	328-8090
Indian Affairs Commission 600 E Blvd Ave Rm 117 *Web:* www.nd.gov	Bismarck	ND	58505	701-328-2428	328-1537
Information Technology Dept 600 E Blvd Ave Dept 112 *Web:* www.nd.gov/itd	Bismarck	ND	58505	701-328-3190	328-3000
Insurance Dept 600 E Blvd Ave Dept 401 *TF:* 800-247-0560 ■ *Web:* www.nd.gov	Bismarck	ND	58505	701-328-2440	328-4880
Labor and Human Rights Dept 600 E Blvd Ave Dept 406 *Web:* www.nd.gov/labor	Bismarck	ND	58505	701-328-2660	328-2031
Legislative Assembly State Capitol 600 E Blvd Ave *Web:* www.legis.nd.gov	Bismarck	ND	58505	701-328-2916	328-3615
Medical Examiners Board 418 E Broadway Ste 12 *Web:* www.ndbomex.org	Bismarck	ND	58501	701-328-6500	328-6505
North Dakota Racing Commission 500 N Ninth St *Web:* www.ndracingcommission.com	Bismarck	ND	58501	701-328-4290	
North Dakota Student Financial Assistance Program 600 E Blvd Ave 10th Fl Dept 215 *Web:* www.ndus.nodak.edu	Bismarck	ND	58505	701-328-2960	328-2961
Office of Governor 600 E Blvd Ave *Web:* governor.nd.gov	Bismarck	ND	58505	701-328-2200	328-2205
Parks & Recreation Dept 1600 E Century Ave Ste 3 *TF:* 800-807-4723 ■ *Web:* www.parkrec.nd.gov	Bismarck	ND	58503	701-328-5357	328-5363
Parole & Probation Div 3100 E Railroad Ave *Web:* www.nd.gov/docr	Bismarck	ND	58501	701-328-6190	328-6651
Public Instruction Dept 600 E Blvd Ave Dept 201 *Web:* www.dpi.state.nd.us	Bismarck	ND	58505	701-328-2260	328-2461
Public Service Commission 600 E Blvd Ave Dept 408 *Web:* www.psc.nd.gov	Bismarck	ND	58505	701-328-2400	328-2410
Real Estate Commission 200 E Main Ave Ste 204 *Web:* www.realestatend.org	Bismarck	ND	58501	701-328-9749	328-9750
Secretary of State 600 E Blvd Ave Dept 108 *TF:* 800-352-0867 ■ *Web:* www.nd.gov/sos	Bismarck	ND	58505	701-328-2900	328-2992
Securities Dept 600 E Blvd Ave Dept 414 *Web:* www.nd.gov	Bismarck	ND	58505	701-328-2910	328-2946
Supreme Court 600 E Blvd Ave Dept 180 *Web:* www.ndcourts.gov	Bismarck	ND	58505	701-328-2221	328-4480
Tax Dept 600 E Blvd Ave *Web:* www.nd.gov	Bismarck	ND	58505	701-328-2770	328-3700
Testing & Safety Div 600 E Blvd Ave *Web:* www.psc.nd.gov	Bismarck	ND	58505	701-328-2400	328-2410
Tourism Div 1600 Eentury Ave Ste 200S *TF:* 800-435-5663 ■ *Web:* www.ndtourism.com	Bismarck	ND	58502	701-328-2525	328-4878
Transportation Dept 608 E Blvd Ave *Web:* www.dot.nd.gov	Bismarck	ND	58505	701-328-2500	328-1420
Treasurer 600 E Blvd Ave Dept 120 *Web:* www.nd.gov/ndtreas	Bismarck	ND	58505	701-328-2643	328-3002
University System 600 E Blvd Ave Dept 215 *Web:* www.ndus.edu	Bismarck	ND	58505	701-328-2960	328-2961
Veterans Affairs Dept 4201 38th St S Ste 104 *TF:* 866-634-8387 ■ *Web:* www.nd.gov	Fargo	ND	58104	701-239-7165	239-7166
Vocational Rehabilitation Div 1237 W Divide Ave Ste 2 *TF:* 800-755-2745 ■ *Web:* www.nd.gov	Bismarck	ND	58501	701-328-8800	328-8969
Workers Compensation 1600 E Century Ave Ste 1000 *TF:* 800-777-5033 ■ *Web:* www.workforcesafety.com	Bismarck	ND	58503	701-328-3800	328-3820

339-36 Ohio

				Phone	Fax
Adjutant's General Dept 2825 W Dublin Granville Rd *Web:* www.ong.ohio.gov	Columbus	OH	43235	614-336-7324	
Administrative Director of the Supreme Court 65 S Front St Fl 5 *Web:* www.supremecourt.ohio.gov	Columbus	OH	43215	614-387-9340	387-9349
Aging Dept 50 W Broad St 9th Fl *Web:* aging.ohio.gov	Columbus	OH	43215	614-466-5500	466-5741
Agriculture Dept 8995 E Main St *TF:* 800-282-1955 ■ *Web:* www.agri.ohio.gov	Reynoldsburg	OH	43068	614-728-6201	728-6310
Arts Council 30 E Broad St Ste 33 *Web:* www.oac.state.oh.us	Columbus	OH	43215	614-466-2613	466-4494
Commerce Dept 77 S High St 23rd Fl *Web:* www.com.state.oh.us	Columbus	OH	43215	614-466-3636	
Consumer Protection Section 30 E Broad St 14th Fl *TF:* 800-282-0515 ■ *Web:* www.ohioattorneygeneral.gov	Columbus	OH	43215	614-466-8831	
Department of Veterans Services 77 S High St 7th Fl *Web:* dvs.ohio.gov	Columbus	OH	43215	614-644-0898	
Dept of Rehabilitation & Correction 770 W Broad St *Web:* www.drc.state.oh.us	Columbus	OH	43222	614-752-1159	
Education Dept 25 S Front St *TF:* 877-644-6338 ■ *Web:* education.ohio.gov	Columbus	OH	43215	614-995-1545	
Emergency Management Agency 2855 W Dublin-Granville Rd *Web:* www.ema.ohio.gov	Columbus	OH	43235	614-889-7150	889-7183
Environmental Protection Agency 122 S Front St PO Box 1049 *Web:* www.epa.state.oh.us	Columbus	OH	43216	614-644-3020	644-3184
Financial Institutions Div 77 S High St 21st Fl *TF:* 866-278-0003 ■ *Web:* com.ohio.gov/fiin	Columbus	OH	43266	614-728-8400	728-0380
Governor 77 S High St 30th Fl *Web:* www.governor.ohio.gov	Columbus	OH	43215	614-466-3555	466-9354
Health Dept 246 N High St *Web:* www.odh.ohio.gov	Columbus	OH	43215	614-466-3543	644-0085
Highway Patrol (OSHP) 1970 W Broad St PO Box 182074 *TF:* 877-772-8765 ■ *Web:* statepatrol.ohio.gov	Columbus	OH	43223	614-466-2660	
Historical Society 1982 Velma Ave *Web:* www.ohiohistory.org	Columbus	OH	43211	614-297-2300	297-2411
Housing Finance Agency 57 E Main St *Web:* www.ohiohome.org	Columbus	OH	43215	614-466-7970	644-5393
Information Technology 30 E Broad St Ste 4040	Columbus	OH	43215	614-466-6930	644-8151
Insurance Dept 50 W Town St Third Fl Ste 300 *TF:* 800-686-1526 ■ *Web:* www.insurance.ohio.gov	Columbus	OH	43215	614-644-2658	
Job & Family Services Dept 30 E Broad St 32nd Fl *Web:* www.jfs.ohio.gov	Columbus	OH	43215	614-466-6282	466-2815
Mental Health Dept 30 E Broad St 8th Fl *TF:* 888-636-4889 ■ *Web:* mha.ohio.gov	Columbus	OH	43215	614-466-2596	752-9453
Motor Vehicles Bureau 1970 W Broad St PO Box 16520 *Web:* www.bmv.ohio.gov	Columbus	OH	43216	614-752-7500	
Natural Resources Dept 2045 Morse Rd *Web:* www.ohiodnr.com	Columbus	OH	43229	614-265-6565	
Office of Governor 77 S High St 30th Fl *Web:* governor.ohio.gov	Columbus	OH	43215	614-466-3396	
Ohio Ethics Commission 30 W Spring St L3 *Web:* www.ethics.ohio.gov	Columbus	OH	43215	614-466-7090	466-8368
Ohio Legislative Information Office 77 S High St *Web:* www.lis.state.oh.us	Columbus	OH	43215	614-728-0711	
Ohio Racing Commission 77 S High St 18th Fl *Web:* www.racing.ohio.gov	Columbus	OH	43215	614-466-2757	466-1900
Ohio Tuition Trust Authority 580 S High St Ste 208 *TF Cust Svc:* 800-233-6734 ■ *Web:* www.collegeadvantage.com	Columbus	OH	43215	614-752-9400	
Ohio Workforce Developement Office 4020 E Fifth Ave PO Box 1618 **Fax Area Code:* 614 ■ *TF:* 888-296-7541 ■ *Web:* www.jfs.ohio.gov/owd	Columbus	OH	43219	888-296-7541	644-7102*
Parks & Recreation Div 2045 Morse Rd Bldg C-3 *TF:* 800-282-7275 ■ *Web:* www.ohiodnr.com	Columbus	OH	43229	614-265-6561	261-8407
Parole Board 1050 Fwy Dr N *Web:* www.drc.state.oh.us	Columbus	OH	43229	614-752-1200	752-1251
Public Utilities Commission 180 E Broad St *Web:* www.puco.ohio.gov	Columbus	OH	43215	614-466-3016	
Regents Board 30 E Broad St 36th Fl *Web:* www.ohiohighered.org	Columbus	OH	43215	614-466-6000	466-5866
Secretary of State 180 E Broad St 16th Fl *Web:* www.sos.state.oh.us	Columbus	OH	43215	614-466-2655	644-0649
Securities Div 77 S High St Ste 22 *Web:* www.com.ohio.gov	Columbus	OH	43215	614-644-7381	
Supreme Court 65 S Front St *Web:* www.sconet.state.oh.us	Columbus	OH	43215	614-387-9530	387-9539
Taxation Dept 30 E Broad St 22nd Fl PO Box 530 *TF:* 888-405-4089 ■ *Web:* tax.ohio.gov	Columbus	OH	43215	614-466-2166	466-6401
Transportation Dept 1980 W Broad St *Web:* dot.state.oh.us	Columbus	OH	43223	614-466-7170	
Travel & Tourism Div PO Box 1001 *TF:* 800-282-5393 ■ *Web:* consumer.discoverohio.com	Columbus	OH	43216	614-466-8844	
Treasurer 30 E Broad St 9th Fl *Web:* www.tos.ohio.gov	Columbus	OH	43215	614-466-2160	

	City	State	ZIP	Phone	Fax
Vital Statistics Unit 246 N High St PO Box 15098 *Web:* www.odh.ohio.gov	Columbus	OH	43215	614-466-2531	
Wildlife Div 2045 Morse Rd Bldg G *TF:* 800-945-3543 ■ *Web:* www.ohiodnr.com/wildlife	Columbus	OH	43229	614-265-6300	
Workers' Compensation Bureau 30 W Spring St *TF:* 800-644-6292 ■ *Web:* www.bwc.ohio.gov	Columbus	OH	43215	614-644-6292	
Youth Services Dept 51 N High St *Web:* www.dys.ohio.gov	Columbus	OH	43215	614-466-4314	752-9859

339-37 Oklahoma

	City	State	ZIP	Phone	Fax
Administrative Office of the Courts 2100 N Lincoln Blvd Ste 3 *Web:* www.ok.gov	Oklahoma City	OK	73105	405-556-9300	
Aging Services Div 312 NE 28th St *Web:* www.okdhs.org/aging	Oklahoma City	OK	73105	405-521-2327	
Agriculture Food & Forestry Dept 2800 N Lincoln Blvd *Web:* www.oda.state.ok.us	Oklahoma City	OK	73105	405-521-3864	
Arts Council 2101 N Lincoln Blvd Ste 640 *Web:* arts.ok.gov	Oklahoma City	OK	73152	405-521-2931	521-6418
Attorney General 313 NE 21st St *Web:* ok.gov/oag	Oklahoma City	OK	73105	405-521-3921	521-6246
Banking Dept 4545 N Lincoln Blvd Ste 164 *Web:* www.ok.gov	Oklahoma City	OK	73105	405-521-2782	522-2993
Chief Medical Examiner 901 N Stonewall Ave *Web:* www.state.ok.us	Oklahoma City	OK	73117	405-239-7141	239-2430
Child Support Enforcement Div PO Box 248822 *TF:* 800-522-2922 ■ *Web:* www.okdhs.org	Oklahoma City	OK	73124	405-522-2273	
Commerce Dept 900 N Stiles Ave *TF:* 800-879-6552 ■ *Web:* www.okcommerce.gov	Oklahoma City	OK	73104	405-815-6552	815-5199
Conservation Commission 2800 N Lincoln Blvd Ste 160 *Web:* www.okcc.state.ok.us	Oklahoma City	OK	73105	405-521-2384	521-6686
Consumer Protection Div 313 NE 21st St	Oklahoma City	OK	73105	405-521-4274	528-1867
Corporation Commission (OCC) 2101 N Lincoln PO Box 52000 *Web:* www.occeweb.com	Oklahoma City	OK	73152	405-521-2211	522-1623
Corrections Dept 3400 N Martin Luther King Ave *Web:* www.ok.gov	Oklahoma City	OK	73111	405-425-2500	425-2886
Development Finance Authority 5900 N Classen Ct *Web:* www.ok.gov	Oklahoma City	OK	73118	405-842-1145	848-3314
Education Dept 2500 N Lincoln Blvd *Web:* www.ok.gov	Oklahoma City	OK	73105	405-521-3301	521-6205
Emergency Management Dept 4600 N Martin Luther King Ave *Web:* www.ok.gov	Oklahoma City	OK	73111	405-521-2481	521-4053
Environmental Quality Dept 707 N Robinson Ave PO Box 1677 *TF:* 800-869-1400 ■ *Web:* www.deq.state.ok.us	Oklahoma City	OK	73101	405-702-1000	702-7101
Health Dept 1000 NE Tenth St *Web:* www.health.state.ok.us	Oklahoma City	OK	73117	405-271-4200	271-3431
Highway Patrol PO Box 11415 *Web:* www.dps.state.ok.us	Oklahoma City	OK	73136	405-425-2424	
Historical Society 800 Nahzi Zuhzi Dr *Web:* www.okhistory.org	Oklahoma City	OK	73105	405-521-2491	521-2492
Housing Finance Agency 100 NW 63rd St Ste 200 *TF:* 800-256-1489 ■ *Web:* www.ohfa.org	Oklahoma City	OK	73116	405-848-1144	
Human Services Dept 2400 N Lincoln Blvd *Web:* www.okdhs.org	Oklahoma City	OK	73105	405-521-3646	521-6458
Indian Affairs Commission 4545 Lincoln Blvd Ste 282 *Web:* www.ok.gov	Oklahoma City	OK	73105	405-521-3828	522-4427
Insurance Dept (OID) 3625 NW 56th Ste 100 *TF:* 800-522-0071 ■ *Web:* www.ok.gov/oid	Oklahoma City	OK	73152	405-521-2828	521-6635
Labor Dept 4001 N Lincoln Blvd *Web:* www.ok.gov	Oklahoma City	OK	73105	405-528-1500	528-5751
Lieutenant Governor 2300 N Lincoln Blvd Ste 211 *Web:* www.ok.gov	Oklahoma City	OK	73105	405-521-2161	522-8694
Mental Health & Substance Abuse Services Dept 1200 NE 13th St PO Box 53277 *Web:* www.odmhsas.org	Oklahoma City	OK	73152	405-522-3908	522-3650
Motor Vehicle Commission 4334 NW Expy Ste 183 *Web:* www.ok.gov	Oklahoma City	OK	73116	405-607-8227	607-8909
National Guard 3501 Military Cir *Web:* www.ok.ngb.army.mil	Oklahoma City	OK	73111	405-228-5000	228-5524
Oklahoma Employment Security Commission PO Box 52003 *Web:* www.ok.gov	Oklahoma City	OK	73152	405-557-5400	557-5355
Oklahoma Ethics Commission 2300 N Lincoln Blvd Rm B5 *Web:* www.ok.gov	Oklahoma City	OK	73105	405-521-3451	521-4905
Oklahoma Legislation Service Bureau 2300 N Lincoln Blvd *Web:* www.oklegislature.gov	State Capitol Bldg	OK	73105	405-521-4081	521-5507
Oklahoma State Regents for Higher Education 655 Research Pkwy Ste 200 *Web:* www.okhighered.org	Oklahoma City	OK	73104	405-225-9100	225-9235
Pardon & Parole Board 120 N Robinson Ave Ste 900W *Web:* www.ok.gov	Oklahoma City	OK	73102	405-521-6600	602-6437
Parks Div PO Box 52002 *TF:* 800-654-8240 ■ *Web:* www.travelok.com	Oklahoma City	OK	73152	405-230-8300	
Personnel Management Office 2101 N Lincoln Blvd Ste G-80 *Web:* www.ok.gov	Oklahoma City	OK	73105	405-521-2177	524-6942
Real Estate Commission 2401 NW 23rd St Ste 18 *Web:* www.ok.gov	Oklahoma City	OK	73107	405-521-3387	521-2189
Rehabilitative Services Dept 5501 N Portland Ave *TF:* 800-845-8476 ■ *Web:* www.okrehab.org	Oklahoma City	OK	73112	405-951-3400	951-3529
Secretary of State 2300 N Lincoln Blvd Ste 101 *Web:* www.sos.ok.gov	Oklahoma City	OK	73105	405-521-3912	521-3771
Securities Dept 204 N Robinson Ave Ste 400 *Web:* www.securities.ok.gov	Oklahoma City	OK	73102	405-280-7700	280-7742
Supreme Court 2100 N Lincoln Blvd Ste 3 *Web:* www.ok.gov	Oklahoma City	OK	73105	405-556-9300	
Tax Commission 2501 N Lincoln Blvd *Web:* www.oktax.state.ok.us	Oklahoma City	OK	73194	405-521-3160	521-3826
Treasurer 2300 N Lincoln Rd Rm 217 *Web:* www.ok.gov	Oklahoma City	OK	73105	405-521-3191	521-4994
Veterans Affairs Dept 2311 N Central Ave *Web:* www.ok.gov	Oklahoma City	OK	73105	405-521-3684	521-6533
Victim Services Unit 313 NE 21st St *Web:* www.oag.ok.gov/oagweb.nsf/vservices.html	Oklahoma City	OK	73105	405-521-3921	521-6246
Vital Records Div 1000 NE 10th St *Web:* www.ok.gov	Oklahoma City	OK	73117	405-271-4040	
Weights & Measures 2800 N Lincoln Blvd *Web:* www.ok.gov	Oklahoma City	OK	73105	405-521-3864	
Wildlife Conservation Dept (ODWC) PO Box 53465 *TF:* 800-522-8039 ■ *Web:* www.wildlifedepartment.com	Oklahoma City	OK	73152	405-521-4660	

339-38 Oregon

	City	State	ZIP	Phone	Fax
Arts Commission 775 Summer St NE Ste 200 *Web:* www.oregonartscommission.org	Salem	OR	97301	503-986-0082	986-0260
Attorney General 1162 Ct St NE Justice Bldg *Web:* www.doj.state.or.us	Salem	OR	97301	503-378-4400	378-4017
Child Support Div 494 State St Ste 300 *Web:* oregonchildsupport.gov	Salem	OR	97301	503-986-6166	986-6158
Children Adults & Families Div (CAF) 500 Summer St NE E62 *Web:* www.oregon.gov	Salem	OR	97301	503-945-5600	373-7032
Community Colleges & Workforce Development Dept 255 Capitol St NE *Web:* www.worksourceoregon.org	Salem	OR	97310	503-378-8648	
Corrections Dept (DOC) 2575 Ctr St NE *Web:* www.oregon.gov/DOC	Salem	OR	97301	503-945-9090	373-1173
Crime Victims Service Div 1162 Ct St NE *TF:* 877-877-9392 ■ *Web:* www.doj.state.or.us/crimev/welcome1.htm	Salem	OR	97301	503-378-4400	378-5738
Dept of Consumer & Business Services 350 Winter St NE PO Box 14480 *Web:* www.oregon.gov	Salem	OR	97309	503-378-4100	378-6444
Dept of Human Services 500 Summer St NE *Web:* www.oregon.gov/DHS	Salem	OR	97301	503-945-5944	378-2897
Dept of Transportation 355 Capitol St NE Ste 135 Rm 222 *TF:* 888-275-6368 ■ *Web:* www.oregon.gov/ODOT	Salem	OR	97301	503-986-4000	986-3432
Driver & Motor Vehicle Services Div 1905 Lana Ave NE *Web:* www.oregon.gov/ODOT/DMV	Salem	OR	97314	503-945-5000	945-5254
Education Dept 255 Capitol St NE	Salem	OR	97310	503-947-5600	
Emergency Management 3225 State St Ste 115 *Web:* www.oregon.gov	Salem	OR	97301	503-378-2911	373-7933
Energy Dept 625 Marion St NE *Web:* oregon.gov	Salem	OR	97301	503-378-4040	373-7806
Environmental Quality Dept 811 SW Sixth Ave *Web:* www.oregon.gov	Portland	OR	97204	503-229-5696	229-6124
Finance & Corporate Securities Div 350 Winter St NE Rm 410 PO Box 14480 *Web:* www.oregon.gov	Salem	OR	97309	503-378-4140	947-7862
Financial Fraud/Consumer Protection Section 1162 Ct St NE *TF:* 877-877-9392 ■ *Web:* www.doj.state.or.us	Salem	OR	97301	503-378-4400	373-7067
Fish & Wildlife Dept (ODFW) 3406 Cherry Ave NE *TF:* 800-720-6339 ■ *Web:* www.dfw.state.or.us	Salem	OR	97303	503-947-6000	947-6042
Forestry Dept 2600 State St Ste 110 *Web:* www.oregon.gov	Salem	OR	97310	503-945-7200	945-7212
Governor 900 Ct St NE Ste 160 *Web:* www.oregon.gov/gov	Salem	OR	97310	503-378-3111	378-6827
Housing & Community Services Dept 725 Summer St NE Ste B *Web:* www.oregon.gov/OHCS	Salem	OR	97301	503-986-2000	986-2020
Insurance Div 350 Winter St NE Rm 440 *Web:* www.cbs.state.or.us	Salem	OR	97301	503-947-7980	378-4351
Labor & Industries Bureau 800 NE Oregon St Ste 1045 *Web:* oregon.gov/boli/pages/index.aspx	Portland	OR	97232	503-731-4200	731-4103
Land Conservation & Development Dept 635 Capitol St NE Ste 150 *Web:* www.oregon.gov	Salem	OR	97301	503-373-0050	378-5518
Legislative Assembly 900 Ct St NE **Fax Area Code:* 503 ■ *TF:* 800-332-2313 ■ *Web:* www.leg.state.or.us	Salem	OR	97301	800-332-2313	373-1527*

	City	State	Zip	Phone	Fax
Measurement Standards Div 635 Capitol St NE *Web:* www.oregon.gov	Salem	OR	97301	503-986-4670	986-4784
Military Dept 1776 Militia Way SE PO Box 14350 *Web:* www.oregon.gov	Salem	OR	97309	503-584-3980	584-3987
Oregon Business Development Dept (OBDD) 775 Summer St NE Ste 200 *TF General:* 800-735-2900 ■ *Web:* www.oregon4biz.com	Salem	OR	97301	503-986-0123	581-5115
Oregon Government Standards & Practices Commission 3218 Pringle Rd SE Ste 220 *Web:* www.oregon.gov	Salem	OR	97302	503-378-5105	373-1456
Oregon Lottery 500 Airport Rd SE *Web:* oregonlottery.org	Salem	OR	97301	503-540-1000	540-1001
Oregon Publication & Distribution Services 900 Ct St NE Rm 49 *Web:* Www.oregonlegislature.gov	Salem	OR	97310	503-986-1360	373-1527
Oregon Student Assistance Commission 1500 Valley River Dr Ste 100 *Web:* oregonstudentaid.gov	Eugene	OR	97401	541-687-7400	
Parks & Recreation Dept (OPRD) 725 Summer St NE Ste C *TF:* 800-551-6949 ■ *Web:* www.oregon.gov/OPRD	Salem	OR	97301	503-986-0707	986-0794
Parole & Post-Prison Supervision Board 2575 Ctr St NE Ste 100 *Web:* www.oregon.gov/BOPPPS	Salem	OR	97301	503-945-0900	373-7558
Public Health Div 800 NE Oregon St Ste 465-B **Fax Area Code:* 503 ■ *Web:* public.health.oregon.gov/PHD	Portland	OR	97232	971-673-1222	731-4031*
Racing Commission 800 NE Oregon St Ste 310 *Web:* www.oregon.gov	Portland	OR	97232	971-673-1555	673-0213
Revenue Dept 955 Ctr St NE *Web:* www.oregon.gov	Salem	OR	97301	503-378-4988	945-8738
Secretary of State 136 State Capitol *Web:* sos.oregon.gov	Salem	OR	97310	503-986-1523	986-1616
Seniors & People with Disabilities Div 500 Summer St NE *Web:* www.oregon.gov	Salem	OR	97301	503-945-5944	581-6198
State Court Administrator Office 1163 State St *Web:* courts.oregon.gov/ojd/osca	Salem	OR	97301	503-986-5500	986-5503
State Police Dept 255 Capitol St NE 4th Fl *Web:* www.oregon.gov	Salem	OR	97310	503-378-3720	378-8282
Supreme Court 1163 State St *Web:* courts.oregon.gov	Salem	OR	97301	503-986-5550	986-5503
Treasurer 350 Winter St NE Ste 100 *Web:* www.oregon.gov	Salem	OR	97301	503-378-4000	373-7051
Veterans' Affairs Dept 700 Summer St NE *Web:* www.oregon.gov	Salem	OR	97301	503-373-2000	373-2362
Vital Records Unit 800 NE Oregon St Ste 225 PO Box 14050 *Web:* public.health.oregon.gov	Portland	OR	97232	971-673-1180	673-1201
Vocational Rehabilitation Services Office (OVRS) 700 Summer St NE E-87 **Fax Area Code:* 503 ■ *TF:* 877-277-0513 ■ *Web:* www.oregon.gov	Salem	OR	97301	800-692-9666	947-5010*
Workers'' Compensation Board 2601 SE 25th St Ste 150 *Web:* www.cbs.state.or.us/wcb	Salem	OR	97302	503-378-3308	373-1684

339-39 Pennsylvania

	City	State	Zip	Phone	Fax
Administrative Office of the Cts (AOPC) 1515 Market St Ste 1414 *Web:* www.pacourts.us/T/AOPC	Philadelphia	PA	19102	215-560-6300	560-6315
Aging Dept 555 Walnut St 5th Fl *Web:* www.aging.state.pa.us	Harrisburg	PA	17101	717-787-7313	783-6842
Agriculture Dept 2301 N Cameron St *Web:* www.agriculture.state.pa.us	Harrisburg	PA	17110	717-772-2853	705-8402
Attorney General Strawberry Sq 16th Fl *Web:* www.attorneygeneral.gov	Harrisburg	PA	17120	717-787-3391	
Banking Dept 17 N Second St Market Square Plz *TF:* 800-722-2657 ■ *Web:* www.banking.state.pa.us	Harrisburg	PA	17101	717-783-4721	
Child Support Enforcement Bureau PO Box 8018 *Web:* www.dpw.state.pa.us	Harrisburg	PA	17105	717-787-2600	787-9706
Community & Economic Development Dept 400 N St 4th Fl *Web:* www.newpa.com	Harrisburg	PA	17120	717-787-3003	787-6866
Conservation & Natural Resources Dept 400 Market St Ste 7 *Web:* www.dcnr.state.pa.us	Harrisburg	PA	17120	717-787-2869	705-2832
Consumer Advocate 555 Walnut St 5th Fl *Web:* www.oca.state.pa.us	Harrisburg	PA	17101	717-783-5048	783-7152
Corrections Dept PO Box 598 *Web:* www.cor.state.pa.us	Camp Hill	PA	17001	717-728-2573	787-0132
Driver & Vehicle Services Bureau 1101 S Front St *Web:* www.dmv.state.pa.us	Harrisburg	PA	17104	717-787-2977	705-1046
Education Dept 333 Market St *Web:* www.pde.state.pa.us	Harrisburg	PA	17126	717-783-6788	783-4517
Emergency Management Agency 2605 I- Dr *Web:* pema.pa.gov	Harrisburg	PA	17110	717-651-2001	651-2021
Environmental Protection Dept PO Box 2063 *Web:* www.dep.state.pa.us	Harrisburg	PA	17105	717-783-2300	783-8926
Fish & Boat Commission 1601 Elmerton Ave *Web:* www.fish.state.pa.us	Harrisburg	PA	17110	717-705-7800	705-7802
Game Commission 2001 Elmerton Ave *Web:* www.pgc.state.pa.us	Harrisburg	PA	17110	717-787-4250	772-2411
General Assembly Capitol Bldg *Web:* www.legis.state.pa.us	Harrisburg	PA	17120	717-787-5920	772-2344
Governor 508 Main Capitol Bldg *Web:* www.governor.state.pa.us	Harrisburg	PA	17120	717-787-2500	772-8284
Health Dept Health & Welfare Bldg PO Box 90 *Web:* www.portal.health.state.pa.us	Harrisburg	PA	17108	717-787-6436	772-6959
Historical & Museum Commission 300 N St *Web:* www.phmc.state.pa.us	Harrisburg	PA	17120	717-787-3362	783-9924
Homeland Security Office 1800 Elmerton Ave *Web:* homelandsecurity.pa.gov	Harrisburg	PA	17110	717-346-4460	
Housing Finance Agency 211 N Front St *Web:* www.phfa.org	Harrisburg	PA	17101	717-780-3800	
Information Technology Office 209 Finance Bldg *Web:* www.oit.state.pa.us	Harrisburg	PA	17120	717-787-5440	787-4523
Insurance Dept 1326 Strawberry Sq **Fax Area Code:* 717 ■ *TF:* 877-881-6388 ■ *Web:* www.ins.state.pa.us	Harrisburg	PA	17120	877-881-6388	783-3898*
Mental Health & Substance Abuse Office PO Box 2675 *Web:* www.dpw.state.pa.us	Harrisburg	PA	17105	717-787-6443	
Military & Veterans Affairs Dept Fort Indiantown Gap Bldg S-0-47 *Web:* www.dmva.state.pa.us	Annville	PA	17003	717-861-8500	861-8314
Office of Governor 200 Capitol Bldg 501 N 3rd St *Web:* www.governor.state.pa.us	Harrisburg	PA	17120	717-787-3300	
Pennsylvania Bill Status 462 Main Capitol Bldg *Web:* www.legis.state.pa.us	Harrisburg	PA	17120	717-787-5920	
Pennsylvania Higher Education Assistance Agency 1200 N Seventh St **Fax Area Code:* 717 ■ *TF:* 800-233-0557 ■ *Web:* www.pheaa.org	Harrisburg	PA	17102	800-233-0557	720-3901*
Pennsylvania State Ethics Commission 309 Finance Bldg PO Box 11470 *TF:* 800-932-0936 ■ *Web:* www.ethics.state.pa.us	Harrisburg	PA	17108	717-783-1610	787-0806
Pennsylvania State System of Higher Education 2986 N Second St *TF:* 800-732-0999 ■ *Web:* www.passhe.edu	Harrisburg	PA	17110	717-720-4000	720-4011
Pennsylvania Workforce Investment Board 901 N Seventh St Ste 103 *Web:* www.paworkforce.state.pa.us	Harrisburg	PA	17120	717-772-4966	
Probation & Parole Board 1101 S Front St Ste 5100 *Web:* www.pbpp.state.pa.us	Harrisburg	PA	17104	717-787-5699	705-1774
Public Utility Commission 400 N St Keystone Bldg PO Box 3265 *TF:* 800-692-7380 ■ *Web:* www.puc.state.pa.us	Harrisburg	PA	17120	717-783-1740	787-6641
Public Welfare Dept PO Box 2675 *Web:* www.dpw.state.pa.us	Harrisburg	PA	17105	717-787-2600	772-2062
Revenue Dept Strawberry Sq 11th Fl *Web:* www.revenue.state.pa.us	Harrisburg	PA	17128	717-783-3680	787-3990
Secretary of the Commonwealth 210 N Office Bldg *Web:* www.dos.state.pa.us	Harrisburg	PA	17120	717-787-5280	787-1734
Securities Commission 17 N Second St *Web:* www.pa.gov	Harrisburg	PA	17101	717-787-2665	
State Parks Bureau PO Box 8551 *TF:* 888-727-2757 ■ *Web:* www.dcnr.state.pa.us	Harrisburg	PA	17105	717-787-6640	787-8817
State Police 1800 Elmerton Ave *Web:* psp.pa.gov	Harrisburg	PA	17110	717-783-5599	
Supreme Court 468 City Hall *Web:* www.pacourts.us	Philadelphia	PA	19107	215-560-6370	
Transportation Dept 400 N St *TF:* 800-932-4600 ■ *Web:* www.dot.state.pa.us	Harrisburg	PA	17120	717-787-2838	
Treasury Dept 129 Finance Bldg *Web:* www.patreasury.gov	Harrisburg	PA	17120	717-787-2465	
Victims Compensation Assistance Program PO Box 1167 *Web:* pccd.pa.gov/pages/default.aspx	Harrisburg	PA	17101	717-783-5153	787-4306
Vital Records Div 101 S Mercer St PO Box 1528 *Web:* www.portal.health.state.pa.us	New Castle	PA	16103	724-656-3100	652-8951
Vocational Rehabilitation Office (OVR) 1521 N Sixth St *TF:* 800-442-6351 ■ *Web:* www.portal.state.pa.us	Harrisburg	PA	17102	717-787-5244	783-5221
Workers Compensation Bureau 1171 S Cameron St Rm 324 *TF:* 800-482-2383 ■ *Web:* www.portal.state.pa.u	Harrisburg	PA	17104	717-783-5421	

339-40 Rhode Island

	City	State	Zip	Phone	Fax
State Government Information 40 Fountain St *Web:* www.ri.gov	Providence	RI	02903	401-222-2000	
Adjutant General's Office 645 New London Ave *Web:* Www.sos.ri.gov	Cranston	RI	02920	401-946-9996	944-1891
Agriculture & Resource Marketing Div 235 Promenade St Rm 370 *Web:* www.dem.ri.gov	Providence	RI	02908	401-222-2781	222-6047
Arts Council 1 Capitol Hill 3rd Fl *Web:* arts.ri.gov	Providence	RI	02908	401-222-3880	222-3018
Attorney General 150 S Main St *Web:* www.riag.state.ri.us/contact	Providence	RI	02903	401-274-4400	222-1331
Board of Governors for Higher Education (RIBGHE) 80 Washington St Shepard Bldg *Web:* www.ribghe.org	Providence	RI	02903	401-456-6000	456-6028
Child Support Services 77 Dorrance St *Web:* www.cse.ri.gov	Providence	RI	02906	401-458-4400	
Children Youth & Families Dept 101 Friendship St *Web:* www.dcyf.state.ri.us	Providence	RI	02903	401-528-3575	528-3590
Consumer Protection Unit 150 S Main St *Web:* www.riag.ri.gov	Providence	RI	02903	401-274-4400	222-5110

Phone Fax

Corrections Dept 40 Howard Ave .... Cranston RI 02920 401-462-1000
Web: www.doc.state.ri.us

Court Administrators Office
250 Benefit St .... Providence RI 02903 401-222-3215
Web: www.courts.ri.gov

Crime Victim Compensation Program
50 Service Ave .... Warwick RI 02886 401-462-7650 222-6140
Web: www.treasury.ri.gov

Economic Development Corp
315 Iron Horse Way Ste 101 .... Providence RI 02908 401-278-9100
Web: commerceri.com

Elderly Affairs Dept
74 W Rd Hazard Bldg 2nd fl .... Cranston RI 02920 401-462-3000
Web: www.google.co.in

Elementary & Secondary Education Dept
255 Westminster St .... Providence RI 02903 401-222-4600 222-6178
Web: www.ride.ri.gov

Emergency Management Agency
645 New London Ave .... Cranston RI 02920 401-946-9996 944-1891
Web: www.riema.ri.gov

Environmental Management Dept
235 Promenade St .... Providence RI 02908 401-222-6800 222-6802
Web: www.dem.ri.gov

General Assembly 82 Smith St .... Providence RI 02903 401-222-2466
Web: www.rilin.state.ri.us

Health Dept 3 Capitol Hill .... Providence RI 02908 401-222-2231 222-6548
Web: www.health.ri.gov

Higher Education Assistance Authority (RIHEAA)
560 Jefferson Blvd .... Warwick RI 02886 401-736-1100 732-3541
TF: 800-922-9855 ■ *Web:* www.riheaa.org

Historical Preservation & Heritage Commission
150 Benefit St .... Providence RI 02903 401-222-2678 222-2968
Web: eisenhowerhouse.com

Housing & Mortgage Finance Corp
44 Washington St .... Providence RI 02903 401-751-5566
Web: www.rhodeislandhousing.org

Human Services Dept
600 New London Ave
Louis Pasteur Bldg, Ste 57 .... Cranston RI 02920 401-462-5300
Web: www.dhs.ri.gov

Library & Information Services Office
1 Capitol Hil 4th fl .... Providence RI 02908 401-574-9300 574-9320
Web: www.olis.ri.gov

Lieutenant Governor 82 Smith St Rm 116 .... Providence RI 02903 401-222-2371 222-2012
Web: www.ltgov.ri.gov

Medical Examiner 48 Orms St .... Providence RI 02908 401-222-5500 222-5517
Web: www.health.ri.gov

Office of the Governor State House .... Providence RI 02903 401-222-2080
Web: www.governor.state.ri.us

Parks & Recreation Div 2321 Hartford Ave .... Johnston RI 02919 401-222-2632
Web: www.riparks.com

Professional Regulation Div
1511 Pontiac Ave Howard Ctr Bldg 70 .... Cranston RI 02920 401-462-8580
Web: www.dlt.ri.gov/profregs

Public Utilities Commission
89 Jefferson Blvd .... Warwick RI 02888 401-941-4500
Web: www.ripuc.org

Rehabilitation Services Office
40 Fountain St .... Providence RI 02903 401-421-7005 222-3574
Web: www.ors.state.ri.us

Rhode Island Bill Status
82 Smith St Rm 217 .... Providence RI 02903 401-222-3580
Web: www.rilin.state.ri.us

Rhode Island Ethics Commission
40 Fountain St .... Providence RI 02903 401-222-3790 222-3382
Web: www.ethics.ri.gov

Rhode Island Labor & Training Dept
1511 Pontiac Ave .... Cranston RI 02920 401-462-8000 462-8872
Web: www.dlt.state.ri.us

Rhode Island Lottery 1425 Pontiac Ave .... Cranston RI 02920 401-463-6500
Web: www.rilot.com

State Police 311 Danielson Pike .... North Scituate RI 02857 401-444-1000 444-1105
Web: risp.ri.gov

Supreme Court 250 Benefit St .... Providence RI 02903 401-222-3272 222-3599
Web: www.courts.ri.gov

Tourism Div 315 Iron Horse Way Ste 101 .... Providence RI 02908 800-556-2484 273-8270*
**Fax Area Code:* 401 ■ *TF:* 800-556-2484 ■ *Web:* www.visitrhodeisland.com

Transportation Dept 2 Capitol Hill .... Providence RI 02903 401-222-2481 222-2086
Web: rhodeislandbids.com

Treasurer 82 Smith St Rm 102 .... Providence RI 02903 401-222-2397 222-6140
Web: www.treasury.ri.gov

Veterans Affairs Div 480 Metacom Ave .... Bristol RI 02809 401-253-8000 254-2320
Web: www.vets.ri.gov

Weights & Measures Office 1511 Pontiac Ave .... Cranston RI 02920 401-462-8570 462-8576
Web: www.dlt.ri.gov/occusafe/weightsmeasures.htm

Worker's Compensation Div
1511 Pontiac Ave Bldg 69 2nd Fl .... Cranston RI 02920 401-462-8100 462-8105
Web: www.dlt.ri.gov/wc

339-41 South Carolina

Phone Fax

State Government Information
1301 Gervais St Ste 710 .... Columbia SC 29201 803-771-0131 771-0131
TF: 866-340-7105 ■ *Web:* sc.gov

Adoption Services Div PO Box 1520 .... Columbia SC 29202 803-898-7561 898-7641
Web: dss.sc.gov

Agriculture Dept 1200 Senate St PO Box 11280 ...... Columbia SC 29211 803-734-2190 734-2192
Web: agriculture.sc.gov

Arts Commission 1800 Gervais St .... Columbia SC 29201 803-734-8696 734-8526
Web: www.state.sc.us

Attorney General 1000 Assembly St .... Columbia SC 29201 803-734-3970 253-6283

Business Carolina Inc (BCI)
1523 Huger St Ste A .... Columbia SC 29201 803-461-3801
Web: www.bcilending.com

Child Support Enforcement Office
3150 Harden St Ext .... Columbia SC 29203 803-898-9210
TF: 800-768-5858 ■ *Web:* www.sc.gov

Commerce Dept 1201 Main St Ste 1600 .... Columbia SC 29201 803-737-0400 737-0418
TF: 800-868-7232 ■ *Web:* www.sccommerce.com

Corrections Dept 4444 Broad River Rd .... Columbia SC 29210 803-896-8500 896-3972
Web: www.doc.sc.gov

Court Administration 1015 Sumter St 2nd Fl .... Columbia SC 29201 803-734-1800 734-1821
Web: www.judicial.state.sc.us

Emergency Management Div (SCEMD)
2779 Fish Hatchery Rd .... West Columbia SC 29172 803-737-8500 737-8570
Web: scemd.org

Health & Environmental Control Dept
2600 Bull St .... Columbia SC 29201 803-898-3432
Web: www.scdhec.gov

Health & Human Services Dept 1801 Main St .... Columbia SC 29201 803-898-2500

Highway Patrol 5400 Broad River Rd bldg 12 .... Columbia SC 29212 803-896-7920 896-7922
Web: www.scdps.gov

Historic Preservation Office
8301 Parklane Rd .... Columbia SC 29223 803-896-6100 896-6167
Web: scdah.sc.gov

Insurance Dept (SCDOI)
1201 Main St Ste 1000 PO Box 100105 .... Columbia SC 29201 803-737-6160 737-6205
Web: www.doi.sc.gov

Labor Licensing & Regulation Dept
110 Centerview Dr .... Columbia SC 29210 803-896-4300 896-4393
Web: www.llr.state.sc.us

Law Enforcement Div
4400 Broad River Rd PO Box 21398 .... Columbia SC 29210 803-896-7001 896-7041
Web: www.sled.sc.gov

Legislature State House PO Box 142 .... Columbia SC 29202 803-212-6200 212-6299
Web: www.scstatehouse.gov

Medical Examiners Board
110 Centerview Dr Ste 202 .... Columbia SC 29210 803-896-4500 896-4515
Web: www.llr.state.sc.us

Mental Health Dept 2414 Bull St PO Box 485 .... Columbia SC 29202 803-898-8581 898-8316
Web: www.state.sc.us/dmh

Motor Vehicles Div PO Box 1498 .... Blythewood SC 29016 803-896-5442
Web: www.scdps.gov

Natural Resources Dept PO Box 167 .... Columbia SC 29202 803-734-4007 734-4300
Web: www.dnr.sc.gov

Office of Governor 1205 Pendleton St .... Columbia SC 29201 803-734-2100 734-5167
Web: governor.sc.gov

Parks Recreation & Tourism Dept
1205 Pendleton St .... Columbia SC 29201 803-734-0156
Web: www.southcarolinaparks.com

Probation Parole & Pardon Services Dept
2221 Devine St Ste 600 PO Box 50666 .... Columbia SC 29250 803-734-9220 734-9440
Web: www.dppps.sc.gov

Professional & Occupational Licensing Boards
110 Centerview Dr .... Columbia SC 29210 803-896-4300 896-4310
Web: www.llr.state.sc.us/pol.asp

Secretary of State 1205 Pendleton St Ste 525 .... Columbia SC 29201 803-734-2170 734-1661
Web: www.scsos.com

Securities Div 1000 Assembly St PO Box 11549 .... Columbia SC 29211 803-734-3970 253-6283
Web: www.scag.gov/scsecurities

Social Services Dept PO Box 1520 .... Columbia SC 29202 803-898-7601 898-7277
Web: dss.sc.gov

South Carolina Commission on Higher Education
1122 Lady St Ste 300 .... Columbia SC 29201 803-737-2260 737-2297
Web: www.che.sc.gov

South Carolina Education Lottery
1333 Main St 4th Fl .... Columbia SC 29201 803-737-2002 737-2005
Web: www.sceducationlottery.com

South Carolina Ethics Commission
5000 Thurmond Mall Ste 250 .... Columbia SC 29201 803-253-4192 253-7539
Web: www.state.sc.us

South Carolina Higher Education Tuition Grants Commission
115 Atrium Wy Ste 102 .... Columbia SC 29203 803-896-1120 896-1126
TF: 877-382-4357 ■ *Web:* www.sctuitiongrants.com

South Carolina State Ports Authority
176 Concord St .... Charleston SC 29401 843-723-8651 577-8710
TF: 800-845-7106 ■ *Web:* www.scspa.com

State Housing Finance & Development Authority
300 Outlet Pointe Blvd Ste C .... Columbia SC 29210 803-896-9001
Web: www.sha.state.sc.us

Supreme Court
1231 Gervais St Supreme Court Bldg .... Columbia SC 29201 803-734-1080 734-1499
Web: dss.sc.gov

Transportation Dept 955 Pk St PO Box 191 .... Columbia SC 29202 803-737-1302 737-2038
Web: www.scdot.org

Treasurer PO Box 11778 .... Columbia SC 29211 803-734-2101 734-2690
Web: www.state.sc.us/treas

Veterans Affairs Div
1205 Pendleton St Ste 463 .... Columbia SC 29201 803-734-0200 734-4014
TF: 800-827-1000 ■ *Web:* va.sc.gov

Victim Assistance Div 1205 Pendleton St .... Columbia SC 29201 803-734-1900 734-1708
Web: www.sova.sc.gov

Vocational Rehabilitation Dept
1410 Boston Ave PO Box 15 .... West Columbia SC 29171 803-896-6500
TF: 800-832-7526 ■ *Web:* www.scvrd.net

Wildlife & Freshwater Fisheries Div
1000 Assembly St PO Box 167 .... Columbia SC 29202 803-734-3886 734-6020
Web: www.dnr.sc.gov/divisions/wildlife.html

Workers' Compensation Commission
1333 Main St # 500 .... Columbia SC 29201 803-737-5700 737-5764
Web: wcc.sc.gov

339-42 South Dakota

	City	State	ZIP	Phone	Fax
State Government Information 500 E Capitol Ave *Web:* www.sd.gov	Pierre	SD	57501	605-773-3011	
Adult Services & Aging Office 700 Governors Dr *Web:* sd.gov	Pierre	SD	57501	605-773-3656	773-6834
Agriculture Dept 523 E Capitol Ave *Web:* sd.gov	Pierre	SD	57501	605-773-3375	773-5926
Arts Council 800 Governors Dr *Web:* www.artscouncil.sd.gov	Pierre	SD	57501	605-773-3131	773-6962
Attorney General 1302 E Hwy 14 *Web:* sd.gov	Pierre	SD	57501	605-773-3215	773-4106
Banking Div 1601 N Harrison Ave Ste 1 *Web:* dlr.sd.gov/banking/default.aspx	Pierre	SD	57501	605-773-3421	773-5367
Child Protection Services 700 Governors Dr *Web:* dss.sd.gov	Pierre	SD	57501	605-773-3227	773-6834
Child Support Div 700 Governors Dr *TF:* 800-286-9145 ■ *Web:* dss.sd.gov	Pierre	SD	57501	605-773-3641	773-7295
Consumer Protection Div 500 E Capitol Ave *Web:* sd.gov	Pierre	SD	57501	605-773-4400	773-4344
Corrections Dept 500 E Capital Ave *Web:* doc.sd.gov	Pierre	SD	57501	605-773-3478	773-3194
Crime Victims' Compensation Program 700 Governors Dr *TF:* 800-696-9476 ■ *Web:* sd.gov	Pierre	SD	57501	605-773-6317	773-6834
DEPARTMENT OF HEALTH 600 E Capitol Ave *TF:* 800-738-2301 ■ *Web:* sd.gov	Pierre	SD	57501	605-773-4961	773-5683
Department of Tribal Relations 302 E Dakota *Web:* www.sdtribalrelations.com	Pierre	SD	57501	605-773-3415	773-6592
Economic Development Office 711 E Wells Ave *TF:* 800-872-6190 ■ *Web:* www.sdreadytowork.com	Pierre	SD	57501	605-773-3301	
Education Dept 700 Governors Dr *Web:* www.doe.sd.gov	Pierre	SD	57501	605-773-3134	773-6139
Emergency Management Office 118 W Capitol Ave *Web:* dps.sd.gov	Pierre	SD	57501	605-773-3231	773-5380
Environment & Natural Resources Dept 523 E Capitol Ave *Web:* sd.gov	Pierre	SD	57501	605-773-3151	773-6035
Finance & Management Bureau 500 E Capitol Ave Rm A-216	Pierre	SD	57501	605-773-3411	773-4711
Governor 500 E Capitol Ave *Web:* sd.gov	Pierre	SD	57501	605-773-3212	773-6873
Highway Patrol Div 118 W Capitol Ave *Web:* dps.sd.gov	Pierre	SD	57501	605-773-3105	773-3018
Housing Development Authority PO Box 1237 *Web:* www.sdhda.org	Pierre	SD	57501	605-773-3181	773-5154
Information & Telecommunications Bureau 700 Governors Dr *Web:* sd.gov	Pierre	SD	57501	605-773-3165	
Insurance Div 445 E Capitol Ave *Web:* dlr.sd.gov	Pierre	SD	57501	605-773-3563	773-5369
Labor Dept 447 Crook St *Web:* www.sdjobs.org	Pierre	SD	57730	605-673-4488	773-4211
Legislature Capitol Bldg 500 E Capitol Ave 3rd Fl *Web:* legis.sd.gov	Pierre	SD	57501	605-773-3251	773-4576
Lieutenant Governor 500 E Capitol Ave *Web:* sd.gov	Pierre	SD	57501	605-773-3661	773-4711
Military & Veterans Affairs Dept 2823 W Main St *Web:* bhr.sd.gov	Rapid City	SD	57702	605-737-6721	737-6677
Motor Vehicle Div 445 E Capital Ave *Web:* dor.sd.gov	Pierre	SD	57501	605-773-3541	773-5129
Pardons & Parole Board 1600 N Dr PO Box 5911 *Web:* doc.sd.gov	Sioux Falls	SD	57117	605-367-5040	
Parks & Recreation Div 523 E Capitol Ave *TF Campground Resv:* 800-710-2267 ■ *Web:* gfp.sd.gov	Pierre	SD	57501	605-773-3391	773-6245
Personnel Bureau 500 E Capitol Ave *Web:* bhr.sd.gov	Pierre	SD	57501	605-773-3148	773-4344
Public Utilities Commission 500 E Capitol Ave *Web:* sd.gov	Pierre	SD	57501	605-773-3201	
Real Estate Commission 221 W Capitol Ave Ste 101 *Web:* sd.gov	Pierre	SD	57501	605-773-3600	773-4356
Regents Board 306 E Capitol Ave Ste 200 *Web:* www.sdbor.edu	Pierre	SD	57501	605-773-3455	
Rehabilitation Services Div 500 E Capitol Ave *TF:* 800-265-9684 ■ *Web:* sd.gov	Pierre	SD	57501	605-773-3195	773-5483
Revenue 445 E Capitol Ave *Web:* dor.sd.gov	Pierre	SD	57501	605-773-3311	773-5129
Secretary of State 500 E Capitol Ave Ste 204 *Web:* www.sdsos.gov	Pierre	SD	57501	605-773-3537	773-6580
Securities Div 445 E Capitol Ave *Web:* sd.gov	Pierre	SD	57501	605-773-4823	773-5953
Social Services Dept 700 Governors Dr *Web:* dss.sd.gov	Pierre	SD	57501	605-773-3165	773-4855
South Dakota Bill Status 500 E Capitol *Web:* legis.sd.gov	Pierre	SD	57501	605-773-3251	
South Dakota Career Ctr Div 116 W Missouri Ave *Web:* www.sdjobs.org	Pierre	SD	57501	605-773-3372	773-6680
South Dakota Gaming Commission 221 W Capitol Ave Ste 101 *Web:* sd.gov	Pierre	SD	57501	605-773-6050	773-6053
State Court Administrator 500 E Capitol Ave *Web:* ujs.sd.gov	Pierre	SD	57501	605-773-8459	773-8437
State Historical Society 900 Governors Dr *Web:* www.history.sd.gov	Pierre	SD	57501	605-773-3458	773-6041
Supreme Court 500 E Capitol Ave *Web:* ujs.sd.gov	Pierre	SD	57501	605-773-3511	773-6128
Tourism Office 711 E Wells Ave *TF:* 800-952-3625 ■ *Web:* www.travelsd.com	Pierre	SD	57501	605-773-3301	
Treasurer 500 E Capitol Ave Ste 212 *Web:* sdtreasurer.gov	Pierre	SD	57501	605-773-3378	773-3115
Weights & Measures Office 118 W Capitol Ave *Web:* dps.sd.gov	Pierre	SD	57501	605-773-3697	773-6631

339-43 Tennessee

	City	State	ZIP	Phone	Fax
Administrative Office of the Cts 511 Union St Ste 600 *Web:* www.tsc.state.tn.us	Nashville	TN	37219	615-741-2687	741-6285
Aging & Disability Commission 500 Deaderick St 8th Fl *Web:* www.state.tn.us/comaging	Nashville	TN	37243	615-741-2056	741-3309
Agriculture Dept 440 Hogan Rd PO Box 40627 *Web:* www.state.tn.us/agriculture	Nashville	TN	37204	615-837-5100	837-5333
Arts Commission 401 Charlotte Ave *Web:* www.tn.gov	Nashville	TN	37243	615-741-1701	741-8559
Attorney General PO Box 20207 *Web:* www.tn.gov	Nashville	TN	37202	615-741-3491	741-2009
Child Support Services Div 400 Deaderick St 12th Fl *TF:* 800-838-6911 ■ *Web:* www.tn.gov	Nashville	TN	37248	615-313-4880	532-2791
Children's Services Dept 436 Sixth Ave N 7th Fl *Web:* www.state.tn.us	Nashville	TN	37243	615-741-9699	
Commerce & Insurance Dept 500 James Robertson Pkwy 5th Fl *Web:* www.state.tn.us/commerce	Nashville	TN	37243	615-741-6007	
Consumer Affairs Div 500 James Robertson Pkwy 5th Fl *Web:* www.state.tn.us	Nashville	TN	37243	615-741-4737	532-4994
Correction Dept 320 Sixth Ave N 4th Fl *Web:* www.state.tn.us	Nashville	TN	37243	615-741-1000	741-4605
Department of Human Resources 505 Deaderick St *Web:* www.state.tn.us	Nashville	TN	37243	615-741-2958	532-0728
Div of Claims Administration 502 Deaderick St *Web:* treasury.tn.gov	Nashville	TN	37243	615-741-2734	532-4979
Economic & Community Development Dept (ECD) 312 Eigth Ave N 11th Fl *TF:* 877-768-6374 ■ *Web:* www.tn.gov/ecd	Nashville	TN	37243	615-741-1888	741-7306
Education Dept 710 James Robertson Pkwy 6th Fl *Web:* www.state.tn.us	Nashville	TN	37243	615-741-2731	532-4791
Emergency Management Agency 3041 Sidco Dr *Web:* www.tn.gov/tema	Nashville	TN	37204	615-741-0001	242-9635
Environment & Conservation Dept 312 Rosa L Parks Ave *Web:* www.state.tn.us/environment	Nashville	TN	37243	615-532-0109	532-0120
Finance & Administration Dept 312 Rosa L Parks Ave *Web:* www.state.tn.us/finance	Nashville	TN	37243	615-741-0320	
Financial Institutions Dept 414 Union St Ste 1000 *Web:* www.tn.gov	Nashville	TN	37219	615-741-2236	
General Assembly 320 Sixth Ave N *Web:* www.legislature.state.tn.us	Nashville	TN	37243	615-741-1000	
Governor State Capitol 1st Fl *Web:* www.tennessee.gov	Nashville	TN	37243	615-741-2001	
Health Dept 425 Fifth Ave N 3rd Fl *Web:* www.state.tn.us	Nashville	TN	37247	615-741-3111	741-2491
Highway Patrol 1150 Foster Ave *Web:* www.state.tn.us	Nashville	TN	37249	615-251-5175	532-1051
Historical Commission 2941 Lebanon Rd *Web:* www.state.tn.us	Nashville	TN	37214	615-532-1550	532-1549
Homeland Security Office 312 Rosa L Parks Ave *Web:* www.tennessee.gov	Nashville	TN	37243	615-532-7825	253-5379
Housing Development Agency 404 James Robertson Pkwy Ste 1114 *Web:* thda.org	Nashville	TN	37243	615-741-2400	
Human Services Dept 400 Deaderick St *Web:* www.state.tn.us	Nashville	TN	37248	615-313-4700	741-4165
Information Resources Office 312 Rosa L Parks Ave *Web:* www.state.tn.us	Nashville	TN	37243	615-741-3700	532-0471
Insurance Div 500 James Robertson Pkwy *Web:* www.tn.gov	Nashville	TN	37243	615-741-2176	532-2788
Mental Health & Developmental Disabilities Dept 425 Fifth Ave N 3rd Fl *TF:* 800-669-1851 ■ *Web:* www.state.tn.us	Nashville	TN	37243	615-532-6500	532-6514
Military Dept 3041 Sidco Dr *Web:* www.tnmilitary.org	Nashville	TN	37204	615-313-0633	313-3129
Probation & Parole Board 404 James Robertson Pkwy Ste 1300 *Web:* www.tennessee.gov/bopp	Nashville	TN	37243	615-741-1673	
Real Estate Commission 500 James Robertson Pkwy Ste 180 *TF:* 800-342-4031 ■ *Web:* www.tn.gov	Nashville	TN	37243	615-741-2273	741-0313
Regulatory Authority 460 James Robertson Pkwy *Web:* www.state.tn.us/tra	Nashville	TN	37243	615-741-2904	
Regulatory Boards Div 500 James Robertson Pkwy *Web:* www.tn.gov	Nashville	TN	37243	615-741-3449	741-6470

	City	State	Zip	Phone	Fax
Rehabilitation Services Div 400 Deaderick St 11th Fl *Web:* www.tn.gov	Nashville	TN	37248	615-313-4700	741-4165
Revenue Dept 500 Deaderick St *Web:* www.state.tn.us/revenue	Nashville	TN	37242	615-741-2461	741-0682
Secretary of State State Capitol 1st Fl *Web:* www.state.tn.us/sos	Nashville	TN	37243	615-741-2819	
Securities Div 500 James Robertson Pkwy Ste 680 *TF:* 800-863-9117 ■ *Web:* www.tennessee.gov	Nashville	TN	37243	615-741-2947	532-8375
State Parks Div 401 Church St 7th Fl *TF:* 888-867-2757 ■ *Web:* tnstateparks.com	Nashville	TN	37243	615-532-0001	
Supreme Court 511 Union St Nashville City Ctr Ste 600 *TF:* 800-448-7970 ■ *Web:* www.tsc.state.tn.us	Nashville	TN	37219	615-741-2687	
Tennessee Bill Status 320 Sixth Ave N 1st Fl *Web:* www.tn.gov/directory	Nashville	TN	37243	615-741-1000	
Tennessee Higher Education Commission 404 James Robertson Pkwy Ste 1900 *Web:* www.state.tn.us	Nashville	TN	37243	615-741-3605	741-6230
Tennessee Labor & Workforce Development Dept 220 French Landing Dr *Web:* www.state.tn.us	Nashville	TN	37243	615-741-6642	741-5078
Tennessee Lottery 200 Athens Way Ste 200 **Fax:* Hum Res ■ *Web:* www.tnlottery.com	Nashville	TN	37228	615-324-6500	*
Tennessee Student Assistance Corp 404 James Robertson Pkwy Ste 1510 *Web:* www.state.tn.us/tsac	Nashville	TN	37243	615-741-1346	741-6101
Tennessee Treasurer Tennessee State Capitol 1st Fl 600 Charlotte Ave *Web:* www.treasury.state.tn.us	Nashville	TN	37243	615-741-2956	
Title & Registration Div 44 Vantage Way Ste 160 *Web:* www.tn.gov/revenue/vehicle	Nashville	TN	37243	615-741-3101	
Tourist Development Dept 312 Eigth Ave N 25th Fl *Web:* www.state.tn.us/tourdev	Nashville	TN	37243	615-741-2159	741-7225
Transportation Dept 505 Deaderick St Ste 700 *Web:* www.tdot.state.tn.us	Nashville	TN	37243	615-741-2848	741-2508
Treasury Dept 600 Charlotte Ave *Web:* www.treasury.state.tn.us	Nashville	TN	37243	615-741-2956	
Veterans Affairs Dept 312 Rosa L Parks Ave 13th Fl *Web:* www.state.tn.us/veteran	Nashville	TN	37243	615-741-2931	
Vital Records Div 421 Fifth Ave N 1st Fl *Web:* www.tn.gov	Nashville	TN	37247	615-741-1763	741-9860
Wildlife Resources Agency PO Box 40747 *Web:* www.state.tn.us/twra	Nashville	TN	37204	615-781-6500	741-4606
Workers Compensation Div 220 French Landing Dr *Web:* tn.gov/maint/tngov/notfound.shtml	Nashville	TN	37243	615-741-6642	

339-44 Texas

	City	State	Zip	Phone	Fax
State Government Information 1501 N Congress Ste 4224 *TF:* 877-452-9060 ■ *Web:* www.texas.gov	Austin	TX	78711	512-936-9500	936-9400
Aging & Disability Services 701 W 51st St Ste W253 *TF:* 888-388-6332	Austin	TX	78751	512-438-3011	438-5885
Agriculture Dept PO Box 12847 **Fax Area Code:* 888 ■ *TF Cust Svc:* 800-835-5832 ■ *Web:* texasagriculture.gov	Austin	TX	78711	512-463-7476	223-8861*
Arts Commission 920 Colorado Ste 501 PO Box 13406 *TF:* 800-252-9415 ■ *Web:* www.arts.texas.gov	Austin	TX	78701	512-463-5535	475-2699
Assistive & Rehabilitation Services Dept 4800 N Lamar Blvd 3rd Fl *Web:* www.sorm.state.tx.us	Austin	TX	78756	512-706-7288	407-3251
Attorney General PO Box 12548 *Web:* www.texasattorneygeneral.gov	Austin	TX	78711	512-463-2191	
Banking Dept 2601 N Lamar Blvd *TF:* 877-276-5554 ■ *Web:* dob.texas.gov	Austin	TX	78705	512-475-1300	475-1313
Child Support Div 300 W 15th St *TF:* 800-252-8014 ■ *Web:* www.texasattorneygeneral.gov	Austin	TX	78701	512-460-6000	475-2994
Comptroller of Public Accounts 111 E 17th St *TF:* 800-531-5441 ■ *Web:* www.cpa.state.tx.us	Austin	TX	78774	512-463-4600	475-0352
Consumer Protection Div PO Box 12548 *TF General:* 800-621-0508 ■ *Web:* www.texasattorneygeneral.gov/consumer	Austin	TX	78711	800-621-0508	
Crime Victims Services Div PO Box 12198 *TF:* 800-983-9933 ■ *Web:* www.texasattorneygeneral.gov	Austin	TX	78711	512-936-1200	320-8270
Criminal Justice Dept PO Box 13084 *Web:* www.tdcj.state.tx.us	Austin	TX	78711	512-475-3250	305-9398
Economic Development PO Box 12428 *Web:* www.texaswideopenforbusiness.com	Austin	TX	78711	512-936-0100	936-0080
Education Agency 1701 N Congress Ave *Web:* www.tea.state.tx.us	Austin	TX	78701	512-463-9734	463-9838
Emergency Management Div PO Box 4087 *Web:* dps.texas.gov	Austin	TX	78773	512-424-2138	424-2444
Environmental Quality Commission (TCEQ) 12100 Pk 35 Cir PO Box 13087 *TF:* 800-735-2989 ■ *Web:* www.tceq.state.tx.us	Austin	TX	78711	512-239-1000	
Family & Protective Services Dept 701 W 51st St PO Box 149030 *Web:* www.dfps.state.tx.us	Austin	TX	78752	512-438-4800	438-3525
General Land Office 1700 N Congress Ave Ste 935 *TF:* 800-998-4456 ■ *Web:* www.glo.texas.gov	Austin	TX	78701	512-463-5001	475-1558
Governor PO Box 12428 *TF:* 800-843-5789 ■ *Web:* www.governor.state.tx.us	Austin	TX	78711	512-463-2000	463-1849
Historical Commission 108 W 16th St *Web:* www.thc.state.tx.us	Austin	TX	78701	512-463-6100	463-8222
Housing & Community Affairs Dept 507 Sabine St PO Box 13941 *Web:* www.tdhca.state.tx.us	Austin	TX	78711	512-475-3800	472-8526
Information Resources Dept 300 W 15th St Ste 1300 *Web:* www.dir.state.tx.us	Austin	TX	78701	512-475-4700	475-4759
Insurance Dept 333 Guadalupe St PO Box 149104 *TF:* 800-252-3439 ■ *Web:* www.tdi.texas.gov	Austin	TX	78714	512-463-6169	475-2005
Legislature State Capitol *Web:* www.capitol.state.tx.us	Austin	TX	78711	512-463-0124	463-0694
Licensing & Regulation Dept PO Box 12157 *Web:* tdlr.texas.gov	Austin	TX	78711	512-463-6599	475-2874
Lieutenant Governor David Dewhurst PO Box 12068 *Web:* www.ltgov.state.tx.us	Austin	TX	78711	512-463-0001	463-0677
Medical Board PO Box 2018 *TF Cust Svc:* 800-248-4062 ■ *Web:* www.tmb.state.tx.us	Austin	TX	78768	512-305-7010	305-7008
Motor Vehicle Div 4000 Jackson Ave PO Box 2293 *TF:* 888-368-4689 ■ *Web:* www.txdmv.gov	Austin	TX	78731	888-368-4689	
Office of Court Administration 205 W 14th St Ste 600 *Web:* www.courts.state.tx.us	Austin	TX	78711	512-463-1625	463-1648
Pardons & Parole Board PO Box 13401 *Web:* www.tdcj.state.tx.us/bpp	Austin	TX	78701	512-936-6351	463-8120
Parks & Wildlife Dept 4200 Smith School Rd *TF:* 800-792-1112 ■ *Web:* www.tpwd.state.tx.us	Austin	TX	78744	512-389-4800	389-4814
Public Safety Dept 5805 N Lamar Blvd *Web:* txdps.state.tx.us	Austin	TX	78752	512-424-2000	424-5708
Public Utility Commission PO Box 13326 *TF:* 888-782-8477 ■ *Web:* www.puc.texas.gov	Austin	TX	78711	512-936-7000	936-7003
Railroad Commission PO Box 12967 *TF:* 877-228-5740 ■ *Web:* www.rrc.state.tx.us	Austin	TX	78711	512-463-7131	463-7161
Secretary of State PO Box 12887 *Web:* www.sos.state.tx.us	Austin	TX	78711	512-463-5770	475-2761
State Securities Board 208 E Tenth St Fl 5 *Web:* www.ssb.state.tx.us	Austin	TX	78701	512-305-8300	305-8310
Supreme Court 201 W 14th St Rm 104 PO Box 12248 *Web:* www.supreme.courts.state.tx.us	Austin	TX	78711	512-463-1312	463-1365
Texas Ethics Commission 201 E 14th St 10th Fl *Web:* www.ethics.state.tx.us	Austin	TX	78701	512-463-5800	463-5777
Texas Higher Education Coordinating Board 1200 E Anderson Ln *Web:* www.thecb.state.tx.us	Austin	TX	78752	512-427-6101	427-6169
Texas Racing Commission 8505 Cross Pk Dr Ste 110 *Web:* txrc.state.tx.us	Austin	TX	78754	512-833-6699	833-6907
Texas Workforce Commission 101 E 15th St *Web:* twc.state.tx.us	Austin	TX	78778	512-463-2222	
Transportation Dept 125 E 11th St *Web:* txdot.gov	Austin	TX	78701	512-463-8585	463-9896
Valadez Adolfo M MD 1100 W 49th St	Austin	TX	78756	512-458-7111	458-7750
Veterans Commission PO Box 12277 *TF:* 800-252-8387 ■ *Web:* www.tvc.state.tx.us	Austin	TX	78711	512-463-5538	475-2395
Vital Statistics Bureau 1100 W 49th St PO Box 12040 **Fax Area Code:* 512 ■ *TF:* 888-963-7111 ■ *Web:* www.dshs.state.tx.us/VS	Austin	TX	78756	888-963-7111	458-7111*
Workers Compensation Commission 7551 Metro Ctr Dr *TF Cust Svc:* 800-252-7031 ■ *Web:* tdi.texas.gov	Austin	TX	78744	512-804-4000	804-4001

339-45 Utah

	City	State	Zip	Phone	Fax
Administrative Office of the Courts PO Box 140241 *Web:* www.utcourts.gov	Salt Lake City	UT	84114	801-578-3800	578-3843
Aging & Adult Services Div 195 N 1950 W Rm 325 *TF:* 877-424-4640 ■ *Web:* www.hsdaas.utah.gov	Salt Lake City	UT	84116	801-538-3910	538-4395
Agriculture & Food Dept 350 N Redwood Rd *Web:* www.ag.utah.gov	Salt Lake City	UT	84116	801-538-7100	538-7126
Arts Council 617 E S Temple *Web:* heritage.utah.gov	Salt Lake City	UT	84102	801-236-7555	236-7556
Attorney General PO Box 142320 *Web:* www.attorneygeneral.utah.gov	Salt Lake City	UT	84114	801-538-9600	538-1121
Child & Family Services Div 195 N 1950 W Rm 225 *TF:* 855-323-3237 ■ *Web:* dcfs.utah.gov	Salt Lake City	UT	84116	801-538-4100	538-3993
Child Support Div 515 E 100 S 8th Fl *Web:* attorneygeneral.utah.gov/childsupport.html	Salt Lake City	UT	84102	801-536-8300	536-8315
Commerce Dept 160 E Broadway Ste 4 *Web:* www.commerce.utah.gov	Salt Lake City	UT	84111	801-530-6701	530-6446
Community & Economic Development Dept 60 E S Temple 3rd Fl *TF:* 855-204-9046 ■ *Web:* business.utah.gov	Salt Lake City	UT	84111	801-538-8680	538-8888
Consumer Protection Div 160 E Broadway *Web:* www.commerce.utah.gov	Salt Lake City	UT	84111	801-530-6601	530-6001
Corrections Dept 14717 S Minuteman Dr *Web:* www.corrections.utah.gov	Draper	UT	84020	801-545-5500	
Crime Victim Reparations Office 350 E 500 S Ste 200 *Web:* www.crimevictim.utah.gov	Salt Lake City	UT	84111	801-238-2360	533-4127
Department of Technology Services 1 State Office Bldg Fl 6 *Web:* www.dts.utah.gov	Salt Lake City	UT	84114	801-537-9000	538-3622
Education Office 250 E 500 S *Web:* schools.utah.gov	Salt Lake City	UT	84111	801-538-7500	538-7521

	City	State	Zip	Phone	Fax
Emergency Services & Homeland Security Div 1110 State Office Bldg *Web:* publicsafety.utah.gov	Salt Lake City	UT	84114	801-538-3400	538-3770
Environmental Quality Dept 195 N 1950 W *TF:* 800-458-0145 ■ *Web:* www.deq.utah.gov	Salt Lake City	UT	84116	801-536-4400	536-0061
Financial Institutions Dept PO Box 146800 *Web:* www.dfi.utah.gov	Salt Lake City	UT	84111	801-538-8830	538-8894
Governor 350 N State St Ste 200 PO Box 142220 *TF:* 800-705-2464 ■ *Web:* www.utah.gov/governor	Salt Lake City	UT	84114	801-538-1000	538-1528
Health Dept PO Box 141010 *Web:* www.health.utah.gov	Salt Lake City	UT	84114	801-538-6003	
Higher Education System 60 S 400 W *Web:* www.utahsbr.edu	Salt Lake City	UT	84101	801-321-7101	321-7199
Highway Patrol 4501 S 2700 W *Web:* www.utah.gov	Salt Lake City	UT	84119	801-965-4518	
Housing Corp 2479 Lake Pk Blvd. *Web:* www.utahhousingcorp.org	West Valley City	UT	84120	801-902-8200	
Human Resource Management Dept State Office Bldg Ste 2120 *Web:* www.dhrm.utah.gov	Salt Lake City	UT	84114	801-538-3025	538-3403
Human Services Dept 195 N 1950 W. *Web:* hs.utah.gov	Salt Lake City	UT	84116	801-538-4171	538-4016
Insurance Dept 3110 State Office Bldg *Web:* www.insurance.utah.gov	Salt Lake City	UT	84114	801-538-3800	538-3829
Labor Commission PO Box 146600 *TF:* 800-530-5090 ■ *Web:* www.laborcommission.utah.gov	Salt Lake City	UT	84114	801-530-6800	530-6390
Legislature State Capitol Complex W Bldg *Web:* www.le.utah.gov	Salt Lake City	UT	84114	801-538-1029	538-1908
Lieutenant Governor PO Box 142325 **Fax Area Code:* 801 ■ *TF:* 800-705-2464 ■ *Web:* www.utah.gov/ltgovernor	Salt Lake City	UT	84114	800-705-2464	538-1133*
Medical Examiner's Office (OME) 48 Medical Dr. *Web:* health.utah.gov/ome	Salt Lake City	UT	84113	801-584-8410	584-8435
Motor Vehicle Div PO Box 30412 *TF:* 800-368-8824 ■ *Web:* dmv.utah.gov	Salt Lake City	UT	84130	801-297-7780	297-3570
Natural Resources Dept 1594 W N Temple Ste 3710 *Web:* seis.utah.edu	Salt Lake City	UT	84116	801-538-7200	538-7315
Occupational & Professional Licensing Div PO Box 146741 *TF:* 866-275-3675 ■ *Web:* www.dopl.utah.gov	Salt Lake City	UT	84111	801-530-6628	530-6511
Office of Tourism 300 N State St *TF:* 800-200-1160 ■ *Web:* www.travel.utah.gov	Salt Lake City	UT	84114	801-538-1900	538-1399
Pardons & Parole Board 448 E Winchester St Ste 300 *Web:* bop.utah.gov	Murray	UT	84107	801-261-6464	261-6481
Parks & Recreation Div 1594 W N Temple Ste 116 *TF:* 800-322-3770 ■ *Web:* www.stateparks.utah.gov	Salt Lake City	UT	84116	801-538-7220	538-7378
Public Service Commission 160 E 300 S PO Box 45585 *Web:* www.psc.state.ut.us	Salt Lake City	UT	84114	801-530-6716	530-6796
Real Estate Div PO Box 146711 *Web:* realestate.utah.gov	Salt Lake City	UT	84114	801-530-6747	526-4387
Rehabilitation Office 250 E 500 S. *TF:* 800-473-7530 ■ *Web:* www.usor.utah.gov	Salt Lake City	UT	84111	801-538-7530	538-7522
Securities Div 160 E Broadway Ste 2 *Web:* securities.utah.gov	Salt Lake City	UT	84111	801-530-6600	530-6980
State Treasurer 315 State Capitol Bldg Ste E. *Web:* www.utah.gov	Salt Lake City	UT	84114	801-538-1042	538-1465
Supreme Court 450 S State St. *Web:* www.utcourts.gov/courts/sup	Salt Lake City	UT	84114	801-238-7967	
Tax Commission 210 N 1950 W *Web:* www.tax.utah.gov	Salt Lake City	UT	84134	801-297-2200	297-3891
Transportation Dept 4501 S 2700 W PO Box 141265 *Web:* www.udot.utah.gov	Salt Lake City	UT	84119	801-965-4000	965-4338
Utah Higher Education Assistance Authority PO Box 145112 *TF:* 877-336-7378 ■ *Web:* www.uheaa.org	Salt Lake City	UT	84114	801-321-7294	366-8431
Utah Sports Commission 201 S Main St Ste 2002 *Web:* www.utahsportscommission.com	Salt Lake City	UT	84111	801-328-2372	328-2389
Veterans' Affairs Office 550 Foothills Blvd Ste 206 *Web:* veterans.utah.gov	Salt Lake City	UT	84108	801-326-2372	326-2369
Vital Records & Statistics Office 288 N 1460 W PO Box 141012 *Web:* www.health.utah.gov/vitalrecords	Salt Lake City	UT	84114	801-538-6105	
Wildlife Resources Div 1594 W N Temple *Web:* wildlife.utah.gov	Salt Lake City	UT	84116	801-538-4700	
Workers' Compensation Fund 100 W Towne Ridge Pkwy *TF:* 800-446-2667 ■ *Web:* www.wcfgroup.com	Sandy	UT	84070	385-351-8000	351-8372

339-46 Vermont

	City	State	Zip	Phone	Fax
Vermont State Government Information 535 Stone Cutters Way Fl 3 Ste 2 *Web:* www.vermont.gov	Montpelier	VT	05602	802-828-1110	
Vermont Aging & Disabilities Dept 103 S Main St. *Web:* www.dail.vermont.gov	Waterbury	VT	05671	802-241-2401	241-2325
Vermont Agriculture Food & Markets Dept 116 State St *Web:* agriculture.vermont.gov	Montpelier	VT	05620	802-828-2430	828-2361
Vermont Arts Council 136 State St *Web:* www.vermontartscouncil.org	Montpelier	VT	05633	802-828-3291	828-3363
Vermont Attorney General 109 State St *Web:* www.state.vt.us	Montpelier	VT	05609	802-828-3171	828-2154
Vermont Banking Div 89 Main St. *Web:* www.dfr.vermont.gov	Montpelier	VT	05620	802-828-3307	828-1477
Vermont Bill Status 115 State St State House *Web:* www.leg.state.vt.us	Montpelier	VT	05633	802-828-2231	828-2424
Vermont Board of Medical Practice 108 Cherry St PO Box 70 *Web:* healthvermont.gov	Burlington	VT	05402	802-657-4220	657-4227
Vermont Chief Medical Examiner 111 Colchester Ave. *Web:* healthvermont.gov/hc/med_exam/med_index.aspx	Burlington	VT	05401	802-863-7320	
Vermont Children & Families Dept 103 S Main St 2nd Fl 5 N. *TF:* 800-786-3214 ■ *Web:* dcf.vermont.gov	Waterbury	VT	05671	802-241-2100	241-2407
Vermont Consumer Assistance Program 146 University Pl *TF:* 800-649-2424 ■ *Web:* www.atg.state.vt.us	Burlington	VT	05405	802-656-3183	656-1423
Vermont Corrections Dept 103 S Main St *Web:* www.doc.state.vt.us	Waterbury	VT	05671	802-241-2442	241-2565
Vermont Court Administrator 111 State St *Web:* www.vermontjudiciary.org	Montpelier	VT	05609	802-828-3278	828-3457
Vermont Crime Victim Services Ctr 58 S Main St. *Web:* www.ccvs.state.vt.us	Waterbury	VT	05676	802-241-1250	241-4337
Vermont Economic Development Dept PO Box 20 *Web:* accd.vermont.gov	Montpelier	VT	05601	802-828-3080	828-3258
Vermont Education Dept 120 State St. *Web:* www.state.vt.us	Montpelier	VT	05620	802-828-3135	828-3140
Vermont Educator Licensing Div 120 State St *Web:* education.vermont.gov	Montpelier	VT	05620	802-828-2445	828-5107
Vermont Emergency Management Office 103 S Main St. *TF:* 800-347-0488 ■ *Web:* dps.vermont.gov	Waterbury	VT	05671	802-241-5000	241-5556
Vermont Environmental Conservation Dept 1 National Life Drive Main 2 *Web:* www.anr.state.vt.us/dec/dec.htm	Montpelier	VT	05620	802-828-1556	244-5141
Vermont Fish & Wildlife Dept 103 S Main St Bldg 10S *Web:* www.anr.state.vt.us	Waterbury	VT	05671	802-241-3700	241-3295
Vermont General Assembly 115 State St *Web:* www.leg.state.vt.us	Montpelier	VT	05633	802-828-2228	828-2424
Vermont Governor 109 State St 5th Fl *Web:* www.vermont.gov	Montpelier	VT	05609	802-828-3333	828-3339
Vermont Health Dept 108 Cherry St *Web:* www.healthvermont.gov	Burlington	VT	05402	802-863-7200	865-7754
Vermont Historic Preservation Div National Life Bldg 6th Fl. *TF:* 800-639-1522 ■ *Web:* accd.vermont.gov	Montpelier	VT	05620	802-828-3213	828-3206
Vermont Insurance Div 89 Main St *Web:* www.dfr.vermont.gov	Montpelier	VT	05620	802-828-3301	
Vermont Labor Dept 5 Green Mountain Dr PO Box 488 *Web:* www.labor.vermont.gov	Montpelier	VT	05601	802-828-4000	828-4022
Vermont Licensing & Professional Regulation Office National Life Bldg N 2nd Fl. *Web:* www.vtprofessionals.org	Montpelier	VT	05620	802-828-2367	828-2368
Vermont Lieutenant Governor State House *Web:* www.ltgov.vermont.gov	Montpelier	VT	05633	802-828-2226	828-3198
Vermont Lottery Commission 1311 US Rt 302 Ste 100 *Web:* wherezit.com	Barre	VT	05641	802-479-5686	479-4294
Vermont Motor Vehicles Dept 120 State St. *Web:* dmv.vermont.gov	Montpelier	VT	05603	802-828-2000	828-2098
Vermont Natural Resources Agency 103 S Main St. *Web:* www.anr.state.vt.us	Waterbury	VT	05671	802-241-3600	244-1102
Vermont Public Service Board 112 State St 4th Fl *Web:* www.state.vt.us/psb	Montpelier	VT	05620	802-828-2358	828-3351
Vermont Secretary of State 128 State St Drawer 9 **Fax Area Code:* 800 ■ *Web:* www.sec.state.vt.us	Montpelier	VT	05633	802-828-2363	439-8683*
Vermont Securities Div 89 Main St. *Web:* www.dfr.vermont.gov	Montpelier	VT	05620	802-828-3420	828-2896
Vermont State Police 103 S Main St. *Web:* vsp.vermont.gov	Waterbury	VT	05671	802-241-5000	241-5551
Vermont Supreme Court 111 State St *Web:* www.vermontjudiciary.org	Montpelier	VT	05609	802-828-3278	828-3457
Vermont Taxes Dept 133 State St *Web:* www.state.vt.us/tax	Montpelier	VT	05609	802-828-2505	828-2701
Vermont Tourism & Marketing Dept 6 Baldwin St PO Box 22 *Web:* www.vermontvacation.com	Montpelier	VT	05633	802-828-3168	828-3163
Vermont Transportation Agency 1 National Life Dr *Web:* vtrans.vermont.gov	Montpelier	VT	05633	802-828-2657	828-2024
Vermont Treasurer 109 State St 4th Fl. *Web:* www.vermonttreasurer.gov	Montpelier	VT	05609	802-828-2301	828-2772
Vermont Veterans Affairs Office 118 State St *TF:* 888-666-9844 ■ *Web:* www.veterans.vermont.gov/ova	Montpelier	VT	05602	802-828-3379	828-5932
Vermont Vital Records Section PO Box 70 *Web:* www.healthvermont.gov	Burlington	VT	05402	802-863-7275	651-1787
Vermont Vocational Rehabilitation Div 103 S Main St. *TF:* 866-879-6757 ■ *Web:* www.vocrehab.vermont.gov	Waterbury	VT	05671	802-241-2186	241-3359

Phone Fax

Vermont Workers' Compensation Div
5 Green Mountain Dr .... Montpelier VT 05601 802-828-2286 828-2195
Web: www.labor.vermont.gov

339-47 Virginia

Phone Fax

Aging & Rehabilitative Services Dept
8004 Franklin Farms Dr .... Richmond VA 23229 804-662-7000 662-9532
TF: 800-552-5019 ■ *Web:* www.vadrs.org

Aging Dept 1610 Forest Ave # 100 .... Richmond VA 23229 804-662-9333 662-9354
Web: www.vda.virginia.gov

Agriculture & Consumer Services Dept
1100 Bank St Ste 210 .... Richmond VA 23219 804-786-3501 371-2945
Web: www.vdacs.virginia.gov

Arts Commission 223 Governor St 2nd Fl .... Richmond VA 23219 804-225-3132 225-4327
Web: arts.virginia.gov

Attorney General 900 E Main St .... Richmond VA 23219 804-786-2071 786-1991
Web: www.oag.state.va.us

Chief Medical Examiner 400 E Jackson St .... Richmond VA 23219 804-786-3174 371-8595
Web: www.vdh.virginia.gov/medexam

Child Support Enforcement Div
730 E Broad St .... Richmond VA 23219 800-468-8894
TF: 800-468-8894 ■ *Web:* www.dss.state.va.us

Corrections Dept 6900 Atmore Dr .... Richmond VA 23225 804-674-3000 674-3509
Web: vadoc.virginia.gov

Criminal Injuries Compensation Fund (CICF)
PO Box 26927 .... Richmond VA 23261 800-552-4007 367-1021*
**Fax Area Code:* 804 ■ *TF:* 800-552-4007 ■ *Web:* www.cicf.state.va.us

Economic Development Partnership
901 E Byrd St .... Richmond VA 23219 804-371-8100 371-8112
Web: www.yesvirginia.org

Education Dept PO Box 2120 .... Richmond VA 23218 804-225-2020 371-2099
Web: www.pen.k12.va.us

Emergency Management Dept 10501 Trade Ct .... Richmond VA 23236 804-897-6500 897-6506
Web: vaemergency.gov

Environmental Quality Dept 629 E Main St .... Richmond VA 23240 804-698-4000 698-4500
Web: www.deq.state.va.us

Financial Institutions Bureau
1300 E Main St Ste 800 PO Box 640 .... Richmond VA 23218 804-371-9657 371-9416
Web: www.scc.virginia.gov

Game & Inland Fisheries Dept
4010 W Broad St .... Richmond VA 23230 804-367-1000 367-0405
Web: www.dgif.virginia.gov

General Assembly
General Assembly Bldg 1000 Bank St .... Richmond VA 23219 804-698-1788
Web: virginiageneralassembly.gov

Governor 1111 E Broad St PO Box 1475 .... Richmond VA 23219 804-786-2211 371-6351
TF: 800-828-1120 ■ *Web:* www.governor.virginia.gov

Health Dept 109 Governor St Ste 13 .... Richmond VA 23219 804-864-7001 864-7022
Web: www.vdh.virginia.gov

Health Professions Dept
9960 Mayland Dr Ste 300 .... Henrico VA 23233 804-367-4400 527-4475
TF: 800-533-1560 ■ *Web:* www.dhp.virginia.gov

Historic Resources Dept 2801 Kensington Ave .... Richmond VA 23221 804-367-2323 367-2391
Web: www.dhr.virginia.gov

Housing Development Authority
601 S Belvidere St .... Richmond VA 23220 804-782-1986
TF: 800-968-7837 ■ *Web:* www.vhda.com

Human Resource Management Dept
101 N 14th St 12th Fl .... Richmond VA 23219 804-225-2131 371-7401
Web: www.dhrm.virginia.gov

Information Technologies Agency (VITA)
11751 Meadowville Ln .... Chester VA 23836 866-637-8482 416-6355*
**Fax Area Code:* 804 ■ *TF:* 866-637-8482 ■ *Web:* www.vita.virginia.gov

Labor & Industry Dept
Main St Centre Bldg 600 E Main St Ste 207 .... Richmond VA 23219 804-371-2327 371-6524
Web: www.doli.virginia.gov

Lieutenant Governor 102 Governor St 1st Fl W .... Richmond VA 23219 804-786-2078 786-7514
Web: www.ltgov.virginia.gov

Mental Health Mental Retardation & Substance Abuse Services Dept
1220 Bank St .... Richmond VA 23219 804-786-3921 371-6638
Web: www.dbhds.virginia.gov

Parole Board 6900 Atmore Dr .... Richmond VA 23225 804-674-3081 674-3284
Web: vpb.virginia.gov

Professional & Occupational Regulation Dept
9960 Mayland Dr # 400 .... Richmond VA 23233 804-367-8500
Web: www.dpor.virginia.gov

Racing Commission 10700 Horsemen's Rd .... New Kent VA 23124 804-966-7400 966-7418
Web: www.vrc.virginia.gov

Secretary of Commerce and Trade
1111 E Broad St PO Box 1475 .... Richmond VA 23219 804-786-7831 371-0250
Web: www.commerce.virginia.gov

Secretary of the Commonwealth
830 E Main St 14th Fl .... Richmond VA 23219 804-786-2441 371-0017
Web: commonwealth.virginia.gov

Social Services Dept 801 E Main St .... Richmond VA 23219 804-726-7000
Web: www.dss.state.va.us

State Corp Commission
1300 E Main St PO Box 1197 .... Richmond VA 23218 804-371-9967 371-9836
Web: www.scc.virginia.gov

State Parks Div 203 Governor St Ste 306 .... Richmond VA 23219 800-933-7275
TF Resv: 800-933-7275 ■ *Web:* dcr.virginia.gov/state-parks

State Police 7700 Midlothian Tpke .... Richmond VA 23235 804-674-2000 674-2936
Web: www.vsp.state.va.us

Supreme Court 100 N Ninth St .... Richmond VA 23219 804-786-2251 786-6249
Web: vcsc.virginia.gov

Taxation Dept 3610 W Broad St Ste 101 .... Richmond VA 23230 804-367-8031 786-3536
Web: www.tax.virginia.gov

Treasury Dept 101 N 14th St Ste 4th .... Richmond VA 23219 804-225-2142 225-3187
Web: www.trs.virginia.gov

Phone Fax

Virginia Community College System
101 N 14th St 15th Fl .... Richmond VA 23219 804-819-4901 819-4766
Web: www.vccs.edu

Virginia Employment Commission
703 E Main St .... Richmond VA 23219 804-786-1485 225-3923
Web: www.vec.virginia.gov

Virginia Lottery 900 E Main St .... Richmond VA 23219 804-692-7777 692-7775
Web: www.valottery.com

Virginia Port Authority 101 W Main St .... Norfolk VA 23510 757-683-8000 683-8500
Web: www.portofvirginia.com

Virginia State Council of Higher Education
101 N 14th St 9th Fl .... Richmond VA 23219 804-225-2600 225-2604
Web: www.schev.edu

Vital Records Div
2001 Maywill St PO Box 1000 .... Richmond VA 23230 804-662-6200 644-2550
TF: 877-572-6333 ■ *Web:* www.vdh.virginia.gov/vitalrec

Workers Compensation Commission 1000 DMV Dr .... Richmond VA 23220 804-205-3603 367-9740
Web: www.vwc.state.va.us

339-48 Washington

Phone Fax

Administrative Office of the Courts
1112 Quince St SE PO Box 41174 .... Olympia WA 98501 360-753-3365

Aging & Disability Services Administration
PO Box 45600 .... Olympia WA 98504 360-725-2300 407-0369
Web: www.altsa.dshs.wa.gov

Agriculture Dept PO Box 42560 .... Olympia WA 98504 360-902-1800 902-2092
Web: www.agr.wa.gov

Arts Commission 711 Capitol Way S Ste 600 .... Olympia WA 98504 360-753-3860 586-5351
Web: www.arts.wa.gov

Attorney General PO Box 40100 .... Olympia WA 98504 360-753-6200 664-0228
Web: www.atg.wa.gov

Child Support Div PO Box 11520 .... Olympia WA 98411 800-442-5437 586-3274*
**Fax Area Code:* 360 ■ *TF:* 800-442-5437 ■ *Web:* www.dshs.wa.gov

Consumer Protection Div
1125 Washington St SE PO Box 40100 .... Olympia WA 98504 360-753-6200
Web: www.atg.wa.gov/page.aspx?id=1792

Corrections Dept PO Box 41100 .... Olympia WA 98504 360-725-8213 664-4056
Web: www.doc.wa.gov

Ecology Dept PO Box 47600 .... Olympia WA 98504 360-407-6000 407-6989
Web: www.ecy.wa.gov

Emergency Management Div
20 Aviation Dr Bldg 20 TA-20 .... Camp Murray WA 98430 253-512-7000
Web: mil.wa.gov

Financial Institutions Dept PO Box 41200 .... Olympia WA 98504 360-902-8703
TF: 877-746-4334 ■ *Web:* www.dfi.wa.gov/cs

Fish & Wildlife Dept 600 Capitol Way N .... Olympia WA 98501 360-902-2200 902-2156
Web: www.wdfw.wa.gov

Governor PO Box 40002 .... Olympia WA 98504 360-902-4111 753-4110
Web: www.governor.wa.gov

Health Dept PO Box 47890 .... Olympia WA 98504 360-236-4501 586-7424
TF: 800-525-0127 ■ *Web:* www.doh.wa.gov

Historical Society 1911 Pacific Ave .... Tacoma WA 98402 253-272-3500 272-9518
TF: 888-238-4373 ■ *Web:* www.washingtonhistory.org

Housing Finance Commission
1000 Second Ave Ste 2700 .... Seattle WA 98104 206-464-7139 587-5113
TF: 800-767-4663 ■ *Web:* www.wshfc.org

Indeterminate Sentence Review Board
PO Box 40907 .... Olympia WA 98504 360-493-9266 493-9287
Web: www.doc.wa.gov

Information Services Dept PO Box 42445 .... Olympia WA 98504 360-902-3550
Web: www.governor.wa.gov

Insurance Commissioner PO Box 40255 .... Olympia WA 98504 360-725-7000 586-3535
Web: www.insurance.wa.gov

Labor & Industries Dept PO Box 44000 .... Olympia WA 98504 360-902-5800 902-4202
Web: www.lni.wa.gov

Legislature 106 Legislative Bldg .... Olympia WA 98504 360-786-7550 786-7520
Web: www.leg.wa.gov

Licensing Dept PO Box 9020 .... Olympia WA 98504 360-902-3600 902-4042
Web: www.dol.wa.gov

Lieutenant Governor 416 Sid Snyder Ave SW .... Olympia WA 98501 360-786-7700 786-7749
Web: www.ltgov.wa.gov

Natural Resources Dept
1111 Washington St SE PO Box 47000 .... Olympia WA 98504 360-902-1000
TF: 800-258-5990 ■ *Web:* www.dnr.wa.gov

Office of Superindent Public Instruction Dept
600 Washington St SE PO Box 47200 .... Olympia WA 98504 360-725-6000 753-6712
Web: www.k12.wa.us

Personnel Dept
1500 Jefferson St S PO Box 44530 .... Olympia WA 98504 360-407-9100 407-9178
Web: www.hr.wa.gov

Professional Educator Standards Board
PO Box 47236 .... Olympia WA 98504 360-725-6275 586-4548
Web: www.pesb.wa.gov

Revenue Dept PO Box 47478 .... Olympia WA 98504 360-705-6714 705-6655
TF: 800-647-7706 ■ *Web:* dor.wa.gov

Secretary of State PO Box 40220 .... Olympia WA 98504 360-902-4151 586-5629
Web: www.sos.wa.gov

Securities Div PO Box 9033 .... Olympia WA 98507 360-902-8760 902-0524
Web: www.dfi.wa.gov/sd

Social & Health Services Dept PO Box 45130 .... Olympia WA 98504 360-902-8400 902-7848
TF: 800-737-0617 ■ *Web:* www.wa.gov/dshs

State Parks & Recreation Commission
1111 Israel Rd SW .... Olympia WA 98504 360-902-8500
TF Campground Resv: 888-226-7688 ■ *Web:* www.parks.wa.gov

State Patrol PO Box 42600 .... Olympia WA 98504 360-753-6540 704-2297*
**Fax:* Hum Res ■ *Web:* www.wsp.wa.gov

Supreme Court 415 12th Ave SW .... Olympia WA 98501 360-357-2077
Web: www.courts.wa.gov

Transportation Dept PO Box 47300 .... Olympia WA 98504 360-705-7000 705-6800
Web: www.wsdot.wa.gov

Phone Fax

Treasurer
416 Sid Snyder Ave SW Rm 230 PO Box 40200 . . . . Olympia WA 98504 360-902-9000 902-9044
Web: www.tre.wa.gov
Utilities & Transportation Commission
1300 S Evergreen Pk Dr SW PO Box 47250 . . . . Olympia WA 98504 360-664-1160 664-1150
TF: 888-333-9882 ■ *Web:* www.utc.wa.gov
Veterans Affairs Dept PO Box 41150 . . . . Olympia WA 98504 360-753-5586 725-2197
TF: 800-562-2308 ■ *Web:* www.dva.wa.gov
Vital Records Div PO Box 47814 . . . . Olympia WA 98504 360-236-4300
Web: www.cdc.gov/nchs/w2w.htm
Vocational Rehabilitation Div PO Box 45340 . . . . Olympia WA 98504 360-438-8000 438-8007
TF: 800-637-5627 ■ *Web:* www.dshs.wa.gov
Washington Bill Status PO Box 40600 . . . . Olympia WA 98504 360-786-7573
TF: 800-562-6000 ■ *Web:* www.leg.wa.gov
Washington Employment Security Dept
212 Maple Pk Ave SE . . . . Olympia WA 98504 360-902-9500
Web: www.esd.wa.gov
Washington Higher Education Coordinating Board
917 Lakeridge Way PO Box 43430 . . . . Olympia WA 98504 360-753-7800 753-7808
Web: www.wsac.wa.gov
Washington Horse Racing Commission
6326 Martin Way Ste 209 . . . . Olympia WA 98516 360-459-6462 459-6461
Web: www.whrc.wa.gov
Washington Public Disclosure Commission
PO Box 40908 . . . . Olympia WA 98504 360-753-1111 753-1112
Web: www.pdc.wa.gov
Washington State Lottery PO Box 43000 . . . . Olympia WA 98504 360-664-4720 664-2630
TF: 800-732-5101 ■ *Web:* www.walottery.com

339-49 West Virginia

Phone Fax

State Government Information 100 Dee Dr . . . . Charleston WV 25311 304-558-3456
Web: www.wv.gov
Accountancy Board 405 Capitol St Ste 908 . . . . Charleston WV 25301 304-558-3557 558-1325
Web: www.boa.wv.gov
Administrative Office of the Courts
1900 Kanawha Blvd E Bldg 1 Rm E-100 . . . . Charleston WV 25305 304-558-0145 558-1212
Web: www.state.wv.us
Agriculture Dept
1900 Kanawha Blvd E Bldg 1 Rm E-28 . . . . Charleston WV 25305 304-558-2201 558-2203
Web: www.wvagriculture.org
Arts Commission
1900 Kanawha Blvd E Cultural Ctr . . . . Charleston WV 25305 304-558-0220 558-2779
Web: www.wvculture.org/arts
Attorney General
1900 Kanawha Blvd E Bldg 1 Rm 26-E . . . . Charleston WV 25305 304-558-2021 558-0140
Web: ago.wv.gov
Board of Medicine 101 Dee Dr Ste 103 . . . . Charleston WV 25311 304-558-2921 558-2084
Web: www.wvdhhr.org
Bureau for Public Health
350 Capitol St Rm 702 . . . . Charleston WV 25301 304-558-2971 558-1035
Web: www.wvdhhr.org/bph
Child Support Enforcement Bureau
231 Capitol St Ste 111 . . . . Charleston WV 25301 304-347-8688 720-9666
TF: 800-571-4864 ■ *Web:* www.wv-childsupport.com
Children & Families Bureau
350 Capitol St Rm R-730 . . . . Charleston WV 25301 304-558-0628 558-4194
TF: 800-642-8589 ■ *Web:* www.wvdhhr.org/bcf
Community Development Div
1900 Kanawha Blvd E . . . . Charleston WA 25311 304-558-2234
TF: 800-982-3386 ■ *Web:* www.wvcommerce.org
Consumer Protection Div
812 Quarrier St 1st Fl . . . . Charleston WV 25301 304-558-8986 558-0184
TF: 800-368-8808 ■ *Web:* www.ago.wv.gov
Corrections Div
112 California Ave Bldg 4 Rm 300 . . . . Charleston WV 25305 304-558-2036 558-5367
Web: www.wvdoc.com
Crime Victims Compensation Fund
1900 Kanawha Blvd E Rm W-334 . . . . Charleston WV 25305 304-347-4850 347-4915
TF: 877-562-6878 ■ *Web:* www.legis.state.wv.us
Dept of Revenue
State Capitol Bldg 1 Rm W-300 . . . . Charleston WV 25305 304-558-1017 558-2324
Web: www.revenue.wv.gov
Development Office
1900 Kanawah Blvd E Bldg 6 Rm 525B . . . . Charleston WV 25305 304-558-2234 558-1189
TF: 800-982-3386 ■ *Web:* www.wvcommerce.org
Div of Natural Resources (DNR)
324 Fourth Ave Bldg 74 . . . . South Charleston WV 25303 304-558-2754 558-2768
Web: www.wvdnr.gov
Education Dept
1900 Kanawha Blvd E Bldg 6 Rm 358 . . . . Charleston WV 25305 304-558-2681 558-0048
Emergency Services Office
1900 Kanawha Blvd E . . . . Charleston WV 25305 304-558-5380
Environmental Protection Dept
601 57th St SE . . . . Charleston WV 25304 304-926-0440 926-0446
Web: www.dep.wv.gov
Historic Preservation Unit
1900 Kanawha Blvd E . . . . Charleston WV 25305 304-558-0220 558-2779
Web: www.wvculture.org/shpo
Housing Development Fund
814 Virginia St E . . . . Charleston WV 25301 304-345-6475
TF: 800-933-9843 ■ *Web:* www.wvhdf.com
Insurance Commission PO Box 50540 . . . . Charleston WV 25305 304-558-3354 558-0412
TF: 888-879-9842 ■ *Web:* www.wvinsurance.gov
Labor Div Capitol Complex 749 B Bldg 6 . . . . Charleston WV 25305 304-558-7890 558-2415
Web: wvlabor.com
Motor Vehicles Div
5707 Maccorkle Ave SE Ste 400 . . . . Charleston WV 25304 304-558-3900
TF: 800-642-9066 ■ *Web:* www.transportation.wv.gov
Office of Governor
State Capitol Bldg 1900 Kanawha Blvd E . . . . Charleston WV 25305 304-558-2000 558-1558
Web: www.governor.wv.gov
Office of Technology 321-323 Capitol St . . . . Charleston WV 25304 304-558-5472
Web: www.technology.wv.gov
Probation & Parole Board
1409 Greenbrier Ste 220 . . . . Charleston WV 25311 304-558-6366 558-5678
Web: paroleboard.wv.gov
Public Service Commission
208 Brooke St PO Box 812 . . . . Charleston WV 25301 304-340-0300 340-0325
TF: 800-344-5113 ■ *Web:* www.psc.state.wv.us
Real Estate Commission
300 Capitol St Ste 400 . . . . Charleston WV 25301 304-558-3555 558-6442
Web: www.wvrec.org
Rehabilitation Services Div
107 Capitol St . . . . Charleston WV 25301 800-642-8207 642-3021
TF: 800-642-8207 ■ *Web:* www.wvdrs.org
Secretary of State
1900 Kanawha Blvd E Bldg 1 Ste 157K . . . . Charleston WV 25305 304-558-6000 558-0900
TF: 866-767-8683 ■ *Web:* www.sos.wv.gov
Securities Div
1900 Kanawha Blvd E Bldg 1 Rm W-100 . . . . Charleston WV 25305 304-558-2257 558-4211
TF: 877-982-9148 ■ *Web:* www.wvsao.gov
State Legislature
State Capitol Complex Rm MB-27 Bldg 1 . . . . Charleston WV 25305 304-347-4836 347-4901
Web: www.legis.state.wv.us
State Parks and Forests 324 4th Ave . . . . Charleston WV 25305 304-558-2764 558-0077
TF: 800-225-5982 ■ *Web:* www.wvstateparks.com
State Police 725 Jefferson Rd . . . . South Charleston WV 25309 304-746-2100
Web: www.wvsp.gov
Supreme Court of Appeals
1900 Kanawha Blvd E Bldg 1 Rm E-317 . . . . Charleston WV 25305 304-558-2601 558-3815
Web: www.courtswv.gov
Tourism Div 90 MacCorkle Ave SW . . . . Charleston WV 25303 800-225-5982
TF: 800-225-5982 ■ *Web:* www.wvtourism.com
Transportation Dept
1900 Kanawha Blvd E Bldg 5 Rm A-109 . . . . Charleston WV 25305 304-558-0444 558-1004
Web: www.wv.gov
Treasurer
1900 Kanawha Blvd E Bldg 1 Ste E-145 . . . . Charleston WV 25305 304-558-5000 558-4097
TF: 800-422-7498 ■ *Web:* www.wvsto.com
Veterans Affairs Div 1321 Plaza E Ste 101 . . . . Charleston WV 25301 304-558-3661 558-3662
TF: 888-838-2332 ■ *Web:* www.veterans.idaho.gov
Vital Statistics 350 Capitol St Rm 165 . . . . Charleston WV 25301 304-558-2931 558-1051
Web: www.wvdhhr.org/bph/oehp/hsc/vr/birtcert.htm
Weights & Measures Div
570 W MacCorkle Ave . . . . Saint Albans WV 25177 304-722-0602 722-0605
West Virginia Bill Status
State Capitol Complex Rm MB27 Bldg 1 . . . . Charleston WV 25305 304-347-4836 347-4901
TF: 877-565-3447 ■ *Web:* www.legis.state.wv.us
West Virginia Ethics Commission
210 Brooks St Ste 300 . . . . Charleston WV 25301 304-558-0664 558-2169
TF: 866-558-0664 ■ *Web:* www.ethics.wv.gov
West Virginia Higher Education Policy Commission
1018 Kanawha Blvd E Ste 700 . . . . Charleston WV 25301 304-558-2101
TF: 888-825-5707 ■ *Web:* wvhepc.com
West Virginia Lottery
900 Pennsylvania Ave . . . . Charleston WV 25302 304-558-0500
Web: www.wvlottery.com
West Virginia Racing Commission
900 Pennsylvania Ave Ste 533 . . . . Charleston WV 25302 304-558-2150 558-6319
Web: www.racing.wv.gov

339-50 Wisconsin

Phone Fax

Aging & Long Term Care Resources Bureau
PO Box 7851 . . . . Madison WI 53707 608-266-2536 267-3203
Web: www.dhs.wisconsin.gov
Agriculture Trade & Consumer Protection Dept
PO Box 8911 . . . . Madison WI 53708 608-224-4889
Web: datcp.wi.gov
Attorney General PO Box 7857 . . . . Madison WI 53707 608-266-1221 267-2779
Web: www.doj.state.wi.us
Board of Regents
1220 Linden Dr 1860 Van Hise Hall . . . . Madison WI 53706 608-262-2324 262-5739
Web: www.wisconsin.edu/bor
Child Support Bureau 201 E Washington Ave . . . . Madison WI 53703 608-266-9909 267-2824
Web: dcf.wisconsin.gov/bcs
Children & Family Services Div
201 E Washington Ave Second Fl PO Box 8916 . . . . Madison WI 53708 608-267-3905 266-6836
Web: www.dcf.wi.gov
Consumer Protection Office
2811 Agriculture Dr PO Box 8911 . . . . Madison WI 53708 608-224-5012
Web: datcp.wi.gov
Corrections Dept PO Box 7925 . . . . Madison WI 53707 608-240-5000 240-3300
Web: doc.wi.gov
Crime Victims Services Office PO Box 7951 . . . . Madison WI 53707 608-264-9497 264-6368
TF: 800-446-6564 ■ *Web:* www.doj.state.wi.us
Department of Safety & Professional Services
PO Box 8935 . . . . Madison WI 53708 608-266-2112 267-0644
Web: dsps.wi.gov
Director of State Courts
16E Capitol Bldg PO Box 1688 . . . . Madison WI 53701 608-266-6828 267-0980
Web: www.wicourts.gov
Economic Development Div
201 W Washington Ave . . . . Madison WI 53703 608-210-6700
Web: inwisconsin.com
Emergency Management Div PO Box 7865 . . . . Madison WI 53707 608-242-3232 242-3247
Web: www.emergencymanagement.wi.gov
Fisheries Management PO Box 7921 . . . . Madison WI 53707 608-267-7498 266-2244
Web: dnr.wi.gov/topic/Fishing
Health Professions Bureau
Dept of Regulation & Licensing PO Box 8935 . . . . Madison WI 53708 608-266-2112 261-7083
Web: dsps.wi.gov

				Phone	Fax
Health Services Dept PO Box 7850	Madison	WI	53707	608-266-1865	266-7882
Web: www.dhs.wisconsin.gov					
Historical Society 816 State St.	Madison	WI	53706	608-264-6400	
Web: www.wisconsinhistory.org					
Housing & Economic Development Authority					
201 W Washington Ave Ste 700	Madison	WI	53703	608-266-7884	267-1099
TF: 800-334-6873 ■ *Web:* www.wheda.com					
Insurance Commission PO Box 7873	Madison	WI	53707	608-266-3585	266-9935
TF: 800-236-8517 ■ *Web:* www.oci.wi.gov					
Legislature State Capitol	Madison	WI	53702	608-266-9960	
TF: 800-362-9472 ■ *Web:* legis.wisconsin.gov					
Lieutenant Governor 19 E State Capitol	Madison	WI	53702	608-266-3516	267-3571
Web: legis.wisconsin.gov					
Motor Vehicles Div 4802 Sheboygan Ave	Madison	WI	53707	608-266-2233	
Web: www.dot.wisconsin.gov/drivers					
Natural Resources Dept					
101 S Webster St PO Box 7921	Madison	WI	53707	608-266-2621	261-4380
Web: dnr.wi.gov					
Office of Governor PO Box 7863	Madison	WI	53707	608-266-1212	267-8983
Web: walker.wi.gov					
Parks & Recreation Bureau					
101 S Webster St PO Box 7921	Madison	WI	53707	608-266-2621	261-4380
TF: 888-936-7463 ■ *Web:* dnr.wi.gov					
Public Instruction Dept					
125 S Webster St PO Box 7841	Madison	WI	53707	608-266-3390	
TF: 800-441-4563 ■ *Web:* www.dpi.state.wi.us					
Public Service Commission					
PO Box 610 N Whitney Way	Madison	WI	53707	608-266-5481	266-3957
Web: psc.wi.gov					
Revenue Dept 2135 Rimrock Rd PO Box 8933	Madison	WI	53708	608-266-6466	266-5718
Web: www.dor.state.wi.us					
Secretary of State 30 W Mifflin Fl 10	Madison	WI	53703	608-266-8888	266-3159
Web: www.sos.state.wi.us					
Securities Div 201 W Washington Ave	Madison	WI	53703	608-266-1064	
State Patrol Div PO Box 7912	Madison	WI	53707	608-266-3212	267-4495
Web: www.dot.wisconsin.gov/statepatrol					
Supreme Court					
110 E Main St Ste 215 PO Box 1688	Madison	WI	53701	608-266-1880	267-0640
Web: www.wicourts.gov					
Teacher Education & Licensing Bureau					
125 S Webster St	Madison	WI	53703	608-266-3390	264-9558
TF: 800-441-4563 ■ *Web:* www.dpi.state.wi.us					
Treasurer PO Box 2114	Madison	WI	53707	855-375-2274	261-6799*
**Fax Area Code:* 608 ■ *TF:* 855-375-2274 ■ *Web:* www.ost.state.wi.us					
Veterans Affairs Dept					
201 W Washington Ave PO Box 7843	Madison	WI	53703	608-266-1311	267-0403
TF: 800-947-8387 ■ *Web:* www.dva.state.wi.us					
Vital Records Office PO Box 309	Madison	WI	53701	608-266-1373	255-2035
Web: www.dhs.wisconsin.gov					
Vocational Rehabilitation Div					
201 East Washington Avenue PO Box 7852	Madison	WI	53707	608-261-0050	266-1133
TF: 800-442-3477 ■ *Web:* dwd.wisconsin.gov					
Wisconsin Bill Status 1 E Main St.	Madison	WI	53708	608-266-9960	
TF: 800-362-9472 ■ *Web:* legis.wisconsin.gov					
Wisconsin Ethics Board					
212 E Washington Ave 3rd Fl	Madison	WI	53703	608-266-8123	264-9319
Web: www.gab.wi.gov					
Wisconsin Lottery PO Box 8941	Madison	WI	53708	608-261-4916	264-6644
Web: www.wilottery.com					
Wisconsin Workforce Development Dept					
201 E Washington Ave	Madison	WI	53702	608-266-3131	266-1784
Web: dwd.wisconsin.gov					
Worker's Compensation Div PO Box 7901	Madison	WI	53707	608-266-1340	267-0394
Web: dwd.wisconsin.gov					

339-51 Wyoming

				Phone	Fax
State Government Information					
State Capitol Bldg 200 W 24th St	Cheyenne	WY	82002	307-777-7841	777-6869
Web: ag.wyo.gov					
Aging Div 6101 Yellowstone Rd N Rm 259B	Cheyenne	WY	82002	307-777-7986	777-5340
TF: 800-442-2766 ■ *Web:* health.wyo.gov					
Agriculture Dept (WDA) 2219 Carey Ave	Cheyenne	WY	82002	307-777-7321	777-6593
Web: wyagric.state.wy.us					
Arts Council 2320 Capitol Ave	Cheyenne	WY	82002	307-777-7742	777-5499
Web: wyoarts.state.wy.us					
Banking Div					
122 W 25th St Herschler Bldg 3rd Fl E	Cheyenne	WY	82002	307-777-7797	777-3555
Web: audit.wyo.gov					
Board of Medicine 130 Hobbs Ave Ste A	Cheyenne	WY	82001	307-778-7053	778-2069
Web: wyomedboard.state.wy.us					
Business Council 214 W 15th St	Cheyenne	WY	82002	307-777-2800	777-2838
Web: www.wyomingbusiness.org					
Certified Public Accountants Board					
325 W 18th St Ste 4	Cheyenne	WY	82002	307-777-7551	777-3796
Community Development Authority PO Box 634	Casper	WY	82602	307-265-0603	266-5414
Web: www.wyomingcda.com					
Consumer Protection Unit 122 W 25th St	Cheyenne	WY	82001	307-777-7874	777-7956
Web: ag.wyo.gov					
Corrections Dept 1934 Wyott Dr Ste 100	Cheyenne	WY	82002	307-777-7208	777-7846
Web: corrections.wy.gov					
Education Dept 2300 Capitol Ave 2nd Fl	Cheyenne	WY	82002	307-777-7675	777-6234
Web: www.edu.wyoming.gov					
Environmental Quality Dept					
122 W 25th St Herschler Bldg	Cheyenne	WY	82002	307-777-7937	777-7682
Web: deq.state.wy.us					
Family Services Dept					
2300 Capitol Ave 3rd Fl Hathaway Bldg	Cheyenne	WY	82002	307-777-7561	777-7747
Web: dfsweb.wyo.gov					
Game & Fish Dept 5400 Bishop Blvd	Cheyenne	WY	82006	307-777-4600	777-4610
Web: wgfd.wyo.gov					
Governor State Capitol 200 W 24th St Rm 124	Cheyenne	WY	82002	307-777-7434	632-3909
Web: governor.wyo.gov					
Health Dept 2300 Capitol Ave Ste 401	Cheyenne	WY	82002	307-777-7656	777-7439
Web: health.wyo.gov					
Highway Patrol (WHP) 5300 Bishop Blvd	Cheyenne	WY	82009	307-777-4301	777-3897
TF: 800-442-9090 ■ *Web:* www.whp.dot.state.wy.us					
Historic Preservation Office					
2301 Central Ave 3rd Fl	Cheyenne	WY	82002	307-777-7697	777-6421
Web: wyoshpo.state.wy.us					
Homeland Security Office					
5500 Bishop Blvd E Door	Cheyenne	WY	82002	307-777-4663	635-6017
Web: wyohomelandsecurity.state.wy.us					
Information Technology Div 2001 Capitol Ave.	Cheyenne	WY	82001	307-777-5003	
Insurance Dept 106 E Sixth Ave	Cheyenne	WY	82001	307-777-7401	777-2446
Web: doi.wyo.gov					
Legislature 213 State Capitol	Cheyenne	WY	82002	307-777-7881	777-5466
Web: legisweb.state.wy.us					
Motor Vehicles Services Div					
5300 Bishop Blvd	Cheyenne	WY	82009	307-777-4375	777-4772
Web: www.dot.state.wy.us					
Probation & Parole Div 700 W 21st St Ste 200	Cheyenne	WY	82001	307-777-7208	
Professional Teaching Standards Board					
1920 Thomes Ave Ste 400	Cheyenne	WY	82002	307-777-7291	
Web: uwyo.edu					
Public Service Commission					
2515 Warren Ave Ste 300	Cheyenne	WY	82002	307-777-7427	777-5700
Web: psc.state.wy.us					
Real Estate Commission					
2020 Carey Ave Ste 702	Cheyenne	WY	82002	307-777-7141	777-3796
Web: www.wyoming.gov					
Revenue Dept Herschler Bldg 2nd Fl W	Cheyenne	WY	82002	307-777-7961	777-7722
Web: revenue.wyo.gov					
Secretary of State 200 W 24th St	Cheyenne	WY	82002	307-777-7378	777-6217
Web: soswy.state.wy.us					
Securities Div 200 W 24th St	Cheyenne	WY	82002	307-777-7370	777-7640
Web: soswy.state.wy.us					
State Parks & Historical Sites Div					
2301 Central Ave	Cheyenne	WY	82002	307-777-6323	
TF: 877-996-7275 ■ *Web:* wyoparks.state.wy.us					
Supreme Court 2301 Capitol Ave	Cheyenne	WY	82002	307-777-7316	777-6129
Web: courts.state.wy.us					
Technical Services Div 2219 Carey Ave	Cheyenne	WY	82001	307-777-7324	777-6593
Web: wyagric.state.wy.us					
Tourism Div 1520 Etchepare Cir.	Cheyenne	WY	82007	307-777-7777	777-2877
TF: 800-225-5996 ■ *Web:* www.wyomingtourism.org					
Transportation Dept 5300 Bishop Blvd	Cheyenne	WY	82009	307-777-4375	777-4163
Web: www.dot.state.wy.us					
Treasurer 200 W 24th St	Cheyenne	WY	82002	307-777-7408	
Web: treasurer.state.wy.us					
Victims Services Div 200 W 24th St Ste 110	Cheyenne	WY	82001	307-777-7200	
Web: ag.wyo.gov					
Vital Records Services Hathaway Bldg	Cheyenne	WY	82002	307-777-7591	
Web: health.wyo.gov					
Vocational Rehabilitation Div					
1510 East Pershing Blvd Ste 1100	Cheyenne	WY	82002	307-777-3700	777-5939
Web: www.wyomingworkforce.org					
Workers'' Safety & Compensation Div					
1510 E Pershing Blvd	Cheyenne	WY	82002	307-777-7159	
Web: wyomingsafety.org					
Workforce Services Dept					
122 W 25th St 2nd Fl E	Cheyenne	WY	82002	307-777-8650	777-7106
Web: www.wyomingworkforce.org					
Wyoming Community College Commission					
2300 Capitol Ave Fl 5 Ste B	Cheyenne	WY	82002	307-777-7763	777-6567
Web: communitycolleges.wy.edu					
Wyoming Legislative Service Office					
3001 E Pershing Blvd	Cheyenne	WY	82002	307-777-7881	777-5466
TF: 800-342-9570 ■ *Web:* legisweb.state.wy.us					

340 GOVERNMENT - US - EXECUTIVE BRANCH

See Also Cemeteries - National p. 1897; Coast Guard Installations p. 1947; Correctional Facilities - Federal p. 2162; Military Bases p. 2770; Parks - National - US p. 2871

				Phone	Fax
Office of the President					
1600 Pennsylvania Ave NW	Washington	DC	20500	202-456-1414	456-2461
Web: www.whitehouse.gov					
Office of the Vice President					
1650 Pennsylvania Ave NW	Washington	DC	20501	202-456-4444	
Web: whitehouse.gov/administration/vice-president-biden					
Council of Economic Advisers					
732 N Capitol St NW	Washington	DC	20401	202-512-1800	
Web: www.whitehouse.gov					
Council on Environmental Quality					
722 Jackson Pl NW	Washington	DC	20506	202-395-5750	456-0753
Web: www.whitehouse.gov/ceq					
Domestic Policy Council					
1600 Pennsylvania Ave NW	Washington	DC	20500	202-456-1111	
Web: whitehouse.gov/administration/eop/dpc					
National Economic Council					
1600 Pennsylvania Ave NW	Washington	DC	20500	202-456-1111	
Web: www.whitehouse.gov/nec					
National Security Council (NSC)					
1600 Pennsylvania Ave NW	Washington	DC	20500	202-456-1414	
Web: www.whitehouse.gov/nsc					
Office of Management & Budget (OMB)					
725 17th St NW	Washington	DC	20503	202-395-3080	395-3888
Web: www.whitehouse.gov/omb					
Office of National AIDS Policy (ONAP)					
The White House	Washington	DC	20502	202-456-4533	
Web: www.whitehouse.gov/onap/aids.html					

Office of Science & Technology Policy
1650 Pennsylvania Ave. ... Washington DC 20504 | Phone: 202-456-4444
Web: www.whitehouse.gov

Office of the US Trade Representative
600 17th St NW ... Washington DC 20508 | Phone: 202-395-7360
Web: www.ustr.gov

President's Foreign Intelligence Advisory Board (PIAB)
White House 1600 Pennsylvania Ave ... Washington DC 20500 | Phone: 202-456-1414 | Fax: 456-2461
Web: www.whitehouse.gov/administration/eop/piab

USA Freedom Corps 1201 New York Ave NW ... Washington DC 20005 | Phone: 202-606-5000
TF: 800-833-3722 ■ *Web:* www.nationalservice.gov

White House Press Secretary
1600 Pennsylvania Ave NW ... Washington DC 20500 | Phone: 202-456-1111 | Fax: 456-2461
Web: www.whitehouse.gov

340-1 US Department of Agriculture

Department of Agriculture (USDA)
1400 Independence Ave SW ... Washington DC 20250 | Phone: 202-720-3631 | Fax: 720-2166
TF: 844-433-2774 ■ *Web:* www.usda.gov

Agricultural Marketing Service
1400 Independence Ave SW ... Washington DC 20250 | Phone: 202-720-5115 | Fax: 720-8477
Web: www.ams.usda.gov

Agricultural Research Service
US Dept of Agriculture
1400 Independence Ave SW ... Washington DC 20250 | Phone: 202-720-3656 | Fax: 720-5427
Web: www.ars.usda.gov

Animal & Plant Health Inspection Service (APHIS)
National Veterinary Services Laboratories
2300 Dayton Ave ... Ames IA 50010 | Phone: 515-663-7200
Web: www.aphis.usda.gov

Center for Nutrition Policy & Promotion (CNPP)
3101 Pk Ctr Dr 10th Fl ... Alexandria VA 22302 | Phone: 703-305-7600 | Fax: 305-3300
TF: 888-779-7264 ■ *Web:* www.cnpp.usda.gov

Co-op State Research Education & Extension Service
1400 Independence Ave SW Ste 2201 ... Washington DC 20250 | Phone: 202-401-4952 | Fax: 720-6486
Web: nifa.usda.gov

Economic Research Service (ERS)
US Dept of Agriculture 1800 M St NW ... Washington DC 20036 | Phone: 202-694-5050 | Fax: 694-5757
Web: www.ers.usda.gov

Farm Service Agency
1400 Independence Ave SW ... Washington DC 20250 | Phone: 202-720-3865
Web: www.fsa.usda.gov

Food & Nutrition Service 3101 Pk Ctr Dr ... Alexandria VA 22302 | Phone: 703-305-2062 | Fax: 305-2908
Web: www.fns.usda.gov
Food Stamp Program 3101 Pk Ctr Dr ... Alexandria VA 22302 | Phone: 703-305-2022 | Fax: 305-2454
TF: 800-221-5689 ■ *Web:* www.fns.usda.gov
Western Region 90 7th St Ste 10-100 ... San Francisco CA 94103 | Phone: 415-705-1310 | Fax: 705-1364
Web: www.fns.usda.gov

Food & Nutrition Service Regional Offices (FNS)
Mid-Atlantic Region 300 Corporate Blvd ... Robbinsville NJ 08691 | Phone: 609-259-5025 | Fax: 259-5185
Web: fns.usda.gov
Midwest Region 77 W Jackson Blvd 20th Fl ... Chicago IL 60604 | Phone: 312-353-6664 | Fax: 886-2475
Web: www.fns.usda.gov
Mountain Plains Region 1244 Speer Blvd Ste 903 ... Denver CO 80204 | Phone: 303-844-0300 | Fax: 844-2160
Web: www.fns.usda.gov
Northeast Region
10 Cswy St Rm 501 Federal Bldg ... Boston MA 02222 | Phone: 617-565-6370 | Fax: 565-6473
Web: www.fns.usda.gov
Southeast Region 61 Forsyth St SW Ste 8T36 ... Atlanta GA 30303 | Phone: 404-562-1801 | Fax: 562-1807
Web: www.fns.usda.gov/fns-regional-offices
Southwest Region 1100 Commerce St Rm 522 ... Dallas TX 75242 | Phone: 214-290-9800 | Fax: 767-0271
Web: www.fns.usda.gov

Food Safety & Inspection Service
1400 Independence Ave SW Rm 331E ... Washington DC 20250 | Phone: 202-720-7025 | Fax: 205-0158
Web: www.fsis.usda.gov

Foreign Agricultural Service
1400 Independence Ave SW ... Washington DC 20250 | Phone: 202-720-3935 | Fax: 690-2159
Web: www.fas.usda.gov

Forest Service (USFS)
1400 Independence Ave SW ... Washington DC 20050 | Phone: 202-205-8333
TF: 800-832-1355 ■ *Web:* www.fs.fed.us

Forest Service Regional Offices
Region 1 (Northern Region) PO Box 7669 ... Missoula MT 59807 | Phone: 406-329-3511 | Fax: 329-3347
Web: www.fs.fed.us
Region 2 (Rocky Mountain Region) 740 Simms St ... Golden CO 80401 | Phone: 303-275-5350 | Fax: 275-5366
Web: www.fs.fed.us
Region 3 (Southwestern Region)
333 Broadway Blvd SE ... Albuquerque NM 87102 | Phone: 505-842-3292
Web: www.fs.fed.us
Region 4 (Intermountain Region) 324 25th St ... Ogden UT 84401 | Phone: 801-625-5306 | Fax: 625-5127
Web: fs.fed.us
Region 5 (Pacific Southwest Region)
1323 Club Dr ... Vallejo CA 94592 | Phone: 707-562-8737
Web: fs.fed.us
Region 6 (Pacific Northwest Region)
333 SW First Ave PO Box 3623 ... Portland OR 97208 | Phone: 503-808-2468 | Fax: 808-2469
Web: fs.fed.us
Region 8 (Southern Region)
1720 Peachtree St Ste 760S ... Atlanta GA 30309 | Phone: 404-347-4177 | Fax: 347-4821
TF: 877-372-7248 ■ *Web:* www.fs.fed.us
Region 9 (Eastern Region)
626 E Wisconsin Ave ... Milwaukee WI 53202 | Phone: 414-297-3600 | Fax: 297-3808
Web: www.fs.fed.us

Grain Inspection Packers & Stockyards Administration
1400 Independence Ave SW Rm 2055-S Bldg ... Washington DC 20250 | Phone: 202-720-0219
Web: www.gipsa.usda.gov

National Agricultural Library
10301 Baltimore Ave Abraham Lincoln Bldg ... Beltsville MD 20705 | Phone: 301-504-5755
Web: www.nal.usda.gov

National Agricultural Statistics Service (NASS)
1400 Independence Ave SW ... Washington DC 20250 | Phone: 202-720-2707 | Fax: 720-9013
TF: 800-727-9540 ■ *Web:* www.nass.usda.gov

Natural Resources Conservation Service
1400 Independence Ave SW Rm 5105A ... Washington DC 20250 | Phone: 202-720-7246 | Fax: 720-7690
Web: www.nrcs.usda.gov

Risk Management Agency
1400 Independence Ave SW MS 0801 ... Washington DC 20250 | Phone: 202-690-2803 | Fax: 690-2818
Web: www.rma.usda.gov

Rural Development
1400 Independence Ave SW ... Washington DC 20250 | Phone: 202-720-9540 | Fax: 720-1725
Web: www.rd.usda.gov

Rural Utilities Service
1400 Independence Ave SW ... Washington DC 20250 | Phone: 202-720-9545
Web: www.rd.usda.gov

Secretary of Agriculture
1400 Independence Ave SW Rm 200A ... Washington DC 20250 | Phone: 202-720-3631 | Fax: 720-2166
Web: www.usda.gov

US Forest Service
Region 10 (Alaska Region) PO Box 21628 ... Juneau AK 99802 | Phone: 907-586-8806 | Fax: 586-7876
Web: www.fs.fed.us

USDA Graduate School 600 Maryland Ave SW ... Washington DC 20024 | Phone: 202-314-3600
Web: cicorp.com

World Agricultural Outlook Board
1400 Independence Ave SW ... Washington DC 20250 | Phone: 202-720-6030
Web: www.usda.gov/oce/commodity

340-2 US Department of Commerce

Department of Commerce
1401 Constitution Ave NW Hoover Bldg ... Washington DC 20230 | Phone: 202-482-4883 | Fax: 482-5168
Web: www.commerce.gov

Bureau of Economic Analysis (BEA)
1441 L St NW ... Washington DC 20005 | Phone: 202-606-9900 | Fax: 606-5311
Web: www.bea.gov

Bureau of Industry & Security
1401 Constitution Ave NW Rm 4065 ... Washington DC 20230 | Phone: 202-622-2480
Web: www.bis.doc.gov

Economic Development Administration
1401 Constitution Ave NW ... Washington DC 20230 | Phone: 202-482-2900
TF: 888-469-3146 ■ *Web:* www.eda.gov

Economic Development Administration Regional Offices
Atlanta 401 W Peachtree St NW Ste 1820 ... Atlanta GA 30308 | Phone: 404-730-3002 | Fax: 730-3025
Web: www.eda.gov
Austin 504 Lavaca St Ste 1100 ... Austin TX 78701 | Phone: 512-381-8144 | Fax: 381-8177
Web: www.eda.gov
Chicago 111 N Canal St Ste 855 ... Chicago IL 60606 | Phone: 312-353-8143 | Fax: 353-8575
Web: www.eda.gov
Denver 410 17th St Ste 250 ... Denver CO 80202 | Phone: 303-844-4715 | Fax: 844-3968
Web: www.eda.gov/contacts.htm
Philadelphia
Curtis Ctr 601 Walnut St Ste 140-S ... Philadelphia PA 19106 | Phone: 215-597-4603
Web: www.eda.gov
Seattle 915 Second Ave Rm 1890 ... Seattle WA 98174 | Phone: 206-220-7660 | Fax: 220-7669
Web: www.eda.gov

Economics & Statistics Administration
1401 Constitution Ave NW ... Washington DC 20230 | Phone: 202-482-0436 | Fax: 482-2552
Web: www.esa.doc.gov

International Trade Administration
1401 Constitution Ave NW ... Washington DC 20230 | Phone: 202-482-3809 | Fax: 482-5819
Web: www.ita.doc.gov

Minority Business Development Agency (MBDA)
1401 Constitution Ave NW ... Washington DC 20230 | Phone: 202-482-1940
Web: www.mbda.gov

Minority Business Development Agency Regional Offices
Atlanta Region 75 5th St NW Ste 300 ... Atlanta GA 30308 | Phone: 404-894-2096
Web: www.mbda.gov
Chicago Region 105 W Adams St Ste 2300 ... Chicago IL 60603 | Phone: 312-353-0182
TF: 888-324-1551 ■ *Web:* www.mbda.gov
Dallas Region
1401 constitution Ave NW Rm 726 ... Washington DC 20230 | Phone: 214-767-8001
Web: www.mbda.gov
New York Region 26 Federal Plaza Ste 3720 ... New York NY 10278 | Phone: 212-264-3262
Web: www.mbda.gov
San Francisco Region
1401 Constitution Ave ... Washington DC 20230 | Phone: 202-482-1940
Web: www.mbda.gov

National Environmental Satellite Data & Information Service
1335 East-West Hwy SSMC1 8th Fl ... Silver Spring MD 20910 | Phone: 301-713-3578 | Fax: 713-1249
Web: www.nesdis.noaa.gov
National Climatic Data Ctr
151 Patton Ave Rm 120 ... Asheville NC 28801 | Phone: 828-271-4800 | Fax: 271-4876
Web: www.ncdc.noaa.gov
National Coastal Data Development Ctr
Bldg 1100 Ste 101 ... Stennis Space Center MS 39529 | Phone: 228-688-2936 | Fax: 688-2010
TF: 866-732-2382 ■ *Web:* www.ncddc.noaa.gov
National Geophysical Data Ctr
E/GC 325 Broadway ... Boulder CO 80305 | Phone: 303-497-6826 | Fax: 497-6513
Web: www.ngdc.noaa.gov
National Oceanographic Data Ctr
1315 East-West Hwy 4th Fl ... Silver Spring MD 20910 | Phone: 301-713-3277 | Fax: 713-3302
Web: www.nodc.noaa.gov

National Institute of Standards & Technology (NIST)
100 Bureau Dr Sp 1070 ... Gaithersburg MD 20899 | Phone: 301-975-6478 | Fax: 926-1630
TF: 800-877-8339 ■ *Web:* www.nist.gov

National Marine Fisheries Service Regional Offices
Alaska Region PO Box 21668 ... Juneau AK 99802 | Phone: 907-586-7221 | Fax: 586-7249
Web: alaskafisheries.noaa.gov
NortheastRegion 1 Blackburn Dr ... Gloucester MA 01930 | Phone: 978-281-9300 | Fax: 281-9333
Web: greateratlantic.fisheries.noaa.gov
Northwest Region 7600 Sand Pt Way NE ... Seattle WA 98115 | Phone: 206-526-6150 | Fax: 526-6426
Web: www.fisheries.noaa.gov

Phone Fax

Pacific Islands Region
1601 Kapiolani Blvd Rm 1110 .... Honolulu HI 96814 808-944-2200 973-2906
TF: 888-674-7411 ■ *Web:* www.fpir.noaa.gov
Southwest Region 501 W Ocean Blvd Ste 4200 ... Long Beach CA 90802 562-980-4000 980-4018
Web: www.nmfs.noaa.gov/ia/permits/contacts.html

National Ocean Service
1305 East-West Hwy .... Silver Spring MD 20910 301-713-3074 713-4269
Web: oceanservice.noaa.gov

National Oceanic & Atmospheric Administration (NOAA)
1401 Constitution Ave NW .... Washington DC 20230 202-482-6090 482-3154
Web: www.noaa.gov

National Sea Grant Program
1315 East-West Hwy SSMC-3 11th Fl .... Silver Spring MD 20910 301-734-1066 713-0799
Web: www.seagrant.noaa.gov

National Technical Information Service (NTIS)
5285 Port Royal Rd .... Springfield VA 22161 703-605-6000 605-6900
TF Orders: 800-553-6847 ■ *Web:* www.ntis.gov

National Telecommunications & Information Administration (NTIA)
1401 Constitution Ave NW Hoover Bldg .... Washington DC 20230 202-482-7002
Web: www.ntia.doc.gov

National Weather Service (NWS)
1325 East-West Hwy .... Silver Spring MD 20910 301-713-0689 713-0662
Web: www.weather.gov
National Hurricane Ctr 11691 SW 17th St .... Miami FL 33165 305-229-4470 553-1901
Web: www.nhc.noaa.gov

National Weather Service Regional Offices
Alaska Region
222 W Seventh Ave Ste 23 Rm 517 .... Anchorage AK 99513 907-271-5088 271-3711
Web: www.arh.noaa.gov
Central Region 7220 NW 101st Terr .... Kansas City MO 64153 816-891-7734
Web: www.weather.gov/organization/regional
Eastern Region 630 Johnson Ave .... Bohemia NY 11716 631-244-0100
Web: weather.gov/erh
Pacific Region 2525 Correa Rd Ste 250 .... Honolulu HI 96822 808-973-5286
Web: www.prh.noaa.gov/pr
Southern Region 819 Taylor St Rm 10A06 .... Fort Worth TX 76102 817-978-1000
Web: www.srh.noaa.gov
Western Region 125 S State St .... Salt Lake City UT 84138 801-524-5133 524-5270
Web: www.wrh.noaa.gov

North American Industry Classification System (NAICS)
US Census Bureau 4600 Silver Hill Rd .... Washington DC 20233 301-763-4636
TF: 800-923-8282 ■ *Web:* www.census.gov/eos/www/naics

Secretary of Commerce
1401 Constitution Ave NW .... Washington DC 20230 202-482-2000
Web: www.commerce.gov

US Census Bureau 4600 Silver Hill Rd .... Washington DC 20233 301-763-6460
Web: www.census.gov

US Census Bureau Regional Offices
Atlanta 101 Marietta St NW Ste 3200 .... Atlanta GA 30303 404-730-3832 730-3835
TF: 800-424-6974 ■ *Web:* www.census.gov
Boston 4 Copley Pl Ste 301 .... Boston MA 02117 617-424-4501 424-0547
TF: 800-562-5721 ■ *Web:* www.census.gov
Chicago 1111 W 22nd St Ste 400 .... Oak Brook IL 60523 630-288-9200 288-9288
TF: 800-865-6384 ■ *Web:* www.census.gov
Denver 6900 W Jefferson Ave Ste 100 .... Denver CO 80235 303-264-0202 969-6777
TF: 800-852-6159 ■ *Web:* www.census.gov
Los Angeles 15350 Sherman Way Ste 300 .... Van Nuys CA 91406 818-267-1700 904-6429
TF: 800-992-3530 ■ *Web:* www.census.gov/rolax/www
New York 32 Old Slip 9th Fl .... New York NY 10005 212-584-3400 478-4800
TF: 800-991-2520 ■ *Web:* www.census.gov/regions
Philadelphia 833 Chestnut St Ste 504 .... Philadelphia PA 19107 215-717-1800 717-0755
TF: 800-262-4236 ■ *Web:* www.census.gov

US Patent & Trademark Office PO Box 1450 .... Alexandria VA 22313 571-272-1000 273-8300
TF: 800-786-9199 ■ *Web:* www.uspto.gov

340-3 US Department of Defense

Phone Fax

Department of Defense (DOD) The Pentagon .... Washington DC 20301 703-545-6700
Web: www.defense.gov

American Forces Information Service (AFIS)
601 N Fairfax St .... Alexandria VA 22314 703-571-3343
Web: www.defense.gov

Defense Commissary Agency 1300 E Ave .... Fort Lee VA 23801 804-734-8000 734-8009
TF: 877-332-2471 ■ *Web:* www.commissaries.com

Defense Contract Audit Agency
8725 John J Kingman Rd Ste 2135 .... Fort Belvoir VA 22060 703-767-3265
TF: 855-414-5892 ■ *Web:* www.dcaa.mil

Defense Contract Management Agency
6350 Walker Ln Ste 300 .... Alexandria VA 22310 888-576-3262
TF: 888-576-3262 ■ *Web:* www.dcma.mil

Defense Information Systems Agency
PO Box 4502 .... Arlington VA 22204 844-247-3457 607-4344*
**Fax Area Code:* 703 ■ *TF:* 844-247-3457 ■ *Web:* www.disa.mil

Defense Intelligence Agency
200 MacDill Blvd .... Washington DC 20340 301-394-5587 394-5356
Web: www.dia.mil

Defense Logistics Agency (DLA)
8725 John J Kingman Rd Ste 1644 .... Fort Belvoir VA 22060 703-767-5200 767-6091
Web: www.dla.mil/Pages/default.aspx

Defense Office of Economic Adjustment
400 Army-Navy Dr Ste 200 .... Arlington VA 22202 703-604-6020
Web: www.oea.gov

Defense Prisoner of War/Missing Personnel Office (DPMO)
2600 Defense Pentagon .... Washington DC 20301 703-699-1169 602-4375
Web: www.dpaa.mil

Defense Security Cooperation Agency
201 12th St S Ste 402 .... Washington DC 20301 703-604-6566
Web: www.dsca.mil

Defense Security Service 27130 Telegraph Rd .... Quantico VA 22314 571-305-6562
Web: www.dss.mil

Defense Technical Information Ctr (DTIC)
8725 John J Kingman Rd Ste 0944 .... Fort Belvoir VA 22060 703-767-9100 767-9183
TF: 800-225-3842 ■ *Web:* www.dtic.mil

Defense Threat Reduction Agency
8725 John T Kingman Rd MS 6201 .... Fort Belvoir VA 22060 703-767-5870 767-4450
TF: 800-701-5096 ■ *Web:* www.dtra.mil

Joint Chiefs of Staff
Chairman
9999 Joint Chiefs of Staff Pentagon .... Washington DC 20318 703-767-8267
Web: www.dtic.mil

Missile Defense Agency
7100 Defense Pentagon .... Washington DC 20301 256-450-1599
Web: www.mda.mil

National Defense University
Fort McNair 300 5th Ave SW .... Washington DC 20319 202-685-4700
Web: ndu.edu

National Security Agency 9800 Savage Rd .... Fort Meade MD 20755 301-688-6524
Web: www.nsa.gov

340-4 US Department of Defense - Department of the Air Force

Phone Fax

Department of the Air Force
1670 Air Force Pentagon .... Washington DC 20330 703-695-9664 693-9601
Web: www.af.mil
North American Aerospace Defense Command
250 Vandenberg St Ste B-016 .... Peterson AFB CO 80914 719-554-6889 554-3165
Web: www.norad.mil

Air Combat Command 205 Dodd Blvd Ste 101 .... Langley AFB VA 23665 757-764-8346
Web: www.acc.af.mil

Air Education & Training Command (AETC)
100 H St Ste 4 .... Randolph AFB TX 78150 210-652-6564 652-2027
Web: www.aetc.af.mil

Air Force Chief of Staff
1670 Air Force Pentagon .... Washington DC 20330 703-571-3343
Web: www.defense.gov

Air Force Materiel Command
4375 Chidlaw Rd Rm N-152 .... Wright-Patterson AFB OH 45433 937-257-1110
Web: www.afmc.af.mil

Air Force Reserve Command
155 Richard Ray Blvd .... Robins AFB GA 31098 478-327-1753 327-0625
Web: www.afrc.af.mil

Air Force Space Command
150 Vandenberg St .... Peterson AFB CO 80914 719-554-3731 554-6013
Web: www.afspc.af.mil

Air Force Special Operations Command
229 Cody Ave Ste 103 .... Hurlburt Field FL 32544 850-884-5515
Web: www.afsoc.af.mil

Air Mobility Command 402 Scott Dr Unit 1M8 .... Scott AFB IL 62225 618-229-7839
Web: www.amc.af.mil

340-5 US Department of Defense - Department of the Army

Phone Fax

Department of the Army 1500 Army Pentagon .... Washington DC 20310 703-697-5131
Web: www.army.mil
US Army Center of Military History
103 Third Ave SW Fort McNair Bldg 35 .... Washington DC 20319 202-685-2727 512-2104
Web: www.history.army.mil

US Army Corps of Engineers 441 G St NW .... Washington DC 20314 202-761-0010 761-1803
Web: www.usace.army.mil

US Army Corps of Engineers Regional Offices
Great Lakes & Ohio River Div 550 Main St .... Cincinnati OH 45202 513-684-3010 684-3755
Web: www.lrd.usace.army.mil
Mississippi Valley Div 1400 Walnut St .... Vicksburg MS 39180 601-634-7783
Web: www.mvd.usace.army.mil
North Atlantic Div
302 General Lee Ave Fort Hamilton .... Brooklyn NY 11252 347-370-4550
Web: www.nad.usace.army.mil
Northwestern Div PO Box 2870 .... Portland OR 97208 503-808-3700 808-3706
Web: www.nwd.usace.army.mil
Pacific Ocean Div Fort Shafter Bldg 525 .... Honolulu HI 96858 808-438-8319 438-2656
Web: www.pod.usace.army.mil
South Atlantic Div 60 Forsyth St SW Rm 9M15 .... Atlanta GA 30303 404-562-5011
Web: www.sad.usace.army.mil
South Pacific Div 1455 Market St .... San Francisco CA 94103 415-503-6514
Web: www.spd.usace.army.mil
Southwestern Div 1100 Commerce St .... Dallas TX 75242 469-487-7007
Web: www.swd.usace.army.mil

US Army Criminal Investigation Command
Public Affairs Office 6010 6th St .... Fort Belvoir VA 22060 703-806-0372
Web: www.cid.army.mil

US Army Forces Command 4700 Knox St .... Fort Bragg NC 28310 910-570-7200 464-5628*
**Fax Area Code:* 404

US Army Intelligence & Security Command
8825 Beulah St .... Fort Belvoir VA 22060 703-428-4965
Web: www.inscom.army.mil

US Army Special Operations Command (USASOC)
2929 Desert Storm Dr .... Fort Bragg NC 28310 910-432-6005 432-1046
Web: www.soc.mil

US Army War College 122 Forbes Ave .... Carlisle PA 17013 717-245-3131 245-4224
TF: 800-453-0992 ■ *Web:* www.carlisle.army.mil

340-6 US Department of Defense - Department of the Navy

Phone Fax

Department of the Navy 1000 Navy Pentagon .... Washington DC 20350 703-695-8400
Web: www.navy.mil

Phone | Fax

Judge Advocate General's Corps
1322 Patterson Ave Ste 3000.......... Washington Navy Yard DC 20374 202-685-5275
Web: www.jag.navy.mil
Medicine & Surgery Bureau 2300 E St NW ...... Washington DC 20372 301-402-8878
Web: www.nlm.nih.gov
Office of Naval Intelligence
4251 Suitland Rd........ Washington DC 20395 301-669-3001
Web: www.oni.navy.mil
Office of Naval Research
1 Liberty Ctr 875 N Randolph St Ste 1425........ Arlington VA 22203 703-696-5031 696-5940
Web: www.onr.navy.mil
Military Sealift Command
914 Charles Morris Ct SE
Washington Navy Yard........ Washington DC 20398 800-793-5784
TF: 800-793-5784
Naval Air Systems Command
47123 Buse Rd Bldg 2272, Ste 075........ Patuxent River MD 20670 301-757-1487
Web: www.navair.navy.mil
Naval Education & Training Command (NETC)
250 Dallas St........ Pensacola FL 32508 850-452-4858
Web: www.netc.navy.mil
Naval Sea Systems Command
1333 Isaac Hull Ave SE
Washington Navy Yard........ Washington DC 20376 202-781-4123
Web: www.navsea.navy.mil
Naval Special Warfare Command
2000 Trident Way........ San Diego CA 92155 619-537-1133 537-1986
Web: www.public.navy.mil
Navy Personnel Command (NPC)
5720 Integrity Dr........ Millington TN 38055 901-874-3165 874-2615
TF: 866-827-5672 ■ *Web:* www.public.navy.mil

340-7 US Department of Defense - US Marine Corps

Phone | Fax

US Marine Corps (USMC)
1555 Southgate Rd
Marine Corps National Capital Region Command .... Arlington VA 22214 703-614-6411 614-6411
Web: www.marines.mil/Pages/Default.aspx
Commandant
3000 Marine Corps Pentagon Rm 4C645........ Washington DC 20350 703-614-4851 693-4414
Web: usmcbirthdayball.com
Public Affairs Div
3000 Marine Corps Pentagon Rm 2B253........ Washington DC 20350 703-693-3088 614-6539
Web: www.hqmc.marines.mil
Marine Corps Recruiting Station
3280 Russell Rd........ Quantico VA 22134 636-532-0522
Web: www.marines.com

340-8 US Department of Education

Phone | Fax

Department of Education
400 Maryland Ave SW........ Washington DC 20202 202-401-2000 401-0689
TF: 800-872-5327 ■ *Web:* www.ed.gov
Inspector General's Fraud & Abuse Hotline
400 Maryland Ave SW........ Washington DC 20202 800-647-8733
TF: 800-647-8733 ■ *Web:* www.ed.gov/about/offices/list/oig/hotline.html
Office of Vocational & Adult Education
400 Maryland Ave SW Room 4W116........ Washington DC 20202 800-872-5327
TF: 800-872-5327 ■ *Web:* www.ed.gov/ovae
Department of Education Regional Offices
Region 1
5 Post Office Sq Ninth Fl Rm 24 POCH Bldg........ Boston MA 02110 617-289-0100
Web: www.ed.gov
Region 10
400 Maryland Ave SW Jackson Federal Bldg........ Washington DC 20202 202-401-2000 872-5327*
**Fax Area Code:* 800 ■ *Web:* www.ed.gov
Region 2 Financial Sq 32 Old Slip 25th Fl........ New York NY 10005 646-428-3906 428-3904
Web: www.ed.gov
Region 3 100 Penn Sq E Ste 505........ Philadelphia PA 19107 215-656-6010 656-6020
Web: www.ed.gov
Region 4
Federal Ctr 61 Forsyth St SW Ste 19T40........ Atlanta GA 30303 404-974-9450 974-9459
Web: www.ed.gov
Region 5 500 W Madison St Ste 1427........ Chicago IL 60661 312-730-1700 730-1704
Web: www.ed.gov
Region 7 8930 Ward Pkwy Ste 2043........ Kansas City MO 64114 816-268-0400 268-0407
Web: www.ed.gov
Region 8 Federal Bldg 1244 Speer Blvd Ste 615........ Denver CO 80204 303-844-3544 844-2524
Web: www.ed.gov
US Dept of Education
Office of Special Education & Rehabilitation Services (OSERS)
400 Maryland Ave SW........ Washington DC 20202 202-401-0418 872-5327*
**Fax Area Code:* 800 ■ *Web:* www2.ed.gov
Region 6 1999 Bryan St Ste 1620........ Dallas TX 75201 214-661-9600 661-9587
TF: 877-521-2172 ■ *Web:* www.ed.gov
National Ctr for Education Statistics
1990 K St NW........ Washington DC 20006 202-502-7300 502-7466
Web: nces.ed.gov
National Institute for Literacy (NIFL)
1775 'I' St NW Ste 730........ Washington DC 20006 202-233-2025 233-2050
TF: 800-228-8813 ■ *Web:* www.lincs.ed.gov
Secretary of Education
400 Maryland Ave SW........ Washington DC 20202 202-401-3000
TF: 800-872-5327 ■ *Web:* www.ed.gov/news/staff/bios/spellings.html

340-9 US Department of Energy

Phone | Fax

Department of Energy (DOE)
1000 Independence Ave SW........ Washington DC 20585 202-586-5450 586-4891
TF: 800-342-5363 ■ *Web:* www.energy.gov
Office of Electricity Delivery & Energy Reliability
1000 Independence Ave SW........ Washington DC 20585 202-586-1411
Web: www.energy.gov/oe
Office of Fossil Energy
1000 Independence Ave SW........ Washington DC 20585 202-586-6660 586-7847
Web: energy.gov
Office of Legacy Management
Office of Stakeholder Relations LM-5........ Washington DC 20585 202-586-3559 586-1540
Web: energy.gov
Energy Information Administration
1000 Independence Ave SW........ Washington DC 20585 202-586-8800 586-0727
Web: www.eia.gov
Federal Energy Regulatory Commission
888 First St NE........ Washington DC 20426 202-502-8004 208-2106
TF: 866-208-3372 ■ *Web:* www.ferc.gov
Federal Energy Regulatory Commission Regional Offices
Atlanta 3700 Crestwood Pkwy NW 9th Fl........ Atlanta GA 30096 678-245-3075 245-3010
Web: www.ferc.gov/contact-us/tel-num/regional/atlanta.asp
Chicago 230 S Dearborn St Rm 3130........ Chicago IL 60604 312-596-4437 596-4460
Web: www.ferc.gov/contact-us/tel-num/regional/chicago.asp
New York 19 W 34th St Ste 400........ New York NY 10001 212-273-5911 631-8124
Web: www.ferc.gov/contact-us/tel-num/regional/newyork.asp
Portland 888 First St NE Fox Tower Ste 550........ Washington DC 20426 202-502-6088 552-2799*
**Fax Area Code:* 503 ■ *TF:* 866-208-3372 ■ *Web:* www.ferc.gov/contact-us/tel-num/regional.asp
San Francisco 100 First St Ste 2300........ San Francisco CA 94105 415-369-3318 369-3322
Web: www.ferc.gov
National Nuclear Security Administration (NNSA)
1000 Independence Ave SW........ Washington DC 20585 202-586-5000 586-4892
Web: www.nnsa.energy.gov
Power Marketing Administrations
Bonneville Power Administration
905 NE 11th Ave........ Portland OR 97232 503-230-3000
TF: 800-282-3713 ■ *Web:* www.bpa.gov
Southeastern Power Administration
1166 Athens Tech Rd........ Elberton GA 30635 706-213-3800 213-3884
Web: energy.gov
Secretary of Energy
1000 Independence Ave SW........ Washington DC 20585 202-586-6210 586-4403
Web: energy.gov/about-us

340-10 US Department of Health & Human Services

Phone | Fax

Department of Health & Human Services (HHS)
330 Independence Ave SW........ Washington DC 20201 202-619-0150
TF: 877-696-6775 ■ *Web:* www.hhs.gov
Department of Health & Human Services Regional Offices
Region 10 701 5th Ave Ste 1600........ Seattle WA 98121 206-615-2010 615-2087
Web: hhs.gov
Region 2 26 Federal Plaza Rm 3835........ New York NY 10278 212-264-4600 264-3620
Web: hhs.gov
Region 4 1301 61 Forsyth St SW Ste 5B95........ Atlanta GA 30303 404-562-7889 562-7899
Web: www.hhs.gov
Region 5 233 N Michigan Ave Ste 1300........ Chicago IL 60601 415-437-8090 353-4144*
**Fax Area Code:* 312
Region 6 1301 Young St Ste 1124........ Dallas TX 75202 214-767-3879 767-3209
Web: www.hhs.gov
Region 7 601 E 12th St........ Kansas City MO 64106 816-426-2821 426-2178
Web: hhs.gov
US Health & Human Services Department
Region 1 200 Independence Ave........ Washington DC 20201 617-565-1500 565-1491
Web: www.hrsa.gov/about/organization/bureaus/oro/region1.html
Region 8 999 18th St S Terr Ste 410........ Denver CO 80202 303-844-6163 844-2019
Web: www.hhs.gov
Region 9 90 7th St Ste 4-100........ San Francisco CA 94103 800-368-1019 437-8329*
**Fax Area Code:* 415 ■ *TF:* 800-368-1019 ■ *Web:* www.hhs.gov
Administration for Children & Families (ACF)
370 L'Enfant Promenade SW........ Washington DC 20447 202-401-9215 401-5450
Web: www.acf.hhs.gov
Administration for Children & Families Regional Offices
Atlanta 61 Forsyth St Ste 4M60........ Atlanta GA 30303 404-562-2800 562-2981
Web: www.acf.hhs.gov/programs/region4
Boston JFK Federal Bldg Rm 2000........ Boston MA 02203 617-565-1020 565-2493
Web: www.acf.hhs.gov
Chicago 233 N Michigan Ave Ste 400........ Chicago IL 60601 312-353-4237 353-2204
Web: www.acf.hhs.gov/programs/region5
Dallas 1301 Young St Ste 914........ Dallas TX 75202 214-767-9648 767-3743
Web: www.acf.hhs.gov/programs/region6
New York 26 Federal Plaza Rm 4114........ New York NY 10278 212-264-2890 264-4881
Web: www.acf.hhs.gov/programs/region2
Philadelphia
150 S Independence Mall W Ste 864........ Philadelphia PA 19106 215-861-4000 861-4070
Web: www.acf.hhs.gov/programs/region3
San Francisco 90 Seventh St 9th Fl........ San Francisco CA 94103 415-437-8400 437-8444
Web: www.acf.hhs.gov/programs/region9
Administration on Aging (AoA)
1 Massachusetts Ave NW........ Washington DC 20201 202-619-0724 357-3555
Web: www.aoa.gov
Administration on Aging Regional Offices (AOA)
Region I JFK Federal Bldg Rm 2075........ Boston MA 02203 617-565-1158
Web: www.aoa.gov
Region V 233 N Michigan Ave Ste 790........ Chicago IL 60601 312-353-5160 886-8533
Web: www.acl.gov
Region VIII
330 Independence Ave SW Ste 4760........ Washington DC 20201 202-401-4634
Web: www.aoa.gov
Regions II & III 26 Federal Plaza Ste 3835........ New York NY 10278 212-264-2976 264-0114
Agency for Healthcare Research & Quality
540 Gaither Rd........ Rockville MD 20850 301-427-1200
TF: 800-358-9295 ■ *Web:* www.ahrq.gov
Agency for Toxic Substances & Disease Registry
4770 Buford Hwy NE........ Atlanta GA 30341 800-232-4636
TF: 800-232-4636 ■ *Web:* www.atsdr.cdc.gov

				Phone	Fax
AIDSinfo PO Box 6303	Rockville	MD	20849	301-519-0459	519-6616
TF: 800-448-0440 ■ *Web:* www.aidsinfo.nih.gov					
Centers for Disease Control & Prevention (CDC)					
1600 Clifton Rd NE	Atlanta	GA	30333	404-639-7000	639-7111
Web: www.cdc.gov					
National Center for Chronic Disease Prevention & Health Promotion (NCCDPHP)					
4770 Buford Hwy NE	Atlanta	GA	30341	800-232-4636	
TF: 800-232-4636 ■ *Web:* www.cdc.gov/nccdphp					
National Center for Emerging & Zoonotic Infectious Diseases					
1600 Clifton Rd	Atlanta	GA	30333	404-639-3311	
TF: 800-232-4636 ■ *Web:* cdc.gov					
National Center for Environmental Health					
4770 Buford Hwy Bldg 101	Atlanta	GA	30341	404-639-3311	
TF: 800-232-4636 ■ *Web:* www.cdc.gov					
National Center for Health Marketing					
1600 Clifton Rd NE	Atlanta	GA	30333	404-639-3311	
TF: 800-311-3435 ■ *Web:* cdc.gov/healthcommunication					
National Center for Health Statistics					
6525 Belcrest Rd	Hyattsville	MD	20782	301-458-4000	
Web: www.cdc.gov					
National Center for HIV/AIDS Viral Hepatitis STD & TB Prevention					
1600 Clifton Rd	Atlanta	GA	30333	800-232-4636	
TF: 800-232-4636 ■ *Web:* www.cdc.gov/NCHHSTP					
National Center for Immunization & Respiratory Diseases					
1600 Clifton Rd NE MS E-05	Atlanta	GA	30333	800-232-4636	
TF: 800-232-4636 ■ *Web:* www.cdc.gov/vaccines					
National Center for Injury Prevention & Control (NCIPC)					
4770 Buford Hwy NE	Atlanta	GA	30341	800-232-4636	
TF: 800-232-4636 ■ *Web:* www.cdc.gov/injury					
National Center for Public Health Informatics					
1600 Clifton Rd NE	Atlanta	GA	30333	800-232-4636	718-2093*
**Fax Area Code:* 404 ■ *TF:* 800-232-4636 ■ *Web:* www.cdc.gov/ncphi					
National Center on Birth Defects & Developmental Disabilities					
1600 Clifton Rd	Atlanta	GA	30329	404-639-3311	
TF: 800-232-4636 ■ *Web:* www.cdc.gov/ncbddd					
National Institute for Occupational Safety & Health					
200 Independence Ave SW	Washington	DC	20201	404-639-3286	
TF: 800-356-4674 ■ *Web:* www.cdc.gov/niosh					
National Office of Public Health Genomics					
4770 Buford Hwy MS K-89	Atlanta	GA	30341	770-488-8510	488-8355
TF: 877-442-9719 ■ *Web:* www.cdc.gov/genomics					
Travelers Health 1600 Clifton Rd NE	Atlanta	GA	30333	800-232-4636	232-3299*
**Fax Area Code:* 888 ■ *TF:* 800-232-4636 ■ *Web:* wwwnc.cdc.gov/travel					
Centers for Medicare & Medicaid Services (CMS)					
7500 Security Blvd	Baltimore	MD	21244	800-633-4227	
TF: 800-633-4227 ■ *Web:* www.cms.gov					
Medicare Hotline 7500 Security Blvd	Baltimore	MD	21244	800-633-4227	
TF: 800-633-4227 ■ *Web:* www.medicare.gov					
Centers for Medicare & Medicaid Services Regional Offices					
Region I JFK Federal Bldg Rm 2325	Boston	MA	02203	617-565-1188	565-1339
Web: www.cms.gov					
Region II 26 Federal Plaza	New York	NY	10278	212-616-2439	380-8855*
**Fax Area Code:* 443 ■ *Web:* cms.gov/regionaloffices					
Region III					
150 S Independence Mall W Ste 216	Philadelphia	PA	19106	215-861-4140	861-4240
Web: www.cms.gov					
Region IV 61 Forsyth St SW Ste 4T20	Atlanta	GA	30303	404-562-1738	380-8945*
**Fax Area Code:* 443 ■ *Web:* www.cms.gov					
Region IX 90 Seventh St Ste 5-300	San Francisco	CA	94105	415-744-3502	744-3517
Web: www.cms.gov					
Region V 233 N Michigan Ave Ste 600	Chicago	IL	60601	410-786-3000	353-0252*
**Fax Area Code:* 312 ■ *Web:* cms.gov/regionaloffices					
Region VI 1301 Young St Ste 714	Dallas	TX	75202	214-767-6427	
Web: www.cms.gov					
Region VII					
Federal Bldg 601 E 12th St Ste 235	Kansas City	MO	64106	303-844-7481	
Web: www.cms.gov					
Region VIII 1600 Broadway Ste 700	Denver	CO	80202	303-844-7035	844-3753
Web: www.cms.gov					
Region X 2201 Sixth Ave Ste 801	Seattle	WA	98121	206-615-2306	
Web: www.cms.gov					
Child Welfare Information Gateway					
1250 Maryland Ave SW 8th Fl	Washington	DC	20024	703-385-7565	385-3206
TF: 800-394-3366 ■ *Web:* www.childwelfare.gov					
Food & Drug Administration (FDA)					
5600 Fishers Ln	Rockville	MD	20857	301-827-2410	443-3100
TF: 888-463-6332 ■ *Web:* www.fda.gov					
Center for Biologics Evaluation & Research					
1401 Rockville Pike Ste 200N MS HFM-4	Rockville	MD	20852	301-827-0372	
Web: www.fda.gov/cber					
Center for Devices & Radiological Health (CDRH)					
10903 New Hampshire Ave WO66-5429	Silver Spring	MD	20993	301-796-7100	847-8149
TF: 800-638-2041 ■ *Web:* www.fda.gov					
Center for Food Safety & Applied Nutrition					
5100 Paint Branch Pkwy	College Park	MD	20740	888-723-3366	
TF: 888-723-3366 ■ *Web:* www.fda.gov					
Center for Veterinary Medicine					
7519 Standish Pl	Rockville	MD	20855	240-276-9000	276-9115
Web: www.fda.gov/cvm					
National Center for Toxicological Research					
3900 N Ctr Rd	Jefferson	AR	72079	870-543-7000	543-7576
TF: 800-638-3321 ■ *Web:* www.fda.gov/nctr					
Food & Drug Administration Regional Offices (FDA)					
Central Region 200 Chestnut St Rm 900	Philadelphia	PA	19106	215-597-4390	597-4660
Web: www.fda.gov					
Northeast Region 158-15 Liberty Ave	Jamaica	NY	11433	718-662-5416	662-5434
Web: www.fda.gov					
Pacific Region 1301 Clay St Ste 1180N	Oakland	CA	94612	877-696-6775	
TF: 877-696-6775 ■ *Web:* www.hhs.gov					
Southwest Region 4040 N Central Expwy Ste 900	Dallas	TX	75204	214-253-4901	253-4960
Web: www.fda.gov					
Health Resources & Services Administration (HRSA)					
5600 Fishers Ln	Rockville	MD	20857	301-443-2216	
TF: 888-275-4772 ■ *Web:* hrsa.gov					

				Phone	Fax
Indian Health Service (IHS)					
801 Thompson Ave Ste 400	Rockville	MD	20852	301-443-1083	443-4794
National Child Care Information & Technical Assistance Ctr (NCCIC)					
9300 Lee Hwy	Fairfax	VA	22031	877-296-2250	
TF: 877-296-2250 ■ *Web:* acf.hhs.gov/programs/occ					
National Clearinghouse for Alcohol & Drug Information					
11426 Rockville Pk PO Box 2345	Rockville	MD	20847	800-729-6686	
TF: 800-729-6686 ■ *Web:* samhsa.gov					
National Hansen's Disease Program (NHDP)					
1770 Physicians Pk Dr	Baton Rouge	LA	70816	800-221-9393	
TF: 800-221-9393 ■ *Web:* hrsa.gov					
National Institutes of Biomedical Imaging & Bioengineering					
National Institute of Biomedical Imaging & Bioengineering (NIBIB)					
6707 Democracy Blvd	Bethesda	MD	20892	301-496-8859	480-0679
Web: www.nibib.nih.gov					
National Institutes of Health (NIH)					
9000 Rockville Pike	Bethesda	MD	20892	301-496-4000	
Web: www.nih.gov					
Center for Scientific Review					
6701 Rockledge Dr MSC 7950	Bethesda	MD	20892	301-435-1115	
Web: www.nih.gov					
Clinical Ctr 10 Ctr Dr Bldg 10	Bethesda	MD	20892	301-496-2563	402-2984
Web: www.cc.nih.gov					
National Cancer Institute					
Public Inquiries Office 6116 Executive Blvd					
Rm 3036A	Bethesda	MD	20892	301-435-3848	
TF: 800-422-6237 ■ *Web:* www.cancer.gov					
National Center for Complementary & Alternative Medicine					
31 Ctr Dr Bldg 31	Bethesda	MD	20892	301-594-7103	
TF: 888-644-6226 ■ *Web:* nccih.nih.gov					
National Center on Minority Health & Health Disparities					
6707 Democracy Blvd Ste 800 Ste 800	Bethesda	MD	20892	301-402-1366	480-4049
Web: www.nimhd.nih.gov					
National Eye Institute 2020 Vision Pl	Bethesda	MD	20892	301-496-5248	402-1065
Web: www.nei.nih.gov					
National Heart Lung & Blood Institute (NHLBI)					
31 Ctr Dr Bldg 31 Rm 5A52 MSC 2486	Bethesda	MD	20892	301-496-5166	402-0818
Web: www.nhlbi.nih.gov					
National Human Genome Research Institute					
31 Ctr Dr Bldg 31 Rm 4B09	Bethesda	MD	20892	301-402-0911	402-2218
Web: www.genome.gov					
National Institute of Arthritis & Musculoskeletal & Skin Diseases					
31 Ctr Dr MSC 2350 Bldg 31 Rm 4C02	Bethesda	MD	20892	301-496-8190	480-2814
Web: www.niams.nih.gov					
National Institute of Dental & Craniofacial Research					
31 Ctr Dr	Bethesda	MD	20892	301-496-3571	402-2185
Web: www.nidcr.nih.gov					
National Institute of Diabetes & Digestive & Kidney Diseases					
31 Ctr Dr MSC 2560	Bethesda	MD	20892	301-496-3583	496-7422
Web: www.niddk.nih.gov					
National Institute of Environmental Health Sciences					
PO Box 12233	Research Triangle Park	NC	27709	919-541-3201	541-2260
Web: www.niehs.nih.gov					
National Institute of General Medical Sciences					
45 Ctr Dr MSC 6200	Bethesda	MD	20892	301-496-7301	
Web: www.nigms.nih.gov					
National Institute of Mental Health					
6001 Executive Blvd Rm 8184 MSC 9663	Bethesda	MD	20892	301-443-4513	443-4279
TF: 866-615-6464 ■ *Web:* www.nimh.nih.gov					
National Institute of Neurological Disorders & Stroke					
PO Box 5801	Bethesda	MD	20824	301-496-5751	
TF: 800-352-9424 ■ *Web:* www.ninds.nih.gov					
National Institute of Nursing Research					
31 Ctr Dr Bldg 31 Rm 5B10	Bethesda	MD	20892	301-496-8230	594-3405
Web: www.ninr.nih.gov					
National Institute on Aging					
31 Ctr Dr Bldg 31 Rm 5C27 MSC 2292	Bethesda	MD	20892	301-496-1752	496-1072
Web: www.nia.nih.gov					
National Institute on Alcohol Abuse & Alcoholism					
5635 Fishers Ln MSC 9304	Bethesda	MD	20892	301-443-3885	443-7043
Web: www.niaaa.nih.gov					
National Institute on Deafness & Other Communication Disorders					
31 Ctr Dr Bldg 31 Rm 3C35	Bethesda	MD	20892	301-496-7243	402-0018
TF: 800-241-1044 ■ *Web:* www.nidcd.nih.gov					
National Institute on Drug Abuse					
6001 Executive Blvd Rm 4123	Bethesda	MD	20892	301-443-6480	
Web: www.drugabuse.gov					
National Library of Medicine					
8600 Rockville Pike Bldg 38	Bethesda	MD	20894	301-594-5983	402-1384
TF: 888-346-3656 ■ *Web:* www.nlm.nih.gov					
Office of Communications & Public Liason					
31 Ctr Dr Bldg 1 Rm 344	Bethesda	MD	20892	301-496-4461	496-0017
Web: www.nih.gov					
Office of Dietary Supplements					
6100 Executive Blvd Ste 3B01	Bethesda	MD	20892	301-435-2920	480-1845
Web: www.ods.od.nih.gov					
Office of Rare Diseases					
6701 Democracy Blvd Ste 1001	Bethesda	MD	20892	301-402-4336	480-9655
Web: www.rarediseases.info.nih.gov					
National Library of Medicine					
Lister Hill National Center for Biomedical Communications					
8600 Rockville Pike Bldg 38A 7th Fl	Bethesda	MD	20894	301-496-4441	480-3035
Web: www.lhncbc.nlm.nih.gov					
National Mental Health Information Ctr					
PO Box 42557	Washington	DC	20015	800-487-4889	747-5470*
**Fax Area Code:* 240 ■ *TF:* 800-487-4889 ■ *Web:* www.samhsa.gov					
National Women's Health Information Ctr					
200 Independence Ave S.W	Washington	DC	20201	800-994-9662	
TF: 800-994-9662 ■ *Web:* www.womenshealth.gov					
NIH Osteoporosis & Related Bone Diseases-National Resource Ctr					
2 AMS Cir	Bethesda	MD	20892	202-223-0344	293-2356
TF: 800-624-2663 ■ *Web:* niams.nih.gov/health_info/bone/default.asp					

Phone Fax

Office of Intergovernmental and External Affairs
Region II 26 Federal Plaza Ste 3835. . . . . New York NY 10278 212-264-4600 264-1324
Web: www.hhs.gov/ophs/rha
Office of Public Health & Science
200 Independence Ave SW Rm 716G. . . . . .Washington DC 20201 202-690-7694 690-6960
TF: 877-696-6775 ■ *Web:* www.hhs.gov/ophs
Office of Public Health & Science Regional Offices
Region 3
150 S Independence Mall W Ste 436. . . . . Philadelphia PA 19106 215-861-4639 861-4617
Web: www.hhs.gov/ash/about-ash/regional-offices/region-3/index.html
Region 4 1301 61 Forsyth St SW Ste 5B95 . . . . .Atlanta GA 30303 404-562-7888 562-7899
Web: www.hhs.gov/ash/about-ash/regional-offices/region-4/index.html
Region 6 1301 Young St Ste 1124. . . . . Dallas TX 75202 214-767-3879 767-3209
Web: www.hhs.gov/ash/about-ash/regional-offices/region-6/index.html
Region I John F Kennedy Federal Bldg Rm 2100. . . . . Boston MA 02203 617-565-1491
Web: www.hhs.gov
Region IX 90 Seventh St Ste 5-100 . . . . .San Francisco CA 94103 415-437-8096 437-8004
Web: www.hhs.gov/about/agencies/iea/regional-offices/region-9/index.html
Region VII 601 E 12th St Rm S-1801. . . . . .Kansas City MO 64106 816-426-3291 426-2178
Web: www.hhs.gov
Region X 2201 Sixth Ave MS RX-11 . . . . .Seattle WA 98121 206-615-2290 615-2481
Office of the Assistant Secretary for Health
Region VIII 999 18th St South Terrace. . . . . Denver CO 80202 303-844-6163 844-2019
Web: www.hhs.gov/ash/about-ash/regional-offices/region-8/index.html
President's Council on Physical Fitness Sports & Nutrition
1101 Wootton Pkwy Ste 560. . . . . .Rockville MD 20852 240-276-9567 276-9860
Web: www.fitness.gov
Secretary of Health & Human Services
200 Independence Ave SW. . . . . .Washington DC 20201 202-690-7000 690-7755
Web: www.hhs.gov/about
Substance Abuse & Mental Health Services Administration (SAMHSA)
1 Choke Cherry Rd. . . . . .Rockville MD 20857 240-276-2000 276-2010
TF: 877-726-4727 ■ *Web:* www.samhsa.gov
Center for Mental Health Services
1 Choke Cherry Ln. . . . . .Rockville MD 20857 877-726-4727 221-4292*
**Fax Area Code:* 240 ■ *TF:* 877-726-4727 ■ *Web:* www.samhsa.gov
Center for Substance Abuse Prevention
1 Choke Cherry Rd. . . . . .Rockville MD 20857 240-276-2420 276-2430
TF: 877-726-4727 ■ *Web:* www.samhsa.gov
Center for Substance Abuse Treatment
1 Choke Cherry Rd PO Box 2345. . . . . .Rockville MD 20857 240-276-2130 221-4292
TF: 877-726-4727 ■ *Web:* www.samhsa.gov
US Surgeon General 1101 Wootton Pkwy Rm 100. . . . . . . Rockville MD 20857 202-205-0143 453-6141*
**Fax Area Code:* 240 ■ *Web:* www.surgeongeneral.gov

340-11 US Department of Homeland Security

Phone Fax

Department of Homeland Security (DHS)
245 Murray Dr SW Bldg 410 .Washington DC 20528 202-282-8000 235-0443*
**Fax Area Code:* 703 ■ *Web:* www.dhs.gov
Ready Campaign 500 C St SW Ste 714 . . . . .Washington DC 20472 800-621-3362 621-3362
TF: 800-621-3362 ■ *Web:* www.ready.gov
Federal Emergency Management Agency (FEMA)
500 C St SW. . . . . .Washington DC 20472 800-621-3362
TF: 800-621-3362 ■ *Web:* www.fema.gov
FEMA for Kids 500 C St SW Ste 714. . . . . .Washington DC 20472 800-621-3362
TF: 800-621-3362 ■ *Web:* www.ready.gov
National Flood Insurance Program
500 C St SW . . . . .Washington DC 20472 888-379-9531 646-2818*
**Fax Area Code:* 202 ■ *TF:* 888-379-9531 ■ *Web:* www.floodsmart.gov
US Fire Administration 16825 S Seton Ave . . . . . Emmitsburg MD 21727 301-447-1000 447-1346
Web: www.usfa.fema.gov
Federal Emergency Management Agency Regional Offices (FEMA)
Region 1 99 High St. . . . . Boston MA 02110 617-956-7551
TF: 877-336-2734 ■ *Web:* www.fema.gov/region-i
Region 10
Federal Regional Ctr 130 228th St SW . . . . .Bothell WA 98021 425-487-4600
Web: www.fema.gov
Region 2 26 Federal Plaza . . . . New York NY 10278 212-680-3600
Web: www.fema.gov
Region 3
1 Independence Mall
615 Chestnut St 6th Fl. . . . . Philadelphia PA 19106 215-931-5500 931-5621
TF: 800-621-3362 ■ *Web:* www.fema.gov
Region 4 3003 Chamblee-Tucker Rd. . . . . .Atlanta GA 30341 770-220-5200 220-5230
Web: www.fema.gov
Region 5 536 S Clark St 6th Fl. . . . . Chicago IL 60605 312-408-5500 408-5234
TF: 877-336-2627 ■ *Web:* www.fema.gov
Region 6 800 N Loop 288 . . . . Denton TX 76209 940-898-5399 898-5325
TF: 800-426-5460 ■ *Web:* www.fema.gov
Region 7 9221 Ward Pkwy. . . . . .Kansas City MO 64114 816-283-7061
Web: www.fema.gov
Region 8
Denver Federal Ctr Bldg 710 PO Box 25267 . . . . .Denver CO 80225 303-235-4900 235-4976
Web: www.fema.gov
Region 9 1111 Broadway Ste 1200 . . . . .Oakland CA 94607 510-627-7100
TF: 877-336-2627 ■ *Web:* www.fema.gov
Federal Law Enforcement Training Ctr
1131 Chapel Crossing Rd. . . . . .Glynco GA 31524 912-267-2100
Web: www.fletc.gov
Secretary of Homeland Security
Naval Security Stn . . . . .Washington DC 20528 202-282-8000
Web: www.dhs.gov/dhspublic
Transportation Security Administration (TSA)
601 S 12th St . . . . .Arlington VA 22202 866-289-9673
TF: 866-289-9673 ■ *Web:* www.tsa.gov
Federal Air Marshal Service 601 S 12th St. . . . . .Arlington VA 22202 866-289-9673
TF: 866-289-9673 ■ *Web:* www.tsa.gov
US Citizenship & Immigration Services Regional Offices
Eastern Region 70 Kimball Ave . . . . .South Burlington VT 05403 800-767-1833
TF: 800-767-1833 ■ *Web:* www.uscis.gov

Phone Fax

US Coast Guard (USCG) 2100 Second St SW. . . . . .Washington DC 20593 202-372-4620 372-4986
Web: www.uscg.mil
Boating Safety Office
2703 Martin Luther King Jr Ave SE
Ste 7501 . . . . .Washington DC 20593 202-372-1062
Web: www.uscgboating.org
Law Enforcement Office 2100 Second St SW. . . . .Washington DC 20593 202-372-2183
Web: www.uscg.mil/hq/cg5/cg531
National Maritime Ctr 100 Forbes Dr. . . . . Martinsburg WV 25404 304-433-3400
TF: 888-427-5662 ■ *Web:* www.uscg.mil
National Pollution Funds Ctr
4200 Wilson Blvd Ste 1000. . . . . .Arlington VA 20598 202-493-6700 493-6900
Web: uscg.mil/ccs/npfc
Navigation Ctr 7323 Telegraph Rd. . . . . .Alexandria VA 22315 703-313-5900 313-5920
Web: www.navcen.uscg.gov
Search & Rescue Office 2100 Second St SW. . . . .Washington DC 20593 202-372-2090 372-2912
Web: uscg.mil/hq/cg5/cg534
US Coast Guard Academy 15 Mohegan Ave . . . . New London CT 06320 860-444-8500 701-6700
TF: 800-883-8724 ■ *Web:* www.cga.edu
US Customs & Border Protection
1300 Pennsylvania Ave NW . . . . .Washington DC 20229 703-526-4200
TF: 877-227-5511 ■ *Web:* www.cbp.gov
US Immigration & Customs Enforcement (ICE)
425 'I' St NW. . . . . .Washington DC 20536 202-514-1900
TF: 866-347-2423 ■ *Web:* www.ice.gov
US Secret Service 245 Murray Dr Bldg 410. . . . . .Washington DC 20223 202-406-5830
Web: www.secretservice.gov

340-12 US Department of Housing & Urban Development

Phone Fax

Department of Housing & Urban Development (HUD)
451 Seventh St SW. . . . . .Washington DC 20410 202-708-0685 619-8153
TF: 800-569-4287 ■ *Web:* www.hud.gov
Public Affairs Office 451 Seventh St SW . . . . .Washington DC 20410 202-708-0980
TF: 800-333-4636 ■ *Web:* www.hud.gov
Department of Housing & Urban Development Regional Offices
Boston 10 Cswy St 3rd Fl . . . . Boston MA 02222 617-994-8200 565-6558
TF: 800-225-5342
Great Plains Region 400 State Ave. . . . . .Kansas City KS 66101 913-551-6857 551-5469
Web: portal.hud.gov
Mid-Atlantic Region 100 Penn Sq E. . . . . Philadelphia PA 19107 215-656-0500 656-3445
TF: 800-225-5342 ■ *Web:* www.hud.gov
New York City Regional Office
26 Federal Plaza Ste 3541 . . . . .New York NY 10278 212-264-8000 264-3068
TF: 800-496-4294 ■ *Web:* portal.hud.gov
Pacific/Hawaii Region
600 Harrison St 3rd Fl. . . . . .San Francisco CA 94107 415-489-6572 436-8412
TF: 800-347-3739 ■ *Web:* portal.hud.gov
Region 5 - Chicago
Federal Bldg 77 W Jackson Blvd . . . . .Chicago IL 60604 312-353-6236 353-5417
Web: portal.hud.gov
Rocky Mountain Region 1670 Bdwy 25th Fl . . . . Denver CO 80202 303-672-5440 672-5004
TF: 800-955-2232 ■ *Web:* portal.hud.gov
Seattle Federal Bldg 909 1st Ave Ste 200. . . . . .Seattle WA 98104 509-368-3200
Web: portal.hud.gov
Southeast/Caribbean Region
5 Points Plaza Bldg 40 Marietta St. . . . . .Atlanta GA 30303 404-331-5136 730-2392
Web: www.hud.gov
Southwest Region
801 N Cherry St Unit 45 Ste 2500 . . . . .Fort Worth TX 76102 817-978-5965 978-5569
Web: www.hud.gov
Government National Mortgage Assn
451 Seventh St SW Rm B-133 .Washington DC 20410 202-708-1535
Web: www.ginniemae.gov
HUD Office of Community Planning & Development
451 7th St SW . . . . .Washington DC 20410 202-708-1112 708-1455
Web: www.hud.gov/offices/cpd
Affordable Housing Programs Office
451 Seventh St SW . . . . .Washington DC 20410 202-708-1112
Web: portal.hud.gov
Block Grant (Disaster Recovery Assistance)
451 Seventh St SW . . . . .Washington DC 20410 202-708-1112 708-1455
Web: portal.hud.gov
HIV/AIDS Housing Office 451 7th St SW . . . . .Washington DC 20410 202-708-1112
Web: portal.hud.gov
Special Needs Assistance Programs Office
451 Seventh St SW . . . . .Washington DC 20410 202-708-1112
Web: portal.hud.gov
HUD Office of Fair Housing & Equal Opportunity
451 Seventh St SW. . . . . .Washington DC 20410 202-708-1112 708-4483
TF: 800-669-9777 ■ *Web:* www.hud.gov/offices/fheo
Housing Discrimination Hotline
451 Seventh St SW . . . . .Washington DC 20410 202-708-1112
TF: 800-333-4636 ■ *Web:* portal.hud.gov
HUD Office of Public & Indian Housing
451 Seventh St SW Rm 4100. . . . . .Washington DC 20410 202-708-0950 619-8478
TF: 800-955-2232 ■ *Web:* portal.hud.gov
Real Estate Assessment Ctr
550 12th St SW Ste 100 . . . . .Washington DC 20410 202-708-1112
TF: 888-245-4860 ■ *Web:* portal.hud.gov
Secretary of Housing & Urban Development
451 Seventh St SW. . . . . .Washington DC 20410 202-708-0417 619-8365
Web: portal.hud.gov

340-13 US Department of the Interior

Phone Fax

Department of the Interior (DOI)
1849 C St NW. . . . . .Washington DC 20240 202-208-3100
Web: www.doi.gov

	City	State	Zip	Phone	Fax
National Park Service (NPS)					
1849 C St NW Rm 1013	Washington	DC	20240	202-208-6843	219-0910
Web: www.nps.gov					
Bureau of Indian Affairs (BIA)					
1849 C St NW MS 4141 MIB	Washington	DC	20240	202-208-7163	208-5320
Web: www.bia.gov					
Bureau of Indian Affairs Regional Offices (BIA)					
Alaska Region 3601 C St Ste 1100	Anchorage	AK	99503	907-271-1536	271-1349
TF: 800-645-8397 ■ *Web:* www.bia.gov					
Eastern Oklahoma Region					
3100 W Peak Blvd PO Box 8002	Muskogee	OK	74402	918-781-4600	781-4604
Web: www.bia.gov					
Eastern Region 545 Marriott Dr Ste 700	Nashville	TN	37214	615-564-6700	564-6701
Web: www.bia.gov					
Great Plains Region 115 Fourth Ave SE	Aberdeen	SD	57401	605-226-7343	226-7446
Web: www.bia.gov					
Midwest Region					
Norman Pointe II Bldg					
5600 W American Blvd Ste 500	Bloomington	MN	55347	612-713-4400	713-4401
Web: www.bia.gov					
Navajo Region 301 W Hill St	Gallup	NM	87301	505-863-8314	863-8324
Web: www.bia.gov					
Northwest Region 911 NE 11th Ave	Portland	OR	97232	503-231-6702	231-2201
Web: www.bia.gov					
Pacific Region 2800 Cottage Way	Sacramento	CA	95825	916-978-6000	978-6099
Web: www.bia.gov					
Rocky Mountain Region 316 N 26th St	Billings	MT	59101	406-247-7943	247-7976
Web: www.bia.gov					
Southern Plains Region PO Box 368	Anadarko	OK	73005	405-247-6673	247-5611
Web: www.indianaffairs.gov					
Southwest Region					
1001 Indian School Rd NW	Albuquerque	NM	87104	505-563-3103	563-3101
Web: www.bia.gov					
Western Region					
2600 N Central Ave FL 8 Ste 310	Phoenix	AZ	85008	602-379-6600	379-4413
Web: www.bia.gov					
Bureau of Land Management (BLM)					
1849 C St NW Rm 5665	Washington	DC	20240	202-208-3801	208-5242
Web: www.blm.gov					
National Wild Horse & Burro Program					
1849 C St NW Rm. 5665	Washington	DC	20240	202-208-3801	
TF: 866-468-7826 ■ *Web:* www.blm.gov					
Bureau of Land Management Regional Offices					
Alaska State Office					
222 W Seventh Ave Ste 13	Anchorage	AK	99513	907-271-5960	271-3684
Web: www.blm.gov					
Arizona State Office 1 N Central Ave Ste 800	Phoenix	AZ	85004	602-417-9200	417-9556
Web: www.blm.gov					
California State Office					
2800 Cottage Way Ste W-1834	Sacramento	CA	95825	916-978-4400	978-4416
Web: www.blm.gov					
Colorado State Office 2850 Youngfield St	Lakewood	CO	80215	303-239-3600	239-3933
Web: www.blm.gov					
Eastern States Office 7450 Boston Blvd	Springfield	VA	22153	703-440-1600	
TF: 800-370-3936 ■ *Web:* www.blm.gov					
Idaho State Office 1387 S Vinnell Way	Boise	ID	83709	208-373-4000	373-3899
Web: www.blm.gov					
Montana State Office 5001 Southgate Dr	Billings	MT	59101	406-896-5000	
Web: www.blm.gov					
Nevada State Office 1340 Financial Blvd	Reno	NV	89502	775-861-6400	861-6606
Web: www.blm.gov					
Oregon/Washington State Office					
333 SW First Ave	Portland	OR	97204	503-808-6001	808-6422
Web: www.blm.gov					
Wyoming State Office					
5353 Yellowstone Rd PO Box 1828	Cheyenne	WY	82003	307-775-6256	775-6129
Web: www.blm.gov					
Bureau of Reclamation 1849 C St NW	Washington	DC	20240	202-513-0501	
Web: www.usbr.gov					
Bureau of Reclamation Regional Offices					
Great Plains Region PO Box 36900	Billings	MT	59107	406-247-7600	247-7604
Web: www.usbr.gov					
Lower Colorado Region PO Box 61470	Boulder City	NV	89006	702-293-8411	293-8333
Web: www.usbr.gov					
Mid-Pacific Region					
2800 Cottage Way Federal Bldg.	Sacramento	CA	95825	916-978-5000	978-5005
Web: www.usbr.gov					
Pacific Northwest Region					
1150 N Curtis Rd Ste 100	Boise	ID	83706	208-378-5012	378-5019
Web: www.usbr.gov					
Upper Colorado Region					
125 S State St Rm 6107	Salt Lake City	UT	84138	801-524-3600	524-5499
Web: www.usbr.gov/uc					
Minerals Management Service					
1849 C St NW Ste 4210	Washington	DC	20240	202-208-3985	208-7242
Web: www.doi.gov					
National Interagency Fire Ctr					
3833 S Development Ave	Boise	ID	83705	208-387-5512	
TF: 877-471-2262 ■ *Web:* www.nifc.gov					
Conservation & Outdoor Recreation Programs					
1849 C St NW Org Code 2220	Washington	DC	20240	202-354-6900	371-5179
Web: www.nps.gov/ncrc					
National Register of Historic Places					
1201 Eye St NW 9th fl	Washington	DC	20005	202-354-2201	371-5197
Web: www.nps.gov/history/index.htm					
National Park Service Regional Offices					
Alaska Region 240 W Fifth Ave Ste 114	Anchorage	AK	99501	907-644-3510	644-3816
Web: nps.gov					
National Park Service Regional Offices Intermountain Region					
12795 W Alameda Pkwy	Denver	CO	80225	303-969-2500	
Web: www.nps.gov					
National Park Service Regional Offices National Capital Region					
1100 Ohio Dr SW	Washington	DC	20242	202-619-7000	619-7220
Web: www.nps.gov/ncro					
National Park Service Regional Offices NortheastRegion					
200 Chestnut St Ste 3	Philadelphia	PA	19106	215-597-7013	597-0815
Web: www.nps.gov					
National Park Service Regional Offices Southeast Region					
100 Alabama St SW 1924 Bldg.	Atlanta	GA	30303	404-507-5600	562-3201
Web: www.nps.gov					
Office of Surface Mining Reclamation & Enforcement					
1951 Constitution Ave NW S Interior Bldg	Washington	DC	20240	202-208-4006	
Web: www.osmre.gov					
Secretary of the Interior 1849 C St NW	Washington	DC	20240	202-208-3100	
Web: www.doi.gov					
US Board on Geographic Names					
12201 Sunrise Valley Dr.	Reston	VA	20192	703-648-4552	648-4549
Web: geonames.usgs.gov					
US Fish & Wildlife Service (USFWS)					
1849 C St NW	Washington	DC	20240	202-208-4717	208-6965
TF: 800-344-9453 ■ *Web:* www.fws.gov					
US Fish & Wildlife Service Regional Offices					
Alaska Region 1011 E Tudor Rd.	Anchorage	AK	99503	907-786-3309	786-3495
Web: www.fws.gov					
California & Nevada Region					
2800 Cottage Way	Sacramento	CA	95825	916-414-6464	414-6486
Web: www.fws.gov					
Great Lakes/Big Rivers Region					
5600 American Blvd W Ste 900	Bloomington	MN	55437	612-713-5360	713-5280
TF: 800-877-8339 ■ *Web:* www.fws.gov/midwest					
Mountain-Prairie Region 134 Union Blvd	Lakewood	CO	80228	303-236-7905	236-8295
Web: www.fws.gov/mountain-prairie					
NortheastRegion 300 Westgate Ctr Dr	Hadley	MA	01035	413-253-8200	253-8308
Web: www.fws.gov					
Pacific Region					
Eastside Federal Complex 911 NE 11th Ave	Portland	OR	97232	503-231-6838	231-6161
Web: www.fws.gov/pacific					
Southeast Region 1875 Century Blvd Ste 400	Atlanta	GA	30345	404-679-4000	679-4006
Web: www.fws.gov/southeast					
Southwest Region					
500 Gold Ave SW PO Box 1306	Albuquerque	NM	87102	505-248-6911	248-6910
Web: www.fws.gov/southwest					
US Geological Survey (USGS)					
12201 Sunrise Valley Dr.	Reston	VA	20192	703-648-6723	
TF: 888-275-8747 ■ *Web:* www.usgs.gov					
Ask USGS 12201 Sunrise Valley Dr.	Reston	VA	20192	703-648-5953	
TF: 888-275-8747 ■ *Web:* usgs.gov					

340-14 US Department of Justice

	City	State	Zip	Phone	Fax
Department of Justice (DOJ)					
950 Pennsylvania Ave NW	Washington	DC	20530	202-514-2007	514-5331
Web: www.justice.gov					
Antitrust Div 950 Pennsylvania Ave NW.	Washington	DC	20530	202-514-2401	616-2645
Web: www.justice.gov					
Civil Div 950 Pennsylvania Ave NW.	Washington	DC	20530	202-514-3301	514-8071
Web: www.justice.gov					
Civil Rights Div 950 Pennsylvania Ave NW	Washington	DC	20530	202-514-4609	
Web: www.justice.gov					
Community Relations Service 600 E St NW	Washington	DC	20530	202-305-2935	305-3009
Web: www.justice.gov					
Criminal Div 601 D St NW	Washington	DC	20530	202-514-0296	
Web: www.justice.gov					
Environment & Natural Resources Div					
950 Pennsylvania Ave NW	Washington	DC	20530	202-514-2701	514-0557
Web: www.justice.gov					
National Security Div					
950 Pennsylvania Ave NW	Washington	DC	20530	202-514-1057	
Web: www.justice.gov					
Office of Information & Privacy					
1425 New York Ave NW Ste 11050	Washington	DC	20530	202-514-3642	514-1009
Web: www.justice.gov					
Public Affairs Office					
950 Pennsylvania Ave NW	Washington	DC	20530	202-514-2000	
Web: www.justice.gov					
Tax Div 950 Pennsylvania Ave NW 4th Fl	Washington	DC	20530	202-514-2901	514-5479
Web: www.justice.gov					
Department of Justice Antitrust Div Regional Office					
Dallas Field Office 1601 Elm St Ste 4950	Dallas	TX	75201	214-880-9401	353-8856*
**Fax Area Code:* 202 ■ *Web:* www.justice.gov					
Department of Justice Antitrust Div Regional Offices					
Atlanta Field Office					
Federal Bldg 75 Spring St SW Ste 1176	Atlanta	GA	30303	404-331-7100	331-7110
Web: www.justice.gov/atr					
Chicago Field Office 209 S LaSalle St Ste 600	Chicago	IL	60604	202-353-1555	353-1046*
**Fax Area Code:* 312 ■ *Web:* www.justice.gov					
Cleveland Field Office					
55 Erieview Plaza Ste 700	Cleveland	OH	44114	216-522-4070	522-8332
Web: www.justice.gov					
New York Field Office					
26 Federal Plaza Rm 3630	New York	NY	10278	212-264-0383	264-0678
Web: www.justice.gov/atr					
Philadelphia Field Office					
7th & Walnut St Ste 650	Philadelphia	PA	19106	215-597-7405	597-8838
Web: www.justice.gov					
San Francisco Field Office					
PO Box 36046	San Francisco	CA	94102	415-436-6660	436-6687
Web: www.justice.gov/atr					
Federal Bureau of Prisons 320 First St NW	Washington	DC	20534	202-307-3198	514-6620
Web: www.bop.gov					
Bureau of Alcohol Tobacco Firearms & Explosives (ATF)					
650 Massachusetts Ave NW	Washington	DC	20226	202-927-8210	
Web: www.atf.gov					
Bureau of Alcohol Tobacco Firearms & Explosives Regional Offices					
Atlanta Field Div 2600 Century Pkwy NE	Atlanta	GA	30345	404-417-2600	417-2601
Web: www.atf.gov					

	City	State	Zip	Phone	Fax
Baltimore Field Div 31 Hopkins Plaza 5th Fl *Web:* www.atf.gov/baltimore-field-division	Baltimore	MD	21201	410-779-1700	
Boston Field Div 10 Cswy St Ste 791	Boston	MA	02222	617-557-1200	557-1201
Charlotte Field Div 6701 Carmel Rd Ste 200 *Web:* www.atf.gov	Charlotte	NC	28226	704-716-1800	716-1801
Chicago Field Div 525 W Van Buren St Ste 600 *Web:* atf.gov	Chicago	IL	60607	312-846-7200	846-7201
Columbus Field Div 37 W Broad St Ste 200 *Web:* www.atf.gov	Columbus	OH	43215	614-827-8400	827-8401
Dallas Field Div 1114 Commerce St Rm 303 *Web:* www.atf.gov	Dallas	TX	75242	469-227-4300	227-4330
Denver Field Div 950 17th St Ste 1800 *Web:* www.atf.gov	Denver	CO	80202	303-575-7600	575-7601
Detroit Field Div 1155 Brewery Pk Blvd Ste 300 *Web:* www.atf.gov	Detroit	MI	48207	313-202-3400	202-3445
Houston Field Div 333 W Loop N # 111 *Web:* www.atf.gov	Houston	TX	77024	713-220-2157	
Kansas City Field Div 2600 Grand Ave Ste 280	Kansas City	MO	64108	816-559-0850	559-0831
Louisville Field Div 600 Martin Luther King Pl #322 *Web:* www.atf.gov	Louisville	KY	40202	502-753-3400	753-3401
Miami Field Div 11410 NW 20 St Ste 201 *Web:* www.atf.gov	Miami	FL	33172	305-597-4800	597-4801
Nashville Field Div 5300 Maryland Way Ste 200 *Web:* www.atf.gov/nashville-field-division	Brentwood	TN	37027	615-565-1400	565-1401
New Orleans Field Div 1 Galleria Blvd Ste 1700	Metairie	LA	70001	504-841-7000	841-7159
Philadelphia Field Div 601 Walnut St. *Web:* www.atf.gov	Philadelphia	PA	19106	215-446-7800	446-7811
Phoenix Field Div 201 E Washington St Ste 940 *Web:* www.atf.gov	Phoenix	AZ	85004	602-776-5400	776-5429
Saint Paul Field Div 30 E Seventh St Ste 1900 *Web:* www.atf.gov	Saint Paul	MN	55101	651-726-0200	726-0201
Tampa Field Div 400 N Tampa St Ste 2100 *Web:* www.atf.gov	Tampa	FL	33602	813-202-7300	202-7301
Washington (DC) Field Div 1401 H St NW Ste 900 *Web:* www.atf.gov/field/washington	Washington	DC	20226	202-648-8010	648-8001
Community Oriented Policing Services (COPS) 1100 Vermont Ave NW 10th Fl *TF:* 800-421-6770 ■ *Web:* www.cops.usdoj.gov	Washington	DC	20530	202-514-5328	
Drug Enforcement Administration (DEA) 700 Army-Navy Dr *Web:* www.justice.gov	Arlington	VA	22202	202-307-7596	
DEA Training Academy PO Box 1475 *Web:* justice.gov	Quantico	VA	22134	703-632-5000	
El Paso Intelligence Ctr 11339 Simms St. *Web:* www.justice.gov	El Paso	TX	79908	202-307-1000	
Drug Enforcement Administration Regional Offices					
Atlanta Div Federal Bldg 75 Spring St SW *Web:* www.justice.gov	Atlanta	GA	30303	404-893-7000	
Boston Div 15 New Sudbury St Rm E400 *Web:* www.justice.gov	Boston	MA	02203	617-557-2100	
Chicago Div Federal Bldg 230 S Dearborn St *Web:* www.justice.gov	Chicago	IL	60604	312-353-7875	
Dallas Div 10160 Technology Blvd E *Web:* www.justice.gov	Dallas	TX	75220	214-366-6900	
Detroit Div 431 Howard St *Web:* www.justice.gov	Detroit	MI	48226	313-234-4000	
Houston Div 1433 W Loop S Ste 600 *Web:* www.justice.gov	Houston	TX	77027	713-693-3000	
Los Angeles Div Federal Bldg 255 E Temple St 20th Fl *Web:* www.justice.gov	Los Angeles	CA	90012	213-621-6700	
Miami Div 8400 NW 53rd St *Web:* www.justice.gov	Miami	FL	33166	305-994-4870	
New Orleans Div 3838 N Cswy Blvd Ste 1800 *Web:* www.justice.gov	Metairie	LA	70002	504-840-1100	
New York Div 99 Tenth Ave *Web:* www.justice.gov	New York	NY	10011	212-337-3900	
Philadelphia Div Federal Bldg 600 Arch St Rm 10224 *Web:* www.justice.gov	Philadelphia	PA	19106	215-861-3474	
Phoenix Div 3010 N Second St Ste 301 *Web:* www.justice.gov	Phoenix	AZ	85012	602-664-5600	
Saint Louis Div 317 S 16th St *Web:* www.justice.gov	Saint Louis	MO	63103	314-538-4600	
San Diego Div 4560 Viewridge Ave *Web:* www.justice.gov	San Diego	CA	92123	858-616-4100	
San Francisco Div 450 Golden Gate Ave *Web:* www.justice.gov	San Francisco	CA	94102	415-436-7900	
Seattle Div 400 Second Ave W *Web:* www.justice.gov	Seattle	WA	98119	206-553-5443	
Washington DC Div 800 K St NW Ste 500 *Web:* www.justice.gov	Washington	DC	20001	202-305-8500	514-1009
Executive Office for Immigration Review 5107 Leesburg Pike *Web:* www.justice.gov	Falls Church	VA	22041	703-305-0289	605-0365
Executive Office for US Trustees 441 G St NW Ste 6150	Washington	DC	20530	202-307-1399	307-2397
Federal Bureau of Investigation (FBI) 935 Pennsylvania Ave NW *Web:* www.fbi.gov	Washington	DC	20535	202-324-3000	
Criminal Justice Information Services 1000 Custer Hollow Rd *Web:* fbi.gov/about-us/cjis/cjis	Clarksburg	WV	26306	304-625-4995	
FBI Laboratory 1970 E Parham Rd *Web:* www.fbi.gov	Richmond	VA	23228	804-261-1044	627-4494
Management & Specialty Training Ctr 791 Chambers Rd *Web:* www.bop.gov/about/facilities/training_centers.jsp	Aurora	CO	80011	303-340-7800	
National Institute of Corrections 320 First St NW *TF:* 800-995-6423 ■ *Web:* nicic.gov	Washington	DC	20534	202-307-3106	
National Institute of Corrections Information Cent 11900 E Cornell Ave Unit C *TF:* 800-877-1461 ■ *Web:* nicic.gov	Aurora	CO	80014	800-877-1461	
Federal Bureau of Prisons Regional Offices					
Mid-Atlantic Region 302 Sentinel Dr Ste 200 *Web:* www.bop.gov	Annapolis Junction	MD	20701	301-317-3100	
North Central Region 400 State Ave Ste 800 *Web:* www.bop.gov/about/ro/ncr	Kansas City	KS	66101	913-621-3939	
Northeast Region 200 Chestnut St 7th Fl *Web:* www.bop.gov	Philadelphia	PA	19106	215-521-7301	
South Central Region 4211 Cedar Springs Rd *Web:* www.bop.gov	Dallas	TX	75219	214-224-3389	
Southeast Region 3800 Camp Creek Pk SW Bldg 2000 *Web:* www.bop.gov	Atlanta	GA	30331	678-686-1200	
Foreign Claims Settlement Commission of the US 600 E St NW *Web:* www.justice.gov	Washington	DC	20579	202-616-6975	616-6993
National Criminal Justice Reference Service PO Box 6000 *TF:* 800-851-3420 ■ *Web:* www.ncjrs.gov	Rockville	MD	20849	301-240-7760	240-5830
National Drug Intelligence Ctr 319 Washington St 5th Fl *Web:* www.justice.gov	Johnstown	PA	15901	814-532-4601	532-4690
Office of Justice Programs (OJP) 810 Seventh St NW *Web:* ojp.gov	Washington	DC	20531	202-307-0703	
Bureau of Justice Assistance 810 Seventh St NW *TF:* 888-744-6513 ■ *Web:* www.bja.gov	Washington	DC	20531	202-616-6500	305-1367
Community Capacity Development Office 810 Seventh St NW *Web:* ojp.gov/ccdo	Washington	DC	20531	202-307-5933	
National Institute of Justice 810 Seventh St NW *Web:* www.nij.gov	Washington	DC	20531	202-307-2942	
Office for Victims of Crime 810 Seventh St NW 8th Fl *TF:* 800-363-0441 ■ *Web:* ojp.gov/ovc	Washington	DC	20531	202-307-5983	514-6383
Office of Juvenile Justice & Delinquency Prevention (OJJDP) 810 Seventh St NW *Web:* www.ojjdp.gov	Washington	DC	20531	202-307-5911	307-2093
Office of Special Counsel for Immigration-Related Unfair Employment Practices 950 Pennsylvania Ave NW *TF:* 800-255-7688 ■ *Web:* www.justice.gov	Washington	DC	20038	202-616-5594	616-5509
Office of the Pardon Attorney 145 N St NE Rm 5E *Web:* www.justice.gov	Washington	DC	20530	202-616-6070	616-6069
Office of Tribal Justice 950 Pennsylvania Ave NW *Web:* www.justice.gov	Washington	DC	20530	202-514-2000	
Office on Violence Against Women 145 N St Ste 10W 121 *Web:* justice.gov/ovw	Washington	DC	20530	202-307-6026	307-2277
US Marshals Service 401 Courthouse Square *TF General:* 800-336-0102 ■ *Web:* www.usmarshals.gov	Alexandria	VA	22314	202-307-9100	
US National Central Bureau of INTERPOL (INTERPOL) 600 E St NW Ste 600 *Web:* www.justice.gov	Washington	DC	20530	202-616-9000	616-8400
US Parole Commission 5550 Friendship Blvd Rm 420 *TF:* 888-585-9103 ■ *Web:* www.justice.gov	Chevy Chase	MD	20815	301-492-5990	

340-15 US Department of Labor

	City	State	Zip	Phone	Fax
Department of Labor (DOL) 200 Constitution Ave NW *TF:* 866-487-2365 ■ *Web:* www.dol.gov	Washington	DC	20210	202-693-4650	
Job Corps 200 Constitution Ave NW Ste N4463 *TF:* 800-733-5627 ■ *Web:* www.jobcorps.gov	Washington	DC	20210	202-693-3000	693-2767
Office of Administrative Law Judges 200 Constitution Ave NW Ste 400 N *TF:* 877-889-5627 ■ *Web:* www.oalj.dol.gov	Washington	DC	20210	202-693-7300	693-7365
Public Affairs Office 200 Constitution Ave NW. *TF:* 866-487-2365 ■ *Web:* www.dol.gov	Washington	DC	20210	202-693-4650	693-5057
Department of Labor Regional Offices					
Region 1 - Boston JFK Federal Bldg Ste 525 *Web:* www.dol.gov	Boston	MA	02203	617-565-2072	
Region 10-Seattle 300 Fifth Ave Ste 1280 *Web:* www.osha.gov	Seattle	WA	98104	206-757-6700	757-6705
Region 2 - New York 201 Varick St Rm 983 *Web:* www.dol.gov	New York	NY	10014	646-264-3650	
Region 3 - Philadelphia 170 S Independence Mall W Ste 631E West *Web:* www.dol.gov	Philadelphia	PA	19106	215-861-4860	861-4867
Region 3 Atlanta 400 W Bay St Rm 63A *Web:* www.dol.gov	Jacksonville	FL	32202	904-351-0551	351-0560
Region 5 - Chicago 230 S Dearborn St *Web:* www.doleta.gov	Chicago	IL	60604	312-596-5400	596-5401
Region 6 Dallas Federal Bldg 525 S Griffin St Rm 407 *Web:* www.dol.gov/owcp/contacts/dallas/arf.htm	Dallas	TX	75202	972-850-2409	850-2401

				Phone	Fax
Region 8 - Denver 1999 Broadway Ste 1620 *Web:* www.dol.gov	Denver	CO	80202	303-844-1286	844-1283
Employment & Training Administration 200 Constitution Ave NW *TF:* 866-487-2365 ■ *Web:* www.doleta.gov	Washington	DC	20210	866-487-2365	
US Dept of Labor 200 Constitution Ave NW *Web:* www.dol.gov/vets	Washington	DC	20210	202-693-4700	693-4754
Bureau of International Labor Affairs 200 Constitution Ave NW *Web:* www.dol.gov/ilab	Washington	DC	20210	202-693-4770	693-4780
Bureau of Labor Statistics 2 Massachusetts Ave NE *TF:* 800-877-8339 ■ *Web:* www.bls.gov	Washington	DC	20212	202-691-5200	691-7890
Consumer Price Index 2 Massachusetts Ave NE *TF:* 800-877-8339 ■ *Web:* www.bls.gov/cpi	Washington	DC	20212	202-691-5200	691-6325
Bureau of Labor Statistics Regional Offices					
Mid-Atlantic Information Office 170 S Independence Mall W Ste 610 E *Web:* www.bls.gov/ro3	Philadelphia	PA	19106	215-597-3282	861-5720
Midwest Information Office 230 S Dearborn St Ste 960 *Web:* www.bls.gov	Chicago	IL	60604	312-353-1880	353-1886
Mountain-Plains Information Office 2300 Main St Ste 1190 *TF:* 800-487-9004 ■ *Web:* www.bls.gov/ro7	Kansas City	MO	64108	816-285-7000	285-7009
New England Information Office JFK Federal Bldg Ste E-310 *Web:* www.bls.gov/ro1	Boston	MA	02203	617-565-2327	565-4182
New York-New Jersey Information Office 201 Varick St Rm 808 **Fax Area Code:* 212 ■ *TF:* 800-877-8339 ■ *Web:* www.bls.gov/ro2	New York	NY	10014	646-264-3600	337-2532*
Southeast Information Office 61 Forsyth St *TF:* 800-347-3764 ■ *Web:* www.bls.gov	Atlanta	GA	30303	404-893-4222	893-4221
Southwest Information Office Federal Bldg 525 Griffin St Rm 221 **Fax Area Code:* 214 ■ *Web:* www.bls.gov/ro6	Dallas	TX	75202	972-850-4800	767-8881*
Western Information Office PO Box 193766 *Web:* www.bls.gov	San Francisco	CA	94119	415-625-2270	625-2351
Employee Benefits Security Administration 200 Constitution Ave NW Rm S2524 *Web:* www.dol.gov/ebsa	Washington	DC	20210	202-693-8300	219-5526
Employment & Training Administration Regional Offices					
Region 3- Atlanta Federal Ctr 61 Forsyth St SW Rm 6M12 **Fax Area Code:* 404 ■ *TF:* 877-872-5627 ■ *Web:* www.doleta.gov/regions/reg03	Atlanta	GA	20210	877-872-5627	302-5382*
Region 4- Dallas Federal Bldg 525 Griffin St Rm 317 *Web:* www.doleta.gov/regions/reg04	Dallas	TX	75202	972-850-4600	850-4605
Region 5 - Chicago Federal Bldg 230 S Dearborn St 6th Fl *Web:* www.doleta.gov/regions/reg05	Chicago	IL	60604	312-596-5400	596-5401
Region I - Boston 25 New Sudbury St Rm E-350 *Web:* www.doleta.gov/regions/reg01bos	Boston	MA	02203	617-788-0170	788-0101
Region II-Philadelphia 170 S Independence Mall W Ste 825 E *Web:* www.doleta.gov	Philadelphia	PA	19106	215-861-5200	861-5260
Employment Standards Administration 200 Constitution Ave NW Rm S2321 *TF:* 866-487-2365 ■ *Web:* www.dol.gov	Washington	DC	20210	202-693-0200	
Office of Labor-Management Standards (OLMS) 200 Constitution Ave NW Rm N-1519 *TF:* 866-487-2365 ■ *Web:* www.dol.gov/olms	Washington	DC	20210	866-487-2365	
Office of Workers" Compensation Programs 200 Constitution Ave Ste S3524	Washington	DC	20210	202-693-8673	
Wage & Hour Div 200 Constitution Ave NW *Web:* doleta.gov	Washington	DC	20210	202-693-0051	
Labor Racketeering & Fraud Investigations Office 200 Constitution Ave NW Rm S5014 *Web:* www.oig.dol.gov/olrfi.htm	Washington	DC	20210	202-693-5100	
Mine Safety & Health Administration (MSHA) 1100 Wilson Blvd *TF:* 800-746-1553 ■ *Web:* www.msha.gov	Arlington	VA	22209	202-693-9400	693-9401
Coal Mine Safety & Health Office 1100 Wilson Blvd *Web:* www.msha.gov/programs/coal.htm	Arlington	VA	22209	202-693-9500	
Metal & Non-Metal Mine Safety & Health Office 1100 Wilson Blvd *Web:* www.msha.gov/programs/metal.htm	Arlington	VA	22209	202-693-9600	693-9601
National Mine Health & Safety Academy 1301 Airport Rd *Web:* www.msha.gov	Beaver	WV	25813	304-256-3100	256-3324
Occupational Safety & Health Administration (OSHA) 200 Constitution Ave NW *TF:* 800-321-6742 ■ *Web:* www.osha.gov	Washington	DC	20210	202-693-1999	693-1659
Occupational Safety & Health Administration Regional Offices					
Region 1 JFK Federal Bldg Rm E-340 *TF:* 800-321-6742 ■ *Web:* www.osha.gov/oshdir/r01.html	Boston	MA	02203	617-565-9860	565-9827
Region 10 300 Fifth Ave Ste 1280 *TF Help Line:* 800-321-6742 ■ *Web:* www.osha.gov/oshdir	Seattle	WA	98104	206-757-6700	757-6705
Region 2 201 Varick St Ste 670 *TF:* 800-321-6742 ■ *Web:* www.osha.gov/oshdir/r02.html	New York	NY	10014	212-337-2378	337-2371
Region 3 Curtis Ctr 170 S Independence Mall W Ste 740W *TF:* 800-321-6742 ■ *Web:* www.osha.gov	Philadelphia	PA	19106	215-861-4900	861-4904
Region 4 61 Forsyth St SW Rm 6T50 **Fax Area Code:* 404 ■ *Web:* www.osha.gov/oshdir/r04.html	Atlanta	GA	30303	678-237-0400	562-2295*
Region 5 230 S Dearborn St Rm 3244 *Web:* www.osha.gov/oshdir/r05.html	Chicago	IL	60604	312-353-2220	353-7774
Region 6 525 Griffin St Ste 602 *Web:* www.osha.gov/oshdir/r06.html	Dallas	TX	75202	972-850-4145	850-4149
Region 7 2300 Main St Suite 1010 2 Pershing Square Bldg *Web:* www.osha.gov/oshdir/r07.html	Kansas City	MO	64108	816-283-8745	283-0547
Region 8 1244 Speer Blvd Ste 551 Cesar Chavez Memorial Bldg *Web:* www.osha.gov/oshdir/r08.html	Denver	CO	80204	720-264-6550	264-6585
Region 9 90 Seventh St Ste 18100 *Web:* www.osha.gov/oshdir/r09.html	San Francisco	CA	94103	415-625-2547	625-2534
Office of Disability Employment Policy 200 Constitution Ave NW Ste S1303 *TF:* 866-633-7365 ■ *Web:* www.dol.gov/odep	Washington	DC	20210	202-693-7880	693-7888
Secretary of Labor 200 Constitution Ave NW Rm S2018 *TF:* 866-487-2365 ■ *Web:* www.dol.gov	Washington	DC	20210	202-693-6000	693-6111
Women's Bureau 200 Constitution Ave NW Rm S3002 *TF:* 800-827-5335 ■ *Web:* www.dol.gov/wb	Washington	DC	20210	202-693-6710	
Women's Bureau Regional Offices					
Region 1 JFK Federal Bldg Rm 525-A *Web:* www.dol.gov/wb	Boston	MA	02203	617-565-1988	565-1986
Region 10 1111 Third Ave Ste 620 *TF:* 800-827-5335 ■ *Web:* www.dol.gov	Seattle	WA	98101	206-553-1534	553-5085
Region 2 201 Varick St Rm 602 *TF:* 800-827-5335 ■ *Web:* www.dol.gov/wb	New York	NY	10014	212-337-2389	337-2394
Region 3 200 Constitution Ave NW Ste 631E **Fax Area Code:* 215 ■ *TF:* 800-827-5335 ■ *Web:* www.dol.gov/wb	Washington	DC	20210	866-487-2365	861-4867*
Region 4 Sam Nunn Federal Ctr 61 Forsyth St SW Ste 6B75 *TF:* 800-827-5335 ■ *Web:* www.dol.gov	Atlanta	GA	30303	404-562-2336	562-2413
Region 5 Federal Bldg 230 S Dearborn St Rm 1022 *TF:* 800-827-5335 ■ *Web:* www.dol.gov	Chicago	IL	60604	312-353-6985	353-6986
Region 6 Federal Bldg 525 Griffin St Ste 735 *TF:* 800-827-5335 ■ *Web:* www.dol.gov/wb	Dallas	TX	75202	972-850-4700	850-4706
Region 7 2300 Main St Ste 1050 *TF:* 800-827-5335 ■ *Web:* www.dol.gov	Kansas City	MO	64108	816-285-7233	285-7237
Region 8 1999 Broadway Ste 1620 PO Box 46550 *TF:* 800-827-5335 ■ *Web:* www.dol.gov/wb	Denver	CO	80201	303-844-1286	844-1283
Region 9 90 Seventh St Ste 2650 *TF:* 800-827-5335 ■ *Web:* www.dol.gov	San Francisco	CA	94103	415-625-2638	625-2641

340-16 US Department of State

				Phone	Fax
Department of State 2201 C St NW *Web:* www.state.gov	Washington	DC	20520	202-647-4000	647-3344
Bureau of Consular Affairs 2201 C St NW SA-29 *TF:* 888-407-4747 ■ *Web:* travel.state.gov	Washington	DC	20520	202-501-4444	
Office of Children's Issues SA-17 9th Fl *TF:* 888-407-4747 ■ *Web:* www.travel.state.gov	Washington	DC	20522	202-501-4444	485-6221
Passport Services 1111 19th St NW Ste 500 *TF:* 888-874-7793 ■ *Web:* travel.state.gov	Washington	DC	20524	877-487-2778	
Bureau of Diplomatic Security DS Public Affairs 2201 C St NW *Web:* www.state.gov	Washington	DC	20522	571-345-2502	
Bureau of East Asian & Pacific Affairs 2201 C St NW Rm 2236 *Web:* www.state.gov/p/eap	Washington	DC	20520	202-895-3500	
Colorado Passport Agency *Colorado Agency* 3151 S Vaughn Way Ste 600 *TF:* 888-874-7793 ■ *Web:* travel.state.gov	Aurora	CO	80014	877-487-2778	
Foreign Service Institute 4000 Arlington Blvd Rt 50 *Web:* www.state.gov/m/fsi	Arlington	VA	22204	703-302-6703	
International Boundary & Water Commission - US & Mexico 4171 N Mesa Ste C-100 *TF:* 800-262-8857 ■ *Web:* www.ibwc.state.gov	El Paso	TX	79902	915-832-4101	832-4190
International Boundary Commission - US & Canada 2000 L St NW Ste 615 *Web:* www.internationalboundarycommission.org	Washington	DC	20036	202-736-9102	632-2008
Passport Services Regional Offices					
Boston Agency 10 Cswy St Rm 247 Tip O'Neill Federal Bldg *TF:* 877-487-2778 ■ *Web:* www.travel.state.gov	Boston	MA	02222	877-487-2778	
Chicago Agency Kluczynski Federal Bldg 230 S Dearborn St 18th Fl **Fax Area Code:* 888 ■ *TF:* 877-487-2778 ■ *Web:* www.travel.state.gov	Chicago	IL	60604	877-487-2778	874-7793*
Connecticut Agency 850 Canal St *TF:* 877-487-2778 ■ *Web:* www.travel.state.gov	Stamford	CT	06902	877-487-2778	
Honolulu Agency 300 Ala Moana Bldg Ste 1-330 *TF:* 877-487-2778 ■ *Web:* www.travel.state.gov	Honolulu	HI	96850	877-487-2778	
Los Angeles Agency 11000 Wilshire Blvd Ste 1000 *TF:* 877-487-2778 ■ *Web:* www.travel.state.gov	Los Angeles	CA	90024	877-487-2778	
New Orleans Agency 365 Canal St Ste 1300 *TF:* 877-487-2778 ■ *Web:* travel.state.gov/content/passports/en/passports/information/where-to-apply/agencies/new-orleans.html	New Orleans	LA	70130	877-487-2778	
New York Agency 376 Hudson St 10th Fl *TF:* 877-487-2778 ■ *Web:* www.travel.state.gov	New York	NY	10014	877-487-2778	
Philadelphia Agency US Custom House 200 Chesnut St Rm 103 *TF:* 877-487-2778 ■ *Web:* www.travel.state.gov	Philadelphia	PA	19106	877-487-2778	
San Francisco Agency 95 Hawthorne St 5th Fl *TF:* 877-487-2778 ■ *Web:* www.travel.state.gov	San Francisco	CA	94105	877-487-2778	
Seattle Agency 300 Fifth Ave Ste 800 *Web:* www.state.gov/m/ds/rls/rpt/18892.htm	Seattle	WA	98104	206-393-0740	393-0739

Phone Fax

Washington (DC) Agency
600 19th St NW 1st Floor Sidewalk Level .... Washington DC 20006 877-487-2778
TF: 877-487-2778 ■ *Web:* www.travel.state.gov
Secretary of State 2201 C St NW .... Washington DC 20520 202-647-4000
Web: www.state.gov
Bureau of Intelligence & Research
2201 C St NW .... Washington DC 20520 202-895-3500
Web: www.state.gov/s/inr
Office of the Chief of Protocol
2201 C St NW .... Washington DC 20520 202-647-1735
Web: www.state.gov/s/cpr
Office of the Coordinator for Counterterrorism
2201 C St NW Rm 2206 .... Washington DC 20520 202-895-3500
Web: www.state.gov/s/ct
U.S Department of State Diplomacy in action
Houston Agency
Federal Bldg 1919 Smith St Ste 1100 .... Houston TX 77002 713-654-0401 209-3470
Web: www.state.gov/m/ds/rls/rpt/18892.htm
Under Secretary for Arms Control & International Security
Bureau of International Security & Nonproliferatio
2201 C St NW Rm 2236 .... Washington DC 20520 202-647-5116
Web: www.state.gov
Bureau of Verification Compliance & Implementation
2201 C St NW Rm 2236 .... Washington DC 20520 202-647-5116
Web: www.state.gov
Under Secretary for Democracy & Global Affairs
Bureau of Democracy Human Rights & Labor
2201 C St NW Rm 7802 .... Washington DC 20520 202-647-5116
Web: www.state.gov
Under Secretary for Political Affairs
Bureau of European & Eurasian Affairs
2201 C St NW Rm 2236 .... Washington DC 20520 202-647-5116
Web: www.state.gov/p/eur
Bureau of International Organization Affairs
2201 C St NW .... Washington DC 20520 202-647-9600
Web: www.state.gov/p/io
Bureau of Near Eastern Affairs
2201 C St NW Rm 2236 .... Washington DC 20520 202-647-7209
Web: www.state.gov/p/nea
Bureau of Western Hemisphere Affairs
2201 C St NW .... Washington DC 20520 202-647-4000
Web: www.state.gov/p/wha
Under Secretary for Public Diplomacy & Public Affairs
Bureau of Educational & Cultural Affairs
301 Fourth St SW .... Washington DC 20547 202-453-8800
Web: eca.state.gov
Bureau of Public Affairs
2201 C St NW Rm 2206 .... Washington DC 20520 202-647-8411 647-3344
Web: www.state.gov

340-17 US Department of Transportation

Phone Fax

Department of Transportation (DOT)
1200 New Jersey Ave SE .... Washington DC 20590 202-366-4000
Web: www.transportation.gov
Federal Aviation Administration (FAA)
800 Independence Ave SW .... Washington DC 20591 866-835-5322
TF: 866-835-5322 ■ *Web:* www.faa.gov
Accident Investigation Office
800 Independence Ave SW Rm 840 .... Washington DC 20591 202-267-9612
Web: www.faa.gov/about/office_org/headquarters_offices/avs
Aircraft Certification Service
800 Independence Ave SW Ste 800 E .... Washington DC 20591 202-267-8235 267-5364
Web: www.faa.gov/about/office_org/headquarters_offices/avs/offices/air
Commercial Space Transportation Office
800 Independence Ave SW .... Washington DC 20591 202-267-7793 267-5450
Web: www.faa.gov
FAA Academy
Mike Monroney Aeronautical Ctr
6500 S MacArthur Blvd .... Oklahoma City OK 73169 405-954-6900 954-3018
Web: www.faa.gov
Flight Standards Service
800 Independence Ave SW Rm 821 .... Washington DC 20591 202-267-8237 267-5230
Web: www.faa.gov/about/office_org/headquarters_offices/avs
Great Lakes Region 2300 E Devon Ave .... Des Plaines IL 60018 847-294-7272 294-7036
Web: www.faa.gov
International Aviation Office
800 Independence Ave SW .... Washington DC 20591 202-385-8900 267-7198
Web: www.faa.gov
Mike Monroney Aeronautical Ctr
6500 S MacArthur Blvd .... Oklahoma City OK 73125 405-954-4821
Web: www.faa.gov/about/office_org
Safety Hotline 800 Independence Ave SW .... Washington DC 20591 800-255-1111
TF: 800-255-1111 ■ *Web:* www.faa.gov
William J Hughes Technical Ctr
Bldg 300 4th Fl G34 .... Atlantic City NJ 08405 609-485-6675 485-4667
Web: www.faa.gov/about/office_org/tc
Federal Aviation Administration Northwest Mountain Region
1601 Lind Ave SW .... Renton WA 98057 425-227-2001
TF: 800-220-5715 ■ *Web:* www.faa.gov
Federal Aviation Administration Regional Offices (FAA)
Alaskan Region 222 W Seventh Ave Ste 14 .... Anchorage AK 99513 907-271-5438 271-2851
Web: www.faa.gov
Central Region Federal Bldg 901 Locust St ...... Kansas City MO 64106 816-329-3050
Web: www.faa.gov
Eastern Region 159-30 Rockaway Blvd .... Jamaica NY 11434 718-553-3001
Web: www.faa.gov
New England Region
12 New England Executive Pk .... Burlington MA 01803 781-238-7020 238-7608
Web: www.faa.gov/airports/new_england
Western Pacific Region 15000 Aviation Blvd .... Lawndale CA 90261 310-725-7800 725-6811
Web: www.faa.gov/airports/western_pacific

Phone Fax

Federal Aviation Administration Southern Region
1701 Columbia Ave .... College Park GA 30337 404-305-5000
Web: www.faa.gov
Federal Highway Administration (FHWA)
400 Seventh St SW .... Washington DC 20590 202-366-0660
Web: www.fhwa.dot.gov
National Highway Institute
4600 Fairfax Dr Ste 800 .... Arlington VA 22203 703-235-0500 235-0593
TF: 877-558-6873 ■ *Web:* www.nhi.fhwa.dot.gov
Federal Motor Carrier Safety Administration (FMCSA)
1200 New Jersey Ave SE .... Washington DC 20590 800-832-5660
TF: 800-832-5660 ■ *Web:* www.fmcsa.dot.gov
Federal Railroad Administration
1200 New Jersey Ave Se .... Washington DC 20590 202-493-6014
Web: www.fra.dot.gov
Federal Railroad Administration Regional Offices (FRA)
Region 1 55 Broadway Room 1077 .... Cambridge MA 02142 617-494-2302 494-2967
TF: 800-724-5991 ■ *Web:* www.fra.dot.gov
Region 2
Baldwin Tower Ste 660 1510 Chester Pike .... Crum Lynne PA 19022 610-521-8200 521-8225
TF: 800-724-5992 ■ *Web:* www.fra.dot.gov
Region 3 61 Forsyth St SW Ste 16T20 .... Atlanta GA 30303 404-562-3800 562-3830
TF: 800-724-5993 ■ *Web:* www.fra.dot.gov
Region 4 200 W Adams St .... Chicago IL 60606 312-353-6203 886-9634
TF: 800-724-5040 ■ *Web:* www.fra.dot.gov
Region 5 4100 International Plaza Ste 450 .... Fort Worth TX 76109 817-862-2200 862-2204
Web: www.fra.dot.gov
Region 6 901 Locust St Ste 464 .... Kansas City MO 64106 816-329-3840 329-3867
TF: 800-724-5996 ■ *Web:* www.fra.dot.gov
Region 7 801 'I' St Ste 466 .... Sacramento CA 95814 916-498-6540 498-6546
Web: www.fra.dot.gov
Region 8 703 Broadway St Ste 650 .... Vancouver WA 98660 360-696-7536 696-7548
TF: 800-724-5998 ■ *Web:* www.fra.dot.gov
Federal Transit Administration
1200 New Jersey Ave SE .... Washington DC 20590 202-366-4043 366-9854
Web: www.transit.dot.gov/about/regional-offices/regional-offices
Federal Transit Administration Regional Offices
Region 1 55 Broadway Ste 920 .... Cambridge MA 02142 617-494-2055 494-2865
Web: www.transit.dot.gov/about/regional-offices/regional-offices
Region 10 Federal Bldg 915 2nd Ave Ste 3142 .... Seattle WA 98174 206-220-7954 220-7959
Web: www.transit.dot.gov
Region 2 1 Bowling Green Rm 429 .... New York NY 10004 212-668-2170 668-2136
Web: www.transit.dot.gov/about/regional-offices/regional-offices
Region 3 1760 Market St Ste 500 .... Philadelphia PA 19103 215-656-7100 656-7260
Web: www.transit.dot.gov/about/regional-offices/regional-offices
Region 4 230 Peachtree St NW Ste 800 .... Atlanta GA 30303 404-865-5600 865-5605
Web: www.transit.dot.gov
Region 5 200 W Adams St Ste 320 .... Chicago IL 60606 312-353-2789 886-0351
Web: www.transit.dot.gov
Region 6 819 Taylor St Rm 8A36 .... Fort Worth TX 76102 817-978-0550 978-0575
Web: www.transit.dot.gov
Region 7 901 Locust St Ste 404 .... Kansas City MO 64106 816-329-3920 329-3921
Web: www.transit.dot.gov
Region 8 12300 W Dakota Ave 1st fl .... Lakewood CO 80228 720-963-3300 963-3333
Web: www.transit.dot.gov
Region 9 201 Mission St Ste 1650 .... San Francisco CA 94105 415-744-3133 744-2726
Web: www.transit.dot.gov
Maritime Administration (MARAD)
1200 New Jersey Ave SE .... Washington DC 20590 202-366-5807
TF Hotline: 800-996-2723 ■ *Web:* www.marad.dot.gov
Div of Gulf Operations
500 Poydras St Ste 1223 .... New Orleans LA 70130 504-589-2000 589-6559
Web: www.marad.dot.gov
National Maritime Resource & Education Ctr (NMREC)
1200 New Jersey Ave SE .... Washington DC 20590 202-366-9595
Web: www.marad.dot.gov
US Merchant Marine Academy
300 Steamboat Rd .... Kings Point NY 11024 516-773-5387 773-5509
TF: 866-546-4778 ■ *Web:* www.usmma.edu
Maritime Administration Regional Offices
Great Lakes Region PO Box 1156 .... Chicago IL 60690 312-353-1032 353-1036
Web: www.marad.dot.gov/about-us/gateway-offices/great-lakes-gateway-office
North Atlantic Region 1 Bowling Green Rm 418 .... New York NY 10004 212-668-3330
Web: www.marad.dot.gov
Western Region 201 Mission St Ste 2200 ..... San Francisco CA 94105 415-744-3125 744-2576
Web: marad.dot.gov
National Highway Traffic Safety Administration (NHTSA)
1200 New Jersey Ave SE .... Washington DC 20590 202-366-9550 366-6916
TF: 888-327-4236 ■ *Web:* www.nhtsa.gov
National Center for Statistics & Analysis
1200 New Jersey Ave SE .... Washington DC 20590 202-366-1503 366-7078
TF: 800-934-8517 ■ *Web:* www.nhtsa.gov
Vehicle Research & Test Ctr
10820 SR 347 PO Box B37 .... East Liberty OH 43319 937-666-4511 666-3590
TF: 800-262-8309 ■ *Web:* www.nhtsa.gov
National Highway Traffic Safety Administration Regional Offices (NHTSA)
NHTSA Region 1 Volpe Ctr Kendall Sq MS 903 .... Cambridge MA 02142 617-494-3427 494-3646
Web: www.nhtsa.gov
NHTSA Region 10 915 Second Ave Ste 3140 .... Seattle WA 98174 206-220-7640 220-7651
Web: www.nhtsa.gov
NHTSA Region 2
222 Mamaroneck Ave Ste 204 .... White Plains NY 10605 914-682-6162 682-6239
Web: www.nhtsa.gov
NHTSA Region 3
1200 New Jersey Ave Ste 6700 .... Washington DC 20590 888-327-4236 962-2770*
**Fax Area Code:* 410 ■ *TF:* 888-327-4236 ■ *Web:* www.nhtsa.gov
NHTSA Region 4 61 Forsyth St SW .... Atlanta GA 30303 404-562-3739 562-3763
Web: www.nhtsa.gov
NHTSA Region 5 1200 New Jersey Ave SE ...... Washington DC 20590 708-503-8822 503-8991
Web: www.nhtsa.gov
NHTSA Region 6 819 Taylor St Rm 8A38 .... Fort Worth TX 76102 817-978-3653 978-8339
Web: www.nhtsa.gov
NHTSA Region 7 901 Locust St Rm 466 .... Kansas City MO 64106 816-329-3900 329-3910
Web: www.nhtsa.gov

Phone Fax

NHTSA Region 8 12300 W Dakota Ave Ste 140 Lakewood CO 80228 720-963-3100 963-3124
Web: www.nhtsa.gov

NHTSA Region 9 201 Mission St Ste 2230 San Francisco CA 94105 415-744-3089 744-2532
Web: www.nhtsa.gov

Pipeline & Hazardous Materials Safety Administration (PHMSA)
1200 New Jersey Ave SE 2nd Fl Washington DC 20590 202-366-4433 366-3666
Web: www.phmsa.dot.gov

Office of Hazardous Materials Safety
1200 New Jersey Ave SE Washington DC 20590 202-366-4433 366-5713
TF: 800-467-4922 ■ *Web:* phmsa.dot.gov

Office of Pipeline Safety
1200 New Jersey Ave SE E Bldg 2nd Fl Washington DC 20590 202-366-4595 366-4566
Web: phmsa.dot.gov

Pipeline & Hazardous Materials Safety Administration Regional Offices (PHMSA)

Central Region (Pipeline)
901 Locust St Rm 462 Kansas City MO 64106 816-329-3800 329-3831
Web: www.phmsa.dot.gov/about/region.html

Eastern Region (Pipeline)
820 Bear Tavern Rd Ste 103 West Trenton NJ 08628 609-989-2256 882-1209
Web: www.phmsa.dot.gov/about/region.html

Southern Region 233 Peachtree St NE Ste 602 Atlanta GA 30303 404-832-1140 832-1168
Web: www.phmsa.dot.gov/about/region.html

Southwest Region 8701 S Gessner Rd Ste 900 Houston TX 77074 713-272-2820 272-2821
Web: www.phmsa.dot.gov

Western Region (Pipeline)
12300 W Dakota Ave Ste 110 Lakewood CO 80228 720-963-3160 963-3161
Web: www.phmsa.dot.gov/about/region.html

Research & Innovative Technology Administration (RITA)
1200 New Jersey Ave SE Washington DC 20590 202-366-7582 366-3759
TF: 800-853-1351 ■ *Web:* www.rita.dot.gov

Bureau of Transportation Statistics
1200 New Jersey Ave SE Washington DC 20590 202-366-1270
TF: 800-853-1351 ■ *Web:* www.rita.dot.gov

Office of Research Development & Technology
1200 New Jersey Ave SE Washington DC 20590 800-853-1351 366-3759*
**Fax Area Code:* 202 ■ *TF:* 800-853-1351 ■ *Web:* www.rita.dot.gov/rdt

Volpe National Transportation Systems Ctr
55 Broadway Cambridge MA 02142 617-494-2000
Web: www.volpe.dot.gov

Saint Lawrence Seaway Development Corp
1200 New Jersey Ave SE Washington DC 20590 202-366-0091 366-7147
TF: 800-785-2779 ■ *Web:* www.seaway.dot.gov

Secretary of Transportation
1200 New Jersey Ave SE Washington DC 20590 855-368-4200
TF: 855-368-4200 ■ *Web:* www.transportation.gov

Surface Transportation Board 395 E St SW Washington DC 20423 202-245-0245 245-0461
Web: www.stb.dot.gov

340-18 US Department of the Treasury

Phone Fax

Department of the Treasury
1500 Pennsylvania Ave NW Washington DC 20220 202-622-2000 622-6415
TF: 800-359-3898 ■ *Web:* www.treasury.gov

Treasurer of the US
1500 Pennsylvania Ave NW Washington DC 20220 202-622-2000 622-6464
Web: www.treasury.gov

Alcohol & Tobacco Tax & Trade Bureau
1310 G St NW Ste 300 Washington DC 20220 202-453-2000
TF: 877-882-3277 ■ *Web:* www.ttb.gov

Bureau of Engraving & Printing
14th & C Sts SW Washington DC 20228 877-874-4114 874-3177*
**Fax Area Code:* 202 ■ *TF:* 877-874-4114 ■ *Web:* www.moneyfactory.gov

Bureau of the Public Debt PO Box 7015 Parkersburg WV 26106 800-722-2678
TF: 800-722-2678

TreasuryDirect PO Box 7015 Parkersburg WV 26106 304-480-7711
TF: 800-722-2678 ■ *Web:* www.savingsbonds.gov

Comptroller of the Currency 250 E St SW Washington DC 20219 202-874-5000 874-5221
TF Cust Svc: 800-613-6743 ■ *Web:* www.occ.treas.gov

Financial Crimes Enforcement Network
2070 Chain Bridge Rd PO Box 39 Vienna VA 22182 703-905-3591
Web: www.fincen.gov

Financial Management Service
401 14th St SW Washington DC 20227 202-874-6950
Web: www.fms.treas.gov

Internal Revenue Service (IRS)
1111 Constitution Ave NW Washington DC 20224 202-622-9511
TF: 800-829-1040 ■ *Web:* www.irs.gov

Appeals Office 77 K St NE Washington DC 20002 202-803-9000
Web: www.irs.gov

Taxpayer Advocate Service
77 K St NE Ste 1500 Washington DC 20002 202-803-9000 810-2125*
**Fax Area Code:* 855 ■ *TF:* 877-777-4778 ■ *Web:* www.irs.gov/advocate

Wage & Investment Div 401 W Peachtree St NW Atlanta GA 30308 404-338-7060
Web: www.irs.gov

Secretary of the Treasury
1500 Pennsylvania Ave NW Washington DC 20220 202-622-2000 622-6415
Web: www.treasury.gov

US Mint 801 Ninth St NW Washington DC 20220 202-354-7462
TF Cust Svc: 800-872-6468 ■ *Web:* www.usmint.gov

Denver 320 W Colfax Ave Denver CO 80204 303-405-4761
Web: www.usmint.gov

Philadelphia 151 N Independence Mall E Philadelphia PA 19106 215-408-0112
Web: www.usmint.gov

San Francisco 155 Hermann St San Francisco CA 94102 415-575-8000
TF: 800-872-6468 ■ *Web:* www.usmint.gov

West Point (NY) PO Box 37 West Point NY 10996 800-872-6468
TF: 800-872-6468 ■ *Web:* usmint.gov

340-19 US Department of Veterans Affairs

Phone Fax

Department of Veterans Affairs (VA)
810 Vermont Ave NW Washington DC 20420 202-461-7600
TF Cust Svc: 800-827-1000 ■ *Web:* www.va.gov

Public & Intergovernmental Affairs Office
810 Vermont Ave NW Washington DC 20420 800-273-8255 273-7635*
**Fax Area Code:* 202 ■ *TF:* 800-273-8255 ■ *Web:* www1.va.gov/opa

National Center for Post-Traumatic Stress Disorder
215 N Main St White River Junction VT 05009 802-296-5132 296-5135
Web: www.ptsd.va.gov

National Cemetery Administration
810 Vermont Ave NW Washington DC 20420 202-565-4964
Web: www.cem.va.gov

Secretary of Veterans Affairs
810 Vermont Ave NW Washington DC 20420 202-461-7600
Web: www1.va.gov/opa/bios

Board of Veterans' Appeals
810 Vermont Ave NW Washington DC 20420 800-923-8387 343-1889*
**Fax Area Code:* 202 ■ *TF:* 800-923-8387 ■ *Web:* www.bva.va.gov

Center for Minority Veterans
810 Vermont Ave Ste 570 Washington DC 20420 202-461-6191 724-7117
Web: ova.dc.gov

Center for Women Veterans
810 Vermont Ave NW Washington DC 20420 800-827-1000 273-7092*
**Fax Area Code:* 202 ■ *TF:* 800-827-1000 ■ *Web:* www1.va.gov/womenvet

Veterans Benefits Administration
810 Vermont Ave NW Washington DC 20420 800-827-1000 275-5947*
**Fax Area Code:* 202 ■ *TF:* 800-827-1000 ■ *Web:* benefits.va.gov

Veterans Canteen Service
1 Jefferson Barracks Rd Bldg 25 Saint Louis MO 63125 314-652-4100 845-1201
Web: www.va.gov

Veterans Health Administration
810 Vermont Ave NW Washington DC 20420 202-273-5400
TF: 800-827-1000 ■ *Web:* www2.va.gov

Gulf War Veterans Information
50 Irving St NW Washington DC 20422 800-313-2232
TF: 800-313-2232 ■ *Web:* gulfwarvets.com

Office of Research & Development
810 Vermont Ave NW MC 12 Washington DC 20420 800-827-1000 254-0460*
**Fax Area Code:* 202 ■ *TF:* 800-827-1000 ■ *Web:* www.research.va.gov

340-20 US Independent Agencies Government Corporations & Quasi-Official Agencies

Included also among these listings are selected Federal Boards, Committees, and Commissions.

Phone Fax

Federal Election Commission 999 E St NW Washington DC 20463 202-694-1100
TF: 800-424-9530 ■ *Web:* www.fec.gov

US Office of Government Ethics
1201 New York Ave NW Ste 500 Washington DC 20005 202-482-9300 482-9237
Web: www.oge.gov

Advisory Council on Historic Preservation
401 F St NW Ste 308 Washington DC 20001 202-606-8503 606-8647
Web: www.achp.gov

American Battle Monuments Commission
Courthouse Plaza II Ste 500
2300 Clarendon Blvd Arlington VA 22201 703-696-6900 696-6666
Web: www.abmc.gov

Architectural & Transportation Barriers Compliance Board
1331 F St NW Ste 1000 Washington DC 20004 202-272-0080 272-0081
TF: 800-872-2253 ■ *Web:* www.access-board.gov

Broadcasting Board of Governors
330 Independence Ave SW Washington DC 20237 202-203-4545 203-4585
Web: www.bbg.gov

International Broadcasting Bureau
330 Independence Ave SW Washington DC 20237 202-203-4000
Web: www.bbg.gov

Voice of America 330 Independence Ave SW Washington DC 20237 202-203-4959
Web: www.voanews.com

Central Intelligence Agency (CIA)
Office of Public Affairs Washington DC 20505 703-482-0623 482-1739
Web: www.cia.gov

Commission of Fine Arts
401 F St NW Ste 312 Washington DC 20001 202-504-2200 504-2195
Web: www.cfa.gov

Commission on Presidential Scholars
Dept of Education Washington DC 20202 202-401-0961 260-7464
Web: www.ed.gov/programs/psp/commission.html

Commission on Security & Cooperation in Europe
234 Ford House Office Bldg 3rd & D Sts SW Washington DC 20515 202-225-1901 226-4199
Web: www.csce.gov

Committee for Purchase from People Who Are Blind or Severely Disabled
1421 Jefferson Davis Hwy
Jefferson Plaza 2 Ste 10800 Arlington VA 22202 703-603-7740 603-0655
Web: www.abilityone.gov

Committee on Foreign Investments in the US
Dept of the Treasury Office of International Investment
1500 Pennsylvania Ave NW Washington DC 20220 202-622-2000 622-2000
Web: www.treasury.gov

Commodity Futures Trading Commission
1155 21 St NW 1155 21 St NW Washington DC 20581 202-418-5000 418-5521
TF: 866-366-2382 ■ *Web:* www.cftc.gov

Commodity Futures Trading Commission Regional Offices

Central Region 525 W Monroe St Chicago IL 60661 312-596-0700 596-0713
Web: www.cftc.gov

Eastern Region 140 Broadway 19th Fl New York NY 10005 646-746-9700 746-9938
Web: www.cftc.gov

Phone | Fax

Southwestern Region
2 Emanuel Cleaver II Blvd Ste 300 Kansas City MO 64112 816-960-7700 960-7750
Web: www.cftc.gov

Consumer Product Safety Commission (CPSC)
4340 E W Hwy Ste 502 Bethesda MD 20814 301-504-7923 504-0051
TF: 800-638-2772 ■ *Web:* www.cpsc.gov

Coordinating Council on Juvenile Justice & Delinquency Prevention
810 Seventh St NW Washington DC 20531 202-307-5911 307-2093
Web: www.juvenilecouncil.gov

Corp for National & Community Service
AmeriCorps USA 1201 New York Ave NW Washington DC 20525 202-606-5000
TF: 800-833-3722 ■ *Web:* www.nationalservice.gov
Learn & Serve America
1201 New York Ave NW Washington DC 20525 202-606-5000
TF: 800-833-3722 ■ *Web:* www.nationalservice.gov
Senior Corps 1201 New York Ave NW Washington DC 20525 202-606-5000
TF: 800-833-3722 ■ *Web:* www.nationalservice.gov

Court Services & Offender Supervision Agency for the District of Columbia
633 Indiana Ave NW Washington DC 20004 202-220-5300 220-5350
Web: www.csosa.gov

Defense Nuclear Facilities Safety Board
625 Indiana Ave NW Ste 700 Washington DC 20004 202-694-7000
TF: 800-788-4016 ■ *Web:* www.dnfsb.gov

Denali Commission 510 L St Ste 410 Anchorage AK 99501 907-271-1414 271-1415
TF: 888-480-4321 ■ *Web:* www.denali.gov

Environmental Protection Agency (EPA)
1200 Pennsylvania Ave NW Washington DC 20460 202-564-4700 501-1450
TF: 888-372-8255 ■ *Web:* www.epa.gov
US National Response Team
1200 Pennsylvania Ave NW Washington DC 20593 202-267-2675
TF: 800-424-9346 ■ *Web:* www.nrt.org

Environmental Protection Agency Regional Offices
Region 1 1 Congress St Ste 1100 Boston MA 02114 617-918-1111 918-0101
TF: 888-372-7341 ■ *Web:* www.epa.gov
Region 10 1200 Sixth Ave Ste 900 Seattle WA 98101 206-553-1200 553-0059
TF: 800-424-4372 ■ *Web:* www.epa.gov
Region 2 290 Broadway New York NY 10007 212-637-3000
Web: www.epa.gov
Region 3 1650 Arch St Philadelphia PA 19103 215-814-5000
TF: 800-438-2474 ■ *Web:* www.epa.gov
Region 4 Federal Ctr 61 Forsyth St SW Atlanta GA 30303 404-562-9900 562-8174
TF: 800-241-1754 ■ *Web:* www.epa.gov
Region 5 77 W Jackson Blvd Chicago IL 60604 312-353-2000
Web: www.epa.gov
Region 6 1445 Ross Ave Ste 1200 Dallas TX 75202 214-665-2200 665-2182
TF: 800-887-6063 ■ *Web:* www.epa.gov
Region 7 901 N Fifth St Kansas City KS 66101 913-551-7003
Web: www.epa.gov
Region 8 1595 Wynkoop St Denver CO 80202 303-312-6312
TF: 800-227-8917 ■ *Web:* www.epa.gov
Region 9 75 Hawthorne St San Francisco CA 94105 415-947-8000 947-3598
TF: 866-372-9378 ■ *Web:* www.epa.gov

Equal Employment Opportunity Commission (EEOC)
1801 L St NW Washington DC 20507 202-663-4191
TF: 800-669-4000 ■ *Web:* www.eeoc.gov

Equal Employment Opportunity Commission Regional Offices
Atlanta District 100 Alabama St SW Ste 4R30 Atlanta GA 30303 800-669-6820 562-6909*
**Fax Area Code:* 404 ■ *TF:* 800-669-6820 ■ *Web:* www.eeoc.gov
Birmingham District
1130 22nd St S Ste 2000 Birmingham AL 35205 205-212-2100 212-2105
TF: 800-669-4000 ■ *Web:* www.eeoc.gov
Charlotte District 129 W Trade St Ste 400 Charlotte NC 28202 704-344-6682 344-6734
TF: 800-669-4000 ■ *Web:* www.eeoc.gov
Chicago District 500 W Madison St Ste 2800 Chicago IL 60661 312-353-2713 353-4041
TF: 800-669-4000 ■ *Web:* www.eeoc.gov
Dallas District 207 S Houston St 3rd Fl Dallas TX 75202 214-253-2700 253-2720
TF: 800-669-4000 ■ *Web:* www.eeoc.gov
Houston District 1201 Louisiana St 6th Fl Houston TX 77002 800-669-4000 651-4987*
**Fax Area Code:* 713 ■ *TF:* 800-669-4000 ■ *Web:* www.eeoc.gov
Indianapolis District
101 W Ohio St Ste 1900 Indianapolis IN 46204 317-226-7212 226-7953
Web: www.eeoc.gov
Los Angeles District
255 E Temple St 4th Fl Los Angeles CA 90012 800-669-4000 894-1118*
**Fax Area Code:* 213 ■ *TF:* 800-669-4000 ■ *Web:* www.eeoc.gov
Miami District 2 S Biscayne Blvd Ste 2700 Miami FL 33131 305-808-1740 808-1834
Web: www.eeoc.gov
New York District 33 Whitehall St 5th Fl New York NY 10004 212-336-3620 336-3790
TF: 866-408-8075 ■ *Web:* www.eeoc.gov
Philadelphia District
801 Market St Ste 1300 Philadelphia PA 19107 800-669-4000 440-2606*
**Fax Area Code:* 215 ■ *TF:* 800-669-4000 ■ *Web:* www.eeoc.gov/field/philadelphia
Phoenix District 3300 N Central Ave Ste 690 Phoenix AZ 85012 602-640-5000 640-5071
Web: www.eeoc.gov
Saint Louis District
1222 Spruce St Rm 8.100 Saint Louis MO 63103 314-539-7800 539-7894
TF: 800-669-4000 ■ *Web:* www.eeoc.gov
San Francisco District
450 Golden Gate Ave 5 W PO Box 36025 San Francisco CA 94102 800-669-4000 522-3415*
**Fax Area Code:* 415 ■ *TF:* 800-669-4000 ■ *Web:* www.eeoc.gov

Export-Import Bank of the US
811 Vermont Ave NW Washington DC 20571 202-565-3946
TF: 800-565-3946 ■ *Web:* www.exim.gov

Farm Credit Administration
1501 Farm Credit Dr McLean VA 22102 703-883-4000 734-5784
Web: www.fca.gov

Farm Credit Administration Regional Offices
Bloomington (MN) Field Office
1501 Farm Credit Dr McLean VA 22102 952-854-7151
Web: www.fca.gov
Dallas Field Office
511 E Carpenter Fwy Ste 650 Irving TX 75062 972-869-0550
Web: fca.gov
Denver Field Office 3131 S Vaughn Way Ste 250 Aurora CO 80014 303-696-9737
Web: www.fca.gov
McLean Field Office 1501 Farm Credit Dr McLean VA 22102 703-883-4056 883-4056
Web: www.fca.gov
Sacramento Field Office
2180 Harvard St Ste 300 Sacramento CA 95815 916-648-1118
Web: www.fca.gov

Federal Acctg Standards Advisory Board
441 G St NW Ste 6814 Washington DC 20548 202-512-7350 512-7366
Web: www.fasab.gov

Federal Communications Commission (FCC)
445 12th St SW Washington DC 20554 888-225-5322 418-0232*
**Fax Area Code:* 202 ■ *TF:* 888-225-5322 ■ *Web:* www.fcc.gov

Federal Deposit Insurance Corp
550 17th St NW Washington DC 20429 202-898-7192
TF: 877-275-3342 ■ *Web:* www.fdic.gov

Federal Deposit Insurance Corp Regional Offices
Atlanta Area Office 10 Tenth St NW Ste 800 Atlanta GA 30309 678-916-2200
TF: 800-765-3342 ■ *Web:* www.fdic.gov
Boston Area Office
15 Braintree Hill Office Pk Ste 300 Braintree MA 02184 781-794-5500
TF: 866-728-9953 ■ *Web:* www.fdic.gov
Chicago Area Office
300 S Riverside Plaza Ste 1700 Chicago IL 60606 312-382-6000
TF: 800-944-5343 ■ *Web:* www.fdic.gov
Dallas Area Office 1601 Bryan St Dallas TX 75201 214-754-0098
TF: 800-568-9161 ■ *Web:* www.fdic.gov
Kansas City Area Office
2345 Grand Blvd Ste 1200 Kansas City MO 64108 816-234-8000
TF: 800-209-7459 ■ *Web:* www.fdic.gov
Memphis Area Office 5100 Poplar Ave Ste 1900 Memphis TN 38137 901-685-1603
TF: 800-210-6354 ■ *Web:* www.fdic.gov
New York Area Office 350 5th Ave Ste 1200 New York NY 11215 917-320-2500
TF: 800-334-9593 ■ *Web:* fdic.gov
San Francisco Area Office
25 Jessie St at Ecker Sq Ste 2300 San Francisco CA 94105 415-546-0160
TF: 800-756-3558 ■ *Web:* www.fdic.gov

Federal Financing Bank
Dept of the Treasury
1500 Pennsylvania Ave NW Washington DC 20220 202-622-2470 622-0707
Web: www.treasury.gov

Federal Housing Finance Board
400 7th St SW Washington DC 20024 202-649-3800 649-1071
Web: www.fhfa.gov

Federal Labor Relations Authority
1400 K St NW Washington DC 20424 202-357-6029 482-6724
Web: www.flra.gov

Federal Labor Relations Authority Regional Offices
Atlanta Region 225 Peachtree St NE Atlanta GA 30303 404-331-5300 331-5280
Web: www.flra.gov
Boston Region Federal Bldg 10 Cswy St Ste 472 Boston MA 02222 617-565-5100 565-6262
Web: www.flra.gov
Chicago Region 55 W Monroe St Ste 1150 Chicago IL 60603 312-886-3465 886-5977
Web: www.flra.gov
Dallas Region 525 S Griffin St Ste 926 LB-107 Dallas TX 75202 214-767-6266 767-0156
Web: www.flra.gov
Denver Region 1391 Speer Blvd # 300 Denver CO 80204 303-844-5224 844-2774
Web: flra.gov
San Francisco Region
901 Market St Ste 470 San Francisco CA 94103 415-356-5000 356-5017
Web: www.flra.gov/ogc_ro_sf
Washington (DC) Region 1400 K St NW 2nd Fl Washington DC 20424 202-357-6029 482-6724
Web: www.flra.gov

Federal Laboratory Consortium for Technology Transfer
950 Kings Hwy N Ste 208 Cherry Hill NJ 08034 856-667-7727 667-8009
Web: www.federallabs.org

Federal Maritime Commission
800 N Capitol St NW Washington DC 20573 202-523-5725 523-0014
Web: www.fmc.gov

Federal Maritime Commission Regional Offices
Los Angeles Area 800 N Capital St NW Washington DC 20573 310-514-4905 514-3931
Web: www.fmc.gov
New Orleans Area 1515 Poydras St New Orleans LA 70112 504-589-6662
Web: www.fmc.gov
South Florida Area PO Box 813609 Hollywood FL 33081 954-963-5362 963-5630
Web: www.fmc.gov

Federal Mediation & Conciliation Service
2100 K St NW Washington DC 20427 202-606-8100 606-4251
Web: www.fmcs.gov

Federal Mediation & Conciliation Service Regional Offices
Eastern Region
6161 Oak Tree Blvd Ste 120 Independence OH 44131 216-520-4800
Web: www.fmcs.gov/internet
Western Region 1300 Godward St Ste 3950 Minneapolis MN 55413 612-331-6670 331-5272
Web: www.fmcs.gov

Federal Mine Safety & Health Review Commission
601 New Jersey Ave NW Washington DC 20001 202-434-9900 434-9944
Web: www.fmshrc.gov

Federal Retirement Thrift Investment Board
1250 H St NW Washington DC 20005 202-942-1600
Web: www.frtib.gov

Federal Trade Commission (FTC)
600 Pennsylvania Ave NW Washington DC 20580 202-326-2222
TF: 877-382-4357 ■ *Web:* www.ftc.gov
National Do Not Call Registry
600 Pennsylvania Ave NW Washington DC 20580 888-382-1222
TF: 888-382-1222 ■ *Web:* www.ftc.gov

Federal Trade Commission Regional Offices
East Central Region
1111 Superior Ave Ste 200 Cleveland OH 44114 216-263-3455 263-3426
TF: 877-382-4357 ■ *Web:* www.ftc.gov
Midwest Region 55 W Monroe St Ste 1825 Chicago IL 20580 877-382-4357
TF: 877-382-4357 ■ *Web:* www.ftc.gov/about-ftc/bureaus-offices/regional-offices/midwest-region

Phone Fax

NortheastRegion 1 Bowling Green Ste 318 .... New York NY 10004 212-607-2829 607-2822
TF: 877-382-4357 ■ Web: www.ftc.gov
Northwest Region 915 Second Ave Rm 2896......... Seattle WA 98174 877-382-4357
TF: 877-382-4357 ■ Web: www.ftc.gov
Southeast Region 60 Forsyth St SW .... Atlanta GA 30303 404-656-1390 656-1379
TF: 877-282-4357 ■ Web: www.ftc.gov
Southwest Region 1999 Bryan St Ste 2150 .... Dallas TX 75201 877-382-4357
TF: 877-382-4357 ■ Web: www.ftc.gov
Western Region 901 Market St Ste 570 .... San Francisco CA 94103 877-382-4357 824-4380*
*Fax Area Code: 310 ■ TF: 877-382-4357 ■
Web: ftc.gov/about-ftc/bureaus-offices/regional-offices/western-region

General Services Administration (GSA)
1275 F St NE .... Washington DC 20417 202-501-0800
Web: www.gsa.gov
Federal Citizen Information Center PO Box 100...... Pueblo CO 81009 888-878-3256
TF: 888-878-3256 ■ Web: publications.usa.gov
Regulatory Information Service Ctr
1800 F St NW Rm 3039....................... Washington DC 20405 202-482-7340
Web: www.gsa.gov

General Services Administration Regional Offices
Region 1 - New England
10 Cswy St Rm 1010
Thomas P O'Neill Federal Bldg .... Boston MA 02222 617-565-5860
TF: 866-734-1727 ■ Web: www.gsa.gov
Region 10 - Northwest/Arctic 400 15th St SW....... Auburn WA 98001 253-931-7000
Web: www.gsa.gov
Region 11 - National Capital Region
301 Seventh St SW .... Washington DC 20407 202-708-9100
Web: www.gsa.gov
Region 2 - Northeast & Caribbean
26 Federal Plaza.............................. New York NY 10278 212-264-2600
Web: www.gsa.gov
Region 3 - Mid-Atlantic
Strawbridge Bldg 20 N 8th St .... Philadelphia PA 19107 215-446-5100
TF: 800-333-4636 ■ Web: www.gsa.gov
Region 4 - Southeast Sunbelt
1800 F St NW Ste 600.......................... Washington DC 20405 800-333-4636 331-0931*
*Fax Area Code: 404 ■ TF: 800-333-4636 ■ Web: www.gsa.gov
Region 5 - Great Lakes 230 S Dearborn St......... Chicago IL 60604 312-886-8900 886-8901
Web: www.gsa.gov
Region 6 - Heartland 1800 F St NW............ Washington DC 20405 816-823-5320 926-7513
Web: www.gsa.gov
Region 7 - Greater Southwest
819 Taylor St................................. Fort Worth TX 76102 817-978-2321
Web: www.gsa.gov
Region 8 - Rocky Mountain
Denver Federal Ctr Bldg 41 .... Denver CO 80225 303-236-7329
TF: 888-999-4777 ■ Web: www.gsa.gov
Region 9 - Pacific Rim
450 Golden Gate Ave .... San Francisco CA 94102 530-756-3082
Web: www.gsa.gov

Harry S Truman Scholarship Foundation
712 Jackson Pl NW .... Washington DC 20006 202-395-4831 395-6995
Web: www.truman.gov

Indian Arts & Crafts Board
Dept of the Interior 1849 C St NW
MS 2528-MIB.................................. Washington DC 20240 202-208-3773 208-5196
TF: 888-278-3253 ■ Web: www.doi.gov/iacb

Inter-American Foundation (IAF)
901 N Stuart St 10th Fl........................... Arlington VA 22203 703-306-4301 306-4365
Web: www.iaf.gov

Interagency Council on Homelessness
409 Third St SW Ste 310 .... Washington DC 20024 202-708-4663
Web: www.usich.gov

Japan-US Friendship Commission
1201 15th St NW Ste 330....................... Washington DC 20005 202-653-9800 653-9802
Web: www.jusfc.gov

Joint Board for the Enrollment of Actuaries
Internal Revenue Service SE:OPR
1111 Constitution Ave NW .... Washington DC 20224 202-622-8229 622-8300
Web: www.irs.gov

Legal Services Corp 3333 K St NW 3rd Fl........... Washington DC 20007 202-295-1500 337-6797
Web: www.lsc.gov

Marine Mammal Commission
4340 E W Hwy Ste 700............................ Bethesda MD 20814 301-504-0087 504-0099
Web: www.mmc.gov

Merit Systems Protection Board (MSPB)
1615 M St NW .... Washington DC 20419 202-653-7200 653-7130
TF: 800-209-8960 ■ Web: www.mspb.gov

Merit Systems Protection Board Regional Offices (MSPB)
Atlanta Region 401 W Peachtree St NW 10th Fl....... Atlanta GA 30308 404-730-2755 730-2767
TF: 800-209-8960 ■ Web: www.mspb.gov
Central Region 230 S Dearborn St 31st Fl .... Chicago IL 60604 312-353-2923 886-4231
Web: www.mspb.gov
Denver Field Office 165 S Union Blvd Ste 318..... Lakewood CO 80228 303-969-5101 969-5109
TF: 800-209-8960 ■ Web: www.mspb.gov
New York Field Office
26 Federal Plaza Rm 3137-A .... New York NY 10278 212-264-9372 264-1417
Web: www.mspb.gov
Northeastern Region
1601 Market St Ste 1700..................... Philadelphia PA 19103 215-597-9960 597-3456
Web: mspb.gov
Washington (DC) Region
1800 Diagonal Rd Ste 205...................... Alexandria VA 22314 703-756-6250 756-7112
Web: www.mspb.gov
Western Region 201 Mission St Ste 2310 ..... San Francisco CA 94105 415-904-6772 904-0580
Web: www.mspb.gov

Migratory Bird Conservation Commission
5275 Leesburg Pike .... Falls Church VA 22203 703-358-1716
Web: www.fws.gov

Millenium Challenge Corp 875 15th St NW......... Washington DC 20005 202-521-3600
Web: www.mcc.gov

Morris K Udall Foundation 130 S Scott Ave............ Tucson AZ 85701 520-901-8500 670-5530
Web: www.udall.gov

Phone Fax

National Aeronautics & Space Administration (NASA)
300 E St SW .... Washington DC 20546 202-358-0001 358-3469
Web: www.nasa.gov

National Archives & Records Administration (NARA)
8601 Adelphi Rd.............................. College Park MD 20740 866-272-6272 837-0483*
*Fax Area Code: 301 ■ TF: 866-272-6272 ■ Web: www.archives.gov
Archival Research Catalog
8601 Adelphi Rd .... College Park MD 20740 866-272-6272
TF: 866-272-6272 ■ Web: archives.gov/research/search
Office of Presidential Libraries
8601 Adelphi Rd Rm 2200.................... College Park MD 20740 301-837-3250 837-3199
Web: www.archives.gov
Office of the Federal Register
800 N Capitol St NW Ste 700-K................. Washington DC 20002 202-741-6000
TF: 877-684-6448 ■ Web: www.archives.gov/federal-register

National Archives & Records Administration Regional Offices
Central Plains Region 400 W Pershing Rd....... Kansas City MO 64108 816-268-8000
Web: www.archives.gov
Great Lakes Region 7358 S Pulaski Rd .... Chicago IL 60629 773-948-9001 948-9050
Web: www.archives.gov/great-lakes
Mid Atlantic Region 900 Market St .... Philadelphia PA 19107 215-606-0100 606-0116
Web: www.archives.gov/midatlantic
Northeast Region 380 Trapelo Rd .... Waltham MA 02452 781-663-0130 663-0154
TF: 866-406-2379 ■ Web: www.archives.gov
Pacific Alaska Region 6125 Sand Pt Way NE......... Seattle WA 98115 206-336-5115 336-5112
TF: 866-325-7208 ■ Web: www.archives.gov
Pacific Region 1000 Commodore Dr .... San Bruno CA 94066 650-238-3500 238-3507
Web: www.archives.gov
Southeast Region 5780 Jonesboro Rd............. Morrow GA 30260 770-968-2100 968-2547
Web: www.archives.gov/southeast
Southwest Region
501 W Felix St Bldg 1 PO Box 6216 .... Fort Worth TX 76115 817-551-2051
Web: www.archives.gov/southwest

National Capital Planning Commission
401 Ninth St NW N Lobby Ste 500................ Washington DC 20004 202-482-7200 482-7272
Web: www.ncpc.gov

National Council on Disability (NCD)
1331 F St NW Ste 850 .... Washington DC 20004 202-272-2004 272-2022
Web: www.ncd.gov

National Credit Union Administration
1775 Duke St .... Alexandria VA 22314 703-518-6300 518-6319
TF Fraud Hotline: 800-827-9650 ■ Web: ncua.gov

National Credit Union Administration Regional Offices
Region 1 9 Washington Sq Washington Ave Ext ...... Albany NY 12205 518-862-7400 862-7420
Web: ncua.gov
Region 2 1775 Duke St Ste 4206................ Alexandria VA 22314 703-518-6300 519-4620
Web: www.ncua.gov
Region 3 7000 Central Pkwy Ste 1600.............. Atlanta GA 30328 678-443-3000 443-3020
Web: ncua.gov
Region 4 4807 Spicewood Springs Rd Ste 5200...... Austin TX 78759 512-342-5600 342-5620
Web: ncua.gov
Region 5 1230 W Washington St Ste 301 .... Tempe AZ 85281 602-302-6000 302-6024
Web: ncua.gov

National Endowment for the Arts (NEA)
1100 Pennsylvania Ave NW .... Washington DC 20506 202-682-5400
Web: www.arts.gov

National Endowment for the Humanities (NEH)
400 7th St SW .... Washington DC 20506 202-606-8400 606-8282
TF: 800-634-1121 ■ Web: www.neh.gov

National Indian Gaming Commission
1441 L St NW Ste 9100 .... Washington DC 20005 202-632-7003 632-7066
Web: www.nigc.gov

National Labor Relations Board (NLRB)
1099 14th St NW .... Washington DC 20570 202-273-1991
TF: 866-667-6572 ■ Web: www.nlrb.gov

National Labor Relations Board Regional Offices
Region 1 10 Cswy St 6th Fl .... Boston MA 02222 617-565-6700 565-6725
TF: 866-667-6572 ■ Web: www.nlrb.gov
Region 10 233 Peachtree St NE Ste 1000 .... Atlanta GA 30303 404-331-2896 331-2858
Web: www.nlrb.gov
Region 11 4035 University Pkwy Ste 200 .... Winston-Salem NC 27106 336-631-5201 631-5210
TF: 866-667-6572 ■ Web: www.nlrb.gov
Region 12 201 E Kennedy Blvd Ste 530............. Tampa FL 33602 813-228-2641 228-2874
Web: www.nlrb.gov
Region 13 200 W Adams St.................... Chicago IL 60606 312-353-7570 886-1341
Web: www.nlrb.gov
Region 14 1222 Spruce St Rm 8.302........... Saint Louis MO 63103 314-539-7770 539-7794
TF: 866-667-6572 ■ Web: www.nlrb.gov
Region 15 1515 Poydras St Rm 610 .... New Orleans LA 70112 504-589-6361 589-4069
Web: www.nlrb.gov
Region 16
Federal Bldg 819 Taylor St Rm 8A24.............. Fort Worth TX 76102 817-978-2921 978-2928
TF: 866-667-6572 ■ Web: www.nlrb.gov
Region 17 8600 Farley St Ste 100 .... Overland Park KS 66212 913-967-3000 967-3010
Web: www.nlrb.gov
Region 18 330 Second Ave S Ste 790 .... Minneapolis MN 55401 612-348-1757 348-1785
TF: 866-667-6572 ■ Web: www.nlrb.gov
Region 19 915 Second Ave # 2948 .... Seattle WA 98174 206-220-6300 220-6305
Web: www.nlrb.gov
Region 2 26 Federal Plaza Rm 3614 .... New York NY 10278 212-264-0300 264-2450
Web: www.nlrb.gov
Region 20 901 Market St Ste 400 .... San Francisco CA 94103 415-356-5130 356-5156
TF: 866-667-6572 ■ Web: www.nlrb.gov
Region 21 888 S Figueroa St 9th Fl........... Los Angeles CA 90017 213-894-5200 894-2778
Web: www.nlrb.gov
Region 22 20 Washington Pl 5th Fl............... Newark NJ 07102 973-645-2100 645-3852
Web: www.nlrb.gov
Region 24 525 FD Roosevelt Ave Ste 1002 .... San Juan PR 00918 787-766-5347 766-5478
Web: www.nlrb.gov
Region 25 575 N Pennsylvania St Ste 238...... Indianapolis IN 46204 317-226-7381 226-5103
TF: 866-667-6572 ■ Web: www.nlrb.gov
Region 26 80 Monroe Ave Ste 350 .... Memphis TN 38103 901-544-0018 544-0008
Web: www.nlrb.gov

Phone | Fax

Region 27 600 17th St 7th Fl N Tower . . . Denver CO 80202 303-844-3551 844-6249
Web: www.nlrb.gov
Region 28 2600 N Central Ave Ste 1800 . . . Phoenix AZ 85004 602-640-2160 640-2178
Web: www.nlrb.gov
Region 29 1 Metrotech Ctr N # A . . . Brooklyn NY 11201 718-330-7713 330-7579
Web: www.nlrb.gov
Region 3
Niagara Ctr Bldg 130 S Elmwood Ave Ste 630 . . . Buffalo NY 14202 716-551-4931 551-4972
TF: 866-667-6572 ■ *Web:* www.nlrb.gov
Region 30 310 W Wisconsin Ave Ste 700 . . . Milwaukee WI 53203 414-297-3861 297-3880
Web: www.nlrb.gov
Region 31 11150 W Olympic Blvd Ste 700 . . . Los Angeles CA 90064 310-235-7352 235-7420
TF: 866-667-6572 ■ *Web:* www.nlrb.gov
Region 32 1301 Clay St Rm 300N . . . Oakland CA 94612 510-637-3300 637-3315
Web: www.nlrb.gov
Region 34 450 Main St . . . Hartford CT 06103 860-240-3522 240-3564
Web: nlrb.gov
Region 4 615 Chestnut St 7th Fl . . . Philadelphia PA 19106 215-597-7601 597-7658
Web: www.nlrb.gov
Region 5 103 S Gay St 8th Fl . . . Baltimore MD 21202 410-962-2822 962-2198
Web: www.nlrb.gov
Region 6 1000 Liberty Ave Rm 904 . . . Pittsburgh PA 15222 412-395-4400 395-5986
Web: www.nlrb.gov
Region 7 477 Michigan Ave Rm 300 . . . Detroit MI 48226 313-226-3200 226-2090
Web: www.nlrb.gov
Region 8 1240 E Ninth St Rm 1695 . . . Cleveland OH 44199 216-522-3715 522-2418
TF: 866-667-6572 ■ *Web:* www.nlrb.gov
Region 9 550 Main St Rm 3003 . . . Cincinnati OH 45202 513-684-3686 684-3946
TF: 866-667-6572 ■ *Web:* www.nlrb.gov

National Mediation Board
1301 K St NW Ste 250E . . . Washington DC 20005 202-692-5000
Web: www.nmb.gov

National Railroad Passenger Corp
60 Massachusetts Ave NE . . . Washington DC 20002 202-906-3741 906-3285
TF: 800-872-7245 ■ *Web:* www.amtrak.com

National Science Foundation (NSF)
4201 Wilson Blvd . . . Arlington VA 22230 703-292-5111 292-9232
TF: 800-877-8339 ■ *Web:* www.nsf.gov

National Transportation Safety Board (NTSB)
490 L'Enfant Plaza SW . . . Washington DC 20594 202-314-6000 314-6293
Web: www.ntsb.gov

No Greater Love 1750 New York Ave NW . . . Washington DC 20006 202-783-4665

Nuclear Regulatory Commission Regional Offices
Region 1 2100 Renaissance Blvd . . . King of Prussia PA 19406 610-337-5000
TF: 800-432-1156 ■ *Web:* www.nrc.gov
Region 2 61 Forsyth St SW Ste 23T85 . . . Atlanta GA 30303 404-562-4400 562-4900
TF: 800-577-8510 ■ *Web:* www.nrc.gov
Region 3 2443 Warrenville Rd Ste 210 . . . Lisle IL 60532 630-829-9500 515-1078
TF: 800-522-3025 ■ *Web:* www.nrc.gov
Region 4 1600 E Lamar Blvd . . . Arlington TX 76011 817-860-8100
TF: 800-952-9677 ■ *Web:* www.nrc.gov

Nuclear Waste Technical Review Board (NWTRB)
2300 Clarendon Blvd Ste 1300 . . . Arlington VA 22201 703-235-4473 235-4495
Web: www.nwtrb.gov

Occupational Safety & Health Review Commission
1120 20th St NW 9th Fl . . . Washington DC 20036 202-606-5400 606-5050
Web: www.oshrc.gov

Occupational Safety & Health Review Commission Regional Offices
Atlanta Region 100 Alabama St SW Rm 2R90 . . . Atlanta GA 30303 404-562-1640 562-1650
TF: 800-321-6742 ■ *Web:* www.oshrc.gov

Office of Compliance
110 Second St SE Rm LA 200 . . . Washington DC 20540 202-724-9250 426-1913
Web: www.compliance.gov

Office of Personnel Management (OPM)
1900 E St NW . . . Washington DC 20415 202-606-1800
Web: www.opm.gov

Office of Special Counsel
1730 M St NW Ste 218 . . . Washington DC 20036 202-254-3600 653-5151
TF: 800-872-9855 ■ *Web:* www.osc.gov

Office of Special Counsel Regional Offices
Dallas Field Office
525 Griffin St Rm 824 PO Box 103 . . . Dallas TX 75202 214-747-1519
TF: 800-872-9855 ■ *Web:* www.osc.gov
San Francisco Bay Area Field Office
Federal Bldg 1301 Clay St Ste 1220-N . . . Oakland CA 94612 510-637-3460 637-3474
TF: 800-872-9855 ■ *Web:* www.osc.gov

Office of the National Counterintelligence Executive (ONCIX)
LX/ICC-B . . . Washington DC 20511 571-204-6537
Web: ncsc.gov

Overseas Private Investment Corp (OPIC)
1100 New York Ave NW . . . Washington DC 20527 202-336-8400 408-9859
Web: www.opic.gov

Peace Corps 1111 20th St NW . . . Washington DC 20526 202-692-1040
TF: 800-424-8580 ■ *Web:* www.peacecorps.gov

Peace Corps Regional Offices
Atlanta Regional Office 1111 20th St NW . . . Washington DC 20526 404-562-3456 562-3455
TF: 855-855-1961 ■ *Web:* www.peacecorps.gov
Chicago Regional Office
55 W Monroe St Ste 450 . . . Chicago IL 60603 312-353-4990 353-4192
TF: 800-424-8580 ■ *Web:* www.peacecorps.gov
Dallas Regional Office
1100 Commerce St Ste 427 . . . Dallas TX 75242 855-855-1961 253-5401*
**Fax Area Code: 214* ■ *TF:* 855-855-1961 ■ *Web:* www.peacecorps.gov
Denver Regional Office 1999 Broadway Ste 2205 . . . Denver CO 80202 855-855-1961
TF: 855-855-1961 ■ *Web:* www.peacecorps.gov
Los Angeles Regional Office
2361 Rosecrans Ave Ste 155 . . . El Segundo CA 90245 310-356-1100 356-1125
TF: 800-424-8580 ■ *Web:* www.peacecorps.gov
Mid-Atlantic Regional Office
1525 Wilson Blvd Ste 100 . . . Arlington VA 22209 202-692-1040
TF: 800-424-8580 ■ *Web:* www.peacecorps.gov
New York Regional Office
201 Varick St Ste 1025 . . . New York NY 10014 212-352-5440 352-5441
TF: 800-424-8580 ■ *Web:* www.peacecorps.gov
Northwest Regional Office
1601 Fifth Ave Ste 605 . . . Seattle WA 98101 206-553-5490 553-2343
TF: 800-424-8580 ■ *Web:* www.peacecorps.gov
San Francisco Regional Office
1301 Clay St Ste 620-N . . . Oakland CA 94612 510-452-8444 452-8441
TF: 800-424-8580 ■ *Web:* www.peacecorps.gov

Pension Benefit Guaranty Corp
1200 K St NW . . . Washington DC 20005 202-326-4000 326-4047
TF Cust Svc: 800-400-7242 ■ *Web:* www.pbgc.gov

Postal Regulatory Commission
901 New York Ave NW Ste 200 . . . Washington DC 20268 202-789-6800 789-6891
Web: www.prc.gov

Presidio Trust
103 Montgomery St PO Box 29052 . . . San Francisco CA 94129 415-561-5300 561-5315

Railroad Retirement Board 844 N Rush St . . . Chicago IL 60611 312-751-4300 751-7136
TF: 877-772-5772 ■ *Web:* www.rrb.gov/general/contact_us.asp

Securities & Exchange Commission (SEC)
100 F St NE . . . Washington DC 20549 202-942-8088 772-9295
TF: 800-732-0330 ■ *Web:* www.sec.gov
Office of Investor Education & Advocacy
100 F St NE . . . Washington DC 20549 202-942-8088 772-9295
Web: sec.gov/servlet/sec/investor

Securities & Exchange Commission Regional Offices
Atlanta Regional Office
3475 Lenox Rd NE Ste 1000 . . . Atlanta GA 30326 404-842-7600
Web: www.sec.gov
Boston Regional Office 33 Arch St 23rd Fl . . . Boston MA 02110 617-573-8900
Web: www.sec.gov/contact/addresses.htm
Chicago Regional Office
175 W Jackson Blvd Ste 900 . . . Chicago IL 60604 312-353-7390 353-7398
Web: www.sec.gov
Denver Regional Office
1801 California St Ste 1500 . . . Denver CO 80202 303-844-1000 844-1010
Web: www.sec.gov
Fort Worth Regional Office
801 Cherry St, Unit 18 . . . Fort Worth TX 76102 817-978-3821
Web: sec.gov
Los Angeles Regional Office
5670 Wilshire Blvd 11th Fl . . . Los Angeles CA 90036 323-965-3998 965-3815
Web: www.sec.gov
Miami Regional Office 801 Brickell Ave Ste 1800 . . . Miami FL 33131 305-982-6300
Web: www.sec.gov
New York Regional Office
3 World Financial Ctr Ste 400 . . . New York NY 10281 212-336-1100
Web: www.sec.gov
Philadelphia Regional Office
Mellon Independence Ctr 701 Market St . . . Philadelphia PA 19106 215-597-3100
Web: www.sec.gov
Salt Lake Regional Office
15 W S Temple St Ste 1800 . . . Salt Lake City UT 84101 801-524-5796
Web: sec.gov
San Francisco Regional Office
44 Montgomery St Ste 2600 . . . San Francisco CA 94104 415-705-2500
Web: sec.gov

Selective Service System 1515 Wilson Blvd . . . Arlington VA 22209 847-688-6888
TF: 888-655-1825 ■ *Web:* www.sss.gov

Selective Service System Regional Offices
Region 1 PO Box 94638 . . . Palatine IL 60094 847-688-6888
TF: 888-655-1825 ■ *Web:* www.sss.gov
Region 2 PO Box 94638 . . . Palatine IL 60094 847-688-6888
TF: 888-655-1825 ■ *Web:* www.sss.gov

Small Business Administration (SBA)
409 Third St SW . . . Washington DC 20416 202-205-6600 205-6802
TF: 800-827-5722 ■ *Web:* www.sba.gov
National Women's Business Council
409 Third St SW Ste 210 . . . Washington DC 20024 202-205-3850 205-6825
Web: www.nwbc.gov

Small Business Administration Regional Offices (SBA)
Region 1 10 Cswy St Ste 265A . . . Boston MA 02222 617-565-8416 565-8420
Web: www.sba.gov/about-offices-list/3
Region 10 2401 Fourth Ave Ste 400 . . . Seattle WA 98121 206-553-5676 553-4155
Web: www.sba.gov
Region 10 701 Fifth Ave Ste 2900 . . . Seattle WA 98104 206-615-2236
TF: 800-772-1213 ■ *Web:* www.ssa.gov
Region 3 1150 First Ave Ste 1001 . . . King Of Prussia PA 19406 610-382-3092
Web: www.sba.gov/about-offices-list/3
Region 4 233 Peachtree St NE Ste 1800 . . . Atlanta GA 30303 404-331-4999 331-2354
Web: www.sba.gov/about-offices-list/3
Region 5 500 W Madison St Ste 1150 . . . Chicago IL 60661 312-353-0357 353-3426
Web: www.sba.gov/about-offices-list/3
Region 6 4300 Amon Carter Blvd Ste 108 . . . Fort Worth TX 76155 817-684-5581 684-5588
Web: www.sba.gov
Region 6 1301 Young St . . . Dallas TX 75202 214-767-9401 767-8986
TF: 800-772-1213 ■ *Web:* www.ssa.gov/dallas
Region 7 100 Walnut Ste 530 . . . Kansas City MO 64106 816-426-4840 426-4848
Web: www.sba.gov
Region 8 721 19th St Ste 426 . . . Denver CO 80202 303-844-2607 292-3582*
**Fax Area Code: 202* ■ *Web:* sba.gov
Region 9 330 N Brand Blvd Ste 1200 . . . Glendale CA 91203 818-552-3437 481-0344*
**Fax Area Code: 202* ■ *Web:* www.sba.gov

Social Security Administration (SSA)
6401 Security Blvd . . . Baltimore MD 21235 410-965-8904
TF: 800-772-1213 ■ *Web:* www.ssa.gov

Social Security Administration Regional Offices
Region 1 JFK Federal Bldg Rm 1900 . . . Boston MA 02203 617-565-2870 565-2143
Web: www.ssa.gov/boston
Region 2 26 Federal Plaza Rm 40-102 . . . New York NY 10278 212-264-4036
TF: 800-772-1213 ■ *Web:* www.ssa.gov/ny
Region 4 61 Forsyth St SW Ste 23T30 . . . Atlanta GA 30303 800-772-1213
TF: 800-772-1213 ■ *Web:* www.ssa.gov/atlanta
Region 5 600 W Madison St PO Box 8280 . . . Chicago IL 60680 312-575-4050
TF: 800-772-1213 ■ *Web:* www.ssa.gov

				Phone	Fax
Social Security Advisory Board 400 Virginia Ave SW Ste 625 ... Web: www.ssab.gov	Washington	DC	20024	202-475-7700	475-7715
State Justice Institute (SJI) 11951 Freedom Drive Ste 1020 ... Web: www.sji.gov	Reston	VA	20190	571-313-8843	313-1173
Susquehanna River Basin Commission 1721 N Front St ... Web: www.srbc.net	Harrisburg	PA	17102	717-238-0423	238-2436
Tennessee Valley Authority (TVA) 400 W Summit Hill Dr ... Web: www.tva.gov	Knoxville	TN	37902	865-632-2101	
US Agency for International Development (USAID) 1300 Pennsylvania Ave NW ... Web: www.usaid.gov	Washington	DC	20523	202-712-0000	216-3524
US Arctic Research Commission 4350 N Fairfax Dr Ste 510 ... Web: www.arctic.gov	Arlington	VA	22203	703-525-0111	525-0114
US Chemical Safety & Hazard Investigation Board 2175 K St NW Ste 400 ... Web: csb.gov	Washington	DC	20037	202-261-7600	261-7650
US Commission on Civil Rights 624 Ninth St NW ... Web: www.usccr.gov	Washington	DC	20425	202-376-7700	376-7672
US Commission on Civil Rights Regional Offices					
Central Regional Office 400 State Ave Ste 908 ... Web: www.usccr.gov	Kansas City	KS	66101	913-551-1400	551-1413
Eastern Regional Office 624 Ninth St NW Ste 700 ... Web: www.usccr.gov	Washington	DC	20425	202-376-7700	376-7672
Midwestern Regional Office 55 W Monroe St Ste 410 ... TF: 800-552-6843 ■ Web: www.usccr.gov	Chicago	IL	60603	312-353-8311	353-8324
Rocky Mountain Regional Office 1700 Broadway ... Web: www.usccr.gov	Denver	CO	80290	303-866-1040	866-1050
Southern Regional Office 61 Forsyth St SW Ste 1840 T ... Web: www.usccr.gov	Atlanta	GA	30303	404-562-7000	562-7004
Western Regional Office 300 N Los Angeles St Ste 2010 ... Web: www.usccr.gov	Los Angeles	CA	90012	213-894-3437	894-0508
US Commission on International Religious Freedom (USCIRF) 800 N Capitol St NW Ste 790 ... Web: www.uscirf.gov	Washington	DC	20002	202-523-3240	523-5020
US Election Assistance Commission 1201 New York Ave NW Ste 300 ... TF: 866-747-1471 ■ Web: www.eac.gov	Washington	DC	20005	202-566-3100	566-3127
US General Services Administration (GSA) 1275 First St NW ... Web: www.gsa.gov/portal/category/100000	Washington	DC	20405	202-208-7642	
US General Services Administration 1800 F St NW ... TF: 800-488-3111 ■ Web: www.usa.gov	Washington	DC	20405	800-488-3111	
US Institute of Peace 2301 Constitution Ave NW ... Web: www.usip.org	Washington	DC	20037	202-457-1700	429-6063
US International Trade Commission 500 E St SW ... Web: www.usitc.gov	Washington	DC	20436	202-205-2000	
US Postal Service (USPS) 475 L'Enfant Plaza W SW ... TF Cust Svc: 800-275-8777 ■ Web: www.usps.com	Washington	DC	20260	202-268-2000	
US Trade & Development Agency 1000 Wilson Blvd Ste 1600 ... Web: www.ustda.gov	Arlington	VA	22209	703-875-4357	875-4009
Vietnam Education Foundation (VEF) 2111 Wilson Blvd Ste 700 ... Web: home.vef.gov	Arlington	VA	22201	703-351-5053	351-1423

341 GOVERNMENT - US - JUDICIAL BRANCH

				Phone	Fax
Federal Judicial Ctr 1 Columbus Cir NE ... Web: www.fjc.gov	Washington	DC	20544	202-502-4000	
Judicial Conference of the US 1 Columbus Cir NE ... Web: www.uscourts.gov/judconf.html	Washington	DC	20544	202-502-2600	
Judicial Panel on Multidistrict Litigation Thurgood Marshall Federal Judiciary Bldg 1 Columbus Cir NE Rm G-255 N Lobby ... Web: www.jpml.uscourts.gov	Washington	DC	20544	202-502-2800	502-2888
Supreme Court of the US 1st St NE 1 1st St NE ... Web: www.supremecourt.gov	Washington	DC	20543	202-479-3000	479-3472
US Court of Appeals for the Armed Forces 450 E St NW ...	Washington	DC	20442	202-761-1448	761-4672
US Court of Appeals for Veterans Claims 625 Indiana Ave NW Ste 900 ... Web: www.uscourts.cavc.gov	Washington	DC	20004	202-501-5970	501-5848
US Court of Federal Claims 717 Madison Pl NW ... Web: www.uscfc.uscourts.gov	Washington	DC	20005	202-357-6400	
US Court of International Trade 1 Federal Plaza ... Web: www.cit.uscourts.gov	New York	NY	10278	212-264-2800	264-1085
US Sentencing Commission Thurgood Marshall Federal Judiciary Bldg 1 Columbus Cir NE S Lobby ... Web: www.ussc.gov	Washington	DC	20002	202-502-4500	
US Tax Court 400 Second St NW ... Web: www.ustaxcourt.gov	Washington	DC	20217	202-521-0700	

341-1 US Appeals Courts

				Phone	Fax
Federal Circuit 717 Madison Pl NW ... Web: www.cafc.uscourts.gov	Washington	DC	20439	202-275-8000	
US Court of Appeals					
Circuit 9 PO Box 193939 ... Web: www.ca9.uscourts.gov	San Francisco	CA	94119	415-355-8000	
District of Columbia Circuit 333 Constitution Ave NW US Courthouse ... Web: www.cadc.uscourts.gov	Washington	DC	20001	202-216-7000	
Eight Circuit 111 S Tenth St Rm 22.329 ... Web: www.ca8.uscourts.gov	Saint Louis	MO	63102	314-244-2400	244-2780
Eleventh Circuit 56 Forsyth St NW ... Web: www.ca11.uscourts.gov	Atlanta	GA	30303	404-335-6100	335-6270
Fifth Circuit 600 Camp St ... Web: www.ca5.uscourts.gov	New Orleans	LA	70130	504-310-7700	
First Circuit 1 Courthouse Way Ste 2500 ... Web: www.ca1.uscourts.gov	Boston	MA	02210	617-748-9057	
Fourth Circuit US Courthouse Annex 1100 E Main St ... Web: www.ca4.uscourts.gov	Richmond	VA	23219	804-916-2700	
Second Circuit US Courthouse 40 Foley Sq ... Web: www.ca2.uscourts.gov	New York	NY	10007	212-857-8500	
Seventh Circuit 219 S Dearborn St Ste 2722 ... Web: www.ca7.uscourts.gov	Chicago	IL	60604	312-435-5850	
Sixth Circuit 100 E Fifth St ... Web: www.ca6.uscourts.gov	Cincinnati	OH	45202	513-564-7000	
Tenth Circuit 1823 Stout St ... Web: www.ca10.uscourts.gov	Denver	CO	80202	303-844-3157	
Third Circuit US Courthouse 601 Market St ... Web: www.ca3.uscourts.gov	Philadelphia	PA	19106	215-597-2995	

341-2 US Bankruptcy Courts

				Phone	Fax
District Court of the Virgin Islands					
US Virgin Islands US Courthouse 5500 Veterans Dr Rm 310 ... Web: www.vid.uscourts.gov	Saint Thomas	VI	00802	340-774-0640	775-8075
US Bankruptcy Court					
Alabama Middle 1 Church St ... Web: www.almb.uscourts.gov	Montgomery	AL	36104	334-954-3800	954-3819
Alabama Northern 1800 Fifth Ave N Rm 120 ... Web: www.alnb.uscourts.gov	Birmingham	AL	35203	205-714-4000	
Alabama Southern 201 St Louis St ... Web: www.alsb.uscourts.gov	Mobile	AL	36602	251-441-5391	441-6286
Alaska 605 W Fourth Ave Ste 138 ... TF: 800-859-8059 ■ Web: www.akb.uscourts.gov	Anchorage	AK	99501	907-271-2655	
Arizona 230 N First Ave Ste 101 ... Web: www.azb.uscourts.gov	Phoenix	AZ	85003	602-682-4000	
Arkansas 300 W Second St ... Web: www.arb.uscourts.gov	Little Rock	AR	72201	501-918-5500	918-5520
California Central 255 E Temple St ... Web: www.cacb.uscourts.gov	Los Angeles	CA	90012	213-894-3118	
California Eastern 501 'I' St Ste 3-200 ... Web: www.caeb.uscourts.gov	Sacramento	CA	95814	916-930-4400	
California Northern 235 Pine St 24th Fl ... Web: www.canb.uscourts.gov	San Francisco	CA	94104	415-268-2300	
California Southern 325 W F St ... Web: www.casb.uscourts.gov	San Diego	CA	92101	619-557-5620	
Central District of Illinois 600 E Monroe St 2nd Fl Rm 226 ... Web: www.ilcb.uscourts.gov	Springfield	IL	62701	217-492-4551	
Colorado US Custom House 721 19th St ... Web: www.cob.uscourts.gov	Denver	CO	80202	720-904-7300	
Connecticut 450 Main St 7th Fl ... Web: www.ctb.uscourts.gov	Hartford	CT	06103	860-240-3675	
Delaware 824 N Market St 3rd Fl ... Web: www.deb.uscourts.gov	Wilmington	DE	19801	302-252-2900	
District of Columbia 333 Constitution Ave NW ... Web: www.dcb.uscourts.gov	Washington	DC	20001	202-354-3280	
District of Hawaii 1132 Bishop St ... Web: www.hib.uscourts.gov	Honolulu	HI	96813	808-522-8100	522-8120
District of Rhode Island The Federal Ctr 380 Westminster Mall 6th Fl ... Web: www.rib.uscourts.gov	Providence	RI	02903	401-626-3100	626-3150
Eastern District of Tennessee 800 Market St Ste 330 ... Web: www.tneb.uscourts.gov	Knoxville	TN	37902	865-545-4279	
Eastern District of Texas 110 N College Ave 9th Fl ... Web: www.txeb.uscourts.gov	Tyler	TX	75702	903-590-3200	
Eastern District of Washington 904 W Riverside Ave Ste 304 ... TF: 800-519-2549 ■ Web: www.waeb.uscourts.gov	Spokane	WA	99201	509-353-2404	
Florida Middle 801 N Florida Ave Ste 727 ... Web: www.flmb.uscourts.gov	Tampa	FL	33602	813-301-5162	
Florida Northern 110 E Pk Ave Ste 100 ... Web: www.flnb.uscourts.gov	Tallahassee	FL	32301	850-521-5001	
Florida Southern 51 SW First Ave ... Web: www.flsb.uscourts.gov	Miami	FL	33130	305-714-1800	
Georgia Middle 433 Cherry St PO Box 1957 ... Web: www.gamb.uscourts.gov	Macon	GA	31202	478-752-3506	
Georgia Northern 75 Spring St SW ... Web: www.ganb.uscourts.gov	Atlanta	GA	30303	404-215-1000	

Court	City	State	Zip	Phone	Fax
Georgia Southern 125 Bull St *Web:* www.gasb.uscourts.gov	Savannah	GA	31401	912-650-4100	
Idaho 550 W Fort St *Web:* www.id.uscourts.gov	Boise	ID	83724	208-334-1074	
Illinois Southern 750 Missouri Ave *Web:* www.ilsb.uscourts.gov	East Saint Louis	IL	62201	618-482-9400	
Indiana Northern 401 S Michigan St *Web:* www.innb.uscourts.gov	South Bend	IN	46601	574-968-2100	
Indiana Southern 46 E Ohio St *Web:* www.insb.uscourts.gov	Indianapolis	IN	46204	317-229-3800	229-3801
Kansas 401 N Market St Rm 167 *Web:* www.ksb.uscourts.gov	Wichita	KS	67202	316-269-6637	
Kentucky Eastern 100 E Vine St Ste 200 *Web:* www.kyeb.uscourts.gov	Lexington	KY	40507	859-233-2608	
Kentucky Western 601 W Broadway Ste 450 *Web:* www.kywb.uscourts.gov	Louisville	KY	40202	502-627-5700	
Louisiana Eastern 500 Poydras St Ste B-601 *Web:* www.laeb.uscourts.gov	New Orleans	LA	70130	504-589-7878	
Louisiana Middle 707 Florida St Ste 119 *Web:* www.lamb.uscourts.gov	Baton Rouge	LA	70801	225-389-0211	
Louisiana Western 300 Fannin St Ste 2201 *Web:* www.lawb.uscourts.gov	Shreveport	LA	71101	318-676-4267	
Maine 537 Congress St 2nd Fl *Web:* www.meb.uscourts.gov	Portland	ME	04101	207-780-3482	780-3679
Massachusetts 5 Post Office Sq *Web:* www.mab.uscourts.gov/mab	Boston	MA	02109	617-748-5300	
Michigan Eastern 211 W Fort St Ste 2100 *Web:* www.mieb.uscourts.gov	Detroit	MI	48226	313-234-0065	
Michigan Western 1 Div Ave N Rm 200 *Web:* www.miwb.uscourts.gov	Grand Rapids	MI	49503	616-456-2693	
Minnesota 300 S Fourth St 7W US Courthouse *TF:* 866-260-7337 ■ *Web:* www.mnb.uscourts.gov	Minneapolis	MN	55415	612-664-5260	
Mississippi Northern 703 Hwy 145 N *Web:* www.msnb.uscourts.gov	Aberdeen	MS	39730	662-369-2596	
Mississippi Southern PO Box 2448 *Web:* www.mssb.uscourts.gov	Jackson	MS	39225	601-608-4600	
Missouri Eastern 111 S Tenth St 4th Fl *TF:* 866-803-9517 ■ *Web:* www.moeb.uscourts.gov	Saint Louis	MO	63102	314-244-4500	244-4990
Missouri Western 400 E Ninth St Rm1510 *Web:* www.mow.uscourts.gov	Kansas City	MO	64106	816-512-1800	
Montana 400 N Main St *Web:* www.mtb.uscourts.gov	Butte	MT	59701	406-497-1240	
Nebraska 111 S 18th Plaza Ste 1125 *Web:* www.neb.uscourts.gov	Omaha	NE	68102	402-661-7444	
Nevada 300 Las Vegas Blvd S *Web:* www.nvb.uscourts.gov	Las Vegas	NV	89101	702-388-6257	
New Hampshire 1000 Elm St 10th Fl *Web:* www.nhb.uscourts.gov	Manchester	NH	03101	603-222-2600	222-2697
New Jersey PO Box 1352 *Web:* www.njb.uscourts.gov	Newark	NJ	07102	973-645-4764	
New Mexico 333 Lomas Blvd N.W. *Web:* www.nmd.uscourts.gov	Albuquerque	NM	87102	505-348-2000	348-2028
New York Eastern 271 Cadman Plaza E *Web:* www.nyeb.uscourts.gov	Brooklyn	NY	11201	347-394-1700	
North Carolina Eastern 1760-A Parkwood Blvd *Web:* www.nceb.uscourts.gov	Wilson	NC	27893	252-237-0248	
North Carolina Middle 101 S Edgeworth St Fl 1 *Web:* www.ncmb.uscourts.gov	Greensboro	NC	27401	336-358-4000	
North Carolina Western 401 W Trade St PO Box 34189 *Web:* www.ncwb.uscourts.gov	Charlotte	NC	28234	704-350-7500	
North Dakota 655 First Ave N Ste 210 *Web:* www.ndb.uscourts.gov	Fargo	ND	58102	701-297-7100	
Northern District of Illinois 219 S Dearborn St *Web:* www.ilnb.uscourts.gov	Chicago	IL	60604	312-435-5694	
Northern District of Iowa 425 Second St SE Ste 800 *Web:* www.ianb.uscourts.gov	Cedar Rapids	IA	52401	319-286-2200	286-2280
Northern District of New York 445 Broadway Ste 330 *Web:* www.nynb.uscourts.gov	Albany	NY	12207	518-257-1661	
Ohio Northern 201 Superior Ave *Web:* www.ohnb.uscourts.gov	Cleveland	OH	44114	216-615-4300	
Ohio Southern 120 W Third St *Web:* www.ohsb.uscourts.gov	Dayton	OH	45402	937-225-2516	
Oklahoma Eastern 111 W Fourth St PO Box 1347 *Web:* www.okeb.uscourts.gov	Okmulgee	OK	74447	918-758-0126	756-9248
Oklahoma Northern 224 S Boulder Ave Rm 105 *Web:* www.oknb.uscourts.gov	Tulsa	OK	74103	918-699-4000	
Oklahoma Western 215 Dean A McGee Ave *Web:* www.okwb.uscourts.gov	Oklahoma City	OK	73102	405-609-5700	
Oregon 1001 SW Fifth Ave Rm 700 *Web:* www.orb.uscourts.gov	Portland	OR	97204	503-326-1500	
Pennsylvania Eastern 900 Market St Ste 400 *Web:* www.paeb.uscourts.gov	Philadelphia	PA	19107	215-408-2800	
Pennsylvania Middle 197 S Main St *TF:* 877-298-2053 ■ *Web:* www.pamb.uscourts.gov	Wilkes-Barre	PA	18701	570-831-2500	829-0249
Pennsylvania Western 5414 US Steel Tower 600 Grant St *Web:* www.pawb.uscourts.gov	Pittsburgh	PA	15219	412-644-2700	644-6512
Puerto Rico 300 Calle Del Recinto Sur *Web:* www.prb.uscourts.gov	San Juan	PR	00901	787-977-6000	977-6008
South Carolina 1100 Laurel St *Web:* www.scb.uscourts.gov	Columbia	SC	29201	803-765-5436	
South Dakota 400 S Phillips Ave Rm 104 *Web:* www.sdb.uscourts.gov	Sioux Falls	SD	57104	605-357-2430	357-2401
Southern District of Iowa 110 E Ct Ave Ste 300 *Web:* www.iasb.uscourts.gov	Des Moines	IA	50306	515-284-6230	284-6303
Southern District of New York US Custom House 1 Bowling Green *Web:* www.nysb.uscourts.gov	New York	NY	10004	212-668-2870	668-2878
Tennessee Middle 701 Broadway Rm 170 *Web:* www.tnmb.uscourts.gov	Nashville	TN	37203	615-736-5584	736-2305
Tennessee Western 200 Jefferson Ave Ste 413 *Web:* www.tnwb.uscourts.gov	Memphis	TN	38103	901-328-3500	
Texas Northern 1100 Commerce St Rm 1254 *TF:* 800-442-6850 ■ *Web:* www.txnb.uscourts.gov	Dallas	TX	75242	214-753-2000	
Texas Southern PO Box 61010 *Web:* www.txs.uscourts.gov	Houston	TX	77208	713-250-5500	
Texas Western 615 E Houston St Rm 597 PO Box 1439 *Web:* www.txwb.uscourts.gov	San Antonio	TX	78205	210-472-6720	472-5196
Utah 350 S Main St Rm 301 *Web:* www.utb.uscourts.gov	Salt Lake City	UT	84101	801-524-6687	524-4409
Vermont 67 Merchants Row PO Box 6648 *Web:* www.vtb.uscourts.gov	Rutland	VT	05702	802-776-2000	776-2020
Virginia Eastern 200 S Washington St *Web:* www.vaeb.uscourts.gov	Alexandria	VA	23219	804-916-2400	
Virginia Western 210 Church Ave SW Rm 200 *Web:* www.vawb.uscourts.gov	Roanoke	VA	24011	540-857-2391	857-2873
Washington Western 700 Stewart St Ste 6301 *Web:* www.wawb.uscourts.gov	Seattle	WA	98101	206-370-5200	
West Virginia Northern 1125 Chapline St Third Fl PO Box 70 *Web:* www.wvnb.uscourts.gov	Wheeling	WV	26003	304-233-1655	233-0185
West Virginia Southern 300 Virginia St E Rm 3200 *Web:* www.wvsb.uscourts.gov	Charleston	WV	25301	304-347-3003	
Western District of New York 100 State St *Web:* www.nywb.uscourts.gov	Rochester	NY	14614	585-613-4200	
Wisconsin Eastern US Courthouse 517 E Wisconsin Ave Rm 126 *TF:* 877-781-7277 ■ *Web:* www.wieb.uscourts.gov	Milwaukee	WI	53202	414-297-3291	
Wisconsin Western 120 N Henry St Rm 340 PO Box 548 *Web:* www.wiwb.uscourts.gov	Madison	WI	53701	608-264-5178	
Wyoming 2120 Capitol Ave Ste 6004 *Web:* www.wyb.uscourts.gov	Cheyenne	WY	82001	307-433-2200	

341-3 US District Courts

Court	City	State	Zip	Phone	Fax
United States District Court *Western District of Michigan* 110 Michigan St NW 399 Federal Bldg *Web:* www.miwd.uscourts.gov	Grand Rapids	MI	49503	616-456-2381	
United States District Court, Central District 312 N Spring St *Web:* www.cacd.uscourts.gov	Los Angeles	CA	90012	213-894-1565	
US District Court Alabama Northern 1729 Fifth Ave N *Web:* www.alnd.uscourts.gov	Birmingham	AL	35203	205-278-1700	
US District Court Arizona 401 W Washington St Ste 130 *Web:* www.azd.uscourts.gov	Phoenix	AZ	85003	602-322-7200	
US District Court Arkansas Western 30 S Sixth St *Web:* www.arwd.uscourts.gov	Fort Smith	AR	72901	479-783-6833	783-6308
US District Court California Eastern 501 I St *Web:* www.caed.uscourts.gov	Sacramento	CA	95814	916-930-4000	
US District Court California Northern 450 Golden Gate Ave PO Box 36060 *Web:* www.cand.uscourts.gov	San Francisco	CA	94102	415-522-2000	
US District Court California Southern 880 Front St Rm 4290 *Web:* www.casd.uscourts.gov	San Diego	CA	92101	619-557-6348	702-9900
US District Court Colorado 901 19th St *TF:* 800-359-8699 ■ *Web:* www.cod.uscourts.gov/Home.aspx	Denver	CO	80294	303-844-3433	335-2040
US District Court Connecticut 141 Church St *Web:* www.ctd.uscourts.gov	New Haven	CT	06510	203-773-2140	773-2334
US District Court Delaware 844 N King St Ste 18 *Web:* www.ded.uscourts.gov	Wilmington	DE	19801	302-573-6170	
US District Court District of Columbia 333 Constitution Ave NW # 6822 *Web:* www.dcd.uscourts.gov	Washington	DC	20001	202-354-3000	
US District Court Florida Middle 401 W Central Blvd Ste 1200 *Web:* www.flmd.uscourts.gov	Orlando	FL	32801	407-835-4200	
US District Court Florida Southern 301 N Miami Ave *Web:* www.flsd.uscourts.gov	Miami	FL	33128	305-523-5100	
US District Court for the District of Alaska 222 W Seventh Ave Ste 4 *TF:* 866-243-3814 ■ *Web:* www.akd.uscourts.gov	Anchorage	AK	99513	907-677-6100	
US District Court Georgia Middle 475 Mulberry St PO Box 128 *Web:* www.gamd.uscourts.gov	Macon	GA	31202	478-752-3497	752-3496
US District Court Georgia Northern 75 Spring St SW *Web:* www.gand.uscourts.gov	Atlanta	GA	30303	404-215-1600	
US District Court Georgia Southern PO Box 8286 *Web:* www.gasd.uscourts.gov	Savannah	GA	31412	912-650-4020	

				Phone	Fax
US District Court Guam 520 W Soledad Ave 4th Fl *Web:* www.gud.uscourts.gov	Hagatna	GU	96910	671-473-9100	
US District Court Hawaii 300 Ala Moana Blvd Rm C-338 *Web:* www.hid.uscourts.gov	Honolulu	HI	96850	808-541-1300	
US District Court Idaho 550 W Fort St. *Web:* www.id.uscourts.gov	Boise	ID	83724	208-334-1361	
US District Court Illinois Central 600 E Monroe St. *Web:* www.ilcd.uscourts.gov	Springfield	IL	62701	217-492-4020	492-4028
US District Court Illinois Northern 219 S Dearborn St 20th Fl *Web:* www.ilnd.uscourts.gov	Chicago	IL	60604	312-435-5670	
US District Court Illinois Southern 750 Missouri Ave *Web:* www.ilsd.uscourts.gov	East Saint Louis	IL	62201	618-482-9371	482-9383
US District Court Indiana Northern 204 S Main St. *Web:* www.innd.uscourts.gov	South Bend	IN	46601	574-246-8000	
US District Court Indiana Southern 46 E Ohio St *Web:* www.insd.uscourts.gov	Indianapolis	IN	46204	317-229-3700	229-3959
US District Court Iowa Northern 101 First St SE *Web:* www.iand.uscourts.gov	Cedar Rapids	IA	52401	319-286-2300	286-2301
US District Court Iowa Southern PO Box 9344 *Web:* www.iasd.uscourts.gov	Des Moines	IA	50306	515-284-6248	284-6418
US District Court Kansas 500 State Ave *Web:* www.ksd.uscourts.gov	Kansas City	KS	66101	913-735-2200	551-6942
US District Court Kentucky Eastern 101 Barr St *Web:* www.kyed.uscourts.gov	Lexington	KY	40507	859-233-2503	
US District Court Kentucky Western 601 W Broadway Rm 106 *Web:* www.kywd.uscourts.gov	Louisville	KY	40202	502-625-3500	625-3880
US District Court Louisiana Eastern 500 Poydras St Rm C-151 *Web:* www.laed.uscourts.gov	New Orleans	LA	70130	504-589-7650	589-7697
US District Court Louisiana Middle 777 Florida St Ste 139 *Web:* www.lamd.uscourts.gov	Baton Rouge	LA	70801	225-389-3500	389-3501
US District Court Louisiana Western 300 Fannin St Ste 1167 *Web:* www.lawd.uscourts.gov	Shreveport	LA	71101	318-676-4273	676-3962
US District Court Maine 156 Federal St *Web:* www.med.uscourts.gov	Portland	ME	04101	207-780-3356	
US District Court Maryland 101 W Lombard St *Web:* www.mdd.uscourts.gov	Baltimore	MD	21201	410-962-2600	
US District Court Massachusetts 1 Courthouse Way Ste 2300 *Web:* www.mad.uscourts.gov	Boston	MA	02210	617-748-9152	
US District Court Michigan Eastern 231 W Lafayette Blvd *Web:* www.mied.uscourts.gov	Detroit	MI	48226	313-234-5005	
US District Court Minnesota 300 S Fourth St Ste 202 *Web:* www.mnd.uscourts.gov	Minneapolis	MN	55415	612-664-5000	664-5033
US District Court Mississippi Northern 911 Jackson Ave E Rm 369 *Web:* www.msnd.uscourts.gov	Oxford	MS	38655	662-234-1971	236-5210
US District Court Mississippi Southern PO Box 23552 *TF:* 866-517-7682 ■ *Web:* www.mssd.uscourts.gov	Jackson	MS	39201	601-965-4439	
US District Court Missouri Eastern 111 S Tenth St Ste 3.300 *Web:* www.moed.uscourts.gov	Saint Louis	MO	63102	314-244-7900	244-7909
US District Court Missouri Western 400 E Ninth St *Web:* www.mow.uscourts.gov	Kansas City	MO	64106	816-512-5000	
US District Court Montana PO Box 8537 *Web:* www.mtd.uscourts.gov	Missoula	MT	59807	406-542-7260	542-7272
US District Court Nebraska 111 S 18th Plaza Ste 1152 *TF:* 866-220-4381 ■ *Web:* www.ned.uscourts.gov	Omaha	NE	68102	402-661-7350	661-7387
US District Court Nevada 333 Las Vegas Blvd S. *Web:* www.nvd.uscourts.gov	Las Vegas	NV	89101	702-464-5400	
US District Court New Hampshire 55 Pleasant St Rm 110 *Web:* www.nhd.uscourts.gov	Concord	NH	03301	603-225-1423	
US District Court New Jersey 50 Walnut St *Web:* www.njd.uscourts.gov	Newark	NJ	07101	973-645-3730	
US District Court New Mexico 333 Lomas Blvd NW *Web:* www.nmcourt.fed.us	Albuquerque	NM	87102	505-348-2000	
US District Court New York Northern 100 S Clinton St PO Box 7367 *Web:* www.nynd.uscourts.gov	Syracuse	NY	13261	315-234-8500	
US District Court New York Southern 500 Pearl St *Web:* www.nysd.uscourts.gov	New York	NY	10007	212-805-0136	
US District Court New York Western 2 Niagara Sq *Web:* www.nywd.uscourts.gov	Buffalo	NY	14202	716-551-4211	551-4850
US District Court North Carolina Eastern PO Box 25670 *Web:* www.nced.uscourts.gov	Raleigh	NC	27611	919-645-1700	645-1750
US District Court North Carolina Middle 324 W Market St 4th Fl. *Web:* www.ncmd.uscourts.gov	Greensboro	NC	27401	336-332-6000	332-6060
US District Court North Carolina Western 401 W Trade St. *TF:* 866-851-1605 ■ *Web:* www.ncwd.uscourts.gov	Charlotte	NC	28202	704-350-7400	
US District Court North Dakota PO Box 1193 *Web:* www.ndd.uscourts.gov	Bismarck	ND	58502	701-530-2300	530-2312
US District Court Northern District Of Florida 111 N Adams St *Web:* www.flnd.uscourts.gov	Tallahassee	FL	32301	850-521-3501	521-3656
US District Court Ohio Northern 801 W Superior Ave *Web:* www.ohnd.uscourts.gov	Cleveland	OH	44113	216-357-7000	357-7040
US District Court Ohio Southern 85 Marconi Blvd *Web:* www.ohsd.uscourts.gov	Columbus	OH	43215	614-719-3000	
US District Court Oklahoma Eastern PO Box 607 *Web:* www.oked.uscourts.gov	Muskogee	OK	74402	918-684-7920	684-7902
US District Court Oklahoma Northern 333 W Fourth St *TF:* 866-213-1957 ■ *Web:* www.oknd.uscourts.gov	Tulsa	OK	74103	918-699-4700	
US District Court Oklahoma Western 200 NW Fourth St Rm 1210 *Web:* www.okwd.uscourts.gov	Oklahoma City	OK	73102	405-609-5000	609-5099
US District Court Oregon 1000 SW Third Ave Ste 740 *Web:* www.ord.uscourts.gov	Portland	OR	97204	503-326-8000	
US District Court Pennsylvania Eastern 601 Market St *Web:* www.paed.uscourts.gov	Philadelphia	PA	19106	215-597-7704	597-6390
US District Court Pennsylvania Middle 235 N Washington Ave PO Box 1148 *Web:* www.pamd.uscourts.gov	Scranton	PA	18501	570-207-5600	207-5650
US District Court Pennsylvania Western 700 Grant St *Web:* www.pawd.uscourts.gov	Pittsburgh	PA	15219	412-208-7500	
US District Court Puerto Rico 150 Carlos Chardon Ave Rm 150 Federal Bldg. *Web:* www.prd.uscourts.gov	San Juan	PR	00918	787-772-3000	766-5693
US District Court South Carolina 1845 Assembly St. *Web:* www.scd.uscourts.gov	Columbia	SC	29201	803-765-5816	
US District Court South Dakota 400 S Phillips Ave Rm 128 *Web:* www.sdd.uscourts.gov	Sioux Falls	SD	57104	605-330-6600	330-6601
US District Court Tennessee Eastern 800 Market St Ste 130 *Web:* www.tned.uscourts.gov	Knoxville	TN	37902	865-545-4228	545-4247
US District Court Tennessee Middle 801 Broadway Rm 800 *Web:* www.tnmd.uscourts.gov	Nashville	TN	37203	615-736-5498	736-7488
US District Court Tennessee Western 167 N Main St Rm 242 *Web:* www.tnwd.uscourts.gov	Memphis	TN	38103	901-495-1200	495-1250
US District Court Texas Eastern 211 W Ferguson St. *Web:* www.txed.uscourts.gov	Tyler	TX	75702	903-590-1000	
US District Court Texas Northern 1100 Commerce St Rm 1452 *Web:* www.txnd.uscourts.gov	Dallas	TX	75242	214-753-2200	753-2266
US District Court Texas Southern PO Box 61010 *Web:* www.txs.uscourts.gov	Houston	TX	77208	713-250-5500	
US District Court US Virgin Islands 3013 Estate Golden Rock *Web:* www.vid.uscourts.gov	Saint Croix	VI	00820	340-773-1130	773-1563
US District Court Utah 350 S Main St Rm 150 *Web:* www.utd.uscourts.gov	Salt Lake City	UT	84101	801-524-6100	526-1175
US District Court Vermont 11 Elmwood Ave Rm 506 PO Box 945 *TF:* 800-837-8718 ■ *Web:* www.vtd.uscourts.gov	Burlington	VT	05402	802-951-6301	
US District Court Virginia Eastern 401 Courthouse Sq 2nd Fl *Web:* www.vaed.uscourts.gov	Alexandria	VA	22314	703-299-2100	
US District Court Virginia Western 180 W. Main St Rm 104 *Web:* www.vawd.uscourts.gov	Abingdon	VA	24210	540-857-5100	857-5110
US District Court Washington Eastern 920 W Riverside Ave Ste 840 *Web:* www.waed.uscourts.gov	Spokane	WA	99201	509-458-3400	458-3420
US District Court Washington Western 700 Stewart St *Web:* www.wawd.uscourts.gov	Seattle	WA	98101	206-370-8400	
US District Court West Virginia Northern 300 Third St PO Box 1518 *Web:* www.wvnd.uscourts.gov	Elkins	WV	26241	304-636-1445	636-5746
US District Court West Virginia Southern 300 Virginia St E Ste 2400 *Web:* www.wvsd.uscourts.gov	Charleston	WV	25301	304-347-3000	
US District Court Wisconsin Eastern 517 E Wisconsin Ave *Web:* www.wied.uscourts.gov	Milwaukee	WI	53202	414-297-3372	
US District Court Wisconsin Western 120 N Henry St Rm 320 PO Box 432 *Web:* www.wiwd.uscourts.gov	Madison	WI	53701	608-264-5156	264-5925
US District Court Wyoming 2120 Capitol Ave 2nd Fl *Web:* www.wyd.uscourts.gov	Cheyenne	WY	82001	307-433-2120	433-2152

341-4 US Supreme Court

	City	State	Zip	Phone	Fax
Roberts John G Jr US Supreme Ct Bldg 1 1st St NE *TF:* 800-772-1213 ■ *Web:* www.supremecourt.gov	Washington	DC	20543	202-479-3000	479-3472
Breyer Stephen G US Supreme Ct Bldg 1 1st St NE *Web:* www.supremecourt.gov	Washington	DC	20543	202-479-3000	
Ginsburg Ruth Bader US Supreme Ct Bldg 1 1st St NE *Web:* www.supremecourt.gov	Washington	DC	20543	202-479-3000	
Kennedy Anthony M US Supreme Ct Bldg 1 1st St NE *TF:* 800-772-1213 ■ *Web:* www.supremecourt.gov	Washington	DC	20543	202-479-3000	479-3472
Scalia Antonin US Supreme Ct Bldg 1 1st St NE *TF:* 800-772-1213 ■ *Web:* www.supremecourt.gov	Washington	DC	20543	202-479-3000	479-3472
Stevens John Paul US Supreme Ct Bldg 1 1st St NE *TF:* 800-772-1213 ■ *Web:* www.supremecourt.gov	Washington	DC	20543	202-479-3000	479-3472
Thomas Clarence US Supreme Ct Bldg 1 1st St NE *Web:* www.supremecourt.gov	Washington	DC	20543	202-479-3000	

342 GOVERNMENT - US - LEGISLATIVE BRANCH

See Also Legislation Hotlines p. 2646

	City	State	Zip	Phone	Fax
Calgary Economic Development 731 First St SE *TF:* 888-222-5855 ■ *Web:* www.calgaryeconomicdevelopment.com	Calgary	AB	T2G2G9	403-221-7831	
Collingwood Events 45 Saint Paul St *Web:* www.collingwood.ca	Collingwood	ON	L9Y3P1	705-445-4811	
Congressional Budget Office Ford House Office Bldg 4th Fl *Web:* www.cbo.gov	Washington	DC	20515	202-226-2602	
Government Accountability Office (GAO) 441 G St NW *Web:* www.gao.gov	Washington	DC	20548	202-512-4800	
Atlanta Office 2635 Century Pkwy Ste 700 *Web:* www.gao.gov	Atlanta	GA	30345	404-679-1900	679-1819
Boston Office 10 Cswy St Rm 575 *Web:* www.gao.gov	Boston	MA	02222	617-788-0500	788-0505
Dallas Office 1999 Bryan St Ste 2200 *Web:* www.gao.gov	Dallas	TX	75201	214-777-5600	777-5758
Dayton Office 2196 D St Area B Bldg 39 *Web:* www.gao.gov	Wright-Patterson AFB	OH	45433	937-258-7900	258-7118
Denver Office 1244 Speer Blvd Ste 800 *Web:* www.gao.gov	Denver	CO	80204	303-572-7306	572-7433
Huntsville Office 6767 Old Madison Pike Bldg 5 Ste 520 *Web:* www.gao.gov	Huntsville	AL	35806	256-922-7500	971-9240
Los Angeles Office 350 S Figueroa St Ste 1010 *Web:* www.gao.gov	Los Angeles	CA	90071	213-830-1000	830-1180
Norfolk Office 5029 Corporate Woods Dr Ste 300 *Web:* www.gao.gov	Virginia Beach	VA	23462	757-552-8100	552-8197
San Francisco Office 301 Howard St Ste 1200 *Web:* www.gao.gov	San Francisco	CA	94105	415-904-2000	904-2111
Seattle Office 701 Fifth Ave Ste 2700 *Web:* www.gao.gov	Seattle	WA	98104	206-287-4800	287-4872
Library of Congress (LOC) 101 Independence Ave SE *Web:* www.loc.gov	Washington	DC	20540	202-707-5000	
American Folklife Ctr 101 Independence Ave SE *Web:* www.loc.gov/folklife	Washington	DC	20540	202-707-5510	707-2076
Congressional Research Service 101 Independence Ave SE *Web:* www.loc.gov/crsinfo	Washington	DC	20540	202-707-5507	707-5643
Law Library of Congress 101 Independence Ave SE *Web:* loc.gov/law/index.html	Washington	DC	20540	202-707-5079	707-1820
National Library Service for the Blind & Physically Handicapped 1291 Taylor St NW *TF:* 888-657-7323 ■ *Web:* www.loc.gov/nls	Washington	DC	20011	202-707-5100	707-0712
THOMAS: Legislative Information on the Internet 101 Independence Ave SE *Web:* loc.gov	Washington	DC	20540	202-707-5000	
US Copyright Office 101 Independence Ave SE *TF:* 877-476-0778 ■ *Web:* www.copyright.gov	Washington	DC	20559	202-707-3000	
Port of Belledune 112 Shannon Dr *Web:* www.portofbelledune.ca	Belledune	NB	E8G2W2	506-522-1200	
Societe Des Traversiers Du Quebec 250 Rue Saint-Paul *Web:* www.traversiers.com	Quebec	QC	G1K9K9	418-643-2019	
Tourism Abbotsford Society 34561 Delair Rd *TF:* 888-332-2229 ■ *Web:* www.tourismabbotsford.ca	Abbotsford	BC	V2S2E1	604-859-1721	
US Government Accountability Office (US GAO) *Chicago Office* 200 W Adams St Ste 700 *Web:* www.gao.gov	Chicago	IL	60606	312-220-7600	220-7726
US Government Printing Office Bookstore (GPO) 732 N Capitol St NW *TF:* 866-512-1800 ■ *Web:* bookstore.gpo.gov	Washington	DC	20401	202-512-1800	512-2104
US House of Representatives 100 Cannon House Office Bldg *Web:* www.house.gov	Washington	DC	20515	202-225-3121	225-1904
US Senate 455 Dirksen Senate Office Bldg *Web:* www.senate.gov	Washington	DC	20510	202-224-3121	

342-1 US Congressional Committees

	City	State	Zip	Phone	Fax
Select Committee on Ethics 220 Hart Bldg *Web:* www.ethics.senate.gov/public/index.cfm/home	Washington	DC	20510	202-224-2981	224-7416
Energy and Commerce, The *Energy & Commerce Committee* 2125 Rayburn Bldg *Web:* www.energycommerce.house.gov	Washington	DC	20515	202-225-2927	
United States Senate Special Committee on Aging G31 Dirksen Senate Office Bldg *Web:* aging.senate.gov	Washington	DC	20510	202-224-5364	224-9926
US Congress *Joint Committee on Printing* 1309 Longworth House Office Bldg *Web:* cha.house.gov	Washington	DC	20515	202-225-8281	
Joint Committee on Taxation, The 502 Ford House Office Bldg *Web:* www.jct.gov	Washington	DC	20515	202-225-3621	
Joint Economic Committee G-01 Dirksen Bldg *Web:* www.jec.senate.gov	Washington	DC	20510	202-224-5171	224-0240
US House of Representatives 100 Cannon House Office Bldg *Web:* www.house.gov	Washington	DC	20515	202-225-3121	225-1904
Agriculture Committee 1301 Longworth Bldg *Web:* www.agriculture.house.gov	Washington	DC	20515	202-225-2171	225-0917
Armed Services Committee 2120 Rayburn House Office Bldg *Web:* www.armedservices.house.gov	Washington	DC	20515	202-225-4151	225-0858
Budget Committee 207 Cannon House Office Bldg *Web:* www.budget.house.gov	Washington	DC	20515	202-226-7270	
Committee on Education & Labor 2181 Rayburn Bldg *Web:* edworkforce.house.gov	Washington	DC	20515	202-225-4527	
Committee on Natural Resources 1324 Longworth Bldg *Web:* naturalresources.house.gov	Washington	DC	20515	202-225-6065	225-1031
Government Reform Committee 2157 Rayburn House Office Bldg *Web:* oversight.house.gov	Washington	DC	20515	202-225-5074	225-3974
Homeland Security Committee 176 Ford House Office Bldg *Web:* homeland.house.gov	Washington	DC	20515	202-226-8417	226-3399
House Administration Committee 1309 Longworth Bldg *Web:* cha.house.gov	Washington	DC	20515	202-225-2061	226-2774
House Committee on Foreign Affairs 2170 Rayburn Bldg *Web:* foreignaffairs.house.gov	Washington	DC	20515	202-225-5021	225-2035
Judiciary Committee 2138 Rayburn Bldg *Web:* www.judiciary.house.gov	Washington	DC	20515	202-225-3951	225-7680
Rules Committee H-312 Capitol Bldg *Web:* www.rules.house.gov	Washington	DC	20515	202-225-9191	225-1061
Small Business Committee 2361 Rayburn Bldg *Web:* www.smallbusiness.house.gov	Washington	DC	20515	202-225-5821	
Transportation & Infrastructure Committee 2165 Rayburn Bldg *Web:* transportation.house.gov	Washington	DC	20515	202-225-9446	
Veterans Affairs Committee 335 Cannon Bldg *Web:* veterans.house.gov	Washington	DC	20515	202-225-3527	
Ways & Means Committee 1102 Longworth Bldg *Web:* www.waysandmeans.house.gov	Washington	DC	20515	202-225-3625	225-2610
US Senate 455 Dirksen Senate Office Bldg *Web:* www.senate.gov	Washington	DC	20510	202-224-3121	
Agriculture Nutrition & Forestry Committee 328A Russell Senate Office Bldg *Web:* agriculture.senate.gov	Washington	DC	20510	202-224-2035	228-2125
Budget Committee 624 Drksen Senate Bldg *Web:* budget.senate.gov	Washington	DC	20510	202-224-0642	
Commerce Science & Transportation Committee Dirksen Senate Office Bldg SD-508 *Web:* www.commerce.senate.gov	Washington	DC	20510	202-224-5115	
Committee on Finance 219 Dirksen Senate Office Bldg *Web:* finance.senate.gov	Washington	DC	20510	202-224-4515	228-0554
Committee on Veterans Affairs 412 Russell Bldg *Web:* veterans.senate.gov	Washington	DC	20510	202-224-9126	
Energy & Natural Resources Committee 304 Dirksen Senate Bldg *Web:* energy.senate.gov	Washington	DC	20510	202-224-4971	224-6163
Environment & Public Works Committee 410 Dirksen Senate Office Bldg *Web:* www.epw.senate.gov/public	Washington	DC	20510	202-224-8832	
Foreign Relations Committee 446 Dirksen Senate Office Bldg *Web:* foreign.senate.gov	Washington	DC	20510	202-224-4651	
Homeland Security & Governmental Affairs Committee 340 Dirksen Senate Office Bldg *Web:* www.hsgac.senate.gov	Washington	DC	20510	202-224-2627	

				Phone	Fax
Judiciary Committee					
224 Dirksen Senate Office Bldg	Washington	DC	20510	202-224-5225	
Web: www.judiciary.senate.gov					
Rules & Administration Committee					
305 Russell Senate Office Bldg	Washington	DC	20510	202-224-6352	
Web: www.rules.senate.gov/public					
US Senate Committee on Indian Affairs					
838 Hart Bldg	Washington	DC	20510	202-224-2251	228-2589
Web: indian.senate.gov					
US Senate Select Committee on Intelligence					
211 Hart Senate Office Bldg	Washington	DC	20510	202-224-1700	224-1772
Web: intelligence.senate.gov					

342-2 US Senators, Representatives, Delegates

The circled letter S denotes that a listing is for a senator.

Alabama

				Phone	Fax
Aderholt Robert (Rep R - AL)					
235 Cannon House Office Bldg.	Washington	DC	20515	202-225-4876	
Web: aderholt.house.gov					
Brooks Mo (Rep R - AL)					
1230 Longworth Bldg	Washington	DC	20515	202-225-4801	225-4392
Web: brooks.house.gov					
Byrne Bradley (Rep R - AL) 119 Cannon HOB	Washington	DC	20515	202-225-4931	225-0562
Web: byrne.house.gov					
Palmer Gary (Rep R - AL)					
206 Cannon House Office Bldg.	Washington	DC	20515	202-225-4912	225-2082
Web: palmer.house.gov					
Roby Martha (Rep R - AL) 428 Cannon Bldg	Washington	DC	20515	202-225-2901	225-8913
Web: roby.house.gov					
Rogers Mike (Rep R - AL) 324 Cannon Bldg	Washington	DC	20515	202-225-3261	226-8485
Web: mikerogers.house.gov					
Ⓢ Sessions Jeff (Sen R - AL)					
326 Russell Bldg	Washington	DC	20510	202-224-4124	224-3149
Web: www.sessions.senate.gov					
Sewell Terri A (Rep D - AL)					
1133 Longworth Bldg	Washington	DC	20515	202-225-2665	226-9567
Web: sewell.house.gov					
Ⓢ Shelby Richard C (Sen R - AL)					
304 Russell Bldg	Washington	DC	20510	202-224-5744	224-3416
Web: www.shelby.senate.gov					

Alaska

				Phone	Fax
Ⓢ Murkowski Lisa (Sen R - AK) 709 Hart Bldg	Washington	DC	20510	202-224-6665	224-5301
Web: www.murkowski.senate.gov					
Ⓢ Sullivan Daniel (Sen R - AK)					
702 Hart Senate Office Bldg	Washington	DC	20510	202-224-3004	224-6501
Web: www.sullivan.senate.gov					
Young Don (Rep R - AK) 2314 Rayburn Bldg	Washington	DC	20515	202-225-5765	225-0425
Web: donyoung.house.gov					

American Samoa

				Phone	Fax
Radewagen Amata (Rep R - AS)					
1339 Longworth House Office Bldg	Washington	DC	20515	202-225-8577	225-8757
Web: radewagen.house.gov					

Arizona

				Phone	Fax
Franks Trent (Rep R - AZ)					
2435 Rayburn Bldg	Washington	DC	20515	202-225-4576	225-6328
Web: franks.house.gov					
Gallego Ruben (Rep D - AZ)					
1218 Longworth House Office Bldg	Washington	DC	20515	202-225-4065	
Web: rubengallego.house.gov					
Gosar Paul A (Rep R - AZ) 504 Cannon Bldg	Washington	DC	20515	202-225-2315	226-9739
Web: gosar.house.gov					
Grijalva Raul (Rep D - AZ)					
1511 Longworth Bldg	Washington	DC	20515	202-225-2435	225-1541
Web: grijalva.house.gov					
Ⓢ Jeff Flake (Sen R - AZ)					
413 Russell Senate Office Bldg	Washington	DC	20510	202-224-4521	228-0515
Web: www.flake.senate.gov					
Kirkpatrick Ann (Rep D - AZ)					
201 Cannon HOB	Washington	DC	20515	202-225-3361	225-3462
Web: kirkpatrick.house.gov					
Ⓢ McCain John (Sen R - AZ)					
218 Russell Senate Office Bldg	Washington	DC	20510	202-224-2235	228-2862
Web: www.mccain.senate.gov					
McSally Martha (Rep R - AZ)					
1029 Longworth House Office Bldg	Washington	DC	20515	202-225-2542	225-0378
Web: mcsally.house.gov					
Salmon Matt (Rep R - AZ)					
2349 Rayburn Bldg	Washington	DC	20515	202-225-2635	226-4386
Web: salmon.house.gov					
Schweikert David (Rep R - AZ)					
409 Cannon House Office Bldg	Washington	DC	20515	202-225-2190	225-0096
Web: schweikert.house.gov					
Sinema Krysten (Rep D - AZ)					
1237 Longworth Bldg	Washington	DC	20515	202-225-9888	225-9731
Web: sinema.house.gov					

Arkansas

				Phone	Fax
Ⓢ Boozman John (Sen R - AR)					
141 Hart Senate Office Bldg	Washington	DC	20510	202-224-4843	228-1371
Web: www.boozman.senate.gov					
Ⓢ Cotton Tom (Sen R - AR)					
124 Russell Senate Office Bldg	Washington	DC	20510	202-224-2353	
Web: www.cotton.senate.gov					
Crawford Rick (Rep R - AR)					
1711 Longworth Bldg	Washington	DC	20515	202-225-4076	225-5602
Web: crawford.house.gov					
Hill French (Rep R - AR)					
1229 Longworth House Office Bldg	Washington	DC	20515	202-225-2506	225-5903
Web: hill.house.gov					
Westerman Bruce (Rep R - AR)					
130 Cannon House Office Bldg.	Washington	DC	20515	202-225-3772	225-1314
Web: westerman.house.gov					
Womack Steve (Rep R - AR)					
1119 Longworth HOB	Washington	DC	20515	202-225-4301	225-5713
Web: womack.house.gov					

California

				Phone	Fax
Aguilar Pete (Rep D - CA)					
1223 Longworth HOB	Washington	DC	20515	202-225-3201	226-6962
Web: aguilar.house.gov					
Bass Karen (Rep D - CA) 408 Cannon Bldg	Washington	DC	20515	202-225-7084	225-2422
Web: bass.house.gov					
Becerra Xavier (Rep D - CA)					
1226 Longworth Bldg	Washington	DC	20515	202-225-6235	225-2202
Web: becerra.house.gov					
Bera Ami (Rep D - CA) 1535 Longworth Bldg.	Washington	DC	20515	202-225-5716	226-1298
Web: bera.house.gov					
Ⓢ Boxer Barbara (Sen D - CA)					
112 Hart Senate Bldg	Washington	DC	20510	202-224-3553	
Web: www.boxer.senate.gov					
Brownley Julia (Rep D - CA)					
1019 Longworth Bldg	Washington	DC	20515	202-225-5811	225-1100
Web: juliabrownley.house.gov					
Calvert Ken (Rep R - CA)					
2205 Rayburn Bldg	Washington	DC	20515	202-225-1986	225-2004
Web: calvert.house.gov					
Capps Lois (Rep D - CA) 2231 Rayburn Bldg	Washington	DC	20515	202-225-3601	225-5632
Web: capps.house.gov					
Cardenas Tony (Rep D - CA)					
1508 Longworth Bldg	Washington	DC	20515	202-225-6131	225-0819
Web: cardenas.house.gov					
Chu Judy (Rep D - CA) 2423 Rayburn HOB	Washington	DC	20515	202-225-5464	225-5467
Web: chu.house.gov					
Cook Paul (Rep R - CA)					
1222 Longworth Bldg	Washington	DC	20515	202-225-5861	
Web: cook.house.gov					
Costa Jim (Rep D - CA)					
1314 Longworth Bldg	Washington	DC	20515	202-225-3341	225-9308
Web: costa.house.gov					
Davis Susan (Rep D - CA)					
1214 Longworth HOB	Washington	DC	20515	202-225-2040	225-2948
Web: www.house.gov/susandavis					
Denham Jeff (Rep R - CA)					
1730 Longworth Bldg	Washington	DC	20515	202-225-4540	225-3402
Web: denham.house.gov					
DeSaulnier Mark (Rep D - CA)					
327 Cannon HOB	Washington	DC	20515	202-225-2095	225-5609
Web: desaulnier.house.gov					
Eshoo Anna G (Rep D - CA) 241 Cannon Bldg.	Washington	DC	20515	202-225-8104	225-8890
Web: eshoo.house.gov					
Farr Sam (Rep D - CA) 1126 Longworth Bldg	Washington	DC	20515	202-225-2861	225-6791
Web: www.farr.house.gov					
Ⓢ Feinstein Dianne (Sen D - CA)					
331 Hart Bldg	Washington	DC	20510	202-224-3841	228-3954
Web: www.feinstein.senate.gov					
Garamendi John (Rep D - CA)					
2438 Rayburn Bldg	Washington	DC	20515	202-225-1880	225-5914
Web: garamendi.house.gov					
Hahn Janice (Rep D - CA) 404 Cannon Bldg	Washington	DC	20515	202-225-8220	226-7290
TF: 855-328-7332 ■ *Web:* hahn.house.gov					
Honda Mike (Rep D - CA)					
1713 Longworth Bldg	Washington	DC	20515	202-225-2631	225-2699
Web: honda.house.gov					
Huffman Jared (Rep D - CA)					
1630 Longworth Bldg	Washington	DC	20515	202-225-5161	225-5163
Web: huffman.house.gov					
Hunter Duncan D (Rep R - CA)					
2429 Rayburn HOB	Washington	DC	20515	202-225-5672	225-0235
Web: hunter.house.gov					
Issa Darrell (Rep R - CA)					
2269 Rayburn HOB	Washington	DC	20515	202-225-3906	225-3303
Web: issa.house.gov					
Knight Steve (Rep R - CA)					
1023 Longworth HOB	Washington	DC	20515	202-225-1956	
Web: knight.house.gov					
LaMalfa Doug (Rep R - CA) 322 Cannon HOB	Washington	DC	20515	202-225-3076	
Web: lamalfa.house.gov					
Lee Barbara (Rep D - CA)					
2267 Rayburn Bldg	Washington	DC	20515	202-225-2661	225-9817
Web: lee.house.gov					
Lieu Ted (Rep D - CA) 415 Cannon HOB	Washington	DC	20515	202-225-3976	
Web: lieu.house.gov					
Lofgren Zoe (Rep D - CA)					
1401 Longworth Bldg	Washington	DC	20515	202-225-3072	
Web: lofgren.house.gov					
Lowenthal Alan (Rep D - CA)					
108 Cannon HOB	Washington	DC	20515	202-225-7924	225-7926
Web: lowenthal.house.gov					
Matsui Doris O (Rep D - CA)					
2311 Rayburn HOB	Washington	DC	20515	202-225-7163	225-0566
Web: matsui.house.gov					

Name / Address	City	State	Zip	Phone	Fax
McCarthy Kevin (Rep R - CA) 2421 Rayburn Bldg *Web:* kevinmccarthy.house.gov	Washington	DC	20515	202-225-2915	225-2908
McClintock Tom (Rep R - CA) 2331 Rayburn HOB *Web:* mcclintock.house.gov	Washington	DC	20515	202-225-2511	225-5444
McNerney Jerry (Rep D - CA) 1210 Longworth Bldg *Web:* mcnerney.house.gov	Washington	DC	20515	202-225-1947	225-4060
Napolitano Grace (Rep D - CA) 1610 Longworth *Web:* napolitano.house.gov	Washington	DC	20515	202-225-5256	225-0027
Nunes Devin (Rep R - CA) 1013 Longworth Bldg Ste 1013 *Web:* nunes.house.gov	Washington	DC	20515	202-225-2523	225-3404
Pelosi Nancy (Rep D - CA) 233 Cannon HOB *Web:* pelosi.house.gov	Washington	DC	20515	202-225-4965	225-4188
Peters Scott (Rep D - CA) 1122 Longworth HOB *Web:* scottpeters.house.gov	Washington	DC	20515	202-225-0508	225-2558
Rohrabacher Dana (Rep R - CA) 2300 Rayburn Bldg *Web:* rohrabacher.house.gov	Washington	DC	20515	202-225-2415	225-0145
Roybal-Allard Lucille (Rep D - CA) 2330 Rayburn Bldg *Web:* roybal-allard.house.gov	Washington	DC	20515	202-225-1766	226-0350
Royce Ed (Rep R - CA) 2310 Rayburn HOB *Web:* www.royce.house.gov	Washington	DC	20515	202-225-4111	226-0335
Ruiz Raul (Rep D - CA) 1319 Longworth Bldg *Web:* ruiz.house.gov	Washington	DC	20515	202-225-5330	225-1238
Sanchez Linda (Rep D - CA) 2329 Rayburn HOB *Web:* lindasanchez.house.gov	Washington	DC	20515	202-225-6676	226-1012
Sanchez Loretta (Rep D - CA) 1114 Longworth Bldg *Web:* www.lorettasanchez.house.gov	Washington	DC	20515	202-225-2965	225-5859
Schiff Adam (Rep D - CA) 2411 Rayburn Bldg *Web:* schiff.house.gov	Washington	DC	20515	202-225-4176	225-5828
Sherman Brad (Rep D - CA) 2242 Rayburn Bldg *Web:* sherman.house.gov	Washington	DC	20515	202-225-5911	225-5879
Speier Jackie (Rep D - CA) 2465 Rayburn HOB *Web:* speier.house.gov	Washington	DC	20515	202-225-3531	226-4183
Swalwell Eric (Rep D - CA) 129 Cannon HOB *Web:* swalwell.house.gov	Washington	DC	20515	202-225-5065	
Takano Mark (Rep D - CA) 1507 Longworth Bldg *Web:* takano.house.gov	Washington	DC	20515	202-225-2305	225-7018
Thompson Mike (Rep D - CA) 231 Cannon Bldg *Web:* mikethompson.house.gov	Washington	DC	20515	202-225-3311	225-4335
Torres Norma (Rep D - CA) 516 Cannon HOB *Web:* torres.house.gov	Washington	DC	20515	202-225-6161	225-8671
Valadao David (Rep R - CA) 1004 Longworth Bldg *Web:* valadao.house.gov	Washington	DC	20515	202-225-4695	225-3196
Vargas Juan (Rep D - CA) 1605 Longworth Bldg *Web:* vargas.house.gov	Washington	DC	20515	202-225-8045	225-2772
Walters Mimi (Rep R - CA) 236 Cannon HOB *Web:* walters.house.gov	Washington	DC	20515	202-225-5611	225-9177
Waters Maxine (Rep D - CA) 2221 Rayburn Bldg *Web:* waters.house.gov	Washington	DC	20515	202-225-2201	225-7854

Colorado

Name / Address	City	State	Zip	Phone	Fax
●Bennet Michael F (Sen D - CO) 261 Hart Senate Office Bldg *Web:* www.baldwin.senate.gov	Washington	DC	20510	202-224-5852	224-9787
Buck Ken (Rep R - CO) 416 Cannon HOB *Web:* buck.house.gov	Washington	DC	20515	202-225-4676	225-5870
Coffman Mike (Rep R - CO) 2443 Rayburn Bldg *Web:* coffman.house.gov	Washington	DC	20515	202-225-7882	226-4623
DeGette Diana (Rep D - CO) 2368 Rayburn Bldg *Web:* degette.house.gov	Washington	DC	20515	202-225-4431	225-5657
●Gardner Cory (Sen R - CO) 354 Russell Senate Office Bldg *Web:* www.gardner.senate.gov	Washington	DC	20510	202-224-5941	224-6524
Lamborn Doug (Rep R - CO) 2402 Rayburn Bldg *Web:* lamborn.house.gov	Washington	DC	20515	202-225-4422	226-2638
Perlmutter Ed (Rep D - CO) 1410 Longworth Bldg *Web:* perlmutter.house.gov	Washington	DC	20515	202-225-2645	225-5278
Polis Jared (Rep D - CO) 1433 Longworth Bldg *Web:* polis.house.gov	Washington	DC	20515	202-225-2161	226-7840
Tipton Scott (Rep R - CO) 218 Cannon Bldg *Web:* tipton.house.gov	Washington	DC	20515	202-225-4761	226-9669

Connecticut

Name / Address	City	State	Zip	Phone	Fax
●Blumenthal Richard (Sen D - CT) 706 Hart Senate Office Bldg *Web:* www.blumenthal.senate.gov	Washington	DC	20510	202-224-2823	224-9673
Courtney Joe (Rep D - CT) 2348 Rayburn Bldg *Web:* courtney.house.gov	Washington	DC	20515	202-225-2076	225-4977
DeLauro Rosa L (Rep D - CT) 2413 Rayburn Bldg *Web:* delauro.house.gov	Washington	DC	20515	202-225-3661	225-4890
Esty Elizabeth (Rep D - CT) 405 Cannon HOB **Fax Area Code:* 860 ■ *Web:* esty.house.gov	Washington	DC	20515	202-225-4476	225-7289*
Himes Jim (Rep D - CT) 1227 Longworth HOB *Web:* himes.house.gov	Washington	DC	20515	202-225-5541	225-9629
Larson John B (Rep D - CT) 1501 Longworth Bldg *Web:* www.larson.house.gov	Washington	DC	20515	202-225-2265	225-1031
●Murphy Christopher (Sen D - CT) 136 Hart Senate Office Bldg *Web:* www.murphy.senate.gov	Washington	DC	20510	202-224-4041	224-9750

Delaware

Name / Address	City	State	Zip	Phone	Fax
Carney John (Rep D - DE) 1406 Longworth Bldg *Web:* johncarney.house.gov	Washington	DC	20515	202-225-4165	
●Carper Thomas R (Sen D - DE) 513 Hart Bldg *Web:* www.carper.senate.gov	Washington	DC	20510	202-224-2441	228-2190
●Coons Christopher A (Sen D - DE) 127A Russell Bldg *Web:* www.coons.senate.gov	Washington	DC	20510	202-224-5042	

District of Columbia

Name / Address	City	State	Zip	Phone	Fax
Norton Eleanor Holmes (Rep D - DC) 2136 Rayburn Bldg *Web:* www.norton.house.gov	Washington	DC	20515	202-225-8050	225-3002

Florida

Name / Address	City	State	Zip	Phone	Fax
Bilirakis Gus M (Rep R - FL) 2112 Rayburn HOB *Web:* bilirakis.house.gov	Washington	DC	20515	202-225-5755	225-4085
Buchanan Vern (Rep R - FL) 2104 Rayburn Bldg *Web:* buchanan.house.gov	Washington	DC	20515	202-225-5015	226-0828
Castor Kathy (Rep D - FL) 205 Cannon Bldg *Web:* castor.house.gov	Washington	DC	20515	202-225-3376	225-5652
Clawson Curt (Rep R - FL) 228 Cannon House Office Bldg *Web:* clawson.house.gov	Washington	DC	20515	202-225-2536	226-0439
Corrine Brown (Rep D - FL) 2111 Rayburn HOB *Web:* corrinebrown.house.gov	Washington	DC	20515	202-225-0123	
Crenshaw Ander (Rep R - FL) 2161 Rayburn HOB *Web:* crenshaw.house.gov	Washington	DC	20515	202-225-2501	225-2504
Curbelo Carlos (Rep R - FL) 1429 Longworth HOB *Web:* curbelo.house.gov	Washington	DC	20515	202-225-2778	
DeSantis Ron (Rep R - FL) 308 Cannon HOB *Web:* desantis.house.gov	Washington	DC	20515	202-225-2706	226-6299
Deutch Ted (Rep D - FL) 2447 Rayburn Bldg *Web:* teddeutch.house.gov	Washington	DC	20515	202-225-3001	225-5974
Diaz-Balart Mario (Rep R - FL) 440 Cannon HOB *Web:* mariodiazbalart.house.gov	Washington	DC	20515	202-225-4211	225-8576
Frankel Lois (Rep D - FL) 1037 Longworth Bldg *TF:* 866-264-0957 ■ *Web:* frankel.house.gov	Washington	DC	20515	202-225-9890	
Graham Gwen (Rep D - FL) 1213 Longworth HOB *Web:* graham.house.gov	Washington	DC	20515	202-225-5235	225-5615
Grayson Alan (Rep D - FL) 303 Cannon HOB *Web:* grayson.house.gov	Washington	DC	20515	202-225-9889	225-9742
Hastings Alcee L (Rep D - FL) 2353 Rayburn Bldg *Web:* www.alceehastings.house.gov	Washington	DC	20515	202-225-1313	225-1171
Jolly David (Rep R - FL) 1728 Longworth HOB *Web:* jolly.house.gov	Washington	DC	20515	202-225-5961	225-9764
Mica John (Rep R - FL) 2187 Rayburn Bldg *Web:* mica.house.gov	Washington	DC	20515	202-225-4035	226-0821
Miller Jeff (Rep R - FL) 336 Cannon Bldg *Web:* jeffmiller.house.gov	Washington	DC	20515	202-225-4136	225-3414
Murphy Patrick (Rep D - FL) 211 Cannon HOB *Web:* patrickmurphy.house.gov	Washington	DC	20515	202-225-3026	225-8398
●Nelson Bill (Sen D - FL) 716 Hart Bldg *Web:* www.billnelson.senate.gov	Washington	DC	20510	202-224-5274	228-2183
Nugent Richard (Rep R - FL) 1727 Longworth Bldg *Web:* nugent.house.gov	Washington	DC	20515	202-225-1002	226-6559
Posey Bill (Rep R - FL) 120 Cannon Bldg *Web:* posey.house.gov	Washington	DC	20515	202-225-3671	225-3671
Rooney Tom (Rep R - FL) 2160 Rayburn HOB *Web:* rooney.house.gov	Washington	DC	20515	202-225-5792	225-3132
Ros-Lehtinen Ileana (Rep R - FL) 2206 Rayburn Bldg *Web:* ros-lehtinen.house.gov	Washington	DC	20515	202-225-3931	225-5620
Ross Dennis (Rep R - FL) 229 Cannon Bldg *Web:* dennisross.house.gov	Washington	DC	20515	202-225-1252	226-0585

Name / Address	City	State	Zip	Phone	Fax
●Rubio Marco (Sen R - FL) 284 Russell Bldg *Web:* www.rubio.senate.gov	Washington	DC	20510	202-224-3041	
Wasserman Schultz Debbie (Rep D - FL) 1114 Longworth HOB *Web:* wassermanschultz.house.gov	Washington	DC	20515	202-225-7931	226-2052
Webster Daniel (Rep R - FL) 1039 Longworth Bldg *Web:* webster.house.gov	Washington	DC	20515	202-225-2176	225-0999
Wilson Frederica (Rep D - FL) 208 Cannon Bldg *Web:* wilson.house.gov	Washington	DC	20515	202-225-4506	226-0777
Yoho Ted (Rep R - FL) 511 Cannon Bldg *Web:* yoho.house.gov	Washington	DC	20515	202-225-5744	225-3973

Georgia

Name / Address	City	State	Zip	Phone	Fax
Allen Rick (Rep R - GA) 513 Cannon HOB *Web:* allen.house.gov	Washington	DC	20515	202-225-2823	225-3377
Bishop Sanford D Jr (Rep D - GA) 2407 Rayburn HOB *Web:* bishop.house.gov	Washington	DC	20515	202-225-3631	225-2203
Carter Buddy (Rep R - GA) 432 Cannon HOB *Web:* buddycarter.house.gov	Washington	DC	20515	202-225-5831	226-2269
Collins Doug (Rep R - GA) 1504 Longworth HOB *Web:* dougcollins.house.gov	Washington	DC	20515	202-225-9893	226-1224
Graves Tom (Rep R - GA) 2442 Rayburn HOB *Web:* tomgraves.house.gov	Washington	DC	20515	202-225-5211	225-8272
Hice Jody (Rep R - GA) 1516 Longworth HOB *Web:* hice.house.gov	Washington	DC	20515	202-225-4101	226-0776
●Isakson Johnny (Sen R - GA) 131 Russell Bldg *Web:* www.isakson.senate.gov	Washington	DC	20510	202-224-3643	228-0724
Johnson Henry C "Hank" Jr (Rep D - GA) 2240 Rayburn Bldg *Web:* hankjohnson.house.gov	Washington	DC	20515	202-225-1605	226-0691
Lewis John (Rep D - GA) 343 Cannon Bldg *Web:* johnlewis.house.gov	Washington	DC	20515	202-225-3801	225-0351
Loudermilk Barry (Rep R - GA) 238 Cannon HOB *Web:* loudermilk.house.gov	Washington	DC	20515	202-225-2931	225-2944
●Perdue David (Sen R - GA) 383 Russell Senate Office Bldg *Web:* www.perdue.senate.gov	Washington	DC	20510	202-224-3521	228-1031
Price Tom (Rep R - GA) 100 Cannon Bldg *Web:* tomprice.house.gov	Washington	DC	20515	202-225-4501	225-4656
Scott Austin (Rep R - GA) 2417 Rayburn HOB *Web:* austinscott.house.gov	Washington	DC	20515	202-225-6531	225-3013
Scott David (Rep D - GA) 225 Cannon Bldg *Web:* davidscott.house.gov	Washington	DC	20515	202-225-2939	225-4628
Westmoreland Lynn A (Rep R - GA) 2202 Rayburn HOB *Web:* westmoreland.house.gov	Washington	DC	20515	202-225-5901	225-2515
Woodall Robert (Rep R - GA) 1724 Longworth HOB *Web:* woodall.house.gov	Washington	DC	20515	202-225-4272	225-4696

Guam

Name / Address	City	State	Zip	Phone	Fax
Bordallo Madeleine (Rep D - GU) 2441 Rayburn Bldg *Web:* bordallo.house.gov	Washington	DC	20515	202-225-1188	226-0341

Hawaii

Name / Address	City	State	Zip	Phone	Fax
Gabbard Tulsi (Rep D - HI) 1609 Longworth HOB *Web:* gabbard.house.gov	Washington	DC	20515	202-225-4906	225-4987
●Hirono Mazie K (Sen D - HI) 330 Hart Bldg *Web:* www.hirono.senate.gov	Washington	DC	20510	202-224-6361	224-2126
●Schatz Brian (Sen D - HI) 722 Hart Bldg *Web:* www.schatz.senate.gov	Washington	DC	20510	202-224-3934	228-1153
Takai Mark (Rep D - HI) 422 Cannon HOB *Web:* takai.house.gov	Washington	DC	20515	202-225-2726	225-0688

Idaho

Name / Address	City	State	Zip	Phone	Fax
●Crapo Mike (Sen R - ID) 239 Dirksen Bldg *Web:* www.crapo.senate.gov	Washington	DC	20510	202-224-6142	228-1375
Labrador Raul R (Rep R - ID) 1523 Longworth Bldg *Web:* labrador.house.gov	Washington	DC	20515	202-225-6611	225-3029
●Risch James E (Sen R - ID) 483 Russell Bldg *Web:* www.risch.senate.gov	Washington	DC	20510	202-224-2752	224-2573
Simpson Mike (Rep R - ID) 2312 Rayburn Bldg *Web:* simpson.house.gov	Washington	DC	20515	202-225-5531	225-8216

Illinois

Name / Address	City	State	Zip	Phone	Fax
Bost Mike (Rep R - IL) 1440 Longworth HOB *Web:* bost.house.gov	Washington	DC	20515	202-225-5661	225-0285
Bustos Cheri (Rep D - IL) 1009 Longworth Bldg *Web:* bustos.house.gov	Washington	DC	20515	202-225-5905	
Davis Danny K (Rep D - IL) 2159 Rayburn Bldg *Web:* www.davis.house.gov	Washington	DC	20515	202-225-5006	225-5641
Davis Rodney (Rep R - IL) 1740 Longworth Bldg *Web:* rodneydavis.house.gov	Washington	DC	20515	202-225-2371	226-0791
Dold Bob (Rep R - IL) 221 Cannon HOB *Web:* dold.house.gov	Washington	DC	20515	202-225-4835	225-0837
Duckworth Tammy (Rep D - IL) 104 Cannon Bldg *Web:* duckworth.house.gov	Washington	DC	20515	202-225-3711	
●Durbin Richard J (Sen D - IL) 711 Hart Bldg *Web:* www.durbin.senate.gov	Washington	DC	20510	202-224-2152	228-0400
Foster Bill (Rep D - IL) 1224 Longworth Bldg *Web:* foster.house.gov	Washington	DC	20515	202-225-3515	225-9420
Gutierrez Luis (Rep D - IL) 2408 Rayburn Bldg *Web:* gutierrez.house.gov	Washington	DC	20515	202-225-8203	225-7810
Hultgren Randy (Rep R - IL) 2455 Rayburn HOB *Web:* hultgren.house.gov	Washington	DC	20515	202-225-2976	225-0697
Kelly Robin (Rep D - IL) 1239 Longworth HOB *Web:* robinkelly.house.gov	Washington	DC	20515	202-225-0773	225-4583
Kinzinger Adam (Rep R - IL) 1221 Longworth Bldg *Web:* kinzinger.house.gov	Washington	DC	20515	202-225-3635	225-3521
●Kirk Mark (Sen R - IL) 524 Hart Bldg *Web:* www.kirk.senate.gov	Washington	DC	20510	202-224-2854	228-4611
Lipinski Daniel (Rep D - IL) 1717 Longworth Bldg *Web:* www.lipinski.house.gov	Washington	DC	20515	202-225-5701	225-1012
Quigley Mike (Rep D - IL) 2458 Rayburn HOB *Web:* quigley.house.gov	Washington	DC	20515	202-225-4061	225-5603
Roskam Peter J (Rep R - IL) 2246 Rayburn HOB *Web:* roskam.house.gov	Washington	DC	20515	202-225-4561	225-1166
Roskam, Peter J. (Rep R - IL) 2246 Rayburn HOB *Web:* roskam.house.gov	Washington	DC	20515	202-225-4561	
Rush Bobby L (Rep D - IL) 2188 Rayburn HOB *Web:* rush.house.gov	Washington	DC	20515	202-225-4372	226-0333
Schakowsky Jan (Rep D - IL) 2367 Rayburn Bldg *Web:* schakowsky.house.gov	Washington	DC	20515	202-225-2111	226-6890
Shimkus John (Rep R - IL) 2452 Rayburn Bldg *Web:* shimkus.house.gov	Washington	DC	20515	202-225-5271	225-5880

Indiana

Name / Address	City	State	Zip	Phone	Fax
Brooks Susan W (Rep R - IN) 1505 Longworth Bldg *Web:* susanwbrooks.house.gov	Washington	DC	20515	202-225-2276	225-0016
Bucshon Larry (Rep R - IN) 1005 Longworth Bldg *Web:* bucshon.house.gov	Washington	DC	20515	202-225-4636	225-3284
Carson Andre (Rep D - IN) 2453 Rayburn Bldg *Web:* carson.house.gov	Washington	DC	20515	202-225-4011	225-5633
●Coats Daniel (Sen R - IN) 493 Russell Bldg *Web:* www.coats.senate.gov	Washington	DC	20510	202-224-5623	228-1820
●Donnelly Joe (Sen D - IN) 720 Hart Bldg *Web:* www.donnelly.senate.gov	Washington	DC	20510	202-224-4814	224-5011
Messer Luke (Rep R - IN) 508 Cannon Bldg *Web:* messer.house.gov	Washington	DC	20515	202-225-3021	
Rokita Todd (Rep R - IN) 236 Cannon Bldg *Web:* rokita.house.gov	Washington	DC	20515	202-225-5037	226-0544
Stutzman Marlin (Rep R - IN) 2418 Rayburn HOB *Web:* stutzman.house.gov	Washington	DC	20515	202-225-4436	226-9870
Visclosky Peter (Rep D - IN) 2328 Rayburn Bldg *Web:* visclosky.house.gov	Washington	DC	20515	202-225-2461	225-2493
Walorski Jackie (Rep R - IN) 419 Cannon Bldg *Web:* walorski.house.gov	Washington	DC	20515	202-225-3915	225-6798
Young Todd (Rep R - IN) 1007 Longworth Bldg *Web:* toddyoung.house.gov	Washington	DC	20515	202-225-5315	226-6866

Iowa

Name / Address	City	State	Zip	Phone	Fax
Blum Rod (Rep R - IA) 213 Cannon HOB *Web:* blum.house.gov	Washington	DC	20515	202-225-2911	
●Ernst Joni (Sen R - IA) 111 Russell Senate Office Bldg *Web:* www.ernst.senate.gov	Washington	DC	20510	202-224-3254	224-9369
●Grassley Chuck (Sen R - IA) 135 Hart Bldg *Web:* www.grassley.senate.gov	Washington	DC	20510	202-224-3744	224-6020
King Steve (Rep R - IA) 2210 Rayburn Bldg *Web:* steveking.house.gov	Washington	DC	20515	202-225-4426	225-3193
Loebsack David (Rep D - IA) 1527 Longworth Bldg *Web:* loebsack.house.gov	Washington	DC	20515	202-225-6576	226-0757
Young David (Rep R - IA) 515 Cannon HOB *Web:* davidyoung.house.gov	Washington	DC	20515	202-225-5476	

Kansas

Name / Address	City	State	Zip	Phone	Fax
Huelskamp Tim (Rep R - KS) 1110 Longworth HOB	Washington	DC	20515	202-225-2715	225-5124
Web: huelskamp.house.gov					
Jenkins Lynn (Rep R - KS) 1526 Longworth HOB	Washington	DC	20515	202-225-6601	225-7986
Web: lynnjenkins.house.gov					
ⓈMoran Jerry (Sen R - KS) 521 Dirksen Senate Office Bldg	Washington	DC	20510	202-224-6521	228-6966
Web: www.moran.senate.gov					
Pompeo Mike (Rep R - KS) 436 Cannon HOB	Washington	DC	20515	202-225-6216	225-3489
Web: pompeo.house.gov					
ⓈRoberts Pat (Sen R - KS) 109 Hart Bldg.	Washington	DC	20510	202-224-4774	224-3514
Web: www.roberts.senate.gov					
Yoder Kevin (Rep R - KS) 215 Cannon Bldg	Washington	DC	20515	202-225-2865	
Web: yoder.house.gov					

Kentucky

Name / Address	City	State	Zip	Phone	Fax
Barr Andy (Rep R - KY) 1432 Longworth Bldg	Washington	DC	20515	202-225-4706	
Web: barr.house.gov					
Guthrie S Brett (Rep R - KY) 2434 Rayburn HOB	Washington	DC	20515	202-225-3501	226-2019
Web: guthrie.house.gov					
Massie Thomas (Rep R - KY) 314 Cannon Bldg	Washington	DC	20515	202-225-3465	225-0003
Web: massie.house.gov					
ⓈMcConnell Mitch (Sen R - KY) 317 Russell Bldg	Washington	DC	20510	202-224-2541	224-2499
Web: www.mcconnell.senate.gov					
ⓈPaul Rand (Sen R - KY) 167 Russell Senate Office Bldg	Washington	DC	20510	202-224-4343	
Web: www.paul.senate.gov					
Rogers Harold (Rep R - KY) 2406 Rayburn Bldg	Washington	DC	20515	202-225-4601	225-0940
Web: halrogers.house.gov					
Whitfield Ed (Rep R - KY) 2184 Rayburn Bldg	Washington	DC	20515	202-225-3115	225-3547
Web: whitfield.house.gov					
Yarmuth John A (Rep D - KY) 403 Cannon Bldg	Washington	DC	20515	202-225-5401	225-5776
Web: yarmuth.house.gov					

Louisiana

Name / Address	City	State	Zip	Phone	Fax
Abraham Ralph (Rep R - LA) 417 Cannon HOB	Washington	DC	20515	202-225-8490	225-5639
Web: abraham.house.gov					
Boustany Charles W Jr (Rep R - LA) 1431 Longworth Bldg	Washington	DC	20515	202-225-2031	225-5724
Web: boustany.house.gov					
ⓈCassidy Bill (Sen R - LA) 703 Hart Senate Office Bldg	Washington	DC	20510	202-224-5824	224-9735
Web: www.cassidy.senate.gov					
Fleming John (Rep R - LA) 2182 Rayburn HOB	Washington	DC	20515	202-225-2777	225-8039
Web: fleming.house.gov					
Graves Garret (Rep R - LA) 204 Cannon HOB	Washington	DC	20515	202-225-3901	225-7313
Web: garretgraves.house.gov					
Richmond Cedric (Rep D - LA) 240 Cannon Bldg	Washington	DC	20515	202-225-6636	225-1988
Web: richmond.house.gov					
Scalise Steve (Rep R - LA) 2338 Rayburn Bldg	Washington	DC	20515	202-225-3015	226-0386
Web: scalise.house.gov					
ⓈVitter David (Sen R - LA) 516 Hart Bldg.	Washington	DC	20510	202-224-4623	228-5061
Web: www.vitter.senate.gov					

Maine

Name / Address	City	State	Zip	Phone	Fax
ⓈCollins Susan M (Sen R - ME) 413 Dirksen Bldg	Washington	DC	20510	202-224-2523	224-2693
Web: www.collins.senate.gov					
ⓈKing Angus S Jr (Sen I - ME) 133 Hart Senate Office Bldg	Washington	DC	20510	202-224-5344	
Web: www.king.senate.gov					
Pingree Chellie (Rep D - ME) 2162 Rayburn HOB	Washington	DC	20515	202-225-6116	225-5590
Web: pingree.house.gov					
Poliquin Bruce (Rep R - ME) 426 Cannon HOB	Washington	DC	20515	202-225-6306	225-2943
Web: poliquin.house.gov					

Maryland

Name / Address	City	State	Zip	Phone	Fax
ⓈCardin Benjamin L (Sen D - MD) 509 Hart Bldg	Washington	DC	20510	202-224-4524	224-1651
Web: www.cardin.senate.gov					
Cummings Elijah (Rep D - MD) 2230 Rayburn HOB	Washington	DC	20515	202-225-4741	225-3178
Web: cummings.house.gov					
Delaney John (Rep D - MD) 1632 Longworth Bldg	Washington	DC	20515	202-225-2721	
Web: delaney.house.gov					
Edwards Donna F (Rep D - MD) 2445 Rayburn Bldg	Washington	DC	20515	202-225-8699	225-8714
Web: donnaedwards.house.gov					
Harris Andy (Rep R - MD) 1533 Longworth Bldg	Washington	DC	20515	202-225-5311	225-0254
Web: harris.house.gov					
Hoyer Steny H (Rep D - MD) 1705 Longworth Bldg	Washington	DC	20515	202-225-4131	225-4300
Web: hoyer.house.gov					
ⓈMikulski Barbara A (Sen D - MD) 503 Hart Bldg	Washington	DC	20510	202-224-4654	224-8858
Web: www.mikulski.senate.gov					
Ruppersberger Dutch (Rep D - MD) 2416 Rayburn Bldg	Washington	DC	20515	202-225-3061	225-3094
Web: ruppersberger.house.gov					
Sarbanes John P (Rep D - MD) 2444 Rayburn Bldg	Washington	DC	20515	202-225-4016	225-9219
Web: sarbanes.house.gov					
Van Hollen Chris (Rep D - MD) 1707 Longworth Bldg	Washington	DC	20515	202-225-5341	225-0375
Web: vanhollen.house.gov					

Massachusetts

Name / Address	City	State	Zip	Phone	Fax
Capuano Michael E (Rep D - MA) 1414 Longworth Bldg	Washington	DC	20515	202-225-5111	225-9322
Web: www.house.gov/capuano					
Clark Katherine (Rep D - MA) 1721 Longworth HOB	Washington	DC	20515	202-225-2836	
Web: katherineclark.house.gov					
Keating William (Rep D - MA) 315 Cannon Bldg	Washington	DC	20515	202-225-3111	225-5658
Web: keating.house.gov					
Kennedy III Joseph P (Rep D - MA) 306 Cannon HOB	Washington	DC	20515	202-225-5931	225-0182
Web: kennedy.house.gov					
Lynch Stephen F (Rep D - MA) 2369 Rayburn HOB	Washington	DC	20515	202-225-8273	225-3984
Web: lynch.house.gov					
ⓈMarkey Edward J (Sen D - MA) 255 Dirksen Senate Office Bldg	Washington	DC	20510	202-224-2742	
Web: www.markey.senate.gov					
McGovern James (Rep D - MA) 438 Cannon Bldg	Washington	DC	20515	202-225-6101	225-5759
Web: mcgovern.house.gov					
Moulton Seth (Rep D - MA) 1408 Longworth HOB	Washington	DC	20515	202-225-8020	225-5915
Web: moulton.house.gov					
Neal Richard E (Rep D - MA) 341 Cannon HOB	Washington	DC	20515	202-225-5601	225-8112
Web: neal.house.gov					
Tsongas Niki (Rep D - MA) 1714 Longworth HOB	Washington	DC	20515	202-225-3411	226-0771
Web: tsongas.house.gov					
ⓈWarren Elizabeth (Sen D - MA) 317 Hart Bldg	Washington	DC	20510	202-224-4543	
Web: www.warren.senate.gov					

Michigan

Name / Address	City	State	Zip	Phone	Fax
Amash Justin (Rep R - MI) 114 Cannon Bldg	Washington	DC	20515	202-225-3831	225-5144
Web: amash.house.gov					
Benishek Dan (Rep R - MI) 514 Cannon Bldg	Washington	DC	20515	202-225-4735	225-4710
Web: benishek.house.gov					
Bishop Mike (Rep R - MI) 428 Cannon HOB	Washington	DC	20515	202-225-4872	225-5820
Web: mikebishop.house.gov					
Candice, Miller (Rep R- MI) 320 Cannon HOB	Washington	DC	20515	202-225-2106	
Web: candicemiller.house.gov/					
Conyers Jr John (Rep D - MI) 2426 Rayburn Bldg	Washington	DC	20515	202-225-5126	225-0072
Web: conyers.house.gov					
Dingell Debbie (Rep D - MI) 116 Cannon HOB	Washington	DC	20515	202-225-4071	226-0371
Web: debbiedingell.house.gov					
Huizenga Bill (Rep R - MI) 1217 Longworth Bldg	Washington	DC	20515	202-225-4401	226-0779
Web: huizenga.house.gov					
Kildee Daniel (Rep D - MI) 227 Cannon Bldg	Washington	DC	20515	202-225-3611	
Web: dankildee.house.gov					
Lawrence Brenda (Rep D - MI) 1237 Longworth HOB	Washington	DC	20515	202-225-5802	226-2356
Web: lawrence.house.gov					
Levin Sander (Rep D - MI) 1236 Longworth Bldg	Washington	DC	20515	202-225-4961	226-1033
Web: levin.house.gov					
Moolenaar John (Rep R - MI) 117 Cannon HOB	Washington	DC	20515	202-225-3561	225-9679
Web: moolenaar.house.gov					
ⓈPeters Gary (Sen D - MI) Hart Senate Office Bldg Ste 724	Washington	DC	20510	202-224-6221	
Web: www.peters.senate.gov					
ⓈStabenow Debbie (Sen D - MI) 731 Hart Senate Office Bldg	Washington	DC	20510	202-224-4822	228-0325
Web: www.stabenow.senate.gov					
Trott Dave (Rep R - MI) 1722 Longworth HOB	Washington	DC	20515	202-225-8171	225-2667
Web: trott.house.gov					
Upton Fred (Rep R - MI) 2183 Rayburn Bldg	Washington	DC	20515	202-225-3761	225-4986
Web: upton.house.gov					

				Phone	Fax
Walberg Tim (Rep R - MI) 2436 Rayburn Bldg *Web:* walberg.house.gov	Washington	DC	20515	202-225-6276	225-6281

Minnesota

				Phone	Fax
Ellison Keith (Rep D - MN) 2263 Rayburn Bldg *Web:* ellison.house.gov	Washington	DC	20515	202-225-4755	225-4886
Emmer Tom (Rep R - MN) 503 Cannon HOB *Web:* emmer.house.gov	Washington	DC	20515	202-225-2331	225-6475
●Franken Al (Sen D - MN) 309 Hart Bldg *Web:* www.franken.senate.gov	Washington	DC	20510	202-224-5641	
Kline John (Rep R - MN) 2439 Rayburn Bldg *Web:* kline.house.gov	Washington	DC	20515	202-225-2271	225-2595
●Klobuchar Amy (Sen D - MN) 302 Hart Bldg *Web:* www.klobuchar.senate.gov	Washington	DC	20510	202-224-3244	228-2186
McCollum Betty (Rep D - MN) 2256 Rayburn HOB *Web:* mccollum.house.gov	Washington	DC	20515	202-225-6631	225-1968
Nolan Rick (Rep D - MN) 2366 Rayburn HOB *Web:* nolan.house.gov	Washington	DC	20515	202-225-6211	225-0699
Paulsen Erik (Rep R - MN) 127 Cannon Bldg *Web:* paulsen.house.gov	Washington	DC	20515	202-225-2871	225-6351
Peterson Collin C (Rep D - MN) 2204 Rayburn HOB *Web:* collinpeterson.house.gov	Washington	DC	20515	202-225-2165	225-1593
Walz Timothy J (Rep D - MN) 1034 Longworth Bldg *Web:* walz.house.gov	Washington	DC	20515	202-225-2472	225-6351

Mississippi

				Phone	Fax
●Cochran Thad (Sen R - MS) 113 Dirksen Bldg *Web:* www.cochran.senate.gov	Washington	DC	20510	202-224-5054	
Harper Gregg (Rep R - MS) 307 Cannon Bldg *Web:* harper.house.gov	Washington	DC	20515	202-225-5031	225-5797
Kelly Trent (Rep R - MS) 1427 Longworth HOB *Web:* trentkelly.house.gov	Washington	DC	20515	202-225-4306	225-3549
Palazzo Steven (Rep R - MS) 331 Cannon Bldg *Web:* palazzo.house.gov	Washington	DC	20515	202-225-5772	225-7074
Thompson Bennie G (Rep D - MS) 2466 Rayburn Bldg *Web:* benniethompson.house.gov	Washington	DC	20515	202-225-5876	225-5898
●Wicker Roger F (Sen R - MS) 555 Dirksen Bldg *Web:* www.wicker.senate.gov	Washington	DC	20510	202-224-6253	228-0378

Missouri

				Phone	Fax
●Blunt Roy (Sen R - MO) 260 Russell Bldg *Web:* www.blunt.senate.gov	Washington	DC	20510	202-224-5721	224-8149
Clay William "Lacy" Jr (Rep D - MO) 2428 Rayburn HOB *Web:* lacyclay.house.gov	Washington	DC	20515	202-225-2406	226-3717
Cleaver Emanuel (Rep D - MO) 2335 Rayburn Bldg *Web:* cleaver.house.gov	Washington	DC	20515	202-225-4535	225-4403
Graves Sam (Rep R - MO) 1415 Longworth Bldg *Web:* graves.house.gov	Washington	DC	20515	202-225-7041	225-8221
Hartzler Vicky (Rep R - MO) 2235 Rayburn HOB *Web:* hartzler.house.gov	Washington	DC	20515	202-225-2876	225-0148
Long Billy (Rep R - MO) 1541 Longworth Bldg *Web:* long.house.gov	Washington	DC	20515	202-225-6536	225-5604
Luetkemeyer Blaine (Rep R - MO) 2440 Rayburn Bldg *Web:* luetkemeyer.house.gov	Washington	DC	20515	202-225-2956	225-5712
●McCaskill Claire (Sen D - MO) 730 Hart Senate Office Bldg *Web:* www.mccaskill.senate.gov	Washington	DC	20510	202-224-6154	228-6326
Smith Jason (Rep R - MO) 1118 Longworth HOB *Web:* jasonsmith.house.gov	Washington	DC	20515	202-225-4404	226-0326
Wagner Ann (Rep R - MO) 435 Cannon Bldg *Web:* wagner.house.gov	Washington	DC	20515	202-225-1621	

Montana

				Phone	Fax
●Daines Steve (Sen R - MT) 320 Hart Senate Office Bldg *Web:* www.daines.senate.gov	Washington	DC	20510	202-224-2651	
●Tester Jon (Sen D - MT) 311 Hart Senate Office Bldg *Web:* www.tester.senate.gov	Washington	DC	20510	202-224-2644	224-8594
Zinke Ryan (Rep R - MT) 113 Cannon House Office Bldg. *Web:* zinke.house.gov	Washington	DC	20515	202-225-3211	225-5687

Nebraska

				Phone	Fax
Ashford Brad (Rep D - NE) 107 Cannon HOB *Web:* ashford.house.gov	Washington	DC	20515	202-225-4155	226-5452
●Fischer Deb (Sen R - NE) 454 Russell Senate Office Bldg *Web:* www.fischer.senate.gov	Washington	DC	20510	202-224-6551	228-1325
Fortenberry Jeff (Rep R - NE) 1514 Longworth Bldg *Web:* fortenberry.house.gov	Washington	DC	20515	202-225-4806	225-5686
●Sasse Ben (Sen R - NE) 386A Russell Senate Office Bldg *Web:* www.sasse.senate.gov	Washington	DC	20510	202-224-4224	
Smith Adrian (Rep R - NE) 2241 Rayburn Bldg *Web:* adriansmith.house.gov	Washington	DC	20515	202-225-6435	225-0207

Nevada

				Phone	Fax
Amodei Mark (Rep R - NV) 332 Cannon HOB *Web:* amodei.house.gov	Washington	DC	20515	202-225-6155	225-5679
Hardy Cresent (Rep R - NV) 430 Cannon HOB *Web:* hardy.house.gov	Washington	DC	20515	202-225-9894	225-9783
Heck Joe (Rep R - NV) 132 Cannon Bldg *Web:* heck.house.gov	Washington	DC	20515	202-225-3252	225-2185
●Heller Dean (Sen R - NV) 324 Hart Bldg *Web:* www.heller.senate.gov	Washington	DC	20510	202-224-6244	228-6753
●Reid Harry (Sen D - NV) 522 Hart Bldg *Web:* www.reid.senate.gov	Washington	DC	20510	202-224-3542	224-7327
Titus Dina (Rep D - NV) 401 Cannon Bldg *Web:* titus.house.gov	Washington	DC	20515	202-225-5965	

New Hampshire

				Phone	Fax
●Ayotte Kelly (Sen R - NH) 144 Russell Bldg *Web:* www.ayotte.senate.gov	Washington	DC	20510	202-224-3324	224-4952
Guinta Frank (Rep R - NH) 326 Cannon HOB *Web:* guinta.house.gov	Washington	DC	20515	202-225-5456	225-5822
Kuster Ann (Rep D - NH) 137 Cannon Bldg *Web:* kuster.house.gov	Washington	DC	20515	202-225-5206	225-2946
●Shaheen Jeanne (Sen D - NH) 506 Hart Senate Office Bldg *Web:* www.shaheen.senate.gov	Washington	DC	20510	202-224-2841	228-3194

New Jersey

				Phone	Fax
●Booker Cory A (Sen D - NJ) 359 Dirksen Senate Office Bldg *Web:* www.booker.senate.gov/?p=contact	Washington	DC	20510	202-224-3224	224-8378
Frelinghuysen Rodney (Rep R - NJ) 2306 Rayburn HOB *Web:* frelinghuysen.house.gov	Washington	DC	20515	202-225-5034	
Garrett Scott (Rep R - NJ) 2232 Rayburn Bldg *Web:* garrett.house.gov	Washington	DC	20515	202-225-4465	225-9048
Lance Leonard (Rep R - NJ) 2352 Rayburn HOB *Web:* lance.house.gov	Washington	DC	20515	202-225-5361	225-9460
LoBiondo Frank (Rep R - NJ) 2427 Rayburn Bldg *Web:* lobiondo.house.gov	Washington	DC	20515	202-225-6572	225-3318
MacArthur Tom (Rep R - NJ) 506 Cannon HOB *Web:* macarthur.house.gov	Washington	DC	20515	202-225-4765	225-0778
●Menendez Robert (Sen D - NJ) 528 Hart Bldg *Web:* menendez.senate.gov	Washington	DC	20510	202-224-4744	
Norcross Donald (Rep D - NJ) 1531 Longworth HOB *Web:* norcross.house.gov	Washington	DC	20515	202-225-6501	225-6583
Pallone Frank Jr (Rep D - NJ) 237 Cannon Bldg *Web:* pallone.house.gov	Washington	DC	20515	202-225-4671	225-9665
Pascrell Bill Jr (Rep D - NJ) 2370 Rayburn Bldg *Web:* pascrell.house.gov	Washington	DC	20515	202-225-5751	225-5782
Payne Jr Donald (Rep D - NJ) 103 Cannon Bldg *Web:* payne.house.gov	Washington	DC	20515	202-225-3436	225-4160
Sires Albio (Rep D - NJ) 2342 Rayburn Bldg *Web:* sires.house.gov	Washington	DC	20515	202-225-7919	226-0792
Smith Chris (Rep R - NJ) 2373 Rayburn Bldg *Web:* chrissmith.house.gov	Washington	DC	20515	202-225-3765	225-7768
Watson Coleman Bonnie (Rep D - NJ) 126 Cannon HOB *Web:* watsoncoleman.house.gov	Washington	DC	20515	202-225-5801	225-6025

New Mexico

				Phone	Fax
●Heinrich Martin (Sen D - NM) 303 Hart Senate Office Bldg *Web:* www.heinrich.senate.gov	Washington	DC	20510	202-224-5521	228-2841
Lujan Ben R (Rep D - NM) 2446 Rayburn Bldg *Web:* lujan.house.gov	Washington	DC	20515	202-225-6190	226-1528
Lujan Grisham Michelle (Rep D - NM) 214 Cannon Bldg *Web:* lujangrisham.house.gov	Washington	DC	20515	202-225-6316	225-4975
Pearce Steve (Rep R - NM) 2432 Rayburn Bldg *Web:* pearce.house.gov	Washington	DC	20515	202-225-2365	225-9599

				Phone	Fax
ⓈUdall Tom (Sen D - NM) 531 Hart Senate Office Bldg *Web:* www.tomudall.senate.gov	Washington	DC	20510	202-224-6621	

New York

				Phone	Fax
Clarke Yvette D (Rep D - NY) 2351 Rayburn Bldg *Web:* clarke.house.gov	Washington	DC	20515	202-225-6231	226-0112
Collins Chris (Rep R - NY) 1117 Longworth Bldg *Web:* chriscollins.house.gov	Washington	DC	20515	202-225-5265	225-5910
Crowley Joseph (Rep D - NY) 1436 Longworth Bldg *Web:* crowley.house.gov	Washington	DC	20515	202-225-3965	
Donovan Daniel (Rep R - NY) 1725 Longworth HOB *Web:* donovan.house.gov	Washington	DC	20515	202-225-3371	
Engel Eliot (Rep D - NY) 2462 Rayburn HOB *Web:* engel.house.gov	Washington	DC	20515	202-225-2464	225-5513
Gibson Chris (Rep R - NY) 1708 Longworth Bldg *Web:* gibson.house.gov	Washington	DC	20515	202-225-5614	225-1168
ⓈGillibrand Kirsten E (Sen D - NY) 478 Russell Bldg *Web:* www.gillibrand.senate.gov	Washington	DC	20510	202-224-4451	228-0282
Hanna Richard (Rep R - NY) 319 Cannon Bldg *Web:* hanna.house.gov	Washington	DC	20515	202-225-3665	225-1891
Higgins Brian (Rep D - NY) 2459 Rayburn Bldg *Web:* higgins.house.gov	Washington	DC	20515	202-225-3306	226-0347
Israel Steve (Rep D - NY) 2457 Rayburn Bldg *Web:* israel.house.gov	Washington	DC	20515	202-225-3335	225-4669
Jeffries Hakeem (Rep D - NY) 1607 Longworth HOB *Web:* jeffries.house.gov	Washington	DC	20515	202-225-5936	
Katko John (Rep R - NY) 1123 Longworth HOB *Web:* katko.house.gov	Washington	DC	20515	202-225-3701	225-4042
King Pete (Rep R - NY) 339 Cannon Bldg *Web:* peteking.house.gov	Washington	DC	20515	202-225-7896	226-2279
Lowey Nita (Rep D - NY) 2365 Rayburn Bldg. *Web:* lowey.house.gov	Washington	DC	20515	202-225-6506	225-0546
Maloney Carolyn (Rep D - NY) 2308 Rayburn Bldg *Web:* maloney.house.gov	Washington	DC	20515	202-225-7944	225-4709
Maloney Sean Patrick (Rep D - NY) 1529 Longworth Bldg *Web:* seanmaloney.house.gov	Washington	DC	20515	202-225-5441	225-3289
Meeks Gregory W (Rep D - NY) 2234 Rayburn Bldg *Web:* meeks.house.gov	Washington	DC	20515	202-225-3461	226-4169
Meng Grace (Rep D - NY) 1317 Longworth Bldg *Web:* meng.house.gov	Washington	DC	20515	202-225-2601	225-1589
Nadler Jerrold (Rep D - NY) 2109 Rayburn HOB *Web:* nadler.house.gov	Washington	DC	20515	202-225-5635	225-6923
Rangel Charles B (Rep D - NY) 2354 Rayburn Bldg *Web:* rangel.house.gov	Washington	DC	20515	202-225-4365	225-0816
Reed Tom (Rep R - NY) 2437 Rayburn HOB *Web:* reed.house.gov	Washington	DC	20515	202-225-3161	226-6599
Rice Kathleen (Rep D - NY) 1508 Longworth HOB *Web:* kathleenrice.house.gov	Washington	DC	20515	202-225-5516	225-5758
ⓈSchumer Charles E (Sen D - NY) 322 Hart Bldg *Web:* www.schumer.senate.gov	Washington	DC	20510	202-224-6542	228-3027
Serrano Jose E (Rep D - NY) 2227 Rayburn Bldg *Web:* serrano.house.gov	Washington	DC	20515	202-225-4361	225-6001
Slaughter Louise (Rep D - NY) 2469 Rayburn Bldg *Web:* www.louise.house.gov	Washington	DC	20515	202-225-3615	225-7822
Stefanik Elise (Rep R - NY) 512 Cannon HOB *Web:* stefanik.house.gov	Washington	DC	20515	202-225-4611	
Tonko Paul D (Rep D - NY) 2463 Rayburn Bldg *Web:* tonko.house.gov	Washington	DC	20515	202-225-5076	225-5077
Velazquez Nydia M (Rep D - NY) 2302 Rayburn Bldg *Web:* velazquez.house.gov	Washington	DC	20515	202-225-2361	226-0327
Zeldin Lee (Rep R - NY) 1517 Longworth HOB *Web:* zeldin.house.gov	Washington	DC	20515	202-225-3826	225-3143

North Carolina

				Phone	Fax
Adams Alma (Rep D - NC) 222 Cannon HOB *Web:* adams.house.gov	Washington	DC	20515	202-225-1510	225-1512
ⓈBurr Richard (Sen R - NC) 217 Russell Senate Office Bldg *Web:* www.burr.senate.gov	Washington	DC	20510	202-224-3154	
Butterfield GK (Rep D - NC) 2305 Rayburn Bldg *Web:* butterfield.house.gov	Washington	DC	20515	202-225-3101	225-3354
Ellmers Renee (Rep R - NC) 1210 Longworth HOB *Web:* ellmers.house.gov	Washington	DC	20515	202-225-4531	225-5662
Foxx Virginia (Rep R - NC) 2350 Rayburn Bldg *Web:* foxx.house.gov	Washington	DC	20515	202-225-2071	225-2995
Holding George (Rep R - NC) 507 Cannon Bldg *Web:* holding.house.gov	Washington	DC	20515	202-225-3032	
Hudson Richard (Rep R - NC) 429 Cannon Bldg *Web:* hudson.house.gov	Washington	DC	20515	202-225-3715	
Jones Walter B (Rep R - NC) 2333 Rayburn Bldg *Web:* jones.house.gov	Washington	DC	20515	202-225-3415	225-3286
McHenry Patrick T (Rep R - NC) 2334 Rayburn Bldg *Web:* mchenry.house.gov	Washington	DC	20515	202-225-2576	225-0316
Meadows Mark (Rep R - NC) 1024 Longworth HOB *Web:* meadows.house.gov	Washington	DC	20515	202-225-6401	226-6422
Pittenger Robert (Rep R - NC) 224 Cannon Bldg *Web:* pittenger.house.gov	Washington	DC	20515	202-225-1976	225-3389
Price David (Rep D - NC) 2108 Rayburn Bldg *Web:* price.house.gov	Washington	DC	20515	202-225-1784	225-2014
Rouzer David (Rep R - NC) 424 Cannon HOB *Web:* rouzer.house.gov	Washington	DC	20515	202-225-2731	225-5773
ⓈTillis Thom (Sen R - NC) 185 Dirksen Senate Office Bldg *Web:* www.tillis.senate.gov	Washington	DC	20510	202-224-6342	228-2563
Walker Mark (Rep R - NC) 312 Cannon HOB *Web:* walker.house.gov	Washington	DC	20515	202-225-3065	225-8611

North Dakota

				Phone	Fax
Cramer Kevin (Rep R - ND) 1032 Longworth Bldg *Web:* cramer.house.gov	Washington	DC	20515	202-225-2611	226-0893
ⓈHeitkamp Heidi (Sen D - ND) SH-110 Hart Senate Office Bldg *Web:* www.heitkamp.senate.gov	Washington	DC	20510	202-224-2043	224-7776
ⓈHoeven John (Sen R - ND) 338 Russell Bldg *Web:* www.hoeven.senate.gov	Washington	DC	20510	202-224-2551	224-7999

Northern Mariana Islands

				Phone	Fax
Sablan Gregorio (Rep D - MP) 423 Cannon Bldg *TF:* 877-446-3465 ■ *Web:* sablan.house.gov	Washington	DC	20515	202-225-2646	226-4249

Ohio

				Phone	Fax
Beatty Joyce (Rep D - OH) 133 Cannon HOB *Web:* beatty.house.gov	Washington	DC	20515	202-225-4324	225-1984
Boehner John A (Rep R - OH) 1011 Longworth Bldg *Web:* boehner.house.gov	Washington	DC	20515	202-225-6205	225-0704
ⓈBrown Sherrod (Sen D - OH) 713 Hart Bldg *Web:* www.brown.senate.gov	Washington	DC	20510	202-224-2315	228-6321
Chabot Steve (Rep R - OH) 2371 Rayburn Bldg *Web:* chabot.house.gov	Washington	DC	20515	202-225-2216	225-3012
Fudge Marcia L (Rep D - OH) 2344 Rayburn Bldg *Web:* fudge.house.gov	Washington	DC	20515	202-225-7032	225-1339
Gibbs Bob (Rep R - OH) 329 Cannon Bldg *Web:* gibbs.house.gov	Washington	DC	20515	202-225-6265	225-3394
Johnson Bill (Rep R - OH) 1710 Longworth Bldg *Web:* billjohnson.house.gov	Washington	DC	20515	202-225-5705	225-5907
Jordan Jim (Rep R - OH) 1524 Longworth Bldg *Web:* jordan.house.gov	Washington	DC	20515	202-225-2676	226-0577
Joyce David (Rep R - OH) 1535 Longworth Bldg *Web:* joyce.house.gov	Washington	DC	20515	202-225-5731	225-3307
Kaptur Marcy (Rep D - OH) 2186 Rayburn Bldg *Web:* www.kaptur.house.gov	Washington	DC	20515	202-225-4146	225-7711
Latta Robert E (Rep R - OH) 2448 Rayburn Bldg *Web:* latta.house.gov	Washington	DC	20515	202-225-6405	225-1985
ⓈPortman Rob (Sen R - OH) 448 Russell Bldg *Web:* www.portman.senate.gov	Washington	DC	20510	202-224-3353	224-9075
Renacci Jim (Rep R - OH) 328 Cannon HOB *Web:* renacci.house.gov	Washington	DC	20515	202-225-3876	225-3059
Ryan Tim (Rep D - OH) 1421 Longworth Bldg. *Web:* timryan.house.gov	Washington	DC	20515	202-225-5261	225-3719
Stivers Steve (Rep R - OH) 1022 Longworth Bldg *Web:* stivers.house.gov	Washington	DC	20515	202-225-2015	225-3529
Tiberi Pat (Rep R - OH) 1203 Longworth HOB *Web:* tiberi.house.gov	Washington	DC	20515	202-225-5355	226-4523
Turner Michael (Rep R - OH) 2239 Rayburn Bldg *Web:* turner.house.gov	Washington	DC	20515	202-225-6465	225-6754

	City	State	Zip	Phone	Fax
Wenstrup Brad (Rep R - OH) 1318 Longworth HOB *Web:* wenstrup.house.gov	Washington	DC	20515	202-225-3164	225-1992

Oklahoma

	City	State	Zip	Phone	Fax
Bridenstine Jim (Rep R - OK) 216 Cannon Bldg *Web:* bridenstine.house.gov	Washington	DC	20515	202-225-2211	
Cole Tom (Rep R - OK) 2467 Rayburn HOB *Web:* cole.house.gov	Washington	DC	20515	202-225-6165	225-3512
●Inhofe James M (Sen R - OK) 205 Russell Bldg *Web:* www.inhofe.senate.gov	Washington	DC	20510	202-224-4721	228-0380
●Lankford James (Sen R - OK) 316 Hart Senate Office Bldg *Web:* www.lankford.senate.gov	Washington	DC	20510	202-224-5754	
Lucas Frank (Rep R - OK) 2405 Rayburn HOB *Web:* lucas.house.gov	Washington	DC	20515	202-225-5565	225-8698
Mullin Markwayne (Rep R - OK) 1113 Longworth Bldg *Web:* mullin.house.gov	Washington	DC	20515	202-225-2701	225-3038
Russell Steve (Rep R - OK) 128 Cannon HOB *Web:* russell.house.gov	Washington	DC	20515	202-225-2132	226-1463

Oregon

	City	State	Zip	Phone	Fax
Blumenauer Earl (Rep D - OR) 1111 Longworth Bldg *Web:* blumenauer.house.gov	Washington	DC	20515	202-225-4811	225-8941
Bonamici Suzanne (Rep D - OR) 439 Cannon Bldg *Web:* bonamici.house.gov	Washington	DC	20515	202-225-0855	225-9497
DeFazio Peter (Rep D - OR) 2134 Rayburn Bldg *Web:* www.defazio.house.gov	Washington	DC	20515	202-225-6416	
●Merkley Jeff (Sen D - OR) 313 Hart Bldg *Web:* www.merkley.senate.gov	Washington	DC	20510	202-224-3753	228-3997
Schrader Kurt (Rep D - OR) 2431 Rayburn HOB *Web:* schrader.house.gov	Washington	DC	20515	202-225-5711	225-5699
Walden Greg (Rep R - OR) 2185 Rayburn Bldg *Web:* walden.house.gov	Washington	DC	20515	202-225-6730	225-5774
●Wyden Ron (Sen D - OR) 221 Dirksen Bldg *Web:* www.wyden.senate.gov	Washington	DC	20510	202-224-5244	228-2717

Pennsylvania

	City	State	Zip	Phone	Fax
Barletta Lou (Rep R - PA) 115 Cannon Bldg *Web:* barletta.house.gov	Washington	DC	20515	202-225-6511	226-6250
Boyle Brendan (Rep D - PA) 118 Cannon HOB *Web:* boyle.house.gov	Washington	DC	20515	202-225-6111	226-0611
Brady Robert (Rep D - PA) 102 Cannon Bldg *Web:* www.brady.house.gov	Washington	DC	20515	202-225-4731	225-0088
Cartwright Matthew (Rep D - PA) 1419 Longworth Bldg *Web:* cartwright.house.gov	Washington	DC	20515	202-225-5546	226-0996
●Casey Robert P Jr (Sen D - PA) 393 Russell Bldg *Web:* www.casey.senate.gov	Washington	DC	20510	202-224-6324	228-0604
Costello Ryan (Rep R - PA) 427 Cannon HOB *Web:* costello.house.gov	Washington	DC	20515	202-225-4315	
Dent Charles W (Rep R - PA) 2211 Rayburn HOB *Web:* dent.house.gov	Washington	DC	20515	202-225-6411	226-0778
Doyle Mike (Rep D - PA) 239 Cannon Bldg *Web:* doyle.house.gov	Washington	DC	20515	202-225-2135	225-3084
Fattah Chaka (Rep D - PA) 2301 Rayburn Bldg *Web:* fattah.house.gov	Washington	DC	20515	202-225-4001	225-5392
Fitzpatrick Michael G (Rep R - PA) 2400 Rayburn Bldg *Web:* fitzpatrick.house.gov	Washington	DC	20515	202-225-4276	225-9511
Kelly Mike (Rep R - PA) 1519 Longworth Bldg *Web:* kelly.house.gov	Washington	DC	20515	202-225-5406	225-3103
Marino Tom (Rep R - PA) 410 Cannon Bldg *Web:* marino.house.gov	Washington	DC	20515	202-225-3731	225-9594
Meehan Pat (Rep R - PA) 434 Cannon HOB *Web:* meehan.house.gov	Washington	DC	20515	202-225-2011	226-0280
Murphy Tim (Rep R - PA) 2332 Rayburn Bldg *Web:* murphy.house.gov	Washington	DC	20515	202-225-2301	225-1844
Perry Scott (Rep R - PA) 1207 Longworth HOB *Web:* perry.house.gov	Washington	DC	20515	202-225-5836	226-1000
Pitts Joseph R (Rep R - PA) 420 Cannon Bldg *Web:* pitts.house.gov	Washington	DC	20515	202-225-2411	225-2013
Rothfus Keith (Rep R - PA) 1205 Longworth HOB *Web:* rothfus.house.gov	Washington	DC	20515	202-225-2065	225-5709
Shuster Bill (Rep R - PA) 2268 Rayburn HOB *Web:* shuster.house.gov	Washington	DC	20515	202-225-2431	225-2486
Thompson Glenn W (Rep R - PA) 124 Cannon Bldg *Web:* thompson.house.gov	Washington	DC	20515	202-225-5121	225-5796
●Toomey Patrick J (Sen R - PA) 248 Hart Bldg *Web:* www.toomey.senate.gov	Washington	DC	20510	202-224-4254	228-0284

Puerto Rico

	City	State	Zip	Phone	Fax
Pierluisi Pedro (Rep D - PR) 2410 Rayburn HOB *Web:* pierluisi.house.gov	Washington	DC	20515	202-225-2615	225-2154

Rhode Island

	City	State	Zip	Phone	Fax
Cicilline David (Rep D - RI) 2244 Rayburn HOB *Web:* cicilline.house.gov	Washington	DC	20515	202-225-4911	225-3290
Langevin Jim (Rep D - RI) 109 Cannon Bldg *Web:* langevin.house.gov	Washington	DC	20515	202-225-2735	225-5976
●Reed Jack (Sen D - RI) 728 Hart Bldg *Web:* www.reed.senate.gov	Washington	DC	20510	202-224-4642	224-4680
●Whitehouse Sheldon (Sen D - RI) 530 Hart Bldg *Web:* www.whitehouse.senate.gov	Washington	DC	20510	202-224-2921	228-6362

South Carolina

	City	State	Zip	Phone	Fax
Clyburn James E (Rep D - SC) 242 Cannon House Office Bldg *Web:* clyburn.house.gov	Washington	DC	20515	202-225-3315	225-2313
Duncan Jeff (Rep R - SC) 106 Cannon HOB *Web:* jeffduncan.house.gov	Washington	DC	20515	202-225-5301	225-3216
Gowdy Trey (Rep R - SC) 1404 Longworth Bldg *Web:* gowdy.house.gov	Washington	DC	20515	202-225-6030	226-1177
●Graham Lindsey (Sen R - SC) 290 Russell Bldg *Web:* www.lgraham.senate.gov	Washington	DC	20510	202-224-5972	224-3808
Mulvaney Mick (Rep R - SC) 2419 Rayburn HOB *Web:* mulvaney.house.gov	Washington	DC	20515	202-225-5501	225-0464
Rice Tom (Rep R - SC) 223 Cannon HOB *Web:* rice.house.gov	Washington	DC	20515	202-225-9895	225-9690
Sanford Mark R (Rep R - SC) 2201 Rayburn HOB *Web:* sanford.house.gov	Washington	DC	20515	202-225-3176	
●Scott Tim (Sen R - SC) 520 Hart Senate Office Bldg *TF:* 855-425-6324 ■ *Web:* www.scott.senate.gov	Washington	DC	20510	202-224-6121	228-5143
Wilson Joe (Rep R - SC) 2229 Rayburn Bldg *Web:* joewilson.house.gov	Washington	DC	20515	202-225-2452	225-2455

South Dakota

	City	State	Zip	Phone	Fax
Noem Kristi (Rep R - SD) 2422 Rayburn HOB *Web:* noem.house.gov	Washington	DC	20515	202-225-2801	225-5823
●Rounds Mike (Sen R - SD) 502 Hart Senate Office Bldg *Web:* www.rounds.senate.gov	Washington	DC	20510	202-224-5842	
●Thune John (Sen R - SD) 511 Dirksen Bldg *Web:* www.thune.senate.gov	Washington	DC	20510	202-224-2321	228-5429

Tennessee

	City	State	Zip	Phone	Fax
●Alexander Lamar (Sen R - TN) 455 Dirksen Bldg *Web:* www.alexander.senate.gov	Washington	DC	20510	202-224-4944	228-3398
Black Diane (Rep R - TN) 1131 Longworth HOB *Web:* black.house.gov	Washington	DC	20515	202-225-4231	225-6887
Blackburn Marsha (Rep R - TN) 2266 Rayburn Bldg *Web:* blackburn.house.gov	Washington	DC	20515	202-225-2811	225-3004
Cohen Steve (Rep D - TN) 2404 Rayburn Bldg *Web:* cohen.house.gov	Washington	DC	20515	202-225-3265	225-5663
Cooper Jim (Rep D - TN) 1536 Longworth Bldg *Web:* www.cooper.house.gov	Washington	DC	20515	202-225-4311	226-1035
●Corker Bob (Sen R - TN) 425 Dirksen Bldg *Web:* www.corker.senate.gov	Washington	DC	20510	202-224-3344	228-0566
DesJarlais Scott (Rep R - TN) 413 Cannon Bldg *Web:* desjarlais.house.gov	Washington	DC	20515	202-225-6831	226-5172
Duncan John J Jr (Rep R - TN) 2207 Rayburn Bldg *Web:* duncan.house.gov	Washington	DC	20515	202-225-5435	225-6440
Fincher Stephen (Rep R - TN) 2452 Rayburn HOB *Web:* fincher.house.gov	Washington	DC	20515	202-225-4714	225-1765
Fleischmann Chuck (Rep R - TN) 230 Cannon HOB *Web:* fleischmann.house.gov	Washington	DC	20515	202-225-3271	225-3494
Roe Phil (Rep R - TN) 407 Cannon Bldg *Web:* roe.house.gov	Washington	DC	20515	202-225-6356	225-5714

Texas

	City	State	Zip	Phone	Fax
Babin Brian (Rep R - TX) 316 Cannon HOB *Web:* babin.house.gov	Washington	DC	20515	202-225-1555	226-0396

Phone Fax

Barton Joe (Rep R - TX) 2107 Rayburn Bldg .... Washington DC 20515 202-225-2002 225-3052
Web: joebarton.house.gov

Brady Kevin (Rep R - TX) 301 Cannon Bldg .... Washington DC 20515 202-225-4901 225-5524
Web: kevinbrady.house.gov

Burgess Michael (Rep R - TX)
2336 Rayburn Bldg. .... Washington DC 20515 202-225-7772 225-2919
Web: burgess.house.gov

Carter John (Rep R - TX)
2110 Rayburn Bldg. .... Washington DC 20515 202-225-3864 225-5866
Web: carter.house.gov

Castro Joaquin (Rep D - TX)
212 Cannon HOB .... Washington DC 20515 202-225-3236 225-1915
Web: castro.house.gov

Conaway K Michael (Rep R - TX)
2430 Rayburn Bldg. .... Washington DC 20515 202-225-3605 225-1783
Web: conaway.house.gov

Ⓢ Cornyn John (Sen R - TX) 517 Hart Bldg .... Washington DC 20510 202-224-2934 228-2856
Web: www.cornyn.senate.gov

Ⓢ Cruz Ted (Sen R - TX) 404 Russell Bldg .... Washington DC 20510 202-224-5922
Web: www.cruz.senate.gov

Cuellar Henry (Rep D - TX)
2209 Rayburn Bldg. .... Washington DC 20515 202-225-1640 225-1641
Web: cuellar.house.gov

Culberson John (Rep R - TX)
2372 Rayburn Bldg. .... Washington DC 20515 202-225-2571 225-4381
Web: culberson.house.gov

Doggett Lloyd (Rep D - TX)
2307 Rayburn HOB. .... Washington DC 20515 202-225-4865
Web: doggett.house.gov

Farenthold Blake (Rep R - TX)
1027 Longworth HOB .... Washington DC 20515 202-225-7742 226-1134
Web: farenthold.house.gov

Flores Bill (Rep R - TX)
1030 Longworth HOB .... Washington DC 20515 202-225-6105 225-0350
Web: flores.house.gov

Gohmert Louie (Rep R - TX)
2243 Rayburn Bldg. .... Washington DC 20515 202-225-3035 226-1230
Web: gohmert.house.gov

Granger Kay (Rep R - TX)
1026 Longworth HOB .... Washington DC 20515 202-225-5071 225-5683
Web: kaygranger.house.gov

Green Al (Rep D - TX) 2347 Rayburn Bldg .... Washington DC 20515 202-225-7508 225-2947
Web: algreen.house.gov

Green Gene (Rep D - TX) 2470 Rayburn Bldg .... Washington DC 20515 202-225-1688 225-9903
Web: green.house.gov

Hensarling Jeb (Rep R - TX)
2228 Rayburn Bldg. .... Washington DC 20515 202-225-3484 226-4888
Web: hensarling.house.gov

Hinojosa Ruben (Rep D - TX)
2262 Rayburn Bldg. .... Washington DC 20515 202-225-2531 225-5688
Web: hinojosa.house.gov

Hurd Will (Rep R - TX) 317 Cannon HOB .... Washington DC 20515 202-225-4511 225-2237
Web: hurd.house.gov

Jackson Lee Sheila (Rep D - TX)
2252 Rayburn Bldg. .... Washington DC 20515 202-225-3816 225-3317
Web: jacksonlee.house.gov

Johnson Eddie Bernice (Rep D - TX)
2468 Rayburn Bldg. .... Washington DC 20515 202-225-8885 226-1477
Web: ebjohnson.house.gov

Johnson Sam (Rep R - TX) 2304 Rayburn HOB .... Washington DC 20515 202-225-4201 225-1485
Web: samjohnson.house.gov

Marchant Kenny (Rep R - TX)
2313 Rayburn HOB. .... Washington DC 20515 202-225-6605 225-0074
Web: marchant.house.gov

McCaul Michael T (Rep R - TX)
131 Cannon Bldg .... Washington DC 20515 202-225-2401 225-5955
Web: mccaul.house.gov

Neugebauer Randy (Rep R - TX)
1424 Longworth Bldg. .... Washington DC 20515 202-225-4005 225-9615
Web: randy.house.gov

O'Rourke Beto (Rep D - TX)
1330 Longworth Bldg. .... Washington DC 20515 202-225-4831
Web: orourke.house.gov

Olson Pete (Rep R - TX) 2133 Rayburn HOB .... Washington DC 20515 202-225-5951 225-5241
Web: olson.house.gov

Poe Ted (Rep R - TX) 2412 Rayburn Bldg. .... Washington DC 20515 202-225-6565 225-5547
Web: poe.house.gov

Ratcliffe John (Rep - TX) 325 Cannon HOB .... Washington DC 20515 202-225-6673 225-3332
Web: ratcliffe.house.gov

Sessions Pete (Rep R - TX)
2233 Rayburn Bldg. .... Washington DC 20515 202-225-2231 225-5878
Web: sessions.house.gov

Smith Lamar (Rep R - TX)
2409 Rayburn Bldg. .... Washington DC 20515 202-225-4236 225-8628
Web: lamarsmith.house.gov

Thornberry Mac (Rep R - TX)
2208 Rayburn Bldg. .... Washington DC 20515 202-225-3706 225-3486
Web: thornberry.house.gov

Veasey Marc (Rep D - TX) 414 Cannon Bldg .... Washington DC 20515 202-225-9897 225-9702
Web: veasey.house.gov

Vela Filemon (Rep D - TX) 437 Cannon Bldg .... Washington DC 20515 202-225-9901 225-9770
Web: vela.house.gov

Weber Randy (Rep R - TX) 510 Cannon Bldg .... Washington DC 20515 202-225-2831 225-0271
Web: weber.house.gov

Williams Roger (Rep R - TX)
1323 Longworth Bldg. .... Washington DC 20515 202-225-9896
Web: williams.house.gov

Utah

Phone Fax

Bishop Rob (Rep R - UT) 123 Cannon Bldg .... Washington DC 20515 202-225-0453 225-5857
Web: robbishop.house.gov

Chaffetz Jason (Rep R - UT)
2236 Rayburn Bldg. .... Washington DC 20515 202-225-7751 225-5629
Web: chaffetz.house.gov

Ⓢ Hatch Orrin G (Sen R - UT) 104 Hart Bldg .... Washington DC 20510 202-224-5251 224-6331
Web: www.hatch.senate.gov

Ⓢ Lee Mike (Sen R - UT)
361A Russell Senate Office Bldg. .... Washington DC 20510 202-224-5444 228-1168
Web: www.lee.senate.gov

Love Mia (Rep R - UT) 217 Cannon HOB .... Washington DC 20515 202-225-3011 225-5638
Web: love.house.gov

Stewart Chris (Rep R - UT)
323 Cannon Bldg .... Washington DC 20515 202-225-9730
Web: stewart.house.gov

Vermont

Phone Fax

Ⓢ Leahy Patrick J (Sen D - VT)
437 Russell Bldg .... Washington DC 20510 202-224-4242 224-3479
Web: www.leahy.senate.gov

Ⓢ Sanders Bernard (Sen I - VT)
332 Dirksen Bldg .... Washington DC 20510 202-224-5141 228-0776
Web: www.sanders.senate.gov

Welch Peter (Rep D - VT)
2303 Rayburn House Office Bldg .... Washington DC 20515 202-225-4115 225-6790
Web: www.welch.house.gov

Virgin Islands

Phone Fax

Plaskett Stacey (Rep D - VI)
509 Cannon HOB .... Washington DC 20515 202-225-1790 225-5517
Web: plaskett.house.gov

Virginia

Phone Fax

Beyer Don (Rep D - VA) 431 Cannon HOB .... Washington DC 20515 202-225-4376 225-0017
Web: beyer.house.gov

Brat Dave (Rep R - VA) 330 Cannon HOB .... Washington DC 20515 202-225-2815 225-0011
Web: brat.house.gov

Comstock Barbara (Rep R - VA)
226 Cannon HOB .... Washington DC 20515 202-225-5136 225-0437
Web: comstock.house.gov

Connolly Gerald E "Gerry" (Rep D - VA)
2238 Rayburn HOB .... Washington DC 20515 202-225-1492 225-3071
Web: connolly.house.gov

Forbes J Randy (Rep R - VA)
2135 Rayburn Bldg. .... Washington DC 20515 202-225-6365 226-1170
Web: forbes.house.gov

Goodlatte Bob (Rep R - VA)
2309 Rayburn Bldg. .... Washington DC 20515 202-225-5431 225-9681
Web: goodlatte.house.gov

Griffith Morgan (Rep R - VA)
1108 Longworth Bldg .... Washington DC 20515 202-225-3861 225-0076
Web: morgangriffith.house.gov

Hurt Robert (Rep R - VA) 125 Cannon HOB. .... Washington DC 20515 202-225-4711 225-5681
Web: hurt.house.gov

Ⓢ Kaine Tim (Sen D - VA)
231 Russell Senate Office Bldg. .... Washington DC 20510 202-224-4024 228-6363
Web: www.kaine.Senate.gov

Rigell Scott (Rep R - VA) 418 Cannon Bldg .... Washington DC 20515 202-225-4215 225-4218
Web: rigell.house.gov

Scott Robert C (Rep D - VA)
1201 Longworth Bldg .... Washington DC 20515 202-225-8351 225-8354
Web: www.bobbyscott.house.gov

Ⓢ Warner Mark R (Sen D - VA)
475 Russell Bldg .... Washington DC 20510 202-224-2023
Web: www.warner.senate.gov

Wittman Robert J (Rep R - VA)
2454 Rayburn Bldg. .... Washington DC 20515 202-225-4261 225-4382
Web: www.wittman.house.gov

Washington

Phone Fax

Ⓢ Cantwell Maria (Sen D - WA)
511 Hart Senate Office Bldg .... Washington DC 20510 202-224-3441 228-0514
Web: www.cantwell.senate.gov

DelBene Suzan (Rep D - WA)
318 cannon Bldg .... Washington DC 20515 202-225-6311 226-1606
Web: delbene.house.gov

Heck Denny (Rep D - WA) 425 Cannon Bldg .... Washington DC 20515 202-225-9740 225-0129
Web: dennyheck.house.gov

Herrera Beutler Jaime (Rep R - WA)
1130 Longworth Bldg .... Washington DC 20515 202-225-3536 225-3478
Web: herrerabeutler.house.gov

Kilmer Derek (Rep D - WA)
1520 Longworth HOB .... Washington DC 20515 202-225-5916
Web: kilmer.house.gov

Larsen Rick (Rep D - WA) 2113 Rayburn HOB .... Washington DC 20515 202-225-2605 225-4420
Web: larsen.house.gov

McDermott Jim (Rep D - WA)
1035 Longworth Bldg .... Washington DC 20515 202-225-3106 225-6197
Web: mcdermott.house.gov

McMorris Rodgers Cathy (Rep R - WA)
203 Cannon Bldg .... Washington DC 20515 202-225-2006 225-3392
Web: mcmorris.house.gov

Ⓢ Murray Patty (Sen D - WA)
154 Russell Bldg .... Washington DC 20510 202-224-2621 224-0238
Web: www.murray.senate.gov

Phone | Fax

Newhouse Dan (Rep R - WA)
1641 Longworth HOB .... Washington DC 20515 202-225-5816 225-3251
Web: newhouse.house.gov
Reichert David G (Rep R - WA)
1127 Longworth Bldg .... Washington DC 20515 202-225-7761 225-4282
Web: reichert.house.gov
Smith Adam (Rep D - WA) 2264 Rayburn HOB .... Washington DC 20515 202-225-8901 225-5893
Web: adamsmith.house.gov

West Virginia

Phone | Fax

●Capito Shelley Moore (R - WV)
172 Russell Senate Office Bldg .... Washington DC 20510 202-224-6472
Web: www.capito.senate.gov
●Capito, Shelley Moore (Sen R - WV)
172 Russell Senate Office Bldg .... Washington DC 20510 202-224-6472
Web: www.capito.senate.gov/contact/contact-shelley
Jenkins Evan (Rep R - WV) 502 Cannon HOB .... Washington DC 20515 202-225-3452 225-9061
Web: evanjenkins.house.gov
●Manchin Joe III (Sen D - WV)
306 Hart Bldg .... Washington DC 20510 202-224-3954 228-0002
Web: www.manchin.senate.gov
McKinley David (Rep R - WV)
412 Cannon Bldg .... Washington DC 20515 202-225-4172 225-7564
Web: mckinley.house.gov
Mooney Alex (Rep R - WV)
1232 Longworth HOB .... Washington DC 20515 202-225-2711 225-7856
Web: mooney.house.gov

Wisconsin

Phone | Fax

●Bladwin Tammy (Sen D - WI) 717 Hart Bldg .... Washington DC 20510 202-224-5653 224-9787
Web: www.baldwin.senate.gov
Duffy Sean P (Rep R - WI)
1208 Longworth Bldg .... Washington DC 20515 202-225-3365 225-3240
Web: duffy.house.gov
Grothman Glenn (Rep R - WI)
501 Cannon HOB .... Washington DC 20515 202-225-2476 225-2356
Web: grothman.house.gov
●Johnson Ron (Sen R - WI) 328 Russell Bldg .... Washington DC 20510 202-224-5323 228-6965
Web: www.ronjohnson.senate.gov
Kind Ron (Rep D - WI) 1502 Longworth Bldg .... Washington DC 20515 202-225-5506 225-5739
Web: kind.house.gov
Moore Gwen (Rep D - WI) 2245 Rayburn Bldg. .... Washington DC 20515 202-225-4572 225-8135
Web: gwenmoore.house.gov
Pocan Mark (Rep D - WI) 313 Cannon Bldg .... Washington DC 20515 202-225-2906 225-6942
Web: pocan.house.gov
Ribble Reid (Rep R - WI)
1513 Longworth Bldg .... Washington DC 20515 202-225-5665 225-5729
Web: ribble.house.gov
Ryan Paul (Rep R - WI)
1233 Longworth Bldg .... Washington DC 20515 202-225-3031 225-3393
Web: paulryan.house.gov
Sensenbrenner F James (Rep R - WI)
2449 Rayburn Bldg .... Washington DC 20515 202-225-5101 225-3190
Web: sensenbrenner.house.gov

Wyoming

Phone | Fax

●Barrasso John (Sen R - WY)
307 Dirksen Bldg .... Washington DC 20510 202-224-6441 224-1724
Web: www.barrasso.senate.gov
●Enzi Michael B (Sen R - WY)
379A Russell Bldg .... Washington DC 20510 202-224-3424 228-0359
Web: www.enzi.senate.gov
Lummis Cynthia M (Rep R - WY)
2433 Rayburn HOB .... Washington DC 20515 202-225-2311 225-3057
TF: 888-879-3599 ■ *Web:* lummis.house.gov

343 GOVERNORS - STATE

Listings for governors are organized by state names.

Phone | Fax

Bentley Robert (R) 600 Dexter Ave .... Montgomery AL 36130 334-242-7100 353-0004
Web: www.governor.alabama.gov/
Walker Bill (I) State Capitolÿ PO Box 110001 .... Juneau AK 99811 907-465-3500 465-3532
Web: gov.state.ak.us/
Moliga Lolo Matalasi (I)
Executive Office Bldg 3rd Flr. .... Pago Pago AS 96799 684-633-4116 633-2269
Ducey Doug (R)
State Capitolÿ 1700 W Washington .... Phoenix AZ 85007 602-542-4331 542-7601
Web: www.azgovernor.gov/
Hutchinson Asa (R) State Capitolÿ Rm 250 .... Little Rock AR 72201 501-682-2345 682-1382
Web: governor.arkansas.gov/
Brown Edmund G. Jr. (D)
State Capitol Bldg Ste 1173 .... Sacramento CA 95814 916-445-2841 558-3160
Web: gov.ca.gov
Hickenlooper John (D) 136 State Capitolÿ .... Denver CO 80203 303-866-2471 866-2003
Web: www.colorado.gov/governor/
Malloy Dan (D) 210 Capitol Aveÿ .... Hartford CT 06106 800-406-1527 524-7395*
**Fax Area Code: 860* ■ *TF:* 800-406-1527 ■ *Web:* www.ct.gov/governor/
Markell Jack (D) Legislative Hallÿ .... Dover DE 19901 302-744-4101 739-2775
Web: governor.delaware.gov/
Scott Rick (R)
PL 05 The Capitolÿ 400 S Monroe St .... Tallahassee FL 32399 850-488-7146 487-0801
Web: www.flgov.com/
Deal Nathan (R) 203 State Capitolÿ .... Atlanta GA 30334 404-656-1776 657-7332
Web: gov.georgia.gov/
Calvo Eddie Baza (R)
Executive Chamberÿ PO Box 2950 .... Agana GU 96932 671-472-8931 477-4826
Web: governor.guam.gov/
Ige David (D)
Executive Chambersÿ State Capitol. .... Honolulu HI 96813 808-586-0034 586-0006
Web: governor.hawaii.gov/
Otter C. L. "Butch" (R) 700 W Jeffersonÿ 2nd Fl. .... Boise ID 83702 208-334-2100 334-2175
Web: gov.idaho.gov/
Rauner Bruce (R)
State Capitolÿ 207 Statehouse .... Springfield IL 62706 217-782-0244 524-4049
Web: www2.illinois.gov/gov/Pages/default.aspx
Pence Mike (R) Statehouse .... Indianapolis IN 46204 317-232-4567 233-3378
Web: www.in.gov/gov/
Branstad Terry E. (R) State Capitolÿ .... Des Moines IA 50319 515-281-5211 281-6611
Web: governor.iowa.gov/
Brownback Sam (R) 300 SW 10th Ave ÿ Ste 212S .... Topeka KS 66612 785-296-3232 296-7973
Web: www.governor.ks.gov/
Bevin Matt (R) 700 Capitol Ave Ste 100ÿ .... Frankfort KY 40601 502-564-2611 564-0437
Web: governor.ky.gov/
Edwards John Bel (D) PO Box 94004 .... Baton Rouge LA 70804 225-342-7015 342-7099
Web: www.gov.louisiana.gov/
LePage Paul (R) #1 State House Sta .... Augusta ME 04333 207-287-3531 287-1034
Web: www.maine.gov/governor/
Hogan Larry (R) 100 State Cir .... Annapolis MD 21401 410-974-3901 974-3275
Web: www.gov.state.md.us/
Baker Charlie (R)
State House Office of the Governorÿ Rm 360 .... Boston MA 02133 617-725-4005 727-9725
Web: www.mass.gov/governor/
Snyder Rick (R) PO Box 30013 .... Lansing MI 48909 517-373-3400 335-6863
Web: www.michigan.gov/gov
Dayton Mark (D)
130 State Capitolÿ75 Rev.
Dr. Martin Luther KingÿJr. Blvd .... St. Paul MN 55155 651-201-3400 797-1850
Web: www.governor.state.mn.us/
Bryant Phil (R) PO Box 139ÿ .... Jackson MS 39205 601-359-3150 359-3741
Web: www.governorbryant.com/
Nixon Jeremiah W. (Jay) (D)
Capitol Bldg Room 218 PO Box 720 .... Jefferson City MO 65102 573-751-3222 526-3291
Web: governor.mo.gov/
Bullock Steve (D) PO Box 200801 .... Helena MT 59620 406-444-3111 444-5529
Web: governor.mt.gov/
Ricketts Pete (R) PO Box 94848ÿ .... Lincoln NE 68509 402-471-2244 471-6031
Web: www.governor.nebraska.gov/
Sandoval Brian (R) Capitol Buildingÿ .... Carson City NV 89701 775-684-5670 684-5683
Web: gov.nv.gov/
Hassan Maggie (D) State House 107 N Main St .... Concord NH 03301 603-271-2121 271-7680
Web: www.governor.nh.gov/
Christie Christopher (R)
The State Houseÿ PO Box 001 .... Trenton NJ 08625 609-292-6000 777-2922
Web: www.state.nj.us/governor/
Martinez Susana (R) State Capitolÿ 4th Fl .... Santa Fe NM 87501 505-476-2200 476-2226
Web: www.governor.state.nm.us/
Cuomo Andrew (D) State Capitolÿ .... Albany NY 12224 518-474-8390
Web: www.governor.ny.gov/
McCrory Pat (R) 20301 Mail Service Ctr .... Raleigh NC 27699 919-814-2000
Web: www.governor.state.nc.us/
Dalrymple Jack (R) 600 E Boulevard Ave .... Bismarck ND 58505 701-328-2200 328-2205
Web: governor.nd.gov/
Torres Ralph Deleon Guerrero (R)
PO Box 10007ÿ .... Saipan MP 96950 670-664-2280 664-2211
Web: gov.mp/
Kasich John (R) 77 S High St 30th Fl .... Columbus OH 43215 614-466-3555 466-9354
Web: governor.ohio.gov/
Fallin Mary (R)
Capitol Bldg 2300 Lincoln Blvd.
Rm. 212 .... Oklahoma City OK 73105 405-521-2342 521-3353
Web: www.gov.ok.gov/
Brown Kate (D)
State Capitol Room 160 900 Court St N .... Salem OR 97301 503-378-4582 378-8970
Web: www.oregon.gov/gov/pages/index.aspx
Wolf Tom (D)
Main Capitol Buildingÿ Rm 225ÿ .... Harrisburg PA 17120 717-787-2500 772-8284
Web: governor.pa.gov/
Alejandro Garcia Padilla PO Box 9020082 .... San Juan PR 00902 787-721-7000
Web: www.fortaleza.pr.gov/
Raimondo Gina (D) State House .... Providence RI 02903 401-222-2080 222-8096
Web: www.governor.state.ri.us/
Haley Nikki R. (R) 1205 Pendleton Stÿ .... Columbia SC 29201 803-734-2100 734-5167
Web: governor.sc.gov/
Daugaard Dennis (R) 500 East Capitol St .... Pierre SD 57501 605-773-3212 773-4711
Web: sd.gov/governor/
Haslam Bill (R) State Capitolÿ .... Nashville TN 37243 615-741-2001 532-9711
Web: www.state.tn.us/governor/
Abbott Greg (R) PO Box 12428 .... Austin TX 78711 512-463-2000 463-5571
Web: gov.texas.gov/
Herbert Gary Richard (R)
Utah State Capitolÿ Ste 200 .... Salt Lake City UT 84114 801-538-1000 538-1557
Web: www.utah.gov/governor/
Shumlin Peter (D)
109 State St Pavilion Office Bldg .... Montpelier VT 05609 802-828-3333 828-3339
Web: www.vermont.gov/governor/
Mapp Kenneth (I)
Government House
21-22 Kongens Gade Charlotte Amalie .... St. Thomas VI 00802 340-774-0001 693-4374
Web: www.gov.vi/governor.html
McAuliffe Terry (D) State Capitolÿ 3rd Fl .... Richmond VA 23219 804-786-2211 371-6351
Web: governor.virginia.gov/
Inslee Jay (D) PO Box 40002 .... Olympia WA 98504 360-902-4111 753-4110
Web: www.governor.wa.gov/
Tomblin Earl Ray (D) 1900 Kanawha St .... Charleston WV 25305 304-558-2000 342-7025
Web: www.governor.wv.gov/
Walker Scott (R) 115 E State Capitol .... Madison WI 05370 608-266-1212 267-8983
Web: walker.wi.gov/

Phone Fax

Mead Matthew (R) State Capitol Bldg Rm 124 ... Cheyenne WY 82002 307-777-7434 632-3909
Web: governor.wy.gov/

344 GRAPHIC DESIGN

See Also Typesetting & Related Services p. 3276

Phone Fax

1 Stop Design Shop Inc 30 BB Sixth Rd ... Woburn MA 01801 781-938-3866
Web: www.1stopdesign.com

1185 Design Inc 941Emerson St ... Palo Alto CA 94301 650-325-4804
Web: www.1185design.com

1K Studios LLC 3400 W Olive Ave Ste 300 ... Burbank CA 91505 818-531-3800
Web: weareonek.com

24 Hour Co 6521 Arlington Blvd ... Falls Church VA 22042 703-533-7209
Web: www.24hrco.com

3 Strikes Inc 1905 Elizabeth Ave ... Rahway NJ 07065 732-382-3820
Web: www.3strikes.com

300 Feet Out 1035 Folsom St ... San Francisco CA 94103 415-551-2377
Web: www.300feetout.com

530medialab 115 W 4th St Ste C1 ... Long Beach CA 90802 562-624-5888
Web: 530medialab.com

A Media Web & Graphic Design
2200 Adeline St Ste 320 ... Oakland CA 94607 510-763-5442
Web: www.amedianysf.com

ABBTECH Professional Resources Inc
45625 Willow Pond Plz ... Sterling VA 20164 703-450-5252
Web: www.abbtech.com

Accent Imaging Inc 8121 Brownleigh Dr ... Raleigh NC 27617 919-782-3332
Web: www.accentimaging.com

Active Imagination Inc 1434 W Alabama St ... Houston TX 77006 713-528-6100
Web: www.aimagination.com

Adcetera Design Studio Inc 3000 Louisiana St ... Houston TX 77006 713-522-8006
Web: www.adcetera.com

Adcolor Inc 950 Brookstown Ave ... Winston-Salem NC 27101 336-727-0309
Web: www.adcolornc.com

Adrenalin Inc 54 W 11th Ave ... Denver CO 80204 303-454-8888
TF: 888-757-5646 ■ *Web:* www.goadrenalin.com

Aec Reprographics and Design Center
1501 S Yale St Ste 101 ... Flagstaff AZ 86001 928-774-8787
Web: www.aecrepro.com

Aesthetic Visual Solutions Inc
7565 Commercial Way ... Henderson NV 89011 702-248-7122

Akoya 2325 E Carson St ... Pittsburgh PA 15203 412-481-3958
Web: www.akoyaonline.com

Albarella Design Inc
100 Bridgepoint Dr ... South Saint Paul MN 55075 651-552-8966
Web: www.albarella.com

Aljon Graphics 1721 E Lambert Rd C ... La Habra CA 90631 562-694-3144
Web: www.aljongraphics.com

Allsopp Design Inc 587 Bay Rd ... South Hamilton MA 01982 978-468-1556
Web: allsoppdesign.com

American Fleet & Retail Graphics Inc
780 S Milliken Ave Ste G ... Ontario CA 91761 909-937-7570
Web: www.amgraph.biz

Anabliss Inc 4055 Tejon St Ste 203 ... Denver CO 80211 303-825-4441
Web: anabliss.com

Anfield Inc 5625 Dillard Dr Ste 217 ... Cary NC 27518 919-851-8681

Anthem 537 E Pete Rose Way Ste 100 ... Cincinnati OH 45202 513-784-0066
Web: www.anthemww.com

Armada Group Inc, The 325 Soquel Ave Ste A ... Santa Cruz CA 95062 800-408-2120
TF: 800-408-2120 ■ *Web:* www.thearmadagroup.com

Art Display Co Inc
401 Hampton Park Blvd ... Capitol Heights MD 20743 240-765-1400
Web: www.artdisplayco.com

Art4Orm Inc 2636 NW 26th Ave Ste 201 ... Portland OR 97210 503-228-1399
Web: www.art4orm.com

Austin Graphics Inc 1198 2nd Ave E ... Owen Sound ON N4K2J1 519-376-2116
Web: www.austingraphics.ca

Avid Inc 50 Founders Plz ... East Hartford CT 06108 860-528-1988
Web: www.avidinc.com

B&B Image Group 1712 Marshall St NE ... Minneapolis MN 55413 612-788-9461
TF: 888-788-9461 ■ *Web:* www.bbimagegroup.com

Basicgrey LLC 377 Marshall Way ... Layton UT 84041 801-544-1116
Web: www.basicgrey.com

Bbr Creative Inc 300 Rue Beauregard ... Lafayette LA 70508 337-233-1515
Web: www.bbrcreative.com

Be Original 1520 Lk Louella Rd ... Suwanee GA 30024 770-813-9933
Web: beoriginal.com

Bendsen Signs & Graphics Inc 2901 N Woodford ... Decatur IL 62526 217-877-2345 877-2347
Web: www.bsg1946.com

BrandEquity International 7 Great Meadow Rd ... Newton MA 02462 800-969-3150
TF: 800-969-3150 ■ *Web:* www.brandequity.com

Brandscope 700 N Sacramento Blvd ... Chicago IL 60612 773-772-9300
Web: www.thinkkaleidoscope.com

Bruce Mau Design Inc 469C King St W ... Toronto ON M5V3M4 416-306-6401
Web: www.brucemaudesign.com

Busse Design USA Inc 5857 Chabot Ct ... Oakland CA 94618 510-596-9422
Web: www.bussedesign.com

C & K Commercial Development LLC
76 Eastern Blvd ... Glastonbury CT 06033 860-652-0300
Web: www.cashman-katz.com

Cactus Punch Inc 4955 N Shamrock Pl ... Tucson AZ 85705 520-622-8460
Web: www.myembroideries.com

Candid Litho Printing Ltd
25-11 Hunters Point ... Long Island NY 11101 212-431-3800
Web: www.candidlitho.com

Canyon Graphics Inc 6680 Cobra Way ... San Diego CA 92121 858-646-0444
Web: www.canyongraphics.com

Capstone Production Group 1638 S Saunders St ... Raleigh NC 27603 919-838-8030
Web: capstoneproductiongroup.com

Card USA Inc 2500 Hollywood Blvd Ste 212 ... Hollywood FL 33020 954-862-1300
Web: www.cardusa.com

Phone Fax

Cg Design Concepts
1150 N Highland Ave Ste 3 ... Fullerton CA 92835 714-871-7342
Web: www.cgdesignconcepts.com

Champion Awards Inc 3649 Winplace Rd ... Memphis TN 38118 901-365-4830
Web: www.gochampion.net

Classic Display Inc 80 Fountain St Ste 1 ... Pawtucket RI 02860 401-721-2240
Web: www.classicdisplay.com

Corporate Visions Inc
1020 19th St NW Ste LL20 ... Washington DC 20036 202-833-4333 833-4332
Web: www.corpvisions.com

Cosgrove Associates Inc
747 Third Ave Fl 16 ... New York NY 10017 212-888-7202
Web: www.cosgroveny.com

Cottonimages.Com Inc 10481 Nw 28th St ... Miami FL 33172 305-251-2560
TF: 888-642-7999 ■ *Web:* www.cottonimages.com

Create One for Me Inc 4416 Nw 99th Ave ... Sunrise FL 33351 954-746-5199
Web: www.createoneforme.com

Creative Assoc 1 Snoopy Pl ... Santa Rosa CA 95403 707-546-7121 526-7361

Curran & Connors Inc 40 Adams Ave Ste 20 C ... Hauppauge NY 11788 631-435-0400 435-0422
Web: www.curran-connors.com

Cyclone Interactive Multimedia Group Inc
535 Albany St Ste 402-A ... Boston MA 02118 617-350-8834
Web: www.cycloneinteractive.com

Danilo Black Inc 36 Gramercy Park E Ste 5N ... New York NY 10003 646-827-8313
Web: www.daniloblack.net

DataChambers LLC 3302 Old Lexington Rd ... Winston-Salem NC 27107 336-499-6000
Web: www.datachambers.com

David Berman Developments 340 Selby Ave ... Ottawa ON K2A3X6 613-728-6777
TF: 800-665-1809 ■ *Web:* www.davidberman.com

Del Tec Packaging Inc 4020 Pelham Ct ... Greenville SC 29606 864-288-7390
Web: www.del-tec.com

Democrat Printing & Lithographing Company Inc
6401 Lindsey Rd ... Little Rock AR 72206 501-374-0271
Web: www.democratprinting.com

Depersico Creative Group 1 Raymond Dr ... Havertown PA 19083 610-789-4400
Web: www.depersico.com

Design Alliance Inc 520 N Washington St ... Alexandria VA 22314 703-838-9894
Web: www.designalliance.com

Design Partners Inc 338 Main St ... Racine WI 53403 262-637-2233
Web: www.design-partners.com

DesignWrite Inc 189 Wall St ... Princeton NJ 08540 609-924-1116
Web: dwrite.com

Deutsch Design Works Inc
10 Arkansas St Ste K ... San Francisco CA 94107 415-487-8520
Web: www.ddw.com

Direct Edge Media Inc 430 W Collins Ave ... Orange CA 92867 714-221-8686
Web: directedgemedia.com

Donaldson Group Inc, The 88 Hopmeadow St ... Simsbury CT 06089 860-658-9777
Web: www.donaldson-group.com

Drum Creative 35 Cessna Ct ... Greenville SC 29607 864-254-6096
Web: drumcreative.com

Duggal Visual Solutions Inc 29 W 23th St ... New York NY 10010 212-924-8100
Web: m.duggal.com

Easypak Llc 24 Jytek Dr ... Leominster MA 01453 978-516-9155
Web: www.easypak.net

Envision Media Inc 331 Soquel Ave Ste 100 ... Santa Cruz CA 95062 831-429-5400
Web: www.envisionmedia.com

envisionit media Inc 153 W Ohio St ... Chicago IL 60654 312-236-2000
Web: envisionitagency.com

Exordium Group Inc, The
25670 Chapin Rd ... Los Altos Hills CA 94022 435-940-0600
Web: www.exordiumgroup.com

Falk Harrison Creative Inc 1300 Baur Blvd ... St. Louis MO 63132 314-531-1410
Web: falkharrison.com

Fineline Graphics & Design Inc
1820 Bellomy St ... Santa Clara CA 95050 408-261-7676
Web: finelinegd.com

Firstbase Services Ltd 34609 Delair Rd ... Abbotsford BC V2S2E1 604-850-5334
TF: 800-758-2922 ■ *Web:* www.firstbase.ca

Flexy Foam 12315 Colony Ave ... Chino CA 91710 909-465-5555

Focal Point LLC, The 501 14th St Ste 200 ... Oakland CA 94612 510-208-1760
Web: www.thefocalpoint.com

GANCOM Inc 209 Senate Ave ... Camp Hill PA 17011 717-763-7387
Web: www.gancom.com

General Theming Contractors LLC
3750 Courtright Ct ... Columbus OH 43227 614-252-6342

Genesys Creative Inc
500 Queens Quay W Ste 103e ... Toronto ON M5V3K8 416-595-9823
Web: www.genesisxd.com

Gerard Design 28371 Davis Pkwy Ste 100 ... Warrenville IL 60555 630-355-0775
Web: www.gerardagency.com

Girvin Inc 121 Stewart St Ste 212 ... Seattle WA 98101 206-674-7808 674-7909
Web: www.girvin.com

Glad Works 545 Pawtucket Ave ... Pawtucket RI 02860 401-724-4523
Web: www.gladworks.com

Goldmark Group Inc, The 1155 Bloomfield Ave ... Clifton NJ 07012 973-777-5720
TF: 800-632-9632 ■ *Web:* www.goldmarkgroup.com

Gordley Design Group Inc 2540 N Tucson Blvd ... Tucson AZ 85716 520-327-6077
Web: www.gordleydesign.com

Graphic Reproduction
1381 Franquette Ave Bldg B1 ... Concord CA 94520 925-674-0900
TF: 800-498-9939 ■ *Web:* www.graphic4u.com

Graphics Service Bureau 370 Park Ave S ... New York NY 10010 212-684-3600
Web: www.gsbinc.net

Gravity Switch Inc 89 Market St ... Northampton MA 01060 413-586-9596
Web: www.gravityswitch.com

Group 22 Inc 1205 E Grand Ave ... El Segundo CA 90245 310-322-2210
Web: www.group22.com

GSP Marketing Technologies Inc
14055 46th St N Ste 1112 ... Clearwater FL 33760 727-532-0647
Web: www.gspretail.com

H & H Graphics Inc 854 N Prince St ... Lancaster PA 17603 717-393-3941
TF: 866-338-7569 ■ *Web:* www.hhgraphicsgroup.com

Company	City	State	ZIP	Phone	Fax
Handelan-pedersen 1453 N Ashland Ave *Web:* www.hpdesign.net	Chicago	IL	60622	312-664-1200	
Holiday Image Inc 760 First St *Web:* www.holidayimagellc.com	Harrison	NJ	07074	718-369-3212	
Homer Group, The 2605 Egypt Rd *Web:* www.homergroup.com	Trooper	PA	19403	610-539-8400	
Hotcards Com Inc 2400 Superior Ave *Web:* www.hotcards.com	Cleveland	OH	44114	216-241-4040	
Howard Design Group 707 State Rd Ste 103 *Web:* howarddesign.com	Princeton	NJ	08540	609-924-1106	
Huck Group Inc, The 510 W Sixth St Ste 1100 *Web:* www.thehuckgroup.com	Los Angeles	CA	90014	213-955-8080	
Hudson Printing & Graphic Design 611 S Mobberly Ave *TF:* 800-530-4888 ■ *Web:* www.hudsonprint.com	Longview	TX	75602	903-758-1773	
Hunt Design Assoc Inc 25 N Mentor Ave *Web:* www.huntdesign.com	Pasadena	CA	91106	626-793-7847	
Idamerica 941 Corporate Ln *Web:* idamerica.com	Chesapeake	VA	23320	757-549-2300	
Imprimis Group Inc 4835 Lyndon B Johnson Fwy *TF:* 888-772-9682 ■ *Web:* www.imprimis.com	Dallas	TX	75244	972-419-1700	419-1799
Internet Exposure Inc 1101 Washington Ave S *Web:* www.iexposure.com	Minneapolis	MN	55415	612-333-2606	
J Allan Writing & Design Studios LLC 115 12th Ave Ne *Web:* www.jallanstudios.com	Saint Petersburg	FL	33701	727-822-2526	
Jaguar Design Studio Inc 9039 Soquel Dr *Web:* www.jaguardesignstudio.com	Aptos	CA	95003	831-662-9991	
Jarrett Industries of The Carolinas Inc 11511 Cronridge Dr *Web:* www.jarrettindustries.com	Owings Mills	MD	21117	410-581-0303	
JK Design Inc 465 Amwell Rd *Web:* www.jkdesign.com	Hillsborough	NJ	08844	908-428-4700	
Johnson - Rauhoff Inc 2525 Lk Pine Dr *Web:* www.johnson-rauhoff.com	Saint Joseph	MI	49085	269-428-3377	
Kane Graphical Corp 2255 W Logan Blvd *Fax Area Code: 773 ■ *TF:* 800-992-2921 ■ *Web:* www.kanegraphical.com	Chicago	IL	60647	800-992-2921	384-1207*
Kass Uehling Inc 333 Seventh Ave *Web:* www.kassuehling.com	New York	NY	10001	212-465-9206	
Kathoderay Media Inc 20 Country Estates Rd *Web:* www.kathoderay.com	Greenville	NY	12083	518-966-5600	
Kessler Crane Inc 1901 Western Ave Ste *Web:* www.kesslercrane.com	Plymouth	IN	46563	574-936-3341	
Kiku Obata & Co 6161 Delmar Blvd Ste 200 *Web:* www.kikuobata.com	Saint Louis	MO	63112	314-361-3110	
LAM Design Associates Inc 409 Manville Rd *Web:* www.lamdesign.com	Pleasantville	NY	10570	914-773-7600	
Lansmont Corp Ryan Ranch Research Pk 17 Mandeville Ct *TF:* 800-526-7666 ■ *Web:* www.lansmont.com	Monterey	CA	93940	831-655-6600	
Larsen Design Office Inc 7101 York Ave S Ste 120 *Web:* www.larsen.com	Minneapolis	MN	55435	952-835-2271	
Lautze & Lautze Cpas & Financial Consult 111 W SAINT JOHN St Ste 1010 *Web:* www.lautze.com	San Francisco	CA	95113	415-543-6900	
Lebowitz Gould Design Inc 150 W 30th St 1202 *Web:* lgd-inc.com	New York	NY	10001	212-695-5700	
Leroy & Clarkson 211 Centre St Rm 5I *Web:* www.leroyandclarkson.com	New York	NY	10013	212-431-9291	
Lindsay Hill Design C-5 Shipway Pl *Web:* lindsayhilldesign.com	Charlestown	MA	02129	617-886-0255	
Lucas Color Card 4900 N Santa Fe Ave *TF:* 888-845-8227 ■ *Web:* lucascolorcard.com	Oklahoma City	OK	73118	405-524-1811	
Marena Studio 12W 23rd St *Web:* www.marenastudios.com	New York	NY	10010	212-243-3070	
Marquand Books Inc 1402 3rd Ave Ste 300 *Web:* www.marquandbooks.com	Seattle	WA	98101	206-624-2030	
Matrix 2 Inc 1903 NW 97th Ave *Web:* www.matrix2advertising.com	Miami	FL	33172	305-591-7672	
McClung Cos Inc 550 Commerce Ave *Web:* www.mcclungco.com	Waynesboro	VA	22980	540-949-8139	
McDill Design 626 N Water St Ste 2 *Web:* www.mcdilldesign.com	Milwaukee	WI	53202	414-277-8111	
Mentus 6755 Mira Mesa Blvd Ste 123-137 *Web:* www.mentus.com	San Diego	CA	92121	858-455-5500	
Mercury Mambo 1107 S Eighth St *Web:* www.mercurymambo.com	Austin	TX	78704	512-447-4440	
Metro Creative Graphics Inc 519 Eigth Ave *TF:* 800-223-1600 ■ *Web:* mcg.metrocreativeconnection.com/publish/newmcc/index.php	New York	NY	10018	212-947-5100	714-9139
Midnight Oil Creative Llc 3800 W Vanowen St Ste 101 *Web:* www.midnightoilcreative.com	Burbank	CA	91505	818-295-6300	
Mike Davis & Associates Inc 15505 Long Vista Dr # 200 *TF:* 888-836-8442 ■ *Web:* www.imagecraftexhibits.com	Austin	TX	78728	512-836-8442	
Milkshake Media LP 2210 S Congress Ave *Web:* www.milkshakemedia.com	Austin	TX	78704	512-474-7777	
Newhall Klein Inc 6109 W Kl Ave *TF:* 866-639-4255 ■ *Web:* www.newhallklein.com	Kalamazoo	MI	49009	269-544-0844	
OAI Corp 4545 W Hillsborough Ave *Web:* www.oaicorp.com	Tampa	FL	33614	813-888-8796	
Object Design Comms Inc 8212 Old Courthouse Rd Ste A *Web:* www.objectdc.com	Vienna	VA	22182	703-917-0023	
ODA 660 York St Ste 101 *Web:* www.odasf.com	San Francisco	CA	94110	415-970-8400	

Company	City	State	ZIP	Phone	Fax
Oden & Associates Inc 119 S Main St Ste 300 *Web:* www.oden.com	Memphis	TN	38103	901-578-8055	
Odopod Inc 385 Grove St *Web:* www.odopod.com	San Francisco	CA	94102	415-436-9980	
Off The Wall Company Inc 4814 Bethlehem Pk *Web:* www.offthewall.net	Telford	PA	18969	215-453-9400	
Offwhite 521 Ft St *TF:* 800-606-1610 ■ *Web:* www.offwhite.com	Marietta	OH	45750	740-373-9010	
Ogle Design 12512 N Gray Rd *Web:* ogle-design.com	Carmel	IN	46033	317-843-1102	
Optima Graphics Inc 1540 Fencorp Ct *Web:* www.optimagfx.com	Fenton	MO	63026	636-349-3396	
Otherwise Inc 1144 W Randolph St *Web:* otherwiseinc.com	Chicago	IL	60607	312-226-1144	
Outside Source Inc 7202 E 71st St *Web:* outsidesource.com	Indianapolis	IN	46256	317-842-4853	
Par-Tech Inc 139 Premier Dr *Web:* www.partechgss.com	Lake Orion	MI	48359	248-276-0213	
Peggy Lauritsen Design Grp Inc 125 Main St Se Ste 340 *Web:* www.pldg.com	Minneapolis	MN	55414	612-623-4200	
Phase 3 Marketing & Communications 3560 Atlanta Industrial Dr *Web:* www.phase3media.com	Atlanta	GA	30331	404-367-9898	
Phinney Bischoff Design House Inc 614 Boylston Ave E *Web:* www.pbdh.com	Seattle	WA	98102	206-322-3484	
Phoenix Creative Services Inc 611 N 10th St Ste 700 *Web:* www.phoenixcreative.com	Saint Louis	MO	63101	314-421-5646	
Pigeon Brands Inc 179 John St 2nd Fl *Web:* www.pigeonbrands.com	Toronto	ON	M5T1X4	905-338-8300	
Pixels & Dots Llc 3181 Linwood Ave Ste 20 *Web:* www.pixelsanddots.com	Cincinnati	OH	45208	513-405-3687	
Pixels & Ink Inc 1210 Queen St Unit 5 *Web:* www.pixelsandink.com	Alexandria	VA	22314	703-548-3426	
Plastic Package Inc 4600 Beloit Dr *Web:* www.plasticpack.com	Sacramento	CA	95838	916-921-3399	
Plexipixel Inc 227 9th Ave N Ste B *Web:* www.plexipixel.com	Seattle	WA	98109	206-781-1405	
Premedia Group LLC 1185 Revolution Mill Dr Ste 1-16 *Web:* www.premediagroup.com	Greensboro	NC	27405	336-274-2421	
Primary Color Systems Corp 265 Briggs Ave *Web:* www.primarycolor.com	Costa Mesa	CA	92626	949-660-7080	
Primary Design Inc 57 Wingate St 4th Fl *Web:* primarydesign.com/	Haverhill	MA	01832	978-373-1565	
Print Room 4633 E Broadway Blvd *Web:* www.theprintroom.com	Tucson	AZ	85711	520-327-5354	
Printing House Ltd, The 1403 Bathurst St *TF:* 800-874-0870 ■ *Web:* www.tph.ca	Toronto	ON	M5R3H8	416-536-6113	
ProWolfe Partners Inc 1121 Olivette Executive Pkwy *Web:* www.prowolfe.com	St. Louis	MO	63132	314-983-9600	
Ps Graphics & Promotions 5991 Monticello Dr *Web:* psgp.com	Montgomery	AL	36117	334-270-9481	
Psyop Inc 45 Howard St 5th Fl *Web:* www.psyop.com	New York	NY	10013	212-533-9055	
Pudik Graphics Inc 111 Oakwood Rd *Web:* www.pudik.com	East Peoria	IL	61611	309-694-2900	
Purered Creative 5243 Royal Woods Pkwy *Web:* www.purered.net	Tucker	GA	30084	770-491-3353	
Q Prime Inc 729 Seventh Ave Lbby *Web:* www.qprime.com	New York	NY	10019	212-302-9790	
QuadSystems LLC N61 W23044 Harry's Way *TF:* 866-246-7693 ■ *Web:* www.quadsystems.com	Sussex	WI	53089	866-246-7693	
Rage Unlimited Inc 1715 Pearl St *Web:* rageunlimited.com	Boulder	CO	80302	303-444-6506	
Red Hill Studios 1017 E St Ste C *Web:* www.redhillstudios.com	San Rafael	CA	94901	415-457-0440	
Rgi Inc 2245 Gilbert Ave Ste 103 *Web:* rgidesign.com	Cincinnati	OH	45206	513-221-2121	
River City Studio Inc 116 W 3rd St Ste 102 *Web:* www.rivercitystudio.com	Kansas City	MO	64105	816-474-3922	
Rocket Communications Inc 81 Langton St Unit 12 *Web:* rocketcom.com	San Francisco	CA	94103	415-863-0101	
RosettaNet 1851 E First St Ste 1050 *Web:* www.rosettanet.org	Santa Ana	CA	92705	714-480-3820	
Sametz Blackstone Assoc 40 W Newton St Blackstone Sq *Web:* www.sametz.com	Boston	MA	02118	617-266-8577	
Sanger & Eby Design LLC 501 Chestnut St *Web:* www.sangereby.com	Cincinnati	OH	45203	513-784-9046	
Savage Design Group Inc 4203 Yoakum Blvd Fl 4 *Web:* www.savagebrands.com	Houston	TX	77006	713-522-1555	
Schafer Condon Carter Inc 1029 W. Madison *Web:* www.sccadv.com	Chicago	IL	60607	312-464-1666	
ScienceMedia Inc 6450 Lusk Blvd Ste E206 *Web:* sciencemedia.com	San Diego	CA	92121	858-625-9261	
Screen Works Inc 3970 Image Dr *TF:* 800-536-9111 ■ *Web:* screenworksinc.com	Dayton	OH	45414	937-264-9111	
Selbert Perkins Design 432 Culver Blvd *Web:* www.selbertperkins.com	Playa Del Rey	CA	90293	310-822-5223	
Sequel Studio LLC 12 W 27th St *Web:* sequelstudio.com	New York	NY	10001	212-994-4320	
Signature Graphics Inc 1000 Signature Dr *TF:* 800-356-3235 ■ *Web:* www.signaturegraphicsinc.com	Porter	IN	46304	219-926-4994	926-7231
Silver Oaks Communications 824 17th St *Web:* www.silveroaks.com	Moline	IL	61265	309-797-9898	

Phone Fax

Skidmore Inc 301 W 4 St Ste 300 ... Royal Oak MI 48067 248-591-2600
Web: www.skidmorestudio.com

Snavely Associates Ltd
112 West Foster Ave Ste 401 ... State College PA 16804 814-234-3672
Web: www.snavelyassociates.com

Solid Light Inc 438 S Third St ... Louisville KY 40202 502-562-0060
Web: www.solidlight-inc.com

Sonjara Inc 207 Park Ave ... Falls Church VA 22046 571-297-6383
Web: www.sonjara.com

Spire Inc 65 Bay St ... Boston MA 02125 617-350-8837 350-9951
TF: 877-350-8837 ■ *Web:* www.spire.net

Spyglass Creative Inc
1639 Hennepin Ave 100 ... Minneapolis MN 55403 612-486-5959
Web: www.spyglasscreative.com

Staiman Design 17 Warren Rd 23b ... Pikesville MD 21208 410-580-0100
Web: www.staiman.com

Store Decor Co, The 5050 Boyd Blvd ... Rowlett TX 75088 972-475-4404
Web: www.thestoredecor.com

Studio 101 4995 Avalon Ridge Pkwy Ste 100 ... Atlanta GA 30071 404-350-1700
Web: www.studio101.com

Studio Graphique Inc
13110 Shaker Sq Ste 101 ... Cleveland OH 44120 216-921-0750
Web: www.studiographique.com

Studio One Digital Inc
180 N Wabash Ave Ste 300 ... Chicago IL 60601 312-376-3300
Web: studio1digital.com

Studio360 Inc 1400 20th Ave ... Seattle WA 98122 206-382-0360
Web: www.studio360.com

Subia Corp 6612 Gulton Ct NE ... Albuquerque NM 87109 505-345-2636
TF: 800-275-2636 ■ *Web:* www.brilliantdigitalprinting.com

Susan Davis International
1101 K St Nw Ste 400 ... Washington DC 20005 202-408-0808
Web: www.susandavis.com

SW!TCH Studio Inc 1835 E Sixth St Ste 18 ... Tempe AZ 85281 480-966-2211
Web: www.switchstudio.com

Tagline Communications Inc
6230 Wilshire Blvd Ste 1231 ... Los Angeles CA 90048 323-857-5337
Web: www.tagline.com

Tailored Marketing 401 Wood St Ste 902 ... Pittsburgh PA 15222 412-281-1442
Web: www.tailoredmarketing.com

Terrapin Systems LLC
1201 Seven Locks Rd Ste 300 ... Rockville MD 20854 301-530-9106
Web: www.terpsys.com

Theprinters.com 3500 E College Ave ... State College PA 16801 814-237-7600
TF: 800-359-2097 ■ *Web:* www.theprinters.com

Think Big Solutions LLC 4995 Monaco St ... Commerce CO 80022 303-286-7200
Web: thinkbigsolutions.com

Think Tank Studio Inc 1226 Turner St Ste D ... Clearwater FL 33756 727-441-4396
Web: thinktankstudio.com

Toky Branding & Design 3139 Olive St ... Saint Louis MO 63103 314-534-2000
Web: toky.com

Tolleson Design Inc 560 Pacific Ave ... San Francisco CA 94133 415-626-7796
Web: tolleson.com

Tonic Studios Inc 476 Broome St Ste 6B ... New York NY 10013 212-431-0260
Web: www.tonicstudios.com

Toolbox Studios Inc 454 Soledad St ... San Antonio TX 78205 210-225-8269
Web: toolboxstudios.com

Toolhouse Design Co
2925 Roeder Ave Ste 200 ... Bellingham WA 98225 360-676-9275
Web: www.toolhouse.com/

Tribe Design LLC 1420 Mcilhenny St ... Houston TX 77004 713-523-5119
Web: www.tribedesign.com

Unimac Graphics 350 Michele Pl ... Carlstadt NJ 07072 201-372-1000 372-0699
Web: www.unimacgraphics.com

Vango Graphics Inc 1371 S Inca St ... Denver CO 80223 303-722-6109
TF: 877-722-6168 ■ *Web:* vango-graphics.com

Visible Innovations 8561 Acadia Dr ... Sagamore Hills OH 44067 216-225-0589
Web: visinno.com

Vista Color Imaging
4770 Van Epps Rd Unit 101 ... Brooklyn Hts OH 44131 216-651-2830
Web: www.vistacolorimaging.com

Vista Graphics Inc
1264 Perimeter Pkwy ... Virginia Beach VA 23454 757-422-8979
Web: www.vistagraphicsinc.com/agency-vg.php

Visual Citi Inc 770 Railroad Ave ... West Babylon NY 11704 631-482-3030
Web: visualciti.com

Visual Goodness Inc 25 W 26th St ... New York NY 10122 212-463-8248
Web: www.visualgoodness.com

Wallace Church Inc 330 E 48th St ... New York NY 10017 212-755-2903
Web: www.wallacechurch.net

Werremeyer Floresca Inc 15 N Gore Ave ... Saint Louis MO 63119 314-963-0505
Web: www.werremeyer.com

Wesco Graphics Inc 410 E Grant Line Rd Ste B ... Tracy CA 95376 209-832-1000 832-7800
Web: www.wescographics.com

West Canadian Digital Imaging Inc
200 - 1601 Ninth Ave SE ... Calgary AB T2G0H4 403-245-2555
TF: 800-267-2555 ■ *Web:* www.westcanadian.com

Weymouth Design 332 Congress St ... Boston MA 02210 617-542-2647
Web: www.weymouthdesign.com

William Fox Munroe Inc 3 E Lancaster Ave ... Shillington PA 19607 610-775-4521
TF: 800-344-2402 ■ *Web:* wfoxm.com

Xplane Corp 926 NW 13th Ave Ste 220 ... Portland OR 97209 503-224-5228
Web: www.xplane.com

Zamboo LLC 4079A Redwood Ave ... Los Angeles CA 90066 310-822-4643
Web: zamboo.com

Zen Design Group Ltd 2850 Coolidge Hwy ... Berkley MI 48072 248-398-5209
Web: www.zendesigngroup.com

Zoltun Studios Inc 10 Bedford Sq Ste 200 ... Pittsburgh PA 15203 412-488-2623
Web: zoltun.com

345 GROCERY STORES

See Also Bakeries p. 1838; Convenience Stores p. 2148; Gourmet Specialty Shops p. 2354; Health Food Stores p. 2458; Ice Cream & Dairy Stores p. 2555; Wholesale Clubs p. 3312

Phone Fax

85C Bakery Caf 2700 Alton Pkwy ... Irvine CA 92606 949-553-8585
Web: www.85cafe.us

A-Pac Manufacturing Company Inc
2719 Courier NW ... Grand Rapids MI 49534 616-791-7222
Web: www.polybags.com

A.G. Ferrari Foods 2000 N Loop Rd ... Alameda CA 94502 510-346-2100 351-2672
TF: 877-878-2783 ■ *Web:* www.agferrari.com

Acme Markets Inc 75 Valley Stream Pkwy ... Malvern PA 19355 610-889-4000
TF: 877-932-7948 ■ *Web:* www.acmemarkets.com

Adam Matthews Inc 2104 Plantside Dr ... Louisville KY 40299 502-499-2253
Web: www.adammatthews.com

Advanced Orthomolecular Research Inc
3900 - 12 St Ne ... Calgary AB T2E8H9 403-250-9997
TF: 800-387-0177 ■ *Web:* www.aor.ca

Akins Harvest Foods 106 F St Sw ... Quincy WA 98848 509-787-4421
Web: www.harvestfoodsnw.com

Alameda Natural Grocery 1650 Park St Unit L ... Alameda CA 94501 510-865-1500
Web: www.alamedanaturalgrocery.com

Alaska Commercial Co 550 W 64th Ave Ste 200 ... Anchorage AK 99518 907-273-4600
TF: 800-563-0002 ■ *Web:* acvaluecenter.com

ALDI Inc 1200 N Kirk Rd ... Batavia IL 60510 630-879-8100 879-8114
TF: 800-366-2324 ■ *Web:* www.aldi.us

Allen's of Hastings Inc 1115 W Second St ... Hastings NE 68901 402-463-5633 463-5730
Web: www.allensuperstore.com

Alliance Foods Inc 605 W Chicago Rd ... Coldwater MI 49036 517-278-2396 278-7936
Web: www.alliance-foods.com

Amax Nutrasource Inc
14291 E Don Julian Rd ... City Of Industry CA 91746 626-961-6600
TF: 800-893-5306 ■ *Web:* www.amaxnutrasource.com

American Consumers Inc 55 Hannah Way ... Rossville GA 30741 706-861-3347 861-3364
Web: shoprite-ga.com

American Metal Market LLC
225 Park Ave S 6th Fl ... New York NY 10003 212-213-6202
Web: www.amm.com

Andersen Bakery Inc 30703 San Clemente St ... Hayward CA 94544 510-429-7100
Web: www.andersenbakery.com

Archon Group LP 6011 Connection Dr ... Irving TX 75039 972-368-2200

Arkansas Poly Inc 1248 S 28th St ... Van Buren AR 72956 479-474-5036
Web: www.arkpoly.com

Arlans Market Inc 6500 Fm 2100 ... Crosby TX 77532 281-328-4868
Web: www.arlansmarket.com

Ascenta Health Ltd 4-15 Garland Ave ... Dartmouth NS B3B0A6 902-435-7329 435-3513
TF: 866-224-1775 ■ *Web:* www.ascentahealth.com

Autry Greer & Sons Inc 2850 W Main St ... Mobile AL 36612 251-457-8655 456-3744
TF: 800-999-7750 ■ *Web:* www.greers.com

B&R Stores Inc 4554 W St ... Lincoln NE 68503 402-464-6297
Web: www.russmarket.com

B. Green & Co 1300 S Monroe St ... Baltimore MD 21230 410-539-6134
Web: www.bgreenco.com

Balls Food Stores Inc 5300 Speaker Rd ... Kansas City KS 66106 913-321-4223
Web: www.henhouse.com

Banner Wholesale Grocers Inc
3000 S Ashland Ave Ste 300 ... Chicago IL 60608 312-421-2650
Web: www.bannerwholesale.com

Bashas Inc 22402 S Bashas Rd ... Chandler AZ 85248 480-895-9350 895-5371*
**Fax:* PR ■ *TF:* 800-755-7292 ■ *Web:* www.bashas.com

Beckmann's Old World Bakery Ltd
104 Bronson St Ste 6 ... Santa Cruz CA 95062 831-423-9242
Web: www.beckmannsbakery.com

Belmont Village LP 8554 Katy Fwy Ste 200 ... Houston TX 77024 713-463-1700
Web: www.belmontvillage.com

Berkot Super Foods 20005 Wolf Rd ... Mokena IL 60448 708-479-7411
Web: www.berkotfoods.com

Best Yet Market Inc 1 Lexington Ave ... Bethpage NY 11714 516-570-5300
Web: bestmarket.com

BI-LO LLC PO Box B ... Jacksonville SC 32203 800-768-4438
TF: 800-967-9105 ■ *Web:* www.bi-lo.com

Big Saver Foods Inc 4260 Charter St ... Vernon CA 90058 323-582-7222 582-2331
Web: www.bigsaverfoods.com

Big Y Foods Inc 2145 Roosevelt Ave ... Springfield MA 01102 413-784-0600
TF Cust Svc: 800-828-2688 ■ *Web:* www.bigy.com

BioCell Technology LLC
4695 Macarthur Ct 11th Fl ... Newport Beach CA 92660 714-632-1231
Web: www.biocelltechnology.com

Biotab Nutraceuticals Inc
401 E Huntington Dr ... Monrovia CA 91016 626-775-6334

Bloomfield Bakers 16100 Foothill Blvd ... Azusa CA 91702 626-610-2253

Bodega Latina Corp 14601B Lakewood Blvd ... Paramount CA 90723 562-616-8800
Web: elsupermarkets.com

Body By Jake Global LLC
11611 San Vicente Blvd Ste 515 ... Los Angeles CA 90049 310-571-7101

Bordner PJ Company Inc 2100 Wales Rd NE ... Massillon OH 44646 330-832-7522

Bosselman Inc
3123 W Stolley Park Rd Ste A ... Grand Island NE 68801 308-381-2800
Web: www.bosselman.com

Boyer's Food Markets Inc 301 S Warren St ... Orwigsburg PA 17961 570-366-1477
Web: www.boyersfood.com

Breadbox Food Stores Inc
10636 HaRdin Vly Rd ... Knoxville TN 37932 865-531-3299
Web: conocophillips.com

Bristol Farms 915 E 230th St ... Carson CA 90745 310-233-4700 233-4701
Web: www.bristolfarms.com

Brookshire Bros Ltd 1201 Ellen Trout Dr ... Lufkin TX 75904 936-634-8155 279-3374*
**Fax Area Code:* 979 ■ *TF:* 855-467-7837 ■ *Web:* www.brookshirebrothers.com

Phone Fax

Brookshire Grocery Co 1600 W SW Loop 323 .... Tyler TX 75701 903-534-3000 534-2240
Web: brookshires.com
Buds Salads 2428 Harrison Ave. .... Dallas TX 75215 214-428-1200
Web: www.buds-salads.com
Buehler Food Markets Inc
1401 Old Mansfield Rd. .... Wooster OH 44691 330-264-4355
Web: www.buehlers.com
Buffalo Services Inc 2100 Veterans Blvd. .... Mccomb MS 39648 601-249-3013
Web: www.buffaloservices.com
Bulk Foods.com 3040 Hill Ave .... Toledo OH 43607 419-531-6887
Web: www.bulkfoods.com
Busch's Inc 2240 S Main St. .... Ann Arbor MI 48103 734-214-8088
Web: www.buschs.com
Byrd Cookie Company Inc 6700 Waters Ave. .... Savannah GA 31406 912-355-1716
TF: 800-291-2973 ■ *Web:* www.byrdcookiecompany.com
C & K Markets Inc 615 Fifth St. .... Brookings OR 97415 541-469-3113 469-6717
Web: www.ckmarket.com
Cache Creek Foods LLC 411 Pioneer Ave .... Woodland CA 95776 530-662-1764
Web: www.cachecreekfoods.com
Cajun Kettle Foods 698 Saint George Ave .... New Orleans LA 70121 504-733-8800
Web: www.kajunkettle.com
Calhoun Enterprises 4155 Lomac St Ste G .... Montgomery AL 36106 334-272-4400 272-7799
Web: calhounent.com
Camellia Foods
1300 Diamond Springs Rd .... Virginia Beach VA 23455 757-855-3371 855-3423
Capital Markets Advisors LLC
1 Great Neck Rd Ste 1 .... Great Neck NY 11021 516-487-9815
Web: www.capmark.org
Capital Markets Cooperative LLC
814 A1A N Ste 303 .... Ponte Vedra Beach FL 32082 904-543-0052
Web: www.capmkts.org
Capitol Distributing Inc
3500 E Commercial Ct .... Meridian ID 83642 208-888-5112 888-5989
TF: 800-769-5659 ■ *Web:* www.capitoldist.com
Capri IGA Foodliner 224 E Harris Ave .... Greenville IL 62246 618-664-0022 664-4629
Caramagno Foods Co 14255 Dequindre St .... Detroit MI 48212 313-869-8200
Web: www.caramagnofoods.com
Cardenas Markets Inc 2501 E Guasti Rd. .... Ontario CA 91761 909-923-7426
Web: cardenasmarkets.com
Carmines Gourmet Market
2401 Pga Blvd .... Palm Beach Gardens FL 33410 561-775-0105
Web: www.carmines.com
Casey's Foods Inc 130 Holly Hills Mall Rd .... Hindman KY 41822 630-369-1686
Web: www.caseysfoods.com
Cefco Convenience Stores Inc
6261 Central Pointe Pkwy PO Box 1287 .... Temple TX 76504 254-791-0009 791-0018
Web: www.cefcostores.com
Chief Super Market Inc 1340 W High St Ste E .... Defiance OH 43512 419-782-0950 782-6047
Web: chiefmarkets.com
City Market 555 Sandhill Ln .... Grand Junction CO 81505 970-241-0750
Web: www.citymarket.com
ClearFreight Inc 880 Apollo St Ste 101 .... El Segundo CA 90245 310-726-0400
Web: clearfreight.com
Clements Marketplace Inc 2575 E Main Rd .... Portsmouth RI 02871 401-683-0180
Web: www.clementsmarket.com
Coborn's Inc 1445 E Hwy 23 .... Saint Cloud MN 56304 320-252-4222 252-0014
Web: www.cobornsinc.com
Cogo's Co 2589 Boyce Plz Rd. .... Pittsburgh PA 15241 412-257-1550
Web: www.cogos.com
Cohn Wholesale Fruit & Grocery
3511 Camino Del Rio S Ste 306 .... San Diego CA 92108 619-528-1113
Community Food Coop 908 W Main St .... Bozeman MT 59715 406-587-4039
Web: www.bozo.coop
Compare Plaza 1050 E Main St. .... Bridgeport CT 06608 203-366-9060
Web: www.comparesupermarkets.com
Convenient Food Mart 123 Gateway Blvd N .... Elyria OH 44035 440-322-6301
Web: myconvenient.com
Covington Foods Inc
419 Fourth St PO Box 206 .... Covington IN 47932 765-793-2470 793-0209
Creative Foods Corp
200 Garden City Plz Ste 505 .... Garden City NY 11530 516-746-6800
Web: www.creativefoodscorp.com
Creditera 5300 Richmond Rd. .... Bedford OH 44146 216-763-3200
Web: www.davesmarkets.com
Crosbys Markets Inc 125 Canal St .... Salem MA 01970 978-745-3571
Web: www.crosbysmarkets.com
Cub Foods 2612 S Broadway St .... Alexandria MN 56308 320-762-1158
Web: www.cub.com/stores/view-store.1007697.html
Cub Foods Stores 421 S Third St .... Stillwater MN 55082 651-439-7200 439-7200
Web: www.cub.com
Cubby's Inc 9230 Mormon Bridge Rd .... Omaha NE 68152 402-453-2468 453-4513
Web: www.cubbys.com
Culpepper & Company Inc 201 Haley Rd .... Ashland VA 23005 804-752-7171
Web: www.rrsfoodservice.com
Custom Poly Bag Inc 9465 Edison St NE .... Alliance OH 44601 330-935-2408
Web: www.custompolybag.com
CW Brower Inc 413 S Riverside Dr .... Modesto CA 95354 209-523-5447
D'Agostino Supermarkets Inc
1385 Boston Post Rd .... Larchmont NY 10538 914-833-4000
Web: www.dagnyc.com
Dan's Supermarket Inc
835 S Washington St Ste 4 .... Bismarck ND 58504 701-258-2127
Web: www.dansupermarket.com
Dari-Mart Stores Inc 125 E Sixth Ave .... Junction City OR 97448 541-998-2388
Web: www.darimart.com
Dean & DeLuca Brands Inc 560 Broadway .... New York NY 10012 212-226-6800
Web: www.deandeluca.com
Del Real Foods LLC 11041 Inland Ave .... Mira Loma CA 91752 951-681-0395
Web: delrealfoods.com
Delaware Supermarkets Inc
1600 W Newport Pk .... Wilmington DE 19804 302-999-1801
Web: www.wsfs.net

Phone Fax

Delsea Shop Rite PO Box 7812 .... Edison NJ 08818 856-691-9395 713-4176*
**Fax Area Code:* 518 ■ *Web:* www.shoprite.com
DeMoulas Super Markets Inc 875 E St .... Tewksbury MA 01876 978-851-8000
Web: mydemoulas.net
Derico of East Amherst Corp
18 Limestone Dr .... Williamsville NY 14221 716-810-0400
Dierbergs Markets Inc
16690 Swingley Ridge Rd. .... Chesterfield MO 63017 636-532-8884 532-8759
Web: www.dierbergs.com
Donelans Super Mkt 248 Great Rd. .... Acton MA 01720 978-635-9893
Web: www.donelans.com
Dorignac's Food Ctr 725 Focis St .... Metairie LA 70005 504-837-4650 832-8944
Web: dorignacs.com
Dorothy Lane Market Inc 2710 Far Hills Ave .... Dayton OH 45419 937-299-3561 299-3568
Web: www.dorothylane.com
Double 8 Foods Inc 2201 E 46th St .... Indianapolis IN 46205 317-253-3417 257-0209
Web: www.double8foods.com
Doug's Supermarket Inc 310 Main Ave NE .... Warroad MN 56763 218-386-1246
Web: www.dougssupermarket.com
Downs Tony Food Co 418 Benzel Ave Sw. .... Madelia MN 56062 507-642-3203
Web: tonydownsfoods.com
Draeger's Super Markets Inc
222 E Fourth Ave .... San Mateo CA 94401 650-685-3715 244-6548
Web: www.draegers.com
Easy Way Food Stores Inc
4545 S Mendenhall Rd .... Memphis TN 38141 901-527-6256 462-3965
Econo Foods 1600 Stephenson .... Iron Mountain MI 49801 906-774-1911
TF: 877-295-4558 ■ *Web:* www.econotnc.com
El Matador Foods Inc 7201 Bayway Dr .... Baytown TX 77520 281-424-4555
TF: 800-470-2447 ■ *Web:* www.elmatadorfoods.com
El Metate Mercado 125 N Rancho Santiago Blvd .... Orange CA 92869 714-771-5527
Web: www.elmetate.com
El Rancho Inc 2600 McCree Rd Ste 100 .... Garland TX 75041 972-526-7300
Web: www.elranchoinc.com
Erla Foods Inc 6233 Church St .... Cass City MI 48726 989-872-5100
Essential Baking Co, The 5601 First Ave S .... Seattle WA 98108 206-545-3804
Web: www.essentialbaking.com
EuroPharma Inc 955 Challenger Dr. .... Green Bay WI 54311 920-406-6500
TF: 866-598-5487 ■ *Web:* www.europharmausa.com
EW James & Sons Inc 1308-14 Nailling Dr .... Union City TN 38261 731-885-0601
Web: www.ewjamesandsons.com
Fairplay Inc 4640 S Halsted St .... Chicago IL 60609 773-247-3077
Web: www.fairplayfoods.com
Fancy Foods Inc
Bldg B-12 Hunts Point Cooperative Market .... Bronx NY 10474 718-617-3000
Web: www.fancyfoodsinc.com
Father's Table LLC, The 2100 Country Club Rd .... Sanford FL 32771 407-324-1200
Web: www.thefatherstable.com
FBC Industries Inc 110 E Ave H .... Rochelle IL 61068 815-562-8169
Web: www.fbcindustries.com
Federated Group Inc
3025 W Salt Creek Ln .... Arlington Heights IL 60005 847-577-1200 632-8302
TF: 800-234-0011 ■ *Web:* www.fedgroup.com
Field Fresh Foods Inc 14805 S San Pedro St .... Gardena CA 90248 310-719-8422
Web: www.fieldfresh.com
Fiesta Mart Inc 5235 Katy Fwy .... Houston TX 77007 713-869-5060 869-6197
Web: www.fiestamart.com
Finagle-a-Bagel Inc 77 Rowe St .... Auburndale MA 02466 617-213-8400
Web: www.finagleabagel.com
First Coast Energy LLP
7014 A C Skinner Pkwy Ste 290 .... Jacksonville FL 32256 904-596-3200 596-8550
Web: www.dailysstores.com
Fluid Market Strategies Inc
625 SW Broadway Ste 300 .... Portland OR 97205 503-808-9003
Food City 1005 N Arizona Ave .... Chandler AZ 85224 480-857-2198
TF: 800-755-7292 ■ *Web:* www.myfoodcity.com
Food Country USA 566 E Main St .... Abingdon VA 24210 276-628-3332
Web: foodcountryusainc.com
Food for Thought Inc 10704 Oviatt Rd. .... Honor MI 49640 231-326-5444
Web: www.foodforthought.net
Food Giant Supermarkets 120 Industrial Dr .... Sikeston MO 63801 573-471-3500 472-3135
Web: foodgiant.com
Foodland Super Market Ltd 3536 Harding Ave .... Honolulu HI 96816 808-732-0791 737-6952
Web: www.foodland.com
Foods of All Nations 2121 Ivy Rd. .... Charlottesville VA 22903 434-296-6131
Web: www.foodsofallnations.com
Fowler Foods Inc 139 Southwest Dr. .... Jonesboro AR 72401 870-935-6032
Freed'S Super Markets Inc
2024 Swamp Pk .... Gilbertsville PA 19525 610-326-4189
Web: freedsmarket.com
Fresh Encounter Inc 317 W Main Cross St .... Findlay OH 45840 419-422-8090 424-3932
Web: www.freshencounter.com
FreshDirect Inc 23-30 Borden Ave .... Long Island NY 11101 718-928-1000
TF: 866-511-1240 ■ *Web:* www.freshdirect.com
Friendly Express # 14 507 City Blvd .... Waycross GA 31503 912-285-7703
Web: friendlyexpress.com
Frontera Foods Inc 449 N Clark St Ste 205 .... Chicago IL 60654 312-595-1624
TF: 800-509-4441 ■ *Web:* www.fronterafiesta.com
Fry's Food Stores of Arizona Inc
500 S 99th Ave .... Tolleson AZ 85353 866-221-4141
TF: 866-221-4141 ■ *Web:* www.frysfood.com
Fuel South Inc 3020 Harris Rd .... Waycross GA 31503 912-284-0264
G & J Land & Marine Food Distributors
506 Front St .... Morgan City LA 70380 985-385-2620
TF: 800-256-9187 ■ *Web:* www.gjfood.com
G & W Foods Inc 2041 Railroad Dr .... Willow Springs MO 65793 417-469-4000
Web: gwfoodsinc.com
Gary & Leos Inc 730 First St .... Havre MT 59501 406-265-1404
Web: garyandleos.com
GE Foodland Inc 1105 E Beltline Rd .... Carrollton TX 75006 972-245-0470
Web: elrodscostplus.com
Gelson's Markets 2020 S Central Ave .... Compton CA 90220 310-638-2842 631-0950
Web: www.gelsons.com

Company	City	State	ZIP	Phone	Fax
Gerland Corp 3131 Pawnee St *Web:* www.gerlands.com	Houston	TX	77054	713-746-3600	746-3621
GermanDeli.com 601 Westport Pkwy, Ste 100 *TF:* 877-437-6269 ■ *Web:* www.germandeli.com	Grapevine	TX	76051	817-410-9955	
Gerrity's Supermarket Inc 950 N S Rd *Web:* www.gerritys.com	Scranton	PA	18504	570-342-4144	
Giant Eagle Inc 101 Kappa Dr *TF Cust Svc:* 800-553-2324 ■ *Web:* www.gianteagle.com	Pittsburgh	PA	15238	412-963-6200	968-1615
Giant Food Inc 8301 Professional Pl Ste 115 **Fax Area Code:* 301 ■ **Fax:* Cust Svc ■ *TF:* 888-469-4426 ■ *Web:* www.giantfood.com	Landover	MD	20785	888-469-4426	618-4998*
Giant Food Stores Inc 1149 Harrisburg Pike **Fax:* Mail Rm ■ *TF:* 888-814-4268 ■ *Web:* www.giantfoodstores.com	Carlisle	PA	17013	717-249-4000	960-1356*
Gold Standard Baking Inc 3700 S Kedzie Ave Ste A *Web:* www.gsbaking.com	Chicago	IL	60632	773-523-2333	
Golub Corp 461 Nott St **Fax Area Code:* 518 ■ *TF:* 800-666-7667 ■ *Web:* pricechopper.com	Schenectady	NY	12308	800-666-7667	379-3515*
Goodsons' Supermarkets Inc US Rt 52	Welch	WV	24801	304-436-8481	
Gordys County Market Downtown 212 Bay St *Web:* www.gordysinc.com	Chippewa Falls	WI	54729	715-726-2500	
GPM Investments LLC 8565 Magellan Pkwy Ste 400 *Web:* www.fasmart.com	Richmond	VA	23227	804-730-1568	
Grade A Markets Inc 563 Newfield Ave *Web:* shoprite.com	Stamford	CT	06905	203-356-1662	961-8135
Grandma's Bakery Inc 1765 Buerkle Rd *Web:* www.grandmasbakery.com	White Bear Lake	MN	55110	651-779-0707	
Greenleaf Inc 1955 Jerrold Ave *Web:* www.greenleafsf.com	San Francisco	CA	94124	415-647-2991	
GreenLine Foods Inc 4575 W Main St PO Box 727 *Web:* www.greenlinefoods.com	Guadalupe	CA	93434	419-353-2326	
Groupon Inc 600 W Chicago Ave Ste 620 *Web:* www.groupon.com	Chicago	IL	60654	312-676-5773	
Gs Foods Inc 5925 S Alcoa Ave *TF:* 800-273-6637 ■ *Web:* www.gsfoods.com	Vernon	CA	90058	323-581-6161	589-2106
Haggen Inc 2900 Woburn St *Web:* www.haggen.com	Bellingham	WA	98226	360-676-5300	
Hancock County Co-op Oil Assn 245 State St *TF:* 800-924-2667 ■ *Web:* www.hancockcountycoop.com	Garner	IA	50438	641-923-2635	
Harmons Grocery 3540 South 4000 West *Web:* www.harmonsgrocery.com	West Valley City	UT	84120	801-969-8261	964-1299
Harps Food Stores Inc 918 S Gutensohn Rd *Web:* www.harpsfood.com	Springdale	AR	72762	479-751-7601	751-3625
Harris Teeter Inc 701 Crestdale Rd PO Box 10100 *TF Cust Svc:* 800-432-6111 ■ *Web:* www.harristeeter.com	Matthews	NC	28105	704-844-3100	
Hastings Co-op Creamery Co 1701 Vermillion St PO Box 217 *Web:* www.hastingscreamery.com	Hastings	MN	55033	651-437-9414	437-3547
Heinen's Inc 4540 Richmond Rd **Fax Area Code:* 216 ■ *TF:* 855-475-2300 ■ *Web:* www.heinens.com	Cleveland	OH	44128	855-475-2300	514-4788*
Hennings Super Market Inc 290 Main St *Web:* henningsmarket.com	Harleysville	PA	19438	215-256-9533	
Herb Pharm LLC 20260 Williams Hwy *Web:* www.herb-pharm.com	Williams	OR	97544	541-846-6262	
Hi Nabor Supermarket Inc 7201 Winbourne Ave *Web:* hinabor.com	Baton Rouge	LA	70805	225-357-1448	
Highland Park Market of Farmington LLC 317 Highland St *Web:* www.highlandparkmarket.com	Manchester	CT	06040	860-646-4277	
Hiller Inc 24359 Northwestern Hwy Ste 150 *Web:* www.hillersmarkets.com	Southfield	MI	48075	248-355-2122	
Holly Poultry Inc 2221 Berlin St *TF:* 800-342-9464 ■ *Web:* www.hollypoultry.com	Baltimore	MD	21230	410-727-6210	
Hollywood Super Market Inc 2670 W Maple Rd *Web:* hollywoodmarkets.com	Troy	MI	48084	248-643-6770	643-0309
Homeland Stores 5857 Northwest Expy *Web:* www.homelandstores.com	Oklahoma City	OK	73132	405-721-6721	
Honey Baked Ham Company of Ohio 11935 Mason Montgomery Rd *Web:* www.honeybaked.com	Cincinnati	OH	45249	513-583-9700	
Hornbacher's 2510 N Broadway *Web:* www.hornbachers.com	Fargo	ND	58102	701-293-5444	
Houchens Industries Inc 700 Church St *Web:* houchensindustries.com	Bowling Green	KY	42101	270-843-3252	
House of Webster Inc, The 1013 N Second St *Web:* www.houseofwebster.com	Rogers	AR	72756	479-636-4640	
Hyatts Market Inc 70 Mchann Rd	Addison	AL	35540	256-747-6005	
IGA Inc 8725 W Higgins Rd Ste 350 *TF:* 800-321-5442 ■ *Web:* www.iga.com	Chicago	IL	60631	773-693-4520	693-4533
Ingles Markets Inc 2913 US Hwy 70 W *NASDAQ: IMKTA* ■ *TF:* 800-635-5066 ■ *Web:* www.ingles-markets.com	Black Mountain	NC	28711	828-669-2941	
International Bakers Service Inc 1902 N Sheridan St *Web:* www.internationalbakers.com	South Bend	IN	46628	574-287-7111	
International Gourmet Foods Inc 7520 Fullerton Rd *TF:* 800-522-0377 ■ *Web:* www.igf-inc.com	Springfield	VA	22153	703-569-4520	
International Plastics Inc 185 Commerce Ctr *TF:* 800-820-4722 ■ *Web:* interplas.com	Greenville	SC	29615	864-297-8000	
InVite Health Inc 1 Garden State Plz *TF:* 800-349-0929 ■ *Web:* www.invitehealth.com	Paramus	NJ	07652	201-587-2222	
Ira Higdon 150 IGA WAY PO Box 488 *Web:* irahigdongc.com	Cairo	GA	39828	229-377-1272	377-8756
JA Mktg Inc 18160 Cottonwood Rd	Sun River	OR	97707	541-593-8113	
Jafco Foods 820 Turnpike St *Web:* www.jafcofoods.com	North Andover	MA	01845	978-989-0012	
Jamac Frozen Foods 570 Grand St *Web:* www.jamacfoods.com	Jersey City	NJ	07302	201-333-6200	
Jamba Juice Co 6475 Christie Ave Ste 150 *Web:* www.jambajuice.com	Emeryville	CA	94608	510-596-0100	
Jerry's Foods 5125 Vernon Ave S *Web:* www.jerrysfoods.com	Edina	MN	55436	952-929-2685	
Jerry's Supermarkets Inc 532 W Jefferson Blvd *Web:* www.supermarket.com	Dallas	TX	75208	214-941-8110	
JJ Cassone Bakery Inc 202 S Regent St *Web:* www.jjcassonebakery.com	Port Chester	NY	10573	914-939-1568	
Joe Caputo & Sons Inc 959 E Oakton St *Web:* www.joecaputoandsons.com	Des Plaines	IL	60018	847-827-6700	
Jons International Market Place 5315 Santa Monica Blvd *Web:* www.jonsmarketplace.com	Los Angeles	CA	90029	323-460-4646	
JSB Industries Inc 130 Crescent Ave *Web:* www.muffintown.com	Chelsea	MA	02150	617-846-1565	
K-VA-T Food Stores Inc PO Box 1158 *TF:* 800-826-8451 ■ *Web:* www.foodcity.com	Abingdon	VA	24212	276-623-5100	
Karns Quality Foods Ltd 6001 Allentown Blvd *Web:* www.karns.com	Harrisburg	PA	17112	717-545-4731	
Kennies Market Inc 217 W Middle St *Web:* www.kenniesmarket.com	Gettysburg	PA	17325	717-334-2179	
Kessler's Food & Liquor 615 Sixth Ave SE *Web:* kesslersgrocery.com	Aberdeen	SD	57401	605-225-1692	
King Kullen Grocery Company Inc 185 Central Ave *Web:* www.kingkullen.com	Bethpage	NY	11714	516-733-7100	827-6325
Kirby Foods Inc 4102-B Fieldstone Rd *Web:* www.kirbyfoods.com	Champaign	IL	61826	217-352-2600	352-9394
Klass Ingredients Inc 3885 N Buffalo St *TF:* 800-662-6577 ■ *Web:* www.klassingredients.com	Orchard Park	NY	14127	716-662-6665	662-0285
KM Supermarkets Inc 851 Marketplace Dr *Web:* www.mackenthuns.com	Waconia	MN	55387	952-442-2512	
Kobayashi Travel Service 650 Iwilei Rd *Web:* www.kobay.com	Honolulu	HI	96817	808-593-9387	
Kowalski Companies Inc 1261 Grand Ave *Web:* www.kowalskis.com	St. Paul	MN	55105	651-698-3366	
Krist Oil Co 303 Selden Rd *Web:* www.kristoil.com	Iron River	MI	49935	906-265-6144	
Kroger Co 1014 Vine St *NYSE: KR* ■ *TF:* 800-576-4377 ■ *Web:* www.kroger.com	Cincinnati	OH	45202	513-762-4000	
KTA Super Stores 321 Keawe St *Web:* ktastores.com	Hilo	HI	96720	808-935-3751	
Kuukpik Corp PO Box 89187 *TF:* 866-480-6220 ■ *Web:* www.kuukpik.com	Nuiqsut	AK	99789	907-480-6220	
La Cena Fine Foods Ltd 4 Rosol Ln *Web:* www.lacenafoods.com	Saddle Brook	NJ	07663	201-797-4600	
La Fortaleza Inc 501 N Ford Blvd *Web:* www.la-fortaleza.com	Los Angeles	CA	90022	323-261-1211	
La Michoacana Meat Market Inc 4717 Telephone Rd *Web:* www.lamichoacanameatmarket.com	Houston	TX	77087	713-645-4202	
La Valle Food Co 10 Henry St *Web:* www.lavalleus.com	Teterboro	NJ	07608	201-462-0300	
Lake Erie Frozen Foods Co 1830 Orange Rd *TF:* 800-766-8501 ■ *Web:* www.leffco.net	Ashland	OH	44805	419-289-9204	
Landis Supermarket Inc 2685 County Line Rd *Web:* www.landismarket.com	Telford	PA	18969	215-723-1157	
Leevers Foods 501 Main St *Web:* www.leeversfoods.com	Cavalier	ND	58220	701-265-4011	
Leevers Supermarkets Inc 2195 N Hwy 83 Unit AA *Web:* www.leevers.com	Franktown	CO	80116	303-814-8646	814-8645
Life Force International Corp 495 Raleigh Ave *TF:* 800-531-4877 ■ *Web:* lifeforce.net	El Cajon	CA	92064	858-218-3200	
Lion Supermarket 1710 Tully Rd *Web:* www.lionsupermarket.com	San Jose	CA	95122	408-238-4451	
Loblaw Cos Ltd 1 President's Choice Cir *TF:* 888-495-5111 ■ *Web:* www.loblaw.ca/en.html	Brampton	ON	L6Y5S5	905-459-2500	861-2387
Loblaws Inc 12 St Clair Ave E *Web:* www.loblaws.ca	Toronto	ON	M4T1L7	416-960-8108	
Lorann Oils 4518 Aurelius Rd *TF:* 800-862-8620 ■ *Web:* www.lorannoils.com	Lansing	MI	48910	517-882-0215	
Lowe's 1804 Hall Ave *Web:* www.lowesmarket.com	Littlefield	TX	79339	806-385-3366	385-8629
Lowes Food Stores Inc 1381 Old Mill Cir Ste 200 *TF:* 800-669-5693 ■ *Web:* www.lowesfoods.com	Winston-Salem	NC	27103	336-659-0180	768-4702
Lund Food Holdings Inc 4100 W 50th St	Edina	MN	55424	952-927-3663	915-2600
Marjon Specialty Foods Inc 3508 Sydney Rd *Web:* www.marjonspecialtyfoods.com	Plant City	FL	33567	813-752-3482	
Market Basket Inc, The 813 Franklin Lakes Rd *Web:* www.marketbasket.com	Franklin Lakes	NJ	07417	201-891-2000	
Market Grocery Co 16 Forest Pkwy Bldg K *Web:* www.marketgrocery.com	Forest Park	GA	30297	404-361-8620	361-3773
Market Hall Foods 5655 College Ave Ste 201 *Web:* www.rockridgemarkethall.com	Oakland	CA	94618	510-250-6000	
Mars Supermarkets Inc 9627 Philadelphia Rd *Web:* www.marsfood.com	Rosedale	MD	21237	410-590-0500	
Martin & Bayley Inc 1311 A W Main *TF:* 800-876-2511 ■ *Web:* www.martinandbayley.com	Carmi	IL	62821	618-382-2334	382-8956
Martin's Marketplace 130 Tichenal Way *Web:* martinsmarketplace.com	Cashmere	WA	98815	509-782-3801	782-2212
McClancy Seasoning Co 1 Spice Rd *TF:* 800-843-1968 ■ *Web:* www.mcclancy.com	Fort Mill	SC	29707	803-548-2366	
McFarling Foods Inc 333 W 14th St *Web:* www.mcfarling.com	Indianapolis	IN	46202	317-635-2633	
Mckeever Enterprises Inc 4216 S Hocker Dr	Independence	MO	64055	816-478-3095	

Company / Address	City	State	Zip	Phone	Fax
Meijer Inc 2929 Walker Ave NW *TF:* 800-543-3704 ■ *Web:* www.meijer.com	Grand Rapids	MI	49544	616-453-6711	791-2572
Meijer Stores Inc 2929 Walker Ave NW *TF:* 800-543-3704 ■ *Web:* www.meijer.com	Grand Rapids	MI	49544	616-453-6711	
Merchants Grocery Co 800 Maddox Dr PO Box 1268 *TF:* 877-897-9893 ■ *Web:* www.merchants-grocery.com	Culpeper	VA	22701	540-825-0786	825-9016
Metabolic Maintenance Products Inc 68994 N Pine St *Web:* www.metabolicmaintenance.com	Sisters	OR	97759	541-549-7800	
Milam's Market 11 N Royal Poinciana Blvd Ste 100 *Web:* www.milamsmarkets.com	Miami Springs	FL	33166	305-884-4870	
Milford Markets Inc Dba Shoprite of Milford 155 Cherry St	Milford	CT	06460	203-882-5280	
Miner'S Inc 5065 Miller Trunk Hwy *Web:* superonefoods.com	Hermantown	MN	55811	218-729-5882	
Mississippi Market Natural Foods Coop 1500 W Seventh St *Web:* www.msmarket.coop	Saint Paul	MN	55102	651-690-0507	
Montalvan Sales Inc 2225 S Castle Harbour Pl *Web:* www.montalvans.com	Ontario	CA	91761	909-930-5670	
Morasch Meats Inc 4050 NE 158th Ave *Web:* moraschmeats.com	Portland	OR	97230	503-257-9821	
Mother's Market & Kitchen 1890 Newport Blvd *TF:* 800-595-6667 ■ *Web:* www.mothersmarket.com	Costa Mesa	CA	92627	949-631-4741	
Mountain Fresh Supermarket 2203 SR- 118	Hunlock Creek	PA	18621	570-477-2988	
National Fruit Flavor Company Inc 935 Edwards Ave *Web:* www.nationalfruitflavor.com	New Orleans	LA	70123	504-733-6757	
Natural Healthy Concepts 310 N Westhill Blvd *TF:* 866-505-7501 ■ *Web:* www.naturalhealthyconcepts.com	Appleton	WI	54914	920-968-2350	
Nature's Best 6 Pt Dr Ste 300 *TF:* 800-800-7799 ■ *Web:* www.naturesbest.net	Brea	CA	92821	714-255-4600	255-4691
New French Bakery Inc, The 828 Kasota Ave SE *Web:* www.newfrenchbakery.com	Minneapolis	MN	55414	612-455-7500	
New Leaf Community Markets Inc 1101 Pacific Ave *Web:* www.newleaf.com	Santa Cruz	CA	95060	831-466-9060	
Newport Avenue Market 1121 Nw Newport Ave *Web:* www.newportavemarket.com	Bend	OR	97703	541-382-3940	
Nino Salvaggio International Marketplace 27900 Harper Ave *Web:* www.ninosalvaggio.com	St Clair Shores	MI	48081	586-778-3650	
Norman Bros Produce Inc 7621 SW 87th Ave *Web:* www.normanbrothers.com	Miami	FL	33173	305-274-9363	596-4541
Norrenberns Foods Inc 205 E Harnett St	Mascoutah	IL	62258	618-566-7010	566-2366
Northgate Gonzalez Inc 1201 N Magnolia Ave *Web:* www.northgatemarkets.com	Anaheim	CA	92801	714-778-3784	778-3295
Novelty Inc 351 W Muskegon Dr *Web:* www.noveltyinc.com	Greenfield	IN	46140	317-462-3121	
Nugget Markets 157 Main St *Web:* www.nuggetmarket.com	Woodland	CA	95695	530-662-5479	668-1246
Nutrition Formulators Inc 10407 N Commerce Pkwy *Web:* www.nutritionformulators.com	Miramar	FL	33025	954-272-2220	
Oasis Foods Inc 2222 Kirkman St	Lake Charles	LA	70601	337-439-5262	
Oceana Natural Foods Coop 159 Se Second St *Web:* www.oceanafoods.org	Newport	OR	97365	541-265-8285	
Oleson's Foods Inc 3850 N Long Lk Rd Ste A *Web:* www.olesonsfoods.com	Traverse City	MI	49684	231-947-6510	
Orange Street Food Farm 701 S Orange St *Web:* orangestreetfoodfarm.com	Missoula	MT	59801	406-543-3188	
Orcas International Inc 9 Lenel Rd *Web:* orcasnaturals.com	Landing	NJ	07850	973-448-2801	
Organic Avenue LLC 116 Suffolk St *Web:* www.organicavenue.com	New York	NY	10002	917-675-7361	
Osborne Bros 201 Eddings Ln *Web:* osbornefoods.com	Nashville	TN	37214	615-885-7338	
Our Time Ltd 2100 Dorr St *Web:* www.ourtime.com	Toledo	OH	43607	419-537-1666	
Overwaitea Food Group 19855 92A Ave *TF:* 800-242-9229 ■ *Web:* www.owfg.com	Langley	BC	V1M3B6	604-888-1213	
Pacific Supermarket Inc 1420 Southgate Ave	Daly City	CA	94015	650-994-1688	
Peapod LLC 9933 Woods Dr *TF:* 800-573-2763 ■ *Web:* www.peapod.com/index.jhtml	Skokie	IL	60077	847-583-9400	583-9494
Penn Dutch Foods 3201 N State Rd 7 *Web:* www.penn-dutch.com	Margate	FL	33063	954-974-3900	
People's Food Co-op 315 Fifth Ave S *Web:* www.peoplesfoodcoop.com	La Crosse	WI	54601	608-784-5798	
PercuVision LLC 765 N Hamilton Rd Ste 260A *Web:* www.percuvision.com	Gahanna	OH	43230	614-337-8700	
Perlmart Inc 954 Rt 166 *Web:* shoprite.com	Toms River	NJ	08753	732-341-0700	
Petrey W L Wholesale Company Inc 10345 Petrey Hwy *Web:* www.petrey.com	Luverne	AL	36049	334-230-5674	335-2422
Pick N Save 6950 W State St *Web:* www.picknsave.com	Wauwatosa	WI	53213	414-475-7181	
Piggly Wiggly Carolina Company Inc PO Box 118047 *TF:* 800-243-9880 ■ *Web:* thepig.net	Charleston	SC	29423	843-554-9880	745-2730
Piggly Wiggly Midwest LLC 2215 Union Ave *Web:* pigglywiggly.com	Sheboygan	WI	53081	920-457-4433	
Plum Market Corp 30777 Northwestern Hwy Ste 301 *Web:* www.plummarket.com	Farmington Hills	MI	48334	248-706-1600	
Pressed Juicery LLC 1550 17Th St *Web:* www.pressedjuicery.com	Santa Monica	CA	90404	310-477-7171	
Provigo Inc 400 Ave Suite Croix *Web:* www.provigo.ca	Saint-laurent	QC	H4L5P3	514-383-3000	
Public Market of Newington LLC 437 New Britain Ave *Web:* publicmarketnewington.com	Newington	CT	06111	860-667-1454	
Publix Super Markets Inc 3300 Publix Corporate Pkwy *TF PR:* 800-242-1227 ■ *Web:* www.publix.com	Lakeland	FL	33811	863-688-1188	
Pumper's Premium Stores Inc 4931 Earle Morris Hwy *Web:* www.pumperspremium.com	Easley	SC	29642	864-306-2999	
Pure Essence Laboratories Inc 6155 S Sandhill Rd Ste 200 *Web:* www.pureessencelabs.com	Las Vegas	NV	89120	702-990-7400	
Rainbow Grocery Co-op Inc 1745 Folsom St *TF:* 877-720-2667 ■ *Web:* rainbow.coop	San Francisco	CA	94103	415-863-0620	
Raley's 500 W Capitol Ave PO Box 15618 **Fax:* Cust Svc ■ *TF:* 800-925-9989 ■ *Web:* www.raleys.com	Sacramento	CA	95852	916-373-3333	373-0881*
Ralphs Grocery Co 1014 Vine St *TF Cust Svc:* 800-576-4377 ■ *Web:* www.ralphs.com	Cincinnati	OH	45202	800-576-4377	
Real Food Company Inc 3060 Fillmore St *Web:* www.realfoodco.com	San Francisco	CA	94123	415-567-6900	
Redner's Markets Inc 3 Quarry Rd *Web:* www.rednersmarkets.com	Reading	PA	19605	610-926-3700	926-6327
Reliable Self-Service Market 36 Circuit Av PO Box 542 *Web:* thereliablemarket.com	Oak Bluffs	MA	02557	508-693-1102	
Remke Markets Inc 1299 Cox Ave *Web:* www.remkes.com	Erlanger	KY	41018	859-594-3400	
Resource Plus 9636 Heckscher Dr *TF:* 888-678-8966 ■ *Web:* www.resourcep.com	Jacksonville	FL	32226	888-678-8966	
RF Owens Company Inc 1062 Broadway *Web:* www.trucchis.com	Raynham	MA	02767	508-824-7514	
Rhema Health Products Ltd 1751 Brigantine Dr *Web:* www.rhemahealthproducts.com	Coquitlam	BC	V3K7B4	604-516-0199	
Rice Epicurean Markets Inc 5333 Gulfton St *Web:* www.riceepicurean.com	Houston	TX	77081	713-662-7700	662-7757
Rico Foods Inc 578 E 19th St *Web:* www.ricofood.com	Paterson	NJ	07514	973-278-0589	
Riedel Marketing Group 5327 E Pinchot Ave *Web:* 4rmg.com	Phoenix	AZ	85018	602-840-4948	
Riesbeck Food Markets Inc 48661 National Rd *Web:* www.riesbeckfoods.com	Saint Clairsville	OH	43950	740-695-7050	695-7555
Road Ranger LLC 4930 E State St *Web:* www.roadrangerusa.com	Rockford	IL	61108	815-387-1700	387-7884
Roasterie Inc, The 1204 W 27th St *TF:* 800-376-0245 ■ *Web:* www.theroasterie.com	Kansas City	MO	64108	816-931-4000	
Roche Bros Supermarkets Inc 70 Hastings St *Web:* rochebros.com	Wellesley Hills	MA	02481	781-235-9400	235-3153
Rock Cave IGA Junction of Rt 4 and Rt 20 *Web:* www.rockcaveiga.com	Rock Cave	WV	26234	304-924-5296	
Rockdale Grocery Inc 994 Institute St NW *Web:* www.pigglywiggly-atl.com	Conyers	GA	30012	770-922-9209	
Ronetco Supermarkets Inc Morris Canal Plz - 1070 Rt 46	Ledgewood	NJ	07852	973-927-8300	
Rosauers Super Markets Inc 1815 W Garland Ave *Web:* www.rosauers.com	Spokane	WA	99205	509-326-8900	328-2483
Rouse's Enterprises LLC 1301 Saint Mary St *Web:* www.rouses.com	Thibodaux	LA	70301	985-447-5998	
Royals Food Town 135 South Main *Web:* royalsfoodtown.com	Loa	UT	84747	435-836-2841	
Sacramento Natural Foods Cooperative Inc 1900 Alhambra Blvd *Web:* sacfood.coop	Sacramento	CA	95816	916-455-2667	
Safeway Inc 5918 Stoneridge Mall Rd *NYSE: SWY* ■ *Web:* www.safeway.com	Pleasanton	CA	94588	925-467-3000	467-3323
Sage V Foods LLC 12100 Wilshire Blvd Ste 605 *Web:* www.sagevfoods.com	Los Angeles	CA	90025	310-820-4496	
Santos Enterprises 5400 Alameda Ave *Web:* www.foodcityep.com	El Paso	TX	79905	915-779-3641	
Save Mart Supermarkets Inc PO Box 4278 *Web:* www.savemart.com	Modesto	CA	95352	209-577-1600	
Save-A-Lot Ltd 100 Corporate Office Dr *Web:* www.save-a-lot.com	Earth City	MO	63045	314-592-9100	592-9619
Schnuck Markets Inc 11420 Lackland Rd *TF:* 800-264-4400 ■ *Web:* www.schnucks.com	Saint Louis	MO	63146	314-994-4400	994-4465
Scolari's Food & Drug Co 950 Holman Way *Web:* www.scolaristores.com	Sparks	NV	89431	775-575-1381	
Seashore Food Distributors Inc 1 Satt Blvd PO Box 235 *Web:* www.seashorefood.com	Rio Grande	NJ	08242	609-886-3100	
Sedano's Supermarkets 3140 W 76 St *Web:* www.sedanos.com	Hialeah	FL	33018	305-824-1034	556-6981
Shady Maple Farm Market Inc 1324 Main St *Web:* www.shady-maple.com	East Earl	PA	17519	717-354-4981	
Sharp Shopper 2475 S Main St Ste A *Web:* www.sharpshopper.net	Harrisonburg	VA	22801	540-434-8848	
Sharp Shopper Inc 1100 Sharp Ave *Web:* sharpshopper.net	Ephrata	PA	17522	717-733-9555	
Shop 'n Save 10461 Manchester Rd **Fax:* Hum Res ■ *TF:* 800-428-6974 ■ *Web:* www.shopnsave.com	Kirkwood	MO	63122	314-984-0900	984-1350*
Shoppers Food & Pharmacy 10501 Martin Luther King Jr Hwy *TF:* 800-866-0514 ■ *Web:* www.shoppersfood.com	Bowie	MD	20720	240-544-0180	544-0187
ShopRite PO Box 7812 **Fax Area Code:* 732 ■ *TF:* 800-746-7748 ■ *Web:* www.shoprite.com	Edison	NJ	08818	800-746-7748	251-9519*
ShopRite Supermarkets Inc 600 York St *TF:* 800-746-7748 ■ *Web:* www.shoprite.com	Elizabeth	NJ	07207	908-527-3300	

Company	Address	City	State	ZIP	Phone	Fax
Shun Fat Supermarket Inc	421 N Atlantic Blvd	Monterey Park	CA	91754	626-308-3998	
	Web: www.shunfatsupermarket.com					
Silva International Inc	523 N Ash St	Momence	IL	60954	815-472-3535	
	Web: silva-intl.com					
Simek's Inc	940 Hastings Ave	Saint Paul Park	MN	55071	651-459-5578	
	Web: www.simeks.com					
Smart & Final Inc	600 Citadel Dr	Commerce	CA	90040	323-869-7500	869-7865
	TF: 800-894-0511 ■ *Web:* www.smartandfinal.com					
Sobeys Inc	115 King St	Stellarton	NS	B0K1S0	902-752-8371	
	Web: www.sobeys.com					
Spivey Enterprises Inc	6148 Brookshire Blvd	Charlotte	NC	28216	704-399-4802	393-1940
	Web: www.quikshoppe.com					
Starco Impex Inc	2710 S 11th St	Beaumont	TX	77701	866-740-9601	842-5650*
	**Fax Area Code:* 888 ■ *TF:* 866-740-9601 ■ *Web:* www.starcoimpex.com					
Stater Bros Markets Inc	301 S Tippecanoe Ave	San Bernardino	CA	92408	909-733-5000	
	Web: www.staterbros.com					
Sterling Extract Company Inc	10929 Franklin Ave Ste V	Franklin Park	IL	60131	847-451-9728	
	Web: www.sterlingextractcompany.com					
Stop & Shop Supermarket Co	1385 Hancock St	Quincy	MA	02169	781-397-0006	
	TF: 800-767-7772 ■ *Web:* www.stopandshop.com					
Strack & Van Til Super Market Inc	9632 Cline Ave	Highland	IN	46322	219-924-6932	
	Web: www.strackandvantil.com					
Sullivan's Foods	425 First St	Savanna	IL	61074	815-273-4511	
	Web: www.sullivansfoods.net					
Sunnyway Foods Inc	212 N Antrim Way	Greencastle	PA	17225	717-597-7121	
	Web: www.sunnywayfoods.com					
Sunset Food Mart Inc	1812 Green Bay Rd	Highland Park	IL	60035	847-432-5500	
	Web: sunsetfoods.com					
Sunshine Market Inc	2901 Campbell Ave	Lynchburg	VA	24501	434-846-7862	
	Web: sunshinemarket.com					
Sunterra Quality Food Markets Inc	1851 Sirocco Dr SW Ste 200	Calgary	AB	T3H4R5	403-266-2820	
	Web: www.sunterramarket.com					
Super A Foods	7200 Dominion Cir	Commerce	CA	90040	323-869-0600	722-0911
	Web: www.superafoods.com					
Super H Mart Inc	2550 Pleasant Hill Rd	Duluth	GA	30096	678-543-4000	
	TF: 877-427-7386 ■ *Web:* www.hmart.com					
Super King Market 2	2716 N San Fernando Rd	Los Angeles	CA	90065	323-225-0044	
	Web: www.superkingmarkets.com					
Supermercado Mi Tierra LLC	9520 International Blvd	Oakland	CA	94603	510-567-8617	
	TF: 800-225-9902 ■ *Web:* supermercadomitierra.com					
Supermercados Selectos Inc	HC 80 Box 7305	Dorado	PR	00646	787-275-2165	
	Web: www.selectospr.com					
SUPERVALU Inc	7075 Flying Cloud Dr	Eden Prairie	MN	55344	952-828-4000	
	NYSE: SVU ■ *TF Cust Svc:* 877-322-8228 ■ *Web:* www.supervalu.com					
Supreme Mfg Company Inc	5 Connerty Ct	East Brunswick	NJ	08816	732-254-0087	
	TF: 800-772-7632 ■ *Web:* www.supreme-mfg.com					
Sure Save Supermarkets Ltd	16-128 Orchid Land Dr	Keaau	HI	96749	808-966-9009	966-6200
	Web: www.suresave.com					
Synergy Worldwide Inc	2162 W Grove Pkwy Ste 100	Pleasant Grove	UT	84062	801-769-7800	
	Web: us.synergyworldwide.com					
Tamura Superette Inc	86-032 Farrington Hwy	Waianae	HI	96792	808-696-3321	
	Web: tamurasupermarket.com					
Tate's Bake Shop Inc	43 N Sea Rd	Southampton	NY	11968	631-283-9830	
	Web: www.tatesbakeshop.com					
Tates Supermarket Inc	120 Fourth St	Clymer	PA	15728	724-254-4420	
	Web: tatesmarket.com					
Theodoro Baking Company Inc	6038 N Lindbergh Blvd	Hazelwood	MO	63042	314-731-3777	
Thruway Food Market & Shopping Ctr	78 Oak St	Walden	NY	12586	845-778-3535	
	Web: www.shopthruway.com					
Thurland Reay Family Investment Co	2100 N Kolb Rd	Tucson	AZ	85715	520-298-2391	
Tilton Market Inc	1524 Tilton Rd	Northfield	NJ	08225	609-641-5118	
	Web: tiltonmarket.com					
Tom's Food Markets	738 Munson Ave	Traverse City	MI	49686	231-947-7175	
	Web: www.toms-foodmarkets.com					
Tony's Finer Foods Inc	3607 W Fullerton Ave	Chicago	IL	60647	773-278-8355	
	Web: tonysfreshmarket.com					
Tops Industries Inc	797 Twin View Blvd	Redding	CA	96003	530-242-0200	
Total Wine & More	11325 Seven Locks Rd Ste 214	Potomac	MD	20854	301-795-1000	
	Web: www.totalwine.com					
Town & Country Markets Inc	20148 Tenth Ave NE	Poulsbo	WA	98370	360-779-1881	
	Web: central-market.com					
Trader Joe's Co	800 S Shamrock Ave	Monrovia	CA	91016	626-599-3700	
	Web: www.traderjoes.com					
Treasure Island Foods Inc	3460 N Broadway	Chicago	IL	60657	773-327-4265	
	Web: www.tifoods.com					
Tribeca Oven Inc	447 Gotham Pkwy	Carlstadt	NJ	07072	201-935-8800	
	Web: tribecaoven.com					
Ukrop's Super Markets Inc	2001 Maywill St Ste 100	Richmond	VA	23230	804-340-3000	
	Web: www.ukropshomestylefoods.com					
United Coop	N7160 Raceway Rd	Beaver Dam	WI	53916	920-887-1756	
	Web: www.unitedcooperative.com					
United Fresh Potato Growers Of Idaho Inc	6109 So. Yellowstone Hwy	Idaho Falls	ID	83402	208-535-8500	
	Web: www.unitedpotato.com					
United Supermarkets Ltd	7830 Orlando Ave	Lubbock	TX	79423	806-791-0220	791-7476
	Web: www.unitedtexas.com					
United Supermarkets of Oklahoma Inc	600 E Broadway St	Altus	OK	73521	580-482-1184	
	Web: www.unitedok.com					
Uwajimaya Inc	600 Fifth Ave S	Seattle	WA	98104	206-624-6248	405-2996
	Web: www.uwajimaya.com					
Value Added Products Coop	2101 College Blvd	Alva	OK	73717	580-327-0400	
	Web: www.vapcoop.com					
Village Pantry LLC	9800 Crosspoint Blvd	Indianapolis	IN	46256	317-594-2100	
	Web: www.marsh.net					
Village Super Market Inc	733 Mountain Ave	Springfield	NJ	07081	973-467-2200	
	NASDAQ: VLGEA ■ *TF:* 800-746-7748 ■ *Web:* www.shoprite.com					
Vita Coco	38 W 21St St	New York	NY	10010	212-206-0763	
	Web: www.vitacoco.com					
Vita Health Products Inc	150 Beghin Ave	Winnipeg	MB	R2J3W2	204-661-8386	663-8386
	Web: www.vitahealth.ca					
VitaDigest.com	20687-2 Amar Rd Ste 258	Walnut	CA	91789	877-848-2168	
	TF: 877-848-2168 ■ *Web:* www.vitadigest.com					
Vyse Gelatin Co	5010 Rose St	Schiller Park	IL	60176	847-678-4780	
	Web: www.vyse.com					
Waldbaums	2 Paragon Dr	Montvale	NJ	07645	866-443-7374	
	TF: 866-443-7374					
Walts Food Centers	16145 S State St	South Holland	IL	60473	708-333-5500	
	Web: www.waltsfoods.com					
Warrenton Oil Co	2299 S Spoede	Truesdale	MO	63383	636-456-3346	
	Web: www.fastlane-cstore.com					
Wedge Community Co-Op Inc	2105 Lyndale Ave S	Minneapolis	MN	55405	612-871-3993	871-0734
	TF: 800-535-4555 ■ *Web:* www.wedge.coop					
Wegmans Food Markets Inc	1500 Brooks Ave PO Box 30844	Rochester	NY	14603	585-328-2550	464-4626*
	**Fax:* Mail Rm ■ *TF:* 800-934-6267 ■ *Web:* www.wegmans.com					
Weis Markets	1000 S Second St PO Box 471	Sunbury	PA	17801	866-999-9347	
	NYSE: WMK ■ *TF:* 866-999-9347 ■ *Web:* www.weismarkets.com					
Westborn Inc	21755 Michigan Ave	Dearborn	MI	48124	313-274-6100	
	Web: www.westbornmarket.com					
Western Bagel Baking Corp	7814 Sepulveda Blvd	Van Nuys	CA	91405	818-786-5847	787-3221
	TF: 800-555-0882 ■ *Web:* www.westernbagel.com					
Western Beef Inc	47-05 Metropolitan Ave	Ridgewood	NY	11385	718-417-3770	
	Web: www.westernbeef.com					
Western Supermarkets	2614 19th St S	Birmingham	AL	35209	205-879-3471	879-3476
	Web: www.westernsupermarkets.com					
Whittle & Mutch Inc	712 Fellowship Rd	Mount Laurel	NJ	08054	856-235-1165	
	Web: www.wamiflavor.com					
Wickens Herzer Panza Cook & Batista Co	35765 Chester Rd	Avon	OH	44011	440-930-8000	
	Web: www.wickenslaw.com					
WinCo Foods Inc	PO Box 5756	Boise	ID	83705	208-377-0110	
	TF: 888-674-6854 ■ *Web:* www.wincofoods.com					
Wing Hing Foods Inc	2539 E Philadelphia St	Ontario	CA	91761	855-734-2742	
	TF: 855-734-2742 ■ *Web:* www.winghing.com					
Winn-Dixie Stores Inc	5050 Edgewood Ct	Jacksonville	FL	32254	904-783-5000	783-5294
	Web: www.winndixie.com					
Woodman'S Food Market Inc	2631 Liberty Ln	Janesville	WI	53545	608-754-8382	
	Web: woodmans-food.com					
Woods Supermarkets Inc	703 E College Ave	Bolivar	MO	65613	417-326-7601	
	Web: www.woodssupermarket.com					
Zallie Supermarkets	1230 Blackwood-Clementon Rd	Clementon	NJ	08021	856-627-6501	627-8650
ZeaVision LLC	716-I Crown Industrial Ct	Chesterfield	MO	63005	314-628-1000	
	TF: 866-833-2800 ■ *Web:* www.eyepromise.com/zeavision					
Zija International Inc	3300 N Ashton Blvd	Lehi	UT	84043	801-494-2300	
	Web: www.drinklifein.com					
Zups Food Market	303 E Sheridan St	Ely	MN	55731	218-365-3188	
	Web: www.zups.com					

346 GYM & PLAYGROUND EQUIPMENT

Company	Address	City	State	ZIP	Phone	Fax
American Athletic Inc (AAI)	200 American Ave	Jefferson	IA	50129	515-386-3125	386-4566
	TF: 800-247-3978 ■ *Web:* www.americanathletic.com					
American Playground Corp	2328 Jefferson St	Anderson	IN	46016	765-642-0288	649-7162
	TF: 800-541-1602 ■ *Web:* american-playground.net					
BCI Burke Company Inc	660 Van Dyne Rd	Fond du Lac	WI	54937	920-921-9220	921-9566
	TF: 800-356-2070 ■ *Web:* www.bciburke.com					
Columbia Cascade Co	1300 SW Sixth Ave Ste 310	Portland	OR	97201	503-223-1157	223-4530
	TF: 800-547-1940 ■ *Web:* www.timberform.com					
Grounds For Play Inc	1401 E Dallas St	Mansfield	TX	76063	800-552-7529	477-1140*
	**Fax Area Code:* 817 ■ *TF:* 800-552-7529 ■ *Web:* www.groundsforplay.com					
Jaypro Sports Inc	976 Hartford Tpke	Waterford	CT	06385	860-447-3001	444-1779
	TF Cust Svc: 800-243-0533 ■ *Web:* www.jaypro.com					
Landscape Structures Inc	601 Seventh St S	Delano	MN	55328	763-972-3391	972-3185
	TF: 800-328-0035 ■ *Web:* www.playlsi.com					
Miracle Recreation Equipment Co	878 Hwy 60	Monett	MO	65708	417-235-6917	235-6816
	TF: 800-523-4202 ■ *Web:* miracle-recreation.com					
PlayCore Inc	401 Chestnut St Ste 410	Chattanooga	TN	37402	877-762-7563	425-3124*
	**Fax Area Code:* 423 ■ *TF:* 877-762-7563 ■ *Web:* www.playcore.com					
Playworld Systems Inc	1000 Buffalo Rd	Lewisburg	PA	17837	570-522-9800	522-3030
	TF: 800-233-8404 ■ *Web:* playworld.com					
School-Tech Inc	745 State Cir	Ann Arbor	MI	48108	800-521-2832	654-4321
	TF: 800-521-2832 ■ *Web:* www.school-tech.com					
SportsPlay Equipment Inc	5642 Natural Bridge Ave	Saint Louis	MO	63120	314-389-4140	389-9034
	TF: 800-727-8180 ■ *Web:* www.sportsplayinc.com					

347 GYPSUM PRODUCTS

Company	Address	City	State	ZIP	Phone	Fax
American Gypsum Co	3811 Turtle Creek Blvd Ste 1200	Dallas	TX	75219	214-530-5500	530-5635
	TF: 866-439-5800 ■ *Web:* www.americangypsum.com					

Phone Fax

Canadian Gypsum Company Inc
350 Burnhamthorpe Rd W 5th Fl .... Mississauga ON L5B3J1 905-803-5600 803-5688
TF: 800-565-6607 ■ *Web:* www.usg.com

CertainTeed Gypsum 2424 Lakeshore Rd W .... Mississauga ON L5J1K4 905-823-9881 823-4860
TF: 800-233-8990 ■ *Web:* www.certainteed.com

Eagle Materials Inc
3811 Turtle Creek Blvd Ste 1100 .... Dallas TX 75219 214-432-2000 432-2100
NYSE: EXP ■ *Web:* www.eaglematerials.com

KCG Inc 15720 W 108th St Ste 100 .... Lenexa KS 66219 913-438-4142
Web: www.rewmaterials.com

Lafarge North America Inc
8700 W Bryn Mawr Ave Ste 300.................... Chicago VA 60631 703-480-3600 480-3899
Web: www.lafarge-na.com

National Gypsum Co 2001 Rexford Rd .... Charlotte NC 28211 704-365-7300 329-6421*
**Fax Area Code:* 800 ■ *TF:* 800-628-4662 ■ *Web:* nationalgypsum.com

PABCO Gypsum 37851 Cherry St.................. Newark CA 94560 510-792-9555
TF: 877-449-7786 ■ *Web:* www.pabcogypsum.com

Southern Wall Products Inc 1827 Fellowship Rd......... Tucker GA 30084 770-938-0121
Web: www.ruco.com

USG Corp 550 W Adams St.......................... Chicago IL 60661 312-436-4000 672-4093
NYSE: USG ■ *TF:* 800-874-4968 ■ *Web:* www.usg.com

348 HAIRPIECES, WIGS, TOUPEES

Phone Fax

Aderans Hair Goods Inc
Simplicity Hair Extensions
9135 Independence Ave...................... Chatsworth CA 91311 877-413-5225
TF Sales: 877-413-5225 ■ *Web:* www.simplicityhair.com

Afro World Hair Goods Inc
7276 Natural Bridge Rd .... Normandy MO 63121 314-474-0151
Web: www.afroworld.com

Alkinco PO Box 278 .... New York NY 10116 212-719-3070 764-7804
TF: 800-424-7118 ■ *Web:* www.alkincohair.com

Eva Gabor International Ltd
5900 Equitable Rd .... Kansas City MO 64120 816-231-3700
Web: virtualrealityhair.com

Freeda Wigs 779 E Newyork Ave.................... Brooklyn NY 11203 718-771-2000
Web: www.freeda.com

Headcovers Unlimited 35 Tiffany Plz................. Ardmore OK 73401 580-226-5871
Web: www.headcovers.com

Headstart Hair For Men Inc
3395 Cypress Gardens Rd .... Winter Haven FL 33884 863-324-5559 324-5673
TF: 800-645-6525 ■ *Web:* www.headstarthairformen.com

Henry Margu Inc 540 Commerce Dr.................. Yeadon PA 19050 610-622-0515
Web: www.henrymargu.com

HPH Corp 1529 SE 47th Terr....................... Cape Coral FL 33904 239-540-0085
TF: 800-654-9884 ■ *Web:* www.discounthairpiece.com

Jacquelyn Wigs 15 W 37th St 4th Fl.................. New York NY 10018 212-302-2266
TF: 800-272-2424 ■ *Web:* www.jacquelynwigs.com

Jean Paree Weegs Inc
4041 South 700 East Ste 2 .... Salt Lake City UT 84107 800-422-9447
TF Orders: 800-422-9447 ■ *Web:* www.jeanparee.com

Jon Renau Collection 2510 Island View Way .... Vista CA 92081 760-598-0067 598-1205
TF: 800-462-9447 ■ *Web:* www.jonrenau.com

Louis Ferre Inc 302 Fifth Ave Ste 10................. New York NY 10001 212-239-1600
TF: 800-695-1061 ■ *Web:* www.louisferre.com

National Fiber Technology LLC 300 Canal St .... Lawrence MA 01840 978-686-2964
TF Cust Svc: 800-842-2751 ■ *Web:* www.nftech.com

Peggy Knight Solutions Inc 1750 Bridgeway.......... Sausalito CA 94965 415-289-1777
TF: 800-997-7753 ■ *Web:* www.peggyknight.com

Rene Of Paris 9135 Independence Ave 9th Fl........ Chatsworth CA 90212 800-353-7363
TF Sales: 800-353-7363 ■ *Web:* www.reneofparis.com

Wig America Co 27317 Industrial Blvd................ Hayward CA 94545 510-887-9579 887-9574
TF: 800-338-7600 ■ *Web:* www.wigamerica.com

World of Wigs 2305 E 17th St..................... Santa Ana CA 92705 714-547-4461 547-6063
TF: 800-794-5572 ■ *Web:* www.worldofwigs.com

YK International Co 3246 W Montrose Ave............ Chicago IL 60618 773-583-5270
TF: 800-266-5254 ■ *Web:* chicago.enquira.com

349 HANDBAGS, TOTES, BACKPACKS

See Also Leather Goods - Personal p. 2645; Luggage, Bags, Cases p. 2688; Sporting Goods p. 3193; Tarps, Tents, Covers p. 3215

Phone Fax

Accurate Flannel Bag Co 468 Totowa Ave .... Paterson NJ 07522 929-356-6791 689-6774*
**Fax Area Code:* 973

Dow Cover Co Inc 373 Lexington Ave............... New Haven CT 06513 203-469-5394 469-5394
TF: 800-735-8877 ■ *Web:* www.dowcover.com

Kate Spade 135 5th Ave.......................... New York NY 10010 212-358-0420
TF: 866-999-5283 ■ *Web:* www.katespade.com

LBU Inc 217 Brook Ave .... Passaic NJ 07055 973-773-4800 773-6005
Web: www.lbuinc.com

Ohio Bag Corp 6044 Rossmoor Lakes Ct.......... Boynton Beach FL 33437 561-736-3131 735-0150
Web: www.ohiobag.com

Vera Bradley Designs 2208 Production Rd .... Fort Wayne IN 46808 260-482-4673 484-2278
TF: 800-975-8372 ■ *Web:* www.verabradley.com

350 HARDWARE - MFR

Phone Fax

A-jax Company Inc 1500 E Eighth St .... Jacksonville FL 32206 904-353-4783
Web: www.ajaxco.com

Ababa Bolt 1466 - 1 Pioneer Way .... El Cajon CA 92020 619-440-1781

Aceco 4419 Federal Way.............................. Boise ID 83716 208-343-7712
TF: 800-359-7012 ■ *Web:* www.aceco.com

Phone Fax

Acorn Manufacturing Company Inc
457 School St..................................... Mansfield MA 02048 800-835-0121
TF: 800-835-0121 ■ *Web:* www.acornmfg.com

Acryline USA Inc 2015 Becancour .... Lyster QC G0S1V0 800-567-0920
TF: 800-567-0920 ■ *Web:* www.acryline.ca

Adams Rite Manufacturing Co
10027 S 51st St Ste 102............................ Phoenix AZ 85044 909-632-2300
TF: 800-872-3267 ■ *Web:* www.adamsrite.com

Advanced Integration LLC
4601 Hilton Corporate Dr .... Columbus OH 43232 614-863-2433
Web: www.advint.com

AEHI Inc 14586 Central Ave .... Chino CA 91710 909-606-6998 606-6885
Web: www.aehiinc.com

AGM Container Controls Inc
3526 E Ft Lowell Rd .... Tucson AZ 85716 520-881-2130 881-4983
TF: 800-995-5590 ■ *Web:* www.agmcontainer.com

Airtronics Inc 1822 S Research Loop .... Tucson AZ 85710 520-881-3982
Web: www.airtronicsinc.com

Akron Hardware 170 Main Ave......................... Akron CO 80720 970-345-6600

AL Hansen Manufacturing Co 701 Pershing Rd....... Waukegan IL 60085 847-244-8900 244-7222
Web: www.alhansen.com

Albion Industries Inc 800 N Clark St.................. Albion MI 49224 517-629-9441
TF: 800-835-8911 ■ *Web:* albioncasters.com

Allied Fastener & Tool Inc 1130 Ng St .... Lake Worth FL 33460 561-585-2113
TF: 877-353-3731 ■ *Web:* alliedfastener.com

AluminArt Products Ltd 1 Summerlea Rd............ Brampton ON L6T4V2 905-791-7521
Web: www.aluminart.com

American Bolt & Screw Manufacturing Corp
601 Kettering Dr .... Ontario CA 91761 909-390-0522
TF: 800-325-0844 ■ *Web:* www.absfasteners.com

AmerTac 1 Rt 17 S .... Saddle River NJ 07458 201-934-3224 934-3224
Web: www.amertac.com

Antenna Factory Inc 931 Albion Ave............. Schaumburg IL 60193 312-242-1727

AO Precision Mfg LLC 1870 Mason Ave .... Daytona Beach FL 32117 386-274-5882
Web: www.aopmfg.com

Architectural Builders Hardware Manufacturing
1222 Ardmore Ave Apt W............................... Itasca IL 60143 630-875-9900
Web: www.abhmfg.com

Architectural Building Supply Co
2965 S Main St.............................. Salt Lake City UT 84115 801-486-3481
Web: www.absdoors.com

Aretech LLC 21730 Red Rum Dr Ste 112................ Ashburn VA 20147 571-292-8889
Web: www.aretechllc.com

Arrow Lock Co 100 Arrow Dr..................... New Haven CT 06511 800-839-3157 421-6615
TF: 800-839-3157 ■ *Web:* www.arrowlock.com

ASCO Sintering Co 2750 Garfield Ave................ Commerce CA 90040 323-725-3550
Web: www.ascosintering.com

Asi Technologies 209 Progress Dr............ Montgomeryville PA 18936 215-661-1002
Web: www.asidrives.com

Assa Abloy of Canada Ltd 160 Four Vly Dr............ Vaughan ON L4K4T9 905-738-2466
TF: 800-461-3007 ■ *Web:* www.assaabloy.ca

ASSA Inc 110 Sargent Dr .... New Haven CT 06511 203-624-5225 892-3256*
**Fax Area Code:* 800 ■ *TF:* 800-235-7482 ■ *Web:* www.assalock.com

ATCO Products Inc 189-V Frelinghuysen Ave .... Newark NJ 07114 973-242-5757 242-0131
Web: www.atcoproducts.com

Attwood Corp 1016 N Monroe St.......................... Lowell MI 49331 616-897-9241 897-8358
TF: 844-808-5704 ■ *Web:* www.attwoodmarine.com

Automotive Racing Products Inc
1863 Eastman Ave .... Ventura CA 93003 805-339-2200 650-0742
TF: 800-826-3045 ■ *Web:* www.arp-bolts.com

AWNEX Inc 260 Valley St Ste 100 .... Ball Ground GA 30107 770-704-7140
Web: www.awnexinc.com

Bad Dog Tools 24 Broadcommon Rd..................... Bristol RI 02809 401-253-1330
TF: 800-252-1330 ■ *Web:* baddogtools.com

Baden Steelbar & Bolt Corp
852 Big Sewickly Crk Rd R........................... Sewickley PA 15143 724-266-3003 266-1619
Web: www.badensteel.com

Baier Marine Company Inc 2920 Airway Ave........ Costa Mesa CA 92626 800-455-3917
TF: 800-455-3917 ■ *Web:* www.baiermarine.com

Baklund R&D LLC 13835 200th St .... Hutchinson MN 55350 320-587-0743
Web: www.baklund.com

Baldwin Hardware Corp 841 E Wyomissing Blvd .... Reading PA 19611 610-777-7811
TF: 800-566-1986 ■ *Web:* www.baldwinhardware.com

Band-It-IDEX Inc 4799 Dahlia St........................ Denver CO 80216 303-320-4555 333-6549
TF: 800-525-0758 ■ *Web:* www.band-it-idex.com

Barnhill Bolt Company Inc
2500 Princeton Dr Ne........................... Albuquerque NM 87107 505-884-1808
TF: 800-472-3900 ■ *Web:* www.barnhillbolt.com

Baron Mfg Company LLC 1200 Capitol Dr............. Addison IL 60101 630-628-9110 628-9141
TF: 800-368-8585 ■ *Web:* www.baronsnaps.com

Bay Standard Manufacturing Inc
24485 Marsh Creek Rd........................... Brentwood CA 94513 925-634-1181
Web: www.baystandard.com

Beacon Fasteners & Components
198 W Carpenter Ave .... Wheeling IL 60090 847-541-0404
Web: www.beaconfasteners.com

Becknell Wholesale I LP 504 E 44th St.............. Lubbock TX 79404 806-747-3201
Web: www.becknell.com

Belwith International Ltd
3100 Broadway Ave .... Grandville MI 49418 800-235-9484
TF: 800-235-9484 ■ *Web:* www.belwith.com

Berenson Corp 2495 Main St .... Buffalo NY 14214 716-833-2402
TF: 800-333-0578 ■ *Web:* www.berensonhardware.com

Best Access Systems 6161 E 75th St .... Indianapolis IN 46250 317-849-2250
TF: 855-365-2407 ■ *Web:* www.bestaccess.com

Bete Fog Nozzle Inc 50 Greenfield St............... Greenfield MA 01301 413-772-0846 772-6729
TF: 800-235-0049 ■ *Web:* www.bete.com

Blum Inc 7733 Old Plank Rd........................... Stanley NC 28164 704-827-1345 827-0799
TF: 800-438-6788 ■ *Web:* www.blum.com

Bomar Inc PO Box 1200........................ Charlestown NH 03603 603-826-5791 826-4125

Bommer Industries Inc PO Box 187 .... Landrum SC 29356 864-457-3301 457-2487
TF: 800-334-1654 ■ *Web:* www.bommer.com

Phone | Fax

Bostwick-Braun Co, The 7349 Crossleigh Ct .... Toledo OH 43617 419-259-3600
Web: www.bostwick-braun.com

Bourdon Forge Company Inc 99 Tuttle Rd .... Middletown CT 06457 860-632-2740 632-7247
Web: www.bourdonforge.com

Brainerd Mfg Company Inc
140 Business Pk Dr .... Winston-Salem NC 27107 336-769-4077
TF: 800-652-7277 ■ *Web:* www.libertyhardware.com

Bronze Craft Corp 37 Will St .... Nashua NH 03060 603-883-7747 883-0222
TF: 800-488-7747 ■ *Web:* www.bronzecraft.com

Bud K 475 Us Hwy 319 S .... Moultrie GA 31768 229-985-1667
Web: www.budk.com

Cal Fasteners Inc 4300 E Miraloma Ave .... Anaheim CA 92807 714-854-1715
Web: www.cfi1.com

Cal-Royal Products Inc
6605 Flotilla St .... City Of Commerce CA 90040 323-888-6601
TF: 800-876-9258 ■ *Web:* www.cal-royal.com

Cassidy-Tricker Industrial Sales
1608 Hwy 13 W .... Burnsville MN 55337 952-882-6338
Web: cassidytricker.com

Central Indiana Hardware Company Inc
9190 Corporation Dr .... Indianapolis IN 46256 317-558-5700
Web: www.cih-indy.com

CH Briggs Hardware Company Inc
2047 Kutztown Rd .... Reading PA 19605 610-929-6969
Web: www.chbriggs.com

Chamberlain Group 845 Larch Ave .... Elmhurst IL 60126 630-279-3600 530-6091
Web: www.chamberlaingroup.com

Charles Leonard Inc 145 Kennedy Dr .... Hauppauge NY 11788 631-273-6700 273-6777
TF: 800-999-7202 ■ *Web:* www.charlesleonard.com

Charles Leonard Western Inc
235 W 140th St .... Los Angeles CA 90061 310-715-7464
Web: clnational.com

Charles Mcmurray Co 2520 N Argyle Ave .... Fresno CA 93727 559-292-5751
Web: www.charlesmcmurray.com

Chicago Hardware & Fixture Co
9100 Parklane Ave .... Franklin Park IL 60131 847-455-6609 455-0012
Web: www.chicagohardware.com

Chicago Nut & Bolt Inc 150 Covington Dr .... Bloomingdale IL 60108 630-529-8600
TF: 888-529-8600 ■ *Web:* www.cnb-inc.com

Circle Bolt & Nut Company Inc
158 Pringle St .... Kingston PA 18704 570-718-6001
TF: 800-548-2658 ■ *Web:* circlebolt.com

Circor Aerospace Inc 2301 Wardlow Cir .... Corona CA 92880 951-270-6200
Web: www.circoraerospace.com

Clampco Products Inc 1743 Wall Rd .... Wadsworth OH 44281 330-336-8857
Web: clampco.com

Classic Brass Inc 2051 Stoneman Cir .... Lakewood NY 14750 716-763-1400
TF: 800-869-3173 ■ *Web:* www.classic-brass.com

Cloud-rider Designs Ltd 1260 Eighth Ave .... Regina SK S4R1C9 306-761-2119
TF: 800-632-1255 ■ *Web:* www.cloud-rider.com

Coast Tool Co 2099 edison ave .... San leandro CA 94577 510-569-1945
TF: 888-675-3737 ■ *Web:* www.coasttool.com

Cobra Anchors Corp 504 Mount-Laurel Ave .... Temple PA 19560 610-929-5764
Web: www.cobraanchors.com

Colonial Bronze Co 511 Winsted Rd .... Torrington CT 06790 860-489-9233 355-7903*
**Fax Area Code:* 800 ■ *TF All:* 800-355-7903 ■ *Web:* www.colonialbronze.com

Columbia River Knife & Tool Inc
18348 SW 126th Pl .... Tualatin OR 97062 503-685-5015
Web: www.crkt.com

Component Hardware Group Inc
1890 Swarthmore Ave .... Lakewood NJ 08701 732-363-4700 364-8110
TF: 800-526-3694 ■ *Web:* www.componenthardware.com

CompX International Inc 5430 LBJ Fwy Ste 1700 .... Dallas TX 75240 972-448-1400 448-1408
NYSE: CIX ■ *Web:* www.compx.com

Controlled Kinematics Inc
46740 Lakeview Blvd .... Fremont CA 94538 408-945-1616
Web: www.ckinematics.com

Cooper Hand Tools Inc 3535 Glenwood Ave .... Raleigh NC 27612 919-781-7200
Web: www.cooperhandtools.com

Corbin Russwin Inc 225 Episcopal Rd .... Berlin CT 06037 860-225-7411
TF: 800-438-1951 ■ *Web:* www.corbinrusswin.com

Cordova Bolt Inc 5601 Dolly Ave .... Buena Park CA 90621 714-739-7500
Web: www.cordovabolt.com

Craft Inc 1929 County St PO Box 3049 .... South Attleboro MA 02703 508-761-7917 399-7240
TF: 800-827-2388 ■ *Web:* craft-inc.myshopify.com

Crown Industrial 213 Michelle Ct .... San Francisco CA 94080 650-952-5150
Web: www.crown-industrial.com

Daemar Inc 861 Cranberry Ct .... Oakville ON L6L6J7 905-847-6500
TF: 800-387-7115 ■ *Web:* www.daemar.com

Dahl Bros Canada Ltd 2600 S Sheridan Way .... Mississauga ON L5J2M4 905-822-2330
TF: 800-268-5355 ■ *Web:* dahlvalve.com

Dayton Superior Corp 1125 Byers Rd .... Miamisburg OH 45342 937-866-0711
TF: 800-745-3700 ■ *Web:* www.daytonsuperior.com

DE-STA-CO 1025 Doris Rd .... Auburn Hills MI 48326 248-836-6700 836-6741*
**Fax:* Sales ■ *TF:* 888-337-8226 ■ *Web:* www.destaco.com

Desch Drive Technology Limited Partnership
240 Shearson Cres .... Cambridge ON N1T1J6 519-621-4560
Web: www.desch.de

Detmar Corp 2001 W Alexandrine Ave .... Detroit MI 48208 313-831-1155
Web: www.detmarcorp.com

Dixie Industries 3510 N Orchard Knob Ave .... Chattanooga TN 37406 423-698-3323
TF: 800-933-4943 ■ *Web:* cmforge.com

Dize Company Inc, The 1512 S Main St .... Winston-salem NC 27127 336-722-5181
Web: www.dizecompany.com

Dooley Enterprises Inc 1198 N Grove St Ste A .... Anaheim CA 92806 714-630-6436
Web: www.dooleyenterprises.com

Door Engineering & Mfg LLC 400 Cherry St .... Kasota MN 56050 507-931-6910
TF: 800-959-1352 ■ *Web:* www.doorengineering.com

DORMA Group North America Dorma Dr .... Reamstown PA 17567 717-336-3881 336-2106
TF: 800-523-8483 ■ *Web:* www.dorma.com

Dortronics Systems Inc
1668 Sag Harbor Tpke .... Sag Harbor NY 11963 631-725-0505
Web: www.dortronics.com

Doug Mockett & Company Inc 1915 Abalone Ave .... Torrance CA 90501 310-318-2491
TF: 800-523-1269 ■ *Web:* www.mockett.com

Driv-Lok Inc 1140 Park Ave .... Sycamore IL 60178 815-895-8161
Web: www.driv-lok.com

Drivekore Inc 101 Wesley Dr .... Mechanicsburg PA 17055 717-697-7440
TF: 800-382-1311 ■ *Web:* www.drivekore.com

Duo Fast Northeast 22 Tolland St .... East Hartford CT 06108 860-289-6861
TF: 888-399-5712

Dynamation Research Inc 2301 Pontius Ave .... Los Angeles CA 90064 310-477-1224
TF: 800-726-7997 ■ *Web:* www.dynamationresearch.com

East Teak Trading Group Inc 1106 Drake Rd .... Donalds SC 29638 864-379-2111 793-7835*
**Fax Area Code:* 360 ■ *TF:* 800-338-5636 ■ *Web:* www.eastteak.com

Eastern Co, The 112 Bridge St PO Box 460 .... Naugatuck CT 06770 203-729-2255 723-8653
NASDAQ: EML ■ *Web:* www.easterncompany.com

Eberhard Hardware Manufacturing Ltd
1523 Bellmill Rd .... Tillsonburg ON N4GOC9 519-688-3443
TF: 800-567-3344 ■ *Web:* www.eberhardcanada.com

Eberhard Mfg Co PO Box 368012 .... Cleveland OH 44149 440-238-9720 572-2732
TF: 800-334-6706 ■ *Web:* www.eberhard.com

ECA Medical Instruments Inc
1107 Tourmaline Dr .... Newbury Park CA 91320 805-376-2509
Web: www.ecamedical.com

Edgewood Building Supply Company Inc
1580 E Epler Ave .... Indianapolis IN 46227 317-786-9208
Web: www.edgewoodbuildingsupply.com

Eklind Tool Comany Inc 11040 King St .... Franklin Park IL 60131 847-994-8550
Web: www.eklindtool.net

Emka Inc 1961 Fulling Mill Rd .... Middletown PA 17057 717-986-1111
Web: www.emkausa.com

Emtek Products Inc
15250 Stafford St .... City of Industry CA 91744 626-961-0413 336-2812
TF: 800-356-2741 ■ *Web:* www.emtek.com

Engineered Products Co (EPCO)
601 Kelso St PO Box 108 .... Flint MI 48506 810-767-2050 767-5084
TF: 888-414-3726 ■ *Web:* www.epcohardware.com

Entagon Inc 9805 Vly View Rd .... Eden Prairie MN 55344 952-941-5305
Web: entagon.com

ER Wagner Mfg Company Inc 4611 N 32nd St .... Milwaukee WI 53209 414-871-5080 449-8228
TF: 800-558-5596 ■ *Web:* www.erwagner.com

Erie Bolt Corp 1325 Liberty St .... Erie PA 16502 814-456-4287
Web: www.ebcind.com

ESPE Mfg Company Inc 9220 Ivanhoe St .... Schiller Park IL 60176 847-678-8950 678-0253
TF Cust Svc: 800-367-3773 ■ *Web:* www.electricalinsulationguys.com

Fastbolt Corp 200 Louis St .... South Hackensack NJ 07606 201-440-9100
TF: 800-631-1980 ■ *Web:* www.fastboltcorp.com

Fastenal Company Caok 5130 N Hwy 167 .... Catoosa OK 74015 918-266-8954
Web: fastenal.com

Faultless Caster 3438 Briley Pk Blvd N .... Nashville TN 37207 800-322-7359 322-9329
TF Cust Svc: 800-322-7359 ■ *Web:* www.faultlesscaster.com

Folger Adam Security Inc 4634 S Presa St .... San Antonio TX 78223 210-533-1231 533-2211
TF: 888-745-0530 ■ *Web:* www.southernfolger.com

Fortune Brands Home & Hardware Inc
520 Lk Cook Rd .... Deerfield IL 60015 847-484-4400
Web: www.fbhs.com

Freud America Inc 218 Feld Ave .... High Point NC 27263 336-434-3171
TF: 800-334-4107 ■ *Web:* www.freudtools.com

Fulton Corp 303 Eigth Ave .... Fulton IL 61252 800-252-0002 589-4433*
**Fax Area Code:* 815 ■ *TF:* 800-252-0002 ■ *Web:* www.fultoncorp.com

G G Schmitt & Sons Inc 2821 Old Tree Dr .... Lancaster PA 17603 717-394-3701 291-9739
TF: 866-724-6488 ■ *Web:* www.ggschmitt.com

Garelick Manufacturing Co
644 Second St .... Saint Paul Park MN 55071 651-459-9795
Web: www.garelick.com

Genie Co 1 Door Dr PO Box 67 .... Mount Hope OH 44660 800-354-3643
TF: 800-354-3643 ■ *Web:* www.geniecompany.com

Georg Fischer LLC 2882 Dow Ave .... Tustin CA 92780 714-731-8800
Web: gfps.com/content/gfps/country_us.html

Grabber Construction Products Inc
20 West Main St Ct Ste 200 .... Alpine UT 84004 925-680-0777
Web: www.grabberman.com

Granite Security Products Inc
4801 Esco Dr .... Fort Worth TX 76140 469-735-4901
TF: 877-948-6723 ■ *Web:* www.winchestersafes.com

Grass America Inc 1202 Hwy 66 S .... Kernersville NC 27284 800-334-3512
TF: 800-334-3512 ■ *Web:* www.grassusa.com

Gray Tools Canada Inc 299 Orenda Rd .... Brampton ON L6T1E8 905-457-3014 457-1050
Web: www.graytools.com

Great Lakes Power Products Inc
7455 Tyler Blvd .... Mentor OH 44060 440-951-5111
Web: www.glpower.com

H & B Mechanical Inc 111 Cal Ave .... Barstow CA 92311 760-256-8401

H & C Tool Supply Corp 235 Mount Read Blvd .... Rochester NY 14611 585-235-5700
TF: 800-323-4624 ■ *Web:* www.hctoolsupply.com

H & L Advantage Inc 3500 Busch Dr SW .... Grandville MI 49418 616-532-1012
Web: hladvantage.com

HA Guden Company Inc 99 Raynor Ave .... Ronkonkoma NY 11779 631-737-2900 737-2933
TF: 800-344-6437 ■ *Web:* www.guden.com

Hager Co 139 Victor St .... Saint Louis MO 63104 314-772-4400 782-0149*
**Fax Area Code:* 800 ■ **Fax:* Sales ■ *TF:* 800-325-9995 ■ *Web:* www.hagerco.com

Halex Corp 750 S Reservoir St .... Pomona CA 91766 909-622-3537
TF: 800-576-1636 ■ *Web:* www.halexcorp.com

Hamilton Caster & Manufacturing Co
1637 Dixie Hwy .... Hamilton OH 45011 513-863-3300 863-5508
Web: www.hamiltoncaster.com

Hampton Products International Corp
50 Icon .... Foothill Ranch CA 92610 949-472-4256
TF: 800-562-5625 ■ *Web:* www.hamptonproducts.com

Hardware Sales Inc 2034 James St .... Bellingham WA 98225 360-734-6140
Web: www.hardwaresales.net

Hartwell Corp 900 Richfield Rd .... Placentia CA 92870 714-993-4200 579-4419
Web: www.hartwellcorp.com

Company	City	State	Zip	Phone	Fax
Helton Industries Ltd 30840 Peardonville Rd — *TF:* 877-300-7412 ■ *Web:* www.heltonindustries.com	Abbotsford	BC	V2T6K2	604-854-3660	
Hi Tech Seals Inc 9211-41 Ave — *TF:* 800-661-6055 ■ *Web:* www.hitechseals.com	Edmonton	AB	T6E6R5	780-438-6055	434-5866
Highland Threads Inc 11700 Gloger St — *Web:* www.highlandthreads.com	Houston	TX	77039	281-986-5100	986-5151
Hindley Mfg Company Inc 9 Havens St — *TF:* 800-323-9031 ■ *Web:* www.hindley.com	Cumberland	RI	02864	401-722-2550	722-3083
HL-A Company Inc 902 Ravenwood Dr — *Web:* www.hla.com.my	Selma	AL	36701	334-874-9010	
HMC Holdings LLC 1605 Old Rt 18 Ste 4-36	Wampum	PA	16157	724-535-1080	
Hoppe North America Inc 205 E Blackhawk Dr — *Web:* www.us.hoppe.com	Fort Atkinson	WI	53538	920-563-2626	
Hudson Lock Inc 81 Apsley St — **Fax Area Code:* 978 ■ *TF:* 800-434-8960 ■ *Web:* www.hudsonlock.com	Hudson	MA	01749	800-434-8960	562-9859*
Hydraflow Inc 1881 W Malvern Ave — *Web:* hydraflow.com	Fullerton	CA	92833	714-773-2600	773-6351
Ideal Pipe Ltd Box 100 - 1100 Ideal Dr — *Web:* www.idealpipe.ca	Thorndale	ON	N0M2P0	519-473-2669	
Imperial Carbide Inc 10826 Mercer Pk — *Web:* www.imperialcarbide.com	Meadville	PA	16335	814-724-3732	
Industrial Nut Corp 1425 Tiffin Ave — *Web:* www.industrialnut.com	Sandusky	OH	44870	419-625-8543	
Ingenium Aerospace LLC 5389 International Dr — *Web:* www.ingeniumaerospace.com	Rockford	IL	61109	815-525-2000	
Inpower LLC 3555 Africa Rd — *TF:* 866-548-0965 ■ *Web:* www.inpowerdirect.com	Galena	OH	43021	740-548-0965	
Intermotive Inc 986 S Canyon Way — *Web:* www.intermotive.net	Colfax	CA	95713	530-346-1801	
Inventory Sales Co 9777 Reavis Rd — *TF:* 866-417-3801 ■ *Web:* www.inventorysales.com	St Louis	MO	63123	314-776-6200	
Isoflux Inc 10 Vantage Point Dr Ste 4 — *Web:* www.isofluxinc.com	Rochester	NY	14624	585-349-0640	
Jacknob Corp 290 Oser Ave PO Box 18032 — *TF:* 800-424-7495 ■ *Web:* www.jacknob.com	Hauppauge	NY	11788	631-546-6560	231-0330
Jacob Holtz Co 10 Industrial Hwy MS-6 Airport Business Complex B — *TF:* 800-445-4337 ■ *Web:* www.jacobholtz.com	Lester	PA	19029	215-423-2800	634-7454
James L Howard & Company Inc 10 Britton Dr — *Web:* www.jameslhoward.com	Bloomfield	CT	06002	860-242-3581	
Jarvis Caster Co 881 Lower Brownsville Rd — *TF:* 800-995-9876 ■ *Web:* www.jarviscaster.com	Jackson	TN	38301	800-995-9876	
Jiffy-tite Company Inc 4437 Walden Ave — *Web:* www.jiffy-tite.com	Lancaster	NY	14086	716-681-7200	
Job Shop Managers 28966 Hancock Pkwy — *Web:* www.skmindustries.com	Valencia	CA	91355	661-294-8373	
Jonathan Engineered Solutions 410 Exchange St Ste 200 — *Web:* www.jonathanengr.com	Irvine	CA	92602	714-665-4400	368-7002
Kaba Ilco Corp 400 Jeffreys Rd — *TF:* 800-334-1381 ■ *Web:* www.kaba-ilco.com	Rocky Mount	NC	27804	252-446-3321	446-4702
Kaba Mas 749 W Short St — *Web:* www.mas-hamilton.com	Lexington	KY	40508	859-253-4744	
Kanebridge Corp 153 Bauer Dr — *TF:* 888-222-9221 ■ *Web:* www.kanebridge.com	Oakland	NJ	07436	201-337-2300	
Kason Industries Inc 57 Amlajack Blvd — *TF:* 800-935-3550 ■ *Web:* www.kasonind.com	Newnan	GA	30265	770-304-3000	251-4854
Keystone Electronics Corp 31-07 20th Rd — *TF:* 800-221-5510 ■ *Web:* www.keyelco.com	Astoria	NY	11105	718-956-8900	956-9040
Knape & Vogt Manufacturing Co 2700 Oak Industrial Dr NE — *TF:* 800-253-1561 ■ *Web:* www.knapeandvogt.com	Grand Rapids	MI	49505	616-459-3311	459-3290
Kw Automotive North Americaine 1075 N Ave — *Web:* www.kwsuspensions.com	Sanger	CA	93657	559-875-0222	
Larson Hardware Manufacturing Co PO Box E — *Web:* www.larsonhardware.com	Sterling	IL	61081	815-625-0503	625-8786
LE Johnson Products Inc 2100 Sterling Ave — *TF:* 800-837-5664 ■ *Web:* www.johnsonhardware.com	Elkhart	IN	46516	574-293-5664	294-4697
Le Smith Co 1030 E Wilson St PO Box 766 — *TF:* 888-537-6484 ■ *Web:* www.lesmith.com	Bryan	OH	43506	419-636-4555	
Liberty Hardware Mfg Corp 140 Business Pk Dr — **Fax Area Code:* 336 ■ *TF:* 800-542-3789 ■ *Web:* www.libertyhardware.com	Winston-Salem	NC	27107	800-542-3789	769-1839*
Lockmasters Security Institute 2101 John C Watts Dr — *TF:* 800-654-0637 ■ *Web:* www.lockmasters.com	Nicholasville	KY	40356	859-885-6041	
Magnus Mobility Systems Inc 1912 Wbusiness Ctr Dr — *Web:* www.magnusinc.com	Orange	CA	92867	714-771-2630	
Mansfield Industries Inc 1776 Harrington Memorial Rd — *Web:* mansfieldec.com	Mansfield	OH	44903	419-524-1300	
Master Lock Company LLC 137 W Forest Hill Ave PO Box 927 — *TF:* 800-464-2088 ■ *Web:* www.masterlock.com	Oak Creek	WI	53154	800-464-2088	308-9245
Medeco Security Locks Inc 3625 Alleghany Dr — **Fax Area Code:* 800 ■ *TF:* 800-839-3157 ■ *Web:* www.medeco.com	Salem	VA	24153	540-380-5000	421-6615*
Metabo Corp 1231 Wilson Dr — *Web:* metabo.us	West Chester	PA	19380	610-436-5900	
Milan Tool Corp 8989 Brookpark Rd — *Web:* www.milantool.com	Cleveland	OH	44129	216-661-1078	
MJL Enterprises LLC 2748 Sonic Dr — *Web:* www.mjl-enterprises.com	Virginia Beach	VA	23453	757-963-8740	
Mountz Inc 1080 N 11th St — *TF:* 888-925-2763 ■ *Web:* www.mountztorque.com	San Jose	CA	95112	408-292-2214	
Murray Corp 260 Schilling Cir — *Web:* www.murraycorp.com	Hunt Valley	MD	21031	410-771-0380	771-5576
MW Mcwong International Inc 1921 Arena Blvd	West Sacramento	CA	95834	916-371-8080	
Nagel Chase Inc 2323 Delaney Rd — *TF:* 800-323-4552 ■ *Web:* www.paysoncasters.com	Gurnee	IL	60031	800-323-4552	
Nik-O-Lok Co 3130 N Mitthoeffer Rd — *TF:* 800-428-4348 ■ *Web:* www.nikolok.com	Indianapolis	IN	46235	317-899-6955	899-6977
Norshield Corp 3232 Mobile Hwy — *TF:* 855-859-3716 ■ *Web:* www.norshield.net	Montgomery	AL	36108	334-551-0650	
Norton Industries Inc 20670 Corsair Blvd — *Web:* nortonclamps.com	Hayward	CA	94545	510-786-3638	786-3082
NYC Dot 50 21st St	Brooklyn	NY	11232	718-965-3539	
OceanWorks International Inc 11611 Tanner Rd Ste A — *Web:* www.oceanworks.com	Houston	TX	77041	281-598-3940	
OMG Inc 153 Bowles Rd — *Web:* www.omgroofing.com	Agawam	MA	01001	413-789-0252	
Omnia Industries Inc Cedar Grove Plant 5 Cliffside Dr — *Web:* www.omniaindustries.com	Cedar Grove	NJ	07009	973-239-7272	
Otto Dukes Construction Supply Solutions 2556 Agnes St — *Web:* www.ottodukestools.com	Corpus Christi	TX	78405	361-883-0921	
P M Industrial Supply Co 9613 Canoga Ave — *TF:* 800-382-3684 ■ *Web:* www.pmindustrial.com	Chatsworth	CA	91311	818-341-9180	
Paneloc Corp PO Box 547 — *TF:* 800-394-6711 ■ *Web:* www.paneloc.com	Farmington	CT	06034	860-677-6711	677-8606
ParkDistributors Inc 347 Railroad Ave — *Web:* www.parkdistributors.com	Bridgeport	CT	06604	203-366-7200	
Payson Casters Inc 2323 N Delaney Rd — *TF:* 800-323-4552 ■ *Web:* www.paysoncasters.com	Gurnee	IL	60031	847-336-6200	782-0158
PCA Aerospace Inc 17800 Gothard St — *Web:* www.pcaaerospace.com	Huntington Beach	CA	92647	714-841-1750	
PDQ Manufacturing 2754 Creek Hill Rd — *TF:* 800-441-9692 ■ *Web:* www.pdqlocks.com	Leola	PA	17540	717-656-4281	
PE Guerin Inc 23 Jane St — *Web:* www.peguerin.com	New York	NY	10014	212-243-5270	727-2290
Peco Fasteners Inc 1218 Six Flags Rd — *Web:* www.thesefa.com	Austell	GA	30168	770-745-1300	
Perko Inc 16490 NW 13th Ave — *Web:* www.perko.com	Miami	FL	33169	305-621-7525	620-9978
PL Porter Co 3000 Winona Ave — *TF:* 888-236-5165 ■ *Web:* www.craneae.com	Burbank	CA	91504	818-526-2600	842-6117
Polar Hardware Manufacturing Co 1813 W Montrose Ave — *Web:* www.polarmfg.com	Chicago	IL	60613	773-935-8600	935-8749
PolyPortables Inc 99 Crafton Dr — *Web:* www.polyportables.com	Dahlonega	GA	30533	706-864-3776	
Prime-Line Products Inc 26950 San Bernardino Ave — *Web:* primeline.net	Redlands	CA	92374	909-887-8118	
Process Development & Control Inc 1075 Montour W Industrial Park — *Web:* www.pdcvalve.com	Coraopolis	PA	15108	724-695-3440	
Prospect Fastener Corp 1295 Kyle Ct — *Web:* www.prospectfastener.com	Wauconda	IL	60084	847-526-2950	
Purdy Corp 101 Prospect Ave — *TF:* 800-547-0780 ■ *Web:* www.purdy.com	Cleveland	OH	44115	800-547-0780	
Qual-Craft Industries PO Box 559 — *TF:* 800-231-5647 ■ *Web:* www.qualcraft.com	Stoughton	MA	02072	781-344-1000	
Railway Specialties Corp 2979 State Rd — *Web:* www.railwayspecialties.com	Croydon	PA	19021	215-788-9242	
Renovator's Supply Inc Renovators Old ML — *TF:* 800-659-2211 ■ *Web:* www.rensup.com	Millers Falls	MA	01349	413-423-3300	423-3800
Riback Supply Co 2412 Business Loop 70 E PO Box 937 — *Web:* www.riback.com	Columbia	MO	65205	573-875-3131	449-8738
Robert H Peterson Co 14724 Proctor Ave — *Web:* www.rhpeterson.com	City Of Industry	CA	91746	626-369-5085	
Rockford Process Control Inc 2020 Seventh St — *TF:* 800-228-3779 ■ *Web:* rockfordprocess.com	Rockford	IL	61104	815-966-2000	966-2026
Rockwood Manufacturing Co 300 Main St — *Web:* www.rockwoodmfg.com	Rockwood	PA	15557	814-926-2026	
Rocky Mountain Hardware Inc 1020 Airport Way PO Box 4108 — *TF:* 888-788-2013 ■ *Web:* www.rockymountainhardware.com	Hailey	ID	83333	208-788-2013	788-2577
Rohrback Cosasco Systems Inc 11841 E Smith Ave — *Web:* cosasco.com	Santa Fe Springs	CA	90670	562-949-0123	
Roll Master 920 Schriewer — *Web:* www.roll-master.com	Seguin	TX	78155	830-386-0991	
Rousseau Metal Inc 105 Ave De Gasp Ouest — *TF:* 866-463-4270 ■ *Web:* www.rousseaumetal.com	St Jean-Port-Joli	QC	G0R3G0	418-598-3381	598-6776
Routeware Inc 16575 SW 72nd Ave — *Web:* www.routeware.com	Portland	OR	97224	503-906-8500	
Rutherford Controls Int'l Corp 210 Shearson Crescent — *TF:* 800-265-6630 ■ *Web:* www.rutherfordcontrols.com	Cambridge	ON	N1T1J6	519-621-7651	
RWM Casters Co PO Box 668 — **Fax Area Code:* 704 ■ *TF:* 800-634-7704 ■ *Web:* www.rwmcasters.com	Gastonia	NC	28053	800-634-7704	868-4205*
S Parker Hardware Manufacturing Corp PO Box 9882 — *TF:* 800-772-7537 ■ *Web:* www.sparker.com	Englewood	NJ	07631	201-569-1600	569-1082
Safemark Systems LP 2101 Park Ctr Dr Ste 125 — *Web:* www.safemark.com	Orlando	FL	32835	407-299-0044	
Salice America Inc 2123 Crown Centre Dr — *TF:* 800-222-9652 ■ *Web:* www.saliceamerica.com	Charlotte	NC	28227	704-841-7810	
Sandy Valley Fasteners LLC 528 Broadway St — *Web:* www.sandyvalleyfasteners.com	Paintsville	KY	41240	606-788-0222	

	City	State	Zip	Phone	Fax
Sargent & Greenleaf Inc 1 Security Dr *TF:* 800-826-7652 ■ *Web:* www.sargentandgreenleaf.com	Nicholasville	KY	40356	859-885-9411	885-3063
Sargent Manufacturing Co 100 Sargent Dr *TF:* 800-727-5477 ■ *Web:* www.sargentlock.com	New Haven	CT	06511	800-727-5477	
Saturn Fasteners Inc 425 S Varney St *TF:* 800-947-9414 ■ *Web:* www.saturnfasteners.com	Burbank	CA	91502	818-846-7145	
Savant Manufacturing Inc 2930 Hwy 383 PO Box 520 *TF:* 800-326-6880 ■ *Web:* www.savantmfg.com	Kinder	LA	70648	337-738-5896	738-3215
Seastrom Mfg Company Inc 456 Seastrom St *TF:* 800-634-2356 ■ *Web:* www.seastrom-mfg.com	Twin Falls	ID	83301	208-737-4300	
Sebewaing Tool & Engineering Co 415 Union St *TF:* 800-453-2207 ■ *Web:* sebewaingtool.com	Sebewaing	MI	48759	989-883-2000	
Securitron Magnalock Corp 10027 S 51st St Ste 102 **Fax Area Code:* 866 ■ *TF Sales:* 800-624-5625 ■ *Web:* www.securitron.com	Phoenix	AZ	85044	623-582-4626	582-4641*
Security Door Controls Inc 801 Avenida Acaso *Web:* www.sdcsecurity.com	Camarillo	CA	93012	805-494-0622	
Selby Furniture Hardware Company Inc 321 Rider Ave *Web:* www.selbyhardware.com	Bronx	NY	10451	718-993-3700	993-3143
Shepherd Caster Corp 203 Kerth St *TF:* 800-253-0868 ■ *Web:* www.shepherdcasters.com	Saint Joseph	MI	49085	269-983-7351	
Shepherd's Home Hardware Ltd 3525 Mill St *Web:* www.shepherdshardware.com	Armstrong	BC	V0E1B0	250-546-3002	
Sherwood Windows Ltd 37 Iron St *TF:* 800-770-5256 ■ *Web:* www.sherwoodwindows.com	Toronto	ON	M9W5E3	416-675-3262	
Signature Hardware 2700 Crescent Springs Pike *TF:* 866-855-2284 ■ *Web:* www.signaturehardware.com	Erlanger	KY	41017	859-647-7564	431-4012
Simpson Strong-Tie Company Inc 5956 W Las Positas Blvd *TF:* 800-925-5099 ■ *Web:* www.strongtie.com	Pleasanton	CA	94588	925-560-9000	847-1597
Smith Fastener Co 3613 Florence Ave *Web:* smithfast.com	Bell	CA	90201	323-587-0382	
Southco Inc 210 N Brinton Lk Rd PO Box 0116 *Web:* www.southco.com	Concordville	PA	19331	610-459-4000	459-4012
Spalding Hardware Ltd 1616 10 Ave SW *TF:* 800-837-0850 ■ *Web:* spaldinghardware.com	Calgary	AB	T3C0J5	800-837-0850	
Spokane Hardware Supply Inc 2001 E Trent Ave *TF:* 800-888-1663 ■ *Web:* www.spokane-hardware.com	Spokane	WA	99202	509-535-1663	
Staples National Advantage 21 S Middlesex Ave *Web:* www.staples.com	Monroe Township	NJ	08831	609-395-1400	
Starborn Industries Inc 45 Mayfield Ave *Web:* www.starbornindustries.com	Edison	NJ	08837	732-381-9800	
Storm Industries Inc & Affiliated Co 23223 Normandie Ave *Web:* stormind.com	Torrance	CA	90501	310-534-5232	
Storms Welding & Manufacturing Inc 513 W Lake St S PO Box 76 *Web:* stormsweldingmfg.com	Cologne	MN	55322	952-466-3343	
Suncor Stainless Inc 70 Armstrong Rd *TF:* 800-218-7702 ■ *Web:* suncorstainless.com	Plymouth	MA	02360	508-732-9191	
Sunex International Inc 100 Roe Rd *TF:* 800-833-7869 ■ *Web:* www.sunextools.com	Travelers Rest	SC	29690	864-834-8759	
Superior Metal Products 713 Maple St *Web:* amtrim.com	Wapakoneta	OH	45895	419-739-4401	
SW Anderson Co 2425 Wisconsin Ave *Web:* swaco.com	Downers Grove	IL	60515	630-964-2600	
Swissomation Inc 112 Marschall Creek Rd *Web:* www.swissomation.com	Fredericksburg	TX	78624	830-997-6565	
Tepro Inc 590 Baxter Ln *Web:* www.tepro.com	Winchester	TN	37398	931-967-5189	
Tides Marine Inc 3251 SW 13th Dr *TF:* 800-420-0949 ■ *Web:* tidesmarine.com	Deerfield Beach	FL	33442	954-420-0949	
Tiffin Metal Products Co 450 Wall St *TF:* 800-537-0983 ■ *Web:* www.tiffinmetal.com	Tiffin	OH	44883	800-537-0983	
Tompkins Industries Inc 1912 E 123rd St *Web:* www.tompkinsind.com	Olathe	KS	66061	913-764-8088	
TriLink Saw Chain LLC 4400 Commerce Cir *Web:* www.trilinksawchain.com	Atlanta	GA	30336	404-419-2900	
Trimark Corp PO Box 350 *TF:* 800-447-0343 ■ *Web:* www.trimarkcorp.com	New Hampton	IA	50659	641-394-3188	
Trimco/Builders Brass Works 3528 Emery St *TF:* 800-637-8746 ■ *Web:* www.trimcobbw.com	Los Angeles	CA	90023	323-262-4191	264-7214
Truth Hardware Inc 700 W Bridge St **Fax:* Cust Svc ■ *TF Cust Svc:* 800-866-7884 ■ *Web:* www.truth.com	Owatonna	MN	55060	507-451-5620	451-5655*
TS Distributors Inc 4404 Windfern Rd *TF:* 800-392-3655 ■ *Web:* www.tsdistributors.com	Houston	TX	77041	832-467-5400	467-5454
Unicorp 291 Cleveland St *TF:* 800-526-1389 ■ *Web:* www.unicorpinc.com	Orange	NJ	07050	973-674-1700	674-3803
United Rotorcraft Solutions LLC 1942 N Trinity St *Web:* www.airmethods.com	Decatur	TX	76234	940-627-0626	
Universal Tool Company Inc 33 Rose Pl	Springfield	MA	01104	413-732-4807	
Urania Engineering Company Inc 198 S Poplar St *Web:* www.uraniaeng.com	Hazleton	PA	18201	570-455-7531	
Velko Hinge Inc 9325 Kennedy Ct *Web:* www.velko.com	Munster	IN	46321	219-924-6363	
Voss Industries Inc 2168 W 25th St *Web:* www.vossind.com	Cleveland	OH	44113	216-771-7655	771-2887
Vulcan Threaded Products 10 Crosscreek Trl *Web:* vulc.com	Pelham	AL	35124	205-620-5100	
Watts Industries (Canada) Inc 5435 N Service Rd *Web:* www.wattscanada.ca	Burlington	ON	L7L5H7	905-332-4090	
Weber-Knapp Co 441 Chandler St *TF:* 800-828-9254 ■ *Web:* www.weberknapp.com	Jamestown	NY	14701	716-484-9135	484-9142
Weiser Lock A Masco Co 19701 Da Vinci *TF:* 800-677-5625 ■ *Web:* www.weiserlock.com	Lake Forest	CA	92610	800-677-5625	
Wharton Hardware & Supply 7724 N Crescent Blvd *Web:* www.whartonhardware.com	Pennsauken	NJ	08110	856-662-6935	
Whiteside Manufacturing Company Inc 309 Hayes St *Web:* www.whitesidemfg.com	Delaware	OH	43015	740-363-1179	
Wolverine Coil Spring Co 818 Front Ave NW *Web:* www.wolverinecoilspring.com	Grand Rapids	MI	49504	616-459-3504	
Woodbury Box Company Inc 301 Mcintosh Pkwy *TF:* 800-722-2061 ■ *Web:* www.chiefmanufacturing.net	Thomaston	GA	30286	800-722-2061	
Wright Tool Company Inc 1 Wright Dr *TF:* 800-321-2902 ■ *Web:* www.wrighttool.com	Barberton	OH	44203	330-848-0600	
Yale Residential Security Products Inc 100 Yale Ave *TF Cust Svc:* 800-438-1951 ■ *Web:* www.yaleresidential.com	Lenoir City	TN	37771	800-438-1951	
Yale Security Inc.ÿ 1902 Airport Rd *TF:* 800-438-1951 ■ *Web:* www.yaleresidential.com	Monroe	NC	28110	800-438-1951	338-0965
Yardley Products Corp 10 W College Ave *TF:* 800-457-0154 ■ *Web:* www.yardleyproducts.com	Yardley	PA	19067	215-493-2723	493-6796

351 HARDWARE - WHOL

	City	State	Zip	Phone	Fax
Aarch Caster & Equipment 314 Axminister Dr *TF:* 888-349-0220 ■ *Web:* www.aarchcaster.com	Fenton	MO	63026	636-349-0220	
Ace Bolt & Screw Co 200 Brooklyn Ave	San Antonio	TX	78215	210-226-0244	226-5037
Action Bolt & Tool Co (WURTH) 2051 E Blue Heron Blvd *TF:* 800-423-0700 ■ *Web:* www.actionboltandtool.com	Riviera Beach	FL	33404	561-845-8800	845-0255
Action Fasteners 265 Edinburgh Dr *Web:* www.actionfasteners.com	Moncton	NB	E1E2K9	506-857-8950	
Adtec Digital 408 Russell St *Web:* www.adtecdigital.com	Nashville	TN	37206	615-256-6619	
Aero-Space Southwest Inc 21450 N Third Ave *TF:* 800-289-2779 ■ *Web:* www.aerospacesw.com	Phoenix	AZ	85027	623-582-2779	
All State Fastener Corp 15460 E 12 Mile Rd *Web:* www.allstatefastener.com	Roseville	MI	48066	586-773-5400	
All-Pro Fasteners Inc 1916 Peyco Dr N *TF:* 800-361-6627 ■ *Web:* www.all-profasteners.com	Arlington	TX	76001	817-467-5700	467-5365
Allied International 13207 Bradley Ave *TF General:* 800-533-8333 ■ *Web:* www.alliedtools.com	Sylmar	CA	91342	818-364-2333	
Associated Steel Corp 18200 Miles Rd **Fax Area Code:* 216 ■ *TF:* 800-321-9300 ■ *Web:* www.associatedsteel.com	Cleveland	OH	44128	800-321-9300	475-6067*
Baer Supply Co 909 Forest Edge Dr *TF:* 800-944-2237 ■ *Web:* www.baersupply.com	Vernon Hills	IL	60061	847-913-2237	913-2230
Bargain Supply Co 844 E Jefferson St *TF:* 800-322-5226 ■ *Web:* www.bargainsupply.com	Louisville	KY	40206	502-562-5000	562-5051
Barnett Inc 801 W Bay St *TF:* 888-803-4467 ■ *Web:* www.e-barnett.com	Jacksonville	FL	32204	904-384-6530	
Bashlin Industries Inc PO Box 867 *Web:* www.bashlin.com	Grove City	PA	16127	724-458-8340	458-8342
Behringer Saws Inc 721 Hemlock Rd *Web:* www.behringersaws.com	Morgantown	PA	19543	610-286-9777	
Better Home Products Ltd 534 Eccles Ave *Web:* www.betterhomeproducts.com	South San Francisco	CA	94080	650-827-9270	
Blish-Mize Co 223 S Fifth St *TF:* 800-995-0525 ■ *Web:* www.blishmize.com	Atchison	KS	66002	913-367-1250	367-0667
Block Iron & Supply Co Po Box 557 *Web:* www.blockiron.com	Oshkosh	WI	54903	920-231-8645	
Bolt Products Inc 16725 E Johnson Dr *Web:* www.boltproducts.com	City Of Industry	CA	91745	626-961-4401	
Bostwick-Braun Co PO Box 912 *TF:* 800-777-9640 ■ *Web:* bostwick-braun.com	Toledo	OH	43697	419-259-3600	259-3959
Buckeye Tools & Supply Company Inc 400 Gargrave Rd *Web:* www.buckeyetools.com	Dayton	OH	45449	937-847-8888	
Builders Hardware & Supply Company Inc 1516 15th Ave W *TF:* 800-828-1437 ■ *Web:* www.builders-hardware.com	Seattle	WA	98119	206-281-3700	281-3747
Bunting Door & Hardware Co 9351G Philadelphia Rd *Web:* www.buntingdoor.com	Baltimore	MD	21237	410-574-8123	
Burgess Sales & Supply Inc 2121 W Morehead St *Web:* www.burgesssales.com	Charlotte	NC	28208	704-333-8933	
Carson's Nut-Bolt & Tool Co 301 Hammett St Ext *Web:* www.carsons-nbt.com	Greenville	SC	29609	864-242-4720	
Cascade Wholesale Hardware Inc 5650 NW *TF General:* 800-877-9987 ■ *Web:* www.cascade.com	Hillsboro	OR	97124	503-614-2600	629-5793
Casey Products 11230 Katherine Xing Ste 400 *Web:* www.caseyproducts.com	Woodridge	IL	60517	630-960-3360	
Caster Technology Corp 11552 Markon Dr *TF:* 866-547-8090 ■ *Web:* www.castertech.com	Garden Grove	CA	92841	714-893-6886	
Charter Industries 2255 29th St S E *Web:* www.charterindustries.com	Grand Rapids	MI	49508	616-245-3388	
Colorado Fasteners and Specialty Tools Inc 570 Turner Dr Ste C *Web:* www.coloradofasteners.com	Durango	CO	81303	970-749-2992	
Commando Products Inc 420A Blue Ridge Ext *Web:* www.commandoproducts.com	Grandview	MO	64030	816-966-8889	
Compatico Inc 4710 44th St SE *TF:* 800-336-1772 ■ *Web:* www.compatico.com	Grand Rapids	MI	49512	616-940-1772	
Concept Electronics Inc 6243 Renoir Ave *Web:* www.ceibr.com	Baton Rouge	LA	70806	225-927-8614	

Phone | Fax

Conveyer & Caster Corp 3501 Detroit Ave .... Cleveland OH 44113 216-631-4448
TF: 800-777-0600 ■ *Web:* www.cc-efi.com

Custom Stud Inc 8415 220th St W .... Lakeville MN 55044 952-985-7000
Web: www.customstud.com

Delta Fastener Corp 7122 Old Katy Rd ....Houston TX 77024 713-868-2351
Web: www.deltafastener.com

Denver Wire Rope & Supply Inc 4100 Dahlia St ....Denver CO 80216 303-377-5166
TF: 800-873-3697 ■ *Web:* denverwirerope.com

Desoto Sales Inc 20945 Osborne St............... Canoga Park CA 91304 818-998-0853 998-7542
TF: 800-826-9779 ■ *Web:* www.desotosales.com

Deutscher & Daughter Inc 10507 150th St. ....Jamaica NY 11435 718-291-5600
Web: www.dddoors.com

Digi-Trax Corp 650 Heathrow Dr .... Lincolnshire IL 60069 847-613-2100
Web: www.americanrealtybrokers.com

Dixie Construction Products Inc
970 Huff Rd NW ....Atlanta GA 30318 404-351-1100 350-2359
TF: 800-992-1180 ■ *Web:* www.dixieconstruction.com

Do it Best Corp 6502 Nelson Ave .... Fort Wayne IN 46803 260-748-5300
Web: www.doitbest.com

Earnest Machine Products Co 12502 Plz Dr......... Cleveland OH 44130 216-362-1100 362-9970
TF: 800-327-6378 ■ *Web:* www.earnestmachine.com

EB Bradley Co 5080 S Alameda St.................Los Angeles CA 90058 323-585-9201 585-5414
TF: 800-533-3030 ■ *Web:* www.ebbradley.com

Emhart Teknologies Inc
50 Shelton Technology Ctr PO Box 859................ Shelton CT 06484 203-924-9341 925-3109
Web: www.stanleyengineeredfastening.com

Excelta Corp 60 Easy St............................Buellton CA 93427 805-686-4686
Web: www.excelta.com

Fastec Industrial
2219 Eddie Williams Rd ....Johnson City TN 37601 800-837-2505 975-2544*
*Fax Area Code: 423 ■ *TF:* 800-837-2505 ■ *Web:* www.fastecindustrial.com

Fastenal Co 2001 Theurer Blvd .... Winona MN 55987 507-454-5374 453-8049
NASDAQ: FAST ■ *TF:* 877-507-7555 ■ *Web:* www.fastenal.com

Faucet Queens Inc 650 Forest Edge Dr .... Vernon Hills IL 60061 847-478-2800 821-0277
Web: faucetqueen.com

Frost Cutlery Company LLC 6861 Mtn View Rd .... Ooltewah TN 37363 423-894-6079
Web: www.frostcutlery.com

Fry Fastening Systems 2150 Waycross Rd .... Cincinnati OH 45240 513-851-2233
Web: www.frysys.com

General Fasteners Co 37584 Amrhein Rd Ste 150 .... Livonia MI 48150 734-452-2400 452-2257
TF: 800-945-2658 ■ *Web:* www.genfast.com

Handy Hardware Wholesale Inc
8300 Tewantin Dr ....Houston TX 77061 713-644-1495
TF: 800-364-3835 ■ *Web:* www.handyhardware.com

Hans Johnsen Co 8901 Chancellor Row................... Dallas TX 75247 214-879-1550 879-1520
TF Sales: 800-879-1515 ■ *Web:* www.hjc.com

Harbor Freight Tools
3491 Mission Oaks Blvd...........................Camarillo CA 93011 805-445-4791
TF: 800-444-3353 ■ *Web:* www.harborfreight.com

Hardware Distribution Warehouses Inc (HDW)
6900 Woolworth Rd ....Shreveport LA 71129 318-686-8527 455-3598*
*Fax Area Code: 662 ■ *TF Cust Svc:* 800-256-8527 ■ *Web:* www.hdwinc.com

Hardware Suppliers of America Inc (HSI)
1400 E Fire Tower Rd........................... Greenville NC 27858 800-334-5625 334-5635
TF: 800-334-5625 ■ *Web:* www.hardwaresuppliers.com

Hawaii Nut & Bolt Inc 905 Ahua St................ Honolulu HI 96819 808-834-1919
TF: 800-764-6887 ■ *Web:* www.hawaiinutandbolt.com

Hayes Bolt & Supply Inc 2950 National Ave .... San Diego CA 92113 619-231-5966
Web: www.hayesbolt.com

Hillman Group Inc 10590 Hamilton Ave .... Cincinnati OH 45231 513-851-4900 851-4997
TF: 800-800-4900 ■ *Web:* www.hillmangroup.com

Hodell-natco Industries Inc 7825 Hub Pkwy........... Cleveland OH 44125 216-447-0165 447-5078
TF: 800-321-4862 ■ *Web:* www.hodell-natco.com

Home Depot Supply
3100 Cumberland Blvd Ste 1480 ....Atlanta GA 30339 770-852-9000
TF: 855-615-8372 ■ *Web:* www.hdsupply.com

Horizon Distribution Inc PO Box 1021 .... Yakima WA 98907 509-453-3181 457-5769
Web: www.horizondistribution.com

House-Hasson Hardware Inc
3125 Water Plant Rd.............................Knoxville TN 37914 865-525-0471
TF: 800-333-0520 ■ *Web:* www.househasson.com

Indufast Industrial Fasteners Ltd
111b-81 Golden Dr............................ Coquitlam BC V3K6R2 604-464-6164
Web: indufast.com

Industrial Hardware & Specialties Inc
17B Kentucky Ave.................................. Paterson NJ 07503 973-684-4010
TF: 800-684-4010 ■ *Web:* www.industrialhardware.com

Infinity Fasteners Inc 11028 Strang Line Rd ....Lenexa KS 66215 913-438-2252
Web: www.infinityfasteners.com

Interline Brands Inc 801 W Bay St.................Jacksonville FL 32204 904-421-1400 358-2486
Web: www.interlinebrands.com

J & E Supply & Fastner Company Inc
1903 SE 59th St ....Oklahoma City OK 73129 405-670-1234
TF: 800-677-7922 ■ *Web:* www.jandesupply.com

J.G. Edelen Company Inc 8901 Kelso Dr ....Baltimore MD 21221 410-918-1200
Web: www.jgedelen.com

Jay Cee Sales & Rivet Inc
32861 Chesley Dr............................... Farmington MI 48336 248-478-2150
TF: 800-521-6777 ■ *Web:* www.rivetsinstock.com

Jensen Distribution Services PO Box 3708........... Spokane WA 99220 800-234-1321 838-2432*
*Fax Area Code: 509 ■ *TF General:* 800-234-1321 ■ *Web:* www.jensenonline.com

JSJ Corp 700 Robbins Rd........................ Grand Haven MI 49417 616-842-6350 847-3112
Web: www.jsjcorp.com

JSJ Corp Dake Div 724 Robbins Rd .... Grand Haven MI 49417 616-842-7110 842-0859
TF: 800-846-3253 ■ *Web:* www.dakecorp.com

Karl W Richter Inc 350 Middlefield Rd................. Toronto ON M1S5B1 416-757-8951
TF: 877-597-8665 ■ *Web:* www.kwrtools.com

Kentec Inc 3250 Centerville Hwy.................... Snellville GA 30039 770-985-1907 985-6989
TF: 800-241-0148 ■ *Web:* www.southerncarlson.com

Key Fasteners Corp 525 Key Way Dr .... Berne IN 46711 260-589-2626
Web: adamswells.com

Leight Sales Company Inc 1051 E Artesia Blvd .... Carson CA 90746 310-223-1000 604-4702

Phone | Fax

Long-Lewis Hardware Co 430 Ninth St N ....Birmingham AL 35203 205-322-2561
Web: www.long-lewis.com

Max Tool Inc 119b Citation Ct.....................Birmingham AL 35209 205-942-2466 942-7144
TF: 800-783-6298 ■ *Web:* www.maxtoolinc.com

MaxTool 5798 Ontario Mills Pkwy .... Ontario CA 91764 909-568-2800
Web: www.maxtool.com

Mclendon Hardware Inc 440 Rainier Ave S..............Renton WA 98057 425-235-3555 264-1511
Web: www.mclendons.com

Monroe Hardware Co 101 N Sutherland Ave .... Monroe NC 28110 704-289-3121 289-2838
TF: 800-222-1974 ■ *Web:* www.monroehardware.com

Nbs Corp 3100 E Slauson Ave..........................Vernon CA 90058 323-923-1627
Web: www.nbsfasteners.com

Norwood Hardware & Supply Company Inc
2906 Glendale Milford Rd......................... Cincinnati OH 45241 513-733-1175
Web: www.norwoodhardware.com

Oasis Stage Werks Inc
249 S Rio Grande St.......................... Salt Lake City UT 84101 801-363-0364
TF: 800-952-6865 ■ *Web:* www.oasis-stage.com

Okee Industries Inc 91 Shield St............... West Hartford CT 06110 860-953-1234
Web: www.okee.net

Omaha Wholesale Hardware Co PO Box 3628 ....Omaha NE 68102 402-444-1673 444-1664
TF: 800-238-4566 ■ *Web:* www.omahawh.com

Onity Inc 2232 Northmont Pkwy Ste 100 .... Duluth GA 30096 800-424-1433
TF: 800-424-1433 ■ *Web:* region.onity.com

Orgill Inc 3742 Tyndale Dr.........................Memphis TN 38125 901-754-8850 752-8989
TF: 800-347-2860 ■ *Web:* www.orgill.com

Parts Assoc Inc 12420 Plz Dr......................... Parma OH 44130 216-433-7700 433-9051
TF: 800-321-1128

Portland Bolt & Manufacturing Company Inc
3441 NW Guam St ....Portland OR 97210 503-227-5488
Web: www.portlandbolt.com

Ram Tool & Supply Co 3620 Eigth Ave S............Birmingham AL 35222 205-714-3300 322-6348
Web: www.ram-tool.com

Ram Winch & Hoist Management LLC
14603 Chrisman Rd ....Houston TX 77039 281-999-8665
Web: www.ramwinch.com

Regitar USA Inc 2575 Container Dr................ Montgomery AL 36109 334-244-1885 244-1901
TF: 877-734-4827 ■ *Web:* www.regitar.com

Repairclinic.com Inc 48600 Michigan Ave ....Canton MI 48188 734-495-3079 495-3842
TF: 800-269-2609 ■ *Web:* www.repairclinic.com

Ryobi Technologies Inc
1428 Pearman Dairy Rd ....Anderson SC 29625 800-525-2579 261-9435*
*Fax Area Code: 864 ■ *TF:* 800-525-2579 ■ *Web:* www.ryobitools.com

Serv-a-lite Products Inc 3451 Morton Dr........... East Moline IL 61244 800-800-4900 851-4997*
*Fax Area Code: 513 ■ *TF:* 800-800-4900 ■ *Web:* www.hillmangroup.com

Signal Industrial Products Corp
1601 Cowart St.................................. Chattanooga TN 37408 423-756-4980
TF: 800-728-1326 ■ *Web:* www.signalproducts.com

Silicone Specialties Inc 430 S Rockford Ave ....Tulsa OK 74120 918-587-5567
TF: 888-243-0672 ■ *Web:* www.ssicm.com

Specialty Bolt & Screw Inc 235 Bowles Rd ....Agawam MA 01001 413-789-6700 789-9340
TF: 800-322-7878 ■ *Web:* www.specialtybolt.com

Standard Supply & Distributing Co
1431 Regal Row .... Dallas TX 75247 214-630-7800 630-1894
TF: 800-460-7801 ■ *Web:* www.standardsupplyhvac.com

Star Stainless Screw Co 30 W End Rd ....Totowa NJ 07512 973-256-2300

Supply Technologies LLC 6065 Parkland Blvd .... Cleveland OH 44124 440-947-2100 947-2299
TF: 800-695-8650 ■ *Web:* supplytechnologies.com

Techni-Tool Inc
1547 N Trooper Rd PO Box 1117................... Worcester PA 19490 610-941-2400 828-5623
TF Cust Svc: 800-832-4866 ■ *Web:* www.techni-tool.com

Thruway Fasteners Inc
2910 Niagara Falls Blvd .... North Tonawanda NY 14120 716-694-1434 694-3865*
*Fax: Sales ■ *Web:* www.thruwayfasteners.com

Tomarco Contractor Specialties Inc
14848 Northam St .... La Mirada CA 90638 714-523-1771 523-1284
Web: www.tomarco.com

Triangle Fastener Corp 1925 Preble Ave .... Pittsburgh PA 15233 412-321-5000 321-7838
TF General: 800-486-1832 ■ *Web:* www.trianglefastener.com

Tripac Fasteners 475 Klug Cir....................... Corona CA 92880 951-280-4488
Web: tripaconline.com

United Hardware Distributing Co
5005 Nathan Ln N................................Plymouth MN 55442 763-559-1800
Web: www.unitedhardware.com

Wallace Hardware Company Inc
5050 S Davy Crockett Pkwy PO Box 6004 .... Morristown TN 37815 423-586-5650
TF: 800-776-0976 ■ *Web:* www.wallacehardware.com

Wurth Revcar Fasteners Inc 3845 Thirlane Rd .... Roanoke VA 24019 877-999-8784
TF: 877-999-8784 ■ *Web:* www.wurthrevcar.com

Wurth Service Supply Inc 4935 W 86th St..........Indianapolis IN 46268 317-704-1000 668-2264*
*Fax Area Code: 716 ■ *Fax: Cust Svc ■ *Web:* www.servicesupply.com

WW Grainger Inc 100 Grainger Pkwy .... Lake Forest IL 60045 847-535-1000
NYSE: GWW ■ *TF:* 888-361-8649 ■ *Web:* www.grainger.com

352 HEALTH CARE PROVIDERS - ANCILLARY

See Also Home Health Services p. 2476; Hospices p. 2484; Vision Correction Centers p. 3296

Phone | Fax

Amedisys Inc
5959 S Sherwood Forest Blvd Ste 300............. Baton Rouge LA 70816 225-292-2031 292-8163
NASDAQ: AMED ■ *TF:* 800-464-0020 ■ *Web:* www.amedisys.com

American Family Care 3700 Cahaba Beach Rd........Birmingham AL 35242 205-403-8902
TF: 800-258-7535 ■ *Web:* www.americanfamilycare.com

American Red Cross In Greater New York (Inc)
520 W 49th St..................................New York NY 10019 877-733-2767
TF: 877-733-2767 ■ *Web:* www.redcross.org

AmeriHealth Mercy Health Plan
8040 Carlson Rd Ste 500........................Harrisburg PA 17112 717-651-3540 937-8776*
*Fax Area Code: 215 ■ *TF:* 888-991-7200 ■ *Web:* amerihealthcaritaspa.com

AmSurg Corp 1A Burton Hills Blvd.................. Nashville TN 37215 615-665-1283 665-0755
NASDAQ: AMSG ■ *TF:* 800-945-2301 ■ *Web:* www.amsurg.com

	City	State	Zip	Phone	Fax
Aptium Oncology 8201 Beverly Blvd.	Los Angeles	CA	90048	323-866-3340	
Web: www.aptiumoncology.com					
CareSource 230 N Main St	Dayton	OH	45402	937-224-3300	
TF: 800-488-0134 ■ *Web:* www.caresource.com					
Central Washington Comprehensive Mental Health					
PO Box 959	Yakima	WA	98907	509-575-4084	
Web: www.cwcmh.org					
Children's Bureau of Southern California					
1910 Magnolia Ave.	Los Angeles	CA	90004	213-342-0100	
TF: 800-730-3933 ■ *Web:* www.all4kids.org					
DaVita Inc 1551 Wewatta St.	Denver	CO	80202	303-405-2100	
NYSE: DVA ■ *TF:* 800-310-4872 ■ *Web:* www.davita.com					
Denver Rescue Mission 6100 Smith Rd	Denver	CO	80216	303-297-1815	295-1566
Web: www.denverrescuemission.org					
Fresenius Medical Care North America					
920 Winter St	Waltham	MA	02451	781-699-9000	
TF: 800-662-1237 ■ *Web:* www.freseniusmedicalcare.us/en/home					
Hanger Orthopedic Group Inc					
10910 Domain Dr Ste 300	Austin	TX	78758	512-777-3800	
TF: 877-442-6437 ■ *Web:* www.hanger.com					
HealthDrive Corp 888 Worcester St	Wellesley	MA	02482	888-964-6681	662-0859
TF: 888-964-6681 ■ *Web:* www.healthdrive.com					
HealthSouth Corp					
3660 Grandview Pkwy Ste 200	Birmingham	AL	35243	205-967-7116	969-4740*
NYSE: HLS ■ **Fax:* Hum Res ■ *TF:* 800-765-4772 ■ *Web:* healthsouth.com					
Healthways Inc 701 Cool Springs Blvd.	Franklin	TN	37067	800-327-3822	665-7697*
NASDAQ: HWAY ■ **Fax Area Code:* 615 ■ *TF:* 800-327-3822 ■ *Web:* www.healthways.com					
Hooper Holmes Inc 170 Mt Airy Rd	Basking Ridge	NJ	07920	908-766-5000	
NYSE: HH ■ *Web:* www.hooperholmes.com					
Hudson River Healthcare Inc 1037 Main St.	Peekskill	NY	10566	914-734-8800	734-8808
Web: www.hrhcare.org					
MedCath Inc 10720 Sikes Pl Ste 300	Charlotte	NC	28277	704-708-6600	708-5035
NASDAQ: MDTH ■ *TF:* 800-461-9330 ■ *Web:* www.medcath.com					
Miracle-Ear Inc 5000 Cheshire Pkwy N	Minneapolis	MN	55446	800-464-8002	268-4365*
**Fax Area Code:* 763 ■ *TF:* 800-464-8002 ■ *Web:* www.miracle-ear.com					
Open Door Family Medical Ctr Inc					
165 Main St	Ossining	NY	10562	914-941-1263	
Web: www.opendoormedical.org					
Orion HealthCorp Inc					
1805 Old Alabama Rd Ste 350	Roswell	GA	30076	678-832-1800	832-1888
OTC: ORNH ■ *Web:* www.orionhealthcorp.com					
Radiation Therapy Services Inc					
2270 Colonial Blvd.	Fort Myers	FL	33907	239-931-7275	
TF: 800-437-1619 ■ *Web:* 21co.com					
SCAN Health Plan					
3800 Kilroy Airport Way Ste 100	Long Beach	CA	90806	562-989-5100	989-5200
TF: 800-247-5091 ■ *Web:* www.scanhealthplan.com					
Shapco Inc 1666 20th St Ste 100.	Santa Monica	CA	90404	310-264-1666	264-1675
Symbion Inc 40 Burton Hills Blvd Ste 500	Nashville	TN	37215	615-234-5900	234-5998
Web: www.symbion.com					
United Surgical Partners International Inc (USPI)					
15305 Dallas Pkwy	Addison	TX	75001	972-713-3500	
Web: www.uspi.com					
Unity Physician Group Pc 1155 W Third St	Bloomington	IN	47404	812-333-2731	331-6585
Web: www.unitypg.com					
US Physical Therapy					
1300 W Sam Houston Pkwy S Ste 300	Houston	TX	77042	713-297-7000	297-7090
NYSE: USPH ■ *TF:* 800-580-6285 ■ *Web:* corporate.usph.com					

353 HEALTH CARE SYSTEMS

See Also General Hospitals - US p. 2496

Health Care Systems are one or more hospitals owned, leased, sponsored, or managed by a central organization. Single-hospital systems are not included here; however, some large hospital networks or alliances may be listed.

	City	State	Zip	Phone	Fax
Addus HealthCare Inc 2401 S Plum Grove Rd.	Palatine	IL	60067	847-303-5300	303-5376
NASDAQ: ADUS ■ *TF:* 888-233-8746 ■ *Web:* www.addus.com					
Adventist Health 2100 Douglas Blvd	Roseville	CA	95661	916-781-2000	
TF: 877-336-3566 ■ *Web:* www.adventisthealth.org					
Albert Einstein Healthcare Network					
5501 Old York Rd	Philadelphia	PA	19141	215-456-7890	456-8539
TF: 800-346-7834 ■ *Web:* www.einstein.edu					
Alexian Bros Health System					
3040 Salt Creek Ln	Arlington Heights	IL	60005	847-818-7600	
Web: www.alexianbrothershealth.org					
Allina Health System 710 E 24th St.	Minneapolis	MN	55404	612-813-3600	
Web: www.allinahealth.org					
American Caresource Holdings Inc					
222 W. LAS COLINAS BLVD Ste 500N.	IRVING	TX	75039	800-370-5994	980-2560*
NASDAQ: ANCI ■ **Fax Area Code:* 972 ■ *TF:* 800-370-5994					
American Kidney Stone Management Ltd (AKSM)					
797 Thomas Ln.	Columbus	OH	43214	614-447-0281	
TF: 800-637-5188 ■ *Web:* www.aksm.com					
American Renal Assoc Inc 66 Cherry Hill Dr	Beverly	MA	01915	978-922-3080	
TF: 877-997-3625 ■ *Web:* www.americanrenal.com					
AmeriHealth Casualty					
1700 Market St Ste 700	Philadelphia	PA	19103	215-587-1901	587-1826
Web: www.amerihealthcasualty.com					
Amery Regional Medical Ctr 265 Griffin St E.	Amery	WI	54001	715-268-8000	268-0311
TF: 800-424-5273 ■ *Web:* www.amerymedicalcenter.org					
Ancilla Systems Inc 1419 S Lk Pk Ave	Hobart	IN	46342	219-947-8500	947-4037
Web: www.ancilla.org					
ApolloMD Inc 5665 New Northside Dr Ste 320	Atlanta	GA	30328	770-874-5400	874-5433
Web: www.apollomd.com					
Appalachian Regional Healthcare Service (ARH)					
80 Hospital Dr PO Box 8086.	Barbourville	KY	40906	859-226-2440	
TF: 888-654-0015 ■ *Web:* www.arh.org					
Ardent Health Services					
1 Burton Hills Blvd Ste 250	Nashville	TN	37215	615-296-3000	296-6005
Web: www.ardenthealth.com					
Ascension Health 4600 Edmundson Rd	Saint Louis	MO	63134	314-733-8000	733-8000
Web: ascension.org					
Aurora Health Care Inc					
750 W Virginia St PO Box 341880	Milwaukee	WI	53234	414-647-3000	649-7982
Web: www.aurorahealthcare.org					
Avera Health 3900 W Avera Dr	Sioux Falls	SD	57108	605-322-4700	322-4799
Web: www1.avera.org					
Banner Health 1441 N 12th St.	Phoenix	AZ	85006	602-495-4000	495-4728
TF: 866-451-3399 ■ *Web:* www.bannerhealth.com					
Baptist Health South Florida Inc					
5000 University Dr	Coral Gables	FL	33146	786-662-7000	
TF: 800-622-2838 ■ *Web:* www.baptisthealth.net					
Baptist Healthcare System 4007 Kresge Way	Louisville	KY	40207	502-897-8100	
Web: www.baptisthealth.com/pages/home.aspx					
Baptist Memorial Health Care Corp					
350 N Humphreys Blvd.	Memphis	TN	38120	901-227-5920	
TF: 800-422-7847 ■ *Web:* www.baptistonline.org					
Baylor Health Care System 3500 Gaston Ave.	Dallas	TX	75246	214-820-0111	
Web: www.baylorhealth.com					
Benedictine Health System					
503 E Third St Ste 400	Duluth	MN	55805	218-786-2370	786-2373
TF: 800-833-7208 ■ *Web:* www.bhshealth.org					
BJC HealthCare 4901 Forest Pk Ave	Saint Louis	MO	63108	314-286-2000	
Web: www.bjc.org					
Bon Secours Health System Inc					
1505 Marriottsville Rd	Marriottsville	MD	21104	410-442-5511	442-1082
Web: www.bshsi.com					
California Family Health Council Inc (CFHC)					
3600 Wilshire Blvd Ste 600	Los Angeles	CA	90010	213-386-5614	368-4410
Web: www.cfhc.org					
CAMC Health System Inc 501 Morris St.	Charleston	WV	25301	304-388-5432	
Web: www.camc.org					
CareGroup Inc 375 Longwood Ave	Boston	MA	02215	617-975-5000	
Web: www.caregroup.org					
Carolinas HealthCare System					
1000 Blythe Blvd PO Box 32861.	Charlotte	NC	28232	704-355-2000	
Web: www.carolinashealthcare.org					
Catholic Health Initiatives					
1999 Broadway Ste 2600	Denver	CO	80202	303-298-9100	
Web: catholichealthinitiatives.net					
Catholic Healthcare Partners					
615 Elsinore Pl	Cincinnati	OH	45202	513-639-2800	639-2700*
**Fax:* Hum Res ■ *TF:* 877-700-4647 ■ *Web:* mercy.com					
Catholic Healthcare West					
185 Berry St Ste 300.	San Francisco	CA	94107	415-438-5500	438-5724
Web: www.dignityhealth.org					
Centra Health Inc 1920 Atherholt Rd	Lynchburg	VA	24501	434-947-3000	947-4706
TF: 800-947-5442 ■ *Web:* www.centrahealth.com					
Chase Brexton Health Services Inc					
1001 Cathedral St.	Baltimore	MD	21201	410-837-2050	
Web: www.chasebrexton.org					
Chesapeake Medical Systems Inc					
118 Cedar St.	Cambridge	MD	21613	410-228-0221	228-4561
Web: chesapeakemedicalsystems.com					
Childhaven 316 Broadway	Seattle	WA	98122	206-624-6477	621-8374
Web: www.childhaven.org					
Christiana Care Health System					
501 W 14th St.	Wilmington	DE	19801	302-366-1929	
TF: 855-250-9594 ■ *Web:* www.christianacare.org					
CHRISTUS Health 6363 N Hwy 161 Ste 450	Irving	TX	75038	214-492-8500	
Web: www.christushealth.org					
CHRISTUS Schumpert Health System					
1 St Mary Pl	Shreveport	LA	71101	318-681-4500	681-6954
TF: 844-444-8440 ■ *Web:* christushealthsb.org					
CHRISTUS Spohn Health System					
1702 Santa Fe St	Corpus Christi	TX	78404	361-881-3000	883-6478
TF: 800-247-6574 ■ *Web:* www.christusspohn.org					
Community Health Systems Inc					
4000 Meridian Blvd	Franklin	TN	37067	615-465-7000	
NYSE: CYH ■ *TF:* 888-373-9600 ■ *Web:* www.chs.net					
Community Services Group (CSG)					
320 Highland Dr PO Box 597	Mountville	PA	17554	717-285-7121	285-2658
TF: 877-907-7970 ■ *Web:* www.csgonline.org					
Covenant Health System 3615 19th St.	Lubbock	TX	79410	806-725-0000	725-0324
Web: www.covenanthealth.org					
Covenant Health Systems Inc					
100 Ames Pond Dr Ste 102	Tewksbury	MA	01876	781-861-3535	851-0828*
**Fax Area Code:* 978 ■ *Web:* www.covenanthealth.net					
Crozer-Keystone Health System (CKHS)					
190 W Sproul Rd	Springfield	PA	19064	610-328-8700	328-8725
TF: 800-254-3258 ■ *Web:* www.crozerkeystone.org					
DCH Health System 809 University Blvd E	Tuscaloosa	AL	35401	205-759-7111	
Web: www.dchsystem.com					
Detroit Medical Ctr (DMC) 4707 St Antoine	Detroit	MI	48201	313-745-6035	966-2040
Web: www.dmc.org					
Eastern Maine Healthcare Systems (EMHS)					
43 Whiting Hill Rd	Brewer	ME	04412	207-973-7050	973-7139
TF: 844-364-4473 ■ *Web:* www.emhs.org					
Edinburg Ctr Inc, The 1040 Waltham St	Lexington	MA	02421	781-862-3600	863-5903
Web: www.edinburgcenter.org					
Fairview Health Services					
2450 Riverside Ave.	Minneapolis	MN	55454	612-672-6000	
TF: 800-824-1953 ■ *Web:* www.fairview.org					
Franciscan Missionaries of Our Lady Health System (FMOLHS)					
4200 Essen Ln	Baton Rouge	LA	70809	225-923-2701	926-4846
Web: www.fmolhs.org					
General Health System (GHS)					
3600 Florida Blvd.	Baton Rouge	LA	70806	225-387-7000	
Web: www.brgeneral.org					
Great Plains Health Alliance Inc					
625 Third St	Phillipsburg	KS	67661	785-543-2111	
TF: 800-432-2779 ■ *Web:* www.gpha.com					
Greenville Hospital System (GHS)					
701 Grove Rd	Greenville	SC	29605	864-455-8976	455-6218
TF: 877-447-4636 ■ *Web:* www.ghs.org					
Guthrie Healthcare System 1 Guthrie Sq	Sayre	PA	18840	570-887-4401	887-4666
TF: 888-448-8474 ■ *Web:* www.guthrie.org					

	City	State	Zip	Phone	Fax
HCA Holdings Inc 1 Pk Plz *NYSE:* HCA ■ *Web:* www.hcahealthcare.com	Nashville	TN	37203	615-344-9551	
HCA Midwest Health System 903 E 104th St Ste 500 *TF:* 800-386-9355 ■ *Web:* www.hcamidwest.com	Kansas City	MO	64131	816-508-4000	
Health Net Of Arizona Inc 1230 W Washington St *TF:* 800-291-6911 ■ *Web:* www.healthnet.com	Tempe	AZ	85281	602-794-1400	
Healtheast 559 Capitol Blvd *Web:* www.healtheast.org	Saint Paul	MN	55103	651-232-2000	232-2315
Henry Ford Health System 1 Ford Pl. **Fax Area Code:* 313 ■ *TF:* 800-436-7936 ■ *Web:* www.henryford.com	Detroit	MI	48202	800-436-7936	874-6380*
Hospital Sisters Health System 4936 Laverna Rd. *Web:* www.hshs.org	Springfield	IL	62707	217-523-4747	
IASIS Healthcare Corp 117 Seaboard Ln Bldg E *TF:* 877-898-6080 ■ *Web:* www.iasishealthcare.com	Franklin	TN	37067	615-844-2747	846-3006
ICG Link Inc 7003 Chadwick Dr Ste 111 *TF:* 877-397-7605 ■ *Web:* www.icglink.net	Brentwood	TN	37027	615-370-1530	370-9997
Infirmary Health System Inc (IHS) 5 Mobile Infirmary Cir *Web:* www.mobileinfirmary.org	Mobile	AL	36607	251-435-2400	660-8348
Inova Health System 8110 Gatehouse Rd **Fax Area Code:* 703 ■ *TF:* 855-694-6682 ■ *Web:* www.inova.org	Falls Church	VA	22042	855-694-6682	504-6607*
Integrated Healthcare Holdings Inc 1301 N Tustin Ave *OTC:* IHCH ■ *Web:* www.ihhioc.com	Santa Ana	CA	92705	714-953-3652	953-3384
INTEGRIS Health Inc 3300 NW Expy *TF:* 888-951-2277 ■ *Web:* www.integrisok.com	Oklahoma City	OK	73112	405-951-2277	949-3623
Intermountain HealthCare 36 S State St. *TF Hum Res:* 800-843-7820 ■ *Web:* www.intermountainhealthcare.org	Salt Lake City	UT	84111	801-442-2000	
Iowa Health System 1200 Pleasant St *Web:* www.unitypoint.org	Des Moines	IA	50309	515-241-6161	241-5059
Island Peer Review Organization Inc (IPRO) 1979 Marcus Ave *Web:* www.ipro.org	New Hyde Park	NY	11042	516-326-7767	328-2310
Johns Hopkins Health System (JHH) 600 N Wolfe St *Web:* www.hopkinsmedicine.org	Baltimore	MD	21287	410-955-5000	
Kindred Healthcare Inc 680 S Fourth Ave. *NYSE:* KND ■ *TF:* 800-545-0749 ■ *Web:* www.kindredhealthcare.com	Louisville	KY	40202	502-596-7300	
LifePoint Health 330 Seven Springs Way *NASDAQ:* LPNT ■ *TF:* 888-982-9144 ■ *Web:* www.lifepointhealth.net	Brentwood	TN	37027	615-920-7000	
Lifespring Inc 460 Spring St *TF:* 800-456-2117 ■ *Web:* lifespringhealthsystems.org	Jeffersonville	IN	47130	812-280-2080	
Mayo Clinic: Benavente Luis A MD 200 SW First St *Web:* www.mayoclinic.org	Rochester	MN	55905	507-284-2511	284-0161
MedCath Inc 10720 Sikes Pl Ste 300 *NASDAQ:* MDTH ■ *TF:* 800-461-9330 ■ *Web:* www.medcath.com	Charlotte	NC	28277	704-708-6600	708-5035
MedStar Health 5565 Sterrett Pl 5th Fl *TF:* 877-772-6505 ■ *Web:* www.medstarhealth.org	Columbia	MD	21044	410-772-6500	
Memorial Health Services Inc 7677 Ctr Ave. *Web:* www.memorialcare.org	Huntington Beach	CA	92647	562-933-1800	
Memorial Hermann Healthcare System 7600 Beechnut St *Web:* www.memorialhermann.org	Houston	TX	77074	713-456-4280	
Methodist Health Care System 6565 Fannin St. **Fax:* Admitting ■ *TF:* 877-726-9362 ■ *Web:* www.houstonmethodist.org	Houston	TX	77030	713-790-3311	790-4885*
Methodist Healthcare Inc 1265 Union Ave *Web:* www.methodisthealth.org	Memphis	TN	38104	901-516-7000	
Methodist Healthcare Ministries of South Texas Inc 4507 Medical Dr. *TF:* 800-959-6673 ■ *Web:* www.mhm.org	San Antonio	TX	78229	210-692-0234	614-7563
Methodist Hospitals of Dallas 1441 N Beckley Ave *TF:* 800-725-9664 ■ *Web:* www.methodisthealthsystem.org	Dallas	TX	75203	214-947-8181	947-6501
MultiCare Health System 315 ML King Jr Way PO Box 5299 *Web:* www.multicare.org	Tacoma	WA	98415	253-697-1950	403-1180
New Ctr Community Mental Health Services 2051 W Grand Blvd *Web:* www.newcentercmhs.org	Detroit	MI	48208	313-961-3200	
New York City Health & Hospitals Corp 125 Worth St *Web:* www.nyc.gov/html/hhc/html/home/home.shtml	New York	NY	10013	212-788-3339	
North Broward Hospital District 303 SE 17th St *Web:* www.browardhealth.org	Fort Lauderdale	FL	33316	954-473-7458	355-4966
Northwestern Counseling & Support Services Inc 107 Fisher Pond Rd *TF:* 800-834-7793 ■ *Web:* www.ncssinc.org	Saint Albans	VT	05478	802-524-6554	527-7801
Novant Health Inc 3333 Silas Creek Pkwy *Web:* www.novanthealth.org	Winston-Salem	NC	27103	336-718-5000	
OhioHealth Corporate Offices 1087 Dennison Ave 3rd Fl *Web:* www.ohiohealth.com	Columbus	OH	43201	614-788-8860	
Optimus Health Care Inc 982 E Main St *Web:* www.optimushealthcare.org	Bridgeport	CT	06608	203-696-3260	339-7677
OSF Healthcare System 800 NE Glen Oak Ave *Web:* www.osfhealthcare.org	Peoria	IL	61603	309-655-2850	655-6869
Palomar Pomerado Health 15615 Pomerado Rd *TF:* 800-628-2880 ■ *Web:* www.palomarhealth.org	Poway	CA	92064	858-613-4000	
Partners HealthCare System Inc 800 Boylston St Ste 1150 *Web:* www.partners.org	Boston	MA	02199	617-278-1000	278-1049
Planned Parenthood of Indiana Inc 200 S Meridian St PO Box 397	Indianapolis	IN	46206	317-637-4343	637-4344
Portland Clinic, The 800 SW 13th Ave *Web:* www.theportlandclinic.com	Portland	OR	97205	503-221-0161	
Premier Inc 12255 El Camino Real *TF:* 877-777-1552 ■ *Web:* www.premierinc.com	San Diego	CA	92130	858-481-2727	481-8919
Provena Health 19065 Hickory Creek Dr Ste 310	Mokena	IL	60448	708-478-7900	
Providence Health & Services 4800 37th Ave SW **Fax Area Code:* 509 ■ *Web:* www2.providence.org	Seattle	WA	98126	206-937-4600	474-4882*
Riverside Health System 701 Town Ctr Dr Ste 1000 *Web:* riversideonline.com	Newport News	VA	23606	757-534-7000	534-7087
Riverside-San Bernardino County Indian Health Inc (RSBCIH) 11555 1/2 Potrero Rd *TF:* 800-732-8805 ■ *Web:* www.rsbcihi.org	Banning	CA	92220	951-849-4761	849-5631
Rush System for Health 1653 W Congress Pkwy *Web:* www.rush.edu	Chicago	IL	60612	312-942-5000	942-5831
Saint Francis Care 114 Woodland St *Web:* www.stfranciscare.org	Hartford	CT	06105	860-714-4000	
Schumacher Group 200 Corporate Blvd Ste 201 **Fax Area Code:* 337 ■ *TF:* 800-893-9698 ■ *Web:* www.schumacherclinical.com	Lafayette	LA	70508	800-893-9698	371-4477*
Scranton Counseling Ctr Inc 326 Adams Ave *Web:* www.scrantonscc.org	Scranton	PA	18503	570-348-6100	
Scripps Health 4275 Campus Pt Ct. *TF:* 800-727-4777 ■ *Web:* www.scripps.org	San Diego	CA	92121	800-727-4777	
Sea Mar Community Health Ctr 1040 S Henderson St *TF:* 855-289-4503 ■ *Web:* www.seamar.org	Seattle	WA	98108	206-763-5277	788-3204
Senior Whole Health LLC (SWH) 58 Charles St *TF:* 888-794-7268 ■ *Web:* www.seniorwholehealth.com	Cambridge	MA	02141	617-494-5353	494-5599
Sentara Healthcare 6015 Poplar Hall Dr **Fax:* Mktg ■ *Web:* www.sentara.com	Norfolk	VA	23502	757-455-7000	455-7964*
Sharp Healthcare 8695 Spectrum Ctr Blvd. *Web:* www.sharp.com	San Diego	CA	92123	858-499-4000	499-5237
Shriners Hospitals for Children 2900 N Rocky Pt Dr **Fax:* Hum Res ■ *TF:* 800-237-5055 ■ *Web:* www.shrinershospitalsforchildren.org	Tampa	FL	33607	813-281-0300	281-8174*
Sisters of Charity of Saint Augustine Health System 2475 E 22nd St *Web:* www.sistersofcharityhealth.org	Cleveland	OH	44115	216-696-5560	696-2204
Sisters of Mary of the Presentation Health System 1202 Page Dr SW PO Box 10007 *Web:* www.smphs.org	Fargo	ND	58106	701-237-9290	235-0906
Sisters of Mercy Health System 14528 S Outer Forty Ste 100 *Web:* www.mercy.net	Chesterfield	MO	63017	314-628-3656	
Sisters of the Holy Family of Nazareth Sacred Heart Province 310 N River Rd	Des Plaines	IL	60016	847-298-6760	803-1941
Southern Illinois Healthcare 1239 E Main St *TF:* 866-744-2468 ■ *Web:* www.sih.net	Carbondale	IL	62902	618-457-5200	
SSM Healthÿ 1000 N Lee Ave. **Fax Area Code:* 405 ■ *TF:* 866-203-5846 ■ *Web:* www.ssmhealthillinois.com	Oklahoma City	OK	73102	618-242-4600	272-6477*
St. Elizabeth's Medical Ctr 736 Cambridge St. *Web:* steward.org	Brighton	MA	02135	617-789-3000	
St. John Medical Ctr 1923 S Utica Ave *Web:* stjohnhealthsystem.com	Tulsa	OK	74104	918-744-2345	
Summit Medical Group 1 Diamond Hill Rd *Web:* www.summitmedicalgroup.com	Berkeley Heights	NJ	07922	908-273-4300	790-6593
Suncoast Ctr Inc PO Box 10970 *Web:* www.suncoastcenter.com	Saint Petersburg	FL	33733	727-327-7656	323-8978
SunLink Health Systems Inc 900 Cir 75 Pkwy Ste 1120 *NYSE:* SSY ■ *Web:* www.sunlinkhealth.com	Atlanta	GA	30339	770-933-7000	933-7010
Sutter Health 2200 River Plaza *TF:* 888-888-6044 ■ *Web:* www.sutterhealth.org	Sacramento	CA	95833	916-733-8800	
Tenet Healthcare Corp 1445 Ross Ave *NYSE:* THC ■ *Web:* www.tenethealth.com	Dallas	TX	75202	469-893-2000	
Terros Inc 3003 N Central Ave Ste 200 *Web:* www.terros.org	Phoenix	AZ	85012	602-222-9444	
Texas Health Resources 612 E. Lamar Blvd Ste 900 *TF:* 877-847-9355 ■ *Web:* www.texashealth.org	Arlington	TX	76011	877-847-9355	
TheraCare 116 W 32nd St 8th Fl *TF:* 800-505-7000 ■ *Web:* www.theracare.com	New York	NY	10001	212-564-2350	564-5896
Trinity Health 27870 Cabot Dr *Web:* www.trinity-health.org	Novi	MI	48377	248-489-6000	
Trinity Health System 380 Summit Ave. *Web:* www.trinityhealth.com	Steubenville	OH	43952	740-283-7000	283-7104
Truman Medical Ctr 2301 Holmes St. *Web:* www.trumed.org	Kansas City	MO	64108	816-404-1000	
United Health Centers of The San Joaquin Valley 650 Zediker Ave PO Box 790 *Web:* public.uhcofsjv.org	Parlier	CA	93648	559-646-6618	646-6614
United Health Services Hospitals 10-42 Mitchell Ave *Web:* www.uhs.net	Binghamton	NY	13903	607-762-2200	762-3203
United Medical Corp 603 Main St *Web:* unitedmedical.com	Windermere	FL	34786	407-876-2200	876-3065
Universal Health Services Inc 367 S Gulph Rd *NYSE:* UHS ■ *TF:* 800-347-7750 ■ *Web:* www.uhsinc.com	King of Prussia	PA	19406	610-768-3300	
University Health Network 190 Elizabeth St *Web:* www.uhn.ca	Toronto	ON	M5G2C4	416-340-4907	
University of California Health System 1111 Franklin St **Fax:* Hum Res ■ *Web:* www.universityofcalifornia.edu	Oakland	CA	94607	510-987-9200	987-0894*
University of Maryland Medical System 22 S Greene St *TF:* 800-492-5538 ■ *Web:* www.umm.edu	Baltimore	MD	21201	410-328-8667	
University of Pittsburgh Medical Ctr Health System 200 Lothrop St *TF:* 800-533-8762 ■ *Web:* www.upmc.com	Pittsburgh	PA	15213	412-647-2345	
University of Texas System Office of Health Affairs 601 Colorado St *Web:* utsystem.edu/offices/health-affairs	Austin	TX	78701	512-499-4224	499-4313

Phone *Fax*

Valeo Behavioral Health Care Inc
5401 SW Seventh St .... Topeka KS 66606 785-233-1730
Web: www.valeotopeka.org

Vanguard Health Systems Inc
20 Burton Hills Blvd Ste 100 .... Nashville TN 37215 615-665-6000 665-6059
Web: www.tenethealth.com

Vantage Health Plan Inc 130 Desiard St Ste 300 .... Monroe LA 71201 318-361-0900
TF: 888-823-1910 ■ *Web:* www.vantagehealthplan.com

Venice Family Clinic 604 Rose Ave .... Venice CA 90291 310-392-8630 392-6642
Web: www.venicefamilyclinic.org

Veterans Health Administration
810 Vermont Ave NW .... Washington DC 20420 202-273-5400
TF: 800-827-1000 ■ *Web:* www2.va.gov

Vibra Healthcare 4550 Lena Dr .... Mechanicsburg PA 17055 717-591-5700 591-5710
Web: www.vibrahealthcare.com

Virginia Commonwealth University Medical Ctr (VCU)
1250 E Marshall St .... Richmond VA 23298 804-828-9000
Web: www.vcuhealth.org

Virtua Health
401 Rt 73 N 50 Lake Center Dr Ste 401 .... Marlton NJ 08053 856-355-0010
Web: www.virtua.org

VistaCare Inc 3350 Riverwood Pkwy Ste 1400 .... Atlanta GA 30339 770-951-6450
Web: www.gentiva.com

Washington County Mental Health Services Inc (WCMHS)
PO Box 647 .... Montpelier VT 05601 802-229-0591 223-8623
TF: 800-649-2642 ■ *Web:* www.wcmhs.org

West Oakland Health Council Inc (WOHC)
700 Adeline St .... Oakland CA 94607 510-835-9610
Web: www.wohc.org

West Penn Allegheny Health System
4800 Friendship Ave .... Pittsburgh PA 15224 800-994-6610 359-3933*
**Fax Area Code:* 412 ■ *TF:* 800-994-6610 ■ *Web:* ahn.org

West Tennessee Healthcare 620 Skyline Dr .... Jackson TN 38301 731-541-5000 541-5195
Web: wth.org

Wheaton Franciscan Healthcare 3801 Spring St .... Racine WI 53405 262-687-4011
TF: 877-304-6332 ■ *Web:* www.mywheaton.org

William Beaumont Hospital
3601 W 13-Mile Rd .... Royal Oak MI 48073 248-551-5000
Web: www.beaumont.edu

Yakima Neighborhood Health Services (YNHS)
12 S Eigth St PO Box 2605 .... Yakima WA 98907 509-454-4143 454-3651
Web: www.ynhs.org

354 HEALTH & FITNESS CENTERS

See Also Spas - Health & Fitness p. 3187; Weight Loss Centers & Services p. 3311

Phone *Fax*

Ace Golf Inc 820 S Kings Ave .... Brandon FL 33511 813-651-4653
Web: www.ace-golf.com

Alaska Club Inc, The 5201 E Tudor Rd .... Anchorage AK 99507 907-337-9550
Web: www.thealaskaclub.com

Algoma University College
1520 Queen St E .... Sault Sainte Marie ON P6A2G4 705-949-2301
TF: 888-254-6628 ■ *Web:* algomau.ca

Any Body Fitness LLC
6513 Kingston Pk Ste 100 .... Knoxville TN 37919 865-247-6705
Web: www.anybodyfit.com

Anytime Fitness Inc 12181 Margo Ave S .... Hastings MN 55033 651-438-5000
Web: www.anytimefitness.com

Asheville Racquet Club Inc
200 Racquet Club Rd .... Asheville NC 28803 828-274-3361
Web: ashevilleracquetclub.com

Asphalt Green Inc 555 E 90th St .... New York NY 10128 212-369-8890
Web: www.agtri.com

Athletic Clubs of America LLC
2920 E Zion Rd .... Fayetteville AR 72703 479-587-0500
Web: www.fayac.com

Atlanta Athletic Club
1930 Bobby Jones Dr .... Johns Creek GA 30097 770-448-2166
Web: www.atlantaathleticclub.org

Atlantic Club, The 1904 Atlantic Ave .... Manasquan NJ 08736 732-223-2100
Web: www.theatlanticclub.com

Auberge et spa Le Nordik Inc
16 ch Nordik .... Old Chelsea QC J9B2P7 819-827-1111
TF: 866-575-3700 ■ *Web:* www.lenordik.com

AXIS Personal Trainers Inc
550 Ravenswood Ave .... Menlo Park CA 94025 650-463-1920
Web: www.axispt.com

Balance 2200 California St NW .... Washington DC 20008 202-797-0021
Web: www.balancegym.com

Bally Fitness 8700 W Bryn Mawr Ave .... Chicago IL 60631 773-380-3000
Web: www.ballyfitness.com

Bar Method, The 3333 Fillmore St .... San Francisco CA 94123 415-441-6333
Web: barmethod.com

Barry's Bootcamp
1106 N La Cienega Blvd Ste 104 .... West Hollywood CA 90069 310-360-6262
Web: www.barrysbootcamp.com

Bay Club Company, The 150 Greenwich St .... San Francisco CA 94111 415-433-2200
Web: bayclubs.com/sanfrancisco

Beacon Consulting Group Inc
125 High St 25th Fl .... Boston MA 02110 617-523-4030
Web: www.beaconcgi.com

Belle Fourche Area Community Center
1111 National St .... Belle Fourche SD 57717 605-892-2467
Web: www.bellefourche.org

Big Fitness 5 Progress St .... Seekonk MA 02771 401-885-5200
TF: 800-383-2008 ■ *Web:* www.bigfitness.com

Blast Fitness Group LLC 452 Lexington St .... Auburndale MA 02466 617-916-5683
Web: blastfitness.com

Body Logic Fitness Studio
14205 Meridian Ave E Ste A4 .... Puyallup WA 98373 253-841-1285

Phone *Fax*

Body Tech 19815 La Grange Rd .... Mokena IL 60448 708-478-5054
Web: bodytechtotalfitness.com

Bosse Sports 141 Boston Post Rd .... Sudbury MA 01776 978-443-4613
Web: bossesports.com

Boulevard Club The 1491 Lk Shore Blvd W .... Toronto ON M6K3C2 416-532-3341
Web: www.boulevardclub.com

Boylan Indoor Tennis 4000 Saint Francis Dr .... Rockford IL 61103 815-877-4273
Web: www.boylan.org

Brick Bodies Fitness Services Inc
201 Old Padonia Rd .... Cockeysville MD 21030 410-252-8058 560-3299
TF: 866-952-7425 ■ *Web:* www.brickbodies.com

Broadwater Athletic Clubs & Hot Springs
4920 W Us Hwy 12 .... Helena MT 59601 406-443-5777
Web: www.thebroadwater.com

Calgary Winter Club 4611 14 St Nw .... Calgary AB T2K1J7 403-289-5511
Web: www.calgarywinterclub.com

Canlan Ice Sports Corp 6501 Sprott st .... Burnaby BC V5B3B8 604-736-9152
Web: www.icesports.com

Capital City Club Inc 7 John Portman Blvd .... Atlanta GA 30303 404-523-8221
Web: www.capitalcityclub.org

Chelsea Piers Sports & Entertainment Complex
23rd St & Hudson River .... New York NY 10011 212-336-6400 336-6130
Web: www.chelseapiers.com

City of Kamloops 105 Seymour St .... Kamloops BC V2C2C6 250-828-3439
Web: www.kamloops.ca

Club Metro Usa LLC 1400 Hooper Ave .... Toms River NJ 08753 732-864-1999

Clubsport of San Ramon
350 Bollinger Canyon Ln .... San Ramon CA 94582 925-735-8500 735-7916
Web: www.clubsportsr.com

Columbia Athletic Clubs 2930 228th Ave SE .... Sammamish WA 98075 425-313-0123
Web: www.columbiaathletic.com

Contours Express Inc 156 Imperial Way .... Nicholasville KY 40356 855-589-9662 241-2234*
**Fax Area Code:* 859 ■ *TF:* 855-589-9662 ■ *Web:* www.contoursexpress.com

Coop's Health & Fitness Club Inc
19 Gladys Dr .... Greenville SC 29607 864-288-2667
Web: www.coopsfitness.com

Core Club, The 66 E 55th St .... New York NY 10022 212-486-6600
Web: www.thecoreclub.com

Corporate Fitness Works Inc
1200 16th St N .... St Petersburg FL 33705 301-417-9697
TF: 855-417-9697 ■ *Web:* www.corporatefitnessworks.com

Courthouse Fitness 451 Division St Ste 200 .... Salem OR 97301 503-588-2582
Web: courthousefit.com

Crossgates Recreation Inc 200 N Military Rd .... Slidell LA 70461 985-643-3500
Web: crossgatesclub.com

Crunch Fitness International 220 W 19th St .... New York NY 10011 212-370-0998
TF: 888-227-8624 ■ *Web:* www.crunch.com

D1 Sports Holdings LLC 7115 S Springs Dr .... Franklin TN 37067 615-778-1893
Web: www.d1sportstraining.com

Defined Fitness 4930 Mcleod Rd Ne .... Albuquerque NM 87109 505-888-7097
Web: www.defined.com

Denver Athletic Club 1325 Glenarm Pl .... Denver CO 80204 303-534-1211
Web: www.denverathleticclub.cc

Detroit Athletic Club 241 Madison St .... Detroit MI 48226 313-963-9200 963-8891
Web: www.thedac.com

Dumbell Man Fitness Equipment, The
655 Hawaii Ave .... Torrance CA 90503 310-381-2900
TF: 800-432-6266 ■ *Web:* www.dumbellman.com

East Bank Club 500 N Kingsbury St .... Chicago IL 60654 312-527-5800 644-3868
Web: www.eastbankclub.com

Equinox Fitness Holdings Inc 895 Broadway .... New York NY 10003 212-677-0180 777-9510
TF: 866-332-6549 ■ *Web:* www.equinox.com

Estancia Club 27998 N 99th Pl .... Scottsdale AZ 85262 480-473-4400
Web: www.estanciaclub.com

Fig Garden Swim & Racquet Club
4722 N Maroa Ave .... Fresno CA 93704 559-222-4816
Web: www.fig-garden.com

Findlay Country Club Pro. Shop
1500 Country Club Dr .... Findlay OH 45840 419-422-9263
Web: www.findlaycc.com

Fitcorp 800 Boylston St .... Boston MA 02199 617-262-2050
Web: www.fitcorp.com

Fitness Ctr 1914 Round Barn Rd .... Champaign IL 61821 217-356-1616 356-7920
Web: www.fitcen.com

Fitness Depot 1808 Lower Roswell Rd .... Marietta GA 30068 770-971-6828 565-7119
TF: 800-974-6828 ■ *Web:* www.thefitnessdepot.com

Fitness Formula Ltd 619 W Jackson .... Chicago IL 60661 312-648-4666
Web: ffc.com

Flex Hr 10700 Medlock Bridge Rd Ste 206 .... Johns Creek GA 30097 770-814-4225 814-4123
TF: 877-735-3947 ■ *Web:* www.flexhr.com

G & G Fitness Equipment Inc
7350 Transit Rd .... Williamsville NY 14221 716-633-2527
TF: 800-537-0516 ■ *Web:* www.livefit.com

Gaston County Family Ymca 3210 Union Rd .... Gastonia NC 28056 704-865-2193
Web: www.gastonymca.org

Gestion Riviere du Diable Inc
4280 Montee Ryan .... Mont Tremblant QC J8E1S4 819-425-9595
Web: www.scandinave.com

Get In Shape For Women 75 Second Ave Ste 220 .... Needham MA 02494 781-444-1913
Web: www.getinshapeforwomen.com

Global Fitness Center Inc 215 Hamilton St .... Leominster MA 01453 978-537-2100
Web: www.globalfitnesscenter.com

GoodLife Fitness
355 Wellington St PO Box 23091 .... London ON N6A3N7 519-433-0601
Web: www.goodlifefitness.com

Green Valley Recreation Inc
921 W Via Rio Fuerte .... Green Valley AZ 85614 520-393-0360
Web: www.gvrec.org

Greenwood Athletic Club
5801 S Quebec St .... Greenwood Village CO 80111 303-770-2582 850-9219
Web: www.greenwoodathleticclub.com

Hamilton Area YMCA Inc
1315 Whitehorse-Mercerville Rd .... Hamilton NJ 08619 609-581-9622
Web: www.hamiltonymca.org

Phone Fax

Harbor Bay Club 200 Packet Landing Rd. Alameda CA 94502 510-521-5414
Web: harborbayclub.com

Healthridge Fitness Center LLC
17800 W 106th St. Olathe KS 66061 913-888-0505
Web: healthridgefitness.com

Healthtrax Fitness & Wellness
2345 Main St Glastonbury CT 06033 860-652-7066 652-7066
TF: 800-998-0880 ■ *Web:* www.healthtrax.com

Hiatus Spa & Retreat 5560 W Lovers Ln Ste 250 Dallas TX 75209 214-352-4111
Web: hiatusspa.com

Ice Specialty Entertainment Inc
409 Santa Monica Blvd Ste E Santa Monica CA 90401 805-520-7465
Web: www.iceoplex.com

In-Shape Health Clubs 1016 E Bianchi Rd. Stockton CA 95210 209-472-2231
Web: www.inshapeclubs.com

India Community Center Inc
555 Los Coches St Milpitas CA 95035 408-934-1130
Web: www.indiacc.org

Inspiring Wellness LLC
665 S Orange Ave Ste 7 Sarasota FL 34236 941-953-5000
Web: www.babybootcamp.com

Iron Tribe Franchise LLC 300 27th St S Birmingham AL 35233 205-226-8669
TF: 855-226-8699 ■ *Web:* irontribefitness.com

Issaquah Swimming Pool 50 Se Clark St Issaquah WA 98027 425-837-3350
Web: ci.issaquah.wa.us

It Healthtrack Inc 6500 Main St Ste 3 Williamsville NY 14221 716-630-0063
Web: ithealthtrack.com

Jonas Fitness Inc 16969 n texas ave Webster TX 77598 800-324-9800
TF: 800-324-9800 ■ *Web:* www.jonasfitness.com

Jordan Essentials 1106 eaglecrest st Nixa MO 65714 417-724-9690
Web: www.jordanessentials.com

Kimberly Spa 4130 S 144th St. Omaha NE 68137 402-614-8400
Web: kimberlyspaomaha.com

Kinderdance International Inc
5238 Valleypointe Pkwy Roanoke VA 24019 321-984-4448 984-4490
TF: 800-554-2334 ■ *Web:* www.kinderdance.com

KoKo Fitness Inc 300 Ledgewood Pl Ste 200 Rockland MA 02370 781-753-9495
Web: www.kokofitclub.com

LA Fitness International 2880 Michelle Dr. Irvine CA 92606 714-505-8958
Web: www.lafitness.com

Lady of America Franchise Corp
500 E Broward Blvd Ste 1650 Fort Lauderdale FL 33394 954-217-8660
Web: www.ladyofamerica.com

Lake Hills Golf Club Inc 1930 Clubhouse Way Billings MT 59105 406-252-9244
Web: www.lakehillsgolf.com

Lake Merced Golf & Country Club
2300 Junipero Serra Blvd Daly City CA 94015 650-755-2233
Web: www.lmgc.org

Lake Shore Athletic Club Inc
2401 NW 94th St Vancouver WA 98665 360-574-1991
Web: www.lsac.com

Landings Club Inc 71 Green Island Rd Savannah GA 31411 912-598-8050
Web: www.landingsclub.com

Las Vegas 51s, The 850 Las Vegas Blvd N Las Vegas NV 89101 702-386-7200
Web: www.milb.com/index.jsp

Las Vegas Athletic Club
2655 S Maryland Pkwy Ste 201 Las Vegas NV 89109 702-734-8944
Web: www.lvac.com

Les entreprises energie Cardio
1040 Michele-Bohec Blvd Ste 300 Blainville QC J7C5E2 450-979-3613
Web: www.energiecardio.com

Lexington Health Care Ctr 17 Cornelia Dr Lexington NC 27292 336-242-1349 862-7855*
**Fax Area Code:* 781

Lifecnter Plus Lf. Heath Fitnes
5133 Darrow Rd Hudson OH 44236 330-655-2377
Web: www.lifecenterplus.com

Litchfield Park Recreation
100 N Old Litchfield Rd Litchfield Park AZ 85340 623-935-9040
Web: www.litchfield-park.org

Little Gym International Inc
7001 N Scottsdale Rd Paradise Valley AZ 85253 888-228-2878
TF General: 888-228-2878 ■ *Web:* www.thelittlegym.com

Livermore Valley Tennis Club II
2000 Arroyo Rd Livermore CA 94550 925-443-7700
Web: www.lvtc.com

Louisville Athletic Club LLC
9565 Taylorsville Rd Louisville KY 40299 502-753-0999
Web: athleticclubs.org

Lucille Roberts Health Clubs Inc
143 Fulton St New York NY 10038 212-267-3730
Web: www.lucilleroberts.com

Makoy Center Inc 5462 Center St Hilliard OH 43026 614-777-1211
Web: www.makoy.com

Matrix Fitness Systems Corp
1600 Landmark Dr Cottage Grove WI 53527 608-839-8686
Web: www.matrixfitness.com

Mdr Fitness Corp 14101 Nw Fourth St Sunrise FL 33325 954-845-9500
TF: 866-521-7337 ■ *Web:* www.mdr.com

Merritt Athletic Clubs
2076 Lord Baltimore Dr Baltimore MD 21244 410-298-8700
Web: www.merrittclubs.com

Milwaukee Athletic Club 758 N Broadway Milwaukee WI 53202 414-273-5080 273-4118
Web: www.macwi.org

Missouri Athletic Club
405 Washington Ave. Saint Louis MO 63102 314-231-7220
Web: www.mac-stl.org

Mountain Empire Family Medicine 31115 Hwy 94 Campo CA 91906 619-445-6200
Web: www.mtnhealth.org

Mountainside Fitness 9745 W Happy Vly Rd Peoria AZ 85383 623-561-5525
Web: www.mountainsidefitness.com

Move Your Mind a Fitness First
2100 Tremont Ctr Columbus OH 43221 614-486-0575

Multnomah Athletic Club 1849 SW Salmon St. Portland OR 97205 503-223-6251 525-8998
Web: www.themac.com

Phone Fax

National Institute for Fitness & Sport Inc, The
250 University Blvd Indianapolis IN 46202 317-274-3432
Web: www.nifs.org

Naturopathica Spa 74 Montauk Hwy Ste 23. East Hampton NY 11937 631-329-2525
Web: www.naturopathica.com

Nautilus Entertainment Design Inc
1010 Pearl St Ste Three La Jolla CA 92037 858-456-6395
Web: www.n-e-d.com

New Castle Community y 20 W Washington St. New Castle PA 16101 724-658-4766
Web: www.ncymca.org

New Orleans Zephyrs, The 6000 Airline Dr. Metairie LA 70003 504-734-5155
Web: www.milb.com/index.jsp

New York Junior Tennis League Inc
5812 Queens Blvd Ste 1 Woodside NY 11377 718-786-7110
Web: www.nyjtl.org

New York Sports Club 888 Seventh Ave 25th Fl New York NY 10106 212-246-6700 246-8422
Web: www.mysportsclubs.com

Nifty After Fifty LLC 12572 Vly View Garden Grove CA 92845 714-823-4400
Web: niftyafterfifty.com

Nu Image MedSpa Inc
3753 Howard Hughes Pkwy Las Vegas NV 89169 702-784-5922

Omni Fitness Club 40 E Norton St Muskegon MI 49444 231-739-3391

Palisades Tennis Club 1171 Jamboree Rd Newport Beach CA 92660 949-644-6900
Web: palisadestennis.com/ptc

Peak Physique Inc 67 Holly Hill Ln Greenwich CT 06830 203-625-9595

Peoplefit Health & Fitness Center
237 Lexington St Ste 110 Woburn MA 01801 781-932-9332
TF: 855-784-4663 ■ *Web:* peoplefit.net

Philadelphia Sports Clubs 888 Seventh Ave. New York NY 10106 212-246-6700 246-8422
Web: www.mysportsclubs.com

Pivotal Health & Fitness LLC
1401 Sam Rittenberg Blvd Charleston SC 29845 843-571-5858
Web: www.pivotalfitness.com

Platte County Community Center North
3101 Running Horse Rd Platte City MO 64079 816-858-0114
Web: www.kansascityymca.org

Poway Pilates 14053 Midland Rd. Poway CA 92064 858-748-7864
Web: powaypilates.net

Powerhouse Gym International
355 S Old Woodward Ste 150. Birmingham MI 48009 248-476-2888 530-9816*
**Fax Area Code:* 249 ■ *Web:* www.powerhousegym.com

Prairie Life Fitness 2275 S 132nd St. Omaha NE 68144 402-691-8546
Web: www.prairielife.com

Premier & Curzons Fitness Clubs
5100 Dixie Rd. Mississauga ON L4W1C9 905-602-9912
TF: 866-371-7307

Ridgewood Racquet Club 249 Ackerman Ave. Ridgewood NJ 07450 201-652-1991
Web: www.ridgewoodracquet.com

River Oaks Country Club Inc
1600 River Oaks Blvd Houston TX 77019 713-529-4321
Web: www.riveroakscc.net

Rivers Club Inc 301 Grant St. Pittsburgh PA 15219 412-391-5227 391-5016
Web: www.clubcorp.com

Riviera Fitness Centers 3908 Veterans Blvd. Metairie LA 70002 504-454-5855 454-7717
Web: www.rivierafitnesscenters.com

Rock Sports Complex LLC, The
7900 W Crystal Ridge Dr Franklin WI 53132 414-529-7676
Web: www.skicrystalridge.com

Royal Fox Country Club
4405 Royal And Ancient Dr. Saint Charles IL 60174 630-584-4000
Web: www.royalfoxcc.com

Sailfish Club of Florida Inc, The
1338 N Lake Way Palm Beach FL 33480 561-844-0206
Web: www.sailfishclub.com

Scotch Malt Whiskey Society 10210 Nw 50th St Sunrise FL 33351 954-749-2440
TF: 800-990-1991 ■ *Web:* www.smwsa.com

Scripps Ranch Swim & Racquet Club
9875 Aviary Dr San Diego CA 92131 858-271-6222
Web: srsrc.com

Seahorse Fitness Inc 69 Columbia St New York NY 10002 212-254-3651
Web: www.seahorseswimclub.com

Seattle Athletic Club 2020 Western Ave Seattle WA 98121 206-443-1111
Web: www.sacdt.com

Seattle Tennis Club 922 Mcgilvra Blvd E. Seattle WA 98112 206-324-3200
Web: seattletennisclub.org

Sensor Dynamics Inc 4568 Enterprise St Fremont CA 94538 510-623-1459
Web: sensordynamics.com

Shockoe Commerce Group LLC
11 S 12th St 4th Fl Richmond VA 23219 804-343-3441
TF: 866-570-0498 ■ *Web:* www.shockoecommerce.com

Skoah Metrotown Inc 4800 Kingsway Ste 103 Burnaby BC V5H4J2 604-433-0200
Web: skoah.com

Somerset Patriots Baseball Club
1 Patriots Park Bridgewater NJ 08807 908-252-0700
Web: somersetpatriots.com

Somerset Valley Ymca 2 Green St. Somerville NJ 08876 908-722-4567
Web: www.somersetcountyymca.org

Spalon Montage 600 Market St Ste 270 Chanhassen MN 55317 952-915-2900
Web: www.spalon.com

Sport Fit Bowie Racquet & Fitness Club Inc
100 Whitemarsh Park Dr. Bowie MD 20715 301-262-4553
Web: sportfitclubs.com

Sport&Health Clubs LLC
1800 Old Meadow Rd Ste 300 Mclean VA 22102 703-556-6550
Web: www.sportandhealth.com

Sportsmen of Stanislaus Club 819 Sunset Ave Modesto CA 95351 209-578-5801
Web: www.sosclub.com

Talisman Centre 2225 Macleod Trl SE Calgary AB T2G5B6 403-233-8393
Web: www.talismancentre.com

Tennis Equities Inc 77 Kensico Dr. Mount Kisco NY 10549 914-241-0797
Web: www.sawmillclub.com

				Phone	Fax
Trail Smoke Eaters Hockey Club 1051 Victoria St *Web:* www.trailsmokeeaters.com	Trail	BC	V1R3T3	250-364-9994	
Trailhead Athletic Club LLC 7900 E Eagle Crest Dr. *Web:* www.thetrailhead.org	Mesa	AZ	85207	480-832-6900	
Transalta Tri Leisure Centre 221 Jennifer Heil Way *Web:* www.trileisure.com	Spruce Grove	AB	T7X4J5	780-960-5080	
TuffStuff Fitness Equipment Inc 13971 Norton Ave. *TF:* 888-884-8275 ■ *Web:* www.tuffstuffitness.com	Chino	CA	91710	909-629-1600	
Vitense Golfland 5501 Schroeder Rd *Web:* www.vitense.com	Madison	WI	53711	608-271-1411	
Washington Sports Clubs 888 Seventh Ave *Web:* www.mysportsclubs.com	New York	NY	10106	212-246-6700	246-8422
Washington Tennis Services Inc 3200 Tower Oaks Blvd *Web:* www.wtsinternational.com	Rockville	MD	20852	301-622-7800	622-3373
Wellbridge Co 6140 Greenwood Plaza Blvd *Web:* www.wellbridge.com	Greenwood Village	CO	80111	303-866-0800	813-4197
Whirl Wynn Fitness LLC 36 S Charles St Ste 203	Baltimore	MD	21201	410-539-7401	
Winnetka Community House 620 Lincoln Ave *Web:* winnetkacommunityhouse.org	Winnetka	IL	60093	847-446-0537	
Work Out World 762 SR- 18 *TF:* 888-564-6969 ■ *Web:* www.workoutworld.com	Brunswick	NJ	08816	732-390-7390	
World Health 7222 Edgemont Blvd NW *TF:* 866-278-4131 ■ *Web:* worldhealth.ca	Calgary	AB	T3A2X7	403-239-4048	
X 3 Sports 2343 Windy Hill Rd Se *Web:* x3sports.com	Marietta	GA	30067	678-903-0100	
XSport Fitness Inc 6420 W Fullerton Ave. *Web:* www.xsportfitness.com	Chicago	IL	60707	773-237-5730	
YMCA of Rock River Valley 200 Y Blvd *Web:* rockriverymca.org	Rockford	IL	61107	815-489-1252	

355 HEALTH FOOD STORES

				Phone	Fax
Christopher Enterprises 155 West 2050 North **Fax Area Code:* 801 ■ *TF:* 800-453-1406 ■ *Web:* www.drchristopher.com	Spanish Fork	UT	84660	800-453-1406	794-6801*
Ginsberg's Foods Inc 29 Ginsberg Ln PO Box 17 *TF:* 800-999-6006 ■ *Web:* www.ginsbergs.com	Hudson	NY	12534	518-828-4004	828-5653
GNC Inc 300 Sixth Ave 14th Fl *NYSE: GNC* ■ *TF:* 877-462-4700 ■ *Web:* www.gnc.com	Pittsburgh	PA	15222	877-462-4700	
Juice It Up! Franchise Corp 17915 Sky Pk Cir Ste J *TF:* 888-705-8423 ■ *Web:* www.juiceitup.com	Irvine	CA	92614	949-475-0146	475-0137
Netrition Inc 25 Corporate Cir Ste 118 *TF:* 888-817-2411 ■ *Web:* www.netrition.com	Albany	NY	12203	518-464-0765	456-9673
Ream's Food Stores 160 E Claybourne Ave *Web:* www.reamsfoods.com	Salt Lake City	UT	84115	801-485-8451	
Vincit Group, The 412 Georgia Ave Ste 300 *Web:* www.vincitgroup.com	Chattanooga	TN	37403	423-265-7090	265-9070
Whole Foods Market Inc 550 Bowie St. *NASDAQ: WFM* ■ *TF:* 888-992-6227 ■ *Web:* www.wholefoodsmarket.com	Austin	TX	78703	512-477-4455	482-7000

356 HEALTH & MEDICAL INFORMATION - ONLINE

				Phone	Fax
At Health Inc 7829 Center Blvd SE *TF:* 888-284-3258 ■ *Web:* www.athealth.com	Snoqualmie	WA	98065	425-292-0329	
BabyCenter LLC 163 Freelon St. *TF:* 866-241-2229 ■ *Web:* www.babycenter.com	San Francisco	CA	94107	415-537-0900	537-0909
Body, The 250 W 57th St *Web:* www.thebody.com	New York	NY	10107	212-541-8500	541-4911
Drgreene.com 9000 Crow Canyon Rd Ste S220 *Web:* www.drgreene.com	Danville	CA	94506	925-964-1793	
eMedicine.com Inc 8420 W Dodge Rd Ste 402 *TF:* 866-241-9601 ■ *Web:* emedicine.medscape.com	Omaha	NE	68114	402-341-3222	341-3336
Medicine Online Inc 18800 Delaware St Ste 650 *Web:* www.medicineonline.com	Huntington Beach	CA	92648	714-848-0444	242-1484
MedlinePlus National Library of Medicine 8600 Rockville Pk *TF:* 888-346-3656 ■ *Web:* www.nlm.nih.gov/medlineplus	Bethesda	MD	20894	301-594-5983	402-1384
Pain.com *Dannemiller Memorial Educational Foundation* 5711 NW Pkwy *TF:* 800-328-2308 ■ *Web:* www.pain.com	San Antonio	TX	78246	210-572-2512	
PubMed US National Library of Medicine 8600 Rockville Pike **Fax Area Code:* 301 ■ *TF:* 888-346-3656 ■ *Web:* www.ncbi.nlm.nih.gov	Bethesda	MD	20894	888-346-3656	402-1384*
Scientific Technologies Corp 4400 E Broadway Blvd Ste 705 *Web:* www.stchome.com	Tucson	AZ	85711	520-202-3333	202-3340
WebMD 111 Eigth Ave Ste 7 *Web:* www.webmd.com	New York	NY	10011	212-624-3700	

HEATING EQUIPMENT - ELECTRIC

See Air Conditioning & Heating Equipment - Residential p. 1722

357 HEATING EQUIPMENT - GAS, OIL, COAL

See Also Air Conditioning & Heating Equipment - Commercial/Industrial p. 1720; Air Conditioning & Heating Equipment - Residential p. 1722; Boiler Shops p. 1865; Furnaces & Ovens - Industrial Process p. 2338

				Phone	Fax
Aerco International Inc 159 Paris Ave *TF:* 800-526-0288 ■ *Web:* www.aerco.com	Northvale	NJ	07647	201-768-2400	784-8073
Appalachian Stove & Fabricators Inc 329 Emma Rd *Web:* www.appalachianstove.com	Asheville	NC	28806	828-253-0164	
Aquatherm Industries Inc 1940 Rutgers University Blvd **Fax Area Code:* 732 ■ *TF:* 800-535-6307 ■ *Web:* www.warmwater.com	Lakewood	NJ	08701	800-535-6307	905-9899*
Atlantis Energy Systems Inc 4517 Industry St *Web:* www.atlantisenergy.com	Poughkeepsie	NY	12603	916-438-2930	
Barnes & Jones Corp 91 Pacella Pk Dr *Web:* www.barnesandjones.com	Randolph	MA	02368	781-963-8000	963-3322
Besicorp Ltd 1151 Flatbush Rd *Web:* www.besicorp.com	Kingston	NY	12401	845-336-7700	336-7172
BFS Industries LLC 200 Industrial Dr *Web:* www.bfs-ind.com	Butner	NC	27509	919-575-6711	575-4275
Bosch Thermotechnology 340 Mad River Pk *TF:* 800-283-3787 ■ *Web:* www.bosch-climate.us	Waitsfield	VT	05673	800-283-3787	
Burner Systems International Inc (BSI) 3600 Cummings Rd *Web:* www.burnersystems.com	Chattanooga	TN	37419	423-822-3600	822-2223
Burnham Holdings Inc 1241 Harrisburg Ave PO Box 3245 *Web:* www.burnhamholdings.com	Lancaster	PA	17604	717-390-7800	
Charles A Hones Inc 607 Albany Ave PO Box 518 *Web:* www.charlesahones.com	North Amityville	NY	11701	631-842-8886	842-9300
Cool Earth Solar Inc 4659 Las Positas Rd Ste C *Web:* www.coolearthsolar.com	Livermore	CA	94551	925-454-8506	
Cool Energy Inc 5541 Central Ave Ste 172 *Web:* coolenergy.com	Boulder	CO	80301	303-442-2121	
Cryoquip Inc 25720 Jefferson Ave *Web:* www.cryoquip.com	Murrieta	CA	92562	951-677-2060	677-2066
Ebner Furnaces Inc 224 Quadral Dr. *Web:* ebner.cc/home	Wadsworth	OH	44281	330-335-1600	335-1605
Electro-Flex Heat Inc 5 Northwood Rd *TF:* 800-585-4213 ■ *Web:* www.electroflexheat.com	Bloomfield	CT	06002	860-242-6287	242-7298
Embassy Industries Inc 315 Oser Ave. *Web:* www.embassyind.com	Hauppauge	NY	11788	631-694-1800	694-1832
Empire Comfort Systems Inc 918 Freeburg Ave *TF:* 800-851-3153 ■ *Web:* www.empirecomfort.com	Belleville	IL	62222	618-233-7420	233-7097
Freeman Gas Inc 1186 Asheville Hwy. *TF:* 800-277-5730 ■ *Web:* www.freemangas.com	Spartanburg	SC	29303	864-582-5475	582-0937
Fulton Cos 972 Centerville Rd *Web:* www.fulton.com	Pulaski	NY	13142	315-298-5121	298-6390
Hayward Pool Products Inc 620 Div St *Web:* www.hayward-pool.com	Elizabeth	NJ	07207	908-351-5400	351-5675
Hearth & Home Technologies Inc 7571 215th St W. *TF:* 888-427-3973 ■ *Web:* www.hearthnhome.com	Lakeville	MN	55044	952-985-6000	985-6005
Heat Controller Inc 1900 Wellworth Ave *Web:* www.heatcontroller.com	Jackson	MI	49203	517-787-2100	787-9341
John Zink Company LLC 11920 E Apache St *TF:* 800-421-9242 ■ *Web:* www.johnzink.com	Tulsa	OK	74116	918-234-1800	234-2700
Johnston Boiler Co 300 Pine St **Fax:* Cust Svc ■ *Web:* www.johnstonboiler.com	Ferrysburg	MI	49409	616-842-5050	842-1854*
LB White Company Inc W 6636 LB White Rd. *TF:* 800-345-7200 ■ *Web:* www.lbwhite.com	Onalaska	WI	54650	608-783-5691	783-6115
Meeder Equipment Co 12323 Sixth St. *TF:* 800-423-3711 ■ *Web:* www.meeder.com	Rancho Cucamonga	CA	91739	909-463-0600	463-0102
New Buck Corp 8000 Hwy 226 S PO Box 69 *Web:* www.buckstove.com	Spruce Pine	NC	28777	828-765-6144	765-0462
New Yorker Boiler Company Inc PO Box 10 *Web:* www.newyorkerboiler.com	Hatfield	PA	19440	215-855-8055	855-8229
North American Mfg Company Ltd 4455 E 71st St *Web:* combustion.fivesgroup.com/about-us/about-combustion.html	Cleveland	OH	44105	216-271-6000	641-7852
Parker Boiler Co 5930 Bandini Blvd *Web:* www.parkerboiler.com	Los Angeles	CA	90040	323-727-9800	722-2848
Power Flame Inc 2001 S 21st St PO Box 974 *Web:* www.powerflame.com	Parsons	KS	67357	620-421-0480	421-0948
Powrmatic Inc 2906 Baltimore Blvd PO Box 439 *TF:* 800-966-9100 ■ *Web:* www.powrmatic.com	Finksburg	MD	21048	410-833-9100	833-7971
ProVision solar Inc 69 Railroad Ave Ste A-7 *Web:* www.provisiontechnologies.com	Hilo	HI	96720	808-969-3281	
Rasmussen Iron Works Inc 12028 E Philadelphia St *TF:* 888-301-0440 ■ *Web:* www.rasmussen.biz	Whittier	CA	90601	562-696-8718	698-3510
Raypak Inc 2151 Eastman Ave *TF:* 800-438-4328 ■ *Web:* www.raypak.com	Oxnard	CA	93030	805-278-5300	278-5468
Reimers Electra Steam Inc 4407 Martinsburg Pk PO Box 37 **Fax Area Code:* 800 ■ *TF:* 800-872-7562 ■ *Web:* www.reimersinc.com	Clear Brook	VA	22624	540-662-3811	726-4215*
Rite Engineering & Manufacturing Corp 5832 Garfield *Web:* www.riteboiler.com	Commerce	CA	90040	562-862-2135	861-9821
Roberts-Gordon Inc 1250 William St PO Box 44 *TF:* 800-828-7450 ■ *Web:* www.rg-inc.com	Buffalo	NY	14240	716-852-4400	852-0854
RW Beckett Corp PO Box 1289 *TF:* 800-645-2876 ■ *Web:* www.beckettcorp.com	Elyria	OH	44036	440-327-1060	327-1064

Phone Fax

Schwank Inc 2 Schwank Way at Hwy 56N ... Waynesboro GA 30830 877-446-3727 554-9390*
*Fax Area Code: 706 ■ TF: 877-446-3727 ■ Web: www.schwankgroup.com

Smith Cast Iron Boilers 260 N Elm St ... Westfield MA 01085 413-562-9631 562-3799
Web: www.westcastboilers.com

Spectrolab Inc 12500 Gladstone Ave ... Sylmar CA 91342 818-365-4611 361-5102
TF: 800-936-4888 ■ Web: www.spectrolab.com

Taco Inc 1160 Cranston St ... Cranston RI 02920 401-942-8000 564-9436*
*Fax Area Code: 905 ■ *Fax: Cust Svc ■ TF: 888-778-2733 ■ Web: www.taco-hvac.com

Templeton Coal Co 701 Wabash Ave ... Terre Haute IN 47807 812-232-7037 232-3752
Web: templetoncoal.com

Thermal Solutions LLC PO Box 3244 ... Lancaster PA 17604 717-239-7642 501-5212*
*Fax Area Code: 877 ■ TF: 800-860-5726 ■ Web: www.thermalsolutions.com

Utica Boilers Inc PO Box 4729 ... Utica NY 13504 866-847-6656 797-3762*
*Fax Area Code: 315 ■ TF: 800-325-5479 ■ Web: www.uticaboilers.com

Water Furnace International Inc
9000 Conservation Way ... Fort Wayne IN 46809 260-478-5667 747-5780*
*Fax: Hum Res ■ TF: 800-222-5667 ■ Web: www.waterfurnace.com

Wayne Combustion Systems 801 Glasgow Ave ... Fort Wayne IN 46803 260-425-9200 424-0904
TF: 855-929-6327 ■ Web: www.waynecombustion.com

Weil-McLain Co 500 Blaine St ... Michigan City IN 46360 219-879-6561 879-4025
Web: www.weil-mclain.com

Williams Comfort Products 250 W Laurel St ... Colton CA 92324 909-825-0993 824-8009
TF: 866-677-8444 ■ Web: www.williamscomfortprod.com

Zeeco Inc 22151 E 91st St S ... Broken Arrow OK 74014 918-258-8551 251-5519
Web: www.zeeco.com

358 HEAVY EQUIPMENT DISTRIBUTORS

See Also Farm Machinery & Equipment - Whol p. 2280; Industrial Equipment & Supplies (Misc) - Whol p. 2556

Phone Fax

4Rivers Equipment 3763 Monarch St ... Frederick CO 80516 303-833-5900
TF: 800-490-6162 ■ Web: 4riversequipment.com

Able Die Casting Corp 3907 Wesley Ter ... Schiller Park IL 60176 847-678-1991
Web: www.ablediecasting.com

Absolute Machine Tools Inc
7420 Industrial Pkwy ... Lorain OH 44053 440-960-6911
Web: www.absolutemachine.com

Ace Industries Inc 6295 McDonough Dr ... Norcross GA 30093 770-441-0898
Web: www.aceindustries.com

Acer Group 2320 E. Valencia Dr ... Fullerton CA 92831 714-632-9701
Web: acergroup.com

ACI Controls Inc 295 Main St ... West Seneca NY 14224 716-675-9450
Web: www.aci-controls.com

Action Lift Inc 1 Memco Dr ... Pittston PA 18640 570-655-2100
Web: actionliftinc.com

Adams Air & Hydraulics Inc 7209 E Adamo Dr ... Tampa FL 33619 813-626-4128
TF: 800-282-4165 ■ Web: www.adamsair.com

Adept Corp 4601 N Susquehanna Trl ... York PA 17406 717-266-3606
TF: 800-451-2254 ■ Web: adeptcorp.com

Admar Supply Co Inc 1950 Brighton Henriett ... Rochester NY 14623 585-272-9390 272-9165
TF: 800-836-2367 ■ Web: www.admarsupply.com

Advanced Specialty Products
428 Clough St ... Bowling Green OH 43402 419-354-2844 352-9663
Web: www.aspohio.com

Advent Electric Inc 301 E Fourth St ... Bridgeport PA 19405 610-277-6610
Web: www.advent-elect.com

Aerial Rigging & Leasing Inc
2940 Drane Field Rd ... Lakeland FL 33811 863-607-9100
Web: www.aerialrigging.com

Aero Grinding Inc 28300 Groesbeck Hwy ... Roseville MI 48066 586-774-6450
Web: aerogrinding.com

Agar Corp Inc 5150 Tacoma Dr ... Houston TX 77041 832-476-5100 476-5299
Web: www.agarcorp.com

Air Center Inc 2175 Stephenson Hwy ... Troy MI 48083 248-619-7800
TF: 800-247-2959 ■ Web: teamaircenter.com

Air Center Inc, The 270 Monroe Ave ... Kenilworth NJ 07033 908-858-5788
Web: www.aircenternj.com

AJ Jersey Inc
125 Saint Nicholas Ave ... South Plainfield NJ 07080 908-754-7333
Web: www.ajjersey.net

Ajacs Die Sales Corp 3855 Linden Ave SE ... Grand Rapids MI 49548 616-452-1469
Web: www.ajacs.com

AKG of America Inc 7315 Oakwood St Ext ... Mebane NC 27302 919-563-4286
Web: www.akg-america.com

Akhurst Machinery Ltd
1669 Foster's Way (Annacis Island) ... Delta BC V3M6S7 604-540-1430
TF: 888-265-4336 ■ Web: akhurst.com

ALBA Enterprises Inc
10260 Indiana Ct ... Rancho Cucamonga CA 91730 909-941-0600
Web: www.albaent.com

Alban Tractor Co 8531 Pulaski Hwy ... Baltimore MD 21237 410-686-7777 780-3481*
*Fax: Hum Res ■ TF: 800-492-6994 ■ Web: www.albancat.com

Allendorph Specialties Inc 201 Stanton St ... Broussard LA 70518 337-232-0503
Web: www.allendorph.com

Alta Equipment Co 28775 Beck Rd ... Wixom MI 48393 248-449-6700
TF: 800-261-9642 ■ Web: www.altaequipment.com

Amj Industries Inc 4000 Auburn St Unit 104 ... Rockford IL 61101 815-654-9000
Web: amjindustries.com

Amp Machinery Systems Inc
1098 Chetwood Dr ... Carol Stream IL 60188 630-213-8970
Web: www.ampmachinery.com

Ams Controls Inc
12180 Prichard Farm Rd ... Maryland Heights MO 63043 314-344-3144
Web: www.amscontrols.com

AmTex Machine Products Inc
4517 Brittmoore Rd ... Houston TX 77041 713-896-4488 896-6363
Web: amtexmachine.com

Anderson America Corp
10710 Southern Loop Blvd ... Pineville NC 28134 704-522-1823
Web: www.andersonamerica.com

Phone Fax

Anderson Equipment Co 1000 Washington Pk ... Bridgeville PA 15017 412-343-2300 504-4251*
*Fax: Sales ■ TF: 800-414-4554 ■ Web: www.andersonequip.com

Anderson Machinery Company Inc
6535 Leopard St ... Corpus Christi TX 78409 361-289-6043 289-6047
Web: www.andersonmachinerytexas.com

Andrews & Hamilton Company Inc
3829 S Miami Blvd ... Durham NC 27703 919-787-4100
TF: 800-443-6866 ■ Web: www.storageequip.com

Aoa Products LLC 3711 King Rd ... Toledo OH 43617 419-350-1244
Web: www.aoaproductsllc.com

Apex Packing & Rubbr Co
1855 New Hwy Ste D ... Farmingdale NY 11735 631-420-8150
TF: 800-645-9110 ■ Web: apexgaskets.com

Aquatec Inc 1235 Shappert Dr ... Machesney Park IL 61115 815-654-1500
Web: www.aquatecinc.com

Argo Sales Ltd 717-7th Ave SW Ste 1300 ... Calgary AB T2P0Z3 403-265-6633
Web: www.argosales.com

Aring Equipment Company Inc
13001 W Silver Spring Dr ... Butler WI 53007 262-781-3770 779-2737
Web: www.aringequipment.com

Arnold Machinery Co
2975 West 2100 South ... Salt Lake City UT 84119 801-972-4000 972-4374
TF Cust Svc: 800-821-0548 ■ Web: www.arnoldmachinery.com

Arnold Supply Inc 2409 Pasadena Blvd ... Pasadena TX 77502 713-477-3333
Web: www.arnoldsupply.com

ASAP Industries LLC 908 Blimp Rd ... Houma LA 70363 985-851-7272
Web: asapind.net

Astro Craft Inc 7509 Spring Grove Rd ... Spring Grove IL 60081 815-675-1500
Web: www.astrocraft.com

Attica Hydraulic Exchange Inc
48175 Gratiot Ave ... Chesterfield MI 48051 586-949-4240
Web: www.ahx1.com

Avantech Inc 95-A Sunbelt Blvd ... Columbia SC 29203 803-407-7171
Web: www.avantechinc.com

Bacon-Universal Company Inc 918 Ahua St ... Honolulu HI 96819 808-839-7202 834-8110
TF: 800-352-3508 ■ Web: www.baconuniversal.com

Bailey Company Inc, The 501 Cowan St ... Nashville TN 37207 615-242-0351
Web: www.baileycompany.com

BalTec Corp 121 Hillpointe Dr Ste 900 ... Canonsburg PA 15317 724-873-5757
Web: www.baltecorporation.com

Balzer Pacific Equipment Co
2136 SE Eigth Ave ... Portland OR 97214 503-232-5141 232-9556
TF: 800-442-0966 ■ Web: www.balzerpacific.com

Bane Machinery Inc PO Box 541355 ... Dallas TX 75354 214-352-2468 352-2460
TF: 800-594-2263 ■ Web: www.banemachinery.com

Baron Oilfield Supply Ltd 9515-108 St ... Grande Prairie AB T8V5R7 780-532-5661
TF: 888-532-5661 ■ Web: www.baronoilfield.ca

Belt Tech Industrial Inc 2574 E 700 S ... Washington IN 47501 812-644-7623
TF: 877-554-2358 ■ Web: belttech1.com

Benchmark Automation LLC 380 Commerce Blvd ... Bogart GA 30622 706-208-0814
Web: www.benchmarkautomation.net

Berco of America Inc W229 N1420 Wwood Dr ... Waukesha WI 53186 262-524-2222
Web: www.bercoamerica.com

Bertelkamp Automation Inc 6321 Baum Dr ... Knoxville TN 37919 865-588-7691
Web: www.bertelkamp.com

Best Swivel Joints LP 9298 Baythorne Dr ... Houston TX 77041 713-690-4511
Web: www.bestswivel.com

Bevco Sales International Inc 9354 194 St ... Surrey BC V4N4E9 604-888-1455
TF: 800-663-0090 ■ Web: bevco.net

Bevel Design Company Inc
8600 La Salle Rd Ste 330 ... Towson MD 21286 443-279-9900
Web: beveldesign.com

Biar Inc 2506 S Philippe Ave ... Gonzales LA 70737 225-647-4300
Web: www.biar.us/index.html

Birmingham-Toledo Inc 3620 Vann Rd ... Birmingham AL 35235 205-655-1881
Web: birminghamtoledo.com

BLT Enterprises Inc 501 Spectrum Cir ... Oxnard CA 93030 805-278-8220
Web: www.blt-enterprises.com

Blue Giant Equipment Corp
85 Heart Lk Rd South ... Brampton ON L6W3K2 905-457-3900
TF: 800-668-7078 ■ Web: www.bluegiant.com

Boldt Machinery Inc 4803 Pittsburgh Ave ... Erie PA 16509 814-833-9836
Web: boldtmachinery.com

Brandeis Machinery & Supply Co
1801 Watterson Trl ... Louisville KY 40299 502-493-4380 499-3180
Web: www.brandeismachinery.com

Branom Instrument Co 5500 Fourth Ave South ... Seattle WA 98108 206-762-6050
Web: www.branom.com

Brenner-Fiedler & Associates Inc
4059 Flat Rock Dr ... Riverside CA 92505 562-404-2721
Web: www.brenner-fiedler.com

Buckeye Pumps Inc 1311 Freese Works Pl ... Galion OH 44833 419-468-7866
Web: www.buckeyepumps.com

Burckhardt Compression (US) Inc
7240 Brittmoore Rd Ste 100 ... Houston TX 77041 281-582-1050
Web: www.burckhardtcompression.com

Burns Controls Co 13735 Beta Rd ... Dallas TX 75244 972-233-6712
TF: 800-442-2010 ■ Web: www.burnscontrols.com

Busch LLC 516 Viking Dr ... Virginia Beach VA 23452 757-463-7800
Web: www.buschvacuum.com/us/en

C M S North America 4095 Korona Ct Se ... Caledonia MI 49316 616-698-9970
TF: 800-931-6083 ■ Web: www.cmsna.com

C s Precision Manufacturing Inc
140028 Lockwood Rd ... Gering NE 69341 308-436-2099
Web: cspecisionmfg.com

Came Americas Automation LLC
11345 Nw 122nd St ... Medley FL 33178 305-433-3307
Web: www.came-americas.com

Cameron Instruments Inc 173 Woolwich St ... Guelph ON N1H3V4 519-824-7111
TF: 888-863-8010 ■ Web: cameroninstruments.com

Canimex Inc 285 Saint-Georges St ... Drummondville QC J2C4H3 819-477-1335
TF: 855-777-1335 ■ Web: www.canimex.com

				Phone	Fax
Capital Equipment & Handling Inc 1100 Cottonwood Ave *Web:* www.cehwi.com	Hartland	WI	53029	262-369-5500	
Cardinal Machinery Inc 7535 Appling Ctr Dr *Web:* www.cardinalmachinery.com	Memphis	TN	38133	901-377-3107	
Carotek Inc 700 Sam Newell Rd PO Box 1395 *Web:* www.carotek.com	Matthews	NC	28106	704-844-1100	
Cascade Controls Northwest 19785 NE San Raffael St *Web:* www.cascade-nw.com	Portland	OR	97230	503-252-3116	
Casco Equipment Corp 4141 Flat Rock Dr *Web:* www.cascoequip.com	Riverside	CA	92505	951-324-8500	
Cast Products Inc 4200 N Nordica Ave *Web:* castproducts.com	Norridge	IL	60706	708-457-1500	
Caster Concepts Inc 16000 E Michigan Ave *Web:* www.casterconcepts.com	Albion	MI	49224	517-629-8838	
CFE Equipment Corp 818 Widgeon Rd *Web:* www.cfeequipment.com	Norfolk	VA	23513	757-858-2660	
Chandler Instruments Company LLC 2001 N Indianwood Ave *Web:* www.chandlereng.com	Broken Arrow	OK	74012	918-250-7200	
Chase-Logeman Corp 303 Friendship Dr *Web:* www.chaselogeman.com	Greensboro	NC	27409	336-665-0754	
Cherry's Industrial Equipment 600 Morse Ave *TF:* 800-350-0011 ■ *Web:* cherrysind.com	Elk Grove Village	IL	60007	800-350-0011	
Cisco Air Systems Inc 214 27th St *Web:* www.ciscoair.com	Sacramento	CA	95816	916-444-2525	
Clarke Power Services Inc 3133 E Kemper Rd *Web:* www.clarkepowerservices.com	Cincinnati	OH	45241	513-771-2200	
Clausing Industrial Inc 1819 N Pitcher St *Web:* www.clausing-industrial.com	Kalamazoo	MI	49007	269-345-7155	
Cleveland Bros Equipment Company Inc 5300 Paxton St *TF:* 866-551-4602 ■ *Web:* www.clevelandbrothers.com	Harrisburg	PA	17111	717-564-2121	
Coair Inc 85 Rue Des Buissons *Web:* www.coair.com	Levis	QC	G6V5B6	418-835-0141	
Coast Pneumatics 8055 E Crystal Dr *Web:* coastpneumatics.com	Anaheim	CA	92807	714-921-2255	
Colby Equipment Company Inc 3048 Ridgeview Dr *TF:* 800-443-2981 ■ *Web:* www.colbyequipment.com	Indianapolis	IN	46226	317-545-4221	
Coleman Instrument Co 11575 Goldcoast Dr *TF:* 800-899-5745 ■ *Web:* www.colemaninstrument.com	Cincinnati	OH	45249	513-489-5745	
Colonial Saw Company Inc 122 Pembroke St *Web:* www.csaw.com	Kingston	NY	02364	781-585-4364	
Colorid LLC 20480 Chartwls Ctr Dr *TF:* 888-682-6567 ■ *Web:* www.colorid.com	Cornelius	NC	28031	704-987-2238	
Columbia Specialty Company Inc 5875 Obispo Ave *Web:* www.columbiaspecialty.com	Long Beach	CA	90805	562-634-6425	
Conmaco/Rector LP 1602 Engineers Rd *Web:* www.conmaco.com	Belle Chasse	LA	70037	504-394-7330	393-8715
Contractors Cargo Co 500 S Alameda St *Web:* contractorscargo.com	Compton	CA	90221	310-609-1957	309-1767
Control Southern Inc 3850 Lakefield Dr *Web:* www.controlsouthern.com	Suwanee	GA	30024	770-495-3100	
Conveyor Handling Company Inc 6715 Santa Barbara Ct *Web:* www.conveyorhandling.com	Elkridge	MD	21075	410-379-2700	
Cooke Sales & Service Company Inc 1422 Washington St *Web:* www.cookesales.com	Chillicothe	MO	64601	660-646-1166	646-0381
Copylite Products Corp 4061 SW 47th Ave *Web:* www.copylite.com	Fort Lauderdale	FL	33314	954-581-2470	
Coughlin Equipment Company Inc 2221 E Hwy 66 *Web:* coughlinequipment.com	El Reno	OK	73036	405-262-9101	
Cressman Tubular Products Corp 3939 Beltline Rd Ste 460 *Web:* www.cressmantubular.com	Addison	TX	75001	214-352-5252	
CU ink Inc 612 Swede St *Web:* www.cuink.com	Norristown	PA	19401	484-690-0212	
Cummins Central Power LLC 10088 S 136th St *Web:* www.cumminscentralpower.com	Omaha	NE	68138	402-551-7678	
DC Equipment Inc 57 Old Mill Rd *Web:* www.dcequipmentinc.com	Geraldine	AL	35974	256-659-4707	
Delta Electric Inc 207 Riverview Ave *Web:* www.deltaelectricwv.com	Logan	WV	25601	304-752-4625	
Delta Materials Handling Inc 4676 Clarke Rd *Web:* www.deltamat.com	Memphis	TN	38141	901-795-7230	
Delta t Systems Inc 2171 State Rd 175 *TF:* 800-733-4204 ■ *Web:* deltatsys.com	Richfield	WI	53076	262-628-0331	
Den-Con Tool Co 5354 S I-35 *Web:* www.dencon.com	Oklahoma City	OK	73129	405-670-5942	
Diacarb Tools Inc 2525 Rue De Miniac *Web:* www.diacarb.com	Saint-laurent	QC	H4S1E5	514-331-4360	
Diamond Equipment Inc 1060 E Diamond Ave *TF:* 800-258-4428 ■ *Web:* www.diamondequipment.com	Evansville	IN	47711	812-425-4428	421-1036
Diesel Engine & Parts Co 8123 Hillsboro *Web:* www.depco.com	Houston	TX	77029	713-675-6100	
Dixon Group Canada Ltd 2200 Logan Ave *Web:* canada.dixonvalve.com	Winnipeg	MB	R2R0J2	204-633-5650	
Dove Equipment Company Inc 723 Sabrina Dr *Web:* www.doveequipment.com	East Peoria	IL	61611	309-694-6228	
Doverco Inc 2111 32e Ave *Web:* www.doverco.ca	Montreal	QC	H8T3J1	514-420-6060	
Durkin Equipment Company Inc 2383 Chaffee Dr *Web:* www.durkininc.com	Saint Louis	MO	63146	314-432-2040	
Dynamic Automation 4525 Runway St *Web:* www.dynamicautomation.com	Simi Valley	CA	93063	805-584-8476	
Eagle Power & Equipment Corp 953 Bethlehem Pk *Web:* www.eaglepowerandequipment.com	Montgomeryville	PA	18936	215-699-5871	
Eagle Scaffolding Services Inc 67 Mill St *Web:* www.eaglescaffolding.com	Amityville	NY	11701	631-842-1700	
Easy Automation Inc 102 Mill St *Web:* www.easy-automation.com	Welcome	MN	56181	507-728-8214	
Ecoa Industrial Products 5051 NW 37th Ave *TF:* 800-433-3833 ■ *Web:* www.ecoalifts.com	Miami	FL	33142	800-433-3833	
Edm Department Inc 1261 Humbracht Cir Ste A *Web:* edmdept.com	Bartlett	IL	60103	630-736-0531	
Eggelhof Inc 1999 Kolfahl St *Web:* www.eggelhof.com	Houston	TX	77023	713-923-2101	
Electrocut-Pacific 993 E San Carlos Ave *Web:* electrocutpacific.com	San Carlos	CA	94070	650-591-8718	
Elliott & Frantz Inc 450 E Church Rd *TF:* 800-220-3025 ■ *Web:* www.elliottfrantz.com	King Of Prussia	PA	19406	610-279-5200	
Ellison Educational Equipment Inc 25862 Commercentre Dr *Web:* www.ellison.com	Lake Forest	CA	92630	949-598-8822	
Empire Southwest Co 1725 S Country Club Dr *TF:* 800-367-4731 ■ *Web:* www.empire-cat.com	Mesa	AZ	85210	480-633-4000	633-4000
Enertechnix Inc PO Box 469 *Web:* www.enertechnix.com	Maple Valley	WA	98038	425-432-1589	
Equipment Depot Ltd 4100 S Interstate 35 *Web:* www.eqdepot.com	Waco	TX	76706	254-662-4322	
EquipNet Inc 5 Dan Rd *Web:* www.equipnet.com	Canton	MA	02021	781-821-3482	
Erb Equipment Co Inc 200 Erb Industrial Dr *TF:* 800-634-9661 ■ *Web:* www.erbequipment.com	Fenton	MO	63026	636-349-0200	349-4426
Estes Equipment Company Inc 2007 Polk St *Web:* www.estes-equipment.com	Chattanooga	TN	37407	423-756-0090	
Everyday Technologies Inc 2005 Campbell Rd *Web:* www.everydaytech.com	Sidney	OH	45365	937-492-4171	
Exact Metrology Inc 11575 Goldcoast Dr *TF:* 866-722-2600 ■ *Web:* www.exactmetrology.com	Cincinnati	OH	45246	513-831-6620	
F&H Food Equipment Co 1526 S Enterprise Ave *Web:* www.fhfoodequipment.com	Springfield	MO	65804	417-881-6114	
Falcon Executive Aviation Inc 4766 E Falcon Dr *TF:* 800-237-2359 ■ *Web:* www.falconaviation.com	Mesa	AZ	85215	480-832-0704	
Faris Machinery Co 5770 E 77th Ave *Web:* www.farismachinery.com/default.htm	Commerce	CO	80022	303-289-5743	
Feenaughty Machinery Co 4800 NE Columbia Blvd *Web:* www.feenaughty.com	Portland	OR	97218	503-282-2566	
FLAIR Flexible Packaging Corp 4100 72 Ave SE *Web:* www.flairpackaging.com	Calgary	AB	T2C2C1	403-207-3226	
Flint Machine Tools Inc 3710 Hewatt Ct *Web:* www.flintmachine.com	Snellville	GA	30039	770-985-2626	
Flodraulic Group Inc 3539 N 700 W *Web:* www.flodraulicgroup.com	Greenfield	IN	46140	317-890-3700	
Florida Aquastore & Utility Construction Inc 4722 NW Boca Raton Blvd Ste C-102 *Web:* www.florida-aquastore.com	Boca Raton	FL	33431	561-994-2400	
Florida Handling Systems Inc 2651 State Rd 60 W *TF:* 800-664-3380 ■ *Web:* www.fhsinc.com	Bartow	FL	33830	863-534-1212	
Flow Dynamics & Automation Inc 1024 11th Ct W *Web:* www.flowdynamics.net	Birmingham	AL	35204	205-581-1200	
Flow Solutions Inc 4401 S Pinemont Ste 208 *Web:* www.flowsolutionsinc.com	Houston	TX	77041	713-939-7000	
Foley Equipment Co 1550 SW St *Fax: Sales ■ *Web:* www.foleyeq.com	Wichita	KS	67213	316-943-4211	943-0896*
FORCE America Inc 501 E Cliff Rd *Web:* www.forceamerica.com	Burnsville	MN	55337	952-707-1300	
Fordia Inc 2745 de Miniac Ville Saint Laurent *TF:* 800-768-7274 ■ *Web:* www.fordia.com	Saint Laurent	QC	H4S1E5	514-336-9211	
Formers by Ernie Inc 7905 Almeda Genoa Rd Ste B *TF:* 866-991-3455 ■ *Web:* www.formersbyernie.net	Houston	TX	77075	713-991-3455	
Foxx Equipment Co 421 Southwest Blvd *TF:* 800-821-2254 ■ *Web:* foxxequipment.com	Kansas City	MO	64108	816-421-3600	
Franks Supply Company Inc 3311 Stanford Dr NE *TF:* 800-432-5254 ■ *Web:* www.franks-supply.com	Albuquerque	NM	87107	505-884-0000	884-1787
G. & M. Die Consulting Company Inc 284 Richert Rd *Web:* www.gmdiecasting.com	Wood Dale	IL	60191	630-595-2340	
G.N. Plastics Company Ltd 345 Old Trunk 3 *Web:* www.gnplastics.com	Chester	NS	B0J1J0	902-275-3571	
Gammon Technical Products Inc 2300 Hwy 34 *Web:* www.gammontech.com	Manasquan	NJ	08736	732-223-4600	
Garden State Engine & Equipment Co 3509 US Hwy 22 *TF:* 800-479-3857 ■ *Web:* gseecrane.com	Somerville	NJ	08876	908-534-5444	534-5623
General Equipment & Supplies Inc 4300 Main Ave *TF:* 800-437-2924 ■ *Web:* www.genequip.com	Fargo	ND	58103	701-282-2662	364-2190
General Oil Equipment Company Inc 60 John Glenn Dr *Web:* www.goe-amhfab.com	Amherst	NY	14228	716-691-7012	
Genesis Automation Inc 3480 Swenson Ave *Web:* www.genesisautomation.com	St. Charles	IL	60174	630-587-0444	
Gil-Mar Manufacturing Company Inc 7925 Ronda Dr *Web:* www.gil-mar.com	Canton	MI	48187	734-459-4803	
Gill Services Inc 650 Aldine Bender Rd *Web:* www.gillservicesinc.com	Houston	TX	77060	281-820-5400	
Gilmore Services Inc 31 E Fairfield Dr *Web:* www.gilmoreservices.com	Pensacola	FL	32501	850-434-1054	

Company	City	State	Zip	Phone	Fax
Giuffre Bros Cranes Inc 6635 S 13th St *Web:* giuffre.com	Milwaukee	WI	53221	414-764-9200	
Glauber Equipment Corp 1600 Commerce Pkwy. *TF:* 888-452-8237 ■ *Web:* www.glauber.com	Lancaster	NY	14086	716-681-1234	
Global Equipment Marketing Inc PO Box 810483 *TF:* 866-750-8662 ■ *Web:* www.globalmagnetics.com	Boca Raton	FL	33481	561-750-8662	750-9507
Global Oil Tools Inc 5343 Hwy 311 *Web:* globaloiltools.com	Houma	LA	70360	985-868-3404	
GMW Associates Inc 955 Industrial Rd *Web:* www.gmw.com	San Carlos	CA	94070	650-802-8292	
Golden Equipment Co 721 Candelaria NE *Web:* www.goldenequipment.com	Albuquerque	NM	87107	505-345-7811	345-0401
GPM Inc 4432 Venture Ave *Web:* virginiachamber.com	Duluth	MN	55811	218-722-9904	
Green Line Hose & Fittings (B.C.) Ltd 1477 Derwent Way *TF:* 800-665-5444 ■ *Web:* www.greenlinehose.com	Delta	BC	V3M6N3	604-525-6700	
Grimstad S84w18887 Enterprise Dr *TF:* 877-474-6782 ■ *Web:* www.grimstad.com	Muskego	WI	53150	414-422-2300	
H Gr Industrial Surplus 20001 Euclid Ave *TF:* 866-447-7117 ■ *Web:* www.hgrinc.com	Euclid	OH	44117	216-486-4567	
Hales Machine Tool Inc 2730 Niagara Ln N *Web:* halesmachinetool.com	Minneapolis	MN	55447	763-553-1711	
Hammond Drives & Equipment Inc 8527 Midland Rd *TF:* 888-695-2239 ■ *Web:* www.hammondeqp.com	Freeland	MI	48623	989-695-2239	
Handi-Ramp 510 N Ave *TF:* 800-876-7267 ■ *Web:* www.handiramp.com	Libertyville	IL	60048	847-680-7700	
Hartwig Inc 10617 Trenton Ave *Web:* www.hartwiginc.com	Saint Louis	MO	63132	314-426-5300	
Hayes Pump Inc 66 Old Powder Mill Rd I *Web:* www.hayespump.com	West Concord	MA	01742	978-369-8800	
Heavy Machines Inc 3926 E Rains Rd *TF:* 888-366-9028 ■ *Web:* www.heavymachinesinc.com	Memphis	TN	38118	901-260-2200	
Hei-Tek Automation LLC 21602 N Second Ave Ste 4 *Web:* www.heitek.com	Phoenix	AZ	85027	602-269-7931	
Henderson Sewing Machine Company Inc Waits Dr Industrial Park *TF:* 800-824-5113 ■ *Web:* www.hendersonsewing.com	Andalusia	AL	36420	334-222-2451	
Heritage Equipment Co 9000 Heritage Dr *Web:* www.heritage-equipment.com	Plain City	OH	43064	614-873-3941	
Hibon Inc 12055 Cote de Liesse *Web:* www.hibon.com	Dorval	QC	H9P1B4	514-631-3501	
HO Penn Machinery Co Inc 122 Noxon Rd **Fax:* Mktg ■ *Web:* www.hopenn.com	Poughkeepsie	NY	12603	845-452-1200	452-3458*
Hoffman Equipment Inc 300 S Randolphville Rd *Web:* www.hoffmanequip.com	Piscataway	NJ	08854	732-752-3600	968-8371
Hooper Handling Inc 5590 Camp Rd *TF:* 800-649-5590 ■ *Web:* www.hooperhandling.com	Hamburg	NY	14075	716-649-5590	
Hydra-Fab Fluid Power Inc 3585 Laird Rd Unit 5 *TF:* 866-466-9866 ■ *Web:* www.hydrafab.com	Mississauga	ON	L5L5Z8	905-569-1819	
Hydraulic Controls Inc 4700 San Pablo Ave *Web:* www.hydraulic-controls.com	Emeryville	CA	94608	510-658-8300	
Identity Automation LP 8833 N Sam Houston Pkwy W *TF:* 877-221-8401 ■ *Web:* www.identityautomation.com	Houston	TX	77064	877-221-8401	
Idesco Corp 37 W 26th St *Web:* www.idesco.com	New York	NY	10010	212-889-2530	
ILMO Products Company Inc 7 Eastgate Dr *TF:* 888-243-9353 ■ *Web:* www.ilmoproducts.com	Jacksonville	IL	62650	217-245-2183	
Improved Construction Methods 1040 N Redmond Rd *TF:* 877-494-5793 ■ *Web:* www.improvedconstructionmethods.com	Jacksonville	AR	72076	877-494-5793	
Indexing Technologies Inc 37 Orchard St *Web:* www.ititooling.com	Ramsey	NJ	07446	201-934-6333	
Inline Services Inc 27731 Commercial Park Rd *Web:* www.inlineservices.com	Tomball	TX	77375	281-401-8142	
Innovasys 36735 Metro Ct *Web:* innovasys1.com	Sterling Heights	MI	48312	586-795-3000	
Innovent Air Handling Equipment 60 28th Ave N *TF:* 877-218-4129 ■ *Web:* innoventair.com	Minneapolis	MN	55411	612-877-4800	
J C Bamford Excavators Ltd 2000 Bamford Blvd *Web:* www.jcbna.com	Pooler	GA	31322	912-447-2000	447-2299
J.L. Souser & Associates Inc 3495 Industrial Dr. *Web:* www.jlsautomation.com	York	PA	17402	717-505-3800	
JACO Environmental Inc PO Box 14307 *Web:* www.jacoinc.net	Mill Creek	WA	98082	425-398-6200	
James W Bell Company Inc 1720 I Ave NE. *Web:* jwbell.biz	Cedar Rapids	IA	52402	319-362-1151	362-4876
Janell Inc 6130 Cornell Rd. *TF:* 888-489-9111 ■ *Web:* www.janell.com	Cincinnati	OH	45242	513-489-9111	
Jasper Engineering & Equipment Co 3800 Fifth Ave W Ste1 *Web:* www.jaspereng.com	Hibbing	MN	55746	218-262-3421	
JC Smith Inc 345 Peat St *Web:* www.jcsmithinc.com	Syracuse	NY	13210	315-428-9903	428-9841
Jobe & Company Inc 7677 Canton Ctr Dr *Web:* www.jobeandcompany.com	Baltimore	MD	21224	410-288-0560	
John Fabick Tractor Co 1 Fabick Dr *TF Cust Svc:* 800-845-9188 ■ *Web:* www.fabickcat.com	Fenton	MO	63026	636-343-5900	343-4910
Kann Enterprises Inc 209 Amendodge Dr *Web:* www.kannenterprises.com	Shorewood	IL	60404	815-609-7170	
KBC Tools & Machinery Inc 6300 18 Mile Rd. *Web:* www.kbctools.com	Sterling Heights	MI	48314	586-979-0500	
Kc Robotics Inc 9000 Le Saint Dr. *Web:* www.kcrobotics.com	Fairfield	OH	45014	513-860-4442	
KDR Supply Inc PO Box 10130 *Web:* www.kdrsupply.com	Liberty	TX	77575	936-336-6267	336-1034
Kfm International Industries 14145 Proctor Ave Ste 7	La Puente	CA	91746	626-369-9566	
Kibble Equipment 1150 S Victory Dr *TF:* 800-624-8983 ■ *Web:* www.kibbleeq.com	Mankato	MN	56001	507-387-8201	388-3565
Kraus Global Inc 25 Paquin Rd. *Web:* www.krausglobal.com	Winnipeg	MB	R2J3V9	204-663-3601	
Kwm Gutterman 795 S Larkin Ave. *Web:* kwmgutterman.com	Rockdale	IL	60436	815-725-9205	
Larmar Industries 3700 S County Rd W # 1295. *Web:* www.larmarindustries.com	Odessa	TX	79765	432-561-8700	
Leavitt Machinery & Rentals Inc 24389 Fraser Hwy. *TF:* 877-850-6499 ■ *Web:* www.leavittmachinery.com	Langley	BC	V2Z2L3	604-607-4450	
Lift Technologies Inc 7040 S Hwy 11 *Web:* www.lift-tekelecar.com	Westminster	SC	29693	864-647-1119	
Liftow Ltd 3150 American Dr *Web:* m.liftow.com	Toronto	ON	L4V1B4	905-677-3270	
Lincoln Contractors Supply Inc 11111 W Hayes Ave *Web:* www.lincolncontractorssupply.com	Milwaukee	WI	53227	414-541-1327	
Lumitron Inc 10503 Timberwood Cir Ste 120 *Web:* www.lumitron-ir.com	Louisville	KY	40223	502-423-7225	
M G America Inc 31 Kulick Rd *Web:* mgamerica.com	Fairfield	NJ	07004	973-808-8185	
M R L Equipment Company Inc PO Box 31154 *TF:* 877-788-2907 ■ *Web:* www.markritelines.com	Billings	MT	59107	406-869-9900	
M&h Plastics Inc 485 Brooke Rd *Web:* www.mhplastics.com	Winchester	VA	22603	540-504-0030	
M&M Pump & Supply Inc 1125 Olivette Executive Pkwy Ste 110 *TF:* 800-369-1450 ■ *Web:* www.mandmpump.com	St. Louis	MO	63132	314-395-8122	
M.G. Newell Corp 301 Citation Ct *TF:* 800-334-0231 ■ *Web:* www.mgnewell.com	Greensboro	NC	27409	336-393-0100	
M.H. Equipment Co 2001 E Hartman Rd *TF:* 888-564-2191 ■ *Web:* www.mhequipment.com	Chillicothe	IL	61523	309-579-8020	
MacAllister Machinery Company Inc 7515 E 30th St *Web:* www.macallister.com	Indianapolis	IN	46219	317-545-2151	860-3310
Machinery & Equipment Company Inc 3401 Bayshore Blvd *TF:* 800-227-4544 ■ *Web:* www.machineryandequipment.com	Brisbane	CA	94005	415-467-3400	
Machining Time Savers Inc 1338 S State College Pkwy. *Web:* www.mtscnc.com	Anaheim	CA	92806	714-635-7373	
Mack Pump & Equipment Company Inc 12005 S Spaulding School Dr *Web:* www.mackpump.com	Plainfield	IL	60585	815-439-2030	
Magnus Equipment 4500 Beidler Rd *TF:* 800-394-8964 ■ *Web:* www.magnusequipment.com	Willoughby	OH	44094	440-942-8488	
Main Line Supply Company Inc 300 N Findlay St *Web:* www.mainlinesupply.com	Dayton	OH	45403	937-254-6910	
Maltz Sales Company Inc 67 Green St *TF:* 800-370-0439 ■ *Web:* www.maltzsales.com	Foxboro	MA	02035	508-203-2400	
Mamata Usa LLC 2275 Cornell Ave. *Web:* www.mamatausa.com	Montgomery	IL	60538	630-801-2320	
Mantissa Corp 616 Pressley Rd *Web:* www.mantissacorporation.com	Charlotte	NC	28217	704-525-1749	
Markem-Imaje Inc 5448 Timberlea Blvd *TF:* 800-267-5108 ■ *Web:* www.markem-imaje.com	Mississauga	ON	L4W2T7	800-267-5108	
Mason West Inc 1601 E Miraloma Ave *Web:* www.masonwest.com	Placentia	CA	92870	714-630-0701	
Material Motion Inc 203 Rio Cir *Web:* www.materialmotion.com	Decatur	GA	30030	404-237-6127	
Mbb Enterprises 3352 W Grand Ave. *Web:* www.mbbmasonry.com	Chicago	IL	60651	773-278-7100	
Mckinney Petroleum Equipment Inc 3926 Halls Mill Rd *TF:* 800-476-7867 ■ *Web:* mckinneypetroleum.com	Mobile	AL	36693	251-661-8800	
McQuade & Bannigan Inc 1300 Stark St. *Web:* www.mqb.com	Utica	NY	13502	315-724-7119	
Mecor Inc 1567 Elmhurst Rd *Web:* mecor.net	Elk Grove Village	IL	60007	847-690-0777	
Medley Material Handling Company Inc 4201 Will Rogers Pkwy. *Web:* www.medleycompany.com	Oklahoma City	OK	73108	405-946-3453	
Mesa Equipment & Supply Co 7100 Second St NW *Web:* mesaequipment.com	Albuquerque	NM	87107	505-345-0284	
Methods Machine Tools Inc 65 Union Ave *TF:* 877-668-4262 ■ *Web:* www.methodsmachine.com	Sudbury	MA	01776	978-443-5388	
Miami Industrial Trucks Inc 2830 E River Rd *Web:* www.mitlift.com	Dayton	OH	45439	937-293-4194	
Michigan Arc Products Corp 2040 Austin Dr. *Web:* www.micharc.com	Troy	MI	48083	248-740-8066	
Miller-Bradford & Risberg Inc W250 N6851 Hwy 164 *Web:* www.miller-bradford.com	Sussex	WI	53089	262-246-5700	
Milton CAT 554 Maple St. *Web:* www.miltoncat.com	Hopkinton	NH	03229	603-746-4611	
Mississippi Valley Equipment Company Inc 1198 Pershall Rd *TF:* 800-325-8001 ■ *Web:* www.mve-stl.com	Saint Louis	MO	63137	314-869-8600	869-6862
Mister Safety Shoes Inc 6-2300 Finch Ave W *TF:* 800-707-0051 ■ *Web:* www.mistersafetyshoes.com	Toronto	ON	M9M2Y3	416-746-3000	
Mobile Parts Inc 2472 Evans Rd PO Box 327. *TF:* 800-461-4055 ■ *Web:* www.mobileparts.com	Val Caron	ON	P3N1P5	705-897-4955	
Modern Automation Inc 134 Tennsco Dr *TF:* 800-921-9705 ■ *Web:* www.modernautomation.com	Dickson	TN	37055	615-446-1990	
Monroe Tractor & Implement Company Inc 1001 Lehigh Stn Rd *TF:* 866-683-5338 ■ *Web:* www.monroetractor.com	Henrietta	NY	14467	585-334-3867	334-0001

Company	City	State	Zip	Phone	Fax
Moodie Implement Co 80335 US Hwy 87 W *TF:* 877-278-5531 ■ *Web:* www.moodieimplement.com	Lewistown	MT	59457	406-538-5433	
Multi-shifter Inc 11110 Park Charlotte Blvd *Web:* www.multi-shifter.com	Charlotte	NC	28278	704-588-9611	
Mustang Tractor & Equipment Co 12800 NW Fwy *TF:* 800-256-1001 ■ *Web:* www.mustangcat.com	Houston	TX	77040	713-460-2000	
Nixon-Egli Equipment Company Inc 2044 S Vineyard Ave *Web:* www.nixon-egli.com	Ontario	CA	91761	909-930-1822	
Norco Inc 1125 W Amity Rd *Web:* www.norco-inc.com	Boise	ID	83705	208-336-1643	
Numatic Engineering Inc 7915 Ajay Dr. *Web:* www.numaticengineering.com	Sun Valley	CA	91352	818-768-1200	
O'keefe Elevator Company Inc 1402 Jones St. *TF:* 800-369-6317 ■ *Web:* www.okeefe-elevator.com	Omaha	NE	68102	402-345-4056	
Ohio Machinery Co 3993 E Royalton Rd *TF:* 800-837-6200 ■ *Web:* www.ohiocat.com	Broadview Heights	OH	44147	440-526-6200	526-9513
Ohio Tool Systems Inc 3863 Congress Pkwy. *Web:* www.ohiotool.com	Richfield	OH	44286	330-659-4181	
Oldenburg Group Inc 1717 W Civic Dr. *Web:* www.oldenburggroup.com	Milwaukee	WI	53209	414-977-1717	977-1700
Omnilift Inc Warwick Commons Industrial Park 1938 Stout Dr *Web:* www.omnilift-inc.com	Warminster	PA	18974	215-443-9090	
Optimal Engineering Systems 6901 Woodley Ave *TF:* 888-777-1826 ■ *Web:* oesincorp.com	Van Nuys	CA	91406	818-222-9200	
Owen Equipment Co 13101 NE Whitaker Way *Web:* www.owenequipment.com	Portland	OR	97230	503-255-9055	
Oxford Alloys Inc 2632 Tee Dr *TF:* 800-562-3355 ■ *Web:* www.oxfordalloys.com	Baton Rouge	LA	70814	225-273-4800	
P & W Sales Inc 405 N Hwy 135 *Web:* www.p-wsales.com	Kilgore	TX	75662	903-984-2102	
Pacific Integrated Handling Inc 10215 Portland Ave *Web:* www.pacificintegrated.com	Tacoma	WA	98445	253-535-5888	
Parlec Inc 101 Perinton Pkwy *Web:* www.parlec.com	Fairport	NY	14450	585-425-4400	
Patten Industries Inc 635 W Lake St. *TF:* 877-688-6812 ■ *Web:* www.pattencat.com	Elmhurst	IL	60126	630-279-4400	279-7892
PCE Pacific Inc 2525 223rd St SE *Web:* www.pcepacific.com	Bothell	WA	98021	425-487-9600	
Petersen Inc 1527 North 2000 West *TF:* 800-410-6789 ■ *Web:* www.peterseninc.com	Ogden	UT	84404	801-732-2000	
Pfeiffer Vacuum Inc 24 Trafalgar Sq *Web:* www.pfeiffer-vacuum.com	Nashua	NH	03063	603-578-6500	
Pierce Pump Company LP 9010 John W Carpenter Fwy. *Web:* www.piercepump.com	Dallas	TX	75247	214-320-3604	
Pipe Valves Inc 1200 E Fifth Ave *Web:* www.pipevalves.com	Columbus	OH	43219	614-294-4971	
Piping Resources Inc 4502 F St *Web:* www.pipingresources.com	Omaha	NE	68117	402-738-8100	
Plasterer Equipment Company Inc 2550 E Cumberland St *Web:* www.plasterer.com	Lebanon	PA	17042	717-273-2616	
Pme Equip Inc 304 Garden Oaks Blvd	Houston	TX	77018	507-289-2229	
Pneumatic & Hydraulic Systems Company Inc 1338 Petroleum Pkwy. *TF:* 877-836-1999 ■ *Web:* pneumaticandhydraulic.com	Broussard	LA	70518	337-839-1999	
Pompaction Inc 119 Blvd Hymus *Web:* www.pompaction.com	Pointe-claire	QC	H9R1E5	514-697-8600	
Power & Industrial Air Systems 5281 Hamilton Blvd *Web:* www.pias-usa.com	Allentown	PA	18106	610-395-3242	
Power Motive Corp 5000 Vasquez Blvd *TF:* 800-627-0087 ■ *Web:* www.powermotivecorp.com	Denver	CO	80216	303-355-5900	388-9328
Precise Printing Equipment 1024 E Arlee Pl	Anaheim	CA	92805	714-991-0427	
Precision Hydraulic Cylinders Inc 196 N Hwy 41 PO Box 1589 *Web:* www.phc-global.com	Beulaville	NC	28518	910-298-0100	
Premier Pump & Supply Inc 19 Fruite St *Web:* www.premierpumponline.com	Belmont	NH	03220	603-528-3100	
Primary Flow Signal Inc 800 Wellington Ave *Web:* www.pfsflowproducts.com	Cranston	RI	02910	401-461-6366	
Proconex Management Group Inc 103 Enterprise Dr *Web:* www.proconexdirect.com	Royersford	PA	19468	610-495-1835	
Profile Food Ingredients LLC 1151 Timber Dr *TF:* 877-632-1700 ■ *Web:* profilefoodingredients.com	Elgin	IL	60123	847-622-1700	
Pronghorn Controls Ltd 101 4919 72 Ave SE *Web:* pronghorn.ca	Calgary	AB	T2C3H3	403-720-2526	
Prospec Technologies Inc 3235 Wharton Way *Web:* prospectech.com	Mississauga	ON	L4X2B6	905-629-3100	
Prosys Industries Inc 47576 Halyard Dr *Web:* prosys-group.com	Plymouth	MI	48170	734-207-3710	
PV Fluid Products 11245 - Vly Ridge Dr NW Suit 322 *Web:* www.pvfluid.com	Calgary	AB	T3B5V4	403-640-0331	
Quality Flow Systems Inc 800 Sixth St NW *Web:* qtsi.net	New Prague	MN	56071	952-758-9445	
Quality Hydraulics & Pneumatics Inc 1415 Wilhelm Rd *Web:* www.qualityhydraulics.com	Mundelein	IL	60060	847-680-8400	
Quest Engineering Inc 2300 Edgewood Ave South *TF:* 800-328-4853 ■ *Web:* www.questenginc.com	Minneapolis	MN	55426	952-546-4441	
Quickdraft Inc 1525 Perry Dr Sw *Web:* www.quickdraft.com	Canton	OH	44710	330-477-4574	
R R Floody Co 5065 27th Ave *TF:* 800-678-6639 ■ *Web:* rrfloody.com	Rockford	IL	61109	815-399-1931	
R&M Materials Handling Inc 4501 Gateway Blvd *TF:* 800-955-9967 ■ *Web:* www.rmhoist.com	Springfield	OH	45502	937-328-5100	
Rajason Tools Inc 11664 County Rd 42 *Web:* www.rajasontools.com	Tecumseh	ON	N8N2M1	519-979-1263	
Ralph W. Earl Company Inc 5930 E Molloy Rd *Web:* www.rwearl.com	Syracuse	NY	13211	315-454-4431	
Rasmussen Equipment Co 3333 West 2100 South *TF:* 800-453-8032 ■ *Web:* www.rasmussenequipment.com	Salt Lake City	UT	84119	801-972-5588	
Raymond of New Jersey LLC 1000 Brighton St *Web:* www.raymond-nj.com	Union	NJ	07083	908-624-9570	
RBI Corp 10201 Cedar Ridge Dr *TF:* 800-444-7370 ■ *Web:* www.rbicorp.com	Ashland	VA	23005	800-444-7370	
RDO Equipment Co 3401 38th St S *TF:* 800-342-4643 ■ *Web:* www.rdoequipment.com	Fargo	ND	58104	701-282-5400	282-8220
Rego-fix Tool Corp 7752 Moller Rd *Web:* www.rego-fix.com	Indianapolis	IN	46268	317-870-5959	
Rencor Controls Inc 21 Sullivan Pkwy. *TF:* 866-472-7030 ■ *Web:* rencor.com	Fort Edward	NY	12828	518-747-4171	
Ri-go Lift Truck Ltd 175 Courtland Ave *Web:* www.rigolift.com	Concord	ON	L4K4T2	905-738-8094	
Rish Equipment Co PO Box 330 *Web:* www.rish.com	Bluefield	WV	24701	304-327-5124	327-8821
RJM Sales Inc 454 Park Ave *TF:* 800-752-9055 ■ *Web:* rjmsales.com	Scotch Plains	NJ	07076	908-322-7880	
Rk Controls 5901 Corvette St. *TF:* 877-305-8451 ■ *Web:* www.rkcontrols.com	Commerce	CA	90040	323-887-7066	
Road Machinery Co 4710 E ElWood St Ste 6 *Web:* www.roadmachinery.com	Phoenix	AZ	85034	602-252-7121	253-9690
Roberts Technology Group Inc 120 New Britain Blvd *Web:* rtgpkg.com	Chalfont	PA	18914	215-822-0600	
Roland Machinery Co 816 N Dirksen Pkwy *TF:* 800-252-2926 ■ *Web:* www.rolandmachinery.com	Springfield	IL	62702	217-789-7711	744-7314
Rosenboom Machine & Tool Inc 1530 Western Ave. *Web:* www.rosenboom.com	Sheldon	IA	51201	712-324-4854	
Rowlands Sales Company Inc Butler Industrial Park *Web:* www.rowlands.com	Hazleton	PA	18201	570-455-5813	
Rudd Equipment Co 4344 Poplar Level Rd. *TF:* 800-527-2282 ■ *Web:* www.ruddequipment.com	Louisville	KY	40213	502-456-4050	459-8695
Ryder Material Handling 210 Annagem Blvd *Web:* rydermaterialhandling.com	Mississauga	ON	L5T2V5	905-565-2100	
S & s Industrial Equipment & Supply Company Inc 7 Chelten Way *TF:* 800-282-3506 ■ *Web:* www.sandsindustrial.com	Trenton	NJ	08638	609-695-3800	
Sardee Industries Inc 5100 Academy Dr Ste 400 *Web:* www.sardee.com	Lisle	IL	60532	630-824-4200	
SDT North America Inc PO Box 682 *TF:* 800-667-5325 ■ *Web:* www.sdtnorthamerica.com	Cobourg	ON	K9A4R5	905-377-1313	
Sellers Equipment Inc 400 N Chicago St *Web:* www.sellersequipment.com	Salina	KS	67401	785-823-6378	823-8083
Sequoia Equipment Company Inc PO Box 2747 *Web:* www.sequoiaequipment.com	Fresno	CA	93745	559-441-1122	441-0454
Shannahan Crane & Hoist Inc 11695 Wakeside Crossing Ct *Web:* www.shannahancrane.com	Saint Louis	MO	63146	314-965-2800	
Shredder Company LLC, The 7380 Doniphan Dr	Canutillo	TX	79835	915-877-3814	
Sidel Systems Usa Inc 12500 El Camino Real *TF:* 800-668-5003 ■ *Web:* www.sidelsystems.com	Atascadero	CA	93422	805-462-1250	
Sielc Technologies 65 E Palatine Rd Ste 221 *Web:* www.sielc.com	Prospect Heights	IL	60070	847-229-2629	
Simark Controls Ltd 10509-46 St S E Ste 10509 *TF:* 800-565-7431 ■ *Web:* www.simarkcontrols.com	Calgary	AB	T2C5C2	403-236-0580	
Single Source Technologies Inc 2600 Superior Ct *Web:* www.singlesourcetech.com	Auburn Hills	MI	48326	248-232-6232	
SMW Autoblok Corp 285 Egidi Dr *Web:* www.smwautoblok.com	Wheeling	IL	60090	847-215-0591	
Southeastern Equipment Company Inc 10874 E Pike Rd *TF:* 800-798-5438 ■ *Web:* www.southeasternequip.com	Cambridge	OH	43725	740-432-6303	432-3303
Southwest Materials Handling Company Inc 4719 Almond St *TF:* 866-674-6067 ■ *Web:* www.swmhc.com	Dallas	TX	75247	214-630-1375	
SpanTech LLC 1115 Cleveland Ave PO Box 369 *Web:* www.spantechllc.com	Glasgow	KY	42141	270-651-9166	
Sparktech Inc 1308 Chisholm Trail Ste 105 *Web:* sparktechinc.com	Round Rock	TX	78681	512-716-3131	
Speco Inc 3946 Willow Rd *Web:* speco.com	Schiller Park	IL	60176	847-678-4240	
SPI Health & Safety inc 60 Rue Gaston-Dumoulin *Web:* www.spi-s.com	Blainville	QC	J7C0A3	450-420-2012	
Stamford Scientific International Inc 4 Tucker Dr. *Web:* www.ssiaeration.com	Poughkeepsie	NY	12603	845-454-8171	
Stan Houston Equipment Co 501 S Marion Rd *TF:* 800-952-3033 ■ *Web:* www.stanhouston.com	Sioux Falls	SD	57106	605-336-3727	336-7860
Staubli Corp 201 Pkwy W Hillside Park *Web:* www.staubli.com	Duncan	SC	29334	864-433-1980	
Stoffel Equipment Company Inc 7764 N 81st St *TF:* 800-354-7502 ■ *Web:* www.stoffelequip.com	Milwaukee	WI	53223	414-354-7500	
Stowers Machinery Corp 6301 Old Rutledge Pike NE *Web:* www.stowerscat.com	Knoxville	TN	37924	865-546-1414	595-1030

	City	State	Zip	Phone	Fax
Sugino Corp 1380 Hamilton Pkwy *Web:* www.suginocorp.com	Itasca	IL	60143	630-250-8585	
Sun Packaging Technologies Inc 2200 NW 32nd St Ste 1700 *Web:* www.sunpkg.com	Pompano Beach	FL	33069	954-978-3080	
Svf Flow Controls Inc 13560 Larwin Cir *Web:* www.svf.net	Santa Fe Springs	CA	90670	562-802-2255	
Swift Saw & Tool Supply Company Inc 1200 171st St *Web:* swiftsaw.com	Hazel Crest	IL	60429	708-335-0550	
SYMTECH Inc 100 Sunbeam Rd *Web:* www.symtech-usa.com	Spartanburg	SC	29303	864-578-7101	
Systec Conveyor Corp 10010 Conveyor Dr *Web:* www.systecconveyors.com	Indianapolis	IN	46235	317-890-9230	
Tcm America Inc 107 Mcqueen St	West Columbia	SC	29172	803-791-5205	
Technical Packaging Services 276 Four Sisters Rd *Web:* technicalpackagingservice.com	South Burlington	VT	05403	802-355-4838	
Tecnara Tooling Systems Inc 12535 McCann Dr *Web:* www.tecnaratools.com	Santa Fe Springs	CA	90670	562-941-2000	
Texas Gauge & Control Inc 7575 Dillon St *Web:* www.texasgauge.com	Houston	TX	77061	713-641-2282	
Texas Welders Supply Company Inc 5515 W Richey Rd *Web:* www.twsco.com	Houston	TX	77066	231-880-4200	
Thompson & Johnson Equipment Company Inc 6926 Fly Rd *Web:* www.thompsonandjohnson.com	East Syracuse	NY	13057	315-437-2881	
Tinker Omega Manufacturing LLC 2424 Columbus Rd *Web:* tinkeromega.com	Springfield	OH	45503	937-322-2272	
Tipco Punch Inc 1 Coventry Rd *TF:* 800-544-8444 ■ *Web:* www.tipcopunch.com	Brampton	ON	L6T4B1	905-791-9811	
Tishma Innovations LLC 101 E State Pkwy *Web:* www.tminn.com	Schaumburg	IL	60173	847-884-1805	
Titan Machinery 644 East Beaton Dr *TF:* 800-548-7747 ■ *Web:* www.titanmachinery.com	West Fargo	ND	58078	701-356-0130	
Toll Gas & Welding Supply 3005 Niagara Ln N *TF:* 877-865-5427 ■ *Web:* tollgas.com	Plymouth	MN	55447	763-551-5300	
Tool Technology Distributors Inc 3110 Osgood Ct *TF:* 800-335-8437 ■ *Web:* www.tooltechnology.com	Fremont	CA	94539	510-656-8220	
Toolmex Corporation Inc 1075 Worcester Rd *Web:* www.eisontmx.com	Natick	MA	01760	508-653-8897	
Toromont Industries Ltd 3131 Hwy 7 W PO Box 5511 *TSE: TIH* ■ *Web:* toromontcat.com	Concord	ON	L4K1B7	416-667-5511	
Transnorm System Inc 2810 Ave E E *Web:* www.transnorm.com	Arlington	TX	76011	972-606-0303	
TranTek Automation Corp 2470 N Aero Park Ct *Web:* www.trantekautomation.com	Traverse City	MI	49686	231-946-6270	
Tri Star Industrial Co 1645 W Buckeye Rd *Web:* www.tristaraz.com	Phoenix	AZ	85007	602-252-0554	
Triflo International Inc 1000 FM 830 *TF:* 800-332-0993 ■ *Web:* www.triflo.com	Willis	TX	77318	936-856-8551	
Trio Pac Inc 386 Rue Mcarthur *Web:* www.triopac.com	Montreal	QC	H4T1X8	514-733-7793	
Turner Designs Hydrocarbon Instruments Inc 2023 N Gateway Ste 101 *Web:* www.oilinwatermonitors.com	Fresno	CA	93727	559-253-1414	
Tuson Corp 475 Bunker Ct *Web:* www.tuson.com	Vernon Hills	IL	60061	847-816-8800	
Tyler Equipment Corp 251 Shaker Rd *TF:* 800-292-6351 ■ *Web:* www.tylerequipment.com	East Longmeadow	MA	01028	413-525-6351	525-5909
U.S. Materials Handling Corp 2231 NY-5 *Web:* www.usmaterialshandling.com	Utica	NY	13502	315-732-4111	
Unisearch Associates Inc 96 Bradwick Dr *Web:* www.unisearch-associates.com	Concord	ON	L4K1K8	905-669-3547	
US Equipment Company Inc 8311 Sorensen Ave *TF:* 800-255-4731 ■ *Web:* www.usequipmentco.com	Santa Fe Springs	CA	90670	800-255-4731	
Valin Corp 555 E California Ave *TF:* 800-774-5630 ■ *Web:* www.valin.com	Sunnyvale	CA	94086	408-730-9850	730-1363
Valley Litho Supply Inc 1047 Haugen Ave *TF:* 800-826-6781 ■ *Web:* valleylithosupply.com	Rice Lake	WI	54868	800-826-6781	
VARGO Companies 3709 Pkwy Ln *Web:* www.vargosolutions.com	Hilliard	OH	43026	614-876-1163	
Verosonic 590 Telser Rd Ste B *Web:* www.verosonic.com	Lake Zurich	IL	60047	847-540-9257	
Victor L Phillips Co 4100 Gardner Ave *TF:* 800-878-9290 ■ *Web:* www.vlpco.com	Kansas City	MO	64120	816-241-9290	241-1738
Vinson Process Controls Company LP 2747 Highpoint Oaks Dr *Web:* www.vpcco.com	Lewisville	TX	75067	972-459-8200	
Vmc Technologies Inc 1788 Northwood Dr *Web:* www.vmctech.com	Troy	MI	48084	248-786-3000	
W.D. Matthews Machinery Co 901 Center St *Web:* www.wdmatthews.com	Auburn	ME	04210	207-784-9311	
Wajax Corp 3280 Wharton Way *TSE: WJX* ■ *Web:* www.wajax.com	Mississauga	ON	L4X2C5	905-212-3300	624-6020
Wajax Industrial Components LP 2200 52 Nd Ave *TF:* 866-546-3267 ■ *Web:* www.wajax-industrial-components.ca	Lachine	QC	H8T2Y3	514-636-3333	
Wallace b e Products Corp 71 N Bacton Hill Rd *TF:* 800-553-5438 ■ *Web:* www.wallacecranes.com	Frazer	PA	19355	610-647-1400	
Watts Equipment Co 17547 Comconex Rd *Web:* www.wattsequipment.com	Manteca	CA	95336	209-825-1700	
Weldstar Inc 1750 Mitchell Rd *Web:* www.weldstar.com	Aurora	IL	60505	630-859-3100	
West Side Tractor Sales Co 1400 W Ogden Ave *Web:* www.westsidetractorsales.com	Naperville	IL	60563	630-355-7150	355-7173
Westbrook Engineering 23501 Mound Rd *TF:* 800-899-8182 ■ *Web:* www.westbrook-eng.com	Warren	MI	48091	586-759-3100	
Western States Equipment Co 500 E Overland Rd PO Box 38 *Web:* www.westernstatescat.com	Meridian	ID	83642	208-888-2287	884-2314
White's Farm Supply Inc 4154 State Rt 31 *TF:* 800-633-4443 ■ *Web:* www.whitesfarmsupply.com	Canastota	NY	13032	315-697-2214	697-8024
Winchester Equipment Co 121 Indian Hollow Rd **Fax Area Code:* 540 ■ *TF:* 800-323-3581 ■ *Web:* www.winchesterequipment.com	Winchester	VA	22603	800-323-3581	665-3058*
Wisconsin Lift Truck Corp 3125 Intertech Dr *Web:* www.wisconsinlift.com	Brookfield	WI	53045	262-781-8010	
Wojanis Inc 1001 Montour W Ind Park *TF:* 800-345-9024 ■ *Web:* www.wojanis.com	Coraopolis	PA	15108	724-695-1415	
WOODCO USA 773 McCarty Dr *Web:* www.woodcousa.com	Houston	TX	77029	713-672-9491	
World Oil Tools Inc 72 Technology Way SE *Web:* www.worldoiltools.com	Calgary	AB	T3S0B9	403-720-5155	
Wynright Corp 2500 York Rd *Web:* www.wynright.com	Elk Grove	IL	60007	847-595-9400	
Wyoming Machinery Co 5300 Old W Yellowstone Hwy *TF:* 800-244-0527 ■ *Web:* www.wyomingcat.com	Casper	WY	82604	307-472-1000	261-4491
Yaro Supply Co Drawer Ste 750608 *Web:* www.yaro.com	Dayton	OH	45475	937-859-6100	

359 HELICOPTER TRANSPORT SERVICES

See Also Air Charter Services p. 1719; Ambulance Services p. 1733

	City	State	Zip	Phone	Fax
Accel Aviation Accessories LLC 11900 Lacy Ln *TF:* 877-999-2391 ■ *Web:* www.accelaviation.com	Fort Myers	FL	33966	877-999-2391	
Aerospace Maintenance Solutions LLC 8759 Mayfield Rd *Web:* aerospacellc.com	Chesterland	OH	44026	440-729-7703	
Air Logistics Inc 4605 Industrial Dr *TF:* 800-365-6771 ■ *Web:* www.bristowgroup.com	New Iberia	LA	70560	337-365-6771	364-8222
Aircoastal Helicopters Inc 2615 Lantana Rd Ste J	Lantana	FL	33462	561-642-6840	642-5393
Bristow Alaska Inc 1915 Donald Ave *TF:* 800-686-4080 ■ *Web:* www.bristowgroup.com	Fairbanks	AK	99701	907-452-1197	452-4539
Carson Helicopters 952 Blooming Glen Rd *TF:* 800-523-2335 ■ *Web:* www.carsonhelicopters.com	Perkasie	PA	18944	215-249-3535	249-1352
CHC Helicopter Corp 4740 Agar Dr *Web:* www.chc.ca	Richmond	BC	V7B1A3	604-276-7500	
Coastal Helicopters Inc 8995 Yandukin Dr *TF:* 800-789-5610 ■ *Web:* www.coastalhelicopters.com	Juneau	AK	99801	907-789-5600	
Columbia Helicopters Inc 14452 Arndt Rd NE *Web:* www.colheli.com	Aurora	OR	97002	503-678-1222	678-1222
Corporate Air Technology 1250 Aviation Ave Ste 125 *Web:* corpairtech.com	San Jose	CA	95110	408-977-0990	
Corporate Helicopters of San Diego 3753 John J Montgomery Dr Ste 2 *TF:* 800-345-6737 ■ *Web:* www.corporatehelicopters.com	San Diego	CA	92123	858-505-5650	874-3038
Cougar Helicopters Inc St John's International Airport 40 Craig Dobbins' Way *Web:* www.cougar.ca	Saint John's	NL	A1A4Y3	709-758-4800	758-4850
Eagle Copters Ltd 823 Mctavish Rd NE *TF:* 800-564-6469 ■ *Web:* www.eaglecopters.com	Calgary	AB	T2E7G9	403-250-7370	
Helicopter Transport Services Inc (HTS) 701 Wilson Pt Rd *Web:* www.htshelicopters.com	Baltimore	MD	21220	410-391-7722	686-4507
Helinet Aviation Services LLC 16303 Waterman Dr *Web:* www.helinet.com	Van Nuys	CA	91406	818-902-0229	902-9278
Highland Helicopters Ltd 4240 Agar Dr *Web:* www.highland.ca	Richmond	BC	V7B1A3	604-273-6161	273-6088
Island Express Helicopter Service 1175 Queens Hwy S *TF Cust Svc:* 800-228-2566 ■ *Web:* www.islandexpress.com	Long Beach	CA	90802	310-510-2525	
Kim Davidson Aviation Inc 2701 Airport Ave *Web:* www.kdasmo.com	Santa Monica	CA	90405	310-391-6293	
Maytag Aircraft Corp 6145 Lehman Dr Ste 300 *Web:* www.maytagaircraft.com	Colorado Springs	CO	80918	719-593-1600	
Midwest Helicopter Airways Inc 525 Executive Dr *TF:* 800-323-7609 ■ *Web:* www.midwesthelicopters.com	Willowbrook	IL	60527	630-325-7860	325-3313
Miraco Inc 102 Maple St *Web:* www.miracoinc.com	Manchester	NH	03103	603-665-9449	
PHI Inc 2001 SE Evangeline Thwy PO Box 90808 *NASDAQ: PHII* ■ *TF:* 866-815-7101 ■ *Web:* www.phihelico.com	Lafayette	LA	70508	337-235-2452	235-1357
Repairtech International Inc 16134 Saticoy St *Web:* www.repairtechinternational.com	Van Nuys	CA	91406	818-989-2681	
San Joaquin Helicopters 1407 S Lexington *Web:* www.sjhelicopters.com	Delano	CA	93215	661-725-1898	725-5401
Vertical Aviation 15035 N 73rd St Ste B	Scottsdale	AZ	85260	480-991-6558	907-2759
Victoria International Airport 1962 Canso Rd *TF:* 866-844-4354 ■ *Web:* www.vih.com	North Saanich	BC	V8L5V5	250-656-3987	655-6839
VIH Logging Ltd 1962 Canso Rd *TF:* 866-844-4354 ■ *Web:* www.vih.com	North Saanich	BC	V8L5V5	250-656-3987	655-6839

Phone Fax

Wiggins Airways Inc 1 Garside Way .... Manchester NH 03103 603-629-9191 665-9644
Web: www.wiggins-air.com

Yellowhead Helicopters Ltd 3010 Selwyn Rd .... Valemount BC V0E2Z0 250-566-4401 566-4333
TF: 888-566-4401 ■ Web: www.yhl.ca

360 HOLDING COMPANIES

See Also Conglomerates p. 2059

A holding company is a company that owns enough voting stock in another firm to control management and operations by influencing or electing its board of directors.

360-1 Airlines Holding Companies

Phone Fax

Alaska Air Group Inc
19300 International Blvd. .... Seattle WA 98188 206-433-3200 392-7825
NYSE: ALK ■ Web: www.alaskaair.com

AMR Corp
4333 Amon Carter Blvd PO Box 619616. .... Fort Worth TX 76155 817-963-1234 967-4162
OTC: AAMRQ ■ Web: www.aa.com

ExpressJet Holdings Inc 990 Toffie Terrac .... Atlanta GA 30354 404-856-1000
Web: www.expressjet.com

Frontier Airlines Inc 7001 Tower Rd .... Denver CO 80249 720-374-4200 374-4621
TF: 800-265-5505 ■ Web: www.flyfrontier.com

JetBlue Airways Corp 118-29 Queens Blvd. .... Forest Hills NY 11375 718-286-7900
NASDAQ: JBLU ■ TF: 800-538-2583 ■ Web: www.jetblue.com

Republic Airways Holdings Inc
8909 PuRdue Rd Ste 300 .... Indianapolis IN 46268 317-484-6000
NASDAQ: RJET ■ Web: rjet.com

360-2 Bank Holding Companies

Phone Fax

1st Constitution Bancorp
2650 Rt 130 & Dey Rd .... Cranbury NJ 08512 609-655-4500 655-5653
NASDAQ: FCCY ■ Web: www.1stconstitution.com

215 Holding Co 215 S 11th St. .... Minneapolis MN 55403 612-332-4732
Web: ffmbank.com

Access National Corp
1800 Robert Fulton Dr Ste 310. .... Reston VA 20191 703-871-2100 766-3386
NASDAQ: ANCX ■ TF: 800-931-0370 ■ Web: www.accessnationalbank.com

Accuristix 2844 Bristol Cir. .... Oakville ON L6H6G4 905-829-9927 491-3001
TF: 866-356-6830 ■ Web: www.accuristix.com

Activar Inc 7808 Creekridge Cir. .... Minneapolis MN 55439 952-944-3533
Web: www.activar.com

Allegheny Valley Bank 5137 Butler St. .... Pittsburgh PA 15201 412-781-1464 781-6474
OTC: AVLY ■ TF: 888-397-3742 ■ Web: www.avbpgh.com

Alpine Bank of Colorado
2200 Grand Ave .... Glenwood Springs CO 81601 970-945-2424 947-1242
TF: 888-425-7463 ■ Web: www.alpinebank.com

AMB Financial Corp 8230 Hohman Ave. .... Munster IN 46321 219-836-5870 836-5883
OTC: AMFC ■ TF: 800-436-5113 ■ Web: www.ambfinancial.com

Amboy Bancorp 3590 US Hwy 9 S .... Old Bridge NJ 08857 732-591-8700 591-0705
TF: 800-942-6269 ■ Web: www.amboybank.com

Amegy Bancorp Inc 4400 Post Oak Pkwy. .... Houston TX 77027 713-235-8800
Web: amegybank.com

Ameri-Force Inc
9485 Regency Sq Blvd Ste 300. .... Jacksonville FL 32225 904-353-1773
Web: www.ameriforce.com

Ameriana Bancorp 2118 Bundy Ave. .... New Castle IN 47362 765-529-2230 521-7628
NASDAQ: ASBI ■ TF: 866-844-7584

American National Bank 628 Main St. .... Danville VA 24541 434-792-5111 792-1582
NASDAQ: AMNB ■ TF: 800-240-8190 ■ Web: www.amnb.com

American River Bankshares
3100 Zinfandel Dr Ste 450 .... Rancho Cordova CA 95670 800-544-0545
NASDAQ: AMRB ■ TF: 800-544-0545 ■ Web: www.americanriverbank.com

American State Bank 1401 Ave Q .... Lubbock TX 79401 806-767-7000
TF: 800-531-1401 ■ Web: www.prosperitybankusa.com

Ames National Corp 405 Fifth St PO Box 846 .... Ames IA 50010 515-232-6251 663-3033
NASDAQ: ATLO ■ Web: www.amesnational.com

Anchor BanCorp Wisconsin Inc 25 W Main St .... Madison WI 53707 608-252-8700 252-1889*
NYSE: ABCW ■ *Fax: Hum Res ■ TF: 800-252-6246 ■ Web: www.anchorbank.com

Andrew R Mancini Assoc Inc 129 Odell Ave .... Endicott NY 13760 607-754-7070 786-0410
Web: andrewmancini.com

Andrus Transportation Services LLC
3185 East Deseret Dr North .... Saint George UT 84790 435-673-1566
TF: 800-888-5838 ■ Web: www.andrustrans.com

Annapolis Bancorp Inc 1000 Bestgate Rd. .... Annapolis MD 21401 410-224-4455 278-6265*
NASDAQ: ANNB ■ *Fax Area Code: 800 ■ TF: 800-555-5455 ■ Web: www.fnb-online.com

Arrow Financial Corp 250 Glen St .... Glens Falls NY 12801 518-415-4307
NASDAQ: AROW ■ TF: 800-937-5449 ■ Web: www.arrowfinancial.com

Associated Banc-Corp 1200 Hansen Rd .... Green Bay WI 54304 920-491-7000
NYSE: ASB ■ TF PR: 800-236-2722 ■ Web: www.associatedbank.com

Astoria Financial Corp
1 Astoria Federal Plz. .... Lake Success NY 11042 516-327-3000
NYSE: AF ■ Web: astoriafederal.com

Atlantic Coast Bank (ACFC) 505 Haines Ave .... Waycross GA 31501 912-283-4711
NASDAQ: ACFC ■ TF: 800-342-2824 ■ Web: www.atlanticcoastbank.net

Bancorp Rhode Island 1 Turks Head Pl. .... Providence RI 02903 401-456-5000
NASDAQ: BARI ■ Web: www.bankri.com

BancorpSouth Inc 2910 W Jackson St .... Tupelo MS 38801 662-680-2000 678-7263
NYSE: BXS ■ TF: 888-797-7711 ■ Web: www.bancorpsouth.com

Bank Capital Corp 5055 N 32nd St .... Phoenix AZ 85018 602-992-5055
Web: biltmorebankaz.com

Bank Independent 710 S Montgomery Ave .... Sheffield AL 35660 256-386-5000
TF: 877-865-5050 ■ Web: www.bibank.com

Bank Mutual Corp 4949 W Brown Deer Rd. .... Milwaukee WI 53223 414-354-1500 251-0580*
NASDAQ: BKMU ■ *Fax Area Code: 608 ■ TF: 844-256-8684 ■ Web: www.bankmutual.com

Bank of Commerce Holdings
1901 Churn Creek Rd. .... Redding CA 96002 530-224-3333
NASDAQ: BOCH ■ TF: 800-421-2575 ■ Web: www.reddingbankofcommerce.com

Phone Fax

Bank of Hawaii Corp 130 Merchant St 20th Fl. .... Honolulu HI 96813 888-643-3888
NYSE: BOH ■ TF: 888-643-3888 ■ Web: www.boh.com

Bank of New York Mellon Corp, The 1 Wall St. .... New York NY 10286 212-495-1784
NYSE: BK ■ Web: www.bnymellon.com

Bank of South Carolina Corp
256 Meeting St. .... Charleston SC 29401 843-724-1500 723-1513
NASDAQ: BKSC ■ TF: 800-523-4175 ■ Web: www.banksc.com

Bank of the Ozarks Inc
12615 Chenal Pkwy PO Box 8811 .... Little Rock AR 72211 501-978-2265
NASDAQ: OZRK ■ TF: 800-628-3552 ■ Web: www.bankozarks.com

BankAtlantic Bancorp Inc
401 E Las Olas Blvd Ste 800. .... Fort Lauderdale FL 33301 954-940-4000
Web: www.bbxcapital.com

Banner Bank PO Box 907 .... Walla Walla WA 99362 509-527-3636
NASDAQ: BANR ■ TF: 800-272-9933 ■ Web: www.bannerbank.com

Bar Harbor Bankshares
82 Main St PO Box 400 .... Bar Harbor ME 04609 207-288-3314 288-2626
NYSE: BHB ■ TF: 888-853-7100 ■ Web: www.bhbt.com

Barnes Transportation Services Inc
2309 Whitley Rd. .... Wilson NC 27895 800-898-5897 291-2787*
*Fax Area Code: 252 ■ TF: 800-898-5897 ■ Web: www.barnestransport.com

Bay Bank 2328 W Joppa Rd .... Lutherville MD 21093 410-494-2580
NASDAQ: BYBK ■ TF: 800-222-6566 ■ Web: www.baybankmd.com

BB & T Corp 200 W Second St. .... Winston-Salem NC 27101 336-733-1470
NYSE: BBT ■ TF: 800-226-5228 ■ Web: bbt.investorroom.com/corporate-information

BBCN Bank 3731 Wilshire Blvd Ste 1000. .... Los Angeles CA 90010 213-639-1700 235-3033
NASDAQ: NARA ■ TF: 888-811-6272 ■ Web: www.bbcnbank.com

BCB Bancorp Inc 104-110 Ave C .... Bayonne NJ 07002 201-823-0700 339-0403
NASDAQ: BCBP ■ Web: www.bcbcommunitybank.com

Beck-Ford Construction LP 6750 MayaRd Rd .... Houston TX 77041 713-896-7774 937-1942
Web: www.beck-ford.com

Benny Whitehead Inc 3265 S Eufaula Ave. .... Eufaula AL 36027 334-687-8055 687-1345
TF: 800-633-7617 ■ Web: www.bwitruck.com

Berkshire Bancorp Inc 160 Broadway .... New York NY 10038 212-791-5362
NASDAQ: BERK ■ Web: www.berkbank.com

Berkshire Hills Bancorp Inc 24 N St .... Pittsfield MA 01201 413-443-5601 443-3587
NYSE: BHLB ■ TF: 800-773-5601 ■ Web: www.berkshirebank.com

Big Spring School District 45 Mt Rock Rd .... Newville PA 17241 717-776-2000
Web: www.bigspringsd.org

Blackburn Radio Inc 700 Richmond St Ste 102. .... London ON N6A5C7 519-679-8680
Web: blackburnradio.com

Bmo Bankcorp Inc 111 W Monroe St. .... Chicago IL 60603 888-340-2265
TF: 888-340-2265 ■ Web: www.bmoharris.com

BMO Harris Bank 770 N Water St .... Milwaukee WI 53202 414-765-7569
NYSE: BMO ■ Web: www.bmoharris.com

BNC Bancorp 1226 Eastchester Dr. .... High Point NC 27265 336-476-9200 889-8451
NASDAQ: BNCN ■ Web: www.bankofnc.com

BNCCORP Inc 322 E Main Ave .... Bismarck ND 58501 701-250-3040 222-3653
OTC: BNCC ■ Web: www.bnccorp.com

Bomaine Corp 20731 S Fordyce Ave. .... Carson CA 90810 310-537-1979

Boston Private Financial Holdings Inc
10 Post Office Sq .... Boston MA 02109 617-912-1900
NASDAQ: BPFH ■ TF: 855-738-8916 ■ Web: www.bostonprivate.com

Brannen Banks Of Florida Inc PO Box 1929 .... Inverness FL 34451 352-726-1221 726-1156
TF: 866-546-8273 ■ Web: www.brannenbanks.com

Bridge Capital Holdings
55 Almaden Blvd Ste 200 .... San Jose CA 95113 408-423-8500 423-8520
NASDAQ: BBNK ■ TF General: 866-273-4265 ■ Web: www.bridgebank.com

Bridge Community Bank 200 S Cherry .... Mechanicsville IA 52306 563-432-7291
Web: bankatbridge.com

Broadway Financial Corp
4800 Wilshire Blvd .... Los Angeles CA 90010 323-634-1700 634-1728
NASDAQ: BYFC ■ TF: 888-988-2265 ■ Web: www.broadwayfederalbank.com

Brookline Bank PO Box 470469 .... Brookline MA 02445 617-730-3520
NASDAQ: BRKL ■ TF Cust Svc: 877-668-2265 ■ Web: www.brooklinebank.com

Brunswick Bank & trust
439 Livingston Ave. .... New Brunswick NJ 08901 732-247-5800 247-0292
Web: www.brunswickbank.com

Bryn Mawr Bank Corp 801 Lancaster Ave .... Bryn Mawr PA 19010 610-525-1700 520-7278*
NASDAQ: BMTC ■ *Fax: Cust Svc ■ TF: 855-381-2631 ■ Web: www.bmtc.com

C & F Financial Corp
802 Main St PO Box 391 .... West Point VA 23181 804-843-4584 843-3017
NASDAQ: CFFI ■ TF: 800-583-3863 ■ Web: cffc.com

Camden National Corp 2 Elm St .... Camden ME 04843 207-236-8821 236-6256
NYSE: CAC ■ TF: 800-860-8821 ■ Web: www.camdennational.com

Capital City Bank Group Inc PO Box 900. .... Tallahassee FL 32302 850-402-7500
NASDAQ: CCBG ■ TF: 888-671-0400 ■ Web: www.ccbg.com

Capital Directions Inc 322 S Jefferson St. .... Mason MI 48854 517-676-0500

Capitol Bancorp Ltd 200 N Washington Sq .... Lansing MI 48933 517-487-6555
OTC: CBCRQ ■ Web: www.capitolbancorp.com

Capitol City Bancshares Inc 562 Lee St SW .... Atlanta GA 30311 404-752-6067
TF: 866-758-6395

Capitol Federal Financial 700 Kansas Ave. .... Topeka KS 66603 785-235-1341
NASDAQ: CFFN ■ TF: 888-822-7333 ■ Web: www.capfed.com

Cardinal Financial Corp
8270 Greensboro Dr Ste 500 .... McLean VA 22102 703-584-3400 584-3518*
NASDAQ: CFNL ■ *Fax: Hum Res ■ TF: 800-473-3247 ■ Web: www.cardinalbank.com

Career Path Training Corp
11300 Fourth St N Ste 200. .... St Petersburg FL 33716 727-342-6420
Web: www.careerpathtraining.com

Carolina Bank Holdings Inc
101 N Spring St .... Greensboro NC 27401 336-288-1898 387-4359
NASDAQ: CLBH ■ TF: 800-472-3272 ■ Web: www.carolinabank.com

Caruso Affiliated Holdings LLC
101 The Grove Dr .... Los Angeles CA 90036 323-900-8100
Web: www.carusoaffiliated.com

Carver Bancorp Inc 75 W 125th St. .... New York NY 10027 718-230-2900
NASDAQ: CARV ■ Web: www.carverbank.com

Cascade Bancorp 1100 NW Wall St .... Bend OR 97701 541-385-6205
NASDAQ: CACB ■ TF Cust Svc: 877-617-3400 ■ Web: www.botc.com

Cathay General Bancorp Inc
777 N Broadway .... Los Angeles CA 90012 213-625-4700 625-1368
NASDAQ: CATY ■ TF: 800-922-8429 ■ Web: www.cathaybank.com

Phone Fax

Center Financial Corp 3435 Wilshire Blvd Los Angeles CA 90010 213-365-0114
Web: taxpayer.net
Central Bank 101 W Commercial St Lebanon MO 65536 417-532-2151 532-2001
Web: www.fscb.com
Central Federal Corp 601 Main St Wellsville OH 14895 330-666-7979 666-7959
NASDAQ: CFBK ■ *TF:* 866-668-4606 ■ *Web:* www.cfbankonline.com
Central Pacific Financial Corp PO Box 3590 Honolulu HI 96811 808-544-0500 544-0500
NYSE: CPF ■ *TF:* 800-342-8422 ■ *Web:* www.centralpacificbank.com
Central Valley Community Bancorp
7100 N Financial Dr Ste 101 Fresno CA 93720 559-298-1775 298-1483
NASDAQ: CVCY ■ *TF:* 866-294-9588 ■ *Web:* www.cvcb.com
Century Bancorp Inc 400 Mystic Ave Medford MA 02155 781-393-4160
NASDAQ: CNBKA ■ *TF:* 866-823-6887 ■ *Web:* www.centurybank.com
CFS Bancorp Inc 707 Ridge Rd Munster IN 46321 219-513-5123 770-7572*
NASDAQ: CITZ ■ **Fax Area Code:* 317 ■ *TF:* 866-622-1370 ■ *Web:* www.firstmerchants.com
Charter Enterprises LLC
1255 Corporate Ctr Dr Ste PH402 Monterey Park CA 91754 323-269-6868
Web: www.charterbbq.com
Chemical Financial Corp 333 E Main St Midland MI 48640 989-839-5350
NASDAQ: CHFC ■ *TF:* 800-867-9757 ■ *Web:* www.chemicalbankmi.com
Citizens & Northern Corp 90-92 Main St Wellsboro PA 16901 570-724-3411 724-6395
NASDAQ: CZNC ■ *Web:* cnbankpa.com
Citizens Financial Group Inc 1 Citizens Dr Riverside RI 02915 401-456-7000
TF: 800-922-9999 ■ *Web:* www.citizensbank.com
Citizens Holding Co
521 Main St PO Box 209 Philadelphia MS 39350 601-656-4692
NASDAQ: CIZN ■ *Web:* www.thecitizensbankphila.com
Citizens South Banking Corp
519 S New Hope Rd PO Box 2249 Gastonia NC 28054 704-868-5200 825-7723*
NASDAQ: CSBC ■ **Fax:* Hum Res ■ *Web:* www.parksterlingbank.com
City Holding Co 25 Gatewater Rd Charleston WV 25313 304-769-1100
NASDAQ: CHCO ■ *Web:* www.bankatcity.com
Clifton Savings Bancorp Inc
1433 Van Houten Ave Clifton NJ 07013 973-473-2200
NASDAQ: CSBK ■ *TF:* 888-562-6727 ■ *Web:* www.cliftonsavings.com
CNB Financial Corp 1 S Second St PO Box 42 Clearfield PA 16830 814-765-9621 765-8294
NASDAQ: CCNE ■ *TF:* 800-492-3221 ■ *Web:* www.cnbbank.bank
Colorado Business Bank 821 17th St Denver CO 80202 303-293-2265
TF: 800-574-4714 ■ *Web:* cobizbank.com
Columbia Bank 1301 A St Ste 800 Tacoma WA 98402 253-305-1900
NASDAQ: COLB ■ *TF:* 800-305-1905 ■ *Web:* www.columbiabank.com
Commercial National Financial Corp
900 Ligonier St Latrobe PA 15650 724-539-3501
OTC: CNAF ■ *TF:* 800-803-2265 ■ *Web:* www.cnbthebankonline.com
Community Bank Shares of Indiana Inc
101 W Spring St New Albany IN 47150 812-944-2224
NASDAQ: YCB ■ *TF:* 866-944-2004 ■ *Web:* www.yourcommunitybank.com
Community Bank System Inc
5790 Widewaters Pkwy Syracuse NY 13214 315-445-2282
NYSE: CBU ■ *TF:* 800-847-2911 ■ *Web:* www.communitybankna.com
Community Bankshares Inc
5570 DTC Pkwy Greenwood Village CO 80111 720-529-3336
Web: www.cobnks.com
Community First Bank Na PO Box 39 Forest OH 45843 419-273-2595
Web: www.com1stbank.com
Community Investors Bancorp Inc
119 S Sandusky Ave Bucyrus OH 44820 419-562-7055 562-5516
OTC: CIBN ■ *TF:* 800-222-4955 ■ *Web:* www.ffcb.com
Community Shores Bank Corp
1030 W Norton Ave Muskegon MI 49441 231-780-1800 780-3006
OTC: CSHB ■ *TF:* 888-853-6633 ■ *Web:* www.communityshores.com
Community State Bank 208 N Ctr Shelbina MO 63468 573-588-4101 588-4408
Web: www.commbankonline.com
Community West Bancshares 445 Pine Ave Goleta CA 93117 805-692-5821 692-8902
NASDAQ: CWBC ■ *Web:* www.communitywest.com
Compass Bancshares Inc 15 S 20th St Birmingham AL 35233 205-297-3584 297-3702
TF: 800-266-7277 ■ *Web:* www.bbvacompass.com
Connecticut Bank & Trust Co
58 State House Sq Hartford CT 06103 860-246-5200
Web: www.berkshirebank.com
ConnectOne Bancorp, Inc 2455 Morris Ave Union NJ 07083 908-206-2907
NASDAQ: CNBC
Contrans Corp 1179 Ridgeway Rd Woodstock ON N4V1E3 519-421-4600
Web: www.contrans.ca
Country Club Bank 2310 S Fourth St Leavenworth KS 66048 913-682-2300
Web: www.countryclubbank.com
Crazy Woman Creek Bancorp Inc PO Box 1020 Buffalo WY 82834 307-684-5591 684-7854
TF: 877-684-2766 ■ *Web:* www.buffalofed.com
Crofutt & Smith Moving & Storage
1 Lenel Rd PO Box 8001 Landing NJ 07850 973-347-7200 347-8143
Cullen/Frost Bankers Inc
100 W Houston St San Antonio TX 78205 210-220-4011
NYSE: CFR ■ *TF:* 800-562-6732 ■ *Web:* www.frostbank.com
CVB Financial Corp
701 N Haven Ave PO Box 51000 Ontario CA 91764 909-980-4030
NASDAQ: CVBF ■ *TF:* 888-222-5432 ■ *Web:* www.cbbank.com
Davidson Pipe Supply Company Inc
5002 Second Ave Brooklyn NY 11232 718-439-6300
Dickinson Financial Corp
1111 Main St Ste 1600 Kansas City MO 64105 816-472-5244 412-0070
Dime Community Bancshares Inc
209 Havemeyer St Brooklyn NY 11211 718-782-6200
NASDAQ: DCOM ■ *TF:* 800-321-3463 ■ *Web:* www.dime.com
Doral Financial Corp 1441 F D Roosevelt Ave San Juan PR 00920 787-749-4949 749-4191
NYSE: DRL ■ *TF:* 866-296-3743 ■ *Web:* www.snl.com
Eagle Bancorp Inc 7815 Woodmont Ave Bethesda MD 20814 240-497-2044 986-8529*
NASDAQ: EGBN ■ **Fax Area Code:* 301 ■ *TF:* 800-364-8313 ■ *Web:* www.eaglebankcorp.com
East West Bancorp Inc 1881 W Main St Alhambra CA 91801 626-308-2012
NASDAQ: EWBC ■ *TF:* 888-895-5650 ■ *Web:* www.eastwestbank.com
Eastern Bank Corp 265 Franklin St Boston MA 02110 617-897-1008
TF Cust Svc: 800-327-8376 ■ *Web:* www.easternbank.com
Eastern Virginia Bankshares Inc
330 Hospital Rd Tappahannock VA 22560 804-443-8400 445-1047
NASDAQ: EVBS ■ *TF General:* 866-296-3743 ■ *Web:* www.snl.com

Phone Fax

Enterprise Bancorp Inc 222 Merrimack St Lowell MA 01852 978-459-9000 656-5813
NASDAQ: EBTC ■ *Web:* www.enterprisebanking.com
Enterprise Financial Services Corp
150 N Meramec Ave Clayton MO 63105 314-725-5500
NASDAQ: EFSG ■ *TF:* 800-396-8141 ■ *Web:* www.enterprisebank.com
Evanov Communications Inc 5312 Dundas St W Toronto ON M9B1B3 416-213-1035
Web: www.evanovradio.com
Evans Bancorp Inc 1 Grimsby Dr Hamburg NY 14075 716-926-2000 926-2005*
NYSE: EVBN ■ **Fax:* Hum Res ■ *TF:* 866-310-0763 ■ *Web:* www.evansbank.com
F & M Bank & Trust Co 505 Broadway Hannibal MO 63401 573-221-6424
Web: bankfm.com
Farmer State Bank of Sublette
303 S Pennsylvania Ave PO Box 20 Sublette IL 61367 815-849-5242
TF: 866-269-1722 ■ *Web:* www.sublettebank.com
Farmers Capital Bank Corp PO Box 309 Frankfort KY 40602 502-227-1668 227-1692
NASDAQ: FFKT ■ *TF:* 800-776-9437 ■ *Web:* www.farmerscapital.com
Fauquier Bankshares Inc 10 Courthouse Sq Warrenton VA 20186 540-347-2700 349-2093
NASDAQ: FBSS ■ *TF:* 800-638-3798 ■ *Web:* www.tfb.bank
FFD Financial Corp 321 N Wooster Ave Dover OH 44622 330-364-7777 364-7779
OTC: FFDF ■ *TF:* 800-558-3424 ■ *Web:* www.onlinefirstfed.com
FFW Corp 1205 N Cass St Wabash IN 46992 260-563-3185 563-4841
OTC: FFWC ■ *TF:* 800-377-4984 ■ *Web:* www.crossroadsbanking.com
Fidelity Federal Bancorp 18 NW Fourth St Evansville IN 47708 812-424-0921 469-2150
OTC: FDLB ■ *TF:* 800-280-8280 ■ *Web:* www.unitedfidelity.com
Financial Institutions Inc 220 Liberty St Warsaw NY 14569 585-786-1100
NASDAQ: FISI ■ *TF:* 866-296-3743 ■ *Web:* www.snl.com
First American Bank Corp
1650 Louis Ave Elk Grove Village IL 60009 847-952-3700
TF: 866-449-1150 ■ *Web:* www.firstambank.com
First BanCorp PO Box 9146 San Juan PR 00908 787-725-2511
NYSE: FBP ■ *TF:* 866-695-2511 ■ *Web:* www.1firstbank.com/pr/es
First Bancorp 341 N Main St Troy NC 27371 910-576-6171 576-1070
NASDAQ: FBNC ■ *TF:* 800-548-9377 ■ *Web:* localfirstbank.com
First Bancorp of Indiana Inc
5001 Davis Lant Dr Evansville IN 47715 812-492-8100
OTC: FBPI
First Bancshares Inc 142 E First St Mountain Grove MO 65711 417-926-5151 926-4362
NYSE: FBSI ■ *Web:* www.firsthomesavingsbank.com
First Banctrust Corp 101 S Central Ave Paris IL 61944 217-465-6381 465-0234
OTC: FIRT ■ *TF:* 800-228-6381 ■ *Web:* www.firstbanktrust.com
First Banks Inc 135 N Meramec Ave Clayton MO 63105 314-854-4600
TF: 800-760-2265 ■ *Web:* www.firstbanks.com
First Busey Corp 100 W University Ave Champaign IL 61820 217-365-4516
NASDAQ: BUSE ■ *TF:* 800-672-8739 ■ *Web:* www.busey.com
First Citizens Bancorp Inc PO Box 29 Columbia SC 29202 919-716-4588 931-8519*
OTC: FCBN ■ **Fax Area Code:* 803 ■ *TF:* 888-612-4444 ■ *Web:* www.firstcitizens.com
First Citizens BancShares Inc
4300 Six Forks Rd Raleigh NC 27609 919-716-7000
NASDAQ: FCNCA ■ *Web:* www.firstcitizens.com
First Citizens Bank
350 S Beverly D Ste 150 Beverly Hills CA 90212 888-323-4732
TF: 888-323-4732 ■ *Web:* www.firstcitizens.com
First Citizens National Bank Charitable Foundation
PO Box 1708 Mason City IA 50402 641-423-1600 423-4600
TF: 800-423-1602 ■ *Web:* www.firstcitizensnb.com
First Commonwealth Financial Corp
601 Philadelphia St Indiana PA 15701 724-349-7220
NYSE: FCF ■ *TF:* 800-711-2265 ■ *Web:* www.fcbanking.com
First Community Bank 420 Second Ave SW Cullman AL 35055 256-734-4863 737-8900
Web: www.fcbcullman.com
First Community Corp (FCC) 5455 Sunset Blvd Lexington SC 29072 803-951-0555
NASDAQ: FCCO ■ *TF:* 800-829-6372 ■ *Web:* www.firstcommunitysc.com
First Defiance Financial Corp
601 Clinton St Defiance OH 43512 419-782-5015
NASDAQ: FDEF ■ *TF:* 800-472-6292 ■ *Web:* www.fdef.com
First Financial Bancorp (FFB)
255 E Fifth St Ste 700 Cincinnati OH 45202 877-322-9530
NASDAQ: FFBC ■ *TF:* 877-322-9530 ■ *Web:* www.bankatfirst.com
First Financial Bankshares Inc PO Box 701 Abilene TX 79604 325-627-7155 627-7393
NASDAQ: FFIN ■ *TF:* 888-588-2623 ■ *Web:* www.ffin.com
First Financial Corp
1 First Financial Plz Terre Haute IN 47807 812-238-6000 232-5336
NASDAQ: THFF ■ *TF:* 800-511-0045 ■ *Web:* www.first-online.com
First FSB of Frankfort
216 W Main St PO Box 535 Frankfort KY 40602 502-223-1638 223-7136
TF: 888-818-3372 ■ *Web:* www.ffsbfrankfort.com
First Horizon National Corp 165 Madison Memphis TN 38103 901-523-4444
NYSE: FHN ■ *TF:* 800-489-4040 ■ *Web:* www.firsthorizon.com
First Interstate Bancsystem Inc
401 N 31st St Billings MT 59101 406-255-5000
NASDAQ: FIBK ■ *TF:* 888-752-3341 ■ *Web:* www.firstinterstatebank.com
First M & F Corp 221 E Washington St Kosciusko MS 39090 662-289-5121
NASDAQ: FMFC
First Merchants Corp 200 E Jackson St Muncie IN 47305 765-747-1500 741-7283*
NASDAQ: FRME ■ **Fax:* Mktg ■ *TF:* 800-205-3464 ■ *Web:* www.firstmerchants.com
First Midwest Bancorp Inc 1 Pierce Pl Ste 1500 Itasca IL 60143 630-875-7200
NASDAQ: FMBI ■ *TF:* 800-322-3623 ■ *Web:* firstmidwest.com
First National Bank
4220 William Penn Hwy Monroeville PA 15146 800-555-5455
TF: 800-555-5455 ■ *Web:* www.fnb-online.com
First National Bank of Tennessee
214 E Main St Livingston TN 38570 931-823-1261
Web: www.fnbotn.com
First National Lincoln Corp
223 Main St PO Box 940 Damariscotta ME 04543 207-563-3195 563-3356
TF: 800-564-3195 ■ *Web:* www.thefirstbancorp.com
First National of Nebraska Inc PO BOX 2490 Omaha NE 68197 402-341-0500 938-5302
TF: 800-688-7070 ■ *Web:* www.firstnational.com
First Niles Financial Inc 55 N Main St Niles OH 44446 330-652-2539 652-0911
NYSE: FNFI
First of Long Island Corp 10 Glen Head Ave Glen Head NY 11545 516-671-4900 676-7900
NASDAQ: FLIC ■ *TF:* 800-554-8969 ■ *Web:* www.fnbli.com
First Security Group Inc 531 Broad St Chattanooga TN 37402 423-266-2000
NASDAQ: FSGI ■ *Web:* www.fsgbank.com

Phone Fax

First South Bancorp Inc 1311 Carolina Ave .... Washington NC 27889 252-946-4178 946-3873
NASDAQ: FSBK ■ *TF:* 800-946-4178 ■ *Web:* www.firstsouthnc.com

First Southern Bank 301 S Ct St .... Florence AL 35630 256-718-4200 718-4296
TF General: 800-625-7131 ■ *Web:* www.firstsouthern.com

First State Bank 730 Harry Sauner Rd .... Hillsboro OH 45133 937-393-9170
TF General: 800-987-2566 ■ *Web:* www.fsb4me.com

First Trinity Financial Corp
7633 E 63rd Pl Ste 230. .... Tulsa OK 74133 918-249-2438
Web: www.firsttrinityfinancial.com

First United Corp 19 S Second St. .... Oakland MD 21550 888-692-2654 334-5784*
NASDAQ: FUNC ■ **Fax Area Code:* 301 ■ **Fax:* Hum Res ■ *TF:* 888-692-2654 ■ *Web:* www.mybank4.com

First West Virginia Bancorp Inc
1701 Warwood Ave. .... Wheeling WV 26003 304-277-1100
NYSE: FWV ■ *Web:* snl.com

FirstFed Bancorp Inc
1630 Fourth Ave N PO Box 340 .... Bessemer AL 35020 205-428-8472 428-8652
TF: 800-436-5112 ■ *Web:* www.firstfedbessemer.com

Flushing Financial Corp
1979 Marcus Ave .... New Hyde Park NY 11042 718-961-5400
NASDAQ: FFIC ■ *TF:* 800-581-2889 ■ *Web:* www.flushingbank.com

German American Bancorp 711 Main St .... Jasper IN 47546 812-482-1314 482-0758
NASDAQ: GABC ■ *TF:* 800-482-1314 ■ *Web:* www.germanamerican.com

Glacier Bancorp Inc PO Box 27...................... Kalispell MT 59903 406-756-4200
NASDAQ: GBCI ■ *TF:* 800-735-4371 ■ *Web:* www.glacierbank.com

Great American Bancorp Inc 1311 S Neil St .... Champaign IL 61820 217-356-2265 356-2502
OTC: GTPS ■ *TF:* 800-962-4284 ■ *Web:* www.greatamericanbancorp.com

Greene County Bancorp Inc 302 Main St. .... Catskill NY 12414 518-943-2600 943-3756
NASDAQ: GCBC ■ *TF:* 888-439-4272 ■ *Web:* thebankofgreenecounty.com

GreenHouse Holdings Inc
5171 Santa Fe St Ste I .... San Diego CA 92109 858-273-2626

Greenwood Racing Inc 3001 St Rd .... Bensalem PA 19020 215-639-9000
TF: 888-238-2946 ■ *Web:* www.parxracing.com

Guaranty Bancshares Inc
100 W Arkansas St PO Box 1158 .... Mount Pleasant TX 75455 903-572-9881 572-9658
TF: 888-572-9881 ■ *Web:* www.gnty.com

Hancock Holding Co 2510 14th St. .... Gulfport MS 39501 228-868-4727
TF: 800-522-6542

Hanmi Bank 3660 Wilshire Blvd Ste PH-A. .... Los Angeles CA 90010 213-382-2200 384-8608
TF: 877-808-4266 ■ *Web:* www.hanmi.com

Harleysville Savings Financial Corp
271 Main St .... Harleysville PA 19438 215-256-8828 513-9393
NASDAQ: HARL ■ *TF:* 888-256-8828 ■ *Web:* www.harleysvillesavings.com

Harrell Bancshares Inc 1325 Hwy 278 Byp. .... Camden AR 71701 870-837-8300

Hawthorn Bancshares Inc
300 SW Longview Blvd. .... Lees Summit MO 64081 816-347-8100
NASDAQ: HWBK ■ *Web:* www.exchangebancshares.com

Heartland Financial USA Inc 1398 Central Ave .... Dubuque IA 52001 563-589-2100
NASDAQ: HTLF ■ *TF:* 888-739-2100 ■ *Web:* www.htlf.com

Heritage Bank 101 N Main St .... Jonesboro GA 30236 770-478-8881 478-8929
TF: 866-971-0106 ■ *Web:* www.heritagebank.com

Heritage Bank 201 Fifth Ave SW. .... Olympia WA 98501 360-943-1500
TF: 800-455-6126 ■ *Web:* www.heritagebankwaonline2.com

Heritage Commerce Corp 150 Almaden Blvd .... San Jose CA 95113 408-947-6900 947-6910
NASDAQ: HTBK ■ *TF:* 800-468-9716 ■ *Web:* www.heritagecommercecorp.com

Heritage Financial Corp 201 Fifth Ave SW............ Olympia WA 98501 360-943-1500
NASDAQ: HFWA ■ *TF:* 800-962-4284 ■ *Web:* www.hf-wa.com

HF Financial Corp 225 S Main Ave. .... Sioux Falls SD 57104 605-333-7556 333-7621
NASDAQ: HFFC ■ *TF:* 800-244-2149 ■ *Web:* www.homefederal.com

High Country Bancorp Inc
7360 W Hwy 50 PO Box 309 .... Salida CO 81201 719-539-2516 530-8881
OTC: HCBC ■ *TF:* 800-201-0557 ■ *Web:* www.highcountrybank.net

HMN Financial Inc 1016 Civic Ctr Dr NW .... Rochester MN 55901 507-535-1309 346-7140
NASDAQ: HMNF ■ *TF:* 888-257-2000 ■ *Web:* www.hmnf.com

Home City Financial Corp
2454 N Limestone St .... Springfield OH 45503 937-390-0470 390-0876
OTC: HCFL ■ *TF:* 866-421-2331 ■ *Web:* www.homecityfederal.com

Home Federal Bank 1602 Cumberland Ave .... Middlesboro KY 40965 606-248-1095 242-1010*
OTC: HFBA ■ **Fax:* Hum Res ■ *TF:* 800-354-0182 ■ *Web:* www.homefederalbank.com

Home Loan Financial Corp 413 Main St. .... Coshocton OH 43812 740-622-0444 623-6000
OTC: HLFN ■ *Web:* www.homeloansavingsbank.com

HopFed Bancorp Inc
2700 Ft Campbell Blvd .... Hopkinsville KY 42240 270-885-1171 889-0313
NASDAQ: HFBC ■ *Web:* www.bankwithheritage.com

Horizon Bank 515 Franklin Sq .... Michigan City IN 46360 219-874-9245
Web: www.horizonbank.com

HSBC North America Holdings Inc
2700 Sanders Rd .... Prospect Heights IL 60070 847-564-5000
TF: 800-975-4722 ■ *Web:* www.hsbc.com

Hulman & Co 900 Wabash Ave .... Terre Haute IN 47807 812-232-9446
Web: www.clabbergirl.com

Huntington Bancshares Inc 7 Easton Oval .... Columbus OH 43219 800-480-2265
NASDAQ: HBAN ■ *TF:* 800-480-2265 ■ *Web:* www.huntington.com

IBERIABANK Corp 200 W Congress St .... Lafayette LA 70501 800-968-0801
NASDAQ: IBKC ■ *TF:* 800-968-0801 ■ *Web:* www.iberiabank.com

Independent Bank Corp 230 W Main St .... Ionia MI 48846 616-527-2400 527-4004
NASDAQ: IBCP ■ *TF:* 888-300-3193 ■ *Web:* www.independentbank.com

International Bancshares Corp
1200 San Bernardo Ave .... Laredo TX 78040 956-722-7611 726-6637
NASDAQ: IBOC ■ *Web:* www.ibc.com

ISCAR Metals 300 Wway Pl......................... Arlington TX 76018 817-258-3200 258-3221
Web: www.iscarmetals.com

Jacksonville Bancorp Inc
1211 W Morton Ave .... Jacksonville IL 62650 217-245-4111
NASDAQ: JXSB ■ *Web:* www.jacksonvillesavings.com

Jeffersonville Bancorp
4866 State Rt 52 PO Box 398 .... Jeffersonville NY 12748 845-482-4000 482-3544
OTC: JFBC ■ *Web:* www.jeffbank.com

Johnson Financial Group Inc
555 Main St Ste 400. .... Racine WI 53403 262-619-2790
Web: johnsonbank.com

Joy State Bank 101 W Main St. .... Joy IL 61260 309-584-4146 584-4148
Web: joystatebank.com

Phone Fax

Keweenaw Financial Corp 235 Quincy St .... Hancock MI 49930 906-482-0404 482-4403
TF: 866-482-0404 ■ *Web:* www.snb-t.com

KeyCorp 127 Public Sq. .... Cleveland OH 44114 216-689-8481
NYSE: KEY ■ *TF:* 800-539-9055 ■ *Web:* www.key.com

Koss-Winn Bancshares Inc
101 N Main St .... Buffalo Center IA 50424 641-562-2696

Lake Sunapee Bank 9 Main St PO Box 29 .... Newport NH 03773 603-863-5772 863-5025
TF: 800-281-5772 ■ *Web:* www.lakesunbank.com

Lakeland Bancorp Inc 250 Oak Ridge Rd .... Oak Ridge NJ 07438 973-697-2000 697-8385
NASDAQ: LBAI ■ *TF:* 866-224-1379 ■ *Web:* www.lakelandbank.com

Lakeland Financial Corp 202 E Ctr St. .... Warsaw IN 46580 574-267-6144
NASDAQ: LKFN ■ *TF:* 800-827-4522 ■ *Web:* www.lakecitybank.com

Lexington B & L Financial Corp
205 S 13th St PO Box 190 .... Lexington MO 64067 660-259-2247 259-2384
Web: www.bl-bank.com

Linkous Construction Company Inc
1661 Aaron Brenner Dr Ste 207 .... Memphis TN 38120 901-754-0700 754-0302
Web: www.linkousconstruction.com

LNB Bancorp Inc 457 Broadway .... Lorain OH 44052 440-989-3348 244-9507
NASDAQ: LNBB ■ *TF:* 800-860-1007 ■ *Web:* www.northwestsavingsbank.com

Logansport Financial Corp 723 E Broadway. .... Logansport IN 46947 574-722-3855 722-3857
OTC: LOGN ■ *TF:* 800-541-9154 ■ *Web:* www.logansportsavings.com

Lumber Industries Inc 5809 Kennett Pk. .... Wilmington DE 19807 302-655-9651

Macatawa Bank Corp
10753 Macatawa Dr PO Box 3119 .... Holland MI 49424 616-820-1444 494-7644
NASDAQ: MCBC ■ *TF:* 877-820-2265 ■ *Web:* www.macatawabank.com

Malaga Financial Corp
2514 Via Tejon .... Palos Verdes Estates CA 90274 310-375-9000 373-3615
OTC: MLGF ■ *TF:* 866-275-2677 ■ *Web:* www.malagabank.com

Matec Instrument Cos Inc 56 Hudson St. .... Northborough MA 01532 508-393-0155
Web: www.matec.com

MB Financial Inc 6111 N River Rd .... Rosemont IL 60018 888-422-6562
NASDAQ: MBFI ■ *TF:* 888-422-6562 ■ *Web:* www.mbfinancial.com

MBT Financial Corp 102 E Front St .... Monroe MI 48161 734-241-3431
NASDAQ: MBTF ■ *TF:* 800-321-0032 ■ *Web:* www.mbandt.com

Mercantil Commercebank Holding Corp
220 Alhambra Cir .... Coral Gables FL 33134 305-460-8701 460-4010*
**Fax:* Cust Svc ■ *Web:* www.commercebankfl.com

Mercantile Bank 200 N 33rd St PO Box 3455 .... Quincy IL 62305 217-223-7300
NYSE: MBCR ■ *TF:* 800-405-6372 ■ *Web:* www.mercantilebk.com

Mercantile Bank Corp 310 Leonard St NW......... Grand Rapids MI 49504 616-406-3000
NASDAQ: MBWM ■ *TF:* 888-345-6296 ■ *Web:* www.mercbank.com

Merchants Bancshares Inc PO Box 1009 .... Burlington VT 05402 802-658-3400
NASDAQ: MBVT ■ *TF:* 800-322-5222 ■ *Web:* www.mbvt.com

Mesa Systems Inc 681 Railroad Blvd. .... Grand Junction CO 81505 970-241-6450
TF: 800-654-3225 ■ *Web:* www.mesasystemsinc.com

Mid Country Financial Corp PO Box 4164 .... Macon GA 31208 478-746-8222
Web: www.midcountryfinancial.com

Mid Penn Bancorp Inc 349 Union St. .... Millersburg PA 17061 717-692-2133 692-4861
NASDAQ: MPB ■ *TF:* 866-642-7736 ■ *Web:* midpennbank.com

MidSouth Bancorp Inc 102 Versailles Blvd .... Lafayette LA 70501 337-237-8343 267-4316
NYSE: MSL ■ *TF:* 800-213-2265 ■ *Web:* www.midsouthbank.com

MidWestOne Financial Group Inc
102 S Clinton St PO Box 1700 .... Iowa City IA 52240 319-356-5800 356-5849
NASDAQ: MOFG ■ *TF Cust Svc:* 800-247-4418 ■ *Web:* ir.midwestone.com

Millennium Bankshares Corp
21430 Cedar Dr Ste 200 .... Sterling VA 20164 703-464-0100 464-0064
OTC: MBVA

Miner-Dederick Construction LLP 1532 Peden .... Houston TX 77006 713-529-3001
Web: www.minerdederick.com

MutualFirst Financial Inc 110 E Charles St .... Muncie IN 47305 765-747-2800
NASDAQ: MFSF ■ *TF:* 800-382-8031 ■ *Web:* bankwithmutual.com

NASB Financial Inc 12520 S 71 Hwy .... Grandview MO 64030 816-765-2200 316-4504
NASDAQ: NASB ■ *TF:* 800-677-6272 ■ *Web:* www.nasb.com

National Bankshares Inc 101 Hubbard St. .... Blacksburg VA 24060 540-951-6300
NASDAQ: NKSH ■ *TF:* 800-552-4123 ■ *Web:* www.nationalbankshares.com

National Penn Bancshares Inc PO Box 547 .... Boyertown PA 19512 800-822-3321
NASDAQ: NPBC ■ *TF:* 800-822-3321 ■ *Web:* www.nationalpenn.com

NBT Bancorp Inc 52 S Broad St .... Norwich NY 13815 607-337-2265 336-7538
NASDAQ: NBTB ■ *TF:* 800-628-2265 ■ *Web:* www.nbtbancorp.com

Nico Trading LLC 222 W Adams St. .... Chicago IL 60606 312-253-8000
Web: www.citigroup.com

North State Bank Inc 6204 Falls of Neuse Rd .... Raleigh NC 27609 919-787-9696 719-4481
TF: 877-357-2265 ■ *Web:* www.northstatebank.com

Northbridge Financial Corp
105 Adelaide St W Ste 700. .... Toronto ON M5H1P9 416-350-4400
TF: 855-620-6262 ■ *Web:* www.nbfc.com

Northeast Bancorp 500 Canal St .... Lewiston ME 04240 207-786-3245 782-7230
NASDAQ: NBN ■ *TF:* 800-284-5989 ■ *Web:* www.northeastbank.com

Northeast Indiana Bancorp Inc
648 N Jefferson St .... Huntington IN 46750 260-356-3311
OTC: NIDB ■ *TF:* 800-550-3372 ■ *Web:* firstfedhuntington.com

Northern States Financial Corp
1601 N Lewis Ave. .... Waukegan IL 60085 847-244-6000
OTC: NSFC ■ *TF:* 800-339-4432 ■ *Web:* www.norstatesbank.com

Northwest Bancorp Inc PO Box 128 .... Warren PA 16365 814-728-7263
TF: 800-859-1000 ■ *Web:* www.northwestsavingsbank.com

Oak Park School District (OPSD) 13900 Granzon ...... Oak Park MI 48237 248-336-7700 336-7738
Web: www.oakparkschools.org

Ocwen Financial Corp
1661 Worthington Rd Ste 100
PO Box 24737 .... West Palm Beach FL 33409 561-681-8000
NYSE: OCN ■ *TF:* 800-746-2936 ■ *Web:* www.ocwen.com

Ohio Valley Banc Corp 420 Third Ave .... Gallipolis OH 45631 740-446-2631 446-4643
NASDAQ: OVBC ■ *TF:* 800-468-6682 ■ *Web:* www.ovbc.com

Old Point Financial Corp
1 W Mellen St PO Box 3392 .... Hampton VA 23663 757-728-1200
NASDAQ: OPOF ■ *TF:* 800-952-0051 ■ *Web:* www.oldpoint.com

Old Second Bancorp Inc 37 S River St .... Aurora IL 60506 630-892-0202 892-9630*
NASDAQ: OSBC ■ **Fax:* Mktg ■ *TF:* 877-866-0202 ■ *Web:* www.oldsecond.com

Opus Bank 19900 MacArthur Blvd 12th Fl .... Irvine CA 92612 949-250-9800
TF: 855-678-7226 ■ *Web:* www.opusbank.com

Phone Fax

Owen Community Bank 279 E Morgan St ....Spencer IN 47460 812-829-2095 829-3069
TF: 800-690-2095 ■ *Web:* owencom.com

Pacific & Western Credit Corp
140 Fullarton St Ste 2002..........................London ON N6A5P2 519-645-1919 645-2060
TSE: PWC ■ *Web:* www.pwbank.com

Pacific Mercantile Bancorp
949 S Coast Dr Ste 105 ....Costa Mesa CA 92626 714-438-2600 438-1088
NASDAQ: PMBC ■ *TF General:* 877-450-2265 ■ *Web:* www.pmbank.com

Pacific Premier Bancorp Inc
1600 Sunflower Ave ....Costa Mesa CA 92626 714-431-4000
NASDAQ: PPBI ■ *TF:* 888-388-5433 ■ *Web:* www.ppbi.com

Pagnotti Enterprises Inc
46 Public Sq Ste 600 ....Wilkes-Barre PA 18701 570-825-8700
Web: www.jeddocoal.com

Paradise Ventures Inc 2901 Rigsby Ln...........Safety Harbor FL 34695 727-726-1115
Web: www.paradisedev.com

Park Bancorp Inc 5400 S Pulaski Rd ....Chicago IL 60632 773-582-8616 434-6043
OTC: PFED ■ *TF:* 888-727-5333 ■ *Web:* www.parkfed.com

Park Bank 7540 W Capitol Dr ....Milwaukee WI 53216 414-466-8000
Web: www.parkbankonline.com

Park National Bank 50 N Third St PO Box 3500 .... Newark OH 43058 740-349-8451
NYSE: PRK ■ *TF:* 888-791-8633 ■ *Web:* www.parknationalcorp.com

Pathfinder Bancorp Inc 214 W First St...............Oswego NY 13126 315-343-0057 342-9403
NASDAQ: PBHC ■ *TF:* 800-811-5620 ■ *Web:* www.pathfinderbank.com

Patriot National Bancorp Inc 900 Bedford St......... Stamford CT 06901 203-251-7200 324-8804
NASDAQ: PNBK ■ *TF:* 888-728-7468 ■ *Web:* bankpatriot.com

Peapack-Gladstone Bank
500 Hills Dr Ste 300 PO Box 700 .... Bedminster NJ 07921 908-234-0700 781-2046
NASDAQ: PGC ■ *TF:* 800-742-7595 ■ *Web:* www.pgbank.com

Peoples Bancorp Inc 138 Putnam St..................Marietta OH 45750 740-373-3155 374-2020*
NASDAQ: PEBO ■ **Fax:* Mail Rm ■ *TF:* 800-374-6123 ■ *Web:* www.peoplesbancorp.com

Peoples Bancorp of North Carolina Inc
518 W 'C' St .... Newton NC 28658 828-464-5620 466-5043
NASDAQ: PEBK ■ *TF:* 800-948-7195 ■ *Web:* www.peoplesbanknc.com

Pinnacle Bancshares Inc 1811 Second Ave............Jasper AL 35501 205-221-4111 221-8860
OTC: PCLB ■ *Web:* www.pinnaclebancshares.com

Placeteco inc 3763 Burrill St .... Shawinigan QC G9N6T6 819-539-8808 539-9224
Web: www.placeteco.com

PlainsCapital Corp 2323 Victory Ave Ste 1400 .... Dallas TX 75219 214-252-4100
TF: 866-762-8392 ■ *Web:* www.plainscapital.com

PNC Financial Services Group Inc
249 Fifth Ave 1 PNC Plz...........................Pittsburgh PA 15222 412-762-2000
NYSE: PNC ■ *TF:* 877-762-2000 ■ *Web:* www.pnc.com

Premier Community Bankshares Inc
4095 Valley Pk ....Winchester VA 22602 540-869-6600
Web: nasdaq.com

Premier Financial Bancorp Inc
2883 Fifth Ave .... Huntington WV 25702 304-522-1645
NASDAQ: PFBI

Princeton National Bancorp Inc
606 S Main St.....................................Princeton IL 61356 309-662-4444 872-0247*
OTC: PNBC ■ **Fax Area Code:* 815 ■ *TF:* 888-897-2276 ■ *Web:* www.hbtbank.com

PrivateBancorp Inc 120 S LaSalle St..................Chicago IL 60603 800-662-7748
NASDAQ: PVTB ■ *TF:* 800-662-7748 ■ *Web:* theprivatebank.com

Prosperity Bancshares Inc 1301 N Mechanic ....El Campo TX 77437 979-543-1426 543-1906
NYSE: PB ■ *TF:* 800-862-9098 ■ *Web:* www.prosperitybankusa.com

Provident Bank 3756 Central Ave.....................Riverside CA 92506 951-686-6060
NASDAQ: PROV ■ *TF:* 800-442-5201 ■ *Web:* www.providentbankmortgage.com

Provident Community Bancshares Inc
2700 Celanese Rd................................. Rock Hill SC 29732 803-325-9400
OTC: PCBS ■ *Web:* www.provcombank.com

Pulaski Financial Corp 12300 Olive Blvd .... Saint Louis MO 63141 314-878-2210
NASDAQ: PULB ■ *TF:* 888-649-3320 ■ *Web:* www.pulaskibank.com

Quad City Bank & Trust 3551 Seventh St ....Moline IL 61265 309-736-3580
NASDAQ: QCRH ■ *TF:* 866-676-0551 ■ *Web:* www.qcbt.com

Rabobank International 245 Pk Ave.................New York NY 10167 212-916-7800 818-0233
Web: rabobank.com

RBC Centura Banks Inc PO Box 1220............Rocky Mount NC 27802 800-769-2553
TF: 800-769-2553 ■ *Web:* www.rbcbankusa.com

Reece-Campbell Inc 320 S Wayne Ave .... Cincinnati OH 45215 513-542-4600 542-4753

Regions Financial Corp 1900 Fifth Ave N...........Birmingham AL 35203 866-688-0658
NYSE: RF ■ *TF:* 866-688-0658 ■ *Web:* www.regions.com

Renasant Corp 209 Troy St PO Box 709.................Tupelo MS 38802 662-680-1001
NASDAQ: RNST ■ *TF Cust Svc:* 800-680-1601 ■ *Web:* www.renasantbank.com

Republic Bancorp Inc 601 W Market St...............Louisville KY 40202 502-584-3600 561-7188
NASDAQ: RBCAA ■ *TF:* 888-540-5363 ■ *Web:* www.republicbank.com

Republic First Bancorp Inc
50 S 16th St Ste 2400........................ Philadelphia PA 19102 215-735-4422
NASDAQ: FRBK ■ *TF:* 888-875-2265 ■ *Web:* www.myrepublicbank.com

Richline Group Inc 6701 Nob Hill Rd...................Tamarac FL 33321 800-327-1808
TF: 800-327-1808 ■ *Web:* www.richlinegroup.com

Riverview Bancorp Inc
900 Washington St Ste 900 ....Vancouver WA 98660 360-693-6650 693-6275
NASDAQ: RVSB ■ *Web:* www.riverviewbank.com

S&T Bancorp Inc 800 Philadelphia St................. Indiana PA 15701 724-349-1800 465-6874*
NASDAQ: STBA ■ **Fax:* Cust Svc ■ *TF:* 800-325-2265 ■ *Web:* www.stbank.com

Salisbury Bancorp Inc
5 Bissell St PO Box 1868........................... Lakeville CT 06039 860-435-9801 435-0631
NASDAQ: SAL ■ *TF:* 800-222-9801 ■ *Web:* www.salisburybank.com

Sandy Spring Bancorp Inc 17801 Georgia Ave............Olney MD 20832 301-774-6400 483-6701
NASDAQ: SASR ■ *TF:* 800-399-5919 ■ *Web:* www.sandyspringbank.com

SCBT Financial Corp 950 John C Calhoun Dr........ Orangeburg SC 29115 803-534-2175
NASDAQ: SCBT ■ *TF:* 800-277-2175 ■ *Web:* www.southstatebank.com

Seacoast Banking Corp of Florida
PO Box 9012 PO Box 9012...............................Stuart FL 34995 772-287-4000 288-6012
NASDAQ: SBCF ■ *TF All:* 800-706-9991 ■
Web: www.seacoastbanking.com/corporateprofile.aspx?iid=100425

Shore Bancshares Inc 18 E Dover St...................... Easton MD 21601 410-822-1400
NASDAQ: SHBI ■ *Web:* www.shorebancshares.com

Sierra Bancorp 86 N Main St PO Box 1930 .... Porterville CA 93257 559-782-4900
NASDAQ: BSRR ■ *TF:* 888-454-2265 ■ *Web:* bankofthesierra.com

Simmons First National Corp 501 Main St..........Pine Bluff AR 71601 870-541-1000
NASDAQ: SFNC ■ *TF:* 866-246-2400 ■ *Web:* www.simmonsfirst.com

Phone Fax

South Street Financial Corp
103 N Second St PO Box 489........................ Albemarle NC 28001 704-982-9184 983-1308
OTC: SSFC ■ *Web:* bankofnc.com

Southern Banc Company Inc 221 S Sixth St .... Gadsden AL 35901 256-543-3860 543-3864
OTC: SRNN ■ *Web:* www.sobanco.com

Southern Missouri Bancorp Inc
531 Vine St.....................................Poplar Bluff MO 63901 573-778-1800
NASDAQ: SMBC ■ *TF:* 855-452-7272 ■ *Web:* www.bankwithsouthern.com

SouthFirst Bancshares Inc
126 N Norton Ave PO Box 167 .... Sylacauga AL 35150 256-245-4365 245-6341
OTC: SZBI ■ *TF:* 800-239-1492 ■ *Web:* www.southfirst.com

Southside Bancshares Inc 1201 S Beckham Ave.......... Tyler TX 75701 903-531-7111 535-4549
NASDAQ: SBSI ■ *TF:* 877-639-3511 ■ *Web:* www.southside.com

Southwest Bancorp Inc
608 S Main St PO Box 1988........................Stillwater OK 74076 888-762-4762
NASDAQ: OKSB ■ *TF:* 888-762-4762 ■ *Web:* www.banksnb.com

Southwest Georgia Financial Corp
201 First St SE...................................Moultrie GA 31768 229-985-1120 980-2211*
NYSE: SGB ■ **Fax:* Hum Res ■ *TF:* 888-683-2265 ■ *Web:* www.sgfc.com

Spitzer Management Inc 150 E Bridge St...............Elyria OH 44035 440-323-4671
Web: www.spitzer.com

SSMB Pacific Holding Company Inc
1755 Adams Ave.................................. San Leandro CA 94577 510-836-6100
Web: www.norcalkw.com

Suffolk Bancorp 4 W Second St PO Box 9000 .... Riverhead NY 11901 631-208-2200 727-3210
NASDAQ: SUBK ■ *Web:* www.scnb.com

Sun Bancorp Inc (SNBC) 226 Landis Ave.............. Vineland NJ 08360 800-786-9066
NASDAQ: SNBC ■ *TF:* 800-786-9066 ■ *Web:* www.sunnationalbank.com

Sunshine Financial Inc 1400 E Park Ave........... Tallahassee FL 32301 850-219-7200
TF: 800-468-3993 ■ *Web:* sunshinesavingsbank.com

SunTrust Banks Inc 303 Peachtree St NE...............Atlanta GA 30308 404-588-7711 335-2686
NYSE: STI ■ *TF:* 800-786-8787 ■ *Web:* www.suntrust.com

Sussex Bank 200 Munsonhurst Rd .... Franklin NJ 07416 973-827-2914
NASDAQ: SBBX ■ *TF:* 800-511-9900 ■ *Web:* www.sussexbank.com

SVB Financial Group 3005 Tasman Dr............. Santa Clara CA 95054 408-654-7400 496-2405
NASDAQ: SIVB ■ *TF:* 800-760-9644 ■ *Web:* www.svb.com

SY Bancorp Inc 1040 E Main St ....Louisville KY 40206 502-582-2571
NASDAQ: SYBT ■ *TF:* 800-625-9066 ■ *Web:* www.syb.com

Synovus Financial Corp
1111 Bay Ave Ste 500 PO Box 120...................Columbus GA 31902 706-649-2311 641-6555
NYSE: SNV ■ *TF:* 888-796-6887 ■ *Web:* www.synovus.com

Tatum Development Corp 11 Pkwy Blvd........... Hattiesburg MS 39401 601-544-6043

TCF Financial Corp 801 Marquette Ave .... Minneapolis MN 55402 612-823-2265
NYSE: TCB ■ *Web:* www.tcfbank.com

Teche Holding Co 1120 Jefferson Terr ....New Iberia LA 70560 337-560-7151 365-7130
NYSE: TSH

Texas Regional Bancshares Inc
3900 N Tenth St 11th Fl PO Box 5910 ....McAllen TX 78502 956-631-5400

TF Financial Corp 3 Penns Trail..................... Newtown PA 18940 215-579-4000
NASDAQ: THRD ■ *Web:* www.3rdfedbank.com

Timberland Bancorp Inc 624 Simpson Ave........... Hoquiam WA 98550 360-533-4747 533-4743
NASDAQ: TSBK ■ *TF:* 800-562-8761 ■ *Web:* www.timberlandbank.com

Titonka Bancshares Inc PO Box 309 .... Titonka IA 50480 515-928-2142 928-2042
TF: 866-985-3247 ■ *Web:* www.tsbbank.com

Tower Financial Corp 116 E Berry St............. Fort Wayne IN 46802 800-731-2265
NASDAQ: TOFC ■ *TF:* 800-731-2265 ■ *Web:* oldnational.com

TriCo Bancshares 63 Constitution Dr....................Chico CA 95973 530-898-0300
NASDAQ: TCBK ■ *TF:* 800-922-8742 ■ *Web:* www.tcbk.com

Trustco Bank Corp NY PO Box 1082 .... Schenectady NY 12301 518-377-3311
NASDAQ: TRST ■ *TF:* 800-670-3110 ■ *Web:* www.trustcobank.com

Trustmark National Bank
248 E Capitol St PO Box 291 ....Jackson MS 39201 601-208-5111
NASDAQ: TRMK ■ *TF Cust Svc:* 800-243-2524 ■ *Web:* www.trustmark.com

UBT Bancshares Inc 823 Broadway .... Marysville KS 66508 785-562-2333

UMB Financial Corp 1010 Grand Blvd.............Kansas City MO 64106 816-860-7000
NASDAQ: UMBF ■ *TF:* 800-821-2171 ■ *Web:* www.umb.com

Umpqua Holdings Corp
1 SW Columbia St Ste 1200........................Portland OR 97258 503-727-4100
NASDAQ: UMPQ ■ *TF:* 866-486-7782 ■ *Web:* www.umpquabank.com

Union Bankshares Inc 20 Lower Main St.............Morrisville VT 05661 802-888-6600
NASDAQ: UNB ■ *TF:* 866-862-1891 ■ *Web:* www.unionbankvt.com

United Bancorp Inc 201 S Fourth St ....Martins Ferry OH 43935 740-633-0445 633-1448
NASDAQ: UBCP ■ *TF:* 888-275-5566 ■ *Web:* www.unitedbancorp.com

United Bancshares Inc
100 S High St PO Box 67.....................Columbus Grove OH 45830 419-659-2141 659-2069
NASDAQ: UBOH ■ *TF:* 800-837-8111 ■ *Web:* www.theubank.com

United Community Banks Inc PO Box 398........... Blairsville GA 30514 706-781-2265 745-8960
NASDAQ: UCBI ■ *TF:* 866-270-7100 ■ *Web:* www.ucbi.com

United Community Financial Corp
PO Box 1111 ....Youngstown OH 44501 330-742-0500 742-0532
NASDAQ: UCFC ■ *TF:* 877-272-7661 ■ *Web:* ir.ucfconline.com

United Security Bancshares Inc
PO Box 249 ....Thomasville AL 36784 334-636-5424
NASDAQ: USBI ■ *TF:* 866-546-8273 ■ *Web:* www.firstusbank.com

Unity Bancorp Inc 64 Old Hwy 22 .... Clinton NJ 08809 908-730-7630 730-9430
NASDAQ: UNTY ■ *TF:* 800-618-2265 ■ *Web:* www.unitybank.com

Universal Enterprises Inc 8030 SW Nimbus .... Beaverton OR 97008 503-644-8723
TF: 800-547-5740 ■ *Web:* www.ueitest.com

University Bancorp Inc 2015 Washtenaw Ave......... Ann Arbor MI 48104 734-741-5858 741-5859
OTC: UNIB ■ *Web:* www.university-bank.com

Univest Corp of Pennsylvania
14 N Main St PO Box 64197......................... Souderton PA 18964 877-723-5571
NASDAQ: UVSP ■ *TF:* 877-723-5571 ■ *Web:* www.univest.net

US Bancorp 800 Nicollet Mall .... Minneapolis MN 55402 651-466-3000
NYSE: USB ■ *TF Cust Svc:* 800-872-2657 ■ *Web:* www.usbank.com

Valley National Bancorp 1455 Valley Rd .... Wayne NJ 07470 973-305-8800
NYSE: VLY ■ *TF:* 800-522-4100 ■ *Web:* valleynationalbank.com

Veteran's Truck Line Inc
800 Black Hawk Dr................................Burlington WI 53105 262-539-3400 539-2720
TF: 800-456-9476 ■ *Web:* www.vetstruck.com

VIST Financial Corp
PO Box 6219 PO Box 6219......................... Wyomissing PA 19610 610-926-7632
NASDAQ: VIST ■ *TF:* 888-238-3330 ■ *Web:* www.vistbank.com

Company	City	State	Zip	Phone	Fax
Washington Federal Inc 425 Pike St *NASDAQ: WAFD* ■ *TF:* 800-324-9375 ■ *Web:* www.washingtonfederal.com	Seattle	WA	98101	206-624-7930	467-0524
Washington Trust Bancorp Inc 23 Broad St *NASDAQ: WASH* ■ *TF:* 800-475-2265 ■ *Web:* www.washtrust.com	Westerly	RI	02891	401-348-1200	348-1470
Wayne Bank 717 Main St *TF:* 800-598-5002 ■ *Web:* www.waynebank.com	Honesdale	PA	18431	570-253-1455	253-3725
Wayne Savings Bancshares Inc 151 N Market St *NASDAQ: WAYN* ■ *TF:* 800-414-1103 ■ *Web:* www.waynesavings.com	Wooster	OH	44691	330-264-5767	264-5908
Webster City Federal Bancorp 820 Des Moines St *NYSE: WCFB* ■ *TF:* 866-519-4004 ■ *Web:* otcmarkets.com	Webster City	IA	50595	515-832-3071	
Webster Financial Corp PO Box 10305 *NYSE: WBS* ■ *TF:* 800-325-2424 ■ *Web:* www.websteronline.com	Waterbury	CT	06726	800-325-2424	
West Bancorp Inc PO Box 65020 *NASDAQ: WTBA* ■ *TF:* 800-810-2301 ■ *Web:* www.westbankstrong.com	West Des Moines	IA	50265	515-222-2300	222-2346
West Side Unlimited Corp 4201 16th Ave SW *TF:* 800-373-2957 ■ *Web:* www.westsideunlimited.com	Cedar Rapids	IA	52404	319-390-4466	
Westfield Financial Inc 141 Elm St *NASDAQ: WFD* ■ *TF:* 800-995-5734 ■ *Web:* www.westfieldbank.com	Westfield	MA	01085	413-568-1911	562-7939
Westwood Holdings Group Inc 200 Crescent Ct Ste 1200 *NYSE: WHG* ■ *TF:* 800-687-0372 ■ *Web:* www.westwoodgroup.com	Dallas	TX	75201	214-756-6900	756-6979
Winona National Bankÿÿÿ PO Box 499 *TF:* 800-546-4392 ■ *Web:* www.winonanationalbank.com	Winona	MN	55987	507-454-4320	
Wintrust Financial Corp 9700 W Higgins Rd Ste 800 *NASDAQ: WTFC* ■ *Web:* www.wintrust.com	Rosemont	IL	60018	847-939-9000	
WSFS Financial Corp 500 Delaware Ave *NASDAQ: WSFS* ■ *TF:* 888-973-7226 ■ *Web:* www.wsfsbank.com	Wilmington	DE	19801	302-792-6000	
WTB Financial Corp PO Box 2127 *TF:* 800-788-4578 ■ *Web:* www.watrust.com	Spokane	WA	99210	800-788-4578	
WVS Financial Corp 9001 Perry Hwy *NASDAQ: WVFC* ■ *Web:* www.wvsbank.com	Pittsburgh	PA	15237	412-364-1911	

360-3 Holding Companies (General)

Company	City	State	Zip	Phone	Fax
A-Mark Precious Metals Inc 429 Santa Monica Blvd Ste 230 *Web:* www.amark.com	Santa Monica	CA	90401	310-587-1485	319-0317
Access Industries Inc 730 Fifth Ave *Web:* www.accessindustries.com	New York	NY	10019	212-247-6400	
Acuity Brands Inc 1170 Peachtree St NE Ste 2400 *NYSE: AYI* ■ *Web:* www.acuitybrands.com	Atlanta	GA	30309	404-853-1400	
Advanced Disposal Services Inc 90 Fort Wade Rd *Web:* www.advanceddisposal.com	Ponte Vedra Beach	FL	32081	904-737-7900	
AeroCare Holdings Inc 3325 Bartlett Blvd *Web:* www.aerocareusa.com	Orlando	FL	32811	407-206-0040	
Affiliated Managers Group Inc (AMG) 600 Hale St *NYSE: AMG* ■ *Web:* www.amg.com	Prides Crossing	MA	01965	617-747-3300	
Agri-Fab Inc 809 S Hamilton St *Web:* www.agri-fab.com	Sullivan	IL	61951	217-728-8388	
Alex Lee Inc PO Box 800 *Web:* www.alexlee.com	Hickory	NC	28603	828-725-4424	323-4435
Alliance Holdings Gp LP 1717 S Boulder Ave Ste 400 *NASDAQ: AHGP* ■ *Web:* www.ahgp.com	Tulsa	OK	74119	918-295-1415	295-7361
Alliance Holdings Inc 1021 Old York Rd 3rd Fl *Web:* www.allianceholdings.com	Abington	PA	19001	215-706-0873	
Allied Systems Holdings Inc 2302 Parklake Dr NE *Web:* www.alliedholdings.com	Atlanta	GA	30345	404-373-4285	
Alpine Group Inc 1 Meadowlands Plz *Web:* www.alpine-group.net	East Rutherford	NJ	07073	201-549-4400	
Alpine Valley Ski Area 6775 East Highland Rd *Web:* www.skialpinevalley.com	White Lake	MI	48383	248-887-2180	
Alutiiq LLC 3909 Arctic Blvd Ste 400 *TF:* 800-829-8547 ■ *Web:* www.alutiiq.com	Anchorage	AK	99503	907-222-9500	222-9501
American Standard Cos Inc 1 Centennial Ave *TF:* 800-442-1902 ■ *Web:* www.americanstandard-us.com	Piscataway	NJ	08855	800-442-1902	
AMETEK Inc 1100 Cassatt Rd PO Box 1764 *NYSE: AME* ■ **Fax Area Code:* 215 ■ *TF:* 800-473-1286 ■ *Web:* www.ametek.com	Berwyn	PA	19312	610-647-2121	323-9337*
Amtex Corp 832 East Walnut St *Web:* www.amtexcorp.com	Garland	TX	75040	972-276-7626	276-5105
ANSA McAL (US) Inc 11403 NW 39 th St *Web:* www.ansamcal.com	Doral	FL	33178	305-599-8766	
Apollo Athletics Inc 1428 S Central Park Ave *Web:* www.apolloathletics.com	Anaheim	CA	92802	714-533-8118	
Arden Group Inc 2020 S Central Ave *NASDAQ: ARDNA* ■ **Fax:* Hum Res	Compton	CA	90220	310-638-2842	631-0950*
Arellano Construction Co 7051 SW 12th St *Web:* www.ohlarellano.com/en	Miami	FL	33144	305-994-9901	
Arpin International Group Inc 4372 Post Rd *Web:* www.arpinintl.com	East Greenwich	RI	02818	401-885-4600	
Atlas Concrete Inc 335 8 Ave SW Ste 850 *Web:* www.atlasconcrete.com	Calgary	AB	T2P1C9	403-297-0550	
Atlas Copco North America LLC 7 Campus Dr Ste 200 *TF:* 800-732-6762 ■ *Web:* www.atlascopco.us	Parsippany	NJ	07054	973-397-3432	397-3414
Atlas World Group Inc 1212 St George Rd *TF:* 800-252-8885 ■ *Web:* www.atlasvanlines.com	Evansville	IN	47711	812-424-2222	421-7129
Augusta National Inc 2604 Washington Rd *Web:* masters.com	Augusta	GA	30904	706-667-6000	736-2321
AUS Inc 155 Gaither Dr *Web:* ausinc.com	Mount Laurel	NJ	08054	856-234-9200	
Austin Industries Inc 3535 Travis St Ste 300 **Fax:* Acctg ■ *Web:* www.austin-ind.com	Dallas	TX	75204	214-443-5500	443-5581*
Bayer 6 W Belt Rd *Web:* www.bayer.us	Wayne	NJ	07470	862-404-3000	
Benetech Inc 2245 Sequoia Dr *Web:* benetechglobal.com	Aurora	IL	60506	630-844-1300	
Berggruen Holdings Inc 1114 Ave of the Americas 41st Fl *Web:* www.berggruenholdings.com	New York	NY	10036	212-380-2230	
Bertelsmann Inc 1540 Broadway 24th Fl *Web:* www.bertelsmann.com	New York	NY	10036	212-782-1000	782-1010
Biglari Holdings Inc 175 E Houston St Ste 1300 *NYSE: BH* ■ *Web:* www.biglariholdings.com	San Antonio	TX	78205	210-344-3400	
Block Communications Inc 405 Madison Ave Ste 2100 *Web:* www.blockcommunications.com	Toledo	OH	43604	419-724-6212	724-6167
Blount International Inc 4909 SE International Way **Fax:* Hum Res ■ *Web:* www.blount.com	Portland	OR	97222	503-653-8881	653-4402*
Blue Sky Industries Inc 1230 Monterey Pass Rd *Web:* www.blueskyindustries.com	Monterey Park	CA	91754	213-620-9950	
Blue Tee Corp 250 Park Ave S *Web:* www.bluetee.com	New York	NY	10003	212-598-0880	
Bluestone Industries Inc 100 Cranberry Creek Dr *Web:* www.bluestoneindustries.com	Beckley	WV	25801	304-252-8528	
Boca Resorts 501 E Camino Real *TF:* 888-543-1277 ■ *Web:* www.bocaresort.com	Boca Raton	FL	33432	561-447-3000	447-3183
Boler Co 500 Pk Blvd Ste 450 *Web:* hendrickson-intl.com	Itasca	IL	60143	630-773-9111	773-9121
Boral Industries Inc 200 Mansell Ct E Ste 310 *Web:* boral.com.au	Roswell	GA	30076	770-645-4500	645-2888
Brandt Holdings Co 4650 26th Ave S Ste E *Web:* www.brandtholdings.com	Fargo	ND	58104	701-237-6000	
Brose North America Inc 3933 Automation Ave *Web:* www.brose.com	Auburn Hills	MI	48326	248-339-4000	339-4099
Bruckmann Rosser Sherrill & Company LLC 126 E 56th St 29th Fl *Web:* www.brs.com	New York	NY	10022	212-521-3700	
BT Conferencing Inc 150 Newport Ave. Ext, Ste 301 *TF:* 866-770-8777 ■ *Web:* www.btconferencing.com	North Quincy	MA	02171	866-770-8777	
C D Henderson Construction Services Ltd 1985 Forest Ln *Web:* www.cdhenderson.com	Garland	TX	75042	972-272-5466	
California Sports Inc 555 N Nash St	El Segundo	CA	90245	310-426-6000	426-6115
Cameron Holdings Corp 1200 Prospect St *Web:* www.cameron-holdings.com	La Jolla	CA	92037	858-551-1335	551-1343
Camino Modular Systems Inc 89 Carlingview Dr *Web:* www.caminomodular.com	Toronto	ON	M9W5E4	416-675-2400	675-2424
Campers Inn Inc 35 Robert Milligan Pkwy *Web:* www.campersinn.com	Merrimack	NH	03054	603-883-1082	
Cardinal Health Inc 7000 Cardinal Pl *NYSE: CAH* ■ *Web:* www.cardinalhealth.com/en.html	Dublin	OH	43017	614-757-5000	757-6000
CBRL Group Inc PO Box 787 *TF:* 800-333-9566 ■ *Web:* www.crackerbarrel.com	Lebanon	TN	37088	800-333-9566	
CenturyTel Inc 100 Centurylink Dr PO Box 4065 *NYSE: CTL* ■ *TF:* 877-290-5458 ■ *Web:* www.centurylink.com	Monroe	LA	71211	318-388-9000	
CGF Industries Inc 2420 N Woodlawn Bldg 100 Ste A *Web:* www.cgcpi.com	Wichita	KS	67220	316-691-4500	691-4545
CIC Group Inc 530 Maryville Centre Dr Ste 100 *Web:* www.cicgroup.com	Saint Louis	MO	63141	314-682-2900	
Citigroup Inc 399 Pk Ave *NYSE: C* ■ *Web:* citigroup.com	New York	NY	10043	212-559-1000	
Clayton Holdings LLC 100 BeaRd Sawmill Rd Ste 200 *TF:* 877-291-5301 ■ *Web:* www.clayton.com	Shelton	CT	06484	203-926-5600	926-5757
Comcast Corp 1701 JFK Blvd *NASDAQ: CMCSA* ■ *TF:* 800-266-2278 ■ *Web:* www.xfinity.com	Philadelphia	PA	19103	215-665-1700	981-7790
ConAgra Foods Inc 1 ConAgra Dr *NYSE: CAG* ■ **Fax:* Hum Res ■ *TF:* 877-266-2472 ■ *Web:* www.conagrafoods.com	Omaha	NE	68102	402-240-4000	595-4707*
CONSOL Energy Inc 1000 Consol Energy Dr *NYSE: CNX* ■ *TF:* 800-544-8024 ■ *Web:* www.consolenergy.com	Canonsburg	PA	15317	724-485-4000	
Consolidated Communications Holdings Inc 121 S 17th St *NASDAQ: CNSL* ■ *Web:* consolidated.com	Mattoon	IL	61938	217-235-3311	235-3311
Cooper Neff Group Inc 555 Croton Rd Ste 100 *Web:* www.cooperneff.com	King Of Prussia	PA	19406	610-491-1400	
Cortec Group 200 Park Ave 20th Fl *Web:* www.cortecgroup.com	New York	NY	10017	212-370-5600	
Courier-Life Inc 1 Metrotech Ctr Ste 1001 *Web:* www.brooklyndaily.com	Brooklyn	NY	11201	718-260-2500	
CPI Wire Cloth & Screens Inc 2425 Roy Rd *Web:* cpiwirecloth.com	Pearland	TX	77581	281-485-2300	485-8837
CraftWorks Restaurants & Brewery Inc 201 W Main St Ste 301 *Web:* www.craftworksrestaurants.com	Chattanooga	TN	37408	423-424-2000	
Crestview Partners LP 667 Madison Ave 10th Fl *Web:* www.crestview.com	New York	NY	10065	212-906-0700	
Crown Group Inc, The 2111 Walter Reuther Dr *Web:* www.thecrowngrp.com	Warren	MI	48091	586-575-9800	
CUI Global Inc 20050 SW 112th Ave *NASDAQ: CUI* ■ *TF:* 800-275-4899 ■ *Web:* www.cuiglobal.com	Tualatin	OR	97062	503-612-2300	
Dectron International Inc 4300 Poirier Blvd *TF:* 888-332-8766	Montreal	QC	H4R2C5	514-334-9609	334-9184

Company / Address	City	State	Zip	Phone	Fax
Del Toro Loan Servicing Inc 2300 Boswell Rd Ste 215 *Web:* www.deltoroloanservicing.com	Chula Vista	CA	91914	619-474-5400	
Delhaize America Inc 2110 Executive Dr PO Box 1330 **Fax:* Hum Res ■ *Web:* www.delhaizegroup.com	Salisbury	NC	28145	704-633-8250	645-4499*
Deluxe Corp 3680 N Victoria St *NYSE: DLX* ■ *TF:* 800-328-7205 ■ *Web:* ww.deluxe.com	Shoreview	MN	55126	651-483-7111	
Dicke Safety Products 1201 Warren Ave *TF:* 877-891-0050 ■ *Web:* www.dicketool.com	Downers Grove	IL	60515	630-969-0050	
Dl Rogers Corp 5013 Davis Blvd *Web:* dlrrestaurants.com	North Richland Hills	TX	76180	817-428-2077	
DNP America LLC 335 Madison Ave 3rd Fl *Web:* www.dnpamerica.com	New York	NY	10017	212-503-1060	
Downing Partners Inc 5150 E Yale Cir	Denver	CO	80222	303-830-6622	
Duchossois Industries Inc 845 Larch Ave *Web:* duch.com	Elmhurst	IL	60126	630-279-3600	
Dundee Bancorp Inc 1 Adelaide St E Ste 2100 *Web:* www.dundeecorp.com	Toronto	ON	M5C2V9	416-863-6990	363-4536
E & A Industries Inc 101 W Ohio St Ste 1350 *Web:* ea-companies.com	Indianapolis	IN	46204	317-684-3150	681-5068
E Boyd & Associates Inc PO Box 99189 *Web:* www.eboyd.com	Raleigh	NC	27624	919-846-8000	
Edward B Howlin Inc 2880 Dunkirk Way *Web:* ebhowlin.com	Dunkirk	MD	20754	301-855-8900	
Elecsys Corp 846 N Mart-Way Ct *NASDAQ: ESYS* ■ *Web:* www.elecsyscorp.com	Olathe	KS	66061	913-647-0158	647-0132
Elvis Presley Enterprises Inc 3734 Elvis Presley Blvd *TF:* 800-238-2000 ■ *Web:* www.elvis.com	Memphis	TN	38116	901-332-3322	344-3101
Envision Healthcare 6200 S Syracuse Way Ste 200 *Web:* www.evhc.net	Greenwood Village	CO	80111	303-495-1200	
EquiLend Holdings LLC 17 State St 9th Fl *Web:* www.equilend.com	New York	NY	10004	212-901-2200	
ESCO Technologies Inc 9900A Clayton Rd *NYSE: ESE* ■ *TF:* 800-368-5948 ■ *Web:* www.escotechnologies.com	Saint Louis	MO	63124	314-213-7200	213-7250
Esmark Steel Group 2500 Euclid Ave *TF:* 800-323-0340 ■ *Web:* www.esmark.com	Chicago Heights	IL	60411	708-756-0400	
Evergreen Shipping Agency (America) Corp 1 Evertrust Plz *Web:* www.evergreen-america.com	Jersey City	NJ	07302	201-761-3000	761-3011
Eyak Corp, The 360 W Benson Blvd Ste 210 *TF:* 800-478-7161 ■ *Web:* eyakcorporation.com	Anchorage	AK	99503	907-334-6971	
FedEx Corp 3610 Hacks Cross Rd *NYSE: FDX* ■ *TF:* 800-463-3339 ■ *Web:* www.fedex.com	Memphis	TN	38125	901-369-3600	
Felchar Manufacturing Corp 196 Corporate Dr *Web:* www.felchar.com	Binghamton	NY	13904	607-723-4076	
Ferrara International Logistics Inc 1319 N Broad St *Web:* www.ferrarainternational.com	Hillside	NJ	07205	908-282-9440	
Field & Stream Licenses Company LLC 18 Kings Hwy N	Westport	CT	06880	203-221-0050	
Florens Container Services (USA) Ltd 275 Battery St Ste 800 *Web:* www.florens.com	San Francisco	CA	94111	415-348-2800	
Forge Industries Inc 4450 Market St	Youngstown	OH	44512	330-782-8301	
Fresh Del Monte Produce Co 241 Sevilla Ave PO Box 149222 *NYSE: FDP* ■ *TF Cust Svc:* 800-950-3683 ■ *Web:* www.freshdelmonte.com	Coral Gables	FL	33134	305-520-8400	567-0320
GCI Affiliated Cos 20875 Crossroads Cir Ste 100 *Web:* gcionline.com	Waukesha	WI	53186	262-798-5080	
George Weston Ltd 22 St Clair Ave E *TSE: WN* ■ *TF:* 800-564-6253 ■ *Web:* www.weston.ca	Toronto	ON	M4T2S7	416-922-2500	922-4395
Global Entertainment Corp 6751 N Sunset Blvd Ste 200 *OTC: GNTP* ■ *Web:* www.globalentertainment2000.com	Glendale	AZ	85305	480-994-0772	994-0759
Global Trading & Sourcing Corp 1587 College Park Business Ctr Rd *Web:* www.gtsco.com	Orlando	FL	32804	407-532-7600	
Gower Corp 355 Woodruff Rd *Web:* www.gower.co.uk	Greenville	SC	29607	864-234-4829	
GreenPointe Holdings LLC 7807 Baymeadows Rd E Ste 205 *Web:* www.greenpointellc.com	Jacksonville	FL	32256	904-996-2485	
GSC Enterprises Inc 130 Hillcrest Dr PO Box 638 *Web:* www.grocerysupply.com	Sulphur Springs	TX	75483	903-885-7621	885-6928
Gulf & Ohio Railways Inc 422 W Cumberland Ave PO Box 2408 *Web:* www.gulfandohio.com	Knoxville	TN	37901	865-525-9400	
GVW Group LLC (GVW) 625 Roger Williams Ave *Web:* www.gvwgroup.com	Highland Park	IL	60035	847-681-8417	681-8515
H Enterprises International Inc 120 S Sixth St	Minneapolis	MN	55402	612-340-8849	339-2690
Haram-Christensen Corp 125 Asia Pl *Web:* www.haramchris.com	Carlstadt	NJ	07072	201-507-8544	
Harold Import Company Inc 747 Vassar Ave *Web:* www.haroldskitchen.com	Lakewood	NJ	08701	732-367-2800	
Hartz Group Inc, The 667 Madison Ave **Fax Area Code:* 212 ■ *Web:* www.hartzmountain.com	New York	NY	10065	201-348-1200	838-8845*
Hayman Capital Management LP 2101 Cedar Springs Rd Ste 1400 *Web:* www.haymancapitalmanagement.com	Dallas	TX	75201	214-347-8050	
Heartland Industrial Partners LP 177 Broad St 10th Fl *Web:* www.heartlandpartners.com	Stamford	CT	06901	203-327-1202	
Hendricks Holding Company Inc 690 Third St *Web:* hendricksholding.com	Beloit	WI	53511	608-362-8000	
Hines Corp 1218 Pontaluna Rd Ste B *Web:* www.hinescorp.com	Spring Lake	MI	49456	231-799-6240	799-6298
Hitch Enterprises Inc 309 Northridge Cir PO Box 1308 *TF:* 800-951-2533 ■ *Web:* www.hitchok.com	Guymon	OK	73942	580-338-8575	
Home Capital Group Inc 145 King St W Ste 2300 *TSE: HCG* ■ *TF:* 800-990-7881 ■ *Web:* www.homecapital.com	Toronto	ON	M5H1J8	416-360-4663	363-7611
Horizon Holding Inc 6101 S 58th St Ste B *Web:* www.horizonholding.com	Lincoln	NE	68516	402-421-6400	
Hunt Consolidated Inc 1900 N Akard St *TF:* 800-424-9300 ■ *Web:* www.huntoil.com	Dallas	TX	75201	214-978-8000	978-8888
Icahn Enterprises LP 767 Fifth Ave 47th Fl *NASDAQ: IEP* ■ *TF:* 800-255-2737 ■ *Web:* www.ielp.com	New York	NY	10153	212-702-4300	750-5841
ICD Group International Inc 600 Madison Ave Ste 1800 *Web:* www.icdgroup.com	New York	NY	10022	212-644-1500	
InfoPro Inc 8200 Greensboro Dr Ste 1450 *Web:* www.infopro.net	Mclean	VA	22102	703-226-2520	
InstaMed Communications LLC 1880 John F Kennedy Blvd 12th Fl *Web:* www.instamed.com	Philadelphia	PA	19103	215-789-3680	
International Textile Group 804 Green Vly Rd Ste 300 *Web:* www.itg-global.com	Greensboro	NC	27408	336-379-6220	
Investors Management Corp 5151 Glenwood Ave *Web:* investorsmanagement.com	Raleigh	NC	27612	919-881-5200	
IsoRay Medical Inc 350 Hills St Ste 106 *TF:* 877-447-6729 ■ *Web:* www.isoray.com	Richland	WA	99354	509-375-1202	375-3473
ITC Holding Company LLC 1791 O G Skinner Dr Ste A *Web:* www.itchold.com	West Point	GA	31833	706-645-9482	
Jacobs Industries Inc 8096 Excelsior Blvd *Web:* www.jacobsinteractive.com	Hopkins	MN	55343	612-339-9500	
JC Horizon Ltd 825 E State St *Web:* www.jchorizonltd.com	Ontario	CA	91761	626-446-1819	
JMK International 4800 Bryant Irvin Ct	Fort Worth	TX	76107	817-737-3703	735-1669
Joseph Cory Holdings LLC 150 Meadowlands Pkwy 3rd Fl *Web:* www.corycompanies.com	Secaucus	NJ	07094	201-795-1000	
Joy Global Inc 100 E Wisconsin Ave Ste 2780 PO Box 554 *NYSE: JOY* ■ *Web:* www.joyglobal.com	Milwaukee	WI	53202	414-319-8500	
Kawasaki Heavy Industries USA Inc 60 E 42nd St Ste 2501 *Web:* www.khi.co.jp	New York	NY	10165	212-759-4950	759-6421
Keller Group Inc, The 1 Northfield Plz Ste 510 *Web:* www.kellergroupinc.com	Northfield	IL	60093	847-446-7550	
Kingman Group Corp, The 14010 Live Oak Ave *Web:* www.kingman.com	Baldwin Park	CA	91706	626-430-2300	
Kurt Orban Partners LLC 111 Anza Blvd Ste 350 *Web:* www.kurtorbanpartners.com	Burlingame	CA	94010	650-579-3959	
Kyocera International Inc 8611 Balboa Ave *TF:* 877-248-4237 ■ *Web:* global.kyocera.com	San Diego	CA	92123	858-576-2600	569-9412
Legacy Investments Inc 5910 N Central Expy	Dallas	TX	75206	214-750-1522	
Lenny's Franchisor LLC 8295 Tournament Dr Ste 200 *Web:* www.lennys.com	Memphis	TN	38125	901-753-4002	
Liberty Diversified International Inc 5600 Hwy 169 N *TF:* 800-421-1270 ■ *Web:* www.libertydiversified.com	New Hope	MN	55428	763-536-6600	536-6685
Liberty Media Holding Corp 12300 Liberty Blvd *Web:* www.libertymedia.com	Englewood	CO	80112	720-875-5400	
Lightfoot Capital Partners LP 725 Fifth Ave 19th Fl *Web:* www.lightfootcapital.com	New York	NY	10022	212-993-1280	
Louise Paris Ltd 1407 Broadway 14th Fl *Web:* www.louiseparis.com	New York	NY	10018	212-354-5411	
M Group Inc 187 S Old Woodward Ste 200 *Web:* www.mgroupinc.com	Birmingham	MI	48009	248-540-8843	
Magnum Hospitality 1515 Cass St Ste D *Web:* www.magnumhospitality.com	Traverse City	MI	49684	231-932-1633	
Mainsail Partners 1 Front St Ste 3000 *Web:* www.mainsailpartners.com	San Francisco	CA	94111	415-391-3150	
Manifold Capital Corp 140 Broadway 47th Fl *OTC: MANF* ■ *Web:* www.aca.com	New York	NY	10005	212-375-2000	375-2100
Marin Investments Ltd 700 W Georgia St Ste 3010 *Web:* www.marin.ca	Vancouver	BC	V7Y1B6	604-687-1450	
Marsh & McLennan Cos Inc 1166 Ave of the Americas *NYSE: MMC* ■ *TF:* 866-374-2662 ■ *Web:* www.mmc.com	New York	NY	10036	212-345-5000	
Maxco Inc 836 Centennial Way Ste 170	Lansing	MI	48917	517-627-1734	627-4951
McKesson Corp 1 Post St *NYSE: MCK* ■ *TF:* 800-482-3784 ■ *Web:* www.mckesson.com	San Francisco	CA	94104	415-983-8300	
MDC Holdings Inc 4350 S Monaco St Ste 500 *NYSE: MDC* ■ *TF:* 888-500-7060 ■ *Web:* www.richmondamerican.com	Denver	CO	80237	303-773-1100	771-3461
MediaTech Capital Partners LLC 70 E 55th St 21st Fl *Web:* www.mediatechcapital.com	New York	NY	10022	212-759-3022	
MediaTek USA Inc 120 Presidential Way *Web:* www.mediatek.com	Woburn	MA	01801	781-503-8000	
Medisys Health Network Inc 8900 Van Wyck Expy *Web:* medisyshealth.org	Jamaica	NY	11418	718-206-6000	
Mel Foster Company Inc 7566 Market Pl Dr *Web:* melfoster.com	Eden Prairie	MN	55344	952-941-9790	
Merco Group Inc, The 7711 N 81st St	Milwaukee	WI	53223	414-365-2600	
Minnwest Corp 14820 Hwy 7 Ste 200 *Web:* www.minnwest.com	Minnetonka	MN	55345	952-545-8815	

Company	City	State	ZIP	Phone	Fax
Mondial International Corp 101 Secor Ln PO Box 8369 *Web:* mondialgroup.com	Pelham Manor	NY	10803	914-738-7411	738-7521
Moore Tool Company Inc 800 Union Ave	Bridgeport	CT	06607	203-366-3224	
Najafi Cos LLC 2525 E Camelback Rd *Web:* najafi.com	Phoenix	AZ	85016	602-476-0600	
Nanco-Nancy Sales Company Inc 22 Willow St	Chelsea	MA	02150	617-884-1700	
Nashville Shores Holdings LLC 4001 Bell Rd *Web:* www.nashvilleshores.com	Hermitage	TN	37076	615-889-7050	
NBC Universal Inc 30 Rockefeller Plaza *Web:* www.nbcuniversal.com	New York	NY	10112	212-664-4444	664-4085
Neenan Company LLP, The 2607 Midpoint Dr *Web:* www.neenan.com	Fort Collins	CO	80525	970-493-8747	
NewMarket Corp 330 S Fourth St *NYSE: NEU* ■ *TF:* 800-625-5191 ■ *Web:* www.newmarket.com	Richmond	VA	23219	804-788-5000	788-5688
NextWave Wireless Inc 10350 Science Ctr Dr Ste 210 *OTC: WAVE* ■ *TF:* 800-461-9330 ■ *Web:* www.nextwave.com	San Diego	CA	92121	858-731-5300	731-5301
Nordenia International 14591 State Hwy 177 *Web:* www.mondigroup.com	Jackson	MO	63755	573-335-4900	335-6172
North American Stainless Inc 6870 Hwy 42 East *TF:* 800-499-7833 ■ *Web:* www.northamericanstainless.com	Ghent	KY	41045	502-347-6000	347-6001
Nustar GP Holdings LLC PO Box 781609 *NYSE: NSH* ■ *TF:* 800-866-9060 ■ *Web:* www.nustargpholdings.com	San Antonio	TX	78248	210-918-2000	
NVE Pharmacueticals 15 Whitehall Rd *Web:* www.stacker2.com	Andover	NJ	07821	973-786-7862	
Octal Corp 125 Galway Pl Unit B & C *Web:* www.octalcorporation.com	Teaneck	NJ	07666	201-862-1010	
OKI Developments Inc 1416 112th Ave NE *TF:* 877-465-3654 ■ *Web:* www.okigolf.com	Bellevue	WA	98004	425-454-2800	646-6999
Omega International Inc 1937 NE Loop 410 Ste 200 *TF:* 888-558-0701 ■ *Web:* omegaco.com	San Antonio	TX	78217	210-805-8808	
Omnicom Group Inc 437 Madison Ave *NYSE: OMC* ■ **Fax:* Hum Res ■ *Web:* www.omnicomgroup.com	New York	NY	10022	212-415-3600	415-3530*
Orca Bay Sports & Entertainment 800 Griffiths Way *Web:* canucks.nhl.com	Vancouver	BC	V6B6G1	604-899-7400	899-7401
Orlando Endodontic Specialists 610 N Mills Ave Nbr 210 *Web:* www.midfloridarootcanals.com	Orlando	FL	32803	407-423-7667	
Otc Global Holdings 5151 San Felipe Ste 2200 *TF:* 877-737-8511 ■ *Web:* www.otcgh.com	Houston	TX	77056	713-358-5450	
Otsuka America Inc 1 Embarcadero Ctr Ste 2020 *Web:* otsuka-america.com	San Francisco	CA	94111	415-986-5300	
Otter Tail Corp 4334 18th Ave SW PO Box 9156 *NASDAQ: OTTR* ■ **Fax Area Code:* 701 ■ *TF:* 866-410-8780 ■ *Web:* www.ottertail.com	Fargo	ND	58106	218-739-8479	232-4108*
Owl Cos 2465 Campus Dr *Web:* www.owlcompanies.com	Irvine	CA	92612	949-797-2000	660-4936
Pace Resources Inc 445 West Philadelphia St PO Box 15040 *Web:* paceresourcesfcu.virtualcu.net	York	PA	17405	717-852-1390	852-1391
Pacific Echo Inc 23540 Telo Ave *Web:* www.pacificecho.com	Torrance	CA	90505	310-539-1822	
Pacific Food Importers Inc 2323 Airport Way S *Web:* www.pacificfoodimporters.com	Seattle	WA	98134	206-682-2740	
Paragon Gaming Corp 6650 Via Austi Pkwy Ste 150 *Web:* paragongaming.com	Las Vegas	NV	89119	702-631-5161	
Pearson Inc 1330 Ave of the Americas 7th Fl *Web:* www.pearson.com	New York	NY	10019	212-641-2400	641-2500
Penney Group Inc 1309 Topsail Rd Sta A *Web:* www.penneygroup.ca	St. John's	NL	A1B3N4	709-782-3404	
Pennsylvania Macaroni Co 2010 Penn Ave # 12 *Web:* www.pennmac.com	Pittsburgh	PA	15222	412-471-8330	
Petra Industries Inc 2101 S Kelly Ave *Web:* www.petra.com	Edmond	OK	73013	405-216-2100	
Phazar Corp 101 SE 25th Ave *NASDAQ: ANTP* ■ *Web:* www.antennaproducts.com	Mineral Wells	TX	76067	940-325-3301	325-0716
PHC Inc 200 Lake St Ste 102 *Web:* phc-inc.com	Peabody	MA	01960	978-536-2777	
Phillips Service Industries Inc 11878 Hubbard *Web:* www.psi-online.com	Livonia	MI	48150	734-853-5000	853-5032
Phosphate Holdings Inc 100 Web Ste 4 *Web:* www.missphosphates.com	Madison	MS	39110	601-898-9004	
Platinum Group of Cos Inc 9121 Oakdale Ave Sute 201 *Web:* www.platinumgroup.org	Chatsworth	CA	91311	818-721-3800	721-3811
Pro-Dex Inc 2361 McGaw Ave *NASDAQ: PDEX* ■ *TF:* 800-562-6204 ■ *Web:* www.pro-dex.com	Irvine	CA	92614	800-562-6204	
Relco LLC 2331 Third Ave *Web:* www.relco.net	Willmar	MN	56201	320-231-2210	
Rema Foods Inc 140 Sylvan Ave *Web:* www.remafoods.net	Englewood Cliffs	NJ	07632	201-947-1000	
Resource Land Holdings LLC 1530 16th St Ste 300 *Web:* www.rlholdings.com	Denver	CO	80202	720-723-2850	
Revlon Inc 237 Pk Ave *NYSE: REV* ■ *TF:* 800-473-8566 ■ *Web:* www.revlon.com	New York	NY	10017	212-527-4000	
Reyes Holdings LLC 6250 North River Rd Ste 9000 *Web:* www.reyesholdings.com	Rosemont	IL	60018	847-227-6500	227-6550
Riverstone Holdings LLC 712 Fifth Ave 36th Fl *Web:* www.riverstonellc.com	New York	NY	10019	212-993-0076	
RLJ Companies LLC, The 3 Bethesda Metro Ctr Ste 1000 *Web:* www.rljcompanies.com	Bethesda	MD	20814	301-280-7700	
Rock Island Capital LLC 1415 W 22nd St Ste 1250 *Web:* www.rockislandcapital.com	Oak Brook	IL	60523	630-413-9136	
Rosen's Diversified Inc 1120 Lake Ave PO Box 933 *Web:* www.rosensdiversifiedinc.com	Fairmont	MN	56031	507-238-6001	
RSCC Aerospace & Defense 680 Hayward St *Web:* www.rsccaerodefense.com	Manchester	NH	03103	603-622-3500	
Sabre Holdings Corp 3150 Sabre Dr *Web:* www.sabre.com	Southlake	TX	76092	682-605-1000	
Sandstone Group Inc 223 N Water St Ste 500 *Web:* www.diachemix.com	Milwaukee	WI	53202	414-902-6700	
Sandvik Inc 1702 Nevins Rd *TF:* 800-726-3845	Fair Lawn	NJ	07410	201-794-5000	794-5165
Saxco International LLC 200 Gibraltar Rd Ste 101 *Web:* www.saxcointl.com	Horsham	PA	19044	215-443-8100	
Sbeeg Holdings LLC 8000 Beverly Blvd *Web:* sbe.com	Los Angeles	CA	90048	323-655-8000	
Schaefer Marine Inc 158 Duchaine Blvd *Web:* schaefermarine.com	New Bedford	MA	02745	508-995-9511	
Schuff International Inc 420 S 19th Ave *OTC: SHFK* ■ *Web:* www.schuff.com	Phoenix	AZ	85009	602-252-7787	
Sears Holdings Corp 3333 Beverly Rd *NASDAQ: SHLD* ■ *Web:* www.searsholdings.com	Hoffman Estates	IL	60179	847-286-2500	
SGS North America Inc 201 State Rt 17 N *TF:* 800-645-5227 ■ *Web:* www.sgsgroup.us.com	Rutherford	NJ	07070	201-508-3000	508-3183
Shamrock Cos Inc, The 24090 Detroit Rd *Web:* www.shamrockcompanies.net	Westlake	OH	44145	440-899-9510	250-2180
Shamrock Holdings Inc 3500 W Olive Ave *Web:* www.shamrock.com	Burbank	CA	91505	818-845-4444	
SHC International Inc 1031 Aldridge Rd Ste I *Web:* www.shc-intl.com	Vacaville	CA	95688	707-448-6076	
Shenandoah Telecommunications Co 500 Shentel Way *NASDAQ: SHEN* ■ *TF:* 800-743-6835 ■ *Web:* www.shentel.com	Edinburg	VA	22824	540-984-5224	984-3438
Siebert Financial Corp 885 Third Ave *NASDAQ: SIEB* ■ *TF:* 877-327-8379 ■ *Web:* www.siebertnet.com	New York	NY	10022	212-644-2400	486-2784
Simon Golub & Sons Inc 5506 Sixth Ave S *Web:* www.simongolub.com	Seattle	WA	98108	206-762-4800	
Simpson Investment Co 917 E 11th St *Web:* simpson.com	Tacoma	WA	98421	253-779-6400	280-9000
Sky Holding Company LLC 850 Montgomery St Ste 200 *Web:* www.jacksonsquareaviation.com	San Francisco	CA	94133	415-821-8300	
Solis Capital Partners LLC 23 Corporate Plz Ste 215 *Web:* www.soliscapital.com	Newport Beach	CA	92660	949-296-2440	
Strata Products Worldwide LLC 8995 Roswell Rd Ste 200 *Web:* www.strataworldwide.com	Sandy Springs	GA	30350	770-321-2500	
Sumitomo Canada Ltd (SCL) 150 King St W Ste 2304 *Web:* www.sumitomocanada.com	Toronto	ON	M5H1J9	416-860-3800	365-3141
Sumitomo Corp of America 600 Third Ave 42nd Fl *TF:* 877-980-3283 ■ *Web:* www.sumitomocorp.com	New York	NY	10016	212-207-0700	207-0456
Sunroad Marina Partners LP 955 Harbor Island Dr *Web:* www.sdmarina.com	San Diego	CA	92101	619-574-0736	
Suntory International Corp 600 Third Ave Ste 2101 *Web:* www.suntory.com	New York	NY	10016	212-891-6600	
Superior Group Inc 100 Front St	West Conshohocken	PA	19428	610-397-2040	397-2041
Tabar Inc 251 Greenwood Ave *Web:* www.tabarinc.com	Bethel	CT	06801	203-748-5242	
TAPO Ventures LLC 195 N Harbor Dr Ste 4601 *Web:* www.tapoventures.com	Chicago	IL	60601	312-540-1333	
Taylor Corp 1725 Roe Crest Dr *Web:* www.taylorcorp.com/Pages/default.aspx	North Mankato	MN	56003	507-625-2828	386-2031
Teijin Holdings USA 600 Lexington Ave 27th Fl *Web:* teijin.com	New York	NY	10022	212-308-8744	308-8902
Telephone & Data Systems Inc 30 N La Salle St Ste 4000 *NYSE: TDS* ■ *TF:* 877-337-1575 ■ *Web:* www.tdsinc.com/home/default.aspx	Chicago	IL	60602	312-630-1900	630-9299
Telesystem Ltd 1250 Rene-Levesque Blvd W Ste 3800 *Web:* www.telesystem.ca	Montreal	QC	H3B4W8	514-397-9797	397-1569
Thompson Investment Management Inc 918 Deming Way 3rd Fl *Web:* www.thompsonim.com	Madison	WI	53717	608-827-5700	
Thought Convergence Inc 11300 W Olympic Blvd Ste 900 *Web:* www.thoughtconvergence.com	Los Angeles	CA	90064	310-909-7900	
Thrall Enterprises Inc 180 N Stetson Ave	Chicago	IL	60601	312-621-8200	
ThyssenKrupp Elevator 9280 Crestwyn Hills Dr *TF:* 877-230-0303 ■ *Web:* www.thyssenkruppelevator.com	Memphis	TN	38125	901-261-1800	
Toma & Assoc Inc 41 Summit St	Jackson	CA	95642	209-223-0156	
Toyota Motor North America Inc 601 Lexington Ave 49th Fl *TF:* 800-331-4331 ■ *Web:* www.toyota.com	New York	NY	10022	800-331-4331	
Transtar Inc 1200 Penn Ave Ste 300 *Web:* www.tstarinc.com	Pittsburgh	PA	15222	412-433-7835	
Tredegar Corp 1100 Boulders Pkwy *NYSE: TG* ■ *TF:* 800-411-7441 ■ *Web:* www.tredegar.com	North Chesterfield	VA	23225	804-330-1000	330-1177
Trian Partners 280 Pk Ave **Fax:* Mail Rm ■ *Web:* www.trianpartners.com	New York	NY	10017	212-451-3000	451-3134*
Trump Organization 725 Fifth Ave *Web:* www.trump.com	New York	NY	10022	212-832-2000	935-0141
TSI Holding Co 999 Executive Pkwy Dr	Saint Louis	MO	63141	314-628-6000	628-6099
Turner Corp 375 Hudson St *Web:* www.turnerconstruction.com	New York	NY	10014	212-229-6000	

Phone Fax

UM Holding Co 56 N Haddon Ave PO Box 200 ... Haddonfield NJ 08033 856-354-2200
Web: www.umholdings.com
Unilever Canada Ltd 160 Bloor St E Ste 1500 ... Toronto ON M4W3R2 416-964-1857
Web: www.unilever.ca
Union Pacific Corp 1400 Douglas St ... Omaha NE 68179 402-544-5000
NYSE: UNP ■ *TF:* 888-870-8777 ■ *Web:* www.up.com
United Co, The 1005 Glenway Ave ... Bristol VA 24201 276-466-3322 645-1404
Vector Group Ltd 100 SE Second St 32nd Fl ... Miami FL 33131 305-579-8000 579-8001
NYSE: VGR ■ *Web:* www.vectorgroupltd.com
VENSURE Employer Services Inc
4140 E Baseline Rd Ste 201 ... Mesa AZ 85206 800-409-8958
TF: 800-409-8958 ■ *Web:* www.vensureinc.com
Viking Group Inc
3033 Orchard Vista Dr Se Ste 308 ... Grand Rapids MI 49546 616-831-6448
Web: vikinggroupinc.com
Warnaco Group Inc 501 Seventh Ave ... New York NY 10018 212-287-8000
NYSE: WRC ■ *Web:* www.pvh.com
Warren Equities Inc 27 Warren Way ... Providence RI 02905 401-781-9900 461-7160
TF: 866-867-4075 ■ *Web:* www.warreneq.com
Warren Technology Inc 2050 W 73 St ... Hialeah FL 33016 305-556-6933
Web: www.warrenhvac.com
WebMD Health Holdings Inc
111 Eigth Ave 7th Fl ... New York NY 10011 212-624-3700
NASDAQ: WBMD ■ *Web:* www.webmd.com
WEDGE Group Inc 1415 Louisiana St Ste 3000 ... Houston TX 77002 713-739-6500
TF: 888-563-5383 ■ *Web:* www.wedgegroup.com
WESCO International Inc
225 W Stn Sq Dr Ste 700 ... Pittsburgh PA 15219 412-454-2200 454-2505
NYSE: WCC ■ *Web:* www.wesco.com
West Texas Gas Inc 211 N Colorado St ... Midland TX 79701 432-682-4349 682-4024
Web: westtexasgas.com
Williams Cos Inc 1 Williams Ctr ... Tulsa OK 74103 918-573-2000
NYSE: WMB ■ *TF:* 800-945-5426 ■ *Web:* co.williams.com
Wood Resources LLC
100 Northfield St Ste 203 ... Greenwich CT 06830 203-622-9138 622-0151
Web: www.atlasholdingsllc.com
Worthington Direct Holdings LLC
6301 Gaston Ave Ste 670 ... Dallas TX 75214 800-599-6636
TF: 800-599-6636 ■ *Web:* www.worthingtondirect.com
WRB Enterprises 1414 W Swann Ave Ste 201 ... Tampa FL 33606 813-251-3737
Web: wrbenterprises.com
YRC Worldwide Inc 10990 Roe Ave ... Overland Park KS 66211 913-696-6100
NASDAQ: YRCW ■ *TF:* 800-846-4300 ■ *Web:* www.yrc.com
Zahava Group Inc 7525 Britannia Park Pl ... San Diego CA 92154 619-671-0001
Web: www.zahavagroup.com

360-4 Insurance Holding Companies

Phone Fax

Affirmative Insurance Holdings Inc
4450 Sojourn Dr Ste 500 ... Addison TX 75001 972-728-6300
OTC: AFFM ■ *Web:* www.affirmativeholdings.com
AFLAC Inc 1932 Wynnton Rd ... Columbus GA 31999 706-323-3431
NYSE: AFL ■ *TF:* 800-992-3522 ■ *Web:* www.aflac.com
AIG SunAmerica Inc 21650 Oxnard St ... Woodland Hills CA 91367 800-445-7862
TF: 800-445-7862 ■ *Web:* www-1000.aig.com
Allstate Corp 2775 Sanders Rd ... Northbrook IL 60062 847-402-5000
NYSE: ALL ■ *TF:* 800-255-7828 ■ *Web:* www.allstate.com
AMBAC Financial Group Inc
1 State St Plz 15th Fl ... New York NY 10004 212-668-0340 509-9190
OTC: ABKFQ ■ *TF:* 800-221-1854 ■ *Web:* www.ambac.com
American Fidelity Assurance Co
2000 N Classen Blvd ... Oklahoma City OK 73106 405-523-2000
TF: 800-654-8489 ■ *Web:* americanfidelity.com
American Financial Group Inc 301 E 4th St ... Cincinnati OH 45202 513-579-2121 579-2580
NYSE: AFG ■ *Web:* www.afginc.com
Americo Life Inc 300 W 11th St ... Kansas City MO 64105 816-391-2000 391-2083
TF General: 800-231-0801 ■ *Web:* www.americo.com
Anthem Insurance Cos Inc
120 Monument Cir Ste 200 ... Indianapolis IN 46204 317-488-6000 488-6028*
**Fax:* Hum Res ■ *TF:* 800-331-1476 ■ *Web:* www.anthem.com
Aon Corp 200 E Randolph St ... Chicago IL 60601 312-381-1000
TF: 877-384-4276 ■ *Web:* www.aon.com
Assicurazioni Generali US Branch
250 Greenwich St 33rd Fl ... New York NY 10007 212-602-7600 587-9537
Web: www.generaliusa.com
Assurant Group 11222 Quail Roost Dr ... Miami FL 33157 305-253-2244
TF: 800-852-2244 ■ *Web:* www.assurant.com
Assurant Inc 1 Chase Manhattan Plz ... New York NY 10005 212-859-7000
NYSE: AIZ ■ *Web:* www.assurant.com
Atlantic American Corp 4370 Peachtree Rd NE ... Atlanta GA 30319 404-266-5500
NASDAQ: AAME ■ *Web:* www.atlam.com
Bexil Corp 11 Hanover Sq ... New York NY 10005 212-785-0400 363-1101
OTC: BXLC ■ *TF:* 800-937-5449 ■ *Web:* www.bexil.com
Capitol Transamerica Corp
1600 Aspen Commons ... Middleton WI 53562 608-829-4200 829-7409*
**Fax:* Hum Res ■ *TF:* 800-475-4450 ■ *Web:* www.capspecialty.com
Chubb Corp 15 Mountain View Rd ... Warren NJ 07059 908-903-2000 903-2027*
NYSE: CB ■ **Fax:* Mail Rm ■ *TF:* 800-252-4670 ■ *Web:* www.chubb.com
CIGNA Corp 1601 Chestnut St ... Philadelphia PA 19192 215-761-1000
NYSE: CI ■ *Web:* www.cigna.com
Cincinnati Financial Corp
6200 S Gilmore Rd ... Fairfield OH 45014 513-870-2000
NASDAQ: CINF ■ *Web:* cinfin.com
Citizens Financial Corp
12910 Shelbyville Rd Ste 300 ... Louisville KY 40243 502-244-2420
OTC: CFIN ■ *TF:* 800-843-7752 ■ *Web:* www.citizensfinancialcorp.com
CNA Financial Corp 333 S Wabash Ave ... Chicago IL 60604 312-822-5000
NYSE: CNA ■ *TF:* 800-262-4357 ■ *Web:* www.cna.com
Conseco Inc 11825 N Pennsylvania St ... Carmel IN 46032 866-595-2255
NYSE: CNO ■ *TF:* 866-595-2255 ■ *Web:* www.conseco.com

Phone Fax

CUNA Mutual Group 5910 Mineral Pt Dr ... Madison WI 53705 608-238-5851
TF: 800-937-2644 ■ *Web:* www.cunamutual.com
Delphi Financial Group Inc
1105 N Market St Ste 1230 ... Wilmington DE 19801 302-478-5142
NYSE: DFG ■ *Web:* www.delphifin.com
Deutsche Bank Americas Holding Corp
60 Wall St ... New York NY 10005 212-250-2500
Web: www.db.com
Donegal Group Inc 1195 River Rd ... Marietta PA 17547 717-426-1931
NASDAQ: DGICA ■ *TF:* 800-877-0600 ■ *Web:* www.donegalgroup.com
EMC Insurance Group Inc 717 Mulberry St ... Des Moines IA 50309 515-280-2511
NASDAQ: EMCI ■ *TF:* 800-447-2295 ■ *Web:* www.emcins.com
Everest Re Group Ltd
477 Martinsville Rd PO Box 830 ... Liberty Corner NJ 07938 908-604-3000 604-3322
TF: 800-269-6660 ■ *Web:* www.everestre.com
Fairfax Financial Holdings Ltd
95 Wellington St W Ste 800 ... Toronto ON M5J2N7 416-367-4941 367-4946
Web: www.fairfax.ca
Farmers Insurance Group
4680 Wilshire Blvd ... Los Angeles CA 90010 323-932-3200
TF: 800-435-7764 ■ *Web:* farmers.com
FBL Financial Group Inc
5400 University Ave ... West Des Moines IA 50266 515-225-5400
NYSE: FFG ■ *Web:* www.fblfinancial.com
Federated Insurance Cos
121 E Pk Sq PO Box 328 ... Owatonna MN 55060 507-455-5200
TF: 800-533-0472 ■ *Web:* federatedinsurance.com
GMAC Insurance Holdings Inc
PO Box 3199 ... Winston-Salem NC 27102 888-293-5108
TF: 888-293-5108 ■ *Web:* nationalgeneral.com
Hallmark Financial Services Inc
777 Main St Ste 1000 ... Fort Worth TX 76102 817-348-1600 348-1815
NASDAQ: HALL ■ *Web:* www.hallmarkgrp.com
Harleysville Group Inc 355 Maple Ave ... Harleysville PA 19438 215-256-5000 256-5678*
NASDAQ: HGIC ■ **Fax:* Mktg ■ *TF:* 800-523-6344 ■ *Web:* www.harleysvillegroup.com
Hartford Financial Services Group Inc
690 Asylum Ave ... Hartford CT 06115 860-547-5000
NYSE: HIG ■ *TF:* 866-553-5663 ■ *Web:* www.thehartford.com
HCC Insurance Holdings Inc 13403 NW Fwy ... Houston TX 77040 713-462-1000 462-4210
Web: www.hcc.com
HealthMarkets Inc 9151 Blvd 26 ... North Richland Hills TX 76180 817-255-5200
Web: www.healthmarketsinc.com
Horace Mann Educators Corp
1 Horace Mann Plz ... Springfield IL 62715 217-789-2500 788-5161
NYSE: HMN ■ *TF:* 800-999-1030 ■ *Web:* www.horacemann.com
Investors Title Co 121 N Columbia St ... Chapel Hill NC 27514 919-968-2200
NASDAQ: ITIC ■ *TF:* 800-326-4842 ■ *Web:* invtitle.com
John Hancock Financial Services Inc
601 Congress St ... Boston MA 02210 617-663-3000 663-4790*
**Fax:* PR ■ *Web:* www.johnhancock.com
Kansas City Life Insurance Co
3520 Broadway ... Kansas City MO 64111 816-753-7000 753-4902
NASDAQ: KCLI ■ *TF:* 800-821-6164 ■ *Web:* www.kclife.com
Kingsway America Inc (KAI)
150 NW Pt Blvd ... Elk Grove Village IL 60007 847-700-9100 700-9170
TF: 800-232-0631 ■ *Web:* kaiadvantage.com
Legal & General America Inc
1701 Research Blvd ... Rockville MD 20850 301-279-4800 294-6960*
**Fax:* Cust Svc ■ *TF:* 800-638-8428 ■ *Web:* www.lgamerica.com
Lifetime Healthcare Cos, The 165 Ct St ... Rochester NY 14647 585-454-1700 238-4233
Web: www.lifethc.com
Lincoln National Corp (LNC)
150 N Radnor-Chester Rd ... Radnor PA 19087 484-583-1400 448-3962*
NYSE: LNC ■ **Fax Area Code:* 215 ■ **Fax:* PR ■ *TF:* 877-275-5462 ■ *Web:* www.lfg.com
Manulife Financial Corp 200 Bloor St E ... Toronto ON M4W1E5 416-926-3000 926-5410
NYSE: MFC ■ *TF:* 800-795-9767 ■ *Web:* www.manulife.com
Markel Corp 4521 Highwoods Pkwy ... Glen Allen VA 23060 800-431-1270 662-7535*
NYSE: MKL ■ **Fax Area Code:* 855 ■ *TF:* 877-566-6323 ■ *Web:* markelinsurance.com
MBIA Inc 113 King St ... Armonk NY 10504 914-273-4545
NYSE: MBI ■ *Web:* www.mbia.com
Meadowbrook Insurance Group Inc
26255 American Dr ... Southfield MI 48034 248-358-1100 358-1614
NYSE: MIG ■ *TF:* 800-482-2726 ■ *Web:* www.meadowbrookinsgrp.com
Midland Co 7000 Midland Blvd ... Amelia OH 45102 800-543-2644
TF: 800-759-9008 ■ *Web:* www.amig.com
Munich Reinsurance America Inc
555 College Rd E PO Box 5241 ... Princeton NJ 08543 609-243-4200 243-4257
Web: www.munichre.com/us
Mutual of Omaha Co 3300 Mutual of Omaha Plz ... Omaha NE 68175 402-342-7600
TF: 800-775-6000 ■ *Web:* www.mutualofomaha.com
Navigators Group Inc 1 Penn Plz 32nd Fl ... New York NY 10119 212-244-2333 244-4077
NASDAQ: NAVG ■ *TF:* 866-408-1922 ■ *Web:* www.navigators-insurance.com
Pacific Mutual Holding Co
700 Newport Ctr Dr ... Newport Beach CA 92660 949-219-3011 219-7614
TF: 800-347-7787 ■ *Web:* www.pacificlife.com
Penn-America Group Inc 420 S York Rd ... Hatboro PA 19040 215-443-3600
Web: www.penn-america.com
Phoenix Cos Inc, The
1 American Row PO Box 5056 ... Hartford CT 06102 860-403-5000
NYSE: PNX ■ *TF:* 800-628-1936 ■ *Web:* www.phoenixwm.phl.com
PICO Holdings Inc 7979 Ivanhoe Ave Ste 301 ... La Jolla CA 92037 858-456-6022 456-6480
NASDAQ: PICO ■ *TF:* 888-389-3222 ■ *Web:* www.picoholdings.com
PMA Capital Corp 380 Sentry Pkwy ... Blue Bell PA 19422 610-397-5298 397-5422
Web: www.pmacompanies.com
PMI Group Inc 3003 Oak Rd ... Walnut Creek CA 94597 800-288-1970
OTC: PMI ■ *TF:* 800-288-1970 ■ *Web:* www.pmi-us.com
ProAssurance Corp 100 Brookwood Pl Ste 300 ... Birmingham AL 35209 205-877-4400 802-4799*
NYSE: PRA ■ **Fax:* Cust Svc ■ *TF:* 800-282-6242 ■ *Web:* www.proassurance.com
Protective Life Corp 2801 Hwy 280 S ... Birmingham AL 35223 205-268-1000
NYSE: PL ■ *TF:* 800-333-3418 ■ *Web:* www.protective.com
Reinsurance Group of America Inc
1370 Timberlake Manor Pkwy ... Chesterfield MO 63017 636-736-7000 736-7150
NYSE: RGA ■ *TF:* 800-985-4326 ■ *Web:* www.rgare.com

Phone Fax

RLI Corp 9025 N Lindbergh Dr .... Peoria IL 61615 309-692-1000 692-1068
NYSE: RLI ■ *TF Cust Svc:* 800-331-4929 ■ *Web:* www.rlicorp.com

Scottish Re Inc
14120 Ballantyne Corporate Pl Ste 300 .... Charlotte NC 28277 704-542-9192 542-5744
Web: www.scottishre.com

Securian Financial Group Inc
400 and 401 Robert St N .... Saint Paul MN 55101 651-665-3500 665-4488
Web: www.securian.com

Security Benefit Group of Cos
1 Security Benefit Pl .... Topeka KS 66636 785-438-3000 368-1772*
**Fax:* Cust Svc ■ *TF:* 800-888-2461 ■ *Web:* www.securitybenefit.com

Selective Insurance Group Inc
40 Wantage Ave .... Branchville NJ 07890 973-948-3000 948-0292
NASDAQ: SIGI ■ *TF:* 800-777-9656 ■ *Web:* www.selective.com

StanCorp Financial Group Inc
1100 SW Sixth Ave .... Portland OR 97204 800-368-1135
NYSE: SFG ■ *TF:* 800-368-1135 ■ *Web:* standard.com

Summit Holding Southeast Inc PO Box 600 .... Gainesville GA 30503 678-450-5825
TF: 800-971-2667 ■ *Web:* www.summitholdings.com

Sun Life Financial Inc 150 King St W .... Toronto ON M5H1J9 416-979-9966
TSE: SLF ■ *TF:* 877-786-5433 ■ *Web:* www.sunlife.com

Torchmark Corp 3700 S Stonebridge Dr .... McKinney TX 75070 972-569-4000 569-3282
NYSE: TMK ■ *TF:* 877-577-3899 ■ *Web:* www.torchmarkcorp.com

Transatlantic Holdings Inc 80 Pine St .... New York NY 10005 212-365-2200 365-2362*
NYSE: TRH ■ **Fax:* Claims ■ *Web:* www.transre.com

Travelers Cos Inc 385 Washington St .... Saint Paul MN 55102 651-310-7911
NYSE: TRV ■ *TF:* 800-328-2189 ■ *Web:* www.travelers.com

ULLICO Inc 1625 Eye St NW .... Washington DC 20006 800-431-5425
TF: 800-431-5425 ■ *Web:* www.ullico.com

United Fire Group
118 Second Ave SE PO Box 73909 .... Cedar Rapids IA 52407 319-399-5700 399-5499
TF: 800-332-7977 ■ *Web:* www.unitedfiregroup.com

United Trust Group Inc (UTGI)
5250 S Sixth St .... Springfield IL 62705 217-241-6410 241-6578
OTC: UTGN ■ *TF:* 800-323-0050 ■ *Web:* www.utgins.com

Universal American Corp (UAFC)
44 S Broadway Ste 1200 .... White Plains NY 10601 914-934-5200 934-0700
NYSE: UAM ■ *TF:* 866-249-8668 ■ *Web:* www.universalamerican.com

UnumProvident Corp 1 Fountain Sq .... Chattanooga TN 37402 423-294-1011 872-8999*
**Fax Area Code:* 410 ■ *TF:* 800-262-0018 ■ *Web:* www.unum.com

Voya Services Co 5780 Powers Ferry Rd NW .... Atlanta GA 30327 770-980-5100
Web: www.voya.com

Western & Southern Financial Group
400 Broadway .... Cincinnati OH 45202 513-629-1800 629-1212
TF: 800-333-5222 ■ *Web:* www.westernsouthern.com

White Mountains Insurance Group Ltd
80 S Main St .... Hanover NH 03755 603-640-2200 643-4592
NYSE: WTM ■ *TF:* 866-295-3762 ■ *Web:* www.whitemountains.com

WR Berkley Corp 475 Steamboat Rd .... Greenwich CT 06830 203-629-3000
NYSE: WRB ■ *Web:* www.wrbc.com

360-5 Utilities Holding Companies

Phone Fax

AGL Resources Inc 10 Peachtree Pl PO Box 4569 .... Atlanta GA 30309 404-584-4000
NYSE: GAS ■ *TF Cust Svc:* 866-977-4278 ■ *Web:* www.aglresources.com

ALLETE Inc 30 W Superior St .... Duluth MN 55802 218-279-5000
NYSE: ALE ■ *TF:* 800-228-4966 ■ *Web:* www.allete.com

Ameren Corp 1901 Chouteau Ave .... Saint Louis MO 63103 314-621-3222
NYSE: AEE ■ *TF:* 800-552-7583 ■ *Web:* ameren.com

American Electric Power Company Inc
1 Riverside Plz .... Columbus OH 43215 614-716-1000
NYSE: AEP ■ *TF Cust Svc:* 800-277-2177 ■ *Web:* www.aep.com

American States Water Co
630 E Foothill Blvd .... San Dimas CA 91773 909-394-3600
NYSE: AWR ■ *TF:* 800-999-4033 ■ *Web:* www.aswater.com

American Water Works Co Inc
1025 Laurel Oak Rd .... Voorhees NJ 08043 856-346-8200 346-8360
NYSE: AWK ■ *TF:* 888-282-6816 ■ *Web:* www.amwater.com

Artesian Resources Corp 664 Churchmans Rd .... Newark DE 19702 302-453-6900 453-6957
NASDAQ: ARTNA ■ *TF:* 800-332-5114 ■ *Web:* www.artesianwater.com

Atmos Energy Corp 5430 LBJ Fwy Ste 1800 .... Dallas TX 75240 972-934-9227
NYSE: ATO ■ *TF:* 888-286-6700 ■ *Web:* www.atmosenergy.com

Black Hills Corp 625 Ninth St .... Rapid City SD 57701 605-721-1700 721-2596*
NYSE: BKH ■ **Fax:* Hum Res ■ *TF:* 866-264-8003 ■ *Web:* www.blackhillscorp.com

CenterPoint Energy Inc 1111 Louisiana St .... Houston TX 77002 713-207-1111
NYSE: CNP ■ *TF Cust Svc:* 800-495-9880 ■ *Web:* www.centerpointenergy.com

CH Energy Group Inc 284 S Ave .... Poughkeepsie NY 12601 845-452-2000
NYSE: CHG ■ *TF:* 800-527-2714 ■ *Web:* www.chenergygroup.com

CMS Energy Corp 1 Energy Plz .... Jackson MI 49201 517-788-0550
NYSE: CMS ■ *TF:* 800-477-5050 ■ *Web:* www.cmsenergy.com

Connecticut Water Service Inc 93 W Main St .... Clinton CT 06413 860-669-8636 664-8081*
NASDAQ: CTWS ■ **Fax:* Cust Svc ■ *TF:* 800-286-5700 ■ *Web:* www.ctwater.com

Consolidated Edison Inc 4 Irving Pl .... New York NY 10003 212-460-4600
NYSE: ED ■ *TF:* 800-752-6633 ■ *Web:* coned.com

Dominion Resources Inc 120 Tredegar St .... Richmond VA 23219 804-819-2000 819-2233
NYSE: D ■ *TF:* 800-552-4034 ■ *Web:* www.dom.com

DPL Inc 1065 Woodman Dr .... Dayton OH 45432 800-736-3001
NYSE: DPL ■ *TF:* 800-433-8500 ■ *Web:* www.dplinc.com

DTE Energy Co 1 Energy Plz .... Detroit MI 48226 313-235-4000
NYSE: DTE ■ *TF:* 800-477-4747 ■ *Web:* www.dteenergy.com

Duke Energy Corp PO Box 70516 .... Charlotte NC 28201 704-594-6200 382-3781*
NYSE: DUK ■ **Fax:* Hum Res ■ *Web:* m.duke-energy.com

Duquesne Light Holdings Inc
411 Seventh Ave .... Pittsburgh PA 15219 412-393-7000 393-7000
TF: 888-393-7000 ■ *Web:* www.duquesnelight.com

Dynegy Inc 601 Travis St Ste 1400 .... Houston TX 77002 713-507-6400
NYSE: DYN ■ *TF:* 800-633-4704 ■ *Web:* www.dynegy.com

Edison International 2244 Walnut Grove Ave .... Rosemead CA 91770 626-302-1212
NYSE: EIX ■ *TF Cust Svc:* 800-655-4555 ■ *Web:* www.edison.com

Energen Corp 605 Richard Arrington Blvd N .... Birmingham AL 35203 205-326-2700
NYSE: EGN ■ *TF:* 800-654-3206 ■ *Web:* www.energen.com

Entergy Corp 639 Loyola Ave .... New Orleans LA 70113 504-576-4000
NYSE: ETR ■ *TF:* 800-368-3749 ■ *Web:* www.entergy.com

FirstEnergy Corp 76 S Main St .... Akron OH 44308 800-633-4766
NYSE: FE ■ *TF:* 800-633-4766 ■ *Web:* www.firstenergycorp.com

FPL Group Inc
NextEra Energy Inc 700 Universe Blvd .... Juno Beach FL 33408 561-694-4000 694-4620
NYSE: NEE ■ *TF:* 888-218-4392 ■ *Web:* www.nexteraenergy.com

Great Plains Energy Inc
1200 Main St PO Box 418679 .... Kansas City MO 64106 816-556-2200
NYSE: GXP ■ *Web:* www.greatplainsenergy.com

Holly Energy Partners LP
100 Crescent Ct Ste 1600 .... Dallas TX 75201 214-871-3555
TF: 800-642-1687 ■ *Web:* www.hollyenergy.com

IDACORP Inc 1221 W Idaho St .... Boise ID 83702 208-388-2200
NYSE: IDA ■ *Web:* www.idacorpinc.com

MidAmerican Energy Holdings Co
666 Grand Ave PO Box 657 .... Des Moines IA 50303 800-329-6261
TF: 800-329-6261 ■ *Web:* www.midamerican.com

National Fuel Gas Co 6363 Main St .... Williamsville NY 14221 716-857-7000 857-7206
NYSE: NFG ■ *TF Cust Svc:* 800-365-3234 ■ *Web:* nationalfuelgas.com

National Grid USA Service Company Inc
25 Research Dr .... Westborough MA 01582 508-389-2000
TF: 800-548-8000 ■ *Web:* www.nationalgridus.com

New Jersey Resources Corp 1415 Wyckoff Rd .... Wall NJ 07719 732-938-1000
NYSE: NJR ■ *TF:* 800-221-0051 ■ *Web:* www.njresources.com

NSTAR 800 Boylston St .... Boston MA 02199 617-424-2000
NYSE: NST ■ *TF:* 800-592-2000 ■ *Web:* nstar.com

OGE Energy Corp 321 N Harvey St .... Oklahoma City OK 73102 405-553-3000
NYSE: OGE ■ *TF:* 800-272-9741 ■ *Web:* www.oge.com

PG & E Corp 77 Beale St 24th Fl .... San Francisco CA 94105 415-267-7000 973-8719*
NYSE: PCG ■ **Fax:* Hum Res ■ *TF:* 800-743-5000 ■ *Web:* www.pgecorp.com

Pinnacle West Capital Corp 400 N Fifth St .... Phoenix AZ 85004 602-250-1000
NYSE: PNW ■ *TF:* 800-457-2983 ■ *Web:* www.pinnaclewest.com

PNM Resources Inc Alvarado Sq .... Albuquerque NM 87158 505-241-2700
NYSE: PNM ■ *TF:* 888-342-5766 ■ *Web:* www.pnmresources.com

PPL Corp 2 N Ninth St .... Allentown PA 18101 610-774-5151
NYSE: PPL ■ *TF:* 800-342-5775 ■ *Web:* www.pplweb.com

Progress Energy Inc 410 S Wilmington St .... Raleigh NC 27601 919-546-6111 546-2920
NYSE: PGN ■ *TF:* 800-452-2777 ■ *Web:* progress-energy.com

Public Service Enterprise Group Inc 80 Pk Plz .... Newark NJ 07102 973-430-7000
NYSE: PEG ■ *TF Cust Svc:* 800-436-7734 ■ *Web:* www.pseg.com

Puget Energy Inc 10885 NE Fourth St .... Bellevue WA 98004 425-454-6363
Web: www.pugetenergy.com/pages/terms.html

Questar Corp
333 S State St PO Box 45433 .... Salt Lake City UT 84145 801-324-5000
NYSE: STR ■ *TF:* 800-323-5517 ■ *Web:* www.questarcorp.com

RGC Resources Inc
519 Kimball Ave PO Box 13007 .... Roanoke VA 24016 540-777-4427
NASDAQ: RGCO ■ *Web:* www.rgcresources.com

SCANA Corp 220 Operation Way .... Cayce SC 29033 803-217-9000 933-8224
NYSE: SCG ■ *TF:* 800-251-7234 ■ *Web:* www.scana.com

Sempra Energy Corp 101 Ash St .... San Diego CA 92101 619-696-2000
NYSE: SRE ■ *TF:* 800-411-7343 ■ *Web:* www.sempra.com

SJW Corp 110 W Taylor St .... San Jose CA 95110 408-279-7900 279-7917
NYSE: SJW ■ *Web:* www.sjwater.com

Southern Co 30 Ivan Allen Jr Blvd NW .... Atlanta GA 30308 404-506-5000
NYSE: SO ■ *Web:* www.southernco.com

Tokyo Gas Co Ltd 1540 Broadway Ste 3920 .... New York NY 10036 646-865-0577 865-0592
Web: www.tokyo-gas.co.jp

UGI Corp 460 N Gulph Rd PO Box 858 .... King Of Prussia PA 19406 610-337-1000
NYSE: UGI ■ *Web:* www.ugicorp.com

Unitil Corp 6 Liberty Ln W .... Hampton NH 03842 603-772-0775 773-6605
NYSE: UTL ■ *TF:* 800-852-3339 ■ *Web:* www.unitil.com

Vectren Corp
211 NW Riverside Dr PO Box 209 .... Evansville IN 47702 812-491-4000
NYSE: VVC ■ *TF:* 800-227-1376 ■ *Web:* www.vectren.com

Westar Energy Inc 818 S Kansas Ave .... Topeka KS 66612 785-575-6300
NYSE: WR ■ *TF:* 800-383-1183 ■ *Web:* www.westarenergy.com

WGL Holdings Inc 101 Constitution Ave NW .... Washington DC 20080 703-750-2000 664-7317*
NYSE: WGL ■ **Fax Area Code:* 301 ■ *TF:* 800-645-3751 ■ *Web:* www.wglholdings.com

Wisconsin Energy Corp 231 W Michigan St .... Milwaukee WI 53203 414-221-2345
NYSE: WEC ■ *TF General:* 800-242-9137 ■ *Web:* www.wecenergygroup.com/message.htm

361 HOME FURNISHINGS - WHOL

Phone Fax

A & J Washroom Accessories Inc
509 Temple Hill Rd .... New Windsor NY 12553 845-562-3332
Web: www.ajwashroom.com

AA Importing Co Inc 7700 Hall St .... Saint Louis MO 63147 314-383-8800 383-2608
TF Cust Svc: 800-325-0602 ■ *Web:* www.aaimporting.com

Adjust-A-Brush 10445 49th St N .... Clearwater FL 33762 727-571-1234
Web: www.adjust-a-brush.com

Adleta Co 1645 Diplomat Dr Ste 200 .... Carrollton TX 75006 972-620-5600 620-5666
TF: 800-423-5382 ■ *Web:* www.adleta.com

Aerolite Extrusion Company Inc
4605 Lk Park Rd .... Youngstown OH 44512 330-782-1127
Web: www.aeroext.com

Ag Russell Knives Inc 2900 S 26th St .... Rogers AR 72758 479-631-0130
Web: www.agrussell.com

Allure Home Creation Co Inc 85 Fulton St .... Boonton NJ 07005 973-402-8888 334-2383
Web: www.allurehome.com

American Accessories International Inc
550 W Main St Ste 825 .... Knoxville TN 37902 865-525-9100 525-0889
Web: americanaccessoriesintl.com

Amero Foods Manufacturing Corp
9445 Washington Blvd N .... Laurel MD 20723 301-498-0912
Web: www.pastryonline.com

Apn Healthcare Inc 308 Centennial Blvd .... Edmond OK 73013 405-341-6945
Web: www.apnhealthcare.com

Phone | Fax

Architex International
3333 Commercial Ave .... Northbrook IL 60062 847-205-1333
TF: 800-621-0827 ■ *Web:* www.architex-ljh.com

Artistic Stone Kitchen & Bath Inc
2973 Teagarden St .... San Leandro CA 94577 510-483-1298
Web: www.artisticstoneinc.com

Ashton Company Inc, The 1510 Primewest Pkwy .... Katy TX 77449 281-578-0165
Web: www.ashtoncompany.com

Atlantic Lighting & Supply Company Inc
218 Ottley Dr Ne .... Atlanta GA 30324 404-872-3521
Web: www.atlanticlightingandsupply.com

Atlantic Scale Co Inc 136 Washington Ave .... Nutley NJ 07110 973-661-7090 661-3651
Web: atlanticscale.com

B & F System Inc 3920 S Walton Walker .... Dallas TX 75236 214-333-2111 333-1511
TF: 877-586-2926 ■ *Web:* www.bnfusa.com

Barcalounger Corp
2829 W Andrew Johnson Hwy Ste 210 .... Morristown TN 37814 423-289-1040
Web: www.barcalounger.com

Beetling Design Corp 2131 Hartley Ave .... Coquitlam BC V3K6Z3 604-525-6777
Web: www.beetling.com

Bellino Fine Linens 18 W Forest Ave .... Englewood NJ 07631 201-568-5255
Web: bellinofinelinens.com

Beme International LLC 7333 Ronson Rd .... San Diego CA 92111 858-751-0580
Web: www.beme.net

Bettendorf-Stanford 1370 W Main St .... Salem IL 62881 618-548-3555
TF: 800-548-2253 ■ *Web:* www.bettendorfstanford.com

Bishop Distributing Co 5200 36th St SE .... Grand Rapids MI 49512 800-748-0363 942-6073*
**Fax Area Code:* 616 ■ *TF Cust Svc:* 800-748-0363 ■ *Web:* www.bishopdistributing.com

Bisque Imports 1 Belmont Ave .... Belmont NC 28012 704-829-9290
TF: 888-568-5991 ■ *Web:* www.bisqueimports.com

Blaze Fireplaces of Northern California Inc
101 Cargo Way .... San Francisco CA 94124 415-495-2002
Web: www.blazefireplaces.com

Boston Warehouse Trading Corp 59 Davis Ave .... Norwood MA 02062 781-769-8550 769-9468
TF: 800-811-2672 ■ *Web:* www.bwtc.com

BR Funsten & Co 5200 Watt Ct Ste B .... Fairfield CA 94534 209-825-5375 825-4916
TF: 888-261-2871 ■ *Web:* www.brfunsten.com

C & F Enterprises Inc 819 Bluecrab Rd .... Newport News VA 23606 757-310-6100
TF: 888-889-9868 ■ *Web:* www.cnfei.com

C Bennett Building Supply Inc
1700 W Terra Ln .... O'Fallon MO 63366 636-379-9886
Web: www.cbennett.net

Caber Sure Fit Inc
25A E Pearce St Unit 1 .... Richmond Hill ON L4B2M9 905-886-5849 886-5917
TF: 800-520-3152

CAC China 30 Camptown Rd .... Maplewood NJ 07040 973-371-4300
Web: www.chinacac.com

Cambridge Silversmith Ltd 116 Lehigh Dr .... Fairfield NJ 07004 973-227-4400 227-5600
TF: 800-890-3366 ■ *Web:* www.cambridgesilversmiths.com

Carlton Group Inc 120 Landmark Dr .... Greensboro NC 27409 336-668-7677
TF: 800-722-7824 ■ *Web:* www.carltonscale.com

Carlton Scale 196 Industrial Dr .... Roanoke VA 24019 540-992-6095
Web: carltonscale.com

Carnations Home Fashions Inc 53 Jeanne Dr .... Newburgh NY 12550 212-679-6017
TF: 800-866-8949 ■ *Web:* www.carnationhomefashions.com

Carolina Scales Inc 929 N Lucas St .... West Columbia SC 29169 803-739-4360
Web: www.carolinascales.com

Carpentree Inc 2724 N Sheridan Rd .... Tulsa OK 74115 918-582-3600
Web: carpentree.com

Casual Cushion Corp 1686 Overview Dr .... Rock Hill SC 29730 803-329-2932
Web: www.casualcushion.com

Caye Home Furnishings LLC
1201 W Bankhead St .... New Albany MS 38652 662-534-4762
Web: www.cayefurniture.com

CCA Global Partners 4301 Earth City Expy .... Earth City MO 63045 314-506-0000 626-3444*
**Fax Area Code:* 603 ■ *TF:* 800-466-6984 ■ *Web:* www.ccaglobalpartners.com

CDC Distributors 10511 Medallion Dr .... Cincinnati OH 45241 513-771-3100 771-2920
TF: 800-678-2321 ■ *Web:* cdcdist.com

Champion Safe Co Inc 2055 S Larsen Pkwy .... Provo UT 84606 801-377-7199 377-7195
Web: www.championsafe.com

Christopher Guy
12670 World Plz Ln Bldg 62 Ste 2 .... Fort Myers FL 33907 239-939-9838
Web: www.christopherguy.com

Classic Blind Ltd 2801 Brasher Ln Ste 100 .... Bedford TX 76021 817-540-9300

Clayworks Ltd 629 Bedford Hwy .... Halifax NS B3M2L6 902-445-4453
Web: clayworks.ca

Clipper Mill Inc 404 Talbert St .... Daly City CA 94014 415-330-2400
Web: www.clippermill.com

Company C Inc 102 Old Tpke Rd .... Concord NH 03301 603-226-4460
Web: www.companyc.com

Component Design Northwest Inc
2355 NW Vaughn St .... Portland OR 97210 503-225-0900
Web: www.cdn-timeandtemp.com

Cook's Corner
19152 Santiago Canyon Rd .... Trabuco Canyon CA 92679 949-858-0266
Web: cookscorners.com

Cookshack 2304 N Ash St .... Ponca City OK 74601 580-765-3669
TF: 800-423-0698 ■ *Web:* cookshack.com

Cool Gear International LLC
10 Cordage Park Cir .... Plymouth MA 02360 855-393-2665
TF: 855-393-2665 ■ *Web:* www.coolgearinc.com

Decorative Crafts Inc 50 Chestnut St .... Greenwich CT 06830 203-531-1500 531-1590
TF: 800-431-4455 ■ *Web:* www.decorativecrafts.com

Delande Lighting 22 New Derby St .... Salem MA 01970 978-744-2609
Web: delandelighting.com

Derr Flooring Company Inc
525 Davisville Rd PO Box 912 .... Willow Grove PA 19090 215-657-6300 657-9830
TF: 800-523-3457 ■ *Web:* www.derrflooring.com

Designer Blinds 4500 S 76th Cir .... Omaha NE 68127 402-331-2283

Dial Lighting Gallery
2240 Kaluaopalena St Ste C .... Honolulu HI 96819 808-845-7811

Dimock Gould & Co 190 22nd St .... Moline IL 61265 309-797-0650

Phone | Fax

Dormify Inc 10101 Molecular Dr .... Rockville MD 20850 413-367-6439
Web: www.dormify.com

Down Under Linen & Bedding Ctr
5170 Dixie Rd .... Mississauga ON L4W1E3 905-624-5854
TF: 888-624-6484 ■ *Web:* downunderbedding.com

Down-Lite International Inc 8153 Duke Blvd .... Mason OH 45040 513-229-3696
Web: www.downlite.com

Dumdum Nelida 5925 N Sacramento Ave .... Chicago IL 60659 773-561-6776

EJ Welch Company Inc 13735 Lakefront Dr .... Earth City MO 63045 314-739-2273
Web: www.ejwelch.com

Ekornes Inc 615 Pierce St .... Somerset NJ 08873 732-302-0097
Web: www.ekornes.com

Erickson's Flooring & Supply Company Inc
1013 Orchard St .... Ferndale MI 48220 248-543-9663
Web: www.ericksonsfloors.com

Fabricut Inc 9303 E 46th St .... Tulsa OK 74145 918-622-7700 664-8919
TF: 800-999-8200 ■ *Web:* www.fabricut.com

Farrey's Wholesale Hardware Company Inc
1850 NE 146th St .... North Miami FL 33181 305-947-5451
TF: 888-854-5483 ■ *Web:* www.farreys.com

Finial Company Inc, The
4030 La Reunion Pkwy Ste 100 .... Dallas TX 75212 214-678-0805
Web: www.thefinialcompany.com

Fusion Hardware Group
5730 Oakbrook Pkwy Ste 105 .... Norcross GA 30093 678-990-1676
Web: www.fusionhardware.com

Galleher Corp 9303 Greenleaf Ave .... Santa Fe Springs CA 90670 562-944-8885
Web: www.galleher.com

Gary Draper & Associates of Atlanta Inc
5665 New Northside Dr Nw Ste 100 .... Atlanta GA 30328 404-256-3601
Web: www.draperandassociates.com

GBI Tile & Stone Inc 3120 Airway Ave .... Costa Mesa CA 92626 949-567-1880
Web: www.gbitile.com

General Floor Industries Inc
190 Benigno Blvd .... Bellmawr NJ 08031 856-931-0012
Web: www.generalfloor.com

Georgia Flooring Outlet 1660 Hwy 155 S .... Mcdonough GA 30253 770-474-9270
Web: www.georgiaflooringoutlet.com

Georgian Plantation Shutter Co
455 Wilbanks Dr .... Ball Ground GA 30107 678-454-1100
TF: 888-684-0382 ■ *Web:* www.georgianshutters.com

Gina B & Company Inc
23811 Aliso Creek Rd Ste 130 .... Laguna Niguel CA 92677 949-643-1430
Web: www.ginab.com

Gourmet Settings Inc
245 W Beaver Creek Rd Ste 10 .... Richmond Hill ON L4B1L1 905-707-0336
Web: www.gourmetsettings.com

Halstead International Inc
Halstead Bldg 15 Oakwood Ave Ste 1 .... Norwalk CT 06850 203-299-3100

Heath Ceramics Ltd 400 Gate Five Rd .... Sausalito CA 94965 415-332-3732
Web: www.heathceramics.com

Hendee Enterprises Inc 9350 S Point Dr .... Houston TX 77054 713-796-2322 796-0494
Web: www.hendee.com

Hendrix Batting Co 2310 Surrett Dr .... High Point NC 27263 336-431-1181
Web: hendrixbatting.com

Heritage Lace Inc 309 S St .... Pella IA 50219 641-628-4949
Web: www.heritagelace.com

Home Design Outlet Center 400 County Ave .... Secaucus NJ 07094 800-701-0388
TF: 800-701-0388 ■ *Web:* www.homedesignoutletcenter.com

Home Essentials & Beyond Inc
200 Theodore Conrad Dr .... Jersey City NJ 07305 732-590-3600
TF: 800-417-6218 ■ *Web:* www.homeessentials.com

Horizons Window Fashions Inc
1705 Waukegan Rd .... Waukegan IL 60085 800-858-2352
TF: 800-858-2352 ■ *Web:* horizonshades.com

Hosley International Inc
20530 Stony Island Ave .... Lynwood IL 60411 708-758-1000

Innovative Hearth Products
2701 S Harbor Blvd .... Santa Ana CA 92704 866-328-4537
TF: 866-328-4537 ■ *Web:* www.fmiproducts.com

Jackson George N Ltd 1139 Mcdermot Ave .... Winnipeg MB R3E0V2 204-786-3821
TF: 800-665-8978 ■ *Web:* www.jackson.ca

Jacobs Trading Co 8090 Excelsior Blvd .... hopkins MN 55343 763-843-2000 843-2101
Web: www.jacobstrading.com

James G Hardy & Co 24919 148th Rd .... Jamaica NY 11422 212-689-6680

Jay Franco & Sons Inc 295 Fifth Ave 3rd Fl .... New York NY 10016 212-679-3022 685-4864
Web: www.jfranco.com

JJ Haines & Company Inc
6950 Aviation Blvd .... Glen Burnie MD 21061 800-922-9248 760-4045*
**Fax Area Code:* 410 ■ *TF:* 800-922-9248 ■ *Web:* www.jjhaines.com

John Matouk Company Inc 11 E 26th St .... New York NY 10010 212-683-9242
Web: www.matouk.com

Johnson Window Films Inc 20655 Annalee Ave .... Carson CA 90746 310-631-6672
Web: www.johnsonwindowfilms.com

Kanawha Scales & Systems Inc
Rock Branch Industrial Pk 303 Jacobson Dr .... Poca WV 25159 304-755-8321
TF: 800-955-8321 ■ *Web:* www.kanawhascales.com

Kashmir Fabrics + Furnishings
3191 Commonwealth Dr .... Dallas TX 75247 214-631-8040
Web: www.kasmirfabrics.com

Keeco LLC 30736 Wiegman Rd .... Hayward CA 94544 510-324-8800
Web: keecohome.com

Kiefer Specialty Flooring Inc
2910 Falling Waters Blvd .... Lindenhurst IL 60046 847-245-8450
TF: 800-322-5448 ■ *Web:* kieferusa.com

Kitchen Art The Store for Cook
1550 Win Hentschel Blvd .... West Lafayette IN 47906 765-497-3878
Web: k-art.com

Klaff's Inc 28 Washington St .... South Norwalk CT 06854 203-866-1603
Web: www.klaffs.com

KovalWilliamson 11208 47th Ave W .... Mukilteo WA 98275 425-347-4249
Web: www.kwawest.com

Kozy Heat Fireplace 204 Industrial Park Rd .... Lakefield MN 56150 507-662-6641

				Phone	Fax
Kraus USA Inc 160 Amsler Ave *Web:* www.krausflooring.com	Shippenville	PA	16254	814-226-9300	
L Bornstein & Co Inc 321 Washington St. *TF:* 800-842-1111	Somerville	MA	02143	617-776-3555	
Lacera Rajco International 375 County Ave Ste 653	Secaucus	NJ	07094	201-583-0303	
Lambs & Ivy Inc 2040-2042 E Maple Ave *Web:* lambsivy.com	El Segundo	CA	90245	310-322-3800	
Lanz Cabinet Shop Inc 3025 W Seventh Pl *TF:* 800-788-6332 ■ *Web:* www.lanzcabinets.com	Eugene	OR	97402	541-485-4050	
Legendary Whitetails 820 Enterprise Dr *TF:* 800-875-9453 ■ *Web:* www.deergear.com	Slinger	WI	53086	800-875-9453	
Legends of England 3520 Roberts Cut Off Rd *TF:* 800-578-1065 ■ *Web:* www.alchemyofengland.com	Fort Worth	TX	76114	817-236-3141	
Leisure World Pool & Hearth Inc 406 E 16th Ave *Web:* www.leisureworldkc.com	Kansas City	MO	64116	816-221-1731	
Les Meubles Saint Damase Inc 246 rue Principale St-Damase Comt. *Web:* www.st-damase.com	St-damase	QC	J0H1J0	450-797-3702	
Lighting Unlimited LLC 4211 Richmond Ave *Web:* www.lulighting.com	Houston	TX	77027	713-626-4025	
Lillian August Designs Inc 32 Knight St. *Web:* www.lillianaugust.com	Norwalk	CT	06851	203-847-3314	
Longust Distributing Inc 2432 W Birchwood Ave **Fax Area Code:* 800 ■ *TF:* 800-352-0521 ■ *Web:* www.longust.com	Mesa	AZ	85202	480-820-6244	352-0526*
Lonseal Inc 928 E 238th St *TF:* 800-832-7111 ■ *Web:* www.lonseal.com	Carson	CA	90745	310-830-7111	830-9986
Luigi Bormioli 5 Walnut Grove Dr Ste 140 *Web:* www.luigibormioli.com	Horsham	PA	19044	215-672-7111	
Lumisolution Inc 162 Av Du Sacre-Coeur *Web:* lumisolution.com	Quebec	QC	G1N2W2	418-522-5693	
M Block & Sons Inc 5020 W 73rd St *TF:* 800-621-8845 ■ *Web:* www.mblock.com	Bedford Park	IL	60638	708-728-8400	728-0022
M Tm Molded Products 3370 Obco Ct *Web:* www.mtmcase-gard.com	Dayton	OH	45414	937-890-7461	
Macy's Home Store 7 W Seventh St. *Web:* www.macysinc.com	Cincinnati	OH	45202	212-695-4400	
Manduka LLC 345 S Douglas St *Web:* www.manduka.com	El Segundo	CA	90245	310-426-1495	
Mason Mfg LLC 1645 N Railroad Ave *Web:* www.masonmfg.com	Decatur	IL	62524	217-422-2770	
Maxtex Inc 3620 Francis Cir *TF:* 800-241-1836 ■ *Web:* www.maxtexinc.com	Alpharetta	GA	30004	770-772-6757	
Maytex Mills Inc 261 Fifth Ave 17th Fl. *Web:* www.maytex.com	New York	NY	10016	212-684-1191	
MDS N30 W22377 Green Rd Ste C *TF:* 888-523-2611 ■ *Web:* www.midwestdesignersupply.com	Waukesha	WI	53186	888-523-2611	
Modus Furniture International 5410 McConnell Ave *Web:* www.modusfurniture.com	Los Angeles	CA	90066	310-827-2129	
More Space Place Inc 5040 140th Ave N *TF:* 888-731-3051 ■ *Web:* www.morespaceplace.com	Clearwater	FL	33760	888-731-3051	
Morrison Terrebonne Lumber Center LLC 605 Barataria Ave *Web:* www.lumbercenter.com	Houma	LA	70360	985-879-1597	
National Credit Adjusters LLC 327 W Fourth Ave *Web:* internationalhomescookware.com	Hutchinson	KS	67501	620-665-7708	
National Glass Ltd 5744 198th St. *TF:* 800-663-8168 ■ *Web:* www.natglass.com	Langley	BC	V3A7J2	604-530-2311	
Naturwood Home Furnishings Inc 2711 Mercantile Dr. *Web:* www.naturwood.com	Rancho Cordova	CA	95742	916-638-2424	
New Buffalo Corp 1220 N Price Rd. *Web:* www.buffalotools.com	St Louis	MO	63132	636-532-9888	
Northern States Metals Co 3207 Innovation Pl *Web:* extrusions.com	Youngstown	OH	44509	330-799-1855	
O Dell Corp 13833 Indian Mound Rd *Web:* www.odellcorp.com	Ware Shoals	SC	29692	864-861-2222	
Ohio Valley Flooring Inc 5555 Murray Ave *Web:* www.ovf.com	Cincinnati	OH	45227	513-561-3399	
Omega Moulding Company Ltd 1 Saw Grass Dr *TF:* 800-289-6634 ■ *Web:* www.omegamoulding.com	Bellport	NY	11713	800-289-6634	
OneCoast Network LLC 230 Spring St Ste 1800 *TF:* 866-592-5514 ■ *Web:* www.onecoast.com	Atlanta	GA	30303	866-592-5514	469-9517
Peking Handicraft Inc 1388 San Mateo Ave. *Web:* www.pkhc.com	South San Francisco	CA	94080	650-871-3788	871-3781
Phoenix AMD International Inc 41 Butler Ct *Web:* www.phoenixamd.com	Bowmanville	ON	L1C4P8	905-427-7440	
Pinnacle Frames & Accents Inc 12303 Technology Boulevard Ste 950 *Web:* nielsenbainbridgegroup.com/pinnacle/home	Austin	TX	78727	512-506-8844	506-3933
Pompanoosuc Mills Corp Route 5 PO Box 238 *TF:* 800-757-4061 ■ *Web:* www.pompy.com	East Thetford	VT	05043	800-757-4061	
Primelite Manufacturing Corp 407 S Main St. *Web:* primelite-mfg.com	Freeport	NY	11520	516-868-4411	
PRO-MART Industries Inc 17421 Von Karman Ave *Web:* www.deltanovaltd.com	Irvine	CA	92614	949-428-7700	
Quiltcraft Industries Inc 1230 E Ledbetter Dr. *Web:* quiltcraft.com	Dallas	TX	75216	214-376-1841	376-1852
Regent Products Corp 8999 Palmer St *TF:* 800-583-1002 ■ *Web:* www.regentproducts.com	River Grove	IL	60171	708-583-1000	
Revere Mills Inc 2860 S River Rd Ste 250 *Web:* www.reveremills.com	Des Plaines	IL	60018	847-759-6800	
Revman International Inc 350 Fifth Ave 70th Fl *Web:* www.revman.com	New York	NY	10118	212-278-0300	
RF Supply Inc 3102 63rd Ave E *Web:* www.rfsupply.com	Bradenton	FL	34203	941-755-3622	
Robert Gordon Industries Ltd 1500 Plz Ave. *Web:* www.gordonsinclair.com	New Hyde Park	NY	11040	516-354-8888	
Roberts Container Corp, The 9131 Oakdale Ave Ste 110 *Web:* www.robertscontainer.com	Chatsworth	CA	91311	818-727-1700	
Santec Inc 3501 Challenger St. *TF:* 800-284-4050 ■ *Web:* www.santecfaucet.com	Torrance	CA	90503	310-542-0063	
Scalehouse, The 974 Rd E	Schuyler	NE	68661	402-352-3686	
Scene Weaver 649 Rosewood Dr Ste B *Web:* www.sceneweaver.com	Columbia	SC	29201	803-252-0662	
Selective Enterprises Inc 10701 Texland Blvd *TF:* 800-334-1207 ■ *Web:* www.unitedsupplyco.com	Charlotte	NC	28273	704-588-3310	
Sewing Source Inc, The PO Box 639 *TF:* 800-849-6945 ■ *Web:* www.thesewingsourceinc.com	Spring Hope	NC	27882	252-478-3900	
Shaheen Carpet Mills Inc 3742 US Hwy 41 NW PO Box 167 *Web:* temp.shaheencarpet.com	Resaca	GA	30735	706-629-9544	625-5341
Shavel Assoc 13 Roszel Rd *Web:* www.shavel.com	Princeton	NJ	08540	609-452-1800	
Shelving Inc 32 S Squirrel Rd *TF:* 800-637-9508 ■ *Web:* www.shelving.com	Auburn Hills	MI	48326	248-852-8600	
Sobel Westex Inc 2670 Western Ave **Fax Area Code:* 702 ■ *TF:* 888-887-6235 ■ *Web:* www.sobelwestex.com	Las Vegas	NV	89109	888-887-6235	735-4957*
SOG Specialty Knives & Tools LLC 6521 212th St SW *TF:* 888-405-6433 ■ *Web:* www.sogknives.com	Lynnwood	WA	98036	425-771-6230	
Southern Moulding & Supply Co 7040 Battle Dr Nw. *Web:* www.southernmoulding.com	Kennesaw	GA	30152	770-422-3949	
Southern Tile Distributors Inc 4590 Village Ave. *TF:* 800-333-8970 ■ *Web:* www.southerntile.com	Norfolk	VA	23502	757-855-8041	
Springs Window Fashions LP 7549 Graber Rd. *TF:* 877-792-0002 ■ *Web:* www.springswindowfashions.com	Middleton	WI	53562	608-836-1011	
Star Extruded Shapes Inc 7055 Herbert Rd. *Web:* www.starext.com	Canfield	OH	44406	330-533-9863	
Star Tech Glass Inc 1835 N Major Ave *Web:* startechglass.com	Chicago	IL	60639	773-745-0800	
Stephen Miller Gallery 800 Santa Cruz Ave *TF:* 888-566-8833 ■ *Web:* www.stephenmillergallery.com	Menlo Park	CA	94025	650-327-5040	
Sterling Cut Glass Company Inc 5020 Olympic Blvd. *TF:* 800-543-1317 ■ *Web:* www.sterlingcutglass.com	Erlanger	KY	41018	859-283-2333	
Sunshine Drapery & Interior Fashions LLC WorkRm 11800 Adie Rd *Web:* www.sunshinedrapery.com	Maryland Heights	MO	63043	314-569-2980	
Susquehanna Glass 731 Ave H. *Web:* www.susquehannaglass.com	Columbia	PA	17512	717-684-2155	
SZCO Supplies Inc 2713 Merchant Dr. *Web:* szco.com	Baltimore	MD	21230	410-368-8300	
T & A Supply Company Inc 6821 S 216th St Bldg A PO Box 927 **Fax Area Code:* 206 ■ *TF:* 800-562-2857 ■ *Web:* www.tasupply.com	Kent	WA	98032	253-872-3682	282-3796*
T & L Distributing LP 7350 Langfield Rd *Web:* www.tldistributing.com	Houston	TX	77092	713-461-7802	932-6790
Tailored Living LLC 1927 N Glassell St *TF:* 866-675-8819 ■ *Web:* www.tailoredliving.com	Orange	CA	92865	866-675-8819	
TeleBrands Corp 79 Two Bridges Rd *Web:* www.telebrands.com	Fairfield	NJ	07004	973-244-0300	
Thomas West Inc 470 Mercury Dr *Web:* www.thomaswest.com	Sunnyvale	CA	94085	408-481-9200	
Thompson Olde Inc 3250 Camino Del Sol *TF:* 800-827-1565 ■ *Web:* www.oldethompson.com	Oxnard	CA	93030	805-983-0388	983-1849
Three Hands Corp 13259 Ralston Ave *TF:* 800-443-5443 ■ *Web:* www.threehands.com	Sylmar	CA	91342	818-833-1200	833-1212
Turf Store.com 237 Boling Industrial Way Se *Web:* www.turfstore.com	Calhoun	GA	30701	706-629-1675	
Twin-Star International Inc 1690 S Congress Ave Ste 210 *Web:* www.twinstarhome.com	Delray Beach	FL	33445	561-330-3201	
Vertex China 131 Brea Canyon Rd. *Web:* www.vertexchina.com	Walnut	CA	91789	909-622-3333	
Virginia Tile Co 28320 Plymouth Rd. *TF:* 877-356-7461 ■ *Web:* www.virginiatile.com	Livonia	MI	48150	734-762-2400	
Wanke Cascade Co 6330 N Cutter Cir *TF:* 800-365-5053 ■ *Web:* www.wanke.com	Portland	OR	97217	503-289-8609	285-5640
Weightech 1649 Country Elite Dr. *TF:* 800-457-3720 ■ *Web:* www.weightechinc.com	Waldron	AR	72958	479-637-4182	
WMF Americas Inc 3512 Faith Church Rd *TF:* 800-966-3009 ■ *Web:* wmfamericas.com/shop	Indian Trail	NC	28079	704-882-3898	893-2198
WoodCrafters Home Products LLC 3700 Camino de Verdad *Web:* www.woodcrafters-tx.com	Weslaco	TX	78596	956-647-8300	
WOWindows LLC PO Box 581 *Web:* www.wowindows.com	Cranford	NJ	07016	908-272-1011	
Yves Delorme Inc 1725 Broadway St *Web:* www.yvesdelorme.com	Charlottesville	VA	22902	434-979-3911	
Zodax Inc 14040 Arminta St. *Web:* www.zodax.com	Panorama City	CA	91402	818-785-5626	

362 HOME FURNISHINGS STORES

See Also Department Stores p. 2191; Furniture Stores p. 2344

				Phone	Fax
A B C Awning & Venetian Blind Corp 858 Saint Andrews Blvd *Web:* www.abcfence.net	Charleston	SC	29407	843-766-6311	

Company	City	State	ZIP	Phone	Fax
AAA Glass & Mirror Co 3300 McCart. *Web:* www.aaa-glass.com	Fort Worth	TX	76110	817-924-4444	
ABL Lights Inc 660 Golf Club Blvd *Web:* abllights.com	Mosinee	WI	54455	715-693-1530	
Able Electric Service 2626 Electronic Ln *Web:* www.ableelectricservice.com	Dallas	TX	75220	214-350-5721	
AC Products Co 4299 S Apple Creek Rd *Web:* www.acproducts.com	Apple Creek	OH	44606	330-698-1105	
Adco Container Co 9959 Canoga Ave *Web:* www.adcocontainer.com	Chatsworth	CA	91311	818-998-2565	
Alconex Specialty Products Inc 4204 W Ferguson Rd *Web:* www.alconex.com	Fort Wayne	IN	46809	260-744-3446	
Allen & Allen Company Inc 202 Culebra Ave *Web:* www.lumberhardware.com	San Antonio	TX	78201	210-733-9191	
Alliance Scale Inc 1020 Turnpike St *Web:* www.alliancescale.com	Canton	MA	02021	781-828-8507	
Altmeyer Home Stores Inc 6515 Rt 22 *TF:* 800-394-6628 ■ *Web:* www.bedbathhome.com	Delmont	PA	15626	724-468-3434	468-3233
Amcon Block & Precast Inc 2211 Hwy 10 S *TF:* 888-251-6030 ■ *Web:* www.amconblock.com	Saint Cloud	MN	56304	320-251-6030	
American Made Cutlery 905 Industrial Rd *Web:* americanmadecutlery.com	Waverly	IA	50677	319-352-2080	
American Scale Service & Supply Co 8590 W 14th Ave *Web:* www.ameriscale.com	Lakewood	CO	80215	303-232-5656	
Ann Clark Ltd 453 Quality Ln. *Web:* www.annclarkcookiecutters.com	Rutland	VT	05701	802-773-7886	
Anna's Linens Inc 3550 Hyland Ave *TF:* 866-266-2728	Costa Mesa	CA	92626	714-850-0504	
Art Material Services Inc 625 Joyce Kilmer Ave *TF:* 888-522-5526 ■ *Web:* www.artmaterialsservice.com	New Brunswick	NJ	08901	732-545-8888	
Associated Energy Systems 8621 S 180th St *Web:* www.aes4home.com	Kent	WA	98032	425-251-9190	
Bath & Beyond, The 77 Connecticut St *Web:* www.bathandbeyond.com	San Francisco	CA	94107	415-552-5001	
Bauerware LLC 3886 17th St. *TF:* 877-864-5662 ■ *Web:* bauerware.com	San Francisco	CA	94114	415-864-3886	
Beacon Products LLC 2041 58th Ave Cir E *TF:* 800-345-4928 ■ *Web:* www.beaconproducts.com	Bradenton	FL	34203	800-345-4928	
Bed Bath & Beyond Inc 650 Liberty Ave *NASDAQ: BBBY* ■ *TF:* 800-462-3966 ■ *Web:* www.bedbathandbeyond.com	Union	NJ	07083	908-688-0888	
Belden Brick & Supply Company Inc 620 Leonard St Nw *Web:* www.beldenbrickandsupply.com	Grand Rapids	MI	49504	616-459-8367	
Bergin Glass Impressions Inc 2511 Napa Vly Corporate Dr Ste 111 *Web:* www.berginglass.com	Napa	CA	94558	707-224-0111	
Besco Electric Supply Co 711 S 14th St. **Fax Area Code:* 352 ■ *TF:* 800-541-6618 ■ *Web:* www.bescoelectric.com	Leesburg	FL	34748	800-541-6618	365-0554*
Bilotta Home Center Inc 564 Mamaroneck Ave *Web:* bilotta.com	Mamaroneck	NY	10543	914-381-7734	
Bishop Hearth & Home Inc 1948 Vanderhorn Dr *Web:* www.bishophome.com	Memphis	TN	38134	901-384-0070	
Bitterman Scales LLC 413 Radcliff Rd *TF:* 877-464-3009 ■ *Web:* www.bittermanscales.com	Willow Street	PA	17584	717-464-3009	
Blade HQ 400 South 1000 East Ste E *Web:* www.bladehq.com	Lehi	UT	84043	801-768-0232	
Blanco America Inc 110 Mount Holly By-Pass *TF:* 800-451-5782 ■ *Web:* www.blanco-germany.com/en_us/en_us/home.html	Lumberton	NJ	08048	800-451-5782	
Bridge Kitchenware Inc B 198 Mt Pleasant Ave *Web:* www.bridgekitchenware.com	East Hanover	NJ	07936	212-688-4220	
Bristol Aluminum 5514 Bristol Emilie Rd *TF:* 800-338-5532 ■ *Web:* www.bristolaluminum.com	Levittown	PA	19057	215-946-3160	
Burlington Coat Factory 1830 Rt 130 N *TF:* 855-355-2875 ■ *Web:* burlingtoncoatfactory.com	Burlington	NJ	08016	609-387-7800	
Byers Choice Ltd 4355 County Line Rd *Web:* www.byerschoice.com	Chalfont	PA	18914	215-822-6700	
Cabinet Outlet Inc 1168 N 50th Pl *Web:* milwaukeecabinetry.com	Milwaukee	WI	53208	414-771-1960	771-3638
Cadco Ltd 145 Colebrook River Rd. *Web:* www.cadco-ltd.com	Winsted	CT	06098	860-738-2500	
Calvert Retail LP 100 W Rockland Rd Ste A PO Box 302 *Web:* www.calvertretail.com	Montchanin	DE	19710	302-622-8811	622-8602
Candela Controls Inc 751 Business Park Blvd Ste 101 *Web:* www.candelacontrols.com	Winter Garden	FL	34787	407-654-2420	
Cape & Island Kitchens Inc 99 State Rd Rte 3A *Web:* capekitchens.com	Sagamore Beach	MA	02562	508-888-4762	
Cardinal Scale Manufacturing Company Inc 203 E Daugherty St PO Box 151 *Web:* www.cardinalscale.com	Webb City	MO	64870	417-673-4631	
Carolina Brush Manufacturing Company Inc 3093 Northwest Blvd *Web:* www.carolinabrush.com	Gastonia	NC	28052	704-867-0286	
Carolina Supplyhouse Inc 218 Second Loop Rd. *Web:* www.thesupplyhouse.com	Florence	SC	29504	843-662-0702	
Central Boiler Inc 20502 160th St *Web:* www.centralboiler.com	Greenbush	MN	56726	218-782-2575	
Challenger Lighting Company Inc 2475 Alft Ln *Web:* challengerlighting.com	Elgin	IL	60124	847-717-4700	
CHF Home Furnishings 104 S Orchard St *Web:* www.shopchf.com	Boise	ID	83705	208-343-7769	
Chintz & Co 1720 Store St *Web:* www.chintz.com	Victoria	BC	V8W1V5	250-381-2404	
Clarion Bathware Inc 44 Amsler Ave. *Web:* www.clarionbathware.com	Shippenville	PA	16254	814-226-5374	
Classic Containers Inc 1700 S Hellman Ave *Web:* www.classiccontainers.com	Ontario	CA	91761	909-930-3610	
Clearlight Glass & Mirror Inc 1318 Shields Rd *Web:* www.clearlightglass.com	Kernersville	NC	27284	336-993-7300	
CMC America Corp 210 S Center St *Web:* cmc-america.com	Joliet	IL	60436	815-726-4336	
COAST Products Inc 8033 NE Holman St. *Web:* www.coastportland.com	Portland	OR	97218	503-234-4545	
Container Store, The 500 Freeport Pkwy. *TF:* 800-733-3532 ■ *Web:* www.containerstore.com	Coppell	TX	75019	972-538-6000	
Conway Glass Tinting Plus 701 Sixth St. *Web:* conwayglasstinting.net	Conway	AR	72032	501-450-7587	
Cost Plus Inc 200 Fourth St. *NASDAQ: CPWM* ■ *TF:* 877-967-5362 ■ *Web:* www.worldmarket.com	Oakland	CA	94607	510-893-7300	893-3681
Crystal Blanc 225 Gap Way. *Web:* www.jcharles.com	Erlanger	KY	41018	859-283-0039	
Cs Illumination Inc 1210 Kestone Way Ste A&B *Web:* csillumination.com	Vista	CA	92081	760-477-1244	
Cutlery & More LLC 135 Prairie Lk Rd *TF:* 800-650-9866 ■ *Web:* www.cutleryandmore.com	East Dundee	IL	60118	800-650-9866	
Dacra Glass 3333 N Commerce Dr *Web:* www.dacraglass.com	Muncie	IN	47303	765-286-3855	
Dale Tiffany Inc 14765 Firestone Blvd *Web:* www.daletiffany.com	La Mirada	CA	90638	714-739-2700	
Dcxcavation Inc 10641 Prospect Ave *Web:* dcxcavation.com	Santee	CA	92071	619-312-1550	
DD Traders Inc Dba Demdaco 5000 W 134th St.	Leawood	KS	66209	913-402-6800	
Delfin Design & Manufacturing Inc 23301 Antonio Pkwy. **Fax Area Code:* 800 ■ *Web:* www.delfinfs.com	Rancho Santa Margarita	CA	92688	949-888-4644	354-7919*
Design Specialties Inc 11100 W Heather Ave *Web:* www.glassfireplacedoors.com	Milwaukee	WI	53224	414-371-1200	
Design Within Reach Inc 711 Canal St 3rd fl 3rd Fl *OTC: DWRI* ■ *TF:* 800-944-2233 ■ *Web:* www.dwr.com	Stamford	CT	06902	203-614-0600	614-0845
DirectBuy Inc 8450 Broadway *TF:* 800-320-3462 ■ *Web:* www.directbuy.com	Merrillville	IN	46410	219-736-1100	755-6279
Eagle Microsystems Inc 366 Cir of Progress Dr *Web:* www.eaglemicrosystems.com	Pottstown	PA	19464	610-323-2250	
Edward Joy Electric 905 Canal St *Web:* www.edwardjoyelectric.com	Syracuse	NY	13210	315-474-3361	479-8604
Elite Lighting Company Inc 412 S Cypress St *Web:* www.elitelighting.com	Mullins	SC	29574	843-464-7681	
Eurokera North America Inc 140 Southchase Blvd *Web:* www.eurokera.com	Fountain Inn	SC	29644	864-963-8082	
Euromarket Designs Inc 1250 Techny Rd **Fax Area Code:* 630 ■ *Web:* www.crateandbarrel.com	Northbrook	IL	60062	847-272-2888	527-1448*
F M Brush Manufacturing Co 7002 72nd Pl *Web:* www.fmbrush.com	Glendale	NY	11385	718-821-5939	
Fashion Glass & Mirrors 585 S Interstate 35 E *Web:* www.fashionglass.com	Desoto	TX	75115	972-223-8936	
Fireplace & Bar-B-Q Center Inc 10470 Metcalf Ave *Web:* fireplacecenterkc.com	Overland Park	KS	66212	913-383-2286	
Fleetwood Aluminum Products Inc 395 Smitty Way *Web:* www.fleetwoodusa.com	Corona	CA	92879	951-279-1070	
Force Flow Inc 2430 Stanwell Dr *TF:* 800-893-6723 ■ *Web:* www.forceflow.com	Concord	CA	94520	800-893-6723	
Foreston Trends Inc 1483 W Via Plata St *Web:* www.forestontrends.com	Long Beach	CA	90810	310-952-8500	
Framed on Madison Inc 976 Lexington Ave Frnt 2 *Web:* framedonmadison.com	New York	NY	10021	212-734-4680	
Gas Turbine Controls Corp 466 Saw Mill River Rd *Web:* www.gasturbinecontrols.com	Ardsley	NY	10502	914-693-0830	
GEARYS Beverly Hills 351 N Beverly Dr. *TF:* 800-793-6670 ■ *Web:* www.gearys.com	Beverly Hills	CA	90210	310-273-4741	
Ginkgo International 8102 Lemont Rd Ste 1100 *Web:* www.ginkgoint.com	Woodridge	IL	60517	630-910-5244	
Glassybaby LLC 3406 E Union St *Web:* www.glassybaby.com	Seattle	WA	98122	206-518-9071	
Gracious Home 1220 Third Ave. *TF:* 800-338-7809 ■ *Web:* www.gracioushome.com	New York	NY	10021	212-517-6300	
Grand Rapids Scale Company Inc 4215 Stafford Ave Sw *TF:* 800-348-5701 ■ *Web:* www.grmetrology.com	Grand Rapids	MI	49548	616-538-7080	
Grand View Glass & Metal Inc 2134 S Green Privado. *Web:* www.grandviewglass.com	Ontario	CA	91761	909-923-9544	
Granite City Electric Supply Co 19 Quincy Ave. *TF:* 800-850-9400 ■ *Web:* www.granitecityelectric.com	Quincy	MA	02169	617-472-6500	472-8661
Gump's 135 Post St. *TF:* 800-766-7628 ■ *Web:* www.gumps.com	San Francisco	CA	94108	415-982-1616	984-9374
Habitat Housewares 3801 Old Seward Hwy Ste 7 *TF:* 800-770-1856 ■ *Web:* www.habitathousewares.com	Anchorage	AK	99503	907-561-1856	563-5863
Halverson Co 235 Paxton Ave *Web:* www.halversoncompany.com	Salt Lake City	UT	84101	801-467-9423	
Hammacher Schlemmer & Co 9307 N Milwaukee Ave. **Fax Area Code:* 847 ■ *TF:* 800-321-1484 ■ *Web:* www.hammacher.com	Niles	IL	60714	800-321-1484	581-8616*
Home Accents Mart 5521 McFarland Blvd	Northport	AL	35476	205-339-6550	
HomeGoods Inc 770 Cochituate Rd. *Web:* www.homegoods.com	Framingham	MA	01701	508-390-1000	
HomePortfolio Inc 288 Walnut St Ste 300 *Web:* www.homeportfolio.com	Newton	MA	02460	617-965-0565	965-4082

Phone Fax

Hussong Manufacturing Company Inc
204 Industrial Park Rd .... Lakefield MN 56150 507-662-6641
TF: 800-253-4904 ■ *Web:* www.kozyheat.com

Hy Cite Corp 333 Holtzman Rd .... Madison WI 53713 608-273-3373
Web: www.hycite.com

Interface Logic Systems Inc
3311 E Livingston Ave .... Columbus OH 43227 614-236-8388
Web: www.interfacelogic.com

Iron-a-way Inc 220 W Jackson St .... Morton IL 61550 309-266-7232
Web: www.ironaway.com

J & D Interiors Inc 8300 Briarwood St Ste A .... Anchorage AK 99518 907-349-9685
Web: jdinteriors.com

Jackalope Pottery 2820 Cerrillos Rd .... Santa Fe NM 87507 505-471-8539
Web: www.jackalope.com

Jetta Corp 425 Centennial Blvd .... Edmond OK 73013 405-340-6661
Web: www.jettacorp.com

Kino Flo Inc 2840 N Hollywood Way .... Burbank CA 91505 818-767-6528
Web: www.kinoflo.com

Kirkland's Inc 5310 Maryland Way .... Brentwood TN 37027 877-541-4855
NASDAQ: KIRK ■ *TF:* 877-541-4855 ■ *Web:* www.kirklands.com

Kitchen & Bath Design Studio
914 S Kerr Ave .... Wilmington NC 28403 910-332-4656
Web: www.kandbgalleries.com

Kitchen & Bath Studios Inc
7001 Wisconsin Ave .... Chevy Chase MD 20815 301-657-1636
Web: kitchenbathstudios.com

Kitchen 24 1608 N Cahuenga Blvd .... Los Angeles CA 90028 323-465-2424
Web: www.kitchen24.info

Kitchen Collection Inc 71 E Water St .... Chillicothe OH 45601 740-773-9150 774-0590
TF General: 888-548-2651 ■ *Web:* www.kitchencollection.com

Kitchen Craft International
4129 United Ave .... Mount Dora FL 32757 352-483-7600
Web: www.cookforlife.com

Kitchen Fantasy 27576 Ynez Rd Ste H9 .... Temecula CA 92591 951-693-4264 693-4265
Web: www.kitchenfantasy.com

Kitchen Supply Co 7540 W Roosevelt Rd .... Forest Park IL 60130 708-383-5990
Web: www.kitchensupply.com

Kiva Kitchen & Bath Holdings LLC
6225 Burnet Rd .... Austin TX 78757 512-454-4526
Web: www.kivahome.com

Kuhn Rikon Corp 46 Digital Dr Ste 5 .... Novato CA 94949 415-883-1101
Web: ch.kuhnrikon.com

Kwik-Covers LLC 811 Ridge Rd .... Webster NY 14580 585-787-9620
TF: 866-586-9620 ■ *Web:* kwikcovers.com

Lamps Plus Inc 20250 Plummer St .... Chatsworth CA 91311 818-886-5267
Web: lampsplus.com

LB Sales Assoc LLC 50 Plant St .... New London CT 06320 860-437-3953

LEDdynamics Inc 44 Hull St .... Randolph VT 05060 802-728-4533
Web: www.leddynamics.com

Leed - Himmel Industries Inc
75 Leeder Hill Dr .... Hamden CT 06517 203-287-6662
Web: www.leed-himmel.com

Lematic Inc 2410 W Main St .... Jackson MI 49203 517-787-3301
Web: www.lematic.com

Light Lines Inc 3337 Rauch St .... Houston TX 77029 713-673-7502
Web: lightlines.net

Lighting By Gregory LLC 158 Bowery .... New York NY 10012 212-226-4156
Web: www.lightingbygregory.com

Lighting Zone Inc 17354 Hawthorne Blvd .... Torrance CA 90504 310-921-9495
Web: www.dreamonlighting.com

Lindamar Industries Inc
1603 Commerce Way .... Paso Robles CA 93446 805-237-1910
TF: 800-235-1811 ■ *Web:* www.lindamarindustries.com

Linon Home Dcor Products Inc 22 Jericho Tpke .... Mineola NY 11501 516-699-1000 699-1001
Web: www.linon.com

Litelab Corp 251 Elm St .... Buffalo NY 14203 716-856-4491
TF: 800-238-4120 ■ *Web:* www.litelab.com

Los Angeles Lighting Manufacturing Company Inc
10141 Olney St .... El Monte CA 91731 626-454-8300
Web: www.lalighting.com

Luxury Bath Liners Inc
1958 Brandon Ct .... Glendale Heights IL 60139 630-295-9084
Web: www.luxurybath.com

Lynx Grills Inc 5895 Rickenbacker Rd .... Commerce CA 90040 323-838-1770
TF: 888-289-5969 ■ *Web:* www.lynxgrills.com

Mason Structural Steel Inc
7500 Northfield Rd .... Walton Hills OH 44146 440-439-1040
TF: 800-686-1223 ■ *Web:* www.masonsteel.com

Mattress Firm Inc 5815 Gulf Fwy .... Houston TX 77023 713-923-1090
TF: 800-821-6621 ■ *Web:* www.mattressfirm.com

Measurement Systems International Inc
14240 Interurban Ave S Ste 200 .... Seattle WA 98168 206-433-0199
Web: www.msiscales.com

Michael C Fina Inc 545 Fifth Ave .... New York NY 10022 212-557-2500
TF: 800-289-3462 ■ *Web:* www.michaelcfina.com

Moline Machinery LLC 114 S Central Ave .... Duluth MN 55807 218-624-5734
Web: www.moline.com

Moxie Pictures 18 E 16th St Fl 4 .... New York NY 10003 212-807-6901
Web: www.moxiepictures.com

Nautical Furnishings Inc
60 NW 60th St .... Fort Lauderdale FL 33309 954-771-1100
Web: www.nauticalfurnishings.com

Nevada Contract Carpet 6840 W Patrick Ln .... Las Vegas NV 89118 702-362-3033 362-5455
Web: nevadacontractcarpet.abbeycarpet.com

New Brunswick International Inc
76 Veronica Ave .... Somerset NJ 08873 732-828-3633
Web: www.nbidigi.net

Notoco Industries LLC 10380 Airline Hwy .... Baton Rouge LA 70816 225-292-1303
Web: www.notocoind.com

Nova Lighting Inc 6323 Maywood Ave .... Huntington Park CA 90255 323-277-6266
Web: www.novalamps.com

OCS Checkweighers Inc 2350 Hewatt Rd .... Snellville GA 30039 678-344-8030
Web: www.ocs-cw.com

Ortega Kitchen and Bath 2834 Clovis Rd .... Lubbock TX 79415 806-763-5777
Web: www.ortegakitchenandbath.com

Panaram International 126 Greylock Ave .... Belleville NJ 07109 973-751-1100
Web: www.usatowl.com

Perdue Inc 5 W Forsyth St # 100 .... Jacksonville FL 32202 904-737-5858
Web: www.perdueoffice.com

Pier 1 Imports Inc 100 Pier 1 Pl .... Fort Worth TX 76102 817-252-8000 252-8174
NYSE: PIR ■ *TF:* 800-245-4595 ■ *Web:* www.pier1.com

Point Lighting Corp 61 W Dudley Town Rd .... Bloomfield CT 06002 860-243-0600
Web: www.pointlighting.com

Precision Solutions Inc 2525 Tollgate Rd .... Quakertown PA 18951 215-536-4400
Web: www.precisionsolutionsinc.com

Redi Floors Inc 1791 Williams Dr .... Marietta GA 30066 770-590-7334
Web: www.redi-floors.com

Restoration Hardware Inc
2900 N MacArthur Dr Ste 100 .... Tracy CA 95376 800-910-9836
TF: 800-910-9836 ■ *Web:* www.restorationhardware.com

Royal Oak Kitchens & Baths
32790 Woodward Ave .... Royal Oak MI 48073 248-549-2944
Web: www.royaloakkitchen.com

SCHOTT North America Inc 615 Hwy 68 .... Sweetwater TN 37874 423-337-3522
Web: www.us.schott.com/flatglass/english

Seattle Lighting Fixture Co
222 Second Ave Ext S .... Seattle WA 98104 206-622-4736 221-1962*
**Fax Area Code:* 503 ■ *TF Cust Svc:* 800-689-1000 ■ *Web:* www.seattlelighting.com

Sentran LLC 4355 E Lowell St Ste F .... Ontario CA 91761 909-605-1544
TF: 888-545-8988 ■ *Web:* www.sentranllc.com

Shiffler Equipment Sales Inc 745 S St .... Chardon OH 44024 440-285-9175
Web: www.chairglides.com

Smoky Mountain Knife Works Inc
2320 Winfield Dunn Pkwy PO Box 4430 .... Sevierville TN 37864 865-453-5871
Web: www.smkw.com

Soft Tex Manufacturing Co 100 N Mohawk St .... Cohoes NY 12047 518-235-3645
Web: www.bedpillows.com

Southern Wholesale Flooring Company Inc
955B Cobb Pl Blvd .... Kennesaw GA 30144 770-514-7110
TF: 800-282-7590 ■ *Web:* www.swfloor.com

Springboard Biodiesel LLC 2282 Ivy St .... Chico CA 95928 530-894-1793
Web: www.springboardbiodiesel.com

Sunteca Systems Inc 2 Ave A .... Leetsdale PA 15056 412-749-5200

Supply New England Inc 123 East St .... Attleboro MA 02703 508-222-5555
Web: www.supplynewengland.com

Sur La Table 5701 Sixth Ave S Ste 486 .... Seattle WA 98108 800-243-0852
TF: 800-243-0852 ■ *Web:* www.surlatable.com

Surrey Satellite Technology US LLC
345 Inverness Dr S Ste 100 .... Englewood CO 80112 303-790-0653
Web: www.sst-us.com

Switch Lighting & Design LLC 1207 Vine St .... Cincinnati OH 45202 513-721-8100
Web: www.switchcollection.com

System Scale Corp 4393 W 96th St .... Indianapolis IN 46268 317-876-9335
Web: www.system-scale.com

Timberlane Inc 150 Domorah Dr .... Montgomeryville PA 18936 215-616-0600
TF: 800-250-2221 ■ *Web:* www.timberlane.com

TJX Cos Inc 770 Cochituate Rd .... Framingham MA 01701 508-390-1000
NYSE: TJX ■ *TF:* 800-926-6299 ■ *Web:* www.tjx.com

Topaz Lighting Corp 925 Waverly Ave .... Holtsville NY 11742 631-758-5507
TF: 800-666-2852 ■ *Web:* www.topaz-usa.com

Totalcomp Scales & Components
13-01 Pollitt Dr Ste 2 .... Fair Lawn NJ 07410 201-797-2718
TF: 800-631-0347 ■ *Web:* www.totalcomp.com

Transducer Techniques Inc 42480 Rio Nedo .... Temecula CA 92590 951-719-3965
Web: www.transducertechniques.com

Tri State Distributors Inc 550 E First Ave .... Spokane WA 99202 509-455-8300
Web: www.tristatedistributors.com

Triple Dot Corp 3302 S Susan St .... Santa Ana CA 92704 714-241-0888
Web: www.triple-dot.com

Vaxcel International Co 121 E N Ave .... Carol Stream IL 60188 630-682-8767
Web: www.vaxcelusa.com

Villeroy & Boch Tableware Ltd
3535 Us Hwy 1 .... Princeton NJ 08540 800-536-2284
TF: 800-536-2284 ■ *Web:* www.villeroy-boch.com

Visionaire Lighting LLC
19645 Rancho Way .... Rancho Dominguez CA 90220 310-512-6480
Web: www.visionairelighting.com

Waterford Wedgwood USA Inc 1330 Campus Pkwy .... Wall NJ 07753 732-938-5800
Web: wedgwood.com

Wells Rug Service Inc 49 Bank St .... Morristown NJ 07960 973-539-3800
Web: www.wellsrug.com

Williams-Sonoma Inc 3250 Van Ness Ave .... San Francisco CA 94109 415-421-7900
NYSE: WSM ■ *TF:* 800-838-2589 ■ *Web:* www.williams-sonomainc.com

Williamsburg Pottery 6692 Richmond Rd .... Williamsburg VA 23188 757-564-3326
Web: www.williamsburgpottery.com

Winsome Trading Inc
16111 Woodinville Redmo .... Woodinville WA 98072 425-483-8888 483-4141
Web: www.winsomewood.com

World Class Lighting 14350 60th St N .... Clearwater FL 33760 727-524-7661
TF: 877-499-6753 ■ *Web:* www.worldclasslighting.com

Z Gallerie Inc 1855 W 139th St .... Gardena CA 90249 310-630-1200 630-1289
TF: 800-358-8288 ■ *Web:* www.zgallerie.com

Zephyr Aluminum LLC
625 Second St PO Box 4906 .... Lancaster PA 17603 717-397-3618
Web: www.zephyraluminum.com

Zimman'S Inc 80 Market St .... Lynn MA 01901 781-598-9432
Web: zimmans.com

363 HOME HEALTH SERVICES

See Also Hospices p. 2484

Phone Fax

A & A Home Health Services
1240 Blalock Rd Ste 210 .... Houston TX 77055 713-783-8803

A Plus Family Care 4538 Callaghan Rd .... San Antonio TX 78228 210-342-2819

Phone Fax

A-1 Action Nursing Care Inc
3508 Greencastle Rd ... Burtonsville MD 20866 301-890-7575
Web: a1actionnursingcare.com

Abarca Health LLC 650 ave munoz rivera ... San juan PR 00918 787-523-1212
Web: www.abarcahealth.com

Abbi Home Care Inc 6453 SW Blvd ... Benbrook TX 76132 817-377-0889 377-0890
TF: 877-383-2224 ■ *Web:* abbihomecare.com

AdCare Health Systems Inc 1145 Hembree RD ... Roswell GA 30076 678-869-5116
NYSE: ADK ■ *Web:* www.adcarehealth.com

Advantage Home Health Care Inc
4008 N Wheeling Ave ... Muncie IN 47304 765-284-1211
TF: 800-884-5088 ■ *Web:* www.advantagehhc.com

Affinity Home Health Care Inc
121 Sandwich St ... Plymouth MA 02360 508-732-8988
Web: affinityhomehealthcare.com

Agape Primary Care
3030 Towne Centre Dr Ste 200 ... Mesquite TX 75150 972-681-8420
Web: www.agapehomehealth.com

Alacare Home Health & Hospice
2400 John Hawkins Pkwy ... Birmingham AL 35244 205-981-8000 981-8743
TF: 800-852-4724 ■ *Web:* www.alacare.com

Alaska Native Tribal Health Consortium Inc
4000 Ambassador Dr ... Anchorage AK 99508 907-729-1900
Web: anthc.org

All About Kids Home Health
2102 W. Teege Ave ... Harlingen TX 78550 956-412-3337
Web: allaboutkidshomehealth.com

Allcare Medical Inc 125 Newtown Rd Ste 300 ... Plainview NY 11803 800-244-4660
TF: 800-244-4660

Allied Healthcare International Inc
245 Pk AVe 39th Fl ... New York NY 10167 212-750-0064 750-7221
Web: www.alliedhealthcare.com

Almost Family Inc
9510 Ormsby Stn Rd Ste 300 ... Louisville KY 40223 502-891-1000 891-8067
NASDAQ: AFAM ■ *TF:* 800-828-9769 ■ *Web:* www.almostfamily.com

Alphavax Inc 2 Triangle Dr ... Research Triangle Park NC 27709 919-595-0400
Web: www.alphavax.com

Altamed Health Services Corp
500 Citadel Dr Ste 490 ... Los Angeles CA 90040 323-725-8751
TF: 877-462-2582 ■ *Web:* www.altamed.org

Alterna-Care 319 E Madison St # 3n ... Springfield IL 62701 217-525-3733
Web: alterna-care.com

Altura Homecare & Rehab
4308 Carlisle Blvd NE Ste 202 ... Albuquerque NM 87107 505-881-0425
Web: www.alturahomecare.com

Amedisys Inc
5959 S Sherwood Forest Blvd Ste 300 ... Baton Rouge LA 70816 225-292-2031 292-8163
NASDAQ: AMED ■ *TF:* 800-464-0020 ■ *Web:* www.amedisys.com

American HomePatient Inc
5200 Maryland Way Ste 400 ... Brentwood TN 37027 615-221-8884 373-9932
TF: 800-890-7271 ■ *Web:* www.ahom.com

Americare Certified Special Services Inc
5923 Strickland Ave ... Brooklyn NY 11234 718-535-3100
Web: www.americareny.com

AmeriCare Medical Inc 1938 Woodslee Dr ... Troy MI 48083 248-280-2020
Web: www.americaremedical.com

AMERIS Health Systems LLC
1114 17th Ave S Ste 205 ... Nashville TN 37212 615-327-4440
Web: www.amerishealth.com

Amerita Inc 20 Fairbanks Ste 173 ... Irvine CA 92618 949-273-6528
Web: www.ameritaiv.com

Androscoggin Home Health Services Inc
PO Box 819 ... Lewiston ME 04243 207-777-7740
TF: 800-482-7412 ■ *Web:* www.ahch.org

Angel Healthcare 5828 Balcones Dr Ste 105 ... Austin TX 78731 512-453-6449

Angel Medical Systems Inc
1163 Shrewsbury Ave Ste E ... Shrewsbury NJ 07702 732-542-5551
Web: www.angel-med.com

Anova Home Health Care Services Inc
1229 Silver Ln Ste 201 ... Pittsburgh PA 15136 412-859-8801
Web: www.anovahomehealth.com

Anthelio Healthcare Solutions Inc
5400 LBJ Fwy Ste 200 ... Dallas TX 75240 214-257-7000 257-7042
TF: 855-268-4354 ■ *Web:* www.antheliohealth.com

Anthem Heatlh Services Inc 57 Karner Rd ... Albany NY 12205 518-862-1247

Any-Time Home Care Inc
127 S Broadway PO Box 995 ... Nyack NY 10960 845-353-8280
Web: anytimehomecare.com

Apria Healthcare Group Inc
26220 Enterprise Ct ... Lake Forest CA 92630 949-639-2000
TF: 800-277-4288 ■ *Web:* www.apria.com

Ariste Medical Inc 20 S Dudley Ste 900 ... Memphis TN 38103 510-410-1880
Web: www.aristemedical.com

Arizona Bridge To Independent Living
5025 E Washington St Ste 200 ... Phoenix AZ 85034 602-256-2245
Web: ability360.org

ARK Diagnostics Inc 48089 Fremont Blvd ... Fremont CA 94538 510-270-6270 270-6298
TF: 877-869-2320 ■ *Web:* www.ark-tdm.com

Aroostook Home Health Services
658 Main St Ste 2 ... Caribou ME 04736 207-492-8290 492-8245
TF: 877-688-9977 ■ *Web:* aroostookhomehealthservices.com

Around The Clock Care 5353 Truxtun Ave ... Bakersfield CA 93309 661-324-4277
Web: www.bakersfieldcare.com

Back Home Again Inc 291 N State Rd 2 ... Valparaiso IN 46383 219-477-4333

Bayada Nurses Home Care Specialists
290 Chester Ave ... Moorestown NJ 08057 856-231-1000 231-1955
TF: 877-591-1527 ■ *Web:* www.bayada.com

Bios Cos 309 E Dewey ... Sapulpa OK 74066 918-227-8390
Web: bioscorp.com

Brandywine Nursing & Rehabilitation Ctr Inc
505 Greenbank Rd ... Wilmington DE 19808 302-998-0101
Web: www.brandywinenursing.org

Bravo Wellness LLC
20445 Emerald Pkwy Dr SW Ste 400 ... Cleveland OH 44135 216-658-9500
Web: www.bravowell.com

Phone Fax

Cadence Health 25 N Winfield Rd ... Winfield IL 60190 630-315-8000
Web: www.cadencehealth.org

Calea Ltd 2785 Skymark Ave Unit 2 ... Mississauga ON L4W4Y3 905-238-1234
TF: 888-909-3299 ■ *Web:* www.calea.ca

CanCare Health Services Inc
45 Sheppard Ave E Ste 204 ... Toronto ON M2N5W9 416-226-6995
TF: 877-226-6995 ■ *Web:* www.cancarehealth.com

Care Partners 68 Sweeten Creek Rd ... Asheville NC 28803 828-252-2255
TF: 800-627-1533 ■ *Web:* www.carepartners.org

Carecycle Solutions LLC 3406 Main St ... Dallas TX 75226 214-698-0600
Web: carecyclesolutions.net

Carelinc Medical Equipment & Supply Company LLC
89 - 54th St SW ... Grand Rapids MI 49548 616-249-2273
Web: www.carelincmed.com

Carepoint Partners LLC
8280 Montgomery Rd Ste 101 ... Cincinnati OH 45236 513-891-6666
Web: carepointpartners.com

Caresource Health Plan 740 SE Seventh St ... Grants Pass OR 97526 541-471-4106
TF: 888-460-0185 ■ *Web:* www.mripa.org

Carestar Inc 5566 Cheviot Rd ... Cincinnati OH 45247 513-618-8300
TF: 866-834-4712 ■ *Web:* carestar.com

Carter Healthcare 3105 S Meridian Ave ... Oklahoma City OK 73119 405-947-7700 947-7300
TF: 888-951-1112 ■ *Web:* www.carterhealthcare.com

Casepro Inc 21738 Hardy Oak Blvd ... San Antonio TX 78258 210-496-8050 496-8970
TF: 888-999-2594 ■ *Web:* caseproinc.com

Central Home Health Care Inc
20245 W 12 Mile Rd Ste 100 ... Southfield MI 48076 248-569-5410
Web: centralhomecare.com

Central Vermont Home Health & Hospice
600 Granger Rd ... Barre VT 05641 802-223-1878
TF: 800-286-1219 ■ *Web:* www.cvhhh.org

Charity Home Health Services Inc
500 Carson Plz Ste 228 ... Carson CA 90746 310-527-4339
Web: charityhhs.com

Cheer Inc 546 S Bedford St ... Georgetown DE 19947 302-856-5187
Web: cheerde.com

Christian Homes Inc 200 N Postville Dr ... Lincoln IL 62656 217-732-9651 732-8686
TF: 800-535-8717 ■ *Web:* www.christianhomes.org

Cole Home Healthcare of Houston Inc
16835 Deer Creek Dr Ste 220 ... Spring TX 77379 281-379-7052
Web: colehealthcare.com

ComForcare Senior Services Inc
2520 Telegraph Rd Ste 100 ... Bloomfield Hills MI 48302 248-745-9700 745-9763
TF: 800-886-4044 ■ *Web:* www.comforcare.com

Comfort Caregivers Inc
6501 E Greenway Pkwy Ste 103 ... Scottsdale AZ 85254 602-482-7777
Web: www.comfortcaregivers.com

Commonwealth Health Corporation Inc
800 Park St ... Bowling Green KY 42101 270-745-1500
TF: 800-786-1581 ■ *Web:* www.chc.net

Confident Care Corp
3 University Plz Dr Ste 340 ... Hackensack NJ 07601 201-498-9400 498-1556
TF: 866-839-2273 ■ *Web:* www.confidentcarecorp.com

Continucare Corp 7200 Corporate Ctr Dr Ste 600 ... Miami FL 33126 305-500-2000 500-2080
TF: 866-312-7154 ■ *Web:* www.continucare.com

Coon Memorial Home Health 1411 Denver Ave ... Dalhart TX 79022 806-244-8738
Web: www.dhchd.org

Coram Healthcare Corp 555 17th St Ste 1500 ... Denver CO 80202 800-267-2642 298-0043*
**Fax Area Code: 303* ■ *TF:* 800-267-2642 ■ *Web:* www.coramhc.com

Delaware Hospice Inc 3515 Silverside Rd ... Wilmington DE 19810 302-478-5707 479-2586
TF: 800-838-9800 ■ *Web:* www.delawarehospice.org

Dependable Nurses of Phoenix Inc
1120 S Swan Rd ... Tucson AZ 85711 520-721-3822
Web: www.dependablenurses.com

Dermatran Health Solutions 1504 market st ... Redding CA 96001 855-675-5210
TF: 855-675-5210

Divine Healthcare Network
856 Univerity Ave W ... St Paul MN 55104 651-665-9795
Web: divinecorporation.com

E-Bizdocs Inc 85 Broadway ... Menands NY 12205 518-456-1011
Web: www.ebizdocs.net

Ejq Home Health Care Inc 800 Middle Ave ... Elyria OH 44035 440-323-7004
Web: ejqhomehealthcare.com

ELJ Inc D/B/A Millennium Medical Supply
1500 Clarksville St ... Paris TX 75460 903-739-8539

Episcopal Health Services Inc
327 Beach 19th St ... Far Rockaway NY 11691 718-869-7000 869-8507
Web: www.ehs.org

Exceptional Home Care LLP 1510 E Grande Blvd ... Tyler TX 75703 903-533-0290
Web: ehctx.com

Fletcher'S Medical Supplies Inc
6851 S Distribution Ave ... Jacksonville FL 32256 904-387-4481 389-6965
TF: 855-541-7809 ■ *Web:* fletchermedical.com

Gateway to Care 3611 Ennis St ... Houston TX 77004 713-783-4616
Web: gatewaytocare.org

Gem Health Care Services Inc-services De Sant Gem Inc
304-383 Parkdale Ave ... Ottawa ON K1Y4R4 613-761-7474
Web: www.gemhealthcare.com

General Healthcare Resources Inc
2250 Hickory Rd Ste 240 ... Plymouth Meeting PA 19462 610-834-1122 834-7525
TF: 800-879-4471 ■ *Web:* www.ghresources.com

Genesis Home Care Inc 116 E Heritage Dr ... Tyler TX 75703 903-509-3374
TF: 800-947-0273 ■ *Web:* genesishomecare.net

Gentiva Health Services Inc
3350 Riverwood Pkwy Ste 1400 ... Atlanta GA 30339 770-951-6450
NASDAQ: GTIV ■ *Web:* www.gentiva.com

Global Medical Solutions Ltd
14140 Ventura Blvd ... Sherman Oaks CA 91423 818-783-2915
Web: globalmedicalsolutions.com

Griswold Special Care Inc
717 Bethlehem Pike Ste 300 ... Erdenheim PA 19038 215-402-0200 277-3820*
**Fax Area Code: 469* ■ *TF:* 855-303-9470 ■ *Web:* www.griswoldhomecare.com

				Phone	Fax
Gurwin Jewish Nursing & Rehabilitation Ctr 68 Hauppauge Rd *Web:* www.gurwin.org	Commack	NY	11725	631-715-2000	715-2940
Hamacher Resource Group LLC 8801 W Heather Ave *TF:* 800-888-0889 ■ *Web:* hamacher.com	Milwaukee	WI	53224	800-888-0889	
HCA Gulf Coast 7400 Fannin Ste 650 *Web:* hcagulfcoast.com	Houston	TX	77054	713-852-1500	
Health Services of Coshocton County 230 S Fourth St *Web:* healthservicescoshocton.com	Coshocton	OH	43812	740-622-7311	
Health Systems 2000 1901 Oak Park Blvd *Web:* www.hhc2000.com	Lake Charles	LA	70601	337-562-1140	
Help At Home Inc 1 N State St Ste 800 *TF:* 800-404-3191 ■ *Web:* www.helpathome.com	Chicago	IL	60602	312-762-0900	704-0022
Henry Street Settlement 265 Henry St *Web:* www.henrystreet.org	New York	NY	10002	212-766-9200	
Homcare Inc 875 W Summit Ave *Web:* homcareinc.com	Muskegon	MI	49441	231-755-6951	
Home Aides of Central New York Inc 723 James St *Web:* homeaidescny.org	Syracuse	NY	13203	315-476-4295	
Home Bound Healthcare Inc 1615 Vollmer Rd *TF:* 800-444-7028 ■ *Web:* www.homeboundhealth.com	Flossmoor	IL	60422	708-798-0800	
Home Care & Elder Services 2141 NW Fillmore Ave *Web:* homecareserv.com	Corvallis	OR	97330	541-757-0214	
Home Care Network Inc 190A E Spring Vly Rd *Web:* www.hcnmidwest.net	Centerville	OH	45458	937-435-1142	
Home Care Partners 1234 Massachusetts Ave NW Ste C-1002 *Web:* www.homecarepartners.org	Washington	DC	20005	202-638-2382	
Home Health Corp of America Inc *Healthcare Investment Corp of America* 620 Freedom Business Ctr Ste 105 *Web:* www.healthinvcorp.com	King of Prussia	PA	19406	484-690-1200	751-9100
Home Healthcare, Hospice & Community Services Inc 312 Marlboro St *Web:* www.hcsservices.org	Keene	NH	03431	603-352-2253	
Home Instead Inc 13323 California St *TF:* 888-484-5759 ■ *Web:* www.homeinstead.com	Omaha	NE	68154	402-498-4466	498-5757
Home IV Care & Nutritional Service 30 Ebco Cir Ste 102 *TF:* 800-552-6576	Waynesboro	VA	22980	800-552-6576	
Home Staff Inc 5517 N Cumberland Ave Ste 915 *TF:* 800-806-6924 ■ *Web:* homestaffinc.com	Chicago	IL	60656	773-467-6002	
Home Staff LLC 40 Millbrook St *Web:* www.homestaffma.com	Worcester	MA	01606	508-755-4600	
Homecare Homebase LLC 6688 N Central Expy Ste 1200 *Web:* www.hchb.com	Dallas	TX	75206	214-239-6700	
Homecare of Mid Missouri Inc 102 W Reed St *Web:* www.homecaremo.org	Moberly	MO	65270	660-263-1517	
Homewatch International Inc 7100 E Belleview Ave Ste 303 *TF:* 800-777-9770 ■ *Web:* www.homewatchcaregivers.com	Greenwood Village	CO	80111	303-758-5111	
Hosanna Health Care 1001 N Conway Ave	Mission	TX	78572	956-519-1000	
Hospice Atlanta-Visiting Nurse Health System 1244 Pk Vista Dr *TF:* 866-374-4776 ■ *Web:* www.vnhs.org	Atlanta	GA	30319	404-869-3000	215-6005
Hospital Cooperative Laundry Inc 6225 E 38th Ave *Web:* hospitalcooperative.com	Denver	CO	80207	303-329-6662	
Inovalon Inc 4321 Collington Rd *Web:* medassurant.com	Bowie	MD	20716	301-809-4000	
IntegraCare Holdings Inc 2559 SW Grapevine Pkwy Ste 300 *TF:* 800-735-2988 ■ *Web:* www.integracarehh.com	Grapevine	TX	76051	817-310-4999	
Intercity Home Care 11 Dartmouth St *Web:* intercityhomecare.com	Malden	MA	02148	781-321-6300	
Interim HealthCare Inc 1601 Sawgrass Corporate Pkwy *TF:* 800-338-7786 ■ *Web:* www.interimhealthcare.com	Sunrise	FL	33323	954-858-6000	858-2720
Invacare Canada L P 570 Matheson Blvd E Unit 8 *Web:* www.invacare.ca	Mississauga	ON	L4Z4G4	905-890-8300	
Ira G Steffy & Son Inc 460 Wenger Dr *Web:* www.iragsteffyandson.com	Ephrata	PA	17522	717-733-2001	733-0971
Kelly Home Care Services Inc 999 W Big Beaver Rd *TF:* 800-755-8636 ■ *Web:* homehealthcareagencies.com	Troy	MI	48084	248-362-4444	
Knoxville Hospital & Clinics 1002 S Lincoln St *Web:* www.knoxvillehospital.org	Knoxville	IA	50138	641-842-2151	
Korman Healthcare LLC 5783 W Erie St *Web:* www.kormanhealthcare.com	Chandler	AZ	85226	480-365-0222	
Lakewood Health System 49725 County 83 *TF:* 800-525-1033 ■ *Web:* lakewoodhealthsystem.com	Staples	MN	56479	218-894-1515	
Lamoille Home Health & Hospice 54 Farr Ave *Web:* www.lhha.org	Morrisville	VT	05661	802-888-4651	
Laurel Rehabilitation Services 216 Haddon Ave Ste 702 *Web:* laurelrehab.com	Westmont	NJ	08108	856-869-7360	
LHC Group LLC 901 Hugh Wallis Rd S *NASDAQ: LHCG* ■ *TF:* 866-542-4768 ■ *Web:* www.lhcgroup.com	Lafayette	LA	70508	337-289-8188	289-8168
LHP Hospital Group Inc 2400 Dallas Pkwy Ste 450 *Web:* www.lhphospitalgroup.com	Plano	TX	75093	972-943-1700	
Lifecare Alliance 1699 W Mound St *Web:* www.lifecarealliance.org	Columbus	OH	43223	614-278-3130	
LifeCare Solutions Inc 10119 Carroll Canyon Rd *Web:* www.lifecaresoln.com	San Diego	CA	92131	858-444-2800	
Lifelink Foundation Inc 409 Bayshore Blvd *TF:* 800-262-5775 ■ *Web:* www.lifelinkfoundation.org	Tampa	FL	33606	813-253-2640	
Lifetime Care 3111 Winton Rd S *Web:* www.lifetimecare.org	Rochester	NY	14623	585-214-1000	
Lincare Holdings Inc 19387 US 19 N *NASDAQ: LNCR* ■ *Web:* www.lincare.com	Clearwater	FL	33764	727-530-7700	532-9692
Living Assistance Services Inc 937 Haverford Rd Ste 200 *TF:* 800-365-4189 ■ *Web:* www.livingassistance.com	Bryn Mawr	PA	19010	800-365-4189	
Long Term Solutions Inc 235 W Central St *Web:* www.longtermsol.com	Natick	MA	01760	508-907-6290	
Longwood Management Corp 4032 Wilshire Blvd Ste 600	Los Angeles	CA	90010	213-389-6900	
Loving Hands Home Care Services Inc 1777 Hamilton Ave *Web:* lovinghandshmcare.com	San Jose	CA	95125	408-266-8331	
Mackenzie Eason & Associates 3023 S University Dr Ste 230 *TF:* 866-392-3139 ■ *Web:* mackenzieeason.com	Fort Worth	TX	76109	817-922-9152	
MaineHealth 110 Free St *Web:* www.mainehealth.com	Portland	ME	04101	207-661-7001	
Mains'l Services Inc 7000 78th Ave N *TF:* 800-441-6525 ■ *Web:* www.mainsl.com	Brooklyn Park	MN	55445	800-441-6525	
MDX Medical Inc 210 Clay Ave Ste 140 *Web:* www.vitals.com	Lyndhurst	NJ	07071	201-842-0760	
Med Team Home Health Care 131 S Beckham Ave *TF:* 800-825-2873 ■ *Web:* med-team.com	Tyler	TX	75702	903-592-9747	
Med-Staff Oklahoma LLC 8321 E 61st St Ste 221	Tulsa	OK	74133	918-317-0270	
MedCure Inc 12013 NE Marx *Web:* www.medcure.org	Portland	OR	97220	503-257-9100	
Medical Cost Management Corp 105 W Adams St Ste 2200 *Web:* www.medicalcost.com	Chicago	IL	60603	312-236-2694	
Medical Ctr at Princeton Home Care 905 Herrontown Rd *TF:* 877-932-8395 ■ *Web:* www.princetonhcs.org	Princeton	NJ	08540	609-497-4900	737-6506
Medical Metrics Inc 2121 Sage Rd Ste 300 *Web:* www.medicalmetrics.com	Houston	TX	77056	713-850-7500	
Medical Services of America Inc (MSA) 171 Monroe Ln **Fax Area Code: 888* ■ *TF:* 800-845-5850 ■ *Web:* www.msa-corp.com	Lexington	SC	29072	803-957-0500	342-6190*
Medistar Home Health 347 Moreau St *Web:* www.medistarhomehealth.com	Marksville	LA	71351	318-253-0014	
Mehling & Associates Inc 9846 Hwy 31 E *Web:* www.athomehealth.org	Tyler	TX	75705	903-592-8001	
Mena Hospital Commission 311 Morrow St N *TF:* 800-394-6185 ■ *Web:* www.menaregional.com	Mena	AR	71953	479-394-2534	
Meridian Health System Inc 1967 Hwy 34, Bldg C, Ste 104 *TF:* 800-560-9990 ■ *Web:* www.meridianhealth.com	Wall	NJ	07719	800-560-9990	
MeritCare Health System Inc 720 4th St N *Web:* www.meritcare.com	Fargo	ND	58102	701-234-2000	
Metro Pavia Health System Inc MaraMar Plz Bldg Avenida San Patricio Ste 950-960 *TF:* 888-882-0882 ■ *Web:* www.metropavia.com	Guaynabo	PR	00968	888-882-0882	
Millenium Home Health Care Inc 370 Reed Rd Ste 319 *Web:* www.mhomehealth.com	Broomall	PA	19008	610-543-4126	
Minnesota Visiting Nurse Agency 2000 Summer St *Web:* www.mvna.org	Minneapolis	MN	55413	612-617-4600	617-4782
Miracle Healthcare LLC 3354 E Broad St Ste H *Web:* www.miraclehealthcolumbus.com	Columbus	OH	43213	937-324-2194	
Mitchell County Hospital Health Systems 400 W Eighth St P O Box 399 *Web:* www.mchks.com	Beloit	KS	67420	785-738-9590	
National Home Health Care Corp 700 White Plains Rd Ste 275 *TF:* 800-422-4661 ■ *Web:* www.nhhc.net	Scarsdale	NY	10583	914-722-9000	722-9239
Netmd Business Inc 38935 Ann Arbor Rd *Web:* netmdbusiness.com	Livonia	MI	48150	734-805-0460	
New Choices Inc 2501 18th St Ste 201 *TF:* 888-355-5502 ■ *Web:* newchoicesinc.com	Bettendorf	IA	52722	563-355-5502	
New Millenium Home Health 6031 Cleveland Ave *Web:* nmilleniumhomehealth.com	Columbus	OH	43231	614-882-7782	
New York Health Care Inc 33 W Hawthorne Ave 3rd Fl *OTC: BBAL* ■ *TF:* 888-978-6942 ■ *Web:* www.nyhc.com	Valley Stream	NY	11580	718-375-6700	
Nizhoni Health Systems LLC 5 Middlesex Ave *Web:* nizhonihealth.com	Somerville	MA	02145	617-623-3211	
No Ordinary Moments Inc 16742 Gothard St Ste 115 *Web:* noordinarymoments.com	Huntington Beach	CA	92647	714-848-3800	
Noble Visiting Nurse and Hospice Services Inc 77 Mill St Ste 207 *Web:* noblehospice.org	Westfield	MA	01085	413-562-7049	
North Los Angel County Regional Ctr 15400 Sherman Way Ste 170 *TF:* 800-430-4263 ■ *Web:* www.nlacrc.org	Van Nuys	CA	91406	818-778-1900	756-6140
Nurse On Call Inc 1926 10th Ave N Ste 400 *Web:* www.nurseoncallfl.com	Lake Worth	FL	33461	561-586-9148	
Nurses Unlimited Inc 4100 E Piedras Dr Ste 105 *Web:* nursesunlimited.com	San Antonio	TX	78228	210-732-4184	
Nursing Enterprises Inc 5101 Wisconsin Ave N.W. Ste 250 *Web:* www.nursingenterprises.com	Washington	DC	20016	202-526-2400	
NutraBella Inc 1875 S Grant St Ste 305 *Web:* www.bellybarproducts.com	San Mateo	CA	94402	650-212-3559	

Phone | Fax

Ohel Children's Home & Family Services Inc
4510 16th Ave — Brooklyn NY 11204 — 718-851-6300
TF: 800-603-6435 ■ *Web:* www.ohelfamily.org

Olmsted Medical Center 210 Ninth St SE — Rochester MN 55904 — 507-288-3443
Web: www.olmmed.org

Ontario Medical Supply Ltd 1100 Algoma Rd — Ottawa ON K1B0A3 — 613-244-8620
TF: 800-804-1112 ■ *Web:* www.oms.ca

Onyx Capital Holdings Inc
10843 Meadow Garden Ct — Las Vegas NV 89135 — 702-233-8056

Optimae LifeServices Inc
301 W Burlington Ave. — Fairfield IA 52556 — 641-472-1684
Web: www.optimaelifeservices.com

Optimal Hospice Care
1675 Chester Ave Ste 401 — Bakersfield CA 93309 — 661-716-4000
Web: www.optimalcares.com

Outreach Healthcare Inc 269 W Renner Pkwy — Richardson TX 75080 — 972-840-7360
Web: www.outreachhealth.com

Passport Program-western
925 Euclid Ave Ste 600. — Cleveland OH 44115 — 216-621-0303
TF: 800-626-7277 ■ *Web:* www.psa10a.org

Pathways Home Health Hospice & Private Duty
585 N Mary Ave — Sunnyvale CA 94085 — 408-730-5900
Web: www.pathwayshealth.org

Pediatric Home Respiratory Services Inc
2800 Cleveland Ave N — Roseville MN 55113 — 651-642-1825
Web: www.pediatrichomeservice.com

Pediatric Services of America Inc
310 Technology Pkwy. — Norcross GA 30092 — 770-441-1580
TF: 800-408-4442 ■ *Web:* www.psahealthcare.com

Pegasus Home Health Care 132 N Maryland Ave. — Glendale CA 91206 — 818-551-1932
Web: www.pegasushomecare.com

Pentec Health Inc 4 Creek Pkwy Ste A. — Marcus Hook PA 19061 — 610-494-8700
Web: www.pentechealth.com

People Care Inc 116 W 32nd St 15th Fl — New York NY 10001 — 212-631-7300
Web: www.peoplecare.com

Perfect Home Care Inc 4210 Middlebrook Dr — Fort Worth TX 76103 — 817-534-9600
Web: www.perfecthomecare.net

Personal Care Inc 321 Sycamore St. — Decatur GA 30030 — 404-373-2727
Web: personalcare.net

Personal-Touch Home Care Inc
186-18 Hillside Ave — Jamaica NY 11432 — 718-468-2500 — 681-2550*
**Fax Area Code:* 412 ■ **Fax:* Hum Res ■ *TF:* 888-275-4147 ■ *Web:* www.pthomecare.com

Phoenix Home Care Inc 3033 S Kansas Expy — Springfield MO 65807 — 417-881-7442
Web: phoenixhomehc.com

Pioneers Medical Center 345 Cleveland St — Meeker CO 81641 — 970-878-5047
Web: pioneershospital.org

Platinum Home Health Care Inc
4903 W 95th St. — Oak Lawn IL 60453 — 708-229-9338
Web: platinumhomehealthcare.com

Pmd Healthcare 6620 grant way — Allentown PA 18106 — 484-664-7600
Web: spiropd.com

Prairie River Home Care Inc
25 1st Ave NE Ste 200 — Buffalo MN 55313 — 507-252-9844
Web: www.prhomecare.com

PreCheck Inc 2500 E T C Jester Blvd Ste. — Houston TX 77008 — 800-999-9861
TF: 800-999-9861 ■ *Web:* www.precheck.com

Preferred Homecare Infusion LLC
4601 E Hilton Ave Ste 100 — Phoenix AZ 85034 — 480-446-9010
Web: preferredhomecare.com

Premier Homecare Inc 6123 Montrose Rd — Rockville MD 20852 — 301-984-1742
Web: www.jssa.org

Prevea Health Services Inc
2710 Executive Dr. — Green Bay WI 54304 — 920-496-4700
Web: www.prevea.com

Pro-care Home Health Limited 122 W Union St — Hartford KY 42347 — 270-298-3112
Web: www.christiancarecommunities.org

Promera Health 61 accord park dr — Norwell MA 02061 — 888-878-9058
TF: 888-878-9058 ■ *Web:* www.promerasports.com

PRS Inc 1761 Old Meadow Rd Ste 100 — McLean VA 22102 — 703-536-9000 — 448-3723
Web: www.prsinc.org

Pulse Home Health Care Inc
2325 Severn Ave Ste 5 — Metairie LA 70001 — 504-831-7778
Web: pulsehomehealthcare.com

Qchc Inc 200 narrows pkwy — Birmingham AL 35242 — 205-437-1512
Web: www.qchcweb.com

Qualchoice of Arkansas Inc
12615 Chenal Pkwy Ste 300. — Little Rock AR 72211 — 501-228-7111
Web: www.qualchoice.com

Richard A Urbanek Jr DDS Ms Pa
5 Eureka Cir Ste B. — Wichita Falls TX 76308 — 940-696-2002

Right at Home Inc 6464 Crt St Ste 150 — Omaha NE 68106 — 402-697-7537 — 697-0289
TF: 877-697-7537 ■ *Web:* www.rightathome.net

Scarab Behavioral Health Services LLC
3203 Brick Church Pk. — Nashville TN 37207 — 615-262-7822
Web: scarabhealth.com

Selfhelp Community Services Inc
520 Eigth Ave 5th Fl — New York NY 10018 — 866-735-1234
TF: 866-735-1234 ■ *Web:* www.selfhelp.net

Sitters & More Inc 125 A Stonebridge Blvd — Jackson TN 38305 — 731-660-0001
Web: sittersandmore.com

Society'S Assets Inc
5200 Washington Ave Ste 225 — Racine WI 53406 — 262-637-9128
TF: 800-378-9128 ■ *Web:* societysassets.org

Solano Coalition for Bett
1 Harbor Ctr Ste 270. — Suisun City CA 94585 — 707-863-4440
TF: 800-978-7547 ■ *Web:* www.solanocoalition.org

Sta-Home Hospice 406 Briarwood Dr Bldg 200 — Jackson MS 39206 — 601-956-5100 — 956-3003
TF: 800-782-4663 ■ *Web:* www.sta-home.com

Star Multi Care Services Inc
115 Broad Hollow Rd Ste 275. — Melville NY 11747 — 631-424-7827 — 427-5466
TF: 877-920-0600 ■ *Web:* www.starmulticare.com

Stowell Associates Select Staff Inc
4485 N Oakland Ave — Milwaukee WI 53211 — 414-963-2600
Web: caremanagedhomecare.com

SunCrest Healthcare Inc
9510 Ormsby Station Rd Ste 300 — Louisville KY 40223 — 615-627-9267
TF: 800-845-6987 ■ *Web:* www.omnihha.com

Sunrise Home Health Services
3200 Broadway Blvd Ste 260 — Garland TX 75043 — 972-278-1414
TF: 800-296-7823 ■ *Web:* sunrisehomehealth.com

TeleVital Inc 1309 Harefield Ct — San Jose CA 95131 — 408-441-6732
Web: www.televital.com

Texas Visiting Nurse Service Ltd
814 E Tyler — Harlingen TX 78550 — 956-412-1401
Web: tvnsltd.com

Todd's Companion Plus Inc
6123 Green Bay Rd Ste 250 — Kenosha WI 53142 — 262-605-4700

Umbrella Medical Systems 505 walnut st — Kansas City MO 64106 — 816-437-7265
Web: www.umbrella-ms.com

Umc Home Health 1301 50th St Ste 9. — Lubbock TX 79412 — 806-747-5377
Web: www.umchealthsystem.com

Valley Endodontics Ltd 1100 N Lynndale Dr. — Appleton WI 54914 — 920-731-4484
Web: valleyendo.com

Verecom Technologies Inc 61 Broadway — New York NY 10006 — 888-562-2468
TF: 888-562-2468 ■ *Web:* www.verecom.com

Visiting Nurse Assn of Morris County (Inc)
175 South St. — Morristown NJ 07960 — 973-539-1216
TF: 800-938-4748 ■ *Web:* www.vnannj.org

VITAS Healthcare Corp
100 S Biscayne Blvd Ste 400 — Miami FL 33131 — 305-374-4143
TF: 866-418-4827 ■ *Web:* www.vitas.com

Vna of Rhode Island 475 Kilvert St — Warwick RI 02886 — 401-574-4900 — 490-8870
TF: 800-638-6274 ■ *Web:* vnari.org

WakeMed Health & Hospitals 3000 New Bern Ave — Raleigh NC 27610 — 919-350-8000
Web: lake-medical.com

Whole Health Products LLC
17301 W Colfax Ave Ste 110 — Golden CO 80401 — 303-684-9618
Web: www.wholehealth.com

Williamsville Suburban LLC 193 S Union Rd — Buffalo NY 14221 — 716-276-1900
Web: www.facebook.com/pages/williamsville-suburban-llc/159706000718409

Wise Regional Health System 2000 S FM 51 — Decatur TX 76234 — 940-627-5921
Web: www.wisehealthsystem.com

WorldMed Assist 1230 Mtn Side Ct — Concord CA 94521 — 866-999-3848
TF: 866-999-3848 ■ *Web:* www.worldmedassist.com

364 HOME IMPROVEMENT CENTERS

See Also Construction Materials p. 2094

Phone | Fax

Above Security Inc
955 Michele-Bohec Blvd Ste 244 — Blainville QC J7C5J6 — 450-430-8166
TF: 866-430-8166 ■ *Web:* www.abovesecurity.com

Ace Hardware Corp 2200 Kensington Ct — Oak Brook IL 60523 — 630-990-6600
Web: www.acehardware.com

Ace Hardware Corporation
1056 W Grand Ave — Grover Beach CA 60523 — 805-489-0158 — 489-2971
Web: www.acehardware.com/home/index.jsp

Al's Garden Art Inc 311 W Citrus — Colton CA 92324 — 909-424-0221
Web: www.alsgardenart.com

Alaska Industrial Hardware Inc
2192 Viking Dr — Anchorage AK 99501 — 907-276-7201 — 258-3054
TF: 800-478-7201 ■ *Web:* store.aihalaska.com

Alene Candles LLC 51 Scarborough Ln — Milford NH 03055 — 603-673-5050
Web: www.alene.com

Ankmar LLC 4200 Monaco St. — Denver CO 80216 — 303-321-6051
Web: www.dhpace.com

Arlington Coal & Lumber Company Inc
41 Pk Ave — Arlington MA 02476 — 781-643-8100 — 643-7414
TF: 800-649-8101 ■ *Web:* www.arlcoal.com

Ashland Lumber Company Inc 134 Front St. — Ashland MA 01721 — 508-881-2660

Atlanta Hardwood Corp 5596 Riverview Rd SE — Mableton GA 30126 — 404-792-2290
TF: 800-476-5393 ■ *Web:* www.hardwoodweb.com

Beisser's Inc 3705 SE Beisser Dr — Grimes IA 50111 — 515-986-4422
Web: www.beisserlumber.com

Belknap White Group Inc, The
111 Plymouth St. — Mansfield MA 02048 — 508-337-2700
Web: www.belknapwhite.com

Beronio Lumber Co 2525 Marin St. — San Francisco CA 94124 — 415-824-4300 — 824-3706
Web: www.beronio.com

Big B Lumberteria 6600 Brentwood Blvd — Brentwood CA 94513 — 925-634-2442 — 634-9839
Web: www.bigblumber.com

Big L Corp 620 S Main St PO Box 134 — Sheridan MI 48884 — 989-291-3232 — 291-3421
Web: www.big-l-lumber.com

Bloedorn Lumber Company Inc PO Box 1077 — Torrington WY 82240 — 307-532-2151 — 532-3760
Web: www.bloedornlumber.com

BMC West Corp 11670 W Franklin Rd. — Boise ID 83709 — 208-331-4300
Web: buildwithbmc.com

Brunsell Bros Ltd 4611 W Beltline Hwy — Madison WI 53711 — 608-275-7171 — 275-7179
Web: www.brunsell.com

Busy Beaver Bldg Centers 2940 Library Rd — Pittsburgh PA 15234 — 412-882-6633 — 882-6833
TF: 800-732-0999 ■ *Web:* www.busybeaver.com

CanWel Building Materials Group Ltd
609 Granville St Ste 1100. — Vancouver BC V7Y1G6 — 604-432-1400
Web: www.canwel.com

Cape Cod Lumber Co Inc 225 Groveland St — Abington MA 02351 — 781-878-0715 — 871-6726
Web: capecodlumber.com

Carlisle Wide Plank Floors Inc 1676 Route 9 — Stoddard NH 03464 — 603-446-3937
Web: www.wideplankflooring.com

Carter Lumber Co Inc 601 Tallmadge Rd. — Kent OH 44240 — 330-673-6100 — 287-1806*
**Fax Area Code:* 765 ■ *Web:* www.carterlumber.com

Center BMW 5201 Van Nuys Blvd — Sherman Oaks CA 91401 — 818-907-9995
Web: centerbmw.com

Chinook Lumber Inc 17606 SR- 9 SE. — Snohomish WA 98296 — 360-668-8800 — 863-6498
Web: www.chinooklumber.com

Choo Choo Build-it Mart 325 Commerce Loop — Vidalia GA 30475 — 912-537-8964 — 537-4839
Web: vnscorp.com

Company	City	State	Zip	Phone	Fax
City Mill Company Ltd 660 N Nimitz Hwy *Web:* www.citymill.com	Honolulu	HI	96817	808-533-3811	
Colonial Mills Inc 560 Mineral Spring Ave. *Web:* www.colonialmills.com	Pawtucket	RI	02904	401-724-6279	
Columbia Showcase & Cabinet Co 11034 Sherman Way *Web:* www.columbiashowcase.com	Sun Valley	CA	91352	818-765-9710	
CoMc LLC 13423 F St *Web:* www.snapstone.com	Omaha	NE	68137	402-505-7627	
Dixieline Lumber Company Inc 3250 Sports Arena Blvd *Web:* www.dixieline.com	San Diego	CA	92110	619-224-4120	225-8192
Doug Ashy Building Materials Inc 1801 Rees St *Web:* www.dougashy.com	Breaux Bridge	LA	70517	337-332-5201	332-5226
Dukes Lumber Company Inc 28504 Dukes Lumber Rd *Web:* dukeslumber.com	Laurel	DE	19956	302-875-7551	
Economy Lumber 720 Camden Ave. *Web:* www.economylumber.com	Campbell	CA	95008	408-378-5231	378-0258
Elementis Specialties Inc 329 Wyckoffs Mill Rd *Web:* www.elementis-specialties.com	Hightstown	NJ	08520	609-443-2000	443-2422
Evanston Lumber Co 1001 Sherman Ave *Web:* www.evanstonlumber.com	Evanston	IL	60202	847-864-7700	
Evergreen Lumber & Truss Inc 84 Central Industrial Row *Web:* www.evergreentruss.com	Purvis	MS	39475	601-794-8404	
Fabrica International Inc 3201 S Susan St *Web:* www.fabrica.com	Santa Ana	CA	92704	949-261-7181	
Fire Rock Products LLC 3620 Ave C *Web:* www.firerock.us	Birmingham	AL	35064	205-639-5000	
Future Home Technology Inc 33 Ralph St	Port Jervis	NY	12771	845-856-9033	
Ganahl Lumber Co 1220 E Ball Rd *Web:* www.ganahl.com	Anaheim	CA	92805	714-772-5444	772-0639
Gemmy Industries Corp 117 Wrangler Dr *Web:* gemmy.com	Coppell	TX	75019	972-538-4200	
Grossman's Inc 90 Hawes Way *Web:* www.bargain-outlets.com	Stoughton	MA	02072	781-297-3300	297-0180
H2O Concepts International Inc 1518 W Knudsen Dr Ste 100 *Web:* www.h2oconcepts.com	Phoenix	AZ	85027	623-582-5222	
Hacienda Home Centers Inc 1255 Bosque Farms Blvd *TF:* 800-944-0704	Bosque Farms	NM	87068	505-869-2637	869-2197
Hayward Lumber Co 429 Front St. *Web:* www.haywardlumber.com	Salinas	CA	93901	831-755-8800	755-8821
Herrman Lumber Co 1917 S State Hwy N *Web:* www.herrmanlumber.com	Springfield	MO	65802	417-862-3737	
Home Depot Inc 2455 Paces Ferry Rd NW *NYSE:* HD ■ *TF Cust Svc:* 800-553-3199 ■ *Web:* www.homedepot.com	Atlanta	GA	30339	770-433-8211	
Jackson Lumber & Millwork Company Inc PO Box 449 *Web:* www.jacksonlumber.com	Lawrence	MA	01842	978-686-4141	
Jones Cassity Inc 302 Pine Tree Rd *Web:* www.cassityjones.com	Longview	TX	75604	903-759-0736	759-1406
JP Flooring Systems Inc 9097 Union Centre Blvd *Web:* www.jpflooring.com	West Chester	OH	45069	513-346-4300	
Junior's Bldg Materials Inc 7574 Battlefield Pkwy *Web:* www.juniorsbuildingmaterials.com	Ringgold	GA	30736	706-937-3400	937-4100
Lampert Yards Inc 1850 Como Ave *Web:* lampertlumber.com	Saint Paul	MN	55108	651-695-3600	695-3601
Len-Co Lumber Corp 1445 Seneca St *TF:* 800-258-4585 ■ *Web:* www.lencobuffalo.com	Buffalo	NY	14210	716-822-0243	822-1821
Liese Lumber Company Inc 319 E Main St *Web:* www.lieselumber.com	Belleville	IL	62220	618-234-0105	
Linen Chest Inc 4455 AutoRt Des Laurentides *TF:* 800-363-3832 ■ *Web:* www.linenchest.com	Laval	QC	H7L5X8	514-341-7077	
Lowe's Cos Inc 1000 Lowe's Blvd *NYSE:* LOW ■ *TF:* 800-445-6937 ■ *Web:* www.lowes.com	Mooresville	NC	28117	704-758-1000	
Lowe's Home Centers Inc PO Box 1111 *TF:* 800-445-6937 ■ *Web:* www.lowes.com	North Wilkesboro	NC	28656	800-445-6937	
Manta Group Ltd, The 1300-350 Bay St *TF:* 866-626-8247 ■ *Web:* www.mantaconsulting.com	Toronto	ON	M5H2S6	416-483-5166	
MarJam Supply Co Inc 20 Rewe St *Web:* www.marjam.com	Brooklyn	NY	11211	718-388-6465	989-0029
Marson & Marson Lumber Inc PO Box 218 *Web:* www.marsonandmarson.com	Leavenworth	WA	98826	509-548-5829	548-6372
Martin Door Manufacturing Inc 2828 South 900 West *TF:* 800-388-9310 ■ *Web:* www.martindoor.com	Salt Lake City	UT	84119	801-973-9310	688-8182
Matthew Hall Lumber Co 127 Sixth Ave N *Web:* www.mathewhall.com	Saint Cloud	MN	56302	320-252-1920	
McCoy's Bldg Supply 1350 IH 35 N *Web:* www.mccoys.com	San Marcos	TX	78666	512-353-5400	
Menard Inc 5101 Menard Dr *Web:* www.menards.com	Eau Claire	WI	54703	715-876-5911	876-2868
Montalbano Lumber Company Inc 1309 Houston Ave *Web:* www.montalbanolumber.com	Houston	TX	77007	713-228-9011	228-8222
National Lumber 71 Maple St *TF:* 800-370-9663 ■ *Web:* www.national-lumber.com	Mansfield	MA	02048	508-339-8020	339-4518
Northern Lights Enterprises Inc 3474 Andover Rd *Web:* www.northernlightscandles.com	Wellsville	NY	14895	585-593-1200	
Northern Tool & Equipment Co 2800 Southcross Dr W *TF Cust Svc:* 800-222-5381 ■ *Web:* www.northerntool.com	Burnsville	MN	55306	952-894-9510	894-1020
Olshan Lumber Co PO Box 1274 *Web:* www.olshanlumber.com	Houston	TX	77251	713-225-5551	220-9400
Orchard Supply Hardware 6450 Via del Oro *Web:* www.osh.com	San Jose	CA	95119	408-281-3500	
Pandel Inc 21 River Dr *TF:* 800-537-3868 ■ *Web:* www.pandel.com	Cartersville	GA	30120	770-382-1034	
Paramount Builders Inc 501 Central Dr *TF:* 888-340-9002 ■ *Web:* www.paramountbuilders.com	Virginia Beach	VA	23454	757-340-9000	
Pilgrim Home & Hearth LLC 5600 Imhoff Dr Ste G *Web:* www.pilgrimhearth.com	Concord	CA	94520	707-746-1200	
Preston Feather Building Ctr PO Box 637 *Web:* www.prestonfeather.com	Petoskey	MI	49770	231-347-2501	
Preverco Inc 285 Rue De Rotterdam *TF:* 877-667-2725 ■ *Web:* www.preverco.com	Saint-augustin-de-desmaures	QC	G3A2E5	418-878-8930	
Reisterstown Lumber Co, The PO Box 337 *TF:* 800-289-8739 ■ *Web:* www.reisterstownlumber.com	Reisterstown	MD	21136	410-833-1300	833-6803
Rocky Mountain Prestress 5801 Pecos St *Web:* www.rmpprestress.com	Denver	CO	80221	303-480-1111	
RONA Inc 220 Ch du Tremblay *TSE:* RON ■ *TF:* 877-599-5900 ■ *Web:* www.rona.ca	Boucherville	QC	J4B8H7	514-599-5100	
Seigle's 1331 Davis Rd *Web:* www.seigles.com	Elgin	IL	60123	847-742-2000	697-6521
Shane Homes Ltd 5661 Seventh St NE *Web:* www.shanehomes.com	Calgary	AB	T2E8V3	403-536-2200	
Simonson Properties Co 535 1st St NE *TF:* 888-843-8789 ■ *Web:* www.simonson-lumber.com	Saint Cloud	MN	56304	320-252-9385	
Sleep Country Canada LP 140 Wendell Ave *Web:* www.sleepcountry.ca	North York	ON	M9N3R2	416-242-4774	
Sliters PO Box 130 *Web:* www.sliters.com	Somers	MT	59932	406-857-3306	857-3369
Sneades Ace Home Center Inc 1750 Prosper Ln *Web:* acehardware.com	Owings	MD	20736	410-257-2963	
Solutioninc Technologies Ltd 5692 Bloomfield St *TF:* 888-496-2221 ■ *Web:* www.solutioninc.com	Halifax	NS	B3K1T2	902-420-0077	
Stanton Carpet Corp 211 Robbins Ln *TF:* 888-809-2989 ■ *Web:* www.stantoncarpet.com	Syosset	NY	11791	516-822-5878	
Star Lumber & Supply 325 S W St *Web:* www.starlumber.com	Wichita	KS	67213	316-942-2221	
Stenerson Bros Lumber Co 1702 First Ave N *Web:* www.stenersonlumber.com	Moorhead	MN	56560	218-233-3437	233-2819
Stratford Building Supply Inc 215 Railroad St *Web:* stratfordbuilding.com	Stratford	WI	54484	715-687-4125	
Sutherland Lumber Co 4000 Main St *Web:* www.sutherlands.com	Kansas City	MO	64111	816-756-3000	360-2195
Tri Supply Co 7410 Eastex Fwy *Web:* www.trisupplyhometeam.com	Beaumont	TX	77708	409-835-7966	
True Value Co 8600 W Bryn Mawr Ave *Web:* www.truevaluecompany.com	Chicago	IL	60631	773-695-5000	
Viola Bros Inc 180 Washington Ave *Web:* www.violabros.com	Nutley	NJ	07110	973-667-7000	667-2048
Watson Building Supplies Inc 50 Royal Group Crescent Unit 2 *Web:* www.watsonbuildingsupplies.com	Vaughan	ON	L4H1X9	905-669-1898	
WE Aubuchon Company Inc 95 Aubuchon Dr *TF:* 800-431-2712 ■ *Web:* www.hardwarestore.com	Westminster	MA	01473	978-874-0521	874-2096
Wheelwright Lumber Co 3127 S Midland Dr *Web:* www.wheelwrightlumberco.com	Ogden	UT	84401	801-627-0850	
Williams Lumber & Home Centers 6760 Rt 9 *Web:* www.williamslumber.com	Rhinebeck	NY	12572	845-876-7011	

365 HOME INSPECTION SERVICES

Company	City	State	Zip	Phone	Fax
A2Z Field Services LLC 7450 Industrial Pkwy Ste 105 *Web:* www.a2zfieldservices.com	Plain City	OH	43064	614-873-0211	
AmeriSpec Inc 3839 Forest Hill Irene Rd *TF:* 877-769-5217 ■ *Web:* www.amerispec.com	Memphis	TN	38125	901-820-8500	
BrickKicker Inc 849 N Ellsworth St *Fax Area Code: 630 ■ *TF:* 800-821-1820 ■ *Web:* www.brickkicker.com	Naperville	IL	60563	800-821-1820	420-2270*
Digital Inspections 804 Nw Buchanan Ave Ste A *Web:* www.digitalinspections.com	Corvallis	OR	97330	541-752-7233	
EVS-US Inc 319 Garlington Rd Ste B4 *Web:* www.evs-sm.com	Greenville	SC	29615	864-288-9777	
Field Service Express Inc 3336 E 32nd St Ste 208 *Web:* fsx.com	Tulsa	OK	74135	918-744-9679	
HomeTeam Inspection Service Inc 575 Chamber Dr *Fax Area Code: 513 ■ *TF:* 800-598-5297 ■ *Web:* www.hometeam.com	Milford	OH	45150	800-598-5297	831-6010*
HouseMaster 92 E Main St Ste 301 *TF:* 800-526-3939 ■ *Web:* www.housemaster.com	Somerville	NJ	08876	732-469-6565	469-7405
Infralogix 1315 Jamestown Rd Ste 201 *Web:* www.infralogix.com	Williamsburg	VA	23185	757-229-2965	
Insparisk LLC 71-19 80th St Ste 8205 *TF:* 888-464-6772 ■ *Web:* www.insparisk.com	Glendale	NY	11385	888-464-6772	
Inspection Depot Inc 7700 Sq Lk Blvd Unit 2 *Web:* www.inspectiondepot.com	Jacksonville	FL	32256	904-425-0001	
iv3 Solutions Corp 50 Minthorn Blvd Ste 301 *TF:* 877-995-2651 ■ *Web:* www.iv3solutions.com	Markham	ON	L3T7X8	877-995-2651	
Koury Engineering & Testing Inc 14280 Euclid Ave *Web:* www.kouryengineering.com	Chino	CA	91710	310-851-8685	
Metalcare Inspection Services Inc 291 Macalpine Cres *Web:* metalcare.com	Fort Mcmurray	AB	T9H4Y4	780-715-1889	
Milrose Consultants Inc 498 Seventh Ave *Web:* www.milrose.com	New York	NY	10018	212-643-4545	

				Phone	Fax
National Property Inspections Inc (NPI) 9375 Burt St Ste 201 *Fax Area Code: 800 ■ TF: 800-333-9807	Omaha	NE	68114	402-333-9807	933-2508*
Parc Environmental 2706 S Railroad Ave Web: parcenvironmental.com	Fresno	CA	93725	559-233-7156	
Quality Control Inspection Inc 40 Tarbell Ave. Web: qcigroup.com	Cleveland	OH	44146	440-359-1900	
Remote Access Technology Inc 61 Atlantic St TF: 877-356-2728 ■ Web: www.rat.ca	Dartmouth	NS	B2Y4P4	902-434-4405	
Southwest Inspection & Testing 441 Commercial Way Web: www.southwesttesting.com	La Habra	CA	90631	562-941-2990	
TesTex Inc 535 Old Frankstown Rd Web: www.testex-ndt.com	Pittsburgh	PA	15239	412-798-8990	
World Inspection Network International Inc 12345 Lk City Way NE Ste 365 TF: 800-309-6753 ■ Web: www.wini.com	Seattle	WA	98125	800-309-6753	

366 HOME SALES & OTHER DIRECT SELLING

				Phone	Fax
4Life Research 9850 South 300 West TF Sales: 888-454-3374 ■ Web: www.4life.com	Sandy	UT	84070	801-256-3102	562-3611
Acquireo.com 14584 Baseline Ave Ste 300142 Web: www.acquireo.com	Fontana	CA	92336	909-266-0840	
Advocare International Lp 2801 Summit Ave. TF: 800-542-4800	Plano	TX	75074	972-665-5800	
Affiliate Venture Group Inc 11325 Sadler Green Ln. Web: www.affiliateventuregroup.com	Glen Allen	VA	23060	804-501-9411	
Alpine Valley Water Company Inc 10341 Julian Dr Web: www.alpinevalleyps.com	Cincinnati	OH	45215	513-672-3400	
Amway Corp 7575 Fulton St E TF: 800-253-6500 ■ Web: www.amway.com	Ada	MI	49355	616-787-4000	787-7550
Arrowsight Inc 45 Kensico Dr 2nd Fl Web: arrowsight.com	Mount Kisco	NY	10549	212-869-8282	
Ataway Exchange 10474 Armstrong St Web: atawayexchange.com	Fairfax	VA	22030	703-934-4700	
Audience Partners LLC 414 Commerce Dr Ste 100 Web: www.audiencepartners.com	Fort Washington	PA	19034	484-928-1010	
Avon Products Inc 1345 Ave of the Americas NYSE: AVP ■ TF Cust Svc: 800-367-2866 ■ Web: www.avon.com	New York	NY	10017	212-282-7000	
Bacarella Transportation Service 225 Masarik Ave Web: www.btxair.com	Stratford	CT	06615	203-375-1180	
Basch Subscriptions Inc 10 Ferry St Ste 429 Web: www.basch.com	Concord	NH	03301	603-229-0662	
Beefeaters Inc 5801 West Side Avenue	North Bergen	NJ	07047	416-438-1108	
Cargo Control USA Inc 911 Fields Dr. Web: www.cargocontrolusa.com	Sanford	NC	27330	919-775-5059	
Chapelwood United Methodist Church 11140 Greenbay St. Web: www.chapelwood.org	Houston	TX	77024	713-465-3467	
Chemready Filter Corp 9594 Velvetleaf Cir	San Ramon	CA	94582	925-735-0414	
Color Me Beautiful 7000 Infantry Ridge Rd Ste 200 *Fax Area Code: 703 ■ TF: 800-265-6763 ■ Web: www.colormebeautiful.com	Manassas	VA	20109	800-265-6763	471-0127*
Colorado Prime Foods 500 Bi-County Blvd Ste 400 *Fax: Cust Svc ■ TF: 800-365-2404 ■ Web: www.reordermenu.com	Farmingdale	NY	11735	631-694-1111	694-4064*
Conklin Company Inc 551 Valley Pk Dr TF: 800-888-8838 ■ Web: www.conklin.com	Shakopee	MN	55379	952-445-6010	496-4281
Consumer Brands LLC 120 Vantis Ste 570 Web: www.consumerbrands.com	Aliso Viejo	CA	92656	949-356-1300	
Corbin Turf & Ornamental Supply 1105 Old Buncombe Rd TF: 800-476-4504 ■ Web: corbinturf.com	Greenville	SC	29617	864-233-2113	
Delaney Educational Enterprises Inc 1455 W Morena Blvd Web: deebooks.com	San Diego	CA	92110	619-275-0063	
Desane & Associates 310 Prospect Ave Apt 134 Web: www.desaneinc.com	Hackensack	NJ	07601	201-342-0909	
Dew-El Corp 10841 Paw Paw Dr TF: 800-443-3935 ■ Web: dew-el.com	Holland	MI	49424	616-396-6554	396-6669
Digital Air Strike Co 932 Hamlin Court Web: digitalairstrike.com	Sunnyvale	CA	94089	408-220-6500	
Eaccess Solutions Inc 407 N Quentin Rd Web: eaccess.com	Palatine	IL	60067	847-991-7190	
EICC Inc 5100 W 41st St Web: www.eiccoalition.org	Cicero	IL	60804	708-496-1170	
Email Co, The 15 Kainona Ave TF: 877-933-6245 ■ Web: theemailcompany.com	Toronto	ON	M3H3H4	877-933-6245	
Eureka Water Co 729 SW Third St. Web: ozarkah2o.com	Oklahoma City	OK	73109	405-235-8474	
F G Quality Supply Inc 41 N Hillside Ave.	Hillside	IL	60162	708-449-0300	
Fabulous Specialties Inc 600 Livingston Ave.	Livingston	NJ	07039	973-535-6300	
Farrar Pump & Machinery Company Inc 1701 S Big Bend Blvd. Web: farrarpump.com	Saint Louis	MO	63117	314-644-1050	
Fleet Feet Inc 406 E Main St Web: fleetfeetsports.com	Carrboro	NC	27510	919-942-3102	
Fosdick Fulfillment Corp 26 Barnes Industrial Park Rd Web: www.fosdickfulfillment.com	North Wallingford	CT	06492	203-269-0211	
Funville Mobile Carnival 415 Plainview Heights Cir Web: funvilleisfun.com	Greeneville	TN	37745	423-638-9818	
Getconnect 14114 Dallas Pkwy Ste 430 TF: 888-200-1831 ■ Web: www.getconnect.com	Dallas	TX	75254	888-200-1831	
Gibraltar Trade Ctr Inc 237 N River Rd Web: www.gibraltartrade.com	Mt Clemens	MI	48043	586-465-6440	
Ginger G 1015 crocker st.	Los angeles	CA	90021	213-765-8397	
Golden Neo-Life Diamite International 3500 Gateway Blvd *Fax Area Code: 510 ■ TF: 800-432-5842 ■ Web: us.gnld.com	Fremont	CA	94538	800-432-5842	657-7563*
Goldshield Elite 1501 Northpoint Pkwy	West Palm Beach	FL	33407	561-615-4701	
Hp2 Inc 1630 E Bethany Home Rd. Web: hp2promo.com	Phoenix	AZ	85016	602-235-9099	
Hunter Events 1686 Union St Ste 305 Web: hunterproductionssf.com	San Francisco	CA	94123	415-563-8704	
iFollo LLC 8461 Trails Dr Web: www.iFollo.com	Park City	UT	84098	435-655-1511	
Image Iv Systems Inc 512 S Varney St TF: 800-473-5424 ■ Web: imageiv.com	Burbank	CA	91502	818-841-0756	
Inbox Group LLC 2100 W Northwest Hwy Ste 114-1135 Web: www.inboxgroup.com	Grapevine	TX	76051	214-530-5972	
Insight Public Sector Inc 444 Scott Dr. Web: www.ips.insight.com	Bloomingdale	IL	60108	630-924-6801	
iSyndica USA Inc 20A Northwest Blvd Ste 190 Web: www.isyndica.com	Nashua	NH	03063	603-452-7671	
It Fitz Tools Inc 2064 Trlwood Dr W	Burleson	TX	76028	817-295-3093	
Janco Supply Company Inc 723 N Highland Ave	Aurora	IL	60506	630-896-4651	
JAZD Markets Inc 3 Dundee Park Ste 102	Andover	MA	01810	978-470-4620	
JR Watkins Inc 150 Liberty St PO Box 5570 TF: 800-243-9423 ■ Web: www.jrwatkins.com	Winona	MN	55987	507-457-3300	452-6723
Kabam Inc 795 Folsom St Ste 600 Web: kabam.com	San Francisco	CA	94107	415-391-0817	
Kaeser & Blair Inc 4236 Grissom Dr TF: 800-642-0790 ■ Web: kaeser-blair.com	Batavia	OH	45103	800-642-0790	
KMA One 6815 Meadowridge Ct TF: 888-500-2536 ■ Web: www.kmaone.com	Alpharetta	GA	30005	770-886-4000	
Kwik Kafe Company Inc 204 Furnace St TF: 800-533-4066 ■ Web: www.kwikkafeco.com	Bluefield	VA	24605	276-322-4691	
Lonestar Badge & Sign 301 Quail Run Web: lonestarbadge.com	Martindale	TX	78655	512-357-2261	
M80 Services Inc 2894 Rowena Ave Web: www.m80im.com	Los Angeles	CA	90039	323-644-7800	
Magnets.com 51 Pacific Ave Ste 4 TF: 866-229-8237 ■ Web: www.magnets.com	Jersey City	NJ	07304	866-229-8237	
Mail Shark 4125 New Holland Rd TF: 888-457-4275 ■ Web: www.themailshark.com	Mohnton	PA	19540	888-457-4275	
Mannatech Inc 600 S Royal Ln Ste 200 NASDAQ: MTEX ■ Web: us.mannatech.com	Coppell	TX	75019	972-471-7400	471-8191
Mary Kay Inc PO Box 799045 *Fax: Cust Svc ■ TF Cust Svc: 800-627-9529 ■ Web: www.marykay.com	Dallas	TX	75379	972-687-6300	687-1608*
MCH Inc 601 E Marshall St. Web: www.mchdata.com	Sweet Springs	MO	65351	660-335-6373	
Melaleuca Inc 3910 S Yellowstone Hwy *Fax Area Code: 888 ■ TF Sales: 800-282-3000 ■ Web: www.melaleuca.com	Idaho Falls	ID	83402	208-522-0700	528-2090*
Mid-West Marketing Inc 239 Hwy 61 Web: mwmktg.espwebsite.com	Bloomsdale	MO	63627	573-483-2577	483-9747
Midwest Railcar Repair Inc 25965 482nd Ave. Web: www.mwrail.com	Brandon	SD	57005	605-582-8300	
Modern Office Methods Inc 4747 Lk Forest Dr. Web: momnet.com	Cincinnati	OH	45242	513-791-0909	
Mt Shasta Spring Water Company Inc 1878 Twin View Blvd TF: 800-922-6227 ■ Web: www.mtshastaspringwater.com	Redding	CA	96003	530-246-8800	
Noevir USA Inc 1095 Main St TF: 800-872-8817 ■ Web: www.noevirusa.com	Irvine	CA	92614	949-660-1111	660-7168
North American Membership Group Inc (NAMG) 12301 Whitewater Dr Web: www.namginc.com	Minnetonka	MN	55343	952-936-9333	
Nutrilite Products Inc 5600 Beach Blvd PO Box 5940 Web: www.nutrilite.com	Buena Park	CA	90621	714-562-6200	736-7610
Office VP Inc 207 Ridge Harbor Dr P.O. Box 401 Web: www.officevp.com	Spicewood	TX	78669	830-693-1429	
OnMark Solutions LLC 27780 Berringer Run Web: www.onmarksolutions.com	Cleveland	OH	44145	440-328-8245	
Pampered Chef Ltd 1 Pampered Chef Ln *Fax Area Code: 630 ■ TF: 888-687-2433 ■ Web: www.pamperedchef.com	Addison	IL	60101	888-687-2433	261-8522*
Partylite Gifts Inc 59 Armstrong Rd TF: 888-999-5706 ■ Web: www.partylite.com	Plymouth	MA	02360	508-830-3100	732-5818
Perfect Parties Usa 147 Summit St Unit 6 Web: www.perfectpartiesusa.com	Peabody	MA	01960	978-977-0500	
Poly Expert Inc 850 ave Munck TF: 877-384-5060 ■ Web: www.polyexpert.com	Laval	QC	H7S1B1	514-384-5060	
PostcardMania 2145 Sunnydale Blvd Bldg 101 TF: 800-628-1804 ■ Web: www.postcardmania.com	Clearwater	FL	33765	800-628-1804	
Princess House Inc 470 Miles Standish Blvd. TF Sales: 800-622-0039 ■ Web: www.princesshouse.com	Taunton	MA	02780	508-823-0711	880-1335
Prism Assoc Inc 9747 Business Park Ave Ste 217 Web: callprism.com	San Diego	CA	92131	858-695-7099	
Private Party Consignments 11344 Interstate 10 E Web: rvconsignment.com	Baytown	TX	77523	281-303-3000	
Qivana 5255 Edgewood Dr TF: 888-874-8262 ■ Web: www.qivana.com	Provo	UT	84604	888-874-8262	
Rak Medical Inc 340 Duquesne Way Web: rakmedical.com	Sewickley	PA	15143	412-741-2880	
Ravenswood Special Events 1100 W Cermak Rd Unit C411 Web: www.ravenswoodevents.com	Chicago	IL	60608	312-633-2600	

Phone | Fax

Razorgator 4216 3/4 Glencoe Ave Marina Del Rey CA 90292 310-481-3400
Web: razorgator.com

Redi-Direct Marketing Inc 5 Audrey Pl Fairfield NJ 07004 973-808-4500
Web: www.redidirect.com

Reliv International Inc
136 Chesterfield Industrial Blvd Chesterfield MO 63005 636-537-9715 537-9753
NASDAQ: RELV ■ *TF:* 800-735-4887 ■ *Web:* www.reliv.com

Rena Ware International Inc
15885 NE 28th St Bellevue WA 98008 425-881-6171 882-7500
Web: www.renaware.com

Repforce Inc 530 Turner Industrial Way Aston PA 19014 610-485-7800
Web: repforce.com

Rexair Inc 50 W Big Beaver Rd Ste 350 Troy MI 48084 248-643-7222 643-7676
Web: www.rainbowsystem.com

S Klahr Inc 45 Randolph Dr Dix Hills NY 11746 631-462-9630

Saladmaster Inc 230 Westway Pl Ste 101 Arlington TX 76018 817-633-3555 633-5544
TF: 800-765-5795 ■ *Web:* www.saladmaster.com

Select Publishing Inc 6417 Normandy Ln Madison WI 53719 608-277-5787
Web: www.selectpub.com

Shaklee Corp 4747 Willow Rd Pleasanton CA 94588 925-924-2000 924-2862
TF: 800-742-5533 ■ *Web:* www.shaklee.com

SK Food Group Inc 4600 37th Ave SW Seattle WA 98126 206-935-8100
TF: 800-722-6290 ■ *Web:* skfoodgroup.com

Smartpak Equine LLC 40 Grissom Rd Ste 500 Plymouth MA 02360 774-773-1000
TF: 888-752-5171 ■ *Web:* www.smartpakequine.com

Specialty Merchandise Corp
996 Flower Glen St Simi Valley CA 93065 805-578-5500
TF Orders: 800-345-4762 ■ *Web:* www.smartlivingcompany.com

Stampin Up 12907 South 3600 West Riverton UT 84065 801-257-5400
Web: stampinup.com

Starfish Junction Productions Llc
226 N Fehr Way Bay Shore NY 11706 631-940-7290
Web: www.starfishjunction.com

StarGreetz Inc 2036 Armacost Ave 2nd Fl Los Angeles CA 90025 310-806-6450
Web: corp.stargreetz.com

Success Motivation International Inc
4567 Lakeshore Dr Waco TX 76710 254-776-9966 776-1230
TF Sales: 888-391-0050 ■ *Web:* www.success-motivation.com

Sunrider International 1625 Abalone Ave Torrance CA 90501 310-781-3808
TF Orders: 888-278-6743 ■ *Web:* www.sunrider.com

Talk Fusion 1319 kingsway rd Brandon FL 33510 813-651-4030
Web: www.talkfusion.com

Tebons Gas & Auto Service Inc
7415 N Harlem Ave Niles IL 60714 847-647-9800
Web: tebonsgas.com

Technifax Office Solutions
3220 Keller Springs Rd Carrollton TX 75006 972-478-2800 478-2812
Web: technifaxdfw.com

Terco Supply 12725 Ross Ave Chino CA 91710 909-628-4694

Thirty-One Gifts LLC 3425 Morse Crossing Columbus OH 43219 614-414-4300
Web: thirtyonegifts.com

Top Dog Express Car Wash
401 S SR 434 Altamonte Springs FL 32714 407-636-9112
Web: topdogexpresscarwash.com

TouchPoint Technologies LLC
2319 Oak Myrtle Ln Ste 104 Wesley Chapel FL 33544 877-898-6824
TF: 877-898-6824 ■ *Web:* www.touchpointtechnologies.com

TouchVision Inc 11095 Knott Ave Ste E Cypress CA 90630 714-886-5300
Web: touchvision.com

Towsleys Inc 1424 Dewey St Manitowoc WI 54220 920-683-7400
Web: www.towsleys.com

Tru-Brew Coffee Service Inc
387 Springdale Ave Hatboro PA 19040 215-441-0110

University Subscription Service
1213 Butterfield Rd Downers Grove IL 60515 630-960-3233 960-3246

Unparalleled Productions Inc
1672 Greenwich St San Francisco CA 94123 415-673-8581
Web: www.unparalleledproductions.com

VC Enterprises Ltd 2025 Olive Ave Sibley IA 51249 712-724-6256

Vector Marketing Co 322 Houghton Ave Olean NY 14760 800-828-0448
TF: 800-828-0448 ■ *Web:* www.vectoroncampus.com

Verndale Corp, The 28 Damrell St Ste 300 Boston MA 02127 866-942-8376
TF: 866-942-8376 ■ *Web:* www.verndale.com

Vita Motivator Company Inc PO Box 8139 Englewood NJ 07631 201-530-0277

Vorwerk USA Company LP 1964 Corporate Sq Longwood FL 32750 407-830-9988
Web: www.vorwerk.com

We Buy Guitars LLC 705 Bedford Ave Bellmore NY 11710 516-221-0563
Web: webuyguitars.org

WEBCARGO Inc
800 Pl Victoria
Ste 2603 Tour de la bourse CP 329 Montreal QC H4Z1G8 866-905-0123
TF: 866-905-0123 ■ *Web:* www.webcargo.net

WebEyeCare Inc 10 Canal St Ste 302 Bristol PA 19007 888-536-7480
TF: 888-536-7480 ■ *Web:* www.webeyecare.com

Winfield Micro Systems Inc
2333 Wisconsin Ave Downers Grove IL 60515 630-960-5515
Web: winfieldmicro.com

YourAreaCode LLC 6242 28th St Ste B Grand Rapids MI 49546 616-622-2000
Web: www.yourareacode.com

367 HOME WARRANTY SERVICES

Phone | Fax

American Home Shield
889 Ridge Lake Blvd PO Box 851 Memphis TN 38120 901-537-8000 537-8005
TF: 800-776-4663 ■ *Web:* www.ahs.com

Asset Marketing Systems Insurance Services LLC
15050 Ave of Science San Diego CA 92128 888-303-8755
TF: 888-303-8755 ■ *Web:* amsfmo.com

Blue Ribbon Home Warranty Inc
95 S Wadsworth Blvd Lakewood CO 80226 303-986-3900 986-3152
TF: 800-571-0475 ■ *Web:* blueribbonhomewarranty.com

Cross Country Home Services
1625 NW 136th Ave Ste 200 Sunrise FL 33323 954-845-2468 845-2264
TF Cust Svc: 800-778-8000 ■ *Web:* www.cchs.com

Cypress Care Inc 2736 Meadow Church Rd Ste 300 Duluth GA 30097 800-419-7191
TF: 800-419-7191 ■ *Web:* www.cypresscare.com

First American Home Buyers Protection Corp
7833 Haskell Ave PO Box 10180 Van Nuys CA 91410 818-781-5050 772-1151*
**Fax Area Code: 800* ■ *TF:* 800-444-9030 ■ *Web:* www.homewarranty.firstam.com

Home Security of America Inc
310 N Midvale Blvd Madison WI 53705 800-367-1448 638-1741*
**Fax Area Code: 877* ■ *TF:* 800-367-1448 ■ *Web:* www.onlinehsa.com

Warrantech Corp Inc 2200 Hwy 121 Bedford TX 76021 817-785-6601
TF: 800-833-8801 ■ *Web:* www.warrantech.com

368 HORSE BREEDERS

See Also Livestock Improvement Services p. 1718

Phone | Fax

AgSource Cooperative Services Inc
135 Enterprise Dr Post Office Box 930230 Verona WI 53593 608-845-1900
Web: www.agsource.com

Airdrie Stud Inc
2641 Old Frankfort Pk PO Box 487 Midway KY 40347 859-873-7270 873-6140
Web: www.airdriestud.com

Ashford Stud 5095 Frankfort Rd Versailles KY 40383 859-873-7088 879-5756
Web: www.coolmore.com

Claiborne Farm 703 Winchester Rd Paris KY 40361 859-233-4252 987-0008
Web: www.clabornefarm.com

Country Life Farm 319 Old Joppa Rd Bel Air MD 21014 410-879-1952 879-6207
Web: www.countrylifefarm.com

Darby Dan Farm 3225 Old Frankfort Pk Lexington KY 40510 859-254-0424 281-6612
TF: 888-321-0424 ■ *Web:* www.darbydan.com

Gainesway Farm 3750 Paris Pk Lexington KY 40511 859-293-2676 299-9371
Web: www.gainesway.com

Glencrest Farm 1576 Moores Mill Rd PO Box 4468 Midway KY 40347 859-233-7032 233-9404
TF: 800-903-0136 ■ *Web:* www.glencrest.com

Grant's Farm 10501 Gravois Rd Saint Louis MO 63123 314-843-1700
Web: anheuser-busch.com

Lancaster DHIA 1592 Old Line Rd Manheim PA 17545 717-665-5960
Web: www.lancasterdhia.com

Lane's End Farm 1500 Midway Rd PO Box 626 Versailles KY 40383 859-873-7300 873-3746
Web: www.lanesend.com

Margaux Farm LLC
596 Moores Mill Rd PO Box 4220 Midway KY 40347 859-846-4433 846-4486
Web: www.margauxfarm.com

Mill Ridge Farm 2800 Bowman Mill Rd Lexington KY 40513 859-231-0606 255-6010
TF: 800-950-6397 ■ *Web:* www.millridge.com

Millford Farm 4852 Midway Rd PO Box 4351 Midway KY 40347 859-846-4705 846-4226
Web: www.millford.com

Northview Stallion Station
55 Northern Dancer Dr Chesapeake City MD 21915 410-885-2855
Web: www.northviewstallions.com

Old Frankfort Stud 360 Watts Ferry Rd Frankfort KY 40601 859-233-1717

Pin Oak Stud
830 Grassy Spring Rd PO Box 68 Versailles KY 40383 859-873-1420 873-2391
Web: www.pinoakstud.com

Pork Champ Llc 1136 Coldicott Hill Rd Lucasville OH 45648 740-493-2164
Web: ringlerenergy.com

Stone Farm 200 Stoney Pt Rd Paris KY 40361 859-987-3737 987-1474
Web: www.stonefarm.com

Sugar Maple Farm 5 Sugar Ln Poughquag NY 12570 845-221-0575

Three Chimneys Farm PO Box 114 Midway KY 40347 859-873-7053 873-5723
Web: www.threechimneys.com

Vinery Kentucky LLC 4241 Spurr Rd Lexington KY 40511 859-455-9388 455-9588

Wimbledon Farm 1725 Walnut Hill Rd Lexington KY 40515 859-272-0636 271-1435

Windfall Farms 4710 Flying Paster Ln Paso Robles CA 93446 805-239-0711

Windfields Farm 2525 DeLong Rd Lexington KY 40515 859-273-3050 273-3035

WinStar Farm LLC 3001 Pisgah Pk Versailles KY 40383 859-873-1717 873-1612
Web: www.winstarfarm.com

369 HORTICULTURAL PRODUCTS GROWERS

See Also Garden Centers p. 2349; Seed Companies p. 3176

Phone | Fax

Ades & Gish Nurseries
2222 N Twin Oaks Vly Rd San Marcos CA 92069 760-410-0400 410-0433
Web: www.agnurseries.com

Aldershot of New Mexico Inc
4884 S Main St Mesilla Park NM 88047 575-523-8621

Alex R Masson Inc 12819 198th St Linwood KS 66052 913-301-3281 301-3288
Web: www.armasson.com

Altman Specialty Plants Inc
3742 Blue BiRd Canyon Rd Vista CA 92084 760-744-8191 744-8835
TF: 800-773-7667 ■ *Web:* www.altmanplants.com

Ameri-Cal Floral Inc
94 San Miguel Canyon Rd Watsonville CA 95076 831-728-4205
Web: www.americal.com

Aris Horticulture Inc 115 Third St SE Barberton OH 44203 800-232-9557 745-3098*
**Fax Area Code: 330* ■ *TF:* 800-232-9557 ■ *Web:* www.arishort.com

Battlefield Farms Inc 23190 Clarks Mtn Rd Rapidan VA 22733 800-722-0744 854-6486*
**Fax Area Code: 540* ■ *TF:* 800-722-0744 ■ *Web:* www.battlefieldfarms.com

Bay City Flower Company Inc
2265 Cabrillo Hwy S Half Moon Bay CA 94019 650-726-5535
TF Sales: 800-399-5858 ■ *Web:* www.baycityflower.com

Bell Nursery Inc 3838 Bell Rd Burtonsville MD 20866 301-421-1500
Web: www.bellnursery.com

Bettinger Farms Inc 11602 Frankfort Rd Swanton OH 43558 419-829-2771 202-2125*
**Fax Area Code: 567* ■ *TF:* 855-629-7661 ■ *Web:* bettingersgreenhouse.com

Blue Ridge Growers Inc
21409 Germanna Hwy Stevensburg VA 22741 540-399-1636
Web: www.blueridgegrowers.com

Company / Address	City	State	Zip	Phone	Fax
Burgett Floral Inc 868 Fuller NE *TF:* 800-404-2999 ■ *Web:* www.burgettflorist.com	Grand Rapids	MI	49503	616-456-1999	
California Pajarosa 133 Hughes Rd PO Box 684 *Web:* www.pajarosa.com	Watsonville	CA	95077	831-722-6374	722-1316
CD Ford & Sons Inc PO Box 300 *TF:* 800-383-4661 ■ *Web:* www.cdford.com	Geneseo	IL	61254	309-944-4661	944-3703
Color Spot Nurseries Inc 2575 Olive Hill Rd **Fax Area Code:* 800 ■ *TF:* 800-554-4065 ■ *Web:* www.colorspot.com	Fallbrook	CA	92028	760-695-1480	250-5135*
Colorama Wholesale Nursery 1025 N Todd Ave *Web:* coloramanursery.com	Azusa	CA	91702	626-969-3585	
Costa Nursery Farms Inc 21800 SW 162nd Ave *TF:* 800-327-7074 ■ *Web:* www.costafarms.com	Miami	FL	33170	800-327-7074	
Cuthbert Greenhouses Inc 4900 Hendron Rd *TF:* 800-321-1939 ■ *Web:* cuthbertgreenhouse.com	Groveport	OH	43125	614-836-3866	836-3767
Dallas Johnson Greenhouse Inc 2802 Twin City Dr *TF:* 800-445-4794 ■ *Web:* www.djgreenhouses.com	Council Bluffs	IA	51501	712-366-0407	
Dan Schantz Farm & Greenhouses LLC 8025 Spinnerstown Rd *TF:* 800-451-3064 ■ *Web:* www.danschantz.com	Zionsville	PA	18092	610-967-2181	
DeLeon's Bromeliads Co 13745 SW 216th St *TF:* 800-448-8649 ■ *Web:* www.deleons4color.com	Miami	FL	33170	305-238-6028	235-2354
Dramm & Echter Inc 1150 Quail Gardens Dr *TF:* 800-854-7021 ■ *Web:* www.drammechter.com	Encinitas	CA	92024	760-436-0188	436-2974
Ever-Bloom Inc 4701 Foothill Rd *TF:* 800-388-8112 ■ *Web:* www.ever-bloom.com	Carpinteria	CA	93013	805-684-5566	
Farmers West 5300 Foothill Rd *TF:* 800-549-0085 ■ *Web:* www.farmerswest.com	Carpinteria	CA	93013	805-684-5531	684-1528
Garden State Growers 99 Locust Grove Rd *TF:* 800-288-8484 ■ *Web:* www.gardenstategrowers.com	Pittstown	NJ	08867	908-730-8888	730-6676
Green Circle Growers Inc 51051 US Hwy 20 *Web:* www.greencirclegrowers.com	Oberlin	OH	44074	440-775-1411	774-1465
Green Valley Floral Co 24999 Potter Rd *TF:* 800-228-1255 ■ *Web:* www.greenvalleyfloral.com	Salinas	CA	93908	831-424-7691	424-4473
Greenleaf Nursery Co 28406 Hwy 82 **Fax Area Code:* 800 ■ *TF:* 800-331-2982 ■ *Web:* www.greenleafnursery.com	Park Hill	OK	74451	918-457-5172	407-5550*
Harts Nursery of Jefferson Inc 4049 Jefferson-Scio Rd *TF:* 800-356-9335 ■ *Web:* www.hartsnursery.com	Jefferson	OR	97352	541-327-3366	
Ingleside Plantation Nurseries 5870 Leedstown Rd *Web:* inglesidenurseries.com	Oak Grove	VA	22443	804-224-7111	224-2032
Johannes Flowers Inc 4990 Foothill Rd *TF:* 800-365-9476 ■ *Web:* www.johannesflowers.com	Carpinteria	CA	93013	805-684-5686	566-2199
Kerry's Nursery Inc 21840 SW 258th St *TF:* 800-331-9127 ■ *Web:* www.kerrys.com	Homestead	FL	33031	800-331-9127	
Knox Nursery Inc 940 Avalon Rd **Fax Area Code:* 407 ■ *TF:* 800-441-5669 ■ *Web:* www.knoxnursery.com	Winter Garden	FL	34787	800-441-5669	290-1702*
Kocher Flower Growers 950 Brittany Rd	Encinitas	CA	92024	760-436-1458	
Kurt Weiss Greenhouses Inc 95 Main St *TF:* 800-344-7805 ■ *Web:* www.kurtweiss.com	Center Moriches	NY	11934	631-878-2500	878-2553
Layser's Flowers Inc 501 W Washington Ave *Web:* www.laysersflowers.com	Myerstown	PA	17067	717-866-5746	866-6099
Matsui Nursery Inc 1645 Old Stage Rd *TF:* 800-793-6433 ■ *Web:* www.matsuinursery.com	Salinas	CA	93908	831-422-6433	422-2387
McLellan Botanicals 2352 San Juan Rd **Fax Area Code:* 415 ■ *TF:* 800-467-2443 ■ *Web:* www.taisucoamerica.com	Aromas	CA	95004	800-467-2443	543-6836*
Metrolina Greenhouses Inc 16400 Huntersville-Concord Rd *TF:* 800-543-3915 ■ *Web:* www.metrolinagreenhouses.com	Huntersville	NC	28078	704-875-1371	875-6741
Mid American Growers Inc 14240 Greenhouse Ave	Granville	IL	61326	815-339-6831	339-2747
Nurserymen's Exchange 2651 N Cabrillo Hwy *TF General:* 800-227-5229 ■ *Web:* www.rocketfarms.com	Half Moon Bay	CA	94019	650-712-4195	712-4290
Ocean Breeze International (OBI) 3910 Via Real *TF:* 888-715-8888 ■ *Web:* www.oceanbreezeintl.com	Carpinteria	CA	93013	805-684-1747	684-0235
Oglevee Ltd 152 Oglevee Ln	Connellsville	PA	15425	724-628-8360	628-7270
Panzer Nursery Inc 17980 W Baseline Rd *TF:* 888-212-5327 ■ *Web:* www.panzernursery.com	Beaverton	OR	97006	503-645-1185	629-9023
Parks Bros Farm Inc 6733 Parks Rd *TF:* 800-334-5770 ■ *Web:* www.parksbrothers.com	Van Buren	AR	72956	479-474-1125	
Paul Ecke Ranch Inc 527 Encinitas Ste 104 *Web:* www.ecke.com	Encinitas	CA	92024	760-753-1134	
Petitti Garden Centers 24964 Broadway Ave *Web:* www.petittigardencenter.com	Oakwood Village	OH	44146	440-439-6511	439-7736
Post Gardens Inc 21189 Huron River Dr *TF:* 800-834-4630	Rockwood	MI	48173	734-379-9688	
Rockwell Farms Inc 332 Rockwell Farms Rd *TF:* 800-635-6576 ■ *Web:* www.rockwellfarms.com	Rockwell	NC	28138	800-635-6576	
Sedan Floral Inc 406 S School St PO Box 339 *Web:* www.sedanfloral.com	Sedan	KS	67361	620-725-3111	725-5257
Silver Terrace Nurseries Inc 501 N St	Pescadero	CA	94060	650-879-2110	
Smith Gardens Inc 4164 Meridian St Ste 400 *TF:* 800-755-6256 ■ *Web:* www.smithgardens.com	Bellingham	WA	98226	360-733-4671	
Speedling Inc 4447 Old 41 Hwy S **Fax Area Code:* 813 ■ *TF Cust Svc:* 800-881-4769 ■ *Web:* www.speedling.com	Ruskin	FL	33570	800-881-4769	645-8123*
Sun Valley Floral Farms Inc 3160 Upper Bay Rd **Fax Area Code:* 707 ■ *TF:* 800-747-0396 ■ *Web:* www.sunvalleyfloral.com	Arcata	CA	95521	800-747-0396	826-8708*
Sunshine Foliage World 2060 Steve Roberts Special *Web:* www.sunshinefoliageworld.com	Zolfo Springs	FL	33890	863-735-0501	
Van Wingerden International Inc 4112 Haywood Rd *Web:* www.natures-heritage.com	Mills River	NC	28759	828-891-4116	
Westerlay Orchids 3504 Via Real *Web:* www.westerlayorchids.com	Carpinteria	CA	93013	805-684-5411	684-5414
Westland Floral Co 1400 Cravens Ln *Web:* www.westlandfloral.com	Carpinteria	CA	93013	805-684-4011	
White's Nursery & Greenhouses Inc 3133 Old Mill Rd *Web:* www.whitesnursery.com	Chesapeake	VA	23323	757-487-2300	
Woodburn Nursery & Azaleas 13009 McKee School Rd NE *TF Sales:* 888-634-2232 ■ *Web:* www.woodburnnursery.com	Woodburn	OR	97071	503-634-2231	634-2238
Worthington Farms Inc 3661 BallaRds Crossroads Rd *Web:* www.worthingtonfarms.com	Greenville	NC	27834	252-756-3827	756-9442
Young's Plant Farm PO Box 3410 *TF:* 800-304-8609 ■ *Web:* www.youngsplantfarm.com	Auburn	AL	36830	800-304-8609	

370 HOSE & BELTING - RUBBER OR PLASTICS

See Also Automotive Parts & Supplies - Mfr p. 1830

Company / Address	City	State	Zip	Phone	Fax
ABC Industrie PO Box 77 *TF:* 800-426-0921 ■ *Web:* www.abc-industries.net	Warsaw	IN	46581	574-267-5166	267-2045
AdChem Manufacturing Technologies Inc 369 Progress Dr *Web:* www.acmtct.com	Manchester	CT	06042	860-645-0592	
Advanced Technology Products Inc 12740 State Rt 4 *Web:* atp4pneumatics.com	Milford Center	OH	43045	937-349-4055	
Aero Rubber Company Inc 8100 W 185th St **Fax Area Code:* 800 ■ *TF:* 800-662-1009 ■ *Web:* www.aerorubber.com	Tinley Park	IL	60487	708-430-4900	662-4400*
American Hose & Rubber Co 3645 E 44th St *TF:* 800-272-7537 ■ *Web:* amhose.com	Tucson	AZ	85713	520-514-1666	
Ammeraal Beltech USA 7501 N St Louis Ave *TF Cust Svc:* 800-323-4170 ■ *Web:* www.ammeraalbeltech.com	Skokie	IL	60076	847-673-6720	673-6373
Apache Hose & Belting Co Inc 4805 Bowling St SW *TF Sales:* 800-553-5455 ■ *Web:* www.apache-inc.com	Cedar Rapids	IA	52404	319-365-0471	365-2522
Atco Rubber Products Inc 7101 Atco Dr *TF:* 800-877-3828 ■ *Web:* www.atcoflex.com	Fort Worth	TX	76118	817-595-2894	
Atcoflex Inc 14261 172nd Ave *Web:* www.atcoflexinc.com	Grand Haven	MI	49417	616-842-4661	842-4623
Belterra Corp 1638 Fosters Way *TF:* 888-860-5600 ■ *Web:* www.belterra.ca	Delta	BC	V3M6S6	604-540-1950	
Belting Industries Company Inc 20 Boright Ave *TF:* 800-843-2358 ■ *Web:* www.beltingindustries.com	Kenilworth	NJ	07033	908-272-8591	272-3825
Carlstar Group LLC, The 725 Cool Springs Blvd Ste 500 *TF:* 866-773-2926 ■ *Web:* www.carlstargroup.com	Franklin	TN	37067	615-503-0220	503-0228
Chemprene Inc 483 Fishkill Ave *TF:* 800-431-9981 ■ *Web:* www.chemprene.com	Beacon	NY	12508	845-831-2800	831-4639
Cobon Plastics Corporation 90 S St *TF:* 800-360-1324 ■ *Web:* www.cobonplastics.com	Newark	NJ	07114	973-344-6330	
Coilhose Pneumatics Inc 19 Kimberly Rd *TF:* 800-424-9300 ■ *Web:* www.coilhose.com	East Brunswick	NJ	08816	732-390-8480	390-9693
Colorite Plastics Co 101 Railroad Ave *Web:* tekni-plex.com	Ridgefield	NJ	07657	201-941-2900	
Cooper Tire & Rubber Co 701 Lima Ave *NYSE:* CTB ■ *TF:* 800-854-6288 ■ *Web:* www.coopertire.com	Findlay	OH	45840	419-423-1321	424-4108
Copper State Rubber of Arizona Inc 750 S 59th Ave *Web:* copperstaterubber.com	Phoenix	AZ	85043	602-269-5927	269-8106
Cosmoflex Inc 4142 Industrial Dr	Hannibal	MO	63401	573-221-0242	221-9290
Dormont Manufacturing Co 6015 Enterprise Dr *TF:* 800-367-6668 ■ *Web:* www.dormont.com	Export	PA	15632	800-367-6668	
Dynacraft Co 650 Milwaukee Ave N *Web:* dynacraftnet.com	Algona	WA	98001	253-333-3000	333-3041
Eaton Corp 1111 Superior Ave Eaton Ctr *Web:* www.eaton.com	Cleveland	OH	44114	216-523-5000	
Fenner Drives 311 W Stiegel St *TF Sales:* 800-243-3374 ■ *Web:* www.fennerdrives.com	Manheim	PA	17545	717-665-2421	664-8214
Flexaust Co 1510 Armstrong Rd **Fax Area Code:* 800 ■ *TF:* 800-343-0428 ■ *Web:* www.flexaust.com	Warsaw	IN	46580	574-267-7909	382-8464*
Flexfab LLC 1699 W M-43 Hwy *Web:* www.flexfab.com	Hastings	MI	49058	269-945-2433	945-4802
Freelin-Wade Co 1730 NE Miller St *TF:* 888-373-9233 ■ *Web:* www.freelin-wade.com	McMinnville	OR	97128	503-434-5561	472-1989
Gates Corp 1551 Wewatta St *TF:* 800-709-6001 ■ *Web:* www.gates.com	Denver	CO	80202	303-744-1911	744-4000
Habasit ABT Inc 150 Industrial Pk Rd *TF:* 800-522-2358 ■ *Web:* www.habasit.com	Middletown	CT	06457	860-632-2211	632-1710
Habasit Belting Inc 1400 Clinton St *TF:* 800-325-1585 ■ *Web:* www.habasit.com	Buffalo	NY	14206	716-824-8484	
HBD/Thermoid Inc 1301 W Sandusky Ave *TF:* 800-543-8070 ■ *Web:* www.hbdthermoid.com	Bellefontaine	OH	43311	937-593-5010	593-4354
Industrial Rubber Works 1700 Nicholas Blvd *TF:* 800-852-1855 ■ *Web:* www.abbottrubber.com	Elk Grove Village	IL	60007	847-952-1800	
Jason Industrial Inc 340 Kaplan Dr *Web:* www.jasonindustrial.com	Fairfield	NJ	07004	973-227-4904	227-1651
JGB Enterprises Inc 115 Metropolitan Dr *Web:* www.jgbhose.com	Liverpool	NY	13088	315-451-2770	451-8503
Key Fire Hose Corp (KFH) PO Box 7107 *TF:* 800-447-5666 ■ *Web:* keyhose.com	Dothan	AL	36302	334-671-5532	671-5616
Legg Company Inc 325 E Tenth St **Fax Area Code:* 316 ■ *TF Sales:* 800-835-1003 ■ *Web:* www.leggbelting.com	Halstead	KS	67056	800-835-1003	835-3218*
Lockwood Products Inc 5615 Willow Ln *TF:* 800-423-1625 ■ *Web:* www.loc-line.com	Lake Oswego	OR	97035	503-635-8113	635-2844
Mattracks Systems 202 Cleveland Ave E *TF:* 877-436-7800 ■ *Web:* www.mattracks.com	Karlstad	MN	56732	218-436-7000	
Mercer Rubber Co 350 Rabro Dr *Web:* www.mercer-rubber.com	Hauppauge	NY	11788	631-582-1524	348-0279

				Phone	Fax
Mulhern Belting Inc 148 Bauer Dr *TF:* 800-253-6300 ■ *Web:* www.mulhernbelting.com	Oakland	NJ	07436	201-337-5700	337-6540
NewAge Industries Inc 145 James Way *TF:* 800-506-3924 ■ *Web:* www.newageindustries.com	SouthHampton	PA	18966	215-526-2300	526-2190
Nichirin Tennessee Inc 1620 Old Belfast Rd *Web:* www.nichirincanada.com	Lewisburg	TN	37091	931-359-5709	
Parker Fluid Connectors Group 6035 Parkland Blvd *TF General:* 800-272-7537 ■ *Web:* parker.com	Cleveland	OH	44124	216-896-3000	896-4000
Performance Polymer Technologies Co 8801 Washington Blvd Ste 109 *Web:* www.pptech.com	Roseville	CA	95678	916-677-1414	677-1474
Plastiflex Company Inc 601-C E Palomar St Ste 424 *Web:* www.plastiflex.com	Chula Vista	CA	91911	619-662-8792	
Ro-Lab American Rubber Co Inc 8830 W Linne Rd *TF:* 800-678-0726 ■ *Web:* www.rolabamerican.com	Tracy	CA	95304	209-836-0965	
Rubber Enterprises Inc 2083 Reek Rd *Web:* www.rubberenterprises.com	Imlay City	MI	48444	810-724-2400	
Salem-Republic Rubber Co 475 W California Ave *TF:* 800-686-4199 ■ *Web:* www.salem-republic.com	Sebring	OH	44672	330-938-9801	938-9809
Shuster Corp 4 Wright St *Web:* www.shustercorp.com	New Bedford	MA	02740	508-999-3261	
Snap-Tite Inc 8325 Hessinger Dr *Web:* www.snap-tite.com	Erie	PA	16509	814-838-5700	
Sparks Belting Co 3800 Stahl Dr SE *TF:* 800-451-4537 ■ *Web:* www.sparksbelting.com	Grand Rapids	MI	49546	616-949-2750	949-8518
Swan Hose 1201 Delaware Ave *TF:* 800-848-8707 ■ *Web:* www.swanhose.com	Marion	OH	43302	800-848-8707	
Tigerflex Corp 801 Estes Ave *Web:* tiger-poly.com	Elk Grove Village	IL	60007	847-640-8366	640-8372
Titeflex Corp 603 Hendee St *TF:* 800-765-2525 ■ *Web:* www.titeflex.com	Springfield	MA	01139	413-739-5631	788-7593
Unaflex LLC 1350 S Dixie Hwy E *TF:* 800-327-1286 ■ *Web:* www.unaflex.com	Pompano Beach	FL	33064	954-943-5002	946-3583
US Rubber Corp 211 East Loop 336 *Web:* www.usrubbercorp.com	Conroe	TX	77301	936-756-1977	756-1674
Voss Belting & Specialty Co 6965 N Hamlin Ave *Web:* www.vossbelting.com	Lincolnwood	IL	60712	847-673-8900	673-1408

371 HOSPICES

See Also Specialty Hospitals p. 2527

Alabama

				Phone	Fax
Aliceville Manor 703 17th St Nw *Web:* alicevillemanornursinghome.com	Aliceville	AL	35442	205-373-6307	
HomeCare of East Alabama Medical Ctr 665 Opelika Rd *TF:* 866-542-4768 ■ *Web:* www.lhcgroup.com	Auburn	AL	36830	334-826-3131	
Hospice of Cullman County 1912 Alabama Hwy 157 *Web:* www.crmchospital.com/our_services/all_services/hospice.aspx	Cullman	AL	35058	256-737-2000	
Hospice of Marshall County 408 Martling Rd *TF:* 888-334-9336 ■ *Web:* www.hospicemc.org	Albertville	AL	35951	256-891-7724	891-7754
Hospice of the Valley 240 Johnston St SE *TF:* 877-260-3657 ■ *Web:* www.hospiceofthevalley.net	Decatur	AL	35601	256-350-5585	350-5567
Hospice of West Alabama 3851 Loop Rd *TF:* 877-362-7522 ■ *Web:* hospiceofwestalabama.org	Tuscaloosa	AL	35404	205-523-0101	523-0102
Oakview Manor 929 Mixon School Rd *Web:* www.oakviewmanor.com	Ozark	AL	36360	334-774-2631	

Alaska

				Phone	Fax
Hospice of Anchorage 2612 E Northern Lights Blvd *Web:* www.hospiceofanchorage.org	Anchorage	AK	99508	907-561-5322	561-0334

Alberta

				Phone	Fax
AgeCare Ltd 105 20 Sunpark Plz SE *Web:* www.agecare.ca	Calgary	AB	T2X3T2	403-873-3200	
Carewest 10301 Southport Ln SW Southport Tower *Web:* carewestwebsite.wordpress.com	Calgary	AB	T2W1S7	403-943-8140	

Arizona

				Phone	Fax
Hospice Family Care 1550 S Alma School Rd *Web:* www.hfc-az.com	Mesa	AZ	85210	480-461-3144	844-9711
Hospice of Arizona 19820 N Seventh Ave Ste 130 *TF:* 888-330-8560 ■ *Web:* www.americanhospice.com	Phoenix	AZ	85027	602-678-1313	242-2178
Infinity Hospice Care LLC 5110 N 40th St Ste 107 *Web:* www.infinityhospicecare.com	Phoenix	AZ	85018	602-381-0375	

Arkansas

				Phone	Fax
Arkansas Hospice 14 Parkstone Cir *TF:* 877-257-3400 ■ *Web:* www.arkansashospice.org	North Little Rock	AR	72116	501-748-3333	
Greenhurst Nursing Center 226 Skyler Dr *Web:* greenhurst.net	Charleston	AR	72933	479-965-7373	
Hospice Home Care 2200 S Bowman *TF:* 800-479-1219 ■ *Web:* www.hospicehomecare.com	Little Rock	AR	72211	501-296-9043	296-9978
Hospice of the Ozarks 701 Burnett Dr *Web:* www.baxterregional.org	Mountain Home	AR	72653	870-508-1000	

British Columbia

				Phone	Fax
Baptist Housing 6165 Hwy 17 Ste 125 *Web:* www.baptisthousing.org	Delta	BC	V4K5B8	604-940-1960	
Port Coquitlam Senior Citizens' Housing Society 2111 Hawthorne Ave *Web:* www.hawthornecare.com	Port Coquitlam	BC	V3C1W3	604-941-4051	

California

				Phone	Fax
Agemark Corp 2614 Telegraph Ave *Web:* agemark.com	Berkeley	CA	94704	510-548-6600	
All Saints Health Care 11810 Saticoy St *Web:* www.allsaints-subacute.com	North Hollywood	CA	91605	818-982-4600	
Arcadia Convalescent Hospital Inc 1601 S Baldwin Ave *Web:* www.arcadiahealthcarecenter.com	Arcadia	CA	91007	626-445-2170	
Broncus Medical Inc 1400 N Shoreline Blvd Ste 8 *Web:* www.broncus.com	Mountain View	CA	94043	650-428-1600	
Citrus Valley Hospice 820 N Phillips Ave *Web:* www.cvhp.org/our_facilities/hospice_home_health.aspx	West Covina	CA	91791	626-859-2263	
Community Hospice Inc 4368 Spyres Way *TF:* 866-645-4567 ■ *Web:* www.hospiceheart.org	Modesto	CA	95356	209-578-6300	578-6391
Compass Health Inc 200 S 13th St Ste 208 *Web:* www.compass-health.com	Grover Beach	CA	93433	805-474-7010	
Country Hills Health Care Inc 1580 Broadway *Web:* www.countryhills.com	El Cajon	CA	92021	619-441-8745	
Desert Hospital Hospice of the Desert Communities 1150 N Indian Canyon Dr	Palm Springs	CA	92262	760-323-6642	327-8086
Elizabeth Hospice 150 W Crest St *TF:* 800-797-2050 ■ *Web:* www.elizabethhospice.org	Escondido	CA	92025	760-737-2050	796-3781
Golden State Health Centers Inc 13347 Ventura Blvd *Web:* www.goldenstatehealth.com	Sherman Oaks	CA	91423	818-385-3200	
Hayes Convalescent Hospital 1250 Hayes St *Web:* www.hayesconvalescent.com	San Francisco	CA	94117	415-931-8806	
Hinds Hospice 1616 W Shaw Ste C-1 *TF:* 800-400-4677 ■ *Web:* www.hindshospice.org	Fresno	CA	93711	559-248-8591	222-4782
Hoffmann Hospice of the Valley 8501 Brimhall Rd Bldg 100 *TF:* 888-833-3900 ■ *Web:* www.hoffmannhospice.org	Bakersfield	CA	93312	661-410-1010	410-1110
Hospice by the Bay 1902 Van Ness Ave 2nd Fl *Web:* hospicebythebay.org	San Francisco	CA	94109	415-626-5900	
Hospice By the Bay 17 E Sir Francis Drake Blvd *Web:* www.hospicebythebay.org	Larkspur	CA	94939	415-927-2273	
Hospice Caring Project of Santa Cruz County 940 Disc Dr *Web:* www.hospicesantacruz.org	Scotts Valley	CA	95066	831-430-3000	430-9272
Hospice of Redlands Community Hospital 350 Terracina Blvd *TF:* 888-397-4999 ■ *Web:* redlandshospital.org	Redlands	CA	92373	909-335-5643	
Hospice of San Joaquin 3888 Pacific Ave *Web:* www.hospicesj.org	Stockton	CA	95204	209-957-3888	957-3986
Livingston Memorial Visiting Nurse Assn Hospice 1996 Eastman Ave Ste 101 *TF:* 800-830-8881 ■ *Web:* www.lmvna.org	Ventura	CA	93003	805-642-1608	642-2320
Marina Care Center 5240 Sepulveda Blvd *Web:* www.marinacare.com	Culver City	CA	90230	310-391-7266	
MBK Senior Living Ltd 4 Park Plz Ste 400 *Web:* www.mbkseniorliving.com	Irvine	CA	92614	949-242-1400	
Mission Hospice Inc of San Mateo County 1670 S Amphlett Blvd Ste 300 *Web:* www.missionhospice.org	San Mateo	CA	94402	650-554-1000	554-1001
Seasons Hospice & Palliative Care of California-Orange 750 The City Dr *TF:* 877-508-0644 ■ *Web:* www.seasons.org	Orange	CA	92868	714-980-0900	
Torrance Memorial Home Health & Hospice 3330 Lomita Blvd *Web:* www.torrancememorial.org	Torrance	CA	90505	310-784-3739	
Visiting Nurses 222 E Canon Perdido St	Santa Barbara	CA	93101	805-690-6202	568-5178
VITAS Healthcare Corp of California 990 W 190th St Ste 120 *TF:* 800-582-9533 ■ *Web:* www.vitas.com	Torrance	CA	90502	305-374-4143	
VITAS Healthcare Corp of California 16830 Ventura Blvd Ste 100 *TF:* 800-582-9533 ■ *Web:* www.vitas.com	Los Angeles	CA	91436	818-385-0273	
VITAS Healthcare Corp of California 310 Commerce Ste 200 *Web:* www.vitas.com	Irvine	CA	92602	714-921-2273	
VITAS Healthcare Corp of California 9655 Granite Ridge Dr Ste 300 *TF:* 866-418-4827 ■ *Web:* www.vitas.com	San Diego	CA	92123	858-499-8901	
VITAS Healthcare Corp of San Gabriel Cities 1343 N Grand Ave *TF:* 866-418-4827 ■ *Web:* www.vitas.com	Covina	CA	91724	866-418-4827	
VNA & Hospice of Northern California 1900 Powell St Ste 300 *TF:* 800-698-1273 ■ *Web:* www.suttercareathome.org	Emeryville	CA	94608	510-450-8596	347-6874

	City	State	ZIP	Phone	Fax
VNA & Hospice of Southern California 150 W First St Ste 270 *TF:* 888-357-3574 ■ *Web:* www.vnasocal.org	Claremont	CA	91711	909-624-3574	624-1559
VNA California 6235 River Crest Dr Ste L *Web:* vnacalifornia.org	Riverside	CA	92507	951-413-1200	
West Anaheim Extended Care 645 S Beach Blvd. *Web:* www.westanaheimec.com	Anaheim	CA	92804	714-821-1993	
Woodruff Convalescent 17836 Woodruff Ave *Web:* www.woodruffconvalescent.com	Bellflower	CA	90706	562-925-8457	

Colorado

	City	State	ZIP	Phone	Fax
Centura Home Care & Hospice 1391 Speer Blvd Ste 600 *Web:* www.centurahealthathome.org	Denver	CO	80204	303-561-5000	
Denver Hospice, The 501 S Cherry St Ste 700 *Web:* www.thedenverhospice.org	Denver	CO	80246	303-321-2828	321-7171
Hospice & Palliative Care of Northern Colorado 2726 W 11th St Rd *TF:* 800-564-5563 ■ *Web:* www.hospiceofnortherncolorado.org	Greeley	CO	80634	970-352-8487	475-0037
Hospice & Palliative Care of Western Colorado 2754 Compass Dr Ste 377 *TF:* 866-310-8900 ■ *Web:* www.hopewestco.org	Grand Junction	CO	81506	970-241-2212	257-2400
Hospice of Boulder County 2594 Trlridge Dr E *TF:* 877-986-4766 ■ *Web:* www.trucare.org	Lafayette	CO	80026	303-449-7740	
Mantey Heights Rehabilitation & Care Centre 2825 Patterson Rd *Web:* www.fivestarseniorliving.com/communities/co/grand-junction/mantey-heights-rehabilitation-care-center	Grand Junction	CO	81506	970-242-7356	
New Dawn Memory Care 2000 S Blackhawk St. *Web:* www.newdawnal.com	Aurora	CO	80014	303-997-2929	
Sangre de Cristo Hospice 1207 Pueblo Blvd Way *Web:* socohospice.org	Pueblo	CO	81005	719-542-0032	

Connecticut

	City	State	ZIP	Phone	Fax
Abbott Terrace Health Ctr 135 South Rd *Web:* athenahealthcare.com	Farmington	CT	06032	203-755-4870	
Connecticut Hospice 100 Double Beach Rd **Fax:* Hum Res ■ *Web:* www.hospice.com	Branford	CT	06405	203-315-7500	315-7561*
Hospice of Southeastern Connecticut Inc 227 Dunham St. *TF:* 877-654-4035 ■ *Web:* www.hospicesect.org	Norwich	CT	06360	860-848-5699	848-6898
iCare Management LLC 341 Bidwell St. *Web:* www.icaremanagement.com	Manchester	CT	06040	860-570-2140	
Regional Hospice of Western Connecticut 30 Milestone Rd *Web:* www.danbury.org/hospice	Danbury	CT	06810	203-702-7400	792-1402
Visiting Nurse & Health Services of Connecticut Inc 8 Keynote Dr. *Web:* www.vnhsc.org	Vernon	CT	06066	860-872-9163	
Visiting Nurse & Hospice Care of Southwestern Connecticut 1266 E Main St. *Web:* vnhcsw.org	Stamford	CT	06902	203-276-3000	

Delaware

	City	State	ZIP	Phone	Fax
Compassionate Care Hospice of Delaware 702 Wilmington Ave. *TF General:* 800-219-0092 ■ *Web:* www.cchnet.net	Wilmington	DE	19805	302-993-9090	993-9094
Milton & Hattie Kutz Home Inc, The 704 River Rd. *Web:* kutzhome.org	Wilmington	DE	19809	302-764-7000	

Florida

	City	State	ZIP	Phone	Fax
Angels Unaware Inc, The 4918 W Linebaugh Ave *Web:* www.angelsunaware.com	Tampa	FL	33624	813-963-2529	
Avante Group Inc 4601 Sheridan St Ste 540N *Web:* www.avantecenters.com	Hollywood	FL	33021	954-987-7180	
Avow Hospice Inc 1095 Whippoorwill Ln. *Web:* www.avowcares.org	Naples	FL	34105	239-261-4404	
Bigbend Hospice 1723 Mahan Ctr Blvd *TF:* 800-772-5862 ■ *Web:* www.bigbendhospice.org	Tallahassee	FL	32308	850-878-5310	
Catholic Hospice Inc 14875 NW 77th Ave Ste 100. *Web:* www.catholichealthservices.org	Miami Lakes	FL	33014	305-822-2380	824-0665
Chapters Health System 12973 Telecom Pkwy Ste 100. *TF:* 866-204-8611 ■ *Web:* www.chaptershealth.org	Temple Terrace	FL	33637	813-871-8111	
Community Hospice of Northeast Florida 4266 Sunbeam Rd *TF:* 866-274-6614 ■ *Web:* www.communityhospice.com	Jacksonville	FL	32257	904-268-5200	
Covenant Hospice 5041 N 12th Ave. *TF:* 800-541-3072 ■ *Web:* www.choosecovenant.org/hospice	Pensacola	FL	32504	850-433-2155	202-5803
Gramercy Park Nursing Center Inc 17475 S Dixie Hwy. *Web:* seniorsmanagement.com	Miami	FL	33157	305-255-1045	
Gulfside Hospice Inc 6224 Lafayette St *TF:* 800-561-4883 ■ *Web:* www.ghppc.org	New Port Richey	FL	34652	727-845-5707	
Hope Hospice 9470 HealthPark Cir *TF:* 800-835-1673 ■ *Web:* www.hopehospice.org	Fort Myers	FL	33908	239-482-4673	
Hospice & VNA of the Florida Keys 1319 William St *Web:* www.hospicevna.com	Key West	FL	33040	305-294-8812	
Hospice by the Sea 1531 W Palmetto Pk Rd *TF:* 800-633-2577 ■ *Web:* www.hospice1.org	Boca Raton	FL	33486	561-395-5031	
Hospice Care of South Florida 7270 NW 12th St PH 6	Miami	FL	33126	305-591-1606	591-1618
Hospice of Lake & Sumter Inc 2445 Ln Pk Rd. *TF:* 888-728-6234 ■ *Web:* cshospice.org	Tavares	FL	32778	352-343-1341	
Hospice of Marion County 3231 SW 34th Ave *TF:* 888-482-5018 ■ *Web:* www.hospiceofmarion.com	Ocala	FL	34474	352-873-7400	873-7435
Hospice of Northeast Florida 4266 Sunbeam Rd *TF:* 866-253-6681 ■ *Web:* www.communityhospice.com	Jacksonville	FL	32257	904-268-5200	407-6090
Hospice of Palm Beach County 5300 E Ave *TF:* 800-287-4722 ■ *Web:* www.hpbc.com	West Palm Beach	FL	33407	561-848-5200	863-2955
Hospice of Saint Francis Inc 1250 Grumman Pl Ste B *TF:* 866-269-4240 ■ *Web:* www.hospiceofstfrancis.com	Titusville	FL	32780	321-269-4240	
Hospice of the Comforter 480 W Central Pkwy **Fax:* Admissions ■ *TF:* 877-696-6775 ■ *Web:* www.hospiceofthecomforter.org	Altamonte Springs	FL	32714	407-682-0808	303-0721*
Hospice of the Florida Suncoast 5771 Roosevelt Blvd. *Web:* thehospice.org	Clearwater	FL	33760	727-586-4432	
Hospice of the Treasure Coast 5090 Dunn Rd *TF:* 800-299-4677 ■ *Web:* www.tchospice.org	Fort Pierce	FL	34981	772-462-8900	
Hospice of Volusia/Flagler 3800 Woodbriar Trl	Port Orange	FL	32129	386-322-4701	
Lifepath Hospice 3010 W Azeele St *TF:* 800-209-2200 ■ *Web:* www.chaptershealth.org	Tampa	FL	33609	813-877-2200	872-7037
Lourdes-Noreen Mckeen Residence For Geriatric Care Inc 315 S Flagler Dr *Web:* www.lourdesmckeen.org	West Palm Beach	FL	33401	561-655-8544	
Marrinson Group Inc 1701 NE 26th St *Web:* www.marrinson.com	Fort Lauderdale	FL	33305	954-566-8353	
MorseLife Inc 4847 Fred Gladstone Dr *Web:* www.morselife.org	West Palm Beach	FL	33417	561-471-5111	
Opis Management Resources 10150 Highlands Manor Dr Ste 300 *Web:* www.opismr.com	Tampa	FL	33610	813-558-6600	
Pines of Sarasota Inc 1501 N Orange Ave. *Web:* pinesofsarasota.com	Sarasota	FL	34236	941-365-0250	
Tidewell Hospice 5955 Rand Blvd *TF:* 800-959-4291 ■ *Web:* tidewellhospice.org	Sarasota	FL	34238	941-552-7500	925-0969
Treasure Coast Hospice 1201 SE Indian St *TF:* 800-299-4677 ■ *Web:* www.tchospice.org	Stuart	FL	34997	772-403-4500	
Visiting Nurse Assn of the Treasure Coast 1110 35th Ln *TF:* 800-749-5760 ■ *Web:* www.vnatc.com	Vero Beach	FL	32960	772-567-5551	569-4174
VITAS Healthcare Corp 201 South Biscayne Blvd Ste 400. *TF:* 877-379-8451 ■ *Web:* www.vitas.com	Miami	FL	33131	305-374-4143	
VITAS Healthcare Corp of Central Florida 5151 Adanson St Ste 200 *Web:* www.vitas.com	Orlando	FL	32804	407-875-0028	
VITAS Hospice Care 201 S Biscayne Blvd Ste 400 *TF General:* 800-582-9533 ■ *Web:* www.vitas.com	Miami	FL	33131	305-374-4143	

Georgia

	City	State	ZIP	Phone	Fax
Columbus Hospice 7020 Moon Rd *Web:* www.columbushospice.com	Columbus	GA	31909	706-569-7992	
Heyman HospiceCare 420 E Second Ave *TF:* 800-324-1078 ■ *Web:* www.floyd.org	Rome	GA	30161	706-509-3200	
Hospice Atlanta-Visiting Nurse Health System 1244 Pk Vista Dr. *TF:* 866-374-4776 ■ *Web:* www.vnhs.org	Atlanta	GA	30319	404-869-3000	215-6005
Hospice of NE Georgia Medical Ctr 2150 Limestone Pkwy Ste 222 *TF:* 888-572-3900 ■ *Web:* www.nghs.com	Gainesville	GA	30501	770-533-8888	219-8887
Hospice of Southwest Georgia 114 A Mimosa Dr *TF:* 800-290-6567 ■ *Web:* www.archbold.org	Thomasville	GA	31792	229-584-5500	
Hospice Savannah Inc PO Box 13190. *TF:* 888-355-4911 ■ *Web:* www.hospicesavannah.org	Savannah	GA	31416	912-355-2289	
Marsh's Edge 136 Marsh's Edge Ln *Web:* marshs-edge.com	St. Simons Island	GA	31522	912-291-2000	
Pine Pointe Hospice & Palliative Care 6261 Peak Rd *TF:* 800-211-1084 ■ *Web:* mccg.org	Macon	GA	31210	478-633-5660	633-6247
Trinity Hospital of Augusta 2803 Wrightsboro Rd Ste 38 *TF:* 800-999-6673 ■ *Web:* www.trinityofaugusta.com	Augusta	GA	30909	706-729-6000	
United Hospice of Atlanta 1626 Jeurgens Ct *TF:* 800-222-0321 ■ *Web:* pruitthealth.com	Norcross	GA	30093	770-279-6200	

Hawaii

	City	State	ZIP	Phone	Fax
Convalescent Center of Honolulu 1900 Bachelot St *Web:* ccoh.us	Honolulu	HI	96817	808-531-5302	
Hospice Hawaii 860 Iwilei Rd *Web:* www.hospicehawaii.org	Honolulu	HI	96817	808-924-9255	922-9161
Hospice of Hilo 1011 Waianuenue Ave *Web:* www.hospiceofhilo.org	Hilo	HI	96720	808-969-1733	969-4863
St. Francis Healthcare Systems 2226 Liliha St PO Box 29700 *Web:* www.stfrancishawaii.org	Honolulu	HI	96820	808-547-6883	

Idaho

	City	State	ZIP	Phone	Fax
Life's Doors Hospice 420 S Orchard St	Boise	ID	83705	208-344-6500	344-6590

Illinois

Phone | Fax

Advocate Hospice
1441 Branding Ave Ste 200 .... Downers Grove IL 60515 630-963-6800 963-6877
Web: www.advocatehealth.com

Big Meadows 1000 Longmoor Ave .... Savanna IL 61074 815-273-2238
Web: www.bigmeadows.biz

Blessing Health System PO Box 7005 .... Quincy IL 62305 217-223-1200
Web: www.blessinghospital.org

Carle Hospice 611 W Park St .... Urbana IL 61801 217-383-3311
TF: 800-239-3620 ■ *Web:* www.carle.org

Clare Oaks 825 Carillon Dr .... Bartlett IL 60103 630-372-1983
Web: www.clareoaks.com

CNS Home Health & Hospice
690 E N Ave Ste 100.................... Carol Stream IL 60188 630-665-7000
Web: www.cnshomehealth.org

Enlivant 330 N Wabash Ave Ste 3700.................... Chicago IL 60611 312-725-7000
Web: www.enlivant.com

Family Hospice of Belleville Area
5110 W Main St .... Belleville IL 62226 618-277-1800 277-1074
Web: www.familyhospice.org

Harbor Light Hospice
800 Roosevelt Rd Bldg C Ste 206.................... Glen Ellyn IL 60137 630-300-3716 942-0118
TF: 800-419-0542 ■ *Web:* harborlighthospice.com

Harmony Nursing & Rehabilitation Center Inc
3919 W Foster Ave .... Chicago IL 60625 773-588-9500
Web: www.harmonychicago.com

Holly Hill Nursing Home 203 Lafayette St .... Anna IL 62906 618-833-3322

Hospice of Kankakee Valley Inc
482 Main St Nw .... Bourbonnais IL 60914 815-939-4141
TF: 855-871-4695 ■ *Web:* hkvcares.org

Hospice of Lincolnland 1000 Health Ctr Dr.................... Mattoon IL 61938 800-454-4055 347-7197*
**Fax Area Code:* 217 ■ *TF:* 800-454-4055 ■ *Web:* www.sarahbush.org/hospice

Hospice of Southern Illinois
305 S Illinois St .... Belleville IL 62220 618-235-1703
TF: 800-233-1708 ■ *Web:* hospice.org

Joliet Area Community Hospice
250 Water Stone Cir .... Joliet IL 60431 815-740-4104 740-4107
TF: 800-360-1817 ■ *Web:* www.joliethospice.org

Little Company of Mary Home Based Services
9800 SW Hwy.................... Oak Lawn IL 60453 708-229-4663 499-5975
Web: www.lcmh.org

Maple Lawn Homes 700 N Main St .... Eureka IL 61530 309-467-2337
Web: www.maple-lawn.com

Northwoods Care Centre 2250 Pearl St .... Belvidere IL 61008 815-544-0358
Web: www.northwoodscare.com

Oak Trace 200 Village Dr.................... Downers Grove IL 60516 630-769-6100
Web: www.lifespacecommunities.com/chicago-senior-living/downers-grove

OSF Hospice 2265 W Altorfer Dr .... Peoria IL 61615 800-673-5288 683-7855*
**Fax Area Code:* 309 ■ *TF:* 800-673-5288 ■ *Web:* www.osfhealthcare.org/services/home-care

Petersen Health Care Inc 830 W Trlcreek Dr .... Peoria IL 61614 309-691-8113
Web: www.petersenhealthcare.net

Rainbow Hospice 444 N NW Hwy Ste 145 .... Park Ridge IL 60068 847-685-9900 685-6390
Web: www.rainbowhospice.org

River Bluff Nursing Home 4401 N Main St.................... Rockford IL 61103 815-877-8061
Web: rbnh.org

Smith Crossing 10501 Emilie Ln Ofc.................... Orland Park IL 60467 708-326-2300
Web: smithcrossing.org

Unity Hospice 700 S Clinton St Ste 210 .... Chicago IL 60607 312-427-6000 427-6004
TF: 888-949-1188 ■ *Web:* www.unityhospice.com

Victorian Village 12600 Renaissance Cir.................... Homer Glen IL 60491 708-301-0800
Web: www.provinet.com

Wealshire 170 Jamestown Ln .... Lincolnshire IL 60069 224-543-7070

Indiana

Phone | Fax

Center for Hospice Care Inc
111 Sunnybrook Ct.................... South Bend IN 46637 574-243-3100 243-3134
TF: 800-413-9083 ■ *Web:* www.cfhcare.org

Holy Cross Village At Notre Dame Inc
54515 State Rd 933 N PO Box 303.................... Notre Dame IN 46556 574-287-1838
Web: www.holycrossvillage.com

Hosparus Inc 502 Hausfeldt Ln .... New Albany IN 47150 812-945-4596 945-4733
TF: 800-895-5633 ■ *Web:* www.hosparus.org

Hospice of the Calumet Area 600 Superior Ave .... Munster IN 46321 219-922-2732 922-1947
TF: 888-303-0180 ■ *Web:* www.hospicecalumet.org

Iowa

Phone | Fax

Cedar Valley Hospice
2101 Kimball Ave Ste 401 .... Waterloo IA 50702 319-272-2002 272-2071
TF: 800-617-1972 ■ *Web:* www.cvhospice.org

Hospice of Siouxland 4300 Hamilton Blvd .... Sioux City IA 51104 712-233-4100 233-1123
TF: 800-383-4545 ■ *Web:* www.hospiceofsiouxland.com

Luther Manor 3131 Hillcrest Rd.................... Dubuque IA 52001 563-588-1413
Web: www.luthermanor.com

Mercy Medical Center North Iowa
1000 4th St SW .... Mason City IA 50401 641-428-6208
TF: 800-297-4719 ■ *Web:* www.mercynorthiowa.com

Kansas

Phone | Fax

Bethesda Home 408 E Main St .... Goessel KS 67053 620-367-2291
Web: www.bethesdahome.org

Harry Hynes Memorial Hospice 313 S Market St........ Wichita KS 67202 316-265-9441 265-6066
TF: 800-767-4965 ■ *Web:* www.hynesmemorial.org

Phone | Fax

Hilltop Lodge Retirement Community
815 N Independence.................... Beloit KS 67420 785-738-3516
Web: www.hilltoplodgeretirementcomm.org

Hospice of Reno County 1600 N Lorraine.......... Hutchinson KS 67502 620-665-2473 669-5959
TF: 800-267-6891 ■
Web: hutchregional.com/locations-services/hospice-homecare-reno-county

Medicine Lodge Memorial Hospital
710 N Walnut St .... Medicine Lodge KS 67104 620-886-3771
Web: www.mlmh.net

Midland Hospice Care 200 SW Frazier Cir .... Topeka KS 66606 785-232-2044 232-5567
TF: 800-491-3691 ■ *Web:* www.midlandcareconnection.org

Kentucky

Phone | Fax

Community Hospice 1480 Carter Ave.................... Ashland KY 41101 606-329-1890 329-0018
TF: 800-926-6184 ■ *Web:* www.communityhospicecares.org

Davco Rest Home Resident 2526 W 10th St........ Owensboro KY 42301 270-684-1705
Web: www.fernterrace.com

Heritage Hospice
120 Enterprise Dr PO Box 1213 .... Danville KY 40423 859-236-2425
TF: 800-203-6633 ■ *Web:* www.heritagehospice.com

Hospice of Lake Cumberland 100 Pkwy Dr .... Somerset KY 42503 606-679-4389
TF: 800-937-9596 ■ *Web:* www.hospicelc.org

Hospice of Southern Kentucky
5872 Scottsville Rd.................... Bowling Green KY 42104 270-782-3402
TF: 800-344-9479 ■ *Web:* www.hospicesoky.org

Hospice of the Bluegrass
2312 Alexandria Dr.................... Lexington KY 40504 859-276-5344 223-0490
TF: 800-876-6005 ■ *Web:* www.hospicebg.com

Lourdes Homecare & Hospice 2855 Jackson St .... Paducah KY 42003 270-444-2262
TF: 800-870-7460 ■ *Web:* www.elourdes.com

Mountain Manor of Paintsville
1025 Euclid Ave .... Paintsville KY 41240 606-789-5808
Web: www.mountainmanorofpaintsville.com

Saint Anthony's Hospice 2410 S Green St .... Henderson KY 42420 270-826-2326 831-2169
TF: 866-380-2326 ■ *Web:* www.stanthonyshospice.org

Louisiana

Phone | Fax

CommCare Corp
601 Poydras St 2755 Pan American Life Center
.... New Orleans LA 70130 504-324-8950
TF: 877-792-5434 ■ *Web:* www.commcare.com

Forest Haven Nursing & Rehabilitation Center LLC
171 Thrasher Dr.................... Jonesboro LA 71251 318-259-2729
Web: www.foresthavennursingandrehab.com

Hospice of Acadiana
2600 Johnston St Ste 200 .... Lafayette LA 70503 337-232-1234 232-1297
TF: 800-738-2226 ■ *Web:* www.hospiceacadiana.com

Hospice of Baton Rouge 9063 Siegen Ln .... Baton Rouge LA 70810 225-767-4673 769-8113
TF: 888-447-0433 ■ *Web:* www.hospicebr.org

Hospice of South Louisiana 6500 W Main St.......... Houma LA 70360 985-868-3095 868-3910
Web: www.glendalehealthcare.com

Magnolia Estates 1511 Dulles Dr.................... Lafayette LA 70506 337-216-0950
Web: www.centralcontrolmgmt.com

Maryland

Phone | Fax

Calvert County Nursing Center Inc
85 Hospital Rd .... Prince Frederick MD 20678 410-535-2300
Web: calvertcountynursingcenter.org

Carroll Hospice 292 Stoner Ave .... Westminster MD 21157 410-871-8000
Web: carrollcountytimes.com

Coastal Hospice & Palliative Care
2604 Old Ocean City Rd PO Box 1733 .... Salisbury MD 21804 410-742-8732 548-5669
TF: 800-780-7886 ■ *Web:* www.coastalhospice.org

Collingswood Nursing Facilities Inc
299 Hurley Ave.................... Rockville MD 20850 301-762-8900
Web: www.collingswoodnursing.com

Gilchrist Hospice Care
11311 McCormick Rd.................... Hunt Valley MD 21031 443-849-8200
TF: 800-735-2258 ■ *Web:* www.gilchristhospice.org

Hospice of the Chesapeake 445 Defense Hwy.......... Annapolis MD 21401 410-987-2003 837-1505*
**Fax Area Code:* 443 ■ *TF General:* 877-462-1101 ■ *Web:* www.hospicechesapeake.org

Montgomery Hospice 1355 Piccard Dr Ste 100.......... Rockville MD 20850 301-921-4400 921-4433
TF: 800-994-6610 ■ *Web:* www.montgomeryhospice.org

Nexion Health Inc 6937 Warfield Ave.................... Sykesville MD 21784 410-552-4800
Web: www.nexion-health.com

Richey Joseph Hospice 838 N Eutaw St .... Baltimore MD 21201 410-523-2150
Web: www.josephricheyhospice.org

Stella Maris Hospice Care Program
2300 Dulaney Vly Rd .... Timonium MD 21093 410-252-4500 560-9693
Web: www.stellamaris.org

Massachusetts

Phone | Fax

Baystate Visiting Nurse Assn & Hospice
50 Maple St .... Springfield MA 01103 413-794-6411
TF: 800-249-8298 ■ *Web:* www.baystatehealth.org

Community VNA 10 Emory St .... Attleboro MA 02703 508-222-0118 226-8939
TF: 800-220-0110 ■ *Web:* www.communityvna.com

Hospice & Palliative Care of Cape Cod Inc
765 Attucks Ln .... Hyannis MA 02601 508-957-0200 957-0229
TF: 800-642-2423 ■ *Web:* hopehealthco.org

Hospice Care 100 Sylvan Rd.................... Woburn MA 01801 781-569-2888 279-4677
TF: 866-279-7103 ■ *Web:* www.vnahospicecare.org

Hospice Life Care 575 Beech St.................... Holyoke MA 01040 413-533-3923
Web: holyokevna.org

				Phone	Fax
Hospice of the North Shore 75 Sylvan St Ste B102 *TF:* 888-283-1722 ■ *Web:* caredimensions.org	Danvers	MA	01923	978-774-7566	774-4389
Island Terrace Nursing Home 57 Long Point Rd *Web:* islandterrace.com	Lakeville	MA	02347	508-947-0151	
Merrimack Valley Hospice 360 Merrimack St Bldg 9 *Fax Area Code: 978 ■ *TF:* 800-933-5593 ■ *Web:* www.homehealthfoundation.org	Lawrence	MA	01843	800-933-5593	552-4401*
Norwell Knoll Nursing Home 329 Washington St	Norwell	MA	02061	781-659-4901	
Old Colony Hospice 1 Credit Union Way *TF:* 800-370-1322 ■ *Web:* www.oldcolonyhospice.org	Randolph	MA	02368	781-341-4145	297-7345
Penacook Place Foundation Inc 150 Water St *Web:* www.penacookplace.org	Haverhill	MA	01830	978-374-0707	
VNA & Hospice of Cooley Dickinson 168 Industrial Dr *Web:* www.vnaandhospice.org	NorthHampton	MA	01060	413-584-1060	

Michigan

				Phone	Fax
Angela Hospice Home Care 14100 Newburgh Rd *TF General:* 866-464-7810 ■ *Web:* www.angelahospice.org	Livonia	MI	48154	734-464-7810	464-6930
Arbor Hospice & Home Care 2366 Oak Vly Dr *TF:* 888-992-2273 ■ *Web:* www.arborhospice.org	Ann Arbor	MI	48103	734-662-5999	662-2330
Gogebic Medical Care Facility 402 N St *Web:* www.gogebicmedicalcare.com	Wakefield	MI	49968	906-224-9811	
Grandvue Medical Care Facility 1728 S Peninsula Rd *Web:* grandvue.org	East Jordan	MI	49727	231-536-2286	
Hospice at Home 4025 Health Pk Ln *TF:* 800-717-3811 ■ *Web:* www.lakelandhealth.org/hospice-at-home-cares	Saint Joseph	MI	49085	269-429-7100	428-3499
Hospice Care of Southwest Michigan 222 N Kalamazoo Mall Ste 100 *Web:* www.hospiceswmi.org	Kalamazoo	MI	49007	269-345-0273	
Hospice of Henry Ford Health System 2799 W Grand Blvd *TF:* 800-436-7936 ■ *Web:* www.henryford.com	Detroit	MI	48202	248-585-5270	
Hospice of Holland Inc 270 Hoover Blvd *TF:* 800-255-3522 ■ *Web:* www.hollandhospice.org	Holland	MI	49423	616-396-2972	396-2808
Hospice of Lansing 4052 Legacy Pkwy Ste 200 *TF:* 877-882-4500 ■ *Web:* www.lansinghospice.org	Lansing	MI	48911	517-882-4500	882-3010
Hospice of Michigan 400 Mack Ave *TF:* 888-247-5701 ■ *Web:* www.hom.org	Detroit	MI	48201	313-578-5000	578-6380
Hospice of North Ottawa Community 1309 Sheldon Rd *Web:* www.noch.org/main.aspx?id=115	Grand Haven	MI	49417	616-842-3600	
Leisure Living Management Inc 3196 Kraft Ave SE Ste 200 *Web:* www.leisure-living.com	Grand Rapids	MI	49512	616-464-1564	
Medilodge of Monroe LLC 481 Village Green Ln *Web:* www.medilodge.com	Monroe	MI	48162	734-242-6282	
Mercy Hospice 281 Enterprise Ct Ste 200	Bloomfield Hills	MI	48302	248-452-5300	
MidMichigan Home Care 3007 N Saginaw Rd *TF:* 800-852-9350 ■ *Web:* www.midmichigan.org	Midland	MI	48640	989-633-1400	
Munson Healthcare 1105 Sixth St *TF:* 800-468-6766 ■ *Web:* www.munsonhealthcare.org	Traverse City	MI	49684	231-935-5000	
Pathways 200 W Spring St *Web:* www.pathwaysup.org	Marquette	MI	49855	906-225-1181	
Pediatric Special Care Inc 17040 W 12 Mile Rd Ste 200 *TF:* 800-282-7337 ■ *Web:* www.pediatricspecialcare.com	Southfield	MI	48076	248-557-4800	

Minnesota

				Phone	Fax
Auburn Manor 501 Oak St N *Web:* www.auburnhomes.org	Chaska	MN	55318	952-448-9303	
Fairview Hospice 2450 26th Ave S *TF:* 800-285-5647 ■ *Web:* www.fairview.org	Minneapolis	MN	55406	612-728-2455	728-2400
Health Partners 8170 33rd Ave S *TF:* 800-247-7015 ■ *Web:* healthpartners.com	Minneapolis	MN	55425	952-883-6877	
Lakeside Medical Center Inc 129 Sixth Ave SE *Web:* lmc-pcac.com	Pine City	MN	55063	320-629-2542	
Luther Memorial Home 221 Sixth St SW *Web:* www.luthermemorialhome.org	Madelia	MN	56062	507-642-3271	
Maple Lawn Nursing Home 400 7th St *Web:* www.maplelawn.org	Fulda	MN	56131	507-425-2571	
Mount Olivet Careview Home 5517 Lyndale Ave S *Web:* mtolivethomes.org	Minneapolis	MN	55419	612-827-5677	
North Memorial Home Health & Hospice 3500 France Ave N Ste 101 *Web:* northmemorial.com	Robbinsdale	MN	55422	763-520-5200	
Southview Acres Health Care Center Inc 2000 Oakdale Ave *Web:* www.southviewacres.com	Saint Paul	MN	55118	651-451-1821	

Mississippi

				Phone	Fax
Delta Area Hospice Care Ltd 522 Arnold Ave	Greenville	MS	38701	662-335-7040	335-7027
Hospice Ministries 450 Towne Ctr Blvd *TF:* 800-273-7724 ■ *Web:* www.hospiceministries.org	Ridgeland	MS	39157	601-898-1053	
Mid-Delta Health Systems Inc 405 N Hayden St *Web:* www.middelta.com	Belzoni	MS	39038	662-247-1254	

Missouri

				Phone	Fax
Fair View Nursing Home 1714 W 16th St *TF:* 877-222-4114 ■ *Web:* fairviewnursinghomesedalia.com	Sedalia	MO	65301	660-827-1594	
Gatesworth at One Mcknight Place, The 1 Mcknight Pl *Web:* thegatesworth.com	Saint Louis	MO	63124	314-993-0111	
Heartland Hands-Hope Hospice 137 N Belt Hwy *TF:* 800-443-1143 ■ *Web:* www.mymosaiclifecare.org	Saint Joseph	MO	64506	816-271-7190	271-7672
Kansas City Hospice & Palliative Care 9221 Ward Pkwy Ste 100 *Web:* www.kchospice.org	Kansas City	MO	64114	816-363-2600	523-0068
Macon County Nursing Home District 701 Sunset Hills Dr *Web:* www.lochhaven.com	Macon	MO	63552	660-385-3113	
Odyssey Healthcare of Kansas City 4911 S Arrowhead Dr *TF:* 800-944-4357 ■ *Web:* gentiva.com	Independence	MO	64055	816-795-1333	
Ozark Riverview Manor Inc 1200 W Hall St *Web:* www.ormanor.com	Ozark	MO	65721	417-581-6025	
Saint Luke's Home Care & Hospice 3100 Broadway St Ste 1000 *TF:* 888-303-7576 ■ *Web:* saintlukeshealthsystem.org	Kansas City	MO	64111	816-756-1160	756-0838
SSM Hospice 2 Harbor Bend Ct *TF:* 800-835-1212 ■ *Web:* ssmhealth.com/system	Lake Saint Louis	MO	63367	314-989-2700	
St. Agnes Home 10341 Manchester Rd *Web:* carmelitedcj.org	Kirkwood	MO	63122	314-965-7616	
VNA Hospice Care (VNA) 11440 Olive Blvd Ste 200 *TF:* 800-392-4740 ■ *Web:* www.vnastl.com	Creve Coeur	MO	63141	314-918-7171	918-8054
VNA of Greater St Louis *Hospice Care* 11440 Olive Blvd Ste 200 *TF:* 800-392-4740 ■ *Web:* www.vnastl.com	Creve Coeur	MO	63141	314-918-7171	918-8054

Montana

				Phone	Fax
Peace Hospice of Montana 1101 26th St S	Great Falls	MT	59405	406-455-3040	455-3070

Nebraska

				Phone	Fax
Edgewood Vista 214 Piper St *Web:* edgewoodseniorliving.com	Grand Island	NE	68803	308-384-0717	
Hands of Heartland 211 Galvin Rd N *Web:* handsofheartland.com	Bellevue	NE	68005	402-933-0680	
Lincoln Specialty Care Center 1128 Lincoln Mall Ste 100 *Web:* www.lincolndocs.com	Lincoln	NE	68501	402-436-2350	
Nye Senior Services LLC 2230 N Somers Ave *Web:* nyehealthservices.com	Fremont	NE	68025	402-753-1400	
Sunrise Country Manor 610 224th *Web:* sunrisecountrymanor.com	Milford	NE	68405	402-761-3230	
Visiting Nurse Assn 12565 W Ctr Rd Ste 100 *TF:* 800-456-8869 ■ *Web:* www.thevnacares.org	Omaha	NE	68144	402-342-5566	342-5587

Nevada

				Phone	Fax
Family Home Hospice 1701 W Charleston Blvd *TF:* 800-748-6773	Las Vegas	NV	89102	702-242-7000	383-9826
Nathan Adelson Hospice 4141 Swenson St *Web:* www.nah.org	Las Vegas	NV	89119	702-733-0320	
Saint Mary's Hospice of Northern Nevada 3605 Grant Dr	Reno	NV	89509	775-770-3081	

New Hampshire

				Phone	Fax
Concord Regional Visiting Nurse Assoc Hospice Program 30 Pillsbury St *TF:* 800-924-8620 ■ *Web:* www.crvna.org	Concord	NH	03301	603-224-4093	227-7525
Home Health & Hospice Care 7 Executive Park Dr *TF:* 800-887-5973 ■ *Web:* www.hhhc.org	Merrimack	NH	03054	603-882-2941	883-1515

New Jersey

				Phone	Fax
Center for Hope Hospice 1900 Raritan Rd *Web:* www.centerforhope.com	Scotch Plains	NJ	07076	908-889-7780	889-5172
Compassionate Care Hospice 21-00 Rt 208 S *TF:* 800-844-4774 ■ *Web:* cchnet.net	Fair Lawn	NJ	07410	201-796-5600	
Greenwood House 53 Walter St *Web:* www.greenwoodhouse.org	Ewing	NJ	08628	609-883-5391	
Heath Village 430 Schooley's Mtn Rd *Web:* heathvillage.com	Hackettstown	NJ	07840	908-852-4801	
Hospice of New Jersey 400 Broadacres Dr 1St Fl *TF:* 800-501-0451 ■ *Web:* www.americanhospice.com	Bloomfield	NJ	07003	973-893-0818	893-0828
Hospice Program of Hackensack University Medical Ctr 25 E Salem St	Hackensack	NJ	07601	201-342-7766	489-7275
Karen Ann Quinlan Hospice 99 Sparta Ave *TF:* 800-882-1117 ■ *Web:* www.karenannquinlanhospice.org	Newton	NJ	07860	973-383-0115	383-6889
Leisure Chateau Care Center Inc 962 River Ave *Web:* leisurechateau.com	Lakewood	NJ	08701	732-370-8600	

Phone Fax

Lighthouse Hospice
1040 Kings Hwy N Ste 100. . . . . Cherry Hill NJ 08034 856-414-1155 414-1313
TF General: 888-467-7423 ■ Web: www.lighthousehospice.net

Medford Care Center 185 Tuckerton Rd . . . . . Medford NJ 08055 856-983-8500
Web: www.medfordcare.com

Oakland Care Center Inc 20 Breakneck Rd. . . . . Oakland NJ 07436 201-337-3300
Web: oaklandrehabhc.com

Riverview Estates 303 Bank Ave . . . . . Riverton NJ 08077 856-829-2274
Web: www.riverviewestates.org

Saint Barnabas Hospice & Palliative Care Ctr
95 Old Short Hills Rd . . . . . West Orange NJ 07052 973-322-4800 322-4795
Web: www.barnabashealth.org

Samaritan Hospice 5 Eves Dr Ste 300 . . . . . Marlton NJ 08053 856-596-1600 596-7881
TF: 800-229-8183 ■ Web: www.samaritannj.org

South Jersey Healthcare HospiceCare
2848 S Delsea Dr Bldg 1 . . . . . Vineland NJ 08360 800-770-7547
TF: 800-770-7547 ■ Web: www.inspirahealthnetwork.org

VNA of Central Jersey (VNACJ)
176 Riverside Ave. . . . . Red Bank NJ 07701 800-862-3330
TF: 800-862-3330 ■ Web: www.vnahg.org

New Mexico

Phone Fax

Mesilla Valley Hospice 299 Montana Ave. . . . . Las Cruces NM 88005 575-525-5757 527-2204
Web: www.mvhospice.org

New York

Phone Fax

Amsterdam Nursing Home Corp
1060 Amsterdam Ave . . . . . New York NY 10025 212-316-7700
Web: www.amsterdamcares.com

Anderson Center For Autism Inc
4885 Route 9 PO Box 367 . . . . . Staatsburg NY 12580 845-889-4034
Web: www.andersoncenterforautism.org

Catskill Area Hospice & Palliative Care Inc
1 Birchwood Dr. . . . . Oneonta NY 13820 607-432-6773
TF: 800-306-3870 ■ Web: www.cahpc.org

Community Hospice of Albany 445 New Karner Rd . . . . . Albany NY 12205 518-724-0200 724-0299
Web: communityhospice.org

Crown Nursing Home Associates Inc
3457 Nostrand Ave. . . . . Brooklyn NY 11229 718-535-5100
Web: www.crowncares.com

East End Hospice
481 Westhampton-Riverhead Rd
PO Box 1048 . . . . . WestHampton Beach NY 11978 631-288-8400 288-8492
TF: 877-513-0099 ■ Web: www.eeh.org

Good Shepherd Hospice
200 Belle Terre Rd 1st Fl . . . . . Port Jefferson NY 11777 631-465-6363 465-6533
Web: goodshepherdhospice.chsli.org

Highland Nursing Home Inc 182 Highland Rd . . . . . Massena NY 13662 315-769-9956
Web: www.highlandnursinghome.com

HomeCare & Hospice 1225 W State St . . . . . Olean NY 14760 716-372-5735
TF: 800-339-7011 ■ Web: www.homecare-hospice.org

Hospicare of Tompkins County 172 E King Rd . . . . . Ithaca NY 14850 607-272-0212 272-0237
Web: www.hospicare.org

Hospice & Palliative Care of Buffalo
225 Como Pk Blvd . . . . . Cheektowaga NY 14227 716-686-1900 686-8181
Web: www.hospicebuffalo.com

Hospice Care in Westchester & Putnam Inc
540 White Plains Rd Ste 300 . . . . . Tarrytown NY 10591 914-666-4228 666-0378
Web: www.vnahv.org

Hospice Care Inc
4277 Middle Settlement Rd . . . . . New Hartford NY 13413 315-735-6484 793-8852
TF: 800-317-5661 ■ Web: www.hospicecareinc.org

Hospice Care Network 99 Sunnyside Blvd . . . . . Woodbury NY 11797 516-832-7100 832-7160
TF: 800-405-6731 ■ Web: hospicecarenetwork.org

Hospice Chautauqua County
20 W Fairmount Ave. . . . . Lakewood NY 14750 716-753-5383
Web: www.hospicechautco.org

Hospice Family Care 550 E Main St . . . . . Batavia NY 14020 585-343-7596 343-7629
TF: 800-719-7129 ■ Web: www.homecare-hospice.org

Hospice of Jefferson County
425 Washington St. . . . . Watertown NY 13601 315-788-7323 788-9653
Web: jeffersonhospice.org

Hospice of Orange & Sullivan Counties
800 Stony Brook Ct . . . . . Newburgh NY 12550 845-561-6111 561-2179
TF: 800-924-0157 ■ Web: www.hospiceoforange.com

Hospice of Saint Lawrence Valley
6805 State Hwy 11 . . . . . Potsdam NY 13676 315-265-3105
TF: 888-827-1000 ■ Web: www.seriousillness.org

Hospice of Westchester
1025 Westchester Ave Ste 200 . . . . . White Plains NY 10604 914-682-1484 682-9425
Web: www.hospiceofwestchester.com

Maplewood Nursing Home Inc 100 Daniel Dr . . . . . Webster NY 14580 585-872-1800
Web: m.visitmaplewood.com

Nathan Littauer Hospital & Nursing Home
99 E State St. . . . . Gloversville NY 12078 518-773-5505
Web: www.nlh.org

Niagara Hospice 4675 Sunset Dr . . . . . Lockport NY 14094 716-439-4417
TF: 800-662-1220 ■ Web: www.niagarahospice.org

Nursing Personnel Homecare Inc
175 S Ninth St . . . . . Brooklyn NY 11211 718-218-8991
Web: www.nursingpersonnelhomecare.com

Orchard Manor Inc 600 Bates Rd. . . . . Medina NY 14103 585-798-4100
Web: orchardmanor.com

United Hospice of Rockland 11 Stokum Ln. . . . . New City NY 10956 845-634-4974 634-7549
Web: www.hospiceofrockland.org

Visiting Nurse Service of New York Hospice Care
1250 Broadway 7th Fl. . . . . New York NY 10001 212-609-1900 290-3933
Web: www.vnsny.org

VNS Hospice of Suffolk 505 Main St. . . . . Northport NY 11768 631-261-7200 261-1985
Web: www.visitingnurseservice.org

Newfoundland And Labrador

Phone Fax

TLC Nursing & Homecare Services Ltd
25 Anderson Ave . . . . . St. John's NL A1B3E4 709-726-3473
Web: www.tlcnursingandhomecare.com

North Carolina

Phone Fax

Caldwell Hospice & Palliative Care
902 Kirkwood St NW . . . . . Lenoir NC 28645 828-754-0101
Web: www.caldwellhospice.org

CarePartners Mountain Area Hospice
PO Box 5779 . . . . . Asheville NC 28813 828-255-0231 255-2944
TF: 800-627-1533 ■ Web: www.carepartners.org

Covenant Care Home
600 Mount Moriah Church Rd . . . . . Lumberton NC 28360 910-738-7777
TF: 877-708-7689 ■ Web: www.covenantcareathome.org

FirstHealth Hospice 5 Aviemore Dr . . . . . Pinehurst NC 28374 910-715-6000
Web: www.firsthealth.org

Four Seasons Hospice & Palliative Care
571 S Allen Rd . . . . . Flat Rock NC 28731 828-692-6178 233-0351
TF: 866-466-9734 ■ Web: www.fourseasonscfl.org

Hospice & Palliative Care of Cabarrus County
5003 Hospice Ln . . . . . Kannapolis NC 28081 704-935-9434 935-9435
Web: www.hpccc.org

Hospice & Palliative CareCenter
101 Hospice Ln . . . . . Winston-Salem NC 27103 336-768-3972 659-0461
TF: 888-876-3663 ■ Web: www.hospicecarecenter.org

Hospice at Charlotte 1420 E Seventh St . . . . . Charlotte NC 28204 704-375-0100 375-8623
Web: www.hpccr.org

Hospice at Greensboro 2500 Summit Ave. . . . . Greensboro NC 27405 336-621-2500 621-4516
Web: www.hospicegso.org

Hospice of Alamance Caswell
914 Chapel Hill Rd . . . . . Burlington NC 27215 336-532-0100
TF: 800-588-8879 ■ Web: www.hospiceac.org

Hospice of Burke County 1721 Enon Rd. . . . . Valdese NC 28690 828-879-1601 879-3500
Web: www.burkehospice.org

Hospice of Cleveland County
951 Wendover Heights Dr. . . . . Shelby NC 28150 704-487-4677 481-8050
Web: www.hospicecares.cc

Hospice of Gaston County
258 E Garrison Blvd PO Box 3984 . . . . . Gastonia NC 28054 704-861-8405 865-0590
Web: www.gastonhospice.org

Hospice of Randolph County 416 Vision Dr. . . . . Asheboro NC 27203 336-672-9300 672-0868
Web: www.hospiceofrandolph.org

Hospice of Rockingham County Inc
2150 NC Hwy 65 PO Box 281. . . . . Wentworth NC 27375 336-427-9022 427-9030
Web: www.hospiceofrockinghamcounty.com

Hospice of Rowan County Inc 720 Grove St . . . . . Salisbury NC 28144 704-637-7645
Web: hospicecarecenter.org

Hospice of Rutherford County
374 Hudlow Rd PO Box 336. . . . . Forest City NC 28043 828-245-0095 248-1035
TF: 800-218-2273 ■ Web: www.hospiceofrutherford.org

Hospice of Stanly County 960 N First St. . . . . Albemarle NC 28001 704-983-4216 983-6662
TF: 800-230-4236 ■ Web: www.hospiceofstanly.org

Hospice of the Piedmont
1801 Westchester Dr . . . . . High Point NC 27262 336-889-8446
Web: hospiceofthepiedmont.org

Hospice of Union County 700 W Roosevelt Blvd. . . . . Monroe NC 28110 704-292-2100 292-2190
Web: www.carolinashealthcare.org

Hospice of Wake County Inc 250 Hospice Cir. . . . . Raleigh NC 27607 919-828-0890
TF: 888-900-3959 ■
Web: transitionslifecare.org/redirected-from-hospicofwake-org

Kitty Askins Hospice Ctr 107 Handley Pk Ct. . . . . Goldsboro NC 27534 919-735-5887 735-5948
TF: 800-692-4442 ■ Web: www.3hc.org

Lower Cape Fear Hospice & Life Care
1414 Physicians Dr . . . . . Wilmington NC 28401 910-796-7900 796-7901
TF: 800-733-1476 ■ Web: www.hospiceandlifecarecenter.org

Palliative CareCenter & Hospice of Catawba Valley
3975 Robinson Rd . . . . . Newton NC 28658 828-466-0466 466-8862
Web: www.catawbaregionalhospice.org

Richmond County Hospice 1119 N US Hwy 1 . . . . . Rockingham NC 28379 910-997-4464 895-7476
TF: 800-322-2997

University Health Systems Hospice
521 E Myers St. . . . . Ahoskie NC 27910 252-332-3392

North Dakota

Phone Fax

Hospice of the Red River Valley
1701 38th St S Ste 101. . . . . Fargo ND 58103 701-356-1500
TF: 800-237-4629 ■ Web: www.hrrv.org

Ohio

Phone Fax

Anna Maria of Aurora Inc 889 N Aurora Rd . . . . . Aurora OH 44202 330-562-6171
Web: www.annamariaofaurora.com

Bridge Home Health & Hospice
15100 Birchaven Ln . . . . . Findlay OH 45840 419-423-5351 423-8967
TF: 800-982-3306 ■ Web: www.bvhealthsystem.org

Columbus West Park Nursing & Rehabilitation Center
1700 Heinzerling Dr . . . . . Columbus OH 43223 614-274-4222
Web: columbuswestpark.com

Community New Life Hospice
5255 N Abbe Rd . . . . . Sheffield Village OH 44035 440-934-1458
Web: mercyonline.org

Concord Care Center of Toledo Inc
3121 Glanzman Rd . . . . . Toledo OH 43614 419-385-6616

Phone Fax

Country Court Nursing Center
1076 Coshocton Ave .... Mount Vernon OH 43050 740-397-4125
Web: countrycourt.com

Eliza Bryant Village 7201 Wade Park Ave .... Cleveland OH 44103 216-361-6141
Web: www.elizabryant.org

FairHope Hospice & Palliative Care Inc
282 Sells Rd.................................. Lancaster OH 43130 740-654-7077 654-6321
TF: 800-994-7077 ■ *Web:* www.fairhopehospice.org

Graceworks Lutheran Services
6430 Inner Mission Way............................ Dayton OH 45459 937-433-2140
Web: www.graceworks.org

Hamlet Village 200 Hamlet Hills Dr Ofc .... Chagrin Falls OH 44022 440-247-4201
Web: www.hamletretirement.com

Heartland Hospice Services 333 N Summit St............ Toledo OH 43604 419-252-5500 252-6404
TF: 800-366-1232 ■ *Web:* www.hcr-manorcare.com

Hill View Retirement Center
1610 Twenty-Eighth St........................... Portsmouth OH 45662 740-354-3135
Web: www.hillviewretirement.org

Homereach Hospice 800 McConnell Dr............... Columbus OH 43214 614-566-5377
TF: 800-837-2455 ■ *Web:* www.ohiohealth.com

Hospice of Central Ohio 2269 Cherry Vly Rd .... Newark OH 43055 740-344-0311
TF: 800-804-2505 ■ *Web:* www.hospiceofcentralohio.org

Hospice of Cincinnati 4360 Cooper Rd.............. Cincinnati OH 45242 513-891-7700 792-6980
TF: 800-691-7255 ■ *Web:* www.hospiceofcincinnati.org

Hospice of Dayton 324 Wilmington Ave................. Dayton OH 45420 937-256-4490 256-9802
TF: 800-653-4490 ■ *Web:* www.hospiceofdayton.org

Hospice of Medina County 5075 Windfall Rd........... Medina OH 44256 330-722-4771 722-5266
TF: 800-700-4771 ■ *Web:* www.hospiceofmedina.org

Hospice of Miami County 550 Summit Ave Ste 101......... Troy OH 45373 937-335-5191
TF: 800-372-0009 ■ *Web:* www.hospiceofmiamicounty.org

Hospice of North Central Ohio 1050 Dauch Dr .... Ashland OH 44805 419-281-7107
TF: 800-952-2207 ■ *Web:* www.hospiceofnorthcentralohio.org

Hospice of Northwest Ohio
30000 E River Rd .... Perrysburg OH 43551 419-661-4001 661-4015
TF: 866-661-4001 ■ *Web:* www.hospicenwo.org

Hospice of the Cleveland Clinic
6801 Brecksville Rd Ste 10...................... Independence OH 44131 216-444-9819 520-1973
TF: 800-263-0403 ■ *Web:* my.clevelandclinic.org

Hospice of the Valley 5190 Market St............. Youngstown OH 44512 330-788-1992 788-1998
Web: www.hospiceofthevalley.com

Hospice of the Western Reserve
300 E 185th St .... Cleveland OH 44119 216-383-2222 383-3750
TF: 800-707-8922 ■ *Web:* www.hospicewr.org

Hospice of Visiting Nurse Service
3358 Ridgewood Rd .... Akron OH 44333 330-665-1455 668-4680
TF: 800-335-1455 ■ *Web:* www.vnsa.com

Meadow Wind Health Care Center Inc
300 23rd St NE................................. Massillon OH 44646 330-833-2026
Web: www.meadowwind.net

Mercy Medical Ctr Hospice 7568 Whipple Ave NW....... Canton OH 44720 330-492-8803 649-4399
Web: cantonmercy.org

Piqua Manor 1840 W High St .... Piqua OH 45356 937-773-0040
Web: piquamanor.com

Quaker Heights Nursing Home Inc
514 High St .... Waynesville OH 45068 513-897-6050
TF: 800-319-1317 ■ *Web:* www.quakerheights.org

State of the Heart Home Health & Hospice
1350 N Broadway .... Greenville OH 45331 937-548-2999 548-7144
TF: 800-417-7535 ■ *Web:* www.stateoftheheartcare.org

Stein Hospice Service 1912 Hayes Ave Ste 3 .... Sandusky OH 44870 419-625-5269 625-5761
TF: 800-625-5269 ■ *Web:* www.steinhospice.org

Universal Home Health & Hospice Care
701 S Main St................................ Bellefontaine OH 43311 937-593-1605
Web: www.uhcinc.org

Valley Hospice Inc 380 Summit Ave .... Steubenville OH 43952 740-284-4440 284-4478
TF: 877-467-7423 ■ *Web:* www.valleyhospice.org

Villa Camillus Inc, The
10515 E River Rd .... Columbia Station OH 44028 440-236-5091
Web: www.the-villa-camillus.com

Visiting Nurse Assn of Ohio 2500 E 22nd St .... Cleveland OH 44115 216-931-1400 694-4182
TF: 877-698-6264 ■ *Web:* www.vnaohio.org

Wexner Heritage Village 1151 College Ave .... Columbus OH 43209 614-231-4900
Web: www.whv.org

Oklahoma

Phone Fax

English Village Manor Nursing Home
1515 Canterbury Blvd................................ Altus OK 73521 580-477-1133
Web: englishvillagemanor.net

Fairview Fellowship Home For Senior Citizens Inc
605 E State Rd .... Fairview OK 73737 580-227-3783
Web: www.fellowshiphome.com

Good Shepherd Hospice
4350 Will Rogers Pkwy Ste 400 .... Oklahoma City OK 73108 405-943-0903
Web: www.goodshepherdhospice.com

Grace Hospice 6400 S Lewis Ave Ste 1000................ Tulsa OK 74136 918-744-7223
TF: 800-659-0307 ■ *Web:* www.gracehospice.com

Hospice of Oklahoma County
4334 NW Expy Ste 106........................ Oklahoma City OK 73116 405-848-8884 841-4899
Web: integrisok.com

Perry Green Valley Nursing Home Inc
1103 Birch St .... Perry OK 73077 580-336-2285
Web: greenvalleyhealthcare.net

Ontario

Phone Fax

All Seniors Care Living Centres Ltd
175 Bloor St E Ste 601............................ Toronto ON M4W3R8 416-323-3773
Web: www.allseniorscare.com

Amica at City Centre
380 Princess Royal Dr .... Mississauga ON L5B4M9 905-803-8100
Web: www.amica.ca

Baycrest Centre For Geriatric Care
3560 Bathurst St.................................. Toronto ON M6A2E1 416-785-2500
Web: www.baycrest.org

Chartwell Master Care LP
100 Milverton Dr Ste 700...................... Mississauga ON L5R4H1 905-501-9219
Web: chartwell.com

Elliott Community The 170 Metcalfe St................. Guelph ON N1E4Y3 519-822-0491
Web: www.elliottcommunity.org

Perley & Rideau Veterans' Health Centre
1750 Russell Rd .... Ottawa ON K1G5Z6 613-526-7170
Web: www.perleyrideau.ca

Revera Long Term Care Inc 55 Standish Ct .... Mississauga ON L5R4B2 519-376-3212
Web: www.reveraliving.com

Schlegel Villages Inc
325 Max Becker Dr Ste 201 .... Kitchener ON N2E4H5 519-571-1873
Web: schlegelvillages.com

Oregon

Phone Fax

Hospice of Bend-La Pine 2075 NE Wyatt Ct .... Bend OR 97701 541-382-5882
Web: www.partnersbend.org

Lovejoy Hospice 939 SE Eigth St .... Grants Pass OR 97526 541-474-1193 474-3035
TF: 888-758-8569 ■ *Web:* lovejoyhospice.org

West Hills Village Senior Residence
5711 Sw Multnomah Blvd .... Portland OR 97219 503-245-7621
Web: www.westhillssenior.com

Willamette Valley Hospice 1015 Third St NW........... Salem OR 97304 503-588-3600 363-3891
TF: 800-555-2431 ■ *Web:* www.wvh.org

Pennsylvania

Phone Fax

Berks VNA 1170 Berkshire Blvd .... Wyomissing PA 19610 855-843-8627 378-9762*
**Fax Area Code:* 610 ■ *TF:* 855-843-8627 ■ *Web:* www.hhcminc.org

Celtic Healthcare 150 Scharberry Ln.................... Mars PA 16046 800-355-8894 931-4288
TF: 800-355-8894 ■ *Web:* www.celtichealthcare.com

Chandler Hall Hospice 99 Barclay St................ Newtown PA 18940 215-860-4000 860-3458
TF: 888-603-1973 ■ *Web:* ch.kendal.org

Compassionate Care Hospice
3331 St Rd Ste 410.............................. Bensalem PA 19020 215-245-3525 245-3540
TF: 800-584-8165 ■ *Web:* www.cchnet.net

Erwine Home Health & Hospice
270 Pierce St Ste 101............................. Kingston PA 18704 570-288-1013
Web: erwineshomehealth.com

Family Hospice & Palliative Care
50 Moffett St.................................... Pittsburgh PA 15243 412-572-8800 572-8827
TF: 800-513-2148 ■ *Web:* familyhospicepa.org

Forbes Hospice 4800 Friendship Ave.............. Pittsburgh PA 15224 412-578-5000
TF: 800-381-8080 ■ *Web:* ahn.org

Geisinger Columbia Montour Hospice
410 Glenn Ave .... Bloomsburg PA 17815 570-784-1723
Web: www.geisinger.org/for-patients/services-specialties/hospice

Golden Hill Nursing Home Inc
520 Friendship St............................... New Castle PA 16101 724-654-7791
Web: goldenhill.com

Harlee Manor Nursing & Rehabilitation Center
463 W Sproul Rd .... Springfield PA 19064 610-544-2200
Web: harleemanor.com

Holy Redeemer Home Care & Hospice
12265 Townsend Rd Ste 400 .... Philadelphia PA 19154 888-678-8678
TF: 888-678-8678 ■ *Web:* www.holyredeemer.com

Hospice of Central Pennsylvania
1320 Linglestown Rd .... Harrisburg PA 17110 717-732-1000 732-5348
TF: 866-779-7374 ■ *Web:* www.hospiceofcentralpa.org

Hospice of Lancaster County
685 Good Dr PO Box 4125......................... Lancaster PA 17604 717-295-3900 391-9582
TF: 888-236-9563 ■ *Web:* www.hospiceandcommunitycare.org

Lehigh Valley Hospice
2166 S 12th St Ste 401........................... Allentown PA 18103 610-969-0300 969-0326
TF: 888-584-2273 ■ *Web:* www.lvhn.org

Meadow View Nursing Center 1404 Hay St.............. Berlin PA 15530 814-267-4212
Web: meadowview.net

Misericordia Nursing & Rehabilitation Center
998 S Russell St....................................... York PA 17402 717-755-1964
Web: mn-rc.org

Nsa Nursing Solutions America
2055 State St .... East Petersburg PA 17520 717-560-3863
Web: nsinursingsolutions.com

St. John Diakon Hospice 1201 N Church St........... Hazleton PA 18202 570-450-1500
Web: diakon.org

SUN Home Health Services Inc
61 Duke St PO Box 232 .... Northumberland PA 17857 570-473-8320 473-3070
TF: 888-478-6227 ■ *Web:* www.sunhomehealth.com

VITAS Healthcare Corp of Pennsylvania
1787 Sentry Pk W Bldg 16 Ste 400................ Blue Bell PA 19422 305-374-4143
TF: 800-582-9533 ■ *Web:* www.vitas.com

VNA 154 Hindman Rd .... Butler PA 16001 724-282-6806 282-7517
TF: 877-862-6659 ■
Web: lutheranseniorlife.org/senior-living/locations/vna-western-pennsylvania-butler

VNA Hospice & Home Health of Lackawanna County
301 Delaware Ave.................................. Olyphant PA 18447 570-383-5180 383-5189
TF: 800-936-7671 ■ *Web:* www.vnahospice.org

York County Cerebral Palsy Home Inc Proj
2050 Barley Rd.. York PA 17408 717-767-6463
Web: www.margaretemoul.org

Quebec

Phone Fax

Vigi Sante Ltee 197 Thornhill............. Dollard-des-ormeaux QC H9B3H8 514-684-0930
Web: www.vigisante.com

Rhode Island

Phone Fax

Home Hospice Care of Rhode Island
1085 N Main St ... Providence RI 02904 401-415-4200
TF: 800-338-6555 ■ *Web:* www.hopehospiceri.org

South Carolina

Phone Fax

Hospice Community Care PO Box 993 ... Rock Hill SC 29731 803-329-1500 329-5935
TF: 800-895-2273 ■ *Web:* www.hospicecommunitycare.org
Hospice of the Upstate 1835 Rogers Rd ... Anderson SC 29621 864-224-3358 328-1132
TF: 800-261-8636 ■ *Web:* www.hospicehouse.net
HospiceCare of the Piedmont
408 W Alexander Ave ... Greenwood SC 29646 864-227-9393 227-9377
Web: www.hospicepiedmont.org
McLeod Hospice 1203 E Cheves St ... Florence SC 29506 843-777-2564
TF: 800-768-4556 ■ *Web:* www.mcleodhealth.org
Mercy Hospice of Horry County
PO Box 50640 ... Myrtle Beach SC 29579 843-236-2282 347-5535
Open Arms Hospice 1836 W Georgia Rd ... Simpsonville SC 29680 864-688-1700 688-1705
TF: 866-473-6276 ■ *Web:* www.openarmshospice.org
Palmetto Health Home Care & Hospice
1400 Pickens St ... Columbia SC 29202 803-296-3100 296-3320
TF: 800-238-1884 ■ *Web:* www.palmettohealth.org

South Dakota

Phone Fax

Dougherty Hospice House
4509 Prince of Peace Pl ... Sioux Falls SD 57103 605-322-7705
Web: www.avera.org

Tennessee

Phone Fax

Alive Hospice Inc 1718 Patterson St ... Nashville TN 37203 615-327-1085 321-8902
TF: 800-327-1085 ■ *Web:* www.alivehospice.org
Amedisys Hospice 209 10th Ave S Ste 512 ... Nashville TN 37203 423-587-9484 587-9408
TF: 800-659-2633 ■ *Web:* www.amedisys.com
Baptist Trinity Home Care & Hospice
6019 Walnut Grove Rd ... Memphis TN 38120 901-226-5000
TF: 800-422-7847 ■ *Web:* www.baptistonline.org
Hospice of Chattanooga 4411 Oakwood Dr ... Chattanooga TN 37416 423-892-4289
TF: 800-267-6828 ■ *Web:* www.hospiceofchattanooga.org
Methodist Alliance Hospice
6400 Shelby View Dr Ste 101 ... Memphis TN 38134 901-516-1999
TF: 800-541-8277 ■ *Web:* www.methodisthealth.org
Obion County Nursing Home
1084 E County Home Rd ... Union City TN 38261 731-885-9065
Web: obioncountynursinghome.com
Sycamores Terrace Retirement
1427 Lebanon Pk ... Nashville TN 37210 615-242-2412
Web: www.sycamoresterrace.com

Texas

Phone Fax

AseraCare Hospice of Austin 14205 Burnet Rd ... Austin TX 78728 512-218-9890 218-9288
TF: 800-332-3982 ■ *Web:* www.aseracare.com
AseraCare Hospice of Milwaukee
7160 Dallas Pkwy Ste 400 ... Plano TX 75024 262-785-1356
TF: 800-598-5132 ■ *Web:* www.aseracare.com
Cartmell Home for Aged Inc
2212 W Reagan St ... Palestine TX 75801 903-727-8500
Web: cartmellhome.org
Cedar Lake Nursing Home 1611 W Royall Blvd ... Malakoff TX 75148 903-489-1702
Web: cedarlakenursing.com
CHRISTUS Spohn Hospice
6200 Saratoga Blvd Bldg B Ste 104 ... Corpus Christi TX 78414 361-994-3400 785-5390*
**Fax Area Code: 210 ■ TF: 844-444-8440 ■ Web:* www.christushomecare.org
CHRISTUS VNA 4241 Woodcock Dr # A100 ... San Antonio TX 78228 210-785-5200
Web: www.christushomecare.org
Community Hospice of Texas
6100 Western Pl Ste 150 ... Fort Worth TX 76107 817-870-2795
TF: 800-226-0373 ■ *Web:* www.chot.org
Daybreak Venture LLC 401 N Elm St ... Denton TX 76201 940-387-4388
Web: www.daybreakventure.com
Golden Acres 2525 Centerville Rd ... Dallas TX 75228 214-327-4503
Web: www.goldenacresliving.com
Hendrick Hospice Care 1682 Hickory St ... Abilene TX 79601 325-677-8516 675-5031
TF: 800-622-8516 ■ *Web:* www.hendrickhospice.org
Home Hospice of Grayson County 505 W Ctr St ... Sherman TX 75090 903-868-9315 893-2772
TF: 888-233-7455 ■ *Web:* www.homehospice.org
Hope Hospice 611 N Walnut Ave ... New Braunfels TX 78130 830-625-7500 606-1388
TF: 800-499-7501 ■ *Web:* www.hopehospice.net
Hospice at the Texas Medical Ctr
1905 Holcombe Blvd ... Houston TX 77030 713-467-7423
TF: 800-630-7894 ■ *Web:* www.houstonhospice.org
Hospice Austin
4107 Spicewood Springs Rd Ste 100 ... Austin TX 78759 512-342-4700 795-9053
TF: 800-445-3261 ■ *Web:* www.hospiceaustin.org
Hospice Brazos Valley 502 W 26th St ... Bryan TX 77803 979-821-2266 821-0041
TF: 800-824-2326 ■ *Web:* www.hospicebrazosvalley.org
Hospice Care Team 1708 N Amburn Rd Ste C ... Texas City TX 77591 409-938-0070 938-1509
Web: www.hospicecareteam.org
Hospice House Foundation Inc
903 n sam houston ave ... Odessa TX 79761 432-580-0067
TF: 877-428-3581 ■ *Web:* www.homehospicewtx.com

Phone Fax

Hospice of East Texas 4111 University Blvd ... Tyler TX 75701 903-266-3400
TF: 800-777-9860 ■ *Web:* www.hospiceofeasttexas.org
Hospice of El Paso 1440 Miracle Way ... El Paso TX 79925 915-532-5699 532-7822
Web: www.hospiceelpaso.org
Hospice of Midland 911 W Texas Ave ... Midland TX 79701 432-682-2855 682-2989
TF: 800-339-1180 ■ *Web:* hospicemidland.org
Hospice of San Angelo
36 E Twohig St PO Box 471 ... San Angelo TX 76903 325-658-6524 658-8895
TF: 800-499-6524 ■ *Web:* www.hospiceofsanangelo.org
Hospice of South Texas 605 E Locust Ave ... Victoria TX 77901 361-572-4300 570-1147
TF: 800-874-6908 ■ *Web:* www.hospiceofsouthtexas.org
Hospice of Wichita Falls
4909 Johnson Rd ... Wichita Falls TX 76310 940-691-0982 691-1608
TF: 800-378-2822 ■ *Web:* www.hospiceofwf.org
James L. West Alzheimer Center
1111 Summit Ave ... Fort Worth TX 76102 817-877-1199
Web: www.jameslwest.org
Lubbock Regional Mental Health Mental Retardation Center
1602 10th St ... Lubbock TX 79401 806-766-0310
TF: 800-687-7581 ■ *Web:* www.lubbockmhmr.org
Methodist Retirement Communities
1440 Lk Front Cir Ste 110 ... The Woodlands TX 77380 281-363-2600
Web: www.mrcaff.org
Park Manor of Quail Valley
2350 Fm 1092 Rd ... Missouri City TX 77459 281-499-9333
Web: parkmanor-quailvalley.com
Sensibill 6115 Camp Bowie Blvd Ste 260 ... Fort Worth TX 76116 817-731-7771
Southwest LTC 1518 Legacy Dr Ste 110 ... Frisco TX 75034 817-222-6000
Web: greenoaks.seniorcarecentersltc.com
St. James House of Baytown 5800 W Baker Rd ... Baytown TX 77520 281-425-1200
Web: www.stjameshouse.org
VITAS Healthcare Corp
4848 Loop Central Dr Ste 650 ... Houston TX 77081 713-663-7777
TF: 800-582-9533 ■ *Web:* www.vitas.com
VITAS Healthcare Corp
8401 Datapoint Dr Ste 300 ... San Antonio TX 78229 210-348-4300
TF: 800-938-4827 ■ *Web:* www.vitas.com

Utah

Phone Fax

Orem Rehabilitation & Nursing Center
575 East 1400 South ... Orem UT 84097 801-225-4741
Web: www.oremrehab.com

Virginia

Phone Fax

Capital Hospice Inc 2900 Telestar Ct ... Falls Church VA 22042 703-538-2065 538-2165
TF: 855-571-5700 ■ *Web:* www.capitalcaring.org
Good Samaritan Hospice 2408 Electric Rd ... Roanoke VA 24018 540-776-0198 776-0841
TF: 888-466-7809 ■ *Web:* www.goodsamhospice.com
Hospice of the Piedmont
675 Peter Jefferson Pkwy Ste 300 ... Charlottesville VA 22911 434-817-6900 245-0187
TF: 800-975-5501 ■ *Web:* www.hopva.org
Hospice of the Rapidan
1200 Sunset Ln Ste 2320 ... Culpeper VA 22701 540-825-4840
Web: www.hotr.org
Mary Washington Hospice
5012 Southpoint Pkwy ... Fredericksburg VA 22407 540-741-1667
TF: 800-257-1667 ■ *Web:* www.marywashingtonhealthcare.com
Willows at Meadow Branch, The
1881 Harvest Dr ... Winchester VA 22601 540-667-3000
Web: www.thewillows-mb.com

Washington

Phone Fax

Evergreen Hospice Services
12822 124th Ln NE ... Kirkland WA 98034 425-899-1070 899-1033
TF: 877-980-7500 ■ *Web:* www.evergreenhealth.com
Harbors Home Health & Hospice 201 Seventh St ... Hoquiam WA 98550 360-532-5454
TF: 800-772-1319 ■ *Web:* myhhhh.org
Hospice of Spokane 121 S Arthur St ... Spokane WA 99202 509-456-0438
TF: 800-467-7423 ■ *Web:* www.hospiceofspokane.org
Kin On Health Care Center 4416 S Brandon St ... Seattle WA 98118 206-721-3630
Web: kinon.org
Milestone Retirement Communities LLC
201 NE Park Plz Dr Ste 105 ... Vancouver WA 98684 360-882-4500
Web: www.milestoneretirement.com
Prestige Care Inc 7700 NE Pkwy Dr Ste 300 ... Vancouver WA 98662 360-735-7155
Web: www.prestigecare.com
Providence Hospice & Home Care of Snohomish County
2731 Wetmore Ave ... Everett WA 98201 425-261-4800
Web: washington.providence.org
Providence Hospice of Seattle
425 Pontius Ave N Ste 300 ... Seattle WA 98109 206-320-4000 320-7333
TF: 888-782-4445 ■ *Web:* www2.providence.org
Providence Sound Home Care & Hospice
3432 S Bay Rd NE ... Olympia WA 98506 360-459-8311
TF: 800-869-7062 ■ *Web:* www2.providence.org
Tri-Cities Chaplaincy 2108 W Entiat Ave ... Kennewick WA 99336 509-783-7416 735-7850
Web: www.tricitieschaplaincy.org
Whatcom Hospice Foundation
2901 Squalicum Pkwy Ste 11 ... Bellingham WA 98225 360-733-1231 788-6858
Web: whatcomhospice.org

West Virginia

Phone Fax

Hospice of Huntington 1101 Sixth Ave ... Huntington WV 25701 304-529-4217 523-6051
TF: 800-788-5480 ■ *Web:* www.hospiceofhuntington.org

Phone Fax

Hospice of the Panhandle
330 Hospice Ln . . . . Kearneysville WV 25430 304-264-0406 264-0409
TF: 800-345-6538 ■ *Web:* www.hospiceotp.org

Kanawha Hospice Care 1606 Kanawha Blvd W. . . . . Charleston WV 25387 304-768-8523
TF: 800-560-8523 ■ *Web:* www.hospicecarewv.org

Nella's Nursing Home Inc 200 Whiteman Ave. . . . . Elkins WV 26241 304-636-2033
Web: nellasofcrystalsprings.com

Wisconsin

Phone Fax

Aurora VNA Zilber Family Hospice
1155 N Honey Creek Pkwy . . . . Wauwatosa WI 53213 414-615-5900
TF: 888-206-6955 ■ *Web:* www.aurorahealthcare.org

Beloit Regional Hospice 655 Third St Ste 200 . . . . Beloit WI 53511 608-363-7421 363-7426
TF: 877-363-7421 ■ *Web:* www.beloitregionalhospice.com

Fond Du Lac Lutheran Home Inc
244 N Macy St . . . . Fond Du Lac WI 54935 920-921-9520
Web: www.lutheranhomesfonddulac.org

Gundersen Lutheran at Home HomeCare & Hospice
914 Green Bay St . . . . La Crosse WI 54601 608-775-8400
TF General: 800-362-9567 ■ *Web:* www.gundersenhealth.org

Horizon Home Care & Hospice
11400 W Lake Park Dr . . . . Milwaukee WI 53224 414-365-8300 365-8330
Web: www.horizonhch.com

Hospice Alliance
10220 Prairie Ridge Blvd . . . . Pleasant Prairie WI 53158 262-652-4400 652-4516
TF: 800-830-8344 ■ *Web:* www.hospicealliance.org

HospiceCare 5395 E Cheryl Pkwy . . . . Madison WI 53711 608-276-4660 276-4672
TF: 800-553-4289 ■ *Web:* www.agrace.org

Milwaukee Protestant Home For The Aged
2505 E Bradford Ave. . . . . Milwaukee WI 53211 414-963-6151
Web: eastcastleplace.com

Newcastle Place Inc
12600 N Port Washington Rd . . . . Mequon WI 53092 262-387-8800
Web: www.newcastleplacelcs.com

St. Joseph Residence 107 E Beckert Rd . . . . New London WI 54961 920-982-5354
Web: stjosephresidence.com

Theda Care at Home 3000 E College Ave. . . . . Appleton WI 54915 920-969-0919 969-0020
TF: 800-984-5554 ■ *Web:* www.thedacare.org

Unity Hospice 2366 Oak Ridge Cir . . . . De Pere WI 54115 920-338-1111 338-8111
TF: 800-990-9249 ■ *Web:* www.unityhospice.org

VITAS Healthcare Corp
2675 N Mayfair Rd Ste 500. . . . . Wauwatosa WI 53226 414-257-2600
TF: 866-418-4827 ■ *Web:* www.vitas.com

Wyoming

Phone Fax

Central Wyoming Hospice Program
319 S Wilson St . . . . Casper WY 82601 307-577-4832 577-4841
Web: www.cwhp.org

372 HOSPITAL HOSPITALITY HOUSES

Phone Fax

Alegent Creighton Health Hospitality House
7105 Newport Ave . . . . Omaha NE 68154 402-572-2900

American Cancer Society Hope Lodge of Baltimore
636 W Lexington St . . . . Baltimore MD 21201 410-547-2522 539-8890
TF: 888-227-6333 ■ *Web:* www.cancer.org

American Cancer Society Hope Lodge of Buffalo
197 Summer St. . . . . Buffalo NY 14222 716-882-9244
Web: www.cancer.org

American Cancer Society Hope Lodge of Charleston
269 Calhoun St. . . . . Charleston SC 29401 843-958-0930 958-9054
TF: 800-227-2345 ■ *Web:* www.cancer.org

American Cancer Society Hope Lodge of Marshfield
611 W Doege St . . . . Marshfield WI 54449 715-486-9100
Web: www.cancer.org

American Cancer Society Hope Lodge of Rochester
411 Second St NW . . . . Rochester MN 55901 507-529-4673
Web: www.cancer.org

American Cancer Society Hope Lodge Worcester
7 Oak St . . . . Worcester MA 01609 508-792-2985 753-3986
TF: 800-227-2345 ■ *Web:* www.cancer.org

American Cancer Society Joe Lee Griffin Hope Lodge
1104 Ireland Way . . . . Birmingham AL 35205 205-558-7860
TF: 800-227-2345 ■ *Web:* www.cancer.org

American Cancer Society Joseph S. & Jeannette M. Silber Hope Lodge
11432 Mayfield Rd . . . . Cleveland OH 44106 216-844-4673 844-2959
Web: www.cancer.org

American Cancer Society Winn-Dixie Hope Lodge
250 Williams St NW . . . . Atlanta GA 30303 404-327-9200
TF: 800-227-2345 ■ *Web:* www.cancer.org

Arbor House 300 Main St. . . . . Lewiston ME 04240 207-795-0111
Web: www.cmmc.org

Atlanta Hospital Hospitality House
1815 S Ponce De Leon Ave NE. . . . . Atlanta GA 30307 404-377-6333 377-0668
TF: 855-286-9658 ■ *Web:* www.atlhhh.org

Bannister Family House 406 Dickinson St . . . . San Diego CA 92103 619-543-7977 543-7937
TF: 800-926-8273 ■ *Web:* health.ucsd.edu

Barnes Lodge 4520 Clayton Ave . . . . Saint Louis MO 63110 314-652-4319
TF: 800-551-3492 ■ *Web:* www.barnesjewish.org

Baylor Plaza Hotel 3600 Gaston Ave . . . . Dallas TX 75246 800-422-9567
TF: 800-422-9567 ■ *Web:* www.baylorhealth.com

Beacon House 19 Myrtle St. . . . . Boston MA 02114 617-523-8295
Web: rogerson.org

Beacon House 1301 N Third St . . . . Marquette MI 49855 906-225-7100 225-4903
TF: 800-562-9753 ■ *Web:* www.upbeaconhouse.org

Blount Hospitality House 610 Madison St . . . . Huntsville AL 35801 256-534-7014
Web: www.blounthospitalityhouse.org

Phone Fax

Brent's Place 11980 E 16th Ave . . . . Aurora CO 80010 303-831-4545 831-4567
Web: www.brentsplace.org

Caring House Inc 2625 Pickett Rd . . . . Durham NC 27705 919-490-5449
Web: www.caringhouse.com

Carolyn Scott Rainbow House 7815 Harney St . . . . Omaha NE 68114 402-955-7815
TF: 800-642-8822 ■ *Web:* www.childrensomaha.org

Carpenter Hospitality House 121 Fifth Ave NE . . . . Hickory NC 28601 828-324-4544

Casa Esperanza 1005 Yale NE . . . . Albuquerque NM 87106 505-246-2700 277-9876
TF: 866-654-1338 ■ *Web:* casanm.org

Children's Hope House
7922 W Jefferson Blvd . . . . Fort Wayne IN 46804 260-459-8550
TF: 800-706-9941 ■ *Web:* childrenshopefw.org

Children's House at Johns Hopkins
1915 McElderry St . . . . Baltimore MD 21205 410-614-2560 614-2568
TF: 800-933-5470 ■ *Web:* believeintomorrow.org

Conine Clubhouse 1005 Joe DiMaggio Dr . . . . Hollywood FL 33021 954-265-5324
TF: 866-532-4362 ■
Web: www.jdch.com/html/at-the-hospital/connie-clubhouse/index.html

Cynthia C. & William E. Perry Pavilion
9400 Turkey Lake Rd . . . . Orlando FL 32819 321-842-8844 842-8871
TF: 800-447-1435 ■ *Web:* www.orlandohealth.com/drpphillipshospital

Danielle House 160 Riverside Dr. . . . . Binghamton NY 13905 607-724-1540 724-1540
Web: www.daniellehouse.org

Devon Nicole House 21 Autumn St 5th Fl . . . . Boston MA 02215 617-355-8457
Web: childrenshospital.org

Doorways, The 612 E Marshall St. . . . . Richmond VA 23219 804-828-6901 827-7213
Web: www.thedoorways.org

Family House Inc 1509 N Knoxville Ave. . . . . Peoria IL 61603 309-685-5300 685-8122
Web: www.familyhousepeoria.org

Fisher House Inc 7323 Hwy 90 W Ste 107 . . . . San Antonio TX 78227 210-673-7500 673-7579
Web: www.fisherhouseinc.org

Francis Cheney Family Place
2650 Siskiyou Blvd. . . . . Medford OR 97504 541-789-5876
Web: www.asante.org

Gary's House 97 State St . . . . Portland ME 04101 207-535-1320

Gift of Life Transplant House
705 Second St SW . . . . Rochester MN 55902 507-288-7470 281-9888
TF: 800-479-7824 ■ *Web:* www.gift-of-life.org

Hanson House 380 E Paseo El Mirador . . . . Palm Springs CA 92262 760-416-5070 416-5071
Web: www.hansonhouse.org

Holland's Rose 132 Griegos Rd NW . . . . Albuquerque NM 87107 505-345-2020 345-5464
Web: www.hollandsrose.com

Hope Lodge Hershey Pennsylvania
125 Lucy Ave . . . . Hummelstown PA 17036 717-533-5111 533-2587
Web: www.cancer.org

Hospital Hospitality House of Louisville
120 W Broadway. . . . . Louisville KY 40202 502-625-1360 625-1363
Web: www.hhhlouisville.org

Hospital Hospitality House of SW Michigan Inc
527 W S St . . . . Kalamazoo MI 49007 269-341-7811 341-7817
Web: www.hhhkz.org

Hospitality House of Charlotte
1400 Scott Ave . . . . Charlotte NC 28203 704-376-0060 376-0059
Web: www.hospitalityhouseofcharlotte.org

Hospitality House of Methodist Hospital Foundation
990 Oak Ridge Tpke PO Box 2529 . . . . Oak Ridge TN 37830 865-835-5261
Web: www.mmcoakridge.com

Hospitality House of Tulsa 1135 S Victor Ave . . . . Tulsa OK 74014 918-794-0088
Web: www.hhtulsa.org

Hubbard House, The 29 W Miller St. . . . . Orlando FL 32806 407-649-6886 849-6447
TF: 800-648-3818 ■ *Web:* www.orlandohealth.com

Huntington Hospital Hospitality House
2801 S Staunton Rd . . . . Huntington WV 25702 304-522-1832

Inn at Cherry Hill 500 17th Ave. . . . . Seattle WA 98122 206-320-2164 320-3526
Web: www.swedish.org

Inn at Virginia Mason 1006 Spring St. . . . . Seattle WA 98104 206-583-6453
TF: 800-283-6453 ■ *Web:* www.innatvirginiamason.com

Jenn's House Inc 3250 S Cedar Crest Blvd . . . . Emmaus PA 18049 610-965-1777
Web: www.jennshouse.org

Kathy's House Inc 600 N 103 St. . . . . Milwaukee WI 53226 414-453-8290 453-8292
Web: www.kathys-house.org

Kevin Guest House 782 Ellicott St . . . . Buffalo NY 14203 716-882-1818 882-1291
Web: www.kevinguesthouse.com

Kohl's House at Children's Memorial Hospital
225 E Chicago Ave . . . . Chicago IL 60611 312-227-4000 227-9456
TF: 800-543-7362 ■ *Web:* www.luriechildrens.org

Mario Pastega Guest House
3505 NW Samaritan Dr. . . . . Corvallis OR 97330 541-768-4650
TF: 800-863-5241 ■ *Web:* www.samhealth.org

Molly's House 430 SE Osceola St . . . . Stuart FL 34994 772-223-6659 223-9990
Web: www.mollyshouse.org

Munson Manor Hospitality House
1220 Medical Campus Dr. . . . . Traverse City MI 49684 231-935-2300
Web: www.munsonhealthcare.org

Nebraska House 983285 Nebraska Medical Ctr . . . . Omaha NE 68198 402-559-5000 559-3434
TF: 800-401-4444 ■ *Web:* www.nebraskamed.com/transplant

Pay It Forward House 719 Somonauk St. . . . . Sycamore IL 60178 815-762-4882
Web: www.payitforwardhouse.org

Quantum House 987 45th St . . . . West Palm Beach FL 33407 561-494-0515 494-0522
Web: www.quantumhouse.org

Quincy Hospitality House 1129 Oak St. . . . . Quincy IL 62301 217-228-3022
Web: www.blessinghospital.org

Rathgeber Hospitality House
1615 12th St. . . . . Wichita Falls TX 76301 940-764-2400 764-2456
Web: www.rathgeberhospitalityhouse.org

Rose Hill Hospitality House
605 26 1/2 Rd. . . . . Grand Junction CO 81506 970-243-7968
Web: stmarygj.org

Rosenbaum Family House
30 Family House Dr PO Box 8228 . . . . Morgantown WV 26506 304-598-6094 598-6412
TF: 855-988-2273 ■ *Web:* wvuhealthcare.com/wvuh/404

Sarah House Inc 100 Roberts Ave. . . . . Syracuse NY 13207 315-475-1747
Web: sarahsguesthouse.org

	City	State	Zip	Phone	Fax
Seton Guest Ctr 2131 W Third St *Web:* stvincent.verity.org	Los Angeles	CA	90057	213-484-7767	207-5816
Seton League House 3207 Medical Pkwy *Web:* www.seton.net	Austin	TX	78705	512-324-1999	
Stanton Hospitality House 1617 Roxie Ave. *Web:* www.capefearvalley.com	Fayetteville	NC	28304	910-615-4000	
Steven's Hope for Children Inc 1014 W Foothill Blvd Ste B. *TF:* 866-378-3836 ■ *Web:* www.stevenshope.org	Upland	CA	91786	909-373-0678	981-4578
Sumner Foundation Hospitality House 406 Steam Plant Rd	Gallatin	TN	37066	615-452-4009	
Travis & Beverly Cross Guest Housing Ctr 9320 SW Barnes Rd *TF:* 888-550-1575 ■ *Web:* www.oregon.providence.org	Portland	OR	97225	503-216-1575	216-6283
Veterans Guest House 880 Locust St *Web:* www.veteransguesthouse.org	Reno	NV	89502	775-324-6958	324-6071
Zachary & Elizabeth Fisher House 111 Rockville Pk Ste 420 **Fax Area Code:* 513 ■ *TF:* 888-294-8560 ■ *Web:* www.fisherhouse.org/houses	Rockville	MD	20850	888-294-8560	487-6661*

373 HOSPITAL HOSPITALITY HOUSES - RONALD MCDONALD HOUSE

	City	State	Zip	Phone	Fax
Ronald McDonald House (RMH) 2524 N State St *Web:* www.rmhcms.org	Jackson	MS	39216	601-981-5683	981-3613
Akron 245 Locust St *TF:* 800-262-0333 ■ *Web:* www.akronchildrens.org	Akron	OH	44302	330-253-5400	253-5477
Albany 139 S Lake Ave *TF:* 866-244-8464 ■ *Web:* www.rmhcofalbany.org	Albany	NY	12208	518-438-2655	459-6529
Albuquerque 1011 Yale Ave NE *TF:* 877-842-8960 ■ *Web:* www.rmhc-nm.org	Albuquerque	NM	87106	505-842-8960	764-0412
Amarillo 1501 Streit Dr *Web:* rmhc.org	Amarillo	TX	79106	806-358-8177	
Ann Arbor 1600 Washington Heights *TF:* 800-544-8684 ■ *Web:* www.rmh-annarbor.org	Ann Arbor	MI	48104	734-994-4442	994-4919
Atlanta 795 Gatewood Rd NE *Web:* www.armhc.org	Atlanta	GA	30329	404-315-1133	315-7873
Austin 1315 Barbara Jordan Blvd. *Web:* rmhc-ctx.org	Austin	TX	78723	512-472-9844	472-5465
Baltimore 635 W Lexington St *Web:* www.rmhcbaltimore.org	Baltimore	MD	21201	410-528-1010	727-6177
Bangor 654 State St. *Web:* rmhcmaine.org	Bangor	ME	04401	207-942-9003	990-2984
Bend 1700 NE Purcell Blvd *Web:* rmhcofcentraloregon.org	Bend	OR	97701	541-318-4950	318-4994
Billings 1144 N 30th St	Billings	MT	59101	406-256-8006	
Birmingham 1700 Fourth Ave S. *Web:* www.rmhca.org	Birmingham	AL	35233	205-638-7255	638-7256
Bismarck 609 N Seventh St *Web:* rmhcbismarck.org	Bismarck	ND	58501	701-258-8551	258-5076
Boise 101 Warm Springs Ave *Web:* www.rmhcidaho.org	Boise	ID	83712	208-336-5478	336-0587
Boston 229 Kent St *Web:* www.ronaldmcdonaldhouseboston.org	Brookline	MA	02446	617-734-3333	
Buffalo 780 W Ferry St. *Web:* rmhcwny.org	Buffalo	NY	14222	716-883-1177	881-9312
Burlington 16 S Winooski Ave *Web:* www.rmhcvt.org	Burlington	VT	05401	802-862-4943	862-2175
Calgary 111 W Campus Pl NW *Web:* www.ahomeawayfromhome.org	Calgary	AB	T3B2R6	403-240-3000	240-1277
Camden 550 Mickle Blvd. *Web:* www.ronaldhouse-snj.org	Camden	NJ	08103	856-966-4663	966-1190
Chapel Hill 101 Old Mason Farm Rd *Web:* www.rmh-chapelhill.org	Chapel Hill	NC	27517	919-913-2040	951-0123
Charleston 81 Gadsden St. *Web:* www.rmhcharleston.org	Charleston	SC	29401	843-723-7957	722-2204
Charlottesville 300 Ninth St SW. *Web:* www.rmhcharlottesville.org	Charlottesville	VA	22903	434-295-1885	295-7735
Chattanooga 200 Central Ave. *TF:* 855-670-4787 ■ *Web:* www.rmhchattanooga.com	Chattanooga	TN	37403	423-778-4300	778-4350
Chicago 211 E Grand Ave *Web:* www.rmhccni.org	Chicago	IL	60611	312-888-2500	
Chicago 1301 W 22nd St Ste 905 *Web:* www.rmhccni.org	Oak Brook	IL	60523	630-623-5300	
Chicago Tripp Ave PO Box 7002 *Web:* www.rmhccni.org	Hines	IL	60141	708-327-2273	327-6000
Cleveland 10415 Euclid Ave *TF:* 800-223-2273 ■ *Web:* www.rmhcleveland.org	Cleveland	OH	44106	216-229-5758	229-0556
Colorado Springs 311 N Logan Ave. *Web:* www.rmhcs.org	Colorado Springs	CO	80909	719-471-1814	471-7147
Columbus 1959 Hamilton Rd. *Web:* www.rmhcwga.org	Columbus	GA	31904	706-321-0033	321-0034
Corpus Christi 3402 Ft Worth St *Web:* www.corpuschristirmhc.org	Corpus Christi	TX	78411	361-854-4073	854-9174
Dallas 4707 Bengal St *Web:* www.rmhdallas.org	Dallas	TX	75235	214-631-7354	631-1527
Danville 100 N Academy Ave PO Box 300 *Web:* www.rmhdanville.org	Danville	PA	17821	570-271-6300	271-8182
Des Moines 1441 Pleasant St *Web:* rmhdesmoines.org	Des Moines	IA	50314	515-243-2111	280-3111
Detroit 3911 Beaubien *Web:* www.rmhc-detroit.org	Detroit	MI	48201	313-745-5909	993-0399
Durham 506 Alexander Ave *TF:* 866-244-8464 ■ *Web:* www.rmhdurhamwake.org	Durham	NC	27705	919-286-9305	286-7307
Edmonton 7726 107 St NW *Web:* rmhcna.org	Edmonton	AB	T6E4K3	780-439-5437	433-6201
El Paso 300 E California St *Web:* www.rmhc.org	El Paso	TX	79902	915-542-1522	
Falls Church 3312 Gallows Rd. *TF:* 855-227-7435 ■ *Web:* rmhcdc.org	Falls Church	VA	22042	703-698-7080	698-7745
Fargo 1234 Broadway *Web:* www.rmhcfargo.org	Fargo	ND	58102	701-232-3980	234-9582
Fort Lauderdale 15 SE 15th St *Web:* rmhcsouthflorida.org	Fort Lauderdale	FL	33316	954-828-1822	828-1824
Fort Myers 16100 Roserush Ct *TF:* 800-435-7352 ■ *Web:* www.rmhcswfl.org	Fort Myers	FL	33908	239-437-0202	437-3521
Fort Worth 1004 Seventh Ave *Web:* www.rmhfw.org	Fort Worth	TX	76104	817-870-4942	870-0254
Galveston 301 14th St *TF:* 800-275-2946 ■ *Web:* www.rmhg.org	Galveston	TX	77550	409-762-8770	
Grand Rapids 1323 Cedar St NE *Web:* rmhwesternmichigan.org	Grand Rapids	MI	49503	616-776-1300	776-0368
Greater Cincinnati 350 Erkenbrecher Ave. *Web:* www.rmhcincinnati.org	Cincinnati	OH	45229	513-636-7642	636-4887
Greenville 529 Moye Blvd *Web:* www.rmhenc.org	Greenville	NC	27834	252-847-5435	
Hamilton 1510 Main St W *Web:* www.rmhchamilton.ca	Hamilton	ON	L8S1E3	905-521-9983	521-9515
Hershey 745 W Governor Rd *TF:* 800-732-0999 ■ *Web:* www.rmhc-centralpa.org	Hershey	PA	17033	717-533-4001	533-1299
Honolulu 1970 Judd Hillside Rd *Web:* ronaldhousehawaii.org	Honolulu	HI	96822	808-973-5683	955-8794
Houston 1907 Holcombe Blvd *Web:* www.ronaldmcdonaldhousehouston.org	Houston	TX	77030	713-795-3500	
Huntington 1500 17th St *TF:* 855-227-7435 ■ *Web:* www.mchouse.org	Huntington	WV	25701	304-529-1122	529-2970
Iowa City 730 Hawkins Dr *Web:* rmhc-easterniowa.org	Iowa City	IA	52246	319-356-3939	353-6873
Jacksonville 824 Children's Way *Web:* www.rmhjax.org	Jacksonville	FL	32207	904-807-4663	
Johnson City 418 N State of Franklin Rd *Web:* rmhc.org	Johnson City	TN	37604	423-975-5437	
Joplin 3402 S Jackson Ave PO Box 2688 *Web:* www.rmhjoplin.org	Joplin	MO	64804	417-624-2273	624-0270
Kansas City 2502 Cherry St *TF:* 888-353-4537 ■ *Web:* www.rmhckc.org	Kansas City	MO	64108	816-842-8321	842-7033
Knoxville 1705 W Clinch Ave. *Web:* www.knoxrmhc.org	Knoxville	TN	37916	865-637-7475	525-7942
Lansing 121 S Holmes St	Lansing	MI	48912	517-485-9303	349-0850
Las Vegas 2323 Potosi St *TF:* 888-248-1561 ■ *Web:* www.rmhlv.com	Las Vegas	NV	89146	702-252-4663	252-7345
Little Rock 1009 Wolfe St. *Web:* rmhclittlerock.org	Little Rock	AR	72202	501-374-1956	
Loma Linda 11365 Anderson St. *Web:* rmhcsc.org/lomalinda	Loma Linda	CA	92354	909-558-8300	558-0300
Long Branch 131 Bath Ave. *Web:* www.rmh-cnj.org	Long Branch	NJ	07740	732-222-8755	
Los Angeles (LARMH) 4560 Fountain Ave. *Web:* rmhcsc.org/losangeles	Los Angeles	CA	90029	323-644-3000	669-0552
Macon 1160 Forsyth St *Web:* www.rmhccga.org	Macon	GA	31201	478-746-4090	746-0580
Madera 9161 Randall Way *Web:* www.rmhccv.org	Madera	CA	93636	559-447-6770	
Madison 2716 Marshall Ct	Madison	WI	53705	608-232-4660	232-4670
Marshfield 803 W N St. *Web:* www.rmhc-marshfield.org	Marshfield	WI	54449	715-387-5899	389-5991
Memphis 535 Alabama Ave *Web:* rmhc-memphis.org	Memphis	TN	38105	901-529-4055	523-0315
Minneapolis 818 Fulton St SE *Web:* rmhtwincities.org	Minneapolis	MN	55414	612-331-5752	331-1255
Missoula 1 Kroc Dr	Oak Brook	IL	60523	406-541-7646	
Montreal 5800 Hudson Rd. *Web:* www.manoirmontreal.qc.ca	Montreal	QC	H3S2G5	514-731-2871	739-8823
Morgantown 841 Country Club Dr. *Web:* www.rmhcmorgantown.org	Morgantown	WV	26505	304-598-0050	599-0780
New Brunswick 145 Somerset St *Web:* www.rmh-cnj.org	New Brunswick	NJ	08901	732-249-1222	
New Haven 501 George St *Web:* www.rmhc-ctma.org/ronald-mcdonald-house-connecticut	New Haven	CT	06511	203-777-5683	777-3082
New Hyde Park 267-07 76th Ave *Web:* www.rmhlongisland.org	New Hyde Park	NY	11040	718-343-5683	343-5798
New Orleans 4403 Canal St **Fax Area Code:* 630	New Orleans	LA	70119	504-486-6668	623-7488*
New York 405 E 73rd St. *Web:* www.rmh-newyork.org	New York	NY	10021	212-639-0100	
Norfolk 404 Colley Ave *Web:* www.rmhcnorfolk.org	Norfolk	VA	23507	757-627-5386	622-0534
Northwest Ohio 3883 Monroe St *Web:* www.rmhctoledo.org	Toledo	OH	43606	419-471-4663	479-6961
Oklahoma City 1301 NE 14th St. *Web:* rmhc-okc.org	Oklahoma City	OK	73117	405-424-6873	424-0919
Omaha 620 S 38th Ave	Omaha	NE	68105	402-346-9377	346-9468
Orange 383 S Batavia St *Web:* rmhcsc.org/orangecounty	Orange	CA	92868	714-639-3600	516-3697
Orlando 2201 Alden Rd *Web:* www.ronaldmcdonaldhouseorlando.org	Orlando	FL	32803	407-898-6127	
Orlando 1630 Kuhl Ave *Web:* www.ronaldmcdonaldhouseorlando.org	Orlando	FL	32806	407-581-1289	
Ottawa 407 Smyth Rd. *Web:* www.rmhottawa.com	Ottawa	ON	K1H8M8	613-737-5523	737-5524
Palo Alto 520 Sand Hill Rd *Web:* www.ronaldhouse.net	Palo Alto	CA	94304	650-470-6000	470-6018
Pasadena 763 S Pasadena Ave *Web:* rmhcsc.org/pasadena	Pasadena	CA	91105	626-585-1588	585-1688
Pensacola 5200 Bayou Blvd. *Web:* www.rmhc-nwfl.org	Pensacola	FL	32503	850-477-2273	
Philadelphia 3925 Chestnut St. *TF:* 800-723-0999 ■ *Web:* www.philarmh.org	Philadelphia	PA	19104	215-387-8406	386-4977
Phoenix 501 E Roanoke Ave *TF:* 877-333-2978 ■ *Web:* www.rmhcphoenix.com	Phoenix	AZ	85004	602-264-2654	264-5670
Pittsburgh 451 44th St. *Web:* www.rmhcpgh.org	Pittsburgh	PA	15201	412-362-3400	362-8540

			Phone	Fax
Portland 250 Brackett St ... Portland	ME	04102	207-780-6282	780-0198
Portland 2115 SW River Pkwy ... Portland	OR	97201	971-230-0808	243-2969*
**Fax Area Code:* 503 ■ *Web:* www.rmhcoregon.org				
Portland 2620 N Commercial Ave ... Portland	OR	97227	971-230-6700	
Web: www.rmhcoregon.org				
Providence 45 Gay St ... Providence	RI	02905	401-274-4447	751-3730
TF: 888-353-4537 ■ *Web:* www.rmhprovidence.org				
Richmond 2330 Monument Ave ... Richmond	VA	23220	804-355-6517	358-3153
Web: www.rmhc-richmond.org				
Rio Grande Valley, The 1720 Treasure Hills Blvd ... Harlingen	TX	78550	956-412-7200	412-6300
Web: www.rmhcrgv.org				
Roanoke 2224 S Jefferson St ... Roanoke	VA	24014	540-857-0770	857-9584
Web: rmhc-swva.org				
Rochester 333 Westmoreland Dr ... Rochester	NY	14620	585-442-5437	442-7330
Web: www.rmhcrochester.org				
Sacramento 2555 49th St ... Sacramento	CA	95817	916-734-4230	734-4238
Web: www.rmhcnc.org				
Saint Louis 4381 W Pine Blvd ... Saint Louis	MO	63108	314-531-6601	531-6353
Web: www.rmhcstl.com				
Saint Louis 3450 Pk Ave ... Saint Louis	MO	63104	314-773-1100	773-2053
Web: www.rmhcstl.com				
San Antonio 227 Lewis St ... San Antonio	TX	78212	210-223-6014	
Web: ronaldmcdonaldhouse-sa.org				
San Antonio 4803 Sid Katz Dr ... San Antonio	TX	78229	210-614-2554	614-2905
Web: www.rmhcsanantonio.org				
San Diego 2929 Children's Way ... San Diego	CA	92123	858-467-4750	467-4757
Web: www.rmhcsd.org				
San Francisco 1640 Scott St ... San Francisco	CA	94115	415-673-0891	673-1335
Web: www.ronaldhouse-sf.org				
Saskatoon 1011 University Dr ... Saskatoon	SK	S7N0K4	306-244-5700	244-3099
Web: www.rmh.sk.ca				
Scranton 332 Wheeler Ave ... Scranton	PA	18510	570-969-8998	969-8991
Web: rmhscranton.org				
Seattle 5130 40th Ave NE ... Seattle	WA	98105	206-838-0600	
TF: 866-987-9330 ■ *Web:* www.rmhcseattle.org				
Spokane 1015 W Fifth Ave ... Spokane	WA	99204	509-624-0500	624-3267
Web: www.rmhcspokane.org				
Springfield 34 Chapin Terr ... Springfield	MA	01107	413-794-5683	
Web: www.rmhc-ctma.org/ronald-mcdonald-house-springfield				
Springfield 949 E Primrose St ... Springfield	MO	65807	417-886-0225	
Web: www.rmhcozarks.org				
Tallahassee 712 E Seventh Ave ... Tallahassee	FL	32303	850-222-0056	222-0086
Web: www.rmhctallahassee.org				
Tampa 35 Columbia Dr ... Tampa	FL	33606	813-254-2398	254-8891
Web: rmhctampabay.org				
Temple 2415 S 47th St ... Temple	TX	76504	254-770-0910	770-1622
Web: rmhc-temple.com				
Topeka 825 SW Buchanan St ... Topeka	KS	66606	785-235-6852	
Web: www.rmhctopeka.org				
Toronto 26 Gerrard St E ... Toronto	ON	M5T1W5	416-977-0458	977-8807
Web: www.rmhctoronto.ca				
Tucson 1 Kroc Dr ... Oak Brook	IL	60523	520-326-0060	
Web: www.rmhctucson.org				
Tulsa 6102 S Hudson Ave ... Tulsa	OK	74136	918-496-2727	496-2762
Web: www.rmhtulsa.org				
Washington 3727 14th St NE ... Washington	DC	20017	202-529-8204	635-3578
Web: rmhcdc.org				
Wauwatosa 8948 W Watertown Plank Rd ... Wauwatosa	WI	53226	414-475-5333	475-6342
Web: rmhcmilwaukee.org				
Wilmington 1901 Rockland Rd ... Wilmington	DE	19803	302-656-4847	
TF: 888-656-4847 ■ *Web:* www.rmhde.org				
Winnipeg 566 Bannatyne Ave ... Winnipeg	MB	R3A0G7	204-774-4777	774-2160
Web: www.rmhmanitoba.org				
Winston-Salem 419 S Hawthorne Rd ... Winston-Salem	NC	27103	336-723-0228	723-0302
TF: 855-227-7435 ■ *Web:* www.rmhws.org				
Ronald McDonald House - Midtown 1110 N Emporia St ... Wichita	KS	67214	316-269-4420	269-0665
Web: www.rmhcwichita.org				
Ronald McDonald House - Sleepy Hollow 520 N Rutan ... Wichita	KS	67208	316-687-2000	
Web: www.rmhcwichita.org				
Ronald McDonald House BC 4567 Heather St ... Vancouver	BC	V5Z0C9	604-736-2957	736-5974
Web: www.rmhbc.ca				
Ronald McDonald House Charities (RMHC) 1 Kroc Dr ... Oak Brook	IL	60523	630-623-7048	623-7488
TF: 855-670-4787 ■ *Web:* www.rmhc.org				
Atlanta 5420 Peachtree Dunwoody Rd ... Sandy Springs	GA	30342	404-847-0760	
Web: www.armhc.org				
Dayton 555 Valley St ... Dayton	OH	45404	937-224-0047	
Web: rmhc.org				
Gainesville 1600 SW 14th St ... Gainesville	FL	32608	352-374-4404	335-5325
TF: 800-435-7352 ■ *Web:* www.rmhcncf.org				
Halifax 1133 Tower Rd ... Halifax	NS	B3H2Y7	902-429-4044	429-8650
Web: rmhatlantic.com				
Reno 323 Maine St ... Reno	NV	89502	775-322-4663	
Web: www.rmhc-reno.com				
Sioux City 2500 Nebraska St ... Sioux City	IA	51104	712-255-4084	255-4281
Web: rmhc-siouxland.org				
Springfield 610 N Seventh St ... Springfield	IL	62702	217-528-3314	528-6084
Web: www.rmhc-centralillinois.org				
Ronald McDonald House Charities of Central Ohio 711 E Livingston Ave ... Columbus	OH	43205	614-227-3700	227-3765
Web: www.rmhc-centralohio.org				
Ronald McDonald House Charities of Denver Inc 1300 E 21st Ave ... Denver	CO	80205	303-832-2667	832-3802
Web: www.ronaldhouse.org				
Ronald McDonald House Charities of Kentuckiana (RMHC) 550 S First St ... Louisville	KY	40202	502-581-1416	581-0037
Web: www.rmhc-kentuckiana.org				
Ronald McDonald House Charities of Nashville *Nashville* 2144 Fairfax Ave ... Nashville	TN	37212	615-343-4000	343-4004
Web: www.rmhcnashville.com				
Ronald McDonald House Charities of the Southwest 3413 Tenth St ... Lubbock	TX	79415	806-744-8877	744-3652
Web: www.rmhcsouthwest.com				
Ronald McDonald House Charities's *Salt Lake City* 935 E Temple ... Salt Lake City	UT	84102	801-363-4663	363-0092
Web: www.rmhslc.org				
Ronald McDonald House of Columbia 2955 Colonial Dr ... Columbia	SC	29203	803-254-3181	254-8688
Web: www.rmhcofcolumbia.org				
Ronald McDonald House of Southwestern Ontario 741 Base Line Rd E ... London	ON	N6C2R6	519-685-3232	
Web: www.rmhlondon.ca				

374 HOSPITALS

See Also Health Care Providers - Ancillary p. 2453; Health Care Systems p. 2454; Hospices p. 2484; Veterans Nursing Homes - State p. 3292

HOSPITALS - DEVELOPMENTAL DISABILITIES

374-1 Children's Hospitals

			Phone	Fax
Alfred I duPont Hospital for Children 1600 Rockland Rd ... Wilmington	DE	19803	302-651-4000	651-4224*
**Fax:* Admitting ■ *Web:* www.nemours.org				
Arkansas Children's Hospital 1 Children's Way ... Little Rock	AR	72202	501-364-1100	364-1452
Web: www.archildrens.org				
Arnold Palmer Hospital for Children & Women 92 W Miller St ... Orlando	FL	32806	407-649-9111	
TF: 800-648-3818 ■ *Web:* www.orlandohealth.com				
Bradley Hospital 1011 Veterans Memorial Pkwy ... East Providence	RI	02915	401-432-1000	432-1500
Web: www.bradleyhospital.org				
Children's Healthcare of Atlanta at Egleston 1405 Clifton Rd NE ... Atlanta	GA	30322	404-785-6000	
TF: 888-785-7778 ■ *Web:* www.choa.org				
Children's Healthcare of Atlanta at Scottish Rite 1001 Johnson Ferry Rd NE ... Atlanta	GA	30342	404-785-5252	
TF: 888-785-7778 ■ *Web:* www.choa.org				
Children's Hospital 200 Henry Clay Ave ... New Orleans	LA	70118	504-899-9511	896-9708*
**Fax:* Admitting ■ *TF:* 800-299-9511 ■ *Web:* www.chnola.org				
Children's Hospital & Medical Ctr 8200 Dodge St ... Omaha	NE	68114	402-955-5400	955-4046*
**Fax:* Admitting ■ *Web:* childrensomaha.org				
Children's Hospital & Research Ctr at Oakland 747 52nd St ... Oakland	CA	94609	510-428-3000	450-5884*
**Fax:* Admitting ■ *Web:* www.childrenshospitaloakland.org				
Children's Hospital Boston 300 Longwood Ave ... Boston	MA	02115	617-355-6000	
Web: www.childrenshospital.org				
Children's Hospital Medical Ctr of Akron 1 Perkins Sq ... Akron	OH	44308	330-543-1000	543-3146*
**Fax:* Admitting ■ *TF:* 800-262-0333 ■ *Web:* www.akronchildrens.org				
Children's Hospital of Alabama 1600 Seventh Ave S ... Birmingham	AL	35233	205-939-9100	
Web: childrensal.org				
Children's Hospital of Michigan 3901 Beaubien Blvd ... Detroit	MI	48201	313-745-5437	993-0385*
**Fax:* Admitting ■ *Web:* www.dmc.org				
Children's Hospital of Orange County 455 S Main St ... Orange	CA	92868	714-997-3000	
Web: www.choc.org				
Children's Hospital of Philadelphia 3400 Civic Ctr Blvd ... Philadelphia	PA	19104	215-590-1000	
Web: www.chop.edu				
Children's Hospital of Pittsburgh 4401 Penn Ave ... Pittsburgh	PA	15224	412-692-5325	
Web: www.chp.edu				
Children's Hospital of the King's Daughters 601 Children's Ln ... Norfolk	VA	23507	757-668-7000	
Web: www.chkd.org				
Children's Hospital of Wisconsin 9000 W Wisconsin Ave ... Milwaukee	WI	53226	414-266-2000	266-2547*
**Fax:* Admitting ■ *Web:* www.chw.org				
Children's Hospitals & Clinics Minneapolis 2525 Chicago Ave ... Minneapolis	MN	55404	612-813-6000	813-6807
TF: 866-225-3251 ■ *Web:* childrensmn.org				
Children's Institute of Pittsburgh 1405 Shady Ave ... Pittsburgh	PA	15217	412-420-2400	420-2200
TF: 877-433-1109 ■ *Web:* www.amazingkids.org				
Children's Medical Ctr 1 Children's Plaza ... Dayton	OH	45404	937-641-3000	641-3326*
**Fax:* Admitting ■ *TF:* 800-228-4055 ■ *Web:* www.childrensdayton.org				
Children's Medical Ctr of Dallas 1935 Medical District Dr ... Dallas	TX	75235	214-456-7000	456-2197
Web: www.childrens.com				
Children's Memorial Hospital 2300 Children's Plz ... Chicago	IL	60614	312-227-4000	
Web: www.luriechildrens.org				
Children's Mercy Hospital & Clinics 2401 Gillham Rd ... Kansas City	MO	64108	816-234-3000	
TF: 866-512-2168 ■ *Web:* www.childrensmercy.org				
Children's National Medical Ctr (CNMC) 111 Michigan Ave NW ... Washington	DC	20010	202-476-5000	
TF: 800-884-5433 ■ *Web:* www.childrensnational.org				
Children's Specialized Hospital 150 New Providence Rd ... Mountainside	NJ	07092	908-233-3720	233-4967
TF: 888-244-5373 ■ *Web:* www.childrens-specialized.org				
Cincinnati Children's Hospital Medical Ctr 3333 Burnet Ave ... Cincinnati	OH	45229	513-636-4200	636-3733*
**Fax:* Admitting ■ *TF:* 800-344-2462 ■ *Web:* www.cincinnatichildrens.org				

Name / Address	City	State	Zip	Phone	Fax
Connecticut Children's Medical Ctr 282 Washington St	Hartford	CT	06106	860-545-9000	
Web: www.connecticutchildrens.org					
Cook Children's Medical Ctr 801 Seventh Ave	Fort Worth	TX	76104	682-885-4000	885-4229
Web: cookchildrens.org					
Copper Hills Youth Ctr 5899 Rivendell Dr	West Jordan	UT	84081	800-776-7116	569-2959*
*Fax Area Code: 801 ■ *TF:* 800-776-7116 ■ *Web:* www.copperhillsyouthcenter.com					
Covenant Children's Hospital (CCH) 4015 22nd Pl	Lubbock	TX	79410	806-725-0000	
Web: covenanthealth.org/about-us/facilities/childrenshospital/default					
Crittenton Children's Ctr 10918 Elm Ave	Kansas City	MO	64134	816-765-6600	767-4101
Web: www.saintlukeshealthsystem.org					
CS Mott Children's Hospital 1500 E Medical Ctr Dr	Ann Arbor	MI	48109	734-936-4000	763-7736
TF: 800-211-8181 ■ *Web:* www.med.umich.edu					
Devereux 1291 Stanley Rd NW PO Box 1688	Kennesaw	GA	30156	678-303-5233	
TF: 800-342-3357 ■ *Web:* www.devereux.org					
Devereux Cleo Wallace 8405 Church Ranch Blvd	Westminster	CO	80021	303-466-7391	466-0904*
*Fax: Admitting ■ *TF:* 800-456-2536 ■ *Web:* www.devereux.org					
Devereux Hospital & Children's Ctr of Florida 8000 Devereux Dr	Melbourne	FL	32940	321-242-9100	
TF: 800-338-3738 ■ *Web:* devereux.org					
Driscoll Children's Hospital 3533 S Alameda St	Corpus Christi	TX	78411	361-694-5000	694-5010
TF: 800-324-5683 ■ *Web:* www.driscollchildrens.org					
East Tennessee Children's Hospital 2018 Clinch Ave PO Box 15010	Knoxville	TN	37901	865-541-8000	
Web: www.etch.com					
Franciscan Hospital for Children 30 Warren St	Boston	MA	02135	617-254-3800	779-1119
Web: franciscanchildrens.org					
Gillette Children's Specialty Healthcare 200 E University Ave	Saint Paul	MN	55101	651-291-2848	229-3999
TF: 800-719-4040 ■ *Web:* www.gillettechildrens.org					
Gulf Coast Treatment Ctr 1015 Mar-Walt Dr	Fort Walton Beach	FL	32547	850-863-4160	863-8576
TF: 800-537-5433 ■ *Web:* www.gulfcoastyouthservices.com					
Hawthorn Ctr 18471 Haggerty Rd	Northville	MI	48167	248-349-3000	349-8259
TF: 855-444-3911 ■ *Web:* michigan.gov					
Helen DeVos Children's Hospital 100 Michigan St NE	Grand Rapids	MI	49503	616-391-9000	391-3105
TF: 800-222-1222 ■ *Web:* www.helendevoschildrens.org					
HSC Pediatric Ctr 1731 Bunker Hill Rd NE	Washington	DC	20017	202-832-4400	529-1646
TF: 800-226-4444 ■ *Web:* www.hschealth.org/medical-programs-therapy					
JD McCarty Ctr for Children with Developmental Disabilities 2002 E Robinson St	Norman	OK	73071	405-307-2800	307-2801
TF: 800-777-1272 ■ *Web:* jdmc.org					
Kennedy Krieger Institute 707 N Broadway	Baltimore	MD	21205	443-923-9200	923-9425
TF: 800-873-3377 ■ *Web:* www.kennedykrieger.org					
KidsPeace Orchard Hills Campus 5300 Kids Peace Dr	Orefield	PA	18069	800-257-3223	
TF: 800-257-3223 ■ *Web:* www.kidspeace.org					
Larabida Children's Hospital & Research Ctr 6501 S Promontory Dr E 65th St at Lk Michigan	Chicago	IL	60649	773-363-6700	
Web: www.larabida.org					
Lucile Packard Children's Hospital (LPCH) 725 Welch Rd	Palo Alto	CA	94304	650-497-8000	497-8968*
*Fax: Admitting ■ *TF:* 800-995-5724 ■ *Web:* stanfordchildrens.org					
Mary Bridge Children's Hospital & Health Ctr 317 Martin Luther King Jr Way	Tacoma	WA	98405	253-403-1400	403-1247
TF: 800-552-1419 ■ *Web:* www.multicare.org					
Massachusetts Hospital School 3 Randolph St	Canton	MA	02021	781-828-2440	821-4086
Web: mhsf.us					
Medical University of South Carolina Children's Hospital 165 Ashley Ave	Charleston	SC	29425	843-792-2300	
Web: www.musckids.org					
Miami Children's Hospital 3100 SW 62nd Ave	Miami	FL	33155	305-666-6511	663-8466
TF: 800-432-6837 ■ *Web:* www.nicklauschildrens.org/home					
Mount Washington Pediatric Hospital 1708 W Rogers Ave	Baltimore	MD	21209	410-578-8600	
Web: www.mwph.org					
New York City Children's Ctr-Queens Campus (NYCCC) 74-03 Commonwealth Blvd	Bellerose	NY	11426	718-264-4500	740-0968
TF: 800-597-8481 ■ *Web:* www.omh.ny.gov					
Phoenix Children's Hospital 1919 E Thomas Rd	Phoenix	AZ	85016	602-546-1000	933-0628
TF: 888-908-5437 ■ *Web:* www.phoenixchildrens.org					
Primary Children's Medical Ctr 100 N Medical Dr	Salt Lake City	UT	84113	801-662-1000	
Web: www.intermountainhealthcare.org					
Rady Children's Hospital (RCH) 3020 Children's Way MC 5101	San Diego	CA	92123	858-576-1700	966-5859*
*Fax: Library ■ *TF:* 800-788-9029 ■ *Web:* www.rchsd.org					
Saint Louis Children's Hospital 1 Children's Pl	Saint Louis	MO	63110	314-454-6000	
TF: 800-427-4626 ■ *Web:* www.stlouischildrens.org					
Seattle Children's Hospital 4800 Sand Pt Way NE	Seattle	WA	98105	206-987-2000	987-5060*
*Fax: Admitting ■ *TF:* 866-987-2000 ■ *Web:* www.seattlechildrens.org					
Shriners Hospitals for Children Boston 51 Blossom St	Boston	MA	02114	617-722-3000	523-1684
TF: 800-255-1916 ■ *Web:* www.shrinershospitalsforchildren.org					
Shriners Hospitals for Children Canada 1529 Cedar Ave	Montreal	QC	H3G1A6	514-842-4464	842-7553
TF: 800-361-7256 ■ *Web:* shrinershospitalsforchildren.org					
Shriners Hospitals for Children Chicago 2211 N Oak Pk Ave	Chicago	IL	60707	773-622-5400	
Web: www.shrinershq.org					
Shriners Hospitals for Children Cincinnati 3229 Burnet Ave	Cincinnati	OH	45229	513-872-6000	872-6999
TF: 800-875-8580 ■ *Web:* shrinershospitalcincinnati.org					
Shriners Hospitals for Children Erie 1645 W Eigth St	Erie	PA	16505	814-875-8700	875-8756
TF: 800-873-5437 ■ *Web:* shrinershospitalsforchildren.org					
Shriners Hospitals for Children Galveston 2900 Rocky Pt Dr	Tampa	Fl	33607	813-281-0300	
TF: 844-739-0849 ■ *Web:* shrinershospitalsforchildren.org					
Shriners Hospitals for Children Greenville 950 W Faris Rd	Greenville	SC	29605	864-271-3444	271-4471
TF: 800-361-7256 ■ *Web:* www.shrinershospitalsforchildren.org					
Shriners Hospitals for Children Honolulu 1310 Punahou St	Honolulu	HI	96826	808-941-4466	
Web: www.shrinershq.org					
Shriners Hospitals for Children Houston 6977 Main St	Houston	TX	77030	713-797-1616	
Web: www.shrinershq.org					
Shriners Hospitals for Children Lexington 1900 Richmond Rd	Lexington	KY	40502	859-266-2101	268-5636
TF: 800-668-4634 ■ *Web:* shrinershospitalsforchildren.org					
Shriners Hospitals for Children Los Angeles 3160 Geneva St	Los Angeles	CA	90020	213-388-3151	387-7528*
*Fax: Admitting ■ *TF:* 888-486-5437 ■ *Web:* losangelesshrinershospital.org					
Shriners Hospitals for Children Northern California 2425 Stockton Blvd	Sacramento	CA	95817	916-453-2000	
Web: www.shrinershq.org					
Shriners Hospitals for Children Philadelphia 3551 N Broad St	Philadelphia	PA	19140	215-430-4000	430-4079
TF: 800-281-4050 ■ *Web:* www.shrinershospitalsforchildren.org					
Shriners Hospitals for Children Portland 3101 SW Sam Jackson Pk Rd	Portland	OR	97239	503-241-5090	
Web: www.shrinershospitalsforchildren.org					
Shriners Hospitals for Children Salt Lake City Fairfax Rd & Virginia St	Salt Lake City	UT	84103	801-536-3500	536-3782
TF: 800-313-3745 ■ *Web:* www.shrinershospitalsforchildren.org					
Shriners Hospitals for Children Shreveport 3100 Samford Ave	Shreveport	LA	71103	318-222-5704	424-7610
Web: www.shrinershospitalsforchildren.org					
Shriners Hospitals for Children Spokane 911 W Fifth Ave	Spokane	WA	99204	509-455-7844	
Web: www.shrinershq.org					
Shriners Hospitals for Children Tampa 12502 N Pine Dr	Tampa	FL	33612	813-972-2250	240-3113*
*Fax Area Code: 864 ■ *Fax: Admitting ■ *TF:* 800-237-5055 ■ *Web:* shrinershospitalsforchildren.org					
Shriners Hospitals for Children Twin Cities 2025 E River Pkwy	Minneapolis	MN	55414	612-596-6100	
Web: www.shrinershq.org					
SSM Cardinal Glennon Children's Hospital 1465 S Grand Blvd	Saint Louis	MO	63104	314-577-5600	
Web: www.cardinalglennon.com					
Streamwood Behavioral Health Ctr 1400 E Irving Pk Rd	Streamwood	IL	60107	630-837-9000	837-2639
TF: 800-272-7790 ■ *Web:* www.streamwoodhospital.com					
Texas Children's Hospital 6621 Fannin St	Houston	TX	77030	832-824-1000	825-3058
TF: 800-364-5437 ■ *Web:* texaschildrens.org					
Texas Scottish Rite Hospital for Children 2222 Welborn St	Dallas	TX	75219	214-559-5000	559-7447
TF: 800-421-1121 ■ *Web:* www.tsrhc.org					
Valley Children's Healthcare 9300 Valley Children's Pl	Madera	CA	93636	559-353-3000	353-8888*
*Fax: Admitting ■ *Web:* www.childrenscentralcal.org					
Wolfson Children's Hospital 800 Prudential Dr	Jacksonville	FL	32207	904-202-8000	
Web: www.wolfsonchildrens.org					
Women's & Children's Hospital of Buffalo 219 Bryant St	Buffalo	NY	14222	716-878-7000	888-3979*
*Fax: Admitting ■ *TF:* 800-462-7653 ■ *Web:* www.kaleidahealth.org					
Youth Villages Inner Harbour 4685 Dorsett Shoals Rd	Douglasville	GA	30135	770-852-6333	
TF: 800-255-8657 ■ *Web:* www.youthvillages.org					

374-2 General Hospitals - Canada

				Phone	Fax
Aberdeen Hospital 835 E River Rd	New Glasgow	NS	B2H3S6	902-752-7600	755-2356
Web: www.aberdeenhealthfoundation.com					
Battlefords Union Hospital 1092 107th St	North Battleford	SK	S9A1Z1	306-446-6600	
Web: buhfoundation.com					
Belleville General Hospital 265 Dundas St E	Belleville	ON	K8N5A9	613-969-7400	968-8234
TF: 800-483-2811 ■ *Web:* www.qhc.on.ca					
Brandon Regional Health Ctr 150 McTavish Ave E	Brandon	MB	R7A2B3	204-578-4000	578-4937
Web: www.brandonrha.mb.ca					
British Columbia's Women's Hospital & Health Centre 4500 Oak St	Vancouver	BC	V6H3N1	604-875-2424	
TF: 888-300-3088 ■ *Web:* www.bcwomens.ca					
Brockville General Hospital 75 Charles St	Brockville	ON	K6V1S8	613-345-5645	
TF: 800-567-7415 ■ *Web:* www.bgh-on.ca					
Burnaby Hospital 3935 Kincaid St	Burnaby	BC	V5G2X6	604-453-1910	
Web: www.fraserhealth.ca					
Cambridge Memorial Hospital 700 Coronation Blvd	Cambridge	ON	N1R3G2	519-621-2330	740-4938
Web: www.cmh.org					
Campbell River Hospital 375 Second Ave	Campbell River	BC	V9W3V1	250-850-2141	
Web: www.viha.ca					
Centre de sant et de services sociaux d'Argenteuil 145 boul Providence	Lachute	QC	J8H4C7	450-562-3761	566-3316
Web: csssargenteuil.qc.ca					
Centre de Sante de la MRC de Maskinonge 41 Boul Comtois	Louiseville	QC	J5V2H8	819-228-2731	228-0425
Web: www.csssm.qc.ca					
Centre Hospitalier Affilie Universitaire de Quebec-Pavillon Saint-Sacrement 1050 Ch Sainte-Foy	Quebec	QC	G1S4L8	418-682-7511	682-7877*
*Fax: Admissions ■ *Web:* www.cha.quebec.qc.ca					

Hospital	City	Prov	Postal Code	Phone	Fax
Centre Hospitalier d'Amqui 135 Rue de l'Hopital *Web:* www.chamqui.com	Amqui	QC	G5J2K5	418-629-2211	629-4498
Centre Hospitalier Hotel-Dieu d'Amos 622 4e Rue O *Web:* csssea.ca	Amos	QC	J9T2S2	819-732-3341	
Centre Hospitalier Hotel-Dieu de Roberval 450 Rue Brassard *Web:* www.csssdomaineduroy.com	Roberval	QC	G8H1B9	418-275-0110	275-6202
Centre Hospitalier Le Gardeur 911 Montee des Pionniers *TF:* 888-654-7525 ■ *Web:* www.csss.sudlanaudiere.ca	Terrebonne	QC	J6V2H2	450-654-7525	470-2640
Centre Hospitalier Mount Sinai 5690 Cavendish Blvd *Web:* sinaimontreal.ca	Montreal	QC	H4W1S7	514-369-2222	369-2225
Centre Hospitalier Pierre Boucher 1333 Boul Jacques-Cartier E *TF:* 866-277-3553	Longueuil	QC	J4M2A5	450-468-8111	465-4369
Centre Hospitalier Regional du Grand Portage 75 Rue St Henri *Web:* csssrivieredulou p.qc.ca	Riviere-du-Loup	QC	G5R2A4	418-868-1010	868-1035
Centre Hospitalier Regional du Suroit 150 Rue St Thomas *Web:* centrejeunessemonteregie.qc.ca	Salaberry-de-Valleyfield	QC	J6T6C1	450-371-9920	371-7454
Chatham-Kent Health Alliance 80 Grand Ave W PO Box 2030 *Web:* www.ckha.on.ca	Chatham	ON	N7M5L9	519-352-6400	436-2522
Children's Hospital of Eastern Ontario 401 Smyth Rd *TF:* 866-797-0007 ■ *Web:* www.cheo.on.ca	Ottawa	ON	K1H8L1	613-737-7600	738-4866
Chilliwack General Hospital 45600 Menholm Rd *Web:* www.fraserhealth.ca	Chilliwack	BC	V2P1P7	604-795-4141	795-4110
CHU Sainte-Justine 3175 Ch de la Cote-Sainte-Catherine *TF:* 888-235-3667 ■ *Web:* www.chusj.org/fr/accueil	Montreal	QC	H3T1C5	514-345-4931	345-4760
Colchester Regional Hospital 207 Willow St *TF:* 800-460-2110 ■ *Web:* www.cehha.nshealth.ca	Truro	NS	B2N5A1	902-893-4321	893-5559
Concordia Hospital 1095 Concordia Ave *TF:* 888-315-9257 ■ *Web:* www.concordiahospital.mb.ca	Winnipeg	MB	R2K3S8	204-667-1560	667-1049
Cornwall Community Hospital 840 McConnell Ave *TF:* 866-263-1560 ■ *Web:* www.cornwallhospital.ca	Cornwall	ON	K6H5S5	613-938-4240	930-4502
Credit Valley Hospital 2200 Eglinton Ave W *TF:* 877-292-4284 ■ *Web:* www.cvh.on.ca	Mississauga	ON	L5M2N1	905-813-2200	813-4444
CSSS du Lac des Deux-Montagnes 520 Boul Sauve *Web:* www.moncsss.com	Saint-Eustache	QC	J7R5B1	450-473-6811	473-6966
Cypress Regional Hospital 2004 Saskatchewan Dr *Web:* www.cypressrha.ca	Swift Current	SK	S9H5M8	306-778-9400	
Dartmouth General Hospital 325 Pleasant St *Web:* www.cdha.nshealth.ca	Dartmouth	NS	B2Y3S3	902-465-8539	
Delta Hospital Foundation 5800 Mtn View Blvd *Web:* www.dhfoundation.ca	Delta	BC	V4K3V6	604-940-9695	940-9670
Dr Georges L Dumont Regional Hospital 330 University Ave *Web:* vitalitenb.ca	Moncton	NB	E2A1A9	506-862-4000	
Eagle Ridge Hospital & Health Care Centre 475 Guildford Way *Web:* www.fraserhealth.ca	Port Moody	BC	V3H3W9	604-461-2022	461-9972
Foothills Medical Centre (FMC) 1403 29th St NW **Fax Area Code:* 403 ■ *Web:* www.albertahealthservices.ca	Calgary	AB	T2N2T9	780-342-2000	944-1663*
Glace Bay Healthcare Facility (GBHF) 300 S St *Web:* www.cbdha.nshealth.ca	Glace Bay	NS	B1A1K9	902-849-5511	842-9775
Grace General Hospital 300 Booth Dr *Web:* www.gracehospital.ca	Winnipeg	MB	R3J3M7	204-837-0111	831-0029
Grand River Hospital Kitchener-Waterloo Health Centre 835 King St W PO Box 9056 *Web:* www.grhosp.on.ca	Kitchener	ON	N2G1G3	519-749-4300	749-4208
Greater Niagara General Hospital 5546 Portage Rd *Web:* www.niagarahealth.on.ca	Niagara Falls	ON	L2E6X2	905-378-4647	358-8435
Grey Bruce Health Services 1800 Eigth St E PO Box 1800 *Web:* www.gbhs.on.ca	Owen Sound	ON	N4K6M9	519-376-2121	372-3942
Guelph General Hospital 115 Delhi St *Web:* www.gghorg.ca	Guelph	ON	N1E4J4	519-822-5350	837-6773
Hamilton Health Sciences 1200 Main St W *Web:* www.hamiltonhealthsciences.ca	Hamilton	ON	L8N3Z5	905-521-2100	
Headwaters Health Care Centre 100 Rolling Hills Dr *Web:* www.headwatershealth.ca	Orangeville	ON	L9W4X9	519-941-2410	942-0483
Health Sciences Centre 820 Sherbrook St *Web:* www.hsc.mb.ca	Winnipeg	MB	R3A1R9	204-787-3661	787-3341
High River Hospital 560 Ninth Ave W *Web:* albertahealthservices.ca	High River	AB	T1V1B3	403-652-2200	652-0199
Hopital Brome Missisquoi-Perkins 950 Rue Principale *Web:* www.santemonteregie.qc.ca/lapommeraie/services/lieux/detail/hopital-bmp.fr.html#.V6G7367l7rd	Cowansville	QC	J2K1K3	450-266-4342	263-8669
Hopital Charles LeMoyne (HCLM) 3120 boul Taschereau *Web:* santemonteregie.qc.ca/champlaincharleslemoyne/index.fr.html	Greenfield Park	QC	J4V2H1	450-466-5000	466-5038
Hopital de Papineau 500 Rue Belanger *Web:* www.cssspapineau.qc.ca	Gatineau	QC	J8L2M4	819-986-3341	
Hopital du Haut-Richelieu 920 Boul du Seminaire N	Saint-Jean-sur-Richelieu	QC	J3A1B7	450-359-5000	359-5251
Hopital Jean-Talon 1385 Jean-Talon St E	Montreal	QC	H2E1S6	514-495-6767	495-6771
Hopital Sainte-Croix 570 Rue Heriot	Drummondville	QC	J2B1C1	819-478-6464	478-6455
Hopital Santa Cabrini 6887 rue Chtelain	Montreal	QC	H1T3X7	514-252-1535	
Hospital Complex Sagamie, The 305 Ave St Vallier CP 5006 *Web:* www.usherbrooke.ca	Chicoutimi	QC	G7H5H6	418-541-1000	541-1168
Hospital Gatineau 909 boul de la Verandrye *Web:* www.csssgatineau.qc.ca	Gatineau	QC	J8P7H2	819-966-6100	
Hotel Dieu Hospital 166 Brock St *TF:* 855-544-3400 ■ *Web:* www.hoteldieu.com	Kingston	ON	K7L5G2	613-544-3310	
Hotel-Dieu d'Arthabaska 5 Rue des Hospitalieres *Web:* www.csssae.qc.ca	Victoriaville	QC	G6P6N2	819-357-2030	758-7281
Hotel-Dieu de Sorel 400 Ave Hotel-Dieu *Web:* fondationhoteldieusorel.org	Sorel-Tracy	QC	J3P1N5	450-746-6003	746-6082
Hotel-Dieu Grace Hospital 1030 Ouellette Ave *Web:* www.hdgh.org	Windsor	ON	N9A1E1	519-973-4411	258-5120
James Paton Memorial Hospital 125 Trans Canada Hwy *Web:* centralhealth.nl.ca	Gander	NL	A1V1P7	709-256-2500	256-7800
Jeffrey Hale - St Brigid's Hospital 1250 ch Sainte-Foy *TF:* 888-984-5333 ■ *Web:* jhsb.ca	Quebec	QC	G1S2M6	418-684-5333	684-5333
Joseph Brant Memorial Hospital (JBMH) 1230 N Shore Blvd *TF:* 800-810-0000 ■ *Web:* www.josephbranthospital.ca	Burlington	ON	L7S1W7	905-632-3730	336-6480
Kelowna General Hospital (KGH) 2268 Pandosy St *TF:* 888-877-4442 ■ *Web:* www.interiorhealth.ca	Kelowna	BC	V1Y1T2	250-862-4000	862-4020
Kootenay Boundary Regional Hospital 1200 Hospital Bench *Web:* www.interiorhealth.ca	Trail	BC	V1R4M1	250-368-3311	
Lachine General Hospital 650 16th Ave	Lachine	QC	H8S3N5	514-637-7789	
Lacombe Hospital & Care Centre 5430 47th Ave *Web:* www.albertahealthservices.ca	Lacombe	AB	T4L1G8	403-782-3336	782-2818
Lake of the Woods District Hospital (LWDH) 21 Sylvan St *Web:* www.lwdh.on.ca	Kenora	ON	P9N3W7	807-468-9861	468-3939
Lakeridge Health Bowmanville 47 Liberty St S *Web:* www.lakeridgehealth.on.ca	Bowmanville	ON	L1C2N4	905-623-3331	743-5943
Lakeridge Health Oshawa 1 Hospital Ct *TF:* 866-338-1778 ■ *Web:* www.lakeridgehealth.on.ca	Oshawa	ON	L1G2B9	905-576-8711	721-4736
Lakeshore General Hospital (LGH) 160 Stillview Ste 5209 *Web:* www.fondationlakeshore.ca	Pointe-Claire	QC	H9R2Y2	514-630-2081	
Langevin Pierre Dr 2705 Laurier Blvd	Quebec	QC	G1V4G2	418-656-4141	654-2247
Langley Memorial Hospital 22051 Fraser Hwy *Web:* www.fraserhealth.ca	Langley	BC	V3A4H4	604-534-4121	534-8283
Lions Gate Hospital 231 E 15th St *TF:* 800-984-1131 ■ *Web:* www.vch.ca	North Vancouver	BC	V7L2L7	604-988-3131	984-5838
London Health Sciences Centre 800 Commissioners Rd E PO Box 5010 *Web:* www.lhsc.on.ca	London	ON	N6A5W9	519-685-8500	685-8127
London Health Sciences Centre Victoria Campus 800 Commissioners Rd E *Web:* www.lhsc.on.ca	London	ON	N6C6B5	519-685-8500	685-8127
Markham Stouffville Hospital *Markham* 381 Church St PO Box 1800 *Web:* www.msh.on.ca	Markham	ON	L3P7P3	905-472-7000	472-7086
Medical Clinic of North Texas 9003 Airport Fwy Ste 300 *Web:* www.mcnt.com	North Richland	TX	76180	817-514-5200	514-5210
Medicine Hat Regional Hospital 666 Fifth St SW *Web:* albertahealthservices.ca	Medicine Hat	AB	T1A4H6	403-529-8000	529-8998
Misericordia Community Hospital & Health Centre 16940 87th Ave	Edmonton	AB	T5R4H5	780-735-2000	735-2774
Mission Memorial Hospital 7324 Hurd St *Web:* www.fraserhealth.ca	Mission	BC	V2V3H5	604-826-6261	826-9513
Moncton Hospital, The 135 MacBeath Ave *Web:* horizonnb.ca	Moncton	NB	E1C6Z8	506-857-5111	857-5545
Montfort Hospital 713 Montreal Rd *TF:* 866-670-4621 ■ *Web:* www.hopitalmontfort.com	Ottawa	ON	K1K0T2	613-746-4621	748-4914
Montreal Heart Institute 5000 Belanger St E *TF:* 855-922-6387 ■ *Web:* www.icm-mhi.org	Montreal	QC	H1T1C8	514-376-3330	593-2540
Mount Saint Joseph Hospital 3080 Prince Edward St *Web:* providencehealthcare.org	Vancouver	BC	V5T3N4	604-874-1141	
Mount Sinai Hospital 600 University Ave **Fax:* PR ■ *Web:* www.mountsinai.on.ca	Toronto	ON	M5G1X5	416-596-4200	586-4807*
Nanaimo Regional General Hospital 1200 Dufferin Crescent	Nanaimo	BC	V9S2B7	250-755-7691	
Norfolk General Hospital 365 W St *Web:* www.ngh.on.ca	Simcoe	ON	N3Y1T7	519-426-0750	429-6998
North Bay Regional Health Centre 50 College Dr PO Box 2500 *Web:* www.nbrhc.on.ca	North Bay	ON	P1B5A4	705-474-7525	
North York General Hospital (NYGH) 4001 Leslie St **Fax:* Hum Res ■ *Web:* www.nygh.on.ca	North York	ON	M2K1E1	416-756-6000	756-6738*
Northern Lights Regional Health Centre (NLRHC) 7 Hospital St *Web:* www.albertahealthservices.ca	Fort McMurray	AB	T9H1P2	780-791-6161	
Oakville-Trafalgar Memorial Hospital 327 Reynolds St *Web:* www.haltonhealthcare.on.ca	Oakville	ON	L6J3L7	905-845-2571	338-4636
Orillia Soldiers' Memorial Hospital (OSMH) 170 Colborne St W **Fax:* Admissions ■ *Web:* www.osmh.on.ca	Orillia	ON	L3V2Z3	705-325-2201	325-7953*
Peace Arch Hospital 15521 Russell Ave *Web:* www.pahfoundation.ca	White Rock	BC	V4B2R4	604-535-4520	541-5820
Peace River Community Health Centre 10101 68th St *Web:* www.albertahealthservices.ca	Peace River	AB	T8S1T6	780-624-7500	
Pembroke Regional Hospital 705 MacKay St *TF:* 866-996-0991 ■ *Web:* www.pemreghos.org	Pembroke	ON	K8A1G8	613-732-2811	732-9986
Penticton Regional Hospital (PRH) 550 Carmi Ave *Web:* www.interiorhealth.ca	Penticton	BC	V2A3G6	250-492-4000	492-9068

Phone | Fax

Perth-Smiths Falls District Hospital
60 Cornelia St W — Smiths Falls ON K7A2H9 613-283-2330 283-8990
Web: www.psfdh.on.ca

Peter Lougheed Centre 3500 26th Ave NE — Calgary AB T1Y6J4 403-943-4555 943-4878
Web: www.albertahealthservices.ca

Peterborough Regional Health Ctr
1 Hospital Dr — Peterborough ON K9J7C6 705-743-2121 876-5107
Web: www.prhc.on.ca

Powell River General Hospital
5000 Joyce Ave — Powell River BC V8A5R3 604-485-3211 485-3243
Web: www.vch.ca

Prince County Hospital
65 Roy Boapes Ave PO Box 3000 — Summerside PE C1N2A9 902-438-4200 432-2551
Web: www.pchcare.com

Queensway-Carleton Hospital 3045 Baseline Rd — Ottawa ON K2H8P4 613-721-4700 721-2000
Web: www.qch.on.ca

Red Deer Regional Hospital Centre
3942 50th A Ave — Red Deer AB T4N4E7 403-343-4422 343-4866
Web: www.albertahealthservices.ca

Richmond Hospital 7000 Westminster Hwy — Richmond BC V6X1A2 604-278-9711
Web: www.vch.ca

Ridge Meadows Hospital 11666 Laity St — Maple Ridge BC V2X7G5 604-463-4111
Web: www.fraserhealth.ca

Rimbey Hospital & Care Centre
5228 50th Ave PO Box 440 — Rimbey AB T0C2J0 403-843-2271 843-2506
Web: albertahealthservices.ca

Riverside Campus of Ottawa Hospital
1967 Riverside Dr — Ottawa ON K1H7W9 613-738-7100 761-5292
Web: www.ottawahospital.on.ca

Ross Memorial Hospital (RMH) 10 Angeline St N — Lindsay ON K9V4M8 705-324-6111 328-2817
TF: 800-510-7365 ■ *Web:* www.rmh.org

Rouge Valley Ajax & Pickering 580 Harwood Ave S — Ajax ON L1S2J4 905-683-2320
TF: 866-752-6989 ■ *Web:* www.rougevalley.ca

Royal Alexandra Hospital 10240 Kingsway Ave — Edmonton AB T5H3V9 780-735-4111
Web: www.albertahealthservices.ca

Royal Columbian Hospital
330 E Columbia St — New Westminster BC V3L3W7 604-520-4253 520-4827
Web: www.fraserhealth.ca

Royal Inland Hospital 311 Columbia St — Kamloops BC V2C2T1 250-374-5111
Web: rihfoundation.ca

Royal University Hospital 103 Hospital Dr — Saskatoon SK S7N0W8 306-655-1000
Web: saskatoonhealthregion.ca

Royal Victoria Hospital 201 Georgian Dr — Barrie ON L4M6M2 705-728-9802 728-0982
Web: www.rvh.on.ca

Royal Victoria Hospital 687 Pine Ave W — Montreal QC H3A1A1 514-934-1934
Web: www.muhc.ca/pfv/rvh

Saint Boniface General Hospital (SBGH)
409 Tache Ave — Winnipeg MB R2H2A6 204-233-8563 231-0041*
**Fax:* Hum Res ■ *Web:* www.saintboniface.ca

Saint John Regional Hospital
400 University Ave PO Box 2100 — Saint John NB E2L4L2 506-648-6000 648-6957
Web: en.horizonnb.ca

Saint Joseph's General Hospital 2137 Comox Ave — Comox BC V9M1P2 250-339-2242 339-1432
Web: www.sjghcomox.ca

Saint Joseph's Health Centre
Guelph 100 Westmount Rd — Guelph ON N1H5H8 519-824-6000
Web: www.sjhcg.ca
London 268 Grosvenor St — London ON N6A4V2 519-646-6100 646-6054
Web: www.sjhc.london.on.ca
Toronto 30 The Queensway — Toronto ON M6R1B5 416-530-6000 530-6243
Web: www.stjoestoronto.ca

Saint Joseph's Healthcare Hamilton
50 Charlton Ave E — Hamilton ON L8N4A6 905-522-1155 521-6140
Web: stjoes.ca

Saint Joseph's Lifecare Centre
99 Wayne Gretzky Pkwy — Brantford ON N3S6T6 519-751-7096 753-7996
TF: 888-699-7817 ■ *Web:* www.sjlc.ca

Saint Mary's General Hospital
911 Queen's Blvd — Kitchener ON N2M1B2 519-744-3311 749-6426
Web: www.smgh.ca

Saint Mary's Hospital Ctr 3830 Lacombe Ave — Montreal QC H3T1M5 514-345-3511 734-2636
Web: www.smhc.qc.ca

Saint Michael's Hospital 30 Bond St — Toronto ON M5B1W8 416-360-4000 864-5870
TF: 866-797-0000 ■ *Web:* www.stmichaelshospital.com

Saint Paul's Hospital 1702 20th St W — Saskatoon SK S7M0Z9 306-655-5000 655-5555

Saint Thomas-Elgin General Hospital
189 Elm St — Saint Thomas ON N5R5C4 519-631-2020 631-1825
Web: www.stegh.on.ca

Saskatoon City Hospital 701 Queen St — Saskatoon SK S7K0M7 306-655-8000
TF: 855-655-7612 ■ *Web:* www.saskatoonhealthregion.ca

Scarborough Hospital Birchmount campus
3030 Birchmount Rd — Scarborough ON M1W3W3 416-495-2400 495-2562
Web: www.tsh.to

Scarborough Hospital General Div
3050 Lawrence Ave E — Scarborough ON M1P2V5 416-438-2911 431-8204
Web: www.tsh.to

Seven Oaks General Hospital
2300 McPhillips St — Winnipeg MB R2V3M3 204-632-7133 697-2106
Web: sogh.ca

Sir Mortimer B Davis Jewish General Hospital
3755 Cote Sainte-Catherine — Montreal QC H3T1E2 514-340-8222 340-7530
Web: www.jgh.ca

Southlake Regional Health Centre
596 Davis Dr — Newmarket ON L3Y2P9 905-895-4521 830-5972
Web: www.southlakeregional.org

Stanton Territorial Health Authority (S)
550 Byrne Rd PO Box 10 — Yellowknife NT X1A2N1 867-669-4224 669-4128
Web: stha.hss.gov.nt.ca

Stratford General Hospital
46 General Hospital Dr — Stratford ON N5A2Y6 519-272-8210 271-7137
TF: 888-275-1102 ■ *Web:* www.hpha.ca

Sunnybrook Health Sciences Centre
Sunnybrook Campus 2075 Bayview Ave — Toronto ON M4N3M5 416-480-6100
Web: www.sunnybrook.ca
Women & Babies research program
76 Grenville St — Toronto ON M5S1B2 416-323-6400
Web: www.sunnybrook.ca

Surrey Memorial Hospital 13750 96th Ave — Surrey BC V3V1Z2 604-588-3381 585-5669
Web: www.fraserhealth.ca

Thunder Bay Regional Health Sciences Centre
980 Olvier Rd — Thunder Bay ON P7B6V4 807-684-6000 684-5890
Web: tbrhsc.net/programs_&_services/cancer_care/dap.asp

Timmins & District Hospital 700 Ross Ave E — Timmins ON P4N8P2 705-267-2131 267-6311
TF: 888-340-3003 ■ *Web:* www.tadh.com

Toronto General Hospital 200 Elizabeth St — Toronto ON M5G2C4 416-340-3111
Web: www.uhn.ca

Toronto Western Hospital 399 Bathurst St — Toronto ON M5T2S8 416-603-2581 603-5434
Web: www.uhn.ca

Trillium Health Centre 100 Queensway W — Mississauga ON L5B1B8 905-848-7100
Web: www.trilliumhealthcentre.org

University of Alberta Hospital
8440 112th St — Edmonton AB T6G2B7 780-407-8822 407-7418
Web: www.albertahealthservices.ca

Valley Regional Hospital 150 Exhibition St — Kentville NS B4N5E3 902-678-7381 679-1904
Web: www.avdha.nshealth.ca

Vancouver General Hospital
11th Floor, 601 West Broadway — Vancouver BC V5Z4C2 604-875-4111 875-5701
Web: www.vch.ca

Vernon Jubilee Hospital 2101 32nd St — Vernon BC V1T5L2 250-545-2211 545-5602
Web: www.interiorhealth.ca

Victoria General Hospital 2340 Pembina Hwy — Winnipeg MB R3T2E8 204-477-3347 261-0223
Web: www.vgh.mb.ca

Welland County General Hospital 65 Third St — Welland ON L3B4W6 905-732-6111 732-3268
Web: www.niagarahealth.on.ca

West Coast General Hospital
3949 Port Alberni Hwy — Port Alberni BC V9Y4S1 250-731-1370
Web: www.viha.ca

West Parry Sound Health Centre
6 Albert St — Parry Sound ON P2A3A4 705-746-9321 746-7364
Web: www.wpshc.com

Western Memorial Regional Hospital
1 Brookfield Ave PO Box 2005 — Corner Brook NL A2H6J7 709-637-5000
Web: www.westernhealth.nl.ca

Windsor Regional Hospital Metropolitan Campus (WRH)
1995 Lens Ave — Windsor ON N8W1L9 519-254-5577 254-3458
Web: www.wrh.on.ca

Windsor Regional Hospital Western Campus (WRHWC)
1453 Prince Rd — Windsor ON N9C3Z4 519-254-5577 254-2317*
**Fax:* Acctg ■ *Web:* www.wrh.on.ca

Woodstock General Hospital 270 Riddell St — Woodstock ON N4S6N6 519-421-4211 421-4238*
**Fax:* Admitting ■ *Web:* www.wgh.on.ca

Yarmouth Regional Hospital (YRH)
60 Vancouver St — Yarmouth NS B5A2P5 902-742-3541 742-0369*
**Fax:* Admitting ■ *Web:* www.swndha.nshealth.ca/pages/yrh.htm

York Central Hospital 10 Trench St — Richmond Hill ON L4C4Z3 905-883-1212 883-2455
Web: www.mackenziehealth.ca

374-3 General Hospitals - US

Alabama

Phone | Fax

Andalusia Regional Hospital (ARH)
849 S Three Notch St PO Box 760 — Andalusia AL 36420 334-222-8466 427-0349
Web: www.andalusiaregional.com

Athens-Limestone Hospital 700 W Market St — Athens AL 35611 256-233-9292 233-9278
Web: www.athenslimestonehospital.com

Baptist Medical Ctr South 2105 E S Blvd — Montgomery AL 36116 334-288-2100
Web: www.baptistfirst.org

Bryan W Whitfield Memorial Hospital
105 Hwy 80 E PO Box 890 — Demopolis AL 36732 334-289-4000
Web: www.bwwmh.com

Cooper Green Hospital 1515 Sixth Ave S — Birmingham AL 35233 205-930-3200 930-3497

Coosa Valley HomeCare 315 W Hickory St — Sylacauga AL 35150 256-208-0087
Web: lhcgroup.com

Crestwood Medical Ctr 1 Hospital Dr — Huntsville AL 35801 256-429-4000
Web: www.crestwoodmedcenter.com

Cullman Regional Medical Ctr (CRMC)
1912 Alabama Hwy 157 PO Box 1108 — Cullman AL 35058 256-737-2000 737-2005
Web: www.crmchospital.com

DCH Regional Medical Ctr
809 University Blvd E — Tuscaloosa AL 35401 205-759-7111
Web: dchsystem.com/our_facilities/dch_regional_medical_center.aspx

Decatur General Hospital 1201 Seventh St SE — Decatur AL 35601 256-341-2000 341-2557
Web: decaturmorganhospital.net

DeKalb Regional Medical Ctr
200 Medical Ctr Dr — Fort Payne AL 35968 256-845-3150
Web: www.dekalbregional.com

East Alabama Medical Ctr 2000 Pepperell Pkwy — Opelika AL 36801 334-749-3411
Web: www.eamc.org

Eliza Coffee Memorial Hospital (ECM)
205 Marengo St — Florence AL 35630 256-768-9191 768-9420
Web: www.chgroup.org/ecm

Flowers Hospital 4370 W Main St — Dothan AL 36305 334-793-5000 836-1888
TF: 877-456-9617 ■ *Web:* www.flowershospital.com

Gadsden Regional Medical Ctr
1007 Goodyear Ave — Gadsden AL 35903 256-494-4000 494-4474
Web: www.gadsdenregional.com

Helen Keller Hospital
1300 S Montgomery Ave — Sheffield AL 35660 256-386-4196 386-4469
Web: www.helenkeller.com

Highlands Medical Ctr 380 Woods Cove Rd — Scottsboro AL 35768 256-259-4444
Web: www.highlandsmedcenter.com

Huntsville Hospital 101 Sivley Rd — Huntsville AL 35801 256-265-1000 265-2585
Web: www.huntsvillehospital.org

	City	State	Zip	Phone	Fax
Jackson Hospital 1725 Pine St. *Web:* www.jackson.org	Montgomery	AL	36106	334-293-8000	
Lanier Health Services (LHS) 4800 48th St **Fax:* Admissions ■ *Web:* www.lanierhospital.com	Valley	AL	36854	334-756-1400	756-6698*
Marshall Medical Ctr South (MMCS) 2505 US Hwy 431 *Web:* mmcenters.com	Boaz	AL	35957	256-593-8310	
Medical Ctr Enterprise (MCE) 400 N Edwards St *TF:* 800-994-6610 ■ *Web:* www.mcehospital.com	Enterprise	AL	36330	334-347-0584	
Mobile Infirmary Medical Ctr (MIMC) 5 Mobile Infirmary Cir *Web:* www.mobileinfirmary.org	Mobile	AL	36607	251-435-2400	
Northeast Alabama Regional Medical Ctr 400 E Tenth St *Web:* www.rmccares.org	Anniston	AL	36207	256-235-5121	
Northport Medical Ctr 2700 Hospital Dr *TF:* 866-840-0750 ■ *Web:* www.dchsystem.com	Northport	AL	35476	205-333-4500	333-4522
Parkway Medical Center Hospital 1874 Beltline Rd *Web:* www.parkwaymedicalcenter.com	Decatur	AL	35601	256-350-2211	
Providence Hospital 6801 Airport Blvd **Fax:* Admitting ■ *Web:* www.providencehospital.org	Mobile	AL	36608	251-633-1000	633-1679*
Quality of Life Health Services Inc 1411 Piedmont Cutoff PO Box 97 *TF:* 888-490-0131 ■ *Web:* www.qolhs.org	Gadsden	AL	35902	256-492-0131	
Riverview Regional Medical Ctr 600 S Third St *Web:* www.riverviewregional.com	Gadsden	AL	35901	256-543-5200	543-5888
Saint Vincent's Hospital 810 St Vincent's Dr *Web:* www.stvhs.com	Birmingham	AL	35205	205-939-7000	
Southeast Alabama Medical Ctr 1108 Ross Clark Cir *Web:* www.samc.org	Dothan	AL	36301	334-793-8111	677-4901
Springhill Medical Ctr 3719 Dauphin St *Web:* www.springhillmedicalcenter.com	Mobile	AL	36608	251-344-9630	
Thomas Hospital 750 Morphy Ave *TF:* 800-422-2027 ■ *Web:* www.infirmaryhealth.org/hospitals/thomas-hospital	Fairhope	AL	36532	251-928-2375	435-6261
UAB Medical West 995 Ninth Ave SW *TF:* 800-994-6610 ■ *Web:* www.medicalwesthospital.org	Bessemer	AL	35022	205-481-7000	481-7994
University of South Alabama Children & Women's Hospital 1700 Ctr St **Fax:* Admitting ■ *Web:* www.usahealthsystem.com	Mobile	AL	36604	251-415-1000	415-1002*
University of South Alabama Medical Ctr 2451 Fillingim St *Web:* www.usahealthsystem.com	Mobile	AL	36617	251-471-7000	
Vaughan Regional Medical Ctr 1015 Medical Ctr Pkwy *TF:* 800-994-6610 ■ *Web:* www.vaughanregional.com	Selma	AL	36701	334-418-4100	

Alaska

	City	State	Zip	Phone	Fax
Alaska Native Medical Ctr (ANMC) 4315 Diplomacy Dr *TF Admitting:* 800-478-6661 ■ *Web:* www.anmc.org	Anchorage	AK	99508	907-563-2662	729-1984
Alaska Regional Hospital 2801 Debarr Rd *Web:* www.alaskaregional.com	Anchorage	AK	99508	907-276-1131	
Fairbanks Memorial Hospital 1650 Cowles St *Web:* bannerhealth.com	Fairbanks	AK	99701	907-452-8181	
Providence Alaska Medical Ctr 3200 Providence Dr *Web:* www.providence.org	Anchorage	AK	99508	907-562-2211	

Arizona

	City	State	Zip	Phone	Fax
Banner Baywood Medical Ctr 6644 E Baywood Ave *Web:* www.bannerhealth.com	Mesa	AZ	85206	480-981-2000	981-4198
Banner Boswell Medical Ctr 10401 W Thunderbird Blvd *Web:* www.bannerhealth.com	Sun City	AZ	85351	623-977-7211	
Banner Del E Webb Memorial Hospital 14502 W Meeker Blvd *TF:* 800-254-4357 ■ *Web:* www.bannerhealth.com	Sun City West	AZ	85375	623-214-4000	214-4105
Banner Desert Medical Ctr 1400 S Dobson Rd *Web:* www.bannerhealth.com	Mesa	AZ	85202	480-512-3000	
Banner Good Samaritan Medical Ctr 1111 E McDowell Rd *Web:* www.bannerhealth.com	Phoenix	AZ	85006	602-239-2000	
Banner Thunderbird Medical Ctr (BTMC) 5555 W ThunderbiRd Rd *Web:* www.bannerhealth.com	Glendale	AZ	85306	602-839-2000	865-5930
Carondelet Saint Joseph's Hospital 350 N Wilmot Rd *Web:* www.carondelet.org	Tucson	AZ	85711	520-873-3968	
Carondelet St. Mary's Hospital 1601 W St Mary's Rd *Web:* www.carondelet.org/home/hospitals-locations/st.-marys-hospital.aspx	Tucson	AZ	85745	520-872-3000	
Casa Grande Regional Medical Ctr (CGRMC) 1800 E Florence Blvd *Web:* bannerhealth.com/casagrande	Casa Grande	AZ	85122	520-381-6300	381-6435
Chandler Regional Hospital 475 S Dobson Rd *TF:* 877-728-5414 ■ *Web:* hospitals.dignityhealth.org	Chandler	AZ	85224	480-728-3000	728-3875
Flagstaff Medical Ctr 1200 N Beaver St *Web:* www.flagstaffmedicalcenter.com	Flagstaff	AZ	86001	928-779-3366	947-3299
Havasu Regional Medical Ctr 101 Civic Ctr Ln *Web:* www.havasuregional.com	Lake Havasu City	AZ	86403	928-855-8185	
HonorHealth John C. Lincoln Medical Center 250 E Dunlap Ave *Web:* www.honorhealth.com/locations/hospitals/john-c-lincoln-medical-center	Phoenix	AZ	85020	602-943-2381	
Kingman Regional Medical Ctr (KRMC) 3269 Stockton Hill Rd *TF:* 877-757-2101 ■ *Web:* www.azkrmc.com	Kingman	AZ	86409	928-757-2101	757-0604
La Paz Regional Hospital Inc 1200 W Mohave Rd *Web:* www.lapazhospital.org	Parker	AZ	85344	928-669-9201	
Maricopa Medical Ctr 2601 E Roosevelt St *TF:* 866-749-2876 ■ *Web:* www.mihs.org	Phoenix	AZ	85008	602-344-5011	344-0719
Maryvale Hospital 5102 W Campbell Ave *Web:* www.abrazohealth.com	Phoenix	AZ	85031	623-848-5000	
Mayo Clinic Hospital 5777 E Mayo Blvd *TF:* 888-266-0440 ■ *Web:* mayoclinic.org/patient-visitor-guide	Phoenix	AZ	85054	480-342-2000	
Northwest Medical Ctr (NMC) 6200 N La Cholla Blvd *Web:* www.northwestmedicalcenter.com	Tucson	AZ	85741	520-742-9000	
Paradise Valley Hospital 3929 E Bell Rd *Web:* www.abrazohealth.com	Phoenix	AZ	85032	602-923-5000	923-5657
Phoenix Baptist Hospital 2000 W Bethany Home Rd *Web:* www.abrazohealth.com	Phoenix	AZ	85015	602-249-0212	
Saint Luke's Medical Ctr 1800 E Van Buren St *Web:* www.stlukesmedcenter.com	Phoenix	AZ	85006	602-251-8100	251-8207
Scottsdale Osborn Medical Center 7400 E Osborn Rd *Web:* www.honorhealth.com	Scottsdale	AZ	85251	480-882-4000	
Scottsdale Shea Medical Center 9003 E Shea Blvd *Web:* www.honorhealth.com	Scottsdale	AZ	85260	480-323-3000	
Tempe Saint Luke's Hospital (TSLH) 1500 S Mill Ave *Web:* www.tempestlukeshospital.com	Tempe	AZ	85281	480-784-5500	
Tucson Medical Ctr 5301 E Grant Rd *TF:* 800-526-5353 ■ *Web:* www.tmcaz.com	Tucson	AZ	85712	520-327-5461	
University Medical Ctr 1501 N Campbell Ave *Web:* www.uahealth.com	Tucson	AZ	85724	520-694-0111	694-4085
University Physicians Healthcare Hospital at Kino Campus (UPH) 2800 E Ajo Way *Web:* www.uahealth.com	Tucson	AZ	85713	520-874-2000	
US Public Health Service Phoenix Indian Medical Ctr 4212 N 16th St *Web:* usphs.gov	Phoenix	AZ	85016	602-263-1200	263-1618
Yavapai Regional Medical Ctr 1003 Willow Creek Rd *TF:* 877-843-9762 ■ *Web:* www.yrmc.org	Prescott	AZ	86301	928-445-2700	
Yuma Regional Medical Ctr 2400 S Ave A *Web:* www.yumaregional.org	Yuma	AZ	85364	928-344-2000	336-7337

Arkansas

	City	State	Zip	Phone	Fax
Arkansas Methodist Medical Ctr 900 W KingsFwy *Web:* www.myammc.org	Paragould	AR	72451	870-239-7000	239-7202
Baptist Health Medical Ctr 3333 Spring Hill Dr *Web:* www.baptist-health.com	North Little Rock	AR	72117	501-202-3000	
Baxter Regional Medical Ctr 624 Hospital Dr *TF:* 800-695-3627 ■ *Web:* www.baxterregional.org	Mountain Home	AR	72653	870-424-1000	
Conway Regional Hospital 2302 College Ave *TF:* 800-245-3314 ■ *Web:* www.conwayregional.org	Conway	AR	72032	501-329-3831	
Crittenden Regional Hospital 200 Tyler St	West Memphis	AR	72301	870-735-1500	732-7710
Helena Regional Medical Ctr 1801 ML King Dr *Web:* www.helenarmc.com	Helena	AR	72342	870-338-5800	
Jefferson Regional Medical Ctr (JRMC) 1600 W 40th Ave *Web:* www.jrmc.org	Pine Bluff	AR	71603	870-541-7100	
Medical Ctr of South Arkansas 700 W Grove St *Web:* www.themedcenter.net	El Dorado	AR	71730	870-863-2000	863-5442
Mercy Health System of Northwest Arkansas 2710 Rife Medical Ln *Web:* www.mercy.net	Rogers	AR	72758	479-338-8000	
National Park Medical Ctr 1910 Malvern Ave *Web:* www.nationalparkmedical.com	Hot Springs National Park	AR	71901	501-321-1000	620-1450
North Arkansas Regional Medical Ctr 620 N Willow St *Web:* www.narmc.com	Harrison	AR	72601	870-365-2000	
North metro Medical Ctr 1400 Braden St *Web:* www.northmetromed.com	Jacksonville	AR	72076	501-985-7000	
Northwest Medical Ctr 609 W Maple Ave *Web:* www.northwesthealth.com	Springdale	AR	72764	479-751-5711	
Ouachita County Medical Ctr (OCMC) PO Box 797 *TF:* 877-836-2472 ■ *Web:* www.ouachitamedcenter.com	Camden	AR	71711	870-836-1000	836-1522
Saint Bernard's Medical Ctr 225 E Jackson Ave *Web:* www.sbrmc.com	Jonesboro	AR	72401	870-972-4100	
Saint Mary's Regional Medical Ctr 1808 W Main St *Web:* www.saintmarysregional.com	Russellville	AR	72801	479-968-2841	968-8189
Saint Vincent Infirmary Medical Ctr 2 St Vincent Cir *Web:* www.stvincenthealth.com	Little Rock	AR	72205	501-552-3000	
Saline Memorial Hospital 1 Medical Pk Dr *Web:* www.salinememorial.org	Benton	AR	72015	501-776-6000	776-6019
Sparks Regional Medical Ctr (SRMC) 1001 Towson Ave *Web:* www.sparkshealth.com	Fort Smith	AR	72901	479-441-4000	441-5397
UAMS Medical Ctr 4301 W Markham St *TF:* 877-467-6560 ■ *Web:* www.uams.edu	Little Rock	AR	72205	501-686-7000	
White River Medical Ctr 1710 Harrison St *Web:* www.whiteriverhealthsystem.com	Batesville	AR	72501	870-262-1200	262-1458

California

Phone Fax

Alameda County Medical Center-Highland Campus
1411 E 31st St .... Oakland CA 94602 510-437-4800
Web: www.alamedahealthsystem.org

Alameda County Medical Ctr - Fairmont Hospital
15400 Foothill Blvd .... San Leandro CA 94578 510-895-4200
Web: www.alamedahealthsystem.org

Alhambra Hospital 100 S Raymond Ave.......... Alhambra CA 91801 626-570-1606
Web: www.alhambrahospital.com

Alta Bates Summit Medical Ctr (ABSMC)
2450 Ashby Ave .... Berkeley CA 94705 510-204-4444
Web: www.altabatessummit.org

Alvarado Hospital Medical Ctr
6655 Alvarado Rd.......... San Diego CA 92120 619-287-3270 229-7020
TF: 800-258-2723 ■ *Web:* www.alvaradohospital.com

Anaheim Memorial Medical Ctr
1111 W La Palma Ave.......... Anaheim CA 92801 714-774-1450 999-6027*
**Fax:* Admitting ■ *Web:* www.memorialcare.org

Antelope Valley Hospital 1600 W Ave J.......... Lancaster CA 93534 661-949-5000
Web: www.avhospital.org

Arrowhead Regional Medical Ctr
400 N Pepper Ave.......... Colton CA 92324 909-580-1000 580-6214
TF: 855-422-8029 ■ *Web:* www.arrowheadmedcenter.org

Bakersfield Memorial Hospital
420 34th St.......... Bakersfield CA 93301 661-327-4647 326-0706*
**Fax:* Admitting ■ *Web:* www.bakersfieldmemorial.org

Baldwin Park Medical Ctr
1011 Baldwin Pk Blvd.......... Baldwin Park CA 91706 626-851-1011 851-5101
Web: healthy.kaiserpermanente.org

Bellflower Doctors Medical Center
9542 E Artesia Blvd .... Bellflower CA 90706 562-804-8112 925-4413

Beverly Hospital 309 W Beverly Blvd .... Montebello CA 90640 323-726-1222 725-4338
Web: www.beverly.org

Brotman Medical Ctr 3828 Delmas Terr .... Culver City CA 90231 310-836-7000
Web: www.brotmanmedicalcenter.com

California Hospital Medical Ctr
1401 S Grand Ave.......... Los Angeles CA 90015 213-748-2411
Web: www.chmcla.org

California Pacific Medical Ctr
3700 California St.......... San Francisco CA 94118 415-600-6000
Web: www.cpmc.org

California Pacific Medical Ctr Davies Campus
Castro & Duboce Sts .... San Francisco CA 94114 415-600-6000
Web: www.cpmc.org

California Pacific Medical Ctr Pacific Campus
2333 Buchanan St .... San Francisco CA 94115 415-600-6000
Web: www.cpmc.org

Cedars-Sinai Medical Ctr (CSMC)
8700 Beverly Blvd.......... Los Angeles CA 90048 310-423-3277 123-0105*
**Fax:* Admitting ■ *TF:* 800-233-2771 ■ *Web:* cedars-sinai.edu

Centinela Hospital Medical Ctr
555 E Hardy St .... Inglewood CA 90301 310-673-4660 677-0535
Web: www.centinelamed.com

Chapman Medical Center 2601 E Chapman Ave .... Orange CA 92869 714-633-0011 532-4345
Web: www.chapman-gmc.com

Citrus Valley Medical Ctr Inter-Community Campus
210 W San BernaRdino Rd .... Covina CA 91723 626-331-7331
Web: www.cvhp.org

Coast Plaza Doctors Hospital Inc
13100 Studebaker Rd.......... Norwalk CA 90650 562-868-3751
Web: avantihospitals.com

Coastal Communities Hospital
2701 S Bristol St .... Santa Ana CA 92704 714-754-5454 754-5556*
**Fax Area Code:* 754 ■ *Web:* www.coastalcommhospital.com

Community Hospital of Long Beach
1720 Termino Ave .... Long Beach CA 90804 562-498-1000 498-4434
TF: 800-994-6610

Community Hospital of San Bernardino (CHSB)
1805 Medical Ctr Dr.......... San Bernardino CA 92411 909-887-6333 887-6468
Web: www.chsb.org

Community Hospital of the Monterey Peninsula (CHOMP)
23625 Holman Hwy .... Monterey CA 93940 831-624-5311 625-4948
TF: 888-452-4667 ■ *Web:* www.chomp.org

Community Memorial Hospital 147 N Brent St .... Ventura CA 93003 805-652-5011 667-2895
Web: www.cmhhospital.com

Community Regional Medical Ctr 2823 Fresno St .... Fresno CA 93721 559-459-6000
Web: www.communitymedical.org

Contra Costa Health Services
2500 Alhambra Ave .... Martinez CA 94553 925-370-5000 370-5138
TF: 877-661-6230 ■ *Web:* www.cchealth.org/medical_center

Dameron Hospital Assn (DHA) 525 W Acacia St.......... Stockton CA 95203 209-944-5550
Web: www.dameronhospital.org

Desert Regional Medical Ctr
1150 N Indian Canyon Dr.......... Palm Springs CA 92262 760-323-6511 864-9577
TF: 800-491-4990 ■ *Web:* www.desertregional.com

Doctors Medical Ctr 1441 Florida Ave.......... Modesto CA 95350 209-578-1211 576-3680
Web: www.dmc-modesto.com

Dominican Hospital (DH) 1555 Soquel Dr.......... Santa Cruz CA 95065 831-462-7700
TF: 866-466-1401 ■ *Web:* www.dominicanhospital.org

Downey Regional Medical Ctr
11500 Brookshire Ave .... Downey CA 90241 562-904-5000
Web: pihhealth.org

Eden Medical Ctr (EMC) 20103 Lk Chabot Rd.......... Castro Valley CA 94546 510-537-1234
Web: www.edenmedicalcenter.org

Eisenhower Medical Ctr
39000 Bob Hope Dr .... Rancho Mirage CA 92270 760-340-3911 773-4396
Web: www.emc.org

El Centro Regional Medical Ctr
1415 Ross Ave .... El Centro CA 92243 760-339-7100
Web: www.ecrmc.org

Phone Fax

Emanuel Medical Ctr (EMC) 825 Delbon Ave.......... Turlock CA 95382 209-667-4200
Web: www.emanuelmedicalcenter.org

Enloe Medical Ctr 1531 Esplanade .... Chico CA 95926 530-332-7300 899-2067
TF: 800-822-8102 ■ *Web:* www.enloe.org

Family Healthcare Network 305 E Ctr Ave.......... Visalia CA 93291 559-737-4700
Web: www.fhcn.org

Feather River Hospital (FRH) 5974 Pentz Rd .... Paradise CA 95969 530-877-9361 876-2160
Web: www.adventisthealth.org/feather-river/pages/default.aspx

Foothill Presbyterian Hospital
250 S Grand Ave.......... Glendora CA 91741 626-963-8411
Web: www.cvhp.org

Fountain Valley Regional Hospital & Medical Ctr
17100 Euclid St .... Fountain Valley CA 92708 714-966-7200 966-8039
TF: 866-904-6871 ■ *Web:* www.fountainvalleyhospital.com

Fremont Medical Ctr 970 Plumas St.......... Yuba City CA 95991 530-751-4000
Web: www.frhg.org

Garden Grove Hospital & Medical Ctr
12601 Garden Grove Blvd.......... Garden Grove CA 92843 714-537-5160 741-3322
Web: www.gardengrovehospital.com

Garfield Medical Ctr
525 N Garfield Ave .... Monterey Park CA 91754 626-573-2222 571-8972
Web: www.garfieldmedicalcenter.com

Glendale Adventist Medical Ctr
1509 Wilson Terr .... Glendale CA 91206 818-409-8000
Web: www.adventisthealth.org/glendale/pages/default.aspx

Glendale Memorial Hospital & Health Ctr
1420 S Central Ave.......... Glendale CA 91204 818-502-1900
Web: www.glendalememorialhospital.org

Good Samaritan Hospital 2425 Samaritan Dr.......... San Jose CA 95124 408-559-2011 559-2675*
**Fax:* Admitting ■ *Web:* www.goodsamsanjose.com

Good Samaritan Hospital
1225 Wilshire Blvd.......... Los Angeles CA 90017 213-977-2121 977-2149
Web: www.goodsam.org

Greater El Monte Community Hospital (GEMCH)
1701 Santa Anita Ave .... South El Monte CA 91733 626-579-7777 350-0368
Web: www.greaterelmonte.com

Harbor-UCLA Medical Ctr 1000 W Carson St.......... Torrance CA 90509 310-222-2345
Web: www.humc.edu

Henry Mayo Newhall Memorial Hospital
23845 McBean Pkwy .... Valencia CA 91355 661-253-8000 253-8142
Web: www.henrymayo.com

Hoag Hospital Irvine (HHI) 16200 Sand Canyon Ave .... Irvine CA 92618 949-764-4624
TF: 800-309-9729 ■ *Web:* www.hoag.org

Hoag Memorial Hospital Presbyterian
1 Hoag Dr.......... Newport Beach CA 92658 949-764-4624
Web: www.hoag.org

Hollywood Presbyterian Medical Ctr
1300 N Vermont Ave.......... Los Angeles CA 90027 213-413-3000
Web: www.hollywoodpresbyterian.com

Huntington Memorial Hospital
100 W California Blvd.......... Pasadena CA 91109 626-397-5000
Web: www.huntingtonhospital.com

John F Kennedy Memorial Hospital
47-111 Monroe St .... Indio CA 92201 760-347-6191 775-8014
Web: www.jfkmemorialhosp.com

John Muir Medical Ctr (JMMC)
1601 Ygnacio Valley Rd .... Walnut Creek CA 94598 925-939-3000 308-8944
TF: 844-398-5376 ■ *Web:* www.johnmuirhealth.com

Kaiser Permanente 401 Bicentennial Way.......... Santa Rosa CA 95403 707-571-4000
Web: health.kaiserpermanente.org

Kaiser Permanente Fontana Medical Ctr
9961 Sierra Ave .... Fontana CA 92335 909-427-5000
Web: health.kaiserpermanente.org

Kaiser Permanente Foundation Hospital
9400 E Rosecrans Ave .... Bellflower CA 90706 562-461-3000 267-7524*
**Fax Area Code:* 510 ■ *TF:* 866-279-8954

Kaiser Permanente Harbor City Medical Ctr
25825 S Vermont Ave.......... Harbor City CA 90710 310-325-5111 517-2234
TF: 800-464-4000 ■ *Web:* healthy.kaiserpermanente.org

Kaiser Permanente Hayward Medical Ctr
27400 Hesperian Blvd .... Hayward CA 94545 510-784-4000 784-4722

Kaiser Permanente Hospital
441 N Lakeview Ave .... Anaheim CA 92807 714-279-4000 279-5590
TF: 800-464-4000 ■ *Web:* healthy.kaiserpermanente.org

Kaiser Permanente Los Angeles Medical Ctr
4867 Sunset Blvd .... Los Angeles CA 90027 323-783-4011 783-7227
Web: healthy.kaiserpermanente.org

Kaiser Permanente Medical Center-Santa Teresa
250 Hospital Pkwy .... San Jose CA 95119 408-972-7000 972-7156*
**Fax:* Cust Svc ■ *Web:* healthy.kaiserpermanente.org/html/kaiser/index.shtml

Kaiser Permanente Medical Center-South Sacramento
6600 Bruceville Rd .... Sacramento CA 95823 916-688-2000 688-2978
TF: 800-464-4000 ■ *Web:* mydoctor.kaiserpermanente.org

Kaiser Permanente Medical Center-West Los Angeles
6041 Cadillac Ave.......... Los Angeles CA 90034 323-857-2000
Web: kaiserpermanente.org

Kaiser Permanente Medical Ctr
4647 Zion Ave .... San Diego CA 92120 619-528-5000
Web: health.kaiserpermanente.org

Kaiser Permanente Medical Ctr
710 Lawrence Expy.......... Santa Clara CA 95051 408-851-1717
TF: 800-464-4000 ■ *Web:* www.kaisersantaclara.org

Kaiser Permanente Medical Ctr
1200 El Camino Real .... South San Francisco CA 94080 650-742-2000 742-3046
TF: 800-464-4000 ■ *Web:* healthy.kaiserpermanente.org

Kaiser Permanente Medical Ctr San Francisco
2425 Geary Blvd.......... San Francisco CA 94115 415-833-2000
Web: healthy.kaiserpermanente.org

Kaiser Permanente Panorama City Medical Ctr
13652 Cantara St .... Panorama City CA 91402 818-375-2000
Web: healthy.kaiserpermanente.org

Kaiser Permanente Riverside Medical Ctr
10800 Magnolia Ave.......... Riverside CA 92505 951-353-2000 353-3055
TF Cust Svc: 800-464-4000 ■ *Web:* kaiserpermanente.org

Name / Address	City	State	ZIP	Phone	Fax
Kaiser Permanente Vallejo Medical Ctr 975 Sereno Dr *Web:* kaiserpermanente.org	Vallejo	CA	94589	707-651-1000	651-2026
Kaiser Permanente Walnut Creek Medical Ctr 1425 S Main St *TF:* 800-464-4000 ■ *Web:* mydoctor.kaiserpermanente.org	Walnut Creek	CA	94596	925-295-4000	
Kaweah Delta Hospital 400 W Mineral King Ave *TF:* 800-717-5670 ■ *Web:* www.kaweahdelta.org	Visalia	CA	93291	559-624-2000	
Kern Medical Ctr 1700 Mt Vernon Ave **Fax:* Admitting ■ *Web:* www.kernmedical.com	Bakersfield	CA	93306	661-326-2000	326-2969*
La Palma Intercommunity Hospital 7901 Walker St *Web:* www.lapalmaintercommunityhospital.com	La Palma	CA	90623	714-670-7400	
Lakewood Regional Medical Ctr 3700 S St *Web:* www.lakewoodregional.com	Lakewood	CA	90712	562-531-2550	
Lifelong Medical Care Inc PO Box 11247 *Web:* www.lifelongmedical.org	Berkeley	CA	94712	510-981-4100	
Lodi Memorial Hospital 975 S Fairmont Ave *TF:* 800-323-3360 ■ *Web:* www.lodihealth.org	Lodi	CA	95240	209-334-3411	274-0634
Loma Linda University Medical Ctr 11234 Anderson St *TF:* 877-558-6248 ■ *Web:* lomalindahealth.org	Loma Linda	CA	92354	909-558-4000	558-0308
Long Beach Memorial Medical Ctr 2801 Atlantic Ave *Web:* www.memorialcare.org	Long Beach	CA	90806	562-933-2000	933-1336
Los Alamitos Medical Ctr 3751 Katella Ave *Web:* www.losalamitosmedctr.com	Los Alamitos	CA	90720	562-598-1311	
Los Robles Hospital & Medical Ctr (LRHMC) 215 W Janss Rd *Web:* www.losrobleshospital.com	Thousand Oaks	CA	91360	805-497-2727	370-4666
Madera Community Hospital 1250 E Almond Ave *Web:* www.maderahospital.org	Madera	CA	93637	559-675-5555	
Marian Medical Ctr 1400 E Church St *Web:* www.marianmedicalcenter.org	Santa Maria	CA	93454	805-739-3000	739-3060
Marin General Hospital 250 Bon Air Rd *TF:* 888-996-9644 ■ *Web:* www.maringeneral.org	Greenbrae	CA	94904	415-925-7000	925-7317
Marina Del Rey Hospital 4650 Lincoln Blvd *TF:* 888-600-5600 ■ *Web:* www.marinahospital.com	Marina del Rey	CA	90292	310-823-8911	
Memorial Medical Ctr (MMC) 1700 Coffee Rd *Web:* www.memorialmedicalcenter.org	Modesto	CA	95355	209-526-4500	
Mendocino Coast District Hospital 700 River Dr *Web:* www.mcdh.org	Fort Bragg	CA	95437	707-961-1234	
Mercy General Hospital 4001 J St *Web:* hospitals.dignityhealth.org	Sacramento	CA	95819	916-453-4545	
Mercy Hospitals of Bakersfield Truxtun Campus (MHB) 2215 Truxtun Ave *Web:* www.mercybakersfield.org	Bakersfield	CA	93301	661-632-5000	
Mercy Medical Ctr Merced Community Campus 333 Mercy Ave *Web:* www.mercymercedcares.org	Merced	CA	95340	209-564-5000	
Mercy San Juan Medical Ctr 6501 Coyle Ave *Web:* hospitals.dignityhealth.org	Carmichael	CA	95608	916-537-5000	
Mercy Southwest Hospital 400 Old River Rd	Bakersfield	CA	93311	661-663-6000	
Methodist Hospital of Sacramento 7500 Hospital Dr *Web:* hospitals.dignityhealth.org	Sacramento	CA	95823	916-423-3000	
Methodist Hospital of Southern California 300 W Huntington Dr *TF:* 888-388-2838 ■ *Web:* www.methodisthospital.org	Arcadia	CA	91007	626-898-8000	462-2688
Mission Hospital Regional Medical Ctr Inc 27700 Medical Ctr Rd *Web:* www.mission4health.com	Mission Viejo	CA	92691	949-364-1400	
Natividad Medical Ctr (NMC) 1441 Constitution Blvd *Web:* www.natividad.com	Salinas	CA	93906	831-755-4111	755-6254
North County Health Services 150 Valpreda Rd *Web:* www.nchs-health.org	San Marcos	CA	92069	760-736-6767	
Northeast Valley Health Corp 1172 N Maclay Ave *Web:* www.nevhc.org	San Fernando	CA	91340	818-898-1388	365-4031
Northern Inyo Hospital 150 Pioneer Ln *Web:* www.nih.org	Bishop	CA	93514	760-873-5811	873-6734
Northridge Hospital Medical Center-Roscoe Blvd Campus 18300 Roscoe Blvd *Web:* www.northridgehospital.org	Northridge	CA	91328	818-885-8500	885-5321
O'Connor Hospital 2105 Forest Ave *Web:* oconnor.verity.org	San Jose	CA	95128	408-947-2500	947-2887
Olive View Medical Ctr (OVMC) 14445 Olive View Dr *Web:* uclaoliveview.org	Sylmar	CA	91342	818-364-1555	
Olympia Medical Ctr 5900 W Olympic Blvd **Fax Area Code:* 323 ■ *Web:* www.olympiamc.com	Los Angeles	CA	90036	310-657-5900	932-5163*
Orange Coast Memorial Medical Ctr (OCMMC) 9920 Talbert Ave *TF:* 877-597-4777 ■ *Web:* www.memorialcare.org	Fountain Valley	CA	92708	714-378-7000	229-5399
Oroville Hospital (OH) 2767 Olive Hwy *Web:* www.orovillehospital.com	Oroville	CA	95966	530-533-8500	
Pacific Clinics 800 S Santa Anita Ave *Web:* www.pacificclinics.org	Arcadia	CA	91006	626-254-5000	
PAMC Ltd 531 W College St *Web:* www.pamc.net	Los Angeles	CA	90012	213-624-8411	
Parkview Community Hospital Medical Ctr (PCHMC) 3865 Jackson St *Web:* www.pchmc.org	Riverside	CA	92503	951-688-2211	352-5484
Peninsula Hospital 1501 Trousdale Dr *Web:* www.mills-peninsula.org	Burlingame	CA	94010	650-696-5400	
Pioneer Medical Group Inc 17777 Ctr Ct Dr N Ste 400 *Web:* www.pioneermedicalgroup.com	Cerritos	CA	90703	562-229-9452	
Pioneers Memorial Healthcare District (PMHD) 207 W Legion Rd *Web:* www.pmhd.org	Brawley	CA	92227	760-351-3333	344-4401
Placentia-Linda Hospital 1301 N Rose Dr *TF:* 888-754-9729 ■ *Web:* www.placentialinda.com	Placentia	CA	92870	714-993-2000	961-8427
Pomerado Hospital 15615 Pomerado Rd *Web:* www.palomarhealth.org	Poway	CA	92064	858-613-4000	
Pomona Valley Hospital Medical Ctr 1798 N Garey Ave *Web:* www.pvhmc.org	Pomona	CA	91767	909-865-9500	865-9796
Presbyterian Intercommunity Hospital 12401 Washington Blvd *Web:* pihhealth.org	Whittier	CA	90602	562-698-0811	
Providence Holy Cross Medical Ctr 15031 Rinaldi St *Web:* providence.org/losangeles/facilities/holycross.htm	Mission Hills	CA	91345	818-365-8051	898-4688
Providence Saint Joseph Medical Ctr 501 S Buena Vista St *Web:* california.providence.org	Burbank	CA	91505	818-843-5111	
Queen of the Valley Medical Ctr 1000 Trancas St *Web:* www.thequeen.org	Napa	CA	94558	707-252-4411	
Redlands Community Hospital Foundation PO Box 3391 *TF:* 888-397-4999 ■ *Web:* www.redlandshospital.org	Redlands	CA	92373	909-335-5500	
Regional Medical Ctr of San Jose (RMCSJ) 225 N Jackson Ave *Web:* www.regionalmedicalsanjose.com	San Jose	CA	95116	408-259-5000	729-2884
Rideout Memorial Hospital 726 Fourth St *TF:* 888-923-3800 ■ *Web:* www.frhg.org	Marysville	CA	95901	530-749-4300	751-4226
Riverside Community Hospital 4445 Magnolia Ave *Web:* riversidecommunityhospital.com	Riverside	CA	92501	951-788-3000	788-3659
Riverside County Regional Medical Ctr 26520 Cactus Ave *Web:* www.rcrmc.org	Moreno Valley	CA	92555	951-486-4000	
Ronald Reagan Medical Ctr 757 Westwood Plaza *Web:* www.uclahealth.org	Los Angeles	CA	90095	310-825-9111	825-7271
Roseville Medical Ctr 1 Medical Plz *Web:* www.sutterroseville.org	Roseville	CA	95661	916-781-1000	781-1210
Saddleback Memorial Medical Ctr 24451 Health Ctr Dr *Web:* www.memorialcare.org	Laguna Hills	CA	92653	949-837-4500	
Saint Agnes Medical Ctr 1303 E Herndon Ave *Web:* www.samc.com	Fresno	CA	93720	559-450-3000	450-3990
Saint Bernardine Medical Ctr 2101 N Waterman Ave *Web:* www.stbernardinemedicalcenter.org	San Bernardino	CA	92404	909-883-8711	881-4546
Saint Francis Medical Ctr 3630 E Imperial Hwy **Fax:* Admitting ■ *Web:* stfrancis.verity.org	Lynwood	CA	90262	310-900-8900	900-4505*
Saint Francis Memorial Hospital 900 Hyde St **Fax:* Admitting ■ *Web:* www.saintfrancismemorial.org	San Francisco	CA	94109	415-353-6000	353-6631*
Saint Helena Hospital 10 Woodland Rd *Web:* www.adventisthealth.org/napa-valley/pages/default.aspx	Saint Helena	CA	94574	707-963-3611	
Saint John's Hospital & Health Ctr 2121 Santa Monica Blvd *Web:* california.providence.org/saint-johns	Santa Monica	CA	90404	310-829-5511	829-8295
Saint Joseph Hospital 1100 W Stewart Dr *Web:* www.sjo.org	Orange	CA	92868	714-633-9111	
Saint Joseph Hospital 2700 Dolbeer St *Web:* www.stjosepheureka.org	Eureka	CA	95501	707-445-8121	
Saint Joseph's Medical Ctr 1800 N California St *Web:* www.stjosephscares.org	Stockton	CA	95204	209-943-2000	
Saint Jude Medical Ctr 101 E Valencia Mesa Dr *Web:* www.stjudemedicalcenter.org	Fullerton	CA	92835	714-871-3280	
Saint Mary Medical Ctr 1050 Linden Ave *Web:* www.stmarymedicalcenter.org	Long Beach	CA	90813	562-491-9000	
Saint Mary's Medical Ctr 450 Stanyan St *Web:* www.stmarysmedicalcenter.org	San Francisco	CA	94117	415-668-1000	
Saint Rose Hospital 27200 Calaroga Ave *Web:* www.strosehospital.org	Hayward	CA	94545	510-264-4000	887-7421
Saint Vincent Medical Ctr 2131 W Third St *Web:* stvincent.verity.org	Los Angeles	CA	90057	213-484-7111	
Salinas Valley Memorial Hospital (SVMH) 450 E Romie Ln *TF:* 800-813-4673 ■ *Web:* www.svmh.com	Salinas	CA	93901	831-757-4333	
San Antonio Community Hospital 999 San BernaRdino Rd *Web:* www.sarh.org/?utm_source=sach&utm_medium=banner&utm_campaign=redirect	Upland	CA	91786	909-985-2811	985-7659
San Dimas Community Hospital 1350 W Covina Blvd *Web:* www.sandimashospital.com	San Dimas	CA	91773	909-599-6811	305-5678
San Francisco General Hospital Medical Ctr 1001 Potrero Ave Ste 1E21 *TF:* 800-723-7140 ■ *Web:* psych.ucsf.edu/sfgh	San Francisco	CA	94110	415-206-8426	206-8942
San Gabriel Valley Medical Ctr 438 W Las Tunas Dr *Web:* www.sgvmc.com	San Gabriel	CA	91776	626-289-5454	
San Joaquin Community Hospital 2615 Eye St *Web:* www.adventisthealth.org/sjch/pages/default.aspx	Bakersfield	CA	93301	661-395-3000	869-6962
San Joaquin General Hospital (SJGH) 500 W Hospital Rd	French Camp	CA	95231	209-468-6000	468-6339*
Santa Barbara Cottage Hospital PO Box 689 *Web:* www.cottagehealth.org	Santa Barbara	CA	93102	805-682-7111	
Santa Clara Valley Medical Ctr 751 S Bascom Ave *Web:* www.scvmc.org	San Jose	CA	95128	408-885-5000	

Phone | Fax

Santa Monica UCLA Medical Ctr
1250 16th St. Santa Monica CA 90404 310-319-4000
Web: www.uclahealth.org/homepage_sanmon.cfm?id=265

Santa Rosa Memorial Hospital (SRMH)
1165 Montgomery Dr Santa Rosa CA 95405 707-546-3210
Web: stjosephhealth.org/about-us

Scripps Green Hospital
10666 N Torrey Pines Rd La Jolla CA 92037 858-455-9100
TF: 800-727-4777 ■ *Web:* www.scripps.org

Scripps Memorial Hospital-Encinitas
354 Santa Fe Dr Encinitas CA 92024 760-753-6501
Web: www.scripps.org/locations/hospitals__scripps-memorial-hospital-encinitas

Scripps Memorial Hospital-La Jolla
9888 Genesee Ave La Jolla CA 92037 800-727-4777
TF: 800-727-4777 ■
Web: www.scripps.org/locations/hospitals__scripps-memorial-hospital-la-jolla

Scripps Mercy Hospital 4077 Fifth Ave. San Diego CA 92103 619-294-8111
Web: www.scripps.org

Sequoia Hospital 170 Alameda Ave Redwood City CA 94062 650-369-5811
Web: www.sequoiahospital.org

Seton Medical Ctr 1900 Sullivan Ave. Daly City CA 94015 650-992-4000
TF: 800-371-2176 ■ *Web:* seton.verity.org

Sharp Chula Vista Medical Ctr
751 Medical Ctr Ct Chula Vista CA 91911 619-482-5800
Web: www.sharp.com/hospital

Sharp Grossmont Hospital (SGH)
5555 Grossmont Ctr Dr La Mesa CA 91942 619-740-6000
TF: 800-827-4277 ■ *Web:* www.sharp.com/grossmont

Sharp Memorial Hospital 7901 Frost St San Diego CA 92123 858-939-3400
Web: sharp.com

Shasta Regional Medical Ctr (SRMC)
1100 Butte St Redding CA 96001 530-244-5400 244-5119
Web: www.shastaregional.com

Sherman Oaks Hospital & Health Ctr
4929 Van Nuys Blvd Sherman Oaks CA 91403 818-981-7111
Web: www.shermanoakshospital.org

Sierra Nevada Memorial Hospital
155 Glasson Way Grass Valley CA 95945 530-274-6000
Web: www.snmh.org

Sierra View District Hospital (SVDH)
465 W Putnam Ave Porterville CA 93257 559-784-1110 788-6135
Web: www.sierra-view.com

Sierra Vista Regional Medical Ctr (SVRMC)
1010 Murray Ave San Luis Obispo CA 93405 805-546-7600
TF: 866-904-6871 ■ *Web:* www.sierravistaregional.com

Simi Valley Hospital (SVH)
2975 N Sycamore Dr Simi Valley CA 93065 805-955-6000 955-6072*
Web: www.adventisthealth.org/simi-valley-hospital/pages/default.aspx

Sonora Regional Medical Ctr (SRMC)
1000 Greenly Rd Sonora CA 95370 209-536-5000
TF Compliance: 877-336-3566 ■
Web: www.adventisthealth.org/sonora-regional/pages/default.aspx

Summit Medical Ctr 350 Hawthorne Ave Oakland CA 94609 510-655-4000
Web: www.sutterhealth.org

Sutter Auburn Faith Community Hospital (SAFH)
11815 Education St Auburn CA 95602 530-888-4500 886-6611
TF: 800-478-8837 ■ *Web:* www.sutterauburnfaith.org

Sutter General Hospital 2801 L St Sacramento CA 95816 916-454-2222
Web: www.sutterhealth.org

Sutter Health Sacramento Sierra Region
2801 L St Sacramento CA 95816 916-454-2222
Web: www.checksutterfirst.org

Sutter Medical Ctr of Santa Rosa
3325 Chanate Rd Santa Rosa CA 95404 707-576-4006
TF: 800-651-5111 ■ *Web:* www.suttersantarosa.org

Sutter Memorial Hospital 5151 F St. Sacramento CA 95819 916-454-3333
Web: www.sutterhealth.org

Sutter Solano Medical Ctr (SSMC)
300 Hospital Dr Vallejo CA 94589 707-554-4444 648-3227
Web: www.suttersolano.org

Temple Community Hospital
235 N Hoover St Los Angeles CA 90004 213-382-7252
Web: www.templecommunityhospital.com

Torrance Memorial Medical Ctr
3330 Lomita Blvd Torrance CA 90505 310-325-9110 784-4801
TF: 866-843-2572 ■ *Web:* www.torrancememorial.org

Tri-City Medical Ctr 4002 Vista Way Oceanside CA 92056 760-724-8411 940-4050
Web: www.tricitymed.org

Tri-City Regional Medical Ctr
21530 S Pioneer Blvd. Hawaiian Gardens CA 90716 562-860-0401 924-5871
Web: www.tcrmc.org

Tulare Regional Medical Ctr 869 N Cherry Tulare CA 93274 559-685-3462
Web: www.tulareregional.org

UC Irvine Healthcare 101 the City Dr S Orange CA 92868 714-456-7890
TF: 877-824-3627 ■ *Web:* www.ucirvinehealth.org

UCSF Medical Ctr 505 Parnassus Ave San Francisco CA 94143 415-476-1000
Web: www.ucsfhealth.org

Ukiah Valley Medical Ctr 275 Hospital Dr Ukiah CA 95482 707-462-3111 463-7384
Web: www.adventisthealth.org/ukiah-valley

University of California Davis Medical Ctr
2315 Stockton Blvd Sacramento CA 95817 916-734-2011 734-8080*
**Fax:* Admitting ■ *Web:* www.ucdmc.ucdavis.edu

Valley Presbyterian Hospital
15107 Vanowen St Van Nuys CA 91405 818-782-6600 902-5703
Web: www.valleypres.org

Ventura County Medical Center
3291 Loma Vista Rd Ventura CA 93003 805-652-6000
TF: 800-369-7437 ■
Web: www.vchca.org/hospitals/ventura-county-medical-center

Verdugo Hills Hospital 1812 Verdugo Blvd. Glendale CA 91208 818-790-7100 952-4616
Web: www.uscvhh.org

West Anaheim Medical Ctr (WAMC)
3033 W Orange Ave Anaheim CA 92804 714-827-3000 229-6813
Web: westanaheimmedctr.com

Phone | Fax

West Hills Hospital & Medical Center
7300 Medical Centre Dr West Hills CA 91307 818-676-4000
Web: westhillshospital.com

Western Medical Ctr Anaheim (WMCA)
1025 S Anaheim Blvd Anaheim CA 92805 714-533-6220
Web: www.westernmedanaheim.com

Western Medical Ctr Santa Ana
1001 N Tustin Ave Santa Ana CA 92705 714-953-3500 953-3613
Web: www.westernmedicalcenter.com

White Memorial Medical Ctr
1720 Cesar E Chavez Ave Los Angeles CA 90033 323-268-5000
Web: www.adventisthealth.org/white-memorial/pages/default.aspx

Whittier Hospital Medical Ctr
9080 Colima Rd Whittier CA 90605 562-945-3561 693-6811
TF: 800-613-4291 ■ *Web:* www.whittierhospital.com

Woodland Healthcare 1325 Cottonwood St. Woodland CA 95695 530-662-3961
Web: hospitals.dignityhealth.org

Woodland Hills Medical Center
5601 De Soto Ave. Woodland Hills CA 91365 818-719-2000
Web: kaiserpermanente.org

Colorado

Phone | Fax

Arkansas Valley Regional Medical Ctr (AVRMC)
1100 Carson Ave La Junta CO 81050 719-384-5412 383-6005
TF: 877-696-6775 ■ *Web:* www.avrmc.org

Avista Adventist Hospital
100 Health Pk Dr Louisville CO 80027 303-673-1000
Web: avistahospital.org

Boulder Community Hospital (BCH)
1100 Balsam Ave Boulder CO 80301 303-440-2273 440-2278*
**Fax:* Admitting ■ *Web:* www.bch.org

Denver Health Medical Ctr (DHMC) 777 Bannock St Denver CO 80204 303-436-6000
Web: www.denverhealth.org

Exempla Lutheran Medical Ctr
8300 W 38th Ave Wheat Ridge CO 80033 303-425-4500
Web: sclhealthsystem.org

Exempla Saint Joseph Hospital
1835 Franklin St. Denver CO 80218 303-837-7111 837-7123
Web: sclhealthsystem.org

Littleton Adventist Hospital
7700 S Broadway Littleton CO 80122 303-730-8900
Web: www.mylittletonhospital.org

Longmont United Hospital (LUH)
1950 Mountain View Ave Longmont CO 80501 303-651-5111 678-4050
Web: www.luhcares.org

McKee Medical Ctr 2000 N Boise Ave. Loveland CO 80538 970-669-4640 635-4112
Web: www.bannerhealth.com

Medical Ctr of Aurora (MCA) 1501 S Potomac St Aurora CO 80012 303-695-2600
Web: www.auroramed.com

Memorial Health System (MHS)
Central 1400 E Boulder St Colorado Springs CO 80909 719-365-5000 848-5551*
**Fax Area Code:* 720 ■ **Fax:* Admissions ■ *TF:* 877-422-3648 ■
Web: www.uchealth.org/southerncolorado/pages/default.aspx

Mercy Medical Ctr 1010 Third Springs Blvd Durango CO 81301 970-247-4311
TF: 800-345-2516 ■ *Web:* www.mercydurango.org

North Colorado Medical Ctr 1801 16th St Greeley CO 80631 970-352-4121 350-6644
Web: www.bannerhealth.com

North Suburban Medical Ctr (NSMC)
9191 Grant St Thornton CO 80229 303-451-7800 450-4458
TF: 877-647-7440 ■ *Web:* www.northsuburban.com

OnCure Medical Corp
188 Inverness Dr W Ste 650 Englewood CO 80112 303-643-6500 643-6560
Web: www.oncure.com

Parkview Medical Ctr 400 W 16th St Pueblo CO 81003 719-584-4000 584-7376
TF: 800-543-4046 ■ *Web:* www.parkviewmc.com

Penrose Hospital 2222 N Nevada Ave Colorado Springs CO 80907 719-776-5000
TF: 800-398-2045 ■ *Web:* www.penrosestfrancis.org

Porter Adventist Hospital 2525 S Downing St Denver CO 80210 303-778-1955 778-5252
Web: www.porterhospital.org

Poudre Valley Hospital 1024 S Lemay Ave Fort Collins CO 80524 970-495-7000
TF: 800-994-6610 ■
Web: www.uchealth.org/northerncolorado/pages/default.aspx

Presbyterian-Saint Luke's Medical Ctr
1719 E 19th Ave Denver CO 80218 303-839-6000 869-2428
Web: www.pslmc.com

Rose Medical Ctr 4567 E Ninth Ave Denver CO 80220 303-320-2121
TF: 866-746-4282 ■ *Web:* www.rosemed.com

Saint Anthony Central Hospital
11600 W Second Pl Lakewood CO 80228 720-321-0000
Web: www.stanthonyhosp.org

Saint Mary's Hospital & Regional Medical Ctr
2635 N Seventh St Grand Junction CO 81502 800-458-3888
TF: 800-458-3888 ■ *Web:* stmarygj.org

Saint Mary-Corwin Medical Ctr
1008 Minnequa Ave Pueblo CO 81004 719-557-4000
TF: 800-228-4039 ■ *Web:* www.stmarycorwin.org

San Luis Valley Regional Medical Ctr
106 Blanca Ave. Alamosa CO 81101 719-589-2511
Web: www.sanluisvalleyhealth.org

Swedish Medical Ctr 501 E Hampden Ave. Englewood CO 80113 303-788-5000 788-6265
Web: www.swedishhospital.com

University of Colorado Hospital
12605 E 16th Ave Aurora CO 80045 720-848-0000
Web: www.uchealth.org/metrodenver/pages/default.aspx

Connecticut

Phone | Fax

Bridgeport Hospital 267 Grant St. Bridgeport CT 06610 203-384-3000 384-3046
Web: www.bridgeporthospital.org

Bristol Hospital (BH) 41 Brewster Rd Bristol CT 06010 860-585-3000 585-3853
Web: www.bristolhospital.org

Phone Fax

Charlotte Hungerford Hospital (CHH)
540 Litchfield St . . . Torrington CT 06790 860-496-6666 482-8627
Web: charlottehungerford.org
Danbury Hospital (DH) 24 Hospital Ave . . . Danbury CT 06810 203-739-7000
TF: 800-516-3658 ■ *Web:* www.danburyhospital.org
Greenwich Hospital 5 Perryridge Rd . . . Greenwich CT 06830 203-863-3000 863-3845
TF: 800-657-8355 ■ *Web:* www.greenwichhospital.org
Griffin Hospital 130 Div St . . . Derby CT 06418 203-735-7421 732-7569
Web: www.griffinhealth.org
Hartford Hospital 80 Seymour St . . . Hartford CT 06102 860-545-5000 545-3622
TF: 800-545-7664 ■ *Web:* www.harthosp.org
Hospital of Saint Raphael 1450 Chapel St . . . New Haven CT 06511 203-789-3000
TF: 888-700-6543 ■ *Web:* www.ynhh.org
Johnson Memorial Hospital
201 Chestnut Hill Rd . . . Stafford Springs CT 06076 860-684-4251 749-2201
Web: www.jmmc.com
Lawrence & Memorial Hospital
365 Montauk Ave . . . New London CT 06320 860-442-0711
Web: www.lmhospital.org
Manchester Memorial Hospital 71 Haynes St. . . . Manchester CT 06040 860-646-1222
Web: townofmanchester.org
Middlesex Hospital 28 Crescent St . . . Middletown CT 06457 860-358-6000 358-2626
TF: 800-548-2394 ■ *Web:* www.middlesexhospital.org
Milford Hospital (MH) 300 Seaside Ave. . . . Milford CT 06460 203-876-4000 876-4220
Web: www.milfordhospital.org
New Britain General Campus 100 Grand St . . . New Britain CT 06050 860-224-5011
Web: thocc.org
Norwalk Hospital 34 Maple St . . . Norwalk CT 06856 203-852-2000
Web: www.norwalkhospital.org
Rockville General Hospital 31 Union St. . . . Vernon CT 06066 860-872-0501 872-5393
Web: www.echn.org
Saint Francis Hospital & Medical Ctr
114 Woodland St . . . Hartford CT 06105 860-714-4000
TF: 800-993-4312 ■ *Web:* www.stfranciscare.org
Saint Mary's Hospital 56 Franklin St. . . . Waterbury CT 06706 203-709-6000 709-3238
Web: www.stmh.org
Saint Vincent's Medical Ctr 2800 Main St . . . Bridgeport CT 06606 203-576-6000 576-5345
TF: 877-255-7847 ■ *Web:* www.stvincents.org
Stamford Hospital 30 Shelburne Rd. . . . Stamford CT 06904 203-276-1000
Web: www.stamfordhealth.org
University of Connecticut Health Ctr
John Dempsey Hospital 263 Farmington Ave . . . Farmington CT 06030 860-679-2000 679-1255
TF: 800-535-6232 ■ *Web:* health.uconn.edu
Veterans Admin Medical Center
555 Willard Ave . . . Newington CT 06111 860-666-6951 667-6764
Waterbury Hospital 64 Robbins St. . . . Waterbury CT 06721 203-573-6000 573-6161
Web: waterburyhospital.org
William W Backus Hospital 326 Washington St. . . . Norwich CT 06360 860-889-8331 823-1501
Web: backushospital.org
Windham Community Memorial Hospital (WCMH)
112 Mansfield Ave . . . Willimantic CT 06226 860-456-9116 456-6838
Web: www.windhamhospital.org
Yale-New Haven Hospital 20 York St . . . New Haven CT 06504 203-688-4242
Web: www.ynhh.org

Delaware

Phone Fax

Bayhealth Medical Ctr 21 W Clarke Ave. . . . Milford DE 19963 302-430-5738
TF: 877-453-7107 ■ *Web:* www.bayhealth.org
Beebe Medical Ctr 424 Savannah Rd. . . . Lewes DE 19958 302-645-3300 645-3405
Web: beebehealthcare.org
Christiana Hospital 4755 Ogletown-Stanton Rd. . . . Newark DE 19718 302-733-1000
Web: www.christianacare.org
Kent General Hospital 640 S State St . . . Dover DE 19901 302-674-4700 674-2202
TF: 888-761-8300 ■ *Web:* www.bayhealth.org
Nanticoke Memorial Hospital
801 Middleford Rd . . . Seaford DE 19973 302-629-6611
Web: www.nanticoke.org
Saint Francis Hospital 7th N Clayton St . . . Wilmington DE 19805 302-421-4100
Web: www.stfrancishealthcare.org

District of Columbia

Phone Fax

George Washington University Hospital
900 23rd St NW . . . Washington DC 20037 202-715-4000
TF: 888-449-3627 ■ *Web:* www.gwhospital.com
Howard University Hospital
2041 Georgia Ave. . . . Washington DC 20060 202-865-6100 865-1360
Web: huhealthcare.com
Providence Hospital 1150 Varnum St NE . . . Washington DC 20017 202-269-7000 269-7160
Web: www.provhosp.org
Washington Hospital Ctr 110 Irving St NW. . . . Washington DC 20010 202-877-7000 877-7826
TF: 855-546-1686 ■ *Web:* www.medstarhealth.org

Florida

Phone Fax

Aventura Hospital 20900 Biscayne Blvd. . . . Aventura FL 33180 305-682-7000
TF: 800-523-5772 ■ *Web:* www.aventurahospital.com
Baptist Hospital 1000 W Moreno St. . . . Pensacola FL 32501 850-434-4011 434-4702
Web: www.ebaptisthealthcare.org
Baptist Hospital of Miami 8900 SW 88th St. . . . Miami FL 33176 786-596-1960 598-5910*
**Fax Area Code:* 305 ■ *TF:* 800-994-6610 ■ *Web:* www.baptisthealth.net
Baptist Medical Ctr 800 Prudential Dr. . . . Jacksonville FL 32207 904-202-2000
TF: 800-222-1222 ■ *Web:* www.baptistjax.com
Bay Medical Ctr 615 N Bonita Ave . . . Panama City FL 32401 850-769-1511
TF: 800-268-2435 ■ *Web:* www.baymedical.org
Blake Medical Ctr 2020 59th St W. . . . Bradenton FL 34209 941-792-6611
Web: www.blakemedicalcenter.com

Phone Fax

Boca Raton Regional Hospital
800 Meadows Rd . . . Boca Raton FL 33486 561-395-7100 955-4884
Web: www.brrh.com
Brandon Regional Hospital 119 Oakfield Dr. . . . Brandon FL 33511 813-681-5551
Web: www.brandonhospital.com
Brooksville Regional Hospital
17240 Cortez Blvd . . . Brooksville FL 34601 352-796-5111 544-5711
TF: 844-455-8708 ■ *Web:* bayfrontbrooksville.com
Capital Regional Medical Ctr (CRMC)
2626 Capital Medical Blvd . . . Tallahassee FL 32308 850-325-5000 325-5198
TF: 800-994-6610 ■ *Web:* www.capitalregionalmedicalcenter.com
Central Florida Regional Hospital
1401 W Seminole Blvd . . . Sanford FL 32771 407-321-4500
Web: www.centralfloridaregional.com
Charlotte Regional Medical Ctr
809 E Marion Ave . . . Punta Gorda FL 33950 941-639-3131 637-2579
Web: bayfrontcharlotte.com
Citrus Memorial Hospital
502 W Highland Blvd . . . Inverness FL 34452 352-726-1551
Web: www.citrusmh.com
Cleveland Clinic Hospital
2950 Cleveland Clinic Blvd . . . Weston FL 33331 954-689-5000 689-5165
TF: 866-293-7866 ■ *Web:* my.clevelandclinic.org
Community Hospital 5637 Marine Pkwy . . . New Port Richey FL 34652 727-848-1733
Web: medicalcentertrinity.com
Coral Gables Hospital Inc (CGH)
3100 Douglas Rd . . . Coral Gables FL 33134 305-445-8461 441-6879
TF: 866-728-3677 ■ *Web:* www.coralgableshospital.com
Coral Springs Medical Ctr
3000 Coral Hills Dr. . . . Coral Springs FL 33065 954-344-3000
Web: www.browardhealth.org
Delray Medical Ctr (DMC) 5352 Linton Blvd. . . . Delray Beach FL 33484 561-498-4440 495-3103
Web: www.delraymedicalctr.com
DeSoto Memorial Hospital Inc
900 N Robert Ave . . . Arcadia FL 34266 863-494-3535 494-8400
Web: www.dmh.org
Doctors Hospital Sarasota 5731 Bee Ridge Rd . . . Sarasota FL 34233 941-342-1100
Web: www.doctorsofsarasota.com
Doctors' Hospital 5000 University Dr. . . . Coral Gables FL 33146 786-308-3000 308-3402
Web: www.baptisthealth.net
Edward White Hospital
2323 Ninth Ave N . . . Saint Petersburg FL 33713 727-323-1111 328-6226
Web: www.edwardwhitehospital.com
Fawcett Memorial Hospital
21298 Olean Blvd . . . Port Charlotte FL 33952 941-629-1181 627-6141
Web: www.fawcetthospital.com
Florida Hospital Heartland Medical Ctr
4200 Sun 'n Lake Blvd PO Box 9400 . . . Sebring FL 33871 863-314-4466 402-3415
TF: 800-756-4447 ■ *Web:* floridahospital.com
Florida Hospital North Pinellas
1395 S Pinellas Ave . . . Tarpon Springs FL 34689 727-942-5000
Web: www.floridahospital.com
Florida Hospital Oceanside
264 S Atlantic Ave . . . Ormond Beach FL 32176 386-672-4161
Web: www.floridahospital.com
Florida Hospital Orlando 601 E Rollins St . . . Orlando FL 32803 407-303-2800
Web: www.floridahospital.com
Florida Hospital Zephyrhills
7050 Gall Blvd . . . Zephyrhills FL 33541 813-788-0411
Web: www.floridahospital.com
Fort Walton Beach Medical Ctr (FWBMC)
1000 Mar-Walt Dr. . . . Fort Walton Beach FL 32547 850-862-1111
Web: www.fwbmc.com
Gulf Coast Medical Ctr 13681 Doctors Way . . . Fort Myers FL 33912 239-343-1000
TF: 800-809-9906 ■ *Web:* www.leememorial.org/facilities/gcmcenter.asp
Gulf Coast Medical Ctr 449 W 23rd St . . . Panama City FL 32405 850-769-8341
Web: www.gcmc-pc.com
Health First Cape Canaveral Hospital
701 W Cocoa Beach Cswy . . . Cocoa Beach FL 32931 321-799-7111 434-6103
Web: www.health-first.org
Holmes Regional Medical Ctr
1350 Hickory St . . . Melbourne FL 32901 321-434-7000 727-1200
TF: 800-716-7737 ■ *Web:* www.health-first.org
Holy Cross Hospital
4725 N Federal Hwy . . . Fort Lauderdale FL 33308 954-771-8000 492-5741
TF: 888-419-3456 ■ *Web:* www.holy-cross.com
Homestead Hospital 975 Baptist Way . . . Homestead FL 33033 786-243-8000
Web: www.baptisthealth.net
Imperial Point Medical Ctr
6401 N Federal Hwy . . . Fort Lauderdale FL 33308 954-776-8500
Web: www.browardhealth.org
Indian River Medical Ctr 1000 36th St. . . . Vero Beach FL 32960 772-567-4311 562-5628
Web: www.indianrivermedicalcenter.com
Jackson Hospital 4250 Hospital Dr . . . Marianna FL 32446 850-526-2200 482-6374
Web: www.jacksonhosp.com
Jackson Memorial Hospital 1611 NW 12th Ave. . . . Miami FL 33136 305-585-1111 326-9470
Web: www.jacksonhealth.org
Jupiter Medical Ctr 1210 S Old Dixie Hwy . . . Jupiter FL 33458 561-263-2234
Web: www.jupitermed.com
Kendall Regional Medical Ctr 11750 SW 40th St . . . Miami FL 33175 305-223-3000
Web: www.kendallmed.com
Lakeland Regional Health
1324 Lakeland Hills Blvd . . . Lakeland FL 33805 863-687-1100 687-1214
Web: mylrh.org
Largo Medical Center - Indian Rocks Rd Campus
2025 Indian Rocks Rd. . . . Largo FL 33774 727-581-9474 586-7106
Lawnwood Regional Medical Ctr (LRMC)
1700 S 23rd St . . . Fort Pierce FL 34950 772-461-4000 460-1353
Web: www.lawnwoodmed.com
Lower Keys Medical Ctr 5900 College Rd. . . . Key West FL 33040 305-294-5531 294-8065
TF: 800-355-2470 ■ *Web:* www.lkmc.com
Manatee County Rural Health Services Inc (MCRHS)
12271 US Hwy 301 . . . Parrish FL 34219 941-776-4000
Web: www.mcrhs.org

				Phone	Fax
Manatee Memorial Hospital 206 Second St E	Bradenton	FL	34208	941-746-5111	745-6862
TF: 844-854-9613 ■ *Web:* www.manateememorial.com					
Martin Memorial Health Systems (MMHS) 200 SE Hospital Ave PO Box 9010	Stuart	FL	34994	772-287-5200	223-5946
TF: 800-368-3375 ■ *Web:* www.martinhealth.org					
Mease Dunedin Hospital 601 Main St	Dunedin	FL	34698	727-733-1111	734-6887
Memorial Hospital of Tampa 2901 W Swann Ave	Tampa	FL	33609	813-873-6400	874-8685
Web: www.memorialhospitaltampa.com					
Memorial Hospital Pembroke (MHP) 7800 Sheridan St	Pembroke Pines	FL	33024	954-962-9650	
Web: www.memorialpembroke.com					
Memorial Hospital West 703 N Flamingo Rd	Pembroke Pines	FL	33028	954-436-5000	
Web: www.memorialwest.com					
Memorial Regional Hospital 3501 Johnson St	Hollywood	FL	33021	954-987-2000	
Web: www.memorialregional.com					
Mercy Hospital 3663 S Miami Ave	Miami	FL	33133	305-854-4400	285-2173
Web: www.mercymiami.com					
Morton Plant Hospital 300 Pinellas St	Clearwater	FL	33756	727-462-7000	
TF: 800-229-2273 ■ *Web:* www.baycare.org					
Mount Sinai Medical Ctr 4300 Alton Rd	Miami Beach	FL	33140	305-674-2121	674-2007
Web: www.msmc.com					
NCH Healthcare System 350 Seventh St N	Naples	FL	34102	239-436-5000	436-5914
Web: www.nchmd.org					
NCH North Naples Hospital 11190 Health Park Blvd	Naples	FL	34110	239-552-7000	
Web: nchmd.org					
North Broward Medical Ctr 201 E Sample Rd	Deerfield Beach	FL	33064	954-941-8300	
Web: www.browardhealth.org					
North Florida Regional Medical Ctr 6500 Newberry Rd	Gainesville	FL	32605	352-333-4000	333-4800
Web: www.nfrmc.com					
North Okaloosa Medical Ctr (NOMC) 151 E Redstone Ave	Crestview	FL	32539	850-689-8100	
Web: www.northokaloosa.com					
North Shore Medical Ctr 1100 NW 95th St	Miami	FL	33150	305-835-6000	835-6163
TF: 800-984-3434 ■ *Web:* www.northshoremedical.com					
Northside Hospital 6000 49th St N	Saint Petersburg	FL	33709	727-521-4411	521-5007
Web: www.northsidehospital.com					
Northwest Medical Ctr (NWMC) 2801 N SR 7	Margate	FL	33063	954-978-4000	
Web: www.northwestmed.com					
Oakhill Hospital 11375 Cortez Blvd	Brooksville	FL	34613	352-596-6632	597-6387
TF: 877-442-2362 ■ *Web:* www.oakhillhospital.com					
Ocala Regional Medical Ctr (ORMC) 1431 SW First Ave	Ocala	FL	34478	352-401-1000	
Web: www.ocalahealthsystem.com/about/ocala-regional-medical-center.dot					
Orange Park Medical Ctr 2001 Kingsley Ave	Orange Park	FL	32073	904-276-8500	
Web: www.orangeparkmedical.com					
Orlando Regional Medical Ctr (ORMC) 1414 Kuhl Ave	Orlando	FL	32806	321-841-5111	
TF: 800-424-6998 ■ *Web:* www.orlandohealth.com					
Orlando Regional South Seminole Hospital 555 W State Rd 434	Longwood	FL	32750	407-767-1200	
Web: www.orlandohealth.com/southseminolehospital					
Osceola Regional Medical Ctr 700 W Oak St	Kissimmee	FL	34741	407-846-2266	518-3616
Web: www.osceolaregional.com					
Pacer Corp 14100 Palmetto Frontage Rd Ste 110	Miami Lakes	FL	33016	305-828-7660	828-2551
Web: www.pacerco.com					
Palm Beach Gardens Medical Ctr 3360 Burns Rd	Palm Beach Gardens	FL	33410	561-622-1411	694-7160
Web: www.pbgmc.com					
Palms of Pasadena Hospital 1501 Pasadena Ave S	Saint Petersburg	FL	33707	727-381-1000	341-7570
Web: www.palmspasadena.com					
Palms West Hospital (PWH) 13001 Southern Blvd	Loxahatchee	FL	33470	561-798-3300	791-2535
TF: 877-549-9337 ■ *Web:* www.palmswesthospital.com					
Parrish Medical Ctr 951 N Washington Ave	Titusville	FL	32796	321-268-6111	268-6231
Web: www.parrishmed.com					
Peace River Regional Medical Ctr 2500 Harbor Blvd	Port Charlotte	FL	33952	941-766-4122	
TF: 888-941-2495 ■ *Web:* bayfrontcharlotte.com					
Physicians Regional Medical Center 6101 Pine Ridge Rd	Naples	FL	34119	239-348-4000	
Web: physiciansregional.com					
Raulerson Hospital 1796 Hwy 441 N	Okeechobee	FL	34972	863-763-2151	824-2991
TF: 877-549-9337 ■ *Web:* www.raulersonhospital.com					
Regional Medical Ctr Bayonet Point 14000 Fivay Rd	Hudson	FL	34667	727-819-2929	869-5491
Web: www.rmchealth.com					
Sacred Heart Hospital of Pensacola 5151 N Ninth Ave	Pensacola	FL	32504	850-416-7000	416-7337
TF: 800-874-1026 ■ *Web:* www.sacred-heart.org					
Saint Anthony's Hospital 1200 Seventh Ave N	Saint Petersburg	FL	33705	727-825-1100	825-1230
Web: baycare.org/sah					
Saint Joseph's Hospital 3001 W ML King Jr Blvd	Tampa	FL	33607	813-870-4000	870-4639
TF: 800-232-6372					
Saint Lucie Medical Ctr 1800 SE Tiffany Ave	Port Saint Lucie	FL	34952	772-335-4000	398-3608
Web: www.stluciemed.com					
Sarasota Memorial Hospital 1700 S Tamiami Trl	Sarasota	FL	34239	941-917-9000	917-1716
TF: 800-764-8255 ■ *Web:* www.smh.com					
Sebastian River Medical Ctr 13695 US Hwy 1	Sebastian	FL	32976	772-589-3186	
Web: www.srmcenter.com					
Seven Rivers Regional Medical Ctr (SRRMC) 6201 N Suncoast Blvd	Crystal River	FL	34428	352-795-6560	795-8369
Web: www.sevenriversregional.com					
Shands Hospital at the University of Florida 1600 SW Archer Rd	Gainesville	FL	32610	352-265-0111	627-4173
TF: 855-483-7546 ■ *Web:* ufhealth.org					
South Bay Hospital 4016 Sun City Ctr Blvd	Sun City Center	FL	33573	813-634-3301	
Web: www.southbayhospital.com					
South Florida Baptist Hospital 301 N Alexander St	Plant City	FL	33563	813-757-1200	757-8209
Web: www.sjbhealth.org/home_south.cfm?id=587					
South Miami Hospital 6200 SW 73rd St	Miami	FL	33143	786-662-4000	
Web: www.baptisthealth.net					
Southwest Florida Regional Medical Ctr 2727 Winkler Ave	Fort Myers	FL	33901	239-939-8457	
Web: www.leememorial.org					
St. Petersburg General Hospital 6500 38th Ave N	Saint Petersburg	FL	33710	727-384-1414	341-4889
TF: 800-733-0610 ■ *Web:* www.stpetegeneral.com					
Tampa General Hospital 1 Tampa General Cir	Tampa	FL	33606	813-844-7000	
Web: www.tgh.org					
Town & Country Hospital 6001 Webb Rd	Tampa	FL	33615	813-888-7060	887-5112
TF: 866-463-7449 ■ *Web:* tampacommunityhospital.com					
UF Health Jacksonville 655 W Eigth St	Jacksonville	FL	32209	904-244-0411	
Web: ufhealthjax.org					
University Community Hospital 3100 E Fletcher Ave	Tampa	FL	33613	813-971-6000	615-8100
Web: www.floridahospital.com					
University Community Hospital Carrollwood 7171 N Dale Mabry Hwy	Tampa	FL	33614	813-932-2222	
Web: www.floridahospital.com					
University Hospital 7201 N University Dr	Tamarac	FL	33321	954-721-2200	724-6575
Web: www.uhmchealth.com					
Venice Regional Medical Ctr (VRMC) 540 The Rialto	Venice	FL	34285	941-485-7711	483-7699
Web: www.veniceregional.com					
West Boca Medical Ctr (WBMC) 21644 State Rd 7	Boca Raton	FL	33428	561-488-8000	488-8105
Web: www.westbocamedctr.com					
West Florida Hospital 8383 N Davis Hwy	Pensacola	FL	32514	850-494-4000	
Web: www.westfloridahospital.com					
Westside Regional Medical Ctr 8201 W Broward Blvd	Plantation	FL	33324	954-473-6600	476-3974
Web: www.westsideregional.com					
Winter Haven Hospital 200 Ave F NE	Winter Haven	FL	33881	863-293-1121	292-4376
Web: baycare.org/winter-haven-hospital					
Wuesthoff Medical Ctr Rockledge 110 Longwood Ave	Rockledge	FL	32955	321-636-2211	597-9629*
**Fax Area Code:* 818 ■ *TF:* 877-456-9617 ■ *Web:* www.wuesthoff.com					

Georgia

				Phone	Fax
Athens Regional Medical Ctr (ARMC) 1199 Prince Ave	Athens	GA	30606	706-475-7000	
Web: www.athenshealth.org					
Atlanta Medical Ctr 303 Pkwy Dr NE	Atlanta	GA	30312	404-265-4000	265-3903
Candler Hospital 5353 Reynolds St	Savannah	GA	31405	912-819-6000	
Web: www.sjchs.org					
Coffee Regional Medical Ctr (CRMC) 1101 Ocilla Rd	Douglas	GA	31533	912-384-1900	
Web: www.coffeeregional.org					
Coliseum Medical Ctr 350 Hospital Dr	Macon	GA	31217	478-765-7000	742-1247
Web: www.coliseumhealthsystem.com					
Colquitt Regional Medical Ctr (CRMC) 3131 S Main St PO Box 40	Moultrie	GA	31768	229-985-3420	
TF: 888-262-2762 ■ *Web:* www.colquittregional.com					
Doctors Hospital 3651 Wheeler Rd	Augusta	GA	30909	706-651-3232	651-2041
Web: www.doctors-hospital.net					
Dodge County Hospital 901 Griffin Ave	Eastman	GA	31023	478-448-4000	
Web: www.dodgecountyhospital.com					
East Georgia Regional Medical Ctr (EGRMC) 1499 Fair Rd	Statesboro	GA	30458	912-486-1000	871-2354
TF: 844-455-8708 ■ *Web:* www.eastgeorgiaregional.com					
Eastside Medical Ctr 1700 Medical Way	Snellville	GA	30078	770-979-0200	736-2395
Web: www.eastsidemedical.com					
Emory Crawford Long Hospital 550 Peachtree St NE	Atlanta	GA	30308	404-686-4411	
Web: www.emoryhealthcare.org					
Emory University Hospital 1364 Clifton Rd	Atlanta	GA	30322	404-712-2000	
Web: www.emoryhealthcare.org					
Fairview Park Hospital 200 Industrial Blvd	Dublin	GA	31021	478-275-2000	
Web: www.fairviewparkhospital.com					
Floyd Medical Ctr 304 Turner McCall Blvd	Rome	GA	30165	706-509-5000	
TF: 866-874-2772 ■ *Web:* www.floyd.org					
Grady Health System 80 Jesse Hill Jr Dr SE	Atlanta	GA	30303	404-616-1000	
Web: www.gradyhealth.org					
Gwinnett Medical Ctr Lawrenceville 1000 Medical Ctr Blvd	Lawrenceville	GA	30046	678-312-1000	
Web: www.gwinnettmedicalcenter.org					
Hamilton Medical Ctr 1200 Memorial Dr PO Box 1168	Dalton	GA	30720	706-272-6000	
Web: www.hamiltonhealth.com					
Houston Medical Ctr 1601 Watson Blvd	Warner Robins	GA	31093	478-922-4281	
Web: www.hhc.org					
Hughes Spalding Children's Hospital 35 Jesse Hill Jr Dr Se	Atlanta	GA	30303	404-785-9500	785-6021
Web: www.choa.org/hughesspalding					
John D Archbold Memorial Hospital 915 Gordon Ave	Thomasville	GA	31792	229-228-2000	
TF: 800-341-1009 ■ *Web:* www.archbold.org					
Meadows Regional Medical Ctr (MRMC) 1 Meadows Pkwy	Vidalia	GA	30474	912-535-5555	
Web: www.meadowsregional.org					
Medical Ctr, The 710 Ctr St	Columbus	GA	31901	706-571-1000	571-1216
Web: www.columbusregional.com/columbuscontentpage.aspx?nd=2053					
Memorial Health University Medical Ctr 4700 Waters Ave	Savannah	GA	31404	912-350-8000	350-7073
Web: www.memorialhealth.com					

	City	State	Zip	Phone	Fax
Memorial Hospital of Adel 706 N Parrish Ave *Web:* www.memorialofadel.com	Adel	GA	31620	229-896-8000	896-8001
Navicent Health 777 Hemlock St *Web:* www.mccg.org	Macon	GA	31201	478-633-1000	
Newton Medical Ctr 5126 Hospital Dr NE *Web:* www.piedmont.org	Covington	GA	30014	770-786-7053	385-4256
North Fulton Hospital 3000 Hospital Blvd *TF:* 877-228-3638 ■ *Web:* www.wellstar.org/locations/pages/wellstar-north-fulton-hospital.aspx?modal=true	Roswell	GA	30076	770-751-2500	751-2912
Northeast Georgia Health System Inc (NGHS) 743 Spring St NE *Web:* www.nghs.com	Gainesville	GA	30501	770-535-3553	219-5437
Northside Hospital 1000 Johnson Ferry Rd NE *Web:* www.northside.com	Atlanta	GA	30342	404-851-8000	851-6010
Oconee Regional Medical Ctr 821 N Cobb St *Web:* www.oconeeregional.com	Milledgeville	GA	31061	478-454-3505	454-3555
Palmyra Medical Centers (PMC) 2000 Palmyra Rd. *Web:* beta.ehc.com	Albany	GA	31701	229-434-2000	434-2563
Phoebe Putney Memorial Hospital 417 W Third Ave PO Box 3770 *TF:* 877-312-1167	Albany	GA	31706	229-312-1000	889-7384
Phoebe Sumter Medical Ctr 1048 E Forsyth St *Web:* www.phoebehealth.com/phoebe-sumter-medical-center/phoebe-sumter-medical-center-home-phoe-be-sumter	Americus	GA	31709	229-924-6011	
Piedmont Healthcare 1133 Eagle's Landing Pkwy *Web:* www.piedmont.org	Stockbridge	GA	30281	678-604-1000	604-5580
Piedmont Hospital 1968 Peachtree Rd NW *Web:* www.piedmont.org	Atlanta	GA	30309	404-605-5000	609-6661
Piedmont Newnan Hospital (PNH) 60 Hospital Rd *Web:* www.piedmont.org	Newnan	GA	30263	770-400-1000	
Redmond Regional Medical Ctr 501 Redmond Rd *Web:* www.redmondregional.com	Rome	GA	30165	706-291-0291	291-0971
Rockdale Medical Ctr (RMC) 1412 Milstead Ave NE *Web:* www.rockdalemedicalcenter.org	Conyers	GA	30012	770-918-3000	918-3104
Saint Francis Hospital 2122 Manchester Expy *Web:* www.mystfrancis.com	Columbus	GA	31904	706-596-4000	596-4481
Saint Joseph's Hospital of Atlanta 5665 Peachtree Dunwoody Rd NE *Web:* www.emoryhealthcare.org	Atlanta	GA	30342	404-851-7001	851-7339
Saint Mary's Health Care System 1230 Baxter St *TF:* 800-233-7864 ■ *Web:* www.stmarysathens.org	Athens	GA	30606	706-389-3000	
South Georgia Medical Ctr 2501 N Patterson St *Web:* www.sgmc.org	Valdosta	GA	31602	229-333-1000	
Southeast Georgia Health System Brunswick Campus 2415 Parkwood Dr *TF:* 844-882-7227 ■ *Web:* www.sghs.org	Brunswick	GA	31520	912-466-7000	466-7013
Southern Regional Medical Ctr 11 Upper Riverdale Rd SW *Web:* www.southernregional.org	Riverdale	GA	30274	770-991-8000	
Tanner Medical Ctr 705 Dixie St *Web:* www.tanner.org	Carrollton	GA	30117	770-836-9666	
Tift Regional Medical Ctr 1641 Madison Ave *TF:* 800-648-1935 ■ *Web:* www.tiftregional.com	Tifton	GA	31794	229-382-7120	
University Health Care System 1350 Walton Way *TF:* 866-591-2502 ■ *Web:* www.universityhealth.org	Augusta	GA	30901	706-722-9011	774-4500
Upson Regional Medical Ctr 801 W Gordon St *Web:* www.urmc.org	Thomaston	GA	30286	706-647-8111	646-3310
Wayne Memorial Hospital (WMH) 865 S First St *Web:* www.wmhweb.com	Jesup	GA	31545	912-427-6811	
Wellstar Cobb Hospital 3950 Austell Rd *Web:* www.wellstar.org	Austell	GA	30106	770-732-4000	
Wellstar Douglas Hospital 8954 Hospital Dr *Web:* www.wellstar.org	Douglasville	GA	30134	770-949-1500	
Wellstar Kennestone Hospital 677 Church St. *Web:* www.wellstar.org	Marietta	GA	30060	770-793-5000	
West Georgia Medical Ctr 1514 Vernon Rd *Web:* www.wghs.org	LaGrange	GA	30240	706-882-1411	

Hawaii

	City	State	Zip	Phone	Fax
Castle Medical Ctr 640 Ulukahiki St *Web:* www.adventisthealth.org/castle/pages/castle-home.aspx	Kailua	HI	96734	808-263-5500	
Hilo Medical Ctr 1190 Waianuenue Ave *Web:* www.hmc.hhsc.org	Hilo	HI	96720	808-932-3000	974-4746
Kaiser Permanente Medical Ctr 3288 Moanalua Rd *Web:* kaiserpermanente.org	Honolulu	HI	96819	808-432-0000	432-7736
Kuakini Health System 347 N Kuakini St *Web:* www.kuakini.org	Honolulu	HI	96817	808-536-2236	547-9547
Maui Memorial Hospital 221 Mahalani St *TF:* 800-427-5940 ■ *Web:* www.mmmc.hhsc.org	Wailuku	HI	96793	808-244-9056	242-2443
Queen's Medical Ctr, The 1301 Punchbowl St. *Web:* www.queensmedicalcenter.org	Honolulu	HI	96813	808-691-7171	
Wilcox Memorial Hospital (WMH) 3-3420 Kuhio Hwy *TF:* 877-709-9355 ■ *Web:* www.hawaiipacifichealth.org	Lihue	HI	96766	808-245-1100	

Idaho

	City	State	Zip	Phone	Fax
Eastern Idaho Regional Medical Ctr (EIRMC) 3100 Channing Way *Web:* www.eirmc.com	Idaho Falls	ID	83404	208-529-6111	529-7021
Portneuf Medical Ctr 651 Memorial Dr. *Web:* www.portmed.org	Pocatello	ID	83201	208-239-1000	
Saint Alphonsus Regional Medical Ctr 1055 N Curtis Rd *TF:* 877-401-3627 ■ *Web:* www.saintalphonsus.org	Boise	ID	83706	208-367-2121	
Saint Joseph Regional Medical Ctr 415 Sixth St *Web:* www.sjrmc.org	Lewiston	ID	83501	208-743-2511	
West Valley Medical Ctr 1717 Arlington Ave **Fax Area Code:* 877 ■ *TF:* 866-270-2311 ■ *Web:* www.westvalleymedctr.com	Caldwell	ID	83605	208-459-4641	865-9738*

Illinois

	City	State	Zip	Phone	Fax
Adventist Hinsdale Hospital 120 N Oak St. *Web:* www.keepingyouwell.com/facilities/hinsdale	Hinsdale	IL	60521	630-856-9000	
Adventist La Grange Memorial Hospital (ALMH) 5101 S Willow Springs Rd *Web:* www.keepingyouwell.com/facilities/lagrange	La Grange	IL	60525	708-245-9000	
Advocate BroMenn Medical Ctr (ABMC) 1304 Franklin Ave. *Web:* www.advocatehealth.com/bromenn/default.cfm?id=1	Normal	IL	61761	309-454-1400	
Advocate Christ Medical Ctr 4440 W 95th St *Web:* www.advocatehealth.com	Oak Lawn	IL	60453	708-684-8000	
Advocate Condell Medical Ctr (ACMC) 801 S Milwaukee Ave *Web:* www.advocatehealth.com/condell	Libertyville	IL	60048	847-362-2900	362-1721
Advocate Good Samaritan Hospital 3815 Highland Ave *Web:* www.advocatehealth.com	Downers Grove	IL	60515	630-275-5900	
Advocate Good Shepherd Hospital (AGSH) 450 W Hwy 22 *Web:* www.advocatehealth.com/gshp	Barrington	IL	60010	847-381-9600	
Advocate Illinois Masonic Medical Ctr 836 W Wellington Ave *Web:* www.advocatehealth.com	Chicago	IL	60657	773-975-1600	
Advocate Lutheran General Hospital 1775 W Dempster St. *Web:* www.advocatehealth.com	Park Ridge	IL	60068	847-723-2210	723-2285
Advocate Sherman Hospital 1425 N Randall Rd *TF:* 800-397-9000 ■ *Web:* www.advocatehealth.com/sherman	Elgin	IL	60123	847-742-9800	
Advocate South Suburban Hospital (SSUB) 17800 S Kedzie Ave *Web:* www.advocatehealth.com/ssub	Hazel Crest	IL	60429	708-799-8000	213-0100
Advocate Trinity Hospital 2320 E 93rd St *Web:* www.advocatehealth.com/trin	Chicago	IL	60617	773-967-2000	
Alexian Bros Medical Ctr 800 Biesterfield Rd *TF:* 800-432-5005 ■ *Web:* www.alexianbrothershealth.org	Elk Grove Village	IL	60007	847-437-5500	981-5774
Alton Memorial Hospital 1 Memorial Dr. *TF:* 800-994-6610 ■ *Web:* www.altonmemorialhospital.org	Alton	IL	62002	618-463-7311	463-7290
Anderson Hospital 6800 SR 162 *Web:* www.andersonhospital.org	Maryville	IL	62062	618-288-5711	
Blessing Hospital Broadway at 11th St. *TF:* 866-460-3933 ■ *Web:* www.blessinghospital.org	Quincy	IL	62301	217-223-8400	223-6891
Carle Foundation Hospital 611 W Pk St. *Web:* www.carle.org	Urbana	IL	61801	217-383-3311	383-3137
Centegra Memorial Medical Ctr 3701 Doty Rd. *TF:* 877-236-8347 ■ *Web:* www.centegra.org	Woodstock	IL	60098	815-338-2500	
Centegra Northern Illinois Medical Ctr 4201 Medical Ctr Dr *Web:* www.centegra.org	McHenry	IL	60050	815-344-5000	
Central DuPage Hospital 25 N Winfield Rd. *TF:* 800-223-9776 ■ *Web:* www.cdh.org	Winfield	IL	60190	630-933-1600	933-1550
CGH Medical Ctr (CGHMC) 100 E LeFevre Rd *TF:* 800-625-4790 ■ *Web:* www.cghmc.com	Sterling	IL	61081	815-625-0400	625-4825
Decatur Memorial Hospital 2300 N Edward St. *TF:* 866-364-3600 ■ *Web:* www.dmhcares.com	Decatur	IL	62526	217-876-8121	876-2615
Delnor-Community Hospital (DCH) 300 Randall Rd. *TF:* 800-223-9776 ■ *Web:* www.delnor.com	Geneva	IL	60134	630-208-3000	718-2650
Edward Hospital 801 S Washington St. *Web:* www.eehealth.org	Naperville	IL	60540	630-527-3000	
Evanston Hospital 2650 Ridge Ave. *TF:* 888-364-6400 ■ *Web:* www.northshore.org/about-us/organization-profile/#EH	Evanston	IL	60201	847-570-2000	
FHN Memorial Hospital 1045 W Stephenson St *TF:* 800-747-4131 ■ *Web:* www.fhn.org	Freeport	IL	61032	815-599-6000	
Franciscan St. James Health - Olympia Fields 20201 S Crawford Ave *Web:* www.franciscanalliance.org/hospitals/olympiafields/pages/default.aspx	Olympia Fields	IL	60461	708-747-4000	503-3270
Galesburg Cottage Hospital (GCH) 695 N Kellogg St *Web:* www.cottagehospital.com	Galesburg	IL	61401	309-343-8131	
Gateway Regional Medical Ctr (GRMC) 2100 Madison Ave *TF General:* 800-422-6237 ■ *Web:* www.gatewayregional.net	Granite City	IL	62040	618-798-3000	
Genesis Medical Ctr Illini Campus 801 Illini Dr *TF:* 800-250-6020 ■ *Web:* www.genesishealth.com	Silvis	IL	61282	309-792-9363	792-4274
GlenOaks Hospital 701 Winthrop Ave. *TF:* 866-751-7127 ■ *Web:* www.keepingyouwell.com	Glendale Heights	IL	60139	630-545-8000	545-3920
Gottlieb Memorial Hospital 701 W N Ave *Web:* www.gottliebhospital.org	Melrose Park	IL	60160	708-681-3200	
Graham Hospital 210 W Walnut St *Web:* www.grahamhealthsystem.org	Canton	IL	61520	309-647-5240	649-5101
Highland Park Hospital 777 Pk Ave W *Web:* www.northshore.org	Highland Park	IL	60035	847-432-8000	
Holy Cross Hospital 2701 W 68th St *Web:* www.holycrosshospital.org	Chicago	IL	60629	773-884-9000	884-8001
Illinois Valley Community Hospital 925 W St *Web:* www.ivch.org	Peru	IL	61354	815-223-3300	224-6763
Ingalls Memorial Hospital 1 Ingalls Dr. *Web:* www.ingalls.org	Harvey	IL	60426	708-333-2300	
Katherine Shaw Bethea Hospital 403 E First St *TF:* 800-582-9731 ■ *Web:* www.ksbhospital.com	Dixon	IL	61021	815-288-5531	285-5859

Phone Fax

Kishwaukee Community Hospital
1 Kish Hospital Dr ... DeKalb IL 60115 815-756-1521 753-5661*
*Fax Area Code: 888 ■ *TF:* 800-397-1521 ■ *Web:* www.kishhealth.org

Lake Forest Hospital
660 N Westmoreland Rd ... Lake Forest IL 60045 847-234-5600 234-8056
Web: www.lakeforesthospital.com

Lincoln Park Hospital 550 W Webster Ave ... Chicago IL 60614 773-883-2000 883-5168

Little Company of Mary Hospital & Health Care Centers
2800 W 95th St ... Evergreen Park IL 60805 708-422-6200 425-9756
Web: www.lcmh.org

Loretto Hospital 645 S Central Ave ... Chicago IL 60644 773-626-4300 854-5518
Web: www.lorettohospital.org

Louis A Weiss Memorial Hospital
4646 N Marine Dr ... Chicago IL 60640 773-878-8700
Web: weisshospital.com

Loyola University Medical Ctr
2160 S First Ave ... Maywood IL 60153 888-584-7888
TF: 888-584-7888 ■ *Web:* www.luhs.org

MacNeal Hospital 3249 S Oak Pk Ave ... Berwyn IL 60402 708-783-9100
TF: 888-622-6325 ■ *Web:* www.macneal.com

Memorial Hospital 4500 Memorial Dr ... Belleville IL 62226 618-233-7750
Web: www.memhosp.com

Memorial Hospital of Carbondale
405 W Jackson St ... Carbondale IL 62902 618-549-0721 529-0449
Web: www.sih.net

Memorial Medical Ctr 701 N First St ... Springfield IL 62781 217-788-3000 788-5591
Web: www.memorialmedical.com

Mercy Hospital & Medical Ctr (MHMC)
2525 S Michigan Ave ... Chicago IL 60616 312-567-2000 567-7054
Web: www.mercy-chicago.org

Methodist Hospital of Chicago (MHC)
5025 N Paulina St ... Chicago IL 60640 773-271-9040
Web: www.methodistchicago.org

Methodist Medical Ctr of Illinois
221 NE Glen Oak Ave ... Peoria IL 61636 309-672-5522
Web: unitypoint.org/peoria

Metro South Medical Ctr
12935 S Gregory St ... Blue Island IL 60406 708-597-2000
Web: www.metrosouthmedicalcenter.com

Morris Hospital 150 W High St ... Morris IL 60450 815-942-2932 942-3154
TF: 877-743-3123 ■ *Web:* www.morrishospital.org

Mount Sinai Hospital Medical Ctr of Chicago
California Ave 15th St ... Chicago IL 60608 773-542-2000
TF: 877-448-7848 ■ *Web:* www.sinai.org

North Shore Skokie Hospital 9600 Gross Pt Rd ... Skokie IL 60076 847-677-9600
Web: www.northshore.org/emergency-medicine/skokie-hospital

Northwest Community Hospital
800 W Central Rd ... Arlington Heights IL 60005 847-618-1000 618-5209
Web: www.nch.org

Norwegian-American Hospital
1044 N Francisco St ... Chicago IL 60622 773-292-8200 278-3531
TF: 877-624-9333 ■ *Web:* www.nahospital.org

OSF Saint Anthony Medical Ctr
5666 E State St ... Rockford IL 61108 815-226-2000 395-5449
TF: 800-343-3185 ■ *Web:* www.osfhealthcare.org/saint-anthony

OSF Saint Francis Medical Ctr
530 NE Glen Oak Ave ... Peoria IL 61637 309-655-2000 655-2303
TF: 888-627-5673 ■ *Web:* www.osfhealthcare.org/saint-francis

OSF Saint Joseph Medical Ctr
2200 E Washington St ... Bloomington IL 61701 309-662-3311
Web: www.osfhealthcare.org/st-joseph

OSF Saint Mary Medical Ctr
3333 N Seminary St ... Galesburg IL 61401 309-344-3161 451-8278
TF: 877-795-0416 ■ *Web:* www.osfhealthcare.org/st-mary

Our Lady of Resurrection Medical Ctr
5645 W Addison St ... Chicago IL 60634 847-493-3500 794-7651*
*Fax Area Code: 773 ■ *Web:* www.presencehealth.org

Palos Community Hospital
12251 S 80th Ave ... Palos Heights IL 60463 708-923-4000
Web: www.paloscommunityhospital.org

Passavant Area Hospital (PAH)
1600 W Walnut St ... Jacksonville IL 62650 217-245-9541
Web: www.passavanthospital.com

Pekin Hospital 600 S 13th St ... Pekin IL 61554 309-347-1151 353-0908
Web: www.pekinhospital.org

Presence Saint Joseph Medical Ctr (PSJMC)
333 N Madison St ... Joliet IL 60435 815-725-7133 741-7579
Web: www.presencehealth.org/stjoes

Proctor Hospital 5409 N Knoxville Ave ... Peoria IL 61614 309-691-1000 683-6190
Web: unitypoint.org/peoria/default.aspx

Resurrection Medical Ctr 7435 W Talcott Ave ... Chicago IL 60631 773-774-8000
Web: www.presencehealth.org

Riverside Medical Ctr (RMC) 350 N Wall St ... Kankakee IL 60901 815-933-1671 935-7823
Web: www.riversidehealthcare.org

Rockford Memorial Hospital
2400 N Rockton Ave ... Rockford IL 61103 815-971-5000
Web: www.rockfordhealthsystem.org

Roseland Community Hospital 45 W 111th St ... Chicago IL 60628 773-995-3000
Web: roselandhospital.org

Rush Oak Park Hospital (ROPH) 520 S Maple Ave ... Oak Park IL 60304 708-383-9300
Web: www.roph.org

Rush University Medical Ctr
1653 W Congress Pkwy ... Chicago IL 60612 312-942-5000 942-3212
Web: www.rush.edu

Rush-Copley Medical Ctr (RCMC) 2000 Ogden Ave ... Aurora IL 60504 630-978-6200
TF: 866-426-7539 ■ *Web:* www.rushcopley.com

Saint Alexius Medical Ctr
1555 Barrington Rd ... Hoffman Estates IL 60169 847-843-2000 490-2570
Web: www.alexianbrothershealth.org

Saint Anthony's Memorial Hospital
503 N Maple St ... Effingham IL 62401 217-342-2121
Web: www.stanthonyshospital.org

Saint John's Hospital 800 E Carpenter St ... Springfield IL 62702 217-544-6464
TF: 855-228-4438 ■ *Web:* www.st-johns.org

Saint Mary of Nazareth Hospital Ctr
2233 W Div St ... Chicago IL 60622 312-770-2000 770-3391
Web: www.presencehealth.org

Saint Mary's Hospital 1800 E Lk Shore Dr ... Decatur IL 62521 217-464-2966
Web: www.stmarysdecatur.com

Sarah Bush Lincoln Health Ctr (SBLHC)
1000 Health Ctr Dr PO Box 372 ... Mattoon IL 61938 217-258-2525 258-4117
TF: 800-345-3191 ■ *Web:* www.sarahbush.org

South Shore Hospital (SSH) 8012 S Crandon Ave ... Chicago IL 60617 773-356-5000 768-0749
Web: www.southshorehospital.com

St. Bernard Hospital & Health Care Ctr
326 W 64th St ... Chicago IL 60621 773-962-3900 962-4219
Web: www.stbernardhospital.com

Swedish Covenant Hospital
5145 N California Ave ... Chicago IL 60625 773-878-8200
Web: www.swedishcovenant.org

SwedishAmerican Hospital 1401 E State St ... Rockford IL 61104 815-968-4400 966-3999
TF: 800-322-4724 ■ *Web:* www.swedishamerican.org

Thorek Memorial Hospital 850 W Irving Pk Rd ... Chicago IL 60613 773-525-6780 975-6703
Web: thorek.org

Touchette Regional Hospital (TRH)
5900 Bond Ave ... Centreville IL 62207 618-332-3060 332-5256
Web: www.touchette.org

Trinity Medical Ctr West Campus (TMC)
2701 17th St ... Rock Island IL 61201 309-779-2800 779-2303
Web: www.unitypoint.org

University of Chicago Medical Ctr
5841 S Maryland Ave ... Chicago IL 60637 773-702-1000 702-4846
TF: 888-824-0200 ■ *Web:* www.uchospitals.edu

University of Illinois Medical Ctr
1740 W Taylor St ... Chicago IL 60612 312-996-3900 996-7049
TF: 866-600-2273 ■ *Web:* hospital.uillinois.edu

Vista Medical Ctr 1324 N Sheridan Rd ... Waukegan IL 60085 847-360-3000
Web: www.vistahealth.com

Vista West Ctr 2615 Washington St ... Waukegan IL 60085 847-249-3900 360-4109
Web: www.vistahealth.com/stmcvmh

West Suburban Hospital Medical Ctr
3 Erie Ct ... Oak Park IL 60302 708-383-6200
TF: 866-938-7256 ■ *Web:* www.westsuburbanmc.com/home.aspx

Westlake Hospital 1225 W Lake St ... Melrose Park IL 60160 708-681-3000
Web: westlakehosp.com/home.aspx

Indiana

Phone Fax

Clark Memorial Hospital (CMH)
1220 Missouri Ave ... Jeffersonville IN 47130 812-282-6631 283-6330
Web: www.clarkmemorial.org

Columbus Regional Hospital 2400 E 17th St ... Columbus IN 47201 812-379-4441
TF: 800-841-4938 ■ *Web:* www.crh.org

Community Hospital 901 Macarthur Blvd ... Munster IN 46321 219-836-1600
Web: www.comhs.org

Community Hospital Anderson (CHA)
1515 N Madison Ave ... Anderson IN 46011 765-298-4242 298-5848
TF: 800-777-7775 ■ *Web:* www.communityanderson.com

Community Hospital East
1500 N Ritter Ave ... Indianapolis IN 46219 317-355-1411 355-1668
Web: ecommunity.com

Community Westview Hospital
3630 Guion Rd ... Indianapolis IN 46222 317-920-8439
Web: www.westviewhospital.org

De Kalb Memorial Hospital Inc
1316 E Seventh St ... Auburn IN 46706 260-925-4600
Web: dekalbhealth.com

Deaconess Hospital 600 Mary St ... Evansville IN 47747 812-450-5000 450-2155
TF: 800-677-3422 ■ *Web:* www.deaconess.com

Elkhart General Hospital 600 E Blvd ... Elkhart IN 46514 574-294-2621 523-3495
Web: www.egh.org

Fayette Regional Health System (FRHS)
1941 Virginia Ave ... Connersville IN 47331 765-825-5131 827-7980
Web: www.fayetteregional.org

Floyd Memorial Hospital 1850 State St ... New Albany IN 47150 812-944-7701 949-5642
TF: 800-423-1513 ■ *Web:* floydmemorial.com

Franciscan St. Elizabeth Health
1501 Hartford St ... Lafayette IN 47904 765-423-6011
TF: 800-371-6011 ■ *Web:* www.franciscanalliance.org/pages/default.aspx

Franciscan St. Margaret Health
5454 Hohman Ave ... Hammond IN 46320 219-932-2300 933-2585
Web: www.franciscanalliance.org/hospitals/pages/stmargarethealth.aspx

Good Samaritan Hospital 520 S Seventh St ... Vincennes IN 47591 812-882-5220 885-3918
Web: www.gshvin.org

Hendricks Regional Health Danville
1000 E Main St ... Danville IN 46122 317-745-4451
Web: www.hendricks.org

Henry County Memorial Hospital (HCM)
1000 N 16th St ... New Castle IN 47362 765-521-0890 521-1555
Web: www.hcmhcares.org

Howard Regional Health System Main Campus (HRHS)
3500 S Lafountain St ... Kokomo IN 46902 765-453-0702
Web: ecommunity.com/howard

Indiana University Hospital
550 N University Blvd ... Indianapolis IN 46202 317-274-5000
TF: 800-248-1199 ■ *Web:* www.iuhealth.org

IU Health Ball Memorial Hospital
2401 W University Ave ... Muncie IN 47303 765-747-3111 741-2848
Web: www.iuhealth.org

Johnson Memorial Hospital (JMH)
1125 W Jefferson St ... Franklin IN 46131 317-736-3300 736-2692
Web: www.johnsonmemorial.org

King's Daughters' Hospital
1373 E State Rd 62 ... Madison IN 47250 812-801-0800 801-0680
Web: www.kdhmadison.org

Name / Address	City	State	Zip	Phone	Fax
La Porte Hospital (LPH) 1007 Lincolnway PO Box 250 *TF:* 800-235-6204 ■ *Web:* www.iuhealth.org/laporte	La Porte	IN	46350	219-326-1234	325-5403
Lutheran Hospital of Indiana 7950 W Jefferson Blvd *TF:* 800-444-2001 ■ *Web:* www.lutheranhospital.com	Fort Wayne	IN	46804	260-435-7001	
Major Hospital 150 W Washington St *Web:* www.mymhp.org	Shelbyville	IN	46176	317-392-3211	
Margaret Mary Community Hospital Inc 321 Mitchell Ave PO Box 226 *TF:* 800-562-5698 ■ *Web:* www.mmhealth.org	Batesville	IN	47006	812-934-6624	934-5373
Marion General Hospital (MGH) 441 N Wabash Ave *Web:* www.mgh.net	Marion	IN	46952	765-662-4000	651-7351
Memorial Hospital & Health Care Ctr 800 W Ninth St *TF:* 800-852-7279 ■ *Web:* www.mhhcc.org	Jasper	IN	47546	812-996-2345	
Memorial Hospital of South Bend 615 N Michigan St *TF:* 800-850-7913 ■ *Web:* www.qualityoflife.org	South Bend	IN	46601	574-647-1000	647-3670
Methodist Hospital 600 Grant St *Web:* www.methodisthospitals.org	Gary	IN	46402	219-886-4000	886-4688
Methodist Hospital 1701 N Senate Blvd PO Box 1367 *TF:* 800-899-8448 ■ *Web:* www.iuhealth.org/methodist	Indianapolis	IN	46202	317-962-2000	962-0304
Parkview Hospital 2200 Randallia Dr *TF:* 888-737-9311 ■ *Web:* www.parkview.com	Fort Wayne	IN	46805	260-373-4000	
Reid Hospital & Health Care Services 1100 Reid Pkwy *Web:* www.reidhosp.com	Richmond	IN	47374	765-983-3000	983-3260
Riverview Hospital 395 Westfield Rd *TF:* 800-523-6001 ■ *Web:* riverview.org	Noblesville	IN	46060	317-773-0760	
Saint Catherine Hospital 4321 Fir St *Web:* www.comhs.org	East Chicago	IN	46312	219-392-1700	
Saint Joseph Hospital 700 Broadway *TF:* 800-258-0974 ■ *Web:* www.lutheranhealth.net	Fort Wayne	IN	46802	260-425-3000	
Saint Joseph Regional Medical Ctr Mishawaka 5215 Holy Cross Pkwy *Web:* www.sjmed.com	Mishawaka	IN	46545	574-335-5000	
Saint Mary Medical Ctr 1500 S Lk Pk Ave *Web:* www.comhs.org/stmary	Hobart	IN	46342	219-942-0551	947-6037
Saint Mary's Medical Ctr of Evansville 3700 Washington Ave *Web:* www.stmarys.org/smlocation	Evansville	IN	47750	812-485-4000	
Schneck Medical Ctr 411 W Tipton St *TF:* 800-234-9222 ■ *Web:* www.schneckmed.org	Seymour	IN	47274	812-522-2349	
St. Vincent Dunn Hospital 1600 23rd St *Web:* www.stvincent.org	Bedford	IN	47421	812-275-3331	
Terre Haute Regional Hospital (THRH) 3901 S Seventh St **Fax Area Code:* 877 ■ *TF:* 866-270-2311 ■ *Web:* www.regionalhospital.com	Terre Haute	IN	47802	812-232-0021	865-9738*
Union Hospital 1606 N Seventh St *Web:* www.myunionhospital.org/unionhospital	Terre Haute	IN	47804	812-238-7000	
Urology of Indiana LLC 679 E County Line Rd *Web:* www.urologyin.com	Greenwood	IN	46143	317-885-1250	
Wishard Health Services 1001 W Tenth St *Web:* eskenazihealth.edu	Indianapolis	IN	46202	317-639-6671	630-7678
Witham Memorial Hospital 2605 N Lebanon St *Web:* witham.org	Lebanon	IN	46052	765-485-8000	
Women's Health Partnership PC 11595 N Meridian St Ste 110 *Web:* www.obgynindiana.com	Carmel	IN	46032	317-575-7300	575-7333

Iowa

Name / Address	City	State	Zip	Phone	Fax
Allen Memorial Hospital 1825 Logan Ave *TF:* 888-343-4165 ■ *Web:* unitypoint.org/waterloo/default.aspx	Waterloo	IA	50703	319-235-3941	235-3906
Broadlawns Medical Ctr 1801 Hickman Rd *TF:* 866-904-5755 ■ *Web:* www.broadlawns.org	Des Moines	IA	50314	515-282-2200	282-8874
Buena Vista Regional Medical Ctr PO Box 309 *TF:* 877-401-8030 ■ *Web:* www.bvrmc.org	Storm Lake	IA	50588	712-732-4030	
Covenant Medical Ctr 3421 W Ninth St *Web:* www.wheatoniowa.org	Waterloo	IA	50702	319-272-8000	
Dallas County Hospital 610 10th St *TF:* 800-877-7541 ■ *Web:* www.dallascohospital.org	Perry	IA	50220	515-465-3547	
Finley Hospital 350 N Grandview Ave *TF:* 800-582-1891 ■ *Web:* www.unitypoint.org	Dubuque	IA	52001	563-582-1881	589-2562
Genesis Medical Ctr 1227 E Rusholme St *Web:* www.genesishealth.com	Davenport	IA	52803	563-421-1000	421-6500
Great River Medical Ctr 1221 S Gear Ave *Web:* www.greatrivermedical.org	West Burlington	IA	52655	319-768-1000	768-3266
Iowa Methodist Medical Ctr (IMMC) 1200 Pleasant St *Web:* unitypoint.org/desmoines/iowa-methodist-medical-center.aspx	Des Moines	IA	50309	515-241-6212	
Jennie Edmundson Hospital 933 E Pierce St *Web:* www.bestcare.org	Council Bluffs	IA	51503	712-396-6000	
Keokuk Area Hospital 1600 Morgan St *Web:* www.keokukhealthsystems.org	Keokuk	IA	52632	319-524-7150	524-5317
Madison County Healthcare System 300 Hutchings St *Web:* www.madisonhealth.com	Winterset	IA	50273	515-462-2373	462-5132
Mary Greeley Medical Ctr 1111 Duff Ave *Web:* www.mgmc.org	Ames	IA	50010	515-239-2011	239-2007
Mercy Hospital 800 Mercy Dr *Web:* chihealth.com	Council Bluffs	IA	51503	712-328-5000	
Mercy Iowa City 500 E Market St *TF:* 800-637-2942 ■ *Web:* www.mercyiowacity.org	Iowa City	IA	52245	319-339-0300	339-3788
Mercy Medical Ctr (MMC) 801 Fifth St *TF:* 800-352-3559 ■ *Web:* www.mercysiouxcity.com	Sioux City	IA	51102	712-279-2010	279-2034
Mercy Medical Ctr 1111 Sixth Ave *TF:* 800-637-2993 ■ *Web:* www.mercydesmoines.org	Des Moines	IA	50314	515-247-3121	
Mercy Medical Ctr 701 Tenth St SE *Web:* www.mercycare.org	Cedar Rapids	IA	52403	319-398-6011	398-6912
Mercy Medical Ctr 250 Mercy Dr *Web:* www.mercydubuque.com	Dubuque	IA	52001	563-589-8000	589-8073
Mercy Medical Ctr North Iowa 1000 Fourth St SW *TF:* 800-433-3883 ■ *Web:* www.mercynorthiowa.com	Mason City	IA	50401	641-428-7000	
Orange City Area Health System 1000 Lincoln Cir SE *TF:* 800-808-6264 ■ *Web:* www.ochealthsystem.org	Orange City	IA	51041	712-737-4984	
Ottumwa Regional Health Ctr 1001 Pennsylvania Ave *TF:* 800-933-6742 ■ *Web:* www.ottumwaregionalhealth.com	Ottumwa	IA	52501	641-684-2300	684-2324
Saint Luke's Hospital (SLH) 1026 A Ave NE *Web:* unitypoint.org/cedarrapids/default.aspx	Cedar Rapids	IA	52406	319-369-7211	369-8105
Saint Luke's Regional Medical Ctr 2720 Stone Pk Blvd *TF:* 800-352-4660 ■ *Web:* www.unitypoint.org	Sioux City	IA	51104	712-279-3500	279-7958
Trinity Regional Medical Ctr (TRMC) 802 Kenyon Rd *Web:* www.unitypoint.org	Fort Dodge	IA	50501	515-573-3101	573-8710
University of Iowa Hospitals & Clinics 200 Hawkins Dr *Web:* uihealthcare.org	Iowa City	IA	52242	319-356-1616	356-3862

Kansas

Name / Address	City	State	Zip	Phone	Fax
Coffeyville Regional Medical Ctr 1400 W Fourth St *TF:* 800-540-2762 ■ *Web:* www.crmcinc.com	Coffeyville	KS	67337	620-251-1200	252-1651
Hays Medical Ctr (HMC) 2220 Canterbury Dr *TF:* 800-248-0073 ■ *Web:* haysmed.com	Hays	KS	67601	785-650-2759	
Hutchinson Regional Healthcare System 1701 E 23rd Ave *TF:* 800-267-6891 ■ *Web:* hutchregional.com	Hutchinson	KS	67502	620-665-2000	
Lawrence Memorial Hospital (LMH) 325 Maine St *TF:* 800-749-4144 ■ *Web:* www.lmh.org	Lawrence	KS	66044	785-505-5000	
Menorah Medical Ctr 5721 W 119th St *Web:* www.menorahmedicalcenter.com	Overland Park	KS	66209	913-498-6000	
Mercy Health Ctr Fort Scott 401 Woodland Hills Blvd *Web:* mercy.net	Fort Scott	KS	66701	620-223-2200	223-5327
Newman Regional Health 1201 W 12th Ave *Web:* www.newmanrh.org	Emporia	KS	66801	620-343-6800	
Olathe Medical Ctr 20333 W 151st St *Web:* www.olathehealth.org	Olathe	KS	66061	913-791-4200	791-4313
Overland Park Regional Medical Ctr 10500 Quivira Rd *Web:* www.oprmc.com	Overland Park	KS	66215	913-541-5000	
Pratt Regional Medical Ctr Corp 200 Commodore St *TF:* 877-572-2787 ■ *Web:* www.prmc.org	Pratt	KS	67124	620-672-7451	672-2113
Providence Medical Ctr 8929 Parallel Pkwy *TF:* 800-281-7777 ■ *Web:* www.providencekc.com	Kansas City	KS	66112	913-596-4000	596-4801
Robert J Dole VA Medical Center 5500 E Kellogg St *TF:* 888-878-6881 ■ *Web:* www.wichita.va.gov/index.asp	Wichita	KS	67218	316-685-2221	651-3666
Saint Catherine Hospital (SCH) 401 E Spruce St *Web:* stcatherinehosp.org	Garden City	KS	67846	620-272-2222	272-2566
Saint Francis Health Ctr 1700 SW Seventh St *TF:* 855-578-3726 ■ *Web:* www.stfrancistopeka.org	Topeka	KS	66606	785-295-8000	
Saint John Hospital Inc of Kansas 3500 S Fourth St *Web:* www.providencekc.com	Leavenworth	KS	66048	913-680-6000	680-6013
Salina Regional Health Ctr 400 S Santa Fe Ave *Web:* www.srhc.com	Salina	KS	67401	785-452-7000	452-6963
Shawnee Mission Medical Ctr 9100 W 74th St *Web:* www.shawneemission.org	Shawnee Mission	KS	66204	913-676-2000	676-7792
St. Rose Ambulatory & Surgery Center 3515 Broadway St *Web:* www.stroseasc.org	Great Bend	KS	67530	620-792-2511	
Stormont-Vail Regional Health Ctr 1500 SW Tenth Ave *TF:* 800-432-2951 ■ *Web:* www.stormontvail.org	Topeka	KS	66604	785-354-6000	354-6926
University of Kansas Hospital 3901 Rainbow Blvd *Web:* www.kumed.com	Kansas City	KS	66160	913-588-1227	588-5785
Via Christi Regional Medical Ctr 929 N St Francis St	Wichita	KS	67214	316-268-5000	291-7999
Wesley Medical Ctr 550 N Hillside St *TF:* 800-362-0288 ■ *Web:* www.wesleymc.com	Wichita	KS	67214	316-962-2000	962-7076
Western Plains Medical Complex 3001 Ave A *Web:* www.westernplainsmc.com	Dodge City	KS	67801	620-225-8400	225-8403

Kentucky

Name / Address	City	State	Zip	Phone	Fax
ARH Regional Medical Ctr 100 Medical Ctr Dr *Web:* www.arh.org	Hazard	KY	41701	606-439-1331	439-6682
Baptist Health 1 Trillium Way *TF:* 800-395-4435 ■ *Web:* www.baptisthealth.com	Corbin	KY	40701	606-528-1212	528-3223
Baptist Health Louisville 4000 Kresge Way **Fax Area Code:* 859 ■ *TF:* 800-489-3002 ■ *Web:* www.baptisthealth.com/louisville/pages/default.aspx	Louisville	KY	40207	502-897-8100	276-3765*
Baptist Health Paducah (WBH) 2501 Kentucky Ave **Fax Area Code:* 859 ■ *TF:* 877-271-4176 ■ *Web:* www.baptisthealth.com/paducah/pages/default.aspx	Paducah	KY	42003	270-575-2100	276-3765*

Hospital	City	State	ZIP	Phone	Fax
Clark Regional Medical Ctr Inc 175 Hospital Dr *Web:* www.clarkregional.org	Winchester	KY	40391	859-745-3500	
Ephraim McDowell Regional Medical Ctr 217 S Third St	Danville	KY	40422	859-239-1000	239-6709
Frankfort Regional Medical Ctr 299 King's Daughters Dr *TF:* 888-696-4505 ■ *Web:* www.frankfortregional.com	Frankfort	KY	40601	502-875-5240	226-7936
Greenview Regional Hospital 1801 Ashley Cir *TF:* 800-605-1466 ■ *Web:* tristargreenviewregional.com	Bowling Green	KY	42104	270-793-1000	
Hardin Memorial Hospital 913 W Dixie Ave *Web:* www.hmh.net	Elizabethtown	KY	42701	270-737-1212	
Harlan ARH Hospital 81 Ballpark Rd *TF:* 800-274-9375 ■ *Web:* www.arh.org	Harlan	KY	40831	606-573-8100	
Highlands Regional Medical Ctr 5000 KY Rt 321 *Web:* www.hrmc.org	Prestonsburg	KY	41653	606-886-8511	
Jackson Purchase Medical Ctr 1099 Medical Ctr Cir *TF:* 800-994-6610 ■ *Web:* www.jacksonpurchase.com	Mayfield	KY	42066	270-251-4100	251-4507
Jennie Stuart Medical Ctr 320 W 18th St PO Box 2400 *TF:* 800-887-5762 ■ *Web:* www.jsmc.org	Hopkinsville	KY	42241	270-887-0100	
Kindred Hospital Louisville 1313 St Anthony Pl *Web:* www.kindredlouisville.com	Louisville	KY	40204	502-587-7001	587-0060
King's Daughters Medical Ctr 2201 Lexington Ave *TF:* 888-377-5362 ■ *Web:* www.kdmc.com	Ashland	KY	41101	606-408-4000	
Lake Cumberland Regional Hospital 305 Langdon St *Web:* lakecumberlandhospital.com	Somerset	KY	42503	606-679-7441	678-9919
Lourdes Hospital 1530 Lone Oak Rd *Web:* www.elourdes.com	Paducah	KY	42003	270-444-2444	
Meadowview Regional Medical Ctr (MRMC) 989 Medical Pk Dr *Web:* www.meadowviewregional.com	Maysville	KY	41056	606-759-5311	
Medical Ctr, The 250 Pk St *Web:* www.mcbg.org	Bowling Green	KY	42101	270-780-2660	
Methodist Hospital 1305 N Elm St *TF:* 888-318-1498 ■ *Web:* www.methodisthospital.net	Henderson	KY	42420	270-827-7700	827-7402
Middlesboro Appalachian Regional Hospital 3600 W Cumberland Ave *Web:* arh.org/locations/middlesboro.aspx	Middlesboro	KY	40965	606-242-1100	248-1018
Muhlenberg Community Hospital 440 Hopkinsville St *Web:* www.mchky.org	Greenville	KY	42345	270-338-8000	338-8278
Murray-Calloway County Hospital 803 Poplar St *Web:* www.murrayhospital.org	Murray	KY	42071	270-762-1100	767-3600
Norton Audubon Hospital 1 Audubon Plz Dr *Web:* www.nortonhealthcare.com	Louisville	KY	40217	502-636-7111	
Norton Hospital 200 E Chestnut St *Web:* www.nortonhealthcare.com	Louisville	KY	40202	502-629-8000	629-8417
Norton Suburban Hospital 4001 Dutchmans Ln *Web:* www.nortonhealthcare.com	Louisville	KY	40207	502-893-1000	
Our Lady of Bellefonte Hospital 1000 St Christopher Dr *Web:* www.olbh.com	Ashland	KY	41101	606-833-3333	
Owensboro Medical Health Systems (OMHS) 811 E Parish Ave PO Box 20007 *TF:* 877-888-6647 ■ *Web:* www.owensborohealth.org	Owensboro	KY	42303	270-688-2000	
Pikeville Medical Ctr 911 Bypass Rd *Web:* www.medicalleader.org	Pikeville	KY	41501	606-218-4509	
Pineville Community Hospital 850 Riverview Ave *Web:* www.pinevillecommunityhospital.com	Pineville	KY	40977	606-337-3051	337-4284
Saint Claire Regional Medical Ctr 222 Medical Cir *Web:* www.st-claire.org	Morehead	KY	40351	606-783-6500	
Saint Joseph Hospital 1 St Joseph Dr *Web:* kentuckyonehealth.org	Lexington	KY	40504	859-313-1000	
Saint Joseph Hospital East 150 N Eagle Creek Dr *Web:* kentuckyonehealth.org	Lexington	KY	40509	859-967-5000	
Saints Mary & Elizabeth Hospital 1850 Bluegrass Ave *Web:* www.kentuckyonehealth.org/st-mary-st-elizabeth-hospital	Louisville	KY	40215	502-361-6000	361-6799
Taylor Regional Hospital 1700 Old Lebanon Rd *Web:* www.tchosp.org	Campbellsville	KY	42718	270-465-3561	465-5386
TJ Samson Community Hospital 1301 N Race St *TF:* 800-651-5635 ■ *Web:* www.tjsamson.org	Glasgow	KY	42141	270-651-4444	
UK Good Samaritan Hospital 310 S Limestone St *Web:* ukhealthcare.uky.edu	Lexington	KY	40508	859-226-7000	226-7154
University of Kentucky Chandler Medical Ctr 800 Rose St *Web:* www.mc.uky.edu	Lexington	KY	40536	859-323-5000	323-2044
University of Louisville Hospital 530 S Jackson St *TF:* 800-891-0947 ■ *Web:* www.kentuckyonehealth.org	Louisville	KY	40202	502-562-3000	
Whitesburg Appalachian Regional Hospital (ARH) 240 Hospital Rd *Web:* arh.org/locations/whitesburg.aspx	Whitesburg	KY	41858	606-633-3500	
Williamson ARH Hospital 260 Hospital Dr *TF General:* 888-654-0015 ■ *Web:* arh.org/locations/williamson.aspx	South Williamson	KY	41503	606-237-1700	237-1701

Louisiana

Hospital	City	State	ZIP	Phone	Fax
Baton Rouge General Medical Ctr (BRGMC) 3600 Florida Blvd *Web:* www.brgeneral.org	Baton Rouge	LA	70806	225-387-7000	
CHRISTUS Schumpert Highland 1453 E Bert Kouns *TF:* 888-681-4138 ■ *Web:* christushealthsb.org	Shreveport	LA	71105	318-681-4500	
Dauterive Hospital 600 N Lewis St *Web:* www.dauterivehospital.com	New Iberia	LA	70563	337-365-7311	
Earl K Long Medical Ctr 5825 Airline Hwy *Web:* legis.state.la.us	Baton Rouge	LA	70805	225-358-1000	
East Jefferson General Hospital (EJGH) 4200 Houma Blvd *TF:* 866-280-7737 ■ *Web:* www.ejgh.org	Metairie	LA	70006	504-454-4000	
Glenwood Regional Medical Ctr 503 McMillan Rd *Web:* www.grmc.com	West Monroe	LA	71291	318-329-4200	329-4710
Homer Memorial Hospital 620 E College St *Web:* www.homerhospital.com	Homer	LA	71040	318-927-2024	
Huey P Long Medical Ctr 352 Hospital Blvd PO Box 5352 *Web:* lsuhscshreveport.edu	Pineville	LA	71361	318-448-0811	
Iberia Medical Ctr (IMC) 2315 E Main St *Web:* www.iberiamedicalcenter.com	New Iberia	LA	70560	337-364-0441	374-7641
Lady of The Sea General Hospital (LOSGH) 200 W 134th Pl *Web:* www.losgh.org	Cut Off	LA	70345	985-632-6401	632-8263
Lafayette General Medical Ctr 1214 Coolidge Blvd *Web:* lafayettegeneral.com	Lafayette	LA	70505	337-289-7991	289-8671
Lake Charles Memorial Health System (LCMH) 1701 Oak Pk Blvd *Web:* www.lcmh.com	Lake Charles	LA	70601	337-494-3000	
Lakeview Regional Medical Ctr 95 Judge Tanner Blvd *Web:* www.lakeviewregional.com	Covington	LA	70433	985-867-3800	
Lane Regional Medical Ctr 6300 Main St *Web:* www.lanermc.org	Zachary	LA	70791	225-658-4000	658-4287
Louisiana State University Health Sciences Ctr (LSUHSC) 1501 Kings Hwy *Web:* www.lsuhscshreveport.edu/lsuhealthshreveport/lsuhealthshreveport.aspx	Shreveport	LA	71130	318-675-5000	
Minden Medical Ctr 1 Medical Plz *Web:* www.mindenmedicalcenter.com	Minden	LA	71055	318-377-2321	
Natchitoches Parish Hospital 501 Keyser Ave *TF:* 888-728-8383 ■ *Web:* www.natchitocheshospital.org	Natchitoches	LA	71457	318-214-4200	
North Oaks Health System (NOHS) PO Box 2668 *Web:* www.northoaks.org	Hammond	LA	70404	985-345-2700	230-7655
Northern Louisiana Medical Ctr 401 E Vaughn St *Web:* www.northernlouisianamedicalcenter.com	Ruston	LA	71270	318-254-2100	
NorthShore Regional Medical Ctr (NRMC) 100 Medical Ctr Dr *Web:* www.ochsner.org/locations/north_shore	Slidell	LA	70461	985-649-7070	
Ochsner Clinic Foundation Hospital 1514 Jefferson Hwy *TF:* 800-343-0269 ■ *Web:* www.ochsner.org	New Orleans	LA	70121	504-842-3000	394-0840
Ochsner Medical Ctr Baton Rouge 17000 Medical Ctr Dr *Web:* www.ochsner.org	Baton Rouge	LA	70816	225-752-2470	
Ochsner Medical Ctr West Bank 2500 Belle Chasse Hwy *TF:* 800-231-5257 ■ *Web:* www.ochsner.org	Gretna	LA	70056	504-391-5454	
Our Lady of Lourdes Regional Medical Ctr 4801 Ambassador Caffery Pkwy *Web:* lourdesrmc.com/pages/home.aspx	Lafayette	LA	70508	337-470-2000	
Our Lady of the Lake Regional Medical Ctr 5000 Hennessy Blvd **Fax:* Admissions ■ *Web:* ololrmc.com/pages/home.aspx	Baton Rouge	LA	70808	225-765-6565	765-5290*
Rapides Regional Medical Ctr 211 Fourth St *Web:* www.rapidesregional.com	Alexandria	LA	71301	318-769-3000	449-7575
River Oaks Hospital 1525 River Oaks Rd W *TF:* 800-366-1740 ■ *Web:* www.riveroakshospital.com	New Orleans	LA	70123	504-734-1740	733-3229
River Parishes Hospital 500 Rue De Sante *TF:* 800-231-5275 ■ *Web:* www.ochsner.org	Laplace	LA	70068	985-652-7000	
Saint Patrick Hospital of Lake Charles 524 Dr Michael DeBakey Dr *Web:* christusstpatrick.org	Lake Charles	LA	70601	337-436-2511	491-7157
Saint Tammany Parish Hospital 1202 S Tyler St *Web:* www.stph.org	Covington	LA	70433	985-898-4000	898-4394
Savoy Medical Ctr 801 Poinciana Ave *Web:* www.savoymedical.com	Mamou	LA	70554	337-457-3135	
Slidell Memorial Hospital (SMH) 1001 Gause Blvd *Web:* slidellmemorial.org	Slidell	LA	70458	985-643-2200	
St. Francis Medical Center 3421 Medical Pk Dr *Web:* stfran.com/pages/home.aspx	Monroe	LA	71203	318-966-4000	966-7737
Teche Regional Medical Ctr 1125 Marguerite St *Web:* www.techeregional.com	Morgan City	LA	70380	985-384-2200	
Terrebonne General Medical Ctr (TGMC) 8166 Main St *TF:* 888-850-6270 ■ *Web:* www.tgmc.com	Houma	LA	70360	985-873-4141	873-5306
Thibodaux Regional Medical Ctr (TRMC) 602 N Acadia Rd *TF:* 800-822-8442 ■ *Web:* thibodaux.com	Thibodaux	LA	70301	985-447-5500	446-5033
Touro Infirmary 1401 Foucher St *Web:* www.touro.com	New Orleans	LA	70115	504-897-7011	897-8769
Tulane Medical Ctr (TMC) 1415 Tulane Ave *TF:* 800-588-5800 ■ *Web:* www.tulanehealthcare.com	New Orleans	LA	70112	504-988-5263	

				Phone	Fax
University Hospital (MCLNO) 2021 Perdido St *Web:* www.lsuhospitals.org	New Orleans	LA	70112	504-903-3000	
University Medical Ctr 2390 W Congress St *Web:* lafayettegeneral.com	Lafayette	LA	70506	337-261-6000	
West Calcasieu Cameron Hospital 701 E Cypress St *Web:* www.wcch.com	Sulphur	LA	70663	337-527-7034	
West Jefferson Medical Ctr 1101 Medical Ctr Blvd *Web:* www.wjmc.org	Marrero	LA	70072	504-349-1134	349-6299
Willis-Knighton Medical Ctr (WKMC) 2600 Greenwood Rd *Web:* www.wkhs.com/home.aspx	Shreveport	LA	71103	318-212-4000	212-4195

Maine

				Phone	Fax
Aroostook Medical Ctr, The (TAMC) 140 Academy St *Web:* www.tamc.org	Presque Isle	ME	04769	207-768-4000	768-4116
Central Maine Medical Ctr 300 Main St *Web:* www.cmmc.org	Lewiston	ME	04240	207-795-0111	
Eastern Maine Medical Ctr 489 State St *Web:* www.emmc.org	Bangor	ME	04401	207-973-7000	973-7348
Franklin Community Health Network 111 Franklin Health Commons *TF:* 800-398-6031 ■ *Web:* www.fchn.org	Farmington	ME	04938	207-778-6031	778-2548
Maine General Medical Ctr (MGMC) *Augusta* 361 Old Belgrade Rd *Web:* www.mainegeneral.org	Augusta	ME	04330	207-626-1000	621-8801
Maine Medical Ctr (MMC) 22 Bramhall St *TF:* 877-339-3107 ■ *Web:* www.mmc.org	Portland	ME	04102	207-662-0111	
Brighton Campus 335 Brighton Ave. *Web:* www.mmc.org/mmc_body.cfm?id=2291	Portland	ME	04102	207-775-4000	
Mercy Hospital 144 State St *TF:* 800-293-6583 ■ *Web:* www.mercyhospital.org	Portland	ME	04101	207-879-3000	879-3429
Mid Coast Hospital 123 Medical Ctr Dr *TF:* 800-994-6610 ■ *Web:* www.midcoasthealth.com	Brunswick	ME	04011	207-729-0181	721-1230
Miles Memorial Hospital 35 Miles St *Web:* www.mileshealthcare.org	Damariscotta	ME	04543	207-563-1234	563-4572
Northern Maine Medical Ctr (NMMC) 194 E Main St *Web:* www.nmmc.org	Fort Kent	ME	04743	207-834-3155	834-2949
Penobscot Bay Medical Ctr 4 Glen Cove Dr # 101 Ste 202 *Web:* www.penbayhealthcare.org	Rockport	ME	04856	207-596-8000	
Saint Mary's Regional Medical Ctr 93 Campus Ave *Web:* www.stmarysmaine.com	Lewiston	ME	04240	207-777-8100	777-8800
Southern Maine Medical Ctr (SMMC) 1 Medical Ctr Dr PO Box 626 *Web:* smhc.org	Biddeford	ME	04005	207-283-7000	283-7020
St. Joseph Healthcare 360 Broadway PO Box 403 *Web:* www.stjoeshealing.org	Bangor	ME	04402	207-262-1000	262-1240

Maryland

				Phone	Fax
Anne Arundel Medical Ctr 2001 Medical Pkwy *Web:* www.aahs.org	Annapolis	MD	21401	443-481-1000	
Baltimore Washington Medical Ctr 301 Hospital Dr *TF:* 800-994-6610 ■ *Web:* www.mybwmc.org	Glen Burnie	MD	21061	410-787-4000	595-1958
Braddock Hospital 12500 Willowbrook Rd *TF:* 888-369-1122 ■ *Web:* www.wmhs.com	Cumberland	MD	21502	240-964-7000	
Carroll Hospital Ctr 200 Memorial Ave *Web:* carrollhospitalcenter.org	Westminster	MD	21157	410-848-3000	871-7474
Doctors Community Hospital (DCH) 8118 Good Luck Rd *Web:* www.dchweb.org	Lanham	MD	20706	301-552-8118	552-8521
Franklin Square Hospital Ctr 9000 Franklin Sq Dr *TF:* 888-404-3549 ■ *Web:* www.medstarhealth.org	Baltimore	MD	21237	443-777-7000	777-7904
Frederick Memorial Hospital 400 W Seventh St **Fax:* Admitting ■ *Web:* www.fmh.org	Frederick	MD	21701	240-566-3300	566-3066*
Good Samaritan Hospital of Maryland 5601 Loch Raven Blvd *TF:* 855-633-5655 ■ *Web:* www.medstarhealth.org	Baltimore	MD	21239	410-532-8000	
Greater Baltimore Medical Ctr (GBMC) 6701 N Charles St *Web:* www.gbmc.org	Baltimore	MD	21204	443-849-2000	849-8679
Harbor Hospital Ctr 3001 S Hanover St *TF:* 800-280-9006 ■ *Web:* www.medstarhealth.org	Baltimore	MD	21225	410-350-3200	354-4440
Holy Cross Hospital 1500 Forest Glen Rd *TF:* 800-358-9001 ■ *Web:* www.holycrosshealth.org	Silver Spring	MD	20910	301-754-7000	754-7012
Howard County General Hospital 5755 Cedar Ln *TF:* 866-323-4615 ■ *Web:* www.hopkinsmedicine.org	Columbia	MD	21044	410-740-7890	740-7610
Johns Hopkins Bayview Medical Ctr 4940 Eastern Ave *Web:* www.hopkinsmedicine.org	Baltimore	MD	21224	410-550-0100	550-7996
Johns Hopkins Hospital 600 N Wolfe St *Web:* www.hopkinsmedicine.org/the_johns_hopkins_hospital	Baltimore	MD	21287	410-955-5000	
Laurel Regional Hospital (LRH) 7300 Van Dusen Rd *Web:* dimensionshealth.org	Laurel	MD	20707	301-725-4300	497-7953
Maryland General Hospital 827 Linden Ave *Web:* ummidtown.org	Baltimore	MD	21201	410-225-8000	462-5834
Memorial Hospital at Easton (MHE) 219 S Washington St	Easton	MD	21601	410-822-1000	820-7831
Mercy Medical Ctr (MMC) 345 St Paul Pl. *TF:* 800-636-3729 ■ *Web:* www.mdmercy.com	Baltimore	MD	21202	410-332-9000	962-1303
Meritus Health 11116 Medical Campus Rd *TF:* 800-735-2258 ■ *Web:* www.meritushealth.com	Hagerstown	MD	21742	301-790-8000	
Montgomery General Hospital 18101 Prince Philip Dr *Web:* www.medstarhealth.org	Olney	MD	20832	301-774-8882	
Northwest Hospital Ctr 5401 Old Ct Rd *TF:* 800-876-1175 ■ *Web:* www.lifebridgehealth.org	Randallstown	MD	21133	410-521-2200	
Peninsula Regional Medical Ctr 100 E Carroll St *TF:* 800-543-7780 ■ *Web:* www.peninsula.org	Salisbury	MD	21801	410-546-6400	543-7102
Prince George's Hospital Ctr 3001 Hospital Dr *Web:* princegeorgeshospital.org	Cheverly	MD	20785	301-618-2000	
Saint Agnes HealthCare 900 S Caton Ave. *TF:* 800-875-8750 ■ *Web:* www.stagnes.org	Baltimore	MD	21229	410-368-6000	
Saint Joseph Medical Ctr (SJMC) 7601 Osler Dr *Web:* www.stjosephtowson.com	Towson	MD	21204	410-337-1000	
Saint Mary's Hospital 25500 Pt Lookout Rd *TF:* 855-633-0231 ■ *Web:* www.medstarhealth.org	Leonardtown	MD	20650	301-475-8981	475-5388
Shady Grove Adventist Hospital 9901 Medical Ctr Dr	Rockville	MD	20850	301-279-6000	
Sinai Hospital of Baltimore 2401 W Belvedere Ave *Web:* www.sinai-balt.com	Baltimore	MD	21215	410-601-9000	
Southern Maryland Hospital Ctr 7503 Surratts Rd **Fax:* Admissions ■ *Web:* www.medstarsouthernmaryland.org	Clinton	MD	20735	301-868-8000	868-5015*
Suburban Hospital 8600 Old Georgetown Rd *Web:* hopkinsmedicine.org/suburban_hospital	Bethesda	MD	20814	301-896-3100	493-5583
Total Health Care Inc 1501 Div St. *Web:* www.totalhealthcare.org	Baltimore	MD	21217	410-383-8300	728-4412
Union Hospital 106 Bow St *Web:* www.uhcc.com	Elkton	MD	21921	410-398-4000	
Union Memorial Hospital 201 E University Pkwy *Web:* www.medstarhealth.org	Baltimore	MD	21218	410-554-2000	554-2652
University of Maryland Shore Regional Health 501 S Union Ave. *Web:* umuch.org	Havre de Grace	MD	21078	443-843-5000	
Upper Chesapeake Medical Ctr 500 Upper Chesapeake Dr *Web:* umuch.org/?	Bel Air	MD	21014	443-643-1000	
Washington Adventist Hospital 7600 Carroll Ave. *Web:* www.adventisthealthcare.com	Takoma Park	MD	20912	301-891-7600	891-5991

Massachusetts

				Phone	Fax
Anna Jaques Hospital (AJH) 25 Highland Ave *Web:* www.ajh.org	Newburyport	MA	01950	978-463-1000	463-1250
Baystate Franklin Medical Ctr 164 High St *Web:* www.baystatehealth.org	Greenfield	MA	01301	413-773-0211	
Baystate Medical Ctr 759 Chestnut St *Web:* www.baystatehealth.org	Springfield	MA	01199	413-794-0000	
Berkshire Medical Ctr 725 N St *Web:* www.berkshirehealthsystems.org	Pittsfield	MA	01201	413-447-2000	447-2206
Beth Israel Deaconess Hospital-Milton 199 Reedsdale Rd. *Web:* www.bidmilton.org	Milton	MA	02186	617-696-4600	696-7380
Beth Israel Deaconess Medical Ctr (BIDMC) 330 Brookline Ave *TF:* 800-667-5356 ■ *Web:* www.bidmc.org	Boston	MA	02215	617-667-7000	
Beverly Hospital 85 Herrick St *Web:* www.beverlyhospital.org	Beverly	MA	01915	978-922-3000	
Boston Medical Ctr 1 Boston Medical Ctr Pl *Web:* www.bmc.org	Boston	MA	02118	617-638-8000	
Brockton Hospital 680 Centre St *Web:* www.signature-healthcare.org	Brockton	MA	02302	508-941-7000	
Cambridge Hospital 1493 Cambridge St *Web:* www.challiance.org	Cambridge	MA	02139	617-665-1000	
Cape Cod Hospital 27 Pk St *TF:* 800-545-5014 ■ *Web:* www.capecodhealth.org/capecodhospital	Hyannis	MA	02601	508-771-1800	
Charlton Memorial Hospital 363 Highland Ave *Web:* www.southcoast.org	Fall River	MA	02720	508-679-3131	
Cooley Dickinson Hospital 30 Locust St *Web:* www.cooley-dickinson.org	NorthHampton	MA	01060	413-582-2000	582-2952
Emerson Hospital 133 Old Rd To 9 Acre Corner *Web:* www.emersonhospital.org	Concord	MA	01742	978-369-1400	287-3655
Falmouth Hospital 100 Terr Heun Dr *Web:* www.capecodhealth.org	Falmouth	MA	02540	508-548-5300	
Faulkner Hospital 1153 Centre St *Web:* www.brighamandwomensfaulkner.org	Jamaica Plain	MA	02130	617-983-7000	524-8663
Good Samaritan Medical Ctr 235 N Pearl St *Web:* steward.org	Brockton	MA	02301	508-427-3000	
Harrington Memorial Hospital (HMH) 100 S St *TF:* 800-416-6072 ■ *Web:* www.harringtonhospital.org	Southbridge	MA	01550	508-765-9771	765-3147
HealthAlliance Leominster Hospital 60 Hospital Rd *Web:* umassmemorialhealthcare.org/umass-memorial-medical-center	Leominster	MA	01453	978-466-2000	
Heywood Hospital 242 Green St *Web:* www.heywood.org	Gardner	MA	01440	978-632-3420	630-6529
Holy Family Hospital 70 E St *Web:* steward.org	Methuen	MA	01844	978-687-0151	688-7689
Holyoke Medical Ctr 575 Beech St *Web:* www.holyokehealth.com	Holyoke	MA	01040	413-534-2500	534-2633
Hubbard Regional Hospital 340 Thompson Rd *Web:* harringtonhospital.org	Webster	MA	01570	508-943-2600	
Jordan Hospital 275 Sandwich St. *TF:* 800-256-7326 ■ *Web:* bidplymouth.org	Plymouth	MA	02360	508-746-2000	

Phone Fax

Lahey Clinic Foundation Inc 41 Mall Rd Burlington MA 01805 781-744-8000
TF: 800-524-3955 ■ *Web:* www.lahey.org

Lawrence General Hospital 1 General St Lawrence MA 01842 978-683-4000 946-8059
Web: www.lawrencegeneral.org

Lawrence Memorial Hospital of Medford
170 Governors Ave Medford MA 02155 781-306-6000
Web: www.hallmarkhealth.org

Lowell General Hospital (LGH) 295 Varnum Ave Lowell MA 01854 978-937-6000 937-6869
Web: www.lowellgeneral.org

Massachusetts General Hospital 55 Fruit St Boston MA 02114 617-726-2000
Web: www.massgeneral.org

Melrose-Wakefield Hospital 585 Lebanon St Melrose MA 02176 781-979-3000 979-3015
Web: www.hallmarkhealth.org

Mercy Medical Ctr 271 Carew St Springfield MA 01104 413-748-9000 781-7217
Web: www.mercycares.com

MetroWest Medical Ctr 115 Lincoln St Framingham MA 01702 508-383-1000 383-1166
TF: 800-357-6060 ■ *Web:* www.mwmc.com
Leonard Morse Campus 67 Union St Natick MA 01760 508-650-7000
Web: www.mwmc.com

Milford Regional Medical Ctr 14 Prospect St Milford MA 01757 508-473-1190 473-2744
Web: www.milfordregional.org

Morton Hospital & Medical Ctr
88 Washington St Taunton MA 02780 508-828-7000 824-6941
Web: www.mortonhospital.org

Mount Auburn Hospital (MAH) 330 Mt Auburn St Cambridge MA 02138 617-492-3500 491-0678
Web: www.mountauburnhospital.org

New England Baptist Hospital
125 Parker Hill Ave Boston MA 02120 617-754-5000 734-7804
TF: 855-370-6324 ■ *Web:* www.nebh.org

Newton-Wellesley Hospital 2014 Washington St Newton MA 02462 617-243-6000 243-6954
Web: www.nwh.org

North Adams Regional Hospital (NARH)
71 Hospital Ave North Adams MA 01247 413-664-5000 664-5028
Web: www.nbhealth.org

North Shore Medical Ctr 81 Highland Ave Salem MA 01970 978-741-1200
Web: northshorephysicians.org

Quincy Medical Ctr 114 Whitwell St Quincy MA 02169 617-773-6100 376-1604
Web: steward.org

Saint Anne's Hospital 795 Middle St Fall River MA 02721 508-674-5600
Web: steward.org

Saint Elizabeth's Medical Ctr
736 Cambridge St Brighton MA 02135 617-789-3000
Web: www.semc.org

Saint Luke's Hospital of New Bedford
101 Page St New Bedford MA 02740 508-997-1515
TF: 800-497-1727 ■ *Web:* www.southcoast.org/stlukes

Saint Vincent Hospital-Worcester Medical Ctr
123 Summer St Worcester MA 01608 508-363-5000
TF: 877-633-2368 ■ *Web:* www.stvincenthospital.com

South Shore Hospital 55 Fogg Rd South Weymouth MA 02190 781-340-8000 337-3768
TF: 800-439-2370 ■ *Web:* www.southshorehospital.org

Southboro Medical Group Inc
24 Newton St Southborough MA 01772 508-481-5500 460-3221
Web: www.southboromedical.com

Sturdy Memorial Hospital 211 Pk St Attleboro MA 02703 508-222-5200
Web: www.sturdymemorial.org

Tufts Medical Ctr (TMC) 800 Washington St Boston MA 02111 617-636-5000 636-8199
TF: 866-220-3699 ■ *Web:* www.tuftsmedicalcenter.org/default

UMass Memorial Medical Ctr
Bone Marrow Transplant Program
55 Lake Ave N Worcester MA 01655 508-334-1000 334-7983
Web: umassmemorialhealthcare.org/umass-memorial-medical-center
Memorial Campus 119 Belmont St Worcester MA 01605 508-334-1000
Web: umassmemorialhealthcare.org/umass-memorial-medical-center
University Campus 55 Lake Ave N Worcester MA 01655 508-334-1000
Web: umassmemorialhealthcare.org/umass-memorial-medical-center

Union Hospital 500 Lynnfield St Lynn MA 01904 781-581-9200 477-3840
Web: nsmc.partners.org

Upham's Corner Health Ctr 500 Columbia Rd Dorchester MA 02125 617-287-8000 282-8625
Web: uphamscornerhealthcenter.org

Whidden Memorial Hospital 103 Garland St Everett MA 02149 617-389-6270
Web: www.challiance.org

Winchester Hospital 41 Highland Ave Winchester MA 01890 781-729-9000 756-2908
Web: www.winchesterhospital.org

Michigan

Phone Fax

Allegan General Hospital 555 Linn St Allegan MI 49010 269-673-8424 686-4239
Web: www.aghosp.org

Allegiance Health 205 NE Ave Jackson MI 49201 517-788-4800
TF: 800-872-6480 ■ *Web:* www.allegiancehealth.org

Alpena Regional Medical Ctr
1501 W Chisholm St Alpena MI 49707 989-356-7000 356-7305
TF: 800-556-8842 ■ *Web:* www.alpenaregionalmedicalcenter.org

Barnes-Jewish Saint Peters Hospital
4901 Forest Park Ave St. Louis MI 63108 314-747-9322
Web: www.bjc.org

Bay Regional Medical Ctr (BRMC)
1900 Columbus Ave Bay City MI 48708 989-894-3000
TF: 800-656-3950 ■ *Web:* www.mclaren.org

Borgess Medical Ctr 1521 Gull Rd Kalamazoo MI 49048 269-226-7000 226-5966
Web: www.borgess.com

Botsford Hospital
28050 Grand River Ave Farmington Hills MI 48336 248-471-8000 471-8896
Web: www.botsford.org

Bronson Methodist Hospital 601 John St Kalamazoo MI 49007 269-341-7654 341-8314
TF: 800-276-6766 ■ *Web:* www.bronsonhealth.com

Chelsea Community Hospital 775 S Main St Chelsea MI 48118 734-475-1311 475-4066
Web: stjoeschelsea.org

Community Health Ctr of Branch County (CHCBC)
274 E Chicago St Coldwater MI 49036 517-279-5400 279-8830
Web: www.chcbc.com

Phone Fax

Covenant Medical Ctr Cooper 700 Cooper Ave Saginaw MI 48602 989-583-0000
Web: www.covenanthealthcare.com

Crittenton Hospital
1101 W University Dr Rochester Hills MI 48307 248-652-5000
Web: www.crittenton.com

Detroit Receiving Hospital & University Health Ctr
4201 St Antoine Blvd Detroit MI 48201 313-745-3000 745-3455
Web: www.dmc.org/detroitreceiving

Dickinson County Healthcare System
1721 S Stephenson Ave Iron Mountain MI 49801 906-774-1313 582-5599*
**Fax Area Code:* 501 ■ *Web:* www.dchs.org

Eaton Rapids Medical Ctr 1500 S Main St Eaton Rapids MI 48827 517-663-2671
Web: www.eatonrapidsmedicalcenter.org

Emergency Physicians Medical Group Pc Inc
2000 Green Rd Ste 300 Ann Arbor MI 48105 734-995-3764 995-2913
Web: www.epmgpc.com

Garden City Hospital (GCH) 6245 Inkster Rd Garden City MI 48135 734-458-3300 421-3530
Web: www.gch.org

Henry Ford Bi-County Hospital
13355 E Ten-Mile Rd Warren MI 48089 586-759-7300
Web: hospital-data.com

Henry Ford Hospital 2799 W Grand Blvd Detroit MI 48202 313-916-2600
TF: 800-999-4340 ■ *Web:* www.henryford.com

Henry Ford Macomb Hospital
15855 19-Mile Rd Clinton Township MI 48038 586-263-2300 263-2614
Web: henryford.com/homepage_macomb.cfm?id=48346

Henry Ford Wyandotte Hospital
2333 Biddle Ave Wyandotte MI 48192 734-246-6000
Web: henryford.com/homepage_wyandotte.cfm?id=37472&otopid=33690

Holland Community Hospital 602 Michigan Ave Holland MI 49423 616-392-5141 394-3572
Web: www.hollandhospital.org

Hurley Medical Ctr 1 Hurley Plz Flint MI 48503 810-262-9000 762-6585
TF: 800-336-8999 ■ *Web:* www.hurleymc.com

Huron Valley Sinai Hospital (HVSH)
1 William Carls Dr Commerce MI 48382 248-937-3300
Web: www.hvsh.org

Ingham Regional Medical Ctr
401 W Greenlawn Ave Lansing MI 48910 517-975-6000
Web: www.mclaren.org

Lakeland Medical Center-Niles
31 N St Joseph Ave Niles MI 49120 269-683-5510 683-2337
TF: 800-968-0115 ■ *Web:* www.lakelandhealth.org

Lapeer Regional Hospital 1375 N Main St Lapeer MI 48446 810-667-5500 667-5582
TF: 888-327-0671 ■ *Web:* www.mclaren.org

Marquette General Hospital
580 W College Ave Marquette MI 49855 906-228-9440 225-3084
Web: www.mgh.org

McLaren Regional Medical Ctr
401 S Ballenger Hwy Flint MI 48532 810-342-2000 342-2428
Web: www.mclaren.org

Memorial Healthcare Ctr 826 W King St Owosso MI 48867 989-723-5211 725-7902
TF: 800-206-8706 ■ *Web:* www.memorialhealthcare.org

Mercy General Health Partners
Muskegon Campus 1500 E Sherman Blvd Muskegon MI 49444 231-672-2000
TF: 800-368-4125 ■ *Web:* www.mercyhealthmuskegon.com

Mercy Hospital Cadillac 400 Hobart St Cadillac MI 49601 231-876-7473
Web: www.munsonhealthcare.org

Mercy Memorial Hospital (MMH) 718 N Macomb St Monroe MI 48162 734-240-8400
Web: www.mercymemorial.org

Metro Health Hospital 5900 Byron Ctr Ave Wyoming MI 49519 616-252-7200 252-0630
TF: 800-968-0051 ■ *Web:* www.metrohealth.net

MidMichigan Medical Ctr 4005 Orchard Dr Midland MI 48670 989-839-3000 839-1399
Web: www.midmichigan.org

Mount Clemens General Hospital
1000 Harrington Blvd Mount Clemens MI 48043 586-493-8000
Web: www.mclaren.org

Munson Medical Ctr 1105 Sixth St Traverse City MI 49684 231-935-5000
Web: www.munsonhealthcare.org

Oakwood Annapolis Hospital 33155 Annapolis Rd Wayne MI 48184 734-467-4000 467-4017
TF: 800-543-9355 ■ *Web:* www.oakwood.org

Oakwood Heritage Hospital 10000 Telegraph Rd Taylor MI 48180 313-295-5000 295-5085
TF: 800-543-9355 ■ *Web:* www.oakwood.org

Oakwood Hospital & Medical Ctr
18101 Oakwood Blvd Dearborn MI 48124 313-593-7000 436-2038
TF: 800-543-9355 ■ *Web:* www.oakwood.org

Oakwood Southshore Medical Ctr 5450 Fort St Trenton MI 48183 734-671-3800 671-3891
TF: 800-543-9355 ■ *Web:* www.oakwood.org

POH Regional Medical Ctr 50 N Perry St Pontiac MI 48342 248-338-5000 338-5667
TF: 888-327-0671 ■ *Web:* www.mclaren.org

Port Huron Hospital (PHH)
1221 Pine Grove Ave Port Huron MI 48060 810-987-5000 502-1567*
**Fax Area Code:* 877 ■ *TF:* 888-327-0671 ■ *Web:* www.mclaren.org/porthuron/porthuron.aspx

Saint John Macomb-Oakland Hospital
Oakland Ctr 27351 Dequindre Rd Madison Heights MI 48071 248-967-7000
Web: www.stjohnprovidence.org/oakland

Saint Joseph Mercy Ann Arbor
5301 McAuley Dr Ypsilanti MI 48197 734-712-3456 712-3855
TF: 866-522-8268 ■ *Web:* www.stjoeshealth.org

Saint Joseph Mercy Hospital Port Huron
2601 Electric Ave Port Huron MI 48060 810-985-1500 985-1579

Saint Joseph Mercy Oakland
44405 Woodward Ave Pontiac MI 48341 248-858-3000 858-3155
TF: 800-396-1313 ■ *Web:* www.stjoesoakland.org

Saint Mary Mercy Hospital 36475 Five-Mile Rd Livonia MI 48154 734-655-4800
TF: 800-464-7492 ■ *Web:* www.stmarymercy.org

Saint Mary's Health Care
200 Jefferson St SE Grand Rapids MI 49503 616-685-5000
Web: www.mercyhealthsaintmarys.com

Scheurer Hospital Inc 170 N Caseville Rd Pigeon MI 48755 989-453-3223 856-2209
TF: 800-690-9972 ■ *Web:* www.scheurer.org

Sinai Grace Hospital 6071 W Outer Dr Detroit MI 48235 313-966-3300 966-3160
TF: 888-362-2500 ■ *Web:* www.sinaigrace.org

Sparrow Health System 1215 E Michigan Ave Lansing MI 48912 517-364-1000 364-8002
TF: 800-772-7769 ■ *Web:* www.sparrow.org

Phone | Fax

Spectrum Health Blodgett Campus
100 Michigan St NE ... Grand Rapids MI 49503 616-774-7444 391-1883
TF: 866-989-7999 ■ *Web:* www.spectrumhealth.org

St Mary's of Michigan (STMH)
800 S Washington Ave ... Saginaw MI 48601 989-907-8115
TF: 877-738-6672 ■ *Web:* www.stmarysofmichigan.org

St. John Detroit Riverview Ctr
7733 E Jefferson Ave ... Detroit MI 48214 866-501-3627
TF: 866-501-3627 ■ *Web:* www.stjohnprovidence.org

St. John Providence 28000 Dequindre ... Warren MI 48092 586-573-5000
TF: 866-501-3627 ■ *Web:* www.stjohnprovidence.org

St. John Providence Health System
28000 Dequindre ... Warren MI 48092 866-501-3627
TF: 866-501-3627 ■ *Web:* www.stjohnprovidence.org

Three Rivers Health 701 S Health Pkwy ... Three Rivers MI 49093 269-278-1145
Web: www.threeriversheaIth.org

University Hospital 1500 E Medical Ctr Dr ... Ann Arbor MI 48109 734-936-4000 936-9437
Web: www.med.umich.edu

Minnesota

Phone | Fax

Abbott Northwestern Hospital
800 E 28th St ... Minneapolis MN 55407 612-863-4000 863-5667
TF: 800-582-5175 ■ *Web:* www.allinahealth.org

Affiliated Community Medical Centers (ACMC)
101 Willmar Ave SW ... Willmar MN 56201 320-231-5000
TF: 888-225-6580 ■ *Web:* www.acmc.com

Cambridge Medical Ctr (CMC) 701 S Dellwood St ... Cambridge MN 55008 763-689-7700
TF: 800-252-4133 ■ *Web:* www.allinahealth.org

Douglas County Hospital (DCH) 111 17th Ave E ... Alexandria MN 56308 320-762-1511 762-6120
Web: www.dchospital.com

Essentia Health 502 E Second St ... Duluth MN 55805 218-786-8376 720-6406
TF: 855-469-6532 ■ *Web:* www.essentiahealth.org

Fairview Ridges Hospital - Burnsville
2450 Riverside Ave ... Minneapolis MN 55454 952-892-2000
Web: www.fairview.org

Fairview Southdale Hospital 6401 France Ave S ... Edina MN 55435 952-924-5000
Web: www.fairview.org/hospitals/southdale/index.htm

Fairview University Medical Ctr Mesabi
750 E 34th St ... Hibbing MN 55746 218-262-4881 362-6619
TF: 888-870-8626 ■ *Web:* www.range.fairview.org

Glacial Ridge Hospital Foundation Inc
10 Fourth Ave SE ... Glenwood MN 56334 320-634-4521 634-2269
TF: 866-667-4747 ■ *Web:* www.glacialridge.org

Hennepin County Medical Ctr (HCMC)
701 Pk Ave ... Minneapolis MN 55415 612-873-3000 904-4214
Web: www.hcmc.org

Lake Region Hospital 712 S Cascade St ... Fergus Falls MN 56537 218-736-8000
TF: 800-439-6424 ■ *Web:* www.lrhc.org

Mayo Clinic 200 First St SW ... Rochester MN 55905 507-284-2511 284-0161
Web: mayoclinic.org

Mayo Clinic Health System Austin
1000 First Dr NW ... Austin MN 55912 507-433-7351
TF: 888-609-4065 ■ *Web:* mayoclinichealthsystem.org

Mayo Clinic Health System Southwest Minnesota
1025 Marsh St ... Mankato MN 56001 507-625-4031
TF: 800-327-3721 ■ *Web:* mayoclinichealthsystem.org

Mercy Hospital 4050 Coon Rapids Blvd ... Coon Rapids MN 55433 763-236-6000
Web: www.allinahealth.org

Methodist Hospital 6500 Excelsior Blvd ... Minneapolis MN 55426 952-993-5000
Web: www.parknicollet.com

Mille Lacs Health System 200 Elm St N ... Onamia MN 56359 320-532-3154
TF: 877-535-3154 ■ *Web:* www.mlhealth.org

North Memorial Health Care
3300 Oakdale Ave N ... Robbinsdale MN 55422 763-520-5200 520-1454
Web: www.northmemorial.com

Regions Hospital 640 Jackson St ... Saint Paul MN 55101 651-254-3456 254-9426
Web: www.regionshospital.com

Rice Memorial Hospital 301 Becker Ave SW ... Willmar MN 56201 320-235-4543
Web: www.ricehospital.com

Ridgeview Medical Ctr (RMC) 500 S Maple St ... Waconia MN 55387 952-442-2191 442-6524
TF: 800-967-4620 ■ *Web:* www.ridgeviewmedical.org

Rochester Methodist Hospital 201 W Ctr St ... Rochester MN 55902 507-284-2511 284-1445
Web: mayoclinic.org

Saint Cloud Hospital 1406 Sixth Ave ... Saint Cloud MN 56303 320-251-2700 255-5711
TF: 800-835-6652 ■ *Web:* www.centracare.com

Saint John's Hospital 1575 Beam Ave ... Maplewood MN 55109 651-232-7000
TF: 888-477-4221 ■ *Web:* www.st-johns.org/stjohns/home.aspx

Saint Luke's Hospital & Regional Trauma Ctr
915 E First St ... Duluth MN 55805 218-249-5555 932-6871*
*Fax Area Code: 816 ■ *TF:* 866-261-5915 ■ *Web:* www.saintlukeshealthsystem.org/services

Saint Mary's Hospital 1216 Second St SW ... Rochester MN 55902 507-255-5123 255-3125
Web: mayoclinic.org

Sanford Health 1300 Anne St NW ... Bemidji MN 56601 218-751-5430 333-5880
Web: www.nchs.com

United Hospital 333 N Smith Ave ... Saint Paul MN 55102 651-241-8000
TF: 800-869-1320 ■ *Web:* www.allinahealth.org

Unity Hospital 550 Osborne Rd ... Fridley MN 55432 763-236-4111
Web: www.allinahealth.org

University of Minnesota Medical Ctr Fairview - University Campus
500 Harvard St ... Minneapolis MN 55455 612-273-3000 273-1919
TF: 800-688-5252 ■ *Web:* www.mhealth.org

Mississippi

Phone | Fax

Baptist Medical Ctr 1225 N State St ... Jackson MS 39202 601-968-1000
TF: 800-948-6262 ■ *Web:* www.mbhs.org

Baptist Memorial Hospital DeSoto
7601 Southcrest Pkwy ... Southaven MS 38671 662-772-4000
Web: www.baptistonline.org

Phone | Fax

Baptist Memorial Hospital Golden Triangle
2520 Fifth St N ... Columbus MS 39703 662-244-1000 244-1651
TF: 800-422-7847 ■ *Web:* www.baptistonline.org

Baptist Memorial Hospital North Mississippi
2301 S Lamar Blvd ... Oxford MS 38655 662-232-8100 232-8391
Web: www.baptistonline.org

Baptist Memorial Hospital Union County
200 Hwy 30 W ... New Albany MS 38652 662-538-7631 538-2591
Web: www.baptistonline.org

Bolivar Medical Ctr 901 Hwy 8 E PO Box 1380 ... Cleveland MS 38732 662-846-2496 846-2380
Web: www.bolivarmedical.com

Central Mississippi Medical Ctr
1850 Chadwick Dr ... Jackson MS 39204 601-376-1000
Web: www.merithealthcentral.com

Delta Regional Medical Ctr (DRMC)
1400 E Union St ... Greenville MS 38703 662-378-3783
Web: www.deltaregional.com

Forrest General Hospital 6051 US Hwy 49 ... Hattiesburg MS 39402 601-288-7000 288-4180
TF: 800-503-5980 ■
Web: www.forresthealth.org/our-locations/forrest-general-hospital

George County Hospital PO Box 607 ... Lucedale MS 39452 601-947-3161
Web: www.georgeregional.com

Greenwood Leflore Hospital 1401 River Rd ... Greenwood MS 38930 662-459-7000
Web: www.glh.org

Grenada Lake Medical Ctr (GLMC) 960 Avent Dr ... Grenada MS 38901 662-227-7000
Web: www.glmc.net

Jeff Anderson Regional Medical Ctr
2124 14th St ... Meridian MS 39301 601-553-6000
Web: www.jarmc.org

King's Daughters Medical Ctr 427 Hwy 51 N ... Brookhaven MS 39601 601-833-6011
Web: www.kdmc.org

Magnolia Regional Health Ctr 611 Alcorn Dr ... Corinth MS 38834 662-293-1000 293-7667
Web: www.mrhc.org

Memorial Hospital at Gulfport 4500 13th St ... Gulfport MS 39501 228-867-4000 867-4747
Web: www.gulfportmemorial.com

Merit Health Biloxi 150 Reynoir St ... Biloxi MS 39530 228-432-1571 436-1205
Web: www.merithealthbiloxi.com

Merit Health Gilmore Memorial (GMRMC)
1105 Earl Frye Blvd ... Amory MS 38821 662-256-7111
Web: www.merithealthgilmore.com

Merit Health Rankin 350 Crossgates Blvd ... Brandon MS 39042 601-825-2811 824-8519
Web: www.merithealthrankin.com

North Mississippi Medical Ctr
830 S Gloster St ... Tupelo MS 38801 662-377-3000 377-3564
Web: www.nmhs.net/tupelo

Northwest Mississippi Regional Medical Ctr
1970 Hospital Dr ... Clarksdale MS 38614 662-627-3211
Web: www.merithealthnorthwestms.com

Oktibbeha County Hospital 400 Hospital Rd ... Starkville MS 39759 662-323-4320
Web: www.och.org

River Region Medical Ctr 2100 Hwy 61 N ... Vicksburg MS 39183 601-883-5000 883-5196
Web: www.riverregion.com

Rush Foundation Hospital 1314 19th Ave ... Meridian MS 39301 601-483-0011 703-4427
Web: www.rushhealthsystems.org

Saint Dominic-Jackson Memorial Hospital
969 Lakeland Dr ... Jackson MS 39216 601-200-2000 200-6800
Web: www.stdom.com

Singing River Hospital 2809 Denny Ave ... Pascagoula MS 39581 228-809-5000
Web: www.mysrhs.com

South Central Regional Medical Ctr (SCRMC)
1220 Jefferson St ... Laurel MS 39440 601-426-4000
Web: www.scrmc.com

Southwest Mississippi Regional Medical Ctr
215 Marion Ave ... McComb MS 39648 601-249-5500 249-1709
Web: www.smrmc.com

University of Mississippi Medical Ctr
2500 N State St ... Jackson MS 39216 601-984-1000 984-4125
Web: www.umc.edu

Wesley Medical Ctr 5001 Hardy St ... Hattiesburg MS 39402 601-268-8000
TF: 877-456-9617 ■ *Web:* www.wesley.com

Missouri

Phone | Fax

Barnes-Jewish Hospital
1 Barnes-Jewish Hospital Plz ... Saint Louis MO 63110 314-362-5000
Web: www.barnesjewish.org

Boone Hospital Ctr 1600 E Broadway ... Columbia MO 65201 573-815-8000
Web: www.boone.org

Bothwell Regional Health Ctr 601 E 14th St ... Sedalia MO 65301 660-826-8833
Web: www.brhc.org

Capital Region Medical Ctr
1125 Madison St ... Jefferson City MO 65101 573-632-5000 632-5880
Web: www.crmc.org

Centerpoint Medical Ctr 19600 E 39th St ... Independence MO 64057 816-698-7000 698-7003
Web: www.centerpointmedical.com

Cox Hospital North 1423 N Jefferson Ave ... Springfield MO 65802 417-269-3000
Web: www.coxhealth.com

Cox Medical Center South
3801 S National Ave ... Springfield MO 65807 417-269-6000
Web: www.coxhealth.com

DesPeres Hospital
2345 Dougherty Ferry Rd ... Saint Louis MO 63122 314-966-9100 966-9274
TF: 888-457-5203 ■ *Web:* www.desPereshospital.com

Freeman Health System 1102 W 32nd St ... Joplin MO 64804 417-347-1111
Web: www.freemanhealth.com

Golden Valley Memorial Hospital
1600 N Second St ... Clinton MO 64735 660-885-5511 885-8496
TF: 888-225-6903 ■ *Web:* www.gvmh.org

Hannibal Regional Hospital 6500 Hospital Dr ... Hannibal MO 63401 573-248-1300
TF: 888-426-6425 ■ *Web:* www.hrhonline.org

Jefferson Regional Medical Ctr (JRMC)
Hwy 61 S PO Box 350 ... Crystal City MO 63019 636-933-1000
Web: www.mercy.net

Phone *Fax*

Kindred Hospital - Saint Louis
4930 Lindell Blvd .... Saint Louis MO 63108 314-361-8700 361-1210
Web: www.kindredstlouis.com

Lake Regional Health System
54 Hospital Dr .... Osage Beach MO 65065 573-348-8000 348-8326
Web: www.lakeregional.com

Liberty Hospital 2525 Glenn Hendren Dr .... Liberty MO 64068 816-781-7200 781-7550
TF: 800-344-3829 ■ *Web:* www.libertyhospital.org

Mercy 1235 E Cherokee .... Springfield MO 65804 417-820-2000 820-6996
TF: 800-909-8326 ■ *Web:* www.mercy.net

Mercy 615 S New Ballas Rd .... Saint Louis MO 63141 314-251-6000
Web: www.mercy.net

Mineral Area Regional Medical Ctr (WARMC)
1101 Weber Rd Ste 302 .... Farmington MO 63640 573-756-4581
Web: www.mineralarearegional.com

Missouri Baptist Hospital of Sullivan
751 Sappington Bridge Rd .... Sullivan MO 63080 573-468-4186 860-2696
TF: 800-939-2273 ■ *Web:* www.missouribaptistsullivan.org

Missouri Baptist Medical Ctr
3015 N Ballas Rd .... Saint Louis MO 63131 314-996-5000 996-5373
TF: 800-392-0936 ■ *Web:* www.missouribaptist.org

Missouri Delta Medical Ctr 1019 N Main St .... Sikeston MO 63801 573-471-1600
Web: www.missouridelta.com

North Kansas City Hospital
2800 Clay Edwards Dr .... North Kansas City MO 64116 816-691-2000 346-7020
Web: www.nkch.org

Ozarks Medical Ctr 1100 N Kentucky Ave .... West Plains MO 65775 417-256-9111 257-6770
Web: www.ozarksmedicalcenter.com

Parkland Health Ctr 1101 W Liberty St .... Farmington MO 63640 573-756-6451
TF: 800-734-3944 ■ *Web:* www.parklandhealthcenter.org

Poplar Bluff Regional Medical Ctr
2620 N Westwood Blvd .... Poplar Bluff MO 63901 573-785-7721
TF: 855-444-7276 ■ *Web:* www.poplarbluffregional.com

Poplar Bluff Regional Medical Ctr South Campus
3100 Oak Grove Rd............................. Poplar Bluff MO 63901 855-444-7276
TF: 855-444-7276 ■ *Web:* www.poplarbluffregional.com

Research Medical Ctr 2316 E Meyer Blvd........... Kansas City MO 64132 816-276-4000 276-4387
Web: researchmedicalcenter.com

Saint Alexius Hospital
Broadway Campus 3933 S Broadway........... Saint Louis MO 63118 314-865-7000 865-7983
TF: 800-245-1431 ■ *Web:* www.stalexiushospital.com

Saint Anthony's Medical Ctr
10010 Kennerly Rd............................ Saint Louis MO 63128 314-525-1000 525-1228
TF: 800-554-9550 ■ *Web:* www.stanthonysmedcenter.com

Saint Francis Medical Ctr
211 St Francis Dr .... Cape Girardeau MO 63703 573-331-3000 331-5009
Web: sfmc.net

Saint Joseph Health Ctr
1000 Carondelet Dr .... Kansas City MO 64114 816-942-4400
Web: www.carondelethealth.org

Saint Louis University Hospital
3635 Vista Ave .... Saint Louis MO 63110 314-577-8000 577-8003
Web: www.sluhospital.com

Saint Luke's Hospital
232 S Woods Mill Rd .... Chesterfield MO 63017 314-434-1500
Web: www.stlukes-stl.com

Saint Luke's Hospital 4401 Wornall Rd............. Kansas City MO 64111 816-932-2000 932-5990
Web: www.saintlukeshealthsystem.org

Saint Mary's Health Ctr
6420 Clayton Rd.......................... Richmond Heights MO 63117 314-768-8000 768-8011
Web: www.ssmhealth.com

Saint Mary's Medical Ctr
201 NW Rd Mize Rd .... Blue Springs MO 64014 816-228-5900 655-5408
Web: www.stmaryskc.com

Skaggs Community Health Ctr
545 Branson Landing Blvd PO Box 650 .... Branson MO 65615 417-335-7000 334-1505
TF: 800-994-6610 ■ *Web:* www.skaggs.net

Southeast Missouri Hospital (SMH)
1701 Lacey St............................... Cape Girardeau MO 63701 573-334-4822
TF: 800-800-5123 ■ *Web:* www.sehealth.org

SSM Health 620 E Monroe St...................... Mexico MO 65265 573-582-5000
TF: 844-776-9355 ■
Web: www.ssmhealthmidmo.com/locations/stmarysaudrain

SSM Saint Joseph Health Ctr
300 First Capitol Dr .... Saint Charles MO 63301 636-949-7077
Web: www.ssmhealth.com

Truman Medical Ctr Hospital Hill
2301 Holmes St .... Kansas City MO 64108 816-404-1000
Web: www.trumed.org

Twin Rivers Regional Medical Ctr (TRRMC)
1301 First St.................................... Kennett MO 63857 573-888-4522 888-5525
Web: www.twinriversregional.com

University Hospital 1 Hospital Dr.................. Columbia MO 65212 573-882-4141 884-4174
Web: www.muhealth.org

US Medical Ctr for Federal Prisoners
1900 W Sunshine St............................ Springfield MO 65807 417-862-7041 837-1711
Web: www.bop.gov

Montana

Phone *Fax*

Benefis Health Care
West Campus 1101 26th St S .... Great Falls MT 59405 406-455-5000 455-3530
Web: www.benefis.org

Benefis HealthSystems
East Campus 1101 26th St S .... Great Falls MT 59405 406-455-5000 455-4587
TF: 800-648-6632 ■ *Web:* www.benefis.org

Billings Clinic 2800 Tenth Ave N.................... Billings MT 59101 406-238-2501
TF: 800-332-7156 ■ *Web:* www.billingsclinic.com

Bozeman Deaconess Hospital 915 Highland Blvd...... Bozeman MT 59715 406-585-5000 585-1070
Web: www.bozemandeaconess.org

Community Medical Ctr 2827 Ft Missoula Rd .... Missoula MT 59804 406-728-4100
Web: www.communitymed.org

Holy Rosary Healthcare 2600 Wilson St............. Miles City MT 59301 406-233-2600 233-4214
TF: 800-843-3820 ■ *Web:* www.holyrosaryhealthcare.org

Kalispell Regional Medical Ctr
310 Sunnyview Ln .... Kalispell MT 59901 406-752-5111 756-2703
TF: 800-228-1574 ■ *Web:* www.krh.org

Livingston Healtcare 504 S 13th St................ Livingston MT 59047 406-222-3541 222-5099
Web: www.livingstonhealthcare.org

Saint James Healthcare 400 S Clark St .... Butte MT 59701 406-723-2500
Web: www.stjameshealthcare.org

Saint Patrick Hospital 500 W Broadway St............ Missoula MT 59802 406-543-7271 329-5693
Web: montana.providence.org/hospitals/st-patrick

St. Luke Community Hospital (Inc)
107 Sixth Ave SW................................. Ronan MT 59864 406-676-4441
Web: www.stlukehealthnet.org

Nebraska

Phone *Fax*

Bryan LGH Medical Ctr East 1600 S 48th St .... Lincoln NE 68506 402-481-7333
TF: 800-742-7844 ■ *Web:* www.bryanhealth.com

Bryan LGH Medical Ctr West 2300 S 16th St........... Lincoln NE 68502 402-481-1111
Web: www.bryanhealth.com

Creighton University Medical Ctr 601 N 30th St ....Omaha NE 68131 402-449-4000 449-5020
TF: 800-368-5097 ■ *Web:* www.creighton.edu

Faith Regional Health Services
2700 W Norfolk Ave .... Norfolk NE 68701 402-371-4880 644-7468
Web: www.frhs.org

Fremont Area Medical Ctr 450 E 23rd St.............Fremont NE 68025 402-721-1610 727-3656
Web: www.famc.org

Good Samaritan Hospital 10 E 31st St ....Kearney NE 68847 308-865-7100 865-2913
TF: 800-277-4306 ■ *Web:* chihealthgoodsamaritan.org

Immanuel Medical Ctr 6901 N 72nd St.................Omaha NE 68122 402-572-2121
Web: chihealth.com/immanuel-medical-center

Mary Lanning Memorial Hospital
715 N St Joseph Ave .... Hastings NE 68901 402-463-4521
Web: www.marylanning.org

Midlands Community Hospital
11111 S 84th St .... Papillion NE 68046 402-593-3000
TF: 855-524-4001 ■ *Web:* chihealth.com

Nebraska Medical Ctr, The 4350 Dewey Ave...........Omaha NE 68105 402-552-2000 552-3267
TF: 800-922-0000 ■ *Web:* www.nebraskamed.com

Nebraska Methodist Hospital 8303 Dodge St...........Omaha NE 68114 402-354-4000 354-8735
Web: www.bestcare.org

Regional West Medical Ctr 4021 Ave B.............Scottsbluff NE 69361 308-635-3711 630-1815
Web: www.rwhs.org

Saint Elizabeth Regional Medical Ctr
555 S 70th St .... Lincoln NE 68510 402-219-8000 219-8973
Web: www.chihealthstelizabeth.com

University of Nebraska Medical Ctr
42nd and Emile...................................Omaha NE 68198 402-559-4000
TF: 877-726-4727 ■ *Web:* www.unmc.edu

Nevada

Phone *Fax*

Carson Tahoe Hospital 1600 Medical Pkwy ....Carson City NV 89703 775-445-8000
Web: www.carsontahoehospital.com

Desert Springs Hospital Medical Ctr
2075 E Flamingo Rd............................. Las Vegas NV 89119 702-733-8800
Web: www.desertspringshospital.com

MountainView Hospital 3100 N Tenaya Way .... Las Vegas NV 89128 702-255-5000 255-5074
Web: www.mountainview-hospital.com

Northern Nevada Medical Ctr 2375 E Prater Way ....Sparks NV 89434 775-331-7000
Web: www.nnmc.com

Renown Regional Medical Ctr 1155 Mill St .... Reno NV 89502 775-982-4100
Web: www.renown.org

Saint Mary's Regional Medical Ctr
235 W Sixth St .... Reno NV 89503 775-770-3000 770-7474
Web: www.saintmarysreno.com

Saint Rose Dominican Hospital
Rose de Lima Campus 102 E Lk Mead Blvd...... Henderson NV 89015 702-564-2622
Web: www.strosehospitals.org/medical_services/our_hospitals/185510

Summerlin Hospital Medical Ctr
657 Town Ctr Dr............................... Las Vegas NV 89144 702-233-7000
Web: www.summerlinhospital.com

Sunrise Hospital & Medical Ctr
3186 S Maryland Pkwy........................... Las Vegas NV 89109 702-731-8000 731-8739
Web: www.sunrisehospital.com

University Medical Ctr
1800 W Charleston Blvd......................... Las Vegas NV 89102 702-383-2000
Web: www.umcsn.com

Valley Hospital Medical Ctr 620 Shadow Ln.......... Las Vegas NV 89106 702-388-4000
Web: www.valleyhospital.net

New Hampshire

Phone *Fax*

Catholic Medical Ctr (CMC) 100 McGregor St....... Manchester NH 03102 603-668-3545 663-6989
TF: 800-437-9666 ■ *Web:* www.catholicmedicalcenter.org

Cheshire Medical Ctr 590 Ct St...................... Keene NH 03431 603-354-5400 354-5402
Web: www.cheshire-med.com

Concord Hospital 250 Pleasant St .... Concord NH 03301 603-225-2711 224-6527
Web: www.concordhospital.org

Dartmouth-Hitchcock Medical Ctr
1 Medical Ctr Dr.............................. Lebanon NH 03756 603-650-5000 650-8765
Web: www.dartmouth-hitchcock.org

Elliot Hospital 1 Elliot Way Ste 100 .... Manchester NH 03103 603-627-1669 624-2297
TF: 800-922-4999 ■ *Web:* www.elliothospital.org

Exeter Hospital 5 Alumni Dr.......................... Exeter NH 03833 603-580-6668 778-6592
Web: www.exeterhospital.com

Frisbie Memorial Hospital 11 Whitehall Rd.......... Rochester NH 03867 603-332-5211 335-8488
Web: www.frisbiehospital.com

Name / Address	City	State	ZIP	Phone	Fax
Lakes Region General Hospital 80 Highland St. *Web:* www.lrgh.org	Laconia	NH	03246	603-524-3211	527-2887
Parkland Medical Ctr 1 Parkland Dr *Web:* www.parklandmedicalcenter.com	Derry	NH	03038	603-432-1500	421-2111
Portsmouth Regional Hospital 333 Borthwick Ave *TF:* 800-685-8282 ■ *Web:* www.portsmouthhospital.com	Portsmouth	NH	03801	603-436-5110	
Saint Joseph Hospital 172 Kinsley St *TF:* 800-222-1222 ■ *Web:* www.stjosephhospital.com	Nashua	NH	03061	603-882-3000	
Southern New Hampshire Medical Ctr 8 Prospect St PO Box 2014 *Web:* snhhs.org	Nashua	NH	03061	603-577-2000	
Speare Memorial Hospital Assn 16 Hospital Rd *Web:* www.spearehospital.com	Plymouth	NH	03264	603-536-1120	
Wentworth-Douglass Hospital 789 Central Ave. *TF:* 877-201-7100 ■ *Web:* www.wdhospital.com	Dover	NH	03820	603-742-5252	740-2242

New Jersey

Name / Address	City	State	ZIP	Phone	Fax
Atlantic Health System 475 South St *Web:* www.atlantichealth.org	Morristown	NJ	07960	973-971-5000	290-7561
Atlanticare Regional Medical Ctr 1925 Pacific Ave *Web:* atlanticare.org	Atlantic City	NJ	08401	609-344-4081	569-7020
Bayonne Medical Center 29th St & Ave E *Web:* bayonnemedicalcenter.org	Bayonne	NJ	07002	201-858-5000	858-5000
Bayshore Community Hospital 727 N Beers St *Web:* www.bayshorehospital.org	Holmdel	NJ	07733	732-739-5900	888-7334
Bergen Regional Medical Ctr 230 E Ridgewood Ave *Web:* www.bergenregional.com	Paramus	NJ	07652	201-967-4000	967-4277
Cape Regional Medical Ctr Inc (CRMC) 2 Stone Harbor Blvd *Web:* www.caperegional.com	Cape May Court House	NJ	08210	609-463-2000	
Capital Health System at Fuld 750 Brunswick Ave *Web:* www.capitalhealth.org	Trenton	NJ	08638	609-394-6000	394-6687
Capital Health System at Mercer 446 Bellevue Ave *Web:* www.capitalhealth.org	Trenton	NJ	08618	609-394-4000	
CentraState Medical Ctr 901 W Main St *Web:* www.centrastate.com	Freehold	NJ	07728	732-431-2000	462-5129
Chilton Hospital 97 W Pkwy *Web:* www.chiltonhealth.org	Pompton Plains	NJ	07444	973-831-5000	831-5516
Christ Hospital 176 Palisade Ave *Web:* www.carepointhealth.org	Jersey City	NJ	07306	201-795-8200	
Clara Maass Medical Ctr 1 Clara Maass Dr *Web:* www.barnabashealth.org	Belleville	NJ	07109	973-450-2000	
Columbus Hospital 495 N 13th St *Web:* www.columbusltach.org	Newark	NJ	07107	973-587-7777	587-7829
Community Medical Ctr (CMC) 99 Hwy 37 W *TF:* 888-724-7123 ■ *Web:* www.barnabashealth.org	Toms River	NJ	08755	732-557-8000	557-8935
Cooper University Hospital 3 Cooper Plz *TF:* 800-826-6737 ■ *Web:* www.cooperhealth.org	Camden	NJ	08103	856-342-2000	
East Orange General Hospital 300 Central Ave *Web:* www.evh.org	East Orange	NJ	07018	973-672-8400	
Englewood Hospital & Medical Ctr 350 Engle St *Web:* www.englewoodhospital.com	Englewood	NJ	07631	201-894-3000	894-1473
Hackensack University Medical Ctr 30 Prospect Ave *Web:* hackensackumc.org	Hackensack	NJ	07601	201-996-2000	489-7275
Hoboken University Medical Ctr 308 Willow Ave *Web:* www.carepointhealth.org	Hoboken	NJ	07030	201-418-1000	
Holy Name Hospital 718 Teaneck Rd *Web:* www.holyname.org	Teaneck	NJ	07666	201-833-3000	227-6048
Hunterdon Medical Ctr 2100 Westcott Dr *Web:* www.hunterdonhealthcare.org	Flemington	NJ	08822	908-788-6100	788-6111
Irvington General Hospital 95 Old Short Hills Rd **Fax Area Code: 973* ■ *TF:* 888-724-7123 ■ *Web:* www.barnabashealth.org	West Orange	NJ	07052	888-724-7123	322-6361*
Jersey City Medical Ctr 355 Grand St. *Web:* www.barnabashealth.org/jersey-city-medical-center.aspx	Jersey City	NJ	07302	201-915-2000	915-2002
Jersey Shore University Medical Ctr 1945 Rt 33 *TF:* 800-560-9990 ■ *Web:* www.jerseyshoreuniversitymedicalcenter.com	Neptune	NJ	07753	732-775-5500	751-5120
JFK Medical Ctr 65 James St *Web:* www.jfkmc.org	Edison	NJ	08818	732-321-7000	
Kennedy Health System-Cherry Hill 2201 Chapel Ave W *TF:* 866-224-0264 ■ *Web:* www.kennedyhealth.org	Cherry Hill	NJ	08002	856-488-6500	488-6526
Kimball Medical Ctr 600 River Ave *Web:* www.barnabashealth.org	Lakewood	NJ	08701	732-363-1900	886-4406
Lifeline Medical Assoc LLC 99 Cherry Hill Rd Ste 220 *TF:* 800-845-2785 ■ *Web:* www.lma-llc.com	Parsippany	NJ	07054	973-316-0307	
Lourdes Medical Ctr of Burlington County 218 Sunset Rd *Web:* www.lourdesnet.org	Willingboro	NJ	08046	609-835-2900	
Memorial Hospital of Salem County 310 Woodstown Rd *Web:* www.mhschealth.com	Salem	NJ	08079	856-935-1000	
Monmouth Medical Ctr 300 Second Ave. *TF:* 888-724-7123 ■ *Web:* www.barnabashealth.org	Long Branch	NJ	07740	732-222-5200	
Morristown Medical Ctr 100 Madison Ave *TF:* 877-310-7226 ■ *Web:* www.atlantichealth.org	Morristown	NJ	07960	973-971-5000	
Muhlenberg Regional Medical Ctr Park Ave & Randolph Rd *Web:* jfkmc.org/jfk-muhlenberg-campus	Plainfield	NJ	07060	908-668-2000	
Newark Beth Israel Medical Ctr 201 Lyons Ave *Web:* www.barnabashealth.org	Newark	NJ	07112	973-926-7000	
Newton Memorial Hospital (NMH) 175 High St. *Web:* atlantichealth.org/newton	Newton	NJ	07860	973-383-2121	
Ocean Medical Ctr (OMC) 425 Jack Martin Blvd. *TF:* 800-560-9990 ■ *Web:* www.oceanmedicalcenter.com/omc	Brick	NJ	08724	732-840-2200	840-3284
Our Lady of Lourdes Medical Ctr 1600 Haddon Ave *TF:* 888-568-7337 ■ *Web:* www.lourdesnet.org	Camden	NJ	08103	856-757-3500	757-3611
Overlook Medical Ctr 99 Beauvoir Ave *Web:* www.atlantichealth.org	Summit	NJ	07902	908-522-2000	
Palisades Medical Ctr 7600 River Rd **Fax:* Admitting ■ *Web:* www.palisadesmedical.org	North Bergen	NJ	07047	201-854-5000	854-5272*
Raritan Bay Medical Ctr 530 New Brunswick Ave *Web:* www.rbmc.org	Perth Amboy	NJ	08861	732-442-3700	
Riverview Medical Ctr 1 Riverview Plz *Web:* www.meridianhealth.com/rmc.cfm	Red Bank	NJ	07701	732-741-2700	
Robert Wood Johnson University Hospital 1 Robert Wood Johnson Pl *TF:* 888-637-9584 ■ *Web:* www.rwjuh.edu	New Brunswick	NJ	08901	732-828-3000	937-8837
Robert Wood Johnson University Hospital at Rahway (RWJUHR) 865 Stone St. **Fax Area Code: 609* ■ *Web:* www.rwjuhr.com	Rahway	NJ	07065	732-381-4200	586-7900*
RWJ University Hospital at Hamilton 1 Hamilton Health Pl *Web:* www.rwjhamilton.org	Hamilton	NJ	08690	609-586-7900	584-6429
Saint Barnabas Medical Ctr 94 Old Short Hills Rd *TF:* 888-724-7123 ■ *Web:* www.barnabashealth.org	West Orange	NJ	07052	973-322-5000	
Saint Clare's Hospital 25 Pocono Rd *Web:* www.saintclares.com	Denville	NJ	07834	973-625-6000	625-6037
Saint Francis Medical Ctr 601 Hamilton Ave *TF:* 888-216-3293 ■ *Web:* www.sfmc.net	Trenton	NJ	08629	609-599-5000	
Saint Joseph's Regional Medical Ctr 703 Main St *Web:* www.stjosephshealth.org	Paterson	NJ	07503	973-754-2000	754-2208
Saint Michael's Medical Ctr 111 Central Ave *Web:* www.smmcnj.org	Newark	NJ	07102	973-877-5000	
Saint Peter's University Hospital 254 Easton Ave *Web:* www.saintpetershcs.com	New Brunswick	NJ	08901	732-745-8600	
Shore Memorial Hospital 1 E New York Ave *Web:* shoremedicalcenter.org	Somers Point	NJ	08244	609-653-3500	
SJH Elmer Hospital 501 W Front St *Web:* www.inspirahealthnetwork.org	Elmer	NJ	08318	856-363-1000	
SJH Regional Medical Ctr (SJHRMC) 1505 W Sheman Ave *TF:* 800-770-7547 ■ *Web:* www.inspirahealthnetwork.org	Vineland	NJ	08360	856-641-8000	
Somerset Medical Ctr (SMC) 110 Rehill Ave *TF:* 888-637-9584 ■ *Web:* rwjuh.edu	Somerville	NJ	08876	908-685-2200	685-2894
Southern Jersey Family Medical Centers Inc 860 S White Horse Pke *Web:* www.sjfmc.org	Hammonton	NJ	08037	609-567-0200	
St. Joseph's Wayne Hospital 224 Hamburg Tpke *Web:* www.stjosephshealth.org	Wayne	NJ	07470	973-942-6900	389-4044
Trinitas Hospital 225 Williamson St. *Web:* www.trinitashospital.com	Elizabeth	NJ	07207	908-994-5000	
Underwood-Memorial Hospital 509 N Broad St *Web:* inspirahealthnetwork.org	Woodbury	NJ	08096	856-845-0100	
Union Hospital 1000 Galloping Hill Rd *Web:* www.barnabashealth.org	Union	NJ	07083	908-964-7333	
University Medical Ctr at Princeton (UMCP) 253 Witherspoon St *TF:* 877-932-8935 ■ *Web:* princetonhcs.org	Princeton	NJ	08540	609-497-4304	497-4306
University of Medicine & Dentistry of New Jersey					
Graduate School of Biomedical Sciences (GSBS) 185 S Orange Ave MSB B640 *Web:* rbhs.rutgers.edu	Newark	NJ	07107	973-972-4511	
University Hospital, The 150 Bergen St C- 431 *Web:* www.uhnj.org	Newark	NJ	07103	973-972-4300	
Valley Health System 223 N Van Dien Ave *TF:* 800-825-5391 ■ *Web:* www.valleyhealth.com	Ridgewood	NJ	07450	201-447-8000	
Virtua Voorhees 303 Lippincott Dr 4th Fl *Web:* www.virtua.org	Voorhees	NJ	08053	856-322-3000	
Virtua-Memorial Hospital Burlington County 175 Madison Ave *Web:* www.virtua.org	Mount Holly	NJ	08060	609-267-0700	
Warren Hospital 185 Roseberry St *Web:* www.warrenhospital.org	Phillipsburg	NJ	08865	908-859-6700	
West Jersey Hospital Berlin 100 Townsend Ave *Web:* www.virtua.org	Berlin	NJ	08009	856-322-3000	

New Mexico

Name / Address	City	State	ZIP	Phone	Fax
Carlsbad Medical Ctr 2430 W Pierce St *Web:* www.carlsbadmedicalcenter.com	Carlsbad	NM	88220	505-887-4100	
Eastern New Mexico Medical Ctr 405 W Country Club Rd *TF:* 800-222-1222 ■ *Web:* www.enmmc.com	Roswell	NM	88201	575-622-8170	
Gallup Indian Medical Ctr 516 E Nizhoni Blvd	Gallup	NM	87301	505-722-1000	722-1397
Gila Regional Medical Ctr 1313 E 32nd St. **Fax Area Code: 505* ■ *Web:* www.grmc.org	Silver City	NM	88061	575-538-4000	538-9714*
Lea Regional Medical Ctr 5419 N Lovington Hwy *TF:* 877-492-8001 ■ *Web:* www.learegionalmedical.com	Hobbs	NM	88240	575-492-5000	492-5505
Lovelace Medical Ctr 5400 Gibson Blvd SE *TF:* 888-281-6531 ■ *Web:* www.lovelace.com	Albuquerque	NM	87108	505-262-7000	727-8000
Memorial Medical Ctr 2450 S Telshor Blvd *Web:* www.mmclc.org	Las Cruces	NM	88011	575-522-8641	

				Phone	Fax
MountainView Regional Medical Ctr 4311 E Lohman Ave *Web:* www.mountainviewregional.com	Las Cruces	NM	88001	575-556-7600	556-7619
Nor-Lea General Hospital Inc 1600 N Main Ave *Web:* www.nor-lea.org	Lovington	NM	88260	575-396-6611	
Plains Regional Medical Ctr 2100 N ML King Blvd *TF:* 800-923-6980 ■ *Web:* www.phs.org	Clovis	NM	88101	505-769-2141	
Presbyterian Espanola Hospital 1010 Spruce St *Web:* www.phs.org	Espanola	NM	87532	505-753-7111	
Presbyterian Hospital 1100 Central Ave SE *TF:* 888-977-2333 ■ *Web:* www.phs.org	Albuquerque	NM	87106	505-841-1234	462-7756
Presbyterian Kaseman Hospital 8300 Constitution Ave NE *TF:* 800-356-2219 ■ *Web:* www.phs.org	Albuquerque	NM	87110	505-291-2000	
Rehoboth McKinley Christian Hospital 1900 Redrock Dr *Web:* www.rmch.org	Gallup	NM	87301	505-863-7000	863-5806
Saint Vincent Regional Medical Ctr 455 St Michael's Dr *Web:* www.stvin.org	Santa Fe	NM	87505	505-983-3361	820-5210
San Juan Regional Medical Ctr 801 W Maple St *Web:* www.sanjuanregional.com	Farmington	NM	87401	505-609-2000	
University Hospital 2211 Lomas Blvd NE **Fax:* Admitting ■ *Web:* hospitals.unm.edu	Albuquerque	NM	87106	505-272-2111	272-0122*

New York

				Phone	Fax
Albany Medical Ctr 47 New Scotland Ave *Web:* www.amc.edu	Albany	NY	12208	518-262-3125	
Albany Memorial Hospital 600 Northern Blvd *Web:* www.nehealth.com	Albany	NY	12204	518-471-3221	
Alice Hyde Medical Ctr 133 Pk St *Web:* www.alicehyde.com	Malone	NY	12953	518-483-3000	481-2320
Arnot Ogden Medical Ctr 600 Roe Ave *Web:* www.arnothealth.org	Elmira	NY	14905	607-737-4100	737-4447
Auburn Memorial Hospital 17 Lansing St *Web:* www.auburnhospital.org	Auburn	NY	13021	315-255-7011	255-7382
Aurelia Osborn Fox Memorial Hospital 1 Norton Ave *Web:* www.bassett.org	Oneonta	NY	13820	607-432-2000	
Bassett Healthcare Network 1 Atwell Rd *TF:* 800-227-7388 ■ *Web:* www.bassett.org	Cooperstown	NY	13326	607-547-3456	547-3921
Bellevue Hospital Ctr 462 First Ave *Web:* nyc.gov	New York	NY	10016	212-562-4141	562-4036
Beth Israel Medical Ctr First Ave & 16th St *Web:* www.bethisraelny.org	New York	NY	10003	212-420-2000	
Bon Secours Community Hospital 160 E Main St *TF:* 866-522-4984 ■ *Web:* www.bonsecourscommunityhosp.org	Port Jervis	NY	12771	845-858-7000	858-7415
BronxCare Family Wellness Center 1276 Fulton Ave *TF:* 877-451-9361 ■ *Web:* www.bronxcare.org	Bronx	NY	10456	718-590-1800	
Brookdale University Hospital & Medical Ctr 1 Brookdale Plz *Web:* www.brookdalehospital.org	Brooklyn	NY	11212	718-240-5000	240-5042
Brookhaven Memorial Hospital Medical Ctr 101 Hospital Rd *Web:* www.brookhavenhospital.org	Patchogue	NY	11772	631-654-7100	
Brooklyn Hospital Ctr 121 DeKalb Ave *Web:* www.tbh.org	Brooklyn	NY	11201	718-250-8000	
Brooks Memorial Hospital 529 Central Ave *Web:* www.brookshospital.org	Dunkirk	NY	14048	716-366-1111	
Buffalo General Hospital 100 High St *TF:* 800-506-6480 ■ *Web:* www.kaleidahealth.org	Buffalo	NY	14203	716-859-5600	
Catskill Regional Medical Ctr 68 Harris-Bushville Rd PO Box 800 *TF:* 888-846-5945 ■ *Web:* www.crmcny.org	Harris	NY	12742	845-794-3300	794-3240
Cayuga Medical Ctr 101 Dates Dr *Web:* www.cayugamed.org	Ithaca	NY	14850	607-274-4011	274-4527
Claxton-Hepburn Medical Ctr 214 King St **Fax:* Hum Res ■ *TF:* 888-220-0042 ■ *Web:* www.claxtonhepburn.org	Ogdensburg	NY	13669	315-393-3600	393-8506*
Clifton Springs Hospital & Clinic 2 Coulter Rd *TF:* 888-786-4347 ■ *Web:* www.cliftonspringshospital.com	Clifton Springs	NY	14432	315-462-9561	462-3492
Columbia Memorial Hospital 71 Prospect Ave *TF:* 866-539-1370 ■ *Web:* www.columbiamemorialhealth.org	Hudson	NY	12534	518-828-7601	828-9980
Coney Island Hospital 2601 Ocean Pkwy *Web:* www.nyc.gov/html/hhc/coneyisland/html/home/home.shtml	Brooklyn	NY	11235	718-616-3000	616-4512
Corning Hospital 176 Denison Pkwy E *TF:* 877-750-2042 ■ *Web:* www.guthrie.org	Corning	NY	14830	607-937-7200	937-7693
Cortland Regional Medical Ctr (CRMC) 134 Homer Ave PO Box 2010 *Web:* www.cortlandregional.org	Cortland	NY	13045	607-756-3500	756-3590
Crouse Hospital 736 Irving Ave *Web:* www.crouse.org	Syracuse	NY	13210	315-470-7111	
CVPH Medical Ctr (CPVH) 75 Beekman St *Web:* www.cvph.org	Plattsburgh	NY	12901	518-561-2000	561-0881
De Graff Memorial Hospital 445 Tremont St *Web:* www.kaleidahealth.org	North Tonawanda	NY	14120	716-694-4500	
Eastern Long Island Hospital Assn, The 201 Manor Pl *Web:* www.elih.org	Greenport	NY	11944	631-477-1000	
Ellis Hospital 1101 Nott St *Web:* www.ellismedicine.org/home/ellishospitalmain.aspx	Schenectady	NY	12308	518-243-4000	
Elmhurst Hospital Ctr 79-01 Broadway *Web:* nyc.gov	Elmhurst	NY	11373	718-334-4000	334-5161
Erie County Medical Ctr 462 Grider St *Web:* www.ecmc.edu	Buffalo	NY	14215	716-898-3000	898-5178
Faxton Saint Luke's Healthcare *Faxton Campus* 1676 Sunset Ave *Web:* www.faxtonstlukes.com	Utica	NY	13502	315-624-6000	
Saint Luke's Campus 1656 Champlin Ave *Web:* www.faxtonstlukes.com	New Hartford	NY	13413	315-624-6000	
FF Thompson Hospital 350 Parrish St *Web:* www.thompsonhealth.com	Canandaigua	NY	14424	585-396-6000	
Flushing Hospital Medical Ctr 4500 Parsons Blvd *Web:* www.flushinghospital.org	Flushing	NY	11355	718-670-5000	670-3077
Forest Hills Hospital (FHH) 102-01 66th Rd	Forest Hills	NY	11375	718-830-4000	275-0950
Geneva General Hospital 196 N St *Web:* www.flhealth.org	Geneva	NY	14456	315-787-4000	
Glen Cove Hospital 101 St Andrews Ln *Web:* www.northshorelij.com/body.cfm?id=53	Glen Cove	NY	11542	516-674-7300	
Glens Falls Hospital 100 Pk St *TF:* 800-994-6610 ■ *Web:* www.glensfallshospital.org	Glens Falls	NY	12801	518-926-1000	926-1919
Good Samaritan Hospital 255 Lafayette Ave *Web:* www.goodsamhosp.org	Suffern	NY	10901	845-368-5000	368-5430
Harlem Hospital Ctr 506 Lenox Ave *Web:* nyc.gov	New York	NY	10037	212-939-1000	939-1974
Highland Hospital of Rochester 1000 S Ave *Web:* www.urmc.rochester.edu	Rochester	NY	14620	585-473-2200	341-8350
Hudson Valley Hospital Ctr 1980 Crompond Rd *Web:* www.hvhc.org	Cortlandt Manor	NY	10567	914-737-9000	
Interfaith Medical Ctr 1545 Atlantic Ave *Web:* www.interfaithmedical.com	Brooklyn	NY	11213	718-613-4000	613-4101
Ira Davenport Memorial Hospital Inc 7571 State Rt 54 *Web:* www.arnothealth.org	Bath	NY	14810	607-776-8500	
Jacobi Medical Ctr 1400 Pelham Pkwy S *Web:* www.nychealthandhospitals.org	Bronx	NY	10461	718-918-5700	
Jamaica Hospital Medical Ctr 8900 Van Wyck Expy *Web:* www.jamaicahospital.org	Jamaica	NY	11418	718-206-6000	657-0545
John T Mather Memorial Hospital 75 N Country Rd *Web:* www.matherhospital.org	Port Jefferson	NY	11777	631-473-1320	476-2792
Kenmore Mercy Hospital 2950 Elmwood Ave *Web:* www.chsbuffalo.org/body.cfm?id=49	Kenmore	NY	14217	716-706-2112	447-6090
Kings County Hospital Ctr 451 Clarkson Ave *Web:* www1.nyc.gov	Brooklyn	NY	11203	718-245-3131	613-8019
Kingsbrook Jewish Medical Ctr 585 Schenectady Ave *Web:* www.kingsbrook.org	Brooklyn	NY	11203	718-604-5000	604-5243
Lawrence Hospital 55 Palmer Ave *Web:* nyplawrence.org	Bronxville	NY	10708	914-787-1000	787-3113
Lenox Hill Hospital 100 E 77th St *Web:* www.northwell.edu/find-care/locations/lenox-hill-hospital	New York	NY	10021	212-434-2000	
Lincoln Medical & Mental Health Ctr 234 E 149th St *Web:* nyc.gov	Bronx	NY	10451	718-579-5016	
Little Falls Hospital 140 Burwell St *Web:* www.bassett.org	Little Falls	NY	13365	315-823-1000	
Long Beach Medical Ctr 455 E Bay Dr *Web:* longbeachmedicalcenter.org	Long Beach	NY	11561	516-897-1000	
Long Island College Hospital (LICH) 339 Hicks St *TF:* 800-227-8922 ■ *Web:* www.downstate.edu/lich	Brooklyn	NY	11201	718-780-1000	270-4775
Lutheran Medical Ctr (LHC) 150 55th St *Web:* lutheranhealthcare.org/main/home.aspx	Brooklyn	NY	11220	718-630-7000	
Maimonides Medical Ctr (MMC) 4802 Tenth Ave *Web:* www.maimonidesmed.org	Brooklyn	NY	11219	718-283-6000	635-8157
Mercy Hospital of Buffalo 565 Abbott Rd *Web:* www.chsbuffalo.org	Buffalo	NY	14220	716-826-7000	
Mercy Medical Ctr 1000 N Village Ave PO Box 9024 *Web:* mercymedicalcenter.chsli.org	Rockville Centre	NY	11571	516-705-2525	705-1406
MidHudson Regional Hospital 241 N Rd *Web:* www.midhudsonregional.org	Poughkeepsie	NY	12601	845-483-5000	485-3762
Millard Fillmore Gates Cir Hospital 726 Exchange St *Web:* www.kaleidahealth.org	Buffalo	NY	14210	716-859-8000	
Montefiore Medical Ctr 111 E 210th St *Web:* www.montefiore.org	Bronx	NY	10467	718-920-4321	920-8543
Mount Saint Mary's Hospital 5300 Military Rd *Web:* www.chsbuffalo.org/facilities/hospitals/mountstmaryshospital	Lewiston	NY	14092	716-297-4800	298-2001
Mount Sinai Medical Ctr, The 1 Gustave L Levy Pl *TF:* 800-637-4627 ■ *Web:* www.mountsinai.org	New York	NY	10029	212-241-6500	731-3418
Mount Sinai of Queens 25-10 30th Ave *TF:* 800-968-7637 ■ *Web:* www.mshq.org	Astoria	NY	11102	718-932-1000	278-1786
Mount Vernon Hospital 12 N Seventh Ave	Mount Vernon	NY	10550	914-664-8000	632-2927
Nassau University Medical Ctr 2201 Hempstead Tpke *Web:* www.ncmc.edu	East Meadow	NY	11554	516-572-0123	
New York Community Hospital 2525 Kings Hwy *Web:* www.nych.com	Brooklyn	NY	11229	718-692-5300	
New York Downtown Hospital 170 William St *Web:* nyp.org	New York	NY	10038	212-312-5000	
New York Hospital Medical Ctr of Queens 56-45 Main St *Web:* www.nyhq.org	Flushing	NY	11355	718-670-2000	661-7704
New York Methodist Hospital 506 Sixth St *Web:* www.nym.org	Brooklyn	NY	11215	718-780-3000	965-4324
New York Presbyterian Hospital 525 E 68th St *TF:* 888-694-5700 ■ *Web:* www.nyp.org	New York	NY	10021	212-746-5454	746-4293

Name / Address	City	State	Zip	Phone	Fax
Newark-Wayne Community Hospital 1250 Driving Pk Ave *Web:* www.rochestergeneral.org	Newark	NY	14513	315-332-2427	332-2371
Niagara Falls Memorial Medical Ctr 621 Tenth St *Web:* www.nfmmc.org	Niagara Falls	NY	14302	716-278-4000	278-4054
North Central Bronx Hospital 3424 Kossuth Ave **Fax Area Code:* 917 ■ *TF:* 877-207-2134 ■ *Web:* nyc.gov	Bronx	NY	10467	718-519-5000	639-2473*
North Fork Radiology PC 1333 Roanoke Ave Ste 202 *Web:* www.northforkrad.com	Riverhead	NY	11901	631-727-2755	
North Shore University Hospital 300 Community Dr *TF:* 888-214-4065 ■ *Web:* www.northshorelij.com/body.cfm?ID=51	Manhasset	NY	11030	516-562-0100	562-2352
Northern Westchester Hospital 400 E Main St *TF:* 877-469-4362 ■ *Web:* www.nwhc.net	Mount Kisco	NY	10549	914-666-1200	
Nyack Hospital 160 N Midland Ave *Web:* www.nyackhospital.org	Nyack	NY	10960	845-348-2000	348-2160
NYU Langone Medical Ctr 550 First Ave *Web:* www.med.nyu.edu	New York	NY	10016	212-263-7300	263-8460
Olean General Hospital 515 Main St *Web:* www.ogh.org	Olean	NY	14760	716-373-2600	375-6393
Oneida Healthcare Ctr 321 Genesee St *Web:* www.oneidahealthcare.org	Oneida	NY	13421	315-363-6000	361-2043
Orange Regional Medical Ctr 60 Prospect Ave *TF:* 888-321-6762 ■ *Web:* www.ormc.org	Middletown	NY	10940	845-343-2424	333-1560
Arden Hill Campus 4 Harriman Dr *Web:* www.ormc.org	Goshen	NY	10924	845-333-1000	
Oswego Hospital 110 W Sixth St *Web:* oswegohealth.org	Oswego	NY	13126	315-349-5511	349-5732
Our Lady of Lourdes Memorial Hospital 169 Riverside Dr *Web:* www.lourdes.com	Binghamton	NY	13905	607-798-5111	798-5989
Park Ridge Hospital 1555 Long Pond Rd	Rochester	NY	14626	585-723-7000	368-3888
Peconic Bay Medical Ctr 1300 Roanoke Ave *Web:* www.pbmchealth.org	Riverhead	NY	11901	631-548-6000	548-6048
Peninsula Hospital Ctr (PHC) 51-15 Beach Ch Dr	Far Rockaway	NY	11691	718-734-2000	
Phelps Memorial Hospital Ctr (PMHC) 701 N Broadway *Web:* www.phelpshospital.org	Sleepy Hollow	NY	10591	914-366-3000	
Putnam Hospital Ctr 670 Stoneleigh Ave *Web:* www.health-quest.org	Carmel	NY	10512	845-279-5711	
Queens Hospital Ctr 82-68 164th St **Fax Area Code:* 212 ■ *TF:* 888-692-6116 ■ *Web:* nyc.gov	Jamaica	NY	11432	718-883-3000	274-4988*
Richmond University Medical Ctr 355 Bard Ave *Web:* rumcsi.org	Staten Island	NY	10310	718-818-1234	
Rochester General Health System (RGHS) 1425 Portland Ave *TF:* 877-922-5465 ■ *Web:* www.rochestergeneral.org	Rochester	NY	14621	585-922-4000	
Rome Memorial Hospital 1500 N James St *Web:* www.romehosp.org	Rome	NY	13440	315-338-7000	338-7695
Saint Catherine of Siena Medical Ctr 50 Rt 25 A	Smithtown	NY	11787	631-862-3000	862-3105
Saint Elizabeth Medical Ctr 2209 Genesee St *Web:* www.stemc.org	Utica	NY	13501	315-798-8100	798-8344
Saint James Mercy Hospital 411 Canisteo St *Web:* www.stjamesmercy.org	Hornell	NY	14843	607-324-8000	324-8115
Saint John's Riverside Hospital *ParkCare Pavilion* 2 Pk Ave *Web:* www.riversidehealth.org	Yonkers	NY	10703	914-964-7300	
Saint Joseph's Hospital 555 E Market St *Web:* www.arnothealth.org	Elmira	NY	14901	607-737-4499	737-7837
Saint Joseph's Hospital Health Ctr 301 Prospect Ave *TF:* 888-785-6371 ■ *Web:* www.sjhsyr.org	Syracuse	NY	13203	315-448-5111	
Saint Joseph's Medical Ctr (SJMC) 127 S Broadway *Web:* saintjosephs.org	Yonkers	NY	10701	914-378-7000	
Saint Luke's Cornwall Hospital *Cornwall Campus* 19 Laurel Ave	Cornwall	NY	12518	845-534-7711	
Saint Mary's Hospital 427 Guy Pk Ave *Web:* www.smha.org	Amsterdam	NY	12010	518-842-1900	841-7158
Saint Mary's Hospital 1300 Massachusetts Ave *Web:* www.stmarysmadison.com	Troy	NY	12180	518-268-5000	
Saint Peter's Health Care Services 315 S Manning Blvd *Web:* www.sphcs.org	Albany	NY	12208	518-525-1550	
Samaritan Hospital 2215 Burdett Ave *Web:* www.nehealth.com	Troy	NY	12180	518-271-3300	
Samaritan Medical Ctr 830 Washington St *TF:* 877-888-6138 ■ *Web:* www.samaritanhealth.com	Watertown	NY	13601	315-785-4000	
Saratoga Hospital 211 Church St *Web:* www.saratogahospital.org	Saratoga Springs	NY	12866	518-587-3222	580-4122
Sisters of Charity Hospital of Buffalo 2157 Main St *Web:* www.chsbuffalo.org/facilities/hospitals/soch	Buffalo	NY	14214	716-862-1000	
Sisters of Charity Hospital, St. Joseph Campus 2605 Harlem Rd *Web:* www.chsbuffalo.org	Cheektowaga	NY	14225	716-891-2400	862-2006
South Nassau Communities Hospital 1 Healthy Way *TF:* 877-768-8462	Oceanside	NY	11572	516-632-3000	377-5385
Southampton Hospital 240 Meeting House Ln *Web:* www.southamptonhospital.org	SouthHampton	NY	11968	631-726-8200	283-5730
Staten Island University Hospital 475 Seaview Ave *Web:* www.siuh.edu	Staten Island	NY	10305	718-226-9000	226-8255
Stony Brook University Hospital (SBUH) 101 Nicolls Rd *Web:* www.stonybrookmedicine.edu	Stony Brook	NY	11794	631-444-4000	444-6649
Strong Memorial Hospital *Stem Cell Transplantation Ctr* 601 Elmwood Ave *Web:* www.urmc.rochester.edu	Rochester	NY	14642	585-275-1941	275-5590
University of Rochester Medical Ctr 601 Elmwood Ave *TF:* 800-999-6673 ■ *Web:* www.urmc.rochester.edu	Rochester	NY	14642	585-275-2100	273-1118
United Memorial Medical Ctr 127 N St *Web:* www.ummc.org	Batavia	NY	14020	585-343-6030	344-7434
University Hospital SUNY Upstate Medical University 750 E Adams St *TF:* 877-464-5540 ■ *Web:* upstate.edu/hospital	Syracuse	NY	13210	315-464-5540	
Upstate University Hospital at Community General 4900 Broad Rd *Web:* upstate.edu	Syracuse	NY	13215	315-492-5011	492-5418
Vassar Bros Medical Ctr 45 Reade Pl *TF:* 877-729-2444 ■ *Web:* www.health-quest.org	Poughkeepsie	NY	12601	845-454-8500	
Westchester Medical Ctr 100 Woods Rd *Web:* www.westchestermedicalcenter.com	Valhalla	NY	10595	914-493-7000	
White Plains Hospital Ctr 41 E Post Rd *Web:* www.wphospital.org	White Plains	NY	10601	914-681-0600	681-2902
Winthrop University Hospital 259 First St *Web:* www.winthrop.org	Mineola	NY	11501	516-663-0333	663-2946
Woodhull Medical & Mental Health Ctr 760 Broadway *Web:* nyc.gov	Brooklyn	NY	11206	718-963-8000	963-8999

North Carolina

Name / Address	City	State	Zip	Phone	Fax
Alamance Regional Medical Ctr 1240 Huffman Mill Rd *Web:* www.armc.com	Burlington	NC	27215	336-538-7000	538-7425
Annie Penn Hospital 618 S Main St *TF:* 866-391-2734 ■ *Web:* www.conehealth.com	Reidsville	NC	27320	336-951-4000	951-4561
Anson Community Hospital 500 Morven Rd *Web:* carolinashealthcare.org	Wadesboro	NC	28170	704-994-4500	
Betsy Johnson Regional Hospital 803 Tilghman Dr, Ste 100 PO Box 1706 *Web:* myharnetthealth.org	Dunn	NC	28334	910-892-7161	
Caldwell Memorial Hospital 321 Mulberry St SW *Web:* www.caldwellmemorial.org	Lenoir	NC	28645	828-757-5100	757-5247
Cape Fear Hospital 5301 Wrightsville Ave *Web:* www.nhrmc.org	Wilmington	NC	28403	910-452-8100	
Cape Fear Valley Medical Ctr (CFVMC) 1638 Owen Dr PO Box 2000 *Web:* www.capefearvalley.com	Fayetteville	NC	28304	910-609-4000	609-6160
CarolinaEast Health System 2000 Neuse Blvd *Web:* www.carolinaeasthealth.com	New Bern	NC	28561	252-633-8111	
Carolinas Medical Center-NorthEast 920 Church St N *TF:* 800-575-1275 ■ *Web:* www.carolinashealthcare.org	Concord	NC	28025	704-403-1275	403-3000
Carolinas Medical Center-University 8800 N Tryon St *TF:* 800-821-1535 ■ *Web:* www.carolinashealthcare.org	Charlotte	NC	28262	704-863-6000	863-6236
Carolinas Medical Ctr 1000 Blythe Blvd *Web:* www.carolinashealthcare.org	Charlotte	NC	28203	704-355-2000	
Carolinas Medical Ctr Mercy 2001 Vail Ave *TF:* 800-821-1535 ■ *Web:* www.carolinashealthcare.org	Charlotte	NC	28207	800-821-1535	
Carolinas Medical Ctr Union (CMCU) 600 Hospital Dr *Web:* www.carolinashealthcare.org	Monroe	NC	28112	704-283-3100	
Carteret General Hospital 3500 Arendell St PO Box 1619 *Web:* www.carterethealth.org	Morehead City	NC	28557	252-808-6000	808-6573
Catawba Valley Medical Ctr 810 Fairgrove Church Rd SE *Web:* www.catawbavalleymedical.org	Hickory	NC	28602	828-326-3000	326-3371
Central Carolina Hospital 1135 Carthage St *TF:* 800-292-2262 ■ *Web:* www.centralcarolinahosp.com	Sanford	NC	27330	919-774-2100	774-2295
Columbus Regional Healthcare System 500 Jefferson St *Web:* www.crhealthcare.org	Whiteville	NC	28472	910-642-8011	642-9305
Davis Regional Medical Ctr 218 Old Mocksville Rd PO Box 1823 *Web:* www.davisregional.com	Statesville	NC	28625	704-873-0281	838-7287
Duke Health Raleigh Hospital 3400 Wake Forest Rd *Web:* www.dukeraleighhospital.org	Raleigh	NC	27609	919-954-3000	954-3900
Duke University Hospital 2301 Erwin Rd *Web:* dukemedicine.org	Durham	NC	27710	919-684-8111	
Durham Regional Hospital 3643 N Roxboro Rd *Web:* www.dukeregional.org	Durham	NC	27704	919-470-4000	477-1931
Forsyth Medical Ctr 3333 Silas Creek Pkwy *Web:* novanthealth.org/forsythmedicalcenter.aspx	Winston-Salem	NC	27103	336-718-5000	718-9258
Frye Regional Medical Ctr (FRMC) 420 N Ctr St *Web:* www.fryemedctr.com	Hickory	NC	28601	828-315-5000	315-3901
Grace Hospital 2201 S Sterling St *Web:* www.blueridgehealth.org/grace-hospital.html	Morganton	NC	28655	828-580-5000	
Halifax Regional Medical Ctr 250 Smith Church Rd *Web:* halifaxregional.org	Roanoke Rapids	NC	27870	252-535-8011	535-8466
Heritage Hospital 111 Hospital Dr *Web:* www.vidanthealth.com	Tarboro	NC	27886	252-641-7700	641-7484
High Point Regional Health System (HPRHS) 601 N Elm St PO Box HP-5 *TF:* 877-878-7644 ■ *Web:* www.highpointregional.com	High Point	NC	27262	336-878-6000	
Hugh Chatham Memorial Hospital 180 Parkwood Dr PO Box 560 *Web:* www.hughchatham.org	Elkin	NC	28621	336-527-7000	526-2783

				Phone	Fax
Iredell Health System 557 Brookdale Dr *Web:* www.iredellhealth.org	Statesville	NC	28677	704-873-5661	872-7924
Johnston Memorial Hospital 509 N Bright Leaf Blvd *Web:* www.johnstonhealth.org	Smithfield	NC	27577	919-934-8171	989-7297
Kernodle Clinic Inc 1234 Huffman Mill Rd *Web:* kernodle.duhs.duke.edu	Burlington	NC	27215	336-538-1234	
Lake Norman Regional Medical Ctr 171 Fairview Rd *Web:* www.lnrmc.com	Mooresville	NC	28117	704-660-4000	
Lenoir Memorial Hospital 100 Airport Rd *Web:* www.lenoirmemorial.org	Kinston	NC	28501	252-522-7000	522-7007
Margaret R Pardee Memorial Hospital 800 N Justice St *Web:* www.pardeehospital.org	Hendersonville	NC	28791	828-696-1000	
Maria Parham Medical Ctr 566 Ruin Creek Rd PO Box 59 *Web:* www.mariaparham.com	Henderson	NC	27536	252-438-4143	436-1114
Mission Hospital-St Joseph Campus 428 Biltmore Ave *Web:* mission-health.org	Asheville	NC	28801	828-213-1111	
Moore Regional Hospital 155 Memorial Dr PO Box 3000 *TF:* 866-415-2778 ■ *Web:* www.firsthealth.org	Pinehurst	NC	28374	910-715-1000	428-1567
Morehead Memorial Hospital 117 E King's Hwy *Web:* www.morehead.org	Eden	NC	27288	336-623-9711	623-7660
Moses H Cone Memorial Hospital 1200 N Elm St *TF:* 866-391-2734 ■ *Web:* www.conehealth.com	Greensboro	NC	27401	336-832-7000	832-8192
Nash Health Care Systems (NHCS) 2460 Curtis Ellis Dr *Web:* www.nhcs.org	Rocky Mount	NC	27804	252-443-8000	962-8067
New Hanover Regional Medical Ctr 2131 S 17th St *TF:* 877-228-8135 ■ *Web:* www.nhrmc.org	Wilmington	NC	28401	910-343-7000	452-8799
Northern Hospital of Surry County 830 Rockford St *Web:* www.northernhospital.com	Mount Airy	NC	27030	336-719-7000	
Onslow Memorial Hospital 317 Western Blvd *Web:* www.onslow.org	Jacksonville	NC	28541	910-577-2345	577-2246
Pender Memorial Hospital 507 E Fremont St *TF:* 888-815-5188 ■ *Web:* www.nhrmc.org	Burgaw	NC	28425	910-259-5451	
Pitt County Memorial Hospital 2100 Stantonsburg Rd *Web:* www.vidanthealth.com	Greenville	NC	27835	252-847-4100	847-5147
Presbyterian Hospital Charlotte 200 Hawthorne Ln *Web:* novanthealth.org/presbyterianmedicalcenter.aspx	Charlotte	NC	28204	704-384-4000	384-5600
Randolph Hospital 364 White Oak St PO Box 1048 *Web:* www.randolphhospital.org	Asheboro	NC	27204	336-625-5151	625-4393
Rex Healthcare 4420 Lk Boone Trl *Web:* www.rexhealth.com	Raleigh	NC	27607	919-784-3100	
Richmond Memorial Hospital 925 Long Dr *Web:* www.firsthealth.org	Rockingham	NC	28379	910-417-3000	
Roanoke-Chowan Hospital 500 S Academy St *Web:* www.vidanthealth.com	Ahoskie	NC	27910	252-209-3148	209-3146
Rowan Regional Medical Ctr (RRMC) 612 Mocksville Ave *TF:* 888-844-0080	Salisbury	NC	28144	704-210-5000	210-5562
Rutherford Regional Health System 288 S Ridgecrest Ave *Web:* www.myrutherfordregional.com	Rutherfordton	NC	28139	828-286-5000	
Sampson Regional Medical Ctr 607 Beaman St *Web:* www.sampsonrmc.org	Clinton	NC	28328	910-592-8511	590-2321
Scotland Memorial Hospital 500 Lauchwood Dr *Web:* www.scotlandhealth.org	Laurinburg	NC	28352	910-291-7000	
Southeastern Regional Medical Ctr 300 W 27th St *Web:* www.srmc.org	Lumberton	NC	28358	910-671-5000	671-5200
Stanly Memorial Hospital 301 Yadkin St *Web:* www.stanly.org	Albemarle	NC	28001	704-984-4000	983-3562
Thomasville Medical Ctr 207 Old Lexington Rd *TF:* 888-844-0080 ■ *Web:* novanthealth.org/thomasvillemedicalcenter.aspx	Thomasville	NC	27360	336-472-2000	
Triangle Orthopedic Assoc PA 120 William Penn Plz *TF:* 800-359-3053 ■ *Web:* www.triangleortho.com	Durham	NC	27704	919-220-5255	220-0520
Valdese General Hospital (VGH) 720 Malcolm Blvd Ste 200 *TF:* 800-994-6610 ■ *Web:* www.blueridgehealth.org	Valdese	NC	28690	828-874-2251	397-3226
Wake Forest University Baptist Medical Ctr Medical Ctr Blvd *Web:* www.wakehealth.edu	Winston-Salem	NC	27157	336-716-2011	716-2067
WakeMed Raleigh Campus 3000 New Bern Ave *Web:* www.wakemed.org	Raleigh	NC	27610	919-350-7000	
Watauga Medical Ctr 336 Deerfield Rd *Web:* www.apprhs.org	Boone	NC	28607	828-262-4100	
Wayne Memorial Hospital 2700 Wayne Memorial Dr *Web:* www.waynehealth.org	Goldsboro	NC	27534	919-736-1110	731-6966
Wesley Long Community Hospital 501 N Elam Ave *TF:* 866-391-2734 ■ *Web:* mosescone.com/body.cfm/?id=41	Greensboro	NC	27403	336-832-1000	832-7869
Wilkes Regional Medical Ctr 1370 W D St PO Box 609 *Web:* wilkesregional.com	North Wilkesboro	NC	28659	336-651-8100	
Wilson Medical Ctr 1705 SW Tarboro St *Web:* www.wilsonmedical.com	Wilson	NC	27893	252-399-8040	
Women's Hospital of Greensboro 801 Green Vly Rd *Web:* www.conehealth.com/womens-hospital	Greensboro	NC	27408	336-832-6500	

North Dakota

				Phone	Fax
Altru Hospital 1200 S Columbia Rd *TF:* 800-732-4277 ■ *Web:* www.altru.org	Grand Forks	ND	58201	701-780-5000	
Medcenter One Hospital 300 N Seventh St *TF:* 800-932-8758 ■ *Web:* bismarck.sanfordhealth.org	Bismarck	ND	58501	701-323-6000	323-5221
St. Alexius Medical Ctr 900 E Broadway Ave *TF:* 877-530-5550 ■ *Web:* www.st.alexius.org	Bismarck	ND	58501	701-530-7755	530-8984
Trinity Hospital Saint Joseph's 1 W Burdick Expy *TF:* 800-247-1316 ■ *Web:* www.trinityhealth.org	Minot	ND	58701	701-857-5000	
Trinity Medical Ctr 1 Burdick Expy W PO Box 5020 *TF:* 800-862-0005 ■ *Web:* www.trinityhealth.org	Minot	ND	58702	701-857-5000	

Ohio

				Phone	Fax
Adena Regional Medical Ctr 272 Hospital Rd *Web:* www.adena.org	Chillicothe	OH	45601	740-779-7500	
Affinity Medical Ctr 875 Eigth St NE *TF:* 800-999-6673 ■ *Web:* www.affinitymedicalcenter.com	Massillon	OH	44646	330-832-8761	837-6814
Akron General Medical Ctr 400 Wabash Ave **Fax:* Admitting ■ *TF:* 800-221-4601 ■ *Web:* www.akrongeneral.org	Akron	OH	44307	330-344-6000	344-1752*
Alliance Community Hospital (ACH) 200 E State St *Web:* www.achosp.org	Alliance	OH	44601	330-596-6000	596-7079
Ashtabula County Medical Ctr (ACMC) 2420 Lake Ave *TF:* 866-213-2262 ■ *Web:* www.acmchealth.org	Ashtabula	OH	44004	440-997-2262	997-6644
Atrium Medical Ctr 1 Medical Ctr Dr *TF:* 800-338-4057 ■ *Web:* www.atriummedcenter.org	Middletown	OH	45005	513-424-2111	
Aultman Hospital 2600 Sixth St SW *Web:* www.aultman.org	Canton	OH	44710	330-452-9911	438-6356
Bethesda Hospital 2951 Maple Ave *TF:* 800-322-4762 ■ *Web:* genesishcs.org	Zanesville	OH	43701	740-454-4000	
Bethesda North Hospital 10500 Montgomery Rd *Web:* www.trihealth.com	Cincinnati	OH	45242	513-569-5400	
Blanchard Valley Hospital 1900 S Main St *Web:* www.bvhealthsystem.org	Findlay	OH	45840	419-423-4500	423-5358
Bryan Hospital (CHWC) 433 W High St *Web:* www.chwchospital.org	Bryan	OH	43506	419-636-1131	630-2155
Charles F Kettering Memorial Hospital 3535 Southern Blvd *Web:* www.ketteringhealth.org	Kettering	OH	45429	937-298-4331	
Christ Hospital 2139 Auburn Ave *TF:* 800-527-8919 ■ *Web:* thechristhospital.com	Cincinnati	OH	45219	513-585-2000	585-3200
Clermont Mercy Hospital 3000 Hospital Dr	Batavia	OH	45103	513-732-8200	732-8550
Cleveland Clinic 2049 E 100th St *Web:* my.clevelandclinic.org	Cleveland	OH	44195	216-444-2200	491-7193
Cleveland Clinic 9500 Euclid Ave *TF:* 800-223-2273 ■ *Web:* my.clevelandclinic.org	Cleveland	OH	44195	216-444-2200	444-0271
Clinton Memorial Hospital (CMH) 610 W Main St PO Box 600 *TF:* 800-803-9648 ■ *Web:* www.cmhregional.com	Wilmington	OH	45177	937-382-6611	382-6633
Community Hospital 2615 E High St *Web:* www.community-mercy.org	Springfield	OH	45505	937-325-0531	
Coshocton County Memorial Hospital Assn Inc 1460 Orange St *Web:* www.ccmh.com	Coshocton	OH	43812	740-622-6411	
Deaconess Hospital 311 Straight St **Fax Area Code:* 937 ■ *Web:* www.deaconess-healthcare.com	Cincinnati	OH	45219	513-559-2100	783-5820*
Doctors Hospital 5100 W Broad St *TF:* 800-432-3309 ■ *Web:* www.ohiohealth.com/doctors	Columbus	OH	43228	614-544-1000	
East Liverpool City Hospital (ELCH) 425 W Fifth St *Web:* www.elch.org	East Liverpool	OH	43920	330-385-7200	
Euclid Hospital 18901 Lk Shore Blvd *Web:* my.clevelandclinic.org	Euclid	OH	44119	216-531-9000	692-7488
Fairfield Medical Ctr (FMC) 401 N Ewing St *TF:* 800-548-2627 ■ *Web:* www.fmchealth.org	Lancaster	OH	43130	740-687-8000	
Fairview Hospital 18101 Lorain Ave *TF:* 800-801-2273 ■ *Web:* my.clevelandclinic.org	Cleveland	OH	44111	216-444-0261	476-4064
Firelands Regional Medical Ctr 1111 Hayes Ave *TF:* 800-342-1177 ■ *Web:* www.firelands.com	Sandusky	OH	44870	419-557-7400	557-6977
Fisher-Titus Medical Ctr (FTMC) 272 Benedict Ave *TF:* 800-589-3862 ■ *Web:* www.fisher-titus.org	Norwalk	OH	44857	419-668-8101	
Flower Hospital 5200 Harroun Rd *Web:* www.promedica.org	Sylvania	OH	43560	419-824-1444	882-2342
Fort Hamilton Hospital 630 Eaton Ave *Web:* www.ketteringhealth.org	Hamilton	OH	45013	513-867-2000	
Good Samaritan Hospital 375 Dixmyth Ave *Web:* www.trihealth.com	Cincinnati	OH	45220	513-569-5400	
Good Samaritan Hospital 2222 Philadelphia Dr *Web:* www.goodsamdayton.org	Dayton	OH	45406	937-278-2612	734-8214
Grandview Medical Ctr 405 W Grand Ave *Web:* www.ketteringhealth.org	Dayton	OH	45405	937-395-3963	395-8327
Grant Medical Ctr 111 S Grant Ave *Web:* www.ohiohealth.com	Columbus	OH	43215	614-566-9000	
Greene Memorial Hospital 1141 N Monroe Dr *Web:* ketteringhealth.org	Xenia	OH	45385	937-352-2000	352-3233
Hillcrest Hospital 6780 Mayfield Rd *Web:* my.clevelandclinic.org	Mayfield Heights	OH	44124	440-312-4500	
Holzer Health Systems 100 Jackson Pk *Web:* www.holzer.org	Gallipolis	OH	45631	740-446-5000	446-5522

				Phone	Fax
Jewish Hospital 4777 E Galbraith Rd *Web:* e-mercy.com/jewish-hospital.aspx	Cincinnati	OH	45236	513-686-3000	686-3003
Kaiser Permanente Parma Medical Ctr 12301 Snow Rd *TF:* 800-524-7372 ■ *Web:* kaiserpermanente.org	Cleveland	OH	44130	216-362-2000	362-2093
Knox Community Hospital 1330 Coshocton Rd *Web:* www.kch.org	Mount Vernon	OH	43050	740-393-9000	393-3487
Lakewood Hospital 14519 Detroit Ave *TF:* 866-588-2264 ■ *Web:* my.clevelandclinic.org	Lakewood	OH	44107	216-521-4200	529-7161
Licking Memorial Hospital 1320 W Main St *Web:* www.lmhealth.org	Newark	OH	43055	740-348-4000	348-4106
Lima Memorial Hospital 1001 Bellefontaine Ave *TF:* 877-362-5672 ■ *Web:* www.limamemorial.org	Lima	OH	45804	419-228-3335	226-5013
Lutheran Hospital 1730 W 25th St *Web:* my.clevelandclinic.org	Cleveland	OH	44113	216-696-4300	363-2082
Marietta Memorial Hospital 401 Matthew St *TF:* 800-523-3977 ■ *Web:* mhsystem.org	Marietta	OH	45750	740-374-1400	374-1787
Marion General Hospital (MGH) 1000 McKinley Pk Dr *Web:* www.ohiohealth.com	Marion	OH	43302	740-383-8400	383-8612
Marymount Hospital 12300 McCracken Rd *TF:* 800-801-2273 ■ *Web:* my.clevelandclinic.org	Garfield Heights	OH	44125	216-581-0500	587-8882
Medcentral Health System Mansfield Hospital 335 Glessner Ave *Web:* www.ohiohealth.com/mansfield	Mansfield	OH	44903	419-526-8000	521-7960
Mercer County Joint Township Community Hospital 800 W Main St *TF:* 888-844-2341 ■ *Web:* www.mercer-health.com	Coldwater	OH	45828	419-678-2341	
Mercy Hospital Anderson 7500 State Rd *Web:* e-mercy.com	Cincinnati	OH	45255	513-624-4500	
Mercy Hospital Western Hills 3131 Queen City Ave *Web:* e-mercy.com	Cincinnati	OH	45238	513-389-5000	389-5201
Mercy Medical Ctr 1320 Mercy Dr NW *TF:* 800-223-8662 ■ *Web:* www.cantonmercy.org	Canton	OH	44708	330-489-1000	489-1312
Mercy Regional Medical Ctr 3700 Kolbe Rd *Web:* www.mercyonline.org	Lorain	OH	44053	440-960-4000	
Mercy St Anne Hospital 3404 W Sylvania Ave *Web:* www.mercyweb.org	Toledo	OH	43623	419-407-2663	407-3889
MetroHealth Medical Ctr 2500 MetroHealth Dr *TF:* 800-554-5251 ■ *Web:* www.metrohealth.org	Cleveland	OH	44109	216-778-7800	
Miami Valley Hospital 1 Wyoming St *TF All:* 800-544-0630 ■ *Web:* www.miamivalleyhospital.org	Dayton	OH	45409	937-208-8000	
Mount Carmel Saint Ann's Hospital 500 S Cleveland Ave *Web:* www.mountcarmelhealth.com	Westerville	OH	43081	614-898-4000	
Mount Carmel West Hospital 793 W State St *TF:* 800-346-1009 ■ *Web:* mountcarmelhealth.com	Columbus	OH	43222	614-234-5000	944-5070
Northside Medical Ctr (NMC) 500 Gypsy Ln *Web:* valleycareofohio.net/pages/home.aspx	Youngstown	OH	44501	330-884-1000	
Ohio State University Wexner Medical Center, The 410 W Tenth Ave *Web:* wexnermedical.osu.edu	Columbus	OH	43210	614-293-8652	
ProMedica 2142 N Cove Blvd *TF:* 866-865-4677 ■ *Web:* www.promedica.org	Toledo	OH	43606	419-291-5437	
Riverside Methodist Hospital 3535 Olentangy River Rd *TF:* 800-837-7555 ■ *Web:* www.ohiohealth.com/facilities/riverside	Columbus	OH	43214	614-566-5000	
Robinson Memorial Hospital 6847 N Chestnut St *Web:* www.robinsonmemorial.org	Ravenna	OH	44266	330-297-0811	
Saint Charles Mercy Hospital 2600 Navarre Ave *TF:* 888-987-6372 ■ *Web:* www.mercyweb.org/st_charles.aspx	Oregon	OH	43616	419-696-7200	
Saint Rita's Medical Ctr (SRMC) 730 W Market St *TF:* 800-232-7762 ■ *Web:* ehealthconnection.com/regions/st%5fritas	Lima	OH	45801	419-227-3361	
Saint Thomas Hospital 444 N Main St *TF:* 800-237-8662 ■ *Web:* www.summahealth.org	Akron	OH	44310	330-375-3000	
Saint Vincent Charity Hospital (SVCH) 2351 E 22nd St *TF:* 800-750-0750 ■ *Web:* www.stvincentcharity.com	Cleveland	OH	44115	216-861-6200	
Salem Community Hospital 1995 E State St *Web:* www.salemhosp.com	Salem	OH	44460	330-332-1551	332-7691
Southeastern Ohio Regional Medical Ctr 1341 Clark St *Web:* www.seormc.org	Cambridge	OH	43725	740-439-8000	439-8175
Southern Ohio Medical Ctr (SOMC) 1805 27th St *Web:* www.somc.org	Portsmouth	OH	45662	740-356-5000	
Southwest General Health Ctr 18697 Bagley Rd *Web:* www.swgeneral.com	Middleburg Heights	OH	44130	440-816-8000	816-5348
St. Joseph Health Ctr 667 Eastland Ave SE *Web:* mercy.com	Warren	OH	44484	330-841-4000	
Summa Barberton Hospital 155 Fifth St NE *TF:* 888-905-6071 ■ *Web:* summahealth.org	Barberton	OH	44203	330-615-3000	
Trinity Medical Ctr West 4000 Johnson Rd *TF:* 877-271-4176 ■ *Web:* www.trinityhealth.com	Steubenville	OH	43952	740-264-8000	283-7104
Trumbull Memorial Hospital (TMH) 1350 E Market St *Web:* valleycareofohio.net	Warren	OH	44482	330-841-9011	
UH Parma Medical Center (PCGH) 7007 Powers Blvd *TF:* 855-292-4292 ■ *Web:* www.uhhospitals.org/parma	Parma	OH	44129	440-743-3000	743-4386
Union Hospital 659 Blvd *Web:* www.unionhospital.org	Dover	OH	44622	330-343-3311	364-0951
University Hospital 234 Goodman St *Web:* uchealth.com	Cincinnati	OH	45219	513-584-1000	
University Hospital Bedford Medical Ctr 44 Blaine Ave *Web:* www.uhhospitals.org	Bedford	OH	44146	440-735-3900	735-3631
University Hospitals of Cleveland 11100 Euclid Ave *TF:* 866-844-2273 ■ *Web:* www.uhhospitals.org	Cleveland	OH	44106	216-844-1000	844-7497
University of Toledo Medical Center, The 3000 Arlington Ave *TF:* 800-321-8383	Toledo	OH	43614	419-383-4000	383-3850
Upper Valley Medical Ctr (UVMC) 3130 N County Rd 25-A *TF:* 866-608-3463 ■ *Web:* www.uvmc.com	Troy	OH	45373	937-440-4000	
Wayne HealthCare 835 Sweitzer St *Web:* www.waynehealthcare.org	Greenville	OH	45331	937-548-1141	
Wood County Hospital 950 W Wooster St *Web:* www.woodcountyhospital.org	Bowling Green	OH	43402	419-354-8900	354-8957

Oklahoma

				Phone	Fax
Children's Hospital at OU Medical Ctr, The 1200 N Everett Dr *Web:* www.oumedicine.com	Oklahoma City	OK	73104	405-271-5656	
Claremore Regional Hospital LLC 1202 N Muskogee Pl *Web:* hillcrestclaremore.com	Claremore	OK	74017	918-341-2556	
Comanche County Memorial Hospital 3401 NW Gore Blvd *Web:* www.ccmhonline.com	Lawton	OK	73505	580-355-8620	
Duncan Regional Hospital 1407 Whisenant Dr *Web:* www.duncanregional.com	Duncan	OK	73533	580-252-5300	251-8829
Grady Memorial Hospital 2220 Iowa Ave *TF:* 800-299-9665 ■ *Web:* www.gradymem.org	Chickasha	OK	73018	405-224-2300	779-2413
Hillcrest Medical Ctr 1120 S Utica Ave *Web:* www.hillcrest.com	Tulsa	OK	74104	918-579-1000	
INTEGRIS Baptist Medical Ctr 3300 NW Expy *Web:* www.integrisok.com	Oklahoma City	OK	73112	405-949-3011	
INTEGRIS Baptist Regional Health Ctr 200 Second Ave SW *TF:* 888-951-2277 ■ *Web:* www.integrisok.com	Miami	OK	74355	918-542-6611	540-7605
INTEGRIS Bass Baptist Health Ctr 600 S Monroe *TF:* 888-951-2277 ■ *Web:* integrisok.com/bass-baptist-health-center-enid-ok	Enid	OK	73701	580-233-2300	
INTEGRIS Southwest Medical Ctr 4401 S Western St **Fax Area Code:* 918 ■ *TF:* 888-949-3816 ■ *Web:* www.integrisok.com/southwest	Oklahoma City	OK	73109	405-636-7000	540-7702*
Jackson County Memorial Hospital 1200 E Pecan St *TF:* 800-595-0455 ■ *Web:* www.jcmh.com	Altus	OK	73521	580-379-5000	
McAlester Regional Health Ctr 1 Clark Bass Blvd *Web:* www.mrhcok.com	McAlester	OK	74501	918-426-1800	
Mercy Health Ctr (MHC) 4300 W Memorial Rd *Web:* www.mercy.net	Oklahoma City	OK	73120	405-755-1515	936-5794
Mercy Memorial Health Ctr (MMHC) 1011 14th Ave NW *TF:* 888-637-2937 ■ *Web:* www.mercy.net	Ardmore	OK	73401	580-223-5400	
Muskogee Regional Medical Ctr 300 Rockefeller Dr *Web:* www.eastarhealth.com	Muskogee	OK	74401	918-682-5501	
Norman Regional Hospital 901 N Porter St *Web:* www.normanregional.com	Norman	OK	73071	405-307-1000	307-1076
OSU Medical Ctr 744 W Ninth St *Web:* www.osumc.net	Tulsa	OK	74127	918-599-1000	
OU Medical Ctr Edmond 1 S Bryant St *Web:* www.oumedicine.com	Edmond	OK	73034	405-341-6100	
Saint Anthony Hospital 1000 N Lee St *TF:* 800-227-6964 ■ *Web:* www.saintsok.com	Oklahoma City	OK	73101	405-272-7000	272-6592
Saint Francis Hospital 6161 S Yale Ave *Web:* www.saintfrancis.com	Tulsa	OK	74136	918-494-2200	
Saint Mary's Regional Medical Ctr 305 S Fifth St *Web:* www.stmarysregional.com	Enid	OK	73701	580-233-6100	249-3982
SouthCrest Hospital 8801 S 101st E Ave *Web:* hillcrestsouth.com	Tulsa	OK	74133	918-294-4000	294-4809
Southwestern Medical Ctr (SWMC) 5602 SW Lee Blvd *Web:* www.southwesternmedcenter.com	Lawton	OK	73505	580-531-4700	531-4702
Stillwater Medical Ctr 1323 W Sixth St *Web:* www.stillwater-medical.org	Stillwater	OK	74074	405-372-1480	
Unity Health Ctr 1102 W MacArthur St *Web:* stanthonyshawnee.com	Shawnee	OK	74804	405-273-2270	878-8101
Valley View Regional Hospital 430 N Monte Vista St *Web:* www.mercy.net	Ada	OK	74820	580-332-2323	421-1386

Oregon

				Phone	Fax
Adventist Medical Ctr 10123 SE Market St *Web:* www.adventisthealth.org/nw/pages/default.aspx	Portland	OR	97216	503-257-2500	261-6638
Bay Area Hospital 1775 Thompson Rd *Web:* www.bayareahospital.org	Coos Bay	OR	97420	541-269-8111	
Good Samaritan Regional Medical Ctr 3600 NW Samaritan Dr *TF:* 888-872-0760 ■ *Web:* www.samhealth.org	Corvallis	OR	97330	541-768-5111	
Legacy Emanuel Hospital & Health Ctr 2801 N Gantenbein Ave *TF:* 888-598-4232 ■ *Web:* www.legacyhealth.org	Portland	OR	97227	503-413-2200	413-2428
Legacy Good Samaritan Hospital 1015 NW 22nd Ave *TF:* 800-733-9959 ■ *Web:* www.legacyhealth.org	Portland	OR	97210	503-335-3500	413-6919
Legacy Meridian Park Hospital 19300 SW 65th Ave *Web:* www.legacyhealth.org	Tualatin	OR	97062	503-692-1212	

				Phone	Fax
McKenzie-Willamette Hospital 1460 G St. *Web:* www.mckweb.com	Springfield	OR	97477	541-726-4400	
Mercy Medical Ctr (MMC) 2700 Stewart Pkwy *Web:* www.mercyrose.org	Roseburg	OR	97470	541-673-0611	677-4848
Oregon Health & Science University Hospital 3181 SW Sam Jackson Pk Rd. *TF:* 800-292-4466 ■ *Web:* www.ohsu.edu	Portland	OR	97239	503-494-8311	494-3400
Peace Health Medical Group 1162 Willamette St *Web:* peacehealth.org	Eugene	OR	97401	360-734-5400	253-1781
Providence Medford Medical Ctr 1111 Crater Lk Ave *TF:* 877-541-0588 ■ *Web:* www.oregon.providence.org	Medford	OR	97504	541-732-5000	732-5872
Providence Portland Medical Ctr 4805 NE Glisan St *TF:* 800-833-8899 ■ *Web:* www.oregon.providence.org	Portland	OR	97213	503-215-1111	215-6858
Providence Saint Vincent Medical Ctr 9205 SW Barnes Rd Ste 20 *TF:* 800-677-6752 ■ *Web:* www.oregon.providence.org	Portland	OR	97225	503-216-2401	216-4041
Sacred Heart Medical Ctr 1255 Hilyard St *TF:* 800-288-7444 ■ *Web:* www.peacehealth.org	Eugene	OR	97401	541-686-7300	
Salem Hospital 665 Winter St SE *TF:* 800-876-1718 ■ *Web:* www.salemhealth.org	Salem	OR	97301	800-876-1718	
Samaritan Albany General Hospital 1046 Sixth Ave SW *Web:* www.samhealth.org	Albany	OR	97321	541-812-4000	812-4610
Sky Lakes Medical Ctr 2865 Daggett Ave *Web:* www.skylakes.org	Klamath Falls	OR	97601	541-882-6311	
Tuality Community Hospital 335 SE Eigth Ave *Web:* www.tuality.org	Hillsboro	OR	97123	503-681-1111	
Willamette Falls Hospital 1500 Div St *Web:* oregon.providence.org	Oregon City	OR	97045	503-656-1631	650-6807

Pennsylvania

				Phone	Fax
Abington Memorial Hospital 1200 Old York Rd *Web:* abingtonhealth.org	Abington	PA	19001	215-481-2000	
Albert Einstein Medical Ctr 5501 Old York Rd *TF:* 800-346-7834 ■ *Web:* www.einstein.edu	Philadelphia	PA	19141	800-346-7834	
Allegheny General Hospital 320 E N Ave *Web:* ahn.org	Pittsburgh	PA	15212	412-359-3131	359-8786
Allegheny Health Network 1301 Carlisle St *Web:* ahn.org	Natrona Heights	PA	15065	724-224-5100	226-7385
Altoona Regional Health System Altoona Hospital 620 Howard Ave *TF:* 877-855-8152 ■ *Web:* www.altoonaregional.org	Altoona	PA	16601	814-889-2011	
Aria Health Bucks County Campus 380 N Oxford Vly Rd *Web:* www.ariahealth.org	Langhorne	PA	19047	215-949-5000	
Aria Health System *Frankford Campus* 4900 Frankford Ave *Web:* www.ariahealth.org	Philadelphia	PA	19124	215-831-2000	
Armstrong County Memorial Hospital (ACMH) 1 Nolte Dr *Web:* www.acmh.org	Kittanning	PA	16201	724-543-8500	543-8704
Berwick Hospital Ctr, The 701 E 16th St *Web:* commonwealthhealth.net	Berwick	PA	18603	570-759-5000	759-3473
Bradford Regional Medical Ctr 116 Interstate Pk *Web:* www.brmc.com	Bradford	PA	16701	814-368-4143	368-5722
Brandywine Hospital 201 Reeceville Rd *Web:* www.brandywinehospital.com	Coatesville	PA	19320	610-383-8000	
Bryn Mawr Hospital 130 S Bryn Mawr Ave *Web:* www.mainlinehealth.org/bmh	Bryn Mawr	PA	19010	610-526-3000	
Butler Health System 1 Hospital Way *Web:* butlerhealthsystem.org	Butler	PA	16001	724-283-6666	
Canonsburg General Hospital 100 Medical Blvd *Web:* ahn.org	Canonsburg	PA	15317	724-745-6100	873-5876
Carlisle Regional Medical Ctr 361 Alexander Spring Rd *Web:* carlislermc.com	Carlisle	PA	17015	717-249-1212	249-0770
Chambersburg Hospital 112 N Seventh St *Web:* www.summithealth.org	Chambersburg	PA	17201	717-267-3000	267-7704
Charles Cole Memorial Hospital 1001 E Second St *Web:* www.colememorial.org	Coudersport	PA	16915	814-274-9300	274-0884
Chester County Hospital 701 E Marshall St **Fax:* Admitting ■ *Web:* www.cchosp.com	West Chester	PA	19380	610-431-5000	430-2958*
Chestnut Hill Hospital 8835 Germantown Ave *Web:* www.chestnuthillhealth.com/chestnut-hill-hospital/home.aspx	Philadelphia	PA	19118	215-248-8200	242-2601
Clarion Hospital (CH) 1 Hospital Dr *TF:* 800-522-0505 ■ *Web:* www.clarionhospital.org	Clarion	PA	16214	814-226-9500	226-1224
Clearfield Hospital 809 Tpke Ave PO Box 992 *TF:* 800-281-8000 ■ *Web:* phhealthcare.org	Clearfield	PA	16830	814-765-5341	
Crozer-Chester Medical Ctr (CCMC) 1 Medical Ctr Blvd *Web:* www.crozerkeystone.org	Upland	PA	19013	610-447-2000	
Delaware County Memorial Hospital 501 N Lansdowne Ave *TF:* 877-884-1564 ■ *Web:* www.crozerkeystone.org	Drexel Hill	PA	19026	610-284-8100	
Divine Providence Hospital 1100 Grampian Blvd *Web:* susquehannahealth.org	Williamsport	PA	17701	570-326-8000	
Doylestown Hospital 595 W State St *Web:* www.doylestownhealth.org	Doylestown	PA	18901	215-345-2200	345-2532
DuBois Regional Medical Ctr 100 Hospital Ave *Web:* phhealthcare.org	Du Bois	PA	15801	814-371-2200	
Easton Hospital 250 S 21st St *Web:* www.easton-hospital.com	Easton	PA	18042	610-250-4000	
Einstein at Elkins Park 60 E Township Line Rd *Web:* einstein.edu/locations/einstein-medical-center-elkins-park	Elkins Park	PA	19027	215-663-6000	
Ellwood City Hospital 724 Pershing St *Web:* www.echospital.org	Ellwood City	PA	16117	724-752-0081	752-0966
Evangelical Community Hospital 1 Hospital Dr *Web:* www.evanhospital.com	Lewisburg	PA	17837	570-522-2000	522-4136
Forbes Regional Hospital 2570 Haymaker Rd *Web:* ahn.org	Monroeville	PA	15146	412-858-2000	
Frick Hospital 508 S Church St *TF:* 877-771-1234 ■ *Web:* excelahealth.org	Mount Pleasant	PA	15666	724-547-1500	
Geisinger Health System (CMC) 1800 Mulberry St *Web:* www.geisinger.org	Scranton	PA	18510	570-703-8000	
Geisinger South Wilkes-Barre (GSWB) 25 Church St *Web:* www.geisinger.org	Wilkes-Barre	PA	18765	570-808-3100	
Geisinger Wyoming Valley Medical Ctr 1000 E Mountain Dr *Web:* www.geisinger.org	Danville	PA	17822	570-271-8600	
Gettysburg Hospital 147 Gettys St PO Box 3786 *Web:* wellspan.org/offices-locations/hospitals	Gettysburg	PA	17325	717-334-2121	334-1302
Gnaden Huetten Memorial Hospital 211 N 12th St *Web:* www.ghmh.org	Lehighton	PA	18235	610-377-1300	
Good Samaritan Hospital (GSH) 252 S Fourth St *Web:* www.gshleb.org	Lebanon	PA	17042	717-270-7500	
Grand View Hospital 700 Lawn Ave *Web:* www.gvh.org	Sellersville	PA	18960	215-453-4000	453-9151
Grove City Medical Ctr (GCMC) 631 N Broad St Ext *Web:* www.gcmcpa.org	Grove City	PA	16127	724-450-7000	450-7179
Hahnemann University Hospital 230 N Broad St *Web:* www.hahnemannhospital.com	Philadelphia	PA	19102	215-762-7000	
Hanover Hospital 300 Highland Ave *TF:* 800-673-2426 ■ *Web:* www.hanoverhospital.org	Hanover	PA	17331	717-637-3711	633-2187
Harrisburg Hospital 111 S Front St *TF:* 888-782-5678 ■ *Web:* www.pinnaclehealth.org	Harrisburg	PA	17101	717-782-3131	782-5536
Heart of Lancaster Regional Medical Ctr 1500 Highland Dr **Fax Area Code:* 727 ■ *TF:* 800-999-6673 ■ *Web:* www.lancastermedicalcenters.com	Lititz	PA	17543	717-625-5000	507-3618*
Heritage Valley Health System 1000 Dutch Ridge Rd *TF:* 877-771-4847 ■ *Web:* www.heritagevalley.org	Beaver	PA	15009	724-728-7000	773-4675
Holy Redeemer Hospital & Medical Ctr 1648 Huntingdon Pk *TF:* 800-818-4747 ■ *Web:* www.holyredeemer.com	Meadowbrook	PA	19046	215-947-3000	
Holy Spirit Hospital 503 N 21st St *Web:* www.hsh.org	Camp Hill	PA	17011	717-763-2100	972-7676
Hospital of the University of Pennsylvania 3400 Spruce St *TF:* 800-789-7366 ■ *Web:* www.pennmedicine.org	Philadelphia	PA	19104	215-662-4000	
Indiana Regional Medical Ctr 835 Hospital Rd *Web:* www.indianarmc.org	Indiana	PA	15701	724-357-7000	357-7449
JC Blair Memorial Hospital 1225 Warm Springs Ave *Web:* www.jcblair.org	Huntingdon	PA	16652	814-643-2290	
Jeanes Hospital 7600 Central Ave *Web:* www.jeanes.com	Philadelphia	PA	19111	215-728-2000	
Jefferson Regional Medical Ctr 565 Coal Vly Rd PO Box 18119 *Web:* www.ahn.org/locations/jefferson-hospital	Pittsburgh	PA	15236	412-469-5000	469-7062
Lancaster General Hospital 555 N Duke St *Web:* www.lancastergeneralhealth.org	Lancaster	PA	17604	717-544-5511	544-5966
Lancaster Regional Medical Ctr 250 College Ave *TF:* 877-456-9617 ■ *Web:* www.lancastermedicalcenters.com	Lancaster	PA	17603	717-291-8211	
Lankenau Medical Ctr 100 E Lancaster Ave *TF:* 866-225-5654 ■ *Web:* www.mainlinehealth.org/lh	Wynnewood	PA	19096	484-476-2000	
Lehigh Valley Health Network 700 E Broad St *TF:* 800-528-1234 ■ *Web:* lvhn.org/hazleton	Hazleton	PA	18201	570-501-4000	501-6971
Lower Bucks Hospital 501 Bath Rd *Web:* www.lowerbuckshosp.com	Bristol	PA	19007	215-785-9200	785-9825
Marian Community Hospital (MCH) 100 Lincoln Ave	Carbondale	PA	18407	570-281-1000	
Meadville Medical Ctr (MMC) 751 Liberty St *TF:* 800-254-5164 ■ *Web:* www.mmchs.org	Meadville	PA	16335	814-333-5000	333-9456
Memorial Hospital 325 S Belmont St *TF:* 800-436-4326 ■ *Web:* www.mhyork.org	York	PA	17405	717-843-8623	849-5329
Memorial Medical Ctr 1086 Franklin St *Web:* www.conemaugh.org	Johnstown	PA	15905	814-534-9000	
Mercy Hospital of Philadelphia 501 S 54th St *Web:* www.mercyhealth.org	Philadelphia	PA	19143	215-748-9000	748-9366
Mercy Suburban Hospital (MSH) 2701 De Kalb Pk *Web:* www.mercyhealth.org/suburban	Norristown	PA	19401	610-278-2000	
Methodist Hospital 2301 S Broad St *Web:* hospitals.jefferson.edu/methodist	Philadelphia	PA	19148	215-952-9000	
Monongahela Valley Hospital 1163 Country Club Rd *Web:* www.monvalleyhospital.com	Monongahela	PA	15063	724-258-1000	258-1830
Montgomery Hospital 1301 Powell St *Web:* www.montgomeryhospital.org	Norristown	PA	19401	610-270-2000	
Moses Taylor Hospital 700 Quincy Ave *Web:* commonwealthhealth.net	Scranton	PA	18510	570-340-2100	
Mount Nittany Medical Ctr 1800 E Pk Ave *TF:* 866-686-6171 ■ *Web:* www.mountnittany.org	State College	PA	16803	814-231-7000	

	City	State	Zip	Phone	Fax
Nazareth Hospital 2601 Holme Ave *Web:* www.mercyhealth.org/nazareth	Philadelphia	PA	19152	215-335-6000	335-7740
Northeastern Hospital School of Nursing 2301 E Allegheny Ave *Web:* www.templehealth.org/content/default.htm	Philadelphia	PA	19134	215-291-3000	
Ohio Valley General Hospital 25 Heckel Rd Kennedy Township *Web:* www.ohiovalleyhospital.org	McKees Rocks	PA	15136	412-777-6161	777-6363
Paoli Hospital (PH) 255 W Lancaster Ave *Web:* mainlinehealth.org/paoli	Paoli	PA	19301	610-648-1000	
Penn Presbyterian Medical Ctr (PPMC) 39th & Market Sts *TF:* 800-789-7366 ■ *Web:* pennmedicine.org/penn-presbyterian-medical-center	Philadelphia	PA	19104	215-662-8000	662-9212
Penn State Milton S Hershey Medical Ctr 500 University Dr *TF:* 800-731-3032 ■ *Web:* www.pennstatehershey.org	Hershey	PA	17033	717-531-8521	531-4162
Pennsylvania Hospital 800 Spruce St *TF:* 800-789-7366 ■ *Web:* www.pennmedicine.org	Philadelphia	PA	19107	215-829-3000	
Phoenixville Hospital 140 Nutt Rd *Web:* www.phoenixvillehospital.com	Phoenixville	PA	19460	610-983-1000	
Pinnacle Health Hospital at Community General 4300 Londonderry Rd *TF:* 888-782-5678 ■ *Web:* pinnaclehealth.org	Harrisburg	PA	17109	717-652-3000	
Pocono Medical Ctr 206 E Brown St *Web:* www.poconohealthsystem.org	East Stroudsburg	PA	18301	570-421-4000	476-3469
Pottstown Memorial Medical Ctr (PMMC) 1600 E High St *Web:* www.pottstownmemorial.com	Pottstown	PA	19464	610-327-7000	
Punxsutawney Area Hospital Inc (PAH) 81 Hillcrest Dr *Web:* www.pah.org	Punxsutawney	PA	15767	814-938-1800	
Reading Hospital & Medical Ctr PO Box 16052 *Web:* www.readinghealth.org	Reading	PA	19612	610-988-8000	
Regional Hospital of Scranton 746 Jefferson Ave *Web:* commonwealthhealth.net	Scranton	PA	18510	570-348-7100	348-7639
Riddle Memorial Hospital 1068 W Baltimore Pike **Fax Area Code:* 610 ■ *TF:* 866-225-5654 ■ *Web:* www.mainlinehealth.org	Media	PA	19063	484-227-9400	891-3592*
Robert Packer Hospital 1 Guthrie Sq *TF:* 888-448-8474 ■ *Web:* www.guthrie.org	Sayre	PA	18840	570-888-6666	
Roxborough Memorial Hospital (RMH) 5800 Ridge Ave *Web:* www.roxboroughmemorial.com	Philadelphia	PA	19128	215-483-9900	
Sacred Heart HealthCare System 421 Chew St *TF:* 800-994-6610 ■ *Web:* www.shh.org	Allentown	PA	18102	610-776-4500	
Saint Joseph Medical Ctr 2500 Bernville Rd *Web:* www.thefutureofhealthcare.org	Reading	PA	19605	610-378-2000	
Saint Vincent Health Ctr 232 W 25th St *Web:* ahn.org/locations/saint-vincent-hospital	Erie	PA	16544	814-452-5000	455-1724
Schuylkill Medical Center 420 S Jackson St	Pottsville	PA	17901	570-621-5000	622-8221
Sewickley Valley Hospital 720 Blackburn Rd *Web:* www.heritagevalley.org	Sewickley	PA	15143	412-741-6600	
Sharon Regional Health System 740 E State St *Web:* www.sharonregional.com	Sharon	PA	16146	724-983-3911	983-3842
Soldiers + Sailors Memorial Hospital 32-36 Central Ave *TF:* 800-808-5287 ■ *Web:* www.laurelhs.org	Wellsboro	PA	16901	570-723-7764	
Somerset Hospital 225 S Ctr Ave *Web:* www.somersethospital.com	Somerset	PA	15501	814-443-5000	
Southwest Regional Medical Ctr 350 Bonar Ave *Web:* www.southwestregionalmedical.com	Waynesburg	PA	15370	724-627-3101	627-8653
St. Joseph's Hospital 16th St at Girard Ave *Web:* www.nphs.com	Philadelphia	PA	19130	215-787-9000	
Sunbury Community Hospital (SCH) 350 N 11th St *Web:* www.sunburyhospital.com	Sunbury	PA	17801	570-286-3333	286-3500
Taylor Hospital 175 E Chester Pk *Web:* www.crozerkeystone.org	Ridley Park	PA	19078	610-595-6000	
Temple University Hospital 3401 N Broad St *Web:* www.tuh.templehealth.org	Philadelphia	PA	19140	215-707-2000	707-3679
Temple University Hospital Episcopal Campus 100 E Lehigh Ave *Web:* www.episcopal.templehealth.org	Philadelphia	PA	19125	215-707-1200	707-0953
Thomas Jefferson University Hospital 111 S 11th St *TF:* 800-533-3669 ■ *Web:* hospitals.jefferson.edu	Philadelphia	PA	19107	215-955-6000	955-6464
Uniontown Hospital (UH) 500 W Berkeley St *Web:* www.uniontownhospital.com	Uniontown	PA	15401	724-430-5000	
University of Pittsburgh Medical Ctr (UPMC)					
Horizon 110 N Main St *TF:* 888-447-1122 ■ *Web:* www.upmc.com	Greenville	PA	16125	724-588-2100	
Northwest 100 Fairfield Dr *Web:* www.upmc.com	Seneca	PA	16346	814-676-7600	
Passavant 9100 Babcock Blvd *TF:* 800-533-8762 ■ *Web:* www.upmc.com	Pittsburgh	PA	15237	412-367-6700	
Shadyside 5230 Centre Ave *TF:* 800-533-8762 ■ *Web:* www.upmc.com	Pittsburgh	PA	15232	412-623-2121	
South Side 2000 Mary St *TF:* 800-533-8762 ■ *Web:* www.upmc.com	Pittsburgh	PA	15203	412-488-5550	
UPMC Hamot 201 State St *Web:* www.upmc.com	Erie	PA	16550	814-877-6000	877-6104
UPMC McKeesport 1500 Fifth Ave *Web:* www.upmc.com	McKeesport	PA	15132	412-664-2000	
UPMC Mercy Hospital 1400 Locust St *TF:* 800-446-3797 ■ *Web:* www.upmc.com	Pittsburgh	PA	15219	412-232-8111	232-7380
UPMC Presbyterian 200 Lothrop St *TF:* 877-986-9862 ■ *Web:* www.upmc.com	Pittsburgh	PA	15213	412-647-8762	
Warren General Hospital 2 Crescent Pk W *Web:* www.wgh.org	Warren	PA	16365	814-723-3300	
Washington Hospital, The 155 Wilson Ave *Web:* www.washingtonhospital.org	Washington	PA	15301	724-225-7000	222-7316
Wayne Memorial Hospital (WMH) 601 Pk St *Web:* www.wmh.org	Honesdale	PA	18431	570-253-8100	253-8993
Western Pennsylvania Hospital 4800 Friendship Ave *Web:* ahn.org	Pittsburgh	PA	15224	412-578-5000	
Wilkes-Barre General Hospital 575 N River St *Web:* commonwealthhealth.net	Wilkes-Barre	PA	18764	570-829-8111	
Williamsport Hospital & Medical Ctr 777 Rural Ave *Web:* www.susquehannahealth.org	Williamsport	PA	17701	570-321-1000	
York Hospital 1001 S George St *Web:* www.wellspan.org	York	PA	17405	717-851-2345	851-2968

Rhode Island

	City	State	Zip	Phone	Fax
Kent Hospital 455 Toll Gate Rd *TF:* 800-892-9291 ■ *Web:* www.kentri.org	Warwick	RI	02886	401-737-7000	
KOCH EYE Assoc 566 Toll Gate Rd *Web:* kocheye.com	Warwick	RI	02886	401-738-4800	738-8153
Landmark Medical Ctr 115 Cass Ave *Web:* www.landmarkmedical.org	Woonsocket	RI	02895	401-769-4100	
Memorial Hospital of Rhode Island (MHRI) 111 Brewster St *TF:* 800-647-4362 ■ *Web:* www.mhri.org	Pawtucket	RI	02860	401-729-2000	
Miriam Hospital, The 164 Summit Ave *Web:* www.miriamhospital.org	Providence	RI	02906	401-793-2500	793-7587
Newport Hospital (NH) 11 Friendship St *TF:* 866-401-0002 ■ *Web:* www.newporthospital.org	Newport	RI	02840	401-845-1646	
Rhode Island Hospital 593 Eddy St *Web:* www.rhodeislandhospital.org	Providence	RI	02903	401-444-4000	444-6572
Roger Williams Medical Ctr 825 Chalkstone Ave *Web:* rwmcmedicine.org	Providence	RI	02908	401-456-2000	456-2029
South County Hospital 100 Kenyon Ave *Web:* www.southcountyhealth.org	Wakefield	RI	02879	401-782-8000	783-6330
Westerly Hospital 25 Wells St *TF:* 800-933-5960 ■ *Web:* westerlyhospital.org	Westerly	RI	02891	401-596-6000	348-0350

South Carolina

	City	State	Zip	Phone	Fax
Aiken Regional Medical Centers 302 University Pkwy *TF:* 800-245-3679 ■ *Web:* www.aikenregional.com	Aiken	SC	29801	803-641-5000	641-5000
AnMed Health 800 N Fant St *Web:* www.anmedhealth.org	Anderson	SC	29621	864-512-1000	512-1552
Beaufort Memorial Hospital 955 Ribaut Rd *TF:* 877-532-6472 ■ *Web:* www.bmhsc.org	Beaufort	SC	29902	843-522-5200	
Bon Secours Saint Francis Hospital 2095 Henry Tecklenburg Dr *Web:* rsfh.com	Charleston	SC	29414	843-402-1000	
Carolina Pines Regional Medical Ctr 1304 W Bobo Newsome Hwy *Web:* www.cprmc.com	Hartsville	SC	29550	843-339-2100	
Carolinas Hospital System 805 Pamplico Hwy *Web:* www.carolinashospital.com	Florence	SC	29505	843-674-5000	
Colleton Medical Ctr (CMC) 501 Robertson Blvd *Web:* www.colletonmedical.com	Walterboro	SC	29488	843-782-2000	
Conway Medical Ctr 300 Singleton Ridge Rd *Web:* www.conwaymedicalcenter.com	Conway	SC	29526	843-347-7111	
East Cooper Medical Center 2000 Hospital Dr *Web:* www.eastcoopermedctr.com	Mount Pleasant	SC	29464	843-881-0100	881-4396
Grand Strand Regional Medical Ctr 809 82nd Pkwy *TF:* 800-342-2383 ■ *Web:* www.grandstrandmed.com	Myrtle Beach	SC	29572	843-692-1000	692-1109
Greenville Memorial Hospital 701 Grove Rd *Web:* www.ghs.org	Greenville	SC	29605	864-455-7000	
Hilton Head Regional Medical Ctr 25 Hospital Ctr Blvd *Web:* www.hiltonheadregional.com	Hilton Head Island	SC	29926	843-681-6122	
KershawHealth Medical Ctr 1315 Roberts St PO Box 7003 *Web:* www.kershawhealth.org	Camden	SC	29020	803-432-4311	
Lexington Medical Ctr 2720 Sunset Blvd *Web:* www.lexmed.com	West Columbia	SC	29169	803-791-2000	791-2660
Marion County Medical Ctr 2829 E Hwy 76 *Web:* www.carolinashospitalmarion.com	Mullins	SC	29574	843-431-2000	
Mary Black Memorial Hospital 1700 Skylyn Dr *Web:* www.maryblackhealthsystem.com	Spartanburg	SC	29307	864-573-3000	
McLeod Medical Ctr Dillon 301 E Jackson St *Web:* www.mcleodhealth.org	Dillon	SC	29536	843-774-4111	
McLeod Regional Medical Ctr 555 E Cheves St *Web:* www.mcleodhealth.org	Florence	SC	29506	843-777-2000	
Oconee Medical Campus (OMC) 298 Memorial Dr *Web:* www.ghs.org/locations/oconee-medical-campus	Seneca	SC	29672	864-882-3351	
Palmetto Health Baptist Columbia 1333 Taylor St Ste 6F *Web:* www.palmettohealth.org	Columbia	SC	29201	803-296-5010	
Palmetto Health Baptist Medical Ctr Easley 200 Fleetwood Dr *Web:* www.palmettohealth.org	Easley	SC	29640	864-442-7200	
Palmetto Health Richland 5 Richland Medical Pk *Web:* palmettohealth.org/body.cfm?id=961	Columbia	SC	29203	803-434-7000	
Piedmont Medical Ctr 222 S Herlong Ave *TF:* 800-222-4218 ■ *Web:* www.piedmontmedicalcenter.com	Rock Hill	SC	29732	803-329-1234	329-0979

Phone | Fax

Providence Hospitals 2435 Forest Dr, Columbia SC 29204 803-256-5300 256-5935
TF: 877-256-5381 ■ *Web:* www.yourprovidencehealth.org

Regional Medical Ctr, The
3000 St Matthews Rd, Orangeburg SC 29118 803-395-2200
TF: 800-476-3377 ■ *Web:* www.trmchealth.org

Roper Hospital 316 Calhoun St, Charleston SC 29401 843-724-2000 724-2995
Web: rsfh.com

Self Regional Hospital 1325 Spring St, Greenwood SC 29646 864-725-4111
Web: www.selfregional.org

Spartanburg Regional Medical Ctr (SRMC)
101 E Wood St, Spartanburg SC 29303 864-560-6000 560-3974
TF: 800-318-2596 ■ *Web:* spartanburgregional.com

Springs Memorial Hospital 800 W Meeting St, Lancaster SC 29720 803-286-1214
Web: www.springsmemorial.com

Trident Medical Ctr 9330 Medical Plz Dr, Charleston SC 29406 843-797-7000
TF: 866-492-9085 ■ *Web:* www.tridenthealthsystem.com

Tuomey Regional Medical Ctr
129 N Washington St, Sumter SC 29150 803-774-9000
Web: www.tuomey.com

Upstate Carolina Medical Ctr
1530 N Limestone St, Gaffney SC 29340 864-487-4271
Web: novanthealth.org/gaffneymedicalcenter.aspx

Wallace Thomson Hospital 322 W S St, Union SC 29379 864-301-2000 429-2524
Web: www.wallacethomson.com

South Dakota

Phone | Fax

Avera McKennan Hospital & University Health Ctr
1325 S Cliff Ave PO Box 5045, Sioux Falls SD 57117 605-322-8000
Web: www.avera.org/mckennan

Avera Queen of Peace Hospital
525 N Foster St, Mitchell SD 57301 605-995-2000 995-2441
TF: 888-531-1685 ■ *Web:* www.avera.org/queen-of-peace

Avera Sacred Heart Hospital 501 Summit, Yankton SD 57078 605-668-8000
Web: www.avera.org/sacred-heart

Avera Saint Luke's Hospital 305 S State St, Aberdeen SD 57401 605-622-5000 622-5127
TF: 800-658-3535 ■ *Web:* www.avera.org/st-lukes-hospital

Huron Regional Medical Ctr (HRMC)
172 Fourth St SE, Huron SD 57350 605-353-6200 353-6300
Web: www.huronregional.org

Mobridge Regional Hospital Inc PO Box 580, Mobridge SD 57601 605-845-3692
Web: www.mobridgehospital.org

Prairie Lakes Hospital & Care Ctr
401 Ninth Ave NW, Watertown SD 57201 605-882-7000 882-7607
TF: 877-917-7547 ■ *Web:* www.prairielakes.com

Rapid City Regional Health
353 Fairmont Blvd, Rapid City SD 57701 605-719-1000 719-8988
Web: www.regionalhealth.com

Sanford USD Medical Ctr 1305 W 18th St, Sioux Falls SD 57117 605-333-1000
Web: www.sanfordhealth.org

Tennessee

Phone | Fax

Athens Regional Medical Ctr
1114 W Madison Ave, Athens TN 37303 423-745-1411
Web: starrregional.com

Baptist Memorial Hospital Memphis
6019 Walnut Grove Rd, Memphis TN 38120 901-226-5000 226-5618
Web: www.baptistonline.org

Baptist Memorial Hospital Union City
1201 Bishop St, Union City TN 38261 731-885-2410 884-8603
TF: 800-344-2470 ■ *Web:* www.baptistonline.org/facilities/unioncity

Blount Memorial Hospital
907 E Lamar Alexander Pkwy, Maryville TN 37804 865-983-7211 980-4868
TF: 800-448-0219 ■ *Web:* www.blountmemorial.org

Bristol Regional Medical Ctr
1 Medical Pk Blvd, Bristol TN 37620 423-844-1121
Web: www.wellmont.org/facilities/bristol/wbrmc/wbrmc.html

Centennial Medical Ctr 2300 Patterson St, Nashville TN 37203 615-342-1000 342-1045
Web: tristarcentennial.com

Claiborne County Hospital & Nursing Home
1850 Old Knoxville Rd, Tazewell TN 37879 423-626-4211
Web: www.claibornehospital.org

Cookeville Regional Medical Ctr (CRMC)
1 Medical Ctr Blvd, Cookeville TN 38501 931-528-2541
Web: www.crmchealth.org

Cumberland Medical Ctr (CMC) 421 S Main St, Crossville TN 38555 931-484-9511
Web: www.cmchealthcare.org

Delta Medical Ctr (DMC) 3000 Getwell Rd, Memphis TN 38118 901-369-8100
Web: www.deltamedcenter.com

Dyersburg Regional Medical Ctr
400 E Tickle St, Dyersburg TN 38024 731-285-2410
Web: www.tennova.com

Erlanger Medical Ctr 975 E Third St, Chattanooga TN 37403 423-778-7000
TF: 877-849-8338 ■ *Web:* www.erlanger.org

Fort Sanders Regional Medical Ctr
1901 W Clinch Ave, Knoxville TN 37916 865-541-1111 541-1262
Web: www.fsregional.com

Gateway Medical Ctr (GMC) 651 Dunlop Ln, Clarksville TN 37040 931-502-1000
Web: www.todaysgateway.com/gateway-medical-center/findadoctor.aspx

Henry County Medical Ctr 301 Tyson Ave, Paris TN 38242 731-642-1220 642-9588
Web: www.hcmc-tn.org

Holston Valley Hospital & Medical Ctr
130 W Ravine Rd, Kingsport TN 37660 423-224-4000
Web: www.wellmont.org

Horizon Medical Ctr 111 Hwy 70 E, Dickson TN 37055 615-446-0446
Web: beta.ehc.com

Indian Path Medical Ctr 2000 Brookside Dr, Kingsport TN 37660 423-857-7000
Web: www.mountainstateshealth.com/ipmc

Jackson-Madison County General Hospital
620 Skyline Dr, Jackson TN 38301 731-541-5000
Web: wth.org

Johnson City Medical Ctr
400 N State of Franklin Rd, Johnson City TN 37604 423-431-6111
Web: www.mountainstateshealth.com

Lakeway Regional Hospital (LRH)
726 McFarland St, Morristown TN 37814 423-522-6000 587-8548

Laughlin Memorial Hospital
1420 Tusculum Blvd, Greeneville TN 37745 423-787-5000 787-5083
TF: 800-852-7157 ■ *Web:* www.laughlinmemorial.org

Livingston Regional Hospital 315 Oak St, Livingston TN 38570 931-823-5611
Web: mylivingstonhospital.com

Maury Regional Hospital 1224 Trotwood Ave, Columbia TN 38401 931-381-1111
Web: www.mauryregional.com

Memorial Hospital 2525 Desales Ave, Chattanooga TN 37404 423-495-2525
Web: www.memorial.org

Memorial North Park Hospital 2051 Hamill Rd, Hixson TN 37343 423-495-7100
Web: www.memorial.org

Methodist Hospital South (MHS) 1300 Wesley Dr, Memphis TN 38116 901-516-3700
Web: www.methodisthealth.org/methodist

Methodist Medical Ctr of Oak Ridge
990 Oak Ridge Tpke, Oak Ridge TN 37831 865-835-1000
Web: www.mmcoakridge.com

Methodist North Hospital
3960 New Covington Pk, Memphis TN 38128 901-516-5200
Web: www.methodisthealth.org

Nashville General Hospital 1818 Albion St, Nashville TN 37208 615-341-4000 341-4493
TF: 800-318-2596 ■ *Web:* nashville.gov/hospital-authority.aspx

Northcrest Medical Ctr 100 Northcrest Dr, Springfield TN 37172 615-384-2411 384-1509
Web: www.northcrest.com

Parkridge East Hospital
941 Spring Creek Rd, Chattanooga TN 37412 423-894-7870 855-3648
TF: 800-605-1527 ■ *Web:* www.parkridgeeasthospital.com

Parkridge Medical Ctr 2333 McCallie Ave, Chattanooga TN 37404 423-698-6061 493-1208
Web: www.parkridgemedicalcenter.com

Parkwest Medical Ctr 9352 Pk W Blvd, Knoxville TN 37923 865-373-1000 373-1012
Web: www.treatedwell.com

Premier Medical Group Pc
1850 Business Pk Dr PO Box 3799, Clarksville TN 37043 931-245-7000
Web: www.premiermed.com

Regional Medical Ctr at Memphis
877 Jefferson Ave, Memphis TN 38103 901-545-7100 545-7037
Web: www.regionalonehealth.org

Roane Medical Ctr 412 Devonia St, Harriman TN 37748 865-882-1323
Web: www.covenanthealth.com

Saint Francis Hospital 5959 Pk Ave, Memphis TN 38119 901-765-1000
Web: www.saintfrancishosp.com/en-us/pages/default.aspx

Saint Thomas Hospital 4220 HaRding Rd, Nashville TN 37205 615-222-2111 222-6502
TF: 800-400-5800 ■ *Web:* www.sthealth.com

Skyline Madison Campus 500 Hospital Dr, Madison TN 37115 615-769-5000
Web: tristarskylinemadison.com

Skyline Medical Ctr 3441 Dickerson Pike, Nashville TN 37207 615-769-2000
TF: 800-242-5662 ■ *Web:* tristarskyline.com

Summit Medical Ctr 5655 Frist Blvd, Hermitage TN 37076 615-316-3000 316-4912
Web: tristarsummit.com

Takoma Regional Hospital 401 Takoma Ave, Greeneville TN 37743 423-639-3151 636-2374
Web: www.takoma.org

Tristar Southern Hills Medical Ctr
391 Wallace Rd, Nashville TN 37211 615-781-4000
TF: 800-242-5662 ■ *Web:* tristarsouthernhills.com

Vanderbilt University Medical Ctr
1215 21st Ave S, Nashville TN 37232 615-322-5000 343-7317
TF: 877-936-8422 ■ *Web:* www.mc.vanderbilt.edu

Williamson Medical Ctr (WMC)
4321 Carothers Pkwy, Franklin TN 37067 615-435-5000
Web: www.williamsonmedicalcenter.org

Texas

Phone | Fax

Abilene Regional Medical Ctr
6250 S Hwy 83-84, Abilene TX 79606 325-428-1000 795-2113
Web: www.abileneregional.com

Arlington Memorial Hospital
800 W Randol Mill Rd, Arlington TX 76012 817-960-6100
Web: www.texashealth.org

Baptist Medical Ctr 111 Dallas St, San Antonio TX 78205 210-297-7000
TF: 866-309-2873 ■ *Web:* www.baptisthealthsystem.com

Baylor All Saints Medical Ctr
1400 Eigth Ave, Fort Worth TX 76104 817-926-2544 927-6226
Web: baylorhealth.com

Baylor Medical Center (TMC) 4343 N Josey Ln, Carrollton TX 75010 972-492-1010 394-4783

Baylor Medical Ctr at Garland
2300 Marie Curie Blvd, Garland TX 75042 972-487-5000
Web: baylorhealth.com

Baylor Medical Ctr at Irving
1901 N MacArthur Blvd, Irving TX 75061 972-579-8100 579-5254
Web: www.baylorhealth.com/physicianslocations/irving

Baylor Regional Medical Ctr at Grapevine
1650 W College St, Grapevine TX 76051 817-481-1588
TF: 800-422-9567 ■ *Web:* www.baylorhealth.com

Baylor University Medical Ctr at Dallas
3500 Gaston Ave, Dallas TX 75246 214-820-0111
Web: www.baylorhealth.com

Bayshore Medical Ctr 4000 Spencer Hwy, Pasadena TX 77504 713-359-2000 359-1004
TF: 800-465-4837 ■ *Web:* www.bayshoremedical.com

Ben Taub General Hospital 1504 Taub Loop, Houston TX 77030 713-873-2000
Web: www.harrishealth.org

Brackenridge Hospital 601 E 15th St, Austin TX 78701 512-324-7000
Web: www.seton.net

Brazosport Regional Health System (BRHS)
100 Medical Dr, Lake Jackson TX 77566 979-297-4411 285-1203
Web: brazosportregional.org

Hospital	City	State	ZIP	Phone	Fax
Brownwood Regional Medical Ctr 1501 Burnet Dr *Web:* www.brmc-cares.com	Brownwood	TX	76801	325-646-8541	
Central Texas Medical Ctr (CTMC) 1301 Wonder World Dr *TF:* 800-927-9004 ■ *Web:* www.ctmc.org	San Marcos	TX	78666	512-353-8979	753-3598
CHRISTUS Bossier Medical Ctr 4241 Woodcock Dr Ste A-100 *Web:* www.christushealth.org	San Antonio	TX	78228	210-785-5200	
CHRISTUS Hospital - St Elizabeth 2830 Calder St *TF:* 866-683-3627 ■ *Web:* christussetx.org	Beaumont	TX	77702	409-892-7171	924-3959
CHRISTUS Saint Mary Hospital 3600 Gates Blvd PO Box 3696 *TF:* 866-683-3627 ■ *Web:* christussetx.org	Port Arthur	TX	77642	409-985-7431	989-1033
CHRISTUS Saint Michael Health System 2600 St Michael Dr *Web:* www.christusstmichael.org	Texarkana	TX	75503	903-614-1000	614-2212
CHRISTUS Santa Rosa Hospital 333 N Santa Rosa St *Web:* www.christussantarosa.org	San Antonio	TX	78207	210-704-2011	704-3632
CHRISTUS Spohn Hospital Corpus Christi Shoreline 600 Elizabeth St *Web:* www.christushealth.org	Corpus Christi	TX	78404	361-881-3640	
CHRISTUS Spohn Hospital Corpus Christi-South 5950 Saratoga Blvd *Web:* www.christusspohn.org	Corpus Christi	TX	78414	361-985-5000	
CHRISTUS Spohn Hospital Kleberg 1311 General Cavazos Blvd *Web:* www.christusspohn.org	Kingsville	TX	78363	361-595-1661	
CHRISTUS Spohn Hospital Memorial 2606 Hospital Blvd *Web:* www.christusspohn.org	Corpus Christi	TX	78405	361-902-4000	
Citizens Medical Ctr 2701 Hospital Dr *Web:* citizensmedicalcenter.org	Victoria	TX	77901	361-573-9181	572-5070
Clear Lake Regional Medical Ctr 500 W Medical Ctr Blvd *Web:* www.clearlakermc.com	Webster	TX	77598	281-332-2511	338-3352
Cleveland Regional Medical Ctr 300 E Crockett St *Web:* www.clevelandregionalmedicalcenter.org	Cleveland	TX	77327	281-593-1811	
College Station Medical Ctr 1604 Rock Prairie Rd *Web:* www.csmedcenter.com	College Station	TX	77845	979-764-5100	696-7373
Conroe Regional Medical Ctr 504 Medical Ctr Blvd *TF:* 888-633-2687 ■ *Web:* www.conroeregional.com	Conroe	TX	77304	936-539-1111	
Corpus Christi Medical Ctr 13725 NW Blvd *Web:* www.ccmedicalcenter.com	Corpus Christi	TX	78410	361-761-1000	
Corpus Christi Medical Ctr Bay Area 13725 NW Blvd *Web:* www.ccmedicalcenter.com	Corpus Christi	TX	78412	361-761-1000	
Covenant Medical Ctr 3615 19th St *Web:* www.covenanthealth.org	Lubbock	TX	79410	806-725-0000	
Cypress Fairbanks Medical Ctr 10655 Steepletop Dr *Web:* www.cyfairhospital.com	Houston	TX	77065	281-890-4285	890-5341
Dallas Medical Center 7 Medical Pkwy *Web:* www.dallasmedcenter.com	Dallas	TX	75234	972-888-7000	888-7090
Dallas Regional Medical Ctr (DRMC) 1011 N Galloway Ave **Fax Area Code:* 972 ■ *Web:* www.dallasregionalmedicalcenter.com	Mesquite	TX	75149	214-320-7000	289-9468*
Del Sol Medical Ctr 10301 Gateway W *Web:* www.laspalmasdelsolhealthcare.com/locations-facilities/del-sol-medical-center.aspx	El Paso	TX	79925	915-595-9000	
Denton Regional Medical Ctr 3535 S I-35 E *Web:* www.dentonregional.com	Denton	TX	76210	940-384-3535	384-4702
Detar Hospital Navarro 506 E San Antonio St *Web:* www.detar.com	Victoria	TX	77901	361-575-7441	
Detar Hospital North 101 Medical Dr *Web:* www.detar.com	Victoria	TX	77904	361-573-6100	
Doctors Hospital at White Rock Lake 9440 Poppy Dr *TF:* 866-893-8446 ■ *Web:* www.baylorhealth.com/physicianslocations/whiterock/pages/default.aspx	Dallas	TX	75218	214-820-0111	324-0612
Doctors Hospital of Laredo 10700 McPherson Rd *TF:* 844-244-4874 ■ *Web:* www.doctorshosplaredo.com	Laredo	TX	78045	956-523-2000	523-0444
East Houston Regional Medical Ctr 13111 E Fwy *Web:* www.easthoustonrmc.com	Houston	TX	77015	713-393-2000	
East Texas Medical Ctr Athens 2000 S Palestine St *Web:* www.etmc.org	Athens	TX	75751	903-676-1000	
East Texas Medical Ctr Tyler 1000 S Beckham Ave *Web:* www.etmc.org	Tyler	TX	75701	903-597-0351	535-6334
Edinburg Regional Medical Ctr (ERMC) 1102 W Trenton Rd *TF:* 800-465-5585 ■ *Web:* www.southtexashealthsystem.com	Edinburg	TX	78539	956-388-6000	
Fort Duncan Regional Medical Ctr 3333 N Foster Maldonado Blvd **Fax:* Admissions ■ *Web:* www.fortduncanmedicalcenter.com	Eagle Pass	TX	78852	830-773-5321	872-2549*
Good Shepherd Medical Ctr 700 E Marshall Ave *Web:* www.gsmc.org	Longview	TX	75601	903-315-2000	315-2479
Gulf Coast Medical Ctr (GCMC) 10141 US 59 Rd *Web:* www.gulfcoastmedical.com	Wharton	TX	77488	979-532-2500	282-6190
Harris Methodist Fort Worth 1301 Pennsylvania Ave *Web:* www.texashealth.org	Fort Worth	TX	76104	817-882-2000	
Harris Methodist-HEB 1600 Hospital Pkwy *Web:* www.texashealth.org	Bedford	TX	76022	817-848-4000	
Hendrick Health System 1900 Pine St *Web:* www.hendrickhealth.org	Abilene	TX	79601	325-670-2000	670-4417

Hospital	City	State	ZIP	Phone	Fax
Hillcrest Baptist Medical Ctr 3000 Herring Ave *TF:* 800-793-6030 ■ *Web:* sw.org/location/waco-hillcrest-hospital	Waco	TX	76708	254-202-2000	
Houston Northwest Medical Ctr 710 FM 1960 W *Web:* www.hnmc.com	Houston	TX	77090	281-440-1000	440-2666
Huguley Memorial Medical Ctr 11801 S Fwy *Web:* www.texashealthhuguley.org	Burleson	TX	76028	817-293-9110	568-1298
Hunt Regional Healthcare 4215 Joe Ramsey Blvd *TF:* 855-854-2283 ■ *Web:* www.huntregional.org	Greenville	TX	75401	903-408-5000	408-1669
Huntsville Memorial Hospital 110 Memorial Hospital Dr *Web:* www.huntsvillememorial.com	Huntsville	TX	77340	936-291-3411	
John Peter Smith Hospital 1500 S Main St *Web:* www.jpshealthnet.org	Fort Worth	TX	76104	817-921-3431	
Kingwood Medical Ctr 22999 US Hwy 59 *Web:* www.kingwoodmedical.com	Kingwood	TX	77339	281-348-8000	
Knapp Medical Ctr (KMC) 1401 E Eigth St PO Box 1110 *Web:* www.knappmed.org	Weslaco	TX	78596	956-968-8567	968-0764
Laredo Medical Ctr (LMC) 1700 E Saunders Ave *Web:* www.laredomedical.com	Laredo	TX	78041	956-796-5000	
Las Colinas Medical Ctr 6800 N MacArthur Blvd *Web:* www.lascolinasmedical.com	Irving	TX	75039	972-969-2000	969-2080
Las Palmas Medical Ctr 1801 N Oregon St *Web:* www.laspalmasdelsolhealthcare.com	El Paso	TX	79902	915-521-1200	
Live centre speciality 1111 Gallagher Dr	Sherman	TX	75090	903-870-7000	
Longview Regional Medical Ctr 2901 N Fourth St *Web:* www.longviewregional.com	Longview	TX	75605	903-758-1818	
Mainland Medical Ctr 6801 Emmett Lowry Expy *Web:* www.mainlandmedical.com	Texas City	TX	77591	409-938-5000	
McAllen Medical Ctr 301 W Expy 83 *Web:* www.southtexashealthsystem.com	McAllen	TX	78503	956-632-4000	
Medical City Hospital 7777 Forest Ln *Web:* www.medicalcityhospital.com	Dallas	TX	75230	972-566-7000	566-6560
Medical Ctr Hospital (MCH) 500 W Fourth St *Web:* www.medicalcenterhealthsystem.com	Odessa	TX	79761	432-640-6000	
Medical Ctr of Arlington (MCA) 3301 Matlock Rd *Web:* www.medicalcenterarlington.com	Arlington	TX	76015	817-465-3241	472-4878
Medical Ctr of Lewisville 500 W Main St *Web:* www.lewisvillemedical.com	Lewisville	TX	75057	972-420-1000	
Medical Ctr of McKinney 4500 Medical Ctr Dr *Web:* www.medicalcenterofmckinney.com/home	McKinney	TX	75069	972-569-8000	
Medical Ctr of Plano, The 3901 W 15th St *Web:* www.themedicalcenterofplano.com	Plano	TX	75075	972-596-6800	
Medical Ctr of Southeast Texas, The 2555 Jimmy Johnson Blvd *Web:* www.medicalcentersetexas.com	Port Arthur	TX	77640	409-724-7389	
Memorial Hermann - Texas Medical Ctr 6411 Fannin St *Web:* www.memorialhermann.org	Houston	TX	77030	713-704-4000	
Memorial Hermann Katy Hospital 23900 Katy Fwy *Web:* memorialhermann.org/locations	Katy	TX	77494	281-644-7000	644-7280
Memorial Hermann Memorial City Hospital 921 Gessner Rd **Fax Area Code:* 281 ■ *TF:* 800-526-2121 ■ *Web:* www.memorialhermann.org	Houston	TX	77024	713-242-3000	359-3340*
Memorial Hermann Southwest Hospital 7600 Beechnut St *Web:* www.memorialhermann.org	Houston	TX	77074	713-456-5000	
Methodist Charlton Medical Ctr 3500 W Wheatland Rd *Web:* methodisthealthsystem.org	Dallas	TX	75237	214-947-7777	
Methodist Dallas Medical Ctr 1441 N Beckley Ave *Web:* www.methodisthealthsystem.org	Dallas	TX	75203	214-947-8181	947-3403
Methodist Hospital 6565 Fannin St *Web:* www.houstonmethodist.org	Houston	TX	77030	713-790-3311	441-7465
Methodist Hospital 8109 Fredericksburg Rd *TF:* 800-333-7333 ■ *Web:* sahealth.com	San Antonio	TX	78229	210-575-0355	575-6292
Methodist Hospital System, The 6447 Main St *Web:* www.houstonmethodist.org	Houston	TX	77030	713-790-3333	
Methodist Richardson Medical Ctr 401 W Campbell Rd *Web:* methodisthealthsystem.org	Richardson	TX	75080	972-498-4000	
Metroplex Hospital 2201 S Clear Creek Rd *TF:* 800-926-7664 ■ *Web:* www.mplex.org	Killeen	TX	76549	254-526-7523	526-3483
Metropolitan Methodist Hospital 1310 McCullough Ave *Web:* sahealth.com	San Antonio	TX	78212	210-757-2200	
Midland Memorial Hospital 2200 W Illinois Ave *TF:* 800-833-2916 ■ *Web:* www.midland-memorial.com	Midland	TX	79701	432-685-1111	685-4970
Mission Regional Medical Ctr 900 S Bryan Rd *Web:* www.missionhospital.com	Mission	TX	78572	956-323-9000	323-1360
Mother Frances Hospital 800 E Dawson St *Web:* tmfhc.org	Tyler	TX	75701	903-593-8441	525-1201
Nacogdoches Medical Ctr 4920 NE Stallings Dr *TF:* 866-898-8446 ■ *Web:* www.nacmedicalcenter.com	Nacogdoches	TX	75965	936-569-9481	568-3400
Nacogdoches Memorial Hospital 1204 N Mound St *Web:* www.nacmem.org	Nacogdoches	TX	75961	936-564-4611	568-8588
Navarro Regional Hospital (NRH) 3201 W Hwy 22 *Web:* www.navarrohospital.com	Corsicana	TX	75110	903-654-6800	
Nix Medical Ctr 414 Navarro St *Web:* www.nixhealth.com	San Antonio	TX	78205	210-271-1800	
North Hills Hospital 4401 Booth Calloway Rd *Web:* www.northhillshospital.com	North Richland Hills	TX	76180	817-255-1000	

Phone Fax

Northeast Baptist Hospital
8811 Village Dr. San Antonio TX 78217 210-297-2000 297-0200
Web: www.baptisthealthsystem.com

Northeast Medical Ctr Hospital
18951 Memorial N Humble TX 77338 281-540-7700
Web: www.memorialhermann.org

Northeast Methodist Hospital
12412 Judson Rd San Antonio TX 78233 210-757-7000
Web: www.sahealth.com

Northwest Texas Hospital 1501 S Coulter Amarillo TX 79106 806-354-1000 354-1122
TF: 800-887-1114 ■ *Web:* www.nwths.com

OakBend Medical Ctr 1705 Jackson St Richmond TX 77469 281-341-3000 341-3056
Web: www.oakbendmedcenter.org

Palestine Regional Medical Ctr
2900 S Loop 256 Palestine TX 75801 903-731-1000 731-2236
TF: 800-222-1222 ■ *Web:* www.palestineregional.com

Pampa Regional Medical Ctr 1 Medical Plz Pampa TX 79065 806-665-3721
Web: www.prmctx.com

Paris Regional Medical Ctr 820 Clarksville St. Paris TX 75460 903-785-4521
Web: www.parisregionalmedical.com

Parkland Health & Hospital System
5201 Harry Hines Blvd Dallas TX 75235 214-590-8000
Web: www.parklandhospital.com

Peterson Regional Medical Ctr
551 Hill Country Dr Kerrville TX 78028 830-896-4200
Web: www.petersonrmc.com

Plaza Medical Ctr 900 Eigth Ave Fort Worth TX 76104 817-877-5292 347-1989
Web: www.plazamedicalcenter.com

Presbyterian Hospital of Dallas
8200 Walnut Hill Ln Dallas TX 75231 214-345-6789
Web: www.texashealth.org

Providence Healthcare Network 6901 Medical Pkwy Waco TX 76712 254-751-4000 751-4769
Web: www.providence.net

Rio Grande Regional Hospital 101 E Ridge Rd McAllen TX 78503 956-632-6000
Web: www.riohealth.com

Saint David's Medical Ctr 919 E 32nd St Austin TX 78705 512-476-7111
Web: www.stdavids.com

Saint Joseph Medical Ctr 1401 St Joseph Pkwy Houston TX 77002 713-757-1000 657-7123
Web: www.sjmctx.com

Saint Joseph Regional Health Ctr
2801 Franciscan Dr Bryan TX 77802 979-776-3777
Web: www.st-joseph.org

San Angelo Community Medical Ctr
3501 Knickerbocker Rd San Angelo TX 76904 325-949-9511 947-6550
Web: www.sacmc.com

San Jacinto Methodist Hospital (SJMH)
4401 Garth Rd Baytown TX 77521 281-420-8600 420-8672*
**Fax:* Admitting ■ *Web:* www.houstonmethodist.org

Scott & White Memorial Hospital
2401 S 31st St Temple TX 76508 254-724-2111 724-2786
TF: 800-792-3710 ■ *Web:* www.sw.org

Seton Medical Ctr 1201 W 38th St. Austin TX 78705 512-324-1000
Web: www.seton.net

Shannon Medical Ctr (SMC) 120 E Harris Ave San Angelo TX 76903 325-653-6741 658-8295
TF: 800-368-1019 ■ *Web:* www.shannonhealth.com

Southwest General Hospital (SGH)
7400 Barlite Blvd San Antonio TX 78224 210-921-2000 921-3508
TF: 877-898-6080 ■ *Web:* www.swgeneralhospital.com

Southwestern University Hospital
5151 Harry Hines Blvd Dallas TX 75390 214-645-5555
Web: www.utswmedicine.org

St. David's Round Rock Medical Ctr
2400 Round Rock Ave Round Rock TX 78681 512-341-1000 238-1799
Web: www.stdavids.com

Texas Health Presbyterian Hospital Denton
3000 N I-35 Denton TX 76201 940-898-7000 898-7071
Web: www.texashealth.org

Texas Health Presbyterian Hospital-WNJ Therapy Services
500 N Highland Ave Sherman TX 75092 903-870-4611 870-4409
Web: www.wnj.org

Texas Healthcare PLLC
2821 Lackland Rd Ste 300 Fort Worth TX 76116 817-378-3640 740-8516
TF: 877-238-6200 ■ *Web:* www.txhealthcare.com

Texoma Medical Ctr 5016 S US Hwy 75 Denison TX 75020 903-416-4000
Web: www.texomamedicalcenter.net

Titus Regional Medical Ctr
2001 N Jefferson Ave Mount Pleasant TX 75455 903-577-6000
Web: www.titusregional.com

Tomball Regional Hospital (TRMC)
605 Holderrieth St Tomball TX 77375 281-401-7500
Web: www.tomballregionalmedicalcenter.com

United Regional Hospital
Eighth Street Campus
1600 11th St 2nd Fl. Wichita Falls TX 76301 940-764-7000 766-8711
Web: www.unitedregional.org

University Hospital 4502 Medical Dr San Antonio TX 78229 210-358-4000 358-5936
TF: 866-864-5226 ■ *Web:* www.universityhealthsystem.com

University Medical Ctr 602 Indiana Ave Lubbock TX 79415 806-775-8200
Web: www.umchealthsystem.com

University Medical Ctr of El Paso (UMCEP)
4815 Alameda Ave El Paso TX 79905 915-544-1200
Web: www.umcelpaso.org

University of Texas Health Ctr at Tyler (UTHCT)
11937 US Hwy 271 Tyler TX 75708 903-877-7777
Web: www.uthealth.org

University of Texas Medical Branch Hospitals
301 University Blvd Galveston TX 77555 409-772-1011 772-5119
TF: 800-201-0527 ■ *Web:* www.utmb.edu

Valley Baptist Medical Ctr Brownsville
1040 W Jefferson St Brownsville TX 78520 956-698-5400 541-0712*
**Fax:* Hum Res ■ *TF:* 855-720-7448 ■ *Web:* www.valleybaptist.net/brownsville

Valley Baptist Medical Ctr Harlingen
2101 Pease St. Harlingen TX 78550 956-389-1100 389-1632
Web: www.valleybaptist.net

Valley Regional Medical Ctr
100-A E Alton Gloor Blvd Brownsville TX 78526 956-350-7000
TF: 877-813-6455 ■ *Web:* www.valleyregionalmedicalcenter.com

Wadley Regional Medical Ctr 1000 Pine St. Texarkana TX 75501 903-798-8000 798-8030
Web: www.wadleyhealth.com

West Houston Medical Ctr 12141 Richmond Ave. Houston TX 77082 281-558-3444
Web: westhoustonmedical.com

Woodland Heights Medical Ctr
505 S John Redditt Dr Lufkin TX 75904 936-634-8311 637-8600
TF: 800-222-1222 ■ *Web:* www.woodlandheights.net

Zale Lipshy University Hospital
5151 Harry Hines Blvd Dallas TX 75390 214-645-5555
Web: www.utsouthwestern.edu

Utah

Phone Fax

Alta View Hospital 9660 South 1300 Eest Sandy UT 84094 801-501-2600
Web: www.intermountainhealthcare.org/xp/public/altaview

American Fork Hospital
170 North 1100 East American Fork UT 84003 801-763-3300 855-3548
Web: www.intermountainhealthcare.org

Davis Hospital & Medical Ctr (DHMC)
1600 W Antelope Dr Layton UT 84041 801-807-1000 807-7610
TF: 877-898-6080 ■ *Web:* www.davishospital.com

Intermountain Healthcare Logan Regional Hospital
500 E 1400 N Logan UT 84341 435-716-1000 716-5409
TF: 800-442-4845 ■ *Web:* www.intermountainhealthcare.org

Jordan Valley Medical Center
3460 S Pioneer Pkwy West Valley City UT 84120 801-964-3100 964-3279

Lakeview Hospital 630 E Medical Dr Bountiful UT 84010 801-299-2200
Web: www.lakeviewhospital.com

LDS Hospital 8th Ave & C St Salt Lake City UT 84143 801-408-1100 408-1665
TF: 888-301-3880 ■ *Web:* intermountainhealthcare.org

McKay-Dee Hospital Ctr 4401 Harrison Blvd Ogden UT 84403 801-627-2800
Web: www.intermountainhealthcare.org/hospitals/mckaydee/pages/home.aspx

Mountain View Hospital 1000 East 100 North Payson UT 84651 801-465-7000 465-7170
TF: 877-865-9738 ■ *Web:* www.mvhpayson.com

Ogden Regional Medical Ctr 5475 Adams Ave Pkwy Ogden UT 84405 801-479-2111
TF: 877-870-3745 ■ *Web:* www.ogdenregional.com

Saint Mark's Hospital
1200 East 3900 South Salt Lake City UT 84124 801-268-7111
Web: www.stmarkshospital.com

Salt Lake Regional Medical Ctr
1050 East South Temple Salt Lake City UT 84102 801-350-4111 350-4522
Web: www.saltlakeregional.com

University of Utah Hospital & Clinics
50 N Medical Dr Salt Lake City UT 84132 801-581-2121 585-5280
Web: healthcare.utah.edu

Utah Valley Regional Medical Ctr 1034 N 500 W Provo UT 84604 801-373-7850 357-7780
Web: www.intermountainhealthcare.org/xp/public/uvrmc

Vermont

Phone Fax

Brattleboro Memorial Hospital Inc
17 Belmont Ave Ste 1 Brattleboro VT 05301 802-257-0341 257-8822
TF: 866-972-5266 ■ *Web:* www.bmhvt.org

Central Vermont Medical Ctr (CVMC) 130 Fisher Rd. Berlin VT 05602 802-371-4100
Web: www.cvmc.org

Copley Hospital Inc 528 Washington Hwy Morrisville VT 05661 802-888-8888
TF: 888-833-8329 ■ *Web:* www.copleyvt.org

Rutland Regional Medical Ctr 160 Allen St. Rutland VT 05701 802-775-7111 747-1620
Web: www.rrmc.org

Southwestern Vermont Medical Ctr
100 Hospital Dr Bennington VT 05201 802-442-6361 447-5013
TF: 800-422-6237 ■ *Web:* www.svhealthcare.org/hospital

Springfield Hospital
25 Ridgewood Rd PO Box 2003 Springfield VT 05156 802-885-2151 885-7357
Web: www.springfieldhospital.org

University of Vermont Medical Center, The (FAHC)
111 Colchester Ave. Burlington VT 05401 802-847-0000 656-2790
TF: 800-358-1144 ■ *Web:* www.uvmhealth.org/medcenter/pages/default.aspx

Virginia

Phone Fax

Alleghany Regional Hospital 1 ARH Ln Low Moor VA 24457 540-862-6879
Web: lewisgale.com/locations/lewisgale-hospital-alleghany/index.dot

Augusta Medical Ctr (AMC)
78 Medical Ctr Dr PO Box 1000 Fishersville VA 22939 540-932-4000
TF: 800-932-0262 ■ *Web:* www.augustahealth.com

Bon Secours DePaul Medical Ctr
150 Kingsley Ln Norfolk VA 23505 757-889-5112
Web: bshr.com

Bon Secours Maryview Medical Ctr
3636 High St Portsmouth VA 23707 757-398-4444
Web: bshr.com/facilities/maryview.html

Bon Secours Memorial Regional Medical Ctr
8260 Atlee Rd Mechanicsville VA 23116 804-764-6000 764-6420
TF: 888-455-3766 ■ *Web:* richmond.bonsecours.com

Bon Secours Saint Mary's Hospital
5801 Bremo Rd Richmond VA 23226 804-285-2011 559-0356
TF: 877-342-1500 ■ *Web:* richmond.bonsecours.com

Buchanan General Hospital (BGH)
1535 Slate Creek Rd Grundy VA 24614 276-935-1000 935-1354
Web: www.bgh.org

Carilion New River Valley Medical Ctr
2900 Lamb Cir Christiansburg VA 24073 540-731-2000 731-2505
TF: 800-432-7874 ■ *Web:* www.carilionclinic.org

Carilion Roanoke Community Hospital (CRCH)
101 Elm Ave SE Roanoke VA 24013 540-985-8000
Web: carilionclinic.org

				Phone	Fax
Carilion Roanoke Memorial Hospital 1906 Belleview Ave. *Web:* www.carilionclinic.org	Roanoke	VA	24014	540-981-7000	
Chesapeake Regional Medical Ctr 736 Battlefield Blvd N. *TF:* 800-456-8121 ■ *Web:* www.chesapeakeregional.com	Chesapeake	VA	23320	757-312-8121	312-6154
CJW Medical Ctr 7101 Jahnke Rd *TF:* 800-468-6620 ■ *Web:* hcavirginia.com	Richmond	VA	23225	804-320-3911	323-8049
Community Memorial Healthcenter 412 Bracey Ln. *Web:* vcu-cmh.org	South Hill	VA	23970	434-447-3151	
Danville Regional Medical Ctr 142 S Main St. *TF:* 800-688-3762 ■ *Web:* danvilleregional.com	Danville	VA	24541	434-799-2100	
Fauquier Hospital 500 Hospital Dr. *Web:* www.fauquierhealth.org	Warrenton	VA	20186	540-316-5000	
Halifax Regional Health System (HRHS) 2204 Wilborn Ave. *Web:* www.sentara.com/halifax-southern-virginia/hospitalslocations/locations/sentara-halifax-regional-hospital.aspx	South Boston	VA	24592	434-517-3100	517-3626
Henrico Doctor's Hospital 1602 Skipwith Rd *Web:* hcavirginia.com	Richmond	VA	23229	804-289-4500	289-4801
Inova Alexandria Hospital 4320 Seminary Rd *Web:* www.inova.org	Alexandria	VA	22304	703-504-3000	
Inova Fair Oaks Hospital 3600 Joseph Siewick Dr. *Web:* www.inova.org	Fairfax	VA	22033	703-391-3600	391-3273
Inova Fairfax Hospital 3300 Gallows Rd. *Web:* www.inova.org	Falls Church	VA	22042	703-776-4001	776-6128
Inova Mount Vernon Hospital 2501 Parkers Ln. *Web:* www.inova.org	Alexandria	VA	22306	703-664-7000	
John Randolph Medical Ctr 411 W Randolph Rd. *Web:* hcavirginia.com	Hopewell	VA	23860	804-541-1600	452-3699
Lewis-Gale Medical Ctr 1900 Electric Rd *Web:* lewisgale.com	Salem	VA	24153	540-776-4000	953-5372
Lynchburg General Hospital 1901 Tate Springs Rd. *Web:* web.lynchburgchamber.org	Lynchburg	VA	24501	434-947-3000	
Martha Jefferson Hospital (MJH) 500 Martha Jefferson Dr. *TF:* 888-652-6663 ■ *Web:* www.sentara.com/charlottesville-virginia/hospitalslocations/locations/martha-jefferson-hospital.aspx	Charlottesville	VA	22902	434-654-7000	
Mary Immaculate Hospital 2 Bernardine Dr *Web:* www.bonsecours.com/hampton-roads	Newport News	VA	23602	757-886-6000	
Mary Washington Hospital 1001 Sam Perry Blvd *TF:* 800-395-2455 ■ *Web:* www.marywashingtonhealthcare.com	Fredericksburg	VA	22401	540-741-1100	310-0100
Memorial Hospital 320 Hospital Dr *Web:* www.martinsvillehospital.com	Martinsville	VA	24115	276-666-7200	666-7600
Montgomery Regional Hospital 3700 S Main St. *Web:* lewisgale.com	Blacksburg	VA	24060	540-951-1111	953-5372
Prince William Hospital 8700 Sudly Rd *Web:* novanthealth.org/princewilliammedicalcenter.aspx	Manassas	VA	20110	703-369-8000	396-5297
Reston Hospital Ctr 1850 Town Ctr Pkwy *TF General:* 888-327-8882 ■ *Web:* www.restonhospital.com	Reston	VA	20190	703-689-9000	
Retreat Hospital 2621 Grove Ave. *TF:* 800-888-3627 ■ *Web:* hcavirginia.com	Richmond	VA	23220	804-254-5100	254-5187
Riverside Regional Medical Ctr 500 J Clyde Morris Blvd. *Web:* riversideonline.com	Newport News	VA	23601	757-594-2000	594-2084
Sentara Careplex Hospital 3000 Colliseum Dr. *TF:* 800-736-8272 ■ *Web:* www.sentara.com	Hampton	VA	23666	757-736-1000	
Sentara Leigh Hospital 830 Kempsville Rd. *Web:* www.sentara.com/hospitals	Norfolk	VA	23502	757-261-6000	
Sentara Norfolk General Hospital 600 Gresham Dr Ste 8630 *Web:* www.sentara.com/hospitals	Norfolk	VA	23507	757-388-6105	388-6106
Sentara Obici Hospital 2800 Godwin Blvd *TF:* 800-736-8272 ■ *Web:* www.sentara.com	Suffolk	VA	23434	757-934-4000	934-4284
Sentara Virginia Beach General Hospital 1060 First Colonial Rd *TF:* 800-736-8272 ■ *Web:* www.sentara.com/hospitals	Virginia Beach	VA	23454	757-395-8000	
Sentara Williamsburg Regional Medical Ctr 100 Sentara Cir. *Web:* www.sentara.com	Williamsburg	VA	23188	757-984-6000	
Shore Memorial Hospital 9507 Hospital Ave PO Box 17. *TF:* 800-834-7035 ■ *Web:* www.riversideonline.com/shore	Nassawadox	VA	23413	757-414-8000	414-8633
Smyth County Community Hospital 565 Radio Hill Rd. *Web:* www.mountainstateshealth.com/scch	Marion	VA	24354	276-378-1000	
Southampton Memorial Hospital 100 Fairview Dr *Web:* www.smhfranklin.com	Franklin	VA	23851	757-569-6100	
Southside Community Hospital (SCH) 800 Oak St *Web:* sch.centrahealth.com	Farmville	VA	23901	434-392-8811	392-7654
Southside Regional Medical Ctr 200 Medical Park Blvd *Web:* www.srmconline.com	Petersburg	VA	23805	804-765-5000	
Tidewater Physicians Multispecialty Group PC 860 Omni Blvd Ste 304. *Web:* mytpmg.com	Newport News	VA	23606	757-232-8764	232-8865
Twin County Regional Hospital 200 Hospital Dr. *TF:* 800-295-3342 ■ *Web:* www.tcrh.org	Galax	VA	24333	276-236-8181	
University of Virginia Health System 1215 Lee St *TF:* 800-251-3627 ■ *Web:* www.healthsystem.virginia.edu/toplevel/home/home.cfm	Charlottesville	VA	22908	434-924-0211	982-3759
UVA Culpeper Hospital 501 Sunset Ln *TF:* 866-608-4749 ■ *Web:* www.uvaculpeperhospital.com	Culpeper	VA	22701	540-829-4100	
Virginia Baptist Hospital 3300 Rivermont Ave *TF:* 866-749-4455 ■ *Web:* www.centrahealth.com	Lynchburg	VA	24503	434-947-4000	
Virginia Hospital Ctr 1701 N George Mason Dr. *Web:* www.virginiahospitalcenter.com	Arlington	VA	22205	703-558-5000	
Winchester Medical Ctr 1840 Amherst St *Web:* www.valleyhealthlink.com	Winchester	VA	22601	540-536-8000	

Washington

				Phone	Fax
Auburn Regional Medical Ctr 202 N Div St Plaza 1 *TF:* 866-268-7223 ■ *Web:* www.multicare.org	Auburn	WA	98001	253-833-7711	697-7293
Capital Medical Ctr 3900 Capital Mall Dr SW *TF:* 888-677-9757 ■ *Web:* www.capitalmedical.com	Olympia	WA	98502	360-754-5858	956-2574
Deaconess Medical Ctr 800 W Fifth Ave. *Web:* www.deaconessspokane.com	Spokane	WA	99204	509-458-5800	
Evergreen Hospital Medical Ctr 12040 NE 128th St *Web:* www.evergreenhealth.com	Kirkland	WA	98034	425-899-1000	899-2624
Good Samaritan Hospital (GSH) 407 14th Ave SE *Web:* www.multicare.org/goodsam	Puyallup	WA	98372	253-697-4000	
Grays Harbor Community Hospital 920 Anderson Dr *Web:* www.ghchwa.org	Aberdeen	WA	98520	360-532-5122	
Harrison Memorial Hospital 2520 Cherry Ave *TF:* 866-844-9355 ■ *Web:* www.harrisonhospital.org	Bremerton	WA	98310	360-377-3911	792-6503
Highline Medical Ctr 16251 Sylvester Rd SW *Web:* www.chifranciscan.org/highline-medical-center	Burien	WA	98166	206-244-9970	246-5385
Kadlec Regional Medical Ctr 888 Swift Blvd. *TF:* 800-780-6067 ■ *Web:* www.kadlec.org	Richland	WA	99352	509-946-4611	942-2679
Kennewick General Hospital (KGH) 900 S Auburn St. *Web:* www.trioshealth.org	Kennewick	WA	99336	509-586-6111	586-5892
Legacy Salmon Creek Hospital 2211 NE 139th St *TF:* 877-270-5566 ■ *Web:* www.legacyhealth.org	Vancouver	WA	98686	360-487-1000	487-3459
Lourdes Medical Ctr 520 N Fourth Ave *Web:* www.yourlourdes.com	Pasco	WA	99301	509-547-7704	546-2291
Northwest Hospital & Medical Ctr 1550 N 115th St. *TF:* 877-694-4677 ■ *Web:* www.nwhospital.org	Seattle	WA	98133	206-364-0500	368-1949
Olympic Medical Ctr 939 Caroline St *TF:* 888-362-6260 ■ *Web:* www.olympicmedical.org	Port Angeles	WA	98362	360-417-7000	
Overlake Hospital Medical Ctr 1035 116th Ave NE. *Web:* www.overlakehospital.org	Bellevue	WA	98004	425-688-5000	688-5087
PeaceHealth 1615 Delaware St PO Box 3002 *Web:* www.peacehealth.org	Longview	WA	98632	360-414-2000	
PeaceHealth St Joseph Medical Ctr 2901 Squalicum Pkwy *TF:* 800-541-7209 ■ *Web:* www.peacehealth.org	Bellingham	WA	98225	360-734-5400	738-6393
Peninsula Community Health Services PO Box 960 *Web:* www.pchsweb.org	Bremerton	WA	98337	360-377-3776	373-2096
Proliance Surgeons Inc 805 Madison Ste 901 *Web:* www.proliancesurgeons.com	Seattle	WA	98104	206-264-8100	
Providence Centralia Hospital 914 S Scheuber Rd. *TF Help Line:* 877-736-2803 ■ *Web:* washington.providence.org	Centralia	WA	98531	360-736-2803	330-8614
Providence Everett Medical Ctr *Colby Campus* 1321 Colby Ave. *Web:* www2.providence.org	Everett	WA	98201	425-261-2000	261-4030
Providence Holy Family Hospital 5633 N Lidgerwood St *Web:* www2.providence.org	Spokane	WA	99208	509-482-0111	482-2456
Providence Regional Medical Ctr Everett 916 Pacific Ave. *Web:* www2.providence.org	Everett	WA	98201	425-261-2000	261-4051
Providence Sacred Heart Medical Ctr 101 W Eigth Ave. *TF:* 800-442-8534 ■ *Web:* washington.providence.org	Spokane	WA	99204	509-474-3170	474-4925
Providence Saint Peter Hospital (PSPH) 413 Lilly Rd NE. *TF:* 888-492-9480 ■ *Web:* www2.providence.org	Olympia	WA	98506	360-491-9480	493-4277
Providence St Mary Medical Ctr 401 W Poplar St PO Box 1477 *TF:* 877-215-7833 ■ *Web:* www2.providence.org	Walla Walla	WA	99362	509-525-3320	
Qualis Health PO Box 33400 *TF:* 800-949-7536 ■ *Web:* www.qualishealth.org	Seattle	WA	98133	206-364-9700	368-2419
Saint Joseph Medical Ctr (SJMC) 1717 S J St **Fax Area Code:* 253 ■ *TF:* 888-825-3227 ■ *Web:* chifranciscan.org	Tacoma	WA	98405	888-825-3227	426-6260*
Skagit Valley Hospital 1415 E Kincaid St. *Web:* www.skagitvalleyhospital.org	Mount Vernon	WA	98273	360-424-4111	
Southwest Washington Medical Ctr (SWMC) 400 NE Mother Joseph Pl PO Box 1600 *Web:* peacehealth.org/southwest	Vancouver	WA	98664	360-514-2000	
Swedish Medical Ctr Cherry Hill Campus 500 17th Ave *Web:* www.swedish.org	Seattle	WA	98122	206-320-2000	
Swedish Medical Ctr First Hill 747 Broadway *Web:* www.swedish.org	Seattle	WA	98122	206-386-6000	386-2277
Swedish Medical Ctr/Edmonds 21601 76th Ave W *Web:* www.swedish.org	Edmonds	WA	98026	425-640-4000	640-4010
Tacoma General Hospital 315 MLK Jr Way *TF:* 800-552-1419 ■ *Web:* www.multicare.org	Tacoma	WA	98405	253-403-1000	403-1180
University of Washington Medical Ctr 1959 NE Pacific St. *Web:* www.washington.edu	Seattle	WA	98195	206-685-8973	

				Phone	Fax
UW Medicine Eastside Hospital & Specialty 3100 Northup Way *TF:* 877-520-5000 ■ *Web:* eastside.uwmedicine.org	Bellevue	WA	98004	877-520-5000	
Valley Hospital & Medical Ctr (VHMC) 12606 E Mission Ave *Web:* www.spokanevalleyhospital.com/pages/home.aspx	Spokane Valley	WA	99216	509-924-6650	473-5903
Valley Medical Ctr 400 S 43rd St *TF:* 855-923-4633 ■ *Web:* www.valleymed.org	Renton	WA	98055	425-228-3450	
Virginia Mason Medical Ctr 925 Seneca St *Web:* www.virginiamason.org	Seattle	WA	98101	206-624-1144	
Yakima Regional Medical & Heart Ctr 110 S Ninth Ave *Web:* yakimaregional.com	Yakima	WA	98902	509-575-5000	454-6193
Yakima Valley Memorial Hospital 2811 Tieton Dr *Web:* www.yakimamemorial.org	Yakima	WA	98902	509-575-8000	

West Virginia

				Phone	Fax
Beckley Appalachian Regional Hospital 306 Stanaford Rd *Web:* www.arh.org	Beckley	WV	25801	304-255-3000	
Bluefield Regional Medical Ctr (BRMC) 500 Cherry St *TF:* 800-994-6610 ■ *Web:* www.bluefieldregional.net	Bluefield	WV	24701	304-327-1100	
Cabell Huntington Hospital 1340 Hal Greer Blvd *Web:* www.cabellhuntington.org	Huntington	WV	25701	304-526-2000	
Charleston Area Medical Ctr 501 Morris St *Web:* www.camc.org	Charleston	WV	25301	304-388-5432	388-3604
City Hospital 2500 Hospital Dr *TF:* 888-988-1362 ■ *Web:* www.wvuniversityhealthcare.com	Martinsburg	WV	25401	304-264-1000	260-1437
Davis Memorial Hospital 812 Gorman Ave *TF:* 888-477-6895 ■ *Web:* www.davishealthsystem.org	Elkins	WV	26241	304-636-3300	637-3184
Fairmont General Hospital (FGH) 1325 Locust Ave *Web:* www.fghi.com	Fairmont	WV	26554	304-367-7100	367-7246
Grafton City Hospital Inc 500 Market St *Web:* www.graftonhospital.com	Grafton	WV	26354	304-265-0400	
Greenbrier Valley Medical Ctr 202 Maplewood Ave *Web:* www.gvmc.com	Ronceverte	WV	24970	304-647-4411	647-6010
Logan Regional Medical Ctr 20 Hospital Dr *TF:* 888-982-9144 ■ *Web:* www.loganregionalmedicalcenter.com	Logan	WV	25601	304-831-1101	831-1871
Monongalia General Hospital 1200 JD Anderson Dr *Web:* mongeneral.com	Morgantown	WV	26505	304-598-1200	
Ohio Valley Medical Ctr 2000 Eoff St *Web:* ovmc-eorh.com	Wheeling	WV	26003	304-234-0123	234-8229
Pleasant Valley Hospital 2520 Valley Dr *Web:* www.pvalley.org	Point Pleasant	WV	25550	304-675-4340	
Princeton Community Hospital 122 12th St *Web:* www.pchonline.org	Princeton	WV	24740	304-487-7000	487-2161
Raleigh General Hospital 1710 Harper Rd *Web:* www.raleighgeneral.com	Beckley	WV	25801	304-256-4100	256-4009
Reynolds Memorial Hospital (RMH) 800 Wheeling Ave *Web:* www.reynoldsmemorial.com	Glen Dale	WV	26038	304-845-3211	843-3202
Saint Francis Hospital 333 Laidley St *Web:* www.stfrancishospital.com	Charleston	WV	25301	304-347-6500	
Stonewall Jackson Memorial Hospital (SJMH) 230 Hospital Plaza *TF:* 866-637-0471 ■ *Web:* www.stonewalljacksonhospital.com	Weston	WV	26452	304-269-8000	269-8090
Thomas Memorial Hospital 4605 MacCorkle Ave SW *Web:* www.thomaswv.org	South Charleston	WV	25309	304-766-3600	766-4359
United Hospital Ctr 327 Medical pk Dr *TF:* 800-607-8888 ■ *Web:* www.uhcwv.org	Bridgeport	WV	26330	304-624-2121	
Weirton Medical Ctr 601 Colliers Way *TF:* 800-994-6610 ■ *Web:* www.weirtonmedical.com	Weirton	WV	26062	304-797-6000	797-6176
West Virginia University Hospitals 1 Medical Ctr Dr *Web:* wvumedicine.org	Morgantown	WV	26506	304-598-4200	598-4073
Wetzel County Hospital 3 E Benjamin Dr *Web:* www.wetzelcountyhospital.com	New Martinsville	WV	26155	304-455-8000	455-4259
Wheeling Hospital 1 Medical Pk *Web:* wheelinghospital.org	Wheeling	WV	26003	304-243-3000	

Wisconsin

				Phone	Fax
Appleton Medical Ctr 1818 N Meade St *TF:* 800-236-4101 ■ *Web:* www.thedacare.org	Appleton	WI	54911	920-731-4101	738-6319
Aspirus Wausau Hospital 333 Pine Ridge Blvd *TF:* 800-283-2881 ■ *Web:* www.aspirus.org	Wausau	WI	54401	715-847-2121	847-0095
Aurora Lakeland Medical Ctr (ALMC) W3985 County Rd NN *Web:* www.aurorahealthcare.org	Elkhorn	WI	53121	262-741-2000	
Aurora Sinai Medical Ctr 945 N 12th St *TF:* 888-863-5502 ■ *Web:* www.aurorahealthcare.org	Milwaukee	WI	53201	414-219-2000	
Bay Area Medical Ctr (BAMC) 3100 Shore Dr *TF:* 888-788-2070 ■ *Web:* bamc.org	Marinette	WI	54143	715-735-4200	
Beaver Dam Community Hospital 707 S University Ave *Web:* www.bdch.com	Beaver Dam	WI	53916	920-887-7181	887-7973
Bellin Hospital 744 S Webster Ave *Web:* www.bellin.org	Green Bay	WI	54301	920-433-3500	
Beloit Health System 1969 W Hart Rd *TF:* 800-637-2641 ■ *Web:* www.beloithealthsystem.org	Beloit	WI	53511	608-363-5724	363-5702
Columbia Saint Mary's Hospital 2025 E Newport Ave *Web:* www.columbia-stmarys.org	Milwaukee	WI	53211	414-961-3300	
Columbia Saint Mary's Hospital 2323 N Lake Dr *Web:* www.columbia-stmarys.org	Milwaukee	WI	53211	414-291-1000	
Columbia Saint Mary's Hospital Ozaukee 13111 N Port Washington Rd *TF:* 800-457-6004 ■ *Web:* www.columbia-stmarys.org	Mequon	WI	53097	262-243-7300	
Community Memorial Hospital (CMH) W 180 N 8085 Town Hall Rd *Web:* froedtert.com	Menomonee Falls	WI	53051	262-251-1000	
Elmbrook Memorial Hospital 19333 W N Ave *Web:* www.mywheaton.org/locations/elmbrook_memorial	Brookfield	WI	53045	262-785-2000	
Fort Atkinson Memorial Hospital 611 Sherman Ave E *Web:* www.forthealthcare.com	Fort Atkinson	WI	53538	920-568-5000	
Franciscan Skemp Health Care 700 W Ave S *Web:* mayoclinichealthsystem.org	La Crosse	WI	54601	608-785-0940	
Froedtert Hospital 9200 W Wisconsin Ave *Web:* www.froedtert.com	Milwaukee	WI	53226	414-805-4311	805-7790
Gundersen Lutheran Medical Ctr 1836 S Ave *TF:* 800-362-9567 ■ *Web:* www.gundersenhealth.org	La Crosse	WI	54601	608-782-7300	372-3253
Holy Family Memorial Medical Ctr 2300 Western Ave PO Box 1450 *TF:* 800-994-3662 ■ *Web:* www.hfmhealth.org	Manitowoc	WI	54220	920-320-2011	
Kenosha Medical Ctr 6308 Eigth Ave *TF:* 800-994-6610 ■ *Web:* www.uhsi.org	Kenosha	WI	53143	262-656-2011	
Lakeview Medical Ctr 1100 N Main St *Web:* www.lakeviewmedical.com	Rice Lake	WI	54868	715-234-1515	
Mayo Foundation for Medical Education & Research 1221 Whipple St PO Box 4105 *Web:* mayoclinichealthsystem.org	Eau Claire	WI	54702	715-838-3219	
Memorial Medical Ctr 1615 Maple Ln *TF:* 877-611-1988 ■ *Web:* www.ashlandmmc.com	Ashland	WI	54806	715-685-5500	685-5118
Mercy Hospital & Trauma Ctr 1000 Mineral Pt Ave *TF:* 800-756-4147 ■ *Web:* www.mercyhealthsystem.com	Janesville	WI	53548	608-756-6000	
Mercy Medical Ctr (MMC) 500 S Oakwood Rd *TF:* 800-894-9327 ■ *Web:* www.affinityhealth.org	Oshkosh	WI	54904	920-223-2000	
Ministry Saint Joseph's Hospital (MSJH) 611 St Joseph Ave *Web:* www.ministryhealth.org/sjh/home.nws	Marshfield	WI	54449	715-387-1713	
Monroe Clinic Hospital 515 22nd Ave *TF:* 800-338-0568 ■ *Web:* www.monroeclinic.org	Monroe	WI	53566	608-324-2000	324-1114
Oconomowoc Memorial Hospital 791 Summit Ave *TF:* 800-242-0313 ■ *Web:* www.prohealthcare.org	Oconomowoc	WI	53066	262-569-9400	569-0336
Prairie Du Chien Memorial Hospital 705 E Taylor St *Web:* www.pdcmemorialhospital.org	Prairie Du Chien	WI	53821	608-357-2000	
Richland Hospital Inc, The 333 E Second St *TF:* 888-467-7485 ■ *Web:* www.richlandhospital.com	Richland Center	WI	53581	608-647-6321	647-6325
Sacred Heart Hospital 900 W Clairemont Ave *TF:* 888-445-4554 ■ *Web:* www.sacredheartеauclaire.org	Eau Claire	WI	54701	715-717-4121	
Saint Elizabeth Hospital 1506 S Oneida St *TF:* 800-223-7332 ■ *Web:* www.affinityhealth.org	Appleton	WI	54915	920-738-2000	
Saint Joseph's Hospital 2661 County Hwy I *TF:* 877-723-1811 ■ *Web:* www.stjoeschipfalls.com	Chippewa Falls	WI	54729	715-723-1811	
Saint Mary's Hospital 2251 N Shore Dr *TF Cust Svc:* 800-578-0840 ■ *Web:* www.ministryhealth.org	Rhinelander	WI	54501	715-361-2000	361-2011
Saint Mary's Hospital Medical Ctr 1726 Shawano Ave *TF:* 800-666-5606 ■ *Web:* www.stmgb.org	Green Bay	WI	54303	920-498-4200	
Saint Michael's Hospital 900 Illinois Ave *TF:* 800-420-2622 ■ *Web:* www.ministryhealth.org	Stevens Point	WI	54481	715-346-5000	
Saint Vincent Hospital 835 S Van Buren St *TF:* 800-236-3030 ■ *Web:* www.stvincenthospital.org	Green Bay	WI	54301	920-433-0111	
Southwest Health Ctr Inc 1400 Eastside Rd *Web:* www.southwesthealth.org	Platteville	WI	53818	608-348-2331	
St. Agnes Hospital 430 E Div St *TF:* 800-922-3400 ■ *Web:* www.agnesian.com	Fond du Lac	WI	54935	920-929-2300	
Stoughton Hospital 900 Ridge St *Web:* www.stoughtonhospital.com	Stoughton	WI	53589	608-873-6611	873-2355
Theda Clark Medical Ctr 130 Second St *TF:* 800-236-3122 ■ *Web:* www.thedacare.org	Neenah	WI	54956	920-729-3100	
University of Wisconsin Hospital & Clinics 600 Highland Ave *TF:* 800-323-8942 ■ *Web:* www.uwhealth.org	Madison	WI	53792	608-263-6400	263-9830
Waukesha Memorial Hospital 725 American Ave *TF:* 800-326-2011 ■ *Web:* www.prohealthcare.org	Waukesha	WI	53188	262-928-1000	
West Allis Memorial Hospital 8901 W Lincoln Ave 2nd Fl *Web:* www.aurorahealthcare.org	West Allis	WI	53227	414-328-6000	328-8536
Wheaton Franciscan - Saint Joseph 5000 W Chambers St *Web:* www.mywheaton.org	Milwaukee	WI	53210	414-447-2000	
Wheaton Franciscan Healthcare 3801 Spring St *TF:* 877-304-6332 ■ *Web:* www.mywheaton.org	Racine	WI	53405	262-687-4011	
All Saints 3801 Spring St *TF:* 877-304-6332 ■ *Web:* www.mywheaton.org	Racine	WI	53405	262-687-4011	
Wheaton Franciscan Healthcare - St. Francis 3237 S 16th St *Web:* www.mywheaton.org	Milwaukee	WI	53215	414-647-5000	647-5565

Wyoming

Phone | Fax

Campbell County Memorial Hospital
501 S Burma PO Box 3011 .... Gillette WY 82717 307-688-1000 688-1516*
*Fax: Hum Res ■ Web: www.cchwyo.org

Cheyenne Regional Medical Ctr (CRMC)
214 E 23rd St .... Cheyenne WY 82001 307-634-2273
Web: www.crmcwy.org

Ivinson Memorial Hospital 255 N 30th St .... Laramie WY 82072 307-742-2141 742-2150
TF: 877-858-0990 ■ Web: www2.ivinsonhospital.org

Memorial Hospital of Sweetwater County
1200 College Dr .... Rock Springs WY 82901 307-362-3711
TF General: 866-571-0944 ■ Web: www.sweetwatermemorial.com

Riverton Memorial Hospital LLC
2100 W Sunset Dr .... Riverton WY 82501 307-856-4161 856-9587
TF: 888-982-9144 ■ Web: sagewesthealthcare.com

Sheridan Memorial Hospital 1401 W Fifth St .... Sheridan WY 82801 307-672-1000
Web: www.sheridanhospital.org

Wyoming Medical Ctr 1233 E Second St .... Casper WY 82601 307-577-7201 233-8230
TF: 800-822-7201 ■ Web: wyomingmedicalcenter.org

374-4 Military Hospitals

Phone | Fax

Brooke Army Medical Ctr (BAMC)
3551 Roger Brooke Dr .... Fort Sam Houston TX 78234 210-916-4141
TF: 800-443-2262 ■ Web: www.bamc.amedd.army.mil

Charleston Naval Hospital 110 NNPTC Cir .... Goose Creek SC 29445 843-794-6221
Web: www.med.navy.mil/sites/chas/pages/default.aspx

Colonel Florence A Blanchfield Army Community Hospital
650 Joel Dr .... Fort Campbell KY 42223 270-798-8400

Darnall Army Medical Ctr
36000 Darnall Loop .... Fort Hood TX 76544 254-288-8000 286-7372
TF: 800-305-6421 ■ Web: www.crdamc.amedd.army.mil

David Grant US Air Force Medical Ctr
101 Bodin Cir .... Travis AFB CA 94535 707-423-3735 423-7416
TF: 800-264-3462 ■ Web: www.travis.af.mil/units/dgmc

Dwight David Eisenhower Army Medical Ctr (DDAMC)
300 Hospital Rd .... Fort Gordon GA 30905 706-787-5811 787-5342*
*Fax: Admitting ■ Web: www.ddeamc.amedd.army.mil

Evans Army Community Hospital
1650 Cochran Cir .... Fort Carson CO 80913 719-526-7000
Web: www.evans.amedd.army.mil

Ireland Army Community Hospital
289 Ireland Ave .... Fort Knox KY 40121 502-624-9333 624-9255
Web: www.iach.knox.amedd.army.mil

Irwin Army Community Hospital
600 Caisson Hill Rd .... Fort Riley KS 66442 785-239-7000
Web: iach.amedd.army.mil

Keller Army Community Hospital
900 Washington Rd .... West Point NY 10996 845-938-7992
TF: 800-552-2907 ■ Web: kach.amedd.army.mil

Lyster Army Health Clinic Andrews Ave .... Fort Rucker AL 36362 334-255-7000
Web: lyster.amedd.army.mil/sitepages/home.aspx

Madigan Army Medical Ctr 9040 Jackson Ave .... Tacoma WA 98431 253-968-1110 968-1633*

Martin Army Community Hospital
7950 Martin Loop Bldg 9200 .... Fort Benning GA 31905 706-544-2041
Web: martin.amedd.army.mil

National Naval Medical Ctr
8901 Wisconsin Ave .... Bethesda MD 20889 301-295-4000

Naval Hospital 100 Brewster Blvd .... Camp Lejeune NC 28547 910-450-4300 450-4012
Web: www.med.navy.mil/sites/nhcl/pages/default.aspx

Naval Hospital Bremerton 1 Bo1 Rd .... Bremerton WA 98312 360-475-4000
TF: 800-422-1383 ■ Web: www.med.navy.mil

Naval Hospital Pensacola 6000 W Hwy 98 .... Pensacola FL 32512 850-505-6601 505-6213
Web: www.med.navy.mil

Naval Medical Ctr Portsmouth
620 John Paul Jones Cir .... Portsmouth VA 23708 757-953-5000

Naval Medical Ctr San Diego
34800 Bob Wilson Dr .... San Diego CA 92134 619-532-6400
Web: www.med.navy.mil

Tripler Army Medical Ctr
1 Jarrett White Rd Tripler AMC .... Honolulu HI 96859 808-433-6661 433-4899
TF: 877-880-2184 ■ Web: www.tamc.amedd.army.mil

US Air Force 375th Medical Group
310 W Losey St .... Scott AFB IL 62225 866-683-2778
TF: 866-683-2778 ■ Web: www.scott.af.mil

US Air Force 96th Medical Group
307 Boatner Rd .... Eglin AFB FL 32542 850-883-8600
Web: www.eglin.af.mil/units/eglinhospital.asp

US Air Force Medical Ctr Keesler 81st Medical Group
301 Fisher St .... Keesler AFB MS 39534 228-376-8225 377-9748
Web: www.keesler.af.mil

William Beaumont Army Medical Ctr
5005 N Piedras St .... El Paso TX 79920 915-742-2121
Web: www.wbamc.amedd.army.mil

Winn Army Community Hospital
1061 Harmon Ave .... Fort Stewart GA 31314 912-435-6837

Womack Army Medical Ctr
Bldg 4-2817 Reilly Rd .... Fort Bragg NC 28310 910-907-6000 907-8473
Web: www.wamc.amedd.army.mil

374-5 Psychiatric Hospitals

Listings here include state psychiatric facilities as well as private psychiatric hospitals.

Phone | Fax

Adventist Behavioral Health
14901 Broschart Rd .... Rockville MD 20850 301-251-4500 315-3000
TF: 800-204-8600

Alaska Psychiatric Institute 3700 Piper St .... Anchorage AK 99508 907-269-7100 269-7128
Web: dhss.alaska.gov

Alton Mental Health Ctr 4500 College Ave .... Alton IL 62002 618-474-3200 474-3807
Web: 'www.agacistore.com

Ancora Psychiatric Hospital
301 Spring Garden Rd .... Hammonton NJ 08037 609-561-1700 561-2509
Web: nj.gov

Appalachian Behavioral Healthcare
100 Hospital Dr .... Athens OH 45701 740-594-5000
Web: mha.ohio.gov

Arizona State Hospital 2500 E Van Buren St .... Phoenix AZ 85008 602-244-1331 220-6355
TF: 877-588-5163 ■ Web: www.azdhs.gov/azsh

Arkansas State Hospital
4313 W Markham St .... Little Rock AR 72205 501-686-9000 686-9483
Web: humanservices.arkansas.gov

Atascadero State Hospital
10333 S Camino Real .... Atascadero CA 93422 805-468-2000 468-3386
TF: 844-210-6207 ■ Web: dsh.ca.gov

Aurora Las Encinas Hospital
2900 E Del Mar Blvd .... Pasadena CA 91107 626-795-9901 792-2919
TF: 800-792-2345 ■ Web: www.lasencinashospital.com

Austin State Hospital 4110 Guadalupe St .... Austin TX 78751 512-452-0381 419-2163
TF: 866-407-3773 ■ Web: dshs.state.tx.us

Banner Behavioral Health Hospital
7575 E Earll Dr .... Scottsdale AZ 85251 480-941-7500
TF: 800-254-4357 ■ Web: www.bannerhealth.com

Bellevue Hospital Ctr 462 First Ave .... New York NY 10016 212-562-4141 562-4036
Web: nyc.gov

Belmont Ctr for Comprehensive Treatment
4200 Monument Rd .... Philadelphia PA 19131 215-877-2000
Web: www.einstein.edu

Big Spring State Hospital 1901 N Hwy 87 .... Big Spring TX 79720 432-267-8216 268-7263
Web: dshs.state.tx.us

Brentwood A Behavioral Health Co
1006 Highland Ave .... Shreveport LA 71101 318-678-7500 227-9296
TF: 877-678-7500 ■ Web: www.brentwoodbehavioral.com

Bridgewater State Hospital 20 Admin Rd .... Bridgewater MA 02324 508-279-4500
Web: mass.gov

Bronx Psychiatric Ctr 1500 Waters Pl .... Bronx NY 10461 718-931-0600 862-4858
TF: 800-597-8481 ■ Web: omh.ny.gov

Broughton Hospital 1000 S Sterling St .... Morganton NC 28655 828-433-2111
Web: ncdhhs.gov

BryLin Hospitals 1263 Delaware Ave .... Buffalo NY 14209 716-886-8200
TF: 800-727-9546 ■ Web: www.brylin.com

Buffalo Psychiatric Ctr 400 Forest Ave .... Buffalo NY 14213 716-885-2261 885-4852
TF: 800-597-8481 ■ Web: www.omh.ny.gov

Butler Hospital 345 Blackstone Blvd .... Providence RI 02906 401-455-6200 455-6309*
*Fax: Admitting ■ Web: www.butler.org

Capital District Psychiatric Ctr
75 New Scotland Ave .... Albany NY 12208 518-447-9611 434-0041
Web: www.omh.ny.gov/omhweb/facilities/cdpc

Caro Ctr 2000 Chambers Rd .... Caro MI 48723 989-673-3191 673-6749
TF: 888-556-0490 ■ Web: michigan.gov

Carrier Clinic 252 County Rd 601 .... Belle Mead NJ 08502 908-281-1000
TF: 800-933-3579 ■ Web: carrierclinic.org

Catawba Hospital 5525 Catawba Hospital Dr .... Catawba VA 24070 540-375-4200
TF: 800-451-5544 ■ Web: www.catawba.dbhds.virginia.gov

Cedar Springs Behavioral Health System
2135 Southgate Rd .... Colorado Springs CO 80906 719-633-4114 578-0857
TF: 800-888-1088 ■ Web: cedarspringsbhs.com

Cedarcrest Hospital 525 Russell Rd .... Newington CT 06111 860-666-4613

Central Louisiana State Hospital
242 W Shamrock St .... Pineville LA 71360 318-484-6200 484-6501
TF: 866-666-8335 ■ Web: www.dhh.louisiana.gov

Central State Hospital
26317 W Washington St .... Petersburg VA 23803 804-524-7000
Web: www.csh.dbhds.virginia.gov

Central State Hospital 10510 LaGrange Rd .... Louisville KY 40223 502-253-7000
Web: kentucky.gov

Central Washington Hospital
1201 S Miller St .... Wenatchee WA 98801 509-662-1511
TF: 800-365-6428 ■ Web: www.cwhs.com

Cherry Hospital 201 Stevens Mill Rd .... Goldsboro NC 27530 919-731-3200 731-3785
Web: www.ncdhhs.gov/dsohf/cherry

Chester Mental Health Ctr 1315 Lehman Dr .... Chester IL 62233 618-826-4571
TF: 800-843-6154 ■ Web: www.dhs.state.il.us

Chicago Lakeshore Hospital 4840 N Marine Dr .... Chicago IL 60640 773-878-9700 907-4607
TF Cust Svc: 800-888-0560 ■ Web: www.chicagolakeshorehospital.com

Chicago-Read Mental Health Ctr
4200 N Oak Pk Ave .... Chicago IL 60634 773-794-4000 794-4046
Web: www.dhs.state.il.us

Clarks Summit State Hospital
1451 Hillside Dr .... Clarks Summit PA 18411 570-586-2011 587-7415
Web: dpw.state.pa.us

Clifton T Perkins Hospital Ctr
8450 Dorsey Run Rd .... Jessup MD 20794 410-724-3000 724-3009
TF: 877-463-3464 ■ Web: dhmh.maryland.gov

Coastal Harbor Treatment Ctr
1150 Cornell Ave .... Savannah GA 31406 912-354-3911
Web: coastalharbor.com

College Hospital 10802 College Pl .... Cerritos CA 90703 562-924-9581 809-0981
TF: 800-352-3301 ■ Web: www.collegehospitals.com

College Hospital Costa Mesa
301 Victoria St .... Costa Mesa CA 92627 949-642-2734 574-3320
TF: 800-773-8001 ■ Web: www.collegehospitals.com

Colorado Mental Health Institute at Fort Logan (CMHIFL)
3520 W Oxford Ave .... Denver CO 80236 303-866-7066 866-7101*

Colorado Mental Health Institute at Pueblo (CMHIP)
1600 W 24th St .... Pueblo CO 81003 719-546-4000
Web: www.colorado.gov

Connecticut Valley Hospital
1000 Silver St .... Middletown CT 06457 860-262-5000 262-5989
Web: ct.gov

	City	State	ZIP	Phone	Fax
Creedmoor Psychiatric Ctr 79-25 Winchester Blvd	Queens Village	NY	11427	718-464-7500	264-3636
TF: 800-597-8481 ■ *Web:* www.omh.ny.gov/omhweb/facilities/crpc/facility.htm					
Danville State Hospital 200 State Hospital Dr	Danville	PA	17821	570-271-4500	
Web: dsh.thomas-industriesinc.com					
Del Amo Hospital 23700 Camino Del Sol	Torrance	CA	90505	310-530-1151	
TF: 800-533-5266 ■ *Web:* www.delamohospital.com					
Delaware Psychiatric Ctr 1901 N Dupont Hwy Main Bldg	New Castle	DE	19720	302-255-9399	255-4428
TF: 800-652-2929 ■ *Web:* dhss.delaware.gov					
Dominion Hospital 2960 Sleepy Hollow Rd	Falls Church	VA	22044	703-536-2000	533-9650
Web: www.dominionhospital.com					
Dorothea Dix Hospital 820 S Boylan Ave	Raleigh	NC	27699	919-733-5540	
East Central Regional Hospital *Augusta* 3405 Mike Padgett Hwy	Augusta	GA	30906	706-792-7006	
East Louisiana State Hospital 4502 Hwy 951	Jackson	LA	70748	225-634-0100	
Web: new.dhh.louisiana.gov					
Eastern Louisiana Mental Health System Greenwell Springs Campus 628 N 4th St PO Box 629	Baton Rouge	LA	70802	225-634-0100	
Web: www.dhh.state.la.us					
Eastern State Hospital (ESH) 4601 Ironbound Rd	Williamsburg	VA	23188	757-253-5161	253-5065
TF: 800-994-6610 ■ *Web:* esh.dbhds.virginia.gov					
Elgin Mental Health Ctr 750 S State St	Elgin	IL	60123	847-742-1040	608-8619
Elmira Psychiatric Ctr 100 Washington St	Elmira	NY	14901	607-737-4711	737-9080
TF: 800-597-8481 ■ *Web:* omh.ny.gov					
Essex County Hospital Ctr 204 Grove Ave	Cedar Grove	NJ	07009	973-571-2800	
Web: essexcountynj.org					
Fair Oaks Hospital 5352 Linton Blvd	Delray Beach	FL	33484	561-498-4440	495-3103
TF: 866-904-6871 ■ *Web:* www.delraymedicalctr.com					
Fairfax Hospital 10200 NE 132nd St	Kirkland	WA	98034	425-821-2000	
TF: 800-435-7221 ■ *Web:* www.fairfaxhospital.com					
Fairmount Behavioral Health System 561 Fairthorne Ave	Philadelphia	PA	19128	215-487-4000	
TF: 800-235-0200 ■ *Web:* www.fairmountbhs.com					
Fort Lauderdale Hospital 1601 E Las Olas Blvd	Fort Lauderdale	FL	33301	954-463-4321	453-5497
TF: 800-585-7527 ■ *Web:* www.fortlauderdalehospital.org					
Four Winds Hospital 800 Cross River Rd	Katonah	NY	10536	914-763-8151	
TF: 800-528-6624 ■ *Web:* www.fourwindshospital.com					
Friends Hospital 4641 Roosevelt Blvd	Philadelphia	PA	19124	215-831-4600	
TF: 800-889-0548 ■ *Web:* www.friendshospital.com					
Fulton State Hospital 600 E Fifth St	Fulton	MO	65251	573-592-4100	592-3000
Web: dmh.mo.gov					
GEO Care South Florida State Hospital 800 E Cypress Dr	Pembroke Pines	FL	33025	954-392-3000	
Georgia Regional Hospital at Atlanta 3073 Panthersville Rd	Atlanta	GA	30034	404-243-2100	
Web: dbhdd.georgia.gov					
Georgia Regional Hospital at Savannah 1915 Eisenhower Dr	Savannah	GA	31406	912-356-2011	356-2691
TF: 800-436-7442					
Greater Binghamton Health Ctr 425 Robinson St	Binghamton	NY	13904	607-724-1391	773-4387
Green Oaks Hospital 7808 Clodus Fields Dr	Dallas	TX	75251	972-991-9504	
TF: 800-866-6554 ■ *Web:* www.greenoakspsych.com					
Greystone Park Psychiatric Hospital 59 Koch Ave	Morris Plains	NJ	07950	973-538-1800	
Web: www.nj.gov/humanservices/dmhs/oshm/gpph					
Griffin Memorial Hospital 900 E Main St	Norman	OK	73071	405-321-4880	
TF General: 800-955-3468 ■ *Web:* ok.gov					
H Douglas Singer Mental Health & Development Ctr 4402 N Main St	Rockford	IL	61103	815-987-7096	
Hamilton Ctr Inc PO Box 4323	Terre Haute	IN	47804	812-231-8323	
TF: 800-742-0787 ■ *Web:* www.hamiltoncenter.org					
Hampstead Hospital 218 E Rd	Hampstead	NH	03841	603-329-5311	329-4746
Web: www.hampsteadhospital.com					
Hartgrove Hospital 5730 W Roosevelt Rd	Chicago	IL	60644	773-413-1700	
Web: hartgrovehospital.com					
Havenwyck Hospital 1525 University Dr	Auburn Hills	MI	48326	248-373-9200	377-8160*
**Fax:* Admitting ■ *TF:* 800-401-2727 ■ *Web:* havenwyckhospital.com					
Hawaii State Hospital 45-710 Keaahala Rd	Kaneohe	HI	96744	808-247-2191	247-7335
Heartland Behavioral Healthcare 3000 S Erie St	Massillon	OH	44646	330-833-3135	833-6564
Web: mha.ohio.gov					
Hill Crest Behavioral Health Services 6869 Fifth Ave S	Birmingham	AL	35212	205-833-9000	
TF: 800-292-8553 ■ *Web:* www.hillcrestbhs.com					
Holly Hill Hospital 3019 Falstaff Rd	Raleigh	NC	27610	919-250-7000	231-3231
TF: 800-447-1800 ■ *Web:* www.hollyhillhospital.com					
Horsham Clinic 722 E Butler Pk	Ambler	PA	19002	215-643-7800	654-1148*
**Fax:* Admissions ■ *TF:* 800-237-4447 ■ *Web:* www.horshamclinic.com					
Intracare North Hospital 1120 Cypress Station	Houston	TX	77090	713-790-0949	
Web: www.intracarehospital.com					
Jewish Hospital & St Mary's HealthCare 200 Abraham Flexner Way	Louisville	KY	40202	502-587-4011	479-4350
TF: 800-451-3637					
John J Madden Mental Health Ctr 1200 S First Ave	Hines	IL	60141	708-338-7400	338-7057
Web: illinois.gov					
John Umstead Hospital 1003 12th St	Butner	NC	27509	919-575-7211	575-7013
Kalamazoo Psychiatric Hospital 1312 Oakland Dr	Kalamazoo	MI	49008	269-337-3000	
TF: 888-509-7007 ■ *Web:* michigan.gov					
Kerrville State Hospital 721 Thompson Dr	Kerrville	TX	78028	830-896-2211	792-4926
TF: 888-963-7111 ■ *Web:* dshs.state.tx.us					
Kingsboro Psychiatric Ctr 681 Clarkson Ave	Brooklyn	NY	11203	800-597-8481	221-7633*
**Fax Area Code:* 718 ■ **Fax:* Admitting ■ *TF:* 800-597-8481 ■ *Web:* www.omh.ny.gov					
Lakeside Behavioral Health System 2911 Brunswick Rd	Memphis	TN	38133	901-377-4700	
TF: 800-232-5253 ■ *Web:* lakesidebhs.com					
Langley Porter Psychiatric Institute 401 Parnassus Ave	San Francisco	CA	94143	415-476-7000	476-7320
TF: 800-723-7140 ■ *Web:* psych.ucsf.edu					
Lincoln Medical & Mental Health Ctr 234 E 149th St	Bronx	NY	10451	718-579-5016	
Web: nyc.gov					
McLean Hospital 115 Mill St	Belmont	MA	02478	617-855-2000	
TF: 800-333-0338 ■ *Web:* mcleanhospital.org					
Meadows Psychiatric Ctr 132 The Meadows Dr	Centre Hall	PA	16828	814-364-2161	
TF: 800-641-7529 ■ *Web:* www.themeadows.net					
Meadowview Psychiatric Hospital 595 County Ave	Secaucus	NJ	07094	201-369-5252	
Web: hudsoncountynj.org					
Memorial Hermann Prevention & Recovery Ctr (MHPARC) 3043 Gessner	Houston	TX	77080	713-939-7272	939-7272
TF: 800-464-7272 ■ *Web:* parc.memorialhermann.org					
Mendota Mental Health Institute 301 Troy Dr	Madison	WI	53704	608-301-1000	301-1358
Web: www.dhs.wisconsin.gov					
Menninger Clinic 12301 S Main St PO Box 809045	Houston	TX	77035	713-275-5000	275-5107
TF: 800-351-9058 ■ *Web:* www.menningerclinic.com					
Mental Health Institute 2277 Iowa Ave	Independence	IA	50644	319-334-2583	
Web: independenceia.com					
Metropolitan State Hospital 11401 Bloomfield Ave	Norwalk	CA	90650	562-863-7011	868-6920
Web: dsh.ca.gov					
Middle Tennessee Mental Health Institute 221 Stewarts Ferry Pike	Nashville	TN	37214	615-902-7400	741-8953
TF: 800-770-8277 ■ *Web:* tn.gov					
Milwaukee County Mental Health Complex 9455 Watertown Plank Rd	Milwaukee	WI	53226	414-257-6995	
Web: www.county.milwaukee.gov					
Mississippi State Hospital PO Box 157A	Whitfield	MS	39193	601-351-8000	351-8228
Web: www.msh.state.ms.us					
Moccasin Bend Mental Health Institute 100 Moccasin Bend Rd	Chattanooga	TN	37405	423-265-2271	785-3333
Web: tn.gov					
Mohawk Valley Psychiatric Ctr 1400 Noyes St	Utica	NY	13502	315-738-3800	738-4414
TF: 800-597-8481 ■ *Web:* omh.ny.gov					
Napa State Hospital 2100 Napa-Vallejo Hwy	Napa	CA	94558	707-253-5000	253-5513
TF: 866-762-0972 ■ *Web:* www.dsh.ca.gov					
New Hampshire Hospital 36 Clinton St	Concord	NH	03301	603-271-5200	271-5395
Web: www.dhhs.nh.gov					
New Mexico Behavioral Health Institute 3695 Hot Springs Blvd	Las Vegas	NM	87701	505-454-2100	454-5172*
**Fax:* Admissions ■ *TF:* 800-446-5970 ■ *Web:* nmhealth.org/about/ofm/ltcf/nmbhi					
Norfolk Regional Ctr 1700 N Victory Rd	Norfolk	NE	68702	402-370-3400	
Web: dhhs.ne.gov					
Norristown State Hospital 1001 Sterigere St	Norristown	PA	19401	610-313-1000	313-1013
North Dakota State Hospital 2605 Cir Dr	Jamestown	ND	58401	701-253-3650	253-3999
TF: 888-862-7342 ■ *Web:* www.nd.gov					
North Texas State Hospital 6515 Kemp Blvd	Wichita Falls	TX	76308	940-692-1220	
Northcoast Behavioral Healthcare System *South Campus* 1756 Sagamore Rd PO Box 305	Northfield	OH	44067	330-467-7131	467-2420
Web: mha.ohio.gov					
Northwest Georgia Regional Hospital 705 N Div St	Rome	GA	30165	706-295-6011	
Web: ngoc.com					
Northwest Missouri Psychiatric Rehabilitation Ctr 3505 Frederick Ave	Saint Joseph	MO	64506	816-387-2300	751-8224*
**Fax Area Code:* 573 ■ **Fax:* Admitting ■ *TF:* 800-273-8255					
Oklahoma Forensic Ctr 24800 S 4420 Rd	Vinita	OK	74301	918-256-7841	
Web: ok.gov					
Oregon State Hospital 2600 Ctr St NE	Salem	OR	97301	503-945-2800	945-2807
TF: 800-544-7078 ■ *Web:* oregon.gov					
Patton State Hospital 3102 E Highland Ave	Patton	CA	92369	909-425-7000	425-6370*
**Fax:* Admitting ■ *Web:* dsh.ca.gov					
Peachford Behavioral Health System (PBHS) 2151 Peachford Rd	Atlanta	GA	30338	770-455-3200	
Web: www.peachford.com					
Pembroke Hospital 199 Oak St	Pembroke	MA	02359	781-829-7000	
TF: 800-222-2237 ■ *Web:* arbourhealth.com					
Peninsula Hospital 2347 Jones Bend Rd	Louisville	TN	37777	865-970-9800	
Web: www.peninsulabehavioralhealth.org/hospital					
Pilgrim Psychiatric Ctr 998 Crooked Hill Rd	West Brentwood	NY	11717	631-761-3500	761-2600
TF: 800-597-8481 ■ *Web:* www.omh.ny.gov					
Pine Rest Christian Mental Health Services 300 68th St SE PO Box 165	Grand Rapids	MI	49501	616-455-5000	831-2608*
**Fax:* Hum Res ■ *TF:* 800-678-5500 ■ *Web:* www.pinerest.org					
Poplar Springs Hospital 350 Poplar Dr	Petersburg	VA	23805	804-733-6874	862-6322*
**Fax:* Admitting ■ *TF:* 866-546-2229 ■ *Web:* www.poplarsprings.com					
Psychiatric Institute of Washington 4228 Wisconsin Ave NW	Washington	DC	20016	202-885-5600	885-5614
TF: 800-369-2273 ■ *Web:* www.psychinstitute.com					
Research Psychiatric Ctr 2323 E 63rd St	Kansas City	MO	64130	816-444-8161	
Web: researchpsychiatriccenter.com					
Richard H Hutchings Psychiatric Ctr 620 Madison St	Syracuse	NY	13210	800-690-6639	
TF: 800-690-6639					
Richmond State Hospital (RSH) 498 NW 18th St	Richmond	IN	47374	765-966-0511	939-0622
Web: www.in.gov/fssa/dmha/6914.htm					
Ridge Behavioral Health System 3050 Rio Dosa Dr	Lexington	KY	40509	859-269-2325	
TF: 800-753-4673 ■ *Web:* www.ridgebhs.com					
River Park Hospital 1230 Sixth Ave	Huntington	WV	25701	304-526-9111	
TF: 800-621-2673 ■ *Web:* www.riverparkhospital.net					
Riverview Psychiatric Ctr 250 Arsenal St 11 State House Stn	Augusta	ME	04330	207-624-4600	287-2601
TF: 888-261-6684 ■ *Web:* maine.gov					

	City	State	Zip	Phone	Fax
Rochester Psychiatric Ctr 1111 Elmwood Ave. *Web:* rochesterhealth.com	Rochester	NY	14620	585-241-1200	
Rockland Psychiatric Ctr 140 Old Orangeburg Rd *Fax: Admitting ■ *Web:* omh.ny.gov	Orangeburg	NY	10962	845-359-1000	680-5580*
Rogers Memorial Hospital Inc 34700 Valley Rd *TF:* 800-767-4411 ■ *Web:* www.rogershospital.org	Oconomowoc	WI	53066	262-646-4411	646-3158
Rusk State Hospital 805 N Dickinson Dr *Web:* www.dshs.state.tx.us	Rusk	TX	75785	903-683-3421	683-7400
Saint Elizabeths Hospital 1100 Alabama Ave SE *Web:* www.stelizabethseast.com	Washington	DC	20032	202-299-5000	
San Antonio State Hospital 6711 S Braunfels Ave *Web:* dshs.state.tx.us	San Antonio	TX	78223	210-532-8811	531-7780
San Diego County Psychiatric Hospital 3853 Rosecrans St *Web:* www.sandiegocounty.gov	San Diego	CA	92110	619-692-8200	
Seton Shoal Creek Hospital 3501 Mills Ave. *Web:* www.seton.net	Austin	TX	78731	512-324-2000	
Sharp-Mesa Vista Hospital 7850 Vista Hill Ave *Web:* www.sharp.com	San Diego	CA	92123	858-278-4110	
Sheppard Pratt Health System 6501 N Charles St PO Box 6815 *Web:* www.sheppardpratt.org	Baltimore	MD	21285	443-364-5500	
Sheppard Pratt Health System (SPHS) 6501 N Charles St *Fax: Admissions ■ *TF:* 800-627-0330 ■ *Web:* www.sheppardpratt.org	Baltimore	MD	21285	410-938-3000	938-4532*
South Beach Psychiatric Ctr 777 Seaview Ave. *Web:* omh.ny.gov	Staten Island	NY	10305	718-667-2300	
South Oaks Hospital 400 Sunrise Hwy. *Web:* south-oaks.org	Amityville	NY	11701	631-608-5610	264-5259
Southeast Missouri Mental Health Ctr 1010 W Columbia St *Web:* dmh.mo.gov	Farmington	MO	63640	573-218-6792	218-6785
Southwest Behavioral Health Services Inc 3450 N Third St *Web:* www.sbhservices.org	Phoenix	AZ	85012	602-257-9339	265-8377
Southwestern Virginia Mental Health Institute 340 Bagley Cir *Fax: Admitting ■ *Web:* www.swvmhi.dbhds.virginia.gov	Marion	VA	24354	276-783-1200	783-1216*
Spring Grove Hospital Ctr 55 Wade Ave	Catonsville	MD	21228	410-402-6000	
Spring Harbor Hospital 123 Andover Rd *TF:* 888-524-0080 ■ *Web:* www.springharbor.org	Westbrook	ME	04092	207-761-2200	761-2108
Springfield Hospital Ctr 6655 Sykesville Rd *Fax: Hum Res ■ *TF:* 800-333-7564 ■ *Web:* dhmh.maryland.gov	Sykesville	MD	21784	410-970-7000	970-7024*
Summit Behavioral Healthcare 1101 Summit Rd. *Web:* mha.ohio.gov	Cincinnati	OH	45237	513-948-3600	948-3080
Taunton State Hospital 60 Hodges Ave	Taunton	MA	02780	508-977-3000	
Thomas B Finan Ctr 10102 Country Club Rd SE PO Box 1722 *TF:* 888-854-0035 ■ *Web:* msa.maryland.gov	Cumberland	MD	21502	301-777-2405	777-2364
Timberlawn Mental Health System 4600 Samuell Blvd *TF:* 800-426-4944 ■ *Web:* www.timberlawn.com	Dallas	TX	75228	214-381-7181	388-6453
Torrance State Hospital 121 Longview Dr PO Box 111 *Fax: Admitting ■ *TF:* 866-816-9212 ■ *Web:* www.dpw.state.pa.us/foradults/statehospitals/torrancestatehospital	Torrance	PA	15779	724-459-8000	459-1212*
Trenton Psychiatric Hospital PO Box 7500 *Web:* www.nj.gov	West Trenton	NJ	08628	609-633-1500	
UCLA Neuropsychiatric Institute & Hospital 760 Westwood Plz *Web:* www.semel.ucla.edu	Los Angeles	CA	90095	310-825-0511	
University Behavioral Ctr 2500 Discovery Dr *TF:* 800-999-0807 ■ *Web:* www.universitybehavioral.com	Orlando	FL	32826	407-281-7000	282-7012
Utah State Hospital 1300 E Ctr St *Web:* www.ush.utah.gov	Provo	UT	84606	801-344-4400	344-4225
Walter P Reuther Psychiatric Hospital 30901 Palmer Rd *Fax: Mail Rm ■ *TF:* 877-765-8388 ■ *Web:* michigan.gov	Westland	MI	48186	734-367-8400	722-5562*
Warren State Hospital 33 Main Dr *Web:* dpw.state.pa.us	North Warren	PA	16365	814-723-5500	
Wernersville State Hospital PO Box 300 *Web:* www.dpw.state.pa.us	Wernersville	PA	19565	610-670-4173	
West Oaks Hospital 6500 Hornwood Dr *Web:* westoakshospital.com	Houston	TX	77074	713-995-0909	
Western Mental Health Institute 11100 Hwy 64 W *Fax Area Code: 865 ■ *TF:* 800-770-8277 ■ *Web:* tn.gov	Bolivar	TN	38008	731-228-2000	457-0335*
Western State Hospital 2400 Russellville Rd *Web:* westernstatehospital.ky.gov	Hopkinsville	KY	42240	270-889-6025	
Western State Hospital 1301 Richmond Ave *Web:* www.healthsystem.virginia.edu	Staunton	VA	24401	540-332-8000	332-8144
Western State Hospital 9601 Steilacoom Blvd SW *TF:* 877-501-2233 ■ *Web:* dshs.wa.gov	Tacoma	WA	98498	253-582-8900	756-2963
Westwood Lodge Hospital 45 Clapboardtree St *TF:* 800-222-2237 ■ *Web:* arbourhealth.com	Westwood	MA	02090	781-762-7764	762-0550
William R Sharpe Jr Hospital 936 Sharpe Hospital Rd *TF:* 866-384-5250	Weston	WV	26452	304-269-1210	436-6380
Winnebago Mental Health Institute (WMHI) 1300 S Dr PO Box 9 *Web:* dhs.wisconsin.gov/mh%5fwinnebago	Winnebago	WI	54985	920-235-4910	237-2047
Wyoming State Hospital (WSH) 831 Hwy 150 S *Web:* www.health.wyo.gov/statehospital	Evanston	WY	82930	307-789-3464	789-7213

374-6 Rehabilitation Hospitals

	City	State	Zip	Phone	Fax
Allied Services Rehabilitation Hospital 475 Morgan Hwy *TF:* 888-734-2272 ■ *Web:* www.allied-services.org	Scranton	PA	18508	570-348-1300	341-4548
Bacharach Institute for Rehabilitation 61 W Jimmie Leeds Rd *Web:* www.bacharach.org	Pomona	NJ	08240	609-652-7000	652-7487
Baptist Rehabilitation Germantown 2100 Exeter Rd *Web:* www.baptistonline.org	Germantown	TN	38138	901-757-1350	
Baton Rouge Rehab Hospital 8595 United Plaza Blvd	Baton Rouge	LA	70809	225-927-0567	928-0317
Baylor Institute for Rehabilitation 909 N Washington Ave *Web:* www.baylorhealth.com	Dallas	TX	75246	214-820-9300	
Bryn Mawr Rehab Hospital 414 Paoli Pike *TF:* 888-876-8764 ■ *Web:* www.mainlinehealth.org	Malvern	PA	19355	484-596-5400	
Burke Rehabilitation Hospital 785 Mamaroneck Ave *TF:* 888-992-8753 ■ *Web:* www.burke.org	White Plains	NY	10605	914-597-2500	
Cardinal Hill Healthcare System 2050 Versailles Rd *Web:* www.cardinalhill.org	Lexington	KY	40504	859-254-5701	
Charlotte Institute of Rehabilitation 1100 Blythe Blvd *TF:* 800-634-2256 ■ *Web:* www.carolinashealthcare.org	Charlotte	NC	28203	704-355-4300	
Craig Hospital 3425 S Clarkson St *TF:* 800-247-0257 ■ *Web:* www.craighospital.org	Englewood	CO	80113	303-789-8000	789-8219
Crotched Mountain Rehabilitation Ctr 1 Verney Dr. *Web:* www.cmf.org	Greenfield	NH	03047	603-547-3311	547-3232
Drake Ctr 151 W Galbraith Rd *TF:* 800-948-0003 ■ *Web:* www.uchealth.com/danieldrakecenter	Cincinnati	OH	45216	513-418-2500	
Edwin Shaw Rehab 1621 Flickinger Rd *TF:* 800-221-4601 ■ *Web:* www.akrongeneral.org	Akron	OH	44312	330-784-1271	948-8332
Fairlawn Rehabilitation Hospital 189 May St *Web:* www.fairlawnrehab.org	Worcester	MA	01602	508-791-6351	
Frazier Rehabilitation Institute 220 Abraham Flexner Way *TF:* 800-333-2230 ■ *Web:* kentuckyonehealth.org	Louisville	KY	40202	502-582-7400	582-7477
Gaylord Hospital Gaylord Farms Rd PO Box 400 *TF:* 866-429-5673 ■ *Web:* www.gaylord.org	Wallingford	CT	06492	203-284-2800	294-8705
Good Shepherd Rehabilitation Hospital 850 S Fifth St *Web:* www.goodshepherdrehab.org	Allentown	PA	18103	610-776-3585	
Harmon Medical & Rehabilitation Hospital 2170 E Harmon Ave *Web:* fundltc.com	Las Vegas	NV	89119	702-794-0100	794-0041
HealthSouth Bakersfield Rehabilitation Hospital 5001 Commerce Dr *Web:* healthsouthbakersfield.com	Bakersfield	CA	93309	661-323-5500	
HealthSouth Braintree Rehabilitation Hospital 250 Pond St *Web:* www.healthsouthbraintree.com	Braintree	MA	02184	781-348-2500	356-2748
HealthSouth Chattanooga Rehabilitation Hospital 3660 Grandview Pkwy Ste 200 *TF:* 800-765-4772 ■ *Web:* www.healthsouth.com	Birmingham	AL	35243	205-967-7116	
HealthSouth City View Rehabilitation Hospital 6701 Oakmont Blvd *Web:* healthsouthcityview.com	Fort Worth	TX	76132	817-370-4700	
HealthSouth Deaconess Rehabilitation Hospital 4100 Covert Ave *Web:* healthsouthdeaconess.com	Evansville	IN	47714	812-476-9983	
HealthSouth Harmarville Rehabilitation Hospital 320 Guys Run Rd *TF:* 800-765-4772 ■ *Web:* www.healthsouthharmarville.com	Pittsburgh	PA	15238	412-828-1300	
HealthSouth Hospital of Pittsburgh 320 Guys Run Rd *TF:* 800-765-4772 ■ *Web:* www.healthsouthharmarville.com	Pittsburgh	PA	15238	412-828-1300	
HealthSouth Houston Rehabilitation Institute 13031 Wortham Ctr Dr *Web:* www.healthsouth.com	Houston	TX	77065	832-280-2500	
HealthSouth Humble Rehabilitation Hospital 19002 McKay Dr *Web:* www.healthsouthhumble.com	Humble	TX	77338	281-319-9541	446-8022
HealthSouth Lakeshore Rehabilitation Hospital 3660 Grandview Pkwy Ste 200 *Web:* www.healthsouth.com	Birmingham	AL	35243	205-967-7116	
HealthSouth MountainView Regional Rehabilitation Hospital 1160 Van Voorhis Rd *TF:* 800-388-2451 ■ *Web:* www.healthsouthmountainview.com	Morgantown	WV	26505	304-598-1100	598-1103
HealthSouth Nittany Valley Rehabilitation Hospital 550 W College Ave *TF:* 800-842-6026 ■ *Web:* www.nittanyvalleyrehab.com	Pleasant Gap	PA	16823	814-359-3421	359-5898
HealthSouth Plano Rehabilitation Hospital 2800 W 15th St. *Web:* www.healthsouthplano.com	Plano	TX	75075	972-612-9000	
HealthSouth Reading Rehabilitation Hospital 1623 Morgantown Rd *Web:* www.healthsouthreading.com	Reading	PA	19607	610-796-6000	
HealthSouth Rehabilitation Hospital of Albuquerque 7000 Jefferson St NE *Web:* www.healthsouthnewmexico.com	Albuquerque	NM	87109	505-344-9478	345-6722
HealthSouth Rehabilitation Hospital of Altoona 2005 Vly View Blvd. *TF:* 800-873-4220 ■ *Web:* www.healthsouthaltoona.com	Altoona	PA	16602	814-944-3535	
HealthSouth Rehabilitation Hospital of Arlington 3200 Matlock Rd *Web:* www.healthsoutharlington.com	Arlington	TX	76015	817-468-4000	

				Phone	Fax
HealthSouth Rehabilitation Hospital of Austin 1215 Red River TF: 800-765-4772 ■ Web: www.healthsouthaustin.com	Austin	TX	78701	512-474-5700	
HealthSouth Rehabilitation Hospital of Beaumont 3340 Plz 10 Blvd Web: www.healthsouthbeaumont.com	Beaumont	TX	77707	409-835-0835	835-1401
HealthSouth Rehabilitation Hospital of Columbia 2935 Colonial Dr Web: www.healthsouthcolumbia.com	Columbia	SC	29203	803-254-7777	
HealthSouth Rehabilitation Hospital of Erie 143 E Second St TF: 800-765-4772 ■ Web: healthsoutherie.com	Erie	PA	16507	814-878-1230	878-1470
HealthSouth Rehabilitation Hospital of Fayetteville 153 E Monte Painter Web: www.healthsouth.com	Fayetteville	AR	72703	479-444-2200	
HealthSouth Rehabilitation Hospital of Florence 900 E Cheves St Web: www.healthsouthflorence.com	Florence	SC	29506	843-679-9000	
HealthSouth Rehabilitation Hospital of Fort Smith 1401 S J St Web: www.healthsouthfortsmith.com	Fort Smith	AR	72901	479-785-3300	
HealthSouth Rehabilitation Hospital of Fort Worth 1212 W Lancaster Web: www.healthsouthfortworth.com	Fort Worth	TX	76102	817-870-2336	
HealthSouth Rehabilitation Hospital of Jonesboro 1201 Fleming Ave Web: www.healthsouthjonesboro.com	Jonesboro	AR	72401	870-932-0440	
HealthSouth Rehabilitation Hospital of Kingsport 113 Cassel Dr TF: 800-454-7422 ■ Web: www.healthsouthkingsport.com	Kingsport	TN	37660	423-246-7240	
HealthSouth Rehabilitation Hospital of Largo 901 N Clearwater-Largo Rd Web: healthsouthlargo.com	Largo	FL	33770	727-586-2999	
HealthSouth Rehabilitation Hospital of Memphis 4100 Austin Peay Hwy Web: www.healthsouthnorthmemphis.com	Memphis	TN	38128	901-213-5400	
HealthSouth Rehabilitation Hospital of Montgomery 4465 Narrow Ln Rd Web: www.healthsouthmontgomery.com	Montgomery	AL	36116	334-284-7700	
HealthSouth Rehabilitation Hospital of New Jersey 14 Hospital Dr Web: www.rehabnjtomsriver.com	Toms River	NJ	08755	732-244-3100	
HealthSouth Rehabilitation Hospital of North Alabama 107 Governors Dr Web: healthsouth.com	Huntsville	AL	35801	256-535-2300	
HealthSouth Rehabilitation Hospital of Sarasota 6400 Edgelake Dr Web: healthsouth.com	Sarasota	FL	34240	941-921-8600	
HealthSouth Rehabilitation Hospital of Tallahassee 1675 Riggins Rd Web: www.healthsouthtallahassee.com	Tallahassee	FL	32308	850-656-4800	
HealthSouth Rehabilitation Hospital of Texarkana 515 W 12th St Web: www.healthsouthtexarkana.com	Texarkana	TX	75501	903-735-5011	
HealthSouth Rehabilitation Hospital of Utah 8074 South 1300 East Web: www.healthsouthutah.com	Sandy	UT	84094	801-565-6666	
HealthSouth Rehabilitation Institute of Tucson 2650 N Wyatt Dr Web: www.rehabinstituteoftucson.com	Tucson	AZ	85712	520-325-1300	
HealthSouth Riosa 9119 Cinnamon Hill Web: www.hsriosa.com	San Antonio	TX	78240	210-691-0737	
HealthSouth Sea Pines Rehabilitation Hospital 101 E Florida Ave Web: www.healthsouthseapines.com	Melbourne	FL	32901	321-984-4662	984-4627
HealthSouth Sunrise Rehabilitation Hospital 4399 Nob Hill Rd Web: healthsouthsunrise.com	Sunrise	FL	33351	954-749-0300	746-1562
HealthSouth Treasure Coast Rehabilitation Hospital 1600 37th St Web: healthsouthtreasurecoast.com	Vero Beach	FL	32960	772-778-2100	
HealthSouth Tustin Rehabilitation Hospital 14851 Yorba St Web: tustinrehab.com	Tustin	CA	92780	714-832-9200	
Hillside Rehabilitation Hospital (HRH) 8747 Squires Ln NE Web: valleycareofohio.com	Warren	OH	44484	330-841-3700	
Hospital for Special Care 2150 Corbin Ave Web: www.hfsc.org	New Britain	CT	06053	860-223-2761	612-6304
Howard Regional Health System West Campus Specialty Hospital 829 N Dixon Rd Web: ecommunity.com/howard	Kokomo	IN	46901	765-452-6700	
JFK Johnson Rehabilitation Institute 65 James St Web: www.jfkmc.org/clinical-services	Edison	NJ	08818	732-321-7733	
John Heinz Institute of Rehabilitation Medicine 150 Mundy St Ste 3 Web: allied-services.org	Wilkes-Barre	PA	18702	570-826-3800	826-3898
Kansas Rehabilitation Hospital 1504 SW Eigth Ave Web: www.kansasrehabhospital.com	Topeka	KS	66606	785-235-6600	
Kentfield Rehabilitation Hospital 1125 Sir Francis Drake Blvd Web: www.kentfieldrehab.com	Kentfield	CA	94904	415-456-9680	
Kernan Hospital 2200 Kernan Dr Web: umrehabortho.org	Baltimore	MD	21207	410-448-2500	448-6825
Laguna Honda Hospital & Rehabilitation Ctr 375 Laguna Honda Blvd Web: www.lagunahonda.org	San Francisco	CA	94116	415-759-2300	759-2374
Madonna Rehabilitation Hospital 5401 S St TF: 800-676-5448 ■ Web: www.madonna.org	Lincoln	NE	68506	402-489-7102	
Magee Rehabilitation Hospital 1513 Race St TF: 800-966-2433 ■ Web: www.mageerehab.org	Philadelphia	PA	19102	215-587-3000	568-3736
Marianjoy Rehabilitation Hospital 26 W 171 Roosevelt Rd TF: 800-462-2366 ■ Web: www.marianjoy.org	Wheaton	IL	60187	630-462-4000	
Mary Free Bed Rehabilitation Hospital 235 Wealthy St SE TF: 800-528-8989 ■ Web: www.maryfreebed.com	Grand Rapids	MI	49503	616-242-0300	454-3939
Methodist Rehabilitation Ctr 1350 E Woodrow Wilson Dr *Fax: Admitting ■ TF: 800-223-6672 ■ Web: www.methodistonline.org	Jackson	MS	39216	601-981-2611	364-3465*
Mid-America Rehabilitation Hospital 5701 W 110th St Web: midamericarehabhospital.com	Overland Park	KS	66211	913-491-2400	
Missouri Rehabilitation Ctr 600 N Main St Web: www.muhealth.org	Mount Vernon	MO	65712	417-466-3711	
National Rehabilitation Hospital 102 Irving St NW Web: www.medstarhealth.org	Washington	DC	20010	202-877-1000	877-1602
Navicent Health 3351 Northside Dr Web: www.navicenthealth.org	Macon	GA	31210	478-633-1000	
New England Rehabilitation Hospital of Portland 335 Brighton Ave	Portland	ME	04102	207-775-4000	662-8446
Northeast Rehabilitation Hospital 70 Butler St TF: 800-439-2370 ■ Web: www.northeastrehab.com	Salem	NH	03079	603-893-2900	893-1628
Pinecrest Rehabilitation Hospital 5360 Linton Blvd Web: www.delraymedicalctr.com	Delray Beach	FL	33484	561-495-0400	
Rancho Los Amigos National Rehabilitation Ctr 7601 E Imperial Hwy *Fax: Admitting ■ TF: 877-726-2461 ■ Web: dhs.lacounty.gov/wps/portal/dhs/rancho	Downey	CA	90242	562-401-7111	401-7022*
Rehabilitation Hospital of Indiana 4141 Shore Dr TF: 866-510-2273 ■ Web: www.rhin.com	Indianapolis	IN	46254	317-329-2000	566-9111
Rehabilitation Hospital of the Pacific 226 N Kuakini St Web: www.rehabhospital.org	Honolulu	HI	96817	808-531-3511	544-3335
Rehabilitation Institute of Chicago 345 E Superior St *Fax: Admitting ■ TF Admitting: 800-354-7342 ■ Web: www.ric.org	Chicago	IL	60611	312-238-1000	238-5846*
Rehabilitation Institute of Michigan 261 Mack Blvd Web: www.rimrehab.org	Detroit	MI	48201	313-745-1203	993-0808
Roosevelt Warm Springs Institute for Rehabilitation 6135 Roosevelt Hwy Web: www.rooseveltrehab.org	Warm Springs	GA	31830	706-655-5000	
Sacred Heart Rehabilitation Institute 2323 N Lake Dr Web: www.columbia-stmarys.org	Milwaukee	WI	53211	414-298-6750	
Saint Lawrence Rehabilitation Ctr 2381 Lawrenceville Rd Web: www.slrc.org	Lawrenceville	NJ	08648	609-896-9500	
Saint Luke's Rehabilitation Institute 711 S Cowley St Web: www.st-lukes.org	Spokane	WA	99202	509-473-6000	473-6978
Saint Vincent Rehabilitation Hospital 2201 Wildwood Ave Web: stvincentrehabhospital.com	Sherwood	AR	72120	501-834-1800	
San Joaquin Valley Rehabilitation Hospital 7173 N Sharon Ave Web: www.sanjoaquinrehab.com	Fresno	CA	93720	559-436-3600	436-3688
Shadyside Nursing & Rehabilitation Ctr 5609 Fifth Ave TF: 800-366-1232 ■ Web: manorcare.com	Pittsburgh	PA	15232	412-362-3500	362-1951
Shepherd Ctr 2020 Peachtree Rd NE Web: www.shepherd.org	Atlanta	GA	30309	404-352-2020	350-7341
Siskin Hospital for Physical Rehabilitation 1 Siskin Plaza *Fax Area Code: 630 ■ Web: www.siskinrehab.org	Chattanooga	TN	37403	423-634-1200	792-5636*
Southern Indiana Rehabilitation Hospital 3104 Blackiston Blvd TF: 800-737-7090 ■ Web: www.sirh.org	New Albany	IN	47150	812-941-8300	
Southern Kentucky Rehabilitation Hospital 1300 Campbell Ln Web: www.skyrehab.com	Bowling Green	KY	42104	270-782-6900	
Spalding Rehabilitation Hospital 900 Potomac St TF: 800-367-3309 ■ Web: www.spaldingrehab.com	Aurora	CO	80011	303-367-1166	
Spaulding Rehabilitation Hospital 125 Nashua St TF: 888-774-0055 ■ Web: www.spauldingrehab.org	Boston	MA	02114	617-573-7000	
Sunnyview Rehabilitation Hospital 1270 Belmont Ave Web: www.nehealth.com	Schenectady	NY	12308	518-382-4500	
TIRR Memorial Hermann Hospital 1333 Moursund St TF: 800-447-3422 ■ Web: www.memorialhermann.org	Houston	TX	77030	713-799-5000	
Trinity Mother Frances Rehabilitation Hospital - Tyler 3131 Troup Hwy	Tyler	TX	75701	903-510-7000	510-7005
Trinity Neurological Rehabilitation Ctr 1400 Lindberg Dr Web: trinityneurorehab.com	Slidell	LA	70458	985-641-4985	646-0793
Villa Maria Nursing Center 1050 NE 125th St	North Miami	FL	33161	305-891-8850	891-3361
Walton Rehabilitation Hospital 1355 Independence Dr Web: www.wrh.org	Augusta	GA	30901	706-724-7746	
Warm Springs Rehabilitation Hospital of San Antonio 5101 Medical Dr Web: www.warmsprings.org	San Antonio	TX	78229	717-731-9660	
Warm Springs Specialty Hospital 200 Memorial Dr Web: www.warmsprings.org	Luling	TX	78648	830-875-8400	875-5029
Wesley Rehabilitation Hospital 8338 W 13th St N Web: www.wesleyrehabhospital.com	Wichita	KS	67212	316-729-9999	729-8888

374-7 Specialty Hospitals

Phone | Fax

Barbara Ann Karmanos Cancer Institute
4100 John R St — Detroit MI 48201 — 800-527-6266
TF: 800-527-6266 ■ *Web:* www.karmanos.org

Bascom Palmer Eye Institute 900 NW 17th St — Miami FL 33136 — 305-326-6000
TF: 800-329-7000 ■ *Web:* www.bascompalmer.org/site

Bone & Joint Hospital 1111 N Dewey Ave — Oklahoma City OK 73103 — 405-272-9671
Web: www.boneandjoint.com

Brigham & Women's Hospital 75 Francis St — Boston MA 02115 — 617-732-5500
TF: 800-722-5520 ■ *Web:* www.brighamandwomens.org

Callahan Eye Foundation Hospital
1720 University Blvd — Birmingham AL 35233 — 205-325-8100
Web: uabmedicine.org

Coler-Goldwater Specialty Hospital & Nursing Facility
1 Main St Franklin D Roosevelt Is. — New York NY 10044 — 212-318-8000 318-4370
Web: www.nyc.gov

Cornerstone Hospital of Austin 4207 Burnet Rd — Austin TX 78756 — 512-706-1900
Web: chghospitals.com

Dana-Farber Cancer Institute 44 Binney St — Boston MA 02115 — 617-632-3000 632-5520*
**Fax:* PR ■ *TF:* 866-408-3324 ■ *Web:* www.dana-farber.org

Deborah Heart & Lung Ctr 200 Trenton Rd — Browns Mills NJ 08015 — 609-893-6611 893-1213
Web: www.deborah.org

Delaware Hospital for the Chronically Ill
100 Sunnyside Rd — Smyrna DE 19977 — 302-233-1000
Web: dhss.delaware.gov

Dermatology Assoc of Atlanta
5555 Pchtrdnwyd Ste 190 — Atlanta GA 30324 — 404-256-4457
TF: 800-233-0706 ■ *Web:* www.dermatlanta.com

Doheny Eye Institute 1450 San Pablo St — Los Angeles CA 90033 — 323-442-7100 442-7127
Web: www.doheny.org

Eleanor Slater Hospital 14 Harrington Rd — Cranston RI 02920 — 401-462-2339 462-3204
TF: 800-438-8477 ■ *Web:* www.bhddh.ri.gov

Elmwood Healthcare Ctr & Specialty Hospital (SFHCC)
401 N Broadway — Green Springs OH 44836 — 419-639-2626
Web: elmwoodcommunities.com

Fox Chase Cancer Ctr 333 Cottman Ave — Philadelphia PA 19111 — 215-728-6900 728-2682
TF: 888-369-2427 ■ *Web:* www.foxchase.org

Georgia Cancer Specialists Pc (GCS)
1872 Montreal Rd — Tucker GA 30084 — 770-496-9443 496-9490
TF: 800-491-5991 ■ *Web:* www.gacancer.com

H Lee Moffitt Cancer Ctr & Research Institute
University of S Florida 12902 Magnolia Dr — Tampa FL 33612 — 888-663-3488 745-4064*
**Fax Area Code:* 813 ■ *TF:* 800-456-3434 ■ *Web:* www.moffitt.org

Hebrew Hospital Home Continuum of Care
61 Grasslands Rd — Valhalla NY 10595 — 914-681-8400
Web: www.hebrewhospitalhome.org

Hospice of Washington County Inc
747 Northern Ave — Hagerstown MD 21742 — 301-791-6360
Web: www.hwc-md.org

Hospital for Special Surgery 535 E 70th St — New York NY 10021 — 212-606-1000 606-1930
Web: www.hss.edu

Hughston Orthopedic Hospital 100 Frist Ct — Columbus GA 31908 — 706-494-2100
TF: 855-795-3609 ■ *Web:* columbusregional.com

James Cancer Hospital & Solove Research Institute, The
300 W Tenth Ave Ste 519 — Columbus OH 43210 — 614-293-5066 293-3132
Web: cancer.osu.edu

Kindred Healthcare Inc 700 W Sixth Ave — Anchorage AK 99501 — 413-787-6700
Web: khparkview.com

Kindred Hospital Atlanta 705 Juniper St — Atlanta GA 30308 — 404-873-2871 873-4516
TF: 800-255-0135 ■ *Web:* www.kindredatlanta.com

Kindred Hospital Dallas 9525 Greenville Ave — Dallas TX 75243 — 214-355-2600 355-2630
Web: www.khdallas.com

Kindred Hospital Fort Worth Southwest
7800 Oakmont Blvd — Fort Worth TX 76132 — 817-346-0094 263-4071
Web: www.kindredhospitalfwsw.com

Kindred Hospital Kansas City
8701 Troost Ave — Kansas City MO 64131 — 816-995-2000 995-2171
TF: 800-545-0749 ■ *Web:* www.kindredhospitalkc.com

Lake Taylor Transitional Hospital
1309 Kempsville Rd — Norfolk VA 23502 — 757-461-5001 461-4282
Web: www.laketaylor.org

Leahi Hospital 3675 Kilauea Ave — Honolulu HI 96816 — 808-733-8000 733-7914
TF: 800-845-6733 ■ *Web:* www.hhsc.org

Life Care Hospital of Pittsburgh
225 Penn Ave — Pittsburgh PA 15221 — 412-247-2424 247-2333
Web: lifecare-hospitals.com

Lombardi Comprehensive Cancer Ctr at Georgetown University
3800 Reservoir Rd NW — Washington DC 20007 — 202-444-2198 444-9429
Web: lombardi.georgetown.edu

Magee-Womens Hospital 300 Halket St — Pittsburgh PA 15213 — 412-641-6361
Web: www.magee.edu

Mary Rutan Hospital 205 E Palmer Rd — Bellefontaine OH 43311 — 937-592-5015 592-0207
Web: www.maryrutan.org

Massachusetts Eye & Ear 243 Charles St — Boston MA 02114 — 617-523-7900
Web: www.masseyeandear.org

Matheny Medical & Educational Ctr
65 Highland Ave — Peapack NJ 07977 — 908-234-0011 719-2137
Web: www.matheny.org

MD Anderson Cancer Ctr 1515 Holcombe Blvd — Houston TX 77030 — 713-792-2121
TF: 800-889-2094 ■ *Web:* www.mdanderson.org

Memorial Sloan-Kettering Cancer Ctr
1275 York Ave — New York NY 10065 — 212-639-2000
TF: 800-525-2225 ■ *Web:* www.mskcc.org

Miami Heart Institute
4701 N Meridian Ave — Miami Beach FL 33140 — 305-672-1111
Web: www.msmc.com

Midwestern Regional Medical Ctr (MRMC)
2520 Elisha Ave — Zion IL 60099 — 847-872-4561 872-6419
TF: 800-615-3055 ■ *Web:* www.cancercenter.com

Monroe Community Hospital
435 E Henrietta Rd — Rochester NY 14620 — 585-760-6500 760-6066
Web: www.monroehosp.org

National Jewish Medical & Research Ctr
1400 Jackson St PO Box 17169 — Denver CO 80206 — 303-388-4461
TF: 877-225-5654 ■ *Web:* www.nationaljewish.org

New York Eye & Ear Infirmary 310 E 14th St — New York NY 10003 — 212-979-4000 979-4512
TF: 800-522-4582 ■ *Web:* www.nyee.edu

Oak Forest Hospital of Cook County
15900 S Cicero Ave — Oak Forest IL 60452 — 708-687-7200

Odessa Regional Medical Ctr 520 E Sixth St — Odessa TX 79761 — 432-582-8000
TF: 877-898-6080 ■ *Web:* www.odessaregionalmedicalcenter.com

Orthopaedic Hospital 403 W Adams Blvd — Los Angeles CA 90007 — 213-742-1000 741-8338
Web: ortho-institute.org

Phillips Eye Institute 2215 Pk Ave S — Minneapolis MN 55404 — 612-775-8800
Web: www.allinahealth.org

Piedmont Geriatric Hospital
5001 E Patrick Henry Hwy PO Box 427 — Burkeville VA 23922 — 434-767-4401
Web: www.pgh.dbhds.virginia.gov

Presbyterian Orthopaedic Hospital
1901 Randolph Rd — Charlotte NC 28207 — 704-316-2000
Web: novanthealth.org/presbyterianmedicalcenter.aspx

Princess Margaret Hospital
610 University Ave — Toronto ON M5G2M9 — 416-946-2000
Web: www.uhn.ca

Roswell Park Cancer Institute
Elm and Carlton St — Buffalo NY 14263 — 716-845-2300
TF: 877-275-7724 ■ *Web:* www.roswellpark.org

Runnells Specialized Hospital of Union County
40 Watchung Way — Berkeley Heights NJ 07922 — 908-771-5700 771-0376
Web: www.ucnj.org/government/runnells-specialized-hospital

Saint Vincent Women's Hospital
8111 Township Line Rd — Indianapolis IN 46260 — 317-415-8111 236-8785*
**Fax Area Code:* 765 ■ **Fax:* Admitting ■ *TF:* 800-582-8258 ■ *Web:* www.stvincent.org

Samuel Mahelona Memorial Hospital
4800 Kawaihau Rd — Kapaa HI 96746 — 808-822-4961 823-4100
TF: 800-845-6733 ■ *Web:* www.smmh.hhsc.org

Sidney Kimmel Comprehensive Cancer Ctr at Johns Hopkins
401 N Broadway The Harry & Jeanette Weinberg Bldg
Ste 1100 — Baltimore MD 21231 — 410-955-5222 955-6787
Web: www.hopkinsmedicine.org

Siteman Cancer Ctr 4921 Parkview Pl — Saint Louis MO 63110 — 314-362-5196
TF: 800-600-3606 ■ *Web:* www.siteman.wustl.edu

Specialty Hospital Jacksonville
4901 Richard St — Jacksonville FL 32207 — 904-737-3120 242-5826*
**Fax Area Code:* 615 ■ *Web:* www.specialtyhospitaljax.com

Stanford Cancer Ctr
875 Lake Blake Wilbur Dr — Stanford CA 94305 — 650-498-6000 724-1433
TF: 800-422-6237 ■ *Web:* med.stanford.edu/cancer.html

Stony Point Surgical Ctr 8700 Stony Pt Pkwy — Richmond VA 23235 — 804-775-4500 643-3542
Web: www.stonypointsc.com

Straith Hospital for Special Surgery
23901 Lahser Rd — Southfield MI 48034 — 248-357-3360 357-0915
TF: 800-994-6610 ■ *Web:* www.straithhospital.org

Tewksbury Hospital 365 E St — Tewksbury MA 01876 — 978-851-7321 851-5648*
**Fax:* Mail Rm ■ *Web:* mass.gov

Texas Ctr for Infectious Diseases
2303 SE Military Dr — San Antonio TX 78223 — 210-534-8857 531-4502
TF: 800-839-5864 ■ *Web:* www.dshs.state.tx.us/tcid/default.shtm

Texas Orthopedic Hospital 7401 Main St — Houston TX 77030 — 713-799-8600 794-3580
TF: 866-783-4549 ■ *Web:* www.texasorthopedic.com

UC Davis Cancer Ctr 4501 X St — Sacramento CA 95817 — 916-734-5800 703-5067
TF: 800-362-5566 ■ *Web:* www.ucdmc.ucdavis.edu/cancer

University of Michigan Trauma Burn Ctr
1500 E Medical Ctr Dr — Ann Arbor MI 48109 — 734-936-9666 936-9657
Web: www.traumaburn.org

Vanderbilt-Ingram Cancer Ctr
691 Preston Bldg — Nashville TN 37232 — 615-936-1793 936-5879
Web: www.vicc.org

Veterans Home & Hospital 287 W St — Rocky Hill CT 06067 — 860-529-2571 721-5979*
**Fax:* Admitting ■ *Web:* ct.gov

Villa Feliciana Chronic Disease Hospital
5002 Hwy 10 — Jackson LA 70748 — 225-634-4000 634-4191
Web: dhh.louisiana.gov

Wills Eye 840 Walnut St — Philadelphia PA 19107 — 215-928-3000 928-0634
Web: www.willseye.org

Woman's Hospital 100 Woman's Wy — Baton Rouge LA 70815 — 225-927-1300 924-8110
Web: www.womans.org

Woman's Hospital of Texas 7600 Fannin St — Houston TX 77054 — 713-790-1234 790-0028
Web: www.womanshospital.com

Women & Infants Hospital of Rhode Island
101 Dudley St — Providence RI 02905 — 401-274-1100 453-7666
Web: www.womenandinfants.org

Women's & Children's Hospital (WCH)
4600 Ambassador Caffery Pkwy — Lafayette LA 70508 — 337-521-9100 521-9102
TF: 888-569-8331 ■ *Web:* www.womens-childrens.com

Women's Christian Assn Hospital
207 Foote Ave — Jamestown NY 14701 — 716-487-0141
Web: www.wcahospital.org

374-8 Veterans Hospitals

Listings for veterans hospitals are organized by states, and then by city names within those groupings.

Phone | Fax

Birmingham VA Medical Ctr 700 S 19th St — Birmingham AL 35233 — 205-933-8101 933-4498*
**Fax:* Admitting ■ *Web:* birmingham.va.gov

Tuscaloosa VA Medical Ctr 3701 Loop Rd E — Tuscaloosa AL 35404 — 205-554-2000
TF: 888-269-3045 ■ *Web:* tuscaloosa.va.gov

VA Medical Ctr 2400 Hospital Rd — Tuskegee AL 36083 — 334-727-0550 724-2793
TF: 800-214-8387 ■ *Web:* www.centralalabama.va.gov

	City	State	ZIP	Phone	Fax
Northern Arizona VA Health Care System 500 Hwy 89 N *TF:* 800-949-1005 ■ *Web:* www.prescott.va.gov	Prescott	AZ	86313	928-445-4860	
Southern Arizona Veterans Healthcare System 3601 S Sixth Ave *TF:* 800-470-8262 ■ *Web:* tucson.va.gov	Tucson	AZ	85723	520-792-1450	
Veterans Affairs Medical Ctr 1100 N College Ave *TF:* 800-691-8387 ■ *Web:* www.fayettevillear.va.gov	Fayetteville	AR	72703	479-443-4301	
VA Central California Health Care System 2615 E Clinton Ave *Web:* fresno.va.gov	Fresno	CA	93703	559-225-6100	
Jerry L Pettis Memorial Veterans Affairs Medical Ctr 11201 Benton St *Fax: Admitting ■ *TF:* 800-827-1000	Loma Linda	CA	92357	909-825-7084	422-3140*
Veterans Affairs Long Beach Medical Ctr 5901 E Seventh St *TF:* 888-769-8387 ■ *Web:* www.longbeach.va.gov	Long Beach	CA	90822	562-826-8000	826-5906
VA Greater Los Angeles Healthcare System 11301 Wilshire Blvd *Web:* www.losangeles.va.gov	Los Angeles	CA	90073	310-478-3711	268-3494
Veterans Affairs Medical Ctr 3801 Miranda Ave *Web:* www.paloalto.va.gov	Palo Alto	CA	94304	650-493-5000	852-3228
Veterans Affairs Medical Ctr 3350 La Jolla Village Dr *TF:* 800-331-8387	San Diego	CA	92161	858-552-8585	
San Francisco VA Medical Ctr 4150 Clement St *TF:* 877-487-2838 ■ *Web:* www2.va.gov	San Francisco	CA	94121	415-221-4810	
Denver Veterans Affairs Medical Ctr 1055 Clermont St *Fax: Mail Rm ■ *TF:* 888-336-8262 ■ *Web:* Www.denver.va.gov	Denver	CO	80220	303-399-8020	393-2861*
Grand Junction VA Medical Ctr 2121 N Ave *Web:* grandjunction.va.gov	Grand Junction	CO	81501	970-242-0731	244-1323
Veterans Affairs Medical Ctr 1601 Kirkwood Hwy *TF:* 800-450-8262 ■ *Web:* www.wilmington.va.gov	Wilmington	DE	19805	302-994-2511	
Veterans Affairs Medical Ctr 10000 Bay Pines Blvd *TF:* 888-820-0230 ■ *Web:* www2.va.gov	Bay Pines	FL	33744	727-398-6661	398-9442
Malcom Randall VAMC NF/SGVHS 1601 SW Archer Rd *Fax: Mail Rm ■ *TF:* 800-324-8387 ■ *Web:* www2.va.gov/directory/guide/facility.asp?id=54	Gainesville	FL	32608	352-376-1611	374-6113*
Veterans Affairs Medical Ctr 1201 NW 16th St *TF:* 888-276-1785 ■ *Web:* www.miami.va.gov	Miami	FL	33125	305-324-4455	
Veterans Affairs Medical Ctr 13000 Bruce B Downs Blvd *TF:* 888-716-7787 ■ *Web:* www.va.gov	Tampa	FL	33612	813-972-2000	
Carl Vinson Veterans Affairs Medical Ctr 1826 Veterans Blvd *Fax: Mail Rm ■ *TF:* 800-595-5229 ■ *Web:* va.gov	Dublin	GA	31021	478-272-1210	277-2717*
Veterans Affairs Medical Ctr 500 W Fort St *TF:* 800-273-8255	Boise	ID	83702	208-422-1000	
Veterans Affairs Medical Ctr 820 S Damen Ave *TF:* 888-569-5282 ■ *Web:* www.chicago.va.gov	Chicago	IL	60612	312-569-8387	
Edward Hines Jr Veterans Affairs Hospital 5000 S Fifth Ave PO Box 5000 *Web:* www.hines.va.gov	Hines	IL	60141	708-202-8387	202-2506
Veterans Affairs Medical Ctr 2121 Lake Ave *TF:* 800-360-8387 ■ *Web:* veteransfuneralhomes.com	Fort Wayne	IN	46805	260-426-5431	
Richard L. Roudebush VA Medical Ctr 1481 W Tenth St *TF:* 888-878-6889 ■ *Web:* www1.va.gov/directory/guide/facility.asp?id=62	Indianapolis	IN	46202	317-988-4498	
Veterans Affairs Medical Ctr 3600 30th St *TF:* 800-294-8387 ■ *Web:* www2.va.gov	Des Moines	IA	50310	515-699-5999	699-5862
Veterans Affairs Medical Ctr 601 Hwy 6 W *TF:* 866-687-7382 ■ *Web:* www.iowacity.va.gov	Iowa City	IA	52246	319-338-0581	
Veterans Affairs Outpatient Clinic 1515 W Pleasant St Bldg 1 *TF:* 800-816-8878 ■ *Web:* www.centraliowa.va.gov	Knoxville	IA	50138	641-842-3101	
Dwight D Eisenhower V A Medical Ctr 4101 South 4th St *TF:* 800-952-8387 ■ *Web:* www.leavenworth.va.gov	Leavenworth	KS	66048	913-682-2000	
Colmery-O'Neil Veterans Affairs Medical Ctr 2200 SW Gage Blvd *TF:* 800-574-8387 ■ *Web:* www.topeka.va.gov	Topeka	KS	66622	785-350-3111	350-4336
Alexandria Veterans Affairs Medical Ctr 2495 Shreveport Hwy 71 N *Fax: Hum Res ■ *TF:* 800-375-8387 ■ *Web:* www.alexandria.va.gov	Pineville	LA	71360	318-473-0010	483-5093*
Overton Brooks Veterans Affairs Medical Ctr 510 E Stoner Ave *TF:* 800-863-7441 ■ *Web:* www.shreveport.va.gov	Shreveport	LA	71101	318-221-8411	990-5556
Veterans Affairs Medical Ctr 10 N Greene St *TF:* 800-463-6295 ■ *Web:* veterans.maryland.gov	Baltimore	MD	21201	410-605-7000	605-7904
Edith Nourse Rogers Memorial Veterans Hospital 200 Springs Rd *Web:* en.wikipedia.org	Bedford	MA	01730	415-839-6885	882-0495
Veterans Affairs Medical Ctr 940 Belmont St *TF:* 800-865-3384 ■ *Web:* www2.va.gov	Brockton	MA	02301	508-583-4500	
Veterans Affairs Medical Ctr 150 S Huntington Ave *Fax Area Code: 617 ■ *TF:* 800-273-8255 ■ *Web:* www.va.gov	Jamaica Plain	MA	02130	800-273-8255	278-4508*
Veterans Affairs Medical Ctr 2215 Fuller Rd *Web:* www.annarbor.va.gov	Ann Arbor	MI	48105	734-769-7100	
U.S. Department of Veterans Affairs 325 E 'H' St *TF:* 800-215-8262 ■ *Web:* www.ironmountain.va.gov	Iron Mountain	MI	49801	906-774-3300	
Paragon Health Pc 2318 Gull Rd Ste B *Web:* www.paragonhealthpc.com	Kalamazoo	MI	49048	269-341-4554	381-3063
Veterans Affairs Medical Ctr 1500 Weiss St *TF:* 877-222-8387 ■ *Web:* www.va.gov	Saginaw	MI	48602	989-497-2500	321-4903
Veterans Affairs Medical Ctr 1 Veterans Dr *TF:* 866-414-5058 ■ *Web:* www.minneapolis.va.gov	Minneapolis	MN	55417	612-725-2000	
G.V. (Sonny) Montgomery VA Medical Ctr 1500 E Woodrow Wilson Dr *Fax: Hum Res ■ *Web:* jackson.va.gov	Jackson	MS	39216	601-362-4471	368-3811*
Harry S Truman Memorial Veterans Hospital 800 Hospital Dr *TF:* 877-222-8387 ■ *Web:* columbiamo.va.gov	Columbia	MO	65201	573-814-6000	814-6600
John J Pershing Veterans Affairs Medical Ctr 1500 N Westwood Blvd *TF:* 888-557-8262 ■ *Web:* poplarbluff.va.gov	Poplar Bluff	MO	63901	573-686-4151	778-4559
VA Medical Ctr 3687 Veterans Dr	Fort Harrison	MT	59636	406-442-6410	447-7904
Veterans Affairs Medical Ctr 600 S 70th St *TF:* 866-851-6052 ■ *Web:* veteransfuneralhomes.com	Lincoln	NE	68510	402-489-3802	
Veterans Affairs Medical Ctr 4101 Woolworth Ave *TF:* 800-451-5796 ■ *Web:* Www.nebraska.va.gov	Omaha	NE	68105	402-346-8800	
Sierra NV Healthcare Systems (VA Medical Ctr) 975 Kirman Ave *TF:* 888-838-6256 ■ *Web:* www.reno.va.gov	Reno	NV	89502	775-786-7200	
Veterans Affairs Medical Ctr 718 Smyth Rd *TF:* 800-892-8384 ■ *Web:* www.manchester.va.gov	Manchester	NH	03104	603-624-4366	626-6576
East Orange Campus of the VA New Jersey Health Care System (NJHCS) 385 Tremont Ave *Fax Area Code: 202 ■ *Fax: Hum Res ■ *TF General:* 844-872-4681 ■ *Web:* www.usa.gov	East Orange	NJ	07018	844-872-4681	456-1414*
Veterans Affairs Medical Ctr 151 Knollcroft Rd *Web:* www.va.gov	Lyons	NJ	07939	908-647-0180	
Veterans Affairs Medical Ctr 1501 San Pedro Dr SE *Web:* va.gov	Albuquerque	NM	87108	505-265-1711	256-2855
Stratton Veterans Affairs Medical Ctr 113 Holland Ave *Fax: Admitting ■ *TF:* 800-223-4810 ■ *Web:* www.albany.va.gov	Albany	NY	12208	518-626-5000	626-6709*
Batavia VA Medical Ctr 222 Richmond Ave *TF:* 800-273-8255 ■ *Web:* buffalo.va.gov	Batavia	NY	14020	585-297-1000	297-1069
Bath Veterans Affairs Medical Ctr 76 Veterans Ave *Fax: Admissions ■ *TF:* 877-845-3247 ■ *Web:* www.bath.va.gov	Bath	NY	14810	607-664-4000	664-4915*
James J Peters Veterans Affairs Medical Ctr 130 W Kingsbridge Rd *Web:* bronx.va.gov	Bronx	NY	10468	718-584-9000	741-4571
Veterans Affairs Medical Ctr 3495 Bailey Ave *TF:* 800-532-8387 ■ *Web:* www.buffalo.va.gov	Buffalo	NY	14215	716-834-9200	862-8759
Montrose Campus 2094 Albany Post Rd PO Box 100 *TF:* 800-269-8749 ■ *Web:* www.hudsonvalley.va.gov	Montrose	NY	10548	914-737-4400	788-4244
VA NY Harbor Healthcare System 423 E 23rd St *Web:* nyharbor.va.gov	New York	NY	10010	212-686-7500	951-3375
Veterans Affairs Medical Ctr 79 Middleville Rd *Web:* www.northport.va.gov	Northport	NY	11768	631-261-4400	
Veterans Affairs Medical Ctr 800 Irving Ave *Fax: Admitting ■ *TF:* 800-792-4334 ■ *Web:* syracuse.va.gov	Syracuse	NY	13210	315-425-4400	425-4375*
VA Hudson Valley Health Care System *Castle Point Campus* 41 Castle Pt Rd *TF:* 877-222-8387 ■ *Web:* www.hudsonvalley.va.gov	Wappingers Falls	NY	12590	845-831-2000	838-5193
Veterans Affairs Medical Ctr 1100 Tunnel Rd *TF:* 800-932-6408 ■ *Web:* www.asheville.va.gov	Asheville	NC	28805	828-298-7911	299-2502
Veterans Affairs Medical Ctr 508 Fulton St *TF:* 800-273-8225 ■ *Web:* www.durham.va.gov	Durham	NC	27705	919-286-0411	286-6825
WG Bill Hefner Veterans Affairs Medical Ctr 1601 Brenner Ave *TF:* 800-469-8262 ■ *Web:* www.salisbury.va.gov	Salisbury	NC	28144	704-638-9000	
Veterans Affairs Medical Ctr 3200 Vine St *TF:* 877-829-5500 ■ *Web:* www.fisherhouse.org/houses/house-locations/#Ohio	Cincinnati	OH	45220	513-475-6571	487-6661
Louis Stokes Cleveland Veterans Affairs Medical Ctr 10701 E Blvd *TF:* 888-838-6446 ■ *Web:* cleveland.va.gov	Cleveland	OH	44106	216-791-3800	
Dayton Va Medical Ctr 4100 W Third St *TF:* 800-368-8262 ■ *Web:* dayton.va.gov	Dayton	OH	45428	937-268-6511	262-2187
Veterans Affairs Medical Ctr 921 NE 13th St *TF:* 866-835-5273 ■ *Web:* Www.oklahoma.va.gov	Oklahoma City	OK	73104	405-456-1000	
Veterans Affairs Medical Ctr 913 NW Garden Valley Blvd *TF:* 800-827-1000 ■ *Web:* www2.va.gov	Roseburg	OR	97470	541-440-1000	440-1225
Altoona VA Medical Ctr 2907 Pleasant Vly Blvd *Fax Area Code: 814 ■ *TF:* 877-626-2500 ■ *Web:* www.altoona.va.gov	Altoona	PA	16602	877-626-2500	940-7898*
Erie VA Medical Ctr 135 E 38th St *TF:* 800-274-8387 ■ *Web:* www.erie.va.gov	Erie	PA	16504	814-868-8661	
Veterans Affairs Medical Ctr 1700 S Lincoln Ave *TF:* 800-409-8771 ■ *Web:* www.lebanon.va.gov	Lebanon	PA	17042	800-409-8771	
Veterans Affairs Medical Ctr 7180 Highland Dr *TF:* 866-482-7488	Pittsburgh	PA	15206	412-365-4900	
Veterans Affairs Medical Ctr 830 Chalkstone Ave *TF:* 866-590-2976 ■ *Web:* www.va.gov	Providence	RI	02908	401-273-7100	
Ralph H Johnson Veterans Affairs Medical Ctr 109 Bee St *Web:* charleston.va.gov	Charleston	SC	29401	843-577-5011	
Veterans Affairs Medical Ctr 6439 Garners Ferry Rd *Fax: Mail Rm ■ *TF:* 888-651-2683 ■ *Web:* www.columbiasc.va.gov	Columbia	SC	29209	803-776-4000	695-6862*
Veterans Affairs Medical Ctr 1030 Jefferson Ave *TF:* 800-636-8262 ■ *Web:* va.gov	Memphis	TN	38104	901-523-8990	

Phone Fax

James H Quillen Veterans Affairs Medical Ctr
Corner of Lamont & Veterans Way
PO Box 4000 Mountain Home TN 37684 423-926-1171 979-3519
TF: 877-573-3529 ■ *Web:* www.mountainhome.va.gov

Alvin C York Medical Ctr
3400 Lebanon Pike Murfreesboro TN 37129 615-867-6000
TF: 800-228-4973 ■ *Web:* tennesseevalley.va.gov

Veterans Affairs Medical Ctr
1310 24th Ave S Nashville TN 37212 615-327-4751
TF: 800-228-4973 ■ *Web:* www.va.gov

Thomas E Creek Veterans Affairs Medical Ctr
6010 Amarillo Blvd W Amarillo TX 79106 806-355-9703
TF: 800-687-8262 ■ *Web:* www.amarillo.va.gov

VA Medical Ctr 4500 S Lancaster Rd Dallas TX 75216 214-742-8387 857-1171
TF: 800-849-3597 ■ *Web:* www.northtexas.va.gov

Veterans Affairs Medical Ctr
2002 Holcombe Blvd Houston TX 77030 713-791-1414 794-7218
TF: 800-553-2278 ■ *Web:* www.houston.va.gov

South Texas Veterans Health Care System
7400 Merton Minter St San Antonio TX 78229 210-617-5300
Web: www.southtexas.va.gov

Central Texas Veterans Health Care System
1901 Veterans Memorial Dr Temple TX 76504 254-778-4811
TF: 800-423-2111 ■ *Web:* www2.va.gov

Veterans Affairs Medical Ctr 4800 Memorial Dr Waco TX 76711 254-752-6581
Web: va.gov

Veterans Affairs Medical Ctr
500 Foothill Dr Salt Lake City UT 84148 801-582-1565
TF: 800-613-4012 ■ *Web:* www.visn19.va.gov

White River Junction Veterans Affairs Medical Ctr
215 N Main St White River Junction VT 05009 802-295-9363 296-5138
TF: 866-687-8387 ■ *Web:* www.whiteriver.va.gov

Veterans Affairs Medical Ctr
100 Emancipation Dr Hampton VA 23667 757-728-3100
Web: www.va.gov

Salem Veterans Affairs Medical Ctr
1970 Roanoke Blvd Salem VA 24153 540-982-2463
TF: 888-982-2463 ■ *Web:* va.gov

Veterans Affairs Puget Sound Medical Ctr
1660 S Columbian Way Seattle WA 98108 206-762-1010 764-2270*
**Fax:* Admitting ■ *TF:* 800-329-8387 ■ *Web:* www.pugetsound.va.gov

Veterans Affairs Medical Ctr
77 Wainwright Dr Walla Walla WA 99362 509-525-5200 528-5738*
**Fax Area Code:* 304 ■ **Fax:* Admissions ■ *TF:* 800-827-1000

Veterans Affairs Medical Ctr
200 Veterans Ave Beckley WV 25801 304-255-2121 255-2431
Web: www1.va.gov

Louis A Johnson Veterans Affairs Medical Ctr
1 Medical Ctr Dr Clarksburg WV 26301 304-623-3461 626-7724
TF: 800-733-0512 ■ *Web:* clarksburg.va.gov

Huntington Veterans Affairs Medical Ctr
1540 Spring Valley Dr Huntington WV 25704 304-429-6741 429-0270
TF: 800-827-8244 ■ *Web:* huntington.va.gov

Veterans Affairs Medical Ctr
2500 Overlook Terr Madison WI 53705 608-256-1901 280-7116
TF: 888-478-8321 ■ *Web:* www.madison.va.gov

Tomah Veterans Affairs Medical Ctr
500 E Veterans St Tomah WI 54660 608-372-3971 372-1692*
**Fax:* Admissions ■ *TF:* 800-872-8662 ■ *Web:* tomah.va.gov

375 HOT TUBS, SPAS, WHIRLPOOL BATHS

Phone Fax

Alaglass Swimming Pools
165 Sweet Bay Rd Saint Matthews SC 29135 877-655-7179
TF: 877-655-7179 ■ *Web:* alaglas.com

Atlantic Spas & Billiards 8721 Glenwood Ave Raleigh NC 27617 919-783-7447 783-0146
TF: 800-849-8827 ■ *Web:* www.atlanticspasandbilliards.com

Bath-Tec Inc PO Box 1118 Ennis TX 75120 972-646-5279 646-5688
TF: 800-526-3301 ■ *Web:* www.bathtec.com

Best Bath Systems 723 Garber St Caldwell ID 83605 208-342-6823 333-8657
TF: 866-333-8657 ■ *Web:* bestbath.com

Cal Spas Inc 1462 E Ninth St Pomona CA 91766 909-623-8781 629-0751
TF: 800-225-7727 ■ *Web:* www.calspas.com

Dimension One Spas 2611 Business Pk Dr Vista CA 92081 760-727-7727 734-4425
Web: www.d1spas.com

Galaxy Aquatics Inc
1075 W Sam Houston Pkwy N Ste 210 Houston TX 77043 713-464-0303 464-0399
Web: www.galaxy-aquatics.com

Hydra Baths 1632 West 139th St Gardena CA 90249 714-556-9133 708-0632
Web: www.hydrabaths.com

Hydro Systems Inc 29132 Ave Paine Valencia CA 91355 661-775-0686 775-0668
TF: 800-747-9990 ■ *Web:* www.hydrosystem.com

Jason International Inc
8328 MacArthur Dr North Little Rock AR 72118 501-771-4477 771-2333
TF: 800-255-5766 ■ *Web:* www.jasoninternational.com

Kallista Inc 1227 N Eigth St Ste 2 Sheboygan WI 53081 920-457-4441
TF Cust Svc: 888-452-5547 ■ *Web:* www.kallista.com

Koral Industries Inc 1504 S Kaufman St Ennis TX 75119 972-875-6555 875-9558
TF: 800-627-2441 ■ *Web:* www.koralco.com

Marquis Spas Corp 596 Hoffman Rd Independence OR 97351 503-838-0888 838-3849
TF: 800-275-0888 ■ *Web:* www.marquisspas.com

Master Spas Inc 6927 Lincoln Pkwy Fort Wayne IN 46804 260-436-9100 432-7935
TF: 800-860-7727 ■ *Web:* www.masterspas.com

Plastic Development Co Inc
75 Palmer Industrial Rd PO Box 4007 Williamsport PA 17701 800-451-1420 323-8485*
**Fax Area Code:* 570 ■ *TF:* 800-451-1420 ■ *Web:* www.pdcspas.com

Royal Baths Manufacturing Co
14635 Chrisman Rd Houston TX 77039 281-442-3400 442-1455
TF: 800-826-0074 ■ *Web:* www.royalbaths.com

Spa Manufacturers 6060 Ulmerton Rd Clearwater FL 33760 727-530-9493 539-8151
TF: 877-530-9493 ■ *Web:* www.spamanufacturers.com

Phone Fax

Spurlin Industries Inc 625 Main St Palmetto GA 30268 770-463-1644 463-2932
TF: 800-749-4475 ■ *Web:* www.spurlinindustries.com

Thermo Spas Inc 155 E St Wallingford CT 06492 800-876-0158 265-7133*
**Fax Area Code:* 203 ■ *TF:* 800-876-0158 ■ *Web:* www.thermospas.com

Watertech Whirlpool Bath & Spa
2507 Plymouth Rd Johnson City TN 37601 800-289-8827 926-6438*
**Fax Area Code:* 423 ■ *TF:* 800-289-8827 ■ *Web:* www.watertechtn.com

Watkins Mfg Corp 1280 Pk Ctr Dr Vista CA 92081 800-999-4688
TF: 800-999-4688 ■ *Web:* www.hotspring.com

376 HOTEL RESERVATIONS SERVICES

Phone Fax

AC Central Reservations Inc
201 Tilton Rd London Sq Mall Ste 17B Northfield NJ 08225 609-383-8880 383-8616
TF: 888-227-6667 ■ *Web:* www.acrooms.com

Accommodations Plus Inc 1200 Route 109 Lindenhurst NY 11757 516-798-4444
Web: www.apihotels.com

Advance Reservations Inn Arizona PO Box 950 Tempe AZ 85280 480-990-0682 990-3390
TF: 800-456-0682 ■ *Web:* www.azres.com

Agile Ticketing Solutions 4124 Central Pk Hermitage TN 37076 615-360-6700
Web: tickettogo.com

Alexandria & Arlington Bed & Breakfast Networks (AABBN)
4938 Hampden Ln Ste 164 Bethesda MD 20814 703-549-3415 517-9179*
**Fax Area Code:* 202 ■ *TF:* 888-549-3415 ■ *Web:* www.aabbn.com

Alliance Reservations Network
21640 N 19th Ave Ste C102 Phoenix AZ 85027 602-444-9993 207-4911*
**Fax Area Code:* 515 ■ *TF Cust Svc:* 800-419-1545 ■ *Web:* www.reservetravel.com

Anchorage Alaska Bed & Breakfast Assn (AABBA)
PO Box 242623 Anchorage AK 99524 907-272-5909
TF: 888-584-5147 ■ *Web:* www.anchorage-bnb.com

Annapolis Accommodations 41 Maryland Ave Annapolis MD 21401 410-263-3262 263-1703
Web: www.stayannapolis.com

B & B Agency of Boston
47 Commercial Wharf Ste 3 Boston MA 02110 800-248-9262
TF: 800-248-9262 ■ *Web:* www.boston-bnbagency.com

Bed & Breakfast Assn of Downtown Toronto
PO Box 190 Stn B Toronto ON M5T2W1 416-410-3938 483-8822
Web: www.bnbinfo.com

Bed & Breakfast Atlanta 790 N Ave Ste 202 Atlanta GA 30306 404-875-0525 876-6544
TF: 800-967-3224 ■ *Web:* www.bedandbreakfastatlanta.com

Bed & Breakfast Cape Cod PO Box 2250 Mashpee MA 02649 508-255-3824
TF: 800-556-3815 ■ *Web:* www.bookcapecod.com

Branson's Best Reservations
2875 Green Mtn Dr Branson MO 65616 417-339-2204
TF: 800-335-2555 ■ *Web:* www.bransonbest.com

Branson/Lakes Area Lodging Assn PO Box 430 Branson MO 65615 417-559-3869 335-3643
Web: blala.clubexpress.com

Capitol Reservations
1730 Rhode Island Ave NW Washington DC 20036 202-452-1270 452-0537
TF: 800-619-4337 ■ *Web:* www.visitdc.com

Central Reservation Service of New England Inc
300 Terminal C
Logan International Airport East Boston MA 02128 617-569-3800 561-4840

Colonial Williamsburg Reservation Ctr
PO Box 1776 Williamsburg VA 23187 757-229-1000
TF: 800-447-8679 ■ *Web:* www.history.org

COMM Group Inc 2003 S Easton Rd Ste 100 Doylestown PA 18901 215-348-8775
Web: www.cheapcaribbean.com

Daniel's Group of Companies Inc, The
10520 Seven Mile Rd Caledonia WI 53108 262-835-3553
Web: www.meetings-incentives.com

Greater Miami & The Beaches Hotel Assn (GMBHA)
1674 Meridian Ave Ste 420 Miami Beach FL 33139 305-531-3553 531-8954
Web: gmbha.com

Greater New Orleans Hotel & Lodging Assn
2020 St Charles Ave 5th Fl New Orleans LA 70130 504-525-2264 210-0356
TF: 866-366-1121 ■ *Web:* www.gnohla.com

Hawaii's Best Bed & Breakfasts 571 Pauku St Kailua HI 96734 808-263-3100 262-5030
TF: 800-262-9912 ■ *Web:* www.bestbnb.com

Holiday Inn Express & Suites
5001 Brougham Dr Drayton Valley AB T7A0A1 780-515-9888 514-2734
TF: 877-444-3110 ■ *Web:* www.hiedraytonvalley.com

Hot Rooms 875 N. Michigan Ave Ste 3100 Chicago IL 60611 773-468-7666 649-0559*
**Fax Area Code:* 312 ■ *TF:* 800-468-3500 ■ *Web:* www.hotrooms.com

Jackson Hole Central Reservations (JHCR)
140 E Broadway Ste 24 PO Box 2618 Jackson WY 83001 307-733-4005 733-1286
TF: 888-838-6606 ■ *Web:* www.jacksonholewy.com

Key West Key 726 Passover Ln Key West FL 33040 800-881-7321 294-2974*
**Fax Area Code:* 305 ■ *TF:* 800-881-7321 ■ *Web:* www.keywestkey.com

Know Before You Go Reservations
8000 International Dr Orlando FL 32819 407-352-9813
TF: 800-749-1993 ■ *Web:* www.knowbeforeugo.com

Lasvegastickets.com
5030 Paradise Rd Ste B108 Las Vegas NV 89119 702-597-1588
TF: 800-597-7469 ■ *Web:* lasvegastickets.com

Leading Hotels of the World
485 Lexington Ave Ste 401 New York NY 10017 212-515-5600 515-5899
TF: 800-745-8883 ■ *Web:* www.lhw.com

Luxe Worldwide Hotels
11461 W Sunset Blvd Los Angeles CA 90049 310-440-3090 440-0821
TF: 888-336-3745 ■ *Web:* www.luxehotels.com

Martha's Vineyard & Nantucket Reservations
73 Lagoon Pond Rd Vineyard Haven MA 02568 508-693-7200
Web: www.mvreservations.com

Myrtle Beach Reservation Service
5905 S Kings Hwy Ste 20 Myrtle Beach SC 29575 843-626-9668 448-8143
Web: www.mbhospitality.org

Nantucket Accommodations 2 Windy Way Nantucket MA 02554 508-228-9559 901-4032
TF: 866-743-3330 ■ *Web:* nantucketaccommodations.com

National Corporate Housing
365 Herndon Pkwy Ste 111 Herndon VA 20170 866-229-4720
TF: 866-229-4720 ■ *Web:* www.nationalcorporatehousing.com

				Phone	Fax
New Otani North America Reservation Ctr 120 S Los Angeles St *TF Cust Svc:* 800-421-8795 ■ *Web:* newotani.co.jp	Los Angeles	CA	90012	213-629-1200	473-1416
Ocean City Hotel-Motel-Restaurant Assn PO Box 340 *TF:* 800-626-2326 ■ *Web:* www.ocvisitor.com	Ocean City	MD	21843	410-289-6733	
Private Lodging Service 1978 Coltman Rd *Web:* privatelodgings.com	Cleveland	OH	44106	216-291-1209	
Quikbook 381 Pk Ave S 3rd Fl *TF:* 800-789-9887 ■ *Web:* www.quikbook.com	New York	NY	10016	212-779-7666	779-6120
Resort 2 Me 975 Cass St *TF:* 800-757-5646 ■ *Web:* www.resort2me.com	Monterey	CA	93940	831-642-6622	
San Diego Concierge 4379 30th St Ste 4 *TF:* 800-979-9091 ■ *Web:* www.sandiegoconcierge.com	San Diego	CA	92104	619-280-4121	
San Francisco Reservations 360 22nd St Ste 300	Oakland	CA	94612	510-628-4450	
Stay Aspen Snowmass 425 Rio Grande Pl *TF:* 888-649-5982 ■ *Web:* www.stayaspensnowmass.com	Aspen	CO	81611	970-925-9000	925-9008
Sundance Vacations Inc 264 Highland Park Blvd *Web:* www.sundancevacations.com	Wilkes-Barre	PA	18702	570-820-0900	
Vacation Co 42 New Orleans Rd Ste 102 *TF:* 800-845-7018 ■ *Web:* www.vacationcompany.com	Hilton Head Island	SC	29928	843-686-6100	
Washington DC Accommodations 2201 Wisconsin Ave NW Ste C-120 *TF:* 800-503-3330 ■ *Web:* www.wdcahotels.com	Washington	DC	20007	202-289-2220	
Winter Park Resort 85 Parsenn Rd *TF Resv:* 800-903-7275 ■ *Web:* www.winterparkresort.com	Winter Park	CO	80482	970-726-5514	726-1690
Worldhotels 152 W 57th St 6th Fl *Web:* www.worldhotels.com	New York	NY	10019	212-956-0200	
WorldRes Ltd 15333 N Pima Rd Ste 245	Scottsdale	AZ	85260	480-946-5100	946-0450
Xanterra South Rim LLC 10 Albright St PO Box 699 *Web:* www.grandcanyonlodges.com	Grand Canyon	AZ	86023	928-638-2631	638-9810

377 HOTELS - CONFERENCE CENTER

				Phone	Fax
A-1 Hospitality LLC 7809 W Quinault Ave *Web:* www.hotelsa1.com	Kennewick	WA	99336	509-783-2164	
Ace Hotel & Swim Club 701 e palm canyon dr *Web:* www.acehotel.com	Palm Springs	CA	92264	504-900-1180	
Acoma Business Enterprise I 40 Exit 102 *Web:* www.skycity.com	Acoma	NM	87034	505-552-6017	
Airlie Conference Ctr 6809 Airlie Rd *TF:* 800-288-9573 ■ *Web:* www.airlie.com	Warrenton	VA	20187	540-347-1300	341-3207
Alexandra Apt Hotel 77 Ryerson Ave *Web:* alexandrahotel.com	Toronto	ON	M5T2V4	416-504-2121	
Allen Management 736 Thimble Shoals Blvd *Web:* www.apluslodging.com	Newport News	VA	23606	757-722-2804	
Aloha Surf Hotel, The 444 Kanekapolei St *Web:* www.alohasurfhotelwaikiki.com	Honolulu	HI	96815	808-923-4402	
Amerilodge 1040 W Hamlin Rd *Web:* amerilodgegroup.com	Rochester Hills	MI	48309	248-601-2500	
Aspen Wye River Conference Ctr 600 Aspen Dr *Web:* www.marriott.com	Queenstown	MD	21658	410-827-7400	827-9295
Atlanta Carrier Hotel 56 Marietta St *Web:* www.56marietta.com	Atlanta	GA	30303	404-869-8992	
Auberge Bonaparte 447 St-francois-xavier *Web:* www.bonaparte.com	Montreal	QC	H2Y2T1	514-844-1448	
Avista Hotel Group 5353 Conroy Rd Ste 200 *Web:* www.avistahotels.com	Orlando	FL	32811	407-581-9000	
Avista Resort 300 N Ocean Blvd *Web:* www.avistaresort.com	North Myrtle Beach	SC	29582	843-249-2521	
Avocet Hospitality Group 38 Ctr St *Web:* avocethospitality.com	Folly Beach	SC	29439	843-588-6699	
BALSAMS Grand Resort Hotel, The 1000 Cold Spring Rd *TF:* 800-255-0800 ■ *Web:* www.thebalsams.com	Dixville Notch	NH	03576	800-255-0800	
Banff Centre, The 107 Tunnel Mtn Dr PO Box 1020 *TF:* 800-884-7574 ■ *Web:* www.banffcentre.ca	Banff	AB	T1L1H5	403-762-6100	
Brown Room at Congress Hall 251 Beach Ave *Web:* www.caperesorts.com	Cape May	NJ	08204	609-884-8421	
Brutger Equities Inc 100 4th Ave S *Web:* www.brutgerequities.com	Saint Cloud	MN	56301	320-252-6262	
Cabins Usa Gatlinburg Llc 510 Ski Mountain Rd Ste 6 *Web:* cabinsusagatlinburg.com	Gatlinburg	TN	37738	865-436-5031	
Capstone Development LLC 1200 G St, NW Ste 800 *Web:* www.cstonedevelopment.com	Washington	DC	20005	202-661-3536	
Chaminade 1 Chaminade Ln *TF:* 800-283-6569 ■ *Web:* www.chaminade.com	Santa Cruz	CA	95065	831-475-5600	476-4798
Chateau Elan Resort & Conference Ctr 100 Rue Charlemagne *TF:* 800-233-9463 ■ *Web:* www.chateauelan.com	Braselton	GA	30517	678-425-0900	425-6000
Chattanoogan, The 1201 Broad St *TF:* 877-756-1684 ■ *Web:* www.chattanooganhotel.com	Chattanooga	TN	37402	423-756-3400	756-3404
Chauncey Conference Ctr 1 Chauncey Rd *Web:* www.acc-chaunceyconferencecenter.com	Princeton	NJ	08541	609-921-3600	683-4958
Cheyenne Mountain Conference Resort 3225 Broadmoor Vly Rd *TF:* 800-428-8886 ■ *Web:* www.cheyennemountain.com	Colorado Springs	CO	80906	719-538-4000	
Clarion Hotel & Conference Ctr Antietam Creek 901 Dual Hwy *Web:* www.clarionhagerstown.com	Hagerstown	MD	21740	301-733-5100	733-9192
Club Holdings LLC 11101 W 120th Ave Ste 300 *Web:* www.quintess.com	Broomfield	CO	80021	720-406-1100	
Club Quarters Inc 49 W 45th St *Web:* clubquarters.com	New York	NY	10036	212-575-0006	
Coconut Mallory Resort & Marina 1445 S Roosevelt Blvd *Web:* mallorykeywest.com	Key West	FL	33040	305-292-0017	
Colonial Inn (Reno) 250 N Arlington Ave *Web:* www.colonialgardencourt.com	Reno	NV	89501	775-322-3838	
Concrete Contractors Interstate 12599 Stotler Ct *Web:* seicci.com	Poway	CA	92064	858-679-5550	
Conference Ctr at NorthPointe 100 Green Meadows Dr S *TF:* 866-233-9393 ■ *Web:* www.nwhotelandconferencecenter.com	Lewis Center	OH	43035	614-880-4300	880-4167
Cook Hotel & Conference Ctr 3848 W Lakeshore Dr *TF:* 866-610-2665 ■ *Web:* www.thecookhotel.com	Baton Rouge	LA	70808	225-383-2665	
Country Springs Hotel & Conference Ctr 2810 Golf Rd *TF:* 800-247-6640 ■ *Web:* www.countryspringshotel.com	Pewaukee	WI	53072	262-547-0201	
Crystal Mountain Resort 12500 Crystal Mtn Dr *TF:* 800-968-7686 ■ *Web:* www.crystalmountain.com	Thompsonville	MI	49683	231-378-2000	378-2998
Decatur Hotels LLC 317 Magazine St *Web:* www.decaturhotel.com	New Orleans	LA	70130	504-539-9000	
Decore Hotels 10026 164 St Nw *Web:* decorehotels.com	Edmonton	AB	T5P4Y3	780-481-7578	
Dellisart Lodging LLC 8975 Nesbit Lks Dr *Web:* www.dellisart.com	Alpharetta	GA	30022	770-558-4300	
Delta Sherbrooke Hotel & Conference Centre 2685 Rue King O *TF:* 800-268-1133 ■ *Web:* www.deltahotels.com	Sherbrooke	QC	J1L1C1	819-822-1989	822-8990
Diplomat Hotel Corp 2100 ParkLk Dr N.E. Ste A *Web:* www.diplomathotels.com	Atlanta	GA	30345	770-938-2060	
DNC Parks & Resorts at KSC Inc State Rd 405 *Web:* www.kennedyspacecenter.com	Titusville	FL	32899	321-449-4247	
Dolce Atlanta-Peachtree 201 Aberdeen Pkwy *TF:* 800-983-6523 ■ *Web:* www.dolce.com	Peachtree City	GA	30269	770-487-2666	631-4096
Dolce Hayes Mansion 200 Edenvale Ave *TF:* 866-981-3300 ■ *Web:* www.hayesmansion.com	San Jose	CA	95136	408-226-3200	
Dora Brothers Hospitality Corp 9904 N by Northeast Blvd *Web:* www.dorahotels.com	Fishers	IN	46038	317-578-9000	
Doral Arrowwood Conference Resort 975 Anderson Hill Rd **Fax Area Code:* 914 ■ *TF:* 844-211-0512 ■ *Web:* www.arrowwood.com	Rye Brook	NY	10573	844-214-5500	323-5500*
Doral Park Avenue Hotel 70 Park Ave *Web:* www.doralparkavenue.com	New York	NY	10016	212-687-7050	
Edith Macy Conference Ctr 550 Chappaqua Rd *Web:* www.edithmacy.com	Briarcliff Manor	NY	10510	914-945-8000	945-8009
Edward Adams House Bed & Breakfast 729 S Water St *Web:* edwardadamshousebandb.com	Silverton	OR	97381	503-873-8868	
Emory Conference Ctr Hotel 1615 Clifton Rd *TF:* 800-933-6679 ■ *Web:* www.emoryconferencecenter.com	Atlanta	GA	30329	404-712-6000	712-6025
Evergreen Marriott Conference Resort 4021 Lakeview Dr *TF:* 800-228-9290 ■ *Web:* marriott.com/vanityredirect/atleg	Stone Mountain	GA	30083	770-879-9900	465-3264
Fogelman Executive Conference Ctr 330 Innovation Dr University of Memphis *Web:* www.wilsonhotels.com	Memphis	TN	38152	901-678-2021	678-5329
Founders Inn 5641 Indian River Rd *TF:* 800-926-4466 ■ *Web:* www.foundersinn.com	Virginia Beach	VA	23464	757-424-5511	
Four Points by Sheraton Norwood Hotel & Conference Ctr 1125 Boston-Providence Tpke (Rt 1) *Web:* www.fourpointsnorwood.com	Norwood	MA	02062	781-769-7900	551-3552
Genetti Lycoming Hotel 200 W 4th St *Web:* genetti.com	Williamsport	PA	17701	570-326-6600	
Georgetown University Hotel & Conference Ctr 3800 Reservoir Rd NW *TF:* 888-902-1606 ■ *Web:* www.acc-guhotelandconferencecenter.com	Washington	DC	20057	202-687-3200	687-3297
Glen Cove Mansion Hotel & Conference Ctr 200 Dosoris Ln *TF:* 877-782-9426 ■ *Web:* www.glencovemansion.com	Glen Cove	NY	11542	516-671-6400	705-0147
Gordon Companies Inc 384 Broadway *Web:* www.gordoncompanies.net	Albany	NY	12207	518-462-7411	
Grace Inn, The 10831 S 51st St *Web:* www.graceinn.com	Phoenix	AZ	85044	480-893-3000	
Grandover Resort & Conference Ctr 1000 Club Rd *TF:* 800-472-6301 ■ *Web:* www.grandover.com	Greensboro	NC	27407	336-294-1800	856-9991
Grayl's Hotel 340 Beach Dr NE *Web:* www.graylshotel.com	Saint Petersburg	FL	33701	727-896-1080	
H Hotel, The 111 W Main St *Web:* www.thehhotel.com	Midland	MI	48640	989-839-0500	837-6000
Hamilton Park Hotel & Conference Ctr 175 Pk Ave *TF:* 877-999-3223 ■ *Web:* www.hamiltonparkhotel.com	Florham Park	NJ	07932	973-377-2424	
Hanford Hotels Inc 4 Corporate Plz Ste 102 *Web:* www.hanfordhotels.com	Newport Beach	CA	92660	949-640-8888	
Heritage Hotel 522 Heritage Rd *Web:* www.heritagesouthbury.com	Southbury	CT	06488	203-264-8200	264-5035
Hickory Ridge Marriott Conference Hotel 10400 Fernwood Rd *TF:* 800-334-0344 ■ *Web:* www.marriott.com	Bethesda	IL	20817	301-380-3000	
Hidden Valley Resort & Conference Ctr 1 Craighead Dr PO Box 4420 *TF:* 800-452-2223 ■ *Web:* www.hiddenvalleyresort.com	Hidden Valley	PA	15502	814-443-8000	443-8254

Phone Fax

Hilton Scranton & Conference Ctr
100 Adams Ave. . . . . Scranton PA 18503 570-343-3000 343-8415
TF: 800-445-8667 ■ *Web:* www.hilton.com

Holiday Inn on The Hill, The
415 New Jersey Ave . . . . Washington DC 20001 202-638-1616
Web: www.hionthehilldc.com

Hotel at Auburn University & Dixon Conference Ctr, The
241 S College St. . . . . Auburn AL 36830 334-821-8200 826-8746
TF: 800-228-2876 ■ *Web:* www.auhcc.com

Hotel Park 1125 9th St. . . . . Sacramento CA 95814 916-441-5361
Web: www.hotelpark.org

Hotel Plaza Valleyfield
40 Av Du Centenaire. . . . . Salaberry-de-valleyfield QC J6S3L6 450-373-1990
Web: www.plazavalleyfield.com

Hotel Roanoke & Conference Ctr
110 Shenandoah Ave . . . . Roanoke VA 24016 540-985-5900 853-8264
Web: www.hotelroanoke.com

Hotel Rose 50 Southwest Morrison St . . . . Portland OR 97204 503-221-0711
Web: www.HotelFifty.com

Hotels Etc Inc 7712 Hampton Pl Bldg 11C . . . . Loganville GA 30052 877-967-7283
TF: 877-967-7283 ■ *Web:* www.hotelsetc.com

Howard Johnson Express Inn - Westbury
120 Jericho TurnPk Jericho . . . . Long Island City NY 11753 516-333-9700
Web: www.hojo.com

Hyatt Place New York Midtown South
52-54 W 36th . . . . New York NY 10015 888-492-8847
TF: 888-492-8847 ■ *Web:* www.newyorkmidtown.place.hyatt.com

IBM Palisades Conference Ctr 334 Rt 9 W . . . . Palisades NY 10964 845-732-6000
Web: www.dolcepalisades.com

Imic Hotels 1 Surrey Ct . . . . Columbia SC 29212 803-772-2629
Web: hamptoninn3.hilton.com

Inn at Aspen 38750 Hwy 82. . . . . Aspen CO 81611 800-222-7736 925-9037*
**Fax Area Code:* 970 ■ *TF:* 800-222-7736 ■ *Web:* wyndhamvacationrentals.com

Inn at Virginia Tech & Skelton Conference Ctr
901 Prices Fork Rd. . . . . Blacksburg VA 24061 540-231-8000 231-0146
TF: 877-200-3360 ■ *Web:* www.innatvirginiatech.com

InterContinental Hotel Cleveland
9801 Carnegie Ave . . . . Cleveland OH 44106 216-707-4100
Web: www.ihg.com

InterContinental New York Barclay, The
111 E 48th St . . . . New York NY 10017 212-755-5900
Web: m.intercontinentalnybarclay.com

Islander Resort, The
3161 S Atlantic Ave . . . . Daytona Beach FL 32118 386-761-2335
Web: guyharveyoutpostislamorada.com

Ivey Spencer Leadership Centre
551 Windermere Rd . . . . London ON N5X2T1 519-679-4546 645-0733
TF: 888-678-6926 ■ *Web:* www.iveyspencerleadershipcentre.com

James L Allen Ctr 2169 Campus Dr . . . . Evanston IL 60208 847-467-7000 491-8002
TF: 877-755-2227 ■ *Web:* www.kellogg.northwestern.edu

Kingbridge Centre, The 12750 Jane St. . . . . King City ON L7B1A3 905-833-3086 833-3075
TF: 800-827-7221 ■ *Web:* www.kingbridgecentre.com

Kingsgate Marriott Conference Ctr at the University of Cincinnati
151 Goodman St. . . . . Cincinnati OH 45219 513-487-3800 487-3810
TF: 800-228-9290 ■ *Web:* www.marriott.com/hotels/travel/cvgkg

Kingsmill Resort & Spa
1010 Kingsmill Rd . . . . Williamsburg VA 23185 757-253-1703 253-8246
TF: 800-832-5665 ■ *Web:* www.kingsmill.com

Lakeview Golf Resort & Spa 1 Lakeview Dr. . . . . Morgantown WV 26508 304-594-1111
TF: 800-624-8300 ■ *Web:* www.lakeviewresort.com

Lakeway Inn & Resort 101 Lakeway Dr. . . . . Austin TX 78734 512-261-6600
Web: www.lakewayresortandspa.com

Lansdowne Resort 44050 Woodridge Pkwy . . . . Leesburg VA 20176 703-729-8400 729-4096
TF: 877-513-8400 ■ *Web:* www.lansdowneresort.com

Lodge At Breckenridge, The
112 Overlook Dr. . . . . Breckenridge CO 80424 970-453-9300
TF: 800-736-1607 ■ *Web:* www.thelodgeatbreckenridge.com

Lodge Hotels and Resorts
6889 Rowland Rd Ste 100 . . . . Eden Prairie MN 55344 952-294-2124
Web: www.lodgehotels.com

Lotus Hotels Inc 2525 San Pablo Dam Rd. . . . . San Pablo CA 94806 925-979-5758
Web: www.lotushotels.com

Manidokan Camp and Retreat Center
1600 Harpers Ferry Rd . . . . Knoxville MD 21758 301-834-7244
Web: www.manidokan.org

Marietta Conference Ctr & Resort
500 Powder Springs St. . . . . Marietta GA 30064 770-427-2500 819-3224*
**Fax Area Code:* 678 ■ *TF:* 888-685-2500 ■ *Web:* www3.hilton.com/en/index.html

Marriott Montgomery Prattville at Capitol Hill
2500 Legends Cir. . . . . Prattville AL 36066 334-290-1235 290-2222
TF Resv: 800-593-6429 ■ *Web:* www.marriott.com

Mena Tours and Travel Inc 5209 N Clark St. . . . . Chicago IL 60640 733-275-2125
Web: www.menatourschicago.com

Met Hotel Troy, The 5500 Crooks Rd . . . . Troy MI 48098 248-879-2100
Web: www.themettroy.com

Millennium Broadway Hotel New York
145 W 44th St. . . . . New York NY 10036 212-768-4400 768-0847
TF: 800-622-5569 ■ *Web:* www.millenniumhotels.com

Miramar at Waikiki 2345 Kuhio Ave . . . . Honolulu HI 96815 808-922-2077
Web: miramar-at-waikiki.honoluluhotelshawaii.net

Monarch Ski & Snowboard Area 1 Powder Pl. . . . . Monarch CO 81227 719-539-3573
Web: www.skimonarch.com

Mount st Louis Moonstone Ski Resort Ltd
24 Mt St Louis Rd W Rr 4. . . . . Coldwater ON L0K1E0 905-856-4754
Web: www.skicanada.org

MYGOLA INC 4701 Willard Ave Ste 1703 . . . . Chevy Chase MD 20815 650-353-7778
Web: www.mygola.com

Myrtle Beach Hotels LLC
2808 S Ocean Blvd. . . . . Myrtle Beach SC 29577 843-692-9977
Web: www.myrtlebeachhotels.net

National Ctr for Employee Development (NCED)
2701 E Imhoff Rd . . . . Norman OK 73071 405-366-4420 366-4319
TF: 866-438-6233 ■ *Web:* www.nced.com

Phone Fax

NAV Canada Training & Conference Ctr
1950 Montreal Rd. . . . . Cornwall ON K6H6L2 613-936-5800 936-5010
TF: 877-832-6416 ■ *Web:* www.navcentre.ca

Normandy Hotel, The 2118 Wyoming Ave N.W . . . . Washington DC 20008 202-483-1350
Web: www.doylecollection.com

Oak Brook Hills Marriott Resort
3500 Midwest Rd . . . . Oak Brook IL 60523 630-850-5555 850-5567
TF: 800-228-9290 ■ *Web:* marriott.com/hotels/propertypage/chimc

Oak Ridge Hotel & Conference Ctr
1 Oak Ridge Dr . . . . Chaska MN 55318 952-368-3100 368-1488
TF Sales: 800-737-9588 ■ *Web:* oakridgeminneapolis.com

Ocean Properties Ltd
1001 E Atlantic Ave Ste 202 . . . . Delray Beach FL 33483 561-279-9900
Web: www.oplhotels.com

Omni Royal Orleans Hotel
621 St. Louis St . . . . New Orleans LA 70140 504-529-5333
Web: www.omnihotelneworleans.com

On the Ave Hotel
2178 Broadway 222 W 77th St. . . . . New York NY 10024 212-362-1100
Web: www.ontheave-nyc.com

One South Lake Street LLC One S Lk St. . . . . Reno NV 89501 775-327-4362
Web: www.sienareno.com

Outrigger Kiahuna Plantation Resort
2253 Poipu Rd Ste B . . . . Koloa HI 96756 808-742-6411
Web: kauai-kiahuna.com

Paul J Rizzo Conference Ctr
Rizzo Conference Ctr 150 DuBose House Ln . . . . . Chapel Hill NC 27517 919-913-2098 913-2099
Web: www.rizzoconferencecenter.com

Penn Stater Conference Ctr Hotel
215 Innovation Blvd . . . . State College PA 16803 814-863-5000 863-5002
TF: 800-233-7505 ■ *Web:* www.pshs.psu.edu

Perry South Beach Hotel, The
2377 Collins Ave . . . . Miami Beach FL 33139 305-604-1000
Web: www.perrysouthbeachhotel.com

PNK (River City) LLC
777 River City Casino Blvd. . . . . Saint Louis MO 63125 888-578-7289
TF: 888-578-7289 ■ *Web:* www.rivercity.com

Prestige Resorts & Destinations Ltd
700 E Lk St Second Fl . . . . Wayzata MN 55391 952-473-9559
Web: www.prestigeresorts.com

R David Thomas Executive Conference Ctr (RDTC)
100 Fuqua Dr PO Box 90120 . . . . Durham NC 27708 919-660-6400 660-3607
Web: www.fuqua.duke.edu

Renaissance Portsmouth Hotel & Waterfront Conference Ctr
425 Water St. . . . . Portsmouth VA 23704 757-673-3000 673-3030
TF: 888-839-1775 ■ *Web:* renaissance-hotels.marriott.com

Resort at Squaw Creek
400 Squaw Creek Rd PO Box 3333. . . . . Olympic Valley CA 96146 530-583-6300 581-6632
TF: 800-327-3353 ■ *Web:* www.squawcreek.com

Roaring Run Resort Sales 194 Tannery Rd. . . . . Champion PA 15622 724-593-7837
Web: roaringrunresort.com

Rodd Hotels & Resorts PO Box 432 . . . . Charlottetown PE C1A7K7 902-892-7448
Web: www.roddvacations.com

Rosewood Little Dix Bay
P.O. Box 720 Saint John. . . . . Cruz Bay VI 00831 284-495-5555
Web: www.littledixbay.com

San Ramon Valley Conference Ctr
3301 Crow Canyon Rd . . . . San Ramon CA 94583 925-866-7500
Web: www.sanramonvalleyconferencecenter.com

Saratoga Hilton 534 Broadway . . . . Saratoga Springs NY 12866 518-584-4000 584-7430
TF: 800-445-8667 ■ *Web:* www.hilton.com

Sheraton Long Island Hotel 110 Motor Pkwy. . . . . Smithtown NY 11788 631-231-1100
Web: www.upskylongisland.com

Sheraton New York Hotel & Towers
811 7th Ave . . . . New York NY 10019 212-581-1000
Web: www.sheratonnewyork.com

Sheraton Old San Juan Hotel
100 Calle Brumbaugh. . . . . San Juan PR 00901 787-289-1914
Web: www.sheratonoldsanjuan.com

Skamania Lodge
1131 SW Skamania Lodge Way PO Box 189 . . . . Stevenson WA 98648 509-427-7700 427-2547
TF: 800-221-7117 ■ *Web:* www.destinationhotels.com/skamania

Sky Hospitality LLC
5999 Central Ave Ste 102. . . . . Saint Petersburg FL 33710 727-576-5167
Web: www.skyhospitality.com

Snowbird Ski & Summer Resort
Hwy 210 PO Box 929000 . . . . Snowbird UT 84092 801-742-2222 947-8227
TF: 800-453-3000 ■ *Web:* www.snowbird.com

Sportsmans Hotel & Restaurant 12700 Renovo Rd. . . . . . Renovo PA 17764 570-923-9968
Web: www.sportsmanshotel.com

St. Giles Hotels LLC 120-130 E 39th St . . . . New York NY 10016 212-779-7822
Web: www.stgiles.com

Stevenswood Lodge Llc 8211 N Hwy 1 . . . . Little River CA 95456 707-937-2810
Web: www.stevenswood.com

Stoweflake Mountain Resort & Spa
1746 Mountain Rd PO Box 369 . . . . Stowe VT 05672 802-253-7355 253-6858
TF: 800-253-2232 ■ *Web:* www.stoweflake.com

Summit Group Inc, The
2701 S Minnesota Ave Ste 6. . . . . Sioux Falls SD 57105 605-361-9566
Web: www.thesummitgroupinc.com

Sydell Group Ltd 1170 Broadway. . . . . New York NY 10001 646-307-9600
Web: www.sydellgroup.com

Talaris Conference Ctr 4000 NE 41st St. . . . . Seattle WA 98105 206-268-7000 268-7001
Web: www.talarisconferencecenter.com

Terrapin Management Corp 675 Meadows Rd. . . . . Aspen CO 81611 415-388-5436
Web: www.terrapininvestments.com

TUCSON AZ?HILTON GARDEN INN HOTEL
6575 S Country Club Rd. . . . . Tucson AZ 85756 520-741-0505
Web: hiltongardeninn1.hilton.com

Twin Tier Hospitality LLC 255 Spring St Ste 100 . . . . Sayre PA 18840 570-882-8644
Web: www.twintierhospitality.com

UMPQUA Indian Development Corp
146 Chief Miwaleta Ln . . . . Canyonville OR 97417 541-839-1221
Web: www.uidcorp.com

Phone | Fax

University of Maryland University College Marriott Conference Ctr Hotel
3501 University Blvd E ... Adelphi MD 20783 301-985-7300 985-7517
TF: 800-721-7033 ■ *Web:* www.marriott.com

University Place Conference Ctr & Hotel-Indianapolis
850 W Michigan St ... Indianapolis IN 46202 317-269-9000 278-8176
Web: eventservices.iupui.edu

University Plaza Hotel & Convention Ctr
333 John Q Hammons Pkwy ... Springfield MO 65806 417-864-7333 831-5893
Web: www.upspringfield.com

US Hotels Inc 37 Beach Ave ... Kennebunk ME 04043 207-967-4750
Web: www.ushotelsgroup.com

Vdara Condo Hotel LLC 3950 Las Vegas Blvd ... Las Vegas NV 89119 866-718-2489
TF: 866-718-2489 ■ *Web:* www.vdara.com

Visions Hotels LLC 382 E Second St ... Corning NY 14830 607-962-9868
Web: www.visions-hotels.com

Watergate Hotel, The 2650 VIRGINIA AVE NW ... Washington DC 20037 202-965-2300
Web: thewatergatehotel.com

Whalen's Grindstone Shores Inc
3373 Pointe Aux Barques Rd ... Port Austin MI 48467 989-738-7664
Web: whalensgrindstoneshores.com

White Oaks Conference Resort & Spa
253 Taylor Rd SS4 ... Niagara-on-the-Lake ON L0S1J0 905-688-2550
TF Resv: 800-263-5766 ■ *Web:* www.whiteoaksresort.com

Willard Hotel 1401 pennsylvania ave nw ... Washington DC 20004 202-628-9100
Web: washington.intercontinental.com

Windemere Hotel and Conference Center
2047 S Hwy 92 ... Sierra Vista AZ 85635 520-459-5900
Web: windemerehotel.com

Windsor Hilton Garden Inn 555 Corporate Dr ... Windsor CT 06095 860-688-6400
Web: www.windsor.gardeninn.com

Windsor Suites, The
1700 Benjamin Franklin Pkwy ... Philadelphia PA 19103 215-981-5678
Web: www.thewindsorsuites.com

Woodlands Resort & Conference Ctr, The
2301 N Millbend Dr ... The Woodlands TX 77380 281-367-1100
TF Resv: 800-433-2624 ■ *Web:* www.woodlandsresort.com

Wyndham Peachtree Conference Ctr
2443 Hwy 54 W ... Peachtree City GA 30269 770-487-2000
TF: 800-996-3426 ■ *Web:* www.wyndham.com

Wynn Resorts Holdings LLC
3145 Las Vegas Blvd S ... Las Vegas NV 89109 702-733-4444
Web: www.wynnmacau.com

378 HOTELS - FREQUENT STAY PROGRAMS

Phone | Fax

45 Allen Plaza Development LLC
45 Ivan Allen Jr Blvd ... Atlanta GA 30308 404-582-5800
Web: www.watlantadowntown.com

Aava Whistler Hotel Ltd 4005 Whistler Way ... Whistler BC V0N1B4 604-932-2522
TF: 800-663-5644 ■ *Web:* www.aavawhistlerhotel.com

Afton Alps Inc 6600 Peller Ave S ... Hastings MN 55033 651-436-5245
Web: www.aftonalps.com

Alliance Hospitality Management LLC
1001 Wade Ave Ste 215 ... Raleigh NC 27603 919-791-1801
Web: www.alliancehospitality.com

Alta Mira Recovery Programs LLC
125 Bulkley Ave ... Sausalito CA 94965 415-332-1350
Web: www.altamirarecovery.com

Amara Resort LLC 100 Amara Ln ... Sedona AZ 86336 928-282-4828
Web: www.amararesort.com

Ambassador Hotel Inc 2040 Kuhio Ave ... Honolulu HI 96815 808-941-7777
Web: www.ambassadorwaikiki.com

Americas Best Value Inn
2586 N Slappey Blvd Ste 100 ... Albany GA 31701 805-557-7300
Web: www.americasbestvalueinn.com

Andaz 5th Avenue 485 Fifth Ave 41st St ... New York NY 10017 212-601-1234
Web: www.newyork.5thavenue.andaz.hyatt.com

Apple Farm Bakery 2015 Monterey St ... San Luis Obispo CA 93401 805-544-6100
TF: 800-255-2040 ■ *Web:* www.applefarm.com

Aqua Waikiki Pearl Hotel 415 Nahua St ... Waikiki Beach HI 96815 808-922-1616
Web: www.aquawaikikipearl.com

Ascent Hospitality LLC 3616 S Bogan Rd Ste 201 ... Buford GA 30591 706-529-6900
Web: www.ascent-hospitality.com

Auberge Resorts LLC
591 Redwood Hwy Ste 3150 ... Mill Valley CA 94941 415-380-3460
Web: www.aubergeresorts.com

Avalon Hotel, The 16 E 32nd St ... New York NY 10016 212-299-7000
Web: www.avalonhotelnyc.com

Bavarian Lion Company of California
2777 Fourth St ... Santa Rosa CA 95405 707-545-8530
Web: www.flamingoresort.com

Bay Landing Hotel 1550 Bayshore Hwy Fl 2 ... Burlingame CA 94010 650-259-9000 259-9099
Web: www.baylandinghotel.com

Baywood Hotels Inc 7871 Belle Point Dr ... Greenbelt MD 20770 301-345-8700
Web: www.baywoodhotels.com

BBL Hospitality LLC 302 Washington Ave Ext ... Albany NY 12203 518-640-6464
Web: www.bblhospitality.com

Beach Terrace Motor Inn 3400 Atlantic Ave ... Wildwood NJ 08260 609-522-8100
TF: 800-841-8416 ■ *Web:* www.beachterrace.com

Bear Creek Mountain Resort 101 Doe Mtn Ln ... Macungie PA 18062 610-641-7101
TF: 866-754-2822 ■ *Web:* www.bcmountainresort.com

Belleclaire Hotel Corp 250 W 77th St ... New York NY 10024 212-362-7700
Web: www.hotelbelleclaire.com

Best Western Edgewater 2400 London Rd ... Duluth MN 55812 218-728-3601
Web: www.zmchotels.com

Best Western InnTowner, The
2424 University Ave ... Madison WI 53726 608-233-8778
Web: inntowner.com

BEST WESTERN PLUS Heritage Inn
151 E McLeod Rd ... Bellingham WA 98226 360-647-1912
Web: www.bestwesternheritageinn.com

Phone | Fax

Beverly Hills Plaza Hotel
10300 Wilshire Blvd ... Los Angeles CA 90024 310-275-5575
Web: www.beverlyhillsplazahotel.com

Billings Ventures LP 1801 Majestic Ln ... Billings MT 59102 406-839-9300
Web: www.thebighornresort.com

Bjork Construction Company Inc
4420 Enterprise Pl ... Fremont CA 94538 510-656-4688
Web: www.bjorkconstruction.com

Blue Harbor Resort & Conference Center
725 Blue Harbor Dr ... Sheboygan WI 53081 920-452-2900
Web: www.blueharborresort.com

Bluewater Resort & Casino 11300 Resort Dr ... Parker AZ 85344 928-669-7000
Web: www.bluewaterfun.com

Boston Common Hotel & Conference Center
40 Trinity Pl ... Boston MA 02116 617-933-7700
Web: www.bostoncommonhotel.com

Breakers Hotel & Restaurant
1507 Ocean Ave ... Spring Lake NJ 07762 732-449-7700
Web: www.breakershotel.com

Breckenridge Grand Vacations LLC
PO Box 6879 ... Breckenridge CO 80424 970-547-3630
Web: www.breckenridgegrandvacations.com

Brendan's Camarillo LLC 1755 E Daily Dr ... Camarillo CA 93010 805-383-7528
Web: brendans.com

Broadway Plaza Hotel 1155 Broadway ... New York NY 10001 212-679-7665
TF: 877-504-6835 ■ *Web:* www.broadwayplazahotel.com

Bromley Mountain Ski Resort 3984 Vt Rt 11 ... Peru VT 05152 802-824-5522
Web: www.bromley.com

Buena Vista Motor Inn 1599 Lombard St ... San Francisco CA 94123 415-923-9600
TF: 800-835-4980 ■ *Web:* www.buenavistamotorinn.com

Buffalo Lodging Associates LLC
570 Delaware Ave ... Buffalo NY 14202 716-858-3163
Web: www.buffalolodging.com

Burke Mountain Operating Co
223 Sherburne Lodge Rd ... East Burke VT 05832 802-626-7300
Web: qburke.com

Caneel Bay Inc North Shore Rd ... Cruz Bay VI 00831 340-776-6111
Web: www.caneelbay.com

Capstone Hotel Ltd 320 Paul W Bryant Dr ... Tuscaloosa AL 35401 205-752-3200
Web: www.hotelcapstone.com

Carson Doubletree Hotel Civic Plaza, The
2 Civic Plz ... Carson CA 90745 310-830-9200
Web: www.carsondoubletree.com

Celebrity Hotel Inc 629 Main St ... Deadwood SD 57732 605-578-1909
Web: www.celebritycasinos.com

Champion Hotels LLC 3048 N Grand Blvd ... Oklahoma City OK 73107 405-606-7400
Web: www.championhotels.com

Chena Hot Springs Resort LLC PO Box 58740 ... Fairbanks AK 99711 907-451-8104
Web: www.chenahotsprings.com

Chestnut Mountain Resort 8700 Chestnut Dr ... Galena IL 61036 800-397-1320
TF: 800-397-1320 ■ *Web:* www.chestnutmtn.com

Chicago South Loop Hotel 11 W 26th St ... Chicago IL 60616 312-225-7000
Web: www.chicagosouthloophotel.com

Chimney Rock Inn 800 Thompson Ave ... Bound Brook NJ 08805 732-469-4600
Web: www.chimneyrockinn.com

Choice Hotels Canada Inc
5090 Explorer Dr Ste 500 ... Mississauga ON L4W4T9 905-602-2222
Web: www.choicehotels.ca

Christian Brothers Retreat 4401 Redwood Rd ... Napa CA 94558 707-252-3810
Web: www.christianbrosretreat.com

Christie Lodge PO Box 1196 ... Avon CO 81620 970-845-4504
TF: 888-325-6343 ■ *Web:* www.christielodge.com

Chukchansi Gold Resort & Casino
711 Lucky Ln ... Coarsegold CA 93614 866-794-6946
TF: 866-794-6946 ■ *Web:* chukchansigold.com

Coach Stop Inn, The 4755 Rt 6 ... Wellsboro PA 16901 570-724-5361
Web: www.coachstopinn.com

Comfort Inn & Suites 2201 Hotel Cir S ... San Diego CA 92108 619-881-6200
Web: www.choicehotels.com

Commonwealth Hotels LLC
100 E Rivercenter Blvd Ste 1050 ... Covington KY 41011 859-261-5522
Web: www.commonwealthhotels.com

Conrad Chicago 521 N Rush St ... Chicago IL 60611 312-645-1500
Web: conradhotels3.hilton.com/en/future-openings/chicago.html

Copper Beech Inn, The 46 Main St ... Ivoryton CT 06442 860-767-0330
Web: www.copperbeechinn.com

Coral Hospitality LLC 9180 Galleria Ct Ste 600 ... Naples FL 34109 239-449-1800
Web: www.coralhospitality.com

Country Hearth Inn Inc
50 Glenlake Pkwy NE Ste 350 ... Atlanta GA 30328 770-393-2662
TF: 888-443-2784 ■ *Web:* www.countryhearth.com

Courtyard Anaheim at Disneyland, The
2045 S Harbor Blvd ... Anaheim CA 92802 714-740-2645
Web: www.marriott.com/hotels/travel/laxad-courtyard-anaheim-resort-convention-center

Cromwell Morgan 244 Fifth Ave Ste 2400 ... New York NY 10001 212-726-2994
Web: www.cromwellmorgan.com

Crowne Plaza Hotel St Louis-Clayton
7750 Carondelet Ave Clayton ... Clayton MO 63105 314-726-5400 719-7126
Web: www.cpclayton.com

Crowne Plaza Hotels & Resorts
2701 Summer St ... Stamford CT 06905 203-359-1300
Web: www.ihg.com/crowneplaza/hotels/us/en/stamford/stmcp/hoteldetail

Crowne Plaza Minneapolis Airport West
5401 Green Vly Dr ... Bloomington MN 55437 952-831-8000
Web: www.cpmsp.com

Crowne Plaza Niagara Falls - Fallsview
5685 Falls Ave ... Niagara Falls ON L2E6W7 905-374-4447
TF: 800-263-7135 ■ *Web:* www.niagarafallscrowneplazahotel.com

Crowne Plaza Ravinia
4355 Ashford Dunwoody Rd ... Atlanta GA 30346 770-395-7700
Web: www.cpravinia.com

CS&M Associates 500 Canal St ... New Orleans LA 70130 504-525-2500
Web: www.sheratonneworleans.com

				Phone	Fax
Danfords Hotel & Marina 25 E Broadway	Port Jefferson	NY	11777	800-332-6367	
TF: 800-332-6367 ■ *Web:* www.danfords.com					
Days Inn Hinton-Jasper Hotel 358 Smith St.	Hinton	AB	T7V2A1	780-817-1960	
TF: 800-259-4827 ■ *Web:* www.daysinnhinton.com					
Dearborn Partners LLC 200 W Madison St Ste 1950	Chicago	IL	60606	312-795-1000	
Web: www.dearbornpartners.com					
Decatur Conference Center & Hotel 4191 W US Hwy 36 Wyckles Rd	Decatur	IL	62522	217-422-8800	
Web: www.hoteldecatur.com					
Discovery Inn Hotel 4701 Franklin Ave	Yellowknife	NT	X1A2N6	867-873-4151	
Web: www.discoveryinn.ca					
DKN Hotels LLC 42 Corporate Park Ste 200	Irvine	CA	92606	714-427-4320	
Web: www.dknhotels.com					
Donovan House 1155 14th St NW	Washington	DC	20005	202-737-1200	
Web: www.inndc.com					
DoubleTree 2200 Fwy Blvd	Minneapolis	MN	55430	763-566-8000	
Web: doubletree3.hilton.com/en/hotels/minnesota/doubletree-by-hilton-hotel-minneapolis-north-mspnodt/index.html					
DoubleTree 1707 Hillsborough St	Raleigh	NC	27605	919-828-0811	
Web: www.brownstonehotel.com					
DoubleTree by Hilton Baltimore - BWI Airport 890 Elkridge Landing Rd	Linthicum	MD	21090	410-859-8400	
Web: www.doubletreebwiairporthotel.com					
DoubleTree by Hilton Hotel Bethesda - Washington DC 8120 Wisconsin Ave	Bethesda	MD	20814	301-652-2000	
Web: www.doubletreebethesda.com					
Doubletree by Hilton Hotel Tucson-Reid Park 445 S Alvernon Way	Tucson	AZ	85711	520-881-4200	
Web: www.dtreidpark.com					
Dow Hotel Company LLC, The 16400 Southcenter Pkwy Ste 405	Seattle	WA	98188	206-575-3600	
Web: www.dowhotelco.com					
Easton's Group of Hotels Inc 3100 Steeles Ave E Gateway Centre Ste 601	Markham	ON	L3R8T3	905-940-9409	
Web: www.eastonsgroup.com					
Eastover Hotel & Resort LLC 430 East St.	Lenox	MA	01240	413-637-0625	
Web: www.eastover.com					
Edgewater Beach Resort Management 11212 Front Beach Rd	Panama City	FL	32407	850-235-4044	
Web: www.resortcollection.com/about-edgewater-beach-resort					
Embassy Suites Hotel & Casino-San Juan Puerto Rico 8000 Tartak St Isla Verde Carolina	San Juan	PR	00979	787-791-0505	
Web: embassysuites3.hilton.com/en/hotels/puerto-rico/embassy-suites-by-hilton-san-juan-hotel-and-casino-sjueses/index.html					
Embassy Suites Hotel Orlando - International Drive South 8978 International Dr	Orlando	FL	32819	407-352-1400	
Web: embassysuites3.hilton.com/en/hotels/florida/embassy-suites-by-hilton-orlando-international-drive-convention-center-mcoores/index.html					
Embassy Suites Memphis 1022 S Shady Grove Rd	Memphis	TN	38120	901-684-1777	
Web: www.indianaroof.com					
FairBridge Inns LLC 421 W Riverside Ave Ste 407	Spokane	WA	99201	877-866-8090	
TF: 877-866-8090 ■ *Web:* www.fairbridgeinns.com					
Fairmont Hotel Management Lp 950 Mason St	San Francisco	CA	94108	415-982-6500	
Web: www.tongaroom.com					
Fairmont Olympic Hotel Seattle, The 411 University St	Seattle	WA	98101	206-621-1700	
Web: www.seattleskal.org					
Fairmont San Francisco Hotel, The 950 Mason St	San Francisco	CA	94108	415-772-5000	
TF: 800-257-7544 ■ *Web:* fairmont.com					
Fort William Henry Corp, The 48 Canada St	Lake George	NY	12845	518-668-3081	
Web: www.fortwilliamhenry.com					
Fountain Grove Inn, The 101 Fountaingrove Pkwy	Santa Rosa	CA	95403	707-578-6101	
Web: www.fountaingroveinn.com					
Gainey Suites Hotel 7300 E Gainey	Scottsdale	AZ	85258	480-922-6969	
TF: 800-970-4666 ■ *Web:* www.gaineysuiteshotel.com					
GF Management Inc 1628 John F Kennedy Blvd 8 Penn Ctr 23rd Fl	Philadelphia	PA	19103	215-972-2222	
Web: www.gfhotels.com					
Golden Inn Hotel 7849 Dune Dr	Avalon	NJ	08202	609-368-5155	
Web: www.goldeninn.com					
Grand Hyatt Denver 1750 Welton St.	Denver	CO	80202	303-295-1234	
Web: denver.grand.hyatt.com/en/hotel/home.html					
Grand Hyatt Tampa Bay 2900 Bayport Dr	Tampa	FL	33607	813-874-1234	
Web: tampabay.grand.hyatt.com/en/hotel/home.html					
Grand Pacific Resorts Inc Grand Pacific Plz 5900 Pasteur Ct Ste 200	Carlsbad	CA	92008	760-431-8500	
Web: www.grandpacificresorts.com					
Grand Seas Resort Partners 2424 N Atlantic Ave	Daytona Beach	FL	32118	386-677-7880	
GrandLife Hotels Inc 310 W Broadway	New York	NY	10013	212-965-3000	
TF: 800-965-3000 ■ *Web:* www.grandlifehotels.com					
Great Wolf Lodge of Sandusky LLC 4600 Milan Rd US 250	Sandusky	OH	44870	419-609-6000	
Web: www.greatbearlodge.com					
Green Turtle Bay Inc 239 Jetty Dr	Grand Rivers	KY	42045	270-362-8364	
Web: www.greenturtlebay.com					
Greenwich Hospitality Group LLC 500 Steamboat Rd	Greenwich	CT	06830	203-661-9800	
Web: www.thedelamar.com					
Greenwich Hotel, The 377 Greenwich St.	New York	NY	10013	212-941-8900	
Web: www.thegreenwichhotel.com					
Gulf Bay Hotels Inc 3470 Club Ctr Blvd	Naples	FL	34114	239-732-9400	
Web: www.gulfbay.com					
Gunstock Recreation Area 719 Cherry Vly Rd	Gilford	NH	03249	603-293-4341	
Web: www.gunstock.com					
Hampton Inn Brookhaven 2000 N Ocean Ave	Farmingville	NY	11738	631-732-7300	
Web: hamptoninn3.hilton.com/en/hotels/new-york/hampton-inn-long-island-brookhaven-ispbhhx/index.html					
Hampton Inn (Pittsburgh Pennsylvania) 3315 Hamlet St	Pittsburgh	PA	15213	412-681-1000	
Web: www.pittsburghhamptoninn.com					
Hampton Marina Hotel 700 Settlers Landing Rd	Hampton	VA	23669	757-727-9700	
Web: www.hamptonmarinahotel.com					
Harbor Hotel Provincetown 698 Commercial St Cape Cod	Provincetown	MA	02657	855-447-8696	
TF: 855-447-8696 ■ *Web:* www.harborhotelptown.com					
Harbour Towers Hotel & Suites 345 Quebec St.	Victoria	BC	V8V1W4	250-385-2405	
TF: 800-663-5896 ■ *Web:* www.harbourtowers.com					
Hawkeye Hotels Inc 1601 N Roosevelt Ave	Burlington	IA	52601	319-752-7400	
Web: www.hawkeyehotels.com					
HEI Hospitality LLC 101 Merritt 7 Corporate Park 1st Fl	Norwalk	CT	06851	203-849-8844	
Web: www.heihotels.com					
Hi-lo Motel Cafe & Rv Park 88 S Weed Blvd	Weed	CA	96094	530-938-2904	
Web: www.sisdevco.com					
Highgate Hotels Inc 545 E John Carpenter Fwy Ste 1400	Irving	TX	75062	972-444-9700	
Web: www.highgateholdings.com					
HighPointe Hotel Corp 311 Gulf Breeze Pkwy	Gulf Breeze	FL	32561	850-932-9314	
Web: www.highpointe.com					
Hilton Concord 1970 Diamond Bouleverd	Concord	CA	94520	925-827-2000	
Web: www.concordhilton.com					
Hilton Garden Inn Baton Rouge Airport 3330 Harding Blvd	Baton Rouge	LA	70807	225-357-6177	
Web: www.pinkshell.com					
Hilton Hotel Waco 113 S University Parks Dr.	Waco	TX	76701	254-754-8484	
Web: www.hiltonwaco.com					
Hilton Miami Downtown 1601 Biscayne Blvd	Miami	FL	33132	305-374-0000	
Web: www.hiltonmiamidowntown.com					
Hilton Savannah Desoto 15 E Liberty St	Savannah	GA	31401	912-232-9000	
Web: www.desotohilton.com					
Hilton Suites Winnipeg Airport 1800 Wellington Ave	Winnipeg	MB	R3H1B2	204-783-1700	
Web: www.fortisproperties.com					
Hilton Woodcliff Lake 200 Tice Blvd.	Woodcliff Lake	NJ	07677	201-391-3600	
Web: www.hiltonwoodcliffiake.com					
Hinton Lakeview Inns & Suites 500 Smith St	Hinton	AB	T7V2A1	780-865-2575	
TF: 877-355-3500 ■ *Web:* www.lakeviewhotels.com					
Holiday Inn Ann Arbor-Near the Univ of MI 3600 Plymouth Rd	Ann Arbor	MI	48105	734-769-9800	
Web: www.hiannarbor.com					
Holiday Inn Baltimore Inner Harbor Hotel 301 W Lombard St	Baltimore	MD	21201	410-685-3500	
TF: 877-834-3613 ■ *Web:* www.innerharborhi.com					
Holiday Inn By the Bay 88 Spring St	Portland	ME	04101	207-775-2311	
Web: www.innbythebay.com					
Holiday Inn Los Angeles International Airport 9901 La Cienega Blvd.	Los Angeles	CA	90045	310-649-5151	
Web: www.hilax.com					
Holiday Inn Select Hotel & Suites in Oakville 2525 Wyecroft Rd	Oakville	ON	L6L6P8	905-847-1000	
Web: www.oakvillehotel.com					
Holiday Inn Select in Windsor Canada 1855 Huron Church Rd	Windsor	ON	N9C2L6	519-966-1200	
Web: www.his-windsor.com					
Hoover Dam Lodge Hwy 93	Boulder City	NV	89005	702-293-5000	
Web: www.haciendaonline.com					
Horizon Hotel Resort & Spa Inc 1050 E Palm Canyon Dr	Palm Springs	CA	92264	760-323-1858	
Web: www.thehorizonhotel.com					
Horseshoe Valley Resort Ltd 1101 Horseshoe Vly Rd - Comp 10 RR 1	Barrie	ON	L4M4Y8	705-835-2790	
TF: 800-461-5627 ■ *Web:* www.horseshoeresort.com					
Hotel Blue 717 Central Ave Nw	Albuquerque	NM	87102	505-924-2400	
TF: 877-878-4868 ■ *Web:* www.thehotelblue.com					
Hotel Carter 250 W 43rd St	New York	NY	10036	212-944-6000	
Web: www.carterhotel.com					
Hotel Equities Inc 41 Perimeter Ctr E Ste 510	Atlanta	GA	30346	678-578-4444	
Web: www.hotelequities.com					
Hotel ML, The 915 Rt 73	Mt. Laurel	NJ	08054	856-234-7300	
Web: www.thehotelml.com					
Hotel Modera 515 SW Clay St.	Portland	OR	97201	503-484-1084	
Web: hotelmodera.com					
Hotel of Rivington 107 Rivington St.	New York	NY	10002	212-475-2600	
Web: www.hotelonrivington.com					
Hotel Palomar Washington DC 2121 P St NW	Washington	DC	20037	202-448-1800	
Web: www.hotelpalomar-dc.com					
Hotel Shangri La 1301 Ocean Ave.	Santa Monica	CA	90401	310-394-2791	
TF: 877-999-1301 ■ *Web:* www.shangrila-hotel.com					
Hunt Valley Inn Baltimore 245 Shawan Rd.	Hunt Valley	MD	21031	410-785-7000	
Web: www.huntvalleywyndhamgrand.com					
Hyatt at Fisherman's Wharf 555 N Point St	San Francisco	CA	94133	415-563-1234	
Web: fishermanswharf.centric.hyatt.com/en/hotel/home.html					
Hyatt Chicago Magnificent Mile 633 N Saint Clair St	Chicago	IL	60611	312-787-1234	
Web: www.chicagomagnificentmile.hyatt.com					
Hyatt Dulles 2300 Dulles Corner Blvd	Herndon	VA	20171	703-713-1234	
Web: dulles.regency.hyatt.com/en/hotel/home.html					
Hyatt Gold Passport Program 9805 Q St PO Box 27089	Omaha	NE	68127	800-233-1234	593-4030*
**Fax Area Code:* 402 ■ *TF:* 800-233-1234 ■ *Web:* www.goldpassport.com					
Hyatt Key West Resort & Spa 601 Front St	Key West	FL	33040	305-809-1234	
Web: keywest.hyatt.com					
Hyatt Place East End & Resort Marina 451 E Main St	Riverhead	NY	11901	631-208-0002	
Web: longislandeastend.place.hyatt.com/en/hotel/home.html					
Hyatt Place North Charleston Hotel 7331 Mazyck Rd	North Charleston	SC	29406	843-735-7100	
Web: northcharleston.place.hyatt.com					

Phone Fax

Hyatt Place San Jose Downtown
282 Almaden Blvd ... San Jose CA 95113 408-998-0400
Web: www.sanjose.place.hyatt.com

Hyatt Regency Albuquerque 330 Tijeras NW ... Albuquerque NM 87102 505-842-1234
Web: albuquerque.regency.hyatt.com/en/hotel/home.html

Hyatt Regency Bethesda
1 Bethesda Metro Ctr 7400 Wisconsin Ave ... Bethesda MD 20814 301-657-1234
Web: bethesda.regency.hyatt.com/en/hotel/home.html

Hyatt Regency Boston 1 Ave de Lafayette ... Boston MA 02111 617-912-1234
Web: boston.regency.hyatt.com/en/hotel/home.html

Hyatt Regency Century Plaza
2025 Ave of the Stars ... Los Angeles CA 90067 310-228-1234

Hyatt Regency Columbus 350 N High St ... Columbus OH 43215 614-463-1234
Web: columbus.regency.hyatt.com/en/hotel/home.html

Hyatt Regency Jacksonville Riverfront
225 E Coastline Dr ... Jacksonville FL 32202 904-588-1234
Web: jacksonville.regency.hyatt.com/en/hotel/home.html

Hyatt Regency La Jolla at Aventine
3777 La Jolla Village Dr ... San Diego CA 92122 858-552-1234
Web: lajolla.regency.hyatt.com/en/hotel/home.html

Hyatt Regency Lexington 401 W High St ... Lexington KY 40507 859-253-1234
Web: lexington.regency.hyatt.com/en/hotel/home.html

Hyatt Regency Minneapolis
1300 Nicollet Mall ... Minneapolis MN 55403 612-370-1234
Web: minneapolis.regency.hyatt.com/en/hotel/home.html

Hyatt Regency Montreal 1255 Jeanne-Mance ... Montreal QC H5B1E5 514-982-1234
Web: montreal.regency.hyatt.com/en/hotel/home.html

Hyatt Regency North Dallas
701 E Campbell Rd ... Richardson TX 75081 972-231-9600
Web: northdallas.regency.hyatt.com/en/hotel/home.html

Hyatt Regency Phoenix 122 N Second St ... Phoenix AZ 85004 602-252-1234
Web: phoenix.regency.hyatt.com/en/hotel/home.html

Hyatt Regency Pittsburgh International Airport
1111 Airport Blvd PO Box 12420 ... Pittsburgh PA 15231 724-899-1234
Web: pittsburghairport.regency.hyatt.com/en/hotel/home.html

Hyatt Regency Rochester 125 E Main St ... Rochester NY 14604 585-546-1234
Web: rochester.regency.hyatt.com/en/hotel/home.html

Hyatt Regency San Francisco
5 Embarcadero Ctr ... San Francisco CA 94111 415-788-1234
Web: sanfrancisco.regency.hyatt.com/en/hotel/home.html

Hyatt Regency Santa Clara
5101 Great America Pkwy ... Santa Clara CA 95054 408-200-1234
Web: santaclara.regency.hyatt.com/en/hotel/home.html

Hyatt Regency Savannah 2 W Bay St ... Savannah GA 31401 912-238-1234
Web: savannah.regency.hyatt.com/en/hotel/home.html

Hyatt Regency Suites Atlanta Northwest
2999 Windy Hill Rd ... Marietta GA 30067 770-956-1234
Web: atlantasuites.regency.hyatt.com/en/hotel/home.html

Hyatt Regency Tulsa 100 E Second St ... Tulsa OK 74103 918-582-9000
Web: tulsa.regency.hyatt.com/en/hotel/home.html

Hyatt Regency Valencia 24500 Town Ctr Dr ... Valencia CA 91355 661-799-1234
Web: valencia.regency.hyatt.com/en/hotel/home.html

Hyatt Regency Washington DC on Capitol Hill
400 New Jersey Ave NW ... Washington DC 20001 202-737-1234
Web: washingtondc.regency.hyatt.com/en/hotel/home.html

Indianapolis Marriott Downtown
350 W Maryland St ... Indianapolis IN 46225 317-822-3500
Web: www.indymarriott.com

Inn at Jackson Hole, The
3345 W Village Dr PO Box 328 ... Teton Village WY 83025 307-733-2311
Web: www.innatjacksonhole.com

Inn at Mamas Fish House 799 Poho Pl ... Paia HI 96779 808-579-8488
TF: 800-860-4852 ■ *Web:* mamasfishhouse.com

Inn at USC Columbia South Caolina Hotel
1619 Pendleton St ... Columbia SC 29201 803-779-7779
Web: www.innatusc.com

InterContinental Mark Hopkins San Francisco
999 California St ... San Francisco CA 94108 415-392-3434
Web: www.intercontinentalmarkhopkins.com

InterContinental Montreal
360 St-Antoine St W ... Montreal QC H2Y3X4 514-987-9900
Web: www.montreal.intercontinental.com

Intercontinental San Francisco
888 Howard St ... San Francisco CA 94103 888-811-4273
TF: 888-811-4273 ■ *Web:* www.intercontinentalsanfrancisco.com

InterContinental Stephen F Austin Hotel
701 Congress Ave ... Austin TX 78701 512-457-8800
Web: www.austin.intercontinental.com

JW Marriott Denver Cherry Creek Hotel
150 Clayton Ln ... Denver CO 80206 303-316-2700
Web: www.jwmarriottdenver.com

Keating Hotel, The 432 F St ... San Diego CA 92101 619-814-5700
Web: www.thekeating.com

King George Hotel 334 Mason St ... San Francisco CA 94102 415-781-5050
Web: www.kinggeorge.com

Kontiki Beach Resort 2290 N Fulton Beach Rd ... Rockport TX 78382 361-729-2318 729-3212
TF: 800-388-0649 ■ *Web:* www.kontikibeach.com

KSL Resorts 50-905 Avenida Bermudas ... La Quinta CA 92253 760-564-8000
Web: www.kslresorts.com

Kyo-Ya Company Ltd 2255 Kalakaua Ave ... Honolulu HI 96815 808-931-8600
Web: kyoyahotelsandresorts.com

Lahaina Shores Beach Resort 475 Front St ... Lahaina HI 96761 866-934-9176
TF: 866-934-9176 ■ *Web:* www.lahainashores.com

Lancaster Group Inc, The
3411 Richmond Ave Ste 460 ... Houston TX 77046 713-224-6000
Web: www.lancaster.com

Landmark Hotel Group LLC
4453 Bonney Rd ... Virginia Beach VA 23462 757-213-4380
Web: www.landmarkhotelgroup.com

Landsby, The 1576 Mission Dr Ofc ... Solvang CA 93463 805-688-3121
Web: www.thelandsby.com

LBO Holding Inc Route 302 ... Bartlett NH 03812 603-374-2368
Web: www.attitash.com

LeisureLink Inc 90 S 400 W Ste 300 ... Salt Lake City UT 84101 855-840-2249
TF: 855-840-2249 ■ *Web:* www.leisurelink.com

Liberty Hotel, The 215 Charles St ... Boston MA 02114 617-224-4000
Web: www.libertyhotel.com

Lodge at Big Sky LLC, The 75 Sitting Bull Rd ... Big Sky MT 59716 406-995-7858
Web: www.lodgeatbigsky.com

Lodge at Tiburon, The 1651 Tiburon Blvd ... Tiburon CA 94920 415-435-3133
Web: www.lodgeattiburon.com

London West Hollywood Hotel
1020 N San Vicente Blvd ... West Hollywood CA 90069 866-282-4560
TF: 866-282-4560 ■ *Web:* www.thelondonwesthollywood.com

Lord Amherst Inc 5000 Main St ... Amherst NY 14226 716-839-2200
Web: www.lordamherst.com

Los Gatos Hotel Corp 210 E Main St ... Los Gatos CA 95030 408-335-1700
Web: hotellosgatos.com

LTD Hospitality Group LLC
1564 Crossways Blvd ... Chesapeake VA 23320 757-420-0900
Web: ltdhospitality.com

M Gibson Hotels Group 409 Montbrook Ln ... Knoxville TN 37919 865-539-0588
Web: www.mgibsonhotels.com

Maidstone Hotel, The 207 Main St ... East Hampton NY 11937 631-324-5006
Web: www.themaidstone.com

Maine Course Hospitality Group Inc
15 Main St Ste 210 ... Freeport ME 04032 207-865-6105
Web: www.mchg.com

Manchester Grand Hyatt San Diego
1 Market Pl ... San Diego CA 92101 619-232-1234
Web: www.manchestergrandhyattsandiego.com

Manhattan at Times Square Hotel, The
790 Seventh Ave ... New York NY 10019 212-581-3300
Web: www.manhattanhoteltimessquare.com

Marin Suites Hotel LLC
45 Tamal Vista Blvd ... Corte Madera CA 94925 415-924-3608
Web: www.marinsuites.com

Mark Scott Construction
2835 Contra Costa Blvd ... Pleasant Hill CA 94523 925-944-0502
Web: www.msconstruction.com

Marshall Hotels & Resorts Inc
1315 S Division St ... Salisbury MD 21804 410-749-8464
Web: www.marshallhotels.com

Mayfair Hotel 1256 W Seventh St ... Los Angeles CA 90017 213-484-9789
Web: www.mayfairla.com

McGuires Motor Inn 120 S Telegraph Rd ... Waterford MI 48328 248-682-5100
Web: www.mcguiresmotorinn.com

Meadowmere Resort 74 Main St ... Ogunquit ME 03907 207-646-9661
TF: 800-633-8718 ■ *Web:* www.meadowmere.com

Melrose Hotel Washington DC, The
2430 Pennsylvania Ave NW ... Washington DC 20037 202-955-6400
Web: www.melrosehoteldc.com

Menominee Hotel PO Box 760 ... Keshena WI 54135 715-799-3600
TF: 800-343-7778 ■ *Web:* www.menomineecasinoresort.com

Microtel Inn & Suites 11274 S Fortuna Rd ... Yuma AZ 85367 928-345-1777
Web: www.underhilltransfer.com

Midamerica Hotels Corp
105 S Mount Auburn Rd ... Cape Girardeau MO 63703 573-334-0546
Web: www.midamcorp.com

Midas Hospitality LLC
1804 Borman Cir Dr Ste 100 ... St. Louis MO 63146 314-692-0100
Web: www.midashospitality.com

Mont Saint-Sauveur International Inc
350 Saint-Denis Ave ... Saint-Sauveur QC J0R1R3 450-227-4671
Web: www.montsaintsauveur.com

Mountaineer Inn 3343 Mountain Rd ... Stowe VT 05672 802-253-7525
Web: www.stowemountaineerinn.com

Neil Locke & Associates
550 E Devon Ave Ste 130 ... Itasca IL 60143 630-285-9085
Web: www.neillocke.com

Noble Investment Group Ltd
2000 Monarch Tower 3424 Peachtree Rd NE ... Atlanta GA 30326 404-419-1000
Web: www.nobleinvestment.com

Norfolk Marriott Waterside 235 E Main St ... Norfolk VA 23510 757-627-4200
Web: www.norfolkmarriott.com

Norwich Partners LLC 10 Morgan Dr Ste 1 ... Lebanon NH 03766 603-643-2206
Web: www.norwichpartners.com

Nu Hotel 85 Smith St ... Brooklyn NY 11201 718-852-8585
Web: www.nuhotelbrooklyn.com

Nylo Hotels LLC 260 Peachtree St NW Ste 2301 ... Atlanta GA 30303 404-221-0600
Web: www.nylohotels.com

Oak Plantation Resort & Suites Condominium Association Inc
4090 Enchanted Oaks Cir ... Kissimmee FL 34741 888-411-4141
TF: 888-411-4141 ■ *Web:* www.oakplantationresort.com

Oceanfront Lodging Inc
305 N First St ... Jacksonville Beach FL 32250 904-249-4949
Web: www.bestwesternjacksonvillebeach.com

Oceano Hotel & Spa Half Moon Bay Harbor
280 Capistrano Rd ... Half Moon Bay CA 94019 650-726-5400
Web: www.oceanohalfmoonbay.com

Omni Hotels Select Guest Loyalty Program
11819 Miami St 3rd Fl ... Omaha NE 68164 800-843-6664
TF Cust Svc: 800-843-6664 ■ *Web:* omnihotels.com/loyalty

OTO Development LLC 100 Dunbar St Ste 402 ... Spartanburg SC 29306 864-596-8930
Web: www.otodevelopment.com

Overland Park Convention Center Hotel
6100 College Blvd ... Overland Park KS 66211 913-234-2100
Web: www.opconventioncenter.com

Pacific Plaza Hotels Inc
1000 Marina Village Pkwy Ste 100 ... Alameda CA 94501 510-832-6868
Web: www.pacificplazahotels.com

Paramount Hospitality Management LLC
12562 International Dr ... Orlando FL 32821 321-329-4054
Web: www.paramounthospitality.com

Parke Hotel & Conference Center
1413 Leslie Dr ... Bloomington IL 61704 309-662-4300
Web: www.parkehotel.com

Phone | Fax

Perry Group International
1 Market Plz Ste 3600 ... San Francisco CA 94105 415-434-0135
TF: 800-580-3950 ■ *Web:* www.perrygroup.com

Pharos Hospitality LLC
320 S Tryon St Ste 202 ... Charlotte NC 28202 704-333-1818
Web: www.pharoshospitality.com

Plaza Hotel, The 5th Ave at Central Park S ... New York NY 10019 212-759-3000
TF: 888-850-0909 ■ *Web:* www.theplazany.com

Ponderosa Motor Inn 1206 Trans Canada Hwy ... Golden BC V0A1H0 250-344-2205
Web: www.ponderosamotorinn.bc.ca

Prince Preferred Guest Program
100 Holomoana St ... Honolulu HI 96815 800-774-6234 943-4158*
**Fax Area Code:* 808 ■ *TF:* 800-774-6234 ■ *Web:* www.princepreferred.com

Pueblo Bonito Hotels & Resorts
4350 La Jolla Village Dr ... San Diego CA 92122 858-642-2050
TF: 800-990-8250 ■ *Web:* www.pueblobonito.com

Purple Sage Motel 1501 E Coliseum Dr ... Snyder TX 79549 325-573-5491
Web: www.placestostay.com

Pyramid Hotel Group LLC
1 Post Office Sq Ste 3100 ... Boston MA 02109 617-412-2800
Web: www.pyramidadvisors.com

Raintree Resorts Management Company LLC
PO Box 350 ... Teton Village WY 83025 307-734-9777
TF: 866-352-9777 ■ *Web:* www.tetonclub.com

Ramada Inn Airport
2275 Marina Mile Blvd STATE Rd 84 ... Fort Lauderdale FL 33312 954-584-4000
Web: www.ramadainnairport.com

Ramada Plaza Beach Resort
1500 Miracle Strip Pkwy Se ... Fort Walton Beach FL 32548 850-243-9161
TF: 800-874-8962 ■ *Web:* www.ramadafwb.com

Red Lion Hotel 621 21St St ... Lewiston ID 83501 208-799-1000
TF: 800-232-6730 ■ *Web:* www.redlionlewiston.com

Redbury Hotel, The 1717 Vine St ... Los Angeles CA 90028 323-962-1717
Web: theredbury.com

Resorts of the Canadian Rockies Inc
1505 17th Ave SW ... Calgary AB T2T0E2 403-254-7669
TF: 800-258-7669 ■ *Web:* www.skircr.com

Roedel Companies LLC 1134 Gibbons Hwy ... Wilton NH 03086 603-654-2040
Web: www.roedelcompanies.com

Rosemont Suites 181 W Town St ... Norwich CT 06360 860-889-2671
Web: www.whghotels.com

Royal St Charles Hotel LLC
135 Saint Charles Ave ... New Orleans LA 70130 504-587-3700
Web: www.destinationhotels.com/royal-st-charles

San Jose Airport Hotel LLC 1740 N First St ... San Jose CA 95112 408-793-3300

Sand Pearl Resort LLC
500 Mandalay Ave ... Clearwater Beach FL 33767 727-441-2425
Web: www.sandpearl.com

Saskatoon Inn Hotel & Conference Centre
2002 Airport Dr ... Saskatoon SK S7L6M4 306-242-1440
Web: www.saskatooninn.com

Sea Breeze Ocean View Motel, The
323 State Hwy 3 ... Bar Harbor ME 04609 207-288-3565
Web: www.seabreeze.us

Seattle Marriott Waterfront Hotel
2100 Alaskan Way ... Seattle WA 98121 206-443-5000
Web: www.gowestmarriott.com

Seldovia Native Association Inc
700 E Dimond Blvd ... Anchorage AK 99515 907-868-8006
Web: www.dimondcenterhotel.com

Seven Crown Resorts Inc PO Box 16247 ... Irvine CA 92623 949-588-7400
Web: www.sevencrown.com

Shamin Hotels Inc 2000 Ware Bottom Spring Rd ... Chester VA 23836 804-777-9000
Web: www.shaminhotels.com

Shane's Rib Shack
9404 W Westgate Blvd #C101 ... Glendale AZ 85305 623-877-7427
Web: www.shanesribshack.com

Sheraton Atlanta 165 Courtland St Ne ... Atlanta GA 30303 404-659-6500
Web: www.sheratonatlantahotel.com

Sheraton Columbia Hotel 10207 Wincopin Cir ... Columbia MD 21044 410-730-3900
Web: www.sheratoncolumbia.com

Sheraton Crescent Hotel 2620 W Dunlap Ave ... Phoenix AZ 85021 602-943-8200
Web: www.sheratoncrescent.com

Sheraton Iowa City Hotel 210 S Dubuque St ... Iowa City IA 52240 319-337-4058
Web: www.sheratoniowacity.com

Sheraton Music City Hotel (Nashville Tenn)
777 McGavock Pk ... Nashville TN 37214 615-885-2200
Web: www.sheratonmusiccity.com

Sheraton Nashville Downtown Hotel
623 Union St ... Nashville TN 37219 615-259-2000
Web: www.sheratonnashvilledowntown.com

Sheraton Oklahoma City Hotel
1 N Broadway ... Oklahoma City OK 73102 405-235-2780
Web: www.sheratonokc.com

Sheraton Premiere at Tysons Corner
8661 Leesburg Pk ... Tysons VA 22182 703-448-1234
Web: www.sheratontysonscorner.com

Sheraton Universal Hotel
333 Universal Hollywood Dr ... Universal City CA 91608 818-980-1212
Web: www.sheratonuniversal.com

Silver Lake Resort Owners Association Inc
7751 Black Lk Rd ... Kissimmee FL 34747 407-397-2828
Web: www.takeme2orlando.com

Sky Lodge, The 201 Heber Ave Main St ... Park City UT 84068 435-658-2500
TF: 888-876-2525 ■ *Web:* www.theskylodge.com

Spectra Co 2510 Supply St ... Pomona CA 91767 909-599-0760
Web: www.spectracompany.com

Sree Hotels LLC
Palladium at Piper Glen 5113 Piper Sta Dr
Ste 300 ... Charlotte NC 28277 704-364-6008
Web: www.sree.com

St. Anthony Riverwalk Wyndham Hotel, The
300 E Travis St ... San Antonio TX 78205 210-227-4392
Web: www.thestanthonyhotel.com

Starwood Hotels Preferred Guest Program
111 Westchester Ave ... White Plains NY 10604 512-834-2426
TF: 888-625-4988 ■ *Web:* www.starwoodhotels.com

Sterling Hotel Dallas 1055 Regal Row ... Dallas TX 75247 214-634-8550

Stevens Pass Mountain Resort LLC
Summit Stevens Pass US Hwy 2 ... Skykomish WA 98288 206-812-4510
Web: www.stevenspass.com

Stillman Development International LLC
505 Park Ave Ste 1700 ... New York NY 10022 212-686-2400
Web: www.stillmandevelopment.com

Stonebridge McWhinney LLC
9100 E Panorama Dr Ste 300 ... Englewood CO 80112 303-785-3100
Web: www.stonebridgecompanies.com

Summit Hospitality Group Ltd
3141 John Humphries Wynd Ste 200 ... Raleigh NC 27612 919-787-5100
Web: www.summithospitality.com

Sunshine Village Corp
Calgary Snow Central 1037 11th Ave SW ... Calgary AB T2R0G1 403-705-4000
Web: www.skibanff.com

Sunstream Hotels & Resorts
6231 Estero Blvd ... Fort Myers Beach FL 33931 239-765-4111
TF: 844-652-3696 ■ *Web:* www.sunstream.com

Swissotel Management (USA) LLC
323 E Wacker Dr ... Chicago IL 60601 312-565-0565
Web: www.swissotel.com

Sybaris Clubs International Inc
2430 E Rand Rd ... Arlington Heights IL 60004 847-637-3000
Web: www.sybaris.com

T Bar m Inc 2549 W State Hwy 46 ... New Braunfels TX 78132 830-625-7738
Web: www.tbarm.com

T2 Development LLC
620 Newport Ctr Dr 14th Fl ... Newport Beach CA 92660 949-610-8200
Web: www.t2dev.com

Tahoe Biltmore Lodge & Casino PO Box 115 ... Crystal Bay NV 89402 775-831-0660
TF: 800-245-8667 ■ *Web:* www.tahoebiltmore.com

Terranea Resort & Spa
100 Terranea Way ... Rancho Palos Verdes CA 90275 310-265-2800
TF: 866-547-3066 ■ *Web:* www.terranea.com

Tramz Hotels LLC 776 Mountain Blvd Ste 200 ... Watchung NJ 07069 908-753-7400
Web: www.tramzhotels.com

Trust Hospitality LLC
806 Douglas Rd 4th Fl ... Coral Gables FL 33134 305-537-7040
Web: www.trusthospitality.com

TRYP Hotels Worldwide Inc
395 Rue De La Couronne ... Quebec QC G1K7X4 800-267-2002
TF: 800-267-2002 ■ *Web:* www.hotelpur.com

Turf Hotels Inc 792 Watervliet Shaker Rd ... Latham NY 12110 518-786-0976
Web: www.turfhotels.com

Twin Pine Casino 22223 Hwy 29 PO Box 789 ... Middletown CA 95461 707-987-0197 987-0375
TF: 800-564-4872 ■ *Web:* twinpine.com

UCF Hotel Venture 6800 Lakewood Plz Dr ... Orlando FL 32819 407-503-9000
Web: www.ucfalumni.com

Union Station Hotel 1001 Broadway ... Nashville TN 37203 615-726-1001
Web: www.unionstationhotelnashville.com

Vacationer RV Resort 1581 East Main St ... El Cajon CA 92021 877-626-4409
TF: 877-626-4409 ■ *Web:* www.vacationerrv.com

Value Place LLC 8621 E 21st St N Ste 250 ... Wichita KS 67206 316-631-1370
Web: www.valueplace.com

Vantage Hospitality Group Inc
3300 N University Dr ... Coral Springs FL 33065 954-575-2668
Web: www.joinvantagehotels.com

Virgin River Casino Corp 100 Pioneer Blvd ... Mesquite NV 89027 702-346-7777
Web: www.virginriver.com

W New York- Union Square 201 Park Ave S ... New York NY 10003 212-253-9119
TF: 877-822-0000 ■ *Web:* www.wnewyorkunionsquare.com

Wampanoag Tribe of Gay Head Aquinnah
20 Black Brook Rd ... Aquinnah MA 02535 508-645-9265
Web: www.wampanoagtribe.net

Warner Center Marriott Woodland Hills
21850 Oxnard St ... Woodland Hills CA 91367 818-887-4800
Web: www.warnercentermarriott.com

Washington Jefferson LLC 318 W 51st St ... New York NY 10019 212-246-7550
TF: 888-567-7550 ■ *Web:* www.wjhotel.com

Waterfront Place Hotel 2 Waterfront Pl ... Morgantown WV 26501 304-296-1700
Web: www.waterfrontplacehotel.com

Wedmore Place LLC 5810 Wessex Hundred ... Williamsburg VA 23185 866-933-6673
TF: 866-933-6673 ■ *Web:* www.wedmoreplace.com

Western Camp Services Ltd 7668 - 69 St ... Edmonton AB T6B2J7 780-468-1568 468-1948
Web: www.westerncampservices.com

Westin Atlanta Airport, The 4736 Best Rd ... Atlanta GA 30337 404-762-7676
Web: www.westinatlantaairport.com

Westin Atlanta Perimeter North, The
7 Concourse Pkwy NE ... Atlanta GA 30328 770-395-3900
Web: www.westinatlantanorth.com

Westin Chicago River North, The
320 N Dearborn St ... Chicago IL 60654 312-744-1900
Web: www.westinchicago.com

Westin Governor Morris Hotel, The
2 Whippany Rd ... Morristown NJ 07960 973-539-7300
Web: www.westingovernormorris.com

Westin Long Beach, The 333 E Ocean Blvd ... Long Beach CA 90802 562-436-3000
Web: westinlb.com

Westin Michigan Avenue Hotel
909 N Michigan Ave ... Chicago IL 60611 312-943-7200
Web: www.thewestinmichiganavenue.com

Westin O'Hare, The 6100 N River Rd ... Rosemont IL 60018 847-698-6000
Web: www.westinohare.com

Westin Reston Heights, The
11750 Sunrise Vly Dr ... Reston VA 20191 703-391-9000
Web: www.westinreston.com

Westin San Diego Gaslamp Quarter, The
910 Broadway Cir ... San Diego CA 92101 619-239-2200
Web: www.westingaslamp.com

Phone Fax

Westin Westminster Hotel, The
10600 Westminster Blvd. . . . . Westminster CO 80020 303-410-5000
Web: www.westindenverboulder.com

Westminster Hotel LLC
550 W Mount Pleasant Ave. . . . . Livingston NJ 07039 973-533-0600
Web: www.westminsterhotel.net

Whiteface Lodge, The 7 Whiteface Inn Ln. . . . . Lake Placid NY 12946 518-523-0500
Web: www.thewhitefacelodge.com

Wilderness Hotel & Resort Inc
511 E Adams St . . . . . Wisconsin Dells WI 53965 608-253-9729
Web: www.wildernessresort.com

Wyndham ByRequest Program PO Box 4090. . . . . Aberdeen SD 57401 800-996-3426
TF: 800-996-3426 ■ *Web:* www.wyndham.com

YOTEL 570 Tenth Ave Times Sq. . . . . New York NY 10036 646-449-7700
Web: www.yotel.com/en

379 HOTELS & HOTEL COMPANIES

See Also Casino Companies p. 1893; Corporate Housing p. 2162; Hotel Reservations Services p. 2529; Hotels - Conference Center p. 2530; Hotels - Frequent Stay Programs p. 2532; Resorts & Resort Companies p. 3068

Phone Fax

1859 Historic Hotels Ltd PO Box 59 . . . . . Galveston TX 77553 409-763-8536 763-5304
Web: www.1859historichotels.com

1886 Crescent Hotel & Spa
75 Prospect Ave . . . . . Eureka Springs AR 72632 479-253-9766 253-5296
TF: 877-342-9766 ■ *Web:* www.crescent-hotel.com

21c Museum Hotel 700 W Main St. . . . . Louisville KY 40202 502-217-6300 578-6601*
**Fax Area Code:* 513 ■ *Web:* www.21chotel.com

35th Street Hotel Corp 45 W 35th St. . . . . New York NY 10001 212-947-2500
Web: www.hotelmetronyc.com

500 West Hotel 500 W Broadway . . . . . San Diego CA 92101 619-234-5252 234-5272
Web: www.500westhotelsd.com

70 Park Avenue Hotel 70 Pk Ave at 38th St. . . . . New York NY 10016 212-973-2400 973-2401
TF: 877-707-2752 ■ *Web:* www.70parkave.com

A La Carte Event Pavilion Ltd
4050 Dana Shores Dr . . . . . Tampa FL 33634 813-831-5390

AAA Properties 331 Wall St . . . . . Chico CA 95928 530-895-3500
Web: aaapropertieschico.com

Academy Hotel Colorado Springs, The
8110 N Academy Blvd . . . . . Colorado Springs CO 80920 719-598-5770 598-5965
TF: 800-766-8524 ■ *Web:* www.theacademyhotel.com

Acadia Inn 98 Eden St . . . . . Bar Harbor ME 04609 207-288-3500
TF: 800-638-3636 ■ *Web:* www.acadiainn.com

Acapulco Hotel & Resort
2505 S Atlantic Ave . . . . . Daytona Beach Shores FL 32118 386-761-2210
TF: 855-922-3224 ■ *Web:* acapulcohoteldaytona.com

Accent Inns Vancouver Airport
10551 St Edwards Dr . . . . . Richmond BC V6X3L8 604-273-3311 273-9522
TF: 800-663-0298 ■
Web: www.accentinns.com/vancouver-airport/hotel-directions

Accent Inns Vancouver-Burnaby
3777 Henning Dr . . . . . Burnaby BC V5C6N5 604-473-5000 473-5095
TF: 800-663-0298 ■ *Web:* www.accentinns.com/burnaby/hotel-amenities

Accor North America
4001 International Pkwy . . . . . Carrollton TX 75007 972-360-9000
Web: www.accorhotels-group.com/en.html

Acqua Hotel 555 Redwood Hwy. . . . . Mill Valley CA 94941 415-380-0400 380-9696
TF: 888-662-9555 ■ *Web:* www.marinhotels.com

Acqualina 17875 Collins Ave. . . . . Sunny Isles Beach FL 33160 305-918-8000 918-8100
TF: 877-312-9742 ■ *Web:* www.acqualinaresort.com

Adam's Mark Hotels & Resorts 120 Church St . . . . . Buffalo NY 14202 716-845-5100
Web: www.adamsmark.com

Adams Oceanfront Resort 4 Read St . . . . . Dewey Beach DE 19971 302-227-3030
TF: 800-448-8080 ■ *Web:* www.adamsoceanfront.com

Admiral Fell Inn
888 S Broadway Historic Fell's Pt. . . . . Baltimore MD 21231 410-522-7377 522-0707
TF: 866-583-4162 ■ *Web:* www.harbormagic.com

Admiral on Baltimore 2 Baltimore Ave. . . . . Rehoboth Beach DE 19971 302-227-1300
TF: 888-882-4188 ■ *Web:* www.admiralonbaltimore.com

Adolphus, The 1321 Commerce St . . . . . Dallas TX 75202 214-742-8200 651-3588
TF: 800-221-9083 ■ *Web:* www.hoteladolphus.com

Adventureland Inn 305 34th Ave NW. . . . . Altoona IA 50009 515-265-7321 265-3506
TF: 800-910-5382 ■ *Web:* www.adventurelandpark.com

Affinia Dumont 150 E 34th St. . . . . New York NY 10016 212-481-7600 889-8856
TF: 866-233-4642 ■ *Web:* www.affinia.com

Affinia 50 155 E 50th St. . . . . New York NY 10022 212-751-5710 753-1468
TF: 866-246-2203 ■ *Web:* www.affinia.com

Affinia Chicago 155 E 50th St. . . . . New York NY 10022 212-751-5710 753-1468
TF: 866-246-2203 ■ *Web:* www.affinia.com

Affinia Gardens 215 E 64th St. . . . . New York NY 10065 212-355-1230 758-7858
TF: 866-233-4642 ■ *Web:* www.affinia.com

Affinia Manhattan 371 Seventh Ave. . . . . New York NY 10001 212-563-1800 643-8028
TF: 866-246-2203 ■ *Web:* www.affinia.com

Airport Settle Inn 2620 S Packerland Dr . . . . . Green Bay WI 54313 920-499-1900 499-1973
TF: 800-688-9052 ■ *Web:* www.settle-inn.com

Airtel Plaza Hotel 7277 Valjean Ave. . . . . Van Nuys CA 91406 818-997-7676
TF: 877-939-9268 ■ *Web:* www.airtelplaza.com

Ala Moana Hotel 410 Atkinson Dr . . . . . Honolulu HI 96814 808-955-4811 944-6839
TF: 800-367-6025 ■
Web: www.outrigger.com/hotels-resorts/hawaiian-islands/oahu-waikiki/ala-moana-hotel

Alamo Inn 2203 E Commerce St. . . . . San Antonio TX 78203 210-227-2203 222-2860
Web: alamoinnmotel.com

Albert at Bay Suite Hotel 435 Albert St . . . . . Ottawa ON K1R7X4 613-238-8858 238-1433
TF: 800-267-6644 ■ *Web:* www.albertatbay.com

Alberta Place Suite Hotel 10049 103rd St. . . . . Edmonton AB T5J2W7 780-423-1565 426-6260

Albion Hotel 1650 James Ave . . . . . Miami Beach FL 33139 305-913-1000 674-0507
TF General: 877-782-3557 ■ *Web:* www.rubellhotels.com

Alexis Hotel 1007 First Ave. . . . . Seattle WA 98104 206-624-4844 621-9009
TF: 866-356-8894 ■ *Web:* www.alexishotel.com

Phone Fax

Algonquin Hotel 59 W 44th St. . . . . New York NY 10036 212-840-6800 944-1419
Web: www.thealgonquin.net

Alpenhof Lodge 3255 W Village Dr. . . . . Teton Village WY 83025 307-733-3242
TF: 800-732-3244 ■ *Web:* alpenhoflodgereservations.com

Ambassador Hotel 2308 W Wisconsin Ave. . . . . Milwaukee WI 53233 414-345-5000
TF: 888-322-3326 ■ *Web:* www.ambassadormilwaukee.com

Ambrosia House Tropical Lodging
622 Fleming St . . . . . Key West FL 33040 305-296-9838 296-2425
TF: 800-535-9838 ■ *Web:* www.ambrosiakeywest.com

America's Best Franchising Inc
50 Glenlake Pkwy Ste 350 . . . . . Atlanta GA 30328 770-393-2662
America's Best Inns & Suites
50 Glen Lake Pkwy NE Ste 350 . . . . . Atlanta GA 30328 770-393-2662 393-2480
TF: 800-237-8466 ■ *Web:* www.americasbestinn.com

American Liberty Hospitality Inc
10700 Richmond Ave Ste 120 . . . . . Houston TX 77042 713-977-5556
Web: www.amliberty.com

AmericInn International LLC 250 Lake Dr E. . . . . Chanhassen MN 55317 952-294-5000 294-5001
TF Resv: 800-634-3444 ■ *Web:* www.americinn.com

Ameristar Casino & Hotel
3200 N Ameristar Dr. . . . . Kansas City MO 64161 816-414-7000
TF: 888-777-8700 ■ *Web:* www.ameristar.com

Ameristar Casino Hotel Council Bluffs
2200 River Rd. . . . . Council Bluffs IA 51501 712-328-8888
TF: 866-667-3386 ■ *Web:* www.ameristar.com

Ameritel Inn Boise Towne Square
7965 W Emerald St. . . . . Boise ID 83704 208-378-7000
TF: 800-600-6001 ■ *Web:* www.ameritelinns.com

Ameritel Inn Pocatello
1440 Pocatello Bench Rd . . . . . Pocatello ID 83201 208-234-7500
TF: 800-600-6001 ■ *Web:* www.ameritelinns.com

Amsterdam Hospitality
888 Seventh Ave 20th Fl. . . . . New York NY 10019 212-292-3600 292-7495

Amway Grand Plaza Hotel
187 Monroe Ave NW . . . . . Grand Rapids MI 49503 616-774-2000 776-6489
TF: 800-253-3590 ■ *Web:* www.amwaygrand.com

Anaheim Plaza Hotel & Suites
1700 S Harbor Blvd . . . . . Anaheim CA 92802 714-772-5900 772-8386
TF: 800-631-4144 ■ *Web:* www.anaheimplazahotel.com

Anchor-In 1 S St. . . . . Hyannis MA 02601 508-775-0357 775-1313
Web: anchorin.com

Anchorage Uptown Suites 235 E 2nd Court. . . . . Anchorage AK 99501 907-279-4232
Web: www.anchorageuptownsuites.com

Andaluz 125 Second St NW . . . . . Albuquerque NM 87102 505-242-9090
Web: www.hotelandaluz.com

Andaz San Diego 600 F St. . . . . San Diego CA 92101 619-849-1234 531-7955
TF: 877-489-4489 ■
Web: sandiego.andaz.hyatt.com/hyatt/hotels/index.jsp?null

Andrews Hotel 624 Post St . . . . . San Francisco CA 94109 415-563-6877 928-6919
TF: 800-926-3739 ■ *Web:* www.andrewshotel.com

Angler's Inn 265 N Millward . . . . . Jackson WY 83001 307-733-3682
TF: 800-867-4667 ■ *Web:* anglersinn.net

Antler Inn 43 W Pearl St PO Box 575. . . . . Jackson WY 83001 307-733-2535
TF: 800-483-8667 ■ *Web:* www.townsquareinns.com

Apple Tree Inn 9508 N Div St . . . . . Spokane WA 99218 509-466-3020
TF: 800-323-5796 ■ *Web:* www.appletreeinnmotel.com

Applewood Manor Inn 62 Cumberland Cir . . . . . Asheville NC 28801 828-254-2244 254-0899
TF: 800-442-2197 ■ *Web:* www.applewoodmanor.com

Aqua Bamboo 2425 Kuhio Ave . . . . . Honolulu HI 96815 808-922-7777 943-8555
TF: 855-747-0754 ■ *Web:* www.aquaresorts.com

Aqua Hospitality Corp 445 Seaside Ave . . . . . Honolulu HI 96815 808-923-2345 943-8555
TF: 855-747-0755 ■ *Web:* www.aquaresorts.com

Aqua Hotel & Lounge 1530 Collins Ave. . . . . Miami Beach FL 33139 305-538-4361
Web: www.aquamiami.com

Aqua Waikiki Wave 2299 Kuhio Ave . . . . . Honolulu HI 96815 808-922-1262 943-8555
TF: 855-747-0754 ■ *Web:* www.aquaresorts.com

ARC the Hotel Ottawa 140 Slater St. . . . . Ottawa ON K1P5H6 613-238-2888 235-8421
TF: 800-699-2516 ■ *Web:* www.arcthehotel.com

Arena Hotel 817 The Alameda . . . . . San Jose CA 95126 408-294-6500 294-6585
Web: www.pacifichotels.com

Argonaut Hotel 495 Jefferson St. . . . . San Francisco CA 94109 415-563-0800 563-2800
TF: 866-415-0704 ■ *Web:* www.argonauthotel.com

Arizona Charlie's Boulder Casino & Hotel
4575 Boulder Hwy . . . . . Las Vegas NV 89121 702-951-5800
TF: 888-236-9066 ■ *Web:* www.arizonacharliesboulder.com

Arizona Charlie's Decatur Casino & Hotel
740 S Decatur Blvd. . . . . Las Vegas NV 89107 702-258-5200 258-5192
TF: 888-236-8645 ■ *Web:* www.arizonacharliesdecatur.com

Arizona Inn 2200 E Elm St . . . . . Tucson AZ 85719 800-933-1093 881-5830*
**Fax Area Code:* 520 ■ *TF:* 800-933-1093 ■ *Web:* arizonainn.com

Asano of Hawaii Corp 3159 Koapaka St Ste D. . . . . Honolulu HI 96819 808-836-3939

Ashland Springs Hotel 212 E Main St . . . . . Ashland OR 97520 541-488-1700 488-0240
TF: 888-795-4545 ■ *Web:* www.ashlandspringshotel.com

Ashmore Inn & Suites 4019 S Loop 289 . . . . . Lubbock TX 79423 806-785-0060
Web: www.ashmoreinn.com

Ashton Hotel 610 Main St . . . . . Fort Worth TX 76102 817-332-0100 332-0110
Web: www.theashtonhotel.com

Assiniboine Gordon Inn on the Park
1975 Portage Ave . . . . . Winnipeg MB R3J0J9 204-888-4806 897-9870
Web: gordonhotels.com

Associated Hotels LLC
1 North LaSalle St Ste 1015 . . . . . Chicago IL 60602 312-782-6008 782-2356
Web: www.associatedhotelsllc.com

Asticou Inn 15 Peabody Dr . . . . . Northeast Harbor ME 04662 207-276-3344
TF: 800-258-3373 ■ *Web:* www.asticou.com

Aston Hotels & Resorts
2155 Kalakaua Ave Ste 500 . . . . . Honolulu HI 96815 808-931-1400 931-1414
TF: 800-775-4228 ■ *Web:* www.astonhotels.com

Astor Crowne Plaza 739 Canal St . . . . . New Orleans LA 70130 504-962-0500 962-0503
TF: 877-408-9661 ■ *Web:* www.astorneworleans.com

Astor Hotel, The 924 E Juneau Ave . . . . . Milwaukee WI 53202 414-271-4220 271-6370
TF: 800-558-0200 ■ *Web:* astormilwaukee.com

				Phone	Fax
Atheneum Suite Hotel & Conference Ctr 1000 Brush Ave	Detroit	MI	48226	313-962-2323	962-2424
TF: 800-772-2323 ■ *Web:* www.atheneumsuites.com					
Atlantic Eyrie Lodge 6 Norman Rd	Bar Harbor	ME	04609	800-422-2883	288-8500*
**Fax Area Code:* 207 ■ *TF:* 800-422-2883 ■ *Web:* www.atlanticeyrielodge.com					
Atlantic Palace Suites Hotel 1507 Boardwalk	Atlantic City	NJ	08401	609-344-1200	345-0733
Web: www.atlanticpalacesuites.com					
Atlantic Sands Hotel 101 N Boardwalk	Rehoboth Beach	DE	19971	302-227-2511	
TF: 800-422-0600 ■ *Web:* www.atlanticsandshotel.com					
Atlantic, The 601 N Ft Lauderdale Beach Blvd	Fort Lauderdale	FL	33304	954-567-8020	567-8040
Web: www.atlantichotelfl.com					
Atrium Holding Co 6900 E Camelback Rd Ste 607	Scottsdale	AZ	85251	480-222-6035	
Atrium Hotel 18700 MacArthur Blvd	Irvine	CA	92612	949-833-2770	
TF: 800-854-3012 ■ *Web:* www.atriumhotel.com					
Auberge du Soleil 180 Rutherford Hill Rd	Rutherford	CA	94573	707-963-1211	963-8764
TF: 800-348-5406 ■ *Web:* www.aubergedusoleil.com					
Auberge du Vieux-Port 97 Rue de la Commune E	Montreal	QC	H2Y1J1	514-876-0081	876-8923
TF: 888-660-7678 ■ *Web:* www.aubergeduvieuxport.com					
Auberge Saint-Antoine 8 rue Saint-Antoine	Quebec	QC	G1K4C9	418-692-2211	692-1177
TF: 888-692-2211 ■ *Web:* www.saint-antoine.com					
Austin Hotel & Spa 305 Malvern Ave	Hot Springs	AR	71901	501-623-6600	624-7160
TF: 877-623-6697 ■ *Web:* www.theaustinhotel.com					
Avalon Corporate Furnished Apartments 1553 Empire Blvd	Webster	NY	14580	585-671-4421	671-9771
TF: 800-934-9763 ■ *Web:* www.rochesterfurnished.com					
Avalon Hotel 16 W Tenth St	Erie	PA	16501	814-459-2220	459-2322
TF: 888-295-4949 ■ *Web:* www.avalonerie.com					
Avalon Motel Corp 1529 Broadway	Saugus	MA	01906	781-233-4200	
Web: avalon-motel.com					
Avendra LLC 702 King Farm Blvd Ste 600	Rockville	MD	20850	301-825-0500	825-0497
Web: www.avendra.com					
Avenue Inn & Spa 33 Wilmington Ave	Rehoboth Beach	DE	19971	800-433-5870	
TF: 800-433-5870 ■ *Web:* www.avenueinn.com					
Avenue Plaza Resort 2111 St Charles Ave	New Orleans	LA	70130	504-566-1212	
TF: 800-614-8685 ■ *Web:* www.avenueplazaresort.com					
Ayres Hotel Anaheim 2550 E Katella Ave	Anaheim	CA	92806	714-634-2106	
TF: 800-595-5692 ■ *Web:* www.ayreshotels.com					
Bahama House 2001 S Atlantic Ave	Daytona Beach Shores	FL	32118	888-687-1894	248-0991*
**Fax Area Code:* 386 ■ *TF:* 888-687-1894 ■ *Web:* www.daytonabahamahouse.com					
Balance Rock Inn 21 Albert Meadow	Bar Harbor	ME	04609	207-288-2610	288-5534
TF: 800-753-0494 ■ *Web:* www.balancerockinn.com					
Balboa Park Inn 3402 Pk Blvd	San Diego	CA	92103	619-298-0823	
TF: 800-938-8181 ■ *Web:* www.balboaparkinn.com					
Bally's Casino Tunica 1450 Bally's Blvd	Robinsonville	MS	38664	866-422-5597	
TF: 866-422-5597 ■ *Web:* www.ballystunica.com					
Balmoral Inn 120 Balmoral Ave	Biloxi	MS	39531	228-388-6776	388-5450
TF: 800-393-9131 ■ *Web:* www.balmoralinn.com					
Bar Harbor Hotel-Bluenose Inn 90 Eden St	Bar Harbor	ME	04609	207-288-3348	288-2183
TF: 800-445-4077 ■ *Web:* barharborhotel.com					
Barclay Hotel 1348 Robson St	Vancouver	BC	V5E1C5	604-688-8850	688-2534
Web: www.barclayhotel.com					
Barnstead Inn 349 Bonnet St	Manchester Center	VT	05255	802-362-1619	
TF: 800-331-1619 ■ *Web:* www.barnsteadinn.com					
Baronne Plaza Hotel 201 Baronne St	New Orleans	LA	70112	504-522-0083	
TF: 888-756-0083 ■ *Web:* www.baronneplaza.com					
Barrington Hotel & Suites 263 Shepherd of the Hills Expy	Branson	MO	65616	417-334-8866	336-2585
TF: 800-760-8866 ■ *Web:* www.barringtonhotel.com					
Bavarian Inn 855 N Fifth St	Custer	SD	57730	605-673-2802	
Web: www.bavarianinnsd.com					
Bay Club Hotel & Marina 2131 Shelter Island Dr	San Diego	CA	92106	619-224-8888	225-1604
TF: 800-672-0800 ■ *Web:* www.bayclubhotel.com					
Bay Harbor Inn & Suites *Daddy O Miami* 9660 E Bay Harbor Dr	Bay Harbor Islands	FL	33154	305-868-4141	
Web: www.daddyohotel.com/miami					
Bay Park Hotel 1425 Munras Ave	Monterey	CA	93940	831-649-1020	373-4258
TF Resv: 800-338-3564 ■ *Web:* www.bayparkhotel.com					
Bayfront Inn 138 Avenida Menendez	Saint Augustine	FL	32084	904-824-1681	
Web: www.bayfrontinn.com					
Baymont Inn 4025 McDonald Dr	Dubuque	IA	52003	563-582-3752	
TF: 800-337-0550 ■ *Web:* www.baymontinns.com					
Beach Haven Inn 4740 Mission Blvd	San Diego	CA	92109	858-272-3812	272-3532
Web: www.beachhaveninn.com					
Beach Plaza - Ft Lauderdale 625 N Ft Lauderdale Beach Blvd	Fort Lauderdale	FL	33304	954-566-7631	
Web: 3palmshotels.com					
Beacher's Lodge 6970 A1A S	Saint Augustine	FL	32080	904-471-8849	471-3002
TF: 800-527-8849 ■ *Web:* www.beacherslodge.com					
Beacon Hotel 720 Ocean Dr	Miami Beach	FL	33139	305-674-8200	
TF: 877-674-8200 ■ *Web:* www.beaconsouthbeach.com					
Beacon Hotel & Corporate Quarters 1615 Rhode Island Ave NW	Washington	DC	20036	202-296-2100	
TF: 800-823-1700 ■ *Web:* www.openhospitality.com					
Beaver Creek Lodge 26 Avon Dale Ln	Beaver Creek	CO	81620	970-845-9800	845-8242
TF: 800-525-7280 ■ *Web:* www.beavercreeklodge.net					
Beecher Hill LLC 9991 Beecher Hill Rd	Peshastin	WA	98847	509-548-0559	
TF: 866-414-0559 ■ *Web:* beecherhill.com					
Beechwood Hotel 363 Plantation St	Worcester	MA	01605	508-754-5789	
TF: 800-344-2589 ■ *Web:* www.beechwoodhotel.com					
Bell Tower Hotel 300 S Thayer St	Ann Arbor	MI	48104	734-769-3010	769-4339
TF: 800-562-3559 ■ *Web:* www.belltowerhotel.com					
Bell Tower Inn 1235 Second St SW	Rochester	MN	55902	507-289-2233	289-2233
TF: 800-448-7583 ■ *Web:* www.rochesterlodging.com					
Bellasera Hotel 221 Ninth St S	Naples	FL	34102	239-649-7333	649-6233
TF: 855-990-0301 ■ *Web:* www.sunstream.com/naples/bellasera					
Bellevue Club Hotel 11200 SE Sixth St	Bellevue	WA	98004	425-454-4424	688-3101
TF: 800-579-1110 ■ *Web:* www.bellevueclub.com					
Bellmoor, The 6 Christian St	Rehoboth Beach	DE	19971	302-227-5800	
TF: 800-425-2355 ■ *Web:* www.thebellmoor.com					
Belvedere Hotel 319 W 48th St	New York	NY	10036	212-245-7000	245-4455
TF: 800-492-8122 ■ *Web:* www.newyorkhotel.com					
Ben Lomond Suites LLC 2510 Washington Blvd	Ogden	UT	84401	801-627-1900	394-5342
TF: 877-627-1900 ■ *Web:* benlomondsuites.com					
Benchmark Hospitality International 4 Waterway Sq Ste 300	The Woodlands	TX	77380	281-367-5757	367-1407
Web: www.benchmarkresortsandhotels.com					
Bendel Executive Suites 213 Bendel Rd	Lafayette	LA	70503	337-261-0604	233-4296
Web: www.bendelexec.com					
Benjamin, The 125 E 50th St	New York	NY	10022	212-715-2500	
TF: 866-222-2365 ■ *Web:* www.thebenjamin.com					
Bennett Enterprises Inc PO Box 670	Perrysburg	OH	43552	419-874-1933	
Web: www.bennett-enterprises.com					
Benson, The 309 SW Broadway	Portland	OR	97205	503-228-2000	471-3920
TF: 800-663-1144 ■ *Web:* www.coasthotels.com					
Bentley Hotel New York 500 E 62nd St	New York	NY	10065	212-644-6000	
Web: www.hotelbentleynewyork.com					
Bergen County Community Action Program I 241 Moore St	Hackensack	NJ	07601	201-968-0200	
Web: www.bergencap.org					
Berkeley Hotel, The 1200 E Cary St	Richmond	VA	23219	804-780-1300	648-4728
TF: 888-780-4422 ■ *Web:* www.berkeleyhotel.com					
Bernards Inn 27 Mine Brook Rd	Bernardsville	NJ	07924	908-766-0002	766-4604
TF: 888-766-0002 ■ *Web:* www.bernardsinn.com					
Bernardus Lodge 415 Carmel Valley Rd	Carmel Valley	CA	93924	831-658-3400	659-3529
TF: 800-223-2533 ■ *Web:* www.bernardus.com					
Best Western Chincoteague Island 7105 Maddox Blvd	Chincoteague Island	VA	23336	757-336-6557	336-6558
TF: 800-553-6117 ■ *Web:* www.bestwestern.com					
Best Western International Inc 6201 N 24th Pkwy	Phoenix	AZ	85016	602-957-4200	957-5942*
**Fax:* Mktg ■ *TF:* 800-528-1234 ■ *Web:* www.bestwestern.com					
Best Western Laguna Brisas Spa Hotel 1600 S Coast Hwy	Laguna Beach	CA	92651	949-497-7272	
TF: 888-296-6834 ■ *Web:* www.lagunabrisas.com					
Best Western Victorian Inn 487 Foam St	Monterey	CA	93940	831-373-8000	655-8174
TF: 800-232-4141 ■ *Web:* www.victorianinn.com					
Betsy Hotel 1440 Ocean Dr	Miami Beach	FL	33139	305-531-6100	531-9009
TF: 866-792-3879 ■ *Web:* www.thebetsyhotel.com					
Beverly Heritage Hotel 1820 Barber Ln	Milpitas	CA	95035	408-943-9080	432-8617
Web: www.beverlyheritage.com					
Beverly Hills Hotel 9641 Sunset Blvd	Beverly Hills	CA	90210	310-276-2251	887-2887
TF: 800-650-1842 ■ *Web:* www.dorchestercollection.com					
Beverly Hilton 9876 Wilshire Blvd	Beverly Hills	CA	90210	310-274-7777	285-1313
TF: 800-605-8896 ■ *Web:* www.beverlyhilton.com					
Beverly Wilshire - A Four Seasons Hotel 9500 Wilshire Blvd	Beverly Hills	CA	90212	310-275-5200	274-2851
TF: 800-545-4000 ■ *Web:* www.fourseasons.com/beverlywilshire					
Bienville House Hotel 320 Decatur St	New Orleans	LA	70130	504-529-2345	525-6079
TF: 800-535-7836 ■ *Web:* www.bienvillehouse.com					
Bigelow Management Inc 4640 S Eastern Ave	Las Vegas	NV	89119	702-456-1606	
Web: budgetsuites.com					
Billings C'mon Inn Hotel 2020 Overland Ave	Billings	MT	59102	406-655-1100	
TF: 800-655-1170 ■ *Web:* www.cmoninn.com					
Billings Hotel & Convention Ctr 1223 Mullowney Ln	Billings	MT	59101	406-248-7151	
TF: 800-537-7286 ■ *Web:* www.billingshotel.net					
Biltmore Greensboro Hotel 111 W Washington St	Greensboro	NC	27401	336-272-3474	
TF General: 800-332-0303 ■ *Web:* www.thebiltmoregreensboro.com					
Biltmore Hotel & Suites 2151 Laurelwood Rd	Santa Clara	CA	95054	408-988-8411	
TF: 800-255-9925 ■ *Web:* www.hotelbiltmore.com					
Biltmore Hotel Oklahoma 401 S Meridian Ave	Oklahoma City	OK	73108	405-947-7681	947-4253
TF: 800-522-6620 ■ *Web:* www.biltmoreokc.com					
Biltmore Suites 205 W Madison St	Baltimore	MD	21201	410-728-6550	728-5829
TF: 800-868-5064 ■ *Web:* www.biltmoresuites.com					
Bismarck Expressway Suites 180 E Bismarck Expy	Bismarck	ND	58504	701-222-3311	222-3311
TF: 888-774-5566 ■ *Web:* expresswayhotels.com					
Black Swan Inn 746 E Ctr St	Pocatello	ID	83201	208-233-3051	
Web: www.blackswaninn.com					
Blackfoot Inn 5940 Blackfoot Trl SE	Calgary	AB	T2H2B5	403-252-2253	252-3574
TF: 800-661-1151 ■ *Web:* www.hotelblackfoot.com					
Blacktail Mountain Ski Area LLC 13990 Blacktail Mtn Rd	Lakeside	MT	59922	406-844-0999	
Web: www.blacktailmountain.com					
Blackwell, The 2110 Tuttle Pk Pl	Columbus	OH	43210	614-247-4000	247-4040
TF: 866-247-4003 ■ *Web:* www.theblackwell.com					
Blakely New York 136 W 55th St	New York	NY	10019	212-245-1800	582-8332
TF: 800-735-0710 ■ *Web:* www.blakelynewyork.com					
Blantyre 16 Blantyre Rd PO Box 995	Lenox	MA	01240	413-637-3556	
TF: 844-881-0104 ■ *Web:* blantyre.com					
Blue Horizon Hotel 1225 Robson St	Vancouver	BC	V6E1C3	604-688-1411	688-4461
TF: 800-663-1333 ■ *Web:* www.bluehorizonhotel.com					
Blue Moon Hotel 944 Collins Ave	Miami Beach	FL	33139	305-673-2262	534-1546
TF: 800-553-7739 ■ *Web:* www.bluemoonhotel.com					
Blue Parrot Inn 409 Angela St	Key West	FL	33040	305-296-0033	
TF: 800-549-4430 ■ *Web:* www.blueparrotinn.com					
Bluenose Inn & Suites 636 Bedford Hwy	Halifax	NS	B3M2L8	800-565-2301	
TF: 800-553-5339					
Boardwalk Plaza Hotel 2 Olive Ave	Rehoboth Beach	DE	19971	302-227-7169	227-0561
TF: 800-332-3224 ■ *Web:* www.boardwalkplaza.com					
Bodega Bay Lodge 103 Coast Hwy 1	Bodega Bay	CA	94923	707-875-3525	
TF Resv: 888-875-2250 ■ *Web:* www.bodegabaylodge.com					
Bohemian Hotel Celebration 700 Bloom St	Celebration	FL	34747	407-566-6000	566-1844
TF: 888-249-4007 ■ *Web:* www.celebrationhotel.com					

Phone Fax

Bond Place Hotel 65 Dundas St E .... Toronto ON M5B2G8 416-362-6061
TF: 800-268-9390 ■ *Web:* bondplace.ca

Boomtown Hotel Casino 300 Riverside Dr .... Bossier City LA 71111 318-746-0711
Web: www.boomtownbossier.com

Boone Tavern Hotel of Berea College
100 S Main St. .... Berea KY 40403 859-985-3700 985-3715
TF: 800-366-9358 ■ *Web:* www.boonetavernhotel.com

Borgata Hotel Casino & Spa
1 Borgata Way .... Atlantic City NJ 08401 609-317-1000 317-1039
TF: 877-786-9900 ■ *Web:* www.theborgata.com

Boston Harbor Hotel 70 Rowes Wharf .... Boston MA 02110 617-439-7000 330-9450
TF: 800-752-7077 ■ *Web:* www.bhh.com

Boston Marriott Copley Place
110 Huntington Ave .... Boston MA 02116 617-236-5800
Web: marriott.com

Boston Park Plaza Hotel & Towers 50 Pk Plz. .... Boston MA 02116 617-426-2000
TF: 800-225-2008 ■ *Web:* www.bostonparkplaza.com

Boulder Adventure Lodge (A-Lodge)
91 Four Mile Canyon Rd. .... Boulder CO 80302 435-335-7460
TF: 800-556-3446 ■ *Web:* boulder-utah.com

Boulder Station Hotel & Casino
4111 Boulder Hwy .... Las Vegas NV 89121 702-432-7777 367-6138*
**Fax:* Circulation Desk ■ *TF:* 800-683-7777 ■ *Web:* boulderstation.sclv.com

Bourbon Orleans - A Wyndham Historic Hotel
717 Orleans St .... New Orleans LA 70116 504-523-2222 571-4666
TF: 866-513-9744 ■ *Web:* www.bourbonorleans.com

Bradley Boulder Inn 2040 16th St .... Boulder CO 80302 303-545-5200
Web: www.thebradleyboulder.com

Bradley Inn 3063 Bristol Rd. .... New Harbor ME 04554 207-677-2105 677-3367
TF: 800-942-5560 ■ *Web:* www.bradleyinn.com

Brazilian Court, The 301 Australian Ave .... Palm Beach FL 33480 561-655-7740 655-0801
TF: 800-552-0335 ■ *Web:* www.thebraziliancourt.com

Breakers at Waikiki, The 250 Beach Walk .... Honolulu HI 96815 808-923-3181 923-7174
TF: 800-426-0494 ■ *Web:* www.breakers-hawaii.com

Breakers Hotel & Suites 105 Second St. .... Rehoboth Beach DE 19971 302-227-6688 227-2013
TF: 800-441-8009 ■ *Web:* www.thebreakershotel.com

Breakwater Inn 1711 Glacier Ave .... Juneau AK 99801 888-586-6303 463-4820*
**Fax Area Code:* 907 ■ *TF:* 888-586-6303

Breckinridge Inn 2800 Breckinridge Ln .... Louisville KY 40220 502-456-5050 451-1577
Web: www.breckinridgeinn.com

Brent House Hotel 1512 Jefferson Hwy .... New Orleans LA 70121 504-842-4140 842-4160
TF: 800-535-3986 ■ *Web:* www.brenthouse.com

Bridgewater Hotel 723 First Ave .... Fairbanks AK 99701 800-528-4916 452-6126*
**Fax Area Code:* 907 ■ *TF:* 800-528-4916 ■ *Web:* www.fountainheadhotels.com

Bristol Hotel 1055 First Ave. .... San Diego CA 92101 619-232-6141 232-0118
TF: 800-662-4477 ■ *Web:* www.thebristolsandiego.com

Brookshire Suites 120 E Lombard St .... Baltimore MD 21202 410-625-1300 522-9602
TF: 855-345-5033 ■ *Web:* www.brookshiresuites.com

Brookside Inn 1297 S Perry St .... Castle Rock CO 80104 303-688-2500
Web: www.bsmc.com

Brookstown Inn 200 Brookstown Ave .... Winston-Salem NC 27101 336-725-1120 773-0147
TF: 800-845-4262 ■ *Web:* www.brookstowninn.com

Brookstreet Hotel 525 Legget Dr .... Ottawa ON K2K2W2 613-271-1800
TF: 888-826-2220 ■ *Web:* www.brookstreethotel.com

Brown County Inn 51 State Rd 46 .... Nashville IN 47448 812-988-2291
TF: 800-772-5249 ■ *Web:* www.browncountyinn.com

Brown Hotel, The 335 W Broadway St .... Louisville KY 40202 502-583-1234
TF: 888-888-5252 ■ *Web:* www.brownhotel.com

Brown Palace Hotel 321 17th St .... Denver CO 80202 303-297-3111 312-5900
TF: 800-321-2599 ■ *Web:* www.brownpalace.com

Brown's Wharf Inn 121 Atlantic Ave .... Boothbay Harbor ME 04538 207-633-5440 633-5440
TF: 800-334-8110 ■ *Web:* www.brownswharfinn.com

Bryant Park Hotel 40 W 40th St .... New York NY 10018 212-869-0100 869-4446
TF: 877-640-9300 ■ *Web:* www.bryantparkhotel.com

Buckingham Hotel 101 W 57th St .... New York NY 10019 212-246-1500 262-0698
Web: tripadvisor.com.au

Buckrail Lodge 110 E Karns Ave PO Box 23 .... Jackson WY 83001 307-733-2079 734-1663
Web: www.buckraillodge.com

Budget Host Inn 116 Kenyon Rd W .... Fort Dodge IA 50501 515-955-8501
Web: budgethost.com

Budget Host International
2307 Roosevelt Dr .... Arlington TX 76016 817-861-6088 861-6089
TF: 800-283-4678 ■ *Web:* www.budgethost.com

Budget Suites of America
2770 N Hwy 360 .... Grand Prairie TX 75050 972-647-2500
TF: 866-877-2000 ■ *Web:* www.budgetsuites.com

Buena Vista Suites 8203 World Ctr Dr. .... Orlando FL 32821 407-239-8588 239-1401
TF Resv: 800-537-7737 ■ *Web:* www.thecaribehotelsorlando.com

Business Inn 180 MacLaren St .... Ottawa ON K2P0L3 613-232-1121 232-8143
TF: 800-363-1777 ■ *Web:* thebusinessinn.com

C'mon Inn Grand Forks 3051 32nd Ave S .... Grand Forks ND 58201 701-775-3320
TF: 800-255-2323 ■ *Web:* www.cmoninn.com

Caesars License Company LLC
3655 Las Vegas Blvd S. .... Las Vegas NV 89109 702-946-7000
TF: 877-796-2096 ■ *Web:* www.caesars.com/paris-las-vegas

California Hotel & Casino 12 E Ogden Ave. .... Las Vegas NV 89101 702-385-1222 388-2660
TF: 800-634-6505 ■ *Web:* www.thecal.com

Cambridge Suites Hotel Halifax
1583 Brunswick St .... Halifax NS B3J3P5 902-420-0555 420-9379
TF: 800-565-1263 ■ *Web:* www.cambridgesuiteshalifax.com

Cambridge Suites Hotel Toronto
15 Richmond St E. .... Toronto ON M5C1N2 416-368-1990 601-3751
TF: 800-463-1990 ■ *Web:* www.cambridgesuitestoronto.com

Camino Real El Paso 101 S El Paso St .... El Paso TX 79901 915-534-3050 534-3024
Web: www.caminoreal.com

Camino Real Hotel LLC 2856 E Main St. .... Eagle Pass TX 78852 830-757-8111

Campus Inn & Suites 390 E Broadway .... Eugene OR 97401 541-343-3376 485-9392

Canad Inns - Club Regent Casino Hotel
1415 Regent Ave W .... Winnipeg MB R2C3B2 204-667-5560 667-5913
TF: 888-332-2623 ■ *Web:* www.canadinns.com

Canad Inns Fort Garry 1824 Pembina Hwy .... Winnipeg MB R3T2G2 204-261-7450 261-5433
TF: 888-332-2623 ■ *Web:* www.canadinns.com

Canad Inns Garden City 2100 McPhillips St. .... Winnipeg MB R2V3T9 204-633-0024 697-3377
TF: 888-332-2623 ■ *Web:* www.canadinns.com

Canad Inns Polo Park 1405 St Matthews Ave .... Winnipeg MB R3G0K5 204-775-8791 783-4039
TF: 888-332-2623 ■ *Web:* www.canadinns.com

Canal Park Lodge 250 Canal Pk Dr .... Duluth MN 55802 218-279-6000
TF: 800-777-8560 ■ *Web:* www.canalparklodge.com

Canandaigua Inn on the Lake
770 S Main St. .... Canandaigua NY 14424 585-394-7800 394-5003
TF: 800-228-2801 ■ *Web:* www.theinnonthelake.com

Canary Hotel 31 W Carrillo .... Santa Barbara CA 93101 805-884-0300 884-8153
TF: 866-999-5401 ■ *Web:* www.canarysantabarbara.com

Cannery Casino & Hotel, The
Cannery Casino Resorts LLC
2121 E Craig Rd. .... North Las Vegas NV 89030 702-507-5700
TF: 866-999-4899 ■ *Web:* www.cannerycasinos.com

Canoe Bay PO Box 28 .... Chetek WI 54728 715-924-4594
Web: www.canoebay.com

Cape Cod Irish Village 822 Rt 28 .... S.Yarmouth MA 02664 508-771-0100
Web: www.capecod-irishvillage.com

Capella Hotel Group 3384 Peachtree Rd Ste 375 .... Atlanta GA 30326 404-842-7280
Web: www.capellahotelgroup.com

Capital Hill Hotel & Suites 88 Albert St .... Ottawa ON K1P5E9 613-235-1413 235-6047
TF: 800-463-7705 ■ *Web:* www.capitalhill.com

Capital Hotel 111 W Markham St .... Little Rock AR 72201 501-374-7474 370-7091
TF: 877-637-0037 ■ *Web:* www.capitalhotel.com/site

Capital Hotel Management LLC 548 Cabot St. .... Beverly MA 01915 978-522-7000
Web: www.chmhotel.com

Capitol Hill Hotel 200 C St SE .... Washington DC 20003 202-543-6000 547-2608
Web: capitolhillhotel-dc.com

Capitol Plaza Hotel & Conference Ctr
100 State St .... Montpelier VT 05602 802-223-5252
TF: 800-274-5252 ■ *Web:* www.capitolplaza.com

Capitol Plaza Hotel Jefferson City
415 W McCarty St .... Jefferson City MO 65101 573-635-1234 635-4565
TF: 800-338-8088 ■ *Web:* www.capitolplazajeffersoncity.com

Capt Hirams Resort 1606 Indian River Dr .... Sebastian FL 32958 772-589-4345
TF: 888-447-2671 ■ *Web:* www.hirams.com

Captain Daniel Stone Inn 10 Water St. .... Brunswick ME 04011 207-373-1824
Web: thedanielhotel.com

Caretel Inns of America Inc
910 S Washington Ave .... Royal Oak MI 48067 248-850-7138

Caribbean Cove Hotel & Water Park
3850 Depauw Blvd .... Indianapolis IN 46268 317-872-9790
Web: www.caribbeancovewaterpark.com

Caribe Royale Orlando All-Suites Hotel & Convention Ctr
8101 World Ctr Dr .... Orlando FL 32821 407-238-8000 238-8050
TF Resv: 800-823-8300 ■ *Web:* www.thecaribehotelsorlando.com

Carlson
Radisson Hotels & Resorts
701 Carlson Pkwy .... Minnetonka MN 55305 763-212-5000
TF: 800-333-3333 ■ *Web:* www.carlson.com

Carlson Hotels Worldwide
701 Carlson Pkwy. .... Minneapolis MN 55305 763-212-5000
Web: www.carlsonhotels.com
Country Inns & Suites by Carlson
11340 Blondo St Ste 100 .... Omaha NE 68164 800-600-7275
TF: 800-600-7275 ■ *Web:* www.countryinns.com

Carlton Arms 160 E 25th St .... New York NY 10010 212-679-0680
Web: www.carltonarms.com

Carlton on Madison Ave 88 Madison Ave .... New York NY 10016 212-532-4100 696-9758
TF Resv: 800-601-8500 ■ *Web:* www.carltonhotelny.com

Carlyle Hotel, The
1731 New Hampshire Ave NW .... Washington DC 20009 202-234-3200
TF: 877-301-0019 ■ *Web:* www.carlylehoteldc.com

Carmel River Inn 26600 Oliver Rd .... Carmel CA 93923 831-624-1575
TF: 800-882-8142 ■ *Web:* www.carmelriverinn.com

Carnegie Hotel
1216 W State of Franklin Rd .... Johnson City TN 37604 423-979-6400 979-6424
TF: 866-757-8277 ■ *Web:* www.carnegiehotel.com

Carolina Inn 211 Pittsboro St. .... Chapel Hill NC 27516 919-933-2001
TF: 800-962-8519 ■ *Web:* www.carolinainn.com

Carousel Beachfront Hotel & Suites
11700 Coastal Hwy. .... Ocean City MD 21842 410-524-1000 524-7766
TF: 800-641-0011 ■ *Web:* www.carouselhotel.com

Carousel Inn & Suites 1530 S Harbor Blvd .... Anaheim CA 92802 714-758-0444 772-9960
TF: 800-854-6767 ■ *Web:* www.carouselinnandsuites.com

Carroll Properties Partnership
12734 Kenwood Ln Ste 35 .... Fort Myers FL 33907 239-278-5900
Web: carroll-properties.com

Cartier Place Suite Hotel 180 Cooper St .... Ottawa ON K2P2L5 613-236-5000 238-3842
TF: 800-236-8399 ■ *Web:* www.suitedreams.com

Casa Blanca Motor Lodge Ltd
2728 Victoria Ave .... Brandon MB R7B2V9 204-728-1500

Casa Grande Suite Hotel 834 Ocean Dr .... Miami Beach FL 33139 305-672-7003
Web: www.casagrandesuitehotel.com

Casa Madrona Hotel 801 Bridgeway .... Sausalito CA 94965 415-332-0502 331-3125
TF General: 800-288-0502 ■ *Web:* www.casamadrona.com

Casa Monica Hotel 95 Cordova St. .... Saint Augustine FL 32084 904-827-1888 819-6065
TF Help Line: 800-648-1888 ■ *Web:* www.casamonica.com

Casa Munras Hotel 700 Munras Ave .... Monterey CA 93940 831-375-2411 375-1365
TF: 800-222-2446 ■ *Web:* www.hotelcasamunras.com

Casa Via Mar Inn & Tennis Club
377 W Ch Islands Blvd. .... Port Hueneme CA 93041 805-984-6222 984-9490
Web: www.casaviamar.com

Casablanca Hotel 147 W 43rd St .... New York NY 10036 212-869-1212 391-7585
TF: 888-922-7225 ■ *Web:* www.casablancahotel.com

Cascades Inn 3226 Shepherd of the Hills Expy .... Branson MO 65616 417-335-8424 334-1927
TF: 800-588-8424 ■ *Web:* www.cascadesinn.com

Casino Royale Hotel 3411 Las Vegas Blvd S. .... Las Vegas NV 89109 702-737-3500
TF: 800-854-7666 ■ *Web:* www.casinoroyalehotel.com

Castle in the Sand Hotel
3701 Atlantic Ave .... Ocean City MD 21842 410-289-6846 289-9446
TF: 800-552-7263 ■ *Web:* www.castleinthesand.com

Phone Fax

Castle Inn & Suites 1734 S Harbor Blvd Anaheim CA 92802 714-774-8111 956-4736
TF: 800-227-8530 ■ *Web:* www.castleinn.com

Castle on the Hudson 400 Benedict Ave Tarrytown NY 10591 914-631-1980 631-4612
TF: 800-616-4487 ■ *Web:* www.castleonthehudson.com

Centennial Hotel 96 Pleasant St Concord NH 03301 603-227-9000 225-5031
Web: www.thecentennialhotel.com

Center Court Historic Inn & Cottages
1075 Duval St C-19 Key West FL 33040 305-296-9292
TF: 800-797-8787 ■ *Web:* www.centercourtkw.com

Century Hotel South Beach 140 Ocean Dr Miami Beach FL 33139 305-674-8855
TF: 877-659-8855 ■ *Web:* centurymiamibeach.com

Century Plaza Hotel & Spa 1015 Burrard St Vancouver BC V6Z1Y5 604-687-0575 682-5790
TF: 800-663-1818 ■ *Web:* www.century-plaza.com

Century Suites Hotel 300 SR-446 Bloomington IN 47401 812-336-7777
TF: 800-766-5446 ■ *Web:* www.centurysuites.com

Chamberlain West Hollywood
1000 Westmount Dr West Hollywood CA 90069 310-657-7400 854-6744
TF: 877-686-2082 ■ *Web:* www.chamberlainwesthollywood.com

Chambers Hotel 15 W 56th St New York NY 10019 212-974-5656 974-5657
Web: www.chambershotel.com

Chancellor Hotel on Union Square
433 Powell St San Francisco CA 94102 415-362-2004 362-1403
TF: 800-428-4748 ■ *Web:* www.chancellorhotel.com

Chandler Inn 26 Chandler St Boston MA 02116 617-482-3450 542-3428
TF: 800-842-3450 ■ *Web:* www.chandlerinn.com

Charles Hotel Harvard Square 1 Bennett St Cambridge MA 02138 617-864-1200 864-5715
TF: 800-882-1818 ■ *Web:* www.charleshotel.com

Charles Inn, The 20 Broad St Bangor ME 04401 207-992-2820 992-2826
Web: www.thecharlesinn.com

Charleston Place 205 Meeting St Charleston SC 29401 843-722-4900 722-0728
TF: 888-635-2350 ■ *Web:* belmond.com/charleston-place

Charter at Beaver Creek
120 Offerson Rd PO Box 5310 Avon CO 81620 970-949-6660 949-6709
TF: 800-525-6660 ■ *Web:* www.wyndhamvacationrentals.com

Charter One Hotels & Resorts Inc
2032 Hillview St Sarasota FL 34239 941-364-9224 921-5246
Web: www.charteronehotels.com

Chartwell Hospitality LLC
2000 Meridian Blvd Ste 200 Franklin TN 37067 615-550-1270
Web: www.chartwellhospitality.com

Chase Hotel at Palm Springs
200 W Arenas Rd Palm Springs CA 92262 760-320-8866 323-1501
TF: 877-532-4273 ■ *Web:* www.chasehotelpalmsprings.com

Chase Park Plaza 212 N KingsHwy Blvd Saint Louis MO 63108 314-633-3000 633-3077
TF Resv: 877-587-2427 ■ *Web:* www.chaseparkplaza.com

Chateau du Sureau
48688 Victoria Ln PO Box 577 Oakhurst CA 93644 559-683-6860 683-0800
Web: www.chateausureau.com

Chateau Dupre Hotel 131 Rue Decatur New Orleans LA 70130 504-569-0600
Web: www.bestneworleanshotels.com

Chateau Hotel & Conference Ctr, The
1601 Jumer Dr Bloomington IL 61704 309-662-2020
Web: www.chateauhotel.biz

Chateau Louis Hotel & Conference Centre
11727 Kingsway Edmonton AB T5G3A1 780-452-7770 454-3436
TF: 800-661-9843 ■ *Web:* www.chateaulouis.com

Chateau Marmont Hotel 8221 Sunset Blvd Los Angeles CA 90046 323-656-1010 655-5311
Web: www.chateaumarmont.com

Chateau on the Lake 415 N State Hwy 265 Branson MO 65616 417-334-1161 339-5566
TF: 888-333-5253 ■ *Web:* www.chateauonthelake.com

Chateau Vaudreuil Suites Hotel
21700 Rt Transcanada Hwy Vaudreuil-Dorion QC J7V8P3 450-455-0955 455-6617
TF: 800-363-7896 ■ *Web:* chateauvaudreuil.ca

Chateau Versailles 1659 Sherbrooke St W Montreal QC H3H1E3 514-933-3611
TF: 888-933-8111 ■ *Web:* www.chateauversaillesmontreal.com

Chelsea Savoy Hotel 204 W 23rd St New York NY 10011 212-929-9353 741-6309
TF: 866-929-9353 ■ *Web:* www.chelseasavoynyc.com

Cheshire, The 6300 Clayton Rd Saint Louis MO 63117 314-647-7300 647-0442
Web: www.cheshirestl.com

Chesterfield Hotel 363 Cocoanut Row Palm Beach FL 33480 561-659-5800 659-6707
TF: 800-243-7871 ■ *Web:* www.chesterfieldpb.com

Chestnut Hill Hotel 8229 Germantown Ave Philadelphia PA 19118 215-242-5905 242-8778
TF: 800-628-9744 ■ *Web:* www.chestnuthillhotel.com

Chiltern Inn 11 Cromwell Harbor Rd Bar Harbor ME 04609 207-288-3371
TF: 800-709-0114 ■ *Web:* www.chilterninnbarharbor.com

Chimo Hotel 1199 Joseph Cyr St Ottawa ON K1J7T4 613-744-1060 744-7076
TF: 800-387-9779 ■ *Web:* www.chimohotel.com

Choice Hotels International Inc
10750 Columbia Pk Silver Spring MD 20901 301-592-5000
NYSE: CHH ■ *TF:* 800-424-6423 ■ *Web:* www.choicehotels.com

Choice Hotels International Inc
3033 Hilton Dr Bossier City LA 71111 318-747-2400 747-6822
TF: 800-424-6423 ■ *Web:* www.choicehotels.com/rodeway-inn

Choice Hotels International Inc
9655 Grove Cir N Maple Grove MN 55369 763-494-5556
Web: www.choicehotels.com/cambria

Choice Hotels International, Inc.
997 New Loudon Rd Latham NY 12110 518-785-0931 782-2578
TF: 800-424-6423 ■ *Web:* www.choicehotels.com/clarion

Choice Hotelsÿ 3050 University Pkwy Winston-Salem NC 27105 877-424-6423 714-4578*
**Fax Area Code:* 336 ■ *TF:* 877-424-6423 ■ *Web:* www.choicehotels.com/clarion

Chrysalis Inn & Spa 804 Tenth St Bellingham WA 98225 360-756-1005
TF: 888-808-0005 ■ *Web:* www.thechrysalisinn.com

Churchill Hotel 1914 Connecticut Ave NW Washington DC 20009 202-797-2000 462-0944
TF: 800-424-2464 ■ *Web:* www.thechurchillhotel.com

Cincinnatian Hotel 601 Vine St Cincinnati OH 45202 513-381-3000 651-0256
TF: 800-942-9000 ■ *Web:* www.cincinnatianhotel.com

Circa39 Hotel 3900 Collins Ave Miami Beach FL 33140 305-538-4900 538-4998
Web: www.circa39.com

Circus Circus Hotel & Casino Reno
500 N Sierra St Reno NV 89503 775-329-0711 328-9652
TF: 800-648-5010 ■ *Web:* www.circusreno.com

Circus Circus Hotel Casino & Theme Park Las Vegas
2880 Las Vegas Blvd S Las Vegas NV 89109 702-734-0410
TF Resv: 800-634-3450 ■ *Web:* www.circuscircus.com

City Suites Hotel 933 W Belmont Ave Chicago IL 60657 773-404-3400
Web: www.chicagocitysuites.com

Civic Plaza Hotel 505 Pine St Abilene TX 79601 325-676-0222 676-0513

CJ Grand Hotel & Spa
67585 Hacienda Ave Desert Hot Springs CA 92240 760-329-4488
Web: cjmineralspa.com

Clarendon Hotel & Suites 401 W Clarendon Ave Phoenix AZ 85013 602-252-7363
Web: goclarendon.com

Clayton on the Park 7343 Scottsdale Mall Scottsdale AZ 85251 480-990-7300
Web: www.theclaytononthepark.com

Cleftstone Manor 92 Eden St Bar Harbor ME 04609 207-288-8086
TF: 888-288-4951 ■ *Web:* www.cleftstone.com

Cliff House at Pikes Peak
306 Canyon Ave Manitou Springs CO 80829 888-212-7000
TF: 888-212-7000 ■ *Web:* www.thecliffhouse.com

Clift, The 495 Geary St San Francisco CA 94102 415-775-4700
Web: morganshotelgroup.com

Clinton Inn Hotel 145 Dean Dr Tenafly NJ 07670 201-871-3200 871-3435
TF: 800-275-4411 ■ *Web:* www.clinton-inn.com

Clocktower Inn Hotel 181 E Santa Clara St Ventura CA 93001 805-652-0141 643-1432
Web: www.clocktowerinn.com

ClubHouse Hotel & Suites Sioux Falls
2320 S Louise Ave Sioux Falls SD 57106 605-361-8700 361-5950
TF: 866-534-8700 ■ *Web:* siouxfalls.clubhouseinn.com

Coachman Inn 32959 SR-Hwy 20 Oak Harbor WA 98277 360-675-0727
Web: www.thecoachmaninn.com

Coast Edmonton House Suite Hotel
1090 W Georgia S Ste 900 Vancouver BC V6E3V7 604-682-7982
TF: 800-716-6199 ■ *Web:* www.coasthotels.com

Coast Hotels & Resorts Canada
1090 W Georgia St Vancouver BC V6E3V7 604-682-7982 682-8942
Web: www.coasthotels.com

Coast Hotels & Resorts USA
2003 Western Ave Ste 500 Seattle WA 98121 206-826-2700 826-2701
Web: www.coasthotels.com

Coast Plaza Hotel 1316 33 St Ne Calgary AB T2A6B6 403-248-8888
TF: 800-661-1464 ■ *Web:* www.calgaryplaza.com

Coastal Hotel Group 18525 36th Ave S Seattle WA 98188 206-388-0400 388-0400
Web: www.coastalhotels.com

Coastal Inn Concorde 379 Windmill Rd Dartmouth NS B3A1J6 902-465-7777
TF: 800-565-1565 ■
Web: coastalinns.com/coastal-inn-halifax-dartmouth-ns.php

Coastal Inns Inc 111 Warwick St Box 280 Digby NS B0V1A0 800-401-1155
TF: 800-665-7829 ■ *Web:* www.coastalinns.com

Coastal Palms Hotel 120th St Coastal Hwy Ocean City MD 21842 800-641-0011
TF: 800-641-0011 ■ *Web:* www.coastalpalmshotel.com

Cocca's Inn & Suites
Corner of Wolf Rd & Central Ave Albany NY 12205 518-459-2240 459-9758
TF: 888-426-2227 ■ *Web:* www.coccas.com

Coffee Exchange 207 Wickenden St Providence RI 02903 401-273-1198
TF: 877-263-3334 ■ *Web:* www.coffeexchange.com

Cohasset Harbor Inn 124 Elm St Cohasset MA 02025 781-383-6650
Web: cohassetharborresort.com

Colby Hill Inn 33 The Oaks PO Box 779 Henniker NH 03242 603-428-3281 428-9218
TF: 800-531-0330 ■ *Web:* www.colbyhillinn.com

Colcord Hotel 15 N Robinson Ave Oklahoma City OK 73102 405-601-4300
Web: www.colcordhotel.com

Colgate Inn 1 Payne St Hamilton NY 13346 315-824-2300 824-4500
Web: www.colgateinn.com

College Houses Co-ops 1906 Pearl St Ofc 101 Austin TX 78705 512-476-5678
Web: collegehouses.org

Colonnade Hotel 120 Huntington Ave Boston MA 02116 617-424-7000 424-1717
TF: 800-962-3030 ■ *Web:* www.colonnadehotel.com

Colony Hotel & Cabana Club
525 E Atlantic Ave Delray Beach FL 33483 561-276-4123
Web: www.thecolonyhotel.com

Colony South Hotel 7401 Surratts Rd Clinton MD 20735 301-856-4500 856-4500
Web: www.colonysouth.com

Colorado Belle Hotel & Casino
2100 S Casino Dr Laughlin NV 89029 702-298-4000
TF Resv: 877-460-0777 ■ *Web:* www.coloradobelle.com

Columbia Gorge Hotel 4000 Westcliff Dr Hood River OR 97031 541-386-5566 386-9141
TF: 800-345-1921 ■ *Web:* www.columbiagorgehotel.com

Columbia Hospitality 2223 Alaskan Way Ste 200 Seattle WA 98121 206-239-1800 239-1801
Web: www.columbiahospitality.com

Columbia Sussex Corp
740 Centre View Blvd Crestview Hills KY 41017 859-578-1100 578-1154
Web: www.columbiasussex.com

Columns, The 3811 St Charles Ave New Orleans LA 70115 504-899-9308 899-8170
TF: 800-445-9308 ■ *Web:* www.thecolumns.com

Come Back in 508 E Wilson St Madison WI 53703 608-258-8619
Web: comebackintavern.com

Comfort Inn & Suites Milwaukee
916 E State St Milwaukee WI 53202 414-276-8800 442-1100*
**Fax Area Code:* 916 ■ *TF:* 800-424-6423 ■ *Web:* www.choicehotels.com

Commander Hotel 1401 Atlantic Ave Ocean City MD 21842 888-289-6166
TF: 888-289-6166 ■ *Web:* www.commanderhotel.com

Commonwealth Park Suites Hotel 901 Bank St Richmond VA 23219 804-343-7300
TF: 888-343-7301 ■ *Web:* www.commonwealthparksuites.com

Conch House Heritage Inn 625 Truman Ave Key West FL 33040 305-293-0020
TF: 800-207-5806 ■ *Web:* www.conchhouse.com

Conch House Marina Resort
57 Comares Ave Saint Augustine FL 32080 904-829-8646 829-5414
TF: 800-940-6256 ■ *Web:* www.conch-house.com

Congress Plaza Hotel & Convention Ctr
520 S Michigan Ave Chicago IL 60605 312-427-3800 427-2919
Web: www.congressplazahotel.com

Conrad Motel 100 Conrad Ct Glenville WV 26351 304-462-7316

Contactpointe of Pittsburgh
2593 Wexford Bayne Rd Ste 200 Sewickley PA 15143 412-788-0680
TF: 877-255-4916 ■ *Web:* contactpointe.com

Phone | Fax

Continental Bayside Hotel 146 Biscayne Blvd .... Miami FL 33132 305-358-4555
Web: www.crshotels.com

Cooper Hotel & Conference Ctr
12230 Preston Rd .... Dallas TX 75230 972-386-0306
TF: 800-444-5187 ■ *Web:* www.cooperaerobics.com

Cooper Hotels 1661 Arrion Brainner Dr Ste 200 .... Memphis TN 38120 901-322-1400 322-1403
Web: www.cooperhotels.com

Cooper Hotels 1661 Aaron Brenner Dr Ste 200 .... Memphis TN 38120 901-322-1400
Web: www.cooperhotels.com

Copley Square Hotel 47 Huntington Ave .... Boston MA 02116 617-536-9000 267-3547
TF: 800-225-7062 ■ *Web:* www.copleysquarehotel.com

Cornhusker Hotel, The 333 S 13th St .... Lincoln NE 68508 402-474-7474 474-1847
TF: 866-706-7706 ■ *Web:* www.marriott.com

Cosmopolitan Hotel Toronto 8 Colborne St .... Toronto ON M5E1E1 416-350-2000 350-2460
TF: 800-958-3488 ■ *Web:* www.cosmotoronto.com

Country Hearth 3450 S Clack St .... Abilene TX 79606 325-695-7700
Web: www.countryhearthabilene.com

Country Inn at the Mall 936 Stillwater Ave .... Bangor ME 04401 207-941-0200
TF Resv: 800-244-3961 ■ *Web:* www.countryinnatthemall.net

Country Inn Lake Resort 1332 Airport Rd .... Hot Springs AR 71913 501-767-3535
TF: 800-822-7402 ■ *Web:* www.countryinnlakeresort.com

Courtyard by Marriott Waikiki Beach
400 Royal Hawaiian Ave .... Honolulu HI 96815 808-954-4000 954-4047
Web: marriott.com

Courtyard Fort Lauderdale Beach
440 Seabreeze Blvd .... Fort Lauderdale FL 33316 954-524-8733 525-8145
TF: 888-236-2427 ■ *Web:* www.marriott.com/courtyard/travel.mi

Courtyard San Diego Oceanside
3501 Seagate Way .... Oceanside CA 92056 760-966-1000
Web: marriott.com

Cove Inn 900 Broad Ave S .... Naples FL 34102 239-262-7161 261-6905
TF: 800-255-4365 ■ *Web:* www.coveinnnaples.com

Cowboy Village Resort
120 S Flat Creek Dr PO Box 38 .... Jackson WY 83001 307-733-3121
TF: 800-962-4988 ■ *Web:* www.townsquareinns.com/cowboy-village

Cozy Country Inn 103 Frederick Rd .... Thurmont MD 21788 301-271-7373 271-3107

Craftsman Inn 7300 E Genesee St .... Fayetteville NY 13066 315-637-8000
Web: www.craftsmaninn.com

Creekside Inn 3400 El Camino Real .... Palo Alto CA 94306 650-493-2411 493-6787
TF: 800-492-7335 ■ *Web:* www.greystonehotels.com

Crescent Hotel 403 N Crescent Dr .... Beverly Hills CA 90210 310-247-0505
Web: www.crescentbh.com

Crescent Hotels & Resorts LLC
10306 Eaton Pl Ste 430 .... Fairfax VA 22030 703-279-7820

Crest Hotel & Suites 1670 James Ave .... Miami Beach FL 33139 305-531-0321 531-8180
TF: 800-531-3880 ■ *Web:* www.crestgrouphotels.com

Cresthill Suites Hotel 1415 Washington Ave .... Albany NY 12206 518-454-0007
Web: www.cresthillsuites.com

Crestline Hotels & Resorts
3950 University Dr Ste 301 .... Fairfax VA 22030 571-529-6100 529-6095
Web: www.crestlinehotels.com

Crockett Hotel 320 Bonham St .... San Antonio TX 78205 210-225-6500 225-6251
Web: www.crocketthotel.com

Cross Creek Resort 3815 Pennsylvania 8 .... Titusville PA 16354 814-827-9611
TF: 800-461-3173 ■ *Web:* www.crosscreekresort.com

Crown American Hotels Co Pasquerilla Plz .... Johnstown PA 15907 814-533-4600
TF: 800-245-9295 ■ *Web:* www.crownamericanhotels.com

Crown Reef Resort 2913 S Ocean Blvd .... Myrtle Beach SC 29577 843-626-8077 916-0735
TF: 877-435-9125 ■ *Web:* www.crownreef.com

Crowne Plaza Campbell House
1375 S Broadway Rd .... Lexington KY 40504 859-255-4281 254-4368
Web: www.thecampbellhouse.com

Crowne Plaza Chateau Lacombe
10111 Bellamy Hill .... Edmonton AB T5J1N7 780-428-6611
TF: 800-661-8801 ■ *Web:* www.chateaulacombe.com

Crowne Plaza Hollywood Beach Resort
4000 S Ocean Dr .... Hollywood FL 33019 954-454-4334
Web: cphollywoodbeach.com

Crowne Plaza St Paul Riverfront
11 E Kellogg Blvd .... St Paul MN 55101 651-292-1900
Web: ihg.com

Crowne Plaza Syracuse 701 E Genesee St .... Syracuse NY 13210 315-479-7000 472-2700
TF: 888-227-6963 ■ *Web:* cpsyracuse.com

Crowne Plaza Times Square Manhattan
1605 Broadway .... New York NY 10019 212-977-4000

Crystal Beach Suites & Health Club
6985 Collins Ave .... Miami Beach FL 33141 305-865-9555
TF: 888-643-4630 ■ *Web:* www.crystalbeachsuites.com

Crystal Inn 185 S State St Ste 1300 .... Salt Lake City UT 84111 801-320-7200 320-7201
TF General: 800-662-2525 ■ *Web:* www.crystalinns.com

Crystal Inn Salt Lake City Downtown
230 W 500 S .... Salt Lake City UT 84101 801-328-4466 320-7201
TF: 800-662-2525 ■ *Web:* crystalinns.com

Curtis, The 1405 Curtis St .... Denver CO 80202 303-571-0300 825-4301
TF: 800-525-6651 ■ *Web:* www.thecurtis.com

Custom Hotel 8639 Lincoln Blvd .... Los Angeles CA 90045 310-645-0400 645-0700
TF: 877-287-8601 ■ *Web:* www.jdvhotels.com

Daly Seven Inc 4829 Riverside Dr .... Danville VA 24541 434-822-2161
Web: dalyseven.com

Dan'l Webster Inn 149 Main St .... Sandwich MA 02563 508-888-3622
TF: 800-444-3566 ■ *Web:* www.danlwebsterinn.com

Dauphine Orleans Hotel 415 Dauphine St .... New Orleans LA 70112 504-586-1800 586-1409
TF: 800-521-7111 ■ *Web:* www.dauphineorleans.com

Davenport Hotel, The 10 S Post St .... Spokane WA 99201 509-455-8888 624-4455
TF: 800-899-1482 ■ *Web:* www.davenporthotelcollection.com

David William Hotel Condo Assn
700 Biltmore Way .... Coral Gables FL 33134 305-445-7821
Web: davidwilliamcondo.com

Davidson & Jones Hotel Corp 1207 Front St .... Raleigh NC 27609 919-828-0880
Web: davidsonandjones.com

Days Inns Worldwide Inc
215 W 94th St Broadway .... New York NY 10025 212-866-6400
TF: 800-225-3297 ■ *Web:* www.daysinn.com

Daytona Beach Resort & Conference Ctr
2700 N Atlantic Ave .... Daytona Beach FL 32118 386-672-3770
TF: 800-654-6216 ■ *Web:* www.daytonabeachresort.com

Daytona Inn Beach Resort
219 S Atlantic Ave .... Daytona Beach FL 32118 386-252-3626 255-3680
TF General: 800-874-1822 ■ *Web:* daytonainnbeachresort.com

Dearborn Inn the - A Marriott Hotel
20301 Oakwood Blvd .... Dearborn MI 48124 313-271-2700 271-2700
TF: 800-228-9290 ■ *Web:* www.marriott.com

Deer Path Inn 255 E Illinois Rd .... Lake Forest IL 60045 847-234-2280 234-3352
Web: thedeerpathinn.com

Deerfoot Inn & Casino 1000 11500 35th St SE .... Calgary AB T2Z3W4 403-236-7529 252-4767
TF: 877-236-5225 ■ *Web:* www.deerfootinn.com

Defender Resorts Inc 6301 N Kings Hwy .... Myrtle Beach SC 29572 843-449-1354
Web: defenderresorts.com

Del Monte Lodge Renaissance Rochester Hotel & Spa, The
41 N Main St .... Pittsford NY 14534 585-381-9900 381-9825
TF: 866-237-5979 ■ *Web:* marriott.com/hotels/propertypage/rocdl

DELAMAR Greenwich Harbor 500 Steamboat Rd .... Greenwich CT 06830 203-661-9800
TF: 866-335-2627 ■ *Web:* www.delamargreenwich.com

Delta King Riverboat Hotel 1000 Front St .... Sacramento CA 95814 916-444-5464
TF: 800-825-5464 ■ *Web:* www.deltaking.com

Deluxe Inn Odessa Hotel 1518 S Grant Ave .... Odessa TX 79761 432-333-1486
Web: deluxeinnodessa.com

DePalma Hotel Corp
700 Highlander Blvd Ste 400 .... Arlington TX 76015 817-557-1811 557-4333
Web: www.depalmahotels.com

Desert Inn Resort 900 N Atlantic Ave .... Daytona Beach FL 32118 386-258-6555 238-1635

Desert Riviera Hotel
610 E Palm Canyon Dr .... Palm Springs CA 92264 760-327-5314
TF: 866-270-8322 ■ *Web:* www.desertrivierahotel.com

Destination Hotels & Resorts Inc
10333 E Dry Creek Rd Ste 450 .... Englewood CO 80112 303-799-3830 799-6011
TF: 855-893-1011 ■ *Web:* www.destinationhotels.com

Diamond Head Inn 605 Diamond St .... San Diego CA 92109 858-273-1900 273-8532
TF: 888-478-7829 ■ *Web:* www.diamondheadinn.com

Dimension Development Co 769 Hwy 494 .... Natchitoches LA 71457 318-352-8238 352-8276
Web: www.dimdev.com

Dinah's Garden Hotel 4261 El Camino Real .... Palo Alto CA 94306 650-493-2844 856-4713
TF: 800-227-8220 ■ *Web:* www.dinahshotel.com

Disney's Paradise Pier Hotel
1717 S Disneyland Dr .... Anaheim CA 92802 714-999-0990
Web: www.disneyworld.disney.go.com

Disney's Saratoga Springs Resort & Spa
1960 Broadway St .... Lake Buena Vista FL 32830 407-827-1100 827-4444
Web: disneyworld.disney.go.com/resorts/saratoga-springs-resort-and-spa

Disneyland Hotel 1150 Magic Way .... Anaheim CA 92802 714-778-6600 956-6597
Web: disneyland.disney.go.com

Dockers Inn 3060 Green Mtn Dr .... Branson MO 65616 417-334-3600
Web: www.dockersinn.com

Dolce International 28 W Grand Ave .... Montvale NJ 07645 201-307-8700
Web: www.dolce.com

Dolphin Beach Resort 4900 Gulf Blvd .... Saint Pete Beach FL 33706 727-360-7011 367-5909
TF: 800-237-8916 ■ *Web:* www.dolphinbeach.com

Dolphin Inn 1705 Atlantic Ave .... Virginia Beach VA 23451 757-491-1420
TF: 800-365-3467 ■ *Web:* www.dolphininnhotel.com

Dominion Lodging Inc 658 Roanoke Rd .... Daleville VA 24083 540-992-4077
Web: www.dominionlodging.com

Don Hall's Guesthouse
1313 W Washington Ctr Rd .... Fort Wayne IN 46825 260-489-2524 489-7067
Web: www.donhalls.com

Donatello, The 501 Post St .... San Francisco CA 94102 415-441-7100 441-7100
TF: 800-258-2366 ■ *Web:* www.clubdonatello.org

Dora Hotel Company LLC 10734 Sky Prairie St .... Fishers IN 46037 317-863-5700
Web: www.dorahotelco.com

Doubletree Claremont 555 W Foothill Blvd .... Claremont CA 91711 909-626-2411 624-0756
TF: 800-222-8733 ■ *Web:* www3.hilton.com

Doubletree Hotel 2800 Via Cabrillo Marina .... San Pedro CA 90731 310-514-3344 514-8945
Web: doubletree3.hilton.com/en/hotels/california/doubletree-by-hilton-hotel-san-pedro-port-of-los-angeles-lgbspdt/index.html

Doubletree Hotel Downtown Wilmington Legal District
700 N King St .... Wilmington DE 19801 302-655-0400
TF: 800-222-8733 ■ *Web:* www3.hilton.com

Doubletree North Shore Hotel 9599 Skokie Blvd .... Skokie IL 60077 847-679-7000 679-0904
TF: 800-445-8667 ■ *Web:* www3.hilton.com

Downtown Erie Hotel 18 W 18th St .... Erie PA 16501 814-456-2961 456-7067
TF: 800-832-9101 ■ *Web:* www.downtownneriehotel.com

Drake Hotel, The 140 E Walton Pl .... Chicago IL 60611 312-787-2200 787-1431
TF: 800-553-7253 ■ *Web:* www.thedrakehotel.com

Dream 210 W 55th St .... New York NY 10019 212-247-2000
Web: www.dreamhotels.com

Driftwood Hospitality Management LLC
11770 Us Hwy One Ste 202 .... North Palm Beach FL 33408 561-207-2700
Web: www.driftwoodhospitality.com

Driftwood Hotel 435 Willoughby Ave .... Juneau AK 99801 907-586-2280 586-1034
TF: 800-544-2239 ■ *Web:* www.dhalaska.com

Driftwood Shores Resort 88416 First Ave .... Florence OR 97439 541-997-8263 997-3253
TF: 800-422-5091 ■ *Web:* www.driftwoodshores.com

Driskill Hotel 604 Brazos St .... Austin TX 78701 512-474-5911 474-2214
TF: 800-252-9367 ■ *Web:* www.driskillhotel.com

Drury Hotels Company LLC
721 Emerson Rd Ste 400 .... Saint Louis MO 63141 314-429-2255 429-5166
TF: 800-378-7946 ■ *Web:* www.druryhotels.com

Duane Street Hotel 130 Duane St .... New York NY 10013 212-964-4600 964-4800
Web: www.duanestreethotel.com

Dude Rancher Lodge 415 N 29th St .... Billings MT 59101 406-259-5561 259-0095
Web: www.duderancherlodge.com

Duke Towers- All Condominium Hotel
807 W Trinity Ave .... Durham NC 27701 919-687-4444 683-1215
TF: 866-385-3869 ■ *Web:* www.duketower.com

Duke's 8th Avenue Hotel 630 W Eigth Ave .... Anchorage AK 99501 907-274-6213
TF: 800-478-4837 ■ *Web:* www.dukesalaskahotel.com

Phone Fax

Dunes Manor Hotel 2800 Baltimore Ave. .... Ocean City MD 21842 410-289-1100
TF: 800-523-2888 ■ *Web:* www.dunesmanor.com

Dunhill Hotel 237 N Tryon St. .... Charlotte NC 28202 704-332-4141
TF: 800-354-4141 ■ *Web:* www.dunhillhotel.com

Dunn Hospitality Group LLC
300 SE Riverside Dr Ste 100 .... Evansville IN 47713 812-471-9300
Web: www.dunnhospitalitygroup.com

Dylan Hotel 52 E 41st St .... New York NY 10017 212-338-0500 227-1206*
**Fax Area Code:* 646 ■ *Web:* www.dylanhotel.com

Dynasty Suites 1235 W Colton Ave. .... Redlands CA 92374 909-793-6648 792-5219
TF General: 800-874-8958 ■ *Web:* www.dynastysuites.com

Eagle Mountain House
179 Carter Notch Rd PO Box 804 .... Jackson NH 03846 603-383-9111 383-0854
TF: 800-966-5779 ■ *Web:* www.eaglemt.com

East Canyon Hotel & Spa
288 E Camino Monte Vista .... Palm Springs CA 92262 760-320-1928
TF: 877-324-6835 ■ *Web:* www.eastcanyonps.com

Eastland Park Hotel 157 High St. .... Portland ME 04101 207-775-5411
Web: www.westinportlandharborview.com

Eden House 1015 Fleming St .... Key West FL 33040 800-533-5397
TF: 800-533-5397 ■ *Web:* www.edenhouse.com

Edgewater Beach Hotel 1901 Gulf Shore Blvd N .... Naples FL 34102 888-564-1308 403-2100*
**Fax Area Code:* 239 ■ *TF:* 866-624-1695 ■ *Web:* www.edgewaternaples.com

Edgewater Hotel 2411 Alaskan Way Pier 67 .... Seattle WA 98121 206-728-7000 441-4119
TF: 800-624-0670 ■ *Web:* www.edgewaterhotel.com

Edgewater Resort 200 Edgewater Cir. .... Hot Springs AR 71913 501-767-3311
TF: 800-234-3687 ■ *Web:* www.ewresort.com

Edgewater Resort & Waterpark 2400 London Rd. .... Duluth MN 55812 218-728-3601 728-3727
TF: 800-777-7925 ■ *Web:* www.duluthwaterpark.com

Edmonds Harbor Inn & Suites 130 W Dayton .... Edmonds WA 98020 425-771-5021 672-2880
TF: 800-441-8033 ■ *Web:* www.bestwestern.com

Eisenhower Inn & Conference Ctr
2634 Emmitsburg Rd .... Gettysburg PA 17325 717-334-8121
Web: www.eisenhower.com

EJ Del Monte Corp 909 Linden Ave .... Rochester NY 14625 585-586-3121
Web: delmontehotelgroup.com

El Cortez Hotel & Casino 600 E Fremont St .... Las Vegas NV 89101 702-385-5200
TF: 800-634-6703 ■ *Web:* www.elcortezhotelcasino.com

El Rey Inn 1862 Cerillos Rd .... Santa Fe NM 87505 505-982-1931
TF: 800-521-1349 ■ *Web:* www.elreyinnsantafe.com

El Tovar Hotel 1 Main St .... Grand Canyon AZ 86023 928-638-2631
TF: 888-297-2757 ■ *Web:* www.grandcanyonlodges.com

Elan Hotel 8435 Beverly Blvd .... Los Angeles CA 90048 323-658-6663 658-6640
TF: 866-203-2212 ■ *Web:* www.greystonehotels.com

Elbow River Casino (ERC) 218 18th Ave SE .... Calgary AB T2G1L1 403-289-8880
Web: elbowrivercasino.com

Eldorado Hotel 309 W San Francisco St .... Santa Fe NM 87501 505-988-4455 995-4543
TF: 800-955-4455 ■ *Web:* www.eldoradohotel.com

Eldorado Hotel Casino 345 N Virginia St. .... Reno NV 89501 775-786-5700 322-7124
TF Resv: 800-879-8879 ■ *Web:* www.eldoradoreno.com

Eldridge Hotel 701 Massachusetts St .... Lawrence KS 66044 785-749-5011 749-4512
TF: 800-527-0909 ■ *Web:* www.eldridgehotel.com

Eliot Hotel, The 370 Commonwealth Ave .... Boston MA 02215 617-267-1607 536-9114
TF: 800-443-5468 ■ *Web:* www.eliothotel.com

Elk Country Inn 480 W Pearl St PO Box 1255 .... Jackson WY 83001 307-733-2364
TF: 800-483-8667 ■ *Web:* www.townsquareinns.com

Elvis Presley's Heartbreak Hotel
3677 Elvis Presley Blvd .... Memphis TN 38116 901-332-1000
TF: 877-777-0606 ■ *Web:* www.elvis.com

Embarcadero Resort Hotel & Marina
1000 SE Bay Blvd .... Newport OR 97365 541-265-8521 265-7844
Web: embarcaderoresort.com

Embassy Hotel 610 Polk St .... San Francisco CA 94102 415-673-1404 474-4188
Web: www.theembassyhotelsf.com

Embassy Hotel & Suites 25 Cartier St .... Ottawa ON K2P1J2 613-237-2111 563-1353
TF: 800-661-5495 ■ *Web:* www.ottawaembassy.com/default-en.html

Embassy Suites Chicago Downtown Lakefront
511 N Columbus Dr .... Chicago IL 60611 312-836-5900
Web: embassysuites3.hilton.com

Embassy Suites Columbus-Dublin
5100 Upper Metro Pl .... Dublin OH 43017 614-790-9000
Web: embassysuites3.hilton.com

Emerald Queen Hotel & Casino 5700 Pacific Hwy E .... Fife WA 98424 253-922-2000
TF: 888-820-3555 ■ *Web:* emeraldqueen.com

Emerson Resort & Spa 5340 Rt 28 .... Mount Tremper NY 12457 845-688-2828
TF: 877-688-2828 ■ *Web:* www.emersonresort.com

Emily Morgan Hotel 705 E Houston St. .... San Antonio TX 78205 210-225-5100
TF: 800-824-6674 ■ *Web:* www.emilymorganhotel.com

Empire Landmark Hotel & Conference Centre
1400 Robson St .... Vancouver BC V6G1B9 604-687-0511
TF: 800-830-6144 ■ *Web:* www.empirelandmarkhotel.com

Empress Hotel 7766 Fay Ave. .... La Jolla CA 92037 858-454-3001
Web: www.empress-hotel.com

Enclave Suites of Orlando 6165 Carrier Dr. .... Orlando FL 32819 407-351-1155
TF: 800-457-0077 ■ *Web:* www.enclavesuites.com

Epoque Hotels 2500 NE 135th St Ste 502 .... North Miami FL 33181 305-538-9697
TF: 866-376-7831 ■ *Web:* www.epoquehotels.com

Ethan Allen Hotel 21 Lake Ave Ext .... Danbury CT 06811 203-744-1776 791-9673
TF: 800-742-1776 ■ *Web:* www.ethanallenhotel.com

Euro-American Finance Network Inc
1212 S Main St Ste B .... Wildwood FL 34785 352-504-1641
Web: www.eafninc.com

Euro-Suites Hotel
University Centre 501 Chestnut Ridge Rd .... Morgantown WV 26505 800-678-4837
TF: 800-678-4837 ■ *Web:* www.euro-suites.com

Evergreen Lodge 250 S Frontage Rd W .... Vail CO 81657 970-476-7810 476-4504
TF: 800-284-8245 ■ *Web:* www.evergreenvail.com

Excalibur Hotel & Casino
3850 Las Vegas Blvd S .... Las Vegas NV 89109 702-597-7777 597-7009
TF: 877-750-5464 ■ *Web:* www.excalibur.com

Executive Hotel Vintage Court
650 Bush St .... San Francisco CA 94108 415-392-4666 433-4065
TF: 888-388-3932 ■ *Web:* www.executivehotels.net

Phone Fax

Executive Inn 978 Phillips Ln .... Louisville KY 40209 502-367-6161
TF: 888-205-8144 ■ *Web:* hotelplanner.com

Executive Inn Group Corp
Executive Hotels & Resorts
1080 Howe St 8th Fl .... Vancouver BC V6Z2T1 604-642-5250 642-5255
TF: 866-642-6888 ■ *Web:* www.executivehotels.net

Executive Pacific Plaza Hotel 400 Spring St. .... Seattle WA 98104 206-623-3900 623-2059
TF: 888-388-3932 ■ *Web:* executivehotels.net/downtownseattlehotel

Executive Suite Hotel 4360 SpenaRd Rd. .... Anchorage AK 99517 907-243-6366
TF: 888-315-2378 ■ *Web:* www.executivesuitehotel.com

Expressway Hotels 4303 17th Ave S .... Fargo ND 58103 701-239-4303
TF: 877-239-4303 ■ *Web:* expresswaysuitesfargo.com

Extended Stay America
11525 N Community House Rd Ste 100 .... Charlotte NC 28277 980-345-1600 573-1695*
**Fax Area Code:* 864 ■ *TF:* 800-804-3724 ■ *Web:* www.extendedstayamerica.com

Extended Stay Hotels
Crossland Economy Studios
11525 N Community House Rd Ste 100 .... Charlotte NC 28277 980-345-1600
TF: 800-804-3724 ■ *Web:* www.crosslandstudios.com
Extended StayAmerica
11525 N Community House Rd Ste 100 .... Charlotte NC 28277 980-345-1600
TF: 800-804-3724 ■ *Web:* www.extendedstayamerica.com
StudioPLUS Deluxe Studios
530 Woods Lake Rd .... Greenville SC 29607 864-288-4300
TF: 800-804-3724 ■ *Web:* www.extendedstayamerica.com

Fairbanks Golden Nugget Hotel, The
900 Noble St .... Fairbanks AK 99701 907-452-5141
Web: www.golden-nuggethotel.com

Fairbanks Princess Riverside Lodge
4477 Pikes Landing Rd .... Fairbanks AK 99709 907-455-4477 455-4476
TF: 800-426-0500 ■ *Web:* princesslodges.com

Fairmont Hotels & Resorts Inc
100 Wellington St W TD Ctr Ste 1600 .... Toronto ON M5K1B7 416-874-2600 874-2601
TF General: 800-441-3313 ■ *Web:* www.fairmont.com

Fairmount Hotel, The 401 S Alamo St .... San Antonio TX 78205 210-224-8800 475-0082
TF: 877-229-8808 ■ *Web:* www.thefairmounthotel-sanantonio.com

Falmouth Inn 824 Main St. .... Falmouth MA 02540 508-540-2500
Web: www.falmouthinn.com

Fargo C'mon Inn Hotel 4338 20th Ave SW .... Fargo ND 58103 701-277-9944 277-9117
TF: 800-334-1570 ■ *Web:* www.cmoninn.com

Fearrington House
2000 Fearrington Village Ctr .... Pittsboro NC 27312 919-542-2121
TF: 800-277-0130 ■ *Web:* www.fearrington.com

Federal Square Inn & Extended Stay
8781 Madison Blvd .... Madison AL 35758 256-772-8470 772-0620

Fenwick Inn 13801 Coastal Hwy .... Ocean City MD 21842 410-250-1100 250-0087
TF: 800-492-1873 ■ *Web:* www.fenwickinn.com

Fiesta Henderson 777 W Lk Mead Pkwy .... Henderson NV 89015 702-558-7000
TF: 888-899-7770 ■ *Web:* www.fiestahenderson.sclv.com

Fifteen Beacon Hotel 15 Beacon St. .... Boston MA 02108 617-670-1500 670-6925
Web: www.xvbeacon.com

Figueroa Hotel 939 S Figueroa St .... Los Angeles CA 90015 213-627-8971 689-0305
Web: www.hotelfigueroa.com

Findlay Inn & Conference Ctr
200 E Main Cross St .... Findlay OH 45840 419-422-5682
TF Cust Svc: 800-825-1455 ■ *Web:* www.findlayinn.com

Fireside Inn & Suites 25 Airport Rd. .... West Lebanon NH 03784 603-298-5900 298-0340
TF: 877-258-5900 ■ *Web:* www.firesideinnwestlebanon.com

First Gold Hotel 270 Main St .... Deadwood SD 57732 605-578-9777 578-3979
TF: 800-274-1876 ■ *Web:* www.firstgold.com

First Interstate Inn 20 SE Wyoming Blvd .... Casper WY 82609 307-234-9125

Fisherman's Wharf Inn
22 Commercial St .... Boothbay Harbor ME 04538 207-633-5090 633-5092
TF: 800-628-6872 ■ *Web:* fishermanswharfinn.com

Fitger's Inn 600 E Superior St .... Duluth MN 55802 218-722-8826 722-8826
TF: 888-348-4377 ■ *Web:* www.fitgers.com

Fitzgerald Hotel 620 Post St .... San Francisco CA 94109 415-775-8100
Web: www.fitzgeraldhotel.com

Fitzpatrick Manhattan Hotel
687 Lexington Ave .... New York NY 10022 212-355-0100 355-1371
TF: 800-367-7701 ■ *Web:* www.fitzpatrickhotels.com

Flagship All Suites Resort
60 N Maine Ave .... Atlantic City NJ 08401 609-343-7447
TF: 800-647-7890 ■ *Web:* www.fantasearesorts.com

Foley House Inn 14 W Hull St Chippewa Sq .... Savannah GA 31401 912-232-6622
TF: 800-647-3708 ■ *Web:* www.foleyinn.com

Foot of the Mountain Motel
200 W Arapahoe Ave .... Boulder CO 80302 303-442-5688 442-5719
TF: 866-773-5489 ■ *Web:* www.footofthemountainmotel.com

Foothills Inn 1625 N La Crosse St .... Rapid City SD 57701 605-348-5640 348-0073
TF: 877-428-5666 ■ *Web:* www.thefoothillsinn.com

Fort Garry, The 222 Broadway .... Winnipeg MB R3C0R3 204-942-8251 956-2351
TF: 800-665-8088 ■ *Web:* www.fortgarryhotel.com

Fort Marcy Hotel Suites 321 Kearney Ave .... Santa Fe NM 87501 505-988-2800
TF: 888-667-2775 ■ *Web:* www.allseasonsresortlodging.com

Forum Motor Inn
800-814 Atlantic Ave PO Box 448 .... Ocean City NJ 08226 609-399-8700
Web: www.theforuminoc.homestead.com

Four Points by Sheraton Charlotte
315 E Woodlawn Rd .... Charlotte NC 28217 704-522-0852
TF: 800-368-7764 ■ *Web:* www.starwoodhotels.com

Four Points by Sheraton French Quarter
541 Bourbon St .... New Orleans LA 70130 504-524-7611 524-8273
TF: 866-716-8133 ■ *Web:* www.fourpointsfrenchquarter.com

Four Queens Hotel & Casino 202 Fremont St. .... Las Vegas NV 89101 702-385-4011 387-5158
TF: 800-634-6045 ■ *Web:* www.fourqueens.com

Four Sails Resort Hotel
3301 Atlantic Ave .... Virginia Beach VA 23451 757-491-8100 491-0573
TF: 800-227-4213 ■ *Web:* www.foursails.com

Four Seasons Hotels Inc 1165 Leslie St .... Toronto ON M3C2K8 416-449-1750 441-4374
TF: 800-332-3442 ■ *Web:* www.fourseasons.com

Francis Marion Hotel, The 387 King St .... Charleston SC 29403 843-722-0600 853-2186
TF: 877-756-2121 ■ *Web:* www.francismarionhotel.com

Name	City	State	Zip	Phone	Fax
Franklin, The 164 E 87th St	New York	NY	10128	212-369-1000	369-8000
TF: 800-607-4009 ■ *Web:* www.franklinhotel.com					
Fremont Hotel & Casino 200 Fremont St	Las Vegas	NV	89101	702-385-3232	
TF: 800-634-6460 ■ *Web:* www.fremontcasino.com					
French Quarter Suites Hotel 1119 N Rampart St	New Orleans	LA	70116	504-524-7725	522-9716
TF: 800-457-2253 ■ *Web:* www.frenchquartersuites.com					
Frost Valley Ymca 2000 Frost Vly Rd	Claryville	NY	12725	845-985-2291	
Web: www.frostvalley.org					
Future Inns 30 Fairfax Dr	Halifax	NS	B3S1P1	902-443-4333	
Web: www.futureinns.co.uk					
G6 Hospitality LLC *Motel 6* 4001 International Pkwy	Carrollton	TX	75007	972-360-9000	716-6416
TF: 800-466-8356 ■ *Web:* www.motel6.com					
Galleria Park Hotel 191 Sutter St	San Francisco	CA	94104	415-781-3060	
Web: www.jdvhotels.com					
Galt House Hotel 140 N Fourth St	Louisville	KY	40202	502-589-5200	
TF: 800-843-4258 ■ *Web:* www.galthouse.com					
Galveston Computer Solutions LLC 523 24th St Ste 5	Galveston	TX	77550	409-762-4326	
Web: galvestoncs.com					
Garden City Hotel 45 Seventh St	Garden City	NY	11530	516-747-3000	747-1414
TF: 877-549-0400 ■ *Web:* www.gardencityhotel.com					
Garden Court Hotel 520 Cowper St	Palo Alto	CA	94301	650-322-9000	324-3609
TF: 800-824-9028 ■ *Web:* www.gardencourt.com					
Garden Place Hotel 6461 Transit Rd	Depew	NY	14043	716-683-7990	
TF: 877-456-4097 ■ *Web:* www.salvatores.net/garden_place/index.html					
Gardens Hotel 526 Angela St	Key West	FL	33040	305-294-2661	292-1007
TF: 800-526-2664 ■ *Web:* www.gardenshotel.com					
Gardner Hotel 311 E Franklin Ave	El Paso	TX	79901	915-532-3661	
Web: www.gardnerhotel.com					
Garfield Suites Hotel 2 Garfield Pl	Cincinnati	OH	45202	513-421-3355	421-3729
Garland, The 4222 Vineland Ave	North Hollywood	CA	91602	818-980-8000	766-0112
TF: 800-238-3759 ■ *Web:* www.thegarland.com					
Garrett's Desert Inn 311 Old Santa Fe Trl	Santa Fe	NM	87501	505-982-1851	989-1647
TF: 800-888-2145 ■ *Web:* www.garrettsdesertinn.com					
Gaslamp Plaza Suites 520 E St	San Diego	CA	92101	619-232-9500	238-9945
TF: 800-874-8770 ■ *Web:* www.gaslampplaza.com					
Gastonian, The 220 E Gaston St	Savannah	GA	31401	912-232-2869	232-0710
TF: 800-322-6603 ■ *Web:* www.gastonian.com					
Gateway Hospitality LLC 111 Stonemark Ln Ste 202	Columbia	SC	29210	803-798-7979	
Web: gatewayhospitality.com					
Gateways Inn 51 Walker St	Lenox	MA	01240	413-637-2532	637-1432
TF: 888-492-9466 ■ *Web:* www.gatewaysinn.com					
Gaylord Opryland Hotel & Convention Ctr 2800 Opryland Dr	Nashville	TN	37214	615-889-1000	885-3054
TF: 888-236-2427 ■ *Web:* www.marriott.com					
General Morgan Inn 111 N Main St	Greeneville	TN	37743	423-787-1000	
Web: generalmorganinn.com					
Genesee Grande Hotel 1060 E Genesee St	Syracuse	NY	13210	315-476-4212	471-4663
Web: www.geneseegrande.com					
Geneva on the Lake 1001 Lochland Rd	Geneva	NY	14456	315-789-7190	682-6306
TF: 800-343-6382 ■ *Web:* www.genevaonthelake.com					
George Washington University Inn 824 New Hampshire Ave NW	Washington	DC	20037	202-337-6620	298-7499
TF: 800-424-9671 ■ *Web:* www.gwuinn.com					
Georgetown Inn 1310 Wisconsin Ave	Washington	DC	20007	202-333-8900	333-8308
TF: 866-971-6618 ■ *Web:* www.georgetowninn.com					
Georgian Court Hotel 773 Beatty St	Vancouver	BC	V6B2M4	604-682-5555	682-8830
TF: 800-663-1155 ■ *Web:* www.georgiancourthotelvancouver.com					
Georgian Hotel 1415 Ocean Ave	Santa Monica	CA	90401	310-395-9945	
TF: 800-538-8147 ■ *Web:* www.georgianhotel.com					
Georgian Resort 384 Canada St	Lake George	NY	12845	518-668-5401	668-5870
TF: 800-525-3436 ■ *Web:* www.georgianresort.com					
Georgian Terrace Hotel 659 Peachtree St NE	Atlanta	GA	30308	404-897-1991	724-9116
TF: 800-651-2316 ■ *Web:* www.thegeorgianterrace.com					
Gideon Putnam Resort & Spa 24 Gideon Putnam Rd	Saratoga Springs	NY	12866	518-584-3000	
TF: 800-452-7275 ■ *Web:* www.gideonputnam.com					
Giusto Enterprises Inc 7525 Mission St	Daly City	CA	94014	650-992-7090	
Web: elcaminoinn.com					
Glacier Bay Country Inn 35 Tong Rd	Gustavus	AK	99826	480-725-1168	
Web: www.glacierbayalaska.com					
Glass House Inn 3202 W 26th St	Erie	PA	16506	814-833-7751	833-4222
TF: 800-956-7222 ■ *Web:* www.glasshouseinn.com					
Glen Grove Suites 2837 Yonge St	Toronto	ON	M4N2J6	416-489-8441	440-3065
TF: 800-565-3024 ■ *Web:* www.glengrove.com					
Glendorn 1000 Glendorn Dr	Bradford	PA	16701	814-362-6511	368-9923
TF: 800-843-8568 ■ *Web:* www.glendorn.com					
Glenerin Inn, The 1695 The Collegeway	Mississauga	ON	L5L3S7	905-828-6103	828-0891
TF: 877-991-9971 ■ *Web:* www.glenerininn.com					
Glenmore Inn 2720 Glenmore Trl SE	Calgary	AB	T2C2E6	403-279-8611	236-8035
TF: 800-661-3163 ■ *Web:* www.glenmoreinn.com					
Glidden House 1901 Ford Dr	Cleveland	OH	44106	216-231-8900	231-2130
TF: 866-812-4537 ■ *Web:* www.gliddenhouse.com					
Glorietta Bay Inn 1630 Glorietta Blvd	Coronado	CA	92118	619-435-3101	435-6182
TF: 800-283-9383 ■ *Web:* www.gloriettabayinn.com					
Gold Coast Hotel & Casino 4000 W Flamingo Rd	Las Vegas	NV	89103	702-367-7111	
TF: 800-331-5334 ■ *Web:* www.goldcoastcasino.com					
Goldbelt Hotel Juneau 51 Egan Dr	Juneau	AK	99801	907-586-6900	463-3567
TF: 888-478-6909 ■ *Web:* www.goldbelt.com/subsidiaries/gbhj.html					
Golden Eagle Resort 511 Mountain Rd PO Box 1090	Stowe	VT	05672	802-253-4811	253-2561
TF: 800-626-1010 ■ *Web:* www.goldeneagleresort.com					
Golden Hotel, The 800 11th St	Golden	CO	80401	303-279-0100	279-9353
TF: 800-233-7214 ■ *Web:* www.thegoldenhotel.com					
Goldener Hirsch Inn 7570 Royal St E	Park City	UT	84060	435-649-7770	
TF Cust Svc: 800-252-3373 ■ *Web:* www.goldenerhirschinn.com					
Good Hospitality Services Inc 1051 Southpoint Dr Ste A	Valparaiso	IN	46385	219-462-6265	
Web: goodhsi.com					
Good Hotel *Good Hotel* 112 Seventh St	San Francisco	CA	94103	415-621-7001	626-3974
TF: 800-444-5819 ■ *Web:* www.haiyi-hotels.com/thegoodhotel					
Good-Nite Inn Fremont 4135 Cushing Pkwy	Fremont	CA	94538	510-656-9307	656-9110
TF: 800-648-3466 ■ *Web:* www.goodnite.com					
Goodmanagement 603 Pilot House Dr Ste 225	Newport News	VA	23606	757-596-5215	
Web: www.goodmanagement.com					
Gouverneur Hotel Montreal (Place-Dupuis) 1000 Sherbrooke St W Ste 2300	Montreal	QC	H3A3R3	888-910-1111	
TF: 888-910-1111 ■ *Web:* www.gouverneur.com					
Governor Calvert House 58 State Cir	Annapolis	MD	21401	410-263-2641	268-3613
TF: 800-847-8882 ■ *Web:* www.historicinnsofannapolis.com					
Governor's Inn 700 W Sioux Ave	Pierre	SD	57501	605-224-4200	
TF General: 877-523-0080 ■ *Web:* www.govinn.com					
Governor's Inn 210 Richards Blvd	Sacramento	CA	95811	916-448-7224	448-7382
TF: 800-999-6689 ■ *Web:* www.governorsinnhotel.com					
Governors Inn 209 S Adams St	Tallahassee	FL	32301	850-681-6855	222-3105
Web: thegovinn.org					
Grafton on Sunset 8462 W Sunset Blvd	West Hollywood	CA	90069	323-654-4600	654-5918
TF: 800-821-3660 ■ *Web:* www.graftononsunset.com					
Graham, The 1075 Thomas Jefferson St NW	Washington	DC	20007	202-337-0900	333-6526
TF: 855-341-1292 ■ *Web:* thegrahamgeorgetown.com					
Gramercy Park Hotel 2 Lexington Ave	New York	NY	10010	212-920-3300	673-5890
TF: 866-784-1300 ■ *Web:* www.gramercyparkhotel.com					
Grand America Hotel 555 S Main St	Salt Lake City	UT	84111	801-258-6000	258-6911
TF: 800-621-4505 ■ *Web:* www.grandamerica.com					
Grand Beach Inn (GBI) 198 E Grand Ave	Old Orchard Beach	ME	04064	207-934-4621	
Web: grandbeachinnmaine.com					
Grand Country Inn Grand Country Sq 1945 W Hwy 76	Branson	MO	65616	417-335-3535	
TF: 888-505-4096 ■ *Web:* www.grandcountry.com/lodging					
Grand Del Mar 5300 Grand Del Mar Ct	San Diego	CA	92130	858-314-2000	314-2001
TF: 855-314-2030 ■ *Web:* www.fairmont.com/san-diego					
Grand Gateway Hotel 1721 N LaCrosse St	Rapid City	SD	57701	605-342-8853	342-0663
TF: 866-742-1300 ■ *Web:* www.grandgatewayhotel.com					
Grand Hotel & Suites Toronto 225 Jarvis St	Toronto	ON	M5B2C1	416-863-9000	
Web: www.grandhoteltoronto.com					
Grand Hotel Edmonton 10266 103rd St	Edmonton	AB	T5J0Y8	780-422-6365	
Web: www.thegrandedmonton.ca					
Grand Hotel Minneapolis, The 615 Second Ave S	Minneapolis	MN	55402	612-288-8888	373-0407
TF: 866-843-4726 ■ *Web:* www.grandhotelminneapolis.com					
Grand Hotel of Cape May Beach Ave	Cape May	NJ	08204	609-884-5611	
TF: 800-257-8550 ■ *Web:* www.grandhotelcapemay.com					
Grand Hotel, The 149 State Rt 64	Tusayan	AZ	86023	928-638-3333	
Web: www.grandcanyongrandhotel.com					
Grand Hyatt Washington 1000 H St NW	Washington	DC	20001	202-582-1234	
Web: washingtondc.grand.hyatt.com/en/hotel/home.html					
Grand Oaks Hotel 2315 Green Mountain Dr	Branson	MO	65616	800-553-6423	
TF: 800-553-6423 ■ *Web:* www.grandoakshotel.net					
Grand Summit Hotel 570 Springfield Ave	Summit	NJ	07901	908-273-3000	273-4228
TF: 800-346-0773 ■ *Web:* grandsummit.com					
Grande Colonial 910 Prospect St	La Jolla	CA	92037	888-828-5498	454-5679*
**Fax Area Code:* 858 ■ *TF:* 888-828-5498 ■ *Web:* www.thegrandecolonial.com					
Grandmark Lodging 3300 28th St SW	Grandville	MI	49418	616-534-7641	
Grant Plaza Hotel 465 Grant Ave	San Francisco	CA	94108	415-434-3883	434-3886
TF: 800-472-6899 ■ *Web:* www.grantplaza.com					
Granville Island Hotel 1253 Johnston St	Vancouver	BC	V6H3R9	604-683-7373	683-3061*
**Fax:* Admin ■ *TF Resv:* 800-663-1840 ■ *Web:* www.granvilleislandhotel.com					
Graycote Inn 40 Holland Ave	Bar Harbor	ME	04609	207-288-3044	288-2719
Web: www.graycoteinn.com					
Great Divide Lodge 550 Village Rd PO Box 8059	Breckenridge	CO	80424	970-547-5550	
TF: 888-400-9590 ■ *Web:* www.breckresorts.com					
Green Harbor Resort 182 Baxter Ave	West Yarmouth	MA	02673	508-771-1126	
Web: www.greenharborresort.com					
Green Mountain Inn 18 Main St PO Box 60	Stowe	VT	05672	802-253-7301	253-5096
TF: 800-253-7302 ■ *Web:* www.greenmountaininn.com					
Green Park Inn 9239 Valley Blvd	Blowing Rock	NC	28605	828-414-9230	
Web: www.greenparkinn.com					
Green Valley Ranch Resort Casino & Spa 2300 Paseo Verde Pkwy	Henderson	NV	89052	702-617-7777	
TF Resv: 866-782-9487 ■ *Web:* greenvalleyranch.sclv.com					
Grey Bonnet Inn 831 Rt 100 N	Killington	VT	05751	800-342-2086	775-3371*
**Fax Area Code:* 802 ■ *TF:* 800-342-2086					
Greyfield Inn 4 N Second St Ste 300	Fernandina Beach	FL	32034	904-261-6408	321-0666
TF: 866-401-8581 ■ *Web:* www.greyfieldinn.com					
Grove Hotel, The 245 S Capitol Blvd	Boise	ID	83702	208-333-8000	333-8800
Web: www.grovehotelboise.com					
Guest Inn 2533 N Piccoli Rd	Stockton	CA	95215	209-931-6675	931-8351
Habana Inn 2200 NW 40th St	Oklahoma City	OK	73112	405-525-0730	
TF: 800-988-2221 ■ *Web:* www.habanainn.com					
Habitat Suites 500 E Highland Mall Blvd	Austin	TX	78752	512-467-6000	467-6000
TF: 800-535-4663 ■ *Web:* www.habitatsuites.com					
Hacienda Hotel 525 N Sepulveda Blvd	El Segundo	CA	90245	310-615-0015	615-0217
Hacienda The at Hotel Santa Fe 1501 Paseo del Peralta	Santa Fe	NM	87501	505-955-7805	
TF: 855-825-9876 ■ *Web:* www.hotelsantafe.com/the_hacienda					
Halekulani Hotel 2199 Kalia Rd	Honolulu	HI	96815	808-923-2311	926-8004
TF: 800-367-2343 ■ *Web:* www.halekulani.com					
Half Moon Bay Lodge & Conference Ctr 2400 S Cabrillo Hwy	Half Moon Bay	CA	94019	650-726-9000	726-7951
TF: 800-710-0778 ■ *Web:* pacificahotels.com/halfmoonbaylodge					
Halifax Marriott Harborfront Hotel 1919 Upper Water St	Halifax	NS	B3J3J5	902-421-1700	422-5805
TF: 800-450-4442 ■ *Web:* www.marriott.com/hotels/travel/yhzmc-halifax-marriott-harbourfront-hotel					
Halliburton House Inn 5184 Morris St	Halifax	NS	B3J1B3	902-420-0658	423-2324
TF: 888-512-3344 ■ *Web:* www.thehalliburton.com					
Hallmark Inns & Resorts 15455 Hallmark Dr Ste 200	Lake Oswego	OR	97035	503-635-4555	
TF: 888-448-4449 ■ *Web:* www.hallmarkinns.com					

Phone Fax

Hampton Inn & Suites Atlanta Downtown Hotel
161 Spring St NW....Atlanta GA 30303 404-589-1111
Web: hamptoninn3.hilton.com/en/index.html

Hampton Inn Phoenix-Biltmore
2310 E Highland Ave....Phoenix AZ 85016 602-956-5221

Handlery Union Square Hotel
351 Geary St....San Francisco CA 94102 415-781-7800 781-0216
TF: 800-995-4874 ■ *Web:* www.handlery.com

Hanover Inn 2 E Wheelock St....Hanover NH 03755 603-643-4300 643-4433
TF: 800-443-7024 ■ *Web:* www.hanoverinn.com

Harbor Court Hotel 165 Steuart St....San Francisco CA 94105 415-882-1300 882-1313
TF: 866-792-6283 ■ *Web:* www.harborcourthotel.com

Harbor Court Hotel 550 Light St....Baltimore MD 21202 410-234-0550 659-5925
TF: 800-766-3782 ■ *Web:* www.sonesta.com

Harbor House 28 Pier 21....Galveston TX 77550 409-763-3321 765-6421
Web: www.harborhousepier21.com

Harbor View Hotel
131 N Water St Martha's Vineyard PO Box 7....Edgartown MA 02539 508-627-7000
TF: 800-225-6005 ■ *Web:* www.harbor-view.com

Harborside Hotel & Marina 55 W St....Bar Harbor ME 04609 207-288-5033 288-3661
TF: 800-328-5033 ■ *Web:* www.theharborsidehotel.com

Harborside Inn 1 Christie's Landing....Newport RI 02840 401-846-6600
TF: 800-427-9444 ■ *Web:* www.newportharborsideinn.com

Harborside Inn of Boston 185 State St....Boston MA 02109 617-723-7500 670-6015
Web: www.harborsideinnboston.com

Hard Rock Hotel & Casino Biloxi
777 Beach Blvd....Biloxi MS 39530 228-374-7625 276-7655
TF: 877-877-6256 ■ *Web:* www.hrhcbiloxi.com

Hard Rock Hotel Chicago 230 N Michigan Ave....Chicago IL 60601 312-345-1000
Web: www.hardrockhotelchicago.com

Hard Rock Hotel San Diego 207 Fifth Ave....San Diego CA 92101 619-702-3000 702-3007
TF: 866-751-7625 ■ *Web:* www.hardrockhotelsd.com

Harrah's Council Bluffs
1 Harrahs Blvd....Council Bluffs IA 51501 712-329-6000 329-6491
TF: 800-342-7724 ■ *Web:* www.caesars.com/harrahs-council-bluffs

Harrah's Joliet 151 N Joliet St....Joliet IL 60432 815-740-7800 740-2223
TF: 800-522-4700 ■ *Web:* www.caesars.com/harrahs-joliet

Harraseeket Inn 162 Main St....Freeport ME 04032 207-865-9377
TF: 800-342-6423 ■ *Web:* www.harraseeketinn.com

Harrison Plaza Suite Hotel 409 S Cole Rd....Boise ID 83709 208-376-3608 376-3608

Hartness House Inn 30 Orchard St....Springfield VT 05156 802-885-2115
TF: 800-732-4789 ■ *Web:* hartnesshouse.com

Harvard Square Hotel
110 Mt Auburn St Harvard Sq....Cambridge MA 02138 617-864-5200 864-2409
TF: 800-458-5886 ■ *Web:* www.harvardsquarehotel.com

Harvest Inn 1 Main St....Saint Helena CA 94574 707-963-9463 963-4402
TF: 800-950-8466 ■ *Web:* www.harvestinn.com

Hassayampa Inn 122 E Gurley St....Prescott AZ 86301 800-322-1927 445-8590*
*Fax Area Code: 928 ■ *TF Cust Svc:* 800-322-1927 ■ *Web:* www.hassayampainn.com

Hastings House Country House Hotel
160 Upper Ganges Rd....Salt Spring Island BC V8K2S2 250-537-2362
TF: 800-661-9255 ■ *Web:* www.hastingshouse.com

Hawaiian Inn
2301 S Atlantic Ave....Daytona Beach Shores FL 32118 386-255-5411 253-1209
TF: 800-922-3023 ■ *Web:* www.hawaiianinn.com

Hawthorne Hotel 18 Washington Sq W....Salem MA 01970 978-744-4080
TF: 800-729-7829 ■ *Web:* www.hawthornehotel.com

Hawthorne Inn & Conference Ctr
420 High St....Winston-Salem NC 27101 336-777-3000 777-3282
TF: 877-777-3099 ■ *Web:* www.wakehealth.edu

Hay-Adams Hotel 800 16th St NE....Washington DC 20006 202-638-6600 638-2716
Web: www.hayadams.com

Haywood Park Hotel 1 Battery Pk Ave....Asheville NC 28801 828-252-2522 253-0481
Web: www.haywoodpark.com

Heartland Inns 87-2nd St....Coralville IA 52241 319-351-8132
TF Resv: 800-334-3277 ■ *Web:* www.heartlandinns.com

Heathman Lodge 7801 NE Greenwood Dr....Vancouver WA 98662 360-254-3100
Web: www.heathmanlodge.com

Henley Park Hotel
926 Massachusetts Ave NW....Washington DC 20001 202-638-5200 638-6740
TF: 800-222-8474 ■ *Web:* www.henleypark.com

Henlopen Hotel 511 N Boardwalk....Rehoboth Beach DE 19971 302-227-2551 227-8147
TF: 800-441-8450 ■ *Web:* www.henlopenhotel.com

Heritage Hotels & Resorts Inc
201 Third St NW Ste 1500....Albuquerque NM 87102 505-836-6700
Web: www.heritagehotelsandresorts.com

Heritage Inn 1350 Richmond Rd....Williamsburg VA 23185 757-229-2455

Heritage Inn, The 34521 Postal Ln....Lewes DE 19958 800-669-9399
TF: 800-669-9399 ■ *Web:* www.rehobothheritage.com

Hermitage Hotel 231 Sixth Ave N....Nashville TN 37219 615-244-3121 254-6909
TF: 888-888-9414 ■ *Web:* www.thehermitagehotel.com

Hermosa Inn 5532 N Palo Cristi Rd....Paradise Valley AZ 85253 602-955-8614 955-8299
TF: 800-241-1210 ■ *Web:* www.hermosainn.com

Hershey Entertainment & Resorts Co
27 W Chocolate Ave....Hershey PA 17033 800-437-7439
TF: 800-437-7439 ■ *Web:* www.hersheypa.com

Hershey Lodge 325 University Dr....Hershey PA 17033 717-533-3311 533-9642
TF: 844-330-1802 ■ *Web:* www.hersheylodge.com

HI Development Corp 111 W Fortune St....Tampa FL 33602 813-229-6686
Web: www.hidevelopment.com

Hilgard House Hotel & Suites
927 Hilgard Ave....Los Angeles CA 90024 310-208-3945 208-1972
TF: 800-826-3934 ■ *Web:* www.hilgardhouse.com

Hilltop Inn of Vermont 3472 Airport Rd....Montpelier VT 05602 802-229-5766 229-5766
TF: 877-609-0003 ■ *Web:* www.hilltopinnvt.net

Hilton Anaheim 777 W Convention Way....Anaheim CA 92802 714-750-4321
Web: www3.hilton.com/en/hotels/california/hilton-anaheim-snaahhh/index.html

Hilton Atlanta Northeast
5993 Peachtree Industrial Blvd....Norcross GA 30092 770-447-4747
Web: hilton.com

Hilton Garden Inn (Burlington Canada)
985 Syscon Rd....Burlington ON L7L5S3 905-631-7000
Web: hiltongardeninn3.hilton.com

Phone Fax

Hilton Garden Inn Greenville
108 Carolina Point Pkwy....Greenville SC 29605 864-284-0111
Web: hiltongardeninn3.hilton.com

Hilton Jackson 1001 E County Line Rd....Jackson MS 39211 601-957-2800
Web: www.hiltonjackson.com

Hilton La Jolla Torrey Pines
10950 N Torrey Pines Rd....La Jolla CA 92037 858-558-1500
Web: hilton.com

Hilton Long Beach Hotel & Executive Meeting Center
701 W Ocean Blvd....Long Beach CA 90831 562-983-3400
Web: hiltonlb.com

Hilton Providence 21 Atwells Ave....Providence RI 02903 401-831-3900
Web: hilton.com

Hilton St Louis Hotel at BaLLPark
1 S Broadway....Saint Louis MO 63102 314-421-1776
Web: www3.hilton.com/en/hotels/missouri/hilton-st-louis-at-the-ballpark-stlbvhf/index.html

Hilton Suites Atlanta Perimeter
6120 Peachtree Dunwoody Rd Ne....Atlanta GA 30328 770-668-0808
Web: hilton.com

Hilton Worldwide 7930 Jones Branch Dr....McLean VA 22102 703-883-1000
TF: 800-445-8667 ■ *Web:* www.hiltonworldwide.com

Historic Bullock Hotel 633 Main St....Deadwood SD 57732 800-336-1876
TF: 800-336-1876 ■ *Web:* www.historicbullock.com

Historic French Market Inn
509 Decatur St....New Orleans LA 70130 504-561-5621 581-3802
TF: 800-366-2743 ■ *Web:* www.frenchmarketinn.com

Historic Inns of Annapolis 58 State Cir....Annapolis MD 21401 410-263-2641 268-3613
TF: 800-847-8882 ■ *Web:* www.historicinnsofannapolis.com

HLC Hotels Inc 7080 Abercorn St PO Box 13069....Savannah GA 31416 912-352-4493 352-0314
TF: 800-344-4378 ■ *Web:* www.hlchotels.com

Holiday Inn 301 Government St....Mobile AL 36602 251-694-0100
TF: 888-465-4329 ■ *Web:* www.ihg.com

Holiday Inn Express DFW North
4550 W John Carpenter Fwy....Irving TX 75063 800-465-4329
TF: 800-465-4329 ■ *Web:* www.ihg.com

Holiday Inn Resort Daytona Beach Oceanfront
1615 S Atlantic Ave....Daytona Beach FL 32118 386-255-0921
TF: 800-874-0975 ■ *Web:* www.hiresortdaytona.com

Hollow Inn 278 S Main St....Barre VT 05641 802-479-9313 476-5242
Web: www.hollowinn.com

Hollywood Roosevelt Hotel
7000 Hollywood Blvd....Los Angeles CA 90028 323-466-7000
Web: www.thompsonhotels.com

Hollywood Standard Hotel
8300 Sunset Blvd....West Hollywood CA 90069 323-650-9090
Web: www.standardhotels.com

Homestead Inn 420 Field Pt Rd....Greenwich CT 06830 203-869-7500 869-7502
Web: www.homesteadinn.com

Horton Grand Hotel 311 Island Ave....San Diego CA 92101 619-544-1886
TF: 800-542-1886 ■ *Web:* www.hortongrand.com

Hospitality Inn 3709 NW 39th St....Oklahoma City OK 73112 405-942-7730

Hospitality International Inc
1726 Montreal Cir....Tucker GA 30084 800-251-1962 270-1077*
*Fax Area Code: 770 ■ *TF:* 800-251-1962 ■ *Web:* www.bookroomsnow.com
Master Hosts Inns & Resorts 1726 Montreal Cir....Tucker GA 30084 800-247-4677 270-1077*
*Fax Area Code: 770 ■ *TF:* 800-247-4677 ■ *Web:* www.bookroomsnow.com
Passport Inn 1726 Montreal Cir....Tucker GA 30084 800-251-1962 270-1077*
*Fax Area Code: 770 ■ *TF:* 800-251-1962 ■ *Web:* www.bookroomsnow.com
Red Carpet Inn 1726 Montreal Cir....Tucker GA 30084 800-247-4677 270-1077*
*Fax Area Code: 770 ■ *TF:* 800-247-4677 ■ *Web:* www.bookroomsnow.com
Scottish Inns 1726 Montreal Cir....Tucker GA 30084 800-251-1962 270-1077*
*Fax Area Code: 770 ■ *TF:* 800-251-1962 ■ *Web:* www.bookroomsnow.com

Hospitality Suites Resort
409 N Scottsdale Rd....Scottsdale AZ 85257 480-949-5115
TF: 800-445-5115 ■ *Web:* www.hospitalitysuites.com

Hostmark Hospitality Group
1300 E Woodfield Rd Ste 400....Schaumburg IL 60173 847-517-9100 517-9797
Web: www.hostmark.com

Hotel & Suites Normandin
4700 Pierre-Bertrand Blvd....Quebec QC G2J1A4 418-622-1611 622-9277
TF: 800-463-6721 ■ *Web:* www.hotelnormandin.com

Hotel 1000 1000 First Ave....Seattle WA 98104 206-957-1000 357-9457
TF: 877-315-1088 ■ *Web:* www.hotel1000seattle.com

Hotel 140 140 Clarendon St....Boston MA 02116 617-585-5600 585-5699
TF: 800-714-0140 ■ *Web:* www.hotel140.com

Hotel 43 981 Grove St....Boise ID 83702 208-342-4622 344-5751
TF: 800-243-4622 ■ *Web:* www.hotel43.com

Hotel 71 71 St Pierre St....Quebec QC G1K4A4 418-692-1171
TF: 888-692-1171 ■ *Web:* www.hotel71.ca

Hotel Abri 127 Ellis St....San Francisco CA 94102 415-392-8800
TF: 866-778-6169 ■ *Web:* www.hotelabrisf.com

Hotel Adagio 550 Geary St....San Francisco CA 94102 415-775-5000 775-9388
TF: 855-687-7262 ■ *Web:* www.jdvhotels.com

Hotel Alex Johnson 523 Sixth St....Rapid City SD 57701 605-342-1210
Web: www.alexjohnson.com

Hotel Allegro Chicago 171 W Randolph St....Chicago IL 60601 312-236-0123 236-3440
TF: 800-643-1500 ■ *Web:* www.allegrochicago.com

Hotel Ambassadeur 3401 Blvd Ste-Anne....Quebec QC G1E3L4 418-666-2828 666-2775
TF: 800-363-4619 ■ *Web:* www.hotelambassadeur.ca

Hotel Ambassador 1324 S Main St....Tulsa OK 74119 918-587-8200 587-8208
TF General: 888-408-8282 ■ *Web:* www.ambassadorhotelcollection.com

Hotel Andra 2000 Fourth Ave....Seattle WA 98121 206-448-8600 441-7140
TF: 877-448-8600 ■ *Web:* www.hotelandra.com

Hotel Andrew Jackson 919 Royal St....New Orleans LA 70116 504-561-5881
Web: www.frenchquarterinns.com

Hotel Angeleno 170 N Church Ln....Los Angeles CA 90049 310-476-6411
Web: hotelangeleno.com

Hotel Astor 956 Washington Ave....Miami Beach FL 33139 305-531-8081 531-3193
Web: www.hotelastor.com

Hotel at Old Town Wichita 830 E First St....Wichita KS 67202 316-267-4800 267-4840
TF: 877-265-3869 ■ *Web:* www.hotelatoldtown.com

Name	City	State	ZIP	Phone	Fax
Hotel Avante 860 E El Camino Real *TF:* 800-538-1600 ■ *Web:* jdvhotels.com/hotels/california/silicon-valley-hotels/hotel-avante	Mountain View	CA	94040	650-940-1000	968-7870
Hotel Beacon 2130 Broadway *TF:* 800-572-4969 ■ *Web:* www.beaconhotel.com	New York	NY	10023	212-787-1100	724-0839
Hotel Bedford 118 E 40th St *TF:* 800-221-6881 ■ *Web:* www.hotelbedfordny.com	New York	NY	10016	212-697-4800	697-1093
Hotel Bel-Air 701 Stone Canyon Rd *TF:* 800-648-4097 ■ *Web:* www.dorchestercollection.com	Los Angeles	CA	90077	310-472-1211	276-2251
Hotel Bethlehem 437 Main St *Web:* www.hotelbethlehem.com	Bethlehem	PA	18018	610-625-5000	
Hotel Bijou 111 Mason St *TF:* 877-568-2733 ■ *Web:* www.jdvhotels.com	San Francisco	CA	94102	415-771-1200	
Hotel Blake 500 S Dearborn St *Web:* www.hotelblake.com	Chicago	IL	60605	312-986-1234	
Hotel Boulderado 2115 13th St *TF:* 800-433-4344 ■ *Web:* www.boulderado.com	Boulder	CO	80302	303-442-4344	442-4378
Hotel Burnham 1 W Washington St *TF:* 866-690-1986 ■ *Web:* www.burnhamhotel.com	Chicago	IL	60602	312-782-1111	782-0899
Hotel Captain Cook 939 W Fifth Ave *TF:* 800-843-1950 ■ *Web:* www.captaincook.com	Anchorage	AK	99501	907-276-6000	
Hotel Carlton 1075 Sutter St *Web:* www.jdvhotels.com	San Francisco	CA	94109	415-673-0242	
Hotel Casa del Mar 1910 Ocean Way *Web:* www.hotelcasadelmar.com	Santa Monica	CA	90405	310-581-5533	
Hotel Chateau Bellevue 16 Rue de la Porte *TF:* 877-849-1877 ■ *Web:* www.hoteloldquebec.com/en	Quebec	QC	G1R4M9	418-692-2573	692-4876
Hotel Chateau Laurier 1220 Pl George-V Ouest *TF:* 877-522-8108 ■ *Web:* hotelchateaulaurier.com	Quebec	QC	G1R5B8	418-522-8108	524-8768
Hotel Classique 2815 Laurier Blvd *TF:* 800-463-1885 ■ *Web:* www.hotelclassique.com	Quebec	QC	G1V4H3	418-658-2793	658-6816
Hotel Colorado 526 Pine St *TF:* 800-544-3998 ■ *Web:* www.hotelcolorado.com	Glenwood Springs	CO	81601	970-945-6511	945-7030
Hotel Commonwealth 500 Commonwealth Ave *TF:* 866-784-4000 ■ *Web:* www.hotelcommonwealth.com	Boston	MA	02215	617-933-5000	266-6888
Hotel Congress 311 E Congress St *TF:* 800-722-8848 ■ *Web:* www.hotelcongress.com	Tucson	AZ	85701	520-622-8848	792-6366
Hotel Contessa 306 W Market St *TF:* 866-435-0900 ■ *Web:* www.thehotelcontessa.com	San Antonio	TX	78205	210-229-9222	
Hotel Crescent Court 400 Crescent Ct *Web:* www.rosewoodhotels.com	Dallas	TX	75201	214-871-3200	871-3272
Hotel de Anza 233 W Santa Clara St *TF:* 800-843-3700 ■ *Web:* www.destinationhotels.com/hotel-de-anza	San Jose	CA	95113	408-286-1000	286-0500
Hotel De La Monnaie Owners Association Inc 405 Esplanade Ave *Web:* hoteldelamonnaie.com	New Orleans	LA	70116	504-947-0009	
Hotel Deca 4507 Brooklyn Ave NE *TF:* 800-899-0251 ■ *Web:* www.hoteldeca.com	Seattle	WA	98105	206-634-2000	
Hotel Del Sol 3100 Webster St *TF:* 877-433-5765 ■ *Web:* www.jdvhotels.com	San Francisco	CA	94123	415-921-5520	
Hotel Deluxe 729 SW 15th Ave *TF:* 866-895-2094 ■ *Web:* www.hoteldeluxeportland.com	Portland	OR	97205	503-219-2094	219-2095
Hotel Derek 2525 W Loop S *TF:* 866-292-4100 ■ *Web:* www.hotelderek.com	Houston	TX	77027	713-961-3000	297-4392
Hotel Drisco 2901 Pacific Ave **Fax Area Code:* 510 ■ *TF:* 800-738-7477 ■ *Web:* jdvhotels.com/hotels/california	San Francisco	CA	94115	415-346-2880	832-6228*
Hotel du Pont 11th & Market Sts *TF:* 800-441-9019 ■ *Web:* www.hoteldupont.com	Wilmington	DE	19801	302-594-3100	594-3108
Hotel Durant 2600 Durant Ave *TF:* 800-738-7477 ■ *Web:* www.jdvhotels.com	Berkeley	CA	94704	510-845-8981	832-6228
Hotel Edison 228 W 47th St *TF:* 800-637-7070 ■ *Web:* www.edisonhotelnyc.com	New York	NY	10036	212-840-5000	
Hotel El Convento 100 Cristo St Old San Juan *Web:* www.elconvento.com	San Juan	PR	00901	787-723-9020	
Hotel Elysee 60 E 54th St *Web:* www.elyseehotel.com	New York	NY	10022	212-753-1066	980-9278
Hotel Encanto de Las Cruces 705 S Telshor Blvd *TF:* 866-383-0443 ■ *Web:* www.hotelencanto.com	Las Cruces	NM	88011	575-522-4300	522-4300
Hotel Financial Strategies 468 N Camden Dr Ste 200 *Web:* www.hotelfinancial.com	Beverly Hills	CA	90210	310-247-2101	
Hotel Fort Des Moines 1000 Walnut St *Web:* hotelfortdesmoines.com	Des Moines	IA	50309	515-243-1161	
Hotel Galvez - A Wyndham Historic Hotel 2024 Seawall Blvd *TF:* 800-996-3426 ■ *Web:* www.wyndham.com	Galveston	TX	77550	409-765-7721	
Hotel Gault 449 Rue St-Helene St *Web:* www.hotelgault.com	Montreal	QC	H2Y2K9	514-904-1616	904-1717
Hotel George 15 E St NW *TF General:* 800-546-7866 ■ *Web:* www.hotelgeorge.com	Washington	DC	20001	202-347-4200	347-4213
Hotel Giraffe 365 Pk Ave S at 26th St *Web:* www.hotelgiraffe.com	New York	NY	10016	212-685-7700	685-7771
Hotel Grand Pacific 463 Belleville St *TF:* 800-663-7550 ■ *Web:* www.hotelgrandpacific.com	Victoria	BC	V8V1X3	250-386-0450	380-4475
Hotel Grand Victorian 2325 W Hwy 76 *TF:* 800-324-8751 ■ *Web:* www.hotelgrandvictorian.com	Branson	MO	65616	417-336-2935	
Hotel Granduca 1080 Uptown Pk Blvd *TF:* 888-472-6382 ■ *Web:* www.granducahouston.com	Houston	TX	77056	713-418-1000	418-1001
Hotel Griffon 155 Steuart St *TF:* 800-321-2201 ■ *Web:* www.hotelgriffon.com	San Francisco	CA	94105	415-495-2100	495-3522
Hotel Group, The (THG) 110 James St Ste 102 *Web:* www.thehotelgroup.com	Edmonds	WA	98020	425-771-1788	672-8280
Hotel Highland 1023 20th St S *Web:* www.choicehotels.com/ascend	Birmingham	AL	35205	205-933-9555	933-6918
Hotel Huntington Beach 7667 Ctr Ave *Web:* www.hotelhb.com	Huntington Beach	CA	92647	714-891-0123	
Hotel Icon 220 Main St **Fax Area Code:* 832 ■ *Web:* www.hotelicon.com	Houston	TX	77002	713-224-4266	223-3223*
Hotel Indigo San Diego 509 Ninth Ave *Web:* www.hotelinsd.com	San Diego	CA	92101	619-727-4000	
Hotel Jerome 330 E Main St **Fax Area Code:* 970 ■ *TF:* 855-331-7213 ■ *Web:* hoteljerome.aubergeresorts.com	Aspen	CO	81611	855-331-7213	920-2050*
Hotel Kabuki San Francisco 1625 Post St *Web:* jdvhotels.com/hotels/california/san-francisco-hotels/hotel-kabuki	San Francisco	CA	94115	415-922-3200	
Hotel La Rose 308 Wilson St *TF:* 800-527-6738 ■ *Web:* www.hotellarose.com	Santa Rosa	CA	95401	707-579-3200	579-3247
Hotel Le Bleu 370 Fourth Ave *TF:* 866-427-6073 ■ *Web:* www.hotellebleu.com	Brooklyn	NY	11215	718-625-1500	
Hotel Le Cantlie Suites 1110 Sherbrooke St W *TF:* 800-567-1110 ■ *Web:* www.hotelcantlie.com	Montreal	QC	H3A1G9	514-842-2000	844-7808
Hotel Le Capitole 972 St Jean St *TF:* 800-261-9903 ■ *Web:* www.lecapitole.com	Quebec	QC	G1R1R5	418-694-4444	
Hotel Le Clos Saint-Louis 69 St Louis St *TF:* 800-461-1311 ■ *Web:* www.clossaintlouis.com	Quebec	QC	G1R3Z2	418-694-1311	694-9411
Hotel Le Germain Toronto 30 Mercer St *TF:* 866-345-9501 ■ *Web:* www.legermainhotels.com/en/torontomercer	Toronto	ON	M5V1H3	416-345-9500	345-9501
Hotel Le Marais 717 Conti St *TF:* 800-935-8740 ■ *Web:* www.hotellemarais.com	New Orleans	LA	70130	504-525-2300	
Hotel le Priori 15 du Sault-au-Matelot St *TF:* 800-351-3992 ■ *Web:* www.hotellepriori.com	Quebec	QC	G1K3Y7	418-692-3992	
Hotel Le Soleil 567 Hornby St *TF:* 877-632-3030 ■ *Web:* www.hotellesoleil.com	Vancouver	BC	V6C2E8	604-632-3000	632-3001
Hotel Le St-James 355 St Jacques St *TF:* 866-841-3111 ■ *Web:* www.hotellestjames.com	Montreal	QC	H2Y1N9	514-841-3111	841-1232
Hotel Lombardy 2019 Pennsylvania Ave NW *TF:* 800-424-5486 ■ *Web:* www.hotellombardy.com	Washington	DC	20006	202-828-2600	
Hotel Lord-Berri 1199 Berri St *TF:* 888-363-0363 ■ *Web:* www.lordberri.com	Montreal	QC	H2L4C6	514-845-9236	849-9855
Hotel Los Gatos 210 E Main St *Web:* www.jdvhotels.com	Los Gatos	CA	95030	408-335-1700	335-1750
Hotel Lucia 400 SW Broadway *TF:* 877-225-1717 ■ *Web:* www.hotellucia.com	Portland	OR	97205	503-225-1717	225-1919
Hotel Lumen 6101 Hillcrest Ave *TF:* 800-908-1140 ■ *Web:* www.hotellumen.com	Dallas	TX	75205	214-219-2400	219-2402
Hotel Lusso 808 West Sprague Avenue *TF General:* 800-899-1482 ■ *Web:* www.davenporthotelcollection.com	Spokane	WA	99201	509-747-9750	
Hotel Madera 1310 New Hampshire Ave NW *TF:* 800-546-7866 ■ *Web:* www.hotelmadera.com	Washington	DC	20036	202-296-7600	293-2476
Hotel Majestic 1500 Sutter St *Web:* www.thehotelmajestic.com	San Francisco	CA	94109	415-441-1100	673-7331
Hotel Manoir Victoria 44 Cote du Palais *TF:* 800-463-6283 ■ *Web:* www.manoir-victoria.com	Quebec	QC	G1R4H8	418-692-1030	692-3822
Hotel Maritime Plaza 1155 Guy St	Montreal	QC	H3H2K5	514-932-1411	932-0446
Hotel Mark Twain 345 Taylor St *TF:* 877-854-4106 ■ *Web:* www.hotelmarktwain.com	San Francisco	CA	94102	415-673-2332	
Hotel Marlowe Cambridge 25 Edwind H Land Blvd *TF:* 800-825-7140 ■ *Web:* www.hotelmarlowe.com	Cambridge	MA	02141	617-868-8000	868-8001
Hotel Max 620 Stewart St *TF:* 866-833-6299 ■ *Web:* www.hotelmaxseattle.com	Seattle	WA	98101	206-728-6299	443-5754
Hotel Mead 451 E Grand Ave *TF:* 800-843-6323 ■ *Web:* www.hotelmead.com	Wisconsin Rapids	WI	54494	715-423-1500	423-1510
Hotel Mela 120 W 44th St *TF:* 877-452-6352 ■ *Web:* www.hotelmela.com	New York	NY	10036	212-710-7000	
Hotel Metro 411 E Mason St *TF:* 877-638-7620 ■ *Web:* www.hotelmetro.com	Milwaukee	WI	53202	414-272-1937	
Hotel Monaco Chicago 225 N Wabash Ave *TF:* 866-610-0081 ■ *Web:* www.monaco-chicago.com	Chicago	IL	60601	312-960-8500	960-1883
Hotel Monaco Denver 1717 Champa St *TF:* 800-990-1303 ■ *Web:* www.monaco-denver.com	Denver	CO	80202	303-296-1717	296-1818
Hotel Monaco Portland 506 SW Washington at Fifth Ave *TF:* 866-861-9514 ■ *Web:* www.monaco-portland.com	Portland	OR	97204	503-222-0001	222-0004
Hotel Monaco Salt Lake City 15 West 200 South *TF Resv:* 800-805-1801 ■ *Web:* www.monaco-saltlakecity.com	Salt Lake City	UT	84101	801-595-0000	532-8500
Hotel Monaco Seattle 1101 Fourth Ave *TF:* 800-715-6513 ■ *Web:* www.monaco-seattle.com	Seattle	WA	98101	206-621-1770	621-7779
Hotel Monte Vista 100 N San Francisco St *TF:* 800-545-3068 ■ *Web:* www.hotelmontevista.com	Flagstaff	AZ	86001	928-779-6971	779-2904
Hotel Monteleone 214 Royal St *TF:* 866-338-4684 ■ *Web:* www.hotelmonteleone.com	New Orleans	LA	70130	504-523-3341	
Hotel Murano 1320 Broadway Plz *TF:* 888-862-3255 ■ *Web:* www.hotelmuranotacoma.com	Tacoma	WA	98402	253-238-8000	591-4105
Hotel Nikko San Francisco 222 Mason St *TF:* 866-636-4556 ■ *Web:* www.hotelnikkosf.com	San Francisco	CA	94102	415-394-1111	394-1106
Hotel Northampton 36 King St *TF:* 800-547-3529 ■ *Web:* www.hotelnorthampton.com	NorthHampton	MA	01060	413-584-3100	
Hotel Ocean 1230 Ocean Dr *Web:* www.hotelocean.com	Miami Beach	FL	33139	305-672-2579	672-7665
Hotel Oceana					
Oceana Santa Monica 849 Ocean Ave *Web:* www.hoteloceanasantamonica.com	Santa Monica	CA	90403	310-393-0486	
Santa Barbara 202 W Cabrillo Blvd *TF:* 800-965-9776 ■ *Web:* hotelmilosantabarbara.com	Santa Barbara	CA	93101	805-965-4577	965-9937
Hotel Omni Mont-Royal 1050 Sherbrooke St W *TF:* 800-843-6664 ■ *Web:* www.omnihotels.com	Montreal	QC	H3A2R6	514-284-1110	845-3025
Hotel Orrington 1710 Orrington Ave *TF:* 888-677-4648 ■ *Web:* www.hotelorrington.com	Evanston	IL	60201	847-866-8700	866-8724
Hotel Pacific 300 Pacific St *TF:* 800-554-5542 ■ *Web:* www.hotelpacific.com	Monterey	CA	93940	831-373-5700	373-6921
Hotel Park City (HPC) 2001 Pk Ave *Web:* www.hotelparkcity.com	Park City	UT	84060	435-200-2000	940-5001
Hotel Phillips 106 W 12th St *TF:* 877-704-5341 ■ *Web:* www.hotelphillips.com	Kansas City	MO	64105	816-221-7000	221-3477
Hotel Plaza Athenee 37 E 64th St *TF:* 800-447-8800 ■ *Web:* www.plaza-athenee.com	New York	NY	10065	212-734-9100	772-0958
Hotel Plaza Quebec 3031 Laurier Blvd *TF:* 800-567-5276 ■ *Web:* www.hotelsjaro.com/plazaquebec/index-en.aspx	Sainte-Foy	QC	G1V2M2	418-658-2727	658-6587
Hotel Plaza Real 125 Washington Ave *TF:* 855-752-9273 ■ *Web:* hotelchimayo.com	Santa Fe	NM	87501	505-988-4900	983-9322

Phone | Fax

Hotel Preston 733 Briley Pkwy Nashville TN 37217 615-361-5900
TF: 800-407-4324 ■ *Web:* www.hotelpreston.com

Hotel Provincial 1024 Rue Chartres New Orleans LA 70116 504-581-4995 581-1018
TF: 800-535-7922 ■ *Web:* www.hotelprovincial.com

Hotel Rex 562 Sutter St San Francisco CA 94102 415-433-4434 433-3695
TF Resv: 800-433-4434 ■
Web: jdvhotels.com/hotels/california/san-francisco-hotels/hotel-rex

Hotel Rodney 142 Second St Lewes DE 19958 302-645-6466
TF: 800-824-8754 ■ *Web:* www.hotelrodneydelaware.com

Hotel Roger Williams 131 Madison Ave New York NY 10016 212-448-7000 448-7007
TF Resv: 888-448-7788 ■ *Web:* www.therogernewyork.com

Hotel Rouge 1315 16th St NW Washington DC 20036 202-232-8000 667-9827
TF: 800-738-1202 ■ *Web:* www.rougehotel.com

Hotel Royal Plaza
1905 Hotel Plaza Blvd Lake Buena Vista FL 32830 407-828-2828
TF: 888-662-4683 ■ *Web:* bhotelsandresorts.com/b-walt-disney-world

Hotel Ruby Foo's 7655 Decarie Blvd Montreal QC H4P2H2 514-731-7701
TF: 800-361-5419 ■ *Web:* www.hotelrubyfoos.com

Hotel Saint Francis 210 Don Gaspar Ave Santa Fe NM 87501 505-983-5700 989-7690
TF: 800-529-5700 ■ *Web:* www.hotelstfrancis.com

Hotel Saint Marie 827 Toulouse St New Orleans LA 70112 504-561-8951
TF: 800-366-2743 ■ *Web:* www.hotelstmarie.com

Hotel Saint Pierre 911 Burgundy St New Orleans LA 70116 504-524-4401
Web: www.frenchquarterinns.com

Hotel Saint Regis Detroit 3071 W Grand Blvd Detroit MI 48202 313-873-3000 481-8408
Web: www.hotelstregisdetroit.com

Hotel San Carlos 202 N Central Ave Phoenix AZ 85004 602-253-4121 253-6668
TF: 866-253-4121 ■ *Web:* hotelsancarlos.com

Hotel Santa Barbara 533 State St Santa Barbara CA 93101 805-957-9300 962-2412
TF: 888-259-7700 ■ *Web:* www.hotelsantabarbara.com

Hotel Santa Fe 1501 Paseo de Peralta Santa Fe NM 87501 505-982-1200
TF: 855-825-9876 ■ *Web:* www.hotelsantafe.com

Hotel Sax Chicago 333 N Dearborn St Chicago IL 60610 312-245-0333 640-7779*
*Fax Area Code: 416 ■ *TF:* 855-880-1240 ■ *Web:* www.thompsonhotels.com

Hotel Sepia 3135 Ch St-Louis Sainte-Foy QC G1W1R9 418-653-4941 653-0774
TF: 888-301-6837 ■ *Web:* www.hotelsepia.ca

Hotel Shelley 844 Collins Ave Miami Beach FL 33139 305-531-3341 674-0811
TF: 877-762-3477 ■ *Web:* www.hotelshelley.com

Hotel Solamar 435 Sixth Ave San Diego CA 92101 619-819-9500
TF: 877-230-0300 ■ *Web:* www.hotelsolamar.com

Hotel St Germain 2516 Maple Ave Dallas TX 75201 214-871-2516 871-0740
Web: www.hotelstgermain.com

Hotel st James Inc 109 W 45th St New York NY 10036 212-730-9444
Web: hotel-st-james.hotelapp.me

Hotel Strasburg, The 213 S Holliday St Strasburg VA 22657 540-465-9191 465-4788
TF: 800-348-8327 ■ *Web:* www.hotelstrasburg.com

Hotel Teatro 1100 14th St Denver CO 80202 303-228-1100
TF: 888-727-1200 ■ *Web:* www.hotelteatro.com

Hotel The Queen Mary 1126 Queens Hwy Long Beach CA 90802 562-435-3511
TF: 877-342-0738 ■ *Web:* www.queenmary.com

Hotel Triton 342 Grant Ave San Francisco CA 94108 415-394-0500 394-0555
TF: 800-800-1299 ■ *Web:* www.hoteltriton.com

Hotel Tybee 1401 Strand Ave Tybee Island GA 31328 912-786-7777
Web: www.hoteltybee.com

Hotel Universel 2300 Ch St-Foy Quebec QC G1V1S5 418-653-5250 653-4486
TF: 800-463-4495 ■ *Web:* www.hoteluniversel.qc.ca

Hotel Utica 102 Lafayette St Utica NY 13502 315-724-7829
TF: 877-906-1912 ■ *Web:* www.hotelutica.com

Hotel Valencia Santana Row 355 Santana Row San Jose CA 95128 408-551-0010 551-0550
TF: 866-842-0100 ■ *Web:* www.hotelvalencia-santanarow.com

Hotel Valley Ho 6850 E Main St Scottsdale AZ 85251 480-376-4600 421-7782
TF: 866-882-4484 ■ *Web:* www.hotelvalleyho.com

Hotel Victoria 56 Yonge St Toronto ON M5E1G5 416-363-1666 363-7327
Web: www.hotelvictoria-toronto.com

Hotel Viking 1 Bellevue Ave Newport RI 02840 401-847-3300
TF: 800-556-7126 ■ *Web:* www.hotelviking.com

Hotel Vintage Park 1100 Fifth Ave Seattle WA 98101 206-624-8000 623-0568
TF: 800-853-3914 ■ *Web:* hotelvintage-seattle.com

Hotel Wales 1295 Madison Ave New York NY 10128 212-876-6000 860-7000
TF: 866-925-3746 ■ *Web:* www.hotelwalesnyc.com

Hotel Weatherford, The 23 N Leroux St Flagstaff AZ 86001 928-779-1919 773-8951
Web: www.weatherfordhotel.com

Hotel Wolcott 4 W 31st St New York NY 10001 212-268-2900 563-0096
Web: www.wolcott.com

Hotel XIXe Siecle
Lhotel 262 St Jacques St W Vieux-Quebec QC H2Y1N1 514-985-0019 985-0059
TF: 877-553-0019 ■ *Web:* www.lhotelmontreal.com

Hotel ZaZa Dallas 2332 Leonard St Dallas TX 75201 214-468-8399 468-8397
TF: 800-597-8399 ■ *Web:* www.hotelzaza.com

Hotel ZaZa Houston 5701 Main St Houston TX 77005 713-526-1991 526-0359
TF Resv: 888-880-3244 ■ *Web:* www.hotelzaza.com/houston

Hotel, The 801 Collins Ave Miami Beach FL 33139 305-531-2222 531-3222
Web: www.thehotelofsouthbeach.com

Hotels Unlimited Inc 399 Monmouth St East Windsor NJ 08520 609-632-0006

HP Hotels Inc 1 Chase Corporate Dr Ste 210 Birmingham AL 35244 205-879-7004
TF: 800-576-3467 ■ *Web:* hp-hotels.com

Humphrey's Half Moon Inn & Suites
2303 Shelter Island Dr San Diego CA 92106 619-224-3411 224-3478
TF: 800-542-7400 ■ *Web:* www.halfmooninn.com

Huntington Hotel & Nob Hill Spa
1075 California St San Francisco CA 94108 415-474-5400 474-6227
Web: thescarlethotels.com/huntington-hotel-san-francisco

Hyannis Holiday Motel 131 Ocean St Hyannis MA 02601 508-775-1639 775-1672
TF: 800-423-1551 ■ *Web:* hyannisholiday.com

Hyannis Travel Inn 18 N St Hyannis MA 02601 508-775-8200 775-8201
TF: 800-352-7190 ■ *Web:* www.hyannistravelinn.com

Hyatt Carmel Highlands 120 Highlands Dr Carmel CA 93923 831-620-1234 626-1574
TF: 800-633-7313 ■ *Web:* www.highlandsinn.hyatt.com

Hyatt Fair Lakes Hotel 12777 Fair Lakes Cir Fairfax VA 22033 703-818-1234
Web: fairpo.com

Hyatt Hotels Corp 71 S Wacker Dr Chicago IL 60606 312-750-1234
NYSE: H ■ *TF:* 888-591-1234 ■ *Web:* www.hyatt.com

Grand Hyatt Hotels 71 S Wacker Dr Chicago IL 60606 312-750-1234
TF Resv: 800-233-1234 ■ *Web:* www.hyatt.com

Hyatt Place Hotels 71 S Wacker Dr Chicago IL 60606 312-750-1234
TF: 888-492-8847 ■ *Web:* www.place.hyatt.com

Hyatt Regency Hotels 71 S Wacker Dr Chicago IL 60606 312-750-1234
TF Resv: 800-233-1234 ■ *Web:* www.hyatt.com

Hyatt Summerfield Suites 71 S Wacker Dr Chicago IL 60606 312-750-1234
Web: www.house.hyatt.com

Park Hyatt Hotels 71 S Wacker Dr Chicago IL 60606 312-750-1234
TF Resv: 800-233-1234 ■ *Web:* www.hyatt.com

Hyatt Summerfield Suites Herndon
467 Herndon Pkwy Herndon VA 20170 703-437-5000
Web: herndonreston.house.hyatt.com/en/hotel/home.html

Hyatt Westlake Plaza in ThoUSAnd Oaks
880 S Wlake Blvd Westlake Village CA 91361 805-557-1234
Web: westlake.regency.hyatt.com/en/hotel/home.html

Ilikai Hotel & Suites 1777 Ala Moana Blvd Honolulu HI 96815 808-949-3811 947-0892
TF: 866-536-7973 ■ *Web:* www.ilikaihotel.com

Imperial of Waikiki 205 Lewers St Honolulu HI 96815 808-923-1827 921-7586
TF: 800-347-2582 ■ *Web:* www.imperialofwaikiki.com

Imperial Swan Hotel 4141 S Florida Ave Lakeland FL 33813 863-647-3000
Web: www.imperialswanlakeland.com

Indian Creek Hotel 2727 Indian Creek Dr Miami Beach FL 33140 305-531-2727 531-5651
Web: www.thefreehand.com

Indiana Memorial Union Board
900 E Seventh St Rm 270 Bloomington IN 47405 812-855-4682
Web: www.imu.indiana.edu

Indigo Inn 1 Maiden Ln Charleston SC 29401 843-577-5900
TF: 800-845-7639 ■ *Web:* www.indigoinn.com

Ingleside Inn 200 W Ramon Rd Palm Springs CA 92264 760-325-0046
TF: 800-772-6655 ■ *Web:* www.inglesideinn.com

Inhance Corp 609 Eighth St Fort Madison IA 52627 319-372-4920

Inlet Tower Suites 1200 L St Anchorage AK 99501 907-276-0110 258-4914
TF: 800-544-0786 ■ *Web:* www.inlettower.com

Inn & Spa at Loretto 211 Old Santa Fe Trl Santa Fe NM 87501 505-988-5531 984-7968
TF: 800-727-5531 ■ *Web:* www.destinationhotels.com/inn-at-loretto

Inn Above Tide, The 30 El Portal Sausalito CA 94965 415-332-9535
TF: 800-893-8433 ■ *Web:* innabovetide.com

Inn at Camachee Harbor
201 Yacht Club Dr Saint Augustine FL 32084 904-825-0003 825-0048
TF: 800-688-5379 ■ *Web:* www.camacheeinn.com

Inn at Gig Harbor 3211 56th St NW Gig Harbor WA 98335 253-858-1111 851-5402
TF: 800-795-9980 ■ *Web:* www.innatgigharbor.com

Inn at Harbour Town
7 Lighthouse Ln Hilton Head Island SC 29928 843-363-8100
TF Resv: 800-732-7463

Inn at Henderson's Wharf 1000 Fell St Baltimore MD 21231 410-522-7777
Web: www.hendersonswharf.com

Inn at Lambertville Station
11 Bridge St Lambertville NJ 08530 609-397-4400
Web: www.lambertvillestation.com

Inn at Langley 400 First St PO Box 835 Langley WA 98260 360-221-3033 221-3033
TF: 800-843-3779 ■ *Web:* www.innatlangley.com

Inn at Little Washington
Middle & Main St PO Box 300 Washington VA 22747 540-675-3800 675-3100
Web: www.theinnatlittlewashington.com

Inn at Longshore 260 Compo Rd S Westport CT 06880 203-226-3316
Web: www.innatlongshore.com

Inn at Montchanin Village
528 Montchanin Rd Montchanin DE 19710 302-888-2133 691-0198
TF: 800-269-2473 ■ *Web:* www.montchanin.com

Inn at Montpelier, The 147 Main St Montpelier VT 05602 802-223-2727 223-0722
Web: www.innatmontpelier.com

Inn at Morro Bay 60 State Pk Rd Morro Bay CA 93442 805-772-5651 772-4779
TF: 800-321-9566 ■ *Web:* www.innatmorrobay.com

Inn at Mystic 3 Williams Ave PO Box 526 Mystic CT 06355 860-536-9604
Web: www.innatmystic.com

Inn at National Hall 100 W Putnam Ave Greenwich CT 06830 203-221-1351
Web: www.innatnationalhall.com

Inn at Nichols Village
1101 Northern Blvd Clarks Summit PA 18411 570-587-1135 586-7140
Web: www.nicholsvillage.com

Inn at Otter Crest 301 Otter Crest Loop Otter Rock OR 97369 541-765-2111
TF: 800-452-2101 ■ *Web:* www.innatottercrest.com

Inn at Oyster Point
425 Marina Blvd South San Francisco CA 94080 650-737-7633
Web: www.innatoysterpoint.com

Inn at Pelican Bay 800 Vanderbilt Beach Rd Naples FL 34108 239-597-8777 597-8012
TF: 800-597-8770 ■ *Web:* www.innatpelicanbay.com

Inn at Perry Cabin 308 Watkins Ln Saint Michaels MD 21663 410-745-2200 745-3348
TF: 800-722-2949 ■ *Web:* belmond.com/inn-at-perry-cabin-st-michaels

Inn at Queen Anne 505 First Ave N Seattle WA 98109 206-282-7357
Web: www.innatqueenanne.com

Inn at Reading, The 1040 N Pk Rd Wyomissing PA 19610 610-372-7811 372-4545
TF: 800-383-9713 ■ *Web:* www.innatreading.com

Inn at Saint John 939 Congress St Portland ME 04102 207-773-6481
TF: 800-636-9127 ■ *Web:* www.innatstjohn.com

Inn at Saint Mary's 53993 US Hwy 31-33 N South Bend IN 46637 574-232-4000
Web: www.innatsaintmarys.com

Inn at Sawmill Farm, The
7 Crosstown Rd PO Box 2210 West Dover VT 05356 802-464-8131
Web: www.theinnatsawmillfarm.com

Inn at Spanish Head 4009 SW Hwy 101 Lincoln City OR 97367 541-996-2161 996-4089
TF: 800-452-8127 ■ *Web:* www.spanishhead.com

Inn at Tallgrass, The 2280 N Tara Cir Wichita KS 67226 316-684-3466
Web: www.theinnattallgrass.com

Inn at the Market 86 Pine St Seattle WA 98101 206-443-3600
TF: 800-446-4484 ■ *Web:* www.innatthemarket.com

Inn At The Quay 900 Quayside Dr New Westminster BC V3M6G1 604-520-1776 520-5645
TF: 800-663-2001 ■ *Web:* www.innatwestminsterquay.com

Inn at Union Square 440 Post St San Francisco CA 94102 415-397-3510 989-0529
TF: 800-288-4346 ■ *Web:* www.greystonehotels.com

Name / Address	City	State	Zip	Phone	Fax
Inn at, The Tides, The 800 Coast Hwy 1	Bodega Bay	CA	94923	707-875-2751	875-2669
TF: 800-541-7788 ■ *Web:* www.innatthetides.com					
Inn by the Lake 3300 Lk Tahoe Blvd	South Lake Tahoe	CA	96150	530-542-0330	
TF: 800-877-1466 ■ *Web:* www.innbythelake.com					
Inn of Chicago Magnificent Mile 162 E Ohio St	Chicago	IL	60611	312-787-3100	
Web: www.innofchicago.com					
Inn of Long Beach 185 Atlantic Ave	Long Beach	CA	90802	562-435-3791	436-7510
TF: 800-230-7500 ■ *Web:* www.innoflongbeach.com					
Inn of the Anasazi 113 Washington Ave	Santa Fe	NM	87501	505-988-3030	988-3277
TF: 888-767-3966 ■ *Web:* www.rosewoodhotels.com					
Inn of the Governors 101 W Alameda St	Santa Fe	NM	87501	505-982-4333	989-9149
TF: 800-234-4534 ■ *Web:* www.innofthegovernors.com					
Inn on Biltmore Estate 1 Antler Hill Rd	Asheville	NC	28803	828-225-1600	225-6185
TF: 800-411-3812 ■ *Web:* www.biltmore.com					
Inn on Fifth 699 Fifth Ave S	Naples	FL	34102	239-403-8777	403-8778
TF: 888-403-8778 ■ *Web:* innonfifth.com					
Inn on Gitche Gumee 8517 Congdon Blvd	Duluth	MN	55804	218-525-4979	
TF: 800-317-4979 ■ *Web:* www.innongitchegumee.com					
Inn on Lake Superior 350 Canal Pk Dr	Duluth	MN	55802	218-726-1111	727-3976
TF: 888-668-4352 ■ *Web:* www.theinnonlakesuperior.com					
Inn on the Alameda 303 E Alameda St	Santa Fe	NM	87501	505-984-2121	
TF: 888-984-2121 ■ *Web:* www.innonthealameda.com					
Inn on the Creek 295 N Millward Ave	Jackson	WY	83001	307-739-1565	
Web: bedandbreakfast.com					
Inn on the Paseo 630 Paseo de Peralta	Santa Fe	NM	87501	505-984-8200	
TF: 855-984-8200 ■ *Web:* www.innonthepaseo.com					
Inns at Mill Falls 312 Daniel Webster Hwy	Meredith	NH	03253	800-622-6455	279-6797*
**Fax Area Code:* 603 ■ *TF:* 800-622-6455 ■ *Web:* www.millfalls.com					
Inns of America Suites 755 Raintree Dr	Carlsbad	CA	92011	760-438-6661	
Web: hotelringingbell.com					
InnSuites Hospitality Trust InnSuites Hotels & Suites 475 N Granada Ave	Tucson	AZ	85701	520-622-0923	
TF: 800-842-4242 ■ *Web:* www.innsuites.com					
InnSuites Hotel Tempe/Phoenix Airport 1651 W Baseline Rd	Tempe	AZ	85283	480-897-7900	491-1008
TF: 800-841-4242 ■ *Web:* www.innsuites.com/tempe-hotel.html					
InnSuites Hotel Tucson City Ctr 475 N Granada Ave	Tucson	AZ	85701	520-622-3000	
Web: www.innsuites.com/tucson_citycenter					
InterContinental Hotels Group 3315 Peachtree Rd NE	Atlanta	GA	30326	404-946-9000	946-9001
Web: www.ihg.com					
Crowne Plaza Hotels & Resorts 3 Ravinia Dr Ste 2900	Atlanta	GA	30346	770-604-2000	
Web: ihg.com					
Holiday Inn Hotels & Resorts 3 Ravinia Dr Ste 100	Atlanta	GA	30346	770-604-2000	604-5403
TF: 800-725-8232 ■ *Web:* www.ihgplc.com					
Hotel Indigo 3 Ravinia Dr Ste 100	Atlanta	GA	30346	770-604-2000	604-5403
TF: 800-334-5194 ■ *Web:* www.ihgplc.com					
Staybridge Suites 3 Ravinia Dr Ste 100	Atlanta	GA	30346	770-604-2000	604-5403
TF: 800-465-4329 ■ *Web:* www.ihgplc.com					
InterMountain Management LLC 2390 Tower Dr	Monroe	LA	71201	318-325-5561	
Web: www.intermountainhotels.com					
International Hotel 20 Second Ave SW	Rochester	MN	55902	800-940-6811	285-2767*
**Fax Area Code:* 507 ■ *TF:* 800-940-6811 ■ *Web:* www.towersatkahlergrand.com					
International Hotel of Calgary 220 Fourth Ave SW	Calgary	AB	T2P0H5	403-265-9600	
Web: internationalhotel.ca					
International House Hotel 221 Camp St	New Orleans	LA	70130	504-553-9550	553-9560
TF: 800-633-5770 ■ *Web:* www.ihhotel.com					
Interstate Hotels & Resorts Inc 4501 N Fairfax Dr	Arlington	VA	22203	703-387-3100	
Web: www.interstatehotels.com					
Iroquois New York 49 W 44th St	New York City	NY	10036	212-840-3080	
TF: 800-332-7220 ■ *Web:* www.iroquoisny.com					
Island Hotel, The 690 Newport Ctr Dr	Newport Beach	CA	92660	949-759-0808	759-0568
TF: 866-554-4620 ■ *Web:* www.islandhotel.com					
Jack London Inn 444 Embarcadero W	Oakland	CA	94607	510-444-2032	
TF: 800-549-8780 ■ *Web:* www.jacklondoninn.com					
Jackson Hole Lodge 420 W Broadway PO Box 1805	Jackson	WY	83001	307-733-2992	739-2144
TF: 800-604-9404 ■ *Web:* www.jacksonholelodge.com					
Jailhouse Inn 13 Marlborough St	Newport	RI	02840	401-847-4638	
Web: www.jailhouse.com					
James Chicago, The 55 E Ontario	Chicago	IL	60611	312-337-1000	337-7217
TF: 888-526-3778 ■ *Web:* www.jameshotels.com					
James Gettys Hotel 27 Chambersburg St	Gettysburg	PA	17325	717-337-1334	334-2103
TF: 888-900-5275 ■ *Web:* www.jamesgettyshotel.com					
Jameson Inns					
Jameson Inns 115 Ann Denard Dr	Washington	GA	30673	706-678-7925	
TF: 800-526-3766 ■ *Web:* www.jamesoninns.com					
Janus Hotels & Resorts Inc 2300 Corporate Blvd NW Ste 232	Boca Raton	FL	33431	561-997-2325	997-5331
Web: www.janushotels.com					
Jared Coffin House 29 Broad St	Nantucket	MA	02554	508-228-2400	228-8549
TF Cust Svc: 800-248-2405 ■ *Web:* www.jaredcoffinhouse.com					
JC Resorts LLC 533 Coast Blvd S	La Jolla	CA	92037	858-605-2700	
Web: www.jcresorts.com					
Jefferson Hotel 101 W Franklin St	Richmond	VA	23220	804-788-8000	225-0334
TF: 800-424-8014 ■ *Web:* jeffersonhotel.com					
JHM Hotels Inc 60 Pointe Cir	Greenville	SC	29615	864-232-9944	248-1600*
**Fax:* PR ■ *Web:* www.jhmhotels.com					
John Q Hammons Hotel Management LLC 300 S John Q Hammons Pkwy #900	Springfield	MO	65806	417-864-4300	873-3540
Web: www.jqhhotels.com					
Joie de Vivre Hospitality Inc 530 Bush St Ste 501	San Francisco	CA	94108	415-835-0300	835-0317
Web: www.jdvhotels.com					
Jolly Hotel Madison Towers 22 E 38th St	New York	NY	10016	212-802-0600	447-0747
TF Resv: 888-726-0528 ■ *Web:* www.jollymadison.com					
Jolly Roger Inn 640 W Katella Ave	Anaheim	CA	92802	714-782-7500	
TF: 888-296-5986 ■ *Web:* www.jollyrogerhotel.com					
Jorgenson's Inn & Suites 1714 11th Ave	Helena	MT	59601	406-442-1770	449-0155
Web: www.jorgensonsinn.com					
Kahala Mandarin Oriental Hotel Hawaii Resort 5000 Kahala Ave	Honolulu	HI	96816	808-739-8888	739-8800
TF: 800-367-2525 ■ *Web:* www.kahalaresort.com					
Kawada Hotel 200 S Hill St	Los Angeles	CA	90012	213-621-4455	687-4455
TF: 800-752-9232 ■ *Web:* www.kawadahotel.com					
Kawailoa Development Company LP 1571 Poipu Rd Ste 307 PO Box 369	Koloa	HI	96756	808-742-6300	742-7197
Web: www.kawailoa.com					
Kellogg Hotel & Conference Ctr 219 S Harrison Rd Michigan State University Campus	East Lansing	MI	48824	517-432-4000	353-1872
TF: 800-875-5090 ■ *Web:* kelloggcenter.com					
Kelly Inns Ltd 3205 W Sencore Dr	Sioux Falls	SD	57107	605-965-1440	965-1450
Web: www.kellyinns.com					
Kensington Court Ann Arbor 610 Hilton Blvd	Ann Arbor	MI	48108	734-761-7800	761-1040
TF Orders: 800-344-7829 ■ *Web:* www.kcourtaa.com					
Kensington Park Hotel 450 Post St	San Francisco	CA	94102	415-788-6400	
TF: 800-553-1900 ■ *Web:* www.kensingtonparkhotel.com					
Kensington Riverside Inn 1126 Memorial Dr NW	Calgary	AB	T2N3E3	403-228-4442	228-9608
TF: 877-313-3733 ■ *Web:* www.kensingtonriversideinn.com					
Kent, The 1131 Collins Ave	Miami Beach	FL	33139	305-604-5068	
Web: www.thekenthotel.com					
Keswick Hall 701 Club Dr	Keswick	VA	22947	434-979-3440	977-4171
TF: 888-778-2565 ■ *Web:* www.keswick.com					
Key Lime Inn 725 Truman Ave	Key West	FL	33040	305-294-5229	294-9623
TF: 800-549-4430 ■ *Web:* www.historickeywestinns.com					
Keystone Lodge & Spa 22010 US Hwy 6	Keystone	CO	80435	970-496-3000	
Web: keystoneresort.com					
Killington Grand Resort Hotel & Conference Ctr 4763 Killington Rd	Killington	VT	05751	802-422-5001	
TF: 800-621-6867 ■ *Web:* www.killington.com					
Kimball Terrace Inn 10 Huntington Rd	Northeast Harbor	ME	04662	207-276-3383	
TF: 800-454-6225 ■ *Web:* www.kimballterraceinn.com					
Kimberly Hotel 145 E 50th St	New York	NY	10022	212-755-0400	355-4318
TF: 800-683-0400 ■ *Web:* www.kimberlyhotel.com					
Kimpton Hotel & Restaurant Group 422 SW Broadway	Portland	OR	97205	503-228-1212	228-3598
TF: 800-263-2305 ■ *Web:* www.hotelvintage-portland.com					
Kimpton Hotel & Restaurant Group LLC 222 Kearny St Ste 200	San Francisco	CA	94108	415-397-5572	296-8031
TF: 800-546-7866 ■ *Web:* www.kimptonhotels.com					
Kimpton Hotel & Restaurant Group, LLC 10050 S DeAnza Blvd	Cupertino	CA	95014	415-397-5572	
TF: 800-499-1408 ■ *Web:* www.kimptonhotels.com/boutique-hotels-in-san-francisco					
King Kamehameha's Kona Beach Hotel 75-5660 Palani Rd	Kailua-Kona	HI	96740	808-329-2911	329-4602
TF: 800-367-2111 ■ *Web:* www.konabeachhotel.com					
King Pacific Lodge 255 W First St	North Vancouver	BC	V7M3G8	604-987-5452	
TF: 855-825-9378					
Kings Island Resort & Conference Ctr 5691 Kings Island Dr	Mason	OH	45040	513-398-0115	
Kinseth Hotel Corp 2 Quail Creek Cir	North Liberty	IA	52317	319-626-5600	
Web: www.kinseth.com					
Kinzie Hotel 20 W Kinzie St	Chicago	IL	60654	312-395-9000	
TF: 877-262-5341 ■ *Web:* kinziehotel.com					
Kitano New York 66 Pk Ave E 38th St	New York	NY	10016	212-885-7000	885-7100
TF: 800-548-2666 ■ *Web:* www.kitano.com					
Knickerbocker on, The Lake, The 1028 E Juneau Ave	Milwaukee	WI	53202	414-276-8500	276-3668
Web: www.knickerbockeronthelake.com					
Knob Hill Inn 960 N Main St PO Box 1327	Ketchum	ID	83340	208-726-8010	
TF: 800-526-8010 ■ *Web:* www.knobhillinn.com					
Koko Inn 5201 Ave Q	Lubbock	TX	79412	806-747-2591	747-2591
Kona Kai Resort 1551 Shelter Island Dr	San Diego	CA	92106	619-221-8000	
TF: 800-566-2524 ■ *Web:* www.resortkonakai.com					
L' Appartement Hotel 455 Sherbrooke W	Montreal	QC	H3A1B7	514-284-3634	287-1431
TF: 800-363-3010 ■ *Web:* www.appartementhotel.com					
L'Enfant Plaza Hotel 480 L'Enfant Plaza SW	Washington	DC	20024	202-484-1000	646-4456
Web: www.lenfantplazahotel.com					
L'Ermitage Beverly Hills Hotel 9291 Burton Way	Beverly Hills	CA	90210	310-278-3344	278-8247
TF: 877-235-7582 ■ *Web:* www.viceroyhotelsandresorts.com					
L'Hotel du Vieux-Quebec 1190 St Jean St	Quebec	QC	G1R1S6	418-692-1850	
TF: 800-361-7787 ■ *Web:* www.hvq.com					
L'Hotel Quebec 3115 des Hotels Ave	Sainte-Foy	QC	G1W3Z6	418-658-5120	658-4504
TF: 800-567-5276 ■ *Web:* www.hotelsjaro.com					
La Colombe D'Or Inn 3410 Montrose Blvd	Houston	TX	77006	713-469-4750	524-8923
Web: www.lacolombedor.com					
La Fonda 100 E San Francisco St	Santa Fe	NM	87501	505-982-5511	988-2952
TF: 800-523-5002 ■ *Web:* www.lafondasantafe.com					
La Pensione Hotel 606 W Date St	San Diego	CA	92101	619-236-8000	236-8088
TF: 800-232-4683 ■ *Web:* www.lapensionehotel.com					
La Posada Hotel & Suites 1000 Zaragoza St	Laredo	TX	78040	956-722-1701	
TF Resv: 800-444-2099 ■ *Web:* www.laposada.com					
La Quinta Inn & Suites Secaucus Meadowlands 350 Lighting Way	Secaucus	NJ	07094	201-863-8700	863-6209
TF General: 800-753-3757 ■ *Web:* www.lq.com/en/findandbook/hotel-details.7719.html					
La Valencia Hotel 1132 Prospect St	La Jolla	CA	92037	858-454-0771	456-3921
Web: www.lavalencia.com					
Lafayette Hotel 600 St Charles Ave	New Orleans	LA	70130	504-524-4441	
TF: 800-366-2743 ■ *Web:* www.lafayettehotelneworleans.com					
Lafayette Hotel 101 Front St	Marietta	OH	45750	740-373-5522	
TF: 800-331-9336 ■ *Web:* www.lafayettehotel.com					
Lafayette Hotel & Suites San Diego 2223 El Cajon Blvd	San Diego	CA	92104	619-296-2101	296-0512
TF: 800-468-3531 ■ *Web:* www.lafayettehotelsd.com					
Lafayette Park Hotel 3287 Mt Diablo Blvd	Lafayette	CA	94549	925-283-3700	284-1621
TF: 855-382-8632 ■ *Web:* www.lafayetteparkhotel.com					

Phone | Fax

Lake Louise Inn 210 Village Rd PO Box 209 ... Lake Louise AB T0L1E0 403-522-3791 522-2018
TF: 800-661-9237 ■ *Web:* www.lakelouiseinn.com

Lake Lure Inn & Spa, The 2771 Memorial Hwy ... Lake Lure NC 28746 828-625-2526
TF: 888-434-4970 ■ *Web:* www.lakelure.com

Lake Meritt, The 1800 Madison St ... Oakland CA 94612 510-903-3600
Web: www.thelakemerritt.com

Lake Placid Lodge 144 Lodge Way ... Lake Placid NY 12946 518-523-2700 523-1124
TF: 877-523-2700 ■ *Web:* www.lakeplacidlodge.com

Lakeside Inn 100 N Alexander St ... Mount Dora FL 32757 352-383-4101 385-1615
TF: 800-556-5016 ■ *Web:* www.lakeside-inn.com

Lakeview on the Lake 8696 E Lake Rd ... Erie PA 16511 814-899-6948
TF: 888-558-8439 ■ *Web:* www.lakeviewerie.com

Lakewoods Resort & Lodge 21540 County Hwy M ... Cable WI 54821 715-794-2561
Web: lakewoodsresort.com

Lamothe House Hotel 621 Esplanade Ave ... New Orleans LA 70116 800-535-7815 302-2019*
**Fax Area Code:* 504 ■ *TF:* 800-535-7815 ■ *Web:* www.frenchquarterguesthouses.com

Lamp Post Inn 2424 E Stadium Blvd ... Ann Arbor MI 48104 734-971-8000 971-7483
Web: www.lamppostinn.com

Lamplighter Inn & Suites South
1772 S Glenstone Ave ... Springfield MO 65804 417-882-1113
Web: www.lamplighter-sgf.com

Lancaster Hotel 701 Texas St ... Houston TX 77002 713-228-9500 223-4528
TF: 800-231-0336 ■ *Web:* www.thelancaster.com

Landmark Inn 230 N Front St ... Marquette MI 49855 906-228-2580 228-5676
TF General: 888-752-6362 ■ *Web:* www.thelandmarkinn.com

Langdon Hall Country House Hotel & Spa
1 Langdon Dr ... Cambridge ON N3H4R8 519-740-2100 740-8161
TF: 800-268-1898 ■ *Web:* www.langdonhall.ca

Langham Boston, The 250 Franklin St ... Boston MA 02110 617-451-1900 423-2844
TF: 800-791-7781 ■ *Web:* www.langhamhotels.com

Lantern Lodge Motor Inn 411 N College St ... Myerstown PA 17067 717-866-6536 866-8857
TF: 800-262-5564 ■ *Web:* www.thelanternlodge.com

LaPlaya Resort & Suites
2500 N Atlantic Ave ... Daytona Beach FL 32118 386-672-0990
TF: 800-224-5052 ■ *Web:* laplayadaytona.com

Larkspur Hotels & Restaurants Inc
550 W Hamilton Ave ... Campbell CA 95008 408-364-1514
Web: www.larkspurhotels.com

Las Vegas Sands Corp 3355 Las Vegas Blvd S ... Las Vegas NV 89109 702-414-1000 414-4884
NYSE: LVS ■ *Web:* www.sands.com

LaSalle Hotel 120 S Main St ... Bryan TX 77803 979-822-2000 779-4343
Web: www.lasalle-hotel.com

LaSalle Hotel Properties
3 Bethesda Metro Ctr Ste 1200 ... Bethesda MD 20814 301-941-1500 941-1553
NYSE: LHO ■ *Web:* www.lasallehotels.com

Latham Hotel, The 135 S 17th St ... Philadelphia PA 19103 215-563-7474 568-0110
TF: 877-528-4261

Laurel Inn 444 Presidio Ave ... San Francisco CA 94115 415-346-7431
TF: 800-552-8735 ■
Web: jdvhotels.com/hotels/california/san-francisco-hotels/laurel-inn

Laurel Lodge Enterprises Inc 1909 Harper Rd ... Beckley WV 25801 304-255-0228
Web: lleinc.com

Le Chamois 4557 Blackcomb Way ... Whistler BC V0N1B4 604-932-8700
TF: 866-944-7853 ■ *Web:* www.lechamoiswhistler.com

Le Meridian 20 Sidney St ... Cambridge MA 02139 617-577-0200 494-8366
TF: 800-543-4300 ■ *Web:* starwoodhotels.com

Le Meridien Chambers Minneapolis
901 Hennepin Ave ... Minneapolis MN 55403 612-767-6900 767-6801
TF General: 877-782-0116 ■ *Web:* www.lemeridienchambers.com

Le M,ridien Dallas, The Stoneleigh
2927 Maple Ave ... Dallas TX 75201 214-871-7111
TF: 888-625-4988 ■ *Web:* lemeridiendallasstoneleigh.com

Le Merigot - A JW Marriott Beach Hotel & Spa
1740 Ocean Ave ... Santa Monica CA 90401 310-395-9700 395-9200
TF: 888-539-7899 ■ *Web:* www.marriott.com

Le Montrose Suite Hotel
900 Hammond St ... West Hollywood CA 90069 310-855-1115 657-9192
TF: 800-776-0666 ■ *Web:* www.lemontrose.com

Le Nouvel Montreal Hotel & Spa
1740 Rene-Levesque Blvd W ... Montreal QC H3H1R3 514-931-8841 931-5581
TF: 800-363-6063 ■ *Web:* www.lenouvelhotel.com

Le Parc Suite Hotel 733 NW Knoll Dr ... West Hollywood CA 90069 877-591-9556 659-7812*
**Fax Area Code:* 310 ■ *TF Resv:* 800-578-4837 ■ *Web:* www.leparcsuites.com

Le Pavillon Hotel 833 Poydras St ... New Orleans LA 70112 504-581-3111 620-4130
Web: www.lepavillon.com

Le Port-Royal Hotel & Suites 144 St Pierre St ... Quebec QC G1K8N8 418-692-2777 692-2778
TF: 866-417-2777 ■ *Web:* www.leportroyal.com

Le Richelieu Hotel 1234 Chartres St ... New Orleans LA 70116 504-529-2492 524-8179
TF: 800-535-9653 ■ *Web:* www.lerichelieuhotel.com

Le Saint Sulpice 414 Rue St Sulpice ... Montreal QC H2Y2V5 514-288-1000 288-0077
TF General: 877-785-7423 ■ *Web:* www.lesaintsulpice.com

Leisure Hotels LLC
Leisure Hotel Corp
5000 W 95th St Ste 100 ... Prairie Village KS 66207 913-905-1460
Web: www.leisurehotel.com

Leisure Sports Inc
7077 Koll Ctr Pkwy Ste 110 ... Pleasanton CA 94566 925-600-1966 643-7950*
**Fax Area Code:* 949 ■ *TF:* 888-239-0930 ■ *Web:* clubsports.com

Leland, The 400 Bagley St ... Detroit MI 48226 313-962-2300
Web: theleland.net

Lenox Hotel 61 Exeter St ... Boston MA 02116 617-536-5300 267-1237
TF: 800-225-7676 ■ *Web:* www.lenoxhotel.com

Lenox Hotel & Suites 140 N St ... Buffalo NY 14201 716-884-1700
Web: www.lenoxhotelandsuites.com

Leola Village Inn & Suites 38 Deborah Dr ... Leola PA 17540 717-656-7002 656-7648
TF: 877-669-5094 ■ *Web:* www.theinnatleolavillage.com

Les Mars Hotel 27 N St ... Healdsburg CA 95448 707-433-4211 433-4611
Web: www.hotellesmars.com

Les Suites Hotel Ottawa 130 Besserer St ... Ottawa ON K1N9M9 613-232-2000 232-1242
TF: 866-682-0879 ■ *Web:* www.les-suites.com

Lexington Downtown Hotel & Conference Center
369 W Vine St ... Lexington KY 40507 859-231-9000
Web: www.lexingtondowntownhotel.com

Phone | Fax

Lexington Hotel-George Washington Inn & Conference Ctr
500 Merrimac Trl ... Williamsburg VA 23185 757-259-5500

Library Hotel 299 Madison Ave ... New York NY 10017 212-983-4500 499-9099
TF: 877-793-7323 ■ *Web:* www.libraryhotel.com

Lighthouse Club Hotel 201 60th St ... Ocean City MD 21842 410-524-5400
TF: 888-371-5400 ■ *Web:* fagers.com

Lighthouse Lodge & Suites
1150 Lighthouse Ave ... Pacific Grove CA 93950 800-858-1249 655-4922*
**Fax Area Code:* 831 ■ *TF:* 800-858-1249 ■ *Web:* www.lighthouselodgecottages.com

Linden Row Inn 100 E Franklin St ... Richmond VA 23219 804-783-7000 648-7504
TF: 800-348-7424 ■ *Web:* www.lindenrowinn.com

Listel Hotel, The 1300 Robson St ... Vancouver BC V6E1C5 604-684-8461 684-7092
TF: 800-663-5491 ■ *Web:* www.thelistelhotel.com

Litchfield Plantation
24 Ave of the Oaks ... Pawleys Island SC 29585 843-543-3146
Web: www.litchfieldplantation.net

Little America Hotel & Resort Cheyenne
2800 W Lincolnway ... Cheyenne WY 82009 307-775-8400 775-8425
TF: 800-445-6945 ■ *Web:* www.cheyenne.littleamerica.com

Little America Hotel & Towers Salt Lake City
555 S Main St ... Salt Lake City UT 84101 801-258-6568 596-5911
TF: 800-453-9450 ■ *Web:* www.littleamerica.com

Little America Hotel Flagstaff
2515 E Butler Ave ... Flagstaff AZ 86004 928-779-7900 779-7983
TF: 800-352-4386 ■ *Web:* flagstaff.littleamerica.com

Little America Hotels & Resorts
500 S Main St ... Salt Lake City UT 84101 801-596-5700
TF: 800-281-7899 ■ *Web:* www.littleamerica.com

Little Nell, The 675 E Durant Ave ... Aspen CO 81611 970-920-4600
TF: 888-843-6355 ■ *Web:* www.thelittlenell.com

Lodge & Spa at Cordillera
2205 Cordillera Way ... Edwards CO 81632 970-926-2200 926-2486
TF: 800-877-3529 ■ *Web:* www.cordilleralodge.com

Lodge At Breckenridge, The
112 Overlook Dr ... Breckenridge CO 80424 970-453-9300
TF: 800-736-1607 ■ *Web:* www.thelodgeatbreckenridge.com

Lodge at the Mountain Village
1415 Lowell Ave ... Park City UT 84060 435-649-0800
TF: 800-453-1360 ■ *Web:* visitparkcity.com

Lodge on the Desert 306 N Alvernon Way ... Tucson AZ 85711 520-320-2000 327-5834
TF: 877-498-6776 ■ *Web:* www.lodgeonthedesert.com

LodgeWorks LP 8100 E 22nd St Bldg 500 ... Wichita KS 67226 316-681-5100 681-0905
Web: www.lodgeworks.com

Lodgian Inc 2002 Summit Blvd Ste 300 ... Atlanta GA 30319 404-364-9400 812-3102
NYSE: LGN

Lodging Hospitality Management Corp
111 W Port Plz Ste 500 ... St Louis MO 63146 314-434-9500
Web: www.lhmc.com

Lofts Hotel & Suites 55 E Nationwide Blvd ... Columbus OH 43215 614-461-2663 461-2630
TF General: 877-902-9022 ■ *Web:* www.55lofts.com

Lombardy Hotel, The 111 E Fifth St ... New York NY 10022 212-753-8600
Web: www.lombardyhotel.com

Lone Oak Lodge 2221 N Fremont St ... Monterey CA 93940 831-372-4924 372-4985
TF General: 800-283-5663 ■ *Web:* www.loneoaklodge.com

Long House Alaskan Hotel 4335 Wisconsin St ... Anchorage AK 99517 907-243-2133
TF: 888-243-2133 ■ *Web:* www.longhousehotel.com

Long Island Hotels LLC
1757 Veteran'S Memorial Hwy Ste 22 ... Islandia NY 11749 631-234-9700
Web: www.longislandhotelsllc.com

Longhouse Hospitality 4770 S Atlanta Rd ... Smyrna GA 30080 404-351-9700
Web: www.longhousehospitality.com

Lonsdale Quay Hotel
123 Carrie Cates Ct ... North Vancouver BC V7M3K7 604-986-6111 986-8782
TF: 800-836-6111 ■ *Web:* www.lonsdalequayhotel.com

Lookout Inn 6901 Lookout Rd ... Boulder CO 80301 877-234-4779 530-4573*
**Fax Area Code:* 303 ■ *TF:* 800-530-1513

Lord Elgin Hotel 100 Elgin St ... Ottawa ON K1P5K8 613-235-3333 235-3223
TF: 800-267-4298 ■ *Web:* www.lordelginhotel.ca

Lord Nelson Hotel & Suites 1515 S Pk St ... Halifax NS B3J2L2 902-423-6331 423-7148
TF: 800-565-2020 ■ *Web:* www.lordnelsonhotel.com

Lord Stanley Suites on the Park
1889 Alberni St ... Vancouver BC V6G3G7 604-688-9299 688-9297
TF: 888-767-7829 ■ *Web:* www.lordstanley.com

Los Angeles Athletic Club
431 W Seventh St ... Los Angeles CA 90014 213-625-2211 689-1194
TF: 800-421-8777 ■ *Web:* www.laac.com

Los Willows Inn & Spa
530 Stewart Canyon Rd ... Fallbrook CA 92028 760-731-9400
Web: www.loswillows.com

Lowell Inn 102 N Second St ... Stillwater MN 55082 651-439-1100
Web: www.lowellinn.com

LQ Management LLC 909 Hidden Ridge Ste 600 ... Irving TX 75038 214-492-6600
TF: 800-753-3757 ■ *Web:* www.lq.com
La Quinta Inn & Suites
909 Hidden Ridge Ste 600 ... Irving TX 75038 214-492-6600
TF: 800-753-3757 ■ *Web:* www.lq.com

Luxe Hotel Rodeo Drive 360 N Rodeo Dr ... Beverly Hills CA 90210 310-273-0300 859-8730
TF: 800-468-3541 ■ *Web:* www.luxehotels.com

Luxe Hotel Sunset Blvd 11461 Sunset Blvd ... Los Angeles CA 90049 310-476-6571 471-6310
TF: 800-468-3541 ■ *Web:* www.luxehotels.com

Luxe Worldwide Hotels
11461 W Sunset Blvd ... Los Angeles CA 90049 310-440-3090 440-0821
TF: 888-336-3745 ■ *Web:* www.luxehotels.com

Luxor Hotel & Casino 3900 Las Vegas Blvd S ... Las Vegas NV 89119 702-262-4000 262-4404
TF Resv: 800-288-1000 ■ *Web:* www.luxor.com

LXR Luxury Resorts 501 E Camino Real Blvd ... Boca Raton FL 33432 561-447-5300
Web: www.luxuryresorts.com

MacArthur Place 29 E MacArthur St ... Sonoma CA 95476 707-938-2929 933-9833
TF: 800-722-1866 ■ *Web:* www.macarthurplace.com

Madison Concourse Hotel & Governors Club
1 W Dayton St ... Madison WI 53703 608-257-6000 257-5280
TF: 800-356-8293 ■ *Web:* www.concoursehotel.com

Madison Hotel 79 Madison Ave ... Memphis TN 38103 901-333-1200 333-1210
Web: www.madisonhotelmemphis.com

Name / Address	City	State	Zip	Phone	Fax
Madison Hotel, The 1 Convent Rd *TF:* 800-526-0729 ■ *Web:* www.themadisonhotel.com	Morristown	NJ	07960	973-285-1800	540-8566
Madison the - A Loews Hotel 667 Madison Ave *TF:* 800-235-6397 ■ *Web:* www.loewshotels.com	New York	NY	10065	212-521-2000	
Magic Castle Hotel 7025 Franklin Ave *Web:* magiccastlehotel.com	Los Angeles	CA	90028	323-851-0800	
Magnolia Hotel & Spa, The 623 Courtney St *TF:* 877-624-6654 ■ *Web:* www.magnoliahotel.com	Victoria	BC	V8W1B8	250-381-0999	381-0988
Magnolia Hotel Dallas 1401 Commerce St *TF:* 888-915-1110 ■ *Web:* www.magnoliahotels.com	Dallas	TX	75201	214-915-6500	253-0053
Magnolia Hotel Denver 818 17th St *TF:* 888-915-1110 ■ *Web:* www.magnoliahotels.com	Denver	CO	80202	303-607-9000	607-0101
Magnolia Hotel Houston 1100 Texas Ave *TF:* 888-915-1110 ■ *Web:* www.magnoliahotels.com	Houston	TX	77002	713-221-0011	221-0022
Main Street Station Hotel & Casino 200 N Main St *TF:* 800-713-8933 ■ *Web:* www.mainstreetcasino.com	Las Vegas	NV	89101	702-387-1896	
Maison 140 Beverly Hills 140 Lasky Dr *Web:* maison140.com	Beverly Hills	CA	90212	310-281-4000	281-4001
Maison Dupuy Hotel 1001 Toulouse St *TF:* 800-535-9177 ■ *Web:* www.maisondupuy.com	New Orleans	LA	70112	504-586-8000	
Majestic Hotel 528 W Brompton *Web:* www.majestic-chicago.com	Chicago	IL	60657	773-404-3499	
Malaga Inn 359 Church St *TF:* 800-235-1586 ■ *Web:* malagainn.com	Mobile	AL	36602	251-438-4701	438-4701
Malibu Beach Inn 22878 Pacific Coast Hwy *Web:* www.malibubeachinn.com	Malibu	CA	90265	310-456-6444	456-1499
Mandarin Oriental Hotel Group (USA) 345 California St Ste 1250 *TF:* 800-526-6566 ■ *Web:* www.mandarinoriental.com	San Francisco	CA	94104	415-772-8800	782-3778
Mandarin Oriental Miami 500 Brickell Key Dr *TF:* 800-526-6566 ■ *Web:* www.mandarinoriental.com	Miami	FL	33131	305-913-8288	913-8300
Mandarin Oriental New York 80 Columbus Cir *TF:* 866-801-8880 ■ *Web:* www.mandarinoriental.com	New York	NY	10023	212-805-8800	805-8888
Mandarin Oriental San Francisco 222 Sansome St *TF:* 800-526-6566 ■ *Web:* www.mandarinoriental.com	San Francisco	CA	94104	415-276-9888	433-0289
Mandarin Oriental Washington DC 1330 Maryland Ave SW *TF:* 888-888-1778 ■ *Web:* www.mandarinoriental.com	Washington	DC	20024	202-554-8588	554-8999
Manor House Inn 106 W St *TF:* 800-437-0088 ■ *Web:* www.barharbormanorhouse.com	Bar Harbor	ME	04609	207-288-3759	
Mansfield, The 12 W 44th St *TF:* 800-255-5167 ■ *Web:* www.mansfieldhotel.com	New York	NY	10036	212-277-8700	764-4477
Mansion on Forsyth Park 700 Drayton St *TF:* 888-213-3671 ■ *Web:* www.mansiononforsythpark.com	Savannah	GA	31401	912-238-5158	238-5146
Mansion View Inn & Suites 529 S Fourth St *TF:* 800-252-1083 ■ *Web:* www.mansionview.com	Springfield	IL	62701	217-544-7411	
Maple Hill Farm Bed & Breakfast Inn 11 Inn Rd *TF:* 800-622-2708 ■ *Web:* www.maplebb.com	Hallowell	ME	04347	207-622-2708	622-0655
Marcus Corp 100 E Wisconsin Ave *NYSE: MCS* ■ *Web:* www.marcuscorp.com	Milwaukee	WI	53202	414-905-1000	
Marcus Hotels & Resorts 100 E Wisconsin Ave Ste 1950 *Web:* www.marcushotels.com	Milwaukee	WI	53202	414-905-1200	905-2250
Marina Del Mar Resort & Marina 527 Caribbean Dr *Web:* www.marinadelmarkeylargo.com	Key Largo	FL	33037	305-451-4107	451-1891
Marina Inn at Grande Dunes 8121 Amalfi Pl *TF Resv:* 877-913-1333 ■ *Web:* www.marinainnatgrandedunes.com	Myrtle Beach	SC	29572	843-913-1333	913-1334
Marine Surf Waikiki Hotel 364 Seaside Ave *Web:* www.waikikiview.com	Honolulu	HI	96815	808-779-3261	
Mariner's Point Resort of Cape Cod 425 Grand Ave *Web:* www.marinerspointresort.com	Falmouth	MA	02540	508-457-0300	
Mark Spencer Hotel 409 SW 11th Ave *TF:* 800-548-3934 ■ *Web:* www.markspencer.com	Portland	OR	97205	503-224-3293	223-7848
Mark Twain Hotel 225 NE Adams St *TF:* 866-325-6351 ■ *Web:* www.marktwainhotel.com	Peoria	IL	61602	309-676-3600	636-6118
Market Pavilion Hotel 225 E Bay St *TF:* 877-440-2250 ■ *Web:* www.marketpavilion.com	Charleston	SC	29401	843-723-0500	723-4320
Maron Hotel & Suites 42 Lk Ave Ext *Web:* www.maronhotel.com	Danbury	CT	06811	203-791-2200	
MarQueen Hotel 600 Queen Anne Ave N *Web:* www.marqueen.com	Seattle	WA	98109	206-282-7407	283-1499
Marquesa Hotel 600 Fleming St *TF:* 800-869-4631 ■ *Web:* www.marquesa.com	Key West	FL	33040	305-292-1919	294-2121
Marquette Hotel, The 710 Marquette Ave *TF:* 800-328-4782 ■ *Web:* www.marquettehotel.com	Minneapolis	MN	55402	612-333-4545	288-2188
Marriott Charleston Hotel 170 Lockwood Blvd *TF:* 888-236-2427 ■ *Web:* www.marriott.com	Charleston	SC	29403	843-723-3000	723-0276
Marriott Columbus 800 Front Ave *TF:* 800-455-9261 ■ *Web:* www.marriott.com	Columbus	GA	31901	706-324-1800	576-4413
Ritz-Carlton Hotel Co LLC 4445 Willard Ave Ste 800 *TF:* 800-241-3333 ■ *Web:* www.ritzcarlton.com	Chevy Chase	MD	20815	301-547-4700	
Martha Washington Hotel & Spa, The 150 W Main St *TF:* 888-999-8078 ■ *Web:* www.themartha.com	Abingdon	VA	24210	276-628-3161	628-8885
Maryland Inn 16 Church Cir *TF:* 800-847-8882 ■ *Web:* www.historicinnsofannapolis.com	Annapolis	MD	21401	410-263-2641	268-3613
Matrix Hotel 10640-100 Ave *TF:* 866-465-8150 ■ *Web:* www.matrixedmonton.com	Edmonton	AB	T5J3N8	780-429-2861	
Maumee Bay Lodge & Conference Ctr 1750 Pk Rd Ste 2 *TF:* 800-282-7275 ■ *Web:* www.maumeebaystateparklodge.com	Oregon	OH	43616	419-836-1466	836-2438
Mayfair Hotel & Spa 3000 Florida Ave *TF:* 800-433-4555 ■ *Web:* www.mayfairhotelandspa.com	Coconut Grove	FL	33133	305-441-0000	447-9173
Mayflower Inn 118 Woodbury Rd *TF:* 800-585-7198 ■ *Web:* gracehotels.com/mayflower	Washington	CT	06793	860-868-9466	868-1497
Mayflower Park Hotel 405 Olive Way *TF:* 800-426-5100 ■ *Web:* www.mayflowerpark.com	Seattle	WA	98101	206-623-8700	382-6996
Mayo Clinic 4500 San Pablo Rd *TF:* 888-255-4458 ■ *Web:* www.mayoclinic.org	Jacksonville	FL	32224	904-992-9992	
McCamly Plaza Hotel 50 Capital Ave SW *Web:* www.mccamlyplaza.com	Battle Creek	MI	49017	269-963-7050	
McKibbon Hotel Management Inc 5315 Avion Park Dr Ste 120 *Web:* www.mckibbonhotels.com	Tampa	FL	33607	813-241-2399	
McKinley Grand Hotel 320 Market Ave S *TF:* 844-378-9476 ■ *Web:* www.mckinleygrandhotel.com	Canton	OH	44702	330-454-5000	454-5494
McLure Hotel, The 1200 Market St	Wheeling	WI	26003	304-232-0300	233-1653
MCM Elegante Suites 4250 Ridgemont Dr *TF:* 888-897-9644 ■ *Web:* www.mcmelegantesuites.com	Abilene	TX	79606	325-698-1234	698-2771
Mediterranean Inn 425 Queen Anne Ave N *Web:* www.mediterranean-inn.com	Seattle	WA	98109	206-428-4700	
Meeting Street Inn 173 Meeting St *TF:* 800-842-8022 ■ *Web:* www.meetingstreetinn.com	Charleston	SC	29401	843-723-1882	
Mendocino Hotel & Garden Suites 45080 Main St *Web:* www.mendocinohotel.com	Mendocino	CA	95460	707-937-0511	
Menger Hotel 204 Alamo Plz *TF:* 800-345-9285 ■ *Web:* www.mengerhotel.com	San Antonio	TX	78205	210-223-4361	228-0022
Mercer Hotel 147 Mercer St *TF:* 888-918-6060 ■ *Web:* www.mercerhotel.com	New York	NY	10012	212-966-6060	965-3838
Meridian Plaza Resort 2310 N Ocean Blvd *TF:* 800-323-3011 ■ *Web:* www.meridianplaza.com	Myrtle Beach	SC	29577	843-626-4734	448-4569
Metropolitan Hotel Vancouver 645 Howe St *TF:* 800-667-2300 ■ *Web:* www.metropolitan.com/vanc	Vancouver	BC	V6C2Y9	604-687-1122	643-7267
Metterra Hotel on Whyte 10454 82nd Ave *TF:* 866-465-8150 ■ *Web:* www.metterra.com	Edmonton	AB	T6E4Z7	780-465-8150	465-8174
Meyer Crest Ltd 725 Folger Ave *Web:* www.meyercrest.com	Berkeley	CA	94710	510-845-1077	845-1544
Meyer Jabara Hotels 1601 Belvedere Rd Ste 407 S *TF:* 877-696-8671 ■ *Web:* www.meyerjabarahotels.com	West Palm Beach	FL	33406	561-689-6602	689-4363
Miami International Airport Hotel NW 20th St & Le Jeune Rd *TF:* 800-327-1276 ■ *Web:* usmia2.webhotel.microsdc.us	Miami	FL	33122	305-871-4100	871-0800
Midtown Hotel 220 Huntington Ave *TF:* 800-343-1177 ■ *Web:* www.midtownhotel.com	Boston	MA	02115	617-262-1000	262-8739
Mill Street Inn 75 Mill St *TF:* 800-392-1316 ■ *Web:* www.millstreetinn.com	Newport	RI	02840	401-849-9500	848-5131
Mill Valley Inn 165 Throckmorton Ave *TF:* 855-334-7946 ■ *Web:* www.marinhotels.com	Mill Valley	CA	94941	415-389-6608	389-5051
Mills House Hotel 115 Meeting St *TF:* 800-874-9600 ■ *Web:* www.millshouse.com	Charleston	SC	29401	843-577-2400	
Milner Hotel Boston 78 Charles St S *TF:* 877-645-6377 ■ *Web:* www.milner-hotels.com	Boston	MA	02116	617-426-6220	350-0360
Milner Hotels Inc 1538 Centre St *TF:* 877-645-6377 ■ *Web:* www.milner-hotels.com	Detroit	MI	48226	313-963-3950	962-0410
Minto Place Suite Hotel 185 Lyons St N *TF:* 800-267-3377 ■ *Web:* www.minto.com	Ottawa	ON	K1R7Y4	613-232-2200	232-6962
Mira Monte Inn & Suites 69 Mt Desert St **Fax Area Code: 207* ■ *TF:* 800-553-5109 ■ *Web:* www.miramonte.com	Bar Harbor	ME	04609	800-553-5109	288-3115*
Mirabeau Park Hotel 1100 N Sullivan Rd *TF:* 866-584-4674 ■ *Web:* www.mirabeauparkhotel.com	Spokane Valley	WA	99037	509-924-9000	922-4965
Mirbeau Inn & Spa 851 W Genesee St *TF:* 877-647-2328 ■ *Web:* www.mirbeau.com	Skaneateles	NY	13152	315-685-5006	
Mission Inn 3649 Mission Inn Ave *TF:* 800-843-7755 ■ *Web:* www.missioninn.com	Riverside	CA	92501	951-784-0300	683-1342
Misty Harbor & Barefoot Beach Resort 118 Weirs Rd *TF:* 800-336-4789 ■ *Web:* www.mistyharbor.com	Gilford	NH	03249	603-293-4500	
Miyako Hotel Los Angeles 328 E First St *TF:* 800-228-6596 ■ *Web:* www.miyakoinn.com	Los Angeles	CA	90012	213-617-2000	617-2700
MMI Hotel Group PO Box 320009 *Web:* mmihospitality.com	Jackson	MS	39232	601-936-3666	939-5685
MODA Hotel 900 Seymour St *TF:* 877-683-5522 ■ *Web:* www.modahotel.ca	Vancouver	BC	V6B3L9	604-683-4251	683-0611
Moderne Hotel, The 243 W 55th St *Web:* modernehotelnyc.com	New York	NY	10019	212-397-6767	397-8787
Mojave A Desert Resort 73721 Shadow Mtn Dr *TF Resv:* 800-391-1104 ■ *Web:* www.resortmojave.com	Palm Desert	CA	92260	760-346-6121	674-9072
Molly Pitcher Inn 88 Riverside Ave *TF:* 800-221-1372 ■ *Web:* www.mollypitcher-oysterpoint.com	Red Bank	NJ	07701	732-747-2500	
Monarch Hotel & Conference Ctr 12566 SE 93rd Ave *TF:* 800-492-8700 ■ *Web:* www.monarchhotel.cc	Clackamas	OR	97015	503-652-1515	652-7509
Mondrian Hotel 8440 Sunset Blvd *TF:* 800-525-8029 ■ *Web:* www.morganshotelgroup.com	West Hollywood	CA	90069	323-650-8999	650-5215
Monmouth Plantation 36 Melrose Ave *TF:* 800-828-4531 ■ *Web:* www.monmouthhistoricinn.com	Natchez	MS	39120	601-442-5852	446-7762
Monte Carlo Inn-Airport Suites 7035 Edwards Blvd *TF:* 800-363-6400 ■ *Web:* www.montecarloinns.com	Mississauga	ON	L5T2H8	905-564-8500	564-8400
Monterey Bay Inn 242 Cannery Row *TF:* 800-424-6242 ■ *Web:* www.montereybayinn.com	Monterey	CA	93940	831-373-6242	655-8174
Monterey Hotel 406 Alvarado St *TF:* 800-966-6490 ■ *Web:* www.montereyhotel.com	Monterey	CA	93940	831-375-3184	373-2899
Monterey Inn Resort & Conference Centre 2259 Prince of Wales Dr *TF:* 800-565-1311 ■ *Web:* ramadaottawa.com	Ottawa	ON	K2E6Z8	613-288-3500	226-5900
Monterey Plaza Hotel & Spa 400 Cannery Row *TF:* 800-334-3999 ■ *Web:* www.woodsidehotels.com	Monterey	CA	93940	831-646-1700	
Morgans Hotel 237 Madison Ave *TF:* 800-606-6090 ■ *Web:* www.morganshotelgroup.com	New York	NY	10016	212-686-0300	779-8352
Morgans Hotel Group Co 475 Tenth Ave *NASDAQ: MHGC* ■ **Fax Area Code: 305* ■ *TF:* 800-606-6090 ■ *Web:* www.morganshotelgroup.com	New York	NY	10018	212-277-4100	532-0099*

	City	State	Zip	Phone	Fax
Morris Inn 130 Morris Inn University of Notre Dame *Web:* www.morrisinn.nd.edu	Notre Dame	IN	46556	574-631-2000	631-2340
Morrison-Clark Historic Inn & Restaurant 1015 L St NW *TF:* 800-332-7898 ■ *Web:* www.morrisonclark.com	Washington	DC	20001	202-898-1200	
Mosaic Hotel 125 S Spalding Dr *TF:* 800-463-4466 ■ *Web:* www.mosaichotel.com	Beverly Hills	CA	90212	310-278-0303	
Mosser Hotel 54 Fourth St *TF:* 800-227-3804 ■ *Web:* www.themosser.com	San Francisco	CA	94103	415-986-4400	495-7653
Motel 6 Wichita 465 S Webb Rd *TF:* 800-466-8356 ■ *Web:* www.motel6.com	Wichita	KS	67207	316-684-6363	
Mount View Hotel & Spa 1457 Lincoln Ave *TF:* 800-816-6877 ■ *Web:* www.mountviewhotel.com	Calistoga	CA	94515	707-942-6877	942-6904
Mountain Haus 292 E Meadow Dr *TF:* 800-237-0922 ■ *Web:* www.mountainhaus.com	Vail	CO	81657	970-476-2434	476-3007
Mountain Lake Hotel 115 Hotel Cir *TF:* 800-346-3334 ■ *Web:* www.mtnlakelodge.com	Pembroke	VA	24136	540-626-7121	626-7172
Mountain Villas 9525 W Skyline Pkwy *TF:* 866-688-4552 ■ *Web:* www.mtvillas.com	Duluth	MN	55810	218-624-5784	
Movie Colony Hotel 726 N Indian Canyon Dr *Web:* www.moviecolonyhotel.com	Palm Springs	CA	92262	760-320-6340	320-1640
Muse, The 130 W 46th St *TF:* 877-692-6873 ■ *Web:* www.themusehotel.com	New York	NY	10036	212-485-2400	485-2789
Mutiny Hotel 2951 S Bayshore Dr *TF:* 888-868-8469 ■ *Web:* www.providentresorts.com	Miami	FL	33133	305-441-2100	441-2822
Napa River Inn 500 Main St *TF:* 877-251-8500 ■ *Web:* www.napariverinn.com	Napa	CA	94559	707-251-8500	251-8504
Nassau Inn, The 10 Palmer Sq *Web:* www.nassauinn.com	Princeton	NJ	08542	609-921-7500	921-9385
Nathan Hale Inn & Conference Ctr 855 Bolton Rd *Web:* www.nathanhaleinn.com	Storrs	CT	06268	860-427-7888	427-7850
National Hotel 1677 Collins Ave *TF:* 800-327-8370 ■ *Web:* www.nationalhotel.com	Miami Beach	FL	33139	305-532-2311	534-1426
Nativo Lodge Hotel 6000 Pan American Fwy NE *TF:* 888-628-4861 ■ *Web:* www.hhandr.com	Albuquerque	NM	87109	505-798-4300	798-4305
New Castle Hotels & Resorts 2 Corporate Dr *TF:* 800-321-2211 ■ *Web:* www.newcastlehotels.com	Shelton	CT	06484	203-925-8370	
New Haven Hotel 229 George St *TF:* 800-644-6835 ■ *Web:* www.newhavenhotel.com	New Haven	CT	06510	203-498-3100	498-0911
New Haven Premier Suites Hotel 3 Long Wharf Dr *Web:* newhavenvillagesuites.com	New Haven	CT	06511	203-777-5337	777-2808
New Otani Kaimana Beach Hotel 2863 Kalakaua Ave *TF:* 800-356-8264 ■ *Web:* www.kaimana.com	Honolulu	HI	96815	808-923-1555	922-9404
New York Marriott East Side 525 Lexington Ave *Web:* marriott.com	New York	NY	10017	212-755-4000	
New York Palace Hotel 455 Madison Ave *TF:* 800-697-2522 ■ *Web:* www.lottenypalace.com	New York	NY	10022	212-888-7000	303-6000
New York's Hotel Pennsylvania 401 Seventh Ave *TF:* 800-223-8585 ■ *Web:* www.hotelpenn.com/thehotel.html	New York	NY	10001	212-736-5000	502-8712
New Yorker Hotel 481 Eigth Ave *Web:* www.newyorkerhotel.com	New York	NY	10001	212-971-0101	629-6536
Newport Bay Club & Hotel 337 Thames St PO Box 1440 *Web:* www.newportbayclub.com	Newport	RI	02840	401-849-8600	846-6857
Newport Beach Hotel & Suites 1 Wave Ave *TF:* 800-655-1778 ■ *Web:* www.newportbeachhotelandsuites.com	Middletown	RI	02842	401-846-0310	847-2621
Newport Beachside Hotel & Resort 16701 Collins Ave *TF:* 800-327-5476 ■ *Web:* www.newportbeachsideresort.com	Miami Beach	FL	33160	305-949-1300	
Newport Harbor Corp 366 Thames St *Web:* www.newportharbor.com	Newport	RI	02840	401-848-7010	
Newport Harbor Hotel & Marina 49 America's Cup Ave *TF:* 800-955-2558 ■ *Web:* www.newporthotel.com	Newport	RI	02840	401-847-9000	849-6380
Nine Zero Hotel 90 Tremont St *TF:* 866-906-9090 ■ *Web:* www.ninezero.com	Boston	MA	02108	617-772-5800	772-5810
Nittany Lion Inn 200 W Pk Ave *TF:* 800-233-7505 ■ *Web:* www.pshs.psu.edu	State College	PA	16803	814-865-8500	865-8501
Noble House Hotels & Resorts 600 Sixth St S *Web:* www.noblehousehotels.com	Kirkland	WA	98033	425-827-8737	827-6707
North Forty Resort LLC 3765 Mt Hwy 40 W *Web:* northfortyresort.com	Columbia Falls	MT	59912	406-862-7740	
Northland Properties Corp 310 1755 W Broadway *Web:* www.northland.ca	Vancouver	BC	V6J4S5	604-730-6610	
Norwood Hotel 112 Marion St *TF:* 888-888-1878 ■ *Web:* www.norwood-hotel.com	Winnipeg	MB	R2H0T1	204-233-4475	231-1910
O Henry Hotel 624 Green Vly Rd *TF:* 800-965-8259 ■ *Web:* www.ohenryhotel.com	Greensboro	NC	27408	336-854-2000	854-2223
O Hotel 819 S Flower St *Web:* ohotelgroup.com	Los Angeles	CA	90017	213-623-9904	
O'Neill Hotels & Resorts Management Ltd 1690-401 W Georgia St *Web:* www.oneillhotels.com	Vancouver	BC	V6B5AT	604-684-0444	
Oberlin Inn 10 E College St *Web:* thehotelatoberlin.com	Oberlin	OH	44074	440-775-7001	775-6356
Ocean Five Hotel 436 Ocean Dr *Web:* www.oceanfive.com	Miami Beach	FL	33139	305-532-7093	
Ocean Forest Plaza 5523 N Ocean Blvd *TF General:* 800-845-6701 ■ *Web:* www.sandsresorts.com	Myrtle Beach	SC	29577	843-497-0044	692-5234
Ocean Key Resort 424 Atlantic Ave *TF:* 800-955-9700 ■ *Web:* www.vsaresorts.com	Virginia Beach	VA	23451	757-425-2200	
Ocean Park Hotels Inc 710 Fiero Ln Ste 14	San Luis Obispo	CA	93401	805-544-0812	
Ocean Pointe Suites at Key Largo 500 Burton Dr *TF:* 800-882-9464 ■ *Web:* www.providentresorts.com/ocean-pointe-suites	Tavernier	FL	33070	305-853-3000	853-3007
Ocean Reef Club 35 Ocean Reef Dr Ste 200 *TF:* 888-422-9944 ■ *Web:* www.oceanreef.com	Key Largo	FL	33037	305-367-2611	
Ocean Resort Hotel Waikiki 175 Paoakalani Ave *TF:* 877-367-1912 ■ *Web:* www.castleresorts.com	Honolulu	HI	96815	808-922-3861	922-3773
Ocean Sky Hotel & Resort 4060 Galt Ocean Dr *TF:* 800-678-9022 ■ *Web:* www.oceanskyresort.com	Fort Lauderdale	FL	33308	954-565-6611	564-7730
Ocean Walk Resort 300 N Atlantic *TF:* 888-743-2561 ■ *Web:* www.wyndhamoceanwalk.com	Daytona Beach	FL	32118	386-323-4800	
Oceancliff Hotel & Resort 65 Ridge Rd *Web:* www.newportexperience.com	Newport	RI	02840	401-841-8868	
OHANA Waikiki Beachcomber Hotel 2300 Kalakaua Ave **Fax Area Code:* 800 ■ *TF:* 866-956-4262 ■ *Web:* www.outrigger.com	Honolulu	HI	96815	808-922-4646	622-4852*
Old City House Inn 115 Cordova St *Web:* www.oldcityhouse.com	Saint Augustine	FL	32084	904-826-0113	
Old Mill Toronto 21 Old Mill Rd *TF:* 866-653-6455 ■ *Web:* oldmilltoronto.com	Toronto	ON	M8X1G5	416-236-2641	236-2749
Olde Mill Inn 5835 Dixie Hwy *Web:* oldemillinnofclarkston.com	Clarkston	MI	48346	248-623-0300	
Omaha Downtown Lodging Investors II LLC 1005 Dodge St	Omaha	NE	68102	402-341-4400	
Omni Hotels 4001 Maple Ave *TF:* 800-843-6664 ■ *Web:* www.omnihotels.com	Dallas	TX	75219	402-952-6664	
Omni La Mansion del Rio 112 College St *TF:* 800-292-7300 ■ *Web:* www.omnihotels.com	San Antonio	TX	78205	210-518-1000	226-0389
One Washington Cir Hotel 1 Washington Cir NW *TF:* 800-424-9671 ■ *Web:* www.thecirclehotel.com	Washington	DC	20037	202-872-1680	
Onyx Hotel 155 Portland St *TF:* 866-660-6699 ■ *Web:* www.onyxhotel.com	Boston	MA	02114	617-557-9955	557-0005
Opus Hotel 322 Davie St *TF:* 866-642-6787 ■ *Web:* vancouver.opushotel.com	Vancouver	BC	V6B5Z6	866-642-6787	
Orchard Garden Hotel 466 Bush St *TF:* 888-717-2881 ■ *Web:* www.theorchardgardenhotel.com	San Francisco	CA	94108	415-399-9807	393-9917
Orchard Hotel 665 Bush St *TF:* 888-717-2881 ■ *Web:* www.theorchardhotel.com	San Francisco	CA	94108	415-362-8878	362-8088
Orchards Hotel, The 222 Adams Rd *Web:* www.orchardshotel.com	Williamstown	MA	01267	413-458-9611	458-3273
Orchards Inn of Sedona 254 Hwy N 89 A **Fax Area Code:* 928 ■ *TF:* 855-474-7719 ■ *Web:* www.orchardsinn.com	Sedona	AZ	86336	855-474-7719	282-5710*
Orient Express Hotels Inc 1155 Ave of the Americas *NYSE:* OEH ■ *TF:* 800-237-1236 ■ *Web:* belmond.com	New York	NY	10036	212-302-5055	302-5203
Orlando, The 8384 W Third St *TF:* 800-624-6835 ■ *Web:* www.theorlando.com	Los Angeles	CA	90048	323-658-6600	653-3464
Orleans Las Vegas Hotel & Casino 4500 W Tropicana Ave *TF:* 800-675-3267 ■ *Web:* www.orleanscasino.com	Las Vegas	NV	89103	702-365-7111	
Outrigger Enterprises Group 2375 Kuhio Ave **Fax Area Code:* 303 ■ *TF:* 800-462-6262 ■ *Web:* www.outrigger.com	Honolulu	HI	96815	808-921-6941	369-9403*
Outrigger Hotels & Resorts 2375 Kuhio Ave **Fax:* Sales ■ *TF:* 800-688-7444 ■ *Web:* www.outrigger.com	Honolulu	HI	96815	808-921-6941	926-4368*
Outrigger Waikiki on the Beach 2335 Kalakaua Ave *TF:* 800-688-7444 ■ *Web:* www.outrigger.com	Honolulu	HI	96815	808-923-0711	921-9749
Overlook Lodge PO Box 351 *Web:* www.visitbearmountain.com	Bear Mountain	NY	10911	845-786-2731	786-2543
Owyhee Plaza Hotel 1109 Main St *Web:* www.owyheeplaza.com	Boise	ID	83702	208-343-4611	
Oxford Hotel 1600 17th St *TF:* 800-228-5838 ■ *Web:* www.theoxfordhotel.com	Denver	CO	80202	303-628-5400	
Oxford Palace 745 S Oxford Ave *Web:* www.oxfordhotel.com	Los Angeles	CA	90005	213-389-8000	
Oxford Suites Boise 1426 S Entertainment Ave *TF General:* 888-322-8001 ■ *Web:* www.oxfordsuitesboise.com	Boise	ID	83709	208-322-8000	322-8002
Oxford Suites Spokane Valley 15015 E Indiana Ave *TF:* 866-668-7848 ■ *Web:* www.oxfordsuitesspokanevalley.com	Spokane Valley	WA	99216	509-847-1000	847-1001
Oxford Suites Spokane-Downtown 115 W N River Dr *TF:* 800-774-1877 ■ *Web:* www.oxfordsuitesspokane.com	Spokane	WA	99201	509-353-9000	353-9164
Oyster Point Hotel, The 146 Bodman Pl *TF:* 800-345-3484 ■ *Web:* www.theoysterpointhotel.com	Red Bank	NJ	07701	732-530-8200	747-1875
Pace's Lodging Corp 4265 45th St S Ste 200 *Web:* propertyresourcesgroup.com	Fargo	ND	58104	701-281-9500	281-9501
Pacific Beach Hotel 2490 Kalakaua Ave *TF:* 800-367-6060 ■ *Web:* www.pacificbeachhotel.com	Honolulu	HI	96815	808-922-1233	922-0129
Pacific Edge Hotel 647 S Coast Hwy *Web:* www.pacificedgehotel.com	Laguna Beach	CA	92651	949-494-8566	
Pacific Inn 600 Marina Dr *TF:* 866-466-0300 ■ *Web:* thepacificinn.com	Seal Beach	CA	90740	562-493-7501	596-3448
Pacific Inn Resort & Conference Centre 1160 King George Hwy *TF:* 800-667-2248 ■ *Web:* www.pacificinn.com	Surrey	BC	V4A4Z2	604-535-1432	531-6979
Pacific Shores Inn 4802 Mission Blvd *TF:* 888-478-7829 ■ *Web:* www.pacificshoresinn.com	San Diego	CA	92109	858-483-6300	483-9276
Pacific Terrace Hotel 610 Diamond St *TF:* 800-344-3370 ■ *Web:* www.pacificterrace.com	San Diego	CA	92109	858-581-3500	274-2534
Painted Buffalo Inn 400 W Broadway PO Box 2547 *TF:* 800-288-3866 ■ *Web:* www.paintedbuffaloinn.com	Jackson	WY	83001	307-733-4340	
Palace Casino 158 Howard Ave *TF:* 800-725-2239 ■ *Web:* www.palacecasinoresort.com	Biloxi	MS	39530	228-432-8888	
Palace Hotel 2 New Montgomery St *TF:* 866-716-8136 ■ *Web:* www.sfpalace.com	San Francisco	CA	94105	415-512-1111	543-0671
Palace Station Hotel & Casino 2411 W Sahara Ave *TF Resv:* 800-634-3101 ■ *Web:* palacestation.sclv.com	Las Vegas	NV	89102	702-367-2411	

Phone | Fax

Palmer House Hilton 17 E Monroe St ... Chicago IL 60603 312-726-7500 922-5240
TF: 800-445-8667 ■ *Web:* www.hiltonchicagohotel.com

Palmer Inn, The 3499 US 1 ... Princeton NJ 08540 609-452-2500
Web: www.palmerinnprinceton.com

Palos Verdes Inn
1700 S Pacific Coast Hwy ... Redondo Beach CA 90277 310-316-4211

Pan Pacific Hotel Vancouver
999 Canada Pl Ste 300 ... Vancouver BC V6C3B5 604-662-8111 685-8690
TF: 800-937-1515 ■ *Web:* www.panpacific.com

Pan Pacific Seattle 2125 Terry Ave ... Seattle WA 98121 206-264-8111 654-5049
TF: 877-324-4856 ■ *Web:* www.panpacific.com

Pantages Hotel 200 Victoria St ... Toronto ON M5B1V8 416-362-1777
TF: 866-852-1777 ■ *Web:* www.pantageshotel.com

Par-A-Dice Hotel 21 Blackjack Blvd ... East Peoria IL 61611 309-699-7711
TF: 800-727-2342 ■ *Web:* www.paradicecasino.com

Paragon Hotel Corp
5333 N Seventh St Ste A-100 ... Phoenix AZ 85014 602-248-0811
Web: www.paragonhotels.com

Paramount Hotel 724 Pine St ... Seattle WA 98101 206-292-9500 292-8610
TF: 877-821-2011 ■ *Web:* www.paramounthotelseattle.com

Paramount Hotel 235 W 46th St ... New York NY 10036 212-764-5500 354-5237
TF Resv: 855-234-2074 ■ *Web:* www.nycparamount.com

Paramount Hotel 808 SW Taylor St ... Portland OR 97205 503-223-9900 223-7900
TF: 855-215-0160 ■ *Web:* www.portlandparamount.com

Paramount Hotel Group 710 Rt 46 E Ste 206 ... Fairfield NJ 07004 973-882-0505 882-0043
Web: www.paramounthotelgroup.com

Parc 55 Hotel 55 Cyril Magnin St ... San Francisco CA 94102 415-392-8000
Web: www.parc55hotel.com

Paris Las Vegas 3655 Las Vegas Blvd S ... Las Vegas NV 89109 800-522-4700
TF: 800-342-7724 ■ *Web:* www.totalrewards.com

Park Central Hotel 1010 Houston St ... Fort Worth TX 76102 817-336-2011 336-2011

Park Central New York 870 Seventh Ave ... New York NY 10019 212-247-8000 707-5557
Web: www.parkcentralny.com

Park Central, The 640 Ocean Dr ... Miami Beach FL 33139 305-538-1611 534-7520
Web: www.theparkcentral.com

Park Plaza Hotel Oakland 150 Hegenberger Rd ... Oakland CA 94621 510-635-5300 635-9661
Web: www.redlion.com

Park Shore Waikiki Hotel 2586 Kalakaua Ave ... Honolulu HI 96815 808-954-7426 923-0311
TF: 866-536-7975 ■ *Web:* www.parkshorewaikiki.com

Park South Hotel 124 E 28th St ... New York NY 10016 212-448-0888 448-0811
TF: 800-315-4642 ■ *Web:* www.parksouthhotel.com

Park Vista Resort Hotel
705 Cherokee OrchaRd Rd PO Box 30 ... Gatlinburg TN 37738 865-436-9211 430-7533
TF Sales: 800-227-5622 ■ *Web:* www.parkvista.com

Parkway Inn 125 N Jackson St PO Box 494 ... Jackson WY 83001 800-247-8390
TF: 800-247-8390 ■ *Web:* www.parkwayinn.com

Paso Robles Inn 1103 Spring St ... Paso Robles CA 93446 805-238-2660 238-4707
TF: 800-676-1713 ■ *Web:* www.pasoroblesinn.com

Peabody Memphis 149 Union Ave ... Memphis TN 38103 901-529-4000
TF: 800-732-2639 ■ *Web:* www.peabodymemphis.com

Peabody Orlando 5118 Park Ave Ste 245 ... Memphis TN 38117 901-762-5400 762-5464

Peachtree Hotel Group LLC
2 Premier Plaza 5607 Glenridge Dr Ste 430 ... Atlanta GA 30342 404-497-4111
Web: www.peachtreehotelgroup.com

Peacock Suites 1745 S Anaheim Blvd ... Anaheim CA 92805 714-535-8255 535-8914
TF: 800-522-6401 ■ *Web:* www.shellhospitality.com

Pearl Hotel, The 1410 Rosecrans St ... San Diego CA 92106 619-226-6100 226-6161
Web: www.thepearlsd.com

Peery Hotel 110 West 300 South ... Salt Lake City UT 84101 801-521-4300
TF: 800-331-0073 ■ *Web:* www.peeryhotel.com

Pegasus International Hotel 501 Southard St ... Key West FL 33040 305-294-9323 294-4741
TF: 800-397-8148 ■ *Web:* www.pegasuskeywest.com

Pelham Hotel 444 Common St ... New Orleans LA 70130 504-522-4444
TF: 888-856-4486 ■ *Web:* www.thepelhamhotel.com

Pelican Grand Beach Resort Condominium Associati
2000 N Ocean Blvd ... Fort Lauderdale FL 33305 954-568-9431
TF: 800-525-6232 ■ *Web:* pelicanbeach.com

Penguin Hotel 1418 Ocean Dr ... Miami Beach FL 33139 305-534-9334
TF: 800-499-7964

Peninsula Beverly Hills
9882 S Santa Monica Blvd ... Beverly Hills CA 90212 310-551-2888 788-2319
TF: 800-462-7899 ■ *Web:* www.peninsula.com

Peninsula Chicago 108 E Superior St ... Chicago IL 60611 312-337-2888 751-2888
TF: 866-288-8889 ■ *Web:* www.peninsula.com

Peninsula New York 700 Fifth Ave ... New York NY 10019 212-956-2888 903-3949
TF: 800-262-9467 ■ *Web:* www.peninsula.com

Penn's View Hotel 14 N Front St ... Philadelphia PA 19106 215-922-7600 922-7642
TF: 800-331-7634 ■ *Web:* www.pennsviewhotel.com

Peppermill Hotel & Casino 2707 S Virginia St ... Reno NV 89502 775-826-2121 689-7041
TF: 800-648-6992 ■ *Web:* www.peppermillreno.com

Perfect North Slopes Inc
19074 Perfect Pl Ln ... Lawrenceburg IN 47025 812-537-3754
Web: perfectnorth.com

Petite Auberge 863 Bush St ... San Francisco CA 94108 415-928-6000
Web: jdvhotels.com/hotels/california

Pfister Hotel 424 E Wisconsin Ave ... Milwaukee WI 53202 414-273-8222 273-5025
TF: 800-558-8222 ■ *Web:* www.thepfisterhotel.com

Phillips Beach Plaza Hotel
1301 Atlantic Ave ... Ocean City MD 21842 410-289-9121
TF: 800-492-5834 ■ *Web:* www.beachplazaoc.com

Phoenix Grand Hotel Salem 201 Liberty St SE ... Salem OR 97301 503-540-7800 540-7830
TF: 877-540-7800 ■ *Web:* www.grandhotelsalem.com

Phoenix Hotel 601 Eddy St ... San Francisco CA 94109 415-776-1380
TF: 800-248-9466 ■
Web: jdvhotels.com/hotels/california/san-francisco-hotels/phoenix-hotel

Phoenix Park Hotel 520 N Capitol St ... Washington DC 20001 202-638-6900 393-3236
TF: 800-824-5419 ■ *Web:* www.phoenixparkhotel.com

Piccadilly Inn Airport 5115 E McKinley Ave ... Fresno CA 93727 559-375-7760
Web: www.piccadillyinn.com

Piccadilly Inn Express 2305 W Shaw Ave ... Fresno CA 93711 559-348-5520
Web: www.piccadillyinn.com

Pier 5 Hotel 711 Eastern Ave ... Baltimore MD 21202 410-539-2000 783-1787
TF: 866-583-4162 ■ *Web:* www.harbormagic.com

Pierpont Inn 550 Sanjon Rd ... Ventura CA 93001 805-643-6144 643-9167
Web: www.pierpontinn.com

Pierre, The 2 E 61st St ... New York NY 10065 212-838-8000 940-8109
Web: www.tajhotels.com

Pillar Hotels & Resorts LP
6031 Connection Dr Ste 500 ... Irving TX 75039 972-830-3100
Web: pillarhotels.com

Pillars Hotel at New River Sound
111 N Birch Rd ... Fort Lauderdale FL 33304 954-467-9639 763-2845
TF: 800-241-3333 ■ *Web:* www.pillarshotel.com

Pine Crest Inn 85 Pine Crest Ln ... Tryon NC 28782 828-859-9135
TF: 800-633-3001 ■ *Web:* www.pinecrestinn.com

Pines Lodge 141 Scott Hill Rd ... Beaver Creek CO 81620 970-429-5043 845-7809
TF Resv: 800-859-8242 ■ *Web:* www.pineslodge.rockresorts.com

Pisgah Inn PO Box 749 ... Waynesville NC 28786 828-235-8228
Web: www.pisgahinn.com

Pitcher Inn 275 Main St ... Warren VT 05674 802-496-6350
Web: www.pitcherinn.com

Place D'Armes Hotel 625 St Ann St ... New Orleans LA 70116 504-524-4531
TF: 800-366-2743 ■ *Web:* www.placedarmes.com

Place Louis Riel All-Suite Hotel
190 Smith St ... Winnipeg MB R3C1J8 204-947-6961 947-3029
TF: 800-665-0569 ■ *Web:* www.placelouisriel.com

Plains Hotel, The 1600 Central Ave ... Cheyenne WY 82001 307-638-3311
Web: www.theplainshotel.com

Plantation Inn of New England
295 Burnett Rd ... Chicopee MA 01020 413-592-8200 592-9671

Planters Inn 112 N Market St ... Charleston SC 29401 843-722-2345 577-2125
TF: 800-845-7082 ■ *Web:* www.plantersinn.com

Planters Inn 29 Abercorn St ... Savannah GA 31401 912-232-5678 232-8893
TF: 800-554-1187 ■ *Web:* www.plantersinnsavannah.com

Platinum Hotel 211 E Flamingo Rd ... Las Vegas NV 89169 702-365-5000
TF General: 877-211-9211 ■ *Web:* www.theplatinumhotel.com

Plaza Hotel & Casino 1 Main St PO Box 760 ... Las Vegas NV 89101 702-386-2110
TF: 800-634-6575 ■ *Web:* wwwplazahotelcasinocom

Plaza Inn 900 Medical Arts NE ... Albuquerque NM 87102 505-243-5693 843-6229

Plaza on the River Resort Club Hotel 121 W St ... Reno NV 89501 775-786-2200
TF: 800-628-5974 ■ *Web:* www.plazaresortclub.com

Plaza Square Motor Lodge
2255 Central Blvd ... Brownsville TX 78520 956-546-5104 548-0243

Plaza Suite Hotel Resort 620 S Peters St ... New Orleans LA 70130 800-770-6721 524-2135*
**Fax Area Code:* 504 ■ *TF:* 800-770-6721 ■ *Web:* www.plazaresort.com

Plaza Suites Silicon Valley
3100 Lakeside Dr ... Santa Clara CA 95054 408-748-9800
TF: 800-345-1554 ■ *Web:* www.theplazasuites.com

PLJ Restaurant 333 Fulton St ... San Francisco CA 94102 415-294-8925

Plump Jack's Squaw Valley Inn
1920 Squaw Vly Rd PO Box 2407 ... Olympic Valley CA 96146 530-583-1576 583-1734
TF: 800-323-7666 ■ *Web:* www.plumpjacksquawvalleyinn.com

Point Plaza Suites & Conference Hotel
950 J Clyde Morris Blvd ... Newport News VA 23601 757-599-4460 599-4336
TF: 800-841-1112 ■ *Web:* www.pointplazasuites.com

Pollard, The 2 N Broadway ... Red Lodge MT 59068 406-446-0001
Web: www.thepollard.com

Pontchartrain Hotel 2031 St Charles Ave ... New Orleans LA 70130 504-524-0581
TF: 800-708-6652 ■ *Web:* www.pontchartrainhotel.com

Port Ludlow Assoc LLC 70 Breaker Ln ... Port Ludlow WA 98365 360-437-2101
Web: portludlowresort.com

Port-O-Call Hotel 1510 Boardwalk ... Ocean City NJ 08226 609-399-8812
TF: 800-334-4546 ■ *Web:* www.portocallhotel.com

Portland Harbor Hotel 468 Fore St ... Portland ME 04101 207-775-9090 775-9990
TF: 888-798-9090 ■ *Web:* www.portlandharborhotel.com

Portland Regency Hotel 20 Milk St ... Portland ME 04101 207-774-4200 775-2150
TF: 800-727-3436 ■ *Web:* www.theregency.com

Portofino Hotel & Yacht Club
260 Portofino Way ... Redondo Beach CA 90277 310-379-8481 372-7329
TF: 800-468-4292 ■ *Web:* www.hotelportofino.com

Portofino Inn & Suites Anaheim
1831 S Harbor Blvd ... Anaheim CA 92802 714-782-7600 782-7619
TF Resv: 800-398-3963 ■ *Web:* www.portofinoinnanaheim.com

Portola Plaza Hotel 2 Portola Plaza ... Monterey CA 93940 831-649-4511 649-4511
TF: 888-222-5851 ■ *Web:* www.portolahotel.com

Post Hotel, The
200 Pipestone Rd PO Box 69 ... Lake Louise AB T0L1E0 403-522-3989 522-3966
TF: 800-661-1586 ■ *Web:* www.posthotel.com

Prairie Band Casino & Resort 12305 150th Rd ... Mayetta KS 66509 785-966-7777 966-7799
TF: 888-727-4946 ■ *Web:* www.prairieband.com

Prairie Hotel 700 Prairie Pk Ln ... Yelm WA 98597 360-458-8300 458-8301
Web: www.prairiehotel.com

Preferred Hotel Group
311 S Wacker Dr Ste 1900 ... Chicago IL 60606 312-913-0400 913-5124
Web: preferredhotels.com

Preferred Hotels & Resorts Worldwide Inc
311 S Wacker Dr Ste 1900 ... Chicago IL 60606 312-913-0400 913-5124
TF: 800-650-1281 ■ *Web:* preferredhotels.com

Sterling Hotels Corp 311 S Wacker Dr Ste 1900 ... Chicago IL 60606 312-913-0400 913-5124
Web: preferredhotels.com

Summit Hotels & Resorts
311 S Wacker Dr Ste 1900 ... Chicago IL 60606 312-913-0400 913-5124
TF: 800-650-1281 ■ *Web:* preferredhotels.com

Premier Hotel Times Square, The
133 W 44th St ... New York NY 10036 212-789-7670
Web: millenniumhotels.com

President Abraham Lincoln Hotel & Conference Ctr (PALHACC)
701 E Adams St ... Springfield IL 62701 217-544-8800 544-9607
TF: 855-610-8733 ■ *Web:* doubletree3.hilton.com

Prestige Harbourfront Resort & Convention Centre
251 Harbourfront Dr Ne ... Salmon Arm BC V1E2W7 250-833-5800
TF: 877-737-8443 ■ *Web:* prestigehotelsandresorts.com

Priced Rite Suites 2327 University Ave ... Green Bay WI 54302 920-469-2130
Web: www.pricedritesuites.com

Prince Conti Hotel 830 Conti St ... New Orleans LA 70112 504-529-4172
TF: 800-366-2743 ■ *Web:* www.princecontihotel.com

Phone Fax

Prince George Hotel, The 1725 Market St . . . . . . Halifax NS B3J3N9 902-425-1986
TF: 800-565-1567 ■ *Web:* www.princegeorgehotel.com

Princess Bayside Beach Hotel & Golf Ctr
4801 Coastal Hwy. . . . . . . Ocean City MD 21842 410-723-2900
TF General: 888-622-9743 ■ *Web:* www.princessbayside.com

Princess Royale Oceanfront Hotel & Conference Ctr
9100 Coastal Hwy. . . . . . . Ocean City MD 21842 410-524-7777 524-7787
TF: 800-476-9253 ■ *Web:* www.princessroyale.com

Priory, The 614 Pressley St . . . . . . Pittsburgh PA 15212 412-231-3338
Web: www.thepriory.com

Prism Hotels & Resorts
14800 Landmark Blvd Ste 800 . . . . . . Dallas TX 75254 214-987-9300
Web: www.prismhotels.com

Procaccianti Group, The 1140 Reservoir Ave. . . . . . Cranston RI 02920 401-946-4600

Prospector Hotel 375 Whittier St . . . . . . Juneau AK 99801 907-586-3737 586-1204
Web: www.prospectorhotel.com

Providence Biltmore Hotel 11 Dorrance St . . . . . . Providence RI 02903 800-294-7709
TF: 800-294-7709 ■ *Web:* www.providencebiltmore.com

Publick House Historic Resort
277 Main St Rt 131. . . . . . Sturbridge MA 01566 508-347-3313 347-1460
TF Cust Svc: 800-782-5425 ■ *Web:* www.publickhouse.com

Puffin Inn 4400 SpenaRd Rd . . . . . . Anchorage AK 99517 907-243-4044 248-6853
TF: 800-478-3346 ■ *Web:* puffininn.net

Q Hotel, The 560 Westport Rd. . . . . . Kansas City MO 64111 816-931-0001

Quail Run Lodge 1130 Bob Harman Rd. . . . . . Savannah GA 31408 912-964-1421
Web: www.quailrunlodge.com

Quaintance-Weaver Inc 324 W Wendover Ave . . . . . . Greensboro NC 27408 336-370-0966 370-0965
Web: www.qwrh.com

Quality Hotel-airport 7228 Wminster Hwy. . . . . . Richmond BC V6X1A1 604-244-3051
TF: 877-244-3051 ■ *Web:* qualityhotelvancouverairport.com

Quality Inn Flamingo 1300 N Stone Ave . . . . . . Tucson AZ 85705 520-770-1910 770-0750
Web: www.flamingohoteltucson.com

Quality Inn Halifax Airport Hotel
60 Sky Blvd Halifax International Airport . . . . . . Goffs NS B2T1K3 902-873-3000
TF: 800-667-3333 ■ *Web:* www.airporthotelhalifax.com

Quarterpath Inn & Suites 620 York St . . . . . . Williamsburg VA 23185 757-220-0964
Web: www.quarterpathinnandsuites.com

Quebec Inn 7175 Blvd Hamel Ouest. . . . . . Quebec QC G2G1B6 418-872-9831 872-1336
TF: 800-567-5276 ■ *Web:* www.hotelsjaro.com/quebecinn/index-en.aspx

Queen Anne Hotel 1590 Sutter St. . . . . . San Francisco CA 94109 415-441-2828 775-5212
TF: 800-227-3970 ■ *Web:* www.queenanne.com

Queen Kapiolani Hotel 150 Kapahulu Ave. . . . . . Honolulu HI 96815 808-922-1941
Web: www.queenkapiolani.com

Quimby House Inn 109 Cottage St . . . . . . Bar Harbor ME 04609 207-288-5811
TF: 800-344-5811 ■ *Web:* www.quimbyhouse.com

Quorum Hotels & Resorts
5429 Lyndon B Johnson Fwy #625 . . . . . . Dallas TX 75240 972-458-7265 991-5647
Web: www.quorumhotels.com

Rabbit Hill Inn
48 Lower Waterford Rd PO Box 55 . . . . . . Lower Waterford VT 05848 802-748-5168 748-8342
TF: 800-626-3215 ■ *Web:* www.rabbithillinn.com

Radisson Butler Blvd 4700 Salisbury Rd. . . . . . Jacksonville FL 32256 904-281-9700 281-1957
TF: 888-201-1718 ■ *Web:* www.radisson.com

Radisson Chicago-O'Hare Hotel
1450 E Touhy Ave. . . . . . Des Plaines IL 60018 847-296-8866 296-8268
TF: 888-201-1718 ■ *Web:* www.radisson.com

Radisson Hotel & Suites Fort Mc Murray
435 Gregoire Dr . . . . . . Fort Mcmurray AB T9H4K7 780-743-2400
Web: www.radissonfortmcmurray.com

Radisson Hotel Bloomington Mall of America
1700 American Blvd E . . . . . . Bloomington MN 55425 952-854-8700 854-8701
TF Resv: 800-967-9033 ■
Web: www.radisson.com/bloomington-hotel-mn-55425/mnblmmal

Radisson Hotel Gateway Seattle-Tacoma Airport
18118 International Blvd. . . . . . Seattle WA 98188 206-244-6666 244-6679
Web: www.radisson.com

Radisson Milwaukee North Shore
7065 N Port Washington Rd. . . . . . Milwaukee WI 53217 414-351-6960 351-5194
TF: 800-395-7046 ■ *Web:* www.radisson.com

Raffaello Hotel 201 E Delaware Pl . . . . . . Chicago IL 60611 312-943-5000 924-9158
TF: 800-916-4339 ■ *Web:* www.chicagoraffaello.com

Railroad Pass Hotel & Casino
2800 S Boulder Hwy. . . . . . Henderson NV 89002 702-294-5000 294-0092
TF: 800-654-0877 ■ *Web:* www.railroadpass.com

Ramada Middletown 425 E Main Rd . . . . . . Middletown RI 02842 401-846-3555 846-3666
TF: 800-854-9517 ■ *Web:* ramada.com

Ramada Plaza & Conference Ctr
4900 Sinclair Rd. . . . . . Columbus OH 43229 614-846-0300
TF: 800-272-6232 ■ *Web:* www.ramada.com

Ranch at Steamboat 1800 Ranch Rd. . . . . . Steamboat Springs CO 80487 970-879-3000
TF: 888-686-8075 ■ *Web:* www.ranch-steamboat.com

Ranch Inn 45 E Pearl St . . . . . . Jackson WY 83001 307-733-6363 733-0623
TF: 800-348-5599 ■ *Web:* www.ranchinn.com

Rancho Alegre Lodge
3600 S Pk Loop Rd PO Box 998. . . . . . Jackson WY 83001 307-733-7988
Web: www.ranchoalegre.com

Raphael Kansas City 325 Ward Pkwy . . . . . . Kansas City MO 64112 816-756-3800 802-2131
TF: 800-821-5343 ■ *Web:* www.raphaelkc.com

Red Jacket Beach Resort 39 Todd Rd . . . . . . South Yarmouth MA 02664 508-398-6941 398-1830
TF: 800-227-3263 ■ *Web:* www.redjacketresorts.com

Red Lion Hotels Corp 201 W N River Dr Ste 100. . . . . . Spokane WA 99201 800-733-5466 325-7324*
NYSE: RLH ■ *Fax Area Code: 509 ■ *TF Resv:* 800-733-5466 ■ *Web:* www.redlion.com

Red Lion Inn 30 Main St PO Box 954. . . . . . Stockbridge MA 01262 413-298-5545
Web: www.redlioninn.com

Red Rock Resort Spa & Casino
11011 W Charleston Blvd. . . . . . Las Vegas NV 89135 702-797-7777 797-7890
TF: 866-767-7773 ■ *Web:* redrock.sclv.com

Red Roof Inn 4271 Sidco Dr . . . . . . Nashville TN 37204 615-832-0093
Web: www.redroof.com

Red Roof Inn Monterey 2227 N Fremont St. . . . . . Monterey CA 93940 831-372-7586
Web: www.redroofinnmonterey.com

Red Roof Inn Nashville Airport
510 Claridge Dr . . . . . . Nashville TN 37214 615-872-0735
Web: redroof.com

Phone Fax

Redstone Inn 82 Redstone Blvd. . . . . . Redstone CO 81623 970-963-2526
Web: www.redstoneinn.thegilmorecollection.com

Redstone Inn & Suites 504 Bluff St. . . . . . Dubuque IA 52001 563-582-1894
Web: www.theredstoneinn.com

Regency Fairbanks Hotel 95 Tenth Ave . . . . . . Fairbanks AK 99701 907-459-2700
TF: 800-478-1320 ■ *Web:* www.regencyfairbankshotel.com

Regency House Hotel 140 Rt 23 N. . . . . . Pompton Plains NJ 07444 973-696-0900 696-0201
Web: www.regencyhousehotel.com

Regency Suites Calgary 610 Fourth Ave SW . . . . . . Calgary AB T2P0K1 403-231-1000
TF: 800-468-4044 ■ *Web:* www.regencycalgary.com

Regency Suites Hotel Midtown Atlanta
975 W Peachtree St . . . . . . Atlanta GA 30309 404-876-5003 817-7511
TF: 800-642-3629 ■ *Web:* www.regencysuites.com

Remington Hotel Corp
14185 Dallas Pkwy Ste 1150 . . . . . . Dallas TX 75254 972-980-2700 980-2705
Web: www.remingtonhotels.com

Remington Suite Hotel 220 Travis St . . . . . . Shreveport LA 71101 318-425-5000
TF: 800-444-6750 ■ *Web:* www.remingtonsuite.com

Residence & Conference Centre - Toronto
1760 Finch Ave E . . . . . . Toronto ON M2J5G3 416-491-8811 491-0486
TF: 877-225-8664 ■ *Web:* www.stayrcc.com

Residences on Georgia
101-1288 W Georgia St . . . . . . Vancouver BC V6E4R3 604-891-6101 891-6103
Web: www.respal.com

Rhett House Inn 1009 Craven St. . . . . . Beaufort SC 29902 843-524-9030
TF: 888-480-9530 ■ *Web:* www.rhetthouseinn.com

Richfield Hospitality Services
7600 E OrchaRd Rd Ste 230-S . . . . . . Greenwood Village CO 80111 303-220-2000
Web: www.richfield.com

Richmond, The 1757 Collins Ave . . . . . . Miami Beach FL 33139 305-538-2331 531-9021
TF: 855-627-3767 ■ *Web:* www.richmondhotel.com

Rittenhouse Hotel 210 W Rittenhouse Sq . . . . . . Philadelphia PA 19103 215-546-9000 732-3364
TF: 800-635-1042 ■ *Web:* www.rittenhousehotel.com

Ritz-Carlton Dallas 2121 McKinney Ave . . . . . . Dallas TX 75201 214-922-0200
TF Resv: 800-960-7082 ■ *Web:* www.ritzcarlton.com

Riu Hotel Florida Beach 3101 Collins Ave . . . . . . Miami FL 33140 305-673-5333 673-9335
TF: 888-666-8816 ■ *Web:* www.riu.com

River Inn 924 25th St NW. . . . . . Washington DC 20037 202-337-7600 337-6520
Web: www.theriverinn.com

River Street Inn 124 E Bay St . . . . . . Savannah GA 31401 912-234-6400 234-1478
Web: www.riverstreetinn.com

River Terrace Inn 1600 Soscol Ave . . . . . . Napa CA 94559 707-320-6910
Web: riverterraceinn.com

River's Edge Hotel & Spa
0455 SW Hamilton Ct. . . . . . Portland OR 97239 503-802-5800
Web: www.riversedgehotel.com

River's Edge Resort Cottages 4200 Boat St. . . . . . Fairbanks AK 99709 907-474-0286 474-3665
TF: 800-770-3343 ■ *Web:* www.riversedge.net

Riveredge Resort Hotel 17 Holland St . . . . . . Alexandria Bay NY 13607 315-482-9917 482-5010
TF: 800-365-6987 ■ *Web:* www.riveredge.com

Riverside Hotel 620 E Las Olas Blvd. . . . . . Fort Lauderdale FL 33301 954-467-0671 462-2148
TF: 800-325-3280 ■ *Web:* www.riversidehotel.com

Riverside Inn 1 Fountain Ave. . . . . . Cambridge Springs PA 16403 814-398-4645 398-8161
Web: www.theriversideinn.com

Riverstone Billings Inn 880 N 29th St. . . . . . Billings MT 59101 406-252-6800 252-6800
TF: 800-231-7782 ■ *Web:* www.billingsinn.com

Riverview Plaza Hotel 64 S Water St. . . . . . Mobile AL 36602 251-438-4000 415-0123
Web: marriott.com

Riviera Hotel 1431 Robson St . . . . . . Vancouver BC V6G1C1 604-685-1301 685-1335
TF: 888-699-5222 ■ *Web:* rivieravancouver.com

Road King Inn Columbia Mall
3300 30th Ave S. . . . . . Grand Forks ND 58201 800-707-1391
TF: 800-707-1391

Robert Treat Hotel 50 Pk Pl . . . . . . Newark NJ 07102 973-622-1000 622-6410
TF: 800-569-2300 ■ *Web:* www.rthotel.com

Rock View Resort 1049 Parkview Dr . . . . . . Hollister MO 65672 417-334-4678
TF: 800-375-9530 ■ *Web:* www.rockviewresort.com

Rocklin Park Hotel 5450 China Garden Rd . . . . . . Rocklin CA 95677 916-630-9400 630-9448
TF: 888-630-9400 ■ *Web:* www.rocklinpark.com

Rodeway Inn 1315 N 27th St. . . . . . Billings MT 59101 406-245-4128

Roger Sherman Inn 195 Oenoke Ridge. . . . . . New Canaan CT 06840 203-966-4541 966-0503
Web: www.rogershermaninn.com

Roger Smith Hotel 501 Lexington Ave . . . . . . New York NY 10017 212-755-1400 758-4061
TF: 800-445-0277 ■ *Web:* www.rogersmith.com

Roosevelt Hotel 45 E 45th St . . . . . . New York NY 10017 212-661-9600 885-6161
TF: 888-833-3969 ■ *Web:* www.theroosevelthotel.com

Rose Hotel 807 Main St. . . . . . Pleasanton CA 94566 925-846-8802 846-2272
TF: 800-843-9540 ■ *Web:* www.rosehotel.net

Rosedale on Robson Suite Hotel
838 Hamilton St . . . . . . Vancouver BC V6B6A2 604-689-8033 689-4426
TF: 800-661-8870 ■ *Web:* www.rosedaleonrobson.com

Rosellen Suites at Stanley Park
2030 Barclay St . . . . . . Vancouver BC V6G1L5 604-689-4807 684-3327
TF: 888-317-6648 ■ *Web:* www.rosellensuites.com

Rosen Centre Hotel 9840 International Dr . . . . . . Orlando FL 32819 407-996-9840 996-0865
TF: 800-204-7234 ■ *Web:* www.rosencentre.com

Rosen Hotels & Resorts Inc
9840 International Dr . . . . . . Orlando FL 32819 407-996-9840 996-0865
TF: 800-204-7234 ■ *Web:* www.rosenhotels.com

Rosen Plaza Hotel 9700 International Dr . . . . . . Orlando FL 32819 407-996-9700 354-5774
TF: 800-366-9700 ■ *Web:* www.rosenplaza.com

Rosen Shingle Creek 9939 Universal Blvd. . . . . . Orlando FL 32819 407-996-9939 996-9938
TF: 866-996-9939 ■ *Web:* www.rosenshinglecreek.com

Rosewood Hotels & Resorts
500 Crescent Ct Ste 300. . . . . . Dallas TX 75201 214-880-4200 880-4201
TF: 888-767-3966 ■ *Web:* www.rosewoodhotels.com

Roslyn Claremont Hotel 1221 Old Northern Blvd . . . . . . Roslyn NY 11576 516-625-2700 625-2731
TF: 800-626-9005 ■ *Web:* theroslynhotel.com

Rough Creek Lodge 5165 County Rd 2013 . . . . . . Glen Rose TX 76043 254-965-3700
TF: 877-907-0754 ■ *Web:* www.roughcreek.com

Royal Garden at Waikiki Hotel
440 Olohana St. . . . . . Honolulu HI 96815 808-943-0202
TF: 800-989-0971 ■ *Web:* www.extraholidays.com

Phone Fax

Royal Holiday Beach Resort 1988 Beach Blvd. . . . . Biloxi MS 39531 228-388-7553
TF Resv: 800-874-0402 ■ *Web:* www.holidaybeachresort.com

Royal Hotel South Beach
763 Pennsylvania Ave. . . . . Miami Beach FL 33139 305-673-9009 673-9244
Web: www.royalsouthbeach.com

Royal Park Hotel-brookshire & The Commons
600 E University Dr. . . . . Rochester MI 48307 248-652-2600
TF: 800-339-2761 ■ *Web:* royalparkhotel.net

Royal Regency Hotel 165 Tuckahoe Rd. . . . . Yonkers NY 10710 914-476-6200
TF: 800-215-3858 ■ *Web:* www.royalregencyhotelny.com

Royal Sonesta Hotel Boston
40 Edwin H Land Blvd . . . . Cambridge MA 02142 617-806-4200 806-4232
TF: 800-766-3782 ■ *Web:* www.sonesta.com/boston

Royal Sonesta Hotel New Orleans
800 Iberville St . . . . New Orleans LA 70112 504-586-0300
TF: 800-766-3782 ■ *Web:* www.sonesta.com

Royal Sonesta Hotel New Orleans
300 Bourbon St . . . . New Orleans LA 70130 504-586-0300 586-0335
TF: 800-766-3782 ■ *Web:* sonesta.com/royalneworleans

Royal Suite Lodge 3811 Minnesota Dr. . . . . Anchorage AK 99503 907-563-3114 563-4296

Royal Sun Inn 1700 S Palm Canyon Dr. . . . . Palm Springs CA 92264 760-327-1564
TF: 800-619-4786 ■ *Web:* www.royalsuninn.com

Royalton Hotel 44 W 44th St. . . . . New York NY 10036 212-869-4400 869-8965
TF: 800-606-6090 ■ *Web:* www.morganshotelgroup.com

Ruffin Hotels Lp Dba Long Beach Marriott
4700 Airport Plz Dr. . . . . Long Beach CA 90815 562-425-5210

Rushmore View Inn 610 Hwy 16A . . . . Keystone SD 57751 605-666-4466

Sage Hospitality Resources LLC
1575 Welton St Ste 300 . . . . Denver CO 80202 303-595-7200 595-7219
Web: www.sagehospitality.com

Saint Anthony the - A Wyndham Historic Hotel
300 E Travis St. . . . . San Antonio TX 78205 210-227-4392 227-0915
TF: 800-996-3426 ■ *Web:* www.wyndham.com

Saint Gregory Luxury Hotel & Suites
2033 M St NW . . . . Washington DC 20036 202-530-3600 466-6770
Web: www.capitalhotelswdc.com

Saint James Hotel 330 Magazine St. . . . . New Orleans LA 70130 504-304-4000 304-4444
Web: www.saintjameshotel.com

Saint Michaels Harbour Inn & Marina
101 N Harbor Rd. . . . . Saint Michaels MD 21663 410-745-9001
TF: 800-955-9001 ■ *Web:* www.harbourinn.com

Saint Paul Hotel 350 Market St. . . . . Saint Paul MN 55102 651-292-9292
TF: 800-292-9292 ■ *Web:* www.saintpaulhotel.com

Saint Regis Hotel 602 Dunsmuir St . . . . Vancouver BC V6B1Y6 604-681-1135 683-1126
TF: 800-770-7929 ■ *Web:* www.stregishotel.com

Saint Regis Hotel Winnipeg 285 Smith St . . . . Winnipeg MB R3C1K9 204-942-0171 943-3077
TF: 800-663-7344 ■ *Web:* www.stregishotel.net

Salisbury Hotel 123 W 57th St . . . . New York NY 10019 212-246-1300 977-7752
TF: 888-692-5757 ■ *Web:* www.nycsalisbury.com

Sam's Town Hotel & Casino Shreveport
315 Clyde Fant Pkwy . . . . Shreveport LA 71101 877-770-7867
TF: 877-770-7867 ■ *Web:* www.samstownshreveport.com

Sam's Town Hotel & Gambling Hall
5111 Boulder Hwy . . . . Las Vegas NV 89122 702-456-7777
TF: 800-897-8696 ■ *Web:* www.samstownlv.com

San Carlos Hotel 150 E 50th St. . . . . New York NY 10022 212-755-1800 688-9778
TF: 800-722-2012 ■ *Web:* www.sancarloshotel.com

San Joaquin Hotel 1309 W Shaw Ave. . . . . Fresno CA 93711 559-225-1309
Web: www.sjhotel.com

San Mateo Marriott 1770 S Amphlett Blvd . . . . San Mateo CA 94402 650-653-6000
Web: www.sanmateomarriott.com

Sandman Hotels Inns & Suites
1755 W Broadway Ste 310 . . . . Vancouver BC V6J4S5 604-730-6600 730-4645
Web: www.sandmanhotels.ca

Sands Casino Resort Bethlehem
77 Sands Blvd . . . . Bethlehem PA 18015 877-726-3777
TF: 877-726-3777 ■ *Web:* www.pasands.com

Sands Central Inn 1525 Central Ave. . . . . Hot Springs AR 71901 501-624-1258 624-2800

Sands Ocean Club Resort 9550 Shore Dr. . . . . Myrtle Beach SC 29572 888-999-8485
TF General: 888-999-8485 ■ *Web:* www.sandsresorts.com

Sands Regency Casino Hotel 345 N Arlington Ave . . . . Reno NV 89501 775-348-2200 348-2278*
*Fax: Hum Res ■ *TF Resv:* 800-233-4939 ■ *Web:* www.sandsregency.com

Sandwich Lodge & Resort
54 Rt 6A - Old King's Hwy . . . . Sandwich MA 02563 508-888-2275 888-8102
TF: 800-282-5353 ■ *Web:* sandwichlodge.com

Sanibel Inn 937 E Gulf Dr. . . . . Sanibel FL 33957 239-472-3181
TF: 866-565-5480 ■ *Web:* www.theinnsofsanibel.com

Santa Barbara Inn 901 E Cabrillo Blvd. . . . . Santa Barbara CA 93103 805-966-2285 966-6584
TF: 800-231-0431 ■ *Web:* www.santabarbarainn.com

Santa Maria Inn 801 S Broadway . . . . Santa Maria CA 93454 805-928-7777 928-5690
TF: 800-462-4276 ■ *Web:* www.santamariainn.com

Saratoga Hilton 534 Broadway . . . . Saratoga Springs NY 12866 518-584-4000 584-7430
TF: 800-445-8667 ■ *Web:* www.hilton.com

Satellite Hotel 411 Lakewood Cir. . . . . Colorado Springs CO 80910 719-596-6800
TF: 800-423-8409 ■ *Web:* www.satellitehotel.net

Saunders Hotel Group Ltd 240 Newbury St. . . . . Boston MA 02116 617-861-9000 861-9010
Web: www.saundershotelgroup.net

Savoy Suites Georgetown
2505 Wisconsin Ave NW . . . . Washington DC 20007 202-337-9700
TF: 877-301-0002 ■ *Web:* www.savoysuites.com

Scotsman Inn West 5922 W Kellogg St . . . . Wichita KS 67209 316-943-3800 943-3800
TF: 800-950-7268 ■ *Web:* www.scotsmaninnwichita.com

Sea Chambers Motel 67 Shore Rd. . . . . Ogunquit ME 03907 207-646-9311 646-0938
Web: www.seachambers.com

Sea Gull Motel on the Beach
2613 Atlantic Ave . . . . Virginia Beach VA 23451 757-425-5711
Web: www.seagullinn.net

Sea Ranch Lodge
60 Sea Walk Dr PO Box 44 . . . . The Sea Ranch CA 95497 707-785-2371 785-2917
TF: 800-732-7262 ■ *Web:* www.searanchlodge.com

Sea View Hotel 9909 Collins Ave . . . . Bal Harbour FL 33154 305-866-4441 866-1898
TF: 800-447-1010 ■ *Web:* www.seaview-hotel.com

Seacoast Suites Hotel 5101 Collins Ave. . . . . Miami Beach FL 33140 305-865-5152
Web: www.seacoastsuites.com

Seafarer Motel 2079 Main St . . . . Chatham MA 02633 508-432-1739
Web: www.chathamseafarer.com

Seaport Hotel & World Trade Ctr 1 Seaport Ln. . . . . Boston MA 02210 617-385-4000 385-4001
TF: 877-732-7678 ■ *Web:* www.seaportboston.com

Seaport Marina Hotel
6400 E Pacific Coast Hwy. . . . . Long Beach CA 90803 562-434-8451 598-6028
Web: www.seaportmarinahotel.com

Seaside Inn 541 E Gulf Dr . . . . Sanibel Island FL 33957 239-472-1400
TF: 866-565-5092 ■ *Web:* www.theinnsofsanibel.com

Seattle Convention Ctr Pike Street
1011 Pike St. . . . . Seattle WA 98101 206-682-8282 682-5315
TF: 800-225-5466 ■ *Web:* homewoodsuites3.hilton.com

Sedona Rouge Hotel & Spa 2250 W SR- 89A. . . . . Sedona AZ 86336 928-203-4111
TF: 866-312-4111 ■ *Web:* www.sedonarouge.com

Seelbach Hilton Louisville
500 S Fourth St . . . . Louisville KY 40202 502-585-3200 585-9239
TF: 800-333-3399 ■ *Web:* www.seelbachhilton.com

Senate Luxury Suites 900 SW Tyler St . . . . Topeka KS 66612 785-233-5050
TF: 800-488-3188 ■ *Web:* www.senatesuites.com

Sentinel Hotel 614 SW 11th Ave. . . . . Portland OR 97205 503-224-3400 241-2122
TF: 888-246-5631 ■ *Web:* www.sentinelhotel.com

Serrano Hotel 405 Taylor St . . . . San Francisco CA 94102 415-885-2500 474-4879
TF: 866-575-9941 ■ *Web:* www.serranohotel.com

Setai, The 2001 Collins Ave. Miami Beach FL 33139 305-520-6000
TF: 888-625-7500 ■ *Web:* www.thesetaihotel.com

Seven Gables Inn 26 N Meramec Ave. . . . . Saint Louis MO 63105 314-863-8400 863-8846
Web: sevengablesinn.com

Shades of Green on Walt Disney World Resort
1950 W Magnolia Palm Dr . . . . Lake Buena Vista FL 32830 407-824-3400 824-3665
TF: 888-593-2242 ■ *Web:* www.shadesofgreen.org

Shaner Hotel Group 1965 Waddle Rd. . . . . State College PA 16803 814-234-4460 278-7295*
*Fax: Hum Res ■ *Web:* www.shanercorp.com

Shangri-La Hotel Toronto 188 University Ave. . . . . Toronto ON M5H0A3 647-788-8888
Web: www.shangri-la.com

Shelborne Wyndham Grand South Beach
1801 Collins Ave . . . . Miami Beach FL 33139 305-531-1271 531-2206
Web: www.shelbornewyndhamgrand.com

Shelburne Murray Hill 303 Lexington Ave. . . . . New York NY 10016 212-689-5200 779-7068
TF: 866-233-4642 ■ *Web:* www.affinia.com

Shephard's Beach Resort
619 S Gulfview Blvd . . . . Clearwater Beach FL 33767 727-441-6875
TF: 800-237-8477 ■ *Web:* www.shephards.com

Sheraton Colonial Hotel & Golf Club Boston North
1 Audubon Rd. . . . . Wakefield MA 01880 781-245-9300 245-9300
Web: www.starwoodhotels.com

Sheraton Delfina Santa Monica
530 W Pico Blvd. . . . . Santa Monica CA 90405 310-399-9344 399-2504
TF: 888-625-4988 ■ *Web:* www.lemeridiendelfina.com

Sheraton Gateway Hotel Los Angeles
6101 W Century Blvd . . . . Los Angeles CA 90045 310-642-1111 645-1414
TF: 888-627-7104 ■ *Web:* www.sheratonlax.com

Sheraton Suites Calgary Eau Claire
255 Barclay Parade SW . . . . Calgary AB T2P5C2 403-266-7200
TF: 866-716-8134 ■ *Web:* sheratonsuites.com

Sheridan Pond 8130 S Lakewood Pl . . . . Tulsa OK 74137 918-901-9449
Web: www.sheridanpondapartmentstulsa.com

Sherry-Netherland Hotel 781 Fifth Ave. . . . . New York NY 10022 212-355-2800 319-4306
TF: 877-743-7710 ■ *Web:* t.sherrynetherland.com

Shilo Inn Hotel Salt Lake City
206 SW Temple . . . . Salt Lake City UT 84101 800-222-2244
TF: 800-222-2244 ■ *Web:* www.shiloinns.com

Shilo Inn Suites Hotel Portland Airport
117707 NE Airport Way . . . . Portland OR 97220 503-252-7500 254-0794
TF: 800-222-2244 ■ *Web:* www.shiloinns.com

Shilo Inn Suites Salem 3304 Market St. . . . . Salem OR 97301 503-581-4001 399-9385
TF: 800-222-2244 ■ *Web:* www.shiloinns.com

Shilo Inns Suites Hotels 11600 SW Shilo Ln . . . . Portland OR 97225 503-641-6565
TF: 800-222-2244 ■ *Web:* www.shiloinns.com

Shores Resort & Spa, The
2637 S Atlantic Ave . . . . Daytona Beach Shores FL 32118 386-767-7350 760-3651
Web: www.shoresresort.com

Shutters on the Beach 1 Pico Blvd . . . . Santa Monica CA 90405 310-458-0030
Web: www.shuttersonthebeach.com

Siena Hotel 1505 E Franklin St . . . . Chapel Hill NC 27514 919-929-4000 968-8527
TF: 800-223-7379 ■ *Web:* www.sienahotel.com

Sierra Land Group Inc
801 N Brand Blvd Ste 1010 . . . . Glendale CA 91203 818-247-3681

Sigma Sigma Sigma Foundation
225 N Muhlenberg St . . . . Woodstock VA 22664 540-459-4212
Web: trisigma.org

Silver Cloud Hotel Seattle Broadway
1100 Broadway . . . . Seattle WA 98122 206-325-1400 324-1995
TF: 800-590-1801 ■ *Web:* www.silvercloud.com

Silver Cloud Inn Seattle-Lake Union
1150 Fairview Ave N . . . . Seattle WA 98109 206-447-9500 812-4900
TF General: 800-330-5812 ■ *Web:* www.silvercloud.com

Silver Cloud Inn University District
5036 25th Ave NE . . . . Seattle WA 98105 206-526-5200 522-1450
TF: 800-205-6940 ■ *Web:* www.silvercloud.com

Silver King Hotel 1485 Empire Ave. . . . . Park City UT 84060 435-649-5500
TF: 888-667-2775 ■ *Web:* www.allseasonsresortlodging.com

Silver Smith Hotel & Suites 10 S Wabash Ave. . . . . Chicago IL 60603 312-372-7696 372-7320
TF: 800-979-0084 ■ *Web:* www.silversmithchicagohotel.com

SilverBirch Hotels & Resorts
1600 - 1030 W Georgia St . . . . Vancouver BC V6E2Y3 604-646-2447 431-5802*
*Fax Area Code: 780 ■ *TF:* 800-661-1232 ■ *Web:* www.silverbirchhotels.com

Silverdale Beach Hotel
3073 NW Bucklin Hill Rd . . . . Silverdale WA 98383 360-698-1000 692-0932
TF: 800-544-9799 ■ *Web:* www.silverdalebeachhotel.com

Simonton Court Historic Inn & Cottages
320 Simonton St. . . . . Key West FL 33040 800-944-2687
TF: 800-944-2687 ■ *Web:* www.simontoncourt.com

Sir Francis Drake Hotel 450 Powell St . . . . San Francisco CA 94102 415-392-7755 391-8719
TF: 800-795-7129 ■ *Web:* www.sirfrancisdrake.com

	City	State	ZIP	Phone	Fax
Sise Inn, The 40 Ct St	Portsmouth	NH	03801	603-433-1200	
Web: thehotelportsmouth.com					
Ski Bromont 150 Champlain	Bromont	QC	J2L1A2	450-534-2200	
TF: 866-276-6668 ■ *Web:* www.skibromont.com					
Sky Hotel 709 E Durant Ave	Aspen	CO	81611	970-925-6760	925-6778
TF: 800-882-2582 ■ *Web:* www.theskyhotel.com					
Skyline Hotel 725 Tenth Ave	New York	NY	10019	212-586-3400	
Web: www.skylinehotelny.com					
Smoky Shadows Motel & Conference Ctr					
4215 Pkwy	Pigeon Forge	TN	37863	865-453-7155	453-0308
Web: www.smokyshadows.com					
Snell House 21 Atlantic Ave	Bar Harbor	ME	04609	207-288-8004	
TF: 866-763-5524 ■ *Web:* www.snellhouse.com					
Snowbird Mountain Lodge					
4633 Santeetlah Rd	Robbinsville	NC	28771	828-479-3433	479-3473
TF: 800-941-9290 ■ *Web:* www.snowbirdlodge.com					
Snowy Owl Inn 41 Village Rd	Waterville Valley	NH	03215	603-236-8383	
TF: 800-766-9969 ■ *Web:* www.snowyowlinn.com					
Sofia Hotel 150 W Broadway	San Diego	CA	92101	619-234-9200	544-9879
TF: 800-826-0009 ■ *Web:* www.thesofiahotel.com					
SoHo Grand Hotel 310 W Broadway	New York	NY	10013	212-965-3000	965-3200
TF: 800-965-3000 ■ *Web:* www.sohogrand.com					
SoHo Metropolitan Hotel 318 Wellington St W	Toronto	ON	M5V3T4	416-599-8800	599-8801
TF: 866-764-6638 ■ *Web:* www.metropolitan.com/soho					
Somerset Hills Hotel (SSH) 200 Liberty Corner Rd	Warren	NJ	07059	908-647-6700	647-8053
Web: www.thesomersethillshotel.com					
Somerset Inn 2601 W Big Beaver Rd	Troy	MI	48084	248-643-7800	643-2296
TF: 800-228-8769 ■ *Web:* www.somersetinn.com					
Sonesta Hotel & Suites Coconut Grove					
2889 McFarlane Rd	Miami	FL	33133	305-529-2828	529-2008
TF: 800-766-3782 ■ *Web:* sonesta.com/coconutgrove					
Soniat House 1133 Chartres St	New Orleans	LA	70116	504-522-0570	522-7208
TF: 800-544-8808 ■ *Web:* www.soniathouse.com					
Sophie Station Suites 1717 University Ave	Fairbanks	AK	99709	800-528-4916	479-7951*
**Fax Area Code:* 907 ■ *TF:* 800-528-4916 ■ *Web:* www.fountainheadhotels.com					
South Beach Marina Inn & Vacation Rentals					
232 S Sea Pines Dr	Hilton Head Island	SC	29928	843-671-6498	671-7495
TF: 800-367-3909 ■ *Web:* www.sbinn.com					
South Pier Inn on the Canal 701 Lake Ave S	Duluth	MN	55802	218-786-9007	
TF: 800-430-7437 ■ *Web:* www.southpierinn.com					
South Point Hotel & Casino					
9777 Las Vegas Blvd S	Las Vegas	NV	89183	702-796-7111	
TF: 866-796-7111 ■ *Web:* www.southpointcasino.com					
Southampton Inn 91 Hill St	SoutHampton	NY	11968	631-283-6500	283-6559
TF: 800-832-6500 ■ *Web:* www.southamptoninn.com					
Southernmost On the Beach 508 S St	Key West	FL	33040	305-296-6577	294-2108
TF: 800-354-4455					
Southfork Hotel 1600 N Central Expy	Plano	TX	75074	972-578-8555	423-7147
TF: 877-386-4383					
Southway Inn 2431 Bank St	Ottawa	ON	K1V8R9	613-737-0811	737-3207
TF: 877-688-4929 ■ *Web:* www.southway.com					
Spindrift Inn 652 Cannery Row	Monterey	CA	93940	831-646-8900	655-8174
TF: 800-841-1879 ■ *Web:* www.spindriftinn.com					
Spring Creek Ranch 1800 Spirit Dance Rd	Jackson	WY	83001	307-733-8833	
TF: 800-443-6139 ■ *Web:* www.springcreekranch.com					
St. James Hotel 406 Main St	Red Wing	MN	55066	651-388-2846	
TF: 800-252-1875 ■ *Web:* www.st-james-hotel.com					
St. Julien Hotel & Spa 900 Walnut St	Boulder	CO	80302	720-406-9696	406-9668
TF: 877-303-0900 ■ *Web:* www.stjulien.com					
Stamford Suites 720 Bedford St	Stamford	CT	06901	203-359-7300	359-7304
TF: 866-394-4365 ■ *Web:* www.stamfordsuites.com					
Stanford Court - A Renaissance Hotel					
905 California St	San Francisco	CA	94108	415-989-3500	
Web: www.marriott.com/default.mi					
Stanley Hotel 333 Wonderview Ave	Estes Park	CO	80517	970-586-3371	586-4964
TF: 800-976-1377 ■ *Web:* www.stanleyhotel.com					
Stanyan Park Hotel 750 Stanyan St	San Francisco	CA	94117	415-751-1000	668-5454
Web: www.stanyanpark.com					
Star Island Resort 5000 Ave of the Stars	Kissimmee	FL	34746	407-997-8000	
TF: 800-513-2820 ■ *Web:* www.star-island.com					
Starwood Hotels & Resorts Worldwide Inc					
1111 Westchester Ave	White Plains	NY	10604	914-640-8100	640-8310
NYSE: HOT ■ *TF Cust Svc:* 888-625-5144 ■ *Web:* www.starwoodhotels.com					
Saint Regis Hotels & Resorts					
1111 Westchester Ave	White Plains	NY	10604	914-640-8100	640-8310
TF: 888-625-4988 ■ *Web:* www.starwoodhotels.com					
Westin Hotels & Resorts					
1111 Westchester Ave	White Plains	NY	10604	914-640-8100	640-8310
TF: 888-625-5144 ■ *Web:* www.starwoodhotels.com					
State Plaza Hotel 2117 E St NW	Washington	DC	20037	202-861-8200	
TF: 800-424-2859 ■ *Web:* www.stateplaza.com					
Staten Island Hotel 1415 Richmond Ave	Staten Island	NY	10314	718-698-5000	737-7294
Web: esplanadesi.com					
Sterling Hotel 1300 H St	Sacramento	CA	95814	916-448-1300	448-8066
Web: sterlinghotelsacramento.com					
Stockyards Hotel 109 E Exchange Ave	Fort Worth	TX	76164	817-625-6427	624-2571
TF: 800-423-8471 ■ *Web:* www.stockyardshotel.com					
Stone Castle Hotel & Conference Ctr, The					
3050 Green Mtn Dr	Branson	MO	65616	417-335-4700	335-3906
TF: 800-677-6906 ■ *Web:* bransonstonecastle.com					
Stonebridge Inn					
300 Carriage Way PO Box 5008	Snowmass Village	CO	81615	970-923-2420	923-5889
TF: 800-922-7242 ■ *Web:* www.stonebridgeinn.com					
Stonehedge Inn 160 Pawtucket Blvd	Tyngsboro	MA	01879	978-649-4400	649-9256
Web: www.stonehedgeinnandspa.com					
Stonewall Jackson Hotel & Conference Ctr					
24 S Market St	Staunton	VA	24401	540-885-4848	885-4840
TF: 866-880-0024 ■ *Web:* www.stonewalljacksonhotel.com					
Stoney Creek Inn 101 Mariner's Way	East Peoria	IL	61611	309-694-1300	694-9303
TF: 800-659-2220 ■ *Web:* stoneycreekhotels.com/home.do					
Strater Hotel 699 Main Ave	Durango	CO	81301	970-247-4431	259-2208
TF: 800-247-4431 ■ *Web:* www.strater.com					
Stratford Hotel 242 Powell St	San Francisco	CA	94102	415-397-7080	397-7087
TF: 888-688-0038 ■ *Web:* www.hotelstratford.com					
Strathallan Hotel 550 E Ave	Rochester	NY	14607	585-461-5010	
Web: www.strathallan.com					
Strathcona Hotel 60 York St	Toronto	ON	M5J1S8	416-363-3321	363-4679
TF: 800-268-8304 ■ *Web:* www.thestrathconahotel.com					
Strathcona Hotel, The 919 Douglas St	Victoria	BC	V8W2C2	250-383-7137	
TF: 800-663-7476 ■ *Web:* www.strathconahotel.com					
Stratosphere Tower Hotel & Casino					
2000 S Las Vegas Blvd	Las Vegas	NV	89104	702-380-7777	383-4755*
**Fax:* Sales ■ *TF:* 800-998-6937 ■ *Web:* www.stratospherehotel.com					
Sturbridge Host Hotel & Conference Ctr					
366 Main St	Sturbridge	MA	01566	508-347-7393	347-3944
TF: 800-582-3232 ■ *Web:* www.sturbridgehosthotel.com					
Sugar Magnolia 804 Edgewood Ave NE	Atlanta	GA	30307	404-222-0226	
Web: www.sugarmagnoliabb.com					
Suites at Fisherman's Wharf					
2655 Hyde St	San Francisco	CA	94109	415-771-0200	
TF: 800-227-3608 ■ *Web:* www.shellhospitality.com					
Suites Hotel in Canal Park, The					
325 Lake Ave S	Duluth	MN	55802	218-727-4663	722-0572
TF: 800-794-1716 ■ *Web:* www.thesuitesduluth.com					
Summit Lodge & Spa 4359 Main St	Whistler	BC	V0N1B4	604-932-2778	932-2716
TF: 888-913-8811 ■ *Web:* summitlodge.com					
Sun Viking Lodge					
2411 S Atlantic Ave	Daytona Beach Shores	FL	32118	386-252-6252	252-5463
TF: 800-874-4469 ■ *Web:* www.sunviking.com					
Sunburst Hospitality Corp					
10770 Columbia Pk Ste 200	Silver Spring	MD	20901	301-592-3800	592-3830
Web: www.snbhotels.com					
Suncoast Hotel & Casino 9090 Alta Dr	Las Vegas	NV	89145	702-636-7111	
TF: 877-677-7111 ■ *Web:* www.suncoastcasino.com					
Sundial Boutique Hotel					
4340 Sundial Crescent	Whistler	BC	V0N1B4	604-932-2321	
TF: 800-661-2321 ■ *Web:* www.sundialhotel.com					
Sunrise Suites Resort Key West					
3685 Seaside Dr	Key West	FL	33040	305-296-6661	296-6665
Web: www.sunrisesuiteskeywest.com					
Sunset Inn Travel Apartments					
1111 Burnaby St	Vancouver	BC	V6E1P4	604-688-2474	669-3340
TF: 800-786-1997 ■ *Web:* www.sunsetinn.com					
Sunset Marquis Hotel & Villas					
1200 N Alta Loma Rd	West Hollywood	CA	90069	310-657-1333	652-5300
TF: 800-858-9758 ■ *Web:* www.sunsetmarquis.com					
Sunset Station Hotel & Casino					
1301 W Sunset Rd	Henderson	NV	89014	702-547-7777	
TF: 888-786-7389 ■ *Web:* sunsetstation.sclv.com					
Sunset Tower Hotel 8358 Sunset Blvd	West Hollywood	CA	90069	323-654-7100	
Web: www.sunsettowerhotel.com					
Surf & Sand Resort 1555 S Coast Hwy	Laguna Beach	CA	92651	949-497-4477	494-2897
TF: 877-741-5908 ■ *Web:* www.surfandsandresort.com					
Surfsand Resort 148 W Gower Rd	Cannon Beach	OR	97110	503-436-2274	436-9116
TF: 800-547-6100 ■ *Web:* www.surfsand.com					
Surfside Inn 1211 Atlantic Ave	Virginia Beach	VA	23451	757-428-1183	
TF: 800-437-2497 ■ *Web:* www.virginiabeachsurfside.com					
Surrey Hotel 20 E 76th St	New York	NY	10021	212-288-3700	
TF: 866-233-4642 ■ *Web:* www.affinia.com					
Sutton Place Hotel Edmonton 10235 101st St	Edmonton	AB	T5J3E9	780-428-7111	441-3098
Web: www.suttonplace.com/hotels/sutton-place-hotel-edmonton-edm?property=edm					
Swag, The 2300 Swag Rd	Waynesville	NC	28785	828-926-0430	926-2036
TF: 800-789-7672 ■ *Web:* www.theswag.com					
Sweden House 4605 E State St	Rockford	IL	61108	815-398-4130	
Taj Boston 15 Arlington St	Boston	MA	02116	617-536-5700	
TF: 866-969-1825 ■ *Web:* www.tajhotels.com					
Taj Campton Place 340 Stockton St	San Francisco	CA	94108	415-781-5555	955-5536
TF: 866-969-1825 ■ *Web:* www.tajhotels.com					
Tarsadia Investments,					
620 Newport Ctr Dr	Newport Beach	CA	92660	949-610-8000	
Web: tarsadia.com					
Terminal City Club 837 W Hastings St	Vancouver	BC	V6C1B6	604-681-4121	681-9634
Web: tcclub.com					
Teton Mountain Lodge & Spa					
3385 Cody Ln	Teton Village	WY	83025	307-201-6066	
TF: 800-631-6271 ■ *Web:* www.tetonlodge.com					
Thayer Hotel 674 Thayer Rd	West Point	NY	10996	845-446-4731	446-0338
TF: 800-247-5047 ■ *Web:* www.thethayerhotel.com					
Tickle Pink Inn at Carmel Highlands					
155 Highland Dr	Carmel	CA	93923	831-624-1244	626-9516
TF: 800-635-4774 ■ *Web:* www.ticklepinkinn.com					
Tidewater Inn & Conference Ctr 101 E Dover St	Easton	MD	21601	410-822-1300	820-8847
TF: 800-237-8775 ■ *Web:* www.tidewaterinn.com					
Timbers Hotel, The 4411 Peoria St	Denver	CO	80239	303-373-1444	373-1975
Time, The 224 W 49th St	New York	NY	10019	212-246-5252	245-2305
TF: 877-846-3692 ■ *Web:* www.thetimehotels.com/new-york/default-en.html					
Times Hotel & Suites					
6515 Wilfrid-Hamel Blvd	L'Ancienne-Lorette	QC	G2E5W3	418-877-7788	877-3333
TF: 888-902-4444 ■ *Web:* grandtimeshotel.com					
Tivoli Lodge 386 Hanson Ranch Rd	Vail	CO	81657	970-476-5615	476-6601
TF: 800-451-4756 ■ *Web:* www.tivolilodge.com					
Topaz Hotel 1733 N St NW	Washington	DC	20036	202-393-3000	785-9581
TF: 800-775-1202 ■ *Web:* www.topazhotel.com					
TOWER23 Hotel 723 Felspar St	San Diego	CA	92109	858-270-2323	
Web: www.t23hotel.com					
Town & Country Inn 20 State RT 2	Shelburne	NH	03581	603-466-3315	466-3315
TF General: 800-325-4386 ■ *Web:* www.townandcountryinn.com					
Town & Country Inn & Conference Ctr					
2008 Savannah Hwy	Charleston	SC	29407	843-571-1000	
TF: 800-334-6660 ■ *Web:* www.thetownandcountryinn.com					
Town Inn Suites 620 Church St	Toronto	ON	M4Y2G2	416-964-3311	
TF: 800-387-2755 ■ *Web:* www.towninn.com					
Townsend Hotel 100 Townsend St	Birmingham	MI	48009	248-642-7900	645-9061
TF: 800-548-4172 ■ *Web:* www.townsendhotel.com					
Townsend Manor Inn 714 Main St	Greenport	NY	11944	631-477-2000	477-2371
Web: www.townsendinn.com					

Phone | Fax

Tradewinds Carmel
Mission St at Third Ave .... Carmel By The Sea CA 93921 831-624-2776 624-0634
Web: www.tradewindscarmel.com

Trans World Corp (TWC) 545 Fifth Ave Ste 940..........New York NY 10017 212-983-3355 983-8129
OTC: TWOC ■ *TF:* 877-407-9037 ■ *Web:* www.transwc.com

Travelodge Virginia Beach
1909 Atlantic Ave..............................Virginia Beach VA 23451 757-425-0650
TF: 800-578-7878 ■ *Web:* www.travelodge.com

Tremont Chicago 100 E Chestnut St...................Chicago IL 60611 312-751-1900
TF: 866-716-8147 ■ *Web:* www.tremontchicago.com

Tremont House - A Wyndham Historic Hotel, The
2300 Ship Mechanic Row......................... Galveston TX 77550 409-763-0300
Web: www.wyndham.com

Trianon Old Naples 955 Seventh Ave S ....Naples FL 34102 239-435-9600
TF: 877-482-5228 ■ *Web:* www.trianon.com

Tropical Winds Oceanfront Hotel
1398 N Atlantic Ave ....Daytona Beach FL 32118 386-258-1016 255-6462
TF: 800-245-6099 ■ *Web:* tropicalwindshotel.com

Tropicana Inn & Suites 1540 S Harbor Blvd........... Anaheim CA 92802 714-635-4082 635-1535
TF: 800-828-4898 ■ *Web:* tropicanainn-anaheim.com

Trump International Hotel & Tower
725 Fifth Ave ....New York NY 10022 312-588-8000 299-1150*
**Fax Area Code:* 212 ■ *TF:* 888-448-7867 ■ *Web:* www.trumphotelcollection.com

Tugboat Inn
80 Commercial St PO Box 267................Boothbay Harbor ME 04538 207-633-4434 633-5892
TF: 800-248-2628 ■ *Web:* www.tugboatinn.com

Tuscany Suites & Casino 255 E Flamingo Rd......... Las Vegas NV 89169 702-893-8933 947-5994
TF Resv: 877-887-2261 ■ *Web:* www.tuscanylv.com

TWELVE Atlantic Station 361 17th St.....................Atlanta GA 30363 404-961-1212 961-1221
Web: www.twelvehotels.com

TWELVE Centennial Park 400 W Peachtree St ....Atlanta GA 30308 404-418-1212 418-1221
Web: www.twelvehotels.com

Twin Farms 452 Royalton Tpke PO Box 115 .... Barnard VT 05031 802-234-9999
TF: 800-894-6327 ■ *Web:* www.twinfarms.com

UMass Hotel at the Campus Ctr
1 Campus Ctr Way..Amherst MA 01003 413-549-6000
TF: 877-822-2110 ■ *Web:* www.hotelumass.com

Umstead Hotel & Spa 100 Woodland Pond.................Cary NC 27513 919-447-4000
TF: 866-877-4141 ■ *Web:* www.theumstead.com

Union Station A Wyndham Historic Hotel
PO Box 4090 ....Aberdeen SD 57401 800-996-3426
TF: 800-996-3426 ■ *Web:* www.wyndham.com

University Inn Seattle 4140 Roosevelt Way NE........... Seattle WA 98105 206-632-5055 547-4937
TF: 800-733-3855 ■ *Web:* www.universityinnseattle.com

University Place 310 SW Lincoln St....................Portland OR 97201 503-221-0140 226-6260
TF: 866-845-4647 ■
Web: www.pdx.edu/cegs/university-place-hotel-conference-center

University Plaza Hotel & Conference Ctr
3110 Olentangy River Rd ....Columbus OH 43202 614-267-7461 831-5893*
**Fax Area Code:* 417

University Plaza Hotel & Convention Ctr
333 John Q Hammons Pkwy.........................Springfield MO 65806 417-864-7333 831-5893
Web: www.upspringfield.com

US Grant, The 326 Broadway....................... San Diego CA 92101 619-232-3121 232-3626
TF: 866-716-8136 ■ *Web:* www.usgrant.net

US Suites 4970 Windplay Dr C1.................... El Dorado Hills CA 95762 916-941-7970
TF Cust Svc: 800-877-8483 ■ *Web:* www.ussuites.com

Vacation Resorts International Inc
23041 Avenida De La Carlota Ste 400 .... Laguna Hills CA 92653 949-587-2299
Web: www.vriresorts.com

Valley River Inn 1000 Vly River Way.................. Eugene OR 97401 541-743-1000 683-5121
TF: 800-543-8266 ■ *Web:* www.valleyriverinn.com

Vancouver Extended-Stay Suites
1288 W Georgia St Ste 101 ....Vancouver BC V6E4R3 604-891-6181
Web: www.vancouverextendedstay.com

Vanderbilt Grace 41 Mary St ....Newport RI 02840 401-846-6200 847-7689
TF: 888-826-4255 ■ *Web:* www.gracehotels.com

Varscona Hotel 8208 106th St .... Edmonton AB T6E6R9 780-434-6111 439-1195
TF: 866-465-8150 ■ *Web:* www.varscona.com

Velvet Cloak Inn, The 1505 Hillsborough St............ Raleigh NC 27605 919-828-0333 828-2656
TF: 888-828-0335 ■ *Web:* www.thevelvetcloak.com

Viceroy Palm Springs 415 S BelaRdo Rd...........Palm Springs CA 92262 760-320-4117 329-5739*
**Fax Area Code:* 786 ■ *TF:* 866-781-9923 ■ *Web:* www.viceroyhotelsandresorts.com

Viceroy Santa Monica 1819 Ocean Ave .... Santa Monica CA 90401 310-260-7500 260-7515
TF: 888-622-4567 ■ *Web:* viceroyhotelsandresorts.com

Victoria Inn Winnipeg 1808 Wellington Ave...........Winnipeg MB R3H0G3 204-786-4801 786-1329
TF: 877-842-4667 ■ *Web:* www.vicinn.com

Victoria Regent Hotel, The 1234 Wharf St............. Victoria BC V8W3H9 250-386-2211 386-2622
TF: 800-663-7472 ■ *Web:* www.victoriaregent.com

Victorian Condo-Hotel & Conference Ctr
6300 Seawall Blvd .... Galveston TX 77551 409-740-3555 741-1676
TF: 800-231-6363 ■ *Web:* www.victoriancondo.com

Villa Florence 225 Powell St..................San Francisco CA 94102 415-397-7700 397-1006
TF: 800-553-4411 ■ *Web:* www.villaflorence.com

Villa Royale Inn 1620 Indian Trl.....................Palm Springs CA 92264 760-327-2314
TF: 800-245-2314 ■ *Web:* www.villaroyale.com

Village Latch Inn 101 Hill St PO Box 3000......... SoutHampton NY 11968 631-283-2160 283-3236
TF: 800-545-2824 ■ *Web:* www.villagelatch.com

Villagio Inn & Spa 6481 Washington St............. Yountville CA 94599 707-944-8877
TF: 800-351-1133 ■ *Web:* www.villagio.com

Villas de Santa Fe 400 Griffin St .... Santa Fe NM 87501 505-988-3000 988-4700
Web: www.diamondresorts.com

Villas on the Bay 105 Marine St................Saint Augustine FL 32084 904-599-7301
Web: thevillas.com

Vintage Inn Napa Valley
6541 Washington St.................................. Yountville CA 94599 800-351-1133
TF Cust Svc: 800-351-1133 ■ *Web:* www.vintageinn.com

Vintners Inn 4350 Barnes Rd......................... Santa Rosa CA 95403 707-575-7350 575-1426
TF: 800-421-2584 ■ *Web:* www.vintnersinn.com

Virginian Lodge
750 W Broadway PO Box 1052...................Jackson Hole WY 83001 307-733-2792
TF: 800-262-4999 ■ *Web:* www.virginianlodge.com

Virginian Suites 1500 Arlington Blvd .... Arlington VA 22209 703-522-9600 525-4462
TF: 866-371-1446 ■ *Web:* www.virginiansuites.com

Phone | Fax

Viscount Gort Hotel 1670 Portage Ave.................Winnipeg MB R3J0C9 204-775-0451 772-2161
TF: 800-665-1122 ■ *Web:* www.viscount-gort.com

Viscount Suite Hotel 4855 E Broadway Blvd............ Tucson AZ 85711 520-745-6500 790-5114
TF Resv: 800-527-9666 ■ *Web:* www.viscountsuite.com

Vista Host Inc 10370 Richmond Ave Ste 150............Houston TX 77042 713-267-5800 267-5820
TF: 800-257-3000 ■ *Web:* vistahost.com

Voyageur Inn 200 Viking Dr.........................Reedsburg WI 53959 608-524-6431
Web: www.magnusonhotels.com/Voyageur-Inn-Conference-Center

Voyageur Lakewalk Inn 333 E Superior St .... Duluth MN 55802 218-722-3911
TF: 800-258-3911 ■ *Web:* www.voyageurlakewalkinn.com

Waikiki Gateway Hotel 2070 Kalakaua Ave............ Honolulu HI 96815 808-955-3741
Web: www.waikikigateway.com

Waikiki Parc Hotel 2233 Helumoa Rd .... Honolulu HI 96815 808-921-7272 923-1336
TF: 800-422-0450 ■ *Web:* www.waikikiparc.com

Waikiki Resort Hotel 2460 Koa Ave.................. Honolulu HI 96815 808-922-4911 922-9468
TF: 800-367-5116 ■ *Web:* www.waikikiresort.com

Waldorf Towers, The 100 E 50th St...................New York NY 10022 212-355-3100
TF: 800-925-3673 ■ *Web:* www.waldorfnewyork.com

Warwick Denver Hotel 1776 Grant St ....Denver CO 80203 303-861-2000 832-0320
TF: 800-203-3232 ■ *Web:* warwickhotels.com/denver

Warwick Melrose Hotel 3015 Oak Lawn Ave .... Dallas TX 75219 214-521-5151 521-2470
TF: 800-521-7172 ■ *Web:* warwickhotels.com/dallas

Warwick New York Hotel 65 W 54th St..............New York NY 10019 212-247-2700 247-2725*
**Fax:* Sales ■ *TF:* 800-223-4099 ■ *Web:* warwickhotels.com/new-york

Warwick Regis Hotel San Francisco
490 Geary St................................... San Francisco CA 94102 415-928-7900 441-8788
Web: warwickhotels.com/san-francisco

Warwick Seattle Hotel 401 Lenora St.................. Seattle WA 98121 206-443-4300 448-1662
TF: 800-426-9280 ■ *Web:* warwickhotels.com/seattle

Washington Court Hotel
525 New Jersey Ave NW.........................Washington DC 20001 202-628-2100
TF: 800-321-3010 ■ *Web:* www.washingtoncourthotel.com

Washington Duke Inn & Golf Club
3001 Cameron Blvd ....Durham NC 27705 919-490-0999 688-0105
TF: 800-443-3853 ■ *Web:* www.washingtondukeinn.com

Washington Inn Hotel, The 495 Tenth St..............Oakland CA 94607 510-452-1776 452-4436
Web: www.thewashingtoninn.com

Washington Plaza Hotel
10 Thomas Cir NW
Massachusetts Ave at 14th St.....................Washington DC 20005 202-842-1300 371-9602
TF: 800-424-1140 ■ *Web:* www.washingtonplazahotel.com

Washington Square Hotel 103 Waverly Pl ....New York NY 10011 212-777-9515 979-8373
TF: 800-222-0418 ■ *Web:* www.washingtonsquarehotel.com

Washington Suites 100 S Reynolds St..............Alexandria VA 22304 703-370-9600 370-0467

Waterfront Hotel 10 Washington St....................Oakland CA 94607 510-836-3800
TF: 888-842-5333 ■ *Web:* www.jdvhotels.com

Waters Edge Hotel 25 Main St......................... Tiburon CA 94920 415-789-5999 789-5888
TF: 888-662-9555 ■ *Web:* www.marinhotels.com

Wauwinet, The 120 Wauwinet Rd PO Box 2580.......... Nantucket MA 02584 508-228-0145 228-6712
TF: 800-426-8718 ■ *Web:* www.wauwinet.com

Weber's Inn 3050 Jackson Rd .... Ann Arbor MI 48103 734-769-2500 769-4743
TF Resv: 800-443-3050 ■ *Web:* www.webersinn.com

Wedgewood Hotel 845 Hornby St.................. Vancouver BC V6Z1V1 604-689-7777 608-5348
TF: 800-663-0666 ■ *Web:* www.wedgewoodhotel.com

Wedgewood Resort Hotel 212 Wedgewood Dr.........Fairbanks AK 99701 800-528-4916 451-8184*
**Fax Area Code:* 907 ■ *TF:* 800-528-4916 ■ *Web:* www.fountainheadhotels.com

Wellington Hotel 871 Seventh Ave...................New York NY 10019 212-247-3900 581-1350
TF: 800-652-1212 ■ *Web:* www.wellingtonhotel.com

Wellington Resort 551 Thames St ....Newport RI 02840 401-849-1770 847-6250
TF: 800-228-2968 ■ *Web:* www.wellingtonresort.com

Wentworth Mansion 149 Wentworth St..............Charleston SC 29401 843-853-1886 720-5290
TF: 888-466-1886 ■ *Web:* www.wentworthmansion.com

Western States Lodging
1018 W Atherton Dr .... Taylorsville UT 84123 801-269-0700 269-1512
Web: wslm.biz

Westford Regency Inn & Conference Ctr
219 Littleton Rd .... Westford MA 01886 978-692-8200 692-7403
Web: www.westfordregency.com

Westgate Branson Woods 2201 Roark Vly Rd ....Branson MO 65616 417-334-2324
TF: 877-253-8572 ■
Web: westgatedestinations.com/missouri/branson/westgate-branson-woods

Westgate Painted Mountain Country Club
6302 E McKellips Rd ....Mesa AZ 85215 480-654-3611 654-3613
TF: 888-433-3707 ■
Web: www.westgatedestinations.com/arizona/mesa/westgate-painted-mountain-golf-resort

Westin Houston Downtown, The 1520 Texas Ave.......Houston TX 77002 713-228-1520 228-1555
TF: 800-427-4697 ■ *Web:* www.westinhoustondowntown.com

Westin San Francisco Market Street
50 Third St .... San Francisco CA 94103 415-974-6400 543-8268
Web: www.starwoodhotels.com

Westmark Hotels Inc 300 Elliott Ave W.................Seattle WA 98119 800-544-0970 285-7152*
**Fax Area Code:* 206 ■ *TF:* 800-544-0970 ■ *Web:* www.westmarkhotels.com

Westmont Hospitality Group Inc
5090 Explorer Dr Ste 700.......................... Mississauga ON L4W4T9 905-629-3400 624-7805
Web: www.whg.com

Westmont Hospitality Group Inc
5847 San Felipe St Ste 4650 ....Houston TX 77057 713-782-9100 782-9600
Web: www.whg.com

Westport Inn, The 1595 Post Rd E.................. Westport CT 06880 203-557-8124 254-8439
Web: www.westportinn.com

Wheatleigh 11 Hawthorne Rd .... Lenox MA 01240 413-637-0610 637-4507
Web: wheatleigh.com

White Barn Inn 37 Beach Ave .... Kennebunk ME 04043 207-967-2321 967-1100
Web: www.whitebarninn.com

White Elephant Inn & Cottages 50 Easton St .... Nantucket MA 02554 508-228-2500 325-1195
TF: 800-475-2637 ■ *Web:* www.whiteelephanthotel.com

White Inn, The 52 E Main St........................ Fredonia NY 14063 716-672-2103 672-2107
Web: www.whiteinn.com

White Lodging Services Inc
701 E 83rd Ave....................................Merrillville IN 46410 219-472-2900 756-2902
Web: www.whitelodging.com

White Swan Inn 845 Bush St................... San Francisco CA 94108 415-775-1755
TF: 800-999-9570 ■ *Web:* www.whiteswaninnsf.com

Phone Fax

Whitehall Hotel 105 E Delaware Pl . . . Chicago IL 60611 312-944-6300 944-8552
Web: www.thewhitehallhotel.com
Whitelaw Hotel 808 Collins Ave . . . Miami Beach FL 33139 305-398-7000 398-7010
Web: www.whitelawhotel.com
Whitney the - A Wyndham Historic Hotel
610 Poydras St . . . New Orleans LA 70130 504-581-4222
TF: 800-996-3426 ■ *Web:* www.wyndham.com
Wickaninnish Inn 500 Osprey Ln PO Box 250 . . . Tofino BC V0R2Z0 250-725-3100 725-3110*
*Fax: Resv ■ *TF:* 800-333-4604 ■ *Web:* www.wickinn.com
Wild Palms Hotel 910 E Fremont Ave . . . Sunnyvale CA 94087 408-738-0500 736-8302
Web: www.jdvhotels.com
Williamsburg Lodge 310 S England St . . . Williamsburg VA 23185 757-229-1000
TF Cust Svc: 800-447-8679 ■ *Web:* www.history.org
Willows Historic Palm Springs Inn
412 W Tahquitz Canyon Way . . . Palm Springs CA 92262 760-320-0771 320-0780
TF: 800-966-9597 ■ *Web:* www.thewillowspalmsprings.com
Willows Hotel 555 W Surf St . . . Chicago IL 60657 773-528-8400
TF: 877-207-2111 ■ *Web:* www.willowshotelchicago.com
Willows Lodge 14580 NE 145th St . . . Woodinville WA 98072 425-424-3900 424-2585
TF: 877-424-3930 ■ *Web:* www.willowslodge.com
Wilson Hotel Management Company Inc
8700 Trl Lk Dr W Ste 300 . . . Memphis TN 38125 901-346-8800 346-5808
Web: www.wilsonhotels.com
Windsor Arms Hotel 18 St Thomas St . . . Toronto ON M5S3E7 416-971-9666 921-9121
TF: 877-999-2767 ■ *Web:* www.windsorarmshotel.com
Windsor Capital Group Inc
3000 Ocean Pk Blvd Ste 3010 . . . Santa Monica CA 90405 310-566-1100 566-1199
Web: www.wcghotels.com
Windsor Court Hotel 300 Gravier St . . . New Orleans LA 70130 504-523-6000 596-4513
TF: 888-596-0955 ■ *Web:* www.windsorcourthotel.com
Windsor Hotel 125 W Lamar St . . . Americus GA 31709 229-924-1555 924-1555
Web: www.windsor-americus.com
Winegardner & Hammons Inc 4243 Hunt Rd . . . Cincinnati OH 45242 513-891-1066 794-2590
Web: www.whihotels.com
Wonder View Inn & Suites
50 Eden St PO Box 25 . . . Bar Harbor ME 04609 207-288-3358 288-2005
TF: 888-439-8439 ■ *Web:* www.wonderviewinn.com
Woodloch Pines Inc 731 Welcome Lk Rd . . . Hawley PA 18428 570-685-8000 685-8093
TF: 800-966-3562 ■ *Web:* www.woodloch.com
Woodmark Hotel on Lake Washington
1200 Carillon Pt . . . Kirkland WA 98033 425-822-3700 822-3699
TF: 800-822-3700 ■ *Web:* www.thewoodmark.com
Wort Hotel 50 N Glenwood . . . Jackson WY 83001 307-733-2190 733-2067
TF Cust Svc: 800-322-2727 ■ *Web:* www.worthotel.com
Wyndham Grand Chicago Riverfront
71 E Wacker Dr . . . Chicago IL 60601 312-346-7100 346-1721
Web: wyndhamgrandchicagoriverfront.com
Wyndham Hotel Group
Baymont Inn & Suites 1023 Eighth Ave NW . . . Aberdeen SD 57401 800-337-0550
TF: 800-337-0550 ■ *Web:* www.baymontinns.com
Ramada 949 Route 46 . . . Parsippany NJ 07054 877-212-2733
TF Resv: 877-212-2733 ■ *Web:* www.ramada.com
Travelodge PO Box 4090 . . . Aberdeen SD 57041 312-427-8000
TF Resv: 800-525-4055 ■ *Web:* www.travelodge.com
Wyndham Vacation Resorts 6277 Sea Harbor Dr . . . Orlando FL 32821 800-251-8736
TF: 800-251-8736 ■ *Web:* www.clubwyndham.com
Wyndham Lake Buena Vista
1850 Hotel Plaza Blvd . . . Lake Buena Vista FL 32830 407-828-4444
TF: 800-624-4109 ■ *Web:* www.wyndhamlakebuenavista.com
Wyndham Midtown 45 205 E 45th St . . . New York NY 10017 212-867-5100 867-7878
Web: www.wyndhammidtown45.com
Wyndham Worldwide Corp
Wyndham Hotel Group 22 Sylvan Way . . . Parsippany NJ 07054 973-753-6000 753-6000
NYSE: WYN ■ *Web:* www.wyndhamworldwide.com
Wynfrey Hotel 1000 Riverchase Galleria . . . Birmingham AL 35244 205-705-1234 988-4597
TF: 800-633-7313 ■ *Web:* wynfrey.regency.hyatt.com
Wynn Las Vegas 3131 Las Vegas Blvd S . . . Las Vegas NV 89109 702-770-7000
TF: 877-321-9966 ■ *Web:* www.wynnlasvegas.com
Yankee Inn 461 Pittsfield Lenox Rd . . . Lenox MA 01240 413-499-3700
Web: www.yankeeinn.com
Yankee Peddler Inn 113 Touro St . . . Newport RI 02840 401-846-1323
Web: www.yankeepeddlerinn.com
Yarmouth Resort 343 Main St Rt 28 . . . West Yarmouth MA 02673 508-775-5155
TF: 877-838-3524 ■ *Web:* www.yarmouthresort.com
Yogo Inn 211 E Main St . . . Lewistown MT 59457 406-535-8721 535-8969
TF: 800-860-9646 ■ *Web:* www.yogoinn.com
Yorktowne Hotel 48 E Market St . . . York PA 17401 717-848-1111 845-4707
TF: 800-233-9324 ■ *Web:* www.yorktowne.com

380 ICE - MANUFACTURED

Phone Fax

Arctic Glacier USA Inc
1654 Marthaler Ln . . . West Saint Paul MN 55118 651-455-0410 455-7799
CV Ice Company Inc 83796 Date Ave . . . Indio CA 92201 760-347-3529
Web: www.cvice.com
Dusing Bros Ice Manufacturing Co
3607 Dixie Hwy . . . Elsmere KY 41018 859-727-2720 727-2780
Hanover Foods Corp 1550 York St PO Box 334 . . . Hanover PA 17331 717-632-6000
OTC: HNFSA ■ *TF:* 800-888-4646 ■ *Web:* www.hanoverfoods.com
House of Flavors Inc 110 N William St . . . Ludington MI 49431 231-845-7369 845-7371
TF: 800-930-7740 ■ *Web:* www.houseofflavors.com
Icemakers Inc 3711 Fifth Ct N . . . Birmingham AL 35222 205-591-2791 591-2389
TF General: 800-467-2181 ■ *Web:* www.icemakers.net
Pelesys Learning Systems Inc
Ste 125 - 13500 Maycrest Way . . . Richmond BC V6V2N8 604-233-6268
Web: www.pelesys.com
Pelican Ice & Cold Storage Inc 711 Oxley St . . . Kenner LA 70062 504-602-0013
Web: pelicanice.com
Reddy Ice Holdings Inc
8750 N Central Expy Ste 1800 . . . Dallas TX 75231 214-526-6740 528-1532
OTC: RDDYQ ■ *TF:* 800-683-4423 ■ *Web:* www.reddyice.com

Phone Fax

Toyo Pumps North America Corp
1550 Brigantine Dr . . . Coquitlam BC V5C6H2 604-298-1213
Web: www.toyopumps.com

381 ICE CREAM & DAIRY STORES

Phone Fax

Amy's Ice Creams 3500 Guadalupe St . . . Austin TX 78705 512-458-6895 458-4971
Web: www.amysicecreams.com
Bahama Buck's Original Shaved Ice Co
5123 69th St . . . Lubbock TX 79424 806-771-2189 771-2190
Web: www.bahamabucks.com
Baskin-Robbins Inc 130 Royall St . . . Canton MA 02021 781-737-3000
TF: 800-859-5339 ■ *Web:* www.baskinrobbins.com
Ben & Jerry's Homemade Inc
30 Community Dr . . . South Burlington VT 05403 802-846-1500 846-1538
Web: www.benjerry.com
Carvel Express 200 Glenridge Pt Pkwy Ste 200 . . . Atlanta GA 30342 800-322-4848
TF: 800-322-4848 ■ *Web:* www.carvel.com
Cloverland Green Spring Dairy Inc
2701 Loch Raven Rd . . . Baltimore MD 21218 410-235-4477
TF Orders: 800-492-0094 ■ *Web:* www.cloverlanddairy.com
Cold Stone Creamery Inc
9311 E Via De Ventura . . . Scottsdale AZ 85258 480-362-4800 362-4812
TF Cust Svc: 866-452-4252 ■ *Web:* www.coldstonecreamery.com
Dairy Queen 7505 Metro Blvd . . . Minneapolis MN 55439 952-830-0200 830-0227
TF: 800-883-4279 ■ *Web:* www.dairyqueen.com
Freshens Quality Brands 1750 The Exchange . . . Atlanta GA 30339 678-627-5400 627-5454
Web: www.freshens.com
Kilwins Quality Confections Inc (KQC)
1050 Bay View Rd . . . Petoskey MI 49770 888-454-5946
TF: 888-454-5946 ■ *Web:* www.kilwins.com
Newport Creamery Inc
35 Stockanosset Cross Rd PO Box 8819 . . . Cranston RI 02920 401-946-4000
Web: www.newportcreamery.com
Rita's Water Ice Franchise Co LLC
1401 Bridgetown Pike . . . Feasterville PA 19053 215-322-8774
Web: www.ritasice.com
Royal Crest Dairy Inc 350 S Pearl St . . . Denver CO 80209 303-777-2227 744-9173
TF: 888-226-6455 ■ *Web:* www.royalcrestdairy.com
Stewart's Shops PO Box 435 . . . Saratoga Springs NY 12866 518-581-1201
Web: stewartsshops.com

382 IMAGING EQUIPMENT & SYSTEMS - MEDICAL

See Also Medical Instruments & Apparatus - Mfr p. 2741

Phone Fax

Agfa Corp 611 River Dr . . . Elmwood Park NJ 07407 201-440-2500
TF: 888-274-8626 ■ *Web:* www.agfagraphics.com/gs/usa/en/internet/maings
Alpine Solutions Inc
3222 Corte Malpaso Ste 204 . . . Camarillo CA 93012 805-388-1699
TF: 855-388-1883 ■ *Web:* www.alpinesolutionsinc.com
BrainLAB Inc 3 Westbrook Corp Ctr . . . Westchester IL 60154 708-409-1343 409-1619
TF: 800-784-7700 ■ *Web:* www.brainlab.com
CIVCO Medical Instruments 102 First St . . . Kalona IA 52247 319-656-4447
Web: www.civcomedical.com
Dentsply International Inc
221 W Philadelphia St PO Box 872 . . . York PA 17405 717-845-7511 849-4762
NASDAQ: XRAY ■ *TF:* 800-877-0020 ■ *Web:* www.dentsply.com
Digirad Corp 13950 Stowe Dr . . . Poway CA 92064 858-726-1600 726-1700
NASDAQ: DRAD ■ *TF:* 800-947-6134 ■ *Web:* www.digirad.com
Dornier MedTech America Inc
1155 Roberts Blvd . . . Kennesaw GA 30144 770-426-1315 426-6115
TF: 800-367-6437 ■ *Web:* www.dornier.com
Eastman Kodak Co 343 State St . . . Rochester NY 14650 585-724-4000
OTC: EKDKQ ■ *Web:* www.kodak.com
Fonar Corp 110 Marcus Dr . . . Melville NY 11747 631-694-2929 390-7766
NASDAQ: FONR ■ *Web:* www.fonar.com
Given Imaging Ltd 3950 Shackleford Rd Ste 500 . . . Duluth GA 30096 770-662-0870 662-0510
NASDAQ: GIVN ■ *Web:* www.givenimaging.com
Hitachi Medical Systems America Inc
1959 Summit Commerce Pk . . . Twinsburg OH 44087 330-425-1313 425-1410
TF: 800-800-3106 ■ *Web:* www.hitachimed.com
Hologic Inc 35 Crosby Dr . . . Bedford MA 01730 781-999-7300 280-0669
NASDAQ: HOLX ■ *TF:* 800-523-5001 ■ *Web:* www.hologic.com
Holorad 2929 S Main St . . . Salt Lake City UT 84115 801-983-6075
Web: www.holorad.com
iCAD Inc 98 Spit Brook Rd Ste 100 . . . Nashua NH 03062 603-882-5200 880-3843
NASDAQ: ICAD ■ *TF:* 866-280-2239 ■ *Web:* www.icadmed.com
ImageWorks 250 Clearbrook Rd . . . Elmsford NY 10523 914-592-6100 592-6148
TF: 800-592-6666 ■ *Web:* www.imageworkscorporation.com
Imaging Diagnostic Systems Inc
6531 NW 18th Ct . . . Plantation FL 33313 954-581-9800 979-2420
OTC: IMDS ■ *Web:* www.imds.com
ITT Night Vision & Imaging
7635 Plantation Rd . . . Roanoke VA 24019 540-563-0371 362-4979
TF: 800-448-8678 ■ *Web:* www.nightvision.com
Konica Minolta Medical Imaging
411 Newark Pompton Tpke . . . Wayne NJ 07470 973-633-1500 523-7408
Web: konicaminolta.us
Merge Helathcare 350 N Orleans St 1st Fl . . . Chicago IL 60654 312-565-6868 565-6870
TF: 877-446-3743 ■ *Web:* www.merge.com
Novadaq Technologies Inc
5090 Explorer Dr Ste 202 . . . Mississauga ON L4W4T9 905-629-3822
TSE: NDQ ■ *Web:* www.novadaq.com
One Call Medical Inc (OCM)
20 Waterview Blvd PO Box 614 . . . Parsippany NJ 07054 973-257-1000 257-0044
TF: 800-872-2875 ■ *Web:* www.onecallcm.com
PerkinElmer Inc 940 Winter St . . . Waltham MA 02451 203-925-4602 944-4904
NYSE: PKI ■ *Web:* www.perkinelmer.com

	City	State	Zip	Phone	Fax
Philips 5000 Marina Blvd Ste 100 *TF Cust Svc:* 877-328-2808 ■ *Web:* www.usa.philips.com/healthcare/country-selector.html	Brisbane	CA	94005	650-228-5555	228-5580
Philips Medical Systems 3000 Minuteman Rd *TF:* 800-934-7372 ■ *Web:* www.usa.philips.com/healthcare/country-selector.html	Andover	MA	01810	978-659-3000	
Precision Optics Corp Inc 22 E Broadway *OTC: PEYE* ■ *TF:* 800-447-2812 ■ *Web:* www.poci.com	Gardner	MA	01440	978-630-1800	630-1487
Quest Diagnostics 1311 Calle Batido	San Clemente	CA	92673	949-940-7200	
S & S Technology 10625 Telge Rd *TF:* 800-231-1747 ■ *Web:* www.ssxray.com	Houston	TX	77095	281-815-1300	815-1444
Shimadzu Medical Systems 20101 S Vermont Ave *TF General:* 800-477-1227 ■ *Web:* www.shimadzu.com	Torrance	CA	90502	310-217-8855	217-0661
Siemens Medical Solutions Inc 51 Valley Stream Pkwy **Fax Area Code:* 610 ■ *TF:* 800-888-7436 ■ *Web:* healthcare.siemens.com	Malvern	PA	19355	888-826-9702	219-3124*
Siemens Molecular Imaging Inc 810 Innovation Dr *Web:* healthcare.siemens.com	Knoxville	TN	37932	865-218-2000	218-3000
SonoSite Inc 21919 30th Dr SE *NASDAQ: SONO* ■ *TF:* 888-482-9449 ■ *Web:* www.sonosite.com	Bothell	WA	98021	425-951-1200	951-1201
Stereotaxis Inc 4320 Forest Pk Ave *NASDAQ: STXS* ■ *TF:* 866-646-2346 ■ *Web:* www.stereotaxis.com	Saint Louis	MO	63108	314-678-6100	678-6159
Topcon Medical Systems Inc 111 Bauer Dr *TF:* 800-223-1130 ■ *Web:* www.topconmedical.com	Oakland	NJ	07436	201-599-5100	599-5250
Toshiba America Inc 1251 Ave of the Americas Ste 4100 *TF:* 800-457-7777 ■ *Web:* www.toshiba.com	New York	NY	10020	212-596-0600	593-3875
Toshiba America Medical Systems Inc 2441 Michelle Dr *TF Cust Svc:* 800-521-1968 ■ *Web:* www.medical.toshiba.com	Tustin	CA	92780	714-730-5000	730-4022
Varian Medical Systems Inc 3100 Hansen Way *NYSE: VAR* ■ *TF:* 800-544-4636 ■ *Web:* www.varian.com	Palo Alto	CA	94304	650-493-4000	
Vision-Sciences Inc 40 Ramland Rd S *NASDAQ: VSCI* ■ *TF:* 800-874-9975	Orangeburg	NY	10962	845-365-0600	365-0620
Wolf X-Ray Corp 100 W Industry Ct *TF Cust Svc:* 800-356-9729 ■ *Web:* www.wolfxray.com	Deer Park	NY	11729	631-242-9729	925-5003

383 IMAGING SERVICES - DIAGNOSTIC

	City	State	Zip	Phone	Fax
Alliance Imaging Inc 100 Bayview Cir Ste 400 *TF:* 800-544-3215 ■ *Web:* www.alliancehealthcareservices-us.com	Newport Beach	CA	92660	949-242-5300	
Center for Diagnostic Imaging 5775 Wayzata Blvd Ste 190 *TF:* 800-537-0005 ■ *Web:* mycdi.com	Saint Louis Park	MN	55416	952-541-1840	847-1152
Excel Diagnostic Imaging Clinics 9701 Richmond Ave Ste 122 *Web:* exceldiagnostics.com	Houston	TX	77042	713-781-6200	
Johns Dental Laboratory Inc 423 S 13th St *TF:* 800-457-0504 ■ *Web:* www.johnsdental.com	Terre Haute	IN	47807	812-232-6026	
Medical Resources Inc 1455 Broad St *TF:* 800-537-7272	Bloomfield	NJ	07003	973-707-1100	707-1118
Medquest Assoc Inc 3480 Preston Ridge Rd Ste 600 *Web:* www.mqimaging.com	Alpharetta	GA	30005	678-992-7200	
Memorial MRI & Diagnostic Center LP 1241 Campbell Rd *Web:* www.memorialdiagnostic.com	Houston	TX	77055	713-461-3399	
MNAP Medical Solutions Inc 9908 E Roosevelt Blvd *Web:* mnap.com	Philadelphia	PA	19115	215-464-3300	
Quality Electrodynamics LLC 700 Beta Dr *Web:* www.qualedyn.com	Mayfield Village	OH	44143	440-638-5106	
V-rad Systems Inc 4504 Maple St *Web:* v-radsystems.com	Bellaire	TX	77401	713-667-6056	

384 INCENTIVE PROGRAM MANAGEMENT SERVICES

See Also Conference & Events Coordinators p. 2058

Many of the companies listed here provide travel as a reward for employees or corporate customers in order to boost sales or employee performance. Most of these companies are members of the Society of Incentive & Travel Executives. Some of the companies listed offer merchandise or other types of incentives as well.

	City	State	Zip	Phone	Fax
ADI Meetings & Events 4801 S Lakeshore Dr Ste 108 *Web:* www.adimeetings.com	Tempe	AZ	85282	480-350-9090	350-9393
Beatty Group International 9800 Beaverton Hillsdale Ste 105 *TF:* 800-285-6215 ■ *Web:* www.beattygroup.com	Beaverton	OR	97005	503-644-3340	
Don Jagoda Assoc Inc 100 Marcus Dr *Web:* www.dja.com	Melville	NY	11747	631-454-1800	454-1834
Eaton Incentives Inc 271 Rt 46W Ste H 212-215 *Web:* www.eatonincentives.com	Fairfield	NJ	07004	973-882-7700	
Fields Group Inc 1919 South Blvd Ste 1010	Charlotte	IN	28203	704-372-7855	
Impact Incentives & Meetings Inc 552 Valley Rd Ste 204 *Web:* www.impactincentives.com	West Orange	NJ	07052	973-952-9052	
Incentive Travel & Meetings (ITM) 970 Clementstone Dr Ste 100 *Web:* www.usaitm.com	Atlanta	GA	30342	404-252-2728	252-8328
ITAGroup 4600 Westown Pkwy *TF:* 800-257-1985 ■ *Web:* www.itagroup.com	West Des Moines	IA	50266	800-257-1985	
Marketing Innovators International Inc 9701 W Higgins Rd **Fax Area Code:* 847 ■ *TF:* 800-543-7373 ■ *Web:* www.marketinginnovators.com	Rosemont	IL	60018	800-543-7373	696-3194*
Maxcel Co 13601 Preston Rd E Twr Ste 935 *Web:* www.maxcel.net	Dallas	TX	75240	972-644-0880	680-2488
MotivAction 16355 36th Ave N Ste 100 *Web:* www.motivaction.com	Minneapolis	MN	55446	763-412-3000	
Motivation Through Incentives Inc 10400 W 103 St Ste 10 *TF:* 800-826-3464 ■ *Web:* www.mtievents.com	Overland Park	KS	66214	800-826-3464	
Performance Strategies Inc 6862 Hillsdale Ct *Web:* www.performancestrategies.com	Indianapolis	IN	46250	317-842-0393	578-4711
Premier Incentives 6 Admiral Ln *Web:* www.premierincentives.com	Salem	MA	01970	978-607-0135	
Pro Logic Consumer Marketing Services 1625 S Congress Ave *Web:* www.prologicretail.com/consumer-marketing-services	Delray Beach	FL	33445	561-454-7600	265-2493
Provident Travel 11309 Montgomery Rd *TF:* 800-354-8108 ■ *Web:* www.providenttravel.com	Cincinnati	OH	45249	513-247-1100	
Student Advantage LLC 280 Summer St **Fax Area Code:* 617 ■ *TF:* 800-333-2920 ■ *Web:* www.studentadvantage.com	Boston	MA	02210	800-333-2920	912-2012*
United Incentives Inc 131 N Third St *Web:* www.unitedincentives.com	Philadelphia	PA	19106	215-625-2700	625-2502
Universal Odyssey Inc 1601 Dove St Ste 260 *Web:* www.universalodyssey.com	Newport Beach	CA	92660	949-263-1222	263-0983
USMotivation 7840 Roswell Rd Bldg 100 3rd Fl **Fax Area Code:* 770 ■ *TF:* 866-885-4702 ■ *Web:* www.usmotivation.com	Atlanta	GA	30350	866-885-4702	290-4701*
Vertrue Inc 20 Glover Ave	Norwalk	CT	06850	203-324-7635	674-7080
Viktor Incentives & Meetings 4020 Copper View Ste 130 *TF:* 800-748-0478 ■ *Web:* www.viktorwithak.com	Traverse City	MI	49684	231-947-0882	947-2532

385 INDUSTRIAL EQUIPMENT & SUPPLIES (MISC) - WHOL

	City	State	Zip	Phone	Fax
AaronEquipment Company Inc 735 E Green St PO Box 80 *TF:* 800-492-2766 ■ *Web:* www.aaronequipment.com	Bensenville	IL	60106	630-350-2200	350-9047
Abatix Corp 2400 Skyline Dr Ste 400 *TF:* 800-426-3983 ■ *Web:* www.abatix.com	Mesquite	TX	75149	214-381-0322	388-0443
Accurate Air Engineering Inc 16207 Carmennita Rd *TF:* 800-438-5577 ■ *Web:* www.accurateair.com	Cerritos	CA	90703	562-484-6370	484-6371
Adco Manufacturing Inc 2170 Academy Ave *TF:* 888-608-5946 ■ *Web:* www.adcomfg.com	Sanger	CA	93657	559-875-5563	875-7665
AIM Supply Co 7337 Bryan Dairy Rd *TF:* 800-999-0125 ■ *Web:* www.aimsupply.com	Largo	FL	33777	727-544-6211	544-6211
Aimco 10000 SE Pine St *TF:* 800-852-1368 ■ *Web:* www.aimco-global.com	Portland	OR	97216	800-852-1368	582-9015
Airgas Inc 259 N Radnor-Chester Rd Ste 100 *NYSE: ARG* ■ *TF:* 800-255-2165 ■ *Web:* www.airgas.com	Radnor	PA	19087	610-687-5253	687-1052
Airgas Inc 6055 Rockside Woods Blvd. *Web:* www.airgas.com	Independence	OH	44131	216-642-6600	642-6670
Airgas North Central 1250 W Washington St *Web:* www.airgas.com	West Chicago	IL	60185	630-231-9260	231-7768
AIV LP 7140 W Sam Houston Pkwy N Ste100 *Web:* www.aivinc.com	Houston	TX	77040	713-462-4181	
Alamo Iron Works Inc 943 AT&T Ctr Pkwy *TF:* 800-292-7817 ■ *Web:* www.aiwdirect.com	San Antonio	TX	78219	210-223-6161	704-8351
Allied Automation Inc 5220 E 64th St *Web:* www.allied-automation.com	Indianapolis	IN	46220	317-253-5900	
Ames Supply Co 1936C University Ln	Lisle	IL	60532	630-964-2440	964-0497
AMI Bearings Inc 570 N Wheeling Rd *Web:* www.amibearings.com	Mount Prospect	IL	60056	847-759-0620	
Applied Industrial Technologies Inc 1 Applied Plz Eulid Ave *NYSE: AIT* ■ *Web:* www.applied.com	Cleveland	OH	44115	216-426-4000	
Associated Packaging Inc 435 Calvert Dr *Web:* www.associatedpackaging.com	Gallatin	TN	37066	615-452-2131	452-7890
Atlantic Lift Truck Inc 2945 Whittington Ave *TF:* 800-638-4566 ■ *Web:* www.atlanticlift.com	Baltimore	MD	21230	410-644-7777	
Austin Pump & Supply Co PO Box 17037 *TF:* 800-252-9692 ■ *Web:* www.austinpump.com	Austin	TX	78760	512-442-2348	442-2932
Barnes Distribution 1301 E Ninth St Ste 700 *TF:* 800-726-9626 ■ *Web:* classc.mscdirect.com	Cleveland	OH	44114	216-416-7200	
Bearing Distributors Inc 8000 Hub Pkwy *TF:* 888-423-4872 ■ *Web:* www.bdi-usa.com	Cleveland	OH	44125	216-642-9100	642-9573
Bearing Headquarters Co 2550 S 25th Ave *Web:* www.bearingheadquarters.com	Broadview	IL	60155	708-681-4400	681-4462
Bearings & Drives Inc 607 Lower Poplar St PO Box 4325 *Web:* www.bdindustrial.com	Macon	GA	31208	478-746-7623	742-7836
Bearings Ltd 2100 Pacific St *Web:* www.bearingslimited.com	Hauppauge	NY	11788	631-273-8200	
Berendsen Fluid Power 401 S Boston Ave Ste 1200 *TF:* 800-360-2327 ■ *Web:* www.bfpna.com	Tulsa	OK	74103	918-592-3781	581-5080
Bolttech Mannings 501 Mosside Blvd **Fax Area Code:* 412 ■ *TF:* 888-846-8827 ■ *Web:* www.bolttechmannings.com	North Versailles	PA	15137	724-872-4873	829-1834*
Brake Supply Company Inc 5501 Foundation Blvd *TF:* 800-457-5788 ■ *Web:* www.brake.com	Evansville	IN	47725	812-467-1000	
Brauer Material Handling Systems Inc 226 Molly Walton Dr **Fax Area Code:* 615 ■ *TF:* 800-645-6083 ■ *Web:* www.braueronline.com	Hendersonville	TN	37075	800-645-6083	859-2937*
Briggs Equipment 10540 N Stemmons Fwy *TF:* 800-606-1833 ■ *Web:* www.briggsequipment.us	Dallas	TX	75220	214-630-0808	631-3560

Phone | Fax

Briggs Industrial Equipment
10550 N Stemmons Fwy. Dallas TX 75220 214-630-0808 631-3560
TF: 800-516-9206 ■ *Web:* www.briggsindustrial.com

Brinker Brown Fastener & Supply Inc
12290 Crystal Commerce Loop Fort Myers FL 33966 239-939-3535
Web: www.brinkerbrown.com

C & H Distributors LLC 770 S 70th St Milwaukee WI 53214 414-443-1700 336-1331*
**Fax Area Code:* 800 ■ *TF Sales:* 800-558-9966 ■ *Web:* www.chdist.com

Canadian Bearings Ltd 1600 Drew Rd. Mississauga ON L5S1S5 905-670-6700 670-0459
TF: 800-229-2327 ■ *Web:* www.canadianbearings.com

Carlson Systems Holdings Inc 10840 Harney St. Omaha NE 68154 402-593-5300
Web: www.csystems.com

Carolina Material Handling Services Inc
PO Box 6 Columbia SC 29202 803-695-0149 783-1659
TF: 800-922-6709 ■ *Web:* www.cmhservices.net

Cascade Machinery & Electric Inc
4600 E Marginal Way S Seattle WA 98134 206-762-0500 767-5122
TF: 800-289-0500 ■ *Web:* www.cascade-machinery.com

Cee Kay Supply Co 5835 Manchester Ave Saint Louis MO 63110 314-644-3500 644-4336
Web: www.ceekay.com

Central Power Systems & Services
9200 W Liberty Dr Liberty MO 64068 816-781-8070 781-2207*
**Fax:* Sales ■ *Web:* www.cpower.com

Certified Slings & Supply Inc
PO Box 180127 Casselberry FL 32718 407-331-6677 260-9196
Web: www.certifiedslings.com

Cisco-Eagle 2120 Valley View Ln Dallas TX 75234 972-406-9330 406-9577
TF: 888-877-3861 ■ *Web:* www.cisco-eagle.com

Clean Rooms West Inc 1392 Industrial Dr. Tustin CA 92780 714-258-7700
Web: www.cleanroomswest.com

CMC Construction Services 9103 E Almeda Rd. Houston TX 77054 713-799-1150 799-8431
TF: 877-297-9111 ■ *Web:* www.cmcconstructionservices.com

Cohn & Gregory Inc 5450 Midway Rd Fort Worth TX 76117 817-831-9998
Web: www.cgsupply.com

Conveyco Technologies Inc PO Box 1000 Bristol CT 06011 860-589-8215 583-1384
TF: 800-229-8215 ■ *Web:* www.conveyco.com

Crane Engineering Inc 707 Ford St. Kimberly WI 54136 920-733-4425 733-0211
Web: www.craneengineering.net

Cross Co 4400 Piedmont Pkwy. Greensboro NC 27410 336-856-6000 856-6999
TF: 800-858-1737 ■ *Web:* www.crossco.com

Cummins Southern Plains Inc PO Box 90027 Arlington TX 76004 817-640-6801 640-6852
TF: 800-516-4354 ■ *Web:* www.cummins-sp.com

Cvg International America Inc
7200 NW 19th St Ste 110 Miami FL 33126 305-470-8100 470-8199

Danco Inc 486 Lakewood Rd Waterbury CT 06704 203-753-5121
Web: www.danco-inc.com

Deacon Industrial Supply Co Inc
165 Boro Line Rd King of Prussia PA 19406 610-265-5322 265-6470
TF: 800-726-9800 ■ *Web:* www.deaconind.com

Detroit Pump & Mfg Co 450 Fair St Bldg D. Ferndale MI 48220 248-544-4242 544-4141
TF: 800-686-1662 ■ *Web:* www.detroitpump.com

DoALL Co 1480 S Wolf Rd. Wheeling IL 60090 847-495-6800
Web: www.doall.com

Drago Supply Co 740 Houston Ave Port Arthur TX 77640 409-983-4911 985-6542*
**Fax:* Sales ■ *TF:* 877-609-7975 ■ *Web:* www.dragosupply.com

Dueco N4 W22610 Bluemound Rd Waukesha WI 53186 262-547-8500 547-8407
TF: 800-558-4004

Duncan Industrial Solutions
3450 S MacArthur Blvd Oklahoma City OK 73179 405-688-2300
TF: 800-375-9470 ■ *Web:* www.duncanindustrial.com

Duo-Fast Carolinas Inc
1923 John Crossland Jr Dr. Charlotte NC 28208 704-377-5721
Web: www.duofast.net

DXP Enterprises Inc 7272 Pinemont Dr. Houston TX 77040 713-996-4700 996-4701
NASDAQ: DXPE ■ *TF:* 800-830-3973 ■ *Web:* www.dxpe.com

Eastern Lift Truck Company Inc
549 E Linwood Ave. Maple Shade NJ 08052 856-779-8880 482-8804
TF: 866-980-7175 ■ *Web:* www.easternlifttruck.com

Edgen Corp 18444 Highland Rd. Baton Rouge LA 70809 225-756-9868 756-9868
TF: 866-334-3648 ■ *Web:* www.edgenmurray.com

Ellison Machinery Co
9912 S Pioneer Blvd. Santa Fe Springs CA 90670 562-949-8311 949-9091
Web: www.ellisontechnologies.com

Endries International Inc
714 W Ryan St PO Box 69 Brillion WI 54110 920-756-5381 756-3772
TF: 800-852-5821 ■ *Web:* www.endries.com

Engman-Taylor Company Inc (ETCO)
W142 N9351 Fountain Blvd Menomonee Falls WI 53051 262-255-9300 255-6512
TF: 800-236-1975 ■ *Web:* www.engman-taylor.com

Enpro Inc 121 S LombaRd Rd. Addison IL 60101 630-629-3504 629-3512
TF: 800-323-2416 ■ *Web:* www.enproinc.com

Erie Bearings Company Inc 1432 E 12th St Erie PA 16503 814-453-6871
Web: www.eriebearings.com

Exterran 16666 Northchase Dr Houston TX 77060 281-836-7000
Web: www.exterran.com

Fairmont Supply Co 1001 Consol Energy Dr Canonsburg PA 15317 724-514-3900 261-5310
Web: www.fairmontsupply.com

FCx Performance 3000 E 14th Ave. Columbus OH 43219 614-324-6050 253-2033
TF: 800-253-6223 ■ *Web:* www.fcxperformance.com

Flexlink Systems Inc
6580 Snowdrift Rd Ste 200 Allentown PA 18106 610-973-8200 973-8345
Web: www.flexlink.com

Florida Detroit Diesel-Allison Inc
5040 University Blvd W Jacksonville FL 32216 904-737-7330
TF: 888-812-4440 ■ *Web:* www.fdda.com

Forklifts of Minnesota Inc
2201 W 94th St. Bloomington MN 55431 952-887-5400 881-3030
TF: 800-752-4300 ■ *Web:* www.forkliftsofmn.com

FUJIFILM Graphic System USA Inc 45 Crosby Dr Bedford MA 01730 781-271-4400
TF: 800-755-3854 ■ *Web:* www.fujifilmusa.com

FW Webb Co 160 Middlesex Tpke Bedford MA 01730 781-272-6600 275-3354
TF: 800-343-7555 ■ *Web:* www.fwwebb.com

Gaffney-Kroese Supply Corp
60 Kingsbridge Rd Piscataway NJ 08854 732-885-9000 885-9555
Web: www.gaffney-kroese.com

Ganesh Machinery 20869 Plummer St. Chatsworth CA 91311 818-349-9166
TF: 888-542-6374 ■ *Web:* www.ganeshmachinery.com

Garner 825 E Cooley Ave San Bernardino CA 92408 909-799-3030
Web: www.garnerholt.com

Gas Equipment Company Inc
11616 Harry Hines Blvd Dallas TX 75229 972-241-2333 620-1403
TF: 800-821-1829 ■ *Web:* www.gasequipment.com

General Tool & Supply Co Inc
2705 NW Nicolai St Portland OR 97210 503-226-3411
TF: 800-526-9328 ■ *Web:* www.motionindustries.com

Geneva Scientific Inc 11 N Batavia Ave. Batavia IL 60510 800-338-2697 879-8687*
**Fax Area Code:* 630 ■ *TF:* 800-338-2697 ■ *Web:* www.barcoproducts.com

Genuine Parts Co 2999 Cir 75 Pkwy. Atlanta GA 30339 770-953-1700
NYSE: GPC ■ *Web:* www.genpt.com

Gerotech Inc 29220 Commerce Dr Flat Rock MI 48134 734-379-7788 379-2244
Web: www.gerotechinc.com

Glatt Air Techniques Inc 20 Spear Rd. Ramsey NJ 07446 201-825-8700 825-0389
Web: www.glattair.com

Gosiger Inc 108 McDonough St. Dayton OH 45402 937-228-5174 228-5189
TF: 877-288-1538 ■ *Web:* www.gosiger.com

Greene Rubber Company Inc 20 Cross St Woburn MA 01801 781-937-9909
Web: www.greenerubber.com

H G Makelim Co 219 Shaw Rd. South San Francisco CA 94080 650-873-4757 872-5438
TF: 800-471-0590 ■ *Web:* www.hgmakelim.com

Hagemeyer North America Inc
1460 Tobias Gadson Blvd. Charleston SC 29407 843-745-2400 745-6942
TF: 877-462-7070 ■ *Web:* www.hagemeyerna.com

Haggard & Stocking Assoc
5318 Victory Dr Indianapolis IN 46203 317-788-4661 788-1645
TF: 800-622-4824 ■ *Web:* www.haggard-stocking.com

Hahn Systems Co Inc 6312 SE Ave Indianapolis IN 46203 317-243-3796 244-9079
TF: 800-201-4246 ■ *Web:* www.hahnsystems.com

Harrington Industrial Plastics LLC
14480 Yorba Ave Chino CA 91710 909-597-8641 597-9826
TF: 800-213-4528 ■ *Web:* www.harringtonplastics.com

HD Supply Waterworks Ltd PO Box 1419 Thomasville GA 31799 800-950-7659
TF: 800-492-6909 ■ *Web:* www.hdswaterworks.com

Herc-U-Lift Inc 5655 Hwy 12 W PO Box 69 Maple Plain MN 55359 763-479-2501 479-2296
TF: 800-362-3500 ■ *Web:* www.herculift.com

HJM Precision Inc 9 New Tpke Rd Troy NY 12182 518-235-7407
Web: www.hjmprecision.com

Hope Group 70 Bearfoot Rd Northborough MA 01532 508-393-7660 393-8203
Web: www.thehopegroup.com

Hughes Machinery Co 14400 College Blvd Lenexa KS 66215 913-492-0355 492-1420
Web: www.hughesmachinery.com

Hull Lift Truck Inc 28747 Old US 33 W Elkhart IN 46516 574-293-8651 293-9769
TF: 888-284-0364 ■ *Web:* www.hulllifttruck.com

Hydraulics International Inc
9201 Independence Ave Chatsworth CA 91311 818-998-1231 718-2459
Web: www.hiinet.com

IBT Inc 9400 W 55th St. Merriam KS 66203 913-677-3151 677-3752
TF: 800-332-2114 ■ *Web:* www.ibtinc.com

IKO International Inc
91 Walsh Dr Fox Hill Industrial Park Parsippany NJ 07054 973-402-0254
Web: www.ikont.com

Illinois Auto Electric Co 700 Enterprise St Aurora IL 60504 630-862-3300 862-3137
TF: 800-683-8484 ■ *Web:* www.illinoisautoelectric.com

Indeck Power Equipment Co 1111 Willis Ave Wheeling IL 60090 847-541-8300 541-9984
TF: 800-446-3325 ■ *Web:* www.indeck.com

Indoff Inc 11816 Lackland Rd Saint Louis MO 63146 314-997-1122 812-3932
TF: 800-486-7867 ■ *Web:* www.indoff.com

Industrial Controls Distributors Inc (ICD)
1776 Bloomsbury Ave Ocean NJ 07712 732-918-9000 922-4417
TF Sales: 800-281-4788 ■ *Web:* www.industrialcontrolsonline.com

Industrial Diesel Inc 8705 Harmon Rd Fort Worth TX 76177 817-232-1071 232-0354
TF: 800-323-3659 ■ *Web:* www.industrialdiesel.net

Industrial Supply Solutions Inc
520 Elizabeth St Charleston WV 25311 304-346-5341
Web: www.issimro.com

Innerstave LLC 21660 Eighth St E. Sonoma CA 95476 707-996-8781
Web: www.innerstave.com

Integra Services Technologies Inc
3238 E Pasadena Fwy. Pasadena TX 77503 713-920-2400
Web: www.integratechnologies.com

J. H. Bennett & Company Inc PO Box 8028 Novi MI 48376 248-596-5100 596-0640
TF General: 800-837-5426 ■ *Web:* www.jhbennett.com

Jabo Supply Corp 5164 County Rd 64/66 Huntington WV 25705 304-736-8333 736-8551
TF: 800-334-5226 ■ *Web:* www.jabosupply.com

Jefferds Corp 2070 Winfield Rd Saint Albans WV 25177 304-755-8111
TF: 888-848-6216 ■ *Web:* www.jefferds.com

Kaplan Industries Inc
Route 73 & Morris Ave Maple Shade NJ 08052 856-779-8181
Web: www.kaplanindustries.com

Keen Compressed Gas Company Inc
4063 New Castle Ave New Castle DE 19720 302-594-4545
Web: www.keengas.com

Kemper Equipment Inc 5051 Horseshoe Pk Honey Brook PA 19344 610-273-2066 273-3537
Web: www.kemperequipment.com

Kennametal Inc 1600 Technology Way PO Box 231 Latrobe PA 15650 724-539-5000
NYSE: KMT ■ *TF Cust Svc:* 800-446-7738 ■ *Web:* www.kennametal.com

Kimball Midwest 4800 Robert Rd. Columbus OH 43228 614-219-6100 219-6101
TF: 800-233-1294 ■ *Web:* www.kimballmidwest.com

Knickerbocker Russell Company Inc
4759 Campbells Run Pittsburgh PA 15205 412-494-9233 787-7991
Web: www.knickerbockerrussell.com

Lawson Products Inc 1666 E Touhy Ave Des Plaines IL 60018 847-827-9666 827-1525*
**Fax:* Sales ■ *Web:* www.lawsonproducts.com

Lewis Goetz & Company Inc
1571 Grandview Ave Paulsboro NJ 08066 856-579-1421 579-1429
TF: 800-257-6239 ■ *Web:* www.lewis-goetz.com

Company / Address	City	State	Zip	Phone	Fax
Lewis-Goetz & Co Inc 650 Washington Rd Ste 210	Pittsburgh	PA	15228	412-341-7100	
TF: 800-989-0447 ■ *Web:* www.lewis-goetz.com					
Lipten Company LLC 28054 Ctr Oaks Ct	Wixom	MI	48393	248-374-8910	374-8906
TF: 800-860-0790 ■ *Web:* www.lipten.com					
Lister-Petter Americas Inc 815 E 56 Hwy	Olathe	KS	66061	913-764-3512	764-5493
Web: www.lister-petter.com					
Livingston & Haven 11529 Wilmar Blvd PO Box 7207	Charlotte	NC	28273	704-588-3670	504-2530
Web: www.livhaven.com					
Logan Corp 555 Seventh Ave	Huntington	WV	25701	304-526-4700	526-4747
TF: 888-853-4751 ■ *Web:* www.logancorp.com					
M & L Industries Inc 1210 St Charles St	Houma	LA	70360	985-876-2280	872-9596
TF General: 800-969-0068 ■ *Web:* www.mlind.net					
Mac-Gray Corp 404 Wyman St Ste 400	Waltham	MA	02451	781-487-7600	
NYSE: TUC ■ *TF:* 888-622-4729 ■ *Web:* www.macgray.com					
Machinery Sales Co 17253 Chestnut St	City of Industry	CA	91748	626-581-9211	581-9277
TF: 800-588-8111 ■ *Web:* www.mchysales.com					
Machinery Systems Inc 614 E State Pkwy	Schaumburg	IL	60173	847-882-8085	882-2894
TF: 866-428-1502 ■ *Web:* www.machsys.com					
Mack Boring & Parts Co 2365 US Hwy 22 W	Union	NJ	07083	908-964-0700	964-8475
Web: www.mackboring.com					
Mahar Tool Supply Co Inc 112 Williams St	Saginaw	MI	48605	989-799-5530	799-0830
TF: 800-456-2427 ■ *Web:* www.mahartool.com					
Martin Supply Co 200 Appleton Ave	Sheffield	AL	35660	256-383-3131	389-9447
TF: 800-828-8116 ■ *Web:* www.mscoinc.com					
McCall Handling Co 8801 Wise Ave	Dundalk	MD	21222	410-388-2600	388-2607
TF: 888-870-0685 ■ *Web:* www.mccallhandling.com					
McGill Hose & Coupling Inc 41 Benton Dr PO Box 408	East Longmeadow	MA	01028	413-525-3977	
TF: 800-669-1467 ■ *Web:* www.mcgillhose.com					
McKinley Equipment Corp 17611 Armstrong Ave	Irvine	CA	92614	949-261-9222	
TF: 800-770-6094 ■ *Web:* www.mckinleyequipment.com					
Medart Inc 124 Manufacturers Dr	Arnold	MO	63010	636-282-2300	510-3100*
**Fax Area Code:* 888 ■ *TF Cust Svc:* 800-888-7181 ■ *Web:* www.medartinc.com					
Midway Industrial Supply Inc 51 Wurz Ave	Utica	NY	13502	315-797-6660	
Web: www.midway.ws					
Minnesota Supply Company Inc 6470 Flying Cloud Dr	Eden Prairie	MN	55344	952-828-7300	828-7301
TF: 800-869-1028 ■ *Web:* www.mnsupply.com					
Mitsubishi International Corp 655 Third Ave	New York	NY	10017	212-605-2000	
Web: www.mitsubishicorp.com					
Modern Group Ltd 2501 Durham Rd	Bristol	PA	19007	215-943-9100	943-4978
TF: 800-223-3827 ■ *Web:* www.moderngroup.com					
Motion Industries Inc 1605 Alton Rd	Birmingham	AL	35210	205-956-1122	951-1172
TF: 800-526-9328 ■ *Web:* www.motionindustries.com					
MSC Industrial Direct Co 75 Maxess Rd	Melville	NY	11747	516-812-2000	255-5067*
NYSE: MSM ■ **Fax Area Code:* 800 ■ *TF:* 800-645-7270 ■ *Web:* www.mscdirect.com					
Multiquip Inc 18910 Wilmington Ave	Carson	CA	90746	310-537-3700	537-3927
TF: 800-421-1244 ■ *Web:* www.multiquip.com					
Nachi Robotic Systems Inc 22285 Roethel Dr	Novi	MI	48375	248-305-6545	305-6542
Web: www.nachirobotics.com					
NC Machinery Co 17025 W Valley Hwy	Tukwila	WA	98188	425-251-9800	
TF: 800-562-4735 ■ *Web:* www.ncmachinery.com					
Nebraska Machinery Co Inc 3501 S Jeffers St	North Platte	NE	69101	308-532-3100	
TF: 800-494-9560 ■ *Web:* www.nmc-corp.com					
Nelson-Jameson Inc 2400 E Fifth St PO Box 647	Marshfield	WI	54449	715-387-1151	387-8746
TF: 800-826-8302 ■ *Web:* www.nelsonjameson.com					
New England Industrial Truck Inc 195 Wildwood Ave	Woburn	MA	01801	781-935-9105	
Web: www.neit.com					
Newman's Inc 3003 Texas 225	Pasadena	TX	77503	713-675-8631	675-1589
TF: 800-231-3505					
Nitta Corporation of America 7605 Nitta Dr	Suwanee	GA	30024	770-497-0212	
Web: www.nitta.com					
Nu-Life Environmental Inc PO Box 1527	Easley	SC	29641	864-855-5155	295-2707
TF: 800-654-1752 ■ *Web:* www.nulifeenv.com					
O Berk Co 3 Milltown Ct	Union	NJ	07083	908-851-9500	851-9367
TF: 800-631-7392 ■ *Web:* www.oberk.com					
Pacific Power Group 600 S 56th Pl	Ridgefield	WA	98642	360-887-7400	887-5901
TF: 800-882-3860 ■ *Web:* www.pacificdda.com					
Piping & Equipment Inc 9100 Canniff St	Houston	TX	77017	713-947-9393	
TF: 888-889-9683 ■ *Web:* www.pipingequipment.com					
Poclain Hydraulics Inc PO Box 801	Sturtevant	WI	53177	262-321-0676	554-4860
Web: www.poclain-hydraulics.com					
Premier Equipment Inc 990 Sunshine Ln	Altamonte Springs	FL	32714	407-786-2000	786-2001
Web: www.premierequipment.com					
ProAct Services Corp 1140 Conrad Industrial Dr	Ludington	MI	49431	231-843-2711	
Web: www.proact-usa.com					
Production Tool Supply 8655 E Eight Mile Rd	Warren	MI	48089	586-755-7770	755-4921*
**Fax:* Sales ■ *TF:* 800-366-3600 ■ *Web:* www.pts-tools.com					
Provoast Automation Controls 12635 Danielson Court Ste 205	Poway	CA	92064	858-748-2237	
Web: www.proautocon.com					
R & M Energy Systems 301 Premier Rd	Borger	TX	79007	806-274-5293	
TF Sales: 888-262-8645 ■ *Web:* www.rmenergy.com					
R B M Co 2700 Texas Ave	Knoxville	TN	37921	865-524-8621	546-7326
TF: 800-521-5656 ■ *Web:* www.rbmcompany.com					
Red Ball Oxygen Co Inc 609 N Market	Shreveport	LA	71107	318-425-3211	425-6323
TF: 800-551-8150 ■ *Web:* www.redballoxygen.com					
Rem Sales Inc 910 Gay Hill Rd	Windsor	CT	06095	860-687-3400	687-3401
TF: 877-689-1860 ■ *Web:* www.remsales.com					
Remstar International Inc 41 Eisenhower Dr	Westbrook	ME	04092	800-639-5805	854-1610*
**Fax Area Code:* 207 ■ *TF:* 800-639-5805 ■ *Web:* www.kardexremstar.com					
Renishaw Inc 5277 Trillium Blvd	Hoffman Estates	IL	60192	847-286-9953	286-9974
Web: www.renishaw.com					
Rex Supply Co 3715 Harrisburg Blvd	Houston	TX	77003	713-222-2251	225-5739
TF: 800-369-0669 ■ *Web:* www.rex-supply.com					
RHM Fluid Power Inc 375 Manufacturers Dr	Westland	MI	48186	734-326-5400	326-0339
Web: www.rhmfluidpower.com					
Riekes Equipment Co PO Box 3392	Omaha	NE	68103	402-593-1181	593-9295
TF: 800-856-0931 ■ *Web:* www.riekesequipment.com					
Road Builders Machinery & Supply Company Inc 1001 S Seventh St	Kansas City	KS	66105	913-371-3822	371-3870
Web: www.roadbuildersmachinery.com					
Robert Dietrick Co Inc PO Box 605	Fishers	IN	46038	317-842-1991	842-2698
TF: 866-767-1888 ■ *Web:* www.rd-co.com					
Robert E Morris Co 910 Gay Hill Rd	Windsor	CT	06095	860-687-3300	687-3301
Web: www.robertemorris.com					
Royal Bearing Inc 17719 NE Sandy Blvd	Portland	OR	97230	503-231-0992	
Web: www.royalbearing.com					
RS Hughes Company Inc 1162 Sonora Ct	Sunnyvale	CA	94086	818-686-9111	
TF: 877-774-8443 ■ *Web:* www.rshughes.com					
Ryan Herco Products Corp 3010 N San Fernando Blvd	Burbank	CA	91504	818-841-1141	973-2600
TF: 800-848-1141 ■ *Web:* www.ryanherco.com					
S&K /Air Power 317 Dewitt Ave E	Mattoon	IL	61938	217-258-8500	258-8571
Web: www.skairpower.com					
S. J. Smith Company Inc 3707 W River Dr	Davenport	IA	52802	563-263-1829	324-1336
Web: www.sjsmith.com					
S.l.c. Meter Service Inc 10375 Dixie Hwy	Davisburg	MI	48350	248-625-0667	625-8650
TF: 800-433-4332 ■ *Web:* www.slcmeter.com					
Serenity Packaging Corp 1601 E Main St Ste 2E	Saint Charles	IL	60174	630-762-9870	
Web: www.serenitypkg.com					
Service Motor Co PO Box 170	Dale	WI	54931	920-779-4311	
Web: www.servicemotor.com					
Shively Bros Inc 2919 S Grand Travers St PO Box 1520	Flint	MI	48501	810-232-7401	232-3219
TF: 800-530-9352 ■ *Web:* www.shivelybros.com					
SKS Bottle & Packaging Inc 2600 Seventh Ave Bldg 60 W	Watervliet	NY	12189	518-880-6980	
Web: www.sks-bottle.com					
Smith Power Products Inc 3065 W California Ave	Salt Lake City	UT	84104	801-415-5000	415-5700
TF: 800-658-5352 ■ *Web:* www.smithpowerproducts.com					
So. Cal. Sandbags Inc 12620 Bosley Ln	Corona	CA	92883	951-277-3404	
Web: www.socalsandbags.com					
Sooner Pipe LLC 1331 Lamar St Ste 970 4 Houston Ctr	Houston	TX	77010	713-759-1200	759-0442
TF: 800-888-9161 ■ *Web:* www.soonerpipe.com					
Southern Pump & Tank Co 4800 N Graham St	Charlotte	NC	28269	704-596-4373	599-7700
TF Cust Svc: 800-477-2826 ■ *Web:* www.spatco.com					
Stanley M Proctor Co 2016 Midway Dr	Twinsburg	OH	44087	330-425-7814	
Web: www.stanleyproctor.com					
Star CNC Machine Tool Corp 123 Powerhouse Rd	Roslyn Heights	NY	11577	516-484-0500	484-5820
Web: www.starcnc.com					
Strategic Distribution Inc 1414 Radcliffe St Ste 300	Bristol	PA	19007	215-633-1900	633-4426
TF: 800-322-2644 ■ *Web:* www.sdi.com					
Swift Industrial Power Inc 10917 McBride Ln	Knoxville	TN	37932	865-966-9758	
Web: www.swiftpower.com					
Tech 24 75 Beattie Pl Ste 410	Greenville	SC	29601	864-271-6522	
Web: www.commercialfoodservicerepair.com					
Teeco Products Inc 16881 Armstrong Ave	Irvine	CA	92606	949-261-6295	474-8663
TF: 800-854-3463 ■ *Web:* www.teecoproducts.com					
Temco International Corp 11919 SW 130 St Ste 100	Miami	FL	33186	305-234-7851	
Web: www.temcointl.com					
Tencarva Machinery Company Inc 12200 Wilfong Ct	Midlothian	VA	23112	804-639-4646	639-2400
Web: www.tencarva.com					
Texas Process Equipment Co 5215 Ted St	Houston	TX	77040	713-460-5555	460-4807
TF: 800-828-4114 ■ *Web:* www.texasprocess.com					
TF Hudgins Inc 4405 Directors Row	Houston	TX	77092	713-682-3651	
Web: www.tfhudgins.com					
Timco Rubber Products Inc 12300 Sprecher Ave	Cleveland	OH	44135	216-267-6242	
Web: www.timcorubber.com					
Tool Service Corp 2942 N 117th St	Milwaukee	WI	53226	414-476-7600	
Web: www.toolservice.com					
Total Equipment Co 400 Fifth Ave	Coraopolis	PA	15108	412-269-0999	269-0262
Web: www.totalequipment.com					
Total Filtration Services Inc 2725 Commerce Pkwy	Auburn Hills	MI	48326	248-377-4004	
Web: www.tfsi1.com					
Tox-Pressotechnik LLC 4250 Weaver Pkwy	Warrenville	IL	60555	630-393-0300	393-6800
Web: www.tox-us.com					
Travers Tool Company Inc 128-15 26th Ave	Flushing	NY	11354	718-886-7200	722-0703*
**Fax Area Code:* 800 ■ *TF Cust Svc:* 800-221-0270 ■ *Web:* www.travers.com					
Trio Pines U.S.A. Inc 16233 Heron Ave	La Mirada	CA	90638	714-523-5800	
Web: www.triopines.com					
Troy Belting & Supply Co 70 Cohoes Rd	Watervliet	NY	12189	518-272-4920	
Web: www.troyindustrialsolutions.com					
Turck Inc 3000 Campus Dr	Minneapolis	MN	55441	763-553-7300	553-0708
Web: www.turck.com					
Ulvac Technologies Inc 401 Griffin Brook Dr	Methuen	MA	01844	978-686-7550	689-6300
Web: www.ulvac.com					
Valtra Inc 7141 Paramount Blvd	Pico Rivera	CA	90660	562-949-8625	
TF: 800-989-5244 ■ *Web:* www.valtrainc.com					
Vellano Bros Inc 7 Hemlock St	Latham	NY	12110	518-785-5537	785-5578
TF: 800-342-9855 ■ *Web:* www.vellano.com					
Voto Manufacturers Sales Co 500 N Third St PO Box 1299	Steubenville	OH	43952	740-282-3621	282-5441
TF: 800-848-4010 ■ *Web:* www.votosales.com					
W.P. & R.S. Mars Co 4319 W First St	Duluth	MN	55807	218-628-0303	
Web: www.marssupply.com					
Waukesha-Pearce Industries Inc (WPI) 12320 S Main	Houston	TX	77235	713-723-1050	551-0454
Web: www.wpi.com					

				Phone	Fax

WELSCO Inc 9006 Crystal Hill Rd. North Little Rock AR 72113 501-771-1204
Web: www.welsco.com

Werres Corp 807 E S St. Frederick MD 21701 301-620-4000 662-1028*
**Fax:* Sales ■ *TF:* 800-638-6563 ■ *Web:* www.werres.com

Wilson Supply Co 1302 Conti St. Houston TX 77002 713-237-3700
TF: 800-874-5930

Wind River Holdings LP
555 Croton Rd Croton Rd Corporate Ctr
Ste 300 King Of Prussia PA 19406 610-962-3770
Web: www.windriverholdings.com

Windsor Factory Supply Ltd 730 N Service Rd. Windsor ON N8X3J3 519-966-2202 966-2740
TF: 800-387-2659 ■ *Web:* www.wfsltd.com

Yamazen Inc 735 E Remington Rd. Schaumburg IL 60173 847-490-8130 490-3192
TF: 800-882-8558 ■ *Web:* www.yamazen.com

Yanmar America Corp
101 International Pkwy Adairsville GA 30103 770-877-9894 877-9009
Web: www.yanmar.com

Zatkoff Seals & Packings
23230 Industrial Pk Dr Farmington Hills MI 48335 248-478-2400 478-3392
Web: www.zatkoff.com

Zuckerman Honickman 191 S Gulph Rd King Of Prussia PA 19406 610-962-0100 962-1080
Web: www.zh-inc.com

386 INDUSTRIAL MACHINERY, EQUIPMENT, & SUPPLIES

See Also Conveyors & Conveying Equipment p. 2160; Food Products Machinery p. 2314; Furnaces & Ovens - Industrial Process p. 2338; Machine Shops p. 2688; Material Handling Equipment p. 2732; Packaging Machinery & Equipment p. 2862; Paper Industries Machinery p. 2868; Printing & Publishing Equipment & Systems p. 2988; Rolling Mill Machinery p. 3141; Textile Machinery p. 3241; Woodworking Machinery p. 3315

				Phone	Fax

3G Tech Inc 6910 Hayvenhurst Ave Unit 100 Van Nuys CA 91406 818-510-4709 510-4716
Web: www.gggtech.com

ABB Inc 501 Merritt 7 Norwalk CT 06851 203-750-2200 435-7365
TF Prod Info: 800-626-4999 ■ *Web:* new.abb.com/us

Accu Therm Inc PO Box 249 Monroe City MO 63456 573-735-1060 735-1066
TF: 888-925-4332 ■ *Web:* www.accutherm.com

Acme Electric
N85 W12545 Westbrook Crossing Menomonee Falls WI 53051 910-738-1121 293-7022*
**Fax Area Code:* 262 ■ *TF:* 800-334-5214 ■ *Web:* www.hubbell-acmeelectric.com

Acorn Gencon Plastics Inc
15125 Proctor Ave City of Industry CA 91746 626-968-6681 855-4860
TF: 800-782-7706 ■ *Web:* www.whitehallmfg.com

Adept Technology Inc 5960 Inglewood Dr Pleasanton CA 94588 925-245-3400 960-0452
NASDAQ: ADEP ■ *TF:* 800-292-3378 ■ *Web:* www.adept.com

Advent Design Corp Canal St & Jefferson Ave Bristol PA 19007 215-781-0500 781-0508
Web: adventdesign.com

Aeroglide Corp 100 Aeroglide Dr Cary NC 27511 919-851-2000 851-6029
TF: 800-722-7483 ■ *Web:* www.buhlergroup.com

Airtech International Inc
5700 Skylab Rd Huntington Beach CA 92647 714-899-8100 899-8179
Web: www.airtechintl.com

Alemite LLC
1057-521 Corporate Ctr Dr Ste 100 Fort Mill SC 29715 803-802-0001
TF: 800-267-8022 ■ *Web:* www.alemite.com

Allen-Sherman-Hoff Co 457 Creamery Way Exton PA 19341 484-875-1600 875-2080
Web: www.diamondpower.com

Allentown Equipment 1733 90th St. Sturtevant WI 53177 800-553-3414 884-3070*
**Fax Area Code:* 262 ■ *TF:* 800-553-3414 ■ *Web:* www.putzmeisteramerica.com

Allentown Inc 165 County Rd Allentown NJ 08501 609-259-7951 259-0449
Web: www.allentowninc.com

American Baler Co 800 E Centre St Bellevue OH 44811 419-483-5790 483-3815
TF: 800-843-7512 ■ *Web:* www.americanbaler.com

AO Smith Water Products Co
500 Tennessee Waltz Pkwy Ashland City TN 37015 800-527-1953 792-2163*
**Fax Area Code:* 615 ■ *TF:* 800-527-1953 ■ *Web:* www.hotwater.com

Apache Stainless Equipment Corp
200 W Industrial Dr PO Box 538 Beaver Dam WI 53916 920-356-9900 887-0206
TF: 800-444-0398 ■ *Web:* www.apachestainless.com

Ats Systems Oregon Inc
2121 NE Jack London St Corvallis OR 97330 541-758-3329 758-9022
TF: 800-564-6253 ■ *Web:* www.atsautomation.com

Auto Chlor System 450 Ferguson Dr Mountain View CA 94043 650-967-3085
Web: www.autochlor.com

Azon USA Inc 643 W Crosstown Pkwy Kalamazoo MI 49008 269-385-5942 373-9295
TF: 800-788-5942 ■ *Web:* www.azonintl.com

Bauer-Pileco Inc 100 N FM 3083 E Conroe TX 77303 713-691-3000 691-0089
TF: 800-474-5326 ■ *Web:* www.bauerpileco.com

Besser Co 801 Johnson St Alpena MI 49707 989-354-4111 354-3120
TF: 800-530-9980 ■ *Web:* www.besser.com

Billco Manufacturing Inc
100 Halstead Blvd. Zelienople PA 16063 724-452-7390 452-0217
Web: www.billco-mfg.com

Blower Application Company Inc
N 114 W 19125 Clinton Dr Germantown WI 53022 262-255-5580 255-3446
TF: 800-959-0880 ■ *Web:* www.bloapco.com

Burke E Porter Machinery Co
730 Plymouth Ave NE Grand Rapids MI 49505 616-234-1200 459-1032
Web: www.bepco.com

CHA Industries 4201 Business Ctr Dr Fremont CA 94538 510-683-8554 683-3848*
**Fax:* Sales ■ *Web:* www.chaindustries.com

Charles Ross & Son Co 710 Old Willets Path Hauppauge NY 11788 631-234-0500 234-0691
TF: 800-243-7677 ■ *Web:* www.mixers.com

Chemineer Inc 5870 Poe Ave Dayton OH 45414 937-454-3200 454-3379*
**Fax:* Sales ■ *TF:* 800-643-0641 ■ *Web:* www.chemineer.com

Chemithon Corp 5430 W Marginal Way SW Seattle WA 98106 206-937-9954 932-3786
Web: www.chemithon.com

Chief Automotive Systems Inc
1924 E Fourth St. Grand Island NE 68802 308-384-9747 384-8966*
**Fax:* Mktg ■ *TF:* 800-445-9262 ■ *Web:* www.chiefautomotive.com

				Phone	Fax

Clean Diesel Technologies Inc
4567 Telephone Rd Ste 206 Ventura CA 93003 805-639-9458 707-7746*
NASDAQ: CDTI ■ **Fax Area Code:* 905 ■ *TF:* 800-661-9963 ■ *Web:* www.cdti.com

Clemco Industries Corp I Cable Car Dr Washington MO 63090 636-239-0300 726-7559*
**Fax Area Code:* 800 ■ *Web:* www.clemcoindustries.com

CMA Dishmachines 12700 Knott St Garden Grove CA 92841 714-898-8781
TF: 800-854-6417 ■ *Web:* www.cmadishmachines.com

Corotec Corp 145 Hyde Rd Farmington CT 06032 860-678-0038 674-5229
TF: 800-423-0348 ■ *Web:* www.corotec.com

CUNO Inc 400 Research Pkwy Meriden CT 06450 203-237-5541 238-8701
TF: 800-243-6894 ■ *Web:* www.3m.com

Davis-Ulmer Sprinkler Company Inc
1 Commerce Dr Amherst NY 14228 716-691-3200 691-1230
TF: 877-691-3200 ■ *Web:* www.davisulmer.com

Despatch Industries Inc 8860 207th St W Lakeville MN 55044 952-469-5424 469-4513
TF: 800-726-0110 ■ *Web:* www.despatch.com

Diamond Power International Inc
2600 E Main St. Lancaster OH 43130 740-687-6500 687-4229
TF: 800-848-5086 ■ *Web:* www.diamondpower.com

Dings Co 4740 W Electric Ave. Milwaukee WI 53219 414-672-7830 672-7830
TF: 800-494-1918 ■ *Web:* www.dingsbrakes.com

Dom-Ex LLC 109 Grant St Hibbing MN 55746 218-262-6116 263-8611
Web: www.dom-ex.com

Dresser-Rand
10205 Westheimer Rd W 8 Twr Ste 1000 Houston TX 77042 713-354-6100 354-6110
NYSE: DRC ■ *Web:* www.dresser-rand.com

Dynamic Manufacturing Inc
1930 N Mannheim Rd. Melrose Park IL 60160 708-343-8753 343-8768
Web: www.dynamicmanufacturinginc.com

Easom Automation Systems Inc
32471 Industrial Dr. Madison Heights MI 48071 248-307-0650 307-0701
Web: www.easomeng.com

Ecodyne Ltd 4475 Corporate Dr. Burlington ON L7L5T9 905-332-1404 332-6726
TF: 888-326-3963 ■ *Web:* www.ecodyne.com

EFD Induction Inc 31511 Dequindre Rd Madison Heights MI 48071 248-658-0700 658-0701
Web: www.efd-induction.com

Elliott Tape Inc 1882 Pond Run Auburn Hills MI 48326 248-475-2000 475-5893
Web: www.egitape.com

Enerflex Systems Ltd
1331 Macleod Trail SE Ste 904 Calgary AB T2G0K3 403-387-6377 236-6816
TSE: EFX ■ *TF:* 800-242-3178 ■ *Web:* www.enerflex.com

Energy Sciences Inc 42 Industrial Way Wilmington MA 01887 978-694-9000 694-9046
Web: www.ebeam.com

Engis Corp 105 W Hintz Rd Wheeling IL 60090 847-808-9400 808-9430
TF: 800-993-6447 ■ *Web:* www.engis.com

Equipment Manufacturing Corp (EMC)
14930 Marquardt Ave Santa Fe Springs CA 90670 562-623-9394 623-9342
TF: 888-833-9000 ■ *Web:* www.equipmentmanufacturing.com

FANUC America Corp 3900 W Hamlin Rd Rochester Hills MI 48309 248-377-7000 377-7832
TF: 800-477-6268 ■ *Web:* www.fanucamerica.com/corporate-home.aspx

Farrel Corp 25 Main St. Ansonia CT 06401 203-736-5500 736-5580
TF: 800-800-7290 ■ *Web:* www.farrel-pomini.com

Fluid Management Inc 1023 S Wheeling Rd Wheeling IL 60090 847-537-0880 537-3221
TF: 800-462-2466 ■ *Web:* www.fluidman.com

Formaloy Corp 1080 W Jefferson St Morton IL 61550 309-266-5381

Forward Technology Inc 260 Jenks Ave Cokato MN 55321 320-286-2578 286-2467
TF Cust Svc: 800-307-6040 ■ *Web:* www.forwardtech.com

French Oil Mill Machinery Co 1035 W Greene St Piqua OH 45356 937-773-3420 773-3424
Web: www.frenchoil.com

Fusion Inc 4658 E 355th St Willoughby OH 44094 440-946-3300 942-9083
TF: 800-626-9501 ■ *Web:* www.fusion-inc.com

Gamajet Cleaning Systems Inc 604 Jeffers Cir Exton PA 19341 610-408-9940 408-9945
TF Sales: 877-426-2538 ■ *Web:* www.gamajet.com

General Equipment Co
620 Alexander Dr SW PO Box 334 Owatonna MN 55060 507-451-5510 451-5511
TF Cust Svc: 800-533-0524 ■ *Web:* www.generalequip.com

Genmark Automation Inc 46723 Lakeview Blvd Fremont CA 94538 510-897-3400 942-7561*
**Fax Area Code:* 408 ■ *Web:* www.genmarkautomation.info

George Koch Sons LLC 10 S 11th Ave Evansville IN 47712 812-465-9600 465-9814*
**Fax:* Sales ■ *TF:* 888-873-5624 ■ *Web:* www.kochllc.com

Gerber Scientific Inc 24 Industrial Pk Rd W Tolland CT 06084 860-870-2890
Web: www.gerbertechnology.com

Glastender Inc 5400 N Michigan Rd Saginaw MI 48604 989-752-4275 752-4444
TF: 800-748-0423 ■ *Web:* www.glastender.com

Globe Products Inc 5051 Kitridge Rd Dayton OH 45424 937-233-0233 233-5290
Web: www.globe-usa.com

Glunt Industries Inc 319 N River Rd NW Warren OH 44483 330-399-7585 393-0387
Web: www.glunt.com

Gougler Industries Inc 711 Lake St Kent OH 44240 330-673-5826 677-1616
TF: 800-527-2282 ■ *Web:* www.frdusa.com

Graham Corp 20 Florence Ave Batavia NY 14020 585-343-2216 343-1097
NYSE: GHM ■ *TF Orders:* 800-828-8150 ■ *Web:* www.graham-mfg.com

Gregory Poole Equipment Co
4807 Beryl Rd PO Box 469 Raleigh NC 27606 919-828-0641 890-4621
TF: 800-451-7278 ■ *Web:* www.gregorypoole.com

Grenzebach Corp 10 Herring Rd Newnan GA 30265 770-253-4980 253-5189
Web: www.grenzebach.com

Guzzler Manufacturing Inc
1621 S Illinois St Streator IL 61364 815-672-3171 672-2779*
**Fax:* Sales ■ *Web:* www.guzzler.com

GWI Engineering Inc 1411 Michigan St NE Grand Rapids MI 49503 616-459-8274
Web: www.gwiengineering.com

Hamon Research-Cottrell Inc 58 E Main St. Somerville NJ 08876 908-685-4000 333-2152
TF: 800-445-6578 ■ *Web:* www.hamon-researchcottrell.com

Harrington Hoists Inc 401 W End Ave Manheim PA 17545 717-665-2000 665-2861
TF: 800-233-3010 ■ *Web:* www.harringtonhoists.com

Helgesen Industries Inc 7261 Hwy 60 W Hartford WI 53027 262-673-4444 709-4409
Web: www.helgesen.com

Hfw Industries Inc
196 Philadelphia St PO Box 8 Buffalo NY 14207 716-875-3380 875-3385
TF: 800-937-9311

Hirotec America Inc 4567 Glenmeade Ln Auburn Hills MI 48326 248-836-5100 836-5101
Web: www.hirotecamerica.com

				Phone	Fax
Hosokawa Micron Powder Systems 10 Chatham Rd Web: www.hosokawamicron.co.jp/en/global.html	Summit	NJ	07901	908-273-6360	273-6344
Hosokawa Polymer Systems 63 Fuller Way TF: 800-233-6112 ■ Web: www.polysys.com	Berlin	CT	06037	860-828-0541	829-1313
Husky Injection Molding Systems Ltd 500 Queen St S. TF: 800-465-4875 ■ Web: www.husky.co	Bolton	ON	L7E5S5	905-951-5000	951-5384
Hydro-Thermal Corp 400 Pilot Ct. TF: 800-952-0121 ■ Web: www.hydro-thermal.com	Waukesha	WI	53188	262-548-8900	548-8908
Illinois Tool Works Inc (ITW) 3600 W Lake Ave NYSE: ITW ■ Web: www.itw.com	Glenview	IL	60026	847-724-7500	657-4261
Industrial Fabricators Inc 403 N Cemetery St Web: industrialfabinc.com	Thorp	WI	54771	715-669-5512	669-5514
ITW United Silicone 4471 Walden Ave. Web: www.unitedsilicone.com	Lancaster	NY	14086	716-681-8222	681-8789
Jesco-Wipco Industries Inc 950 Anderson Rd PO Box 388 TF: 800-455-0019 ■ Web: www.jescoonline.com	Litchfield	MI	49252	517-542-2903	542-2501
JV Manufacturing Inc 1603 Burtner Rd. *Fax Area Code: 479	Natrona Heights	PA	15065	724-224-1704	872-0037*
K & B Machine Works Inc 208 Rebecca's Pond Rd Web: www.kb-machine.com	Schriever	LA	70395	985-868-6730	
Kanematsu USA Inc 500 Fifth Ave 29th Fl Web: www.kanematsuusa.com	New York	NY	10110	212-704-9400	704-9483
Kawasaki Robotics Inc 28140 Lakeview Dr Web: robotics.kawasaki.com/en1	Wixom	MI	48393	248-446-4100	446-4200
Kobelco Stewart Bolling Inc (KSBI) 1600 Terex Rd TF: 800-464-0064 ■ Web: www.ksbiusa.com	Hudson	OH	44236	330-655-3111	655-2982
Koch Membrane Systems Inc 850 Main St TF: 888-677-5624 ■ Web: www.kochmembrane.com	Wilmington	MA	01887	978-694-7000	657-5208
Koch-Glitsch Inc 4111 E 37th St N. Web: www.koch-glitsch.com	Wichita	KS	67220	316-828-5110	828-5263
Kois Bros Equipment Company Inc 5200 Colorado Blvd TF: 800-672-6010 ■ Web: www.koisbrothers.com	Commerce	CO	80022	303-298-7370	
Komatsu America Industries LLC 1701 W Golf Rd Ste 300 Web: www.komatsupress.com	Rolling Meadows	IL	60008	847-437-3888	437-1811
Komline-Sanderson Engineering Corp 12 Holland Ave TF: 800-225-5457 ■ Web: www.komline.com	Peapack	NJ	07977	908-234-1000	234-9487
Lawton Industries Inc 4353 Pacific St. TF: 800-692-2600 ■ Web: www.lawtonindustries.com	Rocklin	CA	95677	916-624-7895	624-7898
LDI Industries Inc PO Box 1810 Web: www.ldi-industries.com	Manitowoc	WI	54221	920-682-6877	684-7210
Lee Industries Inc 50 W Pine St. Web: www.leeind.com	Philipsburg	PA	16866	814-342-0461	342-5660
Lesman Instrument Co 135 Bernice Dr TF: 800-953-7626 ■ Web: www.lesman.com	Bensenville	IL	60106	630-595-8400	595-2386
Leviathan Corp 20 Jay St Web: www.leviathancorp.com	Brooklyn	NY	11201	718-701-5718	701-5745
Lightnin 135 Mt Read Blvd TF: 877-247-3797 ■ Web: www.spx.com	Rochester	NY	14611	585-436-5550	436-5589
Ligon Industries LLC 1927 First Ave N 5th Fl. Web: www.ligonindustries.com	Birmingham	AL	35203	205-322-3302	322-3188
Lincoln Industrial Corp 5148 N Hanley Rd *Fax Area Code: 800 ■ *Fax: Cust Svc ■ Web: www.lincolnindustrial.com	Saint Louis	MO	63134	314-679-4200	424-5359*
Littleford Day Inc 7451 Empire Dr TF: 800-365-8555 ■ Web: www.littleford.com	Florence	KY	41042	859-525-7600	525-1446
Lmt USA Inc 1081 S Northpoint Blvd *Fax Area Code: 630 ■ TF: 800-225-0852 ■ Web: www.lmtfette.com	Waukegan	IL	60085	800-225-0852	969-5492*
Marathon Equipment Co PO Box 1798 TF: 800-633-8974 ■ Web: www.marathonequipment.com	Vernon	AL	35592	205-695-9105	695-8813
Mark-Costello Co, The 1145 E Dominguez St. Web: www.mark-costello.com	Carson	CA	90746	310-637-1851	762-2330
Maruka USA Inc 400 Commons Way TF: 800-631-0426 ■ Web: www.marukausa.com	Rockaway	NJ	07866	973-983-1000	983-8647
Materials Transportation Co (MTC) 1408 S Commerce PO Box 1358 TF: 800-433-3110 ■ Web: www.gomtc.com	Temple	TX	76503	254-298-2900	771-0287
McCarty Equipment Co Ltd 1103 Industrial Blvd Web: www.mccartyequipment.com	Abilene	TX	79602	325-691-5558	691-5453
McNeil & NRM Inc 96 E Crosier St. TF: 800-669-2525 ■ Web: www.mcneilnrm.com	Akron	OH	44311	330-253-2525	253-7022
MEGTEC Systems Inc 830 Prosper Rd TF Cust Svc: 800-558-5535 ■ Web: www.megtec.com	De Pere	WI	54115	920-336-5715	339-2784
Metem Corp 700 Parsippany Rd Web: www.metem.com	Parsippany	NJ	07054	973-887-6635	887-1755
MFRI Inc 7720 N Lehigh Ave NASDAQ: MFRI ■ Web: www.mfri.com	Niles	IL	60714	847-966-1000	966-8563
Michigan Fluid Power Inc 4556 Spartan Industrial Dr SW TF: 800-635-0289 ■ Web: www.mifp.com	Grandville	MI	49418	616-538-5700	538-0888
Michigan Wheel Corp 1501 Buchanan Ave SW TF: 800-369-4335 ■ Web: www.miwheel.com	Grand Rapids	MI	49507	616-452-6941	247-0227
Mico Inc 1911 Lee Blvd TF: 800-477-6426 ■ Web: www.mico.com	North Mankato	MN	56003	507-625-6426	625-3212
Micro-Poise Measurment Systems LLC 1624 Englewood Ave TF: 800-428-3812 ■ Web: www.micropoise.com	Akron	OH	44305	330-784-1251	798-0250
Milacron Inc 3010 Disney St. Web: www.milacron.com	Cincinnati	OH	45209	513-487-5000	487-5086
Minuteman International Inc 111 S Rohlwing Rd TF: 800-323-9420 ■ Web: www.minutemanintl.com	Addison	IL	60101	630-627-6900	627-1130
Mississippi Welders Supply Co 5150 W Sixth St. TF: 800-657-4422 ■ Web: www.mwsco.com	Winona	MN	55987	507-454-5231	454-8104
Monroe Environmental Corp 810 W Front St TF: 800-992-7707 ■ Web: www.monroeenvironmental.com	Monroe	MI	48161	734-242-7654	242-5275
Moody-Price LLC 18320 Petroleum Dr *Fax Area Code: 225 ■ TF: 800-272-9832 ■ Web: www.moodyprice.com	Baton Rouge	LA	70809	800-272-9832	763-6005*
Morrell Inc 333 Bald Mtn Rd Web: www.morrellinc.com	Auburn Hills	MI	48326	248-373-1600	373-0612
Mueller Graphic Supply Inc 11475 W Thdore Trcker Way Web: www.muellergraphics.com	Milwaukee	WI	53214	414-475-0990	475-0454
Mueller Steam Specialty 1491 NC Hwy 20 W TF: 800-334-6259 ■ Web: www.muellersteam.com	Saint Pauls	NC	28384	910-865-8241	865-8245
National Super Service Company Inc 3115 Frenchman Rd TF Cust Svc: 800-677-1663 ■ Web: www.nss.com	Toledo	OH	43607	419-531-2121	531-3761
Netzsch Inc 119 Pickering Way Web: pumps.netzsch.com/us	Exton	PA	19341	610-363-8010	363-0971
Neumayer Equipment Company Inc 5060 Arsenal St TF: 800-843-4563 ■ Web: www.neumayerequipment.com	Saint Louis	MO	63139	314-772-4501	772-2311
Nexen Group Inc 560 Oak Grove Pkwy TF: 800-843-7445 ■ Web: www.nexengroup.com	Vadnais Heights	MN	55127	651-484-5900	286-1099
Nilfisk-Advance Inc 14600 21st Ave N. TF Cust Svc: 800-989-2235 ■ Web: www.nilfisk.com/en	Plymouth	MN	55447	800-989-2235	989-6566
Nordson Corp 28601 Clemens Rd NASDAQ: NDSN ■ TF: 800-321-2881 ■ Web: www.nordson.com	Westlake	OH	44145	440-892-1580	892-9507
North Light Color Inc 5008 Hillsboro Ave N Web: www.northlightcolor.com	Minneapolis	MN	55428	763-531-8222	531-8224
Oil & Gas Equipment Corp 8 Rd 350 TF: 800-868-9624 ■ Web: www.ogequip.com	Flora Vista	NM	87415	505-333-2300	333-2301
Oscar Wilson Engines & Parts Inc 826 Lone Star Dr *Fax Area Code: 800 ■ TF: 800-233-3723 ■ Web: www.oscar-wilson.com	O Fallon	MO	63366	636-978-1313	873-6720*
Pall Corp 2200 Northern Blvd. NYSE: PLL ■ TF: 800-645-6532 ■ Web: www.pall.com	East Hills	NY	11548	516-484-5400	801-9754
Parker Industries Inc 1650 Sycamore Ave Web: www.parkerind.com	Bohemia	NY	11716	631-567-1000	567-1355
Parkson Corp 1401 W Cyperess Creek Rd *Fax Area Code: 954 ■ TF: 888-727-5766 ■ Web: www.parkson.com	Fort Lauderdale	FL	33309	888-727-5766	974-6182*
Paul Mueller Co 1600 W Phelps St. OTC: MUEL ■ TF: 800-683-5537 ■ Web: paulmueller.com	Springfield	MO	65802	417-831-3000	831-3528
PDQ Manufacturing Inc 1698 Scheuring Rd TF: 800-227-3373 ■ Web: www.pdqinc.com	De Pere	WI	54115	920-983-8333	983-8330
Peach State Integrated Technologies Inc 3005 Business Pk Dr TF: 800-998-6517 ■ Web: www.peachstate.com	Norcross	GA	30071	678-327-2000	327-2030
Peerless Manufacturing Co 14651 N Dallas Pkwy Ste 500. NASDAQ: PMFG ■ TF: 877-879-7634 ■ Web: www.peerlessmfg.com	Dallas	TX	75254	214-357-6181	351-0194
Pengate Handling Systems Inc 3 Interchange Pl Web: www.pengate.com	York	PA	17406	717-764-3050	764-5854
Permadur Industries Inc 186 Rt 206 S TF: 800-392-0146 ■ Web: www.permadur.com	Hillsborough	NJ	08844	908-359-9767	359-9773
Perry Videx LLC 25 Mount Laurel Rd Web: www.perryvidex.com	Hainesport	NJ	08036	609-267-1600	267-4499
Peterson Machine Tool Inc 1100 N Union St. *Fax Area Code: 620 ■ TF: 800-835-3528 ■ Web: petersonwashandblast.com	Council Grove	KS	66846	800-835-3528	767-6415*
Pfaudler Inc 1000 W Ave. Web: www.pfaudler.com	Rochester	NY	14611	585-235-1000	235-6393
Phillips Machine Service Inc 367 George St. TF: 800-733-1521 ■ Web: www.phillipsmachine.com	Beckley	WV	25801	304-255-0537	255-0565
Phoenix Process Equipment Co 2402 Watterson Trial Web: www.dewater.com	Louisville	KY	40299	502-499-6198	499-1079
Pioneer/Eclipse Corp 1 Eclipse Rd TF Cust Svc: 800-367-3550 ■ Web: pioneereclipse.com	Sparta	NC	28675	336-372-8080	372-2895
Pipe & Tube Supply Inc 1407 N Cypress TF: 800-770-8823 ■ Web: www.pipeandtubesupply.com	North Little Rock	AR	72114	501-372-6556	372-7694
Powerboss Inc 175 Anderson St. Web: powerboss.com	Aberdeen	NC	28315	910-944-2105	944-7409
PPC Industries - Electrostatic Precipitator 3000 E Marshall Ave. Web: www.ppcesp.com	Longview	TX	75601	903-758-3395	758-6487
Premier Safety & Service Inc 2 Industrial Pk Dr TF: 800-828-1080 ■ Web: www.premiersafety.com	Oakdale	PA	15071	724-693-8699	693-8698
PSB Industries Inc PO Box 1318 TF: 800-829-1119 ■ Web: www.psbindustries.com	Erie	PA	16512	814-453-3651	455-9082
PTI Technologies Inc 501 Del Norte Blvd TF: 800-331-2701 ■ Web: www.ptitechnologies.com	Oxnard	CA	93030	805-604-3700	604-3701
Pullman/Holt Corp 10702 N 46th St. Web: www.pullman-holt.com	Tampa	FL	33617	813-971-2223	
R&R Products Inc 3334 E Milber St. TF: 800-528-3446 ■ Web: www.rrproducts.com	Tucson	AZ	85714	520-889-3593	294-1045
R-V Industries Inc 584 Poplar Rd. *Fax: Sales ■ Web: www.rvii.com	Honey Brook	PA	19344	610-273-2457	273-3361*
Retech Systems LLC 100 Henry Stn Rd Web: www.retechsystemsllc.com	Ukiah	CA	95482	707-462-6522	
Roberts Sinto Corp 3001 W Main St Web: www.robertssinto.com	Lansing	MI	48917	517-371-2460	371-4930
Rockford Industrial Welding Supply Inc 4646 Linden Rd TF: 800-226-1904	Rockford	IL	61109	815-226-1900	226-5617
Rotary Lift 2700 Lanier Dr TF: 800-445-5438 ■ Web: www.rotarylift.com	Madison	IN	47250	812-273-1622	
SAES Pure Gas Inc 4175 Santa Fe Rd. Web: www.saespuregas.com	San Luis Obispo	CA	93401	805-541-9299	541-9399
Salem Tools Inc 1602 Midland Rd TF: 800-390-4348 ■ Web: www.salemtools.com	Salem	VA	24153	540-389-0233	375-3807
Salvagnini America Inc 27 Bicentennial Ct. Web: www.salvagnini.com	Hamilton	OH	45015	513-874-8284	874-2229

Phone Fax

Schutte & Koerting LLC 2510 Metropolitan. . . . . Trevose PA 19053 215-639-0900 639-1597
Web: www.s-k.com

Scott Fetzer Co 28800 Clemens Rd . . . . Westlake OH 44145 440-892-3000 892-3033
Web: scottfetzer.com

Senior Flexonics Inc Metal Bellows Div
1075 Providence Hwy. . . . . Sharon MA 02067 781-784-1400 784-1405
Web: www.metalbellows.com

Sentry Equipment & Erectors Inc
13150 E Lynchburg Salem Tpke. . . . . Forest VA 24551 434-525-0769 525-1701
Web: www.sentryequipment.com

Shop-Vac Corp 2323 Reach Rd . . . . Williamsport PA 17701 570-326-0502 321-7089
TF: 800-347-5096 ■ *Web:* www.shopvac.com

SJF Material Handling Equipment
211 Baker Ave. . . . . Winsted MN 55395 320-485-2824 485-2832
TF: 800-598-5532 ■ *Web:* www.sjf.com

Sterling Production Control Units
2280 W Dorothy Ln . . . . Dayton OH 45439 937-299-5594 299-3843
Web: www.pcuinc.com

STI Electronics Inc 261 Palmer Rd . . . . Madison AL 35758 256-461-9191 461-7524
TF: 888-650-3006 ■ *Web:* www.stielectronicsinc.com

Strasbaugh 825 Buckley Rd. . . . . San Luis Obispo CA 93401 805-541-6424 541-6425
OTC: STRB ■ *Web:* www.strasbaugh.com

Super Products LLC 17000 W Cleveland Ave. . . . . New Berlin WI 53151 262-784-7100 784-9561
TF: 800-837-9711 ■ *Web:* www.superproductsllc.com

Superior Crane Corp (SCC)
208 Wilmont Dr PO Box 1464 . . . . Waukesha WI 53189 262-542-0099 542-7767
Web: www.superiorcrane.com

Swiss Precision Instruments Inc
11450 Markon Dr . . . . Garden Grove CA 92841 714-799-1555 842-5164*
**Fax Area Code:* 800 ■ *TF:* 888-774-8200 ■ *Web:* www.swissprec.com

Synventive Molding Solutions Inc
10 Centennial Dr. . . . . Peabody MA 01960 978-750-8065 646-3600
TF: 800-367-5662 ■ *Web:* www.synventive.com

Tennant Co 701 N Lilac Dr. . . . . Minneapolis MN 55422 763-540-1200 540-1437
NYSE: TNC ■ *TF Cust Svc:* 800-553-8033 ■ *Web:* www.tennantco.com

Thermotron Industries Co 291 Kollen Pk Dr. . . . . Holland MI 49423 616-393-4580 392-5643
TF: 800-409-3449 ■ *Web:* www.thermotron.com

Thomas Engineering Inc
575 W Central Rd . . . . Hoffman Estates IL 60192 847-358-5800 358-5817
TF: 800-634-9910 ■ *Web:* www.thomaseng.com

Thompson International Inc PO Box 656. . . . . Henderson KY 42420 270-826-3751 826-3881
Web: www.thompsoninternational.com

Timesavers Inc 11123 89th Ave N . . . . Maple Grove MN 55369 763-488-6600 488-6601
TF: 800-537-3611 ■ *Web:* www.timesaversinc.com

Tool Smith Company Inc
1300 Fourth Ave S PO Box 2384 . . . . Birmingham AL 35233 205-323-2576 323-9060
TF: 800-317-8665 ■ *Web:* www.toolsmith.ws

Tulsa Rig Iron Inc 4457 W 151st PO Box 880 . . . . Kiefer OK 74041 918-321-3330 321-3099
Web: www.tulsarigiron.com

Unified Brands 1055 Mendell Davis Dr. . . . . Jackson MS 39272 888-994-7636 864-7636
TF: 888-994-7636 ■ *Web:* www.unifiedbrands.net

Universal Machine & Engineering Corp
645 Old Reading Pk . . . . Stowe PA 19464 610-323-1810
Web: www.umc-oscar.com

USM Corp 32 Stevens St. . . . . Haverhill MA 01830 978-374-0303 521-5519
TF: 800-361-2056 ■ *Web:* www.usm-americas.com

Vactor Manufacturing Inc 1621 S Illinois St. . . . . Streator IL 61364 815-672-3171 672-2779*
**Fax:* Sales ■ *Web:* www.vactor.com

Vacudyne Inc 375 E Joe Orr Rd. . . . . Chicago Heights IL 60411 708-757-5200 757-7180
TF: 800-459-9591 ■ *Web:* www.vacudyne.com

Van Air Systems Inc 2950 Mechanic St. . . . . Lake City PA 16423 814-774-2631 774-3482
TF: 800-840-9906 ■ *Web:* www.vanairsystems.com

Van Dam Machine Corp 81-B Walsh Dr . . . . Parsippany NJ 07054 973-257-7050 257-7398
Web: www.vandammachine.com

Vermeer Midsouth Inc 1200 Vermeer Cv . . . . Cordova TN 38018 901-758-1928 758-1929
TF: 800-264-4123 ■ *Web:* www.vermeermidsouth.com

Videojet Technologies Inc 1500 Mittel Blvd . . . . Wood Dale IL 60191 630-860-7300 616-3657*
**Fax:* Mktg ■ *TF Cust Svc:* 800-843-3610 ■ *Web:* www.videojet.com

Vulcan Engineering Co 1 Vulcan Dr PO Box 307 . . . . Helena AL 35080 205-663-0732 663-9103
Web: www.vulcangroup.com

W M Sprinkman Corp 4234 Courtney Rd . . . . Franksville WI 53126 262-835-2390 835-4325
TF: 800-816-1610 ■ *Web:* www.sprinkman.com

Welex Inc 1600 Union Meeting Rd. . . . . Blue Bell PA 19422 215-542-8000 542-9841
Web: www.welex.com

Western Hydro Corp 3449 Enterprise Ave . . . . Hayward CA 94545 510-783-9166 732-0250
TF: 800-972-5945 ■ *Web:* www.westernhydro.com

WH Bagshaw Company Inc
1 Pine St Ext PO Box 766 . . . . Nashua NH 03060 603-883-7758 882-2651
TF: 800-343-7467 ■ *Web:* www.whbagshaw.com

Williams Form Engineering Corp
8165 Graphic Dr. . . . . Belmont MI 49306 616-866-0815 866-1810
Web: www.williamsform.com

Windsor K„rcher Group 1351 W Stanford Ave. . . . . Englewood CO 80110 303-762-1800 865-2800
TF: 800-444-7654 ■ *Web:* www.windsorkarchergroup.com

Wood Group Pratt & Whitney Industrial Turbine Services LLC
1460 Blue Hills Ave PO Box 45 . . . . Bloomfield CT 06002 860-286-4600 769-7337
Web: www.wgpw.com

Wright Metal Products Inc
100 Ben Hamby Dr PO Box 6763 . . . . Greenville SC 29606 864-297-6610 281-0594
Web: www.wrightmetalproducts.com

Yale Carolinas Inc (YCI) 9839 S Tryon St. . . . . Charlotte NC 28273 704-588-6930 588-6047
TF: 800-844-1454 ■ *Web:* www.yalecarolinas.com

Young Welding Supply Inc
101 E First St PO Box 700 . . . . Sheffield AL 35660 256-383-5429 383-1385
Web: www.youngwelding.com

387 INFORMATION RETRIEVAL SERVICES (GENERAL)

See Also Investigative Services p. 2596

Phone Fax

2KDirect Inc 3000 Broad St Ste 115 . . . . San Luis Obispo CA 93401 805-597-5000
Web: www.ipromote.com

33Across Inc 229 W 28th St 12th Fl . . . . New York NY 10001 888-297-4094
TF: 888-297-4094 ■ *Web:* www.33across.com

411 Local Search Corp Inc
1200 Eglinton Ave E Ste 300 N York. . . . . Toronto ON M3C1H9 416-849-1432
TF: 866-411-4411 ■ *Web:* www.411.ca

Accesso LLC 1025 Greenwood Blvd Ste 500 . . . . Lake Mary FL 32746 407-333-7311
Web: www.accesso.com

AccuData Holdings Inc
5220 Summerlin Commons Blvd Ste 200. . . . . Fort Myers FL 33907 239-425-4400
Web: www.accudata.com

Acculynk Inc 3225 Cumberland Blvd SE Ste 550 . . . . Atlanta GA 30339 678-894-7010
Web: www.acculynk.com

Acquire Media Corp 3 Becker Farm Rd Ste 401. . . . . Roseland NJ 07068 973-422-0800
Web: www.acquiremedia.com

Acquizition.biz Inc
1100 Rene-Levesque Blvd W 24th Fl . . . . Montreal QC H3B4X9 514-499-0334
TF: 866-499-0334 ■ *Web:* www.acquizition.biz

Adaptive Networks Inc 123 Highland Ave. . . . . Needham MA 02494 781-444-4170
Web: www.adaptivenetworks.com

ADCI of Delaware LLC
5550 Friendship Blvd Ste 340 . . . . Chevy Chase MD 20815 301-951-4423
Web: www.adcit.com

AdMobilize LLC 1680 Michigan Ave Ste 736. . . . . Miami FL 33139 855-236-6245
TF: 855-236-6245 ■ *Web:* www.admobilize.com

Adpay Inc 391 Inverness Pkwy Ste 300-B . . . . Englewood CO 80112 303-268-1527
Web: www.adpay.com

Advantix Solutions Group
1202 Richardson Dr Ste 200. . . . . Richardson TX 75080 866-238-2684
TF: 866-238-2684 ■ *Web:* www.advantixsolutions.com

Aeneas Communications LLC
300 N Cumberland St Ste 200 . . . . Jackson TN 38301 731-554-9200
Web: www.aeneas.com

Aeris 2350 Mission College Blvd Ste 600. . . . . Santa Clara CA 95054 408-557-1993
Web: www.aeris.com

Aerospike Inc
2525 E Charleston Rd Ste 201 . . . . Mountain View CA 94043 408-462-2376
Web: www.aerospike.com

Affant Communication Inc
Affant Communication 3146 Red Hill Ave
Ste 100 . . . . Costa Mesa CA 92626 714-338-7100
Web: www.affant.com

Affinity Circles Inc
701 N Shoreline Blvd 1st Fl . . . . Mountain View CA 94043 650-810-1500
Web: www.affinitycircles.com

Affinity Labs Inc 799 Market St Ste 500 . . . . San Francisco CA 94103 415-365-1400
Web: www.affinitylabs.com

Agentis Inc 222 W Hubbard St. . . . . Chicago IL 60654 630-359-6210
Web: agentisenergy.com

Airborne Mobile Inc 3575 Saint Laurent Blvd . . . . Montreal QC H2X2T7 514-289-9111

Airespring Inc 6060 Sepulveda Blvd Ste 220 . . . . Van Nuys CA 91411 818-786-8990
TF: 888-389-2899 ■ *Web:* www.airespring.com

airG 1133 Melville St Ste 710 . . . . Vancouver BC V6E4E5 604-408-2228
Web: www.airg.com

AirPair Inc 875 Howard St. . . . . San Francisco CA 94103 800-487-0668
TF: 800-487-0668 ■ *Web:* www.airpair.com

Airphrame Inc 25 Taylor St. . . . . San Francisco CA 94102 415-857-5387
Web: www.airphrame.com

Akimbo Systems Inc 411 Borel Ave Ste 100 . . . . San Mateo CA 94402 650-292-3330

Albion Telephone Company Inc 225 W N St . . . . Albion ID 83311 208-673-5335
Web: www.atcnet.net

All Property Management LLC
2505 Third Ave Ste 325 . . . . Seattle WA 98121 206-577-0029
Web: www.allpropertymanagement.com

All Web Leads Inc 7300 FM 2222 Bldg 2 Ste 100 . . . . Austin TX 78730 512-349-7900 349-7910
Web: www.allwebleads.com

Allcharge Inc 15 W 39th St Rm 501 . . . . New York NY 10018 212-679-9445
Web: www.allcharge.com

Allclasses Inc 109 Kingston St 5th Fl. . . . . Boston MA 02111 949-675-4451
Web: allclasses.com

Alli Alliance of Action Sports LLC
150 Harvester Dr Ste 140 . . . . Burr Ridge IL 60527 304-284-0084
Web: www.allisports.com

ALOT Inc 143 Varick St. . . . . New York NY 10013 212-231-2000
Web: www.alot.com

Altocloud Inc 800 W El Camino Real. . . . . Mountain View CA 94040 650-492-5218
Web: www.altocloud.com

American Broadband Communications LLC
153 W Dave Dugas Rd . . . . Sulphur LA 70665 337-583-2111
Web: www.americanbroadband.com

American Robotics Corp
880 Peru Ave Unit 2 . . . . San Francisco CA 94112 562-546-2659
Web: www.swapbox.com

Amernet 315 Montgomery St . . . . San Francisco CA 94104 415-616-5100
Web: www.amer.net

Amigos Library Services 14400 Midway Rd . . . . Dallas TX 75244 972-851-8000 991-6061
TF: 800-843-8482 ■ *Web:* www.amigos.org

Ancero LLC 1001 Briggs Rd Ste 220 . . . . Mount Laurel NJ 08054 856-210-5800
Web: www.ancero.com

AnswerDash Inc
4000 Mason Rd New Ventures Facility Fluke Hall
. . . . Seattle WA 98195 800-311-5786
TF: 800-311-5786 ■ *Web:* www.answerdash.com

AOAExcel Inc 243 N Lindbergh Blvd Fl 1 . . . . St. Louis MO 63141 800-365-2219
TF: 800-365-2219 ■ *Web:* www.aoa.org/aoaexcel?sso=y

Apkudo LLC 3500 Boston St Ste 333 . . . . Baltimore MD 21224 410-777-8612
Web: www.apkudo.com

Apmetrix Inc 5414 Oberlin Dr Ste 200. . . . . San Diego CA 92121 800-490-3184
TF: 800-490-3184 ■ *Web:* www.apmetrix.com

appAttach Inc 401 Parkplace Ctr Ste 305 . . . . Kirkland WA 98033 425-202-5676
Web: www.appattach.com

Applanix Corp 85 Leek Cresent . . . . Richmond Hill ON L4B3B3 905-709-4600
Web: www.applanix.com

appMobi Inc 35-37 E Orange St. . . . . Lancaster PA 17603 717-666-3151

Phone Fax

AppsHosting Inc
13772 Goldenwest St Ste 321 .... Westminster CA 92683 877-625-6610
TF: 877-625-6610

Apptopia Inc 71 Summer St 4th Fl .... Boston MA 02110 617-758-8165
Web: apptopia.com

Arcestra Inc 197 Spadina Ave Ste 200 .... Toronto ON M5T2C8 416-596-9561
Web: www.arcestra.com

Architelos Inc 43622 Merchant Mill Ter .... Leesburg VA 20176 310-418-7162

Ardmore Telephone Company Inc
30190 Ardmore Ave .... Ardmore AL 35739 256-423-2131
Web: www.ardmore.net

Arkadin Inc 5 Concourse Pkwy Ste 1600 .... Atlanta GA 30328 866-551-1432
TF: 866-551-1432 ■ *Web:* www.arkadin.com

AroundWire.Com LLC 18107 Sherman Way Ste 206 .... Reseda CA 91335 888-382-3793
TF: 888-382-3793 ■ *Web:* www.aroundwire.com

Artisan Communications Inc
12400 Hwy W Hwy 71 Ste 350-407 .... Austin TX 78738 512-600-4200
Web: www.artisan.tv

Artsicle Inc 25 W 13th St. .... New York NY 10011 646-470-4219
Web: www.artsicle.com

Ash Creek Enterprises LLC
2226 Black Rock Tpke Ste 202 .... Fairfield CT 06825 203-331-1685
Web: www.ashcreek.com

Association Resource Group
7926 Jones Branch Dr Ste 1150 .... Mc Lean VA 22102 703-734-3500
Web: www.myarg.com

Astor & Sanders
9900 Belward Campus Dr Ste 275 .... Rockville MD 20850 301-838-3420
Web: www.astor-sanders.com

Audability Inc 5915 Airport Rd Ste 700 .... Mississauga ON L4V1T1 416-915-1301
Web: www.audability.com

Audio Authority Corp 2048 Mercer Rd .... Lexington KY 40511 859-233-4599
TF: 800-322-8346 ■ *Web:* www.audioauthority.com

Avangate Inc
555 Twin Dolphin Dr Ste 155 .... Redwood Shores CA 94065 650-249-5280
Web: www.avangate.com

Avfinity LLC 11782 Jollyville Rd. .... Austin TX 78759 512-535-3416
Web: www.avfinity.com

Avvo Inc 705 Fifth Ave S Ste 600 .... Seattle WA 98104 206-734-4111
Web: www.avvo.com

Axiom Education LLC 4 Research Dr .... Shelton CT 06484 203-242-3070
Web: www.axiomeducation.com

Axon Sports LLC 2100 Stewart Ave Ste 201 .... Wausau WI 54401 715-848-1024
Web: www.axonsports.com

Azulstar Inc 1051 Jackson St Ste D .... Grand Haven MI 49417 616-842-2763
Web: www.azulstar.com

Balance Financial Inc
1800 - 112th Ave NE Ste 260-E .... Bellevue WA 98004 425-458-4400
Web: www.balancefinancial.com

BDNA Corp 339 N Bernardo Ave Ste 206 .... Mountain View CA 94043 650-625-9530
Web: www.bdna.com

Beach.com Inc 5 Penn Plz 23rd Fl .... New York NY 10001 212-835-1529
Web: www.beach.com

Beaver Creek Cooperative Telephone Co
15223 Henrici Rd .... Oregon City OR 97045 503-632-3113 632-4159
Web: www.bctelco.com

Beepi 240 Third St Ste 200 .... Los Altos CA 94022 888-542-3374
TF: 888-542-3374 ■ *Web:* www.beepi.com

Best Telecom Inc 262 E End Ave .... Beaver PA 15009 888-365-2273
TF: 888-365-2273 ■ *Web:* www.besttelecom.com

BestTel 360 E. 1st St Ste 904 .... Tustin CA 92780 714-612-7333
Web: www.besttel.net

BigDoor Media Inc 511 Boren Ave N Ste 100 .... Seattle WA 98109 425-296-0805
Web: www.bigdoor.com

BigTent Design Inc
350 Brannan St 3rd Fl. .... San Francisco CA 94107 415-992-6550
Web: www.bigtent.com

Binary Group Inc 1911 Ft Myer Dr Ste 300 .... Arlington VA 22209 571-480-4444 480-4445
Web: www.binarygroup.com

BitNami 650 Mission St 2nd Fl. .... San Francisco CA 94105 415-318-3470
Web: bitnami.com

Bliss Direct Media 641 15Th Ave Ne .... Saint Joseph MN 56374 320-271-1600
TF: 800-578-7947 ■ *Web:* www.blissdirect.com

BlogHer Inc 805 Veterans Blvd Ste 305 .... Redwood City CA 94063 650-363-2564
Web: www.blogher.com

Blogster.com LLC
20545 Ctr Ridge Rd Ste 135 .... Rocky River OH 44116 440-333-7805
Web: www.blogster.com

BloomNet Inc 1 Old Country Rd Ste 500 .... Carle Place NY 11514 866-256-6663
TF: 866-256-6663 ■ *Web:* www.mybloomnet.net

Blue Box Group Inc 119 Pine St Ste 200 .... Seattle WA 98101 800-613-4305
TF: 800-613-4305 ■ *Web:* www.blueboxcloud.com

Blue Jeans Network Inc 516 Clyde Ave .... Mountain View CA 94043 408-550-2828
Web: www.bluejeans.com

Blue Ridge Internet Works
321 E Main St. .... Charlottesville VA 22902 434-817-0707
Web: www.brnets.com

BlueGenesisCom Corp
5915 Airport Rd Ste 1100 .... Mississauga ON L4V1T1 905-673-3232
Web: www.bluegenesis.com

BoardBookit Inc 1 Altoona Pl .... Pittsburgh PA 15228 412-436-5180
Web: www.boardbookit.com

Bobber Interactive Corp
2505 Third Ave Ste 300A .... Seattle WA 98121 206-443-3863
Web: www.bobberinteractive.com

Bocada Inc 5555 Lakeview Dr .... Kirkland WA 98033 425-818-4400 818-4455
TF: 866-262-2321 ■ *Web:* www.bocada.com

BoeFly LLC 50 W 72nd St Ste C6 .... New York NY 10023 800-277-3158
TF: 800-277-3158 ■ *Web:* www.boefly.com

Boston Illiquid Securities Offering Network Inc
205 Portland St Ste 200 .... Boston MA 02114 617-752-1921
Web: www.bison.co

Brand Thunder LLC 6588 Dalmore Ln. .... Dublin OH 43016 614-408-8202
Web: brandthunder.com

Phone Fax

Branding Brand 2313 East Carson St .... Pittsburgh PA 15203 888-979-5018
TF: 888-979-5018 ■ *Web:* www.brandingbrand.com

Broadband Dynamics LLC
8757 E Via De Commercio .... Scottsdale AZ 85258 888-801-1034 801-1038
TF: 888-801-1034 ■ *Web:* www.broadbanddynamics.net

BroadVoice Inc 20847 Sherman Way .... Winnetka CA 91306 978-418-7300
Web: www.broadvoice.com

BuildingSearch.com Inc 90 Railway Ave. .... Campbell CA 95008 408-426-8424
Web: www.buildingsearch.com

BUMP Network Inc 1295 Prospect St Ste A .... La Jolla CA 92037 858-459-4489
Web: www.bump.com

BurrellesLuce
30 B Vreeland Rd PO Box 674 .... Florham Park NJ 07932 973-992-6600 992-7675
TF: 800-631-1160 ■ *Web:* www.burrellesluce.com

Buyers Best Friend Inc 38 Lyon St .... San Francisco CA 94117 415-375-0439
Web: www.bbfdirect.com

Buzzwire Inc 1123 Auraria Pkwy .... Denver CO 80204 720-259-0100 557-0668*
*Fax Area Code: 303

C R T & Associates Inc
806 Hastings St Ste 8 .... Traverse City MI 49686 231-946-1680
Web: www.crt-a.com

C Spire 1018 Highland Colony Pkwy Ste 300 .... Ridgeland MS 39157 855-277-4735
TF: 855-277-4735 ■ *Web:* www.cspire.com

Cal Info 316 W Second St Ste 1102 .... Los Angeles CA 90012 213-687-8710 687-8778
Web: www.calinfo.net

Calient Networks Inc 2665 N First St Ste 204 .... San Jose CA 95134 408-232-6400
Web: www.calient.net

California Regional Multiple Listing Service Inc
3201 W Temple Ave Ste 250 .... Pomona CA 91768 909-859-2040
Web: go.crmls.org

CallDirek 2200 S Dixie Hwy Ste 401 .... Miami FL 33133 866-673-4735
TF: 866-673-4735 ■ *Web:* www.calldirek.com

Camperoo Inc 2900 Weslayan St Ste 545 .... Houston TX 77027 888-538-8809
TF: 888-538-8809 ■ *Web:* www.camperoo.com

Canadian Institute, The 1329 Bay St .... Toronto ON M5R2C4 416-927-7936
Web: www.canadianinstitute.com

CaptainU LLC 5807 S Woodlawn Dr Ste 207 .... Chicago IL 60637 773-834-9097
Web: www.captainu.com

Care Zone Inc 1463 East Republican St Ste 198 .... Seattle WA 98112 888-407-7785
TF: 888-407-7785 ■ *Web:* carezone.com

CARIS-Universal Systems Ltd
115 Waggoners Ln .... Fredericton NB E3B2L4 506-458-8533
Web: www.caris.com

Carriercom Lp 200 s Tenth st .... McAllen TX 78501 956-682-3656
Web: www.carriercom.net

CatholicMatch LLC 211 E Grandview Ave .... Zelienople PA 16063 888-605-3977
TF: 888-605-3977 ■ *Web:* www.catholicmatch.com

Catura Systems Inc
4677 Old Ironsides Dr Ste 180 .... Santa Clara CA 95054 408-986-8933
Web: www.caturasystems.com

CB Information Services Inc
160 Varick St Fl 12 .... New York NY 10013 212-292-3148
Web: www.cbinsights.com

CBT Sports LLC 12 Cadillac Dr Ste 230 .... Brentwood TN 37027 615-879-3786
Web: 247sports.com

CCG Investor Relations Inc
10960 Wilshire Blvd Ste 2050 .... Los Angeles CA 90024 310-477-9800

CCI Communications Inc
155 North 400 West Ste 100 .... Salt Lake City UT 84103 801-994-4100
Web: www.ccicom.com

CCT Telecommunications Inc 1106 E Turner Rd .... Lodi CA 95240 209-365-9500
Web: www.4cct.com

CDNetworks Inc 1919 S Bascom Ave Ste 600 .... Campbell CA 95008 408-228-3700
Web: www.cdnetworks.com

CellularOne 1500 S White Mtn Rd Ste 3 .... Show Low AZ 85901 928-537-0690
Web: www.cellularoneonline.com

ChannelMeter Inc 1061 Market St Ste 504 .... San Francisco CA 94103 510-228-4395
Web: channelmeter.com

CharityUSA.com LLC
600 University St Ste 1000 One Union Square .... Seattle WA 98101 206-268-5400 264-8448
TF: 888-811-5271 ■ *Web:* www.charityusa.com

Chartbeat Inc 826 Broadway 12th St 6th Fl. .... New York NY 10003 646-786-8472
Web: www.chartbeat.com

ChatID Inc 900 Broadway Ste 706 .... New York NY 10003 646-494-5678
Web: www.chatid.com

Chemical Abstracts Service (CAS)
2540 Olentangy River Rd .... Columbus OH 43202 614-447-3600 447-3713
TF: 800-848-6538 ■ *Web:* cas.org

Chirpify Inc 317 SW Alder St Ste 1100 .... Portland OR 97204 503-208-3068
Web: www.chirpify.com

Choose Digital Inc 4040 Aurora St. .... Coral Gables FL 33146 305-443-5981
Web: www.choosedigital.com

CHT Global Corp 2107 N First St Ste 580 .... San Jose CA 95131 408-988-1898
Web: www.chtglobal.com

CIMCO Communications Inc
1901 S Meyers Rd 7th Fl .... Oakbrook Terrace IL 60181 630-691-8080
Web: www.cimco.net

Circle 1 Network Inc 131 W Seeboth St. .... Milwaukee WI 53204 414-271-5437
Web: www.circle1network.com

Citation Communications Inc
1855 Indian Rd Ste 207 .... West Palm Beach FL 33409 561-688-0330
TF: 800-286-5109 ■ *Web:* citation2way.com

Cityfone Telecommunications Inc
3991 Henning Dr Ste 101 .... Burnaby BC V5C6N5 604-298-5900
Web: www.cityfone.net

ClearShot Communications LLC
5 Great Vly Pkwy Ste 333 .... Malvern PA 19355 610-648-3895

clickworker.com Inc PO Box 601 .... Penfield NY 14526 585-210-3912
Web: www.clickworker.com

CloudCheckr Inc 339 East Ave Ste 202-1 .... Rochester NY 14604 585-413-0869
Web: cloudcheckr.com

CloudSway LLC 711 Pacific Ave. .... Tacoma WA 98402 855-212-5683
TF: 855-212-5683 ■ *Web:* www.cloudsway.com

Company	City	State	Zip	Phone	Fax
Clustrix Inc 201 Mission St *Web:* www.clustrix.com	San Francisco	CA	94105	415-501-9560	
Collector Car Network Inc 1345 E Chandler Blvd Ste 101 *Web:* classiccars.com	Phoenix	AZ	85048	480-285-1600	
CollegeDegrees.com LLC 1001 McKinney St Ste 650 *Web:* www.collegedegrees.com	Houston	TX	77002	713-534-1948	
Commnet Wireless LLC 400 Northridge Rd Ste 325 *Web:* www.commnetwireless.com	Atlanta	GA	30350	678-338-5960	
CommSPEED LLC 33725 N Scottsdale Rd *Web:* www.commspeed.net	Scottsdale	AZ	85266	480-305-0584	
Communication Wiring Specialists Inc 8909 Complex Dr Ste F *Web:* www.cwssandiego.com	San Diego	CA	92123	858-278-4545	
Compass Healthcare Marketers 200 princeton S corporate ctr	Ewing	NJ	08628	609-688-8440	
CompleteCampaigns.com Inc 3635 Ruffin Rd 3rd Fl *TF:* 888-217-9600 ■ *Web:* www.completecampaigns.com	San Diego	CA	92123	888-217-9600	
Computers & Tele-Comm Inc 1307 S Sterling Ave *Web:* www.ctcwi.com	Independence	MO	64052	816-252-4080	
ComTech21 1 Barnes Park S *TF:* 877-312-5564 ■ *Web:* www.comtech21.com	Wallingford	CT	06492	877-312-5564	
Comwave Networks Inc 61 Wildcat Rd *TF:* 877-474-6638 ■ *Web:* www.comwave.net	Toronto	ON	M3J2P5	416-663-9700	
ConceptShare Inc 130 Slater St *TF:* 844-227-7848 ■ *Web:* www.conceptshare.com	Ottawa	ON	K1P6E2	613-903-4431	
Conjur Inc 460 Totten Pond Rd *TF:* 855-648-5919 ■ *Web:* www.conjur.net	Waltham	MA	02451	855-648-5919	
ConnXus Inc 5155 Financial Way *Web:* connxus.com	Mason	OH	45040	513-204-2873	
Contingent Network Services LLC 4400 Port Union Rd *Web:* www.contingent.com	West Chester	OH	45011	513-860-2573	
ConvergeOne LLC 3344 Hwy 149 *TF:* 888-321-6227 ■ *Web:* convergeone.com	Eagan	MN	55121	888-321-6227	
Cornerstone SMR Inc 4620 N State Rd 7 Ste 120 *Web:* www.cornerstonesmr.com	Fort Lauderdale	FL	33319	954-714-7030	
Cozi Group Inc 506 Second Ave Ste 800 *Web:* www.cozi.com	Seattle	WA	98104	206-957-8447	
creativeLIVE Inc 757 Thomas St *Web:* www.creativelive.com	Seattle	WA	98109	206-403-1395	
CrossFit Inc 1250 Connecticut Ave NW Ste 200 *Web:* www.crossfit.com	Washington	DC	20036	202-449-8533	
Crosslake Communications 35910 County Rd 66 PO Box 70 *TF:* 800-992-8220 ■ *Web:* www.crosslake.net	Crosslake	MN	56442	218-692-2777	
CU Conferences 8711 Watson Rd Ste 200 *TF:* 888-465-6010 ■ *Web:* www.cuconferences.com	St. Louis	MO	63119	888-465-6010	
Curatel LLC 1605 W Olympic Blvd Ste 800 *TF:* 866-287-2366 ■ *Web:* www.curatel.com	Los Angeles	CA	90015	866-287-2366	
Curriculum Technology LLC 3520 Seagate Way Ste 115 *Web:* www.curriculumtechnology.com	Oceanside	CA	92056	760-295-0863	
Custom Toll Free 10940 Wilshire Blvd 17th Fl *TF:* 800-287-8664 ■ *Web:* www.customtollfree.com	Los Angeles	CA	90024	800-933-3030	
Cybereason Inc 1 Broadway 15th Fl *Web:* www.cybereason.com	Cambridge	MA	02142	781-768-6065	
CypherWorX Inc 3349 Monroe Ave *TF:* 888-685-4440 ■ *Web:* nptrainingworks.com	Rochester	NY	14618	888-685-4440	
DadLabs Inc 4612 Burleson Rd Ste L *Web:* www.dadlabs.com	Austin	TX	78744	512-215-4026	
Dailybreak Inc 100 N Washington St *Web:* www.dailybreak.com	Boston	MA	02114	617-451-1790	
DailyFeats Inc 22 Pearl St	Cambridge	MA	02139	617-714-3833	
DashGo Inc 1620 Broadway Ste C *Web:* www.dashgo.com	Santa Monica	CA	90404	310-997-0675	
Data Center West Inc 739 Welch St *Web:* www.datacenterwest.com	Medford	OR	97501	541-326-4212	
Data Transmission Network Corp 9110 W Dodge Rd Ste 200 *TF:* 800-485-4000 ■ *Web:* www.dtn.com	Omaha	NE	68114	402-390-2328	
DataCore Software Corp 6300 NW Fifth Way Corporate Park *Web:* www.datacore.com	Fort Lauderdale	FL	33309	954-377-6000	
Datadrill Communications Inc 6701 Fairmount Dr Se *Web:* www.datadrill.ca	Calgary	AB	T2H0X6	403-269-7500	
DataGravity Inc 100 Innovative Way Ste 3410 *Web:* www.datagravity.com	Nashua	NH	03062	603-943-8500	
Dataium LLC 2525 Perimeter Pl Dr Ste 105 *TF:* 877-896-3282 ■ *Web:* www.dataium.com	Nashville	TN	37214	877-896-3282	
Dataminr Inc 6 E 32nd St 2nd fl *Web:* www.dataminr.com	New York	NY	10016	646-701-7826	
DataPop Inc 5762 W Jefferson Blvd *Web:* www.datapop.com	Los Angeles	CA	90016	323-302-4987	
DataTrail Inc 6223 2 St SE Ste 205 *Web:* www.datatrail.com	Calgary	AB	T2H1J5	403-253-3651	
Datonics LLC 84 Wooster St Ste 300 *Web:* datonics.com	New York	NY	10012	646-867-0647	
Datotel LLC 710 N Tucker Ste 400 *Web:* www.datotel.com	St. Louis	MO	63101	314-241-9101	
Deal Interactive LLC 3 Park Ave 39th Fl *TF:* 888-415-4888 ■ *Web:* www.dealinteractive.com	New York	NY	10016	888-415-4888	
Dealertrack CentralDispatch Inc 26387 Network Pl *Web:* www.centraldispatch.com	Chicago	IL	60673	858-259-6084	
DealFlow Analytics Inc 131 Jericho Tpke PH3 *Web:* dealflow.com	Jericho	NY	11753	516-876-8006	
Dealmaker Media Inc 5 Lucerne St Ste 2 *Web:* www.dealmakermedia.com	San Francisco	CA	94103	415-864-2885	
Dealtaker Inc 5360 Legacy Dr Ste 115 *Web:* www.dealtaker.com	Plano	TX	75024	214-234-9145	
DebtFolio Inc 35 Braintree Hill Office Park Ste 107 *TF:* 866-876-3654 ■ *Web:* www.geezeo.com	Braintree	MA	06084	866-876-3654	
Declara Inc 977 Commercial St *TF:* 877-216-0604 ■ *Web:* www.declara.com	Palo Alto	CA	94303	877-216-0604	
Delivery.com LLC 199 Water St Fl 23 *Web:* www.delivery.com	New York	NY	10038	212-294-7700	
Demeure Operating Company Ltd 187 King St S Unit 202 *Web:* demeure.com	Waterloo	ON	N2J1R1	519-886-8881	
Desmos Inc 1061 Market St *Web:* www.desmos.com	San Francisco	CA	94103	415-484-5342	
DFT Communications 40 Temple St *TF:* 877-653-3100 ■ *Web:* www.dftcommunications.com	Fredonia	NY	14063	716-673-3000	
Dialink Corp 1660 S Amphlett Blvd Ste 314 *Web:* www.dialink.com	San Mateo	CA	94402	650-691-9330	
Dialog 2250 Perimeter Pk Dr Ste 300 *TF:* 800-334-2564 ■ *Web:* proquest.com	Morrisville	NC	27560	919-804-6400	804-6410
Digital Datavoice Corp (DDV) 1210 Northland Dr Ste 160 *Web:* www.ddvc.com	Mendota Heights	MN	55120	651-994-2284	452-5470
Digital Reef Inc 85 Swanson Rd Ste 310 *Web:* www.digitalreefinc.com	Boxborough	MA	01719	978-893-1000	
Dimensional Insight Inc 60 Mall Rd Ste 210 *Web:* www.dimins.com	Burlington	MA	01803	781-229-9111	
Disqus Inc 301 Howard St Ste 300 *Web:* www.disqus.com	San Francisco	CA	94105	415-738-8848	
DMG Events Inc 3 Stamford Landing Ste 400 46 Southfield Avenue *Web:* www.dmgevents.com	Stamford	CT	06902	203-973-2940	
DocAuto Inc 3500 Pkwy Ln Ste 270 *TF:* 800-362-2886 ■ *Web:* www.docauto.com	Norcross	GA	30092	770-242-6747	
Doctor's Channel LLC, The 1133 Broadway 2nd Fl *Web:* www.thedoctorschannel.com	New York	NY	10010	646-257-5739	
doggyloot LLC 213 N Racine Ave *Web:* www.doggyloot.com	Chicago	IL	60607	312-566-8122	
Domain7 Solutions Inc 33820 S Fraser Way Unit 2A *Web:* www.domain7.com	Abbotsford	BC	V2S2C5	604-855-3772	
DotLoop LLC 700 W Pete Rose Way Ste 446 *Web:* www.dotloop.com	Cincinnati	OH	45203	513-257-0550	
DOTmed.com Inc 29 Broadway Ste 2500 *Web:* www.dotmed.com	New York	NY	10006	212-742-1200	
DoubleVerify Inc 575 Eigth Ave 7th Fl *Web:* www.doubleverify.com	New York	NY	10018	212-631-2111	
DPL Group, The 53 Clark Rd *TF:* 800-561-8880 ■ *Web:* www.dpl.ca	Rothesay	NB	E2E2K9	506-847-2347	847-2348
DrivingSales LLC 8871 S Sandy Pkwy Ste 250 *TF:* 866-943-8371 ■ *Web:* www.drivingsales.com	Sandy	UT	84070	866-943-8371	
Druva Software Inc 150 Mathilda Place, STE 450 *TF:* 888-248-4976 ■ *Web:* www.druva.com	Sunnyvale	CA	94086	888-248-4976	
DSG Tag Systems Inc 5455 152nd St Ste 214 *TF:* 877-589-8806 ■ *Web:* www.dsgtag.com	Surrey	BC	V3S5A5	877-589-8806	
Dubblee Media Inc 1201 BRdway Ste 909 *Web:* lover.ly	New York	NY	10001	646-726-4395	
DVI Communications Inc 11 Park Pl Ste 906 *Web:* www.dvicomm.com	New York	NY	10007	212-267-2929	
EAGLE-Net Alliance 295 Interlocken Blvd Ste 250 *Web:* www.co-eaglenet.net	Broomfield	CO	80021	720-210-9500	
East Kentucky Network LLC 101 Technology Trl *Web:* www.appalachianwireless.com	Ivel	KY	41642	606-477-2355	
Easy Analytic Software Inc 101 Haag Ave *Web:* www.easidemographics.com	Bellmawr	NJ	08031	856-931-5780	
EatStreet Inc 131 W Wilson St Ste 400 *TF:* 866-654-8777 ■ *Web:* eatstreet.com	Madison	WI	53715	866-654-8777	
EBSCO Information Services PO Box 1943 *TF:* 800-758-5995 ■ *Web:* www.ebsco.com	Birmingham	AL	35201	205-991-6600	
EC Suite LLC 2353 W University Dr *Web:* www.ecsuite.com	Tempe	AZ	85281	480-449-8817	
Ecliptic Enterprises Corp 398 W Washington Blvd Ste 100 *Web:* www.eclipticenterprises.com	Pasadena	CA	91103	626-798-2436	
Edison Carrier Solutions 4900 Rivergrade Rd Bldg 2B First Fl *Web:* www.edisoncarriersolutions.com	Irwindale	CA	91706	626-543-8156	
Education Online Services Corp 3303 W Commercial Blvd *Web:* www.educationonlineservices.com	Fort Lauderdale	FL	33309	954-606-5658	
Education.com Inc 333 S B St Unit 101 *Web:* www.education.com	San Mateo	CA	94401	650-366-3380	
Edufii Inc 2078 Parker St Ste 200 *TF:* 800-439-8505 ■ *Web:* edufii.com	San Luis Obispo	CA	93401	800-439-8505	
Eduplanet21 LLC 401 East Winding Hill Rd Ste 200 *Web:* www.eduplanet21.com	Mechanicsburg	PA	17055	717-884-9900	
Efonica FZ-LLC 420 Lexington Ave Ste 518 *Web:* www.efonica.com	New York	NY	10170	212-214-0642	
Ekahau Inc 1851 Alexander Bell Dr Ste 300 *TF:* 866-435-2428 ■ *Web:* www.ekahau.com	Reston	VA	20191	866-435-2428	
Ellipse Communications Inc 14800 Quorum Dr Ste 420 *Web:* www.ellipseinc.com	Dallas	TX	75254	214-237-0199	

				Phone	Fax
ELM Resources 12950 Race Track Rd Ste 201 *TF:* 866-524-8198 ■ *Web:* www.elmresources.com	Tampa	FL	33626	866-524-8198	
Embark Corp 32 E 57th St 18th Fl *Web:* www.embark.com	New York	NY	10022	646-368-8394	
EMC Corporation of Canada 120 Adelaide St W 14th Fl Ste 1400 *TF:* 800-858-1410 ■ *Web:* www.canada.emc.com	Toronto	ON	M5H1T1	416-628-5973	
ENBALA Power Networks Ltd 360 Bay St Ste 401 **Fax Area Code:* 647 ■ *Web:* www.enbala.com	Toronto	ON	M5H2V6	416-623-2626	427-7041*
Endstream Communications LLC 401 E 34Th St *Web:* www.endstream.com	New York	NY	10016	212-786-7289	
Engineering.com Inc 5285 Solar Dr Ste 101 *Web:* www.engineering.com	Mississauga	ON	L4W5B8	905-273-9991	
Enprecis Inc 901 Fifth Ave Ste 820 *Web:* www.enprecis.com	Seattle	WA	98164	206-274-0122	
Environmental Data Resources Inc 440 Wheelers Farms Rd **Fax Area Code:* 800 ■ *TF:* 800-352-0050 ■ *Web:* www.edrnet.com	Milford	CT	06460	203-783-0300	231-6802*
Epicurious LLC 4 Times Sq 17th Fl *Web:* www.epicurious.com	New York	NY	10036	212-381-7057	
eScreen Inc 7500 W 110th St Ste 500 *TF:* 800-881-0722 ■ *Web:* www.escreen.com	Overland Park	KS	66210	913-327-5915	327-8606
ESI Software Inc 1465 Kelly Johnson Blvd Ste 305 *Web:* www.esisoft.us	Colorado Springs	CO	80920	719-638-7033	
ESIS Inc 7920 Arjons Dr Ste H *Web:* www.esisinc.com	San Diego	CA	92126	858-625-0060	
eSnipe Inc 12819 SE 38th St *Web:* www.esnipe.com	Bellevue	WA	98006	425-260-5292	
ESP Solutions Group Inc 8627 N Mopac Ste 400 *Web:* www.espsolutionsgroup.com	Austin	TX	78759	512-879-5300	
EthoStream LLC 10200 Innovation Dr Ste 300 *Web:* www.ethostream.com	Milwaukee	WI	53226	414-223-0473	
Everlaw 2020 Milvia St Ste 220 *TF:* 844-383-7529 ■ *Web:* everlaw.com	Berkeley	CA	94704	844-383-7529	
EverTrue LLC 330 Congress St 2nd Fl *TF:* 855-387-8783 ■ *Web:* www.evertrue.com	Boston	MA	02210	855-387-8783	
Everwise Corp 1178 Broadway 4th Fl *TF:* 888-734-0011 ■ *Web:* www.geteverwise.com	New York	NY	10001	888-734-0011	
EveryScape Inc 65 Chapel St *Web:* www.everyscape.com	Newton	MA	02458	781-250-4800	
Evidentio Inc 11501 Dublin Blvd Ste 200 *Web:* evident.io	Dublin	CA	94568	408-802-0724	
Evisors Inc 55 Broad St Ste 15F *Web:* www.evisors.com	New York	NY	10004	813-384-7677	
Evite LLC 8800 W Sunset Blvd *Web:* www.evite.com	West Hollywood	CA	90069	310-360-2427	
Exactearth Ltd 60 Struck Ct *Web:* www.exactearth.com	Cambridge	ON	N1R8L2	519-622-4445	
Exec Inc 277 Carolina St *Web:* iamexec.com	San Francisco	CA	94103	415-275-8094	
Experis Data Centers Inc 7272 Wisconsin Ave Ste 330 *Web:* www.experisdatacenters.com	Bethesda	MD	20814	240-223-0607	
Expoships LLLP 27598 Riverview Ctr Blvd	Bonita Springs	FL	34134	239-949-5411	
Eyejot Inc 315 5th Ave S Ste 800 *Web:* www.eyejot.com	Seattle	WA	98104	206-274-7374	
ezCater Inc 101 Arch St Ste 1510 *TF:* 800-488-1803 ■ *Web:* www.ezcater.com	Boston	MA	02110	800-488-1803	
Ezzi Net 85 10th Ave Fl 7 *Web:* www.ezzi.net	New York	NY	10011	646-375-3390	
FamilySearch 35 N W Temple St *TF:* 866-406-1830 ■ *Web:* www.familysearch.org	Salt Lake City	UT	84150	866-406-1830	
FamilyTime LLC 101 Merritt Blvd Ste 102 *Web:* www.familytime.com	Trumbull	CT	06611	203-610-8265	
Fanhattan Inc 489 S El Camino Real *Web:* www.vuze.com	San Mateo	CA	94402	650-963-4750	
Fanlala Inc 2099 Mount Diablo Blvd Ste 204 *Web:* www.fanlala.com	Walnut Creek	CA	94596	925-954-1224	
Fidelity ActionsXchange Inc 200 Seaport Blvd *Web:* www.actionsxchange.com	Boston	MA	02210	617-392-2900	
Figment LLC 118 E 64th St *Web:* www.figment.com	New York	NY	10065	212-893-8790	
FirstFuel Software Inc 420 Bedford St Ste 200 *Web:* www.firstfuel.com	Lexington	MA	02420	781-862-6500	
FirstGiving Inc 34 Farnsworth St *Web:* www.firstgiving.com	Boston	MA	02210	617-542-0010	
FishHound LLC 15720 Ventura Blvd Ste 220 *TF:* 800-469-0224 ■ *Web:* www.fishhound.com	Encino	CA	91436	800-469-0224	
Fitocracy Inc 51 E 12th St 4th Fl *Web:* www.fitocracy.com	New York	NY	10003	646-450-3029	
FitOrbit Inc 11611 San Vicente Blvd Ste 515 *Web:* www.fitorbit.com	Los Angeles	CA	90049	424-652-9650	
Flowroute LLC 1221 Second ave *Web:* www.flowroute.com	Seattle	WA	98101	206-641-8000	
Fluidware 12 York St 2nd Fl *TF:* 866-218-5127 ■ *Web:* www.fluidware.com	Ottawa	ON	K1N5S6	866-218-5127	
Flywheel Communications Inc 2501 Harrison St *Web:* www.flywheel.com	San Francisco	CA	94110	415-401-7290	
FMS InfoServ Inc 6053 W Century Blvd 9th Fl *Web:* www.fmsinfoserv.com	Los Angeles	CA	90045	310-981-9510	
FocusVision Worldwide Inc 1266 E Main St *Web:* www.focusvision.com	Stamford	CT	06902	203-961-1715	
FOI Services Inc 704 Quince OrchaRd Rd Ste 275 *TF:* 800-654-1147 ■ *Web:* www.foiservices.com	Gaithersburg	MD	20878	301-975-9400	975-0702
FOIA Group Inc (FGI) 1250 Connecticut Ave NW Ste 200 **Fax Area Code:* 202 ■ *TF:* 888-461-7951 ■ *Web:* www.foia.com	Washington	DC	20036	888-461-7951	347-8419*
FoodLink Online LLC 475 Alberto Way Ste 100 *Web:* www.itradenetwork.com/login	Los Gatos	CA	95032	925-660-1100	
Forex Newscom 55 Water St 50th Fl *TF:* 888-503-6739 ■ *Web:* www.forexnews.com	New York	NY	10041	888-503-6739	
ForSaleByOwnercom Corp 435 N Michigan Ave Fl 5 *Web:* www.forsalebyowner.com	Chicago	IL	60611	312-222-4653	
Fotolia LLC 41 E 11th St 11th Fl *Web:* www.fotolia.com	New York	NY	10003	718-577-1321	
Fotomedia Technologies LLC 155 Fleet St *Web:* www.fotomedialabs.com	Portsmouth	NH	03801	603-570-4843	
Franchise Information Services Inc 4075 Wilson Boulevard Ste 410 *TF:* 800-485-9570 ■ *Web:* www.frandata.com	Arlington	VA	22203	703-740-4700	
Frontier Networks Inc 530 Kipling Ave *TF:* 866-833-2323 ■ *Web:* frontiernetworks.ca	Toronto	ON	M8Z5E3	416-847-5240	252-2301
FTJ FundChoice LLC 2300 Litton Ln Ste 102 *TF:* 800-379-2513 ■ *Web:* www.ftjfundchoice.com	Hebron	KY	41048	800-379-2513	
G3 Telecom Inc 1039 McNicoll Ave *Web:* www.g3telecom.com	Toronto	ON	M1W3W6	416-499-2121	
GDKN Corp 1779 N University Dr Ste 102 *Web:* www.gdkn.com	Pembroke Pines	FL	33024	954-985-6650	
GDS Publishing Ltd 40 Wall St Trump Bldg Ste 5 *Web:* www.gdsinternational.com	New York	NY	10005	212-796-2000	
GEENIUS Inc 4464 Long Lk Rd *Web:* www.geenius.com	Melbourne	FL	32934	321-308-5330	
Genability 221 Main St Ste 400 *Web:* www.genability.com	San Francisco	CA	94105	415-371-0136	
Genius SIS Inc 150 S Pine Island Rd Ste 420 *Web:* www.geniussis.com	Plantation	FL	33324	954-667-7747	
Genus Technologies LLC 6600 France Ave S Ste 425 *Web:* www.genusllc.com	Minneapolis	MN	55435	952-844-2644	
GeoStrut 1374 W 200 S	Lindon	UT	84042	801-356-1311	
Geotab Inc 1081 S Service Rd W *TF:* 877-436-8221 ■ *Web:* www.geotab.com	Oakville	ON	L6L6K3	416-434-4309	
Get It LLC 128 N Pitt St Ste 2 *Web:* www.getit.me	Alexandria	VA	22314	703-880-6630	
Get Smart Content Inc 3000 E Cesar Chavez St *Web:* www.getsmartcontent.com	Austin	TX	78702	512-583-1853	
Getabl Inc 11 Elkins St *Web:* pingup.com	Boston	MA	02127	617-752-1691	
Giant Realm Inc 254 W 31St St 8th Fl *Web:* www.giantrealm.com	New York	NY	10001	212-488-1740	
GigMasters.com Inc 33 S Main St *TF:* 866-342-9794 ■ *Web:* www.gigmasters.com	Norwalk	CT	06854	866-342-9794	
GitHub Inc 548 Fourth St *Web:* github.com	San Francisco	CA	94107	415-448-6673	
Giveanything.com LLC 307 Fifth Ave 4th Fl *Web:* www.giveanything.com	New York	NY	10016	212-689-1200	
GIVINGTRAX 220 Second Ave S Ste 51 *Web:* www.givingtrax.com	Seattle	WA	98104	206-486-0185	
GlobaFone Inc 1950 Lafayette Rd Ste 207 *Web:* globafone.com	Portsmouth	NH	03801	603-433-7232	
Global Science & Technology Inc 7855 Walker Dr Ste 200 *Web:* www.gst.com	Greenbelt	MD	20770	301-474-9696	
GoDaddy Inc 14455 N Hayden Rd *Web:* www.godaddy.com	Scottsdale	AZ	85260	480-505-8800	
Gogo Inc 1250 N Arlington Heights Rd Ste 500 *Web:* www.gogoair.com	Itasca	IL	60143	630-647-1400	
GoodGuide Inc 98 Battery St Ste 400 *Web:* www.goodguide.com	San Francisco	CA	94111	415-732-7722	
Goomzee Corp 4852 Kendrick Pl Ste 1 *Web:* www.goomzee.com	Missoula	MT	59808	406-542-9955	
Graphight 2400 N Lincoln Ave Ste 212 *Web:* rexter.com	Altadena	CA	91001	661-727-3446	
Green Job Interview 3050 Pullman Ave Ste D *Web:* greenjobinterview.com	Costa Mesa	CA	92626	714-444-5500	
Grid4 Communications Inc 2107 Crooks Rd *Web:* www.grid4.com	Troy	MI	48084	248-244-8100	
GridSpeak Corp 555 12th St Ste 2040 *Web:* www.gridspeak.com	Oakland	CA	94607	510-463-8800	
GroupGifting.com Inc 445 Broad Hollow Rd Ste 25 *Web:* www.egifter.com	Melville	NY	11747	516-882-1200	
HarborLink Network Ltd 3131 S Dixie Dr Ste 500 *Web:* www.harborlink.net	Dayton	OH	45439	937-294-2954	
Harris CapRock Communications Inc 4400 S Sam Houston Pkwy E *Web:* www.caprock.com	Houston	TX	77048	832-668-2300	
Havasu Newspapers Inc 2225 Acoma Blvd W *Web:* www.havasunews.com	Lake Havasu City	AZ	86403	928-453-4237	
Healthcare Management Systems Inc (HMS) 3102 W End Ave Ste 400 *TF:* 800-383-3317	Nashville	TN	37203	615-383-7300	383-6093
HELIO LLC 10960 Wilshire Blvd Ste 700 *Web:* www.helio.com	Los Angeles	CA	90024	310-445-7000	
Helixstorm Inc 41619 Margarita Rd Ste 202 *TF:* 888-434-3549 ■ *Web:* www.helixstorm.com	Temecula	CA	92591	888-434-3549	
Helpjuice Inc 211 E Seventh St Ste 620 *TF:* 888-256-0808 ■ *Web:* helpjuice.com	Austin	TX	78701	888-230-3420	
Hibernia Atlantic US LLC 35 Beechwood Rd Melrose Bldg Ste 3C *Web:* www.hiberniaatlantic.com	Summit	NJ	07901	201-454-0777	
Hibernia Networks LLC 25 DeForest Ave Ste 108 *Web:* www.hibernianetworks.com	Summit	NJ	07901	908-516-4200	

Company / Address	City	State	ZIP	Phone	Fax
HipSwap Inc 2436 Second St.	Santa Monica	CA	90405	310-396-5400	
Web: www.hipswap.com					
HireAbility.com LLC 25 Nashua Rd Ste C6	Londonderry	NH	03053	603-432-6653	
Web: www.hireability.com					
Hireology Inc 640 N Lasalle St Ste 650	Chicago	IL	60654	312-253-7870	
Web: www.hireology.com					
Hollywood.com LLC 560 Broadway Ste 404	New York	NY	10012	212-817-9105	
Web: www.hollywood.com					
Homes.com Inc 150 Granby St	Norfolk	VA	23510	866-675-1058	
TF: 866-675-1058 ■ *Web:* www.homes.com					
Host Department LLC 45277 Fremont Blvd Ste 11	Fremont	CA	94538	866-887-4678	
TF: 866-887-4678 ■ *Web:* www.hostdepartment.com					
Hubris Communications Inc 209 N Main	Garden City	KS	67846	620-275-1900	
Web: www.hubris.net					
HyperCube LLC					
3200 W Pleasant Run Rd Ste 300	Lancaster	TX	75146	469-727-1510	
I Am Athlete LLC PO Box 667	Santa Monica	CA	90406	877-462-7979	
TF: 877-462-7979 ■ *Web:* www.imathlete.com					
I-engineeringcom Inc 4 Armstrong Rd Ste 2	Shelton	CT	06484	203-402-0800	
Web: www.i-engineering.com					
IBISWorld Inc 11755 Wilshire blvd 11th fl.	Los Angeles	CA	90025	800-330-3772	
TF: 800-330-3772 ■ *Web:* www.ibisworld.com					
iChange Networks Inc 801 N Harbor	Fullerton	CA	92832	714-447-4098	
Web: www.ichange.com					
ICSA Labs 1000 Bent Creek Blvd Ste 200	Mechanicsburg	PA	17050	717-790-8100	
Web: www.icsalabs.com					
IdeaTek Communications LLC					
10400 E 69th St PO Box 258	Buhler	KS	67522	855-433-2835	
TF: 855-433-2835 ■ *Web:* www.ideatek.com					
Ifonoclast Inc 4620 Fortran Dr Ste 207	San Jose	CA	95134	408-946-9700	
Web: www.phonevite.com					
iForem Inc 350 Marine Pkwy Ste 200	Redwood Shores	CA	94065	650-352-4750	
iLearning Gateway Inc					
2650 Vly View Ln Bldg 1 Ste 200	Dallas	TX	75234	972-488-2298	
Web: www.ilearninggateway.com					
Illuminate Education Inc 47 Discovery Ste 100	Irvine	CA	92618	949-242-0343	
Web: www.illuminateed.com					
ImageShack Corp					
236 N. Santa Cruz Ave. Ste 100	Los Gatos	CA	95030	408-354-5166	
Web: www.imageshack.us					
IMshopping Inc					
4699 Old Ironsides Dr Ste 450	Santa Clara	CA	95054	408-228-4456	
Web: www.imshopping.com					
IMVU Inc PO Box 390012	Mountain View	CA	94039	650-321-8334	
TF: 866-761-0975 ■ *Web:* www.imvu.com					
InComm Conferencing Inc					
208 Harristown Rd Ste 101	Glen Rock	NJ	07452	877-804-2062	
TF: 877-804-2062 ■ *Web:* www.incommconferencing.com					
InDorse Technologies Inc 424 W 33rd St.	New York	NY	10001	646-495-0966	
Information Systems Consulting 401 E East St.	Casper	WY	82601	307-473-8933	
Web: www.isccorp.net					
Information Tycoon LLC					
3424 Peachtree Rd NE Ste 300	Atlanta	GA	30326	404-267-1506	
Web: infotycoon.com					
infoUSA Inc 5711 S 86th Cir	Omaha	NE	68127	800-835-5856	331-1505*
**Fax Area Code:* 402 ■ **Fax:* Sales ■ *TF:* 800-321-0869 ■ *Web:* www.infousa.com					
Infrastructure Networks Inc					
1718 Fry Rd Ste 116	Houston	TX	77084	281-740-3226	
TF: 855-333-4638 ■ *Web:* www.infrastructurenetworks.com					
Innflux LLC 850 W Jackson Blvd Ste 250	Chicago	IL	60607	312-850-3399	
Web: www.innflux.com					
Innovative Telecom Solutions Inc					
9 Vela Way	Edgewater	NJ	07020	800-510-3000	
TF: 800-510-3000 ■ *Web:* www.innovativetel.com					
Insur IQ LLC 2 Corporate Dr Ste 636	Shelton	CT	06484	203-446-8070	
Web: www.insuriq.com					
Integrated Tower Systems 2703 Dawson Rd	Tulsa	OK	74110	918-749-8535	
Web: www.intelcotowers.com					
inTelesystems 17400 Dallas Pkwy	Dallas	TX	75287	972-852-8200	
Web: www.intelesystems.com					
Intelletrace Inc 448 Ignacio Blvd.	Novato	CA	94945	800-618-5877	
TF: 800-618-5877 ■ *Web:* www.intelletrace.com					
Intelsat General Corp					
6550 Rock Spring Dr Ste 450	Bethesda	MD	20817	301-571-1210	
Web: www.intelsatgeneral.com					
Interactive Innovation Group Inc					
413 W Channel Rd	Santa Monica	CA	90402	310-454-3023	
Web: www.panjo.com					
Interactive One Inc 850 Third Ave 3rd Fl.	New York	NY	10022	212-431-4477	
Web: www.interactiveone.com					
International Automotive Technicians' Network Inc					
PO Box 1599	Brea	CA	92822	714-257-1335	
Web: www.iatn.net					
Internet Movie Database Inc 410 Terry Ave N.	Seattle	WA	98109	206-266-7010	
Web: www.imdb.com					
Interschola 1004 Oreilly Ave	San Francisco	CA	94129	415-563-4100	
Web: www.interschola.com					
Iowa Communications Network Inc					
Grimes State Office Bldg 400 E 14th St.	Des Moines	IA	50319	515-725-4692	
Web: icn.iowa.gov					
iPayStation LLC 213 School St Ste 101	Gardner	MA	01440	978-632-6798	
Web: www.paystation.com					
IrishCentral LLC 875 Sixth Ave	New York	NY	10001	212-871-0111	
Web: www.irishcentral.com					
ISLC Inc 14 Savannah Hwy	Beaufort	SC	29906	843-770-1000	
TF: 888-828-4752 ■ *Web:* www.islc.net					
iSnap 808 R St Ste 208	Sacramento	CA	95811	916-333-0330	
Web: www.isnap.com					
ITI TranscenData 5303 DuPont Cir.	Milford	OH	45150	513-576-3900	
Web: www.iti-global.com					
ITworld.com Inc 1 Speen St	Framingham	MA	01701	508-879-0700	
Web: www.itworld.com					
Jibe Mobile Inc 990 N Rengstorff Ave.	Mountain View	CO	94043	650-336-5423	
Web: www.jibemobile.com					
JMD Communications Inc 760 Calle Bolivar	Santurce	PR	00907	787-728-3030	
Web: www.jmdcom.com					
JNJ Mobile Inc 186 S St	Boston	MA	02111	617-542-1614	
Web: www.jnjmobile.com					
Jobaline Inc 620 Kirkland Way Ste 208	Kirkland	WA	98033	425-242-0866	
Web: www.jobaline.com					
Junction Networks Inc 55 Broad St 20th Fl.	New York	NY	10004	212-701-3050	
Web: www.onsip.com					
k-eCommerce 666 St-Martin W Blvd Ste 330	Laval	QC	H7M5G4	514-973-2510	372-5413*
**Fax Area Code:* 888 ■ *Web:* www.k-ecommerce.com					
Kagi Inc 1442-A Walnut St Ste 392	Berkeley	CA	94709	510-658-5244	
Web: www.kagi.com					
Kahuna Inc 555 Bryant St Ste 322	Palo Alto	CA	94301	844-465-2486	
TF: 844-465-2486 ■ *Web:* www.kahuna.com					
Kaleo Software Inc					
2041 Rosecrans Ave Ste 245	El Segundo	CA	90245	888-937-8945	
TF: 888-937-8945 ■ *Web:* www.kaleosoftware.com					
Kalida Telephone Co 121 E Main St PO Box 267	Kalida	OH	45853	419-532-3218	
Web: www.kalidatel.com					
Kaneva Inc 5901-C Peachtree Dunwoody Rd.	Atlanta	GA	30328	678-367-0555	
Web: www.kaneva.com					
Kanjoya Inc 456 Montgomery St Ste 500	San Francisco	CA	94104	650-745-1054	
Web: www.experienceproject.com					
Karma Gaming International Inc					
1498 Lower Water St	Halifax	NS	B3J3R5	902-463-2280	
Web: www.karmagaming.com					
KBA2 Inc 400 Treat Ave Ste E	San Francisco	CA	94110	415-528-5500	
Web: www.crowdoptic.com					
Kiwibox Media Inc 330 W 38th St Ste 1602	New York	NY	10018	212-239-8210	
Web: www.kiwibox.com					
Knew Deal Inc 1528 Woodward Ave 4th Fl	Detroit	MI	48226	313-373-7844	
Web: www.stik.com					
KoinzMedia 1851 McCarthy Blvd Ste 101	Milpitas	CA	95035	408-217-0304	
Web: www.rewardspay.com					
Koozoo Inc 880 Harrison St	San Francisco	CA	94107	415-778-6374	
KORE Telematics Inc					
3700 Mansell Rd Ste 250	Alpharetta	GA	30022	203-478-5281	
Web: www.koretelematics.com					
Kuratur Inc 68 White St Ste 7-315	Red Bank	NJ	07701	732-676-3183	
KX Systems Inc 530 Lytton St 2nd Fl	Palo Alto	CA	94301	650-798-5155	
Web: www.kx.com					
KYCK Inc 619 S Cedar St Ste M	Charlotte	NC	28202	704-951-5925	
Web: www.kyck.com					
Landel Telecom 6830 Via Del Oro Ste 260	San Jose	CA	95119	408-360-0480	
Web: www.landel.com					
LaughStub LLC 2038 Armacost Ave.	Los Angeles	CA	90025	800-927-0939	
TF: 800-927-0939 ■ *Web:* www.laughstub.com					
LD Telecommunications Inc					
2121 Ponce de leon Blvd Ste 2000	Coral Gables	FL	33134	305-358-8952	
Web: www.nexogy.com					
Lexicon International Corp 1400A Adams Rd	Bensalem	PA	19020	215-639-8220	
Web: lexicon-int.com					
LexisNexis Martindale-Hubbell					
121 Chanlon Rd	New Providence	NJ	07974	800-526-4902	
TF: 800-526-4902 ■ *Web:* www.martindale.com					
Liberty Communications Business Office					
413 N Calhoun St	West Liberty	IA	52776	319-627-2145	
Web: www.libertycommunications.com					
LifeShare Technologies LLC					
2177 Intelliplex Dr Ste 150	Shelbyville	IN	46176	317-825-0320	
Web: www.lifesharetech.com					
Lingo Inc 7901 Jones Branch Dr 9th Fl	Mclean	VA	22102	888-546-4699	
TF: 888-546-4699 ■ *Web:* www.lingo.com					
LINQ Services 1200 Steuart St Unit C3	Baltimore	MD	21230	800-421-5467	
TF: 800-421-5467 ■ *Web:* www.linqservices.com					
Linq3 Technologies LLC					
75 Rockefeller Plz 14th Fl	New York	NY	10019	646-837-7070	
Web: www.linq3.com					
LiveRelay Inc					
10815 Rancho Bernardo Rd Ste 300	San Diego	CA	92127	858-348-1710	
Web: www.relaytv.com					
Localstake LLC 212 W Tenth St Ste A480	Indianapolis	IN	46202	317-602-4790	
Web: www.localstake.com					
LocalVox Media Inc 462 Seventh Ave 10th Fl	New York	NY	10018	646-545-3400	
Web: localvox.com					
Loctronix Corp 18815 139th Ave NE Ste C	Woodinville	WA	98072	425-307-3480	
Web: www.loctronix.com					
Logical Net Corp 1462 Erie Blvd.	Schenectady	NY	12305	518-292-4500	
Web: www.logical.net					
Lotsa Helping Hands Inc 118 N Peoria St FL 3	Chicago	IL	60607	301-942-6430	
Web: www.lotsahelpinghands.com					
LOYAL3 Holdings Inc					
150 California St Ste 400	San Francisco	CA	94111	415-981-0700	
Web: www.loyal3.com					
M2M Datasmart Inc					
2010 Jimmy Durante Blvd Ste 220	Del Mar	CA	92014	858-350-5855	
Web: www.m2mdatasmart.com					
Mainstream Data Inc					
375 Chipeta Way Ste B	Salt Lake City	UT	84108	801-584-2800	
Web: www.mainstreamdata.com					
Manhattan Telecommunications Corp					
55 Water St 31st Fl	New York	NY	10041	212-607-2000	
Web: www.mettel.net					
Marcus Evans Inc					
455 N Cityfront Plz Dr The NBC Tower 9th Fl	Chicago	IL	60611	312-540-3000	
Web: www.marcusevans.com					
Market Velocity Inc					
1305 Mall of Georgia Blvd Ste 190	Buford	GA	30519	770-325-6300	
Web: www.marketvelocity.com					
MarketResearch.com					
11200 Rockville Pk Ste 504	Rockville	MD	20852	240-747-3000	747-3004
Web: www.marketresearch.com					

Phone | Fax

Marshall Graphics Systems
1625 Galleria Blvd. Brentwood TN 37027 615-399-8896
Web: www.marshallgraphics.com

MaxTradeIn.com LLC
9102 N Meridian St Ste 450 Indianapolis IN 46260 317-218-3612
Web: www.maxtradein.com

MBO Partners Inc 13454 Sunrise Vly Dr Ste 300 Herndon VA 20171 703-793-6000
Web: www.mbopartners.com

MCNC Inc
3021 E Cornwallis Rd
PO Box 12889 Research Triangle Park NC 27709 919-248-1900
Web: www.mcnc.org

MDSL 1410 Broadway Ste 2101 New York NY 10018 212-201-6199
Web: www.mdsl.com

Media Convergence Group Inc
904 Elm St Ste 208 Columbia MO 65201 573-442-4557
Web: www.newsy.com

Medialets Inc 80 Eighth Ave New York NY 10014 212-300-5670
Web: www.medialets.com

MedTrust Online LLC
14358 N Frank Lloyd Wright Blvd Ste 4 Scottsdale AZ 85260 480-889-8955
Web: www.medtrust-online.com

Meer.net LLC 202 S Randolph Ave Elkins WV 26241 304-636-5722

MeetingOne Corp
501 S Cherry St One Cherry Ctr Ste 1000 Denver CO 80246 303-623-2530
Web: www.meetingone.com

MemberPlanet Inc 23224 Crenshaw Blvd Torrance CA 94065 916-445-1254
Web: www.memberplanet.com

MENTISoftware Solutions LLC
3 Columbus Cir FL 15 New York NY 10019 212-861-2235
Web: www.mentisoftware.com

MerchantCircle Inc 201 Main St Ste 100 Los Altos CA 94022 650-352-1335
Web: www.merchantcircle.com

Merrill DataSite 225 Varick St New York NY 10014 866-399-3770
TF: 866-399-3770

MERX Networks Inc
6 Antares Dr Phase II Unit 103 Ottawa ON K2E8A9 613-727-4900
TF: 800-964-6379 ■ *Web:* www.merx.com

Mesh Systems LLC 12400 N Meridian St Ste 175 Carmel IN 46032 317-661-4800
Web: www.mesh-systems.com

MessageBank LLC 250 W 57Th St Ste 1001 New York NY 10107 212-333-9300
TF: 800-989-8001 ■ *Web:* www.messagebank.com

MexGrocer.com LLC 4060 Morena Blvd Ste C San Diego CA 92117 858-270-0577
Web: www.mexgrocer.com

MindSnacks Inc 1479 Folsom St San Francisco CA 94103 415-400-4626
Web: www.mindsnacks.com

Mixamo Inc 2415 Third St Ste 239 San Francisco CA 94107 415-255-7455
Web: www.mixamo.com

Mobi PCS Inc 733 Bishop St Ste 1200 Honolulu HI 96813 808-723-1111
Web: www.mobipcs.com

Mobile Accord Inc 2150 W 29th Ave 2nd Fl Denver CO 80211 303-531-5505
Web: www.mobileaccord.com

MobileIQ Inc 4800 Baseline Rd Ste E104-247 Boulder CO 80303 866-261-8600
TF: 866-261-8600 ■ *Web:* www.gomobileiq.com

MOGL Loyalty Services Inc
9645 Scranton Rd Ste 110 San Diego CA 92121 888-664-5669
TF: 888-664-5669 ■ *Web:* www.mogl.com

MoJiva Inc 136 Baxter St New York NY 10013 646-862-6201
Web: www.mojiva.com

Moseo Corp 2722 Elake Ave E Seattle WA 98102 206-905-8774
Web: www.seniorhomes.com

Motista Inc 1777 Borel Pl Ste 500 San Mateo CA 94402 650-204-7976
Web: www.motista.com

Mountain Telephone Co 405 Main St West Liberty KY 41472 606-743-3121
TF: 800-939-3121 ■ *Web:* www.mrtc.com

Mpathix Inc 87 Skyway Ave Ste 200 Toronto ON M9W6R3 416-849-4210
Web: www.mpathix.com

MVS Group 1086 Goffle Rd Hawthorne NJ 07506 201-447-1505
Web: www.themvsgroup.com

MYCOM North America Inc
1080 Holcomb Bridge Rd Bldg 200 Ste 350 Roswell GA 30076 770-776-0000
Web: www.mycom-usa.com

MyCorporation Business Services Inc
23586 Calabasas Rd Ste 102 Calabasas CA 91302 818-224-7639
Web: www.mycorporation.com

myITForum.com 6475 Christie Ave Ste 425 Emeryville CA 94608 801-226-8500
Web: www.myitforum.com

MyNewPlace.com 343 Sansome St Ste 700 San Francisco CA 94104 415-348-2009
Web: www.mynewplace.com

NADAguides.com 3186 K Airway Ave Costa Mesa CA 92626 714-556-8511
Web: www.nadaguides.com

National Technical Information Service (NTIS)
5285 Port Royal Rd Springfield VA 22161 703-605-6000 605-6900
TF Orders: 800-553-6847 ■ *Web:* www.ntis.gov

NERAC Inc 1 Technology Dr Tolland CT 06084 860-872-7000 872-6026
Web: www.nerac.com

Netswitch 400 Oy Ste 226 South San Francisco CA 94080 650-583-3066
Web: www.netswitch.net

New Pros Data Inc 155 Hidden Ravines Dr Powell OH 43065 740-201-0410
TF: 800-837-5478 ■ *Web:* www.newpros.com

New Visions Powerline Communications Inc
PO Box 11815 Syracuse NY 13218 315-472-6300
Web: www.nvplc.com

NewCloud Networks 160 Inverness Dr W Englewood CO 80112 855-255-5001
TF: 855-255-5001 ■ *Web:* www.newcloudnetworks.com

Newmark Advertising 15821 Ventura Blvd Ste 570 Encino CA 91436 818-461-0300
Web: www.newmarkad.com

Newsbank Inc 5801 Pelican Bay Blvd Ste 600 Naples FL 34108 239-263-6004 263-3004
TF: 800-243-7694 ■ *Web:* www.newsbank.com

Next Net Media LLC 316 California Ave Ste 804 Reno NV 89509 800-737-5820
TF: 800-737-5820 ■ *Web:* nextnetmedia.com

Nextiva 8800 E Chaparral Rd Ste 300 Scottsdale AZ 85250 602-753-4000
Web: www.nextiva.com

Phone | Fax

nexVortex Inc 510 Spring St Ste 120 Herndon VA 20170 703-579-0200
Web: www.nexvortex.com

Nexxtworks Inc 30798 Us Hwy 19 N Palm Harbor FL 34684 888-533-8353
TF: 888-533-8353 ■ *Web:* www.nexxtworks.com

Niche Directories LLC
909 N Sepulveda Blvd 11th Fl El Segundo CA 90026 877-242-9330
TF: 877-242-9330 ■ *Web:* www.nichedirectories.com

NobelBiz Inc 5973 Avenida Encinas Ste 202 Carlsbad CA 92008 760-405-0105
Web: www.nobelbiz.com

North Africa Journal, The PO Box 1001 Concord MA 01742 508-471-3899
Web: www.north-africa.com

North Florida Broadband Authority
164 Nw Madison St Lake City FL 32055 386-438-5042
Web: www.nfba.net

Northeast Florida Telephone Company Inc
130 N Fourth St Macclenny FL 32063 904-259-2261
Web: www.nefcom.net

Northwest Communications Coop
111 Railroad Ave PO Box 38 Ray ND 58849 701-568-3331
Web: www.nccray.com

Nsight 450 Security Blvd Green Bay WI 54313 920-617-7000
Web: www.nsight.com

Oceus Networks Inc
1895 Preston White Dr Ste 300 Reston VA 20191 703-234-9200
TF: 877-816-2599 ■ *Web:* www.oceusnetworks.com

Ogmento Inc 134 Spring St New York NY 10012 212-226-2736

Oklahoma Telephone & Telegraph Inc
26 N Otis Ave Dustin OK 74839 800-869-1989
TF: 800-869-1989 ■ *Web:* www.oklatel.net

OLogic 544 E Weddell Dr #7 Sunnyvale CA 94089 650-996-1490
Web: www.ologicinc.com

Omitron Inc 7051 Muirkirk Meadows Dr Ste A Beltsville MD 20705 301-474-1700 345-4594
Web: www.omitron.com

On Campus Marketing LLC
10411 Motor City Dr Ste 650 Bethesda MD 20817 301-652-1580
Web: www.ocm.com

OneClass 65 Bloor St E Unit 1902 Toronto ON M4W3L4 855-392-6946
TF: 855-392-6946 ■ *Web:* oneclass.com

OneID Inc 580 Howard St Ste 303 San Francisco CA 94105 415-590-3712
Web: www.oneid.com

OneMorePallet.com
9891 Montgomery Rd Ste 122 Cincinnati OH 45242 855-438-1667
TF: 855-438-1667 ■ *Web:* www.onemorepallet.com

Oneplanetweb Inc 322 E Arrellaga St Santa Barbara CA 93101 805-963-1056

Onvoy Inc 300 S Hwy 169 Ste 700 Minneapolis MN 55426 952-230-4100
Web: www.onvoy.com

Openbay Inc 222 Third St Ste 4000 Cambridge MA 02142 617-398-8888
Web: www.openbay.com

OpenSesame Inc 520 NW Davis St Ste 200 Portland OR 97209 503-808-1268
Web: www.opensesame.com

Optimum Lead Generation LLC
12230 Forest Hill Blvd Ste 200 Wellington FL 33414 561-227-1507

Orbitel Communications LLC
21116 N John Wayne Pkwy Ste B-9 Maricopa AZ 85239 520-568-8890
Web: www.orbitelcom.com

Oricom Internet Inc 400 Rue Nolin Bureau Vanier QC G1M1E7 418-683-4557
Web: orion.oricom.ca

Otelco Inc. 505 Third Ave East Oneonta AL 35121 205-625-3574
Web: www3.otelco.net

OurParents Inc 8521 Leesburg Pk Ste 310 Vienna VA 22182 866-629-1634
TF: 866-629-1634 ■ *Web:* www.ourparents.com

Ovid Technologies Inc
333 Seventh Ave 20th Fl New York NY 10001 646-674-6300 674-6301
TF: 800-950-2035 ■ *Web:* www.ovid.com

Oxford County Telephone & Telegraph Company Inc
491 Lisbon St Lewiston ME 04240 207-333-6900
Web: oxfordnetworks.com

Oxygen Cloud Inc
1600 Seaport Blvd Ste 310 Redwood City CA 94063 650-241-6210
Web: www.oxygencloud.com

P Marshall & Associates LLC
1000 Holcomb Woods Pkwy Ste 210 Roswell GA 30076 678-280-2325
Web: pmass.com

P4RC Inc 10001 Venice Blvd Ste 421 Los Angeles CA 90034 310-621-9555
Web: www.p4rc.com

Pacific Centrex Services Inc
6855 Tujunga Ave North Hollywood CA 91605 818-623-2300
Web: www.pcs1.net

PackLate.com Inc
100 Four Falls Corporate Ctr
Ste 104 West Conshohocken PA 19428 877-472-2552
TF: 877-472-2552 ■ *Web:* packlate.com

Pageplus Cellular 1615 Timberwolf Dr Holland OH 43528 419-382-8603
Web: www.pagepluscellular.com

Paniagua's Enterprises Development Company LLC
6400 Frankford Ave Ste 30 Baltimore MD 21206 410-485-9327
Web: www.paniaguas.net

Paramount Defenses Inc
620 Newport Ctr Dr Ste 1100 Newport Beach CA 92660 949-468-5770
Web: www.paramountdefenses.com

Patent Calls Inc 2802 Flintrock Trace Ste 202 Austin TX 78738 512-371-4120 287-5366
Web: www.patentcalls.com

PayEase Inc 2332 Walsh Ave Santa Clara CA 95051 408-567-9300 567-9370
Web: www.w-phone.com

Peerless Network Inc
222 S Riverside Plz Ste 2730 Chicago IL 60606 312-506-0920
Web: www.peerlessnetwork.com

Phone.com Inc 211 Warren St Ste 116 Newark NJ 07103 973-577-6380
Web: www.phone.com

Pineland Telephone Cooperative Inc
30 S Rountree St Metter GA 30439 912-685-2121
Web: www.pineland.net

				Phone	Fax

Pinnacle Communications Corp
19821 Executive Park Cir ... Germantown MD 20874 301-601-0777
TF: 800-644-9101 ■ *Web:* www.pinnaclecommunications.com

Pixelgate 733 Lakefield Rd Ste A ... Westlake Village CA 91361 805-446-6251
Web: www.pixelgate.net

PK4 Media Inc 1600 E Franklin Ave Ste C ... El Segundo CA 90245 888-320-6281
TF: 888-320-6281 ■ *Web:* www.pk4media.com

PlaceFull Inc 122 S Jackson St Ste 310 ... Seattle WA 98104 206-624-0295
Web: placefull.com

Platfora Inc 1300 S El Camino Real 6th Fl ... San Mateo CA 94402 650-918-1100
Web: www.platfora.com

Plum Analytics Inc 808 Firethorn Cir ... Dresher PA 19025 206-331-7297
Web: www.plumanalytics.com

Pong Marketing & Promotions Inc
201 Creditview Rd ... Woodbridge ON L4L9T1 905-264-3555
Web: www.pongmarketing.com

Popp Telecom Inc 620 Mendelssohn Ave N ... Golden Valley MN 55427 763-797-7900
Web: www.popp.com

Postmasters Inc 701 Brazos St Ste 1616 ... Austin TX 78701 512-693-4040
Web: www.postmaster.io

PresiNET Systems Corp 645 Fort St Ste L109 ... Victoria BC V8W1G2 250-405-5380 405-5362
Web: www.presinet.com

PrestoTech Solutions
4595 Broadmoor Ave Se Ste 200 ... Grand Rapids MI 49512 616-891-4100
Web: www.prestotech.net

PriceWaiter LLC 426 Market St ... Chattanooga TN 37421 855-671-9889
TF: 855-671-9889 ■ *Web:* www.pricewaiter.com

Profisee Group Inc
2520 Northwinds Pkwy Two Northwinds Ctr ... Alpharetta GA 30009 678-202-8990
Web: www.profisee.com

Proformative Inc 99 Almaden Blvd Ste 975 ... San Jose CA 95113 408-400-3993
Web: www.proformative.com

ProofSpace Inc 900 Clancy Ave NE ... Grand Rapids MI 49503 312-933-8823
Web: www.proofspace.com

PropertyMaps Inc 435 Aspen Dr ... Austin TX 78737 512-791-3527
Web: www.propertymaps.com

Pulpo Media Inc 1767 Alcatraz Ave ... Berkeley CA 94703 510-594-2294
Web: www.pulpomedia.com

Pure Auto LLC 164 Market St Ste 250 ... Charleston SC 29401 877-860-7873
TF: 877-860-7873 ■ *Web:* www.purecars.com

Purple Communications Inc 595 Menlo Dr ... Rocklin CA 95765 800-900-9478
TF: 800-900-9478 ■ *Web:* www.purplevrs.com

Qualaroo Inc 1901 Newport Blvd Ste 175 ... Costa Mesa CA 92627 650-485-3415
Web: qualaroo.com

QualVu Inc 12039 W Alameda Pkwy Ste Z-2 ... Lakewood CO 80228 303-640-6222
Web: www.qualvu.com

Quantcast Corp 201 Third St 2nd Fl ... San Francisco CA 94103 415-738-4755
Web: www.quantcast.com

Quantopian Inc 77 Summer St ... Boston MA 02110 617-752-1454
Web: www.quantopian.com

Questia Media America Inc
1 N State St Ste 900 ... Chicago IL 60602 800-889-0097 782-3901*
**Fax Area Code:* 312 ■ *TF:* 800-759-4726 ■ *Web:* www.questia.com

Quizzle LLC 1042 Woodward Ave ... Detroit MI 48226 313-373-3900
Web: www.quizzle.com

Rallyorg 995 Market St 2nd Fl ... San Francisco CA 94105 888-648-2220
TF: 888-648-2220 ■ *Web:* rally.org

RateMyProfessors.com LLC 1515 Broadway ... New York NY 10036 212-654-7763
Web: www.ratemyprofessors.com

RC Telecom Inc 6250 W Tenth St Ste 1 ... Greeley CO 80634 970-356-4572
Web: rctelecom.com

Reachable Inc 855 El Camino Real Ste 260 ... Palo Alto CA 94301 650-324-1400
Web: www.reachable.com

ReadOz LLC 350 W Ontario St Ste 4W ... Chicago IL 60654 312-929-2500
Web: www.readoz.com

Ready Set Work LLC 1487 Dunwoody Dr ... West Chester PA 19380 215-689-4323
Web: www.readysetwork.com

Real Girls Media Network Inc
575 Market St 9th Fl ... San Francisco CA 94105 415-295-8506
Web: www.realgirlsmedia.com

Real Time Translation Inc 1107 Hazeltine Blvd ... Chaska MN 55318 952-479-6180
Web: www.rttmobile.com

RealtyShares Inc 637 Natoma St Ste 5 ... San Francisco CA 94103 415-450-6234
TF: 855-880-6050 ■ *Web:* www.realtyshares.com

Reaslo Inc
5214F Diamond Heights Blvd Ste 217 ... San Francisco CA 94131 888-870-7889
TF: 888-870-7889 ■ *Web:* www.reesio.com

RecordSetter LLC 228 Park Ave S Ste 29280 ... New York NY 10003 646-912-6611
Web: recordsetter.com

RecycleMatch LLC 3375 Westpark Dr Ste 321 ... Houston TX 77005 713-581-0466
Web: www.recyclematch.com

Red Lambda Inc
400 Colonial Ctr Pkwy Ste 270 ... Lake Mary FL 32779 407-682-4940 445-5367*
**Fax Area Code:* 321 ■ *Web:* www.redlambda.com

Redi-Data Inc 5 Audrey Pl ... Fairfield NJ 07004 973-227-4380
Web: www.redidata.com

RefluxMD Inc 10804 Willow Ct Ste B ... San Diego CA 92127 760-668-9904
Web: www.refluxmd.com

RefWorks LLC 7200 Wisconsin Ave Ste 601 ... Bethesda MD 20814 301-961-6700
TF: 800-843-7751 ■ *Web:* www.refworks.com

Regaalo Inc 75 Rochester Ave ... Portsmouth NH 03801 603-570-3200

RelayHealth Corp 1 Post St ... San Francisco CA 94104 404-728-2000
Web: www.relayhealth.com

Reliance Connects 61 W Mesquite Blvd ... Mesquite NV 89027 702-346-5211
Web: www.relianceconnects.com

Rentals Inc 3585 Engineering Dr ... Norcross GA 30092 888-501-7368
TF: 888-501-7368 ■ *Web:* www.rentals.com

rentbits.com Inc 383 Corona St Ste 301 ... Denver CO 80218 303-640-3160
Web: rentbits.com

Reputation Rhino LLC 711 Third Ave 12th Fl ... New York NY 10017 888-975-3331
TF: 888-975-3331 ■ *Web:* reputationrhino.com

Research on Demand Inc 2629 State St ... Santa Barbara CA 93105 805-963-4095

Research Wizard of Tulsa City-County Library
400 Civic Ctr ... Tulsa OK 74103 918-596-7991 596-2598
Web: www.researchwizard.org

Resort Internet
2130 Resort Dr Ste 100 ... Steamboat Springs CO 80487 970-870-1818
Web: www.resortbroadband.com

Resultly LLC 116 W Hubbard St Fl 4 ... Chicago IL 60654 312-273-9400
Web: www.result.ly

Retailigence Corp 2400 Broadway Ste 220 ... Redwood City CA 94063 650-716-4748
Web: retailigence.com

RetailMLS LLC 12 W 23rd St ... New York NY 10010 212-729-1041
Web: retailmls.com

Revestor LLC 505 Montgomery St 11th Fl ... San Francisco CA 94111 415-689-4942
Web: revestor.com

ReviewPush 12885 N Hwy 183 Ste 110A ... Austin TX 78750 512-814-8046
Web: www.reviewpush.com

Rhythm Organism LLC, The
400 N State St Ste 410 ... Chicago IL 60654 312-321-0111
Web: www.fanfueled.com

RidgeviewTel LLC 1880 Industrial Cir Ste C ... Longmont CO 80501 303-309-4005

RightAnswer.com Inc 2900 Rodd St ... Midland MI 48641 989-835-5000
Web: www.rightanswer.com

Rightside Group Ltd
5808 Lk Washington Blvd NE ... Kirkland WA 98033 425-298-2500
Web: www.rightside.co

Rise Broadband 400 Inverness Pkwy Ste 330 ... Englewood CO 80112 303-705-6522
Web: risebroadband.com/?ro=r1

RISQ Inc
625 Rene-Levesque Blvd W Bureau 300 ... Montreal QC H3B1R2 514-845-7181
Web: www.risq.quebec

RivalHealth LLC 6601 Hillsborough St Ste 109 ... Raleigh NC 27606 919-803-6709
Web: www.rivalhealth.com

Riviera Cellular & Telecommunicat PO Box 997 ... Riviera TX 78379 361-296-3232
TF: 877-296-3232 ■ *Web:* www.rivnet.com

RobotsApps.com Inc
50 California St 15th Fl Ste 1500 ... San Francisco CA 94111 415-439-5291
Web: www.robotappstore.com

Rockefeller Group Technology Solutions Inc
1221 Ave of the Americas ... New York NY 10020 212-282-2200
Web: www.rgts.com

Rockhouse Partners LLC
631 Second Ave S Ste 2R ... Nashville TN 37210 615-873-0924
Web: www.rockhousepartners.com

RoundPegg Inc 1215 Spruce St Ste 201 ... Boulder CO 80302 720-663-7344
Web: www.roundpegg.com

SaaS Markets LLC
1720 S Amphlett Blvd Ste 210 ... San Mateo CA 94402 650-458-0748

Salesconx Inc 701 Seventh Ave Ste 9E ... New York NY 10036 212-453-9880
Web: www.salesconx.com

Savant Technology Group Inc
2682 Bishop Dr Ste 210 ... San Ramon CA 94583 925-461-4510
Web: www.savant-us.com

SaveUp Inc 480 Second St Ste 202 ... San Francisco CA 94107 415-578-9949
Web: www.saveup.com

ScanAps 6133 Bristol Pkwy Ste 301 ... Culver City CA 90230 310-670-1700
Web: www.scanaps.com

Schaller Telephone Co 111 w Second st ... Schaller IA 51053 712-275-4211
Web: www.schallertel.net

SchoolDocs LLC 5944 Luther Ln Ste 600 ... Dallas TX 75225 866-311-2293
TF: 866-311-2293 ■ *Web:* www.schooldocs.com

Scoot & Doodle Inc
2625 Middlefield Rd Ste 223 ... Palo Alto CA 94306 888-563-9224
TF: 888-563-9224 ■ *Web:* scootdoodle.com

Scott Enterprises Inc
2225 Downs Dr 6th Fl Exce Stes ... Erie PA 16509 814-868-9500 866-0463
TF: 877-866-3445 ■ *Web:* www.visitscott.com

Scripted Inc 135 Stillman St ... San Francisco CA 94107 800-797-4470
TF: 800-797-4470 ■ *Web:* scripted.com

SECOS Inc 18301 Von Karman Ave Ste 460 ... Irvine CA 92612 949-794-0021
Web: www.secos.com

Sedo.com LLC 161 First St 4th Fl ... Cambridge MA 02142 617-499-7200
Web: www.sedo.com

SeeClickFix Inc 746 Chapel St Ste 207 ... New Haven CT 06510 203-752-0777
Web: www.seeclickfix.com

Seize The Deal LLC
1851 N Greenville Ave Ste 100 ... Richardson TX 75081 866-210-0881
TF: 866-210-0881 ■ *Web:* www.seizethedeal.com

SelectPath Inc 10820 Central Ave SE ... Albuquerque NM 87123 505-275-4601
Web: www.selectpath.com

Sell My Timeshare Now LLC
383 Central Ave Ste 260 ... Dover NH 03820 603-516-0200
TF: 877-815-4227 ■ *Web:* www.sellmytimesharenow.com

Senior-Living.com Inc 8521 Leesburg Pk Ste 310 ... Vienna VA 22182 866-342-4297
TF: 866-342-4297 ■ *Web:* www.seniorliving.net

SERPs Inc 1410 NW Johnson St ... Portland OR 97209 503-683-3470
Web: serps.com

Setel 1165 s Sixth st ... Macclenny FL 32063 904-259-1300
Web: setel.net

Shaadi Karoge Inc 108 W 13th St ... Wilmington DE 19801 510-402-4486
Web: www.shaadikaroge.com

Shapeways BV 419 Park Ave S ... New York NY 10016 718-974-8010
Web: www.shapeways.com

ShopVisible LLC
945 East Paces Ferry Rd Ste 1475 ... Atlanta GA 30326 866-493-7037 745-0790*
**Fax Area Code:* 404 ■ *TF:* 866-493-7037 ■ *Web:* www.shopvisible.com

SilverRail Technologies Inc
300 Trade Ctr Ste 5500 ... Woburn MA 01801 617-934-6786
Web: www.silverrailtech.com

SimpleTuition Inc 268 Summer St Ste 502 ... Boston MA 02210 617-630-6100
Web: simpletuition.com

Skinny Mom Inc 602 Main St Ste 410 ... Cincinnati OH 45202 513-621-6364
Web: skinnymom.com

SkyBlox LLC 244 Peters St Ste 7 ... Atlanta GA 30313 866-632-9685
TF: 866-632-9685 ■ *Web:* www.skyblox.com

Phone Fax

Skype Inc 3210 Porter Dr Palo Alto CA 94304 650-493-7900
Web: www.skype.com

SkyWeaver Inc 1501 Broadway 25th Fl New York NY 10036 646-571-8596
Web: www.skyweaver.com

SlingShot Communications Inc
8723 E Via de Commercio Scottsdale AZ 85258 480-626-8625
Web: www.slingshot.com

Smart Choice Communications LLC
16 W 45Th St New York NY 10036 212-660-7300
Web: www.smartchoiceus.com

SMART IT Services Inc
34715 Van Dyke Ave Sterling Heights MI 48312 586-258-0650
Web: www.smartservices.com

SmartAction Company LLC
390 N Sepulveda Blvd Ste 2150 El Segundo CA 90245 310-776-9200
Web: www.smartaction.com

SmartProcure LLC
700 W Hillsboro Blvd Ste 4-100 Deerfield Beach FL 33441 954-420-9900
Web: smartprocure.us

Smartsat Inc 8222 118th Ave Ste 600 Largo FL 33773 727-535-6880
Web: smartsat.com

Smarty Ants Inc 1400 Rollins Rd Burlingame CA 94010 877-905-2687
TF: 877-905-2687 ■ *Web:* www.smartyants.com

Snapfinger 3025 Windward Plz Ste 150 Alpharetta GA 30005 678-739-4650
Web: www.snapfinger.com

SnapGoods Inc 155 Water St Brooklyn NY 11201 347-651-0845
Web: www.snapgoods.com

Snooth Inc 240 E Roemer Way Santa Maria CA 10016 646-723-4328
Web: www.snooth.com

Social Annex Inc
5301 Beethoven St Ste 260 Los Angeles CA 90066 866-802-8806
TF: 866-802-8806 ■ *Web:* www.socialannex.com

Social Strategy1
5000 Sawgrass Village Cir Ste 30 Ponte Vedra Beach FL 32082 877-771-3366
TF: 877-771-3366 ■ *Web:* www.socialstrategy1.com

SocialChorus 703 Market St Ste 470 San Francisco CA 94103 415-655-2700
Web: www.socialchorus.com

SocialFlow Inc 52 Vanderbilt Ave 12th Fl New York NY 10017 212-883-9844
Web: www.socialflow.com

Sogetel Inc 111, rue du 12-Novembre Nicolet QC J3T1S3 866-764-3835
TF: 866-764-3835 ■ *Web:* www.sogetel.com

SOLOMO Technology Inc
222 W Washington Ave Ste 705 Madison WI 53703 608-220-1900
Web: solomotechnology.com

Sopheon Corp 3001 Metro Dr Bloomington MN 55425 952-851-7500 851-7599
Web: www.sopheon.com

Sorvive Technologies Inc
2090 Buford Hwy Ste 1b Buford GA 30518 770-614-3122
Web: www.sorvive.com

Southwest Communications Inc
4100 N Mulberry Dr Ste 160 Kansas City MO 64116 816-298-4100
TF: 800-383-5533 ■ *Web:* www.scitel.net

SPACECONNECTION Inc, The
10530 Victory Blvd North Hollywood CA 91606 818-754-1100
TF: 800-537-7223 ■ *Web:* www.thespaceconnection.com

SpaceCurve Inc 710 Second Ave Ste 620 Seattle WA 98104 206-453-2225

Spanfeller Media Group Inc
156 Fifth Ave 4th Fl New York NY 10010 646-459-0604
Web: www.spanfellergroup.com

Spectrum Networks Inc 2200 Sixth Ave Ste 905 Seattle WA 98121 206-973-8300

SpeedDate.com Inc PO Box 5545 Redwood City CA 94063 650-692-9000
Web: www.speeddate.com

SpinGo Solutions Inc
14193 S Minuteman Dr Ste 100 Draper UT 84020 877-377-4646
TF: 877-377-4646 ■ *Web:* www.spingo.com

Spira Data Corp 630 - Eigth Ave SW Ste 500 Calgary AB T2P1G6 403-263-6475 263-2513
Web: www.spiradata.com

Sport Ngin LLC 807 Bdwy St NE Ste 300 Minneapolis MN 55413 612-379-1030
Web: www.sportngin.com

Spot411 Technologies Inc 10 Plz Sq Ste C Orange CA 92866 714-771-2050

SpotOn Inc 2350 Kerner Blvd Ste 380 San Rafael CA 94901 877-814-4102
TF: 877-814-4102 ■ *Web:* www.spoton.com

Spredfast Inc 200 W Cesar Chavez Ste 600 Austin TX 78701 512-542-9900
Web: www.spredfast.com

Spreedly Inc 116 W Main St Durham NC 27701 919-432-5008
Web: spreedly.com

Sqrrl Data Inc 275 Third St Cambridge MA 02142 617-902-0784
Web: sqrrl.com

SquaredOut Inc 2900 Bristol St Ste J203 Costa Mesa CA 92626 714-668-0262
Web: www.squaredout.com

Squire Tech Solutions LLC
6304 Fallwater Trl Ste 100 The Colony TX 75056 214-306-6704
Web: www.squiretechsolutions.com

Stage 2 Networks LLC 70 W 40th St 7th Fl New York NY 10018 212-497-8000
Web: stage2networks.com

Star-Tech Inc PO Box 672932 Marietta GA 30006 678-905-1171
Web: www.star-tech.net

StarQuest Software Inc 1288 Ninth St Berkeley CA 94710 510-528-2900
Web: starquest.com

StataCorp LP 4905 Lakeway Dr College Station TX 77845 979-696-4600 696-4601
Web: www.stata.com

Stibo Systems Inc
3550 George Busbee Pkwy NW Ste 350 Kennesaw GA 30144 770-425-3282
Web: www.stibosystems.com

Stickk.com LLC 39 E 30th St Ste 4 New York NY 10016 866-578-4255
TF: 866-578-4255 ■ *Web:* www.stickk.com

StudioNow Inc 4017 Hillsboro Pk Nashville TN 37215 615-577-9400
Web: www.studionow.com

StumbleUpon Inc 301 Brannan St San Francisco CA 94107 415-979-0640
Web: www.stumbleupon.com

StyleCaster Media Group LLC
440 Ninth Avenue11th Floor New York NY 10001 646-300-8350
Web: www.stylecaster.com

Summit Broadband Inc 4558 SW 35th St Orlando FL 32811 407-996-8900
Web: www.summit-broadband.com

Suncast Network Inc
2407 E Oakton St Ste B-10 Arlington Heights IL 60005 847-364-4008
Web: www.suncastv.com

Super Technologies Inc 6005 Keating Rd Pensacola FL 32504 850-433-8555
Web: www.supertec.com

SupportLocal LLC 1062 Delaware St Ste 4 Denver CO 80204 720-432-8160

SupremeBytes LLC PO Box 13746 Columbus OH 43213 614-636-4875
Web: www.supremebytes.com

Sureflix Digital Distribution Inc
229 Yonge St Ste 408 Toronto ON M5B2P9 416-907-7859
Web: www.corporate.sureflix.com

Sutherland Global Services
1160 Pittsford-Victor Rd Pittsford NY 14534 585-586-5757 784-2154
Web: www.sutherlandglobal.com

SystemMetrics Corp 900 Ft St Mall Ste 250 Honolulu HI 96813 808-791-7000
Web: www.platinumlimousinehawaii.com

Tandem Transit LLC
3611 14th Ave 3611 Ste 209 Brooklyn NY 11218 718-689-1303
Web: tandemtransit.com

Tapjoy Inc 111 Sutter St 13th Fl San Francisco CA 94104 415-766-6900
Web: www.tapjoy.com

TargetSpot Inc 149 Fifth Ave 10th Fl New York NY 10010 212-631-0500
Web: www.targetspot.com

Taurad LLC 6733 S Sepulveda Blvd Ste 135 Los Angeles CA 90045 310-281-3360
Web: taurad.com

Technorati Inc 360 Post St Ste 1100 San Francisco CA 94108 415-896-3000
Web: www.technorati.com

Telamon Corp 1000 E 116th St Carmel IN 46032 317-818-6888
Web: www.telamon.com

TelcoIQ 4300 Forbes Blvd Ste 110 Lanham MD 20706 202-595-1500
TF: 877-835-2647 ■ *Web:* www.telcoiq.com

Tele Atlas North America Inc 11 Lafayette St Lebanon NH 03766 603-643-0330
Web: www.tomtom.com

TeleGuam Holdings LLC 624 N Marine Corps Dr Tamuning GU 96913 671-644-4482
Web: www.gta.net

TelePacific Communications
1181 Grier Dr #F Las Vegas NV 89119 702-851-6000
Web: www.telepacific.com

Telephone Electronics Corp 236 E Capitol St Jackson MS 39201 601-354-9070
Web: www.tec.com

TelSpan Inc
101 W Washington St E Tower Ste 1200 Indianapolis IN 46204 800-800-1729
TF: 800-800-1729 ■ *Web:* www.telspan.com

TelTel Inc 2620 Augustine Dr Ste 100 Santa Clara CA 95054 408-970-3318
Web: www.teltel.com

Telx Group Inc, The 1 State St 24th Fl New York NY 10004 212-480-3300
Web: www.telx.com

Tendo Communications
340 Brannan St Ste 500 San Francisco CA 94107 415-369-8200
Web: www.tendocom.com

TennisHub Inc 95 Chestnut St Providence RI 02903 401-626-4280

tenXer Inc 101 Townsend St Ste 209 San Francisco CA 94107 415-500-2982

Therapydia Inc 18 E Blithedale Ave Ste 21 Mill Valley CA 94941 415-389-8677
Web: www.therapydia.com

TheSquareFoot LLC 1776 Yorktown Dr Ste 610 Houston TX 77056 281-701-9697
Web: www.thesquarefoot.com

Thomson Financial 22 Thomson Pl Boston MA 02210 617-856-2000
TF: 888-216-1929 ■ *Web:* www.thomsonreuters.com

TIBCO Software Inc 707 State Rd Ste 212 Princeton NJ 08540 609-683-4002
Web: www.tibco.com/products/automation/application-integration/pattern-matching

TicketBiscuit LLC
1550 Woods of Riverchase Dr Ste 110 Birmingham AL 35244 205-757-8330
Web: www.ticketbiscuit.com

Tie National Accounts 2280 White Oak Ste 108 Aurora IL 60502 630-301-7444
Web: tienational.com

TodoCast Inc
31831 Camino Capistrano Ste 301 San Juan Capistrano CA 92675 866-510-7889
TF: 866-510-7889 ■ *Web:* todocast.tv

Tongal Inc 1918 Main St 2nd Fl Santa Monica CA 90405 310-579-9260
Web: www.tongal.com

Topix LLC 1001 Elwell Ct Palo Alto CA 94303 650-461-8300

TouchLogic Corp 30 Kinnear Ct Ste 602 Richmond Hill ON L4B1K8 877-707-0207
TF: 877-707-0207 ■ *Web:* www.touchlogic.com

Touchstorm LLC 355 Lexington Ave 12th Fl New York NY 10017 877-794-6101
TF: 877-794-6101 ■ *Web:* www.touchstorm.com

Townes Tele-Communications Inc
120 E First St Lewisville AR 71845 870-921-4224
Web: www.walnuthilltel.com

Trada Inc 1023 Walnut St Boulder CO 80302 877-871-1835
TF: 877-871-1835

Transcom Telecommunications Co
3744 Industry Ave Ste 404 Lakewood CA 90712 562-663-2000
Web: www.transcomla.com

TransWorld Network Corp 255 Pine Ave N Oldsmar FL 34677 813-891-4700
Web: www.twncorp.com

Trapit Inc 2390 El Camino Real Ste 220 Palo Alto CA 94306 844-987-2748
TF: 844-987-2748 ■ *Web:* www.trapit.com

Travelport Ltd 300 Galleria Pkwy Atlanta GA 30339 770-563-7400
Web: www.travelport.com

Tribe Networks Inc 208 Utah St San Francisco CA 94103 415-861-2286
Web: www.tribe.net

Trillion Partners Inc
9208 Waterford Centre Blvd Ste 150 Austin TX 78758 512-334-4100
Web: www.trillion.net

Trisys Telecom Inc
215 Ridgedale Ave Ste 2 Florham Park NJ 07932 973-360-2300
Web: www.trisys.com

Trover Inc 307 Third Ave S Ste 520 Seattle WA 98104 206-812-8700
Web: www.trover.com

Truaxis Inc 959 Skyway Rd San Carlos CA 94070 650-654-7440

Phone Fax

True Fit Corp 800 W Cummings Park Ste 6400........... Woburn MA 01801 617-848-3740
Web: www.truefit.com

TruMarx Data Partners Inc
30 S Wacker Dr Ste 2200........................... Chicago IL 60606 312-707-9000
Web: www.trumarx.com

TruSignal LLC 25 6th Ave N........................... St. Cloud MN 56303 855-569-0426
TF: 855-569-0426 ■ *Web:* www.tru-signal.com

TTS LLC 2595 Dallas Pkwy Ste 300...................... Frisco TX 75034 214-778-0800 778-0880
Web: www.tts-us.com

Tungle Corp 410 rue Saint-Nicolas Ste 260............. Montreal QC H2Y2P5 514-678-9181
Web: www.tungle.com

TurfNet Media Network 5276 Wynterhall Way .... Atlanta GA 30338 770-395-9850
Web: www.turfnet.com

Tutum Inc 2302 Environ Way...................... Chapel Hill NC 27517 415-742-2442

Twin Oaks Computing Inc
755 Maleta Ln Ste 203......................... Castle Rock CO 80108 720-733-7906
Web: www.twinoakscomputing.com

Tyze Personal Networks Ltd
210 W Broadway 6th Fl......................... Vancouver BC V5Y3W2 604-628-9594
Web: www.tyze.com

UrbanDaddy Inc 900 Broadway Ste 808 .... New York NY 10003 212-929-7905
Web: www.urbandaddy.com

US Farm Data Inc 10824 Old Mill Rd Ste 8.............. Omaha NE 68154 402-334-1824
Web: www.usfarmdata.com

US News University Connection LLC
9417 Princess Palm Ave............................ Tampa FL 33619 866-442-6587
TF: 866-442-6587 ■ *Web:* www.usnewsuniversitydirectory.com

USA Communications Inc 920 E 56th St Ste B .... Kearney NE 68847 877-234-0102
TF: 877-234-0102 ■ *Web:* www.usacommunications.tv

uShip Inc 205 Brazos St........................... Austin TX 78701 800-698-7447
TF: 800-698-7447 ■ *Web:* www.uship.com

UsingMiles Inc
6400 S Fiddler's Green Cir Ste 975 .... Greenwood Village CO 80111 303-645-0531
Web: www.usingmiles.com

VALMARC Corp 109 Highland Ave.................... Needham MA 02494 339-225-4544
Web: www.valmarc.com

Vanguard Systems Inc
2901 Dutton Mill Rd Ste 220 .... Aston PA 19014 610-891-7703
Web: www.vansystems.com

Vanilla Forums Inc 414 McGill St, Ste 800 .... Montreal QC H2Y1S1 866-845-0815
TF: 866-845-0815 ■ *Web:* www.vanillaforums.com

Vectus Inc
18685 Main St 101 PMB 360................ Huntington Beach CA 92648 866-483-2887
TF: 866-483-2887 ■ *Web:* www.vectus.com

Ventura County Employees' Retirement Association
1190 S Victoria Ave Ste 200......................... Ventura CA 93003 805-339-4250
Web: portal.countyofventura.org

Vermont Telephone Company Inc
354 River St .... Springfield VT 05156 802-885-9000
Web: www.vermontel.com

Vertical Web Media LLC
125 S Wacker Dr Ste 2900.......................... Chicago IL 60606 312-362-9527
Web: www.internetretailer.com

Vessel Metrics LLC 3 Church Cir Ste 325 .... Annapolis MD 21401 888-214-1710
TF: 888-214-1710 ■ *Web:* www.vesselvanguard.com

Vetstreet 780 Township Line Rd .... Yardley PA 19067 215-493-0621
TF: 888-799-8387 ■ *Web:* www.vetstreet.com

Vianet Internet Solutions Inc
128 Larch St Ste 201 .... Sudbury ON P3E5J8 705-675-0402
Web: www.vianet.ca

Vidmaker Inc 612 W Main St Ste 300.................. Madison WI 53703 608-620-6002
Web: www.vidmaker.com

Vinely 1 Kendall Sq Bldg 400 B4202 .... Cambridge MA 02139 888-294-1128
TF: 888-294-1128

Virgin Media Inc 65 Bleecker St 6th Fl................ New York NY 10022 212-906-8440
Web: www.virginmedia.com

VirtualPBX.com Inc 111 N Market St Ste 1000 .... San Jose CA 95113 408-414-7646
Web: www.virtualpbx.com

VirtualWorks Group Inc
5301 N Federal Hwy Ste 230 .... Boca Raton FL 33487 561-327-4900
Web: www.virtualworks.com

Vista Broadband Networks Inc
3020 Santa Rosa Ave .... Santa Rosa CA 95407 707-527-0545
Web: www.vistabroadband.com

Voice123 30 E 23rd St........................... New York NY 10010 212-461-1873
Web: www.voice123.com

VoIP Innovations Inc 8 Penn Ctr W Ste 101 .... Pittsburgh PA 15276 877-478-6471
TF: 877-478-6471 ■ *Web:* www.voipinnovations.com

Voxox Inc 9276 Scranton Rd Ste 300................ San Diego CA 92121 619-900-9000
Web: www.voxox.com

VuFind Inc 1290 Oakmead Pkwy Ste 107............... Sunnyvale CA 94508 408-739-2880
Web: www.vufind.com

Waveguide Inc 10 N Southwood Dr .... Nashua NH 03063 603-598-0096
Web: www.waveguidefiber.com

WAVSYS LLC 101 Broadway Ste 406 .... Brooklyn NY 11249 347-292-8797
Web: www.wavsys.com

WealthForge Holdings Inc
6800 Paragon Pl Ste 237 .... Richmond VA 23230 804-658-5280
Web: www.wealthforge.com

Weblo.com Inc 930-2075 University St .... Montreal QC H3A2L1 514-364-3636
Web: www.weblo.com

WEbook Inc 307 Fifth Ave 7th Fl .... New York NY 10016 646-453-8575
Web: www.webook.com

WebReply.com Inc 1085 Worcester Rd .... Natick MA 01760 508-318-4600
Web: www.webreply.com

WellAware Holdings Inc
2330 N Loop 1604 W Ste 110 .... San Antonio TX 78248 210-816-4600
Web: www.wellaware.us

Wellsphere Inc 2300 Wilson Blvd Ste 600 .... Arlington VA 22201 703-302-1040

WeSpire Inc 125 Kingston St 6th Fl.................... Boston MA 02111 617-531-8970
Web: www.wespire.com

West Coast Green Institute
760 Market St Ste 1028 .... San Francisco CA 94102 415-955-1935
Web: westcoastgreen.com

West Group 610 Opperman Dr......................... Eagan MN 55123 651-687-7000 687-7551
TF Cust Svc: 800-328-4880 ■ *Web:* legalsolutions.thomsonreuters.com

WhamTech Inc 12001 N Central Expy Ste 300 .... Dallas TX 75243 972-991-5700
Web: www.whamtech.com

WhoKnows Inc 425 BRdway St .... Redwood City CA 94063 877-338-2763
TF: 877-338-2763 ■ *Web:* corp.whoknows.com

Wholeshare Inc 2431 Mission St .... San Francisco CA 94110 800-625-4605
TF: 800-625-4605 ■ *Web:* www.wholeshare.com

WibiData Inc 375 Alabama St Ste 350............ San Francisco CA 94110 415-496-9424

Wisetail 212 S Wallace Ave Ste B2.................... Bozeman MT 59715 406-545-4662
Web: www.wisetail.com

Wolfram Alpha LLC 100 Trade Ctr Dr.............. Champaign IL 61820 217-398-0700
Web: www.wolframalpha.com

WyzAnt Inc 1714 N Damen Ave Ste 3N .... Chicago IL 60647 312-646-6365
Web: www.wyzant.com

X17 Inc PO Box 2362 .... Beverly Hills CA 90213 310-230-3332
Web: x17agency.com

Xacti Global LLC 999 W Yamato Rd Ste 100.......... Boca Raton FL 33431 561-989-7400
Web: www.xactiglobal.com

Xtel Communications Inc 401 Rt 73 n .... Marlton NJ 08053 856-596-4000
Web: www.xtel.net

XTRAC LLC 245 Summer St .... Boston MA 02210 855-975-3569
TF: 855-975-3569 ■ *Web:* www.xtracsolutions.com

Ya Sabe Inc 100 Carpenter Dr Ste 135.................. Sterling VA 20164 703-793-3270
Web: www.yasabe.com

Yesware Inc 75 Kneeland St Fl 15...................... Boston MA 02111 855-937-9273
TF: 855-937-9273 ■ *Web:* www.yesware.com

YouDocs Beauty Inc 648 Broadway.................. New York NY 10012 646-449-9445
Web: www.youbeauty.com

YouVisit LLC 20533 Biscayne Blvd Ste 1322........... Aventura FL 33180 866-585-7158
TF: 866-585-7158 ■ *Web:* www.youvisit.com

ZEFR Inc 1621 Abbot Kinney Blvd........................ Venice CA 90291 310-392-3555
Web: zefr.com

Zenfolio Inc 3515-A Edison Way.................. Menlo Park CA 94025 650-412-1888
Web: www.zenfolio.com

Zetta Inc 1362 Borregas Ave .... Sunnyvale CA 94089 650-590-0950
Web: www.zetta.net

Zignal Labs Inc 244 Jackson St 2nd Fl .... San Francisco CA 94111 415-683-7871
Web: www.zignallabs.com

Zindigo Inc
2401 PGA Blvd Ste 280-A .... Palm Beach Gardens FL 33410 561-694-1314
Web: www.zindigo.com

Zooppa.com Inc 911 Western Ave Ste 420............... Seattle WA 98104 206-866-0516
Web: zooppa.com

Ztar Mobile Inc 951 N Walnut Creek Dr Ste C.......... Mansfield TX 76063 214-231-0103
Web: www.ztarmobile.com

ZUUS Media Inc 3 Columbus Cir 15th Fl............. New York NY 10019 646-664-1702

Zypcom Inc 29400 Kohoutek Way Ste 170............ Union City CA 94587 510-324-2501
Web: www.zypcom.com

388 INK

Phone Fax

AJ Daw Printing Ink Co
608 E Compton Blvd E...................... Rancho Dmngz CA 90221 323-723-3253

Braden Sutphin Ink Co 3650 E 93rd St .... Cleveland OH 44105 216-271-2300 271-0515
TF: 800-289-6872 ■ *Web:* www.bsink.com

Central Ink Corp 1100 Harvester Rd .... West Chicago IL 60185 630-231-6500 231-6554
TF: 800-345-2541 ■ *Web:* www.cicink.com

Color Resolutions International
575 Quality Blvd.................................. Fairfield OH 45014 513-552-7200 552-7141
TF: 800-346-8570 ■ *Web:* new.colorresolutions.com

Cudner & O'Connor Co 4035 W Kinzie St............... Chicago IL 60624 773-826-0200 826-0477
Web: www.candocinks.com

Deco Chem Inc 3502 N Home St.................. Mishawaka IN 46545 574-259-3787
TF: 888-332-6465 ■ *Web:* www.decochem.com

Gans Ink & Supply Company Inc
1441 Boyd St .... Los Angeles CA 90033 323-264-2200 264-2916
TF: 800-421-6167 ■ *Web:* www.gansink.com

Independent Ink Inc 13700 Gramercy Pl .... Gardena CA 90249 310-523-4657 329-0943
TF: 800-446-5538 ■ *Web:* www.independentink.com

International Coatings Co 13929 166th St............ Cerritos CA 90703 562-926-1010 926-9486
TF: 800-423-4103 ■ *Web:* www.iccink.com

Kerley Ink Engineers Inc 2700 S 12th Ave .... Broadview IL 60155 708-344-1295 865-5759
Web: www.kerleyink.com

Keystone Printing Ink Co
2700 Roberts Ave.............................. Philadelphia PA 19129 215-228-8100
Web: www.keystoneink.com

Matsui International Company Inc
1501 W 178th St.................................. Gardena CA 90248 310-767-7812 767-7836
TF: 800-359-5679 ■ *Web:* www.matsui-color.com

Nazdar 8501 Hedge Ln Terr.......................... Shawnee KS 66227 913-422-1888 422-2296
TF: 800-767-9942 ■ *Web:* www.nazdar.com

Nor-Cote International Inc
506 Lafayette Ave .... Crawfordsville IN 47933 765-362-9180 364-5408
TF: 800-488-9180 ■ *Web:* www.norcote.com

Polytex 820 E 140th St.................................. Bronx NY 10454 718-402-2000 402-2984
Web: www.polytexink.com

Ranger Industries Inc 15 Park Rd .... Tinton Falls NJ 07724 732-389-3535
Web: www.rangerink.com

Reaxis Inc 941 Robinson Hwy .... Mcdonald PA 15057 800-426-7273
TF: 800-426-7273 ■ *Web:* www.reaxis.com

Sensient Technologies Corp
777 E Wisconsin Ave .... Milwaukee WI 53202 414-271-6755 347-3785
NYSE: SXT ■ *TF:* 800-558-9892 ■ *Web:* www.sensient.com

Sericol Inc 1101 W Cambridge Dr................... Kansas City KS 66103 913-342-4060 342-4752
TF: 800-737-4265 ■ *Web:* www.sericol.com

Siegwerk USA Co 3535 SW 56th St .... Des Moines IA 50321 515-471-2100 471-2200
TF: 800-728-8200 ■ *Web:* www.siegwerk.com

Spectrachem 10 Dell Glen Ave .... Lodi NJ 07644 973-253-3553 253-3663
Web: www.spectrachem.net

				Phone	Fax
Sun Chemical Corp 35 Waterview Blvd. TF: 800-543-2323 ■ Web: www.sunchemical.com	Parsippany	NJ	07054	973-404-6000	404-6001
Superior Printing Ink Co Inc 100 N St Web: www.superiorink.com	Teterboro	NJ	07608	201-478-5600	478-5650
Tonertype of Florida LLC 5313 Johns Rd Ste 210 Web: www.tonertype.com	Tampa	FL	33634	813-915-1300	
Toyo Ink America LLC 1225 N Michael Dr *Fax Area Code: 630 ■ TF General: 866-969-8696 ■ Web: www.toyoink.com	Wood Dale	IL	60191	866-969-8696	628-1769*
U-mark Inc 102 Iowa Ave TF: 866-383-6275 ■ Web: www.umarkers.com	Belleville	IL	62220	618-235-7500	
US Ink Corp 651 Garden St. *Fax: Mktg ■ TF: 800-423-8838 ■ Web: www.sunchemical.com/product/us-ink	Carlstadt	NJ	07072	201-935-8666	933-3728*
Wikoff Color Corp 1886 Merritt Rd. Web: www.wikoff.com	Fort Mill	SC	29715	803-548-2210	548-5728

389 INSULATION & ACOUSTICAL PRODUCTS

				Phone	Fax
Anco Products Inc (API) 2500 S 17th St TF: 800-837-2626 ■ Web: www.ancoproductsinc.com	Elkhart	IN	46517	574-293-5574	295-6235
Applegate Insulation Manufacturing Inc 1000 Highview Dr TF: 800-627-7536 ■ Web: www.applegateinsulation.com	Webberville	MI	48892	517-521-3545	521-3597
CertainTeed Corp 750 E Swedesford Rd TF Prod Info: 800-782-8777 ■ Web: www.certainteed.com	Valley Forge	PA	19482	610-341-7000	341-7777
Claremont Sales Corp 35 Winsome Dr PO Box 430 TF: 800-222-4448 ■ Web: claremontcorporation.com	Durham	CT	06422	860-349-4499	349-7977
CTA Acoustics Inc 100 CTA Blvd Web: www.ctaacoustics.com	Corbin	KY	40701	606-528-8050	528-8074
Dryvit Systems Inc 1 Energy Way TF: 800-556-7752 ■ Web: www.dryvit.com	West Warwick	RI	02893	401-822-4100	822-4510
F Rodgers Corp 7901 National Dr	Livermore	CA	94550	925-960-2300	
Hi-Temp Insulation Inc 4700 Calle Alto Web: www.hi-tempinsulation.com	Camarillo	CA	93012	805-484-2774	484-7551
Industrial Acoustics Company Inc 1160 Commerce Ave Web: www.iacacoustics.com	Bronx	NY	10462	718-931-8000	863-1138
Industrial Insulation Group LLC (IIG) 2100 Line St *Fax Area Code: 912 ■ TF: 800-334-7997 ■ Web: www.jm.com/en/building-materials/industrial-insulation	Brunswick	GA	31520	303-978-2000	267-6096*
Isolatek International Inc 41 Furnace St TF: 800-631-9600 ■ Web: www.cafco.com	Stanhope	NJ	07874	973-347-1200	
ITW Insulation Systems 1370 E 40th St Ste 1 Bldg 7 *Fax Area Code: 713 ■ TF: 800-231-1024 ■ Web: www.itwinsulation.com	Houston	TX	77022	800-231-1024	691-7492*
Johns Manville Corp 717 17th St PO Box 5108 TF Prod Info: 800-654-3103 ■ Web: www.jm.com	Denver	CO	80217	303-978-2000	
Knauf Insulation 1 Knauf Dr TF: 800-825-4434 ■ Web: www.knaufinsulation.com	Shelbyville	IN	46176	317-398-4434	398-3675
MIT International 77 Massachusetts Ave *Fax Area Code: 480 ■ TF General: 800-228-9290 ■ Web: web.mit.edu	Cambridge	TX	02139	617-253-1000	283-1190*
Molded Acoustical Products of Easton Inc 3 Danforth Dr Web: mapeaston.com	Easton	PA	18045	610-253-7135	253-1664
Nu-Wool Company Inc 2472 Port Sheldon Rd TF: 800-748-0128 ■ Web: www.nuwool.com	Jenison	MI	49428	616-669-0100	669-2370
Owens Corning 1 Owens Corning Pkwy NYSE: OC ■ Web: www.owenscorning.com	Toledo	OH	43659	419-248-8000	325-1538
Pittsburgh Corning Corp 800 Presque Isle Dr Web: www.pittsburghcorning.com	Pittsburgh	PA	15239	724-327-6100	387-3806
Premier Manufacturing Corp 12117 Bennington Ave	Cleveland	OH	44135	216-941-9700	941-9719
Rock Wool Manufacturing Co 1400 Seventh Ct PO Box 506 TF Sales: 800-874-7625 ■ Web: www.deltainsulation.com	Leeds	AL	35094	205-699-6121	699-3132
S & S Industries Inc 115 Clemmons Rd *Fax Area Code: 615 ■ Web: www.ssindustries.net	Mount Juliet	TN	37122	914-885-1500	754-8011*
Scott Industries Inc 1573 Hwy 136 W PO Box 7 TF: 800-951-9276 ■ Web: www.scott-mfg.com	Henderson	KY	42419	270-831-2037	831-2039
Soundcoat Co 1 Burt Dr TF: 800-394-8913 ■ Web: www.soundcoat.com	Deer Park	NY	11729	631-242-2200	242-2246
Thermafiber Inc 3711 W Mill St TF: 888-834-2371 ■ Web: www.thermafiber.com	Wabash	IN	46992	260-563-2111	563-7022
Thermwell Products Co 420 Rt 17 S TF: 800-526-5265 ■ Web: www.frostking.com	Mahwah	NJ	07430	201-684-4400	684-1214
TIGHITCO Inc 1375 Seaboard Industrial Blvd Web: www.tighitco.com	Atlanta	GA	30318	404-355-1205	351-4458
Transco Products Inc 1215 E 12th St Ste 2100 Web: www.transcoproducts.com	Streator	IL	61364	312-427-2818	427-4975
Unifrax Corp 2351 Whirlpool St *Fax: Cust Svc ■ Web: www.unifrax.com	Niagara Falls	NY	14305	716-278-3800	278-3904*
Ward Process Inc 311 Hopping Brook Rd Web: www.aapusa.com	Holliston	MA	01746	508-429-1165	429-8543

390 INSURANCE AGENTS, BROKERS, SERVICES

				Phone	Fax
A Plus Benefits Inc 395 West 600 North TF: 800-748-5102 ■ Web: www.aplusbenefits.com	Lindon	UT	84042	801-443-1090	
Abacus Group LLC, The 2541 Lafayette Plz Dr	Albany	GA	31707	229-436-6032	
ACB Insurance Inc 7715 Loma Ct Ste E Web: acb-insurance.com	Fishers	IN	46038	317-915-8601	
Accredited Surety & Casualty Company Inc 4798 New Broad St Ste 200 Web: www.accredited-inc.com	Orlando	FL	32814	407-629-2131	
Accurate Insurance Inc 416 First St Web: accurateinsinc.com	Glenwood	IA	51534	712-527-9106	
Actuarial Systems Corp 15840 Monte St Ste 108 TF: 800-950-2082 ■ Web: www.asc-net.com	Sylmar	CA	91342	800-950-2082	
Adorno-Denker Assoc Inc 4502 Broadway	Long Island	NY	11103	718-278-8660	
Advisornet Financial Inc 701 Fourth Ave S Ste 1500 Web: advisornet.com	Minneapolis	MN	55415	612-347-8600	
Aetna RX Home Delivery LLC 2528 Nw 19th St Web: member.aetna.com	Pompano Beach	FL	33069	954-876-5000	
Affinion Group Inc 6 High Ridge Pk TF: 800-251-2148 ■ Web: www.affiniongroup.com	Stamford	CT	06905	203-956-1000	
Agency Software Inc 215 W Commerce Dr TF: 800-342-7327 ■ Web: www.agencysoftware.com	Hayden Lake	ID	83835	208-762-7188	762-1265
Albert J Marchionne Insurance Agency Inc 11 Independence Ave Web: marchionneinsurance.com	Quincy	MA	02169	617-471-5010	
All Motorists Insurance Agency 5230 Las Virgenes Rd Ste 100 Web: westerngeneral.com	Calabasas	CA	91302	818-880-9070	
Allen Agency 34-36 Elm St PO Box 578	Camden	ME	04843	207-236-4311	236-6647
Alley Rehbaum & Capes Inc 2433 Gulf To Bay Blvd Web: www.arc-insurance.com	Clearwater	FL	33765	727-797-5193	
Alliance Abstract LLC 2 Mott St Ste 605	New York	NY	10013	212-962-2228	
Alliance Brokerage Corp 990 Wbury Rd Web: alliancebrokeragecorp.com	Westbury	NY	11590	516-333-7300	333-5698
Alliance of Transylvanian Saxons 5393 Pearl Rd Web: atsaxons.com	Cleveland	OH	44129	440-842-8442	
Alliance Worldwide Investigative Group Inc 4 Executive Park Dr TF: 800-579-2911 ■ Web: www.allianceinvestigative.com	Clifton Park	NY	12065	518-514-2944	
Allied Solutions LLC 1320 City Ctr Dr Ste 300 Web: alliedsolutions.net	Carmel	IN	46032	317-706-7600	706-7606
Allstate Insurance Co 2955 Pineda Plaza Way Ste 103 Web: agents.allstate.com	Viera	FL	32940	321-242-1002	
Alpena Agency Inc 102 S Third Ave Web: alpenaagency.com	Alpena	MI	49707	989-354-2175	
AM Skier Agency Inc 209 Main Ave Web: amskier.com	Hawley	PA	18428	570-226-4571	
Amano Enzyme USA Company Ltd 1415 Madeline Ln Web: www.amano-enzyme.co.jp	Elgin	IL	60124	847-649-0101	
American Classic Agency 201 Atp Tour Blvd Web: www.aclassic.com	Ponte Vedra	FL	32082	904-285-4030	
American Mutual Share Insurance Corp 5656 Frantz Rd Web: www.excessshare.com	Dublin	OH	43017	614-764-1900	
Amfed Cos LLC 576 Highland Colony Pkwy TF: 800-264-8085 ■ Web: www.amfed.com	Ridgeland	MS	39157	601-853-4949	853-2727
Anchor Financial Group 415 Fallowfield Rd Ste 300 Web: www.anchorfinancialgroup.com	Camp Hill	PA	17011	717-975-0509	
ANCO Insurance 1111 Briarcrest Dr PO Box 3889 *Fax Area Code: 936 ■ TF: 800-749-1733 ■ Web: www.anco.com	Bryan	TX	77802	979-776-2626	327-3219*
Anderson Shumaker Co 824 S Central Ave Web: www.andersonshumaker.com	Chicago	IL	60644	773-287-0874	
Andover Co, The 95 Old River Rd Web: andovercos.com	Andover	MA	01810	978-475-3300	
Andreini & Co 220 W 20th Ave TF: 800-969-2522 ■ Web: www.andreini.com	San Mateo	CA	94403	650-573-1111	378-4361
Andrew G Gordon Inc 306 Washington St TF: 866-243-2259 ■ Web: agordon.com	Norwell	MA	02061	781-659-2262	
Annette Willis Insurance Agency Inc 18401 NW 27th Ave Web: annettewillisinsurance.com	Miami	FL	33056	305-625-2403	
Aon Risk Services Inc 200 E Randolph St TF: 877-384-4276 ■ Web: www.aon.com	Chicago	IL	60601	312-381-1000	701-4580
Arch Capital Group (US) Inc 1 Liberty Plz 53rd Fl	New York	NY	10006	212-651-6500	
Argenia LLC 11524 Fairview Rd TF: 800-482-5968 ■ Web: argenia.com	Little Rock	AR	72212	501-227-9670	
Argus Research Inc. 887 W Marietta St Studio N-108 Web: www.ajg.com/locations/georgia/atlanta-argus	Atlanta	GA	30318	404-846-8883	
Arthur J Gallagher & Co 2 Pierce Pl NYSE: AJG ■ TF: 888-285-5106 ■ Web: www.ajg.com	Itasca	IL	60143	630-773-3800	285-4000
Arthur J. Glatfelter Agency Inc PO Box 2726 TF: 800-233-1957 ■ Web: www.glatfelters.com	York	PA	17405	717-741-0911	741-4160
Ash Brokerage Corp 7609 W Jefferson Blvd Web: www.ashbrokerage.com	Fort Wayne	IN	46804	260-478-0600	
Associated Administrators LLC 911 Ridgebrook Rd Web: www.associated-admin.com	Sparks	MD	21152	410-683-6500	
Associated Agencies Inc 1701 Golf Rd Tower 3 7th Fl Web: www.assocagencies.com	Rolling Meadows	IL	60008	847-427-8400	427-3559
Assurity Life Insurance Co PO Box 82533 TF: 800-869-0355 ■ Web: assurity.com	Lincoln	NE	68501	402-476-6500	
Atkinson & Assoc Insurance Inc 1537 Brantley Rd Bldg C Web: atkinsoninsurance.com	Fort Myers	FL	33907	239-437-5555	
Automated Benefit Services Inc 8220 Irving Rd Web: www.abs-tpa.com	Sterling Heights	MI	48312	586-693-4300	
B C Szerlip Insurance Agency Inc 34 Sycamore Ave Web: bcszerlip.com	Little Silver	NJ	07739	732-842-2020	
Badger Mutual Insurance Co 1635 W National Ave TF: 800-837-7833 ■ Web: www.badgermutual.com	Milwaukee	WI	53204	414-383-1234	
Barney J Belleci 26555 Carmel Rancho Blvd	Carmel	CA	93923	831-624-6466	

Name / Address	City	State	Zip	Phone	Fax
Bateman Gordon & Sands Inc 3050 N Federal Hwy *Web:* bgsagency.com	Lighthouse Point	FL	33064	954-941-0900	
BBR Benefits Solutions LLC 8150 Perry Hwy Ste 100 *Web:* bbrbenefits.com	Pittsburgh	PA	15237	412-847-3100	
Beazley Insurance Company Inc 30 Batterson Park Rd *Web:* www.beazley.com	Farmington	CT	06032	860-677-3700	
Beckerman & Co 430 Lake Ave. *TF:* 800-339-1836 ■ *Web:* www.beckermanco.com	Colonia	NJ	07067	732-499-9200	
Bedford Underwriters Ltd 315 E Mill St *Web:* bedfordunderwriters.com	Plymouth	WI	53073	920-892-8795	
BeneCard Services Inc 3131 Princeton Pike Bldg 2B Ste 103 *Web:* www.benecard.com	Lawrenceville	NJ	08648	609-219-0400	
Benefit & Risk Management Services Inc 10860 Gold Ctr Dr Ste 300 *TF:* 888-326-2555 ■ *Web:* www.brmsonline.com	Rancho Cordova	CA	95670	916-858-2950	
Benefit Communications Inc 2126 21st Ave S. *Web:* benefitcommunications.com	Nashville	TN	37212	615-292-3786	
Benefit Concepts Inc 1173 Brittmoore Rd *Web:* mybciteam.com	Houston	TX	77043	713-722-8779	728-7201
Benefit Resource Group LLC 5985 Home Gardens Dr Ste A. *Web:* benresgroup.com	Reno	NV	89502	775-688-4400	
Benefits Div Inc 125 S Swoope Ave Ste 210 *Web:* benefits-division.com	Maitland	FL	32751	407-629-9085	
Beneplace Inc 11940 Jollyville Rd Ste 300N *Web:* bp.beneplace.com	Austin	TX	78759	512-346-3300	
BeneSys Inc 700 Tower Dr Ste 300 *Web:* www.benesysinc.com	Troy	MI	48098	248-813-9800	
Berkley Risk Administrators Company LLC 222 S Ninth St Ste 1300 *TF:* 800-449-7707 ■ *Web:* www.berkleyrisk.com	Minneapolis	MN	55402	612-766-3000	
Bernheimer-Lincoln Insurance Group 779 Farmington Ave *Web:* bernheimerinsurance.com	West Hartford	CT	06119	860-232-3810	
Bidlake Agency Inc 2905 Millennium Ste 3 *Web:* billingsinsurance.com	Billings	MT	59102	406-245-6224	
Bilbrey Insurance Services Inc 5701 Greendale Rd *TF:* 800-383-0116 ■ *Web:* icapiowa.com	Johnston	IA	50131	800-383-0116	
Bill Farris Insurance Agency Inc 390 Cypress Gardens Blvd *Web:* www.statefarm.com/agent/us/fl/winter-haven/bill-farris-94b3k1ys000	Winter Haven	FL	33880	863-299-2153	
Bischoff Insurance Agency Inc 1300 Oakridge Dr Ste 100 *TF:* 888-229-5558 ■ *Web:* bradbischoff.com	Fort Collins	CO	80525	970-223-9400	
Black Sand Technologies Inc 3316 Bee Cave Rd Ste C *Web:* www.blacksand.com	Austin	TX	78746	512-329-9400	
Bliss Mcknight Inc 2801 E Empire *Web:* blissmcknight.com	Bloomington	IL	61704	309-663-1393	
Block Insurance Agency Inc 2333 Highland St *Web:* blockins.com	Allentown	PA	18104	610-433-4131	433-1531
Body-Borneman Insurance PO Box 584 *Web:* www.body-borneman.com	Boyertown	PA	19512	610-367-1100	367-1140
Boeck & Assoc Inc 930 Town Centre Dr *Web:* boeckinsurance.com	Medford	OR	97504	541-770-9400	
Bogart & Brownell 7648 Standish Pl Ste 320 *Web:* www.bogartandbrownell.com	Rockville	MD	20855	301-444-4500	
Bollinger Insurance 101 JFK Pkwy *Web:* www.bollingerinsurance.com	Short Hills	NJ	07078	973-467-0444	921-2876
Bolte Real Estate Inc & Bolte Insurance Inc 134 E Second St *Web:* bolterealty.com	Port Clinton	OH	43452	419-732-3111	
Bolton & Co 3475 E Foothill Blvd Ste 100 *Web:* www.boltonco.com	Pasadena	CA	91107	626-799-7000	441-3233
Boston Partners Financial Group LLC 138 River Rd Ste 310 *Web:* www.bostonpartnersfinancialgroup.com	Andover	MA	01810	978-689-9303	
Brad Peters Agency Inc 2028 N State St	Belvidere	IL	61008	815-544-2950	
Brady Chapman Holland & Assoc Inc 10055 W Gulf Bank *Web:* bch-insurance.com	Houston	TX	77040	713-688-1500	
Brown & Brown Agency of Insurance Professionals Inc 208 N Mill *Web:* www.bbinsurance.com	Pryor	OK	74361	918-825-3295	
Brown & Brown Inc 220 S Ridgewood Ave. *NYSE: BRO* ■ *Web:* www.bbinsurance.com	Daytona Beach	FL	32114	386-252-9601	
Brown Smith Wallace LLC 6 Cityplace Dr Ste 900 *Web:* bswllc.com	St Louis	MO	63141	314-983-1200	
Bruen Deldin Didio Assoc 3 Starr Ridge Rd *Web:* bddinsurance.com	Brewster	NY	10509	845-279-5151	
Burnham & Flower Group Inc 315 S Kalamazoo Mall *TF:* 888-748-7966 ■ *Web:* bfgroup.com	Kalamazoo	MI	49007	269-381-1173	
Burnham Financial Services LLC 2038 Saranac Ave. *Web:* burnhambenefitadvisors.com	Lake Placid	NY	12946	518-523-8100	
Burns-Fazzi Brock & Associates LLC 1816 E Seventh St *Web:* www.bfbbenefit.com	Charlotte	NC	28204	704-332-2265	
Buursma Agency 728 E Eighth St Ste 4 *Web:* buursmaagency.com	Holland	MI	49423	616-392-2105	
BWD Group LLC 45 Executive Dr *Web:* www.bwd.us	Plainview	NY	11803	516-327-2700	327-2800
Byrnes Agency Inc 394 Lake Rd. *Web:* byrnesagency.com	Dayville	CT	06241	860-774-8549	
C & A Financial Group 2431 Atlantic Ave	Manasquan	NJ	08736	732-528-4800	
C P H & Associates 711 S Dearborn St Unit 205 *TF:* 800-875-1911 ■ *Web:* www.cphins.com	Chicago	IL	60605	312-987-9823	
CAA Saskatchewan 200 N Albert St. *Web:* www.caasask.sk.ca	Regina	SK	S4R5E2	306-791-4314	
Cailor Fleming & Assoc Inc 4610 Market St *TF:* 800-796-8495 ■ *Web:* cailorfleming.com	Youngstown	OH	44512	330-782-8068	
Callbright Corp 6700 Hollister *TF:* 877-462-2552 ■ *Web:* www.callbright.com	Houston	TX	77040	877-462-2552	
CalSurance 681 S Parker St Ste 300 *TF:* 800-762-7800 ■ *Web:* www.calsurance.com	Orange	CA	92868	714-939-0800	939-1641
CAM Administrative Services Inc 25800 Northwestern Hwy Ste 700 *Web:* www.camads.com	Southfield	MI	48075	248-827-1050	
Cantella & Company Inc 28 State St 40th Fl *Web:* www.cantella.com	Boston	MA	02109	617-521-8630	
Capital Analysts Inc 218 Glenside Ave *TF:* 800-242-1421 ■ *Web:* www.capitalanalysts.com	Wyncote	PA	19095	800-242-1421	
Capital Strategies Group Inc 850 Shades Creek Pkwy Ste 300 *Web:* capitalstrategies.net	Birmingham	AL	35209	205-263-2400	
Carl E Mellen & Co 601 W Greenwood Ave *Web:* carlmellen.com	Waukegan	IL	60087	847-244-3500	
Carl Nelson Insurance Agency I 1519 N 11th Ave. *TF:* 800-582-4264 ■ *Web:* carlnelsonins.com	Hanford	CA	93230	559-584-4495	
Carl Warren & Company Inc 770 S Placentia Ave *Web:* www.carlwarren.com	Placentia	CA	92870	714-572-5200	
Carleton Insurance Agency 383 Kings Hwy N *Web:* www.carletoninsurance.com	Cherry Hill	NJ	08034	856-482-6200	
Carol Drake 1913 N Green Vly Pkwy *Web:* caroldrake.com	Henderson	NV	89074	702-361-0300	
Casswood Insurance Agency Ltd 5 Executive Pk Dr *TF:* 800-972-2242 ■ *Web:* www.casswood.com	Clifton Park	NY	12065	518-373-8700	373-8799
Castle Lake Insurance LLC 3385 S Holmes Ave *Web:* castlelakeinsurance.com	Idaho Falls	ID	83404	208-522-7778	
Caterpillar Financial Services Corp 2120 W End Ave *Web:* www.catfinancial.com	Nashville	TN	37203	615-341-1000	
Catholic United Financial 3499 Lexington Ave N *Web:* www.catholicunitedfinancial.org	St Paul	MN	55126	651-490-0170	
CBIZ Benefits & Insurance Services of Maryland Inc 44 Baltimore St. **Fax:* Sales ■ *TF Cust Svc:* 800-615-8418 ■ *Web:* www.cbiz.com	Cumberland	MD	21502	301-777-1500	951-0425*
Century Coverage Corp 76 S Central Ave *Web:* centurycoverage.com	Valley Stream	NY	11580	516-791-1800	
Chamberlin Insurance Group Inc 485 Devon Park Dr Ste 111	Wayne	PA	19087	610-674-0999	
Charles L Crane Agency Co 100 N Broadway Ste 900 *Web:* www.craneagency.com	Saint Louis	MO	63102	314-241-8700	444-4970
Citizens Property Insurance Corp 6676 Corporate Ctr Pkwy *Web:* www.citizensfla.com	Jacksonville	FL	32216	904-296-6105	
Claim Technologies Inc 100 Court Ave Ste 306 *Web:* www.claimtechnologies.com	Des Moines	IA	50309	515-244-7322	
Clark Insurance PO Box 3543 *TF:* 800-773-4300 ■ *Web:* clarkinsurance.com	Portland	ME	04104	207-774-6257	
Clifford & Rano Insurance Agency Inc 57 Cedar St. *TF:* 800-660-8284 ■ *Web:* cliffordrano.com	Worcester	MA	01609	508-752-8284	
CLV Group Inc 485 Bank St Ste 200 *Web:* www.clvgroup.com	Ottawa	ON	K2P1Z2	613-728-2000	
Cna National Warranty Corp 4150 N Drinkwater Blvd Ste 400 *Web:* cnanational.com	Scottsdale	AZ	85251	480-941-1626	
Cobb Strecker Dunphy & Zimmermann Inc 150 S Fifth St Ste 2800 *Web:* www.csdz.com	Minneapolis	MN	55402	612-349-2400	
Columbian Mutual Life Insurance Co Vestal Pkwy E *Web:* www.cfglife.com	Binghamton	NY	13902	607-724-2472	
Combined Specialities International Inc 205 San Marin Dr Ste 5 *Web:* combinedspecialties.com	Novato	CA	94945	415-209-0012	
Combs Insurance Agency Inc 341 S Alaska St. *Web:* combsinsurance.com	Palmer	AK	99645	907-745-2144	
Common Census Inc 90 Bridge St FL 105 *Web:* www.commoncensus.com	Westbrook	ME	04092	207-854-5454	
Concepts Diversified 2509 Kesslersville Rd	Easton	PA	18040	610-250-9996	
Concero Inc 10220 SW Greenburg Rd.	Portland	OR	97223	971-222-1900	222-1919
Concklin Insurance Agency Inc 240 S Wmore Ave. *Web:* concklin.com	Lombard	IL	60148	630-268-1600	
Connecture Inc 18500 W. Corporate Dr Ste 250 *Web:* www.connecture.com	Brookfield	WI	53045	404-879-4600	
Connexus Inc 10000 N Central Expy *Web:* www.idontwanttotravel.com	Dallas	TX	75231	214-443-2600	443-2620
Continental American Insurance Company Inc 2801 Devine St.	Columbia	SC	29205	803-256-6265	
Core-Vens & Company Inc 2301 N Second St *Web:* www.corevensguninsurance.com	Clinton	IA	52732	563-242-5423	
Cornerstone National Insurance Co 3100 Falling Leaf Ct Ste 200 PO Box 6040 *Web:* www.cornerstonenational.com	Columbia	MO	65201	573-817-2481	

Company	City	State	ZIP	Phone	Fax
Corporate Synergies Group LLC 5000 Dearborn Cir Ste 100 *Web:* corpsyn.com	Mount Laurel	NJ	08054	856-813-1500	
Courtesy Insurance Agency 324 W Hefner Rd *Web:* ciaokc.com	Oklahoma City	OK	73114	405-755-4571	
Coverage Inc 4460-P Brookfield Corporate Dr *Web:* coverageinc.com	Chantilly	VA	20151	703-631-8000	
CPI-HR Inc 6830 Cochran Rd *Web:* www.cpihr.com	Solon	OH	44139	440-542-7800	
Cramer Johnson Wiggins & Assoc 1420 Edgewater Dr Ste 200 *Web:* cjw-assoc.com	Orlando	FL	32804	407-849-0044	
Crosby Insurance Inc 8181 E Kaiser Blvd *Web:* crosbyinsurance.com	Anaheim	CA	92808	714-221-5200	
Cross Financial Corp 74 Gilman Rd PO Box 1388 *TF:* 800-999-7345 ■ *Web:* www.crossagency.com	Bangor	ME	04401	207-947-7345	941-0849
Crown Polymers LLC 11111 Kiley Dr *Web:* www.crownpolymers.com	Huntley	IL	60142	847-659-0300	
CSP Information Group Inc 1 Tower Ln Ste 2000 *Web:* www.cspdailynews.com	Oak Brook	IL	60181	630-574-5075	
Cumbre Inc 3333 Concours Ste 5100 *TF:* 800-998-7986 ■ *Web:* www.cumbreinc.com	Ontario	CA	91764	909-484-2456	484-2491
Cunningham Lindsey Group Ltd 3030 Rocky Point Dr Ste 530 *Web:* www.cunninghamlindsey.com	Tampa	FL	33607	813-830-7100	
Curtis Miller Insurance Agency Inc 1800 Blizzard Dr *Web:* curtismillerins.com	Parkersburg	WV	26101	304-485-6431	
CVP Systems Inc 2518 Wisconsin Ave *Web:* www.cvpsystems.com	Downers Grove	IL	60515	630-852-1190	
cynoSure Financial Inc 33490 Harper Ave *Web:* www.cynosurefinancial.com	Clinton Township	MI	48035	586-771-3334	
DailyAccess Corp 307 University Blvd N Bldg 3 Ste 1500 *TF:* 877-859-5735 ■ *Web:* www.dailyaccess.com	Mobile	AL	36688	251-665-1800	
Dale Barton Agency Inc 1100 East 6600 South *TF:* 866-288-1666 ■ *Web:* dalebarton.com	Salt Lake City	UT	84121	801-288-1600	
Daniel & Henry Co 1001 Highlands Plaza Dr W Ste 500 *TF:* 800-256-3462 ■ *Web:* www.danielandhenry.com	Saint Louis	MO	63110	314-421-1525	444-1990
David Chapman Agency Inc 5700 W Mt Hope Rd *Web:* davidchapmanagency.com	Lansing	MI	48917	517-321-4600	
David T Andes 348 Pierce St *Web:* daveandes.com	Kingston	PA	18704	570-288-6471	
David Tate Insurance Agency Inc 2566 N Mcmullen Booth Rd Ste B *Web:* agents.allstate.com	Clearwater	FL	33761	727-796-0408	
Dawson Insurance Agency Inc 721 First Ave N *Web:* dawsonins.com	Fargo	ND	58107	701-237-3311	
Dempsey Insurance Agency Inc 145 Railroad Ave *Web:* demsure.com	Norwood	MA	02062	781-762-0042	
Dennis Mayfield & Associates 720 Oak Cir Dr E *Web:* mayfield-dennis-associates.hub.biz	Greenwich Hills	AL	36609	601-664-9076	
Derek Witham Insurance Agency 685 Salem St	Malden	MA	02148	781-322-2886	
Dibrina Sure Benefits Consulting Inc 62 Frood Rd Ste 302 *Web:* dibrinasure.com	Sudbury	ON	P3C4Z3	705-688-9393	
Dibuduo & Defendis 6873 N W Ave Ste 101 *Web:* dibu.com	Fresno	CA	93711	559-432-0222	
Distinguished Programs Group LLC, The 1180 Ave Of The Americas 16th Fl *TF:* 888-355-4626 ■ *Web:* www.distinguished.com	New York	NY	10036	212-297-3100	
Diversified Brokerage Services Inc 5501 Excelsior Blvd *Web:* www.dbs-lifemark.com	Minneapolis	MN	55416	952-697-5000	
Don Ferderer Insurance 1930 Brea Canyon Rd	Diamond Bar	CA	91765	909-396-1198	
Duke Construction Inc 2600 Broad St Rd *Web:* www.dukeconstructioninc.net	Gum Spring	VA	23065	804-556-6992	
Dyatech LLC 805 S Wheatley St Ste 600 *TF:* 866-651-4222 ■ *Web:* www.dyatech.com	Ridgeland	MS	39157	601-914-1004	
E M Schroeder Agency Inc 294 Town Ctr Dr *Web:* emschroeder.com	Troy	MI	48084	248-689-1020	
Eagan Insurance Agency Inc 2629 N Cswy Blvd *TF:* 888-882-9600 ■ *Web:* www.eaganins.com	Metairie	LA	70002	504-836-9600	836-9621
Eaton & Berube Insurance Agency Inc 365 Nashua St *Web:* www.eatonberube.com	Milford	NH	03055	603-673-0500	
Elant Inc 46 Harriman Dr *TF:* 800-501-3936 ■ *Web:* www.elant.org	Goshen	NY	10924	800-501-3936	
Emery & Webb Inc 989 Main St *TF:* 800-942-5818 ■ *Web:* emerywebb.com	Fishkill	NY	12524	845-896-6727	
Employee benefits News 9221 Ravenna Rd Fl 27 *Web:* www.benefitnews.com	New York	NY	10004	330-425-8399	
Employee Leasing Solutions Inc 1401 Manatee Ave W Ste 600	Bradenton	FL	34205	941-746-6567	
Employer Benefits Inc 31 Keystone Ave *Web:* ebi-nv.com	Reno	NV	89503	775-786-6381	
Employers Insurance Company of Nevada 9790 Gateway Dr Ste 100 *TF:* 888-682-6671 ■ *Web:* www.employers.com	Reno	NV	89521	888-682-6671	
Encon Group Inc 500-1400 Blair Pl *TF:* 800-267-6684 ■ *Web:* www.encon.ca	Ottawa	ON	K1J9B8	613-786-2000	
Endurance Specialty Holdings Ltd 767 Third Ave 5th Fl *NYSE:* ENH ■ *TF:* 855-838-7792 ■ *Web:* www.endurance.bm	New York	NY	10017	212-209-6500	209-6501
EOI Service Company Inc Flex 1820 E First St Ste 400 *Web:* eoiservice.com	Santa Ana	CA	92705	714-935-0503	
Esser Hayes Insurance Group Inc 1811 High Grove *Web:* esserhayes.com	Naperville	IL	60540	630-355-2077	
Evans Ewan & Brady Insurance Agency Inc 2404 Williams Dr *Web:* eebins.com	Georgetown	TX	78628	512-869-1511	
Everett Cash Mutual Insurance Co 10591 Lincoln Hwy *Web:* www.everettcash.com	Everett	PA	15537	814-652-6111	
F.B.P. Insurance Services LLC 130 Theory Ste 200 *Web:* www.preceptgroup.com	Irvine	CA	92617	949-955-1430	
FairMarket Life Settlements Corp 435 Ford Rd Ste 120 *TF:* 866-326-3757 ■ *Web:* www.fairmarketlife.com	St Louis Park	MN	55426	866-326-3757	
Faribo Insurance Agency Inc 1404 Seventh St NW *TF:* 888-923-0430 ■ *Web:* insuranceagencymn.com	Faribault	MN	55021	507-334-3929	
Farmers Fire Insurance Co 2875 Eastern Blvd *TF:* 800-537-0928 ■ *Web:* www.farmersfire.com	York	PA	17402	717-751-4435	
Farmers National Co, The 11516 Nicholas St Ste 100 *Web:* www.farmers-national.com	Omaha	NE	68154	402-496-3276	
Farris Evans Insurance Agency Inc 1568 Union Ave *TF:* 800-395-8207 ■ *Web:* www.farrisevans.com	Memphis	TN	38104	901-274-5424	
Faulkner Pontiac Buick Gmc Truck Inc 705 Autopark Blvd *Web:* www.faulknerauto.com	West Chester	PA	19382	610-436-5600	
FDI Group Inc 39500 High Pointe Blvd Ste 400 *TF:* 800-828-0759 ■ *Web:* www.hcaweb.net	Novi	MI	48375	800-828-0759	
Feingold & Feingold Insurance Agency Inc 22 Elm St *Web:* feingoldco.com	Worcester	MA	01608	508-831-9500	
Financial Designs Ltd 1775 Sherman St Ste 1800 *Web:* www.fdltd.com	Denver	CO	80203	303-832-6100	
First Delta Insurance Inc 400 Plz St PO Box 2398 *Web:* firstdeltarealty.com	West Helena	AR	72390	870-572-1777	
First Investors Financial Services Group Inc 380 Interstate N Pkwy 3rd Fl *Web:* www.fifsg.com	Atlanta	GA	30339	713-977-2600	
First Security Company Inc 212 Third Ave NW *Web:* www.1security.net	Hickory	NC	28601	828-322-4171	322-5094
Flanary Group Inc, The 701 Decatur Ave North *Web:* theflanarygroup.com	Golden Valley	MN	55427	763-545-4564	
Flood & Peterson Insurance Inc 4687 W 18th St *Web:* floodpeterson.com	Greeley	CO	80634	970-356-0123	
Forest Agency Inc 7310 W Madison St *Web:* forestagency.com	Forest Park	IL	60130	708-383-9000	
Fortun Insurance Agency Inc 365 Palermo Ave *TF:* 877-643-2055 ■ *Web:* www.fortuninsurance.com	Coral Gables	FL	33134	305-445-3535	
Fred C Churchinc 41 Wellman St *TF:* 800-225-1865 ■ *Web:* fredcchurch.com	Lowell	MA	01851	978-458-1865	
Fred Loya Insurance 1800 Lee Trevino Ste 201 **Fax Area Code:* 866 ■ *TF:* 800-554-0595 ■ *Web:* www.fredloya.com	El Paso	TX	79936	915-590-5692	685-6260*
Fringe Benefits Management Co 3101 Sessions Rd *TF:* 800-872-0345 ■ *Web:* www.fbmc.com	Tallahassee	FL	32303	850-425-6200	425-6220
Frontier Adjusters of America Inc 4745 N Seventh St Ste 320 *TF:* 800-426-7228 ■ *Web:* www.frontieradjusters.com	Phoenix	AZ	85014	800-426-7228	553-4799
Gallagher Healthcare Insurance Services Inc 12621 Featherwood Dr Ste 300 *Web:* www.ajg.com	Houston	TX	77034	281-674-1420	
Garrison-Ross Agency Inc 602 W Flint PO Box 18 *Web:* www.garrisonross.com	Davison	MI	48423	810-653-2101	
Gaylord Nelson Insurance Agency In 8516 S Pulaski Rd *Web:* gaylordnelson.net	Chicago	IL	60652	773-581-0844	
GCube Insurance Services Inc 3101 Wcoast Hwy Ste 100 *TF:* 877-903-4777 ■ *Web:* www.gcube-insurance.com	Newport Beach	CA	92663	949-515-9981	
Gebco Insurance Assoc 8600 LaSalle Rd Ste 338 *TF:* 800-464-3226 ■ *Web:* www.gogebco.com	Towson	MD	21286	410-668-3100	882-2872
Genatt Associates Inc 3333 New Hyde Park Rd Ste 400 *Web:* www.genatt.com	New Hyde Park	NY	11042	516-869-8666	
Gentle Dental 22 Alpine Ln *Web:* www.gentledental.com	Chelmsford	MA	01824	978-256-7581	
Gerald J Sullivan & Assoc Inc 800 W 6th St Ste 1800 *Web:* gjs.com	Los Angeles	CA	90017	213-626-1000	
Gerrity Baker Williams Inc 3 Goldmine Rd *TF:* 800-548-2329 ■ *Web:* gbwinsurance.com	Flanders	NJ	07836	973-426-1500	
Gibson Insurance Agency Inc 130 S Main St Ste 400 *Web:* gibsonins.com	South Bend	IN	46601	574-245-3500	
Glb Insurance Group of Nevada 4455 S Pecos Rd *Web:* glbins.com	Las Vegas	NV	89121	702-735-9333	
Glenn Miller Insurance Agency Inc 404 E N Ave *Web:* glennmilleragency.com	Northlake	IL	60164	708-562-3404	
Global Warranty Group LLC 500 Middle Country Rd	St. James	NY	11780	631-750-0300	

Phone Fax

Gm Financial Consultants Corp
191 Presidental Blvd Ste W-1 .... Bala Cynwyd PA 19004 610-664-4088
Web: jackgrossman.metlife.com

Goetz Insurors Inc 227 Main St .... Fort Morgan CO 80701 970-867-8246
Web: goetzinsurors.com

Graham Co, The 1 Penn Sq W 25th Fl .... Philadelphia PA 19102 215-567-6300
TF: 888-472-4262 ■ *Web:* www.grahamco.com

Great American Custom Insurance Services Inc
725 S Figueroa St .... Los Angeles CA 90017 213-430-4300 629-8223
Web: www.gamcustom.com

Greene Wealth Management LLC
1301 Fifth Ave Ste 3410 .... Seattle WA 98101 206-623-2200
Web: www.greenewealthmgmt.com

Greene-Hazel & Assoc Inc
10739 Deerwood Park Blvd .... Jacksonville FL 32256 904-398-1234
Web: greenehazel.com

Greene-Niesen Insurance Agency Inc
6810 University Ave .... Middleton WI 53562 608-831-3168
Web: greeneniesen.com

Guy Ezzell Agency Inc 209 E High St .... Lexington KY 40507 859-264-1021

Guy Hurley Blaser & Heuer LLC
1080 Kirts Blvd Ste 500 .... Troy MI 48084 248-519-1400
Web: www.ghbh.com

Haas & Wilkerson Inc
4300 Shawnee Mission Pkwy .... Fairway KS 66205 913-432-4400 432-6159
TF: 800-821-7703 ■ *Web:* www.hwins.com

Hafetz & Assoc LLC 609 New Rd .... Linwood NJ 08221 609-872-0001
Web: hafetzandassociates.com

Hantz Group Inc 26200 America Dr 5th Fl .... Southfield MI 48034 248-304-2855
Web: hantzgroup.com

Harmer Assoc 100 S Wacker Dr Ste 1950 .... Chicago IL 60606 312-407-7180
Web: www.harmer.com

Hauser Agency Inc 16 S Church St .... Mount Pleasant PA 15666 724-547-3536

Headliner Talent Marketing
39398 Moonlight Bay Trl .... Pelican Rapids MN 56572 218-863-1367
Web: headlinertalent.com

Health Network America Inc 745 Hope Rd .... Tinton Falls NJ 07724 732-676-2630
Web: www.healthnetworkamerica.com

HealthSCOPE Benefits Inc
27 Corporate Hill Dr .... Little Rock AR 72205 501-225-1551
TF: 877-240-0135 ■ *Web:* www.healthscopebenefits.com

Healy Group Inc, The 53800 Generations Dr .... South Bend IN 46635 574-271-6000
TF: 800-667-4613 ■ *Web:* www.healygroup.com

Heights Insurance Group Inc
2048 S Hacienda Blvd .... Hacienda Heights CA 91745 626-855-8288
Web: www.kcal.net

Hendricks & Assoc Inc 190 W Huffaker Ln Ste 403 .... Reno NV 89511 775-674-6000
Web: hendricks-inc.com

Herbert H. Landy Insurance Agency Inc
75 Second Ave Ste 410 .... Needham MA 02494 800-336-5422 449-7908*
**Fax Area Code:* 781 ■ *TF:* 800-336-5422 ■ *Web:* www.landy.com

Heuer Insurance Agency Inc
5050 Vista Blvd Ste 101 .... Sparks NV 89436 775-358-5554
Web: heuerinsurance.com

Hibbs Hallmark & Co 501 Shelley Dr .... Tyler TX 75701 800-765-6767 581-5988*
**Fax Area Code:* 903 ■ *TF:* 800-765-6767 ■ *Web:* www.hibbshallmark.com

Hierl Insurance Inc 258 S Main St .... Fond Du Lac WI 54935 920-921-5921
Web: hierl.com

High & Assoc Inc Dba Financial Services Group
105 Old Hewitt Rd Ste 400 .... Waco TX 76712 254-776-7283
Web: highandassociates.net

Hill & Stone Insurance Agency Inc
900 N Shore Dr Ste 225 .... Lake Bluff IL 60044 847-295-3030

Hinkle Insurance Agency Inc
600 Olde Hickory Rd Ste 200 .... Lancaster PA 17601 717-560-9733
TF: 877-408-1418 ■ *Web:* hinkleinsurance.com

Holland Land Title & Abstract Company Inc
110 Pearl St .... Buffalo NY 14202 716-853-6529
Web: hollandtitle.com

Hollis D Segur Inc 156 Knotter Dr .... Cheshire CT 06410 203-699-4500

Holliway Insurance Agency Inc
5765 Olde Wadsworth Blvd .... Arvada CO 80002 303-421-3046

Holmes Murphy & Assoc Inc
3001 Westown Pkwy .... West Des Moines IA 50266 515-223-6800 223-6944
TF: 800-247-7756 ■ *Web:* www.holmesmurphy.com

Hometown Quotes LLC 133 Holiday Ct Ste 207 .... Franklin TN 37067 615-599-5506
Web: www.hometownquotes.com

Horton Group, The 10320 Orland Pkwy .... Orland Park IL 60467 708-845-3000 845-3001
TF: 800-383-8283 ■ *Web:* www.thehortongroup.com

Housing Authority Risk Retention Group Inc
PO Box 189 .... Cheshire CT 06410 203-272-8220
TF: 800-873-0242 ■ *Web:* www.housingcenter.com

Hoyle Holt Allied Services Co 710 W Broadway .... Ardmore OK 73401 580-223-5434

HUB International Insurance Services
1091 N Shoreline Blvd Ste 200 Ste 200 .... Mountain View CA 94043 650-237-3006 472-8000
Web: hubinternational.com

Hub International Ltd
1065 Ave of the Americas .... New York NY 10018 212-338-2000 338-2100
TF: 800-456-5293 ■ *Web:* www.hubinternational.com

Hudson Advisors LLC
2711 N Haskell Ave Ste 1800 .... Dallas TX 75204 214-754-8400
Web: www.hudson-advisors.com

Huggins Actuarial Services Inc
111 Veterans Sq 2nd Fl .... Media PA 19063 610-892-1824
Web: www.hugginsactuarial.com

Human Arc Corp 1457 East 40th St .... Cleveland OH 44103 216-431-5200 431-5201
TF: 800-828-6453 ■ *Web:* www.humanarc.com

Hunt Insurance Agency Inc
12000 S Harlem Ave .... Palos Heights IL 60463 708-361-5300
TF: 800-772-6484 ■ *Web:* thehuntgroup.com

Huntley-Sheehy Inc 520 Olive St .... Marysville CA 95901 530-743-9264
Web: huntley-sheehy.com

Hylant Group 811 Madison Ave .... Toledo OH 43624 419-255-1020 255-7557
TF: 800-249-5268 ■ *Web:* www.hylant.com

Icim Services Inc 1401 H St Nw Fl 10 .... Washington DC 20005 202-682-4150
Web: www.icimutual.com

IIP Insurance Agency Inc 823 Clinton St .... Ottawa IL 61350 815-433-2680
Web: mylocalagent.com

IMA Financial Group Inc
8200 E 32nd St N PO Box 2992 .... Wichita KS 67226 316-267-9221 266-6254
Web: www.imacorp.com

IMPACT Financial Services LLC
381 Riverside Dr Ste 460 .... Franklin TN 37064 615-771-9494
Web: www.impactfinancial.com

Independant Insurance Services In
3956 N Pine St .... Davenport IA 52806 563-383-5555
TF: 800-373-1562 ■ *Web:* yourqcagent.com

Independent Financial Agents Inc 14 Walnut Ave .... Clark NJ 07066 732-815-1202
Web: www.ifaauto.com

Insurance Marketing Center Inc
6101 Executive Blvd Ste 120 .... Rockville MD 20852 301-468-8888
Web: www.imctr.com

Insurance Services Office Inc (ISO)
545 Washington Blvd .... Jersey City NJ 07310 201-469-2000 748-1472*
**Fax:* Hum Res ■ *TF:* 800-888-4476 ■ *Web:* www.verisk.com/iso.html

Insurance Unlimited of La Inc
3111 Ryan St .... Lake Charles LA 70601 337-477-6922
Web: insunlimited.com

InterContinental Insurance Brokers LLC
175 Federal St Ste 725 .... Boston MA 02110 617-648-5100
Web: www.iibweb.com

InterWest Insurance Services Inc
3636 American River Dr 2nd Fl .... Sacramento CA 95864 916-679-2960 979-7992
TF: 800-444-4134 ■ *Web:* www.iwins.com

Iwv Insurance 1310 N Norma St .... Ridgecrest CA 93555 760-446-3544
Web: www.iwvins.com

Izett & Assoc LLC 912 Killian Hill Rd .... Lilburn GA 30047 770-935-9575

J Byrne Agency Inc 5200 New Jersey Ave .... Wildwood NJ 08260 609-522-3406
Web: jbyrneagency.com

J C Taylor Antique Automobile Agency Inc
320 S 69th St .... Upper Darby PA 19082 610-853-1300
Web: www.jctaylor.com

J Smith Lanier & Co 300 W Tenth St .... West Point GA 31833 706-645-2211 643-0606
TF: 800-226-4522 ■ *Web:* www.jsmithlanier.com

Jack Ogren & Company Inc 6929 Hohman Ave .... Hammond IN 46324 219-933-0076
TF: 888-489-4235 ■ *Web:* ogreninsurance.com

Jake A Parrott Insurance Agency Inc
2508 N Herritage St .... Kinston NC 28501 252-523-1041
TF: 800-727-7688 ■ *Web:* parrottins.com

James A Normoyle Insurance Agency
669 Palmetto Ave Ste E .... Chico CA 95926 530-891-1122

James Greene & Assoc Inc 275 W Kiehl Ave .... Sherwood AR 72120 501-834-4001
TF: 800-422-3384 ■ *Web:* jamesgreeneins.com

Jas. D. Collier & Co
606 S Mendenhall Rd Ste 200 .... Memphis TN 38117 800-511-1548 529-2916*
**Fax Area Code:* 901 ■ *TF General:* 800-511-1548 ■ *Web:* www.collierinsurance.com

Jeppesen Marine Inc
15242 NW Greenbrier Pkwy .... Beaverton OR 97006 503-579-1414
Web: www.nobeltec.com

Jim Marshall Insurance Inc
2084 Ninth St Ste D .... Los Osos CA 93402 805-528-4739
Web: jimmarshallinsurance.com

Jimcor Agency 60 Craig Rd .... Montvale NJ 07645 201-573-8200
Web: jimcor.com

Jmd Group LLC 720 Walnut St .... Chattanooga TN 37402 423-265-8111
TF: 866-251-0361 ■ *Web:* jmdgroupllc.com

John Callahan Agency Inc 294 New York Ave .... Huntington NY 11743 631-271-1615
Web: statefarm.com

John E Ernst 126 N 30th St Ste 103 .... Quincy IL 62301 217-223-4127

John F Sutherland & Assoc Ins Svcs Inc
6275 Lusk Blvd .... San Diego CA 92121 858-535-1139

John L Wortham & Son LP 2727 Allen Pkwy .... Houston TX 77019 713-526-3366 526-5872
Web: www.worthaminsurance.com

John Morgan Mclachlan Agency, The
75 E Main St .... Somerville NJ 08876 908-526-4600

John Nuzzo 7428 W Belmont .... Chicago IL 60634 773-889-3900
Web: johnnuzzo.com

Johns Eastern Co Inc
PO Box 110259 Lakewood Branch .... Sarasota FL 34211 941-907-3100 402-7913*
**Fax Area Code:* 813 ■ *TF General:* 877-326-5326 ■ *Web:* www.johnseastern.com

Joseph A Paine Inc 4301 S Pine St Ste 26 .... Tacoma WA 98409 253-472-3055
Web: paineinsurance.com

Joseph Distel & Company Inc 5 Two Mile Rd .... Farmington CT 06032 860-677-6505
Web: distelgroup.com

Joseph P O'Brien Agency Inc
454 New York Ave .... Huntington NY 11743 631-421-0505

KAFL Inc 85 Allen St Ste 300 .... Rochester NY 14608 585-271-6400
TF: 800-272-6488 ■ *Web:* kafl.com

Keenan & Assoc
2355 Crenshaw Blvd Ste 200 PO Box 4328 .... Torrance CA 90501 310-212-3344 212-0300
TF: 800-654-8102 ■ *Web:* www.keenan.com

Keenan Agency Inc, The
6805 Avery Muirfield Dr Ste 200 .... Dublin OH 43016 614-764-7000
Web: keenanins.com

Kelleher Associates LLC
1255 Drummers Ln Four Glenhardie Corporate Ctr
Ste 103 .... Wayne PA 19087 610-293-1115
Web: www.kelleherllc.com

Kelsey National Corp 3030 S Bundy Dr .... Los Angeles CA 90066 310-390-1000
TF: 800-366-5656 ■ *Web:* kelsey.com

Kenney & Assoc 1754 Noirth Washington St .... Naperville IL 60563 630-505-4333

Kentucky National Insurance Co
2709 Old Rosebud Rd .... Lexington KY 40509 859-367-5200 367-5293
Web: www.kynatins.com

Keyes Coverage Inc 5900 Hiatus Rd .... Tamarac FL 33321 954-724-7000
Web: keyescoverage.com

Kraus-Anderson Insurance 420 Gateway Blvd .... Burnsville MN 55337 952-707-8200 890-0535
TF: 800-207-9261 ■ *Web:* www.kainsurance.com

				Phone	Fax
KRW Insurance Agency Inc 338 Memorial Dr *Web:* krw-insurance.com	Crystal Lake	IL	60014	815-459-6300	
Land Title Guarantee Co Inc 3033 E First Ave Ste 600 Ste 600 *Web:* www.ltgc.com	Denver	CO	80206	303-321-1880	322-7603
Landry harris & Co 600 Jefferson St Ste 200 *Web:* www.landryharris.com	Lafayette	LA	70501	337-266-2150	266-2151
Lanz & Mcardle Agency Inc 1022 17th Ave	Monroe	WI	53566	608-325-9126	
Laporte & Assoc Inc 5515 Se Milwaukie Ave. *Web:* laporte-insurance.com	Portland	OR	97202	503-239-4116	
Larry Murphy Insurance Agency Inc 113 E Grand *Web:* larrymurphyinsurance.com	Ponca City	OK	74601	580-767-1520	
Lawley Service Insurance 361 Delaware Ave *TF Cust Svc:* 800-860-5741 ■ *Web:* www.lawleyinsurance.com	Buffalo	NY	14202	716-849-8618	849-8291
Le Mars Insurance Co PO Box 1608 *TF:* 800-545-6480 ■ *Web:* www.lemm.com	Le Mars	IA	51031	800-545-6480	
Leap/Carpenter/Kemps Insurance Agency 3187 Collins Dr *TF:* 800-221-0864 ■ *Web:* lckinsurance.com	Merced	CA	95348	209-384-0727	
Leavell Insurance & Real Estate 117 E Broadway *Web:* leavellinsurance.com	Hobbs	NM	88240	575-393-2550	
leavitt group Enterprises 216 S 200 W *TF:* 800-264-8085 ■ *Web:* www.leavitt.com	Cedar City	UT	84720	435-586-6553	586-1510
Legacy Partners Inc 4000 E Third Ave Ste 600 *Web:* www.legacypartners.com	Foster City	CA	94404	650-571-2250	
Leonard Insurance Services Agency Inc 4244 Mt Pleasant St NW *Web:* leonardinsurance.com	North Canton	OH	44720	330-266-1904	
Lewer Agency Inc 4534 Wornall Rd **Fax Area Code:* 816 ■ *TF:* 800-821-7715 ■ *Web:* www.lewer.com	Kansas City	MO	64111	800-821-7715	561-6840*
Lewis & Assoc Insurance Brokers Inc 700 W Center Ave. *Web:* since1927.com	Visalia	CA	93291	559-733-7272	
Lincoln General Insurance Co 3501 Concord Rd. *TF:* 800-876-3350 ■ *Web:* www.lincolngeneral.com	York	PA	17402	717-757-0000	
Linden Group Health Services Inc 2800 River Rd Ste 310 *Web:* www.lindengrouphealth.com	Des Plaines	IL	60018	847-294-0000	
Linkfield & Cross Agency Inc 1600 E Beltline Ne Ste 211	Grand Rapids	MI	49525	616-447-2777	447-6420
Lipparelli & Assoc Inc 517 Idaho St *Web:* progressive.com	Elko	NV	89801	775-738-7131	
LISI Inc 1600 W Hillsdale Blvd *TF:* 866-570-5474 ■ *Web:* lisibroker.com	San Mateo	CA	94402	650-348-4131	
Lockton Cos 444 W 47th St Ste 900 *Web:* www.lockton.com	Kansas City	MO	64112	816-960-9000	960-9099
Loesel Schaaf Insurance Agency Inc 3537 W 12th St. *TF:* 877-718-9935 ■ *Web:* lsinsure.com	Erie	PA	16505	814-833-5433	
Lombardo Insurance Agency 2096B Silas Deane Hwy *Web:* lombardo-ins.com	Rocky Hill	CT	06067	860-236-6064	
Lone Star Abstract & Title Company Inc 600 N Loraine *Web:* lonestarabstract.com	Midland	TX	79701	432-683-1818	
Loomis Co 850 N Pk Rd *TF:* 800-782-0392 ■ *Web:* www.loomisco.com	Wyomissing	PA	19610	610-374-4040	374-6578
Lovitt & Touche Inc 7202 E Rosewood St Ste 200 PO Box 32702 *TF:* 800-426-2756 ■ *Web:* www.lovitt-touche.com	Tucson	AZ	85710	520-722-3000	722-7245
Loyd Keith Friedlander Partners Ltd 18 Prospect St	Huntington	NY	11743	631-424-2600	
Mack & Associates Ltd 100 N La Salle St Ste 2110 *Web:* www.mackltd.com	Chicago	IL	60602	312-368-0677	
Mackintire Insurance Agency Inc 11 W Main St *Web:* mackintire.com	Westborough	MA	01581	508-366-6161	
Maga Ltd 2610 Lk Cook Rd *TF:* 800-533-6242 ■ *Web:* magaltc.com	Riverwoods	IL	60015	847-940-8866	
Managed Care of America Inc 1910 Cochran Rd Ste 605 *TF:* 800-922-4966 ■ *Web:* www.mcoa.com	Pittsburgh	PA	15220	412-922-2803	
Managed HealthCare Northwest Inc 422 East Burnside St Suite 215 PO Box 4629 *TF:* 800-648-6356 ■ *Web:* www.mhninc.com	Portland	OR	97208	503-413-5800	413-5801
Mark R Veenstra 8501 75th St *Web:* statefarm.com	Kenosha	WI	53142	262-694-4800	
Marsh & Mclennan Agency 250 Pehle Ave **Fax Area Code:* 866 ■ *TF:* 800-669-6330 ■ *Web:* www.mma-ne.com	Saddle Brook	NJ	07663	201-845-6600	795-1158*
Marsh Saldana 1166 Ave of the Americas New York *Web:* latinamerica.marsh.com	New York	NY	10036	787-721-2600	721-1093
Marshall & Sterling Inc 110 Main St *TF:* 800-333-3766 ■ *Web:* marshallsterling.com	Poughkeepsie	NY	12601	845-454-0800	454-0880
Marwood Group LLC 733 Third Ave 11th Fl *Web:* www.marwoodgroup.com	New York	NY	10017	212-532-3651	
Masters & Assoc Insurance Inc 24 E Linden Ave *Web:* mastersins.com	Miamisburg	OH	45343	937-866-3361	
Matson & Cuprill LLC 7361 Kemper Rd Ste B *Web:* matsonandcuprill.com	Cincinnati	OH	45249	513-563-7526	
Mazzeo Agency Inc, The 178 Main St.	Woodbridge	NJ	07095	732-636-5400	
McClone Agency Inc 150 Main St Ste 300	Menasha	WI	54952	920-725-3232	
Mcgohan Brabender Inc 3931 S Dixie Dr *Web:* mcgohanbrabender.com	Dayton	OH	45439	937-293-1600	
McGriff Seibels & Williams Inc 2211 Seventh Ave S *TF:* 800-476-2211 ■ *Web:* www.mcgriff.com	Birmingham	AL	35233	205-252-9871	581-9293

				Phone	Fax
Mcleod Insurance Inc 14425 N Seventh St Ste 100 *Web:* mcleodinsinc.com	Phoenix	AZ	85022	602-843-0005	
Mcsweeney & Ricci Insurance Agency Inc 420 Washington St *Web:* mcsweeneyricci.com	Braintree	MA	02184	781-848-8600	
MedCost Benefit Services LLC 165 Kimel Park Dr *Web:* www.mbstpa.com	Winston-salem	NC	27103	336-774-4400	
Medical Eye Services Inc 345 Baker St E *Web:* www.mesvision.com	Costa Mesa	CA	92626	714-619-4660	
Medical Risk Managers Inc 1170 Ellington Rd *Web:* www.mrm-mgu.com	South Windsor	CT	06074	860-732-3248	
MercyCare Insurance Company Inc 3430 Palmer Dr *Web:* www.mercycarehealthplans.com	Janesville	WI	53547	608-752-3431	
Mesirow Financial Insurance Services Div 353 N Clark St *TF:* 800-453-0600 ■ *Web:* www.mesirowfinancial.com	Chicago	IL	60654	312-595-6200	
MGM Industries Inc 287 Freehill Rd *TF:* 800-476-5584 ■ *Web:* www.mgmindustries.com	Hendersonville	TN	37075	615-824-6572	
MIC Services Insurance Inc 170 Kinnelon Rd - Ste 11 *TF:* 800-355-2662 ■ *Web:* micinsurance.com	Kinnelon	NJ	07405	973-492-2828	
Michael P Randolph 1001 E Wt Harris Blvd. *Web:* agents.allstate.com	Charlotte	NC	28213	704-549-1710	
Michigan Insurance Co 1700 E Beltline Ne PO Box 152120, Ste 100 *TF:* 888-606-6426 ■ *Web:* www.michiganinsurance.com	Grand Rapids	MI	49515	616-447-3600	
MidCap Advisors LLC 1556 Third Ave Ste 410 *Web:* www.midcapadvisors.com	New York	NY	10128	212-722-5683	
Miers Insurance Inc 2222 S 12th St *Web:* miersinsurance.com	Allentown	PA	18103	610-797-7900	
Mike Moss Agency Inc 803 S Dogwood *TF:* 800-447-0163 ■ *Web:* mossins.com	Siloam Springs	AR	72761	479-524-5111	
Miller Buettner & Parrott Inc 1515 S Meridian Rd	Rockford	IL	61102	815-986-0059	
Miller-Lewis Benefit Consultants 121 E Sixth Ave *TF:* 800-734-3198 ■ *Web:* miller-lewis.com	Lancaster	OH	43130	740-654-4055	687-2236
Minnesota Lawyers Mutual Insurance Co 333 S Seventh St Ste 2200 *TF:* 800-422-1370 ■ *Web:* www.mlmins.com	Minneapolis	MN	55402	800-422-1370	305-1510
Mintz Girgan & Brightly Inc 18 W Passaic St *Web:* mgbinsurance.com	Rochelle Park	NJ	07662	201-507-5100	
Mj Insurance Inc 9225 Priority Way W Dr *Web:* mjinsurance.com	Indianapolis	IN	46240	317-805-7500	
MMG Insurance Co 44 Maysville St *Web:* www.mmgins.com	Presque Isle	ME	04769	207-764-6611	
MML Investors Services Inc 1295 State St. *Web:* www.mmlinvestors.com	Springfield	MA	01111	413-737-8400	
Moloney Securities Company Inc 13537 Barrett Pkwy Dr Ste 300 *Web:* www.moseco.com	Manchester	MO	63021	314-909-0600	
Morstan General Agency Inc 600 Community Dr PO Box 4500 *Web:* www.morstan.com	Manhasset	NY	11030	516-488-4747	437-5050
Mother Lode Holding Co 189 Fulweiler Ave *Web:* placertitle.com	Auburn	CA	95603	530-887-2410	
MSI Benefits Group Inc 245 Townpark Dr Ste 100 *TF:* 800-580-1629 ■ *Web:* www.msibenefitsgroup.com	Kennesaw	GA	30144	770-425-1231	425-4722
Multiplan inc 115 Fifth Ave. *TF:* 800-922-4362 ■ *Web:* www.multiplan.com	New York	NY	10003	212-780-2000	780-0420
Murray & Zuckerman Inc 128 Erie Blvd *Web:* mandzinc.com	Schenectady	NY	12305	518-382-5483	
Nansemond Insurance Agency Inc 453 W Washington St. *Web:* nansemondins.com	Suffolk	VA	23434	757-539-3421	
Naomi Taylor-Kenney Insurance Inc 4322 W El Prado Blvd. *Web:* agents.allstate.com	Tampa	FL	33629	813-902-8300	
National Catastrophe Adjusters Inc 9725 Windermere Blvd *Web:* www.ncagroup.com	Fishers	IN	46037	317-915-8888	
National Electronic Attachment Inc 3577 Pkwy Ln Ste 250 *TF:* 800-782-5150 ■ *Web:* www.nea-fast.com	Norcross	GA	30092	770-441-3203	
National Farm Life Insurance Co 6001 Bridge St *TF:* 800-772-7557 ■ *Web:* www.nflic.com	Fort Worth	TX	76112	817-451-9550	
NCCI Holdings Inc 901 Peninsula Corporate Cir *TF Cust Svc:* 800-622-4123 ■ *Web:* www.ncci.com	Boca Raton	FL	33487	561-893-1000	893-1191
Neal W Farinholt 9939 Hibert St. *Web:* nealfarinholt.com	San Diego	CA	92131	858-578-6605	
Nease Lagana Eden & Culley Inc 2100 Riveredge Pkwy *Web:* nlec.com	Atlanta	GA	30328	770-956-1800	
NEBCO Inc 1815 Y St PO Box 80268 *Web:* www.nebraskaash.com	Lincoln	NE	68501	402-434-1212	
Nevada Title Co 2500 N Buffalo Dr Ste 150 *Web:* www.nevadatitle.com	Las Vegas	NV	89128	702-251-5000	
Newbury Corp 222 Ames St. *TF:* 800-688-1825 ■ *Web:* www.ndgroup.com	Dedham	MA	02026	800-688-1825	
Newton One Advisors LLC 131 Continental Dr *Web:* newtonone.com	Newark	DE	19713	302-731-1326	
Norbert Cronin & Co 582 Market St Ste 1104	San Francisco	CA	94104	415-981-2222	
Noridian Administrative Services LLC 901 40th St S Ste 1 *Web:* www.noridian.com	Fargo	ND	58103	503-944-8810	

Phone | Fax

North Star Resource Group Inc
2701 University Ave SE N Star Professional Ctr .... Minneapolis MN 55414 612-617-6000
Web: www.northstarfinancial.com

Northwest Administrators Inc
2323 Eastlake Ave E .... Seattle WA 98102 206-329-4900 726-3209
TF: 877-304-6702 ■ *Web:* www.nwadmin.com

Northwest Insurance Network Inc
330 S Wells St 16th Fl .... Chicago IL 60606 312-427-1777
Web: www.northwestinsurance.com

NSM Insurance Group Inc
555 N Ln Ste 6060 .... Conshohocken PA 19428 610-941-9877
Web: www.nsminc.com

O'Connor Insurance Agency 12101 Olive Blvd .... St Louis MO 63141 314-434-0038
Web: oconnor-ins.com

Omni Life Assocates Inc
375 N Broadway Ste 203 .... Jericho NY 11753 516-938-2465
Web: omniquote.net

Oriska Insurance Co 1310 Utica St .... Oriskany NY 13424 315-768-2726
Web: oriskainsurance.com

Oryx Insurance Brokerage Inc 2 Ct St .... Binghamton NY 13901 607-724-0173 462-6799*
**Fax Area Code:* 888 ■ *Web:* www.oryxinsurance.com

Oswald Cos 1100 Superior Ave Ste 1500 .... Cleveland OH 44114 216-367-8787
TF: 855-467-9253 ■ *Web:* www.oswaldcompanies.com

Otis-Magie Insurance Agency Inc
332 W Superior St Ste 700 .... Duluth MN 55802 218-722-7753 722-7756
TF: 800-241-2425 ■ *Web:* www.otismagie.com

Otsego Mutual Fire Insurance Co
143 Arnold Rd PO Box 40 .... Burlington Flats NY 13315 607-965-8211
Web: otsegomutual.com

Pacesetter Claims Service Inc 2871 N Hwy 167 .... Catoosa Ok 74015 918-665-8887
TF: 888-218-4880 ■ *Web:* www.pacesetterclaims.com

Paradigm Equity Strategies LLC
1611 - A Akron Peninsula Rd .... Akron OH 44313 330-475-1690
TF: 888-249-5727 ■ *Web:* paradigmequity.com

Parker Smith & Feek Inc 2233 112th Ave NE .... Bellevue WA 98004 425-709-3600 709-7460
TF Cust Svc: 800-457-0220 ■ *Web:* www.psfinc.com

Parkville Insurance Services Inc
15242 E Whittier Blvd PO Box 1275 .... Whittier CA 90603 562-945-2702 945-4297
TF: 800-350-2702 ■ *Web:* parkvilleinsurance.com

Paul Cribbs Insurance Agency Inc
3565 N Crossing Cir .... Valdosta GA 31602 229-247-7127
Web: paulcribbs.net

PCC Natural Markets Inc
4201 Roosevelt Way NE .... Seattle WA 98105 206-547-1222
Web: www.pccnaturalmarkets.com

Per-Se Technologies Inc
1145 Sanctuary Pkwy Ste 200 .... Alpharetta GA 30004 770-237-4300
Web: www.per-se.com

Perry Insurance 522 Chickering Rd .... North Andover MA 01845 978-685-7690
Web: perryins.com

Piedmont Community Health Plan Inc
2512 Langhorne Rd .... Lynchburg VA 24501 434-947-4463
TF: 800-400-7247 ■ *Web:* www.pchp.net

Planned Administrators Inc
8906 Two Notch Rd Ste 200 .... Columbia SC 29223 803-462-0151
Web: www.paisc.com

Policemen's Annuity & Benefit Fund of Chicago
221 N LaSalle St Ste 1626 .... Chicago IL 60601 312-744-3891
TF: 800-656-6606 ■ *Web:* www.chipabf.org

POMCO 2425 James St .... Syracuse NY 13206 315-432-9171 432-9171
TF: 800-934-2459 ■ *Web:* www.pomcogroup.com

Preferred Professional Insurance Company Inc
11605 Miracle Hills Dr Ste 200 .... Omaha NE 68154 402-392-1566
Web: www.ppicins.com

Premier Insurance Corp Inc
1326 Cape Coral Pkwy E .... Cape Coral FL 33904 239-542-7101
Web: premierinsurancecorp.com

Premins Company Inc, The 1407 Ave M .... Brooklyn NY 11230 718-375-8300
Web: preminsco.com

Pritchard & Jerden Inc
3565 Piedmont Rd Ste2000 .... Atlanta GA 30305 404-238-9090
Web: pritchardjerden.com

Professional Risk Solutions LLC
37 Mountain Blvd Ste 3 .... Warren NJ 07059 908-834-8401
Web: www.prsbrokers.com

Prospera Financial Services Inc
5429 LBJ Fwy Ste 400 .... Dallas TX 75240 972-581-3000
Web: www.prosperafinancial.com

Protegrity Services Inc
260 Wekiva Springs Rd Ste 1040 .... Longwood FL 32779 407-551-3962 788-0812

PS & Assoc Underwriting Agency Inc
1776 Legacy Cir Ste 104 .... Naperville IL 60563 630-416-0004 416-2246
Web: www.psassociate.com

Purves & Assoc Insurance 500 Fourth St .... Davis CA 95616 530-756-5561
TF: 800-681-2025 ■ *Web:* purvesinsurance.com

Quincy & Company Inc 144 Gould St .... Needham Heights MA 02494 781-431-9600
Web: quincyinsurance.net

R Mcclure Electric 706 Portal St Ste D .... Cotati CA 94931 707-792-2101
Web: rmcclure.com

Rain & Hail LLC 9200 Northpark Dr Ste 250 .... Johnston IA 50131 515-559-1200
Web: www.rainhail.com

Ralph C Mehler Agency Inc
62 E Shenango St .... Sharpsville PA 16150 724-962-5757
Web: mehlerinsurance.com

Rampart Brokerage Corp
1983 Marcus Ave Ste C130 .... New Hyde Park NY 11042 516-538-7000 390-3555
TF: 800-772-6727 ■ *Web:* www.rampartinsurance.com

Rand Insurance Inc 1100 E Putnam Ave .... Riverside CT 06878 203-637-1006
Web: randinsurance.com

Real Estate Errors & Omissions Insurance Corp
1604 700 W Pender St .... Vancouver BC V6C1G8 604-669-0019
Web: www.reeoic.com

Regional Care Inc 905 W 27th St .... Scottsbluff NE 69361 308-635-2260
Web: www.regionalcare.com

Phone | Fax

Reid Jones McRorie & Williams Inc
2200 Executive St PO Box 669248 .... Charlotte NC 28208 704-537-0012
TF: 800-785-2604 ■ *Web:* www.rjmw.com

Reller Risk Management 6315 Fly Rd .... East Syracuse NY 13057 315-432-8210

Renaissance Group 981 Worcester St .... Wellesley MA 02482 800-514-2667
TF: 800-514-2667 ■ *Web:* www.renaissanceins.com

RF Ougheltree & Assoc LLC 1050 Wall St W .... Lyndhurst NJ 07071 201-964-9881
Web: rfoins.com

RH Nicholson & Company Inc
3998 Fair Ridge Dr Ste 200 .... Fairfax VA 22033 703-261-6100
Web: rhnicholson.com

Rhythm Band Instruments LLC
1316 E Lancaster Ave .... Fort Worth TX 76102 817-335-2561
Web: www.rhythmband.com

Richard Hennessy Insurance Agency Inc
6335A SW Capitol Hwy .... Portland OR 97239 503-245-9345
Web: statefarm.com

Rigg Darlington Group Inc, The
14 E Welsh Pool Rd .... Exton PA 19341 484-876-2222

Robert J Hanafin Inc
204 Washington Ave PO Box 509 .... Endicott NY 13760 607-754-3500 754-9797

Robert M Degregorio Insurance Agency Inc
34 Woodside Ave .... Winthrop MA 02152 617-846-3313

Robert Moreno Insurance Services
1400 N Harbor Blvd .... Fullerton CA 92835 714-738-1383
Web: rmismga.com

Robert Runia 1270 East 8600 Souh Ste 8 .... Sandy UT 84094 801-566-5111

Robertson Ryan & Assoc Inc
330 E Kilbourn Ave .... Milwaukee WI 53202 414-271-3575
Web: www.robertsonryan.com

Rosenthal Bros Inc 740 Waukegan Rd Ste 402 .... Deerfield IL 60015 847-940-4300
Web: www.rosenthalbros.com

Roy H Reeve Agency Inc 13400 Main Rd .... Mattituck NY 11952 631-298-4700
Web: www.royreeve.agency

RpmOne Inc 4495 Military Trl Ste 207 .... Jupiter FL 33458 561-741-4447
Web: www.rpmone.com

RSI Insurance Brokers Inc
2801 Bristol St Ste 200 .... Costa Mesa CA 92626 714-546-6616
TF: 800-828-5273 ■ *Web:* rsiinsurancebrokers.com

S L Nusbaum Insurance Agency Inc
500 W 21st St Ste 300 .... Norfolk VA 23517 757-622-4653
Web: nusbauminsurance.com

Sahouri Insurance & Associates Inc
8200 Grnsburg Dr Ste 1550 .... Mclean VA 22102 703-883-0500
TF: 855-242-6660 ■ *Web:* sahouri.com

Santo Insurance & Financial Services Inc
224 Main St .... Salem NH 03079 603-890-6439
Web: santoinsurance.com

SCF Securities Inc 155 E Shaw Ave Ste 102 .... Fresno CA 93710 559-456-6100
Web: www.scfsecurities.com

Scharer Insurance Inc 454 E Ctr St .... Marion OH 43302 740-387-4311
Web: scharerinsurance.com

Scott Danahy Naylon Company Inc (SDN)
300 Spindrift Dr .... Williamsville NY 14221 716-633-3400 633-4306
TF: 800-728-6362 ■ *Web:* www.sdnins.com

Scott N Schumaker 217 E Maple Rd .... Troy MI 48083 248-457-0800
Web: statefarm.com

Sean Wong - State Farm Insurance Agent
7035 Hwy 6 N .... Houston TX 77095 281-550-0555
Web: statefarm.com

Security Escrow & Title Insurance Agency
337 South Main Ste 110 .... Cedar City UT 84720 435-867-0402
TF: 855-319-9820 ■ *Web:* securityescrowutah.com

Selectpath Benefits & Financial Inc
310-700 Richmond St .... London ON N6A5C7 519-675-1177 675-1331
TF: 888-327-5777 ■ *Web:* www.selectpath.ca

Selectquote Insurance Services
595 Market St 10th Fl .... San Francisco CA 94105 415-543-7338 436-7000*
**Fax Area Code:* 800 ■ *TF:* 800-670-3213 ■ *Web:* www.selectquote.com

Self Funding Administrators Corp
339 Busch'S Frontage Rd .... Annapolis MD 21401 410-757-4200

Senior Market Sales Inc (SMS)
8420 W Dodge Rd 5th Fl .... Omaha NE 68114 402-397-3311 397-0455
TF: 800-786-5566 ■ *Web:* www.seniormarketsales.com

Seniority Benefit Group 6365 Riverside Dr .... Dublin OH 43017 614-799-1403
Web: www.senioritybenefitgroup.com

Sherzer & Assoc Insurance Inc
110 Stony Point Rd Ste 120 .... Santa Rosa CA 95401 707-573-1010
Web: www.sherzer.com

Sica Consultants Inc
883 Briarwoods Rd .... Franklin Lakes NJ 07417 201-805-1561
Web: www.sicafletcher.com

SilverStone Group
11516 Miracle Hills Dr Ste 100 .... Omaha NE 68154 402-964-5400 964-5454
TF: 800-288-5501 ■ *Web:* www.silverstonegroup.com

Simkiss Cos 2 Paoli Office Pk PO Box 1787 .... Paoli PA 19301 610-727-5300 727-5414
Web: www.simkiss.com

Sintz & Assoc Inc 57 S Park Blvd .... Greenwood IN 46143 317-889-3000

Smith Nadenbousch Insurance Inc
132 S Queen St .... Martinsburg WV 25401 304-263-3388
Web: smnains.com

Snellings Walters Insurance Agency
1117 Perimeter Ctr W W101 .... Atlanta GA 30338 770-396-9600
Web: www.snellingswalters.com

Southwest Business Corp
9311 San Pedro Ave Ste 600 .... San Antonio TX 78216 210-635-1231
Web: www.swbc.com

SPAAN Tech Inc 311 S Wacker Dr Ste 2400 .... Chicago IL 60606 312-277-8800
Web: www.spaantech.com

SPARTA Insurance Holdings Inc
185 Asylum St Cityplace Ii .... Hartford CT 06103 860-275-6500
Web: www.spartainsurance.com

Stailey Insurance Corp 2084 S Milwaukee St .... Denver CO 80210 303-759-2796
Web: staileycorp.com

Name / Address	City	State	Zip	Phone	Fax
Stallings Crop Insurance Corp PO Box 6100 *TF:* 800-721-7099 ■ *Web:* www.stallingscrop.com	Lakeland	FL	33807	863-647-2747	
Standard Insurance Agency Corp 620 W Pipeline *Web:* www.siatexas.com	Hurst	TX	76053	817-285-1800	
Standard Life Financial Inc 1245 Sherbrooke St W *Web:* www.standardlife.ca	Montreal	QC	H3G1G3	514-499-8855	
Standard Life Investments (USA) Ltd 1 Beacon St 34th Fl *Web:* us.standardlifeinvestments.com	Boston	MA	02108	617-720-7900	
Stanley Mcdonald Agency of Illinois 2018 State Rd *TF:* 800-344-3948 ■ *Web:* armitageinconline.com	La Crosse	WI	54601	608-788-6160	
Stanton Insurance Agency Inc 230 Second Ave Ste 105 *Web:* stantonins.com	Waltham	MA	02451	781-893-3200	
Star Casualty Insurance Company Inc PO Box 451037 *TF:* 877-782-7210 ■ *Web:* www.starcasualty.com	Miami	FL	33134	877-782-7210	
Starkweather & Shepley Inc 60 Catamore Blvd *TF:* 800-854-4625 ■ *Web:* www.starkweathershepley.com	East Providence	RI	02914	401-435-3600	438-0150
Starr Group, The 5005 W Loomis Rd *Web:* starrgroup.com	Greenfield	WI	53220	414-421-3800	
State Farm Mutual Automobile Insurance Co 800 Metairie Rd Ste P *Web:* www.statefarm.com/agent/us/la/metairie/ab-flynt-lfzxz1ys000	Metairie	LA	70005	504-832-4127	
State Mutual Insurance Co 210 E Second Ave *Web:* statemutualinsurance.com	Rome	GA	30161	706-291-1054	
Stephen Mahoney 380 W Portal Ave Ste D *Web:* agents.allstate.com	San Francisco	CA	94127	415-681-7120	
Sterling & Sterling Inc 135 Crossways Park Dr	Woodbury	NY	11797	516-487-0300	
Stieg & Assoc Insurance Inc 3319 Gabel Rd *Web:* stieginsurance.com	Billings	MT	59102	406-656-9666	
Stoner-Johnson Insurance Agency 2330 Airport Hwy *Web:* stonerjohnson.com	Toledo	OH	43609	419-385-3101	
Strassman Insurance Services Inc 26351 Curtiss Wright Pkwy *Web:* strassman.net	Richmond Heights	OH	44143	216-289-1500	
Stratose 2 Concourse Pkwy NE # 300 Ste 300 *Web:* www.coalitionamerica.com	Atlanta	GA	30328	404-459-7201	459-6645
Succession Capital Alliance Insurance Services LLC 4695 MacArthur Ct 10th Fl *Web:* www.successioncapital.com	Newport Beach	CA	92660	949-794-1882	
Sullivan Curtis Monroe 1920 Main St *TF:* 800-427-3253 ■ *Web:* www.sullivancurtismonroe.com	Irvine	CA	92614	949-250-7172	
Summit Financial Resources Inc 4 Campus Dr *Web:* www.summitfinancial.com	Parsippany	NJ	07054	973-285-3600	
Sundel & Milford Inc 11 Scovill St *Web:* sundelmilford.com	Waterbury	CT	06720	203-753-0114	
Surry Insurance Agency & Realty Company Inc 119 W Atkins St *Web:* surryinsurance.com	Dobson	NC	27017	336-386-8228	
Swan & Sons-Morss Company Inc 309 E Water St *TF:* 877-407-1657 ■ *Web:* swanmorss.com	Elmira	NY	14902	607-734-6283	
Synergy Investment Group Ltd 8320 University Exec Park Dr Ste 112 *Web:* synergyinvestments.com	Charlotte	NC	28262	704-333-7637	
Tabb Brockenbrough & Ragland LLC 4905 Dickens Rd *TF:* 800-296-0531 ■ *Web:* www.tbrinsurance.com	Richmond	VA	23230	804-355-7984	
Talladega Insurance Agency 109 Spring St N *Web:* talladega-insurance.com	Talladega	AL	35160	256-362-4153	
Tamrac Group Inc, The 10946 C Beaver Dam Rd *Web:* tamracinsurance.com	Hunt Valley	MD	21030	410-568-1200	
Teachers Protective Mutual Life Insurance Co 116-118 N Prince St *TF:* 800-555-3122 ■ *Web:* www.tpmins.com	Lancaster	PA	17603	717-394-7156	
Tetrault Insurance Agency Inc 4317 Acushnet Ave *TF:* 800-696-9991 ■ *Web:* tetraultinsurance.com	New Bedford	MA	02745	508-995-8365	
Texas Women Ventures 3625 N Hall St Ste 615 *Web:* www.texaswomenventures.com	Dallas	TX	75219	214-444-7890	
Thomas George Associates Ltd 10 Larkfield Rd *Web:* www.tgaltd.com	East Northport	NY	11731	631-261-8800	
Thomas Venturi 5616 Wmontrose Ave	Chicago	IL	60634	773-777-5151	
Three Rivers Holdings Inc Unison Plz 1001 Brinton Rd *Web:* www.unisonhealthplan.com	Pittsburgh	PA	15221	412-858-4000	
Thurston Group LLC John Hancock Ctr 875 N Michigan Ave Ste 3640 *Web:* www.thurstongroup.com	Chicago	IL	60611	312-255-0077	
Title Security of Arizona Inc 6390 E Tanque Verde Rd *Web:* titlesecurity.com	Tucson	AZ	85715	520-885-1600	
Todd Organization Inc, The 24610 Detroit Rd Ste 210 *Web:* www.toddorg.com	Cleveland	OH	44145	440-871-7700	
Toler & Toler Insurance 1564 SR- 160	Gallipolis	OH	45631	740-446-9445	
Total Care Inc 819 S Salina St *Web:* www.totalcareny.com	Syracuse	NY	13202	315-634-5555	
Trans-Century Resources Inc 8716 N Mopac Expy Ste 100 *Web:* www.trans-century.com	Austin	TX	78759	512-345-0280	
Transguard Insurance Company of America Inc 215 S Human Blvd *Web:* www.transguard.com	Naperville	IL	60563	630-864-3500	
TRICOR Insurance & Financial Services Inc 230 W Cherry St *Web:* www.tricorinsurance.com	Lancaster	WI	53813	608-723-6441	
Trimble-Batjer Insurance Assoc 201 S Chadbourne St *Web:* trimble-batjer.com	San Angelo	TX	76903	325-653-6733	
U S Risk Insurance Group Inc 10210 N Central Expy *TF:* 800-926-9155 ■ *Web:* www.usrisk.com	Dallas	TX	75231	214-265-7090	739-1421
Underwriters Safety & Claims Inc 1700 Eastpoint Pkwy *Web:* www.uscky.com	Louisville	KY	40223	502-244-1343	
Uni-Ter Underwriting Management Corp 500 Northridge Rd Ste 330 *Web:* www.usre.com	Atlanta	GA	30350	678-781-2400	
Union Central Life Insurance Co, The 1876 Waycross Rd PO Box 40888 *TF:* 877-546-3863	Cincinnati	OH	45240	877-546-3863	
United Funeral Directors Benefit Life Insurance Co 351 S Sherman Ste 102 *Web:* unitedbenefitsinc.com	Richardson	TX	75081	469-330-2200	
United States Warranty Corp 22 NE 22nd Ave *Web:* www.uswarranty.com	Pompano Beach	FL	33062	954-784-9400	
United Underwriters Inc PO Box 971000 *TF:* 866-686-4833 ■ *Web:* www.uuinsurance.com	Orem	UT	84097	801-226-2662	229-2662
Usasia Insurance Services 319 Union Ave *TF:* 800-372-4822 ■ *Web:* usasia-ins.com	Pomona	CA	91768	909-618-0288	
USI Holdings Corp 200 Summit Lake Dr Ste 350 *Web:* www.usi.com	Valhalla	NY	10595	914-749-8500	749-8550
Van Dyk Group Inc, The 12800 Long Beach Blvd *TF:* 800-222-0131 ■ *Web:* www.vandykgroup.com	Beach Haven	NJ	08008	609-492-1511	492-7643
Van Zandt Emrich & Cary Inc 12401 Plantside Dr *TF:* 800-928-7355 ■ *Web:* www.vzecins.com	Louisville	KY	40299	502-456-2001	454-5137
VanBeurden Insurance Services Inc 1600 Draper St PO Box 67 *Web:* www.vanbeurden.com	Kingsburg	CA	93631	559-897-2975	897-4070
VIVA Health Inc 1222 14th Ave S *TF:* 800-633-1542 ■ *Web:* www.vivahealth.com	Birmingham	AL	35205	205-939-1718	
Wallace Welch Willingham 300 First Ave S 5th Fl *TF:* 800-783-5085 ■ *Web:* www.marineins.com	Saint Petersburg	FL	33701	727-522-7777	521-2902
Weaver Bros Insurance Assoc Inc 4550 Montgomery Ave Ste 300 North Tower *Web:* www.weaverbros.com	Bethesda	MD	20814	301-986-4400	
Weber Insurance Corp 505 Corporate Dr W *TF:* 888-860-0400 ■ *Web:* weberinsurance.com	Langhorne	PA	19047	215-860-0400	
WellCare of Georgia Inc 211 Perimeter Ctr Pkwy Ste 800 *Web:* www.wellcare.com/georgia	Atlanta	GA	30346	678-327-0939	
Weller/Obrien Insurance Services 720 Kelly Ave *Web:* wellerobrien.com	Half Moon Bay	CA	94019	650-726-6328	
Wells Fargo Insurance Inc 600 S Hwy 169 *Web:* www.wellsfargo.com	Saint Louis Park	MN	55426	612-667-5600	667-2681
West Boylston Insurance AgencyInc 12 W Boylston St *Web:* westboylstoninsurance.com	West Boylston	MA	01583	508-835-3877	
West Point Underwriters LLC 7785 66th St *TF:* 800-688-6213 ■ *Web:* westpointuw.com	Pinellas Park	FL	33781	727-507-7565	
Westcor Land Title Insurance Co 201 N New York Ave Ste 200 *Web:* www.wltic.com	Winter Park	FL	32789	407-629-5842	
Western Group Inc 511 W 10Th *Web:* wgiinsurance.com	Pueblo	CO	81003	719-543-3604	
Wharton Group 101 S Livingston Ave *TF:* 800-521-2725 ■ *Web:* www.whartoninsurance.com	Livingston	NJ	07039	973-992-5775	992-6660
White Pigeon Mutual Insurance Assn 105 W Fourth St *Web:* wpigeon.com	Wilton	IA	52778	563-732-2072	
White Planning Group 602 Virginia St E *Web:* whiteplanninggroup.com	Charleston	WV	25301	304-346-3295	
William Gallagher Assoc Investment Services Group Inc (WGA) 470 Atlantic Ave *Web:* www.wgains.com	Boston	MA	02210	617-261-6700	
William Penn Assn 709 Brighton Rd *TF:* 800-848-7366 ■ *Web:* www.williampennassociation.org	Pittsburgh	PA	15233	412-231-2979	
Willis Group Holdings Ltd 200 Liberty St 1 World Financial Ctr *NYSE: WSH* ■ *TF:* 800-234-8596 ■ *Web:* www.willis.com	New York	NY	10281	212-915-8888	915-8511
Wilshire Insurance Co 1206 W Ave J Ste 100 *Web:* www.wilshireinsurance.com	Lancaster	CA	93534	661-940-7300	
Wolverine Mutual Insurance Co 1 Wolverine Way *TF:* 800-733-3320 ■ *Web:* www.wolverinemutual.com	Dowagiac	MI	49047	269-782-3451	
Word & Brown Insurance Administrators Inc 721 S Parker Ste 300 *Web:* www.wordandbrown.com	Orange	CA	92868	714-835-6752	
World Financial Group Inc 11315 Johns Creek Pkwy *Web:* www.worldfinancialgroup.com	Johns Creek	GA	30097	770-453-9300	
XL Capital Group 1540 Broadway *Web:* www.xlgroup.com	New York	NY	10036	212-915-6177	

391 INSURANCE COMPANIES

See Also Home Warranty Services p. 2482; Viatical Settlement Companies p. 3295

391-1 Animal Insurance

Phone *Fax*

Canadian Livestock Insurance
480 University Ave Ste 412 ... Toronto ON M5G1V2 416-510-8191 510-8186
TF: 800-727-1502 ■ *Web:* www.cdnlivestock.ca

Equisport Agency Inc
2306 Eastways Rd PO Box 269 ... Bloomfield Hills MI 48304 248-644-1215 644-1404
TF: 800-432-1215 ■ *Web:* www.equisportagency.com

Henry Equestrian Insurance Brokers
28 Victoria St ... Aurora ON L4G1P9 905-727-1144 727-4986
TF: 800-565-4321 ■ *Web:* www.hep.ca

Merry Rama Insurance 4236 County Hwy 18 ... Delhi NY 13753 607-746-2226 746-2911
Web: www.cattlexchange.com/insurance.htm

Pet's Health Plan 3840 Greentree Ave SW ... Canton OH 44706 800-807-6724
TF: 800-807-6724 ■ *Web:* www.petshealthplan.com

Veterinary Pet Insurance Inc PO Box 2344 ... Brea CA 92822 800-872-7387 989-0533*
**Fax Area Code:* 714 ■ *TF:* 800-872-7387 ■ *Web:* www.petinsurance.com

391-2 Life & Accident Insurance

Phone *Fax*

Acacia Life Insurance Co 7315 Wisconsin Ave ... Bethesda MD 20814 301-280-1000 280-1161*
**Fax:* Cust Svc ■ *TF:* 800-444-1889 ■ *Web:* www.unificompanies.com

Advance Insurance Company of Kansas
1133 SW Topeka Blvd ... Topeka KS 66629 785-273-9804 273-6121
TF: 800-530-5989 ■ *Web:* www.advanceinsurance.com

Aetna Inc 151 Farmington Ave ... Hartford CT 06156 860-273-0123
NYSE: AET ■ *TF:* 800-872-3862 ■ *Web:* www.aetna.com

Alliant Insurance Services Inc
1301 Dove St ... Newport Beach CA 92660 949-756-0271 756-2713
Web: www.alliant.com

Allianz Life Insurance Company of North America
PO Box 1344 ... Minneapolis MN 55416 800-950-5872
TF: 800-950-5872 ■ *Web:* www.allianzlife.com

Allstate Life Insurance Co
3100 Sanders Rd Allstate W Plz ... Northbrook IL 60062 847-402-5000
TF Cust Svc: 800-366-1411 ■ *Web:* www.allstate.com

Amalgamated Life Insurance Co 730 Broadway ... New York NY 10003 212-539-5826
Web: www.amalgamatedlife.com

American Amicable Life Insurance Co PO Box 2549 ... Waco TX 76702 254-297-2777 297-2733
TF: 800-736-7311 ■ *Web:* americanamicable.com

American Equity Investment Life Insurance Co
6000 Westown Pkwy ... West Des Moines IA 50266 515-221-0002 221-9947
TF: 888-221-1234 ■ *Web:* www.american-equity.com

American Family Life Assurance Company of Columbus (AFLAC)
1932 Wynnton Rd ... Columbus GA 31999 706-323-3431 448-8922*
**Fax Area Code:* 800 ■ **Fax:* Cust Svc ■ *TF Cust Svc:* 800-992-3522 ■ *Web:* www.aflac.com

American Family Life Insurance Co
6000 American Pkwy ... Madison WI 53783 608-249-2111 243-4921
TF: 800-692-6326 ■ *Web:* www.amfam.com

American Family Mutual Insurance Co
6000 American Pkwy ... Madison WI 53783 608-249-2111
TF Cust Svc: 800-374-0008 ■ *Web:* www.amfam.com

American Fidelity Life Insurance Co
4060 Barrancas Ave ... Pensacola FL 32507 850-456-7401 453-5440
Web: www.americanfidelitylifeins.com

American Foreign Service Protective Assn
1620 L St ... Washington DC 20036 202-833-4910
Web: www.afspa.org

American Income Life Insurance Co (AIL)
1200 Wooded Acres ... Waco TX 76710 254-761-6400 761-5724
TF: 800-433-3405 ■ *Web:* www.ailife.com

American National Insurance Co 1 Moody Plz ... Galveston TX 77550 409-763-4661 763-4545
NASDAQ: ANAT ■ *Web:* www.americannational.com

American Republic Insurance Co
601 Sixth Ave ... Des Moines IA 50309 800-247-2190 247-2435*
**Fax Area Code:* 515 ■ *TF Cust Svc:* 800-247-2190

American Standard Insurance Company of Wisconsin
6000 American Pkwy ... Madison WI 53783 608-249-2111
TF: 800-692-6326 ■ *Web:* www.amfam.com

American Trust Administrators Inc
255 NW Blue Pkwy Ste 100 ... Lees Summit MO 64063 816-251-7700
Web: www.ataamerica.com

American United Life Insurance Co
1 American Sq 510A PO Box 368 ... Indianapolis IN 46206 317-285-1877
TF: 800-537-6442 ■ *Web:* www.oneamerica.com

Americo Financial Life & Annuity Insurance Co
PO Box 410288 ... Kansas City MO 64141 800-231-0801
TF: 800-231-0801 ■ *Web:* www.americo.com

Ameritas Direct 5900 'O' St ... Lincoln NE 68510 800-555-4655
TF: 800-555-4655 ■ *Web:* www.ameritasdirect.com

Ameritas Life Insurance Corp 5900 'O' St ... Lincoln NE 68510 402-467-1122 467-7935*
**Fax:* Hum Res ■ *TF:* 800-745-1112 ■ *Web:* www.ameritas.com

Anthem Life Insurance Co
6740 N High St Ste 200 ... Worthington OH 43085 614-436-0688
TF: 800-551-7265 ■ *Web:* www.anthem.com

Arch Insurance Group Inc
1 Liberty Plz 53rd Fl ... New York NY 10006 212-651-6500
TF: 866-993-9978 ■
Web: www.archcapgroup.com/insurance/regions/united-states

Assurant Employee Benefits
2323 Grand Blvd ... Kansas City MO 64108 816-474-2345 881-8996
TF: 800-733-7879 ■ *Web:* www.assurantemployeebenefits.com

Phone *Fax*

Aurora National Life Assurance Co
PO Box 4490 ... Hartford CT 06147 800-265-2652 333-2311*
**Fax Area Code:* 803 ■ *TF:* 800-265-2652 ■ *Web:* www.auroralife.com

Axa Distributors LLC
1290 Ave of the Americas ... New York NY 10104 212-314-3731 314-3583

AXA Equitable Life Insurance Co
1290 Ave of the Americas ... New York NY 10104 212-554-1234
Web: us.axa.com

Baltimore Life Cos 10075 Red Run Blvd ... Owings Mills MD 21117 410-581-6600 581-6601*
**Fax:* Claims ■ *TF:* 800-628-5433 ■ *Web:* www.baltlife.com

Bankers Fidelity Life Insurance Co
4370 Peachtree Rd ... Atlanta GA 30319 404-266-5500 266-5699*
NASDAQ: AAME ■ **Fax:* Sales ■ *TF:* 866-458-7504 ■ *Web:* www.bflic.com

Bankers Insurance LLC 4490 Cox Rd ... Glen Allen VA 23060 804-497-3634 643-0938
Web: www.bankersinsurance.net

Bankers Life & Casualty Co
111 E Wacker Dr Ste 2100 ... Chicago IL 60601 312-396-6000
TF: 800-231-9150 ■ *Web:* www.bankerslife.com

Banner Life Insurance Co
1701 Research Blvd ... Rockville MD 20850 301-279-4800
TF: 800-638-8428 ■ *Web:* www.lgamerica.com

Beneficial Financial Group 55 N 300 W ... Salt Lake City UT 84145 801-933-1100 531-3317*
**Fax:* Cust Svc ■ *TF:* 800-233-7979 ■ *Web:* www.beneficialfinancialgroup.com

Benevolent Life Insurance Company Inc
1624 Milam St ... Shreveport LA 71103 318-425-1522 221-1761

Best Life & Health Insurance Co
2505 McCabe Way ... Irvine CA 92614 949-253-4080 222-1004
TF: 800-433-0088 ■ *Web:* www.bestlife.com

Booker T Washington Insurance Co
1728 Third Ave N ... Birmingham AL 35203 205-328-5454 458-3776

Bristol West Insurance Group
5701 Stirling Rd PO Box 229080 ... Davie FL 33314 954-513-2500 316-5275
Web: www.bristolwest.com

Catholic Order of Foresters
355 Shuman Blvd ... Naperville IL 60563 630-983-4900
TF: 800-617-4176 ■ *Web:* catholicforester.org

Central Security Life Insurance Co
2175 N Glenville Dr PO Box 833879 ... Richardson TX 75082 972-699-2770 699-2788
Web: www.cslic.com

Central States Health & Life Company of Omaha
1212 N 96th St ... Omaha NE 68114 402-397-1111
TF: 800-826-6587 ■ *Web:* www.cso.com

CIGNA 900 Cottage Grove Rd ... Hartford CT 06002 860-226-6000 351-3616*
**Fax Area Code:* 800 ■ *TF:* 800-244-6224 ■ *Web:* www.cigna.com

Citizens Insurance Company of America
400 E Anderson Ln ... Austin TX 78752 512-837-7100 836-9785
TF: 800-880-5044 ■ *Web:* www.citizensinc.com

Citizens Security Life Insurance Co
12910 Shelbyville Rd Ste 300 ... Louisville KY 40243 502-244-2420 254-4059
TF: 800-843-7752 ■ *Web:* www.citizenssecuritylife.com

Colonial Life & Accident Insurance Co
1200 Colonial Life Blvd ... Columbia SC 29210 800-325-4368 731-2618*
**Fax Area Code:* 803 ■ *TF:* 800-325-4368 ■ *Web:* www.coloniallife.com

Colonial Penn Life Insurance Co
399 Market St ... Philadelphia PA 19181 215-928-8000
TF: 800-523-9100 ■ *Web:* www.colonialpenn.com

Columbus Life Insurance Co
400 E Fourth St PO Box 5737 ... Cincinnati OH 45201 800-677-9696 361-6939*
**Fax Area Code:* 513 ■ *TF:* 800-677-9595 ■ *Web:* www.columbuslife.com

Companion Life Insurance Co
7909 Parklane Rd Ste 200 ... Columbia SC 29223 803-735-1251 735-0736
TF: 800-753-0404 ■ *Web:* www.companionlife.com

Concord Group Insurance Cos 4 Bouton St ... Concord NH 03301 800-852-3380
TF: 800-852-3380 ■ *Web:* www.concordgroupinsurance.com

Conseco Annuity Assurance Co
11825 N Pennsylvania St ... Carmel IN 46032 866-595-2255
TF: 866-595-2255 ■ *Web:* www.conseco.com

Conseco Senior Health Insurance Co
11825 N Pennsylvania St ... Carmel IN 46032 866-595-2255
TF: 866-595-2255 ■ *Web:* www.conseco.com

Continental Assurance Co 333 S Wabash Ave ... Chicago IL 60604 312-822-5000 260-4376
TF: 800-251-2148 ■ *Web:* www.cna.com

COUNTRY Insurance & Financial Services
1705 Towanda Ave ... Bloomington IL 61701 866-268-6879
TF: 888-211-2555 ■ *Web:* www.countryfinancial.com

Creative Mktg International Corp
11460 Tomahawk Creek Pkwy ... Leawood KS 66211 913-814-0510
TF: 800-992-2642 ■ *Web:* www.creativeone.com

Crump Insurance Services Inc
105 Eisenhower Pkwy ... Roseland NJ 07068 973-461-2100
TF: 800-222-0087 ■ *Web:* crumplifeinsurance.com

Educators Mutual Insurance Assn Utah
852 East Arrowhead Ln ... Salt Lake City UT 84107 801-262-7476
Web: emihealth.com

ELCO Mutual Life & Annuity
916 Sherwood Dr ... Lake Bluff IL 60044 847-295-6000
TF: 888-872-7954 ■ *Web:* www.elcomutual.com

Elite Mktg Group 800 Bering Dr ... Houston TX 77057 713-507-1000
Web: www.elitemktg.net

Epic Life Insurance Co 1765 W Broadway ... Madison WI 53713 608-223-2100 223-2159
TF Sales: 800-236-8809 ■ *Web:* www.epiclife.com

Equitable Life & Casualty Insurance Co
3 Triad Ctr ... Salt Lake City UT 84180 877-358-4060 579-3790*
**Fax Area Code:* 801 ■ *TF Cust Svc:* 877-358-4060 ■ *Web:* www.equilife.com

Erie & Niagara Insurance Assn
8800 Sheridan Dr ... Williamsville NY 14221 716-632-5433
Web: www.enia.com

Erie Family Life Insurance Co
100 Erie Insurance Pl ... Erie PA 16530 814-870-2000 870-4040
TF: 800-458-0811 ■ *Web:* www.erieinsurance.com

Farm Bureau Life Insurance Co
5400 University Ave ... West Des Moines IA 50266 515-225-5400 226-6966*
**Fax:* Hum Res ■ *TF:* 800-247-4170 ■ *Web:* www.fbfs.com

Farm Family Life Insurance Co PO Box 656 ... Albany NY 12201 518-431-5000
TF: 800-948-3276 ■ *Web:* www.farmfamily.com

Phone *Fax*

Farmers New World Life Insurance
3003 77th Ave SE .... Mercer Island WA 98040 206-232-8400 236-6642
Web: farmers.com

Federal Life Insurance Co Mutual
3750 W Deerfield Rd .... Riverwoods IL 60015 847-520-1900 520-1916
TF: 800-233-3750 ■ *Web:* www.federallife.com

Federated Life Insurance Co
121 E Pk Sq PO Box 328 .... Owatonna MN 55060 507-455-5200 455-7840
TF: 800-533-0472 ■ *Web:* federatedinsurance.com

Federated Mutual Insurance Co
121 E Pk Sq PO Box 328 .... Owatonna MN 55060 507-455-5200
TF: 800-533-0472 ■ *Web:* federatedinsurance.com

FEDUSA 13256 66th St N Ste 35 .... Largo FL 33773 727-535-5671 610-1947*
**Fax Area Code:* 866 ■ *Web:* www.directgeneral.com/fed-us-insurance

First UNUM Life Insurance Co
2211 Congress St .... Portland ME 04122 207-575-2211
TF: 800-633-7491 ■ *Web:* www.unum.com

FirstCare 1901 W Loop 289 Ste #9 .... Lubbock TX 79407 806-784-4300
TF: 800-884-4901 ■ *Web:* www.firstcare.com

Gerber Life Insurance Co
1311 Mamaroneck Ave .... White Plains NY 10605 914-272-4000
TF: 800-704-2180 ■ *Web:* www.gerberlife.com

Global Benefits Group Inc
26000 Towne Centre Dr Ste 100 .... Foothill Ranch CA 92610 949-470-2100
Web: www.gbg.com

Go Medico 1515 S 75th St .... Omaha NE 68124 402-391-6900
TF: 800-228-6080 ■ *Web:* gomedico.com

Grange Insurance 671 S High St .... Columbus OH 43206 800-422-0550 445-2337*
**Fax Area Code:* 614 ■ *TF:* 800-422-0550 ■ *Web:* grangeinsurance.com

Great-West Life & Annuity Insurance Co
8515 E OrchaRd Rd .... Greenwood Village CO 80111 303-737-3000
TF: 800-537-2033 ■ *Web:* www.greatwest.com

Great-West Life Assurance Co 100 Osborne St .... Winnipeg MB R3C3A5 204-946-1190
TF: 800-990-6654 ■ *Web:* www.greatwestlife.com

Greek Catholic Union of the USA
5400 Tuscarawas Rd .... Beaver PA 15009 724-495-3400
TF: 800-722-4428 ■ *Web:* www.gcuusa.com

Guarantee Trust Life Insurance Co
1275 Milwaukee Ave .... Glenview IL 60025 847-699-0600 699-2355
TF: 800-338-7452 ■ *Web:* www.gtlic.com

Guardian Life Insurance Company of America
7 Hanover Sq .... New York NY 10004 212-598-8000
TF: 888-600-4667 ■ *Web:* www.guardianlife.com

GuideOne Mutual Insurance Co
1111 Ashworth Rd .... West Des Moines IA 50265 515-267-5000 267-5530*
**Fax:* Hum Res ■ *TF:* 877-448-4331 ■ *Web:* www.guideone.com

Hannover Life Reassurance Co of America
200 South Orange Avenue Ste 1900 .... Orlando FL 32801 407-649-8411
Web: www.hannover-re.com

Harleysville Mutual Insurance Co
355 Maple Ave .... Harleysville PA 19438 215-256-5000
TF: 800-523-6344 ■ *Web:* www.harleysville.com

Hartford Life & Accident Insurance Co
1 Hartford Plz .... Hartford CT 06155 860-547-5000
TF: 877-896-9320 ■ *Web:* www.thehartford.com

Harvey Watt & Co 475 N Central Ave .... Atlanta GA 30354 404-767-7501 761-8326
TF: 800-241-6103 ■ *Web:* www.harveywatt.com

HCC Life Insurance Co
225 Townpark Dr Ste 145 .... Kennesaw GA 30144 770-973-9851 973-9854
TF: 800-447-0460 ■ *Web:* www.hcc.com

Horace Mann Life Insurance Co
1 Horace Mann Plaza .... Springfield IL 62715 217-789-2500 788-5161
TF: 800-999-1030 ■ *Web:* www.horacemann.com

Humana Inc 500 W Main St .... Louisville KY 40202 502-580-1000
NYSE: HUM ■ *TF:* 800-486-2620 ■ *Web:* www.humana.com

Illinois Mutual Life Insurance Co
300 SW Adams St .... Peoria IL 61634 309-674-8255
TF: 800-380-6688 ■ *Web:* www.illinoismutual.com

Indiana Farm Bureau Insurance Co
225 SE St PO Box 1250 .... Indianapolis IN 46206 317-692-7200 692-7009*
**Fax:* Sales ■ *TF:* 800-723-3276 ■ *Web:* www.infarmbureau.com

Industrial Alliance Insurance & Financial Services
1080 Grande Allee W PO Box 1907 Stn Therminus .... Quebec QC G1K7M3 418-684-5000
TF: 800-463-6236 ■ *Web:* ia.ca/individuals

Insurance Marketing Agencies Inc
306 Main St .... Worcester MA 01608 508-753-7233 754-0487
TF: 800-891-1226 ■ *Web:* www.imaagency.com

Investors Heritage Life Insurance Co (IHLIC)
200 Capital Ave PO Box 717 .... Frankfort KY 40602 502-223-2361 875-7084
TF: 800-422-2011 ■ *Web:* www.investorsheritage.com

Jackson National Life Insurance Co
1 Corporate Way .... Lansing MI 48951 517-381-5500
TF: 800-644-4565 ■ *Web:* www.jackson.com

John Hancock Life Insurance Co
1 John Hancock Way Ste 1700 .... Boston MA 02117 617-572-6000
Web: www.johnhancock.com

John Hancock New York 100 Summit Lake Dr .... Valhalla NY 10595 877-391-3748
TF: 800-732-5543 ■ *Web:* www.johnhancock.com

Kilpatrick Life Insurance Co
1818 Marshall St .... Shreveport LA 71101 318-222-0555
Web: www.klic.com

Lafayette Life Insurance Co 400 Broadway .... Cincinnati OH 45202 800-443-8793 362-4900*
**Fax Area Code:* 513 ■ *TF:* 800-443-8793 ■ *Web:* www.llic.com

LDS Group, The PO Box 83480 .... Baton Rouge LA 70884 225-769-9923
Web: www.theldsgroup.com

Life Insurance Co of Alabama 302 Broad St .... Gadsden AL 35901 256-543-2022 543-0019
TF: 800-226-2371 ■ *Web:* www.licoa.com

Lincoln Heritage Life Insurance Co
PO Box 29045 .... Phoenix AZ 85038 800-433-8181 840-0969*
**Fax Area Code:* 602 ■ *TF:* 800-433-8181 ■ *Web:* www.lhlic.com

Lincoln Heritage Life Insurance Co
4343 E Camelback Rd Ste 400 Ste 400 .... Phoenix AZ 85018 602-957-1650 840-0969
TF: 800-438-7180 ■ *Web:* www.lhlic.com

Phone *Fax*

Lincoln National Life Insurance Co
1300 S Clinton St .... Fort Wayne IN 46802 800-454-6265
TF: 800-454-6265 ■ *Web:* www.lfg.com

London Life Insurance Co 255 Dufferin Ave .... London ON N6A4K1 519-432-5281 435-7679
TF: 800-990-6654 ■ *Web:* www.londonlife.com

Loyal American Life Insurance Co
Great American Financial Resources Inc
PO Box 26580 .... Austin TX 78755 800-545-4269
TF: 800-315-5522 ■ *Web:* www.gafri.com

Madison National Life Insurance Company Inc
PO Box 5008 .... Madison WI 53705 608-830-2000 830-2700
TF: 800-356-9601 ■ *Web:* www.madisonlife.com

Medico Group 1515 S 75th St .... Omaha NE 68124 402-391-6900 391-6489
TF: 800-228-6080 ■ *Web:* gomedico.com

MetLife Inc 200 Pk Ave .... New York NY 10166 212-578-2211 578-3320
NYSE: MET ■ *TF:* 800-638-5433 ■ *Web:* global.metlife.com

MetLife Investors Insurance Co
5 Pk Plz Ste 1900 .... Irvine CA 92614 800-848-3854
TF: 800-848-3854 ■ *Web:* metlifepro.metlife.com/index.html

Midland National Life Insurance Co
1 Sammons Plz .... Sioux Falls SD 57193 605-335-5700 335-3621
TF: 800-923-3223 ■ *Web:* midlandnational.com

MML Bay State Life Insurance Co
100 Bright Meadow Blvd .... Enfield CT 06082 860-562-1000
Web: www.massmutual.com

Modern Woodmen of America 1701 First Ave .... Rock Island IL 61201 309-786-6481 793-5547
TF: 800-447-9811 ■ *Web:* www.modern-woodmen.org

Motorists Life Insurance Co 471 E Broad St .... Columbus OH 43215 614-225-8211 225-8365
Web: www.motoristsmutual.com

Mutual Insurance Company of Arizona
PO Box 33180 .... Phoenix AZ 85067 602-956-5276 468-1710
TF: 800-352-0402 ■ *Web:* www.mica-insurance.com

Mutual of America Life Insurance Co
320 Pk Ave .... New York NY 10022 212-224-1600 224-2500*
**Fax:* Mail Rm ■ *TF:* 800-468-3785 ■ *Web:* www.mutualofamerica.com

Mutual of Omaha Insurance Co
Mutual of Omaha Plaza .... Omaha NE 68175 402-342-7600
TF: 800-775-6000 ■ *Web:* www.mutualofomaha.com

Mutual Trust Life Insurance Co
1200 Jorie Blvd .... Oak Brook IL 60522 630-990-1000 990-7083
TF: 800-323-7320 ■ *Web:* www.mutualtrust.com

National Guardian Life Insurance Co (NGL)
2 E Gilman St .... Madison WI 53703 608-257-5611 257-3940
TF: 800-548-2962 ■ *Web:* www.nglic.com

National Mutual Benefit
6522 Grand Teton Plaza .... Madison WI 53719 608-833-1936 833-8714
TF: 800-779-1936 ■ *Web:* www.nmblife.org

National Western Life Insurance Co
850 E Anderson Ln .... Austin TX 78752 512-836-1010 719-0104*
NASDAQ: NWLI ■ **Fax:* Hum Res ■ *TF:* 800-531-5442 ■ *Web:* www.nationalwesternlife.com

Nationwide Life & Annuity Insurance Co
1 Nationwide Pl .... Columbus OH 43215 614-249-7111
TF: 800-882-2822 ■ *Web:* www.nationwide.com

Nationwide Mutual Insurance Co 5100 Rings Rd .... Dublin OH 43017 877-669-6877
TF: 800-543-3747 ■ *Web:* nationwide.com

New England Life Insurance Co 699 Boylston St .... Boston MA 02116 617-585-4574
Web: metlife.com

New York Life Insurance & Annuity Corp
51 Madison Ave .... New York NY 10010 212-576-7000 348-7660*
**Fax Area Code:* 646 ■ **Fax:* Hum Res ■ *TF:* 800-598-2019 ■ *Web:* nylinvestments.com

North Carolina Mutual Life Insurance Co
411 W Chapel Hill St .... Durham NC 27701 919-682-9201 682-1685
TF: 800-626-1899 ■ *Web:* www.ncmutuallife.com

Ohio State Life Insurance Co
PO Box 410288 .... Kansas City MO 64141 800-752-1387
TF: 800-752-1387 ■ *Web:* www.ohiostatelife.com

Old American Insurance Co 3520 Broadway .... Kansas City MO 64111 816-753-7000
TF: 800-733-6242 ■ *Web:* www.oaic.com

OneAmerica Financial Partners Inc (PML)
PO Box 368 .... Indianapolis IN 46206 317-285-1877 285-6462
TF: 800-249-6269 ■ *Web:* www.oneamerica.com

Oxford Life Insurance Co 2721 N Central Ave .... Phoenix AZ 85004 602-263-6666 277-5901
TF Cust Svc: 800-308-2318 ■ *Web:* www.oxfordlife.com

Ozark National Life Insurance Inc
500 E Ninth St .... Kansas City MO 64106 816-842-6300 842-8373
Web: www.ozark-national.com

Pacific Guardian Life Insurance Company Ltd
1440 Kapiolani Blvd Ste 1700 .... Honolulu HI 96814 808-955-2236 942-1284
TF: 800-367-5354 ■ *Web:* www.pacificguardian.com

Pacific Life Insurance Co
700 Newport Ctr Dr .... Newport Beach CA 92660 949-219-3011 219-3706*
**Fax:* Hum Res ■ *TF:* 800-800-7646 ■ *Web:* www.pacificlife.com

Pan-American Life Insurance Co
601 Poydras St .... New Orleans LA 70130 877-939-4550
TF Life Ins: 877-939-4550 ■ *Web:* www.palig.com

Partner Reinsurance Co of the US
1 Greenwich Plaza .... Greenwich CT 06830 203-485-4200 485-4300
TF: 800-831-9146 ■ *Web:* www.partnerre.com

Pekin Life Insurance Co 2505 Ct St .... Pekin IL 61558 309-346-1161
OTC: PKIN ■ *TF:* 800-322-0160 ■ *Web:* www.pekininsurance.com

Penn Insurance & Annuity Co 600 Dresher Rd .... Horsham PA 19044 215-956-8000 956-7699
TF Cust Svc: 800-523-0650 ■ *Web:* www.pennmutual.com

Penn Mutual Life Insurance Co 600 Dresher Rd .... Horsham PA 19044 215-956-8000 956-7699
TF Cust Svc: 800-523-0650 ■ *Web:* www.pennmutual.com

Penn Treaty Network America Insurance Co
3440 Lehigh St .... Allentown PA 18103 800-362-0700 967-4616*
**Fax Area Code:* 610 ■ *TF:* 800-362-0700 ■ *Web:* www.penntreaty.com

Physicians Life Insurance Co 2600 Dodge St .... Omaha NE 68131 402-633-1000
TF: 800-228-9100 ■ *Web:* physiciansmutual.com

Physicians Mutual Insurance Co 2600 Dodge St .... Omaha NE 68131 402-633-1000 633-1604
TF: 800-228-9100 ■ *Web:* physiciansmutual.com

Polish National Alliance of the US of North America
6100 N Cicero Ave .... Chicago IL 60646 773-286-0500
Web: www.pna-znp.org

	City	State	Zip	Phone	Fax
Pro Assurance Corp 1250 23rd St NW Ste 250 *TF:* 800-613-3615 ■ *Web:* www.proassurance.com	Washington	DC	20037	202-969-1866	969-1881
Property-Owners Insurance Co PO Box 30660 *TF:* 800-288-8740 ■ *Web:* auto-owners.com	Lansing	MI	48909	517-323-1200	323-8796
Prudential Financial Inc 751 Broad St *NYSE: PRU* ■ *TF:* 800-843-7625 ■ *Web:* www.prudential.com	Newark	NJ	07102	973-802-6000	367-6476
RBC Liberty Insurance PO Box 789 *TF:* 800-551-8354 ■ *Web:* www.rbcinsurance.com	Greenville	SC	29602	864-609-8111	
Reliable Life Insurance Co 100 King St W PO Box 557 **Fax Area Code:* 866 ■ **Fax:* Claims ■ *TF:* 800-465-0661 ■ *Web:* www.reliablelifeinsurance.com	Hamilton	ON	L8N3K9	905-523-5587	551-1704*
Reliance Standard Life Insurance 2001 Market St Ste 1500 *TF:* 800-351-7500 ■ *Web:* www.reliancestandard.com	Philadelphia	PA	19103	267-256-3500	
Reserve National Insurance Co 601 E Britton Rd *Web:* www.reservenational.com	Oklahoma City	OK	73114	405-848-7931	
Royal State National Insurance Company Ltd 819 S Beretania St *Web:* www.royalstate.com	Honolulu	HI	96813	808-539-1600	
Sabre Healthdirect Inc 590 Alden Rd *TF:* 800-314-3346 ■ *Web:* sabrelife.com	Markham	ON	L3R8N2	905-305-9900	
Savings Bank Life Insurance Company of Massachusetts, The (SBLI) 1 Linscott Rd *Web:* www.sbli.com	Woburn	MA	01801	781-938-3500	
Security Life Insurance Co of America 10901 Red Cir Dr *TF:* 800-328-4667 ■ *Web:* www.securitylife.com	Minnetonka	MN	55343	952-544-2121	945-3419
Security Mutual Life Insurance Co of New York 100 Court St PO Box 1625 **Fax:* Cust Svc ■ *TF:* 800-927-8846 ■ *Web:* www.smlny.com	Binghamton	NY	13901	607-723-3551	723-8665*
Security National Financial Corp (SNFC) 5300 South 360 West Ste 250 PO Box 57250 *NASDAQ: SNFCA* ■ *TF:* 800-574-7117 ■ *Web:* www.securitynational.com	Salt Lake City	UT	84123	801-264-1060	265-9882
Selected Funeral & Life Insurance Co 119 Convention Blvd *Web:* sflic.net	Hot Springs National Park	AR	71902	501-624-2172	
Sentry Life Insurance Co 1800 N Pt Dr *TF:* 800-373-6879 ■ *Web:* www.sentry.com	Stevens Point	WI	54481	715-346-6000	346-7516
Sequoia Insurance Co 31 Upper Ragsdale Dr **Fax Area Code:* 866	Monterey	CA	93940	831-333-9880	632-5246*
Settlers Life Insurance Co 1969 Lee Hwy *TF:* 800-523-2650 ■ *Web:* settlerslife.com	Bristol	VA	24201	276-645-4300	645-4399
Shenandoah Life Insurance Co 2301 Brambleton Ave *TF:* 800-848-5433 ■ *Web:* www.shenlife.com	Roanoke	VA	24015	540-985-4400	985-4444
Slovene National Benefit Society 247 W Allegheny Rd *TF:* 800-843-7675 ■ *Web:* www.snpj.org	Imperial	PA	15126	724-695-1100	
Southern Farm Bureau Life Insurance Co PO Box 78 *Web:* www.sfbli.com	Jackson	MS	39205	601-981-7422	
Southwestern Life Insurance Co 110 W Clinton St Ste 150 **Fax Area Code:* 803	Hobbs	NM	88240	575-393-4577	333-7833*
Standard Life Insurance Company of Indiana 10689 N Pennsylvania St **Fax:* Mktg ■ *TF:* 800-222-3216	Indianapolis	IN	46280	317-574-6201	574-6278*
Standard Security Life Insurance Company of New York 485 Madison Ave 14th Fl *Web:* www.sslicny.com	New York	NY	10022	212-355-4141	644-5786
State Life Insurance Co 1 American Sq PO Box 368 *TF Cust Svc:* 800-537-6442 ■ *Web:* www.oneamerica.com/home	Indianapolis	IN	46206	317-285-2300	285-2380
Sun Life Assurance Company of Canada 1 Sun Life Executive Pk PO Box 9133 *TF:* 800-786-5433 ■ *Web:* www.sunlife.com/us	Wellesley Hills	MA	02481	781-237-6030	
Symetra Life Insurance Co 777 108th Ave Ne Ste 1200 *TF:* 800-574-0233 ■ *Web:* www.symetra.com	Bellevue	WA	98004	425-256-8000	
Texas Life Insurance Co 900 Washington PO Box 830 **Fax:* Sales ■ *TF:* 800-283-9233 ■ *Web:* www.texaslife.com	Waco	TX	76703	254-752-6521	754-7629*
Thrivent Financial for Lutherans 4321 N BallaRd Rd *TF:* 800-847-4836 ■ *Web:* www.thrivent.com	Appleton	WI	54919	920-684-3225	
TIAA-CREF 730 Third Ave *TF:* 866-842-2442 ■ *Web:* www.tiaa.org/public/index.html	New York	NY	10017	212-490-9000	913-2803
Transamerica Occidental Life Insurance Co 1150 S Olive St **Fax:* Mail Rm ■ *TF Cust Svc:* 800-852-4678 ■ *Web:* transamerica.com	Los Angeles	CA	90015	213-742-2111	741-7939*
Trustmark Insurance Co 400 Field Dr *TF:* 888-246-9949 ■ *Web:* www.trustmarkinsurance.com	Lake Forest	IL	60045	847-615-1500	615-3910
United American Insurance Company Inc PO Box 8080 *Web:* www.unitedamerican.com	McKinney	TX	75070	972-529-5085	569-3709
United Heritage Life Insurance Co PO Box 7777 *TF:* 800-657-6351 ■ *Web:* www.unitedheritage.com	Meridian	ID	83680	208-493-6100	466-0825
United Insurance Holdings Corp 360 Central Ave Ste 900 *NASDAQ: UIHC* ■ *TF:* 800-861-4370 ■ *Web:* www.upcinsurance.com	Saint Petersburg	FL	33701	800-295-8016	
United Investors Life Insurance Co 2801 Hwy 280 S *TF:* 800-866-9933 ■ *Web:* www.protective.com	Birmingham	AL	35223	205-268-1000	268-5547
United Life Insurance Co PO Box 73909 *TF:* 800-332-7977 ■ *Web:* www.unitedfiregroup.com	Cedar Rapids	IA	52407	319-399-5700	399-5499
United of Omaha Life Insurance Co Mutual of Omaha Plaza *TF:* 800-775-6000 ■ *Web:* www.mutualofomaha.com	Omaha	NE	68175	402-342-7600	351-2775
United World Life Insurance Co 3300 Mutual of Omaha Plz *TF:* 800-775-6000 ■ *Web:* www.mutualofomaha.com	Omaha	NE	68175	402-342-7600	
USAA Life Insurance Co (USAA) 9800 Fredericksburg Rd **Fax Area Code:* 800 ■ **Fax:* Sales ■ *TF:* 800-531-8000 ■ *Web:* www.usaa.com	San Antonio	TX	78288	210-531-8722	531-8877*
Utica National Insurance Group 180 Genesee St *TF:* 800-274-1914 ■ *Web:* www.uticanational.com	New Hartford	NY	13413	315-734-2000	734-2680
Variable Annuity Life Insurance Co (VALIC) 2929 Allen Pkwy *TF:* 800-448-2542 ■ *Web:* www.valic.com	Houston	TX	77019	800-448-2542	
Washington National Insurance Co 11825 N Pennsylvania St **Fax Area Code:* 800 ■ *TF:* 866-595-2255 ■ *Web:* www.conseco.com	Carmel	IN	46032	866-595-2255	757-6324*
Wawanesa Life Insurance Co 191 Broadway Ste 501 *Web:* wawanesa.com/life/index.html	Winnipeg	MB	R3C3P1	204-985-0684	
Western & Southern Life Insurance Co 400 Broadway **Fax Area Code:* 513 ■ **Fax:* Hum Res ■ *TF:* 800-926-1993 ■ *Web:* www.westernsouthernlife.com	Cincinnati	OH	45202	800-926-1993	629-1212*
Western Fraternal Life Assn (WFLA) 1900 First Ave NE *TF:* 877-935-2467 ■ *Web:* www.wflains.org	Cedar Rapids	IA	52402	319-363-2653	
Western United Life Assurance Co 929 W Sprague Ave PO Box 2290 *TF General:* 800-247-2045 ■ *Web:* www.wula.com	Spokane	WA	99210	509-835-2500	835-3191
Western-Southern Life Assurance Co 400 Broadway **Fax Area Code:* 513 ■ *TF:* 866-832-7719 ■ *Web:* www.westernsouthernlife.com	Cincinnati	OH	45202	866-832-7719	629-1212*
William Penn Life Insurance Co of New York 100 Quentin Roosevelt Blvd *TF:* 800-346-4773 ■ *Web:* www.lgamerica.com	Garden City	NY	11530	516-794-3700	
Woman's Life Insurance Society 1338 Military St PO Box 5020 *TF:* 800-521-9292 ■ *Web:* www.womanslife.org	Port Huron	MI	48061	810-985-5191	985-6970

391-3 Medical & Hospitalization Insurance

Companies listed here provide managed care and/or traditional hospital and medical service plans to individuals and/or groups. Managed care companies typically offer plans as Health Maintenance Organizations (HMOs), Preferred Provider Organizations (PPOs), Exclusive Provider Organizations (EPOs), and/or Point of Service (POS) plans. Other types of hospital and medical service plans offered by companies listed here include indemnity plans and medical savings accounts.

	City	State	Zip	Phone	Fax
AARP Health Care Options PO Box 1017 *TF:* 800-523-5800 ■ *Web:* www.aarphealthcare.com	Montgomeryville	PA	18936	800-523-5800	
Aetna Inc 151 Farmington Ave *NYSE: AET* ■ *TF:* 800-872-3862 ■ *Web:* www.aetna.com	Hartford	CT	06156	860-273-0123	
Aetna US Healthcare Inc 980 Jolly Rd *TF:* 800-872-3862 ■ *Web:* www.aetna.com	Blue Bell	PA	19422	215-775-4800	
AF & L Insurance Co 165 Veterans Way Ste 300 PO Box 5005 *Web:* www.afltc.com	Warminster	PA	18974	215-918-0515	
Alberta Blue Cross 10009 108th St NW *TF:* 800-661-6995 ■ *Web:* www.ab.bluecross.ca	Edmonton	AB	T5J3C5	780-498-8100	425-4627
American Specialty Health Plans 10221 Wateridge Cir *TF:* 800-848-3555 ■ *Web:* www.ashcompanies.com	San Diego	CA	92121	800-848-3555	
Americhoice Corp 8045 Leesburg Pk 6th Fl *Web:* www.americhoice.com	Vienna	VA	22182	703-506-3555	
AMERIGROUP Corp 4425 Corporation Ln *NYSE: AGP* ■ *TF:* 800-600-4441 ■ *Web:* www.amerigroup.com	Virginia Beach	VA	23462	757-490-6900	518-3600
Anthem Blue Cross & Blue Shield 2015 Staples Mill Rd *TF:* 800-451-1527 ■ *Web:* www.anthem.com	Richmond	VA	23230	804-354-7000	
Anthem Blue Cross & Blue Shield Maine 2 Gannett Dr *TF Cust Svc:* 800-482-0966 ■ *Web:* www.anthem.com	South Portland	ME	04106	207-822-7000	822-7375
Anthem Blue Cross & Blue Shield of Connecticut 370 Bassett Rd *TF:* 800-922-1742 ■ *Web:* www.anthem.com	North Haven	CT	06473	800-922-4670	
Anthem Blue Cross & Blue Shield of Nevada 9133 W Russell Rd **Fax Area Code:* 800 ■ *TF:* 800-332-3842 ■ *Web:* www.anthem.com	Las Vegas	NV	89148	702-228-2583	763-3142*
Anthem Blue Cross Blue Shield Colorado 700 Broadway *TF:* 800-654-9338 ■ *Web:* www.anthem.com	Denver	CO	80273	303-831-2131	764-7047
Arkansas Blue Cross Blue Shield PO Box 2181 *TF:* 800-238-8379 ■ *Web:* www.arkansasbluecross.com	Little Rock	AR	72203	501-712-1114	378-2969
AvMed 4300 NW 89th Blvd *TF:* 800-346-0231 ■ *Web:* www.avmed.org	Gainesville	FL	32606	352-372-8400	
Benecaid Health Benefit Solutions Inc 185 The W Mall Ste 800 *TF:* 877-797-7448 ■ *Web:* www.benecaid.com	Toronto	ON	M9C5L5	416-626-8786	
Blue Care Network of Michigan 20500 Civic Ctr Dr **Fax:* Cust Svc ■ *TF:* 800-662-6667 ■ *Web:* bcbsm.com	Southfield	MI	48076	248-799-6400	799-6969*
Blue Cross & Blue Shield of Alabama 450 Riverchase Pkwy E *TF:* 800-292-8868 ■ *Web:* www.bcbsal.org	Birmingham	AL	35244	205-988-2200	
Blue Cross & Blue Shield of Kansas City 2301 Main St **Fax:* Hum Res ■ *TF:* 800-892-6048 ■ *Web:* www.bluekc.com	Kansas City	MO	64108	816-395-2222	395-2726*
Blue Cross & Blue Shield of Michigan 600 Lafayette Blvd E *TF:* 855-237-3501 ■ *Web:* www.bcbsm.com	Detroit	MI	48226	313-225-9000	
Blue Cross & Blue Shield of Mississippi PO Box 1043 *TF:* 800-222-8046 ■ *Web:* www.bcbsms.com	Jackson	MS	39215	601-932-3704	939-7035
Blue Cross & Blue Shield of Montana 560 N Pk Ave PO Box 4309 *TF:* 800-447-7828 ■ *Web:* www.bcbsmt.com	Helena	MT	59604	406-437-5000	

Company	City	State	Zip	Phone	Fax
Blue Cross & Blue Shield of Nebraska 1919 Aksarben Dr PO Box 3248	Omaha	NE	68180	402-982-7000	
TF: 800-422-2763 ■ *Web:* www.nebraskablue.com					
Blue Cross & Blue Shield of New Mexico PO Box 27630	Albuquerque	NM	87125	505-291-3500	
TF: 800-835-8699 ■ *Web:* www.bcbsnm.com					
Blue Cross & Blue Shield of North Carolina 1965 Ivory Creek Blvd	Durham	NC	27702	919-489-7431	765-3521*
**Fax:* Hum Res ■ *TF Cust Svc:* 800-446-8053 ■ *Web:* www.bcbsnc.com					
Blue Cross & Blue Shield of Oklahoma 1215 S Boulder Ave	Tulsa	OK	74119	918-560-3500	
TF Cust Svc: 800-942-5837 ■ *Web:* www.bcbsok.com					
Blue Cross & Blue Shield of Rhode Island 500 Exchange St	Providence	RI	02903	401-459-1000	459-1996
TF: 800-637-3718 ■ *Web:* www.bcbsri.com					
Blue Cross & Blue Shield of Texas Inc 1001 E Lookout Dr	Richardson	TX	75082	972-766-6900	
TF: 800-521-2227 ■ *Web:* www.bcbstx.com					
Blue Cross & Blue Shield of Vermont 445 Industrial Ln	Montpelier	VT	05602	802-223-6131	
TF Cust Svc: 800-247-2583 ■ *Web:* www.bcbsvt.com					
Blue Cross Blue Shield of Arizona 2444 W Las Palmaritas Dr	Phoenix	AZ	85021	602-864-4400	864-4041*
**Fax:* Cust Svc ■ *TF:* 800-232-2345 ■ *Web:* www.azblue.com					
Blue Cross Blue Shield of Delaware PO Box 1991	Wilmington	DE	19899	800-876-7639	
TF: 800-572-4400 ■ *Web:* www.highmarkbcbsde.com					
Blue Cross Blue Shield of Georgia 3350 Peachtree Rd NE	Atlanta	GA	30326	404-842-8000	842-8010
TF Cust Svc: 800-441-2273 ■ *Web:* www.bcbsga.com					
Blue Cross Blue Shield of Illinois 300 E Randolph St	Chicago	IL	60601	312-653-6000	
Web: www.bcbsil.com					
Blue Cross Blue Shield of Kansas 1133 SW Topeka Blvd	Topeka	KS	66629	785-291-7000	290-0711
TF: 800-432-0216 ■ *Web:* www.bcbsks.com					
Blue Cross Blue Shield of Louisiana 5525 Reitz Ave	Baton Rouge	LA	70898	225-295-3307	295-2054
TF: 800-599-2583 ■ *Web:* bcbsla.com					
Blue Cross Blue Shield of Massachusetts 401 Pk Dr	Boston	MA	02215	617-246-5000	636-9494*
**Fax Area Code:* 800 ■ **Fax:* PR ■ *TF:* 800-262-2583 ■ *Web:* www.bluecrossma.com					
Blue Cross Blue Shield of North Dakota 4510 13th Ave S	Fargo	ND	58121	701-282-1100	
TF: 800-342-4718 ■ *Web:* www.bcbsnd.com					
Blue Cross Blue Shield of Wyoming 4000 House Ave	Cheyenne	WY	82001	307-634-1393	778-8582
TF: 800-851-9145 ■ *Web:* www.bcbswy.com					
Blue Cross of California 2 Gannett Dr	South Portland	ME	04106	800-482-0966	438-6811*
**Fax Area Code:* 888 ■ *TF:* 800-999-3643 ■ *Web:* www.anthem.com					
Blue Cross of Idaho 3000 E Pine Ave	Meridian	ID	83642	208-345-4550	331-7311
TF: 800-274-4018 ■ *Web:* www.bcidaho.com					
Blue Cross of Northeastern Pennsylvania 19 N Main St	Wilkes-Barre	PA	18711	800-577-3742	200-6710*
**Fax Area Code:* 570 ■ *TF Cust Svc:* 800-577-3742 ■ *Web:* www.bcnepa.com					
Blue Shield of California 50 Beale St	San Francisco	CA	94105	415-229-5000	229-6230*
**Fax:* Hum Res ■ *Web:* www.blueshieldca.com					
BlueCross BlueShield of Western New York 257 W Genesee St	Buffalo	NY	14240	716-887-6900	887-7912
TF: 800-888-0757 ■ *Web:* bcbswny.com					
Capital District Physicians' Health Plan 500 Patroon Creek Blvd	Albany	NY	12206	518-641-3000	641-3507
TF: 888-258-0477 ■ *Web:* www.cdphp.com					
Capital Health Plan PO Box 15349	Tallahassee	FL	32317	850-383-3333	383-3339
TF: 800-390-1434 ■ *Web:* www.capitalhealth.com					
Capital Management Enterprises Inc 1111 W Dekalb Pk	Wayne	PA	19087	610-265-9600	
Web: www.cms-advisors.com					
CareFirst BlueCross BlueShield 10455 Mill Run Cir	Owings Mills	MD	21117	410-581-3000	
Web: www.carefirst.com					
Carelink Health Plans 500 Virginia St E Ste 400	Charleston	WV	25301	304-348-2900	348-2064
TF: 800-348-2922 ■ *Web:* coventryhealthcare.com					
Cdspi 155 Lesmill Rd	Toronto	ON	M3B2T8	416-296-9401	
TF: 800-561-9401 ■ *Web:* cdspi.com					
Centene Corp 7700 Forsyth Blvd	Saint Louis	MO	63105	314-725-4477	
NYSE: CNC ■ *TF General:* 800-293-0056 ■ *Web:* www.centene.com					
Chiropractic Health Plan of California PO Box 190	Clayton	CA	94517	310-210-5400	844-3124*
**Fax Area Code:* 925 ■ *TF:* 800-995-2442 ■ *Web:* www.chpc.com					
CIGNA Healthcare 900 Cottage Grove Rd	Hartford	CT	06152	860-226-6000	
TF: 800-433-5768 ■ *Web:* www.cigna.com/health					
CIGNA Healthcare of North Carolina Inc 701 Corporate Ctr Dr	Raleigh	NC	27607	919-854-7000	
TF: 800-942-1654 ■ *Web:* www.cigna.com					
Community Care 218 W Sixth St	Tulsa	OK	74119	918-594-5200	594-5209
TF: 800-278-7563 ■ *Web:* www.ccok.com					
CompBenefits Corp 100 Mansell Ct E Ste 400	Roswell	GA	30076	770-552-7101	998-6871*
**Fax:* Cust Svc ■ *TF:* 800-633-1262 ■ *Web:* www.compbenefits.com					
Comprehensive Health Services Inc (CHSI) 10701 Parkridge Blvd Ste 200	Reston	VA	20191	703-760-0700	760-0894
TF: 800-638-8083 ■ *Web:* www.chsmedical.com					
ConnectiCare Inc 175 Scott Swamp Rd	Farmington	CT	06032	860-674-5700	674-5728
TF Cust Svc: 800-251-7722 ■ *Web:* www.connecticare.com					
Coventry Health Care Inc 6705 Rockledge Dr Ste 900	Bethesda	MD	20817	301-581-0600	581-0600*
NYSE: CVH ■ **Fax:* Hum Res ■ *TF:* 866-667-3062 ■ *Web:* www.coventryhealthcare.com					
Coventry Health Care of Delaware Inc 750 Prides Crossing Ste 200	Newark	DE	19713	800-833-7423	
TF: 800-833-7423 ■ *Web:* coventryhealthcare.com					
Coventry Health Care of Georgia Inc 1100 Cir 75 Pkwy Ste 1400	Atlanta	GA	30339	678-202-2100	
TF: 800-470-2004 ■ *Web:* chcgeorgia.coventryhealthcare.com					
Coventry Health Care of Iowa Inc 4320 114th St	Urbandale	IA	50322	515-225-1234	
TF: 800-470-6352 ■ *Web:* chciowa.coventryhealthcare.com					
Coventry Health Care of Kansas Inc 8320 Ward Pkwy	Kansas City	MO	64114	800-969-3343	
TF: 800-969-3343 ■ *Web:* chckansas.coventryhealthcare.com					
Coventry Health Care of Louisiana Inc 1720 S Sykes Dr	Bismarck	ND	58504	800-341-6613	
TF Sales: 800-341-6613 ■ *Web:* chclouisiana.coventryhealthcare.com					
Coventry Health Care of Nebraska Inc 15950 W Dodge Rd Ste 100	Omaha	NE	68164	402-498-9030	
TF: 855-449-2889 ■ *Web:* chcnebraska.coventryhealthcare.com					
Dakotacare 2600 W 49th St PO Box 7406	Sioux Falls	SD	57117	605-334-4000	334-8717
TF: 800-325-5598 ■ *Web:* www.dakotacare.com					
Davis Vision Inc 711 Troy-Schenectady Rd	Latham	NY	12110	800-999-5431	328-4761*
**Fax Area Code:* 888 ■ **Fax:* Claims ■ *TF:* 800-999-5431 ■ *Web:* www.davisvision.com					
Dean Health Insurance Inc 1277 Deming Way	Madison	WI	53717	608-836-1400	827-4212
TF: 800-279-1301 ■ *Web:* www.deancare.com					
Delta Dental Insurance Company of Alaska PO Box 1809	Alpharetta	GA	30023	800-521-2651	
TF: 800-521-2651 ■ *Web:* www.deltadentalins.com					
Delta Dental of Arizona PO Box 43026	Phoenix	AZ	85080	800-352-6132	588-3636*
**Fax Area Code:* 602 ■ *TF:* 800-352-6132 ■ *Web:* www.deltadentalaz.com					
Delta Dental of Arkansas 1513 Country Club Rd PO Box 15965	Sherwood	AR	72120	501-835-3400	835-2733
TF: 800-462-5410 ■ *Web:* www.deltadentalar.com					
Delta Dental of Colorado 4582 S Ulster St Ste 800	Denver	CO	80237	303-741-9300	741-9338
TF: 800-233-0860 ■ *Web:* www.deltadentalco.com					
Delta Dental of Idaho 555 E Parkcenter Blvd PO Box 2870	Boise	ID	83706	208-489-3580	344-4649
TF: 800-356-7586 ■ *Web:* www.deltadentalid.com					
Delta Dental of Indiana PO Box 30416	Lansing	MI	48909	800-524-0149	
TF: 800-524-0149 ■ *Web:* www.deltadentalin.com					
Delta Dental of Iowa 9000 Northpark Dr Ste 13	Johnston	IA	50131	515-261-5500	
TF Cust Svc: 800-544-0718 ■ *Web:* www.deltadentalia.com					
Delta Dental of Kansas 1619 N Waterfront Pkwy PO Box 789769	Wichita	KS	67201	316-264-4511	462-3392
TF: 800-234-3375 ■ *Web:* www.deltadentalks.com					
Delta Dental of Kentucky 10100 Linn Stn Rd PO Box 242810	Louisville	KY	40223	800-955-2030	736-4823*
**Fax Area Code:* 502 ■ *TF Cust Svc:* 800-955-2030 ■ *Web:* www.deltadentalky.com					
Delta Dental of Louisiana PO Box 1803	Alpharetta	GA	30023	800-422-4234	
TF: 800-422-4234 ■ *Web:* www.deltadentalins.com					
Delta Dental of Maryland 1 Delta Dr	Mechanicsburg	PA	17055	717-766-8500	
TF: 800-932-0783 ■ *Web:* www.deltadentalins.com					
Delta Dental of Massachusetts 465 Medford St	Boston	MA	02129	617-886-1000	886-1199
TF Cust Svc: 800-872-0500 ■ *Web:* www.deltadentalma.com					
Delta Dental of Michigan PO Box 30416	Lansing	MI	48909	800-524-0149	
TF: 800-524-0149 ■ *Web:* www.deltadentalmi.com					
Delta Dental of Minnesota PO Box 330	Minneapolis	MN	55440	651-406-5900	
TF: 800-553-9536 ■ *Web:* www.deltadentalmn.org					
Delta Dental of Missouri 12399 Gravois Rd Ste 2	Saint Louis	MO	63127	314-656-3000	656-2900
TF: 800-392-1167 ■ *Web:* www.deltadentalmo.com					
Delta Dental of Montana PO Box 1803	Alpharetta	GA	30023	800-422-4234	
TF: 800-422-4234 ■ *Web:* www.deltadentalins.com					
Delta Dental of New Jersey 1639 State Rt 10	Parsippany	NJ	07054	973-285-4000	285-4141
TF: 800-624-2633 ■ *Web:* deltadentalnj.com					
Delta Dental of New Jersey Inc PO Box 222	Parsippany	NJ	07054	800-452-9310	285-4141*
**Fax Area Code:* 973 ■ *TF:* 800-452-9310 ■ *Web:* deltadentalnj.com					
Delta Dental of New Mexico 2500 Louisiana Blvd NE Ste 600	Albuquerque	NM	87110	505-883-4777	883-7444
TF: 800-999-0963 ■ *Web:* www.deltadentalnm.com					
Delta Dental of New York 1 Delta Dr	Mechanicsburg	PA	17055	717-766-8500	
TF: 800-932-0783 ■ *Web:* www.deltadentalins.com					
Delta Dental of Ohio PO Box 30416	Lansing	MI	48909	800-524-0149	
TF: 800-524-0149 ■ *Web:* www.deltadentaloh.com					
Delta Dental of Oklahoma 16 NW 63rd St Ste 201	Oklahoma City	OK	73116	405-607-2100	607-2190
TF: 800-522-0188 ■ *Web:* www.deltadentalok.org					
Delta Dental of Pennsylvania 1 Delta Dr	Mechanicsburg	PA	17055	800-932-0783	
TF: 800-932-0783 ■ *Web:* www.deltadentalins.com					
Delta Dental of Rhode Island 10 Charles St	Providence	RI	02904	401-752-6000	752-6060*
**Fax:* Cust Svc ■ *TF:* 800-598-6684 ■ *Web:* www.deltadentalri.com					
Delta Dental of South Dakota 720 N Euclid Ave PO Box 1157	Pierre	SD	57501	605-224-7345	224-0909
TF: 800-627-3961 ■ *Web:* www.deltadentalsd.com					
Delta Dental of Tennessee 240 Venture Cir	Nashville	TN	37228	615-255-3175	244-8108
TF Cust Svc: 800-223-3104 ■ *Web:* www.deltadentaltn.com					
Delta Dental of Virginia 4818 Starkey Rd	Roanoke	VA	24014	540-989-8000	725-3890
TF: 800-367-3531 ■ *Web:* www.deltadentalva.com					
Delta Dental of West Virginia 1 Delta Dr	Mechanicsburg	PA	17055	717-766-8500	
TF: 800-932-0783 ■ *Web:* www.deltadentalins.com					
Delta Dental of Wisconsin 2801 Hoover Rd PO Box 828	Stevens Point	WI	54481	715-344-6087	344-9058
TF: 800-236-3713 ■ *Web:* www.deltadentalwi.com					
Delta Dental of Wyoming 6234 Yellowstone Rd PO Box 29	Cheyenne	WY	82009	307-632-3313	632-7309
TF: 800-735-3379 ■ *Web:* www.deltadentalwy.org					
Delta Dental Plan of North Carolina 343 E Six Forks Rd Ste 180	Raleigh	NC	27609	919-832-6015	832-6549
TF: 800-662-8856					
EmblemHealth Co 55 Water St	New York	NY	10041	646-447-5000	
TF: 800-447-8255 ■ *Web:* www.emblemhealth.com					
Excellus BlueCross BlueShield PO Box 22999	Rochester	NY	14692	585-454-1700	
TF: 800-278-1247 ■ *Web:* www.excellusbcbs.com					

	Phone	Fax

Excellus BlueCross BlueShield of Central New York
333 Butternut Dr Syracuse NY 13214 315-671-6400 671-6752*
*Fax: Cust Svc ■ TF: 800-633-6066 ■ Web: www.excellusbcbs.com

EyeMed Vision Care 4000 Luxottica Pl Mason OH 45040 513-765-4321 765-6050
TF: 800-521-3605 ■ Web: portal.eyemedvisioncare.com

Fallon Community Health Plan Inc
10 Chestnut St Ste 7 Worcester MA 01608 508-799-2100 797-9621
TF: 800-333-2535 ■ Web: www.fchp.org

First Choice Health Plan
600 University St Ste 1400 Seattle WA 98101 800-467-5281 667-8062*
*Fax Area Code: 206 ■ *Fax: Cust Svc ■ TF: 800-467-5281 ■ Web: www.fchn.com

First Priority Health 19 N Main St Wilkes-Barre PA 18711 800-822-8753
TF: 800-822-8753 ■ Web: www.bcnepa.com

Foster Thomas Inc 1788 Forest Dr Annapolis MD 21401 800-372-3626
TF: 800-372-3626 ■ Web: www.fosterthomas.com

Geisinger Health Plan 100 N Academy Ave Danville PA 17822 570-271-8760 271-7218
TF: 800-447-4000 ■ Web: www.thehealthplan.com

Great American Supplemental Benefits
PO Box 26580 Austin TX 78755 866-459-4272
TF: 866-459-4272 ■ Web: www.cigna.com

Group Health Co-op 320 Westlake Ave N Ste 100 Seattle WA 98109 206-448-5600 448-2137
TF: 888-901-4636 ■ Web: www.ghc.org

Hanover Insurance Co 440 Lincoln St Worcester MA 01653 508-855-1000 855-6313
TF: 800-853-0456 ■ Web: www.hanover.com

Harvard Pilgrim Health Care Inc
93 Worcester St Wellesley MA 02481 617-509-1000 509-2515
TF: 888-888-4742 ■ Web: www.harvardpilgrim.org

Hawaii Dental Service 700 Bishop St Ste 700 Honolulu HI 96813 808-521-1431 529-9368
TF: 800-232-2533 ■ Web: www.hawaiidentalservice.com

Hawaii Medical Service Assn
818 Keeaumoku St Honolulu HI 96822 808-948-6111 948-5567*
*Fax: Cust Svc ■ TF: 800-776-4672 ■ Web: www.hmsa.com

Health Alliance Plan 2850 W Grand Blvd Detroit MI 48202 313-872-8100 664-5866*
*Fax: Hum Res ■ TF: 800-422-4641 ■ Web: www.hap.org

Health Net Inc 21650 Oxnard St Woodland Hills CA 91367 818-676-6000
NYSE: HNT ■ TF: 800-848-4747 ■ Web: www.healthnet.com

Health Plan of Nevada Inc PO Box 15645 Las Vegas NV 89114 702-242-7716
Web: www.healthplanofnevada.com

Health Tradition Health Plan 1808 E Main St Onalaska WI 54650 608-781-9692
TF: 800-545-8499 ■ Web: www.healthtradition.com

HealthAmerica Pennsylvania Inc
3721 Tecport Dr PO Box 67103 Harrisburg PA 17111 800-788-6445
TF: 800-788-6445 ■ Web: healthamerica.coventryhealthcare.com

HealthCare USA 10 S Broadway Ste 1200 Saint Louis MO 63102 314-241-5300
TF: 800-213-7792 ■ Web: coventryhealthcare.com

HealthPartners Inc PO Box 1309 Minneapolis MN 55440 952-883-5000
TF: 800-883-2177 ■ Web: www.healthpartners.com

Healthplex Inc 333 Earl Ovington Blvd Uniondale NY 11553 516-542-2200 794-3186
TF Cust Svc: 800-468-0608 ■ Web: www.healthplex.com

HealthPlus of Michigan 2050 S Linden Rd Flint MI 48532 810-230-2000
TF: 800-332-9161 ■ Web: www.healthplus.org

Heritage Summit HealthCare of Florida Inc
PO Box 2928 Lakeland FL 33806 863-665-6629 665-5177
TF: 800-282-7644 ■ Web: www.summitholdings.com

Highmark Inc 120 Fifth Ave Pl Pittsburgh PA 15222 412-544-7000 302-7182*
*Fax Area Code: 717 ■ *Fax: Hum Res ■ TF: 800-992-0246 ■ Web: www.highmark.com

Humana Inc 500 W Main St Louisville KY 40202 502-580-1000
NYSE: HUM ■ TF: 800-486-2620 ■ Web: www.humana.com

Humana Military Healthcare Services
500 W Main St Louisville KY 40201 800-444-5445
TF General: 800-444-5445 ■ Web: www.humana-military.com

Independence Blue Cross 1901 Market St Philadelphia PA 19103 800-275-2583 241-0403*
*Fax Area Code: 215 ■ *Fax: Hum Res ■ TF: 800-275-2583 ■ Web: www.ibx.com

Independent Health 511 Farber Lakes Dr Buffalo NY 14221 716-631-3001 635-3838*
*Fax: Hum Res ■ TF: 800-247-1466 ■ Web: www.independenthealth.com

IOA Re Inc 190 W Germantown Pk Ste 200 East Norriton PA 19401 610-940-9000
TF: 800-462-2300 ■ Web: www.ioare.com

Kaiser Foundation Health Plan Inc
1 Kaiser Plz Oakland CA 94612 408-972-3000 271-6493*
*Fax Area Code: 510 ■ TF: 800-464-4000 ■ Web: kaiserpermanente.org

Kaiser Permanente
3495 Piedmont Rd NE Piedmont Ctr Bldg 9 Atlanta GA 30305 404-364-7000
TF: 800-611-1811 ■ Web: medicare.kaiserpermanente.org

Kaiser Permanente 280 W MacArthur Blvd Oakland CA 94611 510-752-1000
TF: 800-464-4000 ■ Web: healthy.kaiserpermanente.org

Kaiser Permanente Colorado Denver/Boulder
2500 S Havanna Aurora CO 80014 303-338-4545
Web: www.kaiserpermanente.org

Kaiser Permanente Hawaii 711 Kapiolani Blvd Honolulu HI 96813 808-432-0000 432-5070
TF: 800-966-5955 ■ Web: kaiserpermanente.org

Kaiser Permanente Northwest
500 NE Multnomah St Ste 100 Portland OR 97232 503-813-2000
TF: 800-813-2000 ■ Web: healthy.kaiserpermanente.org

LA Care Health Plan
555 W Fifth St 29th Fl Los Angeles CA 90013 213-694-1250
TF: 888-839-9909 ■ Web: www.lacare.org

Lexington Veteran Affairs Medical Center
1101 Veterans Dr Lexington KY 40502 859-233-4511
TF: 877-222-8387 ■ Web: lexington.va.gov

Markel American Insurance Co
N14 W23800 Stone Ridge Dr Waukesha WI 53188 262-548-9880
Web: www.markelinsuresfun.com

MEDICA 401 Carlson Pkwy Minnetonka MN 55305 952-992-2900 992-3700*
*Fax: Sales ■ TF Cust Svc: 800-952-3455 ■ Web: www.medica.com

Medical Benefits Mutual Life Insurance Co
1975 Tamarack Rd Newark OH 43058 740-522-8425
TF: 800-423-3151 ■ Web: www.medben.com

Medical Mutual of Ohio 2060 E Ninth St Cleveland OH 44115 216-687-7000 687-6585*
*Fax: Hum Res ■ TF: 800-700-2583 ■ Web: www.medmutual.com

Memorial Health Partners 4700 Waters Ave Savannah GA 31404 912-350-8000 350-5976
TF: 800-537-0690 ■ Web: www.memorialhealth.com

MetLife Inc 200 Pk Ave New York NY 10166 212-578-2211 578-3320
NYSE: MET ■ TF: 800-638-5433 ■ Web: global.metlife.com

Molina Healthcare Inc
200 Oceangate Ste 100 Long Beach CA 90802 562-435-3666 437-7235
NYSE: MOH ■ TF: 888-562-5442 ■
Web: www.molinahealthcare.com/en-us/pages/home.aspx?cookiecheck=true

MVP Health Care 625 State St Schenectady NY 12305 518-370-4793 370-0830*
*Fax: Hum Res ■ TF: 800-777-4793 ■ Web: www.mvphealthcare.com

ODS Cos 601 SW Second Ave Portland OR 97204 503-228-6554 521-7898*
*Fax Area Code: 804 ■ TF: 888-221-0802 ■ Web: ods-security.com/about-ods

Optima Health 4417 Corporation Ln Virginia Beach VA 23462 757-552-7174 552-8919
Web: www.optimahealth.com

Oxford Health Plans LLC 48 Monroe Tpke Trumbull CT 06611 203-459-9100 459-6464
TF: 800-444-6222 ■ Web: www.oxhp.com

Oxford Health Plans (NJ) Inc
111 Wood Ave S Ste 2 Iselin NJ 08830 732-623-1000
TF: 800-201-6920 ■ Web: www.oxhp.com

Pacificare of Texas 6200 NW Pkwy San Antonio TX 78249 210-474-5000
TF: 800-624-7272 ■ Web: uhcwest.com

Paramount Health Care 1901 Indian Wood Cir Maumee OH 43537 419-887-2525
TF: 800-462-3589 ■ Web: www.paramounthealthcare.com

Physicians Plus Insurance Corp
2650 Novation Pkwy Ste 200 Madison WI 53713 608-282-8900
TF: 800-545-5015 ■ Web: www.pplusic.com

Preferred CommunityChoice PPO 218 W Sixth St Tulsa OK 74119 918-594-5200
TF: 800-884-4776 ■ Web: www.ccok.com

Preferred Health Systems Inc
8535 E 21st St N Wichita KS 67206 316-609-2345 609-2346
TF: 800-990-0345 ■ Web: chckansas.coventryhealthcare.com

Premera Blue Cross
7001 220th St SW Mountlake Terrace WA 98043 425-918-4000
TF Cust Svc: 800-722-1471 ■ Web: www.premera.com

Premera Blue Cross Blue Shield of Alaska
2550 Denali St Ste 1404 Anchorage AK 99503 907-258-5065
TF Cust Svc: 800-508-4722 ■ Web: premera.com

Prescription Corp of America
66 Ford Rd Ste 230 Denville NJ 07834 973-983-6300

Priority Health 1231 E Beltline NE Grand Rapids MI 49525 616-942-0954 942-0145
TF: 800-942-0954 ■ Web: www.priorityhealth.com

Regence Blue Cross Blue Shield of Oregon
PO Box 1071 Portland OR 97207 888-675-6570
TF: 888-734-3623 ■ Web: www.regence.com

Regence BlueCross BlueShield of Utah
2890 E Cottonwood Pkwy Salt Lake City UT 84121 801-333-2100 333-6516*
*Fax: Hum Res ■ TF Cust Svc: 800-624-6519 ■ Web: www.regence.com

Rocky Mountain Health Plans
2775 Crossroads Blvd PO Box 10600 Grand Junction CO 81502 970-244-7760 244-7880
TF: 800-843-0719 ■ Web: www.rmhp.org

SafeGuard Health Enterprises Inc
95 Enterprise Ste 100 Aliso Viejo CA 92656 949-425-4300 425-4586
TF: 800-880-1800 ■ Web: www.metlife.com

Sagamore Health Network
11555 N Meridian St Ste 400 Carmel IN 46032 317-573-2886
TF: 800-364-3469 ■ Web: www.sagamorehn.com

Scott & White Health Plan 2401 S 31st St Temple TX 76508 254-298-3000
TF: 800-321-7947 ■ Web: www.sw.org

Sharp Health Plan
4305 University Ave Ste 200 San Diego CA 92105 619-228-2300
TF: 800-359-2002 ■ Web: www.sharphealthplan.com

Sierra Military Health Services Inc
111 Market Pl Ste 410 Baltimore MD 21202 410-547-9040

Spectera Inc
6220 Old Dobbin Ln Liberty 6, Ste 200 Columbia MD 21045 410-265-6033 265-6260
TF: 800-638-3120 ■ Web: www.spectera.com

Trillium Community Health Plan Inc
1800 Millrace Dr Eugene OR 97403 541-431-1950
TF: 800-910-3906 ■ Web: trilliumchp.com

Tufts Associated Health Plans
705 Mt Auburn St Watertown MA 02472 617-972-9400 972-9409
TF: 800-462-0224 ■ Web: www.tuftshealthplan.com

Union Pacific Railroad Employees' Health Systems
1040 North 2200 West Salt Lake City UT 84116 801-595-4300 595-4399
TF: 800-547-0421 ■ Web: www.uphealth.com

UnitedHealth Group Inc 9900 Bren Rd E Minnetonka MN 55343 952-936-1300
NYSE: UNH ■ TF: 800-328-5979 ■ Web: www.unitedhealthgroup.com

Unity Health Insurance 840 Carolina St Sauk City WI 53583 608-643-2491 643-2564
TF: 800-362-3308 ■ Web: www.unityhealth.com

Univera Healthcare 205 Pk Club Ln Buffalo NY 14221 716-847-1480 956-2397*
*Fax Area Code: 800 ■ *Fax: Hum Res ■ TF: 877-883-9577 ■ Web: www.univerahealthcare.com

Universal Care Inc 1600 E Hill St Signal Hill CA 90755 562-424-6200

Va Premier Health Plan Inc
625 Piney Forest Rd Danville VA 24540 434-799-4623
Web: vapremier.com

Voya Services Co 230 Park Ave New York NY 10169 860-580-4646
TF: 855-663-8692 ■ Web: www.voya.com

Washington Dental Service 9706 Fourth Ave NE Seattle WA 98115 206-522-1300 525-2330
TF: 800-367-4104 ■ Web: www.deltadentalwa.com

WellCare Group Inc 8735 Henderson Rd Tampa FL 33634 813-290-6200
TF: 866-765-4385 ■ Web: www.wellcare.com

WellCare Health Plans Inc PO Box 31372 Tampa FL 33631 866-530-9491
TF: 866-530-9491 ■ Web: www.wellcare.com/healthplans/newyork/home.aspx

391-4 Property & Casualty Insurance

	Phone	Fax

Acceptance Insurance Cos Inc
300 W Broadway Ste 1600 Council Bluffs IA 51503 712-329-3600
Web: www.aicins.com

Access Management Group
1100 Northmeadow Pkwy Ste 114 Roswell GA 30076 770-777-6890
Web: www.accessmgt.com

Accident Fund Co
232 S Capitol Ave PO Box 40790 Lansing MI 48901 517-342-4200
TF Mktg: 888-276-0327 ■ Web: www.accidentfund.com

Phone *Fax*

ACE USA 436 Walnut St PO Box 1000 ... Philadelphia PA 19106 215-640-1000 640-2489
TF: 866-357-3797 ■ *Web:* www.acegroup.com

Acuity Insurance 2800 S Taylor Dr ... Sheboygan WI 53081 920-458-9131 458-1618
Web: www.acuity.com

Addison Insurance Co
118 Second Ave SE PO Box 73909 ... Cedar Rapids IA 52401 319-399-5700 399-5499
TF: 800-332-7977 ■ *Web:* www.unitedfiregroup.com

Aegis Security Inc PO Box 3153 ... Harrisburg PA 17105 717-657-9671 657-0340
TF: 800-233-2160 ■ *Web:* www.aegisfirst.com

Agricultural Workers Mutual Auto Insurance Co
PO Box 88 ... Fort Worth TX 76101 817-831-9900 831-7565
TF: 800-772-7424 ■ *Web:* www.agworkers.com

ALLIED Group Inc 1100 Locust St ... Des Moines IA 50391 515-508-4211
TF: 800-532-1436 ■ *Web:* www.alliedinsurance.com

Allied Insurance 1100 Locust St ... Des Moines CA 50391 800-532-1436
TF: 800-532-1436 ■ *Web:* www.alliedinsurance.com

American Agricultural Insurance Co
1501 E Woodfield Rd Ste 300 W ... Schaumburg IL 60173 847-969-2900 969-2752
Web: www.aaic.com

American Commerce Insurance Co
3590 Twin Creeks Dr ... Columbus OH 43204 614-308-3366 308-3365
TF: 800-848-2945 ■ *Web:* www.mapfreinsurance.com

American Family Mutual Insurance Co
6000 American Pkwy ... Madison WI 53783 608-249-2111
TF Cust Svc: 800-374-0008 ■ *Web:* www.amfam.com

American Modern Home Insurance Co
PO Box 5323 ... Cincinnati OH 45201 513-943-7200
TF: 800-543-2644 ■ *Web:* www.amig.com

American National Property & Casualty Co
1949 E Sunshine St ... Springfield MO 65899 417-887-0220 887-1801*
**Fax:* Hum Res ■ *TF:* 800-333-2860 ■ *Web:* www.anpac.com

American Road Insurance Co, The
1 American Rd ... Dearborn MI 48126 313-845-5850 337-9955

American Southern Insurance Co
3715 Northside Pkwy NW Bldg 400 Ste 800 ... Atlanta GA 30327 404-266-9599 266-8327
TF: 800-241-1172 ■ *Web:* www.amsou.com

AMERISAFE Inc 2301 Hwy 190 W ... DeRidder LA 70634 337-463-9052
NASDAQ: AMSF ■ *TF:* 800-256-9052 ■ *Web:* www.amerisafe.com

Amerisure Insurance Co
26777 Halsted Rd Ste 200 ... Farmington Hills MI 48331 248-615-9000 615-8548
TF: 800-257-1900 ■ *Web:* www.amerisure.com

Amica Mutual Insurance Co 100 Amica Way ... Lincoln RI 02865 800-652-6422
TF: 800-652-6422 ■ *Web:* www.amica.com

Arbella Mutual Insurance Co
1100 Crown Colony Dr ... Quincy MA 02169 617-328-2800 328-2970
TF: 800-972-5348 ■ *Web:* www.arbella.com

Arizona Farm Bureau Federation
325 S Higley Rd ... Higley AZ 85296 480-635-3600
Web: www.azfb.org

Armed Forces Insurance Exchange (AFI)
PO Box G ... Fort Leavenworth KS 66027 800-255-6792
TF: 800-255-0187 ■ *Web:* www.afi.org

Armour Risk Management Inc
1880 JFK Blvd Ste 801 ... Philadelphia PA 19103 215-665-5000
Web: www.armourholdings.com

Arrowpoint Capital
Whitehall Corporate Ctr Ste 3
3600 Arco Corporate Dr ... Charlotte NC 28273 704-522-2000
TF: 866-236-7750 ■ *Web:* www.arrowpointcap.com

Associated Industries Of Massachusetts Mutual Insurance Com
PO Box 4070 ... Burlington MA 01803 781-221-1600 270-5599
TF: 866-270-3354 ■ *Web:* www.aimmutual.com

AssuranceAmerica Corp 5500 I- N Pkwy Ste 600 ... Atlanta GA 30328 770-952-0200 952-0258
TF: 800-450-7857 ■ *Web:* www.assuranceamerica.com

Auto-Owners Insurance Co 6101 Anacapri Blvd ... Lansing MI 48917 517-323-1200 323-8796
TF: 800-346-0346 ■ *Web:* www.auto-owners.com

Avemco Insurance Co 411 Aviation Way ... Frederick MD 21701 301-694-5700
TF: 800-874-9125 ■ *Web:* avemco.com

Baldwin & Lyons Inc
111 Congressional Blvd Ste 500 ... Carmel IN 46032 317-636-9800 632-9444
NASDAQ: BWINB ■ *TF:* 800-644-5501 ■ *Web:* www.baldwinandlyons.com

Berkshire Hathaway Group (BHG) 3024 Harney St ... Omaha NE 68131 402-536-3100 298-1915*
**Fax Area Code:* 212 ■ *TF:* 800-223-2064 ■ *Web:* berkshirehathaway.com

Berkshire Hathaway Homestates Cos (BHHC)
PO Box 2048 ... Omaha NE 68103 888-495-8949
TF: 888-495-8949 ■ *Web:* www.bhhc.com

Bituminous Insurance Cos 320 18th St ... Rock Island IL 61201 800-475-4477 786-3847*
**Fax Area Code:* 309 ■ *TF:* 800-475-4477 ■ *Web:* www.bitco.com

Brotherhood Mutual Insurance Co (BMI)
6400 Brotherhood Way PO Box 2589 ... Fort Wayne IN 46825 800-333-3735
TF Cust Svc: 800-333-3735 ■ *Web:* www.brotherhoodmutual.com

Brown & Brown Insurance PO Box 1718 ... Tacoma WA 98401 253-396-5500 396-4500
TF: 800-562-8171 ■ *Web:* www.bbtacoma.com

C Na Insurance 100 Centerview Dr ... Nashville TN 37214 615-871-1400 886-1883

California Casualty Insurance Group
1900 Alameda De Las Pulgas ... San Mateo CA 94403 650-574-4000
TF: 866-680-5143 ■ *Web:* www.calcas.com

Canada Life Assurance Co, The
330 University Ave ... Toronto ON M5G1R8 416-597-1456
TF: 888-252-1847 ■ *Web:* www.canadalife.com

Canal Insurance Co
400 E Stone Ave PO Box 7 ... Greenville SC 29601 800-452-6911 232-5707*
**Fax Area Code:* 864 ■ *TF:* 800-452-6911 ■ *Web:* canalinsurance.com

Capitol Indemnity Corp 1600 Aspen Commons ... Middleton WI 53562 608-829-4200 829-7408
TF: 800-475-4450 ■ *Web:* www.capspecialty.com

Capitol Insurance Cos
1600 Aspen Commons PO Box 5900 ... Middleton WI 53562 608-829-4200 829-7408
TF: 800-475-4450 ■ *Web:* www.capspecialty.com

Carolina Casualty Insurance Co
5011 Gate Pkwy Ste 200 ... Jacksonville FL 32256 904-363-0900 363-8098
TF: 800-874-8053 ■ *Web:* www.carolinacas.com

Central Insurance Cos 800 S Washington St ... Van Wert OH 45891 419-238-1010 238-7626*
**Fax:* Claims ■ *TF:* 800-736-7000 ■ *Web:* www.central-insurance.com

Phone *Fax*

Century-National Insurance Co
12200 Sylvan St PO Box 3999 ... North Hollywood CA 91606 818-760-0880
TF Cust Svc: 800-894-8384 ■ *Web:* www.centurynational.com

Chubb & Son 15 Mountain View Rd ... Warren NJ 07059 908-903-2000 903-2027
TF: 800-252-4670 ■ *Web:* www.chubb.com

Chubb Group of Insurance Cos 15 Mtn View Rd ... Warren NJ 07059 908-903-2000 903-2027
Web: www.chubb.com

Church Mutual Insurance Co 3000 Schuster Ln ... Merrill WI 54452 715-536-5577 539-4650
TF: 800-554-2642 ■ *Web:* www.churchmutual.com

Cincinnati Insurance Co 6200 S Gilmore Rd ... Fairfield OH 45014 513-870-2000
Web: cinfin.com

Civil Service Employees Insurance Co
2121 N California Blvd Ste 989 ... Walnut Creek CA 94596 800-282-6848
TF: 800-282-6848 ■ *Web:* www.cseinsurance.com

Colorado Farm Bureau Mutual Insurance Co
PO Box 5647 ... Denver CO 80217 303-749-7500 660-1694
TF: 800-315-5998 ■ *Web:* www.cfbmic.com

Commerce Insurance Co 211 Main St ... Webster MA 01570 508-943-9000 949-4921
TF: 800-221-1605 ■ *Web:* www.commerceinsurance.com

Community Assn Underwriters of America (CAU)
2 Caufield Pl ... Newtown PA 18940 267-757-7100 757-7410
Web: www.cauinsure.com

Concord Group Insurance Cos 4 Bouton St ... Concord NH 03301 800-852-3380
TF: 800-852-3380 ■ *Web:* www.concordgroupinsurance.com

Continental Casualty Co 333 S Wabash Ave ... Chicago IL 60685 312-822-5000 822-6419
TF: 800-262-2000 ■ *Web:* www.cna.com

Continental Western Group
11201 Douglas Ave ... Urbandale IA 50322 515-473-3000 473-3015*
**Fax:* Hum Res ■ *TF:* 800-235-2942 ■ *Web:* www.cwgins.com

Cornhusker Casualty Co PO Box 2048 ... Omaha NE 68103 888-495-8949
TF: 888-495-8949 ■ *Web:* www.bhhc.com

Country Mutual Insurance Co
1701 Towanda Ave ... Bloomington IL 61701 309-821-3000 821-5160
TF Cust Svc: 888-211-2555 ■ *Web:* www.countryfinancial.com

Crum & Forster Insurance Inc
305 Madison Ave PO Box 1973 ... Morristown NJ 07962 973-490-6600 490-6600*
**Fax:* Hum Res ■ *TF:* 800-690-5520 ■ *Web:* www.cfins.com

Cumberland Insurance Group 633 Shiloh Pike ... Bridgeton NJ 08302 800-232-6992 451-7564*
**Fax Area Code:* 856 ■ *TF:* 800-232-6992 ■ *Web:* www.cumberlandgroup.com

Cumberland Mutual Fire Insurance Co
633 Shiloh Pk ... Bridgeton NJ 08302 800-232-6992 451-7564*
**Fax Area Code:* 856 ■ *TF:* 800-232-6992 ■ *Web:* www.cumberlandgroup.com

Dairyland Insurance Co 1800 N Pt Dr ... Stevens Point WI 54481 715-346-6000 999-4642*
**Fax Area Code:* 800 ■ **Fax:* Sales ■ *TF Sales:* 866-445-5364 ■ *Web:* www.sentry.com

Donegal Mutual Insurance Co
1195 River Rd PO Box 302 ... Marietta PA 17547 717-426-1931 426-7009
TF: 800-877-0600 ■ *Web:* www.donegalgroup.com

Dorinco Reinsurance Co 1320 Waldo Ave ... Midland MI 48642 989-636-0047 638-9963
Web: www.dorinco.com

Economical Insurance Group, The
111 Westmount Rd S PO Box 2000 ... Waterloo ON N2J4S4 519-570-8200 570-8389
TF: 800-265-2180 ■ *Web:* www.economicalinsurance.com

Endurance Reinsurance Corp of America
750 Third Ave Fl 18 & 19 ... New York NY 10017 212-471-2800 471-1748
TF: 888-221-3894 ■ *Web:* endurance.bm

Erie Indemnity Co
Erie Insurance Group 100 Erie Insurance Pl ... Erie PA 16530 814-870-2000 870-3126*
NASDAQ: ERIE ■ **Fax:* Mail Rm ■ *TF:* 800-458-0811 ■ *Web:* www.erieinsurance.com

Erie Insurance Exchange 100 Erie Insurance Pl ... Erie PA 16530 814-870-2000 870-3126
TF: 800-458-0811 ■ *Web:* www.erieinsurance.com

Erie Insurance Property & Casualty Co
100 Erie Insurance Pl ... Erie PA 16530 814-870-2000
TF: 800-458-0811 ■ *Web:* www.erieinsurance.com

Everest Reinsurance Co
477 Martinsville Rd ... Liberty Corner NJ 07938 908-604-3000 604-3322
TF: 800-269-6660 ■ *Web:* www.everestregroup.com

Farm Family Casualty Insurance Co PO Box 656 ... Albany NY 12201 518-431-5000
TF: 800-843-3276 ■ *Web:* www.farmfamily.com

Farmers Alliance Mutual Insurance Co
1122 N Main PO Box 1401 ... McPherson KS 67460 620-241-2200 241-5482
TF: 800-362-1075 ■ *Web:* www.fami.com

Farmers Insurance Exchange
4680 Wilshire Blvd ... Los Angeles CA 90010 323-932-3200 217-1389*
**Fax Area Code:* 877 ■ **Fax:* Hum Res ■ *TF:* 855-808-6599 ■ *Web:* www.farmers.com

Farmers Mutual Hail Insurance Company of Iowa
6785 Westown Pkwy ... West Des Moines IA 50266 515-282-9104 282-1220
TF: 800-247-5248 ■ *Web:* www.fmh.com

Farmers Mutual Insurance Company of Nebraska
1220 Lincoln Mall ... Lincoln NE 68508 402-434-8300
TF: 800-742-7433 ■ *Web:* www.fmne.com

FCCI Insurance Group 6300 University Pkwy ... Sarasota FL 34232 941-907-3224
TF: 800-226-3224 ■ *Web:* www.fcci-group.com

Federated Mutual Insurance Co
121 E Pk Sq PO Box 328 ... Owatonna MN 55060 507-455-5200
TF: 800-533-0472 ■ *Web:* federatedinsurance.com

FEDUSA 13256 66th St N Ste 35 ... Largo FL 33773 727-535-5671 610-1947*
**Fax Area Code:* 866 ■ *Web:* www.directgeneral.com/fed-us-insurance

Fhm Insurance Co
4601 Touchton Rd E Bldg 300 Ste 3150 ... Jacksonville FL 32246 904-724-9890 926-9419*
**Fax Area Code:* 407 ■ *TF:* 800-393-0001 ■ *Web:* www.fhmic.com

Fireman's Fund Insurance Co
1465 N McDowell Blvd ... Petaluma CA 94954 866-386-3932
TF: 866-386-3932 ■ *Web:* www.firemansfund.com

First Insurance Company of Hawaii Ltd
1100 Ward Ave PO Box 2866 ... Honolulu HI 96803 808-527-7777 527-3200
TF: 800-272-5202 ■ *Web:* www.ficoh.com

Florida Family Insurance Services LLC
27599 Riverview Ctr Blvd Ste 100
PO Box 136001 ... Bonita Springs FL 34136 239-495-4700 948-7381
TF: 888-850-4663 ■ *Web:* www.floridafamily.com

Florida Farm Bureau Casualty Insurance Co
5700 SW 34th St ... Gainesville FL 32608 352-378-1321 374-1577
Web: floridafarmbureau.com

Phone Fax

Florida Farm Bureau General Insurance Co
5700 SW 34th St .... Gainesville FL 32608 352-378-1321 374-1577
Web: floridafarmbureau.com

Florida Farm Bureau Insurance Cos
5700 SW 34th St .... Gainesville FL 32608 352-378-1321 374-1577
TF: 866-275-7322 ■ *Web:* floridafarmbureau.com

FM Global 270 Central Ave PO Box 7500 .... Johnston RI 02919 401-275-3000 275-3029
TF: 800-343-7722 ■ *Web:* www.fmglobal.com

Foremost Insurance Co 5600 Beech Tree Ln .... Caledonia MI 49316 800-532-4221
TF: 800-532-4221 ■ *Web:* www.foremost.com

Frankenmuth Insurance 1 Mutual Ave .... Frankenmuth MI 48787 989-652-6121 652-3588
TF: 800-234-4433 ■ *Web:* www.fmins.com

Franklin Mutual Insurance Co 5 Broad St .... Branchville NJ 07826 973-948-3120 948-7190
TF: 800-842-0551 ■ *Web:* www.fmiweb.com

GAINSCO County Mutual Insurance Co
PO Box 199023 .... Dallas TX 75219 972-629-4301
Web: gainsco.com

General Star National Insurance Co
695 E Main St Financial Ctr .... Stamford CT 06901 203-328-5000 328-6423
TF: 800-624-5237 ■ *Web:* www.generalstar.com

Germania Farm Mutual Insurance Assn
507 Hwy 290 E .... Brenham TX 77833 979-836-5224 836-1977
TF: 800-392-2202 ■ *Web:* www.germania-ins.com

Golden Eagle Insurance Corp 525 B St .... San Diego CA 92101 610-832-8240
TF: 888-398-8924 ■ *Web:* libertymutualgroup.com/business

Grain Dealers Mutual Insurance Co
6201 Corporate Dr .... Indianapolis IN 46278 317-388-4500 295-9434
TF: 800-428-7081 ■ *Web:* www.graindealers.com

Grange Mutual Casualty Co 671 S High St .... Columbus OH 43206 800-422-0550
TF: 800-422-0550 ■ *Web:* grangeinsurance.com

Great American Insurance Co 580 Walnut St .... Cincinnati OH 45202 513-369-5000
Web: www.greatamericaninsurancegroup.com

Great Northern Insurance Co 15 Mtn View Rd .... Warren NJ 07059 908-903-2000 903-2027
TF Cust Svc: 800-252-4670 ■ *Web:* www.chubb.com

Great West Casualty Co
1100 W 29th St PO Box 277 .... South Sioux City NE 68776 402-494-2411
TF: 800-228-8602 ■ *Web:* gwccnet.com

Grinnell Mutual Reinsurance Co
4215 Hwy 146 PO Box 790 .... Grinnell IA 50112 641-269-8000 236-2840
TF: 800-362-2041 ■ *Web:* grinnellmutual.com

GuideOne Mutual Insurance Co
1111 Ashworth Rd .... West Des Moines IA 50265 515-267-5000 267-5530*
**Fax:* Hum Res ■ *TF:* 877-448-4331 ■ *Web:* www.guideone.com

Hagerty Insurance Agency LLC
141 River's Edge Dr Ste 200
PO Box 1303 .... Traverse City MI 49684 231-947-6868 941-8227
TF: 877-922-9701 ■ *Web:* www.hagerty.com

Hanover Insurance Co 440 Lincoln St .... Worcester MA 01653 508-855-1000 855-6313
TF: 800-853-0456 ■ *Web:* www.hanover.com

Harco National Insurance Co PO Box 68309 .... Schaumburg IL 60168 800-448-4642 472-6015*
**Fax Area Code:* 847 ■ *TF:* 800-448-4642 ■ *Web:* iat-harco.com

Harleysville Insurance Co of New Jersey
112 W Park Dr .... Mount Laurel NJ 08054 856-642-9779 642-9412*
**Fax:* Claims ■ *TF:* 800-322-5521 ■ *Web:* www.harleysvillegroup.com

Harleysville Worcester Insurance Co
120 Front St Ste 400 .... Worcester MA 01608 508-754-6666 752-7903*
**Fax:* Hum Res ■ *TF:* 800-225-7387 ■ *Web:* www.harleysvillegroup.com

Hartford Casualty Insurance Co
1 Hartford Plaza .... Hartford CT 06155 860-547-5000
Web: www.thehartford.com

Hartford Fire Insurance Co 1 Hartford Plz .... Hartford CT 06115 860-547-5000
Web: www.thehartford.com

Hartford's Omni Auto Plan PO Box 105440 .... Atlanta GA 30348 770-952-4500
TF: 800-243-5860 ■ *Web:* www.thehartford.com

Hingham Mutual Fire Insurance Co 230 Beal St .... Hingham MA 02043 781-749-0841 749-4477
TF: 800-341-8200 ■ *Web:* www.hinghammutual.com

Hortica Insurance
1 Horticultural Ln PO Box 428 .... Edwardsville IL 62025 618-656-4240 656-7581
TF: 800-851-7740 ■ *Web:* www.hortica.com

HSB Group Inc 1 State St .... Hartford CT 06103 860-722-1866 722-5106
TF: 800-472-1866

ICW Group 11455 El Camino Real .... San Diego CA 92130 858-350-2400 350-2704
TF: 800-877-1111 ■ *Web:* www.icwgroup.com

IMT Group, The PO Box 1336 .... Des Moines IA 50266 800-274-3531
TF: 800-274-3531 ■ *Web:* imtins.com

Indiana Farmers Mutual Insurance Co
10 W 106th St .... Indianapolis IN 46290 317-846-4211 848-8629
TF: 800-666-6460 ■ *Web:* www.indianafarmers.com

Injured Workers Insurance Fund
8722 Loch Raven Blvd .... Towson MD 21286 410-494-2000
TF: 800-264-4943 ■ *Web:* www.ceiwc.com

Insurance Company of the West
11455 El Camino Real .... San Diego CA 92130 858-350-2400 350-2616
TF: 800-877-1111 ■ *Web:* www.icwgroup.com

Intact Insurance
700 University Ave Mn 3 Ste 1500 .... Toronto ON M5G0A1 844-489-3768 344-8030*
**Fax Area Code:* 416 ■ **Fax:* Claims ■ *TF:* 877-341-1464

Jacobs Financial Group Inc
300 Summers St Ste 970 .... Charleston WV 25301 304-343-8171
Web: www.thejacobsfinancialgroup.com

James A Scott & Son Inc PO Box 10489 .... Lynchburg VA 24506 434-832-2100 832-2190
TF: 800-365-0101 ■ *Web:* www.scottins.com

Keen Battle Mead & Co (KBMCO)
7850 NW 146th St Ste 200 PO Box 171870 .... Hialeah FL 33016 305-558-1101 822-4722
Web: www.kbmco.com

Kentucky Farm Bureau Mutual Insurance Co
9201 Bunsen Pkwy .... Louisville KY 40220 502-495-5000 495-7703
Web: kyfb.com

Kingstone Companies Inc 1154 Broadway .... Hewlett NY 11557 516-374-7600 295-7216
NASDAQ: KINS ■ *Web:* www.kingstonecompanies.com

Kingsway Financial Services Inc
45 St Clair Ave W Ste 400 .... Toronto ON M4V1K9 416-848-1171 848-1171
NYSE: KFS ■ *Web:* www.kingsway-financial.com

Phone Fax

Koch Supply & Trading LP 4111 E 37th St N .... Wichita KS 67220 713-544-4123 828-5739*
**Fax Area Code:* 316 ■ *Web:* www.kochoil.com

Lexington Insurance Company Inc
99 High St Fl 23 .... Boston MA 02110 617-330-1100
Web: www.lexingtoninsurance.com

Liberty Mutual Group 175 Berkeley St .... Boston MA 02116 617-357-9500
Web: www.libertymutual.com

Lititz Mutual Insurance Co
2 N Broad St PO Box 900 .... Lititz PA 17543 717-626-4751 626-0970
TF: 800-626-4751 ■ *Web:* www.lititzmutual.com

Lumbermen's Underwriting Alliance (LUA)
1905 NW Corporate Blvd PO Box 3061 .... Boca Raton FL 33431 561-994-1900 997-9489*
**Fax:* Hum Res ■ *TF:* 800-327-0630 ■ *Web:* www.lumbermensunderwriting.com

Lykes Insurance Inc 400 N Tampa St .... Tampa FL 33602 813-223-3911 221-1857
Web: www.lykesinsurance.com

Main Street America Group 55 W St .... Keene NH 03431 603-352-4000
TF: 800-258-5310 ■ *Web:* www.msagroup.com

MAPFRE USA Corp 211 Main St .... Webster MA 01570 800-922-8276
TF: 800-922-8276 ■ *Web:* www.commerceinsurance.com

Markel Corp 222 S 15th St StE Ste 1500N .... Omaha NE 68102 888-500-3344 338-2667*
**Fax Area Code:* 866 ■ *TF:* 888-500-3344 ■ *Web:* www.firstcomp.com

Markel Specialty Commercial 4600 Cox Rd .... Glen Allen VA 23060 800-416-4364 527-7915*
**Fax Area Code:* 804 ■ *TF:* 800-416-4364 ■ *Web:* www.markelinsurance.com

Mercer Insurance Group Inc
10 N Hwy 31 PO Box 278 .... Pennington NJ 08534 609-737-0426 737-8719
TF: 800-223-0534 ■ *Web:* www.unitedfiregroup.com

Merchants Insurance Group 250 Main St .... Buffalo NY 14202 716-849-3333 849-3246
TF: 800-462-1077 ■ *Web:* merchantsgroup.com

Mercury Casualty Co 555 W Imperial Hwy .... Brea CA 92821 714-671-6600 857-7116*
**Fax Area Code:* 323 ■ **Fax:* Hum Res ■ *Web:* mercuryinsurance.com

Mercury Insurance Co 555 W Imperial Hwy .... Brea CA 92821 714-671-6600 857-7116*
**Fax Area Code:* 323 ■ **Fax:* Hum Res

Mercury Insurance Group
4484 Wilshire Blvd .... Los Angeles CA 90010 323-937-1060 857-7116
NYSE: MCY ■ *TF:* 800-956-3728 ■ *Web:* www.mercuryinsurance.com

Michigan Millers Mutual Insurance Co
2425 E Grand River Ave PO Box 30060 .... Lansing MI 48912 800-888-1914
TF: 800-888-1914 ■ *Web:* www.mimillers.com

Mid-Continent Group
1437 S Boulder Ave W PO Box 1409 .... Tulsa OK 74119 918-587-7221 588-1293*
**Fax:* Hum Res ■ *TF:* 800-722-4994 ■ *Web:* www.mcg-ins.com

Middlesex Mutual Assurance Co
213 Ct St PO Box 891 .... Middletown CT 06457 800-622-3780
TF: 800-622-3780 ■ *Web:* www.middleoak.com

Midwest Employers Casualty Co
14755 N Outer 40 Dr Ste 300 .... Chesterfield MO 63017 636-449-7000 449-7199
TF: 877-975-2667 ■ *Web:* www.mwecc.com

Millers First Insurance Co 111 E Fourth St .... Alton IL 62002 618-463-3636
TF: 800-558-0500 ■ *Web:* www.millersfirst.com

Montgomery Mutual Insurance Co
13830 Ballantyne Corporate Pl Ste 300 .... Charlotte NC 28277 704-759-7661 544-2971*
**Fax:* Hum Res ■ *TF:* 800-561-0178

Motorists Mutual Insurance Co
471 E Broad St .... Columbus OH 43215 614-225-8211 225-1889*
**Fax Area Code:* 866 ■ *Web:* www.motoristsmutual.com

Mutual of Enumclaw Insurance Co
1460 Wells St .... Enumclaw WA 98022 360-825-2591 825-6885
TF: 800-366-5551 ■ *Web:* www.mutualofenumclaw.com

National Farmers Union Property & Casualty Co
5619 DTC Pkwy Ste 300 .... Greenwood Village CO 80111 303-337-5500 338-2211
TF: 800-347-1961 ■ *Web:* www.farmersunioninsurance.com

National Fire & Marine Insurance Co
3024 Harney St .... Omaha NE 68131 402-536-3000 916-3030
TF: 866-720-7861 ■ *Web:* www.nationalindemnity.com

National Grange Mutual Insurance Co 55 W St .... Keene NH 03431 603-352-4000
TF: 800-258-5310 ■ *Web:* msagroup.com

National Indemnity Co 3024 Harney St .... Omaha NE 68131 402-536-3000 536-3030
Web: www.nationalindemnity.com

National Interstate Corp 3250 I- Dr .... Richfield OH 44286 330-659-8900 659-8901
NASDAQ: NATL ■ *TF:* 800-929-1500 ■ *Web:* www.nationalinterstate.com

Nationwide Mutual Fire Insurance Co
1 Nationwide Plaza .... Columbus OH 43215 614-249-7111 249-9071
TF: 877-669-6877 ■ *Web:* www.nationwide.com

Nationwide Mutual Insurance Co
1 Nationwide Plaza .... Columbus OH 43215 614-249-7111 249-7705*
**Fax:* Cust Svc ■ *TF:* 877-669-6877 ■ *Web:* www.nationwide.com

Nautilus Insurance Group LLC
7233 E Butherus Dr .... Scottsdale AZ 85260 480-951-0905 951-9730
TF: 800-842-8972 ■ *Web:* www.nautilusagents.com

New Era Life Insurance Co PO Box 4884 .... Houston TX 77210 800-552-7879
TF: 800-552-7879 ■ *Web:* www.neweralife.com

New Jersey Manufacturers Insurance Co
301 Sullivan Way .... West Trenton NJ 08628 609-883-1300 882-3457
TF: 800-232-6600 ■ *Web:* www.njm.com

New Mexico Mutual Casualty Co
PO Box 27825 .... Albuquerque NM 87125 505-345-7260 345-0816
TF: 800-788-8851 ■ *Web:* www.nmmcc.com

New York Central Mutual Fire Insurance Co (NYCM)
1899 Central Plz E .... Edmeston NY 13335 800-234-6926 965-2712*
**Fax Area Code:* 607 ■ *TF:* 800-234-6926 ■ *Web:* www.nycm.com

North American Specialty Insurance Co
650 Elm St Ste 600 .... Manchester NH 03101 603-644-6600 644-6613
TF: 800-542-9200 ■ *Web:* swissre.com

North Carolina Farm Bureau Mutual Insurance Co (NCFBMIC)
PO Box 27427 .... Raleigh NC 27611 919-782-1705
Web: www.ncfbins.com

Northern Security Insurance Co PO Box 188 .... Montpelier VT 05601 802-223-2341 229-7646
TF: 800-451-5000 ■ *Web:* www.vermontmutual.com

Northland Insurance Co 385 Washington St .... Saint Paul MN 55102 800-237-9334 310-4949*
**Fax Area Code:* 651 ■ *TF:* 800-237-9334 ■ *Web:* www.northlandins.com

Northwestern Pacific Indemnity Co
15 Mtn View Rd .... Warren NJ 07059 908-903-2000 903-2027
TF Claims: 800-252-4670 ■ *Web:* www.chubb.com

Phone Fax

Odyssey Re Holdings Corp
300 First Stamford Pl .... Stamford CT 06902 203-977-8000 356-0196
TF: 866-745-4440 ■ Web: www.odysseyre.com

Ohio Casualty Insurance Co 9450 SewaRd Rd .... Fairfield OH 45014 513-603-2400 867-3840
TF: 800-843-6446 ■ Web: ohiocasualty-ins.com

Ohio Indemnity Co 250 E Broad St 7th Fl .... Columbus OH 43215 614-228-2800 228-5552
TF: 800-628-8581 ■ Web: www.ohioindemnity.com

Oklahoma Farm Bureau Mutual Insurance Co (OFB)
2501 N Stiles Ave .... Oklahoma City OK 73105 405-523-2300 523-2362
Web: www.okfarmbureau.org

Old Dominion Insurance Co
4601 Touchton Rd E Ste 330 Ste 3400 .... Jacksonville FL 32246 904-642-3000
TF: 800-226-0875 ■ Web: msagroup.com

Old Republic Insurance Co 133 Oakland Ave .... Greensburg PA 15601 724-834-5000 834-4025
Web: orinsco.com

Old Republic International Corp
307 N Michigan Ave .... Chicago IL 60601 312-346-8100
Web: oldrepublic.com

OneBeacon Insurance Group
N 605 US-169 Ste 800 .... Plymouth MN 55441 781-332-7000 332-7904
TF: 800-662-0156 ■ Web: onebeacon.com

Oregon Mutual Insurance Co PO Box 808 .... McMinnville OR 97128 503-472-2141 565-3846
TF: 800-888-2141 ■ Web: www.ormutual.com

Pacific Specialty Insurance Co
3601 Haven Ave .... Menlo Park CA 94025 800-962-1172 780-4820*
*Fax Area Code: 650 ■ TF: 800-962-1172 ■ Web: www.pacificspecialty.com

Peerless Insurance Co 62 Maple Ave .... Keene NH 03431 603-352-3221
TF: 800-542-5385 ■ Web: www.peerless-ins.com

Pekin Insurance (FAIA) 2505 Ct St .... Pekin IL 61558 309-346-1161 346-1589
TF: 800-322-0160 ■ Web: pekininsurance.com

Penn National Insurance Co
2 N Second St PO Box 2361 .... Harrisburg PA 17101 717-234-4941
TF: 800-388-4764 ■ Web: www.pennnationalinsurance.com

Penn-America Insurance Co 3 Bala Plz .... Bala Cynwyd PA 19004 215-443-3600 660-8885*
*Fax Area Code: 610 ■ Web: www.penn-america.com

Pennsylvania Manufacturers Assn Co
380 Sentry Pkwy .... Blue Bell PA 19422 800-222-2749
TF: 800-222-2749 ■ Web: pmacompanies.com

Pharmacists Mutual Insurance Co
808 Hwy 18 W PO Box 370 .... Algona IA 50511 800-247-5930 295-9306*
*Fax Area Code: 515 ■ TF General: 800-247-5930 ■ Web: www.phmic.com/Default.aspx

Philadelphia Consolidated Holding Corp
231 Saint Asaph's Rd Ste 100 .... Bala Cynwyd PA 19004 610-617-7900 617-7940
TF: 877-647-8639 ■ Web: www.phly.com

Philadelphia Contributionship Insurance Co
212 S Fourth St .... Philadelphia PA 19106 215-627-1752 765-4611*
*Fax Area Code: 267 ■ TF Cust Svc: 888-627-1752 ■ Web: www.contributionship.com

Pinnacol Assurance 7501 E Lowry Blvd .... Denver CO 80230 303-361-4000 361-5000
TF: 800-873-7242 ■ Web: www.pinnacol.com

Preferred Employers Group Inc
10800 Biscayne Blvd .... Miami FL 33161 305-899-0404

Preferred Employers Insurance Co
PO Box 85478 .... San Diego CA 92186 866-472-9602 688-3913*
*Fax Area Code: 619 ■ TF Cust Svc: 888-472-9001 ■ Web: www.preferredworkcomp.com

Preferred Mutual Insurance Co
1 Preferred Way .... New Berlin NY 13411 607-847-6161 847-8046*
*Fax: Mail Rm ■ TF: 800-333-7642 ■ Web: www.preferredmutual.com

Princeton Excess & Surplus Lines Insurance Co
555 College Rd E .... Princeton NJ 08543 609-243-4200 243-4257
TF: 800-544-2378 ■ Web: ambest.com

Princeton Insurance Co
746 Alexander Rd PO Box 5322 .... Princeton NJ 08540 609-452-9404 734-8461
TF: 800-334-0588 ■ Web: www.princetoninsurance.com

Progressive Casualty Insurance Co
6300 Wilson Mills Rd Campus E .... Mayfield Village OH 44143 440-461-5000
TF: 800-776-4737 ■ Web: progressive.com

Providence Mutual Fire Insurance Co
340 E Ave .... Warwick RI 02886 401-827-1800 822-1872
TF: 877-763-1800 ■ Web: www.providencemutual.com

Prudential Financial Inc 751 Broad St .... Newark NJ 07102 973-802-6000 367-6476
NYSE: PRU ■ TF: 800-843-7625 ■ Web: www.prudential.com

QBE Holdings Inc Wall St Plz 88 Pine St .... New York NY 10005 212-422-1212 422-1313
TF: 800-362-5448 ■ Web: qbena.com

QBE Reinsurance Corp
88 Pine St Wall St Plz 16th Fl .... New York NY 10005 212-422-1212 422-1313
Web: qbena.com

Quincy Mutual Fire Insurance Co
57 Washington St .... Quincy MA 02169 800-899-1116 899-7790
TF: 800-899-1116 ■ Web: www.quincymutual.com

Republic Western Insurance Co
2721 N Central Ave .... Phoenix AZ 85004 800-528-7134 745-6439*
*Fax Area Code: 602 ■ TF Claims: 800-528-7134 ■ Web: www.repwest.com

RLI Insurance Co 9025 N Lindbergh Dr .... Peoria IL 61615 309-692-1000 692-1068
TF: 800-331-4929 ■ Web: www.rlicorp.com

Royal & SunAlliance Insurance Co of Canada (RSA)
18 York St Ste 800 .... Toronto ON M5J2T8 416-366-7511 367-9869
TF: 800-268-8406 ■ Web: www.rsagroup.ca

RTW Inc
8500 Normandale Lk Blvd Ste 1400
PO Box 390327 .... Bloomington MN 55437 952-893-0403 893-3700
TF Sales: 800-789-2242 ■ Web: www.rtwi.com

Rural Mutual Insurance Company Inc
1241 John Q Hammons Dr PO Box 5555 .... Madison WI 53705 608-836-5525 828-5582
TF: 800-362-7881 ■ Web: www.ruralins.com

Safe Auto Insurance Co
4 Easton Oval PO Box 182109 .... Columbus OH 43219 614-231-0200
TF: 800-723-3288 ■ Web: www.safeauto.com

Safeco Insurance Co of America
1001 Fourth Ave .... Seattle WA 98154 206-545-5000
Web: www.safeco.com

Safety Insurance Group Inc 20 Custom House St .... Boston MA 02110 617-951-0600
NASDAQ: SAFT ■ Web: safetyinsurance.com

Safeway Insurance Group 790 Pasquinelli Dr .... Westmont IL 60559 630-887-8300 887-9886*
*Fax: Hum Res ■ TF: 800-273-0300 ■ Web: www.safewayinsurance.com

Phone Fax

Sagamore Insurance Co
111 Congressional Blvd Ste 500 .... Carmel IN 46032 800-317-9402
TF: 800-317-9402 ■ Web: www.sagamoreinsurance.com

Savers Property & Casualty Insurance Co
11880 College Blvd Ste 500 .... Overland Park KS 66210 800-351-1411 358-1614*
*Fax Area Code: 248 ■ TF: 800-482-2726

Scottsdale Insurance Co
8877 N Gainey Ctr Dr .... Scottsdale AZ 85258 480-365-4000 483-6752
TF: 800-423-7675 ■ Web: www.scottsdaleins.com

Secura Insurance Cos PO Box 819 .... Appleton WI 54912 920-739-3161 739-6795
TF: 800-558-3405 ■ Web: www.secura.net

Seneca Insurance Company Inc
160 Water St 16th Fl .... New York NY 10038 212-344-3000 344-4545
Web: www.senecainsurance.com

Sentry Insurance A Mutual Co
1800 N Pt Dr .... Stevens Point WI 54481 715-346-6000
Web: www.sentry.com

Sentry Insurance Co 2 Technology Park Dr .... Westford MA 01886 800-373-6879 999-4642
TF: 800-373-6879 ■ Web: Www.sentry.com

Sompo Japan Insurance Co of America
777 Third Ave 28th Fl .... New York NY 10017 212-416-1200 416-1205
TF: 800-208-3614 ■ Web: www.sompous.com

Southern Farm Bureau Casualty Insurance Co
1800 E County Line Rd Ste 400 .... Ridgeland MS 39157 601-957-7777 957-4329
Web: www.sfbcic.com

SS Nesbitt & Co Inc 3500 Blue Lake Dr .... Birmingham AL 35243 205-262-2700 262-2701
TF: 800-422-3223 ■ Web: www.ssnesbitt.com

Star Insurance Co 26255 American Dr .... Southfield MI 48034 248-358-4020 358-1614
TF: 800-482-2726

State Auto Property & Casualty Insurance Co
518 E Broad St .... Columbus OH 43215 614-464-5000 719-0866*
*Fax: Hum Res ■ TF: 800-444-9950 ■ Web: www.stateauto.com

State Compensation Insurance Fund
PO Box 8192 .... Pleasanton CA 94588 415-565-1234
TF: 866-721-3498 ■ Web: www.statefundca.com

State Farm Fire & Casualty Co
1 State Farm Plz .... Bloomington IL 61710 309-766-2311
Web: statefarm.com

State Farm Insurance 333 First Commerce Dr .... Aurora ON L4G8A4 877-659-1570
TF: 877-659-1570 ■ Web: www.statefarm.ca

STOPS Inc 8855 Grissom Pkwy .... Titusville FL 32780 321-383-4111 632-2161*
*Fax Area Code: 866 ■ TF: 866-632-2161 ■ Web: www.onecallcm.com

Stratford Insurance Co
400 Parson's Pond Dr .... Franklin Lakes NJ 07417 201-847-8600 847-1010
Web: www.westernworld.com

Swiss Re America Corp 175 King St .... Armonk NY 10504 914-828-8000 828-7000
Web: www.swissre.com

Texas Mutual Insurance Co 6210 E Hwy 290 .... Austin TX 78723 512-224-3800 224-3889
TF: 888-532-5246 ■ Web: www.texasmutual.com

Toa Reinsurance Company of America
177 Madison Ave PO Box 1930 .... Morristown NJ 07962 973-898-9480 898-9495
Web: www.toare.com

Tokio Marine Life 230 Pk Ave .... New York NY 10169 212-297-6600 297-6062
TF: 800-628-2796 ■ Web: www.tokiomarine.us

Topa Insurance Corp
24025 Park Sorrento Ste 300 .... Calabasas CA 91302 310-201-0451
TF: 877-353-8672 ■ Web: www.topains.com

Tower Group Inc 120 Broadway 14th Fl .... New York NY 10271 212-655-2000 655-2199
NASDAQ: TWGP ■ TF: 877-883-6599 ■ Web: www.twrgrp.com

Transcontinental Insurance Co
333 S Wabash Ave CNA Ctr .... Chicago IL 60604 312-822-5000
TF: 800-262-2000 ■ Web: www.cna.com

Transportation Insurance Co 333 S Wabash Ave .... Chicago IL 60604 312-822-5000 822-6419
TF: 800-437-8854 ■ Web: www.cna.com

ULLICO Casualty Co 1625 I St NW .... Washington DC 20006 800-431-5425
TF: 800-431-5425 ■ Web: www.ullico.com

Unico American Corp
23251 Mulholland Dr .... Woodland Hills CA 91364 818-591-9800
TF: 800-669-9800 ■ Web: www.crusaderinsurance.com

Union National Life Insurance
3636 S Sherwood Forest Blvd .... Baton Rouge LA 70816 225-292-7600

Union Standard Insurance Co
122 W Carpenter Fwy Ste 350 .... Irving TX 75039 972-719-2400 719-2401
TF: 800-444-0049 ■ Web: www.usic.com

United Fire & Casualty Co
118 Second Ave SE .... Cedar Rapids IA 52407 319-399-5700 399-5499
NASDAQ: UFCS ■ TF: 800-332-7977 ■ Web: www.unitedfiregroup.com

United Heartland Inc PO Box 3026 .... Milwaukee WI 53201 866-206-5851 787-7701*
*Fax Area Code: 262 ■ TF: 866-206-5851 ■ Web: www.unitedheartland.biz

United National Group
3 Bala Plz E Ste 300 .... Bala Cynwyd PA 19004 610-664-1500 660-8882
TF: 800-333-0352 ■ Web: www.unitednat.com

United National Insurance Co
3 Bala Plz E Ste 300 .... Bala Cynwyd PA 19004 610-664-1500 660-8882
TF: 800-333-0352 ■ Web: www.unitednat.com

Universal Insurance Holding Inc (UIH)
1110 W Commerical Blvd Ste 100 .... Fort Lauderdale FL 33309 800-509-5586
NYSE: UVE ■ TF: 800-509-5586 ■ Web: www.universalinsuranceholdings.com

USA Workers' Injury Network
1250 S Capital of Texas Hwy Bldg 3 Ste 500 .... Austin TX 78746 800-872-0020 328-6785*
*Fax Area Code: 512 ■ TF Cust Svc: 800-872-0020 ■ Web: www.usamco.com

USAA Property & Casualty Insurance Group
9800 Fredericksburg Rd .... San Antonio TX 78288 210-531-8722 531-8877*
*Fax Area Code: 800 ■ TF: 800-531-8722 ■
Web: www.usaa.com/inet/pages/newsroom_factsheets_pnc

Utica First Insurance Co 5981 Airport Rd .... Oriskany NY 13424 315-736-8211 768-4408
TF: 800-456-4556 ■ Web: www.uticafirst.com

Utica National Insurance Group
180 Genesee St .... New Hartford NY 13413 315-734-2000 734-2680
TF: 800-274-1914 ■ Web: www.uticanational.com

Vermont Mutual Insurance Co
89 State St PO Box 188 .... Montpelier VT 05601 802-223-2341 229-7670
TF: 800-451-5000 ■ Web: www.vermontmutual.com

Victoria Insurance 22901 Millcreek Blvd .... Cleveland OH 44122 216-896-6990
TF: 800-888-8424 ■ Web: www.victoriainsurance.com

Company	City	State	Zip	Phone	Fax
Vigilant Insurance Co 15 Mtn View Rd *TF Claims:* 800-252-4670 ■ *Web:* www.chubb.com	Warren	NJ	07059	908-903-2000	903-2027
Wawanesa Insurance 900-191 Broadway **Fax Area Code:* 204 ■ *Web:* www.wawanesa.com	Winnipeg	MB	R3C3P1	858-874-5300	942-7724*
West Bend Mutual Insurance Co 1900 S 18th Ave *TF:* 800-236-5010 ■ *Web:* www.thesilverlining.com	West Bend	WI	53095	262-334-5571	334-9109
Western National Mutual Insurance Co 5350 W 78th St **Fax:* Hum Res ■ *TF:* 800-862-6070 ■ *Web:* www.wnins.com	Edina	MN	55439	952-835-5350	921-3159*
Western Reserve Group, The 1685 Cleveland Rd **Fax:* Hum Res ■ *TF:* 800-362-0426 ■ *Web:* www.wrg-ins.com	Wooster	OH	44691	330-262-9060	262-3259*
Windham Injury Management Group Inc 500 N Comercial St Ste 301 **Fax Area Code:* 866 ■ *Web:* www.windhamgroup.com	Manchester	NH	03101	603-626-5789	404-0557*
Wisconsin Reinsurance Corp 2810 City View Dr *TF:* 800-939-9473 ■ *Web:* www.thewrcgroup.com	Madison	WI	53707	608-242-4500	242-4514
Zenith Insurance Co PO Box 9055 **Fax Area Code:* 877 ■ *TF:* 800-440-5020 ■ *Web:* www.thezenith.com	Van Nuys	CA	91409	818-713-1000	280-4701*

391-5 Surety Insurance

Company	City	State	Zip	Phone	Fax
ACMAT Corp 233 Main St *OTC:* ACMT ■ *Web:* www.acmatcorp.com	New Britain	CT	06051	860-229-9000	
Acstar Insurance Co 233 Main St *Web:* www.acstarins.com	New Britain	CT	06051	860-224-2000	
AMBAC Assurance Corp 1 State St Plaza 15th Fl *TF:* 800-221-1854 ■ *Web:* www.ambac.com	New York	NY	10004	212-658-7470	208-3414
American Public Life Insurance Co 2305 Lakeland Dr PO Box 925 *TF:* 800-256-8606 ■ *Web:* ampublic.com	Jackson	MS	39205	601-936-6600	936-2157
Assurant Solutions 440 Mt Rushmore Rd *Web:* www.assurantsolutions.com	Rapid City	SD	57701	770-763-1000	859-4403
Assured Guaranty Corp 31 W 52nd St *Web:* www.assuredguaranty.com	New York	NY	10019	212-974-0100	581-3268
Balboa Life & Casualty Insurance Co 3349 Michelson Dr Ste 200	Irvine	CA	92612	949-222-8000	222-8716
Bond Pro LLC 1501 E Second Ave *TF:* 888-789-4985 ■ *Web:* www.cumberlandtech.com	Tampa	FL	33605	888-789-4985	
Catholic Mutual Group 10843 Old Mill Rd *TF:* 800-228-6108 ■ *Web:* www.catholicmutual.org	Omaha	NE	68154	402-551-8765	551-2943
Central Insurance Cos 800 S Washington St **Fax:* Claims ■ *TF:* 800-736-7000 ■ *Web:* www.central-insurance.com	Van Wert	OH	45891	419-238-1010	238-7626*
Central States Indemnity Company of Omaha (CSI) 1212 N 96th St *Web:* www.csi-omaha.com	Omaha	NE	68114	402-997-8000	
Century Insurance Group 465 Cleveland Ave **Fax Area Code:* 800 ■ *TF:* 877-855-8462 ■ *Web:* www.meadowbrook.com	Westerville	OH	43082	614-895-2000	832-8793*
Chubb Specialty Insurance 82 Hopmeadow St *TF:* 800-252-4670 ■ *Web:* www.chubb.com	Simsbury	CT	06070	860-408-2000	408-2002
Cincinnati Casualty Co 6200 S Gilmore Rd	Fairfield	OH	45014	513-870-2000	870-2911
CNA Surety Corp 333 S Wabash Ave *NYSE:* L ■ *TF:* 877-672-6115 ■ *Web:* www.cnasurety.com	Chicago	IL	60604	312-822-5000	
Connecticut Medical Insurance Co (CMIC) 80 Glastonbury Blvd Third Fl	Glastonbury	CT	06033	860-633-7788	633-8237
Copic Insurance Co 7351 Lowry Blvd *TF:* 800-421-1834 ■ *Web:* www.callcopic.com/cic	Denver	CO	80230	720-858-6000	858-6001
Dentists Insurance Co 1201 K St 17th Fl **Fax Area Code:* 916 ■ *TF:* 800-733-0634 ■ *Web:* www.tdicinsurance.com	Sacramento	CA	95814	800-733-0633	498-6162*
Doctors' Co, The 185 Greenwood Rd **Fax Area Code:* 707 ■ *TF:* 800-421-2368 ■ *Web:* www.thedoctors.com	Napa	CA	94558	800-421-2368	226-0165*
Euler Hermes ACI 800 Red Brook Blvd 4th Fl *TF:* 877-883-3224 ■ *Web:* eulerhermes.us	Owings Mills	MD	21117	410-753-0753	
Everest Reinsurance Co 477 Martinsville Rd *TF:* 800-269-6660 ■ *Web:* www.everestregroup.com	Liberty Corner	NJ	07938	908-604-3000	604-3322
Federated Mutual Insurance Co 121 E Pk Sq PO Box 328 *TF:* 800-533-0472 ■ *Web:* federatedinsurance.com	Owatonna	MN	55060	507-455-5200	
Financial Guaranty Insurance Co 125 Pk Ave 6th Fl *TF:* 800-352-0001 ■ *Web:* www.fgic.com	New York	NY	10017	212-312-3000	312-3231
Fireman's Fund Insurance Co 1465 N McDowell Blvd *TF:* 866-386-3932 ■ *Web:* www.firemansfund.com	Petaluma	CA	94954	866-386-3932	
First Insurance Company of Hawaii Ltd 1100 Ward Ave PO Box 2866 *TF:* 800-272-5202 ■ *Web:* www.ficoh.com	Honolulu	HI	96803	808-527-7777	527-3200
Great American Insurance Co 580 Walnut St *Web:* www.greatamericaninsurancegroup.com	Cincinnati	OH	45202	513-369-5000	
Hartford Underwriters Insurance Co 1 Hartford Plz *Web:* www.thehartford.com	Hartford	CT	06115	860-547-5000	
Heritage Insurance Managers Inc 922 Isom Rd	San Antonio	TX	78216	210-829-7467	
Illinois State Medical Inter-Insurance Exchange (ISMIE) 20 N Michigan Ave Ste 700 *TF:* 800-782-4767 ■ *Web:* www.ismie.com	Chicago	IL	60602	312-782-2749	782-2023
Insurance Company of the West 11455 El Camino Real *TF:* 800-877-1111 ■ *Web:* www.icwgroup.com	San Diego	CA	92130	858-350-2400	350-2616
International Fidelity Insurance Co (IFIC) 1 Newark Ctr 20th Fl *TF:* 800-333-4167 ■ *Web:* www.ific.com	Newark	NJ	07102	973-624-7200	643-7116
JP Everhart & Co PO Box 2683 *TF:* 888-622-8575 ■ *Web:* txnotaryapplication.com	Waco	TX	76702	888-622-8575	
Kansas Bankers Surety Co 1220 SW Executive Dr	Topeka	KS	66615	785-228-0000	228-0079
Kansas Medical Mutual Insurance Co (KaMMCO) 623 SW Tenth Ave Ste 200 *TF:* 800-232-2259 ■ *Web:* www.kammco.com	Topeka	KS	66612	785-232-2224	232-4704
Lexington Insurance Company Inc 99 High St Fl 23 *Web:* www.lexingtoninsurance.com	Boston	MA	02110	617-330-1100	
Life of the South Insurance Co 10151 Deerwood Pk Blvd Bldg 100 *TF:* 800-888-2738 ■ *Web:* www.life-south.com	Jacksonville	FL	32256	904-350-9660	
Louisiana Medical Mutual Insurance Co 1 Galleria Blvd Ste 700 **Fax Area Code:* 504 ■ *TF:* 800-452-2120 ■ *Web:* www.lammico.com	Metairie	LA	70001	800-452-2120	841-5300*
MBIA Insurance Corp 113 King St *Web:* www.mbia.com	Armonk	NY	10504	914-273-4545	
Media/Professional Insurance Inc 1201 Walnut Ste 1800 *TF:* 866-282-0565 ■ *Web:* www.axiscapital.com	Kansas City	MO	64106	816-471-6118	471-6119
Medical Assurance Inc 100 Brookwood Pl Ste 300 *TF Cust Svc:* 800-282-6242 ■ *Web:* www.proassurance.com	Birmingham	AL	35209	205-877-4400	802-4799
Medical Mutual Group 700 Spring Forest Rd *TF:* 800-662-7917 ■ *Web:* www.medicalmutualgroup.com	Raleigh	NC	27609	919-872-7117	878-7550
Medical Mutual Insurance Company of Maine 1 City Ctr Ste 9 *TF:* 800-942-2791 ■ *Web:* www.medicalmutual.com	Portland	ME	04112	207-775-2791	775-6576
Medical Mutual Liability Insurance Society of Maryland 225 International Cir PO Box 8016 *TF:* 800-492-0193 ■ *Web:* www.medicalmutualofmd.com	Hunt Valley	MD	21030	410-785-0050	785-2631
Medical Protective Co 5814 Reed Rd **Fax Area Code:* 800 ■ *TF:* 800-463-3776 ■ *Web:* www.medpro.com	Fort Wayne	IN	46835	260-485-9622	398-6726*
Mortgage Guaranty Insurance Corp 270 E Kilbourn Ave *TF:* 800-558-9900 ■ *Web:* www.mgic.com	Milwaukee	WI	53202	414-347-6480	
NCMIC Insurance Co 14001 University Ave **Fax Area Code:* 800 ■ *TF:* 800-769-2000 ■ *Web:* www.ncmic.com	Clive	IA	50325	515-313-4500	996-2642*
Norcal Mutual Insurance Company Inc 560 Davis St *TF:* 800-652-1051 ■ *Web:* www.norcalmutual.com	San Francisco	CA	94111	415-397-9700	835-9817
Old Republic Insured Automotive Services Inc 8282 S Memorial Dr *TF:* 800-331-3780 ■ *Web:* www.orias.com	Tulsa	OK	74133	918-307-1000	
Old Republic Surety 445 S Moorlands Rd Ste 200 *TF:* 800-217-1792 ■ *Web:* www.orsurety.com	Brookfield	WI	53005	262-797-2640	797-8353
Pekin Life Insurance Co 2505 Ct St *OTC:* PKIN ■ *TF:* 800-322-0160 ■ *Web:* www.pekininsurance.com	Pekin	IL	61558	309-346-1161	
Penn National Insurance Co 2 N Second St PO Box 2361 *TF:* 800-388-4764 ■ *Web:* www.pennnationalinsurance.com	Harrisburg	PA	17101	717-234-4941	
Pennsylvania Medical Society Liability Insurance Co (PMSLIC) 1700 Bent Creek Blvd PO Box 2080 **Fax Area Code:* 717 ■ *TF:* 800-445-1212 ■ *Web:* www.norcalmutual.com/resources/pmslic	Mechanicsburg	PA	17050	844-466-7225	796-8080*
PMI Mortgage Insurance Co 3003 Oak Rd *Web:* www.pmi-us.com	Walnut Creek	CA	94597	925-658-7878	658-6931
Podiatry Insurance Company of America 3000 Meridian Blvd Ste 400 *TF:* 800-251-5727 ■ *Web:* www.picagroup.com	Franklin	TN	37067	615-984-2005	370-9021
Pre-Paid Legal Services Inc 1 Pre-Paid Way *TF:* 800-654-7757 ■ *Web:* www.legalshield.com	Ada	OK	74820	580-436-1234	
Princeton Insurance Co 746 Alexander Rd PO Box 5322 *TF:* 800-334-0588 ■ *Web:* www.princetoninsurance.com	Princeton	NJ	08540	609-452-9404	734-8461
ProAssurance 20 Allen Ave Ste 430 *TF:* 800-282-6242 ■ *Web:* www.proassurance.com	Saint Louis	MO	63119	314-961-7700	918-0530
ProMutual Group 13th Fl 4th Fl **Fax Area Code:* 617 ■ *TF:* 800-225-6168 ■ *Web:* www.coverys.com	Boston	MA	02111	800-225-6168	330-1748*
Protective Insurance Co 111 Congressional Blvd Ste 500 *TF:* 800-644-5501 ■ *Web:* www.protectiveinsurance.com	Carmel	IN	46032	800-644-5501	
Radian Asset Assurance Inc *Radian Group Inc, The* 335 Madison Ave 25th Fl *TF:* 877-723-4261 ■ *Web:* www.radian.biz	New York	NY	10017	212-983-3100	682-5377
Radian Group Inc 1601 Market St *NYSE:* RDN ■ *TF:* 800-523-1988 ■ *Web:* www.radian.biz	Philadelphia	PA	19103	215-564-6600	
Reciprocal of America 4200 Innslake Dr Ste 102 *TF:* 800-284-8847 ■ *Web:* www.reciprocalgroup.com	Glen Allen	VA	23060	804-747-8600	270-5281
Republic Mortgage Insurance Co 101 N Cherry St Ste 101 **Fax Area Code:* 336 ■ *TF:* 800-999-7642 ■ *Web:* www.rmic.com	Winston-Salem	NC	27101	800-999-7642	661-3275*
RLI Insurance Co 9025 N Lindbergh Dr *TF:* 800-331-4929 ■ *Web:* www.rlicorp.com	Peoria	IL	61615	309-692-1000	692-1068
Rose & Kiernan Inc 99 Troy Rd *TF:* 866-488-6582 ■ *Web:* www.rkinsurance.com	East Greenbush	NY	12061	518-244-4245	244-4262
Securities Investors Protection Corp 805 15th St NW Ste 800 *Web:* www.sipc.org	Washington	DC	20005	202-371-8300	371-6728
State Volunteer Mutual Insurance Co 101 W Pk Dr Ste 300 *TF:* 800-342-2239 ■ *Web:* www.svmic.com	Brentwood	TN	37027	615-377-1999	370-1343
Surety Group Inc 3715 Northside Pkwy NW Ste 1-315 *TF:* 800-486-8211 ■ *Web:* www.suretygroup.com	Atlanta	GA	30327	404-352-8211	351-3237
Texas Hospital Insurance Exchange 8310 N Capital of Texas Hwy Ste 250 *TF:* 800-792-0060 ■ *Web:* www.thie.com	Austin	TX	78731	512-451-5775	451-3101
Texas Lawyers Insurance Exchange (TLIE) 1801 S MoPac Ste 300 *TF:* 800-252-9332 ■ *Web:* www.tlie.org	Austin	TX	78746	512-480-9074	482-8738
Transamerica 4333 Edgewood Rd NE *TF:* 800-852-4678 ■ *Web:* www.transamerica.com	Cedar Rapids	IA	52499	319-355-8511	
Triad Guaranty Insurance Corp 101 S Stratford Rd *TF Cust Svc:* 888-691-8074 ■ *Web:* www.tgic.com	Winston-Salem	NC	27104	336-723-1282	

				Phone	Fax
ULLICO Casualty Co 1625 I St NW *TF:* 800-431-5425 ■ *Web:* www.ullico.com	Washington	DC	20006	800-431-5425	
United Guaranty Corp (UGC) 230 N Elm St **Fax Area Code:* 336 ■ **Fax:* Hum Res ■ *TF:* 800-334-8966 ■ *Web:* www.ugcorp.com	Greensboro	NC	27401	800-334-8966	230-1946*
United National Group 3 Bala Plz E Ste 300 *TF:* 800-333-0352 ■ *Web:* www.unitednat.com	Bala Cynwyd	PA	19004	610-664-1500	660-8882
Utica National Insurance Group 180 Genesee St *TF:* 800-274-1914 ■ *Web:* www.uticanational.com	New Hartford	NY	13413	315-734-2000	734-2680
Victor O Schinnerer & Co Inc 2 Wisconsin Cir Ste 200 *Web:* www.schinnerer.com	Chevy Chase	MD	20815	301-961-9800	951-5444
Vision Financial Corp PO Box 506 **Fax Area Code:* 603 ■ *TF:* 800-793-0223 ■ *Web:* www.visfin.com	Keene	NH	03431	800-793-0223	357-0250*
Warranty Group Inc, The 175 W Jackson 11th Fl *TF:* 800-621-2130 ■ *Web:* www.thewarrantygroup.com	Chicago	IL	60604	312-356-3000	
Western World Insurance Co 400 Parson's Pond Dr *TF:* 888-847-8600 ■ *Web:* www.westernworld.com	Franklin Lakes	NJ	07417	201-847-8600	847-1010
Western World Insurance Group Inc 400 Parson's Pond Dr *Web:* www.westernworld.com	Franklin Lakes	NJ	07417	201-847-8600	847-1010
XL Specialty Insurance Co 70 Seaview Ave **Fax Area Code:* 573 ■ *TF:* 877-263-7995 ■ *Web:* insurance.mo.gov	Stamford	CT	06902	203-964-5200	526-2092*
Zurich North America 1400 American Ln **Fax Area Code:* 877 ■ **Fax:* Claims ■ *TF:* 800-382-2150 ■ *Web:* www.zurichna.com	Schaumburg	IL	60196	847-605-6000	962-2567*

391-6 Title Insurance

Most title insurance companies also provide other real estate services such as escrow, flood certification, appraisals, etc.

				Phone	Fax
Advantage Title Agency Inc 201 Old Country Rd Ste 200 *Web:* www.advantagegroupny.com	Melville	NY	11747	631-424-6100	
Alamo Title Insurance 9600 N Mo Pac Expy Ste 125 *Web:* austintitle.com	Austin	TX	78759	512-459-7222	459-7460
AmeriPoint Title Inc 10101 Reunion Pl Ste 250	San Antonio	TX	78216	210-340-2921	
Attorney's Title Insurance Fund Inc 6545 Corporate Ctr Blvd *TF:* 800-336-3863 ■ *Web:* thefund.com	Orlando	FL	32822	407-240-3863	240-0750
Chicago Title & Trust Co 171 N Clark St **Fax:* Hum Res ■ *TF:* 800-621-1919 ■ *Web:* www.ctic.com	Chicago	IL	60601	312-223-2000	223-2942*
Chicago Title Company of Oregon 10135 SE Sunnyside Rd Ste 300 *Web:* www.chicagotitleoregon.com	Clackamas	OR	97015	503-794-5860	
Commonwealth Land Title Insurance Co 601 Riverside Ave *TF:* 888-866-3684 ■ *Web:* www.cltic.com	Jacksonville	FL	32204	888-866-3684	
Community Title & Escrow Ltd 2600 State St Bldg D *TF:* 800-854-4049 ■ *Web:* communitytitle.net	Alton	IL	62002	618-466-7755	466-7782
Dakota Homestead Title Insurance Co 315 S Phillips Ave *Web:* www.tsptitle.com	Sioux Falls	SD	57104	605-336-0388	996-3270
Entitle Direct Group Inc 281 Tresser Blvd 6th Fl *TF:* 877-936-8485 ■ *Web:* www.entitledirect.com	Stamford	CT	06901	203-724-1150	
Fidelity National Title Group Inc 601 Riverside Ave *TF:* 888-866-3684 ■ *Web:* www.fntg.com	Jacksonville	FL	32204	904-854-8100	357-1007
Fidelity National Title Insurance Co 7025 N Scottsdale Rd *TF:* 888-934-3354 ■ *Web:* www.fntic.com	Scottsdale	AZ	85258	480-344-6400	
Fidelity National Title Insurance Company of Oregon 900 SW Fifth Ave Mezzanine Level *TF:* 888-934-3354 ■ *Web:* www.fntic.com	Portland	OR	97204	503-223-8338	796-6611
First American Corp 1 First American Way *NYSE:* FAF ■ *TF:* 800-854-3643 ■ *Web:* www.firstam.com	Santa Ana	CA	92707	714-250-3000	
GeoVera Holdings Inc 1455 Oliver Rd *Web:* www.geoveraholdingsinc.com	Fairfield	CA	94534	707-863-3700	
Gracy Title Co 524 N Lamar Blvd Ste 200 *Web:* www.gracytitle.com	Austin	TX	78703	512-472-8421	478-6038
Greater Illinois Title Co 120 N La Salle St Ste 900 *Web:* www.gitc.com	Chicago	IL	60602	312-236-7300	236-0284
Hanover Insurance Co 440 Lincoln St *TF:* 800-853-0456 ■ *Web:* www.hanover.com	Worcester	MA	01653	508-855-1000	855-6313
Meridian Title Corp 202 S Michigan St *TF:* 800-777-1574 ■ *Web:* www.meridiantitle.com	South Bend	IN	46601	574-232-5845	289-1514
Mississippi Valley Title Insurance Co 315 Tom Bigbee St *TF:* 800-647-2124 ■ *Web:* www.mvt.com	Jackson	MS	39201	601-969-0222	969-2215
Monroe Title Insurance Corp 47 W Main St *TF:* 800-966-6763 ■ *Web:* www.monroetitle.com	Rochester	NY	14614	585-232-4950	232-4988
North American Title Co 1855 Gateway Blvd Ste 600 *TF:* 800-566-0370 ■ *Web:* www.nat.com/home.aspx	Concord	CA	94520	925-935-5599	933-4851
Northpoint Escrow & Title LLC 10800 NE Eighth St Ste 200 *TF:* 877-678-1678	Bellevue	WA	98004	425-453-8880	
Old Republic National Title Insurance Co (ORTIG) 400 Second Ave S *TF:* 800-328-4441 ■ *Web:* www.oldrepublictitle.com	Minneapolis	MN	55401	612-371-1111	371-1191
Orange Coast Title Company Inc 640 N Tustin Ave Ste 106 *Web:* www.octitle.com	Santa Ana	CA	92705	714-558-2836	
Placer Title Co 2394 Fair Oaks Blvd *Web:* www.placertitle.com	Sacramento	CA	95825	916-973-1002	482-3049
Rattikin Title Co 201 Main St Ste 800 *Web:* rattikintitle.com	Fort Worth	TX	76102	817-332-1171	882-9886
Security Mutual Insurance Co 2417 N Triphammer Rd PO Box 4620 *Web:* www.securitymutual.com	Ithaca	NY	14852	607-257-5000	
Southland Title LLC 6710 Stewart Rd Ste 300 *Web:* www.southlandtitle.net	Galveston	TX	77551	409-744-0727	744-3909
Stewart Information Services Corp 1980 Post Oak Blvd Ste 800 *NYSE:* STC ■ *TF:* 800-729-1900 ■ *Web:* www.stewart.com	Houston	TX	77056	713-625-8100	552-9523
Stewart REI Data Inc 1980 Post Oak Blvd Ste 800 *TF:* 800-729-1900 ■ *Web:* www.stewart.com	Houston	TX	77056	212-922-0050	
Stewart Title & Trust of Phoenix 244 W Osborn Rd **Fax:* Cust Svc ■ *Web:* www.stewartaz.com	Phoenix	AZ	85013	602-462-8000	230-6209*
Stewart Title Guaranty Co 1980 Post Oak Blvd Ste 800 *TF:* 800-729-1900 ■ *Web:* www.stewart.com	Houston	TX	77056	713-625-8100	552-9523
Title Guaranty of Hawaii Inc 235 Queen St *TF:* 800-222-3229 ■ *Web:* www.tghawaii.com	Honolulu	HI	96813	808-533-6261	521-0210
Title Resource Group LLC 3001 Leadenhall Rd *Web:* www.trgc.com	Mount Laurel	NJ	08054	856-914-8500	
Title Resources Guaranty Co (TRGC) 8111 LBJ Fwy Ste 1200 **Fax Area Code:* 888 ■ *TF:* 800-526-8018 ■ *Web:* www.titleresources.com	Dallas	TX	75251	972-644-6500	485-3630*
US Recordings Inc 2925 Country Dr *TF:* 877-272-5250 ■ *Web:* www.usrecordings.com	Little Canada	MN	55117	651-765-6400	
USHEALTH Group Inc 300 Burnett St Ste 200 *TF:* 800-387-9027 ■ *Web:* www.ushealthgroup.com	Fort Worth	TX	76102	800-387-9027	

391-7 Travel Insurance

Most of the companies listed here are insurance agencies and brokerages that specialize in selling travel insurance policies, rather than the insurers who underwrite the policies.

				Phone	Fax
Access America 2805 N Parham Rd *TF:* 800-284-8300 ■ *Web:* www.allianztravelinsurance.com	Richmond	VA	23294	800-284-8300	
All Aboard Benefits 6162 E Mockingird Ln Ste 104 *TF:* 800-462-2322 ■ *Web:* www.allaboardbenefits.com	Dallas	TX	75214	214-821-6677	821-6676
Continental Assurance Co 333 S Wabash Ave *TF:* 800-251-2148 ■ *Web:* www.cna.com	Chicago	IL	60604	312-822-5000	260-4376
Highway To Health Inc 1 Radnor Corporate Ctr Ste 100 **Fax Area Code:* 610 ■ *TF:* 888-243-2358 ■ *Web:* www.hthtravelinsurance.com	Radnor	PA	19087	888-243-2358	254-8797*
Ingle International 460 Richmond St W Ste 100 *TF:* 800-360-3234 ■ *Web:* ingleinternational.com	Toronto	ON	M5V1Y1	416-730-8488	730-1878
Insurance Consultants International 19760 Knights Crossing Ste 1C *TF:* 800-576-2674 ■ *Web:* www.globalhealthinsurance.com	Monument	CO	80132	719-573-9080	
International SOS Assistance Inc 3600 Horizon Blvd Ste 300 *TF:* 800-441-2668 ■ *Web:* www.internationalsos.com	Trevose	PA	19053	215-244-1500	942-8299
Lloyd's America Inc 25 W 53rd St 14th Fl *Web:* www.lloyds.com	New York	NY	10019	212-382-4060	382-4070
Pan-American Life Insurance Co 601 Poydras St *TF Life Ins:* 877-939-4550 ■ *Web:* www.palig.com	New Orleans	LA	70130	877-939-4550	
Travel Insured International 855 Winding Brook Dr PO Box 280568 **Fax Area Code:* 860 ■ *TF:* 800-243-3174 ■ *Web:* www.travelinsured.com	Glastonbury	CT	06033	800-243-3174	528-8005*
Wallach & Company Inc 107 W Federal St *TF:* 800-237-6615 ■ *Web:* www.wallach.com	Middleburg	VA	20118	540-687-3166	687-3172

392 INTERCOM EQUIPMENT & SYSTEMS

				Phone	Fax
Anacom General Corp 1240 S Claudina St **Fax:* Sales ■ *TF:* 800-955-9540 ■ *Web:* www.anacom-medtek.com	Anaheim	CA	92805	714-774-8484	774-7388*
Clear-Com USA 850 Marina Village Pkwy *Web:* www.clearcom.com	Alameda	CA	94501	510-337-6600	
Clever Devices Ltd 300 Crossways Pk Dr *TF:* 800-872-6129 ■ *Web:* www.cleverdevices.com	Woodbury	NY	11797	516-433-6100	
Crest Healthcare Supply 195 Third St *TF:* 800-328-8908 ■ *Web:* www.cresthealthcare.com	Dassel	MN	55325	320-275-3382	275-2306
David Clark Company Inc 360 Franklin St **Fax:* Sales ■ *TF Cust Svc:* 800-298-6235 ■ *Web:* www.davidclark.com	Worcester	MA	01615	508-751-5800	753-5827*
Lee Dan Communications Inc 155 Adams Ave *TF:* 800-231-1414 ■ *Web:* www.leedan.com	Hauppauge	NY	11788	631-231-1414	231-1498

393 INTERIOR DESIGN

				Phone	Fax
20k Group Llc 711 William St Unit 114 *Web:* www.20kgroup.com	Houston	TX	77002	713-224-1877	
24 Asset Management Corp 2020 Camino del Rio N Ste 900 *TF:* 855-414-2424 ■ *Web:* www.24asset.com	San Diego	CA	92108	855-414-2424	
A Caring Exprnce Hm Healthcare 21 Douglas Ave *Web:* www.acaringexperience.com	Providence	RI	02908	401-453-4545	
A-1 Crane Services Ltd 1148 Sta Main *Web:* ncsg.com	Grande Prairie	AB	T8V4B5	780-532-8212	
A.C. Schultes of Maryland Inc 16289 Sussex Hwy *Web:* www.acschultes.com	Bridgeville	DE	19933	410-841-6710	
ABBYY Language Services 880 N McCarthy Blvd *Web:* abbyy-ls.com	Milpitas	CA	95035	856-782-8106	

Company / Address	City	State	Zip	Phone	Fax
ABC Billing Solutions 6305 Wynbrook Way *Web:* www.abcbillingsolutions.com	Raleigh	NC	27612	919-870-5939	
Academy Fire Protection Inc 48-81 Maspeth Ave *Web:* www.academyfire.com	Maspeth	NY	11378	347-473-7200	
Accent 7171 Mercy Rd Ste 200 *TF:* 800-397-7243 ■ *Web:* www.onlineaccent.com	Omaha	NE	68106	402-397-9920	
Accent Office Interiors Inc 2108 Gilliam Ln # 3 *Web:* www.accentoffice.com	Tallahassee	FL	32308	850-386-5201	
Accord Creditor Services LLC PO Box 10005 *TF:* 800-373-0760 ■ *Web:* www.accordcreditorservices.com	Newnan	GA	30271	800-373-0760	
Acorn Design and Manufacturing 24 Terry Ln *Web:* acorndisplay.com	Lebanon	PA	17042	717-964-1111	
AdHub LLC, The 146 Alexander St *TF:* 866-712-2986 ■ *Web:* www.adhub.com	Rochester	NY	14607	585-442-2585	
Advance Central Services Inc 1313 N Market St 10th Fl *Web:* www.newspapersupport.com	Wilmington	DE	19801	302-830-9732	
Advance Graphic Printing Inc Diana St Amelia Industrial Park Lot 18 & 19 *Web:* www.agppr.com	Guaynabo	PR	00968	787-641-5400	
Advance Relocation & Storage Inc 195 Sweet Hollow Rd *Web:* www.theadvancegrp.com	Old Bethpage	NY	11804	212-809-1988	
Advance Response LLC 4950 Hamilton Ave Ste 103 *Web:* www.advanceresponse.com	San Jose	CA	95130	646-263-4214	
Aetna Maintenance Inc 1911 N U.S. Hwy 301 Ste 150 *Web:* www.aetnabuilding.com	Tampa	FL	33619	813-621-6878	
Aftermath Claim Science Inc 4580 Weaver Pkwy Ste 200 *Web:* www.equian.com	Warrenville	IL	60555	630-922-1900	
Agency Spotter Inc 318 Cherokee Ave SE Ste 107 *Web:* www.agencyspotter.com	Atlanta	GA	30312	404-210-5825	
AGR Group Inc 6275 S. Pearl St Ste 100-300 *Web:* www.agrgroupinc.com	Las Vegas	CA	89120	714-245-7151	
Ak-Chin Indian Community 42507 W Peters & Nall Rd *Web:* www.ak-chin.nsn.us	Maricopa	AZ	85238	520-568-1000	
AKA Enterprise Solutions 875 Sixth Ave 20th Fl *Web:* www.akaes.com	New York	NY	10001	212-502-3900	
Alan Ferguson Associates 1212 N Main St *Web:* alanferguson.com	High Point	NC	27262	336-889-3866	
Alberta Workers' Compensation Board 9912-107 St PO Box 2415 *Web:* www.wcb.ab.ca	Edmonton	AB	T5J2S5	780-498-3999	
Aldinger Company Inc 1440 Prudential Dr *Web:* www.aldingercompany.com	Dallas	TX	75235	214-638-1808	
Allen Commercial Industries Inc 11301 Mosier Vly Rd *Web:* www.allen-commercial.com	Euless	TX	76040	817-267-4919	
AllStar Deals Inc 150 Fifth Ave 4th Fl *Web:* www.giftconnect.co	New York	NY	10010	240-876-5388	
AM Technical Solutions Inc 2213 RR 620 N Ste 105 *Web:* www.amts.com	Austin	TX	78734	512-266-7259	
Ambix Manufacturing Inc 71 Hobbs St Ste 104 *Web:* www.ambixllc.com	Conway	NH	03818	603-452-5247	
Amerit Fleet Solutions Inc 1331 N California Blvd Ste 150 *Web:* www.kelleyamerit.com	Walnut Creek	CA	94596	925-444-1389	
Angus Management 1125 Leslie St *Web:* www.angusmanagement.com	Toronto	ON	M3C2J6	604-728-4404	
Ansol Inc 13766 Torrey Glenn Rd *Web:* www.ansolinc.com	San Diego	CA	92129	619-523-2040	
AnswerLive LLC 301 S McDowell St Ste 120 *Web:* www.answerlive.com	Charlotte	NC	28204	704-333-8880	
Apollo Retail Specialists LLC 1234 Tech Blvd *Web:* www.apolloretail.com	Tampa	FL	33619	813-712-2525	
Applied Merchandising Concepts LLC 15 Beechwood Ave *Web:* www.appliedmerchandising.com	New Rochelle	NY	10801	914-738-5200	
ArabMedicare.com PO Box 12547 *Web:* www.arabmedicare.com	Research Triangle Park	NC	27709	919-781-5838	
Aram A. Kaz Co, The 365 Silas Deane Hwy *Web:* www.aramkaz.com	Wethersfield	CT	06109	860-529-6900	
Arch Communications Inc 1327 Hampton Ave *Web:* archcom.net	St. Louis	MO	63139	314-645-8000	
Architrave Interiors Inc 1337 Ocean Ave Ste D *Web:* architraveinteriors.com	Santa Monica	CA	90401	310-395-5657	
Ark TeleServices 2 E Merrick Rd *TF:* 800-898-5367 ■ *Web:* www.arktele.com	Valley Stream	NY	11580	800-898-5367	
ArroHealth 49 Wireless Blvd Ste 140 *Web:* www.arrohealth.com	Hauppauge	NY	11788	631-780-5000	
ARS National Services Inc 201 W Grand Ave *TF:* 800-456-5053 ■ *Web:* www.arsnational.com	Escondido	CA	92025	800-456-5053	
Arvato Digital Services LLC 29011 Commerce Ctr Dr *TF:* 800-223-1478	Valencia	CA	91355	800-223-1478	
Ashland Partners & Company LLP 3549 Lear Way Ste 105 *Web:* www.ashlandpartners.com	Medford	OR	97504	541-857-8800	
Assured Packaging Inc 6080 Vipond Dr *Web:* www.assuredpackaging.com	Mississauga	ON	L5T2V4	905-565-1410	
Asurion Canada Inc 1222 Main St 2nd Fl	Moncton	NB	E1C1H6	506-386-9204	
Atelka Inc 1000 St Antoine St W Ste 500 *Web:* www.atelka.com	Montreal	QC	H3C3R7	514-448-4905	
ATG Technologies Inc 2639 N Monroe St Cedars Bldg B Ste 200 *TF:* 800-775-7790 ■ *Web:* www.patlive.com	Tallahassee	FL	32303	800-775-7790	
ATIS Elevator Inspections LLC 1976 Innerbelt Business Center *Web:* www.atis.com	St. Louis	MO	63114	314-441-3999	
ATL Inc W140 N9504 Fountain Blvd *Web:* www.atlco.com	Menomonee Falls	WI	53051	262-255-6150	
Atlantic Skyline 4605 Brookfield Corporate Dr *Web:* www.atlanticexhibits.com	Chantilly	VA	20151	703-802-6800	
AtoZdatabases com 11211 John Galt Blvd *Web:* www.atozdatabases.com	Omaha	NE	68137	402-939-2030	
Automatika Inc 137 Delta Dr *Web:* www.automatika.com	Pittsburgh	PA	15238	412-968-1022	
Avalon Development Corp 130 Goldstream Rd *Web:* www.avalonalaska.com	Fairbanks	AK	99708	907-457-5159	
Azzur Group LLC 726 Fitzwatertown Rd Ste 6 *Web:* www.azzur.com/consulting	Willow Grove	PA	19090	610-363-0422	
b2b2dot0 Inc 7474 Creedmoor Rd Ste 108 *Web:* www.b2b2dot0.com	Raleigh	NC	27613	919-676-7429	
Baltimore Development Corp 36 S Charles St Ste 2100 *Web:* www.baltimoredevelopment.com	Baltimore	MD	21201	410-837-9305	
Bay Area Exhibits Inc 1735 Technology Dr Ste 250 *Web:* www.baexhibits.com	San Jose	CA	95051	408-566-8888	
Bellwyck Packaging Inc 21 Finchdene Sq *Web:* www.bellwyck.ca	Toronto	ON	M1X1A7	416-752-1210	
BestPass Inc 828 Washington Ave *Web:* www.bestpass.com	Albany	NY	12203	518-458-1579	
Beveridge Seay Inc 2000 P St Nw Ste 700 *Web:* www.bevseay.com	Washington	DC	20036	202-822-3800	
BGO Architects Inc 4245 N Central Expy Ste 300 *Web:* www.bgoarchitects.com	Dallas	TX	75205	214-520-8878	
Bill A. Duffy International Inc 700 Ygnacio Vly Rd Ste 330 *Web:* www.bdasports.com	Walnut Creek	CA	94596	925-279-1040	
BizQuest LLC 2100 E Rt 66 Ste 200 *TF:* 888-280-3815 ■ *Web:* www.bizquest.com	Glendora	CA	91740	888-280-3815	
BlackBridge Geomatics Corp 3528 30th St N *Web:* blackbridge.com	Lethbridge	AB	T1H6Z4	403-381-2800	
Block Vision Holdings Corp 120 W Fayette St Ste 700 *Web:* www.blockvision.com	Baltimore	MD	21201	410-752-0121	
Blue Rhino Studio Inc 3277 Sun Dr *Web:* www.rhinocentral.com	Eagan	MN	55121	651-287-0900	
BlueLink Marketing LLC 306 W 37th St 11th Fl *Web:* www.bluelinkmarketing.com	New York	NY	10018	212-730-5785	
Boardroom Events LLC 5409 Overseas Hwy #295 *Web:* www.boardroomevents.com	Marathon	FL	33050	786-361-0454	
Bonanza Inc 400 E Pine St Ste 215 *Web:* www.bonanza.com	Seattle	WA	98122	425-654-1521	
BorderJump LLC 631 Second Ave S Ste 200 *Web:* www.borderjump.com	Nashville	TN	37210	615-346-9373	
Brady McCasland Inc 2000 Converse Ave *Web:* bradymccasland.com	St. Louis	MO	62203	636-377-0369	
Broadcast Communications Media Inc 3101 Ocean Park Blvd Ste 309 *Web:* www.bcmedia.tv	Santa Monica	CA	90405	310-452-6585	
Broadcast Promotions Inc 1775 Bald Hill Rd	Warwick	RI	02886	401-826-3600	
Builders Design & Leasing Inc 7601 Lindbergh Dr *Web:* www.buildersdesign.com	Gaithersburg	MD	20879	301-590-1100	
Building Service Inc (BSI) W222 N630 Cheaney Rd *TF:* 866-353-3600 ■ *Web:* www.buildingservice.com	Waukesha	WI	53186	262-955-6400	
Byrd Maintenance Services Inc 3172 Hwy 20 West *Web:* www.bmsi1.com	Decatur	AL	35601	256-355-1627	
C m Buck & Associates Inc 6850 Guion Rd *TF:* 800-382-3961 ■ *Web:* www.cmbuck.com	Indianapolis	IN	46268	317-293-5704	
Cama Inc 31 Audubon St *Web:* www.camainc.com	New Haven	CT	06511	203-777-9921	
Canada Media Fund 50 Wellington St E Ste 202 *TF:* 877-975-0766 ■ *Web:* www.cmf-fmc.ca	Toronto	ON	M5E1C8	416-214-4400	
Capitol Security Police Inc Victor Lopez St Ste 703 *Web:* www.capitolsecuritypr.com	Santruce	PR	00906	787-727-1700	
CardTrak LLC 4055 Tamiami Trail *TF:* 800-344-7714 ■ *Web:* www.cardtrak.com	Port Charlotte	FL	33952	800-344-7714	
Carenet Healthcare Services 11845 Interstate 10 W Ste 400 *TF:* 800-809-7000 ■ *Web:* www.callcarenet.com	San Antonio	TX	78230	800-809-7000	
Carr & Assoc 22964 Professional Ln Ste 200	Leawood	KS	66211	913-451-9220	
Cascade Receivables Management LLC 101 Second St Ste 100 *TF:* 888-417-1531 ■ *Web:* www.cascadereceivables.com	Petaluma	CA	94952	888-417-1531	
Cathedral Village 600 E Cathedral Rd *Web:* www.presbyterianseniorliving.org/cathedral-village	Philadelphia	PA	19128	215-487-1300	
CBE Companies Inc 1309 Technology Pkwy *TF:* 800-925-6686 ■ *Web:* www.cbecompanies.com	Cedar Falls	IA	50613	800-925-6686	
CCRA Travel Solutions 5070 Mark IV Pkwy *Web:* www.ccra.com	Fort Worth	TX	76106	682-233-0909	
CDR Fundraising Group 1670 Village Green *Web:* www.cdrfg.com	Crofton	MD	21114	301-858-1500	
Cecconi Simone Inc 1335 Dundas St W *Web:* www.cecconisimone.com	Toronto	ON	M6J1Y3	416-588-5900	
Cedar Graphics Inc 311 Parsons Dr *Web:* www.cedargraphicsinc.com	Hiawatha	IA	52233	319-393-3600	
Center Stage Productions Inc 20-10 Maple Ave *Web:* www.cspdisplay.com	Fair Lawn	NJ	07410	973-423-5000	

				Phone	Fax
Central Credit Services Inc 9550 Regency Sq Blvd Ste 602 *Web:* www.ccscollect.com	Jacksonville	FL	32225	904-724-1800	
CExchange Inc 1100 Venture Ct Ste 120 *Web:* cexchange.com	Carrollton	TX	75006	972-695-2060	
CF Napa 1130 Main St *Web:* www.cfnapa.com	Napa	CA	94559	707-265-1891	
CFS II Inc 2488 E 81st St Ste 500 *Web:* www.cfstwo.com	Tulsa	OK	74137	918-394-3950	
Cgs Motorsports 3227 Producer Way Ste 134 *Web:* www.cgsmotorsports.com	Pomona	CA	91768	909-444-5536	
ChemRite CoPac 19725 W Edgewood Dr Bldg A101 *Web:* www.chemritecopac.com	Lannon	WI	53046	262-255-3880	
Chickasaw Telecommunications Services Inc 5 N McCormick *Web:* stillwater.brightok.net	Oklahoma City	OK	73127	405-694-2000	
Choice Translating Inc ÿ112 S Tryon St Ste 1500 *Web:* www.choicetranslating.com	Charlotte	NC	28284	704-717-0043	
Ci Radar LLC 4046 Wetherburn Way Ste 1 *TF:* 888-421-0617 ■ *Web:* www.ciradar.com	Norcross	GA	30092	678-680-2103	
Cintas Canada Limited 6300 Kennedy Rd *Web:* www.cintas.ca	Mississauga	ON	L5T2X5	905-670-4409	
CISCO Inc 1702 Townhurst Ste 2811 *Web:* www.ciscocollect.com	Houston	TX	77043	713-461-9407	
City of Leawood, Kansas 4800 Town Ctr Dr *Web:* www.leawood.org	Leawood	KS	66211	913-339-6700	
CLASSIC HOSTESS INC 2 Skillman St Ste 313 *TF:* 888-280-6539 ■ *Web:* www.classichostess.com	Brooklyn	NY	11205	888-280-6539	
Clean Uniform Co 1316 S Seventh St *Web:* www.cleanuniform.com	St. Louis	MO	63104	314-421-1220	
Cleanwise Inc 1100 E Woodfield Rd Ste 200 *TF:* 877-255-5230 ■ *Web:* www.cleanwise.com	Schaumburg	IL	60173	877-255-5230	
Cloud 10 Corp 6786 S Revere Pkwy Ste 100 *Web:* www.cloud10corp.com	Centennial	CO	80112	303-952-3215	
Clover Wireless LLC 8900 Research Dr *Web:* www.cloverwireless.com	Irvine	CA	92618	949-783-7979	
CLS Lexi-tech Ltd 10 Dawson Ave *Web:* www.cls-lexitech.com/index.php?/en/home	Moncton	NB	E1A6C8	506-859-5200	
CMD Outsourcing Solutions Inc 729 E Pratt St Ste 700 *Web:* www.cmdosi.com	Baltimore	MD	21202	410-347-5544	
CMS Mid-Atlantic Inc 295 Totowa Rd *TF:* 800-267-1981 ■ *Web:* www.cmsmidatlantic.com	Totowa	NJ	07512	800-267-1981	
CO-OP Financial Services Inc 9692 Haven Ave *TF:* 800-782-9042 ■ *Web:* www.co-opfs.org	Rancho Cucamonga	CA	91730	800-782-9042	
Cobian International Group Inc The Major Bldg at Universal Studios 5728 Major Blvd Ste 601 *Web:* www.cobiangroup.com	Orlando	FL	32819	407-447-1140	
CoinLab Inc 811 1st Ave Ste 480 *TF:* 855-522-2646 ■ *Web:* coinlab.com	Seattle	WA	98104	855-522-2646	
Cole Martinez Curtis & Assoc 4040 Del Rey Ave # 7 *Web:* www.cmcadesign.com	Marina del Rey	CA	90292	310-827-7200	822-5803
CollabWorks 650 El Camino Real Ste O *Web:* collabworks.com	Redwood City	CA	94063	650-368-2523	
Commercial Furniture Interiors Inc 1154 Rt 22 W *Web:* www.cfioffice.com	Mountainside	NJ	07092	908-518-1670	654-8436
Compadre LLC 2105 Donley Drÿ Ste 100 *Web:* compadre.com	Austin	TX	78758	512-334-1000	
Company Voice LLC 930 Harvest Dr Union Meeting Corporate Ctr Ste 100 *Web:* companyvoice.com	Blue Bell	PA	19422	610-636-7656	
Competition Bureau Canada 50 Victoria St *Web:* www.competitionbureau.gc.ca	Gatineau	QC	K1A0C9	819-997-4282	
Connectit Networks Inc 4603 NE St. Johns Rd Ste B *Web:* www.connectitnetworks.com	Vancouver	WA	98661	360-450-0860	
Contact America Inc 2325 Maryland Rd Ste 150 *Web:* www.contact-america.com	Willow Grove	PA	19090	858-459-8438	
Contract Environments Inc 1020 W 18th St *Web:* contractenvironments.net	Wilmington	DE	19802	302-658-0668	
Convince & Convert 4463 Forest Hill Dr *Web:* www.convinceandconvert.com	Bloomington	IN	47401	602-616-1895	
Coregistics 240 Northpoint Pkwy *Web:* www.coregistics.com	Acworth	GA	30102	678-453-5900	
Corix Utilities (U S) Inc 126 N Jefferson St Ste 300 *Web:* www.corix.com	Milwaukee	WI	53202	414-291-6520	
Corporate Solutions Group LLC, The 924 Jupiter Dr *Web:* www.thecsg.com	Incline Village	NV	89452	775-832-5151	
Corrective Education Company LLC 2825 Cottonwood Pkwy Ste 500 *TF:* 877-318-0983 ■ *Web:* www.correctiveeducation.com	Salt Lake City	UT	84121	877-318-0983	
Cosmic Cart Inc 521 Lansdowne Rd *Web:* cosmiccart.com	Charlotte	NC	28270	704-651-8534	
CouponMom Inc, The 4686 Scribner Ct *Web:* www.couponmom.com	Marietta	GA	30062	770-649-0447	
Cova Hotel 655 Ellis St *Web:* www.covahotel.com	San Francisco	CA	94109	415-771-3000	
CPC Laboratories Inc 9300 S Sangamon St *Web:* www.cpcpack.com	Chicago	IL	60620	773-341-7711	
CPS Technology Group LLC 213 BEYNON DR *Web:* www.cpstechnologygroup.com	South Abington Township	PA	18411	570-647-4206	
Credigy Solutions Inc 3715 Davinci Court Ste 200 *Web:* www.credigy.net	Norcross	GA	30092	678-728-7310	
CUNA Strategic Services Inc 5710 Mineral Point Rd *Web:* www.cunastrategicservices.com	Madison	WI	53705	608-231-4340	
Custom Exhibits Corp 1830 N Indianwood Ave *Web:* www.customexhibits.com	Broken Arrow	OK	74012	918-250-2121	
Cyber City Teleservices Ltd 401 Hackensack Ave *Web:* www.cctll.com	Hackensack	NJ	07601	201-487-1616	
D P Brown of Saginaw Inc 2845 Universal Dr *TF:* 877-799-9400 ■ *Web:* www.dpbrowntech.com	Saginaw	MI	48603	989-799-9400	
Dallas Data Center Inc 2636 Walnut Hill Ln Ste 202 *Web:* www.dallasdatacenter.com	Dallas	TX	75229	972-993-8888	
Daroff Design Inc 2121 Market St Ste 1 *Web:* www.daroffdesign.com	Philadelphia	PA	19103	215-636-9900	
DataScan Field Services LLC 5925 Cabot Pkwy *Web:* www.dsfs.com	Alpharetta	GA	30005	770-754-6500	
Davis Inotek Calibration Laboratory 4701 Mount Hope Dr Ste J *Web:* www.inotek.com	Baltimore	MD	21215	410-358-3900	
Dawson Design Associates Inc 315 Second Ave S 300 *Web:* www.dawsondesignassociates.com	Seattle	WA	98104	206-932-3102	
Dawson School 199 N School Ave *Web:* www.dawsonisd.net	Dawson	TX	76639	254-578-1031	
DCL Corp 48641 Milmont Dr *Web:* www.dclcorp.com	Fremont	CA	94538	510-651-5100	
DDM-Digital Imaging Data Processing and Mailing Services LC 1223 William St *Web:* www.ddmdirect.com	Buffalo	NY	14206	716-893-8671	
De Forest Creative Group Ltd 300 W Lk St Ste A1 *Web:* www.deforestgroup.com	Elmhurst	IL	60126	630-834-7200	
Decorating Den Systems Inc 8659 Commerce Dr *TF:* 800-332-3367 ■ *Web:* www.decoratingden.com	Easton	MD	21601	410-822-9001	
Decorative Plant Service Inc 1150 Phelps St *Web:* www.decorative.com	San Francisco	CA	94124	415-826-8181	
Dekra America Inc 3901 Roswell Rd Ste 120 *Web:* www.dekra-na.com	Marietta	GA	30062	770-971-3788	
Denison Yacht Sales Inc 401 SW First Ave Ste 102 *Web:* www.denisonyachtsales.com	Fort Lauderdale	FL	33301	954-763-3971	
DeNuke Services Inc 702 S Illinois Ave Ste B-203 *Web:* www.denuke.com	Oak Ridge	TN	37830	865-483-8620	
Design Phase Inc 1771 S Lakeside Dr *Web:* dphase.com	Waukegan	IL	60085	847-473-0077	
DGM Services Inc 1813 Greens Rd *Web:* www.dgm-usa.com	Houston	TX	77032	281-821-0500	
Digital Dialogue LLC 3252 University Dr Ste 165 *TF:* 800-205-4268 ■ *Web:* www.digital-dialogue.com	Auburn Hills	MI	48326	800-205-4268	
Dinova LLC 11950 Jones Bridge Rd Ste 115-117 *Web:* www.dinova.net	Johns Creek	GA	30005	770-239-1888	
DirectEmployers.com 9002 N Purdue Rd Quad III Ste 100 *TF:* 866-268-6206 ■ *Web:* www.directemployers.com	Indianapolis	IN	46268	317-874-9000	
Display Producers Inc 1260 Zerega Ave *Web:* www.displayproducersinc.com	Bronx	NY	10462	718-904-1200	
Diversegy LLC 2720 N Stemmons Fwy N Tower 10th Fl Ste *Web:* www.diversegy.com	Dallas	TX	75207	214-637-2400	
Drummac Inc 1361 13th Ave S Ste 135 *Web:* www.drummac.com	Jacksonville	FL	32250	904-241-4999	
Duane Morris Government Strategies LLC 243 Adams St *Web:* www.dmgs.com	Johnstown	PA	15901	814-539-9898	
Dwellworks LLC 1317 Euclid Ave 2nd Fl *Web:* www.dwellworks.com	Cleveland	OH	44115	216-682-4200	
East Coast Graphics 125 Wireless Blvd *Web:* www.ecoastgraphics.com	Hauppauge	NY	11788	631-231-9300	
EchoData Services Inc 735 Fox Chase Ste 101 *Web:* www.echodata.com	Coatesville	PA	19320	610-466-2100	
Eclipse Design Technologies Inc 33 W Higgins Rd Ste 650 *Web:* eclipsedt.com	South Barrington	IL	60010	847-844-8822	
eCollect LLC 5000 Euclid Ave Ste 4403 *TF:* 888-569-6001 ■ *Web:* www.ecollectpayments.com	Cleveland	OH	44103	888-569-6001	
Economy Linen & Towel Service Inc 80 Mead St *Web:* www.economylinen.com	Dayton	OH	45402	937-222-4625	
Eg Tax Service 2475 Niagara Falls Blvd *Web:* www.egtax.com	Buffalo	NY	14228	716-632-7886	
Elyse Connolly Inc 23 W 16th St *Web:* www.elyseconnolly.com	New York	NY	10011	212-255-0886	
EML LLC 318 Seaboard Ln Ste 106 *Web:* www.eml1.com	Franklin	TN	37067	615-771-2560	
End-User Computing 4841 MONROE ST Ste 307 *Web:* www.euc.com	Toledo	OH	43623	419-292-2200	
Engage3 Inc 109 Stevenson St Ste 200 *Web:* www.engage3.com	San Francisco	CA	94105	415-240-4819	
ENSA North America Inc 785 Tucker Rd PMB 318 *Web:* www.ensa-northamerica.com	Tehachapi	CA	93561	661-822-3963	
ePerformax Centers Inc 8001 Ctrview Pkwy Third Fl *Web:* www.eperformax.com	Cordova	TN	38018	901-751-4800	
Erik Johnson & Assoc 758 N Larrabee Unit 415 *Web:* www.erikjohnsonassociates.com	Chicago	IL	60654	312-644-2202	645-5883

Company	City	State	ZIP	Phone	Fax
Erlang Technology Inc 2138 Woodson Rd Ste 7 *Web:* www.erlangtech.com	St. Louis	MO	63114	314-428-6500	
EscrowTech International Inc 3290 W Mayflower Way *Web:* www.escrowtech.com	Lehi	UT	84043	801-852-8202	
eSupply Systems LLC 7800 W IH-10 Ste 130 *Web:* www.esupplysystems.com	San Antonio	TX	78230	210-979-6670	
Etheridge Printing Co 4434 Mcewen Rd *TF:* 800-834-2709 ■ *Web:* www.etheridge.com	Dallas	TX	75244	214-827-8151	
Etopolos Design 1560 Fourth St Ste B *Web:* www.etopolos.com	San Rafael	CA	94901	415-845-8897	
Eureka Lighting 225 De Li ge ouest Ste 200 *Web:* www.eurekalighting.com	Montreal	QC	H2P1H4	514-385-3515	
EV Connect Inc 714 W Olympic Blvd Ste 939 *Web:* www.evconnect.com	Los Angeles	CA	90015	310-751-7997	
Event Solutions International Inc 1757 Larchwood Dr *Web:* www.eventman.com	Troy	MI	48083	248-307-9400	
EWIE Company Inc 1099 Highland Dr Ste D *Web:* www.ewie.com	Ann Arbor	MI	48108	734-971-6265	
Exhibit Source Inc, The 145 Wells Ave *Web:* www.theexhibitsource.com	Newton Center	MA	02459	781-449-1600	
Express Packaging of Ohio Inc 301 Enterprise Dr *Web:* www.expresspackaging.net	Newcomerstown	OH	43832	740-498-4700	
Family Centre, The 9912-106 St Northwest Ste 20 *Web:* www.the-family-centre.com	Edmonton	AB	T5K1C5	780-423-2831	
FanBox 919 4th Ave Ste 200 *Web:* www.fanbox.com	San Diego	CA	92101	619-788-1398	
FarCountries com 150 W 25th St, Ste 1203 *Web:* www.farcountries.com	New York	NY	10001	212-255-6550	
Farm First Dairy Cooperative 4001 Nakoosa Trl Ste 100 *Web:* www.farmfirstdairycooperative.com	Madison	WI	53714	608-244-3373	
FCI Lender Services Inc 8180 E Kaiser Blvd *Web:* www.trustfci.com	Anaheim Hills	CA	92808	714-282-2424	
Fifth Sun Inc 495 Ryan Ave *Web:* www.5sun.com	Chico	CA	95973	530-343-8725	
First Reliance Holdings LLC 275 N Pointe Pkwy Ste 60 *TF:* 877-495-8938 ■ *Web:* frholdings.com	Amherst	NY	14228	877-495-8938	
FirstPoint Inc 225 Commerce Pl *Web:* www.firstpointresources.com	Greensboro	NC	27401	336-378-6300	
Fisher Group Inc 3571 South 300 West *TF:* 800-365-8920 ■ *Web:* www.fishergroupinc.com	Salt Lake City	UT	84115	800-365-8920	
Foodie Tout Inc 1777 W Watmaugh Rd *Web:* www.foodietout.com	Sonoma	CA	95476	707-938-8385	
Fortitude Business Solutions LLC PO Box 2095 *TF:* 877-577-2644 ■ *Web:* www.fortitudebusiness.com	Daphne	AL	36526	877-577-2644	
Freedom Lights Our World (FLOW) Inc 1510 Falcon Ledge Dr *Web:* www.flowidealism.org	Austin	TX	78746	512-327-8860	
Frontpoint 233 North 1250 West Ste 203 *Web:* www.frontpoint-it.com	Centerville	UT	84014	801-298-5404	
FulCircle Inc 13333 E 37th Ave *Web:* www.fulcircle.spnet.info	Denver	CO	80239	720-374-3600	
Fusicology LLC 2658 Griffith Park Blvd #128 *Web:* fusicology.com	Los Angeles	CA	90039	323-988-2424	
Fusion Packaging Solutions Inc 3333 Welborn St - Ste 400 *Web:* fusionpkg.com	Dallas	TX	75219	214-747-2004	
G Dc Home 695 Coleman Blvd *Web:* www.gdchome.com	Mount Pleasant	SC	29464	843-849-0711	
G2 Secure Staff LLC 400 E Las Colians Blvd Ste 750 *Web:* www.g2securestaff.com	Irving	TX	75039	972-915-6979	
Gallun Snow 1920 Market St Ste 201 *Web:* www.gallunsnow.com	Denver	CO	80202	303-433-9500	
Gardien Services USA Inc 3700 24th Ave Bldg A *Web:* www.gardien.com	Forest Grove	OR	97116	503-430-8980	
Gary Raub Assoc 4345 Murphy Canyon Rd	San Diego	CA	92123	858-565-2775	
GCS Service Inc 370 Wabasha St N *TF:* 800-822-2303 ■ *Web:* www.equipmentcare.com	St. Paul	MN	55102	800-822-2303	
Gehring LP 24800 Drake Rd *Web:* www.gehring.de/en-us	Farmington Hills	MI	48335	248-478-8060	
Genesis Plastics Welding Inc 720 E Broadway *Web:* www.genesisplasticswelding.com	Fortville	IN	46040	317-485-7887	
Geofiny Technologies LLC 3137 Wrightsville Ave *Web:* www.spectrumnc.com	Wilmington	NC	28403	910-392-1496	
GGLO LLC 1301 First Ave Ste 301 *Web:* www.gglo.com	Seattle	WA	98101	206-467-5828	
GHA design studios 1100 Ave des Canadiens-de-Montr,al Ste 130 *Web:* www.ghadesign.com	Montreal	QC	H3B2S2	514-843-5812	
Globa li 7948 E 23rd Ave *Web:* www.globa.li	Denver	CO	80238	303-895-9583	
Global Building Services Inc 25600 Rye Canyon Rd *Web:* www.globalbuildingservices.com	Santa Clarita	CA	91355	661-295-5065	
Global Contact Services LLC 101 Martin Dr *Web:* www.gcsagents.com	Mount Hope	WV	25880	304-877-0427	
Global Linguist Solutions LLC 3190 Fairview Park Dr Ste 1000 *Web:* www.gls-corp.com	Falls Church	VA	22042	817-224-7807	
Global R&D Consulting Group 3200 Autoroute Laval Ouest *TF:* 866-770-5577 ■ *Web:* www.globalr-d.com	Laval	GA	30022	866-770-5577	
GLP Inc 360 W Superior St *Web:* www.garyleepartners.com	Chicago	IL	60654	312-640-8300	
Goldec Hamm's Manufacturing Ltd 6760 65 Ave *TF:* 800-661-1665 ■ *Web:* www.goldec.com	Red Deer	AB	T4P1A5	403-343-6607	
Good Leads 224 Main St Unit 2B *TF:* 866-894-5323 ■ *Web:* www.goodleads.com	Salem	NH	03079	603-870-8150	
Goodwin & Associates Hospitality Services LLC 11 S Main St Ste 200 *Web:* goodwinhospitality.com	Concord	NH	03301	603-223-0303	
Grant & Weber Inc 26610 Agoura Rd Ste 209 *TF:* 800-333-1656 ■ *Web:* www.grantweber.com	Calabasas	CA	91302	818-871-7700	
GreenSeed Contract Packaging 1025 Paramount Pkwy *Web:* greenseedcp.com	Batavia	IL	60510	630-761-8544	
Grid One Solutions Inc 700 Turner Way Ste 205 *Web:* www.gridonesolutions.com	Aston	PA	19014	484-482-2480	
Groople Inc 1732 Wazee St Ste 202 *Web:* www.groople.com	Denver	CO	80202	817-987-9004	
Growing Leaders Inc 270 Scientific Dr NW Ste 10 *Web:* www.growingleaders.com	Norcross	GA	30092	770-495-3332	
Gumas Advertising LLC 99 Shotwell St *Web:* www.gumas.com	San Francisco	CA	94103	415-621-7575	
Gyford Productions 891 Trademark Dr *Web:* www.standoffsystems.com	Reno	NV	89521	775-829-7272	
H & O Centerless Grinding Inc 45 Bathurst Dr *Web:* www.cylindricalprecision.com	Waterloo	ON	N2V1N2	519-884-0322	
H & P Leasing Inc 550 Hwy 49 S *Web:* www.hptrailerleasing.com	Jackson	MS	39218	601-939-9000	
H Chambers Co 1800 Washington Blvd Ste 111 *Web:* www.chambersusa.com	Baltimore	MD	21230	410-727-4535	727-6982
Haas Environmental Inc 7 Red Lion Rd PO Box 2082 *Web:* www.haasenvironmental.com	Vincentown	NJ	08088	609-859-3100	
Hallcon Corp 5775 Yonge St Ste 1010 *Web:* www.hallconcorp.com	Toronto	ON	M2M4J1	416-964-9191	
Hand Era 2859 104th St *Web:* www.handera.com	Des Moines	IA	50322	515-252-7522	
Hba Architecture Engineering And Interior Design 1 Columbus Ctr Ste 1000 *Web:* www.hbaonline.com	Virginia Beach	VA	23462	757-490-9048	
HELIOS Group Utilities & Facilities Management Inc 2099 Fernand-Lafontaine blvd *Web:* www.helios-group.com	Longueuil	QC	J4G2J4	450-646-1903	
Hi Caliber IT Soluitons 38 VALLEY WOOD DR *Web:* www.hi-caliber-it.com	Somerset	NJ	08873	732-828-7482	
Hignell Printing Ltd 488 Burnell St *Web:* www.hignell.mb.ca	Winnipeg	MB	R3G2B4	204-784-1030	
Hileman Enterprises LLC 2217 E Ninth St Ste 200 *Web:* www.hilemangroup.com	Cleveland	OH	44115	216-923-1445	
Hinduja Global Solutions Inc 4355 Weaver Pkwy Ste 310 *Web:* www.teamhgs.com	Warrenville	IL	60555	309-229-2837	
Hogan Inc J Taylor 308 Libbie Ave *Web:* www.jtaylorhogan.com	Richmond	VA	23226	804-282-4474	
Homeowner Protection Office 1055 W Georgia St Ste 2270 Royal Centre *Web:* www.hpo.bc.ca	Vancouver	BC	V6E3P3	604-646-7055	
hovelstay.com LLC 121 W Lexington Dr *Web:* hovelstay.com	Glendale	CA	91203	818-480-5770	
HPG International Inc 2121 N California Blvd Ste 625 *Web:* www.higginspurchasing.com	Walnut Creek	CA	94596	925-949-5700	
Hrizons 10749 108TH AVE N *Web:* www.hrizons.com	Hanover	MN	55341	612-326-9677	
HROplus com 65 Water St *Web:* www.hroplus.com	Laconia	NH	03246	603-524-8762	
hss LLC 5446 Dixie Hwy *Web:* www.valuepointsolutions.com	Saginaw	MI	48601	989-777-2983	
Hubbuch & Co 324 W Main St *Web:* www.hubbuch.com	Louisville	KY	40202	502-583-2713	582-7375
Hypertec BCDR Inc 9300 Trans Canada Hwy *Web:* www.hypertecbcdr.com	Saint-laurent	QC	H4S1K5	514-745-4540	
iBox Network Inc 8680 Wash Blvd Apt 211 *Web:* www.lightboxnetwork.com	Culver City	CA	90232	323-855-0080	
Ice Services Inc 2606 Ctr St Ste 6A *Web:* www.iceservices.net	Anchorage	AK	99503	907-301-6247	
ICON Creative Technologies Group 202 E Huron St Ste 100	Ann Arbor	MI	48104	734-239-3586	
Id Group LLC, The 2641 Irving Blvd *Web:* www.idgroupdallas.com	Dallas	TX	75207	214-638-6800	
Idea and Design Works LLC 5080 Santa Fe St Ste 106 *Web:* www.idwpublishing.com	San Diego	CA	92109	858-270-1315	
Idem Translations Inc 550 California Ave Ste 310 *Web:* www.idemtranslations.com	Palo Alto	CA	94306	650-858-4336	
Imagine Advertising & Publishing Inc 6141 Crooked Creek Rd *TF:* 866-832-3214 ■ *Web:* www.imagineadv.com	Norcross	GA	30092	770-734-0966	
Imagine IT Inc 1043 Grand Ave Ste 206 *Web:* duralogic.com	Saint Paul	MN	55105	651-204-7222	
iMirus 7715 E 111th St Ste 100 *Web:* www.imirus.com	Tulsa	OK	74133	918-492-0660	
In-Care Network Inc 2906 2nd Ave N *Web:* www.incarenetwork.com	Billings	MT	59101	406-259-9616	
Infinite Scale Design Group LLC 16 E Exchange Pl *Web:* www.infinitescale.com	Salt Lake City	UT	84111	801-363-1881	
Influence Technologies Inc 1342 La Colina Dr *TF:* 877-420-2766 ■ *Web:* influencetech.com	Tustin	CA	92780	877-420-2766	

Company / Address	City	State	Zip	Phone	Fax
InfoSend Inc 4240 E La Palma Ave *Web:* www.infosend.com	Anaheim	CA	92807	714-993-2690	
Infospan Inc 31878 Del Obispo St Ste 118 *Web:* www.infospaninc.com	San Juan Capistrano	CA	92675	949-260-9990	
Infusion Marketing Group LLC 18 Knights Bridge Rd *Web:* www.profitgenerator.com	Sherwood	AR	72120	501-519-1969	
Innovadex LLC 7930 Santa Fe 3rd Fl *TF:* 877-292-7279 ■ *Web:* www.ulprospector.com	Overland Park	KS	66204	913-307-9010	
Inovar Inc 1073 West 1700 North *Web:* www.inovar-inc.com	Logan	UT	84321	435-792-4949	
InsideUp Inc 7940 Silverton Ave Ste 215 *Web:* www.insideup.com	San Diego	CA	92122	858-397-5735	
InstaGift LLC 117 West Glenwood Dr *TF:* 877-870-3463 ■ *Web:* instagift.com	Birmingham	AL	35209	877-870-3463	
InterEx Inc 34 Hunt Rd *Web:* www.interex.com	Amesbury	MA	01913	978-388-8755	
Interiors by Steven G Inc 2818 Centre Port Cir *Web:* www.interiorsbysteveng.com	Pompano Beach	FL	33064	954-735-8223	
Intland GmbH 968 Inverness Way *TF:* 866-468-5210 ■ *Web:* www.intland.com	Sunnyvale	CA	94087	866-468-5210	
Invisible Hand Networks Inc 670 Broadway Ste 302 *TF:* 866-637-5286 ■ *Web:* www.invisiblehand.net	New York	NY	10012	212-400-7416	
ISPN Inc 14303 W 95th St *Web:* www.ispn.net	Lenexa	KS	66215	913-859-9500	
iStores Inc 1212 W Fourth Plain Blvd *Web:* www.istoresinc.com	Vancouver	WA	98660	360-567-2520	
ITW Sexton Can Company Inc 3101 Sexton Rd *Web:* www.sextoncan.com	Decatur	AL	35603	256-355-5850	
J. Krug & Associates Inc 1350 W Northwest Hwy Ste 100 *Web:* www.jkrug.com	Mount Prospect	IL	60056	847-392-8585	
Jameson Group 287 S Robertson Blvd Ste 474 *Web:* www.thejamesongroup.com	Beverly Hills	CA	90211	310-289-5085	
Jamie Gibbs & Associates 120 W 73rd St *Web:* www.jamiegibbsassociates.com	Indianapolis	IN	46260	917-862-5313	
JBS Group Inc 260 S Los Robles Ave Ste 217 *Web:* www.jbshotels.com	Pasadena	CA	91101	626-397-2886	
JDL Technologies Inc 5450 NW 33rd Ave Ft Lauderdale Commerce Ste 106 *Web:* www.jdltech.com	Fort Lauderdale	FL	33309	954-334-0650	
JobDiva 116 John St. Ste 1406 *TF:* 866-562-3482 ■ *Web:* www.jobdiva.com	New York	NY	10038	866-562-3482	
Jomax LLC 14100 N 83rd Ave Ste 235 *TF:* 888-866-0721 ■ *Web:* jomaxrecovery.com	Peoria	AZ	85381	888-866-0721	
K&T Switching Services Inc 3901 Colorado Ave *Web:* www.ktswitching.com	Sheffield Village	OH	44054	440-949-1910	
Kay Green Design Inc 859 Outer Rd *TF:* 800-226-5186 ■ *Web:* www.kaygreendesign.com	Orlando	FL	32814	407-246-7155	426-7873
Kear IT Inc 1510-H Caton Ctr Dr *TF:* 877-532-7481 ■ *Web:* www.kearit.com	Baltimore	MD	21227	877-532-7481	
Kinark Child 500 Hood Rd Ste 200 *Web:* www.kinark.on.ca	Markham	ON	L3R9Z3	905-474-9595	
Kishimoto.Gordon.Dalaya PC 1300 Wilson Blvd Ste 250 *Web:* www.kgdarchitecture.com	Rosslyn	VA	22209	202-338-3800	
L&L Foods Inc 333 N Euclid Way *Web:* llfoodsinc.com	Anaheim	CA	92801	714-254-1430	
Language Scientific Inc 10 Cabot Rd Ste 209 *Web:* www.ricintl.com	Medford	MA	02155	617-621-0940	
LatPro Inc 3980 N Broadway Ste 103-147 *Web:* www.latpro.com	Boulder	CO	80304	954-727-3844	
LBL Architects Inc 1106 W Randol Mill Rd Ste 300 *Web:* www.lblarchitects.com	Arlington	TX	76012	817-265-1510	
LeaseQ LLC 100-D Office Tower Park *Web:* www.leaseq.com	Woburn	MA	01801	781-281-2436	
Legum & Norman Mid-West LLC 4401 Ford Ave 12th Fl *Web:* www.legumnorman.com	Alexandria	VA	22302	703-600-6000	
Lehman Hardware & Appliances Inc 4779 Kidron Rd *TF:* 888-438-5346 ■ *Web:* www.lehmans.com	Dalton	OH	44618	888-438-5346	
Leslie Lewis & Associates 247 Spring St *Web:* www.leslielewisdesign.com	Jeffersonville	IN	47130	812-282-6606	
LeTip International Inc 4838 E Baseline Rd Ste 123 *Web:* www.letip.com	Mesa	AZ	85206	480-264-4600	
Lewellen & Best Displays Inc 101 Knell St *TF:* 800-250-7565 ■ *Web:* lbexhibits.com	Montgomery	IL	60538	630-896-2500	
LexiCode Corp 1720 Dutch Fork Rd Ste F *Web:* www.lexicode.com	Ballentine	SC	29002	803-749-9778	
Life Packaging Technology LLC 2751 Tern Cir Ste A *Web:* www.lifepackagingtechnology.com	Costa Mesa	CA	92626	949-395-8145	
Lime Lab Inc 650 Florida St Ste B *Web:* www.lime-lab.com	San Francisco	CA	94110	415-643-5463	
Linxx Security Inc 272 Bedix Rd Ste 220 *Web:* www.linxxsecurity.com	Virginia Beach	VA	23452	757-222-0300	
Loanio Inc 25 Smith St Ste 301 *TF:* 800-624-8830 ■ *Web:* loanio.com	Nanuet	NY	10954	800-624-8830	
Logic PD Inc 6201 Bury Dr *TF:* 855-461-3802 ■ *Web:* www.logicpd.com	Eden Prairie	MN	55346	952-941-8071	
LUZ Inc 221 Main St Ste 1300 *Web:* www.luz.com	San Francisco	CA	94105	415-981-5890	
M & W Transportation Company Inc 1110 Pumping Sta Rd *Web:* www.mwlginc.com	Nashville	TN	37210	615-256-5755	
Mactus Group 4034 148th Ave NE Bldg K1 *Web:* www.mactusgroup.com	Redmond	WA	98052	425-883-3640	
Mall com 811 Dallas St *Web:* www.mall.com	Houston	TX	77002	512-582-4864	
Managed by Q Inc 50 Eldridge St *Web:* www.managedbyq.com	New York	NY	10002	646-729-6424	
Mancini Duffy 275 Seventh Ave 19th Fl *Web:* www.manciniduffy.com	New York	NY	10001	212-938-1260	
Mandil Inc 846 Elati St *Web:* www.mandilinc.com	Denver	CO	80204	303-892-5805	
Marc-michaels Interior Design Inc 850 E Palmetto Park Rd *Web:* www.marc-michaels.com	Boca Raton	FL	33432	561-362-7037	
Mary Jurek Design Inc 2301 W 205th St Unit 114 *Web:* maryjurekdesign.com	Torrance	CA	90501	310-533-1196	
Matric Group LLC 2099 Hill City Rd *Web:* www.matricgroup.com	Seneca	PA	16346	814-677-0716	
Matrix Companies, The 7162 Reading Rd Ste 250 *TF:* 877-550-7973 ■ *Web:* www.matrixtpa.com	Cincinnati	OH	45237	513-351-1222	
MaxBounty Inc PO Box 17039 *Web:* www.maxbounty.com	Ottawa	ON	K4A4W8	613-834-3955	
mCapitol Management 1341 G St NW Ste 700 *Web:* www.mcapitol.com	Washington	DC	20005	202-296-5354	
MDA Geospatial Services International 13800 Commerce Pkwy *Web:* mdacorporation.com/geospatial/international	Richmond	BC	V6V2J3	604-244-0400	
Med-RT 27758 Santa Margarita Pkwy *Web:* www.med-rt.com	Mission Viejo	CA	92691	949-502-2800	
Mennonite Economic Development Associates of Canada 155 Frobisher Dr Ste I-106 *Web:* www.meda.org	Waterloo	ON	N2V2E1	519-725-1633	
Meta5 Inc 122 W Main St Ste 204 *Web:* www.meta5.us	Babylon	NY	11702	631-587-6800	
Metcalfe Group Inc, The 30405 Solon Rd Unit 5 *Web:* www.metcalfegroup.com	Solon	OH	44139	440-349-5995	
MGM Mirage Design Group Inc 3260 Industrial Rd *TF:* 800-929-1111	Las Vegas	NV	89109	866-761-7111	
Microdynamics Group 1400 Shore Rd *Web:* www.microdg.com	Naperville	IL	60563	630-527-8400	
Midco Connections Inc 4901 E 26th St *Web:* www.midcoconnections.com	Sioux Falls	SD	57110	605-330-4125	
Midwest Telemark International Inc 112 Main St West *Web:* www.mtind.com	Mohall	ND	58761	701-756-6483	
Milestone Technologies Inc 3101 Skyway Ct *Web:* www.milestn.com	Fremont	CA	94539	510-651-2454	
Miller/Zell Inc 4715 Frederick Dr SW *Web:* www.millerzell.com	Atlanta	GA	30336	404-691-7400	699-2189
Minacs Group (USA) Inc, The 34115 W Twelve Mile Rd *Web:* www.minacs.com	Farmington Hills	MI	48331	248-395-8200	
MMS Education 105 TERRY DR Ste 120 *Web:* www.mmseducation.com	Newtown	PA	18940	215-579-8590	
Mo-Tires Ltd 2830 5 Ave N *TF:* 800-774-3888 ■ *Web:* www.mo-tires.com	Lethbridge	AB	T1H0P1	403-329-4533	
Mobium Creative Group 2000 Merchandise Mart *Web:* www.mobium.com	Chicago	IL	60654	312-527-0500	
Monterey Financial Services Inc 4095 Avenida De La Plata *Web:* www.montereyfinancial.com	Oceanside	CA	92056	760-639-3500	
Motor City Computer 1610 E Highwood Dr *Web:* www.motorcitycomputer.com	Pontiac	MI	48340	248-454-2000	
Moureaux Hauspy Design Inc 276 Rue St Jacques *Web:* provencherroy.ca	Montreal	QC	H2Y1N3	514-844-3938	
Msa Planning & Design Consultants Inc 642 Harrison St Fl 3 *Web:* www.msasf.com	San Francisco	CA	94107	415-541-0977	
MSA Solutions Inc 1401 S 52nd St Ste 115 *Web:* msasolutions.net	Tempe	AZ	85281	480-968-2900	
MTI America PO Box 667140 *TF:* 800-553-2155 ■ *Web:* www.mtiamerica.com	Pompano Beach	FL	33066	800-553-2155	
myFreightWorld LLC 7133 W 95th St *TF:* 877-549-9438 ■ *Web:* www.myfreightworld.com	Overland Park	KS	66212	877-549-9438	
National Publisher Services LLC 43 Oak Hills Rd *Web:* www.nps1.com	Edison	NJ	08820	732-548-1667	
NEEBCO Limited Partnership 15 Chenell Dr *Web:* www.neebco.com	Concord	NH	03301	603-228-1133	
NEI Global Relocation Inc 8701 W Dodge Rd *Web:* www.neirelo.com	Omaha	NE	68114	402-397-8486	
NetCenergy Corp 231 Elm St *Web:* www.netcenergy.com	Warwick	RI	02888	401-921-3100	
NetworkElites Services Inc 13657 Jupiter Rd Ste 111 *Web:* www.networkelites.com	Dallas	TX	75238	972-235-3114	
NetworkOmni Multilingual Communications Inc 4353 Park Ter Dr *Web:* www.networkomni.com	Westlake Village	CA	91361	818-706-7890	
Networld Media Group LLC 13100 Eastpoint Park Blvd Ste 100 *TF:* 877-441-7545 ■ *Web:* www.networldalliance.com	Louisville	KY	40223	877-441-7545	
Nfusion Design Studio LLC 400 Fourth Ave S *Web:* www.nfusiondesignstudio.com	Nashville	TN	37201	615-850-5530	
Niermann Weeks Company Inc 760 Generals Hwy *Web:* www.niermannweeks.com	Millersville	MD	21108	410-923-0123	923-0647

Phone Fax

Nitelines USA Inc
3065 Peachtree Industrial Blvd Ste 210 .... Duluth GA 30097 877-337-2563
TF: 877-337-2563 ■ *Web:* www.nitelinesusa.com
Noone & Associates Inc 3 Crossgate Dr......... Mechanicsburg PA 17050 717-458-0482
Web: www.nooneappraisals.com
Noritsu Technical Services
6900 Noritsu Ave .... Buena Park CA 90620 888-435-7448
TF: 888-435-7448 ■ *Web:* www.noritsuservice.com
Ntelligent Networks Inc 5303 S Florida Ave........... Lakeland FL 33813 863-802-9675
Web: www.ntelligentnetworks.com
O'Currance Teleservices Inc
11747 South Lonepeak Pkwy Ste 100.................. Draper UT 84020 801-736-0500
Web: www.ocurrance.com
Oak Brook Golf Club 1200 Oak Brook Rd............ Oak Brook IL 60523 630-990-4233
Web: www.oak-brook.org
OceanGate Inc 1205 Craftsman Way Ste 112............ Everett WA 98201 206-949-2237
Web: www.oceangate.com
Oec Business Interiors 104 E I65 Service Rd N........... Mobile AL 36607 251-471-3368
Web: www.oecbi.com
Ogden Telephone Co 4726 E Weston Rd............. Blissfield MI 49228 517-443-5595
Web: www.ogdentel.com
Omnifics Inc 5845 Richmond Hwy Ste 300............ Alexandria VA 22303 703-548-4040 836-8159
Web: www.omnifics.com
On-Ramp Medical Communications LLC
8770 Purdue Rd............................... Indianapolis IN 46268 317-202-3300
Web: www.frontlineindy.com
OptiCat LLC 8170 S Highland Dr Ste E1................. Sandy UT 84093 801-438-1020
Web: www.opticat.net
Optoro Inc 5001-A Forbes Blvd .... Lanham MD 20706 301-760-7003
Web: www.optoro.com
Orion Foods Inc 4915 W 157th Pl .... Overland Park KS 66224 816-728-2249
Web: orionfoods.com
Oxford Communications LLC
121 S Alfred St Ste 6 .... Alexandria VA 22314 703-535-6712
Web: www.oxfordpromos.com
Pacific Design Engineering (1996) Ltd
8505 Eastlake Dr...................................... Burnaby BC V5A4T7 604-421-1311
Web: www.pde.com
Pacific Office Interiors
5304 Derry Ave Ste U.......................... Agoura Hills CA 91301 818-735-0333
Web: www.poi.bz
Palladeo Inc 900 Western Ave Ste.................. Glendale CA 91201 818-241-5656
Web: www.palladeo.com
Pan-Glo Services 1550 CUSTER AVE Ste.......... San Francisco CA 94124 415-648-3325
Web: www.pan-glo.com
Paragon International Inc
2885 N Berkeley Lk Rd Ste 17 .... Duluth GA 30096 678-481-6762
Web: www.paragonint.net
Paws Up Outfitters 40060 Paws Up Rd .... Greenough MT 59823 406-244-5200
Web: www.pawsup.com
PDS Development 15190 Marsh Ln .... Addison TX 75001 972-497-9000
Perceptis LLC 325 W McBee Ave Ste 300............ Greenville SC 29601 864-214-4360
Web: www.perceptis.com
PerformLine Inc 30 W Park Pl 3rd Fl.............. Morristown NJ 07960 973-590-2305
Web: performline.com
Perry Color Card 685 W Ter Dr.................... San Dimas CA 91773 909-599-7954
Web: www.perrycolorcard.com
Philpotts 40 S School St .... Honolulu HI 96813 808-523-6771 521-9569
Web: www.philpotts.net
Phoenix Engineering & Consulting Inc
110 Londonderry Ct Ste 136-C.................... Woodstock GA 30188 404-216-0140
Web: www.phoenix-engineer.com
Phyle Inventory Control Specialists Inc
4150 Grange Hall Rd .... Holly MI 48442 248-328-5000
Web: www.picsinv.com
Pioneer Magnetics 1745 Berkeley St............ Santa Monica CA 90404 310-829-6751
TF: 800-269-6426 ■ *Web:* www.pioneermagnetics.com
Pivot it Inc 3541 Tracy Dr........................ Santa Clara CA 95051 408-836-9314
Web: www.pivot-it.com
Placemaking Group 505 14th St 5th fl................ Oakland CA 94612 510-835-7900
Web: www.placemakinggroup.com
Plant Affair, The 1931 Blake Ave.................. Los Angeles CA 90039 323-661-4571
Web: plantaffair.com
Plantscape Inc 3101 Liberty Ave .... Pittsburgh PA 15201 412-281-6352
Web: www.plantscape.com
Polygon Network PO Box 4806........................ Dillon CO 80435 800-221-4435
TF: 800-221-4435 ■ *Web:* www.polygon.net
Post Bid Ship Inc 7633 E Acoma Dr .... Scottsdale AZ 85260 480-327-6652
Web: www.postbidship.com
Potawatomi Business Development Corp
3215 W State St Ste 300......................... Milwaukee WI 53208 414-290-9490
Web: www.potawatomibdc.com
Potter-Randall Appraisal District
5701 Hollywood Rd (Loop 335) Po Box 7190 .... Amarillo TX 79114 806-355-8426
Web: www.prad.org
Premier BPO Inc 102 Country Ln Ste B............ Clarksville TN 37043 931-551-8888
Web: www.premierbpo.com
Press-A-Print International LLC
1463 Commerce Way .... Idaho Falls ID 83401 208-523-7620
Web: www.pressaprint.com
Prestige Engineering Resources & Technologies Inc
3630 Thirteen Mile Rd .... Warren MI 48092 586-573-3070
Web: www.prestigeeng.com
Primeritus Financial Services Inc
440 Metroplex Dr................................ Nashville TN 37211 888-833-4238
TF: 888-833-4238 ■ *Web:* www.primeritus.com
ProCore Solutions LLC 1260 Cobb Pkwy N............ Marietta GA 30062 678-355-3550
Web: www.procoresolutions.com
Progrexion Marketing Inc
330 N Cutler Dr .... North Salt Lake UT 84054 801-384-4100
Web: www.progrexion.com
Propco Marketing Inc
8750 West Bryn Mawr Ave Ste 1020.................. Chicago IL 60631 773-463-9193
Web: www.propco.com

Phone Fax

Protectolite Inc 84 Railside Rd...................... Toronto ON M3A1A3 416-444-4484
Web: www.protectolite.com
Pump Audio Inc 5 Pine St .... Tivoli NY 12583 845-757-5555
Web: www.pumpaudio.com
QSS Group Inc 4500 Forbes Blvd Ste 200.............. Lanham MD 20706 301-577-0700
Web: www.qssgroupinc.com
QualiTest Ltd 1139 Post Rd.......................... Fairfield CT 06824 877-882-9540
TF: 877-882-9540 ■ *Web:* www.qualitestgroup.com
Quest Service Group LLC 439 Oak St .... Garden City NY 11530 516-594-7079
Web: www.questservicegroup.com
Quippi Corp 444 S Cedros Ave Ste 410 .... La Jolla CA 92037 888-978-4774
TF: 888-978-4774 ■ *Web:* www.quippi.com
R d Jones & Associates Inc
729 E Pratt St Ste 2000............................ Baltimore MD 21202 410-332-4700
Web: www.rdjones.com
R H K Hydraulic Cylinder Services Inc
13111 159th St.................................... Edmonton AB T5V1H6 780-452-2876
Web: www.rhkhydraulics.com
R.P.C. Contracting Inc
934 W Kitty Hawk Rd .... Kitty Hawk NC 27949 252-261-3336
Web: www.rpccontracting.com
Ravenswood Studio Inc
6900 N Central Pk Ave .... Lincolnwood IL 60712 847-679-2800 679-2805
Web: www.ravenswoodstudio.com
RealtyBid International Inc
3225 Rainbow Dr Ste 248...................... Rainbow City AL 35906 877-518-5600
TF: 877-518-5600 ■ *Web:* www.realtybid.com
Records Consultants Inc
10826 Gulfdale St............................. San Antonio TX 78216 210-348-0927
Web: www.rcitech.com
Recruiting Toolbox PO Box 2573.................. Redmond WA 98073 425-557-2100
TF: 888-823-2030 ■ *Web:* www.recruitingtoolbox.com
RED Inc 298 E First St............................ Idaho Falls ID 83401 208-528-0051
Web: www.redinc.com
Regatta Travel Solutions Inc
325 Winding River Ln Ste 201B.................. Charlottesville VA 22911 800-605-5093
TF: 800-605-5093 ■ *Web:* www.regattatravelsolutions.com
Religence Inc 2090 Green St.................. San Francisco CA 94123 415-771-7473
Web: www.religence.com
Remote Logistics International LLC
6430 Richmond Ave Ste 320 .... Houston TX 77057 713-780-9933
Web: www.remotelogisticsinternational.com
Renbor Sales Solutions Inc
256 Thornway Ave .... Thornhill ON L4J7X8 416-671-3555
TF: 855-257-2537 ■ *Web:* www.sellbetter.ca
Rescraft Plastic Products Inc 9 Woodslee Ave........... Paris ON N3L3V1 519-442-4339
Web: www.rescraft.com
Rev.com Inc 251 Kearny St 8th Fl.............. San Francisco CA 94108 888-369-0701
TF: 888-369-0701 ■ *Web:* www.rev.com/translation
RevenueWire Inc 3962 Borden St Ste 102 .... Victoria BC V8P3H8 250-590-2273
Web: www.revenuewire.com
Rex Pak Ltd 85 Thornmount Dr .... Toronto ON M1B5V3 416-755-3324
Web: www.rexpak.com
RightHand Technologies Inc
6545 N Olmsted Ave................................ Chicago IL 60631 773-774-7600
Web: www.righthandtech.com
RJE Business Interiors Inc
623 Broadway St................................ Cincinnati OH 45202 513-641-3700
Web: www.rjecincy.com
RMW Architecture & Interiors
160 Pine St 4th Fl........................... San Francisco CA 94111 415-781-9800
Web: www.rmw.com
Rocketship Inc 110 South 300 West.................... Provo UT 84601 801-373-1922
Web: www.rocketshipdesign.com
Rockford Mercantile Agency Inc
2502 S Alpine Rd .... Rockford IL 61108 815-229-3328
Web: www.rmacollections.com
Rodriguez Chavez Corp 10543 Fisher Rd .... Houston TX 77041 713-457-0570
Web: www.rchind.com
Rome Research Corp 421 Ridge St .... Rome NY 13440 315-339-0491
Web: www.pargovernment.com
Rosenberger TOTH 6970 Central Hwy.............. Pennsauken NJ 08109 856-662-8700
Web: www.tothtech.com
Run Energy LP 5009 S Danville Dr .... Abilene TX 79602 325-795-1550
Web: www.runenergy.com
Sacor Financial Inc
1911 Douglas Blvd 85-126........................ Roseville CA 95661 866-556-0231
TF: 866-556-0231 ■ *Web:* www.sacor.net
Sales Gauge 1186 Old Marlborough Rd............... Concord MA 01742 781-910-0077
TF: 877-406-0493 ■ *Web:* www.sales-gauge.com
ScentSational Technologies LLC
425 Old York Rd.................................. Jenkintown PA 19046 215-886-7777
Web: www.scentsationaltechnologies.com
Scribendi Inc 405 Riverview Dr Ste 304 .... Chatham ON N7M5J5 519-351-1626
Web: www.scribendi.com
Sea Pearl Seafood Company Inc
14120 Shell Belt Rd .... Bayou La Batre AL 36509 251-824-2129
TF: 800-872-8804 ■ *Web:* sea-pearl.com
Seaborn Health Care PO BOX 41158........... Saint Petersburg FL 33743 727-398-1710
Web: www.seabornhc.com
SellerCrowd Inc
41 St. Marks Pl Appartment 4...................... New York NY 10003 617-680-6161
Web: sellercrowd.com
Service Companies Inc, The
14750 NW 77th Court Ste 100 .... Miami Lakes FL 33016 305-681-8800
Web: www.theservicecompanies.com
Setina Manufacturing Company Inc
2926 Yelm Hwy Se.................................. Olympia WA 98501 800-426-2627
TF: 800-426-2627 ■ *Web:* www.setina.com
Sevenrooms Inc 127 W 24th St 5th Fl .... New York NY 10011 212-242-5607
Web: www.sevenrooms.com
SGT LLC 7207 IBM Dr CLT-3A .... Charlotte NC 28262 704-805-2810
Web: www.sgt-llc.com

Phone Fax

ShareASale.com Inc 15 W Hubbard St Ste 500 .... Chicago IL 60654 312-321-0487
Web: www.shareasale.com

Sheila Greco Associates LLC
174 State Hwy 67 .... Amsterdam NY 12010 518-843-4611
Web: www.sheilagreco.com

Sightly Enterprises Inc
910 Camino Del Mar Ste F .... Del Mar CA 92014 951-225-7000
Web: www.sightly.com

Simard 1212 32nd ave .... Lachine QC H8T3K7 905-670-2005
Web: www.simard.ca

Simple Verity Inc 1218 Third Ave .... Seattle WA 98101 617-905-7467
Web: www.simpleverity.com

Simplegrid Technology Inc 40 Baldwin Rd. .... Parsippany NJ 07054 973-265-2838
Web: www.simplegrid.com

Sky Climber Wind Solutions LLC
1800 Pittsburgh Dr .... Delaware OH 43015 740-203-3900
Web: www.skyclimberwindsolutions.com

Skyline North 1604 Wayneport Rd. .... Macedon NY 14502 315-986-4600
Web: www.skyline.com/upstate-new-york-northern-new-england

Slifer Designs 216 Main St Ste C-100 .... Edwards CO 81632 970-926-8200
Web: www.sliferdesigns.com

Sloan Accoustics Inc
49 Bloomfield Ave Ste 101 .... Mountain Lakes NJ 07046 973-227-3555 227-8731
Web: www.sloanandcompany.com

Smart LLC
Smart TuitionOne Woodbridge Ctr Ste 800. .... Woodbridge NJ 07095 866-395-2986
TF: 866-395-2986 ■ *Web:* www.smarttuition.com

Smart System Technology & Commercialization Center
5450 Campus Dr .... Canandaigua NY 14424 585-919-3000
Web: www.stcmems.com

sortimat Technology 2242 N Palmer Dr .... Schaumburg IL 60173 847-925-1234
Web: www.sortimat.com

Space Inc 3142 E Vantage Point Dr Ste 2. .... Midland MI 48642 989-835-5151
Web: spacewithin.net

Speck Design Inc 600 Battery St. .... Palo Alto CA 94111 650-462-9080
Web: www.speckdesign.com

Spectra Print Corp 3201 Dixon St .... Stevens Point WI 54481 715-344-5175
Web: www.spectraprint.com

Springboard Nonprofit Consumer Credit Management Inc
4351 Latham St .... Riverside CA 92501 888-425-3453
TF: 888-425-3453 ■ *Web:* bkhelp.org

Spyre Solutions Inc
91 Rylander Blvd Ste 7-250 .... Toronto ON M1B5M5 416-444-4924
Web: www.spyresolutions.com

Staffelbach Design Associates Inc
2525 McKinnon Ste 800 .... Dallas TX 75201 214-747-2511
Web: www.staffelbach.com

Star Displays Inc 38w636 Us Hwy 20. .... Elgin IL 60124 847-695-2040
Web: www.starincorporated.com

Star Exhibits & Environments Inc
6920 93rd Ave N. .... Minneapolis MN 55445 763-561-4655
TF: 800-419-7827 ■ *Web:* www.starexhibits.com

State Science & Technology Institute
5015 Pine Creek Dr .... Westerville OH 43081 614-901-1690
Web: www.ssti.org

StreamSend 78 York St .... Sacramento CA 95814 916-326-5407
TF: 877-439-4078 ■ *Web:* www.streamsend.com

StreetLinks LLC 7551 S Shelby St. .... Indianapolis IN 46227 317-215-8800
Web: www.streetlinks.com

Strite Industries Ltd 298 Shepherd Ave. .... Cambridge ON N3C1V1 519-658-9361
Web: www.strite.com

Stroma Service Consulting Inc
19 Legault St .... North Bay ON P1A4K6 705-840-6000
Web: www.stroma.ca

Stromberg Architectural Products Inc
4400 Oneal St. .... Greenville TX 75402 903-454-0904
Web: www.strombergarchitectural.com

Summit Account Resolution 12201 Champlin Dr ...... Champlin MN 55316 763-712-3700
Web: www.summitcollects.com

Sunset Farm Foods Inc 1201 Madison Hwy .... Valdosta GA 31601 229-242-3389
Web: www.sunsetfarmfoods.com

SweetLabs Inc 510 Market St Ste 301. .... San Diego CA 92101 619-269-0150
Web: www.sweetlabs.com

Syspro Technologies Inc 6545 Preston Rd Ste 300. .... Plano TX 75024 214-440-3820
Web: www.sysprotech.com

Take Flight Alaska Inc 1740 E 5TH AVE. .... Anchorage AK 99501 907-274-9943
Web: www.takeflightalaska.com

TaskUs Inc
3233 Donald Douglas Loop S Ste 3 .... Santa Monica CA 90405 888-400-8275
TF: 888-400-8275 ■ *Web:* www.taskus.com

TCG Continuum LLC 4251 Leap Rd. .... Hilliard OH 43026 614-876-8600
Web: www.tcgcontinuum.com

TCS 168 Thatcher Rd .... Greensboro NC 27409 336-632-0860
Web: www.tcsusa.com

TECMA Group LLC, The 2000 Wyoming Ave .... El Paso TX 79903 915-534-4252
Web: www.tecma.com

Tektronix Component Solutions Inc
2905 SW Hocken Ave .... Beaverton OR 97005 503-627-4521
Web: www.tek.com/tektronix-component-solutions

Telvista Inc 1605 LBJ Fwy Ste 200 .... Dallas TX 75234 972-919-7800
Web: www.telvista.com

TernPro Inc 1431 Washington Blvd Apt 1703. .... Detroit MI 48226 888-483-8779
TF: 888-483-8779 ■ *Web:* ternpro.com

Tetra Tech Architects & Engineers
Cornell Business & Technology Park 10 Brown Rd
.... Ithaca NY 14850 607-277-7100
TF: 877-882-7241 ■ *Web:* www.tetratechae.com

ThinkDirect Marketing Group Inc
8285 Bryan Dairy Rd Ste 150 .... Largo FL 33773 727-369-2700
Web: www.tdmg.com

Thomas Pheasant Inc 1029 33rd St NW .... Washington DC 20007 202-337-6596
Web: www.thomaspheasant.com

Thomson Scientific Inc 3501 Market St .... Philadelphia PA 19104 215-386-0100
Web: ipscience.thomsonreuters.com

Phone Fax

Tigerlight Inc 473 West 910 South .... Heber City UT 84032 435-657-9529
Web: www.tigerlight.net

TJ Metzgers Inc 207 Arco Dr .... Toledo OH 43607 419-861-8611
Web: www.metzgers.com

TMP Direct 600 International Dr. .... Mount Olive NJ 07828 800-328-2439
TF: 800-328-2439 ■ *Web:* www.tmpwdirect.com

Total Comfort of Wisconsin Inc
W234 N2830 Paul Rd .... Pewaukee WI 53072 262-523-2500
Web: www.total-mechanical.com

Trading Post of Kittery
301 US Rte 1 PO Box 904. .... Kittery ME 03904 800-872-4867
TF: 800-872-4867 ■ *Web:* www.usaguns.com

Training Industry Inc
401 Harrison Oaks Blvd Ste 300. .... Cary NC 27513 866-298-4203
TF: 866-298-4203 ■ *Web:* www.trainingindustry.com

Trak-1 Technology Co PO Box 52028 .... Tulsa OK 74152 918-779-6500
Web: www.trak-1.com

Transformit Inc 33 Sanford Dr .... Gorham ME 04038 207-856-9911
Web: www.transformit.com

TranslateMedia LLC 414 Broadway 4th Fl .... New York NY 10013 212-796-5636
Web: www.translatemedia.com

TREC Global Inc 115 Providence Blvd .... Kendall Park NJ 08824 707-773-3325
Web: www.trecglobal.com

Triad Creative Group 3130 Intertech Dr. .... Brookfield WI 53045 262-781-3100
Web: www.triadcreativegroup.com

Trinsic Technologies Inc
15843 Opal Fire Dr Ste 100 .... Austin TX 78727 512-410-7308
Web: www.trinsictech.com

tripBAM LLC 7318 Marquette .... Dallas TX 75225 214-363-9630
Web: www.tripbam.com

TrueAccord Corp 148 Townsend St Ste 26 .... San Francisco CA 94107 866-611-2731
TF: 866-611-2731 ■ *Web:* www.trueaccord.com

TS3 LLC 1870 General George Patton Dr. .... Franklin TN 37067 615-523-5300
Web: www.ts3technology.com

Uhl Company Inc 9065 zachary ln n .... Maple grove MN 55369 763-425-7226
TF: 800-815-3820 ■ *Web:* www.uhlcompany.com

Up Communications Services LLC
103 SE Atlantic St. .... Tullahoma TN 37388 931-461-5391
Web: upcomllc.com

UsTrendy INC 1842 Beacon St Ste 404. .... Brookline MA 02445 888-535-1187
TF: 888-535-1187 ■ *Web:* www.ustrendy.com

V. G. Reed & Sons Inc 1002 S 12th St. .... Louisville KY 40210 502-560-0100
Web: www.vgreed.com

Veenendaalcave Inc 1170 Peachtree St NE. .... Atlanta GA 30309 404-881-1811 876-1289
Web: www.vcave.com

VendorSeek com LLC
520 Fellowship Rd Ste 102. .... Mt. Laurel NJ 08054 856-222-9960
Web: www.vendorseek.com

Venuelabs 505 Fifth Ave S Ste 300 .... Seattle WA 98104 425-633-1510
TF: 866-333-7328

Verity Information Systems 307 S Main St .... Pratt KS 67124 620-672-6332
Web: www.aenternet.com

Verve 1127 Gregg St. .... Columbia SC 29201 803-799-0045
Web: www.verveinteriors.com

Viking Client Services Inc
7500 Office Ridge Cir Ste 100 .... Eden Prairie MN 55344 952-944-7575
Web: www.vikingservice.com

Villa Lighting Supply Inc
2929 Chouteau Ave .... Saint Louis MO 63103 800-325-0963 531-8720*
**Fax Area Code: 866* ■ *TF:* 800-325-0963 ■ *Web:* www.villalighting.com

Village Inteteriors 215 S Findlay St. .... Seattle WA 98108 206-768-9600
Web: villageinteriorsdesign.com

VIPdesk Connect Inc 324 N Fairfax St .... Alexandria VA 22314 703-299-4422
Web: www.vipdeskconnect.com

Voith Industrial Services Inc
9395 Kenwood Rd Ste 200 .... Cincinnati OH 45242 513-731-3590
Web: redirect.voith.com

W. Caslon & Company Inc 1240 Jefferson Rd .... Rochester NY 14623 585-239-6063
Web: www.caslon.net

Wachs Valve And Hydrant Services LLC
801 Asbury Dr .... Buffalo Grove IL 60089 224-357-2600
Web: www.wachsus.com

Walker Macy 111 SW Oak St. .... Portland OR 97204 503-228-3122
Web: www.walkermacy.com

Walls 360 Inc 5054 Bond St .... Las Vegas NV 89118 888-244-9969
TF: 888-244-9969 ■ *Web:* www.walls360.com

Walton Signage Corp 3419 E Commerce. .... San Antonio TX 78220 210-886-0644
Web: www.waltonsignage.com

Warranty Life Services Inc
4152 Meridian St Ste 105-29 .... Bellingham WA 98226 888-927-7269
TF: 888-927-7269 ■ *Web:* www.warrantylife.com

Westech Solutions LLC
358 Saw Mill River Rd Ste 15 Millwood .... New Castle NY 10546 914-246-0789
Web: www.westechsolutions.com

Wilson Office Interiors
1444 Oak Lawn Ave Ste 105. .... Dallas TX 75207 972-488-4100 488-8815
Web: www.wilsonoi.com

Wirt Design Group
617 W Seventh St Ste 201 .... Los Angeles CA 90017 213-239-0990
Web: www.wirtdesign.com

WorkersCompensation com LLC
711 N Washington Blvd .... Sarasota FL 34236 941-366-3791
Web: www.workerscompensation.com

Workspace Inc 309 Locust St. .... Des Moines IA 50309 515-288-7090
Web: www.workspaceinc.net

WorldPantry.com Inc 1192 Illinois St. .... San Francisco CA 94107 415-401-0080
Web: www.worldpantry.com

Worldwide Court Reporters
3000 Weslayan St Ste 235 .... Houston TX 77027 713-572-2000
TF: 800-745-1101 ■ *Web:* www.worldwidecourtreporters.com

Wyse Meter Solutions Inc
RPO Newmarket Court PO Box 95530 .... Newmarket ON L3Y8J8 866-681-9465
TF: 866-681-9465 ■ *Web:* www.wysemeter.com

Phone | Fax

xDefenders Inc 1100 Pittsford-Victor Rd. . . . . Pittsford NY 14534 585-385-2770
Web: www.xdefenders.com

Yale Club of New York City, The
50 Vanderbilt Ave . . . . . New York NY 10017 212-716-2100
TF: 800-335-9253 ■ *Web:* www.yaleclubnyc.org

Yazaki Energy 701 E Plano Pkwy Ste 305. . . . . Plano TX 75074 469-229-5443
Web: www.yazakienergy.com

Your Linen Service Inc 875 E Bank St . . . . . Petersburg VA 23804 804-732-3315
Web: yourlinenservice.com

Yub Inc 321 Castro St Ste 1 . . . . . Mountain View CA 94041 650-265-7316
Web: yub.com

Zolan Company LLC, The
9947 E Desert Jewel Dr. . . . . Scottsdale AZ 85255 480-306-5680
Web: www.zolan.com

ZXP Technologies Ltd 409 E Wallisville Rd . . . . . Highlands TX 77562 281-426-8800
Web: www.zxptech.com

394 INTERNET BACKBONE PROVIDERS

Companies that are, in effect, Internet service providers for Internet Service Providers (ISPs).

Phone | Fax

BT Americas Inc 2160 E Grand Ave . . . . . El Segundo CA 90245 408-330-2700 330-2701
TF: 888-767-2988 ■ *Web:* www.globalservices.bt.com

Cogent Communications Group Inc
1015 31st St NW . . . . . Washington DC 20007 202-295-4200 338-8798
NASDAQ: CCOI ■ *TF:* 877-875-4432 ■ *Web:* www.cogentco.com

IDT Corp 520 Broad St . . . . . Newark NJ 07102 973-438-1000
NYSE: IDT ■ *Web:* www.idt.net

iPass Inc 3800 Bridge Pkwy. . . . . Redwood Shores CA 94065 650-232-4100 232-4111
NASDAQ: IPAS ■ *TF:* 877-236-3807 ■ *Web:* www3.ipass.com

Level 3 Communications Inc
1025 Eldorado Blvd . . . . . Broomfield CO 80021 720-888-1000
NYSE: LVLT ■ *TF:* 877-453-8353 ■ *Web:* www.level3.com

nFrame Inc 701 Congressional Blvd Ste 100. . . . . Carmel IN 46032 317-805-3759
TF: 877-570-7827 ■ *Web:* www.expedient.com

SunGard Availability Services
680 E Swedesford Rd . . . . . Wayne PA 19087 484-582-2000 687-4726*
**Fax Area Code:* 610 ■ *TF:* 800-468-7483 ■ *Web:* www.sungardas.com

Verio Inc
8300 E Maplewood Ave Ste 400. . . . . Greenwood Village CO 80111 561-912-2555
TF Sales: 800-438-8374 ■ *Web:* www.verio.com

Verizon Business 1 Verizon Way. . . . . Basking Ridge NJ 07920 908-559-2000
TF Cust Svc: 877-297-7816 ■ *Web:* www.verizonenterprise.com

XO Communications Inc 13865 Sunrise Vly Dr. . . . . Herndon VA 20171 703-547-2000 547-2881
TF: 866-349-0134 ■ *Web:* www.xo.com

395 INTERNET BROADCASTING

Phone | Fax

Audible Inc 1 Washington Pk. . . . . Newark NJ 07102 973-820-0400
TF: 888-283-5051 ■ *Web:* www.audible.com

BankCard Services
3055 Wilshire Blvd 3rd Fl . . . . . Los Angeles CA 90010 213-365-1122
TF: 888-339-0100 ■ *Web:* www.e-bankcard.com

CareerBuilder Inc 200 N LaSalle St Ste 1100. . . . . Chicago IL 60601 773-527-3600
Web: www.careerbuilder.com

Caxy Consulting LLC 212 W Van Buren Ste 100. . . . . Chicago IL 60607 312-207-6200
Web: www.caxy.com

Comedy Central 345 Hudson St . . . . . New York NY 10014 212-767-8600
Web: cc.com

Compugen Inc 100 Via Renzo Dr. . . . . Richmond Hill ON L4S0B8 905-707-2000
TF: 800-387-5045 ■ *Web:* www.compugen.com

CrowdGather Inc
20300 Ventura Blvd Ste 330. . . . . Woodland Hills CA 91364 818-435-2472
Web: www.crowdgather.com

Data com Connect Two Waters Park Dr Ste 250 . . . . . San Mateo CA 94403 650-235-8400
Web: www.jigsaw.com

DigitalTown Inc 11974 Portland Ave. . . . . Burnsville MN 55337 952-890-2362
Web: www.digitaltown.com

Dynanet Corp 8182 Lark Brown Rd Ste 300. . . . . Elkridge MD 21075 443-661-1403
Web: www.dynanetcorp.com

Eventure Interactive Inc
3420 Bristol St Fl 6. . . . . Costa Mesa CA 92626 855-986-5669
TF: 855-986-5669 ■ *Web:* www.eventure.com

Gilbane Report, The 763 Massachusetts Ave. . . . . Cambridge MA 02139 617-497-9443
Web: gilbane.com

iovation Inc 111 SW Fifth Ave Ste 3200 . . . . . Portland OR 97204 503-224-6010
Web: www.iovation.com

Kelliher Samets Volk 212 Battery St . . . . . Burlington VT 05401 802-862-8261
Web: www.ksvc.com

LabRoots Inc
18340 Yorba Linda Blvd Ste 107 . . . . . Yorba Linda CA 92886 714-269-2986
Web: labroots.com

Leads com Inc 10021 Balls Ford Rd Ste 200 . . . . . Manassas VA 20109 703-257-2852
Web: leads.web.com

M3 USA Corp 1215 17th St NW Ste 100. . . . . Washington DC 20036 202-293-2288
Web: usa.m3.com

Mary Fisher Design LLC 1731 Emerson St . . . . . Jacksonville FL 32207 904-398-3699
Web: www.maryfisherdesign.com

MedAltus Inc 3567 County Rd 37. . . . . Bloomfield NY 14469 585-582-1310
Web: www.medaltus.com

MedCAREERS Group Inc 758 E Bethel School Rd . . . . . Coppell TX 75019 972-393-5892
Web: www.medcareersgroup.com

Media Temple Inc
8520 National Blvd Bldg A . . . . . Culver City CA 90232 877-578-4000
TF: 877-578-4000 ■ *Web:* www.mediatemple.net

MediaBrains Inc 720 Goodlette Rd N Ste 400. . . . . Naples FL 34102 239-594-3200
Web: www.mediabrains.com

MeetMe Inc 100 Union Sq Dr . . . . . New Hope PA 18938 215-862-1162
Web: www.meetmecorp.com

Phone | Fax

NeuLion Inc 1600 Old Country Rd . . . . . Plainview NY 11803 516-622-8300
Web: www.neulion.com

Ning Inc
2000 Sierra Point Pkay Ste 1000, 10th Fl. . . . . Brisbane CA 94005 270-514-7000
Web: www.ning.com

Nstreams Technologies Inc 1914 Junction Ave. . . . . San Jose CA 95131 408-734-8889 734-8886

OMT Inc 1-1717 Dublin Ave . . . . . Winnipeg MB R3H0H2 204-786-3994 783-5805
TF: 888-665-0501 ■ *Web:* www.omt.net

ON24 Inc 201 Third St 3rd Fl . . . . . San Francisco CA 94103 415-369-8000 369-8388
Web: www.on24.com

Perfect World Entertainment Inc
101 Redwood Shores Pkwy Ste 400 . . . . . Redwood City CA 94065 650-590-7700
Web: www.perfectworld.com

Real Capital Analytics Inc 110 Fifth Ave . . . . . New York NY 10011 212-387-7103
Web: www.rcanalytics.com

Red Brick Design Inc 150 Westford Rd. . . . . Tyngsboro MA 01879 978-649-4411
Web: www.redbrickdesign.com

Richter10.2 Media Group LLC
600 Cleveland St Bank of America Tower
Ste 920. . . . . Clearwater FL 33755 727-447-3600
Web: www.richter10point2.com

Santeon Group Inc 11720 Plz America Dr Ste 810. . . . . Reston VA 20190 703-970-9200
Web: www.santeon.com

Synacor Inc 40 La Riviere Dr Ste 300 . . . . . Buffalo NY 14202 716-853-1362
Web: www.synacor.com

Tine 4 Learning
6300 Ne First Ave Ste 203 . . . . . Fort Lauderdale FL 33334 954-771-0914
Web: www.time4learning.com

Trulia Inc 535 Mission St Ste 700 . . . . . San Francisco CA 94105 415-648-4358
Web: www.trulia.com

Virurl Inc 137 Bay St Ste 6 . . . . . Santa Monica CA 90405 424-209-2442
Web: www.revenue.com

Weather Decision Technologies Inc
201 David L Boren Blvd Ste 270. . . . . Norman OK 73072 405-579-7675
Web: wdtinc.com

Yodle Inc 330 W 34th St 18th Fl. . . . . New York NY 10001 877-276-5104
TF: 877-276-5104 ■ *Web:* www.yodle.com

396 INTERNET DOMAIN NAME REGISTRARS

Phone | Fax

3rd Alternative Inc 145 Merritts Rd . . . . . Farmingdale NY 11735 516-753-1515
Web: www.3rdalternative.net

@Com Technology LLC 1353 Pine St Ste E. . . . . Walnut Creek CA 94596 480-624-2500
Web: www.atcomtechnology.com

A 1 Nethosting 265 Mar Vista Dr. . . . . Vista CA 92083 760-758-4007
Web: a1nethosting.com

Acbel Polytech Inc 251 Dominion Dr # 103 . . . . . Morrisville NC 27560 919-388-4316
Web: www.acbel.com

Acclinet Corp 490 S Stark Hwy. . . . . Weare NH 03281 603-529-4220
Web: www.acclinet.com

Accuvia Consulting Inc
19636 Club House Rd Ste 120. . . . . Gaithersburg MD 20886 301-944-1220
Web: www.accuvia.com

Acg Tech Systems Inc 6 Rock Is . . . . . Ardmore OK 73401 580-222-4467
Web: www.acgsystem.com

ACT Litigation Services Inc
27200 Tourney Rd Ste 450. . . . . Valencia CA 91355 661-284-6401
Web: discoverready.com

Acumenex Com 2201 Brant St. . . . . Burlington ON L7P3N8 877-788-5028
TF: 877-788-5028 ■ *Web:* www.acumenex.com

AITDomains.com 421 Maiden Ln . . . . . Fayetteville NC 28301 877-549-2881 321-1390*
**Fax Area Code:* 910 ■ *TF:* 877-549-2881 ■ *Web:* ait.com/domains

Alexsys Corp 14 Pebble Pl . . . . . Stoneham MA 02180 781-279-0170
Web: www.alexcorp.com

Alignment Nashville Inc
C/O The Mayor's Office Metropliton Cthouse 1 Public Sq
. . . . . Nashville TN 37201 615-862-5009
Web: www.alignmentnashville.org

All Web Cafe Inc 42 Cassatt Ave . . . . . Berwyn PA 19312 610-644-1240
Web: www.allwebcafe.com/

Allied Infosecurity Inc
1009 W 9th Ave Ste B. . . . . King Of Prussia PA 19406 866-240-0094
TF: 866-240-0094 ■ *Web:* www.alliedinfosecurity.com

Alltek Services 2810 Pkwy St. . . . . Lakeland FL 33811 863-709-0709
Web: www.alltekservices.com

Amann Business Systems Inc
1901 Jefferson Hwy . . . . . New Orleans LA 70121 504-836-6800
Web: amannsystems.com

Amr Consulting LLC 92 Broad St . . . . . Keyport NJ 07735 732-705-5057
Web: www.amrcon.com

Arachne Web Technologies Inc
3324 Alpine Dr . . . . . Ann Arbor MI 48108 734-975-8490
Web: www.arachneweb.com

Arcadia Data Inc 415 E Campbell Ave Ste 220 . . . . . Campbell CA 95008 408-340-5919
Web: www.arcadiadata.com

Ascentek Inc 12 Betnr Industrial Dr. . . . . Pittsfield MA 01201 413-496-9900
Web: www.ascentek.com

ASEC International Inc 267 Riverchase Way . . . . . Lexington SC 29072 803-939-4809
Web: asecinternational.com

aSim Inc, The 1005 Slater Rd Oxford Pl Ste 230. . . . . Durham NC 27703 919-226-3299
Web: www.therasim.com

Astrix Software Technology Inc
Edison Corporate Ctr 175 May St Ste 302 . . . . . Edison NJ 08837 732-661-0400
Web: www.astrixsoftware.com

AT-NET Services Inc
9625-D Southern Pine Blvd . . . . . Charlotte NC 29273 704-831-2500
Web: www.at-net.net

Azalea Software Inc
3400 Harbor Ave SW Ste 411. . . . . Seattle WA 98125 206-336-9575
Web: www.azalea.com

Phone *Fax*

Bankers Data Services Inc 521 W 11th St .... Alma GA 31510 912-632-2060
Web: www.bdsalma.com

Bayshore Technologies Inc
5461 W Waters Ave Ste 900 .... Tampa FL 33634 813-889-8324
Web: www.btfl.com

Beats Music LLC 555 19th St .... San Francisco CA 94417 510-915-1958
Web: beatsmusic.com

Best Registration Services Inc
1418 S Third St .... Louisville KY 40208 502-637-4528
TF: 800-977-3475 ■ *Web:* www.bestregistrar.com

Betawave Corp 706 Mission St Fl 10 .... San Francisco CA 94103 415-738-8706
Web: www.betawave.com

Box Ltd 412 W 14th St .... New York NY 10014 212-965-9555
Web: www.boxstudios.com

Bradford Scott Data Corp
1001 Chestnut Hills Pkwy Ste 1 .... Fort Wayne IN 46814 260-625-5107
Web: www.bradfordscott.com

Carinet 8929 Complex Dr .... San Diego CA 92123 858-974-5080
Web: www.cari.net/

Carter-lambert Divisions Llc
3023 Hubbard Rd Ste 210 .... Landover MD 20785 703-286-0826
Web: www.carterlambert.com

Central Oregon Mall on The Internet, The
25 NW Minnesota Ave Ste 8 .... Bend OR 97701 541-317-3963
Web: www.centraloregonmall.com

Century Computers Inc
500 Ala Moana Blvd WaterFrnt Plz Ste 4-200 .... Honolulu HI 96813 808-585-0444
Web: www.centuryc.com

Cfocus Software Inc 10536 joyceton dr. .... Largo MD 20774 301-499-2650
Web: www.cfocussoftware.com

Chiron Data Systems Inc 1802 Regent Ct .... Denton TX 76210 940-497-3134
Web: www.chirondata.com

Citation Solutions Inc 5450 Nw Central Dr .... Houston TX 77092 713-895-8261
Web: www.citationsolutions.com

Cloudwerx Data Solutions Inc
1440 28th St NE Ste 2 .... Calgary AB T2A7W6 403-538-6659
Web: www.cloudwerx.com

Coley Associates 140 Heimer Rd Ste 400 .... San Antonio TX 78232 210-402-6766
Web: www.coleyinc.com

Colorado Network Staffing Inc
8787 TurnPk Dr .... Westminster CO 80031 303-430-1441
Web: www.conetstaff.com

Cormac Corp 13921 Park Ctr Rd Ste 180 .... Herndon VA 20171 703-793-0931
Web: www.cormac-corp.com

Crescent Design Inc 9932 Mesa Rim Rd # B .... San Diego CA 92121 858-452-3240
Web: www.crescentdesign.com

Cvikota Company Inc, The
2031 32nd St S Ste 100 .... La Crosse WI 54601 608-788-8103
Web: www.thebillingpros.com

Cyber Sytes
19981 Panama Cty Bch Pkwy .... Panama City Beach FL 32413 850-233-5514
Web: www.cysy.com

Cybervillage Networkers
7773 Blueberry Hill Ln .... Ellicott City MD 21043 410-579-1993
Web: www.cybernetworkers.com

Cyberwoven LLC 1523 Huger St Ste B .... Columbia SC 29201 803-376-8899
Web: www.cyberwoven.com

Datacorp 200 W 17th St Ste 115 .... Cheyenne WY 82001 307-634-1808
Web: www.mjdatacorp.com

DataGardens Inc 14956?121 A Ave .... Edmonton AB T5V1A3 780-988-9592
Web: www.datagardens.com

Dataline Systems Inc 2709 Pemberton Dr .... Apopka FL 32703 407-298-1234
Web: www.datalinesys.com

DDC Group Inc, The 55 W TechneCtr Dr Ste B .... Milford OH 45150 631-547-5500
Web: www.datacapture.com

Deep Mile Networks LLC
800 W Broad St Ste 408 .... Falls Church VA 22046 703-635-7983
Web: www.deepmile.com

Dekatron Corp 5895 Allentown Rd .... Camp Springs MD 20746 301-702-1005
Web: www.dekatron.com

Desgraff Multimedia
779 rue Paul-Desruisseaux 2nd Fl .... Sherbrooke QC J1J4L9 819-823-8024
Web: desgraff.com

Digicomm Systems 106 Metairie Lawn Dr 307 .... Metairie LA 70001 504-212-6770
Web: www.digicommsystems.com

Document Imaging Systems Corp
1717 Olive St Ste 300 .... Saint Louis MO 63103 314-436-2800
Web: disccorporation.com

Domain-It! 9891 Montgomery Rd .... Cincinnati OH 45242 513-351-4222 351-8222
TF General: 866-269-2355 ■ *Web:* www.domainit.com

DomainPeople Inc
550 Burrard St Ste 200 Bentall Twr 5 .... Vancouver BC V6C2B5 604-639-1680 688-9013
TF: 877-734-3667 ■ *Web:* www.domainpeople.com

DomainRegistry.com Inc
2301 E. Evesham Rd Ste 204 .... Voorhees NJ 08043 856-335-5950
Web: www.domainregistry.com

Dotster
8100 NE Pkwy Dr Ste 300 PO Box 821066 .... Vancouver WA 98682 360-449-5800 253-4234
TF: 800-401-5250 ■ *Web:* www.dotster.com

Dotster Inc PO Box 821066 .... Vancouver WA 98682 360-253-2210
TF: 800-401-5250 ■ *Web:* www.dotster.com

Dynadot LLC PO Box 345 .... San Mateo CA 94401 650-585-1961 869-2893*
**Fax Area Code:* 415 ■ *TF Cust Svc:* 866-652-2039 ■ *Web:* www.dynadot.com

Dynfed Llc 6724 Wilson Ln .... Bethesda MD 20817 703-627-5950
Web: dynfed.com

E C Wise Inc 101 Glacier Pt Ste D .... San Rafael CA 94901 415-355-9473
Web: www.ecwise.com

e-Business Express Inc
2208 E Enterprise Pkwy .... Twinsburg OH 44087 330-963-7150
Web: e-businessexpress.com

easyDNS 219 Dufferin St Ste 304A .... Toronto ON M6K3J1 416-535-8672
TF: 888-677-4741 ■ *Web:* easydns.com

eeParts com Inc 1505 Wallace Dr Ste 102 .... Carrollton TX 75006 469-574-2333
Web: www.eeparts.com

Elephant Ventures LLC 144 E 44th St Fl 7 .... New York NY 10017 212-730-6710
Web: www.elephantventures.com

EnCirca Inc 400 W Cummings Pk Ste 1725-307 .... Woburn MA 01801 781-942-9975 823-8911
Web: www.encirca.com

ENKI LLC 1049-C El Monte Ave Ste 32 .... Mountain View CA 94040 650-964-9100
Web: www.enkiconsulting.net

eNom Inc 5808 Lake Washington Blvd Ste 300 .... Kirkland WA 98033 425-974-4689 974-4791*
**Fax:* Acctg ■ *Web:* www.enom.com

Etera Solutions Llc 354 TurnPk St Ste 203 .... Canton MA 02021 888-536-6515
TF: 888-536-6515 ■ *Web:* eterasolutions.com

Faster Solutions 10 E Superior St Ste 200 .... Duluth MN 55802 218-733-3936
Web: www.fastersolutions.com

Five Star Computing Inc
6316 Saint Andrews Rd Ste C .... Columbia SC 29212 803-561-0056
Web: ncsetoff.org

FSO Knowledge Xchange LLC 208 Shepard Way ...... Manalapan NJ 07726 732-462-3763
Web: www.fsokx.com

Gemini Duplication Inc 9645 W Grove Ave .... Visalia CA 93291 559-739-7481
Web: geminiduplication.com

Hargrove & Associates
100 N 6th St Ste 720C .... Minneapolis MN 55403 612-436-5500
Web: web.hargrove-epc.com

Hedgehog Hosting 10387 Main St Ste 300 .... Fairfax VA 22030 703-218-4170
Web: www.hedgehoghosting.com

HopeLink 115 Constitution Dr Ste 7 .... Menlo Park CA 94025 650-470-0123
Web: www.hopelink.com

Hostexcellence com 1774 Dividend Dr .... Columbus OH 43228 614-534-1962
Web: www.hostexcellence.com/

HostMySite Inc 650 Pencader Dr .... Newark DE 19702 302-731-4948
Web: www.hostmysite.com

Ideal Data Inc 420 River Rd .... North Arlington NJ 07031 201-998-9440
Web: www.idealdata.com

Imaging & Microfilm Access Inc
150 Knickerbocker Ave Ste E .... Bohemia NY 11716 631-589-8100
Web: www.scanyourdocs.com

Indros Group 1 Meadow St Ste 202 .... Brooklyn NY 11206 718-417-1320
Web: www.indrosgroup.com

Infinet Technologies 249 Oak St .... Collingwood ON L9Y2Y2 705-445-2002
Web: www.infinet-technologies.com

Infinite Dimensions Inc
1760 Reston Pkwy Ste 500 .... Reston VA 20191 703-435-9500
Web: www.infdim.com

Insystech Inc 7064 Infantry Ridge Rd .... Manassas VA 20109 703-657-0472
Web: www.insystechinc.com

Inteliport 103 N Church St .... Hertford NC 27944 252-426-4600
Web: www.inteliport.net

Intrada Technologies 31 Ashler Manor Dr .... Muncy PA 17756 570-321-7370
Web: intradatech.com

iPacesetters LLC 135 Chestnut Ridge Rd .... Montvale NJ 07645 201-391-1500
Web: ipacesetters.com

IPOWER Inc 919 E Jefferson St .... Phoenix AZ 85034 602-716-5398
Web: www.ipower.com

It Pitstop 10120 S Eastern Ave Ste 200 .... Henderson NV 89052 702-777-4445
Web: www.itpitstopinc.com

It Pro Source 2600 Kitty Hawk Rd Ste 115 .... Livermore CA 94551 925-455-7701
Web: www.itprosource.com

It4la Inc 8033 W Sunset Blvd 228 .... West Hollywood CA 90046 323-936-4900
Web: www.it4la.com

Jsa Technologies 201 Main St Ste 1320 .... Fort Worth TX 76102 877-572-8324
TF: 877-572-8324 ■ *Web:* www.jsatech.com

Kinetix Broadband 934 Third St .... Alexandria LA 71301 318-487-8200
Web: www.kbisp.com

Krozak Information Technologies Inc
201 Linton Knoll Ct .... Silver Spring MD 20904 301-384-4340
Web: www.krozak.com

Latisys-Denver LLC 393 Inverness Pkwy .... Englewood CO 80012 303-268-1470
Web: www.latisys.com

Lentech Inc 4405 Westridge Ct Nw .... Albuquerque NM 87114 505-217-9095
Web: www.lentechinc.com

Leonard-design et Genie Web
5275 Boul Wilfrid-hamel .... Quebec QC G2E5M7 418-780-1706
Web: www.leonarddg.com

Liquidprint Inc
7366 N Lincoln Ave Ste 300 .... Lincolnwood IL 60712 847-763-1400
Web: www.liquidprint.com

Livecareer Inc 1432 Washington St .... San Francisco CA 94109 800-652-8430
TF: 800-652-8430 ■ *Web:* www.livecareer.com

MacMicro Inc 29 Williamsburg Close .... Scarsdale NY 10583 914-472-8292
Web: www.macmicro.com

Marker Seven 701 Sutter St Fl 5 .... San Francisco CA 94109 415-447-2841
Web: www.markerseven.com

Market Builder Inc, The 5135 E Ingram St .... Mesa AZ 85205 480-707-0444
Web: www.themarketbuilder.com

Matmoncom 303 W Capitol Ave Ste 150 .... Little Rock AR 72201 501-375-4999
Web: www.matmon.com

Megazone 2485 Boul Sainte-anne .... Quebec QC G1J1Y4 418-948-1700
Web: www.megazone.co.nz

Metaops Inc 30425 Munger Dr .... Livonia MI 48154 734-425-1455
Web: www.metaops.com

Mindbody Online 4051 Broad St Ste 220 .... Sn Luis Obisp CA 93401 877-755-4279
TF: 877-755-4279 ■ *Web:* www.mindbodyonline.com

Moniker Online Services LLC
20 SW 27th Ave Ste 201 .... Pompano Beach FL 33069 800-688-6311
TF: 800-688-6311 ■ *Web:* www.moniker.com

Mother Lode Internet 197A Mono Wy .... Sonora CA 95370 209-536-5800
Web: www.motherlodeinternet.com

Muller Media Conversions Inc 21 Locust St .... Manhasset NY 11030 516-833-3067
Web: mullermedia.com

MyEvent com Inc
221 de la Commune St W Ste 305 .... Montreal QC H2Y2C9 514-282-7747
Web: www.myevent.com

Name.com LLC 2500 E Second Ave 2nd Fl .... Denver CO 80206 720-249-2374 399-3167*
**Fax Area Code:* 303 ■ *TF:* 800-365-0006 ■ *Web:* www.name.com

Name / Address	City	State	Zip	Phone	Fax
Nanavati Consulting Inc 109 Longfellow Dr *Web:* www.nanavaticonsulting.com	Millersville	MD	21108	410-421-5184	
Neo Code Software Ltd 425 Carrall St Ste 540 *Web:* www.neocodesoftware.com	Vancouver	BC	V6B6E3	604-638-0668	
Netbones Inc 2685 Warburton Ave *Web:* www.netbones.com	Santa Clara	CA	95051	408-249-6091	
Netfronts Web Hosting 459 North 300 West Ste 16 *Web:* netfronts.com	Kaysville	UT	84037	801-497-0878	
Netwood Communications 10736 Jefferson Blvd Ste 670 *Web:* www.netwood.net	Culver City	CA	90230	310-442-1530	
Network Solutions LLC 13861 Sunrise Valley Dr Ste 300 *TF:* 800-361-5712 ■ *Web:* www.networksolutions.com	Herndon	VA	20171	703-668-4600	668-5888
New City Media Inc 301 S Main St Ste 207 *Web:* www.insidenewcity.com	Blacksburg	VA	24060	540-552-1320	
Nexonia Inc 21 St Clair Ave E Ste 701 *Web:* www.nexonia.com	Toronto	ON	M4T2T5	416-480-0688	
Nexternal Solutions Inc 785 Grand Ave Ste 216 *Web:* www.nexternal.com	Carlsbad	CA	92008	760-730-9015	
Ngci 1420 N Capitol St Nw *Web:* www.ngciglobal.com	Washington	DC	20002	202-527-9595	
Omedix Inc 15849 N 71st St Ste 100 *TF:* 877-866-3349 ■ *Web:* omedix.com	Scottsdale	AZ	85254	877-866-3349	
OpenTech Systems Inc 405 State Hwy 121 Bypass Bldg C Ste 130 *Web:* www.opentechsystems.com	Lewisville	TX	75067	469-635-1500	
Optistreams 2491 Alluvial Ave Ste 68 *Web:* optistreams.com	Clovis	CA	93611	559-440-6366	
Orange Door Inc 370 San Bruno Ave W Ste E *Web:* www.orangedoorinc.com	San Bruno	CA	94066	650-952-1773	
Oseberg LLC 12 E California Ave Ste 200 *Web:* www.oseberg.io	Oklahoma City	OK	73104	405-618-1647	
Patientree Inc 5115 Joanne Kearney Blvd *Web:* www.patientree.com	Tampa	FL	33619	813-814-4435	
Pen Publishing Interactive Inc 239 s pattie st *Web:* www.collegefans.com	Wichita	KS	67211	316-651-0551	
PicksPal Inc 1957 Landings Dr *Web:* www.pickspal.com	Mountain View	CA	94043	650-964-7137	
Piraeus Consulting LLC 1408 4th Ave, Ste 400 *TF:* 866-747-2387 ■ *Web:* www.piraeusdata.com	Seattle	WA	98101	866-747-2387	
Pointmarc LLC 11911 NE 1st St Ste B-302 *Web:* www.pointmarc.com	Bellevue	WA	98005	425-242-7003	
PPLSolutions LLC 2 N Ninth St PL-2 *Web:* www.pplsolutions.com	Allentown	PA	18101	610-774-2932	
Prescient Digital Media Ltd 80 Sherbourne St Unit 101 *Web:* www.prescientdigital.com	Toronto	ON	M5A2R1	416-926-8800	
Prezza Technologies Inc 1 Mifflin Pl 3rd Fl *Web:* www.prezzatech.com	Cambridge	MA	02138	617-715-9605	
PrimeConnections Contact Solutions LLC 301 Brazos St Ste 615 *TF:* 866-976-2747 ■ *Web:* callprimeconnections.com	Austin	TX	78701	866-976-2747	
Pro-data Control Systems Inc 12405 Sw 93rd Ave *Web:* prodatacontrol.com	Miami	FL	33176	305-256-5666	
Pushtotest 33 n 1st st *Web:* www.pushtotest.com	Campbell	CA	95008	408-871-0122	
Pyron Technologies Inc 216 West Main St Ste 110 *Web:* www.pyrontechnologies.com	Missoula	MT	59802	406-543-9211	
Radiowirenet Inc 314 Lafayette St *Web:* radiowire.net	Jefferson City	MO	65101	573-659-7950	
Rally Point Management LLC 100 Pamela Ann Dr *Web:* www.rallypointmanagement.com	Fort Walton Beach	FL	32547	850-226-7589	
Real Interactive LLC 25 Business Park Dr *Web:* www.starpulse.com	Branford	CT	06405	203-488-8447	
Register.com Inc 575 Eigth Ave 8th Fl *TF:* 888-734-4783 ■ *Web:* www.register.com	New York	NY	10018	888-734-4783	
Retail Equation Inc, The 6430 Oak Canyon *Web:* www.theretailequation.com	Irvine	CA	92618	949-262-5100	
RiskSpan Inc 301 Tresser Blvd Ste 1110 *Web:* www.riskspan.com	Stamford	CT	06901	203-355-1510	
Rm Design Studio Ltd 850 W Bartlett Rd *Web:* www.rmdesignstudio.com	Bartlett	IL	60103	630-540-1222	
Robotech C a d Solutions Inc 2 Marine View Plz Ste 7 *Web:* www.robotechcad.com	Hoboken	NJ	07030	201-792-6300	
Rodine Communications Inc 214 S 3rd St *Web:* rodine.com	Sterling	CO	80751	970-522-5097	
Romeo Computer Co 76005 Van Dyke Rd *Web:* www.romeocomp.com	Bruce Township	MI	48065	586-752-5158	
Rsss Lp 711 N Carancahua St *Web:* hightouchtechnologies.com	Corpus Christi	TX	78475	361-993-1790	
RuleSphere International Inc 327 Still River Rd RT. 110 PO Box 152 *Web:* www.rulesphere.com	Still River	MA	01467	978-456-8253	
RVM Inc 40 Rector St 17th Fl *Web:* www.rvminc.com	New York	NY	10006	212-693-1525	
Rycan Technologies Inc 349 W Main St Ste 4 *Web:* www.rycan.com	Marshall	MN	56258	507-532-3324	
ScaleGrid Inc 4205 148th Ave Northeast Ste 100 *Web:* www.scalegrid.net	Bellevue	WA	98007	425-460-4917	
Scandent Group Inc 340 Interstate N Pkwy Ste 340 *Web:* www.scandent.com	Atlanta	GA	30339	770-303-4448	
Scantek Infomanagement Solutions Inc 1100 Easton Rd *Web:* www.scantek.info	Willow Grove	PA	19090	215-882-5000	
Score Technologies Inc 13 Bow Cir Ste 147 *Web:* scoretechnologies.com	Hilton Head	SC	29928	843-384-9855	
Show Media 6623 Las Vegas Blvd S Ste 370 *Web:* www.showmedia.com	Las Vegas	NV	89119	702-778-5313	
SI Holdings 3267 Bee Caves Rd Ste 107 *TF:* 866-551-4646 ■ *Web:* sysinformation.com	Austin	TX	78746	866-551-4646	
Silex Technology America Inc 64 East Winchester St Ste 330 *Web:* www.silexamerica.com	Murray	UT	84107	801-747-0656	
SolutionStream 249 North 1200 East *Web:* www.solutionstream.com	Lehi	UT	84043	801-492-7700	
Sonoted Llc 1 Trotting Horse Ct *Web:* www.sonoted.com	Catonsville	MD	21228	410-744-3950	
St. Croix Solutions Inc 6033 Culligan Way *Web:* www.stcroixsolutions.com	Minnetonka	MN	55345	952-653-2900	
STARTEL Corp 16 Goodyear *Web:* www.startelcorp.com	Irvine	CA	92618	949-863-8700	
Statement Systems Inc 1900 Diplomat Dr *Web:* www.statementsystems.com	Farmers Branch	TX	75234	214-210-0880	
Steelray Software Llc 1440 dutch valley pl ne *Web:* www.steelray.com	Atlanta	GA	30324	404-806-0160	
SynaMed L L C 555 8th Ave Ste 2210 *Web:* www.synamed.com	New York	NY	10018	212-239-2800	
Synergy Information Tech Group 104 A Republic Ave *Web:* www.synergyitg.com	Lafayette	LA	70508	337-234-5767	
T3 Software Builders Inc 15200 Shady Grove Rd *Web:* www.t3software.com	Rockville	MD	20850	301-296-4452	
Tappln Inc 1525 Fourth Ave Ste 500 *Web:* www.tappin.com	Seattle	WA	98101	206-708-7267	
TeamXbox com 128 Woodhaven Dr *Web:* www.teamxbox.com	Mars	PA	16046	412-555-1212	
Tech Access Corp Inc 635 Portion Rd *Web:* www.techaccesscorp.com	Lake Ronkonkoma	NY	11779	631-654-5080	
Tekstrom Inc 18 Shea Way Ste 101 and 102 Delaware Industrial Park *Web:* www.tekstrom.com	Newark	DE	19713	302-709-5900	
Tele Tech Services 500 Oakbrook Ln *Web:* kfrservices.com	Summerville	SC	29483	843-873-9200	
Terraine Inc 5912-A Toole Dr *TF:* 800-531-1242 ■ *Web:* www.terraine.com	Nashville	TN	37230	800-531-1242	
Terranovanet Inc 913 La Paloma Rd *Web:* www.terranova.net	Key Largo	FL	33037	305-453-4011	
Thin Multimedia Inc 809 B Cuesta Dr Ste 2184 *Web:* www.thinmultimedia.com	Mountain View	CA	94040	408-433-9425	
Thor Systems 2671 Pembroke Rd *Web:* www.thorsystems.net	Hopkinsville	KY	42240	270-890-0500	
Threadpoint LLC 24881 Alicia Pkwy Ste E #310 *TF:* 866-631-1595 ■ *Web:* www.threadpoint.com	Laguna Hills	CA	92653	866-631-1595	
Tiger Technologies LLC PO Box 7596 *Fax Area Code: 866 ■ *Web:* www.tigertech.net	Berkeley	CA	94707	510-527-3131	539-5032*
TISD Inc 1502 E Red river *Web:* tisd.net	Victoria	TX	77901	361-573-1102	
TMC Technologies Inc 2110 Pleasant Valley Rd *Web:* www.tmctechnologies.com	Fairmont	WV	26554	304-368-1862	
Tricom Document Management Inc 2450 Peralta Blvd Ste 222 *Web:* www.tricomdata.com	Fremont	CA	94536	510-494-7800	
United Software Assoc Inc 5674 Stoneridge Dr Ste 100 *Web:* www.usain.com	Pleasanton	CA	94588	925-249-0230	
Versa Shore Inc 102 Strathmore Pl Ste A *Web:* www.versashore.com	Los Gatos	CA	95032	408-355-5363	
Vertices Llc 317 george st. *Web:* www.vertices.com	New brunswick	NJ	89012	732-418-9135	
Vinsys Information Technology Inc 12073 Greywing Sq *Web:* www.vinsysinfo.com	Reston	VA	20191	703-371-4120	
Virtual EM Inc 3055 Plymouth Rd Ste 200 *Web:* www.virtualem.com	Ann Arbor	MI	48105	734-222-4558	
Virtual Forum Inc 463 Main St Ste 3 *Web:* www.virtualforum.com	Little Falls	NJ	07424	973-237-1166	
Voicenet Communications Inc 9810 Ashton Rd *Web:* www.voicenet.com	Philadelphia	PA	19114	215-259-2100	
Voytek Inc 3100 Breckenridge Blvd Ste 120 *Web:* www.voytek.com	Duluth	GA	30096	770-921-7017	
Webapper Services Llc 1172 Cobblestone Ct *Web:* www.webapper.com	Fort Collins	CO	80525	970-223-2278	
Whitecap Canada Inc 200 Yorkland Blvd Ste 920 *Web:* www.whitecapcanada.com	Toronto	ON	M2J5C1	416-490-9900	
Wonder Web 22777 Lyons Ave Ste 215 *Web:* wonderwebusa.com	Santa Clarita	CA	91321	661-254-0861	
Wsi-expert Solutions 6316 Hickory Ridge Blvd *Web:* www.wsiexpertsolutions.com	Baton Rouge	LA	70817	225-341-4956	
X By 2 Inc 35055 W 12 Mile Rd Ste 220 *Web:* www.xby2.com	Farmington Hills	MI	48331	248-538-9292	
Zemoga Inc 120 Old Ridgefield Rd *Web:* www.zemoga.com	Wilton	CT	06897	203-663-6214	
Zibiz Corp 50 Alexander Ct *Web:* www.zibiz.com	Ronkonkoma	NY	11779	631-738-1100	

397 INTERNET SEARCH ENGINES, PORTALS, DIRECTORIES

Company	City	State	Zip	Phone	Fax
About Inc 1440 Broadway 19th Fl *Web:* www.about.com	New York	NY	10018	212-204-4000	
Adknowledge Inc 4600 Madison Ave 10th Fl *Web:* www.adknowledge.com	Kansas City	MO	64112	816-931-1771	
America Online Inc (AOL) 22000 AOL Way *Web:* www.aol.com	Dulles	VA	20166	703-265-1000	
Ancestry 360 W 4800 N *TF:* 800-262-3787 ■ *Web:* www.ancestry.com/cs/myfamily	Provo	UT	84604	801-705-7000	705-7001
Ancestry.com 360 W 4800 N *TF Cust Svc:* 800-262-3787 ■ *Web:* www.ancestry.com	Provo	UT	84604	801-705-7000	705-7001
Ask.com 555 12th St Ste 500 *Web:* www.ask.com	Oakland	CA	94607	510-985-7400	
BioSpace Inc 90 New Montgomery St Ste 414 *TF:* 888-246-7722 ■ *Web:* www.biospace.com	San Francisco	CA	94105	877-277-7585	
CEOExpress Co 1 Broadway 14th Fl *Web:* www.ceoexpress.com	Cambridge	MA	02142	617-482-1200	225-4440
Congress.Org 77 K St NE *Web:* www.congress.org	Washington	DC	20002	715-232-1677	
EarthCam Inc 84 Kennedy St *Web:* www.earthcam.com	Hackensack	NJ	07601	201-488-1111	488-1119
Encyclopedia.com 360 N Michigan Ave Ste 1900 *Web:* www.encyclopedia.com	Chicago	IL	60601	312-224-5000	224-5001
FindLaw 610 Opperman Dr **Fax Area Code:* 800 ■ *Web:* www.findlaw.com	Eagan	MN	55123	651-687-6393	392-6206*
Fine Arts Museums of San Francisco 50 Hagiwara Tea Garden Dr *Web:* deyoung.famsf.org	San Francisco	CA	94118	415-750-3600	
Genealogy.com 360 West 4800 North *TF:* 800-262-3787 ■ *Web:* www.genealogy.com	Provo	UT	84604	801-705-7000	705-7001
Google Inc 1600 Amphitheatre Pkwy *NASDAQ: GOOG* ■ *Web:* www.google.co.in	Mountain View	CA	94043	650-253-0000	253-0001
GourmetSpot StartSport Mediaworks Inc 1840 Oak Ave	Evanston	IL	60201	847-866-1830	866-1880
HighBeam Research Inc 65 E Wacker Pl Ste 400 *Web:* www.highbeam.com	Chicago	IL	60601	312-782-3900	782-3901
HomeAdvisor 14023 Denver W Pkwy Ste 200 *TF:* 800-474-1596 ■ *Web:* www.homeadvisor.com	Golden	CO	80401	303-963-7200	980-3003
Hotelrooms.com Inc 108-18 Queens Blvd *TF:* 800-486-7000 ■ *Web:* www.hotelrooms.com	Forest Hills	NY	11375	718-730-6000	261-4598
HowStuffWorks Inc 675 Ponce De Leon Ave Ste 1500 *Web:* www.howstuffworks.com	Atlanta	GA	30326	404-760-4729	
InfoSpace Inc 601 108th Ave NE Ste 1200 *Web:* www.blucora.com	Bellevue	WA	98004	425-201-6100	201-6150
Internet Archive 300 Funston Ave *Web:* www.archive.org	San Francisco	CA	94118	415-561-6767	840-0391
Jayde.com iEntry Inc 2549 Richmond Rd Second Fl *Web:* www.jayde.com	Lexington	KY	40509	859-514-2720	219-9065
Law Engine 7660-H Fay Avenue Ste 342 *TF:* 800-894-2889 ■ *Web:* www.thelawengine.com	La Jolla	CA	92037	858-456-1234	454-3375
Lycos Inc 52 2nd Ave *Web:* www.lycos.com	Waltham	MA	02451	781-370-2700	370-2886
MagPortal.com PO Box 463 *Web:* www.magportal.com	Bryn Mawr	PA	19010	610-581-7702	
MindEdge Inc 271 Waverley Oaks Rd *Web:* www.mindedge.com	Waltham	MA	02452	781-250-1805	250-1810
Nerd World Media 8 New England Executive Pk	Burlington	MA	01803	781-272-6599	
NewsHub 100 Lombard St Ste 203 *TF:* 800-889-9487 ■ *Web:* nabet700.com	Toronto	ON	M5C1M3	416-536-4827	536-0859
Nursing Ctr 323 Norristown Rd Ste 200 *TF:* 800-346-7844 ■ *Web:* www.nursingcenter.com	Ambler	PA	19002	800-787-8985	
RootsWeb.com 360 W 4800 N *TF:* 800-262-3787 ■ *Web:* www.rootsweb.ancestry.com	Provo	UT	84604	801-705-7000	705-7001
ShoppingSpot 1840 Oak Ave *Web:* www.shoppingspot.com	Evanston	IL	60201	847-866-1830	866-1880
Tucows Inc 96 Mowat Ave *TSE: TC* ■ *TF:* 800-371-6992 ■ *Web:* www.tucows.com	Toronto	ON	M6K3M1	416-535-0123	531-5584
USGS Education United States Geological Survey 12201 Sunrise Vly Dr MS 801 *Web:* education.usgs.gov	Reston	VA	20192	703-648-5953	648-4454
Wired News Wired 520 Third St Ste 305 *TF:* 800-769-4733 ■ *Web:* www.wired.com	San Francisco	CA	94107	800-769-4733	
Yahoo! Inc 701 First Ave *NASDAQ: YHOO* ■ *Web:* about.yahoo.com	Sunnyvale	CA	94089	408-349-3300	349-3301
YELLOWPAGES.com LLC 208 S Akard *TF:* 866-329-7118 ■ *Web:* www.yellowpages.com	Dallas	TX	75202	866-329-7118	

398 INTERNET SERVICE PROVIDERS (ISPS)

Company	City	State	Zip	Phone	Fax
ABT Internet Inc 175 E Shore Rd *TF:* 800-367-3414 ■ *Web:* www.abt.net	Great Neck	NY	11023	516-829-5484	829-2955
Access US 712 N Second St Ste 300 *TF:* 800-638-6373 ■ *Web:* accessus.net	Saint Louis	MO	63102	314-655-7700	655-7701
America Online Inc (AOL) 22000 AOL Way *Web:* www.aol.com	Dulles	VA	20166	703-265-1000	
Aplus.net Internet Services 3680 Victoria St N *TF:* 877-275-8763 ■ *Web:* www.aplus.net	Shoreview	MN	55126	858-410-6929	
AT & T Inc 175 E Houston St PO Box 2933 *NYSE: AT&T* ■ *TF:* 800-351-7221 ■ *Web:* www.att.com	San Antonio	TX	78299	210-821-4105	
Cable One Inc 210 E Earll Drive *TF:* 877-692-2253 ■ *Web:* www.cableone.net	Phoenix	AZ	85012	602-364-6000	364-6010
Cincinnati Bell Inc 221 E Fourth St *NYSE: CBB* ■ *TF:* 800-387-3638 ■ *Web:* www.cincinnatibell.com	Cincinnati	OH	45202	513-397-9900	
ClearSail Communications LLC 3950 Braxton *TF:* 888-905-0888 ■ *Web:* www.clearsail.net	Houston	TX	77063	713-230-2800	
Direct Internet Access 141 Desiard St PO Box 7263 **Fax Area Code:* 888 ■ *TF:* 800-296-2249 ■ *Web:* www.directinternet.net	Monroe	LA	71201	800-296-2249	835-2121*
DSLextreme.com 21540 Plummer St Ste A **Fax Area Code:* 818 ■ *TF:* 866-243-8638 ■ *Web:* www.dslextreme.com	Chatsworth	CA	91311	866-243-8638	206-0326*
EarthLink Inc 1375 Peachtree St NE *NASDAQ: ELNK* ■ **Fax:* Sales ■ *TF:* 866-383-3080 ■ *Web:* www.earthlink.net	Atlanta	GA	30309	404-815-0770	795-1034*
Expedient Communications 810 Parish St *TF:* 877-570-7827 ■ *Web:* www.expedient.com	Pittsburgh	PA	15220	412-316-7800	
Frontline Communications PO Box 98 **Fax Area Code:* 845 ■ **Fax:* Sales ■ *TF:* 888-376-6854 ■ *Web:* www.frontline.net	Orangeburg	NY	10962	888-376-6854	680-6541*
HughesNet 11717 Exploration Ln *TF:* 866-347-3292 ■ *Web:* www.hughesnet.com	Germantown	MD	20876	301-428-5500	428-1868
iSelect Internet Inc 1420 W Kettleman Ln Ste E **Fax Area Code:* 877 ■ *TF:* 877-837-1427 ■ *Web:* www.iselect.net	Lodi	CA	95242	209-334-0496	837-1427*
J2 Interactive LLC 2 13th St *Web:* www.j2interactive.com	Charlestown	MA	02129	617-241-7266	
Net Access Corp 2300 15th St Ste 300 *TF:* 800-638-6336 ■ *Web:* www.cologix.com	Denver	CO	80202	973-590-5000	590-5080
NetZero Inc 21301 Burbank Blvd *TF:* 800-638-9376 ■ *Web:* www.netzero.net	Woodland Hills	CA	91367	818-287-3000	287-3010
New Edge Networks 3000 Columbia House Blvd Ste 106 *TF:* 877-725-3343 ■ *Web:* www.newedgenetworks.com	Vancouver	WA	98661	360-693-9009	
Nova Internet Services Inc PO Box 703696 *Web:* www.novaone.net	Dallas	TX	75370	214-904-9600	357-1431
ProtoSource Network 2511 W Shaw Ave Ste 102 *TF:* 866-490-8600 ■ *Web:* www.psnw.com	Fresno	CA	93711	866-490-8600	
Road Runner Group 60 Columbus Cir 60 Columbus Cir **Fax Area Code:* 704 ■ *TF:* 866-689-3678 ■ *Web:* www.timewarnercable.com	New York	NY	10023	703-345-3422	697-4911*
TOAST.net 4841 Monroe St Ste 307 *TF:* 888-862-7863 ■ *Web:* www.toast.net	Toledo	OH	43623	419-292-2200	474-1762
Verio Inc 8300 E Maplewood Ave Ste 400 *TF Sales:* 800-438-8374 ■ *Web:* www.verio.com	Greenwood Village	CO	80111	561-912-2555	
Verizon Business 1 Verizon Way *TF Cust Svc:* 877-297-7816 ■ *Web:* www.verizonenterprise.com	Basking Ridge	NJ	07920	908-559-2000	
WorldGate Communications Inc 3800 Horizon Blvd Ste 103 *OTC: WGATQ*	Trevose	PA	19053	215-354-5100	

399 INVENTORY SERVICES

Company	City	State	Zip	Phone	Fax
Douglas-Guardian Services Corp 14800 St Mary's Ln *TF:* 800-255-0552 ■ *Web:* www.douglasguardian.com	Houston	TX	77079	281-531-0500	531-1777
MSI Inventory Service Corp PO Box 320129 *TF:* 800-820-1460 ■ *Web:* www.msi-inv.com	Flowood	MS	39232	601-939-0130	939-0061
MST Steel Corp 24417 Groesbeck Hwy *Web:* www.mststeel.com	Warren	MI	48089	586-773-5460	773-5486
WIS International 9265 Sky Park Ct Ste 100 **Fax Area Code:* 905 ■ *TF:* 800-268-6848 ■ *Web:* w3.wisintl.com	San Diego	CA	92123	858-565-8111	677-1945*

400 INVESTIGATIVE SERVICES

See Also Information Retrieval Services (General) p. 2561; Public Records Search Services p. 2994; Security & Protective Services p. 3172

Company	City	State	Zip	Phone	Fax
A Very Private Eye Inc 4589 Southfield Ave *Web:* www.averyprivateeye.com	Orlando	FL	32812	407-273-6646	
Accurate Biometrics Inc 4849 N Milwaukee Ave Ste 101 *Web:* www.accuratebiometrics.com	Chicago	IL	60630	773-685-5699	
Alliance Investigations LLC 240 S Montezuma St Ste 103 *Web:* az-pi.com	Prescott	AZ	86303	928-717-1196	
American Guard Services Inc 1299 E Artesia Blvd *Web:* www.americanguardservices.com	Carson	CA	90746	310-645-6200	
American Professional Services Inc 111 Harrison Ave *Web:* www.americanpi.net	Oklahoma City	OK	73104	405-636-4222	632-7667
Amtex Security Inc 5729 Leopard St Ste 1 *Web:* www.amtexsecurity.com/contactus.html	Corpus Christi	TX	78408	361-882-1222	
ASK Services Inc 42180 Ford Rd Ste 101 *TF:* 888-416-1313 ■ *Web:* www.ask-services.com	Canton	MI	48187	734-983-9040	983-9041
Aurico Reports Inc 116 W Eastman St *TF:* 866-255-1852 ■ *Web:* www.aurico.com	Arlington Heights	IL	60004	866-255-1852	
Bombet Cashio & Assoc 11220 N Harrells Ferry Rd *TF:* 800-256-5333 ■ *Web:* www.bombet.com	Baton Rouge	LA	70816	225-275-0796	272-3631
Camping Investigations 4427 N 27th Ave *TF:* 800-862-8458 ■ *Web:* www.campingcompanies.com	Phoenix	AZ	85017	602-864-7860	

Phone Fax

Capitol Detective Agency 2922 N 18th Pl .... Phoenix AZ 85016 602-265-3462
TF: 800-346-0347

Claims Verification Inc
6700 N Andrews Ave Ste 200 .... Ft. Lauderdale FL 33309 888-284-2000
TF: 888-284-2000 ■ *Web:* www.cvi.com

Culpepper Investigations Po Box 21594 .... El Sobrante CA 94820 510-243-9860

Daniel d Stevens 7618 17th Ave. .... Brooklyn NY 11214 718-234-0005
Web: www.employeescreening.com

Donan Engineering Co Inc
11321 Plantside Dr. .... Louisville KY 40299 800-482-5611 267-6973*
**Fax Area Code:* 502 ■ *TF:* 800-482-5611 ■ *Web:* www.donan.com

Douglas Baldwin & Assoc PO Box 1249 .... La Canada CA 91012 818-952-4433 790-4622
TF: 800-392-3950 ■ *Web:* www.baldwinpi.com

Eastern Security Inc 303 Wyman St Ste 300 .... Waltham MA 02451 888-491-8181
TF: 888-491-8181 ■ *Web:* www.easternsecurityinc.com

Espy Investigate Services 1264 Sapphire Ct .... Ripon CA 95366 209-609-2676
Web: www.espyinvestigations.com

Frasco Investigative Services
444 Washington St Ste 306 .... Woburn MA 01801 781-935-3888
Web: frasco.com

Gregg Investigations Inc
500 E Milwaukee St .... Janesville WI 53545 800-866-1976
TF: 800-866-1976 ■ *Web:* www.gregginvestigations.com

Hettrick Cyr & Assoc Inc 287 Main St .... East Hartford CT 06118 860-568-2999
Web: www.hettrickcyr.com

Hrodey & Assoc 114 W Calhoun St. .... Woodstock IL 60098 815-337-4636
Web: www.hrodey.com

Inquiries Inc 129 N W St .... Easton MD 21601 410-819-3711
TF: 866-987-3767 ■ *Web:* www.inquiriesinc.com

International Investigators Inc
3216 N Pennsylvania St .... Indianapolis IN 46205 317-925-1496 926-1177
TF: 800-403-8111 ■ *Web:* www.iiiweb.net

Internet Crimes Group Inc PO Box 3599 .... Princeton NJ 08543 609-806-5000 806-5001
Web: ithreat.com

Investigative Services Inc 4381 S 153rd Cir .... Omaha NE 68137 402-894-5625 896-0621

Kessler International
45 Rockefeller Plz Ste 2000 .... New York NY 10111 212-286-9100 730-2433
TF: 800-932-2221 ■ *Web:* www.investigation.com

L&R Security Services Inc
3930 Old Gentilly Rd .... New Orleans LA 70126 504-943-3191
Web: www.lrsecurity.com

Lincoln Controls Inc 55 W 39th St Rm 201 .... New York NY 10018 212-545-7705
Web: www.lincolncontrolsinc.com

M2SYS LLC 1050 Crown Pointe Pkwy Ste 850 .... Atlanta GA 30338 770-393-0986
Web: www.m2sys.com

Michael Ramey & Assoc Inc PO Box 744 .... Danville CA 94526 800-321-0505 820-8082*
**Fax Area Code:* 925 ■ *TF:* 800-321-0505 ■ *Web:* www.rameypi.com

North Winds Investigations Inc
119 S Second St PO Box 1654 .... Rogers AR 72756 479-925-1612 878-5989
TF: 800-530-4514 ■ *Web:* www.napps.org

Owens & Assoc Investigations
8765 Aero Dr Ste 306 .... San Diego CA 92123 800-297-1343 297-1343*
**Fax Area Code:* 619 ■ *TF:* 800-297-1343 ■ *Web:* www.owenspi.com

PADIC Inc 1609 E Broadway .... Gainesville TX 76240 940-665-6130 665-7486
Web: www.padic.com

Palmer Investigative Services
624 W Gurley St Ste A .... Prescott AZ 86304 928-778-2951 445-7204
TF: 800-280-2951 ■ *Web:* www.palmerinvestigative.com

PI & Information Services LLC PO Box 157 .... Beaverton OR 97075 503-643-4274 643-5474
Web: www.pi-info.com

Pre-employ.com Inc 2301 Balls Ferry Rd .... Anderson CA 96007 530-378-7680
Web: www.pre-employ.com

Private Eyes Inc 190 N Wiget Ln Ste 220 .... Walnut Creek CA 94598 925-927-3333
Web: www.privateeyesinc.com

Research Assoc Inc 27999 Clemens Rd .... Cleveland OH 44145 440-892-9439 892-9439
TF: 800-255-9693 ■ *Web:* www.researchassociatesinc.com

Rick Johnson & Assoc of Colorado
1649 Downing St .... Denver CO 80218 303-296-2200 296-3038
TF: 800-530-2300 ■ *Web:* www.denverpi.com

Seventrees Corp 2181 M-139 South .... Benton Harbor MI 49022 269-925-8111
Web: www.7trees.com

Shawver & Assoc 6262 Weber Rd Ste 112 .... Corpus Christi TX 78413 361-880-8968 880-8971
Web: www.stxpi.com

Southern Research Company Inc
2850 Centenary Blvd .... Shreveport LA 71104 318-227-9700 424-1801
TF: 888-772-6952 ■ *Web:* www.southernresearchinc.com

Starside Security & Investigation Inc
1930 S Brea Canyon Rd Ste 220 .... Diamond Bar CA 91765 909-396-9999
TF: 888-478-2774 ■ *Web:* www.starside.com

State Information Bureau 842 E Pk Ave .... Tallahassee FL 32301 850-561-3990
Web: www.sibflorida.com

Stewart & Assoc Inc 50 W Douglas St Ste 1200 .... Freeport IL 61032 815-235-3807
TF: 888-310-2840 ■ *Web:* www.bwstewart.com

Thillens Inc 4242 N Elston Ave .... Chicago IL 60618 773-539-4444
Web: www.thillens.com

Vericon Resources Inc
3550 Engineering Dr Ste 225 .... Norcross GA 30092 770-457-9922 457-5006
TF: 800-795-3784 ■ *Web:* www.vericon.com

VTS Investigations LLC PO Box 971 .... Elgin IL 60121 800-538-4464 888-8588*
**Fax Area Code:* 847 ■ *TF:* 800-538-4464 ■ *Web:* www.pichicago.com

Watkins Security Agency of D.c. Inc
5325 E Capitol St Se. .... Washington DC 20019 202-581-2871
Web: thewatkinsgroup.com

Wood & Tait Inc 64-5249 Kauakea Rd .... Kamuela HI 96743 808-885-5090 630-0500*
**Fax Area Code:* 888 ■ *TF:* 800-774-8585 ■ *Web:* www.woodtait.com

401 INVESTMENT ADVICE & MANAGEMENT

See Also Commodity Contracts Brokers & Dealers p. 1996; Investment Guides - Online p. 2611; Mutual Funds p. 2818; Securities Brokers & Dealers p. 3163

Phone Fax

13D Research (USVI) LLC
6115 Estate Smith Bay PO Box 2 Ste 333 .... St Thomas VI 00802 340-775-3330
Web: www.13d.com

300 North Capital LLC 300 N Lake Ave Ste 210 .... Pasadena CA 91101 626-449-8500
Web: www.300northcapital.com

A N Culbertson & Company Inc
1 Boars Head Pointe Ste 101 .... Charlottesville VA 22903 434-972-7766
Web: www.anculbertson.com

A&J Capital Investment Inc
1609 W Valley Blvd Ste 328 .... Alhambra CA 91803 626-289-8887
Web: www.ajcap.com

Aaron Bell International Inc
9101 E Kenyon Ave Ste 2300 .... Denver CO 80237 720-200-0470
Web: www.aaron-bell.com

Aberdeen Asset Management Inc
1735 Market St 32nd Fl .... Philadelphia PA 19103 215-405-5700
Web: www.aberdeen-asset.com

Abingdon Capital Management LLC
1650 Tysons Blvd Ste 1575 .... Mclean VA 22102 703-269-3400
Web: www.abingdoncapital.com

Absolute Investment Advisers LLC
18 Shipyard Dr Ste 3C .... Hingham MA 02043 781-740-1904
Web: www.absoluteadvisers.com

Acadian Asset Management Inc 260 Franklin St .... Boston MA 02110 617-850-3500
Web: www.acadian-asset.com

Acquisitions Northwest Inc
210 SW Morrison Ste 600 .... Portland OR 97204 503-225-0479
Web: www.acquisitionsnw.com

Acumen Capital Finance Partners Ltd
404 Sixth Ave S W Ste 700 .... Calgary AB T2P0R9 403-571-0300
TF: 888-422-8636 ■ *Web:* www.acumencapital.com

Acupay System LLC 30 Broad St 46th Fl .... New York NY 10004 212-422-1222
Web: www.acupay.com

Addison Capital Partners
319 Clematis St Ste 211 .... West Palm Beach FL 33401 561-835-4041
Web: www.addisoncapitalpartners.com

Admedia Partners 3 Park Ave 31st Fl .... New York NY 10016 212-759-1870
Web: www.admediapartners.com

Adroit Investment Management Ltd
12th Fl Canadian Western Bank Pl 10303 Jasper Ave
.... Edmonton AB T5J3N6 780-429-3500
Web: www.adroitinvestments.ca

Advanced Materials Partners Inc
45 Pine St .... New Canaan CT 06840 203-966-6415
Web: www.amplink.com

Advent Capital Management LLC
1065 Ave of the Americas 31st Fl .... New York NY 10018 212-482-1600 480-9655
TF: 888-523-8368 ■ *Web:* www.adventcap.com

Advisory Research Holdings Inc
180 N. Stetson Ave
Ste 5500 180 North Stetson Avenue .... Chicago IL 60601 312-565-1414
Web: www.advisoryresearch.com

Aegis Asset Management Inc
2331 W Lincoln Ave .... Anaheim CA 92801 714-635-9900
Web: www.catanzarite.com

AEL Financial LLC
600 N Buffalo Grove Rd .... Buffalo Grove IL 60089 847-465-2009
Web: aelfinancial.com

AEW Capital Management LP (AEW) 2 Seaport Ln .... Boston MA 02210 617-261-9000 261-9555
Web: www.aew.com

AGF Management Ltd 66 Wellington St W 31st Fl. .... Toronto ON M5K1E9 905-214-8203 214-8243
TF: 800-268-8583 ■ *Web:* www.agf.com

Akanthos Capital Management LLC
21700 Oxnard St Ste 1520 .... Woodland Hills CA 91367 818-883-8270
Web: www.akanthoscapital.com

Aksia LLC 599 Lexington Ave 46th Fl .... New York NY 10022 212-710-5710
Web: www.aksia.com

Aldebaran Capital LLC
10293 N Meridian St Ste 100 .... Indianapolis IN 46290 317-818-7827
TF: 888-742-7827 ■ *Web:* www.aldebarancapital.com

Alderman & Company Capital LLC
20 Silver Brook Rd .... Ridgefield CT 06877 203-244-5680
Web: www.aldermancapital.com

Alembic Global Advisors 780 Third Ave 3rd Fl .... New York NY 10017 212-907-5350
Web: www.alembicglobal.com

Allegheny Investments Ltd
Stone Quarry Crossing 811 Camp Horne Rd
Ste 100 .... Pittsburgh PA 15237 412-367-3880
Web: www.alleghenyfinancial.com

Allegiance Financial Group Inc
2935 Country Dr Ste 102 .... Little Canada MN 55117 651-294-4550
Web: www.afg2000.com

Allegis Residential Services Inc
9340 Hazard Way Ste B2 .... San Diego CA 92123 858-430-5700
Web: aspm-sandiego.com

AllianceBernstein Holding LP (AB)
1345 Ave of the Americas .... New York NY 10105 212-486-5800 969-2293*
NYSE: AB ■ **Fax:* Hum Res ■ *TF Cust Svc:* 800-221-5672 ■ *Web:* www.abglobal.com/home.htm

Allianz Global Investors of America LP
680 Newport Ctr Dr Ste 250 .... Newport Beach CA 92660 415-954-5400
Web: us.allianzgi.com

Allianz Real Estate of America
60 E 42nd St Ste 3710 .... New York NY 10165 203-221-8500
Web: allianz-realestate.com

Alloy Silverstein Financial Services
900 Kings Hwy N Ste 101 .... Cherry Hill NJ 08034 856-667-4100
Web: www.alloysilverstein.com

Company	City	State	ZIP	Phone	Fax
Alpha Windward LLC 200 Lowder Brook Dr Ste 2400 *Web:* www.alphawindward.com	Westwood	MA	02090	781-326-8880	
Alphamark Advisors LLC 250 Grandview Dr Ste 175 *Web:* www.alphamarkadvisors.com	Fort Mitchell	KY	41017	859-957-1803	
Altair Advisers LLC 303 W Madison St Ste 600 *Web:* www.altairadvisers.com	Chicago	IL	60606	312-429-3000	
AltaVista Research LLC 243 Fifth Ave Ste 235 *Web:* www.altavista-research.com	New York	NY	10016	646-435-0569	
Alternative Strategy Advisers LLC 601 Carlson Pkwy Ste 1125 *Web:* www.asallc.com	Minnetonka	MN	55305	952-847-2450	
AM Private Investments Inc 45 Pine St E Wing *Web:* www.aminet.com	New Canaan	CT	06840	203-972-5095	
Ambassador Capital Management LLC 500 Griswold St Ste 2800	Detroit	MI	48226	313-961-3111	
Ambassador Financial Group Inc 1605 N Cedar Crest Blvd Ste 508 *Web:* www.ambfg.com	Allentown	PA	18104	610-351-1633	
American Capital Partners LLC 205 Oser Ave *TF:* 800-393-0493 ■ *Web:* www.americancapitalpartners.com	Hauppauge	NY	11788	631-851-0918	
American Century Investments Inc 4500 Main St PO Box 419200 *Fax: Cust Svc ■ *TF:* 800-345-2021 ■ *Web:* www.americancentury.com	Kansas City	MO	64111	816-531-5575	340-7962*
American Portfolios Holdings Inc 4250 Veterans Memorial Hwy Ste 420E *Web:* www.americanportfolios.com	Holbrook	NY	11741	631-439-4600	
American Research & Management Co 145 Front St *Web:* www.arm-co.com	Marion	MA	02738	508-748-1665	
Ameriprise Financial Inc 834 Ameriprise Financial Ctr *NYSE: AMP* ■ *TF:* 866-673-3673 ■ *Web:* www.ameriprise.com	Minneapolis	MN	55474	612-671-3131	
Ameriprise Financial Services Inc 70100 Ameriprise Financial Ctr *TF:* 866-483-8434 ■ *Web:* www.ameriprise.com	Minneapolis	MN	55474	866-483-8434	
AMI Asset Management Corp 10866 Wilshire Blvd Ste 770 *Web:* www.amiassetmanagement.com	Los Angeles	CA	90024	310-446-2740	
Amivest Capital Management 703 Market St 18th Fl *Fax Area Code: 415 ■ *TF:* 800-541-7774 ■ *Web:* www.wrapmanager.com	San Francisco	CA	94103	800-541-7774	541-9760*
AmSouth Investment Services Inc (AIS) 250 Riverchase Pkwy E 4th Fl *Fax Area Code: 205 ■ *TF:* 866-512-3479 ■ *Web:* www.regions.com	Birmingham	AL	35244	866-512-3479	560-7923*
Amundi Smith Breeden 280 S Mangum St Ste 301 *Web:* www.smithbreeden.com	Durham	NC	27701	919-967-7221	
Analytic Investors LLC 555 W Fifth St 50th Fl *TF:* 800-618-1872 ■ *Web:* www.aninvestor.com	Los Angeles	CA	90013	213-688-3015	688-8856
Anchor Capital Advisors LLC 1 Post Office Sq Ste 3850 *Web:* www.anchorcapital.com	Boston	MA	02109	617-338-3800	
Angeles Investment Advisors LLC 429 Santa Monica Blvd Ste 650 *Web:* www.angelesadvisors.com	Santa Monica	CA	90401	310-393-6300	
Apache Capital Management LLC 230 Park Ave Ste 1518 *Web:* www.apachecapital.com	New York	NY	10169	212-972-0991	
Aperio Group LLC 3 Harbor Dr Ste 315 *Web:* www.aperiogroup.com	Sausalito	CA	94965	415-339-4300	
Apex Capital LLC 25 Orinda Way Ste 300	Orinda	CA	94563	925-253-1800	
Appleton Group Wealth Management LLC 100 W Lawrence St 3/F Apple *TF:* 866-993-7727 ■ *Web:* www.appletongrouponline.com	Wisconsin	WI	54911	920-993-7727	
Appleton Partners Inc 1 Post Office Sq 6th Fl *TF:* 800-338-0745 ■ *Web:* www.appletonpartners.com	Boston	MA	02109	617-338-0700	
Aragon Ventures Inc 1455 Adams Dr Ste 1010 *Web:* www.aragonventures.com	Menlo Park	CA	94025	650-566-8000	
Arbor Capital Management Inc 1400 W Benson Blvd Ste 575 *Web:* www.acminc.com	Anchorage	AK	99503	907-222-7581	
Arcade Partners LLC 62 La Salle Rd Ste 304 *Web:* www.arcadepartners.com	West Hartford	CT	06107	860-236-6320	
Arden Asset Management LLC 375 Park Ave 32nd Fl *Web:* www.ardenasset.com	New York	NY	10152	212-751-5252	
ARGI Investment Services LLC 1914 Stanley Gault Pkwy *TF:* 866-568-9719 ■ *Web:* www.argifinancialgroup.com	Louisville	KY	40223	502-753-0609	
Argos Wealth Advisors LLC 4900 Redwood Rd *Web:* www.argoswealth.com	Napa	CA	94558	707-259-1388	
Aristotle Capital Management LLC 11100 Santa Monica Blvd Ste 1700 *TF:* 877-478-4722 ■ *Web:* www.aristotlecap.com	Los Angeles	CA	90025	310-478-4005	478-8496
Armstrong Shaw Associates Inc 45 Grove St *Web:* www.armstrongshaw.com	New Canaan	CT	06840	203-972-9600	
Arnerich Massena & Associates Inc 2045 NE Martin Luther King Jr Blvd *Web:* www.am-a.com	Portland	OR	97212	503-239-0475	
Ashfield Capital Partners LLC 801 Montgomery St Ste 200 *Web:* www.ashfield.com	San Francisco	CA	94113	415-391-4747	
Assante Financial Management Ltd 4145 N Service Rd Ste 100 *Web:* assante.com	Burlington	ON	L7L6A3	905-335-2291	
Asset Allocation & Management Co 30 W Monroe St 3rd Fl *Web:* www.aamcompany.com	Chicago	IL	60603	312-263-2900	
Asset Consulting Group LLC 231 S Bemiston Ave 14th Fl *Web:* www.acgnet.com	St Louis	MO	63105	314-862-4848	
Asset Strategy Consultants LLC 6 N Park Dr Ste 208 *TF:* 866-344-8282 ■ *Web:* www.assetstrategyconsultants.com	Hunt Valley	MD	21030	410-528-8282	
Assetbuilder Inc 1255 W 15th St Ste 1000 *Web:* assetbuilder.com	Plano	TX	75075	972-535-4040	
AssetMark Inc 1655 Grant St 10th Fl *TF:* 800-664-5345 ■ *Web:* www.assetmark.com	Concord	CA	94520	800-664-5345	
Assurex International 8200 E 32nd St N *Web:* www.truenorth.net	Wichita	KS	67226	316-266-6222	
Atalanta/Sosnoff Capital LLC 101 Pk Ave 6th Fl *Web:* www.atalantasosnoff.com	New York	NY	10178	212-867-5000	922-1820
Atlanta Capital Management Company LLC 1075 Peachtree St NW Ste 2100 *Web:* www.atlcap.com	Atlanta	GA	30309	404-876-9411	872-1672
Atlantic Trust 100 E Pratt St 23rd Fl *TF:* 866-644-4144 ■ *Web:* www.atlantictrust.com	Baltimore	MD	21202	410-539-4660	539-4661
Atlantic-Pacific Capital Inc 102 Greenwich Ave 2nd Fl *Web:* www.apcap.com	Greenwich	CT	06830	203-862-9182	
Attain Capital Management LLC 1 E Wacher Dr 30th Fl *TF:* 800-311-1145 ■ *Web:* attaincapital.com	Chicago	IL	60601	312-604-0926	
Aurora Investment Management LLC 300 N LaSalle St 52nd Fl *Web:* www.aurorallc.com	Chicago	IL	60654	312-762-6700	
Austin Associates LLC 7205 W Central Ave *Web:* www.austinassociates.com	Toledo	OH	43617	419-841-8521	
Avalon Capital Management 495 Seaport Ct Ste 106 *Web:* www.avaloncapital.com	Redwood City	CA	94063	650-306-1500	
Avalon Trust Co 125 Lincoln Ave Ste 301 *Web:* www.avalontrust.com	Santa Fe	NM	87501	505-983-1111	
AXA Rosenberg Investment Management LLC 4 Orinda Way Bldg E *Web:* www.axa-im.com/en/equities/rosenberg-equities	Orinda	CA	94563	925-254-6464	253-0141
AXIS Financial Services Inc 2774 Gateway Rd *Web:* www.axisservicing.com	Carlsbad	CA	92009	760-929-6680	
Ayco Company LP 1 Wall St *Web:* www.ayco.com	Albany	NY	12205	518-464-2000	
Aznar Financial Advisors 21 Lakeview Dr *Web:* www.aznaradvisors.com	Morris Plains	NJ	07950	973-540-8850	
Backstrom McCarley Berry & Company LLC 115 Sansome St Mezzanine A *Web:* www.bmcbco.com	San Francisco	CA	94104	415-392-5505	
Badgley Phelps & Bell Inc 1420 Fifth Ave Ste 3200 *TF:* 800-869-7173 ■ *Web:* badgley.com	Seattle	WA	98101	206-623-6172	
Bahl & Gaynor Inc 212 E Third St Ste 200 *TF:* 800-341-1810 ■ *Web:* www.bahl-gaynor.com	Cincinnati	OH	45202	513-287-6100	287-6110
Bailard Biehl & Kaiser Group 950 Tower Ln Ste 1900 *TF:* 800-224-5273 ■ *Web:* www.bailard.com	Foster City	CA	94404	650-571-5800	573-7128
Baker-Meekins Company Inc, The 1404 Front Ave *Web:* www.bakermeekins.com	Lutherville Timonium	MD	21093	410-823-2600	
Bankers Financial Products Corp 1815 Janesville Ave *Web:* www.rate-watch.com	Fort Atkinson	WI	53538	920-568-1401	
Banorte Securities International Ltd 140 E 45th St 32nd Fl *Web:* www.banortesecurities.com	New York	NY	10017	212-484-5200	
Baring Asset Management Co Inc 470 Atlantic Ave Independence Wharf *Web:* www.barings.com	Boston	MA	02210	617-946-5200	946-5400
Barnum Financial Group 6 Corporate Dr *Web:* www.barnumfinancialgroup.com	Shelton	CT	06484	203-513-6000	
Barometer Capital Management Inc 1 University Ave Ste 1910 Ste 1800 PO Box 25 *Web:* www.barometercapital.ca	Toronto	ON	M5J2P1	416-601-6888	
Barrett & Co 42 Weybosset St Ste 2 *Web:* www.barrett.net	Providence	RI	02903	401-351-1000	
Barrington Research Associates Inc 161 N Clark St Ste 2950 *Web:* brai.com	Chicago	IL	60601	312-634-6000	
Barrow Hanley Mewhinney & Strauss LLC 2200 Ross Ave 31st Fl *Web:* www.barrowhanley.com	Dallas	TX	75201	214-665-1900	
Barry Financial Group Inc 40 Se Fifth St Ste 600 *Web:* www.talkmoney.com	Boca Raton	FL	33432	561-368-9120	
Bartlett & Co 600 Vine St Ste 2100 *TF:* 800-800-4612 ■ *Web:* www.bartlett1898.com	Cincinnati	OH	45202	513-621-4612	621-6462
Batterymarch Financial Management Inc 200 Clarendon St *Web:* www.batterymarch.com	Boston	MA	02116	617-266-8300	266-0633
Battle Road Research Ltd 465 Waverley Oaks Rd Ste 209 *Web:* www.battleroad.com	Waltham	MA	02452	781-894-0705	
Beacon Hill Financial Corp 120 Water St *Web:* www.beaconhillfinancial.com	Boston	MA	02109	617-973-6900	
Beacon Pointe Advisors LLC 500 Newport Ctr Dr Ste 125 *Web:* www.bpadvisors.com	Newport Beach	CA	92660	949-718-1600	
Beacon Trust Co 163 Madison Ave Ste 600 *TF:* 866-377-8090 ■ *Web:* www.beacontrust.com	Morristown	NJ	07960	973-377-8090	
Beck Mack & Oliver LLC 360 Madison Ave 18th Fl *Web:* www.beckmack.com	New York	NY	10017	212-661-2640	
Becker Capital Management Inc 1211 S W Fifth Ave Ste 2185 *TF:* 800-551-3998 ■ *Web:* www.beckercap.com	Portland	OR	97204	503-223-1720	

Phone Fax

Bedell Frazier Investment Counselling LLC
2 Walnut Creek Ctr 200 Pringle Ave
Ste 555 .... Walnut Creek CA 94596 925-932-0344
Web: www.bedellinvest.com

Bedrock Capital Management Inc
5050 El Camino Real Ste 204 .... Los Altos Hills CA 94022 650-964-7024
Web: www.bedrockcap.com

Beecher Investors Inc
1266 E Main St Ste 700R .... Stamford CT 06902 203-539-6281
Web: www.beecherinvestors.com

Bel Air Investment Advisors LLC
1999 Ave of the Stars Ste 2800 .... Los Angeles CA 90067 310-229-1500
Web: www.belair-llc.com

Bell Investment Advisors
1111 Broadway Ste 1630 .... Oakland CA 94607 510-433-1066
TF: 800-700-0089 ■ *Web:* www.bellinvest.com

Benchmark Plus Management LLC 820 A St Ste 700 .... Tacoma WA 98402 253-573-0657
Web: www.bpfunds.com

Benefit Services Group Inc, The
N25 W23050 Paul Rd .... Pewaukee WI 53072 262-521-5700
Web: www.bsg.com

Benefits Plus Consulting Group Inc
1807 Pine St Fl 1 .... Philadelphia PA 19103 215-564-0288
Web: www.consultbenefitsplus.com

Benham & Green Capital Management LLC
1299 Prospect St Ste 301 .... La Jolla CA 92037 858-551-3130

Berkshire Advisors Inc 2240 Ridgewood Rd .... Wyomissing PA 19610 610-376-6970
TF: 800-566-4325 ■ *Web:* www.berkshireadvisors.net

Bernicke & Associates Ltd
4813 Keystone Crossing .... Eau Claire WI 54701 715-832-1173
Web: www.bernicke.com

Bessemer Trust Co 630 Fifth Ave .... New York NY 10111 212-708-9100 265-5826
TF: 866-271-7403 ■ *Web:* www.bessemertrust.com

Beverly Hills Wealth Management LLC
9454 Wilshire Blvd .... Beverly Hills CA 90212 310-859-1600

BG Financial Services Group 160 Main St .... Gloucester MA 01930 978-675-9941
Web: www.nsfgma.com

Birch Hill Investment Advisors LLC
24 Federal St 10th Fl .... Boston MA 02110 617-502-8300
Web: www.birchhilladvisors.com

Bison Capital Asset Management LLC
233 Wilshire Blvd Ste 425 .... Santa Monica CA 90401 310-260-6573
Web: www.bisoncapital.com

BlackRock Inc 40 E 52nd St 25th Fl .... New York NY 10055 212-810-5300
NYSE: BLK ■ *Web:* www.blackrock.com

Blue Point Capital Partners
127 Public Sq Ste 5100 .... Cleveland OH 44114 216-535-4700
Web: www.bluepointcapital.com

Blue Rock Advisors Inc 445 E Lk St Ste 120 .... Wayzata MN 55391 952-229-8700
Web: blue-rock.com

Boenning & Scattergood Inc
200 Barr Harbor Dr Four Tower Bridge
Ste 300 .... West Conshohocken PA 19428 610-832-1212
TF: 800-883-1212 ■ *Web:* www.boenninginc.com

Bogdahn Group, The 4901 Vineland Rd Ste 600 .... Orlando FL 32811 866-240-7932
TF: 866-240-7932 ■ *Web:* www.bogdahngroup.com

Boston Advisors Inc 1 Liberty Sq 10th Fl .... Boston MA 02109 617-348-3100 348-0081
TF: 800-523-5903 ■ *Web:* www.bostonadvisors.com

Boston Family Office LLC, The
88 Broad St 2nd Fl .... Boston MA 02110 617-624-0800
TF: 800-900-4401 ■ *Web:* www.bosfam.com

Boston Financial Data Services
2000 Crown Colony Dr .... Quincy MA 02169 617-483-5000
TF: 888-772-2337 ■ *Web:* www.bostonfinancial.com

Boston Portfolio Advisors Inc
800 Corporate Dr Ste 408 .... Fort Lauderdale FL 33334 954-938-3000
Web: www.bostonportfolio.com

Bouchey Financial Group Ltd 1819 Fifth Ave .... Troy NY 12180 518-720-3333
TF: 800-783-0339 ■ *Web:* www.boucheyfinancial.com

Bowling Portfolio Management LLC
4030 Smith Rd Ste 140 .... Cincinnati OH 45209 513-871-7776
Web: www.bowlingpm.com

Boyar's Intrinsic Value Research LLC
6 E 32nd St 7th Fl .... New York NY 10016 212-995-8300
Web: boyarresearch.com

Boys Arnold & Company Inc
1272 Hendersonville Rd .... Asheville NC 28803 828-274-1542
Web: manageyourinvestments.com

Bragg Financial Advisors Inc
1031 S Caldwell St Ste 200 .... Charlotte NC 28203 704-377-0261
Web: www.braggfinancial.com

Brandes Investment Partners LP
11988 El Camino Real Ste 500 .... San Diego CA 92130 858-755-0239 755-0916
TF: 800-237-7119 ■ *Web:* www.brandes.com

Brandywine Capital Associates
113 East Evans St .... West Chester PA 19380 610-344-2910
TF: 888-344-2920 ■ *Web:* www.brandywinecap.com

Brandywine Global Investment Management LLC
2929 Arch St 8th Fl .... Philadelphia PA 19104 215-609-3500 609-3501
TF: 800-348-2499 ■ *Web:* www.brandywineglobal.com

Branson Fowlkes & Company Inc
3300 Chimney Rock Rd Ste 100-B .... Houston TX 77056 713-780-0606
Web: www.bransonfowlkes.com

Brass Ring Capital Inc
301 Carlson Pkwy Ste 265 .... Minnetonka MN 55305 952-473-2710
Web: www.brassringcapital.com

Breckinridge Capital Advisors Inc
125 High St Oliver St Tower Fl 4 .... Boston MA 02110 617-443-0779
Web: www.breckinridge.com

Brenner Group Inc, The
19200 Stevens Creek Blvd Ste 200 .... Cupertino CA 95014 408-873-3400
Web: thebrennergroup.com

Brentwood Capital Advisors LLC
5000 Meridian Blvd Ste 350 .... Franklin TN 37067 615-224-3830
Web: www.brentwoodcap.com

Phone Fax

Bridgewater Assoc Inc 1 Glendinning Pl .... Westport CT 06880 203-226-3030 291-7300
Web: www.bwater.com

Briggs Capital LLC 858 Washington St Ste 100 .... Dedham MA 02026 781-493-6581
Web: www.briggscapital.com

Brighton Jones LLC 506 Second Ave Ste 1800 .... Seattle WA 98104 206-329-5546
Web: www.brightonjones.com

Brooke Private Equity Associates
84 State St Ste 320 .... Boston MA 02109 617-227-3160
Web: www.brookepea.com

Brookmont Capital Management LLC
2000 McKinney Ave Ste 1230 .... Dallas TX 75201 214-953-0190
Web: www.brookmontcapital.com

Brown &Tedstrom Inc 1700 Broadway Ste 500 .... Denver CO 80290 303-863-7231
TF: 800-883-9361 ■ *Web:* www.brown-tedstrom.com

Brown Bros Harriman & Co 140 Broadway .... New York NY 10005 212-483-1818
Web: www.bbh.com

Brown Investment Advisory & Trust Co
901 S Bond St Ste 400 .... Baltimore MD 21231 410-537-5400
TF: 800-645-3923 ■ *Web:* www.brownadvisory.com

Broyhill Asset Management LLC 800 Golfview Pk .... Lenoir NC 28645 828-758-6100
Web: www.broyhillasset.com

BTS Asset Management Inc
420 Bedford St Ste 340 .... Lexington MA 02420 800-343-3040
TF: 800-343-3040 ■ *Web:* www.btsmanagement.com

Buckhead Capital Management LLC
3330 Cumberland Blvd Ste 650 .... Atlanta GA 30339 404-720-8800
Web: www.buckheadcapital.com

Buckingham Family of Financial Services, The
8182 Maryland Ave Ste 900 .... St Louis MO 63105 314-725-0455

Buckman Buckman & Reid Inc
174 Patterson Ave .... Shrewsbury NJ 07702 732-530-0303
Web: www.buckmanbuckman.com

Burgeonvest Bick Securities Ltd
21 King St W Ste 1100 .... Hamilton ON L8P4W7 905-528-6505
Web: www.burgeonvest.com

Cadence Capital Management
265 Franklin St 4th Fl .... Boston MA 02110 617-624-3500 624-3591
Web: www.cadencecapital.com

Cafa Corporate Finance
4269 Sainte-Catherine W Office 200 .... Westmount QC H3Z1P7 514-989-5508
Web: www.cafa.ca

Calamos Asset Management Inc
2020 Calamos Ct .... Naperville IL 60563 630-245-7200
NASDAQ: CLMS ■ *TF:* 800-582-6959 ■ *Web:* www.calamos.com

Caldwell Trust Co 1400 Ctr Rd Ste Two .... Venice FL 34292 941-493-3600
TF: 800-338-9476 ■ *Web:* www.ctrust.com

Calera Capital
580 California St Ste 2200 .... San Francisco CA 94104 415-632-5200
Web: www.caleracapital.com

Caliber Advisors Inc
514 Via De La Valle Ste 210 .... Solana Beach CA 92075 858-792-8990
Web: www.caliberadvisors.com

California Technology Ventures LLC
670 N Rosemead Blvd Ste 201 .... Pasadena CA 91107 626-351-3700
Web: www.ctventures.com

Callan Assoc Inc
101 California St Ste 3500 .... San Francisco CA 94111 415-974-5060 291-4014
TF: 800-227-3288 ■ *Web:* www.callan.com

Calvert Investment Counsel LLC
4 N Park Dr Ste 201 .... Hunt Valley MD 21030 410-435-3270
Web: www.calvertinvestmentcounsel.com

Cambiar Investors Inc
2401 E Second Ave Ste 500 .... Denver CO 80206 888-673-9950
TF: 888-673-9950 ■ *Web:* www.cambiar.com

Cambria Capital LLC
488 E Winchester St Ste 200 .... Salt Lake City UT 84107 877-226-0477
TF: 877-226-0477 ■ *Web:* www.cambriacapital.com

Cambridge Associates LLC 125 High St .... Boston MA 02110 617-457-7500
Web: www.cambridgeassociates.com

Cambridge Financial Group Inc
4100 Horizons Dr Ste 200 .... Columbus OH 43220 614-457-1530
Web: www.cfginc.net

Camcor Capital Inc 525 Eigth Ave S W Ste 4080 .... Calgary AB T2P1G1 403-508-2950
Web: www.camcorpartners.com

Cameron Thomson Group Ltd 390 Bay St Ste 1706 .... Toronto ON M5H2Y2 416-350-5009
TF: 800-395-9943 ■ *Web:* www.cameronthomson.com

Canaccord Genuity, Research Division
Pacific Centre 609 Granville St Ste 2200
PO Box 10337 .... Vancouver BC V7Y1H2 604-643-7300
Web: www.canaccordgenuity.com

Cantor Fitzgerald Canada Corp
1100 Rene-Levesque Blvd W Ste 1310 .... Montreal QC H3B4N4 514-845-8111
Web: www.versantpartners.com

CapFinancial Partners LLC
4208 Six Forks Rd Ste 1700 .... Raleigh NC 27609 919-870-6822
TF: 800-216-0645 ■ *Web:* www.captrustadvisors.com

Capital Advisors Group Inc
Chatham Ctr 29 Crafts St Ste 270 .... Newton MA 02458 617-630-8100
Web: www.capitaladvisors.com

Capital Advisors Inc 2200 S Utica Pl Ste 150 .... Tulsa OK 74114 918-599-0045
Web: www.capitaladv.com

Capital Alpha Partners LLC
600 Pennsylvania Ave SE Ste 220 .... Washington DC 20003 202-548-0111
Web: www.capalphadc.com

Capital Concepts Group Inc
1030-4720 Kingsway .... Burnaby BC V5H4N2 604-432-7743
Web: www.capitalconcepts.ca

Capital Financial Group Inc
6600 Rockledge Dr 6th Fl .... Bethesda MD 20817 301-468-0100
Web: www.cfginc.com

Capital Group Cos Inc 333 S Hope St .... Los Angeles CA 90071 213-615-0514 486-9217
TF: 800-421-8511 ■ *Web:* thecapitalgroup.com

Capital Growth Management LP
1 International Pl .... Boston MA 02110 617-737-3225
TF: 800-345-4048 ■ *Web:* www.cgmfunds.com

Company / Address	City	State	Zip	Phone	Fax
Capital Innovations LLC 325 Forest Grove Dr Ste 100 *Web:* www.capinnovations.com	Pewaukee	WI	53072	262-746-3100	
Capital Institutional Services Inc 1601 Elm St Ste 3900 *Web:* www.capis.com	Dallas	TX	75201	214-720-0055	
Capital Link Inc 230 Park Ave Ste 1536 *Web:* www.capitallink.com	New York	NY	10169	212-661-7566	
Capital Management Corp, The 4101 Cox Rd Ste 110 *Web:* www.the-cmc.com	Glen Allen	VA	23060	804-270-4000	
Capital Premium Financing Inc 12235 South 800 East *Web:* www.capitalpremium.net	Draper	UT	84020	801-571-0775	
Capital Research & Management Co (CRMC) 333 S Hope St *TF:* 800-421-4225 ■ *Web:* thecapitalgroup.com	Los Angeles	CA	90071	213-486-9200	486-9217
CapitalSouth Growth Fund 4201 Congress St Ste 360 *Web:* www.capitalsouthpartners.com	Charlotte	NC	28209	704-376-5502	
Cappello Capital Corp 100 Wilshire Blvd Ste 1200 *Web:* www.cappellocorp.com	Santa Monica	CA	90401	310-393-6632	
CapTrust Advisors LLC 102 W Whiting St Ste 400 *Web:* www.captrustadv.com	Tampa	FL	33602	813-218-5000	
Carderock Capital Management Inc 2 Wisconsin Cir Ste 510 *Web:* www.carderockcapital.com	Chevy Chase	MD	20815	301-951-5288	
Cardinal Capital Management LLC 4 Greenwich Office Park *Web:* www.cardcap.com	Greenwich	CT	06831	203-863-8990	
Carl Domino Inc 515 N Flagler Dr Ste 702 *Web:* www.carldomino.com	West Palm Beach	FL	33401	561-833-2882	
Carolinas Investment Consulting LLC 5605 Carnegie Blvd Ste 400 *TF:* 800-255-2904 ■ *Web:* www.carolinasinvest.com	Charlotte	NC	28209	704-643-2455	
Carty & Company Inc 6263 Poplar Ave Ste 800 *Web:* www.cartyco.com	Memphis	TN	38119	901-767-8940	
CarVal Investors LLC 9320 Excelsior Blvd 7th Fl *Web:* www.carvalinvestors.com	Hopkins	MN	55343	952-984-3774	
Casey Research LLC 55 NE Fifth Ave *TF:* 888-512-2739 ■ *Web:* www.caseyresearch.com	Delray Beach	FL	33483	602-445-2736	
Casgrain & Company Ltd 1200 Mcgill College Ave 21st Fl *TF:* 800-361-8738 ■ *Web:* www.casgrain.ca	Montreal	QC	H3B4G7	514-871-8080	
Castle Creek Capital LLC 6051 El Tordo *Web:* www.castlecreek.com	Rancho Santa Fe	CA	92067	858-756-8300	
Cavallino LLC 599 Bridgeway *Web:* www.cavallinollc.com	Sausalito	CA	94965	415-285-9300	
Cavanal Hill Investment Management Inc 1 Williams Ctr 15th Fl *Web:* www.axiaim.com	Tulsa	OK	74172	918-588-8688	
Cedar Brook Financial Partners LLC 5885 Landerbrook Dr Ste 200 *Web:* cedarbrookfinancial.com	Cleveland	OH	44124	440-683-9200	
Cedar Financial Advisors Inc 3853 SW Hall Blvd *Web:* www.cedaradvisors.com	Beaverton	OR	97005	503-512-5890	
Centaur Capital Partners LP Southlake Town Sq 1460 Main St Ste 234 *Web:* www.centaurcapital.com	Southlake	TX	76092	817-488-9632	
Central Park Group LLC 805 Third Ave 18th Fl *Web:* www.centralparkgroup.com	New York	NY	10022	212-317-9200	
Century Wealth Management LLC 1770 Kirby Pkwy Ste 117 *TF:* 855-850-5532 ■ *Web:* www.centurywealth.com	Memphis	TN	38138	901-850-5532	
CFS Investment Advisory Services LLC 97 Lackawanna Ave Ste 101 *Web:* www.cfsias.com	Totowa	NJ	07512	973-826-8800	
Cherokee Investment Partners LLC 111 E Hargett St Ste 300 *Web:* www.cherokeefund.com	Raleigh	NC	27601	919-743-2500	
Chevy Chase Trust Co 7501 Wisconsin Ave W Tower Ste 1500W *Web:* www.chevychasetrust.com	Bethesda	MD	20814	240-497-5000	
Childs Company LLC 3438 Peachtree Raod Phipps Tower Ste 1400-B *Web:* www.childscompany.com	Atlanta	GA	30326	404-751-3049	
Churchill Corporate Services 56 Utter Ave *TF:* 800-941-7458 ■ *Web:* www.furnishedhousing.com	Hawthorne	NJ	07506	973-636-9400	636-0179
Cincinnati Asset Management Inc 4350 Glndl Milford Rd 1 *Web:* www.cambonds.com	Cincinnati	OH	45242	513-554-8500	
Cirrus Research LLC 303 S Broadway Ste 212 Tarrytown *Web:* www.cirrus-res.com	New York	NY	10591	914-289-1400	
Citco Fund Services San Francisco Inc 560 Mission St Fl 26 *Web:* www.citco.com	San Francisco	CA	94105	415-228-0390	
Clark Capital Management Group Inc (CCMG) 1650 Market St 1 Liberty Pl 53rd Fl *TF:* 800-766-2264 ■ *Web:* www.ccmg.com	Philadelphia	PA	19103	215-569-2224	569-3639
Clearspring Capital Group 11000 Richmond Ste 550 *Web:* www.clearspringcapitalgroup.com	Houston	TX	77042	713-339-1903	
Cleveland Research Co 1375 East Ninth St Ste 2700 *Web:* www.cleveland-research.com	Cleveland	OH	44114	216-649-7250	
CM Bidwell & Associates Ltd 20 Old Pali Pl *Web:* www.cmbidwellandassociates.com	Honolulu	HI	96817	808-595-1099	
Coastal Credit LLC 3852 Virginia Beach Boulvard *Web:* www.coastalcreditllc.com	Virginia Beach	VA	23452	757-340-6000	
Cohen & Steers Inc 280 Pk Ave 10th Fl *NYSE: CNS* ■ *TF:* 800-330-7348 ■ *Web:* www.cohenandsteers.com	New York	NY	10017	212-832-3232	
Coho Partners Ltd 300 Berwyn Park 801 Cassatt Rd Ste 100 *Web:* www.cohopartners.com	Berwyn	PA	19312	484-318-7575	
Collins Barrow Ottawa LLP 400-301 Moodie Dr *Web:* www.collinsbarrowottawa.com	Ottawa	ON	K2H9C4	613-820-8010	
Collins Capital Management Inc 7077 Bonneval Rd Ste 340 *Web:* www.collinscmi.com	Jacksonville	FL	32216	904-493-7500	
Colony Capital Management 3050 Peachtree Rd NW Ste 200 *Web:* www.colonycapital.com	Atlanta	GA	30305	404-365-5050	523-7877
Columbia Threadneedle Investments 1 Financial Ctr *TF:* 800-426-3750 ■ *Web:* www.columbiathreadneedleus.com	Boston	MA	02111	800-426-3750	
Columbus Cir Investors Inc (CCI) 1 Stn Pl Metro Ctr 8th Fl *Web:* www.columbuscircle.com	Stamford	CT	06902	203-353-6000	
Commonfund Inc 15 Old Danbury Rd *Web:* www.commonfund.org	Wilton	CT	06897	203-563-5000	
Commonwealth Capital Advisors LLC 30 S Wacker Dr 22nd Fl *Web:* www.commonwealthcapital.com	Chicago	IL	60606	808-744-9713	
Commonwealth Financial Network 29 Sawyer Rd **Fax Area Code: 866* ■ *TF:* 800-237-0081 ■ *Web:* www.commonwealth.com	Waltham	MA	02453	781-736-0700	316-8357*
Compak Asset Management 1801 Dove St *TF:* 800-388-9700 ■ *Web:* www.compak.com	Newport Beach	CA	92660	800-388-9700	
Concorde Asset Management LLC 1120 E Long Lk Rd Ste 250 *Web:* www.concordefinancial.com	Troy	MI	48085	248-740-8500	
Conestoga Capital Advisors LLC 259 N Radnor Chester Rd Radnor Ct Ste 120 *TF:* 800-320-7790 ■ *Web:* www.conestogacapital.com	Radnor	PA	19087	484-654-1380	
Conexus Financial Partners LP 721 Rt 202/206 *Web:* www.conexuscapital.com	Bridgewater	NJ	08807	908-231-9101	
Conning Asset Management Co 1 Financial Plaza *Web:* www.conning.com	Hartford	CT	06103	860-299-2000	
Connors Investor Services Inc 1210 Broadcasting Rd Ste 200 *TF:* 877-376-7418 ■ *Web:* www.connorsinvestor.com	Wyomissing	PA	19610	610-376-7418	
Conrad Capital Management Inc 425 Broadhollow Rd *Web:* www.conradcapital.com	Melville	NY	11747	631-439-7878	
Cook Pine Capital LLC 73 Arch St Greenwich 2nd Fl *Web:* www.cookpinecapital.com	Greenwich	CT	06830	203-861-2930	
Cooke & Bieler LP 1700 Market St Ste 3222 *Web:* www.cooke-bieler.com	Philadelphia	PA	19103	215-567-1101	567-1681
Cookson Peirce & Company Inc 555 Grant St Ste 380 *Web:* www.cooksonpeirce.com	Pittsburgh	PA	15219	412-471-5320	
Copeland Capital Management LLC 8 Tower Bridge 161 Washington St Ste 1650 *Web:* www.copelandcapital.com	Conshohocken	PA	19428	484-530-4300	
Corbyn Investment Management Inc 2330 W Joppa Rd Ste 108 *Web:* corbyn.com	Lutherville	MD	21093	410-832-5500	
Cornerstone Advisors Asset Management Inc 74 W Broad St Ste 340 *TF:* 800-923-0900 ■ *Web:* www.cornerstone-companies.com	Bethlehem	PA	18018	610-694-0900	
Cornerstone Advisors Inc 1802 Hamilton St *Web:* www.cornerstoneadvisers.com	Allentown	PA	18104	610-437-1375	
Corporate Development Associates Inc 5335 Far Hills Ave Ste 304 *Web:* www.cda-inc.net	Dayton	OH	45429	937-439-4227	
Coughlin & Company Inc 140 E 19th Ave Ste 700 *Web:* www.coughlinandcompany.com	Denver	CO	80203	303-863-1900	
Courier Capital Corp 1114 Delaware Ave *Web:* www.couriercapital.com	Buffalo	NY	14209	716-883-9595	
Covington Capital Management 601 S Figueroa St Ste 2000 *Web:* www.covingtoncapitalmanagement.com	Los Angeles	CA	90017	213-629-7500	
CPM Group 30 Broad St 37th Fl *Web:* www.cpmgroup.com	New York	NY	10004	212-785-8320	
CPS Investment Advisors 1509 S Florida Ave *Web:* www.cpalliance.com	Lakeland	FL	33803	863-688-1725	
Craig-Hallum Capital Group LLC 222 S Ninth St Ste 350 *Web:* www.craig-hallum.com	Minneapolis	MN	55402	612-334-6300	
Cramer Rosenthal Mcglynn LLC 520 Madison Ave 20th Fl *Web:* www.crmllc.com	New York	NY	10022	212-838-3830	
Crawford Investment Counsel Inc 600 Galleria Pkwy Ste 1650 *Web:* www.crawfordinvestment.com	Atlanta	GA	30339	770-859-0045	
Creative Financial Group (CFG) 16 Campus Blvd *TF:* 800-893-4824 ■ *Web:* creativefinancialgroup.com	Newtown Square	PA	19073	610-325-6100	325-6240
Creative Financial Group Ltd 1000 Abernathy Rd Bldg 400 Ste 1500 *Web:* www.cfgltd.com	Atlanta	GA	30328	770-913-9704	
Creative Global Investments LLC Research Div 115 E 57th St 11th Fl *Web:* cg-inv.com	New York	NY	10022	212-939-7256	
Cremac LLC 78 Delevan St *Web:* www.cremac.com	Brooklyn	NY	11231	718-222-4500	

Phone Fax

Crestwood Advisors LLC 50 Federal St Ste 810. . . . . .Boston MA 02110 617-523-8880
TF: 877-273-7896 ■ *Web:* www.crestwoodadvisors.com

CrossHarbor Capital Partners LLC
1 Boston Pl Ste 2300 . . . . .Boston MA 02108 617-624-8300
Web: www.crossharborcapital.com

Crown Financial Ministries
601 Broad St SE. . . . . .Gainesville GA 30501 770-534-1000
TF: 800-722-1976 ■ *Web:* www.crown.org

CRT Capital Group LLC 262 Harbor Dr. . . . . .Stamford CT 06902 203-569-6400
Web: www.crtllc.com

CSM Capital Corp 625 Madison Ave 3rd Fl . . . . .New York NY 10022 212-400-9550
Web: www.csmcapitalcorp.com

Cullinan Associates Inc
295 N Hubbards Ln 2nd Fl. . . . . .Louisville KY 40207 502-893-0300
TF: 800-611-4841 ■ *Web:* www.cullinan.com

Cumberland Private Wealth Management Inc
99 Yorkville Ave Ste 300. . . . . Toronto ON M5R3K5 416-929-1090
TF: 800-929-8296 ■ *Web:* www.cumberlandprivate.com

Curran Investment Management
30 S Pearl St Omni Plz 9th Fl. . . . . .Albany NY 12207 518-391-4246
TF: 866-432-1246 ■ *Web:* www.curranllc.com

Curtis Financial Group LLC
1 Liberty Pl Ste 4400 1650 Market St. . . . . Philadelphia PA 19103 215-972-2375
Web: www.curtisfinancial.com

Cutler Investment Counsel LLC
525 Bigham Knoll. . . . . .Jacksonville OR 97530 541-770-9000
Web: www.cutler.com

Cypress Capital Group Inc
251 Royal Palm Way Ste 500 . . . . Palm Beach FL 33480 561-659-5889
Web: www.cypresscapitalgroup.com

Cypress Wealth Advisors LLC
101 California St Ste 1025 . . . . San Francisco CA 94111 415-489-2100
Web: www.cypresswealth.com

Dahab Assoc Inc 423 S Country Rd . . . . Bay Shore NY 11706 631-665-6181
Web: www.dahab.com

DailyFX 55 Water St 50th Fl . . . . .New York NY 10041 212-897-7660
TF: 888-503-6739 ■ *Web:* www.dailyfx.com

Dale Scott & Co
650 California St 8th Fl. . . . . San Francisco CA 94108 415-956-1030
Web: www.dalescott.com

Dalton Greiner Hartman Maher & Company LLC
565 Fifth Ave Ste 2101 . . . . .New York NY 10017 212-557-2445 557-4898
Web: www.dghm.com

Dalton Investments LLC
1601 Cloverfield Blvd Ste 5050 N. . . . . Santa Monica CA 90404 424-231-9100
Web: www.daltoninvestments.com

Darrell & King LLC
410 White Gables Ln . . . . Charlottesville VA 22903 434-977-7010
Web: www.darrellandking.com

Davidson & Garrard Inc 810 Main St. . . . . .Lynchburg VA 24505 434-847-6600
Web: dg-g.com

DDJ Capital Management LLC
130 Turner St Bldg 3 Ste 600 . . . . Waltham MA 02453 781-283-8500 283-8555
Web: www.ddjcap.com

Deans Knight Capital Management Ltd
999 W Hastings St Ste 1500. . . . . .Vancouver BC V6C2W2 604-669-0212
Web: www.deansknight.com

Deltec Asset Management LLC
623 Fifth Ave 28th Fl . . . . .New York NY 10022 212-546-6200
Web: www.deltec-ny.com

Denning & Company LLC
1 California St Ste 2800 . . . . San Francisco CA 94111 415-399-3939
Web: www.denningandcompany.com

Denver Investment Advisors LLC
1225 17th St 26th Fl. . . . . .Denver CO 80202 303-312-5000 312-4900
Web: www.denvest.com

Depository Trust Co 55 Water St .New York NY 10041 212-855-1000 855-8707
Web: www.dtcc.com

Design ProfessionalXL Group
2959 Salinas Hwy. . . . . .Monterey CA 93940 831-649-5522
TF: 800-227-4284 ■ *Web:* xlgroup.com

Desjardins Securities Inc
1170 Peel St Ste 300 . . . . Montreal QC H3B0A9 514-987-1749
Web: www2.vmdconseil.ca

Developing World Markets Finance LLP
750 Washington Blvd Ste 500 . . . . Stamford CT 06901 203-655-5453
Web: www.dwmarkets.com

DH Corp Ste 201 939 Eglinton Ave E. Toronto ON M4G4H7 416-696-7700
Web: www.dh.com/cheques

Dimeo Schneider & Assoc LLC
500 W Madision St Ste 3855 . . . . .Chicago IL 60661 312-853-1000 853-3352
Web: www.dimeoschneider.com

Dinosaur Securities LLC
470 Park Ave S 9th Fl. . . . . .New York NY 10016 212-448-9944
Web: www.dinogroup.com

DISCERN Investment Analytics Inc
493 S El Camino. . . . . .San Mateo CA 94402 415-817-9012
Web: www.discern.com

Disciplined Growth Investors Inc
Fifth St Towers 150 S Fifth St Ste 2550 . . . . Minneapolis MN 55402 612-317-4100
Web: www.dginv.com

DL Carlson Investment Group Inc
101 N State St. . . . . Concord NH 03301 603-224-5977
Web: www.carlsoninvest.com

Dodge & Cox 555 California St 40th Fl . . . . San Francisco CA 94104 415-981-1710
Web: www.dodgeandcoxworldwide.com

Don Park LP 842 York Mills Rd . . . . .North York ON M3B3A8 416-449-7275
Web: www.donpark.com

Donald Smith & Company Inc
152 W 57th St 22nd Fl. . . . . .New York NY 10019 212-284-0990
Web: www.donaldsmithandco.com

Donaldson Capital Management LLC
20 NW First St 5th Fl . . . . Evansville IN 47708 812-421-3211
Web: www.dcmol.com

Phone Fax

Dorsey Wright & Associates Inc
1011 Boulder Springs Dr Ste 150. . . . . Richmond VA 23225 804-320-8511
Web: www.dorseywright.com

Dover Financial Research LLC 208 Dover Rd . . . . Westwood MA 02090 781-461-0922
Web: www.doverfr.com

Dragonfly Capital Partners LLC
The Packard Bldg 1310 S Tryon St Ste 109 . . . . Charlotte NC 28203 704-342-3491
Web: www.dragonflycapital.com

Drake Capital Advisors LLC
1 Fawcett Pl Ste 140. . . . . .Greenwich CT 06830 203-861-7500
Web: www.drakeadvisors.com

Driehaus Capital Management Inc 25 E Erie St . . . . .Chicago IL 60611 312-587-3800
TF: 800-688-8819 ■ *Web:* www.driehaus.com

Duff & Phelps Investment Management Co
200 S Wacker Dr Ste 500 . . . . .Chicago IL 60606 312-263-2610
TF: 800-338-8214 ■ *Web:* www.dpimc.com

DUNN Capital Management LLC
309 SE Osceola St Dunn Bldg Ste 350. . . . . .Stuart FL 34994 772-286-4777
Web: www.dunncapital.com

Eagle Asset Management
880 Carillon Pkwy . . . . Saint Petersburg FL 33716 800-237-3101
TF: 800-237-3101 ■ *Web:* www.eagleasset.com

Eagle Global Advisors LLC
5847 San Felipe Ste 930. . . . . .Houston TX 77057 713-952-3550
Web: www.eagleglobal.com

Eagle Investment Systems LLC
65 LaSalle Rd Ste 305 . . . . West Hartford CT 06107 860-561-4602
Web: www.eagleinvsys.com

Earnest Partners LLC
1180 Peachtree St Ste 2300 . . . . .Atlanta GA 30309 404-815-8772 815-8948
TF: 800-322-0068 ■ *Web:* www.earnestpartners.com

Eastbourne Capital Management LLC
1101 Fifth Ave Ste 370. . . . . .San Rafael CA 94901 415-448-1200
Web: www.eastbournecapital.com

Edgar Lomax Co 6564 Loisdale Ct Ste 310. . . . . .Springfield VA 22150 703-719-0026
TF: 866-205-0524 ■ *Web:* www.edgarlomax.com

Eidelman Virant Capital
8000 Maryland Ave Ste 380 . . . . Saint Louis MO 63105 314-727-9686
Web: www.eidelmanvirant.com

Elan Financial Services
225 W Sta Sq Dr Ste 620 . . . . .Pittsburgh PA 15219 877-935-2637
TF: 877-935-2637 ■ *Web:* www.elanfinancialservices.com

Electronic Entertainment Design & Research Inc
2075 Corte Del Nogal Ste B . . . . Carlsbad CA 92011 760-579-7100
Web: www.eedar.com

Eliot Rose Asset Management LLC
1000 Chapel View Blvd Ste 240 . . . . Cranston RI 02920 401-588-5100
TF: 866-585-5100 ■ *Web:* www.eliotrose.com

Elliott Cove Capital Management
1000 Second Ave Ste 1440. . . . . Seattle WA 98104 206-267-2683
Web: www.elliottcove.com

emat Capital Management LLC
7474 N Figueroa St Ste A . . . . .Los Angeles CA 90041 323-255-1333
Web: www.ematcapital.com

Emerald Asset Advisors LLC
2843 Executive Park Dr. . . . . Weston FL 33331 954-385-9624
Web: www.emerald-eas.com

Encima Global LLC 645 Madison Ave 5th Fl. . . . . .New York NY 10022 212-876-4400
Web: www.encimaglobal.com

Encompass Financial Advisors Inc
6107 SW Murray Blvd . . . . Beaverton OR 97008 503-643-8075
Web: fiadvisor.com

Energy Security Analysis Inc
401 Edgewater Pl Ste 640. . . . . .Wakefield MA 01880 781-245-2036
Web: www.esai.com

EnviroCap LLC 2111 W Swann Ave ste 200. . . . . Tampa FL 33606 813-341-3650
Web: www.envirocap.com

Envision Capital Management Inc
11755 Wilshire Blvd 1140 . . . . .Los Angeles CA 90025 310-445-3252
Web: www.envisioncap.com

Epoch Investment Partners Inc
640 Fifth Ave 18th Fl . . . . .New York NY 10019 212-303-7200 202-4948
NASDAQ: EPHC ■ *Web:* www.eipny.com

Essex Investment Management Company LLC
125 High St 29th Fl . . . . .Boston MA 02110 617-342-3200 342-3280
Web: www.essexinvest.com

Estrada Hinojosa & Company Inc
1717 Main St LB47. . . . . Dallas TX 75201 214-658-1670 658-1671
TF: 800-676-5352 ■ *Web:* www.estradahinojosa.com

Europlay Capital Advisors LLC
15260 Ventura Blvd 20th Fl . . . . .Sherman Oaks CA 91403 818-444-4400
Web: www.europlaycapital.com

EVC Group Inc 201 Mission St Ste 1930 . . . . San Francisco CA 94105 415-896-6820
Web: www.evcgroup.com

Evercore Partners Inc 55 E 52nd St . . . . .New York NY 10055 212-857-3100
Web: www.evercore.com

Evergreen Advisors LLC
9256 Bendix Rd Ste 300. . . . . .Columbia MD 21045 410-997-6000
Web: www.evergreenadvisorsllc.com

Evergreen Capital Management LLC
10500 N East 8th Ste 950. . . . . .Bellevue WA 98004 425-467-4600
Web: www.evergreengavekal.com

Excipio Consulting LLC
1216 E Kenosha St . . . . .Broken Arrow OK 74012 918-357-5507
Web: www.excipio.net

Executive Monetary Management LLC
220 E 42nd St 32nd Fl . . . . .New York NY 10017 212-476-5555
Web: www.michaelbolton.com

Exvere Inc 1301 Fifth Ave Ste 3405 . . . . Seattle WA 98101 206-728-1800
Web: www.exvere.com

Fairfield Research Corp
65 Locust Ave Ste 200 . . . . New Canaan CT 06840 203-972-0404
Web: www.frcinvest.com

Company	City	State	Zip	Phone	Fax
Falkenberg Capital Corp 600 S Cherry St Cherry Creek Plz I Ste 1108 *Web:* www.falkenbergcapital.com	Denver	CO	80246	303-320-4800	
Falls River Group LLC 305 Fifth Ave S Ste 206 *Web:* www.fallsrivergroup.com	Naples	FL	34102	239-649-4222	
Farber Financial Group 150 York St Ste 1600 *Web:* www.farberfinancial.com	Toronto	ON	M5H3S5	416-497-0150	
Favus Institutional Research LLC PO Box 1003 *Web:* favusinstitutionalresearch.com	New York	NY	10276	917-952-8158	
Fayez Sarofim & Co 909 Fannin St Ste 2907 *Web:* www.sarofim.com	Houston	TX	77010	713-654-4484	
FCA Corp 791 Town & Country Blvd Ste 250 *Web:* www.fcacorp.com	Houston	TX	77024	713-781-2856	781-7195
FCM Investments 2200 Ross Ave Ste 4600 W *Web:* www.fcminvest.com	Dallas	TX	75201	214-665-6900	665-6940
Federated Investors 1001 Liberty Ave Federated Investors Twr *NYSE:* FII ■ *TF:* 800-245-0242 ■ *Web:* www.federatedinvestors.com	Pittsburgh	PA	15222	412-288-1900	
Feltl & Company Inc 2100 LaSalle Plz 800 LaSalle Ave *Web:* www.feltl.com	Minneapolis	MN	55402	612-492-8800	
FHL Capital Corp 2 N Twentieth St Ste 860 *Web:* www.fhlcapital.com	Birmingham	AL	35203	205-328-3098	
FIC Capital Inc 286 Madison Ave 11th Fl *Web:* www.ficcapital.com	New York	NY	10017	212-679-2100	
Fidelity Investments Institutional Services Company Inc 82 Devonshire St *TF:* 800-343-3548 ■ *Web:* www.fidelity.com	Boston	MA	02109	617-563-9840	
Fiduciary Capital Management Inc PO Box 80 *Web:* www.fcmstablevalue.com	Wallingford	CT	06492	203-269-0440	269-6440
Fiduciary Management Inc of Milwaukee 100 E Wisconsin Ave Ste 2200 *TF:* 800-264-7684 ■ *Web:* www.fiduciarymgt.com	Milwaukee	WI	53202	414-226-4545	226-4522
Financial Dimensions Group 3900 Northwoods Dr *Web:* www.fdg-advisors.com	Saint Paul	MN	55112	651-481-6280	
Financial Resource Group LLC 12900 Preston Rd Ste 100, LB-104 *Web:* financialresourcegroup.co/index.html	Dallas	TX	75230	972-960-7790	
Financial Technology Partners LP 601 California St 22nd Fl *Web:* www.ftpartners.com	San Francisco	CA	94108	415-512-8700	
First Affirmative Financial Network LLC 5475 Mark Dabling Blvd Ste 108 *Web:* www.firstaffirmative.com	Colorado Springs	CO	80918	719-636-1045	
First Fidelity Capital Markets Inc 10463 Stonebridge Blvd Ste 400 *Web:* www.ffidelity.com	Boca Raton	FL	33498	561-558-0730	
First Pacific Advisors Inc 11400 W Olympic Blvd Ste 1200 *TF:* 800-982-4372 ■ *Web:* www.fpafunds.com	Los Angeles	CA	90064	310-473-0225	996-5450
Firsthand Capital Management Inc 150 Almaden Blvd Ste 1250 *Web:* www.firsthandcapital.com	San Jose	CA	95113	408-886-7096	
Fischer Francis Trees & Watts Inc 200 Pk Ave 11th Fl *TF:* 866-392-4090 ■ *Web:* www.fftw.com	New York	NY	10166	212-681-3000	
Fisher Investments 13100 Skyline Blvd *TF:* 800-550-1071 ■ *Web:* www.fi.com	Woodside	CA	94062	800-550-1071	
Flexial Corp 1483 Gould Dr *Web:* www.flexial.com	Cookeville	TN	38506	931-432-1853	
Flexible Plan Investments Ltd 3883 Telegraph Rd Ste 100 *TF:* 800-347-3539 ■ *Web:* www.flexibleplan.com	Bloomfield Hills	MI	48302	248-642-6640	
FMR Corp 82 Devonshire St *TF:* 800-343-3548 ■ *Web:* www.fidelity.com	Boston	MA	02109	800-343-3548	
Fogel Capital Management Inc 453 Riverside Dr *Web:* fogelcapital.com	Stuart	FL	34994	772-223-9686	
Foothills Asset Management Ltd 8767 E Via de Ventura Ste 175 *TF:* 800-663-9870 ■ *Web:* www.faml.net	Scottsdale	AZ	85258	480-777-9870	
Ford Equity Research Inc 11722 Sorrento Vly Rd Ste I *TF:* 800-842-0207 ■ *Web:* www.fordequity.com	San Diego	CA	92121	858-755-1327	
Forefront Analytics LLC 1 Tower Bridge 100 Front St Ste 1111 *Web:* www.forefrontanalytics.com	West Conshohocken	PA	19428	610-341-3900	
Forest Investment Assoc 15 Piedmont Ctr Ste 1250 *Web:* www.forestinvest.com	Atlanta	GA	30305	404-261-9575	261-9574
Formula Growth Ltd 1010 Sherbrooke St W Ste 2300 *TF:* 877-343-6654 ■ *Web:* www.formulagrowth.ca	Montreal	QC	H3A2R7	514-288-5136	
Fort Point Capital Partners LLC 275 Sacramento St 8th Fl *Web:* www.fortpointcap.com	San Francisco	CA	94111	415-625-0909	
Fort Washington Investment Advisors Inc 303 Broadway Ste 1200 *TF:* 888-244-8167 ■ *Web:* www.fortwashington.com	Cincinnati	OH	45202	513-361-7600	
Foster & Motley Inc 7755 Montgomery Rd Ste 100 *Web:* www.fosterandmotley.com	Cincinnati	OH	45236	513-561-6640	
Franklin Park Associates LLC Franklin Park 251 St Asaphs Rd Three Bala Plz Ste 500 W *Web:* www.franklinparkllc.com	Bala Cynwyd	PA	19004	610-822-0500	
Franklin Resources Inc 1 Franklin Pkwy Bdge 970 1st Fl *NYSE:* BEN ■ **Fax:* Hum Res ■ *TF:* 800-632-2301 ■ *Web:* www.franklintempleton.com	San Mateo	CA	94403	650-312-2000	525-7141*
Fredericks Michael & Co 430 Park Ave *Web:* www.fm-co.com	New York	NY	10022	212-732-1600	
Front Street Capital 33 Yonge St Ste 600 *TF:* 800-513-2832 ■ *Web:* www.frontstreetcapital.com	Toronto	ON	M5E1G4	416-364-1990	
Frontier Asset Management LLC 201 N Connor St Ste 250 *Web:* www.frontierasset.com	Sheridan	WY	82801	307-673-5675	
Frontier Investment Management Co 8401 N Central Expy Ste 300 *TF:* 800-553-8034 ■ *Web:* www.frontierinvest.com	Dallas	TX	75225	972-934-2590	
Fundquest 1 Winthrop Sq *Web:* www.fundquestadvisor.com	Boston	MA	02110	617-526-0766	
Gannett Welsh & Kotler LLC 222 Berkeley St 15th Fl *TF:* 800-225-4236 ■ *Web:* www.gwkinvest.com	Boston	MA	02116	617-236-8900	236-1815
Garcia Hamilton & Associates LP 5 Houston Ctr 1401 McKinney Ste 1600 *Web:* www.dhja.com	Houston	TX	77010	713-853-2322	
GARP Research & Securities Co 406 Main St Reisterstown *Web:* www.garpresearch.com	Baltimore	MD	21136	410-764-1300	
Garrison Investment Group LP 1290 Ave of the Americas Ste 914 *Web:* www.garrisoninv.com	New York	NY	10104	212-372-9500	
Gates Capital Management Inc 1177 Ave of the Americas between 45th and 46th Sts 46th Fl *Web:* www.gatescap.com	New York	NY	10036	212-626-1421	
GDBA Investments LLLP 1440 Blake St Ste 310	Denver	CO	80202	720-932-9395	932-9397
Gemini Fund Services LLC 450 Wireless Blvd *Web:* www.geminifund.com	Hauppauge	NY	11788	631-470-2600	
Genus Capital Management Inc 900 W Hastings St 6th Fl *Web:* www.genuscap.com	Vancouver	BC	V6C1E5	604-683-4554	
Georgian Partners 2 St Clair Ave W Ste 1400 *Web:* www.georgianpartners.com	Toronto	ON	M4V1L5	416-868-9696	
Global Cash Card 7 Corporate Park Ste 130 *TF:* 888-220-4477 ■ *Web:* www.globalcashcard.com	Irvine	CA	92606	949-751-0360	
Global Credit Advisers LLC 101 Park Ave 26th Fl *Web:* www.globalcreditadvisers.com	New York	NY	10178	212-949-1860	
Goelzer Investment Management Inc 111 Monument Cir Ste 500 *Web:* www.goelzerinc.com	Indianapolis	IN	46204	317-264-2600	
Goldcrest Investments 2525 McKinnon St Ste 550	Dallas	TX	75201	214-303-1112	
Golden Capital Management LLC 10715 David Taylor Dr Ste 400 *Web:* www.gcm1.com	Charlotte	NC	28262	704-593-1144	
Goldman Sachs Asset Management (GSAM) 200 W St *TF:* 800-526-7384 ■ *Web:* www.goldmansachs.com	New York	NY	10282	212-902-1000	
Gollob Morgan Peddy & Company CPA 1001 Ese Loop 323 Ste 300 *Web:* www.gmpcpa.com	Tyler	TX	75701	903-534-0088	
Goode Investment Management Inc 23220 Shaker Blvd Ste 1700	Shaker Heights	OH	44122	216-771-9000	771-1949
Gould Asset Management LLC 341 W First St Ste 200 *Web:* www.gouldasset.com	Claremont	CA	91711	909-445-1291	
Gramercy Advisors LLC 20 Dayton Ave *Web:* www.gramercyadvisors.com	Greenwich	CT	06830	203-552-1900	
Granahan Investment Management Inc 404 Wyman St Ste 460 *Web:* www.granahan.com	Waltham	MA	02451	781-890-4412	
Granite Point Capital 222 Berkeley St *Web:* www.granitepoint.com	Boston	MA	02116	617-587-7500	
Grantham Mayo Van Otterloo & Company LLC (GMO) 40 Rowes Wharf *Web:* www.gmo.com	Boston	MA	02110	617-330-7500	261-0134
Grassi Investment Management LLC 2350 Mission College Blvd Ste 190 *Web:* www.grassiinvest.com	Santa Clara	CA	95054	650-934-0770	
Gratry & Company LLC 3201 Enterprise Pkwy Ste 495 *Web:* www.gratry.com	Beachwood	OH	44122	216-283-8423	
Graybill Bartz & Thompson 135 S. Cottage Hill *Web:* www.graybillbartz.com	Elmhurst	IL	60126	630-941-9460	832-3491
Great Point Investors LLC 2 Center Plz Ste 410 *Web:* www.gpinvestors.com	Boston	MA	02108	617-526-8800	
Greenhill & Company Inc 300 Pk Ave 23rd Fl *NYSE:* GHL ■ *Web:* www.greenhill.com	New York	NY	10022	212-389-1500	389-1700
Greycroft Partners LLC 292 Madison Ave 41st St *Web:* greycroft.com	New York	NY	10017	212-756-3508	
Greystone Managed Investments Inc 300 Park Centre 1230 Blackfoot Dr *TF:* 800-213-4286 ■ *Web:* www.greystone.ca	Regina	SK	S4S7G4	306-779-6400	
H A M Media Group 1058 N. TAMIAMI Tl Ste 108-302 *Web:* www.hammedia.com	Sarasota	FL	34236	917-407-6014	
Hagerty Peterson & Company LLC 421 N Northwest Hwy Ste 201 *Web:* www.hagertypeterson.com	Barrington	IL	60010	847-277-9900	
Hahn Capital Management LLC 601 Montgomery St Ste 840 *Web:* www.hahncap.com	San Francisco	CA	94111	415-394-6512	
Haidar Capital Management LLC Carnegie Hall Tower 152 W 57th St *Web:* www.haidarcapital.com	New York	NY	10019	212-752-5077	
Hall Capital Partners LLC 1 Maritime Plz 5th Fl *Web:* www.hallcapital.com	San Francisco	CA	94111	415-288-0544	
Halpern Capital Inc 20900 NE 30th Ave Ste 200 *Web:* www.halperncapital.com	Aventura	FL	33180	786-528-1400	
Hamilton Advisors Inc 373 Stanwich Rd *Web:* www.hamiltonadvisors.com	Greenwich	CT	06830	203-629-1112	629-1469

				Phone	Fax
Hamilton Capital Management 5025 Arlington Centre Blvd	Columbus	OH	43220	614-273-1000	
TF: 888-833-5951 ■ *Web:* www.hamiltoncapital.com					
Hanseatic Management Services Inc 5600 Wyoming N E Ste 220	Albuquerque	NM	87109	505-828-2824	
Web: www.hanseaticgroup.com					
Harbour Investments Inc 575 D'Onofrio Dr Ste 300	Madison	WI	53719	608-662-6100	
Web: www.harbourinv.com					
Harrington Investments Inc 1001 Second St Ste 325	Napa	CA	94559	707-252-6166	
Web: harringtoninvestments.com					
Harris Assoc LP 111 South Wacker Dr Ste 4600	Chicago	IL	60606	312-646-3600	
TF: 800-731-0700 ■ *Web:* www.harrisassoc.com					
Hartford Investment Management Co 1 Hartford Plz	Hartford	CT	06155	860-297-6700	
Web: www.himco.com					
Haywood Securities Inc Waterfront Centre 200 Burrard St Ste 700	Vancouver	BC	V6C3L6	604-697-7100	
TF: 800-663-9499 ■ *Web:* www.haywood.com					
HD Vest Financial Services 6333 N State Hwy 161 4th Fl	Irving	TX	75038	972-870-6000	870-6128
TF: 866-218-8206 ■ *Web:* hdvest.com					
HealthEdge Investment Partners 5550 W Executive Dr Ste 230	Tampa	FL	33609	813-490-7100	
Web: www.healthedgepartners.com					
Hedgeye Risk Management LLC 1 High Ridge Park	Stamford	CT	06905	203-562-6500	
Web: www2.hedgeye.com					
Height Analytics LLC 1775 Pennsylvania Ave NW 5th Fl	Washington	DC	20006	202-629-0000	
Web: www.heightllc.com					
Henderson Global Investors 1735 Market St Fl 30	Philadelphia	PA	19103	860-723-8600	
Web: www.henderson.com					
Hengehold Capital Management LLC 6116 Harrison Ave	Cincinnati	OH	45247	513-598-5120	
TF: 877-598-5120 ■ *Web:* www.hengeholdcapital.com					
Hennessee Group LLC 500 Fifth Ave 47th Fl	New York	NY	10110	212-857-4400	
Web: www.hennesseegroup.com					
Herndon Plant Oakley Ltd 800 N Shoreline Blvd Ste 2200 South	Corpus Christi	TX	78401	361-888-7611	888-9342
TF: 800-888-4894 ■ *Web:* www.hpo.com					
Hershey Trust Co 100 Mansion Rd E	Hershey	PA	17033	717-520-1100	
Web: www.hersheytrust.com					
HFI Wealth Management Inc 620 Newport Center Dr Ste 500	Newport Beach	CA	92660	304-876-2619	
Web: www.unitedcp.com/wv1					
HFS Consultants 505 Fourteenth St 5th Fl	Oakland	CA	94612	510-768-0066	
Web: www.hfsconsultants.com					
HGK Asset Management Inc 525 Washington Blvd Newport Tower Ste 2000	Jersey City	NJ	07310	201-659-3700	
Web: www.hgk.com					
Hid Inc 119 Starwood Cir Lot 16	Jacksonville	NC	28540	910-455-6664	
Hillsdale Investment Management Inc 100 Wellington St W Ste 2100 TD Centre	Toronto	ON	M5K1J3	416-913-3900	913-3901
Web: www.hillsdaleinv.com					
Hillview Capital Advisors LLC 777 THIRD AVE 28th Fl	New York	PA	10017	484-708-4720	
Web: www.hillviewcap.com					
HLB Cinnamon Jang Willoughby Metro Tower II Ste 900-4720 Kingsway	Burnaby	BC	V5H4N2	604-435-4317	
Web: www.cjw.com					
Holland Capital Management LP 303 W Madison St Ste 700	Chicago	IL	60606	312-553-4830	553-4848
TF: 800-295-9779 ■ *Web:* www.hollandcap.com					
Horizon Wealth Management 8280 Ymca Plaza Dr Bldg 5	Baton Rouge	LA	70810	225-612-3820	
Web: www.horizonfg.com					
Houston Trust Co 1001 Fannin St Ste 700	Houston	TX	77002	713-651-9400	
Web: www.houstontrust.com					
Howland Capital Management Inc 75 Federal St Ste 1100	Boston	MA	02110	617-357-9110	357-5540
Web: www.howlandcapital.com					
HPA Development Group Inc 7800 Cooper Rd Ste 204	Cincinnati	OH	45242	513-793-2400	
Web: www.hpadg.com					
HSBC Bank USA 452 Fifth Ave	New York	NY	10018	800-975-4722	
TF: 800-975-4722 ■ *Web:* www.banking.us.hsbc.com					
Hughes Capital Management Inc 916 Prince St 3rd Fl	Alexandria	VA	22314	703-684-7222	684-7799
Hyperion Capital Management Inc 200 Vessey St 3 World Financial Ctr	New York	NY	10281	212-549-8400	
TF: 800-497-3746 ■ *Web:* brookfieldim.com					
ICC Capital Management Inc 390 N Orange Ave Ste 2100	Orlando	FL	32801	407-839-8440	
Web: www.icccapital.com					
ICM Asset Management Inc 601 W Main Ave	Spokane	WA	99201	509-455-3588	
TF: 800-488-4075 ■ *Web:* www.icmasset.com					
ICON Advisers Inc 5299 DTC Blvd Ste 1200	Greenwood Village	CO	80111	303-790-1600	
TF: 800-828-4881 ■ *Web:* www.iconadvisers.com					
IGM Financial Inc 447 Portage Ave 1 Canada Ctr	Winnipeg	MB	R3B3H5	888-746-6344	956-7688*
NYSE: IGM ■ **Fax Area Code:* 204 ■ *TF:* 888-746-6344 ■ *Web:* www.investorsgroup.com					
Imperial Capital LLC 2000 Ave of the Stars S Tower 9th Fl	Los Angeles	CA	90067	310-246-3700	
Web: www.imperialcapital.com					
Incentives Advisors LLC 1001 W Southern Ave Ste 135	Mesa	AZ	85210	480-302-6370	
Web: www.incentiveadvisors.com					
Income Research & Management 100 Federal St 30th Fl	Boston	MA	02110	617-330-9333	
Web: www.incomeresearch.com					
Indaba Capital Management LP 1 Letterman Dr Bldg D Ste DM700 The Presidio of San Francisco	San Francisco	CA	94129	415-680-1180	
Web: www.indabacapital.com					
Independent Capital Management 4141 Inland Empire Blvd Ste 301	Ontario	CA	91764	909-948-1608	
Web: www.icmfinancial.com					
Infinity Capital Partners LLC 1355 Peachtree St N E Ste 750	Atlanta	GA	30309	404-458-4448	
Web: www.infinityfunds.com					
Innovest Portfolio Solutions LLC 4643 S Ulster St Ste 1040	Denver	CO	80237	303-694-1900	
Web: www.innovestinc.com					
Institutional Shareholder Services Inc 2099 Gaither Rd Ste 501	Rockville	MD	20850	301-556-0500	
Web: www.issgovernance.com					
Integra Capital Ltd 2020 Winston Park Dr Ste 200	Oakville	ON	L6H6X7	905-829-1131	
TF: 800-363-2480 ■ *Web:* www.integra.com					
Integral Group LLC, The 191 Peachtree St NE Ste 4100	Atlanta	GA	30303	404-224-1860	224-1899
Web: www.integral-online.com					
Integrated Wealth Counsel LLC 5375 Kietzke Ln Ste 210	Reno	NV	89511	831-624-3317	
Web: www.integratedwealth.com					
Intelligent Capital Inc Market at Third St The Hearst Bldg Ste 810	San Francisco	CA	94103	415-974-1000	
Web: www.intelligentcapital.com					
Interlaken Capital Inc 475 Steamboat Rd 2nd Fl	Greenwich	CT	06830	203-629-8750	
Web: www.interlakencapital.com					
International Risk Management Institute Inc 12222 Merit Dr Ste 1600	Dallas	TX	75251	972-960-7693	
Web: www.cvrdallas.com					
InvestAmerica Investment Advisors Inc 101 Second St SE Ste 800	Cedar Rapids	IA	52401	319-363-8249	363-9683
Web: www.investamericaventure.com					
Investcorp International Inc 280 Park Ave Fl 37	New York	NY	10017	212-599-4700	
Web: www.investcorp.com					
Investment Counselors of Maryland LLC 803 Cathedral St	Baltimore	MD	21201	410-539-3838	625-9016
Web: www.icomd.com					
Investment Performance Services LLC 7402 Hodgson Memorial Dr Ste 100	Savannah	GA	31406	912-352-2862	
Web: www.ips-net.com					
Investment Scorecard Inc 601 Grassmere Park Dr Ste 1	Nashville	TN	37211	615-301-1975	
TF: 800-555-6035 ■ *Web:* informais.com					
Investor Growth Capital Inc 1 Rockefeller Plaza Ste 2416	New York	NY	10020	212-515-9000	515-9009
Web: www.investorab.com					
IOS Partners 311 Mendoza Ave	Coral Gables	FL	33134	305-648-2877	
Web: www.iospartners.com					
Ironbound Capital Management LP 902 Carnegie Ctr Ste 300	Princeton	NJ	08540	609-951-5000	
Web: www.ironboundcapital.com					
ISC Group Inc 3500 Oak Lawn Ave Ste 400	Dallas	TX	75219	214-520-1115	
Web: www.iscgroup.com					
Ivory Investment Management LP 11755 Wilshire Blvd Ste 1350	Los Angeles	CA	90025	310-899-7300	
Web: ivorycapital.co					
Jacob Securities Inc 199 Bay St Commerce Court W PO Box 322 Ste 2901	Toronto	ON	M5L1G1	416-866-8300	
Web: www.jacobsecurities.com					
Jacobus Wealth Management Inc 2323 N Mayfair Rd	Milwaukee	WI	53226	414-475-6565	
Web: www.jwmfamilyoffices.com					
Jacuzzi Brands Inc 13925 City Ctr Dr Ste 200	Chino Hills	CA	91709	909-606-1416	
Web: www.jacuzzi.com					
James Investment Research Inc 1349 Fairgrounds Rd	Xenia	OH	45385	937-426-7640	
Web: www.jamesfunds.com					
Janus Capital Management LLC 151 Detroit St	Denver	CO	80206	303-333-3863	
Web: www.janus.com					
Jatheon Technologies Inc British Colonial Bldg 8 Wellington St E Mezzanine Level	Toronto	ON	M5E1C5	416-840-0418	849-9971
TF: 888-528-4366 ■ *Web:* www.jatheon.com					
Jeffrey Matthews Financial Group LLC, The 30B Vreeland Rd Ste 210	Florham Park	NJ	07932	973-805-6222	
TF: 888-467-3636 ■ *Web:* www.jeffreymatthews.com					
Jetstream Capital LLC 12 Cadillac Dr Ste 280	Brentwood	TN	37027	615-425-3400	425-3401
Web: www.jetstreamcapital.com					
JFS Wealth Advisors LLC 1479 N Hermitage Rd	Hermitage	PA	16148	724-962-3200	
Web: www.jfswa.com					
JMG Financial Group Ltd 2301 W 22nd St Ste 300	Oak Brook	IL	60523	630-571-5252	
Web: jmgfinancial.com					
JNBA Financial Advisors Inc 8500 Normandale Lk Blvd Ste 450	Minneapolis	MN	55437	952-844-0995	
Web: jnba.com					
JNK Securities Corp 902 Broadway 20th Fl	New York	NY	10010	212-885-6300	
Web: www.jnksecurities.com					
John Hsu Capital Group Inc 747 Third Ave 26th Fl	New York	NY	10017	212-223-7515	
Web: www.johnhsucapital.com					
John W Bristol & Company Inc 48 Wall St 18th Fl	New York	NY	10005	212-389-5880	
Web: www.jwbristol.com					

Phone | Fax

Johnson Investment Counsel Inc
3777 W Fork Rd ... Cincinnati OH 45247 513-661-3100
TF: 800-541-0170 ■ *Web:* www.johnsoninv.com

Johnston Asset Management Corp
1 Landmark Sq 20th Fl ... Stamford CT 06901 203-324-4722
Web: www.johnstonasset.com

Jones & Roth PC 432 W 11th Ave ... Eugene OR 97401 541-687-2320 485-0960
Web: www.jrcpa.com

JPMorgan Fleming Asset Management PO Box 8528 ... Boston MA 02266 800-480-4111 471-3053*
**Fax Area Code:* 816 ■ *TF:* 800-480-4111 ■
Web: am.jpmorgan.com/us/en/asset-management/gim/adv/home

Jra Financial Advisors
7373 Kirkwood Ct Ste 300 ... Maple Grove MN 55369 763-315-8000
TF: 800-278-5988 ■ *Web:* www.jrafinancial.com

Kalmar Investments Inc
Barley Mill House 3701 Kennett Pk ... Wilmington DE 19807 302-658-7575
Web: www.kalmarinvestments.com

Karr Barth Assoc Inc 40 Monument Rd ... Bala Cynwyd PA 19004 610-660-4459
Web: karr-barthassociates.com

KARVY Global Services (US)
11 Broadway Ste 1568 ... New York NY 10004 212-267-4381
Web: www.karvyglobal.com

Kaspick & Co
203 Redwood Shores Pkwy Ste 300 ... Redwood Shores CA 94065 650-585-4100
Web: www.kaspick.com

Kayne Anderson Capital Advisors LP
1800 Ave of the Stars 3rd Fl ... Los Angeles CA 90067 800-638-1496
TF: 800-638-1496 ■ *Web:* www.kaynecapital.com

KCD Financial Inc 3313 S Packerland Dr Ste E ... De Pere WI 54115 920-347-3400
Web: www.kcdfinancial.com

KCM Investment Advisors LLC
750 Lindaro St Ste 250 ... San Rafael CA 94901 415-461-7788
TF: 888-287-5555 ■ *Web:* www.kcmadvisors.com

KDI Capital Partners LLC
4101 Lk Boone Trl Ste 218 ... Raleigh NC 27607 919-573-4124
Web: www.kdicapitalpartners.com

Keane Capital Management Inc
3440 Toringdon Way Ste 308 ... Charlotte NC 28277 704-364-3250

Keats, Connelly & Associates LLC
3336 N 32nd St Ste 100 ... Phoenix AZ 85018 602-955-5007
Web: www.keatsconnelly.com

Kensico Capital Management Corp
55 RailRoad Ave 2nd Fl ... Greenwich CT 06830 203-862-5800
Web: www.kensicocapital.com

Kerlin Capital Group LLC
555 S Flower St Ste 2750 ... Los Angeles CA 90071 213-627-3300
Web: www.kerlincapital.com

Keystone Capital Corp
3511 Camino Del Rio S Ste 406 ... San Diego CA 92108 619-283-3107
Web: www.keystonecapcorp.com

Keystone Capital Inc 155 N Wacker Dr Ste 4150 ... Chicago IL 60606 312-219-7900
Web: www.keystonecapital.com

Killen Group Inc 1189 Lancaster Ave ... Berwyn PA 19312 610-296-7222
TF: 877-454-5536 ■ *Web:* www.thekillengroup.com

Kirr Marbach & Co Investment Management
621 Washington St ... Columbus IN 47201 812-376-9444
TF: 800-808-9444 ■ *Web:* www.kirrmar.com

Knightsbridge Asset Management LLC
660 Newport Ctr Dr Ste 460 ... Newport Beach CA 92660 949-644-4444
Web: www.knightsb.com

Koler Wealth Management 6400 Pearl Rd ... Parma OH 44130 440-884-7042
Web: www.kolerfinancialgroup.com

Koonce Securities Inc
6550 Rock Spring Dr Ste 600 ... Bethesda MD 20817 301-897-9700
Web: www.koonce.net

Kootenay Savings Financial
300 - 1199 Cedar Ave ... Trail BC V1R4B8 250-368-2686
Web: www.kscu.com

Kornitzer Capital Management Inc
5420 W 61st Pl ... Shawnee Mission KS 66205 913-677-7778
Web: www.kornitzercapitalmanagement.com

Koshinski Asset Management Inc
226 W Eldorado St ... Decatur IL 62522 217-425-6340
Web: www.investment-planners.com

Kubera Partners LLC
1475 Franklin Ave Garden City ... New York NY 11530 212-202-7657
Web: www.kuberapartners.com

Kuhns Brothers 558 Lime Rock Rd ... Lakeville CT 06039 860-435-7000
Web: www.kuhnsbrothers.com

L. Roy Papp & Associates LLP
2201 E Camelback Rd Ste 227B ... Phoenix AZ 85016 602-956-0980
Web: www.roypapp.com

Laird Norton Tyee 801 Second Ave Ste 1600 ... Seattle WA 98104 206-464-5100
TF: 800-426-5105 ■ *Web:* lairdnortonwm.com

Lakeside Capital Management LLC
50 S Sixth St Ste 1460 ... Minneapolis MN 55402 612-243-4400
Web: www.gmbmezz.com

Lampo Group Inc, The 1749 Mallory Ln ... Brentwood TN 37027 615-371-8881
Web: www.daveramsey.com

Lancaster Pollard Investment Advisory Group
65 E State St Ste 1600 ... Columbus OH 43215 614-224-8800
Web: www.lancasterpollard.com

Landaas & Co 411 E Wisconsin Ave 20th Fl ... Milwaukee WI 53202 414-223-1099
TF: 800-236-1096 ■ *Web:* www.landaas.com

Lau Associates LLC
20 Montchanin Rd Ste 110 ... Greenville DE 19807 302-792-5955
Web: www.lauassociates.net

Laurentian Bank Securities Inc
1981 McGill College Ave Ste 100 ... Montreal QC H3A3K3 514-350-2800
TF: 888-350-8577 ■ *Web:* www.vmbl.ca

Lawson Kroeker Investment Management Inc
450 Regency Pkwy Ste 410 ... Omaha NE 68114 402-392-2606
Web: www.lawsonkroeker.com

Lazenby & Associates Inc
2000 N Seventh St ... WestMonroe LA 71291 702-304-9270
Web: www.lazenbyassociates.com

LCG Assoc Inc 400 Galleria Pkwy SE ... Atlanta GA 30339 770-644-0100 644-0105
Web: www.lcgassociates.com

Leconte Wealth Management LLC
703 William Blount Dr ... Maryville TN 37801 865-379-8200
TF: 888-236-6630 ■ *Web:* lecontewealth.com

Leerink Swann & Co 1 Federal St 37th Fl ... Boston MA 02110 800-808-7525
TF: 800-808-7525 ■ *Web:* www.leerink.com

Legend Financial Advisors Inc
5700 Corporate Dr Ste 350 ... Pittsburgh PA 15237 412-635-9210
Web: www.legend-financial.com

Lenox Advisors Inc 530 Fifth Ave ... New York NY 10036 212-536-8700
Web: www.lenoxadvisors.com

Lenox Wealth Management Inc
8044 Montgomery Rd Ste 170 ... Cincinnati OH 45236 513-618-7080
Web: www.lenoxwealth.com

Lexington Wealth Management 12 Waltham St ... Lexington MA 02421 781-860-7745
TF: 800-626-1566 ■ *Web:* www.lexingtonwealth.com

Libbie Agran Financial Services & Seminars
2120 Colorado Ave Ste 100 ... Santa Monica CA 90404 310-586-1828
Web: www.lafs.net

Liberty Lane Service Company LLC Liberty Ln ... Hampton NH 03842 603-929-2600
Web: www.latonaassociates.com

LifeTech Capital 4431 Woodfield Blvd ... Boca Raton FL 33432 561-988-9129
Web: www.lifetechcapital.com

Lighthouse Investment Partners LLC
3801 PGA Blvd Ste 500 ... Palm Beach Gardens FL 33410 561-741-0820
Web: www.lighthousepartners.com

Lineage Capital LLC 399 Boylston St Ste 450 ... Boston MA 02116 617-778-0660
Web: www.lineagecap.com

Linscomb & Williams Inc
1400 Post Oak Blvd Ste 1000 ... Houston TX 77056 713-840-1000
TF: 800-960-1200 ■ *Web:* www.linscomb-williams.com

Litman Gregory Asset Management LLC
100 Larkspur Landing Cir Ste 204 ... Larkspur CA 94939 415-461-8999
Web: www.lginvestment.com

Litman Gregory Research Inc
100 Larkspur Landing Cir Ste 204 ... Larkspur CA 94939 925-254-8999
Web: litmangregory.com

LivePlanet Inc 2644 30th St ... Santa Monica CA 90405 310-664-2400
Web: www.liveplanet.com

Llenroc Capital LLC
781 Lincoln Ave Ste 340 ... San Rafael CA 94901 415-785-3670
Web: www.llenroccap.com

LM Capital Group LLC 750 B St Ste 3010 ... San Diego CA 92101 619-814-1401
Web: www.lmcapital.com

Loeb Enterprises LLC 712 Fifth Ave 14th Fl ... New York NY 10019 646-442-5807
Web: www.loebenterprises.com

Logan Capital Management Inc
6 Coulter Ave Ste 2000 ... Ardmore PA 19003 800-215-1100
TF: 800-215-1100 ■ *Web:* www.logancapital.com

Logan Circle Partners LP
1717 Arch St Ste 1500 ... Philadelphia PA 19103 267-330-0000
Web: www.logancirclepartners.com

Lone Star Funds 2711 N Haskell Ave Ste 1700 ... Dallas TX 75204 214-754-8300
Web: www.lonestarfunds.com

Longview Wealth Management LLC
15268 Boulder Pointe Rd ... Eden Prairie MN 55347 952-906-1289
Web: www.longviewwealth.com

Loomis Sayles & Company Inc LP
PO Box 219594 ... Kansas City MO 64121 800-633-3330
TF: 800-343-2029 ■ *Web:* www.loomissayles.com

Lord & Benoit LLC 1 W Boylston St ... Worcester MA 01605 508-853-6404

Lord Abbett & Co 90 Hudson St ... Jersey City NJ 07302 201-827-2000
TF: 888-522-2388 ■ *Web:* www.lordabbett.com

Mackenzie Financial Corp 180 Queen St W ... Toronto ON M5V3K1 416-922-5322 922-5660
TF: 888-653-7070 ■ *Web:* www.mackenzieinvestments.com

Mackie Research Capital Corp
199 Bay St Commerce Court W Ste 4500 ... Toronto ON M5L1G2 416-860-7600
Web: www.mackieresearch.com

Mackinac Partners LLC
74 W Long Lake Rd Ste 205 ... Bloomfield Hills MI 48304 248-258-6900
Web: www.mackinacpartners.com

Madison Investment Advisors Inc
550 Science Dr ... Madison WI 53711 608-274-0300
TF: 800-767-0300 ■ *Web:* www.madisonadv.com

Magee Thomson Investment Partners LLC
12531 High Bluff Dr Ste 120 ... San Diego CA 92130 858-350-5050
Web: www.mageethomson.com

Magnitude Capital LLC
601 Lexington Ave 56th Fl ... New York NY 10022 212-915-3900
Web: www.magnitudecapital.com

Main Street Advisors LLC 205 E Main St ... Westminster MD 21157 410-840-9200
Web: www.mainstadvisors.com

Mallory Capital Group LLC
19 Old King'S Hwy S Ste 14 ... Darien CT 06820 203-655-1571
Web: www.mallorycapital.com

Manarin Investment Counsel Ltd 505 N 210th St ... Omaha NE 68022 402-330-1166
TF: 800-397-1167 ■ *Web:* www.manarin.com

Manchester Financial Inc
2815 Townsgate Rd Ste 100 ... Westlake Village CA 91361 805-495-4405
TF: 800-492-1107 ■ *Web:* www.mfinvest.com

Mann Armistead & Epperson Ltd
119 Shockoe Slip ... Richmond VA 23219 804-644-1200
Web: www.maeltd.com

Manning & Napier Advisors Inc
290 Woodcliff Dr ... Fairport NY 14450 585-325-6880
Web: www.manning-napier.com

Maplewood Investment Advisors Inc
8750 N Central Expy Ste 715 ... Dallas TX 75231 214-739-5677
Web: www.maplewoodinvestments.com

Phone | Fax

Marco Consulting Group Inc
550 W Washington Blvd Ste 900 . . . Chicago IL 60661 312-575-9000
Web: www.marcoconsulting.com

Mark Asset Management Corp
667 Madison Ave 9th Fl . . . New York NY 10065 212-372-2500
Web: markasset.com

Market Street Partners LLC
477 Pacific Ave . . . San Francisco CA 94133 415-445-3240
Web: www.marketstreetpartners.com

Marketocracy Inc 1208 W Magnolia Ste 236 . . . Fort Worth TX 76104 877-462-4180 777-6181*
**Fax Area Code:* 888 ■ *TF:* 877-462-4180 ■ *Web:* www.marketocracy.com

Marque Millennium Capital Management LLC
850 Third Ave 13th Fl . . . New York NY 10022 212-759-6801
Web: www.marqmil.com

Marquette Asset Management
60 S Sixth St Ste 3900 . . . Minneapolis MN 55402 612-661-3770
TF: 866-661-3770 ■ *Web:* www.marquetteam.com

Marshall & Sullivan Inc
1109 First Ave Ste 200 . . . Seattle WA 98101 206-621-9014
TF: 800-735-7290 ■ *Web:* www.msinvest.com

Martin Capital Management LLP
300 NIBCO Pkwy Ste 301 . . . Elkhart IN 46516 574-293-2077
Web: www.mcmadvisors.com

Marvin & Palmer Assoc Inc
200 Bellevue Pky Ste 220 . . . Wilmington DE 19809 302-573-3570
Web: www.marvinandpalmer.com

Maryanov Madsen Gordon & Campbell CPA
801 E Tahquitz Canyon Way Ste 200
PO Box 1826 . . . Palm Springs CA 92262 760-320-6642 327-6854
Web: www.mmgccpa.com

MatlinPatterson Global Advisers LLC
520 Madison Ave 35 FL . . . New York NY 10022 212-651-9500
Web: www.matlinpatterson.com

Matrix Capital Advisors LLC
200 S Wacker Dr Ste 680 . . . Chicago IL 60606 312-612-6100
Web: matrixcapital.com

Matterhorn Capital Management LLC
3512 Paesanos Pkwy Ste 301 . . . San Antonio TX 78231 210-694-4329
Web: www.matterhorncap.com

Maxim Group LLC 405 Lexington Ave . . . New York NY 10174 212-895-3500
Web: www.maximgrp.com

Mazama Capital Management Inc
1 S W Columbia St Ste 1500 . . . Portland OR 97258 503-221-8725
Web: www.mazamacap.com

McCullough & Associates LLC
101 California St Ste 3260 . . . San Francisco CA 94111 415-956-8700
Web: www.macinv.com

McCutchen Group LLC 925 Fourth Ave Ste 2288 . . . Seattle WA 98104 206-816-6850
Web: www.mccutchengroup.com

McDonnell Investment Management LLC
18W140 Butterfield Rd Ste 1200 . . . Oak Brook IL 60181 630-684-8600
Web: www.mcdmgmt.com

McGlinn Capital Management
850 N Wyomissing Blvd . . . Wyomissing PA 19610 610-374-5125
Web: www.mcglinncap.com

McKinley Capital Management LLC
3301 C St Ste 500 . . . Anchorage AK 99503 907-563-4488
Web: www.mckinleycapital.com

McMorgan & Co LLC 1 Front St Ste 500 . . . San Francisco CA 94111 415-788-9300
Web: www.nylinvestments.com

MCS Financial Advisors 360 E Tenth Ave Ste 200 . . . Eugene OR 97401 541-345-7023
Web: www.mcsfa.com

MD Sass Investor Services Inc
1185 Ave of the Americas 18th Fl . . . New York NY 10036 212-730-2000 764-0381
Web: www.mdsass.com

Megastar Financial Corp 1080 Cherokee St . . . Denver CO 80204 303-321-8800
Web: www.libertyhomefinancial.com

Mellon Capital Management Corp
50 Fremont St Ste 3900 . . . San Francisco CA 94105 415-546-6056 777-5699
Web: www.mcm.com

Mercadien Group
3625 Quakerbridge Rd Ste D . . . Hamilton Township NJ 08619 609-689-9700 838-3331
Web: www.mercadien.com

Mercer Global Advisors Inc
1801 E Cabrillo Blvd . . . Santa Barbara CA 93108 800-898-4642
TF: 800-258-1559 ■ *Web:* www.merceradvisors.com

Mercury Investment Management LLC
88 Union Ctr Ste 1150 . . . Memphis TN 38103 901-521-4200
Web: www.mercuryprop.com

Merit Financial 2201 Bdwy . . . North Bend OR 97459 973-331-5600

Meritage Portfolio Management Inc
7500 College Blvd Ste 1212 . . . Overland Park KS 66210 913-345-7000
Web: www.meritageportfolio.com

Merritt Capital Management Inc
30 Western Ave Ste 101 . . . Gloucester MA 01930 978-282-0035
Web: www.merrittcapitalmanagement.com

Metropolitan West Asset Management LLC
865 S Figueroa St . . . Los Angeles CA 90017 213-244-0000
Web: www.mwamllc.com

MFS Investment Management 500 Boylston St . . . Boston MA 02116 617-954-5000 954-6621
TF: 877-960-6077 ■ *Web:* www.mfs.com

MFX Solutions Inc 1050 17th St NW Ste 550 . . . Washington DC 20036 202-527-9947
Web: www.mfxsolutions.com

MidMark Capital 177 Madison Ave . . . Morristown NJ 07960 973-971-9960 971-9963
Web: www.midmarkcapital.com

Milestone Investments Inc
315 Manitoba Ave Ste 310 . . . Wayzata MN 55391 952-476-8516
Web: www.milestoneusa.com

Millbrook Capital Management Inc
570 Lexington Ave 46th Fl . . . New York NY 10022 212-586-4333
Web: www.millcap.com

Miller-Green Financial Group
1330 Lk Robbins Dr Ste 360 . . . The Woodlands TX 77380 281-364-9100
Web: www.miller-green.com

Phone | Fax

Mission Markets Inc 394 Broadway 6th Fl . . . New York NY 10013 646-837-6877
Web: www.missionmarkets.com

Mission Wealth Management LLC
1123 Chapala St 3rd Fl . . . Santa Barbara CA 93101 805-882-2360
TF: 888-642-7221 ■ *Web:* www.missionwealthmanagement.com

Mitchell & Titus LLP
1 Battery Pk Plz 27th Fl . . . New York NY 10004 212-709-4500 709-4680
Web: www.mitchelltitus.com

MJ Whitman LLC 622 Third Ave 32nd Fl . . . New York NY 10017 212-888-2290
Web: www.mjwhitman.com

MMA Financial LLC 3600 O'Donnell St Ste 600 . . . Baltimore MD 21224 443-263-2900
Web: www.mmacapitalmanagement.com

MoffettNathanson LLC
1180 Ave Of The Americas . . . New York NY 10036 212-519-0020
Web: www.moffettnathanson.com

Monarch Capital Management Inc
127 W Berry St Ste 402 . . . Fort Wayne IN 46802 260-422-2765
Web: www.monarchcapitalmgmt.com

Monitor Clipper Partners LLC
116 Huntington Ave 9th Fl . . . Boston MA 02116 617-638-1100
Web: www.monitorclipper.com

Moody Aldrich Partners LLC 18 Sewall St . . . Marblehead MA 01945 781-639-2750 639-2751
Web: www.moodyaldrich.com

Moody's Corp
250 Greenwich St 7 World Trade Ctr . . . New York NY 10007 212-553-0300
NYSE: MCO ■ *Web:* www.moodys.com

Mooreland Partners LLC
537 Steamboat Rd Ste 200 . . . Greenwich CT 06830 203-629-4400
Web: www.moorelandpartners.com

Morgan Dempsey Capital Management LLC
309 N Water St . . . Milwaukee WI 53202 414-319-1080
Web: www.morgandempsey.com

Morley Financial Services Inc
1300 SW Fifth Ave Ste 3300 . . . Portland OR 97201 503-484-9300
TF: 800-548-4806 ■ *Web:* www.morley.com

Morningstar Inc 22 W Washington St . . . Chicago IL 60606 312-696-6000 696-6009
NASDAQ: MORN ■ *TF Orders:* 800-735-0700 ■ *Web:* www.corporate.morningstar.com

Morrow & Co LLC 470 W Ave . . . Stamford CT 06902 203-658-9400
TF: 800-662-5200 ■ *Web:* morrowco.com

Morton Capital Management
27200 Agoura Rd Ste 200 . . . Calabasas CA 91301 818-222-4727
Web: www.mortoncapital.com

MPS LORIA Financial Planners LLC
7500 S County Line Rd . . . Burr Ridge IL 60527 630-887-4404
Web: www.mpsloria.com

MRB Partners Inc 2001 Rue University Ste 810 . . . Montreal QC H3A2A6 514-558-1515
Web: www.mrbpartners.com

Murray Devine & Company Inc
1650 Arch St Ste 2700 . . . Philadelphia PA 19103 215-977-8700
Web: www.murraydevine.com

National Financial Partners Corp (NFP)
340 Madison Ave 20th Fl . . . New York NY 10173 212-301-4000 301-4001
NYSE: NFP ■ *Web:* www.nfp.com

Navellier Securities Corp 1 E Liberty St Ste 504 . . . Reno NV 89501 775-785-2300
TF: 800-887-8671 ■ *Web:* www.navellier.com

NCM Capital Management Group Inc
2634 Durham Chapel Hill Blvd Ste 206 . . . Durham NC 27707 919-688-0620 683-1352*
**Fax:* Mktg ■ *Web:* www.ncmcapital.com

Neiman Funds Management LLC
6631 Main St . . . Williamsville NY 14221 877-385-2720
TF: 877-385-2720 ■ *Web:* www.neimanfunds.com

Nelson Roberts Investment Advisors LLC
1950 University Ave Ste 202 . . . East Palo Alto CA 94303 650-322-4000
Web: www.nelsonroberts.com

NEPC LLC 255 State St 8th Fl . . . Boston MA 02109 617-374-1300
Web: www.nepc.com

Neuberger Berman LLC 605 Third Ave . . . New York NY 10158 800-223-6448
TF: 800-223-6448 ■ *Web:* www.nb.com

New Constructs LLC
210 Jamestown Park Ste 201 . . . Brentwood TN 37027 615-377-0443
Web: www.newconstructs.com

New Mexico State Investment Council
41 Plz la Prensa . . . Santa Fe NM 87507 505-476-9500
Web: www.sic.state.nm.us

New York Global Group Inc
The Trump Bldg 40 Wall St 38th Fl . . . New York NY 10005 212-566-0499
Web: www.nyggroup.com

Newport Asia LLC
601 California St Ste 1168 . . . San Francisco CA 94108 415-677-8620
Web: www.newportasiallc.com

Newport Private Capital LLC
610 Newport Ctr Dr Ste 600 . . . Newport Beach CA 92660 949-644-7300
Web: www.privatecapital.com

Newsouth Capital Management Inc
999 S Shady Grove Rd Ste 501 . . . Memphis TN 38120 901-761-5561
Web: www.newsouthcapital.com

NGP Energy Capital Management
5221 N O'Connor Blvd Ste 1100 . . . Irving TX 75039 972-432-1440
Web: www.ngpenergycapital.com

Nogales Investors Management LLC
9229 W Sunset Blvd Ste 900 . . . Los Angeles CA 90069 310-276-7439
Web: www.nogalesinvestors.com

NorthCoast Asset Management LLC
1 Greenwich Office Park . . . Greenwich CT 06831 203-532-7000
TF: 800-274-5448 ■ *Web:* www.northcoastam.com

Northern Trust Company of Connecticut
300 Atlantic St Ste 400 . . . Stamford CT 06901 312-630-0779 356-9341*
**Fax Area Code:* 203 ■ *TF:* 866-876-9944 ■ *Web:* www.ntrs.com

Northland Securities Inc
45 S Seventh St Ste 2000 . . . Minneapolis MN 55402 612-851-5900
Web: www.northlandsecurities.com

Northwestern Mutual Investment Services LLC
611 E Wisconsin Ave Ste 300 . . . Milwaukee WI 53202 866-664-7737
TF: 866-664-7737 ■ *Web:* www.northwesternmutual.com

Phone | Fax

Northwood Family Office LP
130 King St W Ste 2250 Toronto ON M5X1C8 416-502-1245
Web: www.northwoodfamilyoffice.com

Nottingham Management Company Inc, The
116 S Franklin St Rocky Mount NC 27804 252-972-9922
Web: www.equityfund.com

Obermeyer Wood Investment Counsel, LLLP
501 Rio Grande Pl Ste 107 Aspen CO 81611 970-925-8747
Web: www.obermeyerwood.com

Oberon Asset Management LLC
51 Wooster St 4th Fl New York NY 10013 917-237-0147
Web: www.oberonasset.com

Odlum Brown Ltd 250 Howe St Ste 1100 Vancouver BC V6C3S9 604-669-1600 844-5342
TF: 866-636-8222 ■ *Web:* www.odlumbrown.com

Off Wall Street Consulting Group Inc
22 Hilliard St Ste 3 Cambridge MA 02138 617-868-7880
Web: www.riverviewpartners.com

Offit Capital Advisors LLC
485 Lexington Ave 24th Fl New York NY 10017 212-588-3276
Web: www.offitcapital.com

Ohio Municipal Advisory Council
9321 Ravenna Rd Ste K Twinsburg OH 44087 330-963-7444
Web: www.ohiomac.com

Old Hill Partners 1120 Boston Post Rd 2nd Fl Darien CT 06820 203-656-3004
Web: www.oldhill.com

Oppenheimer & Company Inc 300 Madison Ave New York NY 10017 212-885-4646
Web: www.opco.com

Opus Capital Management LLC
221 E. 4th St Ste 2700 Cincinnati OH 45202 513-621-6787
Web: www.opusinc.com

Osborne Partners Capital Management LLC
580 California St Ste 1900 San Francisco CA 94104 415-362-5637
TF: 800-362-7734 ■ *Web:* www.osbornepartners.com

Otter Creek Management Inc
222 Lakeview Ave Ste 1100 West Palm Beach FL 33401 561-832-4110
Web: ottercreekmgt.com

Oxford Financial Group Ltd
11711 N Meridian St Ste 600 Carmel IN 46032 317-843-5678
Web: www.ofgltd.com

Pacer Financial Inc 16 Industrial Blvd. Paoli PA 19301 610-644-8100
Web: www.pacerfinancial.com

Pacific Income Advisers Inc
1299 Ocean Ave Second Fl Ste 210 Santa Monica CA 90401 310-393-1424
Web: www.pacificincome.com

Pacific Investment Management Company LLC
840 Newport Ctr Dr. Newport Beach CA 92660 949-720-6000 720-1376
TF: 800-387-4626 ■ *Web:* www.pimco.com

Pacific Vista Capital LLC
2211 Encinitas Blvd Encinitas CA 92024 760-479-0601
Web: www.pacvista.com

Palisades Hudson Financial Group LLC
2 Overhill Rd Ste 100 Scarsdale NY 10583 914-723-5000
Web: www.palisadeshudson.com

Pan American Finance LLC
601 Brickell Key Dr Ste 604 Miami FL 33131 305-577-9799
Web: www.panamfinance.com

Paradigm Capital Inc
95 Wellington St W Ste 2101 Toronto ON M5J2N7 416-361-9892
Web: www.paradigmcapinc.com

Paradigm Financial Advisors LLC
12231 Manchester Rd. Des Peres MO 63131 314-966-3400
Web: www.pfaclient.com

Parady Financial Group Inc
340 Heald Way Ste 226 The Villages FL 32163 352-751-3016
TF: 855-701-4351 ■ *Web:* www.paradyfinancial.com

Park West Asset Management LLC
900 Larkspur Landing Cir Ste 165 Larkspur CA 94939 415-524-2900

Parsons Capital Management Inc
10 Weybosset St Ste 1000 Providence RI 02903 401-521-2440
TF: 888-521-2440 ■ *Web:* www.parsonscapital.com

Partners Capital Investment Group LLC
50 Rowes Wharf 4th Fl Boston MA 02110 617-292-2570
Web: www.partners-cap.com

Payden & Rygel 333 S Grand Ave. Los Angeles CA 90071 213-625-1900 628-8488
TF: 800-572-9336 ■ *Web:* www.payden.com

Peak Financial Management Inc
281 Winter St Ste 160 Waltham MA 02451 781-487-9500
TF: 877-567-9500 ■ *Web:* www.peak-financial.com

Peninsula Asset Management Inc
1111 Third Ave W Ste 340 Bradenton FL 34205 800-269-6417 748-2654*
**Fax Area Code:* 941 ■ *TF:* 800-269-6417 ■ *Web:* www.peninsulaasset.com

Penobscot Investment Management Company Inc
50 Congress St Ste 410 Boston MA 02109 617-227-3111
Web: www.pimboston.com

Pensionmark Retirement Group
24 E Cota St Santa Barbara CA 93101 805-456-6260
Web: www.pensionmark.com

Pentalpha Capital Group LLC
1 Greenwich Office Park N Bldg Greenwich CT 06831 203-660-6100 629-8907
Web: www.pentalphaglobal.com

Peregrine Capital Partners LLC
732 Pittsford-Victor Rd. Pittsford NY 14534 585-218-5220
Web: www.peregrinecapitalpartners.com

Perkins Capital Management Inc 730 E Lake St Wayzata MN 55391 952-473-8367
Web: www.perkinscap.com

Permal Group, The 900 Third Ave 28th Fl New York NY 10022 212-418-6500
Web: www.permal.com

Perryman Financial Advisory Inc
12221 Merit Dr Ste 1660 Dallas TX 75251 972-770-4800
Web: www.billperryman.com

Personal Capital Corp 726 Main St. Redwood City CA 94063 855-855-8005
TF: 855-855-8005 ■ *Web:* www.personalcapital.com

Peter A Sokoloff & Co
550 N Brand Blvd Ste 1650 Glendale CA 91203 818-547-4500
Web: www.sokoloffco.com

Petra Financial Advisors Inc
2 N Cascade Ave Ste 720 Colorado Springs CO 80903 719-636-9000
Web: www.petrafinancial.com

Piedmont Investment Advisors LLC
300 W Morgan St Ste 1200 Durham NC 27701 919-688-8600
Web: www.piedmontinvestment.com

Pillar Financial Advisors LLC
3046 Breckenridge Ln Ste 104 Louisville KY 40220 502-384-3890
Web: www.pillar.net

Pin Oak Investment Advisors Inc
510 Bering Dr Ste 100 Houston TX 77057 713-871-8300
Web: www.pinoakinc.com

Pittenger & Anderson Inc
5533 S 27th St Ste 201 Lincoln NE 68512 402-328-8800
TF: 800-897-1588 ■ *Web:* www.pittand.com

Placemark Investments Inc 16633 Dallas Pkwy Addison TX 75001 972-404-8100
Web: www.placemark.com

PlanMember Financial Corp
6187 Carpinteria Ave Carpinteria CA 93013 805-684-1199
Web: online.planmember.com

Platinum Advisors LLC 1215 K St Ste 1150 Sacramento CA 95814 916-443-8891
Web: www.platinumadvisors.com

Portfolio Strategy Group Inc, The
81 Main St White Plains NY 10601 914-328-6660
Web: www.portfoliostrategygroup.com

Portland Global Advisors LLC
217 Commercial St Ste 400 Portland ME 04101 207-773-2773
Web: portlandglobal.com

Ppm America Inc 225 W Wacker Dr Ste 1200 Chicago IL 60606 312-634-2500
Web: www.ppmamerica.com

Prairie Capital Management LLC
4900 Main St Ste 700 Kansas City MO 64112 816-531-1101
Web: www.prairiecapital.com

Primary Global Research LLC
1975 W El Camino Real Ste 300 Mountain View CA 94040 888-893-1688
TF: 888-893-1688 ■ *Web:* www.pg-research.com

Prime Buchholz & Assoc Inc
273 Corporate Dr Ste 250 Portsmouth NH 03801 603-433-1143 433-8661
Web: www.primebuchholz.com

PRIMECAP Management Co 225 S Lk Ave Ste 400 Pasadena CA 91101 626-304-9222
Web: www.primecapmanagement.com

Primerica Financial Services
3120 Breckinridge Blvd Duluth GA 30099 770-381-1000
TF: 800-257-4725 ■ *Web:* www.primerica.com

Private Advisors LLC 901 E Byrd St Ste 1400 Richmond VA 23219 804-289-6000
Web: www.privateadvisors.com

Producers Financial
5350 Tomah Dr Ste 3800 Colorado Springs CO 80918 719-535-0739
TF: 800-985-5549 ■ *Web:* www.pfnco.com

Progress Investment Management Co
33 New Montgomery St 19th Fl San Francisco CA 94105 415-512-3480 512-3475
Web: www.progressinvestment.com

Provident Advisors LLC 2800 Niagara Ln N. Plymouth MN 55447 952-345-5200

Prudential Financial Inc 751 Broad St Newark NJ 07102 973-802-6000 367-6476
NYSE: PRU ■ *TF:* 800-843-7625 ■ *Web:* www.prudential.com

Pugh Capital Management Inc
520 Pk St Ste 2900 Seattle WA 98101 206-322-4985 322-3025
Web: www.pughcapital.com

Puplava Securities Inc
10809 Thornmint Rd 2nd Fl San Diego CA 92127 858-487-3939
Web: www.puplava.com

Pure Financial Advisors Inc
3131 Camino del Rio N Ste 1550 San Diego CA 92108 619-814-4100
Web: www.purefinancial.com

Putnam Investments 30 Dan Rd PO Box 8383 Canton MA 02021 617-292-1000
TF: 888-478-8626 ■ *Web:* www.putnam.com

PVG Asset Management Corp
24918 Genesee Trl Rd Golden CO 80401 303-526-0548
TF: 800-777-0818 ■ *Web:* www.pvgassetmanagement.com

Pzena Investment Management Inc
120 W 45th St 20th Fl. New York NY 10036 212-355-1600 308-0010
NYSE: PZN ■ *Web:* www.pzena.com

QCI Asset Management 40A Grove St. Pittsford NY 14534 585-218-2060 218-2013
TF: 800-836-3960 ■ *Web:* www.e-qci.com

Quabbin Capital Inc 160 Federal St Boston MA 02110 617-330-9041
Web: www.quabbincapital.com

Quadravest Capital Management Inc
77 King St W Royal Trust Tower Ste 4500 Toronto ON M5K1K7 416-304-4440
Web: www.quadravest.com

Quaker Funds 1180 W Swedesford Rd Ste 150 Berwyn PA 19312 610-455-2200
Web: www.quakerfunds.com

Quantlab Financial LLC
4200 Montrose Blvd Ste 200 Houston TX 77006 713-333-5440
Web: www.quantlab.com

Quantum Capital Management LLC
105 E Mill Rd Northfield NJ 08225 609-677-4949
Web: www.quantumadv.com

Quazar Capital Corp
3535 Plymouth Blvd Ste 210 Minneapolis MN 55447 763-550-9000
Web: quazarcapital.com

Quest Capital Management Inc
8117 Preston Rd Ste 700 Dallas TX 75225 214-691-6090
Web: www.questadvisor.com

Quest Investment Management Inc
1 S W Columbia St Ste 1100 Portland OR 97258 503-221-0158
Web: www.questinvestment.com

Quest Partners LLC 126 E 56th St 19th Fl New York NY 10022 212-838-7222
Web: www.questpartnersllc.com

R N Croft Financial Group Inc
218 Steeles Ave E Thornhill ON L3T1A6 905-695-7777
TF: 877-249-2884 ■ *Web:* www.croftgroup.com

R. M. Davis Inc 24 City Center Portland ME 04101 207-774-0022
Web: www.rmdavis.com

R.H. Bluestein & Co 260 E Brown St Ste 100 Birmingham MI 48009 248-646-4000

	City	State	Zip	Phone	Fax
Radnor Financial Advisors Inc 485 Devon Park Dr Ste 119 *TF:* 888-271-9922 ■ *Web:* www.radnorfinancial.com	Wayne	PA	19087	610-975-0280	
Raffles Capital Group Inc 1 Burning Tree Rd *Web:* www.rafflescapital.com	Greenwich	CT	06830	203-629-5604	
Rampart Investment Management Company LLC 1 International Pl 14th Fl *Web:* www.rimco.com	Boston	MA	02110	617-342-6900	
Raskob Kambourian Financial Advisors Ltd 4100 N First Ave *Web:* www.rkfin.com	Tucson	AZ	85719	520-690-1999	
Raymond James Ltd 2200-925 W Georgia St Cathedral Pl *TF:* 888-545-6624 ■ *Web:* www.raymondjames.ca	Vancouver	BC	V6C3L2	604-659-8000	
RB Milestone Group 125 Park Ave 25th Fl *Web:* www.rbmilestone.com	New York	NY	10168	212-661-0075	
RBC Global Asset Management 225 Franklin St	Boston	MA	02110	617-722-4700	722-4714
RCGT Inc 7950 Asheville Hwy	Spartanburg	SC	29303	864-503-0879	
Real Estate Management Services Group LLC 1100 Fifth Ave S Ste 305 *Web:* www.remsgroup.com	Naples	FL	34102	239-262-3017	
Redhills Ventures LLC 908 Trophy Hills Dr *Web:* www.redhillsventures.com	Las Vegas	NV	89134	702-233-2160	
Regiment Capital Advisors LLC 222 Berkeley St 12th Fl	Boston	MA	02116	617-488-1600	
Renaissance Macro Research LLC 116 E 16th St 12th Fl *Web:* www.renmac.com	New York	NY	10003	212-537-8811	
Retirement Investment Advisors Inc 3001 United Founders Blvd Ste A *Web:* www.wealthtrac.com	Oklahoma City	OK	73112	405-842-3443	
Retirement Plan Advisors LLC 105 W Adams St Ste 2175 *Web:* www.retirementplanadvisors.com	Chicago	IL	60603	312-701-1100	
Retirement System Group Inc 108 Corporate Park Dr *TF:* 855-549-6689	White Plains	NY	10604	212-503-0100	
RG Associates Inc 201 N Charles St Ste 806 *Web:* www.accountingobserver.com	Baltimore	MD	21201	410-783-0672	
RGM Advisors LLC 221 W 6th St Ste 1600 *Web:* www.rgmadvisors.com	Austin	TX	78701	512-807-5000	
Rhodes Computer Services Inc 4324 Washington Rd Ste 103 *Web:* www.rhodesmurphy.com	Evans	GA	30809	706-868-1298	
Rhumbline Advisers Corp 265 Franklin St 21st Fl *Web:* www.rhumblineadvisers.com	Boston	MA	02110	617-345-0434	345-0675
Rice Hall James & Assoc LLC 600 W Broadway Ste 1000 *Web:* www.ricehalljames.com	San Diego	CA	92101	619-239-9005	
Richardson Partners Financial Ltd 1100 One Lombard Pl *Web:* www.rpfl.com	Winnipeg	MB	R3B0X3	204-957-7735	
Richland Investments LLC 4100 Newport Pl Dr Ste 800 *Web:* www.richlandcommunities.com	Newport Beach	CA	92660	949-261-7010	
Richmond Capital Management Inc 10800 Midlothain Tpke Ste 217 *Web:* www.richmondcap.com	Richmond	VA	23235	804-379-8280	
Ridgestone Corp 10880 Wilshire Blvd Ste 910 *Web:* www.ridgestonecorp.com	Los Angeles	CA	90024	310-209-5300	
Rising Results Inc 201 Edward Curry Ave Ste 202 *Web:* www.risingresults.com	Staten Island	NY	10314	718-370-8300	
Riverfront Investment Group LLC 1214 E Cary St *TF:* 866-583-0744 ■ *Web:* www.riverfrontig.com	Richmond	VA	23219	804-549-4800	
RNC Genter Capital Management 11601 Wilshire Blvd 25th Fl *TF:* 800-877-7624 ■ *Web:* www.rncgenter.com	Los Angeles	CA	90025	310-477-6543	479-6406
Roffman Miller Assoc Inc 1835 Market St Ste 500 *TF:* 800-995-1030 ■ *Web:* www.roffmanmiller.com	Philadelphia	PA	19103	215-981-1030	981-0146
Rogge Capital Management LP 401 Congress Ave Ste 2750 *Web:* www.roggecapital.com	Austin	TX	78701	512-322-0909	
Ronald Blue & Company LLC 300 Colonial Ctr Pkwy Ste 300 *TF:* 800-841-0362 ■ *Web:* www.ronblue.com	Roswell	GA	30076	770-280-6000	280-6001
Roncelli Inc 6471 Metro Pkwy *Web:* www.roncelli-inc.com	Sterling Heights	MI	48312	586-264-2060	
Rosenblatt Securities Inc 20 Broad St 26th Fl *Web:* rblt.com	New York	NY	10005	212-607-3100	
Rosenblum-silverman-sutton Sf Inc 1388 Sutter St Ste 725 *Web:* www.rssic.com	San Francisco	CA	94109	415-771-4500	771-0542
Rosenthal Retirement Planning LP 1412 Main St 6th Fl *Web:* www.rrp.com	Dallas	TX	75202	214-752-1000	
Rothschild North America Inc 1251 Ave of the Americas 51st Fl *TF:* 844-726-3863 ■ *Web:* www.rothschild.com	New York	NY	10020	212-403-3500	403-3501
Roundtable Investment Partners LLC 280 Park Ave E 23rd Fl *Web:* www.roundtableip.com	New York	NY	10017	212-488-4700	
Royal Capital Management LLC 623 Fifth Ave 24th Fl	New York	NY	10022	212-920-3400	
Royce & Assoc LLC 745 Fifth Ave *TF:* 800-221-4268 ■ *Web:* www.roycefunds.com	New York	NY	10151	800-221-4268	
RS Investment Management Company LLC 1 Bush St Ste 900 *Web:* www.rsinvestments.com	San Francisco	CA	94104	415-591-2700	

	City	State	Zip	Phone	Fax
RSF Social Finance 1002A O'Reilly Ave *Web:* www.rsfsocialfinance.org	San Francisco	CA	94129	415-561-3900	
Ruane Cunniff & Goldfarb Inc 9 W 57th St Ste 5000 *TF:* 800-686-6884 ■ *Web:* www.sequoiafund.com	New York	NY	10019	212-832-5280	832-5298
Russell Investment Group 1301 Second Ave Ste 18 *TF:* 800-787-7354 ■ *Web:* russellinvestments.com/us	Seattle	WA	98101	800-787-7354	
Russell Investments 1301 Second Ave 18th Fl *TF:* 800-426-7969 ■ *Web:* russellinvestments.com/us	Seattle	WA	98101	206-505-7877	
RW Pressprich & Company Inc Research Div 452 Fifth Ave 12th Fl *Web:* www.pressprich.com	New York	NY	10018	212-832-6200	
RWI Ventures 545 Middlefield Rd Ste 220 *Web:* www.rwigroup.com	Menlo Park	CA	94025	650-543-3300	
Sage Advisory Services Ltd Co 5900 SW Pkwy Bldg 1 Ste 100 *Web:* www.sageadvisory.com	Austin	TX	78735	512-327-5530	
Sage Group LLC, The 11111 Santa Monica Blvd Ste 2200 *Web:* www.sagellc.com	Los Angeles	CA	90025	310-478-7899	
Sage Rutty & Company Inc 100 Corporate Woods Ste 300 *Web:* www.sagerutty.com	Rochester	NY	14623	585-232-3760	
Sagient Research Systems Inc 3655 Nobel Dr Ste 540 *Web:* www.sagientresearch.com	San Diego	CA	92122	858-623-1600	
Samco Capital Markets 4617 Montrose Blvd Ste C202 *Web:* www.samcocap.com	Houston	TX	77006	713-467-7344	
Sampers Financial Inc 79 Midland Ave *Web:* www.sampersfinancial.com	Montclair	NJ	07042	973-744-1014	
Sapers & Wallack Inc 275 Washington St Ste 205 *Web:* www.sapers-wallack.com	Newton	MA	02458	617-225-2600	
Sasco Capital Inc 10 Sasco Hill Rd *Web:* www.sascocap.com	Fairfield	CT	06430	203-254-6800	
Saturna Capital Corp 1300 N State St *TF:* 888-732-6262 ■ *Web:* www.saturna.com	Bellingham	WA	98225	360-734-9900	
Savant Investment Group LLC 461 Second St Ste 925 *Web:* www.savantig.com	San Francisco	CA	94107	415-926-7200	
Saybrook Capital LLC 11400 W Olympic Blvd *Web:* www.saybrook.net	Los Angeles	CA	90064	310-899-9200	
SBV Venture Partners 454 Ruthven Ave	Palo Alto	CA	94301	650-522-0085	
Scharf Investments LLC 5619 Scotts Vly Dr Ste 140 *Web:* www.scharfinvestments.com	Scotts Valley	CA	95066	831-429-6513	
Schechter Wealth Strategies 251 Pierce St *Web:* www.schechterwealth.com	Birmingham	MI	48009	248-731-9500	
Schneider Capital Management Corp 460 E Swedesford Rd Ste 2000 *Web:* schneidercap.com	Wayne	PA	19087	610-687-8080	
Schreiner Capital Management Inc 111 Summit Dr	Exton	PA	19341	610-524-7310	
Schultz Collins Lawson Chambers Inc 455 Market St Ste 1250 *TF:* 877-291-2205 ■ *Web:* www.schultzcollins.com	San Francisco	CA	94105	415-291-3000	
Schultze Asset Management LLC 3000 Westchester Ave Ste 204 *Web:* www.samco.net	Purchase	NY	10577	914-701-5260	
SDL Capital LP 480 San Antonio Rd Ste 200 *Web:* www.sdlventures.com	Mountain View	CA	94040	650-559-9355	
Seamans Capital Management LLC 500 Boylston St Ste 420 *Web:* www.seamanscapital.com	Boston	MA	02116	781-890-5225	
Seaport Group LLC Research Division, The 360 Madison Ave 22nd Fl *Web:* seaportglobal.com	New York	NY	10017	212-616-7700	
Segal Advisors Inc 116 Huntington Ave Fl 8 *Web:* www.segalrc.com	Boston	MA	02116	617-424-7300	
Segal Rogerscasey 1 Parklands Dr *Web:* www.segalrc.com	Darien	CT	06820	203-621-3620	
Segall Bryant & Hamill 540 W Madison St Ste 1900 *TF:* 800-836-4265 ■ *Web:* www.sbhic.com	Chicago	IL	60606	312-474-1222	
Select Portfolio Management Inc 120 Vantis *TF:* 800-445-9822 ■ *Web:* www.selectportfolio.com	Aliso Viejo	CA	92656	949-975-7900	
Sentinel Wealth Management Inc 11710 Plaza America Dr Ste 130 *Web:* www.sentinelwealth.com	Reston	VA	20190	703-787-5770	
Sharenet Inc 5600 Explorer Dr *Web:* www.sharenetinc.com	Mississauga	ON	L4W4Y2	905-206-0884	206-9783
Sheaff Brock Investment Advisors LLC 10401 N Meridian St Ste 100 *TF:* 866-575-5700 ■ *Web:* www.sheaffbrock.com	Indianapolis	IN	46290	317-705-5700	
Sherman Capital Markets LLC 200 Meeting St Ste 206	Charleston	SC	29401	843-266-1717	
Shields & Company Inc 890 Winter St Ste 160 *Web:* www.shieldsco.com	Waltham	MA	02451	781-890-7033	
Shine Investment Advisory Services Inc 9892 Rosemont Ave Ste 100 *Web:* www.shineinvestments.com	Lone Tree	CO	80124	303-740-8600	
Sidus Investment Management LLC 767 Third Ave 15th Fl *Web:* www.sidusfunds.com	New York	NY	10017	212-751-6644	
Sigma Analysis & Management Ltd 101 College St Ste 345 *Web:* www.sigmanalysis.com	Toronto	ON	M5G1L7	416-260-6291	
Signalert Corp 150 Great Neck Rd Ste 301 *TF:* 800-829-6229 ■ *Web:* www.systemsandforecasts.com	Great Neck	NY	11021	516-829-6444	
Signator Investors Inc 197 Clarendon St C-8 *TF:* 800-543-6611 ■ *Web:* www.signatorinvestors.com	Boston	MA	02116	800-543-6611	

				Phone	Fax
Signature Estate & Investment Advisors LLC 2121 Ave Of The Stars Ste 1600 *Web:* www.seia.com	Los Angeles	CA	90067	310-712-2323	
Signia Capital Management LLC 108 N Washington St Ste 305 *Web:* www.signiacapital.com	Spokane	WA	99201	509-789-8970	
Silver Lake Technology Management LLC 2775 Sand Hill Rd Ste 100 *Web:* www.silverlake.com	Menlo Park	CA	94025	650-233-8120	233-8125
Silvercrest Asset Management Group LLC 1330 Ave of the Americas 38th Fl *Web:* www.silvercrestgroup.com	New York	NY	10019	212-649-0600	
Simmons & Company International 700 Louisiana Ste 1900 *Web:* www.simmonspjc.com	Houston	TX	77002	713-236-9999	
Sit Investment Assoc Inc 80 S Eigth St 3300 IDS Ctr *Web:* www.sitinvest.com	Minneapolis	MN	55402	612-332-3223	332-1911
SKBA Capital Management 44 Montgomery St Ste 3500 *Web:* www.skba.com	San Francisco	CA	94104	415-989-7852	989-2114
SKIRITAI Capital LLC 1 Ferry Bldg Ste 255 *Web:* www.skiritai.com	San Francisco	CA	94111	415-677-5460	
Smith Graham & Co 600 Travis St Ste 6900 *TF:* 800-739-4470 ■ *Web:* smithgraham.com	Houston	TX	77002	713-227-1100	
SMS Financial LLC 2645 N 7th Ave *Web:* smsfinancial.net	Phoenix	AZ	85007	602-944-0624	
Sonata Capital Group Inc 2001 Sixth Ave Ste 3410 *Web:* www.sonatacap.com	Seattle	WA	98121	206-256-4400	
Sound Shore Management Inc 8 Sound Shore Dr Ste 180 *TF:* 800-551-1980 ■ *Web:* www.soundshore.com	Greenwich	CT	06830	203-629-1980	
South Texas Money Management Ltd 700 N Saint Mary's Ste 100 *TF:* 800-805-1385 ■ *Web:* stmmltd.com	San Antonio	TX	78205	210-824-8916	
Southeastern Asset Management Inc 6410 Poplar Ave Ste 900 *Web:* www.southeasternasset.com	Memphis	TN	38119	901-761-2474	
SouthernSun Asset Management LLC 6070 Poplar Ave Ste 300 *Web:* www.southernsunam.com	Memphis	TN	38119	901-333-6980	
Sovereign Society, The 98 S E Sixth Ave Ste 2 *TF:* 866-584-4096 ■ *Web:* www.sovereignsociety.com	Delray Beach	FL	33483	888-358-8125	
Speece Thorson Capital Group Inc 225 S Sixth St Ste 2575 *Web:* www.stcapital.com	Minneapolis	MN	55402	612-338-4649	
Spero-Smith Investment Advisers Inc 3601 Green Rd Ste 102 *TF:* 800-794-7545 ■ *Web:* www.sperosmith.com	Cleveland	OH	44122	216-464-6266	
Sperry, Mitchell & Company Inc 595 Madison Ave 30th Fl *Web:* sperrymitchell.com	New York	NY	10022	212-832-6628	
Spire Investment Partners LLC 7918 Jones Branch Dr Ste 750 *TF:* 888-737-8907 ■ *Web:* www.spireip.com	Mclean	VA	22102	703-748-5800	
Springsted Inc 380 Jackson St Ste 300 *Web:* www.springsted.com	Saint Paul	MN	55101	651-223-3000	
Springvale Terrace 8505 Springvale Rd *Web:* www.seaburyresources.org/srj/index.php/housing/springvaleterrace	Silver Spring	MD	20910	301-587-0190	
St. Charles Capital LLC 1400 Sixteenth St Ste 300	Denver	CO	80202	303-339-9099	
Standard Pacific Capital LLC 101 California St 36th Fl *Web:* standardpacific.com	San Francisco	CA	94111	415-352-7100	
Standish Mellon 1 Boston Pl *Web:* www.standish.com	Boston	MA	02108	617-248-6000	248-6050
Stanford Investment Group Inc 2570 W El Camino Real Ste 520 *Web:* www.stanfordinvestment.com	Mountain View	CA	94040	650-941-1717	
Stansberry & Assoc Investment Research LLC 1217 Saint Paul St *TF:* 888-261-2693 ■ *Web:* www.stansberryresearch.com	Baltimore	MD	21202	888-261-2693	
Stanwich Advisors LLC 1 Dock St Ste 602 *Web:* www.stanwichadvisors.com	Stamford	CT	06902	203-406-1099	
StarMine Corp 49 Stevenson St *Web:* starmine.com	San Francisco	CA	94105	415-777-1147	
State Universities Retirement System of Illinois 1901 Fox Dr *TF:* 800-275-7877 ■ *Web:* www.surs.com	Champaign	IL	61820	217-378-8800	
Stellar Capital Management LLC 2200 E Camelback Rd Ste 130 *Web:* www.stellarmgt.com	Phoenix	AZ	85016	602-778-0307	
Sterling Investment Partners 285 Riverside Ave Ste 300 *Web:* www.sterlinglp.com	Westport	CT	06880	203-226-8711	
Sterling Mutuals Inc 880 Ouellette Ave 9th Fl *Web:* www.sterlingmutuals.com	Windsor	ON	N9A1C7	519-256-1002	
Stevens Capital Management LP 201 King Of Prussia Rd Ste 400 *Web:* www.scm-lp.com	Wayne	PA	19087	610-971-5000	
Stoever Glass & Company Inc 30 Wall St *TF:* 800-223-3881 ■ *Web:* stoeverglass.com	New York	NY	10005	800-223-3881	
StoneCreek Capital Inc 18500 Von Karman Ave Ste 590 *Web:* www.stonecreekcapital.com	Irvine	CA	92612	949-752-4580	
StoneRidge Investment Partners LLC 301 Lindenwood Dr Ste 310 *Web:* www.stoneridgeinvestments.com	Malvern	PA	19355	610-647-5253	
Stoneworth Financial LLC 6575 W Loop S Ste 468 *Web:* www.stoneworthfinancial.com	Houston	TX	77401	713-429-1838	
Strategic Financial Alliance Inc, The 2200 Century Pkwy Ste 500 *Web:* www.thesfa.net	Atlanta	GA	30345	678-954-4000	
Stratford Advisory Group Inc 500 W Madison St Ste 2740 *Web:* www.stratfordadvisorygroup.com	Chicago	IL	60661	312-798-3200	
StreetAuthority LLC 4601 Spicewood Springs Rd Bldg 3 Ste 100 *Web:* www.streetauthority.com	Austin	TX	78759	512-501-4001	
StreetInsider.com Inc 280 W Maple Ste 210 *Web:* www.streetinsider.com	Birmingham	MI	48009	248-593-6536	
Stretegic Mktg Ventures Inc 8262 Lees Ridge Rd *Web:* www.smvbpo.com	Warrenton	VA	20186	540-349-8888	
Summit Strategies Inc 8182 Maryland Ave 6th Fl *Web:* www.ssgstl.com	St. Louis	MO	63105	314-727-7211	
SunTrust Banks Inc 25 Pk Pl NE *NYSE: STI* ■ *Web:* suntrust.com	Atlanta	GA	30303	404-588-7610	575-2837
Swarthmore Group 1650 Arch St Ste 2100 *Web:* www.swarthmoregroup.com	Philadelphia	PA	19103	215-557-9300	557-9305
Systematic Financial Management LP 300 Frank W Burr Blvd Seventh Fl Glenpoint Ctr E 7th Fl *TF:* 800-258-0497 ■ *Web:* www.sfmlp.com	Teaneck	NJ	07666	201-928-1982	
T Rowe Price Assoc Inc 100 E Pratt St **Fax:* Cust Svc ■ *TF:* 800-638-7890 ■ *Web:* www3.troweprice.com/usis/corporate/en/home.html	Baltimore	MD	21202	410-345-2000	345-6244*
Tactical Allocation Group LLC 139 S Old Woodward Ave *Web:* www.tagllc.net	Birmingham	MI	48009	248-283-2520	
TAG Associates LLC 75 Rockefeller Plz *Web:* www.tagassoc.com	New York	NY	10019	212-275-1500	275-1510
Takenaka Partners LLC 801 S Figueroa St Ste 620 *Web:* www.takenakapartners.com	Los Angeles	CA	90017	213-891-0060	
Tamarac Inc 701 Fifth Ave 14th Fl *TF:* 866-525-8811 ■ *Web:* www.tamaracinc.com	Seattle	WA	98104	866-525-8811	
TAMRO Capital Partners LLC 1701 Duke St Ste 250 *TF:* 888-816-2925 ■ *Web:* www.tamrocapital.com	Alexandria	VA	22314	703-740-1000	
Taurus Asset Management LLC 590 Madison Ave 35th Fl *Web:* www.taurusassetmanagement.com	New York	NY	10022	212-457-9922	
TCI Wealth Advisors Inc 4011 E Sunrise Dr *TF:* 877-733-1859 ■ *Web:* www.tciwealth.com	Tucson	AZ	85718	520-733-1477	
TE Financial Consultants Ltd 26 Wellington St E Ste 710 *Web:* www.tewealth.com	Toronto	ON	M5E1S2	416-366-1451	
TeamCo Advisers LLC 1 Bush St Ste 550 *Web:* www.teamcoadvisers.com	San Francisco	CA	94104	415-445-9800	
Technomart RGA Inc 401 Washington Ave Ste 1101 *TF:* 800-877-6555 ■ *Web:* www.technomartrga.com	Baltimore	MD	21204	410-828-6555	
Telemus Capital Partners LLC 2 Towne Sq Ste 800 *Web:* www.telemuscapital.com	Southfield	MI	48076	248-827-1800	
Telsey Advisory Group LLC 535 Fifth Ave 12th Fl *Web:* www.telseygroup.com	New York	NY	10017	212-973-9700	
Terry McDaniel & Co 2630 Exposition Blvd Ste 300 *Web:* www.tmcdanco.com	Austin	TX	78703	512-495-9500	
Third Coast Capital Advisors LLC 1 N Franklin St Ste 3200 *Web:* www.thirdcoastca.com	Chicago	IL	60606	312-332-6484	
Third River Capital Management LLC 221 N Lasalle St 32nd Fl Ste 3200 *Web:* www.thirdrivercapital.com	Chicago	IL	60601	312-628-6700	
Thompson Research Group LLC 1033 Demonbreun St Ste 625 *Web:* www.thompsonresearchgroup.com	Nashville	TN	37203	615-891-6200	
Thompson Siegel & Walmsley Inc 6806 Paragon Pl Ste 300 *TF:* 800-697-1056 ■ *Web:* www.tswinvest.com	Richmond	VA	23230	804-353-4500	353-0925
Thoroughbred Financial Services LLC 5110 Maryland Way Ste 300 *Web:* www.thoroughbredfinancial.com	Brentwood	TN	37027	615-371-0001	
TICC Capital Corp 8 Sound Shore Dr Ste 255 *Web:* www.ticc.com	Greenwich	CT	06830	203-983-5275	
Tirschwell & Loewy Inc 400 Park Ave *Web:* www.tirschwellandloewy.com	New York	NY	10022	212-888-7940	
Titlemax of South Carolina Inc 15 Bull St Ste 200 *Web:* www.gmlblaw.com	Savannah	GA	31401	901-236-0578	
TM Capital Corp 641 Lexington Ave 30th Fl *Web:* www.tmcapital.com	New York	NY	10022	212-809-1360	
Tom Johnson Investment Management Inc 201 Robert S Kerr Ave *TF:* 888-404-8546 ■ *Web:* tjim.com	Oklahoma City	OK	73102	405-236-2111	
Torch Energy Advisors Inc (TEAI) 1331 Lamar Ave Ste 1450	Houston	TX	77010	713-650-1246	655-1866
Toyon Associates Inc 1800 Sutter St Ste 600 *Web:* www.toyonassociates.com	Concord	CA	94520	925-685-9312	
Tradition Capital Management LLC 129 Summit Ave *Web:* www.traditioncm.com	Summit	NJ	07901	908-598-0909	
Transamerica Corporation 440 Mamaroneck Ave *Web:* www.divinvest.com	Harrison	NY	10528	914-627-3000	697-3743
Transfer Solutions Inc 550 S Nursery Ave *Web:* www.ts-inc.com	Purcellville	VA	20132	703-777-1126	
Transmarket Group LLC 550 W Jackson Blvd Ste 1300 *Web:* www.transmarketgroup.com	Chicago	IL	60661	312-284-5500	284-5650

				Phone	Fax
Treflie Capital Management 35 Ezekills Holw	Sag Harbor	NY	11963	631-725-2500	
TF: 866-236-3363 ■ *Web:* www.treflie.com					
Trellis Capital Corp 333 Wilson Ave Ste 600	Toronto	ON	M3H1T2	416-398-2299	
Web: www.trelliscapital.com					
Trent Capital Management Inc 3150 N Elm St Ste 204	Greensboro	NC	27408	336-282-9302	
Web: www.trentcapital.com					
Triangle Securities LLC 1301 Annapolis Dr	Raleigh	NC	27608	919-838-3221	
Web: www.trianglesecurities.com					
Trimaran Fund Management LLC 1325 Ave of the Americas	New York	NY	10019	212-616-3700	616-3701
Web: www.trimarancapital.com					
TrimTabs Investment Research 1 Harbor Dr Ste 211	Sausalito	CA	94965	415-324-5873	
Web: www.trimtabs.com					
TripleTree 7601 France Ave S Ste 150	Minneapolis	MN	55435	952-253-5300	
Web: www.triple-tree.com					
Trustmont Financial Group Inc 200 Brush Run Rd Ste A	Greensburg	PA	15601	724-468-5665	
Web: www.trustmontgroup.com					
Tsg Equity Partners LLC 636 Great Rd	Stow	MA	01775	978-461-9900	
Web: www.tsgequity.com					
Turner Investment Partners Inc 1205 Westlakes Dr Ste 100	Berwyn	PA	19312	484-329-2300	
Web: www.turnerinvestments.com					
TYGH Capital Management Inc 1211 S W Fifth Ave Ste 2100	Portland	OR	97204	503-972-0150	
TF: 800-972-0150 ■ *Web:* www.tyghcap.com					
Ullman John & Associates Inc 51 E Market St	Corning	NY	14830	607-936-3785	
Web: www.jgua.com					
Unique Investment Corp 7028 Kearny Dr	Huntington Beach	CA	92648	714-848-5900	
Web: www.uniquepartners.com					
United Capital Financial Advisers LLC 620 Newport Center Dr Ste 500	Newport Beach	CA	92660	949-999-8500	
Web: www.unitedcp.com					
Unity Financial Strategists Inc 100 Wall St 22nd Fl	New York	NY	10005	212-785-4200	
Web: www.unityfinancialadvisors.com					
Univers Workplace Benefits Inc 897 12th St	Hammonton	NJ	08037	609-561-0240	
Web: univers.biz					
US Capital Advisors LLC 1330 Post Oak Blvd Ste 900	Houston	TX	77056	713-366-0500	
Web: www.uscallc.com					
US Global Investors Inc 7900 Callaghan Rd	San Antonio	TX	78229	210-308-1234	308-1223
NASDAQ: GROW ■ *TF:* 800-873-8637 ■ *Web:* www.usfunds.com					
US Renewables Group LLC 2425 Olympic Blvd Ste 4050 W	Santa Monica	CA	90404	310-586-3900	
Web: www.usregroup.com					
USAA Investment Management 9800 Fredericksburg Rd PO Box 659453	San Antonio	TX	78288	800-531-8722	
TF: 800-531-8722 ■ *Web:* www.usaa.com					
Valley Financial Solutions Inc 2847 Penn Forest Blvd Ste 100	Roanoke	VA	24018	540-777-4302	
Web: www.valleyfinancialsolutions.com					
Value Line Asset Management 220 E 42nd St	New York	NY	10017	212-907-1500	
TF: 800-634-3583 ■ *Web:* www.valueline.com					
Van Strum & Towne Inc 505 Sansome St Ste 1001	San Francisco	CA	94111	415-981-3455	
Web: www.vanstrum.com					
Vanguard Group 455 Devon Pk Dr	Wayne	PA	19087	610-669-1000	669-6551
TF: 800-662-7447 ■ *Web:* investor.vanguard.com					
VCI Emergency Vehicle 43 jefferson ave	Berlin	NJ	08009	856-768-2162	
TF: 800-394-2162 ■ *Web:* vciambulances.com					
VectorVest Inc 20472 Chartwell Ctr Dr Ste D	Cornelius	NC	28031	704-895-4095	
Web: www.vectorvest.com					
Verisight Inc 35 Iron Point Cir Ste 100	Folsom	CA	95630	916-932-1800	
Web: verisightgroup.com					
Veritable LP 6022 W Chester Pk	Newtown Square	PA	19073	610-640-9551	
Web: www.finestimage.com					
Vertical Research Partners LLC 6 Landmark Sq Ste 720	Stamford	CT	06901	203-276-5680	
Web: verticalresearchpartners.com					
Virtus Investment Partners Inc 100 Pearl St 9th Fl	Hartford	CT	06103	860-263-4707	
Web: www.virtus.com					
Vontobel Asset Management Inc 1540 Broad Way Ave 38th Fl	New York	NY	10036	212-415-7000	415-7087
TF General: 800-445-8872 ■ *Web:* www.vusa.com					
VSR Financial Services Inc PO Box 26250	Overland Park	KS	66225	913-498-2900	
Web: www.vsrfinancial.com					
VTL Associates LLC 1 Commerce Sq 2005 Market St Ste 2020	Philadelphia	PA	19103	215-854-8181	
Web: www.vtlassociates.com					
WAB Capital LLC 1559 Michael Ln Pacific Palisades	Los Angeles	CA	90272	310-230-8664	
Web: www.growthequities.com					
Waddell & Reed Financial Inc 6300 Lamar Ave	Overland Park	KS	66201	913-236-2000	532-2749*
NYSE: WDR ■ **Fax Area Code: 800* ■ *TF:* 888-923-3355 ■ *Web:* www.waddell.com					
Wade Financial Advisory Inc 2105 S Bascom Ave Ste 110	Campbell	CA	95008	408-369-7399	
Web: www.wadefa.com					
Warwick Investment Management Inc 4444 Carter Creek Pkwy Ste 109	Bryan	TX	77802	979-260-9777	
Web: www.warwickpartners.net					
Washington Capital Management Inc 1301 Fifth Ave Ste 3100	Seattle	WA	98101	206-382-0825	382-0950
Web: www.wcmadvisors.com					
Wasmer Schroeder & Company Inc 600 Fifth Ave S Ste 210	Naples	FL	34102	239-263-6877	263-8146
Web: www.wasmerschroeder.com					
Waters Parkerson & Company LLC 228 St Charles Ave Ste 512	New Orleans	LA	70130	504-581-2022	
Web: www.wpcoinc.com					
WCM Investment Management 281 Brooks St	Laguna Beach	CA	92651	949-380-0200	
Web: www.wcminvest.com					
WE Donoghue & Company Inc 629 Washington St	Norwood	MA	02062	800-642-4276	
TF: 800-642-4276 ■ *Web:* www.donoghue.com					
WE Family Offices LLC 701 Brickell Ave Ste 2100	Miami	FL	33131	305-825-2225	
Web: www.wefamilyoffices.com					
Wealth Conservancy Inc, The 1525 Spruce St Ste 300	Boulder	CO	80302	303-444-1919	
TF: 888-440-1919 ■ *Web:* www.thewealthconservancy.com					
Wealthfront Inc 541 Cowper St	Palo Alto	CA	94301	650-249-4250	
Web: www.wealthfront.com					
Webb Financial Group 7900 Xerxes Ave S Ste 1920	Minneapolis	MN	55431	952-837-3200	
TF: 800-927-9322 ■ *Web:* www.webbfinancial.com					
Wedge Capital Management LLP 301 S College St Ste 2920	Charlotte	NC	28202	704-334-6475	334-3542
Web: www.wedgecapital.com					
Weil Co, The 12555 High Bluff Dr Ste 180	San Diego	CA	92130	858-704-1444	
Web: www.cweil.com					
Weiss Research Inc 15430 Endeavour Dr	Jupiter	FL	33478	800-291-8545	
TF: 800-291-8545 ■ *Web:* www.weissinc.com					
Welch Capital Partners LLC 90 Park Ave	New York	NY	10016	212-754-6077	
Web: www.welchcapital.com					
Wellington Management Company LLP 280 Congress St	Boston	MA	02210	617-951-5000	
Web: www.wellington.com					
Wentworth Hauser & Violich (WHV) 301 Battery St	San Francisco	CA	94111	415-981-6911	288-6153
TF: 800-204-2650 ■ *Web:* www.whv.com					
West Face Capital Inc 2 Bloor St E Ste 3000	Toronto	ON	M4W1A8	647-724-8900	
Web: westfacecapital.com					
Westfield Capital Management Company LP 1 Financial Ctr 24th Fl	Boston	MA	02111	617-428-7100	
Web: www.westfieldcapital.com					
Weston Capital Management Inc 1450 S Bundy Dr	Los Angeles	CA	90025	310-826-0811	
Web: www.westoncap.com					
Wilbanks, Smith & Thomas Asset Management LLC 150 W Main St Ste 1700	Norfolk	VA	23510	757-623-3676	
TF: 800-229-3677 ■ *Web:* www.wstam.com					
Williams, Jones & Associates LLC 717 Fifth Ave Ste 1700	New York	NY	10022	212-935-8750	
Web: www.williamsjones.com					
Willis Investment Counsel Inc 710 Green St	Gainesville	GA	30501	770-718-0706	
Web: www.wicinvest.com					
Wilshire Assoc Inc 1299 Ocean Ave Ste 700	Santa Monica	CA	90401	310-451-3051	458-0520
TF: 855-626-8281 ■ *Web:* www.wilshire.com					
Windlake Capital Advisors LLC 980 N Michigan Ave Ste 1400	Chicago	IL	60611	312-357-0900	
Web: www.windlakeadvisors.com					
Woodmont Investment Counsel LLC 401 Commerce St Ste 5400	Nashville	TN	37219	615-297-6144	
TF: 800-278-8003 ■ *Web:* www.woodmontcounsel.com					
Woodridge Capital 800 Woodlands Pkwy Ste 201	Ridgeland	MS	39157	601-957-6006	
Web: www.woodridge-capital.com					
Woodstock Corp 27 School St Ste 200	Boston	MA	02108	617-227-0600	
Web: www.woodstockcorp.com					
Woodway Financial Advisors 10000 Memorial Dr Ste 650	Houston	TX	77024	713-683-7070	683-0702
Web: www.woodwayfinancial.com					
Workplace Answers LLC 3701 Executive Ctr Dr Ste 201	Austin	TX	78731	866-861-4410	
TF: 866-861-4410 ■ *Web:* www.workplaceanswers.com					
WRA Inc 2169 Francisco Blvd E Ste G	San Rafael	CA	94901	415-454-8868	
Web: www.eahhousing.org					
Wright Investors' Service 440 Wheelers Farms Rd	Milford	CT	06461	203-783-4400	783-4401
TF: 800-232-0013 ■ *Web:* wrightinvestorsservice.com					
XRoads Solutions Group 1821 E Dyer Rd Ste 225	Santa Ana	CA	92705	949-567-1600	
Web: www.xroadsllc.com					
Yacktman Asset Management Co 6300 Bridgepoint Pkwy Bldg 1 Ste 320	Austin	TX	78730	512-767-6700	
TF: 800-835-3879 ■ *Web:* www.yacktman.com					
YHB Investment Advisors Inc 29 S Main St Ste 306	West Hartford	CT	06107	860-561-7050	
Web: www.yhbia.com					
Your Source Private Equity 707 E Northern Ave	Phoenix	AZ	85020	602-343-1700	
Web: www.ysfi.com					
Zebra Capital Management LLC 612 Wheelers Farm Rd	Milford	CT	06461	203-878-3223	
Web: www.zebracapm.com					
Zuk Financial Group 22936 El Toro Rd	Lake Forest	CA	92630	949-472-4550	
Web: www.zukfinancial.com					

402 INVESTMENT COMPANIES - SMALL BUSINESS

The companies listed here conform to the Small Business Administration's standards for investing.

				Phone	Fax
Argentum Group, The 60 Madison Ave Ste 701	New York	NY	10010	212-949-6262	949-8294
Web: www.argentumgroup.com					
Atalanta Investment Company Inc PO Box 7718	Incline Village	NV	89452	775-833-1836	833-1890

Phone | Fax

Bankoh Investment Services Inc
130 Merchant St Ste 850 .... Honolulu HI 96813 808-537-8500
Web: www.boh.com

Brynwood Partners LP
8 Sound Shore Dr Ste 265 .... Greenwich CT 06830 203-622-1790 622-0559
Web: www.brynwoodpartners.com

Center for Innovation
University of N Dakota PO Box 8372 .... Grand Forks ND 58202 701-777-3132 777-2339
Web: www.innovators.net

Cypress Group LLC 437 Madison Ave 33rd Fl. .... New York NY 10022 212-705-0150 705-0199
Web: www.cypressgp.com

El Dorado Ventures 702 Oak Grove Ave .... Menlo Park CA 94025 650-854-1200
Web: www.eldorado.com

Elliott Management 40 W 57th St .... New York NY 10019 212-974-6000
Web: www.elliottmgmt.com

Eos Partners LP 320 Pk Ave 9th Fl .... New York NY 10022 212-832-5800 832-5815
Web: www.eospartners.com

Federal Farm Credit Banks Funding Corp
10 Exchange Pl Ste 1401 .... Jersey City NJ 07302 201-200-8131 200-8109
Web: www.farmcreditfunding.com

Galliard Capital Management Inc
800 La Salle Ave Ste 1100 .... Minneapolis MN 55402 612-667-3220 667-3223
TF: 800-717-1617 ■ *Web:* www.galliard.com

GamePlan Financial Marketing LLC
300 ParkBrooke Pl Ste 200 .... Woodstock GA 30189 678-238-0601 718-1954
TF Cust Svc: 800-886-4757 ■ *Web:* www.gameplanfinancial.com

Gemini Investors LLC 20 William St Ste 250 .... Wellesley MA 02481 781-237-7001 237-7233
Web: www.gemini-investors.com

Hornor Townsend & Kent Inc (HTK)
600 Dresher Rd Ste C1C .... Horsham PA 19044 800-289-9999 956-7750*
**Fax Area Code:* 215 ■ *TF:* 800-289-9999 ■ *Web:* www.htk.com

Impact Seven Inc 147 Lk Almena Dr .... Almena WI 54805 715-357-3334 357-6233
TF: 800-685-9353 ■ *Web:* www.impactseven.org

Inverness Management LLC
21 Locust Ave Ste 1D .... New Canaan CT 06840 203-966-4177
Web: www.invernessmanagement.com

Kansas Venture Capital Inc (KVCI)
10601 Mission Rd Ste 250 .... Leawood KS 66206 913-262-7117 262-3509
Web: www.kvci.com

Kentucky Highlands Investment Corp
362 Old Whitley Rd PO Box 1738 .... London KY 40743 606-864-5175 864-5194
Web: www.khic.org

Marwit Capital LLC
100 Bayview Cir Ste 550 .... Newport Beach CA 92660 949-861-3636 861-3637
Web: www.marwit.com

Mason Wells 411 E Wisconsin Ave Ste 1280 .... Milwaukee WI 53202 414-727-6400 727-6410
Web: www.masonwells.com

MVP Capital Partners
259 N Radnor-Chester Rd Ste 130 .... Radnor PA 19087 610-254-2999
Web: www.meridian-venture.com

Novus Ventures LP
20111 Stevens Creek Blvd Ste 130 .... Cupertino CA 95014 408-252-3900

Physical Optics Corp 1845 W 205th St .... Torrance CA 90501 310-320-3088 320-4667
Web: www.poc.com

RFE Investment Partners 36 Grove St .... New Canaan CT 06840 203-966-2800 966-3109
Web: www.rfeip.com

River Cities Capital Funds
221 E Fourth St Ste 2400 .... Cincinnati OH 45202 513-621-9700 579-8939

Seacoast Capital Partners 55 Ferncroft Rd .... Danvers MA 01923 978-750-1300 750-1301
Web: www.seacoastcapital.com

Sorrento Assoc Inc
12250 El Camino Real Ste 100 .... San Diego CA 92130 858-792-2700 792-5070
Web: www.sorrentoventures.com

Stonehenge Capital Company LLC
236 Third St .... Baton Rouge LA 70801 225-408-3000 408-3090
Web: www.stonehengecapital.com

TPG Capital LP 301 Commerce St Ste 3300 .... Fort Worth TX 76102 817-871-4000 871-4001
Web: www.tpg.com

UMB Capital Corp 1010 Grand Blvd .... Kansas City MO 64106 816-860-7000
TF: 800-821-2171 ■ *Web:* www.umb.com

Vestor Partners LP 607 Cerrillos Rd .... Santa Fe NM 87501 505-988-9100
Web: www.vestor.com

Virginia Capital Partners LLC
1801 Libbie Ave Ste 201 .... Richmond VA 23226 804-648-4802 648-4809
Web: www.vacapital.com

Waterside Capital Corp
2505 Cheyne Walk .... Virginia Beach VA 23454 757-626-1111
OTC: WSCC

403 INVESTMENT COMPANIES - SPECIALIZED SMALL BUSINESS

Companies listed here conform to the Small Business Administration's requirements for investment in minority companies.

Phone | Fax

Accord Financial Corp Ste 1803 77 Bloor St W .... Toronto ON M5S1M2 416-961-0007
Web: www.accordfinancial.com

Al Copeland Investments Inc
1001 Harimaw Ct S .... Metairie LA 70001 504-830-1000 401-0401
TF: 800-401-0401 ■ *Web:* www.alcopeland.com

ALCO Inc 6925 - 104 St .... Edmonton AB T6H2L5 780-435-3502
TF: 800-563-1498 ■ *Web:* www.alcoinc.ca

Appaloosa Management LP
51 John F Kennedy Pkwy .... Short Hills NJ 07078 973-701-7000
Web: www.amlp.com

Arlington Capital Partners
5425 Wisconsin Ave Ste 200 .... Chevy Chase MD 20815 202-337-7500 337-7525
Web: www.arlingtoncap.com

Associated Southwest Investors Inc
6501 Americas Pkwy NE .... Albuquerque NM 87110 505-247-4050 247-1899

Bastion Capital Corp
1901 Ave of the Stars .... Los Angeles CA 90067 310-788-5700 277-7582

Benefits Data Trust 2 Logan Sq Ste 550 .... Philadelphia PA 19103 215-207-9100
Web: bdtrust.org

Phone | Fax

Brentwood Assoc
11150 Santa Monica Blvd Ste 1200 .... Los Angeles CA 90025 310-477-6611 477-1011
Web: www.brentwood.com

Brown Gibbons Lang & Co LLC
1375 E 9th St Ste 2500 .... Cleveland OH 44114 216-241-2800 241-7417
Web: www.bglco.com

Burney Co 121 Rowell Ct .... Falls Church VA 22046 703-241-5611
Web: www.burney.com

Canadian Home Income Plan Corp
1090 Pender St W .... Vancouver BC V6E2N7 604-685-2447
Web: www.chip.ca

Capricorn Management LLC 30 E Elm St .... Greenwich CT 06830 203-861-6600
Web: www.capricornholdings.com

Castle Harlan Inc 150 E 58th St .... New York NY 10155 212-644-8600 207-8042
Web: www.castleharlan.com

Chatham Financial Corp
235 Whitehorse Ln .... Kennett Square PA 19348 610-925-3120
Web: www.chathamfinancial.com

Chatham Lodging Trust
50 Cocoanut Row Ste 200 .... Palm Beach FL 33480 561-802-4477
Web: www.chathamlodgingtrust.com

Chicago Oakbrook Financial Group
903 Commerce Dr Ste 300 .... Oak Brook IL 60523 630-954-5572
Web: www.cofgroup.com

Clayton Dubilier & Rice Inc
375 Pk Ave 18th Fl .... New York NY 10152 212-407-5200 407-5252
Web: www.cdr-inc.com

Community Mortgage Corp 142 Timber Creek Dr. .... Cordova TN 38018 901-759-4400
Web: www.communitymtg.com

Core Realty Holdings LLC
1600 Dove St Ste 450 .... Newport Beach CA 92660 949-863-1031
Web: www.corerealtyholdings.com

Cypress Sharpridge Investments Inc (CYS)
890 Winter St .... Waltham MA 02451 617-639-0440
NYSE: CYS ■ *Web:* www.cysinv.com

Global Banks Premium Income Trust
1375 Kerns Rd .... Burlington ON L7P4S8 905-331-4286
Web: www.portlandic.com

Goldner Hawn Johnson & Morrison Inc (GHJ&M)
90 S Seventh St 3700 Wells Fargo Ctr .... Minneapolis MN 55402 612-338-5912
Web: www.ghjm.com

Ibero American Investors Corp 817 E Main .... Rochester NY 14605 585-256-8900
Web: www.iberoinvestors.com

La Financiere Agricole Du Quebec
1400 Blvd de la Rive-Sud .... Saint-Romuald QC J2X3C7 418-838-5602
Web: www.fadq.qc.ca

Linx Partners LLC 100 Galleria Pkwy Ste 1150 .... Atlanta GA 30339 770-818-0335
Web: www.linxpartners.com

Littlejohn & Company LLC
8 Sound Shore Dr Ste 303 .... Greenwich CT 06830 203-552-3500 552-3550
Web: www.littlejohnllc.com

Madison Capital Partners Corp
500 W Madison St Ste 3890 .... Chicago IL 60661 312-277-0156 277-0163
Web: www.madisoncapitalpartners.net

MBN Corp 812 Memorial Dr NW .... Calgary AB T2N3C8 403-269-2100
Web: www.middlefield.com

MCG Global LLC 300 Long Beach Blvd Ste 13 .... Stratford CT 06615 203-386-0615 386-0771
Web: www.mcgglobal.com

Medallion Capital
3000 W County Rd 42 Ste 301 .... Burnsville MN 55337 952-831-2025 831-2945
Web: www.medallionfinancial.com

Mennonite Savings & Credit Union (Ontario) Ltd
1265 Strasburg Rd .... Kitchener ON N2R1S6 519-746-1010
Web: www.mscu.com

Milestone Growth Fund
527 Marquette Ave Ste 1915 .... Minneapolis MN 55402 612-338-0090
Web: www.milestonegrowth.com

MMG Ventures LP 826 E Baltimore St .... Baltimore MD 21202 410-333-2548
Web: www.mmgcapitalgroup.com

NCA Partners Inc 1200 Westlake Ave N Ste 600 .... Seattle WA 98109 206-689-5615 689-5614
Web: www.nwcap.com

Nitze-Stagen & Company Inc
2401 Utah Ave S Ste 305 .... Seattle WA 98134 206-467-0420 467-0423
Web: www.nitze-stagen.com

Opportunity Capital Corp
2201 Walnut Ave Ste 210 .... Fremont CA 94538 510-795-7000
Web: www.opportunitycapitalpartners.com

Polestar Capital Inc
180 N Michigan Ave Ste 1905 .... Chicago IL 60601 312-984-9090 984-9877
Web: www.polestarvc.com

Princeton Financial Systems LLC
600 College Rd E .... Princeton NJ 08540 609-987-2400 987-9320
Web: www.pfs.com

Pro Mujer Inc 253 W 35th St 11th Fl South .... New York NY 10001 646-626-7000
Web: www.promujer.org

Rainmaker Group Ventures LLC, The
4550 N Point Pkwy Ste 400 .... Alpharetta GA 30022 678-578-5700
Web: www.letitrain.com

Rayonier Inc 225 Water St Ste 1400 .... Jacksonville FL 32202 904-357-9100
Web: www.rayonier.com

RD Legal Funding LLC 45 Legion Dr .... Cresskill NJ 07626 201-568-9007
Web: www.legalfunding.com

Security Credit Services LLC
2653 W Oxford Loop Ste 108 .... Oxford MS 38655 662-281-7220
TF: 866-699-7889 ■ *Web:* www.securitycreditservicesllc.com

Smith Affiliated Capital (SAC)
800 Third Ave 12th Fl .... New York NY 10022 212-644-9440 644-1979
TF: 888-387-3298 ■ *Web:* www.smithcapital.com

Stockbridge Capital Partners LLC
4 Embarcadero Ctr Ste 3300 .... San Francisco CA 94111 415-658-3300
Web: stockbridgerealestate.com

United FCS ACA 2616 US Hwy 45 .... Antigo WI 54409 715-623-7644
Web: www.unitedfcs.com

404 INVESTMENT GUIDES - ONLINE

See Also Buyer's Guides - Online p. 1886

	City	State	Zip	Phone	Fax
Briefing.com Inc 401 N Michigan Ste 2910 *TF General:* 800-752-3013 ■ *Web:* www.briefing.com	Chicago	IL	60611	312-670-4463	670-5761
EDGAR Online Inc 11200 Rockville Pk Ste 310 *NASDAQ: EDGR* ■ *TF:* 800-732-0330 ■ *Web:* edgar-online.com	Rockville	MD	20852	301-287-0300	287-0390
eSignal 3955 Pt Eden Way *TF:* 800-815-8256 ■ *Web:* www.esignal.com	Hayward	CA	94545	510-266-6000	266-6100
FactSet Research Systems Inc 601 Merritt 7 3rd Fl *NYSE: FDS* ■ *TF:* 877-322-8738 ■ *Web:* www.factset.com	Norwalk	CT	06851	203-810-1000	810-1000
Harris myCFO Inc 2200 Geng Rd Ste 100 *TF:* 866-966-1130 ■ *Web:* ctcmycfo.com	Palo Alto	CA	94303	650-210-5000	
Hoover's Inc 5800 Airport Blvd *TF:* 800-486-8666 ■ *Web:* www.hoovers.com	Austin	TX	78752	512-374-4500	374-4501
InvestorPlace.com 2420A Gehman Ln 2420A Gehman Ln *TF:* 800-219-8592 ■ *Web:* www.investorplace.com	Lancaster	PA	17602	800-219-8592	
Motley Fool Inc 2000 Duke St 4th Fl *Web:* www.fool.com	Alexandria	VA	22314	703-838-3665	254-1999
Stockwatch 700 W Georgia St PO Box 10371 *TF:* 800-268-6397 ■ *Web:* www.stockwatch.com	Vancouver	BC	V7Y1J6	604-687-1500	687-0541
TheStreet.com Inc 14 Wall St 15th Fl *NASDAQ: TST* ■ *TF:* 800-562-9571 ■ *Web:* www.thestreet.com	New York	NY	10005	212-321-5000	321-5016
Yahoo! Finance 701 First Ave *Web:* finance.yahoo.com	Sunnyvale	CA	94089	408-349-3300	349-3301

405 INVESTMENT (MISC)

See Also Banks - Commercial & Savings p. 1839; Commodity Contracts Brokers & Dealers p. 1996; Franchises p. 2325; Investment Guides - Online p. 2611; Mortgage Lenders & Loan Brokers p. 2778; Mutual Funds p. 2818; Investment Newsletters p. 2827; Real Estate Investment Trusts (REITs) p. 3049; Royalty Trusts p. 3141; Securities Brokers & Dealers p. 3163; Venture Capital Firms p. 3288

	City	State	Zip	Phone	Fax
ABRY Partners LLC 111 Huntington Ave 29th Fl *TF:* 800-777-3674 ■ *Web:* www.abry.com	Boston	MA	02199	617-859-2959	859-8797
Acacia Research Corp 500 Newport Ctr Dr Ste 700 *NASDAQ: ACTG* ■ *Web:* www.acaciaresearch.com	Newport Beach	CA	92660	949-480-8300	480-8301
Adams Express Co 500 E Pratt St Ste 1300 *NYSE: ADX* ■ *TF:* 800-638-2479 ■ *Web:* www.adamsexpress.com	Baltimore	MD	21202	410-752-5900	
AEA Investors Inc 666 Fifth Ave 36th Fl *Web:* www.aeainvestors.com	New York	NY	10103	212-644-5900	888-1459
Bancroft Fund Ltd 65 Madison Ave Ste 550 *NYSE: BCV*	Morristown	NJ	07960	973-631-1177	631-1313
Barry S. Nussbaum Company Inc 13151 Emily Rd *Web:* www.bncrealestate.com	Dallas	TX	75240	972-437-9900	
Central Securities Corp 630 Fifth Ave Ste 820 *NYSE: CET* ■ *TF:* 866-593-2507 ■ *Web:* www.centralsecurities.com	New York	NY	10111	212-698-2020	
Cerberus Capital Management LP 875 Third Ave *Web:* www.cerberuscapital.com	New York	NY	10022	212-891-2100	
Columbia Ventures Corp (CVC) 12503 SE Mill Plain Blvd Ste 120 *Web:* www.colventures.com	Vancouver	WA	98684	360-816-1840	
Counsel Corp 1211 Ave of the Americas Ste 2902 *NYSE: CXS* ■ *TF:* 866-296-3743 ■ *Web:* www.snl.com	New York	NY	10036	212-696-0100	696-9809
DPEC Capital Inc 135 Fifth Ave *TF:* 844-574-3577 ■ *Web:* finra.org	New York	NY	10010	301-590-6500	
Dundee Wealth Management Inc 1 Adelaide St E *Web:* dundeecorp.com	Toronto	ON	M5C2V9	416-350-3250	
Enerplus Resources Fund 3000 Dome Tower 333 7th Ave SW Ste 3000 *TF:* 800-319-6462 ■ *Web:* www.enerplus.com	Calgary	AB	T2P2Z1	403-298-2200	298-2211
Enstar USA Inc 7035 Halcyon Pk Dr *NASDAQ: ESGR* ■ *Web:* www.enstargroup.com	Montgomery	AL	36117	334-834-5483	
Eureka Growth Capital 1717 Arch St 3420 Bell Atlantic Twr *Web:* www.eurekagrowth.com	Philadelphia	PA	19103	267-238-4200	238-4201
Fairmont Capital Inc 3350 E Birch St Ste 206 *Web:* www.fairmontcapital.com	Brea	CA	92821	714-524-4770	524-4775
Fairview Capital Partners Inc 75 Isham Rd Ste 200 *Web:* www.fairviewcapital.com	West Hartford	CT	06107	860-674-8066	678-5108
Fidelity Investments Charitable Gift Fund PO Box 770001 **Fax Area Code: 877* ■ *TF:* 800-262-6039 ■ *Web:* www.fidelitycharitable.org	Cincinnati	OH	45277	800-262-6039	665-4274*
Forstmann Little & Co 767 Fifth Ave	New York	NY	10153	212-355-5656	759-9059
Fremont Group Inc 199 Fremont St *Web:* www.fremontgroup.com	San Francisco	CA	94105	415-284-8500	
Golden Gate Capital 1 Embarcadero Ctr Fl 39 *Web:* goldengatecap.com	San Francisco	CA	94111	415-983-2700	983-2701
Gores Technology Group 9800 Wilshire Blvd *Web:* www.gores.com	Beverly Hills	CA	90212	310-209-3010	209-3310
Gould Investors LP 60 Cutter Mill Rd Ste 303 *Web:* gouldlp.com	Great Neck	NY	11021	516-466-3100	
Haverford Trust Co 3 Radnor Corp Ctr Ste 450 *TF:* 888-995-1979 ■ *Web:* www.haverfordquality.com	Radnor	PA	19087	610-995-8700	995-8796
Hellman & Friedman LLC 1 Maritime Plaza 12th Fl *Web:* www.hf.com	San Francisco	CA	94111	415-788-5111	788-0176
Highland Capital Management LP 300 Crescent Ct Ste 700 *Web:* www.highlandcapital.com	Dallas	TX	75201	972-628-4100	628-4147
Hold Bros On-Line Capital 10 W 46th St Ste 2450 *Web:* www.holdbrothers.com	New York	NY	10036	212-792-0900	
HomeVestors of America Inc 6500 Greenville Ave Ste 400 *TF:* 866-200-6475 ■ *Web:* www.homevestors.com	Dallas	TX	75206	972-761-0046	761-9022
ICV Capital Partners LLC 810 7th Ave 35th Fl *Web:* naicvc.com	New York	NY	10019	212-455-9600	455-9603
Jll Partners Inc 450 Lexington Ave 31st Fl *Web:* www.jllpartners.com	New York	NY	10017	212-286-8600	286-8626
Kunath Karren Rinne & Atkin LLC 1000 Second Ave Ste 4000 *Web:* www.kkra.com	Seattle	WA	98104	206-621-7400	
Lion Chemical Capital LLC 535 Madison Ave 4th Fl *Web:* www.lionchemicalcapital.com	New York	NY	10022	212-355-5500	
Liquidnet Holdings Inc 498 Seventh Ave 12th Fl *Web:* www.liquidnet.com	New York	NY	10018	646-674-2000	674-2003
Main Street Capital Corp 1300 Post Oak Blvd *NYSE: MAIN* ■ *TF:* 800-966-1559 ■ *Web:* www.mainstcapital.com	Houston	TX	77056	713-350-6000	350-6042
McCown De Leeuw & Co (MDC) 950 Tower Ln Ste 800 *Web:* www.mdcpartners.com	Foster City	CA	94404	650-854-6000	854-0853
Moors & Cabot Inc 111 Devonshire St *TF:* 800-426-0501 ■ *Web:* www.moorscabot.com	Boston	MA	02109	617-426-0500	426-9608
Novitas Capital 435 Devon Pk Dr Ste 801 *Web:* www.novitascapital.com	Wayne	PA	19087	610-293-4075	254-4240
Pembina Pipeline Corp 585 Eighth Ave SW *TSE: PPL* ■ *TF:* 888-428-3222 ■ *Web:* www.pembina.com	Calgary	AB	T2P1G1	403-231-7500	237-0254
Platinum Equity Holdings *Platinum Equity LLC* 360 N Crescent Dr *Web:* www.platinumequity.com	Beverly Hills	CA	90210	310-712-1850	
Provender Capital Group 1841 Broadway	New York	NY	10023	212-271-8888	271-8875
Rand Capital Corp 2200 Rand Bldg *NASDAQ: RAND* ■ *Web:* www.randcapital.com	Buffalo	NY	14203	716-853-0802	854-8480
SCP Private Equity Partners 1200 Liberty Ridge Dr *Web:* www.scppartners.com	Chesterbrook	PA	19087	610-995-2900	975-9546
Sequoia Equities Inc 1777 Botelho Dr Ste 300 *Web:* www.experiencesequoia.com	Walnut Creek	CA	94596	925-945-0900	
Smith Whiley & Co 242 Trumbull St 8th Fl *Web:* www.smithwhiley.com	Hartford	CT	06103	860-548-2513	
Spell Capital Partners LLC 222 S Ninth St Ste 2880 *Web:* www.spellcapital.com	Minneapolis	MN	55402	612-371-9650	371-9651
Superior Plus Income Fund 840-7 Ave SW Ste 1400 *TF:* 866-490-7587 ■ *Web:* www.superiorplus.ca	Calgary	AB	T2P3G2	403-218-2970	218-2973
Technology Ventures Corp 1155 University Blvd SE *Web:* www.techventures.org	Albuquerque	NM	87106	505-246-2882	246-2891
Thomas H Lee Partners 100 Federal St *TF:* 877-456-3427 ■ *Web:* www.thl.com	Boston	MA	02110	617-227-1050	227-3514
Thomas Properties Group Inc 515 S Flower St 6th Fl *NYSE: TPGI*	Los Angeles	CA	90071	213-613-1900	633-4760
Tracinda Corp 150 Rodeo Dr Ste 250	Beverly Hills	CA	90212	310-271-0638	271-3416
Vulcan Inc 505 Fifth Ave S Ste 900 *Web:* www.vulcan.com	Seattle	WA	98104	206-342-2000	342-3000
Welsh Carson Anderson & Stowe 320 Pk Ave Ste 2500 *Web:* www.welshcarson.com	New York	NY	10022	212-893-9500	

406 JANITORIAL & CLEANING SUPPLIES - WHOL

	City	State	Zip	Phone	Fax
Accutemp Products Inc 8415 N Clinton Park *Web:* accutemp.net	Fort Wayne	IN	46825	260-493-0415	
Advanced Vacuum Company Inc 1215 Business Pkwy N *Web:* www.advaco.com	Westminster	MD	21157	410-876-8200	
Alliance Fire Protection Co 2114 E Cedar St *Web:* www.afpc.com	Tempe	AZ	85281	480-966-9178	
Badger Land Car Wash Equipment & Supplies LLC 300A E Oak St *Web:* www.badgerlandcarwashequipment.com	Oak Creek	WI	53154	414-764-4250	
Brady Industries Inc 7055 Lindell Rd *TF:* 800-293-4698 ■ *Web:* www.bradyindustries.com	Las Vegas	NV	89118	702-876-3990	876-1580
C&T Design & Equipment Company Inc 2750 Tobey Dr *TF:* 800-966-3374 ■ *Web:* www.c-tdesign.com	Indianapolis	IN	46219	317-898-9602	
Castle Sprinkler & Alalarm 5117 College Ave *Web:* www.csafire.com	College Park	MD	20740	301-927-7300	
Culinary Depot Inc 2 Melnick Dr *TF:* 888-845-8200 ■ *Web:* www.culinarydepotinc.com	Monsey	NY	10952	888-845-8200	
EXSL/Ultra Labs Inc 30921 Wiegman Rd *Web:* exsl.net	Hayward	CA	94544	510-324-4567	324-8881
Finley Fire Equipment Company Inc 5255 N State Rt 60 NW *Web:* www.finleyfire.com	Mcconnelsville	OH	43756	740-962-4328	
Fitch Co 2201 Russell St *TF:* 800-933-4824 ■ *Web:* www.fitchco.com	Baltimore	MD	21230	410-539-1953	727-2244
I Janvey & Sons Inc 218 Front St *Web:* www.janvey.com	Hempstead	NY	11550	516-489-9300	

Phone | Fax

Industrial Soap Co 722 S Vandeventer Ave .... Saint Louis MO 63110 314-241-6363 533-5556
TF: 800-405-7627 ■ *Web:* www.industrialsoap.com

J. Ennis Fabrics Ltd 12122 - 68 St .... Edmonton AB T5B1R1 800-663-6647
TF: 800-663-6647 ■ *Web:* www.jennisfabrics.com

Kellermeyer Co 475 W Woodland Cir............Bowling Green OH 43402 419-255-3022 255-2752
TF: 800-445-7415

Kenway Distributors Inc
6320 Strawberry Ln ....Louisville KY 40214 502-367-2201 368-5519
Web: www.kenway.net

Mobile Fixture & Equipment Company Inc
1155 Montlimar Dr...............................Mobile AL 36609 251-342-0455
Web: www.mobilefixture.com

Mortech Manufacturing Inc 411 N Aerojet Ave..........Azusa CA 91702 626-334-1471
Web: mortechmfg.com

Rose Products & Services Inc 545 Stimmel Rd....... Columbus OH 43223 614-443-7647 443-2771
TF: 800-264-1568 ■ *Web:* hillyard.com

Sani-Clean Distributors 57 Industrial Way ....Portland ME 04103 207-797-8240

Shadow Beverages & Snacks LLC
4650 E Cotton Ctr Blvd Ste 240 ....Phoenix AZ 85040 480-371-1100
Web: www.shadowbev.com

Standard Companies Inc, The
2601 S Archer Ave ....Chicago IL 60608 312-225-2777
Web: www.thestandardcompanies.com

Taylor Freezers of California
221 Harris Ct ....South San Francisco CA 94080 877-978-4800
TF: 877-978-4800 ■ *Web:* www.taylorfreezers.com

407 JEWELERS' FINDINGS & MATERIALS

Phone | Fax

10G LLC 100 Morey Dr ....Woodridge IL 60517 630-754-2400
Web: www.10g.com

A & D Technology Inc 4622 Runway Blvd .... Ann Arbor MI 48108 734-973-1111
Web: www.aanddtech.com

Absolute Analysis Inc
2393 Teller Rd Ste 109......................... Newbury Park CA 91320 805-376-6048
Web: www.absoluteanalysis.com

Advanced Mechanical Technology Inc
176 Waltham St ....Watertown MA 02472 617-926-6700
Web: www.amti.biz

Affinity Biosensors LLC
1221 Chapala St Ste B .... Santa Barbara CA 93101 805-960-5100
Web: www.lifescaleast.com

Ag Leader Technology Inc 2202 S River Side Dr..........Ames IA 50010 515-232-5363
Web: agleader.com

Amber Precision Instruments Inc
746 San Aleso Ave ....Sunnyvale CA 94085 408-752-0199
Web: www.amberpi.com

AmbiCom Holdings Inc 500 Alder Dr..................Milpitas CA 95035 408-321-0822
Web: www.ambicom.com

American Automatrix Inc 1 Technology Ln .... Export PA 15632 724-733-2000
Web: www.aamatrix.com

Ampex Casting Corp 23 W 47th St 4th Fl.............New York NY 10036 212-719-1318 719-3493

ANDalyze Inc 2109 S Oak St Ste 102................ Champaign IL 61820 217-328-0045
Web: www.andalyze.com

Andrews Industrial Controls 108 Rosslyn Rd .... Carnegie PA 15106 412-279-5335
Web: www.andrewsic.com

Ashcroft Inc 250 E Main St......................... Stratford CT 06614 203-378-8281
Web: www.ashcroftinc.com

Aspect Automation LLC 1185 Willow Lk Blvd......... Saint Paul MN 55110 651-643-3700
Web: www.aspectautomation.com

AutoSeis Inc 2101 Midway Rd Ste 310............. Carrollton TX 75006 972-332-3388
Web: www.autoseis.net

Avalon Vision Solutions LLC
422 Thornton Rd Ste 104 .... Lithia Springs GA 30122 770-944-8445
Web: www.avalonvision.com

B&W Tek Inc 19 Shea Way Ste 301.................... Newark DE 19713 302-368-7824
Web: www.bwtek.com

Best Priced Products Inc 3 Westchester Plz........... Elmsford NY 10523 914-345-3800
Web: www.bpp2.com

Bizerba USA Inc 31 Gordon Rd.....................Piscataway NJ 08854 732-565-6000
Web: www.bizerba.com

Boon Edam Inc 402 McKinney Pkwy.................Lillington NC 27546 910-814-3800
Web: www.boonedam.us

Boulder Innovation Group Inc
4824 Sterling Dr................................. Boulder CO 80301 303-447-0248
Web: www.imageguided.com

BrightSign LLC 16795 Lark Ave Ste 200 .... Los Gatos CA 95032 408-852-9263
Web: www.brightsign.biz

Brooks Instrument LLC 407 W Vine St .... Hatfield PA 19440 215-362-3500
Web: www.brooksinstrument.com

Capstone Metering LLC 1600 Capital Ave Ste 200 ....Plano TX 75074 214-469-1065
Web: www.intellih2o.com

CDEX Inc 4555 S Palo Verde Ste 123................... Tucson AZ 85714 520-745-5172
Web: www.cdex-inc.com

Chauvin Arnoux Inc 15 Faraday Dr.....................Dover NH 03820 603-749-6434
Web: www.aemc.com

Coastal Environmental Systems Inc
820 First Ave S.................................... Seattle WA 98134 206-682-6048
Web: www.coastalenvironmental.com

Comark Instruments Inc
Bldg 50-209 PO Box 500......................... Beaverton OR 97077 503-643-5204
Web: www.comarkinstruments.net

Control Module Inc 89 Phoenix Ave..................... Enfield CT 06082 860-745-2433
Web: www.controlmod.com

COSA Xentaur Corp 84G Horseblock Rd................. Yaphank NY 11980 631-345-3434
Web: www.cosaxentaur.com

Craftstones PO Box 847 ....Ramona CA 92065 760-789-1620 789-3432
Web: www.craftstones.com

Cranesmart Systems Inc 4908 97 St NW .... Edmonton AB T6E5S1 780-437-2986 438-9491
TF: 888-562-3222 ■ *Web:* cranesmart.com

Phone | Fax

CW Brabender Instruments Inc
50 E Wesley St..........................South Hackensack NJ 07606 201-343-8425
Web: www.cwbrabender.com

Cyber-Rain Inc 6345 Balboa Blvd Ste 230 ....Encino CA 91316 877-888-1452
TF: 877-888-1452 ■ *Web:* www.cyber-rain.com

Data Physics Corp 2480 N 1ST ST Ste 100 .... San Jose CA 95131 408-437-0100
Web: www.dataphysics.com

David H Fell & Company Inc
6009 Bandini Blvd ....Commerce CA 90040 323-722-9992 722-6567
TF: 800-822-1996 ■ *Web:* www.dhfco.com

Delta Controls Inc 17850 - 56th Ave .... Surrey BC V3S1C7 604-574-9444 574-7793
Web: www.deltacontrols.com

Delta M Corp 1003 Larsen Dr .... Oak Ridge TN 37830 800-922-0083
TF: 800-922-0083 ■ *Web:* www.deltamcorp.com

DEVAR Inc 706 Bostwick Ave......................Bridgeport CT 06605 203-368-6751
Web: www.devarinc.com

dpiX LLC 1635 Aeroplaza Dr .... Colorado Springs CO 80916 719-457-7700
Web: www.dpix.com

DTN.IQ Inc 9110 W Dodge Rd Ste 200..................Omaha NE 68114 402-390-2328
Web: www.interquote.com

EHT International Inc
1340 Gay Lussac Ste 10......................... Boucherville QC J4B7G4 450-906-0705
Web: www.ehtinternational.com

Embraer Aircraft Maintenance Services Inc
10 Airways Blvd ....Nashville TN 37217 615-367-2100
Web: www.embraerexecutivejets.com

Emme E2MS LLC PO Box 2251 .... Bristol CT 06011 800-396-0523
TF: 800-396-0523 ■ *Web:* www.getemme.com

Environmental Systems Products Inc
7 Kripes Rd.....................................East Granby CT 06026 860-392-2100
Web: www.esp-global.com

ET Water Systems LLC
384 Bel Marin Keys Blvd Ste 145.....................Novato CA 94949 415-945-9383
Web: www.etwater.com

Eyedro Green Solutions Inc
151 Charles St W Ste 100.........................Kitchener ON N2G1H6 226-499-0944
Web: eyedro.com

FBS Inc 3340 W College Ave.......................State College PA 16801 814-234-3437
Web: www.fbsworldwide.com

FCT Assembly Inc 1309 N 17th Ave .... Greeley CO 80631 970-346-8002
Web: www.fctassembly.com

Findings Inc 160 Water St........................... Keene NH 03431 603-352-3717
TF: 800-225-2706 ■ *Web:* leachgarner.com

Fireye Inc 3 Manchester Rd .... Derry NH 03038 603-432-4100
Web: www.fireye.com

Flexstar Technology Inc 1965 Concourse Dr..........San Jose CA 95131 408-643-7000
Web: www.flexstar.com

FoodChek Systems Inc 1414 8 St. S.W. Ste 450......... Calgary AB T2R1J6 403-269-9424
TF: 877-298-0208 ■ *Web:* www.foodcheksystems.com

Fossil Power Systems Inc
10 Mosher Dr Burnside Industrial Park..............Dartmouth AB B3B1N5 902-468-2743
Web: www.fossil.ca

Fugro-Roadware Inc 2505 Meadowvale Blvd........ Mississauga ON L5N5S2 905-567-2870
TF: 800-828-2726 ■ *Web:* www.roadware.com

GeoDigital International Inc
175 Longwood Rd S McMaster Innovation Park
Ste 400A.......................................Hamilton ON L8P0A1 905-667-7204 388-0501*
**Fax Area Code: 250* ■ *Web:* www.geodigital.com

George Kelk Corp 48 Lesmill Rd..................... Toronto ON M3B2T5 416-445-5850
TF: 888-275-5355 ■ *Web:* www.kelk.com

Gordon-Darby Inc 2410 Ampere Dr..................Louisville KY 40299 502-266-5797
Web: www.gordon-darby.com

Governor Control Systems Inc
3101 SW Third Ave.........................Fort Lauderdale FL 33315 954-462-7404
Web: www.govconsys.com

GroundMetrics Inc 4217 Ponderosa Ave Ste A .... San Diego CA 92123 619-786-8023
Web: www.groundmetrics.com

Guardian Interlock Systems of Northeast Georgia Inc
228 Church St ....Marietta GA 30060 770-499-0499
Web: www.guardianinterlock.com

Heat-Timer Corp 20 New Dutch Ln.................... Fairfield NJ 07004 973-575-4004
Web: www.heat-timer.com

Helitune Inc 190 Gordon St..................Elk Grove Village IL 60007 847-228-0985
Web: www.helitune.com

Hortau Inc 3485 Sacramento Dr Ste B .... San Luis Obispo CA 93401 418-839-2852 839-2851
Web: www.hortau.com

Humboldt Manufacturing Co 875 Tollgate Rd .... Elgin IL 60123 708-456-6300
TF: 800-544-7220 ■ *Web:* www.humboldtmfg.com

HydroPoint Data Systems Inc
1720 Corporate Cir...............................Petaluma CA 94954 707-769-9696
Web: www.hydropoint.com

Image Sensing Systems Inc
500 Spruce Tree Centre 1600 University Ave ....St. Paul MN 55104 651-603-7700
Web: www.imagesensing.com

Interocean Systems 3738 Ruffin Rd................San Diego CA 92123 858-565-8400
Web: www.interoceansystems.com

Intoximeters Inc 2081 Craig Rd .... Saint Louis MO 63146 314-429-4000
Web: www.intox.com

IRD LLC 4740 Allmond Ave..........................Louisville KY 40209 502-366-0916
Web: www.irdbalancing.com

James A Murphy & Son Inc
50 Colorado Ave PO Box 3006.................South Attleboro MA 02703 508-761-5060
Web: patch.com/attleboro

JASCO Inc 28600 Mary's Ct .... Easton MD 21601 410-822-1220
Web: www.jascoinc.com

Kahan Jewelry Corp 1156 Ave......................New York NY 10036 212-719-1055

Karbra Co 151 W 46th St 10th Fl ....New York NY 10036 212-736-9300
Web: karbra.com

Kejr Inc 1835 Wall St................................ Salina KS 67401 785-825-1842
Web: geoprobe.com

Kent Scientific Corp 1116 Litchfield St ....Torrington CT 06790 860-626-1172
Web: www.kentscientific.com

Kinemotive Corp 222 Central Ave................. Farmingdale NY 11735 631-249-6440
Web: www.kinemotive.com

Phone Fax

Kratos Analytical Inc
100 Red Schoolhouse Rd Bldg A ... Chestnut Ridge NY 10977 845-426-6700
Web: www.kratos.com

Krohn Industries Inc PO Box 98 ... Carlstadt NJ 07072 201-933-9696 933-9684
TF: 800-526-6299 ■ *Web:* www.krohnindustries.com

Kuster Co 2900 E 29th St ... Long Beach CA 90806 562-595-0661
Web: www.kusterco.com

Labsphere Inc 231 Shaker St ... North Sutton NH 03260 603-927-4266
Web: www.labsphere.com

Lazare Kaplan International Inc
19 W 44th St 16th Fl ... New York NY 10036 212-764-7201
OTC: LKII ■ *Web:* www.lazarediamonds.com

Lee's Morvillo Group 160 Niantic Ave ... Providence RI 02907 401-353-1740
TF: 800-821-1700 ■ *Web:* www.leesmfg.com

Lifeloc Technologies Inc
12441 W 49th Ave Unit 4 ... Wheat Ridge CO 80033 303-431-9500
Web: www.lifeloc.com

LMG Holdings Inc 4290 Glendale Milford Rd ... Blue Ash OH 45242 513-651-9560
Web: www.lifesafer.com

Loadstar Sensors Inc
48501 Warm Springs Blvd Ste 109 ... Fremont CA 94539 510-274-1872
Web: www.loadstarsensors.com

LPA Designs 21 Gregory Dr Ste 140 ... South Burlington VT 05403 802-658-0038
Web: www.lpadesign.com

Magic Novelty Inc 308 Dyckman St ... New York NY 10034 212-304-2777 567-2809
Web: www.magicnovelty.com

Measurement Technology Group Inc
1310 Emerald Rd ... Greenwood SC 29646 864-223-1212
Web: www.redsealmeasurement.com

Meriam Process Technologies Inc
10920 Madison Ave ... Cleveland OH 44102 216-281-1100
Web: www.meriam.com

Met One Instruments Inc
1600 Washington Blvd ... Grants Pass OR 97526 541-471-7111
Web: www.metone.com

Micron Optics Inc 1852 Century Pl NE ... Atlanta GA 30345 404-325-0005
Web: www.micronoptics.com

MicroSense LLC 205 Industrial Ave E ... Lowell MA 01852 978-843-7673
Web: www.microsense.net

Modern Machine & Tool Company Inc
11844 Jefferson Ave ... Newport News VA 23606 757-873-1212
TF: 800-482-1835 ■ *Web:* www.mmtool.com

MRU Instruments Inc 6699 Portwest Dr Ste 130 ... Houston TX 77024 713-426-3260
Web: www.mru-instruments.com

MSP Corp 5910 Rice Creek Pkwy Ste 300 ... Shoreview MN 55126 651-287-8100
Web: www.mspcorp.com

MTI Instruments Inc 325 Washington Ave Ext ... Albany NY 12205 518-218-2550
Web: www.mtiinstruments.com

Nanovea 6 Morgan Ste 156 ... Irvine CA 92618 949-461-9292
Web: nanovea.com

NCI Technologies Inc 636 Cure-Boivin Blvd ... Boisbriand QC J7G2A7 450-434-7222
Web: www.ncitech.ca

New Frontier Electronics Inc
6131 Kellers Church Rd ... Pipersville PA 18947 215-766-1240
Web: www.surgex.com

Newage Testing Instruments Inc
820 Pennsylvania Blvd ... Feasterville PA 19053 215-355-6900
Web: www.hardnesstesters.com

Nidec Avtron Automation Corp
7555 E Pleasant Vly Rd Bldg 100 ... Independence OH 44131 216-642-1230
Web: www.nidec-avtron.com

Northern Digital Inc 103 Randall Dr ... Waterloo ON N2V1C5 519-884-5142
TF: 877-634-6340 ■ *Web:* www.ndigital.com

Nutfield Technology Inc 1 Wall St Ste 115 ... Hudson NH 03051 603-893-6200
Web: www.nutfieldtech.com

OmniMetrix LLC 5225 Belle Wood Ct ... Buford GA 30518 770-209-0012
Web: www.omnimetrix.net

OndaVia Inc 26102 Eden Landing Rd Ste 1 ... Hayward CA 94545 510-887-3180
Web: www.ondavia.com

Optel Vision Inc
2680, boul. du Parc Technologique ... Quebec QC G1P4S6 418-688-0334 688-9397
Web: www.optelvision.com

OptoAtmospherics Inc 1777 Highland Dr Ste B ... Ann Arbor MI 48108 734-975-8777
Web: www.optoatmospherics.com

Paroscientific Inc 4500 148th Ave Ne ... Redmond WA 98052 425-883-8700
Web: www.paroscientific.com

Paul H Gesswein & Co 255 Hancock Ave ... Bridgeport CT 06605 203-366-5400 366-3953
TF: 800-544-2043 ■ *Web:* www.gesswein.com

Piezotech LLC 8431 Georgetown Rd Ste 300 ... Indianapolis IN 46268 317-876-4670
Web: www.piezotechnologies.com

Pillar Innovations LLC 92 Corporate Dr ... Grantsville MD 21536 301-245-4007
Web: www.pillarinnovations.com

Polimaster Inc 2300 Clarendon Blvd Ste 708 ... Arlington VA 22201 703-525-5075
Web: www.polimaster.us

PowerOneData Inc
1201 S Alma School Rd Mesa Financial Ctr
Ste 229 ... Mesa AZ 85210 480-668-0700
Web: www.p1di.com

Precision Specialties Co 1201 East Pecan St ... Sherman TX 75090 800-527-3295 893-2328*
**Fax Area Code:* 903 ■ *TF:* 800-527-3295 ■ *Web:* www.presco.com

Precision Time Systems Inc 349 McKay Rd ... Bolivia NC 28422 910-253-9850
Web: www.precisiontime.com

ProvibTech Inc 11011 Brooklet Dr Ste 300 ... Houston TX 77099 713-830-7601
Web: www.provibtech.com

QualMark Corp 10390 E 48th Ave ... Denver CO 80238 303-254-8800
Web: www.qualmark.com

Rad-Comm Systems Corp 7522 Bath Rd ... Mississauga ON L4T1L2 905-678-6503
Web: www.radcommsystems.com

Radiant Zemax LLC
22908 NE Alder Crest Dr Ste 100 ... Redmond WA 98053 425-844-0152
Web: www.radimg.com

Rainwise Inc 25 Federal St ... Bar Harbor ME 04609 207-288-5169
TF: 800-762-5723 ■ *Web:* www.rainwise.com

Phone Fax

Rees Scientific Corp 1007 Whitehead Rd Ext ... Trenton NJ 08638 609-530-1055
Web: www.reesscientific.com

ReVera Inc 3090 Oakmead Village Dr ... Santa Clara CA 95051 408-510-7400
Web: www.revera.com

Romanoff International Supply Corp
9 Deforest St ... Amityville NY 11701 631-842-2400 842-0028
TF Cust Svc: 800-221-7448 ■ *Web:* www.romanoff.com

Romet Ltd 1080 Matheson Blvd East ... Mississauga ON L4W2V2 905-624-1591 624-5668
TF: 800-387-3201 ■ *Web:* www.rometlimited.com

S Himmelstein & Co 2490 Pembroke Ave ... Hoffman Estates IL 60169 847-843-3300
Web: www.himmelstein.com

Santa Barbara Control Systems
5375 Overpass Rd ... Santa Barbara CA 93111 805-683-8833
Web: www.sbcontrol.com

Satlantic Inc
Richmond Terminal Pier 9 3481 N Marginal Rd ... Halifax NS B3K5X8 902-492-4780
Web: www.satlantic.com

Saunders & Associates LLC
2520 E Rose Garden Ln ... Phoenix AZ 85050 602-971-9977
Web: www.saunders-assoc.com

Schenck AccuRate Inc
746 E Milwaukee St PO Box 208 ... Whitewater WI 53190 262-473-2441
Web: www.accuratefeeders.com

SECO Manufacturing Company Inc 4155 Oasis Rd ... Redding CA 96003 530-225-8155
Web: www.surveying.com

Senet Inc 94 River Rd Ste 101 ... Hudson NH 03051 603-880-8484
Web: www.enertrac.com

Sentient Energy Inc 880 Mitten Rd ... Burlingame CA 94010 650-523-6680
Web: www.sentient-energy.com

SepSensor Inc 257 Simarano Dr Annex II ... Marlborough MA 01752 508-229-2291

SIE Computing Solutions Inc 10 Mupac Dr ... Brockton MA 02301 508-588-6110
TF: 800-926-8722 ■ *Web:* sie-cs.com

Signalisation Ver-Mac Inc 1781 Bresse ... Quebec QC G2G2V2 418-654-1303 654-0517
TF: 888-488-7446 ■ *Web:* www.ver-mac.com

SIX Safety Systems Inc
250031 Mountain View Trail Ste 1 ... Calgary AB T3Z3S3 403-932-7955
Web: www.sixsafetysystems.com

Solmetric Corp 117 Morris St Ste 100 ... Sebastopol CA 95472 707-823-4600
Web: www.solmetric.com

Sotax Corp 2400 Computer Dr ... Westborough MA 01581 508-417-1112
Web: www.sotax.com

Source Production & Equipment Company Inc
113 Teal St ... Saint Rose LA 70087 504-464-9471
Web: www.spec150.com

Space Optics Research Labs LLC
7 Stuart Rd ... Chelmsford MA 01824 978-250-8640
TF: 800-552-7675 ■ *Web:* www.sorl.com

Spectral Applied Research Inc
9078 Leslie St Unit 11 ... Richmond Hill ON L4B3L8 905-326-5040
Web: www.spectral.ca

Sri Instruments Inc 20720 Earl St ... Torrance CA 90503 702-361-2210
Web: www.srigc.com

Strainsert Inc 12 Union Hill Rd ... West Conshohocken PA 19428 610-825-3310
Web: www.strainsert.com

Stuller Settings Inc PO Box 87777 ... Lafayette LA 70598 800-877-7777 444-4741
TF: 800-877-7777 ■ *Web:* www.stuller.com

Sumitomo (SHI) Cryogenics of America Inc
1833 Vultee Sreet ... Allentown PA 18103 610-791-6700
Web: www.shicryogenics.com

Super Systems Inc 7205 Edington Dr ... Cincinnati OH 45249 513-772-0060
Web: www.supersystems.com

SymCom Inc 222 Disk Dr ... Rapid City SD 57701 605-348-5580
TF: 800-843-8848 ■ *Web:* www.symcom.com

TAC Americas Inc 1650 W Crosby Rd ... Carrollton TX 75006 972-323-1111

Tavis Corp 3636 State Hwy 49 S ... Mariposa CA 95338 209-966-2027
Web: www.taviscorp.com

Techmor Inc 19911-D N Cove Rd ... Cornelius NC 28031 336-442-3686
Web: www.techmor.com

Test Evolution Corp 102 S St ... Hopkinton MA 01748 781-644-2111
Web: www.testevolution.com

Testek Inc 28320 Lakeview Dr ... Wixom MI 48393 248-573-4980
Web: www.testek.com

Tornado Spectral Systems
555 Richmond St W Ste 705 Ste 705 ... Toronto ON M5V3B1 416-361-3444
Web: tornado-spectral.com

Unholtz-Dickie Corp 6 Brookside Dr ... Wallingford CT 06492 203-265-3929
Web: www.udco.com

Veris Industries Inc 16640 SW 72nd Ave ... Portland OR 97224 503-598-4564
Web: www.veris.com

Viconics Technologies Inc
9245 Langelier Blvd ... Saint-Leonard QC H1P3K9 514-321-5660
TF: 800-563-5660 ■ *Web:* www.viconics.com

Victor Settings Inc 25 Brook Ave ... Maywood NJ 07607 201-845-4433 712-0818
TF: 800-322-9008 ■ *Web:* www.victorsettings.com

William Goldberg Diamond Corp 589 Fifth Ave ... New York NY 10017 212-980-4343
Web: www.williamgoldberg.com

Wireless Seismic Inc
13100 Southwest Fwy Ste 150 ... Sugar Land TX 77478 832-532-5080
Web: www.wirelessseismic.com

Xensor Corp 4000 Bridge St ... Drexel Hill PA 19026 610-284-2508
Web: www.xensor.com

Zepp Labs Inc 20 S Santa Cruz Ave Ste 102 ... Los Gatos CA 95030 408-884-8077
Web: www.zepp.com

408 JEWELRY - COSTUME

Phone Fax

1928 Jewelry Co 3000 W Empire Ave ... Burbank CA 91504 818-841-1928
TF: 800-227-1928 ■ *Web:* www.1928.com

A & Z Hayward Co 655 Waterman Ave ... East Providence RI 02914 401-438-0550 438-6970
TF: 800-556-7462 ■ *Web:* www.azhayward.com

	City	State	Zip	Phone	Fax
American Ring Company Inc 19 Grosvenor Ave	East Providence	RI	02914	401-438-9060	438-3806
Arden Jewelry Manufacturing Co 10 Industrial Ln *Web:* www.ardenjewelry.com	Johnston	RI	02919	401-274-9800	
C & J Jewelry Company Inc 100 Dupont Dr *TF:* 888-527-4268 ■ *Web:* www.candjjewelry.com	Providence	RI	02907	401-944-2200	
Donald Bruce & Co 3600 N Talman Ave	Chicago	IL	60618	773-477-8100	
FGX International Inc 500 George Washington Hwy *Web:* fgxi.com	Smithfield	RI	02917	401-231-3800	
Gem-Craft Inc 1420 Elmwood Ave	Cranston	RI	02910	401-854-1200	
Jewelry Fashions Inc 385 Fifth Ave *Web:* www.robertrose.com	New York	NY	10016	212-947-7700	
Kirk's Folly 236 Chapman St *Web:* www.kirksfolly.com	Providence	RI	02905	401-941-4300	
Shira Accessories Ltd 28 W 36th St	New York	NY	10018	212-594-4455	
Speidel Corp 1425 Cranston St **Fax Area Code:* 800 ■ *Web:* www.speidel.com	Cranston	RI	02920	401-519-2000	928-2423*
Swank Inc 656 Joseph Warner Blvd *Web:* swankinc.com	Taunton	MA	02780	508-822-2527	

409 JEWELRY - PRECIOUS METAL

	City	State	Zip	Phone	Fax
American Achievement Corp 7211 Cir S Rd *TF:* 800-531-5055 ■ *Web:* www.artcarved.com	Austin	TX	78745	512-444-0571	443-5213
Armbrust International Ltd 735 Allens Ave *Web:* www.armbrustintl.com	Providence	RI	02905	401-781-3300	781-2590
Balfour 7211 Cir S Rd *TF:* 800-225-3687 ■ *Web:* www.balfour.com	Austin	TX	78745	800-225-3687	
Byard F Brogan Inc PO Box 0369 *TF:* 800-232-7642 ■ *Web:* www.bfbrogan.com	Glenside	PA	19038	215-885-3550	885-1366
Danecraft Inc 1 Baker St *Web:* www.danecraft.com	Providence	RI	02905	401-941-7700	
David Yurman Designs Inc 24 Vestry St *Web:* www.davidyurman.com	New York	NY	10013	212-896-1550	
Diablo Mfg Company Inc 900 Golden Gate Terr PO Box 1108 *TF Cust Svc:* 800-551-2233 ■ *Web:* www.diablosilver.com	Grass Valley	CA	95945	530-272-2241	272-2243
Esposito Jewelry Inc 225 DuPont Dr	Providence	RI	02907	401-943-1900	
Gem East Corp 2124 Second Ave *Web:* www.gemeast.com	Seattle	WA	98121	206-441-1700	
Gemveto Jewelry Company Inc 18 E 48th St Ste 502 *Web:* www.gemveto.com	New York	NY	10017	212-755-2522	755-2027
Hammerman Bros Inc 50 W 57th St 12th Fl *TF:* 800-223-6436 ■ *Web:* www.hammermanbrothers.com	New York	NY	10019	212-956-2800	956-2769
Harry Klitzner Co, The 530 Wellington Ave Ste 11 *TF:* 800-621-0161 ■ *Web:* www.klitzner.com	Cranston	RI	02910	800-621-0161	622-9802
Harry Winston Inc 718 Fifth Ave *TF:* 800-988-4110 ■ *Web:* www.harrywinston.com	New York	NY	10019	212-399-1000	489-6715
Ira Green Inc 177 Georgia Ave *TF General:* 800-663-7487 ■ *Web:* www.iragreen.com	Providence	RI	02905	401-467-4770	
Jacmel Jewelry Inc 3030 47th Ave *TF:* 800-945-4300 ■ *Web:* www.jacmel.com	Long Island	NY	11101	800-945-4300	
James Avery Craftsman Inc 145 Avery Rd N *TF:* 800-283-1770 ■ *Web:* www.jamesavery.com	Kerrville	TX	78029	830-895-1122	
Jostens Inc 3601 Minnesota Ave Ste 400 **Fax:* Hum Res ■ *TF:* 800-235-4774 ■ *Web:* www.jostens.com	Minneapolis	MN	55435	952-830-3300	830-3293*
Kinsley & Sons Inc 24 S Church St Ste A *TF General:* 800-468-4428 ■ *Web:* www.gothic-jewelry.com	Union	MO	63084	800-468-4428	
Maui Divers of Hawaii 1520 Liona St *TF:* 800-462-4454 ■ *Web:* www.mauidivers.com	Honolulu	HI	96814	808-946-7979	946-0406
Mtm Recognition Corp 3201 SE 29th St *TF:* 877-686-7464 ■ *Web:* www.mtmrecognition.com	Oklahoma City	OK	73115	405-670-4545	670-0619
Novell Design Studio 2100 Felver Ct **Fax Area Code:* 908 ■ *TF:* 888-668-3551 ■ *Web:* www.novelldesignstudio.com	Rahway	NJ	07065	888-668-3551	245-5090*
OC Tanner Co 1930 S State St **Fax Area Code:* 801 ■ *TF:* 800-453-7490 ■ *Web:* www.octanner.com	Salt Lake City	UT	84115	800-453-7490	493-3013*
Oro-Cal Mfg Company Inc 1720 Bird St *Web:* www.orocal.com	Oroville	CA	95965	530-533-5065	
Ostbye & Anderson Inc 10055 51st Ave N **Fax Area Code:* 877 ■ *TF:* 866-553-1515 ■ *Web:* www.ostbye.com	Minneapolis	MN	55442	763-553-1515	553-1515*
Paris 1624 Knowlton St *Web:* www.paristiaras.com	Cincinnati	OH	45223	513-542-8345	
Relios Inc 6815 Academy Pkwy W NE *TF:* 800-827-6543 ■ *Web:* www.carolynpollack.com	Albuquerque	NM	87109	505-345-5304	
Robert S Fisher & Company Inc 280 Sheffield St *TF:* 800-526-8052 ■ *Web:* www.rsfisher.com	Mountainside	NJ	07092	908-928-0002	928-0092
Stamper Black Hills Gold Jewelry 7201 S Hwy 16 *Web:* www.stamperbhg.com	Rapid City	SD	57702	605-342-0751	343-9783
Stanley Creations Inc 1414 Willow Ave *TF:* 800-220-1414 ■ *Web:* www.stanleycreations.com	Melrose Park	PA	19027	215-635-6200	635-2708
Sunshine Minting Inc 7600 Mineral Dr Ste 700 *TF:* 800-274-5837 ■ *Web:* www.sunshinemint.com	Coeur d'Alene	ID	83815	208-772-9592	772-9739
Tache USA Inc 550 Fifth Ave *Web:* www.tacheusa.com	New York	NY	10036	212-371-1234	852-4961
Terryberry Co 2033 Oak Industrial Dr NE *TF:* 800-253-0882 ■ *Web:* www.terryberry.com	Grand Rapids	MI	49505	616-458-1391	
Tiffany & Co 727 Fifth Ave *NYSE:* TIF ■ *TF Orders:* 800-526-0649 ■ *Web:* www.tiffany.com	New York	NY	10022	212-755-8000	
Trebor Enterprises Ltd 927 W Stephenson St	Freeport	IL	61032	815-235-1700	
Tru-Kay Manufacturing Co 2 Carol Dr	Lincoln	RI	02865	401-333-2105	
Uncas Manufacturing Co 150 Niantic Ave	Providence	RI	02907	401-944-4700	943-2951
Wheeler Mfg Co Inc 107 Main Ave PO Box 629 *TF:* 800-843-1937 ■ *Web:* www.wheelerjewelry.com	Lemmon	SD	57638	605-374-3848	374-3655
Wright & Lato 2100 Felver Ct *TF:* 800-724-1855 ■ *Web:* www.wrightandlato.com	Rahway	NJ	07065	973-674-8700	674-6964

410 JEWELRY STORES

	City	State	Zip	Phone	Fax
Aires Jewelers Co 3 Harrison Ave *Web:* airesjewelers.com	Morris Plains	NJ	07950	973-292-0950	
Alvin Goldfarb Jeweler of Seattle Inc 305 Bellevue Way Ne *Web:* agjeweler.com	Bellevue	WA	98004	425-454-9393	
Argo & Lehne Jewelers Inc 3100 Tremont Rd *Web:* argolehne.com	Columbus	OH	43221	614-457-6261	
Arthur Groom & Company Inc 262 E Ridgewood Ave *Web:* www.arthurgroom.com	Ridgewood	NJ	07450	201-670-0300	
Aucoin-Hart 1525 Metairie Rd *TF:* 800-992-8743 ■ *Web:* aucoinhart.com	Metairie	LA	70005	504-834-9999	
B C Clark Inc 12042 N May Ave *Web:* www.bcclark.com	Oklahoma City	OK	73120	405-755-4040	
Ben Amun Company Inc 246 W 38th St Fl 12a *Web:* www.ben-amun.com	New York	NY	10018	212-944-6480	944-9625
Ben Bridge Jeweler Inc PO Box 1908 *TF Cust Svc:* 888-917-9171 ■ *Web:* www.benbridge.com	Seattle	WA	98111	206-239-6811	
Ben Moss Jewellers 300-201 Portage Ave *TF:* 888-236-6677 ■ *Web:* www.benmoss.com	Winnipeg	MB	R3B3K6	204-947-6682	
Bergstrom Jewelers Inc 1695 W End Blvd *Web:* bergstromjewelers.com	St Louis Park	MN	55416	952-767-0606	
Betteridge Jewelers Inc 117 Greenwich Ave *Web:* www.betteridge.com	Greenwich	CT	06830	203-869-0124	
Birks & Mayors Inc 1240 du Sq-Phillips St *TF:* 800-758-2511 ■ *Web:* www.birksandmayors.com	Montreal	QC	H3B3H4	800-758-2511	
Blue Nile Inc 705 Fifth Ave S Ste 900 *NASDAQ:* NILE ■ *TF:* 800-242-2728 ■ *Web:* www.bluenile.com	Seattle	WA	98104	206-336-6700	
Bluedial.com 3622 N Rancho Dr *Web:* www.bluedial.com	Las Vegas	NV	89130	702-645-5260	
Bobby Wilkerson Inc 222 S Main St *Web:* www.wilkersons.com	Stuttgart	AR	72160	870-673-4441	
Borsheim's Inc 120 Regency Pkwy *TF:* 800-642-4438 ■ *Web:* www.borsheims.com	Omaha	NE	68114	402-391-0400	391-6694
Brian Gavin Diamonds 7322 Southwest Frwy Ste 1810 - Arena One *Web:* www.briangavindiamonds.com	Houston	TX	77074	713-574-6666	
Charm Jewelry Ltd 140 Portland St *Web:* charmdiamondcentres.com	Dartmouth	NS	B2Y1J1	902-463-7177	
Coleman E Adler & Sons Inc 722 Canal St *TF:* 800-925-7912 ■ *Web:* www.adlersjewelry.com	New Orleans	LA	70130	504-523-5292	568-0610
Color Merchants 6 E 45th St Rm 1704 *Web:* www.colormerchants.com	New York	NY	10017	212-682-4788	
Cooper & Company Inc 10179 Commerce Park Dr *Web:* www.dakotawatchsales.com	Cincinnati	OH	45246	513-671-6067	
Corbo Jewelers Inc 58 Pk Ave *Web:* www.corbojewelers.com	Rutherford	NJ	07070	201-438-4454	438-3108
De Von's Jewelers Inc 1689 Arden Way *Web:* www.devonsjewelers.com	Sacramento	CA	95815	916-929-3991	
DGSE Cos Inc 11311 Reeder Rd *NYSE:* DGSE ■ *TF:* 800-527-5307 ■ *Web:* www.dgse.com	Dallas	TX	75229	972-484-3662	
Diamond Cellar Inc 6280 Sawmill Rd *Web:* www.diamondcellar.com	Dublin	OH	43017	614-336-4545	
Don Roberto Jewelers Inc 1020 Calle Recordo Ste 100 *Web:* www.donrobertojewelers.com	San Clemente	CA	92673	949-361-6700	
Dunkin's Diamonds Inc 897 Hebron Rd *TF:* 877-343-4883 ■ *Web:* www.dunkinsdiamonds.com	Heath	OH	43056	877-343-4883	
Ed Levin Inc 52 W Main St *Web:* www.edlevinjewelry.com	Cambridge	NY	12816	518-677-8595	
Elegant Illusions Inc 542 Lighthouse Ave Ste 5 *Web:* www.elegant-illusions.com	Pacific Grove	CA	93950	831-649-1814	649-1001
Ernest Bock Jewelers 226 W Portal Ave	San Francisco	CA	94127	415-681-5362	
Fantasy Diamond Corp 1550 W Carrol Ave *TF:* 800-621-4445 ■ *Web:* endlessdiamond.com	Chicago	IL	60607	312-583-3200	583-3434
Fashion Time 2700 Potomac Mills Cir *Web:* www.shopfashiontime.com	Woodbridge	VA	22192	703-490-1556	
Finks Jewelry Inc 3545 Electric Rd *TF:* 800-699-7464 ■ *Web:* www.finks.com	Roanoke	VA	24018	540-342-2991	344-5385
Firestone & Parson Inc 30 Newbury St	Boston	MA	02116	617-266-1858	
Freeman Jewelers Inc 76 Merchants Row *TF:* 800-451-4167 ■ *Web:* rutlanddowntown.com	Rutland	VT	05701	802-773-2792	
Garfield Refining Co 810 East Cayuga St *TF:* 800-523-0968 ■ *Web:* www.garfieldrefining.com	Philadelphia	PA	19124	800-523-0968	
Gleim The Jeweler Inc 322 University Ave *Web:* www.gleimjewelers.com	Palo Alto	CA	94301	650-323-1331	
GN Diamond LLC 800 Chestnut St *TF:* 800-724-8810 ■ *Web:* www.gndiamond.com	Philadelphia	PA	19107	215-925-0217	
Green Lake Jewelry Works 550 Ne Northgate Way *Web:* www.seattlejewelry.com	Seattle	WA	98125	206-527-1108	
Gregg Ruth & Co 22809 Pacific Coast Hwy *Web:* greggruth.com	Malibu	CA	90265	310-456-1888	
H Stern Jewelers Inc 645 Fifth Ave *TF:* 800-747-8376 ■ *Web:* www.hstern.net	New York	NY	10022	212-688-0300	888-5137
H. E. Murdock Co Inc 88 Main St *TF:* 888-974-1805 ■ *Web:* www.daysjewelers.com	Waterville	ME	04901	207-873-7036	
Haltoms Jewelers 317 Main St *Web:* www.haltoms.com	Fort Worth	TX	76102	817-336-4051	
Handpicked Inc 150 Harbison Blvd Ste C *Web:* www.behandpicked.com	Columbia	SC	29212	803-749-6024	
Harris Originals of NY Inc 800 Prime Pl *Web:* www.harrisjewelry.com	Hauppauge	NY	11788	631-348-0303	

Company	City	State	Zip	Phone	Fax
Harry Ritchie's Jewelers Inc 956 Willamette St *TF Cust Svc:* 800-935-2850 ■ *Web:* www.harryritchies.com	Eugene	OR	97401	541-686-1787	485-8841
Harry Winston Inc 718 Fifth Ave. *TF:* 800-988-4110 ■ *Web:* www.harrywinston.com	New York	NY	10019	212-399-1000	489-6715
Helzberg Diamonds 1825 Swift Ave **Fax:* Sales ■ *TF:* 800-435-9237 ■ *Web:* www.helzberg.com	North Kansas City	MO	64116	816-842-7780	627-1301*
Henry B Ball Co 5254 Dressler Rd NW *Web:* henrybball.com	Canton	OH	44718	330-499-3000	
Husar's House of Fine Diamonds 131 N Main St *Web:* www.husars.com	West Bend	WI	53095	262-334-3453	
Hyde Park Jewelers Inc 3000 E First Ave Ste 243 *Web:* www.hydeparkjewelers.com	Denver	CO	80206	303-333-4446	
Jay Roberts Jewelers 515 Rt 73 S. *TF:* 888-828-8463 ■ *Web:* www.jayrobertsjewelers.com	Marlton	NJ	08053	856-596-8600	
Jewel-Osco 150 Pierce Rd *Web:* www.jewelosco.com	Itasca	IL	60143	630-948-6000	
Jewelers Inc, The 2400 Western Ave *Web:* www.thejewelers.com	Las Vegas	NV	89102	702-382-1234	
Jewelry Concepts Inc 41 Western Industrial Dr.	Cranston	RI	02921	401-228-8586	
JewelryWeb.com Inc 98 Cuttermill Rd Ste 464 **Fax Area Code:* 800 ■ *TF:* 800-955-9245 ■ *Web:* www.jewelryweb.com	Great Neck	NY	11021	516-482-3982	955-2520*
Jewels by Park Lane 100 Commerce Dr *Web:* www.hallenspecialties.com	Schaumburg	IL	60173	847-884-9999	
Kay Jewelers 375 Ghent Rd. *TF:* 800-681-8796 ■ *Web:* www.kay.com	Akron	OH	44333	330-668-5000	668-5187
King's Jewelry & Loan 800 S Vermont Ave. *TF:* 800-378-1111 ■ *Web:* www.kingspawn.com	Los Angeles	CA	90005	213-383-5555	
Lauren Spencer Inc 40 Clairedan Dr *Web:* www.lauren-spencer.com	Powell	OH	43065	614-888-7773	
Lee Michaels Fine Jewelers Inc 11314 Cloverland Ave *Web:* lmfj.com	Baton Rouge	LA	70809	225-291-9094	
Lee Michaels Jewelers Inc 7560 Corporate Blvd. *Web:* www.lmfj.com	Baton Rouge	LA	70809	225-926-4644	
Lester Lampert Corporate 7 E Huron St *Web:* www.lesterlampert.com	Chicago	IL	60611	312-944-6888	
Lori Bonn Jewelery 114 Linden St *TF:* 877-507-4206 ■ *Web:* www.loribonn.com	Oakland	CA	94607	877-507-4206	
Lux Bond & Green Inc 46 Lasalle Rd **Fax Area Code:* 860 ■ *TF:* 800-524-7336 ■ *Web:* www.lbgreen.com	West Hartford	CT	06107	800-524-7336	521-8693*
Magnon Jewelers Inc 606 S Dale Mabry Hwy. *Web:* magnon-jewelers.com	Tampa	FL	33609	813-872-9374	
Mann's Jewelers Inc 2945 Monroe Ave *Web:* www.mannsjewelers.com	Rochester	NY	14618	585-271-4000	
Maria Collection, The 1048 N Pearl St. *Web:* www.themariacollection.com	Bridgeton	NJ	08302	856-453-9523	
Mccarys Jewelers Inc 1409 E 70th St Ste 118. *Web:* mccarys.com	Shreveport	LA	71105	318-798-3050	
Mead Jewelers Inc 1309 13th St. *Web:* meadjewelers.com	Woodward	OK	73801	580-256-6373	
Mervis Diamond Corp 1900 Mervis Way Tyson's Corner *Web:* www.mervisdiamond.com	Vienna	VA	22182	703-448-9000	
Michaels Creative Jewelry 4843 E Ray Rd *Web:* www.michaelscreative.com	Phoenix	AZ	85044	480-598-0306	
Morgan & Co 1131 Glendon Ave *TF:* 800-458-4367 ■ *Web:* www.morganjewellers.com	Los Angeles	CA	90024	310-208-3377	208-6920
Northville Clock & Watch Shop 132 W Dunlap St *Web:* www.clockone.com	Northville	MI	48167	248-349-4938	
Osterman Jewelers 375 Ghent Rd *TF:* 800-844-7130 ■ *Web:* ostermanjewelers.com	Akron	OH	44333	330-668-5000	
Ozel Fine Jewelers 4718 Admiralty Way	Marina Del Rey	CA	90292	310-301-9797	
Painful Pleasures Inc 7410 Coca Cola Dr Ste 108 *Web:* www.painfulpleasures.com	Hanover	MD	21076	410-712-0145	
Peoples Jewellers 1100 Pembroke St E. *Web:* www.peoplesjewellers.com	Pembroke	ON	K8A6Y7	613-735-1536	
Perrywinkles Fine Jewelry 227 Main St. *Web:* www.perrywinkles.com	Burlington	VT	05401	802-865-2624	
Randy'S Jewelry Inc 309 S Main St. *Web:* randys-jewelry.com	O Fallon	MO	63366	636-978-1953	
Reeds Jewelers Inc PO Box 2229 *TF Orders:* 877-406-3266 ■ *Web:* www.reeds.com	Wilmington	NC	28402	910-350-3100	
Reis Nichols Jewelers 789 Us Hwy 31 N *Web:* www.reisnichols.com	Greenwood	IN	46142	317-883-4467	
Republic Metals Corp 12900 NW 38th Ave. *Web:* republicmetalscorp.com	Miami	FL	33054	305-685-8505	
Ringmaster Jewelers Inc 1990 Healy Dr *Web:* ringmasterjewelers.com	Winston-Salem	NC	27103	336-722-2218	
Rogers Jewelry Co PO Box 3151 *TF:* 800-877-4221 ■ *Web:* www.thinkrogers.com	Modesto	CA	95353	800-877-4221	
Ross Simons Jewelers Inc 9 Ross Simons Dr *TF:* 800-835-0919 ■ *Web:* www.ross-simons.com	Cranston	RI	02920	800-835-0919	
Samuels Jewelers 9607 Research Blvd Ste 100 Bldg F *TF:* 877-202-2870 ■ *Web:* www.samuelsjewelers.com	Austin	TX	78759	512-369-1400	
Satya Jewelry Inc 330 Bleecker St *Web:* www.satyajewelry.com	New York	NY	10014	212-243-7313	
Sea of Diamonds.com 606 S Olive St Ste 1026 *Web:* www.steindiamonds.com	Los Angeles	CA	90014	213-226-0150	
Shane Co 9790 E Arapahoe Rd *TF:* 866-467-4263 ■ *Web:* www.shaneco.com	Greenwood Village	CO	80112	866-467-4263	
Shreve Crump & Low Inc 39 Newbury St. *TF:* 800-328-4326 ■ *Web:* www.shrevecrumpandlow.com	Boston	MA	02116	617-267-9100	
Silverberg Jewelry Co 6730 22nd Ave N *Web:* www.silverbergjewelry.com	St Petersburg	FL	33710	727-381-1286	
Simon G Jewelry Inc 528 State St *Web:* www.simongjewelry.com	Glendale	CA	91203	818-500-9697	
Smart Creations Inc 1799 St Johns Ave	Highland Park	IL	60035	847-433-3451	
Smith Jewelers C W 603 Wisconsin Ave. *Web:* www.cwsmithjewelers.com	North Fond Du Lac	WI	54937	920-922-6259	
Sol Jewelry Designs Inc 550 S Hill St Ste 1020 *TF:* 888-323-7772 ■ *Web:* soljewelry.com	Los Angeles	CA	90013	213-622-7772	
Spark Creations Inc 10 W 46th St *Web:* www.sparkcreations.com	New York	NY	10036	212-575-8385	
Sultan Co 500 Ala Moana Blvd Ste 7-210 *Web:* obits.staradvertiser.com	Honolulu	HI	96819	808-833-7772	837-1358
Tapper's Fine Jewelry Inc Orchard Mall 6337 Orchard Lk Rd *Web:* www.tappers.com	West Bloomfield	MI	48322	248-932-7700	
TAWA Supermarket Inc 6281 Regio Ave *Web:* www.99ranch.com	Buena Park	CA	90620	714-521-8899	
Tiffany & Co 727 Fifth Ave. *NYSE:* TIF ■ *TF Orders:* 800-526-0649 ■ *Web:* www.tiffany.com	New York	NY	10022	212-755-8000	
Tiny Jewel Box Inc 1147 Connecticut Ave Nw *Web:* www.tinyjewelbox.com	Washington	DC	20036	202-393-2747	
Trabert & Hoeffer 111 E Oak St *TF:* 800-539-3573 ■ *Web:* www.trabertandhoeffer.com	Chicago	IL	60611	312-787-1654	
Van Cleef & Arpels Inc 744 Fifth Ave *TF:* 877-826-2533 ■ *Web:* www.vancleefarpels.com	New York	NY	10019	212-896-9284	
Ware Jewelers 7268 Eastchase Pkwy *Web:* www.warejewelers.com	Montgomery	AL	36117	334-386-9273	
Wedding Day Diamonds 7901 Penn Ave S *Web:* www.weddingdaydiamonds.com	Bloomington	MN	55431	952-253-0235	
Wedding Ring Shop 1181 Kapiolani Blvd. *Web:* www.weddingringshop.com	Honolulu	HI	96814	808-945-7766	
Wempe Jewelers 700 Fifth Ave. *Web:* www.wempe.com	New York	NY	10019	212-397-9000	
William Crow Jewelry Inc 910 16th St Ste 320 *Web:* williamcrow.com	Denver	CO	80202	303-592-1695	
Wixon Jewelers Inc 9955 Lyndale Ave S *TF:* 800-853-7667 ■ *Web:* wixonjewelers.com	Minneapolis	MN	55420	952-881-8862	
Worthington Jewelers 692 High St *Web:* www.worthingtonjewelers.com	Worthington	OH	43085	614-430-8800	
Ybarras Jewelers Inc 678 N Wilson Way Ste 28	Stockton	CA	95205	209-547-0320	
Zale Corp 6201 15th Ave *NYSE:* ZLC ■ *TF Cust Svc:* 866-249-2593 ■ *Web:* signetjewelers.com	Brooklyn	NY	11219	718-921-8137	
Zales Jewelers Div 901 W Walnut Hill Ln. *TF Cust Svc:* 800-311-5393 ■ *Web:* www.zales.com	Irving	TX	75038	972-580-4000	

411 JEWELRY, WATCHES, GEMS - WHOL

Company	City	State	Zip	Phone	Fax
AH Lisanti Capital Growth LLC 608 Fifth Ave Ste 1200 *Web:* www.ahlisanti.com	New York	NY	10020	212-792-6990	
Alexa's Angels Inc 621 Innovation Cir *Web:* www.alexas-angels.com	Windsor	CO	80550	970-686-7247	
Alishaev Bros Inc 20 W 47th St Ste 203 *TF:* 877-859-6020 ■ *Web:* alishaevbros.com	New York	NY	10036	877-859-6020	
American Time & Signal Co 140 Third St *Web:* www.american-time.com	Dassel	MN	55325	320-275-2101	
Anatometal 411 Ingalls St *Web:* www.anatometal.com	Santa Cruz	CA	95060	831-454-9880	
Anne Koplik Designs Inc 173 Main St. *Web:* annekoplik.com	Brewster	NY	10509	845-279-8244	
Antwerp Diamond Distributors 6 E 45th St Ste 302	New York	NY	10017	212-319-3300	207-8168
Ball Watch USA 1131 Fourth St N. *Web:* www.ballwatchusa.com	Saint Petersburg	FL	33701	727-896-4278	
Barse & Company Inc 7800 John Carpenter Fwy. *Web:* barse.com	Dallas	TX	75247	214-631-0925	
Bead Bazaar USA Inc 687 Lofstrand Ln Ste H *Web:* beadkit.com	Rockville	MD	20850	301-610-6022	
Bennett Brothers Inc 30 E Adams St *Web:* www.bennettbrothers.com	Chicago	IL	60603	312-263-4800	
Broco Products Inc 18624 Syracuse Ave *TF:* 800-321-0837 ■ *Web:* brocoproducts.com	Cleveland	OH	44110	216-531-0880	
Charles & Colvard Ltd 170 Southport Dr. *NASDAQ:* CTHR ■ *TF:* 877-202-5467 ■ *Web:* www.moissanite.com	Morrisville	NC	27560	877-202-5467	
Charles Wolf Couture 579 Fifth Ave Ste 1518	New York	NY	10017	212-371-6130	
Circa Inc 415 Madison Ave 19th Fl *TF:* 877-876-5493 ■ *Web:* circajewels.com	New York	NY	10017	212-486-6013	
Clyde Duneier Inc 415 Madison Ave Fl 6 *Web:* www.clydeduneier.com	New York	NY	10017	212-398-1122	
Combine International Inc 354 Indusco Ct *Web:* combine.com	Troy	MI	48083	248-585-9900	
Continental Coin Corp 5627 Sepulveda Blvd. *TF:* 800-552-6467 ■ *Web:* continentalcoin.com	Van Nuys	CA	91411	818-781-4232	782-6779
Danforth Pewterers Ltd 52 Seymour St *Web:* www.danforthpewter.com	Middlebury	VT	05753	802-388-8666	
Dominion Diamond Corp PO Box 4569 Sta A *Web:* www.ddcorp.ca	Toronto	ON	M5W4T9	416-362-2237	362-2230
EH Ashley & Company Inc 1 White Squadron Rd *TF:* 800-735-7424 ■ *Web:* ehashley.com	Riverside	RI	02915	401-431-0950	
Empire Diamond Corp 350 Fifth Ave Ste 4000 *TF:* 800-728-3425 ■ *Web:* www.dialadiamond.com	New York	NY	10118	212-564-4777	564-4960
Ettika LLC 714 S Hill St Ste 405 *Web:* ettika.com	Los Angeles	CA	90014	213-817-5510	
FAF Inc 26 Lark Industrial Pkwy *Web:* www.faf.com	Greenville	RI	02828	401-949-3000	

	City	State	Zip	Phone	Fax
Frederick Goldman Inc 154 W 14th St *TF:* 800-221-3232 ■ *Web:* www.fgoldman.com	New York	NY	10011	800-221-3232	
Fremada Gold Inc 2 W 45th St Ste 1605 *Web:* www.fremadaspecials.com	New York	NY	10036	212-921-8829	
Gemex Systems Inc 6040 W Executive Dr Ste A *TF:* 866-694-3639 ■ *Web:* www.gemex.com	Mequon	WI	53092	262-242-1111	
Genal Strap Inc 31-00 47th Ave *Web:* voguestrap.com	Long Island	NY	11101	718-706-8700	
Genesis Diamonds Cool Springs LLC 3742 Hillsboro Pk *Web:* genesisdiamonds.net	Nashville	TN	37215	615-269-6996	
Gennaro Inc 1725 Pontiac Ave *Web:* www.gennaroinc.com	Cranston	RI	02920	401-632-4100	
Gepco Ltd SUITE B, 9025 CARLTON HILLS BLVD. *Web:* www.gepcoltd.com	Santee	CA	92071	909-708-4303	
Gerson Co 1450 S Lone Elm Rd *TF:* 800-444-8172 ■ *Web:* www.gersoncompany.com	Olathe	KS	66061	913-262-7400	535-7592
Gottlieb Bros Inc 55 E Washington	Chicago	IL	60602	312-609-2222	
HS Strygler & Company Inc 37 W 20th St Ste 1210	New York	NY	10011	212-727-7840	727-3700
Identification Plates Inc 1555 High Point Dr *TF:* 800-395-2570 ■ *Web:* www.idplates.com	Mesquite	TX	75149	972-216-1616	216-1555
Jeff Cooper Inc 288 Wbury Ave *Web:* www.jeffcooperdesigns.com	Carle Place	NY	11514	516-333-8200	
Jewel-Craft Inc 4122 Olympic Blvd *TF:* 800-525-5482 ■ *Web:* www.jewel-craft.com	Erlanger	KY	41018	859-282-2400	
Joseph Blank Inc 62 W 47th St Ste 808 *TF:* 800-223-7666 ■ *Web:* www.josephblank.com	New York	NY	10036	212-575-9050	302-8521
Just Bead It 9514 Third Ave *Web:* www.justbeadit.net	Stone Harbor	NJ	08247	609-368-0400	
Kabana Inc 616 Indian School Rd NW *Web:* www.kabana.com	Albuquerque	NM	87102	505-843-9330	
Kendra Scott Design Inc 1400 S Congress Ave Ste A-170 *TF:* 866-677-7023 ■ *Web:* www.kendrascott.com	Austin	TX	78704	512-499-8400	499-8414
KMA Sunbelt Trading Corp 3696 Ulmerton Rd *Web:* www.shopidc.com	Clearwater	FL	33762	727-572-7258	
La Vie Parisienne Corp 1837 Lincoln Blvd *Web:* lavieparisienne.com	Santa Monica	CA	90404	310-392-8428	
Lashbrook Designs 131 E 13065 S *TF:* 888-252-7388 ■ *Web:* lashbrookdesigns.com	Draper	UT	84020	888-252-7388	
Leo Wolleman Inc 45 W 45th St 10th Fl *TF:* 800-223-5667 ■ *Web:* www.leowolleman.com	New York	NY	10036	212-840-1881	869-4216
Lyles-De Grazier Co 2050 N Stemmons Fwy Ste 7943 *Web:* www.lylesjewelry.com	Dallas	TX	75207	214-747-3558	
MA Reich & Co Inc 481 Franklin St *Web:* www.mareich.com	Buffalo	NY	14202	716-856-4085	
Merchants Overseas Inc 41 Bassett St	Providence	RI	02903	401-331-5603	
Metal Marketplace International (MMI) 718 Sansom St *TF:* 800-523-9191 ■ *Web:* www.metalmarketplace.com	Philadelphia	PA	19106	215-592-8777	592-8195
Mikimoto (America) Company Ltd 680 Fifth Ave 4th Fl *TF:* 844-341-0579 ■ *Web:* www.mikimotoamerica.com	New York	NY	10019	212-457-4500	
Morgan Advanced Materials 7331 William Ave *Web:* www.morgantechnicalceramics.com	Allentown	PA	18106	610-366-7100	
MR Diamonds Inc 66 W 47th St Window 1A	New York	NY	10036	312-346-3333	
Paramount Sales Company Inc 10140 Gallows Pt Dr	Knoxville	TN	37931	865-470-9977	470-9801
PM Recovery Inc 106 Calvert St *Web:* www.pmrecovery.com	Harrison	NY	10528	914-835-1900	
Prime Time International Inc 135 W 36th St 5th Fl *Web:* www.waitex.com	New York	NY	10018	212-695-5322	
Pugster Inc 2835 Sierra Grande St *Web:* pugster.com	Pasadena	CA	91107	626-356-1881	
Rego Mfg Company Inc 1870 E Mansfield St *Web:* www.regoonline.com	Bucyrus	OH	44820	419-562-0466	
Seno Jewelry LLC 259 W 30th St 10th Fl *TF:* 888-468-0888 ■ *Web:* www.ippolita.com	New York	NY	10001	888-468-0888	
SKL Company Inc 545 Island Rd	Ramsey	NJ	07446	201-825-6633	825-8009
Tacori Enterprises 1736 Gardena Ave *Web:* tacori.com	Glendale	CA	91204	818-863-1536	
Tara Pearls 10 W 46th Ste 600 *Web:* www.tarapearls.com	New York	NY	10036	212-575-8191	
Thunderbird Supply Co 1907 W Historic Rt 66 *Web:* www.thunderbirdsupply.com	Gallup	NM	87301	505-722-4323	722-6736
TSI Accessory Group Inc 8350 Lehigh Ave	Morton Grove	IL	60053	847-965-1700	
United Legwear Company LLC 48 W 38th St *Web:* www.unitedlegwear.com	New York	NY	10018	212-391-4143	
Variety Gem Company Inc 11 W 46th St Fl 3 *Web:* www.varietygem.com	New York	NY	10036	212-921-1820	
World Minerals Inc 130 Castilian Dr *TF:* 800-893-4445 ■ *Web:* www.worldminerals.com	Goleta	CA	93117	805-562-0200	
Yunique Solutions Inc 552 Seventh Ave *Web:* www.yunique.com	New York	NY	10018	212-672-0098	

412 JUVENILE DETENTION FACILITIES

See Also Correctional & Detention Management (Privatized) p. 2162; Correctional Facilities - Federal p. 2162; Correctional Facilities - State p. 2163
Listings are organized alphabetically by states.

LABELS - FABRIC

See Narrow Fabric Mills p. 3243

	City	State	Zip	Phone	Fax
Bethel Youth Facility 301 W Northern Lights Blvd PO Box 1989 *Web:* dhss.alaska.gov	Bethel	AK	99559	907-543-5200	543-2710
Fairbanks Youth Facility 1502 Wilbur St *TF:* 800-478-2686	Fairbanks	AK	99701	907-451-2150	
Johnson Youth Ctr 3252 Hospital Dr *TF:* 800-780-9972 ■ *Web:* dhss.alaska.gov	Juneau	AK	99801	907-586-9433	463-4933
McLaughlin Youth Ctr 2600 Providence Dr *TF:* 800-478-2221 ■ *Web:* dhss.alaska.gov	Anchorage	AK	99508	907-261-4399	261-4308
Nome Youth Facility 804 E Fourth St *Web:* dhss.alaska.gov	Nome	AK	99762	907-443-5434	443-7295
Arkansas Juvenile Access & Treatment Ctr 425 W Capitol Ste 1620 *TF:* 877-727-3468 ■ *Web:* www.arkansas.gov	Little Rock	AR	72201	501-324-8900	324-8904
Jack Jones Jefferson County Juvenile Detention Ctr 101 E Barraque St *Web:* www.jeffcoso.org	Pine Bluff	AR	71611	870-541-5351	
Northwest Arkansas Regional Juvenile Program 36 Johnny Cake Pt Rd *Web:* saysyouth.org	Mansfield	AR	72944	479-928-0166	928-2060
El Paso de Robles Youth Correctional Facility 4545 Airport Rd PO Box 7008 *Web:* www.cdcr.ca.gov	Paso Robles	CA	93447	805-238-4040	227-2569
OH Close Youth Correctional Facility 7650 S Newcastle Rd PO Box 213001 *Web:* cdcr.ca.gov	Stockton	CA	95213	209-944-6391	
Ventura Youth Correctional Facility 3100 Wright Rd *TF:* 866-232-5627 ■ *Web:* www.cdcr.ca.gov	Camarillo	CA	93010	805-485-7951	485-2801
Adams Youth Services Ctr 1933 E Bridge St *Web:* colorado.gov	Brighton	CO	80601	303-659-4450	637-0471
Gilliam Youth Services Ctr 2844 Downing St	Denver	CO	80205	303-291-8951	
Grand Mesa Youth Sevices Ctr 360 28th Rd *Web:* www.colorado.gov	Grand Junction	CO	81501	970-242-1521	242-8127
Lookout Mountain Youth Services Ctr 2901 Ford St *Web:* colorado.gov	Golden	CO	80401	303-866-2471	
Marvin W Foote Youth Services Ctr 13500 E Fremont Pl *Web:* www.colorado.gov	Englewood	CO	80112	303-534-3468	768-7516
Mount View Youth Services Ctr 7862 W Mansfield Pkwy *Web:* www.colorado.gov	Denver	CO	80235	303-987-4502	
Platte Valley Youth Services Ctr 2200 'O' St	Greeley	CO	80631	970-304-6275	304-6228
Pueblo Youth Services Ctr 1406 W 17th St	Pueblo	CO	81003	719-546-4928	
Spring Creek Youth Services Ctr 3190 E Las Vegas St *Web:* www.colorado.gov	Colorado Springs	CO	80906	719-390-2700	
Zebulon Pike Youth Services Ctr 1427 W Rio Grande *Web:* www.colorado.gov	Colorado Springs	CO	80906	303-534-3468	
Connecticut Juvenile Training School 1225 Silver St	Middletown	CT	06457	860-638-2400	
John R Manson Youth Institute 42 Jarvis St	Cheshire	CT	06410	203-806-2500	699-1845
Ferris School 959 Centre Rd *TF:* 800-292-9582 ■ *Web:* kids.delaware.gov	Wilmington	DE	19805	302-993-3800	993-3820
New Castle County Detention Ctr 963 Centre Rd *TF:* 800-969-4357 ■ *Web:* kids.delaware.gov	Wilmington	DE	19805	302-633-3100	995-8393
Stevenson House Detention Ctr 750 N Dupont Hwy	Milford	DE	19963	302-424-8100	422-1535
Bay Regional Juvenile Detention Ctr 450 E 11th St *Web:* www.djj.state.fl.us/programsfacilities/detentioncenters	Panama City	FL	32401	850-872-4706	873-7099
Brevard Regional Juvenile Detention Ctr 5225 DeWitt Ave	Cocoa	FL	32927	321-690-3400	504-0907
Duval Regional Juvenile Detention Ctr 1241 E Eigth St	Jacksonville	FL	32206	904-798-4819	
Hillsborough Regional Juvenile Detention Ctr West 3948 ML King Jr Blvd *Web:* www.djj.state.fl.us/programsfacilities/detentioncenters	Tampa	FL	33614	813-871-7650	871-4764
Leon Regional Juvenile Detention Ctr 2303 Ronellis Dr *Web:* www.djj.state.fl.us/programsfacilities/detentioncenters	Tallahassee	FL	32310	850-488-7672	922-2842
Manatee Regional Juvenile Detention Ctr 1803 Fifth St W *Web:* manateeclerk.com	Bradenton	FL	34205	941-741-3023	
Marion Regional Juvenile Detention Ctr 3040 NW Tenth St	Ocala	FL	34475	352-732-1450	732-1457
Orange Regional Juvenile Detention Ctr 2800 S Bumby Ave *Web:* www.djj.state.fl.us/programsfacilities/detentioncenters	Orlando	FL	32806	407-897-2800	897-2856
Polk Regional Juvenile Detention Ctr 2155 Bob Phillips Rd	Bartow	FL	33830	863-534-7090	
Saint Lucie Regional Juvenile Detention Ctr 1301 Bell Ave	Fort Pierce	FL	34982	772-468-3940	468-4005
Juvenile Corrections Center-Nampa 1650 11th Ave N	Nampa	ID	83687	208-465-8443	465-8484
Juvenile Corrections Center-Saint Anthony 2220 E 600 N PO Box 40	Saint Anthony	ID	83445	208-624-3462	624-0973
Illinois Youth Ctr Harrisburg 1201 W Poplar St **Fax Area Code: 815 ■ Web:* idjj.state.il.us	Harrisburg	IL	62946	618-252-8681	795-6869*
Illinois Youth Ctr Saint Charles 3825 Campton Hills Rd *Web:* www.illinois.gov/idjj/pages/st_charles_iyc.aspx	Saint Charles	IL	60175	630-584-0506	584-1014
Camp Summit Boot Camp 2407 N 500 W *Web:* in.gov	La Porte	IN	46350	219-874-9898	326-9218
Logansport Juvenile Correctional Facility 1118 S St Rd 25 *TF:* 800-800-5556 ■ *Web:* www.in.gov/idoc	Logansport	IN	46947	574-753-7571	732-0729
Plainfield Re-Entry Educational Facility 501 W Main St *Web:* in.gov/idoc	Plainfield	IN	46168	317-839-7751	838-7548
Iowa Juvenile Home 701 S Church St	Toledo	IA	52342	641-484-2560	484-2816
State Training School 3211 Edgington Ave *TF:* 800-362-2178 ■ *Web:* dhs.iowa.gov	Eldora	IA	50627	641-858-5402	858-2416

Phone Fax

Larned Juvenile Correctional Facility
1301 Kansas Hwy 264 .... Larned KS 67550 620-285-0300 285-0301
Topeka Juvenile Correctional Complex
1430 NW 25th St .... Topeka KS 66618 785-354-9800
Mountainview Youth Development Ctr
1182 Dover Rd .... Charleston ME 04422 207-285-0880 285-0836
Web: maine.gov
Cresson Secure Treatment Unit
160 Gould St Ste 300 .... Needham MA 02494 814-886-6903
Web: jri.org
Pine Hills Youth Correctional Facility
4 N Haynes Ave .... Miles City MT 59301 406-232-1377 232-7432
Web: www.cor.mt.gov
Riverside Youth Correctional Facility
2 Riverside Rd PO Box 88 .... Boulder MT 59632 406-225-4500 225-4511
Web: mt.gov
Mountainview Youth Correctional Facility
31 Petticoat Ln .... Annandale NJ 08801 908-638-6191 638-4423
Youth Diagnostic Development Ctrl
4000 Edith NE .... Albuquerque NM 87107 505-841-2400 841-2428
Crossroads Juvenile Ctr 17 Bristol St .... Brooklyn NY 11212 718-495-8160 495-8254
Horizon Juvenile Ctr 560 Brook Ave .... Bronx NY 10455 718-292-0065 401-8109
Web: www1.nyc.gov
Foothills Correctional Institution
5150 Western Ave .... Morganton NC 28655 828-438-5585 438-5598
Web: ncdps.gov
Morrison Correctional Institution
1573 McDonald Church Rd PO Box 169 .... Hoffman NC 28347 910-281-3161 281-3609
Web: www.ncdps.gov
Western Youth Institution 5155 Western Ave .... Morganton NC 28655 828-438-6037 438-6076
Web: doc.state.nc.us
Cuyahoga Hills Juvenile Correctional Facility
4321 Green Rd .... Highland Hills OH 44128 216-464-8200 464-3540
TF: 800-872-3132 ■ *Web:* dys.ohio.gov
Indian River Juvenile Correctional Facility
2775 Indian River Rd SW .... Massillon OH 44648 330-837-4211 837-4740
Web: www.dys.ohio.gov
Ohio Dept of Youth Services 51 N High St .... Columbus OH 43215 614-466-4314
Web: www.dys.ohio.gov
Ohio River Juvenile Correctional Facility
4696 Gallia Pk .... Franklin Furnace OH 45629 740-354-7000
Web: dys.ohio.gov
Scioto Juvenile Correctional Facility
5993 Home Rd .... Delaware OH 43015 740-881-3250 881-5944
Web: dys.ohio.gov
Central Oklahoma Detention Juvenile Ctr
700 S Ninth St .... Tecumseh OK 74873 405-598-2135 598-8713
Web: www.ok.gov
Southwest Oklahoma Juvenile Ctr
300 S Broadway .... Manitou OK 73555 580-397-3511 397-3491
Camp Florence 4859 S Jetty Rd .... Florence OR 97439 541-997-2076
Web: oregon.gov
Camp Tillamook 6820 Barracks Cir .... Tillamook OR 97141 503-842-4243 842-1476
Web: www.oregon.gov
Eastern Oregon Youth Correctional Facility
1800 W Monroe St .... Burns OR 97720 541-573-3133 573-3665
Web: oregon.gov
Hillcrest Youth Correctional Facility
2450 Strong Rd SE .... Salem OR 97302 503-986-0400 986-0406
Web: oregon.gov
MacLaren Youth Correctional Facility
2630 N Pacific Hwy .... Woodburn OR 97071 503-981-9531 982-4439
Web: oregon.gov
Oregon Youth Authority Riverbend (OYA)
58231 Oregon Hwy 244 .... La Grande OR 97850 541-663-8801 663-9181
Web: www.oregon.gov/oya/pages/facilities/riverbend.aspx
Rogue Valley Youth Correctional Facility
2001 NE 'F' St .... Grants Pass OR 97526 541-471-2862 471-2861
Web: oregon.gov
Tillamook Youth Correctional Facility
6700 Officer Row .... Tillamook OR 97141 503-842-2565 842-4918
Web: oregon.gov
Loysville Youth Development Ctr
10 Opportunity Dr .... Loysville PA 17047 717-789-3841 789-5538
New Castle Youth Development Ctr
1745 Frew Mill Rd .... New Castle PA 16101 724-656-7300
South Mountain Secure Treatment Unit
10056 S Mtn Rd .... South Mountain PA 17261 717-749-7904 749-7905
STAR Academy 12279 Brady Dr .... Custer SD 57730 605-673-2521 673-5489
Web: www.doc.sd.gov
Mountain View Youth Development Ctr
809 Peal Ln .... Dandridge TN 37725 865-397-0174 397-0738
Woodland Hills Youth Development Ctr
3965 Stewarts Ln .... Nashville TN 37218 615-532-2000 532-8402
TF: 855-418-1622 ■ *Web:* www.tennessee.gov
Evins Regional Juvenile Ctr
3801 E Monte Cristo Rd .... Edinburg TX 78542 956-289-5500
Gainesville State School 1379 FM 678 .... Gainesville TX 76240 940-665-0701 665-0469
Web: tjjd.texas.gov
Giddings State School
2261 James Turman Rd PO Box 600 .... Giddings TX 78942 979-542-4500 542-0177
Web: www.tjjd.texas.gov/aboutus/facilities.aspx
Woodside Juvenile Rehabilitation Ctr
26 Woodside Dr .... Colchester VT 05446 802-655-4990
Beaumont Juvenile Correctional Ctr
3500 Beaumont Rd .... Beaumont VA 23014 804-556-3316
Bon Air Juvenile Correctional Ctr
1900 Chatsworth Ave .... Bon Air VA 23235 804-323-2550 323-2440
Web: www.djj.virginia.gov
Hanover Juvenile Correctional Ctr
7093 Broadneck Rd .... Hanover VA 23069 804-537-5316 537-5907
Web: djj.virginia.gov
Davis Juvenile Correctional Ctr
141 Forestry Camp Rd .... Davis WV 26260 304-259-5241 259-4851

Phone Fax

Lincoln Hills School W4380 Copper Lk Rd .... Irma WI 54442 715-536-8386 536-8236
Web: doc.wi.gov
Prairie du Chien Correctional Institution
500 E Parrish St .... Prairie du Chien WI 53821 608-326-7828 326-5960
Web: doc.wi.gov

413 LABELS - OTHER THAN FABRIC

Phone Fax

Accurate Dial & Nameplate Inc
329 Mira Loma Ave .... Glendale CA 91204 323-245-9181 243-6793*
**Fax Area Code:* 818 ■ *TF:* 800-400-4455 ■ *Web:* www.accuratedial.com
Acro Labels Inc 2530 Wyandotte Rd .... Willow Grove PA 19090 215-657-5366 657-3325
TF: 800-355-2235 ■ *Web:* www.acrolabels.com
Alcop Adhesive Label Co 826 Perkins Ln .... Beverly NJ 08010 609-871-4400 871-3017
TF: 888-313-3017 ■ *Web:* alcoplabels.com
AME Label Corp 25155 W Ave Stanford .... Valencia CA 91355 661-257-2200 257-7981
TF: 866-278-9268 ■ *Web:* www.amelabel.com
American Law Label Inc
1674 S Research Loop Ste 436 .... Tucson AZ 85710 520-546-6200 546-6203
Web: www.americanlawlabel.com
Arch Crown Tags Inc 460 Hillside Ave .... Hillside NJ 07205 973-731-6300 731-2228
TF: 800-526-8353 ■ *Web:* www.archcrown.com
Avery Dennison Corp
17700 Foltz Industrial Pkwy .... Strongsville OH 44149 440-878-7000
Avery Dennison Corp 207 Goode Ave .... Glendale CA 91203 626-304-2000
NYSE: AVY ■ *TF Cust Svc:* 888-567-4387 ■ *Web:* www.averydennison.com
Best Label Co 2900 Faber St .... Union City CA 94587 510-489-5400 489-2914
TF: 800-637-5333 ■ *Web:* www.bestlabel.com
Blue Ribbon Tag & Label Corp
4035 N 29th Ave .... Hollywood FL 33020 954-922-9292 922-9977
TF: 800-433-4974 ■ *Web:* www.blueribbonlabel.com
Brady Corp 6555 W Good Hope Rd .... Milwaukee WI 53223 414-358-6600 292-2289*
NYSE: BRC ■ **Fax Area Code:* 800 ■ **Fax:* Cust Svc ■ *TF Cust Svc:* 800-541-1686 ■ *Web:* www.bradycorp.com
Brady Identification Solutions
6555 W Good Hope Rd .... Milwaukee WI 53223 414-358-6600 292-2289*
**Fax Area Code:* 800 ■ **Fax:* Cust Svc ■ *TF Cust Svc:* 800-537-8791 ■ *Web:* www.bradyid.com
CCL Label Inc 161 Worcester Rd Ste 502 .... Framingham MA 01701 508-872-4511 756-8555*
**Fax Area Code:* 416 ■ *TF:* 877-240-9772 ■ *Web:* www.cclind.com
Cellotape Inc 47623 Fremont Blvd .... Fremont CA 94538 510-651-5551 651-8091
TF: 800-231-0608 ■ *Web:* www.cellotape.com
Chase Corp 26 Summer St .... Bridgewater MA 02324 781-332-0700 697-6419*
NYSE: CCF ■ **Fax Area Code:* 508 ■ *Web:* www.chasecorp.com
Clamp Swing Pricing Company Inc
8386 Capwell Dr .... Oakland CA 94621 510-567-1600
TF: 800-227-7615 ■ *Web:* clampswing.com
Data Label Inc 1000 Spruce St .... Terre Haute IN 47807 812-232-0408 238-1847
TF: 800-457-0676 ■ *Web:* www.data-label.com
DeskTop Labels 7277 Boone Ave N .... Minneapolis MN 55428 800-241-9730 531-5764*
**Fax Area Code:* 763 ■ *TF:* 800-241-9730 ■ *Web:* www.desktoplabels.com
Discount Labels Inc 4115 Profit Ct .... New Albany IN 47150 800-995-9500 995-9600
TF: 800-995-9500 ■ *Web:* www.discountlabels.com
East West Label Co 1000 E Hector St .... Conshohocken PA 19428 610-825-0410
TF: 800-441-7333 ■ *Web:* www.ewlabel.com
Ennis Inc PO Box D .... Wolfe City TX 75496 972-775-9801 453-2674*
**Fax Area Code:* 800 ■ *TF:* 800-527-1008 ■ *Web:* www.ennis.com/our-products/labels
General Data Co Inc 4354 Ferguson Dr .... Cincinnati OH 45245 513-752-7978 752-6947*
**Fax:* Sales ■ *TF:* 800-733-5252 ■ *Web:* www.general-data.com
Gilbreth Packaging Systems 3001 State Rd .... Croydon PA 19021 800-630-2413 785-4077*
**Fax Area Code:* 215 ■ *TF:* 800-630-2413 ■ *Web:* www.gilbrethusa.com
Grand Rapids Label Co
2351 Oak Industrial Dr NE .... Grand Rapids MI 49505 616-459-8134 459-4543
TF: 800-552-5215 ■ *Web:* www.grlabel.com
Green Bay Packaging Inc 1700 Webster Ct .... Green Bay WI 54302 920-433-5111
TF: 800-236-8400 ■ *Web:* www.gbp.com
Harris Industries Inc
5181 Argosy Ave .... Huntington Beach CA 92649 714-898-8048 898-7108
TF: 800-222-6866 ■ *Web:* www.harrisind.com
Impact Label Corp 3434 S Burdick St .... Kalamazoo MI 49001 269-381-4280 381-1055
TF: 800-820-0362 ■ *Web:* www.impactlabel.com
International Label & Printing Company Inc
2550 United Ln .... Elk Grove Village IL 60007 800-244-1442 595-1747*
**Fax Area Code:* 630 ■ *TF:* 800-244-1442 ■ *Web:* www.internationallabel.com
Label Graphics Company Inc
1225 Carnegie St Ste 104B .... Rolling Meadows IL 60008 847-454-1005 454-1008
Web: labelgraphicscompany.com
Labelmaster Co 5724 N Pulaski Rd .... Chicago IL 60646 773-478-0900
TF: 800-621-5808 ■ *Web:* www.labelmaster.com
Labeltape Inc 5100 Beltway Dr SE .... Caledonia MI 49316 616-698-1830 698-7831
TF: 800-928-4537 ■ *Web:* www.labeltape-inc.com
Lancer Label 301 S 74th St .... Omaha NE 68114 800-228-7074 390-9459*
**Fax Area Code:* 402 ■ *TF Cust Svc:* 800-228-7074 ■ *Web:* www.lancerlabel.com
LGInternational 6700 SW Bradbury Ct .... Portland OR 97224 503-620-0520 620-3296
Web: www.lgintl.com
McCourt Label Co 20 Egbert Ln .... Lewis Run PA 16738 814-362-3851 362-4156
TF: 800-458-2390 ■ *Web:* www.mccourtlabel.com
Morgan Fabrics Corp 4265 Exchange Ave .... Los Angeles CA 90058 323-583-9981 923-2352
Web: www.morganfabrics.com
MPI Label Systems Inc 450 Courtney Rd .... Sebring OH 44672 330-938-2134 938-9878
TF: 800-423-0442 ■ *Web:* www.mpilabels.com
Multi-Color Corp 4053 Clough Woods Dr .... Batavia OH 45103 513-381-1480 381-2240
NASDAQ: LABL ■ *Web:* www.multicolorcorp.com
National Label Company Inc
2025 Joshua Rd .... Lafayette Hill PA 19444 610-825-3250 834-8854
Web: www.nationallabel.com
National Printing Converters Inc
18 S Murphy Ave .... Brazil IN 47834 800-877-6724
TF: 800-877-6724 ■ *Web:* www.npclabels.com
Northeast Data Services 1316 College Ave .... Elmira NY 14901 607-733-5541
Phifer Inc 4400 Kauloosa Ave PO Box 1700 .... Tuscaloosa AL 35401 205-345-2120 759-4450
TF: 800-633-5955 ■ *Web:* www.phifer.com

Phone | Fax

Print-O-Tape Inc 755 Tower Rd ... Mundelein IL 60060 847-362-1476 949-7449
TF: 800-346-6311 ■ *Web:* www.printotape.com

Printed Systems 1265 Gillingham Rd ... Neenah WI 54956 800-352-2332 321-8247*
*Fax Area Code: 888 ■ *Fax: Sales ■ *TF Sales:* 800-352-2332 ■ *Web:* www.psdtag.com

Quikstik Labels 220 Broadway ... Everett MA 02149 617-389-7570 381-9280
TF: 800-225-3496 ■ *Web:* www.qsxlabels.com

Reidler Decal Corp
264 Industrial Pk Rd PO Box 8 ... Saint Clair PA 17970 800-628-7770 429-1528*
*Fax Area Code: 570 ■ *TF:* 800-628-7770 ■ *Web:* www.reidlerdecal.com

Shamrock Scientific Specialty Systems Inc
34 Davis Dr ... Bellwood IL 60104 708-547-9005 248-1907*
*Fax Area Code: 800 ■ *TF:* 800-323-0249 ■ *Web:* www.shamrocklabels.com

Smyth Cos Inc 1085 Snelling Ave N ... Saint Paul MN 55108 651-646-4544 646-8949
TF: 800-473-3464 ■ *Web:* www.smythco.com

Sohn Manufacturing Inc 544 Sohn Dr ... Elkhart Lake WI 53020 920-876-3361 876-2952
Web: www.sohnmanufacturing.com

Spear Inc 5510 Courseview Dr ... Mason OH 45040 513-459-1100 459-1362
Web: www.spearinc.com

Spectrum Label Corp 30803 San Clemente St ... Hayward CA 94544 510-477-0707 477-0787
TF: 800-545-2235 ■ *Web:* www.spectrumlabel.com

Spinnaker Coating Inc 518 E Water St ... Troy OH 45373 937-332-6500 332-6518
TF: 800-543-9452 ■ *Web:* spinnakercoating.com

Strutz International Inc
440 Mars-Valencia Rd PO Box 509 ... Mars PA 16046 724-625-1501 625-3570
Web: www.strutz.com

Tag-It Pacific Inc
21900 Burbank Blvd Ste 270 ... Woodland Hills CA 91367 818-444-4100 444-4105
Web: www.talonzippers.com

Tape & Label Converters Inc
8231 Allport Ave ... Santa Fe Springs CA 90670 562-945-3486 696-8198
TF: 888-285-2462 ■ *Web:* www.stickybiz.com

Tapecon Inc 10 Latta Rd ... Rochester NY 14612 585-621-8400
TF: 800-333-2407 ■ *Web:* www.tapecon.com

TAPEMARK Co 1685 Marthaler Ln ... St Paul MN 55118 651-455-1611 450-8403
TF: 800-535-1998 ■ *Web:* www.tapemark.com

Valmark Industries Inc 7900 National Dr ... Livermore CA 94550 925-960-9900 960-0900
Web: www.valmark.com

Weber Marking Systems Inc
711 W Algonquin Rd ... Arlington Heights IL 60005 847-364-8500 364-8575
TF Sales: 800-843-4242

West Coast Tag & Label Co PO Box 4099 ... West Hills CA 91308 213-748-0244 710-7645*
*Fax Area Code: 818

Whitlam Label Company Inc
24800 Sherwood Ave ... Center Line MI 48015 586-757-5100 757-1243
TF: 800-755-2235 ■ *Web:* www.whitlam.com

Wise Tag & Label Company Inc
1077 Thomas Busch Memorial Hwy ... Pennsauken NJ 08110 856-663-2400 663-8610
Web: www.wisetaglabel.com

Wright Global Graphics 5115 Prospect St ... Thomasville NC 27360 336-472-4200 476-8554
TF: 800-678-9019 ■ *Web:* www.wrightglobalgraphics.com

WS Packaging Group Inc 2571 S. Hemlock Rd ... Green Bay WI 54229 800-818-5481 866-6485*
*Fax Area Code: 920 ■ *TF:* 800-236-3424 ■ *Web:* www.wspackaging.com

414 LABOR UNIONS

Phone | Fax

Actors' Equity Assn 1560 Broadway ... New York NY 10036 212-869-8530 719-9815
Web: www.actorsequity.org

AFT Healthcare 555 New Jersey Ave NW ... Washington DC 20001 202-879-4491
TF: 800-238-1133 ■ *Web:* www.aft.org

Air Line Pilots Assn 535 Herndon Pkwy ... Herndon VA 20170 703-689-2270 232-0438*
*Fax Area Code: 202 ■ *TF:* 877-331-1223 ■ *Web:* www.alpa.org

Alberta Union of Prov Employees
10451 170 St Nw ... Edmonton AB T5P4S7 780-930-3300
Web: www.aupe.org

Allied Pilots Association
14600 Trinity Blvd O'Connell Bldg Ste 500 ... Fort Worth TX 76155 817-302-2272
Web: www.alliedpilots.org

Amalgamated Transit Union (ATU)
10000 New Hampshire Ave ... Silver Spring MD 20903 202-537-1645 244-7824
TF: 888-240-1196 ■ *Web:* www.atu.org

American Federation of Government Employees
80 F St NW ... Washington DC 20001 202-737-8700 639-6441
TF: 888-844-2343 ■ *Web:* www.afge.org

American Federation of Labor & Congress of Industrial Organizations (AFL-CIO)
815 16th St NW ... Washington DC 20006 202-637-5000 637-5058
TF: 877-850-4959 ■ *Web:* www.aflcio.org

American Federation of Musicians of the US & Canada (AFM)
1501 Broadway Ste 600 ... New York NY 10036 212-869-1330 764-6134
TF: 800-762-3444 ■ *Web:* www.afm.org

American Federation of State County & Municipal Employees
1625 L St NW ... Washington DC 20036 202-429-1000 429-1293
Web: www.afscme.org

American Federation of Teachers (AFT)
555 New Jersey Ave NW ... Washington DC 20001 202-879-4400 879-4556*
*Fax: PR ■ *TF:* 800-238-1133 ■ *Web:* www.aft.org

American Federation of Television & Radio Artists (AFTRA)
260 Madison Ave 7th Fl ... New York NY 10016 212-532-0800 532-2242
Web: www.sagaftra.org

American Postal Workers Union
1300 L St NW ... Washington DC 20005 202-842-4200
Web: www.apwu.org

American Train Dispatchers Assn
4239 W 150th St ... Cleveland OH 44135 216-251-7984

Apartment Association
333 W Broadway Ste 101 ... Long Beach CA 90802 562-426-8341
Web: www.apt-assoc.com

Association of Civilian Technicians (ACT)
12620 Lk Ridge Dr ... Woodbridge VA 22192 703-494-4845 494-0961
Web: www.actnat.com

Association of Flight Attendants
501 Third St NW ... Washington DC 20001 202-434-1300 434-1319
Web: afacwa.org

Association of Professional Flight Attendants
1004 W Euless Blvd ... Euless TX 76040 817-540-0108 540-2077
TF: 800-395-2732 ■ *Web:* www.apfa.org

Association of Western Pulp & Paper Workers
1430 SW Clay St ... Portland OR 97208 503-228-7486
Web: www.awppw.org

B C Teachers Federation
100 - 550 W 6th Ave ... Vancouver BC V5Z4P2 604-871-2283
Web: www.bctf.ca

B.C. Government & Service Employees' Union
4911 Canada Way ... Burnaby BC V5G3W3 604-291-9611
TF: 800-663-1674 ■ *Web:* www.bcgeu.ca

Bakery Confectionery Tobacco Workers & Grain Millers International Union
10401 Connecticut Ave ... Kensington MD 20895 301-933-8600 946-8452
Web: www.bctgm.org

Brotherhood of Locomotive Engineers & Trainmen (BLET)
1370 Ontario St Mezzanine Level ... Cleveland OH 44113 216-241-2630 241-6516
TF: 877-772-5772 ■ *Web:* www.ble-t.org

Brotherhood of Maintenance of Way Employees (BMWED)
41475 Gardenbrook Rd ... Novi MI 48375 248-662-2660 662-2659
Web: www.bmwed.org

Brotherhood of Railroad Signalmen
917 Shenandoah Shores Rd ... Front Royal VA 22630 540-622-6522 622-6532
Web: www.brs.org

Canada Labour Congress 2841 Riverside Dr ... Ottawa ON K1V8X7 613-521-3400 521-4655
Web: canadianlabour.ca

Chicago Teachers Union
222 Merchandise Mart Plz Ste 400 ... Chicago IL 60654 312-329-9100 329-6200
Web: www.ctunet.com

Communications Workers of America (CWA)
501 Third St NW ... Washington DC 20001 202-434-1100
Web: www.cwa-union.org

Directors Guild of America
7920 W Sunset Blvd ... Los Angeles CA 90046 310-289-2000 289-2029
TF: 800-421-4173 ■ *Web:* www.dga.org

Federal Education Assn
1201 16th St NW Ste 117 ... Washington DC 20036 202-822-7850
Web: www.feaonline.org

Freelancers Union 20 Jay St Ste 700 ... Brooklyn NY 11201 718-532-1515
Web: www.freelancersunion.org

Glass Molders Pottery Plastics & Allied Workers International Union
608 E Baltimore Pike ... Media PA 19063 610-565-5051 565-0983
TF: 855-670-4787 ■ *Web:* www.gmpiu.org

Graphic Artists Guild Inc
32 Broadway Ste 1114 ... New York NY 10004 212-791-3400 791-0333
Web: www.graphicartistsguild.org

Graphic Communications International Union
1900 L St NW Ste 800 ... Washington DC 20036 202-462-1400
Web: www.teamster.org

Inlandboatmen's Union of the Pacific (IBU)
1711 W Nickerson St Ste D ... Seattle WA 98119 206-284-6001 284-5043
TF: 800-562-6000 ■ *Web:* www.ibu.org

International Alliance of Theatrical Stage Employees Moving Picture Technicians (IATSE)
1430 Broadway 20th Fl ... New York NY 10018 212-730-1770 921-7699
TF: 800-456-3863 ■ *Web:* iatse.net

International Assn of Bridge Structural Ornamental & Reinforcing Iron Workers
1750 New York Ave NW Ste 400 ... Washington DC 20006 202-383-4800 638-4856
TF: 800-368-0105 ■ *Web:* www.ironworkers.org

International Assn of Fire Fighters (IAFF)
1750 New York Ave NW 3rd Fl ... Washington DC 20006 202-737-8484 737-8418
Web: www.iaff.org

International Assn of Heat & Frost Insulators & Asbestos Workers
9602 ML King Jr Hwy ... Lanham MD 20706 301-731-9101 731-5058
Web: www.insulators.org

International Assn of Machinists & Aerospace Workers
9000 Machinists Pl ... Upper Marlboro MD 20772 301-967-4500
Web: www.goiam.org

International Brotherhood of Boilermakers Iron Shipbuilders Blacksmiths Forgers & Helpers
753 State Ave Ste 570 ... Kansas City KS 66101 913-371-2640 281-8101
Web: www.boilermakers.org

International Brotherhood of Electrical Workers
900 Seventh St NW ... Washington DC 20001 202-833-7000
Web: www.ibew.org

International Brotherhood of Police Officers (IBPO)
159 Burgin Pkwy ... Quincy MA 02169 617-376-0220 376-0285*
*Fax: Legal Dept ■ *Web:* www.ibpo.org

International Brotherhood of Teamsters
25 Louisiana Ave NW ... Washington DC 20001 202-624-6800 624-6918*
*Fax: PR ■ *Web:* www.teamster.org

International Chemical Workers Union Council
1655 W Market St Fl 6 ... Akron OH 44313 330-926-1444 926-0816
Web: www.icwuc.org

International Federation of Professional & Technical Engineers
8630 Fenton St Ste 400 ... Silver Spring MD 20910 301-565-9016 565-0018
Web: www.ifpte.org

International Longshore & Warehouse Union
1188 Franklin St 4th Fl ... San Francisco CA 94109 415-775-0533 775-1302
TF: 866-266-0013 ■ *Web:* www.ilwu.org

International Organization of Masters Mates & Pilots
700 Maritime Blvd ... Linthicum Heights MD 21090 410-850-8700 850-0973
TF: 877-667-5522 ■ *Web:* www.bridgedeck.org

International Union of Bricklayers & Allied Craftworkers (BAC)
1776 eye St NW ... Washington DC 20006 202-783-3788 393-0219
TF: 888-880-8222 ■ *Web:* www.bacweb.org

International Union of Elevator Constructors (IUEC)
7154 Columbia Gateway Dr ... Columbia MD 21046 410-953-6150
Web: www.iuec.org

International Union of Operating Engineers
1125 17th St NW ... Washington DC 20036 202-429-9100
Web: www.iuoe.org

International Union of Painters & Allied Trades (IUPAT)
7234 Pkwy Dr ... Hanover MD 21076 410-564-5900
TF: 800-554-2479 ■ *Web:* www.ibpat.org

International Union of Police Assn
1549 Ringling Blvd Ste 600 ... Sarasota FL 34236 941-487-2560 487-2570
TF: 800-247-4872 ■ *Web:* iupa.org

Phone Fax

International Union Security Police & Fire Professionals of America (SPFPA)
25510 Kelly Rd. Roseville MI 48066 586-772-7250 772-9644
TF: 800-228-7492 ■ *Web:* www.spfpa.org

International Union United Automobile Aerospace & Agricultural Implement Workers of America
8000 E Jefferson Ave. Detroit MI 48214 313-926-5000 823-6016
Web: www.uaw.org

Laborers' International Union of North America
905 16th St NW. Washington DC 20006 202-737-8320 737-2754
Web: www.liuna.org

Llorens Pharmaceuticals International Division
7080 NW 37th Ct. Miami FL 33147 305-716-0595
Web: www.llorenspharm.com

Marine Engineers' Beneficial Assn (MEBA)
444 N Capitol St NW Ste 800. Washington DC 20001 202-638-5355 638-5369
Web: mebaunion.org

Michigan Federation of Teachers
2661 E Jefferson Ave. Detroit MI 48207 313-393-2200
Web: www.mftsrp.org

Missouri Afl-cio 227 Jefferson St. Jefferson City MO 65101 573-634-2115
Web: moaflcio.org

Mont Pelerin Capital LLC
660 Newport Ctr Dr Ste 1220. Newport Beach CA 92660 949-706-6707
Web: www.montpelerincapital.com

Mspta 1715 Abbey Rd Ste B. East Lansing MI 48823 517-336-7782
Web: mspta.net

NA of Broadcast Employees & Technicians (NABET-CWA)
501 Third St NW. Washington DC 20001 202-434-1254 434-1426
Web: www.nabetcwa.org

NA of Letter Carriers 100 Indiana Ave NW. Washington DC 20001 202-393-4695 737-1540
Web: www.nalc.org

National Air Traffic Controllers Assn (NATCA)
1325 Massachusetts Ave NW. Washington DC 20005 202-628-5451 628-5767
TF: 800-266-0895 ■ *Web:* www.natca.org

National Alliance of Postal & Federal Employees
1628 11th St NW. Washington DC 20001 202-939-6325 939-6389
Web: www.napfe.com

National Basketball Players Assn (NBPA)
310 Malcolm X Blvd. New York NY 10027 212-655-0880 655-0881
Web: www.nbpa.com

National Conference of Firemen & Oilers
1025 Vermont Ave NW. Washington DC 20005 202-962-0981
Web: www.ncfo.org

National Federation of Federal Employees
805-15th St NW Ste 500. Washington DC 20036 202-216-4420 862-4432
Web: www.nffe.org

National League of Postmasters of the US
5904 Richmond Hwy Ste 500. Alexandria VA 22303 703-329-4550 329-0466
Web: www.postmasters.org

National Organization of Industrial Trade Unions
148-06 Hillside Ave. Jamaica NY 11435 718-291-3434
Web: www.noitu.org

National Rural Letter Carriers' Assn
1630 Duke St 4th Fl. Alexandria VA 22314 703-684-5545 548-8735
Web: www.nrlca.org

National Treasury Employees Union
1750 H St NW 10th Fl. Washington DC 20006 202-572-5500 572-5643
Web: www.nteu.org

National Writers Union (NWU)
256 W 38th St Ste 703. New York NY 10018 212-254-0279 254-0673
Web: www.nwu.org

New York Apple Association Inc
7645 Main St PO Box 350. Fishers NY 14453 585-924-2171
Web: www.nyapplecountry.com

News Media Guild 424 W 33rd St Ste 260. New York NY 10001 212-869-9290 840-0687
Web: www.newsmediaguild.org

Newspaper Guild-Communications Workers of America, The
501 Third St NW 6th Fl. Washington DC 20001 202-434-7177 434-1472
Web: www.newsguild.org

Northern California Laborers Apprenticeship Program
1001 Westside Dr. San Ramon CA 94583 925-828-2513
Web: www.norcalaborers.org

Ocsea-Afscme Local
390 Worthington Rd Ste A. Westerville OH 43082 614-865-4700
TF: 800-969-4702 ■ *Web:* www.ocsea.org

Ohio Federation of Teachers
1251 E Broad St Frnt. Columbus OH 43205 614-258-3240
Web: oh.aft.org

Ontario Nurses Association
85 Grenville St Ste 400. Toronto ON M5S3A2 416-964-8833
TF: 800-387-5580 ■ *Web:* www.ona.org

Pipeline Industry Benefit Fund
4845 S 83rd E Ave. Tulsa OK 74145 918-280-4800
Web: www.pibf.org

Plumbers Local Union No 68 502 Link Rd. Houston TX 77009 713-869-3592

Plumbing Industry Board Trade Education Committee
3711 47th Ave. Long Island NY 11101 718-752-9630
Web: www.ualocal1.org

Power Worker's Union, The 244 Eglinton Ave E. Toronto ON M4P1K2 416-481-4491
TF: 800-958-8798 ■ *Web:* www.pwu.ca

Professional Security Officers Union
3411 E 12th St Ste 200. Oakland CA 94601 510-437-8100 261-2039
Web: www.seiu-usww.org

Road Sprinkler Fitters Local Union 669
7050 Oakland Mills Rd. Columbia MD 21046 410-381-4300
Web: www.sprinklerfitters669.org

RWDSU 30 E 29th St. New York NY 10016 212-684-5300 779-2809
Web: rwdsu.info

Screen Actors Guild (SAG)
5757 Wilshire Blvd. Los Angeles CA 90036 323-954-1600 549-6775
TF: 800-724-0767 ■ *Web:* www.sagaftra.org

Seafarers International Union
5201 Auth Way. Camp Springs MD 20746 301-899-0675 899-7355
TF: 800-252-4674 ■ *Web:* www.seafarers.org

Seiu Local 503 Opeu 488 E 11th Ave Ste B100. Eugene OR 97401 541-342-1055
Web: www.seiu503.org

Phone Fax

Service Employees International Union
1800 Massachusetts Ave NW. Washington DC 20036 202-730-7000
TF: 800-424-8592 ■ *Web:* www.seiu.org

Sheet Metal Workers International Assn (SMWIA)
1750 New York Ave NW 6th Fl. Washington DC 20006 202-783-5880 662-0894
TF: 800-251-7045 ■ *Web:* www.smwia.org

Shopper Local 2222 Sedwick Rd # 102. Durham NC 27713 877-251-4592
TF: 877-251-4592 ■ *Web:* www.shopperlocal.com

Speea 15205 52nd Ave S. Tukwila WA 98188 206-433-0991
Web: speea.org

Transportation Communications International Union
3 Research Pl. Rockville MD 20850 301-948-4910 948-1369
TF: 877-772-5772 ■ *Web:* www.goiam.org

UA Local 486 8100 Sandpiper Cir Ste 200. Nottingham MD 21236 410-866-4380
Web: www.ualocal486.com

Uflac Local 112 Dental In
1571 Beverly Blvd. Los Angeles CA 90026 213-895-4006
Web: www.uflac.org

Unifor 301 Laurier Ave W. Ottawa ON K1P6M6 613-230-5200
TF: 877-230-5201 ■ *Web:* www.cep.ca

Union Of Agricultural Procedures, The
555 Boul Roland-therrien Ste 100. Longueuil QC J4H3Y9 450-679-0530

Union of American Physicians & Dentists
180 Grand Ave Ste 1380. Oakland CA 94612 510-839-0193 763-8756
TF: 800-622-0909 ■ *Web:* www.uapd.com

Union Roofers Health & Welfare
9901 Paramount Blvd Ste 211. Downey CA 90240 562-927-1434

UNITE HERE 275 Seventh Ave. New York NY 10001 212-265-7000
Web: www.unitehere.org

United Assn 3 Park Pl. Annapolis MD 21401 410-269-2000
Web: www.ua.org

United Brotherhood of Carpenters & Joiners of America
101 Constitution Ave NW. Washington DC 20001 202-546-6206 543-5724
TF: 800-530-5090 ■ *Web:* www.carpenters.org

United Electrical Radio & Machine Workers of America
1 Gateway Ctr Ste 1400. Pittsburgh PA 15222 412-471-8919 471-8999
Web: www.ueunion.org

United Farm Workers of America
29700 Woodford Techachpi Rd PO Box 62. Keene CA 93531 661-823-6151 823-6174
Web: www.ufw.org

United Food & Commercial Workers International Union (UFCW)
1775 K St NW. Washington DC 20006 202-223-3111 466-1562
TF: 800-551-4010 ■ *Web:* www.ufcw.org

United Food & Commercial Workers Union Local 555
7095 SW Sandburg St. Tigard OR 97281 503-684-2822
TF: 800-452-8329 ■ *Web:* www.ufcw555.com

United Scenic Artists 29 W 38th St 15th Fl. New York NY 10018 212-581-0300 977-2011
TF: 800-456-3863 ■ *Web:* www.usa829.org

United Steel Workers (USW)
3340 Perimeter Hill Dr. Nashville TN 37211 615-834-8590
Web: www.usw.org

United Steelworkers of America
60 Blvd of the Allies. Pittsburgh PA 15222 412-562-2575 562-2445
Web: www.usw.org

United Transportation Union
14600 Detroit Ave. Cleveland OH 44107 216-228-9400 228-5755
TF: 800-558-8842 ■ *Web:* www.utu.org

Utility Workers Union of America (UWUA)
888 16th St NW Ste 550. Washington DC 20006 202-974-8200 974-8201
Web: www.uwua.net

Willamette Education Service District Employees Association Inc
2611 Pringle Rd Se. Salem OR 97302 503-588-5330
Web: www.ddouglas.k12.or.us

Writers Guild of America East (WGAE)
250 Hudson St. New York NY 10013 212-767-7800 582-1909
Web: www.wgaeast.org

Writers Guild of America West (WGAw)
7000 W Third St. Los Angeles CA 90048 323-951-4000 782-4800
TF: 800-421-4182 ■ *Web:* www.wga.org

415 LABORATORIES - DENTAL

See Also Laboratories - Medical p. 2622

Phone Fax

1 Biotechnology PO Box 758. Oneco FL 34264 941-355-8451 351-0026
TF: 800-951-4246 ■ *Web:* www.1biotechnology.com

A & M Dental Laboratories Inc
425 S Santa Fe St. Santa Ana CA 92705 714-547-8051
Web: www.aandmdental.com

Access Bio Inc 65 Clyde Rd Ste A. Somerset NJ 08873 732-873-4040
Web: www.accessbio.net

Accu Reference Medical Lab
1901 E Linden Ave Unit 4. Linden NJ 07036 908-474-1004
Web: www.accureference.com

Accurate Diagnostic Labs Inc
3000 Hadley Rd. South Plainfield NJ 07080 732-839-3300
Web: www.adlabs.net

ACM Medical Laboratory Inc
160 Elmgrove Park. Rochester NY 14624 585-247-3500
Web: www.acmlab.com

Aculabs Inc 2 Kennedy Blvd. East Brunswick NJ 08816 732-777-2588
Web: www.aculabs.com

Advanced Medical Analysis LLC
1941 Walker Ave. Monrovia CA 91016 626-357-8999

Advanced Radiology PA 7253 Ambassador Rd. Baltimore MD 21244 443-436-1100
Web: www.advancedradiology.com

Affiliated Medical Services Laboratory Inc
2916 E Central Ave. Wichita KS 67214 316-265-4533
Web: www.amsreferencelab.com

Afr Labs LLC
23891 Via Fabricante Ste 607. Mission Viejo CA 92691 949-462-9822
Web: afrlabs.com

Phone Fax

Alcopro Inc 2547 Sutherland Ave. Knoxville TN 37919 865-525-4900
TF: 800-227-9890 ■ *Web:* www.alcopro.com

Alfred Mann Foundation, The
25134 Rye Canyon Loop Valencia CA 91355 661-702-6700
Web: www.aemf.org

American Esoteric Laboratories Inc
1701 Century Ctr Cove Memphis TN 38134 901-405-8200
Web: www.ael.com

American Health Associates
671 Ohio Pk Ste K Cincinnati IN 45245 800-522-7556
TF: 800-522-7556 ■ *Web:* www.thml.com

Ami Imaging Systems Inc
7815 Telegraph Rd Bloomington MN 55438 952-828-0080
Web: www.ami-imaging.com

Any Lab Test Now 235 Bloomfield Dr 110 Bldg B Lititz PA 17543 717-823-6787
Web: www.anylabtestnow.com

Applied Diagnostics Inc
1140 Business Center Dr Ste 370 Houston TX 77043 713-271-4133 271-6885
TF: 855-239-8378 ■ *Web:* www.applieddiagnostics.com

Ascend Clinical LLC 1400 Industrial Way Redwood City CA 94063 650-780-5500
Web: www.ascendclinical.com

Associated Clinical Laboratories 1526 Peach St Erie PA 16501 814-461-2420
Web: www.associatedclinicallabs.com

Aurora Diagnostics LLC
11025 RCA Ctr Dr Ste 300 Palm Beach Gardens FL 33410 561-626-5512
Web: www.auroradx.com

BlueLine Services LLC
448 East 6400 South Ste 425 Salt Lake City UT 84107 801-575-8378
Web: www.blueline-services.com

Boos Dental Laboratory
1000 Boone Ave N Ste 660 Golden Valley MN 55427 763-544-1446 546-1392
TF: 800-333-2667 ■ *Web:* www.dentalservices.net

Boston Endoscopy Center LLC
175 Worcester St (Rte 9) Wellesley Hills MA 02481 617-754-0800
Web: www.gmed.com

Boyce & Bynum Pathology Laboratories PC
200 Portland St Columbia MO 65201 573-886-4600
Web: www.bbpllab.com

BRLI No 2 Acquisition Corp
207 Perry Pkwy Gaithersburg MD 20877 301-519-2100
TF: 888-729-1206 ■ *Web:* www.genedx.com

C D D 11603 Crosswinds Way Ste 100 San Antonio TX 78233 210-590-3033
TF: 888-858-8663 ■ *Web:* www.cddmedical.com

C Dental X Ray 1050 Northgate Dr Ste 110 San Rafael CA 94903 415-472-1323
Web: www.cdental.com

Calgary Laboratory Services
3535 Research Rd NW Calgary AB T2L2K8 403-770-3500
TF: 800-661-3450 ■ *Web:* www.calgarylabservices.com

Calloway Laboratories Inc 12 Gill St Ste 4000 Woburn MA 01801 781-224-9899

Candelis Inc 18821 Bardeen Ave Irvine CA 92612 949-852-1000
Web: www.candelis.com

Carolina Medical Lab 1815 Back Creek Dr Charlotte NC 28213 704-598-8818
TF: 800-963-3522 ■ *Web:* www.cmedlab.com

CBLPath Inc 2100 SE 17th St Ocala FL 34471 352-732-9990
Web: www.cblpath.com

Celdara Medical LLC 16 Cavendish Court DRTC Lebanon NH 03766 617-320-8521
Web: www.celdaramedical.com

Central Coast Pathology Consultants Inc
3701 S Higuera St Ste 200 San Luis Obispo CA 93401 805-541-6033
Web: www.ccpathology.com

Cleveland HeartLab Inc
6701 Carnegie Ave Ste 500 Cleveland OH 44103 866-358-9828
TF: 866-358-9828 ■ *Web:* www.clevelandheartlab.com

Clinical Information Network Inc
8283 N Hayden Rd Hayden Corporate Ctr
Ste 270 Scottsdale AZ 85258 480-422-1811
Web: www.clinicalinfonet.com

Clinical Laboratories of Hawaii LLP
91-2135 Ft Weaver Rd Ste 300 Ewa Beach HI 96706 808-677-7999
Web: www.clinicallabs.com

Clinical Laboratory Partners LLC
129 Patricia M. Genova Dr Newington CT 06111 860-545-2299
Web: www.clinicallaboratorypartners.com

Clinical Pathology Laboratories Inc
9200 Wall St Austin TX 78754 512-339-1275
Web: www.cpllabs.com

Clinical Science Laboratory Inc
51 Francis Ave Mansfield MA 02048 508-339-6106
Web: clinicalsciencelab.com

Coast2Coast Diagnostics Inc
600 N Tustin Ave Ste 110 Santa Ana CA 92705 800-730-9263
TF: 800-730-9263 ■ *Web:* www.c2cdiagnostics.net

Consultants in Laboratory Medicine
3170 W Central Ave Toledo OH 43606 419-534-6600
Web: www.clm-pml.com

ConVerge Diagnostic Services LLC
200 Corporate Pl Ste 7 Peabody MA 01960 978-538-8000
Web: www.converge.com

Cytolab Pathology Services 6825 216th St Sw Lynnwood WA 98036 425-712-8020
TF: 800-845-6167

Delta Pathology Group LLP
2915 Missouri Ave Shreveport LA 71109 318-621-8820
Web: www.deltapathology.com

Dental Technologies Inc (DTI) 5601 Arnold Rd Dublin CA 94568 925-829-3611 828-0153
TF: 800-229-0936 ■ *Web:* www.dtidental.com

Detroit Bio-med Laboratories
23955 Fwy Park Dr Farmington Hills MI 48335 248-471-4111
Web: www.detroitbio.com

Diagnostic Imaging Inc
4 Neshaminy Interplex Ste 209 Trevose PA 19053 215-244-3070
Web: diiradiology.com

Diagnostic Laboratory of Oklahoma LLC
225 N East 97th St Oklahoma City OK 73114 405-608-6100
Web: www.dlolab.com

Diagnostic Laboratory Services Inc
99-859 Iwaiwa St Aiea HI 96701 808-589-5100
Web: www.dlslab.com

Diagnostic Pathology Medical Group Inc
3301 C St Ste 200e Sacramento CA 95816 916-446-0424
Web: www.cafebleu.com

Diagnostic Radiology Associates of Edison
3830 & 3840 Park Ave Edison NJ 08820 732-494-9061

DIATHERIX Laboratories Inc
601 Genome Way Ste 4208 Huntsville AL 35806 256-327-0699
Web: www.diatherix.com

Distinctive Dental Studio Ltd. Inc
1504 Wall St Naperville IL 60563 630-369-4600
TF: 800-552-7890 ■ *Web:* www.ddsltdlab.com

DNA Labs International Inc
240 Sw Natura Ave Deerfield Beach FL 33441 954-426-5163
Web: www.dnalabsinternational.com

Duckworth Pathology Group Inc 1211 Union Ave Memphis TN 38104 901-725-7551

Dynacare Laboratories Inc
9200 W Wisconsin Ave Milwaukee WI 53226 414-805-7600
Web: www.dynacaremilwaukee.com

DynaLifeDX Diagnostic Laboratory Services
10150 - 102 St Ste 200 Edmonton AB T5J5E2 780-451-3702
TF: 800-661-9876 ■ *Web:* www.dynalifedx.com

East Side Clinical Laboratory Inc
10 Risho Ave East Providence RI 02914 401-455-8400
Web: www.esclab.com

Elisa Act Biotechnologies 109 Carpenter Dr Sterling VA 20165 800-553-5472
TF: 800-553-5472 ■ *Web:* www.elisaact.com

Ella Health Inc
1 Lemoyne Sq Plz
Ste 102 (On Camp Hill Bypass Rd) Lemoyne PA 17043 717-695-9464
Web: www.ellahealth.com

ExamWorks Inc 3280 Peachtree Rd Ste 2625 Atlanta GA 30305 404-952-2400
Web: www.examworks.com

Express Diagnostics Int'l Inc
1550 Industrial Dr Blue Earth MN 56013 507-526-3951
Web: www.drugcheck.com

First - Call Medical Inc
574 Boston Rd Unit 11 Billerica MA 01821 978-670-5399
Web: www.fcminc.com

First Dental Health 5771 Copley Dr Ste 101 San Diego CA 92111 800-334-7244
TF: 800-334-7244 ■ *Web:* www.firstdentalhealth.com

Foundation Laboratory 1716 W Holt Ave Pomona CA 91768 909-623-9301
TF: 800-843-7190 ■ *Web:* www.foundationlaboratory.com

Futurewise 816 Second Ave Ste 200 Seattle WA 98104 713-874-1990
Web: www.houstontraining.com

Gamma Dynacare Medical Laboratories Inc
115 Midair Ct Brampton ON L6T5M3 800-668-2714
TF: 800-668-2714 ■ *Web:* www.dynacare.ca

Gene By Gene LTD 1445 N Loop West 820 Houston TX 77008 832-381-5410
Web: www.genebygene.com

Genetic Assays Inc
4711 Trousdale Dr Ste 209 Nashville TN 37220 615-781-0709
Web: www.geneticassays.com

Genetics & IVF Institute Inc
3015 Williams Dr Fairfax VA 22031 703-698-7355
Web: www.givf.com

Genetics Associates Inc
1916 Patterson St Ste 400 Nashville TN 37203 615-327-4532
TF: 800-331-4363 ■ *Web:* www.geneticsassociates.com

Gw Technologies 1245 S Garfield Ave Traverse City MI 49686 231-941-2250
Web: www.goodwillnmi.org

HEALTHeLINK
The Commons at Walden 2568 Walden Ave
Ste 107 Buffalo NY 14225 716-206-0993
Web: www.wnyhealthelink.com

HEALTHEON Inc 201 St Charles Ave Ste 2500 New Orleans LA 70170 504-599-5982
Web: www.healtheoninc.com

Highlands Pathology Consultants Pc
2175 Hwy 75 Ste 4 Blountville TN 37617 423-323-5290
TF: 877-696-6775 ■ *Web:* www.asspalace.com

Histopath Billing 3853 S Alameda St Corpus Christi TX 78411 361-992-4040
Web: www.histopath.com

Imaging Healthcare Specialists Medical Group Inc
6256 Greenwich Dr Ste 150 San Diego CA 92122 866-558-4320
TF: 866-558-4320 ■ *Web:* www.imaginghealthcare.com

Implantech Dental Laboratory
72415 Parkview Dr Palm Desert CA 92260 760-341-7388
Web: www.implantechlab.com

Incyte Diagnostics
13103 E Mansfield Ave Spokane Valley WA 99216 509-892-2700
Web: www.incytepathology.com

Industrial Health Council
3513 Seventh Ave S Birmingham AL 35222 205-326-4109
Web: www.i-h-c.org

Infuse Medical 3369 W Mayflower Ave Ste 100 Lehi UT 84043 801-331-8610
Web: www.infusemed.com

Insight Medical Holdings Ltd
200 Meadowlark Health Ctr 156 St and 89 Ave
Edmonton AB T5R5W9 780-669-2222
Web: www.x-ray.ca

Integrated Regional Laboratories Inc
5361 NW 33rd Ave Ft. Lauderdale FL 33309 800-522-0232
TF: 800-522-0232 ■ *Web:* www.irlfl.com

Interactive Medical Connections Inc
700 Gemini St Ste 110 Houston TX 77058 281-486-4434
TF: 800-480-8040 ■ *Web:* www.edrugfree.com

International Medical Laboratory Inc
6419 Parkland Dr Sarasota FL 34243 941-756-0000
Web: www.internationalmedicallab.com

Interscope Pathology Medical Group Inc
21114 Vanowen St Canoga Park CA 91303 818-992-7848
Web: www.interscopepath.com

Phone | Fax

Kaylor Dental Laboratory Inc
619 N Florence St . . . . . Wichita KS 67212 316-943-3226
TF: 800-657-2549 ■ Web: www.kaylordental.com

Kimball Genetics Inc 8490 Upland Dr Ste 100 . . . . . Englewood CO 80112 800-444-9111
TF: 800-444-9111 ■ Web: www.kimballgenetics.com

KMH Cardiology & Diagnostic Centres
2075 Hadwen Rd . . . . . Mississauga ON L5K2L3 905-855-1860
Web: www.kmhlabs.com

Knight Dental Group 3659 Tampa Rd. . . . . . Oldsmar FL 34677 813-854-3333
Web: www.knightdentalgroup.com

Landmark Imaging Medical Group Inc
11620 Wilshire Blvd Ste 100 . . . . . Los Angeles CA 90025 310-914-7336
Web: www.landmarkimaging.com

Lawson Health Research Institute Inc
268 Grosvenor St . . . . . London ON N6A4V2 519-646-6005
Web: www.lawsonresearch.ca

Lenox Hill Radiology & Medical Imaging Associates PC
61 E 77th St . . . . . New York NY 10075 212-772-3111
Web: www.lenoxhillradiology.com

LifeScan Laboratory Inc 5255 W Golf. . . . . . Skokie IL 60077 800-270-0037
TF: 800-270-0037 ■ Web: lifescanlab.com

Litholink Corp 2250 W Campbell Park Dr . . . . . Chicago IL 60612 312-243-0600
Web: www.litholink.com

Lous Clinical Laboratory Inc 706 Adams Ave . . . . . Odessa TX 79761 432-332-9421
Web: www.drug-screen.com

Main Street Radiology 13625 37th Ave Fl 2 . . . . . Flushing NY 11354 718-428-1500
Web: www.mainstreetradiology.com

Mayo Collaborative Services Inc
3050 Superior Dr NW . . . . . Rochester MN 55901 507-266-5700
Web: www.mayomedicallaboratories.com

Med Fusion LLC
2501 S State Hwy 121 Business Ste 1100 . . . . . Lewisville TX 75067 972-966-7000
Web: www.medfusionservices.com

Medical Instrument Development Laboratories Inc
557 McCormick St . . . . . San Leandro CA 94577 510-357-3952
Web: www.midlabs.com

MEDomics LLC 426 N San Gabriel Ave . . . . . Azusa CA 91702 626-804-3645
Web: www.medomics.com

Metallurgical Technologies Inc PA
160 Bevan Dr . . . . . Mooresville NC 28115 704-663-5108
Web: www.met-tech.com

Mo Bio Laboratories Inc
2746 Loker Ave W Ste A. . . . . . Carlsbad CA 92010 760-929-9911
Web: www.mobio.com

Modern Dental Laboratory USA LLC
13228 SE 30th St Ste C-6. . . . . . Bellevue WA 98005 877-711-8778
TF: 877-711-8778 ■ Web: www.moderndentalusa.com

Molecular Diagnostics Laboratories Inc
632 Russell St . . . . . Covington KY 41011 513-437-3000
Web: www.mdl-labs.com

Molecular Imaging Services Inc 10 Whitaker Ct. . . . . . Bear DE 19701 866-937-8855
TF: 866-937-8855 ■ Web: www.mismedical.com

Moleculera Labs LLC
755 Research Pkwy Ste 410. . . . . . Oklahoma City OK 73104 405-239-5250
Web: www.moleculeralabs.com

MRI Group 2100 Harrisburg Pk. . . . . . Lancaster PA 17601 717-291-1016
TF: 888-674-1377 ■ Web: www.mrigroup.com

Murray Kaizer Dental Laboratory
24 Spring Ln Ste 1 . . . . . Farmington CT 06032 860-677-7700
Web: www.murraykaizer.com

Nakanishi Dental Laboratory Inc
2959 Northup Way . . . . . Bellevue WA 98004 425-822-2245
Web: www.nakanishidentallab.com/

National Center for Drug Free Sport, The
2537 Madison Ave . . . . . Kansas City MO 64108 816-474-8655
Web: www.drugfreesport.com

Navix Diagnostix Inc 100 Myles Standish Blvd . . . . . Taunton MA 02780 508-977-2807
Web: www.navixdiagnostix.com

Nicholas Laboratories LLC
15 Enterprise Ste 550. . . . . . Aliso Viejo CA 92656 949-448-4360

Northern Illinois Clinical Laboratory Ltd
306 Era Dr . . . . . Northbrook IL 60062 847-509-9779
Web: www.nicl.com

O'Brien Dental Lab Inc
4311 SW Research Way . . . . . Corvallis OR 97333 541-754-1238
TF: 800-445-5941 ■ Web: www.obriendentallab.com

OB-GYN Physicians Inc
118 Fairview Dr Ste 100. . . . . . Franklin VA 23851 314-872-7400
Web: www.obgynphysician.com

Occupational Care Consultants
3028 Navarre Ave . . . . . Oregon OH 43616 419-697-6850
Web: www.therapyworks.net

Old Town Endoscopy Center LLC
5500 Greenville Ave Ste 1100. . . . . . Dallas TX 75206 214-646-3470
Web: www.dhat.com

Omega Laboratories Inc 400 N Cleveland Ave . . . . . Mogadore OH 44260 330-628-5748
Web: www.omegalabs.net

OncoMDx Inc 2458 Embarcadero Way. . . . . . Palo Alto CA 94303 650-532-9500
Web: www.oncomdx.com

One Source Toxicology Laboratory Inc
1213 Genoa Red Bluff Rd . . . . . Pasadena TX 77504 713-920-2559
Web: www.onesourcetox.com

Oral Arts Dental Laboratory Inc
3339 Chamblee Dunwoody Rd . . . . . Atlanta GA 30341 770-454-9640
Web: www.oralartsdental.com

OralDNA Labs Inc
7400 Flying Cloud Dr Ste 150 . . . . . Eden Prairie MN 55344 952-400-7772
Web: www.oraldna.com

Orthodent Ltd 311 Viola Ave . . . . . Oshawa ON L1H3A7 905-436-3133
Web: orthodentus.com

Outpatient Imaging Affiliates LLC
4322 Harding Pk Ste 422 . . . . . Nashville TN 37205 615-846-7733
Web: www.oiarad.com

Palo Alto Medical Foundation for Health Care Research & Education, The
795 El Camino Real . . . . . Palo Alto CA 94301 650-853-2974
Web: www.pamf.org

Pathology & Cytology Laboratories Inc
290 Big Run Rd . . . . . Lexington KY 40503 859-278-9513
TF: 800-264-0514 ■ Web: www.pandclab.com

Pathology Group The Mid South
6046 KNIGHT ARNOLD Rd EXT Ste 101. . . . . . Memphis TN 38115 901-542-6800
Web: www.trumbulllabs.com

Pathology Inc 19951 Mariner Ave Ste 150 . . . . . Torrance CA 90503 310-769-0561
Web: www.pathologyinc.com

Pathology Laboratories Inc
1946 N 13th St Ste 301 . . . . . Toledo OH 43604 419-255-4600
Web: www.pathlabs.org

PeaceHealth Laboratories
123 International Way. . . . . . Springfield OR 97477 541-341-8010
Web: www.peacehealthlabs.org

PersonalizeDx 2980 Scott St. . . . . . Vista CA 92081 877-429-6643
TF: 877-429-6643 ■ Web: www.personalizedxlabs.com/2.html

Pharmacogenetics Diagnostic Laboratory LLC
201 E Jefferson St Ste 309 . . . . . Louisville KY 40202 502-569-1584
Web: www.pgxlab.com

Pharmagra Labs Inc 158 Mclean Rd . . . . . Brevard NC 28712 828-884-8656
Web: www.pharmagra.com

Phase 2 Medical Manufacturing Inc
88 Airport Dr. . . . . . Rochester NH 03867 603-332-8900
Web: www.phase2medical.com

Phenopath Laboratories PLLC
551 N 34th St Ste 100 . . . . . Seattle WA 98103 206-374-9000
TF: 888-927-4366 ■ Web: www.phenopath.com

Physicians Laboratory Services Inc 4840 "F" St . . . . . Omaha NE 68117 402-731-4145
Web: www.physlab.com

Physicians Reference Laboratory LLC
7800 W 110th St. . . . . . Overland Park KS 66210 913-338-4070
Web: www.prlnet.com

Pittman Dental Laboratory
2355 Centennial Cir . . . . . Gainesville GA 30504 770-534-4457
Web: www.pittmandental.com

PLUS Diagnostics Inc 825 Rahway Ave . . . . . Union NJ 07083 732-901-7575
Web: www.plusdx.com

Poly-Tech Dental Studio
868 N Garfield Ave . . . . . Montebello CA 90640 323-890-9004
Web: poly.edu

Posca Bros Dental Laboratory Inc
641 W Willow St. . . . . . Long Beach CA 90806 562-427-1811
TF: 800-537-6722 ■ Web: www.poscabrothers.com

Precipio Diagnostics LLC
4 Science Park 3rd Fl . . . . . New Haven CT 06511 203-787-7888
Web: precipiodx.com

Preferred Dental Laboratory Inc
37 Woodland Rd. . . . . . Roseland NJ 07068 973-228-7777
Web: www.preferreddentalgroup.com

Primex Clinical Laboratories Inc
16742 Stagg St Ste 120 . . . . . Van Nuys CA 91406 818-779-0496
Web: www.primexlab.com

Quality Bioresources Inc 1015 N Austin St . . . . . Seguin TX 78155 830-372-4797
TF: 888-674-7224 ■ Web: www.qualbio.com

RadNet Inc 1516 Cotner Ave . . . . . Los Angeles CA 90025 310-445-2800 445-2980
Web: www.radnet.com

Regional Medical Laboratories Inc
175 College St . . . . . Battle Creek MI 49037 269-969-6161
Web: www.glplasticandhandsurgery.com

Reliance Pathology Partners LLC
5755 Hoover Blvd. . . . . . Tampa FL 33634 813-884-2849
Web: www.pims-inc.com

Reproductive Genetics Institute Inc
2825 N Halsted. . . . . . Chicago IL 60657 773-472-4900
Web: www.east-westmedical.net

Roe Dental Laboratory Inc
9565 Midwest Ave . . . . . Garfield Heights OH 44125 216-663-2233 663-2237
TF: 800-228-6663 ■ Web: www.roedentallab.com

Rolling Oaks Radiology Inc
415 Rolling Oaks Dr . . . . . Thousand Oaks CA 91361 805-778-1513
Web: www.rollingoaksradiology.com

Roman Research Inc 800 Franklin St. . . . . . Hanson MA 02341 800-225-8652
TF: 800-225-8652 ■ Web: www.romanresearch.com

Rose Radiology Boot Ranch
4133 Woodlands Pkwy . . . . . Palm Harbor FL 34685 727-781-3888
TF: 877-674-7673 ■ Web: www.roseradiology.com

Sand Lake Imaging 9350 Turkey Lk Rd . . . . . Orlando FL 32819 407-363-2772
Web: www.sandlakeimaging.com

Shiel Medical Laboratory Inc
Brooklyn Navy Yard Bldg 292 63 Flushing Ave
. . . . . Brooklyn NY 11205 718-552-1000
Web: www.shiel.com

Siloam Biosciences LLC 413 Northland Blvd . . . . . Cincinnati OH 45240 513-429-2976
Web: www.siloambio.com

Simonmed Imaging
6900 E Camelback Rd Ste 700 . . . . . Scottsdale AZ 85251 480-614-8555
Web: www.simonmed.com

Slater Technology Fund 3 Davol Sq Ste A340 . . . . . Providence RI 02903 401-831-6633
Web: www.slaterfund.com

Sonic Healthcare USA Inc
9737 Great Hills Trl Ste 100 . . . . . Austin TX 78759 512-439-1600
Web: www.sonichealthcareusa.com

South Bay Expressway LP 1129 La Media Rd. . . . . . San Diego CA 92154 619-661-7070
Web: www.southbayexpressway.com

South Jersey Radiology Associates PA
100 Carnie Blvd . . . . . Voorhees NJ 08043 856-751-5522
Web: www.sjra.com

SPSmedical Supply Corp 6789 W Henrietta Rd. . . . . . Rush NY 14543 585-359-0130
Web: www.spsmedical.com

Stockton Endoscopy Center
415 E Harding Way Ste E . . . . . Stockton CA 95204 209-942-1179
Web: www.stocktonurology.com

Phone | Fax

Studio 2 Digital Dental Design Inc
2405 32nd St SE.................................Kentwood MI 49512 616-957-2140
Web: www.studio2dental.com

Suncoast Pathology Inc 446 Tamiami Trl S ....Venice FL 34285 941-483-3319
Web: www.defevercruisers.com

Touchstone Medical Imaging LLC
5214 Maryland Way Ste 200......................Brentwood TN 37027 615-661-9200
Web: www.touchstoneimaging.com

TriCore Reference Laboratories
1001 Woodward Pl NE ....Albuquerque NM 87102 505-938-8888
Web: www.tricore.org

Truxtun Radiology Medical Group LP
1817 Truxtun Ave ....Bakersfield CA 93301 661-325-6800
Web: www.truxtunrad.com

Utah Imaging Associates Inc
380 N 200 W Ste 209...........................Bountiful UT 84010 801-924-0029
Web: www.utahimaging.com

VantagePoint Laboratory Partners LLC
4980 Carroll Canyon Rd.........................San Diego CA 92121 858-638-8120
Web: www.vpointlabs.com

VDIC Inc 16900 SE 82nd Dr.......................Clackamas OR 97015 503-722-8077
Web: www.vdic.com

Vista Imaging Services Inc
3941 Park Dr Ste 20-463 .... El Dorado Hills CA 95762 415-272-3925
TF: 855-972-9729 ■ *Web:* www.vistaimagingservices.com

Warde Medical Laboratory 300 W Textile Rd.........Ann Arbor MI 48108 734-214-0300
TF: 800-876-6522 ■ *Web:* www.wardelab.com

Weidmann Diagnostic Solutions Inc
4011 Power Inn Rd Ste G ....Sacramento CA 95826 916-455-2284
Web: www.weidmann-diagnostics.com

Weland Clinical Laboratories PC
1911 First Ave SE............................Cedar Rapids IA 52402 319-366-1503
Web: www.welandlaboratories.com

West End Diagnostic Imaging
2425 Bloor St W Ste 103 ....Toronto ON M6S4W4 416-763-4331
Web: www.wedi.ca

Yosemite Pathology Group Inc
2625 Coffee Rd Ste S ....Modesto CA 95355 209-577-1200
Web: www.ypmg.com

416 LABORATORIES - DRUG-TESTING

See Also Laboratories - Medical p. 2622

Phone | Fax

Aerobiology Laboratory Associates Inc
43760 Trade Ctr Pl Ste 100 ....Dulles VA 20166 703-648-9150
Web: www.aerobiology.net

ArcticDx Inc
MaRS Centre S Tower 101 College St Ste 200...........Toronto ON M5G1L7 866-964-5182
TF: 866-964-5182 ■ *Web:* www.arcticdx.com

Bio-Reference Laboratories Inc
481 Edward H Ross Dr ....Elmwood Park NJ 07407 800-229-5227 791-1941*
NASDAQ: BRLI ■ **Fax Area Code:* 201 ■ *TF:* 800-229-5227 ■ *Web:* www.bioreference.com

Drug Detection Laboratories Inc
9700 Business Pk Dr Ste 407.....................Sacramento CA 95827 916-366-3113 366-3917
Web: www.drugdetection.net

DrugScan Inc
200 Precision Rd Ste 200 PO Box 347 ....Horsham PA 19044 800-235-4890
TF: 800-235-4890 ■ *Web:* www.drugscan.com

ElSohly Laboratories Inc 5 Industrial Pk Dr ....Oxford MS 38655 662-236-2609 234-0253
Web: www.elsohly.com

Industrial Laboratories Company Inc, The
4046 Youngfield St...........................Wheat Ridge CO 80033 303-287-9691 287-0964
Web: www.industriallabs.net

LabOne Inc 10101 Renner Blvd ....Lenexa KS 66219 913-888-1770 888-1778*
**Fax:* Sales ■ *TF:* 800-646-7788 ■ *Web:* www.labone.com

MEDTOX Scientific Inc 402 W County Rd D ....Saint Paul MN 55112 651-636-7466
NASDAQ: MTOX ■ *TF:* 800-832-3244 ■ *Web:* www.medtox.com

Mobile Medical Lab Services
6312 Carolina Beach Rd.........................Wilmington NC 28412 910-452-0093
Web: mobilemedicallabservices.com

Moffitt Genetics Corporation Inc
10902 N McKinley Dr................................Tampa FL 33612 813-384-5000
Web: www.m2gen.com

Mri Center Of New England Inc
800 W Cummings Park Ste 1150 ....Woburn MA 01801 781-932-8650
Web: www.mricenter.com

New York Imaging Service Inc
5 Jeanne Dr Ste 3.............................Newburgh NY 12550 845-561-6947
Web: www.nyimagingservice.org

Obetech LLC 800 E Leigh St.......................Richmond VA 23219 804-344-5360
Web: adv36.com

Ocular Systems Inc
Innovation Quarter 101 N Chestnut St
Ste 303...................................... Winston-salem NC 27101 336-784-4603
Web: www.ocularsystemsinc.com

Onsite Health Diagnostics LLC
8445 Freeport Pkwy Ste 500...............................Irving TX 75063 972-823-1600
Web: www.onsitehealthdiagnostics.com

Pathologists' Regional Laboratory
1225 Highland Ave..............................Clarkston WA 99403 509-758-5576
Web: pathregional.com

Pinon Family Practice
2300 E 30th St Bldg C2 ....Farmington NM 87401 505-324-1000
Web: www.pinonfp.com

Sequenom Center for Molecular Medicine LLC
301 Michigan St NE Ste 580.....................Grand Rapids MI 49503 616-391-4330
Web: www.sequenomcmm.com

US Drug Testing Laboratories Inc
1700 S Mt Prospect Rd.........................Des Plaines IL 60018 847-375-0770 375-0775
TF: 800-235-2367 ■ *Web:* www.usdtl.com

Valsource Inc 105 Gottier Dr ....Downingtown PA 19335 610-942-0646
Web: www.valsource.com

417 LABORATORIES - GENETIC TESTING

See Also Laboratories - Medical p. 2622

Phone | Fax

American Red Cross Pacific NorthWest Blood Service
3131 N Vancouver Ave ....Portland OR 97227 503-284-1234
Web: www.redcrossblood.org

Blood Systems Laboratories 2424 W Erie Dr...........Tempe AZ 85282 602-343-7000
TF: 800-288-2199 ■ *Web:* www.bloodsystemslaboratories.org

BRT Laboratories Inc 400 W Franklin St.............Baltimore MD 21201 410-225-9595
TF: 800-765-5170 ■ *Web:* www.brtlabs.com

Center for Genetic Testing at Saint Francis
6465 S Yale Ave ....Tulsa OK 74136 918-502-1720
TF: 877-789-6001 ■ *Web:* www.saintfrancis.com

Commonwealth Biotechnologies Inc
601 Biotech Dr ....Richmond VA 23235 804-648-3820 648-2641
TF: 800-735-9224 ■ *Web:* cbi-biotech.com

DNA Diagnostics Ctr 1 DDC Way.....................Fairfield OH 45014 513-881-7800 881-7803
TF: 800-362-2368 ■ *Web:* www.dnacenter.com

DNA Paternity Lab of Utah
2749 E Parleys Way Ste 100................... Salt Lake City UT 84109 801-466-3872 582-8460
TF: 800-362-5559 ■ *Web:* www.affiliatedgenetics.com

Eurofins Scientific Inc
2200 Rittenhouse St Ste 150 ....Des Moines IA 50321 515-265-1461 266-5453
Web: www.eurofinsus.com

Genetic Profiles Corp
10675 Treena St Ste 103 ....San Diego CA 92131 800-551-7763
TF: 800-551-7763 ■ *Web:* www.geneticprofiles.com

Genetica DNA Laboratories Inc
8740 Montgomery Rd.............................Cincinnati OH 45236 513-985-9777
TF: 800-433-6848 ■ *Web:* www.genetica.com

GenQuest DNA Analysis Laboratory
133 Coney Island Dr...................................Sparks NV 89431 775-358-0652
TF: 877-362-5227 ■ *Web:* www.genquestdnalab.com

Genzyme Genetics 3400 Computer Dr ....Westborough MA 01581 508-898-9001 331-5799*
**Fax Area Code:* 267 ■ *TF:* 800-255-7357 ■ *Web:* www.labcorp.com

Identity Genetics Inc 47927 213th St.................Aurora SD 57002 800-861-1054
TF: 800-861-1054 ■ *Web:* www.identitygenetics.com

Laboratory Corp of America Holdings
358 S Main St...................................Burlington NC 27215 336-584-5171
NYSE: LH ■ *TF:* 800-334-5161 ■ *Web:* www.labcorp.com

LABS Inc 6933 S Revere Pkwy ....Centennial CO 80112 720-528-4750 528-4786
TF: 866-393-2244 ■ *Web:* www.labs-inc.org

Maxxam Analytics Inc 335 LaiRd Rd Ste 2 ....Guelph ON N1G4P7 877-706-7678
TF: 877-706-7678 ■ *Web:* www.maxxam.ca

Medical Genetics Consultants
819 DeSoto St ....Ocean Springs MS 39564 800-362-4363 872-1893*
**Fax Area Code:* 228 ■ *TF:* 800-362-4363 ■ *Web:* www.legalgenetics.com

Memorial Blood Centers (MBC) 737 Pelham Blvd..... Saint Paul MN 55114 651-332-7000 332-7001
TF Cust Svc: 888-448-3253 ■ *Web:* www.mbc.org

Molecular Pathology Laboratory Network Inc
250 E Broadway ....Maryville TN 37804 865-380-9746 380-9191
TF: 800-932-2943 ■ *Web:* www.mplnet.com

NMS Labs 3701 Welsh Rd.......................Willow Grove PA 19090 215-657-4900 657-2972
TF: 800-522-6671 ■ *Web:* www.nmslabs.com

Paternity Testing Corp (PTC) 300 Portland St.........Columbia MO 65201 573-442-9948 442-9870
TF: 888-837-8323 ■ *Web:* www.ptclabs.com

Rhode Island Blood Ctr 405 Promenade St.......... Providence RI 02908 401-453-8360 453-8557
TF: 800-283-8385 ■ *Web:* www.ribc.org

RJ Lee Group Inc 350 Hochberg Rd ....Monroeville PA 15146 724-325-1776 733-1799
Web: rjlg.com

South Texas Blood & Tissue Ctr
6211 IH-10 W...............................San Antonio TX 78201 210-731-5555 731-5501
TF: 800-292-5534 ■ *Web:* southtexasblood.org

State University of New York Upstate Medical University Tissue Typing Laboratory
750 E Adams St ....Syracuse NY 13210 315-464-4775 464-9557
TF: 877-464-5540 ■ *Web:* www.upstate.edu

University of North Texas Health Science Ctr
3500 Camp Bowie Blvd ....Fort Worth TX 76107 817-735-2000 735-5016
TF: 800-687-7580 ■ *Web:* www.unthsc.edu

418 LABORATORIES - MEDICAL

See Also Blood Centers p. 1863; Laboratories - Dental p. 2619; Laboratories - Drug-Testing p. 2622; Laboratories - Genetic Testing p. 2622; Organ & Tissue Banks p. 2861

Phone | Fax

A b C Testing Inc 95 First St PO Box 868............Bridgewater MA 02324 508-697-6068
Web: www.abcndt.com

ABC American Bio-clinical
2730 N Main St Ste 101.........................Los Angeles CA 90031 800-262-1688
TF: 800-262-1688 ■ *Web:* www.abclab.com

Accugenix Inc 223 Lake Dr.............................. Newark DE 19702 302-292-8888
TF: 877-274-8371 ■ *Web:* criver.com/products-services

AdvanDx Inc 400 Tradecenter.........................Woburn MA 01801 781-376-0009
Web: www.advandx.com

Analyte Health Inc 328 S Jefferson St Ste 770...........Chicago IL 60661 312-477-3000
Web: www.analytehealth.com

ANI Pharmaceuticals Inc 210 Main St W .... Baudette MN 56623 302-482-8644
Web: www.anipharmaceuticals.com

Applied Laboratories Inc
3240 N Indianapolis Rd PO Box 2127 ....Columbus IN 47202 812-372-2607 372-2631
Web: www.appliedlabs.com

Ariosa Diagnostics Inc 5945 Optical Ct ....San Jose CA 95138 855-927-4672
TF: 855-927-4672 ■ *Web:* www.ariosadx.com

Arkansas Anatomic Pathology Services pa
411 E Matthews Ave ....Jonesboro AR 72401 870-930-3518
TF: 800-764-0447 ■ *Web:* www.dapsonline.com

Atherotech Inc 201 London Pkwy.................Birmingham AL 35211 800-719-9807
TF: 800-719-9807 ■ *Web:* www.atherotech.com

Phone | Fax

Aurum Ceramic Dental Laboratories Ltd
115 17 Ave SW ... Calgary AB T2S0A1 403-228-5120
TF: 800-665-8815 ■ *Web:* www.aurumgroup.com

Bio-Reference Laboratories Inc
481 Edward H Ross Dr ... Elmwood Park NJ 07407 800-229-5227 791-1941*
NASDAQ: BRLI ■ **Fax Area Code:* 201 ■ *TF:* 800-229-5227 ■ *Web:* www.bioreference.com

BioMarker Strategies LLC
855 N Wolfe St Ste 603 ... Baltimore MD 21205 410-522-1008
Web: www.biomarkerstrategies.com

Biometrix Inc 2419 Ocean Ave ... San Francisco CA 94127 415-333-0522
Web: biometrixinc.com

BioZone Laboratories Inc 580 Garcia Ave ... Pittsburg CA 94565 925-473-1000
Web: www.biozonelabs.com

Biron Groupe Sante Inc 4105-F Blvd Matte ... Brossard QC J4Y2P4 514-866-6146
Web: www.biron.ca

Boval Company LP 505 W Industrial Blvd ... Cleburne TX 76031 817-645-1706
TF: 800-635-1706 ■ *Web:* www.bovalco.com

Calvert Labs 1225 Crescent Green Ste 115 ... Cary NC 27518 919-459-8653
TF: 800-300-8114 ■ *Web:* www.calvertlabs.com

Canadian Medical Laboratories Ltd
6560 Kennedy Rd ... Mississauga ON L5T2X4 800-263-0801
TF: 800-263-0801 ■ *Web:* profilecanada.com

Cell Signaling Technology Inc 3 Trask Ln ... Danvers MA 01923 978-867-2300 867-2400
TF: 877-678-8324 ■ *Web:* www.cellsignal.com

Charlotte Radiological P.A 1701 East Blvd ... Charlotte NC 28203 704-334-7800
Web: www.charlotteradiology.com

CIS Biotech Inc 2675 N Decatur Rd Ste 212 ... Atlanta GA 30033 404-499-0303
Web: www.cisbiotech.com

ClearPath Diagnostics
600 E Genesee St Ste 305 ... Syracuse NY 13202 315-234-3300
Web: www.clearpathdiagnostics.com

Cmi 6704 Guada Coma Dr ... Schertz TX 78154 210-967-6169 967-9233
TF: 800-840-1070 ■ *Web:* www.cmi-satx.com

Cml Healthcare Inc
Unit 1 60 Courtneypark Dr W ... Mississauga ON L5W0B3 905-565-0043
TF: 800-263-0801 ■ *Web:* www.cmlhealthcare.com

Crown Valley Imaging LLC
27401 Los Altos Ste 150 ... Mission Viejo CA 92691 949-367-1010
Web: www.crownvalleyimaging.com

David Chen Md Diagnostic Medical Group Inc
1129 S San Gabriel Blvd ... San Gabriel CA 91776 626-287-6746
Web: www.dmg.net

DIANON Systems Inc 1 Forest Pkwy ... Shelton CT 06484 203-926-7100
TF: 800-328-2666 ■ *Web:* www.dianon.com

DNA Reference Lab Inc
7271 Wurzbach Rd Ste 125 ... San Antonio TX 78240 210-692-3800
Web: www.dnareferencelab.com

Doctors Pathology Services
1253 College Park Dr ... Dover DE 19904 302-677-0000
Web: dpspa.com

Donlevy Laboratories Inc
11165 Delaware Pkwy ... Crown Point IN 46307 219-226-0001
Web: www.donlevylab.com

Doshi Diagnostic Imaging Services PC
560 S Broadway ... Hicksville NY 11801 516-933-2800
Web: www.doshidiagnostic.com

Equipoise Dental Laboratory Inc
85 Portland Ave ... Bergenfield NJ 07621 201-385-4750 385-3280
TF: 800-999-4950 ■ *Web:* www.equipoisedental.com

ESA Biosciences Inc 22 Alpha Rd ... Chelmsford MA 01824 978-250-7000

Focus Diagnostics Inc 11331 Vly View St ... Cypress CA 90630 562-240-6500
Web: m.focusdx.com

Genetrack Biolabs Inc 401-1508 Broadway W ... Vancouver BC V6J1W8 604-325-7282
TF: 888-828-1899 ■ *Web:* www.genetrack.com

Genova Diagnostics 63 Zillicoa St ... Asheville NC 28801 828-253-0621 252-9303*
**Fax:* Cust Svc ■ *TF:* 800-522-4762 ■ *Web:* www.gdx.net

Global Neuro-Diagnostics LP
2670 Firewheel Dr Ste B ... Flower Mound TX 75028 866-848-2522
TF: 866-848-2522 ■ *Web:* www.globalneuro.net

Global Safety & Security Inc
4713 Trenton St ... Metairie LA 70006 504-454-6933

Great Plains Laboratory Inc
11813 W 77th St ... Overland Park KS 66214 913-341-8949
TF: 800-288-0383 ■ *Web:* www.greatplainslaboratory.com

Green Dental Laboratories Inc
1099 Wilburn Rd ... Heber Springs AR 72543 501-362-3132
Web: greendentallab.com

Harmony Dental Lab 758 W Duval St ... Jacksonville FL 32202 904-354-4467
TF: 888-354-3594 ■ *Web:* www.harmonydental.com

Health Network Laboratory 2024 Lehigh St ... Allentown PA 18103 610-402-8170
TF: 877-402-4221 ■ *Web:* www.healthnetworklabs.com

Identigene LLC 2495 South West Temple ... Salt Lake City UT 84115 801-462-1401
TF: 888-404-4363 ■ *Web:* www.dnatesting.com

Igenex 795 San Antonio Rd ... Palo Alto CA 94303 650-424-1191
TF: 800-832-3200 ■ *Web:* www.igenex.com

Keller Laboratories Inc
160 Larkin Williams Industrial Ct ... Fenton MO 63026 636-600-4200
TF: 800-325-3056 ■ *Web:* www.kellerlab.com

LabOne Inc 10101 Renner Blvd ... Lenexa KS 66219 913-888-1770 888-1778*
**Fax:* Sales ■ *TF:* 800-646-7788 ■ *Web:* www.labone.com

Laboratory Corp of America Holdings
358 S Main St ... Burlington NC 27215 336-584-5171
NYSE: LH ■ *TF:* 800-334-5161 ■ *Web:* www.labcorp.com

Lakeland Surgical & Diagnostic Center LLP
1315 N Florida Ave ... Lakeland FL 33805 863-683-2268
Web: www.lsdc.net

LifeLabs Inc 3680 Gilmore Way ... Burnaby BC V5G4V8 604-431-5005
Web: www.lifelabs.com

Machaon Diagnostics Inc 3023 Summit St ... Oakland CA 94609 510-839-5600
Web: www.machaondiagnostics.com

Mcmahon Publishing Group 545 W 45th St ... New York NY 10036 212-957-5300
Web: www.mcmahonmed.com

Phone | Fax

Medical Diagnostic Laboratories LLC
2439 Kuser Rd ... Hamilton NJ 08690 609-570-1000
TF: 877-269-0090 ■ *Web:* www.mdlab.com

Midwest Clinical Laboratories
3267 S 16th St ... Milwaukee WI 53215 414-647-5505 256-5566

National Genetics Institute
2440 S Blvd Ste 235 ... Los Angeles CA 90064 310-996-0036
TF: 800-352-7788 ■ *Web:* www.ngi.com

Nebraska Lablinc LLC 5440 S St Ste 100 ... Lincoln NE 68506 402-484-5462
TF: 866-886-5462 ■ *Web:* www.lablinc.com

NeoGenomics Inc
12701 Commonwealth Dr Ste 9 ... Fort Myers FL 33913 941-923-1949
Web: www.neogenomics.com

NeuroScience Inc 373 280th St ... Osceola WI 54020 715-294-2144
TF: 888-342-7272 ■ *Web:* www.neurorelief.com

NMS Labs 3701 Welsh Rd ... Willow Grove PA 19090 215-657-4900 657-2972
TF: 800-522-6671 ■ *Web:* www.nmslabs.com

Norgen Biotek Corp 3430 Schmon Pkwy ... Thorold ON L2V4Y6 905-227-8848 227-1061
TF: 866-667-4362 ■ *Web:* www.norgenbiotek.com

North Coast Clinical Laboratory Inc
2215 Cleveland Rd ... Sandusky OH 44870 419-626-6012
TF: 800-325-5737 ■ *Web:* www.northcoastlab.com

Northern Diagnostic Laboratories Inc
301A US Route 1 ... Scarborough ME 04074 207-396-7830
Web: www.nordx.org

Opmedic Group Inc
1361 Beaumont Ave Ste 301 ... Mount-royal QC H3P2W3 514-345-8535
TF: 888-776-2732 ■ *Web:* www.groupeopmedic.com

Parkway Clinical Laboratories Inc
3494 Progress Dr ... Bensalem PA 19020 215-245-5112
TF: 800-327-2764 ■ *Web:* www.parkwayclinical.com

Path Logic Inc
950 Riverside Pkwy Ste 90 ... West Sacramento CA 95605 855-291-4528
TF: 855-291-4528 ■ *Web:* www.pathlogic.com

Pathology Ctr, The 8303 Dodge St ... Omaha NE 68114 402-354-4540
Web: thepathologycenter.org

Penta Laboratories 9740 Cozycroft Ave ... Chatsworth CA 91311 818-882-3872
Web: pentalabs.com

PerkinElmer Genetics Inc 90 Emerson Ln ... Bridgeville PA 15017 412-220-2300
Web: www.perkinelmer.com/genetics/index.html

Persante Health Care Inc
130 Gaither Dr Ste 124 ... Mt. Laurel NJ 08054 856-234-0770
Web: www.persante.com

Personal Genome Diagnostics Inc
2809 Boston St Ste 503 ... Baltimore MD 21224 443-602-8833
Web: personalgenome.com

Physician's Automated Laboratory Inc (PALLAB)
9830 Brimhall Rd ... Bakersfield CA 93312 661-829-2260 829-1317
TF: 800-675-2271 ■ *Web:* www.pallab.org

Ponca Tribe 2602 J St ... Omaha NE 68107 402-734-5275
Web: www.poncatribe-ne.org

Princeton Radiology Associates P.A. Inc
3674 Route 27 ... Kendall Park NJ 08824 732-821-5563
Web: www.prapa.com

ProPath Laboratory Inc 1355 River Bend Dr ... Dallas TX 75247 214-638-2000
Web: www.propathlab.com

ProScan Imaging LLC 5400 Kennedy Ave ... Cincinnati OH 45213 513-618-1063
Web: www.proscan.com

Quest Diagnostics at Nichols Institute
33608 Ortega Hwy ... San Juan Capistrano CA 92675 949-728-4000 728-4985*
**Fax:* Hum Res ■ *TF:* 800-642-4657 ■ *Web:* www.questdiagnostics.com

Quest Diagnostics Inc 3 Giralda Farms ... Madison NJ 07940 201-393-5000 462-4169*
NYSE: DGX ■ **Fax:* Cust Svc ■ *TF:* 800-222-0446 ■ *Web:* www.questdiagnostics.com

Scientific Molding Corp Ltd 330 SMC Dr ... Somerset WI 54025 715-247-3500 247-3611
Web: www.smcltd.com

South Bend Medical Foundation
530 N Lafayette Blvd ... South Bend IN 46601 574-234-4176 234-1561
TF: 800-544-0925 ■ *Web:* www.sbmflab.org

Specialty Laboratories Inc 27027 Tourney Rd ... Valencia CA 91355 661-799-6543 799-6634
TF Sales: 800-421-7110 ■ *Web:* www.specialtylabs.com

Strand Analytical Laboratories LLC
5770 Decatur Blvd Ste A ... Indianapolis IN 46241 317-455-2100
Web: stranddiagnostics.com/forensics

Sunrise Medical Laboratories Inc
250 Miller Pl ... Hicksville NY 11801 631-435-1515
TF Cust Svc: 800-782-0282 ■ *Web:* www.sunriselab.com

TeraRecon Inc 4000 E Third Ave Ste 200 ... Foster City CA 94404 650-372-1100
Web: www.terarecon.com

US Laboratory & Radiology Inc 2 Jonathan Dr ... Brockton MA 02301 508-583-2000
Web: www.uslabrad.com

Visalia Medical Lab 5400 West Hillsdale Ave ... Visalia CA 93291 559-562-1222
TF: 800-486-2362 ■ *Web:* www.vmchealth.com

Vista Biologicals Corp 2120-C Las Palmas Dr ... Carlsbad CA 92009 760-438-5058
Web: www.vistabiologicals.com

419 LABORATORY ANALYTICAL INSTRUMENTS

See Also Glassware - Laboratory & Scientific p. 2354; Laboratory Apparatus & Furniture p. 2625

Phone | Fax

Abaxis Inc 3240 Whipple Rd ... Union City CA 94587 510-675-6500 441-6150
NASDAQ: ABAX ■ *TF:* 800-822-2947 ■ *Web:* www.abaxis.com

Actinix Inc 1800 Green Hills Rd Ste 105 ... Scotts Valley CA 95066 831-440-9388
Web: www.actinix.com

Advanced Technical Support Inc
231 Crosswicks Rd ... Bordentown NJ 08505 609-298-2522
Web: www.atsrheosystems.com

Alden Research Laboratory Inc
30 Shrewsbury St ... Holden MA 01520 508-829-6000 829-5939
Web: www.aldenlab.com

Altamira Instruments Inc
149 Delta Dr Ste 200 ... Pittsburgh PA 15238 412-963-6385
Web: www.altamirainstruments.com

	City	State	Zip	Phone	Fax
American Biologics 1180 Walnut Ave	Chula Vista	CA	91911	619-429-8200	429-8004
TF: 800-227-4473 ■ *Web:* www.americanbiologics.com					
Analytical Sensors & Instruments Ltd 12800 Pk One Dr	Sugar Land	TX	77478	281-565-8818	565-8811
Web: www.asi-sensors.com					
Analytical Spectral Devices Inc 2555 55th St Ste 100	Boulder	CO	80301	303-444-6522	
Web: www.asdi.com					
Andor Technology Plc (USA) 425 Sullivan Ave Ste No3	South Windsor	CT	06074	860-290-9211	
Web: www.andor.com					
Ankom Technology 2052 Oneil Rd	Macedon	NY	14502	315-986-8090	
Web: www.ankom.com					
Applied Instrument Technologies Inc 2121 Aviation Dr	Upland	CA	91786	909-204-3700	
Web: www.aitanalyzers.com					
Asylum Research Corp 6310 Hollister Ave	Santa Barbara	CA	93117	805-696-6466	
Web: www.asylumresearch.com					
BBI Source Scientific Inc 7390 Lincoln Way	Garden Grove	CA	92841	714-898-9001	
BD Biosciences 2350 Qume Dr	San Jose	CA	95131	408-432-9475	954-2347
TF: 800-223-8226 ■ *Web:* www.bdbiosciences.com					
Bio/Data Corp PO Box 347	Horsham	PA	19044	215-441-4000	443-8820
TF: 800-257-3282 ■ *Web:* www.biodatacorp.com					
Bioanalytical Systems Inc 2701 Kent Ave	West Lafayette	IN	47906	765-463-4527	497-1102
NASDAQ: BASI ■ *TF:* 800-845-4246 ■ *Web:* www.basinc.com					
BiOptix Inc 1775 38th St	Boulder	CO	80301	303-545-5550	
Web: www.bioptix.com					
BioTek Instruments Inc 100 Tigan St PO Box 998	Winooski	VT	05404	802-655-4740	655-7941
TF: 888-451-5171 ■ *Web:* www.biotek.com					
Biovision Technologies 64 E Uwchlan Ave # 273	Exton	PA	19341	610-524-9740	
Web: www.biovis.com					
Blanke Industries Inc 1099 Brown St Ste 103	Wauconda	IL	60084	847-487-2780	
Web: www.blankeindustries.com					
Block Engineering Inc 377 Simarano Dr	Marlborough	MA	01752	508-251-3100	
Web: www.blockeng.com					
Brinkmann Instruments Inc 1819 Underwood Blvd	Delran	NJ	08075	856-764-7300	
Web: www.lauda-brinkmann.com					
Bruker Daltonics Inc 40 Manning Rd	Billerica	MA	01821	978-663-3660	667-5993
Web: www.bruker.com					
Buehler Ltd 41 Waukegan Rd	Lake Bluff	IL	60044	847-295-6500	295-7979
TF Sales: 800-283-4537 ■ *Web:* buehler.com					
California Analytical Instruments Inc 1312 W Grove Ave	Orange	CA	92865	714-974-5560	282-6280
TF: 800-959-0949 ■ *Web:* www.gasanalyzers.com					
Caliper Life Sciences Inc 68 Elm St	Hopkinton	MA	01748	508-435-9500	435-3439
TF: 800-762-4000 ■ *Web:* www.perkinelmer.com					
CAO Group Inc 4628 Skyhawk Dr	West Jordan	UT	84084	801-256-9282	256-9287
TF: 877-877-9778 ■ *Web:* www.caogroup.com					
CardioGenics Holdings Inc 6295 Northam Dr Unit 8	Mississauga	ON	L4V1W8	905-673-8501	
Web: www.cardiogenics.com					
Cargille-Sacher Laboratories Inc 55 Commerce Rd	Cedar Grove	NJ	07009	973-239-6633	239-6096
Web: www.cargille.com					
CDS Analytical Inc 465 Limestone Rd PO Box 277	Oxford	PA	19363	610-932-3636	932-4158
TF: 800-541-6593 ■ *Web:* www.cdsanalytical.com					
CEM Corp 3100 Smith Farm Rd	Matthews	NC	28104	704-821-7015	821-7894
TF: 800-726-3331 ■ *Web:* www.cem.com					
Cepheid 904 E Caribbean Dr	Sunnyvale	CA	94089	408-541-4191	541-4192
NASDAQ: CPHD ■ *TF:* 888-838-3222 ■ *Web:* www.cepheid.com					
Cetac Technologies Inc 14306 Industrial Rd	Omaha	NE	68144	402-733-2829	733-5292
TF: 800-369-2822 ■ *Web:* www.cetac.com					
CH Technologies (USA) Inc 263 Center Ave Ste 1	Westwood	NJ	07675	201-666-2335	
Web: www.envmed.com					
Chemetrics Inc 4295 Catlett Rd	Calverton	VA	20138	540-788-9026	788-4856
Web: www.chemetrics.com					
Chrom Tech Inc 5995 149th St W Ste 102	Apple Valley	MN	55124	952-431-6000	
TF: 800-822-5242 ■ *Web:* www.chromtech.com					
CMI Inc 316 E Ninth St	Owensboro	KY	42303	270-685-6545	685-6678
TF: 866-835-0690 ■ *Web:* www.alcoholtest.com					
CompuMed Inc 5777 W Century Blvd Ste 360	Los Angeles	CA	90045	310-258-5000	645-5880
TF: 800-421-3395 ■ *Web:* compumed.ning.com					
Corning Inc Life Sciences Div 836 N St Bldg 300 Ste 3401	Tewksbury	MA	01876	978-442-2200	635-2476
TF: 800-492-1110 ■ *Web:* www.corning.com/lifesciences					
CPI International Inc 5580 Skylane Blvd	Santa Rosa	CA	95403	707-525-5788	
Web: www.cpiinternational.com					
CRAIC Technologies Inc 948 N Amelia Ave	San Dimas	CA	91773	310-573-8180	
Web: www.microspectra.com					
Custom Sensors & Technology 531 Axminister Dr	Fenton	MO	63026	636-305-0666	
Web: www.customsensors.com					
Datacolor 5 Princess Rd	Lawrenceville	NJ	08648	609-924-2189	895-7414
TF General: 800-340-1007 ■ *Web:* www.datacolor.com					
Daxor Corp 350 Fifth Ave Ste 7120	New York	NY	10118	212-244-0555	244-0806
NYSE: DXR ■ *Web:* www.daxor.com					
DeltaNu LLC 5452 Old Hwy 130	Laramie	WY	82070	307-745-9148	
Diba Industries Inc 4 Precision Rd	Danbury	CT	06810	203-744-0773	
Web: www.dibaind.com					
Direct Dimensions Inc 10310 S Dolfield Rd	Owings Mills	MD	21117	410-998-0880	
Web: www.dirdim.com					
Eberbach Corp 505 S Maple Rd	Ann Arbor	MI	48103	734-665-8877	
TF: 800-422-2558 ■ *Web:* www.eberbachlabtools.com					
Eckert & Ziegler Isotope Products Inc 24937 Ave Tibbitts	Valencia	CA	91355	661-309-1010	
Web: www.isotopeproducts.com					
EDAX Inc 91 McKee Dr	Mahwah	NJ	07430	201-529-4880	529-3156
Web: www.edax.com					
Entech Instruments Inc 2207 Agate Ct	Simi Valley	CA	93065	805-527-5939	
Web: www.entechinst.com					
Environics Inc 69 Industrial Park Rd E	Tolland	CT	06084	860-872-1111	
Web: www.environics.com					
Environmental Express Ltd 2345A Charleston Regional Pkwy	Charleston	SC	29492	843-881-6560	
Web: www.envexp.com					
Eppendorf North America Inc 1 Cantiague Rd	Westbury	NY	11590	516-334-7500	
Web: www.eppendorf.com/us-en					
Exergen Corp 400 Pleasant St	Watertown	MA	02472	617-923-9900	923-9911
Web: www.exergen.com					
FEI Co 5350 NE Dawson Creek Dr	Hillsboro	OR	97124	503-726-7500	726-2570*
NASDAQ: FEIC ■ **Fax:* Sales ■ *TF Cust Svc:* 866-693-3426 ■ *Web:* www.fei.com					
Fisher Scientific Company Inc 112 Colonnade Rd	Ottawa	ON	K2E7L6	613-226-8874	226-7658
TF: 800-234-7437 ■ *Web:* www.fishersci.ca					
Fluid Imaging Technologies Inc 65 Forest Falls Dr	Yarmouth	ME	04096	207-846-6100	
Web: www.fluidimaging.com					
FORNEY LLC 310 Seven Fields Blvd One Adams Pl	Seven Fields	PA	16046	724-346-7400	
Web: www.forneyonline.com					
Gambro BCT 10811 W Collins Ave	Lakewood	CO	80215	303-231-4357	231-4357
TF: 877-339-4228 ■ *Web:* www.terumobct.com					
Gamma Vacuum LLC 2915 133rd St W	Shakopee	MN	55379	952-445-4841	
Web: www.gammavacuum.com					
Gatan Inc 5794 W Las Positas Blvd	Pleasanton	CA	94588	925-463-0200	463-0204
TF: 888-887-3377 ■ *Web:* www.gatan.com					
GrayWolf Sensing Solutions LLC 6 Research Dr	Shelton	CT	06484	203-402-0477	
TF: 800-218-7997 ■ *Web:* www.wolfsense.com					
Hach Co PO Box 389	Loveland	CO	80539	970-669-3050	669-2932
TF: 800-227-4224 ■ *Web:* www.hach.com					
Hamilton Co 4970 Energy Way	Reno	NV	89502	775-858-3000	
TF: 800-648-5950 ■ *Web:* www.hamiltoncompany.com					
Harvard Bioscience Inc 84 October Hill Rd	Holliston	MA	01746	508-893-8999	429-5732
NASDAQ: HBIO ■ *TF:* 800-272-2775 ■ *Web:* www.harvardbioscience.com					
Helena Laboratories Inc 1530 Lindbergh Dr	Beaumont	TX	77704	409-842-3714	842-3094
TF: 800-231-5663 ■ *Web:* www.helena.com					
Hitachi High Technologies America Inc 10 N Martingale Rd Ste 500	Schaumburg	IL	60173	847-273-4141	273-4407
Web: www.hitachi-hightech.com/us					
Horiba Instruments Inc 17671 Armstrong Ave	Irvine	CA	92614	949-250-4811	250-0924
TF: 800-446-7422 ■ *Web:* www.horiba.com					
hygiena LLC 941 Avenida Acaso	Camarillo	CA	93012	805-388-8007	
TF: 877-494-4364 ■ *Web:* www.hygiena.com					
Illumina Inc 9885 Towne Centre Dr	San Diego	CA	92121	858-202-4500	202-4545
NASDAQ: ILMN ■ *TF:* 800-809-4566 ■ *Web:* www.illumina.com					
Inanovate Inc 2 Davis Dr Ste 13169	Research Triangle Park	NC	27709	919-354-1028	
Web: www.inanovate.com					
Infolab Inc 17400 Hwy 61 N	Clarksdale	MS	38614	662-627-2283	627-1913
Instrumentation Laboratory Inc 180 Hartwell Rd	Bedford	MA	01730	781-861-0710	861-1908
TF Sales: 800-955-9525 ■ *Web:* www.instrumentationlaboratory.com					
IonField Systems LLC 1 Executive Dr Ste 8	Moorestown	NJ	08057	856-437-0330	823-1426
Web: ionfieldsystems.com					
IonSense Inc 999 Broadway Ste 404	Saugus	MA	01906	781-484-1043	
Web: www.ionsense.com					
ISCO Inc 4700 Superior St PO Box 82531	Lincoln	NE	68501	402-464-0231	465-3022*
**Fax:* Cust Svc ■ *TF:* 800-228-4250 ■ *Web:* www.isco.com					
JEOL USA Inc 11 Dearborn Rd	Peabody	MA	01960	978-535-5900	536-2205
Web: www.jeol.co.jp/en					
k-Space Associates Inc 2182 Bishop Cir E	Dexter	MI	48130	734-426-7977	
Web: www.k-space.com					
Kimble Chase Life Science & Research Products LLC 1022 Spruce St	Vineland	NJ	08362	856-692-8500	
Web: www.kimble-chase.com					
Kurt J Lesker Co 1925 Rt 51	Jefferson Hills	PA	15025	412-387-9200	
Web: www.lesker.com					
Labcon North America Inc 3700 Lkeville Hwy	Petaluma	CA	94954	707-766-2100	766-2199
TF: 800-227-1466 ■ *Web:* www.labcon.com					
LaMotte Co 802 Washington Ave	Chestertown	MD	21620	410-778-3100	778-6394
TF: 800-344-3100 ■ *Web:* www.lamotte.com					
Leco Corp 3000 Lakeview Ave	Saint Joseph	MI	49085	269-985-5496	982-8977*
**Fax:* Sales ■ *TF:* 800-292-6141 ■ *Web:* www.leco.com					
Levitt-Safety Ltd 2872 Bristol Cir	Oakville	ON	L6H5T5	905-829-3299	829-2919
Web: www.levitt-safety.com					
Li Cor Inc PO Box 4425	Lincoln	NE	68504	402-467-3576	467-2819
TF: 800-447-3576 ■ *Web:* www.licor.com					
Luminex Corp 12212 Technology Blvd	Austin	TX	78727	512-219-8020	219-5195
NASDAQ: LMNX ■ *TF:* 888-219-8020 ■ *Web:* www.luminexcorp.com					
M. Braun Inc 14 Marin Way	Stratham	NH	03885	603-773-9333	773-0008
Web: www.mbraun.com					
Malvern Instruments Inc 117 Flanders Rd	Westborough	MA	01581	508-768-6400	
Web: www.malvern.com					
Mandel Scientific Company Inc 2 Admiral Pl	Guelph	ON	N1G4N4	519-763-9292	763-2005
TF: 888-883-3636 ■ *Web:* www.mandel.ca					
MassTech Inc 6992 Columbia Gateway Dr	Columbia	MD	21046	443-539-1758	
Web: www.apmaldi.com					
Matrix Technologies Corp 22 Friars Dr	Hudson	NH	03051	603-595-0505	
Web: www.matrixtechcorp.com					
Med-Plus Medical Supplies 17 Vanderbilt Ave	Brooklyn	NY	11205	718-222-4416	
TF: 888-433-2300 ■ *Web:* www.medexsupply.com					
Mettler-Toledo International Inc 1900 Polaris Pkwy	Columbus	OH	43240	614-438-4511	
Web: www.mt.com					
Micromeritics Instrument Corp 1 Micromeritics Dr	Norcross	GA	30093	770-662-3620	662-3696
TF: 800-229-5052 ■ *Web:* www.micromeritics.com					
Microsonic Systems Inc 76 Bonaventura Dr	San Jose	CA	95134	408-844-4980	
Web: www.microsonics.com					
Microtrac Inc 148 Keystone Dr	Montgomeryville	PA	18936	215-619-9920	
Web: www.microtrac.com					

Phone *Fax*

Modal Shop Inc, The 1776 Mentor Ave .... Cincinnati OH 45212 513-351-9919
TF: 800-860-4867 ■ *Web:* www.modalshop.com

Molecular Devices Inc (MDI) 1311 Orleans Dr .... Sunnyvale CA 94089 408-747-1700 747-3601
TF: 800-635-5577 ■ *Web:* www.moleculardevices.com

Monogram Biosciences Inc
345 Oyster Pt Blvd .... South San Francisco CA 94080 650-635-1100 635-1111
TF: 800-777-0177 ■ *Web:* www.monogrambio.com

MPD Inc 316 E Ninth St .... Owensboro KY 42303 270-685-6200 685-6494
TF: 866-225-5673 ■ *Web:* www.mpdinc.com

NanoDrop Technologies LLC
3411 Silverside Rd Bancroft Bldg .... Wilmington DE 19810 302-479-7707
Web: www.nanodrop.com

New Objective Inc 2 Constitution Way .... Woburn MA 01801 781-933-9560
TF: 888-220-2998 ■ *Web:* www.newobjective.com

Nor-Cal Controls Inc 1952 Concourse Dr .... San Jose CA 95131 408-435-0400
Web: www.norcal4air.com

Noran Instruments Inc 5225 Verona Rd .... Madison WI 53711 608-276-6100 273-5045
Web: www.thermofisher.com/en/home.html

Nova Biomedical Corp 200 Prospect St .... Waltham MA 02454 781-894-0800 894-5915
TF Sales: 800-458-5813 ■ *Web:* www.novabio.us

NOVA R & D Inc 1525 Third St Ste C .... Riverside CA 92507 951-781-7332
Web: www.novarad.com

NucSafe Inc 601 Oak Ridge Tpke .... Oak Ridge TN 37830 865-220-5050
Web: www.nucsafe.com

OI Corp 151 Graham Rd PO Box 9010 .... College Station TX 77842 979-690-1711 690-0440
TF: 800-653-1711 ■ *Web:* www.oico.com

Olis Inc 130 Conway Dr Ste A B & C .... Bogart GA 30622 706-353-6547 353-1972
TF: 800-852-3504 ■ *Web:* www.olisweb.com

Pall Life Sciences 600 S Wagner Rd .... Ann Arbor MI 48103 734-665-0651 913-6495
TF: 800-521-1520 ■ *Web:* www.pall.com

PANalytical Inc 117 Flanders Rd .... Westborough MA 01581 508-647-1100
Web: www.panalytical.com

Particle Measuring Systems Inc
5475 Airport Blvd .... Boulder CO 80301 303-443-7100 449-6870
TF Cust Svc: 800-238-1801 ■ *Web:* www.pmeasuring.com

PerkinElmer Inc 940 Winter St .... Waltham MA 02451 203-925-4602 944-4904
NYSE: PKI ■ *Web:* www.perkinelmer.com

Petroleum Analyzer Company LP
8824 Fallbrook Dr .... Houston TX 77064 281-940-1803
Web: www.paclp.com

Phenomenex Inc 411 Madrid Ave .... Torrance CA 90501 310-212-0555 328-7768
Web: www.phenomenex.com

Photo Research Inc 9731 Topanga Canyon Pl .... Chatsworth CA 91311 818-341-5151 725-9770
TF: 877-424-6423 ■ *Web:* www.photoresearch.com

Physical Electronics Inc 18725 Lake Dr E .... Chanhassen MN 55317 952-828-6100 828-6451
Web: www.phi.com

Picarro Inc 480 Oakmead Pkwy .... Sunnyvale CA 94085 408-962-3900
Web: www.picarro.com

Qualigen Inc 2042 Corte Del Nogal .... Carlsbad CA 92011 760-918-9165
Web: www.qualigeninc.com

Quantum Design Inc 6325 Lusk Blvd .... San Diego CA 92121 858-481-4400
Web: www.qdusa.com

QUEST Integrated Inc 19823 58th Pl S .... Kent WA 98032 253-872-9500
Web: www.qi2.com

Real-Time Laboratories LLC
990 S Rogers Cir Ste 5 .... Boca Raton FL 33487 561-988-8826
Web: www.real-timelabs.com

Response Biomedical Corp 1781 75th Ave W .... Vancouver BC V6P6P2 604-456-6010 456-6066
TSE: RBM ■ *TF:* 888-591-5577 ■ *Web:* www.responsebio.com

Sakura Finetek USA Inc 1750 W 214th St .... Torrance CA 90501 310-972-7800 972-7888
TF: 800-725-8723 ■ *Web:* www.sakura-americas.com

Schroer Manufacturing Co 511 Osage Ave .... Kansas City KS 66105 913-281-1500
TF: 800-444-1579 ■ *Web:* www.shor-line.com

Scientific Industries Inc 70 Orville Dr .... Bohemia NY 11716 631-567-4700
TF: 888-850-6208 ■ *Web:* www.scientificindustries.com

SEER Technology Inc
2681 Parleys Way Ste 201 .... Salt Lake City UT 84109 801-746-7888
TF: 877-505-7337 ■ *Web:* www.seertechnology.com

Senova Systems Inc 1230 Bordeaux Dr .... Sunnyvale CA 94089 415-324-8505
Web: www.senovasystems.com

Sentry Equipment Corp
966 Blue Ribbon Cir N .... Oconomowoc WI 53066 262-567-7256 567-4523
Web: www.sentry-equip.com

Sheldon Laboratory Systems Inc
102 Kirk St PO Box 836 .... Crystal Springs MS 39059 601-892-2731
TF: 800-531-7604 ■ *Web:* www.sheldonlabs.com

Shimadzu Scientific Instruments Inc
7102 Riverwood Dr .... Columbia MD 21046 410-381-1227 381-1222
TF: 800-477-1227 ■ *Web:* www.ssi.shimadzu.com

Siskiyou Corp 110 Sw Booth St .... Grants Pass OR 97526 541-479-8697
TF: 877-313-6418 ■ *Web:* www.siskiyou.com

Smart Imaging Technologies Inc
1770 Saint James Pl Ste 414 .... Houston TX 77056 713-589-3500
TF: 877-280-1100 ■ *Web:* www.smartimtech.com

Soilmoisture Equipment Corp 801 S Kellogg Ave .... Goleta CA 93117 805-964-3525
TF: 888-964-0040 ■ *Web:* www.soilmoisture.com

SonoPlot Inc 3030 Laura Ln Ste 120 .... Middleton WI 53562 608-824-9311
Web: www.sonoplot.com

Soquelec Ltd 5757 Cavendish Blvd Ste 540 .... Montreal QC H4W2W8 514-482-6427 482-1929
Web: www.soquelec.com

Sparton Corp 425 N Martingale Rd Ste 2050 .... Schaumburg IL 60173 847-762-5800
TF: 800-772-7866 ■ *Web:* sparton.com

Spectech 106 Union Vly Rd .... Oak Ridge TN 37830 865-482-9948
Web: www.spectrumtechniques.com

Spectra Analysis Inc 257 Simarano Dr .... Marlborough MA 01752 508-281-6232
Web: www.spectra-analysis.com

Spectra Services Inc 6359 Dean Pkwy .... Ontario NY 14519 585-265-4320
TF: 800-955-7732 ■ *Web:* www.spectraservices.com

Spectro Inc 1 Executive Dr Ste 101 .... Chelmsford MA 01824 978-486-0123
Web: spectrosci.com

Spectrum Laboratories Inc
18617 Broadwick St .... Rancho Dominguez CA 90220 310-885-4600 885-4666
TF: 800-634-3300 ■ *Web:* www.spectrumlabs.com

Spectrum Systems Inc 3410 W Nine-Mile Rd .... Pensacola FL 32526 850-944-3392 944-1011
TF: 800-432-6119 ■ *Web:* spectrumsystems.com

STARR Life Sciences Corp
333 Allegheney Ave Ste 300 .... Oakmont PA 15139 866-978-2779
TF: 866-978-2779 ■ *Web:* www.starrlifesciences.com

Stellarnet Inc 14390 Carlson Cir .... Tampa FL 33626 813-855-8687
Web: www.stellarnet.us

Supelco Inc 595 N Harrison Rd .... Bellefonte PA 16823 814-359-3441 325-5052*
**Fax Area Code:* 800 ■ *TF:* 800-247-6628 ■ *Web:* www.sigmaaldrich.com

Supercritical Fluid Technologies Inc
1 Innovation Way .... Newark DE 19711 302-738-3420
Web: www.supercriticalfluids.com

TA Instruments Inc 159 Lukens Dr .... New Castle DE 19720 302-427-4000
Web: www.tainstruments.com

Techne Inc 3 Terri Ln Ste 10 .... Burlington NJ 08016 609-589-2560
Web: www.techneusa.com

Tekran Instruments Corp 230 Tech Ctr Dr .... Knoxville TN 37912 865-688-0688
TF: 888-383-5726 ■ *Web:* www.tekran.com

Teledyne Instruments Inc
16830 Chestnut St .... City Of Industry CA 91748 626-934-1500
Web: www.teledyne-ai.com

Teledyne Leeman Labs Inc 110 Lowell Rd .... Hudson NH 03051 603-886-8400
Web: www.teledyneleemanlabs.com

Teledyne Tekmar Company Inc
4736 Socialville Foster Rd .... Mason OH 45040 513-229-7000
Web: www.teledynetekmar.com

Temptronic Corp 41 Hampden Rd .... Mansfield MA 02048 781-688-2300 688-2301*
**Fax:* Sales ■ *TF Tech Support:* 800-558-5080 ■ *Web:* www.temptronic.com

Thermo Fisher Scientific Inc 81 Wyman St .... Waltham MA 02454 781-622-1000 622-1207
NYSE: TMO ■ *TF:* 800-678-5599 ■ *Web:* www.thermofisher.com

Thinky USA 23151 Verdugo Dr .... Laguna Hills CA 92653 949-768-9001
Web: www.janustechsales.com

Thoren Caging Systems Inc 815 W Seventh St .... Hazleton PA 18201 570-455-5041
Web: www.thoren.com

Toptica Photonics Inc 1286 Blossom Dr Ste 1 .... Victor NY 14564 585-657-6663
TF: 877-277-9897 ■ *Web:* www.toptica.com

Transgenomic Inc 12325 Emmet St .... Omaha NE 68164 402-452-5400 452-5401
OTC: TBIO ■ *TF:* 888-233-9283 ■ *Web:* www.transgenomic.com

Upchurch Scientific Inc 619 Oak St .... Oak Harbor WA 98277 360-679-2528
TF: 800-426-0191 ■ *Web:* www.idex-hs.com

Vernier Software & Technology LLC
13979 SW Millikan Way .... Beaverton OR 97005 503-277-2299
Web: www.vernier.com

WaferGen Bio-systems Inc
7400 Paseo Padre Pkwy .... Fremont CA 94555 510-651-4450
Web: www.wafergen.com

Waters Corp 34 Maple St .... Milford MA 01757 508-478-2000 872-1990
NYSE: WAT ■ *TF:* 800-252-4752 ■ *Web:* www.waters.com

X-ray Instrumentation Associates
8450 Central Ave .... Newark CA 94560 510-494-9020
Web: www.xia.com

XiGo Nanotools Inc 116 Research Dr Ste 39 .... Bethlehem PA 18015 610-849-5090
Web: www.xigonanotools.com

ZAPS Technologies Inc 4314 SW Research Way .... Corvallis OR 97333 541-207-1122
Web: www.zapstechnologies.com

ZTR Control Systems Inc
8050 County Rd 101 East .... Minneapolis MN 55379 855-724-5987
TF: 855-724-5987 ■ *Web:* www.ztr.com

420 LABORATORY APPARATUS & FURNITURE

See Also Glassware - Laboratory & Scientific p. 2354; Laboratory Analytical Instruments p. 2623; Scales & Balances p. 3145

Phone *Fax*

Baker Company Inc 161 Gatehouse Rd PO Box E .... Sanford ME 04073 207-324-8773 324-3869
TF: 800-992-2537 ■ *Web:* www.bakerco.com

Bel-Art Products Inc 661 Rte 23 S .... Wayne NJ 07440 973-694-0500 694-7199
TF: 800-423-5278 ■ *Web:* www.belart.com

Boekel Scientific 855 Pennsylvania Blvd .... Feasterville PA 19053 215-396-8200 396-8264
TF: 800-336-6929 ■ *Web:* www.boekelsci.com

Caliper Life Sciences Inc 68 Elm St .... Hopkinton MA 01748 508-435-9500 435-3439
TF: 800-762-4000 ■ *Web:* www.perkinelmer.com

Cole-Parmer Instrument Co
625 E Bunker Ct .... Vernon Hills IL 60061 847-549-7600 247-2929
TF: 800-323-4340 ■ *Web:* www.coleparmer.com

Comet Technologies Inc 3400 Gilchrist Rd .... Akron OH 44260 330-798-4800
Web: www.yxlon.com

Corning Inc Life Sciences Div
836 N St Bldg 300 Ste 3401 .... Tewksbury MA 01876 978-442-2200 635-2476
TF: 800-492-1110 ■ *Web:* www.corning.com/lifesciences

Durcon Co 8464 Ronda Dr .... Canton MI 48187 734-455-4520
Web: www.durcon.com

Edstrom Industries Inc 819 Bakke Ave .... Waterford WI 53185 262-534-5181 534-5184
TF: 800-558-5913 ■ *Web:* www.edstrom.com

ETS-Lindgren LP 1301 Arrow Pt Dr .... Cedar Park TX 78613 512-531-6400 531-6500
Web: www.ets-lindgren.com

Ika-Works Inc 2635 Northchase Pkwy SE .... Wilmington NC 28405 910-452-7059 452-7693
TF: 800-733-3037 ■ *Web:* www.ika.com

Infolab Inc 17400 Hwy 61 N .... Clarksdale MS 38614 662-627-2283 627-1913

Kalamazoo Technical Furniture
6450 Vly Industrial Dr .... Kalamazoo MI 49009 800-832-5227
TF: 800-832-5227 ■ *Web:* www.teclab.com

Kewaunee Scientific Corp
2700 W Front St PO Box 1842 .... Statesville NC 28687 704-873-7202 873-5160*
NASDAQ: KEQU ■ **Fax:* Sales ■ *TF:* 800-824-6626 ■ *Web:* www.kewaunee.com

Knf Neuberger Inc 2 Black Forest Rd .... Trenton NJ 08691 609-890-8600 890-2838
TF: 800-323-4340 ■ *Web:* www.knf.com

Koch Modular Process Systems LLC
45 Eisenhower Dr .... Paramus NJ 07652 201-267-8670 368-8989
Web: www.modularprocess.com

Lab Fabricators Co 1802 E 47th St .... Cleveland OH 44103 216-431-5444 431-5447
Web: www.labfabricators.com

Company	City	State	ZIP	Phone	Fax
Labconco Corp 8811 Prospect Ave *TF Cust Svc:* 800-821-5525 ■ *Web:* www.labconco.com	Kansas City	MO	64132	816-333-8811	363-0130
Nalge Nunc International 75 Panorama Creek Dr *TF:* 800-625-4327 ■ *Web:* www.thermoscientific.com	Rochester	NY	14625	585-586-8800	586-3294
Omnicell Inc 1201 Charleston Rd *NASDAQ: OMCL* ■ *TF:* 800-850-6664 ■ *Web:* www.omnicell.com	Mountain View	CA	94043	650-251-6100	251-6266
Pacific Combustion Engineering Co 2107 Border Ave *TF:* 800-342-4442 ■ *Web:* www.pacificcombustion.com	Torrance	CA	90501	310-212-6300	212-5333
Parr Instrument Co 211 53rd St *TF:* 800-872-7720 ■ *Web:* www.parrinst.com	Moline	IL	61265	309-762-7716	762-9453
Parter Medical Products Inc 17015 Kingsview Ave *TF:* 800-666-8282 ■ *Web:* www.partermedical.com	Carson	CA	90746	310-327-4417	327-8601
Percival Scientific Inc 505 Research Dr *TF:* 800-695-2743 ■ *Web:* www.percival-scientific.com	Perry	IA	50220	515-465-9363	465-9464
Preston Industries Inc 6600 W Touhy Ave *TF:* 800-229-7569 ■ *Web:* www.polyscience.com	Niles	IL	60714	847-647-0611	647-1155
SKC Inc 863 Vly View Rd *Web:* www.skcinc.com	Eighty Four	PA	15330	724-941-9701	941-1369
Thermal Product Solutions 2821 Old Rt 15 PO Box 150 *TF:* 800-586-2473 ■ *Web:* www.thermalproductsolutions.com	New Columbia	PA	17856	570-538-7200	538-7380
Thermo Fisher Scientific Inc 81 Wyman St *NYSE: TMO* ■ *TF:* 800-678-5599 ■ *Web:* www.thermofisher.com	Waltham	MA	02454	781-622-1000	622-1207
ThermoGenesis Corp 2711 Citrus Rd *NASDAQ: KOOL* ■ *TF:* 800-783-8357 ■ *Web:* cescatherapeutics.com	Rancho Cordova	CA	95742	916-858-5100	858-5199
Thomas Scientific 1654 High Hill Rd PO Box 99 *TF:* 800-345-2100 ■ *Web:* www.thomassci.com	Swedesboro	NJ	08085	856-467-2000	467-3087
Valley City Mfg Co Ltd, The 64 Hatt St *Web:* www.valleycity.com	Dundas	ON	L9H2G3	905-628-2253	628-0753

421 LADDERS

Company	City	State	ZIP	Phone	Fax
ALACO Ladder Co 5167 G St *TF:* 888-310-7040 ■ *Web:* www.alacoladder.com	Chino	CA	91710	909-591-7561	591-7565
Ballymore Co 501 Gunnard Carlson Dr *TF:* 800-762-8327 ■ *Web:* www.ballymore.com	Coatesville	PA	19365	610-593-5062	593-8615
Cotterman Co 130 Seltzer Rd *TF:* 800-552-3337 ■ *Web:* www.cotterman.com	Croswell	MI	48422	810-679-4400	679-4510
Duo-Safety Ladder Corp 513 W Ninth Ave *TF:* 877-386-5377 ■ *Web:* www.duosafety.com	Oshkosh	WI	54902	920-231-2740	231-2460
Lynn Ladder & Scaffolding Company Inc 20 Boston St *TF:* 800-225-2510 ■ *Web:* www.lynnladder.com	Lynn	MA	01904	781-598-6010	593-2915
Putnam Rolling Ladder Inc 32 Howard St *Web:* www.putnamrollingladder.com	New York	NY	10013	212-226-5147	941-1836
Werner Co 93 Werner Rd *TF:* 888-523-3371 ■ *Web:* www.wernerco.com/us	Greenville	PA	16125	888-523-3371	456-8459
Wing Enterprises Inc 1198 N Spring Creek *TF:* 866-872-5901 ■ *Web:* littlegiantladders.com	Springville	UT	84663	801-489-3684	489-3685

422 LANDSCAPE DESIGN & RELATED SERVICES

Company	City	State	ZIP	Phone	Fax
Annco Services Inc 8892 152nd Pl S *Web:* www.anncoservices.com	Delray Beach	FL	33446	561-638-2540	638-3993
Artistic Maintenance Inc 23676 Birtcher Dr *Web:* www.artisticmaintenance.com	Lake Forest	CA	92630	949-581-9817	581-0436
Brickman Group Ltd 375 S Flowers Mill Rd	Langhorne	PA	19047	215-757-9400	891-1259
Cagwin & Dorward Inc 1565 S Novato Blvd Ste B *TF:* 800-891-7710 ■ *Web:* www.cagwin.com	Novato	CA	94947	415-892-7710	897-7864
Chapel Valley Landscape Co 3275 Jennings Chapel Rd *Web:* www.chapelvalley.com	Woodbine	MD	21797	301-924-5400	854-6390
Creative Environments 8920 S Hardy Dr *TF:* 855-777-9305 ■ *Web:* www.creativeenvironments.com	Tempe	AZ	85284	480-458-4100	777-9296
D Schumacher Landscaping Inc 635 Manley St *Web:* www.dschumacher.com	West Bridgewater	MA	02379	508-427-7707	
Davids Clarence & Co 22901 S Ridgeland Ave *Web:* www.clarencedavids.com	Matteson	IL	60443	708-720-4100	720-4200
Environmental Earthscapes Inc 5075 S Swan Rd *TF:* 800-571-1575 ■ *Web:* www.groundskeeper.com	Tucson	AZ	85706	520-571-1575	750-7480
Golden Bear International Inc 11780 US Hwy 1 *Web:* www.nicklaus.com	North Palm Beach	FL	33408	561-626-3900	
Hindsdale Nurseries Inc 7200 S Madison Rd *Web:* www.hinsdalenurseries.com	Willowbrook	IL	60527	630-323-1411	
Horizon Distributors Inc 5214 S 30th St *Web:* www.horizononline.com	Phoenix	AZ	85040	480-337-6750	337-6701
Jensen Corp 1983 Concourse Dr *Web:* www.jensencorp.com	San Jose	CA	95131	408-446-1118	446-4881
Landscape Concepts Management 31745 Alleghany Rd *TF:* 866-655-3800 ■ *Web:* www.landscapeconcepts.com	Grayslake	IL	60030	847-223-3800	223-0169
Landscape Development Inc 28447 Witherspoon Pkwy *Web:* www.landscapedevelopment.com	Valencia	CA	91355	661-295-1970	295-1969
Lied's Landscape Design & Construction N63 W22039 Hwy 74 *Web:* www.lieds.com/design	Sussex	WI	53089	262-246-6901	
Lipinski Landscape & Irrigation Contractors Inc 100 Sharp Rd *TF:* 800-644-6035 ■ *Web:* www.meritservicesolutions.com	Marlton	NJ	08053	800-644-6035	
LMI Landscapes Inc 1437 Halsey Way *Web:* www.lmilandscapes.com	Carrollton	TX	75007	972-446-0020	
Mariani Enterprises Inc 300 Rockland Rd *Web:* www.marianilandscape.com	Lake Bluff	IL	60044	847-234-2172	234-2754
Mariposa Horticultural Enterprises Inc 15529 Arrow Hwy *Web:* mariposa-ca.com	Irwindale	CA	91706	626-960-0196	
Mission Landscape Services Inc 536 E Dyer Rd **Fax Area Code: 714* ■ *TF:* 800-545-9963 ■ *Web:* www.missionlandscape.com	Santa Ana	CA	92707	800-545-9963	668-0119*
Park West Cos Inc 22421 Gilberto Ste A *Web:* www.parkwestlandscape.com	Rancho Santa Margarita	CA	92688	949-546-8300	546-8301
Peoria Landscaping Company Inc 2700 W Cedar Hills Dr *Web:* www.greenview.com	Dunlap	IL	61525	309-243-7761	
Schrickel Rollins & Assoc Inc 1161 Corporate Dr W Ste 200 *Web:* www.sradesign.com	Arlington	TX	76006	817-649-3216	649-7645
Spectrum Care Landscape 27181 Burbank *Web:* www.spectrumcarelandscape.com	Foothill Ranch	CA	92610	949-454-6900	
Summit Landscape Services Inc 12452 Cutten Rd *Web:* www.summitls.com	Houston	TX	77066	281-583-7900	583-7994
SWA Group 2200 Bridgeway Blvd *Web:* www.swagroup.com	Sausalito	CA	94965	415-332-5100	332-0719
Teufel Nursery Inc 3431 NW John Olsen Pl *Web:* www.teufellandscape.com	Hillsboro	OR	97124	503-646-1111	646-1112
Turf Management Systems LLC PO Box 26389 *Web:* www.turfmanagementsystems.com	Birmingham	AL	35260	205-979-8604	979-6063
Underwood Bros 3747 E Southern Ave *Web:* www.aaalandscape.com	Phoenix	AZ	85040	602-437-2690	437-2970
US Lawns 4700 Millenia Blvd Ste 240 *TF:* 800-875-2967 ■ *Web:* www.uslawns.com	Orlando	FL	32839	800-875-2967	
ValleyCrest Cos 24151 Ventura Blvd **Fax Area Code: 888*	Calabasas	CA	91302	818-223-8500	223-8142*

423 LANGUAGE SCHOOLS

See Also Translation Services p. 3260

Company	City	State	ZIP	Phone	Fax
Access International Business Institute 609 E Liberty St *Web:* www.accessesl.org	Ann Arbor	MI	48104	734-994-1456	994-7341
Agape English Language Institute (AELI) 610 Pickens St PO Box 12504 *TF:* 877-476-2354 ■ *Web:* www.aeliusa.com	Columbia	SC	29201	803-799-3452	252-5500
American Academy of English 530 Golden Gate Ave *Web:* www.aae.edu	San Francisco	CA	94102	415-567-0189	567-1475
American Language Communication Ctr 229 W 36th St *Web:* www.learnenglish.com	New York	NY	10018	212-736-2373	947-6403
AmeriSpan Unlimited 1334 Walnut St 6 Fl *TF:* 800-879-6640 ■ *Web:* www.amerispan.com	Philadelphia	PA	19107	215-751-1100	751-1986
Berlitz Languages Inc 400 Alexander Pk *Web:* www.berlitz.com	Princeton	NJ	08540	609-524-2514	514-9689
Boston Academy of English 38 Chauncy St 8th Fl **Fax Area Code: 617* ■ *TF:* 800-704-9313 ■ *Web:* www.bostonacademyofenglish.com	Boston	MA	02111	800-704-9313	695-9349*
Boston Academy of English inc 38 Chauncy St 8th Fl **Fax Area Code: 617* ■ *TF:* 800-704-9313 ■ *Web:* bostonacademyofenglish.com	Boston	MA	02111	800-704-9313	695-9349*
Brandon College 944 Market St 2nd Fl *Web:* www.brandoncollege.com	San Francisco	CA	94102	415-391-5711	391-3918
Colorado School of English 331 14th St *TF:* 877-234-0654 ■ *Web:* www.englishamerica.com	Denver	CO	80202	720-932-8900	932-0315
Converse International School of Languages 636 Broadway Ste 210 *Web:* www.cisl.edu	San Diego	CA	92101	619-239-3363	239-3778
Cultural Ctr for Language Studies 3191 Coral Way Ste 114 *TF:* 800-704-8181 ■ *Web:* www.cclscorp.com	Miami	FL	33145	305-529-2257	443-8538
Diplomatic Language Services LLC 1901 N Ft Myer Dr Ste 600 *Web:* dlsdc.com	Arlington	VA	22209	703-243-4855	243-7003
EC Boston 729 Boylston St *Web:* www.ecenglish.com	Boston	MA	02116	617-247-3033	247-2959
ELS Language Centers 7 Roszel Rd *Web:* www.els.edu	Princeton	NJ	08540	609-759-5910	
Embassy CES 328 Seventh Ave 6th Fl *Web:* embassyenglish.com	New York	NY	10001	212-629-7300	
English Connection Inc 77 Railroad Pl *Web:* esldirectory.com	Saratoga Springs	NY	12866	518-581-1478	
English Language Ctr Inc (ELC) 10850 Wilshire Blvd Ste 210 *Web:* www.elc.edu	Los Angeles	CA	90024	617-536-9788	
ESL Instruction & Consulting Inc 42 Broad St NW *TF:* 877-579-2366 ■ *Web:* www.eslinstruction.com	Atlanta	GA	30303	404-577-2366	577-2360
Global Village English Centres 888 Cambie St *Web:* www.gvenglish.com	Vancouver	BC	V6B2P6	604-684-1118	684-1117
Human International Academy 123 Camino de la Reina W-200 *Web:* www.hiausa.com	San Diego	CA	92108	619-501-8091	
ILSC Education Group Inc, The 555 Richards St *Web:* www.ilsc.com	Vancouver	BC	V6B2Z5	604-689-9095	
inlingua International 551 Fifth Ave *Web:* www.inlinguametrony.com	New York	NY	10176	212-682-8585	

Phone | Fax

Intercultural Communications College
810 Richards St Ste 200 Honolulu HI 96813 808-946-2445 946-2231
Web: www.icchawaii.edu

International Ctr for Language Studies Inc
1133 15th St NW Ste 600 Washington DC 20005 202-639-8800 783-6587
Web: www.icls.edu

International English Institute
640 Spence Ln Ste 121 Nashville TN 37217 615-327-1715 399-9799
Web: www.iei.edu

International House Vancouver
200-1215 W BRdway Ste 2001 Vancouver BC V6H1G7 604-739-9836 739-9839
Web: www.ihvancouver.com

International Language Institute
1717 Rhode Island Ave NW Ste 100 Washington DC 20036 202-362-2505 686-5603
Web: ilidc.com

Internexus 220 South 200 East Ste 200 Salt Lake City UT 84111 801-487-2499
Web: www.internexus.to

Intrax International Institute
600 California St 10th Fl San Francisco CA 94108 415-434-1221 434-5404
Web: www.staffordhouse.com/intrax.htm

Lado International College
401 Ninth St NW Ste C100 Washington DC 20004 202-223-0023 337-1118
Web: lado.edu

Language Academy
200 S Andrews Ave Ste 100 Fort Lauderdale FL 33301 954-462-8373 462-3738
Web: www.languageacademy.com

Language Co 189 W 15th St Edmond OK 73013 405-715-9996 715-1116
Web: www.thelanguagecompany.com

Language Door LLC 18103 Sky Park Cir Ste D2 Irvine CA 92614 310-826-4140
Web: www.languagedoor.com

Language Exchange International
500 NE Spanish River Blvd Ste 19 Boca Raton FL 33431 561-368-3913
Web: www.languageexchange.com

Language Pacifica 585 Glenwood Ave Menlo Park CA 94025 650-321-1840
Web: www.languagepacifica.com

Language Plus Inc 4110 Rio Bravo Ste 202 El Paso TX 79902 915-544-8600 544-8640
Web: www.languageplus.com

Language Studies Canada
124 Eglinton Ave W Ste 400 Toronto ON M4R2G8 416-488-2200 488-2225
Web: www.ecenglish.com

Lingua School Inc
225 E Las Olas Blvd 6th Fl Fort Lauderdale FL 33301 954-577-9955
TF: 888-654-6482 ■ *Web:* www.linguaschool.com

Michigan Language Ctr 309 S State St Ann Arbor MI 48107 734-663-9415 663-9623
Web: www.englishclasses.com

New England School of English
36 John F Kennedy St Cambridge MA 02138 617-864-7170 864-7282
Web: nese.edu

Ordinate Corp 299 S California Ave Ste 300 Palo Alto CA 94306 650-470-3600
Web: www.ordinate.com

Pacific Language Institute
755 Burrard St Ste 300 Vancouver BC V6Z1X6 604-688-8330 688-0638
Web: kaplaninternational.ca

POLY Languages Institute Inc (POLY)
5757 Wilshire Blvd Ste 510 Los Angeles CA 90036 323-933-9399 686-5384
TF: 877-738-5787 ■ *Web:* www.polylanguages.com

Rennert Bilingual 216 E 45th St New York NY 10017 212-867-8700 867-7666
Web: www.rennert.com

Rosemead College of English
8705 E Valley Blvd Rosemead CA 91770 626-285-9668 285-1351
Web: www.rosemeadcollege.edu

Tamwood International College
300-909 Burrard St Vancouver BC V6Z2N2 604-899-4480 899-4481
TF: 866-533-0123 ■ *Web:* www.tamwood.com

University Language Institute
2448 E 81st St Ste 1400 Tulsa OK 74137 918-493-8088 493-8084
Web: www.uli.net

Wisconsin English as a Second Language Institute
19 N Pinckney St Madison WI 53703 608-257-4300 257-4346
Web: www.wesli.com

Zoni Language Centers 22 W 34th St New York NY 10001 212-736-9000 947-8030
Web: www.zoni.com

424 LASER EQUIPMENT & SYSTEMS - MEDICAL

See Also Medical Instruments & Apparatus - Mfr p. 2741

Phone | Fax

BioLase Technology Inc 4 Cromwell Irvine CA 92618 888-424-6527
TF: 800-699-9462 ■ *Web:* www.biolase.com

Candela Corp 530 Boston Post Rd Wayland MA 01778 508-358-7400 358-5602
NASDAQ: CLZR ■ *TF:* 800-733-8550 ■ *Web:* syneron-candela.com

Convergent Laser Technologies 1660 S Loop Rd Alameda CA 94502 510-832-2130 832-1600
Web: www.convergentlaser.com

Cynosure Inc 5 Carlisle Rd Westford MA 01886 978-256-4200 256-6556
NASDAQ: CYNO ■ *TF:* 800-886-2966 ■ *Web:* www.cynosure.com

Iridex Corp 1212 Terra Bella Ave Mountain View CA 94043 650-940-4700 940-4710
NASDAQ: IRIX ■ *TF Cust Svc:* 800-388-4747 ■ *Web:* www.iridex.com

Laserscope 3070 Orchard Dr San Jose CA 95134 408-943-0636 943-1051*
**Fax:* Sales ■ *TF:* 800-878-3399 ■ *Web:* fundinguniverse.com

LaserSight Technologies Inc
931 S Semoran Blvd Ste 204 Winter Park FL 32792 407-678-9900

Lumenis Ltd 2033 Gateway Pl Ste 200 San Jose CA 95110 408-764-3000 764-3999
TF: 877-586-3647 ■ *Web:* www.lumenis.com

Palomar Medical Technologies Inc
15 Network Dr Burlington MA 01803 781-993-2300 993-2330
NASDAQ: PMTI ■ *Web:* www.palmed.com

PhotoMedex Inc
40 Ramland Rd S, 2nd Fl Ste 200 Orangeburg NY 10962 215-619-3600
NASDAQ: PHMD ■ *TF:* 888-966-1010 ■ *Web:* www.photomedex.com

PLC Medical Systems Inc 459 Fortune Blvd Milford MA 01757 508-541-8800 541-7980
Web: www.renalguard.com

Spectranetics Corp 9965 Federal Dr Colorado Springs CO 80921 719-447-2000 447-2022
NASDAQ: SPNC ■ *TF:* 800-231-0978 ■ *Web:* www.spectranetics.com

Phone | Fax

Trimedyne Inc 15091 Bake Pkwy Irvine CA 92618 949-559-5300 855-8206
OTC: TMED ■ *TF:* 800-733-5273 ■ *Web:* www.trimedyne.com

425 LASERS - INDUSTRIAL

Phone | Fax

AGL Corp 2202 N Redmond Rd PO Box 189 Jacksonville AR 72076 501-982-4433 982-0880
TF: 800-643-9696 ■ *Web:* agl-lasers.com

Baublys Control Laser Corp
7101 Tpc Dr Ste 100 Orlando FL 32822 407-926-3500 926-3590
TF: 866-612-8619 ■ *Web:* www.controllaser.com

Coherent Inc 5100 Patrick Henry Dr Santa Clara CA 95054 408-764-4000 764-4000
NASDAQ: COHR ■ *TF Sales:* 800-527-3786 ■ *Web:* www.coherent.com

Continuum 3150 Central Expy Santa Clara CA 95051 408-727-3240 727-3550
TF: 888-532-1064 ■ *Web:* www.continuumlasers.com

Cymer Inc 17075 Thornmint Ct San Diego CA 92127 858-385-7300 385-7100
NASDAQ: CYMI ■ *Web:* www.cymer.com

Electro Scientific Industries Inc
13900 NW Science Pk Dr Portland OR 97229 503-641-4141 671-5544*
NASDAQ: ESIO ■ **Fax:* Claims ■ *TF Cust Svc:* 800-331-4708 ■ *Web:* esi.com

GSI Group Inc 125 Middlesex Tpke Bedford MA 01730 781-266-5700 266-5114
NASDAQ: GSIG ■ *TF:* 800-342-3757 ■ *Web:* www.gsig.com

Ionatron Inc 3590 E Columbia St Tucson AZ 85714 520-628-7415 622-3835
OTC: AERG ■ *Web:* www.appliedenergetics.com

IPG Photonics Corp 50 Old Webster Rd Oxford MA 01540 508-373-1100 373-1103
NASDAQ: IPGP ■ *TF:* 877-980-1550 ■ *Web:* www.ipgphotonics.com

Isomet Corp 5263 Port Royal Rd Springfield VA 22151 703-321-8301 321-8546
OTC: IOMT ■ *Web:* www.isomet.com

Jodon Engineering 62 Enterprise Dr Ann Arbor MI 48103 734-761-4044
Web: www.jodon.com

Kigre Inc 100 Marshland Rd Hilton Head Island SC 29926 843-681-5800 681-4559
Web: www.kigre.com

Laser Excel N6323 Berlin Rd PO Box 279 Green Lake WI 54941 920-294-6544 294-6588
TF: 800-285-6544 ■ *Web:* www.laserexcel.com

Leica Geosystems Inc 3498 Kraft Ave SE Grand Rapids MI 49512 616-977-4189 942-4627
TF Sales: 800-367-9453 ■ *Web:* www.leica-geosystems.com

PRIMA North America Inc 711 E Main St Chicopee MA 01020 413-598-5200
Web: www.prima-na.com

PTR-Precision Technologies Inc 120 Post Rd Enfield CT 06082 860-741-2281 745-7932
Web: www.ptreb.com

Rofin-Sinar Inc 40984 Concept Dr Plymouth MI 48170 734-455-5400 455-5587
NASDAQ: RSTI ■ *Web:* www.rofin.com

STI Optronics Inc 2755 Northup Way Bellevue WA 98004 425-827-0460 828-3517
Web: www.stioptronics.com

Synrad Inc 4600 Campus Pl Mukilteo WA 98275 425-349-3500 349-3667
TF: 800-796-7231 ■ *Web:* www.synrad.com

TRUMPF Group 111 Hyde Rd Farmington CT 06032 860-255-6000 255-6424*
**Fax:* Mktg ■ *Web:* www.trumpf.com

426 LAUNDRY & DRYCLEANING SERVICES

See Also Linen & Uniform Supply p. 2674

Phone | Fax

ACW Management Corp
2527 Echester Dr PO Box 6535 High Point NC 27265 336-841-4188 841-4117
Web: www.acleanerworld.com

Admiral Inc 10 Taylor Ave Annapolis MD 21401 410-267-8381
TF: 800-864-4429 ■ *Web:* www.admiralcleaners.com

Al Phillips the Cleaner
3250 W Ali Baba Ln Ste C-F Las Vegas NV 89118 702-798-7333 798-1731
Web: www.alphillipslv.com

Anton'S Cleaners Inc 500 Clark Rd Tewksbury MA 01876 978-851-3721
Web: antons.com

Apparel Finishing America 250 Belmont Ave Haledon NJ 07508 973-942-6800
Web: www.apparelgroup.org

AW Zengeler Cleaners 550 Dundee Rd Northbrook IL 60062 847-272-6550 272-5465
Web: www.zengelercleaners.com

Best Cleaners Inc 265 Osborne Rd Loudonville NY 12211 518-459-7440
Web: www.bestcleanersny.com

Broadway Laundry Cleaners
548 N Broadway St Greenville MS 38701 662-332-5988
Web: www.linenservice.com

Camelot Cleaners Co 8590 Frederick St Omaha NE 68124 402-393-5257
Web: camelotcleanersomaha.com

Champion Cleaners 2548 Rocky Ridge Rd Vestavia AL 35243 205-824-7737
Web: www.championcleaners.com

Coinmach Service Corp
303 Sunnyside Blvd Ste 70 Plainview NY 11803 516-349-8555 349-9125
TF: 877-264-6622 ■ *Web:* www.cscsw.com

Concord Custom Cleaners
1303 US 127 Byp S Ste A Frankfort KY 40601 859-422-4800
Web: www.concordcustomcleaners.com

Consumer Textile Corp 123 N 4th Clinton OK 73601 580-323-3111

Crown Management Services Inc
1501 N Guillemard St Pensacola FL 32501 850-438-7578 438-9395
TF: 800-844-5280 ■ *Web:* crownlaundry.com

Dependable Clrs & Shirt Ldry 101 Adams St Denver CO 80206 303-322-8822
Web: www.dependablecleaners.com

Division Laundry & Cleaners Inc
6649 Old Hwy 90 W San Antonio TX 78227 210-674-5110 673-8510
Web: divisionlaundry.com

Dove Cleaners Inc 1560 Yonge St Toronto ON M4T2S9 416-413-7900
TF: 866-999-3683 ■ *Web:* www.dovecleaners.com

Dry Cleaning Depot Inc
730 W Broward Blvd Fort Lauderdale FL 33312 954-522-3660
Web: www.drycleaningdepot.com

Dryclean USA Inc 290 NE 68th St Miami FL 33138 305-754-9966 754-8010
Web: www.drycleanusa.com

Imperial Laundry Services LLC 1236 13th St Racine WI 53403 262-632-7997
Web: www.imperiallaundrysystems.com

Phone | Fax

Lapels Dry Cleaning 962 Washington St . . . Hanover MA 02339 781-826-0759
Web: lapelsdrycleaning.com

Lois Inc Dba Brown'S Cleaners
1223 Montana Ave . . . Santa Monica CA 90403 310-451-8531

Marberry Cleaners & Launderers
220 John St . . . North Aurora IL 60542 630-897-0579
Web: www.marberrycleaners.com

Martinizing Dry Cleaning
8944 Columbia Rd Ste J . . . Loveland OH 45140 800-827-0207
TF: 800-827-0207 ■ *Web:* www.martinizing.com

Model Cleaners Uniforms & Apparel LLC
100 Third St . . . Charleroi PA 15022 724-489-9553
Web: www.modeluniforms.com

New System Laundry LLC 432 NE 10th Ave . . . Portland OR 97232 503-232-8181
Web: www.newsystemlaundry.com

North Texas Health Care Laundry Cooperation Assn
1080 Post Paddock . . . Grand Prairie TX 75050 469-916-1150
Web: nthcl.org

Nu-Yale Cleaners 6300 Hwy 62 . . . Jeffersonville IN 47130 812-285-7400 285-7421
TF: 888-644-7400 ■ *Web:* www.nuyale.com

PAC Industries Inc 5341 Jaycee Ave . . . Harrisburg PA 17112 717-657-0407
Web: pacindustries.com

Pressed4Time Inc 8 Clock Tower Pl Ste 110 . . . Maynard MA 01754 800-423-8711 823-8301*
**Fax Area Code:* 978 ■ *TF:* 800-423-8711 ■ *Web:* www.pressed4time.com

Prestige Cleaners Inc 7536 Taggart Ln . . . Knoxville TN 37938 865-938-7701
Web: prestigecleanersinc.net

Pride Cleaners Inc 300 E 51st St . . . Kansas City MO 64112 816-753-8481
Web: www.pridecleaners.com

Rockwood Dry Cleaners 171 Granville St . . . Gahanna OH 43230 614-471-3700
Web: rockwoodcleaners.com

Sloan's Dry Cleaning Inc 3001 N Main St . . . Los Angeles CA 90031 323-225-1303 223-5358

Spic & Span Inc 4301 N Richards St . . . Milwaukee WI 53212 414-964-5050 964-5042
Web: www.spicandspan.com

Spot Lite Cleaners 120 Bradley Rd . . . Madison CT 06443 203-245-9536
Web: www.spotlite.com

Spotless Cleaners Inc 410 Fifth St . . . Dunmore PA 18512 570-346-7577

Star Gold Cleaners Inc 200 Wilson St . . . Brewer ME 04412 207-989-5170
Web: www.goldstarcleaners.com

Sun Country Cleaners Inc 2240 34th Way N . . . Largo FL 33771 727-535-9930
Web: www.suncountrycleaners.com

Superior Health Linens LLC 5005 S Packard Ave . . . Cudahy WI 53110 414-769-0670
Web: www.superiorhealthlinens.com

Swan Super Cleaners Inc 1535 Bethel Rd . . . Columbus OH 43220 614-442-5000
Web: www.swancleaners.com

Swiss Cleaners 35 Windsor Ave PO Box 825 . . . Rockville CT 06066 860-872-0166
Web: www.swisscleaners.com

Up-To-Date Laundry Inc 1221 Desoto Rd . . . Baltimore MD 21223 410-646-0475
Web: www.uptodatelaundry.net

Zips Dry Cleaners
7474 Greenway Center Dr Ste 1200 . . . Greenbelt MD 20770 301-306-1100
Web: www.321zips.com

LAUNDRY EQUIPMENT - HOUSEHOLD

See Appliances - Major - Mfr p. 1737; Appliances - Whol p. 1738

427 LAUNDRY EQUIPMENT & SUPPLIES - COMMERCIAL & INDUSTRIAL

Phone | Fax

Alliance Laundry Systems LLC PO Box 990 . . . Ripon WI 54971 920-748-3121 748-4564
Web: www.alliancelaundry.com

American Dryer Corp 88 Currant Rd . . . Fall River MA 02720 508-678-9000 678-9447
Web: adclaundry.com

Chicago Dryer Co 2200 N Pulaski Rd . . . Chicago IL 60639 773-235-4430 235-4439
Web: www.chidry.com

Coinmach Service Corp
303 Sunnyside Blvd Ste 70 . . . Plainview NY 11803 516-349-8555 349-9125
TF: 877-264-6622 ■ *Web:* www.cscsw.com

Colmac Industries Inc PO Box 72 . . . Colville WA 99114 509-684-4505 684-4500
TF: 800-926-5622 ■ *Web:* www.colmacind.com

Dexter Co 2211 W Grimes Ave . . . Fairfield IA 52556 641-472-5131 472-5131
Web: www.dexter.com

Edro Corp 37 Commerce St . . . East Berlin CT 06023 860-828-0311 828-5984
TF Sales: 800-628-6434 ■ *Web:* www.edrocorp.com

Ellis Corp 1400 W Bryn Mawr Ave . . . Itasca IL 60143 630-250-9222 250-9241
TF: 800-611-6806 ■ *Web:* www.elliscorp.com

Forenta LP 2300 W Andrew Johnson Hwy Ste A . . . Morristown TN 37814 423-586-5370 586-3470
Web: www.forentausa.com

GA Braun Inc 461 E Brighton Ave . . . Syracuse NY 13212 315-475-3123 475-4130
TF: 800-432-7286 ■ *Web:* www.gabraun.com

Kemco Systems Inc 11500 47th St N . . . Clearwater FL 33762 727-573-2323 573-2346
TF: 800-633-7055 ■ *Web:* www.kemcosystems.com

Minnesota Chemical Co 2285 Hampden Ave . . . Saint Paul MN 55114 651-646-7521 649-1101
TF: 800-328-5689 ■ *Web:* www.minnesotachemical.com

Pellerin Milnor Corp 700 Jackson St . . . Kenner LA 70062 504-467-9591 469-1849
Web: www.milnor.com

Rema Dri-Vac Corp 45 Ruby St . . . Norwalk CT 06850 203-847-2464 847-3609
Web: www.remadrivac.com

Thermal Engineering of Arizona Inc
2250 W Wetmore Rd . . . Tucson AZ 85705 520-888-4000 888-4457
TF: 866-832-7278 ■ *Web:* www.teatucson.com

428 LAW FIRMS

See Also Arbitration Services - Legal p. 1740; Legal Professionals Associations p. 1794; Bar Associations - State p. 1849; Litigation Support Services p. 2676

Phone | Fax

A Ble Advocates for Basic Legal Equality Inc
525 Jefferson Ave . . . Toledo OH 43604 419-255-0814
Web: www.lawolaw.org

Phone | Fax

Aafedt, Forde, Gray, Monson & Hager PA
150 S Fifth St Ste 2600 . . . Minneapolis MN 55402 612-339-8965
Web: www.aafedt.com

Abbey, Weitzenberg, Warren & Emery PC
100 Stony Point Rd Ste 200 . . . Santa Rosa CA 95401 707-542-5050
Web: www.abbeylaw.com

Abelson Herron Halpern LLP
333 S Grand Ave Ste 1550 . . . Los Angeles CA 90071 213-402-1900
Web: www.abelsonherron.com

Abraham Watkins Nichols Sorrels Agosto & Friend
800 Commerce St . . . Houston TX 77002 713-222-7211
Web: abrahamwatkins.com

Abrahamson Uiterwyk & Barnes
2639 Mccormick Dr . . . Clearwater FL 33759 727-797-5297
Web: www.theinjurylawyers.com

Acadiana Legal Service Corp 1020 Surrey St . . . Lafayette LA 70501 337-237-4320
Web: www.la-law.org

AccessAlpha Worldwide LLC
630 Davis St Ste 201 . . . Evanston IL 60201 847-475-6000
Web: www.accessalpha.com

Adam Moore Law Firm, The 217 N Second St . . . Yakima WA 98901 509-575-0372
Web: www.adammoorelaw.com

Adams Jhonson & Duncan 3128 Colby Ave . . . Everett WA 98201 425-339-8556
Web: adamslawyers.com

Adelberg, Rudow, Dorf & Hendler LLC
7 Saint Paul St Ste 600 . . . Baltimore MD 21202 410-539-5195
Web: www.adelbergrudow.com

Adelsberger Donna & Associates
2782 Jenkintown Rd . . . Glenside PA 19038 215-576-8690
Web: dlalawyers.com

Advocacy Center for Persons With Disabilities
2728 Centerview Dr Ste 102 . . . Tallahassee FL 32301 850-488-9071
TF: 800-342-0823 ■ *Web:* www.disabilityrightsflorida.org

Ahmad, Zavitsanos, Anaipakos, Alavi & Mensing PC
1 Houston Ctr 1221 McKinney St Ste 3460 . . . Houston TX 77010 713-655-1101
TF: 800-856-8153 ■ *Web:* www.azalaw.com

Ahmuty, Demers & McManus 200 IU Willets Rd . . . Albertson NY 11507 516-294-5433
Web: www.admlaw.com

Akerman Senterfitt 1 SE Third Ave 25th Fl . . . Miami FL 33131 305-374-5600 374-5095
Web: www.akerman.com

Akin Gump Strauss Hauer & Feld LLP
1333 New Hampshire Ave NW . . . Washington DC 20036 202-887-4000 887-4288
Web: www.akingump.com

Alan b Harris Attorney at Law 409 N Texas Ave . . . Odessa TX 79761 432-580-3118
TF: 800-887-1676 ■ *Web:* alanbharris.com

Albert & Mackenzie A Professional Law Corp
28348 Roadside Dr Ste 105 . . . Agoura Hills CA 91301 818-575-9876
Web: www.albmac.com

Alex M Greenberg, DDS PC
18 E 48th St Rm 1702 . . . New York NY 10017 212-319-9700
Web: www.dralexgreenberg.com

Alleman Hall Mccoy Russell & Tuttle LLP
806 S W Broadway Ste 600 . . . Portland OR 97205 503-459-4141
Web: www.ahmrt.com

Allen Dell PA 202 S Rome Ave Ste 100 . . . Tampa FL 33606 813-223-5351
Web: www.allendell.com

Allen, Summers, Simpson, Lillie & Gresham PLLC
80 Monroe Ave Ste 650 . . . Memphis TN 38103 901-763-4200
Web: www.allensummers.com

Alpern Myers Stuart LLC
14 N Sierra Madre St Ste A . . . Colorado Springs CO 80903 719-471-7955
Web: www.coloradolawyers.net

Alston & Bird LLP 1201 W Peachtree St . . . Atlanta GA 30309 404-881-7000 881-7777
Web: www.alston.com

Altschul & Altschul Inc 18 E 12th St Frnt 1 . . . New York NY 10003 212-924-1505
Web: www.altschul.biz

Alvarez, Sambol, Winthrop & Madson PA
390 N Orange Ave . . . Orlando FL 32801 407-210-2796
Web: www.awtspa.com

Alverson, Taylor, Mortensen & Sanders
7401 W Charleston Blvd . . . Las Vegas NV 89117 702-384-7000
Web: www.alversontaylor.com

Amal Law Group LLC
7804 W College Dr Ste 3n . . . Palos Heights IL 60463 708-361-3600
Web: amallaw.com

Amato Legal Search Inc
2321 Old Maple Ct . . . Ellicott City MD 21042 410-750-7550
Web: amatolegalsearch.com

American LegalNet Inc
16501 Ventura Blvd Ste 615 . . . Encino CA 91436 818-817-9225
Web: alncorp.com

Anderson H Thomas 6160 Saint Andrews Rd . . . Columbia SC 29212 803-798-9586
Web: hthomasanderson.com

Anderson, Julian & Hull LLP
C W Moore Plz 250 S Fifth St Ste 700 . . . Boise ID 83707 208-344-5800
Web: www.ajhlaw.com

Anderson, O'Brien, Bertz, Skrenes & Golla
1257 Main St . . . Stevens Point WI 54481 715-344-0890
Web: www.andlaw.com

Anderson, Zeigler, Disharoon, Gallagher & Gray A Professional Corp
50 Old Courthouse Sq 5th Fl . . . Santa Rosa CA 95404 707-545-4910
Web: andersonzeigler.com

Andreou & Casson Ltd 661 W Lk St Ste 2n . . . Chicago IL 60661 312-935-2001
Web: www.andreou-casson.com

Andrew Moore & Associates 1132 Old York Rd . . . Abington PA 19001 215-885-3500
Web: www.moore4law.com

Andrews Kurth LLP
600 Travis St Chase Towers Ste 4200 . . . Houston TX 77002 713-220-4200 220-4285
Web: www.andrewskurth.com

Anglin Flewelling Rasmussen Campbell & Trytten LLP
199 S Los Robles Ste 600 . . . Pasadena CA 91101 626-535-1900
Web: www.afrct.com

Anthony Ostlund Baer & Louwagie PA
3600 Wells Fargo Bldg 90 S Seventh St . . . Minneapolis MN 55402 612-349-6969
Web: anthonyostlund.com

Phone Fax

Arguedas Cassman & Headley 803 Hearst Ave Berkeley CA 94710 510-845-3000
Web: www.achlaw.com

Armbrecht Jackson LLP
63 S Royal St Riverview Plz 13th Fl Mobile AL 36602 251-405-1300
Web: www.ajlaw.com

Armentor Glenn Law Corp 300 Stewart St Lafayette LA 70501 337-233-1471
TF: 800-960-5551 ■ *Web:* www.glennarmentor.com

Armstrong Donohue & Ceppos
204 Monroe St Ste 101 Rockville MD 20850 301-251-0440
Web: www.adclawfirm.com

Arnold & Itkin LLP 6009 Memorial Dr Houston TX 77007 713-222-3800
TF: 888-493-1629 ■ *Web:* www.arnolditkin.com

Arnold & Porter LLP 555 12th St NW Washington DC 20004 202-942-5000 942-5999
Web: www.arnoldporter.com

Arns Law Firm, The 515 Folsom St Fl 3 San Francisco CA 94105 415-495-7800
TF: 800-495-7800 ■ *Web:* www.arnslaw.com

Arthur, Chapman, Kettering, Smetak & Pikala PA
500 Young Quinlan Bldg 81 S Ninth St Minneapolis MN 55402 612-339-3500
Web: www.arthurchapman.com

Ashbaugh Beal LLP
4400 Columbia Ctr 701 Fifth Ave Seattle WA 98104 206-386-5900
Web: ashbaughbeal.com

Asian Pacific American Legal Center of Southern California
1145 Wilshire Blvd Fl 2 Los Angeles CA 90017 213-977-7500
Web: advancingjustice-la.org

Asiatico & Associates Pllc
5850 Granite Pkwy Ste 900 Plano TX 75024 214-570-0700
Web: baalegal.com

Ater Wynne LLP
1331 NW Lovejoy St Lovejoy Bldg Ste 900 Portland OR 97209 503-226-1191
Web: aterwynne.com

Atkinson Andelson Loya Ruud & Romo A Professional Law Corp
12800 Towne Ctr Dr Cerritos CA 90703 562-653-3200
Web: www.aalrr.com

Atkinson Conway & Gagnon Inc
420 L St Ste 500 Anchorage AK 99501 907-276-1700
TF: 800-478-1900 ■ *Web:* www.acglaw.com

Atlas Legal Research Lp
14241 Dallas Pkwy Ste 650 Dallas TX 75205 214-526-8811
Web: www.atlaslegal.com

Attorney Aid Divorce & Bankruptcy Center Inc
3605 Long Beach Blvd Ste 300 Long Beach CA 90807 562-988-0885
TF: 877-905-5297 ■ *Web:* www.attorneyaid.com

Attorney General 120 W Water St Dover DE 19904 302-739-4211

Ausley McMullen 123 S Calhoun St Tallahassee FL 32302 850-224-9115
Web: ausley.com

Austin Davis & Mitchell Attorneys at Law
109 Cherry St Dunlap TN 37327 423-949-4159
Web: austindavismitchell.com

Babcock Law Firm 10101 Siegen Ln Ste 3C Baton Rouge LA 70810 225-819-3737
Web: www.stephenbabcock.com

Backus Meyer & Branch LLP 116 Lowell St Manchester NH 03104 603-668-7272
Web: www.backusmeyer.com

Bailey & Galyen 1901 W Airport Fwy Bedford TX 76021 817-288-1101
Web: www.galyen.com

Bailey & Glasser LLP 209 Capitol St Charleston WV 25301 304-345-6555
Web: www.baileyglasser.com

Bailey Cavalieri LLC
1 Columbus 10 W Broad St Ste 2100 Columbus OH 43215 614-221-3155
Web: baileycav.com

Bailey, Javins & Carter Lc 213 Hale St Charleston WV 25301 304-345-0346
Web: www.baileyjavinscarter.com

Baker & McKenzie LLP
300 E Randolph St Ste 5000 Chicago IL 60601 312-861-8800 861-2899
Web: www.bakermckenzie.com

Baker Botts LLP 910 Louisiana St 1 Shell Plz Houston TX 77002 713-229-1234 229-1522
Web: www.bakerbotts.com

Baker Donelson Bearman Caldwell & Berkowitz PC
165 Madison Ave 1st Tennessee Bldg Ste 2000 Memphis TN 38103 901-526-2000 577-2303
Web: www.bakerdonelson.com

Baker Hostetler LLP
1900 E Ninth St National City Ctr Ste 3200 Cleveland OH 44114 216-621-0200 696-0740
Web: www.bakerlaw.com

Baker Manock & Jensen 5260 N Palm Ste 421 Fresno CA 93704 559-432-5400
Web: www.bakermanock.com

Baker, Keener & Nahra LLP
633 W Fifth St Ste 5500 Los Angeles CA 90071 213-241-0900
Web: www.bknlawyers.com

Balch & Bingham LLP 1710 Sixth Ave N Birmingham AL 35203 205-251-8100
Web: www.balch.com

Baldwin C. Mark Atty. 112 Old Bridge St Jacksonville NC 28540 910-455-4065

Baldwin Haspel Burke & Mayer LLC
Energy Ctr 1100 Poydras St Ste 3600 New Orleans LA 70163 504-569-2900
Web: www.bhbmlaw.com

Ball Janik 101 Sw Main St Ste 1100 Portland OR 97204 503-228-2525
Web: www.bjllp.com

Ball Kirk & Holm Pc 3324 Kimball Ave Waterloo IA 50704 319-234-2638
Web: www.ballkirkholm.com

Ballard Spahr Andrews & Ingersoll LLP
1735 Market St 51st Fl Philadelphia PA 19103 215-665-8500 864-8999
Web: www.ballardspahr.com

Ballon Stoll Bader & Nadler PC
729 Seventh Ave 17th Fl New York NY 10019 212-575-7900
Web: www.ballonstoll.com

Banner & Witcoff Ltd 10 S Wacker Dr Ste 3000 Chicago IL 60606 312-463-5000
Web: bannerwitcoff.com

Barg Coffin Lewis & Trapp LLP
350 California St 22nd Fl San Francisco CA 94104 415-228-5400
Web: www.bargcoffin.com

Baritz & Colman LLP
1075 Broken Sound Pkwy NW Ste 102 Boca Raton FL 33487 561-864-5100
Web: www.baritzcolman.com

Phone Fax

Barkan & Barkan Company LPA
81 S Fourth St Ste 300 Columbus OH 43215 614-461-1551
Web: www.barkanlaw.net

Barker Martin PS 719 Second Ave Ste 1200 Seattle WA 98104 360-756-9806
TF: 888-381-9806 ■ *Web:* www.barkermartin.com

Barley, Snyder, Senft & Cohen LLC
126 E King St Lancaster PA 17602 717-299-5201
Web: www.barley.com

Barlow Garsek & Simon LLP 920 Foch St Fort Worth TX 76107 817-731-4500
Web: www.bgsfirm.com

Barlow, Josephs & Holmes Ltd
101 Dyer St Fl 5 Providence RI 02903 401-273-4446
Web: barjos.com

Barna, Guzy & Steffen Ltd
400 Northtown Financial Plz 200 Coon Rapids Blvd
Coon Rapids MN 55433 763-780-8500
Web: www.bgs.com

Barnes & Thornburg 11 S Meridian St Indianapolis IN 46204 317-236-1313 231-7433
TF: 800-236-1352 ■ *Web:* www.btlaw.com

Barnwell Whaley Patterson & Helms LLC
288 Meeting St Charleston SC 29401 843-577-7700
Web: www.barnwell-whaley.com

Barran Liebman LLP
601 SW Second Ave Ste 2300 Portland OR 97204 503-228-0500
Web: www.barran.com

Barrett & McNagny LLP 215 E Berry St Fort Wayne IN 46802 260-423-9551
Web: www.barrettlaw.com

Barris, Sott, Denn & Driker PLLC
333 W Fort St Ste 1200 Detroit MI 48226 313-965-9725
TF: 877-529-8750 ■ *Web:* www.bsdd.com

Barron & Newburger PC
1212 Guadalupe St Ste 104 Austin TX 78701 512-476-9103
Web: www.bnpclaw.com

Barton, Klugman & Oetting LLP
350 S Grand Ave Ste 2200 Los Angeles CA 90071 213-621-4000
Web: bkolaw.com

Baxter, Baker, Sidle, Conn & Jones PA
120 E Baltimore St Ste 2100 Baltimore MD 21202 410-385-8122
Web: www.bbsclaw.com

Bay Area Legal Aid 1735 Telegraph Ave Oakland CA 94612 510-663-4755
Web: www.baylegal.org

Bayard Firm, The 222 Delaware Ave Ste 900 Wilmington DE 19899 302-655-5000
Web: www.bayardfirm.com

Bazelon Less & Feldman PC
1 S Broad St Ste 1500 Philadelphia PA 19107 215-568-1155
Web: www.bazless.com

BCF LLP 25th Fl 1100 Rene-Levesque Blvd W Montreal QC H3B5C9 514-397-8500
TF: 866-511-8501 ■ *Web:* www.bcf.ca

Bean, Kinney & Korman A Professional Corp
2300 Wilson Blvd
The Navy League Bldg 7th Fl Arlington VA 22201 703-525-4000
Web: www.beankinney.com

Beasley Allen Crow Methvin
218 Commerce St Montgomery AL 36104 334-269-2343
Web: www.beasleyallen.com

Becherer Kannett & Schweitzer
The Water Tower 1255 Powell St Emeryville CA 94608 510-658-3600
Web: bkscal.com

Becket & Lee LLP 16 General Warren Blvd Malvern PA 19355 610-644-7800
Web: www.becket-lee.com

Begley, Carlin & Mandio LLP
680 Middletown Blvd Langhorne PA 19047 215-750-0110
Web: www.begleycarlin.com

Beliveau, Fradette, Doyle & Gallant PA
91 Bay St Manchester NH 03104 603-623-1234
Web: www.beliveau-fradette.com

Bell, Nunnally & Martin
3232 McKinney Ave Ste 1400 Dallas TX 75204 214-740-1400
Web: www.bellnunnally.com

Bennett Jones LLP
855 Second St S W 4500 Bankers Hall E Calgary AB T2P4K7 403-298-3100
Web: www.bennettjones.ca

Bennington Johnson Biermann & Craigmile LLC
3500 Republic Plz 370 17th St Ste 3500 Denver CO 80202 303-629-5200

Berding & Weil LLP
2175 N California Blvd Ste 500 Walnut Creek CA 94596 925-838-2090
TF: 800-838-2090 ■ *Web:* www.berding-weil.com

Berg Hill Greenleaf & Ruscitti LLP
1712 Pearl St Boulder CO 80302 303-402-1600
Web: www.bhgrlaw.com

Berger & Montague PC 1622 Locust St Philadelphia PA 19103 215-875-3000
TF: 800-424-6690 ■ *Web:* www.bergermontague.com

Berkowitz Oliver Williams Shaw & Eisenbrandt LLP
Crown Ctr 2600 Grand Blvd Ste 1200 Kansas City MO 64108 816-561-7007
Web: www.berkowitzoliver.com

Berman Myles L Law Offices
4665 Macarthur Ct Ste 240 Newport Beach CA 92660 949-640-1860
Web: www.topgundui.com

Berndt & Associates PC
30500 Van Dyke Ave Ste 702 Warren MI 48093 586-558-9000
Web: www.berndtlegal.com

Berry & Berry Law Offices 2930 Lakeshore Ave Oakland CA 94610 510-250-0200
Web: berryandberry.com

Best & Flanagan LLP
60 S Sixth St Ste 2700 Minneapolis MN 55402 612-339-7121 339-5897
Web: www.bestlaw.com

Best, Vanderlaan & Harrington
25 E Washington St Ste 800 Chicago IL 60602 312-819-1100
Web: www.bestfirm.com

Beveridge & Diamond PC
1350 I St NW Ste 700 Washington DC 20005 202-789-6000
Web: www.bdlaw.com

Bilicki Law Firm Pc, The 1285 N Main St Jamestown NY 14701 716-664-5600
Web: www.bilickilaw.com

Phone | Fax

Black Mann & Graham LLP
2905 Corporate Cir. Flower Mound TX 75028 972-353-4174
TF: 888-293-0505 ■ *Web:* www.blackmannandgraham.com

Black Srebnick Kornspan & Stumpf PA
201 S Biscayne Blvd Ste 1300 Miami FL 33131 305-371-6421
Web: www.royblack.com

Blackwell Burke PA 431 S Seventh St 2500 Minneapolis MN 55415 612-343-3200
Web: www.blackwellburke.com

Blakinger Byler & Thomas PC 28 Penn Sq Lancaster PA 17603 717-299-1100
Web: www.blakingerthomas.com

Blalock Walters PA 802 11th St W Bradenton FL 34205 941-748-0100
Web: blalockwalters.com

Blaney McMurtry LLP
Maritime Life Tower 2 Queen St E Ste 1500 Toronto ON M5C3G5 416-593-1221
Web: www.blaney.com

Blank Rome LLP 1 Logan Sq 130 N 18th St Philadelphia PA 19103 215-569-5500 569-5555
Web: www.blankrome.com

Blasingame, Burch, Garrard & Ashley PC
440 College Ave Athens GA 30603 706-354-4000
TF: 866-354-3544 ■ *Web:* www.bbgbalaw.com

Blecher & Collins
515 S Figueroa St Ste 1750 Los Angeles CA 90071 213-622-4222
Web: www.blechercollins.com

Blitt & Gaines Pc 661 Glenn Ave Wheeling IL 60090 847-403-4900
TF: 888-920-0620 ■ *Web:* www.blittandgaines.com

Blue Williams LLP
3421 N Causeway Blvd Ste 900 Metairie LA 70002 504-831-4091
TF: 800-326-4991 ■ *Web:* bluewilliams.com

Bodman PLC
1901 Saint Antoine St Sixth Fl at Ford Field
Detroit MI 48226 313-259-7777
Web: www.bodmanlaw.com

Boehl Stopher & Graves LLP
400 W Market St Ste 2300 Louisville KY 40202 502-589-5980
Web: www.bsg-law.com

Boies Schiller & Flexner LLP
5301 Wisconsin Ave NW Washington DC 20015 202-237-2727 237-6131
TF: 877-224-0464 ■ *Web:* bsfllp.com

Bone McAllester Norton PLLC
511 Union St Nashville City Ctr Ste 1600 Nashville TN 37219 615-238-6300
Web: www.bonelaw.com

Boren, Oliver & Coffey LLP
59 N Jefferson St Martinsville IN 46151 765-342-0147
TF: 800-403-9971 ■ *Web:* www.boclawyers.com

Bose McKinney & Evans LLP
111 Monument Cir Ste 2700 Indianapolis IN 46204 317-684-5000 684-5173
Web: www.boselaw.com

Boss Law Firm APLC, The
409 Camino del Rio S Ste 201 San Diego CA 92108 619-234-1776
Web: bosslawfirm.com

Boyle Fredrickson SC 840 N Plankinton Ave Milwaukee WI 53203 414-225-9755
Web: www.boylefred.com

Bracewell & Giuliani LLP
711 Louisiana St Ste 2300 Houston TX 77002 713-223-2300 221-1212
Web: www.bracewelllaw.com

Bradford & Barthel LLP 2518 River Plz Dr. Sacramento CA 95833 916-569-0790 569-0799
Web: www.bradfordbarthel.com

Bradley & Riley PC PO Box 2804 Cedar Rapids IA 52406 319-363-0101
Web: bradleyriley.com

Bradley Arant Boult Cummings LLP
1819 Fifth Ave N. Birmingham AL 35203 205-521-8000
Web: www.bradley.com

Brady Connolly & Masuda Pc
211 Landmark Dr Ste C2 Normal IL 61761 309-862-4914
Web: bcm-law.com

Brann & Isaacson 184 Main St. Lewiston ME 04243 207-786-3566
Web: www.brannlaw.com

Bremer Whyte Brown & O'Meara LLP
20320 SW Birch St 2nd Fl Newport Beach CA 92660 949-221-1000
Web: www.bremerwhyte.com

Brennan Manna & Diamond LLC 75 E Market St Akron OH 44308 330-253-5060
Web: www.bmdllc.com

Brewer & Pritchard 3 Riverway Ste 1800 Houston TX 77024 713-209-2950
TF: 800-445-8710 ■ *Web:* www.bplaw.com

Brian Patrick Conry Pc
534 Sw Third Ave Ste 711 Portland OR 97204 503-274-4430
Web: www.brianpatrickconry.com

Brick Gentry Law Firm
6701 Westown Pkwy Ste 100 West Des Moines IA 50266 515-274-1450
Web: www.brickgentrylaw.com

Bricker & Eckler LLP 100 S Third St Columbus OH 43215 614-227-2300
Web: www.bricker.com

Brock & Scott PLLC
1315 Westbrook Plz Dr. Winston-salem NC 27103 336-760-5526
Web: www.brockandscott.com

Brooklyn Legal Services Corp
105 Court St Fl 3 Brooklyn NY 11201 718-237-5500
Web: www.legalservicesnyc.org/our-program/brooklyn

Brooks, Pierce, McLendon, Humphrey & Leonard LLP
230 N Elm St Ste 2000 Greensboro NC 27401 336-373-8850
Web: www.brookspierce.com

Brown & Charbonneau LLP 420 Exchange Ste 270 Irvine CA 92602 714-505-3000
Web: bc-llp.com

Brown & Connery LLP 360 Haddon Ave. Westmont NJ 08108 856-854-8900
Web: brownconnery.com

Brown & Michaels 400 M T Bank Bldg Ste 400 Ithaca NY 14850 607-256-2000
Web: www.bpmlegal.com

Brown, Garganese, Weiss & D'Agresta PA
111 N Orange Ave Ste 2000 Orlando FL 32802 407-425-9566
Web: www.orlandolaw.net

Brownlee Fryett 396 11th Ave SW Fl 7 Calgary AB T2R0C5 403-232-8408
Web: www.brownleelaw.com

Broyles Kight & Ricafort PC
8250 Haverstick Rd Ste 100 Indianapolis IN 46240 317-571-3600
TF: 888-834-2692 ■ *Web:* www.bkrlaw.com

Phone | Fax

Buchalter Nemer Pc 1000 Wilshire Blvd Los Angeles CA 90017 213-891-0700 896-0400
Web: www.buchalter.com

Buchanan Ingersoll & Rooney PC
301 Grant St 1 Oxford Ctr 20th Fl Pittsburgh PA 15219 412-562-8800 562-1041
TF: 800-444-6738 ■ *Web:* www.bipc.com

Budd Larner P C 150 John F Kennedy Pkwy Short Hills NJ 07078 973-379-4800 379-7734
Web: www.buddlarner.com

Bull, Housser & Tupper LLP
900 Howe St Ste 900 Vancouver BC V6Z2M4 604-687-6575
TF: 866-687-6575 ■ *Web:* www.bht.com

Bullivant Houser Bailey PC
888 SW Fifth Ave Ste 300 Portland OR 97204 503-228-6351
Web: www.bullivant.com

Burch & Cracchiolo PA 702 E Osborn Rd Ste 200 Phoenix AZ 85014 602-274-7611
Web: www.bcattorneys.com

Burch Porter & Johnson Pllc 130 N Ct Ave Memphis TN 38103 901-524-5000 524-5024
Web: www.bpjlaw.com

Burg Simpson Eldredge Hersh Jardine PC
40 Inverness Dr E Englewood CO 80112 303-792-5595
Web: www.burgsimpson.com

Burns Burns Walsh & Walsh pa 704 Topeka Ave. Lyndon KS 66451 785-828-4418
TF: 888-528-3186 ■ *Web:* bbwwlaw.com

Bush Ross PA 1801 N Highland Ave Tampa FL 33602 813-224-9255
Web: www.bushross.com

Butch Quinn Rosemurgy Jardis Burkhart Lewandowski & Miller Pc
816 Ludington St Escanaba MI 49829 906-786-4422
Web: www.bqrlaw.com

Bybel Rutledge LLP 1017 Mumma Rd Lemoyne PA 17043 717-731-1700
Web: www.bybelrutledge.com

Cabaniss, Johnston, Gardner, Dumas & O'Neal LLP
Park Pl Tower 2001 Park Pl N Ste 700 Birmingham AL 35203 205-716-5200
Web: www.cabaniss.com

Cable Huston Benedic
1001 Sw Fifth Ave Ste 2000 Portland OR 97204 503-224-3092
Web: www.cablehuston.com

Caesar, Rivise, Bernstein, Cohen & Pokotilow Ltd
12th Fl 1635 Market St Philadelphia PA 19103 215-567-2010
Web: www.caesar.law

Cain Lamarre Casgrain Wells Senc
630 boul Rene-Levesque Ouest Ste 2780 Montreal QC H3B1S6 514-393-4580
Web: www.clcw.ca

Cairncross & Hempelmann PS
524 Second Ave Ste 500 Seattle WA 98104 206-587-0700
Web: www.cairncross.com

Cameron, Hodges, Coleman, LaPointe & Wright PA
111 N Magnolia Ave Ste 1350 Orlando FL 32801 407-841-5030
TF: 888-841-5030 ■ *Web:* www.cameronhodges.com

Campbell, Guin, Williams, Guy & Gidiere LLC
Capitol Park Ctr 2711 University Blvd Tuscaloosa AL 35401 205-633-0200
Web: www.tannerguin.com

Cannon & Dunphy Sc 595 N Barker Rd. Brookfield WI 53045 262-780-7188
Web: www.cannon-dunphy.com

Cantor Colburn LLP 22nd Fl 20 Church St Hartford CT 06103 860-286-2929
Web: www.cantorcolburn.com

Capell & Howard PC 150 S Perry St. Montgomery AL 36104 334-241-8000
Web: capellhoward.com

Carlile Patchen & Murphy LLP 366 E Broad St Columbus OH 43215 614-228-6135 221-0216
Web: www.cpmlaw.com

Carlsmith Ball LLP
1001 Bishop St Ste 2100 PO Box 656 Honolulu HI 96813 808-523-2500 523-0842
Web: www.carlsmith.com

Carlson, Caspers, Vandenburgh & Lindquist
225 S Sixth St Ste 4200 Minneapolis MN 55402 612-436-9600
Web: carlsoncaspers.com

Carlson, Gaskey & Olds A Professional Corp
400 W Maple Rd Ste 350 Birmingham MI 48009 248-988-8360
Web: www.cgolaw.com

Carlton Fields PA
4221 W Boy Scout Blvd Corporate Ctr Three
Ste 1000 Tampa FL 33607 813-223-7000
Web: www.carltonfields.com

Carluccio, Leone, Dimon, Doyle & Sacks LLC
9 Robbins St. Toms River NJ 08753 732-797-1600
Web: cldds.com

Carman Callahan & Ingham LLP
Carman Bldg 280 Main St Farmingdale NY 11735 516-249-3450
Web: www.carmancallahan.com

Carmody Torrance Sandak & Hennessey LLP
50 Leavenworth St Waterbury CT 06721 203-573-1200
Web: carmodylaw.com

Carpenter Lipps & Leland LLP
280 N High St Ste 1300 Columbus OH 43215 614-365-4100
Web: carpenterlipps.com

Carr & Ferrell LLP 120 Constitution Dr. Menlo Park CA 94025 650-812-3400
Web: www.carrferrell.com

Carr McClellan Ingersall Thompson
216 Park Rd Burlingame CA 94010 650-342-9600
Web: www.carr-mcclellan.com

Carter Ledyard & Milburn LLP 2 Wall St Fl 13 New York NY 10005 212-732-3200 732-3232
Web: www.clm.com

Carter Mario Injury Lawyers
176 Wethersfield Ave Hartford CT 06114 860-525-2222
Web: cartermario.com

Casey Gerry Schenk Francavilla Blatt & Penfield LLP
110 Laurel St San Diego CA 92101 619-238-1811
Web: www.caseygerry.com

Casner & Edwards LLP 303 Congress St. Boston MA 02210 617-426-5900
Web: www.casneredwards.com

Cassels Brock & Blackwell LLP
2100 Scotia Plz 40 King St W Toronto ON M5H3C2 416-869-5300
Web: www.casselsbrock.com

Cassin & Cassin LLP 711 Third Ave 20th Fl New York NY 10017 212-972-6161
Web: www.cassinllp.com

Cavanagh Law Firm, The 1850 N Central Ave. Phoenix AZ 85004 602-322-4000 322-4100
TF: 888-824-3476 ■ *Web:* www.cavanaghlaw.com

				Phone	Fax
Cellino & Barnes PC 2500 Main Pl Tower 350 Main St *TF:* 800-888-8888 ■ *Web:* www.cellinoandbarnes.com	Buffalo	NY	14202	716-854-2020	
Center-Battered Womens Services Po Box 1406 *Web:* www.sanctuaryforfamilies.org	New York	NY	10268	212-349-6009	
Cga Law Firm 106 Harrisburg St *Web:* www.cgalaw.com	East Berlin	PA	17316	717-848-4900	
Chaffetz Lindsey LLP 1700 BRdway 33rd Fl *Web:* www.chaffetzlindsey.com	New York	NY	10019	212-257-6960	
Chalker Flores LLP 14951 N Dallas Pkwy Ste 400 *Web:* www.chalkerflores.com	Dallas	TX	75254	817-820-0244	
Chang & Boos 1305 11th St Ste 301 *Web:* www.americanlaw.com	Bellingham	WA	98225	360-671-5945	
Chapman & Intrieri LLP 2236 Mariner Sq Dr Ste 300 *Web:* chapmanandintrieri.com	Alameda	CA	94501	510-864-3600	
Charles d Hankey Law Office PC 434 E New York St *TF:* 800-520-3633 ■ *Web:* www.hankeylawoffice.com	Indianapolis	IN	46202	317-634-8565	
Chasan Leyner & Lamparello A Professional Corp 300 Harmon Meadow Blvd *Web:* www.chasanlaw.com	Secaucus	NJ	07094	201-348-6000	
Cheng Cohen LLC 311 N Aberdeen Ste 400 *Web:* www.chengcohen.com	Chicago	IL	60607	312-243-1701	
Chilivis, Cochran, Larkins & Bever LLP 3127 Maple Dr NE *Web:* www.cclblawyers.com	Atlanta	GA	30305	404-233-4171	
Christensen O'Connor Johnson & Kindness PLLC 1201 Third Ave Ste 3600 *Web:* www.cojk.com	Seattle	WA	98101	206-682-8100	
Clark, Gagliardi & Miller PC 99 Court St *TF:* 800-734-5694 ■ *Web:* www.cgmlaw.com	White Plains	NY	10601	800-734-5694	
Clarke Silverglate PA 799 Brickell Plz Ste 900 *Web:* www.cspalaw.com	Miami	FL	33131	305-377-0700	
Clifford Chance LLP 31 W 52nd St *Web:* www.cliffordchance.com	New York	NY	10019	212-878-8000	878-8375
Cloppert, Latanick, Sauter & Washburn LLP 225 E Broad St Fl 4 *Web:* www.cloppertlaw.com	Columbus	OH	43215	614-461-4455	
Cobb & Cole 149 S Ridgewood Ave Ste 700 *Web:* www.cobbcole.com	Daytona Beach	FL	32114	386-255-8171	
Cocciardi & Associates Inc 4 Kacey Ct *TF:* 800-377-3024 ■ *Web:* www.cocciardi.com	Mechanicsburg	PA	17055	717-766-4500	
Cochran Firm LLC 111 E Main St *TF:* 800-843-3476 ■ *Web:* www.cochranfirm.com	Dothan	AL	36301	334-793-1555	793-8280
Codilis & Associates PC 15W030 N Frontage Rd *Web:* www.codilis.com	Burr Ridge	IL	60527	630-794-5300	
Cohen & Gresser LLP 800 Third Ave *Web:* www.cohengresser.com	New York	NY	10022	212-957-7600	
Cohen & Grigsby Pc 625 Liberty Ave *Web:* www.cohenlaw.com	Pittsburgh	PA	15222	412-297-4900	209-0672
Cohen Highley LLP 255 Queens Ave *TF:* 800-563-1020 ■ *Web:* www.cohenhighley.com	London	ON	N6A5R8	519-672-9330	
Cohen Seglias Pallas Greenhall & Furman PC 30 S 17th St 19th Fl United Plz *Web:* cohenseglias.com	Philadelphia	PA	19103	215-564-1700	
Cohen, Hurkin, Ehrenfeld, Pomerantz & Tenenbaum 25 Chapel St Ste 705 *Web:* www.cohenhurkin.com	Brooklyn	NY	11201	718-596-9000	
Cokinos Bosien & Young PC 2919 Allen Pkwy Ste 1500 *Web:* www.cbylaw.com	Houston	TX	77019	713-535-5500	
Cole Scott & Kissane pa 617 Whitehead St *Web:* www.csklegal.com	Key West	FL	33040	305-294-4440	
Collins & Lacy PC 1330 Lady St 6th Fl *TF:* 888-648-0526 ■ *Web:* www.collinsandlacy.com	Columbia	SC	29201	803-256-2660	
Colten Cummins Watson & Vincent PC 3959 Pender Dr Ste 200 *Web:* www.coltenlaw.com	Fairfax	VA	22030	703-277-9700	
Colucci & Umans Inc 218 E 50th St *Web:* www.colucci-umans.com	New York	NY	10022	212-935-5700	
Coman & Anderson PC 650 Warrenville Rd Ste 500 *Web:* www.comananderson.com	Lisle	IL	60532	630-428-2660	
Connell Foley LLP 85 Livingston Ave *Web:* www.connellfoley.com	Roseland	NJ	07068	973-535-0500	
Connelly Baker Wotring LLP 700 JPMorgan Chase Tower 600 Travis St *Web:* www.connellybaker.com	Houston	TX	77002	713-980-1700	
Conrad & Scherer LLP 633 S Federal Hwy *Web:* www.conradscherer.com	Fort Lauderdale	FL	33301	954-462-5500	
Conrad, Trosch & Kemmy PA 301 S McDowell St Ste 809 *Web:* www.ctklawyers.com	Charlotte	NC	28204	704-553-8221	
Conroy, Simberg, Ganon, Krevans, Abel, Lurvey, Morrow & Schefer PA 3440 Hollywood Blvd 2nd Fl *Web:* www.conroysimberg.com	Hollywood	FL	33021	954-961-1400	
Constangy, Brooks & Smith LLC 230 Peachtree St N W Ste 2400 *Web:* constangy.com	Atlanta	GA	30303	404-525-8622	
Consumer Attorneys of California 770 L St Ste 1200 *Web:* www.caoc.org	Sacramento	CA	95814	916-442-6902	
Conway, Olejniczak & Jerry SC 231 S Adams St *Web:* www.lcojlaw.com	Green Bay	WI	54301	920-437-0476	
Cooch & Taylor 1000 W St The Brandywine Bldg 10th Fl *Web:* www.coochtaylor.com	Wilmington	DE	19801	302-984-3800	
Cooley Godward Kronish LLP 3000 El Camino Real *TF:* 888-654-2411 ■ *Web:* www.cooley.com	Palo Alto	CA	94306	650-843-5000	849-7400

				Phone	Fax
Coon Brent & Associates Law Firm Pc 215 Orleans St *TF:* 866-335-2666 ■ *Web:* bcoonlaw.com	Beaumont	TX	77701	409-835-2666	
Cooper Legal Services Dwayne e Cooper Atty at Law 8411 Tuskin Way *TF:* 800-959-1825 ■ *Web:* cooperlegalservices.com	Indianapolis	IN	46278	317-873-3600	
Copple, Rockey, Mckeever & Schlecht PC LLO 2425 Taylor Ave *TF:* 888-860-2425 ■ *Web:* www.greatadvocates.com	Norfolk	NE	68701	402-371-4300	
Cors & Bassett 537 E Pete Rose Way Ste 400 *Web:* www.corsbassett.com	Cincinnati	OH	45202	513-852-8200	
Cory Watson Crowder & DeGaris 2131 Magnolia Ave *Web:* www.cwcd.com	Birmingham	AL	35205	205-328-2200	
Costello, Porter, Hill, Heisterkamp, Bushnell & Carpenter LLP Security Bldg 704 St Joseph St *Web:* www.costelloporter.com	Rapid City	SD	57709	605-343-2410	
Couch White LLP 540 Broadway *Web:* www.couchwhite.com	Albany	NY	12201	518-426-4600	
Covington & Burling LLP 1201 Pennsylvania Ave NW *Web:* www.cov.com	Washington	DC	20004	202-662-6000	662-6291
Covington Patrick Hagins Stern & Lewis pa Law Firm 211 Pettigru St *Web:* covpatlaw.com	Greenville	SC	29601	864-242-9000	
Cowles & Thompson A Professional Corp 901 Main St Ste 3900 *Web:* www.cowlesthompson.com	Dallas	TX	75202	214-672-2000	672-2020
Cox Smith Matthews Inc 112 E Pecan St Ste 1800	San Antonio	TX	78205	210-554-5516	
Cozen O'Connor 1900 Market St *TF:* 800-523-2900 ■ *Web:* www.cozen.com	Philadelphia	PA	19103	215-665-2000	665-2013
Craige Brawley Liipfert & Walker LLP 110 Oakwood Dr Ste 300 *Web:* www.craigebrawley.com	Winston-Salem	NC	27103	336-725-0583	
Cranfill Sumner & Hartzog LLP 5420 Wade Park Blvd Ste 300	Raleigh	NC	27607	919-828-5100	
Cravath Swaine & Moore LLP 825 Eigth Ave Worldwide Plz *Web:* www.cravath.com	New York	NY	10019	212-474-1000	474-3700
Critchfield, Critchfield & Johnston Ltd 225 N Market St *Web:* www.ccj.com	Wooster	OH	44691	330-264-4444	
Crivello Carlson Sc 710 N Plankinton Ave Ste 500 *Web:* www.crivellocarlson.com	Milwaukee	WI	53203	414-271-7722	
Crowley Fleck PLLP 490 N 31st St Ste 500 *Web:* www.crowleyfleck.com	Billings	MT	59101	406-252-3441	
Cruser & Mitchell LLP 275 Scientific Dr *Web:* cmlawfirm.com	Norcross	GA	30092	404-881-2622	
Cullen, Weston, Pines & Bach LLP 122 W Washington Ave Ste 900 *TF:* 866-443-8661 ■ *Web:* www.cwpb.com	Madison	WI	53703	608-807-0752	
Cummings & Lockwood LLC 8000 Health Ctr Blvd Ste 300 *Web:* www.cl-law.com	Bonita Springs	FL	34135	239-947-8811	
Curtin & Heefner 250 N Pennsylvania *Web:* www.curtinheefner.com	Morrisville	PA	19067	215-736-2521	
Dale L Buchanan & Associates PC 6576 E Brainerd Rd *TF:* 800-813-8783 ■ *Web:* dalebuchanan.com	Chattanooga	TN	37421	423-894-2552	
Daley & Heft LLP 462 Stevens Ave Ste 201 *Web:* daleyheft.com	Solana Beach	CA	92075	858-755-5666	
Daniel & Stark Law Offices 100 W William Joel Bryan Pkwy *TF:* 800-474-1233 ■ *Web:* www.danielstarklaw.com	Bryan	TX	77803	254-776-6200	
Daniels & Porco LLP 517 Route 22 *Web:* www.danielsporco.com	Pawling	NY	12564	845-855-5900	
Dann, Dorfman, Herrell & Skillman PC 1601 Market St Ste 2400 *Web:* www.ddhs.com	Philadelphia	PA	19103	215-563-4100	
Dascenzo Intellectual Property Law PC 1000 S W Broadway Ste 1555 *Web:* www.dascenzoiplaw.com	Portland	OR	97205	503-224-7529	
Davenport, Evans, Hurwitz & Smith LLP 206 W 14th St *Web:* dehs.com	Sioux Falls	SD	57101	605-336-2880	
Davidson, Davidson & Kappel LLC 589 Eighth Ave 16th Fl *Web:* www.ddkpatent.com	New York	NY	10018	212-736-1940	
Davies Pearson PC 920 Fawcett Ave *TF:* 800-439-1112 ■ *Web:* www.dpearson.com	Tacoma	WA	98401	253-620-1500	
Davis & Gilbert 1740 Broadway *Web:* www.dglaw.com	New York	NY	10019	212-468-4800	
Davis & Wilkerson Pc 5113 SW Pk Ste 115 *Web:* www.dwlaw.com	Austin	TX	78735	512-482-0614	
Davis Graham & Stubbs LLP 1550 17th St Ste 500 *Web:* www.dgslaw.com	Denver	CO	80202	303-892-9400	893-1379
Davis Law Firm 10500 Heitage Blvd Ste 102 *TF:* 800-770-0127 ■ *Web:* www.jeffdavislawfirm.com	San Antonio	TX	78201	210-444-4444	
Davis Polk & Wardwell 450 Lexington Ave *Web:* www.davispolk.com	New York	NY	10017	212-450-4000	701-5800
Davis Wright Tremaine LLP 1201 Third Ave #2200 *Web:* www.dwt.com	Seattle	WA	98101	206-622-3150	757-7700
Dawda, Mann, Mulcahy & Sadler PLC 39533 Woodward Ave Ste 200 *Web:* www.dmms.com	Bloomfield Hills	MI	48304	248-642-3700	
Day Pitney LLP 242 Trumbull St *TF:* 866-667-6572 ■ *Web:* www.daypitney.com	Hartford	CT	06103	860-275-0100	275-0343
De Cotiis Fitzpatrick Cole & Wisler LLP 500 Frank W Burr Blvd *Web:* www.decotiislaw.com	Teaneck	NJ	07666	201-928-1100	
Dean Law Group, The 3990 Old Town Ave C-303 *Web:* www.thedeanlawgroup.com	San Diego	CA	92110	619-531-9300	

	City	State	Zip	Phone	Fax
Dean, Ringers, Morgan & Lawton PA 1200 Capital Plz I 201 E Pine St Ste 1200 — *Web:* www.drml-law.com	Orlando	FL	32801	407-422-4310	
Debevoise & Plimpton LLP 919 Third Ave — *Web:* www.debevoise.com	New York	NY	10022	212-909-6000	909-6836
Dechert LLP 2929 Arch St Cira Ctr — *TF:* 800-328-4880 ■ *Web:* www.dechert.com	Philadelphia	PA	19104	215-994-4000	994-2222
Degan, Blanchard & Nash A Professional Law Corp 400 Poydras St Ste 2600 — *Web:* www.degan.com	New Orleans	LA	70130	504-529-3333	
Deily Mooney & Glastetter LLP 8 Thurlow Ter — *Web:* www.deilylawfirm.com	Albany	NY	12203	518-436-0344	
Delahousaye Angela Law Offices 1655 N Main St Ste 260 — *Web:* www.delahousayelaw.com	Walnut Creek	CA	94596	925-944-3300	
Delaney, Wiles, Hayes, Gerety, Ellis & Young Inc 1007 W Third Ave Ste 400 — *Web:* www.delaneywiles.com	Anchorage	AK	99501	907-279-3581	
Dennis, Corry, Porter & Smith LLP 14 Piedmont Ctr 3535 Piedmont Rd NE Ste 900 — *TF:* 800-735-0838 ■ *Web:* www.dcplaw.com	Atlanta	GA	30305	404-365-0102	
Deutsch Williams Brooks DeRensis & Holland PC 1 Design Ctr Pl Ste 600 — *Web:* www.dwboston.com	Boston	MA	02210	617-951-2300	
Deutsch, Kerrigan & Stiles LLP 755 Magazine St — *Web:* www.deutschkerrigan.com	New Orleans	LA	70130	504-581-5141	
DeWitt Ross & Stevens SC 2 E Mifflin St Ste 600 — *Web:* www.dewittross.com	Madison	WI	53703	608-255-8891	
Dickstein Shapiro LLP 1825 Eye St NW — *TF:* 800-203-3447 ■ *Web:* www.dicksteinshapiro.com	Washington	DC	20006	202-420-2200	420-2201
Diederiks & Whitelaw Plc 13885 Hedgewood Dr Ste 317 — *Web:* www.dwpatentlaw.com	Woodbridge	VA	22193	703-583-8300	
DiFrancesco, Bateman, Coley, Yospin, Kunzman, Davis & Lehrer PC 15 Mountain Blvd — *Web:* www.newjerseylaw.net	Warren	NJ	07059	908-757-7800	
Dinkes & Schwitzer 112 Madison Ave Fl 10 — *Web:* www.wsatlaw.com	New York	NY	10016	212-683-3800	
DLA Piper 203 N LaSalle St Ste 1900 — *Web:* www.dlapiper.com	Chicago	IL	60601	312-368-4000	236-7516
Dld Lawyers 150 Alhambra Cir Ph — *Web:* www.dldlawyers.com	Coral Gables	FL	33134	305-443-4850	
Docken & Co 900-800 6 Ave Sw — *TF:* 877-269-3612 ■ *Web:* docken.com	Calgary	AB	T2P3G3	403-269-3612	
Dolden Wallace & Folick 888 Dunsmuir St — *Web:* www.dolden.com	Vancouver	BC	V6C3K4	604-689-3222	
Domengeaux Wright Roy & Edwards LLC 556 Jefferson St Ste 500 — *TF:* 800-375-6186 ■ *Web:* www.wrightroy.com	Lafayette	LA	70501	337-233-3033	
Donald Harris Law Firm 158 Columbus Ave Ste 302 — *Web:* www.donaldharrislawfirm.com	Sandusky	OH	44870	419-621-9388	
Donati Law Firm LLP 1545 Union Ave — *TF:* 800-521-0578 ■ *Web:* www.donatilaw.com	Memphis	TN	38104	901-278-1004	
Donohoe & Stapleton LLC 2781 Zelda Rd — *Web:* donohoeandstapleton.com	Montgomery	AL	36106	334-269-3355	
Donohue Brown Mathewson & Smyth LLC 140 S Dearborn St Ste 800 — *Web:* www.dbmslaw.com	Chicago	IL	60603	312-422-0900	
Dorsey & Whitney LLP 50 S Sixth St Ste 1500 — *TF:* 800-759-4929 ■ *Web:* www.dorsey.com	Minneapolis	MN	55402	612-340-2600	340-2868
Downey Brand LLP 621 Capitol Mall 18th Fl — *Web:* www.downeybrand.com	Sacramento	CA	95814	916-444-1000	
Dozier, Miller, Pollard & Murphy LLP Cameron Brown Bldg 301 S McDowell St Ste 700 — *Web:* doziermillerlaw.com	Charlotte	NC	28204	704-372-6373	
Drake, Loeb, Heller, Kennedy, Gogerty, Gaba, Rodd PLLC 555 Hudson Vly Ave Ste 100 — *Web:* www.drakeloeb.com	New Windsor	NY	12553	845-561-0550	
Dreher Langer & Tomkies LLP 41 S High St Ste 2250 — *Web:* www.dltlaw.com	Columbus	OH	43215	614-628-8000	
Drinker Biddle & Reath LLP 1 Logan Sq Ste 2000 — *Web:* www.drinkerbiddle.com	Philadelphia	PA	19103	215-988-2700	988-2757
Drummond Woodsum LLP 84 Marginal Way Ste 600 — *Web:* www.dwmlaw.com	Portland	ME	04101	207-772-1941	
Duane Morris LLP 30 S 17th St — *Web:* www.duanemorris.com	Philadelphia	PA	19103	215-979-1000	979-1020
DuBois, Sheehan, Hamilton, Levin & Weissman LLC 511 Cooper St — *Web:* www.duboislaw.com	Camden	NJ	08102	856-365-7665	
Dudley & Smith PA 101 Fifth St E Ste 2602 — *Web:* www.dudleyandsmith.com	Saint Paul	MN	55101	651-291-1717	
Dunn Carney Allen Higgins & Tongue LLP 851 SW Sixth Ave Ste 1500 — *Web:* www.dunncarney.com	Portland	OH	97204	503-224-6440	
Dunn Lambert LLC 80 W State Rt 4 — *Web:* www.njbizlawyer.com	Paramus	NJ	07652	201-291-0700	
Dunnington Bartholow & Miller LLP 250 Park Ave — *Web:* www.dunnington.com	New York	NY	10017	212-682-8811	
Durham Jones & Pinegar 111 East Broadway Ste 900 — *Web:* www.durhamjones.com	Salt Lake City	UT	84111	801-415-3000	
Eagleton, Eagleton & Harrison Inc 320 S Boston Ave Ste 1700 — *Web:* www.eehlaw.com	Tulsa	OK	74103	918-584-0462	
Eastham, Watson, Dale & Forney LLP The Niels Esperson Bldg 808 Travis Ste 1300 — *Web:* www.easthamlaw.com	Houston	TX	77002	713-225-0905	
Eastman & Smith Ltd 1 Seagate 24th Fl — *Web:* www.eastmansmith.com	Toledo	OH	43699	419-241-6000	
Eckell, Sparks, Levy, Auerbach, Monte, Sloane, Matthews & Auslander PC 344 W Front St — *Web:* www.eckellsparks.com	Media	PA	19063	610-565-3700	
Edward A. Williamson Law Firm Pllc, The 509 S Church Ave — *Web:* www.eawlaw.com	Philadelphia	MS	39350	601-656-5634	
Edwards, Kenny & Bray 1900 - 1040 W Georgia St — *Web:* www.ekb.com	Vancouver	BC	V6E4H3	604-689-1811	
Einhorn, Harris, Ascher, Barbarito & Frost PC 165 E Main St — *Web:* www.einhornharris.com	Denville	NJ	07834	973-627-7300	
Elarbee , Thompson , Sapp & Wilson LLP 800 International Tower 229 Peachtree St NE — *Web:* www.elarbeethompson.com	Atlanta	GA	30303	404-659-6700	
Elderkin, Martin, Kelly & Messina PC 150 E Eighth St Fl 2 — *Web:* www.elderkinlaw.com	Erie	PA	16501	814-456-4000	
Elliott, Ostrander & Preston PC Union Bank Tower 707 SW Washington St Ste 1500 — *TF:* 866-716-3410 ■ *Web:* www.eoplaw.com	Portland	OR	97205	503-224-7112	
Ellis Ged & Bodden pa 7171 N Federal Hwy — *TF:* 888-342-3476 ■ *Web:* www.ellisandged.com	Boca Raton	FL	33487	561-995-1966	
Ellis Law Group LLP 740 University Ave Ste 100 — *Web:* www.womenlawyers-sacramento.org	Sacramento	CA	95825	916-283-8820	
Ellis, Li & McKinstry PLLC Market Pl Tower 2025 First Ave Ph A — *Web:* www.elmlaw.com	Seattle	WA	98121	206-682-0565	
Ellison, Schneider & Harris LLP 2015 H St — *Web:* www.eslawfirm.com	Sacramento	CA	95814	916-447-2166	
Emerson Thomson & Bennett LLC 1914 Akron Peninsula Rd — *TF:* 800-822-8113 ■ *Web:* www.etblaw.com	Akron	OH	44313	330-434-9999	
Empire Justice Center 1 W Main St Ste 200 — *Web:* www.empirejustice.org	Rochester	NY	14614	585-454-4060	
Engelman Berger PC 3636 N Central Ave Ste 700 — *Web:* www.engelmanberger.com	Phoenix	AZ	85012	602-271-9090	
English, Lucas, Priest & Owsley LLP 1101 College St — *Web:* www.elpolaw.com	Bowling Green	KY	42102	270-781-6500	
Epstein Becker & Green PC 250 Pk Ave — *Web:* www.ebglaw.com	New York	NY	10177	212-351-4500	661-0989
Epstein Cole LLP 393 University Ave — *Web:* www.epsteincole.com	Toronto	ON	M5G1E6	416-862-9888	
Ervin Cohen & Jessup 9401 Wilshire Blvd 9th Fl — *Web:* www.ecjlaw.com	Beverly Hills	CA	90212	310-273-6333	
Escamilla, Poneck & Cruz LLP 850 Riverwalk Pl 700 N St Mary's St — *Web:* www.escamillaponeck.com	San Antonio	TX	78205	210-225-0001	
Evan K Thalenberg Law Offices 216 E Lexington St — *TF:* 800-778-1181 ■ *Web:* ektlaw.com	Baltimore	MD	21202	410-625-9100	
Evans Latham & Campisi 1 Post St Ste 600 — *Web:* www.elc-law.com	San Francisco	CA	94104	415-421-0288	
Ezra Sutton Law Offices 900 Us Hwy 9 N Ste 201 — *Web:* ezrasutton.com	Woodbridge	NJ	07095	732-634-3520	
Faegre & Benson LLP 90 S Seventh St 2200 Wells Fargo Bldg — *TF:* 800-328-4393 ■ *Web:* www.faegrebd.com	Minneapolis	MN	55402	612-766-7000	766-1600
Fafinski Mark & Johnson PA 775 Prairie Center Dr Ste 400 — *Web:* www.fmjlaw.com	Eden Prairie	MN	55344	952-995-9500	
Fann & Petruccelli PA 5100 N Federal Hwy Ste 300 B — *Web:* fplawyers.com	Fort Lauderdale	FL	33308	954-771-4118	
Farah Afaf Vicky 201 E Liberty St Ste 7 — *Web:* vickyfarah.com	Ann Arbor	MI	48104	734-663-9813	
Farr, Farr, Emerich, Hackett & Carr PA Earl D Farr Bldg 99 Nesbit St — *TF:* 855-327-7529 ■ *Web:* www.farr.com	Punta Gorda	FL	33950	941-639-1158	
Farrell Fritz EAB Plz 14th Fl — *Web:* www.farrellfritz.com	Uniondale	NY	11556	516-227-0700	
Farris, Riley & Pitt LLP 2025 Third Ave N Ste 400 — *TF:* 888-580-5176 ■ *Web:* www.frplegal.com	Birmingham	AL	35203	205-324-1212	
Faruki Ireland & Cox PLL 500 Courthouse Plz SW 10 N Ludlow St — *Web:* www.ficlaw.com	Dayton	OH	45402	937-227-3700	
Feldesman Tucker Leifer Fidell LLP 1129 20th St NW Ste 400 — *Web:* www.feldesmantucker.com	Washington	DC	20036	202-466-8960	
Feldman Gale & Weber PA 2 S Biscayne Blvd 1 Biscayne Tower 30th Fl — *Web:* www.feldmangale.com	Miami	FL	33131	305-358-5001	
Feldman, Kramer & Monaco PC 330 Vanderbilt Motor Pkwy — *Web:* www.fkmlaw.com	Hauppauge	NY	11788	631-231-1450	
Fennemore Craig PC 3003 N Central Ave Ste 2600 — *Web:* www.fclaw.com	Phoenix	AZ	85012	602-916-5000	
Ferguson, Case, Orr, Paterson, & Cunningham LLP 1050 S Kimball Rd — *Web:* www.fcopc.com	Ventura	CA	93004	805-659-6800	
Ferrara Fiorenza Larrison Barrett & Reitz PC 5010 Campuswood Dr — *Web:* www.ferrarafirm.com	East Syracuse	NY	13057	315-437-7600	

				Phone	Fax
Fiddler Gonzalez & Rodriguez PSC 254 Munoz Rivera Ave 6th Fl *Web:* www.fgrlaw.com	Hato Rey	PR	00918	787-753-3113	
Fieger Fieger Kenney & Giroux PC 19390 W 10-Mile Rd *Web:* www.fiegerlaw.com	Southfield	MI	48075	248-355-5555	
Field Law 10235 101 St Nw Ste 2000 *TF:* 800-222-6479 ■ *Web:* www.fieldlaw.com	Edmonton	AB	T5J3G1	780-423-3003	
Finkelstein & Partners LLP 1279 Route 300 *Web:* www.lawampm.com	Newburgh	NY	12551	845-562-0203	
Finley, Alt, Smith, Scharnberg, Craig, Hilmes & Gaffney PC 699 Walnut St Ste 1700 *Web:* www.finleylaw.com	Des Moines	IA	50309	515-288-0145	
Fire-Safe Protection Services 1815 Sherwood Forest St *Web:* www.fire-safe.net	Houston	TX	77043	713-722-7800	
Fish & Richardson PC 1 Marina Park Dr *TF:* 800-818-5070 ■ *Web:* www.fr.com	Boston	MA	02110	617-542-5070	542-8906
Fitelson Lasky Aslan & Couture Atty 551 Fifth Ave Rm 605 *Web:* agnesdemilledances.com	New York	NY	10176	212-586-4700	
Fitzpatrick Cella Harper & Scinto 1290 Ave of the Americas *Web:* www.fitzpatrickcella.com	New York	NY	10104	212-218-2100	218-2200
Flaster Greenberg 1810 Chapel Ave W *Web:* www.flastergreenberg.com	Cherry Hill	NJ	08002	856-661-1900	
Fletcher, Heald & Hildreth PLC 1300 N 17th St 11th Fl *Web:* www.fhhlaw.com	Arlington	VA	22209	703-812-0400	
Flicker, Kerin, Kruger & Bissada A Limited Liability Partnership 120 B Santa Margarita Ave *Web:* www.fkkblaw.com	Menlo Park	CA	94025	650-289-1400	
Flook & Graham Pc 11 E Kansas St Ste 100 *Web:* flookandgraham.com	Liberty	MO	64068	816-792-0500	
Foley & Lardner LLP 777 E Wisconsin Ave *TF:* 855-225-5341 ■ *Web:* www.foley.com	Milwaukee	WI	53202	414-271-2400	297-4900
Ford & Harrison LLP 271 17th St NW Ste 1900 *Web:* www.fordharrisonlaw.com	Atlanta	GA	30363	404-888-3800	
Ford Nassen & Baldwin PC 8080 N Central Expy Ste 1600 LB 65 *Web:* www.fordnassen.com	Dallas	TX	75206	214-523-5100	
Fortney Scott LLC 1750 K St Nw Ste 325 *Web:* fortneyscott.com	Washington	DC	20006	202-689-1200	
Foster Pepper Pllc 1111 Third Ave Ste 3400 *TF:* 800-995-5902 ■ *Web:* www.foster.com	Seattle	WA	98101	206-447-4400	447-9700
Foster Swift Collins & Smith 313 S Washington Sq *Web:* www.fosterswift.com	Lansing	MI	48933	517-371-8100	
Foulston & Siefkin LLP 1551 N Waterfront Pkwy Ste 100 *Web:* www.foulston.com	Wichita	KS	67206	316-267-6371	
Fox Galvin LLC 1 S Memorial Dr 12th Fl *Web:* www.foxgalvin.com	St. Louis	MO	63102	314-588-7000	
Fox Rothschild LLP 2000 Market St 10th Fl *Web:* www.foxrothschild.com	Philadelphia	PA	19103	215-299-2000	299-2150
Fraim & Fiorella PC 150 Boush St Ste 601 *Web:* fraimandfiorella.com	Norfolk	VA	23510	757-227-5900	
Framme Law Firm PC 2812 Emerywood Pkwy Ste 220 *Web:* www.frammelaw.com	Richmond	VA	23294	804-649-1334	
Franczek Sullivan Pc 300 S Wacker Dr Ste 3400 *Web:* www.franczek.com	Chicago	IL	60606	312-786-6119	
Frankfurt Kurnit Klein & Selz Pc 488 Madison Ave 10th Fl *Web:* www.fkks.com	New York	NY	10022	212-980-0120	593-9175
Franklin & Prokopik A Professional Corp The B & O Bldg 2 N Charles St Ste 600 *Web:* www.fandpnet.com	Baltimore	MD	21201	410-752-8700	
Fraser Stryker PC LLO 500 Energy Plz 409 S 17th St *TF:* 800-544-6041 ■ *Web:* www.fraserstryker.com	Omaha	NE	68102	402-341-6000	
Fraser Trebilcock Davis & Dunlap PC 124 W Allegan St Ste 1000 *Web:* www.fraserlawfirm.com	Lansing	MI	48933	517-482-5800	
Frederic Dorwart Lawyers Old City Hall 124 E Fourth St *Web:* www.fdlaw.com	Tulsa	OK	74103	918-583-9922	
Fredrickson, Mazeika & Grant LLP 5720 Oberlin Dr *Web:* fmglegal.com	San Diego	CA	92121	858-642-2002	
Freeborn & Peters 311 S Wacker Dr Ste 3000 *Web:* www.freeborn.com	Chicago	IL	60606	312-360-6000	360-6520
Freeland Cooper & Foreman LLP 150 Spear St Ste 1800 *Web:* www.freelandlaw.com	San Francisco	CA	94105	415-541-0200	
Freeman Freeman & Smiley LLP 1888 Century Pk E Ste 1900 *Web:* www.ffslaw.com	Los Angeles	CA	90067	310-255-6100	391-4042
Freund, Freeze & Arnold, A Legal Professional Association 1 S Main St Fifth Third Ctr Ste 1800 *Web:* ffalaw.com	Dayton	OH	45402	937-222-2424	
Friday, Eldredge & Clark LLP 400 W Capitol Ave Ste 2000 *Web:* www.fridayfirm.com	Little Rock	AR	72201	501-376-2011	
Fried Frank Harris Shriver & Jacobson LLP (FFHSJ) 1 New York Plz *Web:* www.friedfrank.com	New York	NY	10004	212-859-8000	859-4000
Friedemann Goldberg LLP 420 Aviation Blvd Ste 201 *Web:* www.frigolaw.com	Santa Rosa	CA	95403	707-543-4900	
Friedman & Feiger LLP 5301 Spring Vly Rd Ste 200 *Web:* www.fflawoffice.com	Dallas	TX	75254	972-788-1400	
Friedman Michael G. Atty. 77 N Bridge St *Web:* www.maurosavolaw.com	Somerville	NJ	08876	908-526-0707	
Frost Brown Todd LLC 201 E Fifth St 2200 PNC Ctr *TF:* 866-559-6446 ■ *Web:* www.frostbrowntodd.com	Cincinnati	OH	45202	513-651-6800	651-6981
Fulbright & Jaworski LLP 1301 McKinney St Ste 5100 *TF:* 866-385-2744 ■ *Web:* www.nortonrosefulbright.com	Houston	TX	77010	713-651-5151	651-5246
Fullerton & Knowles PC 12644 Chapel Rd Ste 206 *Web:* www.fullertonlaw.com	Clifton	VA	20124	703-818-2600	
Fultz Maddox Hovious & Dickens PLC 2700 National City Tower 101 S Fifth St *Web:* www.fmhd.com	Louisville	KY	40202	502-588-2000	
Gagen, McCoy, McMahon, Koss, Markowitz & Raines A Professional Corp 279 Front St *Web:* www.gagenmccoy.com	Danville	CA	94526	925-837-0585	
Gallagher, Gams, Pryor, Tallan & Littrell LLP 471 E Broad St 19th Fl *TF:* 866-378-1624 ■ *Web:* www.ggptl.com	Columbus	OH	43215	614-228-5151	
Gallon Takacs Boissoneault & Schaffer Company LPA Jack Gallon Bldg 3516 Granite Cir *Web:* www.gallonlaw.com	Toledo	OH	43617	419-843-2001	
Galloon e s & Associates 40 W Fourth St Ste 2200 *Web:* esgallon.com	Dayton	OH	45402	937-586-3100	
Galloway, Lucchese, Everson & Picchi A Professional Corp 1676 N California Blvd Ste 500 *Web:* www.glattys.com	Walnut Creek	CA	94596	925-930-9090	
Garan Lucow Miller PC 1000 Woodbridge St *TF:* 800-875-1530 ■ *Web:* www.garanlucow.com	Detroit	MI	48207	313-446-1530	
Garden City Group LLC 105 Maxess Rd *TF:* 888-404-8013 ■ *Web:* www.gardencitygroup.com	Melville	NY	11747	631-470-5000	470-5100
Gardner James Nakken Hugo & Nolan 429 First St *Web:* yololaw.com	Woodland	CA	95695	530-662-7367	
Garfunkel Wild & Travis PC 111 Great Neck Rd Ste 503 *Web:* www.garfunkelwild.com	Great Neck	NY	11021	516-393-2200	
Garganigo, Goldsmith & Weiss 14 Penn Plz Ste 1020 *Web:* www.ggw.com	New York	NY	10122	212-643-6400	
Garland & Mason LLC Manalapan Corporate Plz 195 Rt 9 South *Web:* www.kmrslaw.com	Manalapan	NJ	07726	732-358-2028	358-2029
Garrett & Tully A Professional Corp 225 S Lk Ave Ste 1400 *Web:* www.garrett-tully.com	Pasadena	CA	91101	626-577-9500	
Garvin & Hickey LLC 181 E Livingston Ave *Web:* garvin-hickey.com	Columbus	OH	43215	614-225-9000	
Gary d Mccallister & Associates LLC 120 N La Salle St Ste 2800 *Web:* www.mccallisterlawgroup.com	Chicago	IL	60602	312-345-0611	
Gary K Walch 23801 Calabasas Rd Ste 1019 *Web:* www.walchlaw.com	Calabasas	CA	91302	818-222-3400	
Gates, O'Doherty, Gonter & Guy LLP 15373 Innovation Dr Ste 170 *Web:* gogglaw.com	San Diego	CA	92128	949-769-2481	
Gauntlett & Associates Attorneys at Law 18400 Von Karman Ave Ste 300 *Web:* www.gauntlettlaw.com	Irvine	CA	92612	949-553-1010	
Gawthrop Greenwood PC 17 E Gay St Ste 100 *Web:* www.gawthrop.com	West Chester	PA	19381	610-696-8225	
GCA Law Partners LLP 1891 Landings Dr *Web:* www.gcalaw.com	Mountain View	CA	94043	650-428-3900	
General Code Publishers Corp 72 Hinchey Rd *Web:* www.generalcode.com	Rochester	NY	14624	585-328-1810	
Gentry Locke Rakes & Moore LLP 10 Franklin Rd S E Ste 900 *Web:* www.gentrylocke.com	Roanoke	VA	24011	540-983-9300	
George Warshaw & Associates PC 77 Newbury St Fl 4 *Web:* www.warshawdicarlo.com	Boston	MA	02116	617-262-7800	
Geragos & Geragos PC 644 S Figueroa St *Web:* www.geragos.com	Los Angeles	CA	90017	213-625-3900	625-1600
Gerard Singer Levick & Busch Pc 16200 Addison Rd Ste 140 *Web:* www.singerlevick.com	Addison	TX	75001	972-380-5533	
Germer Gertz LLP 550 Fannin Ste 400 *Web:* www.germer.com	Beaumont	TX	77701	409-654-6700	
Gerrish McCreary Smith PC 700 Colonial Rd Ste 200 *Web:* www.gerrish.com	Memphis	TN	38117	901-767-0900	
Geygan & Geygan Ltd 8050 Hosbrook Rd Ste 107 *Web:* geygan.net	Cincinnati	OH	45236	513-793-6555	
Gibbons PC 1 Gateway Ctr *Web:* www.gibbonslaw.com	Newark	NJ	07102	973-596-4500	596-0545
Gibson Dunn & Crutcher LLP 333 S Grand Ave Ste 4600 *TF:* 888-203-1112 ■ *Web:* www.gibsondunn.com	Los Angeles	CA	90071	213-229-7000	229-7520
Gilbert Kelly Crowley & Jennett LLP 550 S Hope St Ste 2200 *Web:* www.gilbertkelly.com	Los Angeles	CA	90071	213-615-7000	
Gilberti Stinziano Heintz & Smith PC 555 E Genesee St *Web:* www.gilbertilaw.com	Syracuse	NY	13202	315-442-0100	
Gilbride, Tusa, Last & Spillane 31 Brookside Dr PO Box 658 *Web:* www.gtlslaw.com	Greenwich	CT	06836	203-622-9360	
Giles & Lambert PC 1 E Main St *Web:* www.gileslambert.com	Martinsville	VA	24112	276-632-7000	

				Phone	Fax
Gill Elrod Ragon Owen & Sherman pa 425 W Capitol Ave Ste 3800 *Web:* gill-law.com	Little Rock	AR	72201	501-376-3800	
Ginsburg & Misk Attys 21548 Jamaica Ave *Web:* www.gmlawyers.net	Queens Village	NY	11428	718-468-0500	
Giordano, Halleran & Ciesla PC 125 Half Mile Rd *Web:* www.ghclaw.com	Middletown	NJ	07748	732-741-3900	
Gipson Hoffman & Pancione 1901 Ave of The Stars 11th Fl *Web:* www.ghplaw.com	Los Angeles	CA	90067	310-556-4660	356-8945
Gislason & Hunter LLP 2700 S Broadway *TF:* 800-469-0234 ■ *Web:* www.gislason.com	New Ulm	MN	56073	507-354-3111	
Glancy Prongay & Murray LLP 1801 Ave Of The Stars *TF:* 888-773-9224 ■ *Web:* www.glancylaw.com	Los Angeles	CA	90067	310-201-9150	
Glaser Weil Fink Jacobs Howard Avchen & Shapiro LLP 10250 Constellation Blvd 19th Fl *Web:* glaserweil.com	Los Angeles	CA	90067	310-553-3000	556-2920
Gleason Law Offices PC 163 Merrimack St *Web:* www.gleasonlawoffices.com	Haverhill	MA	01830	978-521-4044	
Glinsmann & Glinsmann, Chartered 12 Russell Ave *Web:* mygreencardlawyer.com	Gaithersburg	MD	20877	301-987-0030	
Global Learning Resources Inc 46330 Sentinel Dr *Web:* www.glresources.com	Fremont	CA	94539	510-659-0179	
Glynn & Finley LLP 100 Pringle Ave Ste 500 *Web:* www.glynnfinley.com	Walnut Creek	CA	94596	925-210-2800	
Godfrey & Kahn SC 833 E Michigan St Ste 1800 *Web:* www.gklaw.com	Milwaukee	WI	53202	414-273-3500	
Goehring, Rutter & Boehm 437 Grant St Ste 1424 *Web:* www.grblaw.com	Pittsburgh	PA	15219	412-281-0587	
Goldberg & Connolly G&C Bldg 66 N Village Ave *Web:* www.goldbergconnolly.com	Rockville Centre	NY	11570	516-764-2800	
Goldberg Weisman Cairo 1 E Wacker Dr Ste 3800 *TF:* 800-464-4772 ■ *Web:* www.gwclaw.com	Chicago	IL	60601	312-464-1234	
Goldberg, Persky & White PC 1030 Fifth Ave *Web:* www.gpwlaw.com	Pittsburgh	PA	15219	412-471-3980	
Goldfarb & Lipman LLP 1300 Clay St 11th Fl *Web:* www.goldfarblipman.com	Oakland	CA	94612	510-836-6336	
Goldman Antonetti & Cordova 250 Munoz Rivera Ave Ste 1400 *Web:* www.gaclaw.com	San Juan	PR	00918	787-759-8000	
Goldwater Dube 3500 Boul De Maisonneuve O *Web:* www.goldwaterdube.com	Montreal	QC	H3Z3C1	514-861-4367	
Gonzales Hoblit Ferguson LLP 802 N Carancahua St Ste 2000 *Web:* www.ghf-lawfirm.com	Corpus Christi	TX	78470	361-888-9392	
Goode Casseb Jones Riklin Choate & Watson A Professional Corp 2122 N Main Ave *Web:* www.goodelaw.com	San Antonio	TX	78212	210-733-6030	
Goodell Devries Leech & Dann LLP 1 S St 20th Fl *TF:* 888-229-4354 ■ *Web:* www.gdldlaw.com	Baltimore	MD	21202	410-783-4000	783-4040
Goodman Allen & Filetti PLLC 4501 Highwoods Pkwy Ste 210 *Web:* www.goodmanallen.com	Glen Allen	VA	23060	804-346-0600	
Goodsill Anderson Quinn & Stifel 1099 Alakea St Ste 1800 *Web:* www.goodsill.com	Honolulu	HI	96813	808-547-5600	
Goodwin Procter LLP 53 State St *Web:* www.goodwinprocter.com	Boston	MA	02109	617-570-1000	523-1231
Gordon Feinblatt Rothman Hoffberger & Hollander LLC 233 E Redwood St *Web:* www.gfrlaw.com	Baltimore	MD	21202	410-576-4156	576-4246
Gordon Thomas Honeywell LLP 1201 Pacific Ave Ste 2100 *Web:* www.gth-law.com	Tacoma	WA	98402	253-620-6500	620-6565
Gordon, Fournaris & Mammarella PA 1925 Lovering Ave *Web:* gfmlaw.com	Wilmington	DE	19806	302-652-2900	
Goulston & Storrs 400 Atlantic Ave *Web:* www.goulstonstorrs.com	Boston	MA	02110	617-482-1776	
Goyette & Associates Inc 2366 Gold Meadow Way Ste 200 *Web:* goyetteassociates.com	Gold River	CA	95670	916-851-1900	
Graham Curtin & Sheridan PA 4 Headquarters Plz PO Box 1991 *Web:* www.grahamcurtin.com	Morristown	NJ	07962	973-292-1700	
Graham Lundberg & Peschel 2153 Bethel Rd Se *Web:* www.glpattorneys.com	Port Orchard	WA	98366	360-876-5005	
Grant, Herrmann, Schwartz & Klinger 675 Third Ave *Web:* www.ghsklaw.com	New York	NY	10017	212-682-1800	
Grant, Konvalinka & Harrison PC Republic Ctr 633 Chestnut St Ninth Fl Ste 900 *Web:* www.gkhpc.com	Chattanooga	TN	37450	423-756-8400	
Gravel & Shea 76 St Paul St PO Box 369 *Web:* www.gravelshea.com	Burlington	VT	05402	802-658-0220	
Gravely & Pearson LLP 425 Soledad St Ste 600 *Web:* www.gplawfirm.com	San Antonio	TX	78205	210-472-1111	
Gray Plant Mooty Inc 500 IDS Ctr 80 S Eighth St *Web:* www.gpmlaw.com	Minneapolis	MN	55402	612-632-3000	
Gray, Layton, Kersh, Solomon, Sigmon, Furr & Smith PA 516 S New Hope Rd *Web:* www.gastonlegal.com	Gastonia	NC	28054	704-865-4400	
Greenan, Peffer, Sallander & Lally LLP 6111 Bollinger Canyon Rd Ste 500 *Web:* www.gpsllp.com	San Ramon	CA	94583	925-866-1000	
Greenbaum, Rowe, Smith, Ravin, Davis & Himmel LLP Metro Corporate Campus 99 Wood Ave South *Web:* www.greenbaumlaw.com	Woodbridge	NJ	07095	732-549-5600	
Greenberg Glusker Fields Claman & Machtinger LLP 1900 Ave of the Stars 21st Fl *Web:* www.greenbergglusker.com	Los Angeles	CA	90067	310-553-3610	553-0687
Greer Herz & Adams LLP 2525 S Shore Blvd Ste 203 *Web:* www.greerherz.com	League City	TX	77573	281-480-5278	
Grey Law of Ventura County Inc 3585 Maple St Ste 126 *Web:* www.greylaw.us	Ventura	CA	93003	805-658-2266	
Griffel, Dorshow & Johnson, Chartered 1809 Plymouth Rd Ste 222 *Web:* www.612law3333.com	Hopkins	MN	55305	612-529-3333	
Grossman, Tucker, Perreault & Pfleger PLLC 55 S Commercial St *Web:* gtpp.com	Manchester	NH	03101	603-668-6560	
Group Wellesley 933 Wellesley Rd *Web:* www.groupwellesley.com	Pittsburgh	PA	15206	412-363-3481	
Grower, Ketcham, Rutherford, Bronson, Eide & Telan PA 901 N Lk Destiny Rd Ste 450 *Web:* www.growerketcham.com	Maitland	FL	32751	407-423-9545	
Guida, Slavich & Flores PC 750 N Saint Paul St Ste 200 *Web:* www.guidaslavichflores.com	Dallas	TX	75201	214-692-0009	692-6610
Gullett, Sanford, Robinson & Martin PLLC 150 Third Ave S Ste 1700 *Web:* www.gsrm.net	Nashville	TN	37201	615-244-4994	
Gunster Yoakley & Stewart Pa 777 S Flagler Dr Ste 500 E *TF:* 800-749-1980 ■ *Web:* www.gunster.com	West Palm Beach	FL	33401	561-655-1980	655-5677
Gurstel Chargo LLP 6681 Country Club Dr *TF:* 877-750-6335 ■ *Web:* www.gurstel.com	Golden Valley	MN	55427	763-267-6700	
Gutman, Mintz, Baker & Sonnenfeldt 813 Jericho Tpke *Web:* www.gmbspc.com	New Hyde Park	NY	11040	516-775-7007	
Hagen Wilka & Archer LLP 600 S Main Ave Ste 102 *Web:* hwalaw.com	Sioux Falls	SD	57104	605-334-0005	
Hagens Berman Sobol Shapiro LLP 1918 Eighth Ave Ste 3300 *Web:* www.hbsslaw.com	Seattle	WA	98101	206-623-7292	
Haight Brown & Bonesteel LLP 555 S Flower St *Web:* www.hbblaw.com	Los Angeles	CA	90071	213-542-8000	542-8100
Hailey, McNamara, Hall, Larmann & Papale LLP 1 Galleria Blvd Ste 1400 *Web:* www.hmhlp.com	Metairie	LA	70001	504-836-6500	
Hale Lane Peek Dennison & Howard 5441 Kietzke Ln 2nd Fl *Web:* www.halelane.com	Reno	NV	89511	775-327-3000	
Hall & Evans 1125 17th St Ste 600 *Web:* www.hallevans.com	Denver	CO	80202	303-628-3300	
Hall Render Killian Heath & Lyman Pc 1 American Sq Ste 2000 Ste 2000 *Web:* www.hallrender.com	Indianapolis	IN	46282	317-633-4884	633-4878
Hall, Estill, Hardwick, Gable, Golden & Nelson PC 320 S Boston Ave Ste 200 *Web:* www.hallestill.com	Tulsa	OK	74103	918-594-0400	
Hangley Aronchick Segal & Pudlin PC 1 Logan Sq 18th and Cherry Sts *Web:* www.hangley.com	Philadelphia	PA	19103	215-568-6200	
Hansen, Jacobson, Teller, Hoberman, Newman, Warren, Richman, Rush & Kaller LLP 450 N Roxbury Dr 8th Fl *Web:* www.hjth.com	Beverly Hills	CA	90210	310-271-8777	
Hanson Lulic & Krall LLC 700 Northstar E 608 Second Ave S *Web:* hlk.com	Minneapolis	MN	55402	612-333-2530	
Harbour, Smith, Harris & Merritt 404 N Green St *Web:* www.harbourlaw.com	Longview	TX	75601	903-757-4001	
Hardin, Kundla, McKeon & Poletto PA - A Professional Corp 673 Morris Ave *Web:* www.hkmpp.com	Springfield	NJ	07081	973-912-5222	
Hargreaves & Taylor 750 B St Ste 2300 *Web:* www.htfamlaw.com	San Diego	CA	92101	619-238-5501	
Harman, Claytor, Corrigan & Wellman A Professional Corp PO Box 70280 *TF:* 877-747-4229 ■ *Web:* www.hccw.com	Richmond	VA	23255	804-747-5200	
Harmon Curran Spielberg & Eisenberg 1726 M St Nw Ste 600 *Web:* www.harmoncurran.com	Washington	DC	20036	202-328-3500	
Harper Grey LLP 3200 Vancouver Centre 650 W Georgia St *Web:* www.harpergrey.com	Vancouver	BC	V6B4P7	604-687-0411	
Harrang Long Gary Rudnick PC 360 E 10th Ave Ste 300 *TF:* 800-315-4172 ■ *Web:* www.harrang.com	Eugene	OR	97401	541-485-0220	
Harris Law Firm 1125 17th St Ste 450 *Web:* www.harrisfamilylaw.com	Denver	CO	80202	303-622-5502	
Harris Wyatt & Amala Attorneys at Law 5778 Commercial St Se *TF:* 800-853-2144 ■ *Web:* www.salemattorneys.com	Salem	OR	97306	503-378-7744	
Harrison & Held LLP 333 W Wacker Dr Ste 1700 *Web:* www.harrisonheld.com	Chicago	IL	60606	312-753-6185	

Firm	City	State	ZIP	Phone	Fax
Harrison, Eichenberg & Murphy LLP 155 E Wilbur Rd Ste 200 *Web:* www.hem-law.com	Thousand Oaks	CA	91360	805-495-7379	
Harter Secrest & Emery LLP (HSE) 1600 Bausch & Lomb Pl. *Web:* www.hselaw.com	Rochester	NY	14604	585-232-6500	232-2152
Hartley, Rowe & Fowler PC 6622 Broad St *Web:* www.hrflegal.com	Douglasville	GA	30134	770-920-2000	
Hartline Dacus Barger Dreyer LLP 6688 N Central Expy Ste 1000 *Web:* www.hdbdlaw.com	Dallas	TX	75206	214-369-2100	
Hartman, Simons, Spielman & Wood LLP 6400 Powers Ferry Rd NW Ste 400 *Web:* www.hartmansimons.com	Atlanta	GA	30339	770-955-3555	
Hartnett Law Firm, The 2920 N Pearl St *TF:* 800-900-9702 ■ *Web:* www.hartnettlawfirm.com	Dallas	TX	75201	214-742-4655	
Harwood Lloyd LLC 130 Main St *Web:* www.harwoodlloyd.com	Hackensack	NJ	07601	201-487-1080	
Haverstock & Owens LLP 162 N Wolfe Rd *Web:* hollp.com	Sunnyvale	CA	94086	408-530-9700	
Hawkins Parnell Thackston & Young LLP 4000 SunTrust Plz 303 Peachtree St NE *Web:* www.hptylaw.com	Atlanta	GA	30308	404-614-7400	
Hawley Troxell Ennis & Hawley LLP 877 Main St Ste 1000 *Web:* www.hawleytroxell.com	Boise	ID	83702	208-344-6000	
Haworth, Bradshaw, Stallknecht & Barber Inc 4380 Auburn Blvd *Web:* www.haworthlaw.com	Sacramento	CA	95841	916-484-4354	
Haynes & Boone LLP 2323 Victory Ave #700 *Web:* www.haynesboone.com	Dallas	TX	75219	214-651-5000	651-5940
Haynsworth Sinkler Boyd PA 134 Meeting St 3rd Fl *Web:* www.hsblawfirm.com	Charleston	SC	29402	843-722-3366	
Heard & Smith LLP 3737 Broadway Ste 310 *Web:* www.heardandsmith.com	San Antonio	TX	78209	210-820-3737	
Heavner, Scott, Beyers & Mihlar LLC 111 E Main St Ste 200 *Web:* hsbattys.com	Decatur	IL	62523	217-422-1719	
Heidell, Pittoni, Murphy & Bach LLP 99 Park Ave *Web:* www.hpmb.com	New York	NY	10016	212-286-8585	
Henderson, Caverly, Pum & Charney LLP 12750 High Bluff Dr Ste 300 *Web:* www.hcesq.com	San Diego	CA	92130	858-755-3000	
Henson & Efron PA 220 S Sixth St Ste 1800 *Web:* www.hensonefron.com	Minneapolis	MN	55402	612-339-2500	
Herman Herman Katz & Cotlar LLP 820 Okeefe Ave *TF:* 844-943-7626 ■ *Web:* hhklawfirm.com	New Orleans	LA	70113	504-581-4892	
Herold & Sager, Attorneys at Law 550 Second St Ste 200 *Web:* www.heroldsagerlaw.com	Encinitas	CA	92024	760-487-1047	
Herrick Feinstein LLP 2 Park Ave *Web:* www.herrick.com	New York	NY	10016	212-592-1400	
Hershner Hunter LLP 180 E 11th Ave *Web:* www.hershnerhunter.com	Eugene	OR	97401	541-686-8511	
Hertz Schram & Saretsky Pc 1760 S Telegraph Rd Ste 300 *TF:* 866-775-5987 ■ *Web:* www.hertzschram.com	Bloomfield Hills	MI	48302	248-335-5000	
Heslin, Rothenberg, Farley, & Mesiti PC 5 Columbia Cir *Web:* www.hrfmlaw.com	Albany	NY	12203	518-452-5600	
Heyl Royster Voelker & Allen Pc 124 SW Adams St Ste 600 *Web:* www.heylroyster.com	Peoria	IL	61602	309-676-0400	
Hicken, Scott, Howard & Anderson PA 2150 Third Ave Ste 300 *Web:* www.hshalaw.com	Anoka	MN	55303	763-421-4110	
Hiday & Ricke pa 4100 E Southpoint Dr Ste 3 *Web:* www.hidayricke.com	Jacksonville	FL	32216	904-363-2769	
Hill Ward Henderson 101 E Kennedy Blvd Ste 3700 *Web:* www.hwhlaw.com	Tampa	FL	33602	813-221-3900	
Hill, Farrer & Burrill LLP 300 S Grand Ave 37th Fl *Web:* www.hillfarrer.com	Los Angeles	CA	90071	213-620-0460	
Hillis, Clark, Martin & Peterson PS 1221 Second Ave Ste 500 *Web:* www.hcmp.com	Seattle	WA	98101	206-623-1745	
Hillman, Brown & Darrow PA 221 Duke Of Gloucester St *Web:* www.hbdlaw.com	Annapolis	MD	21401	410-263-3131	
Hinckley Allen & Snyder LLP 28 State St *Web:* www.hinckleyallen.com	Boston	MA	02109	617-345-9000	345-9020
Hinkle Elkouri Law Firm LLC 2000 Epic Ctr 301 N Main St *Web:* hinklaw.com	Wichita	KS	67202	316-267-2000	
Hinman, Howard & Kattell LLP 700 Security Mutual 80 Exchange St *Web:* www.hhk.com	Binghamton	NY	13901	607-723-5341	
Hinshaw & Culbertson LLP 222 N LaSalle St Ste 300 *Web:* www.hinshawlaw.com	Chicago	IL	60601	312-704-3000	704-3001
Hoagland, Longo, Moran, Dunst & Doukas 40 Paterson St *Web:* www.hoaglandlongo.com	New Brunswick	NJ	08903	732-545-4717	
Hochman, Salkin, Rettig, Toscher & Perez PC 9150 Wilshire Blvd Ste 300 *Web:* taxlitigator.com	Beverly Hills	CA	90212	310-281-3200	
Hodes Keating & Pilon 134 N La Salle St Ste 1300 *Web:* www.hkp-customs.com	Chicago	IL	60602	312-553-1440	
Hodgson Russ LLP 140 Pearl St The Guaranty Bldg Ste 100 *Web:* www.hodgsonruss.com	Buffalo	NY	14202	716-856-4000	
Hoffman Alvary & Company LLC 7 Wells Ave Ste 33 *Web:* hoffmanalvary.com	Newton Center	MA	02459	617-758-0500	
Hoffmann & Baron LLP 6900 Jericho Tpke *Web:* www.hbiplaw.com	Syosset	NY	11791	516-822-3550	
Hogan Marren Ltd 321 N Clark St Ste 1301 *Web:* www.hmltd.com	Chicago	IL	60654	312-946-1800	
Holihan Law 1101 N Lk Destiny Rd Ste 275 *Web:* www.holihanlaw.com	Maitland	FL	32751	407-660-8575	
Hopkins & Carley A Law Corp PO Box 1469 *TF:* 800-829-3676 ■ *Web:* www.hopkinscarley.com	San Jose	CA	95109	408-286-9800	998-4790
Horowitt, Darryl J. - Coleman & Horowitt LLP 499 W Shaw Ave Ste 116 *TF:* 800-891-8362 ■ *Web:* www.ch-law.com	Fresno	CA	93704	559-248-4820	
Horton, Oberrecht, Kirkpatrick & Martha, Attorneys At Law A Professional Corp NBC Bldg 225 Broadway Ste 2200 *Web:* www.hortonfirm.com	San Diego	CA	92101	619-232-1183	
Horvitz & Levy LLP 15760 Ventura Blvd Ste 1800 *Web:* horvitzlevy.com	Encino	CA	91436	818-995-0800	
Houser & Allison APC 9970 Research Dr *Web:* www.houser-law.com	Irvine	CA	92618	949-679-1111	
Howard & Howard Attorneys Pc 2950 S State St Ste 360 *Web:* howardandhoward.com	Ann Arbor	MI	48104	248-645-1483	645-1568
Howard N. Sobel Law Offices 507 Kresson Rd *Web:* sobellaw.com	Voorhees	NJ	08043	856-424-6400	
Howard, Kohn, Sprague & FitzGerald LLP 237 Buckingham St *Web:* www.hksflaw.com	Hartford	CT	06126	860-525-3101	
Howrey LLP 1299 Pennsylvania Ave NW	Washington	DC	20004	202-383-6596	
Hudson Cook LLP 7037 Ridge Rd Ste 300 *Web:* www.hudsoncook.com	Hanover	MD	21076	410-684-3200	
Hudson, Mallaney, Shindler & Anderson PC 5015 Grand Ridge Dr Ste 100 *Web:* www.hudsonlaw.net	West Des Moines	IA	50265	515-223-4567	
Hughes Hubbard & Reed LLP 1 Battery Pk Plz *Web:* www.hugheshubbard.com	New York	NY	10004	212-837-6000	422-4726
Hunt Leibert Jacobson PC 50 Weston St *Web:* www.huntleibert.com	Hartford	CT	06120	860-808-0606	
Hunter, Smith & Davis LLP 1212 N Eastman Rd *Web:* www.hsdlaw.com	Kingsport	TN	37664	423-378-8800	
Hunton & Williams LLP 951 E Byrd St Riverfront Plaza E Tower *Web:* www.hunton.com	Richmond	VA	23219	804-788-8200	788-8218
Hurley Rogner Miller Cox 1560 Orange Ave # 500 *Web:* www.hrmcw.com	Winter Park	FL	32789	407-571-7400	
Hurley, Toevs, Styles, Hamblin & Panter PA 4155 Montgomery Blvd Ne *Web:* hurleyfirm.com	Albuquerque	NM	87109	505-888-1188	
Husch Blackwell LLP 4801 Main St Ste 1000 *Web:* www.husch.com	Kansas City	MO	64108	816-983-8000	
Hyland Levin LLP 6000 Sagemore Dr Ste 6301 *Web:* www.hylandlevin.com	Marlton	NJ	08053	856-355-2900	
Hyman Phelps & Mcnamara Pc 700 13th St NW Ste 1200 *Web:* www.hpm.com	Washington	DC	20005	202-737-5600	737-9329
Illinois Legal Aid Online 17 N State St Ste 1590 *Web:* illinoislegalaid.org	Chicago	IL	60602	312-977-9047	
Inner City Law Center 1309 E Seventh St *Web:* www.innercitylaw.org	Los Angeles	CA	90021	213-891-2880	
Innocence Project of Florida Inc 1100 E Park Ave *Web:* www.floridainnocence.org	Tallahassee	FL	32301	850-561-6767	
Iowa Legal Aid 1111 Ninth St Ste 230 *TF:* 800-992-8161 ■ *Web:* www.iowalegalaid.org	Des Moines	IA	50314	515-243-2151	
Iphorgan Ltd 195 Arlington Heights Rd Ste 125 *Web:* iphorgan.com	Buffalo Grove	IL	60089	847-808-5500	
Ipwatch Corp 401 E Tuscaloosa St *Web:* www.ipwatch.com	Florence	AL	35630	256-718-0078	
Irell & Manella LLP 1800 Ave of the Stars Ste 900 *Web:* irell.com	Los Angeles	CA	90067	310-277-1010	203-7199
Iseman Cunningham Riester & Hyde LLP 9 Thurlow Ter *Web:* www.icrh.com	Albany	NY	12203	518-462-3000	
Ivey, Barnum & O'mara LLC 170 Mason St *Web:* www.ibolaw.com	Greenwich	CT	06830	203-661-6000	
Jacko Law Group PC 5920 Friars Rd Ste 208 *TF:* 866-497-2298 ■ *Web:* www.jackolg.com	San Diego	CA	92108	619-298-2880	
Jackson & Hertogs 170 Columbus Ave Fl 4 *Web:* jackson-hertogs.com	San Francisco	CA	94133	415-986-4559	
Jackson DeMarco Tidus & Peckenpaugh Law Corp 2030 Main St 12th Fl *Web:* www.jdtplaw.com	Irvine	CA	92614	949-752-8585	
Jackson Kelly PLLC PO Box 553 *Web:* www.jacksonkelly.com	Charleston	WV	25322	304-340-1172	
Jacob Medinger & Finnegan LLP (JMF) 1270 Ave of the Americas *Web:* jmfnylaw.com	New York	NY	10020	212-524-5000	
Jacobson Holman PLLC 400 Seventh St NW *Web:* www.jhip.com	Washington	DC	20004	202-638-6666	
Jacobson, Hansen, Najarian & Mcquillan 1690 W Shaw Ave Ste 201 *Web:* jhnmlaw.com	Fresno	CA	93711	559-448-0400	

Phone Fax

Jaffe Raitt Heuer & Weiss PC
27777 Franklin Rd Ste 2500 Southfield MI 48034 248-351-3000
Web: www.jaffelaw.com

James Hoyer Newcomer & Smiljanich pa
3301 Thomasville Rd Tallahassee FL 32308 850-325-2680
Web: www.jameshoyer.com

James, McElroy & Diehl PA 600 S College St Charlotte NC 28202 704-372-9870
Web: www.jmdlaw.com

Jameson & Dunagan PC
3890 W Northwest Hwy Ste 550 Dallas TX 75220 214-369-6422
Web: jamesondunagan.com

Jan Dils Attorneys at Law Lc 107 Lb And T Way Logan WV 25601 304-831-0000
Web: www.jandils.com

Jardine, Logan & O'Brien PLLP
8519 Eagle Point Blvd Ste 100 Lake Elmo MN 55042 651-290-6500
Web: www.jlolaw.com

Jaspan Schlesinger Hoffman LLP
300 Garden City Plz Garden City NY 11530 516-746-8000
Web: www.jaspanllp.com

Javitch Block & Rathbone LLP
700 Walnut St Ste 300 Cincinnati OH 45202 513-744-9600

Jeansonne & Remondet LLC
365 Canal St Ste 1600 New Orleans LA 70130 337-237-4370
TF: 800-446-2745 ■ *Web:* www.jeanrem.com

Jeffers, Danielson, Sonn & Aylward PS
2600 Chester Kimm Rd Wenatchee WA 98801 509-662-3685
Web: www.jdsalaw.com

Jenkins Fenstermaker PLLC 325 Eighth St Huntington WV 25701 304-523-2100
TF: 866-617-4736 ■ *Web:* www.jenkinsfenstermaker.com

Jenkins, Wilson, Taylor & Hunt PA
3100 Tower Blvd Ste 1200 Durham NC 27707 919-493-8000
Web: www.jwth.com

Jenner & Block LLP 353 N Clark St Chicago IL 60654 312-222-9350 527-0484
Web: www.jenner.com

Jensen Baird Gardner & Henry 10 Free St Portland ME 04112 207-775-7271
Web: www.jensenbaird.com

John C. Heath, Attorney at Law PLLC
360 N Cutler Dr Salt Lake City UT 84054 800-756-9681
TF: 800-756-9681 ■ *Web:* www.lexingtonlaw.com

Johnson & Bell Ltd 33 W Monroe St Ste 2700 Chicago IL 60603 312-372-0770 372-9818
Web: johnsonandbell.com

Johnston, Allison & Hord PA
1065 E Morehead St Charlotte NC 28204 704-332-1181
Web: www.jahlaw.com

Jones Day 51 Louisiana Ave NW Washington DC 20001 202-879-3939 626-1700
Web: www.jonesday.com

Jones, Allen & Fuquay LLP 8828 Greenville Ave Dallas TX 75243 214-343-7400
Web: www.jonesallen.com

Jordan Price Wall Gray Jones & Carlton PLLC
1951 Clark Ave Raleigh NC 27605 919-828-2501
Web: www.jordanprice.com

Joseph, Greenwald & Laake PA
6404 Ivy Ln Ste 400 Rockville MD 20770 301-220-2200
TF: 877-412-7429 ■ *Web:* www.jgllaw.com

Judicare Wisconsin Inc Attys
401 Fifth St Ste 200 Wausau WI 54403 715-842-1681
Web: www.judicare.org

Kagan Binder PLLC 221 Main St N Ste 200 Stillwater MN 55082 651-351-2900
Web: www.kaganbinder.com

Kahn Soares & Conway LLP 1415 L St Ste 400 Sacramento CA 95814 916-448-3826
Web: www.ksclawyers.com

Karbal, Cohen, Economou, Silk & Dunne LLC
150 S Wacker Dr Ste 1700 Chicago IL 60606 312-431-3700
Web: www.karballaw.com

Karl Truman Law Office LLC
420 Wall St Jeffersonville IN 47130 812-282-8500
Web: www.trumanlaw.com

Katz & Korin PC
The Emelie Bldg 334 N Senate Ave Indianapolis IN 46204 317-464-1100
Web: www.katzkorin.com

Katz Goldstein & Warren Pc
2345 Waukegan Rd Ste 150 Bannockburn IL 60015 847-317-9500
Web: kgwlaw.com

Katz Law Office Ltd 2408 W Cermak Rd Chicago IL 60608 773-847-8982
TF: 866-352-3033 ■ *Web:* katzlawchicago.com

Kaufman Borgeest & Ryan LLP
23975 Park Sorrento Ste 370 Calabasas CA 91302 818-880-0993
Web: kbrlaw.com

Kay Casto & Chaney PLLC
1500 Chase Tower 707 Virginia St E Charleston WV 25301 304-345-8900
Web: www.kaycasto.com

Kaye Scholer LLP 425 Pk Ave New York NY 10022 212-836-8000 836-8689
Web: www.kayescholer.com

Keating Muething & Klekamp Pll
1 E Fourth St Ste 1400 Cincinnati OH 45202 513-579-6400 579-6457
Web: www.kmklaw.com

Keeney, Waite & Stevens
402 W Broadway Ste 1820 San Diego CA 92101 619-238-1661
Web: www.keenlaw.com

Keesal Young & Logan
400 Oceangate PO Box 1730 Long Beach CA 90801 562-436-2000 436-7416
Web: www.kyl.com

Kegler, Brown, Hill & Ritter Company LPA
65 E State St Capitol Sq Ste 1800 Columbus OH 43215 614-462-5400
Web: www.keglerbrown.com

Keker & Van Nest LLP 633 Battery St San Francisco CA 94111 415-391-5400
Web: www.kvn.com

Kell, Alterman & Runstein LLP
520 SW Yamhill St Ste 600 Portland OR 97204 503-222-3531
Web: www.kelrun.com

Keller & Heckman LLP 1001 G St NW Ste 500w Washington DC 20001 202-434-4100 434-4646
Web: www.khlaw.com

Kelley & Ferraro LLP
2200 Key Tower 127 Pub Sq Cleveland OH 44114 216-202-3450
TF: 800-398-1795 ■ *Web:* www.kelley-ferraro.com

Phone Fax

Kelley Drye & Warren LLP 101 Pk Ave New York NY 10178 212-808-7800 808-7897
Web: www.kelleydrye.com

Kellogg, Huber, Hansen, Todd, Evans & Figel PLLC
Sumner Sq 1615 M St NW Ste 400 Washington DC 20036 202-326-7900
Web: www.khhte.com

Kelly Mike Law Group LLC
500 Taylor St Ste 400 Columbia SC 29201 803-726-0123
TF: 866-692-0123 ■ *Web:* www.mklawgroup.com

Kemp & Smith LLP 221 N Kansas Ste 1700 El Paso TX 79901 915-533-4424 546-5360
Web: www.kempsmith.com

Ken Nunn Law Office 104 S Franklin Rd Bloomington IN 47404 812-332-9451
Web: kennunn.com

Killian Jensen & Davis Pc Martin Cheryl
202 N Seventh St Grand Junction CO 81501 970-241-0707
Web: www.killianlaw.com

Kilmer, Voorhees & Laurick PC
732 NW 19th Ave Portland OR 97209 503-224-0055
Web: www.kilmerlaw.com

Kilpatrick Townsend & Stockton LLP
1100 Peachtree St Atlanta GA 30309 404-815-6500 815-6555
Web: www.kilpatricktownsend.com

Kimball, Tirey & St. John LLP
7676 Hazard Ctr Dr Ste 900 San Diego CA 92108 619-234-1690
Web: www.kts-law.com

King & Partners Plc 170 College Ave Ste 230 Holland MI 49423 616-355-0400
Web: www.king-partners.com

King & Schickli PLLC 247 N Broadway Lexington KY 40507 859-252-0889
TF: 888-364-5712 ■ *Web:* www.iplaw1.net

King & Spalding 1180 Peachtree St NE Atlanta GA 30309 404-572-4600 572-5100
Web: www.kslaw.com

King, Krebs & Jurgens PLLC
Capital One Bldg 201 St Charles Ave
45th Fl New Orleans LA 70170 504-582-3800
Web: www.kingkrebs.com

Kinney & Lange PA 312 S Third St Minneapolis MN 55415 612-339-1863
Web: www.kinney.com

Kirby Noonan Lance & Hoge LLP
350 Tenth Ave Ste 1300 San Diego CA 92101 619-231-8666
Web: www.knlh.com

Kirk Rankin Law Office
11501 Georgia Ave Ste 210 Silver Spring MD 20902 301-933-4648
Web: kirkrankin.com

Kirkland & Ellis LLP 200 E Randolph Dr Chicago IL 60601 312-861-2000 861-2200
TF: 800-647-7600 ■ *Web:* www.kirkland.com

Kirkpatrick & Lockhart Preston Gates Ellis LLP
210 Sixth Ave Pittsburgh PA 15222 412-355-6500 355-6501
TF: 800-452-8260 ■ *Web:* www.klgates.com

Kissinger & Fellman PC 3773 Cherry Creek N Dr Denver CO 80209 303-320-6100
Web: www.kandf.com

Kitch Drutchas Wagner Valitutti & Sherbrook Pc
1 Woodward Ave Ste 2400 Detroit MI 48226 313-965-7900
Web: www.kitch.com

Kivell, Rayment & Francis PC
7666 E 61st St Ste 550 Tulsa OK 74133 918-254-0626
Web: www.kivell.com

Kleinfeld, Kaplan & Becker LLP
1140 19th St NW Ste 900 Washington DC 20036 202-223-5120
Web: www.kkblaw.com

Klenda Austerman LLC
1600 Epic Ctr 301 N Main St Wichita KS 67202 316-267-0331
Web: klendalaw.com

Kline & Specter A Professional Corp
1525 Locust St 19th Fl Philadelphia PA 19102 215-772-1000
TF: 800-243-1100 ■ *Web:* www.klinespecter.com

Klinedinst Law 801 K St Fl 28 Sacramento CA 95814 916-444-7573
Web: www.klinedinstlaw.com

Knox McLaughlin Gornall & Sennett PC
120 W Tenth St Erie PA 16501 814-459-2800
Web: kmgslaw.com

Kobayashi, Sugita & Goda LLP, Attorneys at Law
999 Bishop St Ste 2600 Honolulu HI 96813 808-535-5700
Web: www.ksglaw.com

Koenig Jacobsen LLP 16300 Bake Pkwy Irvine CA 92618 949-756-0700
Web: kjattorneys.com

Kohner Mann & Kailas SC
Washington Bldg 4650 N Port Washington Rd Milwaukee WI 53212 414-962-5110
Web: www.kmksc.com

Kominiarek Bressler Harvick & Gudmundson LLC
33 N Dearborn St Ste 1310 Chicago IL 60602 312-322-1111 782-1432
Web: www.kbhglaw.com

Kope & Associates LLC
3900 Market St Ste 201 Camp Hill PA 17011 717-761-7573
Web: www.kopelaw.com

Korshak Kracoff Kong & Sugano LLP
1640 S Sepulveda Blvd Ste 520 Los Angeles CA 90025 310-996-2340
Web: kkks.com

Koskoff, Koskoff & Bieder PC
350 Fairfield Ave Bridgeport CT 06604 203-583-8634
Web: www.koskoff.com

Kotin, Crabtree & Strong LLP 1 Bowdoin Sq Boston MA 02114 617-227-7031
Web: www.kcslegal.com

Kramer, Dillof, Livingston & Moore
217 Broadway Fl 10 New York NY 10007 212-267-4177
Web: kdlm.com

Kream & Kream 536 Broad St Ste 5 East Weymouth MA 02189 781-331-9333
Web: www.kreamandkream.com

Kreis Enderle 8225 Moorsbridge Rd Kalamazoo MI 49003 269-324-3000
Web: www.kreisenderle.com

Kremblas Foster Phillips & Pollick
7632 Slate Ridge Blvd Reynoldsburg OH 43068 614-575-2100
Web: ohiopatent.com

Krieg DeVault Alexander & Capehart
1 Indiana Sq Ste 2800 Indianapolis IN 46204 317-636-4341 636-1507
Web: www.kriegdevault.com

	City	State	ZIP	Phone	Fax
Kring & Chung LLP 38 Corporate Park *Web:* www.kringandchung.com	Irvine	CA	92606	949-261-7700	
Kronick Moskovitz Tiedemann & Girard (KMTG) 400 Capitol Mall Fl 27 *Web:* www.kmtg.com	Sacramento	CA	95814	916-321-4500	321-4555
Krugliak, Wilkins, Griffiths & Dougherty Co 4775 Munson St NW *Web:* www.kwgd.com	Canton	OH	44735	330-497-0700	
Kutak Rock LLP 1650 Farnam St *Web:* www.kutakrock.com	Omaha	NE	68102	402-346-6000	346-1148
Kuzmich Law Firm Pc 335 W Main St *Web:* www.kuzmichlaw.com	Lewisville	TX	75057	972-434-1555	
L. Patrick Mulligan & Associates LPA Co 28 N Wilkinson St *Web:* www.patrickmulligan.com	Dayton	OH	45402	937-228-9790	
Lackey Hershman LLP 3102 Oak Lawn Ave Ste 777 *Web:* www.lhlaw.net	Dallas	TX	75219	214-560-2201	
Lacy Katzen LLP 130 E Main St 2nd Fl *Web:* www.lacykatzen.com	Rochester	NY	14604	585-454-5650	
Ladas & Parry LLP 1040 Ave of the Americas *Web:* www.ladas.com	New York	NY	10018	212-708-1800	246-8959
Lakin Spears LLP Embarcadero Pl 2400 Geng Rd Ste 110 *Web:* www.lakinspears.com	Palo Alto	CA	94303	650-328-7000	
Lamb & Barnosky LLP 534 Broadhollow Rd Ste 210 PO Box 9034 *Web:* www.lambbarnosky.com	Melville	NY	11747	631-694-2300	
Lamb McErlane PC 24 E Market St PO Box 565 *Web:* www.lambmcerlane.com	West Chester	PA	19381	610-430-8000	
Lamson, Dugan & Murray LLP 10306 Regency Pkwy Dr *Web:* www.ldmlaw.com	Omaha	NE	68114	402-397-7300	
Landrum & Shouse LLP 220 W Main St Ste 800 *Web:* www.landrumshouse.com	Lexington	KY	40507	502-589-7616	
Lane & Waterman LLP 220 N Main St Ste 600 *Web:* www.l-wlaw.com	Davenport	IA	52801	563-324-3246	324-1616
Lanier Ford Shaver & Payne PC 2101 W Clinton Ave Ste 102 *Web:* www.lanierford.com	Huntsville	AL	35805	256-535-1100	
Lanier Law Group PA 600 S Duke St *Web:* lanierlawgroup.com	Durham	NC	27701	919-682-2111	
LaRiviere, Grubman PC 19 Upper Ragsdale Dr Ste 200 *Web:* www.lgpatlaw.com	Monterey	CA	93942	831-649-8800	
Larson Berg & Perkins Pllc 105 N Third St *Web:* www.lbplaw.com	Yakima	WA	98901	509-457-1515	
Larson King LLP 30 E Seventh St Ste 2800 *TF:* 877-373-5501 ■ *Web:* www.larsonking.com	Saint Paul	MN	55101	651-312-6500	312-6618
Lashly & Baer PC 714 Locust St *Web:* www.lashlybaer.com	St. Louis	MO	63101	314-621-2939	
Lassiter-Taylor Law Firm, The 6215 Claret Dr *Web:* www.lassiterlawyers.com	Jacksonville	FL	32210	904-779-5585	
Latham & Watkins LLP 885 Third Ave *Web:* www.lw.com	New York	NY	10022	212-906-1200	751-4864
Latimer, Biaggi, Rachid, & Godreau LLP Firstbank Bldg 1519 Ponce de Leon Ave Ste 1205 *Web:* www.lbrglaw.com	San Juan	PR	00902	787-724-0230	
Lavin O'Neil Ricci Cedrone & Disipio 190 N Independence Mall W *Web:* www.lavin-law.com	Philadelphia	PA	19106	215-627-0303	627-2551
Law Society of Manitoba 219 Kennedy St *Web:* www.lawsociety.mb.ca	Winnipeg	MB	R3C1S8	204-942-5571	
Law Weathers & Richardson Pc 333 Bridge St NW *Web:* www.varnumlaw.com/law-weathers	Grand Rapids	MI	49504	616-336-6000	732-1740
Lawson & Weitzen LLP 88 Black Falcon Ave *Web:* www.lawson-weitzen.com	Boston	MA	02210	617-439-4990	
Lawson Lundell LLP 925 W Georgia St Cathedral Pl Ste 1600 *Web:* www.lawsonlundell.com	Vancouver	BC	V6C3L2	604-685-3456	
Lawton & Cates SC 10 E Doty St Ste 400 *TF:* 800-900-4539 ■ *Web:* www.lawtoncates.com	Madison	WI	53703	608-282-6200	
Lawyer Referral Service 123 Remsen St *Web:* www.brooklynbar.org	Brooklyn	NY	11201	718-624-0843	
Leason Ellis LLP 1 Barker Ave 5th Fl *Web:* www.leasonellis.com	White Plains	NY	10601	914-821-9070	
Lee & Hayes PLLC 601 W Riverside Ave Ste 1400 *Web:* www.leehayes.com	Spokane	WA	99201	509-324-9256	
Leete Kosto & Wizner LLC 999 Asylum Ave Ste 202 *Web:* lkwvisa.com	Hartford	CT	06105	860-249-8100	
Legal Aid 126 W Adams St Fl 7 *TF:* 866-356-8371 ■ *Web:* www.jaxlegalaid.org	Jacksonville	FL	32202	904-356-8371	
Legal Aid Bureau Inc 500 E Lexington St *Web:* www.mdlab.org	Baltimore	MD	21202	410-951-7777	
Legal Aid Foundation of Los Angeles 1102 Crenshaw Blvd *Web:* www.lafla.org	Los Angeles	CA	90019	323-801-7991	
Legal Aid Society of Palm Beach County Inc 423 Fern St Ste 200 *TF:* 800-403-9353 ■ *Web:* www.legalaidpbc.org	West Palm Beach	FL	33401	561-655-8944	
Legal Aid Society of San Mateo County, The 30 Twin Dolphin Dr Ste 123 *Web:* www.legalaidsmc.org	Redwood City	CA	94402	650-558-0915	
Lehr Middlebrooks & Vreeland PC 2021 Third Ave N *Web:* www.lehrmiddlebrooks.com	Birmingham	AL	35203	205-326-3002	
Lerman Senter PLLC 2001 L St NW Ste 400 *Web:* www.lermansenter.com	Washington	DC	20006	202-429-8970	
Lerner David Littenberg Krumholz & Mentlik 600 South Ave W *Web:* ldlkm.com	Westfield	NJ	07090	908-654-5000	
Lerner, Sampson & Rothfuss A Legal Professional Association 120 E Fourth St *Web:* www.lsrlaw.com	Cincinnati	OH	45202	513-241-3100	
Lesperance & Martineau 1440 Rue Sainte-catherine O *TF:* 888-273-8387 ■ *Web:* www.l-m.ca	Montreal	QC	H3G1R8	514-861-4831	
Levasseur Dier & Associates Pc 3233 Coolidge Hwy *Web:* www.mortgage-foreclosures.com	Berkley	MI	48072	248-586-1200	
Levine Blaszak Block & Boothby LLP 2001 L St NW Ste 900 *Web:* www.lb3law.com	Washington	DC	20036	202-857-2550	
Lewis & Kappes 1700 One American Sq Box 82053 *Web:* www.lewis-kappes.com	Indianapolis	IN	46282	317-639-1210	
Lewis Brisbois Bisgaard & Smith LLP 221 N Figueroa St Ste 1200 *Web:* lewisbrisbois.com	Los Angeles	CA	90012	213-250-1800	250-7900
Lewis Wagner 501 Indiana Ave #200 *TF:* 800-237-0505 ■ *Web:* www.lewiswagner.com	Indianapolis	IN	46202	317-237-0500	
Liddle & Robinson LLP 800 Third Ave Fl 8 *Web:* www.liddlerobinson.com	New York	NY	10022	212-687-8500	
Lightfoot, Franklin & White LLC The Clark Bldg 400 20th St N *Web:* www.lfwlaw.com	Birmingham	AL	35203	205-581-0700	
Lind, Jensen, Sullivan & Peterson A Professional Association 1300 AT&T Tower 901 Marquette Ave South *Web:* www.lindjensen.com	Minneapolis	MN	55402	612-333-3637	
Lindquist & Vennum PLLP 4200 IDS Ctr 80 S Eighth St *Web:* www.lindquist.com	Minneapolis	MN	55402	612-371-3211	
Linowes & Blocher LLP 7200 Wisconsin Ave Ste 800 *Web:* linowes-law.com	Bethesda	MD	20814	301-654-0504	654-2801
Lippes Mathias Wexler Friedman LLP 665 Main St Ste 300 *Web:* www.lippes.com	Buffalo	NY	14203	716-853-5100	
Lipson, Neilson, Cole, Seltzer & Garin PC 3910 Telegraph Rd Ste 200 *Web:* www.lipsonneilson.com	Bloomfield Hills	MI	48302	248-593-5000	
Lipton Law Center Pc 18930 W 10 Mile Rd *Web:* www.liptonlaw.com	Southfield	MI	48075	248-557-1688	
Liskow & Lewis 701 Poydras St Ste 5000 *Web:* www.liskow.com	New Orleans	LA	70139	504-581-7979	
Little Pedersen Fankhauser LLP 901 Main St Ste 4110 *Web:* www.lpf-law.com	Dallas	TX	75202	214-573-2300	
Littler Mendelson PC 650 California St 20th Fl *TF:* 888-548-8537 ■ *Web:* www.littler.com	San Francisco	CA	94108	415-433-1940	399-8490
Lloyd & McDaniel PLC 11405 Park Rd Ste 200 *TF:* 866-548-2486 ■ *Web:* www.lloydmc.com	Louisville	KY	40223	502-585-1880	
Lloyd Gray Whitehead & Monroe PC 2501 20th Pl S Ste 300 *TF:* 800-967-7299 ■ *Web:* www.lgwmlaw.com	Birmingham	AL	35223	205-967-8822	
Locke Lord Bissell & Liddell LLP (LLBL) 2200 Ross Ave Ste 2200 *Web:* www.lockelord.com	Dallas	TX	75201	214-740-8000	740-8000
Loewinsohn Flegle Deary LLP 12377 Merit Dr Ste 900 *Web:* lfdlaw.com	Dallas	TX	75251	214-572-1700	
Lone Star Legal Aid 1415 Fannin St Ste 300 *Web:* www.gclf.org	Houston	TX	77002	713-652-0077	
Longsworth Law Offices LLC 7030 Pointe Inverness Way Ste 330 *Web:* longsworthlaw.com	Fort Wayne	IN	46804	260-436-1555	
Lopez Mchugh LLP 1123 Admiral Peary Way *TF:* 877-703-7070 ■ *Web:* lopezmchugh.com	Philadelphia	PA	19112	215-952-6910	
Lorber Greenfield & Polito LLP 13985 Stowe Dr *TF:* 800-659-8821 ■ *Web:* lorberlaw.com	Poway	CA	92064	858-513-1020	
Lorge & Lorge Law Firm 501 W Willow St *TF:* 800-529-2946 ■ *Web:* www.lawfirm.net	Bear Creek	WI	54922	715-752-3304	
Lowenstein Sandler PC 65 Livingston Ave St 2 *Web:* www.lowenstein.com	Roseland	NJ	07068	973-597-2500	
Lozano Smith 7404 N Spalding Ave *Web:* www.lozanosmith.com	Fresno	CA	93720	559-431-5600	
Lukins & Annis PS 1600 WA Trust Financial Ctr 717 W Sprague Ave Ste 1600 *Web:* www.lukins.com	Spokane	WA	99201	509-455-9555	
Lynch, Traub, Keefe & Errante A Professional Corp 52 Trumbull St *TF:* 888-692-7403 ■ *Web:* www.ltke.com	New Haven	CT	06506	203-787-0275	
Lynn Todd m 12350 Jefferson Ave Ste 300 *Web:* www.pwhd.com	Newport News	VA	23602	757-223-4573	
Lyons & Lyons Attorneys at Law 8310 Princeton Glendale Rd *Web:* www.lyonsandlyonslaw.com	West Chester	OH	45069	513-777-2222	
Macdonald Devin PC 3800 Renaissance Tower 1201 Elm St *Web:* macdonalddevin.com	Dallas	TX	75270	214-744-3300	
MacElree Harvey Ltd 17 W Miner St *Web:* www.macelree.com	West Chester	PA	19381	610-436-0100	
Macera & Jarzyna LLP 1200-427 Laurier Ave W *Web:* www.macerajarzyna.com	Ottawa	ON	K1R7Y2	613-238-8173	
Mackall, Crounse & Moore PLC 1400 AT&T Tower 901 Marquette Ave *Web:* www.mcmlaw.com	Minneapolis	MN	55402	612-305-1400	
Magavern Magavern & Grimm LLP 1100 Rand Bldg *Web:* www.magavern.com	Buffalo	NY	14203	716-856-3500	

Phone Fax

Mahaffey & Gore PC 300 NE First St Oklahoma City OK 73104 405-236-0478
Web: www.mahaffeygorelaw.com

Maher, Guiley & Maher PA
631 W Morse Blvd Ste 200 Winter Park FL 32789 407-839-0866
Web: maherlawfirm.com

Mallilo & Grossman 16309 Northern Blvd Flushing NY 11358 718-461-6633
TF: 866-593-6274 ■ *Web:* www.malliloandgrossman.com

Manatt, Phelps & Phillips
11355 W Olympic Blvd Los Angeles CA 90064 310-312-4000
Web: www.manatt.com

Mandel, Katz & Brosnan LLP
The Law Bldg 210 Rt 303 Valley Cottage NY 10989 845-639-7800
Web: www.mkbllp.com

Manley Deas & Kochalski LLC PO Box 165028 Columbus OH 43216 614-220-5611
Web: mdk-llc.com

Manning Fulton & Skinner PA
3605 Glenwood Ave Raleigh NC 27612 919-787-8880
Web: www.manningfulton.com

Marcari, Russotto, Spencer & Balaban PC
6801 Pleasant Pines Dr Ste 101 Raleigh NC 27613 919-787-9944
Web: www.donmarcari.com

Marcus & Pollack LLP 633 Third Ave 9th fl. New York NY 10017 212-490-2900
Web: marcuspollack.com

Marger Johnson & McCollom PC
210 S W Morrison St Portland OR 97204 503-222-3613
Web: techlaw.com

Margolis Edelstein
170 S Independence Mall W The Curtis Ctr
Ste 400E Philadelphia PA 19106 215-922-1100
Web: www.margolisedelstein.com

Mariani & Reck LLC 83 Broad St New London CT 06320 860-443-5023
Web: www.marianireck.com

Mariscal Weeks Mcintyre & Friedlander Pa
2901 N Central Ave Phoenix AZ 85012 602-285-5000 285-5100
Web: www.dickinson-wright.com

Marnen Mioduszewski Bordonaro Wagner & Sinnott LLC
516 W 10th St Erie PA 16502 814-874-3460
Web: mmbwslaw.com

Marrone, Robinson, Frederick & Foster
111 N First St Ste 300 Burbank CA 91502 818-841-1144
Web: www.mrfflaw.net

Marsh Fischmann & Breyfogle LLP
8055 E Tufts Ave Ste 450 Denver CO 80237 303-770-0051
Web: www.mfblaw.com

Marshall Dennehey Warner Coleman & Goggin
1845 Walnut St Philadelphia PA 19103 215-575-2600 575-0856
Web: www.marshalldennehey.com

Marshall V Miller & Company Pc
4929 Main St Kansas City MO 64112 816-561-4999
Web: www.millerco.com

Marten Law 1191 Second Ave Ste 2200 Seattle WA 98101 206-292-2600
Web: www.martenlaw.com

Martin, Disiere, Jefferson & Wisdom LLP
808 Travis St # 1800 Houston Tx Houston TX 77002 512-610-4400
Web: www.mdjwlaw.com

Martin, Harding & Mazzotti LLP
1222 Troy-Schenectady Rd. Niskayuna NY 12309 518-862-1200
Web: www.1800law1010.com

Martin, Leigh, Laws & Fritzlen Professional Corp
1044 Main St Ste 900 Kansas City MO 64105 816-221-1430
Web: www.martinleigh.com

Martin, Shudt, Wallace, DiLorenzo & Johnson
258 Hoosick St Ste 201 Troy NY 12180 518-272-6565
Web: www.martinshudt.com

Maslon Edelman Borman & Brand LLP
3300 Wells Fargo Ctr 90 S Seventh St Minneapolis MN 55402 612-672-8200
Web: www.maslon.com

Mason, Griffin & Pierson PC
101 Poor Farm Rd Princeton NJ 08540 609-921-6543
Web: www.mgplaw.com

Matheny Sears Linkert & Jaime LLP
3638 American River Dr Sacramento CA 95864 916-978-3434
Web: www.mathenysears.com

Mattioni LLP 1316 Kings Hwy Swedesboro NJ 08085 856-241-9779
Web: www.mattioni.com

Mawicke & Goisman SC 1509 N Prospect Ave Milwaukee WI 53202 414-224-0600
Web: www.dmgr.com

Maxwell Noll Inc 600 S Lk Ave Ste 502 Pasadena CA 91106 626-796-7133
Web: www.maxnoll.com

May, Adam, Gerdes & Thompson LLP
503 S Pierre St Pierre SD 57501 605-224-8803
TF: 800-636-8803 ■ *Web:* www.magt.com

Mazursky Constantine LLC
999 Peachtree St Ste 1500 Atlanta GA 30309 404-888-8820
Web: www.mazconlaw.com

Mazzotta, Sherwood & Vagianelis, P.C.
9 Washington Sq Washington Ave Ext Albany NY 12205 518-452-0941
Web: www.msvlawfirm.com

McAfee & Taft A Professional Corp
2 Leadership Sq 211 N Robinson
Ste 1000 Oklahoma City OK 73102 405-235-9621
TF: 800-235-9621 ■ *Web:* www.mcafeetaft.com

McAndrews Held & Malloy
500 W Madison St 34th Fl Chicago IL 60661 312-775-8000 775-8100
Web: www.mcandrews-ip.com

Mccallum, Hoaglund, Cook & Irby LLP
905 Montgomery Hwy Ste 201 Vestavia AL 35216 205-824-7767
TF: 866-974-8145 ■ *Web:* www.mhcilaw.com

McConnaughhay Duffy Coonrad Pope & Weaver Pa
1709 Hermitage Blvd Ste 200 Tallahassee FL 32308 850-222-8121
Web: www.mcconnaughhay.com

Mccranie, Sistrunk, Anzelmo, Hardy, Maxwell & Mcdaniel PC
909 Poydras St Ste 1000 New Orleans LA 70112 504-831-0946
Web: www.mcsalaw.com

McDermott Will & Emery
227 W Monroe St Ste 4700 Chicago IL 60606 312-372-2000 984-7700
Web: www.mwe.com

Mcdivitt Law Firm 19 E Cimarron St Colorado Springs CO 80903 303-426-4878
Web: mcdivittlaw.com

McDougall Gauley 500-616 Main St Saskatoon SK S7H0J6 306-653-1212
Web: www.mcdougallgauley.com

Mcdowell Rice Smith & Buchanan Pc
605 W 47th St Ste 350 Kansas City MO 64112 816-753-5400 753-9996
Web: www.mcdowellrice.com

McElroy Deutsch & Mulvaney LLP
PO Box 2075 Morristown NJ 07962 973-993-8100 425-0161
Web: www.mdmc-law.com

Mcgarry Bair Pc 32 Market Ave Sw Ste 500 Grand Rapids MI 49503 616-742-3500
Web: www.mcgarrybair.com

Mcginnis Lochridge & Kilgore LLP
600 Congress Ave Austin TX 78701 512-495-6000 495-6093
Web: www.mcginnislaw.com

Mcgowan Hood & Felder LLC 1517 Hampton St Columbia SC 29201 803-779-0100
Web: www.mcgowanhood.com

McGuireWoods LLP 901 E Cary St 1 James Ctr Richmond VA 23219 804-775-1000 775-1061
TF: 877-712-8778 ■ *Web:* www.mcguirewoods.com

McHale & Slavin PA 2855 PGA Blvd Palm Beach Gardens FL 33410 561-625-6575
Web: www.mchaleslavin.com

McKee, Voorhees & Sease PLC
801 Grand Ste 3200 Des Moines IA 50309 515-288-3667
Web: www.ipmvs.com

McKenna Storer 33 N LaSalle St Ste 1400 Chicago IL 60602 312-558-3900
Web: mckenna-law.com

Mckenzie Lake Lawyers LLP 300 Dundas St London ON N6B1T6 519-672-5666
Web: www.mckenzielake.com

McLennan Ross LLP
600 W Chambers 12220 Stony Plain Rd Edmonton AB T5N3Y4 780-482-9200
TF: 800-567-9200 ■ *Web:* www.mross.com

McManis Faulkner
Fairmont Plz 50 W San Fernando St 10th Fl San Jose CA 95113 408-279-8700
Web: www.mcmanislaw.com

Mcmillan & Terry pa
6101 Carnegie Blvd Ste 310 Charlotte NC 28209 704-552-9997
Web: mplawcarolinas.com

McNees Wallace & Nurick LLC
125 N Washington Ave Scranton PA 18503 570-209-7220
Web: www.mcneeslaw.com

McTeague Higbee Case Cohen Whitney & Toker PA
4 Union Park Topsham ME 04086 207-725-5581
Web: www.me-law.com

Meisner & Associates Pc
30200 Telegraph Rd Ste 467 Bingham Farms MI 48025 248-644-4433
TF: 800-470-4433 ■ *Web:* meisner-law.com

Meissner Tierney Fisher & Nichols S.C
111 E Kilbourn Ave 19th Fl Milwaukee WI 53202 414-273-1300
Web: www.mtfn.com

Meltzer Lippe Goldstein & Schissel LLP
190 Willis Ave Mineola NY 11501 516-747-0300
Web: www.mlg.com

Mendes & Mount LLP 750 Seventh Ave New York NY 10019 212-261-8000
Web: www.mendes.com

Merchant & Gould
3200 IDS Ctr 80 S Eighth St Minneapolis MN 55402 612-332-5300
Web: www.merchantgould.com

Merrigan Brandt Ostenso & Cambre pa
25 Ninth Ave N Hopkins MN 55343 952-933-2390
Web: merriganlaw.com

Mesch, Clark & Rothschild PC 259 N Meyer Ave Tucson AZ 85701 520-624-8886
Web: www.mcrazlaw.com

Messa & Associates PC 123 S 22nd St Philadelphia PA 19103 215-568-3500
Web: messalaw.com

Messerli & Kramer PA
1400 Fifth St Towers 100 S Fifth St Minneapolis MN 55402 612-672-3600 672-3777
Web: www.messerlikramer.com

Meyer Unkovic & Scott LLP
535 Smithfield St Ste 1300 Pittsburgh PA 15222 412-456-2800 456-2864
Web: www.muslaw.com

Midkiff, Muncie & Ross PC
300 Arboretum Pl Ste 420 Richmond VA 23236 804-560-9600
Web: www.midkifflaw.com

MidPenn Legal Services 213 A N Front St Harrisburg PA 17101 717-234-0492
Web: www.midpenn.org

Milbank Tweed Hadley & McCloy LLP
1 Chase Manhattan Plaza New York NY 10005 212-530-5000 530-5219
TF: 800-229-0543 ■ *Web:* www.milbank.com

Miller & Chevalier Chartered
655 15th St NW Ste 900 Washington DC 20005 202-626-5800 626-5801
TF: 866-628-4282 ■ *Web:* www.millerchevalier.com

Miller & Luring Company LPa 314 W Main St Troy OH 45373 937-339-2627
Web: www.millerluring.com

Miller & Martin PLLC
832 Georgia Ave Volunteer Bldg Ste 1000 Chattanooga TN 37402 423-756-6600
Web: www.millermartin.com

Miller Canfield Paddock & Stone PLC
150 W Jefferson Ave Ste 2500 Detroit MI 48226 313-963-6420 496-7500
Web: www.millercanfield.com

Miller Johnson Snell & Cummiskey PLC
250 Monroe Ave NW Ste 800 PO Box 306 Grand Rapids MI 49503 616-831-1700 831-1701
TF: 800-772-1213 ■ *Web:* www.millerjohnson.com

Miller Law Firm Pc, The
950 W University Dr Ste 300 Rochester MI 48307 248-841-2200
Web: www.millerlawpc.com

Miller Nash LLP 3400 US Bancorp Tower Portland OR 97204 503-224-5858
Web: www.millernash.com

Miller Russell H. Law Offices
20 Park Rd Ste E Burlingame CA 94010 650-401-8735
Web: www.millerpoliticallaw.com

	Phone	Fax

Miller Stratvert PA
500 Marquette Ave NW Ste 1100 . . . Albuquerque NM 87125 505-842-1950
Web: www.mstlaw.com

Miner, Barnhill & Galland PC 14 W Erie St . . . Chicago IL 60654 312-751-1170
Web: www.lawmbg.com

Minerva & D'agostino PC
107 S Central Ave . . . Valley Stream NY 11580 516-872-7400
Web: mindaglaw.com

Mintz Levin Cohn Ferris Glovsky & Popeo PC
1 Financial Ctr . . . Boston MA 02111 617-542-6000 542-2241
Web: www.mintz.com

Mitchell Williams Selig Gates & Woodyard Pllc
425 W Capitol Ave Ste 1800 . . . Little Rock AR 72201 501-688-8800 688-8807
Web: mitchellwilliamslaw.com

Modrall Sperling Roehl Harris & Sisk P.a
PO Box 2168 . . . Albuquerque NM 87103 505-848-1800
Web: www.modrall.com

Moffatt Thomas Barrett Rock & Fields
101 S Capitol Blvd 10th Fl . . . Boise ID 83702 208-345-2000
Web: www.moffatt.com

Montgomery Little & Soran PC
5445 Dtc Pkwy Ste 800 . . . Greenwood Village CO 80111 303-773-8100 220-0412
Web: www.montgomerylittle.com

Montlick & Associates PC
17 Executive Park Dr Ste 300 . . . Atlanta GA 30329 404-529-6333
Web: www.montlick.com

Moore Ingram Johnson & Steele LLP
Emerson Overlook 326 Roswell Rd . . . Marietta GA 30060 770-429-1499
Web: www.mijs.com

Morgan & Weisbrod 6800 W Loop S Ste 450 . . . Bellaire TX 77401 713-838-0003
TF: 877-898-1581 ■ *Web:* www.morganweisbrod.com

Morgan Lewis & Bockius LLP
1701 Market St . . . Philadelphia PA 19103 215-963-5000 963-5001
TF: 866-963-7137 ■ *Web:* www.morganlewis.com

Morgan Lewis & Bockius LLP 1 Federal St . . . Boston MA 02110 617-951-8000
Web: www.morganlewis.com

Morgan Melhuish Abrutyn
651 W Mount Pleasant Ave Ste 200 . . . Livingston NJ 07039 973-994-2500
Web: www.morganlawfirm.com

Morris Duffy Alonso & Faley
2 Rector St 22nd Fl . . . New York NY 10006 212-766-1888
Web: www.mdafny.com

Morris Polich & Purdy
1055 W Seventh St Ste 2400 . . . Los Angeles CA 90017 213-891-9100 488-1178
Web: www.mpplaw.com

Morrison & Foerster LLP 425 Market St . . . San Francisco CA 94105 415-268-7000 268-7522
Web: www.mofo.com

Morrison Mahoney LLP 250 Summer St . . . Boston MA 02210 617-439-7500 439-7590
Web: www.morrisonmahoney.com

Morrison Scott Alan Law Offices of pa
141 W Patrick St Ste 300 . . . Frederick MD 21701 301-694-6262
TF: 866-220-5185 ■ *Web:* www.samlawoffice.com

Morse, Barnes-Brown & Pendleton PC
CityPoint 230 Third Ave 4th Fl . . . Waltham MA 02451 781-622-5930
Web: www.mbbp.com

Mulherin, Rehfeldt & Varchetto PC
211 S Wheaton Ave Ste 200 . . . Wheaton IL 60187 630-653-9300
Web: www.mrvlaw.com

Mullen & Filippi LLP
1601 Response Rd Ste 300 . . . Sacramento CA 95815 916-442-4503
Web: www.mulfil.com

Muller Muller Richmond Harms Myers & Sgroi Atty
33233 Woodward Ave . . . Birmingham MI 48009 248-645-2440
Web: www.mullerfirm.com

Mullin Hoard & Brown LLP
Amarillo National Plz Two
Ste 800 500 S Taylor Lobby Box Ste 213 . . . Amarillo TX 79101 806-372-5050
Web: www.mullinhoard.com

Munck Wilson Mandala LLP
600 Banner Pl Tower 12770 Coit Rd . . . Dallas TX 75251 972-628-3600
Web: www.munckwilson.com

Munsch Hardt Kopf Harr Pc 500 N Akard St . . . Dallas TX 75201 214-855-7500 855-7584
TF: 800-321-6742 ■ *Web:* www.munsch.com

Murphy & Grantland PA 4406-B Forest Dr . . . Columbia SC 29260 803-782-4100
Web: www.murphygrantland.com

Murphy & McGonigle 4870 Sadler Rd Ste 301 . . . Glen Allen VA 23060 804-762-5320
Web: www.mmlawus.com

Murphy Sullivan Kronk 275 College St . . . Burlington VT 05401 802-861-7000
Web: www.mskvt.com

Murphy, Hesse, Toomey & Lehane LLP
Crown Colony Plz 300 Crown Colony Dr Ste 410 . . . Quincy MA 02169 617-479-5000
Web: www.mhtl.com

Murray, Plumb & Murray 75 Pearl St . . . Portland ME 04101 207-773-5651
Web: www.mpmlaw.com

Musick Peeler & Garrett LLP
1 Wilshire Blvd Ste 2000 . . . Los Angeles CA 90017 213-629-7600
Web: www.musickpeeler.com

Myers, Oliver & Price PC
1401 Central Ave Nw Ste A . . . Albuquerque NM 87104 505-247-9080
Web: moplaw.com

Myers, Widders, Gibson, Jones & Feingold LLP
5425 Everglades St . . . Ventura CA 93003 805-644-7188

Nagle & Associates pa
7780 Brier Creek Pkwy Ste 210 . . . Raleigh NC 27617 919-433-0035
Web: www.naglefirm.com

Nahon, Saharovich & Trotz PLC
488 S Menhenhall Rd . . . Memphis TN 38117 901-683-7000
TF: 800-529-4004 ■ *Web:* www.nstlaw.com

Nason, Yeager, Gerson, White & Lioce PA
3001 PGA Blvd Ste 305 . . . Palm Beach Gardens FL 33401 561-686-3307
Web: nasonyeager.com

Nauman Smith Shissler & Hall LLP
200 N Third St Fl 18 . . . Harrisburg PA 17101 717-236-3010
Web: nssh.com

	Phone	Fax

Neal & Harwell PLC
1 Nashville Pl Ste 2000 150 Fourth Ave N . . . Nashville TN 37219 615-244-1713
Web: www.nealharwell.com

Nelson & Kennard
2180 Harvard St Ste 160 PO Box 13807 . . . Sacramento CA 95815 866-920-2295
TF: 866-920-2295 ■ *Web:* nelson-kennard.com

Nelson Mullins Riley & Scarborough LLP
1320 Main St 17th Fl . . . Columbia SC 29201 803-799-2000 256-7500
TF: 800-237-2000 ■ *Web:* www.nelsonmullins.com

Neuberger Quinn Gielen Rubin Gibber PA
1 South St 27th Fl . . . Baltimore MD 21202 410-332-8550
Web: www.nqgrg.com

Nevada Disability Advocacy & Law Center Inc
2820 W Charleston Blvd Ste 11 . . . Las Vegas NV 89102 702-257-8150
Web: ndalc.org

New Haven Legal Assistance Association Inc
426 State St . . . New Haven CT 06510 203-946-4811
TF: 877-829-5500 ■ *Web:* nhlegal.org

New York Prosecutors Training Institute
107 Columbia St . . . Albany NY 12210 518-432-1100
Web: www.nypti.org

Newmeyer & Dillion LLP
895 Dove St 5th Fl . . . Newport Beach CA 92660 949-854-7000
Web: www.newmeyeranddillion.com

Niedner, Bodeux, Carmichael, Huff, Lenox & Pashos LLP
131 Jefferson St . . . Saint Charles MO 63301 636-949-9300
TF: 888-572-2192 ■ *Web:* www.niednerlaw.com

Nielsen, Merksamer, Parrinello, Gross & Leoni LLP
2350 Kerner Blvd Ste 250 . . . San Rafael CA 94901 415-389-6800
Web: www.nmgovlaw.com

Niles Barton & Wilmer
111 S Calvert St Ste 1400 . . . Baltimore MD 21202 410-783-6300 783-6363
Web: www.nilesbarton.com

Nirenstein, Horowitz & Associates PC
43 Woodland St Ste 520 . . . Hartford CT 06105 860-548-1000
Web: www.preserveyourestate.net

Niro Scavone Haller & Niro Ltd
181 W Madison St Ste 4600 . . . Chicago IL 60602 312-236-0733
Web: www.niroscavone.com

Nisen & Elliott LLC 200 W Adams St Ste 2500 . . . Chicago IL 60606 312-346-7800
Web: www.nisen.com

Nolan & Heller LLP 39 N Pearl St 3rd Fl . . . Albany NY 12207 518-449-3300
Web: www.nolanandheller.com

Norman, Wood, Kendrick & Turner
1130 22nd St S Ridge Park Pl Ste 3000 . . . Birmingham AL 35205 205-328-6643
Web: nwkt.com

Norris, McLaughlin & Marcus PA
721 Route 202-206 . . . Bridgewater NJ 08807 908-722-0700
Web: nmmlaw.com

North Berman & Beebe
1111 14th St Nw Ste 920 . . . Washington DC 20005 202-371-1100
Web: northberman.com

Notaro & Michalos PC 100 Dutch Hill Rd . . . Orangeburg NY 10962 845-359-7700
Web: www.notaromichalos.com

Nowell Amoroso Klein Bierman PA
155 Polifly Rd 3rd Fl . . . Hackensack NJ 07601 201-343-5001

Nuzzo & Roberts LLC 1 Town Ctr . . . Cheshire CT 06410 203-250-2000
Web: www.nuzzo-roberts.com

Nysarc Inc 393 Delaware Ave . . . Delmar NY 12054 518-439-8311 439-1893
TF: 800-735-8924 ■ *Web:* www.nysarc.org

O'Brien, Tanski & Young LLP
CityPlace II 185 Asylum St . . . Hartford CT 06103 860-525-2700
Web: www.otylaw.com

O'connell, Tivin, Miller & Burns LLC
135 S La Salle St Ste 2300 . . . Chicago IL 60603 312-256-8800
Web: www.otmblaw.com

O'donnell Lee Mccowan & Phillips LLC
112 Silver St . . . Waterville ME 04901 207-872-0112
Web: www.odonnellandlee.com

O'hagan Smith & Amundsen
308 W State St Ste 320 . . . Rockford IL 61101 815-987-0441
Web: salawus.com

O'Melveny & Myers LLP
400 S Hope St 10th Fl . . . Los Angeles CA 90071 213-430-6000 430-6407
Web: www.omm.com

O'Reilly Rancilio PC
Sterling Town Ctr 12900 Hall Rd
Ste 350 . . . Sterling Heights MI 48313 586-726-1000
TF: 800-708-3528 ■ *Web:* www.orlaw.com

O'riordan Bethel Law Firm LLP, The
1314 19th St Nw . . . Washington DC 20036 202-822-1720
Web: oriordan-law.com

Ogden, Gibson, Broocks, Longoria & Hall LLP
1900 Pennzoil S Twr . . . Houston TX 77002 713-844-3000
Web: www.ogwbl.com

Ogne Alberts & Stuart Pc 1869 E Maple Rd . . . Troy MI 48083 248-362-3707
Web: oaspc.com

Ohio Legal Assistance Foundation
10 W Broad St Ste 950 . . . Columbus OH 43215 614-715-8560
TF: 800-877-9772 ■ *Web:* www.olaf.org

Oliff & Berridge PLC
277 S Washington St Ste 500 . . . Alexandria VA 22314 703-836-6400
Web: www.oliff.com

Oliver, Price & Rhodes
1212 S Abington Rd . . . Clarks Summit PA 18411 570-585-1200
Web: oprlaw.com

ONeill & Borges
American International Plz 250 Munoz Rivera Ave
Ste 800 . . . San Juan PR 00918 787-764-8181
Web: www.oneillborges.com

Orgain Bell & Tucker LLP 470 Orleans St . . . Beaumont TX 77704 409-838-6412
Web: www.obt.com

Orlans Associates PC 1650 W Big Beaver Rd . . . Troy MI 48084 248-502-1400
Web: www.orlans.com

Phone Fax

Orrick Herrington & Sutcliffe LLP
666 Fifth Ave .... New York NY 10103 212-506-5000 506-5151
TF: 866-342-5259 ■ *Web:* www.orrick.com

Otten Johnson Robinson Neff & Ragonetti PC
950 17th St Ste 1600 .... Denver CO 80202 303-825-8400 825-6525
Web: www.ottenjohnson.com

Pachulski Stang Ziehl Young & Jones Professional Corp
10100 Santa Monica Blvd. .... Los Angeles CA 90067 310-277-6910
Web: pszjlaw.com

Paine, Hamblen, Coffin, Brooke & Miller LLP
717 W Sprague Ave Washington Trust Financial Ctr
Ste 1200 .... Spokane WA 99201 509-455-6000
Web: www.painehamblen.com

Paladin Law Group LLP 1176 Blvd Way .... Walnut Creek CA 94595 925-947-5700
Web: www.paladinlaw.com

Pallett Valo LLP 77 City Ctr Dr Ste 300 .... Mississauga ON L5B1M5 905-273-3300
TF: 800-323-3781 ■ *Web:* www.pallettvalo.com

Parker McCay PA
9000 Midlantic Dr Ste 300 .... Mount Laurel NJ 08054 856-596-8900
Web: www.parkermccay.com

Parker Poe Adams & Bernstein LLP
3 Wachovia Ctr 401 S Tryon St Ste 3000 .... Charlotte NC 28202 704-372-9000
TF: 866-602-5893 ■ *Web:* www.parkerpoe.com

Parker Stanbury LLP
444 S Flower St Ste 1900 .... Los Angeles CA 90071 619-528-1259
Web: www.parkstan.com

Parker, Kern, Nard & Wenzel
1111 E Herndon Ave Ste 202 .... Fresno CA 93720 559-449-2558
Web: pknwlaw.com

Parlee McLaws LLP
3400 Petro-Canada Centre 150-6th Ave SW .... Calgary AB T2P3Y7 403-294-7000
Web: www.parlee.com

Parr Brown Gee & Loveless 101 S 200 E Ste 700 .... Slc UT 84111 801-532-7840
Web: www.parrbrown.com

Parr Richey Obremsky & Morton
201 N Illinois St Ste 300 .... Indianapolis IN 46204 317-269-2500
TF: 888-337-7766 ■ *Web:* www.parrlaw.com

Parrett, Porto, Parese & Colwell PC
1 Hamden Ctr 2319 Whitney Ave Ste 1-D .... Hamden CT 06518 203-281-2700
Web: www.byxbee.com

Partridge Snow & Hahn LLP 180 S Main St .... Providence RI 02903 401-861-8200
Web: www.psh.com

Passman & Jones
2500 Renaissance Tower 1201 Elm St .... Dallas TX 75270 214-742-2121
Web: www.passmanjones.com

Paul Hastings Janofsky & Walker LLP
515 S Flower St 25th Fl .... Los Angeles CA 90071 213-683-6000 627-0705
Web: www.paulhastings.com

Paul Weiss Rifkind Wharton & Garrison LLP
1285 Ave of the Americas .... New York NY 10019 212-373-3000 757-3990
Web: www.paulweiss.com

PDQ Legal Services 7890 E McClain Dr Ste 3 .... Scottsdale AZ 85260 480-556-6660

Peabody & Arnold LLP 600 Atlantic Ave .... Boston MA 02210 617-951-2100 951-2125
Web: www.peabodyarnold.com

Pearce & Durick 314 E Thayer Ave .... Bismarck ND 58502 701-223-2890
Web: www.pearce-durick.com

Pearne & Gordon LLP
1801 E Ninth St Ste 1200 .... Cleveland OH 44114 216-579-1700
Web: www.pearne.com

Peirson Patterson LLP
2310 W Interstate 20 Ste 100 .... Arlington TX 76017 817-461-5500
Web: www.peirsonpatterson.com

Pellettieri Rabstein & Altman
100 Nassau Pk Blvd .... Princeton NJ 08540 609-520-0900 452-8796
TF: 800-432-5297 ■ *Web:* www.pralaw.com

PennStuart 208 E Main St .... Abingdon VA 24210 276-628-5151
Web: www.pennstuart.com

Pepper Hamilton LLP
3000 Two Logan Sq 18th & Arch St .... Philadelphia PA 19103 215-981-4000 981-4750
Web: www.pepperlaw.com

Perantinides & Nolan Company LPa
80 S Summit St Ste 300 .... Akron OH 44308 330-434-7873
Web: eyemg.com

Perkins Coie LLP 1201 Third Ave Ste 4800 .... Seattle WA 98101 206-359-8000 359-9000
TF: 888-720-8382 ■ *Web:* www.perkinscoie.com

Perkins Thompson & Hinckley
1 Canal Plz Ste 900 .... Portland ME 04101 207-774-2635
Web: perkinsthompson.com

Peter J. Jaensch Immigration 2198 Main St .... Sarasota FL 34237 941-366-9841
Web: visaamerica.com

Peters & Freedman LLP
191 Calle Magdalena Ste 220 .... Encinitas CA 92024 760-436-3441
Web: www.hoalaw.com

Peters Murdaugh Parker Ellzr
123 S Walter St PO Box 1164 .... Walterboro SC 29488 843-549-9544
Web: www.pmped.com

Phelan Hallinan & Schmieg LLP
400 Fellowship Rd Ste 100 .... Mount Laurel NJ 08054 856-813-5500
Web: www.phelanhallinan.com

Phelps Dunbar LLP
Canal Pl 365 Canal St Ste 2000 .... New Orleans LA 70130 504-566-1311
Web: www.phelpsdunbar.com

Philips & Cohen LLP
2000 Massachusetts Ave Nw Ste 100 .... Washington DC 20036 202-833-4567
Web: www.phillipsandcohen.com

Phillips & Webster Pllc Attys
17410 133rd Ave NE ste 301 .... Woodinville WA 98072 425-482-1111
Web: www.justiceforyou.com

Phillips Law Group LLC 1618 Thompson Ave .... Atlanta GA 30344 404-761-6800
Web: www.phillipslawatlanta.com

Phillips Murrah PC
101 N Robinson Ave Corporate Tower
13th Fl .... Oklahoma City OK 73102 405-235-4100
Web: www.phillipsmurrah.com

Pickrel Schaeffer & Ebeling
40 N Main St - Kettering Tower .... Dayton OH 45423 937-223-1130
Web: www.pselaw.com

Pierce & Associates 1 N Dearborn St Ste 1300 .... Chicago IL 60602 312-346-9088
Web: www.atty-pierce.com

Pierce & Shearer LLP
730 Polhemus Rd Ste 101 .... San Mateo CA 94402 650-573-9300
Web: www.pierceshearer.com

Pietragallo Gordon Alfano Bosick & Raspanti LLP
1 Oxford Centre Fl 38 .... Pittsburgh PA 15219 412-263-2000
Web: www.pietragallo.com

Pietrantoni Mendez & Alvarez LLP
Popular Ctr Bldg 208 Ponce de Leon Ave
19th Fl .... San Juan PR 00918 787-274-1212
Web: www.pmalaw.com

Pillsbury Winthrop Shaw Pittman LLP
50 Fremont St .... San Francisco CA 94105 415-983-1000 983-1200
Web: www.pillsburylaw.com

Plews Shadley Racher & Braun LLP
1346 N Delaware St .... Indianapolis IN 46202 317-637-0700
Web: www.psrb.com

Polsinelli Shalton Flanigan Suelthaus PC
700 W 47th St Ste 1000 .... Kansas City MO 64112 816-753-1000 753-1536
TF: 800-422-0893 ■ *Web:* www.polsinelli.com

Porteous, Hainkel & Johnson LLP
704 Carondelet St .... New Orleans LA 70130 504-581-3838
Web: www.phjlaw.com

Portnoff Law Associates Ltd
1000 Sandy Hill Rd Ste 1 .... Norristown PA 19401 484-690-9300
TF: 866-211-9466 ■ *Web:* portnoffonline.com

Porzio Bromberg & Newman PC
100 Southgate Pkwy .... Morristown NJ 07962 973-538-4006
Web: www.pbnlaw.com

Post & Schell PC
4 Penn Ctr 1600 John F Kennedy Blvd .... Philadelphia PA 19103 215-587-1000
Web: postschell.com

Potestivo & Associates PC
811 S Blvd Ste 100 .... Rochester Hills MI 48307 248-853-4400
Web: www.potestivolaw.com

Potter Anderson & Corroon
Hercules Plz 1313 N Market St .... Wilmington DE 19801 302-984-6000
Web: www.potteranderson.com

Powell, Trachtman, Logan, Carrle & Lombardo PC
475 Allendale Rd Ste 200 .... King Of Prussia PA 19406 610-354-9700
Web: www.powelltrachtman.com

Powers Pyles Sutter & Verville PC
1501 M St NW 7th Fl .... Washington DC 20005 202-466-6550
Web: www.ppsv.com

Powers Vincent m & Associates
411 S 13th St Ste 300 .... Lincoln NE 68508 402-474-8000
Web: vincepowerslaw.com

Poyner & Spruill LLP
301 Fayetteville St Ste 1900 .... Raleigh NC 27601 919-783-6400
Web: www.poynerspruill.com

Pray, Walker, Jackman, Williamson, & Marlar
900 Oneok Plz 100 W Fifth St .... Tulsa OK 74103 918-581-5500
Web: www.praywalker.com

Preis & Roy PLC
Versailles Centre 102 Versailles Blvd
Ste 400 .... Lafayette LA 70501 337-237-6062
Web: www.pkrlaw.com

Pressler & Pressler LLP 7 Entin Rd .... Parsippany NJ 07054 973-753-5100
Web: www.pressler-pressler.com

Preti, Flaherty, Beliveau, Pachios & Haley LLC
45 Memorial Cir .... Augusta ME 04330 207-623-5300
Web: www.preti.com

Price Postel & Parma LLP
200 E Carrillo St Fl 4 .... Santa Barbara CA 93101 805-962-0011
Web: www.melfassett.com

Price, Heneveld, Cooper, De Witt & Litton
695 Kenmoor Ave SE .... Grand Rapids MI 49546 616-949-9610
Web: www.priceheneveld.com

Prickett, Jones & Elliott PA
1310 King St Box 1328 .... Wilmington DE 19899 302-888-6500
Web: prickett.com

Pro Bono Partnership
237 Mamaroneck Ave Ste 300 .... White Plains NY 10605 914-328-0674
Web: www.probonopartner.org

Procopio Cory Hargreaves & Savitch LLP
525 B St Ste 2200 .... San Diego CA 92101 619-238-1900 235-0398
Web: www.procopio.com

Proskauer Rose LLP 1585 Broadway .... New York NY 10036 212-969-3000 969-2900
TF: 866-444-3272 ■ *Web:* www.proskauer.com

Provost-Umphrey Law Firm LLP 490 Park St .... Beaumont TX 77704 409-835-6000
Web: www.provostumphrey.com

Quarles & Brady LLP
411 E Wisconsin Ave Ste 2400 .... Milwaukee WI 53202 414-277-5000 271-3552
TF: 800-654-2200 ■ *Web:* www.quarles.com

Quest Discovery Services Inc
981 Ridder Park Dr .... San Jose CA 95131 408-441-7000
Web: www.questds.com

Quine IP Law Group 2033 Clement Ave Ste 200 .... Alameda CA 94501 510-337-7871
Web: www.quinelaw.com

Quinn, Johnston, Henderson, Pretorius & Cerulo Chartered
227 N E Jefferson St .... Peoria IL 61602 309-674-1133
Web: www.quinnjohnston.com

Rachlin & Wolfson LLP 390 Bay St Ste 1500 .... Toronto ON M5H2Y2 416-367-0202
Web: www.rachlinlaw.com

Rad Law Firm 2001 Beach St Ste 600 .... Fort Worth TX 76103 817-465-8733
TF: 800-598-1090 ■ *Web:* www.radlawfirm.com

Radey Thomas Yon & Clark
301 S Bronough St Ste 200 .... Tallahassee FL 32301 850-425-6654
Web: www.radeylaw.com

Ragan & Ragan p C 3100 Rt 138 W .... Wall Township NJ 07719 732-280-4100
Web: www.raganlaw.com

Phone Fax

Rainwater, Holt & Sexton PA
6315 Ranch Dr ... Little Rock AR 72223 800-434-4800
TF: 800-434-4800 ■ *Web:* www.callrainwater.com
Rajkowski Hansmeier Ltd 11 Seventh Ave N ... Saint Cloud MN 56303 320-251-1055
Web: www.rajhan.com
Rankin, Hill, Porter & Clark LLP
23755 Lorain Rd Ste 200 ... North Olmsted OH 44070 216-566-9700
Web: www.rankinhill.com
Rash, Chapman, Schreiber, Leaverton & Morrison LLP
2112 Rio Grande St ... Austin TX 78705 512-477-7543
Web: www.rashchapman.com
Rawle & Henderson
1339 Chestnut St One S Penn Sq The Widener Bldg
16th Fl ... Philadelphia PA 19107 215-575-4200
Web: www.rawle.com
Recordtrak Inc
651 Allendale Rd PO Box 61591 ... King Of Prussia PA 19406 610-992-5000 354-8946
Redmon, Peyton & Braswell LLP
510 King St Ste 301 ... Alexandria VA 22314 703-684-2000
Web: www.rpb-law.com
Reed Smith 435 Sixth Ave ... Pittsburgh PA 15219 412-288-3131 288-3063
Web: www.reedsmith.com
Rees Broome PC 1900 Gallows Rd ... Tysons Corner VA 22182 703-790-1911
Web: www.reesbroome.com
Reicker, Pfau, Pyle & McRoy LLP
1421 State St Ste B ... Santa Barbara CA 93101 805-966-2440
Web: www.reickerpfau.com
Reilly Like & Tenety
179 Little E Neck Rd ... West Babylon NY 11704 631-669-3000
Relin, Goldstein & Crane LLP
28 E Main St Ste 1800 ... Rochester NY 14614 585-325-6202
TF: 888-984-2351 ■ *Web:* www.rgcattys.net
Reminger & Reminger Company LPa
101 W Prospect Ave ... Cleveland OH 44115 216-687-1311 687-1841
TF: 800-486-1311 ■ *Web:* www.reminger.com
Renaud Cook Drury Mesaros PA
1 N Central Ste 900 ... Phoenix AZ 85004 602-307-9900
Web: www.rcdmlaw.com
Rendigs, Fry, Kiely & Dennis LLP
600 Vine St Ste 2650 ... Cincinnati OH 45202 513-381-9200
TF: 800-274-2330 ■ *Web:* www.rendigs.com
Reuben & Junius LLP 1 Bush St Ste 600 ... San Francisco CA 94104 415-567-9000
Web: www.reubenlaw.com
Reynolds, Mirth, Richards & Farmer LLP
Manulife Pl 10180-101 St Ste 3200 ... Edmonton AB T5J3W8 780-425-9510
TF: 800-661-7673 ■ *Web:* www.rmrf.com
Rhoades McKee PC
55 Campau Ave NW Ste 300 ... Grand Rapids MI 49503 616-235-3500 459-5102
Web: www.rhoadesmckee.com
Richard a Kennedy Law Office
3773 Tibbetts St Ste D ... Riverside CA 92506 951-715-5000
Web: www.richardakennedy.com
Richards Layton & Finger PO Box 551 ... Wilmington DE 19899 302-651-7700 651-7701
Web: www.rlf.com
Rieders, Travis, Humphrey, Harris, Waters, Waffenschmidt & Dohrmann
161 W Third St ... Williamsport PA 17701 570-323-8711
Web: www.riederstravis.com
Riemer & Braunstein LLP 3 Ctr Plz 6th Fl ... Boston MA 02108 617-523-9000
Web: www.riemerlaw.com
Riggs Abney Neal Orbison & Lewis Inc
502 W Sixth St Frisco Bldg ... Tulsa OK 74119 918-587-3161
Web: www.riggsabney.com
Riker, Danzig, Scherer, Hyland & Perretti LLP
1 Speedwell Ave ... Morristown NJ 07962 973-538-0800
Web: www.riker.com
Riley Bennett & Egloff LLP
141 E Washington St 4th Fl ... Indianapolis IN 46204 317-636-8000
Web: www.rbelaw.com
Rinke Noonan
US Bank Plz 1015 W St Germain St Ste 300 ... Saint Cloud MN 56302 320-251-6700
Web: www.rinkenoonan.com
Ritchie, Dillard, Davies & Johnson PC
606 W Main St Ste 300 ... Knoxville TN 37902 865-637-0661
Web: www.rddjlaw.com
Rivkin Radler LLP 926 RXR Plz ... Uniondale NY 11556 516-357-3000
Web: www.rivkinradler.com
Robbins Arroyo LLP 600 B St Ste 1900 ... San Diego CA 92101 619-525-3990
Web: www.robbinsarroyo.com
Roberts & Holland LLP 825 Eighth Ave 37th Fl ... New York NY 10019 212-903-8700
Web: www.robertsandholland.com
Robie & Matthai A Professional Corp
Biltmore Tower 500 S Grand Ave 15th Fl ... Los Angeles CA 90071 213-706-8000
Web: www.romalaw.com
Robinson & Geraldo Prof Corp
ÿ1316 Pennsylvania Ave ... Washington DC 20003 717-232-8525
Web: www.rglaw.net
Robinson & Mcelwee Pllc
700 Virginia St E Ste 400 ... Charleston WV 25301 304-344-5800
Web: ramlaw.com
Robinson & Wood Inc 227 N First St ... San Jose CA 95113 408-298-7120
Web: www.robinsonwood.com
Robinson Bradshaw & Hinson Pa
101 N Tryon St Ste 1900 ... Charlotte NC 28246 704-377-2536 378-4000
Web: www.robinsonbradshaw.com
Rodey Dickason Sloan Akin & Robb P A
201 Third St NW Ste 2200 ... Albuquerque NM 87102 505-765-5900 768-7395
TF: 800-226-2935 ■ *Web:* www.rodey.com
Rogers & Lapan PA 355 Windy Ridge Rd ... Chapel Hill NC 27517 919-545-9259
Web: rogerslapan.com
Roig, Kasperovich, Tutan & Woods PA
1255 S Military Trl Ste 100 ... Deerfield Beach FL 33442 954-834-0330
Web: www.roiglawyers.com
Ropes & Gray LLP 1 International Pl ... Boston MA 02110 617-951-7000 951-7050
Web: www.ropesgray.com

Phone Fax

Rose Law Firm A Professional Assn
120 E Fourth St ... Little Rock AR 72201 501-375-9131 375-1309
Web: www.roselawfirm.com
Rosemarie Arnold Law Offices
1386 Palisade Ave ... Fort Lee NJ 07024 201-461-1111
Web: www.rosemariearnold.com
Rosen Law Firm LLC 18 Broad St Ste 201 ... Charleston SC 29401 843-377-1700
Web: www.rosen-lawfirm.com
Rosenn, Jenkins & Greenwald LLP
15 S Franklin St ... Wilkes-Barre PA 18711 570-826-5600
Web: www.rjglaw.com
Ross & Matthews PC 3650 Lovell Ave ... Fort Worth TX 76107 817-255-2000
TF: 800-458-6982 ■ *Web:* www.rossandmatthews.com
Ross, Banks, May, Cron & Cavin PC
7700 San Felipe Ste 550 ... Houston TX 77063 713-626-1200
TF: 866-896-1492 ■ *Web:* www.rossbanks.com
Ross, Brittain & Schonberg Company LPA
Corporate Plz II 6480 Rockside Woods Blvd S
Ste 350 ... Cleveland OH 44131 216-447-1551
Web: www.rbslaw.com
Rossi Kimms & Mcdowell LLC
20609 Gordon Park Sq Ste 150 ... Ashburn VA 20147 703-726-6020
Web: rkmllp.com
Rothberg Logan & Warsco LLP
505 E Washington Blvd ... Fort Wayne IN 46802 260-422-9454
Web: www.rlwlawfirm.com
Rothman Gordon P.C Grant Bldg 3rd Fl ... Pittsburgh PA 15219 412-338-1100
Web: www.rothmangordon.com
Rourke & Blumenthal LLP
495 S High St Ste 450 ... Columbus OH 43215 614-220-9200
Web: www.randbllp.com
Rowley Chapman & Barney Ltd 63 E Main St Ste 501 ... Mesa AZ 85201 480-833-1113
TF: 888-476-8411 ■ *Web:* www.azlegal.com
Royse Law Firm PC 1717 Embarcadero Rd ... Palo Alto CA 94303 650-813-9700
Web: www.rroyselaw.com
Rubin & Levin PC
500 Marott Ctr 342 Massachusetts Ave ... Indianapolis IN 46204 317-634-0300
Web: www.rubin-levin.com
Rush Moore LLP 737 BISHOP St Ste 2400 ... Honolulu HI 96813 808-521-0400 521-0497
Web: www.rmhawaii.com
Ruskin Moscou Faltischek PC
East Tower 15th Fl 1425 RXR Plz ... Uniondale NY 11556 516-663-6600
Web: www.rmfpc.com
Rusty Hardin & Associates LLP
5 Houston Ctr 1401 McKinney Ste 2250 ... Houston TX 77010 713-652-9000
Web: rustyhardin.com
Ryan Smith & Carbine Ltd
Mead Bldg 98 Merchants Row ... Rutland VT 05702 802-786-1000
Web: www.rsclaw.com
Ryley Carlock & Applewhite Pa
1 N Central Ave Ste 1200 ... Phoenix AZ 85004 602-258-7701 257-9582
Web: www.rcalaw.com
Rywant Alvarez Jones Russo & Guyton pa
407 Courthouse Sq ... Inverness FL 34450 352-341-4441
Web: rywantalvarez.com
Saalfeld Griggs PC
Park Pl 250 Church St SE Ste 200 ... Salem OR 97301 503-399-1070
Web: www.sglaw.com
Sachs Waldman Pc 1000 Farmer St ... Detroit MI 48226 313-965-3464
TF: 800-638-6722 ■ *Web:* www.sachswaldman.com
Sackett & Associates 1055 Lincoln Ave ... San Jose CA 95125 408-295-7755
TF: 800-913-3000 ■ *Web:* www.sackettlaw.com
Sacks Tierney PA
4250 N Drinkwater Blvd 4th Fl ... Scottsdale AZ 85251 480-425-2600
Web: www.sackstierney.com
Salvi & Schostok Pc
218 N Martin Luther King Jr Ave ... Waukegan IL 60085 847-249-1227
Web: www.salvilaw.com
Samuels, Miller, Schroeder, Jackson & Sly LLP
225 N Water St Ste 301 ... Decatur IL 62523 217-429-4325
Web: www.samuelsmiller.com
Saul Ewing LLP
Centre Sq W 1500 Market St 38th Fl ... Philadelphia PA 19102 215-972-7777
Web: www.saul.com
Saxe Doernberger & Vita PC 1952 Whitney Ave ... Hamden CT 06517 203-287-2100
Web: www.sdvlaw.com
Schaefer The Law Firm of John f
380 N Old Woodward Ave Ste 320 ... Birmingham MI 48009 248-642-6655
Web: lfjfs.com
Scheef & Stone LLP 500 N Akard St Ste 2700 ... Dallas TX 75201 214-706-4200
Web: www.solidcounsel.com
Schiff Hardin LLP
233 S Wacker Dr 6600 Sears Tower ... Chicago IL 60606 312-258-5500 258-5600
Web: www.schiffhardin.com
Schiller & Knapp LLP 950 New Loudon Rd Ste 109 ... Latham NY 12110 518-786-9069
Web: www.schillerknapp.com
Schindler Cohen & Hochman LLP
100 Wall St 15th Fl ... New York NY 10005 212-277-6300
Web: www.schlaw.com
Schlachman, Belsky & Weiner PA
300 E Lombard St Ste 1100 ... Baltimore MD 21202 410-685-2022
Web: www.sbwlaw.com
Schlichter, Bogard & Denton
100 S Fourth St Ste 900 ... St. Louis MO 63102 314-621-6115
TF: 800-873-5297 ■ *Web:* uselaws.com
Schneiderman & Sherman
23938 Research Dr Ste 300 ... Farmington Hills MI 48335 248-539-7400
TF: 866-867-7688 ■ *Web:* sspclegal.com
Schroeder Group, The
20800 Swenson Dr Ste 475 ... Waukesha WI 53186 262-798-8220
TF: 800-372-3020 ■ *Web:* www.tsglaw.com
Schulte Roth & Zabel LLP 919 Third Ave ... New York NY 10022 212-756-2000 593-5955
Web: www.srz.com
Schwartz Hannum PC 11 Chestnut St ... Andover MA 01810 978-623-0900
Web: shpclaw.com

Phone Fax

Schwartz Semerdjian Ballard & Cauley LLP
101 W Broadway Ste 810 San Diego CA 92101 619-236-8821
Web: www.schwartzsemerdjian.com
Scolaro, Shulman, Cohen, Fetter & Burstein PC
Franklin Sq 507 Plum St Ste 300 Syracuse NY 13204 315-471-8111
Web: www.scolaro.com
Scopelitis , Garvin , Light , Hanson & Feary PLC
600 Republic Centre 633 Chestnut St Chattanooga TN 37450 423-266-2769
Web: www.scopelitis.com
Searcy Denney Scarola Barnhart
Po Box 3626 West Palm Beach FL 33402 561-686-6300
TF: 800-780-8607 ■ *Web:* www.searcylaw.com
Sebaly Shillito & Dyer
1900 Kettering Tower 40 N Main St Dayton OH 45423 937-222-2500
Web: ssdlaw.com
Secrest Wardle Lynch Hampton
Po Box 3040 Farmington Hills MI 48333 248-851-9500
Web: www.secrestwardle.com
Seder & Chandler 339 Main St Burnside Bldg Worcester MA 01608 508-757-7721
Web: www.sederlaw.com
Seed Mackall & Cole LLP
1332 Anacapa St Ste 200 Santa Barbara CA 93101 805-963-0669
Web: seedmackall.com
Selman Breitman LLP 11766 Wilshire Blvd Los Angeles CA 90025 310-445-0800 473-2525
Web: selmanbreitman.com
Seltzer Caplan Mcmahon Vitek
2100 Symphony Towers 750 B St San Diego CA 92101 619-685-3003
Web: www.scmv.com
Serratelli Schiffman Brown & Calhoon
2080 Linglestown Rd Ste 201 Harrisburg PA 17110 717-540-9170
Web: www.skellydrc.com
Settle & Pou PC 3333 Lee Pkwy 8th Fl Dallas TX 75219 214-520-3300
TF: 800-538-4661 ■ *Web:* www.settlepou.com
Seward & Kissel 1 Battery Pk Plaza Ste 19 New York NY 10004 212-574-1200 480-8421
Web: www.sewkis.com
Seyfarth Shaw LLP 131 S Dearborn St Ste 2400 Chicago IL 60603 312-460-5000 460-7000
Web: www.seyfarth.com
Sharp & Cobos PC
4705 Spicewood Springs Rd Ste 100 Austin TX 78759 512-473-2265
Web: sharpcobos.com
Shartsis Friese & Ginsburg LLP
1 Maritime Plz 18th Fl San Francisco CA 94111 415-421-6500 421-2922
Web: www.sflaw.com
Shean Law Offices 1114 N College Ave Bloomington IN 47404 812-332-3643
TF: 877-743-2652 ■ *Web:* www.sheanlaw.com
Shearman & Sterling LLP 599 Lexington Ave New York NY 10022 212-848-4000 848-7179
Web: www.shearman.com
Shepherd, Finkelman, Miller & Shah LLP
65 Main St Chester CT 06412 860-526-1100
Web: www.sfmslaw.com
Sheppard Mullin Richter & Hampton LLP
333 S Hope St 48th Fl Los Angeles CA 90071 213-620-1780 620-1398
Web: www.sheppardmullin.com
Shermeta, Adams & Von Allmen PC
901 Tower Dr Ste 400 Troy MI 48098 248-519-1700
Web: www.shermeta.com
Shernoff Bidart Darras & Echeverria LLP
600 S Indian Hill Blvd Claremont CA 91711 909-621-4935
Web: shernoff.com
Sherrard Kuzz LLP 155 University Ave Toronto ON M5H3B7 416-603-0700
Web: www.sherrardkuzz.com
Shook & Stone Attorneys at Law
710 S Fourth St Las Vegas NV 89101 702-385-2220
Web: www.shookandstone.com
Shook Hardy & Bacon LLP 2555 Grand Blvd Kansas City MO 64108 816-474-6550 421-5547
TF: 855-380-7584 ■ *Web:* www.shb.com
Siben & Siben LLP 90 E Mn St Bay Shore NY 11706 631-665-3400
Web: www.sibensiben.com
Sidley Austin LLP 787 Seventh Ave New York NY 10019 312-853-7000 853-7036
TF: 800-306-5230 ■ *Web:* www.sidley.com
Sieben Polk PA 1640 S Frontage Rd Ste 200 Hastings MN 55033 651-437-3148
TF: 800-620-1829 ■ *Web:* www.siebenpolklaw.com
Siemer, Austin, Resch, Fuhr & Totten
307 N Third St Effingham IL 62401 217-342-9291
Web: siemeraustin.com
Sigman Janssen Stack Sewall & Pitz
303 S Memorial Dr Appleton WI 54911 920-731-5201
Web: www.sigmanlegal.com
Sills Cummis & Gross PC
1 Riverfront Plz The Legal Center Newark NJ 07102 973-643-7000
Web: www.sillscummis.com
Silver & Archibald LLP 997 S Milledge Ave Athens GA 30605 706-548-8122
TF: 877-526-6281 ■ *Web:* silverandarchibald.com
Silver Golub & Teitell LLP 184 Atlantic St Stamford CT 06904 203-325-4491
Web: www.sgtlaw.com
Simmons Perrine Moyer Bergman PLC
115 Third St SE Ste 1200 Cedar Rapids IA 52401 319-366-7641
Web: www.simmonsperrine.com
Simon & Geherin PLLC 1310 S Main St Ste 11 Ann Arbor MI 48104 734-997-0870
Web: www.simongeherin.com
Simpson Thacher & Bartlett LLP
425 Lexington Ave New York NY 10017 212-455-2000 455-2502
Web: www.stblaw.com
Sindel, Sindel & Noble PC
8008 Carondelet Ave Ste 301 Saint Louis MO 63105 314-721-6040
TF: 866-489-5504 ■ *Web:* www.sindellaw.com
Sirote & Permutt Pc
2311 Highland Ave S PO Box 55727 Birmingham AL 35205 205-930-5100 930-5101
Web: www.sirote.com
Siskinds LLP 680 Waterloo St PO Box 2520 London ON N6A3V8 519-672-2121
TF: 877-672-2121 ■ *Web:* www.siskinds.com
Skadden Arps Slate Meagher & Flom LLP
4 Times Sq New York NY 10036 212-735-3000 735-2000
Web: www.skadden.com

Phone Fax

Skoler, Abbott & Presser PC
1 Monarch Pl Ste 2000 Springfield MA 01144 413-737-4753
Web: skoler-abbott.com
Slack & Davis LLP 2705 Bee Caves Rd Ste 220 Austin TX 78746 512-795-8686
TF: 800-455-8686 ■ *Web:* www.slackdavis.com
Slevin & Hart PC
1625 Massachusetts Ave NW Ste 450 Washington DC 20036 202-797-8700
Web: www.slevinhart.com
Slover & Loftus LLP 1224 17th St NW Washington DC 20036 202-347-7170
Web: www.sloverandloftus.com
Slutzky Wolfe & Bailey LLP
2255 Cumberland Pkwy Se Ste 1300 Atlanta GA 30339 770-438-8000
Web: swbatl.com
Smith Bovill Pc 200 Saint Andrews Rd Saginaw MI 48638 989-792-9641
Web: www.smithbovill.com
Smith Hartvigsen PLLC
The Walker Ctr 175 South Main St
Ste 300 Salt Lake City UT 84111 801-413-1600
TF: 877-825-2064 ■ *Web:* www.smithhartvigsen.com
Smith Hulsey & Busey
225 Water St Ste 1800 Jacksonville FL 32202 904-359-7700 359-7708
Web: www.smithhulsey.com
Smith Katzenstein & Furlow LLP
The Corporate Plz 800 Delaware Ave Wilmington DE 19899 302-652-8400
Smith Keller Miner & O'shea
69 Delaware Ave Rm 1212 Buffalo NY 14202 716-855-3611
Web: www.smithminerlaw.com
Smith Mazure Director Wilkins Young & Yagerman PC
111 John St 20th Fl New York NY 10038 212-964-7400
Web: www.smithmazure.com
Smith Peterson Law Office
133 W Broadway PO Box 249 Council Bluffs IA 51503 712-328-1833
Web: www.smithpeterson.com
Smith, Anderson, Blount, Dorsett, Mitchell & Jernigan LLP
2500 First Union Capitol Center Raleigh NC 27602 919-821-1220
Web: www.smithlaw.com
Smith, Sovik, Kendrick & Sugnet PC
250 S Clinton St Ste 600 Syracuse NY 13202 315-474-2911
TF: 800-675-0011 ■ *Web:* www.smithsovik.com
Snell & Wilmer LLP
1 Arizona Ctr 400 E Van Buren St Ste 1900 Phoenix AZ 85004 602-382-6000 382-6070
TF: 800-322-0430 ■ *Web:* www.swlaw.com
Snow Christensen & Martineau
10 Exchange Pl Salt Lake City UT 84111 801-521-9000
Web: www.scmlaw.com
Solem, Mack & Steinhoff PC
3333 S Bannock St Ste 900 Englewood CO 80110 303-761-4900
Web: solemlaw.com
Somach Simmons & Dunn
500 Capitol Mall Ste 1000 Sacramento CA 95814 916-446-7979
Web: www.somachlaw.com
Sorling, Northrup, Hanna, Cullen & et al
607 E Adams St Illinois Bldg Ste 800 Springfield IL 62705 217-544-1144
Web: www.sorlinglaw.com
Southern Environmental Law Center
201 W Main St Ste 14 Charlottesville VA 22902 434-977-4090
Web: www.southernenvironment.org
Sowell Gray Stepp & Laffitte LLC
1310 Gadsden St Columbia SC 29211 803-929-1400
Web: www.sowell.com
Spangler, Jennings & Dougherty PC
8396 Mississippi St Merrillville IN 46410 219-769-2323
Web: www.sjdlaw.com
Spector Gadon & Rosen PC
7 Penn Ctr 7th Fl 1635 Market St Philadelphia PA 19103 215-241-8888
Web: www.lawsgr.com
Spence Law Firm LLC 15 S Jackson St Jackson WY 83001 307-733-7290 733-5248
TF: 800-967-2117 ■ *Web:* www.spencelawyers.com
Spencer Fane Britt & Browne LLP
1000 Walnut St Ste 1400 Kansas City MO 64106 816-474-8100 474-3216
Web: www.spencerfane.com
Spilman Thomas & Battle PLLC
Spilman Cntr 300 Knwh Blv Spilman Ctr Spilman Center
Ste 100 Charleston WV 25301 304-340-3838
TF: 800-967-8251 ■ *Web:* www.spilmanlaw.com
Squire Patton Boggs 2550 M St NW Washington DC 20037 202-457-6000 457-6315
Web: www.pattonboggs.com
Squire Patton Boggs
127 Public Sq 4900 Key Tower Cleveland OH 44114 216-479-8500 479-8780
Web: www.squirepattonboggs.com
St. Onge Steward Johnston & Reens LLC
986 Bedford St Stamford CT 06905 203-324-6155
Web: www.ssjr.com
Stanley, Lande & Hunter A Professional Corp
301 Iowa Ave Ste 400 Muscatine IA 52761 563-264-5000
Web: www.slhlaw.com
Stark & Knoll Company LPA 3475 Ridgewood Rd Akron OH 44333 330-376-3300
Web: www.stark-knoll.com
Stark & Stark 993 Lenox Dr Bldg 2 Lawrenceville NJ 08648 609-896-9060 896-0629
TF: 800-535-3425 ■ *Web:* www.stark-stark.com
Starr & Associates PC
4245 N Central Expy Ste 350 Dallas TX 75205 214-219-8440
Stearns Weaver Miller Weissler Alhadeff & Sitterson P.A.
150 W Flagler St Ste 2200 Miami FL 33130 305-789-3200 789-3395
TF: 866-293-7866 ■ *Web:* stearnsweaver.com
Steele Law Firm p C The 949 County Rt 53 Oswego NY 13126 315-216-4721
TF: 877-496-2687 ■ *Web:* www.thesteelelawfirm.com
Stein Monast LLP 70 rue Dalhousie Bureau 300 Quebec QC G1K4B2 418-529-6531
Web: www.steinmonast.ca
Stein Sperling Bennett De Jong Driscoll & Greenfeig PC
25 W Middle Ln Rockville MD 20850 301-340-2020
Web: www.steinsperling.com
Steptoe & Johnson LLP
1330 Connecticut Ave NW Washington DC 20036 202-429-3000 429-3902
Web: www.steptoe.com

Phone | Fax

Steptoe & Johnson PLLC
400 White Oaks Blvd ... Bridgeport WV 26330 304-933-8000
Web: www.steptoe-johnson.com

Steven Brian Davis Law Offices
12396 World Trade Dr Ste 115 ... San Diego CA 92128 858-451-1004
Web: needattorney.org

Stevens & Lee PC 111 N Sixth St ... Reading PA 19603 610-478-2000
Web: www.stevenslee.com

Stewart Sokol & Gray LLC
2300 Sw First Ave Ste 200 ... Portland OR 97201 503-221-0699
Web: lawssg.com

Stichter, Riedel, Blain & Prosser PA
110 E Madison St Ste 200 ... Tampa FL 33602 813-229-0144
Web: www.srbp.com

Stidham & Associates PSC
401 Lewis Hargett Cir Ste 250 ... Lexington KY 40503 859-219-2255
Web: www.stidhamlaw.com

Stikeman Elliott LLP
1155 Rene-levesque Blvd W 40th Fl ... Montreal QC H3B3V2 514-397-3000
Web: www.stikeman.com

Stoel Rives LLP 760 SW 9th Ave Ste 3000 ... Portland OR 97205 503-224-3380
Web: www.stoel.com

Stokes Lazarus & Carmichael
2018 Power Ferry RD STE 700 ... Atlanta GA 30339 404-352-1465
Web: www.scelaw.com

Stoll Stoll Berne Lokting & Shlachter PC
209 SW Oak St Ste 500 ... Portland OR 97204 503-227-1600
Web: www.ssbls.com

Stone Pigman Walther Wittmann LLC
546 Carondelet St ... New Orleans LA 70130 504-581-3200
Web: www.stonepigman.com

Storch Amini & Munves PC
2 Grand Central Tower 140 E 45th St 25th Fl ... New York NY 10017 212-490-4100
Web: samlegal.com

Strauss & Troy 150 E Fourth St ... Cincinnati OH 45202 513-621-2120 241-8259
Web: www.strausstroy.com

Strip Hoppers Leithart Mcgrath
575 S Third St ... Columbus OH 43215 614-228-6345
Web: columbuslawyer.net

Stroock & Stroock & Lavan LLP 180 Maiden Ln ... New York NY 10038 212-806-5400
Web: www.stroock.com

Stroud, Willink & Howard LLC
25 W Main St Ste 300 PO Box 2236 ... Madison WI 53701 608-257-2281
Web: www.stroudlaw.com

Stueve Siegel Hanson LLP
460 Nichols Rd Ste 200 ... Kansas City MO 64112 816-714-7100
TF: 800-714-0360 ■ *Web:* stuevesiegel.com

Sturgill, Turner, Barker & Moloney PLLC
333 W Vine St Ste 1400 ... Lexington KY 40507 859-255-8581
Web: www.sturgillturner.com

Sughrue Mion PLLC
2100 Pennsylvania Ave NW Ste 800 ... Washington DC 20037 202-293-7060
Web: www.sughrue.com

Suiter Swantz Pc Llo 14301 Fnb Pkwy Ste 220 ... Omaha NE 68154 402-496-0300
Web: www.suiter.com

Sullivan & Cromwell LLP 125 Broad St ... New York NY 10004 212-558-4000 558-3588
Web: www.sullcrom.com

Sullivan Hincks & Conway
120 W 22nd St Ste 100 ... Oak Brook IL 60523 630-573-5021
Web: www.shlawfirm.com

Sulloway & Hollis
9 Capitol St & 29 School St ... Concord NH 03301 603-224-2341
Web: www.sulloway.com

Summit Law Group PLLC
315 Fifth Ave S Ste 1000 ... Seattle WA 98104 206-676-7000
Web: www.summitlaw.com

Sundahl Powers Kapp & Martin LLC
1725 Carey Ave ... Cheyenne WY 82001 307-632-6421
Web: www.spkm.org

Sutherland Asbill & Brennan LLP
999 Peachtree St NE ... Atlanta GA 30309 404-853-8000 853-8806
TF: 855-857-9769 ■ *Web:* www.sutherland.com

Sutin Thayer & Browne
6565 Americas Pkwy N E Two Park Sq
Ste 1000 ... Albuquerque NM 87110 505-883-2500
Web: sutinfirm.com

Swanson & Bratschun LLC 8210 SouthPark Ter ... Littleton CO 80120 303-268-0066
Web: www.sbiplaw.com

Sweeney Law Firm 8109 Lima Rd ... Fort Wayne IN 46818 260-420-3137
TF: 866-793-6339 ■ *Web:* sweeneylawfirm.com

Sweet, Stevens, Katz & Williams LLP
331 E Butler Ave ... New Britain PA 18901 215-345-9111
Web: sweetstevens.com

Szabo, Zelnick & Erickson PC
12610 Lk Ridge Dr ... Woodbridge VA 22192 703-494-7171
Web: zelnickerickson.com

Tabet DiVito & Rothstein LLC
The Rookery Bldg 209 S LaSalle St 7th Fl ... Chicago IL 60604 312-762-9450
Web: www.tdrlawfirm.com

Taggart Morton LLC
2100 Energy Ctr 1100 Poydras St ... New Orleans LA 70163 504-599-8500
Web: www.taggartmortonlaw.com

Taylor Law Offices Pc 122 E Washington Ave ... Effingham IL 62401 800-879-2250
TF: 800-879-2250 ■ *Web:* taylorlaw.net

Taylor Wellons Politz & Duhe Aplc
8550 United Plz Blvd Ste 101 ... Baton Rouge LA 70809 225-387-9888
TF: 877-850-1047 ■ *Web:* www.twpdlaw.com

Taylor, Porter, Brooks & Phillips
451 Florida St 8th Fl ... Baton Rouge LA 70801 225-387-3221
Web: www.taylorporter.com

Teplitsky, Colson LLP 70 Bond St Ste 200 ... Toronto ON M5B1X3 416-365-9320
Web: www.teplitskycolson.com

Terra Law LLP 177 Park Ave 3rd Fl ... San Jose CA 95113 408-299-1200
Web: www.terra-law.com

Texas Legal Services Center Inc
815 Brazos St Ste 1100 ... Austin TX 78701 512-477-6000
TF: 888-343-4414 ■ *Web:* www.tlsc.org

Thompson & Bowie LLP 3 Canal Plz ... Portland ME 04112 207-774-2500
Web: thompsonbowie.com

Thompson & Knight LLP
1700 Pacific Ave Ste 3300 ... Dallas TX 75201 214-969-1700 969-1751
Web: www.tklaw.com

Thompson & McMullan 100 Shockoe Slip ... Richmond VA 23219 804-649-7545
Web: www.t-mlaw.com

Thompson Coe Cousins & irons
700 N Pearl St 25th Fl ... Dallas TX 75201 214-871-8200 871-8209
Web: www.thompsoncoe.com

Thompson Hine LLP
127 Public Sq 3900 Key Ctr ... Cleveland OH 44114 216-566-5500 566-5800
TF: 877-257-3382 ■ *Web:* www.thompsonhine.com

Thompson, O'Brien, Kemp & Nasuti PC
40 Technology Pkwy S Ste 300 ... Norcross GA 30092 770-925-0111
Web: www.tokn.com

Thornton, Davis & Fein PA
1221 Brickell Ave Ste 1600 ... Miami FL 33131 305-446-2646
Web: www.tdflaw.com

Thorp Reed & Armstrong LLP
301 Grant St 14th Fl ... Pittsburgh PA 15219 412-394-7711 394-2555
TF: 800-949-3120 ■ *Web:* clarkhill.com

Thorpe, North & Western LLP
8180 South 700 East Ste 350 ... Sandy UT 84070 801-566-6633
Web: www.tnw.com

Thorsnes Bartolotta McGuire
2550 Fifth Ave 11th Fl ... San Diego CA 92103 619-236-9363
Web: tbmlawyers.com

Timoney Knox LLP 400 Maryland Dr ... Fort Washington PA 19034 215-646-6000
Web: www.timoneyknox.com

Timothy M. Cary & Associates
3300 Cameron Park Dr Ste 2000 ... Cameron Park CA 95682 530-672-7601
Web: carylaw.com

Tompkins Mc Guire Wachenfeld & Barry
100 Mulberry St ... Newark NJ 07102 973-622-3000 623-7780
Web: www.tompkinsmcguire.com

Tousley Brain Stephens PLLC
1700 Seventh Ave Ste 2200 ... Seattle WA 98101 206-682-5600
Web: www.tousley.com

Townsend James r 150 Dufferin Ave ... London ON N6A5N6 519-672-5272
TF: 888-354-0448 ■ *Web:* www.ftgalaw.com

Triplett Woolf & Garretson LLC
2959 N Rock Rd -Ste 300 ... Wichita KS 67226 316-630-8100
Web: www.twgfirm.com

Tripp Scott 110 SE Sixth St 15th Fl ... Fort Lauderdale FL 33301 954-525-7500
Web: www.trippscott.com

Trojan Law Offices
9250 Wilshire Blvd Ste 325 ... Beverly Hills CA 90212 310-777-8399
Web: www.trojanlawoffices.com

Troutman Sanders LLP
600 Peachtree St NE Ste 5200 ... Atlanta GA 30308 404-885-3000 885-3900
Web: www.troutmansanders.com

Tucker Arensberg Inc 1500 1 PPG Pl ... Pittsburgh PA 15222 412-566-1212 594-5619
Web: www.tuckerlaw.com

Tucker Ellis & West LLP 925 Euclid Ave ... Cleveland OH 44115 216-592-5000 592-5009
Web: tuckerellis.com

Tully Rinckey PLLC 441 New Karner Rd ... Albany NY 12205 518-218-7100
Web: www.tullylegal.com

Turner & Burney Pc Attorneys 105 W Public Sq ... Laurens SC 29360 864-984-6565
Web: www.turnerandburney.com

Turner, Padget, Graham & Laney PA
1901 Main St 17th Fl ... Columbia SC 29202 803-254-2200
Web: www.turnerpadget.com

Turocy & Watson LLP
Key Tower 127 Public Sq 57th Fl ... Cleveland OH 44114 216-696-8730
Web: www.thepatentattorneys.com

Twomey, Latham, Shea, Kelley, Dubin & Quartararo LLP
33 W Second St PO Box 9398 ... Riverhead NY 11901 631-727-2180
Web: www.suffolklaw.com

Udall Shumway PLC 1138 N Alma School Rd Ste 101 ... Mesa AZ 85201 480-461-5300
Web: www.udallshumway.com

Ulmer & Berne 1660 W Second St Ste 1100 ... Cleveland OH 44113 216-583-7000
Web: www.ulmer.com

Underwood Attorneys & Counselors at Law
1111 W Loop 289 ... Lubbock TX 79416 806-793-1711
Web: www.uwlaw.com

Unruh, Turner, Burke & Frees PC
17 W Gay St ... West Chester PA 19381 610-692-1371
Web: www.utbf.com

Updike Kelly & Spellacy Pc PO Box 231277 ... Hartford CT 06123 860-548-2600
Web: www.uks.com

Valensi Rose PLC
1888 Century Park E Ste 1100 ... Los Angeles CA 90067 310-277-8011
Web: www.vrmlaw.com

Van Der Hout Brigagliano & Nightingale LLP
180 Sutter St Fl 5 ... San Francisco CA 94104 650-688-6020
Web: www.vblaw.com

Van Winkle Buck Wall Starnes & Davis PA
11 N Market St ... Asheville NC 28801 828-258-2991
Web: www.vwlawfirm.com

Vann & Sheridan LLP
1720 Hillsborough St Ste 200 ... Raleigh NC 27605 919-510-8585
Web: vannattorneys.com

Venable LLP 575 Seventh St NW ... Washington DC 20004 202-344-4000 344-8300
Web: www.venable.com

Ver Ploeg & Lumpkin PA
Miami Twr 100 SE Second St 30th Fl ... Miami FL 33131 305-577-3996
Web: www.vpl-law.com

Vernis & Bowling of Miami PA 1680 NE 135th St ... Miami FL 33181 305-895-3035
Web: www.florida-law.com

Verrill Dana LLP PO Box 586 ... Portland ME 04112 207-774-4000 774-7499
Web: www.verrilldana.com

Firm	City	State	ZIP	Phone	Fax
Victim Rights Law Center Inc 115 Broad St Fl 3 *Web:* www.victimrights.org	Boston	MA	02110	617-399-6720	
Vinson & Elkins LLP 1001 Fannin St 1st City Tower Ste 2500 *TF:* 877-610-2009 ■ *Web:* www.velaw.com	Houston	TX	77002	713-758-2222	758-2346
Visa Law Group 1806 11th St Nw *Web:* www.visalawgroup.com	Washington	DC	20001	202-265-7530	
Vogel Law Firm 218 NP Ave *Web:* www.vogellaw.com	Fargo	ND	58107	701-237-6983	
Vorys Sater Seymour & Pease LLP (VSSP) 52 E Gay St PO Box 1008 *Web:* www.vorys.com	Columbus	OH	43216	614-464-6400	464-6350
Vrdolyak Law Group LLC 741 N Dearborn St *Web:* www.vrdolyak.com	Chicago	IL	60654	312-482-8200	
Wagner Falconer & Judd Ltd 100 S 5th St Ste 800 *Web:* www.wfjlawfirm.com	Minneapolis	MN	55402	612-339-1421	
Wagner Johnston & Rosenthal 5855 Sandy Springs Cir Ste 300 *Web:* www.wjrlaw.com	Atlanta	GA	30328	404-261-0500	
Wagstaff & Cartmell LLP 4740 Grand Ave Ste 300 *Web:* www.wagstaffcartmell.com	Kansas City	MO	64112	816-701-1100	
Wai & Connor LLP 2566 Overland Ave Ste 570 *Web:* www.waiconnor.com	Los Angeles	CA	90064	310-838-6800	
Walker & Jocke Company LPA 231 S Broadway *Web:* www.walkerandjocke.com	Medina	OH	44256	330-721-0000	
Walker, Morgan & Kinard 135 E Main St *Web:* walkermorgan.com	Lexington	SC	29072	803-359-6194	
Wallace Saunders Austin Brown Enochs 200 W Douglas Ave Ste 400 *Web:* wallacesaunders.com	Wichita	KS	67202	316-269-2100	
Waller Lansden Dortch & Davis Nashville City Ctr 511 Union St Ste 2700 *Web:* www.wallerlaw.com	Nashville	TN	37219	615-850-8487	
Walter | Haverfield LLP 1300 Terminal Tower *Web:* www.walterhav.com	Cleveland	OH	44113	216-781-1212	
Walton Lantaff Schroeder & Carson LLP 9350 S Dixie Hwy 10th Fl *Web:* www.atlanticcivil.com	Miami	FL	33156	305-671-1300	
Ward & Smith 1001 College Ct *Web:* www.wardandsmith.com	New Bern	NC	28563	252-672-5400	
Ward, Murray, Pace & Johnson PC 202 E Fifth St *Web:* www.wmpj.com	Sterling	IL	61081	815-625-8200	
Waters & Kraus LLP 3219 McKinney Ave *Web:* www.waterskraus.com	Dallas	TX	75204	214-357-6244	
Watt, Beckworth, Thompson Henneman & Sullivan LLP 1800 Pennzoil Pl 711 Louisiana St *Web:* www.wthllp.com	Houston	TX	77002	713-650-8100	
Weber Gallagher Simpson Stapleton Fires & Newby LLP 2000 Market St Ste 1300 *Web:* www.wglaw.com	Philadelphia	PA	19103	215-972-7900	
Weil Gotshal & Manges LLP 767 Fifth Ave *Web:* www.weil.com	New York	NY	10153	212-310-8000	310-8007
Weiner Lesniak LLP 629 Parsippany Rd *Web:* www.weinerlesniak.com	Parsippany	NJ	07054	973-403-1100	
Weir & Partners LLP The Widener Bldg 1339 Chestnut St Ste 500 *Web:* www.weirpartners.com	Philadelphia	PA	19107	215-665-8181	
WeirFoulds LLP 4100 - 66 Wellington St W Toronto-Dominion Centre PO Box 35 *Web:* www.weirfoulds.com	Toronto	ON	M5K1B7	416-365-1110	
Welborn Sullivan Meck & Tooley 821 17th St Ste 500 *Web:* www.wsmtlaw.com	Denver	CO	80202	303-830-2500	
Welch Gold & Siegel Pc 428 Forbes Ave Ste 1240 *Web:* www.wgspc.com	Pittsburgh	PA	15219	412-391-1014	
Wendel, Rosen, Black & Dean LLP 1111 Broadway 24th Fl *Web:* www.wendel.com	Oakland	CA	94607	510-834-6600	
Westchase Law Group pa 12029 Whitmarsh Ln *Web:* www.westchaselaw.com	Tampa	FL	33626	813-490-5211	
Westman Champlin & Kelly 900 Second Ave S *Web:* www.wck.com	Minneapolis	MN	55402	612-334-3222	
Weston Hurd LLP The Tower at Erieview 1301 E Ninth St Ste 1900 *Web:* www.westonhurd.com	Cleveland	OH	44114	216-241-6602	
Wharton Levin Ehrmantraut & Klein Profit Sharing Plan 104 W St *Web:* www.wlekn.com	Annapolis	MD	21404	410-263-5900	
Wheeler, Van Sickle & Anderson SC 44 E Mifflin St Ste 1000 *Web:* wheelerlaw.com	Madison	WI	53703	608-255-7277	
White Buffalo Club 160 West Gill Ave Ste 200 *TF:* 888-256-8182 ■ *Web:* whitebuffaloclub.com	Jackson	WY	83001	307-734-4900	
Whiteford, Taylor & Preston LLP 7 Saint Paul St *Web:* www.wtplaw.com	Baltimore	MD	21202	410-347-8700	
Whitfield & Eddy PLC 699 Walnut St Ste 2000 *Web:* www.whitfieldlaw.com	Des Moines	IA	50309	515-288-6041	246-1474
Wiggins, Childs, Quinn & Pantazis LLC The Kress Bldg 301 19th St N *Web:* www.wigginschilds.com	Birmingham	AL	35203	205-314-0500	
Wiley Rein LLP 1776 K St N W *Web:* www.wileyrein.com	Washington	DC	20006	202-719-7000	
Wilkinson Barker Knauer LLP 2300 N St NW Ste 700 *Web:* www.wbklaw.com	Washington	DC	20037	202-783-4141	
Willcox, Buyck & Williams PA 248 W Evans St *Web:* www.willcoxlaw.com	Florence	SC	29501	843-662-3258	
William W Price PA 320 Fern St *Web:* www.wpricepa.com	West Palm Beach	FL	33401	561-659-3212	
Williams & Anderson PLC 111 Ctr St Ste 2200 *Web:* williamsanderson.com	Little Rock	AR	72201	501-372-0800	372-6453
Williams & Connolly LLP 725 12th St NW *Web:* www.wc.com	Washington	DC	20005	202-434-5000	434-5029
Williams & Petro Company LLC 338 S High St 2nd Fl *Web:* williamsandpetro.com	Columbus	OH	43215	614-224-0531	
Williams Mullen 1021 E Cary St James Ctr Two *Web:* www.williamsmullen.com	Richmond	VA	23219	804-643-1991	
Williams Parker Harrison Dietz & Getzen Professional Association 200 S Orange Ave *Web:* www.williamsparker.com	Sarasota	FL	34236	941-366-4800	
Williams, Kastner & Gibbs PLLC 2 Union Sq 601 Union St Ste 4100 *Web:* www.williamskastner.com	Seattle	WA	98101	206-628-6600	
Williams, Turner & Holmes PC 200 N Sixth St Ste 103 *TF:* 800-548-6528 ■ *Web:* www.wth-law.com	Grand Junction	CO	81501	970-242-6262	
Willkie Farr & Gallagher LLP 787 Seventh Ave 2nd Fl *Web:* www.willkie.com	New York	NY	10019	212-728-8000	728-8111
Wilmer Cutler Pickering Hale & Dorr LLP 1875 Pennsylvania Ave *Web:* www.wilmerhale.com	Washington	DC	20006	202-663-6000	663-6363
Wilson Elser Moskowitz Edelman & Dicker LLP 150 E 42nd St *Web:* www.wilsonelser.com	New York	NY	10017	212-490-3000	490-3038
Wilson Sonsini Goodrich & Rosati 650 Page Mill Rd *Web:* www.wsgr.com	Palo Alto	CA	94304	650-493-9300	493-6811
Wilson, Sheehy, Knowles, Robertson & Cornelius PC 909 ESE Loop 323 Ste 400 *Web:* www.wilsonlawfirm.com	Tyler	TX	75701	903-509-5000	
Windels Marx Ln Mittendorf LLP 156 W 56th St *Web:* www.windelsmarx.com	New York	NY	10019	212-237-1000	262-1215
Winderweedle, Haines, Ward & Woodman PA 329 Park Ave N Second Fl 32789 Post Office Box 880 *Web:* www.whww.com	Winter Park	FL	32790	407-423-4246	
Winet, Patrick & Weaver 1215 W Vista Way *Web:* www.wpgch.com	Vista	CA	92083	760-758-4261	
Winstead PC 1201 Elm St 5400 Renaissance Tower *Web:* www.winstead.com	Dallas	TX	75270	214-745-5400	
Winthrop & Weinstine PA 225 S Sixth St Ste 3500 *Web:* www.winthrop.com	Minneapolis	MN	55402	612-604-6400	
Wisler Pearlstine LLP 460 Norristown Rd Ste 110 *Web:* www.wislerpearlstine.com	Blue Bell	PA	19422	610-825-8400	
Wojtalewicz Law Firm Ltd 139 N Miles St *Web:* wojtalewiczlawfirm.com	Appleton	MN	56208	320-289-2363	
Wolfe Jones Boswell & Wolfe Hancock & Daniel LLC 905 Bob Wallace Ave Sw *Web:* www.wjb-law.com	Huntsville	AL	35801	256-534-2205	
Wolff, Hill, McFarlin & Herron PA 1851 W Colonial Dr *Web:* www.whmh.com	Orlando	FL	32804	407-648-0058	
Wolk Law Firm, The 1712 Locust St *Web:* wolklawfirm.com	Philadelphia	PA	19103	215-545-4220	
Womble Carlyle Sandridge & Rice PLLC 1 W Fourth St *Web:* www.wcsr.com	Winston-Salem	NC	27101	336-721-3600	721-3660
Wong Fleming PC 821 Alexander Rd Ste 200 *Web:* wongfleming.com	Princeton	NJ	08540	609-951-9520	
Woodcock Washburn LLP 2929 Arch St Fl 12 *TF:* 877-843-4821 ■ *Web:* bakerlaw.com/_wwmerge.html	Philadelphia	PA	19104	215-568-3100	568-3439
Woods Fuller Shultz & Smith 300 S Phillips Ave Ste 300 *Web:* www.woodsfuller.com	Sioux Falls	SD	57117	605-336-3890	
Woods Rogers PLC 10 S Jefferson St Ste 1400 *Web:* www.woodsrogers.com	Roanoke	VA	24011	540-983-7600	
Workman Nydegger PC 60 East South Temple Ste 1000 *Web:* www.wnlaw.com	Salt Lake City	UT	84111	801-533-9800	
Wright Lindsey & Jennings LLP 200 W Capitol Ave Ste 2300 *Web:* www.wlj.com	Little Rock	AR	72201	501-371-0808	376-9442
Wulfsberg, Reese, Colvig & Firstman PC Kaiser Ctr 300 Lakeside Dr 24th Fl *Web:* www.bwslaw.com	Oakland	CA	94612	510-835-9100	
Wyatt Early Harris Wheeler LLP PO Box 2086 *Web:* www.wehwlaw.com	High Point	NC	27261	336-884-4444	
Wyatt Tarrant & Combs PNC Plz 500 W Jefferson St *Web:* www.wyattfirm.com	Louisville	KY	40202	502-589-5235	
Young Clement Rivers LLP 28 Broad St *Web:* www.ycrlaw.com/home.aspx	Charleston	SC	29401	843-577-4000	
Youth Advocate Programs Inc 2007 N Third St PO Box 950 *Web:* www.yapinc.org	Harrisburg	PA	17102	717-232-7580	
Yturri Rose LLP 89 SW Third Ave *Web:* www.yturrirose.com	Ontario	OR	97914	541-889-5368	

				Phone	Fax
Yukevich | Cavanaugh 355 S Grand Ave 15th Fl. *Web:* www.yukelaw.com	Los Angeles	CA	90071	213-362-7777	
Zager Fuchs PC 268 Broad St *Web:* zagerfuchs.com	Red Bank	NJ	07701	732-747-3700	
Zimmerman Reed PLLP 1100 IDS Ctr 80 S Eighth St *Web:* www.zimmreed.com	Minneapolis	MN	55402	612-341-0400	
Zucker Goldberg & Ackerman 200 Sheffield St Ste 101	Mountainside	NJ	07092	908-233-8500	
Zumpano, Patricios & Winker PA 312 Minorca Ave *Web:* www.zpwlaw.com	Coral Gables	FL	33134	305-444-5565	

429 LAWN & GARDEN EQUIPMENT

See Also Farm Machinery & Equipment - Mfr p. 2278

				Phone	Fax
American Lawn Mower Co 2100 N Grandville Ave *Web:* www.americanlawnmower.com	Muncie	IN	47303	765-288-6624	
Ames True Temper Inc 465 Railroad Ave. *TF:* 800-393-1846 ■ *Web:* www.ames.com	Camp Hill	PA	17011	800-393-1846	
Ariens Co 655 W Ryan St *Web:* www.ariens.com	Brillion	WI	54110	920-756-2141	756-2407
Armatron International Inc 15 Highland Ave *TF:* 800-343-3280 ■ *Web:* www.flowtron.com/mm5/merchant.mvc?Screen=CTGY&Store_Code=F&Category_Code=FTPR	Malden	MA	02148	781-321-2300	
Artcraft Company Inc, The 200 John L Dietsch Blvd. *TF:* 800-659-4042 ■ *Web:* www.artcraft.com	North Attleboro	MA	02763	508-695-4042	
Automatic Irrigation Supply Co 4877 SR- 261 *Web:* www.automaticirrigation.com	Newburgh	IN	47630	812-858-1809	
Binkley & Hurst LP 133 Rothsville Stn Rd *TF:* 800-414-4705 ■ *Web:* www.binkleyhurst.com	Lititz	PA	17543	717-626-4705	
Blount Outdoor Products Group 4909 SE International Way *Web:* blount.com	Portland	OR	97222	503-653-8881	653-4402
Bondioli & Pavesi Inc 10252 Sycamore Dr *Web:* bondioli-pavesi.com	Ashland	VA	23005	804-550-2224	
Bosmere Inc 323 Corban Ave SW *Web:* bosmereusa.com	Concord	NC	28025	704-784-1608	
Brinly-Hardy Co 3230 Industrial Pkwy. *TF:* 800-626-5329 ■ *Web:* www.brinly.com	Jeffersonville	IN	47130	812-218-7200	218-6085
Brown Dairy Equipment 6500 W Gerwoude Dr **Fax Area Code:* 989 ■ *Web:* browndairyequip.com	Mc Bain	MI	49657	231-825-4144	269-1953*
California Flexrake Corp 9620 Gidley St *TF:* 800-266-4200 ■ *Web:* www.flexrake.com	Temple City	CA	91780	626-443-4026	443-6887
Carswell Distributing Co 3750 N Liberty St *TF:* 800-929-1948 ■ *Web:* www.carswelldist.com	Winston-Salem	NC	27105	336-767-7700	
CMD Products 1410 Flightline Dr Ste D *TF:* 800-210-9949 ■ *Web:* www.cmdproducts.com	Lincoln	CA	95648	916-434-0228	
Coast Pump Water Technologies Inc 610 Groveland Ave *Web:* www.coastpumpwatertechnology.com	Venice	FL	34285	941-484-3738	
Commerce Corp 7603 Energy Pkwy *TF:* 800-883-0234 ■ *Web:* bfgsupply.com	Baltimore	MD	21226	410-255-3500	
Corona Clipper Inc 22440 Tomasco Canyon Rd. *TF:* 800-234-2547 ■ *Web:* www.coronatoolsusa.com	Corona	CA	92883	951-737-6515	737-6515
Dultmeier Sales LLC 13808 Industrial Rd. *TF:* 888-677-5054 ■ *Web:* www.dultmeier.com	Omaha	NE	68137	402-333-1444	
EarthWay Products Inc 1009 Maple St *TF:* 800-294-0671 ■ *Web:* www.earthway.com	Bristol	IN	46507	574-848-7491	848-4249
Echo Inc 400 Oakwood Rd *TF:* 800-673-1558 ■ *Web:* www.echo-usa.com	Lake Zurich	IL	60047	847-540-8400	540-9741
Emco Wheaton USA Inc 9111 Jackrabbit Rd *Web:* www.emcowheaton.com	Houston	TX	77095	281-856-1300	856-1325
Encore Manufacturing Company Inc 2415 Ashland Ave. *TF:* 800-267-4255 ■ *Web:* www.encoreequipment.com	Beatrice	NE	68310	800-267-4255	
Future Harvest Development Ltd 725 Evans Crt *Web:* futureharvest.com	Kelowna	BC	V1X6G4	250-491-0255	
Gilmour Mfg Group 2537 Daniels St Somerset *TF Cust Svc:* 866-348-5661 ■ *Web:* www.gilmour.com	Madison	WI	53718	866-348-5661	
Grasshopper Co, The 105 Old US Hwy 81 PO Box 637 *Web:* www.grasshoppermower.com	Moundridge	KS	67107	620-345-8621	345-2301
Grassland Equipment & Irrigation Corp 892-898 Troy Schenectady Rd *TF:* 800-564-5587 ■ *Web:* www.grasslandcorp.com	Latham	NY	12110	518-785-5841	785-5740
Green Depot Inc 1 Ivy Hill Rd *TF:* 800-238-5008 ■ *Web:* greendepot.com	Brooklyn	NY	11211	718-782-2991	
Greenscapes Home & Garden Products Inc 200 Union Grove Rd SE *Web:* www.greenscapesinc.net	Calhoun	GA	30701	706-629-6652	
Handy Tv Inc 224 Oxmoor Cir *Web:* www.handytv.com	Birmingham	AL	35209	205-290-0300	
Harnack Co 6016 Nordic Dr. **Fax Area Code:* 800 ■ *TF Cust Svc:* 800-772-2022 ■ *Web:* www.harnack.net	Cedar Falls	IA	50613	319-277-0660	772-2027*
Holt Equipment Co LLC PO Box 436317 *Web:* www.holtgascompression.com	Louisville	KY	40223	502-797-5075	
Howard Price Turf Equipment Inc 18155 Edison Ave. *Web:* www.howardpriceturf.com	Chesterfield	MO	63005	636-532-7000	532-0201
Hutson 306 Andrus Dr. *TF:* 866-488-7662 ■ *Web:* www.hutsoninc.com/h2	Murray	KY	42071	270-886-3994	
Imperial Sprinkler Supply Inc 1485 N Manassero St *Web:* www.imperialsprinklersupply.com	Anaheim	CA	92807	714-792-2925	
Jacobsen 11108 Quality Dr *Web:* www.jacobsen.com	Charlotte	NC	28273	704-504-6600	504-6661
Kanequip Inc 1451 S Second Ave *TF:* 800-359-1108 ■ *Web:* kanequip.com	Dodge City	KS	67801	620-225-0016	
Kenney Corp 8420 Zionsville Rd *Web:* www.kmcturf.com	Indianapolis	IN	46268	317-872-4793	
Kusel Equipment Co 820 W St *Web:* www.kuselequipment.com	Watertown	WI	53094	920-261-4112	
Landmark Equipment Company Inc 1309 Haltom Rd *Web:* www.landmarkeq.com	Fort Worth	TX	76117	972-579-9999	
Lang Diesel Inc 1366 Toulon Ave *Web:* langdieselinc.com	Hays	KS	67601	785-735-2651	
Lawn & Golf Supply Co Inc 647 Nutt Rd PO Box 447 *Web:* www.lawn-golf.com	Phoenixville	PA	19460	610-933-5801	933-8890
Lawn Equipment Parts Co 1475 River Rd *TF:* 800-365-3726 ■ *Web:* www.lepcoonline.com	Marietta	PA	17547	717-426-5200	
Lawn-Boy Inc 8111 S Lyndale Ave. *Web:* www.lawnboy.com	Bloomington	MN	55420	952-888-8801	887-8258
LL Johnson Distributing Co 4700 Holly St *Web:* www.lljohnson.com	Denver	CO	80216	303-320-1270	
Lodi Irrigation 1301 E Armstrong Rd. *TF:* 800-634-7272 ■ *Web:* www.lodiirrigation.com	Lodi	CA	95242	800-634-7272	
MacKissic Inc PO Box 111 *TF:* 800-348-1117 ■ *Web:* www.mackissic.com	Parker Ford	PA	19457	610-495-7181	495-5951
Master Mark Plastics 210 Ampe Dr *TF Cust Svc:* 800-535-4838 ■ *Web:* www.mastermark.com	Paynesville	MN	56362	320-243-7318	
McLane Manufacturing Inc 7110 E Rosecrans Ave *Web:* mclanemower.com	Paramount	CA	90723	562-633-8158	602-0651
Melnor Inc 109 Tyson Dr **Fax Area Code:* 888 ■ *TF:* 877-283-0697 ■ *Web:* www.melnor.com	Winchester	VA	22603	540-722-5600	411-2500*
Mid West Products Inc PO Box 301 *Web:* www.lambertmfg.com	Phillipsburg	OH	45354	937-337-3641	
Midwest Bio-systems Inc 28933 35 E St *TF:* 877-649-2114 ■ *Web:* www.midwestbiosystems.com	Tampico	IL	61283	815-438-7200	
MTD Products Inc 5965 Grafton Rd *TF:* 800-800-7310 ■ *Web:* www.mtdproducts.com	Valley City	OH	44280	330-225-2600	273-4617
Ohio Steel Industries Inc 2575 Ferris Rd *Web:* www.ohiosteel.com	Columbus	OH	43224	614-471-4800	
Oliver M Dean Inc 125 Brooks St *TF:* 800-648-3326 ■ *Web:* www.omdean.com	Worcester	MA	01606	508-856-9100	
Poly-Clip System Corp 1000 Tower Rd *Web:* www.polyclip-usa.com	Mundelein	IL	60060	847-949-2800	
Precision Products Inc 316 Limit St *TF Cust Svc:* 800-225-5891 ■ *Web:* www.precisionprodinc.com	Lincoln	IL	62656	217-735-1590	735-2435
Rio Delmar Enterprises 8338 Elliott Rd *Web:* www.stihldealer.net	Easton	MD	21601	410-822-8866	
Rugg Mfg Company Inc 105 Newton St *TF:* 800-633-8772 ■ *Web:* www.rugg.com	Greenfield	MA	01302	413-773-5471	
Schiller Grounds Care Inc 1028 St Rd *Web:* www.littlewonder.com	Southampton	PA	18966	215-357-5110	
Simplicity Manufacturing Inc PO Box 702 *TF:* 800-837-6836 ■ *Web:* www.simplicitymfg.com	Milwaukee	WI	53201	800-837-6836	
Smithco Inc 34 W Ave *TF:* 877-833-7648 ■ *Web:* www.smithco.com	Wayne	PA	19087	610-688-4009	688-6069
Stens Corp 2424 Cathy Ln *TF:* 800-457-7444 ■ *Web:* www.stens.com	Jasper	IN	47546	812-482-2526	482-1275
Stihl Inc 536 Viking Dr **Fax Area Code:* 303 ■ *TF Cust Svc:* 800-467-8445 ■ *Web:* www.stihlusa.com	Virginia Beach	VA	23452	757-486-9100	340-0377*
Storr Tractor Co 3191 Rt 22 *TF:* 800-526-3802 ■ *Web:* www.storrtractor.com	Branchburg	NJ	08876	908-722-9830	722-9847
Swisher Mower & Machine Company Inc 1602 Corporate Dr *TF:* 800-222-8183 ■ *Web:* www.swisherinc.com	Warrensburg	MO	64093	660-747-8183	747-8650
Toro Co 8111 Lyndale Ave *NYSE:* TTC ■ **Fax Area Code:* 952 ■ *TF:* 888-384-9939 ■ *Web:* www.toro.com	Bloomington	MN	55420	888-384-9939	887-8258*
Toro Company Commercial Products Div 8111 Lyndale Ave *TF Cust Svc:* 800-348-2424 ■ *Web:* www.toro.com	Bloomington	MN	55420	952-888-8801	887-8258
Tuff Torq Corp 5943 Commerce Blvd *TF:* 866-572-3441 ■ *Web:* www.tufftorq.com	Morristown	TN	37814	423-585-2000	585-2003
Weathermatic 3301 W Kingsley Rd *TF:* 888-484-3776 ■ *Web:* www.weathermatic.com	Garland	TX	75041	972-278-6131	271-5710
Wesspur Tree Equipment 2121 Iron St *TF:* 800-268-2141 ■ *Web:* www.wesspur.com	Bellingham	WA	98225	360-734-5242	

430 LEATHER GOODS - PERSONAL

See Also Clothing & Accessories - Mfr p. 1941; Footwear p. 2316; Handbags, Totes, Backpacks p. 2449; Leather Goods (Misc) p. 2646; Luggage, Bags, Cases p. 2688

				Phone	Fax
AD Sutton & Sons Inc 20 W 33rd St *Web:* www.adsutton.com	New York	NY	10001	212-695-7070	947-6253
Bottega Veneta Inc 699 Fifth Ave *Web:* www.bottegaveneta.com	New York	NY	10022	212-371-5511	
Buxton Co 245 Cadwell Dr *TF:* 800-426-3638 ■ *Web:* www.buxton.co	Springfield	MA	01104	413-734-5900	785-1367
Carroll Cos Inc 1640 Old Hwy 421 S *Web:* www.clgco.com	Boone	NC	28607	828-264-2521	264-2633
Coach Inc 516 W 34th St *NYSE:* COH ■ *TF:* 800-444-3611 ■ *Web:* world.coach.com	New York	NY	10001	212-594-1850	594-1682
Dooney & Bourke Inc 1 Regent St **Fax Area Code:* 800 ■ *TF Cust Svc:* 800-347-5000 ■ *Web:* www.dooney.com	East Norwalk	CT	06855	203-853-7515	326-1496*
Jaclyn Inc 197 W Spring Vly Ave *OTC:* JCLY ■ *Web:* www.jaclyninc.com	Maywood	NJ	07607	201-909-6000	
Sharif Designs Ltd 34-12 36th Ave	Long Island	NY	11106	718-472-1100	937-2561
Westport Corp 331 Changdridge Rd *Web:* www.mundiwestport.com	Pine Brook	NJ	07058	973-575-0110	575-8197

431 LEATHER GOODS (MISC)

Phone *Fax*

Action Co 1425 N Tennessee St .... McKinney TX 75069 972-542-8700 562-7300
TF Sales: 800-937-3700 ■ *Web:* www.actioncompany.com

Auburn Leather Co 125 N Caldwell St .... Auburn KY 42206 270-542-4116 542-7107
TF: 800-635-0617 ■ *Web:* www.auburnleather.com

Capitol Saddlery 8121 N Research Blvd .... Austin TX 78758 512-478-9309
Web: capsaddlery.com

Carroll Cos Inc 1640 Old Hwy 421 S .... Boone NC 28607 828-264-2521 264-2633
Web: www.clgco.com

Garlin-Neumann Leathers Company Inc
66-D River Rd .... Hudson NH 03051 603-595-6319 881-9431
Web: leatherusa.com

Gould & Goodrich Leather Inc
709 E McNeil St .... Lillington NC 27546 910-893-2071 893-4742
TF: 800-277-0732 ■ *Web:* www.gouldusa.com

Hunter Company Inc 3300 W 71st Ave .... Westminster CO 80030 303-427-4626
TF: 800-676-4868 ■ *Web:* www.huntercompany.com

Tex Shoemaker & Son Inc 131 S Eucla Ave .... San Dimas CA 91773 909-592-2071 592-2378
Web: www.texshoemaker.com

432 LEATHER TANNING & FINISHING

Phone *Fax*

Agora Leather Products 2101 28th St N .... St Petersburg FL 33713 727-321-0707
Web: agoraleather.com

Bernardo Fashions LLC 463 Seventh Ave 7th Fl .... New York NY 10018 212-594-3900
Web: www.bernardofashions.com

Carville National Leather Corp
10 Knox Ave PO Box 40 .... Johnstown NY 12095 518-762-1634 762-8973

Creative Extrusion & Technologies Inc
230 Elliot St .... Brockton MA 02302 508-587-2290
Web: creativeet.com

Cromwell Leather Company Inc
147 Palmer Ave .... Mamaroneck NY 10543 914-381-0100 381-0046
Web: www.cromwellgroup.com

Eagle Ottawa Leather Company LLC
2930 W Auburn Rd .... Rochester Hills MI 48309 248-853-3122
Web: www.eagleottawa.com

GST AutoLeather Inc
20 Oak Hollow Dr Ste 300 .... Southfield MI 48033 248-436-2300 436-2390
Web: www.gstautoleather.com

Hermann Oak Leather Co 4050 N First St .... Saint Louis MO 63147 314-421-1173 421-6152
TF: 800-325-7950 ■ *Web:* www.hermannoakleather.com

Horween Leather Co 2015 N Elston Ave .... Chicago IL 60614 773-772-2026 772-9235
Web: www.horween.com

Leather Bros Inc 1314 Nabholz Ave .... Conway AR 72034 501-329-9471
Web: www.leatherbrothers.com

Leatherock International Inc
5285 Lovelock St .... San Diego CA 92110 619-299-7625 299-7629
TF: 800-466-6667 ■ *Web:* www.leatherock.com

North American Tanning Corp
248 W 35th St Ste 505 .... New York NY 10001 212-643-1702 967-0068
Web: www.natanning.com

Robus Leather Corp 4010 W 86th St Ste C .... Indianapolis IN 46268 317-704-7000 702-7001
Web: www.robus.com

Seidel Tanning Corp 1306 E Meinecke Ave .... Milwaukee WI 53212 414-562-4030
Web: www.seideltanning.com

Showa Best Glove Inc 579 Edison St .... Menlo GA 30731 800-241-0323
TF: 800-241-0323 ■ *Web:* www.showagroup.com/global

Simco Leather Corp 99 Pleasant Ave .... Johnstown NY 12095 518-762-7100 736-1514

Stahl USA 13 Corwin St .... Peabody MA 01960 978-531-0371 532-9062
Web: www.stahl.com

Wood & Hyde Leather Company Inc
PO Box 786 .... Gloversville NY 12078 518-725-7105 725-5158
Web: www.woodandhyde.com

433 LEGISLATION HOTLINES

Phone *Fax*

Alabama Bill Status-House
State House 11 S Union St .... Montgomery AL 36130 334-242-7600 242-2489
Web: www.legislature.state.al.us

Alabama State Legislature
State House 11 S Union St .... Montgomery AL 36130 334-242-7600
TF: 800-499-3051 ■ *Web:* www.legislature.state.al.us/senate/senate.html

Alaska Bill Status State Capitol MS 3100 .... Juneau AK 99811 907-465-4930 465-2864
Web: www.legis.state.ak.us/basis

Arkansas Bill Status-Senate
State Capitol Rm 320 .... Little Rock AR 72201 501-682-5951
Web: www.arkleg.state.ar.us

California Bill Status-Assembly
State Capitol Rm 3196 .... Sacramento CA 95814 916-445-2323
Web: www.leginfo.ca.gov/bilinfo.html

District of Columbia Bill Status
1350 Pennsylvania Ave NW .... Washington DC 20004 202-724-8080 347-3070
Web: dccouncil.us

Florida Bill Status
111 W Madison St Rm 704 .... Tallahassee FL 32399 850-488-4371
TF: 800-342-1827 ■ *Web:* www.leg.state.fl.us

Georgia Bill Status-House 309 State Capitol .... Atlanta GA 30334 404-656-5015
Web: www.house.ga.gov

Hawaii Bill Status 415 S Beretania St Rm 401 .... Honolulu HI 96813 808-587-0478 587-0793
Web: www.capitol.hawaii.gov

Idaho Bill Status PO Box 83720 .... Boise ID 83720 208-334-2475 334-2125
Web: www.legislature.idaho.gov

Phone *Fax*

Illinois Bill Status 705 Stratton Bldg .... Springfield IL 62706 217-782-3944 524-6059
Web: www.ilga.gov/legislation

Indiana Bill Status
State House 200 W Washington St Ste 220 .... Indianapolis IN 46204 317-233-5293
Web: www.in.gov/apps/lsa/session/billwatch

Kansas Bill Status
300 SW Tenth Ave State Capitol Bldg Rm 343N .... Topeka KS 66612 785-296-2391 296-1153
Web: www.kslegislature.org

Kentucky Bill Status
702 Capitol Ave Rm 424F .... Frankfort KY 40601 502-564-8100
Web: kentuckyhouserepublicans.org

Maryland Dept of Legislative Services
90 State Cir .... Annapolis MD 21401 410-946-5400 946-5405
TF: 800-492-7122 ■ *Web:* www.mlis.state.md.us

Massachusetts Bill Status
1 Ashburton Pl Rm 1611 .... Boston MA 02108 617-727-7030 742-4528
TF: 800-392-6090 ■ *Web:* malegislature.gov

Minnesota Bill Status-Senate
100 Rev Dr Martin Luther King Junior Blvd
.... Saint Paul MN 55155 651-296-2146
Web: www.house.leg.state.mn.us

Mississippi Bill Status PO Box 2611 .... Jackson MS 39215 601-359-2420
Web: billstatus.ls.state.ms.us

Montana Legislative Services
1301 E Sixth Ave PO Box 201706 .... Helena MT 59620 406-444-3064 444-3036
Web: leg.mt.gov

Nevada Bill Status 401 S Carson St .... Carson City NV 89701 775-684-3360 684-3330
TF: 800-978-2878 ■ *Web:* www.leg.state.nv.us

New Hampshire Bill Status 107 N Main St .... Concord NH 03301 603-271-3435
Web: www.gencourt.state.nh.us

New Jersey Bill Status
State House Annex PO Box 068 .... Trenton NJ 08625 609-292-4840 777-2440
TF: 800-792-8630 ■ *Web:* www.njleg.state.nj.us

New Mexico Legislative Council Services
625 Don Gaspar Ave .... Santa Fe NM 87501 505-986-4600
Web: www.nmlegis.gov

New York Bill Status
202 Legislative Office Bldg .... Albany NY 12248 518-455-4218
TF: 800-342-9860 ■ *Web:* www.assembly.state.ny.us

North Carolina Bill Status 16 W Jones St .... Raleigh NC 27601 919-733-4111
Web: www.ncleg.net

North Dakota Legislative Council Services
State Capitol Bldg 600 E Blvd Ave .... Bismarck ND 58505 701-328-2916 328-3615
TF: 800-366-6888 ■ *Web:* www.legis.nd.gov

Ohio Legislative Information Office
77 S High St .... Columbus OH 43215 614-728-0711
Web: www.lis.state.oh.us

Oklahoma Legislation Service Bureau
2300 N Lincoln Blvd .... State Capitol Bldg OK 73105 405-521-4081 521-5507
Web: www.oklegislature.gov

Oregon Publication & Distribution Services
900 Ct St NE Rm 49 .... Salem OR 97310 503-986-1360 373-1527
Web: Www.oregonlegislature.gov

Pennsylvania Bill Status
462 Main Capitol Bldg .... Harrisburg PA 17120 717-787-5920
Web: www.legis.state.pa.us

Rhode Island Bill Status
82 Smith St Rm 217 .... Providence RI 02903 401-222-3580
Web: www.rilin.state.ri.us

South Carolina Bill Status PO Box 142 .... Columbia SC 29201 803-212-6200
Web: www.scstatehouse.gov

South Dakota Bill Status 500 E Capitol .... Pierre SD 57501 605-773-3251
Web: legis.sd.gov

Tennessee Bill Status
320 Sixth Ave N 1st Fl .... Nashville TN 37243 615-741-1000
Web: www.tn.gov/directory

Utah State Legislature
350 North State St Ste 320
PO Box 145115 .... Salt Lake City UT 84114 801-538-1035 538-1728
Web: le.utah.gov/documents/bills.htm

Vermont Bill Status
115 State St State House .... Montpelier VT 05633 802-828-2231 828-2424
Web: www.leg.state.vt.us

Washington Bill Status PO Box 40600 .... Olympia WA 98504 360-786-7573
TF: 800-562-6000 ■ *Web:* www.leg.wa.gov

West Virginia Bill Status
State Capitol Complex Rm MB27 Bldg 1 .... Charleston WV 25305 304-347-4836 347-4901
TF: 877-565-3447 ■ *Web:* www.legis.state.wv.us

Wisconsin Bill Status 1 E Main St .... Madison WI 53708 608-266-9960
TF: 800-362-9472 ■ *Web:* legis.wisconsin.gov

Wyoming Legislative Service Office
3001 E Pershing Blvd .... Cheyenne WY 82002 307-777-7881 777-5466
TF: 800-342-9570 ■ *Web:* legisweb.state.wy.us

434 LIBRARIES

See Also Library Systems - Regional - Canadian p. 2672

Phone *Fax*

Edmonton Public Library Office
7 Sir Winston Churchill Sq Nw .... Edmonton AB T5J2V4 780-496-7000
Web: www.sirsiweb.epl.ca

Coquitlam Public Library
3001 Burlington Dr .... Coquitlam BC V3B6X1 604-554-7323
Web: www.library.coquitlam.bc.ca

Temiskaming Shores City of
545 Lkshore Rd S .... Haileybury ON P0J1K0 705-672-3707
Web: www.temiskamingshores.ca

Library and Archives Canada
550 de la Cite Blvd .... Gatineau QC K1A0N4 613-995-6274
Web: www.collectionscanada.ca

434-1 Medical Libraries

Phone | Fax

Alfred Taubman Medical Library
University of Michigan 1135 E Catherine St
Ann Arbor MI 48109 734-764-1210 763-1473
Web: www.lib.umich.edu

Allen Memorial Medical Library
Case Western Reserve University
11000 Euclid Ave ... Cleveland OH 44106 216-368-3643
Web: www.case.edu/chsl/allen.htm

Allyn & Betty Taylor Library
University of Western Ontario
Natural Sciences Ctr ... London ON N6A5B7 519-661-3168 661-3435
Web: www.lib.uwo.ca/taylor

Augustus C Long Health Sciences Library
Columbia University Medical Ctr
701 W 168th St ... New York NY 10032 212-305-3605
Web: library.cumc.columbia.edu

Boston University School of Medicine Alumni Medical Library
80 E Concord St R-806 ... Boston MA 02118 617-638-1950
Web: www.bumc.bu.edu/busm/about/library

Brown University Sciences Library
201 Thayer St PO Box 'I' ... Providence RI 02912 401-863-3333 863-2753
Web: www.brown.edu

Chandler Medical Ctr Library
500 S Limestone St ... Lexington KY 40506 859-323-5300 323-1040
Web: libraries.uky.edu

Cleveland Health Sciences Library (CHSL)
Case Western Reserve University Robbins Bldg
2109 Adelbert Rd ... Cleveland OH 44106 216-368-4540
Web: www.case.edu/chsl/library/index.html

Coy C Carpenter Library
Wake Forest University School of Medicine
Medical Ctr Blvd ... Winston-Salem NC 27157 336-716-2011 716-2186
Web: www.wakehealth.edu/library

D Samuel Gottesman Library
1300 Morris Pk Ave # 132 ... Bronx NY 10461 718-430-3108 430-8795
Web: library.einstein.yu.edu

Dahlgren Memorial Library
Georgetown University Medical Ctr 3900 Reservoir Rd NW
PO Box 571420 ... Washington DC 20057 202-687-1448 687-1862
Web: dml.georgetown.edu

Dana Biomedical Library Dartmouth College ... Hanover NH 03755 603-650-1658 650-1354
Web: www.dartmouth.edu

Del E Webb Memorial Library
Loma Linda University 11072 Anderson St ... Loma Linda CA 92350 909-558-4550 558-4188
Web: www.llu.edu/llu/library

Duke University Medical Ctr Library
103 Seeley Mudd Bldg DUMC 3702 ... Durham NC 27710 919-660-1150 681-7599
Web: www.mclibrary.duke.edu

Dykes Library
University of Kansas Medical Ctr
2100 W 39th Ave MS 1050 ... Kansas City KS 66106 913-588-7166 588-7304
Web: library.kumc.edu

Francis A Countway Library of Medicine, The
10 Shattuck St ... Boston MA 02115 617-432-2136 432-4739
Web: www.countway.harvard.edu

Frederick L Ehrman Medical Library
New York University Medical Ctr School of Medicine
Medical Science Bldg Elevator B ... New York NY 10016 212-263-5395 263-6534
Web: hsl.med.nyu.edu

George F Smith Library of the Health Sciences
Univ of Medicine & Dentistry of New Jersey
30 12th Ave ... Newark NJ 07101 973-972-4580 972-7474
Web: rbhs.rutgers.edu

George T Harrell Health Sciences Library
Pennsylvania State University College of Medicine
500 University Dr Milton S Hershey Medical ... Hershey PA 17033 717-531-8626 531-8635
Web: med.psu.edu

Gerstein Science Information Centre
University of Toronto
9 King's College Cir
Sigmund Samuel Library Bldg ... Toronto ON M5S1A5 416-978-2280
Web: gerstein.library.utoronto.ca

Hardin Library for the Health Sciences
University of Iowa 100 Hardin Library ... Iowa City IA 52242 319-335-9871 353-3752
Web: www.lib.uiowa.edu/hardin

Harvey Cushing/John Hay Whitney Medical Library
333 Cedar St PO Box 208014 ... New Haven CT 06520 203-785-5352 785-5636
Web: medicine.yale.edu

Himmelfarb Health Sciences Library
George Washington University Medical Ctr
2300 Eye St NW ... Washington DC 20037 202-994-2850 994-4343
Web: himmelfarb.gwu.edu

Houston Academy of Medicine - Texas Medical Ctr Library
1133 John Freeman Blvd ... Houston TX 77030 713-795-4200 790-7052
Web: www.library.tmc.edu

John A Prior Health Sciences Library
Ohio State University 376 W Tenth Ave ... Columbus OH 43210 614-292-4861 292-1920
Web: www.hsl.osu.edu

Kornhauser Health Sciences Library
University of Louisville 500 S Preston St ... Louisville KY 40292 502-852-5771 852-1631
Web: www.louisville.edu

Lamar Soutter Library 55 N Lake Ave ... Worcester MA 01655 508-856-6099 856-5899
Web: library.umassmed.edu

Lane Medical Library
Stanford University Medical Ctr
300 Pasteur Dr Rm L-109 ... Stanford CA 94305 650-723-6831 725-7471
Web: www.lane.stanford.edu

Leon S McGoogan Library of Medicine
University of Nebraska Medical Ctr
986705 Nebraska Medical Ctr ... Omaha NE 68198 402-559-6221
TF: 866-800-5209 ■ *Web:* www.unmc.edu/library

Library of Rush University
Rush University Medical Ctr
600 S Paulina St Ste 571 ... Chicago IL 60612 312-942-5950 942-3143
Web: rushu.libguides.com

Louis Calder Memorial Library
University of Miami School of Medicine R-950
PO Box 016950 ... Miami FL 33101 305-243-6648 325-9670
Web: calder.med.miami.edu

McGill University Life Sciences Library & Osler Library of the History of Medicine
3655 Sir William Osler ... Montreal QC H3G1Y6 514-398-4475 398-3890
Web: www.mcgill.ca

McMaster University Health Sciences Library
1200 Main St W ... Hamilton ON L8N3Z5 905-525-9140 528-3733
Web: hsl.mcmaster.ca

Meharry Medical College Library
1005 DB Todd Blvd ... Nashville TN 37208 615-327-6318 327-6448
Web: www.mmc.edu

Moody Medical Library 914 Market st ... Galveston TX 77555 409-772-2372 202-2689*
**Fax Area Code: 832* ■ *TF:* 866-235-5223

National Institutes of Health (NIH)
9000 Rockville Pike ... Bethesda MD 20892 301-496-4000
Web: www.nih.gov
Library 9000 Rockville Pike Bldg 10 ... Bethesda MD 20892 301-496-4000 402-2984
Web: www.nih.gov
National Library of Medicine
8600 Rockville Pike Bldg 38 ... Bethesda MD 20894 301-594-5983 402-1384
TF: 888-346-3656 ■ *Web:* www.nlm.nih.gov

New York Academy of Medicine Library
1216 Fifth Ave ... New York NY 10029 212-822-7315 423-0266
Web: www.nyam.org/library

Norris Medical Library
University of Southern California
2003 Zonal Ave ... Los Angeles CA 90089 323-442-1111 221-1235
Web: www.usc.edu/hsc/nml

Oregon Health & Science University
Bone Marrow Transplant Program (OHSU)
3181 SW Sam Jackson Pk Rd ... Portland OR 97239 503-494-1617 494-7086
TF: 800-222-1222 ■ *Web:* www.ohsu.edu
Library 3181 SW Sam Jackson Pk Rd ... Portland OR 97239 503-494-3460 494-3322
Web: www.ohsu.edu/xd/education/library

Raymon H Mulford Library
Medical College of Ohio Toledo
3000 Arlington Ave ... Toledo OH 43614 419-383-4225
TF: 800-321-8383 ■ *Web:* www.utoledo.edu/library/mulford/index.html

Robert B Greenblatt MD Library
Medical College of Georgia
1439 Lny Walker Blvd ... Augusta GA 30912 706-721-3441
Web: www.augusta.edu

Robert M Bird Health Sciences Library
OUHSC 1000 Stanton L Young Blvd
PO Box 26901 ... Oklahoma City OK 73126 405-271-2285 271-3297
Web: library.ouhsc.edu

Rosalind Franklin University of Medicine & Science Learning Resource Ctr
3333 Green Bay Rd ... North Chicago IL 60064 847-578-3000
Web: www.rosalindfranklin.edu

Rowland Medical Library
University of Mississippi 2500 N State St ... Jackson MS 39216 601-984-1231 984-1251
Web: www.umc.edu

Rutgers The State University of New Jersey
Camden 406 Penn St ... Camden NJ 08102 856-225-6104 225-6498*
**Fax:* Admissions ■ *Web:* www.camden.rutgers.edu
Library of Science & Medicine
165 Bevier Rd ... Piscataway NJ 08854 732-445-3854 445-5703
Web: www.libraries.rutgers.edu

Ruth Lilly Medical Library
975 W Walnut St IB 100 ... Indianapolis IN 46202 317-274-7182 278-2349
TF: 877-952-1988 ■ *Web:* www.library.medicine.iu.edu

Saint Louis University 221 N Grand Blvd ... Saint Louis MO 63103 314-977-7288 977-7136*
**Fax:* Admissions ■ *TF:* 800-758-3678 ■ *Web:* www.slu.edu

Schaffer Library of the Health Sciences
Albany Medical College 47 New Scotland Ave ... Albany NY 12208 518-262-5586
Web: www.amc.edu/academic/schaffer

Scott Memorial Library
1020 Walnut St Ste 310 ... Philadelphia PA 19107 215-503-8848 923-3203

Southern Illinois University School of Medicine Medical Library (SIU)
801 N Rutledge St PO Box 19625 ... Springfield IL 62794 217-545-2122 545-0988
Web: www.siumed.edu/lib

State University of New York at Buffalo
Health Sciences Library (HSL)
3435 Main St Abbott Hall Rm 102 ... Buffalo NY 14214 716-829-3900 829-2211
TF: 866-432-5849 ■ *Web:* library.buffalo.edu/hsl

State University of New York Upstate Medical University Health Sciences Library
766 Irving Ave ... Syracuse NY 13210 315-464-7087 464-7199
Web: library.upstate.edu

Stony Brook University Health Sciences Library
8034 Suny HSC Level 3 Rm 136 ... Stony Brook NY 11794 631-444-2512 444-6649
Web: library.stonybrook.edu/healthsciences

SUNY Downstate Medical Ctr
Medical Research Library of Brooklyn, The
450 Clarkson Ave PO Box 14 ... Brooklyn NY 11203 718-270-1000 270-7471
Web: www.downstate.edu

Texas A & M University
Rudder Tower Ste 205 ... College Station TX 77843 979-845-8901 458-4617*
**Fax:* Admissions ■ *TF:* 888-890-5667 ■ *Web:* www.tamu.edu
Medical Sciences Library MS 4462 ... College Station TX 77843 979-845-7428
Web: msl.library.tamu.edu

Texas Tech University Health Sciences Ctr
Preston Smith Library of the Health Sciences
3601 Fourth St MS 7781 ... Lubbock TX 79430 806-743-2200 743-2218
Web: www.ttuhsc.edu/libraries/guides/lubbockguide.aspx#welcome

Tompkins-McCaw Library 509 N 12th St ... Richmond VA 23298 804-828-0636 828-6089
Web: www.library.vcu.edu

Tufts University Hirsh Health Sciences Library
145 Harrison Ave ... Boston MA 02111 617-636-6705 636-4039
Web: www.library.tufts.edu/hsl

	Phone	Fax
Uniformed Services University of the Health Sciences Learning Resource Ctr 4301 Jones Bridge Rd ... Bethesda MD 20814	301-295-3350	
Universite de Montreal Bibliotheque de la Sante 2900 Blvd Edouard-Montpetit Rm L623 ... Montreal QC H3T1J4	514-343-6111	343-2350
Web: www.bib.umontreal.ca/sa		
Universite Laval		
Bibliotheque Scientifique Pavillon Alexandre-Vachon 1045 Ave ... Quebec QC G1V0A6	418-656-3967	656-7699
Web: www.bibl.ulaval.ca		
University of Arizona Arizona Health Sciences Library 1501 N Campbell Ave PO Box 245079 ... Tucson AZ 85724	520-626-6125	626-2922
Web: www.ahsl.arizona.edu		
Medical Library 4301 W Markham St Slot 586 ... Little Rock AR 72205	501-686-7000	686-6745
University of California Irvine *Library* PO Box 19557 ... Irvine CA 92623	949-824-6836	824-3644
TF: 800-848-4722 ■ *Web:* www.lib.uci.edu		
University of California San Diego (UCSD) *Biomedical Library* 9500 Gilman Dr ... La Jolla CA 92093	858-534-3253	534-6609
Web: www.libraries.ucsd.edu		
University of California San Diego Medical Ctr Library 200 W Arbor Dr ... San Diego CA 92103	619-543-6222	
Web: health.ucsd.edu		
University of California San Francisco *Kalmanovitz Library* 530 Parnassus Ave ... San Francisco CA 94143	415-476-8293	476-4653
Web: www.library.ucsf.edu		
Library & Center for Knowledge Management 530 Parnassus Ave ... San Francisco CA 94143	415-476-8293	476-4653
Web: www.library.ucsf.edu		
University of Cincinnati 51 Goodman Dr PO Box 670550 ... Cincinnati OH 45267	513-558-4553	558-2910
Web: www.health.uc.edu		
University of Florida Health Science Ctr Libraries 1600 SW Archer Rd PO Box 100206 ... Gainesville FL 32610	352-273-8408	392-2565
Web: www.library.health.ufl.edu		
University of Illinois Chicago *Daley Library* 801 S Morgan St Rm 1-280 ... Chicago IL 60607	312-996-2716	413-0424
Web: www.uic.edu/depts/lib		
Library of the Health Sciences 1750 W Polk St MC 763 ... Chicago IL 60612	312-996-8974	996-1899
Web: www.uic.edu/depts/lib/lhsc		
University of Maryland Baltimore *Health Sciences & Human Services Library (HSHSL)* 601 W Lombard St ... Baltimore MD 21201	410-706-7995	706-8403
Web: www.hshsl.umaryland.edu		
University of Minnesota Twin Cities *Bio-Medical Library* 117 Pleasant St SE ... Minneapolis MN 55455	612-626-4045	
Web: twin-cities.umn.edu		
University of Nebraska Medical Ctr McGoogan Library of Medicine 986705 Nebraska Medical Ctr ... Omaha NE 68198	402-559-4006	
TF: 866-800-5209 ■ *Web:* www.unmc.edu/library		
University of North Carolina Chapel Hill *Davis Library* CB 3900 ... Chapel Hill NC 27514	919-962-1356	843-8936
Web: library.unc.edu		
Health Sciences Library CB 7585 ... Chapel Hill NC 27599	919-962-0800	966-5592
Web: hsl.lib.unc.edu		
University of Ottawa Health Sciences Library 65 University ... Ottawa ON K1N6N5	613-562-5407	
Web: www.biblio.uottawa.ca		
University of Pennsylvania 3451 Walnut St ... Philadelphia PA 19104	215-898-5000	898-9670*
**Fax:* Admissions ■ *TF:* 800-537-5487 ■ *Web:* www.upenn.edu		
Biomedical Library 3610 Hamilton Walk Johnson Pavilion ... Philadelphia PA 19104	215-898-5815	573-4143
Web: www.library.upenn.edu/biomed		
Health Sciences Library 107 Wiggins Rd Ste B-205 ... Saskatoon SK S7N5E5	306-966-5991	966-5918
Web: library.usask.ca/hsl		
University of Tennessee Health Science Ctr *Health Sciences Library & Biocommunications Ctr* 877 Madison Ave ... Memphis TN 38103	901-448-5634	
TF: 877-747-0004 ■ *Web:* www.uthsc.edu		
University of Texas Health Science Ctr San Antonio *Libraries* 7703 Floyd Curl Dr MSC 7940 ... San Antonio TX 78229	210-567-2400	567-2490
Web: www.library.uthscsa.edu		
University of Texas Southwestern Medical Ctr at Dallas Library, The 5323 Harry Hines Blvd ... Dallas TX 75390	214-648-2001	648-2826
TF: 866-645-6455 ■ *Web:* utsouthwestern.edu		
University of Washington Health Sciences Libraries & Information Ctr 1959 NE Pacific St PO Box 357155 ... Seattle WA 98195	206-543-3390	543-8066
Web: hsl.uw.edu		
University of Wisconsin Madison *Ebling Library* 750 Highland Ave ... Madison WI 53705	608-262-2020	262-4732
Web: www.ebling.library.wisc.edu		
Weill Cornell Medical Library Weill Medical College of Cornell University 1300 York Ave ... New York NY 10065	212-746-6050	746-6494
Web: weill.cornell.edu		
West Virginia University PO Box 6009 ... Morgantown WV 26506	304-293-2121	293-3080
TF: 800-344-9881 ■ *Web:* www.wvu.edu		
William E Laupus Health Sciences Library 500 Health Science Dr 600 Moye Blvd Health Sciences Bldg ... Greenville NC 27834	252-744-2230	744-1376
Web: www.ecu.edu/cs-dhs/laupuslibrary		
William H Welch Medical Library Johns Hopkins University 1900 E Monument St ... Baltimore MD 21205	410-955-3410	
Web: welch.jhmi.edu		
WK Kellogg Health Sciences Library 5850 College St Sir Charles Tupper Medical Bldg ... Halifax NS B3H1X5	902-494-2458	494-3798
Web: libraries.dal.ca		
Woodruff Health Sciences Ctr Library *Emory University* 1462 Clifton Rd NE ... Atlanta GA 30322	404-727-8727	727-9821
Web: health.library.emory.edu		
Woodward Biomedical Library 2198 Health Sciences Mall ... Vancouver BC V6T1Z3	604-822-2883	822-5596
Web: woodward.library.ubc.ca		

434-2 Presidential Libraries

	Phone	Fax
Abraham Lincoln Presidential Library & Museum 112 N Sixth St ... Springfield IL 62701	217-557-6250	
TF: 800-610-2094 ■ *Web:* www.alplm.org		
Dwight D Eisenhower Presidential Library & Museum 200 SE Fourth St ... Abilene KS 67410	785-263-6700	263-6715
TF: 877-746-4453 ■ *Web:* www.eisenhower.utexas.edu		
Franklin D Roosevelt Presidential Library & Museum 4079 Albany Post Rd ... Hyde Park NY 12538	845-486-7770	486-1147
TF: 800-337-8474 ■ *Web:* www.fdrlibrary.marist.edu		
George Bush Library & Museum 1000 George Bush Dr W ... College Station TX 77845	979-691-4000	346-1699*
**Fax Area Code:* 214		
Gerald R Ford Library 1000 Beal Ave ... Ann Arbor MI 48109	734-205-0555	205-0571
Web: www.fordlibrarymuseum.gov		
Harry S Truman Presidential Library & Museum 500 W Hwy 24 ... Independence MO 64050	816-268-8200	268-8295
TF: 800-833-1225 ■ *Web:* www.trumanlibrary.org		
Herbert Hoover Presidential Library & Museum 210 Parkside Dr ... West Branch IA 52358	319-643-5301	643-6045
Web: www.hoover.archives.gov		
Jimmy Carter Library & Museum 441 Freedom Pkwy ... Atlanta GA 30307	404-865-7100	865-7102
Web: www.jimmycarterlibrary.gov		
John F Kennedy Presidential Library & Museum Columbia Pt ... Boston MA 02125	617-514-1600	514-1652
TF: 866-535-1960 ■ *Web:* www.jfklibrary.org		
LBJ Library & Museum 2313 Red River St ... Austin TX 78705	512-721-0216	721-0170
TF: 800-874-6451 ■ *Web:* www.lbjlib.utexas.edu		
Richard Nixon Foundation, The 18001 Yorba Linda Blvd ... Yorba Linda CA 92886	714-993-5075	528-0544
Web: www.nixonfoundation.org		
Ronald Reagan Presidential Library & Museum 40 Presidential Dr ... Simi Valley CA 93065	805-522-2977	577-4074
TF: 800-410-8354		
Rutherford B Hayes Presidential Ctr Spiegel Grove ... Fremont OH 43420	419-332-2081	332-4952
TF: 800-998-7737 ■ *Web:* www.rbhayes.org		
William J Clinton Presidential Ctr 1200 President Clinton Ave ... Little Rock AR 72201	501-370-8000	375-0512
Web: www.clintonfoundation.org		
Woodrow Wilson Presidential Library 20 N Coalter St PO Box 24 ... Staunton VA 24401	540-885-0897	886-9874
TF: 888-496-6376 ■ *Web:* www.woodrowwilson.org		

434-3 Public Libraries

Listings for public libraries are alphabetized by city name within each state grouping.

Alabama

	Phone	Fax
Aliceville Public Library (APL) 416 Third Ave NE ... Aliceville AL 35442	205-373-6691	373-3731
Web: pickenslibrary.com		
Auburn Public Library 749 E Thach Ave ... Auburn AL 36830	334-501-3190	
Web: www.auburnalabama.org		
Bay Minette Public Library 205 W Second St ... Bay Minette AL 36507	251-580-1648	937-0339
Web: cityofbayminette.org		
Bessemer Public Library 400 19th St ... Bessemer AL 35020	205-428-7882	
Web: www.bessemerlibrary.org		
Birmingham Public Library 2100 Pk Pl ... Birmingham AL 35203	205-226-3600	226-3731
Web: www.bham.lib.al.us		
Choctaw County Public Library 124 N Academy Ave ... Butler AL 36904	205-459-2542	
Harrison Regional Library 50 Lester St ... Columbiana AL 35051	205-669-3910	669-3940
Web: www.shelbycounty-al.org		
Cullman County Public Library System 200 Clark St NE ... Cullman AL 35055	256-734-1068	734-6902
Web: www.ccpls.com		
Horseshoe Bend Regional Library 207 NW St ... Dadeville AL 36853	256-825-9232	
TF: 855-336-0333 ■ *Web:* www.horseshoebendlibrary.org		
Florence-Lauderdale Public Library (FLPL) 350 N Wood Ave ... Florence AL 35630	256-764-6564	
Web: www.flpl.org		
Gadsden Public Library 254 College St ... Gadsden AL 35901	256-549-4699	
Web: www.gadsdenlibrary.org		
Guntersville Public Library 1240 O'Brig Ave ... Guntersville AL 35976	256-571-7595	
Web: www.guntersvillelibrary.org		
Cheaha Regional Library 935 Coleman St ... Heflin AL 36264	256-463-7125	463-7125
Web: www.cheaharegionallibrary.org		
Hoover Public Library (HPL) 200 Municipal Dr ... Hoover AL 35216	205-444-7800	444-7878
Web: www.hooverlibrary.org		
Hueytown Public Library 1372 Hueytown Rd ... Hueytown AL 35023	205-491-1443	
Web: www.hueytown.com		
Huntsville-Madison County Public Library 915 Monroe St ... Huntsville AL 35801	256-532-5940	
Web: hmcpl.org		
Carl Elliott Regional Library 98 E 18th St ... Jasper AL 35501	205-221-2568	221-2584
Mobile Public Library 701 Government St ... Mobile AL 36602	251-208-7073	208-7137
TF: 877-322-8228 ■ *Web:* www.mplonline.org		
Montgomery City-County Public Library 245 High St ... Montgomery AL 36104	334-240-4999	240-4980
Web: www.mccpl.lib.al.us		

				Phone	Fax
Lawrence County Public Library 401 College St	Moulton	AL	35650	256-974-0883	
Tuscaloosa Public Library 1801 Jack Warner Pkwy *Web:* www.tuscaloosa-library.org	Tuscaloosa	AL	35401	205-345-5820	758-1735
Bradshaw-Chambers County Public Library 3419 20th Ave *Web:* www.chamberscountylibrary.org	Valley	AL	36854	334-768-2161	

Alaska

				Phone	Fax
ZJ Loussac Public Library 3600 Denali St *Web:* www.muni.org	Anchorage	AK	99503	907-343-2975	343-2930
Big Lake Public Library 3140 S Big Lk Rd	Big Lake	AK	99652	907-892-6475	
Fairbanks North Star Borough Public Library 1215 Cowles St **Fax:* Admin ■ *Web:* library.fnsb.lib.ak.us	Fairbanks	AK	99701	907-459-1022	459-1024*
Homer Public Library 500 Hazel Ave *Web:* www.cityofhomer-ak.gov/library	Homer	AK	99603	907-235-3180	235-3136
Juneau Public Libraries 292 Marine Way *TF:* 800-478-4176 ■ *Web:* www.juneau.org	Juneau	AK	99801	907-586-5324	586-3419

Arizona

				Phone	Fax
Apache Junction Public Library 1177 N Idaho Rd *Web:* www.ajpl.org	Apache Junction	AZ	85119	480-983-6012	
Cochise County Library District 100 Quality Hill Rd *Web:* cochise.az.gov	Bisbee	AZ	85603	520-432-8930	432-7339
Chandler Public Library 22 S Delaware St *Web:* www.chandlerlibrary.org	Chandler	AZ	85225	480-782-2800	782-2823
Cottonwood Public Library 100 S Sixth St *Web:* ctwpl.info	Cottonwood	AZ	86326	928-634-7559	634-0253
Flagstaff City-Coconino County Public Library System 300 W Aspen Ave *Web:* www.flagstaffpubliclibrary.org	Flagstaff	AZ	86001	928-213-2330	
Pinal County Library District (PCLD) 92 W Butte Ave *Web:* www.pinalcountyaz.gov/departments/library	Florence	AZ	85132	520-866-6457	866-6533
Southeast Regional Library 775 N Greenfield Rd *Web:* mcldaz.org	Gilbert	AZ	85234	602-652-3000	
Glendale Public Library 5959 W Brown St *Web:* www.glendaleaz.com	Glendale	AZ	85302	623-930-3530	842-4209
Mohave Educational Services Cooperative Inc 625 E Beale St *TF:* 800-742-2437 ■ *Web:* www.mesc.org	Kingman	AZ	86401	928-753-6945	
Mesa Public Library 64 E First St *Web:* www.mesalibrary.org	Mesa	AZ	85201	480-644-3100	
Nogales City/Santa Cruz County Public Library 518 N Grand Ave *Web:* nogalesaz.gov	Nogales	AZ	85621	520-287-3343	287-4823
Page Public Library 479 Lk Powell Blvd *Web:* www.pagepubliclibrary.org	Page	AZ	86040	928-645-4270	
Peoria Public Library 8463 W Monroe St *Web:* www.peoriaaz.gov	Peoria	AZ	85345	623-773-7555	
Maricopa County Library District 2700 N Central Ave Ste 700 *Web:* www.mcldaz.org	Phoenix	AZ	85004	602-652-3000	
Phoenix Public Library 1221 N Central Ave *Web:* www.phoenixpubliclibrary.org	Phoenix	AZ	85004	602-261-8847	261-8836
Safford City - Graham County Library 808 Seventh Ave *Web:* www.cityofsafford.us	Safford	AZ	85546	928-432-4165	348-3209
Pima County Public Library 101 N Stone Ave *TF:* 877-705-5437 ■ *Web:* www.library.pima.gov	Tucson	AZ	85701	520-594-5600	594-5621

Arkansas

				Phone	Fax
Saline County Public Library 1800 Smithers *TF:* 800-476-4466 ■ *Web:* www.saline.lib.ar.us	Benton	AR	72015	501-778-4766	
Arkansas River Valley Regional Library 501 N Front St *Web:* www.arvrls.com	Dardanelle	AR	72834	479-229-4418	229-2595
Barton Library 200 E Fifth St	El Dorado	AR	71730	870-863-5447	
Washington County Library System 1080 W Clydesdale Dr *Web:* www.co.washington.ar.us	Fayetteville	AR	72701	479-442-6253	442-6812
Fort Smith Public Library 3201 Rogers Ave *TF:* 866-660-0885 ■ *Web:* fortsmithlibrary.org	Fort Smith	AR	72903	479-783-0229	
Crowley Ridge Regional Library 315 W Oak St *Web:* www.libraryinjonesboro.org	Jonesboro	AR	72401	870-935-5133	935-7987
William F. Laman Public Library System 2801 Orange St *Web:* www.lamanlibrary.org	North Little Rock	AR	72114	501-758-1720	758-3539
Pope County Library System 116 E Third St *Web:* popelibrary.org	Russellville	AR	72801	479-968-4368	968-3222
White County Public Library 113 E Pleasure St *Web:* whitecountylibraries.org	Searcy	AR	72143	501-268-2449	

California

				Phone	Fax
Alameda Free Library 1550 Oak St *Web:* alamedaca.gov	Alameda	CA	94501	510-747-7777	337-1471
Alhambra Civic Ctr Library 101 S First St *Web:* www.alhambralibrary.org	Alhambra	CA	91801	626-570-5008	457-1104
Anaheim Public Library 500 W Broadway *Web:* www.anaheim.net/902/library	Anaheim	CA	92805	714-765-1880	765-1730
Placer County Library 350 Nevada St *TF:* 800-488-4308 ■ *Web:* www.placer.ca.gov	Auburn	CA	95603	530-886-4500	886-4555
Azusa City Library 729 N Dalton Ave *Web:* www.ci.azusa.ca.us	Azusa	CA	91702	626-812-5232	334-4868
Beale Memorial Library 701 Truxtun Ave *Web:* www.kerncountylibrary.org	Bakersfield	CA	93301	661-868-0701	868-0799
Beaumont Library District 125 E Eigth St	Beaumont	CA	92223	951-845-1357	845-6217
Benicia Public Library 150 E 'L' St *Web:* www.ci.benicia.ca.us	Benicia	CA	94510	707-746-4343	747-8122
Berkeley Public Library 2090 Kittredge St *Web:* www.berkeleypubliclibrary.org	Berkeley	CA	94704	510-981-6100	981-6111
Beverly Hills Public Library 444 N Rexford Dr *Web:* www.beverlyhills.org	Beverly Hills	CA	90210	310-288-2220	278-3387
Burbank Central Library 110 N Glenoaks Blvd *Web:* www.burbank.lib.ca.us	Burbank	CA	91502	818-238-5600	238-5553
City of Carlsbad Library 1250 Carlsbad Village Dr *TF:* 866-230-2273 ■ *Web:* carlsbadca.gov	Carlsbad	CA	92008	760-434-2870	929-0256
Cerritos Civic Ctr 18025 Bloomfield Ave *TF:* 866-402-7433 ■ *Web:* www.cerritos.us	Cerritos	CA	90703	562-916-1350	916-1375
Chula Vista Public Library 365 F St *Web:* www.chulavistaca.gov/departments/library	Chula Vista	CA	91910	619-691-5069	427-4246
Colton Public Library 656 N Ninth St *Web:* ci.colton.ca.us	Colton	CA	92324	909-370-5083	422-0873
Corona Public Library 650 S Main St *Web:* www.coronapubliclibrary.org	Corona	CA	92882	951-736-2381	736-2499
Coronado Public Library 640 Orange Ave *Web:* www.coronado.ca.us	Coronado	CA	92118	619-522-7390	
Covina Public Library 234 N Second Ave *Web:* covinaca.gov	Covina	CA	91723	626-384-5300	
Daly City Public Library 40 Wembley Dr *TF:* 888-227-7669 ■ *Web:* www.dalycity.org	Daly City	CA	94015	650-991-8025	991-8225
Dixon Public Library 230 N First St *Web:* www.dixonlibrary.com	Dixon	CA	95620	707-678-5447	678-3515
Downey City Library (DCL) 11121 Brookshire Ave *TF:* 877-846-3452 ■ *Web:* www.downeyca.org	Downey	CA	90241	562-904-7360	923-3763
Los Angeles County Public Library 7400 E Imperial Hwy *TF:* 888-794-9466 ■ *Web:* www.colapublib.org	Downey	CA	90242	562-940-8462	803-3032
El Centro Public Library 539 State St *TF:* 877-482-5656 ■ *Web:* www.cityofelcentro.org/library	El Centro	CA	92243	760-337-4565	352-1384
Escondido Public Library 239 S Kalmia St *Web:* www.library.escondido.org	Escondido	CA	92025	760-839-4601	741-4255
Humboldt County Library 1313 Third St *Web:* www.humboldtgov.org/1346/public-library	Eureka	CA	95501	707-269-1900	269-1999
Alameda County Library 2450 Stevenson Blvd *TF:* 888-663-0660 ■ *Web:* aclibrary.org	Fremont	CA	94538	510-745-1500	
Fremont Main Library 2400 Stevenson Blvd *TF:* 800-434-0222 ■ *Web:* www.aclibrary.org	Fremont	CA	94538	510-745-1400	797-6557
Fresno County Public Library 2420 Mariposa St *Web:* www.fresnolibrary.org	Fresno	CA	93721	559-600-7323	
Fullerton Public Library 353 W Commonwealth Ave *Web:* www.ci.fullerton.ca.us	Fullerton	CA	92832	714-738-6333	447-3280
Garden Grove Regional Library 11200 Stanford Ave *Web:* www.ocsd.org/ocgov/ocpubliclibraries/librarylocator/gardengroveregional	Garden Grove	CA	92840	714-530-0711	
Glendale Public Library 222 E Harvard St *Web:* www.glendaleca.gov	Glendale	CA	91205	818-548-2030	548-7225
Glendora Public Library & Cultural Ctr 140 S Glendora Ave *TF:* 866-275-3772 ■ *Web:* www.ci.glendora.ca.us	Glendora	CA	91741	626-852-4891	852-4899
Kings County Library 401 N Douty St *Web:* www.kingscountylibrary.org	Hanford	CA	93230	559-582-0261	583-6163
Hayward Public Library 835 C St *Web:* www.library.ci.hayward.ca.us	Hayward	CA	94541	510-293-8685	
Hemet Public Library 300 E Latham Ave *Web:* hemetpubliclibrary.org	Hemet	CA	92543	951-765-2440	
Huntington Beach Public Library (HBPL) 7111 Talbert Ave *TF:* 800-565-0148 ■ *Web:* www.huntingtonbeachca.gov/government/departments/library	Huntington Beach	CA	92648	714-842-4481	375-5180
Inglewood Public Library 101 W Manchester Blvd *Web:* www.cityofinglewood.org/depts/library	Inglewood	CA	90301	310-412-5380	
Amador County Library 530 Sutter St *Web:* www.co.amador.ca.us	Jackson	CA	95642	209-223-6400	223-6303
Lake County Library 1425 N High St *Web:* library.co.lake.ca.us	Lakeport	CA	95453	707-263-8817	
Livermore Public Library 1188 S Livermore Ave *Web:* www.cityoflivermore.net	Livermore	CA	94550	925-373-5500	
Lodi Public Library 201 W Locust St *Web:* www.lodilibraryfoundation.org	Lodi	CA	95240	209-333-5536	
Lompoc Public Library 501 E N Ave *Web:* www.cityoflompoc.com	Lompoc	CA	93436	805-875-8775	
Long Beach Public Library 101 Pacific Ave *Web:* www.lbpl.org	Long Beach	CA	90822	562-570-7500	570-7408
Los Angeles Public Library 630 W Fifth St *Web:* www.lapl.org	Los Angeles	CA	90071	213-228-7000	228-7369
Los Gatos Public Library (LGPL) 110 E Main St *Web:* www.losgatosca.gov	Los Gatos	CA	95030	408-354-8600	354-0578
Santa Clara County Library 14600 Winchester Blvd *TF:* 800-286-1991 ■ *Web:* www.sccl.org	Los Gatos	CA	95032	408-293-2326	364-0161
Madera County Library 121 N 'G' St *Web:* www.madera-county.com	Madera	CA	93637	559-675-7871	

				Phone	Fax
Yuba County Library 303 Second St *Web:* www.co.yuba.ca.us	Marysville	CA	95901	530-749-7380	741-3098
Menlo Park Public Library 800 Alma St *Web:* www.menloparklibrary.org	Menlo Park	CA	94025	650-330-2500	327-7030
Merced County Library 2100 O St *TF:* 866-249-0773 ■ *Web:* www.co.merced.ca.us	Merced	CA	95340	209-385-7643	726-7912
Mill Valley Public Library 375 Throckmorton Ave *Web:* www.millvalleylibrary.org	Mill Valley	CA	94941	415-389-4292	388-8929
Stanislaus County 800 11th St *Web:* www.stanct.org	Modesto	CA	95354	209-530-3100	
Monrovia Public Library 321 S Myrtle Ave *TF:* 888-620-1749 ■ *Web:* www.cityofmonrovia.org	Monrovia	CA	91016	626-256-8274	256-8255
Monterey Public Library 625 Pacific St *TF:* 800-338-0505 ■ *Web:* www.monterey.org	Monterey	CA	93940	831-646-3932	646-5618
Mountain View Public Library 585 Franklin St *Web:* mountainview.gov	Mountain View	CA	94041	650-903-6335	962-0438
Napa City-County Library 580 Coombs St *TF:* 877-848-7030 ■ *Web:* countyofnapa.org	Napa	CA	94559	707-253-4241	253-4615
National City Public Library 1401 National City Blvd *Web:* www.ci.national-city.ca.us	National City	CA	91950	619-470-5800	470-5880
Nevada County Library 980 Helling Way *Web:* mynevadacounty.com/nc/library	Nevada City	CA	95959	530-265-7050	265-9863
Oakland Public Library 125 14th St *Web:* www.oaklandlibrary.org	Oakland	CA	94612	510-238-3144	238-2232
Oceanside Public Library 330 N Coast Hwy *Web:* www.ci.oceanside.ca.us	Oceanside	CA	92054	760-435-5600	
Ontario City Library 215 E C St *Web:* www.ontarioca.gov/library	Ontario	CA	91764	909-395-2004	
Orange Public Library 407 E Chapmen Ave *Web:* www.cityoforange.org/library	Orange	CA	92866	714-288-2400	771-6126
Butte County Library 1820 Mitchell Ave *Web:* www.buttecounty.net/bclibrary	Oroville	CA	95966	530-538-7641	538-7235
Oxnard Public Library (OPL) 251 S 'A' St *Web:* www.oxnardlibrary.net	Oxnard	CA	93030	805-385-7532	385-7526
City of Palm Springs 300 S Sunrise Way *TF:* 800-611-1911 ■ *Web:* www.palmspringsca.gov/government/departments/library	Palm Springs	CA	92262	760-322-7323	
Palmdale City Library 700 E Palmdale Blvd *Web:* cityofpalmdale.org	Palmdale	CA	93550	661-267-5600	
Palo Alto City Library 1213 Newell Rd *Web:* cityofpaloalto.org/gov/depts/lib/default.asp	Palo Alto	CA	94303	650-329-2436	
Pasadena Public Library 285 E Walnut St *Web:* www.cityofpasadena.net	Pasadena	CA	91101	626-744-4052	585-8396
El Dorado County Library 345 Fair Ln *Web:* www.eldoradolibrary.org	Placerville	CA	95667	530-621-5540	
Contra Costa County Library 75 Santa Barbara Rd *TF:* 800-984-4636 ■ *Web:* www.ccclib.org	Pleasant Hill	CA	94523	925-646-6423	646-6461
Pomona Public Library 625 S Garey Ave	Pomona	CA	91766	909-620-2043	620-3713
Porterville Public Library 41 W Thurman Ave *Web:* www.ci.porterville.ca.us/depts/library	Porterville	CA	93257	559-784-0177	781-4396
Rancho Cucamonga Public Library 7368 Archibald Ave *TF:* 800-655-4555 ■ *Web:* www.rcpl.lib.ca.us	Rancho Cucamonga	CA	91730	909-477-2720	477-2721
Tehama County Library 645 Madison St *Web:* tehamacountylibrary.org	Red Bluff	CA	96080	530-527-0604	527-1562
Shasta Public Library 1100 Parkview Ave *Web:* www.shastalibraries.org	Redding	CA	96001	530-245-7250	
AK Smiley Public Library 125 W Vine St *Web:* www.akspl.org	Redlands	CA	92373	909-798-7565	798-7566
Redondo Beach Public Library 303 N Pacific Coast Hwy *Web:* redondo.org	Redondo Beach	CA	90277	310-318-0675	318-3809
Redwood City Public Library 1044 Middlefield Rd *Web:* www.redwoodcity.org/library	Redwood City	CA	94063	650-780-7018	
Richmond Public Library 325 Civic Ctr Plaza *TF:* 800-833-2900 ■ *Web:* www.ci.richmond.ca.us	Richmond	CA	94804	510-620-6555	620-6850
Riverside City Public Library 3581 Mission Inn Ave *TF:* 888-225-7377 ■ *Web:* www.riversideca.gov/library	Riverside	CA	92501	951-826-5201	826-5407
Palos Verdes Library District 701 Silver Spur Rd *Web:* www.pvld.org	Rolling Hills Estates	CA	90274	310-377-9584	
Roseville Public Library 225 Taylor St *Web:* rosevillelibraryfoundation.org	Roseville	CA	95678	916-774-5221	
Sacramento Public Library 828 'I' St *Web:* www.saclibrary.org	Sacramento	CA	95814	916-264-2770	264-2755
John Steinbeck Library 350 Lincoln Ave *Web:* www.salinaspubliclibrary.org	Salinas	CA	93901	831-758-7311	
Calaveras County Library 891 Mtn Ranch Rd *Web:* calaverasgov.us	San Andreas	CA	95249	209-754-6510	
San Bruno Public Library 701 Angus Ave W *Web:* www.sanbruno.ca.gov	San Bruno	CA	94066	650-616-7078	876-0848
San Diego County Library System 5560 Overland Ave Ste 110 *Web:* www.sdcl.org	San Diego	CA	92123	858-694-2415	
San Diego Public Library 820 E St *TF:* 866-470-1308 ■ *Web:* www.sandiego.gov/public-library	San Diego	CA	92101	619-236-5800	236-5878
San Francisco Public Library 100 Larkin St *Web:* www.sfpl.org	San Francisco	CA	94102	415-557-4400	557-4239
San Jose Public Library 150 E San Fernando St *Web:* www.sjpl.org	San Jose	CA	95113	408-808-2000	
City of San Leandro Public Library, The 835 E 14th St *Web:* www.sanleandro.org	San Leandro	CA	94577	510-577-3351	278-3095

				Phone	Fax
San Luis Obispo City-County Library 995 Palm St *Web:* www.slolibrary.org	San Luis Obispo	CA	93401	805-781-5991	
Marin County Free Library 3501 Civic Ctr Dr Ste 414 *Web:* marinlibrary.org	San Rafael	CA	94903	415-499-3220	499-3726
San Rafael Public Library 1400 Fifth Ave *Web:* www.cityofsanrafael.org	San Rafael	CA	94901	415-485-3323	
Orange County Public Library 1501 E St Andrew Pl *Web:* ocpl.org	Santa Ana	CA	92705	714-566-3000	
Santa Ana Public Library 26 Civic Ctr Dr *Web:* www.ci.santa-ana.ca.us/library	Santa Ana	CA	92701	714-647-5250	
Santa Barbara Public Library 40 E Anapamu St *Web:* santabarbaraca.gov	Santa Barbara	CA	93101	805-962-7653	564-5660
Santa Clara City Library 2635 Homestead Rd *Web:* santaclaraca.gov/government/departments/library	Santa Clara	CA	95051	408-615-2900	
Garfield Park Library 705 Woodrow Ave *Web:* www.santacruzpl.org	Santa Cruz	CA	95060	831-427-7713	
Santa Maria Public Library 420 S Broadway *Web:* www.cityofsantamaria.org	Santa Maria	CA	93454	805-925-0994	928-7432
Santa Monica Public Library 1343 Sixth St *Web:* www.smpl.org	Santa Monica	CA	90401	310-458-8608	
Sonoma County Library Third & E Sts *Web:* sonomalibrary.org	Santa Rosa	CA	95404	707-545-0831	
South San Francisco Public Library 840 W Orange Ave *Web:* www.ssf.net	South San Francisco	CA	94080	650-829-3860	829-3866
Stockton-San Joaquin County Public Library (SSJCPL) 605 N El Dorado St *TF:* 866-805-7323 ■ *Web:* www.ssjcpl.org	Stockton	CA	95202	209-937-8416	
Sunnyvale Public Library (SPL) 665 W Olive Ave *Web:* www.sunnyvale.ca.gov/Departments/SunnyvalePublicLibrary.aspx	Sunnyvale	CA	94086	408-730-7300	
Thousand Oaks Library 1401 E Janss Rd *Web:* www.tol.lib.ca.us	Thousand Oaks	CA	91362	805-449-2660	373-6858
Belvedere-Tiburon Public Library 1501 Tiburon Blvd *Web:* www.beltiblibrary.org	Tiburon	CA	94920	415-789-2665	789-2650
Torrance Public Library 3301 Torrance Blvd *Web:* www.torranceca.gov	Torrance	CA	90503	310-618-5959	618-5952
Tulare Public Library 475 N M St *Web:* www.tularepubliclibrary.org	Tulare	CA	93274	559-685-4500	
Mendocino County Library 105 N Main St *Web:* www.co.mendocino.ca.us	Ukiah	CA	95482	707-463-4491	463-5472
Upland Public Library 450 N Euclid Ave *Web:* www.uplandpl.lib.ca.us	Upland	CA	91786	909-931-4200	931-4209
EP Foster Library 651 E Main St *Web:* www.vencolibrary.org	Ventura	CA	93001	805-648-2716	648-3696
Ventura County Libraries 646 County Sq Dr Ste 150 *Web:* www.vencolibrary.org	Ventura	CA	93003	805-477-7331	477-7340
Tulare County Library System 200 W Oak Ave *Web:* www.tularecountylibrary.org	Visalia	CA	93291	559-713-2700	
Watsonville Public Library 275 Main St Ste 100 *Web:* cityofwatsonville.org	Watsonville	CA	95076	831-768-3400	763-4015
Woodland Public Library 250 First St *TF:* 800-321-2752 ■ *Web:* www.cityofwoodland.org/library	Woodland	CA	95695	530-661-5980	666-5408
Yolo County Library 226 Buckeye St *Web:* yolocounty.org	Woodland	CA	95695	530-666-8005	666-8006
Yorba Linda Public Library 18181 Imperial Hwy *Web:* www.ylpl.net	Yorba Linda	CA	92886	714-777-2873	777-0640
Siskiyou County Library 719 Fourth St	Yreka	CA	96097	530-841-4175	
Sutter County Library 750 Forbes Ave *TF:* 800-533-2873 ■ *Web:* co.sutter.ca.us	Yuba City	CA	95991	530-822-7137	671-6539

Colorado

				Phone	Fax
Aurora Public Library 14949 E Alameda Pkwy *Web:* www.odyssey.aurora.lib.co.us	Aurora	CO	80012	303-739-6600	739-6638
Basalt Regional Library 14 Midland Ave *Web:* basaltrld.org	Basalt	CO	81621	970-927-4311	
Boulder Public Library 1001 Arapahoe Ave *Web:* www.boulderlibrary.org	Boulder	CO	80302	303-441-3100	
Mamie Doud Eisenhower Public Library 3 Community Pk Rd *Web:* www.ci.broomfield.co.us	Broomfield	CO	80020	720-887-2300	887-1384
Douglas County Libraries 100 S Wilcox *Web:* douglascountylibraries.org	Castle Rock	CO	80104	303-791-7323	
Pikes Peak Library District PO Box 1579 *Web:* www.ppld.org	Colorado Springs	CO	80901	719-531-6333	
Denver Public Library 10 W 14th Ave Pkwy *Web:* www.denverlibrary.org	Denver	CO	80204	720-865-1111	
Englewood Public Library 1000 Englewood Pkwy Englewood Civic Ctr 1st Fl *TF:* 866-922-9006 ■ *Web:* www.englewoodgov.org	Englewood	CO	80110	303-762-2560	783-6890
Poudre River Public Library 201 Peterson St *Web:* www.poudrelibraries.org	Fort Collins	CO	80524	970-221-6740	
American Alpine Club 710 Tenth St Ste 15 *Web:* americanalpineclub.org	Golden	CO	80401	303-384-0112	
Farr Regional Library 1939 61st Ave *TF:* 888-861-7323 ■ *Web:* www.mylibrary.us	Greeley	CO	80634	970-506-8550	506-8551
Bemis Public Library 6014 S Datura St *Web:* www.littletongov.org	Littleton	CO	80120	303-795-3961	795-3996

				Phone	Fax
Longmont Public Library 409 Fourth Ave *Web:* longmontcolorado.gov	Longmont	CO	80501	303-651-8470	
Bud Werner Memorial Library 1289 Lincoln Ave *Web:* www.steamboatlibrary.org	Steamboat Springs	CO	80487	970-879-0240	
Rangeview Library District 5877 E 120th Ave *TF:* 800-222-3937 ■ *Web:* www.anythinklibraries.org	Thornton	CO	80602	303-288-2001	451-0190
Westminster Public Library 7392 Irving St *Web:* www.ci.westminster.co.us	Westminster	CO	80030	303-430-2400	

Connecticut

				Phone	Fax
Avon Free Public Library 281 Country Club Rd *Web:* www.avonctlibrary.info	Avon	CT	06001	860-673-9712	675-6364
Bridgeport Public Library 925 Broad St *Web:* www.bportlibrary.org	Bridgeport	CT	06604	203-576-7403	576-8255
Bristol Public Library 5 High St *TF:* 877-603-7323 ■ *Web:* bristollib.com	Bristol	CT	06010	860-584-7787	584-7696
Cheshire Public Library 104 Main St *Web:* cheshirelibrary.com	Cheshire	CT	06410	203-272-2245	272-7714
Danbury Public Library 170 Main St *Web:* www.danburylibrary.org	Danbury	CT	06810	203-797-4505	796-1677
Town of East Hampton Senior Center 105 Main St *Web:* www.easthamptonct.org	East Hampton	CT	06424	860-267-4426	
East Hartford Public Library 840 Main St *Web:* www.easthartfordct.gov/library	East Hartford	CT	06108	860-289-6429	291-9166
Enfield Public Library 104 Middle Rd *Web:* www.enfield-ct.gov	Enfield	CT	06082	860-763-7510	763-7514
Fairfield Public Library 1080 Old Post Rd *Web:* www.fairfieldpubliclibrary.org	Fairfield	CT	06824	203-256-3155	
Welles-Turner Memorial Library 2407 Main St *TF:* 800-411-9671 ■ *Web:* www.wtmlib.com	Glastonbury	CT	06033	860-652-7719	652-7721
Groton Public Library 52 Newtown Rd *Web:* www.groton-ct.gov/library	Groton	CT	06340	860-441-6750	448-0363
Hamden Library 2901 Dixwell Ave *Web:* www.hamdenlibrary.org	Hamden	CT	06518	203-287-2686	
Hartford Public Library 500 Main St *Web:* www.hplct.org	Hartford	CT	06103	860-695-6300	722-6900
Mary Cheney Library 586 Main St *Web:* library.townofmanchester.org	Manchester	CT	06040	860-643-2471	643-9453
Meriden Public Library 105 Miller St *TF:* 800-567-0902 ■ *Web:* meridenlibrary.org	Meriden	CT	06450	203-238-2344	238-3647
Milford Public Library 57 New Haven Ave	Milford	CT	06460	203-783-3304	
New Canaan Library 151 Main St *TF:* 800-545-2433 ■ *Web:* www.newcanaanlibrary.org	New Canaan	CT	06840	203-594-5000	594-5026
New Fairfield Free Public Library 2 Brush Hill Rd *TF:* 877-227-7487 ■ *Web:* www.newfairfieldlibrary.org	New Fairfield	CT	06812	203-312-5679	312-5685
Haskins Laboratories Library 300 George St Ste 900 *Web:* www.haskins.yale.edu	New Haven	CT	06511	203-865-6163	
New Haven Free Public Library 133 Elm St *Web:* www.cityofnewhaven.com/library	New Haven	CT	06510	203-946-8130	946-8140
Lucy Robbins Welles Library 95 Cedar St *TF:* 800-842-1423 ■ *Web:* www.newingtonct.gov	Newington	CT	06111	860-665-8700	667-1255
Norwalk Public Library 1 Belden Ave *TF:* 800-382-9463 ■ *Web:* www.norwalklib.org	Norwalk	CT	06850	203-899-2780	866-7982
Plumb Memorial Library 65 Wooster St *Web:* www.sheltonlibrarysystem.org	Shelton	CT	06484	203-924-1580	924-8422
Simsbury Public Library 725 Hopmeadow St *Web:* www.simsburylibrary.info	Simsbury	CT	06070	860-658-7663	658-6732
Southington Public Library 255 Main St *Web:* www.southingtonlibrary.org	Southington	CT	06489	860-628-0947	
Ferguson Library 1 Public Library Plz *Web:* www.fergusonlibrary.org	Stamford	CT	06904	203-964-1000	357-9098
Willoughby Wallace Memorial Library (WWML) 146 Thimble Islands Rd *Web:* www.wwml.org	Stony Creek	CT	06405	203-488-8702	315-3347
Trumbull Library 33 Quality St *Web:* www.trumbullct-library.org	Trumbull	CT	06611	203-452-5197	452-5125
Silas Bronson Library (SBL) 267 Grand St *Web:* www.bronsonlibrary.org	Waterbury	CT	06702	203-574-8222	574-8055
West Hartford Public Library 20 S Main St *Web:* www.westhartfordlibrary.org	West Hartford	CT	06107	860-561-6950	561-6990
Windsor Public Library 323 Broad St *Web:* www.windsorlibrary.com	Windsor	CT	06095	860-285-1910	

Delaware

				Phone	Fax
Kent County Library 2319 S Dupont Hwy *Web:* www.co.kent.de.us/departments/communitysvcs/library	Dover	DE	19901	302-698-6440	698-6441
Hockessin Library 1023 Valley Rd *TF:* 888-352-7722 ■ *Web:* www.nccde.org	Hockessin	DE	19707	302-239-5160	239-1519
New Castle Public Library 424 Delaware St *TF:* 877-225-7351	New Castle	DE	19720	302-328-1995	378-5594
New Castle County Library 750 Library Ave *TF:* 877-225-7351 ■ *Web:* nccde.org	Newark	DE	19711	302-731-7550	731-4019
Rehoboth Beach Public Library 226 Rehoboth Ave *Web:* www.rehobothlibrary.org	Rehoboth Beach	DE	19971	302-227-8044	227-0597
Kirkwood Library 6000 Kirkwood Hwy *TF:* 888-352-7722 ■ *Web:* www.nccde.org	Wilmington	DE	19808	302-995-7663	995-7687
Wilmington Public Library 10 E Tenth St *Web:* wilmington.lib.de.us	Wilmington	DE	19801	302-571-7400	654-9132

District of Columbia

				Phone	Fax
Library of Congress (LOC) 101 Independence Ave SE *Web:* www.loc.gov	Washington	DC	20540	202-707-5000	
Martin Luther King Jr Memorial Library (MLK) 901 G St NW *Web:* www.dclibrary.org	Washington	DC	20001	202-727-0321	
Medicare Payment Advisory Comm 601 New Jersey Ave Nw *Web:* www.medpac.gov	Washington	DC	20001	202-220-3700	

Florida

				Phone	Fax
DeSoto County Library 125 N Hillsboro Ave *Web:* www.myhlc.org	Arcadia	FL	34266	863-993-4851	
Citrus County Library System 425 W Roosevelt Blvd *Web:* www.cclib.org	Beverly Hills	FL	34465	352-746-9077	746-9493
Boca Raton Public Library 400 NW Second Ave *Web:* www.bocalibrary.org	Boca Raton	FL	33432	561-393-7852	
Boynton Beach City Library 208 S Seacrest Blvd *Web:* www.boyntonlibrary.org	Boynton Beach	FL	33435	561-742-6390	
Manatee County Public Library System PO Box 1000 *Web:* www.mymanatee.org	Bradenton	FL	34206	941-748-4501	749-7191
Hernando County Public Library System 238 Howell Ave *Web:* www.hcpl.lib.fl.us	Brooksville	FL	34601	352-754-4043	754-4044
Seminole County Public Library 215 N Oxford Rd *Web:* www.seminolecountyfl.gov/lls/library	Casselberry	FL	32707	407-665-0000	
Clearwater Public Library 100 N Osceola Ave *TF:* 800-342-8060 ■ *Web:* www.myclearwater.com/cpl	Clearwater	FL	33755	727-562-4970	562-4977
Clewiston Public Library System 120 W Osceola Ave *Web:* www.hendrylibraries.org	Clewiston	FL	33440	863-983-1493	983-9194
Central Brevard Library 308 Forest Ave *Web:* www.brevardcounty.us	Cocoa	FL	32922	321-633-1792	633-1806
Volusia County Public Library 105 E Magnolia Ave *Web:* www.volusialibrary.org	Daytona Beach	FL	32114	386-257-6036	
Walton-De Funiak Library 3 Cir Dr *TF:* 800-342-0141 ■ *Web:* co.walton.fl.us	DeFuniak Springs	FL	32435	850-892-3624	892-4438
Delray Beach Library 100 W Atlantic Ave *Web:* www.delraylibrary.org	Delray Beach	FL	33444	561-266-0194	
Broward County Library 100 S Andrews Ave *Web:* www.broward.org/library/pages/default.aspx	Fort Lauderdale	FL	33301	954-357-7444	
Lee County Library 2050 Central Ave *Web:* www.leegov.com/library	Fort Myers	FL	33901	239-479-4636	
Saint Lucie County Library System 2300 Virginia Ave *Web:* www.st-lucie.lib.fl.us	Fort Pierce	FL	34982	772-462-1100	462-2750
Alachua County Library District 401 E University Ave *TF:* 866-341-2730 ■ *Web:* www.aclib.us	Gainesville	FL	32601	352-334-3900	334-3918
John F Kennedy Library (JFKL) 190 W 49th St *TF:* 877-738-5622 ■ *Web:* www.hialeahfl.gov/library	Hialeah	FL	33012	305-821-2700	818-9144
Pasco County Library System 8012 Library Rd *Web:* www.pascolibraries.org	Hudson	FL	34667	727-861-3020	861-3025
Monroe County Public Library System 700 Fleming St *TF:* 877-772-8346 ■ *Web:* keyslibraries.org	Key West	FL	33040	305-292-3595	295-3626
Columbia County Public Library 308 NW Columbia Ave PO Box 1529 *Web:* www.columbiacountyfla.com/default.asp	Lake City	FL	32055	386-758-2101	758-2135
Lake Worth Public Library 15 N 'M' St *Web:* www.lakeworth.org	Lake Worth	FL	33460	561-533-7354	586-1651
Lakeland Public Library 100 Lk Morton Dr *Web:* www.lakelandgov.net/library/home.aspx	Lakeland	FL	33801	863-834-4270	
Leesburg Public Library 100 E Main St *Web:* www.leesburgflorida.gov	Leesburg	FL	34748	352-728-9790	728-9794
Collier County Public Library (CCPL) 2385 Orange Blossom Dr *Web:* www.colliergov.net	Naples	FL	34109	239-593-0177	
North Miami Public Library 835 NE 132nd St *Web:* northmiamifl.gov	North Miami	FL	33161	305-891-5535	892-0843
North Miami Beach Public Library 1601 NE 164th St *Web:* nmblib.com	North Miami Beach	FL	33162	305-948-2970	787-6007
Orange County Library System 101 E Central Blvd *Web:* www.ocls.lib.fl.us	Orlando	FL	32801	407-835-7323	
Flagler County Public Library (FCPL) 2500 Palm Coast Pkwy NW *TF:* 877-863-5244 ■ *Web:* www.flaglercounty.org	Palm Coast	FL	32137	386-446-6763	446-6773
Bay County Public Library 898 W 11th St *Web:* www.nwrls.lib.fl.us	Panama City	FL	32401	850-522-2100	
Northwest Regional Library System 898 W 11th St *Web:* www.nwrls.com	Panama City	FL	32401	850-522-2100	522-2138
West Florida Regional Library 200 W Gregory St *TF:* 800-435-7352 ■ *Web:* www.cityofpensacola.com	Pensacola	FL	32501	850-436-5060	

				Phone	Fax
Helen B Hoffman Plantation Library 501 N Fig Tree Ln *TF:* 800-774-5866 ■ *Web:* plantation.org	Plantation	FL	33317	954-797-2140	797-2767
Gadsden County Public Library 732 Pat Thomas Pkwy *Web:* www.gcpls.org	Quincy	FL	32351	850-627-7106	
Riviera Beach Public Library 600 W Blue Heron Blvd *Web:* rivierabch.com	Riviera Beach	FL	33404	561-845-4195	881-7308
St. Johns County Public Library 1960 N Ponce de Leon Blvd *Web:* www.sjcpls.org	Saint Augustine	FL	32084	904-827-6940	827-6945
Saint Petersburg Public Library 3745 Ninth Ave N *Web:* www.splibraries.org	Saint Petersburg	FL	33713	727-893-7724	
Seminole County Public Library - North Branch 150 N Palmetto Ave *Web:* www.seminolecountyfl.gov/lls/library	Sanford	FL	32771	407-665-1620	330-3120
Selby Public Library 1331 First St *Web:* www.selbylibraryfriends.org	Sarasota	FL	34236	941-365-5228	
Heartland Library Co-op 319 W Ctr Ave *Web:* www.myhlc.org	Sebring	FL	33870	863-402-6716	
Martin County Public Library 2401 SE Monterey Rd *Web:* www.martin.fl.us	Stuart	FL	34996	772-288-5702	219-4959
Leon County Public Library System 200 W Pk Ave *Web:* cms.leoncountyfl.gov/library	Tallahassee	FL	32301	850-487-2665	
Tampa-Hillsborough County Public Library 900 N Ashley Dr *Web:* www.hcplc.org	Tampa	FL	33602	813-273-3652	
Indian River County Library (IRCL) 1600 21st St *Web:* www.irclibrary.org	Vero Beach	FL	32960	772-770-5060	770-5066
Palm Beach County Public Library System 3650 Summit Blvd *Web:* www.pbclibrary.org	West Palm Beach	FL	33406	561-233-2600	
West Palm Beach Public Library 411 Clematis St *TF:* 866-472-7275 ■ *Web:* www.wpb.org	West Palm Beach	FL	33401	561-868-7700	822-1892

Georgia

				Phone	Fax
Dougherty County Public Library 300 N Pine Ave *Web:* www.docolib.org	Albany	GA	31701	229-420-3200	
Athens/Clarke County Library 2025 Baxter St *Web:* athenslibrary.org	Athens	GA	30606	706-613-3650	613-3660
Atlanta-Fulton Public Library 1 Margaret Mitchell Sq *Web:* www.afpls.org/locations/locations2	Atlanta	GA	30303	404-730-1700	730-1990
Augusta-Richmond County Library 823 Telfair St *Web:* ecgrl.public.lib.ga.us	Augusta	GA	30901	706-821-2600	724-6762
Brunswick-Glynn County Regional Library 208 Gloucester St *TF:* 800-222-6748	Brunswick	GA	31520	912-279-3740	261-3849
West Georgia Regional Library 710 Rome St *Web:* www.wgrl.net	Carrollton	GA	30117	770-836-6711	836-4787
Bartow County Public Library 429 W Main St *Web:* www.bartowlibraryonline.org	Cartersville	GA	30120	770-382-4203	
Columbus Public Library 3000 Macon Rd *TF:* 800-652-0782 ■ *Web:* www.cvlga.org/branches/columbus	Columbus	GA	31906	706-243-2669	
Northwest Georgia Regional Library 310 Cappes St *Web:* www.ngrl.org	Dalton	GA	30720	706-876-1360	
DeKalb County Public Library 215 Sycamore St *TF:* 800-677-1116 ■ *Web:* dekalblibrary.org	Decatur	GA	30030	404-370-3070	370-8469
Flint River Regional Library 800 Memorial Dr *Web:* frrls.net	Griffin	GA	30223	770-412-4770	
Clayton County Library System 865 Battle Creek Rd *Web:* claytonpl.org	Jonesboro	GA	30236	770-473-3850	
LaFayette-Walker County Library 305 S Duke St *Web:* www.chrl.org	La Fayette	GA	30728	706-638-2992	638-4028
Gwinnett County Public Library 1001 Lawrenceville Hwy *Web:* www.gwinnettpl.org	Lawrenceville	GA	30046	770-822-4522	
Middle Georgia Regional Library System 1180 Washington Ave *Web:* maconbibb.us	Macon	GA	31201	478-744-0800	621-5823
Cobb County Public Library System 266 Roswell St *Web:* www.cobbcat.org	Marietta	GA	30060	770-528-2320	
Henry County Public Library System 1001 Florence McGarity Blvd *TF:* 877-527-3712 ■ *Web:* www.henry.public.lib.ga.us	McDonough	GA	30252	770-954-2806	954-2808
Sara Hightower Regional Library 205 Riverside Pkwy NE *Web:* rome.shrls.org	Rome	GA	30161	706-236-4600	236-4631
Live Oak Public Libraries 2002 Bull St *Web:* www.liveoakpl.org	Savannah	GA	31401	912-652-3600	652-3638
South Georgia Regional Library 300 Woodrow Wilson Dr *Web:* www.sgrl.org	Valdosta	GA	31602	229-333-0086	333-7669

Idaho

				Phone	Fax
Boise Public Library 715 S Capitol Blvd *Web:* www.boisepubliclibrary.org	Boise	ID	83702	208-384-4076	384-4025
Coeur d'Alene Public Library 702 E Front *Web:* www.cdalibrary.org	Coeur d'Alene	ID	83814	208-769-2315	769-2381
Idaho Falls Public Library 457 W Broadway *Web:* www.ifpl.org	Idaho Falls	ID	83402	208-612-8460	
Lewiston City Library 428 Thain Rd *Web:* www.cityoflewiston.org	Lewiston	ID	83501	208-743-6519	798-4446
Nampa Public Library (NPL) 101 11th Ave S *Web:* nampalibrary.org	Nampa	ID	83651	208-468-5800	465-2277
Marshall Public Library 113 S Garfield Ave *Web:* www.marshallpl.org	Pocatello	ID	83204	208-232-1263	
East Bonner County Library District 1407 W Cedar St *Web:* ebonnerlibrary.org	Sandpoint	ID	83864	208-263-6930	
Twin Falls Public Library 201 Fourth Ave E *Web:* www.twinfallspubliclibrary.org	Twin Falls	ID	83301	208-733-2964	733-2965

Illinois

				Phone	Fax
Addison Public Library 4 Friendship Plaza *Web:* www.addisonlibrary.org	Addison	IL	60101	630-543-3617	
Algonquin Area Public Library District 2600 Harnish *Web:* www.aapld.org	Algonquin	IL	60102	847-658-4343	
Arlington Heights Memorial Library 500 N Dunton Ave *Web:* www.ahml.info	Arlington Heights	IL	60004	847-392-0100	506-2650
Aurora Public Library 1 E Benton St *Web:* www.aurora.lib.il.us	Aurora	IL	60505	630-264-4100	896-3209
Batavia Public Library District 10 S Batavia Ave *Web:* www.batavia.lib.il.us	Batavia	IL	60510	630-879-1393	
Bensenville Community Public Library 200 S Church Rd *Web:* www.bensenville.lib.il.us	Bensenville	IL	60106	630-766-4642	766-0788
Berwyn Public Library (BPL) 2701 S Harlem Ave *Web:* www.berwynlibrary.org	Berwyn	IL	60402	708-795-8000	795-8101
Bloomington Public Library 205 E Olive St *Web:* blpl.ent.sirsi.net	Bloomington	IL	61701	309-828-6091	
Fountaindale Public Library 300 W Briarcliff Rd *Web:* www.fountaindale.org	Bolingbrook	IL	60440	630-759-2102	
Calumet City Public Library 660 Manistee Ave *Web:* calumetcitypl.org	Calumet City	IL	60409	708-862-6220	862-0872
Carbondale Public Library 405 W Main St *Web:* carbondalepubliclibrary.org	Carbondale	IL	62901	618-457-0354	457-0353
Carol Stream Public Library 616 Hiawatha Dr *TF:* 800-829-1040 ■ *Web:* www.cslibrary.org	Carol Stream	IL	60188	630-653-0755	653-6809
Chicago Public Library 400 S State St *Web:* www.chipublib.org	Chicago	IL	60605	312-747-4300	
Gerber/Hart Library & Archives 6500 N Clark St *Web:* www.gerberhart.org	Chicago	IL	60626	773-381-8030	381-8030
Cicero Public Library 5225 W Cermak Rd *Web:* cicerolibrary.org	Cicero	IL	60804	708-652-8084	652-8095
Crystal Lake Public Library 126 W Paddock St *Web:* www.crystallakelibrary.org	Crystal Lake	IL	60014	815-459-1687	
Danville Public Library 319 N Vermilion St *TF:* 866-235-6096 ■ *Web:* www.danville.lib.il.us	Danville	IL	61832	217-477-5220	477-5230
Decatur Public Library 130 N Franklin St *Web:* decaturlibrary.org	Decatur	IL	62523	217-424-2900	233-4071
DeKalb Public Library 309 Oak St *TF:* 888-268-2824 ■ *Web:* www.dkpl.org	DeKalb	IL	60115	815-756-9568	756-7837
Des Plaines Public Library 1501 Ellinwood Ave *TF:* 800-829-1040 ■ *Web:* www.dppl.org	Des Plaines	IL	60016	847-827-5551	827-7974
Downers Grove Public Library 1050 Curtiss St *Web:* www.downersgrovelibrary.org	Downers Grove	IL	60515	630-960-1200	960-9374
Elk Grove Village Public Library 1001 Wellington Ave *TF:* 800-252-8980 ■ *Web:* www.egvpl.org	Elk Grove Village	IL	60007	847-439-0447	439-0475
Elmhurst Public Library 125 S Prospect Ave *Web:* www.elmhurstpubliclibrary.org	Elmhurst	IL	60126	630-279-8696	279-0636
Evanston Public Library 1703 Orrington Ave *TF:* 888-253-7003 ■ *Web:* epl.org	Evanston	IL	60201	847-448-8600	866-0313
Freeport Public Library 100 E Douglas St *Web:* www.freeportpubliclibrary.org	Freeport	IL	61032	815-233-3000	297-8236
Galesburg Public Library 40 E Simmons St *Web:* www.galesburglibrary.org	Galesburg	IL	61401	309-343-6118	343-4877
DuPage Library System 127 S First St *Web:* www.dupagels.lib.il.us	Geneva	IL	60134	630-232-8457	232-0699
Glenview Public Library 1930 Glenview Rd *Web:* www.glenviewpl.org	Glenview	IL	60025	847-729-7500	729-7558
Grande Prairie Public Library 3479 W 183rd St *TF:* 800-321-9511 ■ *Web:* www.grandeprairie.org	Hazel Crest	IL	60429	708-798-5563	798-5874
Highland Park Public Library 494 Laurel Ave *Web:* www.hplibrary.org	Highland Park	IL	60035	847-432-0216	432-9139
Joliet Public Library 150 N Ottawa St *Web:* jolietlibrary.org	Joliet	IL	60432	815-740-2660	740-6161
Kankakee Public Library 201 E Ct St *Web:* www.lions-online.org	Kankakee	IL	60901	815-939-4564	
Lake Villa Illinois Public Library District 1001 E Grand Ave *Web:* www.lvdl.org	Lake Villa	IL	60046	847-356-7711	

				Phone	Fax
Ela Area Public Library District 275 Mohawk Trl *Web:* www.eapl.org	Lake Zurich	IL	60047	847-438-3433	438-9290
Lewis O Flom Lansing Public Library 2750 Indiana Ave *Web:* www.lansingpl.org	Lansing	IL	60438	708-474-2447	474-9466
Lexington Public Library District 207 S Cedar St *Web:* lexington.lib.il.us	Lexington	IL	61753	309-365-7801	
Cook Memorial Public Library District 413-n Milwaukee Ave *Web:* www.cooklib.org	Libertyville	IL	60048	847-362-2330	
Lisle Library District 777 Front St *Web:* www.lislelibrary.org	Lisle	IL	60532	630-971-1675	
Helen M Plum Memorial Library 110 W Maple St *Web:* helenplum.org	Lombard	IL	60148	630-627-0316	627-0336
Maywood Public Library 121 S Fifth Ave *Web:* www.maywood.org	Maywood	IL	60153	708-343-1847	343-2115
McHenry Public Library District 809 N Front St *Web:* mchenrylibrary.org	Mchenry	IL	60050	815-385-0036	
Morton Grove Public Library 6140 Lincoln Ave *Web:* www.mgpl.org	Morton Grove	IL	60053	847-965-4220	965-7903
Mount Prospect Public Library 10 S Emerson St *Web:* www.mppl.org	Mount Prospect	IL	60056	847-253-5675	
Naperville Public Libraries 200 W Jefferson Ave *Web:* www.naperville-lib.org	Naperville	IL	60540	630-961-4100	637-4870
Normal Public Library 206 W College *Web:* www.normalpl.org	Normal	IL	61761	309-452-1757	452-5312
North Chicago Public Library 2100 Argonne Dr *Web:* ncplibrary.org	North Chicago	IL	60064	847-689-0125	689-9117
Northbrook Public Library 1201 Cedar Ln *Web:* northbrook.info	Northbrook	IL	60062	847-272-6224	498-0440
Oak Lawn Public Library 9427 Raymond Ave *Web:* www.olpl.org	Oak Lawn	IL	60453	708-422-4990	422-5061
Oak Park Public Library 834 Lake St *Web:* www.oppl.org	Oak Park	IL	60301	708-383-8200	
Orland Park Public Library 14921 Ravinia Ave *Web:* www.orlandparklibrary.org	Orland Park	IL	60462	708-428-5100	349-8196
Park Forest Public Library 400 Lakewood Blvd *Web:* www.pfpl.org	Park Forest	IL	60466	708-748-3731	748-8829
Park Ridge Public Library 20 S Prospect Ave *Web:* www.parkridgelibrary.org	Park Ridge	IL	60068	847-825-3123	825-0001
Pekin Public Library 301 S Fourth St *Web:* www.pekinpubliclibrary.org	Pekin	IL	61554	309-347-7111	347-6587
Peoria Public Library 107 NE Monroe St *Web:* www.peoriapubliclibrary.org	Peoria	IL	61602	309-497-2135	
Quincy Public Library 526 Jersey St *Web:* www.quincylibrary.org	Quincy	IL	62301	217-223-1309	
Rock Island Public Library 401 19th St *Web:* www.rockislandlibrary.org	Rock Island	IL	61201	309-732-7323	
Rockford Public Library 215 N Wyman St *Web:* www.rockfordpubliclibrary.org	Rockford	IL	61101	815-965-6731	
Schaumburg Township District Library (STDL) 130 S Roselle Rd *Web:* www.schaumburglibrary.org	Schaumburg	IL	60193	847-985-4000	
Shorewood-Troy Public Library District 650 Deerwood Dr *Web:* www.shorewoodtroylibrary.org	Shorewood	IL	60404	815-725-1715	725-1722
Skokie Public Library 5215 Oakton St *Web:* www.skokielibrary.info	Skokie	IL	60077	847-673-7774	673-7797
Lincoln Library 326 S Seventh St *Web:* www.lincolnlibrary.info	Springfield	IL	62701	217-753-4900	
Tinley Park Public Library 7851 Timber Dr *Web:* www.tplibrary.org	Tinley Park	IL	60477	708-532-0160	532-2981
Urbana Free Library 210 W Green St *Web:* www.urbanafreelibrary.org	Urbana	IL	61801	217-367-4057	367-4061
Waukegan Public Library 128 N County St *Web:* www.waukeganpl.org	Waukegan	IL	60085	847-623-2041	
Wheaton Public Library 225 N Cross St *Web:* www.wheaton.lib.il.us	Wheaton	IL	60187	630-668-1374	668-8950
Winnetka-Northfield Public Library District 768 Oak St *Web:* winnetkalibrary.org	Winnetka	IL	60093	847-446-7220	
Woodridge Public Library 3 Plaza Dr *TF:* 800-279-0400 ■ *Web:* www.woodridgelibrary.org	Woodridge	IL	60517	630-964-7899	964-0175

Indiana

				Phone	Fax
Anderson Public Library 111 E 12th St *Web:* www.and.lib.in.us	Anderson	IN	46016	765-641-2456	641-2197
Eckhart Public Library 603 S Jackson St *Web:* www.epl.lib.in.us	Auburn	IN	46706	260-925-2414	
Batesville Memorial Public Library (BMPL) 131 N Walnut St *Web:* www.ebatesville.com/library	Batesville	IN	47006	812-934-4706	934-6288
Bedford Public Library 1323 K St *Web:* www.bedlib.org	Bedford	IN	47421	812-275-4471	
Monroe County Public Library 303 E Kirkwood Ave *Web:* www.monroe.lib.in.us	Bloomington	IN	47408	812-349-3050	349-3051
Wells County Public Library 200 W Washington St *TF:* 800-824-6111 ■ *Web:* www.wellscolibrary.org	Bluffton	IN	46714	260-824-1612	824-3129
Carmel Clay Public Library 55 Fourth Ave SE *TF:* 800-908-4490 ■ *Web:* www.carmel.lib.in.us	Carmel	IN	46032	317-844-3361	571-4285
Charlestown Clark County Public Library 51 Clark Rd *Web:* www.clarkco.lib.in.us	Charlestown	IN	47111	812-256-3337	256-3890
Bartholomew County Public Library 536 Fifth St *Web:* mybcpl.org	Columbus	IN	47201	812-379-1255	
Fayette County Public Library 828 N Grand Ave *TF:* 844-829-3746 ■ *Web:* www.fcplibrary.lib.in.us	Connersville	IN	47331	765-827-0883	825-4592
Harrison County Public Library District 105 N Capital Ave *Web:* www.hcpl.lib.in.us	Corydon	IN	47112	812-738-4110	
Lincoln Heritage Public Library 105 N Wallace St *Web:* www.lincolnheritage.lib.in.us	Dale	IN	47523	812-937-7170	
East Chicago Public Library (ECPL) 2401 E Columbus Dr *Web:* www.ecpl.org	East Chicago	IN	46312	219-397-2453	
Evansville Vanderburgh Public Library 200 SE ML King Jr Blvd *Web:* www.evpl.org	Evansville	IN	47713	812-428-8200	428-8397
Allen County Public Library 900 Library Plaza *TF:* 800-448-6160 ■ *Web:* www.acpl.lib.in.us	Fort Wayne	IN	46802	260-421-1200	421-1386
Frankfort Community Public Library (FCPL) 208 W Clinton St *Web:* myfcpl.org	Frankfort	IN	46041	765-654-8746	654-8747
Johnson County Public Library 401 S State St *Web:* pageafterpage.org	Franklin	IN	46131	317-738-2833	738-9635
Gary Public Library 220 W Fifth Ave *Web:* www.garypubliclibrary.org	Gary	IN	46402	219-886-2484	886-6829
Putnam County Public Library 103 E Poplar St *Web:* pcpl21.org	Greencastle	IN	46135	765-653-2755	653-2756
Hammond Public Library 564 State St *Web:* www.hammond.lib.in.us	Hammond	IN	46320	219-931-5100	931-3474
Federal Home Loan Bank of Indianapolis 8250 Woodfield Crossing Blvd *Web:* www.fhlbi.com	Indianapolis	IN	46240	317-465-0200	
Jasper Public Library 1116 Main St *Web:* jdcpl.lib.in.us	Jasper	IN	47546	812-482-2712	482-7123
Kokomo-Howard County Public Library 220 N Union St *Web:* www.kokomo.lib.in.us	Kokomo	IN	46901	765-457-3242	457-3683
La Porte County Public Library 904 Indiana Ave *Web:* www.laportelibrary.org	La Porte	IN	46350	219-362-6156	362-6158
Tippecanoe County Public Library 627 S St *TF:* 800-542-7818 ■ *Web:* www.tcpl.lib.in.us	Lafayette	IN	47901	765-429-0100	429-0150
LaGrange County Public Library 203 W Spring St *Web:* www.lagrange.lib.in.us	LaGrange	IN	46761	260-463-2841	
Logansport-Cass County Public Library 616 E Broadway *Web:* www.logan.lib.in.us	Logansport	IN	46947	574-753-6383	722-5889
Madison-Jefferson County Public Library 420 W Main St *Web:* www.madison-jeffco.lib.in.us	Madison	IN	47250	812-265-2744	265-2217
Marion Public Library 600 S Washington St *TF:* 877-275-7673 ■ *Web:* www.marion.lib.in.us	Marion	IN	46953	765-668-2900	668-2911
Lake County Public Library 1919 W 81st Ave *Web:* lcplin.org	Merrillville	IN	46410	219-769-3541	769-0690
Mooresville Public Library 220 W Harrison St *Web:* www.mooresvillelib.org	Mooresville	IN	46158	317-831-7323	831-7383
New Albany-Floyd County Public Library 180 W Spring St *Web:* nafclibrary.org	New Albany	IN	47150	812-944-8464	949-3734
New Castle-Henry County Public Library (NCHC) 376 S 15th St *Web:* nchcpl.org	New Castle	IN	47362	765-529-0362	
Jasper County Public Library 208 W Susan St *Web:* www.jasperco.lib.in.us	Rensselaer	IN	47978	219-866-5881	
Morrisson-Reeves Public Library 80 N Sixth St *Web:* mrlinfo.org	Richmond	IN	47374	765-966-8291	962-1318
Jackson County Public Library (JCPL) 303 W Second St *TF:* 877-275-7673 ■ *Web:* www.myjclibrary.org	Seymour	IN	47274	812-522-3412	522-5456
Shelbyville-Shelby County Public Library 57 W Broadway *TF:* 866-466-4438 ■ *Web:* www.myshelbylibrary.org	Shelbyville	IN	46176	317-398-7121	421-2758
Saint Joseph County Public Library 304 S Main St *Web:* www.sjcpl.lib.in.us	South Bend	IN	46601	574-282-4630	
Vigo County Public Library 1 Library Sq *Web:* www.vigo.lib.in.us	Terre Haute	IN	47807	812-232-1113	232-3208
Valparaiso Public Library 103 Jefferson St *Web:* pcpls.org	Valparaiso	IN	46383	219-462-0524	477-4867
Knox County Public Library 502 N Seventh St *Web:* www.kcpl.lib.in.us	Vincennes	IN	47591	812-886-4380	886-0342
West Lafayette Public Library 208 W Columbia St *Web:* www.wlaf.lib.in.us	West Lafayette	IN	47906	765-743-2261	743-0540

Iowa

				Phone	Fax
Ames Public Library 515 Douglas Ave *Web:* www.amespubliclibrary.org	Ames	IA	50010	515-239-5630	232-4571
Kirkendall Public Library 1210 NW Prairie Ridge Dr *Web:* www.ankenyiowa.gov	Ankeny	IA	50023	515-965-6460	289-9122
Bettendorf Public Library 2950 Learning Campus Dr *Web:* www.bettendorflibrary.com	Bettendorf	IA	52722	563-344-4175	344-4185
Burlington Public Library 210 Ct St *Web:* www.burlington.lib.ia.us	Burlington	IA	52601	319-753-1647	229-0406
Cedar Falls Public Library 524 Main St *Web:* www.cedarfallspubliclibrary.org	Cedar Falls	IA	50613	319-273-8643	
Cedar Rapids Public Library 2600 Edgewood Rd SW Ste 330 *Web:* www.crlibrary.org	Cedar Rapids	IA	52404	319-398-5123	398-0476
Clinton Public Library 306 Eigth Ave S *Web:* clintonpubliclibrary.us	Clinton	IA	52732	563-242-8441	242-8162
Council Bluffs Public Library 400 Willow Ave *Web:* www.councilbluffslibrary.org	Council Bluffs	IA	51503	712-323-7553	
Davenport Public Library 321 Main St *Web:* www.davenportlibrary.com	Davenport	IA	52801	563-326-7832	326-7809
Des Moines Public Library 1000 Grand Ave *Web:* dmpl.org	Des Moines	IA	50309	515-283-4152	237-1654
Carnegie-Stout Public Library 360 W 11th St *Web:* www.dubuque.lib.ia.us	Dubuque	IA	52001	563-589-4225	589-4217
Scott County Library System 200 N Sixth Ave *Web:* scottcountylibrary.org	Eldridge	IA	52748	563-285-4794	285-4743
Fort Dodge Public Library 424 Central Ave *Web:* www.fortdodgeiowa.org	Fort Dodge	IA	50501	515-573-8167	573-5422
Iowa City Public Library 123 S Linn St *TF:* 866-862-6877 ■ *Web:* www.icpl.org	Iowa City	IA	52240	319-356-5200	356-5494
Marion Public Library 1095 Sixth Ave *Web:* www.marionpubliclibrary.org	Marion	IA	52302	319-377-3412	377-0113
Marshalltown Public Library 105 W Boone St *Web:* www.marshalltownlibrary.org	Marshalltown	IA	50158	641-754-5738	754-5708
Mason City Public Library 225 Second St SE *Web:* www.mcpl.org	Mason City	IA	50401	641-421-3668	423-2615
Musser Public Library 304 Iowa Ave *Web:* www.musserpubliclibrary.org	Muscatine	IA	52761	563-263-3065	
Newton Public Library (NPL) 100 N Third Ave W PO Box 746 *Web:* newton.lib.ia.us	Newton	IA	50208	641-792-4108	791-0729
Ottumwa Public Library 102 W Fourth St *Web:* ottumwapubliclibrary.org	Ottumwa	IA	52501	641-682-7563	682-4970
Sioux City Public Library 529 Pierce St *Web:* www.siouxcitylibrary.org	Sioux City	IA	51101	712-255-2933	
Urbandale Public Library 3520 86th St *Web:* www.urbandalelibrary.org	Urbandale	IA	50322	515-278-3945	278-3918
West Des Moines Public Library 4000 Mills Civic Pkwy *Web:* www.wdmlibrary.org	West Des Moines	IA	50265	515-222-3400	222-3401

Kansas

				Phone	Fax
Belleville Public Library 1327 19th St *Web:* www.bellevillepl.blogspot.in	Belleville	KS	66935	785-527-5305	527-5305
Finney County Public Library Garden City 605 E Walnut St *Web:* finneylibrary.org	Garden City	KS	67846	620-272-3680	272-3682
Hutchinson Public Library 901 N Main St *Web:* www.hutchpl.org	Hutchinson	KS	67501	620-663-5441	663-9506
Dorothy Bramlage Public Library Junction City 230 W Seventh St *Web:* www.jclib.org	Junction City	KS	66441	785-238-4311	238-7873
Kansas City Kansas Public Library 625 Minnesota Ave *Web:* links.kckpl.org	Kansas City	KS	66101	913-551-3280	279-2032
Lawrence Public Library 707 Vermont St *TF:* 888-657-7323 ■ *Web:* www.lawrence.lib.ks.us	Lawrence	KS	66044	785-843-3833	843-3368
Leavenworth Public Library 417 Spruce St *Web:* leavenworthpubliclibrary.org	Leavenworth	KS	66048	913-682-5666	682-1248
Manhattan Public Library 629 Poyntz Ave *TF:* 800-432-2796 ■ *Web:* mhklibrary.org	Manhattan	KS	66502	785-776-4741	776-1545
Salina Public Library 301 W Elm St *Web:* www.salinapubliclibrary.org	Salina	KS	67401	785-825-4624	823-0706
Johnson County Library PO Box 2933 *TF:* 800-386-8501 ■ *Web:* www.jocolibrary.org	Shawnee Mission	KS	66201	913-826-4600	
Topeka & Shawnee County Public Library 1515 SW Tenth Ave *Web:* www.tscpl.org	Topeka	KS	66604	785-580-4400	580-4496
Wichita Public Library 223 S Main St	Wichita	KS	67202	316-261-8500	262-4540

Kentucky

				Phone	Fax
Boyd County Public Library 1740 Central Ave *Web:* www.thebookplace.org	Ashland	KY	41101	606-329-0518	329-0578
Kenton County Public Library 502 Scott Blvd *Web:* www.kenton.lib.ky.us	Covington	KY	41011	859-962-4060	962-4096
Boyle County Public Library 307 W Broadway *Web:* boylepublib.org	Danville	KY	40422	859-236-8466	236-7692
Hardin County Public Library 100 Jim Owen Dr *Web:* www.hcpl.info	Elizabethtown	KY	42701	270-769-6337	
Paul Sawyier Public Library 319 Wapping St *TF:* 800-829-3676 ■ *Web:* www.pspl.org	Frankfort	KY	40601	502-352-2665	227-2250
Anderson County Public Library 114 N Main St *Web:* www.andersonpubliclibrary.org	Lawrenceburg	KY	40342	502-839-6420	
Lexington Public Library 140 E Main St *Web:* www.lexpublib.org	Lexington	KY	40507	859-231-5504	231-5598
Louisville Free Public Library 301 York St *Web:* www.lfpl.org	Louisville	KY	40203	502-574-1611	
Daviess County Public Library 2020 Frederica St *Web:* www.dcplibrary.org	Owensboro	KY	42301	270-684-0211	684-0218
McCracken County Public Library 555 Washington St *TF:* 866-829-7532 ■ *Web:* www.mclib.net	Paducah	KY	42003	270-442-2510	
Pulaski County Public Library 304 S Main St *Web:* www.pulaskipubliclibrary.org	Somerset	KY	42501	606-679-8401	679-1779

Louisiana

				Phone	Fax
Rapides Parish Library 411 Washington St *Web:* www.rpl.org	Alexandria	LA	71301	318-445-2411	445-6478
East Baton Rouge Parish Library (EBRPL) 7711 Goodwood Blvd *Web:* www.ebrpl.com	Baton Rouge	LA	70806	225-231-3750	
Bossier Parish Library (BPL) 2206 Beckett St *Web:* www.bossierlibrary.org	Bossier City	LA	71111	318-746-1693	746-7768
Saint Bernard Parish Library 2600 Palmisano Blvd *Web:* www.stbernard.lib.la.us	Chalmette	LA	70043	504-279-0448	
Saint Tammany Parish Library 310 W 21st Ave *Web:* www.sttammany.lib.la.us	Covington	LA	70433	985-893-6280	871-1271
Acadia Parish Library 1125 N Parkerson Ave *Web:* www.acadia.lib.la.us	Crowley	LA	70526	337-788-1880	788-3759
Beauregard Parish Library 205 S Washington Ave *TF:* 800-524-6239 ■ *Web:* www.library.beau.org	DeRidder	LA	70634	337-463-6217	462-5434
St. Mary Parish Library 206 Iberia St *Web:* stmary.lib.la.us	Franklin	LA	70538	337-828-1624	828-2329
Washington Parish Library System 825 Free St *Web:* washingtonparishlibrary.info	Franklinton	LA	70438	985-839-7806	839-7808
Terrebonne Parish Library System 151 Library Dr *Web:* www.terrebonne.lib.la.us	Houma	LA	70360	985-876-5861	917-0582
Jefferson Davis Parish Library 118 W Plaquemine St *Web:* www.jefferson-davis.lib.la.us	Jennings	LA	70546	337-824-1210	824-5444
Lafayette Parish Public Library 301 W Congress St *Web:* lafayettepubliclibrary.org	Lafayette	LA	70501	337-261-5787	261-5782
Calcasieu Parish Public Library System 301 W Claude St *Web:* www.calcasieulibrary.org	Lake Charles	LA	70605	337-721-7116	475-8806
Vernon Parish Library 1401 Nolan Trace *TF:* 800-737-2231	Leesville	LA	71446	337-239-2027	238-0666
Livingston Parish Library 20390 Iowa St PO Box 397 *Web:* mylpl.info	Livingston	LA	70754	225-686-2436	686-3888
DeSoto Parish Library 109 Crosby St *Web:* desotoparishlibrary.org	Mansfield	LA	71052	318-872-6100	872-6120
Avoyelles Parish Library 104 N Washington St *Web:* www.avoyelles.lib.la.us	Marksville	LA	71351	318-253-7559	253-6361
Jefferson Parish Library 4747 W Napoleon Ave *Web:* www.jefferson.lib.la.us	Metairie	LA	70001	504-838-1100	838-1110
Webster Parish Library 521 E & W Sts *Web:* www.webster.lib.la.us	Minden	LA	71055	318-371-3080	371-3081
Ouachita Parish Public Library 1800 Stubbs Ave *Web:* www.oplib.org	Monroe	LA	71201	318-327-1490	327-1373
Natchitoches Parish Library 450 Second St *Web:* www.youseemore.com/natchitoches	Natchitoches	LA	71457	318-357-3280	357-7073
Iberia Parish Library 445 E Main St *Web:* iberialibrary.org	New Iberia	LA	70560	337-364-7024	373-0086
Opelousas-Eunice Public Libraries 212 E Grolee St *Web:* opelousaseunicepubliclibrary.org	Opelousas	LA	70570	337-948-3693	
Iberville Parish Library 24605 J Gerald Berret Blvd *Web:* www.iberville.lib.la.us	Plaquemine	LA	70765	225-687-2520	687-9719
Lincoln Parish Library 910 N Trenton St *Web:* www.mylpl.org	Ruston	LA	71270	318-251-5030	
Saint Martin Parish Library 201 Porter St *Web:* stmartinparishlibrary.org/site.php	Saint Martinville	LA	70582	337-394-2207	394-2248
Shreve Memorial Library 424 Texas St *TF:* 866-783-5462 ■ *Web:* www.shreve-lib.org	Shreveport	LA	71101	318-226-5897	226-4780
Evangeline Parish Library 242 W Main St *Web:* evangelinelibrary.org	Ville Platte	LA	70586	337-363-1369	363-2353

Maine

Library	City	State	Zip	Phone	Fax
Auburn Public Library 49 Spring St *Web:* www.auburnpubliclibrary.org	Auburn	ME	04210	207-333-6640	333-6644
Lithgow Public Library 45 Winthrop St *Web:* www.lithgow.lib.me.us	Augusta	ME	04330	207-626-2415	626-2419
Bangor Public Library 145 Harlow St *TF:* 800-442-4293 ■ *Web:* www.bpl.lib.me.us	Bangor	ME	04401	207-947-8336	947-8336
Camden Public Library (CPL) 55 Main St *Web:* www.librarycamden.org	Camden	ME	04843	207-236-3440	236-6673
Lewiston Public Library 200 Lisbon St *Web:* www.lplonline.org	Lewiston	ME	04240	207-513-3004	
Portland Public Library 5 Monument Sq *Web:* www.portlandlibrary.com	Portland	ME	04101	207-871-1700	871-1703

Maryland

Library	City	State	Zip	Phone	Fax
Anne Arundel County Public Library 5 Harry S Truman Pkwy *Web:* aacpl.net	Annapolis	MD	21401	410-222-7371	222-7188
Enoch Pratt Free Library 400 Cathedral St *Web:* www.prattlibrary.org	Baltimore	MD	21201	410-396-5283	396-8134
Harford County Public Library 1221-A Brass Mill Rd *TF:* 800-944-7403 ■ *Web:* www.hcplonline.org	Belcamp	MD	21017	410-575-6761	273-5606
Dorchester County Public Library 303 Gay St *Web:* www.dorchesterlibrary.org	Cambridge	MD	21613	410-228-7331	228-6313
Queen Anne's County Library 121 S Commerce St *Web:* www.quan.lib.md.us	Centreville	MD	21617	410-758-0980	758-0614
Howard County Central Library 10375 Little Patuxent Pkwy *Web:* www.hclibrary.org	Columbia	MD	21044	410-313-7800	313-7864
Allegany County Public Library System 31 Washington St *Web:* www.alleganycountylibrary.info	Cumberland	MD	21502	301-777-1200	777-7299
Caroline County Public Library 100 Market St *TF:* 800-832-3277 ■ *Web:* www.carolib.org	Denton	MD	21629	410-479-1343	479-1443
Talbot County Free Library 100 W Dover St *Web:* www.tcfl.org/library	Easton	MD	21601	410-822-1626	820-8217
Cecil County Public Library (CCPL) 301 Newark Ave *Web:* www.cecil.ebranch.info	Elkton	MD	21921	410-996-1055	996-5604
Frederick County Public Libraries (FCPL) 110 E Patrick St *Web:* www.fcpl.org	Frederick	MD	21701	301-600-1613	
Prince George's County Memorial Library 6532 Adelphi Rd *Web:* pgcmls.info	Hyattsville	MD	20782	301-699-3500	
St. Mary's County Maryland Libraries 23250 Hollywood Rd *Web:* www.stmalib.org	Leonardtown	MD	20650	301-475-2846	884-4415
Ruth Enlow Library 6 N Second St *Web:* www.relib.net	Oakland	MD	21550	301-334-3996	334-4152
Calvert County Public Library 850 Costley Way *Web:* www.calvert.lib.md.us	Prince Frederick	MD	20678	410-535-0291	535-3022
Wicomico County Free Library 122 S Div St *Web:* www.wicomicolibrary.org	Salisbury	MD	21801	410-749-3612	548-2968
Worcester County Library 307 N Washington St *Web:* www.worcesterlibrary.org	Snow Hill	MD	21863	410-632-2600	632-1159
Baltimore County Public Library 320 York Rd *TF:* 800-705-3493 ■ *Web:* www.bcpl.info	Towson	MD	21204	410-887-6100	887-6103
Washington Research Library Consortium Inc, The 901 Commerce Dr *Web:* www.wrlc.org	Upper Marlboro	MD	20774	301-390-2000	
Carroll County Public Library 1100 Green Vly Rd New *Web:* www.library.carr.org	Windsor	MD	21776	410-386-4500	386-4509

Massachusetts

Library	City	State	Zip	Phone	Fax
Agawam Public Library 750 Cooper St *Web:* www.agawamlibrary.org	Agawam	MA	01001	413-789-1550	789-1552
Jones Library Inc 43 Amity St *Web:* www.joneslibrary.org	Amherst	MA	01002	413-256-4090	256-4096
Memorial Hall Library 2 N Main St *Web:* www.mhl.org	Andover	MA	01810	978-623-8400	623-8407
Robbins Library 700 Massachusetts Ave *Web:* robbinslibrary.org	Arlington	MA	02476	781-316-3200	
Attleboro Public Library 74 N Main St *Web:* www.sailsinc.org	Attleboro	MA	02703	508-222-0157	226-3326
Sturgis Library 3090 Main St *Web:* www.sturgislibrary.org	Barnstable	MA	02630	508-362-6636	362-5467
Bellingham Public Library 100 Blackstone St *Web:* www.bellinghamlibrary.org	Bellingham	MA	02019	508-966-1660	966-3189
Beverly Public Library 32 Essex St *Web:* www.noblenet.org	Beverly	MA	01915	978-921-6062	
Billerica Public Library 15 Concord Rd *Web:* www.billericalibrary.org	Billerica	MA	01821	978-671-0948	
Boston Public Library 700 Boylston St Copley Sq *Web:* www.bpl.org	Boston	MA	02116	617-536-5400	
New England Historic Genealogical Society 101 Newbury St *Web:* www.historicbostons.com	Boston	MA	02116	617-536-5740	
Thayer Public Library 798 Washington St *Web:* www.thayerpubliclibrary.org	Braintree	MA	02184	781-848-0405	356-5447
Brockton Public Library 304 Main St *Web:* www.brocktonpubliclibrary.org	Brockton	MA	02301	508-580-7890	580-7898
Brookline Public Library 361 Washington St *Web:* www.brooklinelibrary.com	Brookline	MA	02445	617-730-2370	
Burlington Public Library 22 Sears St *Web:* www.burlington.org	Burlington	MA	01803	781-270-1690	229-0406
Cambridge Public Library 449 Broadway *Web:* www.cambridgema.gov/cpl	Cambridge	MA	02138	617-349-4040	
Centerville Public Library 585 Main St *Web:* www.centervillelibrary.org	Centerville	MA	02632	508-790-6220	790-6218
Chelmsford Public Library 25 Boston Rd *Web:* www.chelmsfordlibrary.org	Chelmsford	MA	01824	978-256-5521	256-8511
Chicopee Public Library 449 Front St *Web:* www.chicopeepubliclibrary.org	Chicopee	MA	01013	413-594-1800	594-1819
Dartmouth Public Libraries 732 Dartmouth St *Web:* www.dplma.org	Dartmouth	MA	02748	508-999-0726	
Moses Greeley Parker Memorial Library 28 Arlington St *Web:* www.dracutlibrary.org	Dracut	MA	01826	978-454-5474	454-9120
Parlin Memorial Library 410 Broadway *Web:* www.noblenet.org/everett	Everett	MA	02149	617-394-2300	389-1230
Millicent Library 45 Ctr St *Web:* www.millicentlibrary.org	Fairhaven	MA	02719	508-992-5342	993-7288
Fall River Public Library 104 N Main St *TF:* 800-331-3764 ■ *Web:* www.sailsinc.org	Fall River	MA	02720	508-324-2700	324-2707
Falmouth Public Library 300 Main St *Web:* www.falmouthpubliclibrary.org	Falmouth	MA	02540	508-457-2555	457-2559
Fitchburg Public Library 610 Main St *Web:* fitchburgpubliclibrary.org	Fitchburg	MA	01420	978-345-9635	
Sawyer Free Library 2 Dale Ave *Web:* www.sawyerfreelibrary.org	Gloucester	MA	01930	978-281-9763	
Holmes Public Library 470 Plymouth St *Web:* holmespubliclibrary.org	Halifax	MA	02338	781-293-2271	294-8518
Haverhill Public Library 99 Main St *Web:* www.haverhillpl.org	Haverhill	MA	01830	978-373-1586	373-8466
Holyoke Public Library 335 Maple St *Web:* www.holyokelibrary.org	Holyoke	MA	01040	413-322-5640	
Hyannis Public Library (HPL) 401 Main St *Web:* www.hyannislibrary.org	Hyannis	MA	02601	508-775-2280	790-0087
Leominster Public Library 30 W St *Web:* www.leominsterlibrary.org	Leominster	MA	01453	978-534-7522	
Cary Memorial Library 1874 Massachusetts Ave *Web:* www.carylibrary.org	Lexington	MA	02420	781-862-6288	862-7355
Pollard Memorial Library 401 Merrimack St *Web:* www.pollardml.org	Lowell	MA	01852	978-970-4120	
Lynn Public Library 5 N Common St *Web:* www.noblenet.org/lynn	Lynn	MA	01902	781-595-0567	592-5050
Malden Public Library 36 Salem St *Web:* www.maldenpubliclibrary.org	Malden	MA	02148	781-324-0218	324-4467
Marlborough Public Library 35 W Main St *Web:* www.marlborough-ma.gov	Marlborough	MA	01752	508-624-6900	485-1494
Ventress Memorial Library 15 Library Plz *Web:* www.ventresslibrary.org	Marshfield	MA	02050	781-834-5535	
Marstons Mills Public Library 2160 Main St *Web:* www.mmpl.org	Marstons Mills	MA	02648	508-428-5175	420-5194
Medford Public Library 111 High St *Web:* www.medfordlibrary.org	Medford	MA	02155	781-395-7950	391-2261
Melrose Public Library 69 W Emerson St *Web:* www.melrosepubliclibrary.org	Melrose	MA	02176	781-665-2313	
Milford Town Library 80 Spruce St *Web:* www.milfordtownlibrary.org	Milford	MA	01757	508-473-2145	
Milton Public Library 476 Canton Ave *Web:* www.miltonlibrary.org	Milton	MA	02186	617-698-5757	
Morse Institute Library 14 E Central St *Web:* www.morseinstitute.org	Natick	MA	01760	508-647-6520	647-6527
Needham Public Library 1139 Highland Ave *Web:* www.town.needham.ma.us	Needham	MA	02494	781-455-7559	455-7591
New Bedford Free Public Library (NBFPL) 613 Pleasant St *TF:* 877-336-2627 ■ *Web:* www.newbedford-ma.gov/library	New Bedford	MA	02740	508-991-6275	991-6368
Newton Free Library 330 Homer St *Web:* newtonfreelibrary.net	Newton Center	MA	02459	617-796-1360	965-8457
Norfolk Public Library, The 139 Main St *Web:* library.virtualnorfolk.org	Norfolk	MA	02056	508-528-3380	528-6417
Richards Memorial Library 118 N Washington St *Web:* rmlonline.org	North Attleboro	MA	02760	508-699-0122	699-0122
Forbes Library 20 W St *Web:* www.forbeslibrary.org	NortHampton	MA	01060	413-587-1012	587-1015
Northborough Free Library 34 Main St *Web:* northboroughlibrary.org	Northborough	MA	01532	508-393-5025	393-5027
Morrill Memorial Library 33 Walpole St PO Box 220 *Web:* www.norwoodlibrary.org	Norwood	MA	02062	781-769-0200	
Osterville Free Library 43 Wianno Ave *Web:* ostervillevillagelibrary.org	Osterville	MA	02655	508-428-5757	428-5557
Peabody Institute Library 82 Main St *Web:* www.peabodylibrary.org	Peabody	MA	01960	978-531-0100	
Berkshire Athenaeum 1 Wendell Ave *Web:* www.berkshire.net	Pittsfield	MA	01201	413-499-9480	499-9489
Plymouth Public Library 132 S St *Web:* plymouthpubliclibrary.org	Plymouth	MA	02360	508-830-4250	
Provincetown Public Library 356 Commercial St *Web:* provincetownlibrary.org	Provincetown	MA	02657	508-487-7094	
Thomas Crane Public Library 40 Washington St *Web:* www.thomascranelibrary.org	Quincy	MA	02169	617-376-1301	

Library	City	State	ZIP	Phone	Fax
Turner Free Library 2 N Main St *Web:* turnerfreelibrary.org	Randolph	MA	02368	781-961-0932	
Reading Public Library 64 Middlesex Ave. *Web:* www.readingpl.org	Reading	MA	01867	781-944-0840	942-9106
Revere Public Library 179 Beach St *Web:* reverepubliclibrary.org	Revere	MA	02151	781-286-8380	
Salem Public Library 370 Essex St *Web:* www.noblenet.org/salem	Salem	MA	01970	978-744-0860	
Saugus Free Public Library 295 Central St. *Web:* www.noblenet.org	Saugus	MA	01906	781-231-4168	231-4169
Sharon Public Library 11 N Main St *Web:* www.townofsharon.net	Sharon	MA	02067	781-784-1578	
Somerville Public Library (SPL) 79 Highland Ave *Web:* www.somervillepubliclibrary.org	Somerville	MA	02143	617-623-5000	
Bacon Free Library 58 Eliot St *Web:* baconfreelibrary.org	South Natick	MA	01760	508-653-6730	
Springfield City Library 220 State St *Web:* www.springfieldlibrary.org	Springfield	MA	01103	413-263-6828	
Stoughton Public Library 84 Pk St *Web:* www.stoughton.org/library-0	Stoughton	MA	02072	781-344-2711	344-7340
Taunton Public Library 12 Pleasant St *Web:* www.tauntonlibrary.org	Taunton	MA	02780	508-821-1411	821-1414
Tewksbury Public Library 300 Chandler St *Web:* www.tewksburypl.org	Tewksbury	MA	01876	978-640-4490	
Lucius Beebe Memorial Library 345 Main St *Web:* www.wakefieldlibrary.org	Wakefield	MA	01880	781-246-6334	246-6385
Walpole Public Library 143 School St *Web:* www.walpolelibrary.org/walpolenew	Walpole	MA	02081	508-660-7340	
Waltham Public Library 735 Main St *Web:* www.waltham.lib.ma.us	Waltham	MA	02451	781-314-3425	647-5873
Watertown Free Public Library 123 Main St. *TF:* 800-829-3676 ■ *Web:* www.watertownlib.org	Watertown	MA	02472	617-972-6431	926-4375
Wayland Free Public Library 5 Concord Rd. *Web:* www.wayland.ma.us	Wayland	MA	01778	508-358-2311	358-5249
Wellesley Free Library 530 Washington St *Web:* www.ci.wellesley.ma.us	Wellesley	MA	02482	781-235-1610	237-4875
Whelden Memorial Library 2401 Meetinghouse Way PO Box 147 *Web:* wheldenlibrary.org	West Barnstable	MA	02668	508-362-2262	362-1344
Westfield Athenaeum 6 Elm St *Web:* www.westath.org	Westfield	MA	01085	413-568-7833	568-0988
Tufts Library 46 Broad St. *TF:* 888-283-3757 ■ *Web:* weymouth.ma.us	Weymouth	MA	02188	781-337-1402	682-6123
Milne Public Library 1095 Main St *Web:* www.milnelibrary.org	Williamstown	MA	01267	413-458-5369	458-3085
Woburn Public Library 45 Pleasant St. *TF:* 800-392-6089 ■ *Web:* www.woburnpubliclibrary.org	Woburn	MA	01801	781-933-0148	938-7860
Woods Hole Public Library 581 Woods Hole Rd PO Box 185 *Web:* woodsholepubliclibrary.org	Woods Hole	MA	02543	508-548-8961	540-1969

Michigan

Library	City	State	ZIP	Phone	Fax
Lenawee County Library 4459 W US 223 *Web:* www.lenawee.lib.mi.us	Adrian	MI	49221	517-263-1011	
Alpena County George N Fletcher Public Library 211 N First Ave. *TF:* 877-737-4106 ■ *Web:* alpenalibrary.org	Alpena	MI	49707	989-356-6188	356-2765
Ann Arbor District Library (AADL) 343 S Fifth Ave *Web:* www.aadl.org	Ann Arbor	MI	48104	734-327-4200	327-8309
Bay County Library System 500 Ctr Ave *Web:* www.baycountylibrary.org	Bay City	MI	48708	989-894-2837	894-2021
Baldwin Public Library 300 W Merrill St. *Web:* www.baldwinlib.org	Birmingham	MI	48009	248-647-1700	
Bloomfield Township Public Library 1099 Lone Pine Rd *TF:* 800-318-2596 ■ *Web:* www.btpl.org	Bloomfield Hills	MI	48302	248-642-5800	642-4175
Cadillac-Wexford County Public Library 411 S Lake St *Web:* www.cadillaclibrary.org	Cadillac	MI	49601	231-775-6541	
Canton Public Library 1200 S Canton Ctr Rd *TF:* 888-988-6300 ■ *Web:* www.cantonpl.org	Canton	MI	48188	734-397-0999	397-1130
Chelsea District Library 221 S Main St *Web:* chelseadistrictlibrary.org	Chelsea	MI	48118	734-475-8732	
Kent District Library 814 W River Ctr Dr NE *TF:* 877-243-2466 ■ *Web:* www.kdl.org	Comstock Park	MI	49321	616-784-2007	647-3908
Henry Ford Centennial Library 16301 Michigan Ave. *Web:* dearbornlibrary.org	Dearborn	MI	48126	313-943-2330	
Detroit Public Library 5201 Woodward Ave *Web:* www.detroitpubliclibrary.org	Detroit	MI	48202	313-481-1300	
East Lansing Public Library 950 Abbott Rd. *Web:* www.elpl.org	East Lansing	MI	48823	517-351-2420	351-9536
Eastpointe Memorial Library 15875 Oak St. *Web:* cityofeastpointe.net	Eastpointe	MI	48021	586-445-5096	
Escanaba Public Library 400 Ludington St. *TF:* 800-992-9012 ■ *Web:* www.uproc.lib.mi.us	Escanaba	MI	49829	906-786-4463	786-0942
Ferndale Public Library 222 E Nine-Mile Rd *Web:* www.ferndale.lib.mi.us	Ferndale	MI	48220	248-546-2504	545-5840
Flint Public Library 1026 E Kearsley St *Web:* fpl.info	Flint	MI	48502	810-232-7111	
Genesee District Library G-4195 W Pasadena Ave. *TF:* 866-732-1120	Flint	MI	48504	810-732-0110	732-3146
Garden City Public Library 31735 Maplewood St *Web:* www.gardencitylib.org	Garden City	MI	48135	734-793-1830	793-1831
Loutit District Library 407 Columbus St *Web:* www.loutitlibrary.org	Grand Haven	MI	49417	616-842-5560	847-0570
Grand Rapids Public Library 111 Library St NE *Web:* grpl.org	Grand Rapids	MI	49503	616-988-5400	
Dickinson County Library 401 Iron Mtn St *Web:* www.dcl-lib.org	Iron Mountain	MI	49801	906-774-1218	
Jackson District Library 244 W Michigan Ave *Web:* www.myjdl.com	Jackson	MI	49201	517-788-4087	
Georgetown Township Library 1525 Baldwin St *Web:* www.georgetown-mi.gov	Jenison	MI	49428	616-457-9620	
Kalamazoo Public Library 315 S Rose St *Web:* www.kpl.gov	Kalamazoo	MI	49007	269-342-9837	553-7921
Orion Township Public Library 825 Joslyn Rd. *TF:* 877-924-7467 ■ *Web:* www.orionlibrary.org	Lake Orion	MI	48362	248-693-3000	693-3009
Capital Area District Library 401 S Capitol Ave. *Web:* www.cadl.org	Lansing	MI	48933	517-367-6300	374-1068
Livonia Public Library 32777 Five Mile Rd *Web:* livoniapubliclibrary.org	Livonia	MI	48154	734-466-2491	458-6011
Madison Heights Public Library 240 W 13 Mile Rd. *Web:* www.madison-heights.org/departments/library	Madison Heights	MI	48071	248-588-7763	
Peter White Public Library 217 N Front St. *TF:* 800-992-9012 ■ *Web:* www.uproc.lib.mi.us	Marquette	MI	49855	906-228-9510	226-1783
Grace A Dow Memorial Library 1710 W St Andrews Rd *Web:* cityofmidlandmi.gov/1208/welcome-to-our-new-website	Midland	MI	48640	989-837-3430	837-3468
Monroe County Library System 3700 S Custer Rd. *TF:* 800-462-2050 ■ *Web:* www.monroe.lib.mi.us	Monroe	MI	48161	734-241-5277	241-4722
Macomb County 1 South Main 8th Floor *Web:* www.makemacombyourhome.com	Mount Clemens	MI	48038	586-469-7001	
Veterans Memorial Library 301 S University Ave **Fax Area Code:* 541 ■ *TF:* 888-520-8103	Mount Pleasant	MI	48858	989-773-3242	247-4411*
Muskegon Area District Library 4845 Airline Rd. *TF:* 877-569-4801 ■ *Web:* www.madl.org	Muskegon	MI	49444	231-737-6248	737-6307
Novi Public Library 45255 W 10 Mile Rd *Web:* www.novilibrary.org	Novi	MI	48375	248-349-0720	349-6520
Owosso Public Library 502 W Main St *Web:* sdl.lib.mi.us	Owosso	MI	48867	989-725-5134	723-5444
Pontiac Public Library 60 E Pike St *Web:* www.pontiac.lib.mi.us	Pontiac	MI	48342	248-758-3942	758-3990
Saint Clair County Library System 210 McMorran Blvd *TF:* 877-987-7323 ■ *Web:* www.sccl.lib.mi.us	Port Huron	MI	48060	810-987-7323	987-7874
Portage District Library 300 Library Ln *Web:* www.portagelibrary.info	Portage	MI	49002	269-329-4544	324-9222
Rochester Hills Public Library 500 Olde Towne Rd *Web:* www.rhpl.org	Rochester	MI	48307	248-656-2900	650-7131
Roseville Public Library 29777 Gratiot Ave *Web:* www.libcoop.net	Roseville	MI	48066	586-445-5407	445-5499
Royal Oak Public Library 222 E Eleven Mile Rd *Web:* ropl.org	Royal Oak	MI	48067	248-246-3700	545-6220
Public Libraries of Saginaw 505 Janes St *Web:* www.saginawlibrary.org	Saginaw	MI	48607	989-755-0904	755-9829
Shelby Township Library 51680 Van Dyke Hwy *Web:* www.shelbytwplib.org	Shelby Township	MI	48316	586-739-7414	726-0535
Southfield Public Library 26300 Evergreen Rd *Web:* www.sfldlib.org	Southfield	MI	48076	248-796-4200	
Sterling Heights Public Library 40255 Dodge Pk Rd *Web:* www.shpl.net	Sterling Heights	MI	48313	586-446-2665	
Troy Public Library 510 W Big Beaver Rd *Web:* www.libcoop.net	Troy	MI	48084	248-524-3538	524-0112
Warren Public Library 5460 Arden *Web:* www.warrenlibrary.net	Warren	MI	48092	586-751-5377	
Waterford Township Public Library 5168 Civic Ctr Dr *TF:* 800-318-2596 ■ *Web:* www.waterfordmi.gov/477/library	Waterford	MI	48329	248-674-4831	674-1910
West Bloomfield Township Public Library 4600 Walnut Lake Rd *Web:* www.wblib.org	West Bloomfield	MI	48323	248-682-2120	232-2333

Minnesota

Library	City	State	ZIP	Phone	Fax
Albert Lea Public Library 211 E Clark St *Web:* alplonline.org	Albert Lea	MN	56007	507-377-4350	
Douglas County Library 720 Fillmore St *Web:* www.douglascountylibrary.org	Alexandria	MN	56308	320-762-3014	
Anoka County Library 711 County Rd 10. *Web:* www.anoka.lib.mn.us	Blaine	MN	55434	763-717-3267	717-3259
Cambridge Public Library 244 S Birch St. **Fax Area Code:* 617 ■ *TF:* 877-721-4862	Cambridge	MN	55008	763-689-7390	349-4287*
Carver County Library 4 City Hall Plaza *Web:* www.carverlib.org	Chaska	MN	55318	952-448-9395	448-9392
Hill Museum & Manuscript Library PO Box 7300 *Web:* www.hmml.org	Collegeville	MN	56321	320-363-3514	
Duluth Public Library 520 W Superior St. *Web:* www.duluthlibrary.org	Duluth	MN	55802	218-730-4200	723-3822
Buckham Memorial Library 11 Div St E *Web:* www.ci.faribault.mn.us	Faribault	MN	55021	507-334-2089	
Library Foundation of Hennepin County, The 300 Nicollet Mall *Web:* www.supporthclib.org	Minneapolis	MN	55401	612-543-8100	

Library	City	State	ZIP	Phone	Fax
Hennepin County Library (HCL) 12601 Ridgedale Dr *Fax Area Code: 952 ■ *Web:* www.hclib.org	Minnetonka	MN	55305	612-543-8800	847-8600*
Lake Agassiz Regional Library (LARL) 118 Fifth St S PO Box 900 *TF:* 800-247-0449 ■ *Web:* www.larl.org	Moorhead	MN	56560	218-233-3757	233-7556
Owatonna Public Library 105 N Elm St. *TF:* 800-657-3864 ■ *Web:* ci.owatonna.mn.us	Owatonna	MN	55060	507-444-2460	444-2465
Rochester Public Library 101 Second St SE. *Web:* www.rochesterpubliclibrary.org	Rochester	MN	55904	507-285-8000	
Great River Regional Library 1300 W St Germain St *Web:* www.griver.org	Saint Cloud	MN	56301	320-650-2500	650-2501
Saint Paul Public Library 90 W Fourth St. *TF:* 888-335-9632 ■ *Web:* www.sppl.org	Saint Paul	MN	55102	651-266-7000	266-7060
Scott County Library System 13090 Alabama Ave S. *TF:* 877-772-8346 ■ *Web:* www.scott.lib.mn.us	Savage	MN	55378	952-707-1770	707-1775
Ramsey County Public Library 4570 N Victoria St *TF:* 888-335-9632 ■ *Web:* www.rclreads.org	Shoreview	MN	55126	651-486-2200	486-2220
Pioneerland Library System 410 SW Fifth St. *Web:* www.pioneerland.lib.mn.us	Willmar	MN	56201	320-235-6106	214-0187
Winona Public Library 151 W Fifth St PO Box 1247. *Web:* www.selco.lib.mn.us	Winona	MN	55987	507-452-4582	452-5842
Washington County Library 8595 Central Pk Pl *TF:* 800-657-3750 ■ *Web:* www.co.washington.mn.us	Woodbury	MN	55125	651-275-8500	275-8509

Mississippi

Library	City	State	ZIP	Phone	Fax
Hancock County Library 312 Hwy 90 *Web:* hancocklibraries.info	Bay Saint Louis	MS	39520	228-467-5282	467-5503
Bolivar County Library 104 S Leflore Ave *TF:* 888-268-8076 ■ *Web:* www.bolivar.lib.ms.us	Cleveland	MS	38732	662-843-2774	843-4701
Columbus-Lowndes County Library 314 N Seventh St	Columbus	MS	39701	662-329-5300	329-5156
Greenwood-Leflore Public Library 405 W Washington St. *Web:* glpls.com	Greenwood	MS	38930	662-453-3634	453-0683
Library of Hattiesburg Petal & Forrest County 329 Hardy St. *Web:* hatt.ent.sirsi.net/client/default2e	Hattiesburg	MS	39401	601-582-4461	
First Regional Library 370 W Commerce St *TF:* 800-446-0892 ■ *Web:* firstregional.org	Hernando	MS	38632	662-429-4439	429-8853
Marshall County Library 109 E Gholson Ave. *Web:* www.marshall.lib.ms.us	Holly Springs	MS	38635	662-252-3823	252-3066
Eudora Welty Library, The 300 N State St *Web:* jhlibrary.org	Jackson	MS	39201	601-968-5811	968-5817
Laurel-Jones County Library 530 Commerce St. *Web:* www.laurel.lib.ms.us	Laurel	MS	39440	601-428-4313	428-4314
Meridian-Lauderdale County Public Library 2517 Seventh St *TF:* 800-318-2596 ■ *Web:* www.meridian.lib.ms.us	Meridian	MS	39301	601-693-6771	486-2260
Jackson-George Regional Library System 3214 S Pascagoula St. *Web:* www.jgrls.org	Pascagoula	MS	39567	228-769-3060	
Pearl River County Library System 900 Goodyear Blvd. *Web:* www.pearlriver.lib.ms.us	Picayune	MS	39466	601-798-5081	798-5082
Starkville Public Library 326 University Dr *Web:* www.starkville.lib.ms.us	Starkville	MS	39759	662-323-2766	323-9140
Warren County-Vicksburg Public Library 700 Veto St. *TF:* 800-721-7222 ■ *Web:* www.warren.lib.ms.us	Vicksburg	MS	39180	601-636-6411	634-4809

Missouri

Library	City	State	ZIP	Phone	Fax
Bowling Green Public Library 201 W Locust St. *Web:* www.bgmopl.org	Bowling Green	MO	63334	573-324-5030	324-6367
Camden County Library District 89 Rodeo Rd PO Box 1320. *Web:* www.ccld.us	Camdenton	MO	65020	573-346-5954	346-1263
Cape Girardeau Public Library 711 N Clark St *Web:* www.capelibrary.org	Cape Girardeau	MO	63701	573-334-5279	334-8334
Daniel Boone Regional Library 100 W Broadway. *TF:* 800-324-4806 ■ *Web:* www.dbrl.org	Columbia	MO	65203	573-443-3161	443-3281
Cass County Public Library 400 E Mechanic St *Web:* www.casscolibrary.org	Harrisonville	MO	64701	816-380-4600	884-2301
Mid-Continent Public Library 15616 E 24 Hwy *TF:* 800-318-2596 ■ *Web:* www.mymcpl.org	Independence	MO	64050	816-836-5200	521-7253
Missouri River Regional Library 214 Adams St. *TF:* 800-949-7323 ■ *Web:* www.mrrl.org	Jefferson City	MO	65101	573-634-2464	634-7028
Joplin Public Library 300 S Main St *Web:* www.joplinpubliclibrary.org	Joplin	MO	64801	417-623-7953	624-5217
ALFA International 2400 Pershing Rd Ste 500 *Web:* www.alfainternational.com	Kansas City	MO	64108	816-471-2121	
Kansas City Public Library, The (KCPL) 14 W Tenth St. *Web:* www.kclibrary.org	Kansas City	MO	64105	816-701-3400	701-3401
Linda Hall Library 5109 Cherry St *TF:* 800-662-1545 ■ *Web:* www.lindahall.org	Kansas City	MO	64110	816-363-4600	926-8790
Kirkwood Public Library 140 E Jefferson Ave *Web:* www.kirkwoodpubliclibrary.org	Kirkwood	MO	63122	314-821-5770	822-3755
Christian County Library 1005 N Fourth Ave *Web:* www.christiancounty.lib.mo.us	Ozark	MO	65721	417-581-2432	581-8855
Saint Louis County Library (SLCL) 1640 S Lindbergh Blvd. *Web:* www.slcl.org	Saint Louis	MO	63131	314-994-3300	
Saint Louis Public Library (SLPL) 1301 Olive St *Web:* www.slpl.org	Saint Louis	MO	63103	314-241-2288	539-0393
St. Louis Public Library 4234 N Grand Blvd. *Web:* www.stlouis-mo.gov/government/city-laws	Saint Louis	MO	63107	314-534-0313	
Saint Charles City County Library District 77 Boone Hill Dr.	Saint Peters	MO	63376	636-441-2300	
Rolling Hills Consolidated Library 1904 N Belt Hwy. *Web:* rhcl.org	St Joseph	MO	64506	816-236-2106	
University City Public Library 6701 Delmar Blvd. *Web:* www.ucpl.lib.mo.us	University City	MO	63130	314-727-3150	727-6005

Montana

Library	City	State	ZIP	Phone	Fax
Parmly Billings Library 510 N Broadway. *Web:* www.ci.billings.mt.us	Billings	MT	59101	406-657-8258	657-8293
Bozeman Public Library 626 E Main St. *Web:* www.bozemanlibrary.org	Bozeman	MT	59715	406-582-2400	582-2424
Butte-Silver Bow Public Library 226 W Broadway *Web:* www.buttepubliclibrary.info	Butte	MT	59701	406-723-3361	
Great Falls Public Library 301 Second Ave N *Web:* www.greatfallslibrary.org	Great Falls	MT	59401	406-453-0349	453-0181
Lewis & Clark Library 120 S Last Chance Gulch *TF:* 800-733-2767 ■ *Web:* www.lclibrary.org	Helena	MT	59601	406-447-1690	447-1687
Missoula Public Library 301 E Main St. *Web:* www.missoula.lib.mt.us	Missoula	MT	59802	406-721-2665	728-5900

Nebraska

Library	City	State	ZIP	Phone	Fax
Bellevue Public Library 1003 Lincoln Rd *Web:* bellevuelibrary.org	Bellevue	NE	68005	402-293-3157	293-3163
Columbus Public Library 2504 14th St.	Columbus	NE	68601	402-564-7116	
Edith Abbott Memorial Library 211 N Washington St *Web:* www.grand-island.com	Grand Island	NE	68801	308-385-5333	385-5339
Hastings Public Library 517 W Fourth St *Web:* hastingslibrary.us	Hastings	NE	68901	402-461-2346	461-2359
Kearney Public Library & Information Ctr 2020 First Ave *Web:* www.cityofkearney.org	Kearney	NE	68847	308-233-3282	233-3291
Lincoln City Libraries 136 S 14th St *Web:* www.lincolnlibraries.org	Lincoln	NE	68508	402-441-8500	
North Platte Public Library 120 W Fourth St. *Web:* ci.north-platte.ne.us	North Platte	NE	69101	308-535-8036	535-8296
Omaha Public Library 215 S 15th St *Web:* www.omaha.lib.ne.us	Omaha	NE	68102	402-444-4800	444-4504

Nevada

Library	City	State	ZIP	Phone	Fax
Carson City Library 900 N Roop St *Web:* carsoncitylibrary.org	Carson City	NV	89701	775-887-2244	887-2273
Douglas County Library 1625 Library Ln. *Web:* douglas.lib.nv.us	Minden	NV	89423	775-782-9841	782-5754
Washoe County Library (WCL) 301 S Ctr St. *Web:* www.washoecountylibrary.us	Reno	NV	89501	775-327-8300	327-8341

New Hampshire

Library	City	State	ZIP	Phone	Fax
Amherst Town Library 14 Main St. *Web:* www.amherstlibrary.org	Amherst	NH	03031	603-673-2288	672-6063
Concord Public Library 45 Green St *Web:* www.concordnh.gov	Concord	NH	03301	603-225-8670	
Derry Public Library 64 E Broadway. *Web:* www.derry.lib.nh.us	Derry	NH	03038	603-432-6140	432-6128
Dover Public Library 73 Locust St. *Web:* www.dover.nh.gov/government/city-operations/library	Dover	NH	03820	603-516-6050	516-6053
Howe Library 13 S St. *Web:* www.thehowe.org	Hanover	NH	03755	603-643-4120	
Hollis Social Library 2 Monument Sq *Web:* hollislibrary.org	Hollis	NH	03049	603-465-7721	465-3507
Manchester City Library 405 Pine St *Web:* www.manchesternh.gov	Manchester	NH	03104	603-624-6550	624-6559
Nashua Public Library 2 Ct St *Web:* www.nashualibrary.org	Nashua	NH	03060	603-589-4600	594-3457
Wing Group LLC 20 Trafalgar Sq Ste 455. *Web:* www.wing-group.com	Nashua	NH	03063	603-589-4076	
Rochester Public Library 65 S Main St *Web:* www.rpl.lib.nh.us	Rochester	NH	03867	603-332-1428	335-7582
Kelley Library 234 Main St *Web:* www.kelleylibrary.org	Salem	NH	03079	603-898-7064	898-8583

New Jersey

Phone | Fax

Atlantic City Free Public Library
1 N Tennessee Ave ... Atlantic City NJ 08401 609-345-2269 345-5570
TF: 800-621-3362 ■ *Web:* acfpl.org

Bayonne Free Public Library 697 Ave C ... Bayonne NJ 07002 201-858-6970
Web: www.bayonnenj.org

Dillon Clarence Public Library
2336 Lamington Rd ... Bedminster NJ 07921 908-234-2325
Web: www.clarencedillonpl.org

Belleville Public Library
221 Washington Ave ... Belleville NJ 07109 973-450-3434 759-6731
Web: www.bellepl.org

Warren County Library 199 Hardwick St ... Belvidere NJ 07823 908-475-6322
Web: warrenlib.com

Bloomfield Public Library 90 Broad St ... Bloomfield NJ 07003 973-566-6200
Web: bplnj.org

Cumberland County Library
800 E Commerce St ... Bridgeton NJ 08302 856-453-2210
Web: www.clueslibs.org

Somerset County Library 1 Vogt Dr ... Bridgewater NJ 08807 908-526-4016 526-5221
TF: 888-313-3532 ■ *Web:* www.somerset.lib.nj.us

Cape May County Library (CMCL)
30 Mechanic St ... Cape May Court House NJ 08210 609-463-6350
Web: www.cmclibrary.org

Clark Public Library 303 Westfield Ave ... Clark NJ 07066 732-388-5999 388-7866

Clifton Public Library 292 Piaget Ave ... Clifton NJ 07011 973-772-5500
Web: www.cliftonpl.org

East Brunswick Public Library
2 Jean Walling Civic Ctr ... East Brunswick NJ 08816 732-390-6950 390-6869
TF: 800-829-1040 ■ *Web:* www.ebpl.org

East Orange Public Library
21 S Arlington Ave ... East Orange NJ 07018 973-266-5600
Web: www.eopl.org

Edison Township Free Public Library
340 Plainfield Ave ... Edison NJ 08817 732-287-2298 819-9134
Web: www.edisonpubliclibrary.net

Elizabeth Public Library 11 S Broad St ... Elizabeth NJ 07202 908-354-6060 354-5845
Web: www.elizpl.org

Englewood Public Library 31 Engle St ... Englewood NJ 07631 201-568-2215
Web: www.englewoodlibrary.org

Maurice M Pine Free Public Library
10-01 Fair Lawn Ave ... Fair Lawn NJ 07410 201-796-3400
Web: www.fairlawnlibrary.org

Hunterdon County Library
314 State Hwy 12 Bldg Ste 3 ... Flemington NJ 08822 908-788-1444 806-4862
Web: www.hclibrary.us

Fort Lee Free Public Library 320 Main St ... Fort Lee NJ 07024 201-592-3614 585-0375
Web: www.bccls.org

Garfield Free Public Library
500 Midland Ave ... Garfield NJ 07026 973-478-3800 478-7162
Web: www.bccls.org

Johnson Public Library 274 Main St ... Hackensack NJ 07601 201-343-4169 343-1395
Web: www.bccls.org

Hoboken Public Library (HPL) 500 Pk Ave ... Hoboken NJ 07030 201-420-2346
Web: hobokenfol.org

Irvington Public Library 5 Civic Sq ... Irvington NJ 07111 973-372-6400 372-6860
Web: www.irvingtonpubliclibrary.org

Jersey City Free Public Library
472 Jersey Ave ... Jersey City NJ 07302 201-547-4501 547-4584
TF: 800-443-0315 ■ *Web:* jclibrary.org

Kearny Public Library 318 Kearny Ave ... Kearny NJ 07032 201-998-2666 998-1141
Web: www.kearnylibrary.org

Mercer County Library System (MCL)
2751 Brunswick Pk ... Lawrenceville NJ 08648 609-882-9246
Web: www.mcl.org

Linden Public Library 31 E Henry St ... Linden NJ 07036 908-298-3830 486-2636
Web: lindenpl.org

Livingston Public Library
10 Robert H Harp Dr ... Livingston NJ 07039 973-992-4600 994-2346
Web: livingston.bccls.org

Long Branch Free Public Library
328 Broadway ... Long Branch NJ 07740 732-222-3900
Web: www.longbranchlib.org

Monmouth County Library (MCL) 125 Symmes Rd ... Manalapan NJ 07726 732-431-7220
Web: www.monmouthcountylib.org

Atlantic County Library-Mays Landing
40 Farragut Ave ... Mays Landing NJ 08330 609-625-2776 625-8143
Web: www.atlanticlibrary.org

Middletown Township Library
55 New Monmouth Rd ... Middletown NJ 07748 732-671-3700 671-5839
Web: www.mtpl.org

South Brunswick Public Library
110 Kingston Ln ... Monmouth Junction NJ 08852 732-329-4000
Web: www.lmxac.org

Mount Arlington Public Library
333 Howard Blvd ... Mount Arlington NJ 07856 973-398-1516
Web: mountarlingtonlibrary.org

Burlington County Library 5 Pioneer Blvd ... Mount Holly NJ 08060 609-267-9660 267-4091
Web: www.bcls.lib.nj.us

Mount Laurel Library
100 Walt Whitman Ave ... Mount Laurel NJ 08054 856-234-7319 234-6916
TF: 888-576-5529 ■ *Web:* www.mtlaurel.lib.nj.us

Gloucester County Library System
389 Wolfert Stn Rd ... Mullica Hill NJ 08062 856-223-6000 223-6039
Web: www.gcls.org

Neptune Public Library 25 Neptune Blvd ... Neptune NJ 07753 732-775-8241 774-1132
Web: www.neptunepubliclibrary.org

New Brunswick Free Public Library
60 Livingston Ave ... New Brunswick NJ 08901 732-745-5108
Web: www.lmxac.org

Phone | Fax

Newark Public Library 5 Washington St ... Newark NJ 07101 973-733-7784
Web: www.npl.org

Sussex County Library 125 Morris Tpke ... Newton NJ 07860 973-948-3660 948-2071
Web: www.sussexcountylibrary.org

North Bergen Free Public Library
8411 Bergenline Ave ... North Bergen NJ 07047 201-869-4715 868-0968
Web: nbpl.org

North Brunswick Public Library
880 Hermann Rd ... North Brunswick NJ 08902 732-246-3545 246-1341
Web: northbrunswicklibrary.org

Nutley Free Public Library 93 Booth Dr ... Nutley NJ 07110 973-667-0405 667-4673
Web: www.bccls.org

Ocean City Public Library
1735 Simpson Ave Ste 4 ... Ocean City NJ 08226 609-399-2434
Web: oceancitylibrary.org

Old Bridge Public Library
1 Old Bridge Plz ... Old Bridge NJ 08857 732-721-5600 607-4816
TF: 800-829-1040 ■ *Web:* www.oldbridgelibrary.org

Orange Public Library 348 Main St ... Orange NJ 07050 973-673-0153 673-1847
Web: www.orangepl.org

Sayreville Free Public Library
1050 Washington Rd ... Parlin NJ 08859 732-727-0212
Web: www.lmxac.org

Parsippany-Troy Hills Public Library
449 Halsey Rd ... Parsippany NJ 07054 973-887-5150 887-5150
Web: www.parsippanylibrary.org

Paterson Free Public Library 250 Broadway ... Paterson NJ 07501 973-321-1223 321-1205
Web: www.patersonpl.org

Pennsauken Free Public Library
5605 N Crescent Blvd ... Pennsauken NJ 08110 856-665-5959 486-0142
Web: www.pennsaukenlibrary.org

Perth Amboy Public Library
196 Jefferson St ... Perth Amboy NJ 08861 732-826-2600 324-8079
Web: ci.perthamboy.nj.us

John F Kennedy Library 500 Hoes Ln ... Piscataway NJ 08854 732-463-1633
Web: piscatawaylibrary.org

Plainfield Public Library 800 Pk Ave ... Plainfield NJ 07060 908-757-1111 754-0063
Web: www.plainfieldlibrary.info

Rahway Public Library 2 City Hall Plz ... Rahway NJ 07065 732-340-1551 340-0393
Web: www.rahwaylibrary.org

Margaret E Heggan Public Library
606 Delsea Dr ... Sewell NJ 08080 856-589-3334
Web: www.hegganlibrary.org

Franklin Township Public Library
485 DeMott Ln ... Somerset NJ 08873 732-873-8700 873-0746
Web: www.franklintwp.org

Teaneck Public Library 840 Teaneck Rd ... Teaneck NJ 07666 201-837-4171 837-0410
TF: 800-245-1377 ■ *Web:* www.teaneck.org

Ocean County Library 101 Washington St ... Toms River NJ 08753 732-349-6200 473-1356
Web: theoceancountylibrary.org

Trenton Public Library 120 Academy St ... Trenton NJ 08608 609-392-7188 695-8631
Web: www.trentonlib.org

Union Township Public Library 1980 Morris Ave ... Union NJ 07083 908-851-5450 851-4671
Web: www.uniontownship.com/379/union-public-library

Union City Public Library 324 43rd St ... Union City NJ 07087 201-866-7500 866-0962
Web: www.uclibrary.org

Vineland Public Library 1058 E Landis Ave ... Vineland NJ 08360 856-794-4244
Web: www.vineland.lib.nj.us

Camden County Library 203 Laurel Rd ... Voorhees NJ 08043 856-772-1636 772-6105
TF: 877-222-3737 ■ *Web:* www.camdencountylibrary.org

Wayne Public Library 461 Valley Rd ... Wayne NJ 07470 973-694-4272
Web: www.waynepubliclibrary.org

West Milford Township Library
1490 Union Vly Rd ... West Milford NJ 07480 973-728-2820 728-2106
Web: www.wmtl.org

West New York Public Library
425 60th St ... West New York NJ 07093 201-295-5135 662-1473
Web: wnypl.org

West Orange Public Library
46 Mt Pleasant Ave ... West Orange NJ 07052 973-736-0198 733-7240
TF: 800-345-7587 ■ *Web:* www.wopl.lib.nj.us

Westfield Memorial Library 550 E Broad St ... Westfield NJ 07090 908-789-4090 789-0921
Web: www.wmlnj.org

Morris County Library (MCL) 30 E Hanover Ave ... Whippany NJ 07981 973-285-6930
Web: www.gti.net/mocolib1

Monroe Township Free Public Library
713 Marsha Ave ... Williamstown NJ 08094 856-629-1212
Web: www.monroetpl.org

Willingboro Public Library
220 Willingboro Pkwy ... Willingboro NJ 08046 609-877-6668 835-1699
TF: 866-321-9571 ■ *Web:* www.willingboro.org

Woodbridge Public Library
George Frederick Plz ... Woodbridge NJ 07095 732-634-4450
Web: www.woodbridge.lib.nj.us

New Mexico

Phone | Fax

Marshall Memorial Library 110 S Diamond Ave ... Deming NM 88030 575-546-9202

Farmington Public Library
2101 Farmington Ave ... Farmington NM 87401 505-599-1270 599-1257
Web: infoway.org

Hobbs Public Library 509 N Shipp St ... Hobbs NM 88240 575-397-9328
Web: www.hobbspubliclibrary.org

Thomas Branigan Memorial Library
200 E Picacho Ave ... Las Cruces NM 88001 575-528-4000 528-4030
Web: www.las-cruces.org

Santa Fe Public Library 145 Washington Ave ... Santa Fe NM 87501 505-955-6780
Web: www.santafelibrary.org

New York

Library	City	State	Zip	Phone	Fax
Albany Public Library (APL) 161 Washington Ave *Web:* www.albanypubliclibrary.org	Albany	NY	12210	518-427-4300	449-3386
Amherst Public Library 350 John James Audubon Pkwy *Web:* buffalolib.org	Amherst	NY	14228	716-689-4922	689-6116
Baldwinsville Public Library 33 E Genesee St *Web:* www.bville.lib.ny.us	Baldwinsville	NY	13027	315-635-5631	635-6760
Suffolk Co-op Library System 627 N Sunrise Service Rd PO Box 9000 *Web:* portal.suffolklibrarysystem.org	Bellport	NY	11713	631-286-1600	286-1647
Brentwood Public Library (BPL) 34 Second Ave *Web:* brentwoodnylibrary.org	Brentwood	NY	11717	631-273-7883	
Bronx Library Ctr 310 E Kings Bridge Rd **Fax Area Code:* 646 ■ *TF:* 800-342-3688	Bronx	NY	10458	718-579-4244	312-4781*
Brooklyn Public Library (BPL) 496 Franklin Ave *Web:* bklynlibrary.org	Brooklyn	NY	11238	718-623-0012	
Buffalo & Erie County Public Library 1 Lafayette Sq *Web:* www.buffalolib.org	Buffalo	NY	14203	716-858-8900	858-6211
Middle Country Public Library 101 Eastwood Blvd *Web:* middlecountrypubliclibrary.org	Centereach	NY	11720	631-585-9393	
Reinstein Public Library 2580 Harlem Rd *Web:* buffalolib.org	Cheektowaga	NY	14225	716-892-8089	
Half Hollow Hills Community Library 55 Vanderbilt Pkwy *Web:* hhhlibrary.org	Dix Hills	NY	11746	631-421-4530	
East Meadow Public Library Front St & E Meadow Ave *Web:* eastmeadow.info	East Meadow	NY	11554	516-794-2570	
East Rochester Public Library 111 W Elm St *Web:* www.libraryweb.org	East Rochester	NY	14445	585-586-8302	
Steele Memorial Library 101 E Church St *Web:* www.steele.lib.ny.us	Elmira	NY	14901	607-733-9173	733-9176
Fayetteville Free Library Inc 300 Orchard St *Web:* fflib.org	Fayetteville	NY	13066	315-637-6374	
Franklin Square Public Library, The 19 Lincoln Rd *Web:* franklinsquarepl.org	Franklin Square	NY	11010	516-488-3444	
Crandall Public Library 251 Glen St *Web:* www.crandalllibrary.org	Glens Falls	NY	12801	518-792-6508	
Greece Public Library 2 Vince Tofany Blvd *Web:* greecepubliclibrary.org	Greece	NY	14612	585-225-8951	
Hamburg Public Library 102 Buffalo St *Web:* buffalolib.org	Hamburg	NY	14075	716-649-4415	649-4160
Hempstead Public Library 115 Nichols Ct *Web:* www.nassaulibrary.org	Hempstead	NY	11550	516-481-6990	481-6719
Islip Public Library 71 Monell Ave *Web:* www.isliplibrary.org	Islip	NY	11751	631-581-5933	
Cornell University School of Hotel Administration Cornell University School of Hotel Aministration *Web:* sha.cornell.edu	Ithaca	NY	14853	607-255-8702	
Finger Lakes Library System 119 E Green St *TF:* 800-909-3557	Ithaca	NY	14850	607-273-4074	273-3618
Tompkins County Public Library 101 E Green St *TF:* 800-772-7267 ■ *Web:* www.tcpl.org	Ithaca	NY	14850	607-272-4557	272-8111
Queens Borough Public Library 89-11 Merrick Blvd *Web:* www.queenslibrary.org	Jamaica	NY	11432	718-990-0700	
Chautauqua-Cattaraugus Library System 106 W Fifth St *Web:* www.cclslib.org	Jamestown	NY	14701	716-484-7135	483-6880
Town of Tonawanda Public Library Kenmore Branch 160 Delaware Rd *Web:* www.buffalolib.org	Kenmore	NY	14217	716-873-2842	873-8416
Buffalo & Erie County Public Library 5466 Broadway *Web:* buffalolib.org	Lancaster	NY	14086	716-683-1120	686-0749
William K Sanford Town Library 629 Albany Shaker Rd *Web:* www.colonie.org	Loudonville	NY	12211	518-458-9274	
Ramapo Catskill Library System 619 Rt 17-M *TF:* 800-327-7343 ■ *Web:* www.rcls.org	Middletown	NY	10940	845-343-1131	
Hendrick Hudson Free Library 185 Kings Ferry Rd *Web:* www.westchesterlibraries.org	Montrose	NY	10548	914-739-5654	
Mount Vernon Public Library 28 S First Ave *Web:* mountvernonpubliclibrary.org	Mount Vernon	NY	10550	914-668-1840	
Medical Lette, The 1000 Main St *Web:* secure.medicalletter.org	New Rochelle	NY	10801	914-235-0500	
Jump Film Editing 625 Broadway 8th Fl 8th Fl *Web:* www.nycjump.com	New York	NY	10012	212-228-7474	
New York Public Library 5th Ave & 42nd St *Web:* www.nypl.org	New York	NY	10018	917-275-6975	
Saturn Production Inc 305 E 86th St *Web:* www.iperceptions.com	New York	NY	10028	212-348-7300	
Niagara Falls Public Library 1425 Main St *Web:* www.niagarafallspubliclib.org	Niagara Falls	NY	14305	716-286-4894	286-4885
Patchogue-Medford Library 54-60 E Main St Ste 60 *Web:* www.pmlib.org	Patchogue	NY	11772	631-654-4700	
Clinton-Essex-Franklin Library System 33 Oak St *Web:* www.cefls.org	Plattsburgh	NY	12901	518-563-5190	563-0421
Mount Pleasant Public Library NY 350 Bedford Rd *Web:* www.mountpleasantlibrary.org	Pleasantville	NY	10570	914-769-0548	
Northern New York Library Network 6721 Us Hwy 11 *TF:* 877-833-1674 ■ *Web:* nnyln.org	Potsdam	NY	13676	315-265-1119	
Mid-Hudson Library System 103 Market St *Web:* www.midhudson.org	Poughkeepsie	NY	12601	845-471-6060	
Brighton Memorial Library 2300 Elmwood Ave *Web:* www.brightonlibrary.org	Rochester	NY	14618	585-784-5300	784-5333
Central Library of Rochester & Monroe County 115 S Ave *Web:* www3.libraryweb.org/home2.aspx	Rochester	NY	14604	585-428-7300	428-8353
Chili Public Library 3333 Chili Ave *Web:* www.libraryweb.org/chili	Rochester	NY	14624	585-889-2200	
Gates Public Library 1605 Buffalo Rd *Web:* www.gateslibrary.org	Rochester	NY	14624	585-247-6446	426-5733
Henrietta Public Library 455 Calkins Rd *Web:* www.hpl.org	Rochester	NY	14623	585-359-7092	334-6369
Irondequoit Public Library 45 Cooper Rd *Web:* www.libraryweb.org/irondequoit	Rochester	NY	14617	585-336-6062	
Southern Adirondack Library System 22 Whitney Pl *Web:* www.sals.edu	Saratoga Springs	NY	12866	518-584-7300	
Mohawk Valley Library System 858 Duanesburg Rd *Web:* www.mvls.info	Schenectady	NY	12306	518-355-2010	
Schenectady County Public Library System 99 Clinton St *Web:* www.scpl.org	Schenectady	NY	12305	518-388-4500	386-2241
Mastics-moriches-shirley Community Library 407 William Floyd Pkwy *Web:* www.communitylibrary.org	Shirley	NY	11967	631-399-1511	
John C Hart Memorial Library 1130 E Main St *Web:* yorktownlibrary.org	Shrub Oak	NY	10588	914-245-5262	245-5936
Saint George Library Ctr 5 Central Ave **Fax Area Code:* 646 ■ *TF:* 800-342-3688	Staten Island	NY	10301	718-442-8560	312-4781*
Onondaga County Public Library 447 S Salina St *Web:* www.onlib.org	Syracuse	NY	13202	315-435-1900	
Nassau Library System 900 Jerusalem Ave *TF:* 800-662-1220 ■ *Web:* www.nassaulibrary.org	Uniondale	NY	11553	516-292-8920	481-4777
Mid-York Library System 1600 Lincoln Ave *Web:* myls.ent.sirsi.net	Utica	NY	13502	315-735-8328	735-0943
Henry Waldinger Memorial Library 60 Verona Pl *Web:* www.nassaulibrary.org	Valley Stream	NY	11582	516-825-6422	
Four County Library System 304 Clubhouse Rd *Web:* www.4cls.org	Vestal	NY	13850	607-723-8236	723-1722
Vestal Public Library 320 Vestal Pkwy E *Web:* www.4cls.org	Vestal	NY	13850	607-754-4244	
Flower Memorial Library 229 Washington St	Watertown	NY	13601	315-785-7705	788-2584
North Country Library System 22072 CR 190 *Web:* web.ncls.org	Watertown	NY	13601	315-782-5540	782-6883
Webster Public Library 980 Ridge Rd ; Webster Plz *Web:* www.websterlibrary.org	Webster	NY	14580	585-872-7075	
West Islip Public Library 3 Higbie Ln *TF:* 866-833-1122 ■ *Web:* www.wipublib.org	West Islip	NY	11795	631-661-7080	661-7137
West Seneca Public Library 1300 Union Rd *Web:* buffalolib.org	West Seneca	NY	14224	716-674-2928	
White Plains Public Library 100 Martine Ave *Web:* whiteplainslibrary.org	White Plains	NY	10601	914-422-1400	422-1462
Yonkers Public Library 1 Larkin Ctr *Web:* www.ypl.org	Yonkers	NY	10701	914-337-1500	

North Carolina

Library	City	State	Zip	Phone	Fax
Randolph Public Library 201 Worth St *Web:* www.randolphlibrary.org	Asheboro	NC	27203	336-318-6800	318-6823
Asheville-Buncombe Library System 67 Haywood St *Web:* www.buncombecounty.org/governing/depts/library	Asheville	NC	28801	828-250-4746	
Transylvania County Library (TCL) 212 S Gaston St *Web:* library.transylvaniacounty.org	Brevard	NC	28712	828-884-3151	
Fontana Regional Library 33 Fryemont Rd *Web:* www.fontanalib.org	Bryson City	NC	28713	828-488-2382	
Pender County Public Library 103 S Cowan St PO Box 879 *Web:* www.pendercountync.gov/government/departments/publiclibrary.aspx	Burgaw	NC	28425	910-259-1234	
May Memorial Library 342 S Spring St *Web:* www.alamancelibraries.org	Burlington	NC	27215	336-229-3588	229-3592
Chapel Hill Public Library 100 Library Dr *Web:* chapelhillpubliclibrary.org	Chapel Hill	NC	27514	919-968-2780	
Charlotte Mecklenburg Library 310 N Tryon St *Web:* cmlibrary.org	Charlotte	NC	28202	704-416-0100	
J C Holliday Library 217 Graham St	Clinton	NC	28328	910-592-4153	
Durham County Library 300 N Roxboro St *Web:* www.durhamcountylibrary.org	Durham	NC	27701	919-560-0100	560-0106
Rockingham County Public Library 527 Boone Rd *Web:* www.rcpl.org	Eden	NC	27288	336-627-1106	623-1258
Cumberland County Public Library 300 Maiden Ln *TF:* 866-488-7386 ■ *Web:* www.cumberland.lib.nc.us	Fayetteville	NC	28301	910-483-1580	486-5372

Phone | Fax

Gaston County Public Library
1555 E Garrison Blvd ... Gastonia NC 28054 704-868-2164 853-0609
TF: 888-241-3115 ■ *Web:* gastonlibrary.org

Greensboro Public Library 219 N Church St ... Greensboro NC 27401 336-373-2471
Web: www.greensboro-nc.gov

Halifax County Library System PO Box 97 ... Halifax NC 27839 252-583-3631 583-8661
Web: www.halifaxnc.libguides.com

H. Leslie Perry Memorial Library
205 Breckenridge St ... Henderson NC 27536 252-438-3316 438-3744
Web: www.perrylibrary.org

Henderson County Public Library
301 N Washington St ... Hendersonville NC 28739 828-697-4725 692-8449
TF: 866-866-2362 ■ *Web:* www.henderson.lib.nc.us

High Point Public Library (HPPL)
901 N Main St ... High Point NC 27262 336-883-3660 883-3636
TF: 877-772-8346 ■ *Web:* www.highpointnc.gov/749/library

Onslow County Public Library
58 Doris Ave E ... Jacksonville NC 28540 910-455-7350 455-1661
TF: 800-351-1697 ■ *Web:* www.onslowcountync.gov/Library

Duplin County Library 107 Bowdens Rd ... Kenansville NC 28349 910-296-2117 296-2172
Web: www.duplincountync.com

Caldwell County Public Library
120 Hospital Ave ... Lenoir NC 28645 828-757-1270 757-1413
Web: ccpl.libguides.com/main

Harnett County Public Library PO Box 1149 ... Lillington NC 27546 910-893-3446 893-3001
Web: harnett.libguides.com/library

Franklin County Library 906 N Main St ... Louisburg NC 27549 919-496-2111 496-1339
Web: www.franklincountync.us

McDowell County Public Library 90 W Ct St ... Marion NC 28752 828-652-3858 652-2098
Web: www.main.nc.us

McDowell County Schools 334 S Main St ... Marion NC 28752 828-652-4535
Web: www.mcdowell.k12.nc.us

Davie County Public Library 371 N Main St ... Mocksville NC 27028 336-753-6030 751-1370
Web: www.daviecountync.gov

Union County Public Library 316 E Windsor St ... Monroe NC 28112 704-283-8184 282-0657
Web: www.union.lib.nc.us

Burke County Public Library 204 S King St ... Morganton NC 28655 828-437-5638 433-1914
Web: www.bcpls.org

New Bern-Craven County Public Library
400 Johnson St ... New Bern NC 28560 252-638-7800 638-7817
Web: newbern.cpclib.org

Catawba County Library 115 W C St ... Newton NC 28658 828-465-8664
Web: www.catawbacountync.gov/library

Richard H Thornton Public Library 210 Main St ... Oxford NC 27565 919-693-1121 693-2244
Web: www.granville.lib.nc.us

Wake County Public Library System
4020 Carya Dr ... Raleigh NC 27610 919-250-1200
Web: www.wakegov.com

Sandhill Regional Library System
412 E Franklin St ... Rockingham NC 28379 910-997-3388
Web: www.ncmail.net

Rowan Public Library PO Box 4039 ... Salisbury NC 28145 704-216-8243 638-3002
Web: www.rowancountync.gov

Brunswick County Library 109 W Moore St ... Southport NC 28461 910-457-6237 457-6977
Web: www.brunswickcountync.gov/library

Iredell County Library PO Box 1810 ... Statesville NC 28687 704-878-3090 878-5449
Web: www.iredell.lib.nc.us

Edgecombe County Memorial Library
909 N Main St ... Tarboro NC 27886 252-823-1141
Web: www.edgecombelibrary.org

Alexander County Library
77 First Ave SW ... Taylorsville NC 28681 828-632-4058
Web: www.alexanderlibrary.org

Montgomery Community College Foundation Inc
1011 Page St ... Troy NC 27371 910-576-6222
Web: www.montgomery.edu

Haywood County Public Library
678 S Haywood St ... Waynesville NC 28786 828-452-5169 452-6746
Web: haywoodlibrary.libguides.com

New Hanover County Public Library
201 Chestnut St ... Wilmington NC 28401 910-798-6301 798-6312
Web: www.nhclibrary.org

Wilson County Public Library 249 W Nash St ... Wilson NC 27893 252-237-5355
TF: 877-321-2652 ■ *Web:* www.wilson-co.com

Forsyth County Public Library
201 N Chestnut St FL 5 ... Winston-Salem NC 27101 336-703-2665 727-2549
TF: 866-345-1884 ■ *Web:* www.forsyth.cc

Gunn Memorial Public Library
161 Main St E ... Yanceyville NC 27379 336-694-6241 694-9846
Web: caswellcountync.gov

North Dakota

Phone | Fax

Bismarck Veterans Memorial Public Library
515 N Fifth St ... Bismarck ND 58501 701-355-1480 221-3729

City of Fargo 200 Third St N ... Fargo ND 58102 701-241-1310
Web: cityoffargo.com/cityinfo/departments/library

Carnegie Regional Library 49 W Seventh St ... Grafton ND 58237 701-352-2754 352-2757
TF: 800-568-5964

Minot Public Library 516 Second Ave SW ... Minot ND 58701 701-852-1045 852-2595
Web: www.minotlibrary.org

Ohio

Phone | Fax

Akron-Summit County Public Library
60 S High St ... Akron OH 44326 330-643-9000
Web: www.ascpl.lib.oh.us

Rodman Public Library 215 E Broadway St ... Alliance OH 44601 330-821-2665
Web: www.rodmanlibrary.com

Phone | Fax

Ashtabula County District Library
335 W 44th St ... Ashtabula OH 44004 440-997-9341 992-7714
Web: www.acdl.info

Clermont County Public Library System
326 Broadway St ... Batavia OH 45103 513-732-2736 732-3177
Web: clermontlibrary.org

Logan County District Library
220 N Main St ... Bellefontaine OH 43311 937-599-4189 599-5503
Web: www.logancountylibraries.org

Bexley Public Library 2411 E Main St ... Bexley OH 43209 614-231-9709
Web: www.bexlib.org

Wood County District Public Library
251 N Main St ... Bowling Green OH 43402 419-352-5104 354-0405
Web: www.wcdpl.lib.oh.us

Guernsey County District Public Library
800 Steubenville Ave ... Cambridge OH 43725 740-432-5946 432-7142
Web: www.gcdpl.lib.oh.us

Stark County District Library
715 Market Ave N ... Canton OH 44702 330-452-0665 452-0403
Web: www.starklibrary.org

Carroll County District Library
70 Second St NE ... Carrollton OH 44615 330-627-2613 627-2523
Web: carrolllibrary.org

Geauga County Public Library
12701 Ravenwood Dr ... Chardon OH 44024 440-286-6811 286-7419
Web: www.geauga.lib.oh.us

Chillicothe & Ross County Public Library
140 S Paint St ... Chillicothe OH 45601 740-702-4145
Web: crcpl.org

Public Library of Cincinnati & Hamilton County
800 Vine St ... Cincinnati OH 45202 513-369-6900
Web: www.cincinnatilibrary.org

Pickaway County District Public Library
1160 N Ct St ... Circleville OH 43113 740-477-1644 474-2855
Web: www.pickawaylib.org

Cleveland Public Library 325 Superior Ave ... Cleveland OH 44114 216-623-2800 623-7015
Web: www.cpl.org

Shaker Heights Public Library
16500 Van Aken Blvd ... Cleveland OH 44120 216-991-2030
Web: www.shakerlibrary.org

Cleveland Heights-University Heights Public Library
2345 Lee Rd ... Cleveland Heights OH 44118 216-932-3600 932-0932
Web: www.heightslibrary.org

Columbus Metropolitan Library
96 S Grant Ave ... Columbus OH 43215 614-645-2275
Web: www.columbuslibrary.org

Dayton Metro Library 215 E Third St ... Dayton OH 45402 937-463-2665
Web: www.daytonmetrolibrary.org

Defiance Public Library 320 Ft St ... Defiance OH 43512 419-782-1456 782-6235
Web: www.defiancelibrary.org

Delaware County District Library
84 E Winter St ... Delaware OH 43015 740-362-3861 369-0196
TF: 866-862-7286 ■ *Web:* www.delawarelibrary.org

Brooke-Gould Memorial Library 301 N. Barron St ... Eaton OH 45320 937-456-4331 456-4774

Euclid Public Library 631 E 222nd St ... Euclid OH 44123 216-261-5300
Web: www.euclidlibrary.org

Findlay Hancock County District Public Library
206 Broadway ... Findlay OH 45840 419-422-1712 422-0638
Web: www.findlaylibrary.org

Birchard Public Library of Sandusky County
423 Croghan St ... Fremont OH 43420 419-334-7101 334-4788
Web: www.birchard.lib.oh.us

Dr Samuel L Bossard Memorial Library
7 Spruce St ... Gallipolis OH 45631 740-446-7323 446-1701
Web: www.bossard.lib.oh.us

Portage County District Library
10482 S St ... Garrettsville OH 44231 330-527-4378 527-4370
TF: 800-500-5179 ■ *Web:* www.portagecounty.lib.oh.us

Lane Public Library 300 N Third St ... Hamilton OH 45011 513-894-7156 894-2718
Web: www.lanepl.org

Highland County District Library
10 Willettsville Pk ... Hillsboro OH 45133 937-393-3114 393-2985
Web: highlandco.org

Hudson Library & Historical Society
96 Library St ... Hudson OH 44236 330-653-6658
Web: www.hudsonlibrary.org

Briggs Lawrence County Public Library
321 S Fourth St ... Ironton OH 45638 740-532-1124
Web: www.briggslibrary.com

Lakewood Public Library 15425 Detroit Ave ... Lakewood OH 44107 216-226-8275 521-4327
Web: lakewoodpubliclibrary.org

Fairfield County District Library
219 N Broad St ... Lancaster OH 43130 740-653-2745
Web: www.fcdlibrary.org

Lebanon Public Library 101 S Broadway ... Lebanon OH 45036 513-932-2665
Web: www.lebanonlibrary.org

Lima Public Library 650 W Market St ... Lima OH 45801 419-228-5113
Web: www.limalibrary.com

Logan-Hocking County District Library
230 E Main St ... Logan OH 43138 740-385-2348 385-9093
Web: www.hocking.lib.oh.us

Lorain Public Library System 351 W Sixth St ... Lorain OH 44052 440-244-1192 244-4888
TF: 800-322-7323 ■ *Web:* lorainpubliclibrary.org

Mansfield-Richland County Public Library
43 W Third St ... Mansfield OH 44902 419-521-3100 525-4750
TF: 877-795-2111 ■ *Web:* www.mrcpl.org

Washington County Public Library
615 Fifth St ... Marietta OH 45750 740-373-1057 373-2860
Web: wcplib.info

Medina County District Library 210 S Broadway ... Medina OH 44256 330-725-0588 725-2053
Web: www.mcdl.info

Middletown Public Library 125 S Broad St ... Middletown OH 45044 513-424-1251
Web: www.midpointelibrary.org

Phone Fax

Holmes County District Public Library (HCDPL)
3102 Glen Dr .... Millersburg OH 44654 330-674-5972 674-1938
Web: www.holmeslibrary.org

Mount Vernon & Knox County Public Library
201 N Mulberry St .... Mount Vernon OH 43050 740-392-2665 397-3866

Perry County District Library
117 S Jackson St .... New Lexington OH 43764 740-342-4194 342-4204
Web: www.pcdl.org

Tuscarawas County Public Library
121 Fair Ave NW .... New Philadelphia OH 44663 330-364-4474 364-8217
Web: www.tusclibrary.org

Newark Public Library 101 W Main St .... Newark OH 43055 740-928-3923
Web: www.newarklibrary.info

Putnam County District Library
136 Putnam Pkwy .... Ottawa OH 45875 419-523-3747 523-6477
Web: www.mypcdl.org

Morely Library 184 Phelps St .... Painesville OH 44077 440-352-3383
Web: www.morleylibrary.org

Cuyahoga County Public Library 2111 Snow Rd. .... Parma OH 44134 216-398-1800
TF: 800-749-5560 ■ *Web:* www.cuyahogalibrary.org

Paulding County Carnegie Library
205 S Main St. .... Paulding OH 45879 419-399-2032 399-2114
Web: www.pauldingcountylibrary.org

Ida Rupp Public Library 310 Madison St. .... Port Clinton OH 43452 419-732-3212
Web: www.idarupp.lib.oh.us

Portsmouth Public Library 1220 Gallia St .... Portsmouth OH 45662 740-354-5688 353-3483
Web: www.portsmouth.lib.oh.us

Clark County Public Library
201 S Fountain Ave .... Springfield OH 45501 937-328-6903 328-6908
Web: www.ccpl.lib.oh.us

Public Library of Steubenville & Jefferson County
407 S Fourth St .... Steubenville OH 43952 740-282-9782 282-2919
Web: www.steubenville.lib.oh.us

Tiffin-Seneca Public Library 77 Jefferson St. .... Tiffin OH 44883 419-447-3751 447-3045
Web: tiffinsenecalibrary.org

Toledo-Lucas County Public Library
325 N Michigan St .... Toledo OH 43604 419-259-5200
Web: www.toledolibrary.org

Troy-Miami County Public Library 419 W Main St .... Troy OH 45373 937-339-0502 335-4880
TF: 866-657-8556 ■ *Web:* www.troypubliclibrary.org

Upper Arlington Public Library
2800 Tremont Rd .... Upper Arlington OH 43221 614-486-9621 486-4530
Web: www.ualibrary.org

Brumback Library 215 W Main St. .... Van Wert OH 45891 419-238-2168 238-3180
Web: www.brumbacklib.com

Wadsworth Public Library 132 Broad St. .... Wadsworth OH 44281 330-334-5761
Web: www.wadsworthlibrary.com

Warren-Trumbull County Public Library
444 Mahoning Ave NW .... Warren OH 44483 330-399-8807 395-3988
Web: www.wtcpl.lib.oh.us

Carnegie Public Library
127 S N St .... Washington Court House OH 43160 740-335-2540 335-2928
Web: www.cplwcho.org

Garnet A Wilson Public Library of Pike County
207 N Market St .... Waverly OH 45690 740-947-4921 947-2918
Web: www.pike.lib.oh.us

Westerville Public Library
126 S State St. .... Westerville OH 43081 614-882-7277 882-4160
TF: 800-816-0662 ■ *Web:* westervillelibrary.org

Greene County Public Library
76 E Market St PO Box 520 .... Xenia OH 45385 937-352-4000 372-4673
Web: greenelibrary.info

Public Library of Youngstown & Mahoning County
305 Wick Ave .... Youngstown OH 44503 330-744-8636 744-2258
Web: libraryvisit.org

Reuben Mc Millan Free Library Association Inc, The
305 Wick Ave .... Youngstown OH 44503 330-744-8636
Web: www.libraryvisit.org

Muskingum County Library System
220 N Fifth St .... Zanesville OH 43701 740-453-0391 455-6357
Web: www.muskingumlibrary.org

Oklahoma

Phone Fax

J W Martin Library 709 Oklahoma Blvd .... Alva OK 73717 580-327-8574
Web: www.nwosu.edu

Bartlesville Public Library
600 S Johnstone Ave .... Bartlesville OK 74003 918-338-4161 337-5338
Web: www.bartlesville.lib.ok.us

Edmond Public Library 10 S Blvd .... Edmond OK 73034 405-341-9282
Web: www.metrolibrary.org

Lawton Public Library 110 SW Fourth St .... Lawton OK 73501 580-581-3450 248-0243
TF: 855-895-8064 ■ *Web:* www.cityof.lawton.ok.us

Southeastern Library System of Oklahoma (SEPLSO)
401 N Second St. .... McAlester OK 74501 918-426-0456 423-5731
TF: 800-215-6494 ■ *Web:* oklibrary.net

Eastern Oklahoma District Library System
814 W Okmulgee St .... Muskogee OK 74401 918-683-2846 683-0436
Web: www.eodls.lib.ok.us

Pioneer Library System
300 Norman Center Court. .... Norman OK 73072 405-801-4500 701-2608
Web: pioneerlibrarysystem.org

Ponca City Library 515 E Grand Ave .... Ponca City OK 74601 580-767-0345 767-0374
TF: 800-522-8165 ■ *Web:* www.poncacityok.gov/index.aspx?nid=155

Stillwater Public Library 1107 S Duck St. .... Stillwater OK 74074 405-372-3633 624-0552
Web: library.stillwater.org

Tulsa City-County Library (TCCL) 400 Civic Ctr .... Tulsa OK 74103 918-549-7323
Web: www.tulsalibrary.org

Tulsa Zoological Park Library 6421 E 36th St N .... Tulsa OK 74115 918-669-6600
Web: www.tulsazoo.org

Ontario

Phone Fax

Waterloo Public Library 35 Albert St .... Waterloo ON N2L5E2 519-886-1310 886-7936
Web: www.wpl.ca

Oregon

Phone Fax

Beaverton City Library 12375 SW Fifth St. .... Beaverton OR 97005 503-644-2197
Web: www.beavertonlibrary.org

Deschutes Public Library 507 NW Wall St. .... Bend OR 97701 541-312-1020 389-2982
TF: 855-268-3767 ■ *Web:* www.deschuteslibrary.org

Coos Bay Public Library 525 W Anderson Ave .... Coos Bay OR 97420 541-269-1101 269-7567
Web: bay.cooslibraries.org

Corvallis-Benton County Library
645 NW Monroe Ave .... Corvallis OR 97330 541-766-6793 766-6915
Web: www.library.ci.corvallis.or.us

Eugene Public Library 100 W Tenth Ave .... Eugene OR 97401 541-682-5450 682-5898
Web: www.eugene-or.gov

Josephine County Library System
200 NW 'C' St PO Box 1684 .... Grants Pass OR 97526 541-476-0571
Web: www.josephinelibrary.org

Hillsboro Public Library
2850 NE Brookwood Pkwy .... Hillsboro OR 97124 503-615-6500
TF: 855-870-0049 ■ *Web:* www.ci.hillsboro.or.us

Klamath County Library 126 S Third St. .... Klamath Falls OR 97601 541-882-8894 882-6166
Web: klamathlibrary.org

Lake Oswego Public Library 706 Fourth St .... Lake Oswego OR 97034 503-636-7628 635-4171
Web: www.ci.oswego.or.us

McMinnville Public Library
225 NW Adams St .... McMinnville OR 97128 503-435-5555
Web: www.maclibrary.org

Jackson County Library System
205 S Central Ave. .... Medford OR 97501 541-774-8679
Web: www.jcls.org

Ledding Library 10660 SE 21st Ave .... Milwaukie OR 97222 503-786-7580 659-9497
Web: www.milwaukieoregon.gov

Clackamas County Library
16201 SE McLoughlin Blvd .... Oak Grove OR 97267 503-655-8543
Web: www.clackamas.us/lib/hours.html

Oregon City Public Library
606 John Adams. .... Oregon City OR 97045 503-657-8269
Web: orcity.org

Multnomah County Library 801 SW Tenth Ave. .... Portland OR 97205 503-988-5123 988-5226
Web: www.multcolib.org

Douglas County Library System
1409 NE Diamond Lk Blvd .... Roseburg OR 97470 541-440-4311
Web: www.dclibrary.us

Salem Public Library 555 Liberty St SE. .... Salem OR 97301 503-588-6071 588-6055
Web: www.cityofsalem.net/departments/library

Springfield Public Library
225 N Fifth St. .... Springfield OR 97477 541-726-3766 726-3747
Web: www.ci.springfield.or.us

Tigard Public Library 13500 SW Hall Blvd .... Tigard OR 97223 503-684-6537
Web: tigard-or.gov

Pennsylvania

Phone Fax

Allentown Public Library 1210 Hamilton St .... Allentown PA 18102 610-820-2400 820-0640
Web: www.allentownpl.org

Altoona Area Public Library 1600 Fifth Ave. .... Altoona PA 16602 814-946-0417 946-3230
Web: www.altoonalibrary.org

LTK Engineering Services Inc 100 W Butler Ave .... Ambler PA 19002 215-542-0700
Web: www.ltk.com

Bethlehem Area Public Library
11 W Church St .... Bethlehem PA 18018 610-867-3761 867-2767
TF: 800-732-0999 ■ *Web:* www.bapl.org

Bucks County Free Library 150 S Pine St. .... Doylestown PA 18901 215-348-9081 348-4760
Web: www.buckslib.org

Erie County Library System 160 E Front St. .... Erie PA 16507 814-451-6900
Web: www.erielibrary.org

Raymond M Blasco MD Memorial Library
160 E Front St. .... Erie PA 16507 814-451-6900
Web: www.erielibrary.org

Chester County Library 450 Exton Sq Pkwy .... Exton PA 19341 610-280-2600
Web: www.ccls.org

Adams County Public Library
140 Baltimore St. .... Gettysburg PA 17325 717-334-5716 334-7992
Web: www.adamslibrary.org

Dauphin County Library System
101 Walnut St. .... Harrisburg PA 17101 717-234-4961 234-7479
Web: www.dcls.org

Cambria County Library System 248 Main St .... Johnstown PA 15901 814-536-5131 536-6905
Web: www.cclsys.org

Lancaster Public Library 125 N Duke St. .... Lancaster PA 17602 717-394-2651 394-3083
Web: www.lancaster.lib.pa.us

Library System of Lebanon County
125 N Seventh St .... Lebanon PA 17046 717-273-7624 273-2719
Web: lclibs.org

Montgomery County-Norristown Public Library
1001 Powell St. .... Norristown PA 19401 610-278-5100 277-0344
Web: mnl.mclinc.org

Oil Creek District Library Ctr
2 Central Ave .... Oil City PA 16301 814-678-3054 676-0359
Web: www.oilcreekdistrictlibrary.org

Osceola Mills Public Library
600 Lingle St .... Osceola Mills PA 16666 814-339-7229

Free Library of Philadelphia
1901 Vine St. .... Philadelphia PA 19103 215-686-5322 563-3628
TF: 800-732-0999 ■ *Web:* www.freelibrary.org

				Phone	Fax
Carnegie Library of Pittsburgh 4400 Forbes Ave *Web:* carnegielibrary.org	Pittsburgh	PA	15213	412-622-3114	
Northland Public Library 300 Cumberland Rd *Web:* www.northlandlibrary.org	Pittsburgh	PA	15237	412-366-8100	
Upper st Clair Township Lbrry 1820 Mclaughlin Run Rd *Web:* www.twpusc.org	Pittsburgh	PA	15241	412-835-5540	
Pottsville Free Public Library 215 W Market St *Web:* www.pottsvillelibrary.org	Pottsville	PA	17901	570-622-8880	622-2157
Reading Public Library 100 S Fifth St *Web:* www.reading.lib.pa.us	Reading	PA	19602	610-655-6355	655-6609
Albright Memorial Library 500 Vine St *Web:* www.lclshome.org	Scranton	PA	18509	570-348-3000	348-3020
Scranton Public Library 500 Vine St *Web:* www.albright.org	Scranton	PA	18509	570-348-3000	
Osterhout Free Library 71 S Franklin St *Web:* osterhout.info	Wilkes-Barre	PA	18701	570-823-0156	
James V Brown Library of Williamsport & Lycoming County 19 E Fourth St *Web:* www.jvbrown.edu	Williamsport	PA	17701	570-326-0536	326-1671
Martin Memorial Library 159 E Market St *Web:* www.yorklibraries.org	York	PA	17401	717-846-5300	848-2330

Rhode Island

				Phone	Fax
Coventry Public Library 1672 Flat River Rd *Web:* www.coventrylibrary.org	Coventry	RI	02816	401-822-9100	822-9133
Cranston Public Library 140 Sockanosset Cross Rd *Web:* www.cranstonlibrary.org	Cranston	RI	02920	401-943-9080	946-5079
Cumberland Public Library 1464 Diamond Hill Rd *Web:* www.cumberlandlibrary.org	Cumberland	RI	02864	401-333-2552	334-0578
East Providence Public Library 41 Grove Ave *Web:* www.eastprovidencelibrary.org	East Providence	RI	02914	401-434-2453	
Marion J Mohr Memorial Library 1 Memorial Ave *Web:* www.mohrlibrary.org	Johnston	RI	02919	401-231-4980	231-4984
Newport Public Library 300 Spring St *Web:* www.newportlibraryri.org	Newport	RI	02840	401-847-8720	842-0841
Pawtucket Public Library 13 Summer St *TF:* 800-359-3090 ■ *Web:* www.pawtucketlibrary.org	Pawtucket	RI	02860	401-725-3714	
Providence Public Library 150 Empire St *Web:* www.provlib.org	Providence	RI	02903	401-455-8000	
Warwick Public Library (WPL) 600 Sandy Ln *Web:* warwicklibrary.org	Warwick	RI	02886	401-739-5440	
West Warwick Public Library System 1043 Main St *Web:* www.wwlibrary.org	West Warwick	RI	02893	401-828-3750	828-8493
Westerly Public Library 44 Broad St *Web:* www.westerlylibrary.org	Westerly	RI	02891	401-596-2877	596-5600
Woonsocket Harris Public Library 303 Clinton St *TF:* 800-359-3090 ■ *Web:* www.woonsocketlibrary.org	Woonsocket	RI	02895	401-769-9044	767-4140

South Carolina

				Phone	Fax
Aiken-Bamberg-Barnwell-Edgefield Regional Library System 314 Chesterfield St *Web:* www.abbe-lib.org	Aiken	SC	29801	803-642-7575	
Anderson County Library 300 S McDuffie St *Web:* www.andersonlibrary.org	Anderson	SC	29621	864-260-4500	
Marlboro County Library 203 Fayetteville Ave *Web:* www.edelmanpubliclibrary.org	Bennettsville	SC	29512	843-479-5630	479-5645
Charleston County Public Library 68 Calhoun St *Web:* www.ccpl.org	Charleston	SC	29401	843-805-6930	727-3741
Chester County Library 100 Ctr St *Web:* www.chesterlibsc.org	Chester	SC	29706	803-377-8145	377-8146
Chesterfield County Library 119 Main St *Web:* chesterfield.lib.sc.us	Chesterfield	SC	29709	843-623-7489	623-3295
Richland County Public Library (RCPL) 1431 Assembly St *Web:* www.richlandlibrary.com	Columbia	SC	29201	803-799-9084	
State Library 1430 Senate St *Web:* www.statelibrary.sc.gov	Columbia	SC	29201	803-734-4611	
Darlington County Library 204 N Main St *Web:* www.darlington-lib.org	Darlington	SC	29532	843-398-4940	398-4942
Dillon County Library 600 E Main St *Web:* dillon.lib.sc.us	Dillon	SC	29536	843-774-0330	774-0733
Pickens County Library 304 Biltmore Rd *Web:* pickens.lib.sc.us	Easley	SC	29640	864-850-7077	850-7088
Florence County Library 509 S Dargan St *Web:* www.florencelibrary.org	Florence	SC	29506	843-662-8424	
Cherokee County Public Library 300 E Rutledge Ave	Gaffney	SC	29340	864-487-2711	487-2752
Greenville County Library 25 Heritage Green Pl *TF:* 866-275-7273 ■ *Web:* www.greenvillelibrary.org	Greenville	SC	29601	864-242-5000	235-8375
Hilton Head Library 11 Beach City Rd *TF:* 800-860-1444 ■ *Web:* beaufortcountylibrary.org	Hilton Head Island	SC	29926	843-255-6500	342-9220
Williamsburg County Library 215 N Jackson St *Web:* www.mywcl.org	Kingstree	SC	29556	843-355-9486	355-9991
Lancaster County Library 313 S White St *Web:* www.lanclib.org	Lancaster	SC	29720	803-285-1502	285-6004
Laurens County Library 1017 W Main St *Web:* lcpl.org	Laurens	SC	29360	864-681-7323	681-0598
Harvin Clarendon County Library 215 N Brooks St *Web:* www.clarendoncountylibrary.com	Manning	SC	29102	803-435-8633	435-8101
Marion County Library (MCL) 101 E Ct St *Web:* www.marioncountylibrary.org	Marion	SC	29571	843-423-8300	423-8302
Berkeley County Library 1003 Hwy 52	Moncks Corner	SC	29461	843-719-4223	719-4732
Chapin Memorial Library 400 14th Ave N *Web:* www.cityofmyrtlebeach.com	Myrtle Beach	SC	29577	843-918-1275	918-1288
Orangeburg County Library (OCL) 510 Louis St *Web:* www.orangeburgcounty.org	Orangeburg	SC	29115	803-531-4636	
York County Library 138 E Black St *Web:* www.yclibrary.org	Rock Hill	SC	29730	803-981-5858	
Dorchester County Library 506 N Parler Ave *Web:* www.dcl.lib.sc.us	Saint George	SC	29477	843-563-9189	563-7823
Spartanburg County Public Library 151 S Church St *Web:* www.infodepot.org	Spartanburg	SC	29306	864-596-3507	596-3518
Sumter County Library 111 N Harvin St *Web:* www.sumtercountylibrary.org	Sumter	SC	29150	803-773-7273	773-4875
Union County Carnegie Library 300 E S St *Web:* www.unionlibrary.org	Union	SC	29379	864-427-7140	
Oconee County Library 501 W S Broad St *Web:* oconeelibrary.org	Walhalla	SC	29691	864-638-4133	
Colleton County Memorial Library 600 Hampton St *Web:* www.colletonlibrary.org	Walterboro	SC	29488	843-549-5621	549-5122

South Dakota

				Phone	Fax
Brookings Public Library 515 Third St *Web:* www.brookingslibrary.org	Brookings	SD	57006	605-692-9407	
RE Rawlins Municipal Library 1000 E Church St	Pierre	SD	57501	605-773-7421	773-7423
Rapid City Public Library (RCPL) 610 Quincy St *Web:* www.rcgov.org/library	Rapid City	SD	57701	605-394-4171	

Tennessee

				Phone	Fax
Cheatham County Public Library 188 County Services Dr Ste 200 **Fax Area Code:* 305	Ashland City	TN	37015	615-792-4828	393-8193*
EG Fisher Public Library 1289 Ingleside Ave *TF:* 800-552-6843 ■ *Web:* fisherlibrary.org	Athens	TN	37303	423-745-7782	745-1763
Sullivan County Public Library 1655 Blountville Blvd PO Box 510 *Web:* sullivancountylibrarytn.org	Blountville	TN	37617	423-279-2714	
Chattanooga-Hamilton County Bicentennial Library 1001 Broad St *Web:* www.lib.chattanooga.gov	Chattanooga	TN	37402	423-757-5310	757-4994
Clarksville Montgomery County Public Library 350 Pageant Ln *TF:* 877-239-6635 ■ *Web:* www.mcgtn.org/library	Clarksville	TN	37040	931-648-8826	648-8831
Cleveland Bradley County Public Library 795 N Church St NE *Web:* www.clevelandlibrary.org	Cleveland	TN	37311	423-472-2163	
Clinton Public Library 118 S Hicks St *Web:* clintonpubliclibrary.org	Clinton	TN	37716	865-457-0519	
Blue Grass Regional Library 104 E Sixth St **Fax Area Code:* 865 ■ *TF:* 888-345-5575	Columbia	TN	38401	931-388-9282	981-4587*
Putnam County Library 50 E Broad St *Web:* www.pclibrary.org	Cookeville	TN	38501	931-526-2416	372-8517
Art Cir Public Library 3 E St *Web:* www.artcirclelibrary.info	Crossville	TN	38555	931-484-6790	484-2350
McIver's Grant Public Library 204 N Mill Ave *Web:* www.dyersburgdyercolibrary.com	Dyersburg	TN	38024	731-285-5032	
Elizabethton-Carter County Public Library 201 N Sycamore St	Elizabethton	TN	37643	423-547-6360	
Williamson County Public Library 1314 Columbia Ave *Web:* wcpltn.org	Franklin	TN	37064	615-595-1243	595-1245
Martin Curtis-Hendersonville Public Library 140 Saundersville Rd	Hendersonville	TN	37075	615-824-0656	
Jacksboro Public Library 585 Main St Ste 201 *Web:* www.jacksboropubliclibrary.org	Jacksboro	TN	37757	423-562-3675	562-9587
Jackson-Madison County Library 433 E Lafayette St *Web:* www.jmcl.tn.org	Jackson	TN	38301	731-425-8600	425-8609
Johnson City Public Library 100 W Millard St *Web:* www.jcpl.net	Johnson City	TN	37604	423-434-4450	434-4469
Kingsport Public Library 400 Broad St *Web:* www.kingsportlibrary.org	Kingsport	TN	37660	423-224-2559	
Lawrence County Public Library 519 E Gaines St *Web:* lawrencecountytn.gov	Lawrenceburg	TN	38464	931-762-4627	766-1597
Lebanon-Wilson County Public Library 108 S Hatton Ave *Web:* www2.youseemore.com/lebanon-wilson/default.asp	Lebanon	TN	37087	615-444-0632	444-0535
Lenoir City Public Library 100 W Broadway St Ste 103	Lenoir City	TN	37771	865-986-3210	
Reelfoot Regional Library Ctr 542 N Lindell St	Martin	TN	38237	731-587-2347	

Library	City	State	Zip	Phone	Fax
Blount County Public Library 508 N Cusick St	Maryville	TN	37804	865-982-0981	
Web: www.blountlibrary.org					
Morristown-Hamblen Public Library 417 W Main St	Morristown	TN	37814	423-586-6410	587-6226
Web: morristownhamblenlibrary.org					
Highland Rim Regional Library Ctr 2118 E Main St	Murfreesboro	TN	37130	615-893-3380	895-6727
Web: tennessee.gov					
Linebaugh Public Library 105 W Vine St	Murfreesboro	TN	37130	615-893-4131	848-5038
Web: www.linebaugh.org					
Nashville Public Library 615 Church St	Nashville	TN	37219	615-862-5800	880-2119
Web: www.library.nashville.org					
Stokely Memorial Library 383 E Broadway	Newport	TN	37821	423-623-3832	623-3832
Oak Ridge Public Library 1401 Oak Ridge Tpke	Oak Ridge	TN	37830	865-425-3455	425-3429
Web: www.oakridgetn.gov/department/library/home					
WG Rhea Library 400 W Washington St	Paris	TN	38242	731-642-1702	
Web: rheapubliclibrary.org					
Giles County Public Library 122 S Second St	Pulaski	TN	38478	931-363-2720	
Web: www.gilescountylibrary.org					
Hawkins County Library System 407 E Main St	Rogersville	TN	37857	423-272-8710	272-9261
Web: www.hawkinslibraries.org					
Sevier County Public Library 408 High St	Sevierville	TN	37862	865-453-3532	365-1667
Web: www.sevierlibrary.org					
Argie Cooper Public Library 100 S Main St	Shelbyville	TN	37160	931-684-7323	685-4848
Web: www.acolibrary.com					
Fayette County Library 216 W Market St	Somerville	TN	38068	901-465-5248	465-5271
TF: 866-465-3591 ■ *Web:* www.fayettetn.us					
County Library 1304 Old Knoxville Rd	Tazewell	TN	37879	423-626-5414	626-9481
Obion County Public Library 1221 E Reelfoot Ave	Union City	TN	38261	731-885-7000	
Web: www.oclibrary.org					
Franklin County Library 105 S Porter St	Winchester	TN	37398	931-967-3706	962-1477
Web: franklincountylibrary.org					

Texas

Library	City	State	Zip	Phone	Fax
Abilene Public Library 202 Cedar St	Abilene	TX	79601	325-677-2474	676-6024
Web: www.abilenetx.com					
Alice Public Library 401 E Third St	Alice	TX	78332	361-664-9506	668-3248
Amarillo Public Library 413 SE Fourth Ave	Amarillo	TX	79101	806-378-3054	378-9327
Web: www.amarillolibrary.org					
Brazoria County Library System 451 N Velasco Ste 250	Angleton	TX	77515	979-864-1505	864-1298
Web: bcls.lib.tx.us					
Arlington Public Library 101 E Abram St	Arlington	TX	76010	817-459-6900	
TF: 888-227-7669 ■ *Web:* www.arlingtonlibrary.org					
Henderson County CW Murchison Memorial Library 121 S Prairieville	Athens	TX	75751	903-677-7295	
Web: www.koha.org					
Austin Public Library 800 Guadalupe St	Austin	TX	78701	512-974-7400	499-7403
Web: library.austintexas.gov					
Beaumont Public Library System 801 Pearl St	Beaumont	TX	77701	409-838-6606	838-6838
Web: beaumonttexas.gov/departments/library					
Howard County Library 500 S Main St	Big Spring	TX	79720	432-264-2260	750-8588*
**Fax Area Code:* 410					
Nancy Carol Roberts Memorial Library 100 Martin Luther King Junior Pkwy	Brenham	TX	77833	979-337-7201	
Web: cityofbrenham.org					
Brownsville Public Library 4320 Southmost Rd	Brownsville	TX	78521	956-548-1055	548-0684
Web: www.bpl.us					
Brownwood Public Library 600 Carnegie Blvd	Brownwood	TX	76801	325-646-0155	646-6503
Web: www.brownwoodpubliclibrary.com					
Bryan Public Library 201 E 26th St	Bryan	TX	77803	979-209-5600	
Web: www.bcslibrary.org					
Van Zandt County Library 317 First Monday Ln	Canton	TX	75103	903-567-4276	
Web: vanzandtlibrary.org					
Carrollton Public Library 4220 N Josey Ln	Carrollton	TX	75010	972-466-4800	466-4722
TF: 888-727-2978 ■ *Web:* www.cityofcarrollton.com/library					
Montgomery County Library 104 I-45 N	Conroe	TX	77301	936-442-7712	788-8398
Web: www.countylibrary.org					
Corpus Christi Public Libraries 805 Comanche St	Corpus Christi	TX	78401	361-826-7000	
Web: www.cclibraries.com					
Corsicana Public Library 100 N 12th St	Corsicana	TX	75110	903-654-4810	
TF: 877-648-2836 ■ *Web:* www.cityofcorsicana.com					
J Erik Jonsson Central Library 1515 Young St	Dallas	TX	75201	214-670-1400	
Web: www.dallaslibrary2.org/central					
Deer Park Public Library 3009 Ctr St	Deer Park	TX	77536	281-478-7208	478-7212
Web: deerparktx.gov					
Val Verde County Library 300 Spring St	Del Rio	TX	78840	830-774-7595	774-7607
Web: www.youseemore.com/vvcl					
Denison Public Library 300 W Gandy St	Denison	TX	75020	903-465-1797	
Web: www.barr.org					
Emily Fowler Central Library 502 Oakland St	Denton	TX	76201	940-349-8752	349-8101
DeSoto Public Library 211 E Pleasant Run Rd Ste C	DeSoto	TX	75115	972-230-9656	230-5797
TF: 800-886-9008 ■ *Web:* www.ci.desoto.tx.us					
Diboll Texas Independent School District 215 N Temple Dr	Diboll	TX	75941	936-829-4718	
Web: www.dibollisd.com					
Duncanville Public Library 201 James Collins Blvd	Duncanville	TX	75116	972-780-5050	780-6426
Web: duncanville.com					
Eagle Pass Public Library 243 Bliss St	Eagle Pass	TX	78852	830-773-2516	
Web: eaglepasstx.us					
Edinburg Public Library 1906 S Closner	Edinburg	TX	78539	956-383-6246	318-3446
Web: www.edinburg.lib.tx.us					
Euless Public Library 201 N Ector Dr	Euless	TX	76039	817-685-1480	
Web: eulesstx.gov					
City of Farmers Branch 13000 William Dodson Pkwy	Farmers Branch	TX	75234	972-247-3131	
Web: www.dallascremations-funerals.com					
Fort Worth Public Library 500 W Third St	Fort Worth	TX	76102	817-392-7323	871-7734
Web: fortworthtexas.gov					
Friendswood Public Library 416 S Friendswood Dr	Friendswood	TX	77546	281-482-7135	482-2685
TF: 800-696-3493 ■ *Web:* www.friendswood.lib.tx.us					
Rosenberg Library 2310 Sealy Ave	Galveston	TX	77550	409-763-8854	763-0275
Web: www.rosenberg-library.org					
Nicholson Memorial Library System 200 N 5th St	Garland	TX	75040	972-205-2000	205-2523
Web: www.nmls.lib.tx.us					
Upshur County Library 702 W Tyler St	Gilmer	TX	75644	903-843-5001	843-3995
Web: countyofupshur.com					
Hood County Public Library 222 N Travis St	Granbury	TX	76048	817-573-3569	573-3969
TF: 800-452-9292 ■ *Web:* www.co.hood.tx.us					
Grapevine Public Library 1201 Municipal Way	Grapevine	TX	76051	817-410-3400	
Web: grapevinetexas.gov					
Greenville Library 1 Lou Finney Ln	Greenville	TX	75401	903-457-2992	457-2961
Web: www.ci.greenville.tx.us					
Haltom City Public Library 4809 Haltom Rd	Haltom City	TX	76117	817-222-7786	834-1446
Web: www.haltomcitytx.com					
Harlingen Public Library 410 76th Dr	Harlingen	TX	78550	956-216-5888	
Rusk County Library (RCL) 106 E Main St	Henderson	TX	75652	903-657-8557	
Web: www.rclib.org					
Harris County Public Library System 8080 El Rio St	Houston	TX	77054	713-749-9000	749-9090
Web: www.hcpl.net					
Houston Public Library 500 McKinney St	Houston	TX	77002	832-393-1313	393-1324
TF: 800-318-2596 ■ *Web:* www.houstonlibrary.org					
Hurst Public Library 901 Precinct Line Rd	Hurst	TX	76053	817-788-7300	590-9515
TF: 800-344-8377 ■ *Web:* hursttx.gov					
Irving Public Library 801 W Irving Blvd	Irving	TX	75060	972-721-2606	721-2463
Web: irving.net/irvingwiki/index.php?title=main_page					
Butt-Holdsworth Memorial Library 505 Water St	Kerrville	TX	78028	830-257-8422	792-5552
Web: www.kerrvilletx.gov					
Robert J Kleberg Public Library 220 N Fourth St	Kingsville	TX	78363	361-592-6381	
Web: kleberglibrary.com					
Laredo Public Library 1120 E Calton Rd	Laredo	TX	78041	956-795-2400	795-2403
Web: www.laredolibrary.org					
Helen Hall Library (HHL) 100 W Walker St	League City	TX	77573	281-554-1111	
Web: www.leaguecity.com					
Lewisville Public Library 1197 W Main St	Lewisville	TX	75067	972-219-3570	219-5094
Web: www.cityoflewisville.com					
Longview Public Library 222 W Cotton St	Longview	TX	75601	903-237-1351	237-1327
Web: www.longviewtexas.gov/2163/library					
Lubbock Public Library 1306 Ninth St	Lubbock	TX	79401	806-775-2835	
Web: www.mylubbock.us/departmental-websites/departments/library/library-home					
Marshall Public Library 300 S Alamo St	Marshall	TX	75670	903-935-4465	
Web: marshalltexas.net					
McAllen Memorial Library 601 N Main St	McAllen	TX	78501	956-688-3300	
Web: www.mcallenlibrary.net					
Mesquite Public Library 300 W Grubb Dr	Mesquite	TX	75149	972-216-6220	216-6740
Web: www.cityofmesquite.com					
Midland County Public Library 301 W Missouri Ave	Midland	TX	79701	432-688-4320	688-4939
Web: www.co.midland.tx.us					
Speer Memorial Library 801 E 12th St	Mission	TX	78572	956-580-8750	580-8756
Web: www.mission.lib.tx.us					
Nacogdoches Public Library 1112 N St	Nacogdoches	TX	75961	936-559-2970	569-8282
TF: 800-252-5400 ■ *Web:* ci.nacogdoches.tx.us					
New Braunfels Public Library 700 E Common St	New Braunfels	TX	78130	830-221-4300	608-2151
TF: 800-434-8013 ■ *Web:* www.nbtexas.org					
North Richland Hills Public Library 9015 Grand Ave	North Richland Hills	TX	76180	817-427-6800	427-6808
Web: www.library.nrhtx.com					
Ector County Library 321 W Fifth St	Odessa	TX	79761	432-332-0633	337-6502
Web: www.ector.lib.tx.us					
Palestine Public Library 2000 S Loop 256 #42	Palestine	TX	75801	903-729-4121	729-4062
Web: www1.youseemore.com/palestine					
Lee Davis Library 8060 Spencer Hwy	Pasadena	TX	77505	281-476-1850	478-2734
Web: www.sanjac.edu					
Pasadena Public Library 1201 Jeff Ginn Memorial Dr	Pasadena	TX	77506	713-477-0276	473-9640
Web: www.ci.pasadena.tx.us					
Pharr Memorial Library 118 S Cage blvd	Pharr	TX	78577	956-787-3966	787-3345
Web: pharr-tx.gov					
Unger Memorial Library 825 N Austin St	Plainview	TX	79072	806-296-1148	
Web: whc.net					
Plano Public Library System 5024 Custer Rd	Plano	TX	75023	972-769-4200	
Web: planolibrary.org					
Port Arthur Public Library 4615 Ninth Ave	Port Arthur	TX	77642	409-985-8838	985-5969
Web: www.pap.lib.tx.us					
Richardson Public Library 900 Civic Ctr Dr	Richardson	TX	75080	972-744-4350	744-5806
TF: 800-735-2989 ■ *Web:* www.cor.net					
George Memorial Library 1001 Golfview Dr	Richmond	TX	77469	281-342-4455	341-2689
Web: www.fortbend.lib.tx.us					
Round Rock Public Library 216 E Main St	Round Rock	TX	78664	512-218-7001	
Web: www.roundrocktexas.gov					
Tom Green County Library System 33 W Beauregard Ave	San Angelo	TX	76903	325-655-7321	
Web: tgclibrary.com					

Library	City	State	ZIP	Phone	Fax
Daughters of the Republic of Texas Library PO Box 1401 *Web:* www.drtl.org	San Antonio	TX	78295	210-225-1071	
Marcive Inc 12100 Crownpoint Dr Ste 160 *Web:* www.marcive.com	San Antonio	TX	78233	210-646-6161	
San Antonio Public Library 600 Soledad St *Web:* www.sanantonio.gov/library	San Antonio	TX	78205	210-207-2500	
San Benito Public Library 101 W Rose St *TF:* 800-444-1187 ■ *Web:* www.cityofsanbenito.com	San Benito	TX	78586	956-361-3860	361-3867
San Marcos Public Library 625 E Hopkins St *Web:* www.ci.san-marcos.tx.us	San Marcos	TX	78666	512-393-8200	754-8131
Sherman Public Library 421 N Travis St *Web:* www.barr.org	Sherman	TX	75090	903-892-7240	
Taylor Public Library 400 Porter St *Web:* www.ci.taylor.tx.us	Taylor	TX	76574	512-352-3434	352-8080
Temple Public Library 100 W Adams Ave *Web:* www.ci.temple.tx.us/417/library	Temple	TX	76501	254-298-5555	
Terrell Public Library 301 N Rockwell Ave *Web:* cityofterrell.org	Terrell	TX	75160	972-551-6663	551-6662
Texarkana Public Library 600 W Third St *Web:* txark.ent.sirsi.net/client/en_us/default	Texarkana	TX	75501	903-794-2149	794-2139
Moore Memorial Public Library 1701 Ninth Ave N *Web:* www.texascity-library.org	Texas City	TX	77590	409-643-5979	948-1106
Colony Public Library, The 6800 Main St *Web:* thecolonytx.gov	The Colony	TX	75056	972-625-1900	
Tyler Public Library 201 S College Ave *Web:* library.cityoftyler.org	Tyler	TX	75702	903-593-7323	531-1329
Waco-McLennan County Library 1717 Austin Ave *TF:* 800-433-7300 ■ *Web:* www.waco-texas.com	Waco	TX	76701	254-750-5941	750-5940
Watauga Public Library 7109 Whitley Rd *Web:* www.cowtx.org	Watauga	TX	76148	817-514-5855	581-3910
Weatherford Public Library 1014 Charles St *TF:* 800-489-0190 ■ *Web:* ci.weatherford.tx.us	Weatherford	TX	76086	817-598-4150	598-4161
Weslaco Public Library 525 S Kansas Ave *Web:* www.weslaco.lib.tx.us	Weslaco	TX	78596	956-968-4533	969-4069
Wharton County Library 1920 N Fulton St *TF:* 800-244-5492 ■ *Web:* www.whartonco.lib.tx.us	Wharton	TX	77488	979-532-8080	532-2792
Wichita Falls Public Library 600 11th St *Web:* www.wfpl.net	Wichita Falls	TX	76301	940-767-0868	

Utah

Library	City	State	ZIP	Phone	Fax
Davis County Library 61 S Main St PO Box 618 *Web:* www.co.davis.ut.us	Farmington	UT	84025	801-451-2322	451-3281
Logan Library 255 N Main St *Web:* library.loganutah.org	Logan	UT	84321	435-716-9123	716-9145
Weber County Library 2464 Jefferson Ave *TF:* 866-678-5342 ■ *Web:* www.weberpl.lib.ut.us	Ogden	UT	84401	801-337-2632	337-2615
Orem Public Library 58 N State St *Web:* lib.orem.org	Orem	UT	84057	801-229-7050	229-7130
Provo City Library 550 N University Ave *TF:* 800-914-8931 ■ *Web:* provolibrary.com	Provo	UT	84601	801-852-6650	852-6688
Washington County Public Library 88 West 100 South *Web:* library.washco.utah.gov	Saint George	UT	84770	435-634-5737	634-5741
Salt Lake City Public Library 210 East 400 South *Web:* www.slcpl.lib.ut.us	Salt Lake City	UT	84111	801-524-8200	322-8196
Salt Lake County Library System 2197 E Ft Union Blvd *Web:* www.slcolibrary.org	Salt Lake City	UT	84121	801-943-4636	942-6323

Vermont

Library	City	State	ZIP	Phone	Fax
Fletcher Free Public Library 235 College St *Web:* www.fletcherfree.org	Burlington	VT	05401	802-863-3403	865-7227
Kellogg-Hubbard Library 135 Main St *Web:* www.kellogghubbard.org	Montpelier	VT	05602	802-223-3338	223-3338

Virginia

Library	City	State	ZIP	Phone	Fax
Washington County Public Library 205 Oak Hill St *Web:* www.wcpl.net	Abingdon	VA	24210	276-676-6222	
Amherst County Virgina 382 S Main St PO Box 370 *Web:* www.countyofamherst.com	Amherst	VA	24521	434-946-9400	946-9348
Arlington County Central Library 1015 N Quincy St *Web:* www.arlingtonva.us	Arlington	VA	22201	703-228-5990	
Bristol Public Library 701 Goode St *Web:* www.bristol-library.org	Bristol	VA	24201	276-645-8780	669-5593
Jefferson-Madison Regional Library 201 E Market St *TF:* 866-979-1555 ■ *Web:* www.jmrl.org	Charlottesville	VA	22902	434-979-7151	971-7035
Pittsylvania County Public Library 24 Military Dr *Web:* www.pcplib.org	Chatham	VA	24531	434-432-3271	432-1405
Chesapeake Public Library 298 Cedar Rd *Web:* www.chesapeake.lib.va.us	Chesapeake	VA	23322	757-410-7100	410-7122
Montgomery-Floyd Regional Library 125 Sheltman St *Web:* www.mfrl.org	Christiansburg	VA	24073	540-382-6965	382-6964
Culpeper County Library 271 Southgate Shopping Ctr *Web:* www2.youseemore.com/culpeper	Culpeper	VA	22701	540-825-8691	825-7486
Danville Public Library 511 Patton St *Web:* readdanvilleva.org	Danville	VA	24541	434-799-5195	
Fairfax County Public Library 12000 Government Ctr Pkwy Ste 324 *Web:* www.fairfaxcounty.gov/library	Fairfax	VA	22035	703-324-3100	222-3193
Augusta County Library 1759 Jefferson Hwy *Web:* www.augustacountylibrary.org	Fishersville	VA	22939	540-885-3961	
Samuels Public Library 330 E Criser Rd *Web:* www.samuelslibrary.net	Front Royal	VA	22630	540-635-3153	
Gloucester County Library 6920 Main St *Web:* gloucesterva.info	Gloucester	VA	23061	804-693-2998	693-1477
Buchanan County Public Library 1185 Poe Town St *Web:* www.bcplnet.org	Grundy	VA	24614	276-935-5721	
Hampton Public Library 4207 Victoria Blvd *Web:* www.hampton.gov	Hampton	VA	23669	757-727-1154	727-1152
Massanutten Regional Library 174 S Main St *Web:* www.mrlib.org	Harrisonburg	VA	22801	540-434-4475	
Henrico County Public Library 1001 N Laburnum Ave *Web:* www.henricolibrary.org	Henrico	VA	23223	804-290-9300	
Appomattox Regional Library 209 E Cawson St *Web:* www.arls.org	Hopewell	VA	23860	804-458-6329	
Russell County Public Library 248 W Main St PO Box 247 *Web:* www.russell.lib.va.us	Lebanon	VA	24266	276-889-8044	889-8045
Loudoun County Public Library Administration 380 Old Waterford Rd *Web:* www.library.loudoun.gov	Leesburg	VA	20175	703-777-0368	771-5620
Lynchburg Public Library 2315 Memorial Ave *Web:* www.lynchburgpubliclibrary.org	Lynchburg	VA	24501	434-455-6300	845-1479
Newport News Public Library System 2400 Washington Ave *Web:* www.nnva.gov	Newport News	VA	23607	757-926-1350	926-1365
Norfolk Public Library 235 E Plume St *Web:* www.norfolkpubliclibrary.org	Norfolk	VA	23510	757-664-7323	664-7320
Petersburg Public Library 201 W Washington St *Web:* www.ppls.org	Petersburg	VA	23803	804-733-2387	733-7972
Portsmouth Public Library 601 Ct St	Portsmouth	VA	23704	757-393-8501	393-5107
Pulaski County Library 60 W Third St *Web:* www.pclibs.org	Pulaski	VA	24301	540-980-7770	980-7775
Richmond Public Library 101 E Franklin St *Web:* www.richmondpubliclibrary.org	Richmond	VA	23219	804-646-7223	
Roanoke County Public Library 3131 Electric Rd *Web:* www.roanokecountyva.gov	Roanoke	VA	24018	540-772-7507	989-3129
Franklin County Library 355 Franklin St *Web:* library.franklincountyva.org	Rocky Mount	VA	24151	540-483-3098	483-6652
Campbell County Public Library 684 Village Hwy PO Box 310 *Web:* campbellcountylibraries.org	Rustburg	VA	24588	434-332-9560	
Tazewell County Public Library 310 E Main St PO Box 929 *Web:* www.tcplweb.org	Tazewell	VA	24651	276-988-2541	988-5980
Bridgeborn LLC 596 Lynnhaven Pkwy Ste 100 *Web:* www.bridgeborn.com	Virginia Beach	VA	23452	757-437-5000	
Virginia Beach Public Library 4100 Virginia Beach Blvd *Web:* vbgov.com/government/departments/libraries	Virginia Beach	VA	23452	757-385-0150	
Williamsburg Regional Library 7770 Croaker Rd *Web:* www.wrl.org	Williamsburg	VA	23188	757-259-4071	259-4077
Lonesome Pine Regional Library 124 Library Rd *Web:* lprlibrary.org	Wise	VA	24293	276-328-8325	
York County Public Library 8500 George Washington Memorial Hwy *Web:* yorkcounty.gov	Yorktown	VA	23692	757-890-3377	890-2956

Washington

Library	City	State	ZIP	Phone	Fax
Anacortes Public Library 1220 Tenth St	Anacortes	WA	98221	360-293-1910	293-1929
Bellingham Public Library 210 Central Ave *Web:* www.bellinghampubliclibrary.org	Bellingham	WA	98225	360-778-7323	
Kitsap Regional Library 1301 Sylvan Way *TF:* 877-883-9900 ■ *Web:* www.krl.org	Bremerton	WA	98310	360-405-9100	405-9156
Everett Public Library 2702 Hoyt Ave *Web:* www.epls.org	Everett	WA	98201	425-257-8010	
King County Library System 960 Newport Way NW *Web:* www.kcls.org	Issaquah	WA	98027	425-369-3224	
Mid-Columbia Libraries 405 S Dayton St *Web:* www.midcolumbialibraries.org	Kennewick	WA	99336	509-586-3156	
Longview Public Library 1600 Louisiana St *Web:* www.longviewlibrary.org	Longview	WA	98632	360-442-5300	442-5954
Puyallup Public Library 324 S Meridian *TF:* 866-862-4232 ■ *Web:* www.cityofpuyallup.org	Puyallup	WA	98371	253-841-5454	841-5483
Richland Public Library 955 Northgate Dr *Web:* www.richland.lib.wa.us	Richland	WA	99352	509-942-7454	942-7447
Seattle Public Library 1000 Fourth Ave *Web:* www.spl.org	Seattle	WA	98104	206-386-4636	386-4119
Spokane Public Library 906 W Main Ave *Web:* www.spokanelibrary.org	Spokane	WA	99201	509-444-5300	444-5365
Pierce County Library System 3005 112th St E *TF:* 800-346-0995 ■ *Web:* www.piercecountylibrary.org	Tacoma	WA	98446	253-536-6500	537-4600

Library	City	State	Zip	Phone	Fax
Tacoma Public Library 1102 Tacoma Ave S *Web:* www.tacomalibrary.org	Tacoma	WA	98402	253-591-5666	591-5470
Timberland Regional Library 415 Tumwater Blvd SW *TF:* 877-284-6237 ■ *Web:* trl.org	Tumwater	WA	98501	360-943-5001	586-6838
Fort Vancouver Regional Library 1007 E Mill Plain Blvd *Web:* www.fvrl.org	Vancouver	WA	98663	360-329-9906	
Walla Walla Public Library 238 E Alder St *Web:* wallawallapubliclibrary.org	Walla Walla	WA	99362	509-527-4550	
North Central Regional Library 16 N Columbia St *Web:* www.ncrl.org	Wenatchee	WA	98801	509-663-1117	
Yakima Valley Regional Library 102 N Third St *Web:* www.yvrl.org	Yakima	WA	98901	509-452-8541	

West Virginia

Library	City	State	Zip	Phone	Fax
Raleigh County Public Library 221 N Kanawha St	Beckley	WV	25801	304-255-0511	255-9161
Craft Memorial Library 600 Commerce St *Web:* craftmemorial.lib.wv.us	Bluefield	WV	24701	304-325-3943	325-3702
Cabell County Public Library 455 Ninth St Plz *Web:* www.cabell.lib.wv.us	Huntington	WV	25701	304-528-5700	528-5701
Ceredo-Kenova Public Library 1200 Oak St *Web:* www.wcpl.lib.wv.us	Kenova	WV	25530	304-453-2462	453-2462
Martinsburg-Berkeley County Public Library 101 W King St *Web:* martinsburg.lib.wv.us	Martinsburg	WV	25401	304-267-8933	267-9720
Morgantown Public Library 373 Spruce St *Web:* morgantown.lib.wv.us	Morgantown	WV	26505	304-291-7425	291-7437
Fayette County Public Library 531 Summit St *TF:* 855-275-5737 ■ *Web:* fayette.lib.wv.us	Oak Hill	WV	25901	304-465-0121	465-5306
Parkersburg & Wood County Public Library 3100 Emerson Ave *TF:* 800-642-8674 ■ *Web:* parkersburg.lib.wv.us	Parkersburg	WV	26104	304-420-4587	420-4589
Mason County Public Library 508 Viand St *Web:* masoncounty.lib.wv.us	Point Pleasant	WV	25550	304-675-0894	675-0895
Jackson County Public Library 208 Church St N *Web:* jackson.park.lib.wv.us	Ripley	WV	25271	304-372-5343	372-7935
Mary H Weirton Public Library 3442 Main St *Web:* www.weirton.lib.wv.us	Weirton	WV	26062	304-797-8510	797-8526
McDowell Public Library 90 Howard St *Web:* mcdowell.lib.wv.us	Welch	WV	24801	304-436-3070	436-8079
Ohio County Public Library 52 16th St *Web:* ohiocountylibrary.org	Wheeling	WV	26003	304-232-0244	232-6848

Wisconsin

Library	City	State	Zip	Phone	Fax
Northern Waters Library Service 3200 E Lakeshore Dr *TF:* 800-228-5684 ■ *Web:* www.nwls.lib.wi.us	Ashland	WI	54806	715-682-2365	685-2704
Beloit Public Library 605 Eclipse Blvd *Web:* www.als.lib.wi.us	Beloit	WI	53511	608-364-2905	364-2907
Brookfield Public Library 1900 N Calhoun Rd *TF:* 866-868-3947 ■ *Web:* www.ci.brookfield.wi.us/index.aspx?NID=38	Brookfield	WI	53005	262-782-4140	796-6670
Chippewa Falls Public Library 105 W Central St *Web:* www.chippewafallslibrary.org	Chippewa Falls	WI	54729	715-723-1146	
Indianhead Federated Library System 1538 Truax Blvd *TF:* 800-321-5427 ■ *Web:* iflsweb.org	Eau Claire	WI	54703	715-839-5082	839-5151
LE Phillips Memorial Public Library 400 Eau Claire St *Web:* www.ecpubliclibrary.info	Eau Claire	WI	54701	715-839-5004	
Southwest Wisconsin Library System 1775 Fourth St *TF:* 866-866-3393 ■ *Web:* www.swls.org	Fennimore	WI	53809	608-822-3393	
Fond du Lac Public Library 32 Sheboygan St *Web:* fdlpl.org	Fond du Lac	WI	54935	920-929-7080	929-7082
Germantown Community Library N112 W16957 Mequon Rd *Web:* germantownlibrarywi.org	Germantown	WI	53022	262-253-7760	253-7763
USS Liberty Memorial Public 1620 11th Ave	Grafton	WI	53024	262-375-5315	375-5317
Brown County Library 515 Pine St *Web:* www.co.brown.wi.us	Green Bay	WI	54301	920-448-4400	448-4388
Greenfield Public Library 5310 W Layton Ave *Web:* www.greenfieldlibrary.org	Greenfield	WI	53220	414-321-9595	321-8595
La Crosse County Library 103 State St *Web:* www.lacrossecountylibrary.org	Holmen	WI	54636	608-526-9600	
Mid Wisconsin Federated Library System 112 Clinton St *TF:* 800-660-6899 ■ *Web:* www.mwfls.org	Horicon	WI	53032	920-485-0833	
Arrowhead Library System 210 Dodge St *TF:* 855-352-9003 ■ *Web:* www.als.lib.wi.us	Janesville	WI	53548	608-758-6690	758-6689
Hedberg Public Library (HPL) 316 S Main St *Web:* www.hedbergpubliclibrary.org	Janesville	WI	53545	608-758-6600	758-6583
Kenosha Public Library 7979 38th Ave *Web:* www.mykpl.info	Kenosha	WI	53142	262-564-6100	564-6370
La Crosse Public Library 800 Main St *Web:* www.lacrosselibrary.org	La Crosse	WI	54601	608-789-7100	789-7106
Madison Public Library 201 W Mifflin St *Web:* www.madisonpubliclibrary.org	Madison	WI	53703	608-266-6300	
S Central Library Syst 4610 S Biltmore Ln *TF:* 855-516-7257 ■ *Web:* www.scls.info	Madison	WI	53718	608-246-7970	
Manitowoc-Calumet Library System 707 Quay St *Web:* www.manitowoclibrary.org	Manitowoc	WI	54220	920-686-3010	
Stephenson Public Library 1700 Hall Ave	Marinette	WI	54143	715-732-7570	732-7575
Marshfield Public Library 211 E Second St *Web:* www.marshfieldlibrary.org	Marshfield	WI	54449	715-387-8494	
Menasha Public Library 440 First St *Web:* www.menashalibrary.org	Menasha	WI	54952	920-967-5166	967-5159
Menomonee Falls Public Library W156 N8436 Pilgrim Rd *Web:* www.mf.lib.wi.us	Menomonee Falls	WI	53051	262-532-8900	532-8939
Menomonie Public Library 600 Wolske Bay Rd *Web:* www.menomonielibrary.org	Menomonie	WI	54751	715-232-2164	232-2324
Middleton Public Library 7425 Hubbard Ave *Web:* www.midlibrary.org	Middleton	WI	53562	608-831-5564	836-5724
Milwaukee Public Library 814 W Wisconsin Ave *TF:* 866-947-7363 ■ *Web:* www.mpl.org	Milwaukee	WI	53233	414-286-3000	286-2798
Neenah Public Library 240 E Wisconsin Ave PO Box 569 *Web:* www.neenahlibrary.org	Neenah	WI	54956	920-886-6315	
New Berlin Public Library 15105 Library Ln *Web:* www.newberlinlibrary.org	New Berlin	WI	53151	262-785-4980	
Oshkosh Public Library 106 Washington Ave *Web:* www.oshkoshpubliclibrary.org	Oshkosh	WI	54901	920-236-5200	
Winnefox Library System 106 Washington Ave *Web:* www.winnefox.org	Oshkosh	WI	54901	920-236-5220	236-5228
Oxford Public Library 129 S Franklin Ave *Web:* www.oxfordlibrary.org	Oxford	WI	53952	608-586-4458	
Racine Public Library 75 Seventh St *TF:* 888-529-0061 ■ *Web:* www.racinelib.lib.wi.us	Racine	WI	53403	262-636-9241	636-9260
River Falls Public Library 115 E Elm St *Web:* www.rfcity.org	River Falls	WI	54022	715-425-0908	
Mead Public Library 710 N Eigth St *Web:* www.meadpl.org	Sheboygan	WI	53081	920-459-3400	459-0204
Portage County Public Library 1001 Main St *Web:* www.uwsp.edu	Stevens Point	WI	54481	715-346-1544	
Door County Library (DCL) 107 S Fourth Ave *Web:* www.doorcountylibrary.org	Sturgeon Bay	WI	54235	920-743-6578	
Superior Public Library 1530 Tower Ave *TF:* 866-894-4899 ■ *Web:* www.ci.superior.wi.us	Superior	WI	54880	715-394-8860	394-8870
Lakeshores Library System (LLS) 725 Cornerstone Crossing Ste C *Web:* www.lakeshores.lib.wi.us	Waterford	WI	53185	262-514-4500	514-4544
Watertown Public Library 100 S Water St *TF:* 800-829-3676 ■ *Web:* www.watertownpubliclibrary.org	Watertown	WI	53094	920-262-4090	261-8943
Waukesha Public Library 321 Wisconsin Ave *Web:* waukeshapubliclibrary.org	Waukesha	WI	53186	262-524-3680	650-2502
Marathon County Public Library (MCPL) 300 N First St *Web:* www.mcpl.us	Wausau	WI	54403	715-261-7200	261-7204
Wauwatosa Public Library 7635 W N Ave *Web:* www.wauwatosalibrary.org	Wauwatosa	WI	53213	414-471-8484	
West Allis Public Library 7421 W National Ave *TF:* 800-877-8339 ■ *Web:* www.westalliswi.gov	West Allis	WI	53214	414-302-8500	302-8545
West Bend Community Memorial Library 630 Poplar St *Web:* www.west-bendlibrary.org	West Bend	WI	53095	262-335-5151	335-5150
McMillan Memorial Library 490 E Grand Ave *Web:* www.mcmillanlibrary.org	Wisconsin Rapids	WI	54494	715-423-1040	423-2665

Wyoming

Library	City	State	Zip	Phone	Fax
Natrona County Public Library 307 E Second St *Web:* natronacountylibrary.org	Casper	WY	82601	307-237-4935	266-3734
Laramie County Public Library 2200 Pioneer Ave *Web:* www.lclsonline.org	Cheyenne	WY	82001	307-634-3561	634-2082
Campbell County Public Library 2101 S 4-J Rd *Web:* ccgov.net/384/library	Gillette	WY	82718	307-682-3223	686-4009
Sweetwater County Library System 300 N First E St *Web:* www.sweetwaterlibraries.com	Green River	WY	82935	307-875-3615	872-3203
Teton County Public Library 125 Virginian Ln *TF:* 800-878-2167 ■ *Web:* www.tclib.org	Jackson	WY	83001	307-733-2164	733-4568
Fremont County Library System 451 N Second St *Web:* fclsonline.org	Lander	WY	82520	307-332-5194	332-3909
Albany County Public Library 310 S Eigth St *Web:* www.albanycountylibrary.org	Laramie	WY	82070	307-721-2580	721-2584

434-4 Special Collections Libraries

Library	City	State	Zip	Phone	Fax
Academy of Motion Picture Arts & Sciences Herrick Library 333 S La Cienega Blvd *Web:* www.oscars.org	Beverly Hills	CA	90211	310-247-3020	
African American Museum & Library in Oakland 659 14th St *Web:* oaklandlibrary.org/locations/african-american-museum-library-oakland	Oakland	CA	94612	510-637-0200	
AIDS Library 1233 Locust St 2nd Fl *TF:* 877-613-4533 ■ *Web:* www.aidslibrary.org	Philadelphia	PA	19107	215-985-4851	985-4492
American Kennel Club Library 260 Madison Ave 4th Fl *Web:* www.akc.org	New York	NY	10016	212-696-8200	696-8281

				Phone	Fax
American Museum of Natural History *Library* Central Pk W at 79th St *Web:* www.amnh.org	New York	NY	10024	212-769-5400	769-5009
Athenaeum of Philadelphia 219 S Sixth St *Web:* www.philaathenaeum.org	Philadelphia	PA	19106	215-925-2688	925-3755
Bentley Historical Library 1150 Beal Ave *TF:* 866-233-6661 ■ *Web:* www.bentley.umich.edu	Ann Arbor	MI	48109	734-764-3482	936-1333
Boston Athenaeum 10 1/2 Beacon St *Web:* www.bostonathenaeum.org	Boston	MA	02108	617-227-0270	
Center for Migration Studies of New York Inc *Library & Archives* 307 E 60th St 4th Fl **Fax Area Code:* 646 ■ *Web:* cmsny.org/archives	New York	NY	10022	212-337-3080	998-4625*
Folger Shakespeare Library 201 E Capitol St SE *Web:* www.folger.edu	Washington	DC	20003	202-544-4600	544-4623
Frank Lloyd Wright Preservation Trust *Special Collections* 931 Chicago Ave **Fax Area Code:* 708 ■ *Web:* flwright.org	Oak Park	IL	60302	312-994-4000	848-1248*
George Eastman House *Menschel Library* 900 E Ave *Web:* www.eastman.org	Rochester	NY	14607	585-271-3361	271-3970
Gettysburg National Military Park Library & Research Ctr 97 Taneytown Rd *Web:* nps.gov/nps/404.htm	Gettysburg	PA	17325	717-334-1124	334-1997
Juilliard School, The *Wallace Library* 60 Lincoln Ctr Plz *Web:* juilliard.edu	New York	NY	10023	212-799-5000	787-9722
Karpeles Manuscript Library 453 Porter Ave *Web:* www.rain.org/~karpeles	Buffalo	NY	14201	716-885-4139	
Library Company of Philadelphia 1314 Locust St *Web:* www.librarycompany.org	Philadelphia	PA	19107	215-546-3181	546-5167
Lincoln Memorial Shrine 125 W Vine St *Web:* www.lincolnshrine.org	Redlands	CA	92373	909-798-7632	
Portsmouth Athenaeum 9 Market Sq *Web:* www.portsmouthathenaeum.org	Portsmouth	NH	03801	603-431-2538	433-8933
Providence Athenaeum 251 Benefit St *Web:* www.providenceathenaeum.org	Providence	RI	02903	401-421-6970	
Redwood Library & Athenaeum 50 Bellevue Ave *Web:* www.redwoodlibrary.org	Newport	RI	02840	401-847-0292	841-5680
Rosenbach Museum & Library 2008-2010 Delancey St *Web:* www.rosenbach.org	Philadelphia	PA	19103	215-732-1600	545-7529
Salem Athenaeum, The 337 Essex St *Web:* www.salemathenaeum.net	Salem	MA	01970	978-744-2540	744-7536
Schomburg Ctr for Research in Black Culture 515 Malcolm X Blvd *Web:* nypl.org	New York	NY	10037	212-491-2200	
Smithsonian Institution Cullman Library 1000 Constitution Ave NW Natural History Bldg *Web:* library.si.edu	Washington	DC	20560	202-633-2240	633-0219
Smithsonian Institution Dibner Library of the History of Science & Technology Smithsonian Institution NMAH 1041 MRC 672 PO Box 37012 *Web:* library.si.edu	Washington	DC	20013	202-633-3872	633-9102
Vietnam Archive, The Texas Tech University PO Box 41041 *Web:* www.vietnam.ttu.edu	Lubbock	TX	79409	806-742-9010	742-0496
Yale University Beinecke Rare Book & Manuscript Library 121 Wall St *Web:* web.library.yale.edu	New Haven	CT	06511	203-432-2977	432-4047

434-5 State Libraries

				Phone	Fax
Alabama Public Library Service 6030 Monticello Dr *Web:* webmini.apls.state.al.us	Montgomery	AL	36130	334-213-3900	213-3993
Alaska State Library PO Box 110571 *Web:* library.alaska.gov	Juneau	AK	99811	907-465-2920	465-2665
Arizona State Library 1700 W Washington St Ste 300 *Web:* www.azlibrary.gov	Phoenix	AZ	85007	602-542-4035	
Arkansas State Library 900 W Capitol Ste 100 *TF:* 866-801-3435 ■ *Web:* www.library.arkansas.gov	Little Rock	AR	72201	501-682-2053	682-1529
California State Library 900 N St *TF:* 800-952-5666 ■ *Web:* www.library.ca.gov	Sacramento	CA	95814	916-654-0261	654-0241
Colorado State Library 201 E Colfax Ave Rm 309 *Web:* www.cde.state.co.us	Denver	CO	80203	303-866-6900	866-6940
Connecticut State Library 231 Capitol Ave *TF:* 866-886-4478 ■ *Web:* www.ctstatelibrary.org	Hartford	CT	06106	860-757-6510	757-6503
Delaware Div of Libraries 497 S Red Haven Ln *TF:* 800-829-4059 ■ *Web:* www.lib.de.us	Dover	DE	19901	302-739-4748	739-6787
Hawaii State Public Library System (HSPLS) 44 Merchant St *Web:* hawaii.sdp.sirsi.net	Honolulu	HI	96813	808-586-3700	586-3715
Idaho Commission for Libraries (ICFL) 325 W State St *TF:* 800-458-3271 ■ *Web:* www.libraries.idaho.gov	Boise	ID	83702	208-334-2150	334-4016
Illinois State Library 300 S Second St *TF:* 800-665-5576 ■ *Web:* www.cyberdriveillinois.com/departments/library/home.html	Springfield	IL	62701	217-782-2994	785-4326
Indiana State Library (ISL) 140 N Senate Ave *Web:* www.in.gov/library	Indianapolis	IN	46204	317-232-3694	232-3728
Iowa State Library 1007 E Grand Ave Ste 214 *Web:* www.statelibraryofiowa.org	Des Moines	IA	50319	515-281-4105	281-6191
Kentucky Dept for Libraries & Archives 300 Coffee Tree Rd *TF:* 800-372-2968 ■ *Web:* www.kdla.ky.gov	Frankfort	KY	40602	502-564-8300	564-5773
Library of Michigan, The 702 W Kalamazoo St PO Box 30007 *TF:* 800-726-7323 ■ *Web:* www.michigan.gov/mde/0,1607,7-140-54504---,00.html	Lansing	MI	48909	517-373-1580	373-4480
Library of Virginia 800 E Broad St *Web:* www.lva.virginia.gov	Richmond	VA	23219	804-692-3500	692-3594
Louisiana State Library 701 N Fourth St *Web:* www.state.lib.la.us	Baton Rouge	LA	70821	225-342-4915	219-4725
Maine State Library 64 State House Stn *Web:* www.maine.gov	Augusta	ME	04333	207-287-5600	287-5615
Massachusetts Board of Library Commissioners 98 N Washington St *TF:* 800-952-7403 ■ *Web:* mblc.state.ma.us	Boston	MA	02114	617-725-1860	725-0140
Missouri State Library 600 W Main St PO Box 387 *Web:* www.sos.mo.gov/library	Jefferson City	MO	65102	573-751-3615	526-1142
Montana State Library (MSL) 1515 E Sixth Ave PO Box 201800 *Web:* home.msl.mt.gov	Helena	MT	59620	406-444-3115	444-0266
Nebraska Library Commission 1200 N St Ste 120 *TF:* 800-307-2665 ■ *Web:* nlc.nebraska.gov	Lincoln	NE	68508	402-471-2045	471-2083
Nevada State Library & Archives (NSLA) 100 N Stewart St *TF:* 800-922-2880 ■ *Web:* www.nsla.nevadaculture.org	Carson City	NV	89701	775-684-3360	684-3311
New Hampshire State Library 20 Pk St *Web:* www.nh.gov	Concord	NH	03301	603-271-2144	271-2205
New York State Library Empire State Plaza *Web:* www.nysl.nysed.gov	Albany	NY	12230	518-474-5355	474-5786
North Dakota State Library (NDSL) 604 E Blvd Ave Dept 250 *TF:* 800-472-2104 ■ *Web:* www.library.nd.gov	Bismarck	ND	58505	701-328-4622	328-2040
Oklahoma Dept of Libraries 200 NE 18th St *TF:* 800-522-8116 ■ *Web:* www.odl.state.ok.us	Oklahoma City	OK	73105	405-521-2502	525-7804
Oregon State Library 250 Winter NE State Library Bldg *Web:* www.oregon.gov/osl	Salem	OR	97301	503-378-4243	588-7119
South Carolina State Library 1430 Senate St *Web:* www.state.sc.us	Columbia	SC	29201	803-734-8666	734-8676
South Dakota State Library 800 Governors Dr *TF:* 800-423-6665 ■ *Web:* www.library.sd.gov	Pierre	SD	57501	605-773-3131	773-4950
State Library of Ohio 274 E First Ave Ste 100 *TF:* 800-686-1532 ■ *Web:* library.ohio.gov	Columbus	OH	43201	614-644-7061	466-3584
Tennessee State Library & Archives 403 Seventh Ave N *TF:* 877-850-4959	Nashville	TN	37243	615-741-2764	741-6471
Texas State Library & Archives Commission PO Box 12927 *Web:* www.tsl.texas.gov	Austin	TX	78711	512-463-5455	
Utah State Library 250 N 1950 W Ste A *TF:* 800-662-9150 ■ *Web:* heritage.utah.gov	Salt Lake City	UT	84116	801-715-6777	715-6767
Vermont Dept of Libraries 109 State St *TF:* 888-350-0950 ■ *Web:* libraries.vermont.gov	Montpelier	VT	05609	802-828-3261	828-2199
Washington State Library PO Box 40220 *Web:* www.sos.wa.gov	Olympia	WA	98504	360-902-4151	586-7575
West Virginia Library Commission 1900 Kanawha Blvd E *TF:* 800-642-9021 ■ *Web:* www.librarycommission.lib.wv.us	Charleston	WV	25305	304-558-2041	558-2044
Wisconsin Department of Public Instruction 125 S Webster St PO Box 7841 *TF:* 800-441-4563 ■ *Web:* dpi.wi.gov	Madison	WI	53707	608-266-3390	267-1052
Wyoming State Library 2800 Central Ave *Web:* www-wsl.state.wy.us	Cheyenne	WY	82001	307-777-6333	777-6289

434-6 University Libraries

Listings for university libraries are arranged by states.

				Phone	Fax
Alabama Agricultural & Mechanical University J F Drake Memorial Learning Resources Ctr PO Box 489 *Web:* www.aamu.edu	Normal	AL	35762	256-372-5000	372-5768
Auburn University 202 Mary Martin Hall **Fax:* Admissions ■ *TF Admissions:* 866-389-6770 ■ *Web:* www.auburn.edu	Auburn University	AL	36849	334-844-6425	844-6436*
Draughon Library 231 Mell St **Fax:* Admin ■ *Web:* www.lib.auburn.edu	Auburn University	AL	36849	334-844-4500	844-4424*
Tuskegee University Ford Motor Co Library/Learning Resource Ctr Hollis Burke Frissell Library Bldg *TF:* 800-622-6531 ■ *Web:* www.tuskegee.edu	Tuskegee	AL	36088	334-727-8894	727-9282
University of Alabama PO Box 870132 **Fax:* Admissions ■ *TF Admissions:* 800-933-2262 ■ *Web:* www.ua.edu	Tuscaloosa	AL	35487	205-348-6010	348-9046*
Gorgas Library Information Ctr First Fl *TF:* 888-764-5603 ■ *Web:* www.lib.ua.edu/libraries/gorgas	Tuscaloosa	AL	35487	205-348-6047	348-0760
UAA/APU Consortium Library 3211 Providence Dr *Web:* www.consortiumlibrary.org	Anchorage	AK	99508	907-786-1848	
University of Alaska Fairbanks PO Box 757480 **Fax:* Admissions ■ *TF:* 800-478-1823 ■ *Web:* www.uaf.edu	Fairbanks	AK	99775	907-474-7500	474-5379*
Rasmuson Library PO Box 756800 *Web:* library.uaf.edu	Fairbanks	AK	99775	907-474-7481	474-6841
Hayden Library 300 E Orange Mall *Web:* www.asu.edu	Tempe	AZ	85281	480-965-3417	965-9169
University of Arizona Library 1510 E University Blvd **Fax:* Admin ■ *Web:* www.library.arizona.edu	Tucson	AZ	85721	520-621-6442	621-9733*
University of Arkansas 232 Silas Hunt Hall **Fax:* Admissions ■ *TF Admissions:* 800-377-8632 ■ *Web:* www.uark.edu	Fayetteville	AR	72701	479-575-5346	575-7515*

	City	State	Zip	Phone	Fax
California Institute of Technology Library					
1200 E California Blvd MC I-32	Pasadena	CA	91125	626-395-3405	792-7540
Web: www.library.caltech.edu					
California Lutheran University Pearson Library					
60 W Olsen Rd	Thousand Oaks	CA	91360	805-493-3250	493-3842
TF: 877-258-3678 ■ *Web:* www.callutheran.edu					
California Polytechnic State University Kennedy Library					
1 Grand Ave Bldg 35	San Luis Obispo	CA	93407	805-756-2305	756-2346
Web: www.lib.calpoly.edu					
California State University Chico					
Meriam Library 400 W First St	Chico	CA	95929	530-898-6502	898-4443
Web: www.csuchico.edu/library					
California State University Dominguez Hills					
Library 1000 E Victoria St	Carson	CA	90747	310-243-3696	516-4219
Web: library.csudh.edu					
California State University Long Beach					
University Library 1250 Bellflower Blvd	Long Beach	CA	90840	562-985-4047	985-1703
Web: www.csulb.edu/library					
California State University Los Angeles					
Kennedy Memorial Library					
5151 State University Dr	Los Angeles	CA	90032	323-343-3988	343-6401
Web: www.calstatela.edu/library					
California State University Northridge					
Oviatt Library 18111 Nordhoff St	Northridge	CA	91330	818-677-2285	677-2676
Web: library.csun.edu					
California State University Sacramento					
Library 2000 State University Dr E	Sacramento	CA	95819	916-278-5679	278-4160
Web: www.library.csus.edu					
California State University San Bernardino					
Pfau Library 5500 University Pkwy	San Bernardino	CA	92407	909-537-3447	537-7079
Web: www.lib.csusb.edu					
California State University San Marcos					
Library 333 S Twin Oaks Vly Rd	San Marcos	CA	92096	760-750-4340	
Web: www.csusm.edu					
California State University Stanislaus					
Library 1 University Cir	Turlock	CA	95382	209-667-3234	667-3164
Web: library.csustan.edu					
Occidental College Clapp Library					
1600 Campus Rd	Los Angeles	CA	90041	323-259-2640	341-4991
Web: www.oxy.edu					
Pepperdine University Payson Library					
24255 Pacific Coast Hwy	Malibu	CA	90263	310-506-4252	506-4117
Web: www.library.pepperdine.edu					
San Francisco State University Leonard Library					
1630 Holloway Ave	San Francisco	CA	94132	415-338-1854	338-1504
Web: www.library.sfsu.edu					
Sonoma State University University Library					
1801 E Cotati Ave	Rohnert Park	CA	94928	707-664-2397	664-2090
Web: library.sonoma.edu					
Stanford University Green Library					
557 Escondido Mall	Stanford	CA	94305	650-723-2300	725-6874
TF: 800-521-0600 ■ *Web:* library.stanford.edu					
University of California Irvine					
Library PO Box 19557	Irvine	CA	92623	949-824-6836	824-3644
TF: 800-848-4722 ■ *Web:* www.lib.uci.edu					
University of California Los Angeles					
Library System					
11334 Charles E Young Research Library	Los Angeles	CA	90095	310-825-4732	
Web: www.library.ucla.edu					
University of California Riverside					
Libraries PO Box 5900	Riverside	CA	92517	951-827-3220	827-3281
Web: libraries.universityofcalifornia.edu					
University of California San Diego (UCSD)					
Biomedical Library 9500 Gilman Dr	La Jolla	CA	92093	858-534-3253	534-6609
Web: www.libraries.ucsd.edu					
Libraries 9500 Gilman Dr Ste 0175-G	La Jolla	CA	92093	858-534-3336	
Web: libraries.ucsd.edu					
University of California San Francisco					
Kalmanovitz Library 530 Parnassus Ave	San Francisco	CA	94143	415-476-8293	476-4653
Web: www.library.ucsf.edu					
University of California Santa Cruz					
McHenry Library 1156 High St	Santa Cruz	CA	95064	831-459-2076	459-8206
Web: www.library.ucsc.edu					
Doheny Memorial Library					
3550 Trousdale Pkwy University Pk Campus	Los Angeles	CA	90089	213-740-4039	740-3488
TF: 800-775-7330 ■					
Web: libraries.usc.edu/locations/doheny-memorial-library					
Colorado State University 200 W Lake St	Fort Collins	CO	80523	970-491-1101	491-7799*
*Fax: Admissions ■ *Web:* www.colostate.edu					
Morgan Library					
501 University Ave 1019 Campus Delivery	Fort Collins	CO	80523	970-491-1833	491-1195
Web: www.lib.colostate.edu					
University of Colorado at Colorado Springs					
Kraemer Family Library					
1420 Austin Bluffs Pkwy PO Box 7150	Colorado Springs	CO	80918	719-255-3295	528-5227
TF: 800-990-8227 ■ *Web:* www.uccs.edu/~library					
University of Denver Westminster Law Library					
2255 E Evans Ave	Denver	CO	80208	303-871-6190	871-6999
Web: www.law.du.edu/library					
University of Northern Colorado Michener Library					
501 20th St	Greeley	CO	80639	970-351-2601	351-2963
Web: www.unco.edu					
Eastern Connecticut State University Smith Library					
83 Windham St	Willimantic	CT	06226	860-465-4506	465-5522
TF: 800-578-1449 ■ *Web:* www.easternct.edu					
Southern Connecticut State University Buley Library					
501 Crescent St	New Haven	CT	06515	203-392-5750	392-5775
Web: libguides.southernct.edu/home					
Trinity College Raether Library					
300 Summit St	Hartford	CT	06106	860-297-2000	297-2251
Web: www.trincoll.edu/depts/library					
University of Connecticut					
2131 Hillside Rd Unit 3088	Storrs	CT	06269	860-486-2000	486-1476*
*Fax: Admissions ■ *Web:* www.uconn.edu					
Babbidge Library 369 Fairfield Rd Unit 2005	Storrs	CT	06269	860-486-2219	486-0584*
*Fax: Admin ■ *TF:* 888-603-9635 ■ *Web:* www.lib.uconn.edu					
Wesleyan University Olin Library					
252 Church St	Middletown	CT	06459	860-685-2660	685-2661
TF: 800-421-1561 ■ *Web:* www.wesleyan.edu					
Yale University Sterling Memorial Library					
120 High St	New Haven	CT	06511	203-432-1775	432-1294
Web: web.library.yale.edu					
University of Delaware Library					
181 S College Ave	Newark	DE	19717	302-831-2965	831-1046
Web: library.udel.edu					
Gallaudet University Library					
800 Florida Ave NE	Washington	DC	20002	202-651-5217	651-5213
TF: 800-995-0550 ■ *Web:* www.gallaudet.edu/library.html					
George Washington University					
2121 'I' St NW	Washington	DC	20052	202-994-1000	994-9619
TF: 866-498-3382 ■ *Web:* www.gwu.edu					
Gelman Library 2130 H St NW	Washington	DC	20052	202-994-6558	
Web: library.gwu.edu					
Georgetown University Lauinger Library					
37th 'O' St NW	Washington	DC	20057	202-687-7452	687-1215
Web: www.library.georgetown.edu					
Barry University 11300 NE Second Ave	Miami Shores	FL	33161	305-899-3000	899-2971*
*Fax: Admissions ■ *TF:* 800-756-6000 ■ *Web:* www.barry.edu					
Barry Memorial Library					
11300 NE Second Ave	Miami Shores	FL	33161	305-899-3000	
TF: 800-756-6000 ■ *Web:* www.barry.edu/libraryservices					
Florida A & M University					
1700 Lee Hall Dr Rm G-7					
Foote-Hilyer Administration Ctr	Tallahassee	FL	32307	850-599-3000	599-3069
TF: 866-642-1198 ■ *Web:* www.famu.edu					
Coleman Memorial Library					
1500 S Martin Luther King Blvd	Tallahassee	FL	32307	850-599-3370	561-2293
TF: 800-540-6754 ■ *Web:* www.famu.edu/library					
Florida Atlantic University (FAU)					
777 Glades Rd	Boca Raton	FL	33431	561-297-3000	297-2758*
*Fax: Admissions ■ *TF Admissions:* 800-299-4328 ■ *Web:* www.fau.edu					
Florida State University Strozier Library					
Rm 314	Tallahassee	FL	32306	850-644-5211	644-5016*
*Fax: Admin ■ *Web:* www.lib.fsu.edu					
Stetson University DuPont-Ball Library					
421 N Woodland Blvd	DeLand	FL	32723	386-822-7183	740-3626
TF: 800-688-0101 ■ *Web:* www.stetson.edu/other/about/libraries.php					
University of Florida Libraries					
PO Box 117001	Gainesville	FL	32611	352-392-0342	392-7251
TF: 877-351-2377 ■ *Web:* www.uflib.ufl.edu					
University of Miami Richter Library					
PO Box 248214	Coral Gables	FL	33124	305-284-3551	284-4027*
*Fax: Admin ■ *TF:* 800-708-6754 ■ *Web:* www.library.miami.edu					
University of North Florida (UNF)					
1UNF Dr Bldg 12	Jacksonville	FL	32224	904-620-1000	620-2719
Web: www.unf.edu/library					
University of South Florida					
Libraries 4202 E Fowler Ave LIB 122	Tampa	FL	33620	813-974-2729	974-5153
Web: www.lib.usf.edu					
University of South Florida Polytechnic					
Lakeland 3433 Winter Lake Rd	Lakeland	FL	33803	863-667-7000	667-7096*
*Fax: Admissions ■ *TF:* 800-873-5636					
Emory University Woodruff Library					
540 Asbury Cir	Atlanta	GA	30322	404-727-6861	727-0805
Web: emory.edu/home/academics/libraries/index.html					
Georgia Institute of Technology Library					
225 N Ave NW	Atlanta	GA	30332	404-894-4500	894-0399
TF: 888-225-7804 ■ *Web:* www.library.gatech.edu					
Mercer University 1400 Coleman Ave	Macon	GA	31207	478-301-2650	301-2828*
*Fax: Admissions ■ *TF:* 800-637-2378 ■ *Web:* www.mercer.edu					
Tarver Library 1300 Edgewood Ave	Macon	GA	31207	478-301-2960	301-2111
Web: libraries.mercer.edu					
University of Georgia Library					
320 S Jackson St	Athens	GA	30602	706-542-0621	542-4144*
*Fax: Admin ■ *TF:* 877-314-5560 ■ *Web:* www.libs.uga.edu					
Valdosta State University Odum Library					
1500 N Patterson St	Valdosta	GA	31698	229-333-5869	219-1362
Web: www.valdosta.edu					
Hawaii Pacific University					
1164 Bishop St Ste 200	Honolulu	HI	96813	808-544-0200	544-1136*
*Fax: Admissions ■ *TF:* 866-225-5478 ■ *Web:* www.hpu.edu					
Meader Library 1060 Bishop St	Honolulu	HI	96813	808-544-0210	521-7998
TF: 866-225-5478 ■ *Web:* www.hpu.edu					
University of Hawaii at Hilo					
Edwin H. Mookini Library 200 W Kawili St	Hilo	HI	96720	808-974-7344	974-4106
Web: hilo.hawaii.edu					
University of Hawaii at Manoa					
Hamilton Library 2500 Campus Rd	Honolulu	HI	96822	808-956-6911	956-7109
Web: www.manoa.hawaii.edu					
Idaho State University Oboler Library					
850 S Ninth Ave Bldg 50 Stop 8089	Pocatello	ID	83209	208-282-2958	282-5847
Web: www.isu.edu/library					
University of Idaho 875 Perimeter Dr	Moscow	ID	83844	208-885-6111	885-9119
TF: 888-884-3246 ■ *Web:* www.uidaho.edu					
Library PO Box 442350	Moscow	ID	83844	208-885-6534	885-6817
Web: www.lib.uidaho.edu					
DePaul University Library					
2350 N Kenmore Ave 10th Fl	Chicago	IL	60616	312-362-8433	362-6186
Web: library.depaul.edu/pages/default.aspx					
Illinois Institute of Technology					
10 W 33rd St	Chicago	IL	60616	312-567-3025	567-6939*
*Fax: Admissions ■ *TF:* 800-448-2329 ■ *Web:* www.iit.edu					
Galvin Library 35 W 33rd St	Chicago	IL	60616	312-567-3616	567-5318
Web: library.iit.edu					
Illinois State University Milner Library					
201 N School St	Normal	IL	61790	309-438-3451	438-3676*
*Fax: Admin ■ *Web:* www.illinoisstate.edu					
Loyola University Chicago					
Cudahy Library 1032 W Sheridan Rd	Chicago	IL	60660	773-508-2632	
Web: libraries.luc.edu/cudahy					

	City	State	ZIP	Phone	Fax
Northeastern Illinois University Williams Library					
5500 N St Louis Ave	Chicago	IL	60625	773-442-4470	442-4531
TF: 800-393-0865 ■ *Web:* www.neiu.edu					
Northern Illinois University University Libraries					
1425 W Lincoln Hwy	DeKalb	IL	60115	815-753-1000	753-9803
Web: www.niu.edu					
Northwestern University Library					
1970 Campus Dr	Evanston	IL	60208	847-491-7658	491-8306
Web: www.library.northwestern.edu					
Southern Illinois University Carbondale Morris Library					
605 Agriculture Dr MC 6632	Carbondale	IL	62901	618-453-2522	453-3440
Web: www.lib.siu.edu					
Southern Illinois University Edwardsville					
Lovejoy Library					
30 Hairpin Dr PO Box 1063	Edwardsville	IL	62026	618-650-4636	650-2717
TF: 888-328-5168 ■ *Web:* www.siue.edu/lovejoylibrary					
University of Chicago Library 1100 E 57th St	Chicago	IL	60637	773-702-8740	702-6623
Web: www.lib.uchicago.edu					
University of Illinois Chicago					
Daley Library 801 S Morgan St Rm 1-280	Chicago	IL	60607	312-996-2716	413-0424
Web: www.uic.edu/depts/lib					
University of Illinois Springfield					
Brookens Library 1 University Plz	Springfield	IL	62703	217-206-6605	
Web: library.uis.edu					
University of Illinois Urbana-Champaign					
Library 1408 W Gregory Dr MC-522	Urbana	IL	61801	217-333-2290	333-2214
Web: www.library.illinois.edu					
Western Illinois University 1 University Cir	Macomb	IL	61455	309-298-1414	298-3111*
**Fax:* Admissions ■ *TF Admissions:* 877-742-5948 ■ *Web:* www.wiu.edu					
Malpass Library 1 University Cir	Macomb	IL	61455	309-298-2762	298-2791
TF: 800-413-6544 ■ *Web:* www.wiu.edu/library					
Cunningham Memorial Library					
510 N 6 1/2 St	Terre Haute	IN	47809	812-237-2580	
TF: 800-851-4279 ■ *Web:* library.indstate.edu					
DePauw University West Library					
11 E Larabee St	Greencastle	IN	46135	765-658-4420	658-4445
TF: 800-447-2495 ■ *Web:* depauw.edu/libraries					
Indiana University Bloomington					
Libraries 1320 E Tenth St	Bloomington	IN	47405	812-855-8028	855-2576
Web: libraries.indiana.edu					
Indiana University South Bend					
Schurz Library					
1700 Mishawaka Ave PO Box 7111	South Bend	IN	46634	574-520-4440	
Web: www.iusb.edu					
Indiana University-Purdue University Fort Wayne					
Helmke Library 2101 E Coliseum Blvd	Fort Wayne	IN	46805	260-481-5404	
Web: usdirectoryfinder.com					
Indiana University-Purdue University Indianapolis					
Library 755 W Michigan St	Indianapolis	IN	46202	317-274-0462	278-2300
TF: 888-422-0499 ■ *Web:* www.ulib.iupui.edu					
Purdue University					
Schleman Hall 475 Stadium Mall Dr	West Lafayette	IN	47907	765-494-1776	494-0544*
**Fax:* Admissions ■ *Web:* www.purdue.edu					
Libraries ADMN 504 W State St	West Lafayette	IN	47907	765-494-2900	494-0156*
**Fax:* Admin ■ *Web:* www.lib.purdue.edu					
University of Notre Dame Hesburgh Library					
221 Hesburgh Library	Notre Dame	IN	46556	574-631-5252	631-6772
Web: www.library.nd.edu					
Drake University Cowles Library					
2507 University Ave	Des Moines	IA	50311	515-271-2111	271-3933
Web: www.library.drake.edu					
Grinnell College Burling Library					
6th Ave High St	Grinnell	IA	50112	641-269-3371	269-4283
TF: 800-247-0113 ■ *Web:* www.grinnell.edu					
Iowa State University Parks Library					
Osborn Dr & Morrill Rd	Ames	IA	50011	515-294-3642	294-5525
Web: www.lib.iastate.edu					
University of Iowa Libraries					
100 Main Library	Iowa City	IA	52242	319-335-5299	335-5900*
**Fax:* Library ■ *Web:* www.lib.uiowa.edu					
Kansas State University Hale Library					
137 Hale Library 1100 Mid-Campus Dr	Manhattan	KS	66506	785-532-3014	532-7415
Web: www.lib.k-state.edu					
Pittsburg State University Axe Library					
1701 S Broadway	Pittsburg	KS	66762	620-235-4882	235-4090
Web: axe.pittstate.edu					
Wichita State University Ablah Library (WSU)					
1845 Fairmount St	Wichita	KS	67260	316-978-3481	978-3048
Web: libraries.wichita.edu					
University of Kentucky Young Library					
500 S Limestone St	Lexington	KY	40506	859-257-0500	257-0505
Web: www.uky.edu					
University of Louisville Ekstrom Library					
2301 S Third St	Louisville	KY	40292	502-852-6747	852-7394
Web: www.louisville.edu					
Grambling State University Lewis Memorial Library (GSU)					
403 Main St PO Box 4256	Grambling	LA	71245	318-274-3354	274-3268
Web: www.gram.edu/research/library					
Louisiana Tech University Prescott Memorial Library					
PO Box 10408	Ruston	LA	71272	318-257-3555	257-2447
TF: 877-557-2575 ■ *Web:* www.latech.edu/library					
Loyola University					
Monroe Library 6363 St Charles Ave	New Orleans	LA	70118	504-864-7111	864-7247
Web: library.loyno.edu					
Nicholls State University Ellender Memorial Library					
906 E First St	Thibodaux	LA	70301	985-448-4646	448-4925
Web: www.nicholls.edu/library					
Northwestern State University Watson Memorial Library					
913 University Pkwy	Natchitoches	LA	71497	318-357-4477	357-4470
TF: 888-540-9657 ■ *Web:* library.nsula.edu					
Southeastern Louisiana University Sims Memorial Library					
SLU 10896	Hammond	LA	70402	985-549-3860	549-3995
Web: www.southeastern.edu					
Tulane University Howard-Tilton Memorial Library					
7001 Freret St	New Orleans	LA	70118	504-865-5131	865-6773
Web: www.library.tulane.edu					
University of New Orleans Long Library					
2000 Lakeshore Dr	New Orleans	LA	70148	504-280-6556	280-7277
Web: www.library.uno.edu					
Xavier University of Louisiana Library					
1 Drexel Dr	New Orleans	LA	70125	504-486-7411	520-7917
Web: www.xula.edu/library					
Bates College Ladd Library 48 Campus Ave	Lewiston	ME	04240	207-786-6226	786-6055
Web: www.bates.edu					
Bowdoin College Hawthorne-Longfellow Library					
3000 College Stn	Brunswick	ME	04011	207-725-3280	725-3083
Web: library.bowdoin.edu					
Colby College Miller Library					
5100 Mayflower Hill	Waterville	ME	04901	207-859-5147	859-5105
Web: libguides.colby.edu					
University of Maine 5713 Chadbourne Hall	Orono	ME	04469	207-581-1110	581-1213*
**Fax:* Admissions ■ *TF Admissions:* 877-486-2364 ■ *Web:* www.umaine.edu					
Fogler Library 5729 Fogler Library	Orono	ME	04469	207-581-1666	581-1653*
**Fax:* Admin ■ *Web:* www.library.umaine.edu					
Johns Hopkins University Sheridan Libraries					
3400 N Charles St	Baltimore	MD	21218	410-516-8335	516-5080
Web: www.library.jhu.edu					
Lewis J. Ort Library 1 Susan Eisel Dr	Frostburg	MD	21532	301-687-4395	687-7069
Web: frostburg.edu/lewis-ort-library					
Salisbury University Blackwell Library					
1101 Camden Ave	Salisbury	MD	21801	410-543-6130	543-6203
TF: 888-543-0148 ■ *Web:* www.salisbury.edu/library					
Towson University Cook Library 8000 York Rd	Towson	MD	21252	410-704-2461	704-3292
Web: cooklibrary.towson.edu					
University of Maryland					
7569 Baltimore Ave	College Park	MD	20742	301-405-1000	314-9693*
**Fax:* Admissions ■ *TF Admissions:* 800-422-5867 ■ *Web:* www.umd.edu					
McKeldin Library McKeldin Library	College Park	MD	20742	301-405-9075	
Web: www.lib.umd.edu					
University of Maryland Baltimore county					
Kuhn Library 1000 Hilltop Cir	Baltimore	MD	21250	410-455-2353	
Web: www.umbc.edu/aok					
Amherst College Frost Library PO Box 5000	Amherst	MA	01002	413-542-2373	542-2662
Web: www.amherst.edu/library					
Boston College Libraries					
140 Commonwealth Ave	Chestnut Hill	MA	02467	617-552-4472	552-0599
Web: www.bc.edu/libraries					
Boston University Mugar Memorial Library					
771 Commonwealth Ave	Boston	MA	02215	617-353-3710	353-2084
Web: www.bu.edu/library					
Bridgewater State College Maxwell Library					
10 Shaw Rd	Bridgewater	MA	02325	508-531-1392	
Web: www.bridgew.edu/library					
College of the Holy Cross Dinand Library					
1 College St	Worcester	MA	01610	508-793-2642	793-2372
TF: 877-433-1843 ■ *Web:* www.holycross.edu					
Harvard University Widener Library					
Hardvar Yard Rm 110	Cambridge	MA	02138	617-495-3650	
Web: harvard.edu					
Northeastern University Snell Library					
360 Huntington Ave	Boston	MA	02115	617-373-2350	373-5409
Web: www.lib.neu.edu					
Simmons College Beatley Library					
300 The Fenway	Boston	MA	02115	617-521-2780	521-3093
TF: 800-831-4284 ■ *Web:* www.simmons.edu					
Suffolk University Sawyer Library					
73 Tremont St	Boston	MA	02108	617-573-8000	573-8756
Web: www.suffolk.edu/sawlib					
Tufts University Tisch Library					
35 Professors Row	Medford	MA	02155	617-627-3345	627-3002
Web: tischlibrary.tufts.edu					
University of Massachusetts Amherst					
Du Bois Library 154 Hicks Way	Amherst	MA	01003	413-545-0284	545-6873
Web: www.library.umass.edu					
University of Massachusetts Boston					
Healey Library 100 Morrissey Blvd	Boston	MA	02125	617-287-5900	287-5955
Web: www.umb.edu					
University of Massachusetts Dartmouth					
Library 285 Old Westport Rd	North Dartmouth	MA	02747	508-999-8675	999-9142
Web: www.lib.umassd.edu					
University of Massachusetts Lowell					
Lydon Library 84 University Ave	Lowell	MA	01854	978-934-3205	934-3014
Web: www.library.uml.edu					
Andrews University James White Library					
4190 Admin Dr	Berrien Springs	MI	49104	269-471-3264	471-6166
TF: 800-253-2874 ■ *Web:* www.andrews.edu/library					
Eastern Michigan University Halle Library					
955 W Cir Dr	Ypsilanti	MI	48197	734-487-0020	487-8861
TF: 888-888-3465 ■ *Web:* emich.edu/library/index.php					
Ferris State University 1201 S State St	Big Rapids	MI	49307	231-591-2000	591-3944*
**Fax:* Admissions ■ *TF:* 800-433-7747 ■ *Web:* www.ferris.edu					
FLITE Library 1010 Campus Dr	Big Rapids	MI	49307	231-591-3602	591-3724
TF: 800-433-7747 ■ *Web:* www.ferris.edu/library					
Grand Valley State University Zumberge Library					
1 Campus Dr	Allendale	MI	49401	616-331-3252	
TF: 800-879-0581 ■ *Web:* www.gvsu.edu/library					
Hope College Van Wylen Library 53 Graves Pl	Holland	MI	49423	616-395-7790	395-7965
TF: 800-968-7850 ■ *Web:* www.hope.edu					
Michigan State University Library					
100 Library	East Lansing	MI	48824	517-353-8700	432-1191
TF: 800-500-1554 ■ *Web:* www.lib.msu.edu					
Saginaw Valley State University Zahnow Library					
7400 Bay Rd	University Center	MI	48710	989-964-4240	964-4383
TF: 800-968-9500 ■ *Web:* www.svsu.edu/library					
University of Michigan 515 E Jefferson St	Ann Arbor	MI	48109	734-764-1817	
Web: www.umich.edu					
Libraries 920 S University Ave	Ann Arbor	MI	48109	734-764-9356	763-5080
Web: www.lib.umich.edu					
University of Michigan Dearborn					
Mardigian Library 4901 Evergreen Rd	Dearborn	MI	48128	313-593-5445	593-5561
TF: 877-619-6650 ■ *Web:* umdearborn.edu					

Phone Fax

Wayne State University Libraries
5150 Anthony Wayne Dr. Detroit MI 48202 313-577-4023 577-5265
Web: library.wayne.edu
Western Michigan University Waldo Library
1903 W Michigan Ave Kalamazoo MI 49008 269-387-5202 387-5077
TF: 866-533-3438 ■ *Web:* www.wmich.edu
Minnesota State University Mankato
Memorial Library PO Box 8419 Mankato MN 56002 507-389-5952 389-5155
TF: 800-722-0544 ■ *Web:* www.lib.mnsu.edu
Saint John's University Alcuin Library
2835 Abbey Plaza Collegeville MN 56321 320-363-2122 363-2126
TF: 800-544-1489 ■ *Web:* csbsju.edu/libraries
University of Minnesota Crookston
UMC Library 2900 University Ave Crookston MN 56716 218-281-8399 281-8080
TF: 800-862-6466 ■ *Web:* www.crk.umn.edu
University of Minnesota Duluth
Kathryn A. Martin Library 416 Library Dr Duluth MN 55812 218-726-8102 726-8019
TF: 866-999-6995 ■ *Web:* www.d.umn.edu/lib
University of Minnesota Morris
Briggs Library 600 E Fourth St. Morris MN 56267 320-589-6176 589-6168
Web: www.morris.umn.edu
University of Minnesota Twin Cities
Bio-Medical Library 117 Pleasant St SE Minneapolis MN 55455 612-626-4045
Web: twin-cities.umn.edu
Wilson Library 309 19th Ave S Minneapolis MN 55455 612-624-3321 626-9353
Web: www.lib.umn.edu/wilson
University of Saint Thomas O'Shaughnessy-Frey Library
2115 Summit Ave Saint Paul MN 55105 651-962-5494 962-5406
TF: 800-328-6819 ■ *Web:* www.stthomas.edu/libraries
Winona State University Krueger Library
PO Box 5838 Winona MN 55987 507-457-5140 457-5594
Web: www.winona.edu/library
University of Mississippi PO Box 1848 University MS 38677 662-915-7211 915-5869*
**Fax:* Admissions ■ *Web:* www.olemiss.edu
Williams Library 1 Library Loop University MS 38677 662-915-7091 915-5734
TF: 800-891-4596 ■ *Web:* www.olemiss.edu
University of Missouri Kansas City
Nichols Library 800 E 51st St Kansas City MO 64110 816-235-1534 333-5584
TF: 800-775-8652 ■ *Web:* www.umkc.edu
Montana State University
Billings 1500 University Dr Billings MT 59101 406-657-2011 657-2302*
**Fax:* Admissions ■ *TF:* 800-565-6782 ■ *Web:* www.msubillings.edu
Library Renne Library PO Box 173320 Bozeman MT 59717 406-994-3171 994-2851
Web: www.lib.montana.edu
University of Montana Missoula
Mansfield Library 32 Campus Dr Missoula MT 59812 406-243-2053 243-4067
TF: 800-240-4939 ■ *Web:* www.lib.umt.edu
Peru State College Library 600 Hoyt St PO Box 10 Peru NE 68421 402-872-3815 872-2311
TF: 800-742-4412 ■ *Web:* www.peru.edu
University of Nebraska Lincoln
Love Memorial Library
318 Love Library PO Box 884100 Lincoln NE 68588 402-472-2848 472-5131
Web: www.libraries.unl.edu
University of Nevada Las Vegas
Lied Library 4505 S Maryland Pkwy Las Vegas NV 89154 702-895-3011
Web: www.unlv.edu
Dartmouth College Baker-Berry Library
6025 Baker-Berry Library Hanover NH 03755 603-646-2704
Web: www.dartmouth.edu/~library/bakerberry
Plymouth State University Lamson Library
17 High St Plymouth NH 03264 603-535-2258 535-2445
Web: library.plymouth.edu
University of New Hampshire
3 Garrison Ave Grant House Durham NH 03824 603-862-1234 862-0077*
**Fax:* Admissions ■ *Web:* www.unh.edu
Dimond Library 18 Library Way Durham NH 03824 603-862-1540 862-0247*
**Fax:* Admin ■ *Web:* www.library.unh.edu
Princeton University Library
1 Washington Rd Princeton NJ 08544 609-258-4820 258-0441*
**Fax:* Library ■ *Web:* library.princeton.edu
Rutgers The State University of New Jersey
Camden 406 Penn St Camden NJ 08102 856-225-6104 225-6498*
**Fax:* Admissions ■ *Web:* www.camden.rutgers.edu
Libraries 169 College Ave New Brunswick NJ 08901 732-932-7505 932-1101
Web: www.libraries.rutgers.edu
William Paterson University Cheng Library
300 Pompton Rd. Wayne NJ 07470 973-720-2541 720-2585
Web: www.wpunj.edu/library
New Mexico State University (NMSU)
MSC-3A PO Box 30001 Las Cruces NM 88003 575-646-3121 646-6330*
**Fax:* Admissions ■ *TF Admissions:* 800-662-6678 ■ *Web:* www.nmsu.edu
Baruch College The William & Anita Newman Library
151 E 25th St New York NY 10010 646-312-1600
Web: www.baruch.cuny.edu
Brooklyn College Library 2900 Bedford Ave Brooklyn NY 11210 718-951-5335 951-4540
Web: library.brooklyn.cuny.edu
Buffalo State College EH Butler Library
1300 Elmwood Ave Buffalo NY 14222 716-878-6314 878-3134
Web: www.buffalostate.edu/library
City College of New York Cohen Library
160 Convent Ave New York NY 10031 212-650-7155 650-7604
Web: www.ccny.cuny.edu/library
Columbia University Butler Library
535 W 114th St. New York NY 10027 212-854-2271 854-9099
Web: library.columbia.edu
Cornell University Olin Library
Olin & Uris Libraries Ithaca NY 14853 607-255-4144 255-6788
Web: olinuris.library.cornell.edu
Fordham University 441 E Fordham Rd Bronx NY 10458 718-817-3240 367-9404*
**Fax:* Admissions ■ *TF:* 800-367-3426 ■ *Web:* www.fordham.edu
Hofstra University Axinn Library
123 Hofstra University Hempstead NY 11549 516-463-5940 463-6387
Web: www.hofstra.edu
Ithaca College Library 953 Danby Rd Ithaca NY 14850 607-274-3206
Web: library.ithaca.edu

New York University Bobst Library
70 Washington Sq S. New York NY 10012 212-998-2500 995-4829
Web: www.library.nyu.edu
Pace University 1 Pace Plz New York NY 10038 212-346-1200 346-1040*
**Fax:* Admissions ■ *TF:* 866-722-3338 ■ *Web:* www.pace.edu
Birnbaum Library 1 Pace Plz New York NY 10038 212-346-1332 346-1516
Web: www.pace.edu/library
Rensselaer Polytechnic Institute Folsom Library
110 Eigth St Troy NY 12180 518-276-6000 276-8559
Web: library.rpi.edu
Rockefeller University
Library 1230 York Ave PO Box 263 New York NY 10065 212-327-8904
Web: rockefeller.edu
State University of New York College at Geneseo
Milne Library 1 College Cir Geneseo NY 14454 585-245-5594 245-5769
Web: www.geneseo.edu
Syracuse University Bird Library
222 Waverly Ave. Syracuse NY 13244 315-443-2093 443-9510*
**Fax:* Admin ■ *TF:* 866-722-7858 ■ *Web:* library.syr.edu
University at Albany University Libraries
1400 Washington Ave. Albany NY 12222 518-442-3600 442-3567
TF: 800-342-4146 ■ *Web:* library.albany.edu
University at Buffalo
University Libraries 433 Capen Hall. Buffalo NY 14260 716-645-2965 645-3844
Web: library.buffalo.edu
University of Rochester River Campus Libraries
755 Library Rd PO Box 270055 Rochester NY 14627 585-275-5804 273-5309
Web: www.library.rochester.edu
Vassar College Library
124 Raymond Ave PO Box 20 Poughkeepsie NY 12604 845-437-5760 437-5864
Web: library.vassar.edu
Appalachian State University
Belk Library 218 College St PO Box 32026 Boone NC 28608 828-262-2300 262-3001*
**Fax:* Administration ■ *TF:* 877-423-0086 ■ *Web:* www.library.appstate.edu
Duke University Perkins Library PO Box 90193 Durham NC 27708 919-660-5800 660-5923
Web: www.library.duke.edu
East Carolina University Joyner Library
E Fifth St. Greenville NC 27858 252-328-6518 328-4834
Web: www.ecu.edu/cs-lib
North Carolina State University Libraries
CB 7111 Raleigh NC 27695 919-515-2843 515-3628*
**Fax:* Admin ■ *TF:* 877-601-0590 ■ *Web:* www.lib.ncsu.edu
University of North Carolina Chapel Hill
Davis Library CB 3900 Chapel Hill NC 27514 919-962-1356 843-8936
Web: library.unc.edu
Wake Forest University Reynolds Library
PO Box 7777 Winston-Salem NC 27109 336-758-4931 758-5605
Web: www.zsr.wfu.edu
University of North Dakota Chester Fritz Library
3051 University Ave Stop 9000 Grand Forks ND 58202 701-777-2189 777-3319
Web: www.library.und.edu
Ashland University Library 509 College Ave Ashland OH 44805 419-289-5400 289-5422
TF: 866-434-5222 ■ *Web:* www.ashland.edu
Bowling Green State University Jerome Library (BGSU)
1001 E Wooster St Bowling Green OH 43403 419-372-2051 372-0475
TF: 866-246-6732 ■ *Web:* bgsu.edu/library.html
Case Western Reserve University kelvin Smith Library
11055 Euclid Ave Cleveland OH 44106 216-368-3506 368-3669
Web: library.case.edu
Denison University Doane Library
400 W Loop Granville OH 43023 740-587-6235 587-6285
TF: 800-336-4766 ■ *Web:* www.denison.edu/library
Kent State University
800 E. Summit St PO Box 5190 Kent OH 44242 330-672-2121 672-2499*
**Fax:* Admissions ■ *TF:* 800-988-5368 ■ *Web:* www.kent.edu
Libraries 1125 Risman Dr Kent OH 44242 330-672-3456 672-4811*
**Fax:* Admin ■ *Web:* www.library.kent.edu
Oberlin College Library 148 W College St. Oberlin OH 44074 440-775-8285 775-8739
Web: home.oberlin.edu
Ohio Northern University Heterick Memorial Library
525 S Main St. Ada OH 45810 419-772-2181 772-1927
TF: 866-943-5787 ■ *Web:* onu.edu/academics/heterick_memorial_library
Ohio State University 154 W 12th Ave. Columbus OH 43210 614-292-3980 292-4818*
**Fax:* Admissions ■ *TF:* 800-426-5046 ■ *Web:* www.osu.edu
Libraries 1858 Neil Ave Mall Columbus OH 43210 614-292-6175 292-7859
TF: 800-555-1212 ■ *Web:* www.library.osu.edu
Ohio University 120 Chubb Hall Athens OH 45710 740-593-1000 593-0560*
**Fax:* Admissions ■ *TF:* 800-858-6843 ■ *Web:* www.ohio.edu
Alden Library Park Pl Athens OH 45701 740-593-2699 593-0138*
**Fax:* Admin ■ *Web:* www.library.ohiou.edu
Shawnee State University Clark Memorial Library
940 Second St Portsmouth OH 45662 740-351-4778
Web: shawnee.edu
University of Cincinnati Langsam Library
PO Box 210033 Cincinnati OH 45221 513-556-1515 556-0325*
**Fax:* Admin ■ *TF:* 866-397-3382 ■ *Web:* www.libraries.uc.edu
University of Library 302 Buchtel Common Akron OH 44325 330-972-5355 972-5106
Web: www.uakron.edu/libraries
University of Toledo Carlson Library
2801 W Bancroft St MS 509 Toledo OH 43606 419-530-2324 530-2726
TF: 800-586-5336 ■ *Web:* www.utoledo.edu/library
Wright State University Dunbar Library
3640 Colonel Glenn Hwy Dayton OH 45435 937-775-4125 775-2356
Web: www.libraries.wright.edu
Xavier University Library
3800 Victory Pkwy Cincinnati OH 45207 513-745-3881 745-1932
TF: 888-468-4509 ■ *Web:* www.xavier.edu/library
Youngstown State University Maag Library
1 University Plz. Youngstown OH 44555 330-941-3675 941-3734
Web: www.maag.ysu.edu
Northeastern State University
Broken Arrow 3100 E New Orleans Broken Arrow OK 74014 918-449-6000 449-6190*
**Fax:* Admissions ■ *Web:* www.nsuba.edu
Vaughan Library 711 N Grand Ave Tahlequah OK 74464 918-456-5511
Web: library.nsuok.edu

Phone | Fax

Oklahoma State University
219 Student Union Bldg Stillwater OK 74078 405-744-5000 744-7092
TF: 800-852-1255 ■ *Web:* www.okstate.edu

Oral Roberts University Library
7777 S Lewis Ave Tulsa OK 74171 918-495-6723 495-6893
TF: 800-678-8876 ■ *Web:* oru.edu/library

University of Oklahoma Bizzell Memorial Library
401 W Brooks St Norman OK 73019 405-325-4142 325-7550*
**Fax:* Admin ■ *Web:* www.libraries.ou.edu

University of Tulsa McFarlin Library
2933 E Sixth St Tulsa OK 74104 918-631-2873 631-3791
Web: www.lib.utulsa.edu

Eastern Oregon University Pierce Library
1 University Blvd La Grande OR 97850 541-962-3579 962-3335
Web: library.eou.edu

Lewis & Clark College Watzek Library
0615 Palatine Hill Rd Portland OR 97219 503-768-7270 768-7282
Web: library.lclark.edu

Oregon State University Valley Library
121 Vly Library Corvallis OR 97331 541-737-3411 737-3453*
**Fax:* Admin ■ *Web:* osulibrary.oregonstate.edu

Pacific University Library
2043 College Way Forest Grove OR 97116 503-352-1400 352-1416
TF: 800-677-6712 ■ *Web:* pacificu.edu/libraries

Portland State University Millar Library
1875 SW Pk Ave Portland OR 97201 503-725-5874
Web: library.pdx.edu

Reed College Library 3203 SE Woodstock Blvd Portland OR 97202 503-777-7702 777-7786
Web: library.reed.edu

Southern Oregon University Hannon Library
1250 Siskiyou Blvd Ashland OR 97520 541-552-6441 552-6429
Web: hanlib.sou.edu

University of Oregon Knight Library
1299 University of Oregon Eugene OR 97403 541-346-3053 346-3485*
**Fax:* Library ■ *Web:* library.uoregon.edu

Western Oregon University Hamersly Library
345 N Monmouth Ave Monmouth OR 97361 503-838-8418 838-8645
TF: 877-877-1593 ■ *Web:* www.wou.edu/provost/library

Willamette University Hatfield Library
900 State St Salem OR 97301 503-370-6312 370-6141
Web: library.willamette.edu

Bucknell University Bertrand Library
69 Coleman Hall Rd Lewisburg PA 17837 570-577-1557 577-3313
Web: www.bucknell.edu/isr

California University of Pennsylvania Louis L Manderino Library
250 University Ave California PA 15419 724-938-4091 938-5901
Web: www.library.calu.edu

Dickinson College Waidner-Spahr Library
PO Box 1773 Carlisle PA 17013 717-245-1397 245-1439
Web: dickinson.edu/homepage/604/library_information_services

Drexel University Hagerty Library
33rd St & Market St Philadelphia PA 19104 215-895-2767 895-2070
TF: 888-278-8825 ■ *Web:* www.library.drexel.edu

East Stroudsburg University Kemp Library
200 Prospect St East Stroudsburg PA 18301 570-422-3465 422-3151
TF: 877-422-1378 ■ *Web:* www.esu.edu/library

Edinboro University of Pennsylvania Baron-Forness Library (EUB)
200 Tartan Rd Edinboro PA 16444 814-732-2273 732-2883
TF: 888-845-2890 ■ *Web:* edinboro.edu/home/page_not_found.dot

Franklin & Marshall College Shadek-Fackenthal Library
450 College Ave Lancaster PA 17604 717-291-4223
TF: 866-366-7655 ■ *Web:* www.fandm.edu

Indiana University of Pennsylvania Stapleton Library
1011 S Dr Indiana PA 15705 724-357-2340 357-4891
TF: 888-342-2383 ■ *Web:* www.iup.edu/library

Lafayette College Skillman Library
710 Sullivan Rd Easton PA 18042 610-330-5151 252-0370
Web: library.lafayette.edu

Pennsylvania State University
201 Shields Bldg University Park PA 16802 814-865-4700 863-7590
Web: www.psu.edu
Libraries 510 Paterno Library University Park PA 16802 814-865-6368 865-3665
Web: www.libraries.psu.edu

Swarthmore College McCabe Library
500 College Ave Swarthmore PA 19081 610-328-8477
Web: www.swarthmore.edu

Temple University Paley Library
1210 W Berks St Philadelphia PA 19122 215-204-8231 204-5201
Web: www.library.temple.edu

University of Pennsylvania Van Pelt Library
3420 Walnut St Philadelphia PA 19104 215-898-7091 898-0559
TF: 877-784-8379 ■ *Web:* www.library.upenn.edu/vanpelt

University of Pittsburgh 4227 Fifth Ave Pittsburgh PA 15260 412-624-4141 648-8815*
**Fax:* Admissions ■ *TF:* 877-999-3223 ■ *Web:* www.pitt.edu
Hillman Library 3960 Forbes Ave Pittsburgh PA 15260 412-648-7710 648-7887
TF: 888-465-4329 ■ *Web:* www.library.pitt.edu

Villanova University Falvey Memorial Library
800 Lancaster Ave Villanova PA 19085 610-519-4270 519-5018
Web: www.library.villanova.edu

Brown University Rockefeller Library
10 Prospect St Providence RI 02912 401-863-2162 863-1272
TF: 877-668-4493 ■ *Web:* www.brown.edu

Salve Regina University McKillop Library
100 Ochre Pt Ave Newport RI 02840 401-341-2291 341-2951
Web: library.salve.edu

University of Rhode Island (URI)
45 Upper College Rd Kingston RI 02881 401-874-1000 874-5523
Web: ww2.uri.edu
Libraries 15 Lippitt Rd Kingston RI 02881 401-874-2666 874-4608
Web: ww2.uri.edu

Clemson University Library
201 Sikes Hall PO Box 343001 Clemson SC 29634 864-656-5186
Web: www.clemson.edu

Francis Marion University Rogers Library
PO Box 100547 Florence SC 29502 800-368-7551
TF: 800-368-7551 ■ *Web:* www.fmarion.edu/rogerslibrary/directory

University of South Carolina
1600 Hampton St Columbia SC 29208 803-777-7000 777-0101*
**Fax:* Admissions ■ *TF:* 800-868-5872 ■ *Web:* www.sc.edu
Cooper Library 1322 Greene St Columbia SC 29208 803-777-2805 777-9503*
**Fax:* Admin ■ *Web:* library.sc.edu

South Dakota State University Briggs Library
N Campus Dr PO Box 2115 Brookings SD 57007 605-688-5106 688-6133
TF: 800-786-2038 ■ *Web:* www.sdstate.edu

Rhodes College Barret Library 2000 N Pkwy Memphis TN 38112 901-843-3000
TF: 800-844-5969 ■ *Web:* www.rhodes.edu

University of Memphis McWherter Library
126 Ned R McWherter Library Memphis TN 38152 901-678-2201 678-8218
TF: 866-670-6147 ■ *Web:* www.memphis.edu

University of Tennessee Chattanooga
Lupton Library
University of Tennessee at Chattanooga
700 Vine St Chattanooga TN 37403 423-425-4501 425-4775
Web: utc.edu/library

University of Tennessee Knoxville
Hodges Library 1015 Volunteer Blvd Knoxville TN 37996 865-974-4351 974-0555
TF: 800-426-9119 ■ *Web:* www.lib.utk.edu

Vanderbilt University Heard Library
419 21st Ave S Nashville TN 37240 615-322-7100 343-8279
Web: www.library.vanderbilt.edu

Abilene Christian University Brown Library (ACU)
760 Library Ct Abilene TX 79699 325-674-2000
TF: 800-460-6228 ■ *Web:* www.acu.edu/academics/library

Angelo State University Henderson Library
2025 S Johnson St San Angelo TX 76909 325-942-2051 942-2198
TF: 800-946-8627 ■ *Web:* www.angelo.edu

Baylor University Moody Memorial Library & Jones Library
PO Box 97148 Waco TX 76798 254-710-2112
Web: www.baylor.edu/lib

McMurry University Jay-Rollins Library
1601 War Hawk Way Abilene TX 79605 325-793-4692
Web: www.mcm.edu/newsite/web/library

Sixth Floor Museum
411 Elm St Ste 120 Dealey Plz Dallas TX 75202 214-747-6660
TF: 888-485-4854 ■ *Web:* www.jfk.org

Stephen F Austin State University Steen Library (SFASU)
1936 N St Nacogdoches TX 75962 936-468-3401
Web: www.sfasu.edu

Texas A & M University
Rudder Tower Ste 205 College Station TX 77843 979-845-8901 458-4617*
**Fax:* Admissions ■ *TF:* 888-890-5667 ■ *Web:* www.tamu.edu
Evans Library 5000 Tamu College Station TX 77843 979-845-5741 845-6238
Web: library.tamu.edu

Texas Christian University Mary Couts Burnett Library
2800 S University Dr Fort Worth TX 76129 817-257-7000 257-7282
TF: 866-321-7428 ■ *Web:* www.tcu.edu

Texas State University San Marcos
Alkek Library 601 University Dr San Marcos TX 78666 512-245-2133 245-3002
Web: www.library.txstate.edu

Texas Tech University Libraries
18th & Boston Ave PO Box 40002 Lubbock TX 79409 806-742-2265 742-0737
TF: 888-270-3369 ■ *Web:* library.ttu.edu

University of Houston 4800 Calhoun Rd Houston TX 77004 713-743-1000 743-9665
Web: www.uh.edu

University of North Texas Libraries
1155 Union Cir PO Box 305190 Denton TX 76203 940-565-2413 565-4949*
**Fax:* Circulation Desk ■ *TF:* 877-872-0264 ■ *Web:* www.library.unt.edu

University of Texas
Allied Health Sciences School
5323 Harry Hines Blvd Dallas TX 75390 214-648-3111 475-7641*
**Fax Area Code:* 512
Libraries PO Box P Austin TX 78713 512-495-4250 495-4347
Web: www.lib.utexas.edu

Brigham Young University 730 E University Pkwy Provo UT 84604 801-422-7700
Lee Library 2060 HBLL Provo UT 84602 801-422-2905 422-0466*
**Fax:* Admin ■ *Web:* www.lib.byu.edu

University of Utah Marriott Library
Marriott Library 295 S 1500 E Salt Lake City UT 84112 801-581-8558 585-3464*
**Fax:* Admin ■ *TF:* 800-458-0145 ■ *Web:* www.lib.utah.edu

Utah State University Merrill-Cazier Library
3000 Old Main Hill Logan UT 84322 435-797-2631 797-2880*
**Fax:* Admin ■ *Web:* www.library.usu.edu

Weber State University 3848 Harrison Blvd Ogden UT 84408 801-626-6000 626-6747
TF: 800-848-7770 ■ *Web:* www.weber.edu
Stewart Library 2901 University Cir Ogden UT 84408 801-626-6403 626-7045
TF: 877-306-3140 ■ *Web:* www.library.weber.edu

Middlebury College Library 110 Storrs Ave Middlebury VT 05753 802-443-5494 443-5698
TF: 800-829-1040 ■ *Web:* www.middlebury.edu

University of Vermont Bailey/Howe Library
538 Main St Burlington VT 05405 802-656-2023 656-4038
Web: library.uvm.edu

Christopher Newport University Smith Library
1 University Pl Newport News VA 23606 757-594-7133
Web: cnu.edu

College of William & Mary Swem Library
PO Box 8794 Williamsburg VA 23187 757-221-3072 221-2635
TF: 800-462-3683 ■ *Web:* www.swem.wm.edu

Emory & Henry College Kelly Library
30450 Armbrister Dr Emory VA 24327 276-944-6208 944-4592
Web: www.ehc.edu

George Mason University 4400 University Dr Fairfax VA 22030 703-993-1000 993-2392
TF: 888-627-6612 ■ *Web:* www.gmu.edu
Fenwick Library 4400 University Dr Fairfax VA 22030 703-993-2240
Web: library.gmu.edu

James Madison University Library
880 Madison Dr MSC 1704 Harrisonburg VA 22807 540-568-6150
Web: www.lib.jmu.edu

Phone | Fax

Radford University McConnell Library
PO Box 6881 ... Radford VA 24142 540-831-5471 831-6138
Web: library.radford.edu

Regent University
Library 1000 Regent University Dr ... Virginia Beach VA 23464 757-352-4916 226-4167
TF: 888-249-1822 ■ *Web:* www.regent.edu/general/library

University of Richmond 28 Westhampton Way ... Richmond VA 23173 804-289-8000 287-6003
TF: 800-700-1662 ■ *Web:* www.richmond.edu
Boatwright Memorial Library
28 Westhampton Way ... Richmond VA 23173 804-289-8454 287-1840
Web: library.richmond.edu

Virginia Commonwealth University Cabell Library
901 Pk Ave PO Box 842033 ... Richmond VA 23284 804-828-1105 828-0151
TF: 844-352-7399 ■ *Web:* library.vcu.edu/about/libraries/cabell

Virginia Polytechnic Institute & State University Libraries
PO Box 90001 ... Blacksburg VA 24062 540-231-6170 231-7808*
**Fax:* Admin ■ *Web:* www.lib.vt.edu

Central Washington University Brooks Library
400 E University Way ... Ellensburg WA 98926 509-963-3682 963-3684
Web: www.lib.cwu.edu

Evergreen State College Evans Library
2700 Evergreen Pkwy NW ... Olympia WA 98505 360-867-6250
Web: www.evergreen.edu/library

Gonzaga University Foley Library
502 E Boone Ave ... Spokane WA 99258 509-323-5931 323-5904
TF: 800-498-5941 ■ *Web:* gonzaga.edu/campus%2dresources

Pacific Lutheran University Mortvedt Library
12180 Pk Ave S ... Tacoma WA 98447 253-535-7500 535-7315
Web: www.plu.edu/~libr

Seattle University Lemieux Library
901 12th Ave ... Seattle WA 98122 206-296-6210 296-2572
TF: 800-426-7123 ■ *Web:* www.seattleu.edu/lemlib

University of Washington Libraries
PO Box 352900 ... Seattle WA 98195 206-543-0242
Web: www.lib.washington.edu

Washington State University PO Box 641040 ... Pullman WA 99164 509-335-3564 335-4902
TF: 888-468-6978 ■ *Web:* www.wsu.edu

West Virginia University PO Box 6009 ... Morgantown WV 26506 304-293-2121 293-3080
TF: 800-344-9881 ■ *Web:* www.wvu.edu
Libraries PO Box 6069 ... Morgantown WV 26506 304-293-2440 293-6638
Web: lib.wvu.edu

Lawrence University Mudd Library
711 E Boldt Way ... Appleton WI 54911 920-832-6750 832-6967
TF: 800-432-5427 ■ *Web:* www.lawrence.edu/library

Marquette University Raynor Memorial Library
1355 W Wisconsin Ave ... Milwaukee WI 53233 414-288-7556 288-5324
TF: 800-876-1715 ■ *Web:* www.marquette.edu/library

University of Wisconsin Eau Claire
McIntyre Library 105 Garfield Ave ... Eau Claire WI 54702 715-836-3715 836-2949
TF: 877-267-1384 ■ *Web:* www.uwec.edu

University of Wisconsin Green Bay
Cofrin Library 2420 Nicolet Dr ... Green Bay WI 54311 920-465-2333 465-2388
Web: www.uwgb.edu/library

University of Wisconsin La Crosse
Murphy Library 1631 Pine St ... La Crosse WI 54601 608-785-8000 785-8639
Web: www.uwlax.edu/murphylibrary

University of Wisconsin Madison
Ebling Library 750 Highland Ave ... Madison WI 53705 608-262-2020 262-4732
Web: www.ebling.library.wisc.edu
Libraries 728 State St ... Madison WI 53706 608-262-3193 265-2754
Web: www.library.wisc.edu

University of Wisconsin Milwaukee (UWM)
Golda Meir Library
2311 E Hartford Ave PO Box 604 ... Milwaukee WI 53211 414-229-4785
Web: www4.uwm.edu

University of Wisconsin Oshkosh
Polk Library 800 Algoma Blvd ... Oshkosh WI 54901 920-424-3334 424-7338
Web: www.uwosh.edu/library

University of Wisconsin Parkside
Library 900 Wood Rd ... Kenosha WI 53141 262-595-2360
Web: www.uwp.edu

University of Wisconsin Stevens Point
University Library 900 Reserve St ... Stevens Point WI 54481 715-346-2540 346-2367
Web: www.uwsp.edu

University of Wisconsin Stout
Library 315 Tenth Ave E ... Menomonie WI 54751 715-232-1215
TF: 866-716-6685 ■ *Web:* www.uwstout.edu/lib

University of Wisconsin Superior
Jim Dan Hill Library PO Box 2000 ... Superior WI 54880 715-394-8343
TF: 877-232-1727 ■ *Web:* www.uwsuper.edu/library

University of Wisconsin Whitewater
Andersen Library 800 W Main St ... Whitewater WI 53190 262-472-5511
Web: library.uww.edu

University of Wyoming Libraries PO Box 3334 ... Laramie WY 82071 307-766-3190 766-2510*
**Fax:* Admin ■ *TF:* 800-442-6757 ■ *Web:* www-lib.uwyo.edu

435 LIBRARY ASSOCIATIONS - STATE & PROVINCE

Phone | Fax

Adriance Memorial Library 93 Market St ... Poughkeepsie NY 12601 845-485-3445
Web: www.poklib.org

Arizona Library Assn (AzLA)
950 E Baseline Rd Ste 104-1025 ... Tempe AZ 85283 480-609-3999 609-3939
Web: www.azla.org

Barrie Public Library 60 Worsley St ... Barrie ON L4M1L6 705-728-1010
Web: library.barrie.ca

Cariboo Regional District
A-180 Third Ave N ... Williams Lake BC V2G2A4 250-392-3351
Web: cariboord.bc.ca

Castle Branch Inc 1845 Sir Tyler Dr ... Wilmington NC 28405 910-815-3880
Web: www.castlebranch.com

Crystal Springs City Water Department
306 W Railroad Ave S ... Crystal Springs MS 39059 601-892-4111
Web: www.crystalspringsmiss.com

Phone | Fax

Deerfield Public Library Inc
920 Waukegan Rd ... Deerfield IL 60015 847-945-3311
Web: deerfieldlibrary.org

El Paso Public Library 501 N Oregon St ... El Paso TX 79901 915-543-5433
Web: elpasolibrary.org

Glen Ellyn Public Library 400 Duane St ... Glen Ellyn IL 60137 630-469-0879
Web: www.gepl.org

Illinois Library Assn (ILA)
33 W Grand Ave Ste 301 ... Chicago IL 60610 312-644-1896 644-1899
TF: 877-565-1896 ■ *Web:* www.ila.org

Indiana Library Federation (ILF)
941 E 86th St Ste 260 ... Indianapolis IN 46240 317-257-2040 257-1389
Web: www.ilfonline.org

Lake Bluff Public Library
123 E Scranton Ave ... Lake Bluff IL 60044 847-234-2540
Web: lakeblufflibrary.org

Lethbridge Public Library 810 5 Ave S ... Lethbridge AB T1J4C4 403-380-7310
Web: www.lethlib.ca

Maryland Library Assn (MLA) 1401 Hollins St ... Baltimore MD 21223 410-947-5090 947-5089
Web: www.mdlib.org

Messaging Solutions LLC
8203 Shoregrove Dr Ste 200 ... Humble TX 77346 281-852-1301
Web: www.messagingsolutions.com

Midlothian Public Library
14701 Kenton Ave ... Midlothian IL 60445 708-535-2027
Web: www.midlothianlibrary.org

Minnesota Library Assn (MLA)
1821 University Ave W Ste S256 ... Saint Paul MN 55104 651-999-5343 917-1835
Web: www.mnlibraryassociation.org

Mishawaka-Penn-Harris Public Library Indiana
209 Lincoln Way E ... Mishawaka IN 46544 574-259-5277
Web: mphpl.org

Montclair Public Library
50 S Fullerton Ave ... Montclair NJ 07042 973-744-0500
Web: www.montclairlibrary.org

Nanuet Public Library 149 Church St ... Nanuet NY 10954 845-623-4281
Web: www.nanuetlibrary.org

Nelson Public Library 34 Arnold Ln ... Bloomfield KY 40004 502-348-3714
Web: www.nelsoncopublib.org

New Jersey Library Assn (NJLA) PO Box 1534 ... Trenton NJ 08607 609-394-8032 394-8164
Web: www.njla.org

New York Library Assn (NYLA)
6021 State Farm Rd ... Guilderland NY 12084 518-432-6952 427-1697
TF General: 800-252-6952 ■ *Web:* www.nyla.org

North Carolina Library Assn (NCLA)
1811 Capital Blvd ... Raleigh NC 27604 919-839-6252 839-6253
Web: www.nclaonline.org

Orangeburg Public Library 20 Greenbush Rd ... Orangeburg NY 10962 845-359-2244
Web: www.orangeburg-library.org

Orcas Island Library District 500 Rose St ... East Sound WA 98245 360-376-4985
Web: orcaslibrary.org

Parkland Community Library
4422 Walbert Ave ... Allentown PA 18104 610-398-1361
Web: www.parklandlibrary.org

Pennsylvania Library Assn (PaLA)
220 Cumberland Pkwy Ste 10 ... Mechanicsburg PA 17055 717-766-7663 766-5440
Web: www.palibraries.org

Perry County Public Library
289 Black Gold Blvd ... Hazard KY 41701 606-436-4747
Web: www.perrycountylibrary.org

Powell River Public Library
4411 Michigan Ave ... Powell River BC V8A2S3 604-485-4796
Web: www.powellriverlibrary.ca

Red Deer Public Library 4818 49 St ... Red Deer AB T4N1T9 403-346-4576
Web: www.rdpl.org

Rockwall County Library
1215 E Yellowjacket Ln ... Rockwall TX 75087 972-204-7700
Web: www.rockwallcountytexas.com

Rocky River Public Library
1600 Hampton Rd ... Rocky River OH 44116 440-333-7610
Web: www.rrpl.org

Rolling Meadows Library
3110 Martin Ln ... Rolling Meadows IL 60008 847-259-6050
Web: www.rmlib.org

Solano County Library 1150 Kentucky St ... Fairfield CA 94533 866-572-7587
TF: 866-572-7587 ■ *Web:* www.solanocounty.com

South Carolina Library Assn (SCLA) PO Box 1763 ... Columbia SC 29202 803-252-1087 252-0589
Web: www.scla.org

South Holland Public Library
16250 Wausau ... South Holland IL 60473 708-331-5262
Web: www.southhollandlibrary.org

St. Albert Public Library 5 St Anne St ... Saint Albert AB T8N3Z9 780-459-1530
Web: www.sapl.ca

State Education Resource Center
25 Industrial Park Rd ... Middletown CT 06457 860-632-1485
TF: 800-842-8678 ■ *Web:* ctserc.org

Tennessee Library Assn (TLA) PO Box 241074 ... Memphis TN 38124 901-485-6952
Web: www.tnla.org

Texas Library Association
3355 Bee Cave Rd Ste 401 ... West Lake Hills TX 78746 512-328-1518
Web: www.txla.org

Vernon Area Public Library District
300 Olde Half Day Rd ... Lincolnshire IL 60069 847-634-3650
Web: vapld.info

Westport Public Library 20 Jesup Rd ... Westport CT 06880 203-291-4800
Web: westportlibrary.org

Wisconsin Library Assn (WLA)
4610 S Biltmore Ln Ste 100 ... Madison WI 53718 608-245-3640 245-3646
Web: wla.memberclicks.net

436 LIBRARY SYSTEMS - REGIONAL - CANADIAN

Phone | Fax

Cape Breton Regional Library 50 Falmouth St. . . . . Sydney NS B1P6X9 902-562-3279 564-0765
Web: cbrl.ca

Centre Regional de Services Aux Bibliotheques Publiques de L'Estrie Inc
4155 Rue Brodeur. . . . . Sherbrooke QC J1L1K4 819-565-9744 565-9157
Web: www.reseaubiblioduquebec.qc.ca

Centre Regional de Services Aux Bibliotheques Publiques de L'Outaouais Inc
2295 Rue St Louis . . . . Gatineau QC J8T5L8 819-561-6008 561-6767

Centre Regional de Services Aux Bibliotheques Publiques de la Monteregie Inc
275 Rue Conrad-Pelletier . . . . La Prairie QC J5R4V1 450-444-5433 659-3364
Web: www.reseaubiblioduquebec.qc.ca

Centre Regional de Services Aux Bibliotheques Publiques des Laurentides Inc
29 Rue Brissette . . . . Sainte-Agathe-des-Monts QC J8C3L1 819-326-6440 326-0885
Web: www.reseaubiblioduquebec.qc.ca

Evergreen Regional Library
55 1st Ave PO Box 1140. . . . . Gimli MB R0C1B0 204-642-7912 642-8319
Web: erlibrary.ca

Lakeland Regional Library 318 Williams Ave. . . . . Killarney MB R0K1G0 204-523-4949 523-7460
Web: www.lakelandregionallibrary.ca

North Ontario Library Service 334 Regent St. . . . . Sudbury ON P3C4E2 705-675-6467 675-2285
TF: 800-461-6348 ■ *Web:* olsn.ca

Palliser Regional Library 366 Coteau St W . . . . Moose Jaw SK S6H5C9 306-693-3669 692-5657
Web: www.palliserlibrary.ca

Provincial Information & Library Resources Board
Eastern Div 48 St Georges Ave. . . . . Stephenville NL A2N1L1 709-737-3508 737-3571
Web: www.nlpl.ca
West Newfoundl and-Labrador Div 4 W St. . . . . Corner Brook NL A2H0C1 709-634-7333 634-7313
Web: www.nlpl.ca

Saint John Regional Library 1 Market Sq. . . . . Saint John NB E2L4Z6 506-643-7220 643-7225
Web: saintjohnlibrary.com

Southeast Regional Library 49 Bison Ave . . . . Weyburn SK S4H0H9 306-848-3100 842-2665
Web: www.southeast.lib.sk.ca

Southwestern Manitoba Regional Library
149 Main St PO Box 670 . . . . Melita MB R0M1L0 204-522-3923 522-3923
Web: www.wix.com

Wapiti Regional Library 145 12th St E . . . . Prince Albert SK S6V1B7 306-764-0712 922-1516
Web: wapitilibrary.ca

Western Manitoba Regional Library
710 Rosser Ave Unit 1 . . . . Brandon MB R7A0K9 204-727-6648 727-4447
Web: www.wmrl.ca

437 LIGHT BULBS & TUBES

Phone | Fax

Advanced Lighting Technologies Inc
7905 Cochran Rd Ste 300. . . . . Glenwillow OH 44139 440-519-0500
TF: 888-440-2358 ■ *Web:* www.adlt.com

AETEK UV Systems 1229 Lakeview Ct . . . . Romeoville IL 60446 630-226-4200 226-4215
TF: 800-333-2304 ■ *Web:* www.americanultraviolet.com

Amglo Kemlight Laboratories Inc
215 Gateway Rd . . . . Bensenville IL 60106 630-350-9470 350-9474
Web: www.amglo.com

Bayco Products Inc 640 Sanden Blvd . . . . Wylie TX 75098 469-326-9400 326-9401
TF: 800-233-2155 ■ *Web:* www.baycoproducts.com

Carley Lamps Inc 1502 W 228th St . . . . Torrance CA 90501 310-325-8474 534-2912
Web: www.carleylamps.com

Eye Lighting International NA
9150 Hendricks Rd. . . . . Mentor OH 44060 440-350-7000 350-7001
TF Cust Svc: 888-665-2677 ■ *Web:* www.eyelighting.com

Hanovia Corp 6 Evans St . . . . Fairfield NJ 07004 973-651-5510 651-5550
Web: www.hanovia-uv.com

Interlectric Corp 1401 Lexington Ave. . . . . Warren PA 16365 814-723-6061 723-1074
TF: 800-722-2184 ■ *Web:* www.interlectric.com

LCD Lighting Inc 37 Robinson Blvd . . . . Orange CT 06477 203-795-1520 795-2874
TF: 800-826-9465 ■ *Web:* www.light-sources.com

Ledtronics Inc 23105 Kashiwa Ct . . . . Torrance CA 90505 310-534-1505 534-1424
TF: 800-579-4875 ■ *Web:* www.led.net

Light Sources Inc 37 Robinson Blvd . . . . Orange CT 06477 203-799-7877 795-5267
TF: 800-826-9465 ■ *Web:* www.light-sources.com

Litetronics International Inc 4101 W 123rd St . . . . Alsip IL 60803 708-389-8000 371-0627
TF: 800-860-3392 ■ *Web:* www.litetronics.com

OSRAM Sylvania Glass Technologies
131 Portsmouth Ave. . . . . Exeter NH 03833 603-772-4331 778-4554
TF: 800-258-8290 ■ *Web:* www.sylvania.com

OSRAM Sylvania Inc 100 Endicott St . . . . Danvers MA 01923 978-777-1900 750-2152
Web: www.sylvania.com

PerkinElmer Inc 940 Winter St . . . . Waltham MA 02451 203-925-4602 944-4904
NYSE: PKI ■ *Web:* www.perkinelmer.com

Philips Lighting Co 200 Franklin Sq Dr . . . . Somerset NJ 08873 800-555-0050
TF: 800-555-0050 ■ *Web:* www.usa.lighting.philips.com

Rogers Corp Durel Div 2225 W Chandler Blvd. . . . . Chandler AZ 85224 480-917-6000 917-6049
Web: www.rogerscorp.com

Sun Ergoline Inc 1 Walter Kratz Dr . . . . Jonesboro AR 72401 888-771-0996 935-3618*
**Fax Area Code:* 870 ■ *TF:* 888-771-0996 ■ *Web:* sunergoline.com

Technical Consumer Products Inc 325 Campus Dr . . . . . . Aurora OH 44202 800-324-1496 995-6188*
**Fax Area Code:* 330 ■ *TF:* 800-324-1496 ■ *Web:* www.tcpi.com

Trojan Inc 198 Trojan St. . . . . Mount Sterling KY 40353 859-498-0526
TF: 800-264-0526 ■ *Web:* www.trojaninc.com

Ushio America Inc 5440 Cerritos Ave. . . . . Cypress CA 90630 714-236-8600 776-3641*
**Fax Area Code:* 800 ■ **Fax:* Mktg ■ *TF:* 800-326-1960 ■ *Web:* www.ushio.com

UVP Inc 2066 W 11th St . . . . Upland CA 91786 909-946-3197 946-3597
TF Cust Svc: 800-452-6788 ■ *Web:* www.uvp.com

Venmar Ventilation Inc 550 Lemire Blvd . . . . Drummondville QC J2C7W9 819-477-6226 475-2660
Web: www.venmar.ca

Venture Lighting International Inc
32000 Aurora Rd . . . . Solon OH 44139 440-248-3510 349-7771
TF: 800-451-2606 ■ *Web:* www.venturelighting.com

438 LIGHTING EQUIPMENT - VEHICULAR

Phone | Fax

Able 2 Products Company Inc PO Box 543 . . . . Cassville MO 65625 417-847-4791 847-2222
TF: 800-641-4098 ■ *Web:* www.able2products.com

Astronics Corp 130 Commerce Way . . . . East Aurora NY 14052 716-805-1599 655-0309
NASDAQ: ATRO ■ *Web:* www.astronics.com

ATC Lighting & Plastics Inc 101 Parker Dr . . . . Andover OH 44003 440-293-4064 293-4591
Web: www.atc-lighting-plastics.com

Aurora Cord & Cable Co 325 S Union St. . . . . Aurora IL 60505 630-851-1616 851-1626
Web: www.auroracord.com

Avtec Inc 6 Industrial Pk . . . . Cahokia IL 62206 618-337-7800 337-7976
TF: 800-552-8832 ■ *Web:* www.avteclighting.com

Bruce Industries Inc 101 Evans Ave . . . . Dayton NV 89403 775-246-0101
Web: www.bruceind.com

Federal Signal Corp Emergency Products Div
2645 Federal Signal Dr. . . . . University Park IL 60466 708-534-3400
TF: 800-264-3578 ■ *Web:* www.fedsig.com

JW Speaker Corp
N 120 W 19434 Freistadt Rd PO Box 1011. . . . . Germantown WI 53022 262-251-6660 251-2918
TF: 800-558-7288 ■ *Web:* www.jwspeaker.com

KC Hilites Inc PO Box 155. . . . . Williams AZ 86046 928-635-2607 635-2486
Web: kchilites.com

Luminator 900 Klein Rd . . . . Plano TX 75074 972-424-6511 423-1540
TF: 800-388-8205 ■ *Web:* luminatortechnologygroup.com/mass-transit

North American Lighting Inc 2275 S Main St . . . . Paris IL 61944 217-465-6600 465-6610
Web: www.nal.com

Nova Electronics Inc 152 S Brent Cir . . . . Walnut CA 91789 860-537-3471 537-0656
Web: www.code3pse.com/c3buzz/read/218/welcome_nova_customers

Peterson Manufacturing Co 4200 E 135th St . . . . Grandview MO 64030 816-765-2000 761-6693
TF: 800-821-3490 ■ *Web:* www.pmlights.com

Soderberg Mfg Company Inc 20821 Currier Rd . . . . Walnut CA 91789 909-595-1291
Web: www.soderberg.aero

Teledyne Lighting & Display Products
12964 Panama St . . . . Los Angeles CA 90066 310-823-5491 574-2070
TF: 800-563-4020 ■ *Web:* www.teledynelighting.com

Truck-Lite Company Inc 310 E Elmwood Ave . . . . Falconer NY 14733 716-665-6214 665-6403
TF Cust Svc: 800-562-5012 ■ *Web:* www.truck-lite.com

Unity Manufacturing Co 1260 N Clybourn Ave. . . . . Chicago IL 60610 312-943-5200 943-5681
Web: www.unityusa.com

Vehicle Safety Mfg LLC 408 Central Ave. . . . . Newark NJ 07107 973-643-3000
TF General: 800-832-7233 ■ *Web:* www.vehiclesafetymfg.com

Whelen Engineering Company Inc
51 Winthrop Rd & Rt 145 . . . . Chester CT 06412 860-526-9504 526-4078
Web: www.whelen.com

439 LIGHTING FIXTURES & EQUIPMENT

Phone | Fax

ALP Lighting Components Inc
6333 Gross Point Rd . . . . Niles IL 60714 773-774-9550 774-9331
Web: alplighting.com

Altman Lighting Inc 57 Alexander St . . . . Yonkers NY 10701 914-476-7987 966-1980
TF: 800-425-8626 ■ *Web:* www.altmanlighting.com

American Fluorescent Corp
2345 Ernie Krueger Cir. . . . . Waukegan IL 60087 847-249-5970 249-2618
TF: 800-873-2326 ■ *Web:* www.afxinc.com

American Louver Co 7700 N Austin Ave . . . . Skokie IL 60077 847-470-3300 966-8074
TF: 800-772-0355 ■ *Web:* www.americanlouver.com

AmerillumBrands 3728 Maritime Way . . . . Oceanside CA 92056 760-727-7675
Web: www.amerillum.com

Antique Street Lamps Inc 2011-B W Rundberg Ln. . . . . Austin TX 78758 512-977-8444 977-9622
Web: antiquestreetlamps.acuitybrands.com

Ashley Lighting Inc 405 Industrial Dr. . . . . Trumann AR 72472 870-483-6181 483-7140
Web: ashleylighting.com

Automatic Power Inc
10810 W Little York Rd Ste 130 . . . . Houston TX 77041 713-228-5208 228-3717
Web: www.automaticpower.com

Big Beam Emergency Systems Inc
290 E Prairie St PO Box 518. . . . . Crystal Lake IL 60039 815-459-6100 459-6126
Web: www.bigbeam.com

Boyd Corp 6325 San Pedro Ave . . . . San Antonio TX 78216 210-344-9222
Web: www.boydlightingsa.com

Boyd Lighting Co 944 Folsom St . . . . San Francisco CA 94107 415-778-4300 778-4319
Web: www.boydlighting.com

Brinkmann Corp 4215 McEwen Rd . . . . Dallas TX 75244 972-387-4939 770-8545
TF: 800-527-0717

California Lighting Sales Inc (CLS)
4900 Rivergrade Rd Ste D110. . . . . Irwindale CA 91706 626-775-6000 775-6001
Web: www.californialightingsales.com

Carlisle & Finch Co 4562 W Mitchell Ave . . . . Cincinnati OH 45232 513-681-6080 681-6226
Web: www.carlislefinch.com

Chapman Mfg Company Inc PO Box 359 . . . . Avon MA 02322 508-588-3200 587-7592
Web: www.chapmanco.com

Commercial Lighting Industries
81161 Indio Blvd . . . . Indio CA 92201 760-343-2704
TF: 800-755-0155 ■ *Web:* www.commercial-lighting.net

Con-Tech Lighting 2783 Shermer Rd. . . . . Northbrook IL 60062 847-559-5500 559-5505
TF: 800-728-0312 ■ *Web:* www.con-techlighting.com

Cooper Industries 600 Travis St Ste 5400 . . . . Houston TX 77002 713-209-8400 209-8995
NYSE: ETN ■ *TF:* 866-853-4293 ■ *Web:* www.cooperindustries.com

Cooper Lighting Inc 1121 Hwy 74 S . . . . Peachtree City GA 30269 770-486-4800 486-4801
Web: www.cooperindustries.com

Corbett Lighting Inc
14508 Nelson Ave . . . . City of Industry CA 91744 626-336-4511 336-5121
TF: 800-533-8769 ■ *Web:* www.corbettlighting.com

Coronet Lighting PO Box 2065. . . . . Gardena CA 90248 310-593-9561
Web: www.coronetlighting.com

	City	State	ZIP	Phone	Fax
CW Cole & Company Inc 2560 Rosemead Blvd *Web:* www.colelighting.com	South El Monte	CA	91733	626-443-2473	443-9253
Dazor Lighting Solutions 2079 Congressional *TF:* 800-345-9103 ■ *Web:* www.dazor.com	Saint Louis	MO	63146	314-652-2400	652-2069
Deaver Industries Inc 3120 Morgan Rd. *Web:* www.deaverind.com	Bessemer	AL	35022	205-426-4309	426-4364
Dual-Lite Inc 701 Millennium Blvd *TF:* 866-898-0131 ■ *Web:* www.dual-lite.com	Greenville	SC	29607	864-678-1000	678-1415
Edison Price Lighting Inc (EPL) 41-50 22nd St *Web:* www.epl.com	Long Island	NY	11101	718-685-0700	786-8530
Electrix Inc 45 Spring St *Web:* www.electrixillumination.com	New Haven	CT	06519	203-776-5577	624-7545
ELK Lighting Creativity 12 Willow Ln **Fax Area Code:* 866 ■ *TF:* 800-613-3261 ■ *Web:* www.elklighting.com/esource/default.aspx?store=elk	Nesquehoning	PA	18240	800-613-3261	613-3264*
Elk Lighting Inc 12 Willow Lane **Fax Area Code:* 800 ■ *TF:* 866-283-1953 ■ *Web:* www.elkhospitality.com	Nesquehoning	PA	18240	866-283-1953	388-6052*
Energy Focus Inc 32000 Aurora Rd *OTC: EFOI* ■ *TF:* 800-327-7877 ■ *Web:* www.energyfocusinc.com	Solon	OH	44139	440-715-1300	715-1314
EZ Electric Inc 1250 Birchwood Dr *Web:* www.ez-electric.com	Sunnyvale	CA	94089	408-734-4282	
Finelite Inc 30500 Whipple Rd *Web:* www.finelite.com	Union City	CA	94587	510-441-1100	441-1510
Fulton Industries Inc 135 E Linfoot St PO Box 377 *TF:* 800-537-5012 ■ *Web:* www.fultonindoh.com	Wauseon	OH	43567	419-335-3015	335-3215
Gardco Lighting 1611 Clovis Barker Rd *TF:* 800-227-0758 ■ *Web:* www.sitelighting.com	San Marcos	TX	78666	512-753-1000	
GE Lighting Systems Inc 3010 Spartanburg Hwy *TF:* 888-694-3533 ■ *Web:* gelighting.com/lightingweb/na	East Flat Rock	NC	28726	828-693-2000	
Good Earth Lighting Inc 5260 Capitol Dr *Web:* www.goodearthlighting.com	Wheeling	IL	60090	847-808-1133	808-0838
HE Williams Inc 831 W Fairview Ave. *TF:* 866-358-4065 ■ *Web:* www.hew.com	Carthage	MO	64836	417-358-4065	358-6015
High End Systems Inc 2105 Gracy Farms Ln *TF:* 800-890-8989 ■ *Web:* www.highend.com	Austin	TX	78758	512-836-2242	837-5290
High Q Lighting Inc 11439 E Lakewood Blvd *Web:* www.hql.net	Holland	MI	49424	616-396-3591	
Hinkley Lighting 12600 Berea Rd *TF:* 800-446-5539 ■ *Web:* www.hinkleylighting.com	Cleveland	OH	44111	216-671-3300	671-4537
Holophane 214 Oakwood Ave PO Box 3004 *TF:* 866-465-6742 ■ *Web:* www.holophane.com	Newark	OH	43058	740-345-9631	
Hubbell Lighting Inc 701 Millennium Blvd *Web:* www.hubbelllighting.com	Greenville	SC	29607	864-678-1000	678-1065
Hydrel 12881 Bradley Ave **Fax Area Code:* 818 ■ *TF:* 866-533-9901 ■ *Web:* hydrel.acuitybrands.com	Sylmar	CA	91342	866-533-9901	362-6548*
Justice Design Group (JDG) 500 S Grand Ave Ste 110 *Web:* www.jdg.com	Los Angeles	CA	90071	213-437-0102	437-0860
Kenall Mfg 1020 Lakeside Dr. *TF:* 800-453-6255 ■ *Web:* www.kenall.com	Gurnee	IL	60031	847-360-8200	360-1781
Kichler Lighting 7711 E Pleasant Vly Rd PO Box 318010 *TF:* 866-558-5706 ■ *Web:* www.kichler.com	Cleveland	OH	44131	866-558-5706	
Kim Lighting Inc 16555 E Gale Ave PO Box 60080 *Web:* www.kimlighting.com	City of Industry	CA	91745	626-968-5666	968-5716
Kirlin Co 3401 E Jefferson Ave *Web:* www.kirlinlighting.com	Detroit	MI	48207	313-259-6400	259-3121
Koehler-Bright Star Inc 380 Stewart Rd *TF Cust Svc:* 800-788-1696 ■ *Web:* www.flashlight.com	Hanover Township	PA	18706	570-825-1900	825-7108
Kurt Versen Co 1 Paragon Dr *Web:* www.kurtversen.com	Montvale	NJ	07645	201-664-8200	664-4801
Kurtzon Lighting Inc 1420 S Talman Ave. *TF:* 800-837-8937 ■ *Web:* www.kurtzon.com	Chicago	IL	60608	773-277-2121	277-9164
Lamplight Farms Inc W140 N4900 Lilly Rd *TF Cust Svc:* 888-473-1088 ■ *Web:* www.tikibrand.com	Menomonee Falls	WI	53051	262-781-9590	781-6774
LC Doane Co 110 Pond Meadow Rd PO Box 700 *Web:* www.lcdoane.com	Ivoryton	CT	06442	860-767-8295	767-1397
Ledalite Architectural Products 19750-92A Ave. *TF:* 800-665-5332 ■ *Web:* www.ledalite.com	Langley	BC	V1M3B2	604-888-6811	888-2003
Legion Lighting Company Inc 221 Glenmore Ave *TF:* 800-453-4466 ■ *Web:* www.legionlighting.com	Brooklyn	NY	11207	718-498-1770	498-0128
Lighting Quotient, The 114 Boston Post Rd *TF:* 800-222-0193	West Haven	CT	06516	203-931-4455	931-4464
Lights of America 611 Reyes Dr. *Web:* www.lightsofamerica.com	Walnut	CA	91789	909-594-7883	594-6758
Lite Energy 780 Salaberry *Web:* www.liteenergy.com	Laval	QC	H7S1H3	450-668-9620	668-9625
Litecontrol 100 Hawks Ave *Web:* www.litecontrol.com	Hanson	MA	02341	781-294-0100	293-2849
Lithonia Lighting 1 Lithonia Way *TF:* 800-858-7763 ■ *Web:* www.lithonia.com	Conyers	GA	30012	770-922-9000	483-2635
LSI Industries Inc 10000 Alliance Rd *NASDAQ: LYTS* ■ *Web:* www.lsi-industries.com	Cincinnati	OH	45242	513-793-3200	984-1335
Lumec Inc 640 Blvd Cur-Boivin *Web:* www.lumec.com	Boisbriand	QC	J7G2A7	450-430-7040	430-1453
Luxo Corp 5 Westchester Plz. **Fax:* Sales ■ *TF:* 800-222-5896 ■ *Web:* glamox.com/luxous	Elmsford	NY	10523	914-345-0067	345-0068*
Mag Instrument Inc 2001 S Hillman Ave. *TF:* 800-289-6241 ■ *Web:* www.maglite.com	Ontario	CA	91761	909-947-1006	947-3116
Manning Lighting 1810 N Ave PO Box 1063 *Web:* www.manningltg.com	Sheboygan	WI	53083	920-458-2184	458-2491
Mario Industries of Virginia Inc 2490 Patterson Ave SW PO Box 3190 *Web:* www.marioindustries.com	Roanoke	VA	24016	540-342-1111	345-4813
Mark Architectural Lighting 3 Kilmer Rd. *Web:* www.marklighting.com	Edison	NJ	08817	732-985-2600	985-8441
Mercury Lighting Products Company Inc 20 Audrey Pl. *TF:* 800-637-2584 ■ *Web:* www.mercltg.com	Fairfield	NJ	07004	973-244-9444	244-9522
Minka Group 1151 W Bradford Ct *TF:* 800-221-7977 ■ *Web:* www.minkagroup.net	Corona	CA	92882	951-735-9220	
Mole-Richardson Company Inc 937 N Sycamore Ave *Web:* www.mole.com	Hollywood	CA	90038	323-851-0111	851-5593
Mule Lighting Inc 46 Baker St *TF:* 800-556-7690 ■ *Web:* www.mulelighting.com	Providence	RI	02905	401-941-4446	941-2929
Multi-Electric Manufacturing Inc 4223 W Lake St *Web:* www.multielectric.com	Chicago	IL	60624	773-722-1900	722-5694
Musco Sports Lighting LLC 100 First Ave W PO Box 808 *TF:* 800-825-6020 ■ *Web:* www.musco.com	Oskaloosa	IA	52577	641-673-0411	673-4852
National Lighting Company Inc 522 Cortlandt St *Web:* www.natltg.com	Belleville	NJ	07109	973-751-1600	751-4931
North Star Lighting Inc 2150 Parkes Dr. *TF:* 800-229-4330 ■ *Web:* www.northstarlightingsite.com	Broadview	IL	60155	708-681-4330	681-4006
Norwell Manufacturing Inc 82 Stevens St *TF:* 800-822-2831 ■ *Web:* www.norwellinc.com	East Taunton	MA	02718	508-823-1751	823-9431
Omniglow LLC 865 Memorial Ave	West Springfield	MA	01089	413-241-6010	543-5470
OSRAM Sylvania Inc 100 Endicott St *Web:* www.sylvania.com	Danvers	MA	01923	978-777-1900	750-2152
Pacific Coast Lighting 20238 Plummer St *TF:* 800-709-9004 ■ *Web:* www.pacificcoastlighting.com	Chatsworth	CA	91311	818-886-9751	886-5751
Paraflex Industries 2006 Inc 222 New Rd *Web:* www.paraflex.com	Parsippany	NJ	07054	973-340-6040	340-6043
Paramount Industries Inc 304 N Howard St. *TF:* 800-521-5405 ■ *Web:* www.paramountlighting.com/index.php	Croswell	MI	48422	810-679-2551	679-4045
Paul C Buff Inc 2725 Bransford Ave *TF:* 800-443-5542 ■ *Web:* www.paulcbuff.com	Nashville	TN	37204	615-383-3982	383-0676
Peerless Lighting Corp 2246 Fifth St *Web:* www.peerlesslighting.com	Berkeley	CA	94710	510-845-2760	845-2776
Philips Canlyte, Inc 3015 Louis Amos *TF All:* 800-668-2770 ■ *Web:* www.lightingproducts.philips.com/documents/webdb2/_message/redirect/ca	Lachine	QC	H8T1C4	514-636-0670	636-0460
Philips Holding USA Inc 1251 Ave of the Americas *TF:* 800-453-6860 ■ *Web:* usa.philips.com	New York	NY	10020	212-536-0500	536-0506
Philips Luminaire 776 S Green St. **Fax Area Code:* 662 ■ **Fax:* Hum Res ■ *TF:* 800-234-1890 ■ *Web:* www.lightingproducts.philips.com/documents/webdb2/_message/redirect/us	Tupelo	MS	38804	800-234-1890	841-5501*
Prescolite Inc 701 Millennium Blvd *TF:* 888-777-4832 ■ *Web:* www.prescolite.com	Greenville	SC	29607	864-678-1000	678-1415
Prudential Ltd 1737 E 22nd St *Web:* www.prulite.com	Los Angeles	CA	90058	213-746-0360	741-8590
Quoizel Inc 6 Corporate Pkwy *Web:* www.quoizel.com	Goose Creek	SC	29445	843-553-6700	553-1002
RAB Lighting 170 Ludlow Ave **Fax Area Code:* 888 ■ *TF:* 888-722-1000 ■ *Web:* www.rabweb.com	Northvale	NJ	07647	201-784-8600	722-1232*
Rejuvenation Inc 2550 NW Nicolai St **Fax Area Code:* 800 ■ *TF:* 888-401-1900 ■ *Web:* www.rejuvenation.com	Portland	OR	97210	503-231-1900	526-7329*
Renova Lighting Systems Inc 20 Middlesex Rd. *TF:* 800-635-6682 ■ *Web:* www.renova.com	Mansfield	MA	02048	401-682-1850	682-1860
Schonbek Worldwide Lighting Inc 61 Industrial Blvd *TF:* 800-836-1892 ■ *Web:* www.swarovski-lighting.com/ws/web/sl_md.html	Plattsburgh	NY	12901	518-563-7500	563-4228
Sea Gull Lighting Products LLC A Generations Brands Co 301 W Washington St. *TF:* 800-347-5483 ■ *Web:* www.seagulllighting.com	Riverside	NJ	08075	856-764-0500	
Sentry Electric 185 Buffalo Ave *Web:* www.sentrylighting.com	Freeport	NY	11520	516-379-4660	378-0624
Sesco Lighting Inc 1133 W Morse Blvd Ste 100 *Web:* www.sescolighting.com	Winter Park	FL	32789	407-629-6100	629-6168
SIMKAR Corp 700 Ramona Ave **Fax:* Cust Svc ■ *TF:* 800-523-3602 ■ *Web:* www.simkar.com	Philadelphia	PA	19120	215-831-7700	831-7703*
Spectrolab Inc 12500 Gladstone Ave *TF:* 800-936-4888 ■ *Web:* www.spectrolab.com	Sylmar	CA	91342	818-365-4611	361-5102
Spring City Electrical Manufacturing Co PO Box 19 *Web:* www.springcity.com	Spring City	PA	19475	610-948-4000	948-5577
Strand Lighting 10911 Petal St. *TF:* 800-733-0564 ■ *Web:* www.strandlighting.com	Dallas	TX	75238	214-647-7880	647-8031
Streamlight Inc 30 Eagleville Rd. *TF:* 800-523-7488 ■ *Web:* www.streamlight.com	Eagleville	PA	19403	610-631-0600	631-0712
Super Sky Products Inc 10301 N Enterprise Dr. *TF:* 800-558-0467 ■ *Web:* www.supersky.com	Mequon	WI	53092	262-242-2000	242-7409
Swivelier Company Inc 600 Bradley Hill Rd *Web:* www.swivelier.com	Blauvelt	NY	10913	845-353-1455	353-1512
Tech Lighting LLC 7400 Linda Ave *TF:* 800-522-5315 ■ *Web:* www.techlighting.com	Skokie	IL	60077	847-410-4400	410-4500
Tri-Lite Inc 1642 N Besly Ct. *TF:* 800-322-5250 ■ *Web:* www.triliteinc.com	Chicago	IL	60642	773-384-7765	384-5115
Troy-CSL Lighting Inc 14508 Nelson Ave *TF:* 800-533-8769 ■ *Web:* www.troy-lighting.com	City of Industry	CA	91744	626-336-4511	330-4266
Western Reflections 261 Commerce Way *TF Cust Svc:* 800-507-8302 ■ *Web:* www.western-reflections.com	Gallatin	TN	37066	615-451-9700	452-0283
Wildwood Lamps & Accents 516 Paul St PO Box 672 *Web:* www.wildwoodlamps.com	Rocky Mount	NC	27803	252-446-3266	977-6669
Wilshire Manufacturing Co 645 Myles Standish Blvd *Web:* wilshiremfg.com	Taunton	MA	02780	508-824-1970	

440 LIME

Company	City	State	ZIP	Phone	Fax
Austin White Lime Company Ltd 4900 Howard Ln *Web:* www.austinwhitelime.com	Austin	TX	78728	512-255-3646	
Carmeuse North America 11 Stanwix St 11th Fl *TF:* 866-243-0965 ■ *Web:* www.carmeusena.com	Pittsburgh	PA	15222	412-995-5500	995-5570
Cheney Lime & Cement 478 Graystone Rd PO Box 160 *TF:* 800-752-8282 ■ *Web:* www.cheneylime.com	Allgood	AL	35013	205-625-3031	625-3032
Graymont Inc 10991 Shellbridge Way Ste 200 *TF:* 866-207-4292 ■ *Web:* www.graymont.com	Richmond	BC	V6X3C6	604-276-9331	276-9337
Martin Limestone Inc PO Box 550 **Fax Area Code:* 814 ■ *Web:* www.martinlimestone.com	Blue Bell	PA	17506	717-354-1300	766-0202*
Martin Marietta Materials Inc 2710 Wycliff Rd *NYSE: MLM* ■ *Web:* www.martinmarietta.com	Raleigh	NC	27607	919-781-4550	
Mercer Lime & Stone Co 50 Abele Rd Ste 1006 *Web:* www.mercerlime.com	Bridgeville	PA	15017	412-220-0316	220-0347
Schildberg Construction Co PO Box 358 *Web:* schildberg.com	Greenfield	IA	50849	641-743-2131	
Texas Lime Co 15865 Farm Rd 1434 PO Box 851 *TF:* 800-772-8000 ■ *Web:* uslm.com	Cleburne	TX	76033	817-641-4433	556-0905
US Lime & Minerals Inc 5429 LBJ Fwy Ste 230 *NASDAQ: USLM* ■ *Web:* www.uslm.com	Dallas	TX	75240	972-991-8400	385-1340

441 LIMOUSINE SERVICES

Company	City	State	ZIP	Phone	Fax
Advantage Limousine Services Inc 8310 Castleford St Ste 200 *Web:* www.advantagelimos.com	Houston	TX	77040	713-983-9991	983-9959
Alliance Limousine Inc 14553 Delano St Ste 210 **Fax Area Code:* 818 ■ *TF:* 800-954-5466 ■ *Web:* www.alliancelimo.net	Van Nuys	CA	91411	800-954-5466	786-8810*
American Coach Limousine 1100 Jorie Blvd Ste 314 *TF:* 888-709-5466 ■ *Web:* www.americancoachlimousine.com	Oak Brook	IL	60523	630-629-0001	
American Limousines Inc 4401 E Fairmount Ave *TF:* 800-787-1690 ■ *Web:* www.amerlimo.com	Baltimore	MD	21224	410-522-0400	
Arizona Limousines Inc 8900 N Central Ave Ste 101 *TF:* 800-678-0033 ■ *Web:* www.arizonalimos.com	Phoenix	AZ	85020	602-267-7097	870-3388
Atlantic Services Group Inc 2131 K St NW *Web:* atlanticservicesgroup.com	Washington	DC	20037	202-466-5050	
Bayview Limousine Service 15701 Nelson Pl S **Fax Area Code:* 425 ■ *TF:* 800-606-7880 ■ *Web:* www.bayviewlimo.com	Seattle	WA	98188	206-824-6200	277-5895*
Carey Executive Limousine 245 University Ave **Fax Area Code:* 770 ■ *TF:* 800-241-3943 ■ *Web:* www.careyatlanta.com	Atlanta	GA	30315	404-223-2000	933-9937*
Carey International Inc 4530 Wisconsin Ave NW *TF:* 800-336-4646 ■ *Web:* www.carey.com	Washington	DC	20016	202-895-1200	895-1251
Classic Touch Limousine Inc 908 N Walnut St *Web:* www.classictouchlimo.com	Bloomington	IN	47404	812-339-7269	
Classic Transportation Group 1600 Locust Ave *TF:* 800-291-8090 ■ *Web:* www.classictrans.com	Bohemia	NY	11716	631-567-5100	
Elite Limousine Service Inc 1059 12th Ave Ste E *TF:* 800-776-2098 ■ *Web:* www.elitelimohawaii.com	Honolulu	HI	96816	808-735-2431	735-5159
Gateway Limousines 1550 Gilbreth Rd *TF:* 800-486-7077 ■ *Web:* gatewayglobalsf.com	Burlingame	CA	94010	650-697-5548	
Gold Coast Limousines 3463 State St Ste 408 *Web:* www.goldcoastlimos.com	Santa Barbara	CA	93105	805-966-5466	
Grand Avenue Limousine LLC 460 Metroplex Dr *Web:* www.grandavenuelimo.com	Nashville	TN	37211	615-375-3031	
International Chauffeured Service Worldwide 53 E 34th St **Fax Area Code:* 877 ■ *TF:* 800-266-5254 ■ *Web:* www.bookalimo.com	New York	NY	10016	212-213-0302	266-5254*
Mears Transportation Group 324 W Gore St *TF:* 800-759-5219 ■ *Web:* www.mearstransportation.com	Orlando	FL	32806	407-422-4561	422-6923
Park Cities Limousine 7129 Harry Hines Blvd *TF:* 888-559-0708 ■ *Web:* www.limodfw.com	Dallas	TX	75235	214-824-0011	827-0136
Pontarelli Limousine Service 2225 W Hubbard St *TF:* 800-322-5466 ■ *Web:* www.pontarelliischicago.com	Chicago	IL	60612	312-226-5466	226-1300
R & R Limousine 4403 Kiln Ct *TF:* 800-582-5576 ■ *Web:* www.rrlimo.com	Louisville	KY	40218	502-458-1862	458-3608
Regency Limousine International 83-03 24th Ave *TF:* 866-302-2201 ■ *Web:* www.regencylimo.com	East Elmhurst	NY	11370	718-507-4000	507-8283
Ritz Transportation 4676 Wynn Rd *Web:* www.awgambassador.com	Las Vegas	NV	89103	702-889-4242	
Royal Coachman Worldwide 88 Ford Rd Ste 26 *TF:* 800-472-7433 ■ *Web:* www.royalcoachman.com	Denville	NJ	07834	973-400-3200	675-4365
Starlite Limousines LLC PO Box 13542 **Fax Area Code:* 617 ■ *TF:* 800-875-4104 ■ *Web:* www.starlitelimos.com	Scottsdale	AZ	85267	480-422-3619	671-0522*
SuperShuttle International Inc 14500 N Northsight Blvd Ste 329 *Web:* www.supershuttle.com	Scottsdale	AZ	85260	480-609-3000	
Teddy's Transportation System Inc 25 Van Zant St *TF:* 800-888-3339 ■ *Web:* teddyslimo.com	Norwalk	CT	06855	203-866-2231	
US Coachways Inc 100 St Mary's Ave Ste 2B *TF:* 800-359-5991 ■ *Web:* www.uscoachways.com	Staten Island	NY	10305	718-477-4242	
Wild Goose Storage LLC 2780 W Liberty Rd Ste 2500 *Web:* www.niskapartners.com	Gridley	CA	95948	530-846-7350	
XYZ Two Way Radio Inc 275 20th St *TF:* 800-535-3377 ■ *Web:* xyzcar.com	Brooklyn	NY	11215	718-499-2007	

442 LINEN & UNIFORM SUPPLY

Company	City	State	ZIP	Phone	Fax
Ace ImageWear 4120 Truman Rd *TF:* 800-366-0564 ■ *Web:* www.aceimagewear.com	Kansas City	MO	64127	816-231-5737	231-3550
Ace-Tex Enterprises 7601 Central St *TF:* 800-444-3800 ■ *Web:* www.ace-tex.com	Detroit	MI	48210	313-834-4000	834-0260
Admiral Linen Service Inc 2030 Kipling St *Web:* www.admiralservices.com	Houston	TX	77098	713-529-2608	
AmeriPride Services Inc 10801 Wayzata Blvd *TF Cust Svc:* 800-750-4628 ■ *Web:* www.ameripride.com	Minnetonka	MN	55305	952-738-4200	738-4252
Apparelmaster 123 Harrison Ave *TF:* 877-543-1678 ■ *Web:* companycasuals.com	Harrison	OH	45030	513-202-1600	202-1660
Arrow Uniform Rental Inc 6400 Monroe Blvd *TF:* 888-332-7769 ■ *Web:* www.arrowuniform.com	Taylor	MI	48180	313-299-5000	299-5093
Bates Troy Health Care Linen Supply 151 Laurel Ave *Web:* www.batestroy.com	Binghamton	NY	13905	607-723-5333	
Berkshire Blanket Inc 44 E Main St *Web:* www.berkshireblanket.com	Ware	MA	01082	413-967-5964	
Capitol Uniform & Linen Service 195 Commerce Way *Web:* www.capitollinen.com	Dover	DE	19904	302-674-1511	
Cintas Corp PO Box 625737 *NASDAQ: CTAS* ■ *TF:* 800-786-4367 ■ *Web:* www.cintas.com	Cincinnati	OH	45262	513-459-1200	
Continental Linen Services 4200 Manchester Rd **Fax Area Code:* 269 ■ *TF:* 800-878-4357 ■ *Web:* www.clsimage.com	Kalamazoo	MI	49001	800-878-4357	343-2515*
Coyne Textile Services Inc 140 Cortland Ave	Syracuse	NY	13202	315-475-1626	
David Hughes Custom Linen 14332 Wadkins Ave *Web:* customlinenservice.com	Gardena	CA	90249	310-324-2465	
Domestic Linen Supply & Laundry Co Inc 30555 NW Hwy *TF:* 800-344-3555 ■ *Web:* www.domesticuniform.com	Farmington Hills	MI	48334	248-737-2000	
Faultless Linen 330 W 19th Ter *Web:* www.faultlesslinen.com	Kansas City	MO	64108	816-421-2373	
FDR Services Corp of New Jersey Inc 44 Newmans Ct *Web:* fdrcorp.com	Hempstead	NY	11550	973-977-9300	
Frette North America Inc 850 Third Ave 10th Fl *Web:* www.cifg.com	New York	NY	10022	212-299-0400	
G & K Services Inc 5995 Opus Pkwy Ste 500 *TF:* 800-452-2737 ■ *Web:* www.gkservices.com	Minnetonka	MN	55343	952-912-5500	912-5999
Healthcare Services Group Inc (HCSG) 3220 Tillman Dr Ste 300 *TF:* 800-486-3289 ■ *Web:* www.hcsgcorp.com	Bensalem	PA	19020	215-639-4274	
Hospital Laundry Services Inc (HLS) 45 W Hintz Rd *Web:* www.hlschicago.com	Wheeling	IL	60090	847-941-7000	
Industrial Towel & Uniform Inc 2700 S 160th St *TF:* 800-767-2487 ■ *Web:* www.ituabsorbtech.com	New Berlin	WI	53151	262-782-1950	782-1802
Iron City Uniform Rental 6640 Frankstown Ave *TF:* 800-532-2010 ■ *Web:* www.ironcityuniform.com	Pittsburgh	PA	15206	412-661-2001	661-9356
Knights Apparel Inc 5475 N Blackstone Rd *Web:* futurespark.com	Spartanburg	SC	29303	864-587-9690	
Kobe Sportswear Inc 791 Tapscott Rd *Web:* kobesportswear.com	Scarborough	ON	M1X1A2	416-754-7024	291-0146
Linens of the Week 713 Lamont St NW *Web:* www.linensoftheweek.com	Washington	DC	20010	202-291-9200	
Majestic Athletic Ltd 2320 Newlins Mill Rd *Web:* www.majesticathletic.com	Easton	PA	18045	610-746-6800	
Medical Linen Service Inc 290 S Maple Ave *Web:* www.completelinen.com	South San Francisco	CA	94080	650-873-1221	
Mickey's Linen & Towel Supply 4601 W Addison St *Web:* mickeyslinen.com	Chicago	IL	60641	773-545-7211	545-9111
Model Coverall Service Inc 100 28th St SE *TF:* 800-968-6491 ■ *Web:* www.modelcoverall.com	Grand Rapids	MI	49548	616-241-6491	241-0677
Morgan Linen Service Inc 145 Broadway Menands *Web:* www.morganlinenservice.com	Albany	NY	12204	518-465-3337	
Morgan Services Inc 323 N Michigan Ave *TF:* 888-966-7426 ■ *Web:* www.morganservices.com	Chicago	IL	60601	312-346-3181	346-0144
Overall Laundry Services Inc 7200 HaRdeson Rd	Everett	WA	98203	425-347-0123	
Prudential Overall Supply PO Box 11210 *TF:* 800-767-5536 ■ *Web:* www.prudentialuniforms.com	Santa Ana	CA	92711	949-250-4855	261-1947
Roscoe Co 3535 W Harrison St *TF Cust Svc:* 888-476-7263 ■ *Web:* www.eroscoe.com	Chicago	IL	60624	773-722-5000	722-0827
Service Linen Supply Inc 903 S Fourth St *Web:* www.servicelinen.com	Renton	WA	98057	425-255-8686	
Sitex Corp 1300 Commonwealth Dr *TF:* 800-278-3537 ■ *Web:* www.sitex-corp.com	Henderson	KY	42420	270-827-3537	
Summit Golf Brands Inc 8 W 40th St 2nd Fl *TF:* 800-926-8010 ■ *Web:* www.summitgolfbrands.com	New York	NY	10018	212-302-7255	
Superior Linen Service 1012 S Ctr St *Web:* suplinen.com	Tacoma	WA	98409	253-383-2636	383-1061
Tennier Industries Inc 978 Rt 45 - Northside Plz	Pomona	NY	10970	845-362-0800	

	City	State	ZIP	Phone	Fax
Textile Care Services Inc 225 Wood Lk Dr SE TF: 800-422-0945 ■ Web: www.textilecs.com	Rochester	MN	55904	800-422-0945	
Unitech Services Group 295 Parker St TF: 800-344-3824 ■ Web: www.unitechus.com	Springfield	MA	01151	413-543-6911	543-6989
US Linen & Uniform Inc 1106 Harding St TF: 888-875-4636 ■ Web: www.uslinen.com	Richland	WA	99352	509-946-6125	
Valiant Products Corp 2727 Fifth Ave W TF Cust Svc: 800-347-2727 ■ Web: www.valiantproducts.com	Denver	CO	80204	303-892-1234	
WH Christian & Sons Inc 22 - 28 Franklin St Web: www.whchristian.com	Brooklyn	NY	11222	718-389-7000	389-9644

443 LIQUOR STORES

	City	State	ZIP	Phone	Fax
21st Amendment Inc 1158 W 86th St Web: www.21stamendment.com	Indianapolis	IN	46260	317-846-1678	
ABC Fine Wines & Spirits 8989 S Orange Ave Web: abcfws.com	Orlando	FL	32824	407-851-0000	
Acker Merrall & Condit Company Inc 160 W 72nd St Web: www.ackerwines.com	New York	NY	10023	212-787-1700	
All Star Wine & Spirits 579 Troy Schenectady Rd Web: www.allstarwine.com	Latham	NY	12110	518-220-9463	
B P Lesky Distributing Company Inc 120 Western Maryland Pkwy	Hagerstown	MD	21740	301-733-0787	
B-21 Liquors Inc 43380 US Hwy 19 N Web: b-21.com	Tarpon Springs	FL	34689	727-937-5049	
Berbiglia Inc 1114 W 103 St Web: www.berbiglia.com	Kansas City	MO	64114	816-942-0070	
Bevmax Wines & Liquors 835 E Main St Web: www.bevmax.com	Stamford	CT	06902	203-357-9151	
BevMo! 1401 Willow Pass Rd Ste 900 Web: www.bevmo.com	Concord	CA	94520	925-609-6000	
Big Red Liquors Inc 1110 N College Ave Web: www.bigredliquors.com	Bloomington	IN	47404	812-332-0653	
Bouchaine Vineyards Inc 1075 Buchli Sta Rd Web: www.bouchaine.com	Napa	CA	94559	707-252-9065	
Bowser's Lucky Dog Casino 3140 Dredge Dr Web: orofinogroup.com	Helena	MT	59602	406-442-1555	
Cap n Cork 1031 Broadway Web: www.capncork.com	Fort Wayne	IN	46802	260-423-1496	
Cheers Liquor Mart 1105 N Circle Dr Web: www.cheersliquormart.com	Colorado Springs	CO	80909	719-574-2244	
Chicago Wine Co 835 N Central Ave Web: www.tcwc.com	Wood Dale	IL	60191	630-594-2972	
Clark Distributing Co 1300 Us Hwy 51 Byp S Web: www.clarkdistributingco.com	Dyersburg	TN	38024	731-285-1500	
Colonial Spirits, The 87 Great Rd Web: colonialspirits.com	Acton	MA	01720	978-263-7775	
Consumer'S Beverages Company Inc 2230 S Park Ave Web: consumersbeverages.com	Buffalo	NY	14220	716-893-7040	
Creekside Cellars 28036 Hwy 74 Web: www.creeksidecellars.net	Evergreen	CO	80439	303-674-5460	
Curtis Liquor Stores Inc 790 Chief Justice Cushing Hwy Web: www.curtisliquors.com	Cohasset	MA	02025	781-383-9800	
Druley Enterprises Inc 3305 N Anthony Blvd # 41 Web: www.belmontbev.com	Fort Wayne	IN	46805	260-424-4604	
Dufry Houston Inc 10300 Nw 19th St Ste 114 Web: www.dufry.com	Doral	FL	33172	305-591-1763	
Eagle Brands Inc 3201 NW 72nd Ave Web: www.eaglebrands.com	Miami	FL	33122	305-599-2337	
Eureka Casino Hotel 275 Mesa Blvd Web: www.eurekamesquite.com	Mesquite	NV	89027	702-346-4600	
Ferry Plaza Wine Merchant Administration Offices 101 The Embarcadero TF: 866-991-9400 ■ Web: www.fpwm.com	San Francisco	CA	94105	415-288-0470	
Fine Wine Brokers 4621 N Lincoln Ave	Chicago	IL	60625	773-989-8166	989-8166
Flanigan's Enterprises Inc 5059 NE 18th Ave NYSE: BDL ■ Web: www.flanigans.net	Fort Lauderdale	FL	33334	954-377-1961	
Foppiano Wine Co 12707 Old Redwood Hwy Web: www.foppiano.com	Healdsburg	CA	95448	707-433-7272	
Fox Run Vineyards 670 State Rt 14 TF: 800-636-9786 ■ Web: www.foxrunvineyards.com	Penn Yan	NY	14527	315-536-4616	
Frank Family Vineyards LLC 1091 Larkmead Ln Web: www.frankfamilyvineyards.com	Calistoga	CA	94515	707-942-0859	
Frey Vineyards Winery 14000 Tomki Rd Web: freywine.com	Redwood Valley	CA	95470	707-485-5177	
Gary's Wine & Marketplace 121 Main St Web: www.garyswine.com	Madison	NJ	07940	973-822-0200	
Gold Standard Enterprises Inc 5100 W Dempster St TF: 888-942-9463 ■ Web: www.binnys.com	Skokie	IL	60077	847-674-4200	568-9905
Goody-Goody Liquors Inc 10301 Harry Hines Blvd Web: www.goodygoody.com	Dallas	TX	75220	214-459-9962	
Grape Wine Company of San Antonio Inc, The 1747 Citadel Plz Ste 112	San Antonio	TX	78209	210-828-2222	
Hart Davis Hart Wine Co 363 W Erie St Ste 500W Web: www.hdhwine.com	Chicago	IL	60654	312-482-9996	
Hartwell Vineyards 5815 Silverado Trl Web: www.hartwellvineyards.com	Napa	CA	94558	707-255-4269	
K & L Wine Merchants 855 Harrison St Web: www.klwines.com	San Francisco	CA	94107	415-896-1734	
Kappy s Liquors 325 Bennett Hwy Web: www.kappys.com	Malden	MA	02148	781-321-1000	
Kings Liquor Inc 2810 W Berry St Web: www.kingsliquor.com	Fort Worth	TX	76109	817-923-3737	
L&N Enterprises Inc 5720 Daltry Ln	Colorado Springs	CO	80906	719-576-7925	
Left Bank Wine Co 4910 Triangle St Web: www.leftbankwine.com	Mc Farland	WI	53558	608-838-8400	
Liquor Barn Inc 4301 Towne Ctr Dr Web: www.liquorbarn.com	Louisville	KY	40241	502-426-4222	
Liquor Mart Inc 1750 15th St Web: www.liquormart.com	Boulder	CO	80302	303-449-3374	
Localwineeventscom 2042 General Alexander Dr Web: www.localwineevents.com	Malvern	PA	19355	610-647-4888	
Luna Vineyards Inc 2921 Silverado Trl Web: www.lunavineyards.com	Napa	CA	94558	707-255-5862	
McDonald Oil Company Inc 1700 Lukken Indus Dr W Web: www.mcdonaldoil.com	Lagrange	GA	30240	706-884-6191	
Midwest Aero Support Inc 1303 Turret Dr Web: www.midwestaerosupport.com	Machesney Park	IL	61115	815-398-9202	
Mozingo Liquors Inc 120 S Sixth St	Hartsville	SC	29550	843-332-6554	332-6921
Old World Gourmet Deli & Wine Shop 117 Us Rt 1 Web: www.oldworldgourmet.com	Freeport	ME	04032	207-865-4477	
Owens Liquors Inc 8000 N Kings Hwy Web: owensliquors.com	Myrtle Beach	SC	29572	843-449-6833	
P J Liquor Whse 4898 Broadway Web: www.pjwine.com	New York	NY	10034	212-567-5500	
Patz & Hall Wine Co 851 Napa Vly Corporate Way Ste A TF: 877-265-6700 ■ Web: www.patzhall.com	Napa	CA	94558	707-265-7700	
Pearlstine Distributors Inc (PDI) 1600 Chrlston Rgonal Pkwy TF: 800-922-1048 ■ Web: sc.soeagle.net	Charleston	SC	29492	843-388-6800	388-6799
Pinkie's Inc 1426 E Eigth St Web: www.pinkiestexas.com	Odessa	TX	79761	432-580-0439	580-0918
Rocky Mountain Wine Co 133 Big Horn Dr Web: www.rockymountainwine.com	Kalispell	MT	59901	406-752-9463	
Saratoga Liquor Company Inc 3215 James Day Ave TF: 800-472-6923 ■ Web: www.saratogaliquor.com	Superior	WI	54880	715-394-4487	
Shafer Vineyards 6154 Silverado Trl Web: www.shafervineyards.com	Napa	CA	94558	707-944-2877	
Sherry-Lehmann Wine & Spirits 505 Pk Ave Web: www.sherry-lehmann.com	New York	NY	10022	212-838-7500	838-9285
Shop 'N Save Liquors 20 Independence Ave Web: shopnsaveliquors.com	Quincy	MA	02169	617-773-2060	786-9797
Sigel's Beverages LP 2960 Anode Ln Web: www.sigels.com	Dallas	TX	75220	214-350-1271	357-3490
Spec's Wines Spirits & Finer Foods 2410 Smith St TF: 888-526-8787 ■ Web: www.specsonline.com	Houston	TX	77006	713-526-8787	526-6129
State Liquor Store 15015 Main St Ste 117 Web: www.liq.wa.gov	Bellevue	WA	98007	360-664-1600	
Touring & Tasting 125 S Quarantina St TF: 800-850-4370 ■ Web: www.touringandtasting.com	Santa Barbara	CA	93103	805-965-2813	965-2873
Twin Liquors Lp 5639 Airport Blvd Web: twinliquors.com	Austin	TX	78751	512-222-0700	
United Package Liquors Inc 6350 Rucker Rd Ste 105 Web: www.unitedpackageliquors.com	Indianapolis	IN	46220	317-205-9266	
Vintage Wines 2277 Westbrooke Dr Web: www.vintwine.com	Columbus	OH	43228	614-876-2580	
Wally's Wine & Spirits 2107 Westwood Blvd Web: www.wallywine.com	Los Angeles	CA	90025	310-475-0606	
Westchester Wine Warehouse 53 Tarrytown Rd Web: www.westchesterwine.com	White Plains	NY	10607	914-824-1400	
Wiederkehr Wine Cellars Inc 3324 Swiss Family Dr TF: 800-622-9463 ■ Web: www.wiederkehrwines.com	Altus	AR	72821	479-468-3551	
Willow Park Wines & Spirits Ltd 10801 Bonaventure Dr SE Web: www.willowpark.net	Calgary	AB	T2J6Z8	403-296-1640	
Wine Cask Inc, The 407 Washington St Web: thewineandcheesecask.com	Somerville	MA	02143	617-623-8656	
Wine Club, The 1431 S Village Way TF: 800-966-5432 ■ Web: www.thewineclub.com	Santa Ana	CA	92705	714-835-6485	
Wine of The Month Club Inc 907 S Magnolia Ave Web: wineofthemonthclub.com	Monrovia	CA	91016	626-303-1690	
Wine.com Inc 114 Sansome St 3rd Fl TF: 800-592-5870 ■ Web: www.wine.com	San Francisco	CA	94104	415-291-9500	248-4400
WineShop At Home 525 Airpark Rd TF: 800-946-3746 ■ Web: www.wineshopathome.com	Napa	CA	94558	707-253-0200	
Zachys Wine & Liquor Inc 16 E Pkwy TF: 800-723-0241 ■ Web: www.zachys.com	Scarsdale	NY	10583	914-723-0241	723-1033

444 LITERARY AGENTS

	City	State	ZIP	Phone	Fax
Aaron M Priest Literary Agency 200 W 41st St 21st Fl Web: aaronpriest.com	New York	NY	10036	212-818-0344	573-9417
Browne & Miller Literary Assoc LLC 410 S Michigan Ave Ste 460 Web: www.browneandmiller.com	Chicago	IL	60605	312-922-3063	
David Black Agency 335 Adams St Ste 2707 Web: www.davidblackagency.com	Brooklyn	NY	11201	718-852-5500	852-5539

Phone | Fax

Dominick Abel Literary Agency Inc
146 W 82nd St Ste 1A ... New York NY 10024 212-877-0710
Web: dalainc.com

Don Congdon Assoc Inc
110 William St Ste 2202 ... New York NY 10038 212-727-2688 727-2688
Web: www.doncongdon.com

Donadio & Olsen Inc 40 W 27th St 5th Fl ... New York NY 10001 212-691-8077
Web: donadio.com

Dystel & Goderich Literary Management
1 Union Sq W Ste 904 ... New York NY 10003 212-627-9100 627-9313
Web: www.dystel.com

Frances Collin Literary Agent PO Box 33 ... Wayne PA 19087 610-254-0555 254-5029
Web: www.francescollin.com

George Borchardt Inc 136 E 57th St ... New York NY 10022 212-753-5785
Web: gbagency.com

Harold Ober Assoc Inc
425 Madison Ave Ste 1001 ... New York NY 10017 212-759-8600 759-9428
Web: www.haroldober.com

Harvey Klinger Inc 300 W 55th St ... New York NY 10019 212-581-7068
Web: www.harveyklinger.com

InkWell Management 521 Fifth Ave Ste 2600 ... New York NY 10175 212-922-3500 922-0535
Web: www.inkwellmanagement.com

Jane Rotrosen Agency 318 E 51st St ... New York NY 10022 212-593-4330 935-6985
Web: janerotrosen.com

Jean V Naggar Literary Agency Inc
216 E 75th St Ste 1E ... New York NY 10021 212-794-1082
Web: www.jvnla.com

Larsen Pomada Literary Agents
1029 Jones St ... San Francisco CA 94109 415-673-0939
Web: www.larsenpomada.com

Lowenstein-Yost Assoc Inc
121 W 27th St Ste 501 ... New York NY 10001 212-206-1630 727-0280
Web: www.lowensteinassociates.com

Manus & Assoc Literary Agency Inc
425 Sherman Ave Ste 200 ... Palo Alto CA 94306 650-470-5151 470-5159
Web: www.manuslit.com

Richard Curtis Assoc Inc
171 E 74th St 2nd Fl ... New York NY 10021 212-772-7363
Web: www.curtisagency.com

Sanford J Greenburger Assoc Inc
55 Fifth Ave ... New York NY 10003 212-206-5600 463-8718
Web: www.greenburger.com

Trident Media Group LLC
41 Madison Ave 36th Fl ... New York NY 10010 212-333-1511
Web: www.tridentmediagroup.com

Wallace Literary Agencies Inc
301 E 79th St Ste 14-J ... New York NY 10075 212-570-9090 772-8979

William Morris Agency
1325 Ave of the Americas ... New York NY 10019 212-586-5100 246-3583
Web: www.wma.com

Writers House 21 W 26th St ... New York NY 10010 212-685-2400
Web: www.writershouse.com

445 LITIGATION SUPPORT SERVICES

Phone | Fax

Al Betz & Assoc Inc 125 Airport Dr Ste 30 ... Westminster MD 21157 410-875-3376 875-2857
TF: 877-402-3376 ■ *Web:* www.albetzreporting.com

Alderson Reporting Co
1155 Connecticut Ave NW Ste 200 ... Washington DC 20036 202-289-2260 289-2221
TF: 800-367-3376 ■ *Web:* www.aldersonreporting.com

Allen and Kimbell Llp
317 E Carrillo St ... Santa Barbara CA 93101 805-963-8611
Web: www.aklaw.net

Allen Norton & Blue P A
121 Majorca Ave 3rd Fl ... Coral Gables FL 33134 305-445-7801
Web: www.anblaw.com

Allied Court Reporters Inc 115 Phenix Ave ... Cranston RI 02920 401-946-5500 946-9228
TF: 888-443-3767 ■ *Web:* www.alliedcourtreporters.com

Allman Spry Davis Leggett & Crumpler
380 Knollwood St Ste 700 ... Winston-salem NC 27103 910-722-2300
Web: www.allmanspry.com

Alterman & Boop Llp 35 Worth St Fl 3 ... New York NY 10013 212-226-2800
Web: www.altermanandboop.com

Arhm f
2525 Ponce De Leon Blvd PO Box 1225 ... Coral Gables FL 33134 305-779-3560
Web: arhmf.com

Arnstein & Lehr LLP
120 S Riverside Plz Ste 1200 ... Chicago IL 60606 312-876-7100
Web: www.arnstein.com

Atkinson-Baker Inc (ABI)
500 N Brand Blvd 3rd Fl ... Glendale CA 91203 818-551-7300
TF: 800-288-3376 ■ *Web:* www.depo.com

Attorneys at Law Vandeventer Black Llp
6 Juniper Trl ... Kitty Hawk NC 27949 252-261-5055
Web: www.vanblk.com

Avante Solutions Inc 728 W Jackson Ste 105 ... Chicago IL 60661 312-715-1080
Web: www.avantesolutions.com

Axley Brynelson LLP
Manchester Pl 2 E Mifflin St Ste ... Madison WI 53703 608-257-5661
Web: www.axley.com

Bachus & Schanker LLC
123 N College Ave Ste 211 ... Fort Collins CO 80524 970-223-9802
Web: coloradolaw.net

Baker Sterchi Cowden Rice Llc
1010 Market St Ste 950 ... Saint Louis MO 63101 314-231-2925
Web: bscr-law.com

Bakke Norman 1200 Heritage Dr ... New Richmond WI 54017 715-246-3800
Web: www.bakkenorman.com

Bartko Zankel Tarrant & Miller
900 Frnt St Ste 300 ... San Francisco CA 94111 415-956-1900
Web: www.bztm.com

Phone | Fax

Beard St Clair Gaffney PA
2105 Coronado St ... Idaho Falls ID 83404 208-523-5171
Web: www.beardstclair.com

Beck and Tysver Pllc
2900 Thomas Ave S Ste 100 ... Minneapolis MN 55416 612-915-9633
Web: bitlaw.com

Beggs & Lane 3 W Garden St 7th Fl ... Pensacola FL 32501 850-432-2451
Web: www.beggslane.com

Benefit Recovery Inc
665 Oakleaf Office Ln 2nd Fl ... Memphis TN 38117 901-380-4949
Web: www.benefitrecoveryinc.com

Berger Singerman PA
350 E Las Olas Blvd Ste 1000 ... Fort Lauderdale FL 33301 954-525-9900
Web: www.bergersingerman.com

Bergeson LLP 303 Almaden Blvd Ste 500 ... San Jose CA 95110 408-291-6200
Web: be-law.com

Berkshire & Blunk 1010 S 120th St Ste 220 ... Omaha NE 68154 402-827-7000
Web: www.berkshire-law.com

Betts Patterson & Mines P S
1 Convention Pl 701 Pk St Ste 1400 ... Seattle WA 98101 206-292-9988
Web: bpmlaw.com

Black McCuskey Souers & Arbaugh
1000 United Bank Plz 220 Mkt Av S ... Canton OH 44702 330-456-8341
Web: bmsa.com

Blitman & King Llp 16 Main St W Ste 500 ... Rochester NY 14614 585-232-5600
Web: www.bklawyers.com

Block Landsman 11 S La Salle St Ste 1600 ... Chicago IL 60603 312-251-1144
Web: www.block-landsman.com

Board of Overseers of The Bar 97 Winthrop St ... Augusta ME 04330 207-623-1121
Web: mebaroverseers.org

Bocarsly Emden Cowan Esmail & Arndt LLP
633 W Fifth St 70th Fl ... Los Angeles CA 90071 213-239-8000
Web: bocarslyemden.com

Boccardo Law Firm Inc, The
111 W Saint John St Ste 400 ... San Jose CA 95113 800-662-9807
TF: 800-662-9807 ■ *Web:* www.boccardo.com

Braff Harris & Sukoneck 305 Broadway Fl 7 ... New York NY 10007 212-822-1478
Web: bhs-law.com

Brent Adams & Associates 119 Lucknow Sq ... Dunn NC 28334 910-892-8177
Web: brentadams.com

Brian Loncar & Associates P c
1104 Travis St ... Wichita Falls TX 76301 877-239-4878
TF: 877-239-4878 ■ *Web:* www.brianloncar.com

Brooks Stevens & Pope P A
5121 Kingdom Way Ste 300 ... Raleigh NC 27607 919-481-9103
Web: www.bsp-pa.com

Brown Greer PLC 115 S 15th St Ste 400 ... Richmond VA 23219 804-521-7200
Web: browngreer.com

Brown Hay & Stephens PO Box 2459 ... Springfield IL 62705 217-544-8491
Web: www.bhslaw.com

Browning Kaleczyc Berry and Hoven P C
800 N Last Chance Gulch Ste 101 ... Helena MT 59601 406-443-6820
Web: www.bkbh.com

Bruneau Group 390 Rideau St ... Ottawa ON K1N9P4 613-562-3646
Web: www.bruneaugroup.com

Brunini
190 E Capitol St The Pinnacle Bldg Ste 100 ... Jackson MS 39201 601-948-3101
Web: www.brunini.com

Burton Neil & Associates
1060 Andrew Dr Ste 160 ... West Chester PA 19380 610-696-2120
Web: www.attorneys-network.com

Cadden & Fuller LLP 114 Pacifica Ste 450 ... Irvine CA 92618 949-788-0827
Web: caddenfuller.com

Callister & Reynolds 823 Las Vegas Blvd S ... Las Vegas NV 89101 702-385-3343
Web: reynoldslawyers.com

Cameron & Mittleman LLP 56 Exchange Ter ... Providence RI 02903 401-331-5700
Web: www.cm-law.com

Caplan and Earnest LLC 1800 Broadway Ste 200 ... Boulder CO 80302 303-443-8010
Web: www.celaw.com

Caraway Watson 307 W 7th St Ste 1000 ... Fort Worth TX 76102 817-870-1717
Web: watsoncaraway.com

Carson Boxberger LLP
301 W Jefferson Blvd Ste 200 ... Fort Wayne IN 46802 260-423-9411
Web: www.carsonboxberger.com

Chace Ruttenberg & Freedman LLP
Wayland Bldg 1 Park Row Ste 300 ... Providence RI 02903 401-453-6400
Web: www.crfllp.com

Chu Ring & Hazel 241 A St Ste 300 ... Boston MA 02210 617-443-9800
Web: www.chu-ring.com

Clayton Environmental Services Inc
808 Walker St ... Columbia TN 38401 931-388-6806
Web: www.claytonenvironmental.com

Cline Williams Wright Johnson & Oldfather L L P
1900 U.S.Bank Bldg 233 S 13th St ... Lincoln NE 68508 402-474-6900
Web: www.clinewilliams.com

Cochran Davis & Associates P C
36 Malaga Cove Plz Palos Verdes Estates
Ste 206 ... California CA 90274 310-373-0900
Web: cochranlaw1.com

Cochran Foley & Associates
15510 Farmington Rd ... Livonia MI 48154 734-425-2400
Web: www.cochranfoley.com

Cohen Placitella & Roth P C
2 Commerce Sq 2001 Market St Ste 2900 ... Philadelphia PA 19103 215-567-3500
Web: www.cprlaw.com

Cohne Rappaport & Segal P C
257 East 200 South Ste 700 ... Salt Lake City UT 84111 801-532-2666
Web: www.crslaw.com

Coleman Sudol Sapone P C 714 Colorado Ave ... Bridgeport CT 06605 203-366-3560
Web: www.patentassets.com

Collen IP Intellectual Property Law P C
80 S Highland Ave ... Ossining NY 10562 914-941-5484
Web: www.collenlaw.com

	City	State	Zip	Phone	Fax
Collins Law Firm P C, The 1770 N Park St Ste 202 *Web:* www.collinslaw.com	Naperville	IL	60563	630-527-1595	
Columbia Legal Services 6 S 2nd St Ste 510 *Web:* www.columbialegal.org	Yakima	WA	98901	509-575-5593	
Common Source LP, The 14500 N Fwy *Web:* www.commonsource.com	Houston	TX	77090	281-260-9220	
Compex Legal Services Inc 325 S Maple Ave *TF Cust Svc:* 800-426-6739 ■ *Web:* www.cpxlegal.com	Torrance	CA	90503	800-426-6739	479-3365
Condon & Forsyth Llp 7 Times Sq 18th Fl *Web:* www.condonlaw.com	New York	NY	10036	212-490-9100	
Conner & Winters 3700 First Pl Tower 15 E Fifth St *Web:* www.cwlaw.com	Tulsa	OK	74103	918-586-5711	
Copeland & Bieger P C 212 W Valley St *Web:* www.copelandbieger.com	Abingdon	VA	24212	276-628-9525	
Courtroom Sciences Inc 4950 N O'Connor Rd *TF:* 800-514-5879 ■ *Web:* www.courtroomsciences.com	Irving	TX	75062	972-717-1773	717-3985
Couzens Lansky Fealk Ellis & Lazar P C 39395 Twelve Mile Rd Ste 200 *Web:* www.couzens.com	Farmington Hills	MI	48331	248-489-8600	
Crary Buchanan Bowdish Bovie Beres Elder & 555 S Colorado Ave Ste 1 *Web:* www.crarybuchanan.com	Stuart	FL	34994	772-287-2600	
Creative Dispute Resolutions LLC 211 Little Quarry Rd *Web:* creativedisputeresolutions.com	Gaithersburg	MD	20878	301-977-8002	
Crosby & Rowell Llp 299 3rd St Fl 2 *Web:* crosbyrowell.com	Oakland	CA	94607	510-267-0300	
Crowe & Dunlevy 20 N Broadway Ave # 1800 20 N Broadway *Web:* www.crowedunlevy.com	Oklahoma City	OK	73102	405-235-7700	
Dalton & Finegold L L P 34 Essex St *Web:* www.dfllp.com	Andover	MA	01810	978-470-8400	
Damon & Morey LLP 298 Main St 1000 Cathedral Pl *Web:* www.damonmorey.com	Buffalo	NY	14202	716-856-5500	
David Robert Ellis pa 275 Clearwater Largo Rd N *Web:* davidellispa.com	Largo	FL	33770	727-518-6544	
Davis Miles P L L C 1550 E McKellips Rd Ste 101 *Web:* www.davismiles.com	Mesa	AZ	85203	480-733-6800	
De Beaubien Knight Simmons Mantzaris & Neal LLP 332 N Magnolia Ave *Web:* www.dbksmn.com	Orlando	FL	32801	407-422-2454	
DecisionQuest 21535 Hawthorne Blvd Ste 310 *TF:* 877-833-2474 ■ *Web:* www.decisionquest.com	Torrance	CA	90503	310-618-9600	618-1122
Defender Association of Philadelphia 1441 Sansom St 12th Fl *Web:* www.philadefender.org	Philadelphia	PA	19102	215-568-3190	
Denton Navarro Rocha & Bernal 2517 N Main Ave *Web:* www.rampage-rgv.com	San Antonio	TX	78212	210-227-3243	
Depobook Reporting Services 1600 G St Ste 101 *TF:* 800-830-8885 ■ *Web:* www.depobook.com	Modesto	CA	95354	209-544-6466	544-6566
DepoNet 2700 Centennial Tower 101 Marietta St 101 Marietta St *Web:* www.esquiresolutions.com	Atlanta	GA	30303	404-495-0777	
Depot Law Office Plc 222 W Apple St Ste 248 *Web:* www.depotlawoffice.com	Hastings	MI	49058	269-945-9557	
Derfner Altman & Wilborn Llc 575 King St Ste B *Web:* www.dawlegal.com	Charleston	SC	29403	843-723-9804	
Deters Benzinger & LaVelle P S C 207 Thomas More Pkwy *Web:* www.dbllaw.com	Crestview Hills	KY	41017	859-341-1881	
Devine Millimet & Branch 111 Amherst St *Web:* www.devinemillimet.com	Manchester	NH	03105	603-669-1000	
Dickie McCamey & Chilcote PC 2 Ppg Pl Ste 400 *Web:* dmclaw.com	Pittsburgh	PA	15222	412-281-7272	
Dixon Howell Westmoreland & Newman Attys 924 Westwood Blvd Ste 850 *Web:* dhwnlaw.com	Los Angeles	CA	90024	310-208-4666	
DOAR Litigation Consulting 170 Earle Ave *TF:* 800-875-8705 ■ *Web:* www.doar.com	Lynbrook	NY	11563	516-823-4000	
Dordick Gary Atty 509 S Beverly Dr *Web:* www.dordicklaw.com	Beverly Hills	CA	90212	310-551-0948	
Douglas & London P C 59 Maiden Ln Fl 6 *TF:* 888-596-9790 ■ *Web:* www.douglasandlondon.com	New York	NY	10038	888-596-9790	
Dowling Aaron Inc 8080 N Palm Ave Third Fl *Web:* bctconsulting.com	Fresno	CA	93711	559-432-4500	
Doyle Quane 571 Hartz Ave *Web:* www.familylawgroup.com	Danville	CA	94526	925-314-2320	
Drew Eckl & Farnham LLP 880 W Peachtree St *Web:* www.deflaw.com	Atlanta	GA	30357	404-885-1400	
Duke Law Firm Pc 1572 Montgomery Hwy Ste 205 *Web:* www.dukelawpc.com	Vestavia Hills	AL	35216	205-823-3900	
E J Leizerman and Associates Llc 717 Madison Ave *Web:* www.leizerman.com	Toledo	OH	43624	419-243-1010	
E3 Communications Inc 43 Ct St Ste 910 *Web:* www.e3communications.com	Buffalo	NY	14202	716-854-8182	
Elias Matz Tiernan & Herrick The Walker Bldg 734 15th St NW 11th Fl *Web:* www.emth.com	Washington	DC	20005	202-347-0300	
Eric Buchanan & Associates Pllc 414 Mccallie Ave *TF:* 877-634-2506 ■ *Web:* www.buchanandisability.com	Chattanooga	TN	37402	877-634-2506	
Esanu Katsky Korins & Siger 605 Third Ave *Web:* www.ekks.com/	New York	NY	10158	212-953-6000	
Esseks Hefter & Angel 108 E Main St *Web:* www.ehalaw.com	Riverhead	NY	11901	631-726-6633	
Fay Sharpe Fagan Minnich & Mckee Llp 1228 Euclid Ave Ste 500 *Web:* www.faysharpe.com	Cleveland	OH	44115	216-861-5582	
Fee Smith Sharp & Vitullo L L P 3 Galleria Tower 13155 Noel Rd Ste 1000 *Web:* www.feesmith.com	Dallas	TX	75240	972-934-9100	
Feingold & Kam 3300 P G A Blvd Ste 410 *Web:* www.fkhearttoheart.net	Palm Beach	FL	33410	561-630-6727	
Fonda & Fraser LLP Watt Plz 1925 Century Park E Ste 1380 *Web:* www.fondafraserlaw.com	Los Angeles	CA	90067	310-553-3320	
Forman Holt Eliades & Ravin LLC 218 State 17 N *Web:* www.formanlaw.com	Rochelle Park	NJ	07662	201-845-1000	
Frantz McConnell & Seymour LLP 550 Main Ave Ste 500 *Web:* www.fmsllp.com	Knoxville	TN	37902	865-546-9321	
FTI Consulting 909 Commerce Rd Ste 1400 *NYSE: FCN* ■ *TF:* 800-334-5701 ■ *Web:* www.fticonsulting.com	Annapolis	MD	21401	410-224-8770	224-9740
Gardner Linn Burkhart & Flory Llp 2851 Charlevoix Dr Se Ste 207 *Web:* vglb.com	Grand Rapids	MI	49546	616-975-5500	
Garlington Lohn Robinson PLLP 350 Ryman St *Web:* www.garlington.com	Missoula	MT	59802	406-523-2500	
Gerner & Kearns Co L P A 335 E 3rd St *Web:* gernerlaw.com	Newport	KY	41071	513-241-7722	
Gibbons & Conley 1333 N California Blvd Ste 110 *Web:* gibbons-conley.com	Walnut Creek	CA	94596	925-932-3600	
Gieger Laborde & Laperouse L L C 1 Shell Sq 701 Poydras St Ste 4800 *Web:* glllaw.com	New Orleans	LA	70139	504-561-0400	
Gilbert & Barnhill pa 503 Belle Hall Pkwy Unit 101 *Web:* gilbertbarnhill.publishpath.com	Mount Pleasant	SC	29464	843-856-9227	
Glast Phillips & Murray 2200 One Galleria Tower 13355 Noel Rd L.B. 48 *Web:* www.glastphillips.com	Dallas	TX	75240	972-419-8300	
Golan & Christie LLP 3 1st National Plz 70 W Madison St Ste 1500 *Web:* www.golanchristie.com	Chicago	IL	60602	312-263-2300	
Goldberg & Osborne 4423 E Thomas Rd Ste 3 *Web:* 1800theeagle.com	Phoenix	AZ	85018	602-808-6200	
Golding Holden & Pope Llp 6701 Carmel Rd Ste 105 *Web:* ghplaw.net	Charlotte	NC	28226	704-374-1600	
Good Wildman Hegness & Walley 5000 Campus Dr *Web:* www.goodwildman.com	Newport Beach	CA	92660	714-833-0633	
Gordon & Silver Ltd 3960 Howard Hughes Pkwy 9th Fl *Web:* www.gordonsilver.com	Las Vegas	NV	89169	702-796-5555	
Gordonderr Llp 2025 1st Ave Ste 500 *Web:* www.gordonderr.com	Seattle	WA	98121	206-382-9540	
Greenberg & Lieberman 314 Philadelphia Ave *Web:* www.aplegal.com	Takoma Park	MD	20912	202-625-7000	
Greenblatt & Laube Pc 200 N 8th St *Web:* greenblattlaube.com	Vineland	NJ	08360	856-691-0424	
Greene & Schermer 1301 6th Ave W Ste 505 *Web:* www.manateelegal.com	Bradenton	FL	34205	941-747-3025	
Greene Espel P L L P 200 S Sixth St Ste 1200 *Web:* www.greene-espel.com	Minneapolis	MN	55402	612-373-0830	
Greenspan Humphrey Lavine Barristers 15 Bedford Rd *Web:* www.15bedford.com	Toronto	ON	M5R2J7	416-868-1755	
Grefe & Sidney P L C 500 W Ct Ave Ste 200 *Web:* www.grefesidney.com	Des Moines	IA	50309	515-245-4300	
Gunderson Palmer Nelson & Ashmore LLP 440 Mount Rushmore Rd *Web:* www.gundersonpalmer.com	Rapid City	SD	57709	605-342-1078	
Habush Habush & Rottier S C US Bank Ctr 777 E Wisconsin Ave Ste 2300 *Web:* habush.com	Milwaukee	WI	53202	414-271-0900	
Hack Piro O'Day Merklinger Wallace & McKenna P A 30 Columbia Tpke *Web:* www.hackpiro.com	Florham Park	NJ	07932	973-301-6500	
Hahn & Bowersock Corp 151 Kalmus Dr Ste L1 **Fax Area Code: 714* ■ *TF:* 800-660-3187 ■ *Web:* www.hahnbowersock.com	Costa Mesa	CA	92626	800-660-3187	662-1398*
Hahn Loeser & Parks LLP 3300 BP Tower 200 Public Sq *Web:* www.hahnloeser.com	Cleveland	OH	44114	216-621-0150	
Hallett & Perrin PC 717 Harwood St Ste 1400 *Web:* www.hallettperrin.com	Dallas	TX	75201	214-922-4132	
Halloran & Sage Llp 1 Goodwin Sq *Web:* halloransage.com	Hartford	CT	06103	860-522-6103	
Harris Beach LLP 99 Garnsey Rd 130 E Main St *Web:* www.harrisbeach.com	Pittsford	NY	14534	585-232-4440	
Hart King & Coldren 200 Sandpointe Ave Ste 400 *Web:* www.hartkinglaw.com	Santa Ana	CA	92707	714-432-8700	
Head Johnson & Kachigian Pc 228 W 17th Pl *Web:* www.hjklaw.com	Tulsa	OK	74119	918-587-2000	
Hecht Solberg Robinson Goldberg & Bagley LLP 1 America Plz 600 W Broadway Ste 800 *Web:* www.hechtsolberg.com	San Diego	CA	92101	619-239-3444	
Heidman Redmond Fredregill Po Box 3086 *Web:* www.heidmanlaw.com	Sioux City	IA	51101	712-255-8838	
HeplerBroom LLC 800 Market St Ste 2300 *Web:* www.heplerbroom.com	St Louis	MO	63101	314-241-6160	

Listing	City	State	ZIP	Phone	Fax
Herrling Clark Hartzheim & Siddall Ltd 800 N Lynndale Dr *Web:* www.herrlingclark.com	Appleton	WI	54914	920-739-7366	
High Swartz Roberts & Seidel 40 E Airy St *Web:* www.highswartz.com	Norristown	PA	19404	610-275-2823	
Hill & Ponton pa 444 Seabreeze Blvd Ste 235 *Web:* www.hillandponton.com	Daytona Beach	FL	32118	386-257-2100	
Hobbs Straus Dean and Walker 117 Park Ave Ste 200 *Web:* hsdwlaw.com	Oklahoma City	OK	73102	405-602-9425	
Hochberg d Peter Co Lpa Patent Attys 1940 E 6th St Ste 600 *Web:* www.dpeterhochberg.com	Cleveland	OH	44114	216-771-3800	
Horn 1600 Steeles Ave W Ste 412 *Web:* www.horn.com	Concord	ON	L4K4M2	905-761-8000	
Hunt & Faherty 40 Delaware Ave. *Web:* hunt-faherty.hub.biz	Lambertville	NJ	08530	609-397-0900	
Hurth Yeager Sisk & Blakemore Llp 4860 Riverbend Rd Ste 2 *Web:* hurth.com	Boulder	CO	80301	303-443-7900	
Hyatt & Weber P A 7 Savings Bank Bldg 200 Westgate Cir Ste 500 *Web:* www.hwlaw.com	Annapolis	MD	21401	410-266-0626	
Jackson & Campbell 1 Lafayette Ctr 1120 20th St NW *Web:* www.jackscamp.com	Washington	DC	20036	202-457-1600	
Jane Rose Reporting 80 Fifth Ave *TF:* 800-825-3341 ■ *Web:* www.janerose.net/janeroseflash.swf	New York	NY	10011	212-727-7773	
Johnson & Mock Attorneys at Law 307 N Oakland Ave *Web:* www.johnsonandmock.com	Oakland	NE	68045	402-685-5647	
Johnstone Adams Bailey Gordon & Harris L L C 1 St Louis St 4th Fl *Web:* www.johnstoneadams.com	Mobile	AL	36602	251-432-7682	
Jordan Schrader Attorneys at Law 2 Ctrpointe Dr Fl 6th *Web:* www.jordanramis.com	Lake Oswego	OR	97035	503-598-7070	
Jury Research Institute 2617 Danville Blvd PO Box 100 *TF:* 800-233-5879 ■ *Web:* www.juryresearchinstitute.com	Alamo	CA	94507	925-932-5663	932-8409
Kaye Rose & Partners Llp 1801 Century Park E Ste 1500 *Web:* www.kayerose.com	Los Angeles	CA	90067	310-551-6555	
Keith d Weiner & Associates Co Lpa 75 Public Sq Ste 400 *Web:* www.weinerlaw.com	Cleveland	OH	44113	216-771-6500	
Kevin Ahrenholz Law Firm 620 Lafayette St Ste 300 *Web:* beecherlaw.com	Waterloo	IA	50703	319-433-0754	
Kitchin Neal Webb Webb & Futrell pa Attys 111 E Washington St *Web:* kitchinlaw.com	Rockingham	NC	28379	910-997-2206	
Korein Tillery LLC 505 N Seveth St Ste 3600 *Web:* www.koreintillery.com	Saint Louis	MO	63101	314-241-4844	
Kucker & Bruh Llp 747 Third Ave *Web:* kbllp.com	New York	NY	10017	212-869-5030	
LA Law Library 301 301 W. First St *Web:* www.lalawlibrary.org	Los Angeles	CA	90012	213-785-2529	
Lake & Cobb Plc 1095 W Rio Salado Pkwy Ste 206 *Web:* www.lakeandcobb.com	Tempe	AZ	85281	480-619-4900	
Larkin Hoffman Daly & Lindgren Ltd 1500 Wells Fargo Plz 7900 Xerxes Ave S *Web:* www.lhdl.com	Bloomington	MN	55431	952-835-3800	
Larzelere Picou Wells Simpson Lonero LLC 2 Lkway Ctr 3850 N Causeway Blvd Ste 1100 *Web:* lpwsl.com	Metairie	LA	70002	504-834-6500	
Lastrapes Spangler & Pacheco 333 Rio Rancho Dr Ne Ste 401 *Web:* www.lsplegal.com	Rio Rancho	NM	87174	505-892-3607	
Lauralee G Westine pa 800 Tarpon Woods Blvd Ste E1 *Web:* lauraleewestine.com	Palm Harbor	FL	34685	727-773-2221	
Lawyers Aid Service Inc 408 W 17th St Ofc 101 *Web:* lawyersaidservice.com	Austin	TX	78701	512-474-2002	
Lawyers Group Advertising Inc 631 S 10th St *Web:* lawyersgroup.com	Las Vegas	NV	89101	702-382-5613	
Lazega Law 13499 Biscayne Blvd Ste 107 *Web:* lazegalaw.com	North Miami	FL	33181	754-263-4252	
Leader & Berkon Llp 630 3rd Ave Fl 17 *Web:* www.leaderberkon.com	New York	NY	10017	212-486-2400	
Leech Tishman Fuscaldo & Lampl LLC Citizens Bank Bldg, 525 William Penn Pl 30th Fl *Web:* www.leechtishman.com	Pittsburgh	PA	15219	412-261-1600	
Legal Aid of West Virginia Inc 327 9th St *Web:* www.wvlegalservices.org	Parkersburg	WV	26101	304-485-7522	
Legal Cost Control Inc 255 Kings Hwy E Ste 3 *Web:* legalcost.com	Haddonfield	NJ	08033	856-216-0800	
Leitner Williams Dooley & Napolitan PLLC 801 Broad St 3rd Fl *Web:* www.leitnerfirm.com	Chattanooga	TN	37402	423-265-0214	
Levene Gouldin & Thompson Llp 450 Plz Dr *Web:* www.lgtllp.com	Vestal	NY	13850	607-763-9200	
Levinson Axelrod 2 Lincoln Ct *Web:* njlawyers.com	Tinton Falls	NJ	07712	732-709-5803	
Lewis Rice & Fingersh L C 500 N Broadway Ste 2000 *Web:* www.lewisrice.com	St. Louis	MO	63102	314-444-7600	
Lombardi Loper & Conant LLP Lk Merritt Plz 1999 Harrison St Ste 2600 *Web:* llcllp.com	Oakland	CA	94612	510-433-2600	
London Fischer Llp 59 Maiden Ln Fl 41 *Web:* www.londonfischer.com	New York	NY	10038	212-972-1000	
Londrigan Potter & Randle P c 1227 S 7th St *Web:* lprpc.com	Springfield	IL	62703	217-544-9823	
Lowe Hauptman Ham & Berner LLP 2318 Mill Rd Ste 1400 *Web:* www.ipfirm.com	Alexandria	VA	22314	703-684-1111	
Lugg and Lugg Law Offices 350 E Water St Box 905 *Web:* lugglaw.com	Lock Haven	PA	17745	570-748-2481	
Lyons Doughty & Veldhuis P c 15 Ashley Pl Ste 2b *Web:* www.ldvlaw.com	Wilmington	DE	19804	302-428-1670	
MacMillan Sobanski & Todd LLC 1 Maritime Plz 720 Water St 5th Fl *Web:* www.mstfirm.com	Toledo	OH	43604	419-255-5900	
Martin & Kieklak Law Firm 2059 N Green Acres Rd *Web:* www.martinlawpartners.com	Fayetteville	AR	72703	479-442-2244	
Mc Donnell Boehnen Hulbert and 1136 Water St Ste 101 *Web:* www.mbhb.com	Port Townsend	WA	98368	360-379-6514	
Mccarthy Smith Law Group 550 W Centre Ave Ste 2 *Web:* wnj.com	Portage	MI	49024	269-488-6330	
McConnell Valdes 270 Munz Rivera Ave *Web:* www.mcvpr.com	Hato Rey	PR	00918	787-759-9292	
McGuire Craddock & Strother P C 3550 Lincoln Plz 500 N Akard St Ste 3550 *Web:* www.mcslaw.com	Dallas	TX	75201	214-954-6800	
Meister Seelig & Fein LLP 125 Park Ave 7th Fl *Web:* www.meisterseelig.com	New York	NY	10017	212-655-3500	
Michael J O'Connor & Associates LLC 608 W Oak St *Web:* www.oconnorlaw.com	Frackville	PA	17931	570-874-3300	
Middleton & Reutlinger 2500 Brown & Williamson Tower *Web:* www.middreut.com	Louisville	KY	40202	502-584-1135	
Mika Meyers Beckett & Jones PLC 900 Monroe Ave Nw *Web:* www.mmbjlaw.com	Grand Rapids	MI	49503	616-632-8000	
Milber Makris Plousadis & Seiden 244 Westchester Ave Ste *Web:* milbermakris.com	White Plains	NY	10604	914-681-8710	
Miles & Stockbridge P C 10 Light St 9th Fl *Web:* www.milesstockbridge.com	Baltimore	MD	21202	410-727-6464	
Miller Morton Caillat & Nevis LLP 25 Metro Dr 7th Fl *Web:* www.millermorton.com	San Jose	CA	95110	408-292-1765	
Morrow Romine & Pearson Pc Atty 122 S Hull St *Web:* www.mrplaw.com	Montgomery	AL	36104	334-262-7707	
Mulvaney Kahan & Barry 401 W A St Fl 17 *Web:* mkblaw.com	San Diego	CA	92101	619-238-1010	
Nathanson & Co 10 Minute Man Hl *Web:* nathansonandcompany.com	Westport	CT	06880	203-227-1816	
Neider & Boucher S C 440 Science Dr *Web:* neiderboucher.com	Madison	WI	53705	608-661-4500	
Nelson Levine de Luca & Hamilton LLC 518 E Township Line Rd Ste 300 *Web:* www.nldhlaw.com	Blue Bell	PA	19422	215-358-5100	
New Mexico Legal Aid 301 Gold Ave Sw Ste 101 *Web:* www.nmlegalaid.org	Albuquerque	NM	87102	505-243-7871	
Newby Pridgen Sartip & Masel Llc 4593 Oleander Dr Ste 100 *Web:* www.newbylaw.com	Myrtle Beach	SC	29577	843-449-9417	
Nexsen Pruet LLC 1230 Main St Ste 700 *Web:* www.nexsenpruet.com	Columbia	SC	29201	803-771-8900	
Norris Injury Lawyers Pc 10 Old Montgomery Hwy Ste 250 *Web:* www.norrisinjurylawyers.com	Birmingham	AL	35209	205-870-8000	
North Penn Legal Services 507 Linden St Ste 300 *Web:* northpennlegal.org	Scranton	PA	18503	570-342-0184	
Novus Law LLC 8770 W Bryn Mawr Ave *TF:* 877-668-8752 ■ *Web:* www.novuslaw.com	Chicago	IL	60631	877-668-8752	
Onder Shelton O'Leary & Peterson LLC 110 E Lockwood Ave *Web:* www.onderlaw.com	Saint Louis	MO	63119	314-963-9000	
Patterson Dilthey Clay Bryson & Anderson LLP 4020 Westchase Blvd *Web:* www.pattersondilthey.com	Raleigh	NC	27607	919-821-4020	
Paul Hanley & Harley Llp 1608 Fourth St Ste 300 *Web:* www.thepaullawfirm.com	Berkeley	CA	94710	510-559-9980	
Perrier & Lacoste L L C 1 Canal Pl 365 Canal St Ste 2550 *Web:* www.perrierlacoste.com	New Orleans	LA	70130	504-212-8820	
Poling Law Offices 101 Ramey Ct *Web:* www.poling-law.com	Beckley	WV	25801	304-255-0191	
Porter Rogers Dahlman & Gordon P C 1 Shoreline Plz 800 N Shoreline Ste 800 S *Web:* www.prdg.com	Corpus Christi	TX	78401	361-880-5808	
Primmer & Piper P C 52 Summer St *Web:* www.primmer.com	St. Johnsbury	VT	05819	802-748-5061	
Priority 1 Consulting 42 Fairview Ln *Web:* www.p1cgroup.com	Plymouth	MA	02360	508-224-5128	

				Phone	Fax
Professional Shorthand Reporters Inc (PSR) 601 Poydras St Ste 1615 *TF:* 800-536-5255 ■ *Web:* www.psrdepo.com	New Orleans	LA	70130	504-529-5255	
Provest Llc 6155 Rockside Rd Ste 402 *Web:* www.provest.us	Cleveland	OH	44131	216-328-0005	
Pure Vegetarian 1110 N Old World 3rd St Ste 600 *Web:* insurancesystems.on.ca	Milwaukee	WI	53203	414-271-7873	
R C Mc Lean & Assoc Inc 210 N Tustin Ave *Web:* www.rcmclean.com	Santa Ana	CA	92705	714-347-1000	
R Rex Parris Law Firm 42220 10th St W Ste 109 *Web:* rrexparris.com	Lancaster	CA	93534	661-272-1445	
Rabinovitz & Associates Pc Attys 721 N 4th Ave Ste 201 *Web:* uits.arizona.edu	Tucson	AZ	85705	520-624-5526	
Ralph Rosenberg Court Reporters Inc 1001 Bishop St Ste 2460 *TF:* 888-524-5888 ■ *Web:* www.hawaiicourtreporters.com	Honolulu	HI	96813	888-524-5888	
Ramey Chandler Quinn & Zito 1 Bering Park 750 Bering Dr Ste 600 *Web:* www.ramey-chandler.com	Houston	TX	77057	713-266-0074	
Randall & Danskin P S 1500 Bank Of America Financial Ctr 60 W Riverside *Web:* www.randalldanskin.com	Spokane	WA	99201	509-747-2052	
Ray Quinney & Nebeker 36 S State St Ste 1400 *Web:* www.rqn.com	Salt Lake City	UT	84111	801-532-1500	
Raymond L Robinson Law Office 1501 Venera Ave Ste 300 *Web:* www.rrobinsonlaw.com	Miami	FL	33146	305-662-7618	
Reed & Agee Law Firm 3633 26th St W *Web:* www.reidagee.com	Bradenton	FL	34205	941-753-9971	
Rees Morrison Associates 4 Hawthorne Ave Ste 2A *Web:* www.reesmorrison.com	Princeton	NJ	08540	973-568-9110	
Rembolt Ludtke LLP 1201 Lincoln Mall Ste 102 *Web:* www.remlud.com	Lincoln	NE	68508	402-475-5100	
Rhoads & Sinon LLP allfirst Bank Bldg, One S Market Sq 12th Fl *Web:* www.rhoads-sinon.com	Harrisburg	PA	17108	717-233-5731	
Robert Allen Law 1441 Brickell Ave Ste 1400 *Web:* www.robertallenlaw.com	Miami	FL	33131	305-372-3300	
Romano Law Offices & Associates 5 Irving St *Web:* romanoandromano.com	Worcester	MA	01609	508-791-8255	
Rubin Licatesi PC 600 Old Cntry Rd Ste 440 *Web:* www.lawyerintl.com	Garden City	NY	11530	718-712-6864	
Salon Marrow Dyckman Newman & Broudy LLP 685 3rd Ave *Web:* www.salonmarrow.com	New York	NY	10017	212-661-7100	
Schmeiser Olsen & Watts Llp 18 E University Dr Ste 101 *Web:* iplawusa.com	Mesa	AZ	85201	480-655-0073	
Schroeter Goldmark & Bender Ps 810 3rd Ave *Web:* sgb-law.com	Seattle	WA	98104	206-622-8000	
Schwabe Williamson & Wyatt Pacwest Ctr 1211 S.W. Fifth Ave Stes 1600-1900 Ste *Web:* www.schwabe.com	Portland	OR	97204	503-222-9981	
Schwartz Levitsky Feldman Ch A 2300 Yonge St Ste 1500 PO Box 2434 *Web:* www.slf.ca	Toronto	ON	M4P1E4	416-785-5353	
Scott Marcus & Associates 121 Johnson Rd Ste 1 *Web:* www.marcuslaw.net	Blackwood	NJ	08012	856-227-0800	
Shawe & Rosenthal LLP 1 S St Ste 1800 *Web:* www.shawe.com	Baltimore	MD	21202	410-752-1040	
Sherrard & Roe PLC 424 Church St Ste 2000 *Web:* sherrardroe.com	Nashville	TN	37219	615-742-4200	
Shimokaji & Associates Pc 8911 Research Dr *Web:* www.shimokaji.com	Irvine	CA	92618	949-788-9961	
Simmons Firm LLC, The 230 W Monroe Ste 2221 *Web:* www.simmonsfirm.com	Chicago	IL	60606	314-518-9911	
Spesia Ayers & Ardaugh 116 N Chicago St Ste 200 *Web:* www.spesia-ayers.com	Joliet	IL	60432	815-726-4311	
Stabinski and Funt pa 757 Nw 27th Ave Fl 3 *Web:* www.stabinski-funt.com	Miami	FL	33125	305-643-1382	
Stahancyk Kent & Hook P C Duniway Plz 2400 SW 4th Ave *TF:* 877-673-7632 ■ *Web:* www.stahancyk.com	Portland	OR	97201	877-673-7632	
Starr Litigation Services Inc 1201 Grand Ave	West Des Moines	IA	50265	515-224-1616	
Stockton & Rickman Llc 191 S Main St *Web:* pacga.org	Clayton	GA	30525	706-782-6100	
Strassburger Mckenna Gutnick & Gefsky 525 3rd St *Web:* www.smgglaw.com	Beaver	PA	15009	724-846-1372	
Stubbs & Perdue P A Two Hannover Sq Ste 1630 *Web:* www.stubbsperdue.com	Raleigh	NC	27602	919-856-9400	
Swartz Campbell LLC 300 Delaware Ave Ste 1410 *Web:* www.swartzcampbell.com	Wilmington	DE	19801	215-564-5190	
Synergy Law Group LLC 730 W Randolph St Ste 600 *Web:* synergylawgroup.com	Chicago	IL	60661	312-454-0292	
Taft Stettinius & Hollister LLP 1800 Firstar Tower 425 Walnut St *Web:* www.taftlaw.com	Cincinnati	OH	45202	513-381-2838	
Tashlik Kreutzer Goldwyn & Crandell P C 40 Cuttermill Rd Ste 200 *Web:* tgcllaw.com	Great Neck	NY	11021	516-466-8005	
Teich Groh & Frost 691 Hwy 33 *Web:* www.teichgroh.com	Trenton	NJ	08619	609-890-1500	
Teschner Law Firm LLC 145 King St Ste 411 *Web:* charlestontaxlaw.com	Charleston	SC	29401	843-937-0027	
Tharrington Smith LLP 150 Fayetteville St Wells Fargo Bldg Ste 1800 *Web:* www.tharringtonsmith.com	Raleigh	NC	27601	919-821-4711	
Thomason Hendrix Harvey Johnson & Mitchell Pllc 40 S Main St Ste 2900 *Web:* www.thomason-hendrix.com	Memphis	TN	38103	901-525-8721	
Trial Behavior Consulting Inc 505 Sansome St Ste 1701 *Web:* www.trialbehavior.com	San Francisco	CA	94111	415-781-5879	
Trilogy Studios Inc 5200 Lankershim Blvd Ste 830 *Web:* www.trilogystudios.com	North Hollywood	CA	91601	818-901-9960	
Tueth-keeney Cooper Mohan Jackstadt Pc 101 W Vandalia St Ste 210 *Web:* www.tuethkeeney.com	Edwardsville	IL	62025	618-692-4120	
Underberg & Kessler LLP 1800 Chase Sq *Web:* underbergkessler.com	Rochester	NY	14604	585-258-2800	
US Legal Support Inc 363 N Sam Houston Pkwy E Ste 900 *TF:* 800-567-8757 ■ *Web:* www.uslegalsupport.com	Houston	TX	77060	713-653-7100	653-7171
Vantage Solutions Llc 350 N La Salle Dr Ste 1122 *Web:* vantage-solutions.com	Chicago	IL	60654	312-440-0602	
Veritext LLC 290 W Mt Pleasant Ave Ste 3200 **Fax Area Code:* 973 ■ *TF:* 800-567-8658 ■ *Web:* www.veritext.com	Livingston	NJ	07039	800-567-8658	410-1313*
Vermont Legal Aid Inc 177 Western Ave Ste 1 *Web:* www.vtlegalaid.org	St Johnsbury	VT	05819	802-748-8721	
VoIPLINK Corp 3029 S Harbor Blvd *Web:* www.voiplink.com	Santa Ana	CA	92704	760-918-9100	
Walshin Martin Inc 70 Saw Mill River Rd *Web:* www.walshin.com	Hastings On Hudson	NY	10706	914-478-4300	
Wapnick and Alverado 6383 Arizona Cir *Web:* www.courtcall.com	Los Angeles	CA	90045	310-342-0888	
Ward Anderson Porritt & Bryant Plc 4190 Telegraph Rd Ste 2300 *Web:* www.wardanderson.com	Bloomfield Hills	MI	48302	248-593-1440	
Warren John m 700 Grand Ave Ste 14 *Web:* warren-john-m.hub.biz	Ridgefield	NJ	07657	816-232-7702	
Waterfall Economidis Caldwell Hanshaw & Villamana P C Williams Ctr 5210 E Williams Cir Ste 800 *Web:* www.wechv.com	Tucson	AZ	85711	520-790-5828	
Watkins & Eager PLLC The Emporium Bldg 400 E Capitol St Ste 300 *Web:* www.watkinseager.com	Jackson	MS	39201	601-948-6470	
Weissman Nowack Curry & Wilco 1 Alliance Ctr 3500 Lenox Rd 4th Fl *Web:* www.wncwlaw.com	Atlanta	GA	30326	404-926-4500	
Weldon Huston & Keyser L L P 28 Park Ave W Bank One Bldg *Web:* www.whkmansfield.com	Mansfield	OH	44902	419-524-9811	
Wilbraham Lawler & Buba 603 Stanwix St Ste 1725 *Web:* www.wlbdeflaw.com	Pittsburgh	PA	15222	412-255-0500	
Wilkes & McHugh P A 1 N Dale Mabry Hwy Ste 800 *TF:* 800-255-5070 ■ *Web:* www.wilkesmchugh.com	Tampa	FL	33609	800-255-5070	
Wimberly Lawson Seale Wright & Daves Pllc 929 W 1st N St *Web:* www.wlswd.com	Morristown	TN	37814	423-587-6870	
Wingfield J e & Associates Pc 700 5th St Nw Ste 300 *Web:* jewingfield.com	Washington	DC	20001	202-789-8000	
Winne Banta Hetherington & Basralian P C Ct Plz N 25 Main St PO Box 647 *Web:* www.winnebanta.com	Hackensack	NJ	07602	201-487-3800	
Wishart Norris Henninger & Pittman P A 6832 Morrison Blvd *Web:* www.wnhplaw.com	Charlotte	NC	28211	704-364-0010	
Woodard Emhardt Moriarty McNett & Henry LLP 111 Monument Cir Ste 3700 *Web:* www.uspatent.com	Indianapolis	IN	46204	317-634-3456	
Wyche Burgess Freeman & Parham 44 E.Camperdown Wy *Web:* www.wyche.com	Greenville	SC	29601	864-242-8200	
Zabel Freeman 1135 Heights Blvd *Web:* zabelfreeman.com	Houston	TX	77008	713-802-9117	
Zeisler & Zeisler P C 558 Clinton Ave *Web:* www.zeislaw.com	Bridgeport	CT	06604	203-368-4234	
Zeldes Needle and Cooper 1000 Lafayette Blvd *Web:* www.znclaw.com	Bridgeport	CT	06601	203-333-9441	
Zimmer Kunz PLLC 310 Grant St Ste 3000 *Web:* zklaw.com	Pittsburgh	PA	15219	412-281-8000	
Zisser Customs Law Group Pc 2297 Niels Bohr Ct Ste 114 *Web:* www.zissergroup.com	San Diego	CA	92154	619-671-0376	

446 LIVESTOCK - WHOL

See Also Cattle Ranches, Farms, Feedlots (Beef Cattle) p. 1715; Hog Farms p. 1716

				Phone	Fax
101 Livestock Market Inc 4400 Hwy 101 *Web:* www.101livestock.com	Aromas	CA	95004	831-726-3303	

Phone | Fax

Adams Cattle LLC 327 S First Ave Broken Bow NE 68822 308-872-6494
Web: www.adamslandandcattle.com

Alabama Livestock Auction Inc Hwy 80 E Uniontown AL 36786 334-628-2371 628-6268
Web: www.allivestock.com

All West Select Sires 450 N Hill Blvd Burlington WA 98233 800-426-2697
TF: 800-426-2697 ■ *Web:* www.allwestselectsires.com

Bales Continental Commission Co
39763 US Hwy 14 PO Box 1337 Huron SD 57350 605-352-8682
Web: www.balesccc.com

Billings Livestock Commission Co
2443 N Frontage Rd Billings MT 59101 406-245-4151
Web: www.billingslivestock.com

Blackfoot Livestock Auction 93 Rich Ln Blackfoot ID 83221 208-785-0500
Web: www.blackfootlivestockauction.com

Blue Grass Stockyard
375 Lisle Industrial Ave PO Box 1023 Lexington KY 40588 859-255-7701 255-5495
TF: 800-621-3972 ■ *Web:* www.bgstockyards.com

Cattle Empire LLC 1174 Empire Cir Satanta KS 67870 620-649-2235
Web: www.cattle-empire.net

Circle X Land & Cattle Company Ltd
3131 Briarcrest Dr Ste 220 Bryan TX 77802 979-776-5760 776-4818
Web: www.bre.com

D & S Cattle Co 2167 FL-66 Zolfo Springs FL 33890 863-735-1112 735-1282

Delta Sales Yard Inc 700 W Fifth St Delta CO 81416 970-874-4612 874-3087
Web: www.deltasalesyard.com

Empire Livestock Marketing LLC
5001 Brittonfield Pkwy East Syracuse NY 13057 315-433-9129 433-0068
TF: 800-462-8802 ■ *Web:* www.empirelivestock.com

Equity Co-op Livestock Sales Assn
401 Commerce Ave Baraboo WI 53913 608-356-8311 356-0117
TF: 800-362-3989 ■ *Web:* www.equitycoop.com

Farmers Livestock Auction Inc
1581 E Emma Ave Springdale AR 72764 479-751-5727 751-5896

Finger Lakes Livestock Exchange Inc
3865 Rts 5 & 20 Geneva Tpke Canandaigua NY 14424 585-394-1515 394-9151
Web: www.fingerlakeslivestockex.com

Four States Livestock Sales
501 E First St Hagerstown MD 21740 301-733-8120 733-7318
Web: fourstateslivestocksales.com

High Plains Livestock Exchange LLC
28601 US Hwy 34 Brush CO 80723 970-842-5115 842-5088
TF: 866-842-5115 ■ *Web:* www.hplivestock.com

Houston Livestock Show & Rodeo Inc
NRG Ctr Three NRG Park Houston TX 77054 832-667-1000
Web: www.rodeohouston.com

Jamestown Livestock Auction
3443 82nd Ave SE Jamestown ND 58401 701-252-2111 252-1520
Web: www.jamestownlivestock.com

Keeneland Association Inc
4201 Versailles Rd Lexington KY 40510 859-254-3412
Web: www.keeneland.com

Kidron Auction Inc 4885 Kidron Rd Kidron OH 44636 330-857-2641 698-3088
Web: kidronauction.com

Lewiston Sales Inc
21241 Dutchmans Crossing Rd Lewiston MN 55952 507-523-2112 523-2400
TF: 800-732-6334 ■ *Web:* www.lewistonsales.com

Lexington Livestock Market Inc
300 Plum Creek Pkwy Lexington NE 68850 308-324-4663
Web: www.lexlivestock.com

Lynch Livestock Co 331 Third St NW Waucoma IA 52171 563-776-3311
TF: 800-468-3178 ■ *Web:* www.lynchlivestock.com

Midwest Land & Cattle Company Inc
503 N Mur-Len Rd Olathe KS 66062 913-782-6677

Midwest Livestock Systems Inc
3600 N Sixth St Beatrice NE 68310 402-223-5281
Web: www.midwestlivestock.com

Miller Livestock Markets Inc
100 Sale Barn Rd Dequincy LA 70633 337-786-2995 786-3270
Web: millerlivestockinc.com

National Commission Assn
2501 Exchange Ave Ste 102 Oklahoma City OK 73108 405-232-3128
Web: www.nationallivestock.com

O & S Cattle Co 100 StockyaRds Rd South Saint Paul MN 55075 651-455-5459 455-8394

Overland Stockyard Inc 10565 Ninth Ave Hanford CA 93230 559-582-0404
Web: www.overlandstockyard.com

Pipestone Livestock Auction Market
1500 Seventh St SE Pipestone MN 56164 507-825-3306
Web: www.pipestonelivestock.com

Prairie Livestock LLC
2139 Barton Ferry Rd PO Box 636 West Point MS 39773 662-494-5651
TF: 800-647-6350 ■ *Web:* www.prairielivestock.net

Producers Livestock Auction Co
1131 N Bell St San Angelo TX 76903 325-653-3371 653-3370
Web: www.producersandcargile.com

Producers Livestock Marketing Assn
4809 S 114th St Omaha NE 68137 402-597-9189 597-9505
TF: 800-257-4046 ■ *Web:* producerslivestock.net

Roswell Livestock Auction Sales Inc
900 N Garden PO Box 2041 Roswell NM 88202 575-622-5580
TF: 800-748-1541 ■ *Web:* www.roswelllivestockauction.com

San Antonio Livestock Exposition Inc
PO Box 200230 San Antonio TX 78220 210-225-0575
Web: www.sarodeo.com

Sheridan Livestock Auction Company Inc
Sale Barn Rd Rushville NE 69360 308-327-2406
Web: sheridanlivestock.com

Stockmen's Livestock Market Inc
1200 E Hwy 50 PO Box 528 Yankton SD 57078 605-665-9641 665-9644
Web: stockmenslivestock.com

Topeka Livestock Auction 601 E Lake St Topeka IN 46571 260-593-2522 593-2258
Web: topekalivestock.com

Turner County Stockyard 1315 US Hwy 41 S Ashburn GA 31714 229-567-3371 567-3785
TF: 800-344-9808 ■ *Web:* turnercountystockyard.com

United Producers Inc 8351 N High St Ste 250 Columbus OH 43235 800-456-3276
TF: 800-456-3276 ■ *Web:* www.uproducers.com

Wayland Hopkins Livestock 3634 Tenth St Wayland MI 49348 269-792-2296 792-8055

Winner Livestock Auction Co
31690 Livestock Barn Rd Winner SD 57580 605-842-0451 842-3562
TF: 800-201-0451 ■ *Web:* www.winnerlivestock.com

Winter Livestock Inc PO Box 909 PO Box 909 Enid OK 73702 580-237-4600 237-4604
Web: www.winterlivestock.com

447 LIVESTOCK & POULTRY FEEDS - PREPARED

Phone | Fax

AC Nutrition 158 N Main St Winters TX 79567 325-754-4546 754-4546
TF: 800-588-3333 ■ *Web:* www.acnutrition.com

ADM Alliance Nutrition Inc 1000 N 30th St Quincy IL 62301 217-222-7100
TF: 800-292-3333 ■ *Web:* www.admani.com

AG Partners Inc 512 S Eigth St PO Box 467 Lake City MN 55041 651-345-3328
TF: 800-772-2990 ■ *Web:* agpartners.net

Ag Processing Inc 12700 W Dodge Rd PO Box 2047 Omaha NE 68103 402-496-7809
TF: 800-247-1345 ■ *Web:* www.agp.com

Agri-King Inc 18246 Waller Rd Fulton IL 61252 815-589-2525
TF: 800-435-9560 ■ *Web:* www.agriking.com

Ahrberg Milling Co 200 S Depot St PO Box 968 Cushing OK 74023 918-225-0267 225-0275
TF: 800-324-0267 ■ *Web:* www.ahrbergmilling.com

AL Gilbert Co 304 N Yosemite Ave Oakdale CA 95361 209-847-1721
Web: farmerswarehouse.com

Alabama Farmers Co-op Inc PO Box 2227 Decatur AL 35601 256-353-6843 350-1770
TF: 888-255-2667 ■ *Web:* www.alafarm.com

Albion Laboratories Inc 101 N Main St Clearfield UT 84015 801-773-4631 773-4633
TF: 800-453-2406 ■ *Web:* www.albionminerals.com

American Proteins Inc 4705 Leland Dr Cumming GA 30041 770-886-2250 886-2296
Web: www.americanproteins.com

Bagdad Roller Mills Inc 5740 Elmburg Rd Bagdad KY 40003 502-747-8968
TF: 800-928-3333 ■ *Web:* www.bagdadrollermillsfeed.com

Belstra Milling Company Inc 424 15th St Demotte IN 46310 800-276-2789 987-5227*
**Fax Area Code: 219* ■ *TF:* 800-276-2789 ■ *Web:* www.belstramilling.com

BioZyme Inc 6010 Stockyards Expy Saint Joseph MO 64504 816-238-3326 238-7549
TF: 800-821-3070 ■ *Web:* www.biozymeinc.com

Blue Seal Feeds Inc 2905 US Hwy 61 N Muscatine IA 52761 866-647-1212
TF Cust Svc: 866-647-1212 ■ *Web:* www.blueseal.com

Buckeye Nutrition 330 E Schultz Ave Dalton OH 44618 800-417-6460
TF: 800-417-6460 ■ *Web:* www.buckeyenutrition.com

Central AG Services 209 N Bridge St Clarissa MN 56440 218-756-2112 756-2451

Circle S Ranch Inc 1604 Cir S Ranch Rd Monroe NC 28112 704-764-7414 764-7646

Cumberland Valley Co-op Assn
908 Mt Rock Rd Shippensburg PA 17257 717-532-2197
TF: 800-488-2197 ■ *Web:* agmap.psu.edu

Cutler-Dickerson Company Inc 507 College Ave Adrian MI 49221 517-265-5191 263-4213
Web: cutlerdickerson.com

D & D Commodities Ltd PO Box 359 Stephen MN 56757 800-543-3308 478-3533*
**Fax Area Code: 218* ■ *TF:* 800-543-3308 ■ *Web:* www.ddcommodities.com

Dairymen's Feed & Supply Co
323 E Washington St Petaluma CA 94952 707-763-1585 763-5239

Darling International Inc
251 O'Connor Ridge Blvd Ste 300 Irving TX 75038 972-717-0300
NYSE: DAR ■ *TF:* 855-327-7761 ■ *Web:* www.darlingii.com

DeKalb Feeds Inc 105 Dixon Ave Rock Falls IL 61071 815-625-4546
Web: dekalbfeeds.com

Diamond V Mills Inc PO Box 74570 Cedar Rapids IA 52407 319-366-0745
TF: 800-373-7234 ■ *Web:* www.diamondv.com

Eagle Roller Mill Co 1101 Airport Rd Shelby NC 28150 704-487-5061 482-1263
TF: 800-223-9108 ■ *Web:* www.eaglerollermill.com

Effingham Equity Inc 201 W Roadway Ave Effingham IL 62401 217-342-4101 347-7601
TF: 800-223-1337 ■ *Web:* theequity.com

Elenbaas Co 411 W Front St Sumas WA 98295 360-988-5811 988-0411
TF: 800-808-6954 ■ *Web:* www.elenbaasco.com

Farmers Co-op Elevator Co
177 W Main St PO Box 108 Cottonwood MN 56229 507-423-5412 423-5551
Web: www.farmerscoopelevator.com

Farmers Co-op Elevator Co
109 Isabella St PO Box 200 Radcliffe IA 50230 515-899-2101 899-2105
Web: www.radcliffecoop.com

Farmers Union Co-op 1913 Co Rd B32 Ossian IA 52161 563-532-9381 532-9389

Feed Products Inc 1000 W 47th Ave Denver CO 80211 303-455-3646 477-6206

First Co-op Assn (FCA)
960 Riverview Dr PO Box 60 Cherokee IA 51012 712-225-5400 225-5493
TF: 877-753-5400 ■ *Web:* www.firstcoop.com

FL Emmert Co Inc 2007 Dunlap St Cincinnati OH 45214 513-721-5808 721-6087
TF: 800-441-3343 ■ *Web:* www.emmert.com

Flint River Mills Inc 1100 Dothan Rd Bainbridge GA 39817 229-246-2232
TF Cust Svc: 800-841-8502 ■ *Web:* frmfeeds.com

FM Brown's Sons Inc
205 Woodrow Ave PO Box 2116 Sinking Spring PA 19608 610-678-4567 678-7023
TF: 800-334-8816 ■ *Web:* www.fmbrown.com

Form-A-Feed Inc (FAF) 740 Bowman St Stewart MN 55385 320-562-2413
TF: 800-422-3649 ■ *Web:* www.formafeed.com

Franklin Feed & Supply Co
1977 Philadelphia Ave Chambersburg PA 17201 717-264-6148 264-7865
Web: franklinhardwareandpetcenter.com

Friona Industries LP
500 S Taylor St Ste 601 Amarillo TX 79101 806-374-1811 374-1324
TF: 800-658-6014 ■ *Web:* www.frionaind.com

Furst-McNess Co 120 E Clark St Freeport IL 61032 815-235-6151 232-9724
TF: 800-435-5100 ■ *Web:* www.mcness.com

Goldsboro Milling Co 938 Millers Chapel Rd Goldsboro NC 27534 919-778-3130
Web: cals.ncsu.edu

Harvest Land Co-op 711 Front St PO Box 278 Morgan MN 56266 507-249-3196
TF: 800-245-5819 ■ *Web:* www.harvestland.com

Hog Slat 315 S Sycamore St Flora IN 46929 574-967-3776
TF: 800-949-4647 ■ *Web:* www.hogslat.com

Hubbard Feeds Inc 111 W Cherry St Ste 500 Mankato MN 56001 507-388-9400
TF: 800-869-7219 ■ *Web:* www.hubbardfeeds.com

Phone Fax

Hunt & Behrens Inc 30 Lakeville St .... Petaluma CA 94952 707-762-4594 762-9164
Web: hbfeeds.com

International Ingredient Corp
150 Larkin Williams Industrial Ct
PO Box 26377 .... Fenton MO 63026 636-343-4111 349-4845
Web: www.iicag.com

JBS United Inc 4310 State Rd 38 W .... Sheridan IN 46069 317-758-4495
TF: 800-382-9909 ■ *Web:* www.jbsunited.com

JD Heiskell & Co 116 W Cedar St.................. Tulare CA 93274 559-685-6100 686-8697
TF: 800-366-1886 ■ *Web:* www.heiskell.com

John A Van Den Bosch Co 4511 Holland Ave........... Holland MI 49424 800-968-6477
TF: 800-968-6477 ■ *Web:* www.vbosch.com

Kay Dee Feed Company Inc 1919 Grand Ave......... Sioux City IA 51106 712-277-2011
TF Cust Svc: 800-831-4815 ■ *Web:* kaydeefeed.com

Keith Smith Company Inc
130 K-Tech Ln PO Box 3800 .... Hot Springs AR 71914 501-760-0100 760-9199
Web: www.keith-smith.com

Kemin Industries Inc 2100 Maury St............... Des Moines IA 50317 515-559-5100 559-5232
TF: 800-777-8307 ■ *Web:* www.kemin.com

Lakeland Animal Nutrition 2801 S Combee Rd .... Lakeland FL 33803 863-665-5722 686-9427

Land O'Lakes Inc Western Feed Div
4001 Lexington Ave N .... Arden Hills MN 55126 800-328-9680
TF: 800-328-9680 ■ *Web:* www.landolakesinc.com

Lucta USA Inc
Pine Meadow Corporate Ctr 950 Technology Way
Ste 110.................................... Libertyville IL 60048 847-996-3400
Web: www.lucta.com

Manna Pro Corp
707 Spirit 40 Pk Dr Ste 150 .... Chesterfield MO 63005 800-690-9908
TF: 800-690-9908 ■ *Web:* www.mannapro.com

Mark Hershey Farms Inc 479 Horseshoe Pk........... Lebanon PA 17042 717-867-4624 867-4313
TF: 888-801-3301 ■ *Web:* www.markhersheyfarms.com

Merrick's Inc 2415 Parview Rd PO Box 620307........ Middleton WI 53562 608-831-3440 836-8943
TF: 800-637-7425 ■ *Web:* www.merricks.com

MFA Inc 201 Ray Young Dr.......................... Columbia MO 65201 573-874-5111 876-5505
Web: www.mfaincorporated.com

Milk Specialties Co
7500 Flying Cloud Dr Ste 500 .... Eden Prairie MN 55344 952-942-7310
TF: 800-323-4274 ■ *Web:* www.milkspecialties.com

Moroni Feed Co 15 East 1900 South.................. Moroni UT 84646 435-436-8225 436-8101

Mountaire Corp PO Box 1320......................... Millsboro DE 19966 302-934-1100
TF: 877-887-1490 ■ *Web:* www.mountaire.com

Mountaire Farms of North Carolina
203 Morris Farm Rd.................................. Candor NC 27229 910-974-3232
Web: mountaire.com

Moyer & Son Inc 113 E Reliance Rd .... Souderton PA 18964 215-799-2000
TF: 866-669-3747 ■ *Web:* www.emoyer.com

NRV Inc N8155 American St.......................... Ixonia WI 53036 920-261-7000 261-1685
TF: 800-558-0002 ■ *Web:* nrvmilk.com

Oberbeck Grain Co 700 Walnut St .... Highland IL 62249 618-654-2387 654-5862
TF: 800-632-2012 ■ *Web:* www.oberbeckgrainco.com

OMCO Inc 214 E Mill St .... Odon IN 47562 812-636-7362 636-4777
TF: 800-525-0272 ■ *Web:* marketplaceindiana.com

Pennfield Corp 2260 Erin Ct PO Box 4366 .... Lancaster PA 17601 717-299-2561 295-8766

Pied Piper Mills Inc 423 E Lake Dr .... Hamlin TX 79520 325-576-3684 576-3460

Preble Feed & Grain Inc 6035 N 400 W .... Preble IN 46782 260-547-4452
Web: kentfeeds.com

Prince Agri Products Inc 229 Radio Rd .... Quincy IL 62306 217-222-8854 222-5098
Web: www.princeagri.com

Prince Minerals 21 W 46th St 14th Fl .... New York NY 10036 646-747-4222
Web: www.princeminerals.com

Producers Co-op Assoc 300 E Buffalo St .... Girard KS 66743 620-724-8241
TF: 800-442-2809 ■ *Web:* www.girardcoop.com

Provimi North America Inc
10 Collective Way.............................. Brookville OH 45309 937-770-2400
TF: 888-522-2420 ■ *Web:* www.provimi-na.com

Quali Tech Inc 318 Lake Hazeltine Dr .... Chaska MN 55318 952-448-5151 448-3603
TF: 800-328-5870 ■ *Web:* www.qualitechco.com

Ragland Mills Inc 14079 Hammer Rd................... Neosho MO 64850 417-451-2510
Web: www.raglandmills.com

Ralco Nutrition Inc 1600 Hahn Rd.................. Marshall MN 56258 800-533-5306 532-5740*
**Fax Area Code:* 507 ■ *TF:* 800-533-5306 ■ *Web:* www.ralconutrition.com

Rangen Inc 115 13th Ave S .... Buhl ID 83316 208-543-6421 543-6090
TF Cust Svc: 800-657-6446 ■ *Web:* www.rangen.com

Seminole Feed 335 NE Watula Ave PO Box 940.......... Ocala FL 34470 352-732-4143
TF: 800-683-1881 ■ *Web:* www.seminolefeed.com

Star Milling Co 24067 Water St........................ Perris CA 92570 951-657-3143 657-3114
TF: 800-733-6455 ■ *Web:* www.starmilling.com

Triple Crown Nutrition Inc
319 Barry Ave S Ste 303........................... Wayzata MN 55391 800-451-9916
TF: 800-451-9916 ■ *Web:* www.triplecrownfeed.com

Trouw Nutrition 115 Executive Dr.................. Highland IL 62249 618-654-2070 654-7012
TF: 800-365-1357 ■ *Web:* trouwnutritionusa.com

Ursa Farmers Co-op Inc 202 W Maple Ave PO Box 8 ....Ursa IL 62376 217-964-2111 964-2260
Web: www.ursacoop.com

Valley Proteins Inc 151 Valpro Dr.................. Winchester VA 22603 540-877-2590 877-3215
Web: www.valleyproteins.com

Vita Plus Corp 2514 Fish Hatchery Rd .... Madison WI 53713 608-256-1988 283-7990
TF: 800-362-8334 ■ *Web:* www.vitaplus.com

Zeigler Bros Inc 400 GaRdner Stn Rd................ Gardners PA 17324 717-677-6181 677-6826
TF: 800-841-6800 ■ *Web:* www.zeiglerfeed.com

448 LOGGING

Phone Fax

B & S Logging Inc 4411 NW Elliott Ln .... Prineville OR 97754 541-447-3175 447-7141

Besse Forest Products Group Inc
933 N Eigth St .... Gladstone MI 49837 906-428-3113
Web: www.bessegroup.com

Canal Wood LLC 2430 Main St......................... Conway SC 29526 843-488-9663
TF: 866-587-1460 ■ *Web:* www.canalwood.com

Phone Fax

Cousineau Inc 3 Valley Rd PO Box 58............. North Anson ME 04958 207-635-4445
TF: 877-268-7463 ■ *Web:* www.cousineaus.com

Crane Mills Inc 22938 S Ave .... Corning CA 96021 530-824-5427 824-3157

Croman Corp 801 Ave C............................ White City OR 97503 541-826-4455
Web: www.croman.net

Freres Lumber Company Inc PO Box 276.............. Lyons OR 97358 503-859-2121
Web: www.frereslumber.com

Green Crow Corp
727 E Eigth St PO Box 2469...................... Port Angeles WA 98362 360-452-3325
Web: www.greencrow.com

Greif Inc 425 Winter Rd .... Delaware OH 43015 740-549-6000 657-6592
NYSE: GEF ■ *TF:* 877-781-9797 ■ *Web:* www.greif.com

Hopkes Logging Company Inc
2235 Hadley Rd N.................................. Tillamook OR 97141 503-842-2491 842-9858

Huffman & Wright Logging Inc
801 SE Third St PO Box 910....................... Canyonville OR 97417 541-839-4251

Midwest Walnut Co 1914 Postevin St .... Council Bluffs IA 51503 712-325-9191 325-0156
TF: 800-592-5688 ■ *Web:* www.midwestwalnut.com

Morbark Inc 8507 S Winn Rd .... Winn MI 48896 989-866-2381
Web: www.morbark.com

Roseburg Forest Products Co PO Box 1088 .... Roseburg OR 97470 541-679-3311
TF: 800-245-1115 ■ *Web:* www.roseburg.com

Sealaska Corp 1 Sealaska Plz Ste 400 .... Juneau AK 99801 907-586-1512 586-2304
Web: www.sealaska.com

Sierra Pacific Industries
19794 Riverside Ave.............................. Anderson CA 96007 530-378-8000 378-8109
Web: spi-ind.com

Swanson Group Inc
2695 Glendale Vly Rd PO Box 250................... Glendale OR 97442 541-832-1121
Web: www.swansongroup.biz

Western Forest Products Inc (WFP)
495 Dunsmuir St Unit 210 .... Nanaimo BC V9R6B9 604-648-4500 681-9584
TSE: WEF ■ *Web:* www.westernforest.com

Yeomans Wood & Timber Inc 714 Empire Expy...... Swainsboro GA 30401 478-237-9940
Web: yeomanswood.com

449 LOGISTICS SERVICES (TRANSPORTATION & WAREHOUSING)

See Also Freight Forwarders p. 2328; Marine Services p. 2726; Rail Transport Services p. 3039; Trucking Companies p. 3271; Commercial Warehousing p. 3303

Phone Fax

A Duie Pyle Inc 650 Westtown Rd................. West Chester PA 19381 610-696-5800
TF: 800-523-5020

Access Business Group 7575 Fulton St E.................. Ada MI 49355 616-787-6000
TF Cust Svc: 800-253-6500 ■ *Web:* www.accessbusinessgroup.com

Accomack County School District
23296 Courthouse Ave PO Box 330 .... Accomac VA 23301 757-787-5754 787-2951
Web: www.accomack.k12.va.us

Acme Wire Products Co 7 Broadway Ave .... Mystic CT 06355 860-572-0511
TF: 800-723-7015 ■ *Web:* www.acmewire.com

ADS Tactical Inc
Lynnwood Plz 621 Lynnhaven Pkwy
Ste 400.................................... Virginia Beach VA 23452 757-481-7758
TF: 800-948-9433 ■ *Web:* www.adsinc.com

Advantage Learning Solutions Inc
160-9521 Franklin Ave.......................... Fort Mcmurray AB T9H3Z7 780-743-5001
Web: www.advantagels.ca

American Cargo Express Inc PO Box 483 .... Elizabeth NJ 07207 908-351-3400 289-2490
Web: www.americancargoexpress.com

AN Deringer Inc 64 N Main St................... Saint Albans VT 05478 802-524-8110 524-5970
TF: 800-448-8108 ■ *Web:* www.anderinger.com

APL Logistics Inc
16220 N Scottsdale Rd Ste 300 .... Scottsdale AZ 85254 866-896-2005 586-4861*
**Fax Area Code:* 602 ■ *TF:* 866-896-2005 ■ *Web:* www.apllogistics.com

Associated Global Systems Inc
3333 New Hyde Pk Rd .... New Hyde Park NY 11042 516-627-8910 627-8851
TF Cust Svc: 800-645-8300 ■ *Web:* www.agsystems.com

Atlantic Bulk Carrier Corp
PO Box 112 .... Providence Forge VA 23140 804-966-5459 966-5081
TF: 800-966-0030 ■ *Web:* www.atlanticbulk.com

Axxess International 1804 Alstep Dr Ste........... Mississauga ON L5S1W1 905-672-0270
Web: axxessintl.com

B-H Transfer Co 750 Sparta Rd PO Box 151.......... Sandersville GA 31082 478-552-5119 552-0384
TF: 800-342-6462 ■ *Web:* www.b-htransfer.com

Bantam Group Inc 50 Bay Colony Dr .... Westwood MA 02090 781-329-2020
Web: www.bantamgroup.com

BDP International Inc 510 Walnut St.............. Philadelphia PA 19106 215-629-8900 629-8940
Web: www.bdpinternational.com

Bender Group 345 Parr Cir .... Reno NV 89512 775-788-8800 788-8811
TF: 800-621-9402 ■ *Web:* www.bendergroup.com

Bestway Systems Inc
5755 Granger Rd Ste 400...................... Independence OH 44131 216-398-6090 398-0674
Web: www.bestwaysystems.com

BOC International Inc 23 Drydock Ave................. Boston MA 02210 617-345-0050
Web: www.bocintl.com

Bridger LLC 2009 Chenault Dr Ste 100 .... Carrollton TX 75001 214-722-6960
Web: www.bridgergroup.com

Bulldog Hiway Express 3390 Buffalo Ave .... Charleston SC 29418 843-744-1651 529-3345
TF: 800-331-9515 ■ *Web:* www.bulldoghiway.com

Capital Returns Inc 6101 N 64th St .... Milwaukee WI 53218 414-967-2800
Web: www.genco.com

Cardinal Logistics Management Corp
5333 Davidson Hwy .... Concord NC 28027 704-786-6125 788-6618
Web: www.cardlog.com

Cargo Solution Express Inc 14589 Valley Blvd.......... Fontana CA 92335 909-350-1644 350-4349
Web: www.cargosolutionexpress.com

Caterpillar Logistics Services Inc
500 N Morton Ave .... Morton IL 61550 309-266-3591
Web: www.caterpillar.com

Cdo Technologies Inc 5200 Sprngfeld St Ste 320......... Dayton OH 45431 937-258-0022 258-1614
TF: 866-307-6616 ■ *Web:* www.cdotech.com

Phone *Fax*

Central Transportation Systems Inc
4105 Rio Bravo Ste 100 .... El Paso TX 79902 800-283-3106
TF: 800-283-3106 ■ *Web:* www.centralsystems.com

CH Robinson Worldwide Inc
14701 Charlson Rd .... Eden Prairie MN 55347 952-683-3950
NASDAQ: CHRW ■ *TF Cust Svc:* 855-229-6128 ■ *Web:* www.chrobinson.com

Clarion Associates Inc 30W Monore St Ste 810 .... Chicago IL 60603 312-630-9400
Web: clarionassociates.com

Classical Academy 975 Stout Rd .... Colorado Springs CO 80921 719-484-0091
Web: www.tcatitans.org

Clean Air Technology Inc 41105 Capital Dr .... Canton MI 48187 800-459-6320 459-9437*
**Fax Area Code:* 734 ■ *TF:* 800-459-6320 ■ *Web:* www.cleanairtechnology.com

Clipper Exxpress Inc
9014 Heritage Pkwy Ste 300 .... Woodridge IL 60517 630-739-0700 739-1817
TF: 800-678-2547 ■ *Web:* www.clippergroup.com

Conley Transport Ii Inc 2104 Eastline Rd .... Searcy AR 72143 501-268-4672
Web: www.conleytransport.com

Cord Moving & Storage 4101 Rider Trl N .... Earth City MO 63045 314-720-2147 291-6127
Web: www.cordmoving.com

Coyote Logistics LLC 191 E Deerpath Rd .... Lake Forest IL 60045 847-295-2424
TF: 877-626-9683 ■ *Web:* www.coyotelogistics.com

Crane Worldwide Logistics LLC 1500 Rankin Rd .... Houston TX 77073 281-443-2777
TF: 888-870-2726 ■ *Web:* www.craneww.com

Customer Insight Group Inc 6711 Secrest Cir .... Arvada CO 80007 303-422-9758
Web: www.customerinsightgroup.com

Daniel F Young Inc 1235 Westlakes Dr Ste 255 .... Berwyn PA 19312 610-725-4000 725-0570
TF: 866-407-0083 ■ *Web:* www.dfyoung.com

Daniel Group Ltd, The
400 Clarice Ave Ste 200 .... Charlotte NC 28204 877-967-4242
TF: 877-967-4242 ■ *Web:* thedanielgroup.com

Danny Herman Trucking Inc PO Box 55 .... Mountain City TN 37683 423-727-9061
TF: 800-251-7500 ■ *Web:* www.dannyherman.com

Datastrait Networks Inc
3021 Harbor Ln N Ste 103 .... Minneapolis MN 55447 763-746-4466
Web: datastrait.com

Dennis K Burke Inc
284 Eastern Ave PO Box 6069 .... Chelsea MA 02150 617-884-7800 884-7638
TF: 800-289-2875 ■ *Web:* www.burkeoil.com

Dependable Highway Express Inc
2440 S 48th Ave .... Phoenix AZ 85043 602-278-4401 278-4473
TF: 800-472-2037 ■ *Web:* www.godependable.com

Distribution & Marking Services Inc (DMSI)
10709 Granite St Ste Q .... Charlotte NC 28273 704-749-7300 749-7301
TF: 844-325-3741 ■ *Web:* www.dmsi.net

Dohrn Transfer Co 625 Third Ave .... Rock Island IL 61201 309-794-0723 794-1693
TF: 888-364-7621 ■ *Web:* www.dohrn.com

DSC Logistics 1750 S Wolf Rd .... Des Plaines IL 60018 800-372-1960 390-7276*
**Fax Area Code:* 847 ■ *TF:* 800-372-1960 ■ *Web:* www.dsclogistics.com

DTI Assoc Inc 2920 S Glebe Rd .... Arlington VA 22206 703-299-1600 706-0474

Eagle Support Services Corp
2705 Artie St Bldg 400 Ste 30 .... Huntsville AL 35805 256-534-2274 534-0606
Web: www.eaglesupport.com

Elert & Associates Telecommunications Consultants Inc
140 3rd St S .... Stillwater MN 55082 651-430-2772
Web: www.elert.com

Elston-Richards Inc
5738 Eagle Dr SE Ste B .... Grand Rapids MI 49512 616-698-2698 698-8090
Web: www.elstonrichards.com

EMBASSY Products & Logistics
PO Box 8066 .... Falls Church VA 22041 703-845-0800 820-9385
Web: www.embassy-usa.com

EnteGreat Inc
1500 Urban Ctr Dr Ste 415 .... Vestavia Hills AL 35242 205-968-3050
Web: www.entegreat.com

Ervin Equipment Inc 608 N Ohio St .... Toledo IL 62468 217-849-3125
Web: www.ervinusa.com

Ethier Associates 736 6 Ave Sw .... Calgary AB T2P3T7 403-234-8960
Web: www.ethier.ca

Exel 570 Polaris Pkwy .... Westerville OH 43082 614-865-8500 865-8875
Web: www.exel.com

Expeditors International of Washington Inc
1015 Third Ave 12th Fl .... Seattle WA 98104 206-674-3400 682-9777
NASDAQ: EXPD ■ *TF:* 800-284-7474 ■ *Web:* www.expeditors.com

Extron Logistics LLC 496 S Abbott Ave .... Milpitas CA 95035 510-353-0177
Web: www.extroninc.com

FedEx Supply Chain Services Inc
5455 Darrow Rd .... Hudson OH 44236 901-369-3600
TF: 800-463-3339 ■ *Web:* www.fedex.com

FedEx Trade Networks Inc
6075 Poplar Ave Ste 300 Third Fl .... Memphis TN 38119 901-684-4800 684-4843
NYSE: FDX ■ *Web:* www.ftn.fedex.com

Flow Consulting Inc 13989 CR 136 .... Live Oak FL 32060 386-362-2009
Web: www.flowconsulting.com

Follow Up Sales Systems
400 S Summit St .... Arkansas City KS 67005 620-442-2460
Web: fussinc.com

Fremont Contract Carriers Inc (FCC)
865 S Bud Blvd .... Fremont NE 68025 800-228-9842 727-8712*
**Fax Area Code:* 402 ■ *TF:* 800-228-9842 ■ *Web:* www.fcc-inc.com

Frontier Logistic Services 1700 N Alameda St .... Compton CA 90222 310-604-8208 604-8135
Web: www.frontier-logistics.com

Gazelles Publishing Inc 21246 Dubois Ct .... Ashburn VA 20147 703-858-2400
Web: www.gazelles.com

Gellman Research Associates Inc
115 W Ave Ste 201 .... Jenkintown PA 19046 215-884-7500
Web: gra-inc.com

Global Logistics
99 W Hawthorne Ave L-12 Valley Stream .... New York NY 11580 516-825-2922 825-1143
Web: www.globallog.com

Griffin Transport Services 5360 Capital Ct .... Reno NV 89502 775-331-8010
TF: 800-361-5028 ■ *Web:* legacyscs.com

Groton-Dunstable Regional School District
PO Box 729 .... Groton MA 01450 978-448-5505 448-9402
Web: www.gdrsd.org

Gypsum Express Ltd
8280 Sixty Rd PO Box 268 .... Baldwinsville NY 13027 315-638-2201
TF: 800-621-7901 ■ *Web:* www.gypsumexpress.com

H E Whitlock Inc 4808 Dillon Dr PO Box 8030 .... Pueblo CO 81008 866-933-0709 544-1832*
**Fax Area Code:* 719 ■ *TF:* 866-933-0709 ■ *Web:* www.hewhitlock.com

Halo Group LLC 39475 13 Mile Rd Ste 201 .... Novi MI 48377 248-489-9500
Web: www.halogroup.us

Hanson Logistics 2900 S State St .... Saint Joseph MI 49085 269-982-1390 982-1506
TF: 888-772-1197 ■ *Web:* www.hansonlogisticsgroup.com

Higher Ed Growth LLC
5400 S Lakeshore Dr Ste 101 .... Tempe AZ 85283 866-433-8532
TF: 866-433-8532 ■ *Web:* www.higheredgrowth.com

Highway Transport Logistics Inc (HTL)
6420 Baum Dr .... Knoxville TN 37919 865-584-8631
Web: www.hytt.com

Horizon Air Freight Inc 152-15 Rockaway Blvd .... Jamaica NY 11434 718-528-3800 949-0655
TF: 800-221-6028 ■ *Web:* www.haf.com

Hoyt, Shepston & Sciaroni Inc
161a Starlite St # B .... South San Francisco CA 94080 650-952-6930
Web: www.hoyt-shepston.com

Hub Group Inc 2000 Clearwater Dr .... Oak Brook IL 60523 630-271-3600 964-6475
NASDAQ: HUBG ■ *TF:* 800-377-5833 ■ *Web:* www.hubgroup.com

InterChez Logistics Systems Inc 600 Alpha Pkwy .... Stow OH 44224 330-923-5080
Web: www.interchez.com

ISC Consultants Inc 345 Hoyt St Ste 1000 .... New York NY 11231 212-477-8800
Web: www.isc.com

J A Moss Construction PO Box 180460 .... Richland MS 39218 601-939-4141 939-4142
Web: www.jamossconstruction.com

James Group International 4335 W Ft St .... Detroit MI 48209 313-841-0070 841-5074
Web: www.jamesgroupintl.com

Jarrett Logistics Systems Inc
1347 N Main St .... Orrville OH 44667 330-682-0099
Web: www.jarrettlogistics.com

JB Hunt Transport Services Inc
615 JB Hunt Corporate Dr .... Lowell AR 72745 479-820-0000 820-8249*
NASDAQ: JBHT ■ **Fax:* Hum Res ■ *TF:* 800-643-3622 ■ *Web:* www.jbhunt.com

Jon Peddie Research Inc 4 Saint Gabrielle Ct .... Tiburon CA 94920 415-435-9368
Web: www.jonpeddie.com

Kenco Group Inc 2001 Riverside Dr .... Chattanooga TN 37406 800-758-3289
TF: 800-758-3289 ■ *Web:* www.kencogroup.com

Kintetsu World Express USA Inc
1 Jericho Plz Ste 100 .... Jericho NY 11753 516-933-7100 933-7731
TF: 800-275-4045 ■ *Web:* www.kweusa.com

Kom International 300 St-Sacrement Ste 307 .... Montreal QC H2Y1X4 514-849-4000 849-8888
Web: www.komintl.com

Kuehne & Nagel Inc 10 Exchange Pl .... Jersey City NJ 07302 201-413-5500 413-5777
TF: 866-914-0444 ■ *Web:* www.kn-portal.com

L&B Transport LLC 708 US190 PO Box 74870 .... Port Allen LA 70767 225-387-0894 387-0126
TF: 800-545-9401 ■ *Web:* www.landbtransport.com

L-3 Vertex Aerospace Llc 555 Industrial Dr S .... Madison MS 39110 601-607-6288
Web: www.l-3com.com

Landstar Logistics Inc
13410 Sutton Pk Dr S .... Jacksonville FL 32224 904-398-9400
TF: 800-872-9400 ■ *Web:* www.landstar.com

LeSaint Logistics 868 W Crossroads Pkwy .... Romeoville IL 60446 630-243-5950
TF: 877-566-9375 ■ *Web:* www.lesaint.com

LJG Partners Inc 680 W Beech St .... San Diego CA 92101 619-232-3000
Web: www.ljg.com

Loggins Logistics Inc 5706 Commerce Sq .... Jonesboro AR 72401 870-932-9231 802-2190
Web: www.logginslogistics.com

Logical Solution Services Inc
200 Union Ave .... Lakehurst NJ 08733 732-657-7777
Web: www.solutionservices.us

Lucas County Educational Service Ctr
2275 Collingwood Blvd .... Toledo OH 43620 419-245-4150 245-4186
Web: www.esclakeeriewest.org

Lynden International Logistics Co
10 Corrine Ct .... Vaughan ON L4K4T7 905-879-0114
Web: www.lynden.com/lilco

M & J Transportation 3536 Nicholson Ave .... Kansas City MO 64120 816-231-6733 231-7645
TF: 866-298-3858 ■ *Web:* www.mjtransportationkc.com

Majestic Transportation 283 Lockhaven Ste 100 .... Houston TX 77073 281-869-8031
Web: www.majestictransportation.com

Matson Logistics Inc 555 12th St .... Oakland CA 94607 510-628-4000
TF: 800-762-8766 ■ *Web:* www.matson.com

Maximus Federal Services Inc
3750 Monroe Ave Ste 702 .... Pittsford NY 14534 585-348-3300
Web: www.medicareappeal.com

McElroy Truck Lines Inc 111 80 Spur PO Box 104 .... Cuba AL 36907 205-392-5579 392-7992
TF: 800-992-7863 ■ *Web:* www.mcelroytrucklines.com

McLaughlin Consulting Group Inc
945 Hamilton Ave .... Menlo Park CA 94025 650-366-5999
Web: www.mcgweb.com

Mercator Transport Group Corp
Ste 220 8200 Boul Decarie Ste 220 .... Montreal QC H4T1M4 514-874-1616
Web: www.corpgmt.com

Meridian IQ 11501 Outlook St Ste 500 .... Overland Park KS 66211 877-246-4909 696-7501*
**Fax Area Code:* 913 ■ *TF:* 877-246-4909 ■ *Web:* www2.miq.com

Meteor Express Inc PO Box 248 .... Scottsboro AL 35768 256-218-3000 259-3990
Web: www.meteorx.com

Metropolitan Trucking Inc (MRTK)
299 Market St .... Saddle Brook NJ 07663 800-967-3278 843-6179*
**Fax Area Code:* 201 ■ *TF:* 800-967-3278 ■ *Web:* www.mtrk.com

MHD Enterprises 9715 Burnet Rd #125 .... Austin TX 78758 512-992-2565
Web: www.mhdenterprises.com

Midwest Specialized Transportation Inc
PO Box 6418 .... Rochester MN 55903 507-424-4838
TF: 800-927-8007 ■ *Web:* www.midspec.com

Millard Refrigerated Services Inc
4715 S 132nd St .... Omaha NE 68137 402-896-6600
Web: www.millardref.com

Miller Bros Express LC 560 West 400 North .... Hyrum UT 84319 435-245-6025
Web: www.mbexlc.com

Company / Address	City	State	ZIP	Phone	Fax
Mitsui & Co (USA) Inc 200 Pk Ave *TF:* 877-248-4237 ■ *Web:* www.mitsui.com/us	New York	NY	10166	212-878-4000	878-4800
Modern Transportation Service Inc 2605 Nicholson Rd *Web:* www.moderntrans.com	Sewickley	PA	15143	412-489-4800	
ModusLink PTS Inc 5233 S Old State Rd 37 *Web:* www.moduslinkptstvboards.com	Bloomington	IN	47401	812-824-9331	
Mount Vernon City School Dist 80 2710 N St *Web:* www.mtv80.org	Mount Vernon	IL	62864	618-244-8080	244-8082
Muscle Shoals City School District 3200 Wilson Dam Rd *Web:* www.mscs.k12.al.us	Muscle Shoals	AL	35661	256-389-2600	389-2662
MySupplyChainGroup LLC 1500 First Ave N Ste A111 *TF:* 888-444-7786 ■ *Web:* www.mysupplychaingroup.com	Birmingham	AL	35203	205-706-4300	
National Distributors Inc 1517 Avco Blvd *TF:* 800-334-9677	Sellersburg	IN	47172	812-246-6306	246-9568
National Freight Inc (NFI) 1515 Burnt Mill Rd *TF General:* 877-634-3777 ■ *Web:* www.natlfreight.com	Cherry Hill	NJ	08003	877-634-3777	
Navigator Development Group Inc 116 S Main St Ste 214 *Web:* www.ndgi.com	Enterprise	AL	36330	334-347-7612	
Navis Logistics Network 6551 S Revere Pkwy Ste 250 **Fax Area Code:* 303 ■ *TF:* 800-344-3528 ■ *Web:* www.gonavis.com	Centennial	CO	80111	800-344-3528	741-6653*
Neuger Communications Group Inc 25 Bridge Sq *Web:* www.neuger.com	Northfield	MN	55057	507-664-0700	
NNR Global Logistics USA Inc 450 E Devon Ave Ste 260 *Web:* www.staffingnetwork.com	Itasca	IL	60143	630-773-1490	
Oakley Transport Inc 101 ABC Rd *TF:* 800-969-8265 ■ *Web:* oakleytransport.com	Lake Wales	FL	33859	863-638-1435	
ODW Logistics Inc 1580 Williams Rd *TF:* 800-743-7062 ■ *Web:* www.odwlogistics.com	Columbus	OH	43207	614-497-1660	497-1426
Odyssey Logistics & Technology Corp 39 Old Ridgebury Rd - N1 *Web:* www.odysseylogistics.com	Danbury	CT	06810	203-448-3900	
Omnitrans Inc 4300 Jean-Talon W *Web:* www.omnitrans.com	Montreal	QC	H4P1W3	514-288-6664	
Open Roads Consulting Inc 103 Watson Rd *Web:* www.openroadsconsulting.com	Chesapeake	VA	23320	757-546-3401	
Panalpina 1776 On-the-Green 67 E Pk Pl *Web:* www.panalpina.com	Morristown	NJ	07960	973-683-9000	254-5712
Park-Ohio Holdings Corp (PKOH) 6065 Parkland Blvd *NASDAQ:* PKOH ■ *Web:* www.pkoh.com	Cleveland	OH	44124	440-947-2000	947-2099
Pegasus Logistics Group Inc 306 Airline Dr Ste 100 *TF:* 800-997-7226 ■ *Web:* www.pegasuslogistics.com	Coppell	TX	75019	469-671-0300	671-0317
Pierce Distribution Services Co PO Box 15600 **Fax Area Code:* 815 ■ *TF:* 800-466-7397 ■ *Web:* www.piercedistribution.com	Loves Park	IL	61132	800-466-7397	636-5660*
Pm2 4210 Saltwater Blvd *Web:* www.pm2online.com	Tampa	FL	33615	813-249-0834	
Ponvia Technology Inc 49-T Sherwood Ter *TF:* 877-217-0875 ■ *Web:* www.ponvia.com	Lake Bluff	IL	60045	877-217-0875	
Promantek Inc 21955 E Tallkid Ave *Web:* www.promantek.com	Parker	CO	80138	303-470-9355	
R.C. Dolner LLC 307 5th Ave 9th Fl *Web:* www.rcdolner.com	New York	NY	10016	212-531-8600	633-1108
Radiant Logistics Inc Third Fl 405 114Th Ave Se *TF:* 800-843-4784 ■ *Web:* www.radiantdelivers.com	Bellevue	WA	98004	425-943-4599	
Red Rock Distributing Co 1 NW 50th St *TF:* 800-323-7109 ■ *Web:* www.redrockdist.com	Oklahoma City	OK	73118	405-677-3373	557-7795
Red Star Oil 802 Purser Dr *TF:* 800-774-6033 ■ *Web:* www.redstaroil.com	Raleigh	NC	27603	919-772-1944	779-8871
Reliant Transportation Inc 4411 S 86th St Ste 101 PO Box 67009 *Web:* www.reliant-transportation.com	Lincoln	NE	68526	402-464-7771	464-8124
Renodis Inc 476 Robert St N *TF:* 866-200-8986 ■ *Web:* www.renodis.com	Saint Paul	MN	55101	651-556-1200	
Ridgewood High School 7500 W Montrose Ave *Web:* www.ridgenet.org	Norridge	IL	60706	708-456-4242	456-0342
RIM Logistics Ltd 200 N Gary Ave *TF:* 888-275-0937 ■ *Web:* www.rimlogistics.com	Roselle	IL	60172	630-595-0610	595-0614
Rinchem Company Inc 6133 Edith Blvd NE *TF:* 888-375-2436 ■ *Web:* www.rinchem.com	Albuquerque	NM	87107	505-345-3655	
ROACO Logistics Services 500 Country Club Dr	Bensenville	IL	60106	630-595-8631	
Rural Health Resource Center 525 S Lake Ave Ste 320 *TF:* 800-997-6685 ■ *Web:* ruralcenter.org	Duluth	MN	55802	218-727-9390	
Ryder System Inc 11690 NW 105th St *NYSE:* R ■ *TF:* 800-297-9337 ■ *Web:* www.ryder.com	Miami	FL	33178	305-500-3726	
S & H Express Inc 400 Mulberry St *TF:* 800-637-9782 ■ *Web:* www.sandhexpress.com	York	PA	17403	717-848-5015	852-8722
Saddle Creek Corp 3010 Saddle Creek Rd *Web:* www.sclogistics.com	Lakeland	FL	33801	863-665-0966	666-8295
Schneider National Inc 3101 S Packerland Dr PO Box 2545 *TF:* 800-558-6767 ■ *Web:* www.schneider.com	Green Bay	WI	54306	920-592-2000	592-3063
School District of Hartford 675 E Rossman St *Web:* www.hartfordjt1.k12.wi.us	Hartford	WI	53027	262-673-3155	673-3548
Scully Oil Company & Service Station 150 E Flint St PO Box 398 *Web:* www.scullyoil.com	Lyndon Station	WI	53944	608-666-2662	666-2239
Sds Consulting Corp 3115 12 St Ne Ste 310 *Web:* www.sdsconsulting.ca	Calgary	AB	T2E7J2	403-221-8077	
Seko Worldwide Inc 1100 Arlington Heights Rd Ste 600 **Fax Area Code:* 518 ■ *TF:* 800-323-1235 ■ *Web:* www.sekologistics.com	Itasca	IL	60143	630-919-4800	785-4594*
Shaker Group Inc, The 862 Albany Shaker Rd *TF:* 800-267-0314 ■ *Web:* www.theshakergroup.com	Latham	NY	12110	518-786-9286	782-7226
Shippers Commonwealth LLC 49 Immigration St Seabreeze Bldg Ste 205 *Web:* www.shipperscommonwealth.com	Charleston	SC	29403	843-805-6607	
Sierra West Express Inc 850 Bergin Way	Sparks	NV	89431	775-355-9595	
Slay Industries Inc 1441 Hampton Ave *TF:* 800-852-7529 ■ *Web:* www.slay.com	Saint Louis	MO	63139	314-647-7529	647-5240
Southeast Delco School District 1560 Delmar Dr *Web:* www.sedelco.org	Folcroft	PA	19032	610-522-4300	
Speegle Construction Inc 210 Government Ave *Web:* www.speegleconstruction.com	Niceville	FL	32578	850-729-2484	
Star Line Trucking Corp 18480 W Lincoln Ave *Web:* www.starlinetrucking.com	New Berlin	WI	53146	262-786-8280	786-0071
Store Opening Solutions (SOS) 800 Middle Tennessee Blvd **Fax Area Code:* 615 ■ *TF:* 877-388-9262 ■ *Web:* www.store-solutions.com	Murfreesboro	TN	37129	877-388-9262	867-4740*
Support Kansas City Inc 5960 Dearborn St Ste 200 *Web:* www.supportkc.org	Mission	KS	66202	913-831-4752	
Survival Systems Training Ltd 40 Mount Hope Ave *TF:* 800-788-3888 ■ *Web:* www.sstl.com	Dartmouth	NS	B2Y4K9	902-465-3888	
Tandet Management Inc 1351 Speers Rd *Web:* www.tandet.com	Oakville	ON	L6L2X5	905-827-4200	
TankLink Corp 1000 E State Pkwy Unit F *Web:* www.tanklink.com	Schaumburg	IL	60173	847-882-0060	
Taylor Protocols Inc 16040 Christensen Rd Ste 315 *TF:* 877-355-8229 ■ *Web:* www.taylorprotocols.com	Tukwila	WA	98188	206-283-8144	
Technical Transportation Inc 1701 W Northwest Hwy Ste 100 **Fax Area Code:* 817 ■ *TF:* 800-852-8726 ■ *Web:* www.techtrans.com	Grapevine	TX	76051	800-852-8726	488-0306*
Thornburg Center for Prof Dev 711 Beacon Dr *Web:* thornburgcenter.blogspot.com	Lake Barrington	IL	60010	847-277-7691	
Thoroughbred Direct Intermodal Services 5165 Campus Dr Ste 400 *TF:* 877-250-2902 ■ *Web:* www.ns-direct.com	Plymouth Meeting	PA	19462	610-567-3360	567-3370
Titan Global Distribution 1100 Corporate Sq Dr *Web:* titan-global.com	Saint Louis	MO	63132	314-817-0051	
TRANSFLO Terminal Services Inc 500 Water St Ste J975 *TF:* 866-872-6735 ■ *Web:* transflo.net	Jacksonville	FL	32202	866-872-6735	
TransMontaigne Inc 1670 Broadway Ste 3100 Ste 3100 *Web:* www.transmontaigne.com	Denver	CO	80202	303-626-8200	626-8228
Transplace 3010 Gaylord Pkwy Ste 200 **Fax Area Code:* 972 ■ *TF:* 866-413-9266 ■ *Web:* www.transplace.com	Frisco	TX	75034	866-413-9266	731-4501*
Transportation Insight LLC 328 First Ave NW *Web:* www.t-insight.com	Hickory	NC	28601	828-485-5210	
Transportation Solutions Inc 1900 Brannan Rd *Web:* www.tsilogistics.com	McDonough	GA	30253	770-474-1555	
Trimar Construction Inc 1720 W Cass St *Web:* 0350766.netsolhost.com	Tampa	FL	33606	813-258-5524	258-4743
TSS Inc 110 E Old Settlers Blvd *TF:* 844-681-8158 ■ *Web:* www.totalsitesolutions.com	Round Rock	TX	78664	512-310-1000	
United Nations International School 24-50 Fdr Dr *Web:* www.unis.org	New York	NY	10010	212-684-7400	
Unitrans International Corp 709 S Hindry Ave *Web:* www.unitrans-us.com	Inglewood	CA	90301	310-410-7676	410-1719
University City School Dst 8136 Groby Rd *Web:* www.ucityschools.org	Saint Louis	MO	63130	314-290-4000	
Uplogix Inc 7600B N Capital of Texas Hwy Ste 220 *Web:* www.uplogix.com	Austin	TX	78731	512-857-7000	
UPS Supply Chain Solutions 12380 Morris Rd *TF:* 800-742-5727 ■ *Web:* www.ups-scs.com	Alpharetta	GA	30005	913-693-6151	
UTi Worldwide Inc 100 Oceangate Ste 1500 *NASDAQ:* UTIW ■ *Web:* www.go2uti.com	Long Beach	CA	90802	562-552-9400	
VectorCSP LLC 405 E Main St *Web:* www.vectorcsp.com	Elizabeth City	NC	27909	252-338-2264	
Vimich Traffic Logistics 12201 Tecumseh Rd E **Fax Area Code:* 519 ■ *TF:* 800-284-1045 ■ *Web:* www.vimich.com	Tecumseh	ON	N8N1M3	800-284-1045	735-4309*
Virginkar & Associates Inc 3350 E Birch St Ste 101 *Web:* www.va-inc.com	Brea	CA	92821	714-993-1000	
W M Schlosser Company Inc 2400 51st Pl *Web:* www.wmschlosser.com	Hyattsville	MD	20781	301-773-1300	773-9263
Wallace & Carey Inc 5445-8 St NE *Web:* www.wacl.com	Calgary	AB	T2K5R9	403-275-7360	
Webb Writes Llc 1904 Frnt St *Web:* www.webbwrites.com	Durham	NC	27705	919-384-8850	
Weber Logistics 13530 Rosecrans Ave *TF:* 855-469-3237 ■ *Web:* www.weberlogistics.com	Santa Fe Springs	CA	90670	855-469-3237	
Whitehall Management Consultants Inc 9815 N 95th St *Web:* www.whitehallmgt.com	Scottsdale	AZ	85258	480-860-5700	
Wilheit Packaging LLC 1527 May Dr *TF:* 800-727-4421 ■ *Web:* www.wilheit.com	Gainesville	GA	30507	770-532-4421	532-8956
Willson International Ltd 2345 Argentia Rd Ste 201 *TF:* 800-754-1918 ■ *Web:* www.willsonintl.com	Mississauga	ON	L5N8K4	905-363-1133	

Phone Fax

Wise Consulting Associates Inc
54 Scott Adam Rd Ste 206 ..... Hunt Valley MD 21030 410-628-0100
TF: 800-654-4550 ■ Web: www.wiseconsulting.com
XPO Logistics Inc 6805 Perimeter Dr ..... Dublin OH 43016 614-923-1400
TF: 800-837-7584 ■ Web: www.xpologistics.com

450 LONG-TERM CARE FACILITIES

See Also Long-Term Care Facilities Operators p. 2687; Retirement Communities p. 3136; Veterans Nursing Homes - State p. 3292
Free-standing facilities accredited by the Joint Commission on Accreditation of Healthcare Organizations. Listings in this category are organized alphabetically by states.

Phone Fax

Canterbury Health Facility
1720 Knowles Rd ..... Phenix City AL 36869 334-291-0485
Northside Health Care 700 Hutchins Ave ..... Gadsden AL 35901 256-543-7101
Web: northsidehealthcare.com
Catalina Care Ctr 2611 N Warren Ave ..... Tucson AZ 85719 520-795-9574
Web: nursingfacilitytucson.com
Coronado Care Ctr 11411 N 19th Ave ..... Phoenix AZ 85029 602-256-7500
Web: www.coronadocare.com
Osborn Health & Rehabilitation
3333 N Civic Ctr Plz ..... Scottsdale AZ 85251 480-994-1333
Web: osbornhealth.com
Casa Colina Ctr for Rehabilitation
255 E Bonita Ave ..... Pomona CA 91769 909-596-7733 596-7845
TF: 800-926-5462 ■ Web: www.casacolina.org
Clear View Sanitarium & Convalescent Ctr
15823 S Western Ave ..... Gardena CA 90247 310-538-2323 538-3509
Web: clearviewcare.com
English Oaks Nursing & Rehabilitation Ctr
2633 W Rumble Rd ..... Modesto CA 95350 209-577-1001 577-0366
Web: lifegen.net
Ensign Group Inc, The
27101 Puerta Real Ste 450 ..... Mission Viejo CA 92691 949-487-9500
NASDAQ: ENSG ■ Web: www.ensigngroup.net
Evergreen Rehabilitation & Care Ctr
2030 Evergreen Ave ..... Modesto CA 95350 209-577-1055
Web: www.evergreencare.com
Extended Care Hospital Westminster
206 Hospital Cir ..... Westminster CA 92683 714-891-2769 580-6196*
*Fax Area Code: 909 ■ TF: 800-236-9747
French Park Care Ctr 600 E Washington Ave ..... Santa Ana CA 92701 714-973-1656 836-4349
Web: frenchparkcarecenter.com
Front Porch Communities & Services
303 N Glenoaks Blvd ..... Burbank CA 91502 800-233-3709
TF: 800-233-3709 ■ Web: www.frontporch.net
Gladstone Care & Rehabilitation Ctr
435 E Gladstone St ..... Glendora CA 91740 626-963-5955 963-8683
Web: www.gladstonecare.com
Grand Terrace Healthcare Ctr
12000 Mt Vernon Ave ..... Grand Terrace CA 92313 909-825-5221 783-4811
Web: grandterracecare.com
Hanford Nursing & Rehabilitation Hospital
1007 W Lacey Blvd ..... Hanford CA 93230 559-582-2871
Web: hfcis.cdph.ca.gov
Heritage Rehabilitation Ctr
21414 S Vermont Ave ..... Torrance CA 90502 310-320-8714 320-1809
Web: heritagerehabcenter.com
Huntington Valley Health Care Ctr
8382 Newman Ave ..... Huntington Beach CA 92647 714-842-5551 848-5359
Web: hvhcc.com
Kisco Senior Living LLC
5790 Fleet St Ste 300 ..... Carlsbad CA 92008 760-804-5900 804-5909
Web: kiscoseniorliving.com
La Jolla Nursing & Rehabilitation Ctr
2552 Torrey Pines Rd ..... La Jolla CA 92037 858-453-5810 452-4301
TF: 800-861-0086 ■
Web: covenantcare.com/locations/la-jolla-nursing-and-rehabilitation-center
La Mariposa Nursing & Rehab
1244 Travis Blvd ..... Fairfield CA 94533 707-422-7750 422-7452
New Orange Hills 5017 E Chapman Ave ..... Orange CA 92869 714-997-7090 997-4631
Web: www.neworangehills.com
Pacific Coast Manor 1935 Wharf Rd ..... Capitola CA 95010 831-476-0770 476-0737
Web: covenantcare.com
Pacifica Nursing & Rehabilitation Ctr
385 Esplanade Ave ..... Pacifica CA 94044 650-993-5576 359-9388
Web: pacificarehab.com
Park Anaheim HealthCare Ctr 3435 W Ball Rd ..... Anaheim CA 92804 714-827-5880 827-5880
Park Regency Care Ctr 1770 W La Habra Blvd ..... La Habra CA 90631 714-773-0750 697-8478*
*Fax Area Code: 562 ■ Web: www.parkregencycare.com
Seton Medical Ctr Coastside
600 Marine Blvd ..... Moss Beach CA 94038 650-563-7100 728-5314
Web: verity.org
Subacute Saratoga Children's Hospital
13425 Sousa Ln ..... Saratoga CA 95070 408-378-8875 378-7419
Web: www.subacutesaratoga.com
Tulare Nursing & Rehabilitation
680 E Merritt Ave ..... Tulare CA 93274 559-686-8581
Web: missioncaregroup.com
Tunnell Ctr for Rehabilitation & Healthcare
1359 Pine St ..... San Francisco CA 94109 415-673-8405
Web: www.tunnellrehab.com
Villa Maria Healthcare Ctr
425 E Barcellus Ave ..... Santa Maria CA 93454 805-922-3558
Web: villamariacarecenter.com
Village Square Nursing & Rehabilitation Ctr
1586 W San Marcos Blvd ..... San Marcos CA 92078 760-471-2986 471-5176
Web: www.villagesquarerehab.com
Windsor Rehabilitation Care Ctr
3806 Clayton Rd ..... Concord CA 94521 925-689-2266
Web: www.windsorcares.com

Phone Fax

Apple Rehab 21 Waterville Rd ..... Avon CT 06001 860-927-5368
Web: www.apple-rehab.com
Avon Health Ctr Inc 652 W Avon Rd ..... Avon CT 06001 860-673-2521
Web: avonhealthcenter.com
Branford Hills Health Care Ctr 189 Alps Rd ..... Branford CT 06405 203-481-6221 483-1893
Web: www.bhhcc.com
Hebrew Health Care Inc 1 Abrahms Blvd ..... West Hartford CT 06117 860-523-3800 523-3949
Web: www.hebrewhealthcare.org
Jewish Senior Services of Fairfield County Inc
175 Jefferson St ..... Fairfield CT 06825 203-365-6400 374-8082
Web: jseniors.org
Manchester Manor Health Care Ctr
385 W Ctr St ..... Manchester CT 06040 860-646-0129
Web: www.manchestermanorct.com
Masonic Healthcare Ctr 22 Masonic Ave ..... Wallingford CT 06492 203-679-5900
Web: masonicare.org
Miller Memorial Community 360 Broad St ..... Meriden CT 06450 203-237-8815
Web: www.millercommunity.org
Montowese Health & Rehabilitation Ctr Inc
163 Quinnipiac Ave ..... North Haven CT 06473 203-624-3303 787-9243
Web: www.montowesehealth.com
Noble Horizons 17 Cobble Rd ..... Salisbury CT 06068 860-435-9851 435-0636
Web: www.noblehorizons.org
Pendleton Health & Rehabilitation Ctr
44 Maritime Dr ..... Mystic CT 06355 860-572-1700
Web: savaseniorcare.com
River Glen Health Care Ctr
162 S Britain Rd ..... Southbury CT 06488 203-264-9600 264-9603
Sharon Health Care Ctr 27 Hospital Hill Rd ..... Sharon CT 06069 860-364-1002 364-0237
Web: athenahealthcare.com
Summit at Plantsville 261 Summit St ..... Plantsville CT 06479 860-628-0364 628-9166
Web: www.athenanh.com/CT_Summit.aspx
Valerie Manor Inc 135 South Rd ..... Farmington CT 06032 860-489-1008
Web: athenahealthcare.com
Village Green of Waterbury 128 Cedar Ave ..... Waterbury CT 06705 203-757-9271 757-2988
Watrous Nursing Ctr 9 Neck Rd ..... Madison CT 06443 203-245-9483 245-4668
TF: 877-696-6775 ■ Web: apple-rehab.com
Waveny Care Ctr 3 Farm Rd ..... New Canaan CT 06840 203-594-5200 594-5327
Web: www.waveny.org
West Hartford Health & Rehabilitation Ctr
130 Loomis Dr ..... West Hartford CT 06107 860-521-8700
Web: www.westhartfordhealth.com
Armed Forces Retirement Home - Washington
3700 N Capitol St NW ..... Washington DC 20011 800-422-9988 541-7519*
*Fax Area Code: 202 ■ TF Admissions: 800-422-9988 ■ Web: www.afrh.gov/afrh
Area Agency On Aging
9549 Koger Blvd Gadsden Bldg Ste 100 ..... St Petersburg FL 33702 727-570-9696 234-4401
TF: 800-963-5337 ■ Web: www.agingcarefl.org
Bay Pointe Nursing Pavilion
4201 31st St S ..... Saint Petersburg FL 33712 727-867-1104 867-9837
Web: baypointenursingpavilion.com
Boca Raton Rehabilitation Ctr
755 Meadows Rd ..... Boca Raton FL 33486 561-391-5200 391-0685
Web: bocaratonhealthandrehab.com
Consulate Health Care at Lake Parker
2020 W Lk Parker Dr ..... Lakeland FL 33805 863-682-7580
Web: www.consulatemgt.com
Consulate Health Care of Brandon
701 Victoria St ..... Brandon FL 33510 813-681-4220
Web: consulatehealthcare.com
Consulate Health Care of Tallahassee
800 Concourse Pkwy S Ste 200 ..... Maitland FL 32751 407-571-1550 571-1599
Web: www.consulatehealthcare.com
Heartland Health Care & Rehabilitation Ctr
5401 Sawyer Rd ..... Sarasota FL 34233 941-925-3427 925-8469
Heartland Health Care Ctr Boynton Beach
3600 Old Boynton Rd ..... Boynton Beach FL 33436 561-736-9992 364-9527
Web: www.heartland-manorcare.com
Heartland Health Care Ctr-South Jacksonville
3648 University Blvd S ..... Jacksonville FL 32216 904-733-7440 448-9425
Web: www.heartland-manorcare.com
Leesburg Health & Rehabiltation LLC
715 E Dixie Ave ..... Leesburg FL 34748 352-728-3020 323-5061
Manatee Springs Care & Rehab
5627 Ninth St E ..... Bradenton FL 34203 941-753-8941 753-7576
Web: manateespringsrehab.com
ManorCare Health Services - Carrollwood
3030 W Bearss Ave ..... Tampa FL 33618 813-968-8777
Web: www.hcr-manorcare.com
River Garden Hebrew Home for the Aged
11401 Old St Augustine Rd ..... Jacksonville FL 32258 904-260-1818 260-9733
TF: 800-468-3571 ■ Web: rivergarden.org
Southern Pines Nursing Ctr
6140 Congress St ..... New Port Richey FL 34653 727-842-8402 841-8060
Web: southernpineshealthcare.com
Magnolia Manor Inc 2001 S Lee St ..... Americus GA 31709 229-924-9352
Web: www.magnoliamanor.com
Uhs Pruitt Corp 1626 Jeurgens Ct ..... Norcross GA 30093 770-279-6200 925-4619
Web: www.pruitthealth.com
Kula Hospital 100 Keokea Pl ..... Kula HI 96790 808-878-1221 878-1791
TF: 800-845-6733 ■ Web: www.hhsc.org
Apostolic Christian Restmor Inc
1500 Parkside Ave ..... Morton IL 61550 309-284-1400 266-7877
Web: www.acrestmor.org
Barton W Stone Christian Home
873 Grove St ..... Jacksonville IL 62650 217-479-3400 243-8553
Web: heritageofcare.com
Brentwood North Nursing & Rehabilitation Ctr
3705 Deerfield Rd ..... Riverwoods IL 60015 847-947-9000
Web: brentwoodnorthrehab.com
Brentwood Subacute Rehabilitation Ctr
5400 W 87th St ..... Burbank IL 60459 708-423-1200
Web: savaseniorcare.com
Community Nursing & Rehabilitation Ctr
1136 N Mill St ..... Naperville IL 60563 630-355-3300

Phone | Fax

Evenglow Lodge Inc 215 E Washington St. . . . . Pontiac IL 61764 815-844-6131
Web: www.evenglowlodge.org

Heritage Enterprises Inc
115 W Jefferson St. . . . . Bloomington IL 61702 309-828-4361
Web: www.heritageofcare.com

John C Proctor Endowment
2724 W Reservoir Blvd. . . . . Peoria IL 61615 309-685-6580 566-4292
Web: proctorplace.org

Lieberman Ctr for Health & Rehabilitation
9700 Gross Pt Rd . . . . Skokie IL 60076 847-674-7210 674-6366
Web: cje.net

ManorCare Health Services - Arlington Heights
715 W Central Rd . . . . Arlington Heights IL 60005 847-392-2020 392-0174
Web: manorcare.com

ManorCare Health Services - Homewood
940 Maple Ave . . . . Homewood IL 60430 708-799-0244 799-1505
Web: www.heartland-manorcare.com

ManorCare Health Services - Oak Lawn East
9401 S Kostner Ave . . . . Oak Lawn IL 60453 708-423-7882 423-7947
Web: www.heartland-manorcare.com

Norridge Health Care & Rehabilitation Centre
7001 W Cullom Ave . . . . Norridge IL 60706 708-457-0700 457-8852

North Adams Home Inc 2259 E 1100th St . . . . Mendon IL 62351 217-936-2137 936-2818
Web: www.northadamshome.org

Oakton Pavilion Healthcare Facility Inc
1660 Oakton Pl. . . . . Des Plaines IL 60018 847-299-5588 493-6525

OSF Saint Clare Home 5533 N Galena Rd . . . . Peoria Heights IL 61616 309-682-5428 682-8478
Web: www.osfhealthcare.org

Plymouth Place Inc 315 N LaGrange Rd . . . . La Grange Park IL 60526 708-354-0340 482-6843
Web: www.plymouthplace.org

Regency Nursing Centre 6631 N Milwaukee Ave . . . . Niles IL 60714 847-647-7444
Web: www.regencyrehabcenter.com

Sherman West Court 1950 Larkin Ave. . . . . Elgin IL 60123 847-742-7070
Web: shermanwestcourt.com

Sherwin Manor Nursing Ctr 7350 N Sheridan Rd. . . . . Chicago IL 60626 773-274-1000
Web: www.sherwinmanor.com

Heritage Ctr 1201 W Buena Vista Rd. . . . . Evansville IN 47710 812-429-0700 429-1849
TF: 800-704-0700 ■ *Web:* www.holidayhealthcare.com

Miller's Merry Manor 612 E 11th St . . . . Rushville IN 46173 765-932-4127 932-3054
Web: millersmerrymanor.com

Miller's Merry Manor 1500 Grant St . . . . Huntington IN 46750 260-356-5713 356-8671
Web: www.millersmerrymanor.com

Miller's Merry Manor 200 26th St. . . . . Logansport IN 46947 574-722-4006
Web: www.millersmerrymanor.com

Northwest Manor Health Care Ctr
6440 W 34th St. . . . . Indianapolis IN 46224 317-293-4930
Web: northwesthealthcare.net

Pyramid Point Post-Acute Rehabilitation Ctr
8530 Township Line Rd . . . . Indianapolis IN 46260 317-876-9955 876-6016
TF: 800-861-0086 ■ *Web:* covenantcare.com/locations

St.Vincent Health 2001 W 86th St. . . . . Indianapolis IN 46260 317-338-2345 338-6491
TF: 866-338-2345 ■ *Web:* www.stvincent.org

Waters of Covington 1600 E Liberty St . . . . Covington IN 47932 765-793-4818
Web: www.watersofcovington.com

Abcm Corp 1320 Fourth St NE PO Box 436 . . . . Hampton IA 50441 641-456-5636 456-2320
Web: www.abcmcorp.com

Edgewood Convalescent Home Inc
513 S Bell St. . . . . Edgewood IA 52042 563-928-6461 928-6462

Monticello Nursing & Rehabilitation Ctr
500 Pinehaven Dr . . . . Monticello IA 52310 319-465-5415
Web: monticellocampus.com

New Hampton Nursing & Rehabilitation Ctr
703 S Fourth Ave . . . . New Hampton IA 50659 641-394-4153 394-5483
Web: www.nhnrc.com

New London Nursing & Rehabilitation Ctr
1611 W Lakes Pkwy . . . . West Des Moines IA 50266 319-367-5753 367-2003
Web: careinitiatives.org

Wheatland Manor Inc 316 E Lincolnway St. . . . . Wheatland IA 52777 563-374-1295
Web: wheatmanor.com

Fountain Circle Care & Rehabilitation Center
200 Glenway Rd . . . . Winchester KY 40391 859-744-1800
Web: www.fountaincirclecare.com

Signature Health Care LLC
12201 Bluegrass Pkwy . . . . Louisville KY 40299 502-568-7800
Web: ltcrevolution.com

Fox Chase Rehabilitation & Nursing Ctr
2015 E W Hwy . . . . Silver Spring MD 20910 301-587-2400
Web: reverafoxchase.com

FutureCare Canton Harbor
1300 S Ellwood Ave . . . . Baltimore MD 21224 410-342-6644
Web: futurecare.com

Keswick Multi-Care Ctr 700 W 40th St. . . . . Baltimore MD 21211 410-235-8860 662-4324
Web: choosekeswick.org

Levindale Hebrew Geriatric Ctr & Hospital
2434 W Belvedere Ave . . . . Baltimore MD 21215 410-601-2400 601-2890
Web: www.lifebridgehealth.org/levindale

ManorCare Health Services - Rossville
6600 Ridge Rd . . . . Baltimore MD 21237 410-574-4950 391-4386
Web: manorcare.com

ManorCare Health Services - Ruxton
7001 N Charles St . . . . Towson MD 21204 410-821-9600 337-8313
Web: manorcare.com

Woodside Ctr 9101 Second Ave . . . . Silver Spring MD 20910 301-588-5544
Web: genesishcc.com

Central Boston Elder Services Inc
2315 Washington St. . . . . Boston MA 02119 617-277-7416 277-2005
TF: 800-922-2275 ■ *Web:* www.centralboston.org

Colonial Nursing & Rehabilitation Inc
125 Broad St. . . . . Weymouth MA 02188 781-337-3121
Web: welchhrg.com

Eastpointe Rehabilitation & Skilled Care Ctr
255 Central Ave . . . . Chelsea MA 02150 617-884-5700
Web: www.eastpointerehab.com

Phone | Fax

Fairview Commons Nursing & Rehabilitation Ctr
151 Christian Hill Rd . . . . Great Barrington MA 01230 413-528-4560
Web: www.fairviewcommons.org

HealthBridge Management
57 Old Road to Nine Acre Corner . . . . Concord MA 01742 203-792-8102 378-7868*
*Fax Area Code: 908 ■ *Fax: Admitting

JML Care Ctr 184 Terr Heun Dr . . . . Falmouth MA 02540 508-457-4621 457-1218
Web: capecodhealth.org

Kindred Transitional Care and Rehabilitation
160 Main St . . . . Walpole MA 02081 508-660-3080 660-1634
Web: www.harringtonrehab.com

Marlborough Hills Healthcare Ctr
121 Northboro Rd E . . . . Marlborough MA 01752 508-485-4040 481-5585

Meadow Green Nursing & Rehabilitation Ctr
45 Woburn St. . . . . Waltham MA 02452 781-899-8600
Web: www.meadowgreen.org

Newton Health Care Ctr 2101 Washington St . . . . Newton MA 02462 617-969-4660 928-0737

North Adams Common Nursing Home
175 Franklin St. . . . . North Adams MA 01247 413-664-4041 664-8447
TF: 800-445-4560 ■ *Web:* www.northadamscommons.org

Peabody Glen Health Care Ctr 199 Andover St . . . . Peabody MA 01960 978-531-0772 531-7809
Web: ma.care-one.com

Port Health Care 113 Low St . . . . Newburyport MA 01950 978-462-7373 462-6510
Web: whittierhealth.com

Sacred Heart Home 359 Summer St. . . . . New Bedford MA 02740 508-996-6751 996-5189
Web: www.dhfo.org

Sherrill House Inc (SH)
135 S Huntington Ave. . . . . Jamaica Plain MA 02130 617-731-2400 731-8671
Web: www.sherrillhouse.org

Vinfen Corp 950 Cambridge St . . . . Cambridge MA 02141 617-441-1800 441-1858
Web: www.vinfen.org

Williamstown Commons Nursing & Rehabilitation Ctr
25 Adams Rd . . . . Williamstown MA 01267 413-458-2111 458-3156
TF: 800-445-4560 ■ *Web:* www.williamstowncommons.org

Wilmington Health Care Ctr 750 Woburn St . . . . Wilmington MA 01887 910-341-3300 658-6470*
*Fax Area Code: 978 ■ *Web:* www.wilmingtonhealth.com

Worcester Skilled Care Ctr 59 Acton St. . . . . Worcester MA 01604 508-791-3147
Web: www.wingatehealthcare.com

Bay County Medical Care Facility
564 W Hampton Rd . . . . Essexville MI 48732 989-892-3591 892-6991
Web: www.baycountymcf.com

Clarkston Specialty Healthcare Ctr
4800 Clintonville Rd. . . . . Clarkston MI 48346 248-674-0903
Web: savaseniorcare.com

Crestmont Health Care Ctr 111 Trealout Dr . . . . Fenton MI 48430 810-629-4105
Web: savaseniorcare.com

Farmington HealthCare Ctr
34225 Grand River Ave. . . . . Farmington MI 48335 248-477-7373 477-2888

Heartland Health Care Ctr Bloomfield Hills
2975 N Adams Rd. . . . . Bloomfield Hills MI 48304 248-645-2900 895-1094*
*Fax Area Code: 614 ■ *Web:* www.hcr-manorcare.com

Heartland Health Care Ctr University
28550 Five Mile Rd . . . . Livonia MI 48154 734-427-8270 427-2135
Web: heartland-manorcare.com

Hope Network 3075 Orchard Vista Dr SE. . . . . Grand Rapids MI 49546 616-301-8000 301-8010
TF: 800-695-7273 ■ *Web:* www.hopenetwork.org

Howell Care Ctr 3003 W Grand River Ave. . . . . Howell MI 48843 517-546-4210 546-9495

Isabella Medical Care Facility
1222 N Dr. . . . . Mount Pleasant MI 48858 989-772-2957 772-3669
Web: mcf.isabellacounty.org

Sanctuary at Bellbrook 873 W Avon Rd . . . . Rochester Hills MI 48307 248-656-6300
Web: www.trinityseniorsanctuary.org/communities/sanctuary-bellbrook

Sunset Hills Health & Rehabilitation Ctr
10954 Kennerly Rd. . . . . Saint Louis MO 63128 314-843-4242 843-4031
Web: sunsethillshrc.com

Good Shepherd Rehabilitation & Nursing Ctr
20 Plantation Dr . . . . Jaffrey NH 03452 603-532-8762 593-0006
Web: www.cc-nh.org

Kindred Transitional Care & Rehabilitation - Greenbriar
55 Harris Rd . . . . Nashua NH 03062 603-888-1573 888-5089
Web: www.greenbriarterrace.com

Pleasant Valley Nursing Ctr 8 Peabody Rd . . . . Derry NH 03038 603-434-1566 434-2299

Camden County Health Services Ctr
425 Woodbury Turnersville Rd. Blackwood NJ 08012 856-374-6600
Web: www.cchsc.com

CareOne At Valley 300 Old Hook Rd . . . . Westwood NJ 07675 201-664-8888
Web: www.care-one.com

Daughters of Miriam Ctr/Gallen Institute
155 Hazel St . . . . Clifton NJ 07011 973-772-3700
Web: www.daughtersofmiriamcenter.org

Linwood Care Ctr 201 New Rd & Central Ave. . . . . Linwood NJ 08221 609-927-6131
Web: www.reveralinwood.com

ManorCare Health Services - Mountainside
1180 Rt 22 W . . . . Mountainside NJ 07092 908-654-0020
TF: 800-366-1232 ■ *Web:* www.hcr-manorcare.com

Somerset Valley Rehab Ctr 1621 Rt 22 W . . . . Bound Brook NJ 08805 732-469-2000
Web: care-one.com

Voorhees Pediatric Facility
1304 Laurel Oak Rd . . . . Voorhees NJ 08043 856-346-3300 346-3462
TF: 888-873-5437 ■ *Web:* www.forkidcare.com

Willow Creek Rehabilitation & Care Ctr
1165 Easton Ave. . . . . Somerset NJ 08873 732-246-4100
Web: reverawillowcreek.com

At Rosewood 284 Troy Rd. . . . . Rensselaer NY 12144 518-286-1621 286-1691
Web: www.rosewoodrehabilitation.com

Clove Lakes Health Care & Rehabilitation Ctr
25 Fanning St. . . . . Staten Island NY 10314 718-289-7900
Web: www.clovelakes.com

Comprehensive Care Management Corp (CCM)
1250 Waters Pl Tower 1 Ste 602. . . . . Bronx NY 10461 877-226-8500
TF: 877-226-8500 ■ *Web:* www.centerlighthealthcare.org

Diamond Hill Nursing & Rehabilitation
100 New Tpke Rd . . . . Troy NY 12182 518-235-1410 426-4792
Web: news10.com

Facility	City	State	Zip	Phone	Fax
Dumont Ctr for Rehabilitation & Nursing Care 676 Pelham Rd *Web:* www.dumontcenter.com	New Rochelle	NY	10805	914-632-9600	632-9247
Golden Gate Rehabilitation & Health Care Ctr 191 Bradley Ave *Web:* goldengaterehab.com	Staten Island	NY	10314	718-698-8800	
Grace Plaza of Great Neck Inc 15 St Paul's Pl *Web:* www.graceplaza.com	Great Neck	NY	11021	516-466-3001	
Haven Manor Health Care Ctr 1441 Gateway Blvd	Far Rockaway	NY	11691	718-471-1500	471-9606
Jewish Home Lifecare 120 W 106th St *TF:* 800-544-0304 ■ *Web:* www.jewishhome.org	New York	NY	10025	212-870-5000	870-4715
Lutheran Social Services 715 Falconer St *Web:* www.lutheran-jamestown.org	Jamestown	NY	14701	716-665-4905	665-8055
Margaret Tietz Ctr for Nursing Care 164-11 Chapin Pkwy *Web:* www.margarettietz.org	Jamaica	NY	11432	718-298-7800	
Mosholu Parkway Nursing & Rehabilitation Ctr 3356 Perry Ave	Bronx	NY	10467	718-655-3568	
Palm Gardens Ctr for Nursing & Rehabilitation 615 Ave C *Web:* www.palmgardenscenter.com	Brooklyn	NY	11218	718-633-3300	
Promenade Rehabilitation & Health Care Ctr 140 Beach 114th St	Rockaway Park	NY	11694	718-945-4600	634-8237
Providence Rest 3304 Waterbury Ave *Web:* www.providencerest.org	Bronx	NY	10465	718-931-3000	863-0185
Robinson Terrace 28652 New York 23 *Web:* www.robinsonterrace.com	Stamford	NY	12167	607-652-7521	652-3362
Saint Mary's Hospital for Children Inc 29-01 216th St *Web:* www.stmaryskids.org	Bayside	NY	11360	718-281-8800	
Victory Lake Nursing Ctr 419 N Quaker Ln *Web:* victorylakenursing.com	Hyde Park	NY	12538	845-229-9177	
Wesley Gardens 3 Upton Pk *Web:* wesleygardens.com	Rochester	NY	14607	585-241-2100	241-2180
Kindred Hospital Greensboro 2401 Southside Blvd *TF:* 877-836-2671 ■ *Web:* www.khgreensboro.com	Greensboro	NC	27406	336-271-2800	271-2734
Long Leaf Medical Treatment Ctr 4761 Ward Blvd	Wilson	NC	27893	252-399-2112	399-2138
Valley Nursing Ctr 581 NC Hwy 16 S *Web:* valleyrehab.com	Taylorsville	NC	28681	828-632-8146	
Arbors East Subacute Nursing & Rehabilitation Ctr 5500 E Broad St *Web:* arborseastskillednursing.com	Columbus	OH	43213	614-575-9003	
Area Agency On Aging 10b Inc 1550 Corporate Woods Pkwy *TF:* 800-421-7277 ■ *Web:* www.directionhomeakroncanton.org	Uniontown	OH	44685	330-896-9172	896-6644
Cedarwood Plaza 12504 Cedar Rd *Web:* lhshealth.com	Cleveland Heights	OH	44106	216-371-3600	371-4661
Columbus Rehabilitation & Subacute Institute 44 S Souder Ave *Web:* columbusrehabskillednursing.com	Columbus	OH	43222	614-228-5900	
Communi Care At Waterford 955 Garden Lk Pkwy *Web:* www.communicarehealth.com	Toledo	OH	43614	419-382-2200	
Deaconess Long Term Care Inc (DLTC) 440 Lafayette Ave *Web:* www.deaconess-healthcare.com	Cincinnati	OH	45220	513-487-3600	
Heartland of Beavercreek 1974 N Fairfield Rd	Dayton	OH	45432	937-429-1106	429-0902
Heartland of Centerburg 212 Fairview Ave *Web:* hcr-manorcare.com	Centerburg	OH	43011	740-625-5774	
Hennis Care Centre 1720 Cross St *TF:* 800-241-1044 ■ *Web:* www.henniscarecentre.com	Dover	OH	44622	330-364-8849	364-2128
Kindred Transitional Care and Rehabilitation 75 McMillen Dr **Fax Area Code: 502* ■ *Web:* www.newarkhealthcare.com	Newark	OH	43055	740-344-0357	596-4095*
ManorCare Health Services - North Olmsted 23225 Lorain Rd *Web:* www.hcr-manorcare.com	North Olmsted	OH	44070	440-779-6900	
St. Augustine Health Ministries 7801 Detroit Ave *Web:* staugministries.org	Cleveland	OH	44102	216-634-7400	643-7483
Villa Angela Nursing Rehabilitation Ctr 5700 Karl Rd *Web:* villa-angela.net	Columbus	OH	43229	614-846-5420	
Walton Manor Health Care Ctr 19859 Alexander Rd *Web:* www.saberhealth.com	Walton Hills	OH	44146	440-652-5212	
Oklahoma Veterans Ctr Norman 1776 E Robinson St *TF:* 800-782-5218 ■ *Web:* www.ok.gov	Norman	OK	73071	405-360-5600	
Golden Living Ctr 350 Old Gilkeson Rd *Web:* www.goldenlivingcenters.com/mt-lebanon	Pittsburgh	PA	15228	412-564-3988	257-8226
Golden LivingCenter - Western Reserve 1521 W 54th St *Web:* local.goldenlivingcenters.com	Erie	PA	16509	814-864-0671	
Greenery Speciality Care 2200 Hill Church-Houston Rd *Web:* greenerysccc.com	Canonsburg	PA	15317	724-745-8000	746-8780
Kindred Hospital Philadelphia 6129 Palmetto St *TF:* 800-654-5988 ■ *Web:* www.kindredphila.com	Philadelphia	PA	19111	215-722-8555	725-8998
Kindred Hospital Pittsburgh 7777 Steubenville Pk *TF:* 800-654-5988 ■ *Web:* www.kindredhospitalpittsburgh.com	Oakdale	PA	15071	412-494-5500	494-5511
Laurel Ctr 125 Holly Rd *Web:* genesishcc.com	Hamburg	PA	19526	610-562-2284	
Liberty Nursing & Rehabilitation Ctr 535 N 17th St *Web:* heartland-manorcare.com	Allentown	PA	18104	610-432-4351	435-4470
Presbyterian SeniorCare-Southminster Place 835 S Main St *Web:* www.srcare.org	Washington	PA	15301	724-222-4300	
Presbyterian SeniorCare-Westminster Place 1215 Hulton Rd *TF:* 877-772-6500 ■ *Web:* www.srcare.org	Oakmont	PA	15139	412-828-5600	
Redstone Highlands Health Care Ctr 6 Garden Ctr Dr *TF:* 800-732-0999 ■ *Web:* www.redstonehighlands.org	Greensburg	PA	15601	724-832-8400	836-3710
Rest Haven-York 1050 S George St *TF:* 800-368-1019 ■ *Web:* www.resthavenyork.com	York	PA	17403	717-843-9866	846-5894
South Mountain Restoration Ctr 10058 S Mountain Rd *Web:* www.dhs.pa.gov/citizens/mentalhealthservices/southmountainrestorationcenter	South Mountain	PA	17261	717-749-3121	
Woodhaven Care Ctr 2400 McGinley Rd *Web:* mywoodhavencarecenter.com	Monroeville	PA	15146	412-856-4770	856-6856
Oak Hill Nursing & Rehabilitation Ctr 544 Pleasant St *Web:* kindredhealthcare.com	Pawtucket	RI	02904	401-725-8888	
Saint Elizabeth Home 1 Saint Elizabeth Way *Web:* www.stelizabethcommunity.org	East Greenwich	RI	02818	401-471-6060	471-6072
Heartland Health Care Ctr Charleston 1800 Eagle Landing Blvd *Web:* www.heartland-manorcare.com	Hanahan	SC	29410	843-553-0656	553-9773
Allen Morgan Health Ctr 177 N Highland Ave *Web:* trezevantmanor.org	Memphis	TN	38111	901-325-4003	
Diversicare Healthcare Services Inc 537 Spring St *Web:* diversicareofdover.com	Dover	TN	37058	931-232-6902	
Diversicare Healthcare Services Inc. 100 Elmhurst Dr *Web:* diversicareofoakridge.com	Oak Ridge	TN	37830	865-481-3367	
Fairfield Nursing & Rehabilitation 420 Moody St *Web:* fairfieldnursingandrehab.com	Fairfield	TX	75840	903-389-1236	
Hearthstone of Round Rock 401 Oakwood Blvd *Web:* www.seniorcarecentersltc.com	Round Rock	TX	78681	512-388-7494	388-2166
Heartland Health Care Ctr Bedford 2001 Forest Ridge Dr *Web:* www.heartland-manorcare.com	Bedford	TX	76021	817-571-6804	267-4176
Kindred Hospital Fort Worth 815 Eigth Ave *Web:* kindredfortworth.com	Fort Worth	TX	76104	817-332-4812	332-8843
Plum Creek Specialty Hospital 5601 Plum Creek Dr	Amarillo	TX	79124	806-351-1000	351-8117
Treemont Nursing & Rehabilitation Ctr 5550 Harvest Hill Rd *Web:* www.treemonthealthcare.com	Dallas	TX	75230	972-661-1862	
South Davis Community Hospital 401 S 400 E *Web:* www.sdch.com	Bountiful	UT	84010	801-295-2361	295-1398
Sunshine Terrace Foundation Inc 248 West 300 North *Web:* www.sunshineterrace.net	Logan	UT	84321	435-752-0411	752-1318
Berkshire Health & Rehabilitation Ctr 705 Clearview Dr *Web:* www.berkshirehealthrehab.com	Vinton	VA	24179	540-982-6691	
James River Convalescent Ctr 540 Aberthaw Ave *Web:* vahs.com	Newport News	VA	23601	757-595-2273	595-2271
Laurels of University Park, The 2420 Pemberton Rd *Web:* www.laurelsofuniversitypark.com	Richmond	VA	23233	804-747-9200	747-1574
Lucy Corr Village 6800 Lucy Corr Blvd *Web:* www.lucycorrvillage.com	Chesterfield	VA	23832	804-748-1511	706-5572
Lynchburg Health & Rehabilitation Ctr 5615 Seminole Ave *Web:* lynchburghealthrehab.com	Lynchburg	VA	24502	434-239-2657	
ManorCare Health Services - Arlington 550 S Carlin Springs Rd *Web:* www.hcr-manorcare.com	Arlington	VA	22204	703-379-7200	
ManorCare Health Services - Fair Oaks 12475 Lee Jackson Memorial Hwy *Web:* manorcare.com	Fairfax	VA	22033	703-352-7172	352-1455
Riverside Regional Convalescent Ctr 1000 Old Denbigh Blvd *Web:* riversideonline.com	Newport News	VA	23602	757-875-2000	875-2036
Westport Health Care Ctr 7300 Forest Avenue	Richmond	VA	23226	804-288-3152	285-9348
Ballard Care & RehabilitationCenter 820 NW 95th St *Web:* genesishcc.com	Seattle	WA	98117	206-782-0100	
Kitsap Mental Health Services 5455 Almira Dr NE *Web:* www.kitsapmentalhealth.org	Bremerton	WA	98311	360-405-4010	
Seattle Medical & Rehabilitation Ctr 555 16th Ave *Web:* seattlemedicalpostacute.com	Seattle	WA	98122	206-324-8200	
Glenwood Park Retirement Village 1924 Glenwood Pk Rd *Web:* www.gwpinc.org	Princeton	WV	24739	304-425-8128	
Brewster Village 3300 W Brewster St *Web:* www.outagamie.org	Appleton	WI	54914	920-832-5400	832-4922
Clement Manor 3939 S 92nd St *Web:* www.clementmanor.com	Greenfield	WI	53228	414-321-1800	
Franciscan Villa 3601 S Chicago Ave *Web:* www.franciscanvilla.org	South Milwaukee	WI	53172	414-764-4100	
Middleton Village Nursing & Rehabilitation Ctr 6201 Elmwood Ave	Middleton	WI	53562	608-831-8300	831-4253

451 LONG-TERM CARE FACILITIES OPERATORS

Phone Fax

Active Day/Senior Care Inc
400 Redland Ct Ste 114 .... Owings Mills MD 21117 866-724-9599
TF: 877-435-3372 ■ *Web:* www.seniorcarectrs.com

Aegis Assisted Living 17602 NE Union Hill Rd .... Redmond WA 98052 425-861-9993
TF: 888-252-3447 ■ *Web:* www.aegisliving.com

American Religious Town Hall Meeting Inc
PO Box 180118 .... Dallas TX 75218 214-328-9828 328-3042
TF: 800-783-9828 ■ *Web:* www.americanreligious.org

Americare Systems Inc 214 N Scott St .... Sikeston MO 63801 573-471-1113
Web: www.americareusa.net

Atria Senior Living Group
300 E Market St Ste 100 .... Louisville KY 40202 502-779-4700
Web: www.atriaseniorliving.com

CabelTel International Corp
1603 Lyndon B Johnson Fwy .... Dallas TX 75234 972-407-8400 522-4240*
**Fax Area Code:* 469 ■ *Web:* www.newconceptenergy.com

Cardinal Ritter Senior Services
7601 Watson Rd .... Saint Louis MO 63119 314-961-8000
Web: www.ccstl.org

Comprehensive Systems Inc 1700 Clark St .... Charles City IA 50616 641-228-4842 228-4675
Web: comprehensivesystems.org

ElderWood Senior Care 7 Limestone Dr .... Williamsville NY 14221 716-633-3900
TF: 888-826-9663 ■ *Web:* www.elderwood.com

Extendicare Inc 3000 Steeles Ave E .... Markham ON L3R9W2 905-470-4000 470-5588
NYSE: EXE ■ *Web:* www.extendicare.com

Five Star Quality Care Inc 400 Centre St .... Newton MA 02458 617-796-8387 796-8385
NYSE: FVE ■ *TF:* 866-230-1286 ■ *Web:* www.fivestarseniorliving.com

Genesis HealthCare Corp
101 E State St .... Kennett Square PA 19348 610-444-6350 925-4000
TF: 800-944-7776 ■ *Web:* www.genesishcc.com

HCF Inc 1100 Shawnee Rd .... Lima OH 45805 419-999-2010 999-6284
Web: www.hcfinc.com

HCR Manor Care 333 N Summit St PO Box 10086 .... Toledo OH 43699 419-252-5500 252-6404*
**Fax:* Hum Res ■ *Web:* www.hcr-manorcare.com

Kindred Healthcare Inc 680 S Fourth Ave .... Louisville KY 40202 502-596-7300
NYSE: KND ■ *TF:* 800-545-0749 ■ *Web:* www.kindredhealthcare.com

Life Care Centers of America Inc
3570 Keith St NW PO Box 3480 .... Cleveland TN 37320 423-472-9585 476-5974
Web: www.lcca.com

National HealthCare Corp
100 E Vine St PO Box 1398 .... Murfreesboro TN 37133 615-890-2020 890-0123
NYSE: NHC ■ *Web:* www.nhccare.com

Odyssey HealthCare Inc 717 N Harwood St .... Dallas TX 75201 214-922-9711
TF: 855-865-5894 ■ *Web:* gentiva.com

Royal Management Corp 665 W N Ave .... Lombard IL 60148 630-458-4700 748-3701
Web: www.lexingtonhealth.com

Sun Healthcare Group Inc
18831 Von Karman Ste 400 .... Irvine CA 92612 949-255-7100
NASDAQ: SUNH ■ *TF:* 800-729-6600

Sunrise Senior Living Inc 7902 Westpark Dr .... McLean VA 22102 703-273-7500 744-1601
NYSE: SRZ ■ *TF:* 800-929-4124 ■ *Web:* www.sunriseseniorliving.com

452 LOTTERIES, GAMES, SWEEPSTAKES

See Also Games & Gaming p. 2348

Phone Fax

7 Cedars Casino 170756 Hwy 101 .... Sequim WA 98382 360-683-7777
Web: www.7cedarsresort.com

Alta Ski Lifts Co
Alta Ski Area Hwy 210 Little Cottonwood Canyon .... Alta UT 84092 801-359-1078
Web: www.alta.com

Arizona Lottery 4740 E University Dr .... Phoenix AZ 85034 480-921-4400
Web: arizonalottery.com

AVI Casino Enterprise Inc
10000 Aha Macav Pkwy .... Laughlin NV 89029 702-535-5555
Web: www.avicasino.com

Bartons Club 93 93 Jackpot .... Jackpot NV 89825 775-755-2341
Web: www.bartonsclub93.com

Bay Mills Resort & Casinos
11386 W Lakeshore Dr .... Brimley MI 49715 906-248-3715
Web: www.baymillscasinos.com

Bishop Paiute Gaming Corp 2742 N Sierra Hwy .... Bishop CA 93514 760-873-4150
Web: www.bishoppaiutetribe.com

Bodines Casino 5650 S Carson St .... Carson City NV 89701 775-885-7777
Web: bodinescarson.com

Boot Hill Casino & Resort
4000 W Comanche St .... Dodge City KS 67801 620-682-7777
Web: boothillcasino.com

British Columbia Lottery Corp (BCLC)
74 W Seymour St .... Kamloops BC V2C1E2 250-828-5500 828-5631
TF: 866-815-0222 ■ *Web:* www.bclc.com

Casino San Pablo of Lytton Rancheria
13255 San Pablo Ave .... San Pablo CA 94806 510-215-7888
Web: www.sanpablolytton.com

Catfish Bend Casinos II LLC
3001 Winegard Dr .... Burlington IA 52601 319-753-2946
TF: 866-792-9948 ■ *Web:* www.thepzazz.com

Cedco 3201 Tremont Ave .... North Bend OR 97459 541-756-0662
Web: www.cedco.net

Chinook Winds Casino Resort
1777 NW 44th St .... Lincoln City OR 97367 541-996-5825
TF: 888-244-6665 ■ *Web:* www.chinookwindscasino.com

Choctaw Casino Resorts 3735 Choctaw Rd .... Durant OK 74701 580-920-0160
TF: 888-652-4628 ■ *Web:* www.choctawcasinos.com

Chumash Casino Resort 3400 E Hwy 246 .... Santa Ynez CA 93460 805-686-0855
TF: 800-248-6274 ■ *Web:* chumashcasino.com

Phone Fax

Cliff Castle Casino 555 W Middle Verde Rd .... Camp Verde AZ 86322 928-567-7999
TF: 800-381-7568 ■ *Web:* www.cliffcastlecasinohotel.com

Colorado Lottery 212 W Third St Ste 210 .... Pueblo CO 81003 719-546-2400 546-5208
TF: 800-999-2959 ■ *Web:* www.coloradolottery.com

Colville Tribal Casinos 729 Jackson St .... Omak WA 98841 509-422-8590
Web: www.colvillecasinos.com

Cypress Bayou Casino
832 Martin Luther King Rd .... Charenton LA 70523 800-284-4386
TF: 800-284-4386 ■ *Web:* www.cypressbayou.com

Delaware State Lottery 1575 McKee Rd Ste 102 .... Dover DE 19904 302-739-5291 739-7586
Web: www.delottery.com

District of Columbia Lottery & Charitable Games Control Board
2101 ML King Jr Ave SE .... Washington DC 20020 202-645-8000
Web: www.dclottery.com

Florida Lottery Dept 250 Marriott Dr .... Tallahassee FL 32301 850-487-7777
Web: www.flalottery.com

Fortune Bay Resort & Casino 1430 Bois Forte Rd .... Tower MN 55790 218-753-6400
TF: 800-992-7529 ■ *Web:* fortunebay.com

Gamesville Inc 100 Fifth Ave .... Waltham MA 02451 781-370-2700
Web: www.gamesville.com

Georgia Lottery Corp
250 Williams St NW Ste 3000 .... Atlanta GA 30303 404-215-5000 215-8871
TF: 800-425-8259 ■ *Web:* www.galottery.com

Grand Lake Casino 24701 S 655 Rd .... Grove OK 74344 918-786-8528
Web: grandlakecasino.com

High Winds Casino 61475 E 100 Rd .... Miami OK 74354 918-541-9463
Web: highwindscasino.com

Ho-chunk Golden Nickel Casino
S3214 County Rd Bd .... Baraboo WI 53913 608-355-7777
Web: www.ho-chunkgaming.com

Idaho Lottery 1199 Shoreline Ln Ste 100 .... Boise ID 83702 208-334-2600 334-2610
TF: 800-432-5688 ■ *Web:* www.idaholottery.com

Illinois Lottery 101 W Jefferson St .... Springfield IL 62702 217-524-6435 877-0436*
**Fax Area Code:* 866 ■ *TF:* 800-252-1775 ■ *Web:* www.illinoislottery.com

Indiana Lottery
201 S Capitol Ave Ste 1100 .... Indianapolis IN 46225 317-264-4800
TF: 800-955-6886 ■ *Web:* www.in.gov

Iowa Lottery 2323 Grand Ave .... Des Moines IA 50312 515-323-4633
Web: www.ialottery.com

Kansas Lottery 128 N Kansas Ave .... Topeka KS 66603 785-296-5700
TF: 800-544-9467 ■ *Web:* kslottery.com

Kentucky Lottery Corp 1011 W Main St .... Louisville KY 40202 502-560-1500 560-1532
TF: 800-937-8946 ■ *Web:* www.kylottery.com

Keweenaw Bay Indian Community
16429 Bear Town Rd .... Baraga MI 49908 906-353-6623
Web: www.ojibwacasino.com

Lco Casino Lodge & Convention Center
13767 W County Rd B .... Hayward WI 54843 715-634-5643
Web: lcocasino.com

Louisiana Lottery Corp 555 Laurel St .... Baton Rouge LA 70801 225-297-2000 297-2005
Web: louisianalottery.com

Lucky Chances Casino 1700 Hillside Blvd .... Colma CA 94014 650-758-2237
Web: www.grubgirl.com

Maryland State Lottery
1800 Washington Blvd Ste 330 .... Baltimore MD 21230 410-230-8790 230-8728
Web: www.mdlottery.com

Massachusetts State Lottery Commission
60 Columbian St .... Braintree MA 02184 781-849-5555 849-5546
Web: www.masslottery.com

Michigan State Lottery
101 E Hillsdale St PO Box 30023 .... Lansing MI 48909 517-335-5600 335-5644
Web: www.michigan.gov/lottery

Minnesota State Lottery 2645 Long Lake Rd .... Saint Paul MN 55113 651-635-8273
Web: www.mnlottery.com

Missouri Lottery
1823 Southridge Dr PO Box 1603 .... Jefferson City MO 65109 573-751-4050 751-5188
Web: www.molottery.com

Mole Lake Casino Lodge & Conference Center
3084 State Hwy 55 .... Crandon WI 54520 715-478-3200
Web: www.molelakecasino.com

Montana Lottery 2525 N Montana Ave .... Helena MT 59601 406-444-5825 444-5830
TF: 800-425-1435 ■ *Web:* www.montanalottery.com

Multi-State Lottery Association
4400 NW Urbandale Dr .... Urbandale IA 50322 515-453-1400
Web: www.musl.com

Nassau Regional Off Track Betting Corp
220 Fulton Ave .... Hempstead NY 11550 516-572-2800
Web: www.nassauotb.com

Nebraska Lottery 1800 "O" St PO Box 98901 .... Lincoln NE 68509 402-471-6100 471-6108
TF: 800-587-5200 ■ *Web:* www.nelottery.com

New Hampshire Lottery Commission
14 Integra Dr .... Concord NH 03301 603-271-3391 271-1160
TF: 800-852-3324 ■ *Web:* www.nhlottery.com

New Jersey Lottery PO Box 041 .... Trenton NJ 08625 609-599-5800 599-5935
Web: www.state.nj.us

New Mexico Lottery
Lottery 4511 Osuna Rd NE PO Box 93190 .... Albuquerque NM 87199 505-342-7600 342-7511
Web: www.nmlottery.com

Ocean's Eleven Casino 121 Brooks St .... Oceanside CA 92054 760-439-6988
Web: www.oceans11.com

Odawa Casino Resort, The 1760 Lears Rd .... Petoskey MI 49770 231-439-1206
Web: www.odawacasino.com

Ohio Lottery Commission 615 W Superior Ave .... Cleveland OH 44113 216-787-3200 787-3313
TF: 800-686-4208 ■ *Web:* www.ohiolottery.com

Ohiya Casino 53142 Hwy 12 .... Niobrara NE 68760 402-857-3860
Web: ohiyacasino.com

Oregon Lottery 500 Airport Rd SE .... Salem OR 97301 503-540-1000 540-1001
Web: oregonlottery.org

Pahrump Nugget Hotel & Gambling Hall
681 S Hwy 160 .... Pahrump NV 89048 775-751-6500
Web: pahrumpnugget.com

Patriot Gaming & Electronics Inc
217 N Lindberg St .... Griffith IN 46319 219-922-6400
Web: patriotgaming.com

Phone Fax

Prairie's Edge Casino Resort
5616 Prairies Edge Ln Granite Falls MN 56241 320-564-2121
Web: www.prairiesedgecasino.com

Rail City Casino 2121 Victorian Ave Sparks NV 89431 775-359-9440
Web: www.railcity.com

Red Hawk Casino 1 Red Hawk Pkwy Placerville CA 95667 530-677-7000

Rhode Island Lottery 1425 Pontiac Ave Cranston RI 02920 401-463-6500
Web: www.rilot.com

River Rock Entertainment Authority
3250 Hwy 128 E Geyserville CA 95441 707-857-2777
TF: 877-883-7777 ■ *Web:* www.riverrockcasino.com

Riverwalk Casino Hotel 1046 Warrenton Rd Vicksburg MS 39180 601-634-0100
TF: 866-615-9125 ■ *Web:* www.riverwalkvicksburg.com

Royal River Casino & Entertainment Complex
607 S Veterans St Flandreau SD 57028 605-997-3746
Web: www.royalrivercasino.com

San Felipe's Casino Hollywood 25 Hagon Rd Algodones NM 87001 505-867-6700
TF: 877-529-2946 ■ *Web:* sanfelipecasino.com

Santa Ana Star Casino 54 Jemez Dam Rd Bernalillo NM 87004 505-867-0000
Web: www.santaanastar.com

Shooting Star Casino Hotel & Event Center
777 Se Casino Rd Mahnomen MN 56557 218-935-2711
TF: 800-453-7827 ■ *Web:* www.starcasino.com

Soboba Casino 23333 Soboba Rd San Jacinto CA 92583 951-665-1000
TF: 866-476-2622 ■ *Web:* soboba.net

South Carolina Education Lottery
1333 Main St 4th Fl Columbia SC 29201 803-737-2002 737-2005
Web: www.sceducationlottery.com

Spirit Lake Casino & Resort
7889 Hwy 57 Saint Michael ND 58370 701-766-4747
Web: spiritlakecasino.net

Stockman's Casino 1560 W Williams Ave Fallon NV 89406 775-423-2117
Web: www.stockmanscasino.com

Sun Ray Park & Casino LLC 39 Rd 5568 Farmington NM 87401 505-566-1200
Web: sunraygaming.com

Suquamish Clearwater Casino & Resort
15347 Suquamish Way Ne Ste A Suquamish WA 98392 360-598-8700
Web: clearwatercasino.com

Tennessee Lottery 200 Athens Way Ste 200 Nashville TN 37228 615-324-6500
Web: www.tnlottery.com

Vermont Lottery Commission
1311 US Rt 302 Ste 100 Barre VT 05641 802-479-5686 479-4294
Web: wherezit.com

Virginia Lottery 900 E Main St Richmond VA 23219 804-692-7777 692-7775
Web: www.valottery.com

Washington State Lottery PO Box 43000 Olympia WA 98504 360-664-4720 664-2630
TF: 800-732-5101 ■ *Web:* www.walottery.com

West Virginia Lottery
900 Pennsylvania Ave Charleston WV 25302 304-558-0500
Web: www.wvlottery.com

Western Canada Lottery Corp
125 Garry St 10th Fl Winnipeg MB R3C4J1 204-942-8217
Web: www.wclc.com

Wisconsin Lottery PO Box 8941 Madison WI 53708 608-261-4916 264-6644
Web: www.wilottery.com

Wyandotte Nation Casino 100 Jackpot Pl Wyandotte OK 74370 918-678-4946
TF: 866-447-4946 ■ *Web:* wyandottecasinos.com

Zdi Gaming Inc 2124 196th St Sw Lynnwood WA 98036 425-775-7991
Web: www.zdigaming.com

453 LUGGAGE, BAGS, CASES

See Also Handbags, Totes, Backpacks p. 2449; Leather Goods - Personal p. 2645

Phone Fax

Anvil Cases 15730 Salt Lake Ave City of Industry CA 91745 626-968-4100 968-1703
TF: 800-359-2684 ■ *Web:* www.anvilcase.com

Award Winner Group 202 W Third St Mount Vernon NY 10550 914-664-7134 668-2858
Web: www.awardwinnergroup.com

Bergman Luggage Co
401 NE Northgate Way Ste 914 Seattle WA 98125 206-365-5775
Web: www.bergmanluggage.com

Brewer-Cantelmo Company Inc
55 W 39th St Ste 205 New York NY 10018 212-244-4600 244-1640
Web: www.brewer-cantelmo.com

Calzone Case Co 225 Black Rock Ave Bridgeport CT 06605 203-367-5766 336-4406
TF Cust Svc: 800-243-5152 ■ *Web:* www.calzonecase.com

CH Ellis Co Inc 2432 SE Ave Indianapolis IN 46201 317-636-3351 635-5140
TF Sales: 800-466-3351 ■ *Web:* www.chellis.com

Coach Inc 516 W 34th St New York NY 10001 212-594-1850 594-1682
NYSE: COH ■ *TF:* 800-444-3611 ■ *Web:* world.coach.com

Delsey Luggage 6735 Business Pkwy Ste A Elkridge MD 21075 410-796-5655
TF: 800-558-3344 ■ *Web:* www.delsey.com

Forward Industries Inc
477 S Rosemary Ave Ste 219 West Palm Beach FL 33401 561-465-0030
Web: www.forwardindustries.com

Johnston Manufacturing Co
19406 E Parlier Ave Reedley CA 93654 559-638-2737

LC Industries 2781 Katherine Wy Elk Grove Village IL 60007 312-455-0500
Web: lewisnclark.com

Leather Specialty Co 1088 Business Ln Naples FL 34110 239-333-1000

Mercury Luggage Manufacturing Co
4843 Victor St Jacksonville FL 32207 904-334-8801 733-9671
TF: 800-874-1885 ■ *Web:* www.mercuryluggage.com

Platt Luggage Inc 4051 W 51st St Chicago IL 60632 773-838-2000 838-2010
TF: 800-222-1555 ■ *Web:* www.plattcases.com/default.asp

RJ Singer International Inc
4801 W Jefferson Blvd Los Angeles CA 90016 323-735-1717
Web: www.rjsinger.com

Royal Case Company Inc 419 E Lamar St Sherman TX 75090 903-868-0288 893-7984
Web: www.royalcase.com

Phone Fax

SKB Corp 434 W Levers Pl Orange CA 92867 714-637-1252 637-0491
TF Sales: 800-410-2024 ■ *Web:* www.skbcases.com

Targus Inc 1211 N Miller St Anaheim CA 92806 714-765-5555 765-5599
TF: 877-482-7487 ■ *Web:* www.targus.com

Travelpro USA 700 Banyan Trl Boca Raton FL 33431 561-998-2824 998-8487
TF: 800-741-7471 ■ *Web:* www.travelpro.com

Zero Manufacturing Inc
500 West 200 North North Salt Lake UT 84054 801-298-5900 292-9450
TF: 800-959-5050 ■ *Web:* www.zerocases.com

454 MACHINE SHOPS

See Also Precision Machined Products p. 2968

Phone Fax

A-1 Jays Machinery 2228 Oakland Rd San Jose CA 95131 408-577-0282
Web: www.a1jays.com

Ability Engineering Technology inc
16140 S Vincennes Ave South Holland IL 60473 708-331-0025
Web: www.abilityengineering.com

Accudynamics LLC 240 Kenneth Welch Dr Lakeville MA 02347 508-946-4545
Web: www.accudynamics.com

Accura Technics LLC 310 Marlboro St Keene NH 03431 603-355-2727
Web: www.accuratechnics.com

Accuturn Corp 6510 Box Springs Blvd Ste A Riverside CA 92507 951-656-6621
Web: www.accuturninc.com

Ace Precision Machining Corp
977 Blue Ribbon Cir N Oconomowoc WI 53066 262-252-4003
Web: www.aceprecision.com

Acme Cryogenics Inc 2801 Mitchell Ave Allentown PA 18103 610-966-4488
TF: 800-422-2790 ■ *Web:* www.acmecryo.com

Acme Industries Inc
1325 Pratt Blvd Elk Grove Village IL 60007 847-296-3346 296-8622
Web: www.acmeind.com

Acro Industries Inc 554 Colfax St Rochester NY 14606 585-254-3661 254-0415
Web: www.acroind.com

Acutec Precision Machining Inc
16891 State Hwy 198 Saegertown PA 16433 814-763-3214 763-3817
Web: www.acutecprecision.com

Addison Precision Manufacturing
500 Avis St Rochester NY 14615 585-254-1386
Web: www.addisonprec.com

Advance Mfg Company Inc
8 Tpke Industrial Rd PO Box 726 Westfield MA 01085 413-568-2411 568-6011
Web: www.advancemfg.com

Advanced Integration Technologies (AIT)
481 N Dean Ave Chandler AZ 85226 480-940-0036 423-8469*
**Fax Area Code:* 972

Advanced Machine & Tool Corp
3706 Transportation Dr Fort Wayne IN 46818 260-489-3572
Web: www.amt-corp.com

Aero Business Group. 9151 S Whittier Wichita KS 67207 316-689-4272
Web: theaerogroup.com

Aero Fab 1600 W 41st St Baltimore MD 21211 410-467-9762
Web: www.netzermetalcraftinc.com

Aerospace Techniques Inc
1100 Country Club Rd Middletown CT 06457 860-347-1200
Web: www.aerospacetechniques.com

AFC Tool Company Inc 4900 Webster St Dayton OH 45414 937-275-8700
Web: www.afctool.com

Airfasco Industries Inc 2655 Harrison Ave Sw Canton OH 44706 330-430-6190
Web: www.airfasco.com

Aitkin Iron Works Inc 301 Bunker Hill Dr Aitkin MN 56431 218-927-2400
Web: www.aiw.com

AJL Manufacturing Corp 100 Holleder Pkwy Rochester NY 14615 585-254-1128 458-6400
Web: www.ajlmfg.com

AJR Industries Inc 117 Gordon St Elk Grove Village IL 60007 847-439-0380 439-0230
Web: www.ajrindustries.com

All Tech Engineering 1030 58th St Sw Wyoming MI 49509 616-406-0681
Web: www.alltech-eng.com

Allied Engineering & Production Corp
2421 Blanding Ave Alameda CA 94501 510-522-1500 522-2868

Alpha Lehigh Tool & Machine Co
41 Industrial Rd Alpha NJ 08865 908-454-6481
Web: www.alphalehigh.com

American Grinding & Machine Co
2000 N Mango Ave Chicago IL 60639 773-889-4343 889-3781
TF: 877-988-4343 ■ *Web:* www.americangrinding.com

American Metal Technologies LLC
8213 Durand Ave Sturtevant WI 53177 262-633-1756
Web: www.amermetals.com

American Precision Prototyping Inc
19503 E Sixth St Tulsa OK 74108 918-266-1004

AMG Inc
301 Jefferson Ridge Pkwy Lynchpin Industrial Ctr
Lynchburg VA 24501 434-385-7525
Web: www.amg-inc.net

Amity Machine of Alburtis 3750 Chestnut Rd Alburtis PA 18011 610-966-3115
Web: www.amityindustries.com

Anderson Machining Service Inc
211 Collins Rd Jefferson WI 53549 920-674-6003
Web: www.basinprecision.com

Anderson Tool & Engineering Co Inc
1735 W 53 St Anderson IN 46013 765-643-6691
Web: www.iupui.edu

Andrew Tool & Machining Inc
15300 28th Ave N Plymouth MN 55447 763-559-0402
Web: www.andrewtool.com

Apparent Technologies Inc
11202 Georgian Dr Unit A Austin TX 78753 512-873-0023
Web: www.apparenttech.com

Archer Screw Products Inc
11341 Melrose Ave Franklin Park IL 60131 847-451-1150
Web: www.archerscrew.com

Company	City	State	ZIP	Phone	Fax
Armec Corp 8113 Beaver Ridge Rd *Web:* armec.us	Knoxville	TN	37931	865-483-9969	
Arwood Machine Corp 95 Parker St. *Web:* www.arwoodmachine.com	Newburyport	MA	01950	978-463-3777	
Autotool 7875 Corporate Blvd *Web:* www.autotoolinc.com	Plain City	OH	43064	614-733-0222	
B & B Precision Manufacturing Inc 310 W Main St. *Web:* www.bbprecision.com	Avon	NY	14414	585-226-6226	
B M C Bil Mac Corp 2995 44th St Sw *Web:* www.bmcbil-mac.com	Grandville	MI	49418	616-538-1930	
B&B Manufacturing Company Inc 27940 Beale Ct *Web:* www.bbmfg.com	Valencia	CA	91355	661-257-2161	
B-tec Solutions Inc 913 Cedar Ave *Web:* www.btecsolutions.com	Croydon	PA	19021	215-785-2400	
Barth Industries Company LP 12650 Brookpark Rd *Web:* www.barth-landis.com	Cleveland	OH	44130	216-267-1950	
Barton Air Fabrications Inc 394 Sherman Ave N *Web:* www.bartonairfab.com	Hamilton	ON	L8L6N7	905-524-2234	526-6580
Bayless Engineering Inc 26100 Ave Hall *Web:* www.baylessengineering.com	Valencia	CA	91355	661-257-3373	
Bayne Machine Works Inc 910 Fork Shoals Rd *Web:* www.baynethinline.com	Greenville	SC	29605	864-288-3877	
Biax-Fiberfilm Corp N1001 Tower View Dr. *Web:* www.biax-fiberfilm.com	Greenville	WI	54942	920-757-9000	
Bley LLC 700 Chase Ave *Web:* acmeind.com	Elk Grove Village	IL	60007	847-290-0117	
Blue Ridge Tool & Machine Company Inc 115 Hollow Oaks Ln *Web:* www.blueridgetool.com	Easley	SC	29642	864-859-4758	
Bob Inc 8740 49th Ave N *Web:* www.bobinc.com	North Minneapolis	MN	55428	763-533-2261	533-1735
Boston Centerless Inc 11 Presidential Way *Web:* www.bostoncenterless.com	Woburn	MA	01801	781-994-5000	
Bradhart Products Inc 7747 Lochlin Dr *Web:* www.bradhart.com	Brighton	MI	48116	248-437-8700	
Brandywine Machine Company Inc 300 Creek Rd *TF:* 800-523-7128 ■ *Web:* www.bramcostainless.com	Downingtown	PA	19335	800-523-7128	
BTL Machine Inc 1168 Sherborn St *Web:* www.btlmachine.com	Corona	CA	92879	951-808-9929	
Burger & Brown Engineering Inc 4500 E 142nd St *TF:* 800-764-3518 ■ *Web:* www.smartflow-usa.com	Grandview	MO	64030	816-878-6675	
Bystronic Inc 200 Airport Rd *Web:* www.bystronic.com	Elgin	IL	60123	847-214-0300	
C & F Tool & Die Co 7206 Eckhert Rd *Web:* www.c-ftool.com	San Antonio	TX	78238	210-522-9310	
Cadence Aerospace 2600 94th St SW Bomarc Industrial Park Ste 150 *Web:* www.cadenceaerospace.com	Everett	WA	98204	425-353-0405	
Cambridge Valley Machining Inc 28 Perry Ln *Web:* www.cvmusa.com	Cambridge	NY	12816	518-677-5617	
Cardo Systems Inc 100 High Tower Blvd *Web:* www.cardowireless.com	Pittsburgh	PA	15205	412-788-4533	
CARMANAH Design & Manufacturing Inc 15050 - 54A Ave Unit 8 *Web:* www.carmanahdesign.com	Surrey	BC	V3S5X7	604-299-3431	
Century Precision Machine Inc 1130 W Grove Ave *Web:* www.centuryindustriesinc.com	Orange	CA	92865	714-637-3691	
Chalmers & Kubeck Inc 150 Commerce Dr *TF:* 800-242-5637 ■ *Web:* www.candk.com	Aston	PA	19014	610-494-4300	485-1484
Chant Engineering 59 Industrial Dr *TF:* 888-567-0983 ■ *Web:* www.chantengineering.com	New Britain	PA	18901	215-230-4260	
Chapel Steel Co 590 N Bethlehem Pk PO Box 1000 *TF:* 800-570-7674 ■ *Web:* www.chapelsteel.com	Lower Gwynedd	PA	19002	215-793-0899	793-0919
Cleveland Tool & Machine 5240 Smith Rd *Web:* www.clevtool.com	Brook Park	OH	44142	216-267-6010	
Cling's Manufacturing 700 W 22nd St *Web:* www.clingsaz.com	Tempe	AZ	85282	480-968-1778	
Cloeren Inc 401 16th St *Web:* www.cloeren.com	Orange	TX	77630	409-886-5820	
CNC Industries Ltd 9331 39 Ave *TF:* 877-262-2343 ■ *Web:* www.cncindustries.com	Edmonton	AB	T6E5T3	780-469-2346	
Columbus Jack Corp 2222 S Third St *Web:* www.columbusjack.com	Columbus	OH	43207	614-443-7492	
Commercial Jet Inc 4600 NW 36 St Miami International Airport Bldg 896 *Web:* www.commercialjet.com	Miami	FL	33166	305-341-5150	
Competitive Engineering Inc 3371 E Hemisphere Loop *Web:* www.ceiglobal.com	Tucson	AZ	85706	520-746-0270	
Complete Prototype Services Inc 44783 Morley Dr *Web:* www.completeprototype.com	Clinton Township	MI	48036	586-469-9155	
Component Engineers Inc 108 N Plains Industrial Rd *Web:* www.componenteng.com	Wallingford	CT	06492	203-269-0557	269-1357
Consolidated Bottle Corp 77 Union St *TF:* 800-561-1354 ■ *Web:* www.consbottle.com	Toronto	ON	M6N3N2	416-656-7777	
Control Alt Design Ltd 1760 Britannia Dr Ste 8 *Web:* www.controlalt.com	Elgin	IL	60124	847-695-4050	
Covert Manufacturing Inc 328 S East St *Web:* www.covertmfg.com	Galion	OH	44833	419-468-1761	
Craft Machine Works Inc 2102 48th St *Web:* www.craftmachine.com	Hampton	VA	23661	757-380-8615	380-9120
Cremach Tech Inc 369 Meyers Cir. *Web:* www.cmtus.com	Corona	CA	92879	951-735-3194	
Custom Air Products & Services Inc 35 Southbelt Industrial Dr. *Web:* www.customairproducts.com	Houston	TX	77047	713-460-9009	
Custom Brackets 32 Alpha Park *TF:* 800-530-2289 ■ *Web:* www.custombrackets.com	Cleveland	OH	44143	440-446-0819	
D&E Machining LTD 150 Industrial Dr *Web:* www.demachining.com	Corry	PA	16407	814-664-3531	
D&G Machine Products Inc 50 Eisenhower Dr *Web:* www.dgmachine.com	Westbrook	ME	04092	207-854-1500	
Daman Industrial Services Inc 754 Kittanning Hollow Rd PO Box 486 *Web:* www.damanindustrial.com	East Brady	PA	16028	724-526-5714	526-5277
De Dietrich Process Systems Inc 244 Sheffield St *Web:* www.ddpsinc.com	Mountainside	NJ	07092	908-317-2585	
Dechert Dynamics Corp 713 W Main St *Web:* www.decherts.com	Palmyra	PA	17078	717-838-1326	838-1525
Digital Machining Systems LLC 929 Ridge Rd *TF:* 800-530-8945 ■ *Web:* www.digitalmachining.com	Duson	LA	70529	337-984-6013	
Downey Grinding Co 12323 Bellflower Blvd *Web:* www.downeygrinding.com	Downey	CA	90242	562-803-5556	803-3237
DP Products Inc 2015 Stone Ave *Web:* www.dpprod.com	San Jose	CA	95125	408-299-0190	
DYE Precision Inc 10637 Scripps Summit Ct. *Web:* dyecnc.com	San Diego	CA	92131	858-536-5183	
Dynomax Inc 1535 Abbott Dr *Web:* www.dynomaxinc.com	Wheeling	IL	60090	847-680-8833	
Ebco Industries Ltd 7851 Alderbridge Way *Web:* www.ebco.com	Richmond	BC	V6X2A4	604-278-5578	
Ebtec Corp 120 Shoemaker Ln. *Web:* www.ebteccorp.com	Agawam	MA	01001	413-786-0393	789-2851
Echo Industrial Inc 1615 Ritner Hwy *Web:* www.echoindustrial.com	Carlisle	PA	17013	717-249-6319	
Edward Segal Inc 360 Reynolds Bridge Rd. *Web:* www.edwardsegalinc.com	Thomaston	CT	06787	860-283-5821	
Egge Machine Company Inc 11707 Slauson Ave. *TF:* 800-866-3443 ■ *Web:* www.egge.com	Santa Fe Springs	CA	90670	562-945-3419	
Electro-Tech Machining 2000 W Gaylord St *Web:* www.etmgraphite.com	Long Beach	CA	90813	562-436-9281	436-9281
Elizabeth Companies, The 601 Linden St. *Fax Area Code: 502 ■ *Web:* www.eliz.com	Mckeesport	PA	15132	412-751-3000	635-7850*
Empire Bakery Equipment 171 Greenwich St. *TF:* 800-878-4070 ■ *Web:* empirebake.com	Hempstead	NY	11550	516-538-1210	
Energetiq Technology Inc 7 Constitution Way *Web:* www.energetiq.com	Woburn	MA	01801	781-939-0763	
Enser Corp 1902 Taylor's Ln *Web:* www.enser.com	Cinnaminson	NJ	08077	856-829-5522	
Erdman Automation Corp 1603 14th St S *Web:* www.eacy.com	Princeton	MN	55371	763-389-9475	
Express Manufacturing Inc 3519 W Warner Ave *Web:* www.eminc.com	Santa Ana	CA	92704	714-979-2228	556-0575
F Ziegler Enterprises Ltd 528 Harrison Ct *Web:* www.fziegler.com	North Fond Du Lac	WI	54937	920-921-4084	
Farmington Engineering Inc 7 Orchard Park Rd. *Web:* www.farmingtoneng.com	Madison	CT	06443	203-245-1100	
Faxon Machining Inc 11101 Adwood Dr *Web:* www.faxon-machining.com	Cincinnati	OH	45240	513-851-4644	
Femco Machine Co 754 S Main St Ext. *TF:* 800-458-3445 ■ *Web:* www.femcomachine.com	Punxsutawney	PA	15767	814-938-9763	938-8332
Fixtureworks LLC 33792 Doreka *TF:* 888-794-8687 ■ *Web:* www.fixtureworks.net	Fraser	MI	48026	586-294-1188	
FM Industries Inc 221 Warren Ave *Web:* www.fmindustries.com	Fremont	CA	94539	510-668-1900	668-1920
Forged Components Inc 14527 Smith Rd *Web:* forgedcomponents.com	Humble	TX	77396	281-441-4088	441-8899
Framingham Welding & Engineering Corp 120 Leland St PO Box 112 *Web:* www.framinghamwelding.com	Framingham	MA	01702	508-875-3563	626-4234
Fraser Manufacturing Corp 7235 Boyington St	Lexington	MI	48450	810-359-5338	359-8731
Furmanite America 101 Old Underwood Rd. *TF:* 800-444-5572 ■ *Web:* www.furmanite.com	La Porte	TX	77571	281-842-5100	842-5111
Gatterdam Industrial Services 114 N 30th St *Web:* www.gatterdam.com	Louisville	KY	40212	502-776-3937	
GBF Enterpnrises Inc 2709 Halladay St *Web:* www.gbfenterprises.com	Santa Ana	CA	92705	714-979-7131	
GCH International Inc 330 Boxley Ave. *Web:* www.gchintl.com	Louisville	KY	40209	502-636-1374	
Gill Manufacturing Ltd 9 Kenview Blvd. *Web:* www.gillmanufacturing.com	Brampton	ON	L6T5G5	905-792-0999	
GKI Inc 6204 Factory Rd *Web:* www.gkitool.com	Crystal Lake	IL	60014	815-459-2330	
Golden State Engineering Inc 15338 Garfield Ave *Web:* www.goldenstateeng.com	Paramount	CA	90723	562-634-3125	
Grand Valley Mfg Co (GVM) 701 E Spring St Bldg 52 *Web:* www.grandvalleymfg.com	Titusville	PA	16354	814-827-2707	827-4349
Granite State Manufacturing Co 124 Joliette St. *TF:* 800-464-7646 ■ *Web:* gogsmgo.com	Manchester	NH	03102	800-464-7646	
Greno Industries Inc 2820 Amsterdam Rd *Web:* www.greno.com	Scotia	NY	12302	518-393-4195	
Groupe Meloche Inc 491 Boul. Des Rables *Web:* www.melocheinc.com	Salaberry-de-valleyfield	QC	J6T6G3	450-371-4646	371-4957

Phone Fax

H & S Swansons' Tool Co 9000 68th St N ... Pinellas Park FL 33782 727-541-3575
Web: www.hsswansons.com
H.M. Dunn Co 3301 House Anderson Rd ... Euless TX 76040 817-283-3722 283-8402
Web: www.hmdunn.com
Haas Automation Inc 2800 Sturgis Rd ... Oxnard CA 93030 805-278-1800 278-2255
TF: 800-331-6746 ■ *Web:* int.haascnc.com
Hamill Manufacturing Co 500 Pleasant Vly Rd ... Trafford PA 15085 724-744-2131
Web: www.hamillmfg.com
Hayward Quartz Technology Inc
1700 Corporate Way ... Fremont CA 94539 510-657-9605
Web: www.haywardquartz.com
Hfw Industries Inc
196 Philadelphia St PO Box 8 ... Buffalo NY 14207 716-875-3380 875-3385
TF: 800-937-9311
Highway Machine Company Inc (HMC)
3010 S Old US Hwy 41 ... Princeton IN 47670 812-385-3639 385-8186
TF: 866-990-9462 ■ *Web:* www.hmcgears.com
Hitachi High Technologies America Inc
10 N Martingale Rd Ste 500 ... Schaumburg IL 60173 847-273-4141 273-4407
Web: www.hitachi-hightech.com/us
HMS Products Co 1200 E Big Beaver Rd ... Troy MI 48083 248-689-8120
Web: www.hmsproducts.com
HNH Mach Inc 110 Towerline Pl ... London ON N6E2T1 519-680-3880
Web: www.hnhmachine.com
Howard Engineering Company Inc
687 Wooster St PO Box 1315 ... Naugatuck CT 06770 203-729-5213 729-3843
Web: www.howardengineering.com
Hti Cybernetics 6701 Center Dr ... Sterling Heights MI 48312 586-826-8346
Web: www.htitool.com
Hughes Supply Company of Thomasville Inc
175 Kanoy Rd PO Box 1003 ... Thomasville NC 27360 336-475-8146 472-0404
TF: 800-747-8141 ■ *Web:* www.hughessupplyco.com
Illinois Machine & Tool Works
1961 Edgewater Dr ... North Pekin IL 61554 309-382-3045 382-2644
IMT Precision Inc 31902 Hayman St ... Hayward CA 94544 510-324-8926
Web: www.imtp.com
Indiana Technology & Mfg Cos
6100 Michigan Rd ... Plymouth IN 46563 574-936-2112
Web: www.itamco.com
Industrial Tool Inc 9210 52nd Ave N ... New Hope MN 55428 763-533-7244
TF Sales: 800-776-4455 ■ *Web:* www.industrial-tool.com
IntriPlex Technologies Inc
751 S Kellogg Ave ... Santa Barbara CA 93117 805-683-3414
Web: www.intri-plex.com
Invena Corp 416 E Fifth St ... Eureka KS 67045 620-583-8630
Web: www.invena.com
Island Timberlands LP 65 Front St 4th Fl ... Nanaimo BC V9R5H9 250-755-3500
Web: www.islandtimberlands.com
J C Steele & Sons Inc 710 S Mulberry St ... Statesville NC 28677 704-872-3681
TF: 800-278-3353 ■ *Web:* www.jcsteele.com
Jamco Aerospace Inc 121 E Industry Ct ... Deer Park NY 11729 631-586-7900
Web: www.jamco-aerospace.com
Janicki Industries Inc 1476 Moore St ... Sedro Woolley WA 98284 360-856-5143
Web: www.janicki.com
JBL Enterprises International Inc
3219 Roymar Rd ... Oceanside CA 92058 760-754-2727
Web: www.jblspearguns.com
Jewell Tool Technology 3129 State St ... Bettendorf IA 52722 563-355-5010
TF: 800-831-8665 ■ *Web:* www.jewellgroup.com
JF Fredericks Tool Company Inc
25 Spring Ln ... Farmington CT 06032 860-677-2646 674-8679
Johnson Technology Corp 2034 Latimer Dr ... Muskegon MI 49442 231-777-2685 773-1397
K & M Machine-Fabricating Inc
20745 Michigan 60 ... Cassopolis MI 49031 269-445-2495 445-3002
Web: www.k-mm.com
Kamet Manufacturing Solutions
171 Commercial St ... Sunnyvale CA 94086 408-522-8000
Web: www.kamet.com
Kay Manufacturing Co 602 State St ... Calumet City IL 60409 708-862-6800 862-8122
Web: www.kaymfg.com
Kenona Industries Inc 3044 Wilson Dr NW ... Grand Rapids MI 49534 616-735-6228
Web: www.kenona.com
Kessington Machine Products Inc
27217 County Rd 6 W ... Elkhart IN 46514 574-266-4500
Web: www.kessington.com
Kewaunee Fabrications LLC 520 N Main St ... Kewaunee WI 54216 920-388-2000 388-0263
Web: www.kewauneefabrications.com
Keystone Honing Co 1000 Industrial Dr ... Titusville PA 16354 814-827-9641
Komar Industries Inc 4425 Marketing Pl ... Groveport OH 43125 614-836-2366
Web: www.komarindustries.com
Kurt Manufacturing Co 5280 Main St NE ... Minneapolis MN 55421 763-572-1500 571-8466*
**Fax:* Sales ■ *TF:* 800-458-7855 ■ *Web:* www.kurt.com
Laser Excel N6323 Berlin Rd PO Box 279 ... Green Lake WI 54941 920-294-6544 294-6588
TF: 800-285-6544 ■ *Web:* www.laserexcel.com
Laser Technologies Inc
1120 N Frontenac Rd ... Naperville IL 60563 630-761-1200
Web: lasertechnologiesinc.com
LaVezzi Precision Inc
999 Regency Dr ... Glendale Heights IL 60139 630-582-1230 582-1238
TF: 800-323-1772 ■ *Web:* www.lavezzi.com
Lb Steel LLC 15700 Lathrop Ave ... Harvey IL 60426 708-331-2600 331-8500
Web: www.lbsteel.com
Leiss Tool & Die Co 801 N Pleasant Ave ... Somerset PA 15501 814-444-1444 445-3456
Web: www.leiss.com
Lemco Tool Corp 1850 Metzger Ave ... Cogan Station PA 17728 570-494-0620 494-0860
TF: 800-233-8713 ■ *Web:* www.lemco-tool.com
LHM Technologies Inc 446 Rowtree Dairy Rd ... Woodbridge ON L4L8H2 905-856-2466 856-2474
Web: www.lhmtech.com
Liburdi Engineering Ltd 400 Hwy 6 N ... Dundas ON L9H7K4 905-689-0734 689-0739
Web: www.liburdi.com
Lindquist Machine Corp 610 Baeten Rd ... Green Bay WI 54304 920-713-4100 499-8482
Web: www.lmc-corp.com

Phone Fax

Lith-O-Roll Corp 9521 Telstar Ave ... El Monte CA 91731 626-579-0340 548-4676*
**Fax Area Code:* 800 ■ *TF:* 800-423-4176 ■ *Web:* www.lithoroll.com
Litton Engineering Laboratories
200 Litton Dr Ste 200 ... Grass Valley CA 95945 530-273-6176
TF: 800-821-8866 ■ *Web:* www.littonengr.com
LKM Industries Inc 44 Sixth Rd ... Woburn MA 01801 781-935-9210
Web: www.lkm.com
Logan Machine Co 1405 Home Ave ... Akron OH 44310 330-633-6163 633-6362
Web: www.loganmachine.com
Mac Machine Company Inc 7209 Rutherford Rd ... Baltimore MD 21244 410-944-6171
Web: www.macmachine.com
Magna Machine & Tool Company Inc
3722 N Messick Rd ... New Castle IN 47362 765-766-5388 766-5300
Web: www.magnamachine.com
Major Tool & Machine Inc 1458 E 19th St ... Indianapolis IN 46218 317-636-6433 634-9420
Web: www.majortool.com
Manor Tool & Manufacturing Co
9200 Ivanhoe St ... Schiller Park IL 60176 847-678-2020 678-6937
Web: www.manortool.com
Manufacturing & Design Technology Inc
1033a Cavalier Blvd ... Chesapeake VA 23323 757-485-8924
Web: www.m-d-t.com
Marberry Machine Co 6210 Cunningham Rd ... Houston TX 77041 713-466-9666
Web: www.marberrymachine.com
Marine Exhaust Systems of Alabama Inc
757 Nichols Ave ... Fairhope AL 36532 251-928-1234 928-1234
Web: www.mesamarine.com
Marmen Inc 845 Berlinguet St ... Trois-rivieres QC G8T8N9 819-379-0453
Web: www.marmeninc.com
Marshall Screw Products Co
3820 Chandler Dr Ne ... Minneapolis MN 55421 800-321-6727
TF: 800-321-6727 ■ *Web:* www.marshallmfg.com
Martinez & Turek Inc 300 S Cedar Ave ... Rialto CA 92376 909-820-6800
Web: www.martinezandturek.com
Marton Precision Manufacturing LLC
1365 S Acacia Ave ... Fullerton CA 92831 714-808-6523
Web: www.martoninc.com
Master Automatic Inc 40485 Schoolcraft Rd ... Plymouth MI 48170 734-414-0500
Web: www.masterautomatic.com
McElroy Manufacturing Inc 833 N Fulton Ave ... Tulsa OK 74115 918-836-8611
Web: www.mcelroy.com
McGill Maintenance Partnership Ltd
6402 E Hwy 332 ... Freeport TX 77542 979-233-5438
Web: www.mcgillmaintenance.com
Mellott Manufacturing Co 13156 Long Ln ... Mercersburg PA 17236 717-369-3125
Web: www.mellottmfg.com
Merit Gage Inc
3954 Meadowbrook Rd St. Louis Park ... Minneapolis MN 55426 952-935-0113 935-2641
Web: www.meritgage.com
Metal Craft Machine & Engineering Inc
13760 Business Ctr Dr ... Elk River MN 55330 763-441-1855
Web: www.metal-craft.com
Metalex Manufacturing Inc 5750 Cornell Rd ... Cincinnati OH 45242 513-489-0507 489-1020
Web: www.metalexmfg.com
Meyer Tool Inc 3055 Colerain Ave ... Cincinnati OH 45225 513-853-4400 853-4439
Web: www.meyertool.com
Michigan Production Machining Inc
16700 23 Mile Rd ... Macomb MI 48044 586-228-9700 228-7347
Web: www.michpro.com
Micro Instrument Corp (MIC)
1199 Emerson St PO Box 60619 ... Rochester NY 14606 585-458-3150 254-0922
TF: 800-200-3150 ■ *Web:* www.microinst.com
Micro Machine Company LLC 2429 N Burdick ... Kalamazoo MI 49007 269-388-2440
Web: www.micromachineco.com
Micro-Tronics Inc 2905 S Potter Dr ... Tempe AZ 85282 602-437-8995 431-9480
Web: www.micro-tronics.com
Mid-America Machining Inc 11530 Brooklyn Rd ... Brooklyn MI 49230 517-592-8988
Web: www.mid-americamachining.com
Milltech Manufacturing Co 537 Easy St ... Garland TX 75042 972-276-1786
Web: www.milltechmfg.com
Mitee-bite Products Inc PO Box 430 ... Center Ossipee NH 03814 603-539-4538
Web: www.miteebite.com
Mittler Corp 10 Cooperative Way ... Wright City MO 63390 636-745-7757
Web: www.mittlerbros.com
Morrison Container Handling Solutions
335 W 194th St ... Glenwood IL 60425 708-756-6660
Web: www.morrison-chs.com
Moss Precision Inc 3200 Arden Rd ... Hayward CA 94545 510-785-2235
Web: www.mossprecision.com
Mulgrew Aircraft Components Inc
1810 S Shamrock Ave ... Monrovia CA 91016 626-256-1375
Web: www.mulgrewaircraft.com
MVS Saegertown 1 Crawford St ... Saegertown PA 16433 814-763-2655 763-2069
Web: www.macleanfoggcs.com
Myrmo & Sons Inc 3600 Franklin Blvd ... Eugene OR 97403 541-747-4565 747-6832
Web: www.myrmo.com
Nassau Tool Works Inc 34 Lamar St ... West Babylon NY 11704 631-643-5000 643-5062
Nationwide Precision Products Corp
200 Tech Park Dr ... Rochester NY 14623 585-272-7100
Web: www.nationwideprecision.com
NC Dynamics Inc (NCDI) 3401 E 69th St ... Long Beach CA 90805 562-634-7392 634-6220
Web: www.ncdi.aero
Neosho Trompler Inc
580 S Industrial Dr Stop 1 ... Hartland WI 53029 262-367-5600
Web: www.neoshotrompler.com
New Dimensions Precision Machining Inc
6614 S Union Rd ... Union IL 60180 815-923-8300
Web: www.newdims.com
New Era Ohio LLC 520 W Mulberry St ... Bryan OH 43506 419-633-1616
Web: www.neweraohio.com
Norotos Inc 201 E Alton Ave ... Santa Ana CA 92707 714-662-3113 662-7950
Web: www.norotos.com
Norsco Inc 1816 Ackley Cir ... Oakdale CA 95361 209-845-2327
Web: www.norscoinc.com

Company / Address	City	State	Zip	Phone	Fax
Northstar Machine & Tool Company Inc 4212 Enterprise Cir. *Web:* www.northstaraerospace.com	Duluth	MN	55811	218-720-2920	
Novacro Machining Inc 380 Dewitt Rd *Web:* novacro.com	Stoney Creek	ON	L8E2T2	905-664-2721	
Numerical Precision Inc 2200 Foster Ave. *Web:* www.numericalprecision.com	Wheeling	IL	60090	847-394-3610	394-3962
O & F Machine Products Company Inc 3020 W 20th St PO Box 1363 *Web:* www.ofmachine.com	Joplin	MO	64802	417-623-7476	623-4736
Ohio Fabricators Co 111 N 14th St *Web:* www.ohfab.com	Coshocton	OH	43812	740-622-5922	622-3307
OMW Corp 21 Pamaron Way Ste G *Web:* www.omwcorp.com	Novato	CA	94949	415-382-1669	
Onamac Industries Inc 11504 Airport Rd Bldg G *Web:* www.onamac.com	Everett	WA	98204	425-743-6676	742-2718
OP Schuman & Sons Inc 2001 County Line Rd *Web:* www.opschuman.com	Warrington	PA	18976	215-343-1530	343-1633
Owens Design Inc 47427 Fremont Blvd *Web:* www.owensdesign.com	Fremont	CA	94538	510-659-1800	
Owens Industries Inc 7815 S Sixth St *Web:* www.owensind.com	Oak Creek	WI	53154	414-764-1212	764-6030
P & J Machining Inc 2601 Inter Ave *Web:* www.pnjmachining.com	Puyallup	WA	98372	253-841-0500	
Palcam Technologies Ltd 1300 Ringwell Dr. *Web:* www.palcam.com	Newmarket	ON	L3Y9C7	905-853-1675	853-1584
Paradigm Precision Holdings 404 W Guadalupe Rd	Tempe	AZ	85283	480-839-0501	
Parsons Company Inc 1386 SR- 117 *Web:* www.parsonscompany.com	Roanoke	IL	61561	309-467-9100	
PDC Machines Inc 1875 Stout Dr. *Web:* www.pdcmachines.com	Warminster	PA	18974	215-443-9442	
Peeco 7050 W Ridge Rd *TF:* 800-235-9382 ■ *Web:* www.autodev.com	Fairview	PA	16415	814-474-5561	
Peko Precision Products Inc 1400 Emerson St *Web:* www.pekoprecision.com	Rochester	NY	14606	585-647-3010	647-1366
PEMCO-Naval Engineering Works Inc 3614 Frederic St. *Web:* www.pemco-inc.com	Pascagoula	MS	39567	228-769-7081	
Perfekta Inc 480 E 21st St N. *Web:* www.perfekta-inc.com	Wichita	KS	67214	316-263-2056	263-0106
Peterson Tool Company Inc 739 Fesslers Ln PO Box 100830 *Web:* www.petersontool.com	Nashville	TN	37224	615-242-7341	242-7362
PFI Precision Inc 2011 N Dayton Lakeview Rd *Web:* www.pfiprecision.com	New Carlisle	OH	45344	937-845-3563	
Pioneer Products Inc 1917 S Memorial Dr *Web:* www.pioneerproducts.com	Racine	WI	53403	262-633-6304	633-0465
Poly Cycle Inc 5501 Campbells Run Rd *TF:* 800-394-4333 ■ *Web:* www.polycycle.com	Pittsburgh	PA	15205	412-747-1101	747-0749
Prattville Machine & Tool Company Inc 240 Jubilee Dr 2nd Fl. *Web:* www.prattvillemachine.com	Peabody	MA	01960	978-538-5229	
Precision Gears Inc N 13 W 24705 Bluemound Rd *Web:* www.precisiongears.com	Pewaukee	WI	53072	262-542-4261	542-1592
Precision Machine & Manufacturing Inc 1290 S Bertelsen Rd *Web:* www.premach.com	Eugene	OR	97402	541-484-9841	
Precision Metal Products Inc 307 Pepe's Farm Rd *Web:* www.pmpinc.biz	Milford	CT	06460	203-877-4258	878-8353
Precision Roll Grinders Inc 6356 Chapmans Rd *Web:* www.precisionrollgrinders.com	Allentown	PA	18106	610-395-6966	481-9130
Precision Screw Thread Corp S 82 W 19275 Apollo Dr. *Web:* thepstgroup.com	Muskego	WI	53150	262-679-9000	679-9004
Pro-line Water Screen Services Inc PO Box 2565 *Web:* www.intakescreens.com	Pearland	TX	77588	281-992-6730	
Process Equipment Co 6555 S SR-202 *Web:* www.peco-us.com	Tipp City	OH	45371	937-667-4451	667-9322
Process Fab Inc 15644 Clanton Cir *Web:* www.processfab.com	Santa Fe Springs	CA	90670	562-921-1979	921-3145
Prototype & Plastic Mold Co 35 Industrial Pk Pl *Web:* www.proppm.com	Middletown	CT	06457	860-632-2800	632-2249
Prototype Machine Co 818 Prototype Rd PO Box 249	Flatonia	TX	78941	361-865-3230	
Pyramid Precision Machine Inc 6721 Cobra Way *Web:* www.pyramidprecision.com	San Diego	CA	92121	858-642-0713	
Quality Engineering & Tool Company Inc 380 S Wheatfield St *Web:* qes1.com	York	PA	17403	203-269-5054	
Quality Mfg Company Inc (QMI) PO Box 616 *TF:* 866-460-6459 ■ *Web:* www.qmiky.com	Winchester	KY	40392	859-744-0420	
R & d Machine & Engineering Inc 130 Scarlet Blvd *Web:* www.rdmachine.com	Oldsmar	FL	34677	813-891-9109	
R A Zweig Inc 2500 Ravine Way *Web:* www.zweig-cnc.com	Glenview	IL	60025	847-832-9001	
Ram Precision Industries Inc 11125 Yankee Rd Ste A *Web:* www.ramprecision.com	Dayton	OH	45458	937-885-7700	
Revzero Inc 2431 Galpin Ct Ste 150 *Web:* www.revzeroinc.com	Chanhassen	MN	55317	952-380-9966	
Ridge Engineering Inc 3987 Hampstead Mexico Rd *Web:* www.ridgeeng.com	Hampstead	MD	21074	410-239-7716	239-8710
Rite Track Inc 8655 Rite Track Way *Web:* www.ritetrack.com	West Chester	OH	45069	513-881-7820	
RM Kerner Co 2208 E 33rd St *Web:* www.rmkco.com	Erie	PA	16510	814-898-2000	
RMS-Ross Corp 44325 Yale Rd W *Web:* rmsross-public.sharepoint.com	Chilliwack	BC	V2R4H2	604-792-5911	792-7148
Robinson Metal Inc 1740 Eisenhower Dr. *Web:* www.robinsonmetal.com	De Pere	WI	54115	920-494-7411	
Santinelli International Inc 325 Oser Ave *TF:* 800-644-3343 ■ *Web:* www.santinelli.com	Hauppauge	NY	11788	631-435-3343	
Schaffer Grinding Co 848 S Maple Ave *Web:* www.schaffergrinding.com	Montebello	CA	90640	323-724-4476	724-2635
Scheirer Machine Company Inc 3200 Industrial Blvd *TF:* 800-448-4590 ■ *Web:* www.scheirer.com	Bethel Park	PA	15102	412-833-6500	833-8110
Schmiede Corp 1865 Riley Creek Rd PO Box 1630 *TF:* 800-535-1851 ■ *Web:* www.schmiedecorp.com	Tullahoma	TN	37388	931-455-4801	455-1703
Schwartz Industries Inc 6909 E 11-Mile Rd *Web:* sharedvision.net	Warren	MI	48092	586-759-1777	759-0808
Scicon Technologies Corp 27525 Newhall Ranch Rd *Web:* www.scicontech.com	Valencia	CA	91355	661-295-8630	
Sintel Inc 18437 171st Ave *Web:* www.sintelinc.com	Spring Lake	MI	49456	616-842-6960	
SMF Inc 1550 Industrial Pk. *Web:* www.smf-inc.com	Minonk	IL	61760	309-432-2586	432-2390
Solid Concepts Inc 28309 Ave Crocker *TF:* 888-311-1017 ■ *Web:* www.stratasysdirect.com	Valencia	CA	91355	661-295-4400	257-9311
Sonfarrel Inc 3000-3010 E La Jolla St. *Web:* www.sonfarrel.com	Anaheim	CA	92806	714-630-7280	
South Side Machine Works Inc 3761 Eiler St. *Web:* www.southsidemachine.net	Saint Louis	MO	63116	314-481-7171	481-9271
Southern Prestige Industries Inc 113 Hatfield Rd. *Web:* www.southernprestige.com	Statesville	NC	28625	704-872-9524	
Specialty Bar Products Co 200 Martha St PO Box 127 *Web:* www.specialty-bar.com	Blairsville	PA	15717	724-459-7500	459-0944
St. George Steel Fabrication Inc 1301 East 700 North *Web:* www.stgeorgesteel.com	Saint George	UT	84770	435-673-4856	628-4139
Standard Locknut Inc 1045 E 169th St *TF:* 800-783-6887 ■ *Web:* www.stdlocknut.com	Westfield	IN	46074	317-867-0100	867-4231
Stellar Technology Inc 237 Commerce Dr *Web:* www.stellartech.com	Amherst	NY	14228	716-250-1900	
Steward Machine Company Inc 3911 13th Ave N. *Web:* www.stewardmachine.com	Birmingham	AL	35234	205-841-6461	849-8029
Stewart Assembly & Machining 7234 Blue Ash Rd *Web:* www.pmcworldwide.net	Cincinnati	OH	45236	513-891-9000	
Stillwater Technologies Inc 1040 S Dorset *Web:* www.stlwtr.com	Troy	OH	45373	937-440-2500	
Straton Industries Inc 180 Surf Ave *Web:* www.straton.com	Stratford	CT	06615	203-375-4488	
Supreme Gear Company Inc 17430 Malyn Blvd *Web:* www.dorrisco.com	Fraser	MI	48026	586-294-7625	
Sussek Machine Corp 805 Pierce St *Web:* www.sussek.com	Waterloo	WI	53594	920-478-2126	478-3452
T & K Machine Inc 2220 W Park St *Web:* www.tkparis.com	Paris	TX	75460	903-785-5574	
T & S Machine Shop Inc 1396 Hwy 471 *Web:* www.tandsmachine.com	Brandon	MS	39042	601-825-8627	
T R C Hydraulics Inc 7 Mosher Dr *Web:* www.trchydraulics.com	Dartmouth	NS	B3B1E5	902-468-4605	
Tacoma Screw Products Inc 2001 Center St *Web:* www.tacomascrew.com	Tacoma	WA	98409	253-572-3444	
Tecmotiv (USA) Inc 1500 James Ave *Web:* www.tecmotiv.com	Niagara Falls	NY	14305	716-282-1211	
Tibor Machine Products Inc 7400 W 100th Pl. *Web:* www.tibormachine.com	Bridgeview	IL	60455	708-499-3700	499-6803
Tier One LLC 31 Pecks Ln *TF:* 877-251-2228 ■ *Web:* www.tieronemachining.com	Newtown	CT	06470	203-426-3030	
Total Components Solutions Corp 2080 Tenth St *Web:* www.tcsiowa.com	Rock Valley	IA	51247	712-476-5315	
Tree City Tool 1954 N Montgomery Rd *Web:* www.treecitytool.com	Greensburg	IN	47240	812-663-4196	
Tri-State Machine Inc 3301 Mccolloch St *Web:* www.tri-statemachine.com	Wheeling	WV	26003	304-234-0170	
True Position Technologies Inc 24900 Ave Standford *Web:* www.truepositiontech.com	Valencia	CA	91355	661-294-0030	294-1240
True-Tech Corp 4050 Technology Pl. *Web:* www.true-tech.com	Fremont	CA	94538	510-353-1000	353-9000
TSS Technologies Inc 8800 Global Way *Web:* tsstech.com	West Chester	OH	45069	513-772-7000	772-2938
Tulsa Centerless Bar Processing 1605 N 168th E Ave *Web:* tulsacenterless.com	Tulsa	OK	74116	918-438-0000	
TurboCare Chicopee 2140 Westover Rd	Chicopee	MA	01022	413-593-0500	593-3424
Twin City EDM 7940 Rancher Rd NE *TF:* 800-397-0338 ■ *Web:* www.twincityedm.com	Fridley	MN	55432	763-783-7808	783-7842
Ultra Tech Machinery Inc 297 Ascot Pkwy *Web:* www.utmachinery.com	Cuyahoga Falls	OH	44223	330-929-5544	
UMC Inc 500 Chelsea Rd *Web:* www.ultramc.com	Monticello	MN	55362	763-271-5200	271-5249
Unisource Manufacturing Inc 8040 NE 33rd Dr *TF:* 800-234-2566 ■ *Web:* www.unisource-mfg.com	Portland	OR	97211	503-281-4673	281-5845
Urban Manufacturing Inc 1288 Hickory St. *Web:* www.urban-mfg.com	Pewaukee	WI	53072	262-691-2455	691-8938

Phone / Fax

Usitech Nov Inc
1295 1e Rue Parc Industriel .... Sainte-marie De Beauce QC G6E3T3 418-387-3133
Web: www.usitechnov.com

V W Broaching Service Inc 3250 W Lake St............Chicago IL 60624 773-533-9000
Web: vwbroaching.com

Vaga Industries Inc 2505 Loma Ave .... South El Monte CA 91733 626-442-7436 442-4330
Web: www.vaga.com

Vermont Aerospace Manufacturing Inc
966 Industrial Pwy PO Box 1148 .... Lyndonville VT 05851 802-748-8705 748-8437
Web: www.vtaerospace.com

Vescio Threading Co 14002 Anson Ave.........Santa Fe Springs CA 90670 562-802-1868 802-2073
TF: 800-361-4218 ■ *Web:* www.vesciothreading.com

Vickers Engineering Inc
3604 Glendora Rd PO Box 346......................New Troy MI 49119 269-426-8545 426-8494
Web: www.vickerseng.com

Wahlco Inc 2722 S Fairview St .... Santa Ana CA 92704 714-979-7300 979-0603
TF: 800-423-5432 ■ *Web:* www.wahlco.com

Warren Fabricating & Machining
3240 Mahoning Ave NW.............................Warren OH 44483 330-847-0596
Web: www.warfab.com

Washington Tool & Machine Co
1 S Baird Ave PO Box 873 ....Washington PA 15301 724-225-7470 225-7484
Web: www.washtool.com

Waterbury Swiss Automatics Inc
43 Mattatuck Heights Rd.......................... Waterbury CT 06705 203-573-8584
Web: www.waterburyswiss.com

Wayne Metals LLC 400 E Logan St.................... Markle IN 46770 260-758-3121 758-2521
Web: waynemetals.com

Wayne Trail Technologies Inc
203 E Park St .... Fort Loramie OH 45845 937-295-2120
Web: www.waynetrail.com

Weaver Industries Inc
425 S Fourth St PO Box 326..........................Denver PA 17517 717-336-7507 336-4182
Web: www.weaverind.com

Webber Metal Products Inc
120 Industrial Park Rd ....Cascade IA 52033 563-852-7122
Web: www.webbermetals.com

Weldmac Manufacturing Co 1451 N Johnson Ave ......El Cajon CA 92020 619-440-2300 440-8723
TF: 800-252-1533 ■ *Web:* www.weldmac.com

West Coast Industrial Systems
1995 W Airway Rd .... Lebanon OR 97355 541-451-6677
Web: www.westcoastindustrial.com

West Engineering Company Inc
10106 Louistown Rd..................................Ashland VA 23005 804-798-3966 798-8590
Web: www.west-engineering.net

Whelan Machine & Tool 134 Rochester Dr............Louisville KY 40214 502-364-6370
Web: www.whelanmachine.com

Wilco Machine & Fab Inc 1326 S Broadway .... Marlow OK 73055 580-658-6993 658-6767
Web: www.wilcofab.com

Will-Burt Co 169 S Main St .... Orrville OH 44667 330-682-7015 684-1190
Web: willburt.com

Williams Machine & Tool Company Inc
1009 Schermerhorn Rd...............................Galena KS 66739 620-783-5184
Web: www.wilmaco.com

Wind Turbine Industries Corp
16801 Industrial Cir SE .... Prior Lake MN 55372 952-447-6064
Web: www.windturbine.net

Windham Manufacturing Company Inc
8520 Forney Rd .... Dallas TX 75227 214-388-0511
TF: 888-965-0093 ■ *Web:* www.windhammfg.com

Windings Inc PO Box 566 .... New Ulm MN 56073 507-359-2034
TF: 800-795-8533 ■ *Web:* www.windings.com

Wise Plastics Technologies Inc
3810 Stern Ave..................................Saint Charles IL 60174 847-697-2840
Web: www.wise-hamlin.com

World Class Manufacturing Group Inc, The
1101 S Pine St .... Weyauwega WI 54983 920-867-2527
Web: www.worldcls.com

Wright Plastic Products LLC
201 E Condensery Rd.............................. Sheridan MI 48884 989-291-3211 291-5321
Web: wppllc.com

WSI Industries Inc 213 Chelsea Rd ....Monticello MN 55362 763-295-9202 295-9212
NASDAQ: WSCI ■ *Web:* www.wsiindustries.com

Xtek Inc 11451 Reading Rd ....Cincinnati OH 45241 513-733-7800 733-7939
TF: 888-332-9835 ■ *Web:* www.xtek.com

Yates Industries Inc
23050 E Industrial Dr ....St. Clair Shores MI 48080 586-778-7680
Web: www.yatesind.com

Zach Halopoff Inc 15422 Assembly Ln......... Huntington Beach CA 92649 714-373-3333
Web: www.haloindustries.com

455 MACHINE TOOLS - METAL CUTTING TYPES

See Also Machine Tools - Metal Forming Types p. 2693; Metalworking Devices & Accessories p. 2768

Phone / Fax

Abbco Inc 2401 American Ln..................... Elkgrove Vlg IL 60007 630-595-7115 595-6431
TF: 866-986-6546 ■ *Web:* www.abbcoinc.net

Accurate Boring Co 17420 Malyn Blvd .... Fraser MI 48026 586-294-7555 294-2530
Web: www.accurateboring.com

Acme Manufacturing Co
4240 N Atlantic Blvd.............................. Auburn Hills MI 48326 248-393-7300 393-4060
Web: www.acmemfg.com

Airtronics Gage & Machine Co 516 Slade Ave .... Elgin IL 60120 847-695-0911 695-8745
Web: www.airtronicsgauge.com

Allied Tool Products 9334 N 107th St...............Milwaukee WI 53224 414-355-8280 355-8297
TF: 800-558-5147 ■ *Web:* www.atptools.com

American GFM Corp 1200 Cavalier Blvd ....Chesapeake VA 23323 757-487-2442 487-5274
Web: www.agfm.com

Babin Machine Works Inc 2510 N Ninth St .... Beaumont TX 77703 409-892-1231 892-1236

Bardons & Oliver Inc 5800 Harper Rd........................Solon OH 44139 440-498-5800 498-2001
Web: www.bardonsoliver.com

Phone / Fax

Barnes International Inc
814 Chestnut St PO Box 1203 .... Rockford IL 61105 815-964-8661 964-5074
TF: 800-435-4877 ■ *Web:* www.barnesintl.com

Bourn & Koch Inc 2500 Kishwaukee St................ Rockford IL 61104 815-965-4013 965-0019
Web: www.bourn-koch.com

Bryant Grinder 65 Pearl St..........................Springfield VT 05156 802-885-5161 885-9444
Web: www.bryantgrinder.com

Burr Oak Tool Inc 405 W S St..........................Sturgis MI 49091 269-651-9393 651-4324
Web: www.burroak.com

Carlson Tool & Machine Co 2300 Gary Ln............. Geneva IL 60134 630-232-2460 232-2016
Web: www.carlson-tool.com

Chas G Allen Company Inc 25 Williamsville Rd .... Barre MA 01005 978-355-2911 355-2917
Web: www.chasgallen.com

Continental Machines Inc 5505 W 123rd St ....Savage MN 55378 952-895-6400
Web: continentalhydraulics.com

Crafts Technology 91 Joey Dr ....Elk Grove Village IL 60007 847-758-3100 758-0162
TF: 800-323-6802 ■ *Web:* www.craftstech.net

Darex 210 E Hersey St PO Box 730.....................Ashland OR 97520 541-488-2224 488-2229
TF: 800-597-6170 ■ *Web:* www.darex.com

Davenport Machine Inc 167 Ames St .... Rochester NY 14611 585-235-4545 235-7997
TF: 800-344-5748 ■ *Web:* www.davenportmachine.com

Dayton Machine Tool Co 1314 Webster St..............Dayton OH 45404 937-222-6444 222-6444
Web: www.dmtnet.com

DoALL Co 1480 S Wolf Rd................................Wheeling IL 60090 847-495-6800
Web: www.doall.com

Eagle Tool Co 101 Woodward Ave................ Iron Mountain MI 49801 906-774-0284 774-0342
Web: eaglebroach.com

EH Wachs Co 600 Knightsbridge Pkwy .... Lincolnshire IL 60069 847-537-8800 520-1147*
**Fax:* Sales ■ *TF:* 800-323-8185 ■ *Web:* www.ehwachs.com

Entrust Mfg Technologies Inc
N 58 W 14630 Shawn Cir.................. Menomonee Falls WI 53051 262-252-3802 252-4075
Web: www.entrustmt.com

Everite Machine Products Co
6995 Airport Hwy Ln............................Pennsauken NJ 08110 856-330-6700
Web: www.everite.net

Extrude Hone Corp 235 Industry Blvd.................... Irwin PA 15642 724-863-5900 863-8759
TF: 800-835-3668 ■ *Web:* www.kennametal.com

Flow International Corp 23500 64th Ave S.................Kent WA 98032 253-850-3500 813-9377
NASDAQ: FLOW ■ *TF:* 800-446-3569 ■ *Web:* www.flowwaterjet.com

GF Machining Solutions 560 Bond St............. Lincolnshire IL 60069 847-913-5300 913-5340
TF: 800-282-1336 ■ *Web:* www.gfms.com/content/gfac/country_us/en.html

Gleason Corp 1000 University Ave.................. Rochester NY 14607 585-473-1000 461-4348
TF: 800-727-6333 ■ *Web:* www.gleason.com

Grob Inc 1731 Tenth Ave.................................. Grafton WI 53024 262-377-1400 377-2106
TF: 800-225-6481 ■ *Web:* www.grobinc.com

Hammond Roto-Finish 1600 Douglas Ave............Kalamazoo MI 49007 269-345-7151 345-1710
Web: www.hammondmach.com

Hanchett Manufacturing Inc 906 N State St ....Big Rapids MI 49307 231-796-7678 796-4851
TF: 800-454-7463 ■ *Web:* www.hanchett.com

Hardinge Inc 1 Hardinge Dr................................. Elmira NY 14902 607-734-2281
NASDAQ: HDNG ■ *TF:* 800-843-8801 ■ *Web:* www.hardinge.com

Harrington Tool Co 105 N Rath Ave .... Ludington MI 49431 231-843-3445
Web: harringtontool.net

Hause Machines 809 S Pleasant St ....Montpelier OH 43543 419-485-3158 485-3146
TF: 800-932-8665 ■ *Web:* www.hausemachines.com

Hausermann Abrading Process Co 300 Laura Dr ....Addison IL 60101 630-543-6688 543-6689
Web: www.hausermann.net

Hetran Inc 70 Pinedale Industrial Rd .... Orwigsburg PA 17961 570-366-1411 366-1829
Web: www.hetranb.com

Huffman Corp 1050 Huffman Way......................... Clover SC 29710 803-222-4561 222-7599
TF: 888-483-3626 ■ *Web:* huffman-llc.com

Hurco Cos Inc 1 Technology Way ....Indianapolis IN 46268 317-293-5309 298-2621
NASDAQ: HURC ■ *TF Sales:* 800-634-2416 ■ *Web:* www.hurco.com

Hydromat Inc 11600 Adie Rd.......................... Saint Louis MO 63043 314-432-4644 432-7552*
**Fax:* Sales ■ *Web:* www.hydromat.com

Hypertherm Inc 21 Great Hollow Rd PO Box 5010 ....Hanover NH 03755 603-643-3441 643-5352
TF: 800-643-0030 ■ *Web:* www.hypertherm.com

Hypneumat Inc 5900 W Franklin Dr ....Franklin WI 53132 414-423-7400 423-7414
TF: 800-228-9949 ■ *Web:* www.hypneumat.com

Industrial Steel & Machine Sales Inc
2712 Lackland Dr.................................... Waterloo IA 50702 319-296-1816
Web: www.is-ms.net

John J Adams Die Corp 10 Nebraska St............... Worcester MA 01604 508-757-3894 753-8016

Kaufman Mfg Co 547 S 29th St PO Box 1056...........Manitowoc WI 54221 920-684-6641 686-4103
TF: 800-420-6641 ■ *Web:* www.kaufmanmfg.com

Kennametal Inc 1600 Technology Way PO Box 231........ Latrobe PA 15650 724-539-5000
NYSE: KMT ■ *TF Cust Svc:* 800-446-7738 ■ *Web:* www.kennametal.com

Kitamura Machinery of USA Inc 78 Century Dr........Wheeling IL 60090 847-520-7755 520-7763
Web: www.kitamura-machinery.com

Klingelhofer Corp 165 Mill Ln .... Mountainside NJ 07092 908-232-7200 232-1841
TF: 800-879-5546 ■ *Web:* www.klingelhofer.com

Koike Aronson Inc 635 W Main St PO Box 307 .... Arcade NY 14009 585-492-2400 457-3517
TF: 800-252-5232 ■ *Web:* www.koike.com

Kyocera Tycom Corp 3565 Cadillac.............. Costa Mesa CA 92626 714-428-3600 428-3605
TF: 800-823-7284 ■ *Web:* www.kyoceratycom.com

Lucas Precision LP 13020 St Clair Ave .... Cleveland OH 44108 216-451-5588 451-5174
Web: www.lucasprecision.com

Makino 7680 Innovation Way............................Mason OH 45040 513-573-7200 573-7360
TF: 888-625-4661 ■ *Web:* www.makino.com

McLean Inc 3409 E Miraloma Ave..................... Anaheim CA 92806 714-996-5451 996-5453
TF Cust Svc: 800-451-2424 ■ *Web:* mcleaninc.com

Metal Cutting Corp 89 Commerce Rd .... Cedar Grove NJ 07009 973-239-1100 239-6651
Web: www.metalcutting.com

Metl-Saw Systems Inc 2950 Bay Vista Ct .... Benicia CA 94510 707-746-6200 746-5085
Web: www.metlsaw.com

Monarch Lathes 615 N Oaks Ave PO Box 4609 ....Sidney OH 45365 937-492-4111 492-7958
Web: www.monarchlathe.com

Morgood Tools Inc 940 Millstead Way............... Rochester NY 14624 585-436-8828 436-2426
Web: www.morgood.com

NNT Corp 1320 Norwood Ave ....Itasca IL 60143 630-875-9600 875-8899
TF: 800-556-9999 ■ *Web:* www.nntcorp.com

Company	City	State	ZIP	Phone	Fax
Normac Inc 10 Loop Rd PO Box 69 *Web:* www.normac.com	Arden	NC	28704	828-209-9000	209-9001
North American Products Corp 1180 Wernsing Rd **Fax Area Code:* 800 ■ *TF Cust Svc:* 800-457-7468 ■ *Web:* www.napgladu.com	Jasper	IN	47546	812-482-2000	457-7458*
Ohio Broach & Machine Co 35264 Topps Industrial Pkwy **Fax:* Sales ■ *Web:* www.ohiobroach.com	Willoughby	OH	44094	440-946-1040	946-0725*
Okuma America Corp 11900 W Hall Dr *Web:* www.okuma.com	Charlotte	NC	28278	704-588-7000	588-6503
Oliver of Adrian Inc 1111 E Beecher St PO Box 189 *TF:* 877-668-0885 ■ *Web:* www.oliverinstrument.com	Adrian	MI	49221	517-263-2132	265-8698
P & R Industries Inc 1524 Clinton Ave N *Web:* pandrindustries.com	Rochester	NY	14621	585-266-6725	266-0075
Parker Majestic Inc 300 N Pike Rd *TF:* 866-572-7537 ■ *Web:* www.pennunited.com	Sarver	PA	16055	724-352-1551	353-1196
Peddinghaus Corp 300 N Washington Ave *TF:* 800-786-2448 ■ *Web:* www.peddinghaus.com	Bradley	IL	60915	815-937-3800	937-4003
Pilz Automation Safety LP 7150 Commerce Blvd *Web:* www.pilz.com	Canton	MI	48187	734-354-0272	354-3355
Pioneer Broach Co 6434 Telegraph Rd *TF:* 800-621-1945 ■ *Web:* www.pioneerbroach.com	Los Angeles	CA	90040	323-728-1263	722-1699
PMC Industries Inc 29100 Lakeland Blvd *Web:* www.pmc-colinet.com/default.asp?id=50	Wickliffe	OH	44092	440-943-3300	944-1974
Reno Machine Company Inc 170 Pane Rd *Web:* www.reno-machine.com	Newington	CT	06111	860-666-5641	667-4496
RF Cook Manufacturing Co 4585 Allen Rd *Web:* www.rfcook.com	Stow	OH	44224	330-923-9797	923-8641
Rothenberger USA 4455 Boeing Dr *TF:* 800-545-7698 ■ *Web:* www.rothenberger-usa.com	Rockford	IL	61109	815-397-7617	
Rottler Mfg 8029 S 200th St *TF:* 800-452-0534 ■ *Web:* www.rottlermfg.com	Kent	WA	98032	253-872-7050	395-0230
Royal Master Grinders Inc 143 Bauer Dr *Web:* www.royalmaster.com	Oakland	NJ	07436	201-337-8500	337-2324
RP Machine Enterprises Inc 820 Cochran St *Web:* www.rpmachine.com	Statesville	NC	28677	704-872-8888	872-5777
S & M Machine Service Inc 109 E Highland Dr *TF:* 800-323-1579 ■ *Web:* www.snmmachine.com	Oconto Falls	WI	54154	920-846-8130	846-4803
Saginaw Machine Systems (SMS) 800 N Hamilton St *Web:* www.saginawmachine.com	Saginaw	MI	48602	989-753-8465	753-1751
Savage Saws 31 Commerce St E Haven Industrial Park *Web:* www.savagesaws.com	East Haven	CT	06512	609-267-8501	267-1366
Seneca Falls Technology Group 314 Fall St *Web:* www.sftg.com	Seneca Falls	NY	13148	315-568-5804	568-5800
Servo Products Co 34940 Lakeland Blvd *TF:* 800-521-7359 ■ *Web:* www.servoproductsco.com	Eastlake	OH	44095	440-942-9999	942-9100
Setco Sales Co 5880 Hillside Ave *TF:* 800-543-0470 ■ *Web:* www.setco.com	Cincinnati	OH	45233	513-941-5110	941-6913
SGS Tool Co 55 S Main St **Fax:* Hum Res ■ *Web:* www.sgstool.com	Munroe Falls	OH	44262	330-688-6667	686-2128*
Simmons Machine Tool Corp 1700 N Broadway *Web:* smtgroup.com	Albany	NY	12204	518-462-5431	462-0371
SNK America Inc 1150 Feehanville Dr *TF:* 888-765-6224 ■ *Web:* www.snkamerica.com	Mount Prospect	IL	60056	847-364-0801	364-4363
Southwestern Industries Inc 2615 Homestead Pl *TF:* 800-421-6875 ■ *Web:* www.southwesternindustries.com	Rancho Dominguez	CA	90220	310-608-4422	764-2668
Stephen Bader Co Inc 10 Charles St PO Box 297 *Web:* www.stephenbader.com	Valley Falls	NY	12185	518-753-4456	753-4962
Sunnen Products Co 7910 Manchester Ave **Fax:* Cust Svc ■ *TF:* 800-325-3670 ■ *Web:* www.sunnen.com	Saint Louis	MO	63143	314-781-2100	781-2268*
Technidrill Systems Inc 429 Portage Blvd *TF:* 844-313-7012 ■ *Web:* www.technidrillsystems.com	Kent	OH	44240	330-678-9980	678-9981
Thermal Dynamics Corp 82 Benning St *TF:* 800-752-7621 ■ *Web:* victortechnologies.com	West Lebanon	NH	03784	603-298-5711	298-0558
Thurston Mfg Company Inc 14 Thurber Blvd *Web:* www.thurstonmfg.com	Smithfield	RI	02917	401-232-9100	232-9101
Tiffin Foundry & Machine Inc 423 W Adams St PO Box 37 *Web:* www.tiffinfoundry.com	Tiffin	OH	44883	419-447-3991	447-7969
Tool-Flo Mfg Inc 7803 Hansen Rd *TF:* 800-345-2815 ■ *Web:* www.toolflo.com	Houston	TX	77061	713-941-1080	941-8099
Tornos Technologies US Corp 840 Parkview Blvd *Web:* www.tornos.com	Lombard	IL	60148	630-812-2040	812-2039
Toyoda Machinery USA Inc 316 W University Dr *TF:* 800-257-2985 ■ *Web:* www.toyodausa.com	Arlington Heights	IL	60004	847-253-0340	577-4680
TRU TECH Systems Inc 24550 N River Rd PO Box 46965 *TF:* 877-878-8324 ■ *Web:* www.trutechsystems.com	Mount Clemens	MI	48043	586-469-2700	469-1344
US Tool Grinding Inc 701 S Desloge Dr *TF:* 800-222-1771 ■ *Web:* www.ustg.net	Desloge	MO	63601	573-431-3856	431-6655
Vernon Tool Company Ltd 503 Jones Rd *TF:* 800-452-1542 ■ *Web:* www.vernontool.com	Oceanside	CA	92054	760-433-5860	757-2233
WF Meyers Co 1008 13th St *TF:* 800-457-4055 ■ *Web:* www.wfmeyers.com	Bedford	IN	47421	812-275-4485	275-4488
WF Wells Inc 16645 Heimbach Rd *Web:* wfwells.us	Three Rivers	MI	49093	269-279-5123	279-6337
Whitney Tool Company Inc 906 R St PO Box 545 *TF:* 800-536-1971 ■ *Web:* www.whitneytool.com	Bedford	IN	47421	812-275-4491	275-6458
Wisconsin Machine Tool Corp 3225 Gateway Rd Ste 100 *TF:* 800-243-3078 ■ *Web:* www.machine-tool.com	Brookfield	WI	53045	262-317-3048	317-3079

456 MACHINE TOOLS - METAL FORMING TYPES

See Also Machine Tools - Metal Cutting Types p. 2692; Metalworking Devices & Accessories p. 2768; Rolling Mill Machinery p. 3141; Tool & Die Shops p. 3249

Company	City	State	ZIP	Phone	Fax
Advanced Hydraulics Inc 13568 Vintage Pl *TF:* 888-581-8079 ■ *Web:* www.advancedhydraulicsinc.com	Chino	CA	91710	909-590-7644	590-7049
Amada America Inc 7025 Firestone Blvd *TF:* 800-626-6612 ■ *Web:* www.amada.com	Buena Park	CA	90621	714-739-2111	739-4099
American Actuator Corp (AAC) PO Box 113096 *Web:* www.americanactuator.com	Stamford	CT	06911	203-324-6334	
Anderson Cook Inc 17650 15-Mile Rd *Web:* www.andersoncook.com	Fraser	MI	48026	586-293-0800	
Atlas Technologies Inc 3100 Cotter Ave *Web:* www.atlastechnologies.com	Fenton	MI	48430	810-629-6663	629-8145
Badge A Minit Ltd 345 N Lewis Ave *TF:* 800-223-4103 ■ *Web:* www.badgeaminit.com	Oglesby	IL	61348	815-883-8822	883-9696
Beatty Machine & Mfg Company Inc 940 150th St *Web:* www.beattymachine.com	Hammond	IN	46327	219-931-3000	937-1662
Bedco Inc 4600 Bree Rd *Web:* www.bedcoinc.com	East China	MI	48054	810-329-2292	329-4017
Bliss Clearing Niagara (BCN) 1004 E State St *TF:* 800-642-5477 ■ *Web:* www.bcntechserv.com	Hastings	MI	49058	269-948-3300	948-3313
Bradbury Company Inc 1200 E Cole *TF:* 800-397-6394 ■ *Web:* bradburygroup.com	Moundridge	KS	67107	620-345-6394	345-6381
Bruderer Inc 1200 Hendricks Cswy *Web:* www.bruderer.com	Ridgefield	NJ	07657	201-941-2121	886-2010
CA Lawton Company Inc 1950 Enterprise Way *Web:* www.calawton.com	De Pere	WI	54115	920-337-2470	
Cincinnati Inc 7420 Kilby Rd *Web:* www.e-ci.com	Harrison	OH	45030	513-367-7100	367-7552
Cyril Bath Co 1610 Airport Rd *TF:* 800-801-1418 ■ *Web:* www.cyrilbath.com	Monroe	NC	28110	704-289-8531	289-3932
DR Sperry & Co 623 Rathbone Ave *TF:* 888-997-9297 ■ *Web:* www.drsperry.com	Aurora	IL	60506	630-892-4361	892-1664
Edwards Manufacturing Co 1107 Sykes St *TF:* 800-373-8206 ■ *Web:* www.edwardsironworkers.com	Albert Lea	MN	56007	507-373-8206	373-9433
Emery Corp PO Box 1104 *TF:* 800-255-0537 ■ *Web:* www.emerycorp.com	Morganton	NC	28680	828-433-1536	433-6809
Erie Press Systems 1253 W 12th St PO Box 4061 *TF:* 800-222-3608 ■ *Web:* www.eriepress.com	Erie	PA	16512	814-455-3941	456-4819
FH Peterson Machine Corp 143 S St *Web:* www.fhpetersonmachine.com	Stoughton	MA	02072	781-341-4930	341-6022
GEMCOR Corp 100 Gemcor Dr *Web:* www.gemcor.com	West Seneca	NY	14224	716-674-9300	674-3171
Grant Assembly Technologies 90 Silliman Ave *TF:* 800-227-2150 ■ *Web:* www.grantriveters.com	Bridgeport	CT	06605	203-366-4557	366-0370
Greenerd Press & Machine Company Inc 41 Crown St PO Box 886 *TF:* 800-877-9110 ■ *Web:* www.greenerd.com	Nashua	NH	03061	603-889-4101	889-7601
Heim LP 6360 W 73rd St *TF:* 800-927-9393 ■ *Web:* www.theheimgroup.com	Chicago	IL	60638	708-496-7450	496-7428
Hudson Machinery Worldwide 32 Stevens St	Haverhill	MA	01830	978-373-7295	
Kinefac Corp 156 Goddard Memorial Dr *Web:* www.kinefac.com	Worcester	MA	01603	508-754-6891	756-5342
Lockformer Co 5480 Sixth St SW **Fax Area Code:* 319 ■ *Web:* mestekmachinery.com	Cedar Rapids	IA	52404	630-964-8000	364-3436*
Mate Precision Tooling Inc 1295 Lund Blvd *TF:* 800-328-4492 ■ *Web:* www.matept.com	Anoka	MN	55303	763-421-0230	421-0285
Mega Manufacturing Inc PO Box 457 *TF:* 800-338-5471 ■ *Web:* www.megafab.com	Hutchinson	KS	67504	620-663-1127	
Minster Machine Co 240 W Fifth St PO Box 120 *Web:* www.minster.com	Minster	OH	45865	419-628-2331	628-3517
Murata Machinery USA Inc 2120 Queen City Dr **Fax Area Code:* 704 ■ *TF:* 800-428-8469 ■ *Web:* www.muratec-usa.com	Charlotte	NC	28208	800-428-8469	392-6541*
National Machinery LLC 161 Greenfield St *Web:* www.nationalmachinery.com	Tiffin	OH	44883	419-447-5211	443-2379
NFM Welding Engineers 577 Oberlin Rd SW *Web:* www.nfm.net	Massillon	OH	44647	330-837-3868	837-2230
Oak Products Inc 504 Wade St *Web:* www.oakpresses.com	Sturgis	MI	49091	269-651-8513	651-8513
Pacific Press Technologies 714 Walnut St *TF:* 800-851-3586 ■ *Web:* www.pacific-press.com	Mount Carmel	IL	62863	618-262-8666	262-7000
Pacific Roller Die Co 1321 W Winton Ave *Web:* www.prdcompany.com	Hayward	CA	94545	510-782-7242	887-5639
PHI Inc 14955 E Salt Lk Ave *Web:* www.phi-tulip.com	City of Industry	CA	91746	626-968-9680	333-3610
Presses Inc 6360 W 73rd St *TF:* 800-927-9393 ■ *Web:* www.theheimgroup.com	Chicago	IL	60638	708-496-7400	496-7428
QPI Multipress Inc 2222 S Third St *Web:* www.multipress.com	Columbus	OH	43207	614-228-0185	228-2358
Reed 28 Sword St *TF:* 800-343-6068 ■ *Web:* ptgtools.com	Auburn	MA	01501	508-753-6530	753-0127
Reno Machine Company Inc 170 Pane Rd *Web:* www.reno-machine.com	Newington	CT	06111	860-666-5641	667-4496
Rimrock Corp 1700 Jetway Blvd *Web:* www.rimrockcorp.com	Columbus	OH	43219	614-471-5926	471-7388
Roper Whitney of Rockford Inc 2833 Huffman Blvd **Fax:* Sales ■ *Web:* www.roperwhitney.com	Rockford	IL	61103	815-962-3011	962-2227*
Schleuniger Inc 87 Colin Dr *TF Tech Supp:* 877-902-1470 ■ *Web:* www.schleuniger.com	Manchester	NH	03103	603-668-8117	668-8119
Strippit Inc/LVD 12975 Clarence Ctr Rd *TF:* 800-828-1527 ■ *Web:* www.lvdgroup.com	Akron	NY	14001	716-542-4511	542-5957

				Phone	Fax
Tetrahedron Assoc Inc PO Box 710157 ... San Diego *TF:* 800-958-3872 ■ *Web:* www.tetrahedronassociates.com	CA	92171		619-661-0552	661-0559
Tools for Bending Inc 194 W Dakota Ave ... Denver *TF Cust Svc:* 800-873-3305 ■ *Web:* www.toolsforbending.com	CO	80223		303-777-7170	777-4749
Vamco International 555 Epsilon Dr ... Pittsburgh *Web:* www.vamcointernational.com	PA	15238		412-963-7100	
WA Whitney Co 650 Race St PO Box 1206 ... Rockford *Web:* www.megafab.com	IL	61105		815-964-6771	964-3175
Wabash MPI 1569 Morris St PO Box 298 ... Wabash *Web:* www.wabashmpi.com	IN	46992		260-563-1184	563-1396
Williams White & Co 600 River Dr ... Moline **Fax Area Code:* 309 ■ *TF:* 877-797-7650 ■ *Web:* www.williamswhite.com	IL	61265		877-797-7650	797-7677*
Wysong Inc 4820 US 29 N ... Greensboro *TF:* 800-299-7664 ■ *Web:* www.wysongpartsandservice.com	NC	27405		336-621-3960	621-8360

457 MAGAZINES & JOURNALS

See Also Periodicals Publishers p. 3004

457-1 Agriculture & Farming Magazines

			Phone	Fax
Alfa Corp 2108 E S Blvd ... Montgomery *TF:* 800-964-2532 ■ *Web:* www.alfainsurance.com	AL	36116	334-288-0375	288-0905
American Agriculturist 5227-B Baltimore Pike ... Littlestown *TF:* 800-441-1410 ■ *Web:* farmprogress.com	PA	17340	717-359-0150	359-0250
Beef Magazine 7900 International Dr Ste 300 ... Minneapolis *TF Cust Svc:* 800-722-5334 ■ *Web:* beefmagazine.com	MN	55425	952-851-9329	851-4601
Dairy Herd Management 10901 W 84th Terr ... Lenexa *TF:* 800-255-5113 ■ *Web:* www.dairyherd.com	KS	66214	913-438-8700	438-0695
Farm Bureau Press 10720 Kanis Rd ... Little Rock *Web:* www.arfb.com	AR	72211	501-228-1300	
Farm Industry News 7900 International Dr Ste 300 ... Minneapolis *TF Cust Svc:* 800-722-5334 ■ *Web:* www.farmindustrynews.com	MN	55425	952-851-9329	851-4601
Farm Journal 261 E Broadway PO Box 1167 ... Monticello	MN	55362	763-271-3363	271-3360
Farm Journal 30 S 15th Ste 900 ... Philadelphia *TF:* 800-331-9310 ■ *Web:* www.farmjournalmedia.com	PA	19102	215-557-8900	
Farm Show Magazine 20088 Kenwood Trial ... Lakeville **Fax Area Code:* 952 ■ *TF:* 800-834-9665 ■ *Web:* www.farmshow.com	MN	55044	800-834-9665	469-5575*
Floridagriculture Magazine PO Box 147030 ... Gainesville *Web:* www.floridagriculture.org	FL	32614	352-378-1321	374-1530
Georgia Farm Bureau News 1620 Bass Rd ... Macon *TF:* 800-342-1192 ■ *Web:* www.gfb.org	GA	31210	478-474-8411	474-8750
Hoard's Dairyman Magazine 28 Milwaukee Ave W PO Box 801 ... Fort Atkinson *TF:* 800-245-8222 ■ *Web:* www.hoards.com	WI	53538	920-563-5551	563-7298
Iowa Farm Bureau Spokesman Magazine 5400 University Ave ... West Des Moines *TF:* 866-598-3693 ■ *Web:* iowafarmbureau.com	IA	50266	515-225-5413	225-5419
Kansas Living Magazine 2627 KFB Plz ... Manhattan *TF:* 800-406-3053 ■ *Web:* www.kfb.org	KS	66503	785-587-6000	587-6914
Neighbors Magazine 1324 Chippenham Dr ... Baton Rouge **Fax Area Code:* 334	LA	70808	225-767-8549	284-3957*
Pork Report 1776 NW 114th St PO Box 9114 ... Des Moines *TF:* 800-456-7675 ■ *Web:* www.pork.org	IA	50325	515-223-2600	223-2646
Soybean Digest 7900 International Dr Ste 300 ... Minneapolis *TF Cust Svc:* 800-722-5334 ■ *Web:* www.cornandsoybeandigest.com	MN	55425	952-851-4667	851-4601
Tennessee Farm Bureau News 147 Bear Creek Pike ... Columbia *TF:* 877-876-2222 ■ *Web:* www.tnfarmbureau.org	TN	38401	931-388-7872	388-5818
Texas Agriculture Magazine 7420 Fish Pond Rd PO Box 2689 ... Waco	TX	76710	254-772-3030	
Texas Farm Bureau 7420 Fish Pond Rd PO Box 2689 ... Waco *TF:* 800-488-7872 ■ *Web:* www.texasfarmbureau.org	TX	76710	254-772-3030	
Top Producer Magazine 1818 Market St 31st Fl ... Philadelphia *TF:* 800-320-7992 ■ *Web:* www.agweb.com	PA	19103	800-320-7992	

457-2 Art & Architecture Magazines

			Phone	Fax
AmericanStyle Magazine 3000 Chestnut Ave Ste 304 ... Baltimore *TF:* 800-642-4314 ■ *Web:* www.americanstyle.com	MD	21211	410-889-3093	243-7089
Architectural Digest 4 Times Sq 18th Fl ... New York *TF:* 800-365-8032 ■ *Web:* www.architecturaldigest.com	NY	10036	800-365-8032	
Architectural Record Magazine 2 Penn Plaza 9th Fl ... New York **Fax Area Code:* 212 ■ *TF:* 800-393-6343 ■ *Web:* www.architecturalrecord.com	NY	10121	646-849-7100	904-4256*
Art Calendar 1500 Pk Ctr Dr ... Orlando *Web:* www.professionalartistmag.com	FL	32835	407-563-7000	563-7099
Art in America Magazine 575 Broadway ... New York *TF Cust Svc:* 800-925-8059 ■ *Web:* www.artinamericamagazine.com	NY	10012	212-941-2800	
Artforum International Magazine 350 Seventh Ave 19th Fl ... New York *TF:* 800-966-2783 ■ *Web:* www.artforum.com	NY	10001	212-475-4000	529-1257
Artist's Magazine, The 4700 E Galbraith Rd ... Cincinnati *TF:* 800-422-2550 ■ *Web:* www.artistsnetwork.com	OH	45236	513-531-2222	891-7153
ARTnews Magazine 48 W 38th St 9th Fl ... New York *TF:* 800-284-4625 ■ *Web:* artnews.com	NY	10018	212-398-1690	819-0394
Bomb Magazine 80 Hanson Pl Ste 703 ... Brooklyn *Web:* bombmagazine.org	NY	11217	718-636-9100	636-9200
Design Journal 23371 Mulholland Dr STE 253 ... Woodland Hills *Web:* www.designjournalmag.com	CA	91364	310-394-4394	
Design/Build Business Magazine 3030 Salt Creek Ln Ste 200 ... Arlington Heights *TF:* 800-547-7377 ■ *Web:* www.forresidentialpros.com	IL	60005	847-454-2714	454-2759
HOW Design Magazine 4700 E Galbraith Rd ... Cincinnati *TF Cust Svc:* 800-333-1115 ■ *Web:* www.howdesign.com	OH	45236	513-531-2690	
Inland Architect Magazine 3500 W Peterson Ave Ste 403 ... Chicago *Web:* www.inlandarchitectmag.com	IL	60659	773-866-9900	866-9881
Landscape Architecture Magazine 636 'I' St NW ... Washington	DC	20001	202-898-2444	898-1185
Metropolis Magazine 205 Lexington Ave 17th Fl ... New York *TF:* 800-344-3046 ■ *Web:* www.metropolismag.com	NY	10016	212-627-9977	627-9988
Modernism Magazine 199 George St ... Lambertville *Web:* ragoarts.com	NJ	08530	609-397-4104	
Pastel Journal 4700 E Galbraith Rd ... Cincinnati *TF:* 800-422-2550 ■ *Web:* www.artistsnetwork.com	OH	45236	513-531-2222	891-7153
Southwest Art Magazine 10901 W 120th Ave Ste 350 ... Broomfield *TF:* 877-212-1938 ■ *Web:* www.southwestart.com	CO	80021	303-442-0427	449-0279
Studio Photography & Design Magazine 1233 Janesville Ave ... Fort Atkinson **Fax Area Code:* 800 ■ *Web:* www.imaginginfo.com	WI	53538	631-963-6200	547-7377*
Sunshine Artist Magazine 4075 LB McLeod Rd Ste E ... Orlando *TF:* 800-597-2573 ■ *Web:* www.sunshineartist.com	FL	32811	407-648-7479	648-7454

457-3 Automotive Magazines

			Phone	Fax
American Iron Magazine 1010 Summer St ... Stamford *TF Cust Svc:* 877-693-3572 ■ *Web:* www.aimag.com	CT	06905	203-425-8777	
Automobile Magazine 120 E Liberty St ... Ann Arbor *Web:* www.automobilemag.com	MI	48104	310-531-9900	
AutoWeek Magazine 1155 Gratiot Ave ... Detroit *TF Circ:* 888-288-6954 ■ *Web:* www.autoweek.com	MI	48207	313-446-6000	446-0347
Backroads Magazine 160 Co Rd 521 ... Newton *Web:* www.backroadsusa.com	NJ	07860	973-948-4176	948-0823
Cycle World Magazine 1499 Monrovia Ave ... Newport Beach *TF:* 800-456-3084 ■ *Web:* www.cycleworld.com	CA	92663	949-720-5300	
Easyriders Magazine 28210 Dorothy Dr ... Agoura Hills *TF:* 800-323-3484 ■ *Web:* www.paisanopub.com	CA	91301	818-889-8740	
Friction Zone Magazine 60166 Hop Patch Spring Rd ... Mountain Center *Web:* www.friction-zone.com	CA	92561	951-659-9500	
Grassroots Motorsports Magazine 915 Ridgewood Ave ... Holly Hill *TF:* 800-520-8292 ■ *Web:* www.grassrootsmotorsports.com	FL	32117	386-239-0523	239-0573
Hemmings Motor News 222 Main St ... Bennington *TF:* 800-227-4373 ■ *Web:* www.hemmings.com	VT	05201	802-442-3101	447-9631
Hot Rod Magazine 6420 Wilshire Blvd ... Los Angeles *TF Orders:* 800-800-4681 ■ *Web:* www.hotrod.com	CA	90048	323-782-2000	782-2223
Hot Rod Network 774 S Placentia Ave ... Placentia *TF:* 800-926-8207 ■ *Web:* www.hotrod.com/popular-hot-rodding-magazine	CA	92870	800-926-8207	
Lowrider Magazine 2400 E Katella Ave 11th Fl ... Anaheim *Web:* www.lowrider.com	CA	92806	714-939-2400	978-6390
Motor Trend Magazine 6420 Wilshire Blvd 7th Fl ... Los Angeles *TF:* 800-800-6848 ■ *Web:* www.motortrend.com	CA	90048	323-782-2000	782-2355
Motorcycle Consumer News Magazine 3 Burroughs ... Irvine *TF:* 888-333-0354 ■ *Web:* www.mcnews.com/mcnews	CA	92618	949-855-8822	855-0654
National Speed Sport News Magazine 142 F S Cardigan Way ... Mooresville *TF:* 866-455-2531 ■ *Web:* www.nationalspeedsportnews.com	NC	28117	704-489-5231	
Off-Road Magazine 2400 E Katella Ave 7th fl ... Anaheim *TF:* 877-462-6752 ■ *Web:* www.fourwheeler.com	CA	92806	714-848-8880	978-6390
Road & Track Magazine 1499 Monrovia Ave ... Newport Beach *TF:* 800-835-6422 ■ *Web:* www.roadandtrack.com	CA	92663	949-720-5300	
Stock Car Racing Magazine PO Box 420235 ... Palm Coast *TF:* 800-333-2633 ■ *Web:* www.stockcarracing.com	FL	32142	800-333-2633	

457-4 Boating Magazines

			Phone	Fax
48 Degrees North 6327 Seaview Ave NW ... Seattle *Web:* www.48north.com	WA	98107	206-789-7350	789-6392
Blue Water Sailing Magazine 747 Aquidneck Ave Ste 201 Ste 201 ... Middletown *TF:* 888-800-7245 ■ *Web:* www.bwsailing.com	RI	02842	401-847-7612	845-8580
Boating Life Magazine 460 N Orlando Ave Ste 200 ... Winter Park *Web:* www.boatingmag.com	FL	32789	407-571-4682	
Boating Magazine 1633 Broadway ... New York *Web:* www.boatingmag.com	NY	10019	212-767-4818	
Cruising World Magazine 55 Hammerlund Way ... Middletown *Web:* www.cruisingworld.com	RI	02842	401-845-5100	845-5180
Duncan Mcintosh 18475 Bandilier ... Fountain Valley *Web:* duncanmcintoshco.com	CA	92708	949-660-6150	660-6172
Good Old Boat Magazine 1501 Eigth Ave NW ... Jamestown *Web:* www.goodoldboat.com	ND	58401	701-952-9433	952-9434
PassageMaker Magazine 105 Eastern Ave Ste 203 ... Annapolis *Web:* www.passagemaker.com	MD	21403	410-990-9086	990-9095
Power & Motoryacht Magazine 260 Madison Ave 4th Fl ... New York *TF:* 800-284-8036 ■ *Web:* www.powerandmotoryacht.com	NY	10016	860-767-3200	
SAIL Magazine 98 N Washington St Ste 107 ... Boston *TF:* 877-388-7761 ■ *Web:* www.sailmagazine.com	MA	02114	617-720-8600	723-0911
Sailing World Magazine 55 Hammerlund Way ... Middletown *TF Cust Svc:* 866-436-2460 ■ *Web:* www.sailingworld.com	RI	02842	401-845-5100	845-5180

Phone | Fax

Sea Magazine 17782 Cowan St Ste C .... Irvine CA 92614 949-660-6150 660-6172
TF: 800-873-7327 ■ *Web:* www.seamagazine.com

Yachting Magazine 55 Hammarlund Way .... Middletown RI 02842 800-999-0869
TF: 800-999-0869 ■ *Web:* www.yachtingmagazine.com

457-5 Business & Finance Magazines

Phone | Fax

Advisor Today 2901 Telestar Ct .... Falls Church VA 22042 800-247-4074
TF: 800-247-4074 ■ *Web:* www.advisortoday.com

Alaska Business Monthly
501 W Northern Lights Blvd Ste 100 .... Anchorage AK 99503 907-276-4373 279-2900
TF: 800-770-4373 ■ *Web:* www.akbizmag.com

American Banker Magazine
1 State St Plaza 27th Fl .... New York NY 10004 212-803-8200 843-9600
TF: 800-221-1809 ■ *Web:* www.americanbanker.com

American Journalism Review
University of Maryland
1117 Journalism Bldg
1117 Journalism Bldg Rm 2116 .... College Park MD 20742 301-405-8803
Web: www.ajr.org

Appraisal Journal 200 W Madison Ste 1500 .... Chicago IL 60606 888-756-4624 335-4400*
**Fax Area Code:* 312 ■ *TF:* 888-756-4624 ■ *Web:* www.appraisalinstitute.org

Area Development Magazine
400 Post Ave Ste 304 .... Westbury NY 11590 516-338-0900 338-0100
TF: 800-735-2732 ■ *Web:* www.areadevelopment.com

Arkansas Business LP 122 E Second St .... Little Rock AR 72201 501-372-1443 375-7933
TF: 888-322-6397 ■ *Web:* www.arkansasbusiness.com

Association Management Magazine
1575 'I' St NW .... Washington DC 20005 202-371-0940
TF: 888-950-2723 ■ *Web:* www.asaecenter.org

Atlanta Business Chronicle
3423 Piedmont Rd Ste 400 .... Atlanta GA 30305 404-249-1000 249-1048
Web: www.bizjournals.com

Austin Business Journal
111 Congress Ave Ste 750 .... Austin TX 78701 512-494-2500 494-2525*
**Fax:* Edit ■ *Web:* www.bizjournals.com

Baltimore Business Journal
111 Market Pl Ste 720 .... Baltimore MD 21202 410-576-1161 752-3112
Web: www.bizjournals.com

Banking Strategies Magazine
115 S LaSalle St Ste 3300 .... Chicago IL 60603 312-553-4600
TF: 888-224-0037 ■ *Web:* www.bai.org/bankingstrategies/about.asp

Baton Rouge Business Report
9029 Jefferson Hwy .... Baton Rouge LA 70809 225-928-1700 926-1329
Web: www.businessreport.com

Best's Review Ambest Rd .... Oldwick NJ 08858 908-439-2200 439-3363
Web: www.ambest.com/review

Birmingham Business Journal
2140 11th Ave S Ste 205 .... Birmingham AL 35205 205-322-0000 322-0040
Web: www.bizjournals.com

BizWest 3180 Sterling Cir Ste 201 .... Boulder CO 80301 303-440-4950 440-8954
Web: bizwest.com

BizWest 141 S College Ave .... Fort Collins CO 80524 970-221-5400 221-5432
Web: bizwest.com

Black Enterprise Magazine 130 Fifth Ave .... New York NY 10011 212-242-8000 886-9610
TF Cust Svc: 800-727-7777 ■ *Web:* www.blackenterprise.com

Boston Business Journal 160 Federal St 12th Fl .... Boston MA 02110 617-330-1000 330-1016
Web: www.bizjournals.com

Brandweek Magazine 770 Broadway 7th Fl .... New York NY 10003 646-654-5000
Web: www.adweek.com

British Standards Institution, The
12110 Sunset Hills Rd Ste 200 .... Reston VA 20190 703-437-9000 437-9001
TF: 800-862-4977 ■ *Web:* www.bsigroup.com

Business Facilities Magazine
44 Apple St Ste 3 .... Tinton Falls NJ 07724 732-842-7433 758-6634
TF: 800-524-0337 ■ *Web:* www.businessfacilities.com

Business First 465 Main St .... Buffalo NY 14203 716-854-5822 854-3394
Web: www.bizjournals.com

Business First 455 S Fourth St Ste 278 .... Louisville KY 40202 502-583-1731 587-1703
Web: www.bizjournals.com

Business Insurance Magazine 711 Third Ave .... New York NY 10017 212-210-0100 280-3174*
**Fax Area Code:* 312 ■ *TF:* 877-812-1587 ■ *Web:* www.businessinsurance.com

Business Journal of Milwaukee
825 N Jefferson St Ste 200 .... Milwaukee WI 53202 414-278-7788 278-7028
Web: www.bizjournals.com/milwaukee

Business Journal of Phoenix
101 N First Ave Ste 2300 .... Phoenix AZ 85003 602-230-8400 230-0955
Web: www.bizjournals.com

Business Journal of Portland
851 SW Sixth Ave Ste 500 .... Portland OR 97204 503-274-8733 219-3450
Web: www.bizjournals.com

Business Journal of San Jose
96 N Third St Ste 100 .... San Jose CA 95112 408-295-3800 295-5028
Web: www.bizjournals.com

Business Journal of Tampa Bay
4890 W Kennedy Blvd Ste 850 .... Tampa FL 33609 813-873-8225 876-1827
Web: www.bizjournals.com/tampabay

Business Journal, The 25 E Boardman St .... Youngstown OH 44501 330-744-5023 744-5838
TF: 800-837-6397 ■ *Web:* businessjournaldaily.com

California Real Estate Magazine
525 S Virgil Ave .... Los Angeles CA 90020 213-739-8200 480-7724
TF: 888-811-5281 ■ *Web:* www.car.org

Central New York Business Journal, The
269 W Jefferson St .... Syracuse NY 13202 315-579-3919
TF: 800-836-3539 ■ *Web:* www.cnybj.com

CFO Magazine 253 Summer St .... Boston MA 02210 617-345-9700 951-4090
TF: 800-772-1119 ■ *Web:* ww2.cfo.com

Charlotte Business Journal
1100 S Tryon St Ste 100 .... Charlotte NC 28203 704-973-1100 973-1101*
**Fax:* Edit ■ *Web:* www.bizjournals.com

Phone | Fax

Chief Executive Magazine
1 Sound Shore Dr Ste 100 .... Greenwich CT 06830 203-930-2700 930-2701
Web: www.chiefexecutive.net

Cincinnati Business Courier
101 W Seventh St .... Cincinnati OH 45202 513-621-6665 621-2462
Web: www.bizjournals.com

CIO Magazine
492 Old Connecticut Path PO Box 9208 .... Framingham MA 01701 508-872-0080 879-7784
Web: www.cio.com

Columbus Business First
303 W Nationwide Blvd .... Columbus OH 43215 614-461-4040 365-2980
TF: 800-486-3289 ■ *Web:* www.bizjournals.com

Communications News PO Box 866 .... Osprey FL 34229 941-539-7579
TF: 800-827-9715 ■ *Web:* www.comnews.com

Contract Design Magazine 770 Broadway .... New York NY 10004 800-697-8859 654-7205*
**Fax Area Code:* 646 ■ *TF:* 800-697-8859 ■ *Web:* www.contractdesign.com

Crain's Chicago Business Magazine
150 N Michigan Ave 16th Fl .... Chicago IL 60601 312-649-5200 280-3150
TF: 877-812-1590 ■ *Web:* www.chicagobusiness.com

Crain's Cleveland Business Magazine
700 W St Clair Ave Ste 310 .... Cleveland OH 44113 216-522-1383 694-4264
TF: 888-909-9111 ■ *Web:* www.crainscleveland.com

Crain's Detroit Business Magazine
1155 Gratiot Ave .... Detroit MI 48207 313-446-6000 446-1687
TF: 888-909-9111 ■ *Web:* www.crainsdetroit.com

Crain's New York Business Magazine
685 Third Ave 3rd Fl .... New York NY 10017 212-210-0100 210-0799*
**Fax:* Edit ■ *TF:* 877-824-9379 ■ *Web:* www.crainsnewyork.com

Denver Business Journal 1700 Broadway Ste 515 .... Denver CO 80290 303-837-3500
Web: www.bizjournals.com/denver

Des Moines Business Record 100 Fourth St .... Des Moines IA 50309 515-288-3336
Web: www.businessrecord.com

Drug Topics Magazine
24950 Country Club Blvd Ste 200 .... North Olmsted OH 44070 440-891-2792 891-2735
TF Cust Svc: 877-922-2022 ■ *Web:* drugtopics.modernmedicine.com

E-Commerce Times (ECT) 16133 Ventura Blvd Ste 700 .... Encino CA 91436 818-461-9700 461-9710
TF: 877-328-5500 ■ *Web:* www.ectnews.com

Editor & Publisher Magazine 17782 Cowan Ste C .... Irvine CA 92614 949-660-6150 660-6172
TF: 855-896-7433 ■ *Web:* www.editorandpublisher.com

Enterprise Magazine
825 N 300 W Ste NE220 .... Salt Lake City UT 84103 801-533-0556 533-0684
Web: www.slenterprise.com

Expansion Management Magazine
1300 E Ninth St .... Cleveland OH 44114 216-696-7000
TF: 866-505-7173 ■ *Web:* www.industryweek.com

Fast Company Magazine 7 World Trade Ctr .... New York NY 10007 212-389-5300 389-5496
TF: 800-542-6029 ■ *Web:* www.fastcompany.com

Finance & Commerce
730 Second Ave S US Trust Bldg Ste 100 .... Minneapolis MN 55402 612-333-4244 333-3243
TF: 800-451-9998 ■ *Web:* www.finance-commerce.com

Forbes Magazine 60 Fifth Ave .... New York NY 10011 212-366-8900
TF: 800-295-0893 ■ *Web:* www.forbes.com

Fortune Small Business Magazine (FSB)
1271 Ave of the Americas .... New York NY 10020 212-522-1212
Web: www.money.cnn.com/magazines/fsb

Franchising World Magazine
1501 K St NW Ste 350 .... Washington DC 20005 202-628-8000 628-0812
TF: 800-543-1038 ■ *Web:* www.franchise.org

Futures Magazine 222 S Riverside Plz Ste 620 .... Chicago IL 60606 312-846-4600
Web: www.futuresmag.com

Global Finance Magazine E 20th St .... New York NY 10003 212-447-7900
Web: www.gfmag.com

Grand Rapids Business Journal (GRBJ)
549 Ottawa Ave NW Ste 201 .... Grand Rapids MI 49503 616-459-4545
Web: grbj.com

Greenville Business Magazine
303 Haywood Rd .... Greenville SC 29607 864-271-1105 271-1165
Web: www.greenvillebusinessmag.com

Harvard Business Review 60 Harvard Way .... Boston MA 02163 617-783-7500 783-7555*
**Fax:* Cust Svc ■ *TF:* 800-274-3214 ■ *Web:* www.hbr.org

Health Facilities Management Magazine
155 N Wacker Dr Ste 400 .... Chicago IL 60606 312-893-6800 422-4500
TF: 800-621-6902 ■ *Web:* www.hfmmagazine.com

Hospitals & Health Networks Magazine
155 N Wacker Ste 400 .... Chicago IL 60606 312-893-6800 422-4500
TF: 800-621-6902 ■ *Web:* www.hhnmag.com

Houston Business Journal
1233 W Loop S Ste 1300 .... Houston TX 77027 713-688-8811 963-0482*
**Fax:* Edit ■ *Web:* www.bizjournals.com

HRMagazine 1800 Duke St .... Alexandria VA 22314 703-548-3440 836-0367
TF: 800-283-7476 ■ *Web:* www.shrm.org/hrmagazine

Human Resource Executive Magazine
747 Dresher Rd Ste 500 .... Horsham PA 19044 215-784-0910 784-0275
Web: www.hreonline.com

In Business Magazine 200 River Pl Ste 250 .... Madison WI 53716 608-204-9655 204-9656
Web: www.ibmadison.com

Inc Magazine 7 World Trade Ctr .... New York NY 10007 212-389-5377 389-5379
TF: 800-234-0999 ■ *Web:* www.inc.com

Independent Agent Magazine
127 S Peyton St .... Alexandria VA 22314 800-221-7917
TF: 800-221-7917 ■ *Web:* www.iamagazine.com

Indianapolis Business Journal
41 E Washington St Ste 200 .... Indianapolis IN 46204 317-634-6200 263-5406*
**Fax:* Edit ■ *TF:* 800-428-7081 ■ *Web:* www.ibj.com

Internal Auditor Magazine
247 Maitland Ave .... Altamonte Springs FL 32701 407-937-1100 937-1101
Web: na.theiia.org

Journal of Accountancy 220 Leigh Farm Rd .... Durham NC 27707 888-777-7077 419-5241*
**Fax Area Code:* 919 ■ *TF:* 888-777-7077 ■ *Web:* www.journalofaccountancy.com

Journal of Business 429 E Third Ave .... Spokane WA 99202 509-456-5257 456-0624
Web: www.spokanejournal.com

Journal of Financial Planning Assn
7535 E Hampden Ave Ste 600 .... Denver CO 80231 303-759-4900 759-0749
TF: 800-322-4237 ■ *Web:* www.onefpa.org/journal/pages/default.aspx

Phone Fax

Journal of Property Management
430 N Michigan Ave Chicago IL 60611 800-837-0706 338-4736
TF: 800-837-0706 ■ *Web:* irem.org/home/pagenotfound

Kansas City Business Journal
1100 Main St Ste 210 Kansas City MO 64105 816-421-5900 472-4010
Web: www.bizjournals.com

Law Enforcement Technology Magazine
1233 Janesville Ave Fort Atkinson WI 53538 800-547-7377
TF: 800-547-7377 ■ *Web:* www.officer.com

Leadership Journal 465 Gundersen Dr. Carol Stream IL 60188 630-260-6200
TF: 800-777-3136 ■ *Web:* christianitytoday.com/le

Lodging Magazine 385 Oxford Vly Rd Ste 420 Yardley PA 19067 215-321-9662 321-5124
TF: 800-394-5157 ■ *Web:* www.lodgingmagazine.com

Los Angeles Business Journal
5700 Wilshire Blvd Ste 170 Los Angeles CA 90036 323-549-5225 549-5255
Web: www.labusinessjournal.com

Marketing News 311 S Wacker Dr Ste 5800 Chicago IL 60606 312-542-9000 922-3763
TF: 800-262-1150 ■ *Web:* www.ama.org

Meetings & Conventions Magazine
100 Lighting Way Secaucus NJ 07094 201-902-2000
Web: www.meetings-conventions.com

Memphis Business Journal
80 Monroe Ave Ste 600 Memphis TN 38103 901-523-1000 526-5240
Web: www.bizjournals.com

Mergers & Acquisitions Magazine
1 State St Plz New York NY 10004 212-803-6051
TF Cust Svc: 888-807-8667 ■ *Web:* www.themiddlemarket.com

Midlands Business Journal 1324 S 119th St Omaha NE 68144 402-330-1760 758-9315
Web: www.mbj.com

Minneapolis-Saint Paul Business Journal
333 S Seventh St Ste 350 Minneapolis MN 55402 612-288-2100 288-2121
Web: www.bizjournals.com/twincities

Mississippi Business Journal
200 N Congress St Jackson MS 39201 601-364-1000 364-1007
TF: 800-283-4625 ■ *Web:* www.msbusiness.com

Nashville Business Journal
1800 Church St Ste 300 Nashville TN 37203 615-248-2222 248-6246
Web: www.bizjournals.com

National Assn of Credit Management
8840 Columbia 100 Pkwy Columbia MD 21045 410-740-5560 740-5574
TF: 800-955-8815 ■ *Web:* www.nacm.org

National Association of Housing and Redevelopment Officials
630 'I' St NW Washington DC 20001 202-289-3500 289-8181
TF: 877-866-2476 ■ *Web:* www.nahro.org

National Real Estate Investor Magazine
6151 Powers Ferry Rd NW Ste 200 Atlanta GA 30339 770-955-2500 618-0348
Web: www.nreionline.com

New Accountant Magazine 3525 W Peterson Ave Chicago IL 60659 773-866-9900 866-9881
TF: 888-641-3169 ■ *Web:* www.newaccountantusa.com

New Jersey Business Magazine
310 Passaic Ave Fairfield NJ 07004 973-882-5004 882-4648
Web: www.njbmagazine.com

New Orleans City Business
111 Veterans Memorial Blvd Ste 1440 Metairie LA 70005 504-834-9292 832-3550
Web: www.neworleanscitybusiness.com

Orange County Business Journal (OCBJ)
18500 Von Karman Ave Ste 150 Irvine CA 92612 949-833-8373 833-8751
Web: www.ocbj.com

Orlando Business Journal (OBJ)
255 S Orange Ave Ste 700 Orlando FL 32801 407-649-8470 420-1625
Web: www.bizjournals.com

Palm Beach Daily Business Review
324 Datura St Ste 140 West Palm Beach FL 33401 561-820-2060 820-2077
TF: 800-777-7300 ■ *Web:* www.dailybusinessreview.com

PCBE Inc PO Box 1575 Tacoma WA 98401 253-404-0891 404-0892
TF: 800-540-8322 ■ *Web:* www.businessexaminer.com

Pensions & Investments Magazine
711 Third Ave New York NY 10017 212-210-0100
TF Cust Svc: 888-446-1422 ■ *Web:* www.pionline.com

Pharmaceutical Representative Magazine
641 Lexington Ave 8th Fl New York NY 10022 212-951-6600 951-6604
Web: www.pharmexec.com

Philadelphia Business Journal
400 Market St Ste 1200 Philadelphia PA 19106 215-238-1450 238-9489
Web: www.bizjournals.com/philadelphia

Pittsburgh Business Times
424 S 27th St Ste 211 Pittsburgh PA 15203 412-481-6397 481-9956
Web: www.bizjournals.com/pittsburgh

Print Magazine 10151 Carver Rd Ste 200 Blue Ash OH 45242 513-531-2690
TF: 877-860-9145 ■ *Web:* www.printmag.com

Providence Business News
400 Wminster St Ste 600 Providence RI 02903 401-273-2201 274-6580*
*Fax: Hum Res ■ *Web:* www.pbn.com

Purchasing Magazine 225 Wyman St Waltham MA 02451 888-393-5000
TF: 888-393-5000 ■ *Web:* www.buyerzone.com

Realtor Magazine 430 N Michigan Ave 9th Fl Chicago IL 60611 312-329-8458 329-5978
TF: 800-874-6500 ■ *Web:* www.realtor.org/rmodaily.nsf

Registered Representative Magazine
1166 Ave of the Americas 10th Fl New York NY 10036 212-204-4200
Web: www.penton.com

Rochester Business Journal 45 E Ave Ste 500 Rochester NY 14604 585-546-8303 546-3398
Web: www.rbj.net

Rough Notes Company Inc, The
11690 Technology Dr Carmel IN 46032 317-582-1600 816-1000
TF: 800-428-4384 ■ *Web:* www.roughnotes.com

Sacramento Business Journal 1400 X St Sacramento CA 95818 916-447-7661 444-7779
Web: www.bizjournals.com/sacramento

Sales & Marketing Management Magazine
27020 Noble Rd Excelsior MN 55331 651-292-0165 401-7899*
*Fax Area Code: 952 ■ *Web:* www.salesandmarketing.com

San Antonio Business Journal
8200 IH 10 W Ste 820 San Antonio TX 78230 210-341-3202 341-3031
Web: www.bizjournals.com/sanantonio

San Diego Business Journal
4909 Murphy Canyon Rd Ste 200 San Diego CA 92123 858-277-6359
Web: www.sdbj.com

Self-Employed America Magazine
PO Box 241 Annapolis Junction MD 20701 800-649-6273
TF: 800-649-6273 ■ *Web:* www.nase.org

Selling Power Magazine
1140 International Pkwy Fredericksburg VA 22406 540-752-7000 752-7001
TF: 800-752-7355 ■ *Web:* www.sellingpower.com

Signal Magazine 4400 Fair Lakes Ct Fairfax VA 22033 703-631-6100 631-6188
TF: 800-336-4583 ■ *Web:* www.afcea.org/signal

Sloan Management Review
77 Massachusetts Ave E60-100 Cambridge MA 02139 617-253-7170 258-9739
TF: 800-876-5764 ■ *Web:* www.sloanreview.mit.edu

South Florida Business Journal
6400 N Andrews Ave Ste 200 Fort Lauderdale FL 33309 954-949-7600 949-7591
Web: www.bizjournals.com

Springfield Business Journal
313 Pk Central W Springfield MO 65806 417-831-3238 831-5478
Web: www.sbj.net

Staffdigest Magazine PO Box 384 Alief TX 77411 281-498-2913
Web: www.staffdigest.com

Strategic Finance Magazine
10 Paragon Dr Ste 1 Montvale NJ 07645 201-573-9000 474-1603
TF: 800-638-4427 ■ *Web:* imanet.org

Successful Meetings Magazine
100 Lighting Way Secaucus NJ 07094 201-902-2000
Web: www.successfulmeetings.com

Toledo Business Journal
5301 Southwyck Blvd Ste 104 Toledo OH 43614 419-865-0972 865-2429
Web: www.toledobiz.com

Training Magazine 27020 Noble Rd Excelsior MN 55331 847-559-7596
TF: 877-865-9361 ■ *Web:* www.trainingmag.com

Tri Cities Business Journal
1114 Sunset Dr Ste 2 Johnson City TN 37604 423-854-0140
Web: www.bjournal.com

Triangle Business Journal
3600 Glenwood Ave Ste 100 Raleigh NC 27612 919-878-0010 954-4898
TF: 800-275-9356 ■ *Web:* www.bizjournals.com

Utah Business Magazine
90 S 400 W Ste 650 Salt Lake City UT 84101 801-568-0114
TF: 866-294-1660 ■ *Web:* www.utahbusiness.com

Vancouver Business Journal
1251 Officers Row Vancouver WA 98661 360-695-2442
Web: www.vbjusa.com

Virginia Business Magazine
333 E Franklin St Richmond VA 23219 804-649-6999 649-6311
Web: www.virginiabusiness.com

Washington Business Journal
1555 Wilson Blvd Ste 400 Arlington VA 22209 703-258-0800 258-0802
Web: www.bizjournals.com

Wichita Business Journal
121 N Mead St Ste 100 Wichita KS 67202 316-267-6406 267-8570
Web: www.bizjournals.com

Your Church Magazine 465 Gundersen Dr Carol Stream IL 60188 630-260-6200 260-0114
TF: 877-247-4787 ■ *Web:* www.christianitytoday.com

457-6 Children's & Youth Magazines

Phone Fax

Creative Kids Magazine PO Box 8813 Waco TX 76714 254-756-3337
TF: 800-998-2208 ■ *Web:* www.prufrock.com

Cricket Media Inc 30 Grove St Ste C Peterborough NH 03458 800-821-0115 924-7380*
*Fax Area Code: 603 ■ *TF:* 800-821-0115 ■ *Web:* shop.cricketmedia.com

DECA Dimensions Magazine 1908 Assn Dr Reston VA 20191 703-860-5000 860-4013
Web: www.deca.org

Girls' Life Acqusition Co 4529 Hartford Rd Baltimore MD 21214 410-426-9600
TF: 800-931-2237 ■ *Web:* www.girlslife.com

New Moon Magazine PO Box 161287 Duluth MN 55816 218-878-9673
TF: 800-381-4743 ■ *Web:* www.newmoon.com

Odyssey Magazine 30 Grove St Ste C Peterborough NH 03458 603-924-7209 924-7380
TF: 800-821-0115 ■ *Web:* www.cricketmedia.com/blog

Owl Magazine 10 Lower Spadina Ave Ste 400 Toronto ON M5V2Z2 416-340-2700 340-9769
TF: 800-551-6957 ■ *Web:* www.owlkids.com

Teen People Magazine 1271 Sixth Ave Ste 3540 New York NY 10020 212-522-6699
Web: www.people.com

Turtle Magazine 1100 Waterway Blvd Indianapolis IN 46202 317-634-1100
TF: 800-558-2376 ■ *Web:* uskidsmags.com

Wild Animal Baby Magazine
11100 Wildlife Ctr Dr Reston VA 20190 800-822-9919
TF: 800-822-9919 ■ *Web:* www.nwf.org/wildanimalbaby

Your Big Backyard Magazine
11100 Wildlife Ctr Dr Reston VA 20190 800-822-9919
TF: 800-822-9919 ■ *Web:* www.nwf.org/yourbigbackyard

457-7 Computer & Internet Magazines

Phone Fax

2600 Magazine PO Box 752 Middle Island NY 11953 631-751-2600 474-2677
Web: www.2600.com

Computer Magazine
10662 Los Vaqueros Cir Los Alamitos CA 90720 714-821-8380 821-4010
TF Orders: 800-272-6657 ■ *Web:* www.computer.org

Computers in Libraries Magazine
143 Old Marlton Pk Medford NJ 08055 609-654-6266 654-4309
TF: 800-300-9868 ■ *Web:* www.infotoday.com/cilmag

Computerworld Magazine 1 Speen St Framingham MA 01701 508-879-0700
TF: 800-343-6474 ■ *Web:* www.computerworld.com

eContent Magazine 143 Old Marlton Pike Ste 3 Medford NJ 08055 609-654-6266 654-4309
TF: 800-300-9868 ■ *Web:* www.econtentmag.com

	City	State	Zip	Phone	Fax
Federal Computer Week Magazine 3141 Fairview Pk Dr Ste 777 *TF:* 877-534-2208 ■ *Web:* www.fcw.com	Falls Church	VA	22042	703-876-5100	876-5100
IEEE Computer Graphics & Applications Magazine 10662 Los Vaqueros Cir PO Box 3014 *TF:* 800-272-6657 ■ *Web:* computer.org/portal/web/computingnow/cga	Los Alamitos	CA	90720	714-821-8380	821-4641
IEEE Micro Magazine 10662 Los Vaqueros Cir PO Box 3014 *TF:* 800-272-6657 ■ *Web:* computer.org/portal/web/computingnow/micro	Los Alamitos	CA	90720	714-821-8380	821-4641
Information Today Magazine 143 Old Marlton Pk *TF:* 800-300-9868 ■ *Web:* www.infotoday.com	Medford	NJ	08055	609-654-6266	654-4309
InformationWeek Magazine 600 Community Dr *TF:* 855-569-5945 ■ *Web:* www.informationweek.com	Manhasset	NY	11030	516-562-5000	562-5036
InfoWorld Inc 501 Second St Fl 6 *TF:* 800-227-8365 ■ *Web:* www.infoworld.com	San Francisco	CA	94107	415-243-4344	978-3120
Law Technology News 120 Broadway 5th Fl **Fax Area Code:* 646 ■ *TF Cust Svc:* 800-888-8300 ■ *Web:* legaltechshow.com	New York	NY	10271	212-457-7905	822-5300*
Macworld Magazine 501 Second St Ste 600 *TF Cust Svc:* 800-288-6848 ■ *Web:* www.macworld.com	San Francisco	CA	94107	415-243-0505	442-1891
MultiMedia Schools Magazine 143 Old Marlton Pk *TF:* 800-300-9868 ■ *Web:* www.infotoday.com/mmschools	Medford	NJ	08055	609-654-6266	654-4309
Network Computing Magazine 600 Community Dr *Web:* www.networkcomputing.com	Manhasset	NY	11030	516-562-5000	
Network World Magazine 492 Old Connecticut Path Ste 200 PO Box 9208 *TF:* 800-622-1108 ■ *Web:* www.networkworld.com	Framingham	MA	01701	800-622-1108	
Oracle Magazine 500 Oracle Pkwy **Fax:* Cust Svc ■ *TF:* 800-392-2999 ■ *Web:* www.oracle.com/oramag/index.html	Redwood Shores	CA	94065	650-506-7000	633-2424*
PC World Magazine 501 Second St Ste 600 *Web:* www.pcworld.com	San Francisco	CA	94107	415-243-0505	442-1891
Searcher: The Magazine for Database Professionals 143 Old Marlton Pk *TF:* 800-300-9868 ■ *Web:* www.infotoday.com/searcher	Medford	NJ	08055	609-654-6266	654-4309
Ziff Davis, LLC 28 E 28th St *TF:* 800-289-0429 ■ *Web:* www.ziffdavis.com	New York	NY	10016	212-503-3500	

457-8 Education Magazines & Journals

	City	State	Zip	Phone	Fax
Academe Magazine 1133 19th St NW Ste 200 *TF:* 800-424-2973 ■ *Web:* www.aaup.org	Washington	DC	20036	202-737-5900	737-5526
AEA Advocate Magazine 345 E Palm Ln *TF:* 800-352-5411 ■ *Web:* www.arizonaea.org	Phoenix	AZ	85004	602-264-1774	240-6887
Alabama School Journal 422 Dexter Ave *TF:* 800-392-5839 ■ *Web:* www.myaea.org	Montgomery	AL	36104	334-834-9790	262-8377
American Educator Magazine 555 New Jersey Ave NW *TF:* 800-238-1133 ■ *Web:* www.aft.org	Washington	DC	20001	202-879-4400	
American Teacher Magazine 555 New Jersey Ave NW *TF:* 800-238-1133 ■ *Web:* www.aft.org/publications/american_teacher	Washington	DC	20001	202-879-4400	
Arkansas Educator Magazine 1500 W Fourth St *TF:* 800-632-0624 ■ *Web:* aeaonline.org	Little Rock	AR	72201	501-375-4611	375-4620
California Educator Magazine 1705 Murchison Dr *Web:* www.cta.org	Burlingame	CA	94010	650-697-1400	552-5002
Chronicle of Higher Education, The 1255 23rd St NW Ste 700 *TF:* 800-728-2803 ■ *Web:* www.chronicle.com	Washington	DC	20037	202-466-1000	452-1033
Colorado School Journal 101 W. Colfax Ave Ste 800 *TF:* 800-336-7678 ■ *Web:* www.coloradoea.org	Denver	CO	80202	303-837-1500	
Education Ctr Inc 3515 W Market St Ste 200 *TF:* 800-714-7991 ■ *Web:* www.themailbox.com	Greensboro	NC	27403	336-854-0309	547-1587
Education Week Magazine 6935 Arlington Rd *TF:* 800-346-1834 ■ *Web:* www.edweek.org	Bethesda	MD	20814	301-280-3100	280-3250
Educational Leadership Magazine 1703 N Beauregard St *TF:* 800-933-2723 ■ *Web:* www.ascd.org	Alexandria	VA	22311	703-578-9600	575-5400
Harvard Educational Review 8 Story St 1st Fl *TF:* 877-930-4473 ■ *Web:* www.gse.harvard.edu	Cambridge	MA	02138	617-495-3432	496-3584
ISTA Advocate Magazine 150 W Market St Ste 900 *TF:* 800-382-4037 ■ *Web:* ista-in.org	Indianapolis	IN	46204	317-263-3400	655-3700
Journal of Physical Education Recreation & Dance (JOPERD) 1900 Assn Dr *TF:* 800-213-7193 ■ *Web:* shapeamerica.org	Reston	VA	20191	703-476-3400	476-9527
KEA News 401 Capital Ave *TF:* 800-231-4532 ■ *Web:* www.kea.org	Frankfort	KY	40601	502-875-2889	227-8062
Library Journal 160 Varick St 11th Fl *TF:* 800-588-1030 ■ *Web:* lj.libraryjournal.com	New York	NY	10013	646-380-0700	380-0756
Louisiana Association of Educators 8322 One Kalais Ave *TF:* 800-256-4523 ■ *Web:* www.lae.org	Baton Rouge	LA	70809	225-343-9243	343-9272
MAA FOCUS 1529 18th St NW *TF:* 800-741-9415 ■ *Web:* maa.org/publications/periodicals/maa-focus	Washington	DC	20036	202-387-5200	265-2384
Mailbox Teacher Magazine 3515 W Market St Ste 200 *Web:* www.themailbox.com	Greensboro	NC	27403	336-854-0309	547-1590
Maine Educator Magazine 35 Community Dr *TF:* 800-332-8529 ■ *Web:* centralmaine.com	Augusta	ME	04330	207-622-5866	
MEA Voice Magazine 1216 Kendale Blvd PO Box 2573 *TF:* 800-292-1934 ■ *Web:* www.mea.org	East Lansing	MI	48826	517-332-6551	337-5414
Minnesota Educator Magazine 41 Sherburne Ave *TF:* 800-652-9073 ■ *Web:* educationminnesota.org	Saint Paul	MN	55103	651-227-9541	292-4802
Missouri State Teachers Assn 407 S Sixth St *TF General:* 800-392-0532 ■ *Web:* msta.org	Columbia	MO	65201	573-442-3127	443-5079
MTA Today Magazine 20 Ashburton Pl *TF:* 800-392-6175 ■ *Web:* www.massteacher.org	Boston	MA	02108	617-878-8000	742-7046
NCAE News Bulletin PO Box 27347 *TF:* 800-662-7924 ■ *Web:* www.ncae.org	Raleigh	NC	27611	919-832-3000	829-1626
NCTM News Bulletin 1906 Assn Dr *TF:* 800-235-7566 ■ *Web:* www.nctm.org/news	Reston	VA	20191	703-620-9840	476-2970
New Hampshire Educator Magazine 9 S Spring St *TF:* 866-556-3264 ■ *Web:* www.neanh.org	Concord	NH	03301	603-224-7751	224-2648
New York Teacher Magazine 800 Troy-Schenectady Rd *TF:* 800-342-9810 ■ *Web:* www.nysut.org	Latham	NY	12110	518-213-6000	213-6415
NJEA Review 180 W State St *Web:* www.njea.org	Trenton	NJ	08607	609-599-4561	392-6321
NSEA Voice Magazine 605 S 14th St Ste 200 *TF:* 800-742-0047 ■ *Web:* www.nsea.org	Lincoln	NE	68508	402-475-7611	475-2630
Ohio Education Assn (OEA) 225 E Broad St PO Box 2550 *TF:* 800-282-1500 ■ *Web:* www.ohea.org	Columbus	OH	43216	614-228-4526	228-8771
Oklahoma Education Association 323 E Madison PO Box 18485 *TF:* 800-522-8091 ■ *Web:* www.okea.org/about-oea/contact-the-staff	Oklahoma City	OK	73154	405-528-7785	524-0350
Oregon Education Magazine (OEA) 6900 SW Atlanta St Bldg 1 *TF:* 800-858-5505 ■ *Web:* www.oregoned.org	Portland	OR	97223	503-684-3300	684-8063
Scholastic Coach & Athletic Director Magazine 557 Broadway *TF General:* 800-724-6527 ■ *Web:* www.scholastic.com/coach	New York	NY	10012	212-343-6100	343-6930
Teacher Magazine 6935 Arlington Rd Ste 100 *TF:* 800-346-1834 ■ *Web:* www.edweek.org/tm	Bethesda	MD	20814	301-280-3100	280-3150
Teaching Tolerance Magazine 400 Washington Ave *Web:* www.tolerance.org	Montgomery	AL	36104	334-956-8200	
TSTA Advocate Magazine 316 W 12th St *TF:* 877-275-8782 ■ *Web:* www.tsta.org	Austin	TX	78701	512-476-5355	486-7049
Vermont NEA Today Magazine 10 Wheelock St *TF:* 800-649-6375 ■ *Web:* www.vtnea.org	Montpelier	VT	05602	802-223-6375	223-1253
Virginia Journal of Education 116 S Third St *TF:* 800-552-9554 ■ *Web:* www.veanea.org	Richmond	VA	23219	804-648-5801	775-8379
West Virginia School Journal 1558 Quarrier St *TF:* 800-642-8261 ■ *Web:* www.wvea.org	Charleston	WV	25311	304-346-5315	346-4325
Young Children Magazine 1313 L St NW Ste 500 PO Box 97156 *TF:* 800-424-2460 ■ *Web:* www.naeyc.org	Washington	DC	20005	202-232-8777	328-1846

457-9 Entertainment & Music Magazines

	City	State	Zip	Phone	Fax
American Cinematographer Magazine 1782 N Orange Dr *TF:* 800-448-0145 ■ *Web:* www.theasc.com	Los Angeles	CA	90028	323-969-4333	876-4973
Back Stage Magazine 770 Broadway *Web:* www.backstage.com	New York	NY	10003	212-493-4420	
Bass Player Magazine 28 E 28th St 12th Fl *TF Cust Svc:* 866-246-3595 ■ *Web:* www.bassplayer.com	New York	NY	10016	212-378-0400	378-0470
Broadcast Engineering Magazine 9800 Metcalf Ave *Web:* tvtechnology.com	Overland Park	KS	66212	212-378-0400	
Cadence Magazine Cadence Bldg *Web:* www.cadencebuilding.com	Redwood City	NY	13679	315-287-2852	287-2860
Canadian Musician Magazine 4056 Dorchester Rd **Fax Area Code:* 888 ■ *TF:* 800-363-6336 ■ *Web:* www.canadianmusician.com	Niagara Falls	ON	L2E6M9	905-374-8878	665-1307*
Country Weekly Magazine 118 16th Ave S Ste 230 *Web:* www.countryweekly.com	Nashville	TN	37203	615-259-1111	255-1110
Dance Magazine 333 Seventh Ave 11th Fl *TF:* 800-331-1750 ■ *Web:* www.dancemagazine.com	New York	NY	10001	212-979-4800	
Down Beat Magazine 102 N Haven Rd **Fax Area Code:* 630 ■ *TF:* 800-554-7470 ■ *Web:* www.downbeat.com	Elmhurst	IL	60126	651-251-9682	941-3210*
Dramatics Magazine 2343 Auburn Ave *Web:* www.schooltheatre.org	Cincinnati	OH	45219	513-421-3900	421-7077
Emmy Magazine 5220 Lankershim Blvd *Web:* emmys.com	North Hollywood	CA	91601	818-754-2800	
Entertainment Weekly Magazine 1675 Broadway *TF:* 800-828-6882 ■ *Web:* www.ew.com	New York	NY	10019	212-522-5600	
Film Comment Magazine 165 W 65th St *TF:* 888-313-6085	New York	NY	10023	212-875-5610	875-5636
Grammy Magazine 3030 Olympic Blvd *TF:* 800-423-2017 ■ *Web:* www.grammy.com	Santa Monica	CA	90404	310-392-3777	
Guitar Player Magazine 28 E 28th St 12th Fl *TF Cust Svc:* 800-289-9839 ■ *Web:* www.guitarplayer.com	New York	NY	10016	212-378-0400	
Hollywood Reporter 5055 Wilshire Blvd Ste 600 **Fax:* Edit ■ *TF:* 866-525-2150 ■ *Web:* www.hollywoodreporter.com	Los Angeles	CA	90036	323-525-2000	525-2377*
Hollywood Scriptwriter Magazine PO Box 3761 **Fax Area Code:* 562 ■ *Web:* www.hollywoodscriptwriter.com	Cerritos	CA	90703	310-283-1630	926-2060*
International Musician 120 Walton St *Web:* www.internationalmusician.org	Syracuse	NY	13202	315-422-4488	422-3837
Jazziz Magazine 2650 N Military Trail Ste 140 *TF:* 888-852-9987 ■ *Web:* www.jazziz.com	Boca Raton	FL	33431	561-893-6868	893-6867
JazzTimes Magazine 85 Quincy Ave Ste 2 *TF:* 800-437-5828 ■ *Web:* www.jazztimes.com	Quincy	MA	02169	617-706-9110	536-0102
Keyboard Magazine 28 E 28th St 12th Fl **Fax Area Code:* 555 ■ *TF Cust Svc:* 800-483-2433 ■ *Web:* www.keyboardmag.com	New York	NY	10016	212-378-0400	555-4564*
Live Design 249 W 17th St *TF Sales:* 866-505-7173 ■ *Web:* www.livedesignonline.com	New York	NY	10011	212-204-4272	204-4291

Phone Fax

Metal Edge Magazine 333 Seventh Ave Ste 1100 .... New York NY 10001 212-780-3500
Multichannel News 28 E 28th St 12th Fl .... New York NY 10016 917-281-4700 281-4704
TF Cust Svc: 888-343-5563 ■ *Web:* www.multichannel.com
Opera News Magazine
70 Lincoln Ctr Plaza 6th Fl .... New York NY 10023 212-769-7080 769-8500
Web: operanews.com
Playbill Magazine 525 Seventh Ave Ste 1801 .... New York NY 10018 212-557-5757 682-2932
TF: 800-533-4330 ■ *Web:* www.playbill.com
Pollstar 4697 W Jacquelyn Ave .... Fresno CA 93722 559-271-7900 271-7979*
**Fax:* Edit ■ *TF:* 800-344-7383 ■ *Web:* www.pollstar.com
Rolling Stone Magazine
1290 Ave of the Americas 2nd Fl .... New York NY 10104 800-283-1549
TF: 800-639-3865 ■ *Web:* www.rollingstone.com
TV Guide Magazine LLC
11 West 42nd St 16th Fl .... New York NY 10036 212-852-7500 852-7323
TF: 800-866-1400 ■ *Web:* www.tvguide.com
Video Age International Magazine
216 E 75th St Ste PW .... New York NY 10021 212-288-3933 734-9033
Web: www.videoageinternational.com
Videomaker Magazine 1350 E Ninth St PO Box 4591 .... Chico CA 95927 530-891-8410 891-8443
TF: 800-284-3226 ■ *Web:* www.videomaker.com

457-10 Fraternal & Special Interest Magazines

Phone Fax

AARP the Magazine 601 E St NW .... Washington DC 20049 202-434-3525
TF: 888-687-2277 ■ *Web:* www.aarp.org
AAUW Outlook Magazine 1111 16th St NW .... Washington DC 20036 202-785-7700 872-1425
TF: 800-326-2289 ■ *Web:* www.aauw.org
Adoptive Families Magazine
108 West 39th St Ste 805 .... New York NY 10018 646-366-0830 366-0842
TF: 800-372-3300 ■ *Web:* www.adoptivefamilies.com
American Scholar Magazine
1606 New Hampshire Ave NW .... Washington DC 20009 202-265-3808 986-1601
Web: www.pbk.org
American Spirit 1776 D St NW .... Washington DC 20006 202-628-1776 628-0820
Web: dar.org/national-society/american-spirit-magazine
Columbia Magazine 1 Columbus Plaza .... New Haven CT 06510 203-752-4000 752-4000
TF: 800-380-9995 ■ *Web:* www.kofc.org
Commentary Magazine 561 7th Ave 16th Fl .... New York NY 10018 212-891-1400
TF: 800-829-6270 ■ *Web:* www.commentarymagazine.com
Eagle Magazine 1623 Gateway Cir S .... Grove City OH 43123 614-883-2200 883-2201
TF: 800-648-5080 ■ *Web:* www.foe.com
Elks Magazine 2750 N Lakeview Ave .... Chicago IL 60614 773-755-4700 755-4745
TF: 800-892-8384 ■ *Web:* www.elks.org/elksmag
Gettysburg Review 300 N Washington St .... Gettysburg PA 17325 717-337-6300
Web: www.gettysburgreview.com
Ladies Auxiliary VFW Magazine
406 W 34th St .... Kansas City MO 64111 816-561-8655 931-4753
Web: www.ladiesauxvfw.org
Lion Magazine 300 W 22nd St .... Oak Brook IL 60523 630-571-5466 571-8890
TF Circ: 800-710-7822 ■ *Web:* www.lionsclubs.org
Moose Magazine 155 S International Dr .... Mooseheart IL 60539 630-859-2000
Web: www.mooseintl.org/public/moose_magazine.aspx
Poets & Writers Magazine
90 Broad St Ste 2100 .... New York NY 10004 212-226-3586 226-3963
Web: www.pw.org
Police Times Magazine 6350 Horizon Dr .... Titusville FL 32780 321-264-0911 264-0033
Web: www.aphf.org
Royal Neighbor Magazine 230 16th St .... Rock Island IL 61201 309-788-4561
TF: 800-627-4762 ■ *Web:* www.royalneighbors.org
Scouting Magazine
1325 W Walnut Hill Ln PO Box 152079 .... Irving TX 75015 972-580-2000 580-2079
Web: www.scoutingmagazine.org
Tikkun Magazine 2342 Shattuck Ave Ste 1200 .... Berkeley CA 94704 510-644-1200 644-1255
Web: www.tikkun.org
United Commercial Travellers
1801 Watermark Dr Ste 100 .... Columbus OH 43215 614-228-3276 487-9675
TF: 800-848-0123 ■ *Web:* www.uct.org
WOODMEN Magazine 1700 Farnam St .... Omaha NE 68102 402-342-1890 271-7269
TF: 800-225-3108 ■ *Web:* woodmen.org

457-11 General Interest Magazines

Phone Fax

Alfred Hitchcock Mystery Magazine
44 Wall St Ste 904 .... New York NY 10005 800-220-7443
TF: 800-220-7443 ■ *Web:* www.themysteryplace.com
American Baby Magazine 375 Lexington Ave .... New York NY 10017 212-499-2000
Web: www.parents.com
Asimov's Science Fiction Magazine
267 Broadway 4th Fl .... New York NY 10007 203-866-6688
Web: www.asimovs.com
Atlantic Monthly Magazine
600 New Hampshire Ave NW .... Washington DC 20037 202-266-6000 266-6332
TF Cust Svc: 800-234-2411 ■ *Web:* www.theatlantic.com
Avenue Magazine 79 Madison Ave 16th Fl .... New York NY 10016 212-268-8600
Web: www.avenuemagazine.com
Black Enterprise Magazine 130 Fifth Ave .... New York NY 10011 212-242-8000 886-9610
TF Cust Svc: 800-727-7777 ■ *Web:* www.blackenterprise.com
Booklist Magazine 50 E Huron St .... Chicago IL 60611 800-545-2433
TF: 800-545-2433 ■ *Web:* www.ala.org
Bridal Guide Magazine
330 Seventh Ave 10th Fl .... New York NY 10001 212-838-7733 308-7165
TF: 800-472-7744 ■ *Web:* www.bridalguide.com
Canadian Living Magazine
25 Sheppard Ave W Ste 100 .... Toronto ON M2N6S7 416-733-7600
TF: 800-387-6332 ■ *Web:* www.canadianliving.com
Christianity Today 465 Gundersen Dr .... Carol Stream IL 60188 630-260-6200 260-0114
TF Cust Svc: 800-222-1840 ■ *Web:* christianitytoday.com/iyf

Phone Fax

College Outlook & Career Opportunities Magazine
20 E Gregory Blvd .... Kansas City MO 64114 816-361-0616
TF: 800-274-8867 ■ *Web:* www.mymajors.com
Consumer Reports Magazine 101 Truman Ave .... Yonkers NY 10703 914-378-2000
TF Orders: 800-333-0663 ■ *Web:* www.consumerreports.org
Cook's Illustrated Magazine PO Box 470739 .... Brookline MA 02447 617-232-1000
TF Circ: 800-526-8442 ■ *Web:* www.cooksillustrated.com
Cosmopolitan Magazine 300 W 57th St .... New York NY 10019 212-649-2000
TF: 866-879-6636 ■ *Web:* www.cosmopolitan.com
Country Living Magazine 300 W 57th St .... New York NY 10019 212-649-3204
Web: www.countryliving.com
Country Magazine 1610 North 2nd St Ste 102 .... Milwaukee WI 53212 414-423-0100
TF: 888-861-1265 ■ *Web:* www.country-magazine.com
Cuisine Magazine 2200 Grand Ave .... Des Moines IA 50312 800-311-3995
TF: 800-311-3995 ■ *Web:* www.cuisineathome.com
Delicious Living Magazine
1401 Pearl St Ste 200 .... Boulder CO 80302 303-939-8440 998-9020
Web: deliciousliving.com
Details Magazine 4 Times Sq .... New York NY 10036 212-630-4000
Web: www.gq.com
Ebony Magazine 820 S Michigan Ave .... Chicago IL 60605 312-322-9200
Web: www.ebony.com
Elle Magazine 1633 Broadway 44th Fl .... New York NY 10019 212-903-5000
TF: 800-876-8775 ■ *Web:* www.elle.com
Ellery Queen Mystery Magazine (EQMM)
267 Broadway 4th Fl .... New York NY 10007 800-220-7443
TF: 800-220-7443 ■ *Web:* www.themysteryplace.com/eqmm
Esquire Magazine 300 W 57th St 21st Fl .... New York NY 10019 212-649-4020
Web: www.esquire.com
Essence Magazine 135 W 50th St 4th Fl .... New York NY 10020 800-274-9398 274-9398
TF: 800-274-9398 ■ *Web:* www.essence.com
Family Cir Magazine 375 Lexington Ave 9th Fl .... New York NY 10017 800-627-4444
TF: 800-627-4444 ■ *Web:* www.familycircle.com
Food & Wine Magazine
1120 Ave of the Americas Ste 9 .... New York NY 10036 813-979-6625
TF: 800-333-6569 ■ *Web:* www.foodandwine.com
For the Bride Magazine 222 W 37th St .... New York NY 10018 212-967-0751
Web: www.demetriosbride.com
Franchise Handbook
5555 N Port Washington Rd Ste 305 .... Milwaukee WI 53217 414-882-2878 882-2877*
**Fax Area Code:* 418 ■ *TF:* 800-272-0246 ■ *Web:* franchisehandbook.com
Futurist Magazine 7910 Woodmont Ave Ste 450 .... Bethesda MD 20814 301-656-8274 951-0394
TF: 800-989-8274 ■ *Web:* www.wfs.org
Harper's Bazaar Magazine 300 W 57th St .... New York NY 10019 212-903-5000
Web: www.harpersbazaar.com
Harper's Magazine 666 Broadway 11th Fl .... New York NY 10012 212-420-5720 228-5889
TF: 800-444-4653 ■ *Web:* www.harpers.org
In Touch Weekly Magazine
270 Sylvan Ave .... Englewood Cliffs NJ 07632 201-569-6699
Web: www.intouchweekly.com
Interview Magazine 575 Broadway 5th Fl .... New York NY 10012 212-941-2900 941-2885
TF: 800-925-9574 ■ *Web:* www.interviewmagazine.com
Latina Media Ventures LLC
625 Madison Ave 3rd Fl .... New York NY 10022 212-642-0200 575-3088
TF: 888-489-7753 ■ *Web:* www.latina.com
Lucky Inc 4 Times Sq .... New York NY 10036 614-277-0827
TF: 888-959-5203
Marie Claire Magazine 300 W 57th St 34th Fl .... New York NY 10019 515-282-1607
TF: 800-777-3287 ■ *Web:* www.marieclaire.com
Martha Stewart Living Magazine
601 W 26th St 25th Fl .... New York NY 10001 800-999-6518
TF: 800-999-6518 ■ *Web:* www.marthastewart.com
Men's Journal LLC
1290 Ave of the Americas 2nd Fl .... New York NY 10104 800-677-6367
TF: 800-677-6367 ■ *Web:* www.mensjournal.com
Ms Magazine 1600 Wilson Blvd Ste 801 .... Arlington VA 22209 703-522-4201 522-2219
TF: 866-672-6363 ■ *Web:* www.msmagazine.com
New York Review of Books
435 Hudson St 3rd Fl .... New York NY 10014 212-757-8070 333-5374
TF: 800-354-0050 ■ *Web:* www.nybooks.com
Nylon Magazine 110 Greene St Ste 607 .... New York NY 10012 212-226-6454 226-7738
Web: www.nylon.com
O the Oprah Magazine
5700 Wilshire Blvd Ste 120 .... Los Angeles CA 90036 323-602-5500
Web: www.oprah.com/omagazine
People Magazine
Rockefeller Ctr Time & Life Bldg .... New York NY 10020 212-522-3347 522-0331
TF: 800-541-9000 ■ *Web:* www.people.com/people
Psychology Today Magazine 115 E 23 St 9th Fl .... New York NY 10010 212-260-7210 260-7445*
**Fax:* Edit ■ *TF:* 800-931-2237 ■ *Web:* www.psychologytoday.com
Reminisce Magazine 1610 N 2nd St Ste 102 .... Milwaukee NY 53212 414-423-0100
TF: 888-859-7838 ■ *Web:* www.reminisce.com
Saturday Evening Post, The
1100 Waterway Blvd .... Indianapolis IN 46202 317-634-1100 637-0126
TF: 800-829-5576 ■ *Web:* www.saturdayeveningpost.com
Saveur Magazine 15 E 32nd St 12th Fl .... New York NY 10016 212-219-7400
Web: www.saveur.com
Self Magazine 4 Times Sq .... New York NY 10036 212-286-2860
TF: 800-274-6111 ■ *Web:* www.self.com
Simple & Delicious 5400 S 60th St .... Greendale WI 53129 414-423-0100
TF: 800-344-6913 ■ *Web:* www.tasteofhome.com
Smithsonian Magazine
600 Maryland Ave Ste 6001 .... Washington DC 20024 202-633-6090
TF: 800-766-2149 ■ *Web:* www.smithsonianmag.com
Sun Magazine
8815 Conroy Windermere Rd Ste 130 .... Orlando FL 32835 407-477-2815 293-1179
TF: 888-218-9968 ■ *Web:* www.floridasunmagazine.com
Taste of Home Magazine 5400 S 60th St .... Greendale WI 53129 414-423-0100
TF: 800-344-6913 ■ *Web:* www.tasteofhome.com
This Old House Magazine
135 W 50th St 10th Fl .... New York NY 10020 212-522-9465 522-9435
Web: www.thisoldhouse.com/toh/magazines
Traditional Home Magazine 1716 Locust St .... Des Moines IA 50309 515-284-3762
Web: www.traditionalhome.com

Phone Fax

Utne Reader Magazine 12 N 12th St Ste 400 Minneapolis MN 55403 612-338-5040 338-6043
TF Cust Svc: 800-736-8863 ■ *Web:* www.utne.com

Vanity Fair Magazine 4 Times Sq New York NY 10036 800-365-0635
TF: 800-365-0635 ■ *Web:* www.vanityfair.com

Western Living Magazine
2608 Granville St Ste 560 Vancouver BC V6H3V3 604-877-7732
TF: 800-363-3272 ■ *Web:* www.westernlivingmagazine.com

Wilson Quarterly Magazine
1300 Pennsylvania Ave NW
1 Woodrow Wilson Plaza Washington DC 20004 202-691-4000 691-4247
TF Orders: 888-947-9018 ■ *Web:* www.wilsoncenter.org

Women's Wear Daily Magazine
750 Third Ave 5th Fl New York NY 10017 212-630-4600 630-4580
TF: 800-289-0273 ■ *Web:* www.wwd.com

Working Mother Magazine 2 Park Ave 10th Fl New York NY 10016 212-779-5000
Web: www.workingmother.com

457-12 Government & Military Magazines

Phone Fax

Air Force Magazine 1501 Lee Hwy Arlington VA 22209 703-247-5800 247-5853
TF: 800-727-3337 ■ *Web:* www.afa.org/magazine/aboutmag.asp

Air Force Times Magazine
6883 Commercial Dr Springfield VA 22159 703-750-7400
TF: 800-368-5718 ■ *Web:* www.airforcetimes.com

Airman Magazine 203 Norton St San Antonio TX 78226 210-925-7757 925-7219

ARMY Magazine 2425 Wilson Blvd Arlington VA 22201 703-841-4300 525-9039
TF: 800-336-4570 ■ *Web:* www.ausa.org

FRA Today 125 NW St Alexandria VA 22314 703-683-1400 549-6610
TF: 800-372-1924 ■ *Web:* www.fra.org

Governing Magazine
1100 Connecticut Ave NW Ste 1300 Washington DC 20036 202-862-8802
TF: 800-940-6039 ■ *Web:* www.governing.com

Military & Aerospace Electronics Magazine
98 Spit Brook Rd Nashua NH 03062 847-763-9540 763-9607
Web: www.militaryaerospace.com

Military Engineer Magazine 607 Prince St Alexandria VA 22314 703-549-3800 684-0231
Web: www.same.org

Navy Times Magazine 6883 Commercial Dr Springfield VA 22159 703-750-7400
TF Cust Svc: 800-368-5718 ■ *Web:* www.navytimes.com

Penton Media Inc 1166 Ave 10th Fl New York NY 10036 212-204-4200
Web: www.penton.com

Public Employee Magazine 1625 L St NW Washington DC 20036 202-429-1130 429-1120
TF: 800-792-0045 ■ *Web:* www.afscme.org

Soldier of Fortune Magazine 2135 11th St Boulder CO 80302 303-449-3750
TF: 800-377-2789 ■ *Web:* www.sofmag.com

457-13 Health & Fitness Magazines

Phone Fax

American Fitness Magazine
15250 Ventura Blvd Ste 200 Sherman Oaks CA 91403 818-905-0040
TF: 800-446-2322 ■ *Web:* www.afaa.com

Cooking Light Magazine 2100 Lakeshore Dr Birmingham AL 35209 205-445-6000 445-6600
TF: 800-366-4712 ■ *Web:* www.cookinglight.com

Diabetes Forecast Magazine
1701 N Beauregard St Alexandria VA 22311 703-549-1500
TF: 800-676-4065 ■ *Web:* www.diabetes.org

Fitness Rx for Men Magazine 21 Bennetts Rd Setauket NY 11733 631-751-9696 751-9699
TF: 800-653-1151 ■ *Web:* www.fitnessrxformen.com

Fitness Rx for Women Magazine
21 Bennetts Rd Ste101 Setauket NY 11733 631-751-9696
Web: www.fitnessrxwomen.com

Flex Magazine 21100 Erwin St Woodland Hills CA 91367 412-235-0203
TF: 877-527-8342 ■ *Web:* www.flexonline.com

Heart & Soul Magazine
15480 Annapolis Rd Ste 202-225 Bowie MD 20715 800-834-8813
TF: 800-834-8813 ■ *Web:* www.heartandsoul.com

Ironman Magazine 1701 Ives Ave Oxnard CA 93033 805-385-3500 385-3515
TF: 800-447-0008 ■ *Web:* www.ironmanmagazine.com

MediMedia ManagedÿMarkets
780 Township Line Rd Yardley PA 19067 267-685-2300
Web: www.medimedia.com

Men's Fitness Magazine 1 Pk Ave 3rd Fl New York NY 10016 212-223-8811
Web: www.mensfitness.com

Men's Health Magazine 400 S Tenth St Emmaus PA 18098 610-967-5171
TF: 800-666-2303 ■ *Web:* www.menshealth.com

Ms Fitness Magazine PO Box 2490 White City OR 97503 541-830-0400 830-0410
Web: www.msfitness.com

Muscle & Fitness Hers Magazine
21100 Erwin St Woodland Hills CA 91367 800-340-8954
TF: 800-340-8954 ■ *Web:* www.muscleandfitness.com/muscle-fitness-hers

Prevention Magazine 733 Third Ave Emmaus PA 10017 800-813-8070
TF: 800-813-8070 ■ *Web:* www.prevention.com

Shape Magazine 4 New York Pl New York NY 10004 212-545-4800
Web: www.shape.com

Vegetarian Times
300 N Continental Blvd Ste 650 El Segundo CA 90245 310-356-4100 356-4110
TF: 800-573-1900 ■ *Web:* www.vegetariantimes.com

Yoga Journal Magazine
475 Sansome St Ste 850 San Francisco CA 94111 415-591-0555 591-0733
Web: www.yogajournal.com

457-14 Hobby & Personal Interests Magazines

Phone Fax

American Photo Magazine
1633 Broadway 43rd Fl New York NY 10019 212-767-6000 767-5602
TF: 800-274-4514 ■ *Web:* www.popphoto.com

Antique Trader 700 E State St Iola WI 54990 715-445-2214 445-4087
TF: 800-258-0929 ■ *Web:* www.antiquetrader.com

AOPA Pilot Magazine 421 Aviation Way Frederick MD 21701 301-695-2000 695-2375
TF: 800-872-2672 ■ *Web:* www.aopa.org

Aquarium Fish Magazine 3 Burroughs Irvine CA 92618 949-855-8822 855-3045

Arabian Horse World Magazine
1316 Tamson Dr Ste 101 Cambria CA 93428 805-771-2300 927-6522
TF: 800-955-9423 ■ *Web:* arabianhorseworld.com

Backpacker Magazine 2520 55th St Ste 210 Boulder CO 80301 610-967-8296
Web: www.backpacker.com

Bead & Button Magazine 21027 Crossroads Cir Waukesha WI 53186 262-796-8776 796-1615*
**Fax:* Cust Svc ■ *TF Cust Svc:* 800-533-6644 ■ *Web:* bnb.jewelrymakingmagazines.com

BeadStyle Magazine 21027 Crossroads Cir Waukesha WI 53186 262-796-8776 796-1615*
**Fax:* Cust Svc ■ *TF Cust Svc:* 800-533-6644 ■ *Web:* bds.jewelrymakingmagazines.com

Better Homes & Gardens WOOD Magazine
1716 Locust St Des Moines IA 50309 800-374-9663 551-7114*
**Fax Area Code:* 212 ■ **Fax:* Edit ■ *TF:* 800-374-9663 ■ *Web:* www.woodmagazine.com

Bicycling Magazine 400 S Tenth St Emmaus PA 18098 800-666-2806
TF: 800-666-2806 ■ *Web:* www.bicycling.com

Bird Talk Magazine 3 Burroughs Irvine CA 92618 949-855-8822 855-3045
TF Resv: 800-695-6088 ■ *Web:* www.birdchannel.com

Birds & Blooms Magazine 5400 S 60th St Greendale WI 53129 888-860-8040
TF: 888-860-8040 ■ *Web:* www.birdsandblooms.com

BirdWatching Magazine
25 Braintree Hill Office Pk Ste 404 Braintree MA 02184 877-252-8141
TF: 877-252-8141 ■ *Web:* www.birdwatchingdaily.com

Blood-Horse Magazine PO Box 911088 Lexington KY 40591 859-278-2361 276-4450
TF: 800-866-2361 ■ *Web:* www.bloodhorse.com

Cat Fancy Magazine 3 Burroughs Irvine CA 92618 949-855-8822 855-3045
TF Cust Svc: 800-546-7730 ■ *Web:* www.catchannel.com

Ceramics Monthly
600 N Cleveland Ave Ste 210 Westerville OH 43082 614-794-5867 891-8960
TF: 800-342-3594 ■ *Web:* www.ceramicartsdaily.org

Chess Life Magazine PO Box 3967 Crossville TN 38557 931-787-1234 787-1200
TF Sales: 800-903-8723 ■ *Web:* www.uschess.org

Classic Trains Magazine
21027 Crossroads Cir PO Box 1612 Waukesha WI 53186 262-796-8776 796-1615
TF: 800-533-6644 ■ *Web:* ctr.trains.com

Coin World Magazine 911 S Vandemark Rd Sidney OH 45365 937-498-0800
TF: 866-519-7298 ■ *Web:* www.coinworld.com

COINage Magazine PO Box 6925 Ventura CA 93006 805-644-3824
Web: coinagemag.com

Country Sampler Magazine 707 Kautz Rd Saint Charles IL 60174 630-377-8000 377-8194
Web: www.countrysampler.com

Crafts 'n Things Magazine PO Box 926 Sidney OH 45365 866-222-3621 498-0876*
**Fax Area Code:* 937 ■ *TF:* 866-222-3621 ■ *Web:* craftideas.com

Creating Keepsakes Magazine
14850 Pony Express Rd Bluffdale UT 84065 801-816-8300 816-8301
TF: 888-247-5282 ■ *Web:* www.creatingkeepsakes.com

Crochet World Magazine 306 E Parr Rd Berne IN 46711 260-589-8741
Web: www.crochet-world.com

Daily Racing Form 100 Broadway 7th Fl New York NY 10005 212-366-7600
TF Cust Svc: 800-306-3676 ■ *Web:* www.drf.com

Digital Photographer Magazine
12121 Wilshire Blvd 12th Fl Los Angeles CA 90025 310-820-1500
TF: 800-537-4619 ■ *Web:* www.dpmag.com

Dog Fancy Magazine 3 Burroughs Irvine CA 92618 949-855-8822 855-3045
TF Cust Svc: 800-546-7730

Equus Magazine
656 Quince OrchaRd Rd Ste 600 Gaithersburg MD 20878 301-977-3900 990-9015
TF Cust Svc: 800-829-5910 ■ *Web:* equusmagazine.com/home

Family Handyman Magazine
2915 Commers Dr Ste 700 Eagan MN 55121 800-285-4961
TF: 800-285-4961 ■ *Web:* www.familyhandyman.com

Family Tree Magazine 4700 E Galbraith Rd Cincinnati OH 45236 513-531-2690 422-9686*
**Fax Area Code:* 219 ■ *Web:* www.familytreemagazine.com

Fine Woodworking Magazine
63 S Main St PO Box 5506 Newtown CT 06470 203-426-8171 270-6753
TF: 800-283-7252 ■ *Web:* www.finewoodworking.com

Flying Magazine
460 N. Orlando Ave. Ste 200 Winter Park FL 32789 407-628-4802
TF Cust Svc: 800-678-0797 ■ *Web:* www.flyingmag.com

Horse Illustrated Magazine 3 Burroughs Irvine CA 92618 949-855-8822 580-5668*
**Fax Area Code:* 518 ■ *TF:* 888-588-4677 ■ *Web:* www.horsechannel.com

McCall Patterns Magazine 120 Broadway New York NY 10271 800-782-0323
TF: 800-782-0323 ■ *Web:* www.mccall.com

McCall's Quilting Magazine
741 Corporate Cir Ste A Golden CO 80401 303-215-5600
TF: 800-944-0736 ■ *Web:* www.mccallsquilting.com

Model Airplane News 20 Westport Rd Wilton CT 06897 203-431-9000
TF: 800-988-6488 ■ *Web:* www.modelairplanenews.com

Nuts & Volts Magazine 430 Princeland Ct Corona CA 92879 951-371-8497 371-3052
TF Orders: 800-783-4624 ■ *Web:* www.nutsvolts.com

Outdoor Photographer Magazine
12121 Wilshire Blvd 12th Fl Los Angeles CA 90025 310-820-1500 826-5008
TF Cust Svc: 800-283-4410 ■ *Web:* www.outdoorphotographer.com

Outside Magazine 400 Market St Santa Fe NM 87501 505-989-7100
TF General: 888-909-2382 ■ *Web:* www.outsideonline.com

Paper Crafts Magazine
14512 S Ctr Point Way Ste 600 Bluffdale UT 84065 801-816-8300
TF: 800-727-2387 ■ *Web:* www.papercraftsmag.com

PC Gamer Magazine
4000 Shoreline Ct Ste 400 South San Francisco CA 94080 650-238-2505
TF: 877-404-1337 ■ *Web:* www.pcgamer.com

Popular Mechanics Magazine 300 W 57th St New York NY 10019 212-649-2904
Web: www.popularmechanics.com

Popular Woodworking Magazine
4700 E Galbraith Rd Cincinnati OH 45236 513-531-2690
TF Cust Svc: 877-860-9140 ■ *Web:* www.popularwoodworking.com

Practical Horseman Magazine
656 Quince OrchaRd Rd Ste 600 Gaithersburg MD 20878 301-977-3900 990-9015
Web: practicalhorsemanmag.com

QST Magazine 225 Main St Newington CT 06111 860-594-0200 594-0259
TF: 888-277-5289 ■ *Web:* arrl.org/members-only/page/16609

				Phone	Fax
Quilter's Newsletter Magazine 741 Corporate Cir Ste A *TF:* 800-477-6089 ■ *Web:* www.quiltersnewsletter.com	Golden	CO	80401	303-215-5600	215-5601
Quiltmaker Magazine 741 Corporate Cir Ste A *TF:* 800-388-7023 ■ *Web:* www.quiltmaker.com	Golden	CO	80401	800-881-6634	
Radio Control Boat Modeler 88 Danbury Rd *TF:* 888-235-2021 ■ *Web:* www.airagestore.com	Wilton	CT	06897	203-431-9000	
Rock & Gem Magazine 290 Maple Ct Ste 232 *TF:* 866-377-4666 ■ *Web:* www.rockngem.com	Ventura	CA	93003	805-644-3824	644-3875
Rug Hooking Magazine 5067 Ritter Rd *TF:* 866-375-8626 ■ *Web:* www.rughookingmagazine.com	Mechanicsburg	PA	17055	717-796-0411	
Scale Auto Magazine 21027 Crossroads Cir *TF Cust Svc:* 800-533-6644 ■ *Web:* www.scaleautomag.com	Waukesha	WI	53186	262-796-8776	
Shutterbug Magazine 1419 Chaffee Dr Ste 1 *TF:* 800-829-3340 ■ *Web:* www.shutterbug.com	Titusville	FL	32780	321-269-3212	
Smoke Magazine 26 Broadway *TF:* 800-766-2633 ■ *Web:* www.smokemag.com	New York	NY	10004	212-391-2060	827-0945
Threads Magazine 63 S Main St PO Box 5506 *TF General:* 866-505-4687 ■ *Web:* www.threadsmagazine.com	Newtown	CT	06470	203-426-8171	
Western Horseman Magazine 2112 Montgomery St *Web:* www.westernhorseman.com	Fort Worth	TX	76107	817-737-6397	737-9266
Wine Spectator Magazine 387 Pk Ave S 8th Fl *TF Orders:* 800-752-7799 ■ *Web:* www.winespectator.com	New York	NY	10016	212-684-4224	481-1540
Woodshop News 10 Bokum Rd *TF:* 800-444-7686 ■ *Web:* www.woodshopnews.com	Essex	CT	06426	860-767-8227	767-0645
Woodsmith Magazine 2200 Grand Ave **Fax Area Code:* 515 ■ *TF Cust Svc:* 800-333-5075 ■ *Web:* www.woodsmith.com	Des Moines	IA	50312	800-333-5075	282-6741*

457-15 Law Magazines & Journals

				Phone	Fax
@Law Magazine 8159 E 41st St *Web:* www.nals.org	Tulsa	OK	74145	918-582-5188	582-5907
Advocate Magazine PO Box 895 *Web:* www.isb.idaho.gov	Boise	ID	83701	208-334-4500	
Alabama Lawyer Magazine 415 Dexter Ave *TF:* 800-354-6154 ■ *Web:* www.alabar.org	Montgomery	AL	36104	334-269-1515	261-6310
Arizona Attorney Magazine 4201 N 24th St Ste 200 *TF:* 866-482-9227 ■ *Web:* www.myazbar.org/AZAttorney	Phoenix	AZ	85016	602-252-4804	271-4930
Arkansas Lawyer Magazine 2224 Cottondale Ln *TF:* 800-609-5668 ■ *Web:* arkbar.com	Little Rock	AR	72202	501-375-4606	375-4901
Bench & Bar of Minnesota Magazine 600 Nicollet Mall Ste 380 *TF:* 800-366-4812 ■ *Web:* mnbenchbar.com	Minneapolis	MN	55402	612-333-1183	333-4927
California Bar Journal 180 Howard St *Web:* www.calbar.ca.gov	San Francisco	CA	94105	415-538-2000	
California Lawyer Magazine 44 Montgomery St Ste 250 *Web:* www.dailyjournal.com	San Francisco	CA	94104	415-296-2400	296-2400
Colorado Lawyer Magazine 1900 Grant St 9th Fl *TF:* 800-332-6736 ■ *Web:* www.cobar.org/tcl/index.cfm	Denver	CO	80203	303-860-1115	830-3990
Connecticut Lawyer Magazine 30 Bank St PO Box 350 *Web:* www.ctbar.org	New Britain	CT	06050	860-223-4400	223-4488
Florida Bar Journal 651 E Jefferson St *TF:* 800-342-8060 ■ *Web:* www.floridabar.org	Tallahassee	FL	32399	850-561-5600	681-3859
Georgia Bar Journal 104 Marietta St NW Ste 100 *TF:* 866-773-2782 ■ *Web:* gabar.org	Atlanta	GA	30303	404-527-8700	527-8717
Harvard Law Review 1511 Massachusetts Ave Gannett House *Web:* www.harvardlawreview.org	Cambridge	MA	02138	617-495-4650	
Hawaii Bar Journal 1100 Alakea St Ste 1000 *TF:* 888-586-1056 ■ *Web:* hsba.org	Honolulu	HI	96813	808-537-1868	521-7936
InsideCounsel 120 Bdwy 5th Fl *Web:* www.insidecounsel.com	New York	NY	10271	312-654-3500	654-3525
Journal of the Kansas Bar Assn 1200 SW Harrison St *TF:* 800-928-3111 ■ *Web:* www.ksbar.org	Topeka	KS	66612	785-234-5696	234-3813
Legal Management: Journal of the Assn of Legal Administrators (ALA) 75 Tri State International Ste 222 *TF:* 877-675-5571 ■ *Web:* www.alanet.org	Lincolnshire	IL	60069	847-267-1252	267-1329
Los Angeles Lawyer Magazine 261 S Figueroa St	Los Angeles	CA	90012	213-627-2727	613-1972
Maine Bar Journal 124 State St PO Box 788 *TF:* 800-475-7523 ■ *Web:* www.mainebar.org	Augusta	ME	04332	207-622-7523	623-0083
Maryland Bar Journal 520 W Fayette St *TF:* 800-492-1964 ■ *Web:* www.msba.org/departments	Baltimore	MD	21201	410-685-7878	685-1016
Michigan Bar Journal 306 Townsend St *TF:* 888-726-3678 ■ *Web:* www.michbar.org/journal	Lansing	MI	48933	517-346-6300	482-6248
Mississippi Lawyer Magazine 643 N State St *Web:* www.msbar.org	Jackson	MS	39202	601-948-4471	355-8635
Montana Lawyer Magazine 7 W Sixth Ave Ste 2B *TF:* 888-385-9119 ■ *Web:* www.montanabar.org	Helena	MT	59601	406-442-7660	442-7763
National Jurist Magazine 7670 Opportunity Rd Ste 105 *Web:* www.nationaljurist.com	San Diego	CA	92111	858-300-3201	
New York Law Journal 120 Broadway 5th Fl *TF:* 877-256-2472 ■ *Web:* www.newyorklawjournal.com	New York	NY	10271	877-256-2472	
New York State Bar News 1 Elk St *TF:* 800-442-3863 ■ *Web:* www.nysba.org	Albany	NY	12207	518-463-3200	463-4276
Oregon State Bar Bulletin, The 16037 SW Upper Boones Ferry Rd PO Box 231935 *TF:* 800-452-8260 ■ *Web:* www.osbar.org/publications/bulletin/bulletin.html	Tigard	OR	97281	503-620-0222	684-1366
Texas Bar Journal 1414 Colorado St Ste 902 *TF:* 800-204-2222 ■ *Web:* www.texasbar.com	Austin	TX	78701	512-463-1463	427-4107
Washington Lawyer Magazine 1101 K St NW Ste 200 *TF:* 877-333-2227 ■ *Web:* www.dcbar.org	Washington	DC	20005	202-737-4700	626-3471
Washington State Bar News 1325 Fourth Ave Ste 600 **Fax Area Code:* 206 ■ *TF:* 800-945-9722 ■ *Web:* www.wsba.org	Seattle	WA	98101	800-945-9722	727-8320*
Yale Law Journal PO Box 208215 *Web:* www.yale.edu/yalelj	New Haven	CT	06520	203-432-1666	432-7482

457-16 Medical Magazines & Journals

				Phone	Fax
Access Magazine 444 N Michigan Ave Ste 3400 *TF:* 800-243-2342 ■ *Web:* adha.org/publications	Chicago	IL	60611	312-440-8900	467-1806
Alaska Medicine Magazine 4107 Laurel St *Web:* commerce.alaska.gov	Anchorage	AK	99508	907-562-0304	561-2063
American Journal of Psychiatry 1000 Wilson Blvd Ste 1825 *TF:* 800-368-5777 ■ *Web:* psychiatryonline.org	Arlington	VA	22209	703-907-7300	907-1085
American Medical News 515 N State St *Web:* www.amednews.com	Chicago	IL	60654	312-464-4429	
Annals of Internal Medicine Magazine 190 N Independence Mall W *TF:* 800-523-1546 ■ *Web:* www.annals.org	Philadelphia	PA	19106	215-351-2400	351-2644
Connecticut Medicine Magazine 160 St Ronan St *TF:* 800-842-8440 ■ *Web:* www.csms.org	New Haven	CT	06511	203-865-0587	865-4997
Dental Economics Magazine 1421 S Sheridan Rd *TF:* 800-331-4463 ■ *Web:* www.dentaleconomics.com	Tulsa	OK	74112	800-331-4463	
Diabetes Advisor Magazine 1701 N Beauregard St *TF:* 800-342-2383 ■ *Web:* www.diabetesforecast.org	Alexandria	VA	22311	800-806-7801	
Family Practice Management 11400 Tomahawk Creek Pkwy *TF:* 800-274-2237 ■ *Web:* aafp.org/journals/fpm.html	Leawood	KS	66211	913-906-6000	906-6075
Hospital Physician Magazine 125 Strafford Ave Ste 220 *Web:* turner-white.com	Wayne	PA	19087	610-975-4541	975-4564
Infection Control Today Magazine 3300 N Central Ave Ste 300 *Web:* www.infectioncontroltoday.com	Phoenix	AZ	85012	480-990-1101	990-0819
Internal Medicine News 5635 Fishers Ln Ste 6000 *TF:* 877-524-9336 ■ *Web:* www.internalmedicinenews.com	Rockville	MD	20852	240-221-2400	221-4400
Journal of Kentucky Medical Assn 4965 US Hwy 42 KMA Bldg Ste 2000 *Web:* www.kyma.org	Louisville	KY	40222	502-426-6200	426-6877
Journal of Practical Nursing (JPN) 1940 Duke St Ste 200 *TF:* 800-655-4845 ■ *Web:* www.napnes.org	Alexandria	VA	22314	703-933-1003	940-4089
Journal of the American Dietetic Assn 1600 John F Kennedy Blvd **Fax Area Code:* 212 ■ *TF:* 800-654-2452 ■ *Web:* www.andjrnl.org	Philadelphia	PA	19103	800-654-2452	633-3820*
Journal of the American Medical Assn (JAMA) PO Box 10946 *TF:* 800-262-2350 ■ *Web:* jama.jamanetwork.com	Chicago	IL	60654	312-670-7827	
Journal of the American Pharmacists Assn 2215 Constitution Ave NW *TF:* 800-237-2742 ■ *Web:* www.pharmacist.com	Washington	DC	20037	202-628-4410	783-2351
Journal of the Louisiana State Medical Society 6767 Perkins Rd Ste 100 *TF:* 800-375-9508 ■ *Web:* www.lsms.org	Baton Rouge	LA	70808	225-763-8500	768-5601
Journal of the Medical Assn of Georgia 1849 The Exchange Ste 200 *TF:* 800-282-0224 ■ *Web:* www.mag.org	Atlanta	GA	30339	678-303-9290	303-3732
Journal of the Mississippi State Medical Assn PO Box 2548 *TF:* 800-898-0251 ■ *Web:* www.msmaonline.com	Ridgeland	MS	39158	601-853-6733	853-6746
Mayo Clinic Proceedings Magazine 200 First St SW Siebens Bldg 7-70 *TF Cust Svc:* 800-654-2452 ■ *Web:* www.mayoclinicproceedings.org	Rochester	MN	55905	507-284-2094	284-0252
Medicine & Health/Rhode Island Magazine 405 Promenade St Ste A *Web:* www.rimed.org	Providence	RI	02908	401-331-3207	751-8050
Missouri Medicine Magazine PO Box 1028 *TF:* 800-869-6762 ■ *Web:* www.msma.org	Jefferson City	MO	65102	573-636-5151	636-8552
Monitor on Psychology 750 First Ave NE *Web:* www.apa.org/monitor	Washington	DC	20002	202-336-5500	
NASW News 750 First St NE Ste 700 *TF:* 800-227-3590 ■ *Web:* www.naswpress.org	Washington	DC	20002	202-408-8600	336-8312
NCMS Bulletin 222 N Person St	Raleigh	NC	27601	919-833-3836	833-2023
New England Journal of Medicine 10 Shattuck St *TF:* 800-843-6356 ■ *Web:* www.nejm.org	Boston	MA	02115	617-734-9800	739-9864
Nursing Spectrum Greater New York/New Jersey Metro Magazine 1721 Moon Lk Blvd Ste 540 *TF:* 800-770-0866 ■ *Web:* www.nurse.com	Hoffman Estates	IL	60169	800-770-0866	
Ohio Medicine Magazine 3401 Mill Run Dr *TF:* 800-766-6762 ■ *Web:* osma.org	Hilliard	OH	43026	614-527-6762	527-6763
Pharmacy Today Magazine 2215 Constitution Ave NW *TF:* 800-237-2742 ■ *Web:* www.pharmacist.com	Washington	DC	20037	202-628-4410	783-2351
Psychotherapy Networker 5135 MacArthur Blvd NW *TF:* 888-851-9498 ■ *Web:* www.psychotherapynetworker.org	Washington	DC	20016	202-537-8950	
Social Work Magazine 750 First St NE Ste 700 *TF:* 800-227-3590 ■ *Web:* www.naswpress.org	Washington	DC	20002	202-408-8600	336-8312
South Dakota State Medical Assn (SDSMA) 2600 W 49th St Ste 200 PO Box 7406 *Web:* sdsma.org	Sioux Falls	SD	57117	605-336-1965	274-3274

	City	State	Zip	Phone	Fax
US Pharmacist Magazine 100 Ave of the Americas *TF:* 800-825-4696 ■ *Web:* www.uspharmacist.com	New York	NY	10013	800-825-4696	
Virginia Medical News 2924 Emerywood Pkwy Ste 300 **Fax Area Code:* 804 ■ *TF:* 800-746-6768 ■ *Web:* www.msv.org	Richmond	VA	23294	800-746-6768	355-6189*
West Virginia Medical Journal PO Box 4106 *TF:* 800-257-4747 ■ *Web:* www.wvsma.com	Charleston	WV	25364	304-925-0342	925-0345

457-17 Political & Current Events Magazines

	City	State	Zip	Phone	Fax
American Prospect 1710 Rhode Island Ave NW 12th Fl *Web:* www.prospect.org	Washington	DC	20036	202-776-0730	
American Spectator Magazine 933 N. Kenmore St Ste 405 *TF:* 800-524-3469 ■ *Web:* www.spectator.org	Arlington	VA	22201	703-807-2011	
Association on American Indian Affairs (AAIA) 966 Hungerford Dr Ste 12-B *Web:* www.indian-affairs.org	Rockville	MD	20850	240-314-7155	314-7159
Commonweal Magazine 475 Riverside Dr Rm 405 *Web:* www.commonwealmagazine.org	New York	NY	10115	212-662-4200	662-4183
Foreign Affairs 58 E 68th St *TF Cust Svc:* 800-829-5539 ■ *Web:* foreignaffairs.com	New York	NY	10065	212-434-9527	
Freeman, The 30 S Broadway *TF Sales:* 800-960-4333 ■ *Web:* www.fee.org	Irvington-on-Hudson	NY	10533	914-591-7230	
Maclean's Magazine 1 Mt Pleasant Rd 11th Fl *TF:* 800-268-9119 ■ *Web:* macleans.ca	Toronto	ON	M4Y2Y5	416-764-1300	764-1332
Mother Jones Magazine 222 Sutter St Ste 600 *TF:* 800-438-6656 ■ *Web:* www.motherjones.com	San Francisco	CA	94108	415-321-1700	321-1701
Nation Magazine 33 Irving Pl 8th Fl *TF Cust Svc:* 800-333-8536 ■ *Web:* www.thenation.com	New York	NY	10003	212-209-5400	982-9000
National Journal 600 New Hampshire Ave NW *TF:* 800-613-6701 ■ *Web:* www.nationaljournal.com	Washington	DC	20037	202-739-8400	833-8069
National Review 215 Lexington Ave 11th Fl *Web:* www.nationalreview.com	New York	NY	10016	212-679-7330	679-6174
New Republic, The 1620 L St NW Ste 300C *TF:* 800-827-1289 ■ *Web:* www.newrepublic.com	Washington	DC	20036	202-508-4444	
Newsweek Magazine 7 Hanover Sq *TF Cust Svc:* 800-631-1040 ■ *Web:* www.newsweek.com	New York	NY	10004	800-631-1040	
Reason Magazine 3415 S Sepulveda Blvd Ste 400 *TF Cust Svc:* 888-732-7668 ■ *Web:* www.reason.com	Los Angeles	CA	90034	310-391-2245	391-4395
Slate Magazine 1707 L St. NW Ste 800 *Web:* www.slate.com	Washington	DC	20036	212-445-5330	
US News & World Report 1050 Thomas Jefferson St NW *TF:* 800-836-6397 ■ *Web:* www.usnews.com	Washington	DC	20007	202-955-2000	

457-18 Religious & Spiritual Magazines

	City	State	Zip	Phone	Fax
B'Nai B'Rith Magazine 2020 K St NW 7th Fl *TF:* 888-388-4224 ■ *Web:* www.bnaibrith.org	Washington	DC	20006	202-857-6600	
Biblical Archaeology Review 4710 41st St NW *TF:* 800-221-4644 ■ *Web:* www.biblicalarchaeology.org	Washington	DC	20016	202-364-3300	364-2636
Body & Soul 42 Pleasant St **Fax Area Code:* 603 ■ *TF:* 800-999-6518 ■ *Web:* www.marthastewart.com	Watertown	MA	02472	617-449-5506	647-0116*
Catholic Digest PO Box 6015 *TF:* 800-678-2836 ■ *Web:* www.catholicdigest.com	New London	CT	06320	860-437-3012	
Charisma Magazine 600 Rinehart Rd *TF:* 800-749-6500 ■ *Web:* www.charismamag.com	Lake Mary	FL	32746	407-333-0600	333-7100
Christianity Today Magazine 465 Gundersen Dr *TF:* 800-999-1704 ■ *Web:* www.christianitytoday.com	Carol Stream	IL	60188	630-260-6200	260-0114
Episcopal Life Magazine 815 Second Ave Episcopal Church Ctr *TF:* 800-334-7626 ■ *Web:* www.episcopalchurch.org	New York	NY	10017	212-716-6000	716-6000
Kashrus Magazine PO Box 204 *Web:* www.kashrusmagazine.com	Brooklyn	NY	11204	718-336-8544	336-8550
Lutheran Magazine 8765 W Higgins Rd **Fax Area Code:* 773 ■ *TF:* 800-638-3522 ■ *Web:* www.livinglutheran.org	Chicago	IL	60631	800-638-3522	380-2409*
Ministries Today Magazine 600 Rinehart Rd *Web:* ministrytodaymag.com	Lake Mary	FL	32746	407-333-0600	333-7100
Moment Magazine 4115 Wisconsin Ave NW Ste 10 *TF:* 800-777-1005 ■ *Web:* www.momentmag.com	Washington	DC	20016	202-363-6422	362-2514
Presbyterians Today Magazine 100 Witherspoon St **Fax Area Code:* 502 ■ *TF:* 800-728-7228 ■ *Web:* www.presbyterianmission.org	Louisville	KY	40202	800-872-3283	569-8632*
Reform Judaism Magazine 633 Third Ave *Web:* reformjudaismmag.org	New York	NY	10017	212-650-4240	
Spiritled Woman - Charisma Magazine 600 Rinehart Rd *Web:* www.charismamag.com/index.php/spiritled-woman	Lake Mary	FL	32746	407-333-0600	333-7100
Today's Christian Woman Magazine 465 Gundersen Dr *TF Orders:* 877-247-4787 ■ *Web:* www.christianitytoday.com/women	Carol Stream	IL	60188	630-260-6200	260-0114
US Catholic Magazine 205 W Monroe *TF Cust Svc:* 800-328-6515 ■ *Web:* uscatholic.org	Chicago	IL	60606	312-236-7782	236-8207

457-19 Science & Nature Magazines

	City	State	Zip	Phone	Fax
American Laboratory 395 Oyster Pt Blvd Ste 321 *Web:* www.americanlaboratory.com	South San Francisco	CA	94080	650-243-5600	
American Scientist Magazine 3106 E NC Hwy 54 PO Box 13975 *TF:* 800-243-6534 ■ *Web:* www.americanscientist.org	Research Triangle Park	NC	27709	919-549-4691	549-0090
Archaeology Magazine 36-36 33rd St *TF:* 877-275-9782 ■ *Web:* www.archaeology.org	Long Island	NY	11106	718-472-3050	472-3051
Audubon Magazine 225 Varick St 7th Fl *TF Cust Svc:* 800-274-4201 ■ *Web:* www.audubon.org	New York	NY	10014	212-979-3000	477-9069
Aviation Week & Space Technology Magazine 1200 G St NW *TF:* 800-525-5003 ■ *Web:* www.aviationweek.com	Washington	DC	20005	800-525-5003	
BioScience 1444 'I' St NW Ste 200 *TF:* 800-992-2427 ■ *Web:* www.aibs.org/bioscience	Washington	DC	20005	202-628-1500	628-1509
BioTechniques 52 Vanderbilt Ave 7th Fl *TF:* 800-606-6246 ■ *Web:* biotechniques.com	New York	NY	10017	212-520-2777	661-5052
E/The Environmental Magazine 28 Knight St PO Box 5098 *TF:* 800-321-6742 ■ *Web:* www.emagazine.com	Norwalk	CT	06851	203-854-5559	866-0602
Friends of the Earth Magazine 1100 15th St NW *TF:* 877-843-8687 ■ *Web:* www.foe.org	Washington	DC	20005	202-783-7400	783-0444
Garden Compass 1660 Union St *Web:* gardencompass.com	San Diego	CA	92101	619-239-2202	
National Parks Magazine 777 Sixth St NW Ste 700 *TF General:* 800-628-7275 ■ *Web:* npca.org/news/magazine	Washington	DC	20001	202-223-6722	454-3333
National Wildlife Magazine 11100 Wildlife Ctr Dr *TF Cust Svc:* 800-822-9919 ■ *Web:* www.nwf.org/nationalwildlife	Reston	VA	20190	703-438-6000	
Natural History Magazine 105 W Hwy 54 Ste 265 **Fax Area Code:* 919 ■ *Web:* www.naturalhistorymag.com	Durham	NC	27713	646-356-6500	933-1867*
Nature National Press Bldg 529 14th St NW Ste 968 *TF:* 800-524-0384 ■ *Web:* www.nature.com	Washington	DC	20045	202-737-2355	628-1609
Orion Magazine 187 Main St *TF:* 888-909-6568 ■ *Web:* www.orionmagazine.org	Great Barrington	MA	01230	413-528-4422	528-0676
Physics Today Magazine 1 Physics Ellipse *TF:* 800-344-6902 ■ *Web:* contact.physicstoday.org	College Park	MD	20740	301-209-3040	209-0842
R & D Magazine 100 Enterprise Dr Ste 600 *Web:* www.rdmag.com	Rockaway	NJ	07866	973-920-7000	
Science Magazine 1200 New York Ave NW *TF:* 866-434-2227 ■ *Web:* www.sciencemag.org	Washington	DC	20005	202-326-6500	842-1065
Science News 1719 N St NW *TF Cust Svc:* 800-552-4412 ■ *Web:* www.sciencenews.org	Washington	DC	20036	202-785-2255	
Scientist, The 400 Market St Ste 1250 *Web:* www.the-scientist.com	Philadelphia	PA	19106	215-351-1660	
Sierra Magazine 85 Second St 2nd Fl *TF:* 866-338-1015 ■ *Web:* www.sierraclub.org/sierra	San Francisco	CA	94105	415-977-5500	977-5794
Sky & Telescope Magazine 90 Sherman St *TF:* 800-253-0245 ■ *Web:* www.skyandtelescope.com	Cambridge	MA	02140	617-864-7360	864-6117
Smithsonian Air & Space Magazine PO Box 37012 *TF Cust Svc:* 800-766-2149 ■ *Web:* www.airspacemag.com	Washington	DC	20013	202-633-6070	633-6085
Tech Briefs Media Group 261 Fifth Ave Ste 1901 *TF:* 888-456-3398 ■ *Web:* www.techbriefs.com	New York	NY	10016	212-490-3999	
Technology Review Magazine 1 Main St 7th Fl *Web:* www.technologyreview.com	Cambridge	MA	02142	617-475-8000	475-8042

457-20 Sports Magazines

	City	State	Zip	Phone	Fax
American Rifleman Magazine 11250 Waples Mill Rd *TF:* 800-672-3888 ■ *Web:* americanrifleman.org	Fairfax	VA	22030	800-672-3888	
Baseball America Magazine 4319 S Alston Ave Ste 103 *Web:* baseballamerica.com	Durham	NC	27713	919-682-9635	682-2880
Bassmaster Magazine 3500 Blue Lake Dr Ste 330 *TF:* 877-227-7872 ■ *Web:* www.bassmaster.com/topics/bassmaster%20magazine	Birmingham	FL	35243	877-227-7872	
Beckett Football Card Monthly 4635 McEwen Rd *Web:* www.beckett.com	Dallas	TX	75244	972-991-6657	991-8930
Climbing Magazine 5720 Flatiron Pkwy *TF:* 800-829-5895 ■ *Web:* www.climbing.com	Boulder	CO	80301	800-829-5895	
Competitor Magazine 9477 Waples St Ste 150 **Fax Area Code:* 858 ■ *TF:* 800-311-1255 ■ *Web:* running.competitor.com	San Diego	CA	92121	800-311-1255	768-6801*
Ducks Unlimited Magazine 1 Waterfowl Way *TF:* 800-453-8257 ■ *Web:* www.ducks.org	Memphis	TN	38120	901-758-3825	758-3850
Florida Sportsman Magazine 2700 S Kanner Hwy *Web:* www.flsportsman.com	Stuart	FL	34994	772-219-7400	
Gaebler Ventures 12301 Whitewater Dr *Web:* www.gaebler.com	Minnetonka	MN	55343	952-936-9333	936-9755
Golf Digest 20 Westport Rd Ste 320 *Web:* www.golfdigest.com	Wilton	CT	06897	203-761-5100	761-5129
Hockey News Magazine 25 Sheppard Ave Ste 100 *TF:* 888-361-9768 ■ *Web:* www.thehockeynews.com	Toronto	ON	M2N6S7	514-848-7000	
In-Fisherman Magazine 7819 Highland Scenic Rd *Web:* www.in-fisherman.com	Baxter	MN	56425	218-829-1648	
Journal of the Philosophy of Sport 1607 N Market St *TF:* 800-747-4457 ■ *Web:* www.humankinetics.com	Champaign	IL	61820	217-351-5076	351-1549
Links Magazine 10 Executive Pk Rd *Web:* www.linksmagazine.com	Hilton Head Island	SC	29928	843-842-6200	842-6233
Salt Water Sportsman Magazine 460 N Orlando Ave Ste 200 *TF:* 800-759-2127 ■ *Web:* www.saltwatersportsman.com	Winter Park	FL	32789	407-628-4802	
Ski Magazine 5720 Flatiron Pkwy *TF:* 888-444-8151 ■ *Web:* www.skinet.com	Boulder	CO	80301	303-253-6300	

Phone Fax

Snow Goer Magazine 10405 6th Ave N Ste 210........Plymouth MN 55441 800-710-5249
TF: 800-710-5249 ■ *Web:* www.snowgoer.com
Sport Fishing Magazine
460 N Orlando Ave Ste 200 ....Orlando FL 32789 800-879-0496
TF: 800-879-0496 ■ *Web:* www.sportfishingmag.com
Sports Afield Magazine
15621 Chemical Ln .... Huntington Beach CA 92649 714-373-4910 894-4949
TF: 800-451-4788 ■ *Web:* www.sportsafield.com
Sports Business Daily
120 W Morehead St Ste 310......................Charlotte NC 28202 704-973-1410 973-1401
TF: 800-829-9839 ■ *Web:* www.sportsbusinessdaily.com
Sports Spectrum Magazine
105 Corporate Blvd Ste 2........................Indian Trail NC 28079 704-821-2971
TF: 866-821-2971 ■ *Web:* www.sportsspectrum.com
Tennis Magazine 814 S Westgate Ste 100...........Los Angeles NY 90049 310-893-5300
Web: www.tennis.com
Travel + Leisure Magazine 225 Liberty St ....New York NY 10281 212-382-5600 373-3681*
**Fax Area Code:* 718 ■ *TF:* 800-452-9292 ■ *Web:* www.travelandleisure.com

457-21 Trade & Industry Magazines

Phone Fax

AAPG Explorer Magazine 1444 S Boulder Ave ....Tulsa OK 74119 918-584-2555 560-2636
TF: 800-364-2274 ■ *Web:* www.aapg.org
Aerospace America Magazine
1801 Alexander Bell Dr Ste 500 ....Reston VA 20191 703-264-7500 264-7551
TF: 800-639-2422 ■ *Web:* www.aiaa.org
Air Conditioning Heating & Refrigeration News
2401 W Big Beaver Rd Ste 700..........................Troy MI 48084 248-362-3700 362-0317
TF: 800-837-8337 ■ *Web:* www.achrnews.com
Air Transport World Magazine
8380 Colesville Rd Ste 500 ....Silver Spring MD 20910 301-755-0200 514-3909*
**Fax Area Code:* 913 ■ *Web:* www.atwonline.com
American Salon Magazine 757 Third Ave 5th Fl........New York NY 10017 323-966-4662
TF: 866-871-0656 ■ *Web:* www.americansalon.com
American Society of Civil Engineers (ASCE)
1801 Alexander Bell Dr...............................Reston VA 20191 703-295-6300 295-6211
TF: 800-548-2723 ■ *Web:* www.asce.org
Automotive Executive Magazine
8400 Westpark Dr.................................McLean VA 22102 703-821-7150
Web: insidenova.com
Automotive News Magazine 1155 Gratiot Ave...........Detroit MI 48207 313-446-0450 446-0383
TF: 877-812-1584 ■ *Web:* www.autonews.com
Bartender Magazine PO Box 158.................Liberty Corner NJ 07938 908-766-6006 766-6607*
**Fax:* Edit ■ *TF Sales:* 800-829-4222 ■ *Web:* www.bartender.com
Builder Magazine 1 Thomas Cir NW Ste 600..........Washington DC 20005 202-452-0800 785-1974
TF: 800-325-6180 ■ *Web:* www.builderonline.com
Building Design & Construction Magazine
3030 W Salt Creek Ln Ste 201 ....Arlington Heights IL 60005 847-391-1000 390-0408
TF: 888-811-3288 ■ *Web:* www.bdcnetwork.com
Chemical Processing Magazine
1501 E. Woodfield Rd Ste 400N..................Schaumburg IL 60173 630-467-1300
TF: 800-343-4048 ■ *Web:* www.chemicalprocessing.com
Chemical Week Magazine
140 E 45th St 2 Grand Central Tower,40th Fl ....New York NY 10017 212-884-9528 884-9514
TF Cust Svc: 866-501-7540 ■ *Web:* www.chemweek.com
Civil Engineering Magazine
1801 Alexander Bell Dr...............................Reston VA 20191 703-295-6300 295-6300*
**Fax:* Edit ■ *TF:* 800-548-2723 ■ *Web:* asce.org
Control Engineering Magazine
2000 Clearwater Dr...............................Oak Brook IL 60523 630-288-8000 288-8580
Web: www.controleng.com
DaySpa Magazine 7628 Densmore Ave ....Van Nuys CA 91406 818-782-7328 782-7450
TF: 800-442-5667 ■ *Web:* www.dayspamagazine.com
Design News 225 Wyman St ....Waltham MA 02451 763-746-2792
TF: 800-869-6882 ■ *Web:* www.designnews.com
Designfax Magazine 2506 Tamiami Trail North.........Nokomis FL 34275 941-966-9521 966-2590
TF: 877-245-6247 ■ *Web:* www.designfax.net
EC & M Magazine 9800 Metcalf Ave..............Overland Park KS 66212 913-967-1782 514-6782
Web: www.ecmweb.com
EDN Magazine 303 Second St....................San Francisco CA 94107 415-947-6000
TF Orders: 800-446-6551 ■ *Web:* www.edn.com
Electronic Component News
100 Enterprise Dr Ste 600........................Rockaway NJ 07866 973-920-7000 607-5488
TF: 877-650-5160 ■ *Web:* www.ecnmag.com
Engineering News-Record (ENR)
350 fifth Ave Ste 6000 ....New York NY 10118 646-849-7100 904-2820*
**Fax Area Code:* 212 ■ *TF:* 877-876-8208 ■ *Web:* www.enr.com
EPRI Journal 3420 Hillview Ave.......................Palo Alto CA 94304 650-855-2121 855-2121
TF: 800-313-3774 ■ *Web:* www.epri.com/journal
Equipment Today Magazine
1233 Janesville Ave ....Fort Atkinson WI 53538 920-563-1677
Fine Homebuilding Magazine
63 S Main St PO Box 5506.........................Newtown CT 06470 203-426-8171 270-6753
TF: 800-283-7252 ■ *Web:* www.finehomebuilding.com
Food Management Magazine 1300 E Ninth St........ Cleveland OH 44114 216-696-7000
Web: www.penton.com
Food Processing Magazine
555 W Pierce Rd Ste 301 ....Itasca IL 60143 630-467-1300 467-1179
TF: 800-755-5505 ■ *Web:* www.foodprocessing.com
Furniture/Today Magazine
7025 Albert Pick Rd Ste 200.....................Greensboro NC 27409 336-605-0121 605-1143
Web: www.furnituretoday.com
Giftware News 704 N Wells St ....Chicago IL 60654 312-849-2220 849-2174
TF: 800-229-1967 ■ *Web:* www.talcott.com
Glass Magazine 8200 Greensboro Dr Ste 302 ....McLean VA 22102 703-442-4890
Web: www.glassmagazine.com
Home Media Retailing
4590 MacArthur Ste 500......................Newport Beach CA 92660 714-759-4661 248-4107*
**Fax Area Code:* 540 ■ **Fax:* Sales ■ *TF:* 800-371-6897 ■ *Web:* www.homemediamagazine.com
Industrial Equipment News 5 Penn Plz ....New York NY 10001 212-695-0500 290-7362
Web: www.thomaspublishing.com

Phone Fax

Inside Self Storage Magazine
3300 N Central Ave Ste 300 ....Phoenix AZ 85012 480-990-1101 990-0819
Web: www.insideselfstorage.com
Institute of Scrap Recycling Industries Magazine
1615 L St NW Ste 6000 ....Washington DC 20036 202-662-8500 626-0900
TF: 800-767-7236 ■ *Web:* www.isri.org
Journal of Petroleum Technology
222 Palisades Creek Dr ....Richardson TX 75080 972-952-9393 952-9435
TF: 800-456-6863 ■ *Web:* www.spe.org
Journal of Protective Coatings & Linings
2100 Wharton St Ste 310 ....Pittsburgh PA 15203 412-431-8300 431-5428
TF: 800-837-8303 ■ *Web:* www.paintsquare.com
Land Line Magazine
1 NW Oodia Dr PO Box 1000....................Grain Valley MO 64029 816-229-5791 443-2227
TF: 800-444-5791 ■ *Web:* www.landlinemag.com
Modern Machine Shop Magazine
6915 Valley Ave ....Cincinnati OH 45244 513-527-8800 527-8801
TF: 800-950-8020 ■ *Web:* www.mmsonline.com
Nailpro Magazine 7628 Densmore Ave................Van Nuys CA 91406 818-782-7328 782-7450
TF: 800-442-5667 ■ *Web:* www.nailpro.com
Nails Magazine 3520 Challenger St ....Torrance CA 90503 310-533-2400 533-2507
TF: 888-624-5744 ■ *Web:* www.nailsmag.com
National Clothesline Magazine
801 Easton Rd Ste 2...........................Willow Grove PA 19090 215-830-8467 830-8490
Web: www.natclo.com
National Fisherman Magazine 121 Free St ....Portland ME 04101 207-842-5600 842-5603
TF: 800-959-5073 ■ *Web:* www.nationalfisherman.com
National Fitness Trade Journal
PO Box 2490 ....White City OR 97503 541-830-0400 830-0410
TF: 877-867-7835 ■
Web: www.msfitness.com/nationalfitness/tradejournal/nftj.html
Natural Products Insider Magazine
3300 N Central Ave Ste 3000.........................Phoenix AZ 85012 480-990-1101 990-0819
Web: www.naturalproductsinsider.com
NewBay Media LLC 28 E 28th St 12th Fl ....New York NY 10016 212-378-0400 378-0470
Web: www.newbaymedia.com
Oil & Gas Journal PO Box 2002 ....Tulsa OK 74101 918-831-9423 831-9482
TF: 800-633-1656 ■ *Web:* www.ogj.com
PHONE+ Magazine 3300 N Central Ave Ste 300..........Phoenix AZ 85012 480-990-1101 990-0819
Web: www.channelpartnersonline.com
Plant Engineering Magazine
2000 Clearwater Dr..............................Oak Brook IL 60523 630-288-8780 288-8781
Web: www.plantengineering.com
Plant Services Magazine
555 W Pierce Rd Ste 301 ....Itasca IL 60143 630-467-1300 467-1120
TF: 800-872-9141 ■ *Web:* www.plantservices.com
Plastics Technology Magazine
6915 Valley Ave ....Cincinnati OH 45244 513-527-8800 527-8801
Web: www.ptonline.com
Pro Lights & Staging News Magazine
6000 S Eastern Ste 14-J............................Las Vegas NV 89119 702-932-5585 932-5584
TF General: 888-667-7438 ■ *Web:* www.plsn.com
Proceedings of the IEEE Magazine
445 Hoes Ln.....................................Piscataway NJ 08855 732-562-5478 562-5456
TF: 800-678-4333 ■ *Web:* www.ieee.org
Product Design & Development Magazine
199 E Badger Rd Ste 201 ....Madison WI 53713 973-920-7000
Web: www.pddnet.com
Professional Surveyor Magazine
20 W Third St...................................Frederick MD 21701 301-682-6101
Web: xyht.com
Qualified Remodeler Magazine
1233 Janesville Ave ....Fort Atkinson WI 53538 732-372-7668 563-1707*
**Fax Area Code:* 920 ■ *TF:* 800-547-7377 ■ *Web:* www.forresidentialpros.com
Quality Progress Magazine
600 N Plankinton Ave PO Box 3005...............Milwaukee WI 53201 414-272-8575 272-1734
TF Cust Svc: 800-248-1946 ■ *Web:* www.asq.org/pub/qualityprogress
Retail Traffic 249 W 17th St.........................New York NY 10011 212-204-4200
Web: nreionline.com
Street & Smith's SportsBusiness Journal
120 W Morehead St Ste 310........................Charlotte NC 28202 704-973-1410 973-1401
Web: www.sportsbusinessdaily.com
Travel Weekly Crossroads Magazine
100 Lighting Way ....Secaucus NJ 07094 201-902-2000
Web: www.travelweekly.com
Trucker's Connection
5400 Laurel Springs Pkwy Ste 103..................Suwanee GA 30024 770-416-0927 253-7086*
**Fax Area Code:* 470
United Mine Workers of America
18354 Quantico Gateway Dr Ste 200 ....Triangle VA 22172 703-291-2400
Web: www.umwa.org
Urban Call Magazine
4265 Brownsboro Rd Ste 225................Winston-Salem NC 27106 336-759-7477 759-7212
Web: www.theurbancall.com
Women's Wear Daily Magazine
750 Third Ave 5th Fl..............................New York NY 10017 212-630-4600 630-4580
TF: 800-289-0273 ■ *Web:* www.wwd.com
Writer's Digest 4700 E Galbraith Rd...............Cincinnati OH 45236 513-531-2690
TF Cust Svc: 800-283-0963 ■ *Web:* www.writersdigest.com

457-22 Travel & Regional Interest Magazines

Phone Fax

Alaska Airlines Magazine
2701 First Ave Ste 250 ....Seattle WA 98121 206-441-5871 448-6939
Web: www.alaskaairlinesmagazine.com
Alaska Magazine
301 Arctic Slope Ave Ste 300......................Anchorage AK 99518 386-246-0444
TF: 800-288-5892 ■ *Web:* www.alaskamagazine.com
Arizona Highways Magazine 2039 W Lewis Ave ....Phoenix AZ 85009 800-543-5432 254-4505*
**Fax Area Code:* 602 ■ *TF:* 800-543-5432 ■ *Web:* www.arizonahighways.com
Atlanta Magazine 260 Peachtree St Ste 300 ....Atlanta GA 30303 404-527-5500 527-5575
Web: www.atlantamagazine.com

	Phone	Fax
Baltimore Magazine 1000 Lancaster St Ste 400 .... Baltimore MD 21202	410-752-4200	625-0280
TF Cust Svc: 800-935-0838 ■ *Web:* www.baltimoremagazine.net		
Buffalo Spree Magazine 100 Corporate Pkwy Ste 220 .... Buffalo NY 14226	716-783-9119	783-9983
TF: 855-697-7733 ■ *Web:* www.buffalospree.com		
Cape Cod Life Magazine 13 Steeple St Ste 204 PO Box 1439 .... Mashpee MA 02649	508-419-7381	477-1225
TF: 800-698-1717 ■ *Web:* www.capecodlife.com		
Caribbean Travel & Life Magazine 460 N Orlando Ave Ste 200 .... Winter Park FL 32789	407-628-4802	628-7061
TF Sales: 800-289-9399 ■ *Web:* www.bonniercorp.com		
Chesapeake Bay Magazine 1819 Bay Ridge Ave Ste 180 .... Annapolis MD 21403	410-263-2662	267-6924
TF: 800-283-2883 ■ *Web:* www.chesapeakeboating.net		
Chicago Life Magazine PO Box 11311 .... Chicago IL 60611	773-549-1523	
Web: www.chicagolife.net		
Chicago Magazine 435 N Michigan Ave Ste 1100 .... Chicago IL 60611	312-222-8999	
TF: 800-999-0879 ■ *Web:* www.chicagomag.com		
Cincinnati Magazine 441 Vine St Ste 200 .... Cincinnati OH 45202	513-421-4300	
Web: www.cincinnatimagazine.com		
Cleveland Magazine 1422 Euclid Ave Ste 730 .... Cleveland OH 44115	216-771-2833	781-6318
TF: 800-210-7293 ■ *Web:* www.clevelandmagazine.com		
Columbus Monthly Magazine 34 South Third St .... Columbus OH 43215	614-888-4567	461-8746
Web: www.columbusmonthly.com		
Connecticut Magazine 35 Nutmeg Dr .... Trumbull CT 06611	203-380-6600	380-6610
TF: 800-645-4328 ■ *Web:* www.connecticutmag.com		
Cruise Travel Magazine 990 Grove St Ste 400 .... Evanston IL 60201	847-491-6440	491-0459
Web: cruisetravelmag.com		
Departures Magazine 1120 Ave of the Americas .... New York NY 10036	212-642-1999	827-6413
TF: 888-424-0106 ■ *Web:* www.departures.com		
Down East 680 Commercial St .... Rockport ME 04856	207-594-9544	594-5144
TF: 800-766-1670 ■ *Web:* downeast.com		
Family Motor Coaching Magazine 8291 Clough Pk .... Cincinnati OH 45244	513-474-3622	474-2332
TF: 800-543-3622 ■ *Web:* www.fmca.com		
Guest Informant Magazine 725 Broad St .... Augusta GA 30901	706-724-0851	
TF: 800-622-6358 ■ *Web:* morris.com		
Hamptons Magazine 67 Hampton Rd Ste 201 .... SouthHampton NY 11968	631-283-7125	283-7854
TF: 866-891-3144 ■ *Web:* www.hamptons-magazine.com		
Hana Hou Magazine (Hawaiian Airlines) 1144 Tenth Ave Ste 401 .... Honolulu HI 96816	808-733-3333	733-3340
TF: 888-733-3336 ■ *Web:* www.hanahou.com		
Home & Away Magazine 10703 J St Ste 100 .... Omaha NE 68127	402-592-5000	
Web: www.homeandawaymagazine.com		
Honolulu Magazine 1000 Bishop St Ste 405 .... Honolulu HI 96813	808-534-7546	
TF: 800-788-4230 ■ *Web:* www.honolulumagazine.com		
Houston LifeStyle Magazine 10707 Corporate Dr Ste 170 .... Stafford TX 77477	281-240-2445	240-5079
TF: 866-505-4456 ■ *Web:* www.houstonlifestyles.com		
Hudson Valley Magazine 2678 S Rd 2nd Fl .... Poughkeepsie NY 12601	845-463-0542	463-1544
Web: www.hvmag.com		
Indianapolis Monthly Magazine 40 Monument Cir Ste 100 .... Indianapolis IN 46204	317-237-9288	684-2080
TF Circ: 888-403-9005 ■ *Web:* www.indianapolismonthly.com		
Inland Empire Magazine 3769 Tibbetts St Ste A .... Riverside CA 92506	951-682-3026	682-0246
Web: www.inlandempiremagazine.com		
InsideFlyer Magazine 1930 Frequent Flyer Pt .... Colorado Springs CO 80915	719-597-8889	
TF: 888-407-4747 ■ *Web:* www.insideflyer.com		
Islands Magazine 460 N Orlando Ave Ste 200 .... Winter Park FL 32789	515-237-3697	
TF: 800-250-1523 ■ *Web:* www.islands.com		
Jacksonville Magazine 1261 King St .... Jacksonville FL 32204	904-389-3622	389-3628
TF: 800-962-0214 ■ *Web:* www.jacksonvillemag.com		
Key Magazine PO Box 111266 .... Memphis TN 38111	901-458-3912	458-5723
TF: 866-636-7447 ■ *Web:* www.keymemphis.com		
Key: This Week in Chicago Magazine 222 W Ontario St Ste 420 .... Chicago IL 60654	312-943-0838	664-6113
TF: 877-866-0966 ■ *Web:* www.keymagazinechicago.com		
Los Angeles Confidential Magazine 717 N Highland Ave Unit 10 .... Los Angeles CA 90038	310-289-7300	289-0444
TF: 866-891-3144 ■ *Web:* www.la-confidential-magazine.com		
Los Angeles Magazine 5900 Wilshire Blvd 10th Fl .... Los Angeles CA 90036	323-801-0100	801-0105*
**Fax:* Edit ■ *TF Cust Svc:* 800-876-5222 ■ *Web:* www.lamag.com		
Louisville Magazine 137 W Muhammad Ali Blvd Ste 102 .... Louisville KY 40202	502-625-0100	625-0109
TF: 866-832-0011 ■ *Web:* www.louisville.com		
Memphis Magazine 460 Tennessee St Ste 200 .... Memphis TN 38103	901-521-9000	521-0129
TF: 800-288-9999 ■ *Web:* www.memphismagazine.com		
Michigan Out-of-Doors Magazine (MOOD) 2101 Wood St PO Box 30235 .... Lansing MI 48912	517-371-1041	
TF: 800-777-6720 ■ *Web:* www.mucc.org		
Midwest Living Magazine 1716 Locust St .... Des Moines IA 50309	515-247-2982	
TF: 800-678-8093 ■ *Web:* www.midwestliving.com		
Milwaukee Magazine 126 N Jefferson St .... Milwaukee WI 53202	414-273-1101	287-4373
TF: 800-662-4818 ■ *Web:* www.milwaukeemag.com		
Minneapolis-Saint Paul Magazine 220 S Sixth St Ste 500 .... Minneapolis MN 55402	612-339-7571	339-5806
TF: 800-999-5589 ■ *Web:* www.mspmag.com		
Mississippi Magazine 5 Lakeland Cir PO Box 16445 .... Jackson MS 39216	601-982-8418	982-8447
Web: www.mismag.com		
MotorHome Magazine 2750 Park View Ct Ste 240 .... Oxnard CA 93036	805-667-4100	
TF Cust Svc: 800-678-1201 ■ *Web:* www.motorhome.com		
National Geographic Traveler Magazine 1145 17th St NW .... Washington DC 20036	202-857-7000	
TF: 800-647-5463 ■ *Web:* nationalgeographic.com		
Nevada Magazine 401 N Carson St .... Carson City NV 89701	775-687-5416	687-6159
TF: 855-729-7117 ■ *Web:* www.nevadamagazine.com		
New Jersey Monthly Magazine 55 Pk Pl PO Box 920 .... Morristown NJ 07963	973-539-8230	538-2953
TF: 888-419-0419 ■ *Web:* www.njmonthly.com		
New Mexico Magazine PO Box 12002 .... Santa Fe NM 87504	800-898-6639	827-6496*
**Fax Area Code:* 505 ■ *TF:* 800-898-6639 ■ *Web:* www.nmmagazine.com		
New Orleans Magazine 110 Veterans Blvd Ste 123 .... Metairie LA 70005	504-828-1380	828-1385
TF Edit: 877-221-3512 ■ *Web:* www.myneworleans.com/new-orleans-magazine		
New York Magazine 75 Varick St .... New York NY 10013	212-508-0700	
TF: 800-678-0900 ■ *Web:* www.nymag.com		
Nob Hill Gazette Fairmont Hotel 950 Mason St, Mezzanine Level .... San Francisco CA 94108	415-227-0190	
Web: www.nobhillgazette.com		
Ohio Magazine 1422 Euclid Ave Ste 730 .... Cleveland OH 44115	216-771-2833	781-6318
TF: 800-210-7293 ■ *Web:* www.ohiomagazine.com		
Orange Coast Magazine 3701 Birch St Ste 100 .... Newport Beach CA 92660	949-862-1133	862-0133
TF: 800-397-8179 ■ *Web:* www.orangecoast.com		
Oregon Coast Magazine 88906 Highway 101 N Ste 2B .... Florence OR 97439	541-997-8401	997-1124
TF: 800-348-8401 ■ *Web:* www.oregoncoastmagazine.com		
Orlando Magazine 801 N Magnolia Ave Ste 201 .... Orlando FL 32803	407-423-0618	237-6258
TF: 866-356-3075 ■ *Web:* www.orlandomagazine.com		
Palm Beach Illustrated Magazine 1000 N Dixie Hwy Ste C .... West Palm Beach FL 33401	561-659-6160	
TF: 800-308-7346 ■ *Web:* www.palmbeachillustrated.com		
Palm Springs Life Magazine 303 N Indian Canyon .... Palm Springs CA 92262	760-325-2333	325-7008
Web: www.palmspringslife.com		
Philadelphia Magazine 1818 Market St 36th Fl .... Philadelphia PA 19103	215-564-7700	656-3500
Web: www.phillymag.com		
Phoenix Magazine 15169 N Scottsdale Ste 310 .... Scottsdale AZ 85254	480-664-3960	664-3962
TF: 866-481-6970 ■ *Web:* www.phoenixmag.com		
Saint Louis Bride Magazine 1006 Olive St Ste 202 .... Saint Louis MO 63101	314-588-8313	
Web: bridestl.com		
San Francisco Magazine 243 Vallejo St .... San Francisco CA 94111	415-398-2800	398-6777
TF: 866-736-2499 ■ *Web:* www.modernluxury.com		
Savannah Magazine PO Box 1088 .... Savannah GA 31402	912-652-0423	525-0611
Web: www.savannahmagazine.com		
Southern Accents Magazine 2100 Lakeshore Dr .... Birmingham AL 35209	205-445-6000	624-2910*
**Fax Area Code:* 678 ■ *TF:* 877-262-5866 ■ *Web:* www.southernliving.com		
Southern Living Magazine 2100 Lakeshore Dr .... Birmingham AL 35209	205-445-6000	445-6700
TF: 800-366-4712 ■ *Web:* www.southernliving.com		
Today's Chicago Woman Magazine 150 E Huron St Ste 1001 .... Chicago IL 60611	312-951-7600	
Web: www.tcwmag.com		
Toronto Life Magazine 111 Queen St E Ste 320 .... Toronto ON M5C1S2	416-364-3333	
Web: www.torontolife.com		
Travel Agent Magazine 757 Third Ave 5th Fl .... New York NY 10017	212-895-8200	895-8210
TF: 855-424-6247 ■ *Web:* www.travelagentcentral.com		
TravelAge West Magazine 11400 W Olympic Blvd Ste 325 .... Los Angeles CA 90064	310-954-2510	954-2525
Web: www.travelagewest.com		
Travelhost Magazine 10701 N Stemmons Fwy .... Dallas TX 75220	972-556-0541	432-8729
TF: 800-527-1782 ■ *Web:* www.travelhost.com		
Tucson Lifestyle Magazine 7000 E Tanque Verde Rd Ste 11 .... Tucson AZ 85715	520-721-2929	721-8665
Web: www.tucsonlifestyle.com		
Vermont Life 1 National Life Dr 6th Fl .... Montpelier VT 05620	802-828-3241	
Web: www.vtlife.com		
Washingtonian Magazine 1828 L St NW Ste 200 .... Washington DC 20036	202-296-3600	785-1822*
**Fax:* Edit ■ *Web:* www.washingtonian.com		
Western Outdoors Magazine 185 Avenida La Pata .... San Clemente CA 92673	949-366-0030	366-0804
TF: 800-290-2929 ■ *Web:* www.wonews.com		
Westways Magazine 3333 Fairview Rd .... Costa Mesa CA 92626	714-885-2376	
Where Chicago Magazine 1165 N Clark St Ste 302 .... Chicago IL 60610	312-642-1896	
Web: www.wheretraveler.com		
Where Washington Magazine 1720 Eye St NW Ste 600 .... Washington DC 20006	202-463-4550	
Web: www.wheretraveler.com		
Yankee Magazine 1121 Main St PO Box 520 .... Dublin NH 03444	603-563-8111	563-8252
TF: 800-288-4284 ■ *Web:* www.yankeemagazine.com		

458 MAGNETS - PERMANENT

	Phone	Fax
Bangor Electronics Co 614 Joy St .... Bangor MI 49013	269-427-7944	
Dexter Magnetic Technologies Inc 1050 Morse Ave .... Elk Grove Village IL 60007	847-956-1140	956-8205
Web: www.dextermag.com		
Electron Energy Corp 924 Links Ave .... Landisville PA 17538	717-898-2294	898-0660
TF: 800-824-2735 ■ *Web:* www.electronenergy.com		
Eneflux Armtek Magnetics Inc 700 Hicksville Rd Ste 110 .... Bethpage NY 11714	516-576-3434	
TF: 877-363-3589 ■ *Web:* www.eamagnetics.com		
Flexmag Industries Inc 107 Industry Rd .... Marietta OH 45750	740-374-8024	374-5068
TF: 800-543-4426 ■ *Web:* www.arnoldmagnetics.com		
Magnaworks Technology Inc 36 Carlough Rd .... Bohemia NY 11716	631-218-3431	
Web: www.magnaworkstechnology.com		
Magnet Technology Inc 1599 Kingsview Dr .... Lebanon OH 45036	513-932-4416	932-4502
Web: www.magtech.cc		
Magnetic Component Engineering Inc 2830 Lomita Blvd .... Torrance CA 90505	800-989-5656	784-3192*
**Fax Area Code:* 310 ■ *TF:* 800-989-5656 ■ *Web:* www.mceproducts.com		

Phone Fax

Magnum Magnetics Corp 801 Masonic Pk Rd .... Marietta OH 45750 740-373-7770 373-2880
TF: 800-258-0991 ■ Web: www.magnummagnetics.com

Mohr Corp PO Box 1600 .... Brighton MI 48114 810-225-9494 225-4634
TF: 800-223-6647 ■ Web: www.mohrcorp.com

National Magnetics Group Inc 1210 Win Dr .... Bethlehem PA 18017 610-867-7600 867-0200
Web: www.magneticsgroup.com

Permanent Magnet Company Inc
4437 Bragdon St .... Lawrence IN 46226 317-547-1336 549-9259

Shin-etsu Magnetics Inc 2372 Qume Dr Ste B .... San Jose CA 95131 408-383-9240 383-9245
Web: www.shinetsumagnetics.com

Thomas & Skinner Inc 1120 E 23rd St .... Indianapolis IN 46205 317-923-2501 923-5919
Web: www.thomas-skinner.com

459 MAIL ORDER HOUSES

See Also Art Supply Stores p. 1746; Book, Music, Video Clubs p. 1867; Checks - Personal & Business p. 1932; Computer Stores p. 2036; Seed Companies p. 3176

Phone Fax

1Mart Corp 570 El Camino Real Ste 150 .... Redwood City CA 94063 650-363-7700
Web: americangene.com

2 Checkoutcom Inc 1785 O'Brien Rd .... Columbus OH 43228 614-921-2450
TF: 877-294-0273 ■ Web: www.2checkout.com

Advanced Image Direct 1415 S Acacia Ave .... Fullerton CA 92831 714-502-3900 502-3901
TF: 800-540-3848 ■ Web: www.advancedimagedirect.com

Aeromedixcom LLC Po Box 14730 .... Jackson WY 83002 307-732-2642
TF: 888-362-7123 ■ Web: www.aeromedix.com

Allied Marketing Group Inc 1555 Regal Row .... Dallas TX 75247 214-915-7000
Web: www.alliedmarketinggroup.com

America's Hobby Ctr Inc
8300 Tonnelle Ave .... North Bergen NJ 07047 201-662-0777

Avanzado Llc 25330 Interchange Ct .... Farmington Hills MI 48335 248-615-0538
Web: www.avzdo.com

Backcountry.com
2607 South 3200 West Ste A .... West Valley City UT 84119 800-409-4502
TF Orders: 800-409-4502 ■ Web: www.backcountry.com

Blueport Commerce Inc 580 Harrison Ave .... Boston MA 02118 617-275-7200
Web: www.furniture.com

Brokers Worldwide 701C Ashland Ave .... Folcroft PA 19032 610-461-3661
TF: 800-624-5287 ■ Web: asendiausa.com

Budco Inc 2004 N Yellowood Ave .... Broken Arrow OK 74012 918-252-3420
Web: www.budcobank.com

Certif-a-gift Company the
1625 E Algonquin Rd .... Arlington Heights IL 60005 847-718-0300
Web: certif-a-gift.com

Chadwick's of Boston 500 Bic Dr Bldg 4 .... Milford CT 06461 877-330-3393
TF: 877-330-3393 ■ Web: www.chadwicks.com

Childcraft Education Corp
1156 Four Star Dr .... Mount Joy PA 17552 800-631-5652 532-4453*
*Fax Area Code: 888 ■ TF: 800-631-5652

Cinmar LLC 5566 W Chester Rd .... West Chester OH 45069 888-263-9850 603-1492*
*Fax Area Code: 513 ■ TF: 888-263-9850 ■ Web: www.frontgate.com

Colony Brands Inc 1112 Seventh Ave .... Monroe WI 53566 608-328-8400 328-8457
Web: www.theswisscolony.net

Country Home Products Inc 75 Meigs Rd .... Vergennes VT 05491 802-877-1200 877-1212
Web: www.chp.com

Crutchfield Corp 1 Crutchfield Pk .... Charlottesville VA 22911 434-817-1000
TF Sales: 888-955-6000 ■ Web: www.crutchfield.com

Current USA Inc 1005 E Woodmen Rd .... Colorado Springs CO 80920 800-848-2848 993-3232
TF Cust Svc: 800-848-2848 ■ Web: www.currentcatalog.com

Daniel Smith Artist Materials PO Box 84268 .... Seattle WA 98124 206-223-9599
TF: 800-426-6740 ■ Web: www.danielsmith.com

Design Toscano Inc 1400 Morse Ave .... Elk Grove Village IL 60007 847-952-0100
TF: 800-525-5141 ■ Web: www.designtoscano.com

Digi-Key Corp 701 Brooks Ave S .... Thief River Falls MN 56701 218-681-6674 681-3380
TF: 800-344-4539 ■ Web: www.digikey.com

E-filliate Inc 11321 White Rock Rd .... Rancho Cordova CA 95742 916-858-1000
Web: www.efilliate.com

ET Wright & Company Inc
1251 First Ave .... Chippewa Falls WI 54729 715-720-4288

EVINE Live Inc 6740 Shady Oak Rd .... Eden Prairie MN 55344 800-676-5523
TF: 800-676-5523 ■ Web: www.evine.com

FarSounder Inc 43 Jefferson Blvd .... Warwick RI 02888 401-784-6700
Web: www.farsounder.com

Fingerhut 6509 Flying Cloud Dr .... Eden Prairie MN 55344 800-208-2500
TF: 800-208-2500 ■ Web: www.fingerhut.com

Forestry Suppliers Inc 205 W Rankin St .... Jackson MS 39201 601-354-3565 292-0165
TF Cust Svc: 800-752-8460 ■ Web: www.forestry-suppliers.com

Gaiam Inc 833 W S Boulder Rd Ste C .... Louisville CO 80027 303-222-3600
NASDAQ: GAIA ■ TF: 877-989-6321 ■ Web: www.gaiam.com

Gardens Alive Inc 5100 Schenley Pl .... Lawrenceburg IN 47025 513-354-1482 354-1484
TF: 800-222-1222 ■ Web: www.gardensalive.com

Hammacher Schlemmer & Co 9307 N Milwaukee Ave .... Niles IL 60714 800-321-1484 581-8616*
*Fax Area Code: 847 ■ TF: 800-321-1484 ■ Web: www.hammacher.com

Hanna Andersson Corp 1010 NW Flanders St .... Portland OR 97209 800-222-0544 222-0544*
*Fax Area Code: 503 ■ TF Cust Svc: 800-222-0544 ■ Web: www.hannaandersson.com

Hanover Direct Inc 1200 Harbor Blvd .... Weehawken NJ 07086 201-863-7300 272-3465

Harry & David Holdings Inc
2500 S Pacific Hwy .... Medford OR 97501 877-322-1200 233-2300
TF Cust Svc: 877-322-1200 ■ Web: www.harryanddavid.com

Hello Direct Inc 77 NE Blvd .... Nashua NH 03062 800-435-5634 456-2566*
*Fax: Sales ■ TF: 800-435-5634 ■ Web: www.hellodirect.com

Houston Numismatic Exchange Inc
2486 Times Blvd .... Houston TX 77005 713-528-2135
Web: www.hnex.com

J Crew Group Inc 770 Broadway .... New York NY 10003 212-209-2500 209-2666
TF: 800-562-0258 ■ Web: www.jcrew.com

Jackson & Perkins 2 Floral Ave .... Hodges SC 29653 800-292-4769
TF Cust Svc: 800-292-4769 ■ Web: www.jacksonandperkins.com

JC Whitney 761 Progress Pkwy .... La Salle IL 61301 866-529-5530 431-6095*
*Fax Area Code: 312 ■ TF: 866-529-5530 ■ Web: www.jcwhitney.com

Phone Fax

JDR Microdevices Inc
229 Polaris Ave Ste 17 .... Mountain View CA 94043 650-625-1400 538-5005*
*Fax Area Code: 800 ■ TF: 800-538-5000 ■ Web: www.jdr.com

Lands' End Inc 1 Lands' End Ln .... Dodgeville WI 53595 800-963-4816
TF Orders: 800-963-4816 ■ Web: www.landsend.com

Levenger 420 S Congress Ave .... Delray Beach FL 33445 561-276-2436 243-3629
TF Cust Svc: 800-544-0880 ■ Web: www.levenger.com

Living Naturally LLC
6230 University Pkwy Ste 301 .... Sarasota FL 34240 941-480-1910
Web: www.livingnaturally.com

LL Bean Inc 15 Casco St .... Freeport ME 04033 207-552-3080 552-3080
TF: 800-341-4341 ■ Web: www.llbean.com

Mary Maxim Inc
2001 Holland Ave PO Box 5019 .... Port Huron MI 48061 810-987-2000 987-5056
TF: 800-962-9504 ■ Web: www.marymaxim.com

Maynards Industries Ltd 1837 Main St .... Vancouver BC V5T3B8 604-876-6787
Web: www.maynards.com

MBI Inc 47 Richards Ave .... Norwalk CT 06857 203-853-2000
Web: www.mbi-inc.com

Miles Kimball Co 250 City Ctr Bldg .... Oshkosh WI 54906 920-231-3800 231-6942
TF Cust Svc: 855-202-7394 ■ Web: www.mileskimball.com

Movies Unlimited Inc 3015 Darnell Rd .... Philadelphia PA 19154 215-637-4444 637-2350
TF: 800-668-4344 ■ Web: www.moviesunlimited.com

Mystic Stamp Co 9700 Mill St .... Camden NY 13316 315-245-2690 385-4919*
*Fax Area Code: 800 ■ TF: 866-660-7147 ■ Web: www.mysticstamp.com

NASCO International Inc
901 Janesville Ave .... Fort Atkinson WI 53538 920-563-2446 563-8296
TF Orders: 800-558-9595 ■ Web: www.enasco.com

National 4-H Council
7100 Connecticut Ave .... Chevy Chase MD 20815 301-961-2800
Web: www.4-h.org

National Wholesale Company Inc
400 National Blvd .... Lexington NC 27292 800-480-4673 249-9326*
*Fax Area Code: 336 ■ TF: 800-480-4673 ■ Web: www.shopnational.com

Newport News Inc 711 Third Ave 4th Fl .... New York NY 10017 212-986-2585
Web: www.spiegel.com

NHT Global Inc
609 Deep Valley Dr Ste 395 .... Rolling Hills Estates CA 90274 972-241-6525
Web: www.nhtglobal.com

Norm Thompson Outfitters Inc
3188 NW Aloclek Dr .... Hillsboro OR 97124 877-718-7899 821-1282*
*Fax Area Code: 800 ■ TF: 800-547-1160 ■ Web: normthompson.blair.com

Northeast Data Services 1316 College Ave .... Elmira NY 14901 607-733-5541

Now Courier Inc PO Box 6066 .... Indianapolis IN 46206 800-543-6066 638-5750*
*Fax Area Code: 317 ■ TF: 800-543-6066 ■ Web: www.nowcourier.com

NRC Sports Inc 603 Pleasant St .... Paxton MA 01612 800-243-5033
TF: 800-243-5033 ■ Web: www.nrcsports.com

One World Direct 10 First Ave E .... Mobridge SD 57601 605-845-7172
Web: www.owd.com

Oriental Trading Company Inc 5455 S 90th St .... Omaha NE 68127 402-596-1200
TF: 800-875-8480 ■ Web: www.orientaltrading.com

Patagonia Inc 259 W Santa Clara St PO Box 150 .... Ventura CA 93001 805-643-8616 648-8020
TF Cust Svc: 800-638-6464 ■ Web: www.patagonia.com

Penzeys Spices Inc 12001 W Capitol Dr .... Wauwatosa WI 53222 414-760-7307
Web: www.penzeys.com

Roaman's 2300 SE Ave .... Indianapolis IN 46283 800-677-0229 266-3393*
*Fax Area Code: 317 ■ TF: 800-677-0229 ■ Web: www.roamans.com

RSVP Direct Inc 1019 Noel Ave .... Wheeling IL 60090 847-215-9054
Web: www.rsvpdirect.net

S & S Worldwide Inc 75 Mill St .... Colchester CT 06415 860-537-3451 537-2563
TF Orders: 800-243-9232 ■ Web: www.ssww.com

Seta Corp 6400 E Rogers Cir .... Boca Raton FL 33499 561-994-2660
Web: www.setacorporation.com

SkyMall Inc 1520 E Pima St .... Phoenix AZ 85034 800-759-6255 254-6075*
*Fax Area Code: 602 ■ TF: 800-759-6255 ■ Web: www.skymall.com

Southern Fulfillment Services LLC
1650 90th Ave .... Vero Beach FL 32966 772-226-3500
Web: www.southernfulfillment.com

Specialty Catalog Corp
400 Manley St .... West Bridgewater MA 02379 508-638-7000 894-0181
TF: 800-364-9060 ■ Web: www.scdirect.com

StubHub Inc 199 Fremont St Fl 4 .... San Francisco CA 94105 415-222-8400
TF: 866-788-2482 ■ Web: www.stubhub.com

Sunnyland Farms Inc PO Box 8200 .... Albany GA 31706 800-999-2488
TF: 800-999-2488 ■ Web: www.sunnylandfarms.com

Super Duper Inc PO Box 24997 .... Greenville SC 29616 864-288-3536 288-3380
Web: www.superduperinc.com

Taymark Inc 4875 White Bear Pkwy .... White Bear Lake MN 55110 651-426-1667
Web: www.handyart.com

Tech4Learning Inc
10981 San Diego Mission Rd Ste 120 .... San Diego CA 92108 619-563-5348
TF: 877-834-5453 ■ Web: www.tech4learning.com

Tog Shop Inc 30 Tozer Rd .... Beverly MA 01915 978-922-2040 755-7557*
*Fax Area Code: 800 ■ TF: 800-767-6666 ■ Web: togshop.blair.com

TravelSmith Outfitters
773 San Marin Dr Ste 2300 .... Novato CA 94945 800-770-3387 950-1656
TF: 800-770-3387 ■ Web: www.travelsmith.com

Unicover Corp 1 Unicover Ctr .... Cheyenne WY 82008 307-771-3000 771-3134
TF Cust Svc: 800-443-4225 ■ Web: www.unicover.com

Unistar-Sparco Computers Inc
7089 Ryburn Dr .... Millington TN 38053 901-872-2272 872-8482
TF: 800-840-8400 ■ Web: www.sparco.com

Van Dyke Supply Co 39771 Sd Hwy 34 .... Woonsocket SD 57385 704-279-7985
TF: 800-279-7985 ■ Web: www.vandykestaxidermy.com

Victorian Trading Co 15600 W 99th St .... Lenexa KS 66219 913-438-3995 724-7697*
*Fax Area Code: 800 ■ TF Cust Svc: 800-700-2035 ■ Web: www.victoriantradingco.com

VPNet Technologies Inc
211 Mount Airy Rd .... Basking Ridge NJ 95035 408-404-1400
Web: www.vpn.com

Wild Wings LLC 2101 S Hwy 61 .... Lake City MN 55041 651-345-5355
TF: 800-445-4833 ■ Web: www.wildwings.com

Williams-Sonoma Inc 3250 Van Ness Ave .... San Francisco CA 94109 415-421-7900
NYSE: WSM ■ TF: 800-838-2589 ■ Web: www.williams-sonomainc.com

	City	State	Zip	Phone	Fax
Wintersilks Inc PO Box 196	Jessup	PA	18434	800-718-3687	
TF: 800-648-7455 ■ *Web:* wintersilks.blair.com					
Women's International Pharmacy Inc PO Box 6468	Madison	WI	53716	608-221-7800	221-7819
TF: 800-279-5708 ■ *Web:* www.womensinternational.com					
Woodcraft Supply LLC 1177 Rosemar Rd	Parkersburg	WV	26105	800-535-4482	428-8271*
**Fax Area Code:* 304 ■ *TF:* 800-535-4482 ■ *Web:* www.woodcraft.com					
Your Electronic Warehouse 2828 Broadway St	Quincy	IL	62301	217-224-6171	
Web: 4electronicwarehouse.com					
Zappos.com 400 E Stewart Ave	Las Vegas	NV	89101	800-927-7671	
TF: 800-927-7671 ■ *Web:* www.zappos.com					

460 MALLS - SHOPPING

	City	State	Zip	Phone	Fax
57th Street Antique Row 875 57th St	Sacramento	CA	95819	916-451-3110	
Web: 57thstreetantiquerow.com					
Adams Avenue Business Assn 4649 Hawley Blvd	San Diego	CA	92116	619-282-7329	282-8751
Web: www.adamsavenuebusiness.com					
Ala Moana Shopping Ctr 1450 Ala Moana Blvd	Honolulu	HI	96814	808-955-9517	955-2193
Web: www.alamoanacenter.com					
Allen Premium Outlets 820 W Stacy Rd	Allen	TX	75013	972-678-7000	
Web: www.premiumoutlets.com					
Almeda Mall Almeda Mall 12200 Gulf Frwy	Houston	TX	77075	713-944-1010	944-5948
Web: www.almedamall.com					
Altamonte Mall 451 E Altamonte Dr	Altamonte Springs	FL	32701	407-830-4422	
Web: www.altamontemall.com					
American Antique Mall 3130 E Grant Rd	Tucson	AZ	85716	520-326-3070	
Web: www.americanantiquemall.com					
Anaheim Indoor Marketplace 1440 S Anaheim Blvd	Anaheim	CA	92805	714-999-0888	999-0885
Web: www.anaheimindoormarketplace.com					
Annapolis Harbour Shopping Center 2512A Solomon'S Island Rd	Annapolis	MD	21401	410-266-5857	
Web: www.annapolisharbourcenter.com					
Antique Mall 1251 S Virginia St	Reno	NV	89502	775-324-4141	
TF: 888-316-6255 ■ *Web:* www.antiquemalls.com					
Antique Village 10203 Chamberlayne Rd	Mechanicsville	VA	23116	804-746-8914	
Web: www.antiquevillageva.com					
Antique World 11111 Main St	Clarence	NY	14031	716-759-8483	
Web: www.antiqueworldmarket.com					
Antiques Mall of Madison 4748 Cottage Grove Rd	Madison	WI	53716	608-222-2049	
Web: www.antiquesmadison.com					
Arizona Mills 5000 Arizona Mills Cir	Tempe	AZ	85282	480-491-7300	491-7400
TF: 877-746-6642 ■ *Web:* simon.com/mall/arizona-mills					
Arrowhead Towne Ctr 7700 W Arrowhead Towne Ctr	Glendale	AZ	85308	623-979-7777	
Web: www.arrowheadtownecenter.com					
Aspen Grove Lifestyle Ctr 7301 S Santa Fe Dr	Littleton	CO	80120	877-225-5337	798-0238*
**Fax Area Code:* 303 ■ *TF:* 877-225-5337					
Augusta Mall 3450 Wrightsboro Rd	Augusta	GA	30909	706-733-1001	
Web: www.augustamall.com					
Aventura Mall 19501 Biscayne Blvd	Aventura	FL	33180	305-935-1110	
Web: aventuramall.com					
Avenues Mall 10300 Southside Blvd	Jacksonville	FL	32256	904-363-3054	363-3058
Web: www.simon.com					
Barton Creek Square Mall 2901 S Capital of Texas Hwy	Austin	TX	78746	512-327-7040	328-0923
Web: www.simon.com					
Battlefield Mall 2825 S Glenstone Ave	Springfield	MO	65804	417-883-7777	883-2641
Web: www.simon.com					
Bayshore Town Center 5800 N Bayshore Dr Ste A256	Glendale	WI	53217	414-963-8780	332-5304
TF: 800-235-4636 ■ *Web:* www.bayshoretowncenter.com					
Bearden Antique Mall 310 Mohican St	Knoxville	TN	37919	865-584-1521	
Bel Air Mall 3299 Bel Air Mall	Mobile	AL	36606	251-478-1893	
Web: www.shopatbelairmall.com					
Belmont Shore 200 Nieto Ave Ste 200-B	Long Beach	CA	90803	562-434-3066	
Web: www.belmontshore.org					
Boulder Arts & Crafts 1421 Pearl St Mall	Boulder	CO	80302	303-443-3683	443-7998
TF: 866-656-2667 ■ *Web:* www.boulderartsandcrafts.com					
Boulevard Mall 3528 S Maryland Pkwy	Las Vegas	NV	89169	702-735-7430	
Web: www.boulevardmall.com					
Boulevard Mall 730 Alberta Dr	Amherst	NY	14226	716-834-8600	
Web: www.boulevard-mall.com					
Boynton Beach Mall 801 N Congress Ave	Boynton Beach	FL	33426	561-736-7902	
TF: 877-746-6642 ■ *Web:* www.simon.com					
Brea Mall 1065 Brea Mall	Brea	CA	92821	714-990-2732	
Web: www.simon.com					
Bronx Council on the Arts 1738 Hone Ave	Bronx	NY	10461	718-931-9500	409-6445
TF: 866-564-5226 ■ *Web:* bronxarts.org					
Buena Park Downtown 8308 On The Mall	Buena Park	CA	90620	714-503-5000	761-0748
Web: www.buenaparkdowntown.com					
Burbank Town Ctr 201 E Magnolia Blvd	Burbank	CA	91502	818-566-8556	566-7936
Web: www.burbanktowncenter.com					
Burlington Mall 75 Middlesex Tpke	Burlington	MA	01803	781-272-8667	
TF: 877-746-6642 ■ *Web:* www.simon.com/mall/?id=146					
Burnsville Ctr 1178 Burnsville Ctr	Burnsville	MN	55306	952-435-8182	
Web: www.burnsvillecenter.com					
Camarillo Premium Outlets 740 E Ventura Blvd	Camarillo	CA	93010	805-445-8520	
Web: www.premiumoutlets.com					
Carlsbad Premium Outlets 5620 Paseo del Norte	Carlsbad	CA	92008	760-804-9000	
Web: www.premiumoutlets.com					
Carolina Place Mall 11025 Carolina Pl Pkwy	Pineville	NC	28134	704-543-9300	
Web: www.carolinaplace.com					
Carousel Mall 295 Carousel Mall	San Bernardino	CA	92401	909-884-0106	
Web: carouselmall.net					
Cary Towne Ctr 1105 Walnut St	Cary	NC	27511	919-467-0145	
Web: www.shopcarytownecentermall.com					
Casino Factory Shoppes LLC 13118 Hwy 61 N	Robinsonville	MS	38664	662-363-1940	363-1941
Castleton Square Mall 6020 E 82nd St	Indianapolis	IN	46250	317-849-9993	849-4689
Web: www.simon.com					
Centralia Square 201 S Pearl	Centralia	WA	98531	360-736-6406	
Web: www.myantiquemall.com/centraliasquare.html					
Centre at Salisbury 2300 N Salisbury Blvd	Salisbury	MD	21801	410-548-1600	
Web: www.centreatsalisbury.com					
Century III Mall 3075 Clairton Rd	West Mifflin	PA	15123	412-653-1222	
Web: www.simon.com					
Chapel Hills Mall 1710 Briargate Blvd	Colorado Springs	CO	80920	719-594-0111	594-6439
Web: www.chapelhillsmall.com					
Charlestowne Mall 3800 E Main St	Saint Charles	IL	60174	630-513-1120	513-1459
Web: www.charlestownemall.com					
Cherry Creek Shopping Ctr 3000 E First Ave	Denver	CO	80206	303-388-3900	
Web: www.shopcherrycreek.com					
Chicago Premium Outlets 1650 Premium Outlets Blvd	Aurora	IL	60502	630-585-2200	
Web: www.premiumoutlets.com					
Christiana Mall 132 Christiana Mal	Newark	DE	19702	302-731-9815	
Web: www.christianamall.com					
Christown Spectrum Mall 1703 W Bethany Home Rd	Phoenix	AZ	85015	602-249-0670	
Web: www.christownspectrum.com					
Cielo Vista Mall 8401 Gateway Blvd W	El Paso	TX	79925	915-779-7071	772-4926
Web: www.simon.com					
Citadel Mall 2070 Sam Rittenberg Blvd Ste 200	Charleston	SC	29407	843-766-8321	
Web: www.citadelmall.net					
Citadel Mall, The 750 Citadel Dr E	Colorado Springs	CO	80909	719-591-2900	
Web: www.shopthecitadel.com					
City Centre 1420 Fifth Ave Ste 212	Seattle	WA	98101	206-624-6851	623-4625
City Market Antique Mall 707 Gervais St	Columbia	SC	29201	803-799-7722	
Clackamas Town Ctr 12000 SE 82nd Ave	Happy Valley	OR	97086	503-653-6913	
Web: www.clackamastowncenter.com					
Clifton Square 3700 E Douglas	Wichita	KS	67208	316-686-2177	686-2266
Web: www.cliftonsquare.com					
Collin Creek Mall 811 N Central Expy	Plano	TX	75075	972-543-0369	
Web: www.collincreekmall.com					
Colonie Ctr Wolf Rd & Central Ave Northway Exit 2E	Albany	NY	12205	518-459-9020	
Web: www.shopatcoloniecenter.com					
Columbia Gorge Premium Outlets 450 NW 257th Way Ste 110	Troutdale	OR	97060	503-669-8060	
Web: www.premiumoutlets.com					
Columbia Place 7201 Two Notch Rd	Columbia	SC	29223	803-788-4678	736-9168
Web: www.shopcolumbiaplace.com/shop/columbia.nsf/index					
Columbiana Centre Mall 100 Columbiana Cir	Columbia	SC	29212	803-732-6255	
Web: www.columbianacentre.com					
Commons, The 1928 S Commons	Federal Way	WA	98003	253-839-6150	946-1413
Web: www.shopthecommonsmall.com					
Complexe Les Ailes 677 Sainte-Catherine St W	Montreal	QC	H3A3T2	514-288-3759	
Web: www.complexelesailes.com					
Concord Mall 4737 Concord Pk	Wilmington	DE	19803	302-478-9271	479-8314
Web: www.concordmall.com					
Concord Mills 8111 Concord Mills Blvd	Concord	NC	28027	704-979-3000	
Web: simon.com/default.aspx					
CoolSprings Galleria 1800 Galleria Blvd	Franklin	TN	37067	615-771-2050	
Web: www.coolspringsgalleria.com					
Copley Place 100 Huntington Ave Ste 100	Boston	MA	02116	617-262-6600	369-5002
TF: 877-746-6642 ■ *Web:* simon.com					
Coral Ridge Mall 1451 Coral Ridge Ave	Coralville	IA	52241	319-625-5522	
Web: www.coralridgemall.com					
Coronado Ctr 6600 Menaul Blvd NE Ste 1	Albuquerque	NM	87110	505-881-2700	
Web: www.coronadocenter.com					
Cotton City Antique Mall 2012 Airport Blvd	Mobile	AL	36606	251-479-9747	
Web: antiquemalls.com					
Crabtree Valley Mall 4325 Glenwood Ave	Raleigh	NC	27612	919-787-2506	787-7108
Web: www.crabtree-valley-mall.com					
Crocker Galleria 50 Post St	San Francisco	CA	94104	415-393-1505	
Web: www.thecrockergalleria.com					
Cross County Shopping Ctr 8000 Mall Walk	Yonkers	NY	10704	914-968-9570	
Web: www.crosscountycenter.com					
Crossgates Mall 1 Crossgates Mall Rd	Albany	NY	12203	518-869-9565	
Web: shopcrossgates.com					
Crossroads Mall 7000 Crossroads Blvd	Oklahoma City	OK	73149	405-631-4422	
Web: www.plazamayorok.com					
Cumberland Mall 1000 Cumberland Mall	Atlanta	GA	30339	770-435-2206	
Web: www.cumberlandmall.com					
Dallas Galleria 13350 Dallas Pkwy	Dallas	TX	75240	972-702-7100	
Web: www.galleriadallas.com					
Dayton Mall 2700 Miamisburg Centerville Rd	Dayton	OH	45459	937-433-9834	
Web: www.daytonmall.com					
Dedham Mall 300 Providence Hwy	Dedham	MA	02026	781-329-1210	
Web: www.dedham-mall.com					
Deerbrook Mall 20131 Hwy 59 N	Humble	TX	77338	281-446-5300	
Web: www.shopdeerbrookmall.com					
Del Amo Fashion Ctr 3525 Carson St	Torrance	CA	90503	310-542-8525	793-9235
TF: 877-746-6642 ■ *Web:* www.simon.com					
Derby City Antique Mall 3819 Bardstown Rd	Louisville	KY	40218	502-459-5151	459-3438
Web: www.derbycityantiquemall.com					
Desert Sky Mall 7611 W Thomas Rd	Phoenix	AZ	85033	623-245-1404	
Web: www.desertskymall.com					
Design Ctr of the Americas (DCOTA) 1855 Griffin Rd	Dania Beach	FL	33004	954-920-7997	
TF: 877-992-9204 ■ *Web:* www.dcota.com					
Dixie Outlet Mall 1250 S Service Rd	Mississauga	ON	L5E1V4	905-278-3494	278-4283
Web: www.dixieoutletmall.com					

Phone Fax

Dolphin Mall 11401 NW 12 St .... Miami FL 33172 305-365-7446 436-9000
Web: www.shopdolphinmall.com
Domain, The 11410 Century Oaks Terr .... Austin TX 78758 512-795-4230 833-5173
Web: www.simon.com
Downtown Tempe Community
310 S Mill Ave Ste A-201 .... Tempe AZ 85281 480-355-6060 968-7882
Web: www.downtowntempe.com
Dutch Square Center 421 Bush River Rd .... Columbia SC 29210 803-772-3864 750-0036
Web: www.dutchsquare.com
East Towne Mall 89 E Towne Mall .... Madison WI 53704 608-244-1387
Web: www.shopeasttowne-mall.com
Eastern Shore Centre
30500 State Hwy 181 .... Spanish Fort AL 36527 251-625-0060 625-0039
Web: easternshorecentre.com
Eastfield Mall 1655 Boston Rd .... Springfield MA 01129 413-543-8000 543-4221
Web: www.eastfieldmall.com
Eastgate Mall 4601 Eastgate Blvd .... Cincinnati OH 45245 513-752-2294
Web: www.shopeastgate-mall.com
Eastland Center 18000 Vernier Rd .... Harper Woods MI 48225 313-371-1501
Web: www.shopeastland.com
Eastland Mall 800 N Green River Rd .... Evansville IN 47715 812-477-4848
Web: www.shopeastlandmall.com
Eastmont Town Ctr 7200 Bancroft Ave Ste 268 .... Oakland CA 94605 510-635-2966
Eastridge Mall 2200 Eastridge Loop Ste 2062 .... San Jose CA 95122 408-238-3600
Web: www.eastridgecenter.com
Eastview Mall 7979 Pittsford-Victor Rd .... Victor NY 14564 585-223-4420
Web: www.eastviewmall.com
Eastwood Mall 5555 Youngstown-Warren Rd .... Niles OH 44446 330-652-6980 544-5929
Web: eastwoodmall.com
Eastwood Towne Ctr 3003 Preyde Blvd .... Lansing MI 48912 517-316-9209 316-9214
Web: www.shopeastwoodtownecenter.com
Edens & Avant 1221 Main St Ste 1000 .... Columbia SC 29201 330-836-9174 836-5139
Edmonton City Centre 10025-102A Ave .... Edmonton AB T5J2Z2 780-426-8444
Web: www.edmontoncitycentre.com
El Con Mall 3601 E Broadway Blvd .... Tucson AZ 85716 520-795-9958
Web: www.elconcenter.com
Ellenton Premium Outlets
5461 Factory Shops Blvd .... Ellenton FL 34222 941-723-1150
TF: 888-267-2121 ■ *Web:* www.premiumoutlets.com
Emerald Square Mall
999 S Washington St .... North Attleboro MA 02760 508-699-7979
Web: www.simon.com/mall/?id=335
Empire Mall, The 5000 Empire Mall .... Sioux Falls SD 57106 605-361-0586 362-0283
Web: simon.com/default.aspx
Enfield Square 90 Elm St .... Enfield CT 06082 860-745-7000 745-3007
Web: shopenfieldmall.com
Essex Shoppes & Cinema 21 Essex Way Ste 107 .... Essex VT 05451 802-878-4200 879-5080
Web: www.essexoutlets.com
Factory at Franklin 230 Franklin Rd .... Franklin TN 37064 615-791-1777 591-2511
Web: www.factoryatfranklin.com
Factory Stores at North Bend
North Bend Premium Outlets
461 S Fork Ave SW Ste E-1 .... North Bend WA 98045 425-888-4505
Web: www.premiumoutlets.com
Fair Oaks Mall 11750 Lee Jackson Hwy .... Fairfax VA 22033 703-359-8300
Web: www.shopfairoaksmall.com
Fairfield Commons 4869 Nine Mile Rd .... Richmond VA 23223 804-222-4167 226-2510
Fairlane Town Ctr 18900 Michigan Ave .... Dearborn MI 48126 800-992-9500
TF: 800-992-9500 ■ *Web:* www.shopfairlane.com
Fallbrook Ctr 6633 Fallbrook Ave .... West Hills CA 91307 818-885-9700 885-0029
TF: 866-718-1649 ■ *Web:* www.ggp.com
Fantastic Indoor Swapmeet
1717 S Decatur Blvd .... Las Vegas NV 89102 702-877-0087
Web: www.fantasticindoorswapmeet.com
Farm, The 5321 S Sheridan Ste 27 .... Tulsa OK 74145 918-622-3860 622-4675
Web: www.farmshoppingcenter.com
Fashion Island Shopping Ctr
401 Newport Ctr Dr .... Newport Beach CA 92660 949-721-2000 720-3350
TF: 855-658-8527 ■ *Web:* www.shopfashionisland.com
Fashion Place 6191 S State St .... Murray UT 84107 801-262-9447
Web: www.fashionplace.com
Fashion Show Mall
3200 Las Vegas Blvd S Ste 600 .... Las Vegas NV 89109 702-369-8382
Web: www.thefashionshow.com
Fashion Valley Mall 7007 Friars Rd .... San Diego CA 92108 619-688-9113 294-8291
Web: www.simon.com
Fayette Mall 3401 Nicholasville Rd Ste 303 .... Lexington KY 40503 859-272-3493
Web: www.shopfayette-mall.com
Festival Flea Market Mall
2900 W Sample Rd .... Pompano Beach FL 33073 954-979-4555
TF: 800-353-2627 ■ *Web:* www.festival.com
Fiesta Mall 1445 W Southern Ave Ste 2104 .... Mesa AZ 85202 480-833-4121
Web: www.shopfiesta.com
Fig Garden Village 790 W Shaw Ave .... Fresno CA 93704 559-412-5296
Web: www.shopfiggardenvillage.com
First Colony Mall 16535 SW Fwy Ste 1 .... Sugar Land TX 77479 281-265-6123
Web: www.firstcolonymall.com
Florida Mall 8001 S Orange Blossom Trl .... Orlando FL 32809 407-851-6255 855-1827
Web: www.simon.com
Foothill Village 1400 S Foothill Dr .... Salt Lake City UT 84108 801-487-6670
Web: www.foothillvillage.com
Foothills Mall 7475 N La Cholla Blvd Ste 133 .... Tucson AZ 85741 520-742-7191
Web: www.shopfoothillsmall.com
Four Seasons Town Centre
410 Four Seasons Town Centre .... Greensboro NC 27427 336-292-0171
Web: www.shopfourseasons.com
Fox River Mall 4301 W Wisconsin Ave .... Appleton WI 54913 920-739-4100
Web: www.foxrivermall.com
Foyer, The 3655 Perkins Rd .... Baton Rouge LA 70808 225-343-3655 343-3652
Franklin Mills 1455 Franklin Mills Cir .... Philadelphia PA 19154 215-632-1500 632-7888
TF General: 877-746-6642 ■ *Web:* simon.com/mall/franklin-mills
Fulton's Folly Antique Mall 920 E Olive Ave .... Fresno CA 93728 559-268-3856

Phone Fax

Galleria at Fort Lauderdale
2414 E Sunrise Blvd .... Fort Lauderdale FL 33304 954-564-1015 566-9976
Web: www.galleriamall-fl.com
Galleria at Pittsburgh Mills
590 Pittsburgh Mills Cir .... Tarentum PA 15084 724-904-9010
Web: www.pittsburghmills.com
Galleria at Sunset
1300 W Sunset Rd Ste 1400 .... Henderson NV 89014 702-434-2409 434-0259
Web: www.galleriaatsunset.com
Galleria at Tyler
1299 Galleria at Tyler St .... Riverside CA 92503 951-351-3112
Web: www.galleriatyler.com
Galleria at White Plains 100 Main St .... White Plains NY 10601 914-682-0111 682-1609
Web: simon.com/default.aspx
Galleria, The 5085 Westheimer Rd Ste 4850 .... Houston TX 77056 713-966-3500 966-3596
Web: www.simon.com
Galleries of Syracuse, The 441 S Salina St .... Syracuse NY 13202 315-475-5351 475-4263
Garden City Center 100 Midway Rd Ste 14 .... Cranston RI 02920 401-942-2800
Web: www.gardencitycenter.com
Garden State Plaza 1 Garden State Plz .... Paramus NJ 07652 201-843-2121
Web: www.westfield.com
Gardens Mall, The 3101 PGA Blvd .... Palm Beach Gardens FL 33410 561-622-2115 694-9380
Web: www.thegardensmall.com
Gardner Village 1100 West 7800 South .... West Jordan UT 84088 801-566-8903
TF: 800-662-4335 ■ *Web:* www.gardnervillage.com
Genesee Valley Ctr 3341 S Linden Rd .... Flint MI 48507 810-732-4000 732-4343
TF: 866-236-1128 ■ *Web:* www.geneseemall.com
Glenbrook Square 4201 Coldwater Rd .... Fort Wayne IN 46805 260-483-2121
Web: www.glenbrooksquare.com
Glendale Galleria 100 W Broadway .... Glendale CA 91210 818-246-6737
Web: www.glendalegalleria.com
Golf Mill Shopping Ctr 239 Golf Mill Ctr .... Niles IL 60714 847-699-1070
Web: www.golfmill.com
Governor's Square 1500 Apalachee Pkwy .... Tallahassee FL 32301 850-877-8106
Web: www.governorssquare.com
Grand Avenue 649 Grand Ave .... Saint Paul MN 55105 651-699-0029 699-7775
Web: www.grandave.com
Grapevine Mills 3000 Grapevine Mills Pkwy .... Grapevine TX 76051 972-724-4900 724-4920
Web: www.simon.com/mall/grapevine-mills
Great Lakes Mall 7850 Mentor Ave .... Mentor OH 44060 440-255-6900
TF: 877-746-6642 ■ *Web:* www.simon.com
Great Mall 447 Great Mall Dr .... Milpitas CA 95035 408-945-4022 945-4027
Web: www.simon.com
Green Acres Mall 2034 Green Acres Mall .... Valley Stream NY 11581 516-561-1157 561-3870
Web: www.greenacresmallonline.com
Green Hills Antique Mall 4108 Hillsboro Pk .... Nashville TN 37215 615-383-9851 383-4886
TF: 888-316-6255
Greenbriar Mall 2841 Greenbriar Pkwy SW .... Atlanta GA 30331 404-344-6611 344-6631
Web: www.shopgreenbriar.com
Greenspoint Mall 12300 IH-45 N Fwy .... Houston TX 77060 281-875-4201
Web: www.greenspointmall.com
Greenway Station 1650 Deming Way .... Middleton WI 53562 608-824-9111
Web: www.greenwayshopping.com
Greenwood Park Mall 1251 US Hwy 31 N .... Greenwood IN 46142 317-881-6758 887-8606
TF: 877-746-6642 ■ *Web:* simon.com/mall?id=165
Grossmont Center 5500 Grossmont Ctr Dr .... La Mesa CA 91942 619-465-2900
Web: www.grossmontcenter.com
Grove, The 189 The Grove Dr .... Los Angeles CA 90036 323-900-8080
TF: 888-315-8883 ■ *Web:* www.thegrovela.com
Gurnee Mills 6170 W Grand Ave .... Gurnee IL 60031 847-263-7500
Web: www.simon.com
Gwinnett Place Mall 2100 Pleasant Hill Rd .... Duluth GA 30096 770-813-6840
Web: www.simon.com
Hamilton Mall 4403 Black Horse Pk .... Mays Landing NJ 08330 609-646-6392 645-7837
Web: www.shophamilton.com
Hamilton Place 2100 Hamilton Pl Blvd .... Chattanooga TN 37421 423-855-0001
Web: www.hamiltonplace.com
Hanes Mall
3320 Silas Creek Pkwy Ste 264 .... Winston-Salem NC 27103 336-765-8323
Web: www.shophanesmall.com
Hanover Mall 1775 Washington St .... Hanover MA 02339 781-826-4392
Web: www.hanovermall.com
Hawthorne Boulevard Cutters
1744 Se Hawthorne Blvd .... Portland OR 97214 503-239-0382
Haywood Mall 700 Haywood Rd .... Greenville SC 29607 864-288-0511 297-6018
Web: www.simon.com
Hickory Hollow Mall 5262 Hickory Hollow Pkwy .... Antioch TN 37013 615-731-3500
Hickory Ridge Mall 6075 Winchester Rd .... Memphis TN 38115 901-795-8844
Web: www.hickoryridge.com
Hillsdale Shopping Ctr 60 31st Ave .... San Mateo CA 94403 650-345-8222 573-5457
Web: www.hillsdale.com
Hilltop Mall 2200 Hilltop Mall Rd .... Richmond CA 94806 510-223-6900
Web: www.shophilltop.com
Historic Old Town Fort Collins
19 Old Town Sq Ste 230 .... Fort Collins CO 80524 970-484-6500
TF: 866-203-5939 ■ *Web:* www.downtownfortcollins.com
Historic Valley Junction
137 Fifth St .... West Des Moines IA 50265 515-222-3642 274-8407
Web: www.valleyjunction.com
Holyoke Mall at Ingleside 50 Holyoke St .... Holyoke MA 01040 413-536-1441
Web: holyokemall.com
Hulen Mall 4800 S Hulen St .... Fort Worth TX 76132 817-294-1200
Web: www.hulenmall.com
Independence Mall 3500 Oleander Dr .... Wilmington NC 28403 910-392-1776
Web: www.shopindependencemall.com
Indianapolis Downtown Antique Mall
1044 Virginia Ave .... Indianapolis IN 46203 317-635-5336
Ingram Park Mall 6301 NW Loop 410 .... San Antonio TX 78238 210-684-9570
TF: 877-746-6642 ■ *Web:* www.simon.com
Irving Mall 3880 Irving Mall .... Irving TX 75062 972-255-0571
TF: 877-746-6642 ■ *Web:* www.simon.com
Janet's Antiques 2545 Central Ave .... Saint Petersburg FL 33713 727-823-5700
Web: thepricefairy.com

Name / Address	City	State	ZIP	Phone	Fax
Jantzen Beach SuperCenter 1405 Jantzen Beach Centre	Portland	OR	97217	503-718-1133	
Jefferson Mall 4801 Outerloop Rd *Web:* www.shopjefferson-mall.com	Louisville	KY	40219	502-968-4101	
Jefferson Valley Mall 650 Lee Blvd *Web:* www.simon.com	Yorktown Heights	NY	10598	914-245-4688	
Katy Mills 5000 Katy Mills Cir *Web:* www.simon.com	Katy	TX	77494	281-644-5015	644-5001
Kenwood Towne Centre 7875 Montgomery Rd *Web:* www.kenwoodtownecentre.com	Cincinnati	OH	45236	513-745-9100	
Kierland Commons 15205 N Kierland Blvd Ste 150 *Web:* www.kierlandcommons.com	Scottsdale	AZ	85254	480-348-1577	
King of Prussia Mall 160 N Gulph Rd *TF:* 877-746-6642 ■ *Web:* simon.com/mall/king-of-prussia-mall	King of Prussia	PA	19406	610-265-5727	265-1640
La Gran Plaza 4200 S Fwy Ste 2500 *Web:* www.lagranplazamall.com	Fort Worth	TX	76115	817-922-8888	
Lafayette Antique Market 3108 Johnston St *Web:* lafayetteantiquemarket.com	Lafayette	LA	70503	337-981-9884	
Lake Buena Vista Factory Stores 15657 S Apopka Vineland Rd Sr 535 *Web:* www.lbvfs.com	Orlando	FL	32821	407-238-9301	
Lakeline Mall 11200 Lakeline Mall Dr *Web:* www.simon.com	Cedar Park	TX	78613	512-257-7467	257-0522
Lakeside Mall 14000 Lakeside Cir *Web:* www.shop-lakesidemall.com	Sterling Heights	MI	48313	586-247-1590	
Lakeside Shopping Center 3301 Veterans Memorial Blvd *Web:* www.lakesideshopping.com	Metairie	LA	70002	504-835-8000	
Lakewood Ctr Mall 500 Lakewood Ctr *Web:* www.shoplakewoodcenter.com	Lakewood	CA	90712	562-633-0437	
Landmark Mall 5801 Duke St *Web:* www.landmarkmall.com	Alexandria	VA	22304	703-354-8405	
Lansing City Market 325 City Market Dr *Web:* www.lansingcitymarket.com	Lansing	MI	48912	517-483-7460	483-7462
Las Vegas Premium Outlets 875 S Grand Central Pkwy *Web:* www.premiumoutlets.com	Las Vegas	NV	89106	702-474-7500	
Lenox Square Mall 3393 Peachtree Rd NE *Web:* www.simon.com	Atlanta	GA	30326	404-233-6767	233-7868
Lexington Market 400 W Lexington St *Web:* www.lexingtonmarket.com	Baltimore	MD	21201	410-685-6169	547-1864
Liberty Tree Mall 100 Independence Way *TF:* 877-746-6642 ■ *Web:* www.simon.com	Danvers	MA	01923	978-777-0794	777-9857
Lincoln Center Shops 374 Lincoln Centre *Web:* www.lincolncentershops.com	Stockton	CA	95207	209-477-4868	
Lincoln Mall 208 Lincoln Mall Dr *Web:* www.lincoln-mall.com	Matteson	IL	60443	708-747-5600	
Lincoln Square Shopping Center 436 Lincoln Sq *Web:* www.lincolnsquarearlington.com	Arlington	TX	76011	817-461-7953	274-5574
Los Cerritos Ctr 239 Los Cerritos Ctr *Web:* www.shoploscerritos.com	Cerritos	CA	90703	562-860-0341	
Lower East Side Business Improvement District 54 Orchard St *Web:* lowereastside.org	New York	NY	10002	212-226-9010	
Lynnhaven Mall 701 Lynnhaven Pkwy Ste 1068 *Web:* www.lynnhavenmall.com	Virginia Beach	VA	23452	757-340-9340	
MacArthur Center 300 Monticello Ave *Web:* www.shopmacarthur.com	Norfolk	VA	23510	757-627-6000	627-6624
Macomb Mall 32233 Gratiot Ave *Web:* www.shopmacombmall.com	Roseville	MI	48066	586-293-7800	
Macon Mall 3661 Eisenhower Pkwy *Web:* maconmall.com	Macon	GA	31206	478-477-8840	
Maine Mall 364 Maine Mall Rd *Web:* www.mainemall.com	South Portland	ME	04106	207-774-0303	
Mall at Cortana 9401 Cortana Pl *Web:* www.cortanamall.com	Baton Rouge	LA	70815	225-927-6747	
Mall at Fairfield Commons 2727 Fairfield Commons *Web:* www.mallatfairfieldcommons.com	Beavercreek	OH	45431	937-427-4300	427-3668
Mall at Greece Ridge, The 271 Greece Ridge Ctr Dr *Web:* www.themallatgreeceridge.com	Rochester	NY	14626	585-225-0430	
Mall at Millenia 4200 Conroy Rd *Web:* www.mallatmillenia.com	Orlando	FL	32839	407-363-3555	363-6877
Mall at Robinson 100 Robinson Centre Dr *Web:* www.shoprobinsonmall.com	Pittsburgh	PA	15205	412-788-0816	788-1156
Mall at Short Hills 1200 Morris Tpke *Web:* www.shopshorthills.com	Short Hills	NJ	07078	973-376-7350	
Mall at Steamtown, The 300 Lackawanna Ave *Web:* www.themallatsteamtown.com	Scranton	PA	18503	570-343-3400	
Mall at Wellington Green 10300 W Forest Hill Blvd *Web:* www.shopwellingtongreen.com	Wellington	FL	33414	561-227-6900	
Mall del Norte 5300 San Dario *Web:* www.malldelnorte.com	Laredo	TX	78041	956-724-8191	
Mall of America 60 E Broadway *Web:* www.mallofamerica.com	Bloomington	MN	55425	952-883-8810	
Mall of Louisiana 6401 Bluebonnet Blvd *Web:* www.mallofiouisiana.com	Baton Rouge	LA	70836	225-761-7228	
Mall Saint Matthews 5000 Shelbyville Rd *Web:* www.mallstmatthews.com	Louisville	KY	40207	502-893-0311	
Mall Saint Vincent 1133 St Vincent Ave Ste 200 *Web:* www.mallstvincent.com	Shreveport	LA	71104	318-227-9880	
Manchester Center 1901 E Shields Ave Ste 203 *Web:* www.manchester-center.com	Fresno	CA	93726	559-227-1901	227-1602
Market, The 2628 S Glenstone Ave	Springfield	MO	65804	417-889-1145	882-0261
Marketplace Mall 1 Miracle Mile Dr *Web:* www.themarketplacemall.com	Rochester	NY	14623	585-424-6220	427-2745
Marshall Square Mall 720 University Ave	Syracuse	NY	13210	315-422-3234	475-2004
Mayfair Mall 2500 N Mayfair Rd *Web:* www.mayfairmall.com	Milwaukee	WI	53226	414-771-1300	
Mazza Gallerie 5300 Wisconsin Ave NW *Web:* www.mazzagallerie.com	Washington	DC	20015	202-966-6114	
McCain Mall 3929 Mccain Blvd *Web:* www.simon.com/mall	North Little Rock	AR	72116	501-758-6317	758-0131
Memorial City Mall 303 Memorial City *Web:* memorialcity.com	Houston	TX	77024	713-464-8640	464-7845
Meridian Mall 1982 W Grand River Ave *Web:* www.meridianmall.com	Okemos	MI	48864	517-349-2031	
Merle Hay Mall 3800 Merle Hay Rd *Web:* www.merlehaymall.com	Des Moines	IA	50310	515-276-8551	276-9227
Mesilla Valley Mall 700 S Telshor Blvd *Web:* www.mesillavalleymall.com	Las Cruces	NM	88011	575-522-1001	522-0956
Meyerland Plaza 420 Meyerland Plaza *TF:* 888-675-2275	Houston	TX	77096	713-349-0245	600-1017
Mic Mac Mall 21 MicMac Blvd *Web:* www.micmacmall.com	Dartmouth	NS	B3A4N3	902-463-5891	469-5268
Mid Rivers Mall 1600 Mid Rivers Mall *Web:* www.shopmidriversmall.com	Saint Peters	MO	63376	636-970-2610	
Midway Mall 3343 Midway Mall *Web:* www.midwaymallshopping.com	Elyria	OH	44035	440-324-5749	
Mill Creek Mall 654 Millcreek Mall *TF:* 800-615-3535 ■ *Web:* www.millcreekmall.net	Erie	PA	16565	814-868-9000	864-1193
Mills at Jersey Gardens, The 651 Kapkowski Rd *TF:* 877-789-2327 ■ *Web:* www.simon.com/mall/the-mills-at-jersey-gardens	Elizabeth	NJ	07201	908-354-5900	
Monroeville Mall 200 Mall Blvd *Web:* www.monroevillemall.com	Monroeville	PA	15146	412-243-8511	
Montclair Plaza 5060 Montclair Plz Ln *Web:* montclairplace.com	Montclair	CA	91763	909-626-2442	
Montgomery Street Antique Mall 2601 Montgomery St *Web:* www.montgomerystreetantiques.com	Fort Worth	TX	76107	817-735-9685	
Moreno Valley Mall 22500 Town Cir Ste 1206 *Web:* www.morenovalleymall.com	Moreno Valley	CA	92553	951-653-1177	
Natick Mall 1245 Worcester St *Web:* www.natickmall.com	Natick	MA	01760	508-655-4800	
NCDA&CS Raleigh Farmers Market 1201 Agriculture St *Web:* www.ncagr.gov/markets/facilities/markets/raleigh	Raleigh	NC	27603	919-733-7417	
Newgate Mall 36th St & Wall Ave *Web:* www.newgatemall.com	Ogden	UT	84405	801-621-1161	
Newpark Mall 2086 Newpark Mall *Web:* www.newparkmall.com	Newark	CA	94560	510-794-5523	
North East Mall 1101 Melbourne St Ste 1000 *TF:* 877-746-6642 ■ *Web:* www.simon.com	Hurst	TX	76053	817-284-3427	595-4471
North Idaho Outlets 4300 W Riverbend Ave	Post Falls	ID	83854	208-773-4556	773-4556
North Market 59 Spruce St *Web:* www.northmarket.com	Columbus	OH	43215	614-463-9664	
North Star Mall 7400 San Pedro Ave *Web:* www.northstarmall.com	San Antonio	TX	78216	210-342-2325	
North Town Mall 4750 N Div St *Web:* www.northtownmall.com	Spokane	WA	99207	509-482-0209	
Northbrook Court 1515 Lake Cook Rd *Web:* www.northbrookcourt.com	Northbrook	IL	60062	847-498-8161	
Northgate Mall 9501 Colerain Ave *Web:* www.mynorthgatemall.com	Cincinnati	OH	45251	513-385-5600	
Northgate Mall 401 NE Northgate Way Ste 210 *Web:* www.simon.com	Seattle	WA	98125	206-362-4777	361-8760
NorthPark Ctr 8687 N Central Expy *Web:* www.northparkcenter.com	Dallas	TX	75225	214-363-7441	363-0195
Northpoint Mall 1000 N Pt Cir *Web:* www.northpointmall.com	Alpharetta	GA	30022	770-740-9273	
Northridge Fashion Ctr 9301 Tampa Ave *Web:* www.northridgefashioncenter.com	Northridge	CA	91324	818-885-9700	
Northridge Mall 796 Northridge Mall *Web:* www.shop-northridge-mall.com	Salinas	CA	93906	831-449-7226	
Northshore Mall 210 Andover St *Web:* www.simon.com	Peabody	MA	01960	978-531-3440	
Northwoods Mall 2150 Northwoods Blvd Unit 60 *Web:* shopnorthwoodsmall.com	North Charleston	SC	29406	843-797-3062	
Oak Hollow Mall 921 Eastchester Dr	High Point	NC	27262	336-886-6255	
Oak Park Mall 11149 W 95th St *Web:* www.thenewoakparkmall.com	Overland Park	KS	66214	913-888-4400	
Oak View Mall 3001 S 144th St *Web:* www.oakviewmall.com	Omaha	NE	68144	402-330-3332	
Oakbrook Shopping Ctr 100 Oakbrook Ctr *Web:* www.oakbrookcenter.com	Oak Brook	IL	60523	630-573-0700	573-0710
Oaks, The 350 W Hillcrest Dr *Web:* www.shoptheoaksmall.com	Thousand Oaks	CA	91360	805-495-2032	
Oakwood Ctr 197 Westbank Expy *Web:* www.oakwoodcenter.com	Gretna	LA	70053	504-361-1550	
Oglethorpe Mall 7804 Abercorn Ext *Web:* www.oglethorpemall.com	Savannah	GA	31406	912-354-7038	
Ohio Valley Mall 67800 Mall Rd *Web:* www.ohiovalleymall.net	Saint Clairsville	OH	43950	740-695-4526	695-4451
Old Mill Antique Mall 310 State St *Web:* oldmillantiquemall.com	West Columbia	SC	29169	803-796-4229	
Old Orchard Ctr 4905 Old Orchard Ctr *Web:* www.westfield.com	Skokie	IL	60077	847-673-6800	
Orland Square 288 Orland Sq *TF:* 877-746-6642 ■ *Web:* www.simon.com/mall/?id=189	Orland Park	IL	60462	708-349-1646	349-8419
Orlando Fashion Square 3201 E Colonial Dr	Orlando	FL	32803	407-896-1132	894-8381
Orlando Premium Outlets 8200 Vineland Ave *Web:* www.premiumoutlets.com	Orlando	FL	32821	407-238-7787	
Outlets at Anthem 4250 W Anthem Way *TF:* 888-482-5834 ■ *Web:* www.outletsanthem.com	Phoenix	AZ	85086	623-465-9500	465-9516
Outlets at Loveland 5661 McWhinney Blvd *Web:* www.outletsatloveland.com	Loveland	CO	80538	970-663-1916	

Phone | Fax

Over-the-Rhine Chamber of Commerce
1431 Walnut St. Cincinnati OH 45202 513-241-2690
Web: www.otrchamber.com

Owings Mills Mall 10300 Mill Run Cir. Owings Mills MD 21117 410-363-7000
Web: www.owingsmillsmall.com

Oxford Valley Mall 225 W Washington St. Indianapolis IN 46204 317-636-1600 750-0469*
*Fax Area Code: 215 ■ *Web:* www.simon.com/mall/oxford-valley-mall

Ozark Antique 200 S 20th St. Ozark MO 65721 417-581-5233
Web: ozarkantiquemall.com

Pacific Place 600 Pine St. Seattle WA 98101 206-405-2655
Web: www.pacificplaceseattle.com

Palmer Square 40 Nassau St. Princeton NJ 08542 609-921-2333 921-3797
Web: www.palmersquare.com

Pandora Quaker Bridge Mall
150 Quaker Bridge Mall. Lawrenceville NJ 08648 609-799-8177 275-6523
Web: www.pandora.net

Paradise Valley Mall 4568 E Cactus Rd. Phoenix AZ 85032 602-996-8840
Web: www.theparadisevalleymall.com

Park City Ctr 142 Pk City Ctr. Lancaster PA 17601 717-393-3851
Web: www.parkcitycenter.com

Park Meadows Retail Resort
8401 Pk Meadows Ctr Dr. Littleton CO 80124 303-792-2533
Web: www.parkmeadows.com

Park Meadows Town Ctr
8401 Pk Meadows Ctr Dr. Lone Tree CO 80124 303-792-2533
Web: www.parkmeadows.com

Park Place 5870 E Broadway Blvd. Tucson AZ 85711 520-747-7575
Web: www.parkplacemall.com

Park Plaza Mall 6000 W Markham St. Little Rock AR 72205 501-664-4956
Web: www.parkplazamall.com

Parks at Arlington 3811 S Cooper St. Arlington TX 76015 817-467-0200 468-5356
Web: www.theparksmallarlington.com/en.html

Parkway Place Mall 2801 Memorial Pkwy SW. Huntsville AL 35801 256-533-0700
Web: www.parkwayplacemall.com

Parmatown Mall 7899 W Ridgewood Dr. Parma OH 44129 440-885-5506 884-9330
Web: www.facebook.com

Patrick Henry Mall 12300 Jefferson Ave. Newport News VA 23602 757-249-4305
Web: www.shoppatrickhenrymall.com

Pearlridge Ctr 98-1005 Moana Lua Rd. Aiea HI 96701 808-488-0981 488-9456
Web: www.pearlridgeonline.com

Pembroke Lakes Mall 11401 Pines Blvd. Pembroke Pines FL 33026 954-436-3311
Web: www.pembrokelakesmall.com

Peninsula Town Ctr
4410 E Claiborne Sq Ste 212. Hampton VA 23666 757-838-1505
Web: www.peninsulatowncenter.com

Penn Square Mall 1901 NW Expy. Oklahoma City OK 73118 405-842-4424
Web: www.simon.com

Perimeter Mall
4400 Ashford-Dunwoody Rd Ste 1360. Atlanta GA 30346 770-394-4270
Web: www.perimetermall.com

Place de la Cite 2600 Laurier Blvd. Quebec QC G1V4T3 418-657-6920 657-6924
Web: www.placedelacite.com

Plaza, The 9500 S Western Ave. Evergreen Park IL 60805 708-422-5454 422-9780

Polaris Fashion Place 1500 Polaris Pkwy. Columbus OH 43240 614-846-1500 846-4617
Web: www.polarisfashionplace.com

Potomac Mills 2700 Potomac Mills Cir. Woodbridge VA 22192 703-496-9301 643-1054
TF: 877-746-6642 ■ *Web:* www.simon.com

Prime Outlets San Marcos 3939 S IH-35. San Marcos TX 78666 512-396-2200
TF: 800-331-5479 ■ *Web:* www.premiumoutlets.com

Princeton Forrestal Village
206 Rockingham Row. Princeton NJ 08540 609-799-7400
Web: pfvillage.com

Provo Towne Centre 1200 Towne Centre Blvd. Provo UT 84601 801-852-2400 852-2405
Web: www.provotownecentre.com

Puente Hills Mall 1600 Azusa Ave. City of Industry CA 91748 626-912-8777 913-2719
Web: www.puentehills-mall.com

Quail Springs Mall 2501 W Memorial Rd. Oklahoma City OK 73134 405-755-6530
Web: www.quailspringsmall.com

Regency Mall 5538 Durand Ave. Racine WI 53406 262-554-7903
Web: www.shopregency-mall.com

Regency Square Mall
9501 Arlington Expy Ste 100. Jacksonville FL 32225 904-725-3830
Web: www.regencysquaremall.com

Reynolda Village 2201 Reynolda Rd. Winston-Salem NC 27106 336-758-5584
Web: www.reynoldavillage.com

Richland Mall 3400 Forest Dr. Columbia SC 29204 803-782-7575
Web: www.richlandmallsc.com

Ridgedale Ctr 12401 Wayzata Blvd. Minnetonka MN 55305 952-541-4864
Web: www.ridgedalecenter.com

Ridgmar Mall 1888 Green Oaks Rd. Fort Worth TX 76116 817-731-6591 763-5146
Web: www.ridgmar.com

River City Antique Mall & Collector's Market
6363 Hearne Ave. Shreveport LA 71108 318-621-1009

River Oaks Ctr 96 River Oaks Ctr Dr. Calumet City IL 60409 708-868-0600
TF: 877-746-6642 ■ *Web:* simon.com/mall?id=190

Riverchase Galleria
2000 Riverchase Galleria Ste 400. Hoover AL 35244 205-985-3020
Web: www.riverchasegalleria.com

Rivergate Mall
1000 Rivergate Pkwy Ste 1. Goodlettsville TN 37072 615-859-3458
Web: www.rivergate-mall.com

RiverTown Crossings 3700 Rivertown Pkwy. Grandville MI 49418 616-257-5000
Web: www.rivertowncrossings.com

Riverwalk Marketplace
500 Port Of New Orleans Pl. New Orleans LA 70130 504-522-1555
Web: riverwalkneworleans.com

Rockaway Townsquare Mall 301 Mt Hope Ave. Rockaway NJ 07866 973-361-4070 361-1561
Web: www.simon.com

Rolling Oaks Mall 6909 N Loop 1604 E. San Antonio TX 78247 210-651-5513
TF: 877-746-6642 ■ *Web:* www.simon.com

Roosevelt Field Mall 630 Old Country Rd. Garden City NY 11530 516-742-8001 742-8004
TF: 877-746-6642 ■ *Web:* www.simon.com

Ross Park Mall 1000 Ross Pk Mall Dr. Pittsburgh PA 15237 412-369-4400
Web: www.simon.com

Saint Clair Square 134 St Clair Sq. Fairview Heights IL 62208 618-632-7567
Web: www.stclairsquare.com

Saint Louis Mills 5555 St Louis Mills Blvd. Hazelwood MO 63042 317-636-1600
Web: www.simon.com

Salem Center 401 Center St NE. Salem OR 97301 503-399-9676 364-1284
Web: www.salemcenter.com

San Jacinto Mall 1496 San Jacinto Mall. Baytown TX 77521 281-421-3908 421-7377
Web: www.sanjacintomall.com

Sangamon Antique Mall
3050 E Sangamon Ave. Springfield IL 62702 217-522-7740

Savannah Mall 14045 Abercorn St. Savannah GA 31419 912-927-7467
Web: www.savannahmall.com

Sawgrass Mills 12801 W Sunrise Blvd. Sunrise FL 33323 954-846-2300 846-2312
Web: www.simon.com

Seattle Premium Outlets 10600 Quil Ceda Blvd. Tulalip WA 98271 360-654-3000
Web: www.premiumoutlets.com

Security Square Mall 6901 Security Blvd. Baltimore MD 21244 410-265-6000 281-1473
Web: www.securitysquare.com

Seminole Towne Ctr 200 Towne Ctr Cir. Sanford FL 32771 407-323-2262
TF: 877-746-6642 ■ *Web:* www.simon.com

Sharpstown Mall 201 Sharpstown Ctr Ste 201. Houston TX 77036 713-777-1111
Web: www.plazamericas.com

Sherwood Mall 5308 Pacific Ave. Stockton CA 95207 209-952-6277
Web: www.sherwoodmall.com

Shop at North Bridge, The 520 N Michigan Ave. Chicago IL 60611 312-327-2300
Web: www.theshopsatnorthbridge.com

ShoppingTown Mall 3649 Erie Blvd E. Dewitt NY 13214 315-446-9159
Web: www.shoppingtownmall.com

Shops at Briargate
1885 Briargate Pkwy. Colorado Springs CO 80920 719-265-6264 268-0738
Web: thepromenadeshopsatbriargate.com

Shops at Hilltop North East & West
Laskin Rd. Virginia Beach VA 23451 757-428-2224
Web: www.hilltopshops.com

Shops at Houston Center 1200 Mckinney Ste 545. Houston TX 77010 713-759-1442
Web: www.shopsathc.com

Shops at La Cantera
15900 La Cantera Pkwy Ste 6698. San Antonio TX 78256 210-582-6255
Web: www.theshopsatlacantera.com

Shops at Liberty Place 1625 Chestnut St. Philadelphia PA 19103 215-851-9055
Web: www.shopsatliberty.com

Shops at Riverwoods 4801 N University Ave. Provo UT 84604 801-802-8430
Web: www.shopsatriverwoods.com

Shops at Tanforan, The 1150 El Camino Real. San Bruno CA 94066 650-873-2000 873-4210
Web: www.theshopsattanforan.com

Shops at Willow Bend 6121 W Pk Blvd Ste 1000. Plano TX 75093 972-202-4900
Web: www.shopwillowbend.com

Shops at Woodlake 725 Woodlake Rd. Kohler WI 53044 920-459-1713
TF: 855-444-2838 ■ *Web:* www.americanclubresort.com

Sierra Vista Mall 1050 Shaw Ave. Clovis CA 93612 559-299-5070
Web: www.sierravistamall.com

Solomon Pond Mall 601 Donald Lynch Blvd. Marlborough MA 01752 508-303-6255 303-0206
TF: 877-746-6642 ■ *Web:* simon.com/mall?id=339

South Bay Galleria
1815 Hawthorne Blvd Ste 201. Redondo Beach CA 90278 310-371-7546
Web: www.southbaygalleria.com

South Coast Plaza 3333 Bristol St. Costa Mesa CA 92626 800-782-8888
TF: 800-782-8888 ■ *Web:* www.southcoastplaza.com

South County Ctr 18 S County Centerway. Saint Louis MO 63129 314-892-8954
Web: www.shopsouthcountycenter.com

South Mall 3300 Lehigh St. Allentown PA 18103 610-791-0606
Web: www.shopsouthmall.com

South Park Mall 2310 SW Military Dr. San Antonio TX 78224 210-921-0534 921-0628
Web: www.visitsouthpark.com

South Plains Mall 6002 Slide Rd. Lubbock TX 79414 806-792-4653
Web: www.southplainsmall.com

South Shore Plaza 250 Granite St. Braintree MA 02184 781-843-8200 843-4708
TF: 877-746-6642 ■ *Web:* www.simon.com

Southcenter Mall 2800 Southcenter Mall. Seattle WA 98188 206-246-7400
Web: www.westfield.com

Southdale Ctr 10 Southdale Ctr. Edina MN 55435 952-925-7874 925-7856
TF: 877-746-6642 ■ *Web:* simon.com/mall?id=1249

Southern Park Mall 7401 Market St. Youngstown OH 44512 330-758-4511
TF: 877-746-6642 ■ *Web:* www.simon.com

Southlake Mall 1000 Southlake Mall. Morrow GA 30260 770-961-1050 961-1113
Web: www.southlakemall.com

Southland Mall 1 Southland Mall Dr. Hayward CA 94545 510-782-3527
Web: www.southlandmall.com

Southland Mall 20505 S Dixie Hwy. Miami FL 33189 305-235-8880 235-7956
Web: www.mysouthlandmall.com

SouthPark Mall 4400 Sharon Rd. Charlotte NC 28211 704-364-4411 364-4913
TF: 888-726-5930 ■ *Web:* www.simon.com

SouthPointe Pavilions 2910 Pine Lake Rd Ste Q. Lincoln NE 68516 402-421-2114 421-2191
TF: 800-733-2767 ■ *Web:* www.southpointeshopping.com

Southport Antique Mall
2028 E Southport Rd. Indianapolis IN 46227 317-786-8246
Web: www.southportantiquemall.net

Southridge Mall 5300 S 76th St. Greendale WI 53129 414-421-1102 421-0492
Web: www.simon.com

Southridge Mall 1111 E Army Post Rd. Des Moines IA 50315 515-287-3881
Web: www.shopsouthridgemall.com

Southwest Ctr Mall 3662 W Camp Wisdom Rd. Dallas TX 75237 972-296-1491 861-5798
Web: swcmall.com

Southwest Plaza Mall
8501 W Bowles Ave Ste 2A-483. Littleton CO 80123 303-973-5300
Web: www.southwestplaza.com

Spokane Valley Mall 14700 E Indiana Ave. Spokane WA 99216 509-926-3700
Web: www.spokanevalleymall.com

Spring Hill Mall 1072 Spring Hill Mall. West Dundee IL 60118 847-428-2200
Web: www.springhillmall.com

Phone Fax

Square One Mall 1201 Broadway . . . Saugus MA 01906 781-233-8787 231-9787
TF: 877-746-6642 ■ *Web:* simon.com/mall?id=340

Stanford Shopping Ctr
660 Stanford Shopping Ctr. . . . Palo Alto CA 94304 650-617-8200
Web: www.simon.com

Staten Island Mall 2655 Richmond Ave. . . . Staten Island NY 10314 718-761-6800 494-6766
Web: www.statenislandmall.com/en.html

Stonebriar Centre 2601 Preston Rd . . . Frisco TX 75034 972-668-6255
Web: www.shopstonebriar.com

Stoneridge Shopping Ctr 1 Stoneridge Mall . . . Pleasanton CA 94588 925-463-2778 463-1467
TF: 877-746-6642 ■ *Web:* simon.com/mall/stoneridge-shopping-center

Stonestown Galleria 3251 20th Ave. . . . San Francisco CA 94132 415-564-8848
TF: 800-326-3264 ■ *Web:* www.stonestowngalleria.com

Stratford Square Mall 152 Stratford Sq. . . . Bloomingdale IL 60108 630-539-1000
Web: stratfordmall.com

Summit Sierra 13925 S Virginia St Ste 212. . . . Reno NV 89511 775-853-7800
Web: www.thesummitonline.com

Sunrise Mall 6041 Sunrise Mall . . . Citrus Heights CA 95610 916-961-7150
Web: www.sunrisemallonline.com

Sunvalley Mall 1 Sunvalley Mall. . . . Concord CA 94520 925-825-0400
Web: www.shopsunvalley.com

SuperMall of the Great Northwest
1101 SuperMall Way . . . Auburn WA 98001 253-833-9500 833-9006
Web: www.outletcollectionseattle.com

Tacoma Mall 4502 S Steele St Ste 1177 . . . Tacoma WA 98409 253-475-4565 472-3413
TF: 877-746-6642 ■ *Web:* www.simon.com/mall/?id=238

Tanger Outlet Ctr San Marcos
4015 S IH-35 Ste 319. . . . San Marcos TX 78666 512-396-7446 396-7449
TF: 800-408-8424 ■ *Web:* www.tangeroutlet.com

Timeless Treasures Antique Mall
433 E Us Hwy 69 . . . Kansas City MO 64119 816-455-9400

Town Ctr at Boca Raton
225 W Washington St Ste 100 . . . Indianapolis IN 46204 561-368-6000 338-0891
Web: www.simon.com

Town Ctr at Cobb
400 Ernest Barrett Pkwy NW Ste 100 . . . Kennesaw GA 30144 770-424-9486 424-7917
Web: www.simon.com

Town East Mall 2063 Town E Mall . . . Mesquite TX 75150 972-270-4431
Web: www.towneastmall.com

Tracy Outlets 1005 E Pescadero Ave. . . . Tracy CA 95304 209-833-1895
Web: www.mytracyoutlets.com

Tri-County Mall 11700 Princeton Pike . . . Cincinnati OH 45246 513-671-0120 671-2931
TF: 866-905-4675 ■ *Web:* tricountymall.com

Tucson Mall 4500 N Oracle Rd . . . Tucson AZ 85705 520-293-7330
Web: www.tucsonmall.com

Tulsa Promenade 4107 S Yale Ave. . . . Tulsa OK 74135 918-627-9282 663-9385
Web: www.tulsapromenade.com

Tyrone Square Mall 6901 Tyrone Sq . . . Saint Petersburg FL 33710 727-345-0126 345-5699
Web: www.simon.com/mall/?id=135

Tysons Corner Ctr 1961 Chain Bridge Rd Ste 305 . . . McLean VA 22102 703-847-7300
TF: 877-247-5223 ■ *Web:* tysonscornercenter.com

Tysons Galleria 2001 International Dr. . . . Mclean VA 22102 703-827-7730
Web: www.tysonsgalleria.com

University Mall 2200 E Fowler Ave . . . Tampa FL 33612 813-971-3465 971-0923
Web: www.universitymalltampa.com

University Park Mall 6501 N Grape Rd . . . Mishawaka IN 46545 574-277-2223 272-5924
TF: 877-746-6642 ■ *Web:* www.simon.com

University Village
2623 NE University Village St. . . . Seattle WA 98105 206-523-0622 525-3859
Web: www.uvillage.com

Valley Fair Mall
3601 South 2700 West. . . . West Valley City UT 84119 801-969-6211 969-6233
Web: www.shopvalleyfairmall.com

Valley Plaza Mall 2701 Ming Ave . . . Bakersfield CA 93304 661-832-2436
Web: www.valleyplazamall.com

Valley River Center 293 Valley River Ctr . . . Eugene OR 97401 541-683-5513 343-2478
Web: www.valleyrivercenter.com

Valley View Ctr Mall 13331 Preston Rd. . . . Dallas TX 75240 972-661-2939 239-1344
Web: www.shopvalleyviewcenter.com

Valley View Mall 4802 Vly View Blvd. . . . Roanoke VA 24012 540-563-4440
Web: www.valleyviewmall.com

Vaughan Mills 1 Bass Pro Mills Dr . . . Vaughan ON L4K5W4 905-879-2110 879-1888
Web: www.vaughanmills.com

Viejas Outlet Ctr 5005 Willows . . . Alpine CA 91901 619-659-2070
TF: 877-303-2695 ■ *Web:* viejas.com

Viewmont Mall 100 Viewmont Mall . . . Scranton PA 18508 570-346-9165
Web: www.shopviewmontmall.com

Village on Venetian Bay
4200 Gulf Shore Blvd N . . . Naples FL 34103 239-261-6100
Web: www.venetianvillage.com

Vinings Jubilee
4300 Paces Ferry Rd Se Ste 245. . . . Atlanta GA 30339 770-438-8080 438-8181
Web: www.viningsjubilee.com

Vintage Faire Mall 3401 Dale Rd Ste 483 . . . Modesto CA 95356 209-527-3401
Web: www.shopvintagefairemall.com

Virginia Ctr Commons
10101 Brook Rd Ste 765. . . . Glen Allen VA 23059 317-636-1600
Web: www.simon.com

Vista Ridge Mall 2401 S Stemmons Fwy . . . Lewisville TX 75067 972-315-3641
Web: www.vistaridgemall.com

Voorhees Town Ctr 2120 Voorhees Town Ctr. . . . Voorhees NJ 08043 856-772-1950
Web: www.voorheestowncenter.com

Walden Galleria 1 Walden Galleria . . . Buffalo NY 14225 716-681-7600
Web: waldengalleria.com

Warwick Mall 400 Bald Hill Rd Ste 100 . . . Warwick RI 02886 401-739-7500 732-6052
Web: www.warwickmall.com

Washington Square Mall
10202 E Washington St . . . Indianapolis IN 46229 317-899-4568
Web: www.simon.com

Washington Square Shopping Ctr
9585 SW Washington Sq Rd . . . Portland OR 97223 503-639-8860
Web: www.shopwashingtonsquare.com

Phone Fax

West County Ctr 80 W County Ctr . . . Des Peres MO 63131 314-288-2020
Web: www.shopwestcountycenter.com

West Oaks Mall 2600 Hwy 6 S . . . Houston TX 77082 281-531-1332 531-1579
Web: www.shopwestoaksmall.com

West Oaks Mall 9401 W Colonial Dr Ste 728 . . . Ocoee FL 34761 407-294-6033
Web: www.westoaksmall.com

West Point Market 1711 W Market St . . . Akron OH 44313 330-864-2151 869-8666
TF: 800-838-2156 ■ *Web:* www.westpointmarket.com

West Ridge Mall 1801 SW Wanamaker Rd. . . . Topeka KS 66604 785-272-5119
Web: www.simon.com

West Shore Plaza 250 W Shore Blvd . . . Tampa FL 33609 813-286-0790 286-1250
Web: www.westshoreplaza.com

West Town Mall 7600 Kingston Pk. . . . Knoxville TN 37919 865-693-0292 531-0503
Web: www.simon.com

West Towne Mall 66 W Towne Mall. . . . Madison WI 53719 608-833-6330
Web: www.shopwesttowne-mall.com

Westchester, The 125 Westchester Ave. . . . White Plains NY 10601 914-421-1333 421-1475
TF: 877-746-6642 ■ *Web:* www.simon.com

Westfarms Mall 1500 New Britian Ave . . . West Hartford CT 06110 860-561-3420
Web: www.shopwestfarms.com

Westfield Broward Mall
8000 W Broward Blvd. . . . Plantation FL 33388 954-473-8100
Web: www.westfield.com

Westfield Century City
10250 Santa Monica Blvd. . . . West Los Angeles CA 90067 310-553-5300
Web: www.westfield.com/centurycity

Westfield Citrus Park 8021 Citrus Pk Dr. . . . Tampa FL 33625 813-926-4644
Web: www.westfield.com

Westfield Countryside
27001 US 19 N Ste 1039 . . . Clearwater FL 33761 727-796-1079
Web: www.westfield.com/countryside

Westfield Downtown Plaza 660 J St. . . . Sacramento CA 95814 916-442-4000 442-3117

Westfield Fashion Square
14006 Riverside Dr. . . . Sherman Oaks CA 91423 818-783-0550
Web: www.westfield.com

Westfield Fox Hills 6000 Sepulveda Blvd. . . . Culver City CA 90230 310-390-5073
Web: www.westfield.com/foxhills

Westfield Hawthorn R 122 Hawthorn Ctr. . . . Vernon Hills IL 60061 847-362-2600
Web: www.westfield.com

Westfield Mission Valley
1640 Camino del Rio N . . . San Diego CA 92108 619-296-6375
Web: www.westfield.com

Westfield Montgomery 7101 Democracy Blvd . . . Bethesda MD 20817 301-469-6000
Web: www.westfield.com/montgomery

Westfield San Francisco Centre
865 Market St PO Box K. . . . San Francisco CA 94103 415-495-5656
Web: www.westfield.com

Westfield Santa Anita
400 S Baldwin Ave Ste 231. . . . Arcadia CA 91007 626-445-6255
Web: www.westfield.com/santaanita

Westfield Sarasota Square 8201 S Tamiami Tr . . . Sarasota FL 34238 941-922-9609
Web: www.westfield.com

Westfield Shoppingtown Annapolis
2002 Annapolis Mall . . . Annapolis MD 21401 410-266-5432
Web: www.westfield.com

Westfield Shoppingtown UTC
4545 La Jolla Village Dr . . . San Diego CA 92122 858-546-8858
Web: www.westfield.com

Westfield Southgate 3501 S Tamiami Trl . . . Sarasota FL 34239 941-955-0900
Web: www.westfield.com

Westfield Topanga
6600 Topanga Canyon Blvd . . . Canoga Park CA 91303 818-594-8740
Web: www.westfield.com

Westfield Trumbull Town Shopping Mall
5065 Main St . . . Trumbull CT 06611 203-372-4500
Web: www.westfield.com

Westfield Valley Fair
2855 Stevens Creek Blvd Ste 2178. . . . Santa Clara CA 95050 408-248-4451
Web: www.westfield.com

WestGate Mall 205 W Blackstock Rd . . . Spartanburg SC 29301 864-574-0264
Web: www.westgate-mall.com

Westlake Ctr 400 Pine St . . . Seattle WA 98101 206-467-1600 467-1603
Web: www.westlakecenter.com

Westland Shopping Ctr 35000 W Warren Rd. . . . Westland MI 48185 734-425-5001 425-9205
Web: www.westlandcenter.com

Westminster Mall 1025 Westminster Mall. . . . Westminster CA 92683 714-898-2558
Web: www.simon.com

Westmoreland Mall 5256 Rt 30 E . . . Greensburg PA 15601 724-836-5025
TF: 800-333-7310 ■ *Web:* www.westmorelandmall.com

White Marsh Mall 8200 Perry Hall Blvd. . . . Baltimore MD 21236 410-931-7100
Web: www.whitemarshmall.com

Willowbrook Mall 1400 Willowbrook Mall . . . Wayne NJ 07470 973-785-1655
Web: www.willowbrook-mall.com

Willowbrook Mall 2000 Willowbrook Mall . . . Houston TX 77070 281-890-8000
Web: www.shopwillowbrookmall.com

Wolfchase Galleria 2760 N Germantown Pkwy . . . Memphis TN 38133 901-381-2769
Web: www.simon.com

Woodbridge Center Mall
250 Woodbridge Ctr Dr . . . Woodbridge NJ 07095 732-636-4600
Web: www.woodbridgecenter.com

Woodburn Premium Outlets 1001 N Arney Rd . . . Woodburn OR 97071 503-981-1900
Web: www.premiumoutlets.com

Woodfield Mall 5 Woodfield Mall . . . Schaumburg IL 60173 847-330-1537 330-0204
Web: www.simon.com/mall/woodfield-mall

Woodland Hills Mall 7021 S Memorial Dr. . . . Tulsa OK 74133 918-250-1449 250-9084
Web: www.simon.com

Woodland Mall 3195 28th St SE. . . . Grand Rapids MI 49512 616-949-0012
Web: www.shopwoodlandmall.com

Yorktown Shopping Ctr 203 Yorktown Ctr. . . . Lombard IL 60148 630-629-7330 629-7334
Web: www.yorktowncenter.com

461 MALTING PRODUCTS

See Also Breweries p. 1876

				Phone	Fax
Briess Malting Co 625 S Irish Rd. Web: www.briess.com	Chilton	WI	53014	920-849-7711	849-4277
Great Western Malting Co 1701 NW Harborside Dr. Web: www.greatwesternmalting.com	Vancouver	WA	98660	360-693-3661	
LE Cooke Co 26333 Rd 140. Web: lecooke.com	Visalia	CA	93292	559-732-9146	732-3702
Premier Malt Products Inc 25760 Groesbeck Hwy Ste 103. TF Cust Svc: 800-521-1057 ■ Web: www.premiermalt.com	Warren	MI	48089	586-443-3355	
Schoenmann Produce Company Inc 6950 Neuhaus St. Web: www.schoenmannproduce.com	Houston	TX	77061	713-923-2728	923-5897
United Canadian Malt Ltd 843 Pk St S. Web: www.unitedcanadianmalt.ca	Peterborough	ON	K9J3V1	705-876-9110	876-9118

462 MANAGED CARE - BEHAVIORAL HEALTH

				Phone	Fax
Allen Group 50 Washington St Ste 503. Web: www.theallengroup.com	Norwalk	CT	06854	203-855-5777	
American Behavioral Benefits Managers 2204 Lakeshore Dr Ste 135. TF: 800-925-5327 ■ Web: www.americanbehavioral.com	Birmingham	AL	35209	205-871-7814	868-9600
Anthem Inc 120 Monument Cir. TF: 800-999-7222 ■ Web: www.antheminc.com	Indianapolis	IN	46204	317-488-6000	
APC Hegeman 8-12 Dietz St Ste 201. Web: www.eap-counseling.com	Oneonta	NY	13820	607-432-9039	
APS Healthcare Inc 8403 Colesville Rd. TF: 800-305-3720 ■ Web: www.apshealthcare.com	Silver Spring	MD	20910	800-305-3720	
APS Healthcare Inc 44 S Broadway Ste 1200. TF: 800-305-3720 ■ Web: www.apshealthcare.com	White Plains	NY	10601	800-305-3720	
Associated Behavioral Health Care Inc 4700 42nd Ave SW Ste 470. TF: 800-858-6702 ■ Web: www.abhc.com	Seattle	WA	98116	206-935-1282	
Bensinger DuPont & Assoc (BDA) 134 N LaSalle St Ste 2200. TF: 800-227-8620 ■ Web: www.bensingerdupont.com	Chicago	IL	60602	312-726-8620	726-1061
CIGNA Behavioral Health Inc 11095 Viking Dr Ste 350. TF: 800-753-0540 ■ Web: www.cignabehavioral.com	Eden Prairie	MN	55344	703-907-7730	
Comprehensive EAP 4 Mt Royal Ave. TF: 800-344-1011 ■ Web: www.compeap.com	Marlborough	MA	01752	800-344-1011	
ComPsych Corp 455 N City Front Plaza Dr NBC Tower 13th Fl. TF: 800-851-1714 ■ Web: www.compsych.com	Chicago	IL	60611	312-595-4000	595-4219
COPE Inc 1120 G St NW Ste 550. TF: 800-247-3054 ■ Web: www.cope-inc.com	Washington	DC	20005	202-628-5100	628-5111
CorpCare Assoc Inc 7000 Peachtree Dunwoody Rd Bldg 4 Ste 300. *Fax Area Code: 770 ■ TF: 800-728-9444 ■ Web: www.corpcareeap.com	Atlanta	GA	30328	800-728-9444	396-9522*
Corporate Care Works 8649 Baypine Rd Ste 101. Web: members.healthadvocate.com	Jacksonville	FL	32256	904-296-9436	296-1511
EAP Consultants Inc 3901 Roswell Rd Ste 340. TF: 800-869-0276 ■ Web: www.eapconsultants.com	Marietta	GA	30062	770-951-9970	953-3174
EAP Systems 500 W Cummings Pk. TF: 800-535-4841 ■ Web: www.theeap.com	Woburn	MA	01801	781-935-8850	
FEI Behavioral Health 11700 W Lk Pk Dr. TF: 800-782-1948 ■ Web: www.feinet.com	Milwaukee	WI	53224	414-359-1055	359-1973
Frontier Health 1167 Spratlin Pk Dr PO Box 9054. Web: www.frontierhealth.org	Gray	TN	37615	423-467-3600	467-3710
Gilsbar Inc PO Box 998. TF: 800-445-7227 ■ Web: www.gilsbar.com	Covington	LA	70434	985-892-3520	898-1500
Holman Group 9451 Corbin Ave. TF: 800-321-2843 ■ Web: www.holmangroup.com	Northridge	CA	91324	818-704-1444	704-9339
Hurst Place 209 Limeridge Rd E. *Fax Area Code: 905 ■ TF: 888-521-8300 ■ Web: www.mohawkssi.com	Hamilton	ON	L9A2S6	289-426-5302	521-8166*
Interface EAP Inc (IEAP) 10370 Richmond Ave Ste 1100 PO Box 421879. TF: 800-324-4327 ■ Web: www.ieap.com	Houston	TX	77042	713-781-3364	784-0425
Magellan Health Services Inc 55 Nod Rd. NASDAQ: MGLN ■ TF: 800-424-4399 ■ Web: www.magellanhealth.com	Avon	CT	06001	860-507-1900	507-1990
Managed Health Network Inc 1600 Los Gamos Dr Ste 300. TF: 800-327-2133 ■ Web: www.mhn.com	San Rafael	CA	94903	800-327-2133	
MENTOR Network, The 313 Congress St 5th Fl. TF: 800-388-5150 ■ Web: www.thementornetwork.com	Boston	MA	02210	617-790-4800	790-4848
MHNet Behavioral Health 9606 N MoPac Exwy Ste 600. TF: 888-646-6889 ■ Web: www.mhnet.com	Austin	TX	78759	888-646-6889	
National Employee Assistance Services Inc N 17 W 24100 Riverwood Dr Ste 300. TF: 800-634-6433 ■ Web: www.empathia.com	Waukesha	WI	53188	262-574-2500	
New Directions Behavioral Health LLC PO Box 6729. *Fax Area Code: 913 ■ TF: 800-624-5544 ■ Web: www.ndbh.com	Leawood	KS	66206	800-624-5544	982-8401*
Perspectives Ltd 20 N Clark St Ste 2650. TF: 800-866-7556 ■ Web: www.perspectivesltd.com	Chicago	IL	60602	312-558-5318	558-1570
Preferred Mental Health Management Inc 401 E Douglas Ave Ste 300. Web: www.pmhm.com	Wichita	KS	67202	316-262-0444	
Providence Service Corp 64 E Broadway. NASDAQ: PRSC ■ TF: 800-747-6950 ■ Web: www.prscholdings.com	Tucson	AZ	85701	520-748-7108	747-9787
Stuecker & Assoc Inc 1930 Bishop Ln Watterson Towers Ste 1001. TF: 800-799-9327 ■ Web: www.stueckerandassoc.com	Louisville	KY	40218	502-452-9227	
United Behavioral Health Inc 425 Market St 27th Fl. TF: 800-888-2998 ■ Web: optum.com	San Francisco	CA	94105	415-547-5000	547-5800
ValueOptions Inc 12369 Sunrise Vly Dr Ste C. TF: 877-334-0077 ■ Web: www.valueoptions.com	Reston	VA	20191	703-390-6800	

463 MANAGEMENT SERVICES

See Also Association Management Companies p. 1748; Educational Institution Operators & Managers p. 2204; Facilities Management Services p. 2277; Hotels & Hotel Companies p. 2536; Incentive Program Management Services p. 2556; Investment Advice & Management p. 2597; Pharmacy Benefits Management Services p. 2938

				Phone	Fax
2 Places At 1 Time Inc 270 Peachtree St 20th Fl. *Fax Area Code: 404 ■ TF: 877-275-2237 ■ Web: www.2placesat1time.com	Atlanta	GA	30303	877-275-2237	800-7888*
2030 Inc 607 Cerrillos Rd. Web: www.architecture2030.org	Santa Fe	NM	87505	505-988-5309	
284 Partners LLC 339 E Liberty Ste 340. Web: www.284partners.com	Ann Arbor	MI	48104	734-369-8723	
360 Technologies Inc 15401 Debba Dr. TF: 888-883-0360 ■ Web: www.360tech.com	Austin	TX	78734	512-266-7360	
3H Group Inc 505 Riverfront Parkway. Web: www.3hgrouphotels.com	Chattanooga	TN	37402	423-499-0497	
3P Partners 5B Park Ln. Web: www.3ppartnersdls.com	Hilton Head Island	SC	29928	843-842-2585	
A Plus Arts Academy 270 S Napoleon Ave. Web: aplusarts.com	Columbus	OH	43213	614-338-0767	
A2F-Consulting LLC 4915 St Elmo Ave Ste 205. Web: www.a2f-c.com	Bethesda	MD	20814	301-907-9400	
AA Consulting Inc 208 5th Ave N.W. Web: www.aa-consulting-inc.com	Mandan	ND	58554	701-663-1181	
AArete LLC One S Dearborn Ste 2100. Web: www.aarete.com	Chicago	IL	60603	312-212-4282	
ABELSoft Inc 3310 S Service Rd. TF: 800-267-2235 ■ Web: www.abelsoft.com	Burlington	ON	L7N3M6	800-267-2235	
Abidance Consulting Corp 5680 Hwy 6 Ste 311. Web: www.abidanceconsulting.com	Missouri City	TX	77459	713-253-8820	
Abrams & Jossel Consulting Inc 39 S Lasalle St Ste 1410. Web: www.ajworkout.com	Chicago	IL	60603	312-629-8585	
Absolute Technologies Inc 4890 E La Palma Ave. Web: www.absolutetechnologies.com	Anaheim	CA	92807	714-692-6570	
ACA Associates Inc 545 Fifth Ave Ste 1009. Web: www.aca-assoc.com	New York	NY	10017	212-808-4424	
Acc Technical Services Inc 106 Dwight Park Cir. TF: 855-484-4500 ■ Web: www.acctek.com	Syracuse	NY	13209	315-484-4500	
Accent Computer Solutions Inc 8438 Red Oak St. Web: www.accentonit.com	Rancho Cucamonga	CA	91730	909-204-4801	
Accompass 1052 Yonge St. TF: 866-969-8588 ■ Web: www.accompass.com	Toronto	ON	M4W2L1	416-969-8588	
Accu-Read Inc PO Box 18277. Web: accureadinc.com	Spokane	WA	99228	509-670-5894	
Ace Products Management G 12801 W Silver Spring Rd. TF: 800-294-9007 ■ Web: www.brandedproducts.com	Butler	WI	53007	262-754-1289	
Acentech Inc 33 Moulton St. Web: www.acentech.com	Cambridge	MA	02138	617-499-8000	
ACES 4140 W 99th St. Web: www.acespower.com	Carmel	IN	46032	317-344-7000	
Acoustic Sounds Inc 1500 S Ninth St. Web: store.acousticsounds.com	Salina	KS	67401	785-825-8609	
Act Too Consulting Inc 917 W Inyokern Rd Ste C. Web: www.acttooconsulting.com	Ridgecrest	CA	93555	760-301-5566	
Act2 Retirement Consulting LLC 5120 Watchwood Path. TF: 866-992-9256 ■ Web: www.act2retirement.com	Columbia	MD	21044	866-992-9256	
Action Pact Inc 7709 W Lisbon Ave. Web: www.actionpact.com	Milwaukee	WI	53222	414-258-3649	
Actuarial Management Resources Inc 4964 University Pkwy. Web: www.actmanre.com	Winston-Salem	NC	27106	336-759-0008	
Adams-Gabbert & Associates LLC 7300 W 110th St Ste 700. Web: www.adamsgabbert.com	Overland Park	KS	66210	913-735-4390	
Addison Whitney Inc 11006 Rushmore Dr Ste 350. Web: addisonwhitney.com	Charlotte	NC	28277	704-347-5700	
Addvantage Group Llc, The 126 E Wing St Ste 132. Web: www.theaddvantagegroup.com	Arlington Heights	IL	60004	847-392-9576	
Adelaide Environmental Health Associates 1511 Route 22. Web: adelaidellc.com	Brewster	NY	10509	845-278-7710	
ADI Technologies Inc 1487 Chain Bridge Rd Ste 204. Web: www.aditechnologies.com	Mclean	VA	22101	703-734-9626	
Adjoined Consulting LLC 5301 Blue Lagoon Dr Ste 700. Web: www.adjoined.com	Miami	FL	33126	305-269-8588	
Adsoft Direct Inc 740 Tunbridge Rd. Web: www.adsoftdirect.com	Danville	CA	94526	925-407-3101	

Company	City	State	Zip	Phone	Fax
Advanced Generation Telecom Group Inc 752 Walker Rd Ste H. *Web:* www.adgentelecom.com	Great Falls	VA	22066	703-757-6757	
Advantech Manufacturing Inc 2450 S Commerce Dr. *Web:* www.advantechmfg.com	New Berlin	WI	53151	262-786-1600	
Advisory Council Inc, The 1 Stiles Rd Ste 105 *Web:* www.tacadvisory.com	Salem	NH	03079	781-791-9582	
AED Inc 6525 Belcrest Rd Ste 526 *Web:* www.aedworld.com	Hyattsville	MD	20782	301-683-2112	
AEGIS Systems Engineering and Technology Partners Corp 1000 W Braddock Rd *Web:* www.asetpartners.com	Alexandria	VA	22302	571-297-1916	
Aeromedevac Inc 681 Kenney St *Web:* www.aeromedevac.com	El Cajon	CA	92020	619-284-7910	
AG Communications LLC 909 Church Hill Rd *Web:* www.agcomm.com	Fairfield	CT	06825	203-373-0599	
AgreeYa Solutions Inc 605 Coolidge Dr *Web:* www.agreeya.com	Folsom	CA	95630	916-294-0075	
Ai Control Systems 90 Water St *Web:* aicontrols.com	Muhlenberg	PA	19605	610-921-9670	
AIB International Inc 1213 Bakers Way PO Box 3999 *Web:* www.aibonline.org	Manhattan	KS	66505	785-537-4750	
AirTrav Inc 10 Delisle Ave 14th Fl Ste 1402 *Web:* www.airtrav.ca	Toronto	ON	M4V3C6	289-346-0071	
Akona Consulting 137 Park Ln Ste 200 *Web:* www.akonasystems.com	Kirkland	WA	98033	425-576-0725	
Aks Infotech Inc 8 declan ct *Web:* aksinfotech.net	Monmouth Junction	NJ	08852	609-301-4607	
Alan B Lancz & Assoc Inc 2400 N Reynolds Rd *Web:* www.ablonline.com	Toledo	OH	43615	419-536-5200	536-5401
Alaris Group Inc 4108 N 79th Ave W *Web:* www.alarisgroup.com	Duluth	MN	55810	218-730-9950	
Alcazar Networks Inc 419 State Ave Ste 3 *TF:* 800-349-6192 ■ *Web:* www.alcazarnetworks.com	Emmaus	PA	18049	484-664-2800	
Alderney Advisors LLC 1 Towne Sq Ste 1870 *Web:* www.alderneyadvisors.com	Southfield	MI	48076	248-504-0690	
Aldo Ventures Inc 7370 Viewpoint Rd *Web:* www.aldo.com	Aptos	CA	95003	831-662-2536	
Allen Evans Klein International 305 Madison Ave Ste 1650 *Web:* www.allenevans.com	New York	NY	10165	212-983-9300	
Allergy Partners Pa 14 McDowell St *Web:* www.allergypartners.com	Asheville	NC	28801	828-277-1300	
Alliance Health Networks 9 Exchange Pl Ste 200 *Web:* www.alliancehealth.com	Salt Lake City	UT	84111	801-355-6002	
Alliance of Professionals & Consultants Inc 8200 Brownleigh Dr *Web:* www.apc-services.com	Raleigh	NC	27617	919-510-9696	510-9668
Alliant Consulting Inc 555 Cajon St Ste A *Web:* www.alliantconsulting.net	Redlands	CA	92373	909-792-8812	
AllMed Healthcare Management Inc 621 SW Alder St Ste 740 *TF:* 888-289-6015 ■ *Web:* allmedmd.com	Portland	OR	97205	503-274-9916	
AllTranstek LLC 1101 W 31st St Ste 200 *Web:* www.alltranstek.com	Downers Grove	IL	60515	630-325-9977	
Allvend Management Corp 800 W Airport Fwy 705 *Web:* www.allvend.com	Irving	TX	75062	972-255-8363	
Altman Vilandrie & Co 53 State St 37th Fl *Web:* www.altvil.com	Boston	MA	02109	617-753-7200	
Altus Consulting Corp 38699 Old Wheatland Rd *TF:* 800-300-4505 ■ *Web:* www.altuscc.com	Waterford	VA	20197	703-929-4000	
Amarillo Economic Development Corp 801 S Fillmore Ste 205 *TF:* 800-333-7892 ■ *Web:* www.amarilloedc.com	Amarillo	TX	79101	806-379-6411	
Ambler Growth Strategy Conslnt 3432 Reading Ave. *Web:* ambler.com	Hammonton	NJ	08037	609-567-9669	
Amc Management Group Inc 34 Abby Rd *Web:* www.amcinc.biz	Farmingdale	NJ	07727	732-938-5457	
AmerAssist Inc 8415 Pulsar Pl *TF:* 877-294-9707 ■ *Web:* www.amerassist.com	Columbus	OH	43240	877-294-9707	
American Dental Partners Inc 401 Edgewater Pl Ste 430 *NASDAQ: ADPI* ■ *TF:* 800-838-6563 ■ *Web:* www.amdpi.com	Wakefield	MA	01880	781-213-6500	224-4216
American Utility Management Inc 2211 S York Rd Ste 320 *TF:* 866-520-1245 ■ *Web:* www.aum-inc.com	Oak Brook	IL	60523	866-520-1245	
AMFM Inc 240 Capitol St Ste 500 *TF:* 800-348-1623 ■ *Web:* www.amfmwv.com	Charleston	WV	25301	304-344-1623	
AMI Environmental 8802 S 135Th St Ste 100 *Web:* www.amienvironmental.com	Omaha	NE	68138	402-397-5001	
amidus LLC Research and Technology Park 1450 S Rolling Rd *Web:* amidus.com	Baltimore	MD	21227	410-926-0520	
Ampls 1164 N Kraemer Pl *Web:* ampls.com	Anaheim	CA	92806	714-630-1313	
AMTEK Information Service Inc 4001 Sherwood *Web:* www.amtekusa.com	Houston	TX	77092	713-956-0100	
AMTIS Inc 12124 High Tech Ave Ste 150 *Web:* www.amtisinc.com	Orlando	FL	32817	407-513-9490	
AMZ Financial Insurance Services LLC 4944 Windplay Dr Ste 115 *Web:* www.amzwebcenter.com	El Dorado Hills	CA	95762	916-939-3765	
Andra Partners LLC 2550 Meridian Blvd Ste 200 *Web:* www.andrapartners.com	Franklin	TN	37067	615-567-8090	
Angie Herbers Inc 1228 Westloop Pl Ste 327	Manhattan	KS	66502	785-320-2349	
Ann Arbor Distribution 1942 Mcgregor Rd *Web:* annarbordist.com	Ypsilanti	MI	48198	734-484-0100	
Annex Wealth Management LLC 12700 W Bluemound Rd Ste 200 *Web:* www.advisorsannex.com	Elm Grove	WI	53122	262-786-6363	
Anvasion Inc 53 Taylor Rd *Web:* anvasion.com	Bethel	CT	06801	203-205-0522	
Appix Inc 7915 Jones Branch Dr *Web:* www.appix.com	Mclean	VA	22102	703-748-3250	
Aptimise Composites LLC 8301 Clinton Park Dr *Web:* aptimise.com	Fort Wayne	IN	46825	260-408-0107	
Apto Solutions Inc 1910 MacArthur Blvd *Web:* www.aptosolutions.com	Atlanta	GA	30318	404-605-0992	
Aqs Management Systems Inc 2167 Northdale Blvd NW *Web:* www.aqsperformance.com	Coon Rapids	MN	55433	651-633-7902	
Archway Marketing Services Inc 19850 S Diamond Lake Rd *TF:* 866-779-9855 ■ *Web:* www.archway.com	Rogers	MN	55374	763-428-3300	488-6801
Arcweb Technologies LLC 234 Market St 5th Fl *TF:* 800-846-7980 ■ *Web:* arcweb.co	Philadelphia	PA	19106	800-846-7980	
ARD Inc 159 Bank St Ste 300	Burlington	VT	05401	802-658-5050	
Area Circulation Inc 5656 Shell Rd	Virginia Beach	VA	23455	757-499-8330	
Ares Management LLC 2000 Ave of the Stars 12th Fl *Web:* www.aresmgmt.com	Los Angeles	CA	90067	310-201-4100	201-4170
Argo Inc 737 N Michigan Ave Ste 2000 *Web:* www.argoconsulting.com	Chicago	IL	60611	312-988-9220	
ARK Solutions Inc 1939 Roland Clarks Pl Ste 300 *Web:* www.arksolutionsinc.com	Reston	VA	20191	703-657-0670	
ARS Technologies Inc 98 N Ward St *Web:* www.arstechnologies.com	New Brunswick	NJ	08901	732-296-6620	
Arthur Agency Inc 104 E Jackson St	Carbondale	IL	62901	618-351-1599	
ASAP Ventures LLC 132 King St Ste 200 *Web:* www.asapventures.com	Alexandria	VA	22314	703-837-5150	
Ascend Analytics LLC 1877 Broadway Ste 706 *Web:* www.ascendanalytics.com	Boulder	CO	80302	303-415-1400	
Ascendiant Capital Group LLC 18881 Von Karman Ave 16th Fl *Web:* www.ascendiant.com	Irvine	CA	92612	949-259-4900	
Ascent LLC 2350 Ball Dr *Web:* www.ascent-corp.com	St. Louis	MO	63146	314-989-1011	
Ashwood Management Partners LLC 435 Occidental Ave *Web:* www.ashwoodmp.com	San Mateo	CA	94402	650-867-0076	
ASR International Corp 580 Old Willets Path *Web:* www.asrintl.com	Hauppauge	NY	11788	631-231-1086	
Assess-IT Inc 273 Pine Wood Ct *Web:* www.assess-it.com	Marietta	GA	30068	510-717-9655	
Asset Communications Inc 1764 Prospector Ave *Web:* assetcommunications.com	Park City	UT	84060	435-645-9108	
Assurance Investment Management LLC 1920 Georgetown Rd *Web:* www.assureim.com	Hudson	OH	44236	330-650-1750	
Astro Studios Inc 348 Sixth St *Web:* www.astrostudios.com	San Francisco	CA	94103	415-487-6787	
ATCO Properties & Management Inc 555 Fifth Ave 16th Fl *Web:* www.atco555.com	New York	NY	10017	212-687-5154	682-7599
Ath Power Consulting Corp 9 Bartlet St *Web:* www.athpower.com	Andover	MA	01810	978-474-6464	
Atrilogy Solutions Group Inc 1 Jenner Ste 240 *Web:* www.atrilogy.com	Irvine	CA	92618	949-777-4700	777-4777
Audit Group Inc, The 16141 Swingley Ridge Rd Ste 310 *Web:* theauditgroup.com	Chesterfield	MO	63017	636-536-6333	
Aurora Systems Consulting Inc 2510 W 237th St Ste 202 *Web:* www.auroraent.com	Torrance	CA	90505	310-530-8260	
Aurora Worldwide Development Corp 215 Martin Luther King Jr Blvd Ste 32 *Web:* www.aurorawdc.com	Madison	WI	53701	608-268-3470	
Authenticity Consulting Inc 4008 Lk Dr Ave N *Web:* www.authenticityconsulting.com	Minneapolis	MN	55422	763-971-8890	
Author Services Inc 7051 Hollywood Blvd *Web:* authorservicesinc.com	Hollywood	CA	90028	323-466-3310	
Auto Profit Masters 250 E Dry Creek Rd *TF:* 866-826-7911 ■ *Web:* autoprofitmasters.com	Littleton	CO	80122	303-795-5838	
Autometric Inc 1320 Central Park Blvd Ste 300 *Web:* active.boeing.com	Fredericksburg	VA	22401	540-785-1028	
Avascent Group, The 1615 L St NW Ste 1200 *Web:* www.avascent.com	Washington	DC	20036	202-452-6990	
Avatar Management Services Inc 8157 Bavaria Dr E *TF:* 800-728-2827 ■ *Web:* www.avatarms.com	Macedonia	OH	44056	330-963-3900	
Aviation Management Systems Inc P.O. Box 899 *Web:* amsinc.aero	Portsmouth	NH	03802	603-431-3362	
Avrick Direct Inc PO Box 1449 *Web:* www.avrickdirect.com	Santa Barbara	CA	93103	805-683-6551	
AwaySys Inc 207 Los Angeles Ave # 105 *Web:* www.awaysys.com	Moorpark	CA	93021	805-242-2007	
AWC Inc 6655 Exchequer Dr *Web:* www.awc-inc.com	Baton Rouge	LA	70809	225-752-1100	751-9029
aWhere Inc 4891 Independence St Ste 275 *Web:* www.awhere.com	Wheat Ridge	CO	80033	303-279-9293	
Axia Strategies Inc 8688 Eagle Creek Cir *Web:* www.axiastrategies.com	Savage	MN	55378	952-945-3535	

Phone | Fax

B3 Solutions LLC
1225 W Beaver St Ste 108 ... Jacksonville FL 32204 904-695-4241
Web: b3solutions.com

Baker Foodservice Design Inc
2220 E Paris Ave Se ... Grand Rapids MI 49546 616-942-4011
Web: www.bakergroup.com

Baker Krizner Financial Planning
2230 N Limestone St ... Springfield OH 45503 937-390-8750
TF: 888-390-8753 ■ *Web:* www.bakerkrizner.com

Bamboo Worldwide Inc 30 N Racine Ste 300 ... Chicago IL 60607 773-227-4848
Web: www.bambooworldwide.com

Bankruptcy Management Solutions Inc
5 Peters Canyon Rd Ste 200 ... Irvine CA 92606 800-634-7734
TF: 800-634-7734 ■ *Web:* www.bmsadvantage.com

Banyan Water Inc 11002-B Metric Blvd ... Austin TX 78758 800-276-1507
TF: 800-276-1507 ■ *Web:* www.banyanwater.com

Barada Associates Inc 130 E Second St ... Rushville IN 46173 765-932-5917
Web: baradainc.com

Barnsider Management Corp
15 A Newbury St Rte 1 ... Danvers MA 01923 978-777-3885
Web: www.barnsiderrestaurants.com

Bartell & Bartell Ltd
432 Rolling Rdg Dr ... State College PA 16801 814-861-6606
Web: bartellbartell.com

Bates Creative Group Llc 1119 E W Hwy ... Silver Spring MD 20910 301-495-8844
Web: www.batescreativegroup.com

Bates White LLC 1300 Eye St N W Ste 600 ... Washington DC 20005 202-408-6110
Web: www.bateswhite.com

BC Johnson Associates LLC
3702 Old Chocolate Bayou Rd ... Manvel TX 77578 281-489-4894
Web: www.bcjohnson.com

Bcn Transportation Services
3650 W Liberty Rd ... Ann Arbor MI 48103 734-994-4100
TF: 800-891-9911 ■ *Web:* www.bcnservices.com

BCT Partners LLC 105 Lock St ... Newark NJ 07103 973-622-0900
Web: www.bctpartners.com

Beacon Partnerships Inc 3303 Saddlestone Ct ... Oakton VA 22124 571-248-1851
Web: www.beaconpartnerships.com

Beaird Group, The
236 S Washington St Ste 208 ... Naperville IL 60540 630-637-0430
Web: www.beairdgroup.com

Bedford Management Co 196 Bedford Ave ... Brooklyn NY 11249 718-388-0025
Web: bedfordmanagement.com

Beghou Consulting 1880 Oak Ave ... Evanston IL 60201 847-864-5480
Web: www.beghouconsulting.com

Belham Management Industries
9307 Monroe Rd ... Charlotte NC 28270 704-847-5400
Web: www.bmienergy.com

Benefact Consulting Group
6285 Northam Dr Ste 200 ... Mississauga ON L4V1X5 855-829-2225
TF: 855-829-2225 ■ *Web:* www.benefact.ca

Benefit Advantage Inc 3431 Commodity Ln ... Green Bay WI 54304 920-339-0351
TF: 800-686-6829 ■ *Web:* www.benefitadvantage.com

Benetrends Inc 1180 Welsh Rd ... North Wales PA 19454 267-498-0059
TF: 866-423-6387 ■ *Web:* www.benetrends.com

Berlin Pacific 400 W 47th Ste 3AB ... New York NY 10036 212-247-2502
Web: www.berlinpacific.com

Bernstein Crisis Management Inc
700 S Myrtle Ave Ste 404 ... Monrovia CA 91016 626-825-3838
Web: www.bernsteincrisismanagement.com

Besen Group LLC, The 10127 Ebenshire Ct ... Oakton VA 22124 703-981-8168
Web: www.thebesengroup.com

Beshenich Muir & Associates LLC
121A Cherokee St ... Leavenworth KS 66048 913-904-1880
Web: www.bma-1.com

Beyond Quota LLC 537 King Muir Rd ... Lake Forest IL 60045 847-234-9475
Web: www.beyond-quota.com

Beyond the Arc Inc 2600 Tenth St Ste 616 ... Berkeley CA 94710 877-676-3743
TF: 877-676-3743 ■ *Web:* www.beyondthearc.com

Bill Dunbar & Associates LLC
2601 Fortune Cir E Ste 301A ... Indianapolis IN 46241 317-247-8014
Web: www.billdunbar.com

Billions Corp, The 3522 W Armitage Ave ... Chicago IL 60647 312-997-9999
Web: billions.com

Biocentric Inc 700 Collings Ave ... Collingswood NJ 08107 856-854-3500
Web: www.biocentricinc.com

BioNJ Inc
1255 Whitehorse-Mercerville Rd Bldg B ?
Ste 514 ... Trenton NJ 08691 609-890-3185
Web: bionj.org

Birner Dental Management Services Inc
1777 S Harrison St Ste 1400 ... Denver CO 80210 303-691-0680 691-0889
TF: 877-898-1083 ■ *Web:* www.perfectteeth.com

Bithgroup Technologies Inc
113 W Monument St ... Baltimore MD 21201 410-962-1188
Web: www.bithgroup.com

BIZDOC Inc 4811 Hardware Dr NE Ste B-2 ... Albuquerque NM 87109 505-338-2069
Web: www.bizdoccapital.com

Bizport Ltd 9 N Third St ... Richmond VA 23219 804-780-1060
Web: www.bizportdoes.com

Black Box Principals Inc 83 Cairns Pl ... Belle Mead NJ 08502 201-914-0374
Web: www.bbprincipals.com

Blackhawk Management Corp 1335 Regents Pk Dr ... Houston TX 77058 281-286-5751 286-5752
Web: www.blackhawkmgmt.com

Blenheim Pharmacal Inc
119 Creamery Rd ... North Blenheim NY 12131 518-827-3121
Web: bpipack.com

BlessingWhite Inc 23 Orchard Rd ... Skillman NJ 08558 908-904-1000
Web: blessingwhite.com

Blue Stone Strategy Group LLC
2214 N Central Ave ITCA/El Encanto Bldg
Ste 130 ... Phoenix AZ 85004 602-307-1994
Web: www.bluestonestrategy.com

Blueline Simulations Llc 218 e bearss ave ... Tampa FL 33613 813-269-7467
Web: www.bluelinesimulations.com

Bluewater Energy Inc
3459 Acworth Due W Rd Ste 206 ... Acworth GA 30101 678-594-2058
Web: bluewaterenergysolutions.com

BMM International LLC 815 Pilot Rd Ste G ... Las Vegas NV 89119 702-407-2420
Web: www.bmm.com

BMS Consulting Inc 209 Starling Ave ... Martinsville VA 24112 276-666-9425
Web: www.bmsbenefits.com

Bolero Associates 1820 W Orangewood Ave ... Orange CA 92868 714-634-4441
Web: www.boleroassociates.com

Bonefish Capital LLC
Rosewood Court 2101 Cedar Springs Rd Ste 1050 ... Dallas TX 75201 214-347-0780
Web: www.bonefishcapital.com

Bonocore Technology Partners LLC
29 Meadow Ridge Dr ... Corte Madera CA 94925 415-806-7008
Web: www.bonocore.com

Boston Benefit Partners LLC
177 Milk St Ste 305 ... Boston MA 02109 617-570-9100
Web: www.bosben.com

Boston Strategies International Inc
445 Washington St ... Wellesley MA 02482 781-250-8150
Web: www.bostonstrategies.com

Bowen Group 10 Ctr St Ste 103 ... Stafford VA 22556 540-658-0490
Web: www.thebowengroup.com

Boyer Consulting Inc 708 Cheyenne Dr ... Naperville IL 60565 630-445-5560
Web: www.boyerconsultinginc.com

Brandon Technology Consulting Inc
3012 Business Park Cir Ste 700 ... Goodlettsville TN 37072 615-757-1200
Web: www.brandontci.com

Brandstream 8353 160th Ave N.E. ... Redmond WA 98052 425-497-1404
Web: www.brandstream.com

Brenton Productions Inc
179 Gasoline Alley Ste 102A ... Mooresville NC 02777 800-572-7798
TF: 800-572-7798 ■ *Web:* www.brentontv.com

Bridges Consulting Inc
2701 Technology Dr Ste 210 ... Annapolis Junction MD 20701 240-646-1100
Web: www.bridges-inc.com

Brillio 100 Town Sq Pl Ste 308 ... Jersey City NJ 07310 800-317-0575
TF: 800-317-0575 ■ *Web:* www.brillio.com

Broadgate Inc 830 Kirts Blvd Ste 400 ... Troy MI 48084 248-918-0110
Web: www.broadgateinc.com

Brookwood Program Management LLC
1819 Peachtree Rd NE Ste 501 ... Atlanta GA 30309 404-350-9988
Web: www.brookwoodpm.com

Browning Phyllis Co
14855 Blanco Rd Ste 403 ... San Antonio TX 78216 210-408-2500
Web: www.phyllisbrowning.com

BSC America Inc 803 Bel Air Rd ... Bel Air MD 21014 800-764-7400
TF: 800-764-7400 ■ *Web:* www.bscamerica.com

Bulk Solutions Inc 4040 Waring Rd ... Lakeland FL 33811 863-248-1136
Web: bulksol.com

Burrus Research Associates Inc
557 Cottonwood Ave ... Hartland WI 53029 262-367-0949
Web: www.theadvantagegame.com

Business Valuation Center LLC
560 Herndon Pkwy Ste 130 ... Herndon VA 20170 703-787-0012
Web: businessvaluationcenter.com

BusinessPlans Inc 432 E Pearl St ... Miamisburg OH 45342 937-865-6501
Web: www.businessplansinc.com

Buy Gitomer 310 Arlington Ave ... Charlotte NC 28203 704-333-1112
Web: www.gitomer.com

Buying Alliance 16 Mtn Ash Trl ... Webster NY 14580 585-671-0650
Web: www.diningalliance.com

Bvs Performance Systems Inc
4060 glass rd NE ... Cedar rapids IA 52402 319-378-8718
Web: www.bvs.com

C d Barnes Associates Inc
3437 Eastern Ave Se ... Grand Rapids MI 49508 616-241-4491
Web: cdbarnes.com

C2 Group LLC
325 Seventh St NW Ste 400 Liberty Pl ... Washington DC 20004 202-567-2900
Web: www.thec2group.com

C2it Consulting Inc 9107 state Rd 142 ... Martinsville IN 46151 317-721-2248
Web: www.c2itconsulting.net

C3 Consulting 2975 Sidco Dr ... Nashville TN 37204 615-371-8612
Web: www.c3-consult.com

C5 Insight Inc
9319 Robert D Snyder Rd Ste 348 ... Charlotte NC 28223 704-895-2500
Web: www.c5insight.com

CALC 235A E Ctr Dr ... Alton IL 62002 618-474-0616
Web: www.calc4it.com

Caled 550 Bercut Dr Ste G ... Sacramento CA 95811 916-448-8252
Web: www.caled.org

Cannon Cochran Management Services Inc
2 E Main St Towne Centre Bldg Ste 208 ... Danville IL 61832 217-446-1089
Web: www.ccmsi.com

Canopach Inc 545 Eighth Ave Ste 401 ... New York NY 10018 347-694-7809
Web: www.canopach.com

Cape Henry Associates Inc
1206 Laskin Rd Ste 100 ... Virginia Beach VA 23451 757-502-7424
Web: www.cape-henry.com

Capgemini US LLC 623 Fifth Ave # 33 ... New York NY 10022 212-314-8000
Web: www.capgemini.com

Capital Realty Advisors Inc
600 Sandtree Dr Ste 109 ... Palm Beach Gardens FL 33403 561-624-5888
TF: 800-940-1088 ■ *Web:* www.capitalrealtyadvisors.com

Capital Review Group
1430 E Missouri Ave Ste B-165 ... Phoenix AZ 85014 602-741-7776
Web: www.capitalreviewgroup.com

Capitol Creag LLC 1300 Penn Ave Nw ... Washington DC 20004 202-355-1028
Web: www.capitolcreag.com

CapSouth Partners 2216 W Main St ... Dothan AL 36301 334-673-8600
Web: www.capsouthpartners.com

Name / Address	City	State	ZIP	Phone	Fax
CapWealth Advisors LLC 3000 Meridian Blvd Ste 250 *Web:* capwealthadvisors.com	Franklin	TN	37067	615-778-0740	
Cardno ChemRisk 25 Jessie St at Ecker Sq Ste 1800 *Web:* www.chemrisk.com	San Francisco	CA	94105	415-896-2400	
Cardon & Assoc Inc 2749 E Covenanter Dr *Web:* cardon.us	Bloomington	IN	47401	812-332-2265	
Careers Inc 208 Ave Ponce De Leon Ste 1100 *Web:* www.careersincpr.com	San Juan	PR	00918	787-764-2298	
Carnahan Group Inc 5005 W Laurel St Ste 204 *Web:* www.carnahangroup.com	Tampa	FL	33607	813-289-2588	
Carolina Advanced Digital Inc 133 Triangle Trade Dr *TF:* 800-435-2212 ■ *Web:* www.cadinc.com	Cary	NC	27513	919-663-2211	
Carpedia International Ltd 75 Navy St *TF:* 877-445-8288 ■ *Web:* www.carpedia.com	Oakville	ON	L6J2Z1	877-445-8288	
Cascadia Managing Brands 1109 First Ave Ste 400 *Web:* www.cascadiaconsulting.com	Seattle	WA	98101	206-343-9759	
Cassara Management Group Inc 2440 Ridgeway Ave Ste 120 *Web:* www.cassaramgi.com	Rochester	NY	14626	585-720-1700	
Caswood Group Inc, The 811 Ayrault Rd Ste 2 *Web:* www.caswood.com	Fairport	NY	14450	585-425-0332	
CAT Technology Inc 377 Rt 17 S Ste # 208 *Web:* www.catamerica.com	Hasbrouck Heights	NJ	07604	201-727-9299	
Catalyst House Inc 32545 Golden Lantern St *Web:* www.catalysthouse.net	Dana Point	CA	92629	949-443-0096	
Catapult Technology Ltd 7500 Old Georgetown Rd 11th Fl **Fax Area Code:* 301 ■ *Web:* catapult.sc3.com	Bethesda	MD	20814	240-482-2100	986-8688*
Catchpole Corp, The 10 High St Ste 502 *TF:* 866-431-2666 ■ *Web:* www.catchpole.com	Boston	MA	02110	781-431-2666	
Cattan Services Group Inc 1006 Haywood Dr *Web:* www.cattan.com	College Station	TX	77845	979-260-7200	
Cavanaugh Tocci Associates Inc 327 Boston Post Rd *Web:* cavtocci.com	Sudbury	MA	01776	978-443-7871	
CBR-Technology Corp 15581 Sunburst Ln *Web:* www.cbrtechnology.com	Huntington Beach	CA	92647	714-901-5740	
Ccg Automation Inc 3868 congress pkwy *Web:* www.ccgautomation.com	Richfield	OH	44286	330-659-5082	
CE Resource Inc 1482 Stone Point Dr Ste 100 *TF:* 800-707-5644 ■ *Web:* www.paragoncet.com	Roseville	CA	95661	800-707-5644	
CEBOS Ltd 5936 Ford Court Ste 203 *Web:* www.cebos.com	Brighton	MI	48116	810-534-2222	
Celenia Software NA Inc 1509 Johnson Ferry Rd Ste 150 *Web:* www.celenia.com	Marietta	GA	30062	404-614-1751	
Cengea Solutions Inc 330 St Mary Ave Ste 1160 *Web:* www.cengea.com	Winnipeg	MB	R3C3Z5	204-957-7566	
Center of Workforce Innovations Inc, The 2804 Boilermaker Ct Ste E *Web:* www.innovativeworkforce.com	Valparaiso	IN	46383	219-462-2940	
Central IQ Inc 14527 Cotswolds Dr *Web:* www.centraliq.com	Tampa	FL	33626	813-920-4001	
Centrilogy Consulting The Vineyard II 1452 Hughes Rd 2nd Fl *Web:* centrilogy.com	Grapevine	TX	76051	817-416-9722	
Centuria Corp 11955 Democracy Dr Ste 1620 *Web:* www.centuria.com	Reston	VA	20190	703-435-4600	
Cenvill Recreation Inc 1601 Forum Pl Ste 500 W Palm Beach *Web:* www.cenrec.com	West Palm Beach	FL	33401	561-640-3133	
Ceregenics Inc 10245 W 34th Ave *Web:* www.ceregenics.com	Wheat Ridge	CO	80033	303-274-9101	
CES USA Inc 235 Remington Blvd Ste H *Web:* www.cesltd.com	Bolingbrook	IL	60440	630-296-8939	
CFOs 2Go Inc 500 Ygnacio Vly Rd Ste 410 *Web:* www.2gocompanies.com	Walnut Creek	CA	94596	925-299-4450	
CFX Inc 588 Broadway Ste 1203 *Web:* www.cfx.com	New York	NY	10012	212-431-5800	
Chagrin Consulting Services 24800 Chagrin Blvd Ste 207 *Web:* www.chagrinconsulting.com	Beachwood	OH	44122	216-514-3301	
Chally Group Worldwide Inc 3123 Research Blvd *TF:* 800-254-5995 ■ *Web:* chally.com	Dayton	OH	45420	937-259-1200	
Chartis Group LLC 220 W Kinzie St 5th Fl *TF:* 877-667-4700 ■ *Web:* www.chartisgroup.com	Chicago	IL	60654	877-667-4700	
Charton Management Inc 373 Timberline Pkwy *Web:* www.charton-mgmt.com	Vienna	WV	26105	304-865-2222	
ChemQuest Group Inc, The 8150 Corporate Dr Ste 250 *Web:* www.chemquest.com	Cincinnati	OH	45242	513-469-7555	
Cherokee Enterprises Inc 14474 Commerce Way *Web:* www.cherokeecorp.com	Miami Lakes	FL	33016	305-828-3353	
Chiro. Advance Services Inc W5240 Oak Hill Rd *Web:* chiroadvance.com	Trego	WI	54888	715-635-5211	
Chugach Management Services Inc 3800 Centerpoint Dr Ste 601 *Web:* www.chugach.com	Anchorage	AK	99503	907-563-8866	
CIC Energy Consulting 150 S Wacker Dr Ste 2400	Chicago	IL	60606	312-466-0500	
Cicero Group LP 515 East 100 South Ste 3000 *Web:* cicerogroup.com	Salt Lake City	UT	84102	801-456-6700	
Cimro of Nebraska 1230 O St Ste 120 *Web:* www.cimronebraska.org	Lincoln	NE	68508	402-476-1399	
CIP Group, The 799 Cambridge St *Web:* www.askcip.com	Cambridge	MA	02142	617-354-0866	
Ciproms Inc 3600 Woodview Trce *Web:* www.ciproms.com	Indianapolis	IN	46268	317-870-0480	
Cirro Energy Services Inc 2745 Dallas Pkwy Ste 200 *TF:* 866-791-1911 ■ *Web:* www.cirroenergy.com	Plano	TX	75093	866-791-1911	
Citent Inc 600 Anton Blvd *Web:* www.citent.com	Costa Mesa	CA	92626	714-436-6100	
CityScan Inc 440 N Wabash Apt 3105 *Web:* cityscan.com	Chicago	IL	60611	312-218-0688	
Clarity Partners LLC 20 N Clark St Ste 3600 *Web:* www.claritypartners.com	Chicago	IL	60602	312-920-0550	
Clark Mc Dowall 404 E 11th St *Web:* www.clarkmcdowall.com	New York	NY	10009	212-473-3737	
Clayton L Scroggins Associates Inc 200 Northland Blvd *TF:* 800-359-3970 ■ *Web:* www.scroggins.com	Cincinnati	OH	45246	513-771-7070	
Cleantech Open, The 336 Portage Rd *TF:* 888-989-6736 ■ *Web:* www.cleantechopen.com	Palo Alto	CA	94306	888-989-6736	
Clear-view Technologies Inc 1722 Ringwood Ave Ste 200 *Web:* www.clear-view-tech.com	San Jose	CA	95131	408-512-3549	
Cleartel Communications Inc 1720 Rt 34 *Web:* www.cleartel.com	Wall	NJ	07719	732-280-6408	
closerlook Inc 212 W Superior St Ste 300 *Web:* www.closerlook.com	Chicago	IL	60654	312-640-3700	
Cloud Strategy Partners LLC 129 Lauren Cir *Web:* www.cloudstrategypartners.com	Scotts Valley	CA	95066	408-857-9872	
Clover Global Group 2431 W Irving Park Rd *TF:* 888-256-8370 ■ *Web:* www.cloverglobal.com	Chicago	IL	60618	773-267-6767	
Clyde Industrial LLC 36445 S Reserve Cir *Web:* www.clydeindustrial.com	Avon	OH	44011	440-653-1062	
Coalition of Health Services Inc 301 S Polk St Ste 740 *Web:* cohs.net	Amarillo	TX	79101	806-337-1700	
Coast Dental Services Inc 4010 W Boy Scout Blvd Ste 1100 *TF:* 800-327-6453 ■ *Web:* www.coastdental.com	Tampa	FL	33607	813-288-1999	289-4500
Cochran, Cochran & Yale LLC 955 E Henrietta Rd *Web:* www.ccy.com	Rochester	NY	14623	585-424-6060	
Cofa Media Inc 2544 Gateway Rd Ste 201 *Web:* www.cofamedia.com	Carlsbad	CA	92009	619-602-2529	
Coffee Solutions Inc 2B Airport Dr Ext *Web:* www.coffeesolutions.net	Hopedale	MA	01747	508-422-9233	
Cogentic LLC 1834 Collins St Ste E *Web:* www.cogentic.com	Tarzana	CA	91356	818-578-6930	
Coker Consulting 2400 Lakeview Pkwy Ste 400 *TF:* 800-345-5829 ■ *Web:* www.cokergroup.com	Alpharetta	GA	30009	800-345-5829	
Colautti Construction Ltd 2575 Sheffield Rd *Web:* www.colauttigroup.com	Ottawa	ON	K1T3V7	613-822-1440	
Combustion Components Assoc Inc 884 MN St *Web:* www.cca-inc.net	Monroe	CT	06468	203-268-3139	261-7697
Commodity Sourcing Group (CSG) 19730 Ralston St	Detroit	MI	48203	313-366-0660	
Commongood Careers Inc 38 Chauncy St Ste 1001 *Web:* commongoodcareers.org	Boston	MA	02111	617-542-1404	
Communibiz Inc Po Box 30062 *TF:* 877-266-0979 ■ *Web:* communibiz.com	Billings	MT	59107	406-259-1252	
Communico Ltd 19 Ludlow Rd *Web:* www.communicoltd.com	Westport	CT	06880	203-226-7117	
Community Eldercare Services LLC 2844 Traceland Dr	Tupelo	MS	38801	662-680-3148	844-6558
Compmanagement Inc PO Box 884 *TF:* 800-825-6755 ■ *Web:* www.compmgt.com	Dublin	OH	43017	614-376-5300	766-6888
Comworks Multi Media 2192 Yorkshire Rd *Web:* www.comworksonline.com	Birmingham	MI	48009	248-649-5454	
Concentra Inc 5080 Spectrum Dr Ste 1200 W **Fax Area Code:* 972 ■ *TF:* 866-944-6046 ■ *Web:* www.concentra.com	Addison	TX	75001	866-944-6046	725-6439*
Conception To Reality Inc 6020 W 91 Ave *Web:* ctr-inc.com	Westminster	CO	80031	303-225-0230	
Concord Promotions Inc 2000 Bloomingdale Rd *Web:* store.concordms.com/concordms/index.html	Glendale Heights	IL	60139	630-893-6453	
Conducive Consulting Inc 3445 Executive Ctr Dr Ste 216 *Web:* www.conducivesi.com	Austin	TX	78731	512-551-0660	
Conger & Elsea Inc 9870 Hwy 92 *Web:* www.conger-elsea.com	Woodstock	GA	30188	770-926-1131	
Conklin & de Decker 62B Cranberry Hwy *Web:* www.conklindd.com	Orleans	MA	02653	508-255-5975	
Conquest Technologies Inc 9250 Rumsey Rd Ste B *Web:* www.conquesttechnologies.com	Columbia	MD	21045	410-740-4448	
ConSol Inc 7407 Tam O'Shanter Dr Ste 200 *Web:* www.consol.ws	Stockton	CA	95210	209-473-5000	
CONSOR Inc 7342 Girard Ave Ste 8 *Web:* www.consor.com	La Jolla	CA	92037	858-454-9091	
Contact International Inc 3201 Old Glnvw Rd 50 *Web:* www.contactamt.com	Wilmette	IL	60091	847-324-4411	
Continuous Learning Group Inc, The 500 Cherrington Pkwy Ste 350 *Web:* www.clg.com	Pittsburgh	PA	15108	412-269-7240	
Conway Management Co 547 Amherst St Ste 106 *Web:* www.conwaymgmt.com	Nashua	NH	03063	603-889-1130	
Cooper Perkins Inc 30 N Ave *Web:* www.cooperperkins.com	Burlington	MA	01803	781-425-6397	

Phone | Fax

Copernicus Learning Ventures
250 W 50th St Fl L-29 ... New York NY 10019 646-215-9772
Web: www.copernicuslp.com

Corizon 105 Westpark Dr Ste 200 ... Brentwood TN 37027 800-729-0069
TF: 800-729-0069 ■ *Web:* www.corizonhealth.com

Cornell Technical Services LLC
9700 Patuxent Woods Dr Ste 140 ... Columbia MD 21046 301-560-2544
Web: www.cts-llc.com

Corporate Healthcare Strategies LLC
280 Granite Run Dr Ste 250 ... Lancaster PA 17601 717-581-8382
Web: www.stoudtadvisors.com

Corporate University Xchange
4900 Ritter Rd Ste 103 ... Mechanicsburg PA 17055 717-395-9267
Web: www.corpu.com

Corps Solutions Llc 42 Masters Mill Ct Ste ... Stafford VA 22556 540-720-5838
Web: www.corps-solutions.com

Cortex Consultants Inc 1218 Langley St ... Victoria BC V8W1W2 250-360-1492
TF: 866-931-1192 ■ *Web:* www.cortex.ca

Corum Group Ltd 19805 N Creek Pkwy Ste 300 ... Bothell WA 98011 425-455-8281
Web: www.corumgroup.com

CorVel Corp 2010 Main St Ste 600 ... Irvine CA 92614 949-851-1473 851-1469
NASDAQ: CRVL ■ *TF:* 888-726-7835 ■ *Web:* www.corvel.com

Corvirtus LLC 1011 N Weber St ... Colorado Springs CO 80903 800-322-5329
TF: 800-322-5329 ■ *Web:* www.corvirtus.com

Courtemanche and Associates
4475 Morris Park Dr Ste B ... Charlotte NC 28227 704-573-4535
Web: www.courtemanche-assocs.com

Coyle Hospitality Group
244 Madison Ave Ste 369 ... New York NY 10016 212-629-2083
Web: www.coylehospitality.com

Craford Benefits Consultants
990 Fifth Ave ... San Rafael CA 94901 415-456-9790
Web: www.craford.com

CRAssoc Inc 8580 Cinderbed Rd Ste 2400 ... Newington VA 22122 703-550-8145
TF: 877-272-8960 ■ *Web:* www.crassoc.com

CRC Sogema Inc
1111 Saint-Charles St W Saint-Charles Complex W Tower
Ste 700 ... Longueuil QC J4K5G4 450-651-2800
Web: crcsogema.com

Creative Support Solutions
5508 W Hwy 290 Ste 203 ... Austin TX 78735 512-330-0701
Web: csssolutions.com

Cresting Wave LLC 300 Lanidex Plz ... Parsippany NJ 07054 973-359-0500
Web: www.crestingwave.com

Critical Business Analysis Inc
134 W S Boundary St ... Perrysburg OH 43551 419-874-0800
Web: cbainc.com

Critigen LLC 7604 Technology Way Ste 300 ... Denver CO 80237 303-706-0990 706-1861
Web: www.critigen.com

CRMPlus Consulting Inc 11531 Meridian Point Dr ... Tampa FL 33626 813-343-2173
Web: www.crmplusconsulting.com

CRO Analytics LLC 6139 Stoney Hill Rd ... New Hope PA 18938 571-436-4835
Web: croanalytics.com

Croner Company Inc, The
1028 Sir Francis Drake Blvd ... Kentfield CA 94904 415-485-5530
Web: www.croner.biz

Cross World Network 10 Van Winkle Rd ... Hudson NY 12534 518-851-6688
Web: www.crossworldnetwork.com

Crowe Paradis Services Corp
400 Riverpark Dr Ste 400 ... North Reading MA 01864 978-664-1524
Web: www.cpscmsa.com

Crown Asset Management LLC
3355 Breckinridge Blvd Ste 132 ... Duluth GA 30096 770-817-6700
Web: www.crownasset.com

Crowned Grace Inc
137 National Plz Ste 300 ... National Harbor MD 20745 321-251-5236
Web: www.crownedgrace.com

CRS Registrars Inc 135 Chesterfield Ln Ste 201 ... Maumee OH 43537 419-861-1686
Web: www.crsregistrars.com

CSG Government Solutions Inc
180 N Stetson Ave Ste 3200 ... Chicago IL 60601 312-444-2760
Web: www.csgdelivers.com

Cullen Coates & Associates 173 Riviera Cir ... Larkspur CA 94939 415-945-9581
Web: www.cullencoates.com

Currie Management Consultants Inc
292 Lincoln St ... Worcester MA 01605 508-752-9229
Web: www.curriemanagement.com

Customer Group LLC, The
47 W Polk St Ste 100-233 ... Chicago IL 60605 312-423-8551
Web: www.customergroup.com

CWS Consulting Group LLC
1005 Boylston St Ste 243 ... Newton Highlands MA 02461 617-314-6527
Web: www.cwsgrp.com

D&S Communications Inc 1355 N Mclean Blvd ... Elgin IL 60123 847-468-8082
Web: www.dscomm.com

D. Pagan Communications Inc
175 Pinelawn Rd Ste 215 ... Melville NY 11747 631-659-2309
Web: www.dpagan.com

D. R. Payne & Associates Inc
119 N Robinson Ave Ste 400 ... Oklahoma City OK 73102 405-272-0511
Web: drpayne.com

Dakno 3101 Poplarwood Ct Ste 108 ... Raleigh NC 27604 919-877-8511
Web: www.dakno.com

Dane Holdings Inc
13529 W Camino del Sol ... Sun City West AZ 85375 623-825-3173
Web: www.daneholdings.com

Data Records Management Services Llc
1400 Husband Rd ... Paducah KY 42003 270-443-1255
Web: www.drmsusa.com

Dataccount Inc 299 Broadway Ste 1016 ... New York NY 10007 212-595-1044
Web: www.dataccount.com

DatamanUSA LLC 6890 S Tucson Way Ste 100 ... Centennial CO 80112 720-248-3121
Web: www.datamanusa.com

DataProfit Corp 330 Whitney Ave ... Holyoke MA 01040 413-536-2766
Web: www.dataprofit.com

Datum Corp 6009 Business Blvd ... Sarasota FL 34240 941-256-8700
Web: www.datumcorporation.com

Davis Demographics & Planning Inc
11850 Pierce St Ste 200 ... Riverside CA 92505 951-270-5211
Web: www.davisdemographics.com

Dci Consulting Group Inc 1920 I St Nw ... Washington DC 20006 202-828-6900
Web: dciconsult.com

DD&F Consulting Group 521 S Rock St ... Little Rock AR 72202 501-374-2600
Web: ddfconsulting.com

De Maximis Inc 450 Montbrook Ln ... Knoxville TN 37919 865-691-5052 691-6485
Web: www.demaximis.com

DealNet Capital Corp 325 Milner Ave Ste 300 ... Toronto ON M1B5N1 855-912-3444
TF: 855-912-3444 ■ *Web:* www.dealnetcapital.com

Decimal Technologies Inc
793 Jean-Paul-Vincent Blvd Ste 202 ... Longueuil QC J4G1R3 450-640-1222
Web: www.decimal.ca

Deep East Texas Council of Governments
274 e lamar st ... Jasper TX 75951 409-384-5704
TF: 800-256-6848 ■ *Web:* www.detcog.org

Deer Park Group Inc 21540 N Inglenook Ln ... Deer Park IL 60010 847-387-8002
Web: www.deerparkinc.com

Deetken Group, The 1755 W Bdwy Ste 501 ... Vancouver BC V6J4S5 604-731-4424
Web: www.deetken.com

Defence Construction Canada
Constitution Sq, 350 Albert St 19th Fl ... Ottawa ON K1A0K3 613-998-9548
Web: www.dcc-cdc.gc.ca

Definity Partners LLC 5191 Natorp Blvd Ste 420 ... Mason OH 45040 513-381-7200
Web: www.definitypartners.com

Delta Partners 32 Burrows Rd ... Ottawa ON K1J6E6 613-747-8121
Web: www.deltapartners.ca

Delta Training Partners Inc
4020 Oleander Dr ... Wilmington NC 28403 910-790-1985
Web: deltatraining.com

Delve Group Inc, The 21 W 46th St Ste 1103 ... New York NY 10036 212-255-3870
Web: delvegroup.com

Denmar Services Inc 605 SW B Ave Ste 2 ... Lawton OK 73501 580-355-8900
Web: www.denmarservices.com

Dental Care Alliance LLC 6240 Lk Osprey Dr ... Sarasota FL 34240 941-955-3150 914-9684
Web: dentalcarealliance.net

Desai Systems Inc 199 Oakwood Ave ... West Hartford CT 06119 860-233-0011
Web: www.desai.com

Design Dimension Inc 901 N W St ... Raleigh NC 27603 919-828-1485
Web: www.designdimension.com

Design Net Technical Products Inc
341 Washington Hwy ... Smithfield RI 02917 401-349-0695
Web: designnettech.com

Development Alternatives Inc (DAI)
7600 Wisconsin Ave Ste 200 ... Bethesda MD 20814 301-771-7600 771-7777
Web: www.dai.com

DevFacto Technologies Inc
2250 Scotia Place Tower 1 10060 Jasper Ave ... Edmonton AB T5J3R8 587-520-9118
TF: 877-323-3832 ■ *Web:* www.devfacto.com

Dickson Consulting 351 Old Babcock Trl ... Gibsonia PA 15044 724-272-1527
Web: www.dicksonconsulting.biz

Digital Street Inc
69550 Highway 111 Ste 201 ... Rancho Mirage CA 92270 866-464-5100
TF: 866-464-5100 ■ *Web:* www.digitalstreets.tv

Dirks, Van Essen & Murray
119 E Marcy St Ste 100 ... Santa Fe NM 87501 505-820-2700
Web: www.dirksvanessen.com

Discover Reinsurance Company Inc
5 Batterson Pk ... Farmington CT 06032 860-674-2660 674-2671

Dispute Resolution Management Inc
132 W Pierpont Ave Ste 400 ... Salt Lake City UT 84101 801-355-1444
Web: www.drmworld.com

Divcon EMS 4325 Elm St Ste 210 ... Dallas TX 75226 214-821-6958
Web: divconems.com

Dka 5713 Corporate Way Ste 100 ... West Palm Beach FL 33407 561-640-9171
Web: www.dkahome.com

Doctors Administrative Solutions LLC
1000 N Ashley Dr Ste 300 ... Tampa FL 33602 813-774-9800
Web: dashealth.com

Dodge County Board of Education PO Box 1029 ... Eastman GA 31023 478-374-3783 374-6697
Web: www.dodge.k12.ga.us

Domain Systems Inc 117 West 200 South ... Farmington UT 84025 801-447-3778
Web: www.domainsi.com

Doran Consulting LLC
3101 Magic Hollow Blvd ... Virginia Beach VA 23453 757-368-2208
Web: doranconsulting.com

Doubleknot Inc 14510 Big Basin Way Ste 106 ... Saratoga CA 95070 408-971-9120
Web: www.doubleknot.com

Dougherty Management Associates Inc
9 Meriam St Ste 4 ... Lexington MA 02420 781-863-1519
Web: www.dmahealth.com

Doyletech Corp 28 Thorncliff Pl Ste 201 ... Ottawa ON K2H6L2 613-226-8900

Dresser & Associates Inc 243 US Route 1 ... Scarborough ME 04074 207-885-0809
TF: 866-885-7212 ■ *Web:* www.dresserassociates.com

DRI Consulting Inc 2 Otter Ln ... North Oaks MN 55127 651-415-1400
Web: www.dric.com

DTE Energy Services 414 S Main St Ste 600 ... Ann Arbor MI 48104 734-302-4800
Web: dtepowerandindustrial.com

DUCK FLATS Pharma LLC 109 S St ... Elbridge NY 13060 315-689-3407
Web: www.dfpharma.com

Ducker Worldwide LLC 1250 Maplelawn Dr ... Troy MI 48084 248-644-0086
Web: www.ducker.com

Dunthorpe Marketing Group Inc
8825 Se 11th Ave ... Portland OR 97202 503-236-4242
Web: www.dunthorpemarketing.com

Dyna Lync Corp 200 Consumer Rd Ste 604 ... Toronto ON M2J4R4 416-398-2000
Web: www.dynalync.ca

Company	City	State	ZIP	Phone	Fax
Dynamic Corporate Solutions Inc 1845 Town Ctr Blvd Ste 525 *Web:* www.dynamiccorp.com	Fleming Island	FL	32003	904-278-5383	
Dynamic Devices 8 Lewis Cir *Web:* dynamicdevices.com	Wilmington	DE	19804	302-994-2401	
Dynamic Links International LLC 8286 Daleview Rd *Web:* dynamiclinksint.com	Cincinnati	OH	45247	513-385-2600	
Eagle Construction Services Inc 1624 Jacksonville Rd *Web:* www.eagle1construction.com	Burlington	NJ	08016	609-239-8000	
Eagle's Flight, Creative Training Excellence Inc 489 Clair Rd W *TF:* 800-567-8079 ■ *Web:* www.eaglesflight.com	Guelph	ON	N1L0H7	519-767-1747	
EASI LLC #1551 E Lincoln Ave *Web:* www.easi.com	Madison Heights	MI	48071	248-582-3800	
Eberline Services Inc 7021 Pan American Fwy NE	Albuquerque	NM	87109	505-262-2694	
Ebridge Consulting Llc 2275 E. Continental Blvd Ste 120 *Web:* www.sibridge.com	Southlake	TX	76092	817-756-6231	
EBUSINESS STRATEGIS LLC 18318 Fern Trl Ctr *TF:* 888-647-3249 ■ *Web:* askebiz.com	Houston	TX	77084	281-647-6183	
eCapital Advisors LLC 7101 W 78th St Ste 220 *Web:* www.ecapitaladvisors.com	Bloomington	MN	55439	952-947-9300	
Eclipse Incentive Marketing Corp 251 S Main St *Web:* www.eimcorp.us	Williamstown	NJ	08094	856-866-2126	
Economic Systems Inc 3120 Frview Pk Dr Ste 500 *Web:* www.econsys.com	Falls Church	VA	22042	703-642-5225	
Ecosphere Environmental Services Inc 776 E Second Ave *Web:* www.ecosphere-services.com	Durango	CO	81301	970-382-7256	
Ecredit com 600 N Pine Is Rd *Web:* www.ecredit.com	Plantation	FL	33324	954-315-0208	
Edelman Berland Inc 1875 Eye St NW Ste 900 *Web:* www.edelmanberland.com	Washington	DC	20006	202-326-1772	
EDG Inc 3900 N Causeway Blvd Ste 700 *Web:* www.edg.net	Metairie	LA	70002	504-455-0858	
Edgemark Partners 4510 cox rd *TF:* 800-488-0289 ■ *Web:* www.edgemarkpartners.com	Glen Allen	VA	23060	804-967-2000	
EdgeStone Consulting Inc Princeton Corporate Ctr 5 Independence Way Ste 300 *Web:* www.edgestone.net	Princeton	NJ	08540	609-514-5190	
EDJ Associates Inc 13873 Park Center Rd Ste 301 *Web:* edjassociates.com	Herndon	VA	20191	703-738-9150	
Eisenbach Consulting LLC 921 Shiloh Rd B-300 *TF:* 800-977-4020 ■ *Web:* www.eisenbachconsulting.com	Tyler	TX	75703	800-977-4020	
Eleven Twenty Limited 3700 Fairway Dr *Web:* www.eleventwenty.com	Woodbury	MN	55125	651-797-3070	
Elitexpo Cargo Systems 845 Commerce Dr *TF:* 800-543-5484 ■ *Web:* elitexpo.com	South Elgin	IL	60177	800-543-5484	
Elliot Rossen & Associates 791 Apple Tree Ln *Web:* www.erossen.com	Highland Park	IL	60035	847-624-5752	
Ellis-harper Advertising Inc 710 Stage Rd *Web:* www.ellisharper.com	Auburn	AL	36831	334-887-6536	
EMI Services Inc 301 A St *Web:* www.emiservices.com	Idaho Falls	ID	83402	208-522-1117	
Empowered Networks Inc 1315 Pickering Pkwy Ste 200 *Web:* empowerednetworks.com	Pickering	ON	L1V7G5	905-837-6585	
EnablePath LLC 2208 Vail Ave *Web:* enablepath.com	Charlotte	NC	28207	704-373-9000	
Enaxis Consulting 9 Greenway Plz Ste 3005 *Web:* www.enaxisconsulting.com	Houston	TX	77046	713-881-9494	
Encore Cbt Co 5900 n high st *Web:* www.encorecbt.com	Columbus	OH	43085	614-888-4179	
Enderle Group Inc 389 Photinia Ln *Web:* www.enderlegroup.com	San Jose	CA	95127	408-272-8560	
Energage Inc 3405 Bonaire Xing *Web:* energage.com	Marietta	GA	30066	770-321-0537	
Energy Ace Inc 160 Clairemont Ave Ste 600 *Web:* www.energyace.com	Decatur	GA	30030	404-378-7800	
Energy Authority Inc, The 301 W Bay St Ste 2600 *Web:* www.teainc.org	Jacksonville	FL	32202	904-356-3900	
Energy Management Solutions Inc 7935 Stone Creek Dr Ste 140 *Web:* www.emsenergy.com	Chanhassen	MN	55317	952-767-7450	
Energy Project, The 1 Larkin Plaza 4th Fl *Web:* theenergyproject.com	Yonkers	NY	10701	914-207-8800	
EnergyWorks Inc 71 Old Mill Bottom Rd N Ste 101 *Web:* www.energyworks.com	Annapolis	MD	21409	410-349-2001	
Enernoc Inc 101 Federal St Ste 1100 *NASDAQ: ENOC* ■ *Web:* www.enernoc.com	Boston	MA	02110	617-224-9900	224-9910
Engineering Management Concepts Inc 5051 Verdugo Way Ste 200 *Web:* www.emc-inc.com	Camarillo	CA	93012	805-484-9082	484-4607
Enigma Marketing Trvl Solutions 8463 castlewood dr *Web:* www.enigma-marketing.com	Indianapolis	IN	46250	317-585-0100	
Enite Management LLC 101 W 13th St *Web:* enitegroup.com	Houston	TX	77008	713-298-6149	
Ensave Energy Performance Inc 65 Millet St Ste 105 *TF:* 800-732-1399 ■ *Web:* www.ensave.com	Richmond	VT	05477	800-732-1399	
Entelechy Enterprises Inc 889 E Shore Dr *Web:* www.unlockit.com	Silver Lake	NH	03875	603-424-1237	
Enterey Inc 9900 Irvine Ctr Dr Ste 100 *TF:* 800-691-2349 ■ *Web:* www.enterey.com	Irvine	CA	92618	800-691-2349	
Envirologic Technologies Inc 2960 Interstate Pkwy *Web:* envirologic.com	Kalamazoo	MI	49048	269-342-1100	
Envisa Inc 281 Pleasant St *Web:* www.envisa.com	Framingham	MA	01701	508-405-1220	
Ephor Group LLC 24 E Greenway Plz Ste 440 *TF:* 800-379-9330 ■ *Web:* www.ephorgroup.com	Houston	TX	77046	800-379-9330	
Epi Marketing Group 30262 Crown Vly Pkwy Ste B458 *Web:* www.epi-marketing.com	Laguna Niguel	CA	92677	949-542-7743	
Equias Alliance LLC 8000 Ctrview Pkwy Ste 525 *Web:* www.equiasalliance.com	Cordova	TN	38018	901-754-4712	
Equitrust Financial Group Ltd 570 Lk Cook Rd Ste 101 *Web:* www.equitrustfinancial.com	Deerfield	IL	60015	847-317-0200	
ERA Herman Group Real Estate 4057 Battleground Ave *Web:* www.hermangroup.com	Greensboro	NC	27410	336-282-9370	
Ergo Resource Management Inc 801 N Huntington St 7 *Web:* ergo-syracuse.com	Syracuse	IN	46567	574-457-8020	
Ernan Roman Direct Marketing Corp 3 Melrose Ln *Web:* erdm.com	Little Neck	NY	11363	718-225-4151	
Essential Management Solutions Llc 1 S 2nd St *Web:* emsolutionsllc.net	Pottsville	PA	17901	570-621-9000	
Ethical Markets Media LLC 10 Carrera St *Web:* www.ethicalmarkets.com	St. Augustine	FL	32084	904-829-3140	
Ethos Risk Services Inc 300 1st Ave S Ste 402 *Web:* ethosrisk.com	St. Petersburg	FL	33701	727-822-9800	
Eventech 1833 alford ave *Web:* www.eventech.com	Los Altos	CA	94024	650-961-7845	
Evidence Based Research Inc 1595 Spring Hill Rd *Web:* www.ebrinc.com	Vienna	VA	22182	703-893-6800	
Evision Systems I Inc 2852 Antoine Dr	Houston	TX	77092	713-807-9555	
Excalibur Associates Inc 8687 W 108th Ave *Web:* www.excaliburassociates.com	Westminster	CO	80021	303-464-1574	
Executive Business Media Inc 825 Old Country Rd *Web:* www.ebmpubs.com	Westbury	NY	11590	516-334-3030	334-3059
Executive Diversity Services Inc 675 S Ln St Ste 305 *Web:* www.executivediversity.com	Seattle	WA	98104	206-224-9293	
Executive Sounding Board Associates Inc 3959 Welsh Rd Ste 354 *Web:* www.esba.com	Willow Grove	PA	19090	215-568-5788	
Expansion Strategies Inc 17 Rollingwood Dr *Web:* www.expansionstrategiesinc.com	New Hartford	NY	13413	315-793-3137	
Expense Reduction Analysts Inc 16479 N Dallas Pkwy Bent Tree Twr II Ste 240 *Web:* www.expensereduction.com	Addison	TX	75001	469-310-2970	
Expotel Hospitality Services LLC 401 Veterans Memorial Blvd Ste 102 *Web:* www.expotelhospitality.com	Metairie	LA	70005	504-212-1492	
Fabrizio, McLaughlin & Associates 2624 NE 15th St *Web:* www.fabriziolee.com	Ft Lauderdale	FL	22314	703-684-4510	
Fair Choice Systems Inc 505 Ct St *Web:* www.fairchoicesystems.com	Brooklyn	NY	11231	646-485-0890	
Falk Marques Group LLC 9 Meriam St Ste 21 *Web:* www.falkmarquesgroup.com	Lexington	MA	02420	781-652-0900	
Family Business Institute Inc, The 4050 Wake Forest Rd Ste 110 *Web:* www.familybusinessinstitute.com	Raleigh	NC	27609	919-783-1880	
Family Circle Tennis Center 161 Seven Farms Dr *Web:* www.familycircletenniscenter.com	Daniel Island	SC	29492	843-856-7900	
Fandel Retail Group 650 Fifth St Ste 405 *Web:* www.fandelretail.com	San Francisco	CA	94107	415-538-8355	
Farr Associates Inc 4194 Mendenhall Oaks Pkwy Ste 101 *Web:* www.farrleadership.com	High Point	NC	27265	336-812-8050	
Fast-Impact Consulting Inc 5190 Neil Rd Ste 430 *Web:* www.fast-impact.com	Reno	NV	89502	775-284-3704	
FCC Services 7951 E Maplewood Ave Ste 225 *TF:* 888-275-3227 ■ *Web:* www.fccservices.com	Greenwood Village	CO	80111	888-275-3227	
FCi Federal Inc 602 S King St Ste 102 *Web:* www.fedconsulting.com	Leesburg	VA	20175	703-443-1888	
Fiedor Van Epps & Associates 964 Fifth Ave *Web:* fiedorvanepps.com	San Diego	CA	92101	619-544-1422	
Fieldman Rolapp & Assoc 19900 Macarthur Blvd *Web:* www.fieldman.com	Irvine	CA	92612	949-660-7300	474-8773
File Keepers LLC 6277 E Slauson Ave *TF:* 800-332-3453 ■ *Web:* www.filekeepers.com	Los Angeles	CA	90040	323-728-3133	728-0867
Fino Consulting LLC 20 W 37th St 12th Fl *Web:* www.finoconsulting.com	New York	NY	10018	212-532-0020	
Firm Consulting Group 2107 W Cass St Ste B *TF:* 877-636-9525 ■ *Web:* www.firmconsultinggrp.com	Tampa	FL	33606	877-636-9525	
First Annapolis Consulting Inc 900 Elkridge Landing Rd Ste 400 *Web:* www.firstannapolis.com	Linthicum	MD	21090	410-855-8500	
First Carolina Management Inc 300 N Winstead Ave *Web:* www.1stcarolina.net	Rocky Mount	NC	27804	252-937-8111	

Company	City	State	ZIP	Phone	Fax
First Health Group Corp *Coventry* 3200 Highland Ave *TF:* 800-247-2898 ■ *Web:* www.firsthealth.com	Downers Grove	IL	60515	630-737-7900	
First Infrastructure LLC 15 Wendover Rd *Web:* www.1stinfrastructure.com	Montclair	NJ	07042	973-783-0088	
First Sun EAP 2711 Middleburg Dr Ste 312 *Web:* www.FirstSunEAP.com	Columbia	SC	29204	803-376-2668	
First Western Advisors 6440 Millrock Dr *Web:* www.fwainvest.com	Salt Lake City	UT	84121	801-930-6500	
Fiserv Credit Processing Services Ste 100 901 International Pkwy *Web:* www.progressdata.com	Lake Mary	FL	32746	407-829-4200	
Fishbait Marketing Llc 1968 Long Creek Rd *Web:* fishbaitmarketing.com	Wadmalaw Island	SC	29487	843-557-0532	
Fishkind & Associates Inc 12051 Corporate Blvd *Web:* www.fishkind.com	Orlando	FL	32817	407-382-3256	
Fitch & Associates LLC 303 Marshall Rd Ste G *Web:* www.fitchassoc.com	Platte City	MO	64079	816-431-2600	
Fitting Group Inc Benedum Trees Bldg 223 4th Ave 11th Fl *Web:* www.fittingroup.com	Pittsburgh	PA	15222	412-434-6934	
Five Point Partners LLC 2526 Mount Vernon Rd Ste B348 *Web:* www.fivepoint.net	Atlanta	GA	30338	404-260-1599	
Five Winds International Inc 20 Paoli Pk *Web:* www.fivewinds.com	Paoli	PA	19301	610-640-2302	
Flatiron Group, The No. 285 Lafayette St Ste 2A *Web:* www.theflatirongroup.com	New York	NY	10012	212-966-8615	
FleetWeather Group, The 2566 Route 52 *Web:* fleetweathergroup.com	Hopewell Junction	NY	12533	845-226-8300	
Fletcher Csi LLC 237 Commerce St *Web:* www.fletchercsi.com	Williston	VT	05495	802-660-9636	
Flippen Group, The 1199 Haywood Dr *TF:* 800-316-4311 ■ *Web:* www.flippengroup.com	College Station	TX	77845	979-693-7660	
Focus Center of Pittsburgh 651 Holiday Dr Plz 5 Ste 300 *Web:* www.fcpresearch.com	Pittsburgh	PA	15220	412-279-5900	
Focus Healthcare Management Inc 720 Cool Springs Blvd	Franklin	TN	37067	615-778-4000	778-0801
Focus Management Group USA Inc 5001 W Lemon St *Web:* www.focusmg.com	Tampa	FL	33609	813-281-0062	
FocusCFO LLC 1010 Jackson Hole Dr Ste 202 *Web:* focuscfo.com	Columbus	OH	43004	614-944-5760	
Foley Carrier Services LLC 140 Huyshope Ave *Web:* www.foleyservices.com	Hartford	CT	06106	860-633-2660	
Fonkoze USA Inc 1718 Connecticut Ave NW Ste 201 *Web:* www.fonkoze.org	Washington	DC	20009	202-628-9033	
Food Concepts Inc 2551 Parmenter St *Web:* foodconcepts.com	Middleton	WI	53562	608-831-5006	
Force Management LLC 10815 Sikes Pl Ste 200 *Web:* www.forcemanagement.com	Charlotte	NC	28277	704-246-2400	
Forte Information Resources LLC 1140 Delaware St *Web:* www.forteinformation.com	Denver	CO	80204	303-321-3888	
Fortune Practice Management 2650 Camino Del Rio N	San Diego	CA	92108	619-564-7402	
Foster Lake & Pond Management Inc 9020 White Oak Rd PO Box 1294 *TF:* 888-525-6348 ■ *Web:* www.fosterlake.com	Garner	NC	27529	919-772-8548	
Franchise Brands LLC 325 Bic Dr *TF:* 800-797-2308 ■ *Web:* www.franchisebrandsllc.com	Milford	CT	06461	800-797-2308	
Franchise Co, The (TFC) 5399 Eglinton Ave W Ste 110 *TF:* 800-294-5591 ■ *Web:* www.thefranchisecompany.com	Etobicoke	ON	M9C5K9	416-620-3960	620-3961
Francorp Inc 20200 Governors Dr *Web:* www.francorp.com	Olympia Fields	IL	60461	708-481-2900	
Freedom Technologies Inc 1100 Wilson Blvd Ste 1200 *Web:* freedomtechnologiesinc.com	Arlington	DC	22209	202-371-2220	
Freeman & Mills Inc 350 S Figueroa St Ste 900 *Web:* www.freemanmills.com	Los Angeles	CA	90071	213-620-9535	
FTR Associates Inc 2881 Grandma Barnes Rd *Web:* ftrintel.com	Nashville	IN	47448	812-988-1699	
Fulcrum Financial Inquiry LLP 888 S Figueroa St Ste 2000 *Web:* www.fulcruminquiry.com	Los Angeles	CA	90017	213-787-4100	
Fuld & Company Inc 131 Oliver St 3rd Fl *Web:* www.fuld.com	Boston	MA	02110	617-492-5900	
Full Life Financial LLC 604 Georgetown Dr *Web:* www.FullLifeFinancial.com	Nashville	TN	37205	615-356-4164	
Fundtech Inc 114 Kathleen Dr *Web:* www.fundtech.com	Syosset	NY	11791	516-496-9885	
Funix Inc 184 Westward Dr *Web:* www.funix.com	Miami	FL	33166	305-884-8800	
Fusion Advisor Network Fusion Financial 555 Taxter Rd Ste 190 *Web:* www.fusionfinancialgroup.com	Elmsford	NY	10523	914-909-1518	
Future Financial Planners Inc 847 Broadway *Web:* ffpinc.com	Bayonne	NJ	07002	201-823-1030	
G.S. Proctor & Associates Inc 14408 Old Mill Rd Ste 201 *Web:* www.gsproctor.com	Upper Marlboro	MD	20772	301-952-8885	
Gap International Inc 700 Old Marple Rd *Web:* www.gapinternational.com	Springfield	PA	19064	610-328-0308	
Gartland & Mellina Group Corp 1385 Broadway Ste 912 *Web:* www.gartlandandmellina.com	New York	NY	10018	212-418-4780	
Gaver Technologies Inc 340 W Patrick St *Web:* www.gtifederal.com	Frederick	MD	21701	301-698-5795	
GCR Inc 2021 Lakeshore Dr Ste 500 *Web:* www.gcrincorporated.com	New Orleans	LA	70122	504-304-2500	
Geehan Group 40 N Main St Ste 1570 *Web:* www.geehangroup.com	Dayton	OH	45423	937-226-1622	
Genscape Inc 445 E Main St Ste 200 *Web:* www.genscape.com	Louisville	KY	40202	502-583-3435	583-3464
Geo-Cleanse International Inc 400 State Rt 34 Ste B *Web:* www.geocleanse.com	Matawan	NJ	07747	908-206-1250	
Geo-instruments Inc 24 Celestial Dr *TF:* 800-477-2506 ■ *Web:* www.geo-instruments.com	Narragansett	RI	02882	800-477-2506	
Geode Partners Inc 15851 N Dallas Pkwy Ste 600 *Web:* www.geodepartners.com	Dallas	TX	75001	214-352-1002	
Georesults Inc 309 Pirkle Ferry Rd *Web:* www.georesults.com	Cumming	GA	30040	770-205-8111	
George Darling Consulting Group Inc Towle Office Bldg 260 Merrimac St *Web:* www.darlingconsulting.com	Newburyport	MA	01950	978-463-0400	
George Mcelroy & Associates Inc 1349 Empire Central Ste 600 *Web:* www.gmainc.com	Dallas	TX	75247	214-905-3700	
GIC Group Inc, The 1434 Duke St *Web:* www.gicgroup.com	Alexandria	VA	22314	703-684-1366	
Gifford Fong Associates Inc 3658 Mount Diablo Blvd Ste 200 *Web:* www.gfong.com	Lafayette	CA	94549	925-299-7800	
GlideSlope LLC 133 W 19th St 6th Fl *Web:* www.theglideslope.com	New York	NY	10011	212-776-1817	
Global Center for Economic Enabling Environments 273 24th Ave *Web:* www.gceee.com	San Francisco	CA	94121	206-877-2460	
Global New Beginnings Inc 4042 W 82nd Ct *Web:* www.gnbiusa.com	Merrillville	IN	46410	219-738-3600	
Global Quality Assurance Inc 11602 Lk Underhill Rd Ste 106 *Web:* www.globalqualityassurance.com	Orlando	FL	32825	407-207-6322	
Global Sage Group LLC Po Box 1431 *Web:* globalsagegroup.com	Salem	NH	03079	603-425-9136	
Global Voyages Group LLC 320 120th Ave NE Ste 100 *Web:* www.globalvoyagesgroup.com	Bellevue	WA	98005	425-637-8558	
Gnarus Advisors LLC 4350 N Fairfax Dr Ste 830 *Web:* www.gnarusllc.com	Arlington	VA	22203	571-384-2444	
Gobbell Hays Partners Inc 10500 E 54th Ave J *Web:* www.ghp1.com	Denver	CO	80239	303-574-0082	
Gordon Energy Solutions LLC 11286 Hadley St *Web:* www.gordonenergysolutions.com	Overland Park	KS	66210	913-451-9539	
Gottlieb Martin & Associates Inc 4932 Sunbeam Rd *TF:* 800-833-9986 ■ *Web:* www.gottlieb.com	Jacksonville	FL	32257	904-346-3088	
Graham-Pelton Consulting Inc 39 Beechwood Rd *Web:* grahampelton.com	Summit	NJ	07901	908-608-1388	
Green Peak Partners PO Box 6064 *Web:* www.greenpeakpartners.com	Denver	CO	80206	303-841-7098	
Green Tape Llc 5300 Dtc Pkwy Ste 450 *Web:* www.greentapellc.com	Greenwood Village	CO	80111	303-221-1306	
Greencastle Associates Consulting LLC 627 Swedesford Rd *Web:* www.greencastleconsulting.com	Malvern	PA	19355	610-640-9958	
Greenline Emeritus Consulting 29 S Lasalle St Ste 333 *Web:* www.greenlineemeritus.com	Chicago	IL	60603	312-436-1883	
GreenTree Financial Group Inc 7951 SW Sixth St Ste 216 *Web:* www.gtfinancial.com	Plantation	FL	33324	954-424-2345	
Greentree Group Inc, The 1360 Technology Court Ste 100 *Web:* www.greentreegroup.com	Dayton	OH	45430	937-490-5500	
Griffin Communitcations Group 3101 Nasa Pkwy Ste L *Web:* www.griffincommgroup.com	Seabrook	TX	77586	281-335-0200	
Group Management Services Inc 3296 Columbia Rd Ste 101 *TF:* 888-823-2084 ■ *Web:* www.groupmgmt.com	Richfield	OH	44286	330-659-0100	659-0150
Groupe BBA Inc 375 Sir-Wilfrid-Laurier Blvd *Web:* www.bba.ca	Mont-saint-hilaire	QC	J3H6C3	450-464-2111	
Grove Consultants International, The 1000 Oreilly Ave *TF:* 800-494-7683 ■ *Web:* www.grove.com	San Francisco	CA	94129	415-561-2500	
Growth Design Corp 225 E St Paul Ave Ste 201 *Web:* www.growthdesign.com	Milwaukee	WI	53202	414-224-0586	
Grudi Associates Inc PO Box 626 *Web:* www.grudiassociates.com	Palmyra	PA	17078	717-838-5022	
Gsg Associates Inc 46 W Dayton St *Web:* www.gsga.net	Pasadena	CA	91105	626-585-1808	
GSVlabs Inc 425 Broadway St *Web:* gsvlabs.com	Redwood City	CA	94063	650-421-2000	
GTMIT Means A Lot 239 Walker St SW *Web:* www.gtmcentral.com	Atlanta	GA	30313	404-522-0486	
Guidant Group Inc 3414 Peachtree Rd NE Ste 375 *Web:* www.guidantgroup.com	Atlanta	GA	30326	404-920-6100	

Phone | Fax

Gulf South Research Corp 8081 G S R I Rd .... Baton Rouge LA 70820 225-757-8088
Web: www.gsrcorp.com

Gupton Marrs International Inc
75 S Broadway Ste 400 .... White Plains NY 10601 434-975-0000
Web: www.guptonmarrs.com

GWN Consulting LLC 1498 Sheridan Run Ct. .... Herndon VA 20170 571-318-1909
Web: www.gwnconsulting.com

H & W Management Co
1021 Majestic Dr Ste 380 .... Lexington KY 40513 859-263-0106
Web: www.hwhotels.com

H S C Foundation Inc 1808 I St Nw .... Washington DC 20006 202-454-1220
Web: www.hschealth.org/foundation

Haines Centre for Strategic Management
1420 Monitor Rd .... San Diego CA 92110 619-275-6528
Web: hainescentre.com

Hale Group Ltd, The 8 Cherry St .... Danvers MA 01923 978-777-9077
Web: www.halegroup.com

Hall Hodges & Associates Inc
700 N Brand Blvd Ste 650 .... Glendale CA 91203 818-244-8930
Web: hall-hodges.com

Handel Group Llc, The 247 Limestone Rd .... Ridgefield CT 06877 917-670-8782
Web: www.handelgroup.com

Harkcon 1390 Chain Bridge Rd 570 .... Mclean VA 22101 800-499-6456
TF: 800-499-6456 ■ *Web:* www.harkcon.com

Harkess-Ord LLC 263 W 38th St Ste 306 .... New York NY 10018 212-704-9989
Web: www.harkess-ord.com

Harlan Consulting Services Inc
2515 Briarpark Dr .... Houston TX 77042 713-464-2484
Web: www.harlanconsulting.com

Hatcher Consultants Inc
2955 SW Wanamaker Dr. Click Here For A Map To Our
.... Topeka KS 66614 785-271-5557
Web: www.hatcherconsultants.com

Hawks Giffels & Pullin (Hgp) Inc
1308 Altamont Rd .... Greenville SC 29608 864-370-0213
Web: hgp-inc.com

Hayes Group International Inc, The
4400 Silas Creek Pkwy Ste 301 .... Winston-salem NC 27104 336-765-6764
Web: www.thehayesgroupintl.com

Hazmed Inc 9410 Annapolis Rd Ste 200 .... Lanham MD 20706 301-577-9339
Web: www.hazmed.com

Hdl Companies 1340 Vly Vista Dr Ste 200 .... Diamond Bar CA 91765 909-861-4335
Web: www.hdlcompanies.com

Health Decisions Inc
2510 Meridian Pkwy Ste 300 .... Durham NC 27713 919-967-1111
Web: www.healthdec.com

HealthAxis Inc 7301 N State Hwy 161 .... Irving TX 75039 972-443-5000 556-0572
TF: 888-974-2947 ■ *Web:* www.healthaxis.com

Healthlinx Transitional Leadership Inc
1404 Goodale Blvd Ste 400 .... Columbus OH 43212 614-444-5400
Web: www.healthlinx.com

Healthtek Solutions Inc 109 E Main St. .... Norfolk VA 23510 757-625-0800
Web: ww12.healthtek.com

Helix Design Inc 175 Lincoln St Unit 201 .... Manchester NH 03103 603-644-1408
Web: www.helixdesign.net

Hempstead & Company Inc 807 Haddon Ave .... Haddonfield NJ 08033 856-795-6026
Web: www.hempsteadco.com

Hexavest Inc
1250 Blvd Ren? L?vesque O. Ste 4200 .... Montreal QC H3B4W8 514-390-8484
Web: www.hexavest.com

Hezel Associates LLC
1201 E Fayette St Ste 44 .... Syracuse NY 13210 315-422-3512
Web: hezelassociates.com

Hg Solutions 3701 S Lawrence St .... Tacoma WA 98409 253-588-2626
TF: 866-988-2626 ■ *Web:* www.hughesgroup.biz

Hidi Rae Consulting Engineers Inc
155 Gordon Baker Rd Ste 200 .... Toronto ON M2H3N5 416-364-2100
Web: www.hidi.com

Higher Dimension Research Inc 570 Hale Ave .... Oakdale MN 55128 651-730-6203
Web: www.superfabric.com

HighQuest Group 300 Rosewood Dr Ste 30 .... Danvers MA 01923 978-887-8800
Web: www.highquestpartners.com

Hill Physicians Medical Group Inc
2409 Camino Ramon PO Box 5080 .... San Ramon CA 94583 925-820-8300 820-8252
TF: 800-445-5747 ■ *Web:* www.hillphysicians.com

Hogan Assessment Systems Inc 2622 E 21st St .... Tulsa OK 74114 918-749-0632
Web: www.hoganassessments.com

Holdsworth Financial Group
40 Eagle Vly ct .... Broadview Heights OH 44147 440-746-8100
Web: www.holdsworthfinancial.com

Holt Marketing Services Inc
3075 Boardwalk Dr Unit 2 .... Saginaw MI 48603 989-791-2475
Web: marketingholt.com

Hornby Zeller Associates Inc 48 4th St Ste 300 .... Troy NY 12180 518-273-1614
Web: www.hornbyzeller.com

Horwath Hotel Tourism & Leisure Consulting
13901 Midway Rd Ste 102-104 .... Dallas TX 75244 972-247-8988
Web: www.horwathhtl.us

Hospicomm Inc 41 N Third St Ste 200 .... Philadelphia PA 19106 215-925-5158
Web: www.hospicomm.com

Hospitality Ventures Management LLC
5 Concourse Pkwy Ste 2828 .... Atlanta GA 30328 404-467-9299 467-1962
Web: www.hvmg.com

Hotchkis & Wiley Capital Management LLC
725 S Figueroa St Fl 39 .... Los Angeles CA 90017 213-430-1000 430-1001
Web: www.hwcm.com

Howard Simon & Associates Inc
304 Saunders Rd .... Riverwoods IL 60015 847-945-0340
TF: 800-424-7526 ■ *Web:* hsimon.com

HowGood Inc 33 Flatbush Ave 5th Fl .... Brooklyn NY 11217 888-601-3015
TF: 888-601-3015 ■ *Web:* howgood.com

Howick Associates 111 N Fairchild St .... Madison WI 53703 608-233-3377
Web: www.howickassociates.com

Phone | Fax

Hoyt Group, The
760 U.S. Hwy One The Hoyt Ctr
Ste 300 .... North Palm Beach FL 33408 561-694-7621
Web: www.hoyt.org

HPM Corp 4304 W 24th Ave Ste 100 .... Kennewick WA 99338 509-737-8939
Web: www.hpmcorporation.com

Hpn Worldwide Inc 119 W Vallette St .... Elmhurst IL 60126 630-941-9030
Web: www.hpn.com

Hru Inc. Technical Resources 3451 Dunckel Rd .... Lansing MI 48911 517-272-5888
TF: 888-205-3446 ■ *Web:* www.hru-tech.com

HRValue LLC 1010 E 20th St .... Tulsa OK 74120 614-266-5926
Web: www.4hrv.com

Hudson Mann Inc
1092 Johnnie Dodds Blvd .... Mount Pleasant SC 29464 843-884-5557
Web: www.hudsonmann.com

Hudson Marine Management Service
4350 Haddonfield Rd # 302 .... Pennsauken NJ 08109 856-486-0800
Web: hudsonanalytix.com

Hurley Communications Inc 1113 Washington St .... Norwood MA 02062 781-762-3313
Web: hurleycommunications.com

Huron Consulting Services LLC
550 W Van Buren St .... Chicago IL 60607 312-583-8700
Web: www.huronconsultinggroup.com

Hurwitz & Associates 13A Highland Cir .... Needham MA 02494 617-597-1724
Web: hurwitz.com

HVS Executive Search 372 Willis Ave .... Mineola NY 11501 516-248-8828
Web: www.hvs.com

Hygieneering Inc 7575 Plz Ct .... Willowbrook IL 60527 630-654-2550
TF: 800-444-7154 ■ *Web:* hygieneering.com

Hypotenuse Enterprises Inc 1545 East Ave .... Rochester NY 14610 585-473-7799
Web: www.hypot.com

ICG Consulting Inc
8570 E Shea Blvd Ste 110 .... Scottsdale AZ 85260 480-607-4040
Web: www.icgconsulting.com

ICM Inc 310 N First St. .... Colwich KS 67030 316-796-0900
TF: 877-456-8588 ■ *Web:* www.icminc.com

iComp LLC 2524 Greenwich St .... San Francisco CA 94123 415-409-2070
Web: www.icomp-llc.com

Icon International Inc
4 Stamford 107 Elm St Plz 15th Fl .... Stamford CT 06902 203-328-2300 328-2333
Web: www.icon-intl.com

Idaho Technology Council Inc
348 W ParkCtr Blvd Ste 200 .... Boise ID 83702 208-514-4542
Web: www.idahotechcouncil.org

Ideas To Go Inc 1 Main St SE 5th Fl .... Minneapolis MN 55414 612-331-1570
Web: www.ideastogo.com

IDOM Inc 55 Madison Ave Ste 400 .... Morristown NJ 07960 973-285-3328
Web: www.idomusa.com

Iec Group 3449 e copper point dr .... Meridian ID 83642 208-947-9522
Web: www.iecgroup.com

ieLinks Inc 2701 E Thomas Rd Ste B .... Phoenix AZ 85016 602-852-0101
Web: ecampuslynx.com

Ignite Venture Partners LLC
34522 N Scottsdale Rd Ste D7239 .... Scottsdale AZ 85266 480-575-9717
Web: www.ignite-vp.com

Ignition Ventures Inc 1 Broadway Fl 14 .... Cambridge MA 02142 617-398-0785
Web: www.ignitionventures.com

IHL Consulting Group 1064 Cedarview Ln .... Franklin TN 37067 615-591-2955
TF: 888-445-6777 ■ *Web:* www.ihlservices.com

IM Group, The 1903 Post Rd Ste 201 .... Fairfield CT 06824 203-307-2151
Web: www.the-imgroup.com

Image Resource Group Inc
130 Pinnacle Point Ct Ste 101 .... Columbia SC 29203 803-790-2121
Web: www.imageresourcegroup.com

Images Graphic Specialties Inc
3730 Canal St .... Fort Myers FL 33916 239-561-6406
Web: www.imagesgs.com

Imagine Business Development
485 Ritchie Hwy Ste 201 .... Severna Park MD 21146 410-544-7878
Web: www.imaginellc.com

IMC Consulting 10529 Old Ct Rd .... Woodstock MD 21163 410-505-4666
Web: www.consultimc.com

IMEX Research 1474 Camino Robles .... San Jose CA 95120 408-268-0800
Web: www.imexresearch.com

Impact Resources Inc 5910 Lone Oak Dr .... Bethesda MD 20814 301-581-9676
Web: www.ir-tech.com

IMS Worldwide Inc 309 Henrietta .... Webster TX 77598 281-554-9099
Web: imsw.com

IMSolutions LLC 3600 Pointe Ctr ct Ste 200 .... Dumfries VA 22026 703-221-2685
Web: www.imsolutionsllc.com

In Touch Business Consultants
11370 66th St 132 .... Largo FL 33773 877-676-5492
TF: 877-676-5492 ■ *Web:* www.affinityconsulting.com

Inc Solayre Inc 4568 N Hiatus Rd .... Sunrise FL 33351 954-749-1220
Web: www.solayre.com

Incentive Group Inc, The
399 Knollwood Rd .... White Plains NY 10603 914-948-0904
Web: www.incentivegroup.com

Indigena Solutions LP
Ste 301 - 800 Carleton Ct .... Delta BC V3M6Y6 604-549-5800
Web: www.indigenasolutions.com

InEdge 9900 Cavendish Blvd Ste 250 .... Montreal QC H4M2V2 514-333-6600
Web: www.inedge.com

INFOCUS Marketing Inc 4245 Sigler Rd .... Warrenton VA 20187 800-708-5478
TF: 800-708-5478 ■ *Web:* www.infocusmarketing.com

Infradant Llc 15715 SE 89th Ct .... Summerfield FL 34491 352-693-3581
Web: www.infradant.com

Initio Inc
2850 W Horizon Ridge Pkwy Ste 200 .... Henderson NV 89052 201-621-0400
Web: initioinc.com

Initium 10300 old cutler rd .... Coral Gables FL 33156 305-665-5212
Web: www.initium.com

Company / Address	City	State	Zip	Phone	Fax
Innerspec Technologies Inc 2940 Perrowville Rd *Web:* www.innerspec.com	Forest	VA	24551	434-948-1301	
Innosight LLC 92 Hayden Ave *Web:* innosight.com	Lexington	MA	02421	781-652-7200	
Innovatia Inc 1 Germain St *Web:* www.innovatia.net	Saint John	NB	E2L4V1	506-640-4000	
Ino.Com Inc 4800 Atwell Rd Discovery Village *Web:* www.ino.com	Shady Side	MD	20764	410-867-2100	
Inovo LLC 202 E Washington St Ste 703 *Web:* www.inovotech.com	Ann Arbor	MI	48104	734-213-2100	
Inprov Ltd 2150 E Continental Blvd *Web:* www.inprov.biz	Southlake	TX	76092	817-748-0300	
Insight Performance Inc 990 Washington St Ste S109 *Web:* www.insightperformance.com	Dedham	MA	02026	781-326-8201	
Insite Managed Solutions LLC 1616 W Cape Coral Pkwy Ste 102 PMB 165 *Web:* insitemanagedsolutions.com	Cape Coral	FL	33914	239-313-1085	
Insperity Inc 19001 Crescent Springs Dr. *TF:* 800-237-3170 ■ *Web:* www.insperity.com/?redirect=true	Kingwood	TX	77339	866-715-3552	
Inspire Excellence 657 n W ave. *Web:* www.inspireexcellence.com	Elmhurst	IL	60126	630-279-7500	
Intech Enterprises Inc 3825 Grant St *Web:* www.intechenterprises.net	Washougal	WA	98671	360-835-8785	
Integra Group Inc 16 Triangle Park Dr Ste 1600 *Web:* www.integragrp.com	Cincinnati	OH	45246	513-326-5600	
Integral Hospitality Solutions LLC 3522 Vann Rd Ste 102 *Web:* www.integralhospitality.com	Birmingham	AL	35235	205-655-2097	
Integrity Group, The PO Box 690423 Ste 500 *Web:* www.go-integrity.com	Houston	TX	77269	281-955-0707	
Intellithink LLC 1225 N 78 St Ste 200 *Web:* www.intelli-think.com	Kansas City	KS	66112	913-766-0303	
Interact Performance Systems Inc 180 N Rverview Dr Ste 165 *Web:* www.inter-ps.com	Anaheim	CA	92808	714-283-8288	
InterDent Inc 9800 S La Cienega Blvd Ste 800 *Web:* www.interdent.com	Inglewood	CA	90301	310-765-2400	765-2456
Interior Move Consultants Inc 5 W 19th St Rm 2c *Web:* www.moveconsultants.com	New York	NY	10011	212-343-8624	
Internovo Inc PO Box 26258 *Web:* www.internovo.com	Collegeville	PA	19426	610-409-9120	
InterSpec LLC 208 Fore St. *Web:* www.e-specs.com	Portland	ME	04101	207-772-6135	
Intertek Westport Technology Center 6700 Portwest Dr *Web:* www.westport1.com	Houston	TX	77024	713-479-8414	
Interval Management Inc 515 Nichols Blvd *Web:* www.qmcorp.com	Sparks	NV	89431	775-355-4040	
Investco Financial Corp 1302 Puyallup St *Web:* www.investco.com	Sumner	WA	98390	253-863-6200	
ipCapital Group Inc 426 Industrial Ave Ste 150 *Web:* www.ipcapitalgroup.com	Williston	VT	05495	802-859-7800	
IPD Analytics LLC 1170 Kane Concourse Ste 300 *Web:* www.ipdanalytics.com	Bay Harbor Islands	FL	33154	305-662-8515	
IQ Systems Inc 5595 Equity Ave Ste 300 *TF:* 866-842-4748 ■ *Web:* www.iqisit.com	Reno	NV	89502	775-352-2301	
Irc Building Sciences Group 2121 Argentia Rd Ste 401 *Web:* www.ircgroup.com	Mississauga	ON	L5N2X4	905-607-7244	
ISPA Inc 1100 Cir 75 Pkwy Ste 242 *Web:* www.ispainc.com	Atlanta	GA	30339	770-690-2900	
ISS Technologies 22 Business Park Cir *Web:* www.isstechnologies.com	Arden	NC	28704	828-684-4248	
Ivy Planning Group 15204 Omega Dr Ste 110 *Web:* www.ivygroupllc.com	Rockville	MD	20850	301-963-1669	
Iwpc 610 Louis Dr. *Web:* www.iwpc.org	Warminster	PA	18974	215-293-9000	
J. Calnan & Assoc Inc 3 Batterymarch Pk 5th fl *Web:* www.jcalnan.com	Quincy	MA	02169	617-801-0200	801-0201
J. Joseph Consulting 21732 Hardy Oak Blvd *Web:* www.jjosephconsulting.com	San Antonio	TX	78258	210-587-2750	
J. P. Farley Corp 29055 Clemens Rd *Web:* www.jpfarley.com	Westlake	OH	44145	440-250-4300	
J.F. Smith Group Inc 735 E Glenn Ave. *Web:* www.jfsg.com	Auburn	AL	36831	334-502-5374	
J.R. Henry Consulting Inc PO BOX 9724 *Web:* www.psmarketing.org	Pittsburgh	PA	15229	412-931-2833	
Jamsan Hotel Management Inc 440 Bedford St *Web:* www.jamsanhotels.com	Lexington	MA	02420	781-863-8500	
Janko Hospitality Llc 3050 Finley Rd Ste 300D-1 *Web:* www.jankohotels.com	Downers Grove	IL	60515	630-434-9400	
Jarlette Health Services 689 Yonge St. *Web:* www.jarlette.com	Midland	ON	L4R2E1	705-526-4238	
Jax Kneppers Associates Inc 2125 Ygnacio Vly Rd *Web:* www.jaxkneppers.com	Walnut Creek	CA	94598	925-933-3914	
Jay Electric Company Inc 5300 E Lake Blvd. *Web:* www.jayelectric.com	Birmingham	AL	35217	205-595-9910	
JCO Group Inc 2408 Butler Way *Web:* jcogroup.com	Round Rock	TX	78664	512-246-9301	
Jdk Management Co Inc 1388 SR- 487 *Web:* www.jdkmgt.com	Bloomsburg	PA	17815	570-784-0111	784-4785
Jenaly Technology Group I 1 greenleaf woods dr *Web:* www.jenaly.com	Portsmouth	NH	03801	603-431-7864	
Jeskell Systems LLC 6201 chevy chase dr. *Web:* www.jeskell.com	Laurel	MD	20707	301-230-1533	
JHPIEGO Corp 1615 Thames St *Web:* www.jhpiego.org	Baltimore	MD	21231	410-537-1800	
JHT Inc 2710 Discovery Dr Ste 100 *Web:* www.jht.com	Orlando	FL	32826	407-381-7797	381-0017
Jim Whitten Roof Consultants LLC Po Box 200925 *Web:* www.jimwhitten.com	Austin	TX	78720	512-250-0999	
Jiten Hotel Management Inc 495 Westgate Dr *Web:* www.jitenhotels.com	Brockton	MA	02301	508-427-1667	
JKM Consulting Inc PO Box 3250 *Web:* www.m2connections.com	Oxford	AL	36203	256-405-0613	
Job Performance Systems Inc 1240 N Pitt St Ste 200 *Web:* www.jps-usa.com	Alexandria	VA	22314	703-683-5805	
JobsOhio 41 S High St Ste 1500 *Web:* jobs-ohio.com	Columbus	OH	43215	614-224-6446	
John Levy Consulting 505 Mesa Rd Ste 1 *Web:* johnlevyconsulting.com	Point Reyes Station	CA	94956	415-663-1818	
Jolt Consulting Group 112 Spring St Ste 301 *TF:* 877-249-6262 ■ *Web:* www.joltconsultinggroup.com	Saratoga Springs	NY	12866	877-249-6262	
Jones Consulting Group LLC, The 3648 Carmel Dr. *Web:* www.jconsultants.net	Troy	MI	48083	248-677-2236	
Jones Group Consulting 3824 Corrales Rd Ste 102 *Web:* jonesgroupcrm.com	Corrales	NM	87048	505-792-4070	
Jones Nale & Mattingly PLC 642 S Fourth Ave Ste 300 *Web:* www.jnmcpa.com	Louisville	KY	40202	502-583-0248	
Jova Solutions 965 Mission St Ste 600 *Web:* www.jovasolutions.com	San Francisco	CA	94103	415-348-1400	
Jurinnov Ltd The Idea Ctr 1375 Euclid Ave Ste 400 *Web:* www.jurinnov.com	Cleveland	OH	44115	216-664-1100	
Justice Solutions of America Inc 467 Lk Howell Rd Stes 201-25 Ste *Web:* www.federalprisonconsultants.com	Maitland	FL	32751	386-341-9212	
K2 Project Control Systems 4330 E W Hwy Ste 320 *Web:* www.k2consulting.com	Bethesda	MD	20814	301-656-2228	
Kahn Consulting Inc 157 Leonard Wood N P.O. Box 1045 *Web:* www.kahnconsultinginc.com	Highland Park	IL	60035	847-266-0722	
Kaleel Jamison Consulting Group Inc, The 5 Third St Ste 230 *Web:* www.kjcg.com	Troy	NY	12180	518-271-7000	
Kaplan Devries Inc 1903 Ashwood Ct *Web:* www.kaplandevries.com	Greensboro	NC	27455	336-288-8200	
kasina LLC 581 Ave of The Americas 5th Fl *Web:* www.kasina.com	New York	NY	10011	212-349-7412	
Kawaller & Company LLC 162 State St *Web:* kawaller.com	Brooklyn	NY	11201	718-694-6270	
Keating Technologies Inc 25 Royal Crest Court Ste 120 *TF:* 877-532-8464 ■ *Web:* www.keating.com	Markham	ON	L3R9X4	905-479-0230	
Kehrer Saltzman & Associates LLC 9218 Skipaway Dr. *Web:* kehrerbielan.com	Waxhaw	NC	28173	704-243-4512	
Keiro Services 325 S Boyle Ave *TF:* 800-366-2624 ■ *Web:* www.keiro.org	Los Angeles	CA	90033	323-980-7555	
Kek Associates Inc 100 Josons Dr *Web:* kekdesign.com	Rochester	NY	14623	585-424-3380	
Keller Fay Group LLC 65 Church St 3rd Fl *Web:* www.kellerfay.com	New Brunswick	NJ	08901	732-846-6800	
Kerdan Group, The 139 Main St. *Web:* www.kerdan.com	Cambridge	MA	02142	617-501-1818	
Kesselrun 8215 Roswell Rd Ste 925	Atlanta	GA	30350	770-640-9100	
Kewin Consulting 62 Twenty Seventh St. *Web:* www.kewin.ca	Toronto	ON	M8W2X4	416-802-2526	
Key West Technologies LLC 101 N Clematis St Ste 308 *Web:* www.keywesttechnologies.com	West Palm Beach	FL	33401	561-282-6160	
Kibel Green Inc 2001 Wilshire Blvd Ste 420 *Web:* kginc.com	Santa Monica	CA	90403	310-829-0255	
KickStart Alliance PO Box 705 *Web:* www.kickstartall.com	Los Altos	CA	94023	650-464-7663	
Kinetic Caf? Inc 934 - 1 Yonge St. *Web:* www.kineticcafe.com	Toronto	ON	M5E1E5	416-899-0761	
Kirby Bates Associates Inc 1 Bala Ave Ste 234 *Web:* www.kirbybates.com	Bala Cynwyd	PA	19004	610-667-1800	
KKO & Associates LLC 5 Vine St *Web:* kko.com	Andover	MA	01810	978-475-4079	
Klemmer & Associates Leaders 1340 commerce st *TF:* 800-577-5447 ■ *Web:* www.klemmer.com	Petaluma	CA	94954	707-559-7722	
KLG Advisors 399 Park Ave 11th Fl *Web:* www.klgadvisors.com	New York	NY	10011	212-514-4600	
Km2 Solutions LLC 100 Park Ave Ste 1600 *Web:* www.km2solutions.com	New York	NY	10017	404-848-8886	
KMGi Corp 4501 7th Ave N *Web:* www.kmgi.com	Saint Petersburg	FL	33713	727-322-9596	
Knapp & Associates International 712 Executive Dr. *Web:* www.knappinternational.com	Princeton	NJ	08540	609-921-3478	

	City	State	Zip	Phone	Fax
Koski Research Inc 7 joost ave Ste 301 *Web:* www.koskiresearch.com	San Francisco	CA	94127	415-334-3400	
Kotter International 5 Bennett St. *TF:* 855-400-4712 ■ *Web:* www.kotterinternational.com	Cambridge	MA	02138	617-600-6787	
Kremer & Associates Inc 6400 Brooktree Ct Ste 240 *Web:* www.kremerassociates.com	Wexford	PA	15090	724-934-0808	
Kromite LLC 36 Four Seasons Ste 301 *Web:* www.kromite.com	Chesterfield	MO	63017	314-878-3200	
Kw Engineering 287 17th St Ste 300 *Web:* www.kw-engineering.com	Oakland	CA	94612	510-834-6420	
L3 Payments LLC 850 Hampshire Rd Ste S *Web:* www.l3payments.com	Westlake Village	CA	91361	805-449-1191	
LaborVoices Inc 690 W Fremont Ave *Web:* www.laborvoices.com	Sunnyvale	CA	94087	925-456-4574	
Lakeside Technologies LLC 7500 W 160th St *Web:* www.lakesidetechnologies.com	Stilwell	KS	66085	913-956-4170	
Lamplighter Financial LLC 502 Cabrillo Ct *Web:* www.lamplighterfinancial.com	Petaluma	CA	94954	415-484-6190	
Lane Bridgers Schill 230 Marter Ave *Web:* lanebridgers.com	Moorestown	NJ	08057	856-638-1855	
Lassus Wherley & Associates Pc 1 Academy St *Web:* www.lassuswherley.com	New Providence	NJ	07974	908-464-0102	
Latitude Consulting Group Inc 100 E Michigan Ave Ste 200 *TF:* 888-577-2797 ■ *Web:* www.latitudecg.com	Saline	MI	48176	888-577-2797	
Lawrence Service Co 1405 Xenium Ln N Ste 250 *Web:* www.lmsvc.com	Plymouth	MN	55441	763-383-5700	
Lead Concepts Inc 1060 Texan Trail *Web:* www.leadconcepts.com	Grapevine	TX	76051	817-421-5803	
Leader Enterprises Inc 1775 Woodstock Rd *Web:* leaderagency.com	Roswell	GA	30075	678-507-1010	
Leading Systems Technologies Inc 2721 Prosperity Ave Ste 100 *Web:* www.leadingsystemstechnologies.com	Fairfax	VA	22031	703-204-0404	
Learning Designs 614 Main St Ste 104 *Web:* www.learningdesigns.com	Park City	UT	84060	435-645-9515	
Learning Network, Inc, The 401 Glenneyre St Ste C *Web:* www.learning.net	Laguna Beach	CA	92651	949-497-1318	
Learning Unlimited 5810 E Skelly Dr Ste 500 *TF:* 888-622-4203 ■ *Web:* learningunlimited.com	Tulsa	OK	74135	918-622-3292	
Leedom & Associates LLC 3700 S Tamiami Trl *Web:* www.twentygroups.com	Sarasota	FL	34239	941-371-7999	
Legal Club of America Corp 7771 W Oakland Park Blvd Ste 217 *TF:* 800-316-5387 ■ *Web:* www.legalclub.com	Sunrise	FL	33351	954-377-0222	
Leland Management Inc 8009 S Orange Ave *Web:* www.lelandmanagement.com	Orlando	FL	32809	407-447-9955	
Level Ii 774 Superior Ave *Web:* www.leveltwo.com	San Leandro	CA	94577	510-569-3299	
Level Up Analytics Inc 277 Castro St *Web:* www.levelupanalytics.com	Mountain View	CA	94041	650-386-5914	
Levin Group Inc 10 New Plant Ct *Web:* www.levingroup.com	Owings Mills	MD	21117	410-654-1234	
LexaMed Ltd 705 Front St *Web:* www.lexamed.net	Toledo	OH	43605	419-693-5307	
Lieberman Management Services Inc 355 W Dundee Rd Ste 110 *Web:* www.liebermanmanagement.com	Buffalo Grove	IL	60089	847-459-0000	
Life Products Solutions Group Llc 1450 Madruga Ave Ste 210 *Web:* www.lpsgroup.com	Miami	FL	33146	305-668-8780	
Lifewings Partners LLC 9198 Crestwyn Hills Dr *TF:* 800-290-9314 ■ *Web:* www.saferpatients.com	Memphis	TN	38125	800-290-9314	
Linchris Hotel Corp 269 Hanover St *Web:* www.linchris.com	Hanover	MA	02339	781-826-8824	826-2411
Lindemann Bentzon Engineering Company Inc 290 Citrus Twr Blvd Ste 200 *Web:* www.lbbe.com	Clermont	FL	34711	352-242-0100	
Lionshare Leadership Group Inc 7065 Moores Ln Ste 200 *Web:* lionshare.org	Brentwood	TN	37027	615-377-4688	
Livelogic L l c 13601 Preston Rd Ste 720e *Web:* www.livelogic.net	Dallas	TX	75240	972-385-8515	
LoBue Associates Inc 1771 E Flamingo Rd A219 Ste 219A89119 *Web:* www.lobue.com	Las Vegas	NV	89119	702-898-6940	
Logapps LLC 103 W Broad St Suit 250 *Web:* logapps.com	Falls Church	VA	22046	703-592-6362	
LogicData 10800 E Bethany Dr Ste 202 *Web:* www.logicdata.com	Aurora	CO	80237	303-694-4400	
Logistics Capital & Strategy LLC 1110 N Glebe Rd Ste 250 *Web:* www.logcapstrat.com	Arlington	VA	22201	703-276-9100	
Loren D Stark Company Inc 10750 Rockley Rd *Web:* www.ldsco.com	Houston	TX	77099	281-498-5777	
Lost Recovery Network Lrni 406 dixon st *TF:* 877-693-1456 ■ *Web:* www.lrni.com	Vidalia	GA	30474	912-537-3901	
Louddoor 1001 harden St Market Place Shopping Ctr Ste 203 *Web:* www.louddoor.com	Columbia	SC	29205	803-765-2995	
Loyalty Methods Inc 80 Yesler Way Ste 310 *Web:* www.loyaltymethods.com	Seattle	WA	98104	206-257-2111	
LS Gallegos & Associates Inc 9137 E Mineral Cir Ste 220 *Web:* www.lsgallegos.com	Centennial	CO	80112	303-790-8474	
LT&T (DW Consulting) 1556 Halford Ave #230 *Web:* www.lighthouse-tours.com	Santa Clara	CA	95051	408-260-5802	
Lunarpages. Inc 1360 N Hancock St *Web:* www.lunarpages.com	Anaheim	CA	92807	714-521-8150	
LWBJ Financial LLC 4200 University Ave Ste 410 *Web:* www.lwbj.com	West Des Moines	IA	50266	515-222-5680	
Lynchval Systems Worldwide Inc 4170 Lafayette Ctr Dr Ste 500 *Web:* www.lynchval.com	Chantilly	VA	20151	703-709-1000	
Lytica Inc 308 Legget Dr Ste 200 *Web:* www.lytica.com	Kanata	ON	K2K1Y6	613-271-1414	
M Corp 947 Enterprise Dr Loft C *Web:* www.the-mcorp.com	Sacramento	CA	95825	916-254-0355	
M L S Data Management Solutions 6115 Camp Bowie Blvd Ste 200 *Web:* www.mlsc.com	Fort Worth	TX	76116	817-804-6900	
M2 Logistics Inc 2413 Hazelwood Ln *TF:* 800-391-5121 ■ *Web:* www.m2logistics.com	Green Bay	WI	54304	920-569-8800	
Macadamian Technologies Inc 165 Rue Wellington *TF:* 877-779-6336 ■ *Web:* www.macadamian.com	Gatineau	QC	J8X2J3	819-772-0300	
MacMunnis Inc 1840 Oak Ave Ste 300 *Web:* www.macmunnis.com	Evanston	IL	60201	847-316-1100	
Macro Management Service 800 Navarro St *Web:* www.macromgt.com	San Antonio	TX	78205	210-226-1047	
Mage LLC 119 Braintree St Ste 505 *Web:* www.mageusa.com	Boston	MA	02134	781-449-8366	
Magee Resource Group LLC 920 Pierremont Rd *Web:* www.mageeresource.com	Shreveport	LA	71106	318-865-8411	
MaguireZay LLC 17194 Preston Rd Ste 102-143 *Web:* maguirezay.com	DALLAS	TX	75248	214-692-5002	
mal Energy International Inc, The 36 Bentley Ave *Web:* www.thermalenergy.com	Ottawa	ON	K2E6T8	613-723-6776	
Management & Engineering Technologies International Inc (METI) 8600 Boeing Dr *Web:* www.meticorp.com	El Paso	TX	79925	915-772-4975	772-2253
Manager Tools LLC 5765-F Burke Centre Pkwy Ste 152 *Web:* www.manager-tools.com	Burke	VA	22015	571-336-6211	
Manorhouse Management Inc 706 Old Stream Rd *Web:* www.manorhouseretirement.com	Manakin Sabot	VA	23103	804-784-7255	
Marakon Associates Inc 1411 Bwy 35th fl *Web:* www.marakon.com	New York	NY	10018	212-520-7120	
Marble A D & Company Inc 375 E Elm St Ste 101 *Web:* www.admarble.com	Conshohocken	PA	19428	484-533-2500	
Mariner Partners Inc 4v1, 1 Germain St *Web:* www.marinerpartners.com	Saint John	NB	E2L5G5	506-642-9000	
Marketech 7915 Westglen Dr *Web:* www.marketechcorp.com	Houston	TX	77063	713-667-7778	
Marketri LLC 58 Charter Oak Dr *Web:* www.marketri.com	Doylestown	PA	18901	215-489-5563	
Marketwell Inc 17 N Rd PO Box 70 *Web:* marketwell.com	Tivoli	NY	12583	845-757-2783	
Markon Inc 400 S Maple Ave Ste 230 *Web:* www.markonsolutions.com	Falls Church	VA	22046	703-884-0030	
Marlin Alliance 3990 Old Town Ave Ste C-205 *Web:* themarlinalliance.com	San Diego	CA	92110	619-450-1717	
Marquis Consulting Services Inc 3821 superior ridge dr *Web:* www.marquis-id.com	Fort wayne	IN	46808	260-497-6437	
Mast Hill Consulting Inc 15 Mast Hill Rd *Web:* www.masthillconsulting.com	Hingham	MA	02043	781-741-5200	
Masters Advisors Inc 32 E Roseville Rd *Web:* www.mastersadvisors.com	Lancaster	PA	17601	717-581-1323	
Material & Contract Services LLC 5820 Stoneridge Mall Rd *TF:* 866-772-9250 ■ *Web:* www.macservices.us	Pleasanton	CA	94588	925-460-0397	
Matter Communications Inc 50 Water St Mill No 3 The Tannery *Web:* www.matternow.com	Newburyport	MA	01950	978-499-9250	
Mattersight Corp 200 S Wacker Ste 3100 **Fax Area Code:* 312 ■ *TF:* 877-235-6925 ■ *Web:* www.mattersight.com	Chicago	IL	60606	877-235-6925	454-3501*
MavenWire LLC 630 Freedom Business Ctr 3rd Fl *TF:* 866-343-4870 ■ *Web:* www.mavenwire.com	King Of Prussia	PA	19406	866-343-4870	
Maximum Potential Inc 2854 Hwy 55 Ste 150 *Web:* www.maximumpotential.com	Saint Paul	MN	55121	651-452-8256	
MBS Outsourcing 1201 Oakridge Dr Ste 320 *Web:* www.mbsoutsourcing.com	Fort Collins	CO	80525	970-224-1016	
McBride Associates Inc 1742 N St NW *Web:* www.mcbrideassociates.com	Washington	DC	20036	202-452-1150	
McCormick Group Inc, The 1440 Central Park Blvd Ste 207 *Web:* www.mccormickgroup.com	Fredericksburg	VA	22401	540-786-9777	
McGraw Wentworth Inc 3331 W Big Beaver Rd Ste 200 *Web:* www.mcgrawwentworth.com	Troy	MI	48084	248-822-8000	
Mcintosh & Associates LLC 1955 Lakeway Dr Ste 270b *Web:* mcintoshassociates.com	Lewisville	TX	75057	214-488-2321	
McLagan Partners Inc 1600 Summer St Ste 601 *Web:* www.mclagan.com	Stamford	CT	06905	203-359-2878	
McLarty Associates 900 17th St NW Ste 800 *Web:* www.maglobal.com	Washington	DC	20006	202-419-1420	
Mcmanis Associates Inc 7518 Diplomat Dr Ste 201 *Web:* mcmanis-monsalve.com	Manassas	VA	20109	703-331-3890	
MDA Leadership Consulting Inc 150 S Fifth St *Web:* www.mdaleadership.com	Minneapolis	MN	55402	612-332-8182	
Medco Enterprises Inc 3530 Wayne Ave	Bronx	NY	10467	718-655-1700	

Phone | Fax

Medcor Inc 4805 W Prime Pkwy ...... McHenry IL 60050 815-363-9500 363-9696
TF: 877-696-6775 ■ *Web:* www.medcor.com

Medefis Inc 10826 Old Mill Rd Suitte 101 ...... Omaha NE 68154 402-393-6333
Web: www.medefis.com

Medexcel USA Inc 484 Temple Hill Rd ...... New Windsor NY 12553 845-565-3700
TF: 800-563-6384 ■ *Web:* www.medexcelusa.com

Medical Strategic Planning Inc
5 Shelbern Dr ...... Lincroft NJ 07738 732-219-5090
Web: www.medsp.com

Medium Blue Search Engine Marketing
670 Eleventh St, NW ...... Atlanta GA 30318 404-525-4420
Web: www.mediumblue.com

Medliance 1839 S Alma School Rd Ste 230 ...... Mesa AZ 85210 480-784-6335
Web: www.medliance.com

Medusind Solutions Inc
31103 Rancho Viejo Rd Ste 2150 ...... San Juan Capistrano CA 92675 949-487-7884
Web: www.medusind.com

Meeting Incentive Experts
61 W 15th St Apt 301 ...... Chicago IL 60605 312-842-3600
Web: www.miexperts.com

Meeting Matters Inc 11 Dougal Ln ...... East Northport NY 11731 631-368-2082
Web: meeting-matters.com

Meeting Solutions Llc 593 N Wolf Rd ...... Wheeling IL 60090 847-808-1818
Web: www.associationandmeetingsolutions.com

Meeting Systems Inc 600 N Curtis Rd Ste 170 ...... Boise ID 83706 208-288-0290
Web: www.meetingsystems.com

Meetings and Events International
1314 Burch Dr ...... Evansville IN 47725 812-471-3000
Web: www.meintl.com

MELE Associates Inc 11 Taft Court Ste 101 ...... Rockville MD 20850 240-453-6990
Web: www.meleassociates.com

Mercatus Energy Advisors LLC
708 Main St Ste 880 ...... Houston TX 77002 713-970-1003
Web: www.mercatusenergy.com

Met-L-Flo Inc 720 Heartland Dr Unit S ...... Sugar Grove IL 60554 630-409-9860
Web: www.metlflo.com

Metasystems Inc 13700 State Rd Ste 1 ...... North Royalton OH 44133 440-526-1454
Web: www.metasystems.com

Metis Strategy LLC
6900 Wisconsin Ave Ste 300 ...... Bethesda MD 20815 301-893-4610
Web: www.metisstrategy.com

Metropolitan Health Networks Inc
777 Yamato Rd Ste 510 ...... Boca Raton FL 33431 561-805-8500
NYSE: MDF ■ *TF:* 800-221-5487 ■ *Web:* www.metcare.com

Metrus Group Inc 953 Route 202 ...... Somerville NJ 08876 908-231-1900
Web: www.metrus.com

Metzner Schneider Associates Inc
6620 Gaston Ave ...... Dallas TX 75214 214-887-6464
Web: www.metzner-schneider.com

MHM Services Inc 1593 Spring Hill Rd Ste 600 ...... Vienna VA 22182 703-749-4600 749-4604
TF: 800-416-3649 ■ *Web:* www.mhm-services.com

Michael Raiser Associates Inc
500 Valley Rd Ste 106 ...... Wayne NJ 07470 973-305-0011
Web: teammra.com

Microalloying International Inc
10175 Harwin Dr Ste 107 ...... Houston TX 77036 713-771-5446
Web: www.microalloying.com

Microbiology & Quality Associates Inc
2341 Stanwell Dr ...... Concord CA 94520 925-270-3800
Web: microqa.com

Mid Ohio Regional Planning Commission
111 Liberty St Ste 100 ...... Columbus OH 43215 614-228-2663
TF: 800-750-0750 ■ *Web:* morpc.org

Mid Peninsula Endoscopy Center
50 S San Mateo Dr Ste 400 ...... San Mateo CA 94401 650-373-1970
Web: www.midpeninsulaendoscopy.com

MIDIOR Consulting Inc 22 Putnam Ave ...... Cambridge MA 02139 617-864-8813
Web: www.midior.com

Midland Community Healthcare Services
600 N Marienfeld St Ste 1090 ...... Midland TX 79701 432-570-0238
Web: www.midlandchs.com

Midpoint National 1263 Southwest Blvd ...... Kansas City KS 66103 913-362-7400

Midwest Consulting Group
5605 N MacArthur Blvd ...... Irving TX 75038 972-910-9200
Web: www.mcginfo.com

Midwest Hospitality Group Inc (MHG)
1220 Brookville Way ...... Indianapolis IN 46239 317-356-4000 356-4004
Web: www.mhghotelsllc.com

Mll Life Inc 1750 Yankee Doodle Rd ...... Eagan MN 55121 651-662-5065
Web: www.selectaccount.com

Mikan Associates Consulting
141 W Jackson Blvd Ste 1520 ...... Chicago IL 60604 847-613-6010
TF: 888-902-1970 ■ *Web:* www.mikanassociates.com

Mindstream LLC 2872 NE 25th Ct ...... Fort Lauderdale FL 33305 954-594-2601
Web: www.mindstreameducation.com

Mission1st Group Inc 1161 Broad St Ste 114 ...... Shrewsbury NJ 07702 732-542-5700
Web: www.mission1st.com

Mitchell Selling Dynamics
1360 Puritan Ave ...... Birmingham MI 48009 248-644-8092
TF: 800-328-9696 ■ *Web:* www.mitchellsell.com

MKP communications Inc 5 E 16th St 3rd Fl ...... New York NY 10003 212-983-5700
Web: www.mkpteam.com

ML Levin & Associates 4927 W 88TH ST ...... Prairie Village KS 66207 913-226-8840
Web: www.mllevin.com

MMG Partners 85 E India Row ...... Boston MA 02110 617-367-2727
Web: www.mmgpartners.com

Modis Inc 10201 Centurion Pkwy N Ste 400 ...... Jacksonville FL 32256 904-360-2300 360-2110
TF: 800-372-2788 ■ *Web:* www.modis.com

Modular Process Control LLC
11477 Olde Cabin Rd Ste 300 ...... Chesterfield MO 63141 636-536-1000
Web: www.mpcenergyllc.com

Montana Manufacturing Extension Center
2310 University Way Bldg 2 ...... Bozeman MT 59715 406-994-3812
Web: www.montana.edu/mmec

Montreal International
380 Saint-Antoine St W Ste 8000 ...... Montreal QC H2Y3X7 514-987-8191
Web: www.montrealinternational.com

Monument Consulting LLC
3957 Westerre Pkwy Ste 330 ...... Richmond VA 23233 804-622-9992
Web: www.monumentconsulting.com

Moreland Associates Corp
2532 Santa Clara Ave Ste 413 ...... Alameda CA 94501 510-748-8146
Web: www.morelandassoc.com

Morgan Clarke Enterprises Inc
119 S Warren St ...... Trenton NJ 08608 609-278-3500
Web: www.morganclarke.com

Mortgage Banking Solutions
Frost Bank Tower 401 Congress Ave Ste 1540 ...... Austin TX 78701 512-977-9900
Web: www.mortgagebankingsolutions.com

Mosaic Financial Partners Inc
140 Geary St 6th Fl ...... San Francisco CA 94108 415-788-1952
Web: mosaicfp.com

Moseley Corp, The 31 Hayward St ...... Franklin MA 02038 508-520-4004
Web: www.moseleycorp.com

Mosser Companies 308 Jessie St ...... San Francisco CA 94103 415-284-9000
Web: www.mosserco.com

Mpa Media 5406 Bolsa Ave ...... Huntington Beach CA 92649 714-230-3150
Web: www.mpamedia.com

MSS Services Inc 14200 Schaeffer Rd ...... Germantown MD 20874 301-528-5531
Web: mssserv.com

Mundy & Associates 140 N 8th St Ste 206 ...... Lincoln NE 68508 402-476-8844
Web: www.mundyandassociates.com

Murfee Meadows Inc
120 Office Park Dr Ste 100 ...... Birmingham AL 35223 205-871-9515
Web: murfeemeadows.com

Mutual Fund Store LLC, The
11095 Metcalf Ave Ste 220 ...... Overland Park KS 66210 800-375-3000
TF: 800-375-3000 ■ *Web:* www.mutualfundstore.com

MVS Inc 3630A Georgia Ave NW ...... Washington DC 20010 202-722-7981
Web: www.mvsconsulting.com

MyLLC.com Inc 5716 Corsa Ave Ste 110 ...... Westlake Village CA 91362 888-886-9552
TF: 888-886-9552 ■ *Web:* www.myllc.com

Napa Networks Inc 245 Stafford Rd West Ste 202 ...... Ottawa ON K2H9E8 613-248-3417
TF: 888-641-1113 ■ *Web:* www.talentmap.com

National Administrators Inc
2003 Jericho Tpke ...... New Hyde Park NY 11040 516-352-0263
Web: www.fnainsurance.com

National Health Management Inc
1660 Park Ave ...... Pittsburgh PA 15213 412-578-7800
Web: www.independencecourt.com

National Quality Assurance - U.S.A. Inc
4 Post Office Sq ...... Acton MA 01720 978-635-9256
Web: www.nqa.com/en-us

Navesink Logistics Inc 32 Marcshire Dr ...... Middletown NJ 07748 732-671-5746
Web: www.logjobs.com

Navigate Power LLC 2211 N Elston Ave Ste 309 ...... Chicago IL 60614 888-601-1789
TF: 888-601-1789 ■ *Web:* navigatepower.com

Navigator Management Partners LLC
450 S Frnt St ...... Columbus OH 43215 614-796-0090
Web: www.navmp.com

Navin, Haffty & Associates LLC
200 Cordwainer Dr Ste 100 ...... Norwell MA 02061 781-871-6770
Web: www.navinhaffty.com

Navtech Seminars & Gps Supply
5501 Backlick Rd Ste 230 ...... Springfield VA 22151 703-256-8900
TF: 800-628-0885 ■ *Web:* www.navtechgps.com

NDA Partners LLC 40 Commerce Ln Ste D ...... Rochelle VA 22738 540-738-2550
Web: www.ndapartners.com

Neilson Associates Inc 42 Blue Stone Dr ...... Chadds Ford PA 19317 610-793-0883
Web: www.neilsonassociates.com

Nellis Management Corp 2940 104th St ...... Urbandale IA 50322 515-252-1742
Web: www.nellismanagement.com

Nelson, Tietz & Hoye Inc
81 S Ninth St Ste 330 ...... Minneapolis MN 55402 612-344-1500
Web: www.nth-inc.com

NeoTech Incubator
6751 Columbia Gateway Dr Ste 500 ...... Columbia MD 21046 410-313-6550
Web: www.hceda.org

Neset Consulting Service Inc 6844 Hwy 40 ...... Tioga ND 58852 701-664-1492
Web: www.nesetconsulting.com

Net (net) Inc
Baker Lofts Bldg 217 E 24th St - Ste 010 ...... Holland MI 49423 616-546-3100
Web: www.netnetweb.com

Net Theory Inc 64 Fulton St Ste 603 ...... New York NY 10038 212-868-5950
Web: www.nettheory.com

Netcracker Technology Corp
95 Sawyer Rd University Ofc Pk III ...... Waltham MA 02453 781-419-3300 419-3301
TF: 800-477-5785 ■ *Web:* www.netcracker.com

Netropole 5630 NE Martin Luther King Jr ...... Portland OR 97211 503-241-3499
Web: www.portlandmanagedservices.com

Network Medical Management Inc
1668 S Garfield Ave 2nd Fl ...... Alhambra CA 91801 626-282-0288
Web: www.networkmedmgmt.com

Neuwing Energy Ventures LLC
913 N Market St Ste 1001 ...... Wilmington DE 19801 302-371-9771
Web: www.neuwingenergy.com

New Age Protection Inc
6551 Loisdale Cty Ste 801 ...... Springfield VA 22150 703-912-3057
Web: www.new-age-inc.com

New Ventures West PO Box 591525 ...... San Francisco CA 94159 800-332-4618
TF: 800-332-4618 ■ *Web:* newventureswest.com

Newport Creative Communications Inc
33 Railroad Ave ...... Duxbury MA 02332 781-934-0586
Web: www.newportcreative.com

Nexgen Product Design & Development
3117 Almond Dr ...... Flower Mound TX 75028 972-333-3870
Web: www.nexgenpd.com

Company	City	State	ZIP	Phone	Fax
NextServices Inc 540 Avis Dr Ste H *Web:* nextservices.net	Ann Arbor	MI	48108	734-677-7700	
NFC Global LLC 240 Gibraltar Rd Ste 150 *Web:* www.nfcglobal.com	Horsham	PA	19044	215-657-0800	
Noninvasive Medical Technologies Inc 6412 S Arville St *Web:* www.nmtinc.org	Las Vegas	NV	89118	702-614-3360	
North Channel Capital LLC 5550 S 59th St Ste 22 *Web:* www.northchannelcapital.wfadv.com	Lincoln	NE	68516	402-421-6500	
Northbridge Group, The 30 Monument Sq Ste 105 *Web:* norbridgeinc.com	Concord	MA	01742	781-266-2600	
Northeast Veterans Business Resource Center Po Box 52113 *Web:* www.nevbrc.org	Boston	MA	02205	617-938-3933	
NorthStar Management Partners LLC 4 Bellows Rd *Web:* www.northstarmp.com	Westborough	MA	01581	508-651-0093	
Novatek Communications Inc 500 Helendale Rd Ste 280 *Web:* www.novatekcom.com	Rochester	NY	14609	585-482-4070	
Novologic Inc 279 W Crogan St *Web:* www.novologic.com	Lawrenceville	GA	30046	770-277-1030	
Nucleus Software Inc 3086 Congressional Office Park Ste 10 *Web:* www.nucleussoftware.com	Kendall Park	NJ	08824	732-503-8412	
Nulayer Inc 72 Fraser Ave Ste 201 *Web:* www.nulayer.com	Toronto	ON	M6K3J7	416-840-4384	
Nussle Group, The 828 Slaters Ln Ste 104 *Web:* www.thenusslegroup.com	Alexandria	VA	22314	202-540-9045	
O'Connor Group Inc, The 10 Stearns Rd *Web:* www.theoconnorgroup.com	Bedford	MA	01730	781-275-2423	
O-H Community Partners Ltd 372 W Ontario St Ste 501 *Web:* ohcommunity.com	Chicago	IL	60654	312-850-0600	
Oak Grove Technologies LLC 4140 Parklake Ave Ste 330 *Web:* www.oakgrovetech.com	Raleigh	NC	27612	919-845-1038	
OB Sports Golf Management LLC 7025 E Greenway Pkwy Ste 550 *Web:* www.obsports.com	Scottsdale	AZ	85254	480-948-1300	
Oconomowoc Residential Programs Inc 1746 Executive Dr *Web:* www.orp.com	Oconomowoc	WI	53066	262-569-5515	
Ohm Systems Inc 10250 Chester Rd *TF:* 800-878-0646 ■ *Web:* www.ohmworld.com	Cincinnati	OH	45215	513-771-0008	771-0101
Olive Grove Consulting 540 Ralston Ave #2c *Web:* theolivegrove.com	Belmont	CA	94002	650-591-4155	
Ologie LLC 447 E Main St *Web:* ologie.com	Columbus	OH	43215	614-221-1107	
Olympique Expert Building Care 26232 Enterprise Ct *TF:* 866-659-6747 ■ *Web:* www.olympique.net	Lake Forest	CA	92630	949-455-0796	
Omega Waste Management Inc 957 Colusa St *Web:* www.omegawaste.com	Corning	CA	96021	530-824-1890	
Omegasys It Consulting 229 16th ST Unit 227 *Web:* omegasysit.com	San Diego	IL	92101	773-857-2751	
Omnex Engineering and Management Inc 315 E Eisenhower Pkwy Ste 110 *Web:* www.omnex.com	Ann Arbor	MI	48108	734-761-4940	
OMNI Management Group LLC 5955 De Soto Ave Ste 100 *Web:* www.omnimgt.com	Woodland Hills	CA	91367	818-906-8300	
On Site Marketing 1901 Strasburg Rd *Web:* www.onsitemarketing.com	Coatesville	PA	19320	610-486-6900	
On-line Taxes Inc 724 Jules St *Web:* olt.com	Saint Joseph	MO	64501	816-232-0095	
One Smooth Stone Inc 5222 Main St *Web:* www.onesmoothstone.com	Downers Grove	IL	60515	630-427-4226	
Onprocess Technology Inc 200 Homer Ave *Web:* www.onprocess.com	Ashland	MA	01721	508-520-2711	
Onset Marketing LLC 28525 Beck Rd Ste 125 *Web:* www.onsetmarketing.com	Wixom	MI	48393	248-596-9788	
Onyx Meetings & Events Inc 7200 W 75th St *Web:* www.onyxmeetingsandevents.com	Overland Park	KS	66204	913-831-7200	
Open Options Corp 1203-20 Erb St W *Web:* www.openoptions.com	Waterloo	ON	N2L1T2	519-884-5898	
Operari Group LLC, The 6800 Park Ten Blvd Ste 170-W *Web:* www.operarigroup.com	San Antonio	TX	78213	210-298-1291	
Optimized Legal Solutions LLC 970 W Valley Pkwy Ste 611 *Web:* www.optimizedlegalsolutions.com	Escondido	CA	92025	760-933-9007	
OPTIMUS | SBR 30 Adelaide St E Ste 600 *Web:* optimussbr.com	Toronto	ON	M5C3G8	416-649-6000	
Opvantek Inc 28 S State St *Web:* www.opvantek.com	Newtown	PA	18940	215-968-7790	
Oregon Health Systems Inc 18150 SW Boones Ferry Rd *Web:* www.ohs-inc.com	Portland	OR	97224	503-639-6080	
Organo Gold International Inc 5505 hovander rd *TF:* 877-674-2661 ■ *Web:* www.organogold.com	Ferndale	WA	98248	877-674-2661	
Oriel Stat A Matrix 1 Quality Pl Edison *Web:* www.orielstat.com	Edison	NJ	08830	732-548-0600	
Orion Registrar Inc 7850 vance dr *TF:* 800-446-0674 ■ *Web:* www.orion4value.com	Arvada	CO	80003	303-456-6010	
Orr & Boss Inc 33900 Harper Ave Ste 103 *Web:* www.orrandboss.com	Clinton Township	MI	48035	586-416-9090	
OST Inc 2001 M St NW Ste 3000 *Web:* www.ostglobal.com	Washington	DC	20036	202-466-8099	

Company	City	State	ZIP	Phone	Fax
Oyster Consulting LLC 4405 Cox Rd Ste 150 *Web:* www.oysterllc.com	Glen Allen	VA	23060	804-965-5400	
P.E.T. Terra Systems Inc 110 Evans Mill Dr *Web:* www.petsystems.com	Dallas	GA	30157	770-445-2233	
P3I Inc 77 Main St *Web:* www.p3i-inc.com	Hopkinton	MA	01748	508-435-7882	
PacLand 1144 Eastlake Ave E Ste 601 *Web:* www.pacland.com	Seattle	WA	98109	206-522-9510	
Pak Technologies Inc 7025 W Marcia Rd *Web:* www.paktech.com	Milwaukee	WI	53223	414-371-3100	
Paladin Associates Inc 4709 Layfield Dr Ste 100B *Web:* www.paladinassociatesinc.com	Dunwoody	GA	30338	770-395-9156	
Palladian Partners Inc 8484 Georgia Ave Ste 200 *Web:* www.palladianpartners.com	Silver Spring	MD	20910	301-650-8660	
Panacea Technologies Inc 160 Commerce Dr Ste 500 *Web:* www.panaceatech.com	Montgomeryville	PA	18936	267-421-5300	
Paradigm Construction Services Inc 771 Jamacha Rd Ste 526 *Web:* www.paradigm-cs.net	El Cajon	CA	92019	858-300-8299	
Paradigm Transportation Solutions Ltd 22 King St S Ste 300 *Web:* www.ptsl.com	Waterloo	ON	N2J1N8	519-896-3163	
Paradigms Consulting Group 1874 Scarth St *Web:* www.paradigm.sk.ca	Regina	CA	95070	408-996-9689	
Paragon Advisors LLC 170 Boston Post Rd Ste 105 *Web:* www.paragonadvisorsllc.com	Madison	CT	06443	203-245-9131	
Paragon Audit & Consulting Inc 50 S Steele St Ste 325 *Web:* www.paragonaudit.com	Denver	CO	80209	720-245-6500	
Paragon Events 352 Northeast Third Ave *Web:* www.paragon-events.com	Delray Beach	FL	33444	561-243-3073	
Park Dietz & Associates Inc 2906 Lafayette Rd *Web:* www.parkdietzassociates.com	Newport Beach	CA	92663	949-723-2211	
Parker Ag Services LLC 53036 N Hwy 71 *Web:* www.parkerag.com	Limon	CO	80828	719-775-9870	
Partnercomm Inc 2304 Interstate 20 W *Web:* www.partnercomm.net	Arlington	TX	76017	817-465-9277	
Pascal Enterprises Inc 2621 State St *Web:* www.pascalent.com	Dallas	TX	75204	214-871-0300	
Path-2 Ventures LLC 223 E Blvd *TF:* 888-692-1057 ■ *Web:* www.path-2.com	Charlotte	NC	28203	888-692-1057	
Pathlore Software Corp 7965 N High St Ste 300 *Web:* www.sumtotalsystems.com	Columbus	OH	43235	614-781-0036	
Patricia Lynch Associates Inc 677 Broadway Ste 305 *Web:* www.plynchassociates.com	Albany	NY	12207	518-432-9220	
Patricia Seybold Group 210 Commercial St *TF:* 855-310-0101 ■ *Web:* www.customers.com	Boston	MA	02109	617-742-5200	742-1028
Patricio Enterprises Inc 125 Wdstream Blvd *Web:* www.patricioenterprises.com	Stafford	VA	22556	703-474-4100	
Paul May & Associates Inc - Since 1987 17220 Browning Dr *Web:* www.paulmayassociates.com	Orland Park	IL	60467	708-479-1111	
Pcg Enterprises Inc 643 Bair Is Rd Ste 212 *Web:* www.pcgfirm.com	Redwood	CA	94063	650-327-8108	
PCI Strategic Management LLC 6811 Benjamin Franklin Dr Ste 200 *Web:* www.pci-sm.com	Columbia	MD	21046	410-312-0885	
PDM Group LLC 27908 Orchard Lk Rd Ste B *Web:* www.thepdmgroup.com	Farmington Hills	MI	48334	248-626-5500	
Peak Organization Inc, The 25 W 31st St Fl 12 *Web:* www.peakorg.com	New York	NY	10001	212-947-6600	
Pediatrix Medical Group Inc 1301 Concord Terr *TF:* 800-243-3839 ■ *Web:* www.pediatrix.com	Sunrise	FL	33323	954-384-0175	838-9961
Pembroke Consulting 1515 Market St Ste 960 PO Box 58757 *Web:* www.pembrokeconsulting.com	Philadelphia	PA	19102	215-523-5700	
Pemco Ltd 1632 S King St Ste 100 *Web:* www.pemco-limited.com	Honolulu	HI	96826	808-949-0414	
PENTA Communications Inc 182 TurnPk Rd Ste 200 *Web:* www.pentamarketing.com	Westborough	MA	01581	508-616-9900	
People Focus Inc 391 Taylor Blvd Ste 110 *Web:* www.peoplefocus.com	Pleasant Hill	CA	94523	925-676-6265	
PeopleWorks Inc 6158 10th Ave *TF:* 888-404-3646 ■ *Web:* www.peopleworksinc.com	Aurelia	IA	51005	888-404-3646	
Peridrome Corp 284 Park Pl *TF:* 877-363-7770 ■ *Web:* www.peridrome.com	Brooklyn	NY	11238	877-363-7770	
Persyst Consulting LLC 12345 Lk City Way NE Ste 396 *Web:* www.persyst.com	Seattle	WA	98125	206-396-5825	
Petrie Raymond, Professional Chartered Accountants LLP 255 Cremazie Blvd E Ste 1000 *Web:* www.petrieraymond.qc.ca	Montreal	QC	H2M1M2	514-342-4740	
PFE Consultants Inc Reservoir Corporate Ctr 144 TurnPk Rd Ste 360 *Web:* pfegroup.com	Southborough	MA	01772	508-683-1400	
PFSweb Inc 505 Millennium Dr Ste 500 *NASDAQ: PFSW* ■ *TF:* 888-330-5504 ■ *Web:* www.pfsweb.com	Allen	TX	75013	972-881-2900	
Pharmacy Healthcare Solutions Inc 1700 Reisterstown Rd Ste 106 *Web:* www.pharmhs.com	Pikesville	MD	21208	410-653-7305	
PharmaNet Consulting 504 Carnegie Ctr *Web:* www.pharmanet.com	Princeton	NJ	08540	609-951-6738	

Phone Fax

PHI Environmental Consulting
4844 Jackson Rd ... Ann Arbor MI 48103 734-332-0800
Web: www.phiconsulting.com

PHM Hospitality Inc 3300 Oak Lawn Ave Ste 408 ... Dallas TX 75219 214-521-0002
Web: phmhospitality.com

PHM International Inc 509 Acacia Ave. ... Sebastian FL 32958 772-388-6496
Web: www.phmintl.com

Phoenix Group of Virginia Inc
630C Woodlake Dr ... Chesapeake VA 23320 757-228-1730
Web: www.phoenix-group.com

Pinnacle Hotels USA Inc
8369 Vickers St Ste 101 ... San Diego CA 92111 858-974-8201
Web: www.pinnaclehotelsusa.com

Pinpoint Technologies
17802 Irvine Blvd Ste 215 ... Tustin CA 92780 714-505-7600
TF: 866-603-7770 ■ *Web:* www.pinpoint-tech.com

Pinsonault Associates LLC
350 Clark Dr 2nd Fl ... Mt. Olive NJ 07828 973-448-8800
Web: www.pinsonault.com

Pinyon Environmental Engineering Resources
9100 W Jewell Ave Ste 200 ... Denver CO 80232 303-980-5200
TF: 888-641-7337 ■ *Web:* www.pinyon-env.com

Pitney Bowes Management Services 90 Pk Ave ... New York NY 10016 212-808-3800
TF: 800-322-8000 ■ *Web:* pitneybowes.com/us

PK Network Communications Inc 11 E 47th St ... New York NY 10017 212-888-4700
Web: www.pknetwork.com

Plainfield Asset Management LLC
60 Arch St 2nd Fl ... Greenwich CT 06830 203-302-1700
Web: www.pfam.com

Plan 365 Inc 3201 Glenwood Ave Ste 300 ... Raleigh NC 27612 919-534-2200
Web: www.plan365inc.com

Planet Consulting LLC 407 N 117th St ... Omaha NE 68154 402-964-1999
Web: www.planetci.com

Planetfone Inc 101 Convention Center Dr ... Pasadena CA 91101 626-792-9978
Web: planetfone.com

Planetmagpie 2762 Bayview Dr ... Fremont CA 94538 408-341-8770
Web: www.planetmagpie.com

Planners Network Inc, The
43418 Business Park Dr ... Temecula CA 92590 703-778-9000
Web: www.yourmeeting.com

Plasencia Group Inc, The
1 N Dale Mabry Hwy Ste 100 ... Tampa FL 33609 813-932-1234
Web: www.tpghotels.com

Playback Now Inc 3139 Campus Dr Ste 700 ... Norcross GA 30071 770-447-0616
TF: 800-241-7785 ■ *Web:* www.playbacknow.com

Plexus Ventures LLC 1701 Waterford Way ... Maple Glen PA 19002 215-542-2727
Web: plexusventures.com

Pln & Associates Inc 15400 Jennings Ln Ste 300 ... Bowie MD 20721 301-390-4635
Web: www.pln-inc.com

Pmalliance Inc
2075 Spencers Way Ste 201 ... Stone Mountain GA 30087 770-938-4947
TF: 866-808-3735 ■ *Web:* www.pm-alliance.com

Pmc Solutions Inc 300 Central Ave SW ... Albuquerque NM 87102 505-842-1099
Web: pmcsolutions.com

PointCross Inc
1291 E Hillsdale Blvd Ste 304 ... Foster City CA 94404 650-350-1900
Web: pointcross.com

Pool Management Group Inc
1210 Warsaw Rd Ste 900 ... Roswell GA 30076 770-993-4665
Web: www.poolmanagementgroup.com

Porter Khouw Consulting Inc PO Box 4028 ... Crofton MD 21114 410-451-3617
Web: www.porterkhouwconsulting.com

Porter Medical Ctr Inc 115 Porter Dr ... Middlebury VT 05753 802-388-4701
TF: 800-994-6610 ■ *Web:* www.portermedical.org

Portico Healthnet 2610 University Ave W ... Saint Paul MN 55114 651-603-5100
TF: 866-489-4899 ■ *Web:* www.porticohealthnet.org

Power Management Concepts LLC
510 Grumman Rd W Ste 211 ... Bethpage NY 11714 516-465-0188
Web: www.powermanage.com

Power Wellness 2055 W Army Trl Rd Ste 124 ... Addison IL 60101 630-570-2600
TF: 877-888-2988 ■ *Web:* www.powerwellness.com

Powers David J & Associates Inc
1871 The Alameda ... San Jose CA 95126 408-248-3500
Web: www.davidjpowers.com

Prairie Quest Inc 4211 Hobson Ct Ste A ... Fort Wayne IN 46815 260-420-7374
Web: www.prairiequest.com

Praxis Consulting Group Inc
9 A/B W Highland Av ... Philadelphia PA 19118 215-753-0303
Web: www.praxiscg.com

Prediction Sciences LLC
3252 Holiday Ct Ste 209 ... La Jolla CA 92037 858-404-0404
Web: www.predict.net

PreferredOne Administrative Services Inc
6105 Golden Hills Dr ... Golden Valley MN 55416 763-847-4000
Web: www.preferredone.com

Premier Prizm Solutions LLC
10 E Stow Rd Ste 100 ... Marlton NJ 08053 856-596-5600
Web: www.prizmllc.com

Previdence Corp 5685 South 1475 East Ste 2b ... Ogden UT 84403 801-409-0904
Web: www.previdence.com

PreviMed Inc 1164 Malibu Dr ... San Jose CA 95157 800-565-3901
TF: 800-565-3901 ■ *Web:* www.previmed.com

PRI Group LLC 600 Thomas Dr ... Bensenville IL 60106 708-492-1777
Web: www.theprigroup.com

Pride Hospitality LLC
2129 S Germantown Rd Ste 1 ... Germantown TN 38138 901-751-2212
Web: www.pridehospitality.com

Primatech Inc 50 Northwoods Blvd. ... Columbus OH 43235 614-841-9800
Web: www.primatech.com

PrimeGenesis LLC 200 W Hill Rd ... Stamford CT 06902 203-323-8501
TF: 866-805-7777 ■ *Web:* www.primegenesis.com

Principal Maritime Management LLC
3530 Post Rd Ste 201 ... Southport CT 06890 203-292-9580
Web: princimar.com

Phone Fax

Prism Companies Inc 2200 Western Court Ste 150 ... Lisle IL 60532 630-324-3400

Pritchard Management Associates Inc
517 Wilson Pl Ste 1000 ... Frederick MD 21702 301-662-7877
Web: www.carlpritchard.com

Private Client Resources LLC
Wilton Corporate Ctr - Riverview 187 Danbury Rd
... Wilton CT 06897 203-210-0047
Web: www.pcrinsights.com

Private Club Associates
2750 Holcomb Bridge Rd Ste 220 ... Alpharetta GA 30022 678-585-9120
Web: www.privateclubassociates.com

Proactive Business Solutions Inc
428 13th St 5th Fl ... Oakland CA 94612 510-302-0120
Web: www.proactiveok.com

Proenergy Services LLC 2031 Adams Rd ... Sedalia MO 65301 660-829-5100
Web: www.proenergyservices.com

Profit Point Inc 24 Ayers St ... North Brookfield MA 01535 435-487-9141
Web: www.profitpt.com

Progesys Inc 4020 Blvd le Corbusier Ste 201 ... Laval QC H7L5R2 450-667-7646
TF: 877-274-8815 ■ *Web:* www.progesys.ca

Project Corps LLC 100 W Harrison St 400 ... Seattle WA 98119 206-932-7077
Web: www.projectcorps.com

ProMedical Inc 3245 SW 34th St ... Ocala FL 34474 352-867-8898
Web: www.promedicalinc.com

ProMetrics Inc 480 American Ave. ... King Of Prussia PA 19406 610-265-6344
Web: www.prometrics.com

Property Tax Advisors LLC 805 King St ... Alexandria VA 22314 703-518-4425
Web: www.propertytaxadvisors.com

Prosci Inc 1367 S Garfield Ave. ... Loveland CO 80537 970-203-9332
Web: www.prosci.com

Prospect Medical Holdings Inc
10780 Santa Monica Blvd Ste 400 ... Los Angeles CA 90025 310-943-4500
TF: 800-708-3230 ■ *Web:* www.prospectmedical.com

Protocol Driven Healthcare Inc
40 Morristown Rd Ste 2D ... Bernardsville NJ 07924 515-277-1376
TF: 888-816-4006 ■ *Web:* www.pdhi.com

Protocol Link Inc
175 E Hawthorn Pkwy Ste 210 ... Vernon Hills IL 60061 847-549-0390
Web: www.protocollink.com

ProtonMedia Inc 1690 Sumneytown Pike Ste 370 ... Lansdale PA 19446 215-631-1401
Web: www.protonmedia.com

Provell Inc
855 Village Center Drive Ste 116 ... North Oaks MN 55127 952-258-2000 258-2100*
**Fax:* Hum Res ■ *TF:* 800-624-2946 ■ *Web:* www.provell.com

PRTM Management Consultants Inc
77 Fourth Ave ... Waltham MA 02451 781-434-1200
Web: www.prtm.com

Psg Consulting Inc Po Box 19212 ... Seattle WA 98119 206-285-2824
Web: psgc.com

Pullan Consulting
4400 Paseo Santa Rosa Ste 110 ... Las Vegas NVÿ 89147 805-558-0361
Web: www.pullanconsulting.com

PurEnergy LLC 4488 Onondaga Blvd ... Syracuse NY 13219 315-448-2266
Web: www.purenergyllc.com

PuroSystems Inc 6001 Hiatus Rd Ste 13 ... Tamarac FL 33321 954-597-1112
Web: www.puroclean.com

Push Product Design 2212 2nd Ave N. ... Birmingham AL 35203 205-328-3112
Web: www.pushpd.com

PV Evolution Labs LLC 1360 Fifth St ... Berkeley CA 94710 415-320-7835
Web: www.pvel.com

PVA Consulting Group Inc
20865 Ch de la Cote Nord Ste 200 ... Boisbriand QC J7E4H5 450-970-1970
TF: 877-970-1970 ■ *Web:* www.pva.ca

Pva Inc 2814 Eric Ln ... Burlington NC 27215 336-217-4600
Web: www.pvaglobal.com

QED Group LLC, The
1820 N Ft Myer Dr Ste 700 ... Arlington VA 22209 202-521-1900
Web: www.qedgroupllc.com

QTEC Solutions Inc 110 N Lincoln Ave Ste 201 ... Corona CA 92882 951-270-5357
Web: www.qtec.us

Quality Administration 14466 N Us Hwy 169 ... Smithville MO 64089 816-532-2090
Web: quality-admin.com

Quality Fuel Networks Inc
15227 herriman blvd ... Noblesville IN 46060 317-774-1076
Web: www.qualityfuel.com

Quality Incentive Co 3962 Willow Lk Blvd. ... Memphis TN 38118 901-367-8200
Web: www.qualityincentivecompany.com

Quality Media Resources Inc
10929 Se 23rd St ... Bellevue WA 98004 425-455-0558
TF: 800-800-5129 ■ *Web:* qmr.com

QuantiTech Inc
7027 Old Madison Pike NW Ste 106 ... Huntsville AL 35806 256-650-6263
Web: www.quantitech.com

Quantum Automation Inc 4400 E La Palma Ave ... Anaheim CA 92807 714-854-0800
Web: www.quantumautomation.com

Quintel Management Consulting Inc
5910 S University Ste C18-193 ... Greenwood Village CO 80121 303-781-4771
Web: www.quintelmc.com

R Ms Risk Management Services
8227 Northwest Blvd Ste 230 ... Indianapolis IN 46278 317-872-8227
Web: rms-safety.com

Radar Media Group Inc
12 Blossom Hill Rd Ste 101a ... Winchester MA 01890 781-721-1910
Web: www.radarmedia.com

Rainmaker 97 Central St Ste 204 ... Lowell MA 01852 978-453-1984
Web: www.rainmaker-partners.com

Ralm Inc 4620 Mercason Rd. ... Fayetteville NC 28311 910-486-4491

Ralph Andersen & Assoc
5800 Stanford Ranch Rd ... Rocklin CA 95765 916-630-4900
Web: www.ralphandersen.com

Ran One Inc 2100 Embarcadero Ste 100 ... Oakland CA 94606 510-535-9730
Web: global.ranone.com

Raving Consulting Co 475 Hill St # G ... Reno NV 89501 775-329-7864
Web: www.ravingconsulting.com

Company / Address	City	State	Zip	Phone	Fax
RBN Energy LLC 2323 S Shepherd Dr Ste 1010	Houston	TX	77019	888-400-9838	
TF: 888-400-9838 ■ *Web:* www.rbnenergy.com					
RCS Services Inc 5506 Mitchelldale St	Houston	TX	77092	713-461-4119	
Web: www.riskcontrolservices.com/c.php?p=1					
ReachForce Inc 9020-I Capital of Texas Hwy N Ste 270	Austin	TX	78759	512-327-9000	
Web: www.reachforce.com					
Reachsolutions Llc 7540 Potomac Fall Rd	Mc Lean	VA	22102	703-893-4114	
Web: www.reachsolutions.com					
Real Story Group, The 3470 Olney-Laytonsville Rd Ste 131	Olney	MD	20832	617-340-6464	
Web: www.realstorygroup.com					
Realstreet Staffing 2500 Wallington Way Ste 208	Marriottsville	MD	21104	410-480-8002	
TF: 877-480-8002 ■ *Web:* www.realstreetstaffing.com					
RealTime Group Inc, The 5217 Tennyson Pkwy Ste 200	Plano	TX	75024	972-985-9100	
Web: therealtimegroup.com					
Record Center Innovations Inc 3919 W Washington St	Phoenix	AZ	85009	602-258-4000	
Web: recordcenterinnovations.com					
Recordflow 1751 e garry ave	Santa Ana	CA	92705	877-896-7350	
TF: 877-896-7350 ■ *Web:* www.recordflow.com					
Rector-Dunan & Assoc 314 E Highland Mall Blvd	Austin	TX	78752	512-454-5262	
Red Rocket Media Group LLC 9351 Eastman Park Dr Ste 200	Windsor	CO	80550	970-674-0079	
Web: www.redrocketmg.com					
Red Spot Interactive 1001 jupiter park dr	Jupiter	FL	33458	800-401-7931	
TF: 800-401-7931 ■ *Web:* www.redspotinteractive.com					
Red Tree inc 820 North 1480 East	Orem	UT	84097	801-655-0200	
Web: www.redtreeleadership.com					
RedHouse Associates LLC 802 Lovett Blvd	Houston	TX	77006	713-338-2151	
Web: www.redhouseassociates.com					
Redmonk LLC 93 S Jackson St	Seattle	WA	98104	866-733-6665	
TF: 866-733-6665 ■ *Web:* www.redmonk.com					
Reema Consulting Services Inc 8106 Hallmark Pl	Gaithersburg	MD	20879	301-793-3055	
Web: reemacsi.com					
Referral Institute Franchise LLC 705 Holly Ave	Rohnert Park	CA	94928	707-780-8110	
Web: www.referralinstitute.com					
Registrar Corp 144 Research Dr	Hampton	VA	23666	757-224-0177	
Web: www.registrarcorp.com					
Reingold Inc 433 E Monroe Ave	Alexandria	VA	22301	202-333-0400	
Web: www.reingold.com					
Reinsel Kuntz Lesher 1330 Broadcasting Rd	Wyomissing	PA	19610	610-376-1595	
Web: www.rklcpa.com					
Reiter Giuliani Group LLC, The 170 Second Ave Ste 3D	New York	NY	10003	212-260-4780	
Web: www.reitergiulianigroup.com					
Relationship One Llc 8009 34th Ave S Ste 300	Minneapolis	MN	55425	763-355-1025	
Web: www.relationshipone.com					
Remodelers Advantage Inc 14440 Cherry Ln Ct Ste 201	Laurel	MD	20707	301-490-5620	
Web: www.remodelersadvantage.com					
Resolve Tech Solutions Inc 100 E Royal Ln Ste 215	Irving	TX	75039	214-310-1020	
Web: www.rtsolinc.com					
Restaurant Partners Inc 1030 N Orange Ave Ste 200	Orlando	FL	32801	407-839-5070	839-3388
Web: www.restaurantpartnersinc.com					
Retirement Advantage Inc, The 47 Park Pl Ste 850	Appleton	WI	54914	888-872-2364	
TF: 888-872-2364 ■ *Web:* www.tra401k.com					
Retrievex Inc 4 1st Ave	Peabody	MA	01960	978-539-3350	
Web: www.retrievex.com					
Return Management Services Inc 800 Berkshire Ln N	Plymouth	MN	55441	952-475-0242	
Web: www.rmsincorporated.com					
Revel Consulting 4020 Lk Washington Blvd NE Ste 210	Kirkland	WA	98033	206-407-3173	
Web: www.revelconsulting.com					
RGFCC Corp 627 Cady Dr	Fort Washington	MD	20744	888-389-1230	
TF: 888-389-1230 ■ *Web:* www.rgfcc.com					
Rgm & Associates 3230 Monument Way	Concord	CA	94518	925-671-7717	
Web: www.rgmassociates.com					
RHA Health Services Inc 17 Church St	Asheville	NC	28801	828-232-6844	665-1921
TF: 866-742-2428 ■ *Web:* www.rhahealthservices.org					
Rhodes Holdings LLC 615 Longview Dr	Sugar Land	TX	77478	281-435-3917	
Web: www.rhodes-holdings.com					
Rhodes-Joseph & Tobiason Advisors LLC 1177 High Ridge Rd	Stamford	CT	06905	203-883-8144	
Web: www.rjtadvisors.com					
Richard Heath & Associates 1320 Harbor Bay Pkwy Ste 140	Alameda	CA	94502	510-748-4330	
Web: www.rhainc.com					
Richards Energy Group 781 S Chiques Rd	Manheim	PA	17545	717-898-6330	
Web: www.richardsenergy.com					
Rideau Inc 473 Deslauriers	Montreal	QC	H4N1W2	800-363-6464	
TF: 800-363-6464 ■ *Web:* www.rideau.com					
River Road Partners LLC 462 S Fourth St Ste 1600	Louisville	KY	40202	520-298-7875	
Web: www.riverroadllc.com					
River West Meeting Associates Inc 3616 N Lincoln Ave	Chicago	IL	60613	773-755-3000	
TF: 888-534-5292 ■ *Web:* www.riverwestmeetings.com					
Riverwood Solutions LLC 70 Willow Rd Ste 100	Menlo Park	CA	94025	650-618-7340	
Web: www.rwsops.com					
Rizzetta & Company Inc 3434 Colwell Ave Ste 200	Tampa	FL	33614	813-933-5571	
Web: www.rizzetta.com					
Robert Ferrilli LLC 41 S Haddon Ave Ste 7	Haddonfield	NJ	08033	888-864-3282	
TF: 888-864-3282 ■ *Web:* ferrilli.com					
Robertson GeoConsultants Inc 580 Hornby St Ste 900	Vancouver	BC	V6C3B6	604-684-8072	
Web: www.rgc.ca					
Rocket-Hire LLC 4537 N Robertson St	New Orleans	LA	70117	504-236-7259	
Web: www.rocket-hire.com					
Roco Rescue 7077 Exchequer Dr	Baton Rouge	LA	70809	225-755-7626	
TF: 800-647-7626 ■ *Web:* www.rocorescue.com					
Rodgers Group Ltd, The 3738 N Tripp Ave	Chicago	IL	60641	773-282-0571	
Web: therodgersgroup.com					
ROI4Sales Inc 3355 Quaas Dr	West Bend	WI	53095	262-338-1851	
Web: www.roi4sales.com					
Roland Berger Strategy Consultants LLC 37000 Woodward Ave Ste 200	Bloomfield Hills	MI	48304	248-729-5000	
Web: www.rolandberger.us					
Romo Incentives Group 1156 Suncast Ln Ste 3	El Dorado Hills	CA	95762	916-941-0350	
Web: www.romoincentivesgroup.com					
Roth Observatory International 120 E 79th St Ste 5C	New York	NY	10075	212-861-9420	
Web: www.askroth.com					
Roundhouse Marketing Services Inc 560 E Verona Ave	Verona	WI	53593	608-497-2550	
Web: www.roundhouse-marketing.com					
Royale Management Services Inc 2319 N Andrews Ave	Fort Lauderdale	FL	33311	954-563-1269	
Web: www.rmsaccounting.com					
RPM Revenue Drivers LLC 140 S Mountain Way Dr	Orem	UT	84058	801-449-0541	
Web: surgefront.com					
Rs Marketing Services LLC 35 Ft Boone Ct	Clayton	NC	27527	919-585-4556	
Web: www.rsmsinsights.com					
RSD Solutions Inc 177 Lincolnshire Dr	Fall River	NS	B2T1P8	902-441-4102	
Web: www.rsdsolutions.com					
Rtm Consulting LLC 3221 Ivy Hills Blvd	Cincinnati	OH	45244	513-236-5585	
Web: www.rtmconsulting.net					
Rubicon Marketing Group Inc 1410 SW Morrison St Ste 850	Portland	OR	97205	503-241-4703	
Web: rubiconmarketing.com					
Rucker & Associates Inc 7009 N Ridge Dr Ste 300	Raleigh	NC	27615	919-873-1268	
Web: www.ruckerassociates.com					
Ruggie Wealth Management 2100 Lk Eustis Dr	Tavares	FL	32778	352-343-2700	
TF: 888-343-2711 ■ *Web:* www.ruggiewealth.com					
Russell Phillips & Associates LLC 500 Cross Keys Office Park	Fairport	NY	14450	585-223-1130	
Web: www.phillipsllc.com					
Russell Stephens LLC 445 S Figueroa St Ste 2600	Los Angeles	CA	90071	213-612-7711	
Web: www.russellstephens.com					
RxResults LLC 320 Executive Court Ste 301	Little Rock	AR	72205	501-367-8402	
Web: rxresults.com					
Ryla Teleservices Inc 2120 Barrett Park Dr NW	Kennesaw	GA	30144	678-322-5000	
Web: www.ryla.com					
S f Association Management Services 655 Beach St Fl 1	San Francisco	CA	94109	415-561-8523	
Web: sf-ams.org					
S4 NetQuest 580 N Fourth St Ste 600	Columbus	OH	43215	614-220-5700	
Web: www.s4netquest.com					
Sales Concepts Inc 610 Hembree Pkwy	Roswell	GA	30076	678-624-9229	
Web: www.salesconcepts.com					
Sales Effectiveness Inc 570 W Crssvlle Rd	Roswell	GA	30075	770-552-6612	
Web: www.saleseffectiveness.com					
Salt Lake Cable & Harness Inc 421 West 900 North	North Salt Lake	UT	84054	801-292-4999	
Web: www.saltlakecable.com					
San Diego Assn of Governments-sandag 401 B St Ste 800	San Diego	CA	92101	619-699-1900	
Web: www.sandag.org					
Sand Cherry Associates Inc 8 Sand Cherry	Littleton	CO	80127	303-933-9494	
Web: www.sandcherryassociates.com					
Satov Consultants Inc 250 The Esplanade Ste 200	Toronto	ON	M5A1J2	416-777-9000	
Web: www.satovconsultants.com					
Scarritt Group Inc 7636 N Oracle Rd Ste 100	Tucson	AZ	85704	520-529-0000	
Web: www.scarrittgroup.com					
Scheibel Halaska 735 N Water St Ste 200	Milwaukee	WI	53202	414-272-6898	
Web: www.trefoilgroup.com					
School Innovations & Advocacy Inc 11130 Sun Ctr Dr Ste 100	Rancho Cordova	CA	95670	877-954-4357	
TF: 877-954-4357 ■ *Web:* www.sia-us.com					
Schroeder Measurement Technologies Inc 25400 Hgwy 19 Ste 285	Clearwater	FL	33763	727-738-8727	
Web: www.smttest.com					
Schrudder Performance Group Inc 7681 Tyler?s Pl Blvd	West Chester	OH	45069	513-755-6000	
Web: schrudderperformance.com					
Schwartz Heslin Group Inc (SHG) 8 Airport Park Blvd	Latham	NY	12110	518-786-7733	
Web: www.shggroup.com					
Scott Sheldon LLC 3985 Medina Rd Ste 220	Medina	OH	44256	330-952-1671	
TF: 877-467-7552 ■ *Web:* www.scott-sheldon.com					
SEA Ltd 7349 Worthington-Galena Rd	Columbus	OH	43085	800-782-6851	
TF: 800-782-6851 ■ *Web:* www.sealimited.com					
SearchDex 17330 Preston Rd Ste 240B	Dallas	TX	75252	214-999-0889	
Web: www.searchdex.com					
Security Risk Solutions Inc 698 Fishermans Bnd	Mount Pleasant	SC	29464	843-647-1556	
Web: www.securityrisksolutions.com					
Select Medical Corp 4714 Gettysburg Rd	Mechanicsburg	PA	17055	717-972-1100	
TF: 888-735-6332 ■ *Web:* www.selectmedical.com					
Sellex International Corp 88 E Broad St Ste 1220	Columbus	OH	43215	614-463-1986	
Web: www.sellexinternational.com					

Phone Fax

Sentry Hospitality Ltd
136 E 57th St Ste 1003 .... New York NY 10022 212-753-5347 688-2772
Web: www.sentryhospitality.com
Seracon Consulting 595 Rosebud Ct .... Saline MI 48176 734-944-1065
Web: www.seraconconsulting.com
Service Intelligence Inc
1061 Red Venture Dr Ste 175 .... Fort Mill SC 29707 800-263-2980
TF: 800-263-2980 ■ *Web:* www.serviceintelligence.com
SET Consulting Inc 5821 Windermere Ln .... Fairfield OH 45014 240-296-0800
Web: www.setconsulting.com
Seton Hotel 144 E 40th St .... New York NY 10016 212-889-5301
TF: 866-697-3866 ■ *Web:* www.setonhotelny.com
Sgv International LLC 8588 Kaity Fwy Ste 200 .... Houston TX 77024 713-647-7555
Web: www.sgvinternational.com
Shade Inc 5049 Russell Cir .... Lincoln NE 68507 402-466-3393
Web: www.shadeinc.com
Shaker Consulting Group Inc
3201 Entp Pkwy Ste 360 .... Cleveland OH 44122 888-485-7633
TF: 888-485-7633 ■ *Web:* shakercg.com
Sharpe Consulting LLC 16913 Macduff Ave .... Olney MD 20832 301-570-5127
Web: www.sharpeconsulting.biz
Sheffield Resource Network
2239 N Hayden Rd .... Scottsdale AZ 85257 480-968-6199
Web: www.sheffieldnet.com
Sheridan Healthcare Inc
1613 NW 136th Ave Ste 200 .... Sunrise FL 33323 800-437-2672 851-1775*
**Fax Area Code:* 954 ■ *TF:* 800-437-2672 ■ *Web:* www.sheridanhealthcare.com
Sherpalo P.O. Box 2627 .... Saratoga CA 95070 415-441-4344
Web: www.sherpalo.com
Shipley Associates Inc 532 North 900 West .... Kaysville UT 84037 801-544-9787
Web: www.shipleywins.com
SIB Development & Consulting Inc
796 Meeting St .... Charleston SC 29403 843-576-3606
Web: www.aboutsib.com
Sierra Coastal Partners Inc
8967 Calvert Ave .... Orangevale CA 95662 916-792-3527
Web: www.sierracoastal.com
Sierra Infosys Inc 6001 Savoy Dr Ste 210 .... Houston TX 77036 713-747-9693
Web: www.sierratec.com
Sigma Breakthrough Technologies Inc
123 N Edward Gary 2nd Fl .... San Marcos TX 78666 512-353-7489
Web: www.sbtionline.com
Signum Group LLC
1900 The Exchange SE Bldg 200 .... Atlanta GA 30339 770-514-8111
Web: www.signumgroup.com
Silliman Associates Inc Thomas
425 N Lee St .... Alexandria VA 22314 703-548-4100
Web: www.tsilliman.com
Simione Healthcare Consultants LLC
4130 Whitney Ave .... Hamden CT 06518 203-287-9288
Web: www.simioneconsultants.com
Simunition Ltd 65 Sandscreen Rd .... Avon CT 06001 860-404-0162
Web: simunition.com
Site Tech Systems 541 Atlantic Ave .... Murrells Inlet SC 29576 843-357-4400
Web: sitetechsystems.com
Slater Partners LLC 204 Galway Dr .... Chapel Hill NC 27517 919-933-6883
Web: www.slaterpartners.com
Smart Inc ÿ400 Poydras St Ste 2305 .... New Orleans LA 70130 504-566-0900
Web: www.smartinc1.com
Smart Work Network Inc
135 S Main St Ste 402 .... Greenville SC 29601 864-233-3007
Web: www.smartworknetwork.com
Smith Research Inc 710 Estate Dr .... Deerfield IL 60015 847-948-0440
Web: www.smithresearch.com
Solomon Hardwick & Associates LLC
1160 Folly Rd .... Charleston SC 29412 843-406-6680
Web: www.solomonhardwick.com
Solutions 21 152 Wabash St .... Pittsburgh PA 15220 866-765-2121
TF: 866-765-2121 ■ *Web:* solutions21.com
Solutions AE Inc 236 Auburn Ave .... Atlanta GA 30303 888-562-4441
TF: 888-562-4441 ■ *Web:* www.solutionsae.org
Somete Group LLC
1316 NEW HAMPSHIRE AVE NW APT 607 .... Washington DC 20036 202-223-4920
Web: www.sometegroup.com
Sound Hospitality Management LLC 270 NE 4th St .... Miami FL 33132 305-374-2050
Web: www.soundhospitality.com
Southern Solutions Group Inc
4305 Poplar Creek Ln .... High Point NC 27265 866-581-6055
TF: 866-581-6055 ■ *Web:* www.ssg-nc.com
Sparus Holdings Inc 4487 S Old Peachtree Rd .... Norcross GA 30071 770-447-0267
Web: www.sparusholdings.com
Spaulding Group Inc, The 33 Clyde Rd Ste 103 .... Somerset NJ 08873 732-873-5700
Web: spauldinggrp.com
SpawGlass Construction Corp 13800 W Rd .... Houston TX 77041 281-970-5300 970-5305
TF: 800-771-0422 ■ *Web:* www.spawglass.com
Specialist Printing & Direct Mail Services
4974 Mercury St .... San Diego CA 92111 760-208-2240
Web: www.specialistonline.com
Spectrum Healthcare Resources Inc
12647 Olive Blvd Ste 600 .... Saint Louis MO 63141 800-325-3982 744-4181*
**Fax Area Code:* 314 ■ **Fax:* Hum Res ■ *TF:* 800-325-3982 ■ *Web:* www.spectrumhealth.com
Speed Consulting LLC 2871 Howard Rd .... Waxahachie TX 75165 972-938-0490
Web: www.speedconsulting.com
Speer & Associates Inc
13010 Morris Rd Ste 6 .... Alpharetta GA 30004 770-396-2528
Web: www.speerandassociates.com
Spencer Shenk Capers & Assoc 1515 W 190th St .... Gardena CA 90248 310-515-7555
Web: www.ssca.com
Sports Technologies Inc 10 Front St .... Collinsville CT 06019 860-693-9561
Web: www.sportstechinc.com
Spyglass Biosecurity Inc 3180 Imjin Rd Ste 157 .... Marina CA 93933 831-883-9838
Web: www.spyglassbio.com
SSA Consultants Inc 9331 Bluebonnet Blvd .... Baton Rouge LA 70810 225-769-2676
TF: 800-634-2758 ■ *Web:* www.consultssa.com

Phone Fax

SST Planners 1501 Wilson Blvd Ste 507 .... Arlington VA 22209 703-875-8787
Web: www.sstplanners.com
St. Michael's Inc 3310 Noble Pond Way .... Woodbridge VA 22193 703-463-9463
Web: www.stmichaelsinc.com
St. Onge Co 1400 Williams Rd .... York PA 17402 717-840-8181
Web: www.stonge.com
Sta 4100 Fairfax Dr Ste 910 .... Arlington VA 22203 703-522-5123
Web: stassociates.com
Staff Leasing Inc
149 Northern Concourse Ste 1 .... Syracuse NY 13212 315-641-3600
Web: www.staffleasing-peo.com
Staffing.org Inc 10 Burchard Ln .... Rowayton CT 06853 203-227-0186
Web: www.staffing.org
Staples Construction Company Inc
1501 Eastman Ave .... Ventura CA 93003 805-658-8786 658-8785
TF: 800-881-4650 ■ *Web:* www.staplesconstruction.com
Star Collaborative Llc 18120 46th Ave N .... Plymouth MN 55446 763-515-7838
Web: www.starcollaborative.com
Steering Group Inc, The
1078 Dixie Belle Ct .... Lawrenceville GA 30045 404-978-2282
Web: www.thesteeringgroup.com
Stephen A Goldman Consulting Services LLC
34 Arlington Ave .... Morris Plains NJ 07950 973-267-5929
Web: www.sagcs.com
Stern Group Inc, The 3314 Ross Pl NW .... Washington DC 20008 202-966-7894
Web: www.sterngroup.biz
Stevenson Systems Inc
27822 El Lazo 100 .... Laguna Niguel CA 92677 949-297-4200
Web: www.stevensonsystems.com
Stieglitz Snyder Architecture
425 Franklin St .... Buffalo NY 14202 716-828-9166
Web: www.stieglitzsnyder.com
Stock & Option Solutions Inc
6399 San Ignacio Ave Ste 100 .... San Jose CA 95119 408-979-8700
TF: 888-767-0199 ■ *Web:* www.sos-team.com
Stonehill Group
527 Marquette Ave S Ste 1850 .... Minneapolis MN 55402 612-436-1360
Web: www.stonehillgrp.com
Stop At Nothing Inc
1400 Marsh Landing Pkwy Ste 107 .... Jacksonville FL 32250 904-249-4410
Web: www.stopatnothing.com
Stop Hunger Now 615 Hillsborough St Ste 200 .... Raleigh NC 27603 919-839-0689
TF: 888-501-8440 ■ *Web:* www.stophungernow.org
Strategos 1110 Burlingame Ave Ste 211 .... Burlingame CA 94010 650-344-1999
Web: www.strategos.com
Strayer Consulting Group Inc
16151 Wood Acres Rd .... Los Gatos CA 95030 408-399-1500
Web: www.strayerconsulting.com
Streebo Inc 10998 S Wilcrest Dr Ste 162 .... Houston TX 77099 832-426-2700
Web: www.streebo.com
Strong-Bridge Consulting LLC
10940 NE 33rd Pl Ste 102 .... Bellevue WA 98004 206-905-4631
Web: www.strong-bridge.com
Studeo Legal 307 W Seventh St Ste 1800 .... Fort Worth TX 76102 817-945-6610
Web: www.studeolegal.com
su mitra Inc 88 Corporate Dr Ste 1614 .... Toronto ON M1H3G6 416-907-6866
Web: www.su-mitra.com
Sudler Property Management
875 N Michigan Ave Ste 3980 .... Chicago IL 60611 312-751-0900
Web: www.sudlerathome.com
Summit Energy Services Inc
10350 Ormsby Pk Pl Ste 400 .... Louisville KY 40223 502-429-3800 753-2248
TF: 866-907-8664 ■ *Web:* www.summitenergy.com
Surge Resources 920 Candia Rd .... Manchester NH 03109 603-623-0007
TF: 800-787-4387 ■ *Web:* www.surgeindustries.com
Sutton Enterprises Inc 424 Diana Ct Ste A .... Bensenville IL 60106 847-445-2098
Web: www.suttonenterprises.com
Swingtide Inc W5775 Nine Indian Trail .... Elkhorn WI 53121 262-742-5455
Web: www.swingtide.com
Swiss Consulting Group 101 W 23 St Ste 2422 .... New York NY 10011 212-288-4858
Web: www.swissconsultinggroup.com
Synaptic Decisions LP 10700 N Fwy Ste 130 .... Houston TX 77037 832-300-9800
Web: www.synapticdecisions.com
Synaptis Inc 150 Cornerstone Dr Ste 201 .... Cary NC 27519 919-844-5840
Web: www.synaptis.com
Syndetics Inc 10395 Democracy Ln .... Fairfax VA 22030 703-273-8350
Web: syndetics-inc.com
Synthesis Professional Services Inc
12339 Carroll Ave .... Rockville MD 20852 301-770-8970
Web: www.synthesisps.com
Szarka Financial Management
29691 Lorain Rd .... North Olmsted OH 44070 440-779-1430
Web: www.szarkafinancial.com
T G P Associates Inc 340 W 39th St Fl 11 .... New York NY 10018 212-695-1010
Web: tgpassociates.com
Table Group Inc 3640 MT Diablo Blvd 202 .... Lafayette CA 94549 925-299-9700
Web: www.tablegroup.com
Tagos Group LLC, The
8 E Greenway Plz Ste 1340 .... Houston TX 77046 713-850-7031
Web: www.tagosgroup.com
Tait Subler LLC 60 S 6th St Ste 2800 .... Minneapolis MN 55402 612-758-2000
Web: www.taitsubler.com
Talent Curve 14 Bridle Path .... Pittsboro NC 27312 866-494-0248
TF: 866-494-0248 ■ *Web:* www.talentcurve.com
Taos Mountain 121 Daggett Dr .... San Jose CA 95134 408-588-1200
Web: www.taos.com
Targeted Learning 706 E Technology Ave Ste 3100 .... Orem UT 84097 801-235-9414
Web: www.targetedlearning.com
Task Management Inc 99 Danbury Rd .... Ridgefield CT 06877 203-438-9777
Web: www.taskmanagement.com
Tax Matrix Technologies 1011 Mumma Rd Ste 101 .... Lemoyne PA 17043 717-975-0143
Web: taxmatrix.com

Phone Fax

Taylor Smith Consulting Llc
16800 Greenspoint Pk Dr ... Houston TX 77060 713-937-3111
Web: www.taylorsmithconsulting.com

TBN Consulting LLC 3301 Brunswick Ave N ... Minneapolis MN 55422 763-971-8057
Web: www.tonynelson.com

Team Quality Services Inc
4483 County Rd 19 Ste B ... Auburn IN 46706 260-572-0060
TF: 866-568-8326 ■ *Web:* teamqualityservices.com

Technosphere 155 N Washington Ave ... Bergenfield NJ 07621 201-384-7400
Web: www.technosphere.com

Tecolote Research Inc
420 S Fairview Ave Ste 201 ... Goleta CA 93117 805-571-6366 571-6377
Web: www.tecolote.com

Tekmasters Llc
4437 brookfield corporate dr ... Chantilly VA 20151 703-349-1110
Web: www.tekmasters.com

Tektivity Inc 119 Third St NE ... Cedar Rapids IA 52401 319-362-3336
Web: www.tektivity.com

Tel-affinity Corp 66 Oak Knoll Ter ... Needham MA 02492 781-433-0451
Web: www.tel-affinity.com

Telaffects Llc 300 primera blvd ... Lake Mary FL 32746 407-936-3130
Web: www.telaffects.com

Telcom Corp
1499 W Palmetto Park Rd Ste 214 ... Boca Raton FL 33486 561-394-5448
TF: 800-394-5448 ■ *Web:* www.telcomcorp.com

Telecom Asset Management LLC
1736 Dolores St ... San Francisco CA 94110 415-923-5800
Web: www.telecomassets.com

Telecom Resources International Inc
10632 N Scottsdale Rd Ste 486 ... Scottsdale AZ 85254 480-391-3800
Web: tri-1.com

TeleProviders Inc
23461 Southpointe Dr Ste 185 ... Laguna Hills CA 92653 888-999-4244
TF: 888-999-4244 ■ *Web:* www.teleproviders.com

TeleSoft Systems 335 Wesley St Ste 203 ... Nanaimo BC V9R2R7 250-760-0142
Web: www.telesoftsystems.ca

Ten Dots LLC 211 E Ocean Blvd Ste 204 ... Long Beach CA 90802 562-590-5067
Web: www.tendots.com

TenStep Inc 4390 Laurian Dr ... Kennesaw GA 30144 770-591-9860
Web: www.tenstep.com

Tero International Inc 1840 Nw 118th St Ste 107 ... Clive IA 50325 515-221-2318
Web: www.tero.com

Texelerate LLC 2119 Delancey St Ste 400 ... Philadelphia PA 19103 215-275-8492
Web: www.texelerate.net

TGC 3200 Travis St ... Houston TX 77006 512-236-8002
Web: www.thegoodmancorp.com

ThinkHR Corp 4457 Willow Rd Ste 120 ... Pleasanton CA 94588 925-225-1100
Web: www.thinkhr.com

Three Rivers Planning & Development District Inc
75 S Main St PO Box 690 ... Pontotoc MS 38863 662-489-2415 489-6815
TF: 877-489-6911 ■ *Web:* www.trpdd.com

TigerSwan Inc 3452 Apex Peakway ... Apex NC 27502 919-439-7110
Web: www.tigerswan.com

Tmi Us 8270 W Charleston Blvd ... Las Vegas NV 89117 702-938-1800
Web: www.tmius.com

Toeroek Associates Inc
300 Union Blvd Ste 520 ... Lakewood CO 80228 303-420-7735
Web: www.toeroek.com

Topside Consulting Group LLC
8105 Madrillon Ct ... Vienna VA 22182 703-442-7508
Web: www.topside-consulting.com

Toptech Groupe Conseil Inc
Parc technologique 2750 Einstein St
Ste 250 ... Quebec City QC G1P4R1 418-650-6143
Web: www.toptech.qc.ca

Total Battery Consulting Inc
13376 Rue Montaigne ... Oregon House CA 95962 530-692-0640
Web: www.totalbatteryconsulting.com

Total Contentz LLC 845 E Easy St Ste 102 ... Simi Valley CA 93065 805-522-5900
Web: www.totalcontentz.com

Total E&P New Ventures Inc
Total Plz 1201 Louisiana Ste 1800 ... Houston TX 77002 713-647-3300
Web: www.usa.total.com

Total Logistics Solutions Inc PO Box 11146 ... Burbank CA 91510 818-353-2962
Web: www.logisticsociety.com

TraceSecurity Inc
6300 Corporate Blvd Ste 200 ... Baton Rouge LA 70809 225-612-2121
Web: www.tracesecurity.com

Traffic Group Inc, The 9900 Franklin Sq Dr ... Baltimore MD 21236 410-931-6600
TF: 800-583-8411 ■ *Web:* www.trafficgroup.com

Tragon Corp 365 Convention Way ... Redwood City CA 94063 650-365-1833
Web: tragon.com

Trainertainment LLC PO Box 2168 ... Keller TX 76248 817-886-4840
Web: trainertainment.net

Trale In 14229 W Commerce Rd ... Daleville IN 47334 765-378-5509
Web: www.trale.com

Tran Cert Marketing Inc
2295 Berry Ln Ste 880 ... Point Roberts WA 98281 360-945-2190
Web: www.trancertmarketing.com

Transverse LLC 620 Congress Ave Ste 200 ... Austin TX 78701 512-279-3119
Web: www.gotransverse.com

Transweave Inc 1333 Gough St Ste 7J ... San Francisco CA 94109 415-441-5271
Web: www.transweave.com

Traver Technologies Ltd
2550 Gray Falls Dr Ste 400 ... Houston TX 77077 281-752-6262
Web: www.travertech.com

Treacy & Co 1220 South St ... Needham MA 02492 781-559-3381
Web: www.treacyandco.com

Treeline Associates 3048 W Clarkston Rd ... Lake Orion MI 48362 248-814-7151
Web: treelineassociates.com

Trellist Inc 117 N Market St ... Wilmington DE 19801 302-778-1300
Web: www.trellist.com

Phone Fax

Trinity River Authority of Texas
5300 s collins st ... Arlington TX 76018 817-467-4343
Web: www.trinityra.org

TriReme Medical Inc
7060 Koll Ctr Pkwy Ste 300 ... Pleasanton CA 94566 925-931-1300
Web: qtvascular.com

Trisoft Technologies Inc
14429 Independence Dr ... Plainfield IL 60544 866-364-7031
TF: 866-364-7031 ■ *Web:* www.etrisoft.com

Trissential Inc
1905 E Wayzata Blvd Ste 333 ... Minneapolis MN 55391 952-595-7970
Web: www.trissential.com

Trp Enterprises Inc
333 Summit Square Ct ... Winston-Salem NC 27101 336-777-1947
Web: www.trpnet.com

Truenorth Development Inc
141 N Ctr St 201 ... Northville MI 48167 248-348-6011
Web: www.truen.com

Trusted Advisor Associates Llc
8 Lapis Cir W Orange ... West Orange NJ 07052 973-898-1579
Web: www.trustedadvisor.com

TST Infrastructure
61 Inverness Dr E Ste 100 ... Englewood CO 80112 303-799-5197
Web: www.tstinfrastructure.com

TTG Consultants 4727 Wilshire Blvd ... Los Angeles CA 90010 323-936-6600
TF: 800-736-8840 ■ *Web:* www.ttgconsultants.com

Tug Mcgraw Foundation 1303 Jefferson St Ste 100b ... Napa CA 94559 707-255-1884
Web: tugmcgraw.org

Turover-Straus Group Inc
4145 S Mccann Ct B ... Springfield MO 65804 417-889-0770
Web: tsgnpd.com

Turpin Sales & Marketing Inc
330 Cold Spring Ave ... West Springfield MA 01089 877-377-7573
TF: 877-377-7573 ■ *Web:* www.turpinsales.com

U S Medical Management LLC
27000 Hills Tech Ct Ste 200 ... Farmington Hills MI 48331 407-474-3717
Web: usmmllc.com

UCI Medical Affiliates Inc
1818 Henderson St ... Columbia SC 29201 803-782-4278 782-3445*
**Fax:* Executive Fax ■ *Web:* www.doctorscare.com

Ulterior Motives International Inc
1081 Ohio Dr Ste 2 ... Plano TX 75093 214-826-0011
Web: www.umi-inc.com

Unemed Corp 986099 Nebraska Medical Center ... Omaha NE 68198 402-559-2468
Web: www.unemed.com

Unemployment Services Corp 50 Salem St ... Wakefield MA 01880 781-246-0262
Web: www.uscorp.com

UniComm Consulting LLC 9745 Rim Rock Cir ... Loomis CA 95650 408-420-5539
Web: www.unicommconsulting.com

Unify Square Inc 411 108th Ave NE ... Bellevue WA 98004 425-865-0700
Web: www.unifysquare.com

Unison Consulting Inc 409 W Huron Ste 400 ... Chicago IL 60610 312-988-3360
Web: www.unison-ucg.com

Unisource NTC 1560 Holly Court Ste 200 ... Thousand Oaks CA 91360 800-736-8470
TF: 800-736-8470 ■ *Web:* www.unisourcentc.com

United Sourcing Alliance
2105 Water Ridge Pkwy Ste 470 ... Charlotte NC 28217 704-697-9695
Web: usa-llc.com

United Temps Inc 1550 S Indiana Ave ... Chicago IL 60605 312-922-8558
Web: unitedhq.com

Urban Futures Inc 3111 N Tustin St Ste 230 ... Orange CA 92865 714-283-9334
Web: www.urbanfuturesinc.com

US-Reports Inc 5802 Wright Dr ... Loveland CO 80538 970-593-9888
Web: www.us-reports.com

USA Risk Group Inc 30 Main St Ste 450 ... Burlington VT 05401 802-371-2220
Web: www.usarisk.com

USAdvisors Network LLC
9531 W 78th St Ste 220 ... Eden Prairie MN 55344 952-829-0000
Web: www.usadvisorsnetwork.com

Ux Consulting Company LLC, The 1401 Macy Dr ... Roswell GA 30076 770-642-7745
Web: www.uxc.com

Valley Small Business Development
7035 N Fruit Ave ... Fresno CA 93711 559-438-9680
Web: www.vsbdc.com

Valtim Inc 1095 Venture Dr ... Forest VA 24551 434-525-3004
Web: www.valtim.com

VanAllen Group Inc, The 179 Glen Eagle Way ... Mcdonough GA 30253 770-507-5001
Web: www.vanallen.com

Vanir Construction Management Inc
4540 Duckhorn Dr Ste 300 ... Sacramento CA 95834 916-575-8887 575-8887
TF: 888-912-1201 ■ *Web:* www.vanir.com

Vaya 2111 Plum St Ste 250 ... Aurora IL 60506 630-906-3046
Web: www.vayapath.com

vCustomer Corp 4040 Lk Washington Blvd NE ... Kirkland WA 98033 206-802-0200
Web: www.vcustomer.com

Vectrus Inc 655 Space Ctr Dr ... Colorado Springs CO 80915 719-591-3600
Web: www.vectrus.com

Veetech PC 113 Centrewest Ct ... Cary NC 27513 919-388-0037
Web: www.veetechpc.com

Vega Energy Partners Ltd 3701 Kirby Ste 1290 ... Houston TX 77098 713-527-0557
Web: www.vegaenergy.com

Vendors Exchange International Inc
8700 Brookpark Rd ... Cleveland OH 44129 216-432-1800
TF: 800-321-2311 ■ *Web:* www.veii.com

Venn Products Group 80 Skyline Dr ... Plainview NY 11803 516-822-1561
Web: www.vennproducts.com

Venture Group Enterprises Inc
2520 Whitehall Park Dr Ste 100 ... Charlotte NC 28273 704-676-0160
Web: www.vgei.com

Veracity Credit Consultants LLC
110 16th St Ste 1000 ... Denver CO 80202 303-893-1801
Web: www.veracitycredit.com

Verax Communications 499 Adams St ... Milton MA 02186 617-698-0088
Web: www.veraxcom.com

				Phone	Fax
Veri-Tax LLC 30 Executive Park Ste 200 Web: www.veri-tax.com	Irvine	CA	92614	949-783-2100	
Verifi Inc 8391 Beverly Blvd Ste 310 Web: www.verifi.com	Los Angeles	CA	90048	323-655-5789	
Verisk Analytics 545 Washington Blvd. NASDAQ: VRSK ■ TF: 800-888-4476 ■ Web: www.verisk.com	Jersey City	NJ	07310	201-469-3000	748-1472
Verity Professionals 2400 Lkeview Pkwy Web: verityprofessionals.com	Alpharetta	GA	30004	404-920-6400	
Vermont Energy Investment Corp 128 Lakeside Ave Ste 401 Web: www.veic.org	Burlington	VT	05401	802-658-6060	
Vertigraph Inc 12959 Jupiter Rd Ste 252 TF: 800-989-4243 ■ Web: www.vertigraph.com	Dallas	TX	75238	214-340-9436	
VetStrategy 30 Whitmore Rd TF: 866-901-6471 ■ Web: www.vetstrategy.com	Woodbridge	ON	L4L7Z4	866-901-6471	
Vetter Health Services Inc 20220 Harney St TF: 800-388-4264 ■ Web: www.vetterhealthservices.com	Elkhorn	NE	68022	402-895-3932	895-8165
Victory Asset Management Co 1050 Mantua Pk Web: www.victoryasset.com	Wenonah	NJ	08090	856-464-3100	
Vikmere Software PO Box 34521 Web: vikmere.com	Los Angeles	CA	90034	310-836-2802	
Visible Inventory Inc 6 Raymond Ave Ste 5b Web: www.visibleinventory.com	Salem	NH	03079	603-894-5858	
VisionQuest National Ltd 600 N Swan Rd Web: www.vq.com	Tucson	AZ	85732	520-881-3950	881-3269
Vistech Corp 11 Grays Farm Rd Web: www.vistechcorp.com	Westport	CT	06880	203-454-0300	
Viteos Capital Market Services Limited 21 Clyde Rd Ste 202 Web: www.viteos.com	Somerset	NJ	08873	732-868-8100	
ViTEX Inc 630 Williamson Rd Web: www.vitex.com	Mooresville	NC	28117	704-663-2544	
Vizant Technologies LLC Brandywine Two Bldg 5 Christy Dr Ste 202 Web: vizant.com	Chadds Ford	PA	19317	610-358-1003	
VizQuest Ventures LLC PO Box 920741 Web: www.vizquest.com	Needham	MA	02492	781-207-0311	
Volt VIEWtech Inc 4761 E Hunter Ave TF: 888-396-9927 ■ Web: www.volt.com	Anaheim	CA	92807	714-695-3377	
Von Lehman & CO 250 Grandview Dr Ste 300 Web: www.vlcpa.com	Fort Mitchell	KY	41017	859-331-3300	
Vortex Advisory Group 220 Pond St Web: advisoryleadership.com/consulting	Hopkinton	MA	01748	508-435-0220	
VStock Transfer LLC 18 Lafayette Pl Web: www.vstocktransfer.com	Woodmere	NY	11598	212-828-8436	
Vx Associates LLC 150 Allen Rd Ste 107 Web: www.vxassociates.com	Liberty Corner	NJ	07938	908-696-7973	
W H Meanor & Associates 216 N Mcdowell St Ste 200 Web: www.whmeanor.com	Charlotte	NC	28204	704-372-7640	
Warren Distribution Inc 727 S 13th St Web: www.warrendistribution.com	Omaha	NE	68102	402-341-9397	977-5754
Warren Management Group Inc, The 1720 Jet Stream Dr Ste 200 Web: warrenmgmt.com	Colorado Springs	CO	80921	719-534-0266	
Warren Whitney Sherwood & Company Inc 7231 Forest Ave Web: www.warrenwhitney.com	Richmond	VA	23226	804-282-9566	
Warshaw Group Inc 540 Bdwy 4th Fl Web: www.warshawgroup.com	New York	NY	10012	212-966-4056	
Wasmer Group, The 2001 Jackson St Web: www.wasmer.com	Alexandria	LA	71301	318-443-6551	
Waypoint Consulting 1450 E Boot Rd Web: www.waypointco.com	West Chester	PA	19380	484-472-8611	
Weber Marketing Group Inc 225 Terry Ave North Ste 400 Web: www.webermarketing.com	Seattle	WA	98109	206-340-6111	
Webwise Learning Inc 2626 E 82nd St Ste 330 Web: webwiselearning.com	Bloomington	MN	55425	952-883-0800	
Wellford Energy Group LLC 555 11th St NW Web: www.wellfordenergy.com	Washington	DC	20004	202-783-9193	
Wesley Peachtree Group Inc, The 1475 Klondike Rd SW Ste 100 Web: www.wpg-inc.com	Conyers	GA	30094	404-874-0555	
Westin Engineering Inc 3100 Zinfandel Dr Ste 300	Rancho Cordova	CA	95670	916-852-2121	852-2311
Westney Consulting Group Inc 1800 W Loop S Ste 1200 Web: www.westney.com	Houston	TX	77027	713-861-0800	
Wheaton Partners LLC 1901 N Roselle Rd Ste 640 Web: www.codemap.com	Schaumburg	IL	60195	847-381-5465	
Whelan Group Inc, The 155 W 19th St Web: www.whelangroup.com	New York	NY	10011	212-727-7332	
Wicklander Zulawski & Associates Inc 4932 Main St TF: 800-222-7789 ■ Web: www.w-z.com	Downers Grove	IL	60515	630-852-6800	
WideNet Consulting Group 11400 SE Sixth St Ste 130 Web: www.widenet-consulting.com	Bellevue	WA	98004	425-643-0366	
William Avery & Associates Inc 3 1/2 N Santa Cruz Ave Ste A Web: www.averyassoc.net	Los Gatos	CA	95030	408-399-4424	
William J Ash Company LLC 3 Brayton Woods Dr Web: www.wjashco.com	Rehoboth	MA	02769	401-965-8850	
William W Rutherford Associates Inc 3102 Maple Ave Ste 450 Web: www.wwrutherford.com	Dallas	TX	75201	214-219-8660	
Willow Group Inc, The 8201 Norman Ctr Dr Ste 115 Web: willowg.com	Bloomington	MN	55437	952-897-3550	
Wilmington Group, The 7040 Wrightsville Ave Web: www.wilmingtongroup.com	Wilmington	NC	28403	910-256-1056	
Wilson Legal Solutions Inc 3817 W chester Pk Web: www.wilsonlegalsol.com	Newtown Square	PA	19073	484-422-0010	
Windward Environmental LLC 200 W Mercer St Ste 401 Web: www.windwardenv.com	Seattle	WA	98119	206-378-1364	
Winfree Marketing & Sales Institute 1905 Arnold Palmer Blvd TF: 800-616-9260 ■ Web: www.winfree.org	Louisville	KY	40245	502-253-0700	
Winning Edge Group LLC 2576 Euclid Crescent E Web: www.group50.com	Upland	CA	91784	909-949-9083	
Winning Proposals Inc 374 Maple Ave E Ste 305 Web: www.win-pros.com	Vienna	VA	22180	703-242-6490	
Winsby Inc 1854 Sherman Ave Web: www.winsbyinc.com	Evanston	IL	60201	847-316-9800	
Wise Agent, The 13014 N Saguaro Blvd Web: www.thewiseagent.com	Fountain Hills	AZ	85268	480-836-0345	
Wolff Group Inc 525 Ottawa Ave Northwest Web: www.wolffgroupinc.com	Grand Rapids	MI	49503	616-458-1449	
Words & Numbers Inc 2050 Rockrose Ave	Baltimore	MD	21211	410-467-7835	
Work Institute LLC, The 1620 Westgate Cir Ste 100 Web: workinstitute.com	Brentwood	TN	37027	615-777-6400	
Worklife Balance com 7845 Landowne Dr Web: www.worklifebalance.com	Atlanta	GA	30350	770-913-0064	
Worldview Solutions Inc 115 S 15th St Ste 400 Web: www.worldviewsolutions.com	Richmond	VA	23219	804-915-7628	
Wwc Enterprises Inc 19145 S Us Hwy 377 Web: www.wwcenterprises.com	Dublin	TX	76446	254-445-0100	
X Dot Inc 4500 Westgrove Dr Ste 395 Web: www.x-dot.com	Addison	TX	75001	972-248-7243	
Xceptional HR Consulting LLC 3108 White Cedar Dr Web: xceptionalhr.com	Moore	OK	73160	405-293-2564	
Xtreme Consulting Group Inc 3500 Carillon Point Web: www.xtremeconsulting.com	Kirkland	WA	98033	425-861-9460	
YAHSGS LLC 3100 George Washington Way Ste 103 Web: www.yahsgs.com	Richland	WA	99354	509-375-5359	
Young Startup Ventures Inc 258 Crafton Ave Web: www.youngstartup.com	Staten Island	NY	10314	718-477-2208	
Youthbuild International 58 Day St Ste 300 Web: www.youthbuild.org	Somerville	MA	02144	617-623-9900	
Zero Technologies LLC 4510 Adams Cir Unit G Web: www.zerowater.com	Bensalem	PA	19020	215-244-0823	
Zerochaos LLC 420 S Orange Ave Ste 600 *Fax Area Code: 877 ■ Web: www.zerochaos.com	Orlando	FL	32801	407-770-6161	888-9376*
Zeus Development Corp 2424 Wilcrest Ste 100 Web: www.zeusintel.com	Houston	TX	77042	713-952-9500	
Zeus Jones 2429 Nicollet Ave S Web: www.zeusjones.com	Minneapolis	MN	55408	612-279-1400	
Zielinski Financial Advisors LLC 2403 High Hammock Rd Web: www.zfinancialadvisors.com	Seabrook Island	SC	29455	843-974-4964	
Zimmet Healthcare Consulting LLC 4006 Us Hwy 9 TF: 877-763-2001 ■ Web: zhealthcare.com	Morganville	NJ	07751	732-970-0733	
Zitter Group, The 290 W Mount Pleasant Ave Ste 2210 Web: www.zitter.com	Livingston	NJ	07039	973-376-1300	
Zoyto Inc 433 Northpark Central Dr Web: www.zoyto.com	Houston	TX	77073	713-300-3000	

464 MANNEQUINS & DISPLAY FORMS

				Phone	Fax
Barnhart Display Inc 1170 Charming St Web: www.barnhartdisplay.com	Maitland	FL	32751	407-637-2060	637-2053
Goldsmith New York at Studio 350 601 W 26th St Ste 350 Web: www.goldsmith-inc.com	New York	NY	10001	212-366-9040	
Ronis Bros 39 Harriet Pl Web: www.ronis.com	Lynbrook	NY	11563	516-887-5266	887-5288
Siegel & Stockman USA 126 W 25th St TF: 888-515-8949 ■ Web: www.siegel-stockman.com	New York	NY	10001	212-633-0138	366-0575
Silvestri Studio Inc 8125 Beach St TF: 800-647-8874 ■ Web: www.silvestricalifornia.com	Los Angeles	CA	90001	323-277-4420	585-0861

465 MARINE SERVICES

See Also Freight Transport - Deep Sea (Domestic Ports) p. 2330; Freight Transport - Deep Sea (Foreign Ports) p. 2331; Freight Transport - Inland Waterways p. 2331; Logistics Services (Transportation & Warehousing) p. 2681

				Phone	Fax
AEP River Operations 16150 Main Cir Dr Ste 400 TF: 800-621-3362	Chesterfield	MO	63017	636-530-2100	530-4100
American Port Service Inc 2901 Childs St Web: www.amports.com	Baltimore	MD	21226	410-350-0400	
Andrie Inc 561 E Western Ave TF: 800-722-2421 ■ Web: www.andrietg.com	Muskegon	MI	49442	231-728-2226	726-6747
Bay Houston Towing Co 2243 Milford St TF: 800-324-3755 ■ Web: www.bayhouston.com	Houston	TX	77253	713-529-3755	529-2591

Phone Fax

Bisso Towboat Company Inc 8237 Oak St . . . . New Orleans LA 70178 504-861-1411 861-9298
Web: www.bissotowing.com

Bunkers International Corp
110 Timberlachen Cir Ste 1012 . . . . Lake Mary FL 32746 407-328-7757 328-0045
Web: www.bunkersinternational.com

Cargo Express Inc 1790 Yardley Stn Dr . . . . Yardley PA 19067 215-493-2662 493-4430

Ceres Terminals Inc 2 Tower Ctr Blvd . . . . East Brunswick NJ 08816 201-974-3800 974-3850
Web: www.ceresglobal.com

Cooper/T Smith Stevedoring Co 118 N Royal St . . . . Mobile AL 36602 251-431-6100
Web: www.coopertsmith.com

Crowley Maritime Corp
9487 Regency Square Blvd. Jacksonville FL 32225 904-727-2200 727-2501
TF: 800-276-9539 ■ *Web:* www.crowley.com

Dix Industries Inc 5500 RL Ostos Rd . . . . Brownsville TX 78521 956-831-4228 831-2559
Web: www.dixshipping.com

Donjon Marine Company Inc 100 Central Ave . . . . Hillside NJ 07205 908-964-8812 964-7426
Web: www.donjon.com

Eagle Marine Industries Inc 1 Riverview Ave. . . . . Sauget IL 62201 618-875-1153 875-1505

Edison Chouest Offshore 16201 E Main St. . . . . Galliano LA 70354 985-601-4444 601-4237
TF: 866-925-5161 ■ *Web:* www.chouest.com

Eller-ITO Stevedoring Company LLC
1007 N America Way . . . . Miami FL 33132 305-379-3700 371-9969
Web: www.ellerito.com

Foss Maritime Co 1151 Fairview Ave N . . . . Seattle WA 98119 800-562-2711
TF: 800-562-2711 ■ *Web:* www.foss.com

G & H Towing Company Inc PO Box 2270 . . . . Galveston TX 77553 409-744-6311
Web: www.gandhtowing.com

General Steamship Agencies Inc
575 Redwood Hwy Ste 200. . . . . Mill Valley CA 94941 415-389-5200 389-9020
TF: 855-859-3123 ■ *Web:* www.gensteam.com

Great Lakes Towing Co 4500 Div Ave. . . . . Cleveland OH 44102 216-621-4854 621-7616
TF: 800-321-3663 ■ *Web:* www.thegreatlakesgroup.com

Hawaii Stevedores Inc 1601 Sand Island Pkwy. . . . . Honolulu HI 96819 808-527-3400
Web: www.hawaiistevedores.com

Hawaiian Tug & Barge
1331 N Nimitz Hwy PO Box 3288. Honolulu HI 96817 808-543-9311
TF: 800-572-2743 ■ *Web:* www.htbyb.com

Higman Marine Services
1980 Post Oak Blvd Ste 1101. . . . . Houston TX 77056 713-552-1101 552-0732
Web: higman.com

Hopkins-Carter Company Inc 3300 NW 21st St. . . . . Miami FL 33142 305-635-7377 633-1310
TF: 800-595-9656 ■ *Web:* www.hopkins-carter.com

Hornbeck Offshore Services Inc
103 Northpark Blvd Ste 300. . . . . Covington LA 70433 985-727-2000 727-2006
NYSE: HOS ■ *TF:* 800-642-9816 ■ *Web:* www.hornbeckoffshore.com

Houston Pilots 203 Deerwood Glen Dr Ste 118. . . . . Deer Park TX 77017 713-645-9620
Web: www.houston-pilots.com

International Transportation Service Inc
1281 Pier J Way . . . . Long Beach CA 90802 562-435-7781 590-6761
Web: www.itslb.com

J. F. Brennan Co Inc 820 Bainbridge. . . . . La Crosse WI 54603 608-784-7173 785-2090
Web: www.jfbrennan.com

James Marine Inc (JMI)
4500 Clarks River Rd PO Box 2305 . . . . Paducah KY 42002 270-898-7392 448-0015
Web: www.jamesmarine.com

Kinder Morgan Bulk Terminals Inc
7116 Hwy 22 . . . . Sorrento LA 70778 225-675-5387
TF: 800-232-1627 ■ *Web:* www.kindermorgan.com

LeBeouf Brothers Towing LLC 124 Dry Dock Rd . . . . Bourg LA 70343 985-594-6691 594-5253
Web: www.lebeouftowing.com

Marquette Transportation Company LLC
5525 Mounes St . . . . New Orleans LA 70123 504-733-5845
TF: 800-735-5845 ■ *Web:* www.marquettetrans.com

McAllister Towing & Transportation Co Inc
17 Battery Pl Ste 1200 . . . . New York NY 10004 212-269-3200 509-1147
TF: 888-774-0400 ■ *Web:* www.mcallistertowing.com

McCabe Hamilton & Renny Company Ltd (MHR)
1130 N Nimitz Hwy Rm A265 . . . . Honolulu HI 96817 808-524-3255 545-3101
Web: www.mhrhawaii.com

Murphy Marine Services Inc
701 Christiana Avenue . . . . Port of Wilmington DE 19801 302-571-4700 571-4702

New Haven Terminal Inc 100 Waterfront St. . . . . New Haven CT 06512 203-468-0805 469-6374

New York State Canal Corp
200 Southern Blvd PO Box 189 . . . . Albany NY 12201 518-436-2700
TF: 800-422-6254 ■ *Web:* www.canals.ny.gov

Nicholson Terminal & Dock Co
360 E Great Lakes. . . . . Ecorse MI 48229 313-842-4300 843-1091
Web: www.nicholson-terminal.com

North Star Terminal & Stevedore Company LLC
790 Ocean Dock Rd . . . . Anchorage AK 99501 907-272-7537 272-8927
Web: www.northstarak.com

Odyssey Marine Exploration Inc
5215 W Laurel St . . . . Tampa FL 33607 813-876-1776 876-1777
NASDAQ: OMEX ■ *TF:* 800-458-4646 ■ *Web:* www.shipwreck.net

Otto Candies LLC 17271 US 90 . . . . Des Allemands LA 70030 504-469-7700 469-7740
Web: www.ottocandies.com

Parker Towing Company Inc PO Box 20908 . . . . Tuscaloosa AL 35402 205-349-1677 758-0061
Web: www.parkertowing.com

Pelicans Perch Marina & Boatyard
40 Audusson Ave Bayou Chico. . . . . Pensacola FL 32507 850-453-3471 457-1662
Web: www.pelicansperchmarina.com

Port of Miami Terminal Operating Company LC
635 Australia Way. . . . . Miami FL 33132 305-416-7600 374-6724
Web: www.pomtoc.com

Ports America Inc
525 Washington Blvd Ste 1660 . . . . Jersey City NJ 07310 732-635-3899 216-9366*
**Fax Area Code:* 201 ■ *Web:* www.portsamerica.com

RMS Titanic Inc 3340 Peachtree Rd NE . . . . Atlanta GA 30326 404-842-2600 842-2626
Web: premierexhibitions.com/exhibitions/3/3/titanic-artifact-exhibition

Rukert Terminals Corp 2021 S Clinton St. . . . . Baltimore MD 21224 410-276-1013
Web: www.rukert.com

Sause Bros 3710 NW Front Ave. . . . . Portland OR 97210 503-222-1811 222-2010
TF: 800-488-4167 ■ *Web:* www.sause.com

Phone Fax

Sea Tow Services International Inc
1560 Youngs Ave PO Box 1178 . . . . Southold NY 11971 631-765-3660
TF: 800-473-2869 ■ *Web:* www.seatow.com

SSA Marine 1131 SW Klickitat Way . . . . Seattle WA 98134 206-623-0304 623-0179
TF: 800-422-3505 ■ *Web:* www.ssamarine.com

Tidewater Inc 601 Poydras St Ste 1900 . . . . New Orleans LA 70130 504-568-1010
NYSE: TDW ■ *TF:* 800-678-8433 ■ *Web:* www.tdw.com

Virginia International Terminals Inc
7737 Hampton Blvd . . . . Norfolk VA 23505 757-440-7000 440-7221
TF General: 800-541-2431 ■ *Web:* www.vit.org

Western Towboat Company Inc 617 NW 40th St. . . . . Seattle WA 98107 206-789-9000 789-9755
Web: www.westerntowboat.com

466 MARKET RESEARCH FIRMS

Phone Fax

1stWEST Financial Corp
1536 Cole Blvd Ste 333 . . . . Lakewood CO 80401 866-670-3443
TF: 866-670-3443 ■ *Web:* www.1stwest.com

3-2-1Launch! 66 Ft Point St . . . . Norwalk CT 06855 203-855-9050
Web: maddockdouglas.com

Abbott Nicholson PC 300 River Pl Ste 3000 . . . . Detroit MI 48207 313-566-2500
Web: www.abbottnicholson.com

Aberdeen Group Inc 451 D St Ste 710. . . . . Boston MA 02210 617-854-5200
TF: 800-577-7891 ■ *Web:* www.aberdeen.com

AbsolutData Technologies Inc
1851 Harbor Bay Pkwy Ste 125 . . . . Alameda CA 94502 510-748-9922
Web: www.absolutdata.com

Abt Assoc Inc 55 Wheeler St. . . . . Cambridge MA 02138 617-492-7100 492-5219
Web: www.abtassociates.com

ACG Research 2112 E Catamaran Dr. . . . . Gilbert AZ 85234 408-200-0967
Web: acgcc.com

Advanced Scientific Concepts Inc
135 E Ortega St. . . . . Santa Barbara CA 93101 805-966-3331
Web: www.advancedscientificconcepts.com

Affirmative Risk Management
P.O. Box 24407 (72221) 4016 Stannus St. 4016 Stannus St
. . . . Little Rock AR 72204 501-228-0900
Web: affirmativeriskmgmt.com

All Media Ventures One Quincy Ln . . . . White Plains NY 10605 917-806-6373
Web: www.allmediaventures.com

Allan R Nelson Engineering (1997) Inc
17510-102 Ave 2nd Fl . . . . Edmonton AB T5S1K2 780-483-3436 489-9557
Web: www.arneng.ab.ca

Alliance Energy Services LLC
318 Armour Rd . . . . Kansas City MO 64116 816-421-5192
Web: www.alliancec3.com

AllSource Analysis Inc
1610 Pace St Unit 900 PMB 135 . . . . Longmont CO 80504 303-210-2529
Web: www.allsourceanalysis.com

Alteris Group LLC 29110 Inkster Rd Ste 100. . . . . Southfield MI 48034 248-477-5560
Web: www.alterisgroup.com

Ameresco Canada Inc 90 Sheppard Ave E. . . . . North York ON M2N3A1 416-512-7700 218-2288
TF: 888-483-7267 ■ *Web:* www.ameresco.ca

AML Partners LLC 4 Grand Cove Way. . . . . Edgewater NJ 07020 201-484-8835
TF: 866-790-5095 ■ *Web:* www.amlpartners.com

Amphenol Optimize Manufacturing Co
528 N Mariposa Rd Bldg. A . . . . Nogales AZ 85621 520-397-7015 397-7014
TF: 800-288-4746 ■ *Web:* www.amphenol-optimize.com

AMTEK Engineering Services Ltd
340 Legget Dr Ste 200 . . . . Ottawa ON K2K1Y6 613-749-3990
Web: www.amtekcdn.com

Andrew Seybold Inc
315 Meigs Rd Ste A-267 . . . . Santa Barbara CA 93109 805-898-2460
Web: www.andrewseybold.com

Answers Research Inc
380 Stevens Ave Ste 214 . . . . Solana Beach CA 92075 858-792-4660
Web: www.answersresearch.com

AQA International LLC 501 Commerce Dr, NE. . . . . Columbia SC 29223 800-281-4384
TF: 800-281-4384 ■ *Web:* www.nsf.org

Arbitron Inc 9705 Patuxent Woods Dr. . . . . Columbia MD 21046 410-312-8000
NYSE: ARB ■ *TF:* 800-543-7300 ■ *Web:* www.arbitron.com

Artafact LLC 43165 Sabercat. . . . . Fremont CA 94539 510-651-9178
Web: www.artafact.com

Attitude Measurement Corp
721 Arbor Way Ste 190. . . . . Blue Bell PA 19422 610-238-9200
Web: www.amcglobal.com

AVMetrics LLC 650 Cochran St Ste 10 . . . . Simi Valley CA 93065 805-421-5056
Web: www.avmetrics.net

Bensussen Deutsch & Assoc Inc (BDA)
15525 Woodinville-Redmond Rd NE . . . . Woodinville WA 98072 425-492-6111 492-7222
TF: 800-451-4764 ■ *Web:* www.bdainc.com

Beroe Inc 338 Raleigh St . . . . Holly Springs NC 27540 919-605-3435
Web: www.beroeinc.com

Biomod Concepts Inc 1821B Lavoisier . . . . Sainte-julie QC J3E1Y6 514-905-5848
Web: www.biomod.com

BioTeknica Inc 250 Bird Rd Ste 216 . . . . Coral Gables FL 33146 305-445-2080
Web: www.bioteknica.com

Bishop & Associates Inc 1209 Fox Glen Dr . . . . St. Charles IL 60174 630-443-2702
Web: www.bishopinc.com

Blackstone Group Inc, The
360 N Michigan Ave Ste 1610 . . . . Chicago IL 60601 312-419-0400
Web: www.bgglobal.com

Boardroom Insiders Inc 4085 26th St . . . . San Francisco CA 94114 415-643-5327
Web: www.boardroominsiders.com

Brand Institute Inc 200 SE First St 12th Fl . . . . Miami FL 33131 305-374-2500
Web: www.brandinst.com

BrandJuice Consulting Inc
1700 E 17th Ave Ste 200 . . . . Denver CO 80218 303-454-3272
Web: brandjuice.com

BraveMatters 3334 W Main St Ste 404. . . . . Norman OK 73072 405-217-0029
Web: www.bravematters.com

Phone | Fax

Bridge Consulting Group LLC
11 Pebble Beach Way ... Washington NJ 07882 908-689-7513
Web: www.bridgeconsultinggroup.net

Bridge Metrics LLC 830 S Greenville Ave ... Allen TX 75002 877-801-7158
TF: 877-801-7158 ■ *Web:* www.bridgemetrics.com

Burke Inc 500 W Seventh St ... Cincinnati OH 45203 513-241-5663 684-7500
Web: www.burke.com

Butler Pappas Weihmuller Katz Craig LLP
80 SW Eighth St Ste 3300 ... Miami FL 33130 305-416-9998
Web: www.butler.legal

Buysight Inc 945 Stewart Dr Ste ... Sunnyvale CA 94085 408-830-0300
Web: www.buysight.com

C & R Research Services Inc
500 N Michigan Ave Ste 1200 ... Chicago IL 60611 312-828-9200 527-3113
TF: 800-543-9393 ■ *Web:* crresearch.com

CúSuite Communications 401 N Cattlemen Rd ... Sarasota FL 34232 941-365-2710
Web: www.c-suitecomms.com

CA Walker Research Solutions Inc
100 W Broadway Ste 1170 ... Glendale CA 91210 626-584-8180 584-8199
Web: www.cawalker.com

Cadence Research & Consulting
360 Via Las Brisas Ste 210 ... Thousand Oaks CA 91320 805-499-8603
Web: www.cadenceresearch.com

Car-Lene Research Inc 430 Lk Cook Rd Ste B ... Deerfield IL 60015 847-940-2000
Web: www.carleneresearch.com

Carnegie Observatories 813 Santa Barbara St ... Pasadena CA 91101 626-577-1122
Web: obs.carnegiescience.edu

CarSmart com 3170 Crow Canyon Pl Ste 270 ... San Ramon CA 94583 925-277-0900
Web: www.carsmart.com

CattleLog 10305 102nd Terrace ... Sebastian FL 32958 866-239-2665
TF: 866-239-2665 ■ *Web:* www.cattlelog.com

Causeit Inc 1631 NE Broadway Ste 249 ... Portland OR 97232 503-493-7332
Web: causeit.org

CBR International Corp
2905 Wilderness Pl Ste 202 ... Boulder CO 80301 720-746-1190
Web: www.cbrintl.com

Cell Resin Technologies 1789 Buerkle Cir ... Saint Paul MN 55110 651-770-9161
Web: cellresin.com

Celula Inc 11011 Torreyana Rd Ste 200 ... San Diego CA 92121 858-875-8800
Web: www.celula-inc.com

Centralized Supply Chain Services LLC
8140 Ward Pkwy ... Kansas City MO 64114 913-438-5552
Web: www.cscscoop.com

Chadwick Martin Bailey Inc 179 S St 3rd Fl ... Boston MA 02111 617-350-8922
Web: www.cmbinfo.com

Clear Seas Research 2401 W Big Beaver Rd ... Troy MI 48084 248-786-1683
Web: clearseas.mobi

Clinical Research Advantage Inc
2141 E Broadway Rd ... Tempe AZ 85282 480-820-5656
Web: www.radiantresearch.com

Coleman Research Inc
909 Aviation Pkwy Ste 400 ... Morrisville NC 27560 919-571-0000
Web: www.colemaninsights.com

Colligent Inc 9266 227th Ave NE ... Redmond WA 98053 615-298-1144
Web: www.colligent.com

comScore Inc 11950 Democracy Dr # 600 ... Reston VA 20190 703-438-2000 438-2051
TF: 866-276-6972 ■ *Web:* www.comscore.com

Connected Nation Inc 444 N Capitol St, NW ... Washington DC 20001 877-846-7710
TF: 877-846-7710 ■ *Web:* www.connectednation.com

Contact 101 Inc 777 N Rainbow Blvd Ste 250 ... Las Vegas NV 89107 888-731-2397
TF: 888-731-2397 ■ *Web:* www.contact-101.com

Corra Group 13011 W Washington Blvd ... Los Angeles CA 90066 310-822-7788
Web: www.corragroup.com

Crompco Corp 1815 Gallagher Rd ... Plymouth Meeting PA 19462 610-278-7203
Web: www.crompco.com

Cross Commerce Media Inc 130 Madison Ave ... New York NY 10016 888-890-0020
TF: 888-890-0020 ■ *Web:* www.collectivei.com

Crystal McKenzie Inc 30 E 20th St Ste 305 ... New York NY 10003 212-598-4567
Web: www.cminyc.com

D m r International Inc 200 W Pk St Ste 104 ... Covington KY 41011 859-655-9200
Web: www.dmrinteractive.com

Datassential 1762 Westwood Blvd Ste 250 ... Los Angeles CA 90024 877-886-3687
TF: 877-886-3687 ■ *Web:* www.datassential.com

Davidson-Peterson Associates Inc
201 Lafayette Center ... Kennebunk ME 04043 207-985-1790
Web: digitalresearch.com

Decision Analyst Inc 604 Ave H E ... Arlington TX 76011 817-640-6166 640-6567
Web: www.decisionanalyst.com

Demand Metric 562 Wellington St ... London ON N6A3R5 519-495-9619
TF: 866-947-7744 ■ *Web:* www.demandmetric.com

Dieringer Research Group Inc, The
200 Bishops Way ... Brookfield WI 53005 262-432-5200
Web: www.thedrg.com

Digital Traffic Systems Inc
6020 Academy Rd NE Ste 202 ... Albuquerque NM 87109 505-881-4470
Web: www.dtsits.com

Directions Research Inc 401 E Ct St ... Cincinnati OH 45202 513-651-2990 651-2998
Web: www.directionsrsch.com

Dodd Creative Group Holding Company Inc
3720 Canton St Ste 100 ... Dallas TX 75226 214-821-6990
Web: doddcreative.com

Dolcera Corp 3555 S El Camino Real Ste 305 ... San Mateo CA 94403 650-425-6772
Web: www.dolcera.com

Dunnhumby USA LLC 444 W Third St ... Cincinnati OH 45202 513-632-1020
Web: www.dunnhumby.com

Durie Tangri LLP 217 Leidesdorff St ... San Francisco CA 94111 415-362-6666
Web: www.durietangri.com

DVFG Advisors LLC 125 E Elm St Ste 300 ... Conshohocken PA 19428 610-234-0500
Web: www.dvfgadvisors.com

DYG Inc 36A Padanaram Rd ... Danbury CT 06811 203-744-9008

EcoStrategy Group 195-B Bryant St ... Palo Alto CA 94301 650-321-6009
Web: www.EcoStrategyGroup.com

Elder Research Inc 300 W Main Ste 301 ... Charlottesville VA 22903 434-973-7673
Web: www.datamininglab.com

Empire Advisory Group Inc
38 Chimney View Ln ... Springfield IL 62707 217-528-0047

EmployeeScreenIQ Inc 24500 Chagrin Blvd ... Cleveland OH 44122 216-514-2800
Web: www.employeescreen.com

Enclude Ltd 1220 19th St NW Ste 200 ... Washington DC 20036 202-822-9100
Web: www.encludesolutions.com

ENLASO Corp 9543 W Emerald St Ste 105 ... Boise ID 83704 208-672-8500
Web: www.enlaso.com

Envirosell Inc 907 Broadway ... New York NY 10010 212-673-9100

eXelate 7 W 22nd St 9th Fl ... New York NY 10010 646-380-4400
TF: 877-896-3282 ■ *Web:* exelate.com

Fashion Snoops Inc 39W 38th St ... New York NY 10018 212-768-8804
Web: www.fashionsnoops.com

FGI Research Inc
6350 Quadrangle Dr Ste 210 ... Chapel Hill NC 27517 919-929-7759
Web: www.fgiresearch.com

Firefly Milward Brown 401 Merritt 7 3rd Fl ... Norwalk CT 06851 203-221-0411 221-0791
Web: www.fireflymb.com

Fox Lawson & Assoc LLC
1335 County Rd D Cir E ... St Paul MN 55109 651-635-0976
Web: www.foxlawson.com

Freedonia Group Inc, The 767 Beta Dr ... Cleveland OH 44143 440-684-9600
Web: freedoniagroup.com

FreeMind Group LLC 423 Brookline Ave ... Boston MA 02215 617-648-0340
Web: www.freemindconsultants.com

Futures Co, The 11 Madison Ave 12th flr ... New York NY 10010 212-896-8112
Web: thefuturescompany.com

Galloway Field Service Inc Dba Galloway Research Service
4751 Hamilton-Wolfe ... San Antonio TX 78229 210-734-4346
Web: gallowayresearch.com

Gallup Inc 1001 Gallup Dr ... Omaha NE 68102 402-951-2003
TF: 888-500-8282 ■ *Web:* gallup.com

Gallup Organization 901 F St NW ... Washington DC 20004 202-715-3030 715-3045
TF: 877-242-5587 ■ *Web:* www.gallup.com

Garcia Research Associates Inc
300 E Magnolia Blvd ... Burbank CA 91502 818-566-7722
Web: www.garciaresearch.com

Gartner Inc 56 Top Gallant Rd ... Stamford CT 06902 203-964-0096 316-6300
NYSE: IT ■ *TF:* 866-471-2526 ■ *Web:* www.gartner.com

GCG Marketing 2421 W Seventh St Ste 400 ... Fort Worth TX 76107 817-332-4600
Web: www.gcgmarketing.com

Geffen Mesher & Co 888 SW Fifth Ave Ste 800 ... Portland OR 97204 503-221-0141
Web: www.gmco.com

GFK Custom Research Inc
8401 Golden Vly Rd ... Minneapolis MN 55427 763-542-0800
Web: gfk.com/us/pages/default.aspx

Global Market Insite Inc
1100 112th Ave Ne Ste 200 ... Bellevue WA 98004 206-315-9300
Web: www.lightspeedgmi.com

Graham & Assoc
3000 Riverchase Galleria Ste 310 ... Birmingham AL 35244 205-443-5399 443-5389
Web: www.grahammktres.com

Gravity Tank Inc 114 W Illinois St Fl 3 ... Chicago IL 60654 312-988-3000
Web: www.gravitytank.com

GRFI Ltd 400 E Randolph St Ste 700 ... Chicago IL 60601 888-856-5161
TF: 888-856-5161 ■ *Web:* grfiltd.com

Guidepoint Global LLC 730 Third Ave 11th Fl ... New York NY 10017 212-375-2980
Web: www.guidepoint.com

Gulf of Maine Research Institute, The
350 Commercial St ... Portland ME 04101 207-772-2321
TF: 866-447-2111 ■ *Web:* www.gmri.org

Harrison Edwards Inc
80 Business Park Dr - Ste 303 ... Armonk NY 10504 914-242-0010
Web: harrison-edwardspr.com

Harry Jernigan CPA Attorney PC
5101 Cleveland St Ste 200 ... Virginia Beach VA 23462 757-490-2200
Web: www.hjlaw.com

Hasd&ic 5575 Ruffin Rd Ste 225 ... San Diego CA 92123 858-614-0200
Web: www.hasdic.org

HCD Research Inc
260 US Hwy 202/31 Ste 1000 ... Flemington NJ 08822 908-788-9393
Web: www.hcdi.net

HealthFocus International
449 Central Ave Ste 205 ... St. Petersburg FL 33701 727-821-7499
Web: www.healthfocus.com

Heliae Development LLC 614 E Germann Rd ... Gilbert AZ 85297 480-424-2875
Web: www.heliae.com

Hotspex Inc 40 Eglinton Ave E Ste 801 ... Toronto ON M4P3A2 416-487-5439
Web: www.hotspex.com

HRA - Healthcare Research & Analytics LLC
400 Lanidex Plz ... Parsippany NJ 07054 973-240-1200
Web: www.hraresearch.com

HTG Peer Groups 653 Oak Rd ... Harlan IA 51537 712-744-3619
Web: www.htgpeergroups.com

i2E Inc
840 Research Pkwy Research Park
Ste 250 ... Oklahoma City OK 73104 405-235-2305
Web: www.i2e.org

IBM Almaden Research Center 650 Harry Rd ... San Jose CA 95120 408-927-1080
Web: www.research.ibm.com/labs/almaden/index.shtml

iCrossing Inc 300 W 57th St ... New York NY 10019 212-649-3900
Web: www.icrossing.com

iData Research Inc 850-777 W Broadway ... Vancouver BC V5Z4J7 604-266-6933
Web: idataresearch.com

IMS Health Inc 485 Lexington Ave FL 26 ... New York NY 10017 203-845-5200
Web: www.imshealth.com

InBios International Inc
562 First Ave S Ste 600 ... Seattle WA 98104 206-344-5821
TF: 866-462-4671 ■ *Web:* www.inbios.com

Infinite Wellness Solutions
3300 Reynolda Rd ... Winston-Salem NC 27106 336-725-8624
Web: www.infinitewellnesssolutions.com

Phone | Fax

Information Resources Inc 150 N Clinton St.......... Chicago IL 60661 312-726-1221
TF: 866-262-5973 ■ *Web:* www.iriworldwide.com

Innerscope Research Inc
98 N Washington St 2nd Fl.......................... Boston MA 02114 617-904-0555
Web: innerscoperesearch.com

Innovairre Communications LLC
825 Hylton Rd.. Pennsauken NJ 08110 856-663-2500
TF: 856-663-2500 ■ *Web:* www.innovairre.com

Institute for Corporate Productivity Inc
411 First Ave S Ste 403 .... Seattle WA 98104 206-624-6565
TF: 866-375-4427 ■ *Web:* www.i4cp.com

Institute for Trend Research 166 King St .... Boscawen NH 03303 603-796-2500
Web: www.itreconomics.com

IntelliQ Research and Strategy Inc
112 W Foster Ave Ste 202C .... State College PA 16801 814-234-2344
Web: www.intelliqresearch.com

Interior Architects Inc 1726 Champa St Ste 100......... Denver CO 80202 303-292-4963
Web: www.interiorarchitects.com

International Data Corp (IDC) 5 Speen St .... Framingham MA 01701 508-872-8200 424-4829
TF: 800-343-4952 ■ *Web:* www.idcresearch.com

Inventis Group Ltd 8400 Sugar Maple Dr Ste 305......... Mason OH 45040 513-518-6691
Web: www.inventisgroup.com

Investment Metrics LLC 3 Parklands Dr .... Darien CT 06820 203-662-8400
Web: www.invmetrics.com

Investorideas com
145 Tyee Dr Number 1573 .... Point Roberts WA 98281 800-665-0411
TF: 800-665-0411 ■ *Web:* www.investorideas.com

Invoke Solutions Inc 375 Totten Pond Rd .... Waltham MA 02451 781-810-2700 810-2750
TF: 866-687-4367 ■ *Web:* www.invoke.com

IPOfferings LLC 799 Dover St..................... Boca Raton FL 33487 561-948-0672
Web: www.ipofferings.com

Ipsos Reid Corp 160 Bloor St E Ste 300 .... Toronto ON M4W1B9 416-324-2900
Web: www.ipsos.ca

Ipsos-ASI Inc 301 Merritt 7 Corporate Pk .... Norwalk CT 06851 203-849-7000
Web: www.ipsos.com

Irving Burton Associates Inc
3150 Fairview Park Dr Ste 301 .... Falls Church VA 22042 703-575-8359
Web: www.ibacorp.us

iSuppli Corp 1700 E Walnut Ave Ste 600............. El Segundo CA 90245 310-524-4000
Web: www.isuppli.com

J. Reckner Associates Inc
587 Bethlehem Pike Ste 800................. Montgomeryville PA 18936 215-822-6220
Web: www.reckner.com

Jantzi-Sustainalytics Inc
215 Spadina Ave Ste 300 .... Toronto ON M5T2C7 416-861-0403
Web: www.sustainalytics.com

JD Power & Assoc
2625 Townsgate Rd Ste 100................. Westlake Village CA 91361 805-418-8000 418-8900
TF: 800-274-5372 ■ *Web:* www.jdpower.com

Jim Jordan & Assoc LP 12941 N Fwy Ste 226.......... Houston TX 77060 281-877-7009
Web: www.jordan-associates.com

Johnson design Group Inc
1550 Norththwest Hwy .... Park Ridge IL 60068 847-298-1650
Web: www.jdg1.com

Kantar Group 501 Kings Hwy E 4th Fl................. Fairfield CT 06825 203-330-5200 330-5201

Kaplan Mrd Inc 31 Chesley Rd .... White Plains NY 10605 914-686-1450
Web: kaplanmrd.com

Kazan, McClain, Abrams, Fernandez, Lyons & Farrise PLC
Jack London Market 55 Harrison St Ste 400............ Oakland CA 94607 877-995-6372
TF: 877-995-6372 ■ *Web:* www.kazanlaw.com

KDPaine & Partners Inc 177 Main St 3rd Fl .... Berlin NH 03570 603-319-1055
Web: www.salienceinsight.com

Keybridge Research LLC
3050 K St NW, Ste 220.......................... Washington DC 20007 202-965-9480
Web: www.keybridgeresearch.com

KL Communications Inc 50 English Plz Ste 6B......... Red Bank NJ 07701 732-224-9991
Web: klcommunications.com

Knowledge Works Inc
5750 Old Orchard Rd Ste 250.......................... Skokie IL 60077 847-853-6117
TF: 866-825-3400 ■ *Web:* www.paynetonline.com

Kyron Inc 139 Forest Ave .... Palo Alto CA 94301 650-888-3608
Web: kyron.com

L2 Inc 155 Wooster St 2nd Fl Ste.................... New York NY 10012 646-525-4153
Web: www.l2thinktank.com

LaneTerralever 425 S Mill Ave....................... Tempe AZ 85281 480-839-1080
Web: terralever.com

LC Risq 555 Saturn Blvd Ste B143 .... San Diego CA 92154 310-406-5684
Web: www.lcrisq.com

Leger, The Research Intelligence Group
507 Pl d'Armes Ste 700 .... Montreal QC H2Y2W8 514-982-2464
Web: leger360.com

Liberty Advisor Group LLC
The Mercantile Exchange 30 S Wacker Dr
22nd Fl.. Chicago IL 60606 312-869-9707
Web: www.libertyadvisorgroup.com

Lieberman Research 98 Cutter Mill Rd .... Great Neck NY 11021 516-829-8880 829-8880
Web: www.liebermanresearch.com

Loan Value Group LLC 47 W River Rd Ste C .... Rumson NJ 07760 732-741-7300
Web: www.loanvaluegroup.com

Lopez Research LLC 2269 Chestnut St........... San Francisco CA 94123 415-894-5781
Web: www.lopezresearch.com

Luth Research Inc 1365 Fourth Ave................. San Diego CA 92101 619-234-5884
Web: www.luthresearch.com

Lyndon Group LLC
220 Newport Ctr Dr Ste 11-529 .... Newport Beach CA 92660 949-494-7722
Web: www.lyndon-group.com

M/A/R/C Research 1660 Westridge Cir.................... Irving TX 75038 972-983-0400 983-0444
TF: 800-884-6272 ■ *Web:* www.marcresearch.com

m2M Strategies LLC
33 Buford Village Way Ste 329......................... Buford GA 30518 678-835-9080
Web: m2mstrategies.com

Maguire Associates Inc
555 Virginia Rd 5 Concord Farms Ste 201............. Concord MA 01742 978-371-1775
Web: www.maguireassoc.com

Phone | Fax

Maher Duessel
DL Clark Bldg 503 Martindale St Ste 600.............. Pittsburgh PA 15212 412-471-5500
Web: www.md-cpas.com

Maier Markey & Justic LLP
222 Bloomingdale Rd Ste 400 .... White Plains NY 10605 914-644-9200
Web: mgroupusa.com

Maillie LLP 1521 Concord Pike Ste 301 .... Wilmington DE 19803 302-358-2371
Web: www.maillie.com

Maritz Canada Inc 6900 Maritz Dr................ Mississauga ON L5W1L8 905-696-9400
Web: aworldmoreloyal.com

Maritz Inc 1375 N Hwy Dr .... Fenton MO 63099 636-827-4000
Web: www.maritz.com

Maritz Research Inc 1355 N Hwy Dr.................. Fenton MO 63099 385-695-2940
TF: 877-462-7489 ■ *Web:* www.maritzcx.com

Market Decisions LLC
75 Washington Ave Ste 206 .... Portland ME 04101 207-767-6440 767-8158
TF: 800-293-1538 ■ *Web:* www.marketdecisions.com

Market Strategies Inc 17430 College Pkwy .... Livonia MI 48152 734-542-7600 542-7620
Web: www.marketstrategies.com

Market Track LLC 233 S Wacker Dr Ste 1801 .... Chicago IL 60606 312-529-5102
Web: www.markettrack.com

Marketing & Planning Systems
501 Boylston St Ste 6101............................ Boston MA 02116 781-642-6277
Web: www.millwardbrownanalytics.com

Marketing Analysts Inc (MAI)
2000 Sam Rittenberg Blvd Ste 3007................. Charlotte NC 29407 704-405-2150
Web: www.mairesearch.com

Marketing Workshop Inc 3725 Da Vinci Ct .... Norcross GA 30092 770-449-6767
Web: www.mwshop.com

MarketVision Research Inc
10300 Alliance Rd Ste 200........................ Cincinnati OH 45242 513-791-3100 794-3500
TF: 800-232-4250 ■ *Web:* www.mv-research.com

Martopia Inc 805 E Main St Ste H .... Saint Charles IL 60174 630-587-9944
Web: www.martopia.com

Mashwork Inc 85 BRd St 18th Fl.................... New York NY 10004 646-201-9124
Web: canvs.tv

Meridian Surveys Ltd 355 16th St W............. Prince Albert SK S6V3V6 306-764-9229
Web: www.meridiansurveys.ca

Micro-Tech Consultants Inc
1686 Jessica Pl .... Santa Rosa CA 95403 707-575-4820
TF: 800-752-8878 ■ *Web:* www.micro-techco.com

Millward Brown Group 33 Bloor St E Ste 701 .... Toronto ON M4W3H1 203-330-2581
Web: www.millwardbrown.com

Millward Brown IntelliQuest
11 Madison Ave 12th Fl .... New York NY 10010 212-548-7200 548-7201
Web: www.millwardbrown.com

MinoTech Engineering Inc
JRD Technology Ctr 242 Sturbridge Rd .... Charlton MA 01507 978-474-8034
Web: www.minotecheng.com

Modellers LLC, The
6995 Union Park Ctr Ste 300 .... Salt Lake City UT 84047 801-290-3800
Web: www.themodellers.com

Monterey Technologies Inc
24600 Silver Cloud Court Ste 103 .... Monterey CA 93940 831-648-0190
Web: www.montereytechnologies.com

MORPACE International Inc
31700 Middlebelt Rd Ste 200................. Farmington Hills MI 48334 248-737-5300 737-5326
TF General: 800-881-1723 ■ *Web:* www.morpace.com

MP2 Energy Texas LLC
21 Waterway Ave Ste 450..................... The Woodlands TX 77380 832-510-1030
Web: www.mp2energy.com

Mustel Research Group Ltd
1505 W Second Ave Ste 402 .... Vancouver BC V6H3Y4 604-733-4213
Web: www.mustelgroup.com

National Research Corp 1245 Q St.................. Lincoln NE 68508 402-475-2525 475-9061
NASDAQ: NRCI ■ *TF:* 800-388-4264 ■ *Web:* www.nationalresearch.com

Nautilus Group, The 15305 Dallas Pkwy .... Addison TX 75001 972-720-6600
Web: www.thenautilusgroup.com

Neal Analytics LLC
3240 Eastlake Ave E Ste 104.......................... Seattle WA 98102 206-286-9200
Web: www.nealanalytics.com

Netpop Research LLC 322 Cortland Ave .... San Francisco CA 94110 415-647-1007
Web: netpop.com

NettResults LLC 3943 Irvine Blvd Ste 303 .... Irvine CA 92602 949-534-9130
Web: www.nettresults.com

NeuroFocus Inc 1200 5th St .... Berkeley CA 94710 510-526-1616
Web: www.neurofocus.com

New Home Trends Inc 4314 148th St SE............... Bothell WA 98012 425-742-8040
Web: www.newhometrends.com

News Generation Inc
7508 Wisconsin Ave Ste 300 .... Bethesda MD 20814 301-664-6448
Web: newsgeneration.com

Nichols Research Inc 333 W El Camino Real .... Sunnyvale CA 94087 408-773-8200
Web: nicholsresearch.com

NIH Research Inc
5411 N University Dr Ste 202.................. Coral Springs FL 33067 954-753-7747
Web: www.nihresearch.com

NineSigma Inc 23611 Chagrin Blvd Ste 320........... Cleveland OH 44122 216-295-4800
Web: ninesigma.com

Norman Hecht Research Inc
20 Crossways Park Dr N Ste 400 .... Woodbury NY 11791 516-496-8866
Web: www.normanhechtresearch.com

NPD Group Inc 900 W Shore Rd .... Port Washington NY 11050 516-625-0700 625-2444
TF: 866-444-1411 ■ *Web:* www.npd.com

OnCard Marketing Inc 276 Fifth Ave Ste 608 .... New York NY 10001 866-996-8729
TF: 866-996-8729 ■ *Web:* www.revtrax.com

OneMedPlace 219 E 83rd St 4 Fl .... New York NY 10028 212-734-1008
Web: www.onemedplace.com

Open Minds 163 York St .... Gettysburg PA 17325 717-334-1329
TF: 877-350-6463 ■ *Web:* www.openminds.com

Opinion Research Corp (ORC)
902 Carnegie Ctr Ste 220.......................... Princeton NJ 08540 800-444-4672 419-1892*
**Fax Area Code: 609* ■ *TF:* 800-444-4672 ■ *Web:* www.orcinternational.com

				Phone	Fax
PGM Inc 1215 South 1680 West *Web:* www.pgminc.com	Orem	UT	84058	801-434-9546	
Pharmakon LLC 475 Martingale Rd Ste 200 *Web:* www.pharmakonllc.com	Schaumburg	IL	60173	847-995-0509	
Point Group, The 5949 Sherry Ln Ste 1800 *Web:* www.thepointgroup.com	Dallas	TX	75225	214-378-7970	378-7967
PQ Media LLC 2 Stamford Landing Ste 100 *Web:* www.pqmedia.com	Stamford	CT	06902	203-921-0368	
Pragati Synergetic Research Inc 801 Moffett Blvd NASA Research Park NASA Ames Research Ctr MS 19-46Q Ste 1010 *Web:* www.pragati-inc.com	Moffett Field	CA	94035	650-625-0274	
PredictWallStreet LLC 1840 41st Ave Ste 102-171 *Web:* www.predictwallstreet.com	Capitola	CA	95010	831-464-0308	
PreTesting Group 38 Franklin St *Web:* www.pretesting.com	Tenafly	NJ	07670	201-569-4800	
PriMetrica Inc 5927 Priestly Dr Ste 111 *Web:* www.primetrica.com	Carlsbad	CA	92008	760-651-0030	
Princeton Survey Research Assoc 600 Alexander Rd *Web:* psrai.com	Princeton	NJ	08540	609-924-9204	
Prinzo Group, The 11260 Deerfield Pkwy Ste 100 *Web:* www.prinzogroup.com	Alpharetta	GA	30004	678-496-4615	
Pro-Tech Energy Solutions LLC 215 Executive Drive *Web:* www.pro-techenergy.com	Moorestown	NJ	08057	908-526-3322	
Propane Resources LLC 6950 Squibb Rd Ste 306 *Web:* www.propaneresources.com	Mission	KS	66201	913-262-8345	
Protelus 11000 Northeast 33rd Pl Ste 320 *Web:* protelus.com	Bellevue	WA	98004	425-284-2299	
Public Partnerships LLC 40 Broad St 4th Fl *Web:* www.publicpartnerships.com	Boston	MA	02109	617-426-2026	
Qualtrics 2250 N University Pkwy Ste 48 C *Web:* www.qualtrics.com	Provo	UT	84604	801-374-6682	
Quixel Research LLC 284 SW Birdshill Rd *Web:* www.quixelresearch.com	Portland	OR	97219	503-699-5133	
R W Wentworth & Co Inc 217 W 18th St *Web:* www.rwwentworth.com	New York	NY	10011	212-627-0467	
RateHub.ca 411 Richmond St E Ste 208 *TF:* 800-679-9622 ■ *Web:* www.ratehub.ca	Toronto	ON	M5A3S5	800-679-9622	
RDA Group 450 Enterprise Ct *TF:* 800-669-7324 ■ *Web:* www.rdagroup.com	Bloomfield Hills	MI	48302	248-332-5000	332-4168
RealityCheck Inc 2033 N Geyer Rd *Web:* www.realitycheckinc.com	Saint Louis	MO	63131	314-909-9095	
Red Privet LLC 215 W Pine St *Web:* www.redprivet.com	Selinsgrove	PA	17870	717-260-5239	
Reis Inc 530 Fifth Ave 5th Fl *NASDAQ: REIS* ■ *TF:* 800-366-7347 ■ *Web:* www.reis.com	New York	NY	10036	212-921-1122	921-2533
Relevancy Group LLC, The 1010 Shenandoah Dr *TF:* 877-972-6886 ■ *Web:* www.relevancygroup.com	Spring Lake	NJ	07762	877-972-6886	
Reputation Institute Inc 230 Park Ave 4th Fl Ste 453 *Web:* reputationinstitute.com	New York	NY	10169	212-495-3855	
Research Director Inc 914 Bay Ridge Rd Ste 215 *Web:* www.researchdirectorinc.com	Annapolis	MD	21403	410-295-6619	268-1915
Research for Good Inc 23316 NE Redmond-Fall City Rd Ste 513 *Web:* www.researchforgood.com	Redmond	WA	98053	647-293-4226	
Research Solutions Inc 5435 Balboa Blvd Ste 202 *Web:* www.reprintsdesk.com	Encino	CA	91316	310-477-0354	
Retail Systems Research LLC 8725 NE 10 Ct *Web:* www.retailsystemsresearch.com	Miami	FL	33138	305-757-1357	
Richard T Kiko Agency Inc 2805 Fulton Dr Nw *Web:* kikoauctions.com	Canton	OH	44718	330-830-4020	
Rincon Research Corp 101 N Wilmot Rd Ste 101 *Web:* rincon.com	Tucson	AZ	85711	520-519-4600	519-4747
Robert d Niehaus Inc 140 E Carrillo St *Web:* www.rdniehaus.com	Santa Barbara	CA	93101	805-962-0611	
Robert Hale & Assoc 5405 Morehouse Dr Ste 320 *Web:* productsstrategy.com	San Diego	CA	92121	858-404-0200	
Rockwood Service Corp 43 Arch St *Web:* www.rockwoodservice.com	Greenwich	CT	06830	203-869-6734	
Roland|Criss 2011 E Lamar Blvd Ste 150 *Web:* rolandcriss.com	Arlington	TX	76006	817-861-7963	
RRC Associates Inc 4940 Pearl E Cir Ste 103 *Web:* rrcassoc.com	Boulder	CO	80301	303-449-6558	
Ruf Strategic Solutions 1533 E Spruce St *TF:* 800-829-8544 ■ *Web:* www.ruf.com	Olathe	KS	66061	800-829-8544	
Salient Corp 203 Colonial Dr *Web:* www.salient.com	Horseheads	NY	14845	607-739-4511	
Sapphire Technologies Inc 6660 Taylor Dr Ste 105 *Web:* www.sapphiretech.org	Red Deer	AB	T4P1Y3	412-798-8990	
Savitz Research Solutions 13747 Montfort Dr Ste 211 *Web:* www.savitzresearch.com	Dallas	TX	75240	972-386-4050	661-3198
Scanner Applications Inc 400 Milford Pkwy *Web:* scanapps.wpengine.com	Milford	OH	45150	513-248-5588	
Schulman Ronca & Bucuvalas Inc 275 Seventh Ave Ste 2700 *Web:* www.srbi.com	New York	NY	10001	212-779-7700	779-7785
SCRI International Inc 2023 N Atlantic Ave Ste 310 *Web:* www.scri.com	Cocoa Beach	FL	32931	321-868-8273	
Sea Fare Group Inc 2360 W Commodore Way Ste 210 *Web:* seafaregroup.com	Seattle	WA	98199	206-789-5741	
Secret Ingredient Marketing 217 Knight Dr *Web:* www.secretingredientmarketing.com	San Rafael	CA	94901	415-963-4000	
Segmedica Inc 935 Sheridan Dr Ste 120 *Web:* segmedica.com	Tonawanda	NY	14150	716-754-8744	
Select Sales & Mktg Inc 549 Mercury Ln	Brea	CA	92821	714-990-3755	
Seneca Consulting Group Inc 111 Smithtown Byp Ste 112 *TF:* 866-442-2472 ■ *Web:* www.senecaconsulting.com	Hauppauge	NY	11788	631-577-4092	
Service 800 Inc 2190 W Wayzata Blvd *Web:* service800.com	Minneapolis	MN	55356	952-475-3747	
Service Performance Insight 6260 Winter Hazel Dr Four Bridges *Web:* www.spiresearch.com	Liberty Township	OH	45044	513-759-5443	
Shapard Research LLC 820 Ne 63rd St Uppr E *Web:* www.shapard.com	Oklahoma City	OK	73105	405-607-4664	
Sharetracker LLC 1480 E Hwy MM *TF:* 866-977-7171 ■ *Web:* www.sharetracker.net	Ashland	MO	65010	866-977-7171	
Sheiness, Glover & Grossman LLP 4544 Post Oak Pl Dr Ste 270 *Web:* www.sgglawyers.com	Houston	TX	77027	713-374-7000	
SiteLogic LLC 111 2nd St NW Ste 506 *Web:* www.sitelogicmarketing.com	Canton	OH	44702	330-445-2890	
Siver Insurance Consultants 9400 Fourth St N Ste 119 *Web:* www.siver.com	St. Petersburg	FL	33702	727-577-2780	
SmartRevenue Inc 263 Tresser Blvd 9th Fl *Web:* smartrevenue.com	Stamford	CT	06901	203-733-9156	
Smith Travel Research Inc 735 E Main St *Web:* www.str.com	Hendersonville	TN	37075	615-824-8664	
SPI Lasers 4000 Burton Dr *Web:* www.spioptics.com	Santa Clara	CA	95054	408-454-1170	
Standards Council of Canada 270 Albert St Ste 200 *TF:* 800-844-6790 ■ *Web:* www.scc.ca	Ottawa	ON	K1P6N7	613-238-3222	
Strategic Analysis Inc 4075 Wilson Blvd Ste 200 *Web:* www.sainc.com	Arlington	VA	22203	703-527-5410	527-5445
Strategy Institute 401 Richmond St W Ste 401 *TF:* 866-298-9343 ■ *Web:* www.strategyinstitute.com	Toronto	ON	M5V3A8	866-298-9343	
Strong & Hanni 102 South 200 East Ste 800 *Web:* www.strongandhanni.com	Salt Lake City	UT	84111	801-532-7080	
Sumex Inc 200 Carnegie Dr Ste 203 *Web:* www.sumex.ca	St. Albert	AB	T8N5A7	780-970-2238	
SuperData Research Inc 116 W 23rd St 5th Fl *Web:* www.superdataresearch.com	New York	NY	10011	646-375-2273	
Survey com 2740 Lantz Ave *Web:* survey.com	San Jose	CA	95124	408-850-1227	
Survey Service Inc 1911 Sheridan Dr *Web:* www.surveyservice.com	Buffalo	NY	14223	716-876-6450	
SurveyMonkey Inc 101 Lytton Ave *Web:* www.surveymonkey.com	Palo Alto	CA	94301	650-543-8400	
Synovate Inc 222 S Riverside Plz	Chicago	IL	60606	312-526-4000	526-4099
Topspin Group Inc 415 Executive Dr *Web:* topspingroup.com	Princeton	NJ	08540	609-252-9515	
TRC Holdings Inc 1300 Virginia Dr Ste 200 *TF:* 800-275-2827 ■ *Web:* www.trchome.com	Fort Washington	PA	19034	215-641-2200	
TrendSource Inc 4891 Pacific Hwy Ste 200 *Web:* www.trendsource.com	San Diego	CA	92110	619-718-7467	
Trinity Green Services LLC 1165 S Stemmons Fwy Ste 100 *Web:* www.trinitygrn.com	Lewisville	TX	75067	214-446-9500	
Trouv? Media Inc 433 Airport Blvd Ste 550 *Web:* www.trouvemedia.com	Burlingame	CA	94010	650-963-2000	
Uniform Industrial Corp 47341 Bayside Pkwy *Web:* uicworld.com	Fremont	CA	94538	510-438-6799	
UniqueLeads com Inc 1128 Royal Palm Beach Blvd Ste 222 *Web:* www.uniqueleads.com	Royal Palm Beach	FL	33411	561-491-2826	
Unity Marketing Inc 206 E Church St *Web:* www.unitymarketingonline.com	Stevens	PA	17578	717-336-1600	
Unmetric Inc 2001 Victoria Rd *TF:* 855-558-5588 ■ *Web:* unmetric.com	Chicago	IL	60060	855-558-5588	
Upham Associates Inc 156 Jersey Black Cir *Web:* valientmarketresearch.com	Rochester	NY	14626	585-227-0247	
Urban Icons Marketing Inc 46 NW 36th St Loft 4 *Web:* www.urbaniconsmarketing.com	Miami	FL	33127	305-438-0107	
Verance Corp 4435 Eastgate Mall Ste 350 *Web:* verance.com	San Diego	CA	92131	858-202-2800	
Veros Systems Inc 5914 Ctyard Dr W Bridgepoint Plz II Ste 190 *Web:* www.verossystems.com	Austin	TX	78730	512-686-2400	
VGMarket LLC 3860 Sheridan St Ste C *Web:* www.vgmarket.com	Hollywood	FL	33021	650-483-8384	
W5 Inc 3211 Shannon Rd *Web:* w5insight.com	Durham	NC	27707	919-932-1117	
Walker Information Inc 301 Pennsylvania Pkwy *TF:* 800-334-3939 ■ *Web:* www.walkerinfo.com	Indianapolis	IN	46280	317-843-3939	843-8584
Wendover Corp 130 S State Rd *Web:* www.wendovercorp.com	Upper Darby	PA	19082	610-449-2056	
West Technology Research Solutions LLC 2247A Old Middlefield Way *Web:* www.wtrs.net	Mountain View	CA	94043	650-940-1196	
Westat Inc 1600 Research Blvd *TF:* 800-669-6820 ■ *Web:* www.westat.com	Rockville	MD	20850	301-251-1500	294-2040
Whale Path Inc P.O.Box 390834 *Web:* whalepath.com	Mountain View	CA	94309	415-286-5577	
Wiese Research Associates Inc 9375 Burt St Ste 100 *Web:* www.wraresearch.com	Omaha	NE	68114	402-391-7734	

Company / Address	City	State	Zip	Phone	Fax
Wilkins Research Services LLC 1730 Gunbarrel Rd — *Web:* www.wilkinsresearch.net	Chattanooga	TN	37421	423-894-9478	
WTI Inc 3737 E Broadway Rd — *Web:* www.wticompanies.com	Phoenix	AZ	85040	602-437-8979	
Xpera Group 10911 Technology Pl Ste 103 — *Web:* www.xperagroup.com	San Diego	CA	92127	858-436-7770	
XtremeEDA Corp 200-25 Holland Ave — *TF:* 800-586-0280 ■ *Web:* www.xtreme-eda.com	Ottawa	ON	K1Y4R9	613-728-5912	
Zagada Markets Inc Caribbean Commercial Bldg 145 Grand Ave — *Web:* www.zagada.com	Coral Gables	FL	33133	305-529-9028	
Zion & Zion Consulting Group 60 E Rio Salado Pkwy Ste 900 — *Web:* www.zionandzion.com	Tempe	AZ	85281	480-751-1007	
Zolato Inc 2801 First Ave Ste 306 — *TF:* 866-557-6716 ■ *Web:* www.discuss.io	Seattle	WA	98121	866-557-6716	

467 MARKING DEVICES

Company / Address	City	State	Zip	Phone	Fax
American Marking Systems Inc 1015 Paulison Ave PO Box 1677 — *TF:* 800-782-6766 ■ *Web:* www.ams-stamps.com	Clifton	NJ	07011	973-478-5600	478-0039
Automark Marking Systems 13475 Lakefront Dr — *Web:* www.automark.com	Earth City	MO	63045	314-739-0430	
Cable Markers Company Inc 13805-C Alton Pkwy — **Fax Area Code:* 949 ■ *TF:* 800-746-7655 ■ *Web:* www.cablemarkers.com	Irvine	CA	92618	800-746-7655	699-1642*
Carco Inc 10333 Shoemaker PO Box 13859 — *Web:* www.carcousa.com	Detroit	MI	48213	313-925-9000	925-9602
CH Hanson Co 2000 N Aurora Rd — *TF:* 800-827-3398 ■ *Web:* www.chhanson.com	Naperville	IL	60563	630-848-2000	848-2515
Cosco Industries Inc 7220 W Wilson Ave — **Fax Area Code:* 800 ■ *TF:* 800-296-8970 ■ *Web:* www.coscoindustries.com	Harwood Heights	IL	60706	708-867-5800	323-0275*
DM Stamps & Specialties Inc 1101 N Riverfront Dr — *Web:* dmstampsdiv.com	Mankato	MN	56001	507-387-4444	387-4447
Excelsior Marking Products 888 W Waterloo Rd — *TF:* 800-433-3615 ■ *Web:* www.excelsiormarking.com	Akron	OH	44314	330-745-2300	745-2333
Hampton Technologies LLC 19 Scouting Blvd — *Web:* www.hamptontech.net	Medford	NY	11763	631-924-1335	
Hitt Marking Devices Inc 3231 W MacArthur Blvd — *TF:* 800-969-6699 ■ *Web:* www.hittmarking.com	Santa Ana	CA	92704	714-979-1405	979-1407
Huntington Park Rubber Stamp 2761 E Slauson Ave PO Box 519 — *TF:* 800-882-0029 ■ *Web:* www.hprubberstamp.com	Huntington Park	CA	90255	323-582-6461	582-8046
Industrial Marking Products 1415 Grovenburg Rd — *Web:* www.industrialmarking.com	Holt	MI	48842	517-699-2160	699-1505
Infosight Corp PO Box 5000 — *TF:* 800-401-0716 ■ *Web:* www.infosight.com	Chillicothe	OH	45601	740-642-3600	642-5001
Jackson Marking Products Co 9105 N Rainbow Ln — *TF:* 800-782-6722 ■ *Web:* www.rubber-stamp.com	Mount Vernon	IL	62864	618-242-1334	242-7732
JP Nissen Co 2544 Fairhill Ave PO Box 339 — *Web:* www.nissenmarkers.com	Glenside	PA	19038	215-886-2025	886-0707
Krengel Enterprises 121 Fulton St	New York	NY	10038	212-239-6677	239-0041
La-Co/Markal Co 1201 Pratt Blvd — **Fax Area Code:* 800 ■ *TF:* 800-621-4025 ■ *Web:* www.laco.com	Elk Grove Village	IL	60007	847-956-7600	448-5436*
Matthews International Corp Marking Products Div 6515 Penn Ave — *TF:* 800-775-7775 ■ *Web:* www.matthewsmarking.com	Pittsburgh	PA	15206	412-665-2500	665-2550
Menke Marking Devices 13253 Alondra Blvd — *TF:* 800-231-6023 ■ *Web:* www.menkemarking.com	Santa Fe Springs	CA	90670	562-921-1380	921-1184
New Method Steel Stamps Inc 31313 Kendall Ave — *TF:* 800-582-0199 ■ *Web:* www.newmethod.org	Fraser	MI	48026	586-293-0200	296-1900
Norwood Marking Systems 2538 Wisconsin Ave — *TF:* 800-626-3464 ■ *Web:* itwnorwood.com	Downers Grove	IL	60515	630-968-0646	968-7672
Saint Paul Stamp Works Inc 87 Empire Dr — *Web:* www.stpaulstamp.com	Saint Paul	MN	55103	651-222-2100	228-1314
Schwaab Inc 11415 W Burleigh St — **Fax Area Code:* 800 ■ *TF:* 800-935-9877 ■ *Web:* www.schwaab.com	Milwaukee	WI	53222	414-771-4150	935-9866*
Schwerdtle Stamp Co 166 Elm St — *TF:* 800-535-0004 ■ *Web:* www.schwerdtle.com	Bridgeport	CT	06604	203-330-2750	330-2760
Signet Marking Devices 3121 Red Hill Ave — *TF:* 800-421-5150 ■ *Web:* www.signetmarking.com	Costa Mesa	CA	92626	714-549-0341	
Stamp-Rite Inc 154 S Larch St — *TF:* 800-328-1988 ■ *Web:* www.stamprite.com	Lansing	MI	48912	517-487-5071	487-6211
Tacoma Rubber Stamp & Sign 919 Market St — *TF:* 800-544-7281 ■ *Web:* www.tacomarubberstamp.com	Tacoma	WA	98402	253-383-5433	383-0649
Volk Corp 23936 Industrial Pk Dr — *TF Cust Svc:* 800-521-6799 ■ *Web:* www.volkcorp.com	Farmington Hills	MI	48335	248-477-6700	478-6884
Wendell's Inc 6601 Bunker Lk Blvd NW PO Box 458 — *TF:* 800-936-3355 ■ *Web:* www.wendellsinc.com	Ramsey	MN	55303	763-576-8200	576-0995

468 MASS TRANSPORTATION (LOCAL & SUBURBAN)

See Also Bus Services - Intercity & Rural p. 1881

Company / Address	City	State	Zip	Phone	Fax
Alameda-Contra Costa Transit District 1600 Franklin St 10th Fl — **Fax:* Cust Svc ■ *TF:* 877-878-8883 ■ *Web:* www.actransit.org	Oakland	CA	94612	510-891-4777	891-4705*
Alaska Marine Highway System 6858 Glacier Hwy PO Box 112505 — *TF:* 800-642-0066 ■ *Web:* www.dot.state.ak.us/amhs	Juneau	AK	99801	907-465-3941	465-2476
Altamont Commuter Express (ACE) 949 E Ch St — *TF:* 800-411-7245 ■ *Web:* www.acerail.com	Stockton	CA	95202	800-411-7245	
Ann Arbor Transportation Authority 2700 S Industrial Hwy — *Web:* www.theride.org	Ann Arbor	MI	48104	734-973-6500	973-6338
Bay Area Rapid Transit District 300 Lakeside Dr — *Web:* www.bart.gov	Oakland	CA	94612	510-464-6000	
BC Transit 520 Gorge Rd E — *Web:* www.bctransit.com	Victoria	BC	V8W2P3	250-385-2551	995-5639
Bi-State Development Agency 707 N First St — *Web:* www.metrostlouis.org	Saint Louis	MO	63102	314-982-1400	
Bonneville Transloaders Inc (BTI) 642 S Federal Blvd — *Web:* www.bonntran.com	Riverton	WY	82501	307-856-7480	856-4623
Caledonia Haulers LLC 420 W Lincoln St PO Box 31 — *TF:* 800-325-4728 ■ *Web:* www.caledoniahaulers.com	Caledonia	MN	55921	507-725-9000	725-9015
Cape Cod Regional Transit Authority (CCRTA) 215 Iyannough Rd PO Box 1988 — *TF:* 800-352-7155 ■ *Web:* www.capecodtransit.org	Hyannis	MA	02601	508-775-8504	775-8513
Capital District Transportation Authority (CDTA) 110 Watervliet Ave — *Web:* www.cdta.org	Albany	NY	12206	518-482-8822	437-8318
Catalina Express Berth 95 — *TF:* 800-481-3470 ■ *Web:* www.catalinaexpress.com	San Pedro	CA	90731	310-519-7971	
Central Florida Regional Transportation Authority (Inc) 455 N Garland Ave — *Web:* www.golynx.com	Orlando	FL	32801	407-841-2279	
Central New York Regional Transportation Authority 200 Cortland Ave — *Web:* www.centro.org	Syracuse	NY	13205	315-442-3400	442-3337
Central Ohio Transit Authority (COTA) 33 N High St — *Web:* www.cota.com	Columbus	OH	43215	614-228-1776	275-5933
Central Puget Sound Regional Transit Authority 401 S Jackson St — **Fax:* Hum Res ■ *TF:* 800-201-4900 ■ *Web:* www.soundtransit.org	Seattle	WA	98104	206-398-5000	689-3360*
Champaign-Urbana Mass Transit District 1101 E University Ave — *Web:* www.cumtd.com	Urbana	IL	61802	217-384-8188	384-8215
Charleston Area Regional Transportation Authority (CARTA) 36 John St — *Web:* www.ridecarta.com	Charleston	SC	29403	843-724-7304	
Chicago Transit Authority (CTA) 567 W Lake St — *Web:* www.transitchicago.com	Chicago	IL	60661	312-664-7200	
Cliff Viessman Inc 215 First Ave PO Box 175 — *TF:* 800-328-2408 ■ *Web:* www.viessmantrucking.com	Gary	SD	57237	605-272-5241	272-5546
Connecticut Transit 100 Leibert Rd — *Web:* www.cttransit.com	Hartford	CT	06141	860-522-8101	247-1810
Dallas Area Rapid Transit Authority (DART) 1401 Pacific Ave PO Box 660163 — *Web:* www.dart.org	Dallas	TX	75202	214-749-3278	
Delaware Transit Corp 119 Lower Beach St Ste 100 — *TF:* 800-652-3278 ■ *Web:* www.dartfirststate.com	Wilmington	DE	19805	302-576-6000	577-6066
Erie Metropolitan Transit Authority (EMTA) 127 E 14th St — *Web:* www.ride-the-e.com	Erie	PA	16503	814-452-3515	
Escambia County Area Transit (ECAT) 1515 W Fairfield Dr — *Web:* www.goecat.com	Pensacola	FL	32501	850-595-3228	595-3222
Fort Wayne Public Transportation Corp 801 Leesburg Rd — *Web:* www.fwcitilink.com	Fort Wayne	IN	46808	260-432-4546	436-7729
Fresno Area Express 2223 G St — *Web:* www.fresno.gov	Fresno	CA	93706	559-621-7433	488-1065
GO Transit 20 Bay St Ste 600 — *TF:* 888-438-6646 ■ *Web:* www.gotransit.com	Toronto	ON	M5J2W3	416-869-3200	869-3525
Gold Coast Transit (GCT) 301 E Third St — *Web:* www.goldcoasttransit.org	Oxnard	CA	93030	805-487-4222	487-0925
Golden Empire Transit District 1830 Golden State Ave — *Web:* www.getbus.org	Bakersfield	CA	93301	661-324-9874	869-6394
Greater Cleveland Regional Transit Authority (RTA) 1240 W Sixth St — *Web:* www.riderta.com	Cleveland	OH	44113	216-566-5285	
Greater Peoria Mass Transit District 407 SW Adams St	Peoria	IL	61602	309-676-4040	676-8373
Greater Portland Transit District 114 Valley St — *Web:* gpmetrobus.net	Portland	ME	04102	207-774-0351	774-6241
GRTC Transit System 301 E Belt Blvd — *Web:* www.ridegrtc.com	Richmond	VA	23224	804-358-3871	342-1933
Horizon Freight System Inc 6600 Bessemer Ave — *TF:* 800-480-6829 ■ *Web:* www.horizonfreightsystem.com	Cleveland	OH	44127	216-341-7410	429-3523
Idaho Milk Transport Inc PO Box 1185 — *Web:* www.idahomilktransport.com	Burley	ID	83318	208-878-5000	878-5001
Inter-Urban Transit Partnership 300 Ellsworth St SW — *Web:* www.ridetherapid.org	Grand Rapids	MI	49503	616-776-1100	456-1941
Intermodal Cartage Co Inc 5707 E Holmes Rd — *Web:* www.imcg.com	Memphis	TN	38141	901-363-0050	432-6174
Karl's Transport Inc PO Box 333 — *TF:* 800-922-8707 ■ *Web:* www.karlstransport.com	Antigo	WI	54409	715-623-2033	623-2791
King County Dept of Transportation 201 S Jackson St — *Web:* www.kingcounty.gov	Seattle	WA	98104	206-684-1481	684-1224
Los Angeles County Metropolitan Transportation Authority 1 Gateway Plz — *TF:* 800-621-7828 ■ *Web:* www.metro.net	Los Angeles	CA	90012	213-922-6000	

Phone Fax

Maryland Transit Administration (MTA)
6 St Paul St. . . . . Baltimore MD 21202 410-539-5000 333-3279
Web: www.mta.maryland.gov

Massachusetts Bay Transportation Authority (MBTA)
10 Pk Plaza Ste 3910. . . . . Boston MA 02116 617-222-5000 222-3340*
*Fax: Mktg ■ *Web:* www.mbta.com

Memphis Area Transit Authority (MATA)
1370 Levee Rd . . . . Memphis TN 38108 901-722-7100 722-7123
Web: www.matatransit.com

Metro Transit 200 NE 21st St . . . . Oklahoma City OK 73105 405-522-8000 297-2111
Web: www.okladot.state.ok.us

Metro Transit 200 Ilsley Ave . . . . Dartmouth NS B3B1V1 902-490-4000 490-6688
Web: www.halifax.ca/metrotransit

Metro Transit 560 Sixth Ave N . . . . Minneapolis MN 55411 612-349-7400
Web: www.metrotransit.org

Metropolitan Atlanta Rapid Transit Authority (MARTA)
2424 Piedmont Rd NE . . . . Atlanta GA 30324 404-848-5000
Web: www.itsmarta.com

Metropolitan Transit Authority of Harris County
1900 Maine . . . . Houston TX 77002 713-739-4000 739-4096
Web: ridemetro.org/news/emergencyalerts/default.aspx

Miami-Dade Transit (MDTA) 701 NW First Ct . . . . Miami FL 33136 305-468-5402 469-5580*
*Fax Area Code: 786 ■ *Web:* miamidade.gov

Milwaukee County Transit System
1942 N 17th St. . . . . Milwaukee WI 53205 414-343-1700 343-1787*
*Fax: Hum Res ■ *Web:* www.ridemcts.com

Mission Petroleum Carriers Inc 8450 Mosley. . . . . Houston TX 77075 713-943-8250 944-6080
TF: 800-737-9911 ■ *Web:* www.mipe.com

Monterey-Salinas Transit (MST) 1 Ryan Ranch Rd . . . . . Monterey CA 93940 831-899-2555
Web: www.mst.org

MV Transportation Inc
5910 N Central Expy Ste 1145 . . . . Dallas TX 75206 972-391-4600 863-8944*
*Fax Area Code: 707 ■ *Web:* www.mvtransit.com

New Jersey Transit Corp 1 Penn Plz E . . . . Newark NJ 07105 973-491-7000 491-8247*
*Fax: Cust Svc ■ *TF Cust Svc:* 800-772-3606 ■ *Web:* www.njtransit.com

Niagara Frontier Transit Metro System Inc
181 Ellicott St Ste 1 . . . . Buffalo NY 14203 716-855-7300 856-2524
TF: 877-294-9434

Norfolk Southern Corp 3 Commercial Pl . . . . Norfolk VA 23510 855-667-3655 629-2361*
NYSE: NSC ■ *Fax Area Code: 757 ■ *Fax: Mktg ■ *TF Cust Svc:* 800-635-5768 ■ *Web:* www.nscorp.com

North County Transit District (NCTD)
810 Mission Rd . . . . Oceanside CA 92054 760-966-6500 967-2001
Web: www.gonctd.com

Northeast Illinois Regional Commuter Railroad Corp
547 W Jackson Blvd . . . . Chicago IL 60661 312-322-6777
Web: www.metrarail.com

Northern Indiana Commuter Transportation District
33 E US Hwy 12 . . . . Chesterton IN 46304 219-926-5744 929-4438
TF: 800-743-3333 ■ *Web:* www.nictd.com

Norwalk Transit District (NTD) 275 Wilson Ave. . . . . Norwalk CT 06854 203-852-0000
Web: www.norwalktransit.com

Oahu Transit Services 811 Middle St . . . . Honolulu HI 96819 808-848-4500 848-4419
Web: www.thebus.org

Office Movers Inc 6500 Kane Way . . . . Elkridge MD 21075 410-799-7704 799-3208
TF: 800-331-4025 ■ *Web:* www.officemovers.com

Orange County Transportation Authority
550 S Main St PO Box 14184. . . . . Orange CA 92863 714-560-6282
Web: www.octa.net

Pace Suburban Bus
550 W Algonquin Rd . . . . Arlington Heights IL 60005 847-364-8130
Web: www.pacebus.com

Packard Transport Inc
24021 S Municipal Dr PO Box 380. . . . . Channahon IL 60410 815-467-9260 467-6939
TF: 800-467-9260 ■ *Web:* www.packardtransport.com

Pierce Transit 3701 96th St SW PO Box 99070 . . . . Lakewood WA 98499 253-581-8000 581-8075
TF: 800-562-8109 ■ *Web:* www.piercetransit.org

Port Authority of Allegheny County
345 Sixth Ave 3rd Fl. . . . . Pittsburgh PA 15222 412-566-5500
Web: www.portauthority.org

Regional Transit Authority (RTA)
2817 Canal St. . . . . New Orleans LA 70118 504-827-8300
Web: www.norta.com

Regional Transit Service Inc
1372 E Main St. . . . . Rochester NY 14609 585-654-0200 352-4596*
*Fax Area Code: 951 ■ *Web:* www.myrts.com

Regional Transit System (RTS)
Station 5 PO Box 490. . . . . Gainesville FL 32627 352-334-2600 334-2607
Web: www.go-rts.com

Regional Transportation Authority
175 W Jackson Blvd Ste 1550 . . . . Chicago IL 60604 312-913-3200
Web: www.rtachicago.com

Regional Transportation Commission of Southern Nevada (RTC)
600 S Grand Central Pkwy Ste 350. . . . . Las Vegas NV 89106 702-676-1500 676-1518
TF: 800-228-3911 ■ *Web:* www.rtcsouthernnevada.com

Regional Transportation District (RTD)
1600 Blake St. . . . . Denver CO 80202 303-628-9000
TF: 800-366-7433 ■ *Web:* www.rtd-denver.com

Reliable Carriers Inc 41555 Koppernick Rd . . . . Canton MI 48187 734-453-6677 453-8609
TF: 800-521-6393 ■ *Web:* www.reliablecarriers.com

Reliable Transportation Specialists Inc
139 Venturi Dr . . . . Chesterton IN 46304 219-926-8850 926-5174
Web: www.reliabletrans.com

Rhode Island Public Transit Authority
265 Melrose St. . . . . Providence RI 02907 401-781-9400
Web: www.ripta.com

Riverside Transit Agency (RTA)
1825 Third St PO Box 59968 . . . . Riverside CA 92517 951-565-5000
TF: 800-800-7821 ■ *Web:* www.riversidetransit.com

Sacramento Regional Transit District
1400 29th St. . . . . Sacramento CA 95816 916-321-2800 444-2156
Web: www.sacrt.com

San Diego Transit Corp 100 16th St . . . . San Diego CA 92101 619-238-0100 696-8159

San Mateo County Transit District
1250 San Carlos Ave PO Box 3006 . . . . San Carlos CA 94070 650-508-6200
TF: 800-660-4287 ■ *Web:* www.smctd.com

Phone Fax

Santa Barbara Metropolitan Transit District
550 Olive St . . . . Santa Barbara CA 93101 805-963-3364 962-4794
Web: www.sbmtd.gov

Santa Clara Valley Transportation Authority (VTA)
3331 N First St . . . . San Jose CA 95134 408-321-5555
TF: 800-894-9908 ■ *Web:* www.vta.org

Sonoma County Transit 355 W Robles Ave. . . . . Santa Rosa CA 95407 707-585-7516
TF: 800-345-7433 ■ *Web:* www.sctransit.com

Southeastern Pennsylvania Transportation Authority (SEPTA)
1234 Market St . . . . Philadelphia PA 19107 215-580-7800
Web: www.septa.org

Southern California Regional Rail Authority
700 S Flower St Ste 2600 . . . . Los Angeles CA 90017 213-452-0200 452-0429
TF: 800-371-5465 ■ *Web:* www.metrolinktrains.com

Steamship Authority PO Box 284 . . . . Woods Hole MA 02543 508-548-5011 548-8410
Web: www.steamshipauthority.com

Suburban Mobility Authority for Regional Transportation (SMART)
535 Griswold St Ste 600 Buhl Bldg . . . . Detroit MI 48226 313-223-2100
TF: 866-962-5515 ■ *Web:* www.smartbus.org

TLD Distribution Company LLC
505 S Seventh Ave . . . . City of Industry CA 91746 310-324-5111 516-3960

Toronto Transit Commission (TTC) 1900 Yonge St. . . . . . Toronto ON M4S1Z2 416-393-4000
Web: www.ttc.ca

Transcare Corp 1 Metrotech Ctr . . . . Brooklyn NY 11201 718-763-8888 209-1381
Web: www.transcare.com

Transit Authority of River City (TARC)
1000 W Broadway. . . . . Louisville KY 40203 502-585-1234 213-3243*

Tri-County Commuter Rail Authority
800 NW 33rd St Ste 100. . . . . Pompano Beach FL 33064 954-942-7245 788-7878
Web: www.tri-rail.com

Tri-County Metropolitan Transportation District of Oregon
4012 SE 17th Ave . . . . Portland OR 97202 503-238-7433 962-6469*
*Fax: Mktg ■ *Web:* www.trimet.org

Utah Transit Authority
3600 S 700 W PO Box 30810. . . . . Salt Lake City UT 84130 801-262-5626
TF: 888-743-3882 ■ *Web:* www.rideuta.com

VIA Metropolitan Transit 800 W Myrtle St . . . . San Antonio TX 78212 210-362-2000 362-2563*
*Fax: Cust Svc ■ *TF:* 866-362-4200 ■ *Web:* www.viainfo.net

Virginia Railway Express (VRE)
1500 King St Ste 202 . . . . Alexandria VA 22314 703-684-1001 684-1313
TF: 800-743-3873 ■ *Web:* www.vre.org

VPSI Inc 1220 Rankin Dr. . . . . Troy MI 48083 248-597-3500 597-3501
TF: 800-826-7433 ■ *Web:* www.vride.com

Washington Metropolitan Area Transit Authority
600 Fifth St NW . . . . Washington DC 20001 202-637-7000
Web: www.wmata.com

Westchester County Dept of Transportation
100 E First St . . . . Mount Vernon NY 10550 914-813-7777
Web: www.co.westchester.ny.us/transportation

Worcester Regional Transit Authority
287 Grove St. . . . . Worcester MA 01605 508-791-9782
Web: therta.com

York County Transportation Authority
1230 Roosevelt Ave . . . . York PA 17404 717-846-5562 848-4853
TF: 800-632-9063 ■ *Web:* www.rabbittransit.org

469 MATCHES & MATCHBOOKS

Phone Fax

DD Bean & Sons Co 207 Peterborough St. . . . . Jaffrey NH 03452 603-532-8311 532-6001*
*Fax: Sales ■ *TF:* 800-366-2824 ■ *Web:* www.ddbean.com

Maryland Match Corp 605 Alluvion St . . . . Baltimore MD 21230 410-752-8164 752-3441
TF: 800-423-0013 ■ *Web:* www.marylandmatch.com

470 MATERIAL HANDLING EQUIPMENT

See Also Conveyors & Conveying Equipment p. 2160

Phone Fax

Abell-Howe Crane Inc
2143 Internationale Pkwy Ste 400. . . . . Woodridge IL 60517 800-366-0068 972-0897*
*Fax Area Code: 630 ■ *TF:* 800-366-0068 ■ *Web:* www.abellhowe.com

Advance Lifts Inc 701 Kirk Rd . . . . Saint Charles IL 60174 630-584-9881 584-9405
TF: 800-843-3625 ■ *Web:* www.advancelifts.com

Air Technical Industries 7501 Clover Ave . . . . Mentor OH 44060 440-951-5191 953-9237
TF: 800-321-9680 ■ *Web:* www.airtechnical.com

American Crane & Equipment Corp
531 Old Swede Rd . . . . Douglassville PA 19518 610-385-6061 385-3191*
*Fax: Sales ■ *TF:* 877-877-6778 ■ *Web:* www.americancrane.com

American Lifts 532 E Baili Ct . . . . Greensburg IN 47240 812-663-4085

American Power Pull Corp
550 W Linfoot St PO Box 109. . . . . Wauseon OH 43567 419-335-7050 335-7070
TF: 800-808-5922 ■ *Web:* www.americanpowerpull.com

ATAP Inc 130 Industry way. . . . . Eastaboga AL 36260 256-362-2221 362-2221
TF: 800-362-2827 ■ *Web:* www.atap.com

Autoquip Corp 1058 W Industrial Rd. . . . . Guthrie OK 73044 405-282-5200 282-8105
TF: 888-811-9876 ■ *Web:* www.autoquip.com

Bayhead Products Corp 173 Crosby Rd . . . . Dover NH 03820 603-742-3000 743-4701
TF: 800-229-4323 ■ *Web:* www.bayheadproducts.com

Berns Co 1250 W 17th St . . . . Long Beach CA 90813 562-437-0471 436-1074
TF: 800-421-3773 ■ *Web:* www.thebernsco.com

BGK Finishing Systems
4131 Pheasant Ridge Dr NE . . . . Minneapolis MN 55449 763-784-0466 784-1362
TF: 800-663-5498 ■ *Web:* www.bgk.com

Breeze-Eastern Corp 35 Melanie Ln . . . . Whippany NJ 07981 973-602-1001
Web: www.breeze-eastern.com

Busse/SJI Corp 124 N Columbus St . . . . Randolph WI 53956 800-882-4995 326-3134*
*Fax Area Code: 920 ■ *TF:* 800-882-4995 ■ *Web:* www.arrowheadsystems.com

Cannon Equipment Co 15100 Business Pkwy . . . . Rosemount MN 55068 651-322-6300 322-1583
Web: www.cannonequipment.com

Cascade Corp 2201 NE 201st Ave. Fairview OR 97024 503-669-6300 669-6716
NYSE: CASC ■ *TF:* 800-227-2233 ■ *Web:* www.cascorp.com

Phone Fax

Clark Material Handling Co
700 Enterprise Dr ... Lexington KY 40510 859-422-6400
TF: 866-252-5275 ■ *Web:* www.clarkmhc.com

Clyde Machines Inc
1150 State Hwy 55 N PO Box 194 ... Glenwood MN 56334 320-634-4503 634-4506
Web: www.clydemachines.com

Columbus McKinnon Corp
140 John James Audubon Pkwy ... Amherst NY 14228 716-689-5400
NASDAQ: CMCO ■ *TF:* 800-888-0985 ■ *Web:* www.cmworks.com

Cozzini Inc 4300 W Bryn Mawr Ave ... Chicago IL 60646 773-478-9700 478-8689
Web: www.cozzini.com

Crane Tech Solutions LLC
2030 Ponderosa St ... Portsmouth VA 23701 757-405-0311 405-0313
Web: www.cranetechsolutions.com

Craneveyor Corp 1524 Potrero Ave ... South El Monte CA 91733 888-501-0050 442-7308*
**Fax Area Code:* 626 ■ *TF:* 888-501-0050 ■ *Web:* www.craneveyor.com

Crosby Group, The 2801 Dawson Rd ... Tulsa OK 74110 918-834-4611 832-0940
TF: 800-772-1500 ■ *Web:* www.thecrosbygroup.com

Crown Equipment Corp 44 S Washington St ... New Bremen OH 45869 419-629-2311 629-2900
Web: www.crown.com

Crysteel Mfg Inc 52182 Ember Rd ... Lake Crystal MN 56055 507-726-2728 726-2559
TF Orders: 800-533-0494 ■ *Web:* www.crysteel.com

Dematic 507 Plymouth Ave NE ... Grand Rapids MI 49505 877-725-7500 913-7701*
**Fax Area Code:* 616 ■ *TF Cust Svc:* 877-725-7500 ■ *Web:* www.dematic.com

Detroit Hoist Co 6650 Sterling Dr N ... Sterling Heights MI 48312 586-268-2600 268-0044
TF: 800-521-9126 ■ *Web:* www.detroithoist.com

Downs Crane & Hoist Company Inc
8827 Juniper St ... Los Angeles CA 90002 323-589-6061 589-6066
TF: 800-748-5994 ■ *Web:* www.downscrane.com

Drake-Scruggs Equipment Inc
2000 S Dirksen Pkwy ... Springfield IL 62703 217-753-3871 753-2760
TF: 877-799-0398 ■ *Web:* www.drake-scruggs.com

Dynacon Inc 831 Industrial Blvd ... Bryan TX 77803 979-823-2690 823-0947
Web: www.dynacon.com

Escalera Inc
708 S Industrial Dr PO Box 1359 ... Yuba City CA 95993 530-673-6318 673-6376
TF: 800-622-1359 ■ *Web:* www.escalera.com

Excalibur Equipment LLC
Gregory Industrial Trucks 285 Eldridge Rd ... Fairfield NJ 07004 973-808-8399 808-8398
Web: www.exequipment.com

Excellon Automation Inc
20001 S Rancho Way ... Rancho Dominguez CA 90220 310-668-7700 668-7800
TF: 800-392-3556 ■ *Web:* www.excellon.com

FL Smidth Inc 2040 Ave C ... Bethlehem PA 18017 610-264-6011 264-6170
TF: 800-523-9482 ■ *Web:* www.flsmidth.com

Genie Industries Inc 18340 NE 76th St ... Redmond WA 98052 425-881-1800 883-3475
TF: 800-536-1800 ■ *Web:* www.genielift.com

Gunnebo-Johnson Corp 1240 N Harvard Ave ... Tulsa OK 74115 918-832-8933 834-0984*
**Fax:* Cust Svc ■ *TF Sales:* 800-331-5460 ■ *Web:* www.gunnebojohnson.com

Harlan Materials Handling Corp
27 Stanley Rd ... Kansas City KS 66115 913-342-5650 321-5802
TF: 800-255-4262 ■ *Web:* www.harlan-corp.com

Harlo Corp PO Box 129 ... Grandville MI 49468 616-538-0550
TF: 800-391-4151 ■ *Web:* www.harlo.com

Harper Trucks Inc PO Box 12330 ... Wichita KS 67277 316-942-1381 942-8508
TF: 800-835-4099 ■ *Web:* www.harpertrucks.com

Heyl & Patterson Inc
2000 Cliff Mine Rd PO Box 36 ... Pittsburgh PA 15230 412-788-9810 788-9822
Web: www.heylpatterson.com

Hilman Inc 12 Timber Ln ... Marlboro NJ 07746 732-462-6277 462-6355
TF Cust Svc: 888-276-5548 ■ *Web:* www.hilmanrollers.com

Indusco Group 1200 W Hamburg St ... Baltimore MD 21230 410-727-0665 727-2538
TF: 800-727-0665 ■ *Web:* www.induscowirerope.com

Industrial Vehicles International Inc (IVI)
6737 E 12th St ... Tulsa OK 74112 918-836-6516 838-9529
Web: www.indvehicles.com

Iowa Mold Tooling Co Inc (IMT) 500 W US Hwy 18 ... Garner IA 50438 641-923-3711 923-6063
TF: 800-247-5958 ■ *Web:* www.imt.com

James Walker Co 7109 Milford Industrial Rd ... Baltimore MD 21215 410-486-3950
Web: jameswalker.com

Kelly Systems Inc 422 N Western Ave ... Chicago IL 60612 312-733-3224 733-6971
TF: 800-258-8237 ■ *Web:* www.kellytubesystems.com

Key Handling Systems Inc
137 W Commercial Ave ... Moonachie NJ 07074 201-933-9333 933-4777
Web: www.keyhandling.com

Konecranes America 7300 Chippewa Blvd ... Houston TX 77086 281-445-2225 445-9355
TF: 800-231-0241 ■ *Web:* www.konecranesusa.com

Kornylak Corp 400 Heaton St ... Hamilton OH 45011 513-863-1277 863-7644
TF: 800-837-5676 ■ *Web:* www.kornylak.com

KWD Manufacturing Co
2230 W Southcross Blvd ... San Antonio TX 78211 210-924-5999 924-6799

Landoll Corp 1900 N St ... Marysville KS 66508 785-562-5381 321-3865*
**Fax Area Code:* 888 ■ **Fax:* Sales ■ *TF Cust Svc:* 800-446-5175 ■ *Web:* www.landoll.com

Leebaw Mfg Company Inc PO Box 553 ... Canfield OH 44406 800-841-8083
TF: 800-841-8083 ■ *Web:* www.leebaw.com

Lift-All Company Inc 1909 McFarland Dr ... Landisville PA 17538 717-898-6615 898-1215*
**Fax:* Cust Svc ■ *TF:* 800-909-1964 ■ *Web:* www.lift-all.com

Liftone 440 E Westinghouse Blvd ... Charlotte NC 28273 855-543-8663
TF: 855-543-8663 ■ *Web:* www.liftone.net

Linde Hydraulics Corp
5089 W Western Reserve Rd ... Canfield OH 44406 330-533-6801 533-6893
Web: www.linde-hydraulics.com/en-gb

Lovegreen Industrial Services Inc
2280 Sibley Ct ... Eagan MN 55122 651-890-1166 890-8370
TF: 800-262-8284 ■ *Web:* www.lovegreen.com

MacCabe Electric Conductors Inc
426 Stump Rd PO Box 590 ... Montgomeryville PA 18936 215-368-9420 368-9220
Web: www.maccabeelectric.com

Magline Inc 1205 W Cedar St ... Standish MI 48658 800-624-5463 879-5399*
**Fax Area Code:* 989 ■ *TF:* 800-624-5463 ■ *Web:* www.magliner.com

Manitex Inc 3000 S Austin Ave ... Georgetown TX 78626 512-942-3000 869-7550
TF: 877-314-3390 ■ *Web:* www.manitex.com

Manitou North America 6401 Imperial Dr ... Waco TX 76712 254-799-0232 799-4433
Web: www.constructionequipment.com

Phone Fax

Matot Inc 2501 Van Buren St ... Bellwood IL 60104 708-547-1888 547-1608
TF: 800-369-1070 ■ *Web:* www.matot.com

Maxon Industries Inc
11921 Slauson Ave ... Santa Fe Springs CA 90670 562-464-0099 771-7713*
**Fax Area Code:* 888 ■ *TF:* 800-227-4116 ■ *Web:* www.maxonlift.com

Mazzella Lifting Technologies
21000 Aerospace Pkwy ... Cleveland OH 44142 440-239-7000 239-7010
TF: 800-362-4601 ■ *Web:* www.mazzellacompanies.com/mazzellalifting

McGuire
W194 N11481 McCormick Dr PO Box 309 ... Germantown WI 53022 518-828-7652 255-9399*
**Fax Area Code:* 262 ■ *TF:* 800-624-8473 ■ *Web:* www.wbmcguire.com

Mertz Mfg LLC 1701 N Waverly St ... Ponca City OK 74601 580-762-5646 767-8411
TF: 800-654-6433 ■ *Web:* www.mertzok.com

Mitsubishi Caterpillar Forklift America Inc
2121 W Sam Houston Pkwy N ... Houston TX 77043 713-365-1000 365-1441
Web: www.mcfa.com

Morris Material Handling Inc
315 W Forest Hill Ave ... Oak Creek WI 53154 414-764-6200 570-2779
TF: 800-933-3001 ■ *Web:* www.morriscranes.com

NACCO Materials Handling Group Inc
5875 Landerbrook Dr Ste 300 ... Cleveland OH 44124 503-721-6000 721-6001
Web: www.hyster-yale.com

Nissan Forklift Corp North America (NFC)
240 N Prospect St ... Marengo IL 60152 815-568-0061 568-0179
Web: www.nissanforklift.com

NMC-Wollard Inc 2021 Truax Blvd ... Eau Claire WI 54703 715-835-3151 835-6625
TF: 800-656-6867 ■ *Web:* www.nmc-wollard.com

North American Industries Inc 80 Holton St ... Woburn MA 01801 781-897-4100 729-3343
TF: 800-847-8470 ■ *Web:* www.naicranes.com

Nutting 450 Pheasant Ridge Dr ... Watertown SD 57201 605-882-3000 688-8464*
**Fax Area Code:* 866 ■ *TF:* 800-533-0337 ■
Web: www.accomhs.com/nutting-industrial-carts-trailers-and-order-picking-platforms

Ohio Magnetics Inc 5400 Dunham Rd ... Maple Heights OH 44137 216-662-8484 662-2911
TF: 800-486-6446 ■ *Web:* www.ohiomagnetics.com

Paceco Corp 25503 Whitesell St ... Hayward CA 94545 510-264-9288 264-9280
Web: www.pacecocorp.com

Paragon Technologies Inc
101 Larry Holmes Dr Ste 500 ... Easton PA 18042 610-252-3205 252-3102
OTC: PGNT ■ *Web:* pgntgroup.com

Pettibone Michigan 1100 Superior Ave ... Baraga MI 49908 906-353-4800 353-6325
TF: 800-467-3884 ■ *Web:* www.gopettibone.com

Positech Corp 191 N Rush Lk Rd ... Laurens IA 50554 712-841-4548 841-4765
TF: 800-831-6026 ■ *Web:* positech.com

Powell Systems Inc
162 Churchill-HubbaRd Rd ... Youngstown OH 44505 330-759-9220 759-9434
Web: www.powellsystems.com

Process Equipment Inc
2770 Welborn St PO Box 1607 ... Pelham AL 35124 205-663-5330 663-6037
TF: 888-663-2028 ■ *Web:* www.processbarron.com

Production Equipment Co 401 Liberty St ... Meriden CT 06450 203-235-5795 563-4150*
**Fax Area Code:* 800 ■ *TF:* 800-758-5697 ■ *Web:* www.peco1938.com

Proserv Anchor Crane Group
455 Aldine Bender PO Box 670965 ... Houston TX 77060 281-405-9048 448-7508
TF: 800-835-2223 ■ *Web:* www.proservanchor.com

PTR Baler & Compactor Co
2207 E Ontario St ... Philadelphia PA 19134 215-533-5100
TF: 800-523-3654 ■ *Web:* www.ptrco.com

Pucel Enterprises Inc 1440 E 36th St ... Cleveland OH 44114 216-881-4604 881-6731
TF: 800-336-4986 ■ *Web:* www.pucelenterprises.com

Raymond Corp 22 S Canal St ... Greene NY 13778 607-656-2311 656-9005
TF General: 800-235-7200 ■ *Web:* www.raymondcorp.com

RKI Inc 2301 Central Pkwy ... Houston TX 77092 713-688-4414 688-8982
TF: 800-346-8988 ■ *Web:* www.rki-us.com

Royal Tractor Co Inc 109 Overland Pk Pl ... New Century KS 66031 913-782-2598
TF: 888-782-7278 ■ *Web:* www.royaltractor.com

Scott Industrial Systems Inc
4433 Interpoint Blvd PO Box 1387 ... Dayton OH 45401 937-233-8146 416-6023*
**Fax Area Code:* 800 ■ *TF:* 800-416-6023 ■ *Web:* www.scottindustrialsystems.com

Shepard Niles 220 N Genesee St ... Montour Falls NY 14865 607-535-7111 535-7323
TF: 800-481-2260 ■ *Web:* www.shepard-niles.com

Sherman & Reilly Inc 400 W 33rd St ... Chattanooga TN 37401 423-756-5300 756-2948
TF Sales: 800-251-7780 ■ *Web:* www.sherman-reilly.com

Snorkel 2009 Roseport Rd ... Elwood KS 66024 785-989-3000 989-3070
Web: www.snorkellifts.com

Solazyme Inc 225 Gateway Blvd ... South San Francisco CA 94080 650-780-4777 989-6700
NASDAQ: SZYM ■ *TF:* 877-917-9075 ■ *Web:* solazymeindustrials.com

Southeast Industrial Equipment Inc
12200 Steele Creek Rd ... Charlotte NC 28273 704-399-9700 393-1714
TF: 866-696-9125 ■ *Web:* www.sielift.com

Southworth Products Corp PO Box 1380 ... Portland ME 04104 207-878-0700 797-4734
TF: 800-743-1000 ■ *Web:* www.southworthproducts.com

Steel King Industries Inc
2700 Chamber St ... Stevens Point WI 54481 715-341-3120 341-8792
TF: 800-826-0203 ■ *Web:* www.steelking.com

Streator Dependable Manufacturing Co
1705 N Shabbona St ... Streator IL 61364 815-672-0551 672-7631
TF: 800-795-0551 ■ *Web:* www.streatordependable.com

Taylor-Dunn Manufacturing Co 2114 W Ball Rd ... Anaheim CA 92804 714-956-4040 956-3130
TF: 800-688-8680 ■ *Web:* www.taylor-dunn.com

TC/American Monorail Inc
12070 43rd St NE ... Saint Michael MN 55376 763-497-7000 497-7001
Web: www.tcamerican.com

Terex Corp 200 Nyala Farm Rd ... Westport CT 06880 203-222-7170 222-7976
NYSE: TEX ■ *Web:* www.terex.com

Terex Corp Crane Div 202 Raleigh St ... Wilmington NC 28412 910-395-8500
TF: 877-794-5284 ■ *Web:* www.terex.com

Terex-Telelect Inc
500 Oakwood Rd PO Box 1150 ... Watertown SD 57201 605-882-4000 882-1842
TF: 800-982-8975 ■ *Web:* www.terex.com

Thern Inc 5712 Industrial Pk Rd PO Box 347 ... Winona MN 55987 507-454-2996 454-5282
TF: 800-843-7648 ■ *Web:* thern.com

Triple/S Dynamics Inc
1031 S Haskell Ave PO Box 151027 ... Dallas TX 75315 214-828-8600 828-8688
TF: 800-527-2116 ■ *Web:* www.sssdynamics.com

Company	City	State	Zip	Phone	Fax
United Central Industrial Supply Company LLC 1241 Volunteer Pkwy Ste 1000 *Web:* www.unitedcentral.net	Bristol	TN	37620	423-573-7300	573-7392
Valley Craft 2001 S Hwy 61 *TF:* 800-328-1480 ■ *Web:* www.valleycraft.com	Lake City	MN	55041	651-345-3386	345-3606
Vibra Screw Inc 755 Union Blvd *Web:* www.vibrascrew.com	Totowa	NJ	07512	973-256-7410	256-7567
WA Charnstrom Co 5391 12th Ave E *TF Cust Svc:* 800-328-2962 ■ *Web:* www.charnstrom.com	Shakopee	MN	55379	800-328-2962	916-3215
Waldon Mfg LLC 201 W Oklahoma Ave *TF:* 866-283-2759 ■ *Web:* www.waldonequipment.com	Fiarview	OK	73737	580-227-3711	
Wayne Engineering Corp 701 Performance Dr *Web:* www.wayneusa.com	Cedar Falls	IA	50613	319-266-1721	266-8207
Wesco Industrial Products Inc 1250 Welsh Rd **Fax Area Code:* 800 ■ *Web:* www.wescomfg.com	North Wales	PA	19454	215-699-7031	346-5511*
Western Hoist Inc 1839 Cleveland Ave *TF:* 888-994-6478 ■ *Web:* www.westernlift.org	National City	CA	91950	619-474-3361	474-8261
Whiting Corp 26000 Whiting Way **Fax Area Code:* 708 ■ *TF:* 800-861-5744 ■ *Web:* www.whitingcorp.com	Monee	IL	60449	800-861-5744	587-2001*
Wiggins Lift Company Inc 2571 Cortez St *TF:* 800-350-7821 ■ *Web:* www.wigginslift.com	Oxnard	CA	93031	805-485-7821	485-5230
WinHolt Equipment Group 141 Eileen Way *TF:* 800-444-3595 ■ *Web:* www.winholt.com	Syosset	NY	11791	516-222-0335	921-0538
Zenar Corp 7301 S Sixth St PO Box 107 *Web:* www.zenarcrane.com	Oak Creek	WI	53154	414-764-1800	764-1267

471 MATTRESSES & ADJUSTABLE BEDS

See Also Household Furniture p. 2341

Company	City	State	Zip	Phone	Fax
Bechik Products Inc 1020 Discovery Rd Ste 150 *TF:* 800-328-6569 ■ *Web:* www.bechik.com	Eagan	MN	55121	651-698-0364	698-1009
Bergad Inc 747 Eljer Way *TF:* 888-476-8664 ■ *Web:* www.bergad.com	Ford City	PA	16226	724-763-2883	
Bowles Mattress Co Inc 1220 Watt St *TF:* 800-223-7509 ■ *Web:* www.bowlesmattress.com	Jeffersonville	IN	47130	812-288-8614	
Classic Sleep Products Inc 8214 Wellmoor Ct *TF:* 877-707-7533 ■ *Web:* www.classicmattress.com	Jessup	MD	20794	410-904-0006	
Comfortex Inc 1680 Wilkie Dr *TF:* 800-445-4007 ■ *Web:* www.comfortexinc.com	Winona	MN	55987	507-454-6579	454-6581
Corsicana Bedding Inc PO Box 1050 *TF:* 800-323-4349 ■ *Web:* www.corsicanabedding.com	Corsicana	TX	75151	903-872-2591	
Cotton Belt Inc 401 E Sater St *TF:* 800-849-4192 ■ *Web:* www.edgecombe.com	Pinetops	NC	27864	252-827-4192	827-5683
Diamond Mattress Company Inc 3112 Las Hermanas St *Web:* www.diamondmattress.com	Compton	CA	90221	310-638-0363	638-2005
Dreamline Mfg Inc 1514 S Second St PO Box 1250 *Web:* www.dreamlinebedding.com	Cabot	AR	72023	501-843-3585	
Englander Northeast 12 Esquire Rd *TF:* 800-370-8700 ■ *Web:* www.englander.com	North Billerica	MA	01862	800-370-8700	
FXI, Inc 1241 Old Temescal Rd *Web:* fxi.com/products/valeo-collection	Corona	CA	92881	951-371-8101	
HomeStyle Industries 1323 11th Ave N *Web:* www.home-style.com	Nampa	ID	83687	208-466-8481	
Imperial Bedding Co 720 11th St PO Box 5347 *TF:* 800-529-3321 ■ *Web:* www.imperialbedding.com	Huntington	WV	25703	304-529-3321	525-5317
Jackson Mattress Company Inc 3154 Camden Rd *TF:* 800-763-7378 ■ *Web:* restonic.com	Fayetteville	NC	28306	910-425-0131	425-1602
Jamison Bedding Inc PO Box 681948 *TF Cust Svc:* 800-255-1883 ■ *Web:* www.jamisonbedding.com	Franklin	TN	37068	615-794-1883	
King Koil Licensing Company Inc 7501 S Quincy St Ste 130 *TF:* 800-525-8331 ■ *Web:* www.kingkoil.com	Willowbrook	IL	60527	800-525-8331	
Kingsdown Inc 126 W Holt St **Fax:* Cust Svc ■ *TF Cust Svc:* 800-354-5464 ■ *Web:* www.kingsdown.com	Mebane	NC	27302	919-563-3531	563-6730*
Kolcraft Enterprises Inc 10832 NC Hwy 211 E *TF Cust Svc:* 800-453-7673 ■ *Web:* www.kolcraft.com	Aberdeen	NC	28315	910-944-9345	
Leggett & Platt Inc Number 1 Leggett Rd PO Box 757 *NYSE:* LEG ■ *TF:* 800-888-4569 ■ *Web:* www.leggett.com	Carthage	MO	64836	417-358-8131	358-6996
Meridian Mattress Factory Inc 200 Rubush Rd PO Box 5127 *Web:* mermat.com	Meridian	MS	39301	601-693-3875	
Northwest Bedding 6102 S Hayford Rd *TF:* 800-456-7686 ■ *Web:* www.nwbedding.com	Spokane	WA	99224	509-244-3000	244-9905
Omaha Bedding Co 4011 S 60th St *TF:* 800-279-9018 ■ *Web:* www.omahabeddingco.com	Omaha	NE	68117	402-733-8600	733-0586
Original Mattress Factory Inc, The 4930 State Rd *Web:* originalmattress.com	Cleveland	OH	44134	216-661-8388	
Palliser Furniture Upholstery Ltd 70 Lexington Park *TF:* 866-444-0777 ■ *Web:* www.palliser.com	Winnipeg	MB	R2G4H2	204-988-5600	988-5604
Paramount Industrial Cos Inc 1112 Kingwood Ave *Web:* www.paramountsleep.com	Norfolk	VA	23502	757-855-3321	855-2029
Park Place Corp 6801 Augusta Rd *Web:* www.parkplacecorp.com	Greenville	SC	29605	864-422-8118	
Restonic Mattress 201 James E Casey Dr *TF:* 800-898-6075 ■ *Web:* www.restonic.com	Buffalo	NY	14206	716-895-1414	895-1416
Restonic Mattress Corp 737 Main St *TF:* 800-898-6075 ■ *Web:* www.restonic.com	Buffalo	NY	14203	800-898-6075	
Riverside Mattress Co 225 Dunn Rd *TF:* 888-288-5195 ■ *Web:* www.riversidemattressinc.com	Fayetteville	NC	28312	910-483-0461	484-2334
Serta Mattress/AW Inc 8415 ARdmore Rd *TF:* 888-557-3782 ■ *Web:* www.serta.com	Landover	MD	20785	301-322-1000	
Simmons Co 1 Concourse Pkwy Ste 800 *Web:* www.simmons.com	Atlanta	GA	30328	770-512-7700	392-2560
Sleep Design 5808 Berry Brook Dr *Web:* sleep-designs.com	Houston	TX	77017	713-227-0121	
Sleep Innovations Inc 187 Rt 36 Ste 101	West Long Branch	NJ	07764	732-263-0800	
Sleep Train Inc 2205 Plz Dr **Fax Area Code:* 866 ■ *TF:* 800-919-2337 ■ *Web:* www.sleeptrain.com	Rocklin	CA	95765	800-919-2337	293-5719*
Southerland Inc 1973 Southerland Dr *TF Cust Svc:* 800-443-1183 ■ *Web:* www.southerlandsleep.com	Nashville	TN	37207	615-226-9650	650-2653
Stress-O-Pedic Mattress Company Inc 2060 S Wineville Ave *Web:* www.stressopedic.com	Ontario	CA	91761	909-605-2010	
Symbol Mattress Co 1814 High Pt Ave *Web:* www.symbolmattress.com	Richmond	VA	23230	804-353-8965	
Tempur Production USA Inc 203 Tempur Pedic Dr Ste 102 *Web:* tempurpedic.com	Duffield	VA	24244	276-431-7150	
Tempur-Pedic International Inc 1713 Jaggie Fox Way *NYSE:* TPX ■ **Fax Area Code:* 859 ■ *TF:* 800-821-6621 ■ *Web:* www.tempurpedic.com	Lexington	KY	40511	800-821-6621	259-9843*
Therapedic International 1375 Jersey Ave *TF:* 800-233-7467 ■ *Web:* www.therapedic.com	North Brunswick	NJ	08902	800-233-7467	
VyMaC Corp W3130 State Rd 59 E	Whitewater	WI	53190	920-568-3130	
White Dove Ltd 3201 Harvard Ave *Web:* www.whitedoveusa.com	Cleveland	OH	44105	216-341-0200	
Winston-Salem Industries for the Blind 7730 N Pt Dr *Web:* www.wsifb.com	Winston-Salem	NC	27106	336-759-0551	759-0990

472 MEASURING, TESTING, CONTROLLING INSTRUMENTS

See Also Electrical Signals Measuring & Testing Instruments p. 2222

Company	City	State	Zip	Phone	Fax
ABB Inc 501 Merritt 7 *TF Prod Info:* 800-626-4999 ■ *Web:* new.abb.com/us	Norwalk	CT	06851	203-750-2200	435-7365
Adcole Corp 669 Forest St *Web:* www.adcole.com	Marlborough	MA	01752	508-485-9100	481-6142
AGR International Inc 615 Whitestown Rd *Web:* www.agrintl.com	Butler	PA	16001	724-482-2163	482-2767
All Weather Inc 1165 National Dr *TF:* 800-824-5873 ■ *Web:* www.allweatherinc.com	Sacramento	CA	95834	916-928-1000	928-1165
AMETEK Aerospace & Defense 50 Fordham Rd **Fax:* Cust Svc ■ *Web:* ametekaerodefense.com	Wilmington	MA	01887	978-988-4771	988-4944*
AMETEK Inc Test & Calibration Instruments Div 8600 Somerset Dr *TF:* 800-733-5427 ■ *Web:* www.ametek.com	Largo	FL	33773	727-538-6132	538-6121
AMETEK US Gauge 820 Pennsylvania Blvd *TF:* 888-631-5454 ■ *Web:* www.ametekusg.com	Feasterville	PA	19053	215-355-6900	354-1802
Beta LaserMike Inc 8001 Technology Blvd *TF:* 800-886-9935 ■ *Web:* www.betalasermike.com	Dayton	OH	45424	937-233-9935	233-7284
Bruel & Kjaer Instruments Inc 2815 Colonnades Ct Ste A *TF:* 800-332-2040 ■ *Web:* www.bkhome.com	Norcross	GA	30071	770-209-6907	448-3246
Cambridge Technology Inc 25 Hartwell Ave *TF:* 800-342-3757 ■ *Web:* www.camtech.com	Lexington	MA	02421	781-541-1600	541-1601
Canberra Industries Inc 800 Research Pkwy *TF Sales:* 800-243-3955 ■ *Web:* www.canberra.com	Meriden	CT	06450	203-238-2351	235-1347
Century Equipment Inc 5959 Angola Rd PO Box 352889 *Web:* www.centuryequip.com	Toledo	OH	43615	419-865-7400	865-8215
Clayton Industries 17477 Hurley St *TF:* 800-423-4585 ■ *Web:* www.claytonindustries.com	City of Industry	CA	91744	626-435-1200	435-0180
Copley Controls Corp 20 Dan Rd *Web:* www.copleycontrols.com	Canton	MA	02021	781-828-8090	828-6547
Crane Nuclear Inc 2825 Cobb International Blvd *TF:* 800-795-8013 ■ *Web:* www.cranenuclear.com	Kennesaw	GA	30152	770-424-6343	429-4750
Cubic Transportation Systems Inc 5650 Kearny Mesa Rd *TF:* 800-937-5449 ■ *Web:* www.cubic.com	San Diego	CA	92111	858-268-3100	292-9987
Danaher Corp 2200 Pennsylvania Ave NW Ste 800 *NYSE:* DHR ■ *TF:* 800-833-9200 ■ *Web:* www.danaher.com	Washington	DC	20037	202-828-0850	828-0860
Davis Instrument Corp 3465 Diablo Ave *TF:* 800-678-3669 ■ *Web:* www.davisnet.com	Hayward	CA	94545	510-732-9229	670-0589
Delta Cooling Towers Inc PO Box 315 *TF:* 800-289-3358 ■ *Web:* www.deltacooling.com	Rockaway	NJ	07866	973-586-2201	586-2243
Dynisco LLC 38 Forge Pkwy *TF General:* 800-396-4726 ■ *Web:* www.dynisco.com	Franklin	MA	02038	508-541-9400	541-6206
Emerson Process Management CSI 835 Innovation Dr *TF:* 800-675-4726 ■ *Web:* www2.emersonprocess.com	Knoxville	TN	37932	865-675-2110	218-1764
Endevco Corp 30700 Rancho Viejo Rd *TF:* 800-982-6732 ■ *Web:* www.endevco.com	San Juan Capistrano	CA	92675	949-493-8181	661-7231
Enidine Inc 7 Centre Dr *TF:* 800-852-8508 ■ *Web:* www.enidine.com	Orchard Park	NY	14127	716-662-1900	662-1909
Fairfield Industries Inc 1111 Gillingham Ln *TF:* 800-231-9809 ■ *Web:* www.fairfieldnodal.com	Sugar Land	TX	77478	281-275-7500	275-7500
Fiber Instruments Sales Inc 161 Clear Rd *TF Sales:* 800-500-0347 ■ *Web:* www.fiberinstrumentsales.com	Oriskany	NY	13424	315-736-2206	736-2285
Fisher Research Laboratory Inc 1465H Henry Brennan Ste H *TF:* 800-685-5050 ■ *Web:* www.fisherlab.com	El Paso	TX	79936	915-225-0333	225-0336
Flowline Inc 10500 Humbolt St *Web:* www.flowline.com	Los Alamitos	CA	90720	562-598-3015	431-8507
Garrett Metal Detectors 1881 W State St *TF:* 800-234-6151 ■ *Web:* www.garrett.com	Garland	TX	75042	972-494-6151	494-1881

Company	City	State	ZIP	Phone	Fax
Geokon Inc 48 Spencer St *Web:* www.geokon.com	Lebanon	NH	03766	603-448-1562	448-3216
Geometrics Inc 2190 Fortune Dr *Web:* www.geometrics.com	San Jose	CA	95131	408-954-0522	954-0902
George Risk Industries Inc 802 S Elm St *OTC:* RSKIA ■ *TF Sales:* 800-523-1227 ■ *Web:* www.grisk.com	Kimball	NE	69145	308-235-4645	235-2609
GFI Genfare 751 Pratt Blvd *TF:* 877-247-3797 ■ *Web:* www.spx.com	Elk Grove Village	IL	60007	847-593-8855	593-1824
Gleason M & M Precision Systems Corp 300 Progress Rd *TF:* 800-727-6333 ■ *Web:* www.gleason.com	Dayton	OH	45449	937-859-8273	859-4452
Goodrich Corp 2730 W Tyvola Rd 4 Coliseum Ctr *NYSE:* GR ■ *TF:* 800-735-7899 ■ *Web:* utcaerospacesystems.com	Charlotte	NC	28217	704-423-7000	423-7002
Herman H Sticht Company Inc 45 Main St Ste 701 *TF:* 800-221-3203 ■ *Web:* www.stichtco.com	Brooklyn	NY	11201	718-852-7602	852-7915
Hexagon Metrology Inc 250 Circuit Dr *TF:* 800-343-7933 ■ *Web:* www.sheffieldmeasurement.com	North Kingstown	RI	02852	401-886-2000	886-2727
Howell Instruments Inc 8945 S Fwy *Web:* www.howellinst.com	Fort Worth	TX	76140	817-336-7411	336-7874
Industrial Dynamics Company Ltd 3100 Fujita St *Web:* www.filtec.com	Torrance	CA	90505	310-325-5633	
Instron Corp 825 University Ave *Web:* www.instron.us	Norwood	MA	02062	781-828-2500	575-5750
Interface Inc 7401 E Butherus Dr *TF:* 800-947-5598 ■ *Web:* www.interfaceforce.com	Scottsdale	AZ	85260	480-948-5555	948-1924
Intra Corp 885 Manufacturers Dr *Web:* www.intra-corp.net	Westland	MI	48186	734-326-7030	326-1410
Isra Surface Vision Inc 4470 Peachtree Lakes Dr *Web:* www.lasorsystronics.com	Duluth	GA	30096	770-449-7776	449-0399
Kavlico Corp 14401 Princeton Ave *Web:* www.kavlico.com	Moorpark	CA	93021	805-523-2000	523-7125
Kinemetrics Inc 222 Vista Ave *Web:* www.kinemetrics.com	Pasadena	CA	91107	626-795-2220	795-0868
Kistler Instrument Corp 75 John Glenn Dr *Web:* www.kistler.com	Amherst	NY	14228	716-691-5100	691-5226
L-3 Avionics Systems 5353 52nd St SE *TF:* 800-253-9525 ■ *Web:* www.l-3avionics.com	Grand Rapids	MI	49512	616-949-6600	
Leica Geosystems Inc 3498 Kraft Ave SE *TF Sales:* 800-367-9453 ■ *Web:* www.leica-geosystems.com	Grand Rapids	MI	49512	616-977-4189	942-4627
Link Engineering Company Inc 43855 Plymouth Oaks Blvd *Web:* www.linkeng.com	Plymouth	MI	48170	734-453-0800	453-0802
Lockheed Martin Sippican 7 Barnabas Rd *Web:* www.sippican.com	Marion	MA	02738	508-748-1160	748-3626
Logis Tech Inc 9450 Innovation Dr Ste 1 *Web:* www.logis-tech.com	Manassas	VA	20110	703-393-0122	
Ludlum Measurements Inc 501 Oak St *TF:* 800-622-0828 ■ *Web:* www.ludlums.com	Sweetwater	TX	79556	325-235-5494	235-4672
Magnetic Analysis Corp 103 Fairview Park Dr *TF:* 800-463-8622 ■ *Web:* www.mac-ndt.com	Elmsford	NY	10523	914-699-9450	703-3790
Marposs Corp 3300 Cross Creek Pkwy *TF:* 888-627-7677 ■ *Web:* www.marposs.com	Auburn Hills	MI	48326	248-370-0404	370-0991
Mason Industries Inc 350 Rabro Dr *Web:* www.mason-industries.com	Hauppauge	NY	11788	631-348-0282	348-0279
Metrix Instrument Co 8824 Fallbrook Dr *TF:* 800-638-7494 ■ *Web:* www.metrixvibration.com	Houston	TX	77064	713-461-2131	559-9417
Metrosonics 1060 Corporate Ctr Dr *TF:* 800-245-0779 ■ *Web:* 3m.com	Oconomowoc	WI	53066	262-567-9157	567-4047
Metrotech Corp 3251 Olcott St *TF:* 800-446-3392 ■ *Web:* www.vivax-metrotech.com	Santa Clara	CA	95054	408-734-1400	734-1415
Morcom International Inc 3656 Centerview Dr Unit 1 *Web:* www.morcom.com	Chantilly	VA	20151	703-263-9305	263-9308
MTS Systems Corp 14000 Technology Dr *NASDAQ:* MTSC ■ *TF Cust Svc:* 800-328-2255 ■ *Web:* www.mts.com	Eden Prairie	MN	55344	952-937-4000	937-4515
Mustang Dynamometer 2300 Pinnacle Pkwy *TF:* 888-468-7826 ■ *Web:* www.mustangdyne.com	Twinsburg	OH	44087	330-963-5400	425-3310
Nanometrics Inc 1550 Buckeye Dr *NASDAQ:* NANO ■ *Web:* www.nanometrics.com	Milpitas	CA	95035	408-545-6000	232-5910
Nextest Systems Corp 875 Embedded Way *Web:* www.teradyne.com	San Jose	CA	95138	408-960-2400	960-7660
Novatron Corp 401 Loop 59	Atlanta	TX	75551	903-799-6560	799-6580
Ohmart/VEGA Corp 4241 Allendorf Dr *TF:* 800-367-5383 ■ *Web:* www.vega.com/home_us	Cincinnati	OH	45209	513-272-0131	272-0133
Oxford Instruments Measurement Systems 300 Bake Ave Ste 150 **Fax Area Code:* 978 ■ *TF:* 800-447-4717 ■ *Web:* www.oxford-instruments.com	Concord	MA	01742	800-447-4717	369-8287*
Perceptron Inc 47827 Halyard Dr *NASDAQ:* PRCP ■ *Web:* www.perceptron.com	Plymouth	MI	48170	734-414-6100	414-4700
Preco Electronics Inc 10335 W Emerald St *TF:* 866-977-7326 ■ *Web:* www.preco.com	Boise	ID	83704	208-323-1000	323-1034
Princeton Gamma-Tech Instruments Inc 303-C College Rd E	Princeton	NJ	08540	609-924-7310	924-1729
Promess Inc PO Box 748 *Web:* www.promessinc.com	Brighton	MI	48116	810-229-9334	229-8125
Radiation Monitoring Devices Inc (RMDINC) 44 Hunt St Ste 2 *Web:* www.rmdinc.com	Watertown	MA	02472	617-668-6800	926-9980
Rochester Gauges Inc of Texas 11616 Harry Hines Blvd *TF:* 800-821-1829 ■ *Web:* www.rochestergauges.com	Dallas	TX	75229	972-241-2161	620-1403
Rudolph Technologies Inc 1 Rudolph Rd PO Box 1000 *NASDAQ:* RTEC ■ *TF:* 877-467-8365 ■ *Web:* www.rudolphtech.com	Flanders	NJ	07836	973-691-1300	
Schmitt Industries Inc 2765 NW Nicolai St *NASDAQ:* SMIT ■ *Web:* www.schmitt-ind.com	Portland	OR	97210	503-227-7908	223-1258
Schneeberger Inc 11 Deangelo Dr *Web:* www.schneeberger.com	Bedford	MA	01730	781-271-0140	275-4749
Sensor Systems LLC 2800 Anvil St N *Web:* www.sensorsllc.com	Saint Petersburg	FL	33710	727-347-2181	347-7520
Sercel Inc 17200 Pk Row *Web:* www.sercel.com	Houston	TX	77084	281-492-6688	579-6555
Setra Systems Inc 159 Swanson Rd *TF:* 800-257-3872 ■ *Web:* www.setra.com	Boxborough	MA	01719	978-263-1400	264-0292
Sierra Monitor Corp 1991 Tarob Ct *OTC:* SRMC ■ *TF:* 888-509-1970 ■ *Web:* www.sierramonitor.com	Milpitas	CA	95035	408-262-6611	262-9042
Smiths Detection 2202 Lakeside Blvd *TF:* 800-297-0955 ■ *Web:* www.smithsdetection.com	Edgewood	MD	21040	410-510-9100	
Sorrento Electronics Inc 4949 Greencraig Ln *TF:* 800-252-1180 ■ *Web:* ga.com	San Diego	CA	92123	858-522-8300	522-8300
SuperFlow Technologies Group 4747 Centennial Blvd *TF:* 800-471-7701 ■ *Web:* www.superflow.com	Colorado Springs	CO	80919	719-471-1746	471-1490
Taber Industries 455 Bryant St *TF:* 800-333-5300 ■ *Web:* www.taberindustries.com	North Tonawanda	NY	14120	716-694-4000	694-1450
Taylor Hobson Inc 1725 Western Dr *Web:* www.taylor-hobson.com	West Chicago	IL	60185	630-621-3099	231-1739
Tel-Instrument Electronics Corp 1 Branca Rd *NYSE:* TIK ■ *Web:* www.telinstrument.com	East Rutherford	NJ	07073	201-933-1600	933-7340
Testing Machines Inc 40 McCullough Dr *TF General:* 800-678-3221 ■ *Web:* www.testingmachines.com	New Castle	DE	19720	302-613-5600	613-5619
Thermo Fisher Scientific Inc 10010 Mesa Rim Rd *NYSE:* TMO ■ *TF:* 800-488-4399 ■ *Web:* www.thermofisher.com	San Diego	CA	92121	858-450-9811	546-1734
Thermo Fisher Scientific Inc 81 Wyman St *NYSE:* TMO ■ *TF:* 800-678-5599 ■ *Web:* www.thermofisher.com	Waltham	MA	02454	781-622-1000	622-1207
Tinius Olsen Testing Machine Company Inc 1065 Easton Rd PO Box 1009 *Web:* www.tiniusolsen.com	Horsham	PA	19044	215-675-7100	441-0899
Topcon Positioning Systems Inc 7400 National Dr *Web:* www.topconpositioning.com	Livermore	CA	94551	925-245-8300	245-8599
Ues Inc 4401 Dayton Xenia Rd *Web:* www.ues.com	Dayton	OH	45432	937-426-6900	429-5413
Unilux Inc 59 N Fifth St *TF:* 800-522-0801 ■ *Web:* www.unilux.com	Saddle Brook	NJ	07663	201-712-1266	712-1366
Vaisala Inc 10-D Gill St *TF:* 888-824-7252 ■ *Web:* www.vaisala.com	Woburn	MA	01801	781-933-4500	933-8029
Verity Instruments Inc 2901 Eisenhower St *Web:* www.verityinst.com	Carrollton	TX	75007	972-446-9990	446-9586
White's Electronics Inc 1011 Pleasant Valley Rd *TF Sales:* 800-999-9147 ■ *Web:* www.whitesdetectors.com	Sweet Home	OR	97386	800-547-6911	

473 MEAT PACKING PLANTS

See Also Poultry Processing p. 2967

Company	City	State	ZIP	Phone	Fax
Abbott's Meat Inc 3623 Blackington Ave *Web:* www.abbottsmeat.com	Flint	MI	48532	810-232-7128	
Abbyland Foods Inc 502 E Linden St PO Box 69 *TF:* 800-732-5483 ■ *Web:* www.abbyland.com	Abbotsford	WI	54405	715-223-6386	223-6388
Academy Packing Company Inc 2881 Wyoming St *Web:* academypackingcompany.com	Dearborn	MI	48120	313-841-4900	
Allen Bros Inc 3737 S Halsted St *TF:* 800-548-7777 ■ *Web:* www.allenbrothers.com	Chicago	IL	60609	773-890-5100	890-9146
Alpine Meats 9850 Lowr Sacramento Rd *TF:* 800-399-6328 ■ *Web:* www.alpinemeats.com	Stockton	CA	95210	209-477-2691	477-1994
American Foods Group Inc 544 Acme St *TF:* 800-345-0293 ■ *Web:* www.americanfoodsgroup.com	Green Bay	WI	54302	920-437-6330	
Atlantic Veal & Lamb Inc 275 Morgan Ave *Web:* atlanticveal.com	Brooklyn	NY	11211	718-599-6400	302-3237
ATRAHAN Transformation Inc 860 Chemin Des Acadiens *Web:* www.atrahan.com	Yamachiche	QC	G0X3L0	819-296-3791	
Birchwood Foods 6009 Goshen Springs Rd *Web:* www.bwfoods.com	Norcross	GA	30071	770-448-9101	
Burnett & Son Meat Co Inc 1420 S Myrtle Ave *Web:* www.burnettandson.com	Monrovia	CA	91016	626-357-2165	357-7115
Cargill Meat Solutions 151 N Main PO Box 2519 **Fax:* Hum Res ■ *Web:* cargill.com	Wichita	KS	67201	316-291-2500	291-2589*
Carolina Packers Inc 2999 S Bright Leaf Blvd *TF:* 800-682-7675 ■ *Web:* www.carolinapackers.com	Smithfield	NC	27577	919-934-2181	989-6794
Central Beef Industry LLC 571 W Kings Hwy	Center Hill	FL	33514	352-793-3671	793-2227
Central Nebraska Packing Inc 2800 E Eigth St *TF Cust Svc:* 800-445-2881 ■ *Web:* www.nebraskabrand.com	North Platte	NE	69103	308-532-1250	532-2744
Cherry Meat Packers Inc 4750 S California Ave	Chicago	IL	60632	773-927-1200	927-1520
Chip Steak & Provision Co 232 Dewey St **Fax Area Code:* 507	Mankato	MN	56001	416-236-1163	388-6279*
Chisesi Bros Meat Packing Co 5221 Jefferson Hwy *TF:* 800-966-3550 ■ *Web:* www.chisesibros.com	New Orleans	LA	70123	504-822-3550	
Clougherty Packing Co 3049 E Vernon Ave **Fax Area Code:* 323 ■ *TF Sales:* 800-846-7635 ■ *Web:* www.farmerjohn.com	Los Angeles	CA	90058	800-846-7635	584-1699*
Comer Packing 1000 Poplar St PO Box 33 *TF:* 800-748-8916	Aberdeen	MS	39730	662-369-9325	369-9375
ConAgra Foods Retail Products Co Deli Foods Group 215 W Field Rd *TF:* 877-266-2472 ■ *Web:* www.conagrafoods.com	Naperville	IL	60563	630-857-1000	
Cougle Commission Co 345 N Aberdeen St *Web:* www.couglefoods.com	Chicago	IL	60607	312-666-7861	
Cudahy Patrick Inc 1 Sweet Apple-Wood Ln *TF:* 800-486-6900 ■ *Web:* www.patrickcudahy.com	Cudahy	WI	53110	414-744-2000	744-2000

	City	State	Zip	Phone	Fax
Curtis Packing Co 2416 Randolph Ave	Greensboro	NC	27406	336-275-7684	275-1901
TF: 800-852-7890 ■ *Web:* www.curtispackingcompany.com					
Dallas City Packing Inc 3049 Morrell St	Dallas	TX	75203	214-948-3901	942-2039
Demakes Enterprises Inc 37 Waterhill St	Lynn	MA	01905	781-592-0016	595-7523
Web: oldneighborhoodfoods.com					
DL Lee & Sons Inc 927 Hwy 32 E	Alma	GA	31510	912-632-4406	632-8298
Web: www.dllee.com					
Eddy Packing Company Inc 404 Airport Dr	Yoakum	TX	77995	361-293-2361	293-2254
TF: 800-292-2361 ■ *Web:* www.eddypacking.com					
Esskay Inc 8422 Bellona Ln Ste 200	Towson	MD	21204	410-823-2100	
Web: www.esskaymeat.com					
Fair Oaks Farms Inc 7600 95th St	Pleasant Prairie	WI	53158	262-947-0320	947-0348
Web: www.fairoaksfarms.com					
Farm Boy Meats 2761 N Kentucky Ave	Evansville	IN	47711	812-425-5231	425-5231
TF: 800-852-3976 ■ *Web:* www.farmboyfoodservice.com					
Food Consulting Co, The 13724 Recuerdo Dr	Del Mar	CA	92014	858-793-4658	
TF: 800-793-2844 ■ *Web:* www.foodlabels.com					
Fresh Mark Inc 1888 Southway St SE	Massillon	OH	44646	330-832-7491	830-3174
Web: www.freshmark.com					
Golden State Foods 18301 Von Karman Ave Ste 1100	Irvine	CA	92612	949-252-2000	252-2080
Web: www.goldenstatefoods.com					
Greater Omaha Packing Company Inc 3001 L St	Omaha	NE	68107	402-731-1700	731-8020
TF: 800-747-5400 ■ *Web:* www.greateromaha.com					
Hansel 'n Gretel Brand Inc 79-36 Cooper Ave	Glendale	NY	11385	718-326-0041	326-2069
Web: www.healthydeli.com					
Harris Ranch Beef Co 16277 S McCall Ave PO Box 220	Selma	CA	93662	800-742-1955	896-3095*
**Fax Area Code:* 559 ■ *TF:* 800-742-1955 ■ *Web:* www.harrisranchbeef.com					
Hatfield Quality Meats Inc 2700 Clemens Rd	Hatfield	PA	19440	215-368-2500	
TF: 800-743-1191 ■ *Web:* www.hatfieldqualitymeats.com					
Isaly's Inc PO Box F	Evans City	PA	16033	724-538-9044	538-3262
Web: www.isalys.com					
J Freirich Foods Inc 815 W Kerr St PO Box 1529	Salisbury	NC	28144	704-636-2621	
TF: 800-554-4788 ■ *Web:* freirich.com					
JBS Five Rivers Cattle Feeding LLC 1770 Promontory Cir	Greeley	CO	80634	970-506-8363	
Web: www.fiveriverscattle.com					
JF O'Neill Packing Company Inc 3120 G St	Omaha	NE	68107	402-733-1200	733-1724
JH Routh Packing Company Inc 4413 W Bogart Rd	Sandusky	OH	44870	419-626-2251	625-4782
TF: 800-446-6759 ■ *Web:* routhpacking.com					
John Morrell & Co 805 E Kemper Rd	Cincinnati	OH	45246	513-346-3540	220-9679*
**Fax Area Code:* 408 ■ **Fax:* Cust Svc ■ *TF:* 800-722-1127 ■ *Web:* www.johnmorrell.com					
L & H Packing Co 647 Steves Ave	San Antonio	TX	78283	210-532-3241	
Web: lhpacking.net					
L Frankel Packing Company Inc 230 N Peoria St	Chicago	IL	60607	312-421-3200	421-6049
Land O'Frost Inc 16850 Chicago Ave	Lansing	IL	60438	708-474-7100	
Web: www.landofrost.com					
Long Prairie Packing Co 10 Riverside Dr	Long Prairie	MN	56347	320-732-2171	552-2107*
**Fax Area Code:* 651 ■ *TF:* 800-996-6440					
Morans Ground Beef Co 3425 E Vernon Ave	Vernon	CA	90058	323-585-0068	
Web: www.moransgroundbeef.com					
Morrilton Packing Company Inc 51 Blue Diamond Dr	Morrilton	AR	72110	501-354-2474	354-2283
TF: 800-264-2475 ■ *Web:* petitjeanmeats.com					
National Beef Packing Co LLC 12200 Ambassador Dr Ste 500 PO Box 20046	Kansas City	MO	64163	800-449-2333	
TF: 800-449-2333 ■ *Web:* www.nationalbeef.com					
Ohio Packing Co 1306 Harmon Ave	Columbus	OH	43223	614-239-1600	237-0885
Web: www.ohiopacking.com					
Olymel LP 2200 Pratte Ave Pratte	Saint-Hyacinthe	QC	J2S4B6	450-771-0400	645-2869
TF: 800-361-7990 ■ *Web:* www.olymel.com					
OSI Industries LLC 1225 Corporate Blvd	Aurora	IL	60505	630-851-6600	692-2340
Web: www.osigroup.com					
Pearl Meat Packing Company Inc 27 York Ave	Randolph	MA	02368	781-228-5100	228-5123
TF: 800-462-3022 ■ *Web:* www.pearlmeat.com					
Plumrose USA Inc 1901 Butterfield Rd Ste 305	Downers Grove	IL	60515	732-624-4040	
TF: 800-526-4909 ■ *Web:* www.plumroseusa.com					
Premium Standard Farms Inc Hwy 65 N PO Box 194	Princeton	MO	64673	660-748-4647	748-7341
Quality Meats & Seafoods 700 Ctr St	West Fargo	ND	58078	701-282-0202	
TF: 800-342-4250 ■ *Web:* www.qualitymeats.com					
Quality Porks International Inc 10404 F Plz	Omaha	NE	68127	402-339-1911	339-8383
Web: www.qpii.com					
Quincy Street Inc 13350 Quincy St	Holland	MI	49424	616-399-3330	399-0952
TF: 800-784-6290 ■ *Web:* www.quincystreetinc.com					
Rochelle Foods Inc 1001 S Main St PO Box 45	Rochelle	IL	61068	815-562-4141	562-4149
Rose Packing Company Inc 65 S Barrington Rd	South Barrington	IL	60010	847-381-5700	381-9436*
**Fax:* Cust Svc ■ *TF:* 800-323-7363 ■ *Web:* www.rosepacking.com					
Sam Hausman Meat Packer Inc 4261 Beacon	Corpus Christi	TX	78403	361-883-5521	883-1003
TF: 800-364-5521 ■ *Web:* www.hausmanfoods.com					
Schenk Packing Co Inc 8204 288th St NW	Stanwood	WA	98292	360-629-6290	629-4451
Web: www.schenkpacking.com					
Sioux-Preme Packing Co 4241 US 75th Ave	Sioux Center	IA	51250	800-735-7675	
TF General: 800-735-7675 ■ *Web:* www.siouxpreme.com					
Smithfield Foods Inc 200 Commerce St	Smithfield	VA	23430	757-365-3000	
NYSE: SFD ■ *Web:* www.smithfieldfoods.com					
Square-H Brands Inc 2731 S Soto St	Los Angeles	CA	90058	323-267-4600	261-7350
Web: www.squarehbrands.com					
Superior Farms 1480 Drew Ave Ste 100	Davis	CA	95618	530-758-3091	757-1184
TF: 800-228-5262 ■ *Web:* www.superiorfarms.com					
Thompson Packers Inc 550 Carnation St	Slidell	LA	70460	985-641-6640	
TF: 800-989-6328 ■ *Web:* www.thompack.com					
Travis Meats Inc 7210 Clinton Hwy PO Box 670	Powell	TN	37849	865-938-9051	938-9211
TF: 800-247-7606 ■ *Web:* www.travismeats.com					
Tyson Fresh Meats Inc 800 Stevens Port Dr	Dakota Dunes	SD	57049	605-235-2061	
TF: 800-416-2269 ■ *Web:* www.tyson.com					
Washington Beef LLC 201 Elmwood Rd	Toppenish	WA	98948	509-865-2121	
Web: www.wabeef.org					
Wolverine Packing Company Inc 2535 Rivard St	Detroit	MI	48207	313-259-7500	568-1909
Web: www.wolverinepacking.com					

474 MEDICAL ASSOCIATIONS - STATE

See Also Health & Medical Professionals Associations p. 1789

	City	State	Zip	Phone	Fax
Alabama Medical Assn 19 S Jackson St	Montgomery	AL	36104	800-239-6272	269-5200*
**Fax Area Code:* 334 ■ *TF:* 800-239-6272 ■ *Web:* www.alamedical.org					
Alaska State Medical Assn 4107 Laurel St	Anchorage	AK	99508	907-562-0304	561-2063
TF: 800-951-8712 ■ *Web:* www.asmadocs.org					
Arizona Medical Assn, The (ArMA) 810 W Bethany Home Rd	Phoenix	AZ	85013	602-246-8901	242-6283
TF: 800-482-3480 ■ *Web:* www.azmed.org					
Arkansas Municipal League 301 W 2nd St	North Little Rock	AR	72114	501-374-3484	
Web: www.arml.org					
Asah 2125 Hwy 33	Trenton	NJ	08690	609-890-1400	
Web: www.asah.org					
California Medical Assn 1201 J St Ste 200	Sacramento	CA	95814	916-444-5532	
Web: www.cmanet.org					
Colorado Medical Society 7351 Lowry Blvd	Denver	CO	80230	720-859-1001	859-7509
TF: 800-654-5653 ■ *Web:* www.cms.org					
Connecticut State Medical Society 160 St Ronan St	New Haven	CT	06511	203-865-0587	
TF: 800-406-1527 ■ *Web:* www.csms.org					
Delmarva Foundation For Medical Care Inc (DFMC) 28464 Marlboro Ave	Easton	MD	21601	410-822-0697	
TF: 800-999-3362 ■ *Web:* delmarvafoundation.org					
Foodbank of Southeastern Virginia 2308 Granby St	Norfolk	VA	23517	757-627-6599	
Web: www.foodbankonline.org					
Global Aquaculture Alliance Ltd Inc 5661 Telegraph Rd Ste 3a	Saint Louis	MO	63129	314-293-5500	
Web: www.gaalliance.org					
Hawaii Medical Assn 1360 S Beretania St	Honolulu	HI	96816	808-536-7702	528-2376
TF: 888-536-2792 ■ *Web:* www.hawaiimedicalassociation.org					
Health Alliance of MidAmerica LLC, The 10401 Holmes Rd Ste 280	Kansas City	MO	64131	816-941-3800	
Web: web.mhanet.com					
Idaho Medical Assn 305 W Jefferson St	Boise	ID	83702	208-344-7888	344-7903
Web: www.idmed.org					
Ihs Professional Services Inc 1632 Byron Nelson Pkwy	Southlake	TX	76092	817-296-1726	
Web: www.ihsps.com					
Illinois State Medical Society 20 N Michigan Ave Ste 700	Chicago	IL	60602	312-782-1654	782-2023
TF: 800-782-4767 ■ *Web:* www.isms.org					
Indiana State Medical Assn 322 Canal Walk	Indianapolis	IN	46202	317-261-2060	261-2076
TF: 800-257-4762 ■ *Web:* www.ismanet.org					
Iowa Medical Society 1001 Grand Ave	West Des Moines	IA	50265	515-223-1401	223-0590
TF: 800-747-3070 ■ *Web:* www.iowamedical.org					
Journal Mississippi State Medical Assn 408 W PkwyPl	Ridgeland	MS	39157	601-853-6733	
Web: msmaonline.com					
Kansas Medical Society 623 SW Tenth Ave	Topeka	KS	66612	785-235-2383	235-5114
TF: 800-332-0156 ■ *Web:* kmsonline.org					
Kentucky Medical Assn 4965 US Hwy 42 KMA Bldg Ste 2000	Louisville	KY	40222	502-426-6200	426-6877
Web: www.kyma.org					
Liberty Institutional Review Board Inc 2024 Larchmont Dr	Deland	FL	32724	386-740-9278	
Web: www.libertyirb.com					
Louisiana State Medical Society 6767 Perkins Rd Ste 100	Baton Rouge	LA	70808	225-763-8500	
TF: 800-375-9508 ■ *Web:* www.lsms.org					
Maine Medical Assn 30 Assn Dr	Manchester	ME	04351	207-622-3374	622-3332
TF: 800-772-0815 ■ *Web:* www.mainemed.com					
Maryland State Medical Society 1211 Cathedral St	Baltimore	MD	21201	410-539-0872	547-0915
TF: 800-492-1056 ■ *Web:* www.medchi.org					
Massachusetts Medical Society (MMS) 860 Winter St	Waltham	MA	02451	781-893-4610	893-8009
TF: 800-322-2303 ■ *Web:* www.massmed.org					
Mea Mft 1232 E Sixth Ave	Helena	MT	59601	406-365-4015	
Web: www.mea-mft.org					
Medical Assn of Georgia (MAG) 1849 The Exchange Ste 200	Atlanta	GA	30339	678-303-9290	303-3732
TF: 800-282-0224 ■ *Web:* www.mag.org					
Michigan State Medical Society 120 W Saginaw St	East Lansing	MI	48823	517-337-1351	337-2490
Web: www.msms.org					
Minnesota Medical Assn 1300 Godward St NE Ste 2500	Minneapolis	MN	55413	612-378-1875	378-3875
Web: www.mnmed.org					
Missouri State Medical Assn 113 Madison St	Jefferson City	MO	65101	573-636-5151	636-8552
TF: 800-869-6762 ■ *Web:* www.msma.org					
Montana Medical Assn 2021 11th Ave Ste 1	Helena	MT	59601	406-443-4000	443-4042
TF: 877-443-4000 ■ *Web:* www.mmaoffice.org					
N Ccrc 2102 Almaden Rd Ste 125	San Jose	CA	95125	408-445-3000	
Web: www.nccrc.org					
National Aamco Dealers Association 7316 Wisconsin Ave Ste 420	Bethesda	MD	20814	240-497-1500	
Web: aamcodealers.org					

				Phone	Fax
Natl Alliance for Media Arts & Culture 145 9th St Ste 230 Web: www.namac.org	San Francisco	CA	94103	415-431-1391	
Nebraska Medical Assn 233 S 13th St Ste 1200 Web: www.nebmed.org	Lincoln	NE	68508	402-474-4472	474-2198
Nevada State Medical Assn (NSMA) 3660 Baker Ln Ste 101 Web: nvdoctors.org	Reno	NV	89509	775-825-6788	825-3202
New Hampshire Medical Society 7 N State St TF: 800-564-1909 ■ Web: www.nhms.org	Concord	NH	03301	603-224-1909	226-2432
New Jersey Medical Society 2 Princess Rd TF: 800-706-7893 ■ Web: www.msnj.org	Lawrenceville	NJ	08648	609-896-1766	
New Jersey Principals and Supervisors Association 12 Centre Dr Web: www.njpsa.org	Monroe Township	NJ	08831	609-860-1200	
New Mexico Medical Society (NMMS) 316 Osuna Rd NE Ste 501 TF: 800-748-1596 ■ Web: www.nmms.org	Albuquerque	NM	87107	505-828-0237	828-0336
New York State Medical Society 865 Merrick Ave PO Box 5404 TF: 800-523-4405 ■ Web: www.mssny.org	Westbury	NY	11590	516-488-6100	488-1267
North Carolina Medical Society 222 N Person St TF: 800-722-1350 ■ Web: www.ncmedsoc.org	Raleigh	NC	27601	919-833-3836	833-2023
North Dakota Medical Assn (NDMA) 1622 I- Ave Web: www.ndmed.org	Bismarck	ND	58503	701-223-9475	223-9476
Ohio State Medical Assn 3401 Mill Run Dr TF: 800-766-6762 ■ Web: www.osma.org	Hilliard	OH	43026	614-527-6762	527-6763
Oregon Medical Assn (OMA) 11740 SW 68th Pkwy Ste 100 TF: 877-605-3229 ■ Web: www.theoma.org	Portland	OR	97223	503-619-8000	619-0609
Ovarian Cancer National Alliance Inc 910 17th St Nw Ste 1190 Web: www.ovariancancer.org	Washington	DC	20006	202-331-1332	
Penna State Education Assn Harrisburg 400 N 3rd St Web: psea.org	Harrisburg	PA	17101	717-255-7000	
Pennsylvania Medical Society 777 E Pk Dr TF: 800-228-7823 ■ Web: www.pamedsoc.org	Harrisburg	PA	17111	717-558-7750	558-7840
Permanente Federation LLC, The 1800 Harrison St 22nd Fl Web: physiciancareers.kp.org	Oakland	CA	94612	510-625-6920	
Pride South Florida 4233 Ne 6th Ave Web: pridesouthflorida.org	Oakland Park	FL	33334	954-561-2020	
Rhode Island Medical Society 235 Promenade St Ste 500 TF: 800-343-7776 ■ Web: www.rimed.org	Providence	RI	02908	401-331-3207	751-8050
Schott Management Group Llc 441 Carlisle Dr Ste D Web: www.schottmanagement.net	Herndon	VA	20170	703-437-9500	
South Carolina Medical Assn 132 W Pk Blvd TF: 800-327-1021 ■ Web: www.scmedical.org	Columbia	SC	29210	803-798-6207	772-6783
South East Health Integration Network 2-48 Dundas St W Web: www.southeastlhin.on.ca	Belleville	ON	K8P1A3	613-967-0196	
St. Louis Area Business Health Coalition 8888 Ladue Rd Ste 250 Web: www.stlbhc.org	Saint Louis	MO	63124	314-721-7800	
Texas Medical Assn 401 W 15th St TF: 800-880-1300 ■ Web: www.texmed.org	Austin	TX	78701	512-370-1300	370-1693
Texas Public Employees Association 512 E 11th St Ste 100 Web: www.tpea.org	Austin	TX	78701	512-476-2691	
Vermont Medical Society 134 Main St TF: 800-640-8767 ■ Web: www.vtmd.org	Montpelier	VT	05601	802-223-7898	223-1201
Virginia Medical Society 4205 Dover Rd TF: 800-746-6768 ■ Web: www.msv.org	Richmond	VA	23221	804-353-2721	355-6189
Washington State Medical Assn 2033 Sixth Ave Ste 1100 TF: 800-552-0612 ■ Web: www.wsma.org	Seattle	WA	98121	206-441-9762	441-5863
West Virginia State Medical Assn 4307 MacCorkle Ave SE PO Box 4106 TF: 800-257-4747 ■ Web: www.wvsma.com	Charleston	WV	25364	304-925-0342	925-0345
Wisconsin State Medical Society 330 E Lakeside St *Fax Area Code: 608 ■ TF: 866-442-3800 ■ Web: www.wisconsinmedicalsociety.org	Madison	WI	53701	866-442-3800	442-3802*
Wyoming Medical Society 122 E 17th St TF: 888-879-3599 ■ Web: www.wyomed.org	Cheyenne	WY	82001	307-635-2424	632-1973

475 MEDICAL & DENTAL EQUIPMENT & SUPPLIES - WHOL

				Phone	Fax
180 Medical Inc 5324 W Reno Ste A Web: www.180medical.com	Oklahoma City	OK	73127	405-702-7700	
480 Biomedical Inc 480 Arsenal St Web: www.480biomedical.com	Watertown	MA	02472	617-393-4600	
A Plus International Inc 5138 Eucalyptus Ave TF: 800-762-1123 ■ Web: www.aplusgroup.net	Chino	CA	91710	909-591-5168	591-0359
A to Z Logos 3947 Catamarca Dr Web: a2zlogos.espwebsite.com	San Diego	CA	92124	858-715-4775	
ABC Home Medical Supply Inc 15 E Uwchlan Ave Ste 430 TF: 866-897-8588 ■ Web: www.abc-med.com	Exton	PA	19341	866-897-8588	
Ace Medical Inc 94-910 Moloalo St TF: 866-678-3601 ■ Web: www.acemedicalinc.com	Waipahu	HI	96797	808-678-3600	678-3604
Advacare Systems 2939 N Pulaski Rd Web: www.advacaresystems.com	Chicago	IL	60641	773-725-8858	
Advanced Diagnostics Inc 2440 Cinnabar Loop Web: www.adialaska.com	Anchorage	AK	99507	907-344-3456	
Advanced Imaging Research Inc 4700 Lakeside Ave Ste 400 Web: www.advimg.com	Cleveland	OH	44114	216-426-1461	
Advanced Medical Equipment Inc 2655 S Dixie Dr Web: www.advancedmedequipment.com	Kettering	OH	45409	937-534-1080	
Adventure Medical Kits LLC 7700 Edgewater Dr Ste 526 Web: www.adventuremedicalkits.com	Oakland	CA	94624	510-261-7414	
Aeroflow Inc 3165 Sweeten Creek Rd TF: 888-345-1780 ■ Web: www.aeroflowinc.com	Asheville	NC	28803	888-345-1780	
Aethon Inc 100 Business Ctr Dr Web: www.aethon.com	Pittsburgh	PA	15205	412-322-2975	
Aktina Medical Physics Corp 360 N Route 9W TF: 888-433-3380 ■ Web: www.aktina.com	Congers	NY	10920	845-268-0101	
Allegro Industries 7221 Orangewood Ave Web: www.allegrosafety.com	Garden Grove	CA	92841	714-899-9855	
Allied 100 LLC 1800 US Hwy 51 N Web: www.aedsuperstore.com	Woodruff	WI	54568	715-358-2329	
Alma Lasers Inc 485 Half Day Rd Ste 100 Web: www.almalasers.com	Buffalo Grove	IL	60089	224-377-2000	
Alpha Imaging Inc 4455 Glenbrook Rd TF: 800-331-7327 ■ Web: www.alpha-imaging.com	Willoughby	OH	44094	440-953-3800	953-1455
Alpha Source Inc 6619 W Calumet Rd Web: www.alphasource.com	Milwaukee	WI	53223	414-760-2222	
Amber Diagnostics Inc 2180 Premier Row TF: 866-919-2959 ■ Web: www.amberusa.com	Orlando	FL	32809	407-438-7847	
Amendia Inc 1755 W Oak Pkwy TF: 877-755-3329 ■ Web: www.amendia.com	Marietta	GA	30062	678-445-3784	
American Medical Alarms Inc 4414 SE 16th Pl Ste 4 Web: www.americanmedicalalarms.com	Cape Coral	FL	33904	239-540-4655	
American Medical ID 949 Wakefield Ste 100 TF: 800-363-5985 ■ Web: www.americanmedical-id.com	Houston	TX	77018	800-363-5985	
American Medical Supplies Inc 751 Park of Commerce Dr Ste 126 Web: www.americandiabetic.com	Boca Raton	FL	33487	561-362-7105	
Ampronix Inc 15 Whatney TF: 800-400-7972 ■ Web: www.ampronix.com	Irvine	CA	92618	949-273-8000	
Anatomy Supply Partners LLC 3655 Atlanta Industrial Dr Bldg 200 Ste 250 Web: www.anatomysupply.com	Atlanta	GA	30331	404-696-6999	
Andersen Products Inc 3202 Caroline Dr Web: www.anpro.com	Haw River	NC	27258	336-376-3000	
Andrew Technologies LLC 1421 Edinger Ave Ste D TF: 888-959-7674 ■ Web: hydrasolve.com	Tustin	CA	92780	888-959-7674	
Andromed Inc 5003 Levy St Web: www.andromed.com	Saint Laurent	QC	H4R2N9	514-336-0043	
Anesthesia Service Inc 1821 N Classen Blvd TF: 800-336-3356 ■ Web: www.anesthesiaservice.com	Oklahoma City	OK	73106	405-525-3588	
Ansar Group Inc, The 240 S Eigth St TF: 888-883-7804 ■ Web: www.ans-hrv.com	Philadelphia	PA	19107	215-922-6088	922-6463
Ansell Sandel Medical Solutions LLC 19736 Dearborn St Web: www.sandelmedical.com	Chatsworth	CA	91311	818-534-2500	
AOSS Medical Supply Inc 4971 Central Ave Web: www.aossmedical.com	Monroe	LA	71203	318-325-8290	
Apelon Inc 100 Danbury Rd Ste 202 Web: www.apelon.com	Ridgefield	CT	06877	203-431-2530	
Applied Medical Technology Inc 8000 Katherine Blvd Web: www.appliedmedical.net	Brecksville	OH	44141	440-717-4000	
Aqueduct Medical Inc 665 Third St Ste 20 TF: 877-365-4325 ■ Web: www.aqueductmedical.com	San Francisco	CA	94107	877-365-4325	
AR Medicom Inc 1200 55th Ave Web: www.medicom.com	Lachine	QC	H8T3J8	514-636-6262	
Arcamed LLC 2801 Ftune Cir E Web: www.arcamed.com	Indianapolis	IN	46241	317-375-7733	
Ardus Medical Inc 11297 Grooms Rd Web: www.ardusmedical.com	Cincinnati	OH	45242	513-469-7867	
Aria Medical 1330 W Blanco Rd Web: www.ariamedical.com	San Antonio	TX	78232	210-281-9602	
Arteriocyte Medical Systems Inc 7100 Euclid Ave Research & Development Ctr Web: www.arteriocyte.com	Cleveland	OH	44103	216-456-9640	
Attentus Medical Sales Inc 5750 N Sam Houston Pkwy E Ste 406 Web: www.attentusmedical.com	Houston	TX	77032	281-776-5188	
Avalign Technologies Inc 272 E Deerpath Rd Ste 208 TF: 855-282-5446 ■ Web: www.avaligntech.com	Lake Forest	IL	60045	855-282-5446	
aycan Medical Systems LLC 693 East Ave Web: www.aycanus.com	Rochester	NY	14607	585-473-1350	
Banyan International Corp 11629 49th Pl W TF: 888-782-8548 ■ Web: www.statkit.com	Mukilteo	WA	98275	325-677-1372	
Bard Electrophysiology Inc 55 Technology Dr	Lowell	MA	01851	978-441-6202	
Benco Dental Co 295 CenterPoint Blvd TF: 800-462-3626 ■ Web: www.benco.com	Pittston	PA	18640	800-462-3626	
BidMed LLC 321 N Clark St Ste 2550 Web: bidmed.com	Chicago	IL	60654	773-840-8140	
Bisco Dental Products (Canada) Inc 2571 Smith St TF: 800-667-8811 ■ Web: www.biscocanada.com	Richmond	BC	V6X2J1	604-276-8662	
BIT MedTech operation 15870 Bernardo Ctr Dr Web: www.calmedtech.com	San Diego	CA	92127	858-613-1200	
Blickman Inc 500 US Hwy 46 E Web: www.blickman.com	Clifton	NJ	07011	973-330-0557	
Block Scientific Inc 1620 Ocean Ave Unit 3 Web: www.blockscientific.com	Bohemia	NY	11716	631-589-1118	

Company / Address	City	State	Zip	Phone	Fax
Blue Belt Technologies Inc 2905 Northwest Blvd Ste 40 — *Web:* www.bluebelttech.com	Plymouth	MN	55441	763-452-4950	
Blue Ridge X-Ray Company Inc 120 Vista Blvd — *TF:* 800-727-7290 ■ *Web:* www.blueridgex-ray.com	Arden	NC	28704	800-727-7290	
Breathe Technologies Inc 175 Technology Dr Ste 100 — *Web:* www.breathetechnologies.com	Irvine	CA	92618	949-988-7700	
BRIT Systems Inc 1909 Hi Line Dr — *Web:* www.brit.com	Dallas	TX	75207	214-630-0636	
Broadley-James Corp 19 Thomas — *Web:* www.broadleyjames.com	Irvine	CA	92618	949-829-5555	
Browns Medical Imaging 9880 Pflumm Rd — *Web:* www.brownsmedicalimaging.com	Lenexa	KS	66215	913-888-6710	
Buffalo Hospital Supply Company Inc 4039 Genesee St — *Web:* www.buffalohospital.com	Buffalo	NY	14225	716-626-9400	626-4307
Burkhart Dental Supply Co 2502 S 78th St — *TF Cust Svc:* 800-562-8176 ■ *Web:* www.burkhartdental.com	Tacoma	WA	98409	253-474-7761	472-4773
Burlington Medical Supplies Inc 3 Elmhurst St — *Web:* www.burmed.com	Newport News	VA	23603	757-888-8994	
Butler Animal Health Supply LLC 400 Metro Pl N — *TF PR:* 888-691-2724 ■ *Web:* www.accessbutler.com	Dublin	OH	43017	614-761-9095	659-1653
Byram Healthcare Centers Inc 120 Bloomingdale Rd — *TF:* 800-354-4054 ■ *Web:* www.byramhealthcare.com	White Plains	NY	10605	914-286-2000	
CAN-med Healthcare 200 Bluewater Rd — *TF:* 800-565-7553 ■ *Web:* www.canmedhealthcare.com	Bedford	NS	B4B1G9	902-455-4649	
Canadian Hospital Specialties ULC 2810 Coventry Rd — *TF:* 800-461-1423 ■ *Web:* www.chsltd.com	Oakville	ON	L6H6R1	905-825-9300	
Capital X-Ray Inc 2189 Notasulga Rd — *Web:* www.capitalxray.com	Tallassee	AL	36078	334-283-8410	
Cardiac Dimensions Inc 5540 Lk Washington Blvd NE — *Web:* www.cardiacdimensions.com	Kirkland	WA	98033	425-605-5900	
CardioGrip Corp 12554 W Bridger St Ste 108 — *Web:* www.zona.com	Boise	ID	83713	208-322-9399	
CardioMed Supplies Inc 199 Saint David St — *TF:* 800-387-9757 ■ *Web:* www.cardiomed.com	Lindsay	ON	K9V5K7	705-328-2518	328-9747
Care Medical Systems 1840 S Central St	Visalia	CA	93277	559-741-9005	
CAREstream Medical Ltd 20133 102 Ave Units 1 — **Fax Area Code:* 888 ■ *Web:* www.carestreammedical.com	Langley	BC	V1M4B4	604-552-5486	310-2187*
Carl Zeiss Canada Ltd 45 Valleybrook D — *Web:* www.zeiss.ca	Toronto	ON	M3B2S6	416-449-4660	449-3524
Carolina Apothecary Inc 726 S Scales St — *Web:* www.carolinaapothecary.com	Reidsville	NC	27320	336-342-0071	
Cascade Orthopedic Supply Inc 2638 Aztec Dr — *Web:* www.cascade-usa.com	Chico	CA	95928	530-879-1500	
Cassling Diagnostic Imaging Inc 13808 F St — *Web:* www.cassling.com	Omaha	NE	68137	402-334-5000	
Castlewood Surgical Inc 91 Main St Ste 302 — *Web:* www.castlewoodsurgical.com	Concord	MA	01742	978-610-6321	
Cbaia 1125 Jefferson Davis Hwy Ste 380 — *Web:* www.cbaia.com	Fredericksburg	VA	22401	540-604-9731	
CCS Medical Inc 1505 LBJ Fwy Ste 600 — *TF:* 800-726-9811 ■ *Web:* www.ccsmed.com	Farmers Branch	TX	75234	800-260-8193	
CellAegis Devices Inc 139 Mulock Ave 1st Fl — *Web:* www.cellaegisdevices.com	Toronto	ON	M6N1G9	647-722-9601	
Centennial Optical Ltd 158 Norfinch Dr — *Web:* www.centennialoptical.com	Toronto	ON	M3N1X6	416-739-8539	
CenTrak Inc 125 Pheasant Run Ste 102 — *Web:* www.centrak.com	Newtown	PA	18940	215-860-2928	
Central Medical Equipment Rentals Inc 2850 Douglas Rd 3rd Fl — *Web:* www.empmed.com	Coral Gables	FL	33134	305-441-0156	
CERAGEM International Inc 3699 Wilshire Blvd Ste 900 — *Web:* www.ceragem.com	Los Angeles	CA	90010	213-480-7070	
Charter Medical Ltd 3948-A Westpoint Blvd — *Web:* www.chartermedical.com	Winston-Salem	NC	27103	336-768-6447	
CHME Inc 289 Foster City Blvd Ste A — *Web:* www.chme.org	Foster City	CA	94404	650-357-8550	
Citagenix Inc 1111 Autoroute Chomedy — *Web:* www.citagenix.com	Laval	QC	H7W5J8	450-688-8699	688-1977
Clarion Medical Technologies Inc 125 Fleming Dr — *Web:* www.clarionmedical.com	Cambridge	ON	N1T2B8	519-620-3900	
Colson Associates Inc 1 N Franklin St Site 2420 — *Web:* www.colsongroup.com	Chicago	IL	60606	312-980-1100	
Columbia Medical Manufacturing LLC 11724 Willake St — *Web:* www.columbiamedical.com	Santa Fe Springs	CA	90670	562-282-0244	
Comedical Inc 7100 Roosevelt Way NE — *Web:* www.comedical.com	Seattle	WA	98115	206-524-7424	
Companion Health Services Inc 284 N St — *Web:* www.companionhealthservices.com	Boston	MA	02113	617-227-0830	
Connect America LLC 2193 W Chester Pk — *TF:* 800-654-6100 ■ *Web:* connectamerica.com	Broomall	PA	19008	800-654-6100	
Core Medical Imaging Inc 6161 Ne 175th St Ste 201 — *TF:* 800-809-9729 ■ *Web:* www.coremedicalimaging.com	Kenmore	WA	98028	425-485-4330	
Cortech Solutions Inc 1409 Audubon Blvd Ste B1 — *Web:* www.cortechsolutions.com	Wilmington	NC	28403	910-362-1143	
Crest Services 3015 Merle Hay Rd Ste 6 — *Web:* crestservices.org	Des Moines	IA	50310	515-331-1200	
Cygnus Manufacturing Company LLC Victory Rd Business Park 491 Chantler Dr — *Web:* www.cmc-usa.com	Saxonburg	PA	16056	724-352-8000	
D&B Industrial Group 21649 Cedar Creek Ave — *Web:* www.dbindustrialgroup.com	Georgetown	DE	19947	302-855-0585	
Dalton Medical Corp 1435 Bradley Ln Ste 100 — *Web:* www.daltonmedical.com	Carrollton	TX	75007	972-418-5129	
Decision Diagnostics Corp 2660 Townsgate Rd Ste 300 — *Web:* www.instacare.net	Westlake Village	CA	91361	805-446-1973	
Dectro International Inc 1000 Blvd du Parc-Technologique — *TF:* 800-463-5566 ■ *Web:* www.dectro.com	Quebec	QC	G1P4S3	418-650-0303	
Dedicated Distribution Inc 640 Miami Ave — *TF:* 800-325-8367 ■ *Web:* www.dedicateddistribution.com	Kansas City	KS	66105	913-371-2200	
Delta Medical Systems Inc W239 N2890 Pewaukee Rd Unit E — *Web:* www.deltamedicalsystems.com	Pewaukee	WI	53072	262-523-2300	
Dentsply Canada Ltd 161 Vinyl Ct — *Web:* www.dentsply.com	Woodbridge	ON	L4L4A3	905-851-6060	
Derma Sciences Inc 214 Carnegie Ctr Ste 100 — *TF:* 800-825-4325 ■ *Web:* www.dermasciences.com	Princeton	NJ	08540	609-514-4744	514-8554
DogLeggs LLC 2104 Thomas View Rd — *Web:* www.dogleggs.com	Reston	VA	20191	703-715-0300	
Dr Fresh Inc 6645 Caballero Blvd — *TF:* 866-373-7371 ■ *Web:* www.drfreshdental.com	Buena Park	CA	90620	714-690-1573	
DRE Inc 1800 Williamson Ct — *Web:* www.dremed.com	Louisville	KY	40223	502-244-4444	
Dukal Corp 2 Flee2od Ct — *Web:* www.dukal.com	Ronkonkoma	NY	11779	631-656-3800	
Dura Medical Equipment Inc 7835 NW 148 St — *Web:* www.bayshoreduramedical.com	Miami Lakes	FL	33016	305-821-1202	
Dynamic Medical Systems Inc 2811 E Ana St — *Web:* www.godynamic.com	Rancho Dominguez	CA	90221	310-928-0251	
Eagle Laboratories Inc 10201-A Trademark St — *Web:* www.eaglelabs.com	Rancho Cucamonga	CA	91730	909-481-0011	
Electra-med Corp 5332 Hill 23 Dr — *Web:* www.electramed.com	Flint	MI	48507	810-232-4856	
Electromek Diagnostic Systems Inc 412 W US Hwy 40 — *Web:* www.electromek.com	Troy	IL	62294	618-667-6761	
elliquence LLC 2455 Grand Ave — *Web:* www.elliquence.com	Baldwin	NY	11510	516-277-9000	
Endomedix Inc 211 Warren St — *Web:* www.endomedix.com	Newark	NJ	07103	848-248-1883	
EndoShape Inc 2450 Central Ave Ste I — *Web:* www.endoshape.com	Boulder	CO	80301	303-951-6898	
Endotec Inc 20 Valley St — *Web:* www.endotec.com	South Orange	NJ	07079	973-762-6100	
Engineered Medical Systems Inc 2055 Executive Dr — *Web:* www.engmedsys.com	Indianapolis	IN	46241	317-246-5500	
Enthermics Inc W164 N9221 Water St — *TF:* 800-862-9276 ■ *Web:* www.enthermics.com	Menomonee Falls	WI	53051	262-251-8356	
Erchonia Corp 2021 Commerce Dr — *Web:* www.erchonia.com	Mckinney	TX	75069	214-544-2227	
Evaheart Medical USA Inc 880 William Pitt Way Ste B1-330 — *Web:* www.evaheart-usa.com	Pittsburgh	PA	15238	412-828-7090	
Evans-Sherratt Co 13050 Northend Ave — *TF:* 800-248-3826	Oak Park	MI	48237	248-584-5500	584-5510
eVent Medical Inc 971 Calle Amanecer Ste 101 — *Web:* www.event-medical.com	San Clemente	CA	92673	949-492-8368	
Evis Medical Equipment Inc 751 Maple Ave — *Web:* www.evismedical.com	Hartford	CT	06114	860-296-3565	
Expeditor Systems Inc 4090 Nine McFarland Dr — *TF:* 800-226-8158 ■ *Web:* www.expeditor.com	Alpharetta	GA	30004	800-226-8158	
Feta Med Inc 530 S Henderson Rd Ste D — *Web:* www.fetamed.com	King Of Prussia	PA	19406	610-205-0010	
First Coast Hearing Clinic Inc 1835 Us Hwy 1 S Ste 121 — *Web:* www.firstcoasthearing.com	Saint Augustine	FL	32084	904-429-3823	
Flanagan Instruments Inc 633 Village Ln N — *Web:* www.flanagan.com	Mandeville	LA	70471	985-626-3786	
FMI Inc 2382 United Ln — *Web:* www.fmimed.com	Elk Grove Village	IL	60007	847-350-1535	
Freedom Designs Inc 2241 N Madera Rd — *Web:* www.freedomdesigns.com	Simi Valley	CA	93065	805-582-0077	
GE Walker Inc 3502-C Queen Palm Dr — *Web:* www.gewalker.com	Tampa	FL	33619	813-623-2481	
Global Medical Imaging LLC 222 Rampart St — *TF:* 800-958-9986 ■ *Web:* www.gmi3.com	Charlotte	NC	28203	800-958-9986	
Global Medical LLC 8332 Bristol Ct Ste 108 — *TF:* 800-528-1001	Jessup	MD	20794	800-528-1001	
Global Resources International Inc 4142 Industry Way — *Web:* www.gri-usa.com	Flowery Branch	GA	30542	678-866-0550	
Goetze Dental 3939 NE 33 Terrace — *TF:* 800-692-0804 ■ *Web:* www.goetzedental.com	Kansas City	MO	64117	816-413-1200	
Griffin Home Health Care Inc 4231 Monroe Rd — *Web:* www.griffinhomehealthcare.com	Charlotte	NC	28205	704-347-1993	
Griswold Machine & Engineering Inc 8530 M 60 — *TF:* 800-248-2054 ■ *Web:* www.gme-shields.com	Union City	MI	49094	517-741-4300	
Grogans Health Care Supply Inc 1016 S Broadway St — *TF:* 800-365-1020 ■ *Web:* www.grogans.com	Lexington	KY	40504	859-254-6661	254-6666
Halyard Health Inc 5405 Windward Pkwy — *Web:* www.halyardhealth.com	Alpharetta	GA	30004	678-425-9273	

				Phone	Fax
Hanson Medical Systems Inc 1954 Howell Branch Rd Ste 203 *TF:* 877-671-3883 ■ *Web:* www.hansonmedicalsystems.com	Winter Park	FL	32792	407-671-3883	
Hardy Diagnostics Inc 1430 W Mccoy Ln *Web:* www.hardydiagnostics.com	Santa Maria	CA	93455	805-346-2766	
Healthcom 1600 W Jackson St *TF:* 800-525-6237 ■ *Web:* www.healthcominc.com	Sullivan	IL	61951	800-525-6237	
Hegele Logistic LLC 1460 Brummel Ave *Web:* www.hegelelogistic.com	Elk Grove	IL	60007	847-690-0430	
Helm Surgical Systems LLC 5895 E Evans Ave Ste 100 *Web:* www.helmsurgical.com	Denver	CO	80222	720-524-1900	
HemaSource Inc 4158 Nike Dr Ste B *Web:* www.hemasource.com	West Jordan	UT	84088	801-280-5151	
Henry Schein Inc 135 Duryea Rd *NASDAQ: HSIC* ■ *TF:* 800-582-2702 ■ *Web:* www.henryschein.com	Melville	NY	11747	631-843-5500	843-5652
Hi-Tech Healthcare Inc 1805 Shackleford Ct Ste 100	Norcross	GA	30093	770-449-6785	
Holt Dental Supply Inc N30 W22383 Green Rd Ste A *Web:* holtdentalsupply.com	Waukesha	WI	53186	262-896-9380	
Home Care Specialists Inc 113 Neck Rd *Web:* www.hcshme.com	Haverhill	MA	01835	978-373-7771	
Hospi Tel Manufacturing Corp 545 N Arlington Ave Ste 7 *TF:* 800-631-0462 ■ *Web:* www.hospitel.com	East Orange	NJ	07017	973-678-7100	
Hospira Healthcare Corp 1111 Dr Frederik-Philips Blvd Ste 600 *Web:* www.hospira.ca	Saint-laurent	QC	H4M2X6	514-905-2600	
HRM USA Inc 1039 Pulinski Rd *Web:* www.heartratemonitorsusa.com	Warminster	PA	18974	215-259-2700	
HyperBranch Medical Technology Inc 800-12 Capitola Dr *Web:* www.hyperbranch.com	Durham	NC	27713	919-433-3325	
IC Medical Inc 2340 W Shangri La Rd *Web:* www.icmedical.com	Phoenix	AZ	85029	623-780-0700	
Indigo ORB Inc 2454 Alton Pkwy *Web:* www.indigo-orb.com	Irvine	CA	92606	949-784-0303	
Innovative Optics Inc 6812 Hemlock Ln *Web:* www.innovativeoptics.com	Maple Grove	MN	55369	763-425-7789	
Instratek Inc 15200 Middlebrook Dr Ste G *Web:* www.instratek.com	Houston	TX	77058	281-890-8020	
Instrumed International Inc 626 Cooper Ct *Web:* www.instrumedinc.biz	Schaumburg	IL	60173	847-908-0292	
Intact Medical Corp 550 Cochituate Rd Ste 25 East Wing Fl 4 *Web:* www.intactmedical.com	Framingham	MA	01701	508-655-7820	
Integra LifeSciences Corp 311 Enterprise Dr *Web:* www.integralife.com/index.aspx?redir=lower%20extremity	Plainsboro	NJ	08536	609-275-5363	
International Manufacturing Group Inc 879 F St Ste 120 *TF:* 800-775-6412	West Sacramento	CA	95605	800-775-6412	
Interplex Medical LLC 25 Whitney Dr *Web:* www.interplexmedical.com	Milford	OH	45150	513-248-5120	
Intrinsic Therapeutics Inc 30 Commerce Way *Web:* www.intrinsic-therapeutics.com	Woburn	MA	01801	781-932-0222	
Invuity Inc 444 De Haro St *Web:* www.invuity.com	San Francisco	CA	94107	415-655-2100	
Iowa Veterinary Supply Co (IVESCO) 124 Country Club Rd	Iowa Falls	IA	50126	641-648-2529	648-5994
Jordan Reses Supply Company LLC 24 Frank Lloyd Wright Dr Ste A3300 *Web:* www.jrsupplyco.com	Ann Arbor	MI	48106	734-213-5528	
Jorgensen Laboratories Inc 1450 Van Buren Ave *TF:* 800-525-5614 ■ *Web:* www.jorvet.com	Loveland	CO	80538	970-669-2500	663-5042
Kapstone Medical LLC 100 E S Main St *Web:* www.kapstonemedical.com	Waxhaw	NC	28173	704-843-7852	
Karl Storz Endoscopy-america Inc 600 Corporate Pt *TF:* 800-321-1304 ■ *Web:* www.karlstorz.com	Culver City	CA	90230	310-338-8100	
KCI Medical Canada Inc 75 Courtneypark Dr W Unit No 2 *TF:* 800-668-5403 ■ *Web:* www.kci-medical.ca	Mississauga	ON	L5W0E3	905-565-7187	
KD Scientific Inc 84 October Hill Rd *Web:* www.kdscientific.com	Holliston	MA	01746	508-429-6809	
Keir Surgical Ltd 408 E Kent Ave S Ste 126 *Web:* www.keirsurgical.com	Vancouver	BC	V5X2X7	604-261-9596	
Kentec Medical Inc 17871 Fitch *TF:* 800-825-5996 ■ *Web:* www.kentecmedical.com	Irvine	CA	92614	949-863-0810	833-9730
Keystone Industries 480 S Democrat Rd *TF:* 800-333-3131 ■ *Web:* www.keystoneindustries.com	Gibbstown	NJ	08027	856-663-4700	224-9444
Laerdal Medical Corp 167 Myers Corners Rd PO Box 1840 *Web:* www.laerdal.com	Wappingers Falls	NY	12590	845-297-7770	
LaserBand LLC 120 S Central Ave Ste 450	St. Louis	MO	63105	314-726-1060	
Leeches USA Ltd 300 Shames Dr *TF:* 800-645-3569 ■ *Web:* www.leechesusa.com	Westbury	NY	11590	516-333-2570	997-4948
LENSAR Inc 2800 Discovery Dr *TF:* 888-536-7271 ■ *Web:* www.lensar.com	Orlando	FL	32826	888-536-7271	
Les Wilkins & Assoc Inc 6850 35th Ave NE *TF:* 800-426-6634 ■ *Web:* www.leswilkins.com	Seattle	WA	98115	206-522-0908	522-5292
Life Systems Inc 515 Trade Ctr Blvd *Web:* www.lifesystemsinc.com	Chesterfield	MO	63005	636-787-2100	
Life-Assist Inc 11277 Sunrise Park Dr *TF:* 800-824-6016 ■ *Web:* www.life-assist.com	Rancho Cordova	CA	95742	800-824-6016	
Logi-D Holding Inc 5550 des Rossignols Blvd *Web:* www.logi-d.net	Laval	QC	H7L5W6	450-628-8800	
Mabis Healthcare Inc 1931 Norman Dr *TF:* 800-526-4753 ■ *Web:* www.mabisdmi.com	Waukegan	IL	60085	800-526-4753	479-7968
Mada Medical Products Inc 625 Washington Ave *TF:* 800-526-6370 ■ *Web:* www.madamedical.com	Carlstadt	NJ	07072	201-460-0454	460-3509
Magnaserv Enterprises Inc 2862 SE Monroe St *Web:* www.magnaserv.com	Stuart	FL	34997	772-219-2229	
Majestic Medical Solutions Inc 17424 Airline Hwy Ste 12 *Web:* majesticms.com	Prairieville	LA	70769	225-677-9867	
Maquet-Dynamed Inc 235 Shields Ct *TF:* 800-227-7215 ■ *Web:* www.maquet-dynamed.com	Markham	ON	L3R8V2	905-752-3300	
Marketlab Inc 6850 Southbelt Dr **Fax Area Code:* 616 ■ *TF:* 866-237-3722 ■ *Web:* marketlab.com	Caledonia	MI	49316	866-237-3722	656-2475*
MAST Biosurgery Inc 6749 Top Gun St Ste 108 *Web:* www.mastbio.com	San Diego	CA	92121	858-550-8050	
Materna Medical Inc 2500 Grant Rd *Web:* www.maternamedical.com	Mountain View	CA	94040	415-254-1031	
Mati Therapeutics Inc 4317 Dunning Ln *Web:* www.matitherapeutics.com	Austin	TX	78746	512-329-6360	
MC Healthcare Products Inc 4658 Ontario St **Fax Area Code:* 905 ■ *TF:* 800-268-8671 ■ *Web:* www.mchealthcare.com	Beamsville	ON	L0R1B4	800-268-8671	563-8680*
MCI Optonix LLC 253 E Washington Ave *Web:* www.mcio.com	Washington	NJ	07882	908-835-0004	
McKesson Medical Group Extended Care 8121 Tenth Ave N **Fax Area Code:* 763 ■ *TF:* 800-328-8111 ■ *Web:* www.mbbnet.umn.edu/company_folder/mckhboc-mgec.html	Golden Valley	MN	55427	800-328-8111	595-6677*
McKesson Medical-Surgical 8741 Landmark Rd *TF:* 800-446-3008 ■ *Web:* www.mckesson.com	Richmond	VA	23228	415-983-8300	
MD International Inc 11300 NW 41st St	Miami	FL	33178	305-669-9003	
Med 4 Home Inc 10800 N Congress Ave *Web:* www.med4home.com	Kansas City	MO	64153	816-801-7400	
MED-EL Corp 2511 Old Cornwallis Rd Ste 100 *Web:* www.medel.com	Durham	NC	27713	919-572-2222	
Med-Fit Systems Inc 3553 Rosa Way *Web:* www.medfitsystems.com	Fallbrook	CA	92028	760-723-9618	
MedaCheck LLC 602 Main St Fourth Fl Ste 401 *Web:* www.medacheck.com	Cincinnati	OH	45202	513-488-1111	
MedAvail Technologies Inc 6665 Millcreek Dr Unit No1 *Web:* www.medavail.com	Mississauga	ON	L5N5M4	905-812-0023	
Medcare Products Inc 151 E Cliff Rd *Web:* medcarelifts.com	Burnsville	MN	55337	952-894-7076	
Medi-Globe Corp 110 W Orion St Ste 136 *Web:* www.mediglobe.com	Tempe	AZ	85283	480-897-2772	
Medical Indicators Inc 1589 Reed Rd *Web:* medicalindicators.com	Pennington	NJ	08534	609-737-1600	
Medical Treatment Systems Inc 6300 Westgate Rd Ste A	Raleigh	NC	27617	919-782-9050	
MedicaMetrix Inc 1 Old Sudbury Rd *Web:* www.medicametrix.com	Wayland	MA	01778	617-694-1713	
MediCapture Inc 580 W Germantown Pk Ste 103 *Web:* www.medicapture.com	Plymouth Meeting	PA	19462	610-238-0700	
Medigroup Services Corp 1360 S Fifth St Ste 334 *Web:* www.medigroup.com	St. Charles	MO	63301	636-947-7555	
Medison Econet Corp 7260 NW 58th St *Web:* www.medisoneconet.com	Miami	FL	33166	305-599-7161	
MedSignals Corp 217 Alamo Plz *Web:* www.medsignals.com	San Antonio	TX	78205	210-222-2067	
MedSupply 5850 E Shields Ave Ste 105 *Web:* www.gomedsupply.net	Fresno	CA	93727	559-292-1540	
MEPS Real-Time Inc 2841 Loker Ave E *Web:* www.mepsrealtime.com	Carlsbad	CA	92010	760-448-9500	
Mercy Surgical Dressing Group Inc 4 Zesta Dr *Web:* www.myinfinitum.com	Pittsburgh	PA	15205	412-788-5200	
Mergenet Solutions Inc 6601 Lyons Rd Ste B1-B4 *Web:* www.mergenetsolutions.com	Coconut Creek	FL	33073	561-208-3770	
Merry X-Ray Corp 4444 Viewridge Ave Ste A *Web:* www.merryxray.com	San Diego	CA	92123	858-565-4472	
Mesa Laboratories Inc 12100 W Sixth Ave *NASDAQ: MLAB* ■ *TF Sales:* 800-992-6372 ■ *Web:* www.mesalabs.com	Lakewood	CO	80228	303-987-8000	987-8989
Micro Bio-Medics Inc 14 Pelham Pkwy	Pelham	NY	10803	914-738-9200	
Midway Dental Supply Inc 701 N Michigan St *Web:* www.midwaydental.com	Lakeville	IN	46536	574-784-2533	
MinXray Inc 3611 Commercial Ave *Web:* www.minxray.com	Northbrook	IL	60062	847-564-0323	
Mio 2930 Arbutus St *TF:* 877-770-1116 ■ *Web:* www.mioglobal.com	Vancouver	BC	V6J3Y9	604-224-9184	
Mizuho OSI Inc 30031 Ahern Ave *Web:* www.mizuhosi.com	Union City	CA	94587	510-429-1500	
Mmar Medical Group Inc 9619 Yupondale Dr *Web:* www.mmarmedical.com	Houston	TX	77080	713-465-2003	465-2818
Mobile Medical International Corp 2176 Portland St PO Box 672 *Web:* www.mobile-medical.com	St. Johnsbury	VT	05819	802-748-2322	
Modo Inc 20325 NW von Neumann Dr Ste 170 *Web:* www.modocarts.com	Beaverton	OR	97006	503-690-1400	
Monarch Medical Imaging Equipment Inc 101 Ellis St *Web:* www.monarchmedical.com	Staten Island	NY	10307	718-317-0124	
Monebo Technologies Inc 1800 Barton Creek Blvd *Web:* www.monebo.com	Austin	TX	78735	512-732-0235	732-0285
Monteris Medical Inc 16305 36th Ave N Ste 200 *Web:* www.monteris.com	Plymouth	MN	55446	763-253-4710	
Moore Medical Corp 389 John Downey Dr **Fax Area Code:* 800 ■ *TF Sales:* 800-234-1464 ■ *Web:* www.mooremedical.com	New Britain	CT	06050	860-826-3600	944-6667*
Nanamed LLC 157 Veterans Dr *Web:* www.nanamed.com	Northvale	NJ	07647	201-383-1101	

Company / Address	City	State	Zip	Phone	Fax
Nashville Dental Inc 1229 Northgate Business Pkwy *Web:* www.nashvilledental.com	Madison	TN	37115	615-868-3911	
National HME Inc 7451 Airport Fwy *Web:* www.nationalhme.com	Richland Hills	TX	76118	817-332-4433	
Nationwide Medical Equipment Inc 1510 Stuart Rd Ste 109 *Web:* www.nme.cc	Cleveland	TN	37312	423-478-7433	
Nbn Infusions 2 Pin Oak Ln Ste 250 *Web:* www.nbnrespiratory.com	Cherry Hill	NJ	08003	856-669-0217	
NCD Corp 33801 Curtis Blvd Ste 100 *Web:* www.ncdcorp.com	Eastlake	OH	44095	440-953-4488	
ndd Medical Technologies Inc 2 Dundee Park *Web:* www.nddmed.com	Andover	MA	01810	978-470-0923	
NEI Treatment Systems LLC 3530 Wilshire Blvd Ste 1130 *Web:* www.nei-marine.com	Los Angeles	CA	90010	213-383-5855	
NeoMed Inc 100 Londonderry Ct Ste 112 *Web:* www.neomedinc.com	Woodstock	GA	30188	770-516-2225	
NeoTract Inc 4473 Willow Rd Ste 100 *Web:* www.neotract.com	Pleasanton	CA	94588	925-401-0700	
Neoventa Medical Inc 226 Lowell St *Web:* www.neoventa.com	Wilmington	MA	01887	978-657-7750	
Nesch LLC 9800 Connecticut Dr *Web:* www.neschllc.com	Crown Point	IN	46307	219-644-3505	
Neta Scientific Inc 4206 Sylon Blvd *Web:* www.netascientific.com	Hainesport	NJ	08036	609-265-8210	
Neuro Kinetics Inc 128 Gamma Dr *Web:* www.neuro-kinetics.com	Pittsburgh	PA	15238	412-963-6649	
Neuro-Tec Inc 975 Cobb Pl Blvd Ste 301 *TF:* 800-554-3407 ■ *Web:* www.neurotec.net	Kennesaw	GA	30144	800-554-3407	
NeuroPace Inc 455 N Bernardo Ave *Web:* www.neuropace.com	Mountain View	CA	94043	650-237-2700	
New Star Lasers Inc 9085 Foothills Blvd *Web:* www.newstarlasers.com	Roseville	CA	95747	916-677-1900	
Nidek Inc 47651 Westinghouse Dr *Web:* usa.nidek.com	Fremont	CA	94539	510-226-5700	
Nihon Kohden America Inc 90 Icon *TF:* 800-325-0283 ■ *Web:* us.nihonkohden.com	Foothill Ranch	CA	92610	949-580-1555	580-1550
Nipro Medical Corp 3150 NW 107th Ave *Web:* www.nipro.com	Miami	FL	33172	305-599-7174	
Niveus Medical Inc 849 Independence Ave Ste C *Web:* www.niveusmedical.com	Mountain View	CA	94043	650-336-7922	
Noraxon U.S.A. Inc 15770 N Greenway-Hayden Loop Ste 100 *Web:* www.noraxon.com	Scottsdale	AZ	85260	480-443-3413	
North American Medical Corp 1649 Sands Pl SE Ste A *Web:* www.namcorporation.com	Marietta	GA	30067	770-541-0012	
North American Rescue LLC 35 Tedwall Ct *Web:* www.narescue.com	Greer	SC	29650	864-675-9800	
Northern X-ray Co 2118 Fourth Ave S *Web:* www.nxcimaging.com	Minneapolis	MN	55404	612-870-1561	
Nova Ortho-Med Inc 1470 Beachey Pl *Web:* www.novamedicalproducts.com	Carson	CA	90746	310-352-3600	
Novocor Medical Systems Inc 8408 Old Deer Trail *Web:* www.novocormed.com	Raleigh	NC	27615	919-368-0522	
novoGI Inc PO Box 12363 *TF:* 866-295-7125 ■ *Web:* www.novogi.com	Atlanta	GA	30355	866-295-7125	
Nuclear Imaging Services LLC 11050 W Little York Rd *Web:* www.nis-mit.com	Houston	TX	77041	832-467-4404	
Numotion Inc 975 Hornet Dr *Web:* www.numotion.com	Hazelwood	MO	63042	314-731-7867	
Nurse Assist Inc 3400 Northern Cross Blvd *Web:* www.nurseassist.com	Fort Worth	TX	76137	817-231-1300	
NuvoMed Inc 2300 E Roy St *Web:* www.nuvomed.com	Seattle	WA	98112	206-999-9387	
Oakworks Inc 923 E Wellspring Rd *TF:* 800-558-8850 ■ *Web:* www.oakworks.com	New Freedom	PA	17349	717-235-6807	235-6798
Odyssey Medical Inc 2975 Brother Blvd *Web:* www.odysseymed.com	Bartlett	TN	38133	901-383-7777	
OEC Medical Systems Inc 384 Wright Brothers Dr *Web:* www.gehealthcare.com	Salt Lake City	UT	84116	801-328-9300	
Omar Medical Supplies Inc Holiday Plz Dr Ste 130 *Web:* www.omarinc.com	Matteson	IL	60443	708-679-0347	
Omega Medical Health Systems Inc 1200 E High St Ste 106 *TF:* 866-716-6342 ■ *Web:* www.omegamedicalsystems.com	Pottstown	PA	19464	866-716-6342	
Omron Healthcare Inc 1925 W Field Ct **Fax:* Cust Svc ■ *TF:* 877-216-1333 ■ *Web:* www.omronhealthcare.com	Lake Forest	IL	60045	847-680-6200	680-6269*
Ondal USA 5140 Commerce Rd *Web:* ondal.com	Richmond	VA	23234	804-279-0320	
Online Engineering Inc 400 N Cedar St *Web:* www.online-engineering.com	Manistique	MI	49854	906-341-0090	
Onyx Medical Corp 1800 N Shelby Oaks Dr *Web:* www.onyxmedical.net	Memphis	TN	38134	901-323-6699	
OptiNose US Inc 1010 Stony Hill Rd Ste 375 *Web:* www.optinose.com	Yardley	PA	19067	267-364-3500	
Optonol Inc P.O. Box 2367 *TF:* 877-707-3937 ■ *Web:* www.optonol.com	Kansas City	KS	66110	877-707-3937	
Oral BioTech 812 Water Ave NE *Web:* www.carifree.com	Albany	OR	97321	541-928-4445	
Oral-B Laboratories 600 Clipper Dr Ste 200 *TF:* 800-566-7252 ■ *Web:* www.oralb.com	Belmont	CA	94002	800-566-7252	
Organ Recovery Systems Inc 1 Pierce Pl Ste 475W *Web:* www.organ-recovery.com	Itasca	IL	60143	847-824-2600	
Ortho Kinematics Inc 7004 Bee Cave Rd Bldg III Ste 315 *Web:* www.orthokinematics.com	Austin	TX	78746	512-334-5490	
Orthodontic Design & Production Inc 1370 Decision St Ste D *Web:* www.odpinc.com	Vista	CA	92083	760-734-3995	
Orthopedic Designs North America Inc 5912 Breckenridge Pkwy Ste F *TF:* 888-635-8535 ■ *Web:* www.odi-na.com	Tampa	FL	33610	888-635-8535	
Otologics LLC 5445 Airport Blvd *Web:* www.otologics.com	Boulder	CO	80301	303-448-9933	
Otto Bock Healthcare North America Inc 2 Carlson Pkwy N Ste 100 *TF:* 800-328-4058 ■ *Web:* www.ottobockus.com	Minneapolis	MN	55447	763-553-9464	
Owens & Minor Inc 9120 Lockwood Blvd *NYSE: OMI* ■ *Web:* www.owens-minor.com	Mechanicsville	VA	23116	804-723-7000	723-7100
Paragon Medical Inc 8 Matchett Industrial Park Dr *Web:* www.paragonmedical.com	Pierceton	IN	46562	574-594-2140	
Parmenter Realty Partners 701 Brickell Ave Ste 2020 *Web:* www.parmco.com	Miami	FL	33131	305-379-7500	
PatientSafe Solutions Inc 5375 Mira Sorrento Pl Ste 500 *Web:* www.patientsafesolutions.com	San Diego	CA	92121	858-746-3100	
Patterson Cos Inc 1031 Mendota Heights Rd *NASDAQ: PDCO* ■ *TF:* 800-328-5536 ■ *Web:* www.pattersondental.com	Saint Paul	MN	55120	651-686-1600	686-9331
Patterson Dental Canada Inc 1205 Henri Bourassa Blvd *Web:* www.pattersondental.com/en-ca	West Montreal	QC	H3M3E6	514-745-4040	745-0596
Pearson Dental Supplies Inc 13161 Telfair Ave **Fax Area Code:* 800 ■ *TF:* 800-535-4535 ■ *Web:* www.pearsondental.com	Sylmar	CA	91342	818-362-2600	835-3100*
Pelvalon Inc 923 Thompson Pl *Web:* www.pelvalon.com	Sunnyvale	CA	94085	650-276-0130	
PenRad Technologies Inc 114 Commerce Cir *Web:* www.penrad.com	Buffalo	MN	55313	763-475-3388	
PerceptiMed Inc 365 San Antonio Rd *Web:* perceptimed.com	Mountain View	CA	94040	650-941-7000	
Perio Sciences LLC 11700 Preston Rd Ste 660 *Web:* www.periosciences.com	Dallas	TX	75230	214-953-6818	
Permobil Inc 6961 Eastgate Blvd **Fax Area Code:* 800 ■ *TF:* 800-736-0925 ■ *Web:* www.permobil.com	Lebanon	TN	37090	615-443-2839	231-3256*
PerSys Medical Co 5310 Elm St *TF:* 888-737-7978 ■ *Web:* www.ps-med.com	Houston	TX	77081	888-737-7978	
Pharmed Corp 24340 Sperry Dr	Westlake	OH	44145	440-835-0660	
Philips Healthcare 22100 Bothell Everett Hwy *Web:* www.dunlee.com	Bothell	WA	98021	425-487-7000	
Physcient Inc 112 S Duke St Ste 4A *Web:* www.physcient.com	Durham	NC	27701	919-686-0300	
PickPoint Corp 4234 Hacienda Dr Ste 101 *Web:* www.pickpoint.com	Pleasanton	CA	94588	925-924-1700	
Pivot Medical Inc 247 Humboldt Courtyard *Web:* www.pivotmedical.com	Sunnyvale	CA	94089	408-774-1452	
Platinum Medical Imaging LLC 1027 SW 30th Ave *TF:* 888-673-5151 ■ *Web:* www.platinummedicalparts.com	Deerfield Beach	FL	33442	888-673-5151	
PMT Corp 1500 Park Rd *Web:* www.pmtcorp.com	Chanhassen	MN	55317	952-470-0866	
Portal Instruments Inc 148 Sidney St *Web:* www.portalinstruments.com	Cambridge	MA	02139	617-500-4348	
Precious Chemicals Company Inc 250 Altamonte Commerce Blvd *Web:* www.captek.com	Altamonte Springs	FL	32714	407-889-8891	
Precise Light Surgical Inc 310 W Hamilton Ave Ste 210 *Web:* www.preciselightsurgical.com	Campbell	CA	95008	408-739-5605	
Precision BioLogic Inc 140 Eileen Stubbs Ave *TF:* 800-267-2796 ■ *Web:* www.precisionbiologic.com	Dartmouth	NS	B3B0A9	902-468-6422	
Precision X-Ray Inc 15 Commerce Dr *Web:* www.pxinc.com	North Branford	CT	06471	203-484-2011	
Prestige Medical Corporation International 8600 Wilbur Ave *TF:* 800-762-3333 ■ *Web:* www.prestigemedical.com	Northridge	CA	91324	818-993-3030	
Prima Tech USA 277 Faison McGowan Rd Ste 2 *TF:* 800-458-7454 ■ *Web:* neogen.com/primatech	Kenansville	NC	28349	910-296-6116	296-0306
PRN Medical Services LLC 2311 W Utopia Rd *Web:* www.symbiusmedical.com	Phoenix	AZ	85027	623-780-8686	
Proa Medical Inc 2512 Artesia Blvd Ste 305-C *Web:* proamedical.com	Redondo Beach	CA	90278	310-592-3046	
Professional Hospital Supply Inc 41980 Winchester Rd *Web:* www.phsyes.com	Temecula	CA	92590	951-296-2600	
ProLabs Inc 137 Herricks Rd	Garden City Park	NY	11040	516-877-9000	
ProMed Molded Products Inc 15600 Medina Rd *Web:* www.promedmolding.com	Plymouth	MN	55447	763-331-3800	
Promex Technologies LLC 3049 Hudson St	Franklin	IN	46131	317-736-0128	
PSS World Medical Inc 4345 Southpoint Blvd *NASDAQ: PSSI* ■ *Web:* www.pssworldmedical.com	Jacksonville	FL	32216	904-332-3000	
Pulsar Vascular Inc 4030 Moorpark Ave Ste 110 *Web:* www.pulsarvascular.com	San Jose	CA	95117	408-260-9264	
Pulse Biomedical Inc 1305 Catfish Ln *Web:* www.qrscard.com	Norristown	PA	19403	610-666-5510	
Radiancy Inc 40 Ramland Rd S Ste 200 *TF:* 888-661-2220 ■ *Web:* www.radiancy.com	Orangeburg	NY	10962	845-398-1647	
Rainier Surgical Inc 1144 29th St NW *Web:* www.rainiersurgical.com	Auburn	WA	98001	253-486-0500	
RedRick Technologies Inc 21624 Adelaide Rd *TF:* 800-340-9511 ■ *Web:* www.redricktechnologies.com	Mount Brydges	ON	N0L1W0	519-264-2400	

				Phone	Fax
Reliable Medical Supply Inc 9401 Winnetka Ave N *Web:* www.reliamed.com	Brooklyn Park	MN	55445	763-255-3800	
Reshape Medical 100 Calle Iglesia *TF:* 844-937-7374 ■ *Web:* reshapeready.com	San Clemente	CA	92672	844-937-7374	
Rgh Enterprises Inc 1810 Summit Commerce Pk *TF:* 800-307-5930 ■ *Web:* www.edgepark.com	Twinsburg	OH	44087	330-963-6998	963-6839
Rigaku Americas Corp 9009 New Trails Dr *Web:* www.rigaku.com	The Woodlands	TX	77381	281-362-2300	364-3628
Roberts Home Medical Inc 20465 Seneca Meadows Pkwy *Web:* www.robertshomemedical.com	Germantown	MD	20876	301-353-0300	
Roka Bioscience Inc 20 Independence Blvd 4th Fl *TF:* 855-765-2246 ■ *Web:* www.rokabio.com	Warren	NJ	07059	908-605-4700	
Saebo Inc 2725 Water Ridge Pkwy Ste 320 Six LakePointe Plaza **Fax Area Code:* 855 ■ *TF:* 888-284-5433 ■ *Web:* www.saebo.com	Charlotte	NC	28217	888-284-5433	414-0037*
SameDay Security Inc 133 S Church St *TF:* 866-572-3274 ■ *Web:* www.lifesupportmedical.com	Las Cruces	NM	88001	866-572-3274	
Savoy Technical Services Inc 4301 Hwy 27 South *TF:* 877-703-3235 ■ *Web:* savoyndt.com	Sulphur	LA	70665	337-558-6071	
SCHAERER MEDICAL USA Inc 675 Wilmer Ave *Web:* www.schaerermayfieldusa.com	Cincinnati	OH	45226	513-561-2241	
SciCan Ltd 1440 Don Mills Rd *Web:* www.scican.com	Toronto	ON	M3B3P9	416-445-1600	
Sebacia Inc 2905 Premiere Pkwy Ste 150 *TF:* 888-935-4411 ■ *Web:* www.sebacia.com	Duluth	GA	30097	888-935-4411	
Securisyn Medical LLC 9150 Commerce Ctr Cir Ste 135 *Web:* www.securisyn.com	Highlands Ranch	CO	80129	303-952-4530	
Seno Medical Instruments Inc 3838 Medical Dr *Web:* www.senomedical.com	San Antonio	TX	78229	210-615-6501	
Shared Imaging LLC 801 Phoenix Lk Ave *Web:* www.sharedimaging.com	Streamwood	IL	60107	630-483-3980	
Shared Service Systems Inc 1725 S 20th St *Web:* www.sharedomaha.com	Omaha	NE	68108	402-536-5300	
Shifamed LLC 745 Camden Ave Ste A *Web:* www.shifamed.com	Campbell	CA	95008	408-637-2150	
Signus Medical LLC 18888 Lake Dr E *Web:* www.signusmedical.com	Chanhassen	MN	55317	952-294-8700	
Simbionix USA Corp 7100 Euclid Ave Baker Electric Bldg Ste 180 *Web:* www.simbionix.com	Cleveland	OH	44103	216-229-2040	
Sinclair Dental Company Ltd 900 Harbourside Dr *Web:* www.sinclairdental.com	North Vancouver	BC	V7P3T8	604-986-1544	
SinuSys Corp 4030 Fabian Way *TF:* 855-474-6879 ■ *Web:* sinusys.com	Palo Alto	CA	94303	650-213-9988	
SLMP LLC 407 Interchange St *Web:* www.statlab.com	Mckinney	TX	75071	972-436-1010	
SmartScrubs LLC 3400 E Mcdowell Rd *TF:* 800-800-5788 ■ *Web:* www.smartscrubs.com	Phoenix	AZ	85008	800-800-5788	
Somagen Diagnostics Inc 9220 25th Ave *TF:* 800-661-9993 ■ *Web:* www.somagen.com	Edmonton	AB	T6N1E1	780-702-9500	438-6595
Specialty Surgical Products Inc 1131 Us Hwy 93 N *TF:* 888-878-0811 ■ *Web:* www.ssp-inc.com	Victor	MT	59875	406-961-0102	
SST Group Inc 309 Laurelwood Rd Ste 20 *Web:* www.sstgroup-inc.com	Santa Clara	CA	95054	408-350-3450	
Strukmyer LLC 1801 Big Town Blvd Ste 100 *Web:* www.strukmyer.com	Mesquite	TX	75149	214-275-9595	
Sun Surgical Supply Co 302 NW Sixth St *Web:* www.sunsurgical.com	Gainesville	FL	32601	352-377-2696	
SureTek Medical 25 Maple Creek Cir Ste B *Web:* www.suretekmedical.com	Greenville	SC	29607	864-299-9743	
Surgical Principals Inc 1625 S Tacoma Way *TF:* 888-801-9251 ■ *Web:* spi.historic1625tacomaplace.com	Tacoma	WA	98409	888-801-9251	
Synapse Biomedical Inc 300 Artino St *Web:* synapsebiomedical.com	Oberlin	OH	44074	440-774-2488	
Synovis Micro Companies Alliance Inc 439 Industrial Ln *Web:* www.synovismicro.com	Birmingham	AL	35211	205-941-0111	
Synthes Spine Inc 325 Paramount Dr *Web:* www.depuysynthes.com	Raynham	MA	02767	508-880-8100	
Sysmex America Inc 1 Nelson C White Pkwy *TF:* 800-379-7639 ■ *Web:* www.sysmex.com	Mundelein	IL	60060	847-996-4500	996-4397
Systagenix Wound Management (US) Inc 400 Crown Colony Ste 302 *Web:* www.systagenix.com	Quincy	MA	02169	617-774-5500	
Talyst Inc 11100 NE Eigth St *Web:* www.talyst.com	Bellevue	WA	98004	425-289-5400	289-5663
TCGRx N1671 Powers Lk Rd *Web:* www.tcgrx.com	Powers Lake	WI	53159	262-279-5307	
Tech West Vacuum Inc 2625 N Argyle Ave *TF:* 800-428-7139 ■ *Web:* www.tech-west.com	Fresno	CA	93727	559-291-1650	
Technical Instrument San Francisco 1826 Rollins Rd *TF:* 866-800-9797 ■ *Web:* www.techinst.com	Burlingame	CA	94010	650-651-3000	
Tegra Medical LLC 9 Forge Park *Web:* www.tegramedical.com	Franklin	MA	02038	508-541-4200	
Tendyne Holdings Inc 2825 Fairview Ave N *Web:* www.tendyne.com	Roseville	MN	55113	651-289-5500	
Tetra Medical Supply Corp 6364 W Gross Pt Rd *TF Cust Svc:* 800-621-4041 ■ *Web:* www.tetramed.com	Niles	IL	60714	847-647-0590	647-9034
Therapy Support Inc 2803 N Oak Grove Ave *Web:* www.therapysupport.com	Springfield	MO	65803	417-890-7165	
Thermedx LLC 31200 Solon Rd Unit 1 *TF:* 888-542-9276 ■ *Web:* www.thermedx.com	Solon	OH	44139	440-542-0883	
Ti Ba Enterprises Inc 25 Hytec Cir *Web:* www.ti-ba.com	Rochester	NY	14606	585-247-1212	
Tiba Medical Inc 2701 NW Vaughn St Ste 470 *Web:* www.tibamedical.com	Portland	OR	97210	503-222-1500	
Tosoh Bioscience Inc 6000 Shoreline Court Ste 101 *Web:* www.diagnostics.us.tosohbioscience.com	South San Francisco	CA	94080	650-615-4970	
TPC Advance Technology Inc 18525 Gale Ave *TF:* 800-560-8222 ■ *Web:* www.tpcdental.com	City Of Industry	CA	91748	626-810-4337	
Trans Med USA Inc 31 Progress Ave *TF:* 800-442-1142 ■ *Web:* www.transmed-usa.com	Tyngsboro	MA	01879	978-649-1970	
Tri State Distribution Inc 600 Vista Dr *TF:* 800-392-9824 ■ *Web:* www.provial.com	Sparta	TN	38583	800-392-9824	
Tri-State Surgical Supply & Equipment Ltd 409 Hoyt St *Web:* tristatesurgical.com	Brooklyn	NY	11231	718-624-1000	
Triangle X-ray Co 4900 Thornton Rd Ste 117 *TF:* 866-763-9729 ■ *Web:* trianglexray.com	Raleigh	NC	27616	919-876-6156	
Tridien Medical Inc 4200 NW 120th Ave *Web:* www.tridien.com	Coral Springs	FL	33065	954-340-0500	
Trudell Medical Group Ltd 758 Third St *TF:* 800-757-4881 ■ *Web:* www.tmml.com	London	ON	N5V5J7	519-685-8800	
Turn-key Medical Inc 365 Sw Fifth Ave *Web:* turn-keymedical.com	Meridian	ID	83642	208-888-1760	
Ultra Solutions Acquisition LLC 1137 E Philadelphia St *Web:* www.ultrasolutions.com	Ontario	CA	91761	909-628-1778	
US Med-Equip Inc 9777 W Gulf Bank Ste 20 *Web:* www.usmedequip.com	Houston	TX	77040	713-983-8860	
USDiagnostics Inc 2007 Bob Wallace Ave *Web:* www.usdiagnostics.com	Huntsville	AL	35805	256-534-4881	
Valeritas Inc 750 Rt 202 S Ste 600 *TF:* 855-384-8848 ■ *Web:* www.valeritas.com	Bridgewater	NJ	08807	908-927-9920	927-9927
Vascular Dynamics Inc 2134 Old Middlefield Way Ste J *Web:* www.vasculardynamics.com	Mountain View	CA	94043	650-963-9370	
Vascular Pathways Inc 1847 Trade Ctr Way	Naples	FL	34109	239-254-0391	
VasoHealthcare Revolution Mill Studios 1150 Revolution Mill Dr Studio 1 *Web:* www.vasohealthcare.com	Greensboro	NC	27405	336-398-8276	
Venta Medical LLC 33170 Central Ave *Web:* ventamedical.com	Union City	CA	94587	510-429-9300	
Ventec Life Systems Inc 19021 120th Ave NE Ste E101 *Web:* www.venteclife.com	Bothell	WA	98011	425-355-8038	
Vista Therapeutics Inc 3900 Paseo del Sol *Web:* www.vistatherapeutics.org	Sante Fe	NM	87507	505-474-3143	
Vital Diagnostics Inc 27 Wellington Rd *Web:* www.vitaldiagnosticsinc.com	Lincoln	RI	02865	401-642-8400	
VWR International 100 Matsonford Rd Bldg 1 Ste 200 *TF:* 800-932-5000 ■ *Web:* us.vwr.com	Radnorpa	PA	19087	610-431-1700	431-9174
W Joe Shaw LTD 4200 Underwood Rd *Web:* www.gosafe.com	La Porte	TX	77571	281-476-5392	
Water-Jel Technologies LLC 50 Broad St *Web:* www.waterjel.com	Carlstadt	NJ	07072	201-806-3040	
Western Drug 3604 San Fernando Rd *Web:* www.westerndrug.com	Glendale	CA	91204	818-956-6691	
Westprime Healthcare 5751 Chino Ave *Web:* www.westprimehealthcare.com	Chino	CA	91710	714-529-2027	
William V MacGill & Co 1000 N LombaRd Rd **Fax Area Code:* 800 ■ *TF:* 800-323-2841 ■ *Web:* www.macgill.com	Lombard	IL	60148	630-889-0500	727-3433*
Xenex Disinfection Services LLC 121 Interpark Ste 104 *Web:* www.xenex.com	San Antonio	TX	78216	210-538-9300	
XLV Diagnostics Inc 290 Munro St Ste 2311 *Web:* xlvdiagnostics.com	Thunder Bay	ON	P7A7T1	807-346-6811	
Z-Medica Corp 4 Fairfield Blvd *Web:* www.z-medica.com	Wallingford	CT	06492	203-294-0000	
Zee Medical Inc 22 Corporate Pk **Fax Area Code:* 949 ■ *TF:* 800-435-7763 ■ *Web:* www.zeemedical.com	Irvine	CA	92606	800-435-7763	252-9649*
Zipline Medical Inc 747 Camden Ave Ste A *Web:* www.ziplinemedical.com	Campbell	CA	95008	408-412-7228	
Zosano Pharma Inc 34790 Ardentech Ct *Web:* www.macroflux.com	Fremont	CA	94555	510-745-1200	

MEDICAL FACILITIES

See Developmental Centers p. 2192; Health Care Providers - Ancillary p. 2453; Hospices p. 2484; Hospitals p. 2493; Imaging Services - Diagnostic p. 2556; Substance Abuse Treatment Centers p. 3211

476 MEDICAL INSTRUMENTS & APPARATUS - MFR

See Also Imaging Equipment & Systems - Medical p. 2555; Medical Supplies - Mfr p. 2745

				Phone	Fax
Accurate Surgical & Scientific Instruments Corp 300 Shames Dr *TF:* 800-645-3569 ■ *Web:* www.accuratesurgical.com	Westbury	NY	11590	516-333-2570	997-4948
Accuray Inc 1310 Chesapeake Terr *NASDAQ: ARAY* ■ *TF:* 888-522-3740 ■ *Web:* www.accuray.com	Sunnyvale	CA	94089	408-716-4600	716-4601
AccuTech LLC 2641 La Mirada Dr *Web:* www.accutech-llc.com	Vista	CA	92081	760-599-6555	
ACIST Medical Systems Inc 7905 Fuller Rd *TF:* 888-667-6648 ■ *Web:* www.acist.com	Eden Prairie	MN	55344	952-941-3507	

	City	State	Zip	Phone	Fax
Acme United Corp 60 Round Hill Rd	Fairfield	CT	06824	203-254-6060	
NYSE: ACU ■ *TF:* 800-835-2263 ■ *Web:* www.acmeunited.com					
Ad-tech Medical Instrument Inc 1901 William St	Racine	WI	53404	262-634-1555	
TF: 800-776-1555 ■ *Web:* www.adtechmedical.com					
AESCULAP Inc 3773 Corporate Pkwy	Center Valley	PA	18034	800-282-9000	791-6886*
**Fax Area Code:* 610 ■ *TF:* 800-282-9000 ■ *Web:* www.aesculapusa.com					
AirClean Systems Inc 3248 Lk Woodard Dr	Raleigh	NC	27604	919-255-3220	
Web: www.aircleansystems.com					
Alfa Scientific Designs Inc 13200 Gregg St	Poway	CA	92064	858-513-3888	
Web: www.alfascientific.com					
Alfa Wassermann Inc 4 Henderson Dr	West Caldwell	NJ	07006	973-882-8630	
Web: www.alfawassermannus.com					
Allied Healthcare Products Inc 1720 Sublette Ave	Saint Louis	MO	63110	314-771-2400	477-7701*
NASDAQ: AHPI ■ **Fax Area Code:* 800 ■ **Fax:* Cust Svc ■ *TF:* 800-444-3954 ■ *Web:* www.alliedhpi.com					
Altimate Medical Inc 262 W First St	Morton	MN	56270	507-697-6393	
TF: 800-342-8968 ■ *Web:* www.easystand.com					
Alto Development Corp 5206 Asbury Rd PO Box 758	Farmingdale	NJ	07727	732-938-2266	
Web: aemedical.com					
Amaranth Medical Inc 1145 Terra Bella Ave Ste A	Mountain View	CA	94043	650-965-3830	
Web: amaranthmedical.com					
Ameritek USA Inc 125 130th St SE Ste 200	Everett	WA	98208	425-379-2580	
Web: www.ameritek.org					
Anchor Products Company Inc 52 Official Rd	Addison	IL	60101	630-543-9124	
Web: www.anchorsurgical.com					
Andersen Sterilizers Inc 3154 Caroline Dr	Haw River	NC	27258	336-376-8622	
Web: www.andcal.com					
Andover Healthcare Inc 9 Fanaras Dr	Salisbury	MA	01952	978-465-0044	462-0003
TF: 800-432-6686 ■ *Web:* www.andovercoated.com					
Antares Pharma Inc 3905 Annapolis Ln N Ste 105	Minneapolis	MN	55447	763-475-7700	
AMEX: AIS ■ *Web:* www.antarespharma.com					
Apex Medical Technologies Inc 10064 Mesa Ridge Court Ste 202	San Diego	CA	92121	858-535-0012	
Web: www.apexmedtech.com					
Aradigm Corp 3929 Pt Eden Way	Hayward	CA	94545	510-265-9000	265-0277
OTC: ARDM ■ *Web:* www.aradigm.com					
Armm Inc 17744 Sampson Ln	Huntington Beach	CA	92647	714-848-8190	
Web: www.armminc.com					
Arrow International Inc 2400 Bernville Rd	Reading	PA	19605	610-378-0136	
Web: www.arrowintl.com					
Artisan Laboratories Inc 2532 Se Hawthorne Blvd	Portland	OR	97214	503-238-6006	
TF: 800-222-6721 ■ *Web:* www.artisandental.com					
Aspen Medical Products 6481 Oak Cyn	Irvine	CA	92618	949-681-0200	681-0222
TF: 800-295-2776 ■ *Web:* www.aspenmp.com					
Asuragen Inc 2150 Woodward St Ste 100	Austin	TX	78744	512-681-5200	681-5201
Web: www.asuragen.com					
Atrion Corp 1 Allentown Pkwy	Allen	TX	75002	972-390-9800	396-7581
NASDAQ: ATRI ■ *Web:* www.atrioncorp.com					
Atrium Medical Corp 5 Wentworth Dr	Hudson	NH	03051	603-880-1433	880-6718
TF: 800-528-7486 ■ *Web:* www.atriummed.com					
Avantec Vascular Corp 605 W California Ave	Sunnyvale	CA	94086	408-329-5400	
Web: www.avantecvascular.com					
B Braun Medical Inc 824 12th Ave	Bethlehem	PA	18018	610-691-5400	997-5510
TF: 800-523-9676 ■ *Web:* www.bbraunusa.com					
Bard Access Systems Inc 605 North 5600 West	Salt Lake City	UT	84116	801-522-5000	
TF: 800-443-5505 ■ *Web:* www.bardaccess.com					
Bard Inc Peripheral Vascular 1625 W Third St	Tempe	AZ	85281	480-894-9515	966-7062
TF: 800-321-4254 ■ *Web:* www.bardpv.com					
Baxter Healthcare Corp 1 Baxter Pkwy	Deerfield	IL	60015	847-948-2000	948-1813*
**Fax Area Code:* 224 ■ *Web:* www.baxter.com					
Baxter International Inc 1 Baxter Pkwy	Deerfield	IL	60015	847-948-2000	948-3948
NYSE: BAX ■ *TF:* 800-422-9837 ■ *Web:* www.baxter.com					
BD Medical 9450 S State St	Sandy	UT	84070	801-565-2300	
TF: 888-237-2762 ■ *Web:* www.bd.com					
Becton Dickinson & Co 1 Becton Dr	Franklin Lakes	NJ	07417	201-847-6800	
NYSE: BDX ■ *TF Cust Svc:* 888-237-2762 ■ *Web:* www.bd.com					
Beekley Corp 1 Prestige Ln	Bristol	CT	06010	860-583-4700	
TF: 800-233-5539 ■ *Web:* www.beekley.com					
Benlan Inc 2760 Brighton Rd Winston Business Park	Oakville	ON	L6H5T4	905-829-5004	
Web: www.benlan.com					
Berkley Medical Resources Inc 700 Mtn View Dr	Smithfield	PA	15478	724-564-5002	
Web: www.business.com					
Best Theratronics Ltd 413 March Rd	Ottawa	ON	K2K0E4	613-591-2100	
TF: 866-792-8598 ■ *Web:* www.theratronics.ca					
Best Vascular 4350 International Blvd Ste A	Norcross	GA	30093	770-717-0904	717-1283
TF: 800-668-6783 ■ *Web:* www.bestvascular.com					
Bio Compression Systems Inc 120 W Commercial Ave	Moonachie	NJ	07074	201-939-0716	
TF: 800-888-0908 ■ *Web:* www.biocompression.com					
BioCardia Inc 125 Shoreway Rd Ste B	San Carlos	CA	94070	650-226-0120	
TF: 800-624-1179 ■ *Web:* www.biocardia.com					
Biocoat Inc 211 Witmer Rd	Horsham	PA	19044	215-734-0888	
Web: www.biocoat.com					
BioCure Inc 2975 Gateway Dr Ste 100	Norcross	GA	30071	678-966-3400	
Web: www.biocure.com					
Biodex Medical Systems Inc 20 Ramsay Rd	Shirley	NY	11967	631-924-9000	924-8355
TF: 800-224-6339 ■ *Web:* www.biodex.com					
Bioflex Low Intensity Laser System 411 Horner Ave	Etobicoke	ON	M8W4W3	416-251-1055	
TF: 888-557-4004 ■ *Web:* www.bioflexlaser.com					
BioMerieux Inc 595 Anglum Rd	Hazelwood	MO	63042	314-731-8500	
TF: 800-634-7656 ■ *Web:* www.biomerieux.com					
Biomet Microfixation Inc 1520 Tradeport Dr	Jacksonville	FL	32218	904-741-4400	741-4500
TF: 800-874-7711 ■ *Web:* www.biomet.com					
Bioseal 167 W Orangethorpe Ave	Placentia	CA	92870	714-528-4695	
TF: 800-441-7325 ■ *Web:* www.biosealnet.com					
Biosense Webster Inc 3333 S Diamond Canyon Rd	Diamond Bar	CA	91765	909-839-8500	468-2905
TF: 800-729-9010 ■ *Web:* www.biosensewebster.com					
Biosign Technologies Inc 14-3715 Laird Rd	Mississauga	ON	L5L0A3	416-218-9800	
Blackburn's Physicians Pharmacy Inc 301 Corbet St	Tarentum	PA	15084	724-224-9100	224-9124
TF: 800-472-2440 ■ *Web:* www.blackburnsmed.com					
Blood Bank Computer Systems Inc 1002 15th St SW Ste 120	Auburn	WA	98001	253-333-0046	
Web: www.bbcsinc.com					
Boston Scientific Corp 1 Boston Scientific Pl	Natick	MA	01760	508-650-8000	272-9444*
NYSE: BSX ■ **Fax Area Code:* 888 ■ **Fax:* Cust Svc ■ *TF:* 888-272-1001 ■ *Web:* www.bostonscientific.com					
Braemar Inc 1285 Corporate Ctr Dr	Eagan	MN	55121	651-286-8620	286-8630
TF: 800-328-2719 ■ *Web:* www.braemarinc.com					
Braff Group, The 1665 Washington Rd Ste 3	Pittsburgh	PA	15228	412-833-5733	
Web: www.thebraffgroup.com					
Braintree Laboratories Inc 60 Columbian St W	Braintree	MA	02185	781-843-2202	
Web: www.braintreelabs.com					
Branan Medical Corp 140 Technology Ste 400	Irvine	CA	92618	949-598-7166	
Web: www.brananmedical.com					
Bunnell Inc 436 Lawndale Dr	Salt Lake City	UT	84115	801-467-0800	
TF: 800-800-4358 ■ *Web:* www.bunl.com					
Cadwell Laboratories Inc 909 N Kellogg St	Kennewick	WA	99336	509-735-6481	783-6503
TF: 800-245-3001 ■ *Web:* www.cadwell.com					
Cambridge Heart Inc 46 Jonspin Rd	Wilmington	MA	01887	978-654-7600	752-1330
TF: 888-226-9283 ■ *Web:* www.cambridgeheart.com					
Cantel Medical Corp 150 Clove Rd 9th Fl	Little Falls	NJ	07424	973-890-7220	890-7270
NYSE: CMN ■ *Web:* www.cantelmedical.com					
CardiacAssist Inc 240 Alpha Dr	Pittsburgh	PA	15238	412-963-7770	
TF: 800-373-1607 ■ *Web:* www.tandemlife.com					
Cardica Inc 900 Saginaw Dr	Redwood City	CA	94063	650-364-9975	364-3134
NASDAQ: CRDC ■ *TF:* 888-544-7194 ■ *Web:* www.cardica.com					
Cardiovascular Systems Inc 1225 Old H 8 NW	St Paul	MN	55112	651-259-1600	
TF: 877-274-0360 ■ *Web:* www.csi360.com					
CareFusion Corp 3750 Torrey View Ct	San Diego	CA	92130	858-617-2000	617-2900
NYSE: CFN ■ *TF:* 888-876-4287 ■ *Web:* www.carefusion.com					
Carestream Health Inc 150 Verona St	Rochester	NY	14608	585-627-1800	
Web: www.carestreamhealth.com					
CAS Medical Systems Inc 44 E Industrial Rd	Branford	CT	06405	203-488-6056	488-9438
NASDAQ: CASM ■ *TF:* 800-227-4414 ■ *Web:* www.casmed.com					
Celsion Corp 10220-L Old Columbia Rd	Columbia	MD	21046	410-290-5390	290-5394
NASDAQ: CLSN ■ *TF:* 888-504-7965 ■ *Web:* www.celsion.com					
Certified Safety Manufacturing Inc 1400 Chestnut Ave	Kansas City	MO	64127	816-483-9090	
Web: www.certifiedsafetymfg.com					
Chad Therapeutics Inc 2975 Horseshoe Dr S Ste 600	Naples	FL	34104	239-687-1285	687-1280
OTC: CHADQ ■ *TF:* 800-423-8870 ■ *Web:* www.chadtherapeutics.com					
Chemlink Laboratories Inc 3960 Royal Dr	Kennesaw	GA	30144	770-499-8008	
Web: chemlinklabs.com					
Clementia Pharmaceuticals Inc 1375 TransCanada Hwy Ste 200	Montreal	QC	H9P2W8	514-940-3600	
Web: clementiapharma.com					
CMP Industries LLC 413 N Pearl St	Albany	NY	12297	518-434-3147	
Web: cmpindustries.com					
Command Medical Products Inc 15 Signal Ave	Ormond Beach	FL	32174	386-672-8116	
Web: www.commandmedical.com					
Compass Animal Health Inc 16703 - 116 Ave NW	Edmonton	AB	T5M3V1	780-451-6517	
Web: www.compass-ah.com					
Composite Manufacturing Inc 970 Calle Amanecer Ste B	San Clemente	CA	92673	949-361-7580	
Web: www.carbonfiber.com					
Computerized Screening Inc 9550 Gateway Dr	Reno	NV	89521	775-359-1191	
Web: www.computerizedscreening.com					
Conmed Corp 525 French Rd	Utica	NY	13502	315-797-8375	438-3051*
NASDAQ: CNMD ■ **Fax Area Code:* 800 ■ **Fax:* Cust Svc ■ *TF:* 800-448-6506 ■ *Web:* www.conmed.com					
ConMed Endoscopic Technologie 525 French Rd	Utica	NY	13502	315-797-8375	797-0321
TF: 800-225-1332 ■ *Web:* www.conmed.com					
CONMED Linvatec 11311 Concept Blvd	Largo	FL	33773	727-392-6464	399-5256*
**Fax:* Cust Svc ■ *TF Cust Svc:* 800-448-6506 ■ *Web:* www.conmed.com					
Cook Inc PO Box 4195	Bloomington	IN	47402	812-339-2235	339-2235
TF: 800-457-4500 ■ *Web:* www.cookmedical.com					
Cook Medical Inc 1186 Montgomery Ln	Vandergrift	PA	15690	724-845-8621	845-2848
TF General: 800-457-4500 ■ *Web:* www.cookmedical.com					
Cook Medical Inc 4900 Bethania Stn Rd	Winston-Salem	NC	27105	336-744-0157	
TF: 800-457-4500 ■ *Web:* www.cookmedical.com					
Cook Medical Inc PO Box 4195	Bloomington	IN	47402	812-339-2235	554-8335*
**Fax Area Code:* 800 ■ *TF:* 800-457-4500 ■ *Web:* www.cookmedical.com					
Cook Urological Inc PO Box 4195	Bloomington	IN	47402	812-339-2235	
TF: 800-457-4500 ■ *Web:* www.cookmedical.com					
Cooper Cos Inc 6140 Stoneridge Mall Rd Ste 590	Pleasanton	CA	94588	925-460-3600	
NYSE: COO ■ *TF:* 888-822-2660 ■ *Web:* www.coopercos.com					
CooperSurgical Inc 95 Corporate Dr	Trumbull	CT	06611	203-929-6321	262-0105*
**Fax Area Code:* 800 ■ **Fax:* Cust Svc ■ *TF:* 800-645-3760 ■ *Web:* www.coopersurgical.com					
Cordis Corp 14201 NW 60th Ave	Miami Lakes	FL	33014	800-447-7585	313-2080*
**Fax Area Code:* 786 ■ *TF:* 800-327-7714 ■ *Web:* www.cordis.com					
Corpak Medsystems Inc 1001 Asbury Dr	Buffalo Grove	IL	60089	847-403-3400	541-9526
TF: 800-323-6305 ■ *Web:* www.corpakmedsystems.com					
CP Medical Inc 803 NE 25th Ave	Portland	OR	97232	503-232-1555	
TF: 800-950-2763 ■ *Web:* www.cpmedical.com					
CR Bard Inc 730 Central Ave	Murray Hill	NJ	07974	908-277-8000	
NYSE: BCR ■ *Web:* www.crbard.com					

Phone Fax

CR Bard Inc Urological Div
8195 Industrial Blvd.............................Covington GA 30014 770-784-6100
TF: 800-526-4455 ■ *Web:* www.bardmedical.com
CRH Medical Corp 999 Canada Pl Ste 578...........Vancouver BC V6C3E1 604-633-1440
Web: www.crhsystem.com
Cutera Inc 3240 Bayshore Blvd.....................Brisbane CA 94005 415-657-5500 330-2444
NASDAQ: CUTR ■ *TF:* 888-428-8372 ■ *Web:* www.cutera.com
Cutting Edge Products LLC 1000 Turk Hill Rd..........Fairport NY 14450 252-830-5577
TF: 800-497-0539 ■ *Web:* www.celasers.com
Dale Medical Products Inc PO Box 1556.............Plainville MA 02762 800-343-3980 695-6587*
**Fax Area Code:* 508 ■ *TF:* 800-343-3980 ■ *Web:* www.dalemed.com
Davol Inc 100 Crossings Blvd............................Warwick RI 02886 800-556-6756
TF Cust Svc: 800-556-6756 ■ *Web:* www.davol.com
Defibtech LLC 741 Boston Post Rd Ste 201.............Guilford CT 06437 203-453-4507
TF: 866-333-4248 ■ *Web:* www.defibtech.com
Delcath Systems Inc 810 Seventh Ave 35th Fl.........New York NY 10019 212-489-2100
Web: www.delcath.com
Diopsys Inc 16 Chapin Rd Ste 912..................Pine Brook NJ 07058 973-244-0622
Web: www.diopsys.com
Disposable Instrument Co
14248 Santa Fe Trl Dr......................Shawnee Mission KS 66215 913-492-6492
Web: www.disposableinstrument.com
Dymedix Corp 5985 Rice Creek Pkwy Ste 201.........Shoreview MN 55126 763-789-8280
Web: www.dymedix.com
Encision Inc 6797 Winchester Cir.....................Boulder CO 80301 303-444-2600 444-2693
OTC: ECIA ■ *TF:* 800-998-0986 ■ *Web:* www.encision.com
Endologix Inc 11 Studebaker...........................Irvine CA 92618 949-457-9546 843-1500*
NASDAQ: ELGX ■ **Fax Area Code:* 877 ■ *TF:* 800-983-2284 ■ *Web:* www.endologix.com
Epimed International Inc
141 Sal Landrio Dr.............................Johnstown NY 12095 518-725-0209
Web: www.epimed.com
Escalon Medical Corp 435 Devon Pk Dr Bldg 100........Wayne PA 19087 610-688-6830
NASDAQ: ESMC ■ *Web:* www.escalonmed.com
Eternity Healthcare Inc Ste 1 8755 Ash St..........Vancouver BC V6P6T3 855-324-1110
TF: 855-324-1110 ■ *Web:* eternityhealthcare.com
Ethicon Endo-Surgery Inc 4545 Creek Rd...........Cincinnati OH 45242 513-337-7000
Web: www.ethicon.com
ev3 Inc 3033 Campus Dr...........................Plymouth MN 55441 763-398-7000 398-7200
TF: 800-716-6700 ■ *Web:* www.ev3.net
First Quality Products Inc 121 N Rd...............Mcelhattan PA 17748 570-769-6900
TF: 800-227-3551 ■ *Web:* www.firstquality.com
G & G Instrument Corp 466 Saw Mill River Rd..........Ardsley NY 10502 914-693-6000 693-6738
Web: www.datacut.com
Gauthier Biomedical Inc 2221 Washington St..........Grafton WI 53024 262-546-0010
Web: www.gauthierbiomedical.com
Gaymar Industries Inc 10 Centre Dr.............Orchard Park NY 14127 716-662-2551
TF: 800-828-7341 ■ *Web:* stryker.com
GEM Edwards Inc
5640 Hudson Industrial Pkwy PO Box 429.............Hudson OH 44236 800-733-7976
TF: 800-733-7976 ■ *Web:* www.gemcomedical.com
Gettig Technologies Inc
1 Streamside Pl E............................Spring Mills PA 16875 814-422-8892 422-8011
Web: springmillsmfg.com
GF Health Products Inc 2935 NE Pkwy.................Atlanta GA 30360 770-447-1609 726-0601*
**Fax Area Code:* 800 ■ *TF:* 800-347-5678 ■ *Web:* www.grahamfield.com
Great Basin Scientific Inc
420 E S Temple Ste A.........................Salt Lake City UT 84111 801-990-1055
TF: 888-360-4022 ■ *Web:* www.gbscience.com
GT Urological LLC 960 E Hennepin Ave............Minneapolis MN 55414 612-379-3578
Web: www.gturological.com
Gyrus ACMI 6655 Wedgwood Rd Ste 160...........Maple Grove MN 55311 763-416-3000
Web: medical.olympusamerica.com
Haemonetics Corp 400 Wood Rd....................Braintree MA 02184 781-848-7100 860-1512*
NYSE: HAE ■ **Fax Area Code:* 800 ■ *TF:* 800-225-5242 ■ *Web:* www.haemonetics.com
Harmac Medical Products Inc 2201 Bailey Ave.........Buffalo NY 14211 716-897-4500 897-0016
Web: www.harmac.com
Hartwell Medical Corp
6354 Corte Del Abeto Ste F.......................Carlsbad CA 92011 760-438-5500
TF: 800-633-5900 ■ *Web:* www.hartwellmedical.com
HeartSine Technologies Inc
121 Friends Ln Ste 400..........................Newtown PA 18940 215-860-8100
Web: heartsine.com
Henry Troemner LLC 201 Wolf Dr....................Thorofare NJ 08086 856-686-1600
TF: 800-352-7705 ■ *Web:* www.troemner.com
Hill-Rom Services Inc 1069 SR 46 E................Batesville IN 47006 812-934-7777 934-8189
TF: 800-267-2337 ■ *Web:* www.hill-rom.com
Hoggan Health Industries Inc
8020 South 1300 West.........................West Jordan UT 84088 801-572-6500
TF: 800-678-7888 ■ *Web:* hogganhealth.net
Hospira Inc 275 N Field Dr.......................Lake Forest IL 60045 224-212-2000
NYSE: HSP ■ *TF:* 877-946-7747 ■ *Web:* www.hospira.com
Hospital Marketing Services Company Inc
162 Great Hill Rd..............................Naugatuck CT 06770 203-723-1466
TF: 800-786-5094 ■ *Web:* www.hmsmedical.com
Hypertension Diagnostics Inc
730 Bldg Ste 295.............................Minneapolis MN 55402 651-687-9999
TF: 888-785-7392 ■ *Web:* www.hypertensiondiagnostics.com
ImaCor Inc 839 Stewart Ave Ste 3.................Garden City NY 11530 516-393-0970
Web: www.imacor.com
Imaging Dynamics Company Ltd
3510 - 29 St. NE.................................Calgary AB T1Y7E5 403-251-9939
Web: www.imagingdynamics.com
Imalux Corp 11000 Cedar Ave Ste 250..............Cleveland OH 44106 216-502-0755
Immunalysis Corp 829 Towne Ctr Dr.................Pomona CA 91767 909-482-0840
Web: immunalysis.com
ImmunoScience Inc 6670 Owens Dr..............Pleasonton CA 94588 925-828-1000
Web: www.immunoscience.com
Implant Sciences Corp 500 Research Dr...........Wilmington MA 01887 978-752-1700 752-1711
OTC: IMSC ■ *TF:* 877-732-7333 ■ *Web:* www.implantsciences.com
IND Diagnostic Inc 1629 Fosters Way..................Delta BC V3M6S7 604-522-1619
InfraReDx Inc 34 Third Ave.......................Burlington MA 01803 781-221-0053
Web: www.infraredx.com

Phone Fax

Ingen Technologies Inc
3410 La Sierra Ave Ste F507......................Riverside CA 92503 951-688-7840
Web: www.ingen-tech.com
Inogen Inc 326 Bollay Dr...............................Goleta CA 93117 805-562-0500
Web: www.inogen.com
Inovise Medical Inc
8770 SW Nimbus Ave Ste D.......................Beaverton OR 97008 503-431-3800
TF: 877-466-8473 ■ *Web:* www.inovise.com
Inrad Inc 4375 Donker Court SE....................Kentwood MI 49512 616-301-7800
Web: www.inrad-inc.com
InSitu Technologies Inc 539 Phalen Blvd...............St Paul MN 55130 651-389-1017
Web: www.insitu-tech.com
Insulet Corp 9 Oak Park Dr..........................Bedford MA 01730 781-457-5000
TF: 800-591-3455 ■ *Web:* investor.insulet.com
Integra LifeSciences Holdings Corp
311 Enterprise Dr..............................Plainsboro NJ 08536 609-275-0500 799-3297
NASDAQ: IART ■ *TF:* 800-654-2873 ■ *Web:* www.integra-ls.com
Interrad Medical Inc 181 Cheshire Ln Ste 100.........Plymouth MN 55441 763-225-6699
Web: www.interradmedical.com
Intersect ENT Inc 1555 Adams Dr.................Menlo Park CA 94025 650-641-2100
Web: www.intersectent.com
Interventional Spine Inc
13700 Alton Pkwy Ste 160...............................Irvine CA 92618 949-472-0006
Web: www.i-spineinc.com
Intuitive Surgical Inc
1266 Kifer Rd Bldg 101.........................Sunnyvale CA 94086 408-523-2100 523-1390
NASDAQ: ISRG ■ *TF:* 888-868-4647 ■ *Web:* www.intuitivesurgical.com
Joerns Healthcare 5001 Joerns Dr..............Stevens Point WI 54481 715-341-3600 457-8827*
**Fax Area Code:* 800 ■ *TF:* 800-826-0270
Johnson Matthey Medical Products
1401 King Rd..................................West Chester PA 19380 610-648-8000 648-8111
TF: 800-442-1405 ■ *Web:* www.jmmedical.com
JPI Healthcare Solutions Inc 52 Newton Plz..........Plainview NY 11803 516-513-1330
Web: www.jpihealthcare.com
Katecho Inc 4020 Gannett Ave.....................Des Moines IA 50321 515-244-1212 244-4912
Web: www.katecho.com
Kensey Nash Corp 735 Pennsylvania Dr..................Exton PA 19341 484-713-2100 713-2900
NASDAQ: KNSY ■ *TF General:* 800-322-2885 ■ *Web:* dsm.com/markets/medical/en_us/home.html
Kinamed Inc 820 Flynn Rd.........................Camarillo CA 93012 805-384-2748
TF: 800-827-5775 ■ *Web:* www.kinamed.com
Kirwan Surgical Products Inc
180 Enterprise Dr..............................Marshfield MA 02050 781-834-9500
TF: 888-547-9267 ■ *Web:* www.ksp.com
Knit Rite Inc 120 Osage Ave.......................Kansas City KS 66105 913-281-4600 281-5455
TF: 800-821-3094 ■ *Web:* www.knitrite.com
Laborie Medical Technologies Inc
6415 Northwest Dr Unit 11......................Mississauga ON L4V1X1 905-612-1170
Web: www.laborie.com
Lake Region Mfg Company Inc
340 Lk Hazeltine Dr...............................Chaska MN 55318 866-899-1392
TF: 866-899-1392 ■ *Web:* www.lakeregionmedical.com
Landice Inc 111 Canfield Ave.......................Randolph NJ 07869 973-927-9010
TF: 800-526-3423 ■ *Web:* www.landice.com
Laserage Technology Corp 3021 N Delany Rd........Waukegan IL 60087 847-249-5900 336-1103
Web: www.laserage.com
LeMaitre Vascular Inc 63 Second AVE.............Burlington MA 01803 781-221-2266
Web: www.lemaitre.com
Life Measurement Inc 1850 Bates Ave..............Concord CA 94520 925-676-6002
Web: www.bodpod.com
Lifescan Canada Ltd 210-4321 Still Creek Dr..........Burnaby BC V5C6S7 604-293-2266
Web: www.lifescan.com/company/world/canada
Links Medical Products Inc 9247 Research Dr...........Irvine CA 92618 949-753-0001
Web: www.linksmed.com
Lucent Medical Systems Inc
811 Kirkland Ave Ste 100..........................Kirkland WA 98033 425-822-3310
Web: www.lucentmedical.com
m2m Imaging Corp
5247 Wilson Mills Rd Ste 252....................Cleveland OH 44143 440-684-9690
Web: www.m2mimaging.com
Mangar Industries Inc 97 Britain Dr..............New Britain PA 18901 215-230-0300
Web: www.mangar.com
MAQUET Cardiac Assist 15 Law Dr..................Fairfield NJ 07004 973-244-6100
TF: 800-777-4222 ■ *Web:* ca.maquet.com
Maxtec Inc 6526 S Cottonwood St...............Salt Lake City UT 84107 801-266-5300
Web: www.maxtecinc.com
Med-I-Pant Inc 9100 Ray Lawson Blvd...............Montreal QC H1J1K8 514-356-1224
Web: www.mipinc.info
Medarray Inc 3915 research park dr................Ann Arbor MI 48108 734-769-1066
Web: www.permselect.com
Medi-Nuclear Corp Inc
4610 Littlejohn St............................Baldwin Park CA 91706 626-960-9822
TF: 800-321-5981 ■ *Web:* www.medinuclear.com
Medica Corp 5 Oak Park Dr..........................Bedford MA 01730 781-275-4892
TF: 800-777-5983 ■ *Web:* www.medicacorp.com
Medical Components Inc 1499 Delp Dr...........Harleysville PA 19438 215-256-4201
Web: www.medcompnet.com
Medical Designs LLC
1210 W 18th St Ste 104.........................Sioux Falls SD 57104 605-376-6008
Web: www.medicaldesignsllc.com
Medical International Technology Inc
1872 Beaulac Ville Saint-Laurent....................Montreal QC H4R2E7 514-339-9355
Web: www.mitcanada.ca
Medical Tactile Inc
5757 Century Blvd Ste 600.......................Los Angeles CA 90045 310-641-8228
Web: www.medicaltactile.com
Medicatech USA Inc 50 Maxwell Ave...................Irvine CA 92618 949-679-2881
Web: www.medicatechusa.com
Medin Corp 90 Dayton Ave Bldg 16C....................Passaic NJ 07055 973-779-2400
Web: www.medin.com
Medivance Inc 321 S Taylor Ave Ste 200.............Louisville CO 80027 303-926-1917
Web: www.medivance.com
MEDNOVUS Inc 664 Hymettus Ave....................Leucadia CA 92024 760-390-1410
Web: www.mednovus.com

				Phone	Fax
Medone Surgical Inc 670 Tallevast Rd *TF:* 866-633-6631 ■ *Web:* www.medone.com	Sarasota	FL	34243	941-359-3129	
Medovations Inc 102 E Keefe Ave *TF:* 800-558-6408 ■ *Web:* www.medovations.com	Milwaukee	WI	53212	414-265-7620	265-7628
MedRx Inc 1200 Starkey Rd Ste 105 *TF:* 888-392-1234 ■ *Web:* www.medrx-usa.com	Largo	FL	33771	727-584-9600	
Medtronic Inc 710 Medtronic Pkwy NE *NYSE: MDT* ■ *TF Cust Svc:* 800-328-2518 ■ *Web:* www.medtronic.com	Minneapolis	MN	55432	763-514-4000	514-4879
Medtronic Neurosurgery 125 Cremona Dr *TF Cust Svc:* 800-468-9710 ■ *Web:* medtronic.com	Goleta	CA	93117	800-633-8766	
Medtronic Perfusion Systems 7611 Northland Dr *TF:* 800-328-3320 ■ *Web:* www.medtronic.com	Brooklyn Park	MN	55428	763-391-9000	
MedVenture Technology Corp 2301 Centennial Blvd *Web:* medventure.com	Jeffersonville	IN	47130	812-280-2400	
Megadyne Medical Products Inc 11506 S State St *TF:* 800-747-6110 ■ *Web:* www.megadyne.com	Draper	UT	84020	801-576-9669	576-9698
Mercury Medical 11300 49th St N *TF:* 800-237-6418 ■ *Web:* www.mercurymed.com	Clearwater	FL	33762	727-573-0088	571-3922
Meridian Medical Technologies Inc 6350 Stevens Forest Rd Ste 301 *TF:* 800-638-8093 ■ *Web:* www.meridianmeds.com	Columbia	MD	21046	443-259-7800	259-7801
Merit Medical Systems Inc 1600 W Merit Pkwy *NASDAQ: MMSI* ■ *TF:* 800-356-3748 ■ *Web:* www.merit.com	South Jordan	UT	84095	801-253-1600	253-1652
Michigan Instruments Inc 4717 Talon Ct SE *Web:* www.michiganinstruments.com	Grand Rapids	MI	49512	616-554-9696	
Micro-Tube Fabricators Inc 250 Lackland Dr *Web:* hhmtf.com	Middlesex	NJ	08846	732-469-7420	469-4314
MicroAire Surgical Instruments Inc 3590 Grand Forks Blvd **Fax Area Code:* 434 ■ *TF:* 800-722-0822 ■ *Web:* www.microaire.com	Charlottesville	VA	22911	800-722-0822	975-4144*
Microflex Corp 2301 Robb Dr *Web:* microflexpublic-ansellhealthcare.msappproxy.net	Reno	NV	89523	775-746-6600	
Microlife USA Inc 1617 Gulf to Bay Blvd Second Fl Ste B *TF:* 888-314-2599 ■ *Web:* www.microlifeusa.com	Clearwater	FL	33755	727-451-0484	
Microline Surgical Inc 800 Cummings Ctr Ste 157-X *Web:* www.microlinesurgical.com	Beverly	MA	01915	978-922-9810	
MicroLumen Inc 1 Microlumen Way *Web:* www.microlumen.com	Oldsmar	FL	34677	813-886-1200	
Micropace EP Inc 3205 W Warner Ave *Web:* www.micropaceep.com	Santa Ana	CA	92704	714-258-7025	
Midi Inc 125 Sandy Dr *Web:* www.midi-inc.com	Newark	DE	19713	302-824-4736	
Midmark Corp 60 Vista Dr *TF:* 800-643-6275 ■ *Web:* www.midmark.com	Versailles	OH	45380	937-526-3662	
MiMedx Group Inc 1775 W Oak Commons Ct Ne *TF:* 888-543-1917 ■ *Web:* www.mimedx.com	Marietta	GA	30062	888-543-1917	
Mindray DS USA Inc 800 MacArthur Blvd *Web:* www.mindray.com	Mahwah	NJ	07430	201-995-8000	
Mindways Software Inc 3001 S Lamar Blvd Ste 302 *Web:* www.qct.com	Austin	TX	78704	512-912-0871	
Minntech Corp 14605 28th Ave N *TF:* 800-328-3345 ■ *Web:* www.medivators.com	Minneapolis	MN	55447	763-553-3300	553-3387
Mizuho America 133 Brimbal Ave *Web:* mizuho.publishpath.com	Beverly	MA	01915	978-921-1718	
Moberg Research Inc 224 S Maple St *Web:* www.moberg.com	Ambler	PA	19002	215-283-0860	
Monroe Wheelchair 388 Old Niskayuna Rd *Web:* www.monroewheelchair.com	Latham	NY	12110	518-783-1653	
Morgan Scientific Inc 151 Essex St *Web:* www.morgansci.com	Haverhill	MA	01832	978-521-4440	
Mott Corp 84 Spring Ln *TF:* 800-289-6688 ■ *Web:* www.mottcorp.com	Farmington	CT	06032	860-747-6333	
MPM Medical Inc 2301 Crown Ct *TF:* 800-232-5512 ■ *Web:* www.mpmmedicalinc.com	Irving	TX	75038	972-893-4090	893-4092
Mui Scientific 145 Traders Blvd E *TF:* 800-303-6611 ■ *Web:* muiscientific.com	Mississauga	ON	L4Z3L3	905-890-5525	
Myelotec Inc 4000 Northfield Way Ste 900 *Web:* www.myelotec.com	Roswell	GA	30076	770-664-4656	
Mytrex Inc 10321 South Beckstead Ln *Web:* www.rescuealert.com	South Jordan	UT	84095	801-571-4121	
Nasiff Associates 841 County Rt 37 *TF:* 866-627-4332 ■ *Web:* nasiff.com	Central Square	NY	13036	315-676-2346	
NDH Medical Inc 11001 Roosevelt Blvd N Ste 800 *Web:* www.ndhmedical.com	St. Petersburg	FL	33716	727-570-2293	
NeoMetrics Inc 2605 Fernbrook Ln N Ste J	Plymouth	MN	55447	763-559-4440	
Neovasc Inc 13700 Mayfield Pl Ste 2135 *Web:* www.neovasc.com	Richmond	BC	V6V2E4	604-270-4344	
Nephros Inc 41 Grand Ave *OTC: NEPH* ■ *Web:* www.nephros.com	River Edge	NJ	07661	201-343-5202	343-5207
Neuroptics Inc 2082 Michelson Dr Ste 450 *Web:* www.neuroptics.com	Irvine	CA	92612	949-250-9792	
Neuros Medical Inc 35010 Chardon Rd Ste 210 *Web:* www.neurosmedical.com	Willoughby Hills	OH	44094	440-951-2565	
New Wave Surgical Corp 3700 NW 124th Ave Ste 135 *Web:* www.newwavesurgical.com	Coral Springs	FL	33605	954-796-4126	
New World Medical Inc 10763 Edison Ct *Web:* www.nwm.vision	Rancho Cucamonga	CA	91730	909-466-4304	
NormaTec Industries LP 44 Glen Ave *Web:* www.normatec.net	Newton Center	MA	02459	617-928-3400	
Nova Technology Corp 29 Magnolia Ave *Web:* www.novatechcorp.com	Manchester	MA	01944	978-525-3066	
NovaBone Products LLC 1551 Atlantic Blvd Ste 105 *Web:* www.novabone.com	Jacksonville	FL	32207	904-807-0140	
Novare Surgical Systems Inc 10440 Bubb Rd Ste A *Web:* www.emvllp.com	Cupertino	CA	95014	408-873-3161	
NovaVision Inc 6401 Congress Ave Ste 140 *Web:* www.novavision.com	Boca Raton	FL	33487	561-558-2000	
Novosci 2021 Airport Rd *TF:* 800-854-0567 ■ *Web:* www.novosci.us	Conroe	TX	77301	281-363-4949	363-7080
Nspire Health Inc 1830 Lefthand Cir *TF:* 800-574-7374 ■ *Web:* www.nspirehealth.com	Longmont	CO	80501	303-666-5555	666-5588
Nubenco Medical 1 Kalisa Way Ste 207 *TF:* 800-633-1322 ■ *Web:* nubenco.com	Paramus	NJ	07652	201-967-9000	
Nutech Medical Inc 2641 Rocky Ridge Ln *Web:* www.nutechmedical.com	Birmingham	AL	35216	205-290-2158	
NuVasive Inc 7475 Lusk Blvd *NASDAQ: NUVA* ■ *TF:* 800-475-9131 ■ *Web:* www.nuvasive.com	San Diego	CA	92121	858-909-1800	909-2000
NuVue Therapeutics Inc 11135 Sedgefield Rd *Web:* www.nuvuetherapeutics.com	Fairfax	VA	22030	703-591-1691	
NxStage Medical Inc 439 S Union St 5th Fl *NASDAQ: NXTM* ■ *TF:* 866-697-8243 ■ *Web:* www.nxstage.com	Lawrence	MA	01843	978-687-4700	
Occk Inc 1710 W Schilling Rd *TF:* 800-526-9731 ■ *Web:* www.occk.com	Salina	KS	67401	785-827-9383	
Oceanic Medical Products Inc 8005 Shannon Industrial Park Ln *Web:* www.oceanicmedical.com	Atchison	KS	66002	913-874-2000	
On Line Controls Inc 9 Kane Industrial Dr A *Web:* onlinecontrols.com	Hudson	MA	01749	978-562-5353	
Optima Neuroscience Inc 13400 Progress Blvd *Web:* www.optimaneuro.com	Alachua	FL	32615	352-371-8281	
Organ Transport Systems Inc 6170 Research Rd Ste 103 *Web:* www.organtransportsystems.com	Frisco	TX	75034	972-987-1312	
Ortho Technology Inc 17401 Commerce Park Blvd *TF:* 800-999-3161 ■ *Web:* www.orthotechnology.com	Tampa	FL	33647	813-991-5896	
Ortho-Clinical Diagnostics Inc 1001 US Rt 202 N PO Box 350 **Fax Area Code:* 585 ■ **Fax:* Cust Svc ■ *TF:* 800-828-6316 ■ *Web:* www.orthoclinical.com	Raritan	NJ	08869	800-828-6316	453-3660*
ORTHOCON Inc 1 Bridge St Ste 121 *TF:* 888-445-6784 ■ *Web:* www.orthocon.com	Irvington	NY	10533	914-357-2600	
OSO BioPharmaceuticals Mfg LLC 4401 Alexander Blvd Ne *Web:* www.osobio.com	Albuquerque	NM	87107	505-923-2112	
Osprey Biomedical Corp 1105 N Market St Ste 1300 *Web:* www.ospreybiomedical.com	Wilmington	DE	19801	310-796-5680	
Osseon LLC 2330 Circadian Way *Web:* www.osseon.com	Santa Rosa	CA	95407	707-636-5940	
Osteogenics Biomedical Inc 4620 71st St *Web:* www.cytoplast.com	Lubbock	TX	79424	806-796-1923	
Osteomed Corp 3885 Arapaho Rd *TF Cust Svc:* 800-456-7779 ■ *Web:* www.osteomedcorp.com	Addison	TX	75001	972-677-4600	677-4601
Oxus America Inc 1685 Northfield Dr *TF:* 888-475-1568 ■ *Web:* www.oxusamerica.com	Rochester Hills	MI	48309	888-475-1568	
Pace Tech Inc 2040 Calumet St *Web:* www.pacetech-med.com	Clearwater	FL	33765	727-442-8118	
Paramit Corp 18735 Madrone Pkwy *Web:* www.paramit.com	Morgan Hill	CA	95037	408-782-5600	782-9991
PARI Respiratory Equipment Inc 2412 PARI Way *Web:* www.pari.com	Midlothian	VA	23112	804-253-7274	
Parker Laboratories Inc 286 Eldridge Rd *Web:* www.parkerlabs.com	Fairfield	NJ	07004	973-276-9500	
Path-Tec LLC 1333-A Belfast Ave *Web:* www.path-tec.com	Columbus	GA	31904	706-569-6368	
PatientKeeper Inc 800 Winter St; *Web:* patientkeeper.com	Waltham	MA	02451	781-373-6100	
Pepin Manufacturing Inc 1875 Hwy 61 South *Web:* www.pepinmfg.com	Lake City	MN	55041	651-345-5655	
Pepose Vision Institute PC 1815 Clarkson Rd *TF:* 877-862-2020 ■ *Web:* www.peposevision.com	Chesterfield	MO	63017	636-728-0111	
Peregrine Surgical Ltd 51 Britain Dr *TF:* 877-348-0456 ■ *Web:* www.peregrinesurgical.com	New Britain	PA	18901	215-348-0456	
PerkinElmer Inc 940 Winter St *NYSE: PKI* ■ *Web:* www.perkinelmer.com	Waltham	MA	02451	203-925-4602	944-4904
Perry Baromedical Corp 3750 Prospect Ave *Web:* www.perrybaromedical.com	Riviera Beach	FL	33404	561-840-0395	
Photo Diagnostic Systems Inc 14 Electronics Ave *Web:* www.photodiagnostic.com	Danvers	MA	01923	978-564-8512	
Pilling Surgical 2917 Weck Dr *TF Cust Svc:* 866-246-6990 ■ *Web:* www.teleflex.com/en/emea/brands/pilling/index.html	Research Triangle Park	NC	27709	919-544-8000	361-3914
PneumRx Inc 530 Logue Ave *Web:* www.pneumrx.com	Mountain View	CA	94043	650-625-8910	
Point Medical Corp 891 E Summit St *Web:* pointmedical.com	Crown Point	IN	46307	219-663-1775	
PointCare Technologies Inc 19 Brigham St Office 9-A *Web:* www.pointcare.net	Marlborough	MA	01752	508-537-9769	
Poly-Vac Inc 253 Abby Rd *Web:* www.polyvac.com	Manchester	NH	03103	603-647-7822	
Polyzen Inc 1041 Classic Rd *Web:* www.polyzen.com	Apex	NC	27539	919-319-9599	
Precision Edge Surgical Products Co 415 W 12th Ave *Web:* www.precisionedge.com	Sault Sainte Marie	MI	49783	906-632-4800	632-5619
Prism Medical Ltd Unit 2 485 Millway Ave *TF:* 877-304-5438 ■ *Web:* www.prismmedicalltd.com	Concord	ON	L4K3V4	416-260-2145	

				Phone	Fax
Prizm Medical Inc 3400 Corporate Way Ste I Web: www.prizm-medical.com	Duluth	GA	30096	770-622-0933	
ProChon Biotech Ltd 400 Trade St Ste 395 Web: www1.prochon.com	Woburn	MA	01801	781-305-5035	
Prodigy Diabetes Care LLC 2701-A Hutchison McDonald Rd PO Box 481928 TF: 800-366-5901 ■ Web: www.prodigymeter.com	Charlotte	NC	28269	800-366-5901	
Profex Medical Products Inc 2224 E Person Ave Web: www.profexmed.com	Memphis	TN	38114	901-452-7485	
Promedica Inc 114 Douglas Rd E TF: 800-899-5278 ■ Web: www.promedica-usa.com	Oldsmar	FL	34677	813-854-1905	
Pronk Technologies Inc 8933 Lankershim Blvd TF: 800-609-9802 ■ Web: www.pronktech.com	Sun Valley	CA	91352	818-768-5600	
Propper Mfg Company Inc 36-04 Skillman Ave TF Cust Svc: 800-832-4300 ■ Web: www.proppermfg.com	Long Island	NY	11101	718-392-6650	482-8909
Prosurg Inc 2195 Trade Zone Blvd Web: prosurg.com	San Jose	CA	95131	408-945-4044	
Proteus Applied Technologies Inc 377 Oyster Point Blvd	South San Francisco	CA	94080	650-588-7774	
Pryor Products 1819 Peacock Blvd TF: 800-854-2280 ■ Web: www.pryorproducts.com	Oceanside	CA	92056	760-724-8244	
PSI Health Solutions Inc 1013 Morse Dr Web: www.psibands.com	Pacific Grove	CA	93950	831-373-7712	
Pulse Needlefree Systems Inc 8210 Marshall Dr Web: www.pulse-nfs.com	Lenexa	KS	66214	913-599-1590	
Qosina Corp 2002-Q Orville Drive N Web: www.qosina.com	Ronkonkoma	NY	11779	631-242-3000	
Quality Tech Services Inc 10525 Hampshire Ave South Web: www.qtspackage.com	Bloomington	MN	55438	952-942-8321	
Radiology Support Devices Inc 1904 E Dominguez St Web: www.rsdphantoms.com	Long Beach	CA	90810	310-518-0527	
Ranfac Corp PO Box 635 Web: www.ranfac.com	Avon	MA	02322	508-588-4400	584-8588
Rapid Pathogen Screening Inc 7227 Delainey Ct Web: www.rpsdetectors.com	Sarasota	FL	34240	941-556-1850	
Reed-Lane Inc 359 Newark-Pompton Tpke Web: reedlane.com	Wayne	NJ	07470	973-709-1090	
ResMed Inc 9001 Spectrum Ctr Blvd NYSE: RMD ■ TF: 800-424-0737 ■ Web: www.resmed.com	San Diego	CA	92123	858-836-5000	836-5501
Revere Healthcare Ltd 112 Carry St Web: www.reverehc.com	Cary	IL	60013	847-516-4900	
Rex Medical LP 1100 E Hector St Ste 245 Web: www.rexmedical.com	Conshohocken	PA	19428	610-940-0665	
ROHO Group, The 100 N Florida Ave Web: roho.com	Belleville	IL	62221	618-277-9173	277-9561
Safety Syringes Inc 2875 Loker Ave E Web: www.safetysyringes.com	Carlsbad	CA	92010	760-918-9908	918-0565
Saint Jude Medical St Jude Medical Inc NYSE: STJ ■ TF: 800-328-9634 ■ Web: www.sjm.com	St Paul	MN	55117	651-756-2000	756-3301
Salter Labs 100 Sycamore Rd TF: 800-421-0024 ■ Web: www.salterlabs.com	Arvin	CA	93203	661-854-3166	854-3850
Sandstrom Trade & Technology Inc 610 Niagara St	Welland	ON	L3B5Y5	905-732-1307	
SANUWAVE Health Inc 11475 Great Oaks Way Ste 150 Web: www.sanuwave.com	Alpharetta	GA	30022	678-581-6843	
Seabrook International LLC 15 Woodworkers Way Web: www.seabrookinternational.com	Seabrook	NH	03874	603-474-1919	474-1833
Sechrist Industries Inc 4225 E La Palma Ave TF: 800-732-4747 ■ Web: www.sechristusa.com	Anaheim	CA	92807	714-579-8400	579-0814
Sekisui Diagnostics LLC 4 Hartwell Pl Web: www.sekisuidiagnostics.com	Lexington	MA	02421	781-652-7800	
Shofu Dental Corp 1225 Stone Dr TF: 800-827-4638 ■ Web: www.shofu.com	San Marcos	CA	92078	760-736-3277	
Siemens Medical Solutions Inc 51 Valley Stream Pkwy *Fax Area Code: 610 ■ TF: 800-888-7436 ■ Web: healthcare.siemens.com	Malvern	PA	19355	888-826-9702	219-3124*
Skyline Medical Inc 2915 Commers Dr Ste 900 Web: www.skylinemedical.com	Eagan	MN	55121	651-389-4800	
Smith & Nephew Inc Endoscopy Div 150 Minuteman Rd TF: 800-343-5717 ■ Web: www.smith-nephew.com	Andover	MA	01810	978-749-1000	749-1599
Smiths Medical MD Inc 1265 Grey Fox Rd TF: 800-258-5361 ■ Web: www.smiths-medical.com	Saint Paul	MN	55112	651-633-2556	628-7459
Sorin Group USA Inc 14401 W 65th Way TF: 800-289-5759 ■ Web: www.sorin.com	Arvada	CO	80004	303-424-0129	467-6584
Sorna Corp 2020 Silver Bell Rd Ste 17 Web: www.sorna.com	Eagan	MN	55122	651-406-9900	
Sound Imaging Corp 14 W Forest Ave Web: www.soundimaging.com	Englewood	NJ	07631	201-816-1414	
Specialty Silicone Fabricators 3077 Rollie Gates Dr TF: 800-394-4284 ■ Web: www.ssfab.com	Paso Robles	CA	93446	805-239-4284	239-0523
Spinesmith Partners 93 Red River St Ste 107 Web: spinesmithusa.com	Austin	TX	78701	512-206-0770	
Starplex Scientific Inc 50 A Steinway Blvd TF: 800-665-0954 ■ Web: www.starplexscientific.com	Etobicoke	ON	M9W6Y3	416-674-7474	
STERIS Corp 5960 Heisley Rd NYSE: STE ■ *Fax: Cust Svc ■ TF: 800-548-4873 ■ Web: www.steris.com	Mentor	OH	44060	440-354-2600	639-4450*
Stromberg LLC 255 Primera Blvd Ste 532 Web: timeclockdepot.3dcartstores.com	Lake Mary	FL	32746	407-333-3282	
Stryker Canada LP 45 Innovation Dr TF: 800-668-8324 ■ Web: www.stryker.ca	Hamilton	ON	L9H7L8	800-668-8324	
Stryker Corp 2825 Airview Blvd NYSE: SYK ■ TF: 800-616-1406 ■ Web: www.stryker.com	Kalamazoo	MI	49002	269-385-2600	385-1062
Suburban Surgical Company Inc 275 Twelfth St Web: www.suburbansurgical.com	Wheeling	IL	60090	847-537-9320	
Synemed Inc 4562 E Second St Ste A Web: www.synemed.com	Benicia	CA	94510	707-745-8386	
Synergetics USA Inc 3845 Corporate Ctr Dr NASDAQ: SURG ■ TF: 800-600-0565 ■ Web: www.synergeticsusa.com	O'Fallon	MO	63368	636-939-5100	939-6885
Techno-Aide Inc 7117 Centennial Blvd TF: 800-251-2629 ■ Web: www.techno-aide.com	Nashville	TN	37209	615-350-7030	350-7879
TERATECH Corp 77-79 Terr Hall Ave TF: 866-837-2766 ■ Web: www.terason.com	Burlington	MA	01803	781-270-4143	
Terumo Cardiovascular Systems Corp 6200 Jackson Rd *Fax Area Code: 800 ■ *Fax: Cust Svc ■ TF: 800-262-3304 ■ Web: www.terumo-us.com	Ann Arbor	MI	48103	734-663-4145	292-6551*
Terumo Medical Corp 2101 Cottontail Ln TF: 800-283-7866 ■ Web: www.terumomedical.com	Somerset	NJ	08873	732-302-4900	302-3083
TFX Medical Inc 50 Plantation Dr TF: 800-548-6600 ■ Web: www.teleflexmedicaloem.com	Jaffrey	NH	03452	603-532-7706	532-6108
TheraTest Laboratories Inc 1111 N Main St Web: theratest.com	Lombard	IL	60148	630-627-6069	
Thermasolutions Inc 1889 Buerkle Rd Web: www.thermasolutions.com	White Bear Lake	MN	55110	651-209-3900	
TherOx Inc 17500 Cartwright Rd Ste 100 Web: www.therox.com	Irvine	CA	92614	949-757-1999	
Thinking Systems Corp 750 94th Ave N Ste 211 Web: www.thinkingsystems.com	Saint Petersburg	FL	33702	727-217-0909	
Titertek Instruments Inc 330 Wynn Dr Ste 100 Web: www.titertek.com	Huntsville	AL	35805	256-859-8600	
Topcon Medical Systems Inc 111 Bauer Dr TF: 800-223-1130 ■ Web: www.topconmedical.com	Oakland	NJ	07436	201-599-5100	599-5250
Trans1 Inc 301 Government Ctr Dr Web: www.trans1.com	Wilmington	NC	28403	910-332-1700	
Transenterix Inc 635 Davis Dr Ste 300 Web: www.transenterix.com	Morrisville	NC	27560	919-765-8400	
TransMedics Inc 200 Minuteman Rd Ste 302 Web: www.transmedics.com	Andover	MA	01810	978-552-0900	
Ultraviolet Devices Inc 26145 Technology Dr Web: www.uvdi.com	Valencia	CA	91355	661-295-8140	
Unilife Corp 250 Cross Farm Ln Web: www.unilife.com	York	PA	17406	717-384-3400	
United States Endoscopy Group Inc 5976 Heisley Rd TF: 800-769-8226 ■ Web: www.usendoscopy.com	Mentor	OH	44060	440-639-4494	639-4494
Urologix Inc 14405 21st Ave N TF: 800-475-1403 ■ Web: www.urologix.com	Minneapolis	MN	55447	763-475-1400	475-1443
Utah Medical Products Inc 7043 S 300 W NASDAQ: UTMD ■ TF: 866-754-9789 ■ Web: www.utahmed.com	Midvale	UT	84047	801-566-1200	566-2062
Vasamed Inc 7615 Golden Triangle Dr Ste A *Fax Area Code: 952 ■ TF: 800-695-2737 ■ Web: www.vasamed.com	Eden Prairie	MN	55344	800-695-2737	944-6022*
Vascular Solutions Inc 6464 Sycamore Ct NASDAQ: VASC ■ *Fax Area Code: 877 ■ TF: 877-979-4300 ■ Web: www.vasc.com	Minneapolis	MN	55369	763-656-4300	656-4251*
Ventana Medical Systems Inc 1910 Innovation Pk Dr TF: 800-227-2155 ■ Web: www.ventana.com	Tucson	AZ	85755	520-887-2155	
Veridex LLC 700 US Hwy Rt 202 S TF: 877-837-4339 ■ Web: www.cellsearchctc.com	Raritan	NJ	08869	877-837-4339	
VirtualScopics Inc 350 Linden Oaks NASDAQ: VSCP ■ Web: www.virtualscopics.com	Rochester	NY	14625	585-249-6231	218-7350
Visicon Technologies Inc 871 Latour Ct Web: www.visicontech.com	Napa	CA	94558	707-259-1300	
Vital Signs Inc 20 Campus Rd TF: 800-932-0760 ■ Web: www3.gehealthcare.com	Totowa	NJ	07512	973-790-1330	790-3307
VitalAire Canada Inc 6990 Creditview Rd Unit 6 TF: 888-629-0202 ■ Web: www.vitalaire.com	Mississauga	ON	L5N8R9	888-629-0202	
Vivosonic Inc 120-5525 Eglinton Ave W TF: 877-255-7685 ■ Web: www.vivosonic.com	Toronto	ON	M9C5K5	416-231-9997	
W A Baum Company Inc 620 Oak St TF: 888-281-6061 ■ Web: www.wabaum.com	Copiague	NY	11726	631-226-3940	
WalkMed Infusion LLC 6555 S Kenton St Ste 304 TF: 800-578-0555 ■ Web: walkmed.com	Centennial	CO	80111	303-420-9569	420-4545
Wells Johnson Co 8000 S Kolb Rd TF: 800-528-1597 ■ Web: www.wellsgrp.com	Tucson	AZ	85756	520-298-6069	
Wexler Surgical Supplies 11333 Chimney Rock Rd TF: 800-414-1076 ■ Web: www.wexlersurgical.com	Houston	TX	77035	713-723-6900	
Zonare Medical Systems Inc 420 N Bernardo Ave Web: www.zonare.com	Mountain View	CA	94043	650-230-2800	

477 MEDICAL SUPPLIES - MFR

See Also Personal Protective Equipment & Clothing p. 2926

				Phone	Fax
A-M Systems Inc 131 Business Park Loop Web: a-msystems.com	Sequim	WA	98382	360-683-8300	
Adhesives Research Inc 400 Seaks Run Rd PO Box 100 TF: 800-445-6240 ■ Web: www.adhesivesresearch.com	Glen Rock	PA	17327	717-235-7979	235-8320
Adroit Medical Systems Inc 1146 CaRding Machine Rd TF: 800-267-6077 ■ Web: www.adroitmedical.com	Loudon	TN	37774	800-267-6077	267-6077
Advanced Orthopro Inc 1820 N Illinois St Web: www.advancedorthopro.com	Indianapolis	IN	46202	317-924-4444	
Advanced Sterilization Products (ASP) 33 Technology Dr *Fax Area Code: 949 ■ *Fax: Sales ■ TF: 888-783-7723 ■ Web: www.aspjj.com	Irvine	CA	92618	888-783-7723	450-6800*

Phone *Fax*

AESCULAP Inc 3773 Corporate Pkwy. . . . . Center Valley PA 18034 800-282-9000 791-6886*
Fax Area Code: 610 ■ *TF:* 800-282-9000 ■ *Web:* www.aesculapusa.com

Agrilectric Power Inc 3063 Hwy 397 . . . . . Lake Charles LA 70615 337-430-0006
Web: www.agrilectric.com

Allergan 2525 Dupont Dr PO Box 19534 . . . . . Irvine CA 92612 714-246-4500 246-6987
TF: 800-347-4500 ■ *Web:* www.allergan.com

Allied Healthcare Products Inc
1720 Sublette Ave. . . . . . Saint Louis MO 63110 314-771-2400 477-7701*
NASDAQ: AHPI ■ *Fax Area Code:* 800 ■ *Fax:* Cust Svc ■ *TF:* 800-444-3954 ■ *Web:* www.alliedhpi.com

Alta Manufacturing Inc 47650 Westinghouse Dr . . . . . Fremont CA 94539 510-668-1870
Web: www.altamfg.com

American Ortho-Tech Inc 1320 Mason Ave. . . . . Daytona Beach FL 32117 386-258-0401
Web: www.americanorthotech.com

American Safety Clothing Inc
30 E Park Ave . . . . . Sellersville PA 18960 215-257-7667
Web: americansafetyclothingmfg.com

AMG Medical Inc 8505 Dalton . . . . . Montreal QC H4T1V5 514-737-5251
TF: 800-363-2381 ■ *Web:* www.amgmedical.com

Animas Corp 200 Lawrence Dr. . . . . . West Chester PA 19380 610-644-8990 644-8717
TF: 877-937-7867 ■ *Web:* www.animas.com

Argentum Medical LLC
3700 N Lk Shore Dr Ste 106 . . . . . Chicago IL 60613 773-281-3252
Web: www.silverlon.com

ARIMED ORTHOTICS & PROSTHETICS Inc
302 Livingston St . . . . . Brooklyn NY 11217 718-875-8754
Web: www.arimed.com

Armstrong Medical Industries Inc
575 Knightsbridge Pkwy . . . . . Lincolnshire IL 60069 847-913-0101 913-0138
TF Cust Svc: 800-323-4220 ■ *Web:* www.armstrongmedical.com

Arthrex Inc 1370 Creekside Blvd . . . . . Naples FL 34108 239-643-5553 598-5534
TF: 800-934-4404 ■ *Web:* www.arthrex.com

ASO LLC 300 Sarasota Ctr Blvd. . . . . . Sarasota FL 34240 941-379-0300 378-9040
Web: www.asocorp.com

Aspen Surgical 6945 Southbelt Dr SE. . . . . . Caledonia MI 49316 616-698-7100 698-0525
TF: 888-364-7004 ■ *Web:* www.aspensurgical.com

Avery Dennison Corp 207 Goode Ave . . . . . Glendale CA 91203 626-304-2000
NYSE: AVY ■ *TF Cust Svc:* 888-567-4387 ■ *Web:* www.averydennison.com

Baxter International Inc 1 Baxter Pkwy . . . . . Deerfield IL 60015 847-948-2000 948-3948
NYSE: BAX ■ *TF:* 800-422-9837 ■ *Web:* www.baxter.com

Baylis Medical Company Inc
5959 Trans-Canada Hwy . . . . . Montreal QC H4T1A1 514-488-9801
TF: 800-850-9801 ■ *Web:* www.baylismedical.com

Becton Dickinson & Co 1 Becton Dr. . . . . . Franklin Lakes NJ 07417 201-847-6800
NYSE: BDX ■ *TF Cust Svc:* 888-237-2762 ■ *Web:* www.bd.com

Beltone Electronics Corp 2601 Patriot Blvd. . . . . . Glenview IL 60026 847-832-3300 769-8417*
Fax Area Code: 952 ■ *TF:* 800-235-8663 ■ *Web:* www.beltone.com

BioHorizons Inc 2300 Riverchase Ctr . . . . . Birmingham AL 35244 205-967-7880 870-0304
TF: 888-246-8338 ■ *Web:* www.biohorizons.com

Biomet Inc 56 E Bell Dr PO Box 587 . . . . . Warsaw IN 46582 574-267-6639 267-8137
TF: 800-348-9500 ■ *Web:* www.biomet.com

BioPro Inc 2929 Lapeer Rd. . . . . . Port Huron MI 48060 810-982-7777
Web: www.bioproimplants.com

Biosystems LLC 651 S Main St. . . . . . Middletown CT 06457 860-344-1079
Web: www.biosystems.com

Bioventus LLC 4721 Emperor Blvd Ste 100. . . . . . Durham NC 27703 919-474-6700
Web: www.bioventusglobal.com

Bristol-Myers Squibb Co 345 Pk Ave . . . . . New York NY 10154 212-546-4000
NYSE: BMY ■ *TF:* 800-332-2056 ■ *Web:* www.bms.com

BSN Medical Inc 5825 Carnegie Blvd. . . . . . Charlotte NC 28209 704-554-9933 331-8785
TF: 800-552-1157 ■ *Web:* www.bsnmedical.com

Burke Inc 1800 Merriam Ln . . . . . Kansas City KS 66106 800-255-4147 722-2614*
Fax Area Code: 913 ■ *TF Sales:* 800-255-4147 ■ *Web:* burkebariatric.com

Capstone Therapeutics Corp
1275 W Washington St Ste 101 . . . . . Tempe AZ 85281 602-286-5520
OTC: CAPS ■ *TF:* 800-937-5520 ■ *Web:* www.capstonethx.com

CarTika Medical Inc
6550 Wedgwood Rd N Ste 300. . . . . . Maple Grove MN 55311 763-545-5188
Web: www.cartikamedical.com

Centurion Medical Products
100 Centurion Way. . . . . . Williamston MI 48895 517-546-5400 546-9388
TF: 800-248-4058 ■ *Web:* www.centurionmp.com

Chattanooga Group 4717 Adams Rd . . . . . Hixson TN 37343 423-870-2281 875-5497
TF: 800-592-7329 ■ *Web:* www.djoglobal.com

ClearCount Medical Solutions Inc
101 Bellevue Rd . . . . . Pittsburgh PA 15229 412-931-7233
Web: www.clearcount.com

Community Surgical Supply Inc
1390 Rt 37 W . . . . . Toms River NJ 08755 732-349-2990 244-7588
TF: 800-349-2990 ■ *Web:* www.communitysurgical.com

Connecticut Hypodermics Inc 519 Main St. . . . . . Yalesville CT 06492 203-265-4881 284-1520
Web: www.connhypo.com

Consensus Orthopedics Inc
1115 Windfield Way Ste 100 . . . . . El Dorado Hills CA 95762 916-355-7100
TF: 800-638-2041 ■ *Web:* www.consensusortho.com

Conventus Orthopaedics Inc
10200 73rd Ave N Ste 122 . . . . . Maple Grove MN 55369 763-515-5000
TF: 855-418-6466 ■ *Web:* www.conventusortho.com

CR Bard Inc 730 Central Ave . . . . . Murray Hill NJ 07974 908-277-8000
NYSE: BCR ■ *Web:* www.crbard.com

Cramer Products Inc 153 W Warren St . . . . . Gardner KS 66030 913-856-7511
TF: 800-345-2231 ■ *Web:* www.cramersportsmed.com

Cyberonics Inc
100 Cyberonics Blvd The Cyberonics Bldg. . . . . . Houston TX 77058 281-228-7262 218-9332
NASDAQ: CYBX ■ *TF:* 800-332-1375 ■ *Web:* www.cyberonics.com

DeRoyal Industries Inc 200 DeBusk Ln. . . . . . Powell TN 37849 865-938-7828 362-1230*
Fax: Hum Res ■ *TF:* 800-251-9864 ■ *Web:* www.deroyal.com

DJ Orthopedics Inc 1430 Decision St. . . . . . Vista CA 92081 760-727-1280 936-6569*
Fax Area Code: 800 ■ *TF:* 800-321-9549 ■ *Web:* www.djoglobal.com

DNA Genotek Inc 2 Beaverbrook Rd . . . . . Kanata ON K2K1L1 613-723-5757
Web: www.dnagenotek.com

Dynarex Corporation 10 Glenshaw St . . . . . Orangeburg NY 10962 845-365-8200 365-8201
TF: 888-335-7500 ■ *Web:* www.dynarex.com

Ehob Inc 250 N Belmont Ave . . . . . Indianapolis IN 46222 317-972-4600 972-4601
TF: 800-899-5553 ■ *Web:* www.ehob.com

Environmental Tectonics Corp
125 James Way . . . . . SouthHampton PA 18966 215-355-9100 357-4000
OTC: ETCC ■ *Web:* www.etcusa.com

Ergodyne Corp 1021 Bandana Blvd E Ste 220. . . . . . Saint Paul MN 55108 651-642-9889 642-1882
TF: 800-225-8238 ■ *Web:* www.ergodyne.com

Exactech Inc 2320 NW 66th Ct. . . . . . Gainesville FL 32653 352-377-1140 378-2617
NASDAQ: EXAC ■ *TF:* 800-392-2832 ■ *Web:* www.exac.com

Female Health Co 515 N State St Ste 2225 . . . . . Chicago IL 60654 312-595-9123
TF: 800-882-6655 ■ *Web:* www.femalehealth.com

Ferno-Washington Inc 70 Weil Way . . . . . Wilmington OH 45177 937-382-1451 382-1191
TF: 800-733-3766 ■ *Web:* www.ferno.com

Fillauer Inc PO Box 5189. . . . . . Chattanooga TN 37406 423-624-0946 629-7936
TF: 800-251-6398 ■ *Web:* www.fillauer.com

Flexible Lifeline Systems Inc
14325 W Hardy Rd . . . . . Houston TX 77060 832-448-2900
Web: www.fall-arrest.com

Freeman Manufacturing Co 900 W Chicago Rd. . . . . . Sturgis MI 49091 269-651-2371 651-8248
TF: 800-253-2091 ■ *Web:* www.freemanmfg.com

Getinge USA Inc 1777 E Henrietta Rd . . . . . Rochester NY 14623 585-475-1400
Web: www.getinge.com/us-ca

GF Health Products Inc 2935 NE Pkwy . . . . . Atlanta GA 30360 770-447-1609 726-0601*
Fax Area Code: 800 ■ *TF:* 800-347-5678 ■ *Web:* www.grahamfield.com

Guided Therapeutics Inc
5835 Peachtree Corners E Ste D. . . . . . Norcross GA 30092 770-242-8723 242-8639
OTC: GTHP ■ *Web:* www.guidedinc.com

Gyrus Medical Inc ENT Div
136 Turnpike Rd. . . . . . Southborough MA 01772 508-804-2600
Web: www.medical.olympusamerica.com

Halyard Health 1400 Holcomb Bridge Rd . . . . . Roswell GA 30076 770-587-8000
Web: www.halyardhealth.com

Halyard Health 20202 Windrow Dr . . . . . Lake Forest CA 92630 949-206-2700
TF: 800-448-3569 ■
Web: www.halyardhealth.com/solutions/pain-management/acute-pain-solutions.aspx

Hanger Orthopedic Group Inc
10910 Domain Dr Ste 300 . . . . . Austin TX 78758 512-777-3800
TF: 877-442-6437 ■ *Web:* www.hanger.com

Hanger Prosthetics & Orthopedics Inc
10910 Domain Dr Ste 300 . . . . . Austin TX 78758 877-442-6437
TF: 877-442-6437 ■ *Web:* www.hanger.com

Hans Rudolph Inc 8325 Cole Pkwy. . . . . . Shawnee KS 66227 913-422-7788
Web: www.rudolphkc.com

Helvoet Pharma Inc 9012 Pennsauken Hwy. . . . . . Pennsauken NJ 08110 856-663-2202 663-2636
TF: 800-874-3586 ■ *Web:* www.datwyler.com

Hermell Products Inc 9 Britton Dr. . . . . . Bloomfield CT 06002 860-242-6550
TF: 800-233-2342 ■ *Web:* www.hermell.com

Hightech American Industrial Laboratories Inc (HAI)
320 Massachusetts Ave . . . . . Lexington MA 02420 781-862-9884 860-7722
Web: www.hailabs.com

Hollister Inc 2000 Hollister Dr. . . . . . Libertyville IL 60048 847-680-1000 680-2123*
Fax: Hum Res ■ *TF:* 800-323-4060 ■ *Web:* www.hollister.com

Hosmer-Dorrance Corp 561 Div St . . . . . Campbell CA 95008 408-379-5151 379-5263
Web: www.hosmer.com

Hospira Inc 275 N Field Dr. . . . . . Lake Forest IL 60045 224-212-2000
NYSE: HSP ■ *TF:* 877-946-7747 ■ *Web:* www.hospira.com

Hoveround Corp
2151 Whitfield Industrial Way. . . . . . Sarasota FL 34243 941-739-6200 388-6912*
Fax Area Code: 800 ■ *TF:* 800-542-7236 ■ *Web:* www.hoveround.com

Howard Leight Industries
7828 Waterville Rd . . . . . San Diego CA 92154 800-430-5490 232-3110*
Fax Area Code: 401 ■ *TF:* 800-430-5490 ■ *Web:* www.howardleight.com

Hy-Tape International Inc PO Box 540. . . . . . Patterson NY 12563 800-248-0101 878-4104*
Fax Area Code: 845 ■ *TF:* 800-248-0101 ■ *Web:* www.hytape.com

ICU Medical Inc 951 Calle Amanecer . . . . . San Clemente CA 92673 949-366-2183 366-8368
NASDAQ: ICUI ■ *TF:* 800-824-7890 ■ *Web:* www.icumed.com

Ideal Tape Co 1400 Middlesex St . . . . . Lowell MA 01851 800-284-3325 458-0302*
Fax Area Code: 978 ■ *TF:* 800-284-3325 ■ *Web:* www.idealtape.com

Independence Technology LLC 45 Technology Dr . . . . . Warren NJ 07059 908-412-2200 412-2205

Invacare Corp 1 Invacare Way. . . . . . Elyria OH 44036 440-329-6000 619-7996*
NYSE: IVC ■ *Fax Area Code:* 877 ■ *TF:* 800-333-6900 ■ *Web:* www.invacare.com

Iowa Veterinary Supply Co (IVESCO)
124 Country Club Rd . . . . . Iowa Falls IA 50126 641-648-2529 648-5994

Johnson & Johnson Consumer Products Co
199 Grandview Rd . . . . . Skillman NJ 08558 908-874-1000
TF: 866-565-2229 ■ *Web:* www.johnsonsbaby.com

Johnson & Johnson Inc 7101 Notre-Dame E. . . . . . Montreal QC H1N2G4 514-251-5100
TF: 800-361-8990 ■ *Web:* www.jnjcanada.com

K-Tube Technologies 13400 Kirkham Way . . . . . Poway CA 92064 858-513-9229 513-9459
TF: 800-394-0058 ■ *Web:* www.k-tube.com

Kinetic Concepts Inc (KCI) PO Box 659508. . . . . . San Antonio TX 78265 800-275-4524 311-9291*
Fax: Hum Res ■ *TF Cust Svc:* 800-275-4524 ■ *Web:* www.kci1.com

Langer Inc 2905 Veterans' Memorial Hwy . . . . . Ronkonkoma NY 11779 800-645-5520
TF: 800-645-5520 ■ *Web:* www.langerbiomechanics.com

Les Composites Motion Inc
160 Armand-Majeau Sud . . . . . Saint-roch-de-l'achigan QC J0K3H0 450-588-6555
Web: www.motioncomposites.com

LPS Industries Inc 10 Caesar Pl. . . . . . Moonachie NJ 07074 201-438-3515 643-0180*
Fax Area Code: 732 ■ *TF Sales:* 800-275-6577 ■ *Web:* www.lpsind.com

M & C Specialties Co 90 James Way. . . . . . SouthHampton PA 18966 215-322-1600 322-1620
TF Cust Svc: 800-441-6996 ■ *Web:* www.mcspecialties.com

Maetta Sciences Inc
75 De Mortagne Blvd Ste 109. . . . . . Boucherville QC J4B6Y4 450-652-4200
Web: www.maetta.ca

MAQUET Cardiovascular LLC 45 Barbour Pond Dr. . . . . . Wayne NJ 07470 973-709-7000
Web: www.maquet.com

Martech Medical Products Inc
1500 Delp Dr . . . . . Harleysville PA 19438 215-256-8833 256-8837
Web: www.martechmedical.com

Medaire Inc 4722 N 24th St Ste 450. . . . . . Phoenix AZ 85016 480-333-3700 333-3592
Web: www.medaire.com

Medical Action Industries Inc (MAI)
500 Expy Dr S. . . . . . Brentwood NY 11717 631-231-4600
NASDAQ: MDCI ■ *TF:* 800-645-7042 ■ *Web:* www.medical-action.com

Phone Fax

Medical Depot Inc 99 Seaview Blvd Port Washington NY 11050 516-998-4600
Web: www.drivemedical.com

Medizone International Inc
4000 Bridgeway Ste 401 Sausalito CA 94965 415-331-0303
Web: www.medizoneint.com

MEDport LLC 23 Acorn St Providence RI 02903 401-273-0444
Web: www.medport-llc.com

MedShape Inc 1575 Northside Dr NW Ste 440 Atlanta GA 30318 404-249-9155
Web: www.medshapesolutions.com

Medtronic Inc 710 Medtronic Pkwy NE Minneapolis MN 55432 763-514-4000 514-4879
NYSE: MDT ■ *TF Cust Svc:* 800-328-2518 ■ *Web:* www.medtronic.com

Medtronic MiniMed Inc 18000 Devonshire St Northridge CA 91325 800-646-4633
TF: 800-646-4633 ■ *Web:* www.medtronicdiabetes.com

Medtronic Powered Surgical Solutions
4620 N Beach St Fort Worth TX 76137 817-788-6400
TF: 800-643-2773 ■
Web: www.medtronic.com/for-healthcare-professionals/business-unit-landing-page

Medtronic Sofamor Danek USA Inc
1800 Pyramid Pl Memphis TN 38132 901-396-3133
Web: www.sofamordanek.com

Medtronic Surgical Technologies
6743 Southpoint Dr N Jacksonville FL 32216 904-296-9600
TF: 800-874-5797 ■ *Web:* www.medtronic.com

Mentor Corp 201 Mentor Dr Santa Barbara CA 93111 805-879-6000
NASDAQ: MENT ■ *TF:* 800-525-0245 ■ *Web:* www.mentorwwllc.com

Merits Health Products Inc 730 NE 19th Pl Cape Coral FL 33909 239-772-0579
Web: www.meritshealth.com

Mettler Electronics Corp 1333 S Claudina St Anaheim CA 92805 714-533-2221
TF: 800-854-9305 ■ *Web:* www.mettlerelectronics.com

Microtek Medical Holdings Inc
13000 Deerfield Pkwy Ste 300 Alpharetta GA 30004 678-896-4400 327-5921*
**Fax Area Code:* 662 ■ *TF:* 800-777-7977 ■ *Web:* www.microtekmed.com

Microtek Medical Inc 512 N Lehmberg Rd Columbus MS 39702 662-327-1863 327-5921
TF: 800-824-3027 ■ *Web:* www.microtekmed.com

MicroVention Inc 1311 Valencia Ave Tustin CA 92780 714-247-8000
TF: 800-990-8368 ■ *Web:* www.microvention.com

Micrus Endovascular 821 Fox Ln San Jose CA 95131 408-433-1400 433-1401

Milestone Scientific Inc 220 S Orange Ave Livingston NJ 07039 973-535-2717 535-2829
OTC: MLSS ■ *TF:* 800-862-1125 ■ *Web:* www.milestonescientific.com

Miracle-Ear Inc 5000 Cheshire Pkwy N Minneapolis MN 55446 800-464-8002 268-4365*
**Fax Area Code:* 763 ■ *TF:* 800-464-8002 ■ *Web:* www.miracle-ear.com

Monaghan Medical Corp
5 Latour Ave Ste 1600 Plattsburgh NY 12901 518-561-7330
TF: 800-833-9653 ■ *Web:* www.monaghanmed.com

Moximed Inc 26460 Corporate Ave Ste 100 Hayward CA 94545 510-887-3300
Web: www.moximed.com

MP Biomedicals LLC 3 Hutton Ctr Dr Ste 100 Santa Ana CA 92707 949-833-2500
TF: 800-633-1352 ■ *Web:* www.mpbio.com

National Fabrication Ctr 9561 Satellite Blvd Orlando FL 32837 407-852-6170
Web: hanger.com

Nearly Me Technologies Po Box 21475 Waco TX 76702 254-662-1752
TF: 800-887-3370 ■ *Web:* www.tgtransforms.com

NELCO Inc 3 Gill St Unit D Woburn MA 01801 781-933-1940 933-4763
TF: 800-635-2613 ■ *Web:* www.nelcoworldwide.com

Nemcomed Inc 801 Industrial Dr Hicksville OH 43526 419-542-7743
Web: www.nemcomed.com

Net Safety Monitoring Inc
2721 Hopewell Pl NE Calgary AB T1Y7J7 403-219-0688
Web: www.net-safety.com

Nice-Pak Products Inc 2 Nice-Pak Pk Orangeburg NY 10962 845-365-1700 365-1717
TF: 800-444-6725 ■ *Web:* www.nicepak.com

Nonin Medical Inc 13700 First Ave N Plymouth MN 55441 763-553-9968 577-5500
Web: www.nonin.com

NorMed 4310 S 131 Pl Ste 160 Seattle WA 98168 800-288-8200 242-3315*
**Fax Area Code:* 206 ■ *TF:* 800-288-8200 ■ *Web:* www.normed.com

Nu-Hope Laboratories Inc 12640 Branford St Pacoima CA 91331 818-899-7711
TF: 800-899-5017 ■ *Web:* www.nu-hope.com

NuOrtho Surgical Inc 151 Martine St Fall River MA 02723 617-848-8999

Ok-1 Manufacturing Co 709 S Veterans Dr Altus OK 73521 580-482-0891
Web: www.ok-1safety.com

Ortho Development Corp 12187 S Business Pk Dr Draper UT 84020 801-553-9991 553-9993
TF: 800-429-8339 ■ *Web:* www.odev.com

OrthoCor Medical Inc 1251 Red Fox Rd Arden Hills MN 55112 952-217-6366
Web: www.orthocormedical.com

Orthofeet Inc 152A Veterans Dr Northvale NJ 07647 201-767-6224
Web: orthofeet.com

Orthofix Inc 1720 Bray Central Dr McKinney TX 75069 469-742-2500 742-2556
TF: 800-527-0404 ■ *Web:* www.orthofix.com

OrthoPediatrics Corp 2850 Frontier Dr Warsaw IN 46582 574-268-6379
Web: www.orthopediatrics.com

OrthoPro LLC
3939 S Wasatch Blvd Ste 19 Salt Lake City UT 84124 866-746-0208
TF: 866-746-0208 ■ *Web:* orthoprollc.com

OrthoSensor Inc 1855 Griffin Rd Ste A-310 Dania Beach FL 33004 954-577-7770
Web: www.orthosensor.com

Osborn Medical Corp 100 W Main St Utica MN 55979 507-932-5028
Web: www.osbornmedical.com

Osteomed Corp 3885 Arapaho Rd Addison TX 75001 972-677-4600 677-4601
TF Cust Svc: 800-456-7779 ■ *Web:* www.osteomedcorp.com

Pac-Kit Safety Equipment Co Inc
57 Chestnut St South Norwalk CT 06854 203-857-5361
Web: www.pac-kit.com

Pacific Medical Inc 1700 N Chrisman Rd Tracy CA 95304 800-726-9180 861-5950
TF: 800-726-9180 ■ *Web:* www.pacmedical.com

Passy-Muir Inc 4521 Campus Dr Pmb 273 Irvine CA 92612 949-833-8255
TF: 800-634-5397 ■ *Web:* www.passy-muir.com

PeelMaster Packaging Corp
6153 W Mulford St Unit C Niles IL 60714 847-966-6161
Web: peelmaster.com

Perma-Type Company Inc 83 NW Dr Plainville CT 06062 860-747-9999 747-1986
Web: www.perma-type.com

Phonic Ear Inc 2080 Lakeville Hwy Petaluma CA 94954 707-769-1110
TF: 800-227-0735 ■ *Web:* www.phonicear.com

Phone Fax

Phygen LLC 2301 Dupont Ave Ste 510 Irvine CA 92612 800-939-7008
TF: 800-939-7008 ■ *Web:* www.phygenspine.com

Physiotherapy Associates Inc
855 Springdale Dr Ste 200 Exton PA 19341 610-644-7824
Web: www.physiocorp.com

PLUS Orthopedics USA Inc
10188 Telesis Ct Ste 300 San Diego CA 92121 858-550-3800
Web: ww11.plusortho.com

Posey Co 5635 Peck Rd Arcadia CA 91006 626-443-3143 767-3933*
**Fax Area Code:* 800 ■ *TF:* 800-447-6739 ■ *Web:* www.posey.com

Precision Dynamics Corp
13880 Del Sur St San Fernando CA 91340 818-897-1111
TF: 800-847-0670 ■ *Web:* www.pdcorp.com

Precision Technology Inc 50 Maple St Norwood NJ 07648 201-767-1600
Web: www.ptiplastics.com

Pride Mobility Products Corp
182 Susquehanna Ave Exeter PA 18643 800-800-8586 655-2990*
**Fax Area Code:* 570 ■ *TF:* 800-800-8586 ■ *Web:* www.pridemobility.com

Pro Orthopedic Devices Inc 2884 E Ganley Rd Tucson AZ 85706 520-294-4401
TF: 800-523-5611 ■ *Web:* www.proorthopedic.com

Prosthetic Design Inc 700 Harco Dr Clayton OH 45315 937-836-1464
TF: 800-459-0177 ■ *Web:* prostheticdesign.com

Rapid Fire Marketing Inc
Ste 1234 311 W Third St Carson City NV 89703 404-261-1196
Web: www.rapid-fire-marketing.com

Redi-Medic Ind 1320 Alberta Ave Saskatoon SK S7K1R5 306-955-8821

Rehab Plus Therapeutic Products 6104 45th St Lubbock TX 79407 806-791-2288

Retractable Technologies Inc 511 Lobo Ln Little Elm TX 75068 972-294-1010 292-3600
NYSE: RVP ■ *TF:* 888-806-2626 ■ *Web:* www.vanishpoint.com

REVA Medical Inc 5751 Copley Dr San Diego CA 92111 858-966-3000
Web: www.revamedical.com

Rockford Medical & Safety Co
2420 Harrison Ave Rockford IL 61108 815-394-0100
Web: www.firensafety.com

Rusch Inc
2917 Weck Dr PO Box 12600 Research Triangle Park NC 27709 919-544-8000 361-3914
TF: 866-246-6990 ■ *Web:* teleflex.com/en/usa/notfound.html

Sas Safety Corp 3031 Gardenia Ave Long Beach CA 90807 562-427-2775 244-1938*
**Fax Area Code:* 800 ■ *TF:* 800-262-0200 ■ *Web:* www.sassafety.com

Siemens Hearing Instruments Inc
10 Constitution Ave PO Box 1397 Piscataway NJ 08855 800-766-4500 562-6696*
**Fax Area Code:* 732 ■ *TF:* 800-766-4500 ■ *Web:* healthcare.siemens.com

Smith & Nephew Inc 1450 E Brooks Rd Memphis TN 38116 901-396-2121 396-9929
TF Cust Svc: 800-238-7538 ■ *Web:* www.smith-nephew.com

Smith & Nephew Inc
970 Lk Carillon Dr 310 Saint Petersburg FL 33716 727-392-1261 392-6914
TF Cust Svc: 800-876-1261 ■ *Web:* smith-nephew.com

Smiths Medical ASD Inc 160 Weymouth St Rockland MA 02370 781-878-8011 878-8201
TF: 800-258-5361 ■ *Web:* www.smiths-medical.com

Smiths Medical MD Inc 1265 Grey Fox Rd Saint Paul MN 55112 651-633-2556 628-7459
TF: 800-258-5361 ■ *Web:* www.smiths-medical.com

Smiths Medical Respiratory Support Products
5200 Upper Metro Pl Ste 200 Dublin OH 43017 214-618-0218 734-0254*
**Fax Area Code:* 614 ■ *TF:* 800-258-5361 ■ *Web:* www.smiths-medical.com

Sonic Innovations Inc 2501 Cottontail Ln Somerset NJ 08873 888-423-7834 365-3000*
**Fax Area Code:* 801 ■ *TF:* 888-678-4327 ■ *Web:* www.sonici.us

Sophono Inc 5744 Central Ave Ste 100 Boulder CO 80301 720-407-5160
Web: sophono.com

Southmedic Inc 50 Alliance Blvd Barrie ON L4M5K3 705-726-9383
TF: 800-463-7146 ■ *Web:* southmedic.com

Span-America Medical Systems Inc
70 Commerce Ctr Greenville SC 29615 864-288-8877 288-8692
NASDAQ: SPAN ■ *TF:* 800-888-6752 ■ *Web:* www.spanamerica.com

Spenco Medical Corp PO Box 2501 Waco TX 76702 800-877-3626
TF: 800-877-3626 ■ *Web:* www.spenco.com

Standard Textile Company Inc
1 Knollcrest Dr Cincinnati OH 45237 513-761-9255 761-0467
TF: 800-999-0400 ■ *Web:* www.standardtextile.com

Starkey Laboratories Inc
6700 Washington Ave S Eden Prairie MN 55344 952-941-6401
TF: 800-328-8602 ■ *Web:* www.starkey.com

STERIS Corp 5960 Heisley Rd Mentor OH 44060 440-354-2600 639-4450*
NYSE: STE ■ **Fax:* Cust Svc ■ *TF:* 800-548-4873 ■ *Web:* www.steris.com

Stryker Endoscopy 5900 Optical Ct San Jose CA 95138 408-754-2000
Web: strykerendo.com

Sunrise Medical Inc 2842 Business Pk Ave Fresno CA 93727 800-333-4000
TF: 800-333-4000 ■ *Web:* www.sunrisemedical.com

Surgical Appliance Industries Inc
3960 Rosslyn Dr Cincinnati OH 45209 800-888-0867 309-9055
TF: 800-888-0867 ■ *Web:* www.saibrands.com

Symmetry Medical Inc 3724 N State Rd 15 Warsaw IN 46582 574-267-8700
NYSE: SMA ■ *Web:* www.symmetrymedical.com

SynCardia Systems Inc 1992 E Silverlake Rd Tucson AZ 85713 520-545-1234
Web: www.syncardia.com

Synovis Life Technologies Inc
2575 University Ave Saint Paul MN 55114 651-796-7300 642-9018
NASDAQ: SYNO ■ *TF:* 800-255-4018 ■ *Web:* www.synovislife.com

Synthes USA 1302 Wrights Ln E West Chester PA 19380 610-719-5000 719-5140*
**Fax:* Hum Res ■ *TF:* 800-523-0322 ■ *Web:* synthes.com

Tamarack Habilitation Technologies Inc
1670 94th Ln NE Blaine MN 55449 763-795-0057
TF: 866-795-0057 ■ *Web:* www.tamarackhti.com

TIDI Products LLC 570 Enterprise Dr Neenah WI 54956 800-521-1314 837-7770
TF: 800-521-1314 ■ *Web:* www.tidiproducts.com

Treen Gloves & Safety Products Ltd
704 Alexander St Vancouver BC V6A1E3 604-253-4588
Web: www.treensafety.com

Trulife 26296 Twelve Trees Ln NW Poulsbo WA 98370 360-697-5656
Web: apexsystemsinc.com

TSO3 Inc 2505 Dalton Ave Quebec QC G1P3S5 418-651-0003 653-5726
TF: 866-715-0003 ■ *Web:* www.tso3.com

Utah Medical Products Inc 7043 S 300 W Midvale UT 84047 801-566-1200 566-2062
NASDAQ: UTMD ■ *TF:* 866-754-9789 ■ *Web:* www.utahmed.com

Company	City	State	Zip	Phone	Fax
Venture Tape Corp 30 Commerce Rd *Web:* venturetape.com	Rockland	MA	02370	781-331-5900	
Vital Signs Inc 20 Campus Rd *TF:* 800-932-0760 ■ *Web:* www3.gehealthcare.com	Totowa	NJ	07512	973-790-1330	790-3307
Volcano Corp 3721 Valley Centre Dr Ste 500 **Fax Area Code:* 916 ■ *TF:* 800-228-4728 ■ *Web:* www.volcanocorp.com	San Diego	CA	92130	800-228-4728	638-8812*
West Pharmaceutical Services Inc 101 Gordon Dr *NYSE: WST* ■ *TF:* 800-345-9800 ■ *Web:* www.westpharma.com	Lionville	PA	19341	610-594-2900	594-3000
Widex Canada Ltd 5041 Mainway *Web:* www.widex.ca	Burlington	ON	L7L5H9	905-315-8303	
Wright & Filippis Inc 2845 Crooks Rd *Web:* www.firsttoserve.com	Rochester Hills	MI	48309	248-829-8292	853-1830
Wright Medical Group Inc 5677 Airline Rd *NASDAQ: WMGI* ■ *TF:* 800-238-7188 ■ *Web:* www.wmt.com	Arlington	TN	38002	901-867-9971	867-9534
Wright Medical Technology Inc 5677 Airline Rd **Fax:* Cust Svc ■ *TF:* 800-238-7188 ■ *Web:* www.wmt.com	Arlington	TN	38002	901-867-9971	867-9534*
Zimmer Inc 1800 W Ctr St PO Box 708 *TF:* 800-613-6131 ■ *Web:* www.zimmer.com	Warsaw	IN	46580	574-267-6131	372-4988

478 MEDICAL TRANSCRIPTION SERVICES

Companies listed here have a national or regional clientele base.

Company	City	State	Zip	Phone	Fax
Acusis LLC 4 Smithfield St *Web:* www.acusis.com	Pittsburgh	PA	15222	412-209-1300	209-1299
ASL Distribution Services Ltd 2160 Buckingham Rd *Web:* www.asldistribution.com	Oakville	ON	L6H6M7	905-829-5141	
Bruce R Smith Limited 973 St Johns Rd W *Web:* www.brsmith.com	Simcoe	ON	N3Y4K1	519-426-0904	
Carrier Services of Tennessee Inc 2534 N Mount Juliet Rd *TF:* 800-825-7508 ■ *Web:* www.carrierservtn.com	Mount Juliet	TN	37122	615-758-9757	
Comtrans 20651 Prism Pl	Phoenix	AZ	92630	602-231-0102	
DCT Chambers Trucking Ltd 600 Waddington Dr *Web:* www.chambersgroup.co	Vernon	BC	V1T8T6	250-549-2157	
Energetic Services Inc Mile 54 Alaska Hwy *Web:* www.energeticservices.com	Fort St. John	BC	V1J4J1	250-785-4761	
FreightPros 3307 Northland Dr Ste 360 *TF:* 888-297-6968 ■ *Web:* www.freightpros.com	Austin	TX	78731	888-297-6968	
Hybrid Transit Systems Inc 818 Dows Rd SE *Web:* www.hybridtrans.com	Cedar Rapids	IA	52403	319-261-0749	
Logistic Professionals Inc 1920 Pennsylvania Ave *Web:* www.logisticpros.com	Mcdonough	GA	30253	770-692-0431	
MediGrafix Inc 9 Fairway Ln Ste C **Fax Area Code:* 888 ■ *TF:* 888-744-1301 ■ *Web:* www.medi-grafix.com	Blythewood	SC	29016	803-261-6387	744-1301*
Moran Towing Corp 50 Locust Ave *Web:* www.morantug.com	New Canaan	CT	06840	203-442-2800	
Multivans Inc 13289 Coleraine Dr *Web:* www.multivans.com	Bolton	ON	L7E3B6	905-857-3171	
Rapid Transcript Inc 4311 Wilshire Blvd *Web:* www.rapidtranscript.com	Los Angeles	CA	90010	323-964-0400	
Southern Motor Carriers Rate Conference Inc 500 Westpark Dr *Web:* www.smc3.com	Peachtree City	GA	30269	770-486-5800	
Thomas Transcription Services Inc PO Box 26613 *TF:* 888-878-2889 ■ *Web:* www.thomastx.com	Jacksonville	FL	32226	904-751-5058	751-5240
Transport Bourret Inc 375 Bd Lemire *Web:* www.bourret.ca	Drummondville	QC	J2B8G8	819-477-2202	
Transport Jacques Auger Inc 860 Archimede St *Web:* www.tja.ca	Levis	QC	G6V7M5	418-835-9266	
TransPro Freight Systems Ltd 8600 Escarpment Way Milton *Web:* www.transprofreight.com	Mississauga	ON	L9T0M1	905-693-0699	
Warren Gibson Ltd 206 Church St South PO Box 100 *TF:* 800-461-4374 ■ *Web:* www.warrengibson.com	Alliston	ON	L9R1T9	705-435-4342	

479 MEDICINAL CHEMICALS & BOTANICAL PRODUCTS

See Also Biotechnology Companies p. 1859; Diagnostic Products p. 2192; Pharmaceutical Companies p. 2934; Pharmaceutical Companies - Generic Drugs p. 2936; Vitamins & Nutritional Supplements p. 3296

Companies listed here manufacture medicinal chemicals and botanical products in bulk for sale to pharmaceutical, vitamin, and nutritional product companies.

Company	City	State	Zip	Phone	Fax
Acic Fine Chemicals Inc 81 St Claire Blvd *TF:* 800-265-6727 ■ *Web:* www.acic.com	Brantford	ON	N3S7X6	519-751-3668	751-1378
AM Todd Co 1717 Douglas Ave *Web:* www.wildflavors.com	Kalamazoo	MI	49007	269-343-2603	343-3399
American Laboratories Inc (ALI) 4410 S 102nd St *Web:* www.americanlaboratories.com	Omaha	NE	68127	402-339-2494	339-0801
Anika Therapeutics Inc 32 Wiggins Ave *NASDAQ: ANIK* ■ *Web:* www.anikatherapeutics.com	Bedford	MA	01730	781-457-9000	305-9720
Apotex Pharmachem Inc 34 Spalding Dr *Web:* www.apotexpharmachem.com	Brantford	ON	N3T6B8	519-756-8942	753-3051
AQ Pharmaceuticals Inc 11555 Monarch St *Web:* www.aqpharmaceuticals.com	Garden Grove	CA	92841	714-903-1000	
Array BioPharma Inc 3200 Walnut St *NASDAQ: ARRY* ■ *TF:* 877-633-2436 ■ *Web:* www.arraybiopharma.com	Boulder	CO	80301	303-381-6600	449-5376
Avanti Polar Lipids Inc 700 Industrial Pk Dr *TF:* 800-227-0651 ■ *Web:* www.avantilipids.com	Alabaster	AL	35007	205-663-2494	663-0756
Bachem Bioscience Inc 3132 Kashiwa St *TF:* 888-422-2436 ■ *Web:* www.bachem.com	Torrance	CA	90505	310-539-4171	
Balchem Corp 52 Sunrise Pk Rd PO Box 600 *NASDAQ: BCPC* ■ *TF:* 877-407-8289 ■ *Web:* www.balchem.com	New Hampton	NY	10958	845-326-5613	326-5742
Bedford Laboratories Inc 300 Northfield Rd *TF:* 800-562-4797	Bedford	OH	44146	440-232-3320	232-6264
Ben Venue Laboratories Inc 300 Northfield Rd *TF General:* 800-989-3320 ■ *Web:* www.benvenue.com	Bedford	OH	44146	440-232-3320	439-6398
Betachem Inc 58 Ware Rd	Upper Saddle River	NJ	07458	201-327-4100	327-9366
BI Nutraceuticals 2550 El Presidio St *Web:* www.botanicals.com	Long Beach	CA	90810	310-669-2100	637-3644
Bio-Botanica Inc 75 Commerce Dr *TF:* 800-645-5720 ■ *Web:* www.bio-botanica.com	Hauppauge	NY	11788	631-231-5522	231-7332
Cambrex Charles City Inc 1205 11th St *Web:* www.cambrex.com	Charles City	IA	50616	641-257-1000	228-4152
Cambrex Corp 1 Meadowlands Plz *NYSE: CBM* ■ *TF:* 866-286-9133 ■ *Web:* www.cambrex.com	East Rutherford	NJ	07073	201-804-3000	804-9852
Cell Marque Corp 6600 Sierra College Blvd *Web:* www.cellmarque.com	Rocklin	CA	95677	916-746-8900	
Charm Sciences Inc 659 Andover St *TF:* 800-343-2170 ■ *Web:* www.charm.com	Lawrence	MA	01843	978-687-9200	687-9216
ChemWerth Inc 1764 Litchfield Tpke *Web:* www.chemwerth.com	Woodbridge	CT	06525	203-387-7794	397-8132
Contract Pharmacal Corp 135 Adams Ave *Web:* www.cpc.com	Hauppauge	NY	11788	631-231-4610	231-4610
Creagen Biosciences Inc 23 Rainin Rd *Web:* www.creagenbio.com	Woburn	MA	01801	781-938-1122	
Cyanotech Corp 73-4460 Queen Kaahumanu Hwy Ste 102 *NASDAQ: CYAN* ■ *TF Sales:* 800-453-1187 ■ *Web:* www.cyanotech.com	Kailua-Kona	HI	96740	808-326-1353	329-4533
Designing Health Inc 28410 Witherspoon Pkwy *TF:* 800-774-7387 ■ *Web:* www.missinglinkproducts.com	Valencia	CA	91355	661-257-1705	
Diosynth RTP Inc 101 J Morris Commons Ln *Web:* www.fujifilmdiosynth.com	Morrisville	NC	27560	919-337-4477	
Down to Earth 2525 S King St *Web:* www.downtoearth.org	Honolulu	HI	96826	808-947-7678	
Elge Inc 1000 Cole Ave *Web:* www.elgeinc.com	Rosenberg	TX	77471	281-342-8228	
Flavine North America Inc 10 Reuten Dr *Web:* www.flavine.com	Closter	NJ	07624	201-768-4190	768-2854
Flora Mfg & Distributing Ltd 7400 Fraser Park Dr *TF:* 888-436-6697 ■ *Web:* www.florahealth.com	Burnaby	BC	V5J5B9	604-436-6000	
Gemini Pharmaceuticals Inc 87 Modular Ave *Web:* www.geminipharm.com	Commack	NY	11725	631-543-3334	543-3335
George Uhe Company Inc 219 River Dr *TF:* 800-850-4075 ■ *Web:* www.uhe.com	Garfield	NJ	07026	201-843-4000	843-7517
Greer Laboratories Inc 639 Nuway Cir NE PO Box 800 *TF Cust Svc:* 800-378-3906 ■ *Web:* www.greerlabs.com	Lenoir	NC	28645	828-754-5327	754-5320
GYMA Laboratories of America Inc 135 Cantiague Rock Rd *Web:* www.gyma.com	Westbury	NY	11590	516-933-0900	933-1075
ICC Industries Inc 460 Pk Ave *TF:* 800-422-1720 ■ *Web:* www.iccchem.com	New York	NY	10022	212-521-1700	521-1970
InCon Processing LLC 970 Douglas Rd *Web:* www.incontech.com	Batavia	IL	60510	630-761-1180	
Interchem Corp 120 Rt 17 N *TF:* 800-261-7332 ■ *Web:* www.interchem.com	Paramus	NJ	07652	201-261-7333	261-7339
Johnson Matthey Pharma Services 25 Patton Rd *TF:* 800-444-8544 ■ *Web:* www.jmpharmaservices.com	Devens	MA	01434	978-784-5000	784-5500
Lannett Company Inc (LCI) 13200 Townsend Rd *NYSE: LCI* ■ *TF:* 800-325-9994 ■ *Web:* www.lannett.com	Philadelphia	PA	19154	215-333-9000	333-9004
Libby Laboratories Inc 1700 Sixth St *Web:* www.libbylabs.com	Berkeley	CA	94710	510-527-5400	527-8687
LycoRed Corp 377 Crane St *TF:* 877-592-6733 ■ *Web:* www.lycored.com	Orange	NJ	07051	973-882-0322	882-0323
Natural Standard 1 Davis Sq *Web:* naturalmedicines.therapeuticresearch.com	Somerville	MA	02144	617-591-3300	
Naturex Inc 375 Huyler St *Web:* www.naturex.com	South Hackensack	NJ	07606	201-440-5000	342-8000
NHK Laboratories Inc 12230 E Florience Ave *TF:* 866-645-5227 ■ *Web:* www.nhklabs.com	Santa Fe Springs	CA	90670	562-944-5400	944-0266
NovaDigm Therapeutics Inc 4201 James Ray Dr Reac 1 Bldg Ste 2200 *Web:* www.novadigm.net	Grand Forks	ND	58202	701-757-5161	335-7121
Nutra Pharma Corp 12502 W Atlantic Blvd *TF:* 877-895-5647 ■ *Web:* www.nutrapharma.com	Coral Springs	FL	33071	954-509-0911	
Nutraceutix Inc 9609 153rd Ave NE *TF:* 800-548-3222 ■ *Web:* www.nutraceutix.com	Redmond	WA	98052	425-883-9518	869-1020
NutriScience Innovations LLC 2450 Reservoir Ave *Web:* www.nutriscienceusa.com	Trumbull	CT	06611	203-372-8877	372-9977
Nutrition 21 Inc 3 Manhattanville Rd *Web:* www.nutrition21.com	Purchase	NY	10577	914-701-4500	696-0860
One Lambda Inc 21001 Kittridge St *TF:* 800-822-8824 ■ *Web:* www.onelambda.com	Canoga Park	CA	91303	818-702-0042	702-6904
Paddock Laboratories Inc 3940 Quebec Ave N *Web:* www.paddocklabs.com	Minneapolis	MN	55427	763-546-4676	
Patheon Inc 2100 Syntex Ct *Web:* www.patheon.com	Mississauga	ON	L5N7K9	905-821-4001	812-6709
PendoPharm Inc 6111 Royalmount *TF Cust Svc:* 866-926-7653 ■ *Web:* www.pendopharm.com	Montreal	QC	H4P2T4	514-340-5045	733-9684
Pharma Tech Industries Inc 1310 Stylemaster Dr *Web:* www.pharma-tech.net	Union	MO	63084	636-583-8664	583-5373
Premier Micronutrient Corp 1801 W End Ave Ste 920 *Web:* www.premiermicronutrient.com	Nashville	TN	37203	615-234-4020	

Phone Fax

Rainbow Light Nutritional Sys Inc
100 Ave Tea .... Santa Cruz CA 95060 800-635-1233 429-0189*
Fax Area Code: 831 ■ *TF:* 800-635-1233 ■ *Web:* www.rainbowlight.com
Sabinsa Corp 20 Lake Dr .... East Windsor NJ 08520 732-777-1111 777-1443
Web: www.sabinsa.com
Salvona Technologies LLC 65 Stults Rd Bldg 1 .... Dayton NJ 08810 609-655-0173
Web: www.salvona.com
Scientific Protein Laboratories Inc
700 E Main St PO Box 158 .... Waunakee WI 53597 608-849-5944 849-4053
TF: 800-334-4775 ■ *Web:* www.spl-pharma.com
Siegfried USA LLC 33 Industrial Pk Rd .... Pennsville NJ 08070 856-678-3601 678-8201
TF Cust Svc: 877-763-8630 ■ *Web:* www.siegfried.ch
Sigma-Aldrich Corp 3050 Spruce St. .... Saint Louis MO 63103 314-771-5765 325-5052*
NASDAQ: SIAL ■ *Fax Area Code:* 800 ■ *TF:* 800-325-3010 ■ *Web:* www.sigmaaldrich.com
Spectrum Laboratory Products Inc
14422 S San Pedro St .... Gardena CA 90248 310-516-8000 516-7512*
*Fax: Cust Svc ■ *TF General:* 800-772-8786 ■ *Web:* www.spectrumchemical.com
SPI Pharma Rockwood Office Park Fl 2 .... Wilmington DE 19809 302-576-8567 789-9755*
Fax Area Code: 800 ■ *TF:* 800-789-9755 ■ *Web:* www.spipharma.com
SST Corp 635 Brighton Rd .... Clifton NJ 07012 973-473-4300 473-4326
TF: 800-222-0921 ■ *Web:* www.sst-corp.com
Starwest Botanicals Inc
11253 Trade Ctr Dr .... Rancho Cordova CA 95742 916-638-8100 638-8293
TF General: 888-273-4372 ■ *Web:* www.starwestherb.com
Terry Laboratories Inc 7005 Technology Dr .... Melbourne FL 32904 321-259-1630 242-0625
TF: 800-367-2563 ■ *Web:* www.terrylabs.com
Tri-K Industries Inc 2 Stewart Ct PO Box 10 .... Denville NJ 07834 973-298-8850 750-9785*
Fax Area Code: 201 ■ *TF:* 800-526-0372 ■ *Web:* www.tri-k.com
TSI Health Sciences Inc
305 S Fourth St E Ste 101 .... Missoula MT 59801 406-549-9123
TF: 877-549-9123 ■ *Web:* www.tsiinc.com
Uluru Inc 4452 Beltway Dr .... Addison TX 75001 214-905-5145 905-5130
Web: www.uluruinc.com
United-Guardian Inc (UGI)
230 Marcus Blvd PO Box 18050 .... Hauppauge NY 11788 631-273-0900 273-0858
NASDAQ: UG ■ *TF:* 800-645-5566 ■ *Web:* www.u-g.com
Vinchem Inc 301 Main St .... Chatham NJ 07928 973-635-4841 635-1459
Web: www.vinchem.com
Wilcox Emporium Warehouse 161 Howard St .... Boone NC 28607 828-262-1221
Web: wilcoxemporium.com

480 METAL - STRUCTURAL (FABRICATED)

Phone Fax

A J Sackett & Sons Co, The
1701 S Highland Ave .... Baltimore MD 21224 410-276-4466
Web: www.ajsackett.com
Able Steel Fabricators Inc 4150 E Quartz Cir. .... Mesa AZ 85215 480-830-2253
Web: www.ablesteel.com
Acme Architectural Products Inc
251 Lombardy St .... Brooklyn NY 11222 718-384-7800
Web: www.acmesalesgroup.com
Aerospace America Inc 900 Harry Truman Pkwy .... Bay City MI 48706 989-684-2121 684-4486
TF: 800-237-6414 ■ *Web:* www.aerospaceamerica.com
Afco Manufacturing Corp
428 Cogshall St PO Box 230 .... Holly MI 48442 248-634-4415 634-6301
Web: www.afcomfg.com
Afco Steel Inc 1423 E Sixth St .... Little Rock AR 72202 501-340-6200 340-6260
Web: www.afcosteel.com
Aircon Corp 2873 Chelsea Ave. .... Memphis TN 38108 901-452-0230
Web: www.aircon-corporation.com
AJ Manufacturing Inc 1217 Oak St .... Bloomer WI 54724 715-568-2204
Web: www.ajdoor.com
All Metals Service & Warehousing Inc
100 All Metals Dr .... Cartersville GA 30120 770-427-7379
Web: www.allmetals.com
Allcan Distributors Inc 12612 - 124 St .... Edmonton AB T5L0N7 780-451-2357
Web: www.allcan.com
Allied Steel Fabricators Inc
4604 148th Ave Ne .... Redmond WA 98052 425-861-9558
Web: www.alliedsteelfab.com
Alloy Engineering Co, The 844 Thacker St .... Berea OH 44017 440-243-6800
Web: www.alloyengineering.com
AmChel Communications Inc 2800 Capital St .... Wylie TX 75098 972-442-1030
TF: 866-388-6959 ■ *Web:* www.amchel.com
American Aerogel Corp
460 Buffalo Rd Ste 200A .... Rochester NY 14611 585-328-2140
Web: www.americanaerogel.com
American BOA Inc 1420 Redi Rd .... Cumming GA 30040 770-889-9400
TF: 800-856-4580 ■ *Web:* www.americanboa.com
American Commercial Inc
200 Bob Morrison Blvd .... Bristol VA 24201 276-466-2743
Web: www.dsiunderground.com
Amerimax Bldg Products Inc 5208 Tennyson Pkwy .... Plano TX 75024 469-366-3200 448-8391*
Fax Area Code: 800 ■ *Web:* www.amerimaxbp.com
Amerimax Home Products Inc
450 Richardson Dr .... Lancaster PA 17603 717-299-3711
TF: 800-347-2586 ■ *Web:* www.amerimax.com
Anasteel & Supply Company LLC
2272 Mabros Industrial Pkwy .... Ellenwood GA 30294 404-675-9501
Web: www.anasteel.com
Anchor Fabrication Ltd 1200 Lawson Rd .... Fort Worth TX 76131 817-498-2521
TF: 800-635-0386 ■ *Web:* anchorfabrication.com
Apex Industries Inc 100 Millennium Blvd .... Moncton NB E1E2G8 506-857-1620
TF: 800-268-3331 ■ *Web:* www.apexindustries.com
Arcadia Mfg Group Inc 80 Cohoes Ave .... Green Island NY 12183 518-434-6213
Web: www.arcadiamfg.com
Artimex Iron Company Inc 315 Cypress Ln .... El Cajon CA 92020 619-444-3155
Web: www.artimexiron.com
ASTECH Engineered Products Inc
3030 Red Hill Ave .... Santa Ana CA 92705 949-250-1000

Phone Fax

Azimuth Three Communications
127 Delta Park Blvd .... Brampton ON L6T5M8 905-793-7793 793-0780
Web: www.az3.com
Baker Metal Products Inc 11140 Zodiac Ln. .... Dallas TX 75229 972-241-3553
Web: bakermetal.com
Baker Tankhead Inc 10405 N fwy .... Fort Worth TX 76177 817-232-8030
Web: www.bakertankhead.com
Baron Metal Industries Inc
101 Ashbridge Cir .... Woodbridge ON L4L3R5 416-749-2111
TF: 800-263-7515 ■ *Web:* www.baronmetal.com
Benson Steel Ltd 72 Commercial Rd .... Bolton ON L7E1K4 905-857-0684
Web: www.bensonsteel.com
Berlin Steel Construction Co
76 Depot Rd PO Box 428 .... Kensington CT 06037 860-828-3531 828-5253
Web: www.berlinsteel.com
Bohn & Dawson Inc
3500 Tree Ct Industrial Blvd .... Saint Louis MO 63122 636-225-5011 825-6111
Web: www.bohnanddawson.com
Boman Kemp Basement Window Systems
2393 South 1900 West .... Ogden UT 84401 801-731-0615
Web: www.boman-kemp.com
Braden Mfg LLC 5199 N Mingo Rd .... Tulsa OK 74117 800-272-3360 272-7414*
Fax Area Code: 918 ■ *TF:* 800-272-3360 ■ *Web:* www.braden.com
Brandywine Valley Fabricators Inc
Brandywine Vly Fab .... Coatesville PA 19320 610-384-7440
Web: www.brandywinevalleyfab.com
Brilex Industries Inc PO Box 749 .... Youngstown OH 44501 330-744-1114 744-1125
Web: www.brilex.com
Brookfield Fabricating Corp
111 Stanbury Industrial Dr .... Brookfield MO 64628 660-258-2214
Web: www.brookfieldfabricating.com
Busch Industries Inc
900 E Paris Ave Se Ste 304 .... Grand Rapids MI 49546 616-957-3737
Web: www.buschindustries.com
C&G Systems Corp 320 E Main St .... Lake Zurich IL 60047 847-816-9700
Web: www.cgsystems.com
Capital Tower & Communications Inc
13330 Amberly Rd .... Waverly NE 68462 402-786-3333
Web: www.capitaltower.com
Cauttrell Enterprises Inc 7618 N Broadway .... St. Louis MO 63147 314-385-4270
Web: www.cauttrellenterprises.com
Center Rock Inc 118 Schrock Dr .... Berlin PA 15530 814-267-7100
Web: www.centerrock.com
Central Aluminum Co 2045 Broehm Rd .... Columbus OH 43207 614-491-5700
Web: www.centralaluminum.com
Central Minnesota Fabricating Inc
2725 W Gorton Ave .... Willmar MN 56201 320-235-4181
TF: 800-839-8857 ■ *Web:* www.cmf-inc.com
Central Steel Fabricators Inc 1843 S 54th Ave .... Cicero IL 60804 708-652-2037
Web: www.centralsteelfab.com
Central Texas Iron Works Inc
1000 Winchell St PO Box 2555 .... Waco TX 76712 254-776-8000 772-5811
Web: www.ctiw.com
CENTRIA 1005 Beaver Grade Rd .... Moon Township PA 15108 412-299-8000 299-8051*
*Fax: Hum Res ■ *TF:* 800-759-7474 ■ *Web:* www.centria.com
Certified Stainless Service Inc
2704 Railroad Ave .... Ceres CA 95307 209-537-4747
Web: www.west-mark.com
Cessco Fabrication & Engineering Ltd
7310-99 St .... Edmonton AB T6E3R8 780-433-9531 432-7899
TF: 800-272-9698 ■ *Web:* www.cessco.ca
Chase Industries Inc
10021 Commerce Park Dr .... Cincinnati OH 45246 513-860-5565
TF: 800-543-4455 ■ *Web:* www.chasedoors.com
Cherubini Metal Works Ltd
570 Wilkinson Ave .... Dartmouth NS B3B0J4 902-468-5630
CHI Overhead Doors Inc 1485 Sunrise Dr .... Arthur IL 61911 217-543-2135
Web: www.chiohd.com
Cives Steel Co 210 Cives Ln .... Winchester VA 22603 540-667-3480
Web: www.cives.com
Clark Steel Fabricators Inc
12610 Vigilante Rd .... Lakeside CA 92040 619-390-1502
Web: www.clarksteelfab.com
Clermont Steel Fabricators LLC
2565 Old SR 32 .... Batavia OH 45103 513-732-6033 732-5344
Web: www.clermontsteel.com
CMC Alamo Steel Co 2784 Old Dallas Rd .... Waco TX 76705 254-799-2471 799-6227
TF: 800-500-0333 ■ *Web:* www.cmc.com
CMC Capitol City Steel 14501 S IH 35 .... Buda TX 78610 512-282-8820 295-2500
TF: 888-682-7337 ■ *Web:* www.cmc.com
CMC Rebar Carolinas 2528 N Chester St. .... Gastonia NC 28052 704-865-8571
Web: www.cmc.com
CMC Rebar Georgia 251 Hosea Rd. .... Lawrenceville GA 30045 770-963-6251 339-6623
TF: 888-682-7337 ■ *Web:* www.cmc.com
Coastal Steel Inc 870 Cidco Rd .... Cocoa FL 32923 321-632-8228
Web: www.coastalsteel.com
Collins Industries Ltd 3740-73 Ave. .... Edmonton AB T6B2Z2 780-440-1414
Web: www.collins-industries-ltd.com
Com-Tech Service Group Inc
17827 Commerce Dr .... Westfield IN 46074 317-867-4486
Web: www.comtechservices.net
Commercial Resins Company Inc
8100 E 96th Ave .... Henderson CO 80640 303-288-3914
Web: commercialresins.com
Compo Steel Products Inc 3637 N Holton St .... Milwaukee WI 53212 414-962-6800
Web: www.composteel.com
Contract Fabricators Inc
105 Rolfing Rd .... Holly Springs MS 38635 662-252-6330
Web: www.contractfab.com
Contractors Material Co
10320 S Medallion Dr .... Cincinnati OH 45241 513-733-3000
Web: www.cmcmmi.com
Cooper STEEL Inc 503 N Hillcrest Dr .... Shelbyville TN 37160 931-684-7962
Web: www.coopersteel.com

Company	City	State	ZIP	Phone	Fax
Cowelco a California Corp 1634 W 14th St *Web:* www.cowelco.com	Long Beach	CA	90813	562-432-5766	
Craig Manufacturing Ltd 96 Mclean Ave *TF:* 800-565-5007 ■ *Web:* www.craig-mfg.com	Hartland	NB	E7P2K5	506-375-4493	
Crane Hill Machine & Fabrication Inc 2476 E Us Hwy 50 *Web:* www.cranehillmachine.com	Seymour	IN	47274	812-358-3534	358-2351
Creative Door Services Ltd 14904 - 135 Ave *Web:* creativedoor.com	Edmonton	AB	T5V1R9	780-483-1789	
Cubic Designs Inc 5487 S Westridge Dr. *Web:* www.cubicdesigns.com	New Berlin	WI	53151	262-789-1966	
Danny Byrd Inc 1416 Sandersville Sharon Rd *Web:* www.dannybyrdinc.com	Laurel	MS	39443	601-649-2524	
Dave Steel Company Inc 40 Meadow Rd. *Web:* www.davesteel.com	Asheville	NC	28803	828-252-2771	
Day Wireless Systems Inc 4700 SE International Way *Web:* www.daywireless.com	Milwaukie	OR	97222	503-659-1240	
Dis-Tran Steel Fabrication LLC 529 Cenla Dr *Web:* www.distran.com	Pineville	LA	71360	318-640-6892	
Discount RampsCom LLC 760 S Indiana Ave. *TF:* 888-651-3431 ■ *Web:* www.discountramps.com	West Bend	WI	53095	262-338-3431	
Don Young Co 8181 Ambassador Row. *TF:* 800-367-0390 ■ *Web:* www.dycwindows.com	Dallas	TX	75247	214-630-0934	630-0406
Dover Tank & Plate Co, The 5725 Crown Rd Nw *Web:* www.dovertank.com	Dover	OH	44622	330-343-4443	
Dropbox Inc 401 S 9th St. *TF:* 888-388-7768 ■ *Web:* www.dropboxinc.com	Ironton	OH	45638	888-388-7768	
Dura-Bond Industries Inc 2658 Puckety Dr. *Web:* www.dura-bond.com	Export	PA	15632	724-327-0280	
Eberl Iron Works Inc 128 Sycamore St *Web:* www.eberliron.com	Buffalo	NY	14204	716-854-7633	
Ejcon Corp 5502 Shawland Rd. *Web:* www.ejcon.com	Jacksonville	FL	32254	904-786-0622	
Energy Steel & Supply Co 3123 John Conley Dr *Web:* www.energysteel.com	Lapeer	MI	48446	810-538-4990	
Ennis Steel Industries Inc 204 Metro Park Blvd. *Web:* www.ennissteel.com	Ennis	TX	75119	972-878-0400	878-9563
Etobicoke Ironworks Ltd 141 Rivalda Rd *TF:* 866-274-6971 ■ *Web:* www.eiw.ca	Weston	ON	M9M2M6	416-742-7111	
Euramax International Inc 303 Research Dr Ste 400 *Web:* www.euramax.com	Norcross	GA	30092	770-449-7066	
Excel Bridge Manufacturing Co 12001 Shoemaker Ave *TF:* 800-548-0054 ■ *Web:* www.excelbridge.com	Santa Fe Springs	CA	90670	562-944-0701	
Exergy LLC 320 Endo Blvd *Web:* www.exergyllc.com	Garden City	NY	11530	516-832-9300	
F & R Installers Corp 63 Flushing Ave Ste 270	Brooklyn	NY	11205	718-855-1600	
Fabco Steel Fabrication Inc 14688 San Bernardino Ave *Web:* www.fabcosteel.com	Fontana	CA	92335	909-350-1535	
Fabral Inc 3449 Hempland Rd *TF:* 800-477-2741 ■ *Web:* www.fabral.com	Lancaster	PA	17601	717-397-2741	397-1040
Fabrication Products Inc 4201 Ne Minnehaha St *Web:* www.fabproducts.com	Vancouver	WA	98661	360-696-1324	
Florig R & J Industrial Company Inc 910 Brook Rd *Web:* www.rjflorig.com	Conshohocken	PA	19428	610-825-6655	825-7424
Franke Kindred Canada Ltd 1000 Kindred Rd **Fax Area Code:* 866 ■ *Web:* www.frankekindred.com	Midland	ON	L4R4K9	705-526-5427	227-3035*
FWT LLC 5750 E Interstate 20 *Web:* fwtllc.com	Fort Worth	TX	76119	817-255-3060	
Garaga Inc 8500 25th Ave *TF:* 800-464-2724 ■ *Web:* www.garaga.com	St Georges	QC	G6A1K5	418-227-2828	227-6282
Gayle Mfg Company Inc 1455 E Kentucky Ave *Web:* gaylemfg.com	Woodland	CA	95776	530-662-0284	
Gerlinger Foundry & Machine Works Inc 1527 Sacramento St *Web:* www.gerlinger.com	Redding	CA	96001	530-243-1053	
Glenco Steel Corp 8657 Live Oak Ave	Fontana	CA	92335	909-854-9000	854-9008
GLM Industries LP 1508 - Eighth St *TF:* 800-661-9828 ■ *Web:* www.glmindustries.com	Nisku	AB	T9E7S6	780-955-2233	
Global Fabrication Inc 235 Beaver Dr *Web:* www.globalfabricationinc.com	Dubois	PA	15801	814-372-1500	
Grain Belt Supply Company Inc PO Box 615 *TF:* 800-447-0522 ■ *Web:* www.grainbeltsupply.com	Salina	KS	67402	785-827-4491	827-4494
Heartland Engineered Products LLC 355 Industrial Dr. *Web:* www.heartlandengineeredproducts.com	Harrison	OH	45030	513-367-0080	
Hemco Industries Inc 2408 Karbach St *Web:* www.hemcoind.com	Houston	TX	77092	713-681-2426	
Herber Aircraft Service Inc 1401 E Franklin Ave *TF:* 800-544-0050 ■ *Web:* www.herberaircraft.com	El Segundo	CA	90245	310-322-9575	
Herrick Corp 3003 E Hammer Ln *Web:* www.herricksteel.com	Stockton	CA	95212	209-956-4751	
Hirschfeld Industries LP 112 W 29th St PO Box 3768 *Web:* www.carolinasteel.com	San Angelo	TX	76903	325-486-4201	486-4380
Hogan Manufacturing Inc (HMI) PO Box 398 *Web:* www.hoganmfg.com	Escalon	CA	95320	209-838-7323	838-7329
Hoosier Tank & Manufacturing Inc 1710 N Sheridan St *Web:* hoosiertank.com	South Bend	IN	46628	574-232-8368	
Hurco Technologies Inc 409 Enterprise St *Web:* hurcotech.com	Harrisburg	SD	57032	605-743-2466	
Hyspan Precision Products Inc 1685 Brandywine Ave *Web:* www.hyspan.com	Chula Vista	CA	91911	619-421-1355	421-1702
Imprex Inc 3260 S 108th St *Web:* imprexusa.com	Milwaukee	WI	53227	414-321-9300	
InterLock Industries Inc 545 S Third St Ste 310 *Web:* www.interlockindustries.com	Louisville	KY	40202	502-569-2007	
International Production Specialists Inc 35006 Washington Ave. *Web:* www.ipstanks.com	Honey Creek	WI	53138	262-534-3130	
IP Systems Inc 2685 Industrial Ln.	Broomfield	CO	80020	303-438-1570	
Irwin Car and Equipment 9953 Broadway St. *Web:* www.irwincar.com	Irwin	PA	15642	724-864-8900	
J V Northwest Inc 390 S Redwood St *Web:* www.jvnw.com	Canby	OR	97013	503-263-2858	
J. C. Macelroy Company Inc PO Box 850 *TF:* 800-622-3576 ■ *Web:* www.macelroy.com	Piscataway	NJ	08855	732-572-7100	572-7112
Jebco Industries Inc 111 Ellis Dr *Web:* jebcoindustries.com	Barrie	ON	L4N8Z3	705-797-8888	797-8887
Jesse Engineering Co 1840 Marine View Dr *TF:* 800-468-3595 ■ *Web:* www.jesseengineering.com	Tacoma	WA	98422	253-922-7433	922-1998
JH Industries Inc 1981 E Aurora Rd *TF:* 800-321-4968 ■ *Web:* www.copperloy.com	Twinsburg	OH	44087	330-963-4105	963-4111
Johnson Bros Metal Forming Co 5744 McDermott Dr *Web:* www.johnsonrollforming.com	Berkeley	IL	60163	708-449-7050	449-0042
Kennedy Tank & Mfg Company Inc 833 E Sumner Ave *Web:* www.kennedytank.com	Indianapolis	IN	46227	317-787-1311	
Kern Steel Fabrication Inc 627 Williams St *Web:* kernsteel.com	Bakersfield	CA	93305	661-327-9588	
Lane Conveyors & Drives Inc 15 Industrial Plz *Web:* www.lanesupplyco.com	Brewer	ME	04412	207-989-4560	
Lapeer Industries Inc 400 Mccormick Dr *Web:* www.lapeerind.com	Lapeer	MI	48446	810-664-1816	
LeJeune Steel Co 118 W 60th St *Web:* www.lejeunesteel.com	Minneapolis	MN	55419	612-861-3321	861-2724
Lexicon Inc 8900 Fourche Dam Pk *Web:* www.lexicon-inc.com	Little Rock	AR	72206	501-490-4200	
Liberty Industries LC 2855 Hwy 261 *Web:* www.towerinnovations.net	Newburgh	IN	47630	812-853-0595	
Lichtenwald-Johnston Iron Works Corp 7840 Lehigh St *Web:* lichtenwald-johnston.com	Morton Grove	IL	60053	847-966-1100	966-1159
Linetec 725 S 75th Ave. *TF:* 888-717-1472 ■ *Web:* www.linetec.com	Wausau	WI	54401	715-843-4100	
Lone Wolf Mfg LLC 19321 Stuebner Airline Rd. *Web:* lonewolfmfg.net	Spring	TX	77379	281-370-3087	
M & J Materials Inc 7561 Gadsden Hwy	Trussville	AL	35173	205-655-7451	655-4100
M-13 Construction Management LLC 775 W Spring Creek Pl *Web:* www.m-13.com	Springville	UT	84663	801-489-3215	
M-5 Steel Manufacturing Inc 1450 Mirasol St *Web:* www.m5steel.com	Los Angeles	CA	90023	323-263-9383	
Magnolia Steel Company Inc PO Box 5007 *Web:* www.magnoliasteel.com	Meridian	MS	39302	601-693-4301	
Maguire Iron Inc 1610 N Minnesota Ave *Web:* www.maguireiron.com	Sioux Falls	SD	57104	605-334-9749	
Manko Window Systems Inc 800 Hayes Dr *TF:* 800-642-1488 ■ *Web:* www.mankowindows.com	Manhattan	KS	66502	785-776-9643	
Mark Steel Corp 1230 West 200 South. *Web:* www.marksteel.net	Salt Lake City	UT	84104	801-521-0670	303-2040
Mascott Equipment Company Inc 435 NE Hancock St. *Web:* www.mascottec.com	Portland	OR	97212	503-282-2587	
Mason Corp 123 W Oxmoor Rd *TF:* 800-868-4100 ■ *Web:* www.masoncorp.com	Birmingham	AL	35209	205-942-4100	
McElroy Metal Inc 1500 Hamilton Rd *TF:* 800-562-3576 ■ *Web:* www.mcelroymetal.com	Bossier City	LA	71111	318-747-8097	747-8657
Merchant & Evans Inc 308 Connecticut Dr *TF:* 800-257-6215 ■ *Web:* www.ziprib.com	Burlington	NJ	08016	609-387-3033	
Merrill Iron & Steel Inc 900 Alderson St. *Web:* www.merrilliron.com	Schofield	WI	54476	715-355-8924	
Met-Con Inc 465 Canaveral Groves Blvd *Web:* www.metconinc.com	Cocoa	FL	32926	321-632-4880	639-0158
Midwest Metal Products Co 2100 W Mt Pleasant Rd **Fax Area Code:* 765 ■ *TF:* 888-741-1044 ■ *Web:* www.midwestmetal.com	Muncie	IN	47302	888-741-1044	741-3167*
Midwest Steeplejacks Inc 4623 Timberline Dr S. *Web:* www.midweststeeplejacks.com	Fargo	ND	58104	701-241-7040	
Miller Metal Fabricators Inc 345 National Ave	Staunton	VA	24401	540-886-5575	
Misa Metal Fabricating Inc 7101 International Dr *Web:* www.misametalfab.com	Louisville	KY	40258	502-933-5555	
Mobility Center Inc 6693 Dixie Hwy *TF:* 866-361-7559 ■ *Web:* www.myamigo.com	Bridgeport	MI	48722	989-777-0910	
Monarch LLC 7050 N 76th St. *Web:* www.monarchcorp.com	Milwaukee	WI	53223	414-353-8820	
Mound Technologies Inc 25 Mound Pk Dr. *Web:* moundtechnologies.com	Springboro	OH	45066	937-748-2937	748-9763
Nabco Entrances Inc S82W18717 Gemini Dr *TF:* 888-679-3319 ■ *Web:* www.nabcoentrances.com	Muskego	WI	53150	262-679-0045	
Nello Capital Inc 211 W Washington St Ste 2000 *TF:* 800-806-3556 ■ *Web:* www.nelloinc.com	South Bend	IN	46601	574-288-3632	
New Way Air Bearings Inc 50 McDonald Blvd *Web:* www.newwayairbearings.com	Aston	PA	19014	610-494-6700	
Norlen Inc 900 Grossman Dr **Fax Area Code:* 713 ■ *Web:* www.norlen.com	Schofield	WI	54476	715-359-0506	359-9935*
North Star Propellers Inc 2317 Newton Ave.	San Diego	CA	92113	619-239-8309	
North State Steel Inc 1010 W Gum Rd *Web:* www.northstatesteel.com	Greenville	NC	27834	252-830-8884	

Company	City	State	ZIP	Phone	Fax
Northeast Towers 199 Brickyard Rd *Web:* www.northeasttowers.com	Farmington	CT	06032	860-677-1999	
Northern Pride Communications Inc 20 Ctr Park Rd *Web:* www.northernpridecommunications.com	Topsham	ME	04086	207-798-5540	
Nucor Corp 1915 Rexford Rd *NYSE: NUE* ■ *TF:* 800-294-1322 ■ *Web:* www.nucor.com	Charlotte	NC	28211	704-366-7000	362-4208
Nucor Corp Vulcraft Div 1501 W Darlington St *Web:* www.vulcraft.com	Florence	SC	29501	843-662-0381	662-3132
Ocean Steel & Construction Ltd 400 Chesley Dr *Web:* www.oceansteel.com	Saint John	NB	E2K5L6	506-632-2600	
Olson & Company Steel Inc 1941 Davis St *Web:* www.olsonsteel.com	San Leandro	CA	94577	510-567-2200	
Optimus Corp 5727 S Lewis Ave Ste 600 *Web:* www.optimus-tulsa.com	Tulsa	OK	74105	918-491-9191	
Ornamental Metal Works Inc 2100 N Woodford St	Decatur	IL	62526	217-428-3446	
Owen Industries Inc 501 Ave H *TF:* 800-831-9252 ■ *Web:* www.owenind.com	Carter Lake	IA	51510	712-347-5500	347-6166
Owen Steel Co 727 Mauney Dr *Web:* www.owensteel.com	Columbia	SC	29201	803-251-7680	251-7613
Ozark Steel Fabricators Inc 1 Ozark Steel Dr *Web:* ozarksteel.com	Farmington	MO	63640	573-756-5741	
Pacificomm Systems LLC 73-5563 Olowalu St Ste B6	Kailua-Kona	HI	96740	808-329-6440	
Paramount Components Ltd 2130 Paramount Cres *Web:* www.paramount.bc.ca	Abbotsford	BC	V2T6A5	604-852-2564	
Parkway Metal Products Inc 130 Rawls Rd *Web:* www.parkwaymetal.com	Des Plaines	IL	60018	847-789-4000	
Paxton & Vierling Steel Co 500 Ave H Carter Lake *TF:* 800-831-9252 ■ *Web:* pvsteelfab.com	Carter Lake	IA	51510	800-831-9252	
Phoenix Fabricators & Erectors Inc 182 S Country Rd 900 E *Web:* www.phoenixtank.com	Avon	IN	46123	317-271-7002	
Pipe Welders Inc 2965 W State Rd 84 *Web:* www.pipewelders.com	Fort Lauderdale	FL	33312	954-587-8400	
Precision Masking Inc 721 Lavoy Rd *Web:* www.precisionmasking.com	Erie	MI	48133	734-848-4200	
Price Steel Ltd 13500 156 St *TF:* 800-661-6789 ■ *Web:* www.pricesteel.com	Edmonton	AB	T5V1L3	780-447-9999	
Processed Metals Innovators LLC 600 21st Ave *TF:* 888-877-7277 ■ *Web:* www.pmillc.com	Bloomer	WI	54724	715-568-1700	
Qualico Steel Co Inc PO Box 149 *TF:* 866-234-5382 ■ *Web:* www.qualicosteel.com	Webb	AL	36376	334-793-1290	794-0996
Quality Machine & Welding Company Inc PO Box 27345 *Web:* www.qmwkx.com	Knoxville	TN	37927	865-524-2162	524-1830
R F R Metal Fabrication Inc 3204 Knotts Grove Rd *Web:* www.rfr-metalfab.com	Oxford	NC	27565	919-693-1354	
Ralston Metal Products Ltd 50 Watson Rd S **Fax Area Code: 519* ■ *TF:* 800-265-7611 ■ *Web:* www.ralstonmetal.com	Guelph	ON	N1L1E2	800-265-7611	836-9763*
Ram Welding Company Inc 93 Rado Dr *Web:* www.ramwelding.com	Naugatuck	CT	06770	203-729-2289	
Ramgen Power Systems LLC 11808 Northup Way Ste W-190 *Web:* www.ramgen.com	Bellevue	WA	98005	425-828-4919	
Ranor Inc 1 Bella Dr *Web:* www.ranor.com	Westminster	MA	01473	978-874-0591	874-2748
Rast Iron Works 12895 Interstate 10 East *Web:* www.rastironworks.com	San Antonio	TX	78154	210-659-6704	659-6791
Rodney Hunt Co 46 Mill St *TF:* 800-448-8860 ■ *Web:* www.rodneyhunt.com	Orange	MA	01364	978-544-2511	544-7204
Roscoe Steel 1501 S 30th St W *Web:* www.truenorthsteel.com	Billings	MT	59102	406-656-2253	
Roth Fabricating Inc 9600 Skyline Dr *Web:* www.rothfabricatinginc.com	Morenci	MI	49256	517-458-7541	
RSDC of Michigan LLC 1775 Holloway Dr *TF:* 877-881-7732 ■ *Web:* www.rsdcmi.com	Holt	MI	48842	877-881-7732	
Safe Harbor Access Systems LLC 211 N Koppers Rd *Web:* www.safe-harbor.com	Florence	SC	29506	843-679-6888	
Schuff Steel Inc 1920 Ledo Rd *TF:* 866-252-4628 ■ *Web:* www.schuff.com	Albany	GA	31707	678-821-7061	
Security Metal Products Corp 5700 Hannum Ave Ste 250 *Web:* www.secmet.com	Culver City	CA	90230	310-641-6690	
Senior Flexonics Inc 300 E Devon Ave *Web:* www.senior-flexonics.com	Bartlett	IL	60103	630-837-1811	
Senior Flexonics Pathway Division 2400 Longhorn Industrial Dr *Web:* www.pathwayb.com	New Braunfels	TX	78130	830-629-8080	
SFI-Gray Steel Ltd 3511 W 12th St *Web:* www.sfigray.com	Houston	TX	77008	713-864-6450	
Shape Corp 1900 Hayes St *Web:* www.shapecorp.com	Grand Haven	MI	49417	616-846-8700	846-3464
Shepard Steel Company Inc 110 Meadow St *Web:* www.shepardsteel.com	Hartford	CT	06114	860-525-4446	
Shure-line Construction Inc PO Box 249 *Web:* www.shure-line.com	Kenton	DE	19955	302-653-4610	
Sims Cab Depot 200 Moulinette Rd *TF:* 800-225-7290 ■ *Web:* www.cabdepot.com	Long Sault	ON	K0C1P0	613-534-2289	
SiteMaster Inc 6914 S Yorktown Ave Ste 210 *Web:* www.sitemaster.com	Tulsa	OK	74136	918-663-2232	
Smardt Chiller Group Inc 1800 Trans Canada Hwy *Web:* www.smardt.com	Dorval	QC	H9P1H7	514-426-8989	
SnowBear Ltd 155 Dawson Rd *Web:* www.snowbear.com	Guelph	ON	N1H1C1	519-767-1115	
Southeast Fabricators Inc 7301 University Blvd E *Web:* www.sefab.com	Cottondale	AL	35453	205-556-3227	
Southern Steel Fabricators Inc 208 Wagon Wheel Rd *Web:* www.southernsteelfab.com	Monroe	LA	71202	318-345-2800	
Southland Steel Fabricators Inc 251 Greensburg St *TF:* 800-738-7734 ■ *Web:* www.southlandsteel.com	Greensburg	LA	70441	225-222-4141	
Specialty Manufacturing LLC 5601 San Francisco Rd NE *Web:* www.wirelesscomponents.com	Albuquerque	NM	87109	505-823-1832	
Speedway Steel Fabrication Inc 501 N Truman Blvd PO Box 8 *Web:* www.speedwaysteel.net	Crystal City	MO	63019	636-931-6500	
Stainless LLC 1140 Welsh Rd Ste 250 *Web:* www.talltowers.com	North Wales	PA	19454	215-631-1400	
Standard Iron Inc 2516 Vance Ave *Web:* www.standardiron.com	Chattanooga	TN	37404	423-756-0940	
Starr Manufacturing Inc 4175 Warren-Sharon Rd *Web:* www.starrmfg.com	Vienna	OH	44473	330-394-9891	
Steel Fabricators LLC 721 NE 44th St **Fax: Sales* ■ *Web:* www.sfab.com	Fort Lauderdale	FL	33334	954-772-0440	938-7527*
Steel Fabricators of Monroe LLC 2101 Booth St Ste 4830 *Web:* www.steelfab.com	Monroe	LA	71201	318-387-9426	
Steele Solutions Inc 9909 S 57th St *TF:* 888-542-5099 ■ *Web:* www.steelesolutions.com	Franklin	WI	53132	414-367-5099	
SteelFab Inc 8623 Old Dowd Rd *Web:* www.steelfab-inc.com	Charlotte	NC	28214	704-394-5376	
Steffes Corp 3050 Hwy 22 N *TF:* 888-783-3337 ■ *Web:* www.steffes.com	Dickinson	ND	58601	701-483-5400	
Structural Steel of Carolina LLC 1725 Vargrave St *Web:* www.steelofcarolina.com	Winston-Salem	NC	27107	336-725-0521	
Structural Steel Services 6210 St Louis St	Meridian	MS	39307	601-483-5381	
Stupp Bros Inc 3800 Weber Rd *TF:* 800-535-9999 ■ *Web:* www.stupp.com	Saint Louis	MO	63125	314-638-5000	638-2660
T. Bruce Sales Inc 9 Carbaugh St *TF:* 800-944-0738 ■ *Web:* www.tbrucesales.com	West Middlesex	PA	16159	724-528-9961	528-2050
TFT Inc 2976 N Florence Ave *Web:* tulsafintube.com	Tulsa	OK	74110	918-834-2366	
Thornton Steel Company Inc 2700 W Pafford St *Web:* www.thorntonsteel.com	Fort Worth	TX	76110	817-926-3324	
Tie Down Engineering Inc 255 Villanova Dr SW *TF:* 800-241-1806 ■ *Web:* www.danforthanchors.com	Atlanta	GA	30336	404-344-0000	
Tower Systems Inc 17226 447th Ave PO Box 1474 *Web:* www.towersystems.com	Watertown	SD	57201	605-886-0930	
Trans-tec Machine Ltd 6320 Ridgemont St *Web:* www.transtecmachine.com	Houston	TX	77087	713-643-9114	
Trinity Steel Fabricators Inc 13430 Northwest Fwy Ste 225 *Web:* www.trinitysteel.com	Trinity	TX	77040	713-460-5556	
Trinity Structural Towers Inc 2525 N Stemmons Fwy *Web:* www.trinitytowers.com	Dallas	TX	75207	214-631-4420	589-8640
Trulite Glass & Aluminum Solutions LLC 800 Fairway Dr Ste 200 *Web:* www.trulite.com	Deerfield Beach	FL	33441	954-724-1775	
Union Metal Corp 1432 Maple Ave NE *Web:* www.unionmetal.com	Canton	OH	44705	330-456-7653	456-0196
United Window & Door Manufacturing Inc 24-36 Fadem Rd *TF:* 800-848-4550 ■ *Web:* www.unitedwindowmfg.com	Springfield	NJ	07081	973-912-0600	
US Tower Corp 1099 W Ropes Ave *Web:* www.ustower.com	Woodlake	CA	93286	559-564-6000	
USP Structural Connectors Inc 703 Rogers Dr *Web:* www.uspconnectors.com	Montgomery	MN	56069	507-364-7333	
Val-Fab Inc 218 Jackson St *TF:* 888-482-5322 ■ *Web:* www.valfab.com	Neenah	WI	54956	920-722-1009	
Vibrant Power Inc 310 Courtneypark Dr E *Web:* www.vibrantpower.com	Mississauga	ON	L5T2S5	905-564-8644	
Vitols Tool & Machine Corp 10082 Sandmeyer Ln *Web:* www.vitolsgroup.com	Philadelphia	PA	19116	215-464-8240	
W & K Steel LLC 98 Antisbury Pl	Rankin	PA	15104	412-271-1620	271-3988
W & W Steel Co 1730 W Reno Ave *Web:* www.wwsteel.com	Oklahoma City	OK	73106	405-235-3621	236-4842
Wabi Iron & Steel Corp 330 Broadwood Ave *Web:* www.wabicorp.com	New Liskeard	ON	P0J1P0	705-647-4383	
Wagner Plate Works LLC 4142 W 49th St *Web:* www.wagnerplateworks.com	Tulsa	OK	74107	918-447-4488	
Wahlcometroflex Inc 29 Lexington St *TF:* 800-272-6652 ■ *Web:* sfpathway.com	Lewiston	ME	04240	207-784-2338	
Waiward Steel Fabricators Ltd 10030 - 34 St *Web:* www.waiward.com	Edmonton	AB	T6B2Y5	780-469-1258	
Walters Metal Fabrication 3660 State Rt 111 *Web:* www.waltersmetalfab.com	Granite City	IL	62040	618-931-5551	
WaUSAu Window & Wall Systems 7800 International Dr *TF:* 877-678-2983 ■ *Web:* www.wausauwindow.com	Wausau	WI	54401	715-845-2161	
Wear - Concepts Inc 106 NW Business Park Ln *Web:* www.wearcon.com	Riverside	MO	64150	816-587-1923	
Wojan Window & Door Corp 217 Stover Rd *TF:* 800-632-9827 ■ *Web:* www.wojan.com	Charlevoix	MI	49720	231-547-2931	
WSF Industries Inc 7 Hackett Dr *TF:* 800-874-8265 ■ *Web:* www.wsf-inc.com	Tonawanda	NY	14150	716-692-4930	

Phone | Fax

Zieman Manufacturing Co 168 S Spruce ... Rialto CA 92376 909-873-0061
Web: www.lci1.com/zieman

Zimmerman Metals Inc 201 E 58th Ave ... Denver CO 80216 303-294-0180
TF: 800-247-4202 ■ *Web:* www.zimmerman-metals.com

481 METAL COATING, PLATING, ENGRAVING

Phone | Fax

A & L Metal Processing 1920 George St ... Sandusky OH 44870 419-627-0022

A-Brite Plating Company Inc
3000 W 121st St ... Cleveland OH 44111 216-252-2995
Web: www.abriteplating.com

Alcoa Inc 201 Isabella St ... Pittsburgh PA 15212 412-553-4545 553-4498
NYSE: AA ■ *TF:* 800-388-4825 ■ *Web:* www.alcoa.com

All Metals Processing of Orange County Inc
8401 Standustrial St ... Stanton CA 90680 714-828-8238 828-4552
Web: www.allmetalsprocessing.com

Allegan Metal Finishing Co 1274 Lincoln Rd ... Allegan MI 49010 269-673-6604
Web: www.amfco.biz

Almond Products Inc 17150 148th Ave ... Spring Lake MI 49456 616-844-1813
Web: www.almondproducts.com

Alumicor Ltd 290 Humberline Dr ... Toronto ON M9W5S2 416-745-4222
TF: 877-258-6426 ■ *Web:* www.alumicor.com

Aluminum Coil Anodizing Corp
501 E Lake St ... Streamwood IL 60107 630-837-4000 837-0814
Web: www.acacorp.com

American Nickeloid Co 2900 Main St ... Peru IL 61354 815-223-0373 223-5344
TF: 800-645-5643 ■ *Web:* www.nickeloid.com

Anomatic Corp 1650 Tamarack Rd ... Newark OH 43055 740-522-2203
Web: www.anomatic.com

Apex Anodizing Nev Inc
280 Coney Island Dr Ste B ... Sparks NV 89431 775-355-8121
Web: apexanodizing.com

Applied Thin-Film Products Inc
3439 Edison Way ... Fremont CA 94538 510-661-4287
Web: www.thinfilm.com

APS Materials Inc 4011 Riverside Dr ... Dayton OH 45405 937-278-6547
Web: www.apsmaterials.com

Archer Wire International Corp
7300 S Narragansett Ave ... Bedford Park IL 60638 708-563-1700 563-1740
Web: www.archerwire.com

Arlington Plating Co 600 S Vermont St ... Palatine IL 60078 847-359-1490
Web: www.arlingtonplating.com

AST Products Inc 9 Linnell Cir ... Billerica MA 01821 978-667-4500
TF: 877-667-4500 ■ *Web:* www.astp.com

ATI Precision Finishing 499 Delaware Ave ... Rochester PA 15074 724-775-1664
Web: www.atimetals.com

Bayou Perma-Pipe Canada Ltd 5233 39th St ... Camrose AB T4V4R5 780-672-2345
Web: www.permapipe.com/marketsegments/coating-solutions

Bel Air Finishing Supply Corp
101 Circuit Dr ... North Kingstown RI 02852 401-667-7902
Web: www.belairfinishing.com

Bennett Metal Products Inc
700 Rackaway St PO Box 34 ... Mount Vernon IL 62864 618-244-1911
Web: bennettmetal.com

BF Inkjet Media Inc 116 Bethea Rd #322 ... Fayetteville GA 30214 770-719-2051
Web: www.bfinkjet.com

BL Downey Company LLC 2125 Gardner Rd ... Broadview IL 60155 708-345-8000
TF: 800-323-1206 ■ *Web:* www.bldowney.com

Bon Chef Inc 205 SR- 94 ... Lafayette NJ 07848 973-383-8848
Web: www.bonchef.com

Bowman Plating Company Inc 2631 126th St ... Compton CA 90222 310-639-4343
Web: www.bowmanplating.com

Bredero Shaw A ShawCor Co
3838 N Sam Houston Pkwy E Ste 300 ... Houston TX 77032 281-886-2350 886-2353
Web: www.brederoshaw.com

Central Metal Finishing Inc
80 Flagship Dr ... North Andover MA 01845 978-685-4811
Web: www.cenmet.com

Certified Enameling Inc 3342 Emery St ... Los Angeles CA 90023 323-264-4403
Web: www.certifiedenameling.com

Certified Metal Finishing Inc
1420 SW 28th Ave ... Pompano Beach FL 33069 954-979-0707
Web: certifiedmetalfinishing.com

Charlotte Anodizing Products Inc
591 E Packard Hwy ... Charlotte MI 48813 517-543-1911
TF: 800-818-6945 ■ *Web:* www.charlotte-anodizing.com

Chem Processing Inc 3910 Linden Oaks Dr ... Rockford IL 61109 815-874-8118
TF: 800-262-2119 ■ *Web:* www.chemprocessing.com

Chemart Co 15 New England Way ... Lincoln RI 02865 401-333-9200 333-1634
TF: 800-521-5001 ■ *Web:* www.chemart.com

Chemline Inc 5151 Natural Bridge Rd ... Saint Louis MO 63115 314-664-2230
Web: www.chemline.net

Chemresearch Company Inc 1101 W Hilton Ave ... Phoenix AZ 85007 602-253-4175
Web: chemresearchco.com

Chicago Metallic Corp 4849 S Austin Ave ... Chicago IL 60638 708-563-4600 222-3744*
**Fax Area Code:* 800 ■ *Web:* www.chicago-metallic.com

Coast Coatings LLC 227 Calle Pintoresco ... San Clemente CA 92672 949-492-9037
Web: www.coastpowdercoating.com

Coast Plating Inc 128 W 154th St ... Gardena CA 90248 323-770-0240
Web: www.coastplating.com

Coastline Metal Finishing Corp
7061 Patterson Dr ... Garden Grove CA 92841 714-895-9099
Web: www.coastlinemetalfinishing.com

Conforma Clad Inc 501 Park E Blvd ... New Albany IN 47150 812-948-2118
Web: www.conformaclad.com

Continental Studwelding Ltd 35 Devon Rd ... Brampton ON L6T5B6 905-792-3650 792-3711
TF: 800-848-9442 ■ *Web:* www.constud.ca

Cork Industries Inc 500 Kaiser Dr ... Folcroft PA 19032 610-522-9550
Web: www.corkind.com

Corrosion Monitoring Services Inc
902 Equity Dr ... Saint Charles IL 60174 630-762-9300
Web: www.cmsinc.us

Craddock Finishing Corp
1400 W Illinois St ... Evansville IN 47710 812-425-2691
Web: www.craddockfinishing.com

Crest Coating Inc 1361 S Allec St ... Anaheim CA 92805 714-635-7090 758-8752
Web: www.crestcoating.com

Crown Tumbling Corp
32571 Stephenson Hwy ... Madison Heights MI 48071 248-588-4990

Crystal Finishing Systems Inc
2610 Ross Ave ... Schofield WI 54476 715-355-5351
Web: www.crystalfinishing.com

CuraFlo British Columbia Ltd
7436 Fraser Park Dr ... Burnaby BC V5J5B9 604-298-7278
Web: www.curaflobc.com

Curtis Metal Finishing Co
6645 Sims Dr ... Sterling Heights MI 48313 586-939-2850
Web: www.curtismetal.com

CVD Diamond Corp 2061 Piper Ln ... London ON N5V3S5 519-457-9903
TF: 877-457-9903 ■ *Web:* www.cvddiamond.com

Deposition Sciences Inc 3300 Coffey Ln ... Santa Rosa CA 95403 707-573-6700 573-6748
TF: 866-433-7724 ■ *Web:* www.depsci.com

Dura Coat Products Inc 5361 Via Ricardo ... Riverside CA 92509 951-341-6500
Web: www.duracoatproducts.com

East Side Plating Inc 8400 SE 26th Pl ... Portland OR 97202 503-654-3774
TF: 800-394-8554 ■ *Web:* www.eastsideplating.com

Electric Coating Technologies (ECT)
4407 Railroad Ave ... East Chicago IN 46312 219-378-1930 378-1933
Web: www.materialsciencescorp.com/electric-coating-technologies

Electro-spec Inc 1800 Commerce Pkwy ... Franklin IN 46131 317-738-9199
Web: www.electro-spec.com

Endura Coatings LLC
42250 Yearego Dr ... Sterling Heights MI 48314 586-739-0101
Web: www.enduracoatings.com

Erler Industries Inc
418 Stockwell St PO Box 219 ... North Vernon IN 47265 812-346-4421 346-1892
Web: www.erler.com

Everlube Products 100 Cooper Cir ... Peachtree City GA 30269 770-261-4800
TF: 800-428-7802 ■ *Web:* everlubeproducts.com

Flame Control Coatings LLC
4120 Hyde Park Blvd ... Niagara Falls NY 14305 716-282-1399
Web: www.flamecontrol.com

Form Grind Corp
30062 Aventura ... Rancho Santa Margarita CA 92688 949-858-7000
Web: www.kellysearch.com

FW Gartner Thermal Spraying Ltd
25 Southbelt Industrial Dr ... Houston TX 77047 713-225-0010
TF: 888-439-4872 ■ *Web:* www.fwgts.com

Galvan Industries Inc 7320 Millbrook Rd ... Harrisburg NC 28075 704-455-5102 455-5215
TF General: 800-277-5678 ■ *Web:* www.galvan-ize.com

General Extrusions Inc 4040 Lk Pk Rd ... Youngstown OH 44512 330-783-0270 788-1250
Web: www.genext.com

General Metal Finishing Company Inc (GMF)
42 Frank Mossberg Dr ... Attleboro MA 02703 508-226-5606
Web: www.pepgenmetal.com

GH International Inc 2540 Rena Rd ... Mississauga ON L4T3C9 905-677-5522
Web: www.ghinternational.ca

Giering Metal Finishing Inc 2655 State St ... Hamden CT 06517 203-248-5583
Web: www.gieringmetalfinishing.com

GM Nameplate Inc 2040 15th Ave W ... Seattle WA 98119 206-284-2200 284-3705
TF: 800-366-7668 ■ *Web:* www.gmnameplate.com

Hadronics Inc 4570 Steel Pl ... Cincinnati OH 45209 513-321-9350
TF: 800-829-0826 ■ *Web:* www.hadronics.com

Heyco Metals Inc 1069 Stinson Dr ... Reading PA 19605 610-926-4131
Web: www.heyco-metals.com

Hydratech Engineered Products LLC
10448 Chester Rd ... Cincinnati OH 45215 513-827-9169
Web: hydratechllc.com

Hytek Finishes Co 8127 S 216th St ... Kent WA 98032 253-872-7160
Web: www.hytekfinishes.com

IBC Coating Technologies 902 Hendricks Dr ... Lebanon IN 46052 765-482-9802
Web: www.ibccoatings.com

Ingot Metal Company Ltd 111 Fenmar Dr ... Weston ON M9L1M3 416-749-1372
TF: 800-567-7774 ■ *Web:* www.ingot.ca

Integrated Surface Technologies Inc
1455 Adams St Ste 1125 ... Menlo Park CA 94025 650-324-1824
Web: www.insurftech.com

Interplex Engineered Products 231 Ferris Ave ... Rumford RI 02916 401-434-6543 399-7655*
**Fax Area Code:* 508 ■ *Web:* www.interplex.com

IonBond LLC 200 Roundhill Dr ... Rockaway NJ 07866 973-586-4700 586-4729
Web: www.ionbond.com

IVC Industrial Coatings Inc
2831 E Industrial Pk ... Brazil IN 47834 812-442-5080
Web: www.teamivc.com

J & M Plating Inc 4500 Kishwaukee St ... Rockford IL 61109 815-964-4975
TF: 877-344-3044 ■ *Web:* www.jmplating.com

John C Dolph Co 320 New Rd ... Monmouth Junction NJ 08852 732-329-2333
Web: www.dolphs.com

KC Jones Plating Co 2845 E Ten Mile Rd ... Warren MI 48091 586-755-4900
Web: www.kcjplating.com

KNS Cos Inc 475 Randy Rd ... Carol Stream IL 60188 630-665-9010 665-1819
Web: www.knscompanies.com

Korns Galvanizing Co 75 Bridge St ... Johnstown PA 15902 814-535-3293
Web: kornsgalvanizing.com

Kuntz Electroplating Inc 851 Wilson Ave ... Kitchener ON N2C1J1 519-893-7680 893-5431
Web: www.kuntz.com

LB Foster Co 415 Holiday Dr ... Pittsburgh PA 15220 800-255-4500
NASDAQ: FSTR ■ *TF:* 800-255-4500 ■ *Web:* www.lbfoster.com

Liberty Coating Company LLC
21 S Steel Rd ... Morrisville PA 19067 215-736-1111
Web: www.libertycoating.com

Liquidmetal Coatings LLC
900 Rockmead Dr Ste 240 ... Kingwood TX 77339 281-359-1283

Company / Address	City	State	ZIP	Phone	Fax
Lorin Industries 1960 S Roberts St	Muskegon	MI	49443	231-722-1631	728-3139
TF: 800-654-1159 ■ *Web:* www.lorin.com					
Magna-Tech Manufacturing Corp 3416 S Hoyt Ave	Muncie	IN	47302	765-284-5050	
Web: www.magnatechmfg.com					
Magnetic Metals Corp 1900 Hayes Ave	Camden	NJ	08105	856-964-7842	963-8569
TF: 800-257-8174 ■ *Web:* www.magneticmetals.com					
Markland Industries Inc 1111 E McFadden Ave	Santa Ana	CA	92705	714-245-2850	
Web: www.marklandindustries.com					
Master Finish Co 2020 Nelson SE PO Box 7505	Grand Rapids	MI	49510	877-590-5819	245-0039*
**Fax Area Code:* 616 ■ *TF:* 877-590-5819 ■ *Web:* www.masterfinishco.com					
Material Sciences Corp (MSC) 2200 E Pratt Blvd	Elk Grove Village	IL	60007	734-207-4444	439-0737*
NASDAQ: MASC ■ **Fax Area Code:* 847 ■ *Web:* www.materialsciencescorp.com					
Max Levy Autograph Inc 2710 Commerce Way	Philadelphia	PA	19154	215-842-3675	
TF: 800-798-3675 ■ *Web:* www.maxlevy.com					
MesoCoat Inc 24112 Rockwell Dr	Euclid	OH	44117	216-453-0866	
Web: www.mesocoat.com					
Metal Arts Finishing Inc 1001 S Lake St	Aurora	IL	60506	630-892-6744	
Metal Cladding Inc 230 S Niagara St	Lockport	NY	14094	800-432-5513	439-4010*
**Fax Area Code:* 716 ■ *TF:* 800-432-5513 ■ *Web:* www.metalcladding.com					
Metal Coatings Corp 3700 Dunvale Rd	Houston	TX	77063	713-977-0123	977-0824
Web: www.metcoat.com					
MetaLPlate Galvanizing LP 1120 39th St N	Birmingham	AL	35234	205-595-4703	
Web: www.metalplate.com					
MetoKote Corp 1340 Neubrecht Rd	Lima	OH	45801	419-996-7800	996-7801
Web: www.metokote.com					
Meziere Enterprises Inc 220 S Hale Ave	Escondido	CA	92029	760-746-3273	
TF: 800-208-1755 ■ *Web:* www.meziere.com					
Microcast Technologies Corp (MTC) 1611 W Elizabeth Ave	Linden	NJ	07036	908-523-9503	523-0910
Web: www.mtcnj.com					
Midwest Products Finishing Company Inc 6194 Section Rd	Ottawa Lake	MI	49267	734-856-5200	856-7267
Web: www.midwestecoat.com					
National Coatings Inc 3520 Rennie School Rd	Traverse City	MI	49685	231-943-2557	943-4262
TF: 888-947-2557 ■ *Web:* www.nationalcoatings.biz					
Nd Industries Inc 1000 N Crooks Rd	Clawson	MI	48017	248-288-0000	288-0022
TF: 800-471-5000 ■ *Web:* www.ndindustries.com					
NOF Metal Coatings NA 275 Industrial Pkwy	Chardon	OH	44024	440-285-2231	285-5009
Web: www.metal-coatings.com					
Nor-Ell Inc 851 Hubbard Ave	Saint Paul	MN	55104	651-487-1441	488-1626
TF: 877-276-4075 ■ *Web:* www.nor-ell.com					
Northern Engraving Corp 803 S Black River St	Sparta	WI	54656	608-269-6911	366-3725
Web: www.norcorp.com					
O E C Graphics Inc 555 W Waukau Ave PO Box 2443	Oshkosh	WI	54902	920-235-7770	235-2252
TF: 800-388-7770 ■ *Web:* www.oecgraphics.com					
Passaic Engraving Company Inc 41 Brook Ave	Passaic	NJ	07055	973-777-0621	
Web: www.passaicengraving.com					
Pioneer Metal Finishing LLC 486 Globe Ave	Green Bay	WI	54304	877-721-1100	884-1790*
**Fax Area Code:* 920 ■ *TF:* 877-721-1100 ■ *Web:* www.pioneermetal.com					
Plasma Ruggedized Solutions Inc 2284 Ringwood Ave Ste A	San Jose	CA	95131	408-954-8405	
TF: 800-994-7527 ■ *Web:* www.plasmarugged.com					
Plasma Technology Inc 1754 Crenshaw Blvd	Torrance	CA	90501	310-320-3373	533-1677
Web: www.ptise.com					
Precision Coating Company Inc 63 Sprague St	Boston	MA	02136	781-329-1420	329-3618
Web: www.precisioncoating.com					
Precision Graphics Inc 21 County Line Rd	Somerville	NJ	08876	908-707-8880	707-8884
Web: www.precisiongraphics.us					
Precoat Metals 1310 Papin St 3rd Fl	Saint Louis	MO	63103	317-462-7761	
Web: www.precoat.com					
Premier Die Casting Co 1177 Rahway Ave	Avenel	NJ	07001	732-634-3000	634-0590
TF: 800-394-3006 ■ *Web:* www.diecasting.com					
Providence Metallizing Company Inc 51 Fairlawn Ave	Pawtucket	RI	02860	401-722-5300	724-3410
Web: www.providencemetallizing.com					
Quick Tanks Inc PO Box 338	Kendallville	IN	46755	260-347-3850	347-3853
Web: www.quicktanks.com					
Rimex Metals (USA) Inc 2850 Woodbridge Ave	Edison	NJ	08837	732-549-3800	549-6435
Web: www.rimexmetals.com					
Roehlen Engraving 5901 Lewis Rd	Sandston	VA	23150	804-222-2821	226-3462
Web: www.standexengraving.com					
Roesch Inc 100 N 24th St	Belleville	IL	62222	800-423-6243	233-1186*
**Fax Area Code:* 618 ■ *TF:* 800-423-6243 ■ *Web:* www.roeschinc.com					
Sapa Inc 7933 NE 21st Ave	Portland	OR	97211	503-802-3000	802-3060
TF: 800-547-0790 ■ *Web:* www.sapagroup.com					
Savon Plating & Powder Coating Inc 17 W Watkins Rd	Phoenix	AZ	85003	602-252-4311	
Web: sav-onplating.com					
Sequa Corp Precoat Metals Div 1310 Papin St 3rd Fl	Saint Louis	MO	63103	314-436-7010	436-7050
Web: www.precoatmetals.com					
Southwest Metal Finishing Inc 2445 S Calhoun Rd	New Berlin	WI	53151	262-784-1919	641-7086
Web: www.swmetalfinishing.com					
Standex International Corp Engraving Group 5901 Lewis Rd	Sandston	VA	23150	804-222-2821	226-3462
Web: www.standexengraving.com					
Sumco Inc 1351 S Girls School Rd	Indianapolis	IN	46231	317-241-7600	248-2352
Web: sumco.com					
Summit Corp of America 1430 Waterbury Rd	Thomaston	CT	06787	860-283-4391	283-4010
Web: www.scact.com					
Techno-Coat Inc 861 E 40th St	Holland	MI	49423	616-396-6446	
Web: www.technocoat.com					
Towne Technologies Inc 6-10 Bell Ave PO Box 460	Somerville	NJ	08876	908-722-9500	722-8394
TF: 800-837-2515 ■ *Web:* www.townetech.com					
Ulterion International Inc 1136 Zion Church Rd	Braselton	GA	30517	706-654-2222	
Web: www.ulterion.com					
Ultra-tech Enterprises Inc 4701 Taylor Rd	Punta Gorda	FL	33950	941-575-2000	
TF: 800-293-2001 ■ *Web:* www.ute-inc.com					
Unicote Corp 33165 Groesbeck Hwy	Fraser	MI	48026	586-296-0700	296-3155
Web: www.unicotecorporation.com					
United Galvanizing Inc 6123 Cunningham Rd	Houston	TX	77041	713-466-4161	
Web: unitedgalvinc.com					
US Chrome Corp 175 Garfield Ave	Stratford	CT	06615	800-637-9019	386-0067*
**Fax Area Code:* 203 ■ *TF:* 800-637-9019 ■ *Web:* www.uschrome.com					
Valley City Plating Co 3353 Eastern Ave SE	Grand Rapids	MI	49508	616-245-1223	
Web: www.brassplater.com					
VAM Drilling USA Inc 6300 Navigation Blvd	Houston	TX	77011	713-844-3700	
Web: www.vallourec.com					
Voigt & Schweitzer Inc 1000 Buckeye Park Rd	Columbus	OH	43207	614-449-8281	
Web: www.hotdipgalvanizing.com					
W & m Manufacturing Inc 1000 N Morton St	Portland	IN	47371	260-726-9800	
Web: www.wmmanufacturing.com					
Watson Grinding & Mfg Co 4525 Gessner Dr	Houston	TX	77041	713-466-3053	466-8992
Web: www.watsongrinding.com					
Westfield Electroplating Company Inc 68 N Elm St	Westfield	MA	01085	413-568-3716	
Web: www.westfieldplating.com					
Whitford Corp PO Box 80	Elverson	PA	19520	610-296-3200	286-3510
Web: www.whitfordww.com					
Whyco Finishing Technologies LLC 670 Waterbury Rd	Thomaston	CT	06787	860-283-5826	
Web: www.whyco.com					
Willington Cos 11 Middle River Dr	Stafford Springs	CT	06076	860-684-4281	
TF: 877-967-4743 ■ *Web:* www.wnpinc.com					
Wismarq Corp 930 Armour Rd	Oconomowoc	WI	53066	262-567-1112	
Web: www.wismarq.com					
Womble Company Inc 12821 Industrial Rd	Houston	TX	77015	713-635-8300	635-5209
Web: www.wombleco.com					
Wright Coating Company Inc 1603 N Pitcher St	Kalamazoo	MI	49007	269-344-8195	
Web: www.wrightcoating.com					
Xccent Inc 5240 257th St	Wyoming	MN	55092	651-462-9200	
Web: www.xccentplay.com					

482 METAL FABRICATING - CUSTOM

Company / Address	City	State	ZIP	Phone	Fax
Afco Industries Inc 3400 Roy St	Alexandria	LA	71302	800-551-6576	
TF: 800-551-6576 ■ *Web:* www.afco-ind.com					
Aldine Metal Products Corp 566 Danbury Rd Ste 1	New Milford	CT	06776	860-350-2552	350-1061
Web: www.aldinemetal.com					
Alpha Sintered Metals Inc 95 Mason Run Rd	Ridgway	PA	15853	814-773-3191	776-1009
Web: www.alphasintered.com					
American Aluminum Co 230 Sheffield St	Mountainside	NJ	07092	908-233-3500	233-3241
Web: www.amalco.com					
Angell & Giroux Inc 2727 Alcazar St	Los Angeles	CA	90033	323-269-8596	
Web: www.angellandgiroux.com					
Applied Engineering Inc 2008 E Hwy 50	Yankton	SD	57078	605-665-4425	665-1479
Web: www.appliedeng.com					
Arlington Metals Corp 11355 Franklin Ave	Franklin Park	IL	60131	847-451-9100	451-9676
Web: www.arlingtonmetals.com					
Ascension Industries 1254 Erie Ave	North Tonawanda	NY	14120	716-693-9381	693-9882
Web: www.asmfab.com					
Associated Steel Workers Ltd 91-156 Kalaeloa Blvd	Kapolei	HI	96707	808-682-5588	682-7392
Autoswage Products Inc 726 River Rd	Shelton	CT	06484	203-929-1401	929-6187
Web: www.autoswage.com					
Brakewell Steel Fabricator Inc 55 Leone Ln	Chester	NY	10918	845-469-9131	469-7618
TF: 888-914-9131 ■ *Web:* www.brakewell.com					
Cerro Fabricated Products Inc 300 Triangle Dr	Weyers Cave	VA	24486	540-234-9252	234-8416
Web: www.cerrofabricated.com					
Chandler Industries Inc 1654 N Ninth St	Montevideo	MN	56265	320-269-8893	269-5827
Web: www.chandlerindustries.com					
Chicago Metal Fabricators Inc 3724 S Rockwell St	Chicago	IL	60632	773-523-5755	523-8680
TF: 877-400-5995 ■ *Web:* www.chicagometal.com					
CMW Inc 70 S Gray St	Indianapolis	IN	46201	317-634-8884	638-2706
Web: www.cmwinc.com					
Compax Inc 1210 N Blue Gum St	Anaheim	CA	92806	714-630-3670	632-1344
Web: www.compaxinc.com					
Cross Bros Inc 5255 Sheila St	Los Angeles	CA	90040	323-266-2000	266-2106
TF: 866-939-1057 ■ *Web:* www.crossbrothersinc.com					
CSM Metal Fabricating & Engineering Inc 1800 S San Pedro St	Los Angeles	CA	90015	213-748-7321	749-5106
TF: 800-272-4806 ■ *Web:* www.csmworks.com					
D & S Manufacturing Inc 301 E Main St	Black River Falls	WI	54615	715-284-5376	284-4084
Web: www.dsmfg.com					
Daniel Tanney Company Inc 3268 Clive Ave	Bensalem	PA	19020	215-639-3131	638-3333
Web: dctanney.com					
Delaco Steel Corp 8111 Tireman Ave	Dearborn	MI	48126	313-491-1200	491-6210
Demsey Manufacturing Co 78 New Wood Rd	Watertown	CT	06795	860-274-6209	274-6209
TF: 800-533-6739 ■ *Web:* www.demseymfg.com					
Fabricated Components Inc PO Box 431	Stroudsburg	PA	18360	570-421-4110	421-2553
TF: 800-233-8163 ■ *Web:* www.fabricatedcomponents.com					
Harford Systems Inc 2225 Pulaski Hwy PO Box 700	Aberdeen	MD	21001	410-272-3400	
Web: harfordsystems.com					
Harris Manufacturing Inc 4775 E Vine Ave	Fresno	CA	93725	559-268-7422	
Web: www.harrismfg.com					

				Phone	Fax
International Extrusions Inc 5800 Venoy Rd *TF:* 800-242-8876 ■ *Web:* www.extrusion.net	Garden City	MI	48135	734-427-8700	427-9319
Johnson Matthey Noble Metals 1397 King Rd *Web:* www.noble.matthey.com	West Chester	PA	19380	610-648-8067	648-8105
Lafayette Quality Products 111 Farabee Dr *Web:* lqp-mfg.com	Lafayette	IN	47905	765-447-3106	
Liquidmetal Technologies Inc (LQMT) 30452 Esperanza *OTC: LQMT* ■ *TF:* 888-203-1112 ■ *Web:* www.liquidmetal.com	Rancho Santa Margarita	CA	92688	949-635-2100	635-2188
LTC Roll & Engineering Co 23500 John Gorsuch Dr *Web:* www.ltcroll.com	Clinton Township	MI	48036	586-465-1023	465-0554
Lucasey Manufacturing Corp 2744 E 11th St PO Box 14023 *TF:* 800-582-2739 ■ *Web:* www.lucasey.com	Oakland	CA	94601	510-534-1435	534-6828
Manufacturers Industrial Group LLC 659 Natchez Trace Dr *Web:* www.migllc.com	Lexington	TN	38351	731-967-0001	968-3320
MarathonNorco Aerospace Inc 8301 Imperial Dr *Web:* www.mnaerospace.com	Waco	TX	76712	254-776-0650	776-6558
Master Metal Products Co 495 Emory St *Web:* www.mastermetalproducts.com	San Jose	CA	95110	408-275-1210	275-0523
Metal Fabricating Corp 10408 Berea Rd *Web:* www.metalfabricatingcorp.com	Cleveland	OH	44102	216-631-2480	631-2453
MP Metal Products Inc W1250 Elmwood Ave *TF:* 800-824-6744 ■ *Web:* www.mpmetals.com	Ixonia	WI	53036	920-261-9650	261-9652
National Sintered Alloys Inc Heritage Pk Rt 145 PO Box 332 *Web:* www.nationalsintered.com	Clinton	CT	06413	860-669-8653	669-5428
Newbrook Machines Inc 16 Mechanic St *Web:* excelco.net	Silver Creek	NY	14136	716-934-2644	
NobelClad 5405 Spine Rd *NASDAQ: BOOM*	Boulder	CO	80301	303-665-5700	604-1897
Nor-Cal Metal Fabricators 1121 Third St *Web:* www.nc-mf.com	Oakland	CA	94607	510-836-1451	208-2838
Progressive Tool & Manufacturing Co 290 Fifth St NE *Web:* www.ptmmn.com	Pine Island	MN	55963	507-356-8345	356-4557
Pulley-Kellam Company Inc 245 Erie St	Huntington	IN	46750	260-356-6326	356-1928
Quaker City Plating (QCP) PO Box 2406 *Web:* www.quakercityplating.com	Whittier	CA	90610	562-945-3721	945-9932
Right Mfg 7949 Stromesa Ct Ste G *Web:* www.rightmfg.com	San Diego	CA	92126	858-566-7002	566-7623
Rose Metal Products Inc 1955 E Div St *Web:* www.rosemetalproducts.com	Springfield	MO	65803	417-865-1676	865-7673
Sommer Metalcraft Corp 315 Poston Dr *TF:* 888-876-6637 ■ *Web:* www.sommermetalcraft.com	Crawfordsville	IN	47933	765-362-6201	
TPI Powder Metallurgy Inc 12030 Beaver Rd *Web:* www.tpipm.com	Saint Charles	MI	48655	989-865-9921	865-9924
Uni-Form Components Co 10703 Sheldon Rd *Web:* www.uniformcomponents.com	Houston	TX	77044	281-456-9310	456-0245
Unifab Corp 5260 Lovers Ln *TF General:* 800-648-9569 ■ *Web:* www.unifabcorp.com	Portage	MI	49002	269-382-2803	382-2825
Unique Aluminum Extrusion LLC 333 Cedar Ave	Middlesex	NJ	08846	732-271-1160	
Weldments Inc 10720 N Second St *Web:* weldmentsinc.com	MACHESNEY PARk	IL	61115	815-633-3393	633-2524
White River Distributors Inc 720 Ramsey *TF:* 800-548-7219 ■ *Web:* www.lpgbobtails.com	Batesville	AR	72501	870-793-2374	793-8230
Wire Products Manufacturing Corp 106 N Genesee St	Merrill	WI	54452	715-536-7144	

483 METAL FORGINGS

				Phone	Fax
A & A Global Industries Inc 17 Stenersen Ln *TF:* 800-638-6000 ■ *Web:* aaglobal.com	Cockeysville	MD	21030	410-252-1020	
Advanced Forming Technology Inc 7040 Weld County Rd 20 *Web:* aftmim.com	Longmont	CO	80504	303-833-6000	
Advanced Metal Components Inc 720 Empire Expy *Web:* www.amcinc.net	Swainsboro	GA	30401	478-237-8994	
Alcoa Wheel Products International 1600 Harvard Ave *TF:* 800-242-9898 ■ *Web:* www.alcoa.com	Cleveland	OH	44105	216-641-3600	
Alken-Ziegler Inc 25575 Brest Rd	Taylor	MI	48180	734-946-4444	
Aluminum Precision Products Inc 3333 W Warner St *TF:* 800-411-8983 ■ *Web:* www.aluminumprecision.com	Santa Ana	CA	92704	714-546-8125	540-8662
Ameri-Forge Group Inc 13770 Industrial Rd *Web:* www.ameriforge.com	Houston	TX	77015	713-393-4200	
AMSTED Industries Inc 180 N Stetson St Ste 1800 *Web:* www.amsted.com	Chicago	IL	60601	312-645-1700	
Anchor-Harvey Components LLC 600 W Lamm Rd *TF:* 888-367-4464 ■ *Web:* www.anchorharvey.com	Freeport	IL	61032	815-233-3833	
ATI Ladish Company Inc 5481 S Packard Ave *Web:* www.atimetals.com	Cudahy	WI	53110	414-747-2611	
Bachman Machine Company Inc 4321 N Broadway *Web:* www.bachmanmachine.com	St Louis	MO	63147	314-231-4221	
Ball Chain Mfg Company Inc 741 S Fulton Ave *Web:* www.ballchain.com	Mount Vernon	NY	10550	914-664-7500	664-7460
Batesville Tool & Die Inc 177 Six Pine Ranch Rd *Web:* btdinc.com	Batesville	IN	47006	812-934-5616	
Berkeley Forge & Tool Inc 1331 E Shore Hwy *Web:* www.berkforge.com	Berkeley	CA	94710	510-526-5034	525-9014
Berkshire Manufactured Products Inc 116 Parker St *Web:* www.berkshiremfp.com	Newburyport	MA	01950	978-462-8161	
Bharat Forge America 2807 S ML King Jr Blvd	Lansing	MI	48910	517-393-5300	393-6256
Bobby Rahal Automotive Group 10701 Perry Hwy *Web:* www.bobbyrahal.com	Wexford	PA	15090	724-935-9300	
Bomco Inc 125 Gloucester Ave *Web:* www.bomco.com	Gloucester	MA	01930	978-283-9000	
Brainerd Industries Inc 680 Precision Ct *TF:* 800-790-0430 ■ *Web:* www.brainerdindustries.com	Miamisburg	OH	45342	937-228-0488	
Braxton Mfg Company Inc 858 Echo Lk Rd *Web:* www.braxtonmfg.com	Watertown	CT	06795	860-274-6781	
Brunk Industries Inc 1225 Sage St *Web:* www.brunkindustries.com	Lake Geneva	WI	53147	262-248-8873	
Buchanan Metal Forming Inc (BMF) 103 W Smith St *Web:* www.bmfcorp.com	Buchanan	MI	49107	269-695-3836	695-3830
Bula Forge & Machine Inc 3001 W 121st St *Web:* www.bulaforge.com	Cleveland	OH	44111	216-252-7600	
Canton Drop Forge Inc 4575 Southway St SW *Web:* www.cantondropforge.com	Canton	OH	44706	330-477-4511	477-2046
Carlton Forge Works Inc 7743 E Adams St *Web:* carltonforgeworks.com	Paramount	CA	90723	562-633-1131	531-8896
CB Kaupp & Sons Inc 6-10 Newark Way *Web:* kaupp-kihm.com	Maplewood	NJ	07040	973-761-4000	
Century Metal Spinning Company Inc 430 Meyer Rd *Web:* www.centurymetalspinning.com	Bensenville	IL	60106	630-595-3900	
Cleveland Die & Manufacturing Co 20303 First Ave *Web:* www.clevelanddie.com	Middleburg Heights	OH	44130	440-243-3404	
Clifford-Jacobs Forging Co 2410 N Fifth St PO Box 830 *Web:* www.clifford-jacobs.com	Champaign	IL	61822	217-352-5172	352-4629
Coining Technologies Inc 400 Kuller Rd *Web:* www.coining.com	Clifton	NJ	07011	973-253-0500	
Consolidated Industries Inc 677 Mixville Rd *Web:* www.forgemetal.com	Cheshire	CT	06410	203-272-5371	272-5672
Continental Forge Company Inc 412 E El Segundo Blvd *Web:* www.cforge.com	Compton	CA	90222	310-603-1014	
Cornell Forge Co 6666 W 66th St *Web:* www.cornellforge.com	Chicago	IL	60638	708-458-1582	728-9883
Corry Forge Co 441 E Main St *Web:* www.ellwoodgroup.com	Corry	PA	16407	814-664-9664	664-9452
Coulter Forge Technology Inc 1494 67th St *Web:* www.coulter-forge.com	Emeryville	CA	94608	510-420-3500	420-3555
DeKalb Forge Co 1832 Pleasant St *Web:* www.dekalbforge.com	DeKalb	IL	60115	815-758-6400	756-6958
Doncasters Storms Forge Div 160 Cottage St *Web:* doncasters.com	Springfield	MA	01104	413-785-1801	
Dowding Industries Inc 449 Marilin St *Web:* www.dowdingindustries.com	Eaton Rapids	MI	48827	517-663-5455	
E M J D Corp 4590 S Windermere St *Web:* emjd.com	Englewood	CO	80110	303-761-5236	
Ellwood City Forge 800 Commercial Ave *TF:* 800-843-0166 ■ *Web:* www.ellwoodcityforge.com	Ellwood City	PA	16117	724-752-0055	752-3449
Erie Forge & Steel Inc 1341 W 16th St *Web:* www.whemco.com/erie_forge_and_steel.aspx	Erie	PA	16502	814-452-2300	
Eyelet Crafters Inc 2712 S Main St *Web:* www.eyeletcrafters.com	Waterbury	CT	06706	203-757-9221	
Fansteel Inc 1746 Commerce Rd *Web:* www.fansteel.com	Creston	IA	50801	641-782-8521	
Federal Flange 4014 Pinemont St *TF:* 800-231-0150 ■ *Web:* www.federalflange.com	Houston	TX	77018	713-681-0606	681-3005
Ferguson Perforating & Wire Co 130 Ernest St *TF:* 800-341-9800 ■ *Web:* www.fergusonperf.com	Providence	RI	02905	401-941-8876	
Fine Line Production 2221 Regal Pkwy *TF:* 800-887-5625 ■ *Web:* www.finelineproduction.com	Euless	TX	76040	817-267-6750	267-6787
Foremost Mfg Company Inc 941 Ball Ave *Web:* www.foremost-mfg.com	Union	NJ	07083	908-687-4646	
Forged Components Inc 14527 Smith Rd *Web:* forgedcomponents.com	Humble	TX	77396	281-441-4088	441-8899
Forged Products Inc (FPI) 6505 N Houston Rosslyn Rd *TF:* 800-876-3416 ■ *Web:* www.fpitx.com	Houston	TX	77091	713-462-3416	460-9404
Forged Vessel Connections Inc 945 Bunker Hill Rd Ste 500 *Web:* www.forgedvesselconn.com	Houston	TX	77024	713-393-4200	
Frontier Metal Stamping Inc 3764 Puritan Way *TF:* 888-316-1266 ■ *Web:* www.frontiermetal.com	Erie	CO	80516	303-458-5129	
GB Manufacturing Co 1120 E Main St *Web:* www.gbmfg.com	Delta	OH	43515	419-822-5323	
Green Bay Drop Forge 1341 State St *TF:* 800-824-4896 ■ *Web:* www.greenbaydropforge.com	Green Bay	WI	54304	920-432-6401	432-0859
H & L Tooth Company Inc 10055 E 56 St N *TF:* 800-458-6684 ■ *Web:* www.hltooth.com	Tulsa	OK	74117	918-272-0951	272-0163
Hammond & Irving Inc 254 N St *Web:* www.hammond-irving.com	Auburn	NY	13021	315-253-6265	253-3136
Hardware & Forging Co 3270 E 79th St *Web:* www.clevelandhardware.com	Cleveland	OH	44104	216-641-5200	
HHI Group Holdings LLC 2727 W 14 Mile Rd *Web:* hhiholdings.net	Royal Oak	MI	48073	248-284-2900	
Hirschvogel Inc 2230 S Third St *Web:* hirschvogel.com	Columbus	OH	43207	614-445-6060	445-7335
Hughes Parker Industries LLC 1604 Mahr Ave *Web:* www.hughesparker.com	Lawrenceburg	TN	38464	931-762-9403	
Hydroform USA Inc 2848 E 208th St *Web:* www.hydroforming.net	Long Beach	CA	90810	310-632-6353	

Company	City	State	Zip	Phone	Fax
Ice Industries Inc 3810 Herr Rd *Web:* www.iceindustries.com	Sylvania	OH	43560	419-842-3600	
Independent Forge Co 692 N Batavia St *Web:* www.independentforge.com	Orange	CA	92868	714-997-7337	997-7546
J & E Earl Manufacturing Co 7925 215th St W *Web:* www.jecompanies.com	Lakeville	MN	55044	952-469-3933	
JD Norman Industries Inc 787 W Belden Ave *Web:* www.jdnorman.com	Addison	IL	60101	630-458-3700	
Jervis B. Webb Co 34375 W 12 Mile Rd *Web:* www.daifuku.com/us	Farmington Hills	MI	48331	248-553-1000	553-1228
Jorgensen Forge Corp 8531 E Marginal Way S *TF:* 800-231-5382 ■ *Web:* www.jorgensenforge.com	Tukwila	WA	98108	206-762-1100	
KAPCO Inc 1000 Badger Cir *Web:* www.kapcoinc.com	Grafton	WI	53024	262-377-6500	
Kerkau Manufacturing Co 1321 S Valley Ctr Dr *TF:* 800-248-5060 ■ *Web:* www.kerkau.com	Bay City	MI	48706	989-686-0350	686-0399
Keystone Forging Co 215 Duke St PO Box 269 *Web:* www.keystoneforging.com	Northumberland	PA	17857	570-473-3524	473-7273
KomTeK Technologies 40 Rockdale St *Web:* www.komtektech.com	Worcester	MA	01606	508-853-4500	853-2753
Kreider Corp 2000 S Yellow Springs St *Web:* www.kreidercorp.com	Springfield	OH	45506	937-325-8787	
Kropp Forge 5301 W Roosevelt Rd **Fax:* Sales ■ *Web:* www.kroppforge.com	Cicero	IL	60804	708-652-6691	652-9144*
L H Thomson Company Inc, The 7800 NE Industrial Blvd *Web:* www.lhthomson.com	Macon	GA	31216	478-788-5052	
Lakeview Forge Co 1725 Pittsburgh Ave *Web:* lakeviewforge.com	Erie	PA	16505	814-454-4518	455-5875
Larsen Mfg LLC 1201 Allanson Rd *Web:* www.larsenmfg.net	Mundelein	IL	60060	847-970-9600	
Lefere Forge & Machine Co 665 Hupp Ave *Web:* www.lefereforge.com	Jackson	MI	49203	517-784-7109	784-0929
Lehigh Heavy Forge Corp 275 Emery St *Web:* www.lhforge.com	Bethlehem	PA	18015	610-332-8100	332-8101
Lenape Forged Products Corp 1334 Lenape Rd *Web:* www.lenapeforge.com	West Chester	PA	19382	610-793-5090	793-3070
Liberty Forge Inc PO Box 1210 *TF:* 800-231-2377 ■ *Web:* www.libertyforgeinc.com	Liberty	TX	77575	800-231-2377	
Machine Specialty & Manufacturing Inc 215 Rousseau Rd *TF:* 800-256-1292 ■ *Web:* www.machine-specialty.com	Youngsville	LA	70592	337-837-0020	837-0062
McKenzie Valve & Machining Co 145 Airport Rd *Web:* www.mckenzievalve.com	McKenzie	TN	38201	731-352-5027	352-3029
McWilliams Forge Company Inc 387 Franklin Ave *Web:* www.mcwilliamsforge.com	Rockaway	NJ	07866	973-627-0200	625-9316
Meadville Forging Co 15309 Baldwin St PO Box 459 *Web:* www.meadforge.com	Meadville	PA	16335	814-332-8200	333-4657
Mercer Forge Corp 200 Brown St *TF:* 800-558-5075	Mercer	PA	16137	724-662-2750	662-5642
Metal Forming & Coining Corp (MFC) 1007 Illinois Ave *Web:* www.mfccorp.com	Maumee	OH	43537	419-893-8748	893-6828
Metal Spinners Inc 800 Growth Pkwy *Web:* www.metalspinners.com	Angola	IN	46703	260-665-2192	
Metalist International Inc 1159 S Pennsylvania Ave *Web:* www.metalist.com	Lansing	MI	48912	517-371-2940	371-3027
Mid-West Forge Corp 17301 St Clair Ave *Web:* www.mid-westforge.com	Cleveland	OH	44110	216-481-3030	481-7288
Millennium Forge Inc 990 W Ormsby Ave *Web:* www.millenniumforge.com	Louisville	KY	40210	502-635-3350	635-3028
MMD Equipment 121 High Hill Rd *TF:* 800-433-1382 ■ *Web:* www.mmdequipment.com	Swedesboro	NJ	08085	856-467-3200	467-5235
Modern Drop Forge Co 13810 S Western Ave *Web:* www.modernforge.com	Blue Island	IL	60406	708-388-1806	597-3633
Moline Forge Inc 4101 Fourth Ave *Web:* www.molineforge.com	Moline	IL	61265	309-762-5506	762-5508
MOLY-COP Canada 250 Andover Crescent *Web:* scaw.co.za	Kamloops	BC	V2C6X2	250-573-7770	
National Flange & Fitting Co 4420 Creekmont Dr	Houston	TX	77091	713-688-2515	688-0205
Nissin Precision North America Inc 375 Union Rd *Web:* nissinoh.com	Eagle wood	OH	45322	937-836-1910	832-1270
Norforge & Machining Inc 195 N Dean St *TF:* 800-839-3706 ■ *Web:* bushnell.illinois.gov	Bushnell	IL	61422	309-772-3124	
Ohio Star Forge Co (OSF) 4000 Mahoning Ave NW *Web:* www.ohiostar.com	Warren	OH	44480	330-847-6360	847-6368
Ohio Valley Manufacturing Inc 1501 Harrington Memorial Rd *Web:* www.ohiovalleymfg.com	Mansfield	OH	44903	419-522-5818	
Omni Manufacturing Inc 901 Mckinley Rd *Web:* www.omnimfg.com	Saint Marys	OH	45885	419-394-7424	
Orchid International Group Inc 94 Belinda Pkwy *Web:* www.orchidinternational.com	Mount Juliet	TN	37122	615-754-6600	
Pacific Forge Inc 10641 Etiwanda Ave *Web:* www.pacificforge.com	Fontana	CA	92337	909-390-0701	390-0708
Parish International Inc PO Box 468 **Fax Area Code:* 979 ■ *Web:* www.parishforge.com	Hempstead	TX	77445	281-463-9233	826-8224*
Performance Stamping Company Inc 20 Lk Marian Rd *TF:* 800-935-0393 ■ *Web:* www.performancestamping.com	Carpentersville	IL	60110	847-426-2233	
Phoenix Forging Company Inc 800 Front St *TF:* 800-444-3674 ■ *Web:* www.phoenixforge.com	Catasauqua	PA	18032	610-264-2861	266-0530
Pinnacle Precision Sheet Metal Corp 5410 E La Palma Ave *Web:* www.pinnacleprecisionsheetmetal.com	Anaheim	CA	92807	714-777-3129	
Pinnacle Precision Technologies LLC 2607 Eaton Ln	Racine	WI	53404	262-632-2232	
Portland Forge 250 E Lafayette St **Fax Area Code:* 219 ■ *Web:* www.atimetals.com	Portland	IN	47371	260-726-8121	726-8021*
Powers & Sons LLC 44700 Helm St *Web:* www.powersandsonsllc.com	Plymouth	MI	48170	734-354-6575	254-9517
Precision Die & Stamping Inc 1704 W 10th St *Web:* www.precisiondie.com	Tempe	AZ	85281	480-967-2038	
Precision Drawn Metals Inc 1345 Plainfield Ave *Web:* www.drawnmetals.com	Janesville	WI	53545	608-755-1495	
Precision Metal Products Inc 850 W Bradley Ave *Web:* www.pmp-elcajon.com	El Cajon	CA	92020	619-448-2711	448-2005
Premier Pan Company Inc 33 Mcgovern Blvd *Web:* www.prestigehomes.com	Crescent	PA	15046	724-457-4220	
Presrite Corp 3665 E 78th St *Web:* www.presrite.com	Cleveland	OH	44105	216-441-5990	441-2644
Quality Filters Inc 7215 Jackson Rd *Web:* qualityfiltersinc.com	Ann Arbor	MI	48103	734-668-0211	
Quick Way Stampings Inc of Texas 915 Stanley Dr *Web:* sheetmetal-fabricating.com	Euless	TX	76040	817-267-1515	
Rago & Son Inc 1029 51st Ave *Web:* www.rago-son.com	Oakland	CA	94601	510-536-5700	
Ralco Industries Inc 2720 Auburn Ct *Web:* www.ralcoind.com	Auburn Hills	MI	48326	248-853-3200	
Randall Bearings Inc 1046 Greenlawn Ave PO Box 1258 *TF:* 800-626-7071 ■ *Web:* www.randallbearings.com	Lima	OH	45802	419-223-1075	228-0200
Riley Gear Corp 1 Precision Dr *Web:* www.rileygear.com	St. Augustine	FL	32092	904-829-5652	
Ritatsu Manufacturing Inc 700 Old Liberty Church Rd	Beaver Dam	KY	42320	270-730-7010	
Royal Die & Stamping Co 125 Mercedes Dr *Web:* www.royaldie.com	Carol Stream	IL	60188	630-766-2685	
Saint Croix Forge Inc 5195 Scandia Trl *TF:* 866-668-7642 ■ *Web:* www.stcroixforge.com	Forest Lake	MN	55025	651-464-8967	
Scot Forge Co 8001 Winn Rd PO Box 8 *TF:* 800-435-6621 ■ *Web:* www.scotforge.com	Spring Grove	IL	60081	847-587-1000	587-2000
Standard Steel LLC 500 N Walnut St *Web:* www.standardsteel.com	Burnham	PA	17009	717-248-4911	248-8050
Steel Industries Inc (SII) 12600 Beech-Daly Rd **Fax Area Code:* 313 ■ *TF:* 877-783-3599 ■ *Web:* www.steelindustriesinc.com	Redford Township	MI	48239	877-783-3599	534-2165*
T & W Forge Inc 970 E 64th St **Fax Area Code:* 330 ■ *Web:* sifco.com	Cleveland	OH	44103	216-881-8600	821-7309*
T&C Stamping Inc 1403 Freeman Ave *Web:* www.tandcstamping.com	Athens	AL	35613	256-233-7383	
Talan Products Inc 18800 Cochran Ave *TF:* 877-419-2805 ■ *Web:* www.talanproducts.com	Cleveland	OH	44110	216-458-0170	
Texas Metal Works Inc 13770 Industrial Rd	Houston	TX	77015	713-222-0139	
TFO Tech Company Ltd 221 State St	Jeffersonville	OH	43128	740-426-6381	426-6511
Thermal Structures Inc (TSI) 2362 Railroad St *Web:* www.thermalstructures.com	Corona	CA	92880	951-736-9911	736-1064
Thoro'Bred Inc 5020 E La Palma Ave **Fax Area Code:* 765 ■ *TF:* 877-585-5152 ■ *Web:* www.thorobredinc.com	Anaheim	CA	92807	714-779-2581	420-7040*
ThyssenKrupp Crankshaft Company LLC 1000 Lynch Rd *Web:* www.thyssenkrupp-forginggroup.com	Danville	IL	61834	217-431-0060	431-8934
Titan Tool & Die Ltd 2801 Howard Ave *Web:* www.titantool.ca	Windsor	ON	N8X3Y1	519-966-1234	
Toledo Metal Spinning Co 1819 Clinton St *Web:* www.toledometalspinning.com	Toledo	OH	43607	419-535-5931	
Toner Machining Technologies Inc 212 E Fleming Dr *Web:* www.tonermachining.com	Morganton	NC	28655	828-432-8007	
Trenton Forging Co 5523 Hoover St *Web:* www.trentonforging.com	Trenton	MI	48183	734-675-1620	675-4839
Trinity Forge Inc 947 Trinity Dr *Web:* www.trinityforge.com	Mansfield	TX	76063	817-473-1515	473-6743
Truelove & Maclean Inc 57 Callender Rd *Web:* www.trueloveandmaclean.com	Watertown	CT	06795	860-274-9600	
Turbine Engine Components Technologies Corp (TECT) 334 Beechwood Rd Ste 304 *Web:* www.tectcorp.com	Ft. Mitchell	KY	41017	229-228-2600	
Unit Drop Forge Company Inc 1903 S 62nd St PO Box 340350 *Web:* www.unitforgings.com	West Allis	WI	53219	414-545-3000	545-6318
United Brass Manufacturers Inc 35030 GoddaRd Rd *Web:* unitedbrass.com	Romulus	MI	48174	734-941-0700	941-0640
Van-Rob Inc 200 Vandorf Sideroad *Web:* www.van-rob.com	Aurora	ON	L4G0A2	905-727-8585	
VH Blackinton & Company Inc 221 John L Dietsch Blvd *Web:* www.blackinton.com	Attleboro	MA	02763	508-699-4436	
Vulcan Spring & Manufacturing Co 501 Schoolhouse Rd *Web:* www.vulcanspring.com	Telford	PA	18969	215-721-1721	
Walker Forge Inc 222 E Erie St Ste 300 *Web:* www.walkerforge.com	Milwaukee	WI	53202	414-223-2000	223-2019
Weber Metals Inc 16706 Garfield Ave *Web:* webermetals.com	Paramount	CA	90723	562-602-0260	602-0468
Western Forge & Flange Co 687 County Rd 2201 *TF:* 800-352-6433 ■ *Web:* www.western-forge.com	Cleveland	TX	77327	281-727-7060	727-7060
Wilton Precision Steel Co 320 W First St *Web:* www.wps01.com	Wilton	IA	52778	563-732-3363	732-3365

Phone | Fax

Wozniak Industries Inc
2 Mid America Plz Ste 706 .... Oakbrook Terrace IL 60181 630-954-3400 954-3605
Web: www.wozniakindustries.com

Wozniak Industries Inc Commercial Forged Products Div
5757 W 65th St. .... Bedford Park IL 60638 708-458-1220 458-9346
TF: 800-637-2695 ■ *Web:* www.commercialforged.com

Wrought Washer Manufacturing Inc
2100 S Bay St. .... Milwaukee WI 53207 414-744-0771
TF: 800-558-5217 ■ *Web:* www.wroughtwasher.com

Wyman-Gordon Forgings (Cleveland) Inc
3097 E 61st St .... Cleveland OH 44127 216-341-0085
Web: www.pccforgedproducts.com/brands/wyman_gordon/america/locations/cleveland/overview

Young Manufacturing Inc 2331 N 42nd St. .... Grand Forks ND 58203 701-772-5541
TF: 800-451-9884 ■ *Web:* www.youngmfg.com

484 METAL HEAT TREATING

Phone | Fax

Aberfoyle Metal Treaters Ltd 18 Kerr Cres .... Guelph ON N0B2J0 519-763-1120 763-1121
Web: www.aberfoyle-mt.com

Advanced Heat Treat Corp 2825 MidPort Blvd. .... Waterloo IA 50703 319-232-5221
Web: ahtweb.com

Aerocraft Heat Treating Co Inc
15701 Minnesota Ave. .... Paramount CA 90723 562-674-2400 633-0364
Web: www.aerocraft-ht.com

Ajax Metal Processing Inc 4651 Bellevue St .... Detroit MI 48207 313-267-2100 267-2110
Web: www.ajaxmetal.com

Akron Steel Treating Co 336 Morgan Ave. .... Akron OH 44311 330-773-8211
TF: 800-364-2782 ■ *Web:* www.akronsteeltreating.com

Alfe Heat Treating Inc
6920 Pointe Inverness Way Ste 140 .... Fort Wayne IN 46804 260-747-9422
Web: www.al-fe.com

Bluewater Thermal Solutions
201 Brookfield Pwy Ste 102 .... Greenville SC 29607 864-990-0050 990-0056
TF: 877-990-0050 ■ *Web:* www.bluewaterthermal.com

Byron Products Inc 3781 Port Union Rd .... Fairfield OH 45014 513-870-9111
Web: www.byronproducts.com

Chem-plate Industries Inc
1800 Touhy Ave .... Elk Grove Village IL 60007 847-640-1600 640-1699
Web: www.chemplateindustries.com

Chicago Flame Hardening Company Inc
5200 Railroad Ave .... East Chicago IN 46312 219-397-6475
Web: www.cflame.com

Commercial Steel Treating Corp
31440 Stephenson Hwy .... Madison Heights MI 48071 248-588-3300 588-3534
Web: www.commercialsteel.com

Curtiss-Wright Corp
10 Waterview Blvd 2nd Fl .... Parsippany NJ 07054 973-541-3700 541-3699
NYSE: CW ■ *TF:* 855-449-0995 ■ *Web:* www.curtisswright.com

East Lind Heat Treat Inc
32045 Dequindre Rd. .... Madison Heights MI 48071 248-585-1415
Web: www.eastlind.com

Euclid Heat Treating Co 1340 E 222nd St. .... Euclid OH 44117 216-481-8444
TF: 800-962-2909 ■ *Web:* www.euclidheattreating.com

Fisher-Barton Inc 1040 S 12th St. .... Watertown WI 53094 920-261-0131 261-4549

Flame Metals Processing Corp
12450 Ironwood Cir .... Rogers MN 55374 763-428-2596 428-3689
Web: flamemetals.com

FPM LLC 1501 S Lively Blvd .... Elk Grove Village IL 60007 847-228-2525 228-5912
TF: 877-437-6432 ■ *Web:* www.fpmht.com

Gibraltar Industries Inc 3556 Lakeshore Rd .... Buffalo NY 14219 716-826-6500 826-1589*
NASDAQ: ROCK ■ **Fax:* Sales ■ *TF:* 800-247-8368 ■ *Web:* www.gibraltar1.com

H & S Heat Treating Co 133 S St N .... Port Robinson ON L0S1K0 905-384-9355
Web: www.hsheat.com

HI TecMetal Group Inc 1101 E 55th St .... Cleveland OH 44103 216-881-8100 426-6690
TF: 877-484-2867 ■ *Web:* www.htg.cc

Hudapack Metal Treating Inc 979 Koopman Ln .... Elkhorn WI 53121 262-723-3345
Web: www.hudapack.com

Industrial Steel Treating Inc 613 Carroll St. .... Jackson MI 49202 800-253-9534 550-7045*
**Fax Area Code:* 866 ■ *TF:* 800-253-9534 ■ *Web:* www.indstl.com

Kowalski Heat Treating Co 3611 Detroit Ave .... Cleveland OH 44113 216-631-4411
Web: www.khtheat.com

Maxco Inc 836 Centennial Way Ste 170. .... Lansing MI 48917 517-627-1734 627-4951

Metal Improvement Company LLC
80 Rt 4 E Ste 310 .... Paramus NJ 07652 201-843-7800 843-3460
Web: cwst.com

Metals Technology Corp 120 N Schmale Rd .... Carol Stream IL 60188 630-221-2500
Web: metalstechnology.com

Miller Consolidated Industries Inc
2221 Arbor Blvd .... Dayton OH 45439 937-294-2681
TF: 800-589-4133 ■ *Web:* www.millerconsolidated.com

Modern Industries Inc 613 W 11th St. .... Erie PA 16501 814-455-8061 453-4382
Web: modernind.com

Nitrex Metal Inc 3474 Poirier Blvd .... Saint-Laurent QC H4R2J5 514-335-7191 335-4160
TF: 877-335-7191 ■ *Web:* www.nitrex.com

Opticote Inc 10455 Seymour .... Franklin Park IL 60131 847-678-8900
Web: www.opticote.com

Pacific Metallurgical Inc 925 Fifth Ave S .... Kent WA 98032 253-854-4241
Web: www.pacmet.com

Paulo Products Company Inc 5711 W Park Ave .... St. Louis MO 63110 314-647-7500
Web: www.americanbrazing.com

Pennsylvania Metallurgical Inc
315 Columbia St. .... Bethlehem PA 18015 610-691-1313
Web: www.pmiheattreat.com

Precision Heat Treating Corp
2711 Adams Ctr Rd .... Fort Wayne IN 46803 260-749-5125
Web: www.phtc.net

Rex Heat Treat 951 W Eigth St PO Box 270 .... Lansdale PA 19446 215-855-1131 855-2028
TF: 800-220-4739 ■ *Web:* www.rexht.com

Riverdale Plating & Heat Treating Inc
680 W 134th St. .... Riverdale IL 60827 708-849-2050
Web: www.rpht.com

Phone | Fax

RMT Woodworth Inc 45755 Five Mile Rd. .... Plymouth MI 48170 734-254-0566
Web: www.rmtwoodworth.com

Robert Wooler Co 1755 Susquehanna Rd. .... Dresher PA 19025 215-542-7600 542-0250
Web: www.robertwooler.com

Solar Atmospheres Inc 1969 Clearview Rd .... Souderton PA 18964 215-721-1502
Web: www.solaratm.com

Specialty Heat Treat Holland
3700 Eastern Ave Se. .... Grand Rapids MI 49508 616-245-0465

Specialty Steel Treating Inc
34501 Commerce Rd .... Fraser MI 48026 586-293-5355 293-5390
Web: sst.net

Stahl Specialty Co 111 E Pacific PO Box 6 .... Kingsville MO 64061 816-597-3322 597-3485
TF: 800-821-7852 ■ *Web:* www.stahlspecialty.com

Super Steel Treating Inc 6227 Rinke .... Warren MI 48091 586-755-9140
Web: www.supersteeltreating.com

TC Industries Inc 3703 S Rt 31. .... Crystal Lake IL 60012 815-459-2400 459-3303
Web: www.tcindustries.com

Texas Heat Treating Inc 155 Texas Ave .... Round Rock TX 78664 512-255-5884 255-8464
TF: 800-580-5884 ■ *Web:* www.texasheattreating.com

Texas Stress Inc 1304 Underwood Rd .... La Porte TX 77571 281-930-0897 930-0992
Web: www.texasstress.com

Thermal-vac Technology Inc 1221 W Struck Ave .... Orange CA 92867 714-997-2601
Web: www.thermal-vac.com

Thortex Inc 15045 N.E. Mason St .... Portland OR 97230 503-654-5726
Web: www.thortexinc.com

Tri-City Heat Treat Co 2020 Fifth St .... Rock Island IL 61201 309-786-2689 786-2691
Web: www.tcht.com

Wall Colmonoy Corp 101 W Girard Ave .... Madison Heights MI 48071 248-585-6400 585-7960
Web: www.wallcolmonoy.com

Ward Aluminum Casting Co 642 Growth Ave .... Fort Wayne IN 46808 260-426-8700 420-1919
Web: www.wardcorp.com

485 METAL INDUSTRIES (MISC)

See Also Foundries - Investment p. 2322; Foundries - Iron & Steel p. 2322; Foundries - Nonferrous (Castings) p. 2324; Metal Heat Treating p. 2756; Metal Tube & Pipe p. 2760; Steel - Mfr p. 3208; Wire & Cable p. 3312

Phone | Fax

Alcoa Inc 390 Park Ave .... New York NY 10022 412-553-4545
TF: 800-523-9596 ■ *Web:* www.alcoa.com

Alcoa Inc 201 Isabella St .... Pittsburgh PA 15212 412-553-4545 553-4498
NYSE: AA ■ *TF:* 800-388-4825 ■ *Web:* www.alcoa.com

Alcoa Primary Metals
900 S Gay St Riverview Twr Ste 1100. .... Knoxville TN 37902 865-594-4700
TF: 800-852-0238 ■ *Web:* www.alcoa.com

Allegheny Technologies Inc
1000 Six PPG Pl. .... Pittsburgh PA 15222 412-394-2800
NYSE: ATI ■ *TF Sales:* 800-258-3586 ■ *Web:* www.atimetals.com

Allvac Inc 2020 Ashcraft Ave PO Box 5030 .... Monroe NC 28110 704-289-4511 289-4018*
**Fax:* Sales ■ *TF:* 800-841-5491 ■ *Web:* www.atimetals.com

Altech LLC 242 America Pl. .... Jeffersonville IN 47130 812-282-8256 280-6070
TF: 800-264-8256 ■ *Web:* www.altecextrusions.com

AMETEK Specialty Metal Products
21 Toelles Rd .... Wallingford CT 06492 203-265-6731 294-0196
Web: www.ametekmetals.com

Ampco Metal Inc
1117 E Algonquin Rd .... Arlington Heights IL 60005 847-437-6000 437-6008
TF: 800-844-6008 ■ *Web:* www.ampcometal.com

Anaheim Extrusion Company Inc
1330 N Kraemer Blvd PO Box 6380 .... Anaheim CA 92806 714-630-3111 630-0443
TF: 800-660-3318 ■ *Web:* www.anaheimextrude.com

Arvinyl Metal Laminates Corp
233 N Sherman Ave .... Corona CA 92882 800-278-4695 371-7118*
**Fax Area Code:* 951 ■ *TF:* 800-278-4695 ■ *Web:* www.arvinyl.com

Audubon Metals LLC 3055 Ohio Dr .... Henderson KY 42420 270-830-6622 830-9987
Web: www.audubonmetals.com

Big River Zinc Corp 2401 Mississippi Ave .... Sauget IL 62201 618-274-5000
TF: 800-274-4002 ■ *Web:* www.bigriverzinc.com

Bolton Metal Products Co 2042 Axemann Rd .... Bellefonte PA 16823 814-355-6217 355-6219
Web: www.boltonmetalproducts.com

Bonnell Aluminum 25 Bonnell St .... Newnan GA 30263 770-253-2020
Web: www.bonlalum.com

Broco Inc 10868 Bell Ct. .... Rancho Cucamonga CA 91730 909-483-3222 483-3233
TF: 800-845-7259 ■ *Web:* www.broco-rankin.com

Bunting Magnetics Co 500 S Spencer Ave .... Newton KS 67114 316-284-2020 283-4975
TF: 800-835-2526 ■ *Web:* buntingmagnetics.com

Cabot Supermetals
1095 Windward Ridge Pkwy Ste 200 .... Alpharetta GA 30005 610-367-1500 297-1498*
**Fax Area Code:* 678 ■ *Web:* www.cabotcorp.com

Cannon Muskegon Corp
2875 Lincoln St PO Box 506 .... Muskegon MI 49441 231-755-1681 755-4975
TF: 800-253-0371 ■ *Web:* cannonmuskegon.com

Cardinal Aluminum Co 6910 Preston Hwy. .... Louisville KY 40219 502-969-9302 969-6910*
**Fax Area Code:* 800 ■ *TF Cust Svc:* 800-398-7833 ■ *Web:* cardinalaluminum.com

Century Aluminum Co
2511 Garden Rd Ste 200 Bldg A. .... Monterey CA 93940 831-642-9300
NASDAQ: CENX ■ *Web:* www.centuryaluminum.com

Century Aluminum of Kentucky
1627 SR 271 N PO Box 500 .... Hawesville KY 42348 270-685-2493
Web: centuryaluminum.com

Certified Alloy Products Inc
3245 Cherry Ave PO Box 90. .... Long Beach CA 90801 562-595-6621
Web: doncasters.com

Chase Brass & Copper Co 14212 Selwyn Dr. .... Montpelier OH 43543 419-485-3193 485-5945*
**Fax:* Mail Rm ■ *TF:* 800-537-4291 ■ *Web:* www.chasebrass.com

Chicago Extruded Metals Co (CXM) 1601 S 54th Ave .... Cicero IL 60804 800-323-8102 780-3479*
**Fax Area Code:* 708 ■ *TF Cust Svc:* 800-323-8102 ■ *Web:* www.cxm.com

Colonial Metals Co 217 Linden St PO Box 311 .... Columbia PA 17512 717-684-2311 684-9555
Web: www.colonialmetalsco.com

Company / Address	City	State	ZIP	Phone	Fax
Columbia Falls Aluminum Co 2000 Alluminum Dr	Columbia Falls	MT	59912	406-892-8400	
Web: www.cfaluminum.com					
Croft LLC 107 Oliver Emmerich Dr	McComb	MS	39648	601-684-6121	
TF: 800-437-8421 ■ *Web:* www.croftllc.com					
Curtis Steel Company LLC (CSC) 6504 Hurst St PO Box 7469	Houston	TX	77008	713-861-4621	861-9718
TF: 800-749-4621 ■ *Web:* www.curtissteelco.com					
Custom Aluminum Products Inc 414 Div St	South Elgin	IL	60177	847-717-5000	741-2266
TF: 800-745-6333 ■ *Web:* www.custom-aluminum.com					
Deringer-Ney Inc 616 Atrium Dr Ste 100	Vernon Hills	IL	60061	847-566-4100	367-6029
Web: www.deringerney.com					
Doe Run Co, The 1801 Pk 270 Dr Ste 300	Saint Louis	MO	63146	314-453-7100	453-7177
TF: 800-356-3786 ■ *Web:* www.doerun.com					
Dynamet Inc 195 Museum Rd	Washington	PA	15301	724-228-1000	229-4195
TF: 800-237-9655 ■ *Web:* www.cartech.com					
Eastern Alloys Inc 11 Henry Henning Dr PO Box 317	Maybrook	NY	12543	845-427-2151	427-5185
Web: www.eazall.com					
Elmet Technologies Inc 1560 Lisbon St	Lewiston	ME	04240	207-333-6100	786-8924
TF: 800-343-8008 ■ *Web:* www.elmettechnologies.com					
Empire Resources Inc 2115 Linwood Ave	Fort Lee	NJ	07024	201-944-2200	944-2226
NYSE: ERS ■ *Web:* www.empireresources.com					
Flat Rock Metal Inc (FRM) 26601 W Huron River Dr PO Box 1090	Flat Rock	MI	48134	734-782-4454	782-5640
Web: www.frm.com					
General Extrusions Inc 4040 Lk Pk Rd	Youngstown	OH	44512	330-783-0270	788-1250
Web: www.genext.com					
Glines & Rhodes Inc 189 E St	Attleboro	MA	02703	508-226-2000	226-7136
TF: 800-343-1196 ■ *Web:* www.glinesandrhodes.com					
Globe Metallurgical Inc County Rd 32 PO Box 157	Beverly	OH	45715	740-984-2361	984-8691
Web: www.glbsm.com/globemetallurgical					
H Kramer & Co 1345 W 21st St	Chicago	IL	60608	312-226-6600	226-4713
TF: 800-621-2305 ■ *Web:* hkramer.com					
Handy & Harman 1133 Westchester Ave Ste N222	White Plains	NY	10604	914-461-1300	
Web: www.handyharman.com					
Haynes International Inc 1020 W Pk Ave PO Box 9013	Kokomo	IN	46904	765-456-6000	456-6905
NASDAQ: HAYN ■ *TF:* 800-354-0806 ■ *Web:* www.haynesintl.com					
HC Starck Inc 45 Industrial Pl	Newton	MA	02461	617-630-5800	
Web: www.hcstarck.com					
Hoeganaes Corp 1001 Taylors Ln	Cinnaminson	NJ	08077	856-829-2220	786-2574*
**Fax:* Hum Res ■ *Web:* www.gkn.com					
Hoover & Strong Inc 10700 Trade Rd	North Chesterfield	VA	23236	800-759-9997	616-9997
TF Cust Svc: 800-759-9997 ■ *Web:* www.hooverandstrong.com					
Hoover Precision Products Inc 2200 Pendley Rd	Cumming	GA	30041	770-889-9223	889-0828
Web: www.hooverprecision.com					
Hussey Copper Ltd 100 Washington St	Leetsdale	PA	15056	724-251-4200	251-4243
TF: 800-733-8866 ■ *Web:* www.husseycopper.com					
Industrial Tectonics Inc 7222 Huron River Dr	Dexter	MI	48130	734-426-4681	426-4701
TF: 866-816-8904 ■ *Web:* www.itiball.com					
Johnson Matthey Inc 435 Devon Pk Dr Ste 600	Wayne	PA	19087	610-971-3000	971-3191
Web: www.matthey.com					
JW Aluminum 435 Old Mt Holly Rd	Mount Holly	SC	29445	877-586-5314	
TF Sales: 877-586-5314 ■ *Web:* www.jwaluminum.com					
Kaiser Aluminum Corp 27422 Portola Pkwy Ste 200	Foothill Ranch	CA	92610	949-614-1740	614-1930
TF Sales: 800-873-2011 ■ *Web:* www.kaiseraluminum.com					
Keystone Powdered Metal Co 251 State St	Saint Marys	PA	15857	814-781-1591	781-7648
Web: www.keystonepm.com					
Light Metals Corp 2740 Prairie St SW	Wyoming	MI	49509	616-538-3030	538-2713
TF: 888-363-8257 ■ *Web:* www.light-metals.com					
Linemaster Switch Corp 29 Plaine Hill Rd	Woodstock	CT	06281	860-974-1000	974-3668*
**Fax Area Code:* 800 ■ *TF:* 800-974-3668 ■ *Web:* www.linemaster.com					
Loxcreen Co Inc, The 1630 Old Dunbar Rd PO Box 4004	West Columbia	SC	29172	803-822-8200	822-8547
TF: 800-330-5699 ■ *Web:* www.loxcreen.com					
Lucas-Milhaupt Inc 5656 S Pennsylvania Ave	Cudahy	WI	53110	414-769-6000	769-1093
TF: 800-558-3856 ■ *Web:* www.lucasmilhaupt.com					
Luvata Appleton LLC 553 Carter Ct	Kimberly	WI	54136	920-749-3820	749-3850
TF: 866-488-0217 ■ *Web:* www.luvata.com					
Luvata Ohio Inc 1376 Pittsburgh Dr	Delaware	OH	43015	740-363-1981	363-3847
TF: 800-749-5510 ■ *Web:* www.luvata.com					
Magnetech Industrial Services Inc 800 Nave Rd SE	Massillon	OH	44646	330-830-3500	830-3520
TF General: 800-837-1614 ■ *Web:* www.magnetech.com					
Magnode Corp 400 E State St	Trenton	OH	45067	513-988-6351	988-6357
Web: www.magnode.com					
Magotteaux Inc 725 Cool Springs Blvd Ste 200	Franklin	TN	37067	615-385-3055	297-6743
Web: www.magotteaux.com					
Maurice Pincoffs Company Inc 1235 N Loop W Ste 510 PO Box 920919	Houston	TX	77292	713-681-5461	681-8521
Web: www.pincoffs.com					
Memry Corp 3 Berkshire Blvd	Bethel	CT	06801	203-739-1100	798-6606
TF: 866-466-3679 ■ *Web:* www.memry.com					
Metallurgical Products Co 810 Lincoln Ave PO Box 598	West Chester	PA	19381	610-696-6770	430-8431
Web: www.metprodco.com					
Metglas Inc 440 Allied Dr	Conway	SC	29526	843-349-7319	349-6815
TF: 800-581-7654 ■ *Web:* www.metglas.com					
Micro Surface Engr Inc 1550 E Slauson Ave	Los Angeles	CA	90011	323-582-7348	582-0934
TF: 800-322-5832 ■ *Web:* www.precisionballs.com					
Midland Industries Inc 1424 N Halsted St	Chicago	IL	60642	312-664-7300	664-7371
TF: 800-662-8228 ■ *Web:* www.zincbig.com					
Mueller Brass Co 2199 Lapeer Ave	Port Huron	MI	48060	810-987-7770	794-1214*
**Fax Area Code:* 616 ■ *TF:* 800-553-3336 ■ *Web:* muellerindustriesipd.com					
Mueller Industries Inc 8285 Tournament Dr Ste 150	Memphis	TN	38125	901-753-3200	753-3251
NYSE: MLI ■ *TF:* 800-348-8464 ■ *Web:* www.muellerindustries.com					
NetShape Technologies Inc 31005 Solon Rd	Solon	OH	44139	440-248-5456	248-5807
Web: www.netshapetech.com					
New England Miniature Ball Corp 163 Greenwood Rd W PO Box 585	Norfolk	CT	06058	860-542-5543	542-5058
Web: www.nemb.com					
NN Inc 2000 Waters Edge Dr Bldg 3 Ste 12	Johnson City	TN	37604	423-743-9151	743-8870
NASDAQ: NNBR ■ *TF:* 877-888-0002 ■ *Web:* nninc.com					
Noranda Aluminum Inc 801 Crescent Ctr Dr Ste 600	Franklin	TN	37067	615-771-5700	771-5701
TF: 800-325-8112 ■ *Web:* www.norandaaluminum.com					
Norandal USA Inc 400 Bill Brooks Dr	Huntingdon	TN	38344	731-986-5011	
Web: norandaaluminum.com					
Norandal USA Inc 1709 Jake Alexander Blvd S	Salisbury	NC	28146	704-633-6020	
Web: norandaaluminum.com					
Novelis North America 3560 Lenox Rd Ste 2000	Atlanta	GA	30326	404-760-4000	
TF: 800-892-1819 ■ *Web:* www.novelis.com					
Nyrstar Clarksville 1800 Zinc Plant Rd PO Box 1104	Clarksville	TN	37041	931-552-4200	552-0471
Web: www.nyrstar.com					
Olin Brass 305 Lewis & Clark Blvd	East Alton	IL	62024	502-873-3000	
Web: www.olinbrass.com					
Patrick Industries Inc Patrick Metals Div 5020 Lincolnway E	Mishawaka	IN	46544	574-255-9692	256-6577
TF: 800-922-9692 ■ *Web:* www.patrickmetals.com					
Penn Aluminum International Inc 1117 N Second St PO Box 490	Murphysboro	IL	62966	618-684-2146	
Web: www.pennaluminum.com					
Precision Engineered Products LLC 262 Broad St	North Attleboro	MA	02760	508-695-7700	695-7700
Web: www.polymet.com					
Revere Copper Products Inc 1 Revere Pk	Rome	NY	13440	315-338-2022	338-2224*
**Fax:* Sales ■ *TF:* 800-448-1776 ■ *Web:* www.reverecopper.com					
Ross Metals Corp 27 W 47th St	New York	NY	10036	800-334-7191	768-3018*
**Fax Area Code:* 212 ■ *TF:* 800-334-7191 ■ *Web:* www.rossmetals.com					
RSR Corp 2777 Stemmons Fwy Ste 1800	Dallas	TX	75207	214-631-6070	631-6146
Web: rsrcorp.com					
Sandvik Special Metals LLC 235407 E SR 397	Kennewick	WA	99337	509-586-4131	582-3552
Web: www.smt.sandvik.com					
Sipi Metals Corp 1720 N Elston Ave	Chicago	IL	60642	773-276-0070	276-7014
Web: www.sipimetals.com					
Southwire Co 1 Southwire Dr	Carrollton	GA	30119	770-832-4242	832-4406
TF: 800-444-1700 ■ *Web:* www.southwire.com					
Special Metals Corp 4317 Middle Settlement Rd	New Hartford	NY	13413	315-798-2900	798-2016*
**Fax:* Sales ■ *TF:* 800-334-8351 ■ *Web:* www.specialmetals.com					
Spectro Alloys Corp 13220 Doyle Path	Rosemount	MN	55068	651-437-2815	438-3714
Web: www.spectroalloys.com					
Taber Extrusions LP 915 S Elmira Ave	Russellville	AR	72802	479-968-1021	968-8645
TF: 800-563-6853 ■ *Web:* www.taberextrusions.com					
Titanium Metals Corp (TIMET) 224 Vly Creek Blvd Ste 200	Exton	PA	19341	610-968-1300	934-5345*
NYSE: TIE ■ **Fax Area Code:* 972 ■ *TF:* 800-753-1550 ■ *Web:* www.timet.com					
Tower Extrusions Ltd 1003 Hwy 79 S PO Box 218	Olney	TX	76374	940-564-5681	564-5033
Web: www.towerextrusion.com					
Tree Island Industries 3933 Boundary Rd	Richmond	BC	V6V1T8	604-524-3744	524-2362
TF: 800-663-0955 ■ *Web:* www.treeisland.com					
US Bronze Powders Inc 408 Rt 202 N	Flemington	NJ	08822	908-782-5454	
Web: www.usbronzepowders.com					
US Magnesium LLC 238 North 2200 West	Salt Lake City	UT	84116	801-532-2043	534-1407
Web: www.usmagnesium.com					
Valimet Inc PO Box 31690	Stockton	CA	95213	209-444-1600	982-1365
Web: www.valimet.com					
Valmont Industries Inc 1 Valmont Plz	Omaha	NE	68154	402-963-1000	
NYSE: VMI ■ *TF:* 800-825-6668 ■ *Web:* www.valmont.com					
Victory White Metal Co 6100 Roland Ave	Cleveland	OH	44127	216-271-1400	271-6430
TF: 800-635-5050 ■ *Web:* www.victorywhitemetal.com					
Wah Chang 1600 Old Salem Rd NE	Albany	OR	97321	541-926-4211	967-6994
TF: 888-926-4211 ■ *Web:* www.atimetals.com					
Wiley Sanders Truck Lines Inc PO Box 707 PO Box 707	Troy	AL	36081	800-392-8017	566-3257*
**Fax Area Code:* 334 ■ *TF:* 800-392-8017 ■ *Web:* www.wileysanders.com					
Worthington Industries 200 Old Wilson Bridge Rd	Columbus	OH	43085	614-438-3210	
NYSE: WOR ■ *Web:* www.worthingtonindustries.com					
Xyron Inc 8465 N 90th St Ste 6	Scottsdale	AZ	85258	480-443-9419	443-0118
TF: 800-793-3523 ■ *Web:* www.xyron.com					

486 METAL PRODUCTS - HOUSEHOLD

Company / Address	City	State	ZIP	Phone	Fax
Acme International Enterprises Inc 400 Lyster Ave	Saddle Brook	NJ	07663	973-416-0400	416-0499
Web: acmeusa.com					
All-Clad Metalcrafters LLC 424 Morganza Rd	Canonsburg	PA	15317	724-745-8300	746-5035
TF Cust Svc: 800-255-2523 ■ *Web:* all-clad.com					
Calphalon Corp PO Box 583	Toledo	OH	43697	800-809-7267	666-2859*
**Fax Area Code:* 419 ■ **Fax:* Sales ■ *TF:* 800-809-7267 ■ *Web:* www.calphalon.com					
G & S Metal Products Company Inc 3330 E 79th St	Cleveland	OH	44127	216-441-0700	441-0736
Web: www.gsmetal.com					
Kitchen-Quip Inc 405 E Marion St	Waterloo	IN	46793	260-837-8311	837-7919
Web: www.kqcasting.com					
Le Creuset of America Inc 114 Bob Gifford Blvd	Early Branch	SC	29916	803-943-4308	943-4510
TF: 877-418-5547					
Lifetime Brands Inc 1000 Steward Ave	Garden City	NY	11530	516-683-6000	683-6116
NASDAQ: LCUT ■ *TF:* 800-252-3390 ■ *Web:* www.lifetimebrands.com					
ME Heuck Co 1600 Beech St	Terre Haute	IN	47804	812-238-5000	
TF Cust Svc: 866-634-3825 ■ *Web:* www.heuck.com					

				Phone	Fax
Meyer Corp 1 Meyer Pl *Fax: PR ■ TF Cust Svc: 800-888-3883 ■ Web: www.meyer.com	Vallejo	CA	94590	707-551-2800	551-2953*
Nordic Ware 5005 Hwy 7 TF: 877-466-7342 ■ Web: www.nordicware.com	Minneapolis	MN	55416	952-920-2888	924-8561
Norpro,Inc 2215 Merrill Creek Pkwy Web: www.wholesale.norpro.com	Everett	WA	98203	425-261-1000	
Regal Ware Inc 1675 Reigle Dr Web: www.regalware.com	Kewaskum	WI	53040	262-626-2121	626-8565
Rena Ware International Inc 15885 NE 28th St Web: www.renaware.com	Bellevue	WA	98008	425-881-6171	882-7500
Saladmaster Inc 230 Westway Pl Ste 101 TF: 800-765-5795 ■ Web: www.saladmaster.com	Arlington	TX	76018	817-633-3555	633-5544
Whitesell Corp 2703 Avalon Ave *Fax: Hum Res ■ TF General: 855-227-4515 ■ Web: www.whitesellcorp.com	Muscle Shoals	AL	35661	256-248-8500	248-8585*
Wilton Armetale Co PO Box 600 *Fax Area Code: 717 ■ TF: 800-779-4586 ■ Web: www.armetale.com	Mount Joy	PA	17552	800-779-4586	653-6573*
Wilton Industries Inc 2240 W 75th St *Fax: Sales ■ TF: 800-794-5866 ■ Web: www.wilton.com	Woodridge	IL	60517	630-963-7100	963-7196*

487 METAL PRODUCTS (MISC)

				Phone	Fax
Accuride International Inc 12311 Shoemaker Ave Web: www.accuride.com	Santa Fe Springs	CA	90670	562-903-0200	903-0208
Aerodyne Alloys LLC 350 Pleasant Vly Rd TF: 800-243-4344 ■ Web: www.aerodynealloys.com	South Windsor	CT	06074	860-289-6011	289-2841
Alexandria Extrusion Co 401 County Rd 22 NW TF: 800-568-6601 ■ Web: alexandriaindustries.com	Alexandria	MN	56308	320-763-6537	763-9250
Aluchem Inc 1 Landy Ln TF: 800-336-8519 ■ Web: www.aluchem.com	Cincinnati	OH	45215	513-733-8519	733-0608
Aluminum Ladder Co 1430 W Darlington St TF: 800-752-2526 ■ Web: www.aluminumladder.com	Florence	SC	29501	843-662-2595	661-0972
Arland Tool & Manufacturing Inc PO Box 207 Web: www.arland.com	Sturbridge	MA	01566	508-347-3368	
Bead Industries Inc 11 Cascade Blvd TF: 800-297-4851 ■ Web: www.beadindustries.com	Milford	CT	06460	203-301-0270	301-0280
BEMSCO Inc 1193 South 400 West Web: www.bemsco.com	Salt Lake City	UT	84101	801-487-7455	
Bobrick Washroom Equipment Inc 11611 Hart St Web: www.bobrick.com	North Hollywood	CA	91605	818-764-1000	765-2700
Carolina Carports Inc 187 Cardinal Ridge Trl TF: 800-670-4262 ■ Web: www.carolinacarportsinc.com	Dobson	NC	27017	800-670-4262	
Ditto Sales Inc 2332 Cathy Ln Web: www.dittosales.com	Jasper	IN	47546	812-482-3043	482-9318
Flinchbaugh Engineering Inc 4387 Run Way TF: 866-967-5334 ■ Web: www.flinchbaughengineering.com	York	PA	17406	717-755-1900	840-3217
General Magnaplate Corp 1331 Us Rt 1 TF: 800-441-6173 ■ Web: www.magnaplate.com	Linden	NJ	07036	908-862-6200	
Gonzalez 29401 Stephenson Hwy Web: www.gonzalez-group.com	Madison Heights	MI	48071	248-548-6010	548-3160
J.a. Reinhardt & Co Inc Spruce Cabin Rd Web: jareinhardt.bethermalandpower.com	Mountainhome	PA	18342	570-595-7491	595-3551
Lechler Inc 445 Kautz Rd *Fax Area Code: 800 ■ TF Cust Svc: 800-777-2926 ■ Web: www.lechlerusa.com	Saint Charles	IL	60174	630-377-6611	444-7069*
Liberty Safe & Security Products Inc 1199 W Utah Ave TF: 800-247-5625 ■ Web: www.libertysafe.com	Payson	UT	84651	801-925-1000	465-2712
Magnetic Instrumentation Inc 8431 Castlewood Dr Web: www.maginst.com	Indianapolis	IN	46250	317-842-7500	849-7600
Metalworking Group Inc 9070 Pippin Rd TF: 800-476-9409 ■ Web: www.metalworkinggroup.com	Cincinnati	OH	45251	513-521-4114	521-2816
Metco Industries Inc 1241 Brusselles St Web: www.metcopm.com	St Mary	PA	15857	814-781-3630	
Muza Metal Products Corp 606 E Murdock Ave Web: www.muzametal.com	Oshkosh	WI	54901	920-236-3535	236-3520
Palmer International Inc PO Box 315 Web: palmerint.com	Skippack	PA	19474	610-584-4241	584-4870
Polar Ware Co 502 Hwy 67 *Fax Area Code: 920 ■ TF Cust Svc: 800-237-3655 ■ Web: www.polarware.com	Kiel	WI	53042	800-237-3655	894-2532*
Powdermet Inc 24112 Rockwell Dr Web: www.powdermetinc.com	Euclid	OH	44117	216-404-0053	
Precision Valve Corp 800 Westchester Ave TF: 866-686-8464 ■ Web: www.precisionglobal.com	Rye Brook	NY	10573	914-969-6500	
Spirol International Corp 30 Rock Ave Web: www.spirol.com	Danielson	CT	06239	860-774-8571	774-2048
Spraying Systems Co PO Box 7900 Web: www.spray.com	Wheaton	IL	60189	630-665-5000	260-0842
Tooling & Equipment International Corp 12550 Tech Ctr Dr Web: www.teintl.com	Livonia	MI	48150	734-522-1422	522-1780
Trinity Industries Inc Head Div 11765 Hwy 6 S Web: www.trinityheads.com	Navasota	TX	77868	936-825-6581	
TST Inc 11601 Etiwanda Ave Web: www.tst-inc.com	Fontana	CA	92337	951-685-2155	685-7806
Viking Materials Inc 3225 Como Ave SE TF General: 800-682-3942 ■ Web: www.vikingmaterials.com	Minneapolis	MN	55414	612-617-5800	623-9070
Visual Planning Corp 71 Meadowbank Dr TF: 800-361-1192	Ottawa	ON	K2G0P4	613-563-8727	563-8730

488 METAL STAMPINGS

See Also Closures - Metal or Plastics p. 1941; Electronic Enclosures p. 2230; Metal Stampings - Automotive p. 2759

				Phone	Fax
Accurate Perforating Co 3636 S Kedzie Ave TF: 800-621-0273 ■ Web: www.accurateperforating.com	Chicago	IL	60632	773-254-3232	254-9453
Acme Metal Cap Inc Co 33-53 62nd St Web: www.acmepans.com	Woodside	NY	11377	718-335-3000	335-3037
Admiral Craft Equipment Corp 940 S Oyster Bay Rd *Fax Area Code: 800 ■ TF: 800-223-7750 ■ Web: www.admiralcraft.com	Hicksville	NY	11801	516-433-3535	447-7751*
AK Stamping Inc 1159 US Rt 22 Web: www.akstamping.com	Mountainside	NJ	07092	908-232-7300	232-5202
Albest Metal Stamping Corp 1 Kent Ave Web: www.albest.com	Brooklyn	NY	11211	718-388-6000	388-0404
Alcoa Inc 201 Isabella St NYSE: AA ■ TF: 800-388-4825 ■ Web: www.alcoa.com	Pittsburgh	PA	15212	412-553-4545	553-4498
Alinabal Inc 28 Woodmont Rd Web: www.alinabal.com	Milford	CT	06460	203-877-3241	874-5063
All New Stamping Co 10801 Lower Azusa Rd TF: 800-877-7775 ■ Web: www.allnewstamping.com	El Monte	CA	91731	800-877-7775	877-8121
American Metalcraft Inc 2074 George St TF: 800-333-9133 ■ Web: www.amnow.com	Melrose Park	IL	60160	708-345-1177	345-5758
American Products LLC 597 Evergreen Rd TF: 855-736-2135 ■ Web: www.amprod.us	Strafford	MO	65757	417-736-2135	736-2662
American Trim 1005 W Grand Ave Web: www.amtrim.com	Lima	OH	45801	419-228-1145	996-4850
APG Cash Drawer LLC 5250 Industrial Blvd NE Web: cashdrawer.com	Minneapolis	MN	55421	763-571-5000	571-5771
Aranda Tooling Inc 15301 Springdale St Web: www.arandatooling.com	Huntington Beach	CA	92649	714-379-6565	379-6570
Argo Products Co 3500 Goodfellow Blvd Web: www.argoproducts.com	Saint Louis	MO	63120	314-385-1803	385-1808
Arrow Tru-Line Inc 2211 S Defiance St TF: 877-285-7253 ■ Web: www.arrowtruline.com	Archbold	OH	43502	419-446-2785	445-2068
Arvin Sango Inc 2905 Wilson Ave Web: www.arvinsango.com	Madison	IN	47250	812-265-2888	273-8339
Assurance Manufacturing Co 9010 Evergreen Blvd Web: www.assurancemfg.com	Minneapolis	MN	55433	763-780-4252	780-8847
Ataco Steel Products Corp PO Box 270 TF: 800-536-4822 ■ Web: www.atacosteel.com	Cedarburg	WI	53012	262-377-3000	377-3452
Atlantic Tool & Die Co (ATD) 19963 Progress Dr Web: www.atlantictool.com	Strongsville	OH	44149	440-238-6931	238-2210
Bazz Houston Co 12700 Western Ave TF: 800-385-9608 ■ Web: www.bazz-houston.com	Garden Grove	CA	92841	714-898-2666	898-1389
Behrens Manufacturing Co 1250 E Sanborn St Web: www.behrensmfg.com	Winona	MN	55987	507-454-4664	452-2106
Bermo Inc 4501 Ball Rd NE Web: www.bermo.com	Circle Pines	MN	55014	763-786-7676	785-2159
Beta Shim Co 11 Progress Dr Web: www.betashim.com	Shelton	CT	06484	203-926-1150	929-5509
Bopp-Busch Mfg Co 545 E Huron Rd Web: www.boppbusch.com	Au Gres	MI	48703	989-876-7121	876-6555
Btd Mfg Inc 1111 13th Ave SE TF: 866-562-3986 ■ Web: www.btdmfg.com	Detroit Lakes	MN	56501	866-562-3986	
Capitol Stampings Corp 2700 W N Ave Web: www.capitolstampings.com	Milwaukee	WI	53208	414-372-3500	372-3535
Clairon Metals Corp 11194 Alcovy Rd Web: www.claironmetals.com	Covington	GA	30014	770-786-9681	786-4183
Clow Stamping Co 23103 County Rd 3 Web: www.clowstamping.com	Merrifield	MN	56465	218-765-3111	765-3904
Cly-Del Mfg Co 151 Sharon Rd	Waterbury	CT	06705	203-574-2100	
Crest Manufacturing Co 5 Hood Dr Web: www.crestmfg.com	Lincoln	RI	02865	401-333-1350	333-0821
Custom Stamping & Manufacturing Inc 4855 Hytech Dr PO Box 14340 Web: www.customstampingmfg.com	Carson City	NV	89706	503-238-3700	
Danco Precision Inc Wheatland & Mellon Sts Web: www.dancoprecision.com	Phoenixville	PA	19460	610-933-8981	935-2011
Danville Metal Stamping Company Inc 20 Oakwood Ave Web: www.danvillemetal.com	Danville	IL	61832	217-446-0647	446-0647
Dayton Rogers Manufacturing Co 8401 W 35 W Service Dr TF: 800-677-8881 ■ Web: www.daytonrogers.com	Minneapolis	MN	55449	763-784-7714	784-7714
Defiance Metal Products 21 Seneca St Web: www.defiancemetal.com	Defiance	OH	43512	419-784-5332	782-0148
Delta Consolidated Industries Inc 4800 Krueger Dr TF: 800-643-0084 ■ Web: www.deltatruckstorage.com	Jonesboro	AR	72401	870-935-3711	935-4994
Diamond Manufacturing Co 243 W Eigth St TF: 800-233-9601 ■ Web: www.diamondman.com	Wyoming	PA	18644	570-693-0300	693-3500
Diamond Perforated Metals Inc 7300 W Sunnyview Ave TF: 800-642-4334 ■ Web: www.diamondperf.com	Visalia	CA	93291	559-651-1889	651-1815
DORMA Architectural Hardware DORMA Dr Drawer AC TF: 800-523-8483 ■ Web: www.dorma.com	Reamstown	PA	17567	717-336-3881	336-2106
Dove Die & Stamping Co 15665 Brookpark Rd Web: www.dovedie.com	Cleveland	OH	44142	216-267-3720	267-7250
Dubuque Stamping & Manufacturing Inc 3190 Jackson St Web: www.dbqstamp.com	Dubuque	IA	52001	563-583-5716	

Company	City	State	Zip	Phone	Fax
Dudek & Bock Spring Mfg Co 5100 W Roosevelt Rd *Web:* www.dudek-bock.com	Chicago	IL	60644	773-379-4100	379-4108
DureX Inc 5 Stahuber Ave. *Web:* www.durexinc.com	Union	NJ	07083	908-688-0800	688-0718
E S Investments LLC 14055 US Hwy 19 N *Web:* www.sunmicrostamping.com	Clearwater	FL	33764	727-536-8822	
East Moline Metal Products Co 1201 Seventh St *Web:* www.emmetal.com	East Moline	IL	61244	309-752-1350	752-1380
Elmira Stamping & Mfg Corp 1704 Cedar St *Web:* www.elmirastamping.com	Elmira	NY	14904	607-734-2058	732-0573
Fraen Corp 80 Newcrossing Rd *Web:* www.fraen.com	Reading	MA	01867	781-205-5300	942-2426
Fuller Box Co 150 Chestnut St. *Web:* www.fullerbox.com	North Attleboro	MA	02760	508-695-2525	695-2187
Fulton Industries Inc 135 E Linfoot St PO Box 377 *TF:* 800-537-5012 ■ *Web:* www.fultonindoh.com	Wauseon	OH	43567	419-335-3015	335-3215
Gasser & Sons Inc 440 Moreland Rd *Web:* www.gasser.com	Commack	NY	11725	631-543-6600	543-6649
Genesee Group Inc 1470 Ave T *Web:* www.geneseegroup.com	Grand Prairie	TX	75050	972-623-2004	623-0404
GMP Metal Products Inc 3883 Delor St *TF:* 800-325-9808 ■ *Web:* www.gmpmetal.com	Saint Louis	MO	63116	314-481-0300	481-1379
Gr Spring & Stamping Inc 706 Bond Ave **Fax Area Code:* 614 ■ *Web:* www.grs-s.com	Grand Rapids	MI	49503	616-453-4491	453-0951*
Griffiths Corp 2717 Niagara Ln N *Web:* www.griffithscorp.com	Minneapolis	MN	55447	763-557-8935	
Guarantee Specialties Inc 9401 Carr Ave	Cleveland	OH	44108	216-451-9744	
Hamrock Inc 12521 Los Nietos Rd *Web:* www.hamrock.com	Santa Fe Springs	CA	90670	562-944-0255	944-5676
Hannibal Industries Inc 3851 S Santa Fe Ave. *TF:* 888-246-7074 ■ *Web:* www.hannibalindustries.com	Los Angeles	CA	90058	323-588-4261	589-5640
Harvey Vogel Manufacturing Co 425 Weir Dr. *Web:* www.harveyvogel.com	Woodbury	MN	55125	651-739-7373	739-8666
Hendrick Manufacturing Co 1 Seventh Ave. **Fax Area Code:* 570 ■ **Fax:* Sales ■ *TF Cust Svc:* 800-225-7373 ■ *Web:* www.hendrickmfg.com	Carbondale	PA	18407	800-225-7373	282-1506*
Heyco Products 1800 Industrial Way N. *TF:* 800-526-4182 ■ *Web:* www.heyco.com	Toms River	NJ	08755	732-286-1800	244-8843
Hobson & Motzer Inc 30 Air Line Dr *TF:* 800-476-5111 ■ *Web:* www.hobsonmotzer.com	Durham	CT	06422	860-349-1756	349-3602
HPL Stampings Inc 425 Enterprise Pkwy *TF:* 800-927-0397 ■ *Web:* www.hplstampings.com	Lake Zurich	IL	60047	847-540-1400	540-1422
HTT Inc. 1828 Oakland Ave. *TF:* 866-270-4710 ■ *Web:* www.htt-inc.com	Sheboygan	WI	53081	920-453-5300	453-5301
Innovative Stamping Corp 2068 E Gladwick St. *TF:* 800-400-0047 ■ *Web:* www.innovative-sys.com	Compton	CA	90220	310-537-6996	537-0312
Jagemann Stamping Co 5757 W Custer St *TF:* 888-337-7853 ■ *Web:* www.jagemann.com	Manitowoc	WI	54220	920-682-4633	682-6002
Ken-Tron Manufacturing Inc PO Box 21250 *TF:* 800-872-9336 ■ *Web:* www.ken-tron.com	Owensboro	KY	42304	270-684-0431	684-0435
Kennedy Manufacturing Co 1260 Industrial Dr *TF:* 800-413-8665 ■ *Web:* buykennedy.com	Van Wert	OH	45891	419-238-2442	238-5644
Kerns Manufacturing Corp 37-14 29th St *Web:* www.kernsmfg.com	Long Island	NY	11101	718-784-4044	786-0534
Keystone Friction Hinge Co 520 Matthews Blvd *Web:* kfhinge.com	South Williamsport	PA	17702	570-323-9479	326-0217
Kickhaefer Mfg Co (KMC) 1221 S Pk St PO Box 348 *TF:* 800-822-6080 ■ *Web:* www.kmcstampings.com	Port Washington	WI	53074	262-377-5030	284-9774
Knaack Manufacturing Co 420 E Terra Cotta Ave *TF:* 800-456-7865 ■ *Web:* www.knaack.com	Crystal Lake	IL	60014	815-459-6020	459-9097
Kromet International Inc 200 Sheldon Dr *Web:* www.kromet.com	Cambridge	ON	N1R7K1	519-623-2511	624-9729
L H Carbide Corp 4420 Clubview Dr *Web:* www.lhindustries.com	Fort Wayne	IN	46804	260-432-5563	432-2503
Larson Tool & Stamping Co 90 Olive St *Web:* www.larsontool.com	Attleboro	MA	02703	508-222-0897	226-7407
Macon Resources Inc 2121 Hubbard Ave *Web:* www.maconresources.org	Decatur	IL	62526	217-875-1910	875-8899
Mass Precision Sheetmetal Inc 2110 Oakland Rd *Web:* www.massprecision.com	San Jose	CA	95131	408-954-0200	954-0288
McAlpin Industries Inc 255 Hollenbeck St *Web:* www.mcalpin-ind.com	Rochester	NY	14621	585-266-3060	266-8091
Meriden Manufacturing Inc PO Box 694 *Web:* www.meridenmfg.com	Meriden	CT	06450	203-237-7481	235-3146
Metal Box International 11600 W King St *Web:* edsal.com	Franklin Park	IL	60131	847-455-8500	455-6030
Metal ComponentsLLC 3281 Roger B Chaffee Memorial Blvd SE *Web:* metalcompinc.com	Grand Rapids	MI	49548	616-252-1900	252-1970
Metal Flow Corp 11694 James St. *Web:* www.metalflow.com	Holland	MI	49424	616-392-7976	392-5814
Micro Stamping Corp 140 Belmont Dr. *Web:* www.microstamping.com	Somerset	NJ	08873	732-302-0800	302-0436
Midland Stamping & Fabricating 9521 W Ainslie St. *Web:* midlandstamping.com	Schiller Park	IL	60176	847-678-7573	
Midwest Wire Products LLC 649 S Lansing Ave PO Box 770 *TF:* 800-445-0225 ■ *Web:* www.wireforming.com	Sturgeon Bay	WI	54235	920-743-6591	743-3777
MJ Celco Inc 3900 Wesley Terr. *Web:* www.mjcelco.com	Schiller Park	IL	60176	847-671-1900	671-1978
New Standard Corp 74 Commerce Way *Web:* www.newstandard.com	York	PA	17406	717-757-9450	757-2312
Niles Mfg & Finishing Inc 465 Walnut St *Web:* www.nilesmfg.com	Niles	OH	44446	330-544-0402	544-8018
Northern Stamping Corp 6600 Chapek Pkwy *Web:* northernstamping.com	Cleveland	OH	44125	216-883-8888	883-8237
Okay Industries Inc 200 Ellis St. *Web:* www.okayind.com	New Britain	CT	06051	860-225-8707	225-7047
P & G Steel Products Company Inc 54 Gruner Rd *Web:* www.pgsteel.com	Buffalo	NY	14227	716-896-7900	896-4129
Pax Machine Works Inc PO Box 338 *Web:* www.paxmachine.com	Celina	OH	45822	419-586-2337	586-7123
Penn United Technology Inc 799 N Pike Rd *TF:* 866-572-7537 ■ *Web:* www.pennunited.com	Cabot	PA	16023	724-352-1507	352-4970
PEP Wauconda 821 W Algonquin *Web:* www.pepwauconda.com	Algonquin	IL	60102	847-658-4588	
Perfection Spring & Stamping Corp 1449 E Algonquin Rd *Web:* www.pss-corp.com	Mount Prospect	IL	60056	847-437-3900	437-1322
Plainfield Cos 24035 Riverwalk Ct *Web:* www.plainfieldprecision.com	Plainfield	IL	60544	815-436-5671	439-2970
Precision Resource 25 Forest Pkwy. *Web:* www.precisionresource.com	Shelton	CT	06484	203-925-0012	926-9010
Prestige Stamping Inc 23513 Groesbeck Hwy *Web:* www.prestigestamping.com	Warren	MI	48089	586-773-2700	773-2700
Quaker Mfg Corp PO Box 449 *Web:* www.quakermfg.com	Salem	OH	44460	330-332-4631	332-1519
Quality Perforating Inc 166 Dundaff St. *TF:* 800-872-7373 ■ *Web:* www.qualityperf.com	Carbondale	PA	18407	570-282-4344	282-4627
Quality Tool & Stamping Company Inc 2642 Mcilwraith St *Web:* www.qtstamping.com	Muskegon	MI	49444	231-733-2538	733-0983
Ramcel Engineering Co 2926 MacArthur Blvd *Web:* www.ramcel.com	Northbrook	IL	60062	847-272-6980	272-7196
RES Mfg Company Inc 7801 N 73rd St *Web:* www.resmfg.com	Milwaukee	WI	53223	414-354-4530	
Rockford Toolcraft Inc 766 Research Pkwy *Web:* www.rockfordtoolcraft.com	Rockford	IL	61109	815-398-5507	398-0132
Saunders Manufacturing Co 65 Nickerson Hill Rd. *TF:* 800-341-4674 ■ *Web:* www.saunders-usa.com	Readfield	ME	04355	207-685-9860	685-9918
Slidematic Products Co 4520 W Addison St. *Web:* www.slidematicproducts.com	Chicago	IL	60641	773-545-4213	545-0797
Small Parts Inc 600 Humphrey St. *Web:* www.smallpartsinc.com	Logansport	IN	46947	574-753-6323	753-6660
Sons Tool Inc 460 Thompson Rd. *Web:* www.sonstool.com	Woodville	WI	54028	715-698-2471	698-2335
Spindustries LLC 1301 La Salle St *Web:* www.lgspin.com	Lake Geneva	WI	53147	262-248-6601	248-1277
Stack-On Products Co 1360 N Old Rand Rd *TF:* 800-323-9601 ■ *Web:* www.stack-on.com	Wauconda	IL	60084	847-526-1611	526-6599
Stamtex Metal Stampings 112 Erie St *Web:* www.stamtexmp.com	Niles	OH	44446	330-652-2558	652-7369
Stanley Spring & Stamping Corp 5050 W Foster Ave *Web:* www.stanleyspring.com	Chicago	IL	60630	773-777-2600	
Steel City Corp 190 N Meridian Rd. *TF:* 800-321-0350 ■ *Web:* www.scity.com	Youngstown	OH	44501	330-792-7663	797-2947
Stewart EFI LLC 45 Old Waterbury Rd. *TF:* 800-393-5387 ■ *Web:* www.stewartefi.com	Thomaston	CT	06787	860-283-8213	283-5610
T & D Metal Products Co 602 E Walnut St *Web:* www.tdmetal.com	Watseka	IL	60970	815-432-4938	432-6271
Taylor Metal Products Co 700 Springmill St *Web:* www.tmpind.com	Mansfield	OH	44903	419-522-3471	525-2948
Tech-Etch Inc 45 Aldrin Rd. *Web:* www.tech-etch.com	Plymouth	MA	02360	508-747-0300	746-9639
Trans-Matic Manufacturing Co 300 E 48th St *Web:* www.transmatic.com	Holland	MI	49423	616-820-2500	820-2702
Trident Precision Manufacturing Inc 734 Salt Rd. *Web:* www.tridentprecision.com	Webster	NY	14580	585-265-2010	265-2386
Triton Industries Inc 1020 N Kolmar Ave *Web:* www.tritonindustries.com	Chicago	IL	60651	773-384-3700	384-8748
Waterloo Industries Inc 139 W Forest Hill Ave. **Fax Area Code:* 414 ■ **Fax:* Cust Svc ■ *TF Cust Svc:* 800-558-5528 ■ *Web:* www.waterlooindustries.com	Oak Creek	WI	53154	800-558-5528	766-6388*
Weiss-Aug Company Inc 220 Merry Ln. *Web:* www.weiss-aug.com	East Hanover	NJ	07936	973-887-7600	887-8109
Winzeler Stamping Co 910 E Main St *Web:* www.winzelerstamping.com	Montpelier	OH	43543	419-485-3147	485-5039
WLS Stamping Co 3292 E 80th St. *Web:* www.wlsstamping.com	Cleveland	OH	44104	216-271-5100	341-3203
Wolverine Metal Stamping Inc 3600 Tennis Ct *Web:* www.wms-inc.com	Saint Joseph	MI	49085	269-429-6600	429-6657
Wozniak Industries Inc 2 Mid America Plz Ste 706 *Web:* www.wozniakindustries.com	Oakbrook Terrace	IL	60181	630-954-3400	954-3605
Wrico Stamping Co 2727 Niagara Ln N *Web:* www.wrico-net.com	Minneapolis	MN	55447	763-559-2288	553-7976

489 METAL STAMPINGS - AUTOMOTIVE

See Also Automotive Parts & Supplies - Mfr p. 1830

Company	City	State	Zip	Phone	Fax
Ada Metal Products Inc 7120 Capitol Dr *Web:* www.adametal.com	Lincolnwood	IL	60712	847-673-1190	673-4860
Advance Engineering Co 7505 Baron Dr. *TF:* 800-497-6388 ■ *Web:* www.adveng.net	Canton	MI	48187	313-537-3500	
AJ Rose Manufacturing Co 38000 Chester Rd *Web:* www.ajrose.com	Avon	OH	44011	440-934-7700	934-2802
American Metal & Plastics Inc 450 32nd St SW *TF:* 800-382-0067 ■ *Web:* www.ampi-gr.com	Grand Rapids	MI	49548	616-452-6061	452-3835

Company	City	State	Zip	Phone	Fax
AMG Industries Inc 200 Commerce Dr. *Fax: Mail Rm ■ *Web:* www.amgindustries.com	Mount Vernon	OH	43050	740-397-4044	397-3092*
Automotive Engineered Products Inc 7149 Mission Gorge Rd *Fax Area Code: 909 ■ *Web:* www.jbaheaders.com	San Diego	CA	92120	619-229-7797	599-6424*
Burkland Inc 6520 S State Rd *Web:* burklandinc.com	Goodrich	MI	48438	810-636-2233	636-7525
C Cowles & Co Inc 83 Water St *TF:* 800-624-4483 ■ *Web:* www.ccowles.com	New Haven	CT	06511	203-865-3117	773-1019
Center Mfg Inc 990 84th St. *Web:* www.mecinc.com	Byron Center	MI	49315	920-387-4500	
Clark Metal Products Co 100 Serrell Dr *Web:* www.clark-metal.com	Blairsville	PA	15717	724-459-7550	459-0207
Concord Tool & Mfg 118 N Groesbeck Hwy. *Web:* www.concordtool.com	Mount Clemens	MI	48043	586-465-6537	465-7301
Cooper-Standard Automotive Inc 39550 Orchard Hill Pl Dr *Web:* www.cooperstandard.com	Novi	MI	48375	248-596-5900	
Decoma International Inc *Magna Exteriors & Interiors* 50 Casmir Ct *Fax Area Code: 248 ■ *TF:* 888-348-2398 ■ *Web:* www.magna.com	Concord	ON	L4K4J5	905-669-2888	528-6450*
Dixien 5286 Cir Dr *Web:* www.dixien.com	Lake City	GA	30260	404-366-7427	
Fisher Corp 1625 W Maple Rd *Web:* www.fisherco.com	Troy	MI	48084	248-280-0808	
Gaffoglio Family Metalcrafters Inc 11161 Slater Ave *Web:* www.metalcrafters.com	Fountain Valley	CA	92708	714-444-2000	
Genco Stamping & Manufacturing Co 2001 Genco Dr *Web:* gencostamping.com	Cookeville	TN	38506	931-528-5574	528-8379
GHSP Co 1250 S Beechtree St *Web:* www.ghsp.com	Grand Haven	MI	49417	616-842-5500	842-7230
Grant Industries Inc 33415 Groesbeck Hwy. *Web:* www.grantgrp.com	Fraser	MI	48026	586-293-9200	293-9346
Hamlin Newco LLC 2741 Wingate Ave *Web:* www.hnmetalstamping.com	Akron	OH	44314	330-753-7791	753-5577
Hatch Stamping Co 635 E Industrial Dr *Web:* www.hatchstamping.com	Chelsea	MI	48118	734-475-8628	475-6255
Hines Group Inc, The 5680 Old Hwy 54 E *Web:* www.thehinesgroup.com	Philpot	KY	42366	270-729-4242	
Honda Precision Parts of Georgia LLC 550 Honda Pkwy. *Web:* www.cevalogistics.com	Tallapoosa	GA	30176	770-574-3400	
Industrial Components Inc *IC Assemblies Inc* 2250 NW 102nd Ave. *Web:* www.icassemblies.com	Miami	FL	33172	305-477-0387	594-7332
ITW Drawform 500 Fairview Rd *Web:* www.drawform.com	Zeeland	MI	49464	616-772-1910	772-9572
ITW Highland 1240 Wolcott St. *Web:* www.itwhighland.com	Waterbury	CT	06722	203-574-3200	754-4019
Lake Air 7709 Winpark Dr. *TF:* 888-785-2422 ■ *Web:* www.lakeairmetals.com	Minneapolis	MN	55427	763-546-0994	546-4469
LMC Industries Inc 100 Manufacturers Dr *Web:* www.lmcindustries.com	Arnold	MO	63010	636-282-8080	282-7114
Logghe Stamping Co 16711 E 13-Mile Rd	Fraser	MI	48026	586-293-2250	293-7202
Marquette Tool & Die Co 3185 S KingsHwy Blvd *Web:* www.marquettetool.com	Saint Louis	MO	63139	314-771-8509	771-7964
Matcor Automotive 401 S Steele St	Ionia	MI	48846	616-527-4050	
McKechnie Vehicle Components (MVC) 27087 Gratiot Ave Fl 2 *Web:* www.mvcusa.com	Roseville	MI	48066	586-491-2600	
Means Industries Inc 3715 E Washington Rd *Web:* www.meansindustries.com	Saginaw	MI	48601	989-754-1433	754-1103
Midway Products Group Inc 1 Lyman E Hoyt Dr *Fax: Sales ■ *Web:* www.midwayproducts.com	Monroe	MI	48161	734-241-7242	384-0811*
Modineer Co 2190 Industrial Dr. *Web:* www.modineer.com	Niles	MI	49120	269-683-2550	683-0750
Moroso Performance Products Inc 80 Carter Dr *Fax: Cust Svc ■ *Web:* www.moroso.com	Guilford	CT	06437	203-453-6571	453-6906*
ODM Tool & Manufacturing Co 9550 Joliet Rd *Web:* www.odmtool.com	McCook	IL	60525	708-485-6130	485-6540
Ogihara America Corp 1480 W McPherson Pk Dr *Web:* www.ogihara.com	Howell	MI	48843	517-548-4900	548-6036
Oshkosh Specialty Vehicles LLC 12770 44th St N *Web:* www.oshkoshsv.com	Clearwater	FL	33762	727-573-0400	
Philippi-Hagenbuch Inc 7424 W Plank Rd *TF:* 800-447-6464 ■ *Web:* www.philsystems.com	Peoria	IL	61604	309-697-9200	697-2400
Pk USA Inc 600 W Northridge Dr *Web:* www.pkusa.com	Shelbyville	IN	46176	317-395-5500	395-5501
Polar ware 502 Hgwy 67 PO Box 366 *TF:* 800-237-3655 ■ *Web:* polarware.com/polarware.htm	Kiel	WI	53402	800-237-3655	
Pridgeon & Clay Inc 50 Cottage Grove St SW *Web:* pridgeonandclay.com	Grand Rapids	MI	49507	616-241-5675	241-1799
Radar Industries 27101 Grosbeck Hwy. *Fax Area Code: 586 ■ *TF:* 800-779-0301 ■ *Web:* shiloh.com	Warren	MI	48089	248-358-3570	758-6445*
Shiloh Industries Corp 880 Steel Dr *Web:* www.shiloh.com	Valley City	OH	44280	330-558-2600	
Spartanburg Steel Products Inc 1290 New Cut Rd PO Box 6428 *TF:* 888-974-7500 ■ *Web:* www.ssprod.com	Spartanburg	SC	29304	864-585-5211	583-5641
Steel Parts Corp 801 Berryman Pk *Web:* steelparts.com	Tipton	IN	46072	765-675-2191	675-4232
Stewart EFI LLC 45 Old Waterbury Rd. *TF:* 800-393-5387 ■ *Web:* www.stewartefi.com	Thomaston	CT	06787	860-283-8213	283-5610
Syracuse Stamping Co 1054 S Clinton St *TF:* 800-581-5555 ■ *Web:* www.syraco.com	Syracuse	NY	13202	315-476-5306	474-8876
Thiel Tool & Engineering Company Inc 4622 Bulwer Ave PO Box 470007 *Web:* www.thieltool.com	Saint Louis	MO	63147	314-241-6121	241-7857
Thomas Engineering Co 7024 Northland Dr *Web:* www.thomasengineering.com	Minneapolis	MN	55428	763-533-1501	533-8091
Tinnerman Palnut Engineered Products (Canada) Corp 686 Parkdale Ave N *Web:* www.tinnermanpalnut.com	Hamilton	ON	L8H5Z4	905-549-4661	
Troy Design & Manufacturing Co (TDM) 12675 Berwyn *Web:* www.troydm.com	Redford	MI	48239	313-592-2300	
TYG Holding USA Inc 1800 N McDonald St	Mckinney	TX	75071	972-542-1828	
United Metal Products Corp 8101 Lyndon St *Web:* www.unitedmetalproducts.com	Detroit	MI	48238	313-933-8750	933-1001
Varbros LLC 16025 Brookpark Rd *Web:* www.varbroscorp.com	Cleveland	OH	44142	216-267-5200	267-5205
Versatube Corp 4755 Rochester Rd *Web:* www.versatubecorp.com	Troy	MI	48085	248-689-7373	689-8293
VIA Motors Inc 165 Mtn Way Dr *Web:* www.viamotors.com	Orem	UT	84058	801-764-9333	
Wellington Industries Inc 39555 S I-94 Service Dr *Web:* www.wellingtonind.com	Belleville	MI	48111	734-942-1060	942-9430
Wisconsin Metal Products Co 1807 DeKovin Ave. *Web:* www.wmpco.com	Racine	WI	53403	262-633-6301	

490 METAL TUBE & PIPE

Company	City	State	Zip	Phone	Fax
Advanced Fabrication Services Inc 420 Oak St *Web:* www.afsenergy.com	Lemoyne	PA	17043	717-763-0286	
AK Tube LLC 30400 E Broadway *TF:* 800-955-8031 ■ *Web:* www.aktube.com	Walbridge	OH	43465	419-661-4150	661-4380
American Cast Iron Pipe Co (ACIPCO) 1501 31st Ave N *TF:* 800-442-2347 ■ *Web:* www.american-usa.com	Birmingham	AL	35207	205-325-7701	
ArcelorMittal Laplace LLC 138 Hwy 3217	Laplace	LA	70068	985-652-4900	
Atlas Tube 1855 E 122nd St. *TF:* 800-733-5683 ■ *Web:* www.atlastube.com	Chicago	IL	60633	773-646-4500	646-6128
Atlas Tubular LP 1710 S Hwy 77 *Web:* www.atlastubular.com	Robstown	TX	78380	361-387-7505	387-4613
Berg Steel Pipe Corp 5315 W 19th St *Web:* www.bergpipe.com	Panama City	FL	32401	850-769-2273	763-9683
Bristol Metals LP 390 Bristol Metals Rd. *Web:* www.brismet.com	Bristol	TN	37620	423-989-4700	
Bull Moose Tube Co 1819 Clarkson Rd Ste 100 *Fax: Sales ■ *TF:* 800-325-4467 ■ *Web:* www.bullmoosetube.com	Chesterfield	MO	63017	636-537-2600	537-5848*
California Steel & Tube 16049 Stephens St *TF:* 800-338-8823 ■ *Web:* californiasteelandtube.com	City of Industry	CA	91745	626-968-5511	369-9660
Canerector Inc 1 Sparks Ave. *Web:* www.canerector.com	North York	ON	M2H2W1	416-225-6240	
Cardinal Mfg Company Inc 225 Eiler Ave PO Box 14127 *Web:* www.cardinalmfg.com	Louisville	KY	40214	502-363-2661	
Cerro Flow Products Inc PO Box 66800 *TF:* 888-237-7611 ■ *Web:* www.cerroflow.com	Saint Louis	MO	63166	618-337-6000	337-6958
Charlotte Pipe & Foundry Co 2109 Randolph Rd *TF:* 800-438-6091 ■ *Web:* www.charlottepipe.com	Charlotte	NC	28207	704-372-5030	348-6450
Clark Precision Machined Components LLC 320 Fourth St *Web:* www.clarkprecision.com	Blawnox	PA	15238	412-828-1210	
CTP Corp 3750 Shelby St *Web:* www.tubeproc.com/ctp-corporation	Indianapolis	IN	46227	317-787-1322	
Davis Wire Corp 5555 Irwindale Ave. *Web:* www.daviswire.com	Irwindale	CA	91706	626-969-7651	
Dixie Pipe Sales Inc 2407 Broiller *TF:* 800-733-3494 ■ *Web:* www.dixiepipe.com	Houston	TX	77054	713-796-2021	799-8628
Earle M Jorgensen Co 10650 S Alameda St *Fax Area Code: 610 ■ *TF Sales:* 800-336-5365 ■ *Web:* www.emjmetals.com	Lynwood	CA	90262	323-567-1122	736-6168*
Energy Alloys LLC 350 Glenborough Ste 300 *TF:* 866-448-9831 ■ *Web:* www.ealloys.com	Houston	TX	77067	832-601-5800	601-5801
Felker Bros Corp 22 N Chestnut Ave *TF:* 800-826-2304 ■ *Web:* www.felkerbrothers.com	Marshfield	WI	54449	715-384-3121	387-6837
Hanna Steel Corp 3812 Commerce Ave PO Box 558 *TF:* 800-633-8252 ■ *Web:* www.hannasteel.com	Fairfield	AL	35064	205-780-1111	783-8368
Hannibal Industries Inc 3851 S Santa Fe Ave. *TF:* 888-246-7074 ■ *Web:* www.hannibalindustries.com	Los Angeles	CA	90058	323-588-4261	589-5640
Hofmann Industries Inc 3145 Shillington Rd *Web:* www.hofmann.com	Sinking Spring	PA	19608	610-678-8051	670-2221
Hydro Aluminum North America 999 Corporate Blvd Ste 100 *Fax Area Code: 410 ■ *TF:* 888-935-5752	Linthicum	MD	21090	888-935-5752	487-8053*
International Metal Hose Co 520 Goodrich Rd *TF:* 800-458-6855 ■ *Web:* www.metalhose.com	Bellevue	OH	44811	419-483-7690	483-8225
J D Rush C Inc 5900 E Lerdo Hwy *Web:* www.jdrush.com	Shafter	CA	93263	661-392-1900	399-2728
Jackson Tube Service Inc 8210 Industry Pk Dr *TF:* 800-543-8910 ■ *Web:* www.jackson-tube.com	Piqua	OH	45356	937-773-8550	773-8806
Leavitt Tube 1717 W 115th St. *TF:* 800-532-8488 ■ *Web:* www.leavitt-tube.com	Chicago	IL	60643	773-239-7700	239-1023
LeFiell Manufacturing Co 13700 Firestone Blvd *TF:* 800-451-5971 ■ *Web:* www.lefiell.com	Santa Fe Springs	CA	90670	562-921-3411	
Lock Joint Tube Inc 515 W Ireland Rd. *Fax: Sales ■ *TF:* 800-257-6859 ■ *Web:* www.ljtube.com	South Bend	IN	46614	574-299-5326	299-3464*

	City	State	Zip	Phone	Fax
Marcegaglia USA Inc 1001 E Waterfront Dr *Web:* www.marcegaglia.com	Munhall	PA	15120	412-462-2185	462-6059
Marlin Steel Wire Products 2640 Merchant Dr *Web:* www.marlinwire.com	Baltimore	MD	21230	410-644-7456	
Mercury Tube Products 3211 W Bear Creek Dr *Web:* merctube.com	Englewood	CO	80110	303-761-1835	781-7307
Morris Coupling Co 2240 W 15th St *TF:* 800-426-1579 ■ *Web:* www.morriscoupling.com	Erie	PA	16505	814-459-1741	453-5155
National Metalwares Inc 900 N Russell Ave *Web:* www.nationalmetalwares.com	Aurora	IL	60506	630-892-9000	892-2573
Naylor Pipe Co 1230 E 92nd St *Web:* www.naylorpipe.com	Chicago	IL	60619	773-721-9400	721-9494
Northwest Pipe Co 12005 N Burgard *NASDAQ: NWPX* ■ *TF:* 800-989-9631 ■ *Web:* www.nwpipe.com	Portland	OR	97203	503-285-1400	
Outokumpu Stainless Pipe Inc 1101 N Main St **Fax Area Code:* 800 ■ *TF:* 800-731-7473 ■ *Web:* www.outokumpu.com	Wildwood	FL	34785	352-748-1313	416-7473*
Parmatech Corp 2221 Pine View Way *Web:* atwcompanies.com/parmatech	Petaluma	CA	94954	707-778-2266	
Pipe Fabricating & Supply Co 1235 N Kraemer Blvd *Web:* www.pipefab.com	Anaheim	CA	92806	714-630-5200	630-1277
Plymouth Tube Co 29 W 150 Warrenville Rd *TF Mktg:* 800-323-9506 ■ *Web:* www.plymouth.com	Warrenville	IL	60555	630-393-3550	393-3551
Porter's Group LLC 1111 Oates Rd *Web:* www.portersfab.com	Bessemer City	NC	28016	704-864-1313	
PTC Alliance Copperleaf Corporate Ctr 6051 Wallace Rd Ext Ste 200 *Web:* www.ptcalliance.com	Wexford	PA	15090	412-299-7900	299-2619
Quality Edge Inc 2712 Walkent Dr NW *TF:* 888-784-0878 ■ *Web:* www.qualityedge.com	Walker	MI	49544	888-784-0878	
Salem Tube Inc 951 Fourth St *Web:* www.salemtube.com	Greenville	PA	16125	724-646-4301	646-4311
Small Tube Products Company Inc PO Box 1017 *Web:* www.smalltubeproducts.com	Duncansville	PA	16635	814-695-4491	695-4304
Southland Tube Inc 3525 Richard Arrington Blvd N *TF:* 800-543-9024 ■ *Web:* www.southlandtube.com	Birmingham	AL	35234	205-251-1884	251-1553
Stupp Corp 12555 Ronaldson Rd *TF:* 800-535-9999 ■ *Web:* www.stuppcorp.com	Baton Rouge	LA	70807	225-775-8800	775-7610
Superior Tube Co 3900 Germantown Pk *Web:* www.superiortube.com	Collegeville	PA	19426	610-489-5200	489-5252
Swepco Tube Corp 1 Clifton Blvd *Web:* www.swepcotube.com	Clifton	NJ	07015	973-778-3000	778-9289
Synalloy Corp 775 Spartan Blvd Ste 102 PO Box 5627 *NASDAQ: SYNL* ■ *TF Orders:* 800-937-5449 ■ *Web:* www.synalloy.com	Spartanburg	SC	29304	864-585-3605	596-1501
Tex-Tube Co 1503 N Post Oak Rd *TF:* 800-839-7473 ■ *Web:* www.tex-tube.com	Houston	TX	77055	713-686-4351	681-5256
Troxel Co Hwy 57 *Web:* www.troxel.com	Moscow	TN	38057	901-877-6875	877-6942
Tube Methods Inc PO Box 460 *TF:* 800-220-2123 ■ *Web:* www.tubemethods.com	Bridgeport	PA	19405	610-279-7700	277-2005
Tube Processing Corp 604 E Le Grande Ave *TF:* 800-295-4119 ■ *Web:* www.tubeproc.com	Indianapolis	IN	46203	317-787-1321	786-3074
Unison LLC 7575 Baymeadows Way *Web:* www.unisonindustries.com	Jacksonville	FL	32256	904-739-4000	739-4093
United Industries Inc 1546 Henry Ave *Web:* www.unitedindustries.com	Beloit	WI	53511	608-365-8891	365-1259
Valmont Industries Inc 1 Valmont Plz *NYSE: VMI* ■ *TF:* 800-825-6668 ■ *Web:* www.valmont.com	Omaha	NE	68154	402-963-1000	
Van Leeuwen Pipe & Tube Inc 2875 64th Ave *Web:* www.vanleeuwen.com	Edmonton	AB	T6P1R1	780-469-7410	
Webco Industries Inc 9101 W 21st St PO Box 100 *OTC: WEBC* ■ *Web:* www.webcoindustries.com	Sand Springs	OK	74063	918-245-2211	245-0306
Welded Tubes Inc 135 Penniman Rd *Web:* www.weldedtubes.com	Orwell	OH	44076	440-437-5144	437-5180
Western Pneumatic Tube LLC 835 Sixth St S *Web:* www.wptube.com	Kirkland	WA	98033	425-822-8271	828-6669
Western Tube & Conduit Corp 2001 E Dominguez St *Web:* www.westerntube.com	Long Beach	CA	90810	310-537-6300	604-9785
Wheatland Tube Co 700 S Dock St *TF:* 800-257-8182 ■ *Web:* www.wheatland.com	Sharon	PA	16146	800-257-8182	
Wieland Metals Inc 567 Northgate Pkwy *Web:* www.wielandus.com	Wheeling	IL	60090	847-537-3990	537-4085
World Resources Co 1600 Anderson Rd *Web:* www.worldresourcescompany.com	Mclean	VA	22102	703-734-9800	
Wytech Industries Inc 960 E Hazelwood Ave *Web:* www.wytech.com	Rahway	NJ	07065	732-396-3900	
Yarde Metals Inc 45 Newell St *TF:* 800-444-9494 ■ *Web:* www.yarde.com	Southington	CT	06489	860-406-6061	406-6040

491 METAL WORK - ARCHITECTURAL & ORNAMENTAL

	City	State	Zip	Phone	Fax
Airolite Company LLC PO Box 410 *Web:* www.airolite.com	Schofield	WI	54476	715-841-8757	841-8773
Alabama Metal Industries Corp (AMICO) 3245 Fayette Ave **Fax:* Sales ■ *TF:* 800-366-2642 ■ *Web:* amicoglobal.com	Birmingham	AL	35208	205-787-2611	780-7838*
Alpha Tech Inc 388 Cane Creek Rd *Web:* www.alpha.com	Fletcher	NC	28732	828-684-9709	
Alvarado Mfg Company Inc 12660 Colony St *TF:* 800-423-4143 ■ *Web:* www.alvaradomfg.com	Chino	CA	91710	909-591-8431	628-1403
American Stair Corp Inc 642 Forestwood Dr **Fax Area Code:* 815 ■ *TF:* 800-872-7824 ■ *Web:* www.americanstair.com	Romeoville	IL	60446	800-872-7824	372-3684*
Ameristar Fence Products Inc 1555 N Mingo Rd *TF:* 888-333-3422 ■ *Web:* www.ameristarfence.com	Tulsa	OK	74116	918-835-0898	
Armstrong Bros Holding Company Inc 8530 M 60	Union City	MI	49094	517-741-4471	
ATAS International Inc 6612 Snowdrift Rd *TF:* 800-468-1441 ■ *Web:* www.atas.com	Allentown	PA	18106	610-395-8445	395-9342
Bedford Machine & Tool Inc 2103 John Williams Blvd *TF:* 800-264-1948 ■ *Web:* www.bedfordmachine.com	Bedford	IN	47421	812-275-1948	
Bil-Jax Inc 125 Taylor Pkwy *TF:* 800-537-0540 ■ *Web:* www.biljax.com	Archbold	OH	43502	419-445-8915	445-0367
Bradley Pulverizer Company Inc 123 S Third St *Web:* www.bradleypulverizer.com	Allentown	PA	18105	610-434-5191	
Brand Energy & Infrastructure Services Inc 1325 Cobb International Dr Ste A-1 **Fax Area Code:* 770 ■ *TF:* 855-746-4477 ■ *Web:* www.beis.com	Kennesaw	GA	30152	678-285-1400	514-0285*
Cherokee Metals Company Inc 5883 Glenridge Dr NE	Atlanta	GA	30328	770-449-1444	559-4933
Chicago Metallic Corp 4849 S Austin Ave **Fax Area Code:* 800 ■ *Web:* www.chicago-metallic.com	Chicago	IL	60638	708-563-4600	222-3744*
Construction Specialties Inc 3 Werner Way *TF:* 800-972-7214 ■ *Web:* c-sgroup.com	Lebanon	NJ	08833	908-236-0800	236-0801
Duvinage Corp 60 W Oak Ridge Dr *TF:* 800-541-2645 ■ *Web:* www.duvinage.com	Hagerstown	MD	21740	301-733-8255	791-7240
Fisher & Ludlow Tru-Weld Grating 2000 Corporate Dr Ste 400 *TF:* 800-334-2047 ■ *Web:* www.nucorgrating.com	Wexford	PA	15090	724-934-5320	934-5348
Goldline International Inc 1601 Cloverfield Blvd 100 S Tower *TF:* 877-376-2646 ■ *Web:* goldline.com	Santa Monica	CA	90404	310-587-1423	319-0265
Hafele America Company Inc 3901 Cheyenne Dr **Fax Area Code:* 800 ■ *TF Cust Svc:* 800-423-3531 ■ *Web:* www.hafele.com	Archdale	NC	27263	336-889-2322	325-6197*
Hapco Inc 26252 Hillman Hwy *TF:* 800-368-7171 ■ *Web:* www.hapco.com	Abingdon	VA	24210	276-628-7171	623-2594
IKG Industries 1514 S Sheldon Rd **Fax Area Code:* 713 ■ *Web:* www.harscoikg.com	Channelview	TX	77530	281-452-6637	378-3987*
Irvine Access Floors Inc 9425 Washington Blvd *TF:* 800-969-8870 ■ *Web:* www.irvineaccessfloors.com	Laurel	MD	20723	301-617-9333	617-9907
Jackburn Manufacturing Inc 438 Church St *Web:* www.jackburn.com	Girard	PA	16417	814-774-3573	774-2854
Jerith Mfg Company Inc 14400 McNulty Rd *TF:* 800-344-2242 ■ *Web:* www.jerith.com	Philadelphia	PA	19154	215-676-4068	676-9756
King Architectural Metals Inc PO Box 271169 *TF:* 800-542-2379 ■ *Web:* kingmetals.com	Dallas	TX	75227	800-542-2379	
Lapmaster International LLC 501 W Algonquin Rd *TF:* 877-352-8637 ■ *Web:* www.lapmaster-wolters.com	Mount Prospect	IL	60056	224-659-7101	
Livers Bronze Co 4621 E 75th Terr *Web:* www.liversbronze.com	Kansas City	MO	64132	816-300-2828	300-0864
MC Machinery Systems Inc 1500 Michael Dr *Web:* www.mcmachinery.com	Wood Dale	IL	60191	630-860-4210	
McGregor Industries Inc 46 Line St *Web:* www.mcgregorindustries.com	Dunmore	PA	18512	570-343-2436	343-4915
Milgo Industrial Inc 68 Lombardi St *Web:* www.milgo-bufkin.com	Brooklyn	NY	11222	718-388-6476	963-0614
MiTek Canada Inc 100 Industrial Rd *Web:* www.mitek.ca	Bradford	ON	L3Z3G7	905-952-2900	952-2901
NSK America Corp 1800 Global Pkwy *TF:* 800-585-4675 ■ *Web:* www.nskamericacorp.com	Hoffman Estates	IL	60192	847-843-7664	
Overly Manufacturing Co 574 W Otterman St *TF:* 800-979-7300 ■ *Web:* www.overly.com	Greensburg	PA	15601	724-834-7300	830-2871
Quickmill Inc 760 Rye St *TF:* 800-295-0509 ■ *Web:* www.quickmill.com	Peterborough	ON	K9J6W9	705-745-2961	745-8130
Spider Staging Corp 365 Upland Dr *TF:* 877-774-3370 ■ *Web:* www.spiderstaging.com	Tukwila	WA	98188	206-575-6445	575-6240
Steel Ceilings Inc 451 E Coshocton St *TF:* 800-848-0496 ■ *Web:* www.steelceilings.com	Johnstown	OH	43031	740-967-1063	967-1478
Superior Aluminum Products Inc 555 E Main St PO Box 430 *TF:* 800-548-8656 ■ *Web:* www.superioraluminum.com	Russia	OH	45363	937-526-4065	526-3904
Swanton Welding & Machining Co 407 Broadway Ave *Web:* www.swantonweld.com	Swanton	OH	43558	419-826-4816	826-0489
T Tech Inc 510 Guthridge Ct *TF:* 800-370-1530 ■ *Web:* t-techtools.com/store	Norcross	GA	30092	770-455-0676	
Tate Access Floors Inc 7510 Montevideo Rd *TF:* 800-231-7788 ■ *Web:* tateinc.com	Jessup	MD	20794	410-799-4200	799-4207
Thyssenkrupp Krause Inc 901 Doris Rd	Auburn Hills	MI	48326	248-340-8000	
Universal Builders Supply Inc (UBS) 27 Horton Ave *Web:* www.ubs1.com	New Rochelle	NY	10801	914-699-2400	699-2609
US Equipment Co 20580 Hoover Rd *Web:* www.usequipment.com	Detroit	MI	48205	313-526-8300	
VELUX America Inc 450 Old BrickyaRd Rd *TF:* 866-358-3589 ■ *Web:* www.veluxusa.com	Greenwood	SC	29648	864-941-4700	943-2631
Vicwest Corp 1296 S Service Rd W *TF:* 800-265-6583 ■ *Web:* www.vicwest.com	Oakville	ON	L6L5T7	905-825-2252	825-2272
Withers Tool Die & Mfg 1238 Veterans Memorial Hwy SE *Web:* www.witherstool.com	Mableton	GA	30126	770-948-2544	
Wolf Robotics LLC 4600 Innovation Dr *TF:* 866-965-3911 ■ *Web:* www.wolfrobotics.com	Fort Collins	CO	80525	970-225-7600	
Wooster Products Inc 1000 Spruce St PO Box 6005 *TF:* 800-321-4936 ■ *Web:* www.wooster-products.com	Wooster	OH	44691	330-264-2844	262-4151

492 METALS SERVICE CENTERS

Company	City	State	ZIP	Phone	Fax
101 Pipe & Casing Inc 30101 Agoura Ct Ste 201 *Web:* www.101pipe.com	Agoura Hills	CA	91301	818-707-9101	
A & B Aluminum & Brass Foundry 11165 Denton Dr *TF:* 800-743-4995 ■ *Web:* www.abfoundryonline.com	Dallas	TX	75229	972-247-3579	247-4981
A & D Constructors Inc 707 Schrader Dr. *Web:* www.adconstructors.com	Evansville	IN	47712	812-428-3708	
A F K Corp 300 Pacific St *Web:* www.afkfoundry.com	Ripon	WI	54971	920-748-2265	
A&B Process Systems Corp 201 S Wisconsin Ave *TF:* 888-258-2789 ■ *Web:* www.abprocess.com	Stratford	WI	54484	715-687-4332	
A-588 & A-572 Steel Co, The 133 Sebago Lk Dr. *Web:* www.a588a572steel.com	Sewickley	PA	15143	412-366-1980	366-3780
Abbott Ball Company Inc 19 Railroad Pl. *Web:* www.abbottball.com	West Hartford	CT	06133	860-236-5901	
ABC Metals Inc 500 W Clinton St. *Fax Area Code: 574 ■ *TF:* 800-238-8470 ■ *Web:* www.abcmetals.com	Logansport	IN	46947	800-238-8470	753-6110*
Ability Metal Co 1355 Greenleaf Ave. *Web:* abilitymetal.com	Elk Grove Village	IL	60007	847-437-7040	
Abt Foam LLC 259 Murdock Rd *TF:* 800-438-6057 ■ *Web:* www.abtdrains.com	Troutman	NC	28166	704-528-9806	
Accent Packaging Inc 10131 FM 2920 Rd *Web:* www.accentwire.com	Tomball	TX	77375	281-251-3700	
Accurate Alloys Inc 5455 Irwindale Ave *TF:* 800-842-2222 ■ *Web:* www.accuratealloys.com	Irwindale	CA	91706	626-338-4012	337-8393
Acid Piping Technology Inc 2890 Arnold Tenbrook Rd. *Web:* www.acidpiping.com	Arnold	MO	63010	636-296-4668	
Acier Picard Inc 3000 Rue De L' Etchemin *TF:* 888-834-0646 ■ *Web:* www.acierpicard.com	Levis	QC	G6W7X6	418-834-8300	
Acme Metals & Steel Supply Inc 14930 S San Pedro St *Web:* www.acmemetalsonline.com	Gardena	CA	90248	310-329-2263	
Acme-Monaco Corp 75 Winchell Dr. *Web:* www.acmemonaco.com	New Britain	CT	06052	860-224-1349	
Action Stainless & Alloys Inc 1505 Halsey Way *TF:* 800-749-2523 ■ *Web:* www.actionstainless.com	Carrollton	TX	75007	972-466-1500	466-0909
ACuPowder International LLC 901 Lehigh Ave *Web:* www.acupowder.com	Union	NJ	07083	908-851-4500	
Advanced Laser Machining Inc 600 Cashman Dr. *Web:* www.laser27.com	Chippewa Falls	WI	54729	715-720-8093	
Advanced Support Products Inc 24227 Fm 2978 Rd. *TF:* 800-941-5737 ■ *Web:* www.aspbase.com	Tomball	TX	77375	281-357-1277	357-0577
Advanced Technology Inc 6106 W Market St. *Web:* www.advtechnology.com	Greensboro	NC	27409	336-668-0488	
AEB International Inc 654 Madison Ave Ste 1809. *Web:* aebint.com	New York	NY	10065	212-752-4647	
Aerex Industries Inc 3504 Industrial 27th St. *Web:* www.aerexglobal.com	Ft Pierce	FL	34946	772-461-0004	
Aerospace Alloys Inc 11 Britton Dr *Web:* aalloys.com	Bloomfield	CT	06002	860-882-0019	
Aladdin Steel Inc PO Box 89 *TF:* 800-637-4455 ■ *Web:* www.aladdinsteel.com	Gillespie	IL	62033	217-839-2121	839-3823
Alaskan Copper & Brass Co 3223 Sixth Ave S. *TF:* 800-552-7661 ■ *Web:* www.alascop.com	Seattle	WA	98134	206-623-5800	382-7335
Alcast Foundry Inc 2910 Fisk Ln *Web:* www.alcast-foundry.com	Redondo Beach	CA	90278	310-542-3581	
Alcoa Inc 201 Isabella St *NYSE: AA* ■ *TF:* 800-388-4825 ■ *Web:* www.alcoa.com	Pittsburgh	PA	15212	412-553-4545	553-4498
Alexandria Industries 401 County Rd 22 NW *Web:* www.alexandriaindustries.com	Alexandria	MN	56308	320-763-6537	
Alfiniti Inc 1152 rue Manic *TF:* 800-334-8731 ■ *Web:* www.alfiniti.com	Chicoutimi	QC	G7K1A2	418-696-2545	
All American Grating Inc 3001 Grand Ave *TF:* 800-962-9692 ■ *Web:* www.aagrating.com	Pittsburgh	PA	15225	412-771-6970	
All Foils Inc 16100 Imperial Pkwy *TF:* 800-521-0054 ■ *Web:* www.allfoils.com	Strongsville	OH	44149	440-572-3645	378-0161
All Metals Industries Inc PO Box 807 *TF:* 800-654-6043 ■ *Web:* www.allmetind.com	Belmont	NH	03220	603-267-7023	267-7025
All Star Metals LLC 101 Box Car Rd. *Web:* allstarmetals.wix.com/asm-v2	Brownsville	TX	78521	956-838-2110	
All State Fabricators Corp 1485 Elmwood Ave *Web:* www.emiindustries.com	Cranston	RI	02910	401-785-3900	
Alliance Corp 2395 Meadowpine Blvd. *TF:* 888-821-4797 ■ *Web:* www.alliancecorporation.ca	Mississauga	ON	L5N7W6	905-821-4797	
Allied Metals Corp 1750 Stephenson Hwy. *Web:* www.alliedmet.com	Troy	MI	48083	248-680-2400	
Allied Sinterings Inc 29 Briar Ridge Rd. *TF:* 877-875-0464 ■ *Web:* alliedsinterings.com	Danbury	CT	06810	877-875-0464	
Alloy Surfaces Company Inc 121 N Commerce Dr Chester Township *Web:* www.alloysurfaces.com	Chester Township	PA	19014	610-497-7979	
Almet Inc 300 Hartzell Rd. *Web:* www.almetinc.com	New Haven	IN	46774	260-493-1556	
Almetals Inc 51035 Grand River Ave. *Web:* www.almetals.com	Wixom	MI	48393	248-348-7722	
Alro Steel Corp 3100 E High St. *TF:* 800-877-2576 ■ *Web:* www.alro.com	Jackson	MI	49204	517-787-5500	787-6390
Alstate Steel Inc 203 Murry Rd Se. *Web:* www.alstatesteel.com	Albuquerque	NM	87105	505-877-5454	
Alton Steel Inc 5 Cut St *Web:* www.altonsteel.com	Alton	IL	62002	618-463-4490	
Alu-Bra Foundry Inc 630 E Green St *Web:* alubra.com	Bensenville	IL	60106	630-766-3112	
Alum-alloy Company Inc 603 S Hope Ave. *Web:* www.webstercorp.com	Ontario	CA	91761	909-986-0410	
Alumawall Inc 1701 S Seventh St Ste 9 *Web:* www.alumawall.com	San Jose	CA	95112	408-292-6353	
Aluminum & Stainless Inc PO Box 3484 *TF:* 800-252-9074 ■ *Web:* www.aluminumandstainless.com	Lafayette	LA	70502	337-837-4381	837-5439
Aluminum Distributing 2930 Sw Second Ave *TF:* 866-825-9271 ■ *Web:* www.adimetal.com	Fort Lauderdale	FL	33315	954-523-6474	
Aluminum Extruded Shapes Inc 10549 Reading Rd *Web:* www.alum-ext.com	Cincinnati	OH	45241	513-563-2205	
Aluminum Extrusions Inc 140 Matthews Dr	Senatobia	MS	38668	662-562-6663	
Aluminum Resources Inc 789 Swan Dr. *Web:* www.aluminumresources.com	Smyrna	TN	37167	615-355-6500	
Aluminum Service Inc Fl 1701 Blount Rd Bldg B. *Web:* www.asibp.com	Pompano Beach	FL	33069	954-979-6774	
American Aluminum Extrusion Company LLC 1 Saint Lawrence Ave *TF:* 877-896-2236 ■ *Web:* www.americanaluminum.com	Beloit	WI	53511	608-361-1800	
American Bin & Conveyor Inc 221 Front St. *Web:* www.americanconveyor.com	Burlington	WI	53105	262-763-0123	
American Chrome Co 518 W Crossroads Pkwy *TF:* 800-562-4488 ■ *Web:* www.americanchrome.com	Bolingbrook	IL	60440	630-685-2200	
American Douglas Metals Inc 783 Thorpe Rd. *TF:* 800-428-0023 ■ *Web:* www.americandouglasmetals.com	Orlando	FL	32824	407-855-6590	857-3290
American Foundry Group Inc 14602 S Grant *Web:* www.americanfoundry.com	Bixby	OK	74008	918-366-4401	
American Steel & Aluminum Company Inc 3545 E Main St. *Web:* www.asafab.com	Grand Prairie	TX	75050	972-264-1533	
American Steel Corp 4884 S Desert View Dr *Web:* www.americansteelcorporation.com	Apache Junction	AZ	85220	480-474-0100	
American Steel Products Inc 5620 Ne 65th Ave. *Web:* www.americansteelonline.com	Portland	OR	97218	503-288-8420	
American Strip Steel Inc 901 Coopertown Rd *Fax Area Code: 908 ■ *TF:* 800-526-1216 ■ *Web:* www.americanstrip.com	Delanco	NJ	08075	800-526-1216	412-1442*
AmeriFab Inc 3501 E Ninth St. *Web:* www.amerifabinc.com	Indianapolis	IN	46201	317-231-0100	
Ameriflex Inc 2390 Railroad St *Web:* www.ameriflex.com	Corona	CA	92880	951-737-5557	
Ameritube Master Distribution LLC 1000 N Hwy 77. *Web:* www.ameritube.com	Hillsboro	TX	76645	254-580-9888	
AMI Metals Inc 1738 General George Patton Dr *TF:* 800-727-1903 ■ *Web:* www.amimetals.com	Brentwood	TN	37027	615-377-0400	377-0103
AmRod Corp 60 Pennsylvania Ave *Web:* www.amrod.com	Kearny	NJ	07032	973-344-3806	
Amstek Metal LLC 2408 W Mcdonough. *TF:* 800-551-9473 ■ *Web:* www.amstekmetal.com	Joliet	IL	60436	815-725-2520	
Amthor Steel 1717 Gaskell Ave. *Web:* www.amthorsteel.com	Erie	PA	16503	814-452-4700	
Anel Corp 3244 Hwy 51 *Web:* www.anelcorp.com	Winona	MS	38967	662-283-1540	
Angstrom Sciences Inc 40 S Linden St. *Web:* www.angstromsciences.com	Duquesne	PA	15110	412-469-8466	
Apel Steel Corp 2345 Second Ave NW *Web:* www.apelsteel.net	Cullman	AL	35058	256-739-6280	
Apex Spring & Stamping Corp 11420 First Ave NW *Web:* www.apexspring.com	Grand Rapids	MI	49534	616-453-5463	
Applied Laser Technologies 8404 Venture Cir *TF:* 888-359-3002 ■ *Web:* www.aplaser.com	Schofield	WI	54476	715-359-3002	
Arbon Steel & Service Co Inc 2355 Bond St *Web:* www.arbonsteel.com	University Park	IL	60484	708-534-6800	534-6826
ArcelorMittal Burns Harbor LLC 250 W US Hwy 12 *Web:* www.arcelormittal.com	Burns Harbor	IN	46304	219-787-2120	
Aristo Cast Inc 7400 Research Dr. *Web:* www.aristo-cast.com	Almont	MI	48003	810-798-2900	
Ark Technologies Inc 3655 Ohio Ave *Web:* www.arktechno.com	Saint Charles	IL	60174	630-377-8855	
Arkansas Steel Associates LLC 2803 Van Dyke Rd *Web:* www.arkansassteel.com	Newport	AR	72112	870-523-3693	
Arnold Steel Company Inc 79 Randolph Rd *Web:* www.arnoldsteel.com	Howell	NJ	07731	732-363-1079	
Art Iron Inc 860 Curtis St. *TF:* 800-472-1113 ■ *Web:* www.artiron.com	Toledo	OH	43609	419-241-1261	725-2027
Artistica Metal Designs Inc 3200 Golf Course Dr. *Web:* artisticahome.com	Ventura	CA	93003	805-850-1100	
ASA Alloys Inc 81 Steinway Blvd. *TF:* 800-387-9166 ■ *Web:* www.asaalloys.com	Etobicoke	ON	M9W6H6	416-213-0000	213-9507
Astralloy Steel Products Inc 1550 Red Hollow Rd. *Web:* www.astralloy.com	Birmingham	AL	35215	205-853-0300	
Astro Shapes Inc 65 Main St *Web:* www.astroshapes.com	Struthers	OH	44471	330-755-1414	
Atlantic Cordage Corp 35 Mileed Way *Web:* www.atlantic-group.com	Avenel	NJ	07001	732-574-0700	

Phone | Fax

Atlas Bronze 445 Bunting Ave.... Trenton NJ 08611 609-599-1402
Web: www.atlasbronze.com

Atlas Steel Products Co 7990 Bavaria Rd.... Twinsburg OH 44087 330-425-1600 425-1611
TF: 800-444-1682 ■ *Web:* www.atlassteel.com

ATW Companies Inc 55 Service Ave.... Warwick RI 02886 401-244-1002
Web: www.atwcompanies.com

Aviotrade Inc 10850 NW 21st St Ste 230 & 240.... Miami FL 33172 305-717-5000
Web: www.aviotrade.com

B E Peterson Inc
40 Murphy Dr Avon Industrial Pk.... Avon MA 02322 508-436-7900
Web: www.bepeterson.com

B&S Aircraft Alloys Inc 10 Aerial Way.... Syosset NY 11791 516-681-2400
Web: www.bsaa.com

Baldwin Intl 30403 Bruce Industrial Pkwy.... Solon OH 44139 440-248-9500
Web: www.baldwininternational.com

Bapko Metal Fabricators Inc 838 N Cypress St.... Orange CA 92867 714-639-9380
Web: www.bapko.com

Basic Metals Inc W180 Nn11819 River Ln.... Germantown WI 53022 262-255-9034 255-9073
TF: 800-989-1996 ■ *Web:* www.basicmetals.com

BC Wire Rope & Rigging 2720 E Regal Park Dr.... Anaheim CA 92806 714-666-8000
TF: 800-669-5919 ■ *Web:* www.bcwirerope.com

Beaver Steel Services Inc 1200 Arch St.... Carnegie PA 15106 412-429-8860
Web: www.beaversteel.com

Beck Aluminum Corp
300 Allen Bradley Dr.... Mayfield Heights OH 44124 216-861-4455
Web: www.beckaluminum.com

Bee Steel Inc
2090 Celebration Dr Ste 209.... Grand Rapids MI 49525 616-363-6694
Web: www.beesteelinc.com

Behringer Corp 17 Ridge Rd.... Branchville NJ 07826 973-948-0226
Web: www.behringersystems.com

Bell Foundry Co 5310 Southern Ave.... Southgate CA 90280 323-564-5701
Web: www.bfco.com

Belmont Metals Inc 330 Belmont Ave.... Brooklyn NY 11207 718-342-4900
Web: www.belmontmetals.com

Benner Metals Corp
1220 S State College Blvd.... Fullerton CA 92831 714-879-6477
Web: www.bennermetals.com

Berg Steel Corp 4306 Normandy Ct.... Royal Oak MI 48073 248-549-6066 549-1374
Web: www.bergsteel.com

Bergkamp Inc 3040 Emulsion Dr.... Salina KS 67401 785-825-1375
Web: www.bergkampinc.com

Berlin Metals LLC 3200 Sheffield Ave.... Hammond IN 46327 219-933-0111 933-0692
TF: 800-754-8867 ■ *Web:* www.berlinmetals.com

Berntsen Brass & Aluminum Foundry Inc
2334 Pennsylvania Ave.... Madison WI 53704 608-249-9233
Web: www.berntsen-foundry.com

Berry Metal Co 2408 Evans City Rd.... Harmony PA 16037 724-452-8040
Web: www.berrymetal.com

Betz Industries Inc 2121 Bristol Ave NW.... Grand Rapids MI 49504 616-453-4429
Web: www.betzindustries.com

Blackburn's Fabrication Inc 2467 Jackson Pk.... Columbus OH 43223 614-875-0784
Web: blackburnsfab.com

Blattner Steel Company Inc
2100 Rust Ave.... Cape Girardeau MO 63703 573-339-1129
Web: www.blattnersteel.com

Bluescope Steel Americas LLC
111 W Ocean Blvd Ste 1370.... Long Beach CA 90802 562-491-1441
Web: www.bhpsteel.com

BMG Metals Inc 950 Masonic Ln.... Richmond VA 23231 804-226-1024 222-3693
TF: 800-552-1510 ■ *Web:* www.bmgmetals.com

Boardman Inc 1135 S McKinley Ave.... Oklahoma City OK 73108 405-634-5434
Web: www.boardmaninc.com

Bobco Metals Co 2000 S Alameda St.... Los Angeles CA 90058 877-952-6226
TF: 877-952-6226 ■ *Web:* bobcometal.com

Bodine Aluminum Inc 2100 Walton Rd.... St. Louis MO 63114 314-423-8200
Web: www.bodinealuminum.com

Bohler-Uddeholm North America
2505 Millenium Dr.... Elgin IL 60124 630-883-3100 883-3101
TF: 800-638-2520 ■ *Web:* www.bucorp.com

Bolduc Leroux Inc
3365 des Entreprises Blvd.... Terrebonne QC J6X4J9 450-477-3413
Web: www.bolducleroux.ca

Bourland & Leverich Supply Co LLC
11707 Hwy 152 W P.O. Box 778.... Pampa TX 79066 806-665-0061
Web: www.bl-supply.com

Bowers Manufacturing Co 6565 S Sprinkle Rd.... Portage MI 49002 269-323-2565
Web: www.bowers-mfg.com

Briteline Extrusions Inc
575 Beech Hill Rd.... Summerville SC 29485 843-873-4410
Web: www.briteline.net

Brodhead Steel Products Co
143 S Linden Ave.... South San Francisco CA 94080 650-871-8251
Web: www.brodheadsteel.com

Brown-Strauss Steel 2495 Uravan St.... Aurora CO 80011 303-371-2200 375-8122
TF Sales: 800-677-2778 ■ *Web:* www.brown-strauss.com

BRT Extrusions Inc 1818 N Main St.... Niles OH 44446 330-544-0244
Web: www.brtextrusions.com

C & K Johnson Industries Inc 1061 Samoa Blvd.... Arcata CA 95521 707-822-7687
Web: www.ckjohnsonind.com

California Steel Services Inc
1212 S Mtn View Ave.... San Bernardino CA 92408 909-796-2222
Web: www.calsteel.com

Camalloy Inc 1960 N Main St.... Washington PA 15301 724-222-2022
Web: www.camalloy.com

Cambridge Street Metal Corp (CSM)
82 Stevens St.... East Taunton MA 02718 508-822-2278 822-4667
TF: 800-254-7580 ■ *Web:* www.csmetal.net

Canada Pipe Company Ltd
1757 Burlington St E PO Box 2849.... Hamilton ON L8N3R5 905-547-3251
Web: www.canadapipe.com

Capitol Steel & Iron LLC 1726 S Agnew.... Oklahoma City OK 73108 405-632-7710
Web: www.capitol-steel.com

Phone | Fax

Carfaro Inc 2075 E State St.... Trenton NJ 08619 609-890-6600
Web: www.carfaro.com

Carley Foundry Inc 8301 Coral Sea St Ne.... Blaine MN 55449 763-780-5123
Web: www.carleyfoundry.com

Central Metal Fabricators Inc 900 Sw 70th Ave.... Miami FL 33144 305-261-6262
Web: www.centralmetalfab.com

Central Metals Inc 1054 S Second St.... Camden NJ 08103 856-963-5844
Web: www.centralmetals.com

Central States Industrial Supply Inc
8720 S 137th Cir.... Omaha NE 68138 402-894-1003
Web: www.centralstatesgroup.com

Century Foundry Inc 339 W Hovey Ave.... Muskegon MI 49444 231-733-1572
Web: www.centuryfoundry.com

CERTEX USA Inc 1721 W Culver St.... Phoenix AZ 85007 602-271-9048
Web: www.certex.com

CFC Canadoil Inc 8000 Market St Ste 100.... Houston TX 77029 713-676-0077
Web: www.cfcfittings.com

Charleston Aluminum LLC 480 Frontage Rd.... Gaston SC 29053 803-939-4600
Web: www.charlestonaluminum.com

Charter Steel Trading Company Inc
4401 W Roosevelt Rd.... Chicago IL 60624 773-522-3100
Web: www.chartersteeltrading.com

Chatham Steel Corp 501 W Boundary St.... Savannah GA 31401 912-233-5751 944-0236
TF: 800-800-1337 ■ *Web:* www.chathamsteel.com

Cherokee Steel Supply 196 Leroy Anderson Dr.... Monroe GA 30655 770-207-4621
TF: 800-729-0334 ■ *Web:* www.cherokeesteel.com

Chicago Tube & Iron Co 1 Chicago Tube Dr.... Romeoville IL 60446 815-834-2500 588-3958
TF Cust Svc: 800-972-0217 ■ *Web:* www.chicagotube.com

Chickasaw Distributors Inc
800 Bering Dr Ste 330.... Houston TX 77057 713-974-2905 974-3109
Web: www.chickasawdistributors.com

City Pipe & Supply Corp PO Box 2112.... Odessa TX 79760 432-332-1541 333-2300
TF: 844-307-4044 ■ *Web:* www.citypipe.com

Classic Sheet Metal Inc 1065 Sesame St.... Franklin Park IL 60131 630-694-0300
Web: www.classic-sheet-metal.com

Clayton Metals Inc 546 Clayton Ct.... Wood Dale IL 60191 800-323-7628 860-1053*
*Fax Area Code: 630 ■ *TF:* 800-323-7628 ■ *Web:* www.claytonmetals.com

Cleveland Steel Container Corp
1840 Enterprise Pkwy.... Twinsburg OH 44087 330-405-3000
Web: www.cscpails.com

CMC Rebar 4846 Singleton Blvd.... Dallas TX 75212 214-428-2861
Web: www.cmc.com

Coast Aluminum & Architectural Inc
30551 Huntwood Ave.... Hayward CA 94544 510-441-6600
Web: www.coastaluminum.com

Coastal Corrosion Control Surveys LLC
10172 Mammoth Ave.... Baton Rouge LA 70814 225-275-6131
TF: 800-894-2120 ■ *Web:* www.coastalcorrosion.com

Coilplus Ohio Inc 4801 Gateway Blvd.... Springfield OH 45502 937-322-4455
Web: coilplusohio.com

Coilplus Pennsylvania Inc
5135 Bleigh St.... Philadelphia PA 19136 215-331-5200 331-9538
Web: www.coilplus.com

Col Pump Company Inc 131 E Railroad St.... Columbiana OH 44408 330-482-1029
Web: www.col-pump.net

Colby Metal Inc 701 Industrial Dr.... Colby WI 54421 715-223-2334
Web: www.colbymetal.com

Collins & Hermann Inc 1215 Dunn Rd.... St. Louis MO 63138 314-869-8000
Web: www.collinsandhermann.com

Columbia Pipe & Supply Co 1120 W Pershing Rd.... Chicago IL 60609 773-927-6600 927-8415
TF: 888-429-4635 ■ *Web:* www.columbiapipe.com

Columbia Steel Inc 2175 N Linden Ave.... Rialto CA 92377 909-874-8840
Web: www.columbiasteelinc.com

Columbus Pipe & Equipment Co
773 E Markison Ave.... Columbus OH 43207 614-444-7871
Web: www.columbuspipe.com

Conestoga Supply Corp 11011 Sheldon Rd.... Houston TX 77044 832-391-9431 456-7574*
*Fax Area Code: 281 ■ *Web:* www.conestogasupply.com

Connect-Air International Inc 4240 'B' St NW.... Auburn WA 98001 253-813-5599
Web: www.connect-air.com

Connector Specialists Inc 175 James Dr E.... St Rose LA 70087 504-469-1659
Web: www.connectorspecialists.com

Consolidated Pipe & Supply Inc
1205 Hilltop Pkwy.... Birmingham AL 35204 205-323-7261 251-7838
Web: www.consolidatedpipe.com

Consolidated Steel Services Inc
632 Glendale Vly Blvd.... Fallentimber PA 16639 814-944-5890 943-8278
TF: 800-237-8783 ■ *Web:* www.csteel.com

Constellium Automotive USA LLC
46555 Magellan Dr.... Novi MI 48377 317-301-4600
Web: www.constellium.com

Consumers Pipe & Supply Co
5832 E 61st St.... Los Angeles CA 90040 323-685-6870 724-3781
TF: 800-338-7473 ■ *Web:* www.consumerspipe.com

Continental Casting LLC 801 Second St.... Monroe City MO 63456 573-735-4577
Web: www.continentalcasting.com

Contractors Steel Co 36555 Amrhein Rd.... Livonia MI 48150 734-464-4000 452-3939*
*Fax: Sales ■ *TF:* 800-521-3946 ■ *Web:* www.contractorssteel.com

CORPAC Steel Products Corp
20803 Biscayne Blvd Ste 502.... Miami FL 33180 305-918-0540
Web: www.corpacsteel.com

Couturier Iron Craft Inc
5050 W River Dr Ne.... Comstock Park MI 49321 616-784-6780
Web: www.couturierironcraft.com

Crestwood Tubulars Inc
9962 Lin-Ferry Dr Ste 207.... St. Louis MO 63123 314-842-8604
Web: www.crestwoodtubulars.com

Crown Extrusions Inc 122 Columbia Court N.... Chaska MN 55318 952-448-3533
Web: www.crownextrusions.com

CSC Inc 1109 Court St.... Medford OR 97501 541-779-1970
Web: www.medfab.com

Cullman Casting Corp 251 County Rd 490.... Cullman AL 35055 256-735-0900
Web: www.cullmancasting.com

Company / Address	City	State	ZIP	Phone	Fax
Cumberland Steel Div 4919 Grant Ave. *Web:* www.cumberlandind.com	Cleveland	OH	44125	216-441-1800	
Dakota Riggers & Tool Supply Inc 704 E Benson Rd *Web:* www.dakotariggers.com	Sioux Falls	SD	57104	605-335-0041	
Damascus Steel Casting Co Blockhouse Rd Run Extn. *TF:* 800-920-2210 ■ *Web:* www.damascussteel.com	New Brighton	PA	15066	724-846-2770	
Dameron Alloy Foundries Inc 927 S Santa Fe Ave. *Web:* www.dameron.net	Compton	CA	90224	310-631-5165	
Decker Steel & Supply Inc 4500 Train Ave. *TF:* 800-321-6100 ■ *Web:* www.deckersteel.com	Cleveland	OH	44102	216-281-7900	281-1441
Delta Metals Company Inc 1388 N Seventh St. *Web:* www.delta-metals.com	Memphis	TN	38107	901-525-5000	575-3322
DenCol 4630 Washington St *Web:* www.dencol.com	Denver	CO	80216	303-295-1683	295-1689
Dennis Steel Inc 1105 Leander Dr *Web:* www.dennissteel.com	Leander	TX	78641	512-259-4001	
Doherty Steel Inc 21110 W 311th St *Web:* www.dohertysteel.com	Paola	KS	66071	913-557-9200	
Domtech Inc 40 East Davis St *TF:* 888-278-8258 ■ *Web:* www.domtech.net	Trenton	ON	K8V6S4	613-394-4884	394-0108
Dubose National Energy Services Inc PO Box 499 *TF:* 800-590-2150 ■ *Web:* www.dubosenes.com	Clinton	NC	28329	910-590-2151	590-3444
Duhig & Company Inc 5071 Telegraph Rd *Web:* www.duhig.com	Los Angeles	CA	90022	323-263-7161	263-7161
DW Clark Inc 692 N Bedford St *Web:* www.dwclark.com	East Bridgewater	MA	02333	508-378-4014	
E-J Enterprises Inc 7280 Baltimore Annapolis Blvd	Glen Burnie	MD	21061	410-625-8200	
Eagle Stainless Tube & Fabrication Inc 10 Discovery Way *Web:* www.eagletube.com	Franklin	MA	02038	508-528-8650	
Eagle Steel Products Inc 3420 Collins Ln *Web:* www.eaglesteelproducts.com	Louisville	KY	40245	502-241-6004	
East Coast Metals 171 Ruth Rd *TF:* 800-355-2060 ■ *Web:* eastcoastmetals.com	Harleysville	PA	19438	215-256-9550	
Eastern Metal Supply Inc 3600 23rd Ave S *Web:* www.easternmetal.com	Lake Worth	FL	33461	561-533-6061	
Eaton Fabricating CoInc 1009 McAlpin Ct *Web:* www.eatonfabricating.com	Grafton	OH	44044	440-926-3121	
Eaton Steel Corp 10221 Capital Ave *TF:* 800-527-3851 ■ *Web:* www.eatonsteel.com	Oak Park	MI	48237	248-398-3434	398-3434
Ed Fagan Inc 769 Susquehanna Ave *TF:* 800-335-6827 ■ *Web:* www.edfagan.com	Franklin Lakes	NJ	07417	201-891-4003	891-3207
Edwards Steel Structural Div 1777 Mckinley Ave	Columbus	OH	43222	614-274-6800	
Effort Foundry Inc 6980 Chrisphalt Dr *Web:* www.effortfoundry.com	Bath	PA	18014	610-837-1837	
Electrosteel USA LLC 270 Doug Baker Blvd. *Web:* www.electrosteelusa.com	Birmingham	AL	35242	205-516-8154	
Engineered Building Products Inc 18 Southwood Dr *Web:* www.ebpfab.com	Bloomfield	CT	06002	860-243-1110	
Erickson Metals Corp 25 Knotter Dr *Web:* www.ericksonmetals.com	Cheshire	CT	06410	203-272-2918	
Erie Steel Treating Inc 5540 Jackman Rd *Web:* www.erie.com	Toledo	OH	43613	419-478-3743	
Everglades Steel Corp 5901 NW 74th Ave *Web:* www.evergladessteel.com	Miami	FL	33166	305-591-9460	
Exploreco International LLC 11930 S Sam Houston Parkway East *Web:* www.exploreco.com	Houston	TX	77089	713-796-6000	
Express Contracting 420 Milam *Web:* www.expressmetalwork.com	San Antonio	TX	78202	210-337-2260	
Extruded Aluminum Corp 7200 Industrial Dr. *Web:* www.extrudedaluminum.com	Belding	MI	48809	616-794-0300	
Extrudex Aluminum Ltd 411 Chrislea Rd *TF:* 800-668-7210 ■ *Web:* www.extrudex.com	Woodbridge	ON	L4L8N4	416-745-4444	
F M C of Plymouth Ohio Inc 500 Donnenwirth Dr *Web:* www.fetzermfg.com	Plymouth	OH	44865	419-687-8237	
FabArc Steel Supply Inc 111 Meadow Ln *Web:* www.fabarc.com	Oxford	AL	36203	256-831-8770	
Fairmount Foundry Inc 25 Second Ave *Web:* fairmountfdry.com	Woonsocket	RI	02895	401-769-1585	
Farwest Steel Corp 2000 Henderson Ave. **Fax:* Hum Res ■ *Web:* www.farweststeel.com	Eugene	OR	97403	541-686-2000	681-7250*
Fay Industries Inc 17200 Foltz Pkwy *Web:* www.fayindustries.com	Strongsville	OH	44149	440-572-5030	
Federal Steel Supply Inc 747 Goddard Ave PO Box 840 *Web:* www.fedsteel.com	Chesterfield	MO	63005	636-537-2393	
Fehr Bros Industries Inc 895 Kings Hwy *Web:* endurancehardware.com	Saugerties	NY	12477	845-246-9525	
Feralloy Corp 8755 W Higgins Rd Ste 970 *Web:* www.feralloy.com	Chicago	IL	60631	773-380-1500	380-1535
Field System Machining Inc 720 Schneider Dr *TF:* 800-789-2814 ■ *Web:* www.fieldsystems.com	South Elgin	IL	60177	847-468-1313	
Flack Steel Ltd 425 W Lakeside Ave Ste 200 *Web:* www.flacksteel.com	Cleveland	OH	44113	216-456-0700	
Fotofabrication Corp 3758 W Belmont Ave *Web:* www.fotofab.com	Chicago	IL	60618	773-463-6211	
Fox Valley Spring Company Inc N915 Craftsmen Dr *TF:* 800-776-2645 ■ *Web:* www.foxvalleyspring.com	Greenville	WI	54942	920-757-7777	
Francis Manufacturing Co 500 E Main St PO Box 400 *Web:* www.francismanufacturing.com	Russia	OH	45363	937-526-4551	
Frontier Aluminum Corp 2480 Railroad St *Web:* www.frontier-aluminum.com	Corona	CA	92880	951-735-1770	
Frontier Steel Company Inc 4990 Grand Ave *Web:* www.frontiersteel.com	Pittsburgh	PA	15225	412-865-4444	865-0030
Fry Steel Company Inc 13325 Molette St *Web:* www.frysteel.com	Santa Fe Springs	CA	90670	562-802-2721	
G & L Manufacturing Inc 1975 Fisk Rd *Web:* www.glmanufacturing.com	Cookeville	TN	38506	931-528-1732	
G B C Inc 190 S Union Blvd *Web:* www.gbcinc.com	Lakewood	CO	80228	303-988-6450	
Galesburg Castings Inc 940 Ave C St *Web:* www.galesburgcastings.com	Galesburg	IL	61401	309-343-6178	
Garston Sign & Screen Printing 570 Tolland St *Web:* www.garston.com	East Hartford	CT	06108	860-289-3040	
Gayle Manufacturing Company Inc 1455 E Kentucky Ave *Web:* www.gaylemfg.com	Woodland	CA	95776	530-662-0284	
GB Tubulars Inc 950 Threadneedle St Ste 130 *TF:* 888-245-3848 ■ *Web:* www.gbtubulars.com	Houston	TX	77079	713-465-3585	
General Steel Inc PO Box 1503 *TF:* 800-476-2794 ■ *Web:* www.steeldeal.com	Macon	GA	31202	478-746-2794	745-8136
Genesis Products Inc 2608 Almac Ct *Web:* www.genesisproductsinc.com	Elkhart	IN	46514	574-266-8292	
George Industries Inc 1 S Page St *Web:* www.georgeindustries.com	Endicott	NY	13760	607-748-3371	
Gerber Metal Supply Co 2 Boundary Rd **Fax Area Code:* 905 ■ *Web:* www.gerbermetal.com	Somerville	NJ	08876	908-823-9150	823-9160*
Gibbs Wire & Steel Company Inc Metals Dr PO Box 520 *TF:* 800-800-4422 ■ *Web:* www.gibbswire.com	Southington	CT	06489	860-621-0121	628-7780
Gilchrist Metal Fabricating Company Inc 18 Park Ave *Web:* www.gmfco.com	Hudson	NH	03051	603-889-2600	
Girard Machine Company Inc 700 Dot St *Web:* www.girardmachine.com	Girard	OH	44420	330-545-9731	
Glidewell Specialties Foundry Company Inc 600 Foundry Rd *Web:* www.glidewell-foundry.com	Calera	AL	35040	205-668-1881	
Global Brass & Copper Inc 475 N Martingale Rd Ste 1050 *Web:* www.gbcmetals.com	Schaumburg	IL	60173	847-240-4700	
Globe Iron Foundry Inc 5649 E Randolph St *Web:* www.globeiron.com	Commerce	CA	90040	323-723-8983	
Golden Aluminum Inc 1405 E 14th St *Web:* goldenaluminum.com	Fort Lupton	CO	80621	303-659-9767	
Gordon Aluminum Industries Inc 1000 Mason St *Web:* www.gordonaluminum.com	Schofield	WI	54476	715-359-6101	
Granite Industries Inc 595 E Lugbill Rd *Web:* www.graniteind.com	Archbold	OH	43502	419-445-4733	
Graphicast Inc 36 Knight St *Web:* www.graphicast.com	Jaffrey	NH	03452	603-532-4481	
Greenpoint Metals Inc 301 Shotwell Dr *Web:* www.greenpointmetals.com	Franklin	OH	45005	937-743-4075	
Griggs Steel Company Inc 1200 Souter Dr *Web:* www.griggssteel.com	Troy	MI	48083	248-298-0540	
H5 Colo 12712 Park Central Dr Ste 200 *Web:* www.h5colo.com	Dallas	TX	75251	469-533-0270	
Hanna Steel Corp 3812 Commerce Ave PO Box 558 *TF:* 800-633-8252 ■ *Web:* www.hannasteel.com	Fairfield	AL	35064	205-780-1111	783-8368
Hansen Architectural Systems 5500 Se Alexander St *TF:* 800-599-2965 ■ *Web:* aluminumrailing.com	Hillsboro	OR	97123	503-356-0959	
Harbor Steel & Supply Corp 1115 E Broadway *Web:* www.harborsteel.com	Muskegon	MI	49444	231-739-7152	
Hardwire LLC 1947 Clarke Ave. *Web:* www.hardwirellc.com	Pocomoke City	MD	21851	410-957-3669	
Hascall Steel Co 4165 Spartan Industrial Dr *Web:* www.hascallsteel.com	Grandville	MI	49418	616-531-8600	
Haven Steel Products Inc 13206 S Willison Rd *Web:* www.havensteel.com	Haven	KS	67543	620-465-2573	
Hawk Steel Industries Inc 4010 S Eden Rd *Web:* www.hawksteel.com	Kennedale	TX	76060	817-483-7511	516-0200
Helfrich Bros Boiler Works Inc 39 Merrimack St *Web:* www.hbbwinc.com	Lawrence	MA	01843	978-683-7244	
Howard Precision Metals Inc PO Box 240127 *TF:* 800-444-0311 ■ *Web:* www.howardprecision.com	Milwaukee	WI	53224	414-355-9611	355-2637
Hugo Neu Corp 120 Fifth Ave Ste 600 *Web:* www.hugoneu.com	New York	NY	10011	646-467-6700	
Hynes Industries 3760 Oakwood **Fax Area Code:* 330 ■ *TF:* 800-321-9257 ■ *Web:* www.hynesindustries.com	Youngstown	OH	44515	800-321-9257	799-9098*
Hytech Spring & Machine Corp 950 Lincoln Pkwy *Web:* www.hytechspring.com	Plainwell	MI	49080	269-685-1768	
Ideal Manufacturing Inc 2011 Harnish Blvd. *Web:* www.idealmfginc.com	Billings	MT	59101	406-656-4360	
IMS Buhrke-Olson 511 W Algonquin Rd *Web:* www.metalstamper.com	Arlington Heights	IL	60005	847-981-7550	
Independence Tube Corp 6226 W 74th St *Web:* www.independencetube.com	Chicago	IL	60638	708-496-0380	
Industrial Door Contractors Inc 820 Mayberry Springs Rd *Web:* www.hangardoor.com	Columbia	TN	38401	931-380-0463	
Industrial Material Corp 7701 Harborside Dr *TF:* 800-701-4462 ■ *Web:* www.industrialmaterial.com	Galveston	TX	77554	409-744-4538	744-1844

Company	City	State	ZIP	Phone	Fax
International Mold Steel Inc 6796 Powerline Dr *TF:* 800-625-6653 ■ *Web:* www.imsteel.com	Florence	KY	41042	859-342-6000	
Iowa Spring Manufacturing & Sales Co 2112 Greene St *Web:* www.iowaspring.com	Adel	IA	50003	515-993-4791	
Ironco Enterprises LLC 1025 E Broadway Rd *Web:* www.ironco.net	Phoenix	AZ	85040	602-243-5750	
J & E Earll Manufacturing 4500 Vly Industrial Blvd S *Web:* www.nybo.com	Shakopee	MN	55379	952-445-4500	
J Rubin & Company Inc 305 Peoples Ave *Web:* rockfordconsulting.com	Rockford	IL	61104	815-964-9471	
JDH Pacific Inc 15301 S Blackburn Ave *Web:* www.jdhpacific.com	Norwalk	CA	90650	562-926-8088	926-8066
John Sakash Company Inc 700 Walnut St *Web:* www.johnsakash.com	Elmhurst	IL	60126	630-833-3940	
JT Fennell Company Inc 1104 N Front St	Chillicothe	IL	61523	309-274-2145	
Kaiser Aluminum Canada Ltd 3021 Gore Rd *Web:* www.kaiseral.com	London	ON	N5V5A9	519-457-3610	
Kansas City Structural Steel Inc 3801 Raytown Rd *Web:* www.kcstructuralsteel.com	Kansas City	MO	64129	816-924-0977	
Kasco Fab Inc 4529 S Chestnut Ave	Fresno	CA	93725	559-442-1018	
Kemeny Overseas Products Corp The Civic Opera Bldg 20 N Wacker Dr Ste 1028 *Web:* www.kemenyoverseas.com	Chicago	IL	60606	312-857-0844	
Ken-Mac Metals Inc 17901 Englewood Dr *TF:* 800-831-9503 ■ *Web:* www.tkmna.com	Cleveland	OH	44130	440-234-7500	234-4459
Kenwal Steel Corp 8223 W Warren Ave *Web:* www.kenwal.com	Dearborn	MI	48126	313-739-1000	739-1001
Key Bellevilles Inc 100 Key Ln *TF:* 800-245-3600 ■ *Web:* www.keybellevilles.com	Leechburg	PA	15656	724-295-5111	
Keystone Profiles Ltd 220 Seventh Ave *Web:* www.keystoneprofiles.com	Beaver Falls	PA	15010	724-506-1500	
KGS Steel Inc 3725 Pine Ln *TF:* 800-533-3846 ■ *Web:* www.kgssteel.com	Bessemer	AL	35022	205-425-0800	
Kirsh Foundry Inc 125 Rowell St *Web:* www.kirshfoundry.com	Beaver Dam	WI	53916	920-887-0395	
Kivort Steel 380 Hudson River Rd *TF:* 800-462-2616 ■ *Web:* www.kivortsteel.com	Waterford	NY	12188	518-590-7233	235-2042
Klein Steel Service 105 Vanguarden Pkwy *TF Cust Svc:* 800-477-6789 ■ *Web:* www.kleinsteel.com	Rochester	NY	14606	585-328-4000	328-0470
KobeWieland Copper Products LLC 3990 US 311 Hwy N *Web:* www.wielandcopper.com	Pine Hall	NC	27042	336-445-4500	
Kovatch Castings Inc 3743 Tabs Dr *Web:* www.kovatchcastings.com	Uniontown	OH	44685	330-896-9944	
Kreher Steel Company LLC 1550 N 25th Ave **Fax Area Code:* 708 ■ *TF:* 800-323-0745 ■ *Web:* www.kreher.com	Melrose Park	IL	60160	800-323-0745	345-8293*
L Smith Cooper International Inc 2867 Vail Ave *Web:* www.smithcooper.com	Commerce	CA	90040	323-890-4455	890-4456
Laclede Chain Manufacturing Company LLC 1549 Fenpark Dr *Web:* www.lacledechain.com	Fenton	MO	63026	636-680-2320	
Laibe Corp 1414 Bates St *Web:* www.laibecorp.com	Indianapolis	IN	46201	317-231-2250	
Landmann Wire Rope Products Inc 1818 Gilbreth Rd Ste 148 *Web:* www.landmannwire.com	Burlingame	CA	94010	650-777-4210	
Lane Steel Co Inc 4 River Rd *Web:* www.lanesteel.com	McKees Rocks	PA	15136	412-777-1700	777-1709
Lapham-Hickey Steel Corp 5500 W 73rd St *TF:* 800-323-8443 ■ *Web:* www.lapham-hickey.com	Chicago	IL	60638	708-496-6111	496-8504
Latrobe Specialty Steel Co 2626 Ligonier St **Fax Area Code:* 302 ■ *TF:* 888-245-7856 ■ *Web:* www.cartech.com	Latrobe	PA	15650	724-537-7711	636-5454*
Lawler Foundry Corp 4908 Powell Ave S *Web:* www.lawlerfoundry.com	Birmingham	AL	35222	205-595-0596	
Lee Steel Corp 45525 Grand River Ave *Web:* www.leesteelcorp.com	Novi	MI	48374	313-925-2100	
LeMar Industries Corp 2070 NE 60th Ave *Web:* www.lemarindustries.com	Des Moines	IA	50313	515-266-7264	
Lexington Steel Corp 5443 W 70th Pl *Web:* www.lexsteel.com	Bedford Park	IL	60638	708-594-9200	
Liberty Casting Company LLC 550 S Liberty Rd *Web:* www.libertycasting.com	Delaware	OH	43015	740-363-1941	
Lindquist Steels Inc 1050 Woodend Rd **Fax Area Code:* 203 ■ *TF:* 800-243-9637 ■ *Web:* www.lindquiststeels.com	Stratford	CT	06615	800-243-9637	386-0132*
Lite Metals Co 700 N Walnut St *Web:* www.litemetals.com	Ravenna	OH	44266	330-296-6110	
Littell LLC 1211 Tower Rd *Web:* www.littell.com	Schaumburg	IL	60173	630-622-4700	
Livingston Pipe & Tube Inc 1612 Rt 4 N *TF:* 800-548-7473 ■ *Web:* www.livingstonpipeandtube.com	Staunton	IL	62088	618-635-8700	635-8720
LMS Reinforcing Steel Group Inc 6320 148th St *TF:* 888-698-2008 ■ *Web:* www.lmsgroup.ca	Surrey	BC	V3S3C4	604-598-9930	
Loeffel Steel Products PO Box 2100 *Web:* www.loeffelsteel.com	Barrington	IL	60011	847-382-6770	382-2487
Loveman Steel Corp 5455 Perkins Rd **Fax Area Code:* 440 ■ *TF:* 800-568-3626 ■ *Web:* www.lovemansteel.com	Bedford Heights	OH	44146	800-568-3626	232-0914*
M C Steel Inc 2 Braco International Blvd *Web:* www.mcsteel.com	Wilder	Ky	41076	859-781-8600	
Maas-Hansen Steel Corp 2435 E 37th St PO Box 58364 *TF:* 800-647-8335 ■ *Web:* www.maashansen.com	Vernon	CA	90058	323-586-0171	
Mac Metal Sales Inc 1650 W Hwy 80 *Web:* www.macmetalsales.com	Somerset	KY	42503	606-678-8331	
Macomb Group Inc, The 6600 E 15 Mile Rd *Web:* www.macombgroup.com	Sterling Heights	MI	48312	586-274-4100	
Magic Steel Sales LLC 4242 Clay Ave SW *Web:* www.magicsteelsales.com	Grand Rapids	MI	49548	616-532-4071	
Majestic Steel USA 5300 Majestic Pkwy *TF:* 800-321-5590 ■ *Web:* www.majesticsteel.com	Cleveland	OH	44146	440-786-2666	786-0576
Mandel Metals Inc 11400 W Addison Ave *Web:* www.mandelmetals.com	Franklin Park	IL	60131	847-455-6606	
Manzi Metals Inc 15293 Flight Path Dr *Web:* www.manzimetals.com	Brooksville	FL	34604	352-799-8211	
Marchant Schmidt Inc 24 W Larsen Dr *Web:* www.marchantschmidt.net	Fond Du Lac	WI	54937	920-921-4760	
Marks Metal Technology Inc 10300 Se Jennifer St *Web:* www.marksmetal.com	Clackamas	OR	97015	503-656-0901	
Marmon/Keystone Corp PO Box 992 *TF:* 800-544-1748 ■ *Web:* www.marmonkeystone.com	Butler	PA	16003	724-283-3000	283-0558
Maruichi American Corp 11529 Greenstone Ave *Web:* www.macsfs.com	Santa Fe Springs	CA	90670	562-903-8600	
Masterloy Products Ltd 5663 Doncaster Rd *Web:* www.masterloy.com	Ottawa	ON	K1G3N4	613-822-1010	
Matenaer Corp 810 Schoenhaar Dr *TF:* 800-254-0873 ■ *Web:* www.matenaer.com	West Bend	WI	53090	262-338-0700	338-3491
Mattsco Supply Co 1111 N 161st E Ave *Web:* www.mattsco.org	Tulsa	OK	74116	918-836-0451	
Maumee Valley Fabricators 4801 Bennett Rd *Web:* www.maumeevalleyfab.com	Toledo	OH	43612	419-476-1411	
Mazel & Company Inc 4300 W Ferdinand St *TF:* 800-525-4023 ■ *Web:* www.mazelandco.com	Chicago	IL	60624	773-533-1600	533-9490
McLanahan Corp 200 Wall St *Web:* www.mclanahan.com	Hollidaysburg	PA	16648	814-695-9807	
McNichols Co 9401 Corporate Lake Dr **Fax Area Code:* 813 ■ *TF:* 877-884-4653 ■ *Web:* www.mcnichols.com	Tampa	FL	33634	877-884-4653	243-1888*
Mead Metals Inc 555 Cardigan Rd *Web:* www.meadmetals.com	St. Paul	MN	55126	651-484-1400	
Medley Steel & Supply Inc 9925 Nw 116th Way *Web:* www.medleysteel.com	Medley	FL	33178	305-863-7480	
Meloon Foundries Inc 1841 Lemoyne Ave *Web:* www.meloon.com	Syracuse	NY	13208	315-454-3231	
Mercer Metals 1249 Ave R *Web:* www.mercermetals.com	Grand Prairie	TX	75050	972-790-1576	
Merfish Pipe & Supply Co PO Box 15879 *TF:* 800-869-5731 ■ *Web:* www.merfish.com	Houston	TX	77220	713-869-5731	867-0738
Merit USA 620 Clark Ave **Fax Area Code:* 925 ■ *TF:* 800-445-6374 ■ *Web:* www.meritsteel.com	Pittsburg	CA	94565	800-445-6374	427-6427*
Metal & Wire Products Co 1065 Salem Pkwy *Web:* www.metalandwire.com	Salem	OH	44460	330-332-9448	
Metal Supermarkets IP Inc 520 Abilene Dr 2nd Fl *TF:* 866-867-9344 ■ *Web:* www.metalsupermarkets.com	Mississauga	ON	L5T2H7	905-362-8226	
Metalcraft of Mayville Inc 1000 Metalcraft Dr *Web:* www.mtlcraft.com	Mayville	WI	53050	920-387-3150	
Metals Supply Company Ltd 5311 Clinton Dr *Web:* deltasteel.com	Houston	TX	77020	713-330-8080	
Metaltech Service Center Inc 9915 Monroe *Web:* www.metaltechsc.com	Houston	TX	77075	713-991-5100	
Metrolina Steel Inc 2601 Westinghouse Blvd *Web:* www.metrolinasteel.com	Charlotte	NC	28273	704-598-7007	897-2173
Metropolitan Alloys Corp 17385 Ryan Rd *Web:* www.metroalloys.com	Detroit	MI	48212	313-366-4443	366-9698
Michigan Extruded Aluminum Corp 205 Watts Rd *Web:* www.extrude.net	Jackson	MI	49203	517-764-5400	
Mid City Steel Fabricating Inc 115 Buchner Pl *Web:* www.mid-citysteel.com	La Crosse	WI	54603	608-782-0770	
Mid South Steel Inc 15 Welborn St *Web:* www.midsouthsteelinc.com	Pelham	AL	35124	205-663-1750	
Midwest Iron & Metal Co Inc 700 S Main St *Web:* www.midwestironandmetal.com	Hutchinson	KS	67504	620-662-0551	
Miller J Walter Company Brass Foundry 411 E Chestnut St *Web:* www.jwaltermiller.com	Lancaster	PA	17602	717-392-7428	
Miller Metals Service Corp 2400 Bond St *Web:* www.millermetals.com	University Park	IL	60484	708-534-7200	534-7211
Miller Technical Services Inc 7444 Haggerty Rd *Web:* www.mtsmedicalmfg.com	Canton	MI	48187	734-738-1970	
Minmetals Inc 120 Schor Ave *Web:* www.minmetalsusa.com	Leonia	NJ	07605	201-809-1898	
Mitsubishi International Corp 655 Third Ave *Web:* www.mitsubishicorp.com	New York	NY	10017	212-605-2000	
Morris Bean & Co 777 E Hyde Rd *Web:* www.morrisbean.com	Yellow Springs	OH	45387	937-767-7301	
Motion Dynamics Corp 5625 Airline Rd *Web:* www.motiondc.com	Fruitport	MI	49415	231-865-7400	
Mountain States Steel Inc 325 S Geneva Rd *Web:* www.mssteel.com	Lindon	UT	84042	801-785-5085	
Mueller Metals LLC 2152 Schwartz Rd *Web:* www.muellermetals.com	San Angelo	TX	76904	325-651-9558	
MultAlloy Inc 8511 Monroe St *TF:* 800-568-9551 ■ *Web:* www.multalloy.com	Houston	TX	77061	800-568-9551	
Murphy & Nolan Inc 340 Peat St PO Box 6689 *TF:* 800-836-6385 ■ *Web:* www.murphynolan.com	Syracuse	NY	13217	315-474-8203	474-8208
Myers & Company Architectural Metals 555 Basalt Ave *Web:* www.myersandco.com	Basalt	CO	81621	970-927-4761	
Napco Steel Inc 1800 Arthur Dr *TF:* 800-292-8010 ■ *Web:* www.napcosteel.com	West Chicago	IL	60185	630-293-1900	293-0881
National Bronze & Metals Inc 2929 W 12th St *Web:* www.nbmmetals.com	Houston	TX	77008	713-869-9600	869-0883

Company	City	State	ZIP	Phone	Fax
National Copper & Smelting Company Inc 3333 Stanwood Blvd. *Web:* www.nationaltube.com	Huntsville	AL	35811	256-859-4510	
National Electronic Alloys Inc 3 Fir Ct *Web:* www.nealloys.com	Oakland	NJ	07436	201-337-9400	337-9698
National Material LP 1965 Pratt Blvd. *Web:* www.nmlp.com	Elk Grove Village	IL	60007	847-284-8464	806-4722
National Specialty Alloys LLC 18250 Keith Harrow Blvd *TF General:* 800-847-5653 ■ *Web:* www.nsalloys.com	Houston	TX	77084	281-345-2115	345-1133
National Tube Supply Co 925 Central Ave *TF:* 800-229-6872 ■ *Web:* www.nationaltubesupply.com	University Park	IL	60466	708-534-2700	534-0200
Nelsen Steel & Wire LP 9400 W Belmont Ave *Web:* www.nelsensteel.com	Franklin Park	IL	60131	847-671-9700	
New Process Steel Corp 5800 Westview Dr *TF:* 800-392-4989 ■ *Web:* www.nps.cc/?pgid=home	Houston	TX	77055	713-686-9631	686-5358
Nikkei MC Aluminum America Inc 6875 S Inwood Dr. *Web:* www.nmaluminum.net	Columbus	IN	47201	812-342-1141	
Nippon Steel USA Inc 1251 Ave of the Americas Ste 2320	New York	NY	10020	212-486-7150	593-3049
NMI Industrial Holdings Inc 8503 Weyand Ave. *Web:* www.nmiindustrial.com	Sacramento	CA	95828	916-635-7030	
Noble Steel Inc 1741 W Lincoln St. *Web:* www.noblesteelinc.com	Phoenix	AZ	85007	602-257-8822	
North American Steel Co 18300 Miles Ave. *TF:* 800-321-9310 ■ *Web:* www.northamerican-steel.com	Cleveland	OH	44128	216-475-7300	475-6143
North Shore Steel 1566 Miles St *Web:* www.nssco.com	Houston	TX	77015	713-453-3533	671-5500
North Star BlueScope Steel LLC 6767 County Rd **Fax Area Code:* 888 ■ *Web:* www.northstarbluescope.com	Delta	OH	43515	419-822-2210	822-2113*
Northeast Air Solutions Inc 3 Lopez Rd *Web:* www.air-eng.com	Wilmington	MA	01887	978-988-2000	988-2200
Northern Metal Fab Inc 510 Vandeberg St *Web:* www.nmfinc.com	Baldwin	WI	54002	715-684-3535	
Northwest Aluminum Specialties Inc 2929 W Second St *TF:* 800-626-2241 ■ *Web:* www.nwaluminum.com	The Dalles	OR	97058	541-296-6161	
Northwest Grating Products Inc 9230 Fourth Ave S *Web:* www.network1000.com	Seattle	WA	98108	206-767-3000	
Nucor Steel Marion Inc 912 Cheney Ave. *Web:* www.nucorhighway.com	Marion	OH	43302	740-383-4011	
O'neal Flat Rolled Metals 1229 S Fulton Ave. *TF:* 800-336-3365 ■ *Web:* www.ofrmetals.com	Brighton	CO	80601	303-654-0300	
O'Neal Steel Inc 744 41st St N **Fax:* Sales ■ *TF:* 800-861-8272 ■ *Web:* www.onealsteel.com	Birmingham	AL	35222	205-599-8000	599-8037*
Oberdorfer LLC 6259 Thompson Rd	Syracuse	NY	13206	315-437-7588	
Ohio Valley Aluminum Company LLC 1100 Brooks Industrial Rd *Web:* www.ovaco.com	Shelbyville	KY	40065	502-633-2783	
Olympic Foundry Inc 5200 Airport Way S *Web:* www.olympicfoundry.com	Seattle	WA	98108	206-764-6200	
Olympic Steel Inc 5096 Richmond Rd *NASDAQ: ZEUS* ■ **Fax:* Sales ■ *TF:* 800-321-6290 ■ *Web:* www.olysteel.com	Bedford Heights	OH	44146	216-292-3800	292-3974*
Omega Steel Co 3460 Hollenberg Dr *Web:* www.assetcontrols.com	Bridgeton	MO	63044	314-209-0992	
OnlineMetals.com 1138 W Ewing *TF:* 800-533-6350 ■ *Web:* www.onlinemetals.com	Seattle	WA	98119	800-533-6350	
Orlando Spring Corp 11131 Winners Cir *Web:* www.orlandospring.com	Los Alamitos	CA	90720	562-594-8411	
Oshkosh Coil Spring Inc 3575 N Main St *Web:* www.oshkoshcoilspring.com	Oshkosh	WI	54901	920-235-7620	
Overseas Development Corp 953 Washington Blvd *Web:* www.overseasdevelopment.com	Stamford	CT	06901	203-964-0111	964-4929
Owen Industries Inc 501 Ave H *TF:* 800-831-9252 ■ *Web:* www.owenind.com	Carter Lake	IA	51510	712-347-5500	347-6166
P & W Industries LLC 68668 Hwy 59 *Web:* www.pandwindustries.com	Mandeville	LA	70470	985-892-2461	
PA Inc 6626 Gulf Fwy *Web:* www.painc.com	Houston	TX	77087	713-570-4900	
Pacesetter Steel Service Inc 1045 Big Shanty Rd *TF:* 800-749-6505 ■ *Web:* www.teampacesetter.com	Kennesaw	GA	30144	770-919-8000	
Pacific Alloy Castings Company Inc 5900 E Firestone Blvd. *Web:* www.pacificalloy.com	South Gate	CA	90280	562-928-1387	
Pacific Industrial Development Corp 4788 Runway Blvd *Web:* www.pidc.com	Ann Arbor	MI	48108	734-930-9292	
Pacific Steel & Recycling 1401 Third St NW. *TF:* 800-889-6264 ■ *Web:* pacific-steel.com	Great Falls	MT	59404	406-771-7222	
Packaging Inc 6775 Shady Oak Rd *Web:* www.packinc.com	Eden Prairie	MN	55344	952-935-3421	
Paco Steel & Engineering Corp 19818 S Alameda St *TF:* 800-421-1473 ■ *Web:* www.pacosteel.com	Rancho Dominguez	CA	90221	310-537-6375	
Palmer Manufacturing 18 N Bechtle Ave *TF:* 800-457-5456 ■ *Web:* www.palmermfg.com	Springfield	OH	45504	937-323-6339	
Paragon Steel Enterprises LLC 4211 County Rd 61 *TF:* 800-411-5677 ■ *Web:* www.pstparagonsteel.com	Butler	IN	46721	260-868-1100	868-1101
Parker Steel Co PO Box 2883 *TF:* 800-333-4140 ■ *Web:* www.metricmetal.com	Toledo	OH	43606	419-473-2481	471-2655
PC Campana Inc 1374 E 28th St *Web:* www.pccampana.com	Lorain	OH	44055	440-246-6500	
Peerless Steel Corp 2450 Austin *TF:* 800-482-3947 ■ *Web:* www.peerlesssteel.com	Troy	MI	48083	248-528-3200	528-9144
Pelco Structural LLC 1501 Industrial Blvd. *Web:* www.pelcostructural.com	Claremore	OK	74017	918-283-4004	
Penn Mar Castings Inc 500 Broadway *Web:* www.pennmarcastings.com	Hanover	PA	17331	717-632-4165	
Pennex Aluminum Company LLC 50 Community St *Web:* www.pennexaluminum.com	Wellsville	PA	17365	717-432-9647	
Pennfab Inc 1431 Ford Rd. *Web:* www.pennfab.com	Bensalem	PA	19020	215-245-1577	
Pentz Design Pattern & Foundry 14823 Main St Ne. *TF:* 800-411-6555 ■ *Web:* www.pentzcastsolutions.com	Duvall	WA	98019	425-788-6490	
Perforated Tubes Inc 4850 Fulton St E *TF:* 888-869-5736 ■ *Web:* www.perforatedtubes.com	Ada	MI	49301	616-942-4550	
Peridot Corp 1072 Serpentine Ln. *Web:* www.peridotcorp.com	Pleasanton	CA	94566	925-461-8830	
Peterson Steel Corp 61 W Mountain St *TF:* 800-325-3245 ■ *Web:* www.petersonsteel.com	Worcester	MA	01606	508-853-3630	853-7485
Phillips & Johnston Inc 21w179 Hill Ave *TF:* 877-411-8823	Glen Ellyn	IL	60137	630-469-8150	469-8048
Phoenix Electronic Enterprises Inc 131 Tillson Ave EXT *Web:* www.phoenixmfg.com	Highland	NY	12528	845-691-7700	691-7759
Phoenix Metals Co 4685 Buford Hwy *TF:* 800-241-2290 ■ *Web:* www.phoenixmetals.net	Norcross	GA	30071	770-447-4211	
Phoenix Tube Company Inc 1185 Win Dr. *Web:* www.phoenixtube.com	Bethlehem	PA	18017	610-865-5337	
Pier Foundry & Pattern Shop Inc 51 State St *Web:* www.pierfoundry.com	Saint Paul	MN	55107	651-222-4461	
Pierce Aluminum 34 Forge Pkwy *Web:* www.piercealuminum.com	Franklin	MA	02038	508-541-7007	541-6077
Pioneer Steel Corp 7447 Intervale St *TF:* 800-999-9440 ■ *Web:* pioneersteel.us	Detroit	MI	48238	313-933-9400	933-1621
Plymouth Foundry Inc 523 W Harrison St *Web:* www.plymouthfoundry.com	Plymouth	IN	46563	574-936-2106	
Polymet Alloys Inc 1701 Providence Pk Ste 100 *Web:* www.polymetalloys.com	Birmingham	AL	35242	205-981-2200	
Portland Products Inc 271 Morse Dr *Web:* www.portlandproducts.com	Portland	MI	48875	517-647-4191	
Posner Industries Inc 8641 Edgeworth Dr. *TF:* 888-767-6377 ■ *Web:* www.posners.com	Capitol Heights	MD	20743	301-350-1000	350-1050
Precision Metal Services Inc 418 Stump Rd. *Web:* www.precisionmetalservices.com	Montgomeryville	PA	18936	215-661-0225	
Precision Steel Manufacturing Corp 1723 Seibel Dr Ne *Web:* precisionsteelmfg.com	Roanoke	VA	24012	540-985-8963	
Precision Steel Warehouse Inc 3500 Wolf Rd *TF:* 800-323-0740 ■ *Web:* www.precisionsteel.com	Franklin Park	IL	60131	847-455-7000	455-1341
Precision Tube Company Inc 287 Wissahickon Ave *Web:* www.precisiontube.com	North Wales	PA	19454	215-699-5801	
Premier Aluminum LLC 3633 S Memorial Dr. *Web:* www.premieraluminum.com	Racine	WI	53403	262-554-2100	
Prince & Izant Co 12999 Plz Dr *Web:* www.princeizant.com	Cleveland	OH	44130	216-362-7000	
PRL Aluminum 14760 Don Julian Rd. *Web:* www.prlaluminum.com	City Of Industry	CA	91746	626-968-7507	
Pro Company Sound Inc 225 Parsons St. *Web:* www.procosound.com	Kalamazoo	MI	49007	269-388-9675	
Process Sensors Corp 113 Cedar St *Web:* www.processsensors.com	Milford	MA	01757	508-473-9901	
Quality Manufacturing Corp 4300 Nw Urbandale Dr *Web:* qualitymfgcorp.com	Urbandale	IA	50322	515-331-4300	
Quality Metals Inc 2575 Doswell Ave *Web:* www.qualitymetalsinc.com	St Paul	MN	55108	651-645-5875	
R&S Steel Co 3811 Joliet St *Web:* www.rssteel.com	Denver	CO	80239	303-321-9660	
Rancocas Metals Corp 35 Indel Ave *TF:* 800-762-6382 ■ *Web:* www.rancocasmetals.com	Rancocas	NJ	08073	609-267-4120	267-5690
Randall Metals Corp 2483 Greenleaf Ave. *Web:* www.randallmetals.com	Elk Grove Village	IL	60007	847-952-9690	
Ranger Steel Supply Corp 1225 N Loop W Ste 650 *Web:* www.rangersteel.com	Houston	TX	77008	713-633-1306	
Rangers Die Casting Co 10828 S Alameda St *TF:* 877-386-9969 ■ *Web:* www.rangersdiecasting.com	Lynwood	CA	90262	310-764-1800	
Ratner Steel Supply Company Inc 2500 W County Rd B *Web:* www.ratnersteel.com	Roseville	MN	55113	651-631-8515	
Rayco Industries Inc 1502 Valley Rd. *TF:* 800-505-7111 ■ *Web:* www.raycoindustries.com	Richmond	VA	23222	804-321-7111	
Redline Industries Inc 8401 Mosley Rd *Web:* www.redlineindustries.com	Houston	TX	77075	713-946-5355	946-0747
Reliance Steel & Aluminum Co 350 S Grand Ave Ste 5100 *NYSE: RS* ■ *Web:* www.rsac.com	Los Angeles	CA	90071	213-687-7700	687-8792
Remelt Sources Inc 27151 Tungsten Rd *Web:* www.remeltsources.com	Cleveland	OH	44132	216-289-4555	289-0939
Rigidized Metals Corp 658 Ohio St. *Web:* www.rigidized.com	Buffalo	NY	14203	716-849-4760	
Rj Torching Inc 5061 Energy Dr *Web:* www.rjtorching.com	Flint	MI	48505	810-785-9759	
RMD Instruments LLC 44 Hunt St *Web:* rmdinc.com	Watertown	MA	02472	617-668-6900	
Robert-James Sales Inc 2585 Walden Ave *Web:* www.rjsales.com	Buffalo	NY	14225	716-651-6000	

Phone Fax

Rochester Aluminum Smelting Canada Ltd
31-35 Freshway Dr ... Concord ON L4K1R9 905-669-1222
Web: www.rochesteraluminum.com

Rockingham Steel Inc
2565 John Wayland Hwy ... Harrisonburg VA 22803 540-433-3000
Web: www.rockinghamsteel.com

Rolled Alloys Inc 125 W Sterns Rd ... Temperance MI 48182 734-847-0561 847-6917
TF: 800-521-0332 ■ *Web:* www.rolledalloys.com

Rolled Steel Products Corp
2187 Garfield Ave ... Los Angeles CA 90040 323-723-8836 888-9866
TF: 800-400-7833 ■ *Web:* www.rolledsteel.com

Ross Aluminum Castings LLC 815 N Oak Ave ... Sidney OH 45365 937-492-4134
Web: www.rossal.com

Ross Casting & Innovation LLC
402 S Kuther Rd PO Box 89 ... Sidney OH 45365 937-497-4500
Web: www.rciwheels.com

Roton Products Inc 660 E Elliott Ave ... Saint Louis MO 63122 314-821-4400
Web: www.roton.com

Rowe Foundry Inc
147 W Cumberland St PO Box 130 ... Martinsville IL 62442 217-382-4135
Web: www.rowefoundry.com

Russel Metals Inc 6600 Financial Dr ... Mississauga ON L5N7J6 905-819-7777 819-7409
TSE: RUS ■ *TF:* 800-268-0750 ■ *Web:* www.russelmetals.com

Russellville Steel Company Inc
PO Box 1538 ... Russellville AR 72811 479-968-2211 968-3486
Web: www.rsvlsteel.com

Ryerson Inc 227 W Monroe St ... Chicago IL 60606 312-292-5000
Web: www.ryerson.com

S & S Steel Services Inc 444 E 29th St ... Anderson IN 46016 765-622-4545 622-4556
Web: www.sssteelservices.com

Sabel Steel Industries Inc 749 N Ct St ... Montgomery AL 36104 334-265-6771 264-3692
Web: www.sabelsteel.com

Sager Metal Strip Company LLC
100 Boone Dr ... Michigan City IN 46360 219-874-3609
Web: www.sagermetal.com

Saginaw Pipe Company Inc
1980 Hwy 31 S PO Box 8 ... Saginaw AL 35137 205-664-3670 838-8069*
**Fax Area Code:* 717 ■ *TF:* 800-433-1374 ■ *Web:* www.saginawpipe.com

Salit Steel Ltd 7771 Stanley Ave ... Niagara Falls ON L2E6V6 905-354-5691
TF: 800-263-7110 ■ *Web:* www.salitsteel.com

Salzgitter Mannesmann International (USA) Inc
1770 St James Pl Ste 500 ... Houston TX 77056 713-386-7900
Web: www.salzgitter-usa.com

Sandvik Process Systems LLC 21 Campus Rd ... Totowa NJ 07512 973-790-1600
Web: www.processsystems.sandvik.com

SB International Inc 3626 N Hall St Ste 910 ... Dallas TX 75219 214-526-4423 526-1503
Web: sbisteel.com

Scandic Spring Inc 700 Montague St ... San Leandro CA 94577 510-352-3700
Web: www.scandic.com

Searing Industries Inc
8901 Arrow Route ... Rancho Cucamonga CA 91730 909-948-3030
Web: www.searingindustries.com

Seneca Foundry Inc
240 Mackinlay Kantor Dr ... Webster City IA 50595 515-832-1722
Web: www.senecafoundry.com

Service Steel Aerospace Corp 4609 70th St E ... Fife WA 98424 800-426-9794
TF: 800-426-9794 ■ *Web:* www.ssa-corp.com

Service Steel Inc
4208 E Schrimsher Lane SW Ste 2B7 ... Huntsville AL 35805 503-224-9500 243-6697

SH Enterprises Inc 4000 Central Dr ... Wausau WI 54401 715-848-1200
Web: www.shenter.com

Shamrock Steel Sales Inc 238 W County Rd S ... Odessa TX 79763 432-337-2317 337-5049
TF: 800-299-2317 ■ *Web:* www.shamrocksteelsales.com

Shannon Precision Fastener LLC
31600 Stephenson Hwy ... Madison Heights MI 48071 248-589-9670
Web: www.shannonpf.com

Sheffield Metals International Inc
5467 Evergreen Pkwy ... Sheffield Village OH 44054 440-934-8500
TF: 800-283-5262 ■ *Web:* www.sheffieldmetals.com

Shultz Steel Company Inc
5321 Firestone Blvd ... South Gate CA 90280 323-564-3281
Web: www.shultzsteel.com

Sibel Ayse Halac Iron Works Inc
21675 Ashgrove Ct ... Sterling VA 20166 703-406-4766
Web: www.sahalac.com

Sierra Aluminum Co 2345 Fleetwood Dr ... Riverside CA 92509 951-781-7800
Web: www.sierraaluminum.com

Sim-Tex LP 20880 FM 362 Rd ... Waller TX 77484 713-450-3940
Web: www.sim-tex.com

Siskin Steel & Supply Co Inc
1901 Riverfront Pkwy ... Chattanooga TN 37408 423-756-3671 756-3671
TF: 800-756-3671 ■ *Web:* www.siskin.com

Skol Manufacturing Co 4444 N Ravenswood Ave ... Chicago IL 60640 773-878-5959
Web: skolmfg.com

Skyline Steel LLC 8 Woodhollow Rd Ste 102 ... Parsippany NJ 07054 866-875-9546
TF: 866-875-9546 ■ *Web:* www.skylinesteel.com

SMC Metal Fabricators Inc 2100 S Oakwood Rd ... Oshkosh WI 54904 920-426-6080
Web: www.smcmetal.com

Smithahn Company Inc 836 E N St ... Bethlehem PA 18017 610-866-4461
Web: smithahn.com

Soleno Inc
1160 Rt 133 CP 837 ... Saint-jean-sur-richelieu QC J2X4J5 450-347-7855
TF: 877-633-7473 ■ *Web:* www.soleno.com

Solidiform Inc 3928 Lawnwood St ... Fort Worth TX 76111 817-831-2626 831-8258
Web: www.solidiform.com

Solon Manufacturing Co 425 Center St ... Chardon OH 44024 440-286-7149
TF: 800-323-9717 ■ *Web:* www.solonmfg.com

South st Paul Steel Supply Company Inc
200 Hardman Ave N ... South Saint Paul MN 55075 651-451-6666
Web: www.sspss.com

Southern Copper & Supply Company Inc
875 Yeager Pkwy ... Pelham AL 35124 205-664-9440
TF: 800-289-2728 ■ *Web:* www.southerncopper.com

Phone Fax

Southern Precision Spring Company Inc
2200 Old Steele Creek Rd ... Charlotte NC 28208 704-392-4393
Web: www.spspring.com

Southern Tank & Manufacturing Inc
1501 Haynes Ave ... Owensboro KY 42303 270-684-2321
Web: www.southerntank.net

Southern Wire Corp 8045 Metro Rd ... Olive Branch MS 38654 662-890-4873
TF: 800-238-0333 ■ *Web:* www.southernwire.com

Southwest Metalsmiths Inc 5026 E Beverly Rd ... Phoenix AZ 85044 602-438-8577
Web: www.swmetalsmiths.com

Southwest Steel Casting Co 600 Foundry Dr ... Longview TX 75604 903-759-3946 759-3224
Web: www.swscc.com

Southwestern Suppliers Inc 6815 E 14th Ave ... Tampa FL 33619 813-626-2193 628-0511
Web: www.sowes.com

Special Metals Inc 6406 S Eastern Ave ... Oklahoma City OK 73129 405-677-7700
Web: www.specialmetalsinc.com

Specialty Metals Corp 8300 S 206th St ... Kent WA 98032 253-398-1730
Web: www.specialtymetalscorp.com

Specialty Pipe & Tube Inc PO Box 516 ... Mineral Ridge OH 44440 330-505-8262 505-8260
TF: 800-842-5839 ■ *Web:* www.specialtypipe.com

Spectra Aluminum Products Inc
95 Reagens Industrial Pkwy ... Bradford ON L3Z2A4 905-778-8093
TF: 866-999-2586 ■ *Web:* www.spectraaluminum.com

St. Louis Cold Drawn Inc 1060 Pershall Rd ... St. Louis MO 63137 314-867-4301
Web: www.stlcd.com

St. Louis Pipe & Supply Inc
17740 Edison Ave ... Chesterfield MO 63005 636-391-2500
Web: www.stlpipesupply.com

St. Marys Foundry 409 E S St ... Saint Marys OH 45885 419-394-3346
Web: www.stmfoundry.com

Standard Wire & Steel Works
16255 Vincennes Ave ... South Holland IL 60473 708-333-8300
Web: www.standardwiresteel.com

State Pipe & Supply Inc
9615 S Norwalk Blvd ... Santa Fe Springs CA 90670 562-695-5555 692-1054
TF: 800-733-6410 ■ *Web:* www.statepipe.com

State Steel Supply Co 214 Court St ... Sioux City IA 51101 712-277-4000
Web: www.statesteel.com

Staub Metals Corp 7747 E Rosecrans Ave ... Paramount CA 90723 562-602-2200 633-1456
TF: 800-447-8282 ■ *Web:* www.staubmetals.com

Steal Network LLC
2181 California Ave Ste 400 ... Salt Lake City UT 84104 801-210-0304
Web: www.stealnetwork.com

Steel & Pipe Supply Co 555 Poyntz Ave ... Manhattan KS 66502 785-587-5100 587-5174
Web: www.spsci.com

Steel Edge Inc (SEI) 716 W Mesquite Ave ... Las Vegas NV 89106 702-386-0023
Web: www.steeledgeinc.com

Steel LLC 405 N Clarendon Ave ... Scottdale GA 30079 404-292-7373
Web: www.steelincga.com

Steel Supply Co, The 5101 Newport Dr ... Rolling Meadows IL 60008 800-323-7571 828-1553
TF: 800-323-7571 ■ *Web:* www.steelsupply.com

Steel Technologies Inc
15415 Shelbyville Rd ... Louisville KY 40245 502-245-2110
Web: www.steeltechnologies.com

Steel Unlimited Inc 456 W Valley Blvd ... Rialto CA 92376 909-873-1222
TF: 800-544-6453 ■ *Web:* www.steelunlimited.com

Steel Warehouse Company Inc
2722 W Tucker Dr ... South Bend IN 46619 574-236-5100 236-5154
TF: 800-348-2529 ■ *Web:* www.steelwarehouse.com

Steel Works LLC, The
1020 Niedringhaus Ave ... Granite City IL 62040 618-452-2833
Web: www.tsw.com

Steelhead Partners LLC
333 - 108th Ave NE Ste 2010 ... Bellevue WA 98004 425-974-3788
Web: www.steelheadpartners.com

SteelSalvor LLC
3027 Marina Bay Dr Ste 350 ... League City TX 77573 281-724-8892
Web: steelsalvor.com

Steelways Inc 401 S Water St ... Newburgh NY 12553 845-562-0860
Web: www.steelwaysinc.com

Sterling Pipe & Tube Inc 5335 Enterprise Blvd ... Toledo OH 43612 419-729-9756
Web: www.sterlingpipeandtube.com

Steven F O'Donnell Inc 6724 Binder Ln ... Elkridge MD 21075 410-796-7968
Web: www.stevenfodonnellinc.com

Steward Steel Inc
1219 E US Hwy 62 PO Box 551 ... Sikeston MO 63801 573-471-2121 471-2336
Web: www.stewardsteel.com

Stewart Amos Steel Inc 4400 Paxton St ... Harrisburg PA 17111 717-564-3931
Web: www.stewart-amos.com

Stripco Inc 56598 Magnetic Dr ... Mishawaka IN 46545 574-256-7800
Web: www.stripco.com

Structurlam Products Ltd
2176 Government St ... Penticton BC V2A8B5 250-492-8912
Web: www.structurlam.com

Sunbelt Metals & Manufacturing Inc
920 S Bradshaw Rd ... Apopka FL 32703 407-889-8960
Web: www.sunbeltmetals.com

Supra Alloys Inc 351 Cortez Cir ... Camarillo CA 93012 805-388-2138 987-6492
TF: 888-647-8772 ■ *Web:* www.supraalloys.com

Sylvania Steel Corp 4169 Holland Sylvania Rd ... Toledo OH 43623 419-885-3838
TF General: 800-435-0986 ■ *Web:* www.sylvaniasteel.com

T&B Tube Co 15525 S LaSalle St ... South Holland IL 60473 708-333-1282
Web: www.tbtube.com

Taco Metals Inc 50 NE 179th St ... Miami FL 33162 305-652-8566 770-2387
TF: 800-653-8568 ■ *Web:* www.tacometals.com

Tarrier Steel Company Inc, The
1379 S 22nd St ... Columbus OH 43206 614-444-4000
Web: www.tarrier.com

Tata Steel International (Americas) Inc
475 N Martingale Rd Ste 400 ... Schaumburg IL 60173 847-619-0400
Web: www.tatasteelamericas.com

Tate Ornamental Inc 411 Industrial Dr ... White House TN 37188 615-672-0348
Web: www.tateornamental.com

				Phone	Fax
Tazewell Machine Works Inc 2015 S Second St. Web: www.tazewellmachine.com	Pekin	IL	61554	309-347-3181	
TCI Aluminum/North Inc 2353 Davis Ave. TF: 800-824-6197 ■ Web: www.tcialuminum.com	Hayward	CA	94545	510-786-3750	786-3302
Tenenbaum Recycling Group 4500 W Bethany Rd. Web: www.trg.net	North Little Rock	AR	72117	501-945-0881	945-3865
Terra Nova Steel & Iron (Ontario) Inc 3595 Hawkestone Rd. TF: 877-427-0269 ■ Web: www.terranovasteel.ca	Mississauga	ON	L5C2V1	905-273-3872	273-6553
Texas Pipe & Supply Co Inc 2330 Holmes Rd. TF: 800-233-8736 ■ Web: www.texaspipe.com	Houston	TX	77051	713-799-9235	799-8701
Texas Steel Processing Inc 5480 Windfern Rd. Web: www.txstl.com	Houston	TX	77041	281-822-3200	
Thermo Vac Inc 201 W Oakwood Rd. Web: www.thermovac.com	Oxford	MI	48371	248-969-0300	
Thompson Aluminum Casting Co 5161 Canal Rd. Web: www.thompsoncasting.com	Cleveland	OH	44125	216-206-2781	
Three D Metals Inc 5462 Innovation Dr. Web: www.threedmetals.com	Valley City	OH	44280	330-220-0451	
ThyssenKrupp Materials NA 22355 W 11 Mile Rd. TF: 800-926-2600 ■ Web: www.tkmna.com	Southfield	MI	48033	248-233-5600	233-5600
Thyssenkrupp Steel North America Inc 22355 W Eleven Mile Rd. Web: www.tksna.com	Southfield	MI	48033	248-233-5614	
Tioga Pipe Supply Company Inc 2450 Wheatsheaf Ln. TF: 800-523-3678 ■ Web: www.tiogapipe.com	Philadelphia	PA	19137	215-831-0700	533-1645
Titan Steel Corp 2500-B Broening Hwy. Web: www.titansteel.com	Baltimore	MD	21224	410-631-5200	631-5220
Titus Steel Co Ltd 6767 Invader Cres. Web: www.titussteel.com	Mississauga	ON	L5T2B7	905-564-2446	
Tollman Spring Company Inc 91 Enterprise Dr. Web: www.tollmanspring.com	Bristol	CT	06010	860-583-1326	
Tomson Steel Co (Inc) PO Box 940. *Fax Area Code: 513 ■ TF: 800-837-3001 ■ Web: www.tomsonsteel.com	Middletown	OH	45042	800-837-3001	420-8610*
Tooling Technology LLC 100 Enterprise Dr. Web: www.toolingtechgroup.com	Fort Loramie	OH	45845	937-295-3672	
Torrance Casting Inc 3131 Commerce St. Web: www.torrancecasting.com	La Crosse	WI	54603	608-781-0600	
Totten Tubes Inc 500 Danlee St. Web: www.tottentubes.com	Azusa	CA	91702	626-812-0220	812-0113
Town & Country Industries 400 W Mcnab Rd. Web: www.tc-alum.com	Fort Lauderdale	FL	33309	954-970-9999	
Toyota Tsusho America Inc 805 Third Ave 16th Fl. Web: www.taiamerica.com	New York	NY	10022	212-355-3600	
Trans World Alloys Co 249 E Gardena Blvd. Web: www.twalloys.com	Gardena	CA	90248	310-217-8777	
Tri Star Metals LLC 375 Village Dr. Web: www.tristarmetals.com	Carol Stream	IL	60188	630-462-7600	
Tri-State Ironworks Inc 175 W Bodley Ave. Web: www.tristateironworks.com	Memphis	TN	38109	901-942-1461	
Tri-Wire Engineering Solutions Inc 890 East St. Web: www.triwire.net	Tewksbury	MA	01876	978-640-6899	
Trident Steel Corp 12825 Flushing Meadows Dr Ste 110. TF: 800-777-9687 ■ Web: www.tridentsteel.com	St. Louis	MO	63131	314-822-0500	
Triple-S Steel Supply LLC 6000 Jensen Dr. TF: 800-231-1034 ■ Web: www.sss-steel.com	Houston	TX	77026	713-697-7105	
Tristate Wire Rope Supply Inc 5246 Wooster Pk. Web: tswr.com	Cincinnati	OH	45226	513-871-8656	
Tubetech North America Inc 900 East Taggart St. Web: www.tubetechnorthamerica.com	East Palestine	OH	44413	330-426-9476	
Tubular Steel Inc 1031 Executive Pkwy Dr. TF: 800-388-7491 ■ Web: www.tubularsteel.com	Saint Louis	MO	63141	314-851-9200	851-9336
Turret Steel Industries Inc 105 Pine St. TF: 800-245-4800 ■ Web: www.turretsteel.com	Imperial	PA	15126	724-218-1014	218-1195
TW Metals Inc PO Box 644. Web: www.twmetals.com	Exton	PA	19341	610-458-1300	
Two Rivers Enterprises 490 River St W. Web: www.stainlesskings.com	Holdingford	MN	56340	320-746-3156	
Ulbrich of Illinois Inc 12340 S Laramie Ave. Web: www.astroplastics.com	Alsip	IL	60803	708-489-9500	
United Alloy Inc 4100 Kennedy Rd. Web: www.unitedalloy.com	Janesville	WI	53545	608-758-4717	
United Aluminum Corp 100 United Dr. TF: 800-243-2515 ■ Web: www.unitedaluminum.com	North Haven	CT	06473	203-239-5881	
United States Brass & Copper Co Inc 1401 Brook Dr. TF: 800-821-2854 ■ Web: www.usbrassandcopper.com	Downers Grove	IL	60515	630-629-9340	629-9350
United Steel Inc 164 School St. Web: www.unitedsteel.com	East Hartford	CT	06108	860-289-2323	
Universal Metals LLC 805 Chicago St. Web: www.umimetals.com	Toledo	OH	43611	419-726-0850	
Universal Steel America Houston Inc 1230 E Richey Rd. Web: www.universalsteelamerica.com	Houston	TX	77073	281-821-7400	
Universal Steel Co 6600 Grant Ave. TF: 800-669-2645 ■ Web: www.univsteel.com	Cleveland	OH	44105	216-883-4972	341-0421
US Metals Inc 19102 Gundle Rd. Web: www.tgrexotics.com	Houston	TX	77073	281-443-7473	443-6748
Usemco 1602 Rezin Rd. Web: www.usemco.com	Tomah	WI	54660	608-372-5911	
Valiant Steel & Equipment Inc 6455 Old Peachtree Rd. TF: 800-939-9905 ■ Web: www.valiantsteel.com	Norcross	GA	30071	770-417-1235	417-1669
Venture Steel Inc 60 Disco Rd. Web: www.venturesteel.com	Etobicoke	ON	M9W1L8	416-798-9396	
Viking Materials Inc 3225 Como Ave SE. TF General: 800-682-3942 ■ Web: www.vikingmaterials.com	Minneapolis	MN	55414	612-617-5800	623-9070
Vista Metals Inc 65 Ballou Blvd. TF: 800-431-4113 ■ Web: www.vismet.com	Bristol	RI	02809	401-253-1772	
Vita Needle Co 919 Great Plain Ave. Web: www.vitaneedle.com	Needham	MA	02492	781-444-1780	
Vital Link Inc 914 Bartlett Rd. Web: www.vitallinkinc.com	Sealy	TX	77474	979-885-4181	
Waconia Manufacturing Inc 33 E Eigth St. Web: www.waconiamfg.com	Waconia	MN	55387	952-442-4450	
Warren Steel Holdings LLC 4000 Mahoning Ave. Web: www.warrensteelholdings.com	Warren	OH	44483	330-847-0487	
Waukegan Steel LLC 1201 Belvidere Rd. Web: www.waukegansteel.com	Waukegan	IL	60085	847-662-2810	
WCJ - Pilgrim Wire LLC 4180 N Port Washington Rd. Web: www.wcjwire.com	Glendale	WI	53212	414-291-9566	
Weber Specialties Co 15230 S Us 131. Web: www.weberspecialties.com	Schoolcraft	MI	49087	269-679-5160	
West Central Steel Inc 110 19th St NW PO Box 1178. TF: 800-992-8853 ■ Web: www.wcsteel.com	Willmar	MN	56201	320-235-4070	235-1816
Westfield Steel Inc 530 State Rd 32 W. *Fax Area Code: 317 ■ TF: 800-622-4984 ■ Web: www.westfieldsteel.com	Westfield	IN	46074	800-622-4984	896-5343*
White Aluminum Products LLC 2101 US Hwy 441. TF: 888-474-5884 ■ Web: www.whitealuminum.com	Leesburg	FL	34748	888-474-5884	
White Star Steel Inc 2200 Harbor Blvd. Web: www.whitestarsteel.com	Houston	TX	77220	713-675-6501	
Whitefab Inc 724 Ave W. Web: www.whitefab.com	Birmingham	AL	35214	205-791-2011	
Whitley Steel Company Inc 610 Us Hwy 301 S. Web: www.whitleysteel.com	Jacksonville	FL	32234	904-289-7471	
Willbanks Metals Inc 1155 NE 28th St. TF: 800-772-2352 ■ Web: www.willbanksmetals.com	Fort Worth	TX	76106	817-625-6161	625-8487
Willerding Welding Company Inc 1270 W Terra Ln. Web: www.willerding.com	O'Fallon	MO	63366	636-272-2366	
Williams Metals & Welding Alloys Inc 125 Strafford Ave Ste 108. Web: www.wmwa.net	Wayne	PA	19087	610-225-0105	
Winchester Metals Inc 195 Ebert Rd. Web: www.steelsupplier.com	Winchester	VA	22603	540-667-9000	
Winter F W Inc & Co 550 Delaware Ave. Web: www.fwwinter.com	Camden	NJ	08102	856-963-7490	
Wire Rope Industries Ltd 5501 Trans-Canada Hwy. TF: 800-565-5501 ■ Web: www.wirerope.com	Pointe-claire	QC	H9R1B7	514-697-9711	
Wiscolift Inc W6396 Speciality Dr. TF: 800-242-3477 ■ Web: www.wiscolift.com	Greenville	WI	54942	920-757-8832	
Wisconsin Steel & Tube Corp 1555 N Mayfair Rd. TF: 800-279-8335 ■ Web: www.wisteeltube.com	Milwaukee	WI	53226	414-453-4441	453-0789
WMK & Co 415 Albert St. Web: www.wmkco.com	Billings	MT	59101	406-256-3200	
Wrisco Industries Inc 355 Hiatt Dr Ste B. TF: 800-627-2646 ■ Web: www.wrisco.com	Palm Beach Gardens	FL	33418	561-626-5700	627-3574

493 METALWORKING DEVICES & ACCESSORIES

See Also Machine Tools - Metal Cutting Types p. 2692; Machine Tools - Metal Forming Types p. 2693; Tool & Die Shops p. 3249

				Phone	Fax
Acme Industrial Co 441 Maple Ave. TF: 800-323-5582 ■ Web: www.acmeindustrial.com	Carpentersville	IL	60110	847-428-3911	428-1820
Advanced Machine & Engineering Co 2500 Latham St. TF: 800-225-4263 ■ Web: www.ame.com	Rockford	IL	61103	815-962-6076	962-6483
AG Davis Gage & Engineering Co 6533 Sims Dr. Web: www.agdavis-aagage.com	Sterling Heights	MI	48313	586-977-9000	977-9190
Alcon Tool Co 565 Crosier St. Web: www.alcontool.com	Akron	OH	44311	330-773-9171	773-8042
Allied Machine & Engineering Corp 120 Deeds Dr. TF: 800-321-5537 ■ Web: www.alliedmachine.com	Dover	OH	44622	330-343-4283	343-4781
American Broach & Machine Co 575 S Mansfield. Web: www.americanbroach.com	Ypsilanti	MI	48197	734-961-0300	961-9999
American Drill Bushings Co (ADB) 5740 Hunt Rd. TF: 800-423-4425 ■ Web: www.americandrillbushing.com	Valdosta	GA	31606	229-253-8928	253-8929
Apex Broach & Machine Co 22862 Hoover Rd. Web: www.apbsi.com	Warren	MI	48089	586-758-2626	758-2627
ASKO Inc 501 W Seventh Ave. TF: 800-321-1310 ■ Web: www.askoinc.com	Homestead	PA	15120	412-461-4110	461-5400
ATI Metal Working Products 1 Teledyne Pl. *Fax Area Code: 800 ■ *Fax: Sales ■ TF: 888-926-4211 ■ Web: www.atimetals.com	La Vergne	TN	37086	615-641-4200	223-2219*
Balax Inc PO Box 96. Web: www.balax.com	North Lake	WI	53064	262-966-2355	966-1028
Besly Cutting Tools Inc 16200 Woodmint Ln. TF: 800-435-2965 ■ Web: www.besly.com	South Beloit	IL	61080	815-389-2231	389-1339
Big Kaiser Precision Tooling Inc 641 Fargo Ave. TF: 888-866-5776 ■ Web: www.bigkaiser.com	Elk Grove Village	IL	60007	847-228-7660	228-0881
Boley Tool & Machine Works Inc 1044 Spring Bay Rd. Web: boleytool.com	East Peoria	IL	61611	309-694-2722	694-7879
Buck Chuck Co 2155 Traversefield Dr. *Fax Area Code: 231 ■ TF: 800-228-2825 ■ Web: www.buckchuckusa.com	Traverse City	MI	49686	800-228-2825	947-4953*

Phone | Fax

Carbro Corp 15724 Condon Ave PO Box 278 .... Lawndale CA 90260 310-643-8400 643-9703
TF: 888-738-4400 ■ *Web:* www.carbrocorp.com

Carl Zeiss Industrial Metrology
6250 Sycamore Ln N .... Maple Grove MN 55369 763-744-2400
TF: 800-327-9735 ■ *Web:* www.zeiss.com

Cincinnati Gilbert Machine Tool Company LLC
3366 Beekman St .... Cincinnati OH 45223 513-541-4815 541-4885
Web: www.cincinnatigilbert.com

CJT Koolcarb Inc 494 Mission St .... Carol Stream IL 60188 630-690-5933 690-6355
TF: 800-323-2299 ■ *Web:* www.cjtkoolcarb.com

Cline Tool & Service Co PO Box 866 .... Newton IA 50208 641-792-7081 792-0309
TF: 866-561-3022 ■ *Web:* www.clinetool.com

Cole Carbide Industries Inc
4930 S Lapeer Rd .... Orion Twp MI 48359 586-757-8700 757-8701
Web: www.colecarbide.com

Deltronic Corp 3900 W Segerstrom Ave .... Santa Ana CA 92704 714-545-5800 545-9548
TF: 800-451-6922 ■ *Web:* www.deltronic.com

Detroit Edge Tool Co 6570 E Nevada St .... Detroit MI 48234 313-366-4120 366-1890
TF: 800-404-2038 ■ *Web:* www.detroitedge.com

Dundick Corp 4616 W 20th St .... Cicero IL 60804 708-656-6363 656-2359
Web: www.dundick.com

Edmunds Gages 45 Spring Ln .... Farmington CT 06032 860-677-2813 677-4243
TF: 800-878-1622 ■ *Web:* www.edmundsgages.com

Enmark Tool & Gage Co Inc 18100 Cross Dr .... Fraser MI 48026 586-293-2797 293-1037
Web: www.enmarktool.com

Forkardt 2155 Traverse Field Dr .... Traverse City MI 49686 231-995-8300 995-8361
TF: 800-544-3823 ■ *Web:* www.forkardt.com

Fullerton Tool Company Inc 121 Perry St .... Saginaw MI 48602 989-799-4550 792-3335
TF: 855-722-7243 ■ *Web:* www.fullertontool.com

Gaiser Tool Co 4544 McGrath St .... Ventura CA 93003 805-644-5583 644-2013
Web: www.gaisertool.com

Garr Tool Co 7800 N Alger Rd .... Alma MI 48801 989-463-6171 463-3609
TF: 800-248-9003 ■ *Web:* www.garrtool.com

General Broach Co 307 Salisbury St .... Morenci MI 49256 517-458-7555
Web: www.generalbroach.com

General Cutting Tools
6440 N Ridgeway Ave .... Lincolnwood IL 60712 847-677-8770 677-8786
Web: www.generalcuttingtools.com

Gilman USA 1230 Cheyenne Ave PO Box 5 .... Grafton WI 53024 262-377-2434 377-9438
TF: 800-445-6267 ■ *Web:* gilmanprecision.com

Glassline Corp PO Box 147 .... Perrysburg OH 43552 419-666-5942 666-1549
Web: www.glassline.com

Glastonbury Southern Gage 46 Industrial Pk Rd .... Erin TN 37061 931-289-4243 242-7142*
**Fax Area Code:* 800 ■ *TF:* 800-251-4243 ■ *Web:* www.gsgage.com

Gleason Corp 1351 Windsor Rd .... Loves Park IL 61111 815-877-8900 877-0264
Web: www.gleason.com

Goss & DeLeeuw Machine Co 100 Harding St .... Kensington CT 06037 860-828-4121
Web: goss-deleeuw.com

Guhring Inc 1445 Commerce Ave .... Brookfield WI 53045 262-784-6730 784-9096
TF: 800-776-6170 ■ *Web:* www.guhring.com

Hanlo Gages & Engineering Co 34403 Glendale .... Livonia MI 48150 734-422-4224 422-2244
Web: www.hanlogages.com

Hannibal Carbide Tool Inc
5000 Paris Gravel Rd .... Hannibal MO 63401 573-221-2775 221-1140
TF: 800-451-9436 ■ *Web:* www.hannibalcarbide.com

Hardinge Inc 1 Hardinge Dr .... Elmira NY 14902 607-734-2281
NASDAQ: HDNG ■ *TF:* 800-843-8801 ■ *Web:* www.hardinge.com

Hayden Twist Drill & Tool Company Inc
22822 Globe St .... Warren MI 48089 586-754-7700 754-3312
TF: 800-521-1780 ■ *Web:* www.haydendrills.com

Heidenhain Corp 333 E State Pkwy .... Schaumburg IL 60173 847-490-1191 490-3931
Web: www.heidenhain.com

High Tech Tool Inc 7803 S Loop E .... Houston TX 77012 713-641-2303 641-6664
Web: www.hightechtool.com

Hoppe Technologies Inc 107 First Ave .... Chicopee MA 01020 413-592-9213 592-4688
Web: www.hoppetech.com

Hougen Manufacturing Inc 3001 Hougen Dr .... Swartz Creek MI 48473 810-635-7111 635-8277
TF Orders: 800-426-7818 ■ *Web:* www.hougen.com

Huron Machine Products Inc
228 SW 21st Terr .... Fort Lauderdale FL 33312 800-327-8186 583-2154*
**Fax Area Code:* 954 ■ **Fax:* Sales ■ *TF:* 800-327-8186 ■ *Web:* www.huronmachine.com

Husqvarna Construction Products
17400 W 119th St .... Olathe KS 66061 800-288-5040 825-0028
TF: 800-288-5040 ■ *Web:* www.husqvarna.com

Industrial Tools Inc (ITI) 1111 S Rose Ave .... Oxnard CA 93033 805-483-1111 483-6302
TF: 800-266-5561 ■ *Web:* www.iti-abrasives.com

Iowa Precision Industries Inc
5480 Sixth St SW .... Cedar Rapids IA 52404 319-364-9181 364-3436
Web: mestekmachinery.com/

Jasco Tools Inc 1390 Mt Read Blvd .... Rochester NY 14606 585-254-7000 254-2655
Web: www.jascotools.com

Jergens Inc 15700 S Waterloo Rd .... Cleveland OH 44110 877-486-1454 481-6193*
**Fax Area Code:* 216 ■ *TF:* 800-537-4367 ■ *Web:* www.jergensinc.com

Kennametal Inc 1600 Technology Way PO Box 231 .... Latrobe PA 15650 724-539-5000
NYSE: KMT ■ *TF Cust Svc:* 800-446-7738 ■ *Web:* www.kennametal.com

KEO Cutters Inc 25040 Easy St .... Warren MI 48089 586-771-2050 771-2062
TF: 888-390-2050 ■ *Web:* www.keocutters.com

Lancaster Knives Inc 165 Ct St .... Lancaster NY 14086 716-683-5050 683-5068
TF: 800-869-9666 ■ *Web:* www.lancasterknives.com

Lovejoy Tool Company Inc 133 Main St .... Springfield VT 05156 802-885-2194 885-9511
TF: 800-843-8376 ■ *Web:* www.lovejoytool.com

Madison Cutting Tools Inc
485 Narragansett Pk Dr .... Pawtucket RI 02861 401-729-0400
Web: www.madisontools.com

Melin Tool Co 5565 Venture Dr Unit C .... Cleveland OH 44130 216-362-4230 521-1558*
**Fax Area Code:* 800 ■ *TF:* 800-521-1078 ■ *Web:* www.endmill.com

Micro 100 Tool Corp 1410 E Pine Ave .... Meridian ID 83642 208-888-7310 888-2106
TF: 800-421-8065 ■ *Web:* www.micro100.com

Micro-vu Corp 7909 Conde Ln .... Windsor CA 95492 707-838-6272 838-3985
Web: www.microvu.com

NED Corp 31 Town Forest Rd .... Oxford MA 01540 800-343-6086 799-2796*
**Fax Area Code:* 508 ■ *TF:* 800-343-6086 ■ *Web:* www.nedkut.com

Phone | Fax

Niagara Cutter Inc 2805 Bellingham Dr .... Troy MI 48083 716-689-8400
TF: 800-832-8326 ■ *Web:* www.niagaracutter.com

North American Tool Corp
215 Elmwood Ave .... South Beloit IL 61080 815-389-2300 872-3299*
**Fax Area Code:* 800 ■ *TF:* 800-872-8277 ■ *Web:* www.natool.com

Onsrud Cutter LP 800 Liberty Dr .... Libertyville IL 60048 847-362-1560 362-5028
TF: 800-234-1560 ■ *Web:* www.onsrud.com

OSG Tap & Die Inc
676 E Fullerton Ave .... Glendale Heights IL 60139 630-790-1400 790-1477
TF: 800-837-2223 ■ *Web:* www.osgtool.com

Phillips Corp 7390 Coca Cola Dr .... Hanover MD 21076 410-564-2929 564-2949
TF: 800-878-4242 ■ *Web:* www.phillipscorp.com

Powers Fasteners Inc 2 Powers Ln .... Brewster NY 10509 914-235-6300 576-6483
TF: 800-524-3244 ■ *Web:* www.powers.com

Precision Grinding & Manufacturing Corp
1305 Emerson St .... Rochester NY 14606 585-458-4300 458-7281
Web: www.pgmcorp.com

Precitech Precision Inc 44 Blackbrook Rd .... Keene NH 03431 603-357-2511 358-6174
Web: www.precitech.com

Products Engineering Corp 2645 Maricopa St .... Torrance CA 90503 310-787-4500 787-4501
Web: www.productsengineering.com

Regal-Beloit Corp 200 State St .... Beloit WI 53511 608-364-8800 364-8818
NYSE: RBC ■ *TF:* 800-672-6495 ■ *Web:* www.regalbeloit.com

Reiff & Nestor Co 50 Reiff St .... Lykens PA 17048 717-453-7113 453-7555
TF: 800-521-3422 ■ *Web:* www.rntap.com

Royal Machine & Tool Corp
4 Willowbrook Dr PO Box Y .... Berlin CT 06037 860-828-6555
Web: www.royalworkholding.com

S-T Industries Inc
301 Armstrong Blvd N PO Box 517 .... Saint James MN 56081 507-375-3211 375-4503
TF: 800-326-2039 ■ *Web:* www.stindustries.com

Scotchman Industries Inc 180 E Hwy 14 .... Philip SD 57567 605-859-2542 859-2499
TF: 800-843-8844 ■ *Web:* www.scotchman.com

Scully Jones Seibert Corp 1901 S Rockwell St .... Chicago IL 60608 773-247-5900

Seco Tools 2805 Bellingham Dr .... Troy MI 48083 248-528-5200 528-5600*
**Fax:* Cust Svc ■ *TF:* 800-832-8326 ■ *Web:* www.secotools.com

Somma Tool Company Inc 109 Scott Rd .... Waterbury CT 06705 203-753-2114 756-5489
Web: www.sommatool.com

Spiralock Corp 25235 Dequindre Rd .... Madison Heights MI 48071 248-543-7800 543-1403
TF: 800-521-2688 ■ *Web:* www.stanleyengineeredfastening.com

Star Cutter Co 23461 Industrial Pk Dr .... Farmington MI 48335 248-474-8200 474-9518
TF: 877-635-3488 ■ *Web:* www.starcutter.com

Starrett Webber Gage Div 24500 Detroit Rd .... Cleveland OH 44145 440-835-0001 892-9555
TF: 800-255-3924 ■ *Web:* www.starrett-webber.com

Stilson Products 15935 Sturgeon St .... Roseville MI 48066 586-778-1100 778-4660
TF: 888-400-5978 ■ *Web:* www.stilsonproducts.com

Strong Tool Co 1251 E 286th St .... Cleveland OH 44132 216-289-2450
Web: mdm.com

Tapmatic Corp 802 S Clearwater Loop .... Post Falls ID 83854 208-773-8048 773-3021
TF General: 800-854-6019 ■ *Web:* www.tapmatic.com

Thread Check Inc 390 Oser Ave .... Hauppauge NY 11788 631-231-1515 231-1625
TF: 800-767-7633 ■ *Web:* www.threadcheck.com

TM Smith Tool International Corp
360 Hubbard Ave .... Mount Clemens MI 48043 586-468-1465 468-7190
TF: 800-521-4894 ■ *Web:* www.tmsmith.com

United Drill Bushing Corp 12200 Woodruff Ave .... Downey CA 90241 562-803-1521 486-3465*
**Fax Area Code:* 800 ■ *TF:* 800-486-3466 ■ *Web:* www.ucc-udb.com

US Drill Head Co 5298 River Rd .... Cincinnati OH 45233 513-941-0300
Web: usdrillhead.com

Utica Enterprises Co
13231 23-Mile Rd .... Shelby Township MI 48315 586-726-4300 726-4316

Viking Drill & Tool Inc 355 State St .... Saint Paul MN 55107 651-227-8911 227-1793
TF: 800-328-4655 ■ *Web:* www.vikingdrill.com

Vulcan Tool Co 730 Lorraine Ave .... Dayton OH 45410 937-253-6194 253-1062
Web: www.vulcancut.com

Walker Magnetics Group Inc 20 Rockdale St .... Worcester MA 01606 508-853-3232 852-8649
TF: 800-962-4638 ■ *Web:* www.walkermagnet.com

Walter USA Inc N22 W23855 Ridgeview Pkwy W .... Waukesha WI 53188 800-945-5554 347-2501*
**Fax Area Code:* 262 ■ *TF:* 800-945-5554 ■ *Web:* www.walter-tools.com

Zagar Inc 24000 Lakeland Blvd .... Cleveland OH 44132 216-731-0500 731-8591
Web: www.zagar.com

Zenith Cutter Co 5200 Zenith Pkwy .... Loves Park IL 61111 815-282-5200 282-5232
TF: 800-223-5202 ■ *Web:* zenithcutter.com

494 METALWORKING MACHINERY

See Also Rolling Mill Machinery p. 3141

Phone | Fax

ADS Machinery Corp 1201 Vine Ave NE .... Warren OH 44483 330-399-3601 399-1190
Web: www.adsmachinery.com

Armstrong Mfg Co 2700 SE Tacoma St .... Portland OR 97202 503-228-8381 228-8384
TF: 800-426-6226 ■ *Web:* www.armstrongblue.com

Artos Engineering Co 21605 Gateway Ct .... Brookfield WI 53045 262-252-4545 252-4544
Web: www.artosengineering.com

ATD Engineering & Machine LLC 533 N Ct St .... Au Gres MI 48703 989-876-7161 876-7162
Web: www.atdemllc.com

Bachi Co 1201 Ardmore Ave .... Itasca IL 60143 630-773-5600 773-5621
Web: www.bachiwinder.com

Balance Technology Inc 7035 Jomar Dr .... Whitmore Lake MI 48189 734-769-2100 769-2542
Web: www.balancetechnology.com

Bartell Machinery Systems LLC
6321 Elmer Hill Rd .... Rome NY 13440 315-336-7600 336-0947
TF: 800-537-8473 ■ *Web:* www.bartellmachinery.com

Belvac Production Machinery Inc
237 Graves Mill Rd .... Lynchburg VA 24502 434-239-0358
TF: 800-423-5822 ■ *Web:* www.belvac.com

Delta Brands Inc (DBI) 2204 Century Ctr Blvd .... Irving TX 75062 972-438-7150 579-0100
Web: www.dbimfg.com

Eagle Technologies Group 9850 Red Arrow Hwy .... Bridgman MI 49106 269-465-6986
Web: www.eagletechnologies.com

Company	City	State	Zip	Phone	Fax
Eubanks Engineering Co 3022 Inland Empire Blvd *TF:* 800-729-4208 ■ *Web:* www.eubanks.com	Ontario	CA	91764	909-483-2456	483-2498
FANTA Equipment Co 6521 Storer Ave. *Web:* www.fantaequip.com	Cleveland	OH	44102	216-281-1515	281-7755
Hogan Manufacturing Inc (HMI) PO Box 398 *Web:* www.hoganmfg.com	Escalon	CA	95320	209-838-7323	838-7329
J.R. Automation Technologies LLC 13365 Tyler St *Web:* www.jrauto.com	Holland	MI	49424	616-399-2168	399-5593
Merrill Tool & Machine Co Inc 21659 Gratiot Rd *Web:* www.merrilltool.com	Merrill	MI	48637	989-643-7981	643-7975
Pannier Corp 207 Sandusky St *TF:* 877-726-6437 ■ *Web:* www.pannier.com	Pittsburgh	PA	15212	412-323-4900	323-4962
Pines Technology 30505 Clemens Rd *TF:* 800-207-2840 ■ *Web:* www.pinestech.com	Westlake	OH	44145	440-835-5553	835-5556
Precision Strip Inc 86 S Ohio St PO Box 104 *Web:* www.precision-strip.com	Minster	OH	45865	419-501-1347	
Red Bud Industries 200 B & E Industrial Dr *TF Cust Svc:* 800-851-4612 ■ *Web:* www.redbudindustries.com	Red Bud	IL	62278	618-282-3801	282-6718
Rowe Machinery & Automation Inc 76 Hinckley Rd *TF:* 800-247-2645 ■ *Web:* www.runwithrowe.com	Clinton	ME	04927	207-426-2351	
Superior Machine Company of South Carolina Inc 692 N Cashua Dr *Web:* www.smco.net	Florence	SC	29502	843-468-9200	
Sweed Machinery Inc 653 Second Ave PO Box 228 *TF Sales:* 800-888-1352 ■ *Web:* www.sweed.com	Gold Hill	OR	97525	541-855-1512	855-1165
Tridan International Inc 130 N Jackson St PO Box 537 *Web:* www.tridan.com	Danville	IL	61834	217-443-3592	443-3894
West Bond Inc 1551 S Harris Ct *Web:* www.westbond.com	Anaheim	CA	92806	714-978-1551	978-0431

495 METERS & OTHER COUNTING DEVICES

Company	City	State	Zip	Phone	Fax
AMETEK Inc Dixson Div 287 27 Rd *TF:* 888-302-0639 ■ *Web:* www.ametekvis.com	Grand Junction	CO	81503	970-242-8863	245-6267
AMETEK Sensor Technology Drexelbrook Div 205 Keith Valley Rd *TF Cust Svc:* 800-553-9092 ■ *Web:* www.drexelbrook.com	Horsham	PA	19044	215-674-1234	674-2731
Auto Meter Products Inc 413 W Elm St *TF:* 866-248-6356 ■ *Web:* www.autometer.com	Sycamore	IL	60178	815-895-8141	895-6786
Badger Meter Inc 4545 W Brown Deer Rd *NYSE: BMI* ■ *TF:* 800-876-3837 ■ *Web:* www.badgermeter.com	Milwaukee	WI	53224	414-355-0400	
Beede Electrical Instrument Co 88 Village St *Web:* www.beede.com	Penacook	NH	03303	603-753-6362	753-6201
Clark-Reliance Corp 16633 Foltz Pkwy *TF:* 800-238-4027 ■ *Web:* www.clarkreliance.com	Strongsville	OH	44149	440-572-1500	572-1500
Duncan Solutions Inc 633 W Wisconsin Ave Ste 1600 *TF:* 888-993-8622 ■ *Web:* www.duncanindustries.com	Milwaukee	WI	53203	888-993-8622	
Electro-Sensors Inc 6111 Blue Cir Dr *NASDAQ: ELSE* ■ *TF:* 800-328-6170 ■ *Web:* www.electro-sensors.com	Minnetonka	MN	55343	952-930-0100	930-0130
Elster American Meter Co 2221 Industrial Rd *TF:* 877-595-6254 ■ *Web:* www.elster-americanmeter.com	Nebraska City	NE	68410	402-873-8200	873-7616
Eugene Ernst Products Company Inc PO Box 925 **Fax Area Code:* 888 ■ *TF:* 800-992-2843 ■ *Web:* www.ernstflow.com	Farmingdale	NJ	07727	732-938-5641	992-2843*
Greenwald Industries 212 Middlesex Ave *TF:* 800-221-0982 ■ *Web:* www.greenwaldindustries.com	Chester	CT	06412	860-526-0800	526-4205
Isspro Inc 2515 NE Riverside Way *Web:* www.issproinc.com	Portland	OR	97211	503-528-3400	249-2999
Laser Technology Inc 7070 S Tucson Way *TF:* 800-280-6113 ■ *Web:* www.lasertech.com	Englewood	CO	80112	303-649-1000	649-9710
Max Machinery Inc 33A Healdsburg Ave *Web:* www.maxmachinery.com	Healdsburg	CA	95448	707-433-2662	433-1818
Maxima Technologies Stewart Warner 1811 Rohrerstown Rd *TF:* 800-676-1837 ■ *Web:* www.maximatecc.com	Lancaster	PA	17601	717-581-1000	569-7247
PMP Corp 25 Security Dr *TF Cust Svc:* 800-243-6628 ■ *Web:* www.pmp-corp.com	Avon	CT	06001	860-677-9656	674-0196
POM Inc 200 S Elmira Ave PO Box 430 *TF:* 800-331-7275 ■ *Web:* www.pom.com	Russellville	AR	72802	479-968-2880	968-2840
Schlumberger Ltd 5599 San Felipe Ste 100 *NYSE: SLB* ■ *Web:* www.slb.com	Houston	TX	77056	713-513-2000	513-2006
Sparling Instruments Company Inc 4097 N Temple City Blvd *TF Sales:* 800-800-3569 ■ *Web:* www.sparlinginstruments.com	El Monte	CA	91731	626-444-0571	444-2314
Teleflex Morse Marine Products 640 N Lewis Rd *Web:* www.tfxmarine.com	Limerick	PA	19468	610-495-7011	
Thomas G Faria Corp 385 Norwich-New London Tpke *TF:* 800-473-2742 ■ *Web:* www.faria-instruments.com	Uncasville	CT	06382	860-848-9271	848-2704

496 MICROGRAPHICS PRODUCTS & SERVICES

Company	City	State	Zip	Phone	Fax
Anacomp Inc 15378 Ave of Science *OTC: ANMP* ■ *Web:* www.anacomp.com	San Diego	CA	92128	858-716-3400	
BMI Imaging Systems 1115 E Arques Ave *TF:* 800-359-3456 ■ *Web:* www.bmiimaging.com	Sunnyvale	CA	94085	408-736-7444	736-4397
Comgraphics Inc 329 W 18th St 10th Fl *Web:* ww3.cgichicago.com	Chicago	IL	60616	312-226-0900	226-9411
Comstor Productivity Ctr Inc 441 W Sharp Ave. *TF:* 800-776-2451 ■ *Web:* www.comstorinc.com	Spokane	WA	99201	509-534-5080	536-0281
DPF Data Services Group Inc 1990 Swarthmore Ave. *TF:* 800-431-4416 ■ *Web:* www.dpfdata.com	Lakewood	NJ	08701	732-370-8840	370-1751
DST Output 5220 Robert J Mathews Pkwy *TF:* 800-441-7587 ■ *Web:* dstsystems.com	El Dorado Hills	CA	95762	916-939-4960	
Eye Communication Systems Inc 455 E Industrial Dr *TF:* 800-558-2153 ■ *Web:* www.eyecom.com	Hartland	WI	53029	262-367-1360	367-1362
HF Group Inc 203 W Artesia Blvd *TF:* 800-421-5000 ■ *Web:* www.hf76.com	Compton	CA	90220	310-605-0755	608-1181
Indus International Inc 340 S Oak St PO Box 890 *TF:* 800-843-9377 ■ *Web:* www.indususa.com	West Salem	WI	54669	608-786-0300	786-0786
Micro Com Systems Ltd 27 E Seventh Ave *Web:* www.microcomsys.com	Vancouver	BC	V5T1M4	604-872-6771	
microMEDIA Imaging Systems Inc 1979 Marcus Ave *Web:* www.imagingservices.com	Lake Success	NY	11042	516-355-0300	355-0316

497 MILITARY BASES

See Also Coast Guard Installations p. 1947

497-1 Air Force Bases

Base	City	State	Zip	Phone	Fax
Altus Air Force Base 305 E Ave *Web:* www.altus.af.mil	Altus Afb	OK	73523	580-482-8100	481-5966
Arnold Air Force Base 100 Kindel Dr Ste B-213 *Web:* www.arnold.af.mil	Arnold	TN	37389	931-454-3000	454-6086
Barksdale Air Force Base Second Bomb Wing Public Affairs *Web:* www.barksdale.af.mil	Barksdale AFB	LA	71110	318-456-1015	
Bolling Air Force Base (BAFB) 20 MacDill Blvd Ste 220 *Web:* www.cnic.navy.mil/regions/ndw/installations/jbab.html	Washington	DC	20032	202-404-3281	
Cannon Air Force Base 110 E Sextant Ave Ste 1150 **Fax Area Code:* 505 ■ *TF:* 877-283-3858 ■ *Web:* www.cannon.af.mil	Cannon AFB	NM	88103	575-784-4131	784-2338*
Columbus Air Force Base 555 Seventh St. *Web:* www.columbus.af.mil	Columbus AFB	MS	39710	662-434-7068	434-7009
Davis-Monthan Air Force Base 5275 E Granite St *Web:* www.dm.af.mil	Davis-Monthan AFB	AZ	85707	520-228-3204	228-5299
Dover Air Force Base 201 Eagle Way *Web:* www.dover.af.mil	Dover AFB	DE	19902	302-677-3372	677-2901
Edwards Air Force Base 305 E Popson Ave *Web:* www.edwards.af.mil	Edwards AFB	CA	93524	661-277-1110	277-2732
Eglin Air Force Base Eglin Blvd *Web:* www.eglin.af.mil	Eglin AFB	FL	32542	850-882-3931	
Eielson Air Force Base 354 Broadway St Unit 2B *TF:* 800-538-6647 ■ *Web:* www.eielson.af.mil	Eielson AFB	AK	99702	907-377-1110	377-1606
Ellsworth Air Force Base 1958 Scott Dr *Web:* www.ellsworth.af.mil	Ellsworth AFB	SD	57706	605-385-5056	385-4668
Fairchild Air Force Base 100 W Ent St Ste 155 *Web:* www.fairchild.af.mil	Fairchild AFB	WA	99011	509-247-1212	247-5640
Goodfellow Air Force Base 351 Kearney Blvd *Web:* www.goodfellow.af.mil	Goodfellow AFB	TX	76908	325-654-3877	654-5414
Grand Forks Air Force Base 344 Sixth Ave Grand Forks AFB	Grand Forks	ND	58205	701-747-3000	
Hanscom Air Force Base Hanscom Dr *Web:* www.hanscom.af.mil	Lincoln	MA	01742	781-377-4441	
Hill Air Force Base 7285 Fourth St Bldg 180 Ste 109 *Web:* www.hill.af.mil	Hill AFB	UT	84056	801-777-5201	
Kirtland Air Force Base 2000 Wyoming Blvd SE Ste A-1 *TF:* 877-246-1453 ■ *Web:* www.kirtland.af.mil	Kirtland AFB	NM	87117	505-846-5991	
Langley Air Force Base 49 Spruce St PO Box 1000 **Fax:* Library ■ *Web:* www.jble.af.mil	Langley AFB	VA	23665	757-764-1110	764-3315*
Laughlin Air Force Base 561 Liberty Dr Ste 3 *TF:* 866-966-1020 ■ *Web:* www.laughlin.af.mil	Laughlin AFB	TX	78843	830-298-5988	298-5047
Little Rock Air Force Base 1250 Thomas Ave *TF:* 800-557-6815 ■ *Web:* www.littlerock.af.mil	Little Rock AFB	AR	72099	501-987-1110	987-6978
Los Angeles Air Force Base 483 N Aviation Blvd Los Angeles AFB *Web:* www.losangeles.af.mil	El Segundo	CA	90245	310-653-1110	
Luke Air Force Base 14185 W Falcon St *TF:* 800-321-1080 ■ *Web:* www.luke.af.mil	Luke AFB	AZ	85309	623-856-5853	856-6013
Malmstrom Air Force Base 7410 Flightline Dr Bldg 300 *TF:* 866-731-4633 ■ *Web:* www.malmstrom.af.mil	Malmstrom AFB	MT	59402	406-731-1110	731-4048
Maxwell Air Force Base 55 Le May Plaza S *TF:* 877-353-6807 ■ *Web:* www.maxwell.af.mil	Maxwell AFB	AL	36112	334-953-2014	953-3379
McConnell Air Force Base 57837 Coffeyville St Ste 271 *TF:* 877-272-7337 ■ *Web:* www.mcconnell.af.mil	McConnell AFB	KS	67221	316-759-6100	759-3148
McGuire Air Force Base 2901 Falcon Ln Rm 235 *Web:* www.jointbasemdl.af.mil	Joint Base McGuire-Dix-Lakehurst	NJ	08641	609-754-2104	754-6999
Minot Air Force Base 201 Summit Dr *Web:* www.minot.af.mil	Minot AFB	ND	58705	701-723-6212	723-6534

Name / Address	City	State	Zip	Phone	Fax
Moody Air Force Base 4343 George St Bldg 904 *Web:* www.moody.af.mil	Moody AFB	GA	31699	229-257-3395	257-4804
Mountain Home Air Force Base 366 Gunfighter Ave Ste 314 *TF:* 855-366-0140 ■ *Web:* www.mountainhome.af.mil	Mountain Home AFB	ID	83648	208-828-6800	828-4205
Nellis Air Force Base 4430 Grissom Ave Ste 107 *Web:* www.nellis.af.mil	Nellis AFB	NV	89191	702-652-2750	652-9838
Offutt Air Force Base 906 Sac Blvd Ste 1 *Web:* www.offutt.af.mil	Offutt AFB	NE	68113	402-294-1110	294-7172
Patrick Air Force Base 1201 Edward H White Ste C-129 *Web:* www.patrick.af.mil	Patrick AFB	FL	32925	321-494-5933	494-7302
Scott Air Force Base 101 Heritage Dr *Web:* www.scott.af.mil	Scott AFB	IL	62225	618-256-1110	
Seymour Johnson Air Force Base 1510 Wright Bros Ave *TF:* 800-525-0102 ■ *Web:* www.seymourjohnson.af.mil	Seymour Johnson AFB	NC	27531	919-722-0027	722-0007
Shaw Air Force Base 517 Lance Ave Ste 106 *TF:* 800-235-7776 ■ *Web:* www.shaw.af.mil	Shaw AFB	SC	29152	803-895-2019	895-2028
Sheppard Air Force Base 419 G Ave Ste 3 *TF:* 877-676-1847 ■ *Web:* www.sheppard.af.mil	Sheppard AFB	TX	76311	940-676-2511	676-4245
Tinker Air Force Base 3001 Staff Dr Ste 1AG85A *Web:* www.tinker.af.mil	Tinker AFB	OK	73145	405-739-2026	739-2882
Tyndall Air Force Base 445 Suwannee Rd 101 *TF:* 800-356-5273 ■ *Web:* www.tyndall.af.mil	Tyndall AFB	FL	32403	850-283-1110	283-3225
Vance Air Force Base 246 Brown Pkwy *TF:* 866-966-1020 ■ *Web:* vance.af.mil	Vance AFB	OK	73705	580-213-7476	213-6376
Vandenberg Air Force Base 706 Washington Ave Bldg 10122 *Web:* www.vandenberg.af.mil	Vandenberg	CA	93437	805-606-3595	606-8303
Whiteman Air Force Base 1081 Arnold Ave Bldg 59 Ste 104 *TF:* 866-363-8667 ■ *Web:* www.whiteman.af.mil	Whiteman AFB	MO	65305	660-687-6123	687-7948
Wright-Patterson Air Force Base 5030 Patterson Pkwy *Web:* www.wpafb.af.mil	Wright-Patterson AFB	OH	45433	937-257-1110	

497-2 Army Bases

Name / Address	City	State	Zip	Phone	Fax
Fort AP Hill 18436 Fourth St *Web:* www.army.mil	Fort AP Hill	VA	22427	804-633-8120	633-8105
Fort Benning 6460Way Ave *Web:* www.benning.army.mil	Fort Benning	GA	31905	706-545-2218	545-1604
Fort Detrick 810 Schreider St *Web:* www.detrick.army.mil	Frederick	MD	21702	301-619-7613	
Fort Gordon 201 Third Ave *Web:* www.gordon.army.mil	Fort Gordon	GA	30905	706-791-0110	791-2061
Fort Hamilton 113 Schum Ave Bldg 113 *Web:* www.hamilton.army.mil	Brooklyn	NY	11252	718-630-4101	630-4717
Fort Hood 761st Tank Battalion Ave Bldg 1001 Rm W105 *Web:* www.hood.army.mil	Fort Hood	TX	76544	254-287-1110	288-2750
Fort Huachuca Smith St Bldg 50010 *Web:* www.huachuca.army.mil	Fort Huachuca	AZ	85613	520-533-7111	533-5008
Fort Jackson 5450 Strom Thurmond Blvd Rm 216 *Web:* jackson.armylive.dodlive.mil	Fort Jackson	SC	29207	803-751-7511	
Fort Knox PO Box 995 *Web:* www.knox.army.mil	Fort Knox	KY	40121	502-624-4985	
Fort Leavenworth 881 Mcclellan Ave *Web:* usacac.army.mil	Fort Leavenworth	KS	66027	913-684-4021	684-3624
Fort Lee 500 Lee Ave *Web:* www.lee.army.mil	Fort Lee	VA	23801	804-765-3000	734-4659
Fort Leonard Wood Bldg 744 *TF:* 800-350-7746 ■ *Web:* www.wood.army.mil	Fort Leonard Wood	MO	65473	573-596-0131	563-4012
Fort Polk 2030 14th St *TF:* 800-752-4658 ■ *Web:* www.jrtc-polk.army.mil	Fort Polk	LA	71459	337-531-2911	531-6014
Fort Riley 405 Pershing Ct *TF:* 800-273-8255 ■ *Web:* www.riley.army.mil	Fort Riley	KS	66442	785-239-2022	239-2592
Fort Sam Houston 3630 Stanley Rd *Web:* www.cs.amedd.army.mil	Fort Sam Houston	TX	78234	210-221-8580	
Fort Story 2600 Tarawa Ct *Web:* www.cnic.navy.mil	Norfolk	VA	23521	757-462-8425	
Joint Base Myer 204 Lee Ave Bldg 59 *Web:* www.army.mil	Fort Myer	VA	22211	703-696-0584	
U.S Army Avitation center of Excellence & Fort Rucker 453 Novosel St Bldg 131 *Web:* www-rucker.army.mil	Fort Rucker	AL	36362	334-255-3400	255-1004

497-3 Marine Corps Bases

Name / Address	City	State	Zip	Phone	Fax
Marine Corps Air Station Beaufort PO Box 55001 *Web:* www.beaufort.marines.mil	Beaufort	SC	29904	843-228-7121	228-6005
Marine Corps Air Station Yuma Shaw Ave Bldg 980 *Web:* mcasyuma.marines.mil	Yuma	AZ	85369	928-269-2252	269-3282
Marine Corps Base Hawaii PO Box 63002 *Web:* www.mcbhawaii.marines.mil	Kaneohe Bay	HI	96863	808-257-8840	257-2511
Marine Corps Base Quantico 3250 Catlin Ave *Web:* www.quantico.marines.mil	Quantico	VA	22134	703-784-2121	
Marine Corps Recruit Depot San Diego 1600 Henderson Ave *Web:* www.marines.mil	San Diego	CA	92145	619-524-1011	
MCRD Parris Island 283 Blvd de France *Web:* mcrdpi.marines.mil	Parris Island	SC	29905	843-228-2111	228-2122

497-4 Naval Installations

Name / Address	City	State	Zip	Phone	Fax
Naval Air Station Fallon 4755 Pasture Rd Bldg 309 *Web:* www.cnic.navy.mil	Fallon	NV	89496	775-426-3333	
Naval Air Station Jacksonville 6801 Roosevelt Blvd *TF:* 800-849-6024 ■ *Web:* www.cnic.navy.mil/jacksonville	Jacksonville	FL	32212	904-542-2338	
Naval Air Station Joint Reserve Base Fort Worth 1510 Chennault Ave *Web:* www.cnic.navy.mil/fortworth	Fort Worth	TX	76113	817-782-5000	
Naval Air Station Joint Reserve Base New Orleans 301 Russell Ave *TF:* 800-729-7327 ■ *Web:* www.cnic.navy.mil	New Orleans	LA	70143	504-678-3254	678-9595
Naval Air Station Key West PO Box 9001 *Web:* www.cnic.navy.mil/keywest	Key West	FL	33040	305-293-2425	
Naval Air Station Kingsville 554 Mccain St *Web:* www.cnic.navy.mil/kingsville	Kingsville	TX	78363	361-516-6146	516-6875
Naval Air Station Lemoore 700 Avenger *Web:* www.cnic.navy.mil/Lemoore	Lemoore	CA	93246	559-998-3300	998-3395
Naval Air Station Meridian 200 Rosenbaum Ave *Web:* cnic.navy.mil	Meridian	MS	39309	601-679-2211	
Naval Air Station North Island PO Box 357033 *Web:* www.cnic.navy.mil	San Diego	CA	92135	619-545-9589	545-6260
Naval Air Station Oceana 1750 Tomcat Blvd *Web:* www.cnic.navy.mil/oceana	Virginia Beach	VA	23460	757-433-3131	
Naval Air Station Patuxent River 22268 Cedar Point Road Bldg 409 *TF:* 877-995-5247 ■ *Web:* cnic.navy.mil/patuxent	Patuxent River	MD	20670	301-342-3000	
Naval Air Station Pensacola 190 Radford Blvd *TF:* 800-628-9466 ■ *Web:* navy-lodge.com	Pensacola	FL	32508	800-628-9466	
Naval Air Station Whiting Field 7550 USS Essex St *Web:* www.cnic.navy.mil	Milton	FL	32570	850-623-7341	
Naval Air Station Willow Grove PO Box 21 *Web:* www.cnic.navy.mil	Willow Grove	PA	19090	215-443-1000	443-6017
Naval Base Kitsap 120 S Dewey St *Web:* www.cnic.navy.mil	Bremerton	WA	98314	360-627-4024	
Naval Base San Diego 3455 Senn Rd *TF:* 877-995-5247 ■ *Web:* www.cnic.navy.mil/sandiego	San Diego	CA	92136	619-556-1011	
Naval Station Everett 2000 W Marine View Dr *Web:* www.cnic.navy.mil	Everett	WA	98207	425-304-3366	304-3096
Naval Station Great Lakes 2601E Paul Jones St *Web:* www.cnic.navy.mil	Great Lakes	IL	60088	847-688-3500	
Naval Station Mayport PO Box 280032 *TF:* 800-872-7245 ■ *Web:* www.cnic.navy.mil/mayport	Mayport	FL	32228	904-270-5401	270-5064
Naval Station Newport 690 Peary St *Web:* www.cnic.navy.mil/newport	Newport	RI	02841	401-841-3456	841-2265
Naval Station Pearl Harbor 4827 Bougainville Dr *Web:* www.cnic.navy.mil	Honolulu	HI	96818	808-474-1999	
Naval Support Activity 58 Bennion Rd *Web:* www.usna.edu	Annapolis	MD	21402	410-293-1000	293-3133
U.S. Fleet Forces Command 1562 Mitscher Ave Ste 250 *TF:* 800-473-3549 ■ *Web:* public.navy.mil	Norfolk	VA	23551	757-836-3630	836-3603

498 MILITARY SERVICE ACADEMIES

Name / Address	City	State	Zip	Phone	Fax
Royal Military College of Canada Stn Forces PO Box 17000 *Web:* www.rmcc-cmrc.ca/en	Kingston	ON	K7K7B4	613-541-6000	541-6599
US Air Force Academy (USAFA) 2304 Cadet Dr Ste 2300 *TF:* 800-443-9266 ■ *Web:* www.usafa.af.mil	Air Force Academy	CO	80840	719-333-1110	333-3644
US Military Academy Admissions Bldg 606 3rd Fl *Web:* www.usma.edu	West Point	NY	10996	845-938-4041	938-8121
US Naval Academy 121 Blake Rd **Fax:* Admissions ■ *TF Admissions:* 888-249-7707 ■ *Web:* www.usna.edu	Annapolis	MD	21402	410-293-1000	293-4348*

499 MILLWORK

See Also Lumber & Building Supplies p. 2095; Doors & Windows - Wood p. 2199; Home Improvement Centers p. 2479; Shutters - Window (All Types) p. 3184

Name / Address	City	State	Zip	Phone	Fax
A & L Handles Inc 244 Shoemaker Rd *Web:* www.alhandles.com	Pottstown	PA	19464	610-323-1516	
Alfab Inc 220 Boll Weevil Cir E *Web:* www.alfabinc.com	Enterprise	AL	36330	334-347-9516	
Allegheny Millwork PBT 104 Commerce Blvd *Web:* www.alleghenymillwork.com	Lawrence	PA	15055	724-873-8700	
Allen Millwork Inc 6969 Fern Loop Ste 106 *Web:* homedesigncentershreveport.com	Shreveport	LA	71105	318-629-5300	629-5301
ALLSCO Building Products Ltd 615 St George Blvd *Web:* www.allsco.com	Moncton	NB	E1E2C2	506-853-8080	853-9344
American Millwork Corp 4840 Beck Dr *Web:* www.americanmillwork.com	Elkhart	IN	46516	574-295-4158	293-5378

Company	City	State	Zip	Phone	Fax
Anderson Wood Products Co 1381 Beech St *Web:* www.andersonwood.com	Louisville	KY	40211	502-778-5591	778-5599
Anlin Industries 1665 Tollhouse Rd *TF:* 800-287-7996 ■ *Web:* www.anlin.com	Clovis	CA	93611	559-322-1531	322-1532
Annandale Millwork Allied Systems 220 Arbor Ct. *Web:* amcasc.com	Winchester	VA	22602	540-665-9600	
Appalachian Wood Products Inc 171 Loop Rd *Web:* www.appwood.com	Clearfield	PA	16830	814-765-2003	765-4751
Arcways Inc 1076 Ehlers Rd *Web:* www.arcways.com	Neenah	WI	54956	920-725-2667	
Bay Industries Inc 2929 Walker Dr. *Web:* www.baycompanies.com	Green Bay	WI	54311	920-406-4000	
Black Millwork Company Inc 220 W Crescent Ave *Web:* www.blackmillwork.com	Allendale	NJ	07401	201-934-0100	
Boiseries Raymond Inc 11880, 56e Ave *TF:* 800-361-6577 ■ *Web:* www.boiseriesraymond.com	Montreal	QC	H1E2L6	514-494-1141	494-9666
Bright Wood Corp 335 NW Hess St PO Box 828. *Web:* www.brightwood.com	Madras	OR	97741	541-475-2243	475-7086
Brochsteins Inc 11530 Main St *Web:* www.brochsteins.com	Houston	TX	77025	713-666-2881	
Brockway-Smith Co (BWAY) 146 Dascomb Rd. **Fax Area Code:* 732 ■ *Web:* www.brosco.com	Andover	MA	01810	978-475-7100	826-0606*
Buffelen Woodworking Co 1901 Taylor Way *TF:* 800-423-8810 ■ *Web:* www.buffelendoor.com	Tacoma	WA	98421	253-627-1191	
Cain Millwork Inc 1 Cain Pkwy *TF:* 800-417-3511 ■ *Web:* www.cainmillwork.com	Rochelle	IL	61068	815-561-9700	
Canamould Extrusions Inc 101a Roytec Rd *TF:* 866-874-6762 ■ *Web:* www.canamould.com	Woodbridge	ON	L4L8A9	905-264-4436	
Carter-Lee ProBuild 1717 W Washington St. *TF:* 800-344-9242 ■ *Web:* probuildindy.com	Indianapolis	IN	46222	317-639-5431	639-6982
Cascade Plastics Co Inc 7009 45th St Ct E *Web:* cascadeplastics.com	Fife	WA	98424	253-922-3460	
Cascade Wood Products Inc PO Box 2429 *TF:* 800-423-3311 ■ *Web:* www.cascadewood.com	White City	OR	97503	541-826-2911	826-3985
Causeway Lumber Co 3318 SW Second Ave *Web:* www.causewaylumber.com	Fort Lauderdale	FL	33315	954-763-1224	
Centennial Windows Ltd 687 Sovereign Rd *Web:* www.centennialwindows.com	London	ON	N5V4K8	519-451-0508	
Central Woodwork Inc 870 Keough Rd *TF:* 800-788-3775 ■ *Web:* www.centralwoodwork.com	Collierville	TN	38017	901-363-4141	542-6187
City Thermo Pane Ltd 420 Industrielle St *Web:* www.citythermopane.com	Beresford	NB	E8K2C2	506-542-1130	542-1139
Colonial Millwork Ltd R.R. 219 *Web:* www.colonialmillwork.com	Beverly	WV	26253	304-636-9338	
Columbia Woodworking Inc 935 Brentwood Rd NE. *Web:* cwwcorp.com	Washington	DC	20018	202-526-2387	526-5163
Commercial & Architectural Products Inc PO Box 250 *TF:* 800-377-1221 ■ *Web:* www.marlite.com	Dover	OH	44622	330-343-6621	343-7296
Conforce International Inc 51A Caldari Rd 2nd Fl	Concord	ON	L4K4G3	416-234-0266	
Contact Industries Inc 9200 SE Sunnybrook Blvd Ste 200. *TF:* 800-547-1038 ■ *Web:* www.contactind.com	Clackamas	OR	97015	503-228-7361	221-1340
Cox Interior Inc 1751 Old Columbia Rd **Fax Area Code:* 270 ■ *TF:* 800-733-1751 ■ *Web:* www.coxinterior.com	Campbellsville	KY	42718	800-733-1751	465-7977*
CW Ohio Inc 1209 Maple Ave. *Web:* www.cwohio.com	Conneaut	OH	44030	440-593-5800	593-4545
Dashwood Industries Ltd 69323 Richmond St *TF:* 800-265-4284 ■ *Web:* www.dashwood.com	Centralia	ON	N0M1K0	519-228-6624	228-2083
Delden Manufacturing Company Inc 3530 N Kimball Dr *TF:* 800-821-3708 ■ *Web:* www.deldenmfg.com	Kansas City	MO	64161	816-413-1600	
Dorris Lumber & Moulding Co, The 2601 Redding Ave *TF:* 800-827-5823 ■ *Web:* www.dorrismoulding.com	Sacramento	CA	95820	916-452-7531	
Dubois Wood Products Inc 707 E Sixth St *Web:* www.duboiswood.com	Huntingburg	IN	47542	812-683-3613	683-3847
Durawood Products Inc 18 Industrial Way *Web:* www.durawood.com	Denver	PA	17517	717-336-0220	
Eastern Millwork Co 3222 Oley Tpke Rd PO Box 4128	Reading	PA	19606	610-779-3550	779-1241
Faubion Associates Inc 1000 Forest Ave *Web:* www.faubionassoc.com	Dallas	TX	75315	214-565-1000	
Fenetres Lapco Inc 12995 Rue Du Parc. *Web:* www.lapcoinc.com	Mirabel	QC	J7J1P3	450-971-0432	
Four C's Holdings Ltd 330 Mackenzie Blvd *Web:* www.casman.ca	Fort Mcmurray	AB	T9H4C4	780-791-9283	
Giffin Interior & Fixture Inc 500 Scotti Dr *Web:* giffininterior.com	Bridgeville	PA	15017	412-221-1166	221-3745
Global Window Solutions 128 Industrial Park Rd *Web:* www.globalwindows.ca	Richibucto	NB	E4W4A4	506-523-4900	
Graves Lumber Co 1315 S Cleveland-Massillon Rd *TF:* 877-500-5515 ■ *Web:* www.graveslumber.com	Copley	OH	44321	330-666-1115	666-1377
Great Lakes Woodworking Co 11345 Mound Rd *Web:* www.g-l-w.com	Detroit	MI	48212	313-892-8500	
Havco Wood Products LLC 3200 E Outer Rd. *Web:* www.havco.com	Scott City	MO	63780	573-334-6024	
HB&G Inc PO Box 589 *TF:* 800-264-4424 ■ *Web:* www.hbgcolumns.com	Troy	AL	36081	334-566-5000	566-4629
Herrick & White Ltd 3 Flat St. *Web:* herrick-white.com	Cumberland	RI	02864	401-658-0440	
Hoff Cos Inc 1840 N Lakes Ave *Web:* www.hoffcompanies.com	Meridian	ID	83646	208-884-2002	884-1115

Company	City	State	Zip	Phone	Fax
Hollywood Woodwork Inc 2951 Pembroke Rd *Web:* www.hollywoodwoodwork.com	Hollywood	FL	33020	954-920-5009	374-0876
Horner Millwork Corp 1255 Grand Army Hwy *TF:* 800-543-5403 ■ *Web:* www.hornermillwork.com	Somerset	MA	02726	508-679-6479	
Huttig Bldg Products Inc (HBP) 555 Maryville University Dr Ste 400 *OTC: HBPI* ■ *TF:* 800-325-4466 ■ *Web:* www.huttig.com	Saint Louis	MO	63141	314-216-2600	216-2601
Imperial Woodworking Co 310 N Woodwork Ln. *Web:* www.imperialwoodworking.com	Palatine	IL	60067	847-358-6920	358-0905
Inline Fibreglass Ltd 30 Constellation Ct *TF:* 866-566-5656 ■ *Web:* www.inlinefiberglass.com	Toronto	ON	M9W1K1	416-679-1171	679-1150
J C Millwork Inc 501 Lakeside Pkwy Ste 150 *Web:* www.jcmillwork.com	Flower Mound	TX	75028	469-702-2570	
Jeld-Wen Inc PO Box 1329 *TF:* 800-535-3936 ■ *Web:* www.jeld-wen.com	Klamath Falls	OR	97601	800-535-3936	
Koshii Maxelum America Inc 12 Van Kleeck Dr *Web:* www.kmamax.com	Poughkeepsie	NY	12602	845-471-0500	
Lafayette Wood-Works Inc 3004 Cameron St *TF:* 800-960-3311 ■ *Web:* www.lafwoodworks.com	Lafayette	LA	70506	337-233-5250	233-1147
Laflamme Doors & Windows Corp 39 Industrielle. *TF:* 800-463-1922 ■ *Web:* www.laflamme.com	St. Apollinaire	QC	G0S2E0	800-463-1922	
LJ Smith Co 35280 Scio-Bowerston Rd *Web:* www.ljsmith.net	Bowerston	OH	44695	740-269-2221	269-9047
Long Island Fireproof Door Inc 1105 Clintonville St *Web:* lifd.com	Whitestone	NY	11357	718-767-8800	
Loudoun Stairs Inc 341 N Maple Ave *Web:* www.loudounstairs.com	Purcellville	VA	20132	703-478-8800	
Louisiana-Pacific Corp 414 Union St Ste 2000 *NYSE: LPX* ■ *TF:* 888-820-0325 ■ *Web:* www.lpcorp.com	Nashville	TN	37219	615-986-5600	986-5666
Mann & Parker Lumber Company Inc, The 335 N Constitution Ave. *TF:* 800-632-9098 ■ *Web:* m-pgoldbrand.com	New Freedom	PA	17349	717-235-4834	235-5547
MCD Innovations 3303 N MCDonald St *Web:* www.mcdinnovations.com	Mckinney	TX	75071	972-548-1850	
Menzner Lumber & Supply Co PO Box 217 **Fax Area Code:* 715 ■ *TF:* 800-257-1284 ■ *Web:* www.menznerhardwoods.com	Marathon	WI	54448	800-257-1284	443-3798*
Michbi Doors Inc 75 Emjay Blvd. *TF:* 800-854-4541 ■ *Web:* www.michbidoors.com	Brentwood	NY	11717	631-231-9050	
Middlebury Hardwood Products Inc 101 Joan Dr PO Box 1429 *Web:* mhpi.us	Middlebury	IN	46540	574-825-9524	
Milliken Millwork Inc 6361 Sterling Dr N *TF:* 800-686-9218 ■ *Web:* www.millikenmillwork.com	Sterling Heights	MI	48312	586-264-0950	264-5430
Mission Bell Manufacturing Inc 16100 Jacqueline Ct. *Web:* www.missionbell.com	Morgan Hill	CA	95037	408-778-2036	
Monarch Industries Inc 99 Main St *Web:* www.monarchinc.com	Warren	RI	02885	401-247-5200	
Nana Wall Systems Inc 707 Redwood Hwy *TF:* 800-873-5673 ■ *Web:* www.nanawall.com	Mill Valley	CA	94941	415-383-3148	
New England Garage Door 15 Campanelli Cir *TF:* 800-676-7734 ■ *Web:* www.wayne-dalton.com	Canton	MA	02021	781-821-2737	
Nickell Moulding Company Inc 3015 Mobile Dr *TF:* 800-838-2151 ■ *Web:* www.nickellmoulding.com	Elkhart	IN	46515	574-264-3129	
Northside Cabinets Inc 301 Millstone Dr *Web:* www.northsidecabinets.com	Hillsborough	NC	27278	919-732-6100	
Ohline Corp 1930 W 139th St.	Gardena	CA	90249	310-327-4630	
Paltech Enterprises Inc 2560 Bing Miller Ln *TF:* 800-949-1006 ■ *Web:* www.paltech-entrps.com	Urbana	IA	52345	319-443-2700	
Parenti & Raffaelli Ltd 215 Prospect Ave E. *Web:* www.parentiwoodwork.com	Mount Prospect	IL	60056	847-253-5550	253-6055
PGM Products LLC 1 Commerce Dr **Fax Area Code:* 846	Barrington	NJ	08007	856-546-0704	546-0539*
Quanex Building Products 2270 Woodale Dr *TF:* 800-233-4383 ■ *Web:* www.quanex.com	Mounds View	MN	55112	763-231-4000	
R Value Inc 2267 N Interstate Ave *Web:* www.indowwindows.com	Portland	OR	97227	503-284-2260	
Randall Bros Inc 665 Marietta St NW *TF Cust Svc:* 800-476-4539 ■ *Web:* www.randallbrothers.com	Atlanta	GA	30313	404-892-6666	875-6102
Raynor Garage Doors 1101 E River Rd. *TF:* 800-472-9667 ■ *Web:* www.raynor.com	Dixon	IL	61021	815-288-1431	
Reeb Millwork Corp 7475 Henry Clay Blvd *TF:* 800-862-8622 ■ *Web:* reeb.com	Liverpool	NY	13088	315-451-6699	
Royal Cup Coffee and Tea 160 Cleage Dr *TF:* 800-366-5836 ■ *Web:* www.royalcupcoffee.com	Birmingham	AL	35217	800-366-5836	
Ruffin & Payne Inc 4200 Vawter Ave *Web:* www.ruffin-payne.com	Richmond	VA	23261	804-329-2691	321-4940
Scenic Solutions 16135 New Ave. *Web:* www.scenicsolutions.com	Lemont	IL	60439	630-243-1804	
Sensitile Systems LLC 1735 Holmes Rd *Web:* www.sensitile.com	Ypsilanti	MI	48197	313-872-6314	
Shanahan's LP 8400-124 St *TF:* 888-591-5999 ■ *Web:* www.shanahans.com	Surrey	BC	V3W6K1	604-591-5111	
Shaw/Stewart Lumber Co 645 Johnson St NE *Web:* www.shawstewartlumberco.com	Minneapolis	MN	55413	612-378-1520	
Shuster's Bldg Components 2920 Clay Pk. **Fax Area Code:* 800 ■ *TF:* 800-676-0640 ■ *Web:* www.shusters.com	Irwin	PA	15642	724-446-7000	676-0640*
Sierra Pacific Industries 19794 Riverside Ave. *Web:* spi-ind.com	Anderson	CA	96007	530-378-8000	378-8109
Somerset Door & Column Co 174 Sagamore St *TF:* 800-242-7916 ■ *Web:* doorandcolumn.com	Somerset	PA	15501	814-444-9427	443-1658
Southern Staircase Inc 6025 Shiloh Rd Ste E *TF:* 800-874-8408 ■ *Web:* artisticstairs-us.com	Alpharetta	GA	30005	770-888-7333	888-7344

	City	State	Zip	Phone	Fax
Southern Woodsmith Inc 40 Monroe Dr *Web:* www.southernwoodsmith.com	Pelham	AL	35124	205-663-5299	
Spruceland Millworks Inc 53016 Hwy 60 Ste 803 *Web:* www.spruceland.ca	Acheson	AB	T7X5A7	780-962-6333	
Standard Lumber Co 1912 Lehigh Ave *Web:* standardlumberco.com	Glenview	IL	60026	847-729-7800	729-8500
Stephenson Millwork Company Inc 210 Harper St NE *Web:* www.stephensonmillwork.com	Wilson	NC	27893	252-237-1141	237-4377
Sundt Construction 2620 S 55th St *TF:* 800-280-3000 ■ *Web:* www.sundt.com	Tempe	AZ	85282	480-293-3000	
Sunrise Mfg. Inc 2665 Mercantile Dr *TF:* 800-748-6529 ■ *Web:* www.sunrisemfg.com	Rancho Cordova	CA	95742	916-635-6262	
Taney Corp 5130 Allendale Ln *Web:* www.taneystair.com	Taneytown	MD	21787	410-756-6671	756-4103
Taylor Bros Inc 905 Graves Mill Rd *Web:* www.taylorbrothers.com	Lynchburg	VA	24502	434-237-8100	237-4227
THV Compozit Windows & Doors 5611 FERN VALLEY Rd *Web:* www.thv.com	Louisville	KY	40228	502-968-2020	
Tru Tech Corp 20 Vaughan Vly Blvd *TF:* 888-760-0099 ■ *Web:* www.trutech.ca	Vaughan	ON	L4H0B1	905-856-0096	
Washington Woodworking Company Inc 2010 Beaver Rd *Web:* www.washingtonwoodworking.com	Landover	MD	20785	301-341-2500	341-2512
Weaber Inc 1231 Mount Wilson Rd *Web:* www.weaberlumber.com	Lebanon	PA	17042	717-867-2212	
Werzalit of America Inc 40 Holly Ave *TF:* 800-999-3730 ■ *Web:* www.werzalitusa.com	Bradford	PA	16701	814-362-3881	362-4237
Western Millwork Inc 2940 W Willetta St *Web:* www.westernmillworkaz.com	Phoenix	AZ	85009	602-233-1921	278-7101
Windebank Woodwork & Design Ltd 538 Culduthel Rd *Web:* www.windebank.ca	Victoria	BC	V8Z1G1	250-380-1416	
Woodfold Manufacturing Inc 1811 18th Ave PO Box 346 *Web:* www.woodfold.com	Forest Grove	OR	97116	503-357-7181	357-7185
Woodgrain Millworks Inc 300 NW 16th St *TF:* 888-783-5485 ■ *Web:* www.woodgrain.com	Fruitland	ID	83619	208-452-3801	452-3800
Woodharbor Doors & Cabinetry Inc 3277 Ninth St SW	Mason City	IA	50401	641-423-0444	423-0345
Young Mfg Company Inc 521 S Main St PO Box 167 *TF:* 800-545-6595 ■ *Web:* youngmanufacturing.com	Beaver Dam	KY	42320	270-274-3306	274-9522

500 MINERAL PRODUCTS - NONMETALLIC

See Also Insulation & Acoustical Products p. 2570

	City	State	Zip	Phone	Fax
Asbury Graphite Mills Inc 405 Old Main St *Web:* asbury.com	Asbury	NJ	08802	908-537-2155	537-2908
Astro Met Inc 9974 Springfield Pk *Web:* www.astromet.com	Cincinnati	OH	45215	513-772-1242	772-9080
Brubaker-Mann Inc 36011 Soap Mine Rd *Web:* brubakermann.com	Barstow	CA	92311	760-256-2520	256-0127
Buffalo Crushed Stone Co Inc 2544 Clinton St *TF:* 800-543-3860 ■ *Web:* buffalocrushedstone.com	Buffalo	NY	14224	716-826-7310	826-1342
Burgess Pigment Company Inc 525 Beck Blvd PO Box 349 *TF:* 800-841-8999 ■ *Web:* www.burgesspigment.com	Sandersville	GA	31082	478-552-2544	552-4274
Christy Refractories Co 4641 McRee Ave *Web:* www.christyco.com	Saint Louis	MO	63110	314-773-7500	773-8371
Consolidated Ceramic Products Inc 838 Cherry St *Web:* www.ccpi-inc.com	Blanchester	OH	45107	937-783-2476	783-2539
Continental Mineral Processing Corp 11817 Mosteller Rd *Web:* www.continentalmineral.com	Cincinnati	OH	45241	513-771-7190	771-9153
Crystex Composites LLC 125 Clifton Blvd *Web:* www.crystexllc.com	Clifton	NJ	07011	973-779-8866	779-2013
Dicaliter / Dicaperlr Minerals, Inc 1 Bala Ave Ste 310 *Web:* dicalite.com	Bala Cynwyd	PA	19004	610-660-8820	660-8817
Dri-Rite Co 11600 S Ave O PO Box 170319 *Web:* www.dririte.com	Chicago	IL	60617	773-409-4127	221-2909
Eagle-Picher Minerals Inc 9785 Gateway Dr Ste 1000 *TF Cust Svc:* 800-228-3865 ■ *Web:* www.epminerals.com	Reno	NV	89521	775-824-7600	824-7601
Ferro Corp Electronic Materials Div 4150 E 56th St *Web:* ferro.com	Cleveland	OH	44105	216-641-8580	
Graphel Corp 6115 Centre Pk Dr PO Box 369 *TF:* 800-255-1104 ■ *Web:* www.graphel.com	West Chester	OH	45071	513-779-6166	779-3057
Graphite Metallizing Corp 1050 Nepperhan Ave *Web:* www.graphalloy.com	Yonkers	NY	10703	914-968-8400	968-8468
Graphite Sales Inc 16710 W Pk Cir Dr *TF:* 800-321-4147 ■ *Web:* www.graphitesales.com	Chagrin Falls	OH	44023	440-543-8221	543-5183
Hill & Griffith Co 1085 Summer St *TF:* 800-543-0425 ■ *Web:* www.hillandgriffith.com	Cincinnati	OH	45204	513-921-1075	244-4199
Hydraulic Press Brick Co 5505 W 74th St *Web:* www.hpbhaydite.com	Indianapolis	IN	46268	317-290-1140	290-1071
JS McCormick Co 503 Hegner Way	Sewickley	PA	15143	412-794-6356	749-2766
Kocour Co 4800 S St Louis Ave *Web:* www.kocour.net	Chicago	IL	60632	773-847-1111	847-3399
La Habra Products Inc 4125 E La Palma Ave Ste 250 *TF:* 866-516-0061 ■ *Web:* www.lahabrastucco.com	Anaheim	CA	92807	714-778-2266	774-2079
Merlex Stucco Co 2911 N Orange-Olive Rd *Web:* www.merlex.com	Orange	CA	92865	714-637-1700	637-4865
Miller & Co LLC 9700 W Higgins Rd Ste 1000 *TF:* 800-727-9847 ■ *Web:* www.millerandco.com	Rosemont	IL	60018	847-696-2400	696-2419
Miller Studio 734 Fair Ave NW *TF:* 800-332-0050 ■ *Web:* miller-studio.com	New Philadelphia	OH	44663	330-339-1100	
Mission Stucco Company Inc 7751 70th St *Web:* missionstucco.net	Paramount	CA	90723	562-634-1400	634-4440
Multicoat Corp 23331 Antonio Pkwy *TF:* 877-685-8426 ■ *Web:* www.multicoat.com	Rancho Santa Margarita	CA	92688	949-888-7100	888-2555
NYCO Minerals Inc 803 Mtn View Dr *Web:* sandb.com/our-brands/nyco	Willsboro	NY	12996	518-963-4262	963-1110
Oil-Dri Corp of America 410 N Michigan Ave Ste 400 *NYSE: ODC* ■ *TF:* 800-645-3747 ■ *Web:* www.oildri.com	Chicago	IL	60611	312-321-1515	321-1271
Sacramento Stucco Co 1550 PkwyBlvd *Web:* www.westernblended.com	West Sacramento	CA	95691	916-372-7442	372-4836
San Jose Delta Assoc Inc 482 Sapena Ct *Web:* www.sanjosedelta.com	Santa Clara	CA	95054	408-727-1448	727-6019
Schundler Co 150 Whitman Ave *Web:* www.schundler.com	Edison	NJ	08817	732-287-2244	287-4185
Silbrico Corp 6300 River Rd *TF:* 800-323-4287 ■ *Web:* www.silbrico.com	Hodgkins	IL	60525	708-354-3350	354-6698
US Diamond Wheel Co 101 Kendall Pt Dr **Fax Area Code:* 630 ■ *TF:* 800-223-0457 ■ *Web:* www.radiac.com	Oswego	IL	60543	800-851-1095	898-1796*
USG Corp 550 W Adams St *NYSE: USG* ■ *TF:* 800-874-4968 ■ *Web:* www.usg.com	Chicago	IL	60661	312-436-4000	672-4093
Von Roll Isola USA 200 Von Roll Dr **Fax: Cust Svc* ■ *TF:* 800-654-7652 ■ *Web:* www.vonroll.com	Schenectady	NY	12306	518-344-7100	344-7288*
Winter Bros Material Co 13098 Gravois Rd *Web:* www.winterbrothersmaterial.com	Saint Louis	MO	63127	314-843-1400	843-1403
Ziegler Chemical & Mineral Corp 366 N Broadway Ste 210 *Web:* www.zieglerchemical.com	Jericho	NY	11753	516-681-9600	

501 MINING - COAL

	City	State	Zip	Phone	Fax
Allen Guthrie Mchugh & Thomas Pllc 500 Lee St E Ste 800	Charleston	WV	25301	304-345-7250	
Alliance Resource Partners LP 1717 S Boulder Ave Ste 400 *NASDAQ: ARLP* ■ *Web:* www.arlp.com	Tulsa	OK	74119	918-295-7600	295-7358
Alpha Natural Resources Inc 1 Alpha Pl PO Box 16429 *OTC: ANR* ■ *TF:* 866-322-5742 ■ *Web:* www.alphanr.com	Bristol	VA	24209	276-619-4410	
Amerikohl Mining Inc 202 Sunset Dr *Web:* www.amerikohl.com	Butler	PA	16001	724-282-2339	282-3226
Amira International 15005 E Layton Pl *Web:* amira.com.au	Aurora	CO	80015	303-400-3982	
Berwind Natural Resources Corp 509 15th St	Windber	PA	15963	814-467-4519	467-4559
BNI Coal Ltd 1637 Burnt Boat Dr PO Box 897 *Web:* www.bnicoal.com	Bismarck	ND	58503	701-222-8828	222-1547
C & K Coal Co 1062 E Main St PO Box 69	Clarion	PA	16214	814-226-6911	226-9517
CanAm Coal Corp 1201-5th St SW Ste 202 *Web:* www.canamcoal.com	Calgary	AB	T2R0Y6	403-262-3797	
Cline Mining Corp Heritage Bldg 181 Bay St Brookfield Pl 3rd Fl *Web:* www.clinemining.com	Toronto	ON	M5J2T3	416-504-7600	
Cloud Peak Energy Inc (RTEA) 505 S Gillette Ave PO Box 3009 **Fax Area Code:* 303 ■ *TF:* 866-470-4300 ■ *Web:* www.cloudpeakenergy.com	Gillette	WY	82717	307-687-6000	262-0604*
Colombia Energy Resources Inc 1 Embarcadero Ctr Ste 500	San Francisco	CA	94111	415-460-1165	
Coteau Properties Co 204 County Rd 15 *Web:* www.nacoal.com	Beulah	ND	58523	701-873-2281	873-7226
DH Blattner & Sons Inc 392 County Rd 50 *Web:* www.dhblattner.com	Avon	MN	56310	320-356-7351	356-7392
Drummond Co Inc PO Box 10246 *Web:* www.drummondco.com	Birmingham	AL	35202	205-945-6300	
East Fairfield Coal Co (EFCC) 10900 S Ave PO Box 217 *Web:* www.eastfairfieldcoal.com	North Lima	OH	44452	330-549-2165	
Emerald Intarnational Corp 6895 Burlington Pk *Web:* www.emeraldcoal.com	Florence	KY	41042	859-525-2522	525-4052
Hepburnia Coal Co PO Box I	Grampian	PA	16838	814-236-0473	236-1624
Holmes Limestone Co 4255 SR 39 *Web:* holmeslimestone.com	Millersburg	OH	44654	330-893-2721	893-2941
James River Coal Co 901 E Byrd St Ste 1600 *Web:* www.jamesrivercoal.com	Richmond	VA	23219	804-780-3000	
Jim Walter Resources Inc 16243 Hwy 216 *Web:* www.walterenergy.com	Brookwood	AL	35444	205-554-6150	
JM Huber Corp 499 Thornall St 8th Fl **Fax: Hum Res* ■ *TF:* 877-418-0038 ■ *Web:* www.huber.com	Edison	NJ	08837	732-549-8600	549-2239*
Knight Hawk Coal LLC 500 Cutler-Trico Rd *TF:* 855-611-2625 ■ *Web:* www.knighthawkcoal.com	Percy	IL	62272	618-426-3662	
Lee Ranch Coal Co PO Box 757	Grants	NM	87020	505-285-4651	
Natural Resource Partners LP 601 Jefferson St Ste 3600 *NYSE: NRP* ■ *TF:* 888-334-7102 ■ *Web:* www.nrplp.com	Houston	TX	77002	713-751-7507	
North American Coal Corp 5340 Legacy Dr Bldg I Ste 300 *Web:* www.nacoal.com	Plano	TX	75024	972-448-5400	
Ohio River Collieries Co 70245 Bannock Uniontown Rd	Bannock	OH	43972	740-968-3582	
Ohio Valley Coal Co 56854 Pleasant Ridge Rd	Alledonia	OH	43902	740-926-1351	926-1615
Pacific Coal Resources Ltd 333 Bay St Ste 1100 *Web:* www.pacificcoal.ca	Toronto	ON	M5H2R2	416-360-8725	
Peabody Energy Corp 701 Market St *NYSE: BTU* ■ *Web:* www.peabodyenergy.com	Saint Louis	MO	63101	314-342-3400	

Phone Fax

Peabody Energy Corp
Peabody Plz 701 Market St.......................... St. Louis MO 63101 314-342-3400
TF: 866-470-4500 ■ *Web:* Www.peabodyenergy.com

Reading Anthracite Co
200 Mahantongo St PO Box 1200 .... Pottsville PA 17901 570-622-5150
Web: www.readinganthracite.com

RG Johnson Company Inc 25 S College St .... Washington PA 15301 724-222-6810 222-6815
Web: rgjohnsoninc.com

Rhino Resource Partners LP
424 Lewis Hargett Cir Ste 250 .... Lexington KY 40503 859-389-6500
Web: www.rhinolp.com

S&B Industrial Minerals North America Inc
920 Cassatt Rd Ste 205 .... Berwyn PA 19312 610-647-1123

SABIA Inc 10911 Technology Pl..................... San Diego CA 92127 858-217-2200
Web: www.sabiainc.com

Sharpe Resources Corp 3258 Mob Neck Rd.......... Heathsville VA 22473 804-580-8107
Web: www.sharperesourcescorporation.com

Stewart Materials 13525 Indrio Rd .... Fort Pierce FL 34945 561-972-4517
Web: stewartmaterials.com

TECO Coal Corp 200 Allison Blvd .... Corbin KY 40701 606-523-4444
Web: www.tecocoal.com

Thunder Basin Coal Co PO Box 406 .... Wright WY 82732 307-939-1300
Web: www.archcoal.com

Usibelli Coal Mine Inc 100 River Rd PO Box 1000 .... Healy AK 99743 907-683-2226 683-2253
Web: www.usibelli.com

Western Energy Co 138 Rosebud Ln PO Box 99 .... Colstrip MT 59323 406-748-5100 748-5181
Web: westmoreland.com

Westmoreland Coal Co
9540 S Maroon Cir Ste 200 .... Englewood CO 80112 719-442-2600 877-9089*
NASDAQ: WLB ■ **Fax Area Code:* 307 ■ *TF:* 855-922-6463 ■ *Web:* www.westmoreland.com

Westmoreland Resource Partners LP
41 S High St.................................... Columbus OH 43215 614-643-0337
Web: westmorelandmlp.com

Westmoreland Resources Inc 100 Sarpy Creek Rd .... Hardin MT 59034 406-342-5201 342-5401
Web: westmoreland.com/location/absaloka-mine-montana

502 MINING - METALS

Phone Fax

Agnico-Eagle Mines Ltd 145 King St E Ste 500 .... Toronto ON M5C2Y7 416-947-1212 367-4681
NYSE: AEM ■ *TF:* 888-822-6714 ■ *Web:* www.agnicoeagle.com

B2 Gold Corp
595 Burrard St Ste 3100 PO Box 49143.............. Vancouver BC V7X1J1 604-681-8371 681-6209
TF: 800-316-8855 ■ *Web:* www.b2gold.com

Badger Mining Corp 409 S Church St PO Box 328 .... Berlin WI 54923 920-361-2388 361-2826
TF: 800-932-7263 ■ *Web:* www.badgerminingcorp.com

Barrick Gold Corp
TD Canada Trust Tower 161 Bay St PO Box 212.......... Toronto ON M5J2S1 416-861-9911 861-2492
NYSE: ABX ■ *TF:* 800-720-7415 ■ *Web:* www.barrick.com

Barrick Goldstrike Mines Inc PO Box 29................. Elko NV 89803 416-861-9911
Web: www.barrick.com

BCM Resources Corp 1040 W Georgia St .... Vancouver BC V6E4H1 604-646-0144
TF: 888-646-0144 ■ *Web:* www.bcmresources.com

Cameco Corp 2121 11th St W .... Saskatoon SK S7M1J3 306-956-6200 956-6201
NYSE: CCO ■ *Web:* www.cameco.com

Chaparral Gold Corp
7950 E Acoma Dr Ste 211.......................... Scottsdale AZ 85260 480-483-9932 483-9926
TSE: IMZ

Cliffs Natural Resources
200 Public Sq Ste 3300 .... Cleveland OH 44114 216-694-5700
Web: www.cliffsnaturalresources.com

Climax Molybdenum Co PO Box 220............. Fort Madison IA 52627 602-366-8100 366-7318*
**Fax:* Hum Res ■ *Web:* www.climaxmolybdenum.com

Corriente Resources Inc
5811 Cooney Rd Unit S209 .... Richmond BC V6X3M1 604-282-7212 282-7568
Web: www.corriente.com

Crown Gold Corp 970 Caughlin Crossing Ste 100 .... Reno NV 89519 775-284-7200
TSE: CWM ■ *Web:* www.crowngoldcorp.com

Crystallex International Corp
8 King St E Ste 1201.............................. Toronto ON M5C1B5 416-203-2448 203-0099
TF: 800-738-1577 ■ *Web:* www.crystallex.com

Eldorado Gold Corp 550 Burrard St .... Vanouver BC V6C2B5 604-687-4018 687-4026
NYSE: ELD ■ *TF:* 888-353-8166 ■ *Web:* www.eldoradogold.com

First Quantum Minerals Ltd
543 Granville St 8th Fl .... Vancouver BC V6C1X8 604-688-6577 688-3818
TSE: FM ■ *TF:* 888-688-6577 ■ *Web:* www.first-quantum.com

General Moly Inc 1726 Cole Blvd Ste 115 .... Lakewood CO 80401 303-928-8599
Web: www.generalmoly.com

Gold Reserve Inc 926 W Sprague Ave Ste 200.......... Spokane WA 99201 509-623-1500 623-1634
TSE: GRZ ■ *TF:* 800-625-9550 ■ *Web:* www.goldreserveinc.com

Goldcorp Inc 666 Burrard St Ste 3400................ Vancouver BC V6C2X8 604-696-3000 696-3001
NYSE: G ■ *TF:* 800-567-6223 ■ *Web:* www.goldcorp.com

Golden Star Resources Ltd
150 King St W Ste 1200............................ Toronto ON M5H1J9 303-830-9000
NYSE: GSS ■ *TF:* 800-553-8436 ■ *Web:* www.gsr.com

Goldfield Corp 1684 W Hibiscus Blvd............... Melbourne FL 32901 321-724-1700
NYSE: GV ■ *Web:* www.goldfieldcorp.com

Hecla Mining Co 800 W Pender St Ste 970............ Vancouver BC V6C2V6 604-682-6201 682-6215
NYSE: HL ■ *TF:* 800-432-5291 ■ *Web:* hecla-mining.com

Hecla Mining Co
6500 N Mineral Dr Ste 200..................... Coeur d'Alene ID 83815 208-769-4100 769-4107
NYSE: HL ■ *Web:* www.hecla-mining.com

Hibbing Taconite Co 4950 County Rd 5 N............... Hibbing MN 55746 218-262-5950
Web: cliffsnaturalresources.com

IAMGOLD Corp 401 Bay St Ste 3200 PO Box 153 .... Toronto ON M5H2Y4 416-360-4710
TSE: IMG ■ *TF:* 888-464-9999 ■ *Web:* www.iamgold.com

IBC Advanced Alloys Corp
570 Granville St Ste 1200.......................... Vancouver BC V6C3P1 604-685-6263
TF: 800-373-3251 ■ *Web:* www.ibcadvancedalloys.com

Imperial Metals Corp 580 Hornby St Ste 200 .... Vancouver BC V6C3B6 604-669-8959 687-4030
TSE: III ■ *Web:* www.imperialmetals.com

Phone Fax

Ivanhoe Mines Ltd 654-999 Canada Pl .... Vancouver BC V6C3E1 604-688-6630 682-2060
Web: www.ivanhoemines.com

Kennecott Uranium Co NW Of Rawlins .... Rawlins WY 82301 307-328-1476

Kimber Resources Inc
800 W Pender St Ste 220 .... Vancouver BC V6C2V6 604-669-2251
Web: invecture.com

Kinross Gold Corp 25 York St 17th Fl.................. Toronto ON M5J2V5 416-365-5123 363-6622
NYSE: KGC ■ *TF:* 866-561-3636 ■ *Web:* www.kinross.com

Kinross Gold USA Inc 5370 Kietzke Ln Ste 102 .... Reno NV 89511 775-829-1000
Web: kinross.com

Materion Corp 6070 Parkland Blvd............. Mayfield Heights OH 44124 216-486-4200 383-4091
NYSE: MTRN ■ *TF:* 800-321-2076 ■ *Web:* www.materion.com

Meridian Gold Co 9670 Gateway Dr Ste 200............... Reno NV 89521 775-850-3777 249-6189*
**Fax Area Code:* 888

Mines Management Inc
905 W Riverside Ave Ste 311 .... Spokane WA 99201 509-838-6050 838-0486
NYSE: MGN ■ *Web:* www.minesmanagement.com

Molycorp Inc 67750 Bailey Rd.................. Mountain Pass CA 92366 760-856-2201 856-2253
Web: www.molycorp.com

NA Degerstrom Inc 3303 N Sullivan Rd .... Spokane WA 99216 509-928-3333 927-2010
Web: www.nadinc.com

New Gold Inc 666 Burrard St Ste 3110 .... Vancouver BC V6C2X8 604-696-4100 696-4110
NYSE: NGD ■ *Web:* www.newgold.com

Newmont Mining Corp
6363 S Fiddler's Green Cir Ste 800 .... Greenwood Village CO 80111 303-863-7414 837-5837
NYSE: NEM ■ *Web:* www.newmont.com

NMC Resource Corp 1111 Melville St Ste 1100........ Vancouver BC V6E3V6 604-643-1730
Web: www.nmcresource.com

Nord Resources Corp 1 W Wetmore Rd Ste 203 .... Tucson AZ 85705 520-292-0266 292-0268

North American Palladium Ltd
1 University Ave Ste 402.......................... Toronto ON M5J2J2 416-360-7590 360-7709
TSE: PDL ■ *TF:* 888-360-7590 ■ *Web:* www.napalladium.com

North American Tungsten Corp Ltd
1188 W Georgia St Ste 1640 .... Vancouver BC V6E4A2 604-684-5300
Web: www.natungsten.com

Northgate Minerals Corp 181 Bay St Ste 3910.......... Toronto ON M5J2T3 647-260-8880
CVE: NXG ■ *Web:* www.auricogold.com

NovaGold Resources Inc
789 W Pender St Ste 720 .... Vancouver BC V6C1H2 604-669-6227 669-6272
NYSE: NG ■ *TF:* 866-699-6227 ■ *Web:* www.novagold.com

Optex Systems Holdings Inc
1420 Presidential Dr........................... Richardson TX 75081 972-644-0722 234-3544
OTC: OPXS ■ *Web:* www.optexsys.com

Pacific Rim Mining Corp
625 Howe St Ste 1050 .... Vancouver BC V6C2T6 604-689-1976
OTC: PFRMF ■ *TF:* 888-775-7097 ■ *Web:* oceanagold.com

Pan American Silver Corp
625 Howe St Ste 1500 .... Vancouver BC V6C2T6 604-684-1175 684-0147
TSE: PAA ■ *Web:* www.panamericansilver.com

Roca Mines Inc 490 - 1122 Mainland Ste 490......... Vancouver BC V6B5L1 604-684-2900
Web: www.rocamines.com

Royal Gold Inc 1660 Wynkoop St Ste 1000.............. Denver CO 80202 303-573-1660 595-9385
NASDAQ: RGLD ■ *Web:* www.royalgold.com

Rubicon Minerals Corp 44 Victoria St Ste 400 .... Toronto ON M5C1Y2 604-623-3333
NYSE: RBY ■ *TF:* 866-365-4706 ■ *Web:* www.rubiconminerals.com

Seabridge Gold Inc 106 Front St E Ste 400 .... Toronto ON M5A1E1 416-367-9292 367-2711
TSE: SEA ■ *Web:* www.seabridgegold.net

Sherritt International Corp 1133 Yonge St .... Toronto ON M4T2Y7 416-924-4551 924-5015
TSE: S ■ *TF:* 800-704-6698 ■ *Web:* www.sherritt.com

Silver Standard Resources Inc
999 W Hastings St Ste 1180......................... Vancouver BC V6C2W2 604-689-3846 689-3847
TSE: SSO ■ *TF:* 888-338-0046 ■ *Web:* www.silverstandard.com

Stillwater Mining Co 1321 Discovery Dr .... Billings MT 59102 406-373-8700 373-8701
NYSE: SWC ■ *Web:* www.stillwatermining.com

Stratcor Inc 1180 Omega Dr Ste 1180................ Pittsburgh PA 15205 412-787-4500 787-5030
Web: vanadium.evraz.com

Sunridge International
16857 Saguaro Blvd.......................... Fountain Hills AZ 85268 480-837-6165

Teck Cominco American Inc
501 N Riverpoint Blvd Ste 300 .... Spokane WA 99202 509-747-6111 747-6111
TF: 866-225-0198 ■ *Web:* www.teck.com

Umetco Minerals Corp 2754 Compass Dr........ Grand Junction CO 81506 970-245-3700

Uranium Resources Inc
405 State Hwy 121 Bypass A-110.................... Lewisville TX 75067 972-219-3330
NASDAQ: URRE ■ *Web:* www.uraniumresources.com

US Energy Corp 877 N Eigth W .... Riverton WY 82501 307-856-9271 857-3050
NASDAQ: USEG ■ *TF:* 800-776-9271 ■ *Web:* www.usnrg.com

Vale 200 Bay St Ste 1600 PO Box 70 .... Toronto ON M5J2K2 416-361-7511 361-7781
Web: www.nickel.vale.com

Vista Gold Corp 7961 Shaffer Pkwy Ste 5 .... Littleton CO 80127 720-981-1185 981-1186
NYSE: VGZ ■ *Web:* www.vistagold.com

Western Copper Corp
1040 W Georgia St FL 15 .... Vancouver BC V6E4H1 604-684-9497 669-2926
TF: 888-966-9995 ■ *Web:* westerncopperandgold.com

Western Nuclear Inc 2801 Youngfield St Ste 340......... Golden CO 80401 303-274-1767

Wharf Resources USA Inc 10928 Wharf Rd .... Lead SD 57754 605-584-1441 584-4188
TF: 800-567-6223 ■ *Web:* goldcorp.com

Woulfe Mining Corp
837 W Hastings St Ste 408........................ Vancouver BC V6C3N6 604-684-6264

503 MINING - MINERALS

503-1 Chemical & Fertilizer Minerals Mining

Phone Fax

American Borate Corp
5700 Cleveland St Ste 350..................... Virginia Beach VA 23462 757-490-2242 490-1548
TF: 800-486-1072 ■ *Web:* www.americanborate.com

New Riverside Ochre Co
75 Old River Rd SE............................ Cartersville GA 30121 770-382-4568
TF Orders: 800-248-0176 ■ *Web:* www.nroonline.com

Phone Fax

Potash Corp 1101 Skokie Blvd. Northbrook IL 60062 847-849-4200 849-4695
TF: 800-667-0403 ■ *Web:* www.potashcorp.com

Searles Valley Minerals
9401 Indian Creek Pkwy Ste 1000 Overland Park KS 66210 913-344-9500 344-9602
TF: 800-637-2775 ■ *Web:* www.svminerals.com

Solvay Chemicals Inc 3333 Richmond Ave Houston TX 77098 713-525-6800 525-7805
TF: 800-765-8292

United Salt Corp 4800 San Felipe St. Houston TX 77056 713-877-2600 877-2609
TF: 800-554-8658 ■ *Web:* www.unitedsalt.com

503-2 Clay, Ceramic, Refractory Minerals Mining

Phone Fax

AMCOL International Corp
2870 Forbs Ave Hoffman Estates IL 60192 847-851-1500 250-3325*
NYSE: ACO ■ **Fax Area Code:* 610 ■ *TF General:* 800-962-8586 ■ *Web:* www.amcol.com

Black Hills Bentonite LLC PO Box 9 Mills WY 82644 307-265-3740
Web: www.bhbentonite.com

Dixie Clay Co 305 Dixie Clay Rd Bath SC 29816 803-593-2592 759-2606*
**Fax Area Code:* 205

Hecla Mining Co
6500 N Mineral Dr Ste 200 Coeur d'Alene ID 83815 208-769-4100 769-4107
NYSE: HL ■ *Web:* www.hecla-mining.com

Holmes Limestone Co 4255 SR 39 Millersburg OH 44654 330-893-2721 893-2941
Web: holmeslimestone.com

I-Minerals Inc 880 - 580 Hornby St Vancouver BC V6C3B6 604-303-6573
TF: 877-303-6573 ■ *Web:* www.imineralsinc.com

Imerys USA Inc 100 Mansell Ct E Ste 300 Roswell GA 30076 770-645-3300 645-3384
TF: 800-843-3222 ■ *Web:* www.imerys-paper.com

Kyanite Mining Corp 30 Willis Mtn Ln. Dillwyn VA 23936 434-983-2085 983-5178
Web: www.kyanite.com

Milwhite Inc 5487 S Padre Island Hwy Brownsville TX 78521 956-547-1970 547-1999
TF: 800-442-0082 ■ *Web:* www.milwhite.com

Riverside Clay Co Inc 201 Truss Ferry Rd Pell City AL 35128 205-338-3366 338-7456
TF: 800-924-0637 ■ *Web:* riversiderefractories.com

Riverside Refractories Inc
201 Truss Ferry Rd Pell City AL 35128 205-338-3366 338-7456
TF: 800-924-0637 ■ *Web:* www.riversiderefractories.com

RT Vanderbilt Company Inc 30 Winfield St Norwalk CT 06855 203-853-1400 853-1452
TF Cust Svc: 800-243-6064 ■ *Web:* www.rtvanderbilt.com

Thiele Kaolin Co PO Box 1056 Sandersville GA 31082 478-552-3951
Web: www.thielekaolin.com

US Silica Co 8490 Progress Dr Ste 300 Frederick MD 21701 304-258-2500
TF: 800-243-7500 ■ *Web:* www.ussilica.com

Wyo-Ben Inc 1345 Discovery Dr Billings MT 59102 406-652-6351 656-0748
TF Cust Svc: 800-548-7055 ■ *Web:* www.wyoben.com

503-3 Minerals Mining (Misc)

Phone Fax

Harborlite 130 Castilian Dr Santa Barbara CA 93117 805-562-0200
TF: 800-893-4445 ■ *Web:* www.worldminerals.com

ILC Resources 3301 106th Cir. Urbandale IA 50322 515-243-8106 244-3200
TF: 800-247-2133 ■ *Web:* www.ilcresources.com

Mountain Province Diamonds Inc
161 Bay St Ste 2315 Toronto ON M5J2S1 416-361-3562 603-8565
TSE: MPV ■ *Web:* www.mountainprovince.com

RT Vanderbilt Company Inc 30 Winfield St Norwalk CT 06855 203-853-1400 853-1452
TF Cust Svc: 800-243-6064 ■ *Web:* www.rtvanderbilt.com

Stornoway Diamond Corp
980 W First St Ste 118 North Vancouver BC V7P3N4 604-983-7750
TSE: SWY ■ *TF:* 877-331-2232 ■ *Web:* www.stornowaydiamonds.com

Vanderbilt Minerals Corp 30 Winfield St Norwalk CT 06855 203-853-1400 853-1452
TF: 800-243-6064 ■ *Web:* www.rtvanderbilt.com

WGI Heavy Minerals Inc
810 E Sherman Ave Coeur d'Alene ID 83814 208-666-6000 666-4000
TSE: WG ■ *TF:* 888-542-7638 ■ *Web:* www.wgiheavyminerals.com

503-4 Sand & Gravel Pits

Phone Fax

Brox Industries Inc 1471 Methuen St. Dracut MA 01826 978-454-9105 805-9720
Web: www.broxindustries.com

Edward C Levy Co 9300 Dix Ave Dearborn MI 48120 313-843-7200 849-9441*
**Fax:* Sales ■ *TF:* 877-938-0007 ■ *Web:* www.edwclevy.com

Elmer Larson LLC 21218 Airport Rd Sycamore IL 60178 815-895-4837 895-4437

ER Jahna Industries Inc 202 E Stuart Ave Lake Wales FL 33853 863-676-9431 676-5137
Web: www.jahna.com

Fisher Sand & Gravel Co 3948 First ST SW Underwood ND 58576 701-442-5600
TF: 800-932-8740 ■ *Web:* www.fisherind.com

Hills Materials Co 3975 Sturgis Rd Rapid City SD 57702 605-394-3300 341-3446
TF: 800-325-7056 ■ *Web:* www.hillsmaterials.com

Hilltop Basic Resources Inc
1 W Fourth St Ste 1100 Cincinnati OH 45202 513-651-5000 684-8222
Web: www.hilltopbasicresources.com

Janesville Sand & Gravel Co (JSG)
1110 Harding St Janesville WI 53547 608-754-7701
TF: 800-955-7702 ■ *Web:* www.jsandg.com

Lafarge North America Inc
8700 W Bryn Mawr Ave Ste 300 Chicago VA 60631 703-480-3600 480-3899
Web: www.lafarge-na.com

LG Everist Inc 300 S Phillips Ave Ste 200 Sioux Falls SD 57117 605-334-5000 334-3656
TF: 800-843-7992 ■ *Web:* www.lgeverist.com

Mark Sand & Gravel Co
525 Kennedy Pk Rd PO Box 458 Fergus Falls MN 56537 218-736-7523 736-2647
TF: 800-427-8316 ■ *Web:* www.marksandgravel.com

Martin Marietta Materials Inc
2710 Wycliff Rd Raleigh NC 27607 919-781-4550
NYSE: MLM ■ *Web:* www.martinmarietta.com

Miles Sand & Gravel Company Inc
400 Valley Ave NE Puyallup WA 98372 253-833-3705 833-3746
Web: www.milessandandgravel.com

Pete Lien & Sons Inc 3401 Universal Dr Rapid City SD 57709 605-342-7224 342-6979
Web: www.petelien.com

Pike Industries Inc 3 Eastgate Pk Rd Belmont NH 03220 603-527-5100 527-5101
TF: 800-283-0803 ■ *Web:* pikeindustries.com

Pounding Mill Quarry Corp
171 St Clair S Crossing Bluefield VA 24605 276-326-1145 322-6805
TF: 888-661-7625 ■ *Web:* www.pmqc.com

Rogers Group Inc 421 Great Cir Rd. Nashville TN 37228 615-242-0585
Web: www.rogersgroupincint.com

Standard Sand & Silica Co
1850 US Highway 17 92 N Davenport FL 33837 863-422-7100 421-7349

Tower Rock Stone Co
19829 Lower Frenchman Rd Sainte Genevieve MO 63670 573-883-7415 883-3067

Unimin Corp 258 Elm St. New Canaan CT 06840 203-966-8880 966-3453
Web: www.unimin.com

US Silica Co 8490 Progress Dr Ste 300 Frederick MD 21701 304-258-2500
TF: 800-243-7500 ■ *Web:* www.ussilica.com

Wendling Quarries Inc
2647 225th St PO Box 230 De Witt IA 52742 563-659-9181 659-3393
Web: www.wendlingquarries.com

Westroc Inc 670 West 220 South Pleasant Grove UT 84062 801-785-5600 785-5600

Whibco Inc 87 E Commerce St. Bridgeton NJ 08302 856-455-9200 455-9009
Web: www.whibco.com

503-5 Stone Quarries - Crushed & Broken Stone

Phone Fax

Aggregate Industries Management Inc
7529 Standish Pl Rockville MD 20855 301-284-3600 284-3645
Web: www.aggregate-us.com

Anderson Columbia Co Inc
871 NW Guerdon St PO Box 1829 Lake City FL 32056 386-752-7585 755-5430
Web: www.andersoncolumbia.com

Ararat Rock Products Co 525 Quarry Rd Mount Airy NC 27030 336-786-4693 786-2189

Braen Stone Co 400 Central Ave PO Box 8310 Haledon NJ 07508 973-595-6250 595-7087
Web: braenstone.com

Brox Industries Inc 1471 Methuen St. Dracut MA 01826 978-454-9105 805-9720
Web: www.broxindustries.com

Cessford Construction Co 3808 Old Hwy 61 Burlington IA 52601 319-753-2297 753-0926
Web: www.omgmidwest.com

Eastern Industries Inc
4401 Camp Meeting Rd Ste 200 Center Valley PA 18034 610-866-0932 867-1886
Web: www.eastern-ind.com

Edward C Levy Co 9300 Dix Ave Dearborn MI 48120 313-843-7200 849-9441*
**Fax:* Sales ■ *TF:* 877-938-0007 ■ *Web:* www.edwclevy.com

ER Jahna Industries Inc 202 E Stuart Ave Lake Wales FL 33853 863-676-9431 676-5137
Web: www.jahna.com

Harney Rock & Paving Co 457 S Date Ave Burns OR 97720 541-573-7855 573-3532
TF: 888-298-2681 ■ *Web:* www.harneyrock.com

HB Mellot Estate Inc 100 Mellott Dr Warfordsburg PA 17267 301-678-2050 678-2051
TF: 800-634-5634 ■ *Web:* www.mellottcompany.com

Hills Materials Co 3975 Sturgis Rd Rapid City SD 57702 605-394-3300 341-3446
TF: 800-325-7056 ■ *Web:* www.hillsmaterials.com

Hunt Midwest Enterprises Inc
8300 NE Underground Dr Kansas City MO 64161 816-455-2500
TF: 800-551-6877 ■ *Web:* www.huntmidwest.com

Hunt Midwest Mining Inc
8300 NE Underground Dr Kansas City MO 64161 816-455-2500 455-4462
TF: 800-551-6877 ■ *Web:* www.huntmidwest.com

JF Shea Company Inc Redding Div
17400 Clear Creek Rd Redding CA 96001 530-246-4292
Web: www.jfshea.com

Lafarge North America Inc
8700 W Bryn Mawr Ave Ste 300 Chicago VA 60631 703-480-3600 480-3899
Web: www.lafarge-na.com

LG Everist Inc 300 S Phillips Ave Ste 200 Sioux Falls SD 57117 605-334-5000 334-3656
TF: 800-843-7992 ■ *Web:* www.lgeverist.com

Martin Marietta Materials Inc
2710 Wycliff Rd Raleigh NC 27607 919-781-4550
NYSE: MLM ■ *Web:* www.martinmarietta.com

Meckley's Limestone Products Inc
1543 State Rt 225 Herndon PA 17830 570-758-3011 758-2400
Web: www.meckleys.com

Meshberger Bros Stone Corp 6311 W St Rd 218 Bluffton IN 46714 260-334-5311 334-5353

Midwest Minerals Inc
709 N Locust St PO Box 412 Pittsburg KS 66762 620-231-8120 235-0840
Web: www.midwestminerals.com

Mulzer Crushed Stone Inc
534 Mozart St PO Box 249 Tell City IN 47586 812-547-7921 547-6757
Web: www.mulzer.com

New Enterprise Stone & Lime Company Inc (NESL)
3912 Brumbaugh Rd PO Box 77 New Enterprise PA 16664 814-766-2211
Web: www.nesl.com

NR Hamm Quarry Inc 609 Perry Pl Perry KS 66073 785-597-5111 597-5117

Pennsy Supply Inc 1001 Paxton St. Harrisburg PA 17104 717-233-4511 238-7312
Web: www.pennsysupply.com

Pike Industries Inc 3 Eastgate Pk Rd Belmont NH 03220 603-527-5100 527-5101
TF: 800-283-0803 ■ *Web:* pikeindustries.com

Pounding Mill Quarry Corp
171 St Clair S Crossing Bluefield VA 24605 276-326-1145 322-6805
TF: 888-661-7625 ■ *Web:* www.pmqc.com

Rogers Group Inc 421 Great Cir Rd. Nashville TN 37228 615-242-0585
Web: www.rogersgroupincint.com

Stoneco Inc 7555 Whiteford Rd. Ottawa Lake MI 49267 734-856-2257
Web: stoneco.net

Syar Industries Inc 2301 Napa Vallejo Hwy Napa CA 94558 707-252-8711 224-5932
Web: syar.com

Phone | Fax

Texas Crushed Stone Co
5300 S IH-35 PO Box 1000 .... Georgetown TX 78627 512-930-0106 244-6055
TF: 800-772-8272 ■ *Web:* www.texascrushedstoneco.com

Tilcon NY Inc 162 Old Mill Rd .... West Nyack NY 10994 845-358-4500
TF: 800-872-7762 ■ *Web:* www.tilconny.com

Tower Rock Stone Co
19829 Lower Frenchman Rd .... Sainte Genevieve MO 63670 573-883-7415 883-3067

Trap Rock Industries Inc 460 River Rd .... Kingston NJ 08528 609-924-0300 497-0135
Web: www.traprock.com

Valley Quarries Inc
297 Quarry Rd PO Box J .... Chambersburg PA 17201 717-267-2244 267-2521
Web: www.valleyquarries.com

Vulcan Materials Co
1200 Urban Ctr Dr PO Box 385014 .... Birmingham AL 35238 205-298-3000
NYSE: VMC ■ *TF:* 800-615-4331 ■ *Web:* www.vulcanmaterials.com

Vulcan Materials Company Western Div
3200 San Fernando Rd .... Los Angeles CA 90065 323-258-2777
NYSE: VMC ■ *TF:* 800-615-4331 ■ *Web:* www.vulcanmaterials.com

Wendling Quarries Inc
2647 225th St PO Box 230 .... De Witt IA 52742 563-659-9181 659-3393
Web: www.wendlingquarries.com

Wyroc Inc 2142 Industrial Ct .... Vista CA 92081 760-727-0878 727-9238
Web: www.wyroc.com

503-6 Stone Quarries - Dimension Stone

Phone | Fax

American Clay Enterprises LLC
2418 Second St SW .... Albuquerque NM 87102 505-243-5300
TF: 866-404-1634 ■ *Web:* www.americanclay.com

Eden Stone Company Inc W4520 Lime Rd .... Eden WI 53019 920-477-2521 477-4700
TF: 800-472-2521 ■ *Web:* edenstone.net

Fletcher Granite Company Inc 534 Groton Rd .... Westford MA 01886 978-692-1312
Web: www.fletchergranite.com

Inter-Rock Minerals Inc 20 Toronto St 12th Fl .... Toronto ON M5C2B8 416-367-3003
Web: inter-rockminerals.net

Liter's Quarry Inc 5918 Haunz Ln .... Louisville KY 40241 502-241-7637 241-9410
Web: www.litersinc.com

LW Rozzo Inc 17200 Pines Blvd .... Pembroke Pines FL 33029 954-435-8501 436-6243

Oldcastle Materials Inc
900 Ashwood Pkwy Ste 700 .... Atlanta GA 30338 770-522-5600 522-5608
Web: www.apac.com

Pounding Mill Quarry Corp
171 St Clair S Crossing .... Bluefield VA 24605 276-326-1145 322-6805
TF: 888-661-7625 ■ *Web:* www.pmqc.com

Swenson Granite Co LLC 369 N State St .... Concord NH 03301 603-672-7827 227-9541
Web: www.swensongranite.com

Tower Rock Stone Co
19829 Lower Frenchman Rd .... Sainte Genevieve MO 63670 573-883-7415 883-3067

Wendling Quarries Inc
2647 225th St PO Box 230 .... De Witt IA 52742 563-659-9181 659-3393
Web: www.wendlingquarries.com

504 MISSILES, SPACE VEHICLES, PARTS

See Also Weapons & Ordnance (Military) p. 3305

Phone | Fax

Advanced Thermal Sciences Corp
3355 E La Palma Ave .... Anaheim CA 92806 714-688-4200
Web: www.atschiller.com

Aerojet PO Box 13222 .... Sacramento CA 95813 916-355-4000 351-8667
Web: www.rocket.com

Aerojet Redmond Rocket Ctr 11411 139th Pl NE .... Redmond WA 98052 425-885-5000 882-5804*
**Fax: Mail Rm* ■ *Web:* www.rocket.com

Applied Aerospace Structures Corp (AASC)
3437 S Airport Way PO Box 6189 .... Stockton CA 95206 209-982-0160 983-3375
Web: www.aascworld.com

Astrotech Corp 401 Congress Ave Ste 1650 .... Austin TX 78701 512-485-9530 485-9531
NASDAQ: ASTC ■ *Web:* www.astrotechcorp.com

Boeing Co, The 100 N Riverside Plz .... Chicago IL 60606 312-544-2000
NYSE: BA ■ *Web:* www.boeing.com

Esterline Mason 13955 Balboa Blvd .... Sylmar CA 91342 818-361-3366 365-6809*
**Fax: Sales* ■ *TF:* 800-232-7700 ■ *Web:* www.esterline.com

Hamilton Sundstrand Corp 1 Hamilton Rd .... Windsor Locks CT 06096 860-654-6000
Web: utcaerospacesystems.com

HITCO Carbon Composites Inc 1600 W 135th St .... Gardena CA 90249 310-527-0700 970-5468
TF: 800-421-5444 ■ *Web:* www.hitco.com

International Launch Services (ILS)
1875 Explorer St Ste 700 .... Reston VA 20190 571-633-7400 633-7500
TF: 800-852-4980 ■ *Web:* www.ilslaunch.com

Kratos Defense & Security Solutions, Inc.
3061 Industry Dr .... Lancaster PA 17603 717-397-2777 397-7079*
**Fax: Sales* ■ *Web:* www.kratosmed.com/page/moved/herley

L'Garde Inc 15181 Woodlawn Ave .... Tustin CA 92780 714-259-0771 259-7822
Web: www.lgarde.com

Leading Technology Composites Inc 2626 W May .... Wichita KS 67213 316-944-0011
Web: www.ltc-ltc.com

Lockheed Martin Corp 6801 Rockledge Dr .... Bethesda MD 20817 301-897-6000
NYSE: LMT ■ *TF:* 866-562-2363 ■ *Web:* www.lockheedmartin.com

Lockheed Martin Space Systems Co Michoud Operations
13800 Old Gentilly Rd .... New Orleans LA 70129 504-257-3311 688-0702*
**Fax Area Code: 613* ■ *TF:* 866-562-2363

Novatronics Inc 677 Erie St .... Stratford ON N5A6V6 519-271-3880
Web: www.novatronics.com

Paragon Space Development Corp
3481 E Michigan St .... Tucson AZ 85714 520-903-1000
Web: www.paragonsdc.com

Pratt & Whitney 17900 Bee Line Hwy .... Jupiter FL 33478 860-565-4321
Web: pw.utc.com

Qualitor Inc 24800 Denso Dr Ste 255 .... Southfield MI 48033 248-204-8600 204-8619
Web: www.qualitorinc.com

Phone | Fax

Reinhold Industries Inc
12827 E Imperial Hwy .... Santa Fe Springs CA 90670 562-944-3281 944-7238
Web: www.reinhold-ind.com

Sea Launch Company LLC 2700 Nimitz Rd .... Long Beach CA 90802 562-951-7000
Web: www.sea-launch.com

Space Vector Corp 9223 Deering Ave .... Chatsworth CA 91311 818-734-2600 428-6249
Web: www.spacevector.com

505 MOBILE HOMES & BUILDINGS

Phone | Fax

American Homestar Corp
2450 S Shore Blvd Ste 300 .... League City TX 77573 281-334-9700 334-6320*
**Fax: Acctg* ■ *TF:* 800-313-5570 ■ *Web:* www.americanhomestar.com

Baker Storey McDonald Properties Inc
3011 Armory Dr Ste 120 .... Nashville TN 37204 615-373-9511
Web: www.bsmproperties.com

Cavalier Home Builders LLC
32 Wilson Blvd Ste 100 .... Addison AL 35540 256-747-1575 747-2344

Cavalier Homes Inc 32 Wilson Blvd PO Box 300 .... Addison AL 35540 800-743-2284
TF: 800-743-2284 ■ *Web:* cavalierhomebuilders.net

Cavco Industries Inc
1001 N Central Ave 8th Fl .... Phoenix AZ 85004 602-256-6263 256-6189
NASDAQ: CVCO ■ *TF:* 800-790-9111 ■ *Web:* www.cavco.com

Champion Enterprises Management Co
755 W Big Beaver Rd Ste 1000 .... Troy MI 48084 910-814-4256
Web: www.championhomes.com

Chariot Eagle Inc 931 NW 37th Ave .... Ocala FL 34475 352-629-7007 629-6920
Web: www.charioteagle.com

Chief Custom Homes 111 Grant St PO Box 127 .... Aurora NE 68818 402-694-5250 694-5873
Web: bonnavilla.com

Commodore Corp 1423 Lincolnway E .... Goshen IN 46526 574-533-7100
Web: www.commodorehomes.com

Deer Valley Homebuilders Inc 205 Carriage St .... Guin AL 35563 205-468-8400
Web: www.deervalleyhb.com

Destiny Industries LLC 250 R W Bryant Rd .... Moultrie GA 31788 866-782-6600
TF: 866-782-6600 ■ *Web:* www.destinyhomebuilders.com

DHS Systems LLC 33 Kings Hwy .... Orangeburg NY 10962 845-359-6066 365-2114
Web: www.drash.com

Fleetwood Homes of Idaho Inc
2611 E Comstock Ave .... Nampa ID 83687 208-466-2438
TF: 800-334-8958 ■ *Web:* fleetwoodhomes.com

Fleetwood Homes of Virginia Inc
90 Weaver St .... Rocky Mount VA 24151 540-483-5171
TF: 866-890-6206 ■ *Web:* www.fleetwoodhomes.com

Franklin Homes Inc 10655 Hwy 43 .... Russellville AL 35653 800-332-4511 331-2203*
**Fax Area Code: 256* ■ *TF:* 800-332-4511 ■ *Web:* www.franklinhomesusa.com

Fuqua Homes Inc 7100 S Cooper St .... Arlington TX 76001 817-465-3211 465-5125

Giles Industries Inc 405 S Broad St .... New Tazewell TN 37825 423-626-7243 626-7243
Web: www.gilesindustries.com

Homark Company Inc
100 Third St PO Box 309 .... Red Lake Falls MN 56750 218-253-2777 253-2116
Web: www.detroiter.com

Hometown America LLC 150 N Wacker Dr Ste 2800 .... Chicago IL 60606 312-604-7500 604-7501
TF: 888-735-4310 ■ *Web:* www.hometownamerica.com

Horton Homes Inc 101 Industrial Blvd .... Eatonton GA 31024 706-485-8506 485-4446
TF: 800-657-4000

Jacobsen Homes 600 Packard Ct .... Safety Harbor FL 34695 727-726-1138
TF: 800-843-1559 ■ *Web:* www.jachomes.com

Liberty Homes Inc 1101 Eisenhower Dr N .... Goshen IN 46526 574-533-0431
OTC: LIBHA ■ *Web:* www.libertyhomesinc.com

Little Valley Homes Inc 45225 Grand River Ave .... Novi MI 48375 231-775-8102
Web: www.lvhomes.net

Luxury Retreats International Inc
5530 St Patrick St Ste 2210 .... Montreal QC H4E1A8 514-393-8844
TF: 877-993-0100 ■ *Web:* www.luxuryretreats.com

Manufactured Housing Enterprises Inc
09302 St Rt 6 Rt 6 .... Bryan OH 43506 419-636-4511 636-4322
TF: 800-821-0220 ■ *Web:* www.mheinc.com

Mark Line Industries Inc
51687 County Rd 133 PO Box 277 .... Bristol IN 46507 574-825-5851 825-9139
Web: www.marklineindustries.com

McGrath RentCorp 5700 Las Positas Rd .... Livermore CA 94551 925-606-9200 453-3200
NASDAQ: MGRC ■ *TF:* 800-962-4284 ■ *Web:* www.mgrc.com

Meridian Mobile Home Park Spaces & Rentals
1801 Meridian St Ofc 18 .... Nashville TN 37207 615-227-1159

Mobile/Modular Express Inc 1301 Trimble Rd .... Edgewood MD 21040 410-676-3700 676-7288*
**Fax: Sales* ■ *Web:* www.mobilemodular.com

Moduline Industries Canada Ltd
1421 Brier Park Crescent NW .... Medicine Hat AB T1C1T8 403-527-1555
Web: www.moduline.ca

Nashua Homes of Idaho Inc PO Box 170008 .... Boise ID 83717 208-345-0222 345-1144
TF: 855-766-0222 ■ *Web:* www.nashuabuilders.com

Nobility Homes Inc 3741 SW Seventh St .... Ocala FL 34474 352-732-5157 732-4203
OTC: NOBH ■ *TF:* 800-476-6624 ■ *Web:* www.nobilityhomes.com

Pacific Mobile Structures Inc
1554 Bishop Rd .... Chehalis WA 98532 360-748-0121
Web: www.pacificmobile.com

R-Anell Custom Homes Inc 235 Anthony Grave Rd .... Crouse NC 28033 704-483-5511 483-5674
TF Cust Svc: 800-951-5511 ■ *Web:* www.r-anell.com

Ritz-Craft Corp of Pennsylvania Inc
15 Industrial Pk Rd .... Mifflinburg PA 17844 570-966-1053 966-9248
TF: 800-326-9836 ■ *Web:* www.ritz-craft.com

River Birch Homes Inc 400 River Birch Dr .... Hackleburg AL 35564 205-935-1997 935-3578
TF: 888-760-3314 ■ *Web:* www.riverbirchhomes.com

Satellite Industries Inc
2530 Xenium Ln N .... Minneapolis MN 55441 800-328-3332 328-3334
TF: 800-328-3332 ■ *Web:* www.satelliteindustries.com

Skyline Corp 2520 By-Pass Rd .... Elkhart IN 46514 574-294-6521
NYSE: SKY ■ *TF:* 800-348-7469 ■ *Web:* www.skylinecorp.com

VFP Inc 1701 Midland Rd PO Box 1809 .... Salem VA 24153 540-977-0500 977-5555
Web: www.vfpinc.com

Phone Fax

Virginia Homes Manufacturing Corp
142 Virginia Homes Ln. .... Boydton VA 23917 434-738-6107 738-6926
Web: www.virginiahomesmfg.com

Wick Buildings 405 Walter Rd. .... Mazomanie WI 53560 855-438-9425 795-2534*
**Fax Area Code:* 608 ■ *TF:* 855-438-9425 ■ *Web:* www.wickbuildings.com

506 MODELING AGENCIES

See Also Modeling Schools p. 2777; Talent Agencies p. 3214

Phone Fax

Cleanevent USA Inc 555 Winderley Pl Ste 3007 .... Maitland FL 32751 407-856-7676
Web: www.cleanevent.com

Click Model Management 129 W 27th St PH .... New York NY 10001 212-206-1717 206-6228*
**Fax:* Resv ■ *Web:* www.clickmodel.com

Creative Trust 2105 Elliston Pl .... Brentwood TN 37027 615-297-5010
Web: www.creativetrust.com

DNA Model Management Inc 555 W 25th St .... New York NY 10001 212-226-0080 226-7711
Web: www.dnamodels.com

Faust Goetz Schenker & Blee
2 Rector St Fl 20 .... New York NY 10006 212-363-6900
Web: www.fgsb.com

FINE Design Group Inc 1005 Sansome St .... San Francisco CA 94111 415-552-9300
Web: www.finedesigngroup.com

Ford Models Inc 111 Fifth Ave 9th Fl .... New York NY 10003 212-219-6500 966-5028
Web: models.fordmodels.com

Gener8 Inc 500 Mercury Dr. .... Sunnyvale CA 94085 650-940-9898
Web: www.gener8.net

Hp Industries Inc 415 W Hickory St. .... Kirksville MO 63501 660-627-2000
Web: hpind.com

IMG Models 304 Pk Ave S PH N .... New York NY 10010 212-253-8884 253-8883
Web: www.imgmodels.com

Jancyn Inc 1912 Lincoln Ave .... San Jose CA 95125 408-267-2600
Web: jancyn.com

LA Models 7700 Sunset Blvd .... Los Angeles CA 90046 323-436-7700
Web: www.latalent.com

Marilyn Model Agency 32 Un Sq E Penthouse .... New York NY 10003 212-260-6500
Web: www.marilynagency.com

Mind Over Eye Inc 1639 11th St Ste 117 .... Santa Monica CA 90404 310-396-4663
Web: www.mindovereye.com

mopeutix Inc, The
9951 Businesspark Ave Ste B .... San Diego CA 92131 858-549-1760
Web: thermopeutix.com

Next Model Management 15 Watts St 6th Fl .... New York NY 10013 212-925-5100 925-5931
Web: www.nextmanagement.com

NPowerNY Inc
3 Metrotech Ctr Mezzanine Brooklyn .... New York NY 10001 212-564-7010
Web: www.npower.org

Osbrink Talent Agency Inc
4343 Lankershim Blvd Ste 100 .... Universal city CA 91602 818-760-0991
Web: www.osbrinkagency.com

Parham Santana Inc 7 W 18th St Fl 7 .... New York NY 10011 212-645-7501
Web: www.parhamsantana.com

Pathwayz Communications Inc 4176 Canyon Dr .... Amarillo TX 79109 806-355-0551
Web: www.pathwayz.com

Pillar of Fire 1302 Sherman St .... Denver CO 80203 303-839-1500
Web: www.pillar.org

San Diego Model Management
438 Camino del Rio S Ste 116 .... San Diego CA 92108 619-296-1018 296-3422
Web: www.sdmodel.com

Teton Gravity Research LLC 1260 NW St. .... Wilson WY 83014 307-734-8192
Web: www.tetongravity.com

TradeFair Group Inc, The
11000 Richmond Ste 690 .... Houston TX 77042 832-242-1969
Web: www.tradefairgroup.com

United Pharma LLC 2317 2319 Moore Ave. .... Fullerton CA 92833 714-738-8999
Web: www.unitedpharmallc.com

Urban Sports & Entertainment Group Llc
19600 W Catawba Ave Ste C301 .... Cornelius NC 28031 704-894-0025
Web: www.urbansportsgroup.net

Wilhelmina Models Inc 300 Pk Ave S .... New York NY 10010 212-473-0700 473-3223
Web: www.wilhelmina.com

Women Management 199 Lafayette St 7th Fl. .... New York NY 10012 212-334-7480 334-7492
TF: 800-838-3006 ■ *Web:* www.womenmanagement.com

507 MODELING SCHOOLS

Phone Fax

5th Wheel Training Institute
536 Brazeau Blvd .... New Liskeard ON P0J1P0 705-647-7202
Web: www.5thwheeltraining.com

Abaris Training Resources Inc
5401 Longley Ln Ste 49 .... Reno NV 89511 775-827-6568
Web: www.abaris.com

Ambiance Models & Talent Inc
1096 Dayton Blvd .... Chattanooga TN 37405 423-265-2121
Web: www.ambiancemodels.com

Auburn Career Center 8140 Auburn Rd. .... Painesville OH 44077 440-357-7542
Web: www.auburncc.org

Barbizon International LLC
3111 N University Dr Ste 1002 .... Coral Springs FL 33065 954-345-4140
Web: www.barbizonmodeling.com

Canadian Valley Technology Center
6505 E Us Hwy 66 .... El Reno OK 73036 405-262-2629
Web: www.cvtech.edu

Celt Inc 3462 Clemmons Rd. .... Clemmons NC 27012 336-712-9906
Web: www.celt-inc.com

Civilian Police International LLC
18980 Upper Belmont Pl W 4th Fl .... Leesburg VA 20176 703-724-5788
Web: www.civilianpolice.com

Phone Fax

Cpr Savers & First Aid Supply
7904 E Chaparral Rd Ste A110-242 .... Scottsdale AZ 85250 480-946-0971
Web: www.cpr-savers.com

District 1199 C Training & Upgrade Fund
100 S Broad St .... Philadelphia PA 19110 215-568-2220
Web: www.1199ctraining.org

ECPI College of Technology
5555 Greenwich Rd .... Virginia Beach VA 23462 757-490-9090
Web: www.ecpi.edu

Frederick Taylor University
346 Rheem Blvd Ste 203 .... Moraga CA 94556 800-988-4622
TF: 800-988-4622 ■ *Web:* www.ftu.edu

Horizon Wellness Group
20 Jerusalem Ave 3rd Fl .... Hicksville NY 11801 516-326-2020
Web: www.horizonhealthfairs.com

Informa 75 W St .... Walpole MA 02081 508-668-0288
Web: informatp.com

Institute-Study of Knowledge
323 Harvard Ave .... Half Moon Bay CA 94019 650-728-3322
Web: iskme.org

Jack b Keenan Inc 1820 Georgetta Dr .... San Jose CA 95125 408-448-4686
Web: www.jackbkeenan.com

Masterdrive 15659 E Hinsdale Dr .... Centennial CO 80112 303-627-4447
Web: www.masterdrive.com

MCN Healthcare Inc 1777 S Harrison St Ste 405 .... Denver CO 80210 303-762-0778
Web: www.mcnhealthcare.com

Mercy College of Ohio 2221 Madison Ave .... Toledo OH 43604 419-251-1313
TF: 888-806-3729 ■ *Web:* www.mercycollege.edu

Mid-Atlantic Clearing House Association Inc, The
1344 Ashton Rd Ste 202 .... Hanover MD 21076 410-859-0090
Web: www.macha.org

Modern American Safety Training-mast
841 Alton Ave .... Columbus OH 43219 614-252-0565
Web: www.mastohio.com

National Massage Therapy Institute LLC
10050 Roosevelt Blvd Ste 8 .... Philadelphia PA 19116 215-969-0320
Web: www.nmti.edu

Northern Alberta Institute of Technology
11762 106 St NW .... Edmonton AB T5G2R1 780-471-6248
Web: www.nait.ca

Pc Professor Computer Training & Repair
7056 Beracasa Way .... Boca Raton FL 33433 561-750-7879
Web: www.pcprofessor.com

Pima Medical Institute 3350 E Grant Rd Ste 200 .... Tucson AZ 85716 520-326-1600
TF: 888-556-7334 ■ *Web:* www.pmi.edu

Portage Lakes Career Center
4401 Shriver Rd .... Uniontown OH 44685 330-896-8200
Web: plcc.edu

Poynter Institute for Media Studies Inc, The
801 Third St South .... St. Petersburg FL 33701 727-821-9494
Web: www.poynter.org

Regional Occupational Programs
300 Dana St .... Fort Bragg CA 95437 707-964-9000
TF: 800-451-9999 ■ *Web:* mcoe.us

Rhino Medical Staffing
2000 E Lamar Blvd Ste 250 .... Arlington TX 76006 817-795-2295
TF: 866-267-4466 ■ *Web:* www.rhinomedical.com

Southern Financial Exchange
1340 Poydras St Ste 2010 .... New Orleans LA 70112 504-525-6779
Web: www.sfe.org

Southwest Applied Technology College
510 West 800 South .... Cedar City UT 84720 435-586-2899
Web: www.swatc.edu

St. Lawrence-Lewis BOCES 40 W Main St .... Canton NY 13617 315-386-4504
Web: www.sllboces.org

St. Luke's College 2720 Pierce St .... Sioux City IA 51104 712-279-3149
Web: www.stlukescollege.edu

TechSherpas Inc 5404 Cypress Ctr Dr Ste 125 .... Tampa FL 33609 813-287-8876
Web: www.techsherpas.com

Villaris Martial Arts 645 Poquonock Ave .... Windsor CT 06095 508-752-0091
Web: www.villarisshrewsbury.com/Contact-Us.html

508 MOPS, SPONGES, WIPING CLOTHS

See Also Brushes & Brooms p. 1877; Cleaning Products p. 1939

Phone Fax

A&B Wiper Supply Inc 5601 Paschall Ave .... Philadelphia PA 19143 215-482-6100 482-6190
TF: 800-333-7247 ■ *Web:* www.bestrags.com

Abco Cleaning Products 6800 NW 36th Ave. .... Miami FL 33147 305-694-2226 694-0451
TF: 888-694-2226 ■ *Web:* www.abcoproducts.com

Acme Sponge & Chamois Company Inc
855 Pine St. .... Tarpon Springs FL 34689 727-937-3222
Web: www.acmesponge.com

Bro-Tex Inc 800 Hampden Ave. .... Saint Paul MN 55114 651-645-5721 646-1876
TF: 800-328-2282 ■ *Web:* www.brotex.com

Butler Home Products LLC
237 Cedar Hill St .... Marlborough MA 01752 508-597-8000 597-8010
TF: 888-318-8521 ■ *Web:* www.cleanerhomeliving.com

Cadie Products Corp 151 E 11th St .... Paterson NJ 07524 973-278-8300 278-0303
Web: www.cadie.com

Colman Wolf Sanitary Supply Co
15201 E 11-Mile Rd .... Roseville MI 48066 586-779-5500
Web: www.theprofgroup.com

Continental Manufacturing Co
305 Rock Industrial Pk Dr. .... Bridgeton MO 63044 314-656-4301 770-9938
TF: 800-325-1051 ■ *Web:* www.continentalcommercialproducts.com

Disco Inc 1895 Brannan Rd .... McDonough GA 30253 770-474-7575 327-5492*
**Fax Area Code:* 800 ■ *TF:* 800-325-1051 ■ *Web:* www.katyindustries.com

Ettore Products Co 2100 N Loop Rd .... Alameda CA 94502 510-748-4130 748-4146
TF: 800-438-8673 ■ *Web:* www.ettore.com

				Phone	Fax
Golden Star Inc 4770 N Belleview Ave Ste 209	Kansas City	MO	64116	816-842-0233	842-1129
TF: 800-821-2792 ■ *Web:* www.goldenstar.com					
Houston Wiper & Mill Supply Co 1234 Kress St	Houston	TX	77020	713-672-0571	673-7637
Web: www.houstonwiperandmill.com					
KLEEN-TEX Industries Inc 101 N Greenwood St Ste C	LaGrange	GA	30240	706-882-0111	298-8336*
**Fax Area Code:* 678 ■ *Web:* www.kleen-tex.com					
L C Industries 1 Signature Dr	Hazlehurst	MS	39083	601-894-1771	
Southern Wipers 100 Fairview Rd	Asheville	NC	28803	704-377-3448	
Tranzonic Cos 26301 Curtiss Wright Pkwy Ste 200	Cleveland	OH	44143	216-535-4300	831-5647
Web: www.tranzonic.com					
United Textile Company Inc 751-143rd Ave	San Leandro	CA	94578	510-276-2288	
TF General: 800-233-0077 ■ *Web:* unitedtextileinc.com					
Wipe-Tex International Corp 110 E 153rd St	Bronx	NY	10451	718-665-0787	665-0787
TF: 800-643-9607 ■ *Web:* www.wipe-tex.com					

509 MORTGAGE LENDERS & LOAN BROKERS

See Also Banks - Commercial & Savings p. 1839

				Phone	Fax
21st Mortgage Corp 620 Market St Ste 100	Knoxville	TN	37902	865-292-2120	
TF: 800-955-0021 ■ *Web:* www.21stmortgage.com					
AAA Financial Corp 4613 N University Dr	Coral Springs	FL	33065	954-344-2530	344-0257
TF: 800-881-2530 ■ *Web:* www.aaafinancial.com					
Advantage Mortgage Group Inc, The 4835 E Cactus Rd Ste 150	Scottsdale	AZ	85254	602-953-6500	
Web: www.tamg.biz					
Ascentium Capital LLC 23970 Hwy 59 N	Kingwood	TX	77339	866-722-8500	
TF: 866-722-8500 ■ *Web:* www.ascentiumcapital.com					
BRT Realty Trust 60 Cutter Mill Rd Ste 303	Great Neck	NY	11021	516-466-3100	
NYSE: BRT ■ *TF:* 800-450-5816 ■ *Web:* www.brtrealty.com					
Canada Deposit Insurance Corp 50 O'Connor St 17th Fl	Ottawa	ON	K1P6L2	613-996-2081	
TF: 800-461-2342 ■ *Web:* www.cdic.ca					
Canada Mortgage & Housing Corp 700 Montreal Rd	Ottawa	ON	K1A0P7	613-748-2000	
Web: www.cmhc.ca					
CapitalSource Inc 5404 Wisconsin Ave	Chevy Chase	MD	20815	301-841-2700	
NYSE: CSE ■ *Web:* www.capitalsource.com					
Central Mortgage Co 801 John Barrow Ste 1	Little Rock	AR	72205	501-716-5600	
Web: www.baanthai.com					
CitiMortgage Inc 1000 Technology Dr	O'Fallon	MO	63368	800-283-7918	
TF Cust Svc: 800-283-7918 ■ *Web:* www.citimortgage.com					
CMLS Financial Ltd Oceanic Plz Bldg Ste 2110 - 1066 W Hastings St	Vancouver	BC	V6E3X2	604-687-2118	
Web: m.cmls.ca					
Community Preservation Corp, The (CPC) 28 E 28th St 9Fl	New York	NY	10016	212-869-5300	
Web: www.communityp.com					
Danburg Management Corp 7700 Congress Ave Ste 3100	Boca Raton	FL	33487	561-997-5777	
Web: www.danburg.com					
Dominion Capital Inc 120 Tredegar St	Richmond	VA	23219	804-819-2000	
Web: dom.com					
Dominion Lending Centres Inc 2215 Coquitlam Ave	Port Coquitlam	BC	V3B1J6	866-928-6810	
TF: 866-928-6810 ■ *Web:* www.dominionlending.ca					
Eastern Light Capital Inc 100 Pine St Ste 560	San Francisco	CA	94111	415-693-9500	693-9501
OTC: ELCI					
EPIC Processing Ltd 2919 Valmont Rd Ste 206	Boulder	CO	80301	303-440-8617	
EverHome Mortgage Co 301 W Bay St	Jacksonville	FL	32202	888-882-3837	281-6380*
**Fax Area Code:* 904 ■ **Fax:* Cust Svc ■ *TF Cust Svc:* 800-669-9721 ■ *Web:* www.everbank.com					
Extraco Technology 1704 N Valley Mills Dr	Waco	TX	76710	254-761-2300	
Web: www.extracomortgage.com					
Fannie Mae 3900 Wisconsin Ave NW	Washington	DC	20016	202-752-7000	
OTC: FNMA ■ *TF:* 800-732-6643 ■ *Web:* www.fanniemae.com					
Fin-West Group 1131 W Sixth St	Ontario	CA	91762	909-595-1996	595-7430
OTC: FMOR					
Financial Fedcorp Inc 6305 Humphreys Blvd	Memphis	TN	38120	901-756-2848	
Web: www.finfedmem.com					
First Eastern Mortgage Corp 100 Brickstone Sq	Andover	MA	01810	978-749-3100	749-3148
TF: 800-777-2240 ■ *Web:* www.firsteastern.com					
First Equity Mortgage Bankers 9300 S Dadeland Blvd Ste 500	Miami	FL	33156	305-666-3333	666-3181
TF: 800-973-3654 ■ *Web:* www.fembi.com					
First Financial Services Inc (FFSI) 6230 Fairview Rd Ste 450	Charlotte	NC	28210	866-506-9090	365-3098*
**Fax Area Code:* 704 ■ *TF:* 866-506-9090 ■ *Web:* www.ffsmortgage.com					
Freddie Mac 8200 Jones Branch Dr	McLean	VA	22102	703-903-2000	903-2759
TF: 800-424-5401 ■ *Web:* www.freddiemac.com					
North Central Region 333 W Wacker Dr Ste 2500	Chicago	IL	60606	312-407-7400	
TF: 800-373-3343 ■ *Web:* www.freddiemac.com					
Northeast Region 8200 Jones Branch Dr	McLean	VA	22102	703-903-2000	903-2759
TF: 800-373-3343 ■ *Web:* www.freddiemac.com					
Southeast/Southwest Region 2300 Windy Ridge Pkwy Ste 200N	Atlanta	GA	30339	770-857-8800	
TF: 800-373-3343 ■ *Web:* www.freddiemac.com					
George Mason Mortgage Corp 4100 Monu Crnr Dr Ste 100	Fairfax	VA	22030	703-273-2600	934-9122
TF: 800-867-6859 ■ *Web:* www.gmmllc.com					
Government National Mortgage Assn 451 Seventh St SW Rm B-133	Washington	DC	20410	202-708-1535	
Web: www.ginniemae.gov					
Guild Mortgage Co 5898 Copley Dr 4th & 5th Fl	San Diego	CA	92111	800-365-4441	
TF: 800-365-4441 ■ *Web:* www.guildmortgage.com					
HomeSteps 500 Plano Pkwy	Carrollton	TX	75010	800-972-7555	
TF: 800-972-7555 ■ *Web:* www.homesteps.com					
HSBC Bank USA 2929 Walden Ave	Depew	NY	14043	800-338-4626	826-1874*
**Fax Area Code:* 817 ■ *TF:* 800-338-4626 ■ *Web:* www.us.hsbc.com					
Huntington Mortgage Co 7575 Huntington Pk Dr	Columbus	OH	43235	614-480-6505	
TF: 800-323-4695 ■ *Web:* huntington.com					
Inland Mortgage Corp 2901 Butterfield Rd	Oak Brook	IL	60523	630-218-8000	
TF: 800-826-8228 ■ *Web:* www.inlandgroup.com					
Intervest Mortgage Investment Co 180 Grand Ave Ste 1400	Oakland	CA	94612	510-622-8500	
Web: www.intervestcref.com					
JI Kislak Inc 7900 Miami Lakes Dr W	Miami Lakes	FL	33016	305-364-4100	
Web: www.kislak.com					
Legg Mason Real Estate Investors Inc 350 S Beverly Dr Ste 300	Beverly Hills	CA	90212	310-234-2100	234-2150
Web: www.lmrei.com					
LendingTree Inc 11115 Rushmore Dr	Charlotte	NC	28277	704-541-5351	541-1824
TF: 800-555-8733 ■ *Web:* www.lendingtree.com					
Lion Inc 200 Martin Ln Ste A	Elk Grove	IL	60007	872-228-5466	577-1441*
**Fax Area Code:* 206 ■ *TF:* 800-867-6320					
loanDepot 26642 Towne Centre Dr	Foothill Ranch	CA	92610	888-337-6888	
TF: 888-337-6888 ■ *Web:* www.loandepot.com					
MedDirect Inc 3200 Broadmoor Ave SE	Grand Rapids	MI	49512	616-940-0500	
Web: www.meddirect.net					
Merix Financial Inc 390 Bay St 18th Fl Ste 500	Toronto	ON	M5H2Y2	877-637-4914	
TF: 877-637-4914 ■ *Web:* www.merixfinancial.com					
Midland Mortgage Co PO Box 26648	Oklahoma City	OK	73126	800-654-4566	767-5500*
**Fax Area Code:* 405 ■ **Fax:* Cust Svc ■ *TF:* 800-654-4566 ■ *Web:* www.mymidlandmortgage.com					
MMA Capital Management LLC (MuniMae) 621 E Pratt St Ste 600	Baltimore	MD	21202	443-263-2900	
OTC: MMAB ■ *TF:* 855-650-6932 ■ *Web:* www.mmacapitalmanagement.com					
Mortgage Investors Group 8320 E Walker Springs Ln	Knoxville	TN	37923	865-691-8910	691-7714
TF: 800-489-8910 ■ *Web:* www.migonline.com					
Mortgage Resources Inc (MRI) 425 S Woods Mill Rd Ste 100	Chesterfield	MO	63017	314-576-5577	576-6071
TF: 800-965-9910					
Mortgage Returns 1335 Strassner Dr	St. Louis	MO	63144	314-989-9100	
Web: www.web.mortgagereturns.com					
National Rural Utilities Co-op Finance Corp 2201 Co-op Way	Herndon	VA	20171	703-709-6700	
TF: 800-424-2954 ■ *Web:* www.nrucfc.coop					
Obsidian Mortgage Corp 35 Grand Marshall Dr 2nd fl	Toronto	ON	M1B5W9	416-283-2377	
Web: www.obsidianmortgages.com					
One Reverse Mortgage LLC 9920 Pacific Heights Blvd Ste 350	San Diego	CA	92121	858-455-9120	
Web: www.onereversemortgage.com					
Origen Financial Inc 27777 Franklin Rd Ste 1700	Southfield	MI	48034	248-746-7000	746-7094
OTC: ORGN ■ *Web:* www.origenfinancial.com					
Payscape Advisors 729 Lambert Dr Ne	Atlanta	GA	30324	888-351-6565	
TF: 888-351-6565 ■ *Web:* payscape.com/offices/atlanta					
PHH Mortgage Corp 3000 Leadenhall Rd	Mount Laurel	NJ	08054	800-210-8849	
TF: 800-210-8849 ■ *Web:* www.phhmortgage.com/business					
Pinnacle Mortgage Group Inc 3605 S Teller St	Lakewood	CO	80235	303-716-9000	
Web: www.pinnacle-mortgage.com					
Platinum Bank 802 W Lumsden Rd	Brandon	FL	33511	813-655-1234	
Web: www.platinumbank.com					
Plaza Home Mortgage Inc 5090 Shoreham Pl Ste 206	San Diego	CA	92122	858-346-1208	677-6741
TF: 866-260-2529 ■ *Web:* www.plazahomemortgage.com					
Portland Housing Center Inc 3233 Ne Sandy Blvd	Portland	OR	97232	503-282-7744	
Web: www.portlandhousingcenter.org					
R-B Financial-mortgages Inc 44028 Mound Rd Ste 3	Sterling Heights	MI	48314	586-254-8435	254-8438
Web: www.rbfinancial.com					
Redwood Trust Inc 1 Belvedere Pl Ste 300	Mill Valley	CA	94941	415-389-7373	
NYSE: RWT ■ *TF:* 866-269-4976 ■ *Web:* www.redwoodtrust.com					
Regions Mortgage Inc 215 Forrest St	Hattiesburg	MS	39401	800-986-2462	
TF: 800-986-2462 ■ *Web:* www.regions.com					
Residential Mortgage LLC 100 Calais Dr	Anchorage	AK	99503	907-222-8800	222-8801
TF: 888-357-2707 ■ *Web:* www.residentialmtg.com					
Ringler Assoc Inc 27422 Aliso Creek Rd Ste 200	Aliso Viejo	CA	92656	949-296-9000	
Web: www.ringlerassociates.com					
Safeguard Properties Inc 7887 Safeguard Cir	Valley View	OH	44125	216-739-2900	
TF: 800-852-8306 ■ *Web:* www.safeguardproperties.com					
Softgate Systems Inc 330 Passaic Ave	Fairfield	NJ	07004	973-830-1575	
TF: 888-477-7297 ■ *Web:* www.softgatesystems.com					
Stanley Jay s & Associates 5313 Mcclanahan Dr Ste G5	North Little Rock	AR	72116	501-758-8029	
Web: jaystanley.com					
Sterling Centrecorp Inc 7827 W Flagler St Ste 305	Miami	FL	33144	305-261-8773	
Web: www.sterlingorganization.com					
Street Capital Financial Corp 1 Yonge St Ste 2401	Toronto	ON	M5E1E5	647-259-7873	
Web: www.streetcapital.ca					
SunTrust Mortgage Inc 1001 Semmes Ave	Richmond	VA	23224	800-634-7928	291-0495*
**Fax Area Code:* 804 ■ **Fax:* Mktg ■ *TF:* 800-634-7928 ■ *Web:* www.suntrust.com/mortgage					
Top Flite Financial Inc 123 E Grand River Ave	Williamston	MI	48895	517-655-2140	
Web: www.teamtopflite.com					
Truwest Credit Union PO Box 3489	Scottsdale	AZ	85271	480-441-5900	
TF: 855-878-9378 ■ *Web:* www.truwest.org					
Universal American Mortgage Co 700 NW 107th Ave	Miami	FL	33172	800-741-8262	837-0427*
**Fax Area Code:* 866 ■ *TF:* 800-741-8262 ■ *Web:* www.uamc.com					

	City	State	ZIP	Phone	Fax
Universal Lending Corp (ULC) 6775 E Evans Ave *TF:* 800-758-4063 ■ *Web:* ulc.com	Denver	CO	80224	800-758-4063	
Vanderbilt Mortgage & Finance Inc 500 Alcoa Trl **Fax Area Code:* 865 ■ *TF:* 800-970-7250 ■ *Web:* www.vmf.com	Maryville	TN	37804	800-970-7250	380-3418*
Velocity Trade 99 Yorkville Ave Ste 210 *Web:* velocitytrade.com	Toronto	ON	M5R3K5	416-855-2800	
Verico Capital Mortgages Inc 106-18 Deakin St *TF:* 877-459-4414 ■ *Web:* www.capitalmortgages.com	Ottawa	ON	K2E8B7	613-228-3888	
Vestin Group Inc 8880 W Sunset Rd # 200 *Web:* www.vestinmortgage.com	Las Vegas	NV	89148	702-227-0965	227-5247
Wells Fargo Home Mortgage 2840 Ingersoll Ave *TF:* 800-401-1957 ■ *Web:* www.wellsfargo.com/mortgage	Des Moines	IA	50312	515-237-5196	

510 MORTUARY, CREMATORY, CEMETERY PRODUCTS & SERVICES

	City	State	ZIP	Phone	Fax
AJ Desmond & Sons Funeral Directors 2600 Crooks Rd *TF:* 800-210-7135 ■ *Web:* www.desmondfuneralhome.com	Troy	MI	48084	248-362-2500	362-0190
Baue Funeral Homes 620 Jefferson St *TF:* 888-724-0073 ■ *Web:* baue.com	Saint Charles	MO	63301	636-940-1000	946-3084
Bradford-O'Keefe Funeral Homes Inc 675 E Howard Ave *Web:* www.bradfordokeefe.com	Biloxi	MS	39530	228-374-5650	
Carriage Services Inc 3040 Post Oak Blvd Ste 300 *NYSE: CSV* ■ *TF:* 866-332-8400 ■ *Web:* www.carriageservices.com	Houston	TX	77056	713-332-8400	
Church & Chapel Metal Arts Inc 2616 W Grand Ave *TF:* 800-992-1234 ■ *Web:* www.church-chapel.com	Chicago	IL	60612	800-992-1234	626-3299
Dignity Memorial 1929 Allen Pkwy *TF:* 800-894-2024 ■ *Web:* www.dignitymemorial.com	Houston	TX	77019	713-522-5141	
Forest Lawn Memorial-Parks & Mortuaries 1712 S Glendale Ave *TF:* 800-204-3131 ■ *Web:* www.forestlawn.com	Glendale	CA	91205	323-254-3131	
Hillside Cemetery Assn 1401 Woodland Ave *Web:* hillsidecemetery.com	Scotch Plains	NJ	07076	908-756-1729	
Inglewood Park Cemetery Inc 720 E Florence Ave *Web:* www.inglewoodparkcemetery.org	Inglewood	CA	90301	310-412-6500	
Kensico Cemetery Inc, The 273 Lakeview Ave *Web:* www.kensico.org	Valhalla	NY	10595	914-949-0347	
Midwest Memorial Group LLC 31300 Southfield Rd Ste 1 *Web:* midwestmemorialgroup.com	Beverly Hills	MI	48025	248-290-0338	
Mount Sinai Memorial Park 5950 Forest Lawn Dr *TF:* 800-600-0076 ■ *Web:* mountsinaiparks.org	Los Angeles	CA	90068	323-469-6000	
Neptune Society 4312 Woodman Ave 3rd Fl *TF:* 888-637-8863 ■ *Web:* www.neptunesociety.com	Sherman Oaks	CA	91423	888-637-8863	
Palm Mortuary Inc 1325 N Main St *Web:* www.palmmortuary.com	Las Vegas	NV	89101	702-464-8300	464-8394
Rabenhorst Funeral Home Inc PO Box 2666 *Web:* www.rabenhorst.com	Baton Rouge	LA	70821	225-383-6831	
Service Corp International 1929 Allen Pkwy *NYSE: SCI* ■ *Web:* www.sci-corp.com	Houston	TX	77019	713-522-5141	
Skyview Memorial Lawn 200 Rollingwood Dr *Web:* www.skyviewmemorial.com	Vallejo	CA	94591	707-644-7474	
Spring Grove Cemetery 4521 Spring Grove Ave *TF:* 888-853-2230 ■ *Web:* www.springgrove.org	Cincinnati	OH	45232	513-681-7526	853-6802
Stewart Enterprises Inc 1333 S Clearview Pkwy *NASDAQ: STEI* ■ *TF:* 877-239-3264 ■ *Web:* sci-corp.com/scicorp/home.aspx	New Orleans	LA	70121	713-522-5141	
StoneMor Partners LP 311 Veterans Hwy *NYSE: STON* ■ *Web:* stonemor.com	Levittown	PA	19056	215-826-2800	
Tucson Cemetery Assn 3015 N Oracle Rd *Web:* evergreenmortuary-cemetery.com	Tucson	AZ	85705	520-888-7470	
Union Cemetery 2505 Minnehaha Ave E *Web:* unioncemeterymn.org	Maplewood	MN	55119	651-739-0466	
Wilson Financial Group Inc 15915 Katy Fwy Ste 500	Houston	TX	77094	281-579-2760	579-9089
Woodlawn Cemetery Inc, The Webster Ave & E 233rd St *TF:* 877-496-6352 ■ *Web:* www.thewoodlawncemetery.org	Bronx	NY	10470	718-920-0500	

511 MOTION PICTURE DISTRIBUTION & RELATED SERVICES

	City	State	ZIP	Phone	Fax
Anchor Bay Entertainment Inc 1699 Stutz Dr *Web:* www.anchorbayentertainment.com	Troy	MI	48084	248-816-0909	
Baker & Taylor Inc 2550 W Tyvola Rd Ste 300 **Fax Area Code:* 704 ■ *TF:* 800-775-1800 ■ *Web:* www.btol.com	Charlotte	NC	28217	800-775-1800	998-3316*
Bridgestone Multimedia Group Inc 300 N McKemy Ave *Web:* gobmg.com	Chandler	AZ	85226	480-940-5777	
Buena Vista Home Entertainment Inc (BVHE) 500 S Buena Vista St *Web:* www.bvhe.com	Burbank	CA	91521	818-560-1000	
Carsey-Werner LLC 16027 Ventura Blvd Ste 600 *Web:* www.carseywerner.com	Encino	CA	91436	818-464-9600	
Crown Media Holdings Inc 12700 Ventura Blvd Ste 200 *NASDAQ: CRWN* ■ *TF:* 800-479-7328 ■ *Web:* www.hallmarkchannel.com	Studio City	CA	91604	818-755-2400	
Current House Productions LLC 3860 Via Del Rey *Web:* chpadvertising.com	Bonita Springs	FL	34134	239-676-7658	
Desert Island Films Inc 30 Portico Wy *Web:* www.desertislandfilms.com	Plymouth	MA	02360	774-773-9223	
Echo Bridge Entertainment LLC 3089 Airport Rd	La Crosse	WI	54603	608-784-6620	
Extreme Reach Inc 75 2nd Ave Ste 720 *NASDAQ: DGIT* ■ **Fax Area Code:* 877 ■ *TF:* 877-769-9382 ■ *Web:* extremereach.com	Needham	MA	02494	781-577-2016	302-8633*
Facets Multimedia Inc 1517 W Fullerton Ave *TF Cust Svc:* 800-331-6197 ■ *Web:* www.facets.org	Chicago	IL	60614	773-281-9075	929-5437
First Run Features 630 Ninth Ave Ste 1213 *TF:* 800-229-8575 ■ *Web:* www.firstrunfeatures.com	New York	NY	10036	212-243-0600	989-7649
IM Global LLC 8322 Beverly Blvd *Web:* www.imglobalfilm.com	Los Angeles	CA	90048	310-777-3590	
Ingram Entertainment Inc 2 Ingram Blvd *TF:* 800-621-1333 ■ *Web:* www.ingramentertainment.com	La Vergne	TN	37089	615-287-4000	
Insight Media 2162 Broadway *TF:* 800-233-9910 ■ *Web:* www.insight-media.com	New York	NY	10024	212-721-6316	799-5309
Kino International Corp 333 W 39th St Rm 503 *TF:* 800-562-3330 ■ *Web:* www.kinolorber.com	New York	NY	10018	212-629-6880	714-0871
Kultur International Films Ltd PO Box 755 *TF:* 888-329-2580 ■ *Web:* kulturvideo.com	Forked River	NJ	08731	888-329-2580	
Lifesize Entertainment & Releasing 194 Elmwood Dr Ste 2 *Web:* www.lifesizeentertainment.com	Parsippany	NJ	07054	973-884-4884	
MPI Media Group 16101 108th Ave *Web:* www.mpimedia.com	Orland Park	IL	60467	708-460-0555	
Native Grounds Nursery & Garden Center 1172A S Mt Shasta Blvd *Web:* nativegrounds.org	Mount Shasta	CA	96067	530-926-0555	
NCircle Entertainment 12740 Hillcrest Ste 120 *Web:* www.ncircleentertainment.com	Dallas	TX	75230	214-891-0300	
Paramount Home Entertainment 5555 Melrose Ave *Web:* paramount.com	Los Angeles	CA	90038	323-956-5000	
Paramount Pictures Corp 5555 Melrose Ave *Web:* www.paramount.com	Los Angeles	CA	90038	323-956-5000	956-0121
Sony Pictures Classics 550 Madison Ave 8th Fl *Web:* sonypictures.com	New York	NY	10022	212-833-8833	833-8570
Sony Pictures Entertainment Inc 10202 W Washington Blvd *TF:* 855-327-7669 ■ *Web:* www.sonypictures.com	Culver City	CA	90232	310-244-4000	840-8888
Timeless Media Group Inc 2480 West 7th Pl *Web:* www.timelessvideo.com	Eugene	OR	97402	541-484-7070	
Todd Street Productions 111 Eighth Ave Fl 16 *Web:* www.toddstreet.com	New York	NY	10011	212-966-5900	
Twentieth Century Fox Home Entertainment Inc 2121 Ave of the Stars Ste 100 **Fax Area Code:* 888 ■ *TF:* 877-369-7867 ■ *Web:* www.foxconnect.com	Los Angeles	CA	90067	310-369-3900	443-4369*
Venaca Inc 450 W 31st St 4th Fl *Web:* www.venaca.com	New York	NY	10001	212-660-2965	
Video Data Bank 112 S Michigan Ave *Web:* www.vdb.org	Chicago	IL	60603	312-345-3550	541-8073
Warner Bros Entertainment Inc 4000 Warner Blvd *TF:* 800-778-7879 ■ *Web:* www.warnerbros.com	Burbank	CA	91522	818-954-1853	954-3817
WRS Motion Picture & Video Laboratory 213 Tech Rd *Web:* www.wrslabs.com	Pittsburgh	PA	15205	412-937-1200	

512 MOTION PICTURE PRE- & POST-PRODUCTION SERVICES

	City	State	ZIP	Phone	Fax
Alpha Cine Labs 9800 40th Ave S	Seattle	WA	98118	206-682-8230	682-6649
American Media International LLC 2609 Tucker St *Web:* ami-media.com	Burlington	NC	27215	336-229-5554	228-1409
Ascent Media Group Inc 520 Broadway 5th Fl *Web:* ascentcapitalgroupinc.com	Santa Monica	CA	90401	310-434-7000	434-7007
Beyond Pix Studios 950 Battery St *Web:* beyondpix.com	San Francisco	CA	94111	415-434-1027	434-1032
Broadway Video Inc 1619 Broadway *Web:* www.broadwayvideo.com	New York	NY	10019	212-265-7600	713-1535
Cafefx 1130 E Clark Ave	Santa Maria	CA	93455	805-922-9479	
Cinema Libre Studio 120 S Victory Blvd 1st Fl *Web:* www.cinemalibrestudio.com	Burbank	CA	91502	818-588-3033	349-9922
Crossman Post Production LLC 35 Lone Hollow *TF:* 888-553-1958 ■ *Web:* www.crossmanpost.com	Sandy	UT	84092	801-553-1958	553-0953
Downstream 1624 NW Johnson St *Web:* www.downstream.com	Portland	OR	97209	503-226-1944	226-1283
Edit Bay 571 N Poplar Ste I *Web:* www.theeditbay.com	Orange	CA	92868	714-978-7878	
Elastic Creative 550 Bryant St	San Francisco	CA	94107	415-495-5595	543-8370
Elevation 905 Bernina Ave *Web:* thisiselevation.com	Atlanta	GA	30307	404-221-1705	
Encore Hollywood 6344 Fountain Ave *Web:* www.encorepost.com	Los Angeles	CA	90028	323-466-7663	
Filmworks/Astro Lab 61 W Erie St *Web:* www.filmworkersastro.com	Chicago	IL	60654	312-280-5500	
FOX Studios 10201 W Pico Blvd *Web:* www.foxstudios.com	Los Angeles	CA	90035	310-369-1000	203-1558
Go Edit Inc 5614 Cahuenga Blvd *TF:* 800-833-9200 ■ *Web:* www.goedit.tv	North Hollywood	CA	91601	818-284-6260	985-6260
HDMG Corp 555 First Ave NE *Web:* www.hdmg.com	Minneapolis	MN	55413	612-224-9500	224-9515
Henninger Media Services Inc 2601a Wilson Blvd *Web:* www.henninger.com	Arlington	VA	22201	703-243-3444	243-5697
Level 3 Post 2901 W Alameda Ave *Web:* www.level3post.com	Burbank	CA	91505	818-840-7200	840-7801

Phone Fax

Mad House 240 Madison Ave 14th Fl ... New York NY 10016 212-867-1515
Web: www.madhousenyc.com

Modern Videofilm Inc 2300 Empire Ave ... Burbank CA 91504 818-840-1700
Web: www.mvfinc.com

Point.360 2701 Media Center Dr ... Los Angeles CA 90065 818-565-1400 847-2503
NASDAQ: PTSX ■ *Web:* www.point360.com

Post Modern Co 2734 Walnut St ... Denver CO 80205 303-539-7001
Web: www.postmodernco.com

Post Modern Group LLC 2941 Alton Pkwy ... Irvine CA 92606 949-608-8700 608-8729
Web: www.postmoderngroup.com

Postworks New York
100 Ave of the Americas 11th Fl ... New York NY 10013 212-894-4000 941-0439
Web: postworks.com

Raleigh Studios Worldwide 5300 Melrose Ave ... Hollywood CA 90038 323-466-3111 871-5600
TF: 888-960-3456 ■ *Web:* www.raleighstudios.com

Rhythm & Hues Inc
5890 W Jefferson Blvd Ste Q ... Los Angeles CA 90016 310-448-7500 448-7600
Web: www.rhythm.com

RPG Productions 632 S Glenwood Pl ... Burbank CA 91506 818-848-0240 848-2257
Web: www.rpgproductions.com

Technicolor Complete Post Inc
6040 Sunset Blvd ... Hollywood CA 90028 323-817-6600
Web: www.technicolor.com

Technicolor USA Inc 10330 N Meridian St ... Indianapolis IN 46290 317-587-3000
Web: www.technicolor.com

Victory Studios 2247 15th Ave W ... Seattle WA 98119 206-282-1776 282-3535
Web: www.victorystudios.com

Video Post & Transfer Inc 2727 Inwood Rd ... Dallas TX 75235 214-350-2676 352-1427
Web: www.videopost.com

WRS Motion Picture & Video Laboratory
213 Tech Rd ... Pittsburgh PA 15205 412-937-1200
Web: www.wrslabs.com

513 MOTION PICTURE PRODUCTION - SPECIAL INTEREST

See Also Animation Companies p. 1736; Motion Picture & Television Production p. 2780

Phone Fax

Active Parenting Publishers
1955 Vaughn Rd Ste 108 ... Kennesaw GA 30144 770-429-0565 429-0334
TF: 800-825-0060 ■ *Web:* www.activeparenting.com

American Educational Products Inc
401 Hickory St PO Box 2121 ... Fort Collins CO 80522 970-484-7445 484-1198
TF: 800-289-9299 ■ *Web:* www.amep.com

Broadview Media Inc 201 S Union St ... Montgomery AL 36104 334-223-5708

Classic Worldwide Productions
5001 E Royalton Rd ... Cleveland OH 44147 440-838-5377
Web: classicworldwide.com

Coastal Training Technologies Corp
500 Studio Dr ... Virginia Beach VA 23452 757-498-9014 498-3657
TF: 866-333-6888 ■ *Web:* www.coastal.com

CRM Learning 2218 Faraday Ave Ste 110 ... Carlsbad CA 92008 760-431-9800 931-5792
TF: 800-421-0833 ■ *Web:* www.crmlearning.com

Gail & Rice Productions Inc
30700 Northwestern Hwy ... Farmington Hills MI 48334 248-799-5000 799-5001
Web: www.gail-rice.com

Hammond Communications Group Inc
173 Trade St ... Lexington KY 40511 859-254-1878 254-4290
TF: 888-424-1878 ■ *Web:* www.hammondcg.com

IMS Productions 4555 W 16th St ... Indianapolis IN 46222 317-492-8770 492-8746
Web: www.imsproductionstv.com

Intaglio LLC
5809 Cross Roads Commerce Pkwy Ste 200 ... Grand Rapids MI 49519 616-243-3300
TF: 800-632-9153 ■ *Web:* www.intaglioav.com

Iris Films 2600 Tenth St Ste 413 ... Berkeley CA 94710 510-845-5415 841-3336
Web: www.irisfilms.org

Keystone Learning Systems LLC
6030 Daybreak Cir Ste A150 116 ... Clarksville MD 21029 410-800-4000 422-7015*
**Fax Area Code: 866* ■ *TF:* 800-949-5590 ■ *Web:* www.keystonelearning.com

Kultur International Films Ltd
PO Box 755 ... Forked River NJ 08731 888-329-2580
TF: 888-329-2580 ■ *Web:* kulturvideo.com

Learning Communications LLC 5520 Trabuco Rd ... Irvine CA 92620 800-622-3610 727-4323*
**Fax Area Code: 949* ■ *TF:* 800-622-3610 ■ *Web:* www.learncom.com

Marcus Productions Inc
3107 Stirling Rd Ste 204 ... Fort Lauderdale FL 33312 954-965-5295
Web: www.marcusproductions.com

Medcom Trainex 6060 Phyllis Dr ... Cypress CA 90630 800-877-1443 898-4852*
**Fax Area Code: 714* ■ *TF Cust Svc:* 800-877-1443 ■ *Web:* www.medcomrn.com

National Film Board of Canada
Stn Centre-Ville PO Box 6100 ... Montreal QC H3C3H5 514-283-9000 283-7564
TF: 800-267-7710 ■ *Web:* www.nfb.ca

New Amsterdam Entertainment Inc
1133 Ave of the Americas Ste 1621 ... New York NY 10036 212-922-1930
Web: www.newamsterdamnyc.com

Nightingale-Conant Corp 6245 W Howard St ... Niles IL 60714 800-557-1660
TF Cust Svc: 800-557-1660 ■ *Web:* www.nightingale.com

PADI Americas 30151 Tomas St ... Rancho Santa Margarita CA 92688 949-858-7234 878-4364*
**Fax Area Code: 800* ■ *TF:* 800-527-8378 ■ *Web:* kaptest.com

Zelo Productions Inc 3 S Newton St ... Denver CO 80219 303-936-8995
Web: www.zeloproductions.com

514 MOTION PICTURE & TELEVISION PRODUCTION

See Also Animation Companies p. 1736; Motion Picture Production - Special Interest p. 2780

Phone Fax

3 Ball Entertainment
3650 Redondo Beach Ave ... Redondo Beach CA 90278 424-236-7500
Web: www.3ballproductions.com

3Play Media Inc 125 CambridgePark Dr ... Cambridge MA 02140 617-764-5189
Web: www.3playmedia.com

495 Productions Inc
4222 W Burbank Blvd 2nd Fl ... Burbank CA 91505 818-840-2750
Web: www.495productions.com

9 Story Entertainment Inc 23 Fraser Ave ... Toronto ON M6K1Y7 416-530-9900
Web: www.9story.com

@radical.media 435 Hudson St 6th Fl ... New York NY 10014 212-462-1500
Web: www.radicalmedia.com

ACT Video Productions Inc
5009 Pacific Hwy East Ste 10-0 ... Fife WA 98424 253-926-2440 926-1130
Web: www.actvp.com

Acutrack Inc 350 Sonic Ave ... Livermore CA 94551 925-579-5000
Web: www.acutrack.com

Adconion Media Group Ltd 950 Tower Ln ... Santa Monica CA 94404 650-802-8871
Web: amobee.com

Adm Productions Inc 40 Seaview Blvd ... Port Washington NY 11050 516-484-6900 621-2531
Web: www.admpro.com

Affiliated Media Inc 445 E Ohio St Ste 305 ... Chicago IL 60611 312-670-7200
Web: www.affiliatedmedia.net

Alcon Entertainment LLC
10390 Santa Monica Blvd Ste 250 ... Los Angeles CA 90025 310-789-3040
Web: www.alconent.com

Alliance Tickets Inc 5178 S Broadway ... Englewood CO 80113 303-781-2220

American Zoetrope 916 Kearny St ... San Francisco CA 94133 415-291-1700
Web: www.zoetrope.com

Animated Story Boards Ltd
1001 Ave of the Americas 24 fl ... New York NY 10018 212-595-0400
Web: www.animatedstoryboards.com

Ann Coppel Productions LLC PO Box 17144 ... Seattle WA 98127 206-282-7720
Web: www.anncoppelproductions.com

Anonymous Content LLC 3532 Hayden Ave ... Culver City CA 90232 310-558-3667
Web: www.anonymouscontent.com

Apostle Pictures 568 Broadway Ste 601 ... New York NY 10012 212-541-4323
Web: www.apostlenyc.com

Arcadia Content 6454 Quinpool Rd Ste 301 ... Halifax NS B3L1A9 902-446-3414
Web: arcadiacontent.com

Ascendant Pictures 406 Wilshire Blvd ... Santa Monica CA 90401 310-288-4600
Web: www.ascendantpictures.com

Associated Television International
4401 Wilshire Blvd ... Los Angeles CA 90010 323-556-5600
Web: www.associatedtelevision.com

Asylum, The 72 E Palm Ave ... Burbank CA 91502 323-850-1214
Web: www.theasylum.cc

Attraction Media Inc
5455 de Gaspe Ave Ste 805 ... Montreal QC H2T3B3 514-846-1222
Web: www.attractionmedia.ca

Audio General Inc (AGI)
1680 Republic Rd ... Huntingdon Valley PA 19006 267-288-0300 288-0301
TF: 866-866-2600 ■ *Web:* www.audiogeneral.com

Audio Video Systems Inc
14120 Sullyfield Cir ... Chantilly VA 20151 703-263-1002 263-0722
TF: 877-287-1175 ■ *Web:* www.avsinc.net

Auritt Communications 555 Eigth Ave Rm 709 ... New York NY 10018 212-302-6230
Web: auritt.com

Aurora Pictures Inc 5249 Chicago Ave ... Minneapolis MN 55417 612-821-6490
TF: 800-346-9487 ■ *Web:* www.aurorapictures.com

Auryn Inc 6033 W Century Blvd Ste 808 ... Los Angeles CA 90045 310-649-4278
Web: www.auryn.com

Automated Media Services Corp
110 Commerce Dr ... Allendale NJ 07401 201-934-6666
Web: www.3gtv.com

Avalanche Creative Svcs Inc 135 W 29th St ... New York NY 10001 212-206-9335
Web: www.avalanchecreative.tv

Avatar Studios Inc 2675 Scott Ave Ste G ... Saint Louis MO 63103 314-533-2242 533-3349
Web: www.avatar-studios.com

B-Reel 401 Broadway 24th Fl ... New York NY 10013 212-966-6186
Web: www.b-reel.com

Badiyan Inc 720 W 94th St ... Minneapolis MN 55420 952-888-5507
Web: www.badiyan.com

Banyan Communications Inc
3569 New Town Lk Dr ... Saint Charles MO 63301 636-946-3456
Web: www.banyancom.com

Bardel Entertainment Inc 548 Beatty St ... Vancouver BC V6B2L3 604-669-5589 669-9079
Web: bardel.ca

Bent Image Lab LLC 2729 SE Division St ... Portland OR 97202 503-228-6206
Web: bentimagelab.com

Best Buys Direct Inc 1044 State Rt 23 Ste 310 ... Wayne NJ 07470 973-628-8100
Web: www.bestbuysdirect.com

Big Deahl Productions Inc 1450 N Dayton St ... Chicago IL 60642 312-573-0733
Web: www.bigdeahl.com

Big Foot Productions Inc 3709 36th Ave ... Long Island NY 11101 718-729-1900 729-8638
Web: www.bigfootnyc.com

Bioquant Image Analysis Corp 5611 Ohio Ave ... Nashville TN 37209 615-350-7866
TF: 800-221-0549 ■ *Web:* www.bioquant.com

Booth Production Services Inc
5768 Remington Dr ... Winston-Salem NC 27104 336-766-1961
Web: www.boothproductionservices.com

BRC Imagination Arts 2711 Winona Ave ... Burbank CA 91504 818-841-8084 841-4996
Web: www.brcweb.com

Brightlight Pictures Inc
2400 Boundary Rd The Bridge Studios ... Burnaby BC V5M3Z3 604-628-3000
Web: www.brightlightpictures.com

Broadcast Sports Inc 7455 Race Rd ... Hanover MD 21076 410-564-2600
Web: broadcastsportsinc.com

Brooksfilms Ltd 9336 W Washington Blvd ... Culver City CA 90232 310-202-3292 202-3225

Bruno White Entertainment Inc
9460 Delegates Dr Ste 101 ... Orlando FL 32837 407-352-5555
Web: www.brunowhite.com

Bullfrog Films Inc 372 Dautrich Rd ... Reading PA 19606 610-779-8226
TF: 800-543-3764 ■ *Web:* www.bullfrogfilms.com

Company	City	State	Zip	Phone	Fax
Bunim/Murray Productions 6007 Sepulveda Blvd *Web:* www.bunim-murray.com	Van Nuys	CA	91411	818-756-5100	
Camelot Entertainment Group 300 Spectrum Center Dr Ste 400 *Web:* www.camelotfilms.com	Irvine	CA	92618	949-754-3030	
Campos Creative Works 1715 14th St *Web:* www.ccwla.com	Santa Monica	CA	90404	310-453-1511	
CAV Distributing Corp 253 Utah Ave *Web:* www.cavd.com	South San Francisco	CA	94080	650-588-2228	
CBS News 524 W 57th St *Web:* www.cbsnews.com	New York	NY	10019	212-975-3247	
CBS Studio Ctr 4024 Radford Ave *Web:* www.cbssc.com	Studio City	CA	91604	818-655-5000	
CBS Television Distribution 2450 Colorado Ave Ste 500E *Web:* www.cbstvd.com	Santa Monica	CA	90404	310-264-3300	264-3301
Center City Film & Video 1503 Walnut St *Web:* www.ccfv.com	Philadelphia	PA	19102	215-568-4134	
CenterStaging Corp 3407 Winona Ave *Web:* www.centerstaging.com	Burbank	CA	91504	818-559-4333	
Cev Multimedia Ltd 1020 SE Loop 289 *TF:* 877-610-5017 ■ *Web:* www.cevmultimedia.com	Lubbock	TX	79404	806-745-8820	
CGI Communications Inc 130 E Main St *TF:* 800-398-3029 ■ *Web:* www.cgicommunications.com	Rochester	NY	14604	585-427-0020	
Chainsaw Inc 1017 N Las Palmas Ave *Web:* www.chainsawedit.com	Los Angeles	CA	90038	323-785-1550	
Checchi Capital Advisors LLC 190 N Canon Dr Ste 402 *Web:* www.goodnewschannel.net	Beverly Hills	CA	90210	310-432-0010	
Chelsea Pictures Inc 33 Bond St Unit 1 *Web:* www.chelsea.com	New York	NY	10012	212-431-3434	
Cinecraft Productions Inc 2515 Franklin Blvd *Web:* www.cinecraft.com	Cleveland	OH	44113	216-781-2300	
Cineflix Media Inc 3510 Saint Laurent Blvd Ste 202 *Web:* www.cineflix.com	Montreal	QC	H2X2V2	514-278-3140	
Cinemavault Releasing Inc 175 Bloor St E S Tower Ste 1011 *Web:* www.cinemavault.com	Toronto	ON	M4W3R8	416-363-6060	
Cinemotion Inc 9062 General Dr *Web:* cinemotioninc.com	Plymouth	MI	48170	734-454-4433	
Cinespace Film Studios 2621 W 15th Pl Ste 100 *Web:* www.cinespace.com	Chicago	IL	60608	416-406-4000	
Cinetel Films 8255 W Sunset Blvd *Web:* cinetelfilms.com	West Hollywood	CA	90046	323-654-4000	
Cintrex Audio Visual 656 Axminster Dr *TF:* 800-325-9541 ■ *Web:* www.cintrexav.com	Fenton	MO	63026	636-343-0178	
CloverLeaf Digital LLC 20 Jay St Ste 213 *Web:* www.cloverleafdigital.com	Brooklyn	NY	11201	718-438-6448	
Collective Digital Studio LLC 8383 Wilshire Blvd Ste 1050 *Web:* www.studio71.com/us?showpopover=true	Beverly Hills	CA	90211	323-370-1500	
Columbia TriStar Motion Picture Group 10202 W Washington Blvd *Fax:* Mail Rm ■ *TF:* 855-327-7669 ■ *Web:* www.sonypictures.com/movies	Culver City	CA	90232	310-244-4000	840-8888*
Communca Inc 31 N Erie St *TF:* 800-800-7890 ■ *Web:* www.communica.world	Toledo	OH	43604	800-800-7890	
Compass Rose Media LLC 105 Locust St *Web:* www.compassrosemedia.com	Santa Cruz	CA	95060	831-457-3533	
Concept Art House Inc 785 Market St Ste 1100 *Web:* www.conceptarthouse.com	San Francisco	CA	94103	415-707-1500	
Concepts Tv Production 328 W Main St *Web:* www.conceptstv.com	Boonton	NJ	07005	973-331-1500	
Contecture International Ltd 17252 Armstrong Ave Ste A *Web:* www.contextureintl.com	Irvine	CA	92614	949-250-0811	
Contrast Creative 2598 Highstone Rd *Web:* www.contrastcreative.com	Cary	NC	27519	919-469-9151	
Cosmic Pictures Inc 1345 Major St *Web:* cosmicpictures.com	Salt Lake City	UT	84115	801-463-3880	
Cox Matthews & Associates Inc 10520 Warwick Ave Ste B-8 *Web:* www.diverseeducation.com	Fairfax	VA	22030	703-385-2981	
Creation Ground Media 999 Clark Ave *Web:* www.creationgroundmedia.com	Mountain View	CA	94040	650-947-7779	
Creative Film Management 430 W 14th St Fl 4 *Web:* www.crmmgt.com	New York	NY	10014	212-685-6070	
Crosswater Digital Media LLC 695 Delaware Ave *Web:* www.crosswater.net	Buffalo	NY	14209	716-884-8486	
Culver Studios 9336 W Washington Blvd *Web:* www.theculverstudios.com	Culver City	CA	90232	310-202-1234	
Curtis 1105 Western Ave *Web:* www.curtisinc.com	Cincinnati	OH	45203	513-621-8895	
Danetracks Inc 7356 Santa Monica Blvd *Web:* www.danetracks.com	West Hollywood	CA	90046	323-512-8160	
Davenport Theatrical Enterprises Inc 254 W 54th St 14th Fl *Web:* www.davenporttheatrical.com	New York	NY	10019	212-874-5348	
David Naylor & Assoc Inc PO Box 93216 *Web:* www.dnala.com	Los Angeles	CA	90093	323-463-2826	
Deluxe Digital Media Management Inc 29125 Ave Paine *Web:* www.bydeluxe.com	Valencia	CA	91355	661-702-5000	
Destination Cinema Inc 4155 Harrison Blvd Ste 201 *Web:* www.destinationcinema.com	Ogden	UT	84403	801-392-5881	
Devlin Video International LLC 1501 Broadway Ste 408 *Web:* www.devlinvideo.com	New York	NY	10036	212-391-1313	
Dick Clark Productions Inc (DCP) 2900 Olympic Blvd *Web:* www.dickclark.com	Santa Monica	CA	90404	310-255-4600	
Digital Domain Productions Inc 300 Rose Ave *Web:* www.digitaldomain.com	Venice	CA	90291	310-314-2800	
Digital FX Inc 6010 Perkins Rd Ste B *Web:* www.digitalfx.tv	Baton Rouge	LA	70808	225-763-6010	
Digital Outpost 2772 Loker Ave W *Web:* www.digitaloutpost.com	Carlsbad	CA	92010	760-431-3575	
Dillon Video & Film Productions Inc 2330 Ne Eigth Rd *Web:* www.dillonvideo.com	Ocala	FL	34470	352-620-0686	
Double r Productions LLC 1621 Connecticut Ave Nw Ste 4 *Web:* www.doublerproductions.com	Washington	DC	20009	202-797-7777	
Downtown Digital Post 401 E Jefferson St *Web:* www.downtowndigitalpost.com	Phoenix	AZ	85004	602-462-6464	
Dreamworks Animation LLC 1000 Flower St *Web:* www.dreamworks.com	Glendale	CA	91201	818-695-5000	
Drury Design Dynamics Inc 49 W 27th St *Web:* www.drurydesign.com	New York	NY	10001	212-213-4600	
Dufferin Gate Productions Inc 20 Butterick Rd *Web:* www.dufferingate.com	Toronto	ON	M8W3Z8	416-252-9998	
E-n-g Mobile Systems Inc-broadcast & Mobilab Divs 2245 Via De Mercados *Web:* www.e-n-g.com	Concord	CA	94520	925-798-4060	
Eastco Multi Media Solutions Inc 3646 California Rd *TF:* 800-365-8273 ■ *Web:* www.eastcomultimedia.com	Orchard Park	NY	14127	716-662-0536	
Edmonds Entertainment 1635 N Cahuenga Blvd *Web:* www.edmondsent.com	Los Angeles	CA	90028	323-860-1520	
Edward R Pressman Film Corp 9469 Jefferson Blvd Ste 119 *Web:* www.pressman.com	Los Angeles	CA	90232	310-450-9692	450-9705
EFILM LLC 1146 N Las Palmas Ave *Web:* www.efilm.com	Hollywood	CA	90038	323-463-7041	
Element Productions Inc 316 Stuart St 4th Fl *Web:* element.cc	Boston	MA	02116	617-779-8808	
Elephant Productions Inc 3404 Guadalupe St *Web:* www.changs.com	Austin	TX	78705	512-302-3130	
Emerging Pictures 49 W 27th St 8th Fl *Web:* www.emergingpictures.com	New York	NY	10019	212-245-6767	
Entertainment Studios Inc 1925 Century Park E 10th Fl *Web:* www.es.tv	Los Angeles	CA	90067	310-277-3500	
EUE/Screen Gems Studios 603 Greenwich St *Web:* euescreengems.com	New York	NY	10014	212-450-1600	
Event Producers Inc 5724 Salmen St *TF:* 866-903-6949 ■ *Web:* eventproducers.com	New Orleans	LA	70123	504-466-4066	
Evil Eye Pictures LLC 665 Third St Ste 503 *Web:* evileyepictures.com	San Francisco	CA	94107	415-777-0666	
Exodus Film Group Inc 1255 Electric Ave *Web:* www.exodusfilmgroup.com	Venice	CA	90291	310-684-3155	
F & F Productions LLC 14333 Myerlake Cir *Web:* fandfhd.tv	Clearwater	FL	33760	727-530-5000	535-6547
FDC Graphics Films Inc 3820 William Richardson Dr *Web:* www.fdcfilms.com	South Bend	IN	46628	574-273-4400	
Fenton Communications Inc 1010 Vermont Ave NW Ste 1100 *Web:* www.fenton.com	Washington	DC	20005	202-822-5200	
Film Workers Club 1006 17th Ave S *Web:* www.filmworkers.com	Nashville	TN	37212	615-322-9337	
First Generation Productions 410 Allentown Dr *Web:* www.firstgencom.com	Allentown	PA	18109	610-437-4300	
Focus Features 65 Bleeker St 3rd Fl *Web:* www.focusfeatures.com	New York	NY	10012	212-539-4000	
Focus Features LLC 1540 2nd St Ste 200 *Web:* www.filminfocus.com	Santa Monica	CA	90401	818-777-8738	
Fortis Films 8581 Santa Monica Blvd Ste 1	West Hollywood	CA	90069	310-659-4533	659-4373
Forward Entertainment 9255 Sunset Blvd Ste 805	Los Angeles	CA	90069	310-278-6700	278-6770
Fox Searchlight Pictures 10201 W Pico Blvd Bldg 38 *Web:* www.foxsearchlight.com	Los Angeles	CA	90035	310-369-6000	
Frantic Films Corp 70 Arthur St Ste 300 *Web:* www.franticfilms.com	Winnipeg	MB	R3B1G7	204-949-0070	
Fresh Air Media PO Box 6078 *Web:* freshairmedia.com	Auburn	CA	95604	530-888-7676	
Fujisankei Communications International Inc 150 E 52nd St 34th Fl *Web:* www.fujisankei.com	New York	NY	10022	212-753-8100	688-0392
FUNimation Entertainment Ltd 1200 Lakeside Pkwy Bldg 1 *Web:* www.funimation.com	Flower Mound	TX	75028	972-355-7300	
Game Creek Video LLC 23 Executive Dr *Web:* www.gamecreekvideo.com	Hudson	NH	03051	603-882-5222	
Garden State Studios 1325 Us Hwy 206	Skillman	NJ	08558	609-688-1004	
Genesis Communications Inc 900 Technology Pkwy Ste 300 *Web:* www.phantomefx.com	Cedar Falls	IA	50613	319-266-3656	
Geomedia Inc 4242 Medical Dr Ste 4200 *Web:* www.geomedia.com	San Antonio	TX	78229	210-614-5900	
Global Digital Media Xchange Inc 5432 W 102nd St	Los Angeles	CA	90045	818-972-0200	
Grace Creek Media Inc 100 Cathedral St Ste 9 *Web:* www.gracecreek.com	Annapolis	MD	21401	410-280-8528	

Company	City	State	Zip	Phone	Fax
Gracie Films 10201 W Pico Blvd Bldg 41/42 *Web:* www.graciefilms.com	Los Angeles	CA	90064	310-369-7222	
Grb Entertainment Inc 13400 Riverside Dr Ste 300 *Web:* grbtv.com	Sherman Oaks	CA	91423	818-728-7600	
Greibok Designs LLC 3 E Read St *Web:* www.greibo.com	Baltimore	MD	21202	410-244-8861	
Gurney Productions Inc 8929 S Sepulveda Blvd Ste 510 *Web:* www.gurneyproductions.com	Los Angeles	CA	90045	310-645-1499	
Guru Studio 500-110 Spadina Ave *Web:* www.gurustudio.com	Toronto	ON	M5V2K4	416-599-4878	
Guthy-Renker Corp 41550 Eclectic St Ste 200 *Web:* www.guthy-renker.com	Palm Desert	CA	92260	760-773-9022	
Half Yard Productions LLC 4922 Fairmont Ave Ste 300 *Web:* www.halfyardproductions.com	Bethesda	MD	20814	240-223-3400	
Harmony Gold Music Inc 7655 W Sunset Blvd *Web:* www.harmonygold.com	Los Angeles	CA	90046	323-851-4900	
Harpo Films Inc 345 N Maple Dr Ste 315 **Fax Area Code:* 312	Beverly Hills	CA	90210	310-278-5559	633-1976*
Harpo Productions Inc 110 N Carpenter *Web:* www.oprah.com	Chicago	IL	60607	312-633-1000	633-1976
Hearst Entertainment & Syndication Group 300 W 57th St *Web:* hearst.com/entertainment	New York	NY	10019	212-969-7553	
Hello World Communications 118 W 22nd St Fl 2 *Web:* www.hwc.tv	New York	NY	10011	212-243-8800	
Hendlin Visual Communications Inc 129 N Second St Ste 101 *Web:* hendin.com	Minneapolis	MN	55401	612-338-1663	
High Speed Productions Inc 1303 Underwood Ave *TF:* 888-520-9099 ■ *Web:* www.juxtapoz.com	San Francisco	CA	94124	415-822-3083	
Hillmann & Carr Inc 2233 Wisconsin Ave Nw Ste 425 *Web:* www.hillmanncarr.com	Washington	DC	20007	202-342-0001	
Hopsports Inc 24715 Ave Rockefeller *Web:* www.hopsports.com	Valencia	CA	91355	661-702-8946	
Horizons Video & Film Inc 4000 Horizons Dr *Web:* www.horizonscompanies.com	Columbus	OH	43220	614-481-7200	
Ian Ryan & Assoc Inc 1400 E Touhy Ave Ste 220 *Web:* www.ianryan.com	Des Plaines	IL	60018	847-803-2050	
Icon Productions 808 Wilshire Blvd *Web:* www.iconmovies.us	Santa Monica	CA	90401	310-434-7300	
ICV Digital Media 3908 Valley Ave Ste A *Web:* www.icvdm.com	Pleasanton	CA	94566	925-426-8230	
Image Recordings 4736 Penn Ave Ste 200 *Web:* www.aspstation.net	Pittsburgh	PA	15224	412-362-4050	
Imagina US 7291 NW 74th St *Web:* www.imaginaus.com	Miami	FL	33166	305-777-1900	
Imaginary Forces LLC 2254 S Sepulveda Blvd *Web:* www.imaginaryforces.com	Los Angeles	CA	90064	323-957-6868	
Imagine Entertainment Inc 9465 Wilshire Blvd *Web:* www.imagine-entertainment.com	Beverly Hills	CA	90212	310-858-2000	
iNDELIBLE Media Corp 535 Eighth Ave 16th Fl	New York	NY	10018	212-629-0802	
Infinitude Creative Group LP 1820 Preston Park Blvd Ste 2100 *Web:* www.nfnitude.com	Plano	TX	75093	972-867-6800	
Inhance Digital Corp 8057 Beverly Blvd Ste 200 *Web:* inhance.com	Los Angeles	CA	90048	323-297-7700	
Interface Media Group Inc 1233 20th St NW *Web:* www.interfacemedia.com	Washington	DC	20036	202-861-0500	
Island Co 312 Clematis St Ste 401 *Web:* www.islandcompany.com	West Palm Beach	FL	33401	561-833-8110	
Jerry Bruckheimer Films 1631 Tenth St *Web:* www.jbfilms.com	Santa Monica	CA	90404	310-664-6260	
Jerry Weintraub Productions 4000 Warner Blvd Bungalow 1	Burbank	CA	91522	818-954-2500	954-1399
Jon Voight Entertainment 10203 Santa Monica Blvd 5th Fl *Web:* www.crystalsky.com	Los Angeles	CA	90067	310-843-0223	553-9895
Jones Film & Video 916 W Sixth St *Web:* www.jonesinc.com	Little Rock	AR	72201	501-372-1981	
Jones Mobile Television 5200 Northshore Dr Ste F *Web:* jmtv.com	North Little Rock	AR	72118	501-376-1993	
Joseph Productions Inc 34525 Glendale St *Web:* www.jpitel.com	Livonia	MI	48150	734-266-0500	
JPL Integrated Communictions Inc 471 Jplwick Dr *Web:* www.jplcreative.com	Harrisburg	PA	17111	717-558-8048	
Just for Laughs Inc 2101 St-Laurent Blvd *Web:* www.hahaha.com	Montreal	QC	H2X2T5	514-845-3155	845-4140
Kantola Productions LLC 55 Sunnyside Ave *TF:* 800-280-1180 ■ *Web:* www.kantola.com	Mill Valley	CA	94941	415-381-9363	
Kartemquin Films Ltd 1901 W Wellington Ave *Web:* www.kartemquin.com	Chicago	IL	60657	773-472-4366	472-3348
Kennetic Productions Inc 5 W. Forsyth St Ste 200 *Web:* www.kenneticproductions.com	Jacksonville	FL	32202	904-464-0041	
Kenwood 75 Varney Pl *Web:* www.kenwoodx.com	San Francisco	CA	94107	415-957-5333	
Key Brand Entertainment Inc 1619 Broadway 9th Fl *Web:* kbeinc.net	New York	NY	10019	917-421-5400	

Company	City	State	Zip	Phone	Fax
Knock Inc 1315 Glenwood Ave *Web:* www.knockinc.com	Minneapolis	MN	55405	612-333-6511	
Lakeshore Entertainment Corp 9268 W Third St *Web:* www.lakeshoreentertainment.com	Beverly Hills	CA	90210	310-867-8000	
Lederle Machine Co 830 Jefferson St *Web:* www.lederle.com	Pacific	MO	63069	636-271-7200	
Limelight Communications Inc 2812 Roesh Way *Web:* www.limelight.com	Vienna	VA	22181	703-242-4596	
Line Plot Productions LLC 146 Mt Auburn St	Cambridge	MA	02138	617-864-8300	
Lions Gate Entertainment Inc 2700 Colorado Ave Ste 200 *Web:* www.lionsgate.com	Santa Monica	CA	90404	310-449-9200	255-3870
Little Earth Productions 2400 Josephine St *Web:* www.littlearth.com	Pittsburgh	PA	15203	412-471-0909	
Logan Media Services LLC 1515 Elm Hill Pk Ste 205 *Web:* www.loganmedia.net	Nashville	TN	37210	615-361-8100	
London Broadcasting Co Inc 5052 Addison Cir *Web:* www.londonbroadcastingcompany.com	Addison	TX	75001	214-730-0151	
Lucasfilm Ltd PO Box 29901 *Web:* www.lucasfilm.com	San Francisco	CA	94129	415-623-1000	
MacNeil Lehrer Productions LLC 2700 Quincy St Ste 250 *Web:* www.macneil-lehrer.com	Arlington	VA	22206	703-998-2170	
Magno Sound Inc 729 Seventh Ave Fl 2 *Web:* magnoscreening.com	New York	NY	10019	212-302-2505	
Maitland Primrose Group Inc 7220 N 16th St Ste c *Web:* www.maitlandprimrose.com	Phoenix	AZ	85020	602-944-0046	
Mandalay Pictures 4751 Wilshire Blvd 3rd Fl *Web:* www.mandalay.com	Los Angeles	CA	90010	323-549-4300	
Mars Hill Productions Inc 4711 Lexington Blvd *Web:* www.mars-hill.org	Missouri City	TX	77459	281-403-1463	403-4463
Maslow Media Group Inc, The 2233 Wisconsin Ave NW Ste 400 *Web:* www.maslowmedia.com	Washington	DC	20007	202-965-1100	
McHenry Creative Services Inc 345 Main St *Web:* www.mchenrycreative.com	Harleysville	PA	19438	215-513-0251	
Media Imagery 7905 Browning Rd Ste 218 *Web:* www.mediaimagery.com	Pennsauken	NJ	08109	856-317-0990	
Media Services Ltd 2510 W Dunlap Ave Ste 250 *Web:* www.msgl.com	Phoenix	AZ	85021	602-674-5800	
Meditech Communications Inc 533 Phalen Blvd *Web:* www.gomeditech.com	Saint Paul	MN	55130	651-636-7350	
Memocast 1801 Bush St *Web:* www.memocast.com	San Francisco	CA	94109	415-673-5122	
Metro Teleproductions Inc 1400 E W Hwy Apt 628 *Web:* www.mtitv.com	Silver Spring	MD	20910	301-608-9077	
Metro-Goldwyn-Mayer Studios Inc (MGM) 245 N Beverly Dr **Fax:* Mktg ■ *Web:* www.mgm.com	Beverly Hills	CA	90210	310-586-8674	586-8670*
MG Studios Inc 2005 Tree Fork Ln Ste 113 *Web:* www.mg-studios.com	Longwood	FL	32750	407-679-9291	
Mills James Inc 3545 Fishinger Blvd *Web:* www.mjp.com	Columbus	OH	43026	614-777-9933	
Minds Eye Entertainment Ltd 480 Henderson Dr *Web:* www.mindseyepictures.com	Regina	SK	S4N6E3	306-359-7618	
MIRA Mobile Television Inc 25749 SW Canyon Creek Rd Ste 100	Wilsonville	OR	97070	503-464-0900	
Mirage Productions Inc 111 Spring St *Web:* www.mirageproductions.com	Newton	NJ	07860	973-300-9477	
Miramax Film NY LLC 2540 Colorado Ave Ste 100E *Web:* www.miramax.com	Santa Monica	CA	90404	310-409-4321	
MMG Corporate Communication Inc 515 W Loveland Ave *Web:* www.mmgonline.com	Loveland	OH	45140	513-677-8787	
Mort Crim Communications Inc 155 W Congress Ste 501 *Web:* mccicorp.com	Detroit	MI	48226	313-481-4700	
MPCA 10635 Santa Monica Blvd *Web:* mpcafilm.com	Los Angeles	CA	90025	310-319-9500	319-9501
Mr Mudd 5225 Wilshire Blvd Ste 604 *Web:* mrmudd.com	Los Angeles	CA	90036	323-932-5656	
Muse Entertainment Enterprises Inc 3451 Rue St-Jacques *Web:* www.muse.ca	Montreal	QC	H4C1H1	514-866-6873	
My Eye Media LLC 3515 W Pacific Ave *Web:* myeyemedia.com	Burbank	CA	91505	818-559-7200	
NAMCO BANDAI Holdings (USA) Inc 5551 Katella Ave *Web:* www.namcobandai.com	Cypress	CA	90630	714-816-9500	
Nancy Glass Productions Inc 211 Rock Hill Rd Ste 201 *Web:* www.nancyglassproductions.com	Bala Cynwyd	PA	19004	610-668-1668	
Nash Entertainment 1438 N Gower St Ste 35 *Web:* www.nashentertainment.com	Los Angeles	CA	90028	323-993-7384	
National Media Services Inc 613 N Commerce Ave *Web:* www.nationalmediaservices.com	Front Royal	VA	22630	540-635-4181	
NBA Entertainment 450 Harmon Meadow Blvd **Fax:* Mail Rm ■ *TF:* 866-648-4668 ■ *Web:* nba.com	Secaucus	NJ	07094	201-865-1500	865-2626*
Nelvana Ltd Corus Quay 25 Dockside Dr *Web:* www.nelvana.com	Toronto	ON	M5A0B5	416-479-7000	
Net Element International Inc 1450 S Miami Ave *Web:* www.netelement.com	Miami	FL	33130	787-993-9650	

Company	City	State	ZIP	Phone	Fax
New Horizons Picture Corp 11600 San Vicente Blvd	Los Angeles	CA	90049	310-820-6733	
New Perspective Productions 2949 Smallman St	Pittsburgh	PA	15201	412-681-1600	
NFL Films Inc 1 Nfl Plz *Web:* www.nflfilms.com	Mt Laurel	NJ	08054	856-222-3500	
Nikitova LLC 203 N Lasalle Ste 2100	Chicago	IL	60601	773-913-8015	
North by Northwest Productions 601 W Broad St *Web:* www.nxnw.net	Boise	ID	83702	208-345-7870	
NTV International Corp 645 Fifth Ave Ste 303 *Web:* www.ntvic.com	New York	NY	10022	212-660-6900	660-6998
Nu Image Inc 6423 Wilshire Blvd *Web:* www.millenniumfilms.com	Los Angeles	CA	90048	310-388-6900	
Omnifilm Entertainment Ltd 111 Water St *Web:* www.omnifilm.com	Vancouver	BC	V6B1A7	604-681-6543	
On-line Video Design Inc 710 Acacia Ave *Web:* www.onlinevid.com	Melbourne	FL	32904	321-676-5677	
Original Productions Inc 308 W Verdugo Ave *Web:* www.amygdalamusic.com	Burbank	CA	91502	818-295-6966	
Orion Multimedia 10397 W Centennial Rd	Littleton	CO	80127	720-891-4839	
Overbrook Entertainment Inc 10202 W Washington Blvd 4th Fl	Culver City	CA	90232	310-432-2400	432-2401
Pacific Title Archives 10717 Vanowen St *TF:* 800-968-9111 ■ *Web:* www.pacifictitlearchives.com	North Hollywood	CA	91605	818-760-4223	
Paradise Fx 6711 Valjean Ave Ste A *Web:* www.paradisefx.com	Van Nuys	CA	91406	818-785-3100	
Paramount Pictures Corp 5555 Melrose Ave *Web:* www.paramount.com	Los Angeles	CA	90038	323-956-5000	956-0121
Participant Media LLC 331 Foothill Rd 3rd Fl *Web:* www.participantmedia.com	Beverly Hills	CA	90210	310-550-5100	
PayReel Inc 24928 Genesee Trl Rd *TF:* 800-352-7397 ■ *Web:* www.payreel.com	Golden	CO	80401	303-526-4900	
PDC Productions 3217 N Flood Ave *Web:* www.pdcproductions.com	Norman	OK	73069	405-360-5130	
People Productions Video Services Inc 1737 15th St Ste 200 *Web:* www.peopleproductions.com	Boulder	CO	80302	303-449-6086	
Phoenix Pictures Inc 10203 W Washington Blvd Ste 400 *Web:* www.phoenixpictures.com	Los Angeles	CA	90067	424-298-2788	298-2588
Pivot Point International Inc 1560 Sherman Ave Ste 700 *Web:* www.pivot-point.com	Evanston	IL	60201	847-866-0500	
Pix System LLC 455 Market St Ste 900 *Web:* www.pixsystem.com	San Francisco	CA	94105	415-357-9720	
Post Modern Inc 100 Ross St Lbby 3 *Web:* www.postmodern-pgh.com	Pittsburgh	PA	15219	412-391-6635	
Pot o Gold Multi-cinema Productions Inc 2201 Rogero Rd *Web:* www.pogusa.com	Jacksonville	FL	32211	904-744-7478	
PRG Nocturne Productions Inc 300 Harvestore Dr *Web:* www.trichromes.com	Dekalb	IL	60115	815-756-9600	
Producers Management Television Pmtv 681 Moore Rd Ste 100 *Web:* pmtv.com	King Of Prussia	PA	19406	610-768-1770	
Production Masters Inc 202 Fifth Ave The Buhl Bldg	Pittsburgh	PA	15222	412-281-8500	
Raleigh Studios 5300 Melrose Ave *Web:* www.raleighstudios.com	Hollywood	CA	90038	310-727-2700	
Reaction Audio Visual - Dallas LLC 9951 Muirlands Blvd *Web:* reactionav.com	Irvine	CA	92618	949-600-8235	
Red Hour Films 629 N La Brea Ave	Los Angeles	CA	90036	323-602-5000	602-5001
Reel FX Inc 301 N Crowdus St *Web:* www.reelfx.com	Dallas	TX	75226	214-979-0961	
Regency Enterprises 10201 W Pico Blvd Bldg 12 *Web:* www.newregency.com	Los Angeles	CA	90035	310-369-8300	969-0470
Regent Entertainment Partnership LP 8411 Preston Rd Ste 650 *Web:* www.regententertainment.com	Dallas	TX	75225	214-373-3434	
Renegade Productions Inc 10950 Gilroy Rd Ste J *Web:* www.getrenegade.com	Hunt Valley	MD	21031	410-667-1400	
Resolution Digital Studios 2226 W Walnut St *Web:* www.rdschicago.com	Chicago	IL	60612	312-846-4226	
Revelations Entertainment Inc 1221 Second St 4th Fl *Web:* revelationsent.com	Santa Monica	CA	90401	310-394-3131	
Revision3 Corp 2415 Third St Ste 232 *Web:* www.revision3.com	San Francisco	CA	94107	415-734-3500	
Revolution Studios 2900 Olympic Blvd *Web:* www.revolutionstudios.com	Santa Monica	CA	90404	310-255-7000	255-7001
RGB Group Inc 4141 N Miami Ave Ste 210 *Web:* www.rgbgroup.com	Miami	FL	33127	305-573-1672	
Richter Studios 1143 W Rundell Pl *Web:* www.richterstudios.com	Chicago	IL	60607	312-861-9999	
Ring of Fire Studios LLC 1702 Olympic Blvd Studio A *Web:* www.ringoffire.com	Santa Monica	CA	90404	310-966-5055	
RKO Pictures Inc 2034 Broadway *Web:* www.rko.com	Santa Monica	CA	90404	310-277-0707	
Rodgers & Hammerstein Organization, The 229 W 28th St 11th Fl *TF:* 800-400-8160 ■ *Web:* www.rnh.com	New York	NY	10001	212-541-6600	
Roush Media 84 E Santa Anita Ave *Web:* www.roush-media.com	Burbank	CA	91502	818-559-8648	
Samson Technologies Inc 45 Gilpin Ave *TF:* 800-372-6766 ■ *Web:* www.samsontech.com	Hauppauge	NY	11788	631-784-2200	
Samuel Goldwyn Films LLC 9570 W Pico Blvd Ste 400 *Web:* www.samuelgoldwynfilms.com	Los Angeles	CA	90035	310-860-3100	
Scanline Vfx La Inc 12950 Culver Blvd *Web:* scanlinevfx.com	Los Angeles	CA	90066	310-827-1555	
Scope Seven Inc 2201 Park Pl Ste 100 *Web:* zoodigital.com/	El Segundo	CA	90245	310-220-3939	
Scott Powers Productions Inc 135 W 29th St Rm 404 *Web:* www.scottpowers.com	New York	NY	10001	212-242-4700	
Script to Screen Productions 200 N Tustin Ave Ste 200 *Web:* www.scripttoscreen.com	Santa Ana	CA	92705	714-558-3971	
Section 8 Post Production Facility LLC 23716 Woodward Ave *Web:* www.section8.com	Pleasant Ridge	MI	48069	248-546-2714	
Sesame Workshop 1 Lincoln Plz *Web:* www.sesameworkshop.org	New York	NY	10023	212-595-3456	
Shaftesbury Films Inc 163 Queen St E Ste 100 *Web:* www.shaftesbury.ca	Toronto	ON	M5A1S1	416-363-1411	
Shooters International Inc 63 Berkeley St *Web:* www.shootersfilm.com	Toronto	ON	M5A2W5	416-862-1959	
Sky High Entertainment 777 Blvd Lebourgneuf Ste 160 *Web:* www.shemovie.com	Quebec	QC	G2J1C3	418-682-1443	
Skylight Studios Video Prodctns 109 Squirrel Ln	Levittown	NY	11756	516-579-0245	
Smithgroup Communications Inc 267 SE 33rd Ave *Web:* smithgrp.com	Portland	OR	97214	503-239-4215	
Smp Communications Corp 7626 E Greenway Rd Ste 100 *TF:* 888-796-3342 ■ *Web:* smpcom.com	Scottsdale	AZ	85260	480-905-4100	
Sonar Entertainment 2121 Ave of the Stars Ste 2150 *Web:* sonarent.com	Los Angeles	CA	90067	212-977-9001	
SonicPool Post Production 6860 Lexington Ave *Web:* www.sonicpool.com	Los Angeles	CA	90038	323-460-4649	
Sony Pictures Entertainment Inc 10202 W Washington Blvd *TF:* 855-327-7669 ■ *Web:* www.sonypictures.com	Culver City	CA	90232	310-244-4000	840-8888
Sony Pictures Television 10202 W Washington Blvd *TF:* 800-327-3325 ■ *Web:* www.sonypictures.com	Culver City	CA	90232	310-244-4000	244-1874
Spark Unlimited Inc 15000 Ventura Blvd Ste 202 *Web:* www.sparkunlimited.com	Sherman Oaks	CA	91403	818-788-1005	
Spyglass Entertainment 245 N Beverly Dr *Web:* www.spyglassent.com	Beverly Hills	CA	90210	310-443-5800	443-5912
StagePost Full Screen Spectrum Media 255 French Landing Dr *Web:* www.stagepost.com	Nashville	TN	37228	615-248-1978	
Stonemar Capital LLC 32 Union Sq E Ste 1100 *Web:* www.stonemarproperties.com	New York	NY	10003	212-324-8306	
Strategic Media Services Inc 1911 North Ft Myer Dr Ste 400 *Web:* www.strategicmediaservices.com	Arlington	VA	20009	202-337-5700	
Stu Segall Productions Inc 4705 Ruffin Rd *Web:* www.stusegall.com	San Diego	CA	92123	858-974-8988	
Sundance Institute 1825 Three Kings Dr *Web:* www.sundance.org	Park City	UT	84060	801-328-3456	
Sunrise Communications 621 Newport Ave *Web:* www.suncom.us	Westmont	IL	60559	630-570-5700	
Sunset Gower Studios 1438 N Gower St *Web:* www.sgsandsbs.com	Hollywood	CA	90028	323-467-1001	
Swank Motion Pictures Inc 10795 Watson Rd *TF:* 888-248-8757 ■ *Web:* www.swank.com	St Louis	MO	63127	314-984-6000	
Team People LLC 180 S Washington St *Web:* www.teampeople.tv	Falls Church	VA	22046	202-587-4111	
Three Leaf Productions 940 Science Blvd Ste C *Web:* www.three-leaf.com	Gahanna	OH	43230	614-626-4941	
Threshold Entertainment Inc 1649 11th St *Web:* www.thethreshold.com	Santa Monica	CA	90404	310-452-8899	
Touchstone Pictures 500 S Buena Vista St *Web:* www.thewaltdisneycompany.com	Burbank	CA	91521	818-560-3300	
Touchstone Television Production LLC 500 S Buena Vista St	Burbank	CA	91521	818-560-1000	
Trailblazer Studios Nc Inc 1610 Midtown Pl *Web:* videofonics.com	Raleigh	NC	27609	919-645-6600	
Tribeca Productions 375 Greenwich St 8th Fl *Web:* www.tribecafilm.com	New York	NY	10013	212-941-4000	941-3997
Troupe Modern Media Design & Production, The 3 Industrial Dr Unit 3 *Web:* www.thetroupe.com	Windham	NH	03087	603-893-4554	
True Blue Productions S Brand Blvd	Los Angeles	CA	90029	323-661-9191	
Two Cats Media Ltd 20 W 22nd St Ste 605 *Web:* www.twocatstv.com	New York	NY	10010	212-929-2085	
Two Little Hands Productions 870 E N Union Ave *Web:* www.signingtime.com	Midvale	UT	84047	801-676-4441	676-4441
Uber Content 1040 N Las Palmas Ave Bldg 7n *Web:* www.ubercontent.com	Los Angeles	CA	90038	212-353-8686	
Ultimatte Corp 20945 Plummer St *Web:* www.ultimatte.com	Chatsworth	CA	91311	818-993-8007	
Ultra Stereo Labs Inc 181 Bonetti Dr *Web:* www.uslinc.com	San Luis Obispo	CA	93401	805-549-0161	
Union Editorial LLC 12200 W Olympic Blvd Ste 140 *Web:* www.unioneditorial.com	Los Angeles	CA	90064	310-481-2200	

Phone Fax

Universal Image Production Inc
20750 Civic Ctr Dr Ste 100........................ Southfield MI 48076 248-357-2247
Web: www.universalimages.com
Universal Studios Inc
100 Universal City Plaza........................ Universal City CA 91608 800-864-8377 866-3600*
*Fax Area Code: 818 ■ *TF:* 800-864-8377 ■ *Web:* www.universalstudios.com
Ventana Productions 1819 L St Nw Ste 100w........ Washington DC 20036 202-785-5112
Web: www.ventanadc.com
Versabar Inc 1111 Engineers Rd.................. Belle Chasse LA 70037 504-392-3200
Web: www.vbar.com
Viacom Entertainment Group 1515 Broadway.......... New York NY 10036 212-258-6000
TF: 800-516-4399 ■ *Web:* www.viacom.com
Video Symphony Entertraining Inc
266 E Magnolia Blvd............................... Burbank CA 91502 818-557-6500
TF: 888-370-7589 ■ *Web:* www.vs.edu
Videobred Inc 1000 Hamilton Ave.................. Louisville KY 40204 502-584-5787
Web: www.videobred.com
Vision Global AR Ltee 80, Queen St Ste 301........... Montreal QC H3C2N5 514-879-0020
TF: 800-667-7690
Vista Electronics Inc
27525 Newhall Ranch Rd........................... Valencia CA 91355 661-294-9820
TF: 800-847-8299 ■ *Web:* vistaelectronics.com
Vista Productions Inc 1804 Anaconda Rd.......... Harrisonville MO 64701 816-380-7750
Web: www.vistaprod.com
Visual Communications Group Inc PO Box 22161....... Eagan MN 55122 303-413-0878
Web: visualcomgroup.com
Visual Eyes Medical Media
31320 Via Colinas Ste 118.................... Westlake Village CA 91362 818-707-9922
Web: www.visualeyes.com
Walden Media LLC 1888 Century Pk E.............. Los Angeles CA 90067 310-887-1000
Web: www.walden.com
Warner Bros Entertainment Inc
4000 Warner Blvd.................................. Burbank CA 91522 818-954-1853 954-3817
TF: 800-778-7879 ■ *Web:* www.warnerbros.com
Warner Bros Television Production Inc
4000 Warner Blvd.................................. Burbank CA 91522 818-954-1853
Web: www2.warnerbros.com
Warner Home Video 4000 Warner Blvd Bldg 168......... Burbank CA 91522 866-373-4389
TF: 866-373-4389 ■ *Web:* www.wbshop.com
WatchMojo Inc 5413 Saint Laurent St Ste 200.......... Montreal QC H2T1S5 514-448-1631
Web: www.watchmojo.com
Weinstein Company LLC, The 345 Hudson St......... New York NY 10014 646-862-3400
Web: www.weinsteinco.com
Western Creative Inc 26135 Plymouth Rd .... Redford MI 48239 313-937-1000
Web: www.westerncreative.com
Winkler Films Inc
190 N Canon Dr Ste 500......................... Beverly Hills CA 90210 310-858-5780
Working Title Films
9720 Wilshire Blvd 4th Fl....................... Beverly Hills CA 90212 310-777-3100
Web: www.workingtitlefilms.com
Worktank Enterprises 3131 We Ste 510................ Seattle WA 98121 206-529-3833
Web: www.worktankseattle.com
Zeitbyte LLC 32 W 22nd St 6th Fl .... New York NY 10010 212-989-4800
Web: www.zeitbyte.com
Zoic Inc 3582 Eastham Dr.......................... Culver City CA 90232 310-838-0770
Web: www.zoicstudios.com
ZONE3 Inc 1055 Rene-Levesque Blvd E 9th Fl .... Montreal QC H2L4S5 514-284-5555
Web: www.zone3.ca

MOTION PICTURE THEATERS

See Theaters - Motion Picture p. 3245

515 MOTOR SPEEDWAYS

Phone Fax

Ace Speedway 3401 Altamahaw Race Track Rd .... Altamahaw NC 27244 336-585-1200 585-1209
Web: www.acespeedway.com
Antioch Speedway 1201 W Tenth St .... Antioch CA 94509 925-779-9220 779-9213
Web: www.antiochspeedway.com
Atco Raceway 1000 Jackson Rd......................... Atco NJ 08004 856-768-2167 753-9604
Web: atcodragway.rocks
Atlanta Dragway 500 E Ridgeway Rd .... Commerce GA 30529 706-335-2301
Web: www.atlantadragway.com
Atlanta Motor Speedway PO Box 500 .... Hampton GA 30228 770-946-4211 946-3928
TF: 877-926-7849 ■ *Web:* www.atlantamotorspeedway.com
Auto Club Speedway 9300 Cherry Ave.................. Fontana CA 92335 909-429-5000 429-5500
TF: 800-944-7223 ■ *Web:* autoclubspeedway.com
Bandimere Speedway 3051 S Rooney Rd .... Morrison CO 80465 303-697-6001 697-0815
TF: 888-737-5253 ■ *Web:* www.bandimere.com
Bloomington Speedway 5185 S Fairfax Rd......... Bloomington IN 47401 812-824-8753 824-7400
Web: www.bloomingtonspeedway.com
Brainerd International Raceway
5523 Birchdale Rd .... Brainerd MN 56401 218-824-7223 824-7240
TF: 866-444-4455 ■ *Web:* www.brainerdraceway.com
Bristol Motor Speedway 151 Speedway Blvd .... Bristol TN 37620 423-989-6933 764-1646
TF: 866-415-4158 ■ *Web:* www.bristolmotorspeedway.com
Carolina Dragway 302 Dragstrip Rd.................... Jackson SC 29803 803-471-2285
TF: 877-471-7223 ■ *Web:* www.houseofhook.com
Chicagoland Speedway 500 Speedway Blvd.............. Joliet IL 60433 815-722-5500 727-7895
TF: 888-629-7223 ■ *Web:* www.chicagolandspeedway.com
Colorado National Speedway 4281 Graden Blvd .... Dacono CO 80514 303-665-4173 828-2403
Web: www.coloradospeedway.com
Columbus Motor Speedway Inc
1841 Williams Rd................................. Columbus OH 43207 614-491-1047 491-6010
Web: www.columbusspeedway.com
Concord Speedway 7940 US Hwy 601........... South Concord NC 28025 704-782-4221 782-4420
Web: www.concordspeedway.net
Corpus Christi Speedway 241 Flato Rd........... Corpus Christi TX 78405 361-289-8847
Web: www.ccspeedway.org
Darlington Raceway 1301 Harry Bird Hwy............ Darlington SC 29532 866-459-7223 395-8920*
*Fax Area Code: 843 ■ *TF:* 866-459-7223 ■ *Web:* www.darlingtonraceway.com

Phone Fax

Daytona International Speedway
1801 W International Speedway Blvd .... Daytona Beach FL 32114 386-254-2700
Web: www.daytonainternationalspeedway.com
Dubuque Fairgrounds Speedway
14569 Old Hwy Rd .... Dubuque IA 52002 563-588-1406
Web: www.dbqfair.com
Eagle Raceway 617 S 238th St.......................... Eagle NE 68347 402-238-2595 238-3768
Web: eagleraceway.com
El Paso Speedway Park 3590 W Picacho .... Las Cruces TX 88007 915-791-8749
Web: www.epspeedwaypark.com
Elko Speedway 26350 France Ave.......................... Elko MN 55020 952-461-7223
Web: www.goelkospeedway.com
Evergreen Speedway 14405 179th Ave SE .... Monroe WA 98272 360-805-6100 805-6110
Web: www.evergreenspeedway.com
Florence Motor Speedway 836 E Smith St......... Timmonsville SC 29161 843-346-7711
Web: www.florencemotorspeedway.com
Gainesville Raceway
11211 N County Rd 225............................ Gainesville FL 32609 352-377-0046 371-4212
Web: gainesvilleraceway.com/
Grandview Speedway 43 Passmore Rd .... Bechtelsville PA 19505 610-754-7688
Web: www.grandviewspeedway.com
Hamilton County Speedway 1200 Bluff St .... Webster City IA 50595 515-832-1443 832-6972
Web: www.hamiltoncospeedway.com
Heart O' Texas Speedway 784 N McLennan Dr .... Elm Mott TX 76640 254-829-2294
Web: www.heartotexspeedway.com
Heartland Park Topeka 7530 SW Topeka Blvd........... Topeka KS 66619 785-862-4781 862-2016
TF: 800-437-2237 ■ *Web:* heartlandpark.com
Hickory Motor Speedway 3130 Hwy 70 SE............. Newton NC 28658 828-464-3655 465-5017
TF: 800-843-8725 ■ *Web:* www.hickorymotorspeedway.com
Holland NASCAR Motorsports Complex
11586 Holland Glenwood Rd .... Holland NY 14080 716-537-2272 537-9749
TF: 866-655-0257 ■ *Web:* www.hollandspeedway.com
Homestead-Miami Speedway 1 Speedway Blvd ..... Homestead FL 33035 305-230-5000 230-5140
Web: www.homesteadmiamispeedway.com
Houston Motorsports Park
11620 N Lk Houston Pkwy .... Houston TX 77044 281-458-1972 458-2836
Web: www.houstonmotorsportspark.com
Houston Raceway Park 2525 FM 565 S .... Baytown TX 77523 281-383-2666 383-3777
Web: www.royalpurpleraceway.com
Kalamazoo Speedway 7656 Ravine Rd .... Kalamazoo MI 49009 269-349-3978
Web: www.kalamazoospeedway.com
Kentucky Speedway 1 Speedway Blvd.................. Sparta KY 41086 859-567-3400 647-4307
TF Resv: 888-652-7223 ■ *Web:* www.kentuckyspeedway.com
Kil-Kare Speedway 1166 Dayton-Xenia Rd .... Xenia OH 45385 937-429-2961
Web: www.kilkare.com
Lacrosse Fairgrounds Speedway
N 4985 Cty Rd M .... West Salem WI 54669 608-786-1525 786-1524
Web: www.lacrossespeedway.com
Langley Speedway 11 Dale Lemonds Dr .... Hampton VA 23666 757-865-7223
Web: www.langley-speedway.com
Las Vegas Motor Speedway
7000 Las Vegas Blvd N.............................. Las Vegas NV 89115 702-644-4444 632-8091
TF: 800-644-4444 ■ *Web:* www.lvms.com
Lime Rock Park 60 White Hollow Rd .... Lakeville CT 06039 860-435-5000 435-5010
TF: 800-722-3577 ■ *Web:* limerock.com
Los Angeles County Fairplex
1101 W McKinley Ave .... Pomona CA 91768 909-623-3111 865-3602
Web: www.fairplex.com
Magic Valley Speedway 04N 150W Jerome............ Jerome ID 83338 208-734-3700 324-9616
Web: www.magicvalleyspeedway.com
Mansfield Motorsports Speedway
100 Crall Rd...................................... Mansfield OH 44903 419-524-0183
Web: www.mansfield-speedway.com
Maple Grove Raceway 30 Stauffer Pk Ln............. Mohnton PA 19540 610-856-7812 856-1601
TF: 877-814-2538 ■ *Web:* www.maplegroveraceway.com
Marion County International Raceway
2303 Richwood-LaRue Rd .... La Rue OH 43332 740-499-3666 499-2185
Web: www.mcir.com
Martinsville Speedway 340 Speedway Rd........... Martinsville VA 24112 877-722-3849 956-2820*
*Fax Area Code: 276 ■ *TF:* 877-722-3849 ■ *Web:* www.martinsvillespeedway.com
Michigan International Speedway 12626 US 12 ...... Brooklyn MI 49230 517-592-6666 592-3848
TF: 800-354-1010 ■ *Web:* www.mispeedway.com
Mid-Ohio Sports Car Course
7721 Steam Corners Rd PO Box 3108 .... Lexington OH 44904 419-884-4000 884-0042
TF: 800-643-6446 ■ *Web:* www.midohio.com
Midway Speedway 22301 Hwy B .... Lebanon MO 65536 417-588-4430
Web: www.lebanonmidwayspeedway.com
Monett Speedway 685 Chapell Dr ....Monett MO 65708 417-236-0600
Web: www.monettspeedway.net
Motordrome Speedway 164 Motordrome Rd........... Smithton PA 15479 724-872-7555
Web: www.motordrome.com
Myrtle Beach Speedway
455 Hospitality Ln .... Myrtle Beach SC 29579 843-236-0500 236-0525
Web: www.myrtlebeachspeedway.com
National Orange Show Events Center
689 SE St .... San Bernardino CA 92408 909-888-6788
Web: www.nosevents.com
New York International Raceway Park
2011 New Rd .... Leicester NY 14481 585-382-3030
Web: www.nyirp.com
Oglethorpe Speedway Park
200 Jesup Rd PO Box 687 .... Pooler GA 31322 912-964-8200 964-9501
Web: www.ospracing.net
Old Bridge Township Raceway Park
230 Pension Rd .... Englishtown NJ 07726 732-446-7800 446-1373
Web: www.etownraceway.com
Oxford Plains Speedway 877 Main St................... Oxford ME 04270 207-539-8865 539-8860
Web: www.oxfordplains.com
Peoria Speedway 3520 W Farmington Rd .... Peoria IL 61604 309-357-3339
Web: www.peoriaspeedway.com
Pocono Raceway Long Pond Rd PO Box 500.......... Long Pond PA 18334 570-646-2300 646-2010
TF: 800-722-3929 ■ *Web:* www.poconoraceway.com
Proctor Speedway 800 N Boundary Ave................ Proctor MN 55810 218-624-0606
Web: www.proctorspeedway.com

				Phone	Fax
Quincy Raceways 8000 Broadway St *Web:* www.quincyraceways.com	Quincy	IL	62305	217-224-3843	224-3859
Riverhead Raceway PO Box 1473 *Web:* www.riverheadraceway.com	Riverhead	NY	11901	631-842-7223	
Road America N 7390 Hwy 67 *TF:* 800-365-7223 ■ *Web:* www.roadamerica.com	Elkhart Lake	WI	53020	920-892-4576	892-4550
Road Atlanta Raceway 5300 Winder Hwy *TF:* 800-849-7223 ■ *Web:* www.roadatlanta.com	Braselton	GA	30517	770-967-6143	
Rockingham Dragway 2153 Hwy US 1 N PO Box 70 *Web:* www.rockinghamdragway.com	Rockingham	NC	28379	910-582-3400	582-8667
Sandusky Speedway 614 W Perkins Ave *Web:* www.sanduskyspeedway.com	Sandusky	OH	44870	419-625-4084	
Saugus Speedway 22500 Soledad Canyon Rd *Web:* www.saugusspeedway.com	Saugus	CA	91350	661-259-3886	259-8534
Sebring International Raceway 113 Midway Dr *TF:* 800-626-7223 ■ *Web:* www.sebringraceway.com	Sebring	FL	33870	863-655-1442	655-1777
Sonoma Raceway Hwy S 37 & 121 *TF:* 800-870-7223 ■ *Web:* www.sonomaraceway.com	Sonoma	CA	95476	707-938-8448	938-8430
South Boston Speedway 1188 James D Hagood Hwy PO Box 1066 *TF:* 877-440-1540 ■ *Web:* www.southbostonspeedway.com	South Boston	VA	24592	434-572-4947	575-8992
South Sound Speedway 3730 183rd Ave SW *Web:* www.southsoundspeedway.com	Rochester	WA	98579	360-858-1464	
Stafford Motor Speedway 55 W St PO Box 105 *Web:* staffordmotorspeedway.com	Stafford Springs	CT	06076	860-684-2783	684-6236
Summit Motorsports Park 1300 Ohio 18 *TF:* 800-729-6455 ■ *Web:* www.summitmotorsportspark.com	Norwalk	OH	44857	419-668-5555	663-0502
Texas Motorplex 7500 W Hwy 287 *TF:* 800-668-6775 ■ *Web:* www.texasmotorplex.com	Ennis	TX	75119	972-878-2641	878-1848
Thompson Speedway 205 E Thompson Rd PO Box 278 *Web:* www.thompsonspeedway.com	Thompson	CT	06277	860-923-2280	923-2398
Viking Speedway Inc PO Box 462 *Web:* www.vikingspeedway.net	Alexandria	MN	56308	320-760-9614	
Volusia Speedway Park 1500 W State Rd **Fax Area Code:* 352 ■ *Web:* bubbaracewaypark.com	De Leon Springs	FL	32130	386-985-4402	622-3126*
Watkins Glen International Inc 2790 CR 16 *Web:* www.theglen.com	Watkins Glen	NY	14891	607-535-2486	535-8918
Winchester Speedway 2656 W State Rd 32 PO Box 31 *Web:* www.winchesterspeedway.com	Winchester	IN	47394	765-584-9701	584-8111

516 MOTOR VEHICLES - COMMERCIAL & SPECIAL PURPOSE

See Also All-Terrain Vehicles p. 1733; Automobiles - Mfr p. 1829; Campers, Travel Trailers, Motor Homes p. 1889; Motorcycles & Motorcycle Parts & Accessories p. 2787; Snowmobiles p. 3187; Weapons & Ordnance (Military) p. 3305

				Phone	Fax
A.r.e. Inc PO Box 1100 *Web:* www.4are.com	Massillon	OH	44648	330-481-1333	730-4545
Accubuilt Inc 2550 Central Pt Pkwy *Web:* www.accubuilt.com	Lima	OH	45804	419-222-1501	222-4450
Allied Body Works Inc 625 S 96th St *TF General:* 800-733-7450 ■ *Web:* www.alliedbody.com	Seattle	WA	98108	206-763-7811	763-8836
Altec Industries Inc 210 Inverness Ctr Dr *Web:* altec.com	Birmingham	AL	35242	205-991-7733	408-8601
American LaFrance Corp 1090 Newtonway	Summerville	SC	29483	843-486-7400	
Art Moehn 2200 Seymour Rd *TF:* 866-495-5942 ■ *Web:* artmoehn.com	Jackson	MI	49201	866-495-5942	
Auto Crane Co PO Box 580697 *TF:* 888-848-5445 ■ *Web:* www.autocrane.com	Tulsa	OK	74158	918-836-0463	834-5979
Auto Truck Inc 1420 Brewster Creek Blvd *TF:* 877-284-4440 ■ *Web:* www.autotruck.com	Bartlett	IL	60103	630-860-5600	860-5631
Bianchi Motors Inc 8430 Peach St *TF:* 866-979-8132 ■ *Web:* www.bianchihonda.com	Erie	PA	16509	814-864-5809	
Blue Bird Corp 402 Blue Bird Blvd *Web:* www.blue-bird.com	Fort Valley	GA	31030	478-825-2021	822-2457
Bob Ross Dealerships, The 85 Loop Rd *Web:* www.bobrossauto.com	Centerville	OH	45459	937-401-2037	428-4083
Bobcat Co 250 E Beaton Dr *Web:* www.bobcat.com	West Fargo	ND	58078	701-241-8700	241-8704
Bristol-Donald Company Inc 50 Roanoke Ave *Web:* www.bristoldonald.com	Newark	NJ	07105	973-589-2640	589-2610
Brumbaugh Body Co 1 Jennifer Rd	Duncansville	PA	16635	814-696-9552	
Carnegie Body Co 9500 Brookpark Rd *TF:* 800-362-1989 ■ *Web:* carnegiefederalbody.com	Cleveland	OH	44129	216-749-5000	749-5740
Champion Bus Inc 331 Graham Rd **Fax:* Mktg ■ *TF:* 800-776-4943 ■ *Web:* www.championbus.com	Imlay City	MI	48444	810-724-6474	724-1844*
Coach & Equipment Manufacturing Corp 130 Horizon Pk Dr PO Box 36 *TF:* 800-724-8464 ■ *Web:* www.coachandequipment.com	Penn Yan	NY	14527	800-724-8464	
Columbia ParCar Corp 1115 Commercial Ave *TF:* 800-222-4653 ■ *Web:* www.parcar.com	Reedsburg	WI	53959	608-524-8888	524-8380
Courtesy Chevrolet Ctr 750 Camino Del Rio N *Web:* www.courtesysandiego.com	San Diego	CA	92108	619-297-4321	
Crane Carrier Co 1925 N Sheridan Rd *Web:* www.cranecarrier.com	Tulsa	OK	74115	918-836-1651	832-7348
Curtis Industries LLC 111 Higgins St **Fax Area Code:* 508 ■ *TF:* 800-343-7676 ■ *Web:* curtisindustries.net	Worcester	MA	01606	800-343-7676	854-3377*
Dealers Truck Equipment Co 2460 Midway St *TF:* 800-259-7569 ■ *Web:* www.dealerstruck.com	Shreveport	LA	71108	318-635-7567	525-0903
Delphi Body Works Inc 313 S Washington St PO Box 30 *Web:* www.delphibodyworks.com	Delphi	IN	46923	765-564-2212	564-4255
Delta-Waseca 5200 Willson Rd *Web:* www.deltawaseca.com	Minneapolis	MN	55424	952-922-5569	922-1195
Diamond Coach Corp 2300 W Fourth St PO Box 489 *TF:* 800-442-4645 ■ *Web:* www.diamondcoach.com	Oswego	KS	67356	620-795-2191	795-2191
Dick Gores Rv World 14590 Duval Pl W *TF:* 800-635-7008 ■ *Web:* www.dickgoresrvworld.com	Jacksonville	FL	32218	904-741-5100	
Douglass Truck Bodies Inc 231 21st St *TF:* 800-635-7641 ■ *Web:* www.douglasstruckbodies.com	Bakersfield	CA	93301	661-327-0258	327-3894
E-ONE Inc 1601 SW 37th Ave *Web:* www.e-one.com	Ocala	FL	34474	352-237-1122	237-1151
E-Z-GO 1451 Marvin Griffin Rd *TF:* 800-241-5855 ■ *Web:* www.ezgo.com	Augusta	GA	30906	800-241-5855	
Ebus Inc 9250 Washburn Rd *TF:* 888-925-4263 ■ *Web:* www.ebus.com	Downey	CA	90242	562-904-3474	
Electric Golf Car Co 3190-B Orange Grove Ave *Web:* www.electricgolfcarcompany.com	North Highlands	CA	95660	916-773-2244	488-8857
Elgin Sweeper Co 1300 W Bartlett Rd *Web:* www.elginsweeper.com	Elgin	IL	60120	847-741-5370	742-3035
Elliott Machine Works Inc 1351 Freese Works Pl *TF:* 800-299-0412 ■ *Web:* www.elliottmachine.com	Galion	OH	44833	419-468-4709	468-4642
Erie Vehicle Co 60 E 51st St *TF:* 888-550-3743 ■ *Web:* erievehicle.com	Chicago	IL	60615	773-536-6300	536-5779
Fisher Engineering 50 Gordon Dr **Fax Area Code:* 866 ■ **Fax:* Hum Res ■ *Web:* www.fisherplows.com	Rockland	ME	04841	207-701-4200	816-7256*
Fleet Engineers Inc 1800 E Keating Ave *TF Cust Svc:* 800-333-7890 ■ *Web:* www.fleetengineers.com	Muskegon	MI	49442	231-777-2537	777-2720
Fleet Equipment Corp 567 Commerce St *TF:* 800-631-0873 ■ *Web:* www.fectrucks.com	Franklin Lakes	NJ	07417	201-337-3294	337-3294
Fontaine Modification Co 9827 Mt Holly Rd *TF:* 800-366-8246 ■ *Web:* fontainemodification.com	Charlotte	NC	28214	704-391-1355	391-1671
Fontaine Truck Equipment Co 7574 Commerce Cir *TF:* 800-874-9780 ■ *Web:* www.fontaine.com	Trussville	AL	35173	205-661-4900	655-9982
Ford of Ocala Inc 2816 NW Pine Ave *TF:* 888-255-1788 ■ *Web:* www.fordofocala.com	Ocala	FL	34475	352-732-4800	
Frank J Zamboni & Company Inc 15714 Colorado Ave *Web:* www.zamboni.com	Paramount	CA	90723	562-633-0751	633-9365
Gary Mathews Motors Inc 1100 Ashland City Rd *Web:* www.garymathewsmotors.com	Clarksville	TN	37040	931-552-7100	
General Body Manufacturing Co 7110 Jensen Dr *TF:* 800-395-8585 ■ *Web:* www.generalbody.com	Houston	TX	77093	713-692-5177	692-0700
General Motors Corp (GMC) 100 Renaissance Ctr *NYSE:* GM ■ *Web:* www.gm.com	Detroit	MI	48265	313-556-5000	
George Heiser Body Company Inc 11210 Tukwila International Blvd	Seattle	WA	98168	206-622-7985	622-7135
Gillig Corp 25800 Clawiter Rd *TF:* 800-735-1500 ■ *Web:* www.gillig.com	Hayward	CA	94545	510-785-1500	785-6819
Gowans-Knight Co Inc 49 Knight St *TF:* 800-352-4871 ■ *Web:* www.gowansknight.com	Watertown	CT	06795	860-274-8801	274-7937
Graham Cadillac 1515 W Fourth St *Web:* www.grahamchevycadillac.com	Mansfield	OH	44906	419-989-4012	
Hackney & Sons Inc 911 W 5th St PO Box 880 *TF:* 800-763-0700 ■ *Web:* www.hackneyandsons.com	Washington	NC	27889	252-946-6521	975-8340
Heil Environmental Ltd 2030 Hamilton Pl Blvd Ste 200 *TF:* 866-367-4345 ■ *Web:* www.heil.com	Chattanooga	TN	37421	423-899-9100	
Hercules Manufacturing Co 800 Bob Posey St *TF:* 800-633-3031 ■ *Web:* www.herculesvanbodies.com	Henderson	KY	42420	270-826-9501	826-0439
Hi-Lex America Inc 5200 Wayne Rd *Web:* www.hi-lex.com	Battle Creek	MI	49037	269-968-0781	
HME Inc 1950 Byron Ctr Ave *Web:* www.firetrucks.com	Wyoming	MI	49519	616-534-1463	534-1967
Holiday Automotive 321 N Rolling Meadows Dr *Web:* www.holidayautomotive.com	Fond Du Lac	WI	54937	920-921-8898	923-8454
Honda of Tiffany Springs 9200 NW Prairie View Rd *Web:* www.hondaoftiffanysprings.com	Kansas City	MO	64153	816-452-7000	452-2651
Johnson Refrigerated Truck Bodies 215 E Allen St *TF Sales:* 800-922-8360 ■ *Web:* www.johnsontruckbodies.com	Rice Lake	WI	54868	715-234-7071	234-4628
Joyce Koons Buick Gmc 10660 Automotive Dr *TF:* 866-755-0072 ■ *Web:* joycekoonsbuickgmc.com	Manassas	VA	20109	866-755-0072	
Kann Manufacturing Corp PO Box 400 *TF:* 800-806-5266 ■ *Web:* www.kannmfg.com	Guttenberg	IA	52052	563-252-2035	252-3069
Kassbohrer All Terrain Vehicles Inc 8850 Double Diamond Pkwy *Web:* www.pistenbullyusa.com	Reno	NV	89521	775-857-5000	857-5010
Kenworth Truck Co 10630 NE 38th Pl *Web:* www.kenworth.com	Kirkland	WA	98033	425-828-5000	828-5070
Kesler-Schaefer Auto Auction Inc 5333 W 46th St PO Box 53203 *TF:* 800-959-5722 ■ *Web:* www.ksaa1.com	Indianapolis	IN	46254	317-297-2300	297-6234
Keystone Chevrolet Inc 8700 Charles Page Blvd *Web:* www.keystonechevrolet.com	Sand Springs	OK	74063	918-245-2201	
Kidron Inc 13442 Emerson Rd *TF:* 800-321-5421 ■ *Web:* www.kidron.com	Kidron	OH	44636	330-857-3011	857-8451
KME Fire Apparatus 68 Sicker Rd *Web:* www.kovatch.com	Latham	NY	12110	518-785-0900	785-1794
Knapheide Mfg Co 1848 Westphalia Strasse PO Box 7140 *Web:* www.knapheide.com	Quincy	IL	62305	217-222-7131	222-5939
Labrie Environmental Group 175 du Pont *TF:* 800-463-6638 ■ *Web:* www.labriegroup.com	Saint-Nicolas	QC	G7A2T3	418-831-8250	831-5255
Laird Noller Ford Inc 2245 SW Topeka Blvd *TF:* 800-632-3673 ■ *Web:* www.nollerford-topeka.com	Topeka	KS	66611	785-235-9211	232-7766
Landmark Ford Inc 12000 SW 66th Ave *Web:* www.landmarkford.com	Tigard	OR	97223	503-639-1131	

				Phone	Fax
Leson Chevrolet Co Inc 1501 Westbank Express *TF:* 877-496-2420 ■ *Web:* lesonauto.com	Harvey	LA	70058	504-366-4381	362-2135
Liberty Toyota Scion 4397 Rt 130 S *TF:* 888-809-7798 ■ *Web:* www.libertytoyota.com	Burlington	NJ	08016	609-386-6300	
Libertyville Chevrolet Inc 1001 S Milwaukee Ave *TF Sales:* 877-520-1807 ■ *Web:* www.libertyvillechevrolet.com	Libertyville	IL	60048	847-281-5330	
Lodal Inc 620 N Hooper St PO Box 2315 **Fax:* Orders ■ *TF:* 800-435-3500 ■ *Web:* www.lodal.com	Kingsford	MI	49802	906-779-1700	779-1160*
Loren Hyundai Inc 1620 Waukegan Rd **Fax Area Code:* 847 ■ *Web:* www.lorenautogroup.com	Glenview	IL	60025	224-766-7189	724-8429*
Lumberton Honda Mitsubishi Inc 301 Wintergreen Dr *TF:* 855-712-9438 ■ *Web:* www.lumbertonhonda.com	Lumberton	NC	28358	910-739-9871	
Luther Brookdale Chevrolet 6701 Brooklyn Blvd *TF:* 800-716-1271 ■ *Web:* www.brookdalechevrolet.com	Brooklyn Center	MN	55429	800-716-1271	
LZ Truck Equipment Inc 1881 Rice St *TF:* 800-247-1082 ■ *Web:* www.lztruckequipment.com	Saint Paul	MN	55113	651-488-2571	488-9857
M K Smith Chevrolet 12845 Central Ave PO Box 455	Chino	CA	91710	909-628-8961	628-6637
M. H. Eby Inc PO Box 127 *TF:* 800-292-4752 ■ *Web:* www.mheby.com	Blue Bell	PA	17506	717-354-4971	355-2114
Maple Shade Mazda 2921 Rt 73 S *Web:* www.msmazda.com	Maple Shade	NJ	08052	856-667-8004	
Marion Body Works Inc 211 W Ramsdell St PO Box 500 *Web:* www.marionbody.com	Marion	WI	54950	715-754-5261	754-5776
Martin Chevrolet 23505 Hawthorne Blvd *Web:* www.martinchevrolet.com	Torrance	CA	90505	310-378-0211	
Martin Chevrolet Sales Inc 8800 Gratiot Rd *Web:* www.martincars.net	Saginaw	MI	48609	989-607-0584	781-1722
Matt Castrucci Auto Mall of Dayton 3013 Mall Pk Dr *TF:* 855-204-5293 ■ *Web:* www.mattcastrucciautomall.com	Dayton	OH	45459	855-204-5293	
Matthews-Hargreaves Chevrolet Co 2000 E12 Mile Rd *Web:* www.mhchevy.com	Royal Oak	MI	48067	248-398-8800	
Mayflower Vehicle System 55 N Garfield St	Norwalk	OH	44857	419-668-8132	
Mc Dermott Auto Group 655 Main St *Web:* mcdermottauto.com	East Haven	CT	06512	203-466-1000	
Mc-Coy-Mills 700 W Commonwealth *TF Sales:* 888-434-3145 ■ *Web:* www.mccoymillsford.com	Fullerton	CA	92832	888-434-3145	
McClinton Chevrolet Co 1325 Seventh St *Web:* mcclintonchevrolet.com	Parkersburg	WV	26101	304-699-2478	
McCluskey Chevrolet Inc 9673 Kings Automall Dr *Web:* www.mccluskeychevrolet.com	Cincinnati	OH	45249	513-761-1111	
McDaniel Motor Co 1111 Mt Vernon Ave *TF:* 877-362-0288 ■ *Web:* mcdanieltoyota.com	Marion	OH	43302	740-389-2355	
McGuire Cadillac Inc 910 Rt 1 N **Fax Area Code:* 732 ■ *TF:* 866-552-4208 ■ *Web:* www.mcguirecadillac.com	Woodbridge	NJ	07095	866-552-4208	326-0385*
McLaughlin Body Co 2430 River Dr *Web:* www.mclbody.com	Moline	IL	61265	309-762-7755	762-7807
McNeilus Cos Inc 524 County Rd 34 E PO Box 70 *TF:* 800-265-1098 ■ *Web:* www.mcneiluscompanies.com	Dodge Center	MN	55927	507-374-6321	374-6394
Medical Coaches Inc 399 County Hwy 58 *Web:* www.medcoach.com	Oneonta	NY	13820	607-432-1333	432-8190
Mel Rapton Inc 3630 Fulton Ave *TF:* 800-529-3053 ■ *Web:* www.melraptonhonda.com	Sacramento	CA	95821	916-482-5400	
Mercedes-Benz Of Cincinnati 8727 Montgomery Rd *Web:* www.mbcincy.com	Cincinnati	OH	45236	513-984-9000	984-9468
Mercedes-Benz USA LLC 11850 Bel-Red Rd *Web:* www.mercedesbenzofbellevue.com	Bellevue	WA	98005	425-455-8535	637-5586
Metro Truck Body Inc 1201 W Jon St *Web:* www.metrotruckbody.com	Torrance	CA	90502	310-532-5570	532-0754
Meyer Truck Equipment 196 W State Rd 56 *Web:* www.meyertruckeq.com	Jasper	IN	47546	812-695-3451	695-3397
Mickey Truck Bodies Inc 1305 Trinity Ave PO Box 2044 *TF:* 800-334-9061 ■ *Web:* www.mickeybody.com	High Point	NC	27261	336-882-6806	889-6712
Mike Castrucci Ford Sales Inc 1020 SR- 28 *TF:* 855-902-6741 ■ *Web:* www.mikecastruccifordmilford.com	Milford	OH	45150	513-831-7010	831-4474
Miller Industries Inc 8503 Hilltop Dr *NYSE:* MLR ■ *TF:* 800-292-0330 ■ *Web:* www.millerind.com	Ooltewah	TN	37363	423-238-4171	238-5371
Momentum Bmw Ltd 10002 SW Fwy **Fax Area Code:* 713 ■ *TF:* 800-731-8114 ■ *Web:* momentumbmw.net	Houston	TX	77074	800-731-8114	596-3210*
Monroe Truck Equipment Inc 1051 W Seventh St *TF:* 800-356-8134 ■ *Web:* www.monroetruck.com	Monroe	WI	53566	608-328-8127	328-4278
Morgan Corp 111 Morgan Way PO Box 588 *TF:* 800-666-7426 ■ *Web:* www.morgancorp.com	Morgantown	PA	19543	610-286-5025	
Morgan Olson Corp 1801 S Nottawa Rd **Fax Area Code:* 800 ■ *TF:* 800-233-4823 ■ *Web:* www.morganolson.com	Sturgis	MI	49091	269-659-0200	624-9005*
Morse Operations Inc 3790 W Blue Herron Blvd *TF:* 800-755-2593 ■ *Web:* www.edmorsehonda.com	Riviera Beach	FL	33404	800-755-2593	
Motor Coach Industries International Co 1700 E Golf Rd Ste 300 *TF:* 800-743-3624 ■ *Web:* www.mcicoach.com	Schaumburg	IL	60173	847-285-2000	285-2066
Murrays Ford Inc 3007 Blinker Pkwy *TF:* 800-371-6601 ■ *Web:* www.murraysford.net	Du Bois	PA	15801	814-371-6600	
Nacarato GMC Truck Inc 519 New Paul Rd *TF:* 888-392-8486 ■ *Web:* www.nacaratotrucks.com	La Vergne	TN	37086	615-280-2800	
Nash Chevrolet Co 630 Scenic Hwy **Fax Area Code:* 770 ■ *Web:* nashchevy.com	Lawrenceville	GA	30046	678-317-2797	822-6668*
Noble Ford Mercury Inc 2406 N Jefferson Way *TF:* 800-496-9984 ■ *Web:* www.nobleford.com	Indianola	IA	50125	515-961-8151	
North Florida Lincoln Mercury 4620 Southside Blvd *TF:* 888-457-1949 ■ *Web:* northfloridalincoln.com	Jacksonville	FL	32216	877-941-1435	
O'Daniel Motor Sales Inc 5611 Illinois Rd *Web:* www.odanielauto.com	Fort Wayne	IN	46804	260-435-5300	435-5467
Obs Inc 1324 WTuscarawas St PO Box 6210 *TF:* 800-362-9592 ■ *Web:* www.obsinc.net	Canton	OH	44706	330-453-3725	580-2429
Olathe Toyota 685 N Rawhide *Web:* www.olathetoyota.com	Olathe	KS	66061	913-780-9919	
Omaha Standard Inc 3501 S 11th St Ste 1 *TF:* 800-279-2201 ■ *Web:* www.palfinger.com	Council Bluffs	IA	51501	712-328-7444	328-8383
Oshkosh Truck Corp 2307 Oregon St *TF:* 800-392-9921 ■ *Web:* www.oshkoshdefense.com	Oshkosh	WI	54903	920-235-9150	
PACCAR Inc 777 106th Ave NE *NASDAQ:* PCAR ■ *Web:* www.paccar.com	Bellevue	WA	98004	425-468-7400	468-8216
PACCAR Inc International Div 777 106th Ave NE 12th Fl *Web:* www.paccar.com	Bellevue	WA	98004	425-468-7400	468-8216
Papa's Dodge Inc 585 E Main St *Web:* www.papasjeep.com	New Britain	CT	06051	860-225-8751	
Parkhurst Manufacturing Co 18999 Hwy Y *TF:* 800-821-7380 ■ *Web:* www.parkhurstmfg.com	Sedalia	MO	65301	660-826-8685	
Parkway Chevrolet Inc 25500 Tomball Pkwy *Web:* www.parkwaychevrolet.com	Tomball	TX	77375	281-351-8211	357-3435
Patriot Buick GMC 4600 E Central Texas Expy *Web:* patriotcars.com	Killeen	TX	76543	254-690-7000	690-7701
Performance Chevrolet Inc 4811 Madison Ave *Web:* www.performancechevy.com	Sacramento	CA	95841	916-331-6777	
Peterbilt Motors Co 1700 Woodbrook St **Fax:* Hum Res ■ *Web:* www.peterbilt.com	Denton	TX	76205	940-591-4000	591-4260*
Pierce Mfg Inc 2600 American Dr PO Box 2017 *TF Cust Svc:* 888-974-3723 ■ *Web:* www.piercemfg.com	Appleton	WI	54912	920-832-3000	832-3353
Pohanka of Salisbury 2007 N Salisbury Blvd *Web:* www.pohankaofsalisbury.com	Salisbury	MD	21801	410-202-3450	
Porter Truck Sales LP 135 McCarty St *TF:* 800-956-2408 ■ *Web:* www.portertrk.com	Houston	TX	77029	713-672-2400	672-7343
Powers-Swain Chevrolet Inc 4709 Bragg Blvd *Web:* pschevy.com	Fayetteville	NC	28303	910-864-9500	
Prevost Car Inc 35 boul Gagnon *TF:* 877-773-8678 ■ *Web:* www.prevostcar.com	Sainte-Claire	QC	G0R2V0	418-883-3391	883-4157
Progressive Chevrolet Co 8000 Hills & Dales Rd *Web:* www.progressivechevrolet.com	Massillon	OH	44646	330-833-8564	
Quad-City Peterbilt Inc 8100 N Fairmount St **Fax Area Code:* 563 ■ *TF:* 866-601-8607 ■ *Web:* www.quadcitypeterbilt.com	Davenport	IA	52806	866-601-8607	391-0195*
R & B Car Company Inc 3811 S Michigan St *TF:* 800-260-1833 ■ *Web:* www.rbcarcompany.com	South Bend	IN	46614	800-260-1833	
R & S/Godwin Truck Body Co LLC 5168 S US Hwy 23 PO Box 420 *TF:* 800-826-7413 ■ *Web:* www.rstruckbody.com	Ivel	KY	41642	606-874-2151	874-9136
R&H Motor Cars Ltd 9727 Reisterstown Rd *TF:* 844-233-2593 ■ *Web:* mercedesbenzofowingsmills.com	Owings Mills	MD	21117	844-233-2593	
Rapid Chevrolet Company Inc 2323 E Mall Dr *TF:* 800-456-2105 ■ *Web:* www.rapidchevrolet.com	Rapid City	SD	57701	605-343-1282	343-5458
Rdk Truck Sales Inc 3214 E Adamo Dr *TF:* 877-735-4636 ■ *Web:* www.rdk.com	Tampa	FL	33605	813-241-0711	241-0414
Reading Truck Body Inc 201 Hancock Blvd **Fax Area Code:* 610 ■ *TF All:* 800-458-2226 ■ *Web:* www.readingbody.com	Reading	PA	19611	800-458-2226	775-3261*
Reed Lallier Chevrolet Inc 4500 Raeford Rd *Web:* reedlallier.com	Fayetteville	NC	28304	910-426-2000	
Ressler Motor Co 8474 Huffine Ln *Web:* www.resslermotors.com	Bozeman	MT	59718	406-587-5501	
RIHM Motor Co 2108 University Ave W *Web:* www.rihmkenworth.com	Saint Paul	MN	55114	651-646-7833	646-0630
RKI Inc 2301 Central Pkwy *TF:* 800-346-8988 ■ *Web:* www.rki-us.com	Houston	TX	77092	713-688-4414	688-8982
Rochester-Syracuse Auto Auction 1826 State Rt 414 PO Box 129 *Web:* www.rsautoauction.com	Waterloo	NY	13165	315-539-5006	539-9508
Rocket Supply Corp 404 N Rt 115 PO Box 98 *TF:* 800-252-6871 ■ *Web:* www.rocketsupply.com	Roberts	IL	60962	800-252-6871	
Rush Truck Center - Lubbock 4515 Ave A *TF:* 888-987-2458 ■ *Web:* rushtruckcenters.com	Lubbock	TX	79404	806-747-2579	747-4171
Rydell Chevrolet Inc 18600 Devonshire St *TF:* 866-697-5167 ■ *Web:* chevynorthridge.com	Northridge	CA	91324	319-234-4601	
Saf-T-Cab Inc PO Box 2587 *TF:* 800-344-7491 ■ *Web:* www.saftcab.com	Fresno	CA	93745	559-268-5541	268-5822
Sanborn Chevrolet Inc 1210 S Cherokee Ln *Web:* www.sanbornchevrolet.com	Lodi	CA	95240	209-642-4954	
Sanders Ford Inc 1135 Lejeune Blvd *TF General:* 888-897-8527 ■ *Web:* sandersfordsales.com	Jacksonville	NC	28540	910-455-1911	
Scania USA Inc 121 Interpark Blvd Ste 601 *TF:* 800-272-2642 ■ *Web:* www.scania.com	San Antonio	TX	78216	210-403-0007	403-0211
Scelzi Equipment Inc 1030 W Gladstone St *TF:* 866-972-3594 ■ *Web:* www.seinc.com	Azusa	CA	91702	626-334-0573	
Schetky Northwest Sales Inc 8430 NE Killingsworth St *TF:* 800-255-8341 ■ *Web:* www.schetkynw.com	Portland	OR	97220	503-287-4141	287-2931
Seagrave Fire Apparatus LLC 105 E 12th St *Web:* www.seagrave.com	Clintonville	WI	54929	715-823-2141	823-5768
Segway Inc 14 Technology Dr *TF:* 866-473-4929 ■ *Web:* www.segway.com	Bedford	NH	03110	603-222-6000	222-6001
Shealy's Truck Ctr Inc 1340 Bluff Rd *TF:* 800-951-8580 ■ *Web:* www.shealytruck.com	Columbia	SC	29201	803-771-0176	771-4879
Skaug Truck Body Works Inc 1404 First St	San Fernando	CA	91340	818-365-9123	365-6634
Smith-Cairns Ford 900 Central Pk Ave *Web:* www.smithcairns.com	Yonkers	NY	10704	914-377-8100	377-8118

Phone | Fax

Snethkamp Chrysler Dodge Jeep Ram
11600 Telegraph Rd . . . Redford MI 48239 313-255-2700
TF: 888-455-6146 ■ *Web:* www.snethkampchryslerjeep.net

Somerset Welding & Steel Inc
10558 Somerset Pk . . . Somerset PA 15501 814-444-3400 443-2621
TF: 800-777-2671 ■ *Web:* www.jjbodies.com

Southern Connecticut Freightliner
15 E Industrial Rd . . . Branford CT 06405 203-481-0373
Web: www.netruck.com

Spartan Motors Inc 1541 Reynolds Rd . . . Charlotte MI 48813 517-543-6400
NASDAQ: SPAR ■ *TF:* 800-937-5449 ■ *Web:* www.spartanmotors.com

STAHL/A Scott Fetzer Co
3201 W Old Lincoln Way . . . Wooster OH 44691 330-264-7441 264-3319
TF: 800-277-8245 ■ *Web:* www.stahltruckbodies.com

Stanford Carr Development LLC
1100 Alakea St 27th Fl . . . Honolulu HI 96813 808-537-5220 537-1801
Web: www.stanfordcarr.com

Steelweld Equipment Company Inc
235 N Service Rd W . . . Saint Clair MO 63077 636-629-3704 629-3734

Sterling McCall Ford 6445 SW Fwy . . . Houston TX 77074 281-588-5000
Web: www.sterlingmccallford.com

Sterling Truck Corp
12120 Telegraph Rd . . . Redford Township MI 48239 800-785-4357
TF Cust Svc: 800-385-4357 ■ *Web:* www.sterlingtrucks.com

Steve Hopkins Inc 2499 Auto Mall Pkwy . . . Fairfield CA 94533 707-427-1000
TF: 877-873-3913 ■ *Web:* www.hopkinsautogroup.com

Steve Landers Toyota
10825 Colonel Glenn Rd . . . Little Rock AR 72204 501-568-5800
TF: 888-314-4350 ■ *Web:* www.landerstoyota.com

Sunbury Motor Co 943 N Fourth St . . . Sunbury PA 17801 570-286-7746
TF: 800-358-8090 ■ *Web:* www.sunburymotors.com

Superior Auto Sales Inc 5201 Camp Rd . . . Hamburg NY 14075 716-649-6695
TF: 866-439-9637 ■ *Web:* www.sascars.com

Superior Motors Inc 282 John C Calhoun Dr . . . Orangeburg SC 29115 877-375-4759
TF: 877-375-4759 ■ *Web:* www.superiormotors.com

Superior Trailer Sales Co 501 Hwy 80 . . . Sunnyvale TX 75182 972-226-3893 226-3899
TF: 800-637-0324 ■ *Web:* www.stsco.com

Supreme Corp 2581 E Kercher Rd PO Box 463 . . . Goshen IN 46528 800-642-4889 642-4540*
**Fax Area Code:* 574 ■ *TF All:* 800-642-4889 ■ *Web:* www.supremecorp.com

Sutphen Corp PO Box 158 . . . Amlin OH 43002 614-889-1005 889-0874
TF: 800-726-7030 ■ *Web:* www.sutphen.com

Svi Inc 440 Mark Leany Dr . . . Henderson NV 89011 702-567-5256 567-3020
Web: www.specialtyvehicles.com

Sweeney Buick 7997 Market St . . . Youngstown OH 44512 877-360-4928
TF: 877-360-4928 ■ *Web:* sweeneycars.com

Ten-8 Fire Equipment Inc
2904 59th Ave Dr E . . . Bradenton FL 34203 941-756-7779 756-2598
TF: 877-989-7660 ■ *Web:* www.ten8fire.com

Thomas Built Buses Inc 1408 Courtesy Rd . . . High Point NC 27260 336-889-4871 881-6509
Web: www.thomasbus.com

Thomson-Macconnell Cadillac Inc
2820 Gilbert Ave . . . Cincinnati OH 45206 513-334-4239
TF: 877-472-0738 ■ *Web:* thomsonmacconnell.com

Thor Industries Inc 419 W Pike St . . . Jackson Center OH 45334 937-596-6111 596-6111*
NYSE: THO ■ **Fax Area Code:* 877 ■ *Web:* thorindustries.com

Tom Nehl Truck Co 417 S Edgewood Ave . . . Jacksonville FL 32254 904-389-3653 384-2467
Web: www.tomnehl.com

Tom Roush Inc 525 W David Brown Dr . . . Westfield IN 46074 317-896-5561
TF: 800-382-4619 ■ *Web:* www.tomroush.com

Town & Country Chrysler Inc
19400 SE McLoughlin Blvd . . . Portland OR 97027 503-722-5000
Web: www.cjdwilsonville.com

Trailercraft Inc 1301 E 64th Ave . . . Anchorage AK 99518 907-563-3238 561-4995
TF: 800-478-3238 ■ *Web:* www.trailercraft.com

Truck Utilities Inc 2370 English St . . . Saint Paul MN 55109 651-484-3305 484-0076
TF: 800-869-1075 ■ *Web:* www.truckutilities.com

Trucks only 550 S Country Club Dr . . . Mesa AZ 85210 480-844-7071
Web: www.trucksonlysales.com

Tymco Inc 225 E Industrial Blvd PO Box 2368 . . . Waco TX 76703 254-799-5546 799-2722
TF: 800-258-9626 ■ *Web:* www.tymco.com

Unicell Body Co 571 Howard St . . . Buffalo NY 14206 716-853-8628 843-8638
TF Cust Svc: 800-628-8914 ■ *Web:* www.unicell.com

United Ford Parts & Distribtion Ctr Inc
12007 E 61st St . . . Broken Arrow OK 74012 918-317-6800
TF: 800-800-9001 ■ *Web:* www.unitedford.com

Universal Ford Sales Inc 10751 W Broad St . . . Glen Allen VA 23060 804-273-9700
Web: www.richmondford.com

Valley Chevrolet Inc 601 Kidder St . . . Wilkes-Barre PA 18702 570-821-2772
TF: 877-207-9214 ■ *Web:* valleychevrolet.com

Viking-Cives USA 14331 Mill St . . . Harrisville NY 13648 315-543-2321 543-2366
Web: www.vikingcives.com

Vista-pro Automotive LLC
15 Century Blvd Ste 600 . . . Nashville TN 37214 615-622-2200 622-2302
TF: 888-250-2676

Volvo Construction Equipment of North America Inc
312 Volvo Way . . . Shippensburg PA 17257 717-532-9181
Web: www.volvoce.com

Volvo Group North America Inc
2900 K St NW Ste 401 . . . Washington DC 20007 336-393-4443
Web: www.volvo.com

Volvo Honolulu 704 Ala Moana Blvd . . . Honolulu HI 96813 888-892-2456
TF: 888-892-2456 ■ *Web:* www.volvohonolulu.com

Volvo Trucks North America Inc
7900 National Service Rd PO Box 26115 . . . Greensboro NC 27402 336-393-2000 393-2362
Web: www.volvotrucks.com

Walton Motors Inc 205 E Pawnee Dr . . . Savannah MO 64485 816-324-3141
Web: www.waltonmotorsinc.com

Weld-Built Body Co Inc 276 Long Island Ave . . . Wyandanch NY 11798 631-643-9700 491-4728
Web: www.weldbuilt.com

Wendle Motors Inc 9000 N Div . . . Spokane WA 99218 888-685-7177 468-4056*
**Fax Area Code:* 509 ■ *TF:* 888-685-7177 ■ *Web:* www.wendle.com

Wentworth Chevytown 107 SE Grand Ave . . . Portland OR 97214 503-200-2482
Web: www.wentworthchevrolet.com

Wheeled Coach Industries Inc
2737 Forsyth Rd . . . Winter Park FL 32792 407-677-7777 679-1337
TF: 800-342-0720 ■ *Web:* www.wheeledcoach.com

Wichita Kenworth Inc 5115 N Broadway . . . Wichita KS 67219 316-838-0867 838-4845
TF: 800-825-5558 ■ *Web:* www.wichitakenworth.com

Woburn Foreign Motors Inc 80-82 Olympia Ave . . . Woburn MA 01801 781-935-3040 938-0225
Web: www.wfab.com

World Wide Motors Inc 3900 E 96th St . . . Indianapolis IN 46240 317-580-6800
Web: www.worldwidemotors.com

Yamaha Golf Cars of California Inc
7275 National Dr Ste D . . . Livermore CA 94550 925-371-5350 371-5311
Web: www.yamahagolfcarsofca.com

York Automotive Group Inc 6019 W Central Ave . . . Toledo OH 43615 866-390-8894 842-7788*
**Fax Area Code:* 419 ■ *TF:* 866-390-8894 ■ *Web:* www.yorkauto.com

517 MOTORCYCLES & MOTORCYCLE PARTS & ACCESSORIES

Phone | Fax

American Honda Motor Company Inc
1919 Torrance Blvd . . . Torrance CA 90501 310-783-3170
TF: 800-999-1009 ■ *Web:* www.honda.com

American Suzuki Motor Corp 3251 Imperial Hwy . . . Brea CA 92821 714-996-7040
Web: www.suzuki.com

Andrews Products Inc 431 Kingston Ct . . . Mount Prospect IL 60056 847-759-0190 759-0848
Web: www.andrewsproducts.com

City Cycle Inc 2222 Cantrell Rd . . . Little Rock AR 72202 501-663-8796
Web: www.competitivecyclist.com

Compositech Inc 5315 Walt Pl . . . Indianapolis IN 46254 317-481-1120
Web: www.zipp.com

Corbin 2360 Technology Pkwy . . . Hollister CA 95023 831-634-1100 634-1059
TF: 800-538-7035 ■ *Web:* www.corbin.com

Cycle Shack Inc
1104 San Mateo Ave . . . South San Francisco CA 94080 650-583-7014 583-9154
Web: www.cycle-shack.com

Edelbrock Corp 2700 California St . . . Torrance CA 90503 310-781-2222 320-1187
TF: 800-739-3737 ■ *Web:* www.edelbrock.com

ElliptiGO Inc 722 Genevieve St Ste O . . . Solana Beach CA 92075 858-876-8677
Web: www.elliptigo.com

Fulmer Co 122 Gayoso Ave . . . Memphis TN 38103 901-525-5711
TF: 844-438-5637 ■ *Web:* www.fulmerhelmets.com

Harley-Davidson Inc 3700 W Juneau Ave . . . Milwaukee WI 53208 414-342-4680 343-4621*
NYSE: HOG ■ **Fax:* Hum Res ■ *Web:* harley-davidson.com

Hed Cycling Products 1735 Terrace Dr . . . Roseville MN 55113 651-653-0202
TF: 888-246-3639 ■ *Web:* www.hedcycling.com

Jenson USA Inc 1615 Eastridge Ave . . . Riverside CA 92507 909-947-9036
Web: www.jensonusa.com

Kawasaki Motors Corp USA PO Box 25252 . . . Santa Ana CA 92799 949-770-0400 460-5600
TF: 866-802-9381 ■ *Web:* www.kawasaki.com

Lehman Trikes Inc 125 Industrial Dr . . . Spearfish SD 57783 605-642-2111 642-1184
CVE: LHT ■ *TF:* 888-394-3357 ■ *Web:* www.lehmantrikes.com

Mag-Knight 18121 117th St SE . . . Snohomish WA 98290 360-805-0100 805-0811
Web: www.mag-knight.com

Motovan Corp 1391 Guy Lussac . . . Boucherville QC J4B7K1 450-449-3903
Web: www.motovan.com

National Cycle Inc 2200 Maywood Dr . . . Maywood IL 60153 708-343-0400 343-0625
TF: 877-972-7336 ■ *Web:* www.nationalcycle.com

Persons Majestic Mfg Co PO Box 370 . . . Huron OH 44839 419-433-9057 433-0182
TF: 800-772-2453 ■ *Web:* www.permaco.com

Polaris Industries Inc 2100 Hwy 55 . . . Medina MN 55340 763-542-0500 542-0599
NYSE: PII ■ *Web:* www.polaris.com

Powroll Motor Performance
13850 Commercial Lp . . . Terrebonne OR 97760 541-923-1290 923-5637

Rivco Products Inc 440 S Pine St . . . Burlington WI 53105 262-763-8222 763-8949
TF: 888-801-8222 ■ *Web:* www.rivcoproducts.com

Rolf Prima Inc 780 Bailey Hill Rd Ste 2 . . . Eugene OR 97402 541-868-1715
Web: www.rolfprima.com

World Bicycle Relief
1333 N Kingsbury Ave 4th Fl . . . Chicago IL 60642 312-664-8800
Web: www.worldbicyclerelief.org

Yamaha Motor Corp USA 6555 Katella Ave . . . Cypress CA 90630 800-656-7695
TF Cust Svc: 800-656-7695 ■ *Web:* www.yamaha-motor.com

MOTORS - FLUID POWER

See Pumps & Motors - Fluid Power p. 3008

518 MOTORS (ELECTRIC) & GENERATORS

See Also Automotive Parts & Supplies - Mfr p. 1830

Phone | Fax

ADS/Transicoil 9 Iron Bridge Dr . . . Collegeville PA 19426 484-902-1100 902-1150
TF: 800-323-7115 ■ *Web:* www.adstcoil.com

Advanced Motors & Drives Inc
6268 E Molloy Rd . . . East Syracuse NY 13057 315-434-9303

Advanced Power & Controls LLC
605 E Alton Ave Ste A . . . Santa Ana CA 92705 714-540-9010 540-5313
Web: www.advancedpowercontrols.com

Advantage Manufacturing Inc 624 S B St . . . Tustin CA 92780 714-505-1166
Web: www.electricmotors.com

Aerotech Inc 101 Zeta Dr . . . Pittsburgh PA 15238 412-967-6440 967-6870
Web: www.aerotech.com

Alliance Winding Equipment Inc
3939 Vanguard Dr . . . Fort Wayne IN 46809 260-478-2200
Web: www.alliance-winding.com

Alltrax Inc 1111 Cheney Creek Rd . . . Grants Pass OR 97527 541-476-3565
Web: www.alltraxinc.com

AMK Drives & Controls Inc
5631 S Laburnum Ave . . . Richmond VA 23231 804-222-0323 222-0339
Web: amk-group.com/en

Phone Fax

AO Smith Corp
11270 W Pk Pl Ste 170 PO Box 245008 Milwaukee WI 53224 414-359-4000 359-4180
NYSE: AOS ■ TF: 800-359-4065 ■ Web: www.aosmith.com

AO Smith Electrical Products Co
531 N Fourth St Tipp City OH 45371 937-667-2431 667-5030
TF: 800-543-9450 ■ Web: www.centuryelectricmotor.com

Arco Electric Products Corp
2325 E Michigan Rd Shelbyville IN 46176 317-398-9713 398-2655
TF: 800-428-4370 ■ Web: www.arco-electric.com

ASMO North America LLC 470 Crawford Rd Statesville NC 28625 704-878-6663
Web: www.asmo-na.com

Aura Systems Inc 1310 E Grand Ave El Segundo CA 90245 310-643-5300 643-7457
OTC: AUSI ■ TF: 800-909-2872 ■ Web: www.aurasystems.com

Autotrol Corp
365 E Prairie St PO Box 557 Crystal Lake IL 60039 815-459-3080 459-3227
TF: 800-228-6207 ■ Web: www.autotrol.com

Aveox Inc 2265A Ward Ave Simi Valley CA 93065 805-915-0200
Web: www.aveox.com

Baldor Electric Co
5711 RS Boreham Jr St PO Box 2400 Fort Smith AR 72901 479-646-4711 648-5792
Web: www.baldor.com

Barta - Schoenewald Inc 3805 Calle Tecate Camarillo CA 93012 805-389-1935 389-1165
Web: www.a-m-c.com

Bluffton Motor Works LLC 410 E Spring St Bluffton IN 46714 260-827-2200
TF: 800-579-8527 ■ Web: www.blmworks.com

Blutek Power Inc 300-1 SR- 17 S Ste B2 Lodi NJ 07644 973-594-1800
Web: www.blutekpower.com

Bodine Electric Co 201 Northfield Rd Northfield IL 60093 773-478-3515 478-3232
TF: 800-726-3463 ■ Web: www.bodine-electric.com

Bosch Rexroth Corp
5150 Prairie Stone Pkwy Hoffman Estates IL 60192 847-645-3600 645-6201
TF: 800-860-1055 ■ Web: www.boschrexroth.com/en/us

Buehler Motor Inc
860 Aviation Pkwy Ste 300 Morrisville NC 27560 919-380-3333 380-3256
Web: www.buehlermotor.com

CALEX Manufacturing Co 2401 Stanwell Dr Concord CA 94520 925-687-4411 687-3333
TF: 800-542-3355 ■ Web: www.calex.com

Calnetix Technologies LLC
16323 Shoemaker Ave Cerritos CA 90703 562-293-1660
Web: www.calnetix.com

Cambridge Pro Fab Inc 470 Franklin Blvd Cambridge ON N1R8G6 519-740-6033
Web: www.cambridgeprofab.com

Composite Motors Acquisition Inc
15460 Aviation Loop Dr Brooksville FL 34604 352-799-2599
Web: compositemotors.com

Continental Electric Motors Inc 23 Sebago St Clifton NJ 07013 800-335-6718
TF: 800-335-6718 ■ Web: www.cecoinc.com

Curtis H Stout Inc 5110 Hollywood Ave Shreveport LA 71109 318-636-7777
Web: www.colinx.com

Custom Sensors & Technologies (CST)
14401 Princeton Ave Moorpark CA 93021 805-552-3599
Web: www.cstsensors.com

DA-TECH Corp 141 Railroad Dr Ivyland PA 18974 215-322-9410
Web: swemco.com

Data Electronic Devices Inc 32 NW Dr Salem NH 03079 603-893-2047 893-2956
Web: www.dataed.com

Dumore Corp 1030 Veterans St Mauston WI 53948 608-847-6420 338-6673*
*Fax Area Code: 800 ■ TF: 888-467-8288 ■ Web: www.dumorecorp.com

EAD Motors Inc 1 Progress Dr Dover NH 03820 603-742-3330 742-3330
Web: www.electrocraft.com

eCycle Inc 7775 Walton Pkwy Ste 250 New Albany OH 43054 610-939-0480
Web: www.e-cycle.com

Electric Apparatus Co 409 Roosevelt St Howell MI 48843 517-546-0520 546-0547
Web: www.elecapp.net

Electric Machinery Company Inc
800 Central Ave NE Minneapolis MN 55413 612-378-8000
Web: www.electricmachinery.com

Electric Motor & Contracting Co Inc
3703 Cook Blvd Chesapeake VA 23323 757-487-2121 487-5983
Web: www.emc-co.com

Electric Motors & Specialties Inc
701 W King St PO Box 180 Garrett IN 46738 260-357-4141 357-3888
Web: www.emsmotors.com

Electro Sales Inc 100 Fellsway W Somerville MA 02145 617-666-0500 628-2800

Elwood Corp High Performance Motors Group
2701 N Green Bay Rd Racine WI 53404 262-637-6591 764-4298*
*Fax Area Code: 414 ■ TF: 800-558-9489 ■ Web: www.elwood.com

Emoteq Corp 10002 E 43rd St S Tulsa OK 74146 918-627-1845 660-0207
Web: www.emoteq.com

ENER-G Rudox 765 State Rt 17 Carlstadt NJ 07072 201-438-0111 438-3403
Web: www.rudox.com

Engine Power Source Inc 348 Bryant Blvd Rock Hill SC 29732 704-944-1999
TF: 800-374-7522 ■ Web: www.enginepowersource.com

Everson Tesla Inc 615 Daniel's Rd Nazareth PA 18064 610-746-1520 746-1520
Web: www.eversontesla.com

Fader Agencies 83 Shore Rd Dartmouth NS B3A1A5 902-466-2333

Faradyne Motors Inc 2077 Division St Palmyra NY 14522 315-502-0125
Web: www.faradynemotors.com

Five Star Electric of Houston Inc
19424 Pk Row Ste 100 Houston TX 77084 281-492-7090
TF: 888-492-7090 ■ Web: vfd.com

FLANDERS Inc 8101 Baumgart Rd PO Box 23130 Evansville IN 47724 812-867-7421
TF: 855-875-5888 ■ Web: www.flandersinc.com

Franklin Electric Co Inc
9255 Coverdale Rd Fort Wayne IN 46809 260-824-2900 824-2909
NASDAQ: FELE ■ TF: 800-962-3787 ■ Web: www.franklin-electric.com

Gamesa Wind US LLC 2050 Cabot Blvd W Langhorne PA 19047 215-710-3100
Web: www.gamesacorp.com

Generac Power Systems Inc PO Box 8 Waukesha WI 53187 262-544-4811 544-4851
TF: 888-436-3722 ■ Web: www.generac.com

Gillette Generators Inc 1340 Wade Dr Elkhart IN 46514 574-264-9639
Web: www.gillettegenerators.com

Glentek Inc 208 Standard St El Segundo CA 90245 310-322-3026 322-7709
TF: 877-470-6742 ■ Web: www.glentek.com

Phone Fax

Hankscraft Inc 300 Wengel Dr Reedsburg WI 53959 608-524-4341 524-4342
Web: www.hankscraft.com

Hannon Co, The 1605 Waynesburg Dr SE Canton OH 44707 330-456-4728 456-3323
Web: www.hanco.com

Hansen Corp 901 S First St Princeton IN 47670 812-385-3415 385-3013
Web: www.hansen-motor.com

Hansome Energy Systems Inc 365 Dalziel Rd Linden NJ 07036 908-862-9044 862-8195

Himoinsa Power Systems Inc 16002 W 110th St Lenexa KS 66219 913-495-5557
TF: 866-710-2988 ■ Web: www.hipowersystems.com

Hostvedt Pavoni Inc 30 S Pine St Doylestown PA 18901 215-489-7300
Web: www.hpisales.com

Hyundai Ideal Electric Co 330 E First St Mansfield OH 44902 419-522-3611
Web: www.idealelectricco.com

Imperial Electric Co 1503 Exeter Rd Akron OH 44306 330-734-3600 734-3601
Web: www.imperialelectric.com

Joliet Equipment Corp 1 Doris Ave Joliet IL 60433 815-727-6606 727-6626
TF: 800-435-9350 ■ Web: www.joliet-equipment.com

Joy Global 4400 West National Ave Milwaukee WI 53214 414-671-4400 671-7604
Web: www.joyglobal.com

Kencoil Inc 2805 Engineers Rd Belle Chasse LA 70037 504-394-4010
Web: www.kencoil.com

Kinetek Inc
1751 Lk Cook Rd ArborLake Ctr Ste 550 Deerfield IL 60015 847-267-4473 945-9645
Web: www.kinetekinc.com

Kirkwood Industries Inc 1239 Rockside Rd Parma OH 44134 216-267-6200 351-3141
Web: www.kirkwood-ind.com

Kollmorgen Corp 203A W Rock Rd Radford VA 24141 540-633-3545 731-5647
Web: www.kollmorgen.com

Kraft Power Corp 199 Wildwood Ave Woburn MA 01801 781-938-9100 933-7812
TF: 800-969-6121 ■ Web: www.kraftpower.com

Kurz Electric Solutions Inc 1325 McMahon Dr Neenah WI 54956 920-886-8200 886-8201
TF: 800-776-3629 ■ Web: www.kurz.com

Leeson Electric Corp 2100 Washington St Grafton WI 53024 262-377-8810
Web: www.leeson.com

Lexel Corp 532 Broadhollow Rd Ste 125 Melville NY 11747 631-501-0700 501-1930
Web: www.lexel.com

Louis Allis Co 645 Lester Doss Rd Warrior AL 35180 205-590-2986 590-1571
Web: louisallis.com

Mabuchi Motor America Corp
3001 W Big Beaver Rd Ste 328 Troy MI 48084 248-816-3100 816-3242
Web: www.mabuchi-motor.co.jp

Mamco Corp 8630 Industrial Dr Franksville WI 53126 262-886-9069 886-4639
Web: www.mamcomotors.com

Marathon Electric Inc
100 E Randolf St PO Box 8003 Wausau WI 54402 715-675-3311
TF: 800-616-7077 ■ Web: www.marathonelectric.com

Martindale Electric Co 1375 Hird Ave Cleveland OH 44107 216-521-8567 521-9476
TF: 800-344-9191 ■ Web: www.martindaleco.com

McMillan Electric Co 400 Best Rd Woodville WI 54028 715-698-2488 698-2297
Web: www.mcmillanelectric.com

Merkle-Korff Industries Inc
25 NW Pt Blvd Ste 900 Elk Grove Village IL 60007 847-439-3760 439-3963
Web: www.merkle-korff.com

Mobile Electric Power Solutions Inc
2714 W Kingsley Rd Garland TX 75041 972-864-1015
Web: www.meps.com

Molon Motor & Coil Corp
300 N Ridge Ave Arlington Heights IL 60005 847-253-6000 259-5491
TF: 800-526-6867 ■ Web: www.molon.com

Morrill Motors Inc 229 S Main Ave Erwin TN 37650 888-743-7001 735-0117*
*Fax Area Code: 423 ■ TF: 888-743-7001 ■ Web: www.morrillmotors.com

Motor Appliance Corp
601 International Ave Washington DC 63090 636-532-3406 532-4609
TF: 800-622-3406 ■ Web: www.macmc.com

Motor Products Owosso Corp 201 S Delaney Rd Owosso MI 48867 800-248-3841 723-6035*
*Fax Area Code: 989 ■ TF: 800-248-3841 ■ Web: www.motorproducts.net

Motor Specialty Inc
2801-17 Lathrop Ave PO Box 081278 Racine WI 53408 262-632-2794 632-8899
Web: www.motorspecialty.com

MTU Onsite Energy Corp 100 Power Dr Mankato MN 56001 507-625-7973 625-2968*
*Fax: Sales ■ TF: 800-325-5450 ■ Web: www.mtuonsiteenergy.com

NetGain Motors Inc 800 S State St Ste 4 Lockport IL 60441 630-243-9100
Web: www.go-ev.com

Nidec America Corp
50 Braintree Hill Pk Ste 110 Braintree MA 02184 781-848-0970 380-3634
Web: www.nidec.com

Nidec Motor Corp 8050 W Florissant Ave Saint Louis MO 63136 888-637-7333
TF: 888-637-7333 ■ Web: www.usmotors.com

Northern Lights Inc 4420 14th Ave N.W. Seattle WA 98107 206-789-3880
Web: www.northern-lights.com

Ohio Electric Motors Inc
30 Paint Fork Rd PO Box 168 Barnardsville NC 28709 828-626-2901 626-2155
Web: www.ohioelectricmotors.com

Peerless Electric Co 1401 W Market St Warren OH 44485 330-399-3651
Web: www.peerlesselectric.com

PennEngineering & Manufacturing Corp
5190 Old Easton Rd Danboro PA 18916 215-766-8853 766-3680
TF: 800-237-4736 ■ Web: www.pemnet.com

Petrotech Inc 151 Brookhollow Esplanade New Orleans LA 70123 504-620-6600
TF: 800-486-8850 ■ Web: www.petrotechinc.com

Phoenix Electric Manufacturing Co
3625 N Halsted St Chicago IL 60613 773-477-8855
Web: www.phoenixelectric.com

Phytron Inc 600 Blair Pk Rd Ste 220 Williston VT 05495 802-872-1600 872-0311
Web: www.phytron.com

Piller Inc 45 Turner Rd Middletown NY 10941 800-597-6937 692-0295*
*Fax Area Code: 845 ■ TF: 800-597-6937 ■ Web: www.piller.com

Polyspede Electronics Company Inc
6770 Twin Hills Ave Dallas TX 75231 214-363-7245 363-7245
TF: 888-476-5944 ■ Web: www.polyspede.com

Prestolite Electric Holding Inc
46200 Port St Plymouth MI 48170 734-582-7200
Web: www.prestolite.com

Phone Fax

ProVision solar Inc 69 Railroad Ave Ste A-7 .... Hilo HI 96720 808-969-3281
Web: www.provisiontechnologies.com

RAE Corp 4615 Prime Pkwy .... McHenry IL 60050 815-385-3500
TF: 800-323-7049 ■ *Web:* www.raemotors.com

Reuland Electric Co 17969 E Railroad St. .... Industry CA 91748 626-854-5193
Web: www.reuland.com

Robin America Inc 905 Telser Rd. .... Lake Zurich IL 60047 847-540-7300
Web: subarupower.com

Rotating Right Inc 6120 Davies Rd NW .... Edmonton AB T6E4M9 780-485-2010

Sacramento Computer Power Inc
829 W Stadium Ln .... Sacramento CA 95834 916-923-2772

Sag Harbor Industries Inc
1668 Sag Harbor Tpke .... Sag Harbor NY 11963 631-725-0440 725-4234
TF: 800-724-5952 ■ *Web:* www.sagharborind.com

Shinano Kenshi Corp 5737 Mesmer Ave .... Culver City CA 90230 818-889-5028 991-6439
TF: 800-755-0752 ■ *Web:* www.shinano.com

SIAG Aerisyn LLC 959 Windtower Dr. .... Chattanooga TN 37402 423-648-3884
Web: www.siag.de

Siemens Power Generation 4400 N Alafaya Trl .... Orlando FL 32826 407-736-4197 736-5009*
**Fax:* Hum Res ■ *Web:* www.energy.siemens.com

Skurka Aerospace Inc
4600 Calle Bolero PO Box 2869 .... Camarillo CA 93011 805-484-8884 482-7771
Web: www.skurka-aero.com

SL-Montevideo Technology Inc
2002 Black Oak Ave .... Montevideo MN 56265 320-269-6562 269-7662
Web: www.slmti.com

Specialty Motors Inc 25060 Ave Tibbitts. .... Valencia CA 91355 661-257-7388 257-7389
TF: 800-232-2612 ■ *Web:* www.specialtymotors.com

Stauffer Diesel Inc 34 Stauffer Ln .... Ephrata PA 17522 717-738-2500
Web: www.staufferdiesel.com

Stella Maris LLC 930 W Pont des Mouton .... Lafayette LA 70507 337-504-5128
Web: www.stellamarisllc.com

Sterling Electric Inc 7997 Allison Ave. .... Indianapolis IN 46268 317-872-0471 872-0907
TF Cust Svc: 800-654-6220 ■ *Web:* www.sterlingelectric.com

Stimple & Ward Co 3400 Babcock Blvd .... Pittsburgh PA 15237 412-364-5200 364-5299
TF: 800-792-6457 ■ *Web:* www.swcoils.com

Swiger Coils Systems Inc 4677 Mfg Rd .... Cleveland OH 44135 216-362-7500 362-1496
TF: 800-321-3310 ■ *Web:* www.swigercoil.com

Tampa Armature Works Inc 6312 78th St .... Riverview FL 33578 813-621-5661
TF: 866-465-8905 ■ *Web:* www.tawinc.com

Toledo Commutator 1101 S Chestnut St .... Owosso MI 48867 989-725-8192 725-5930
Web: toledocommutator.com

Toshiba International Corp
13131 W Little York Rd. .... Houston TX 77041 713-466-0277 896-5240
TF: 800-231-1412 ■ *Web:* www.toshiba.com

TPS Houston Group LLC 7101 John Ralston Rd. .... Houston TX 77044 281-459-2435
Web: www.tpshoustongroup.com

Tri State G & T Association 30739 Dd Rd .... Nucla CO 81424 970-864-7316
Web: www.tristategt.com

Trinity Racing 9242 Hyssop Dr. .... Rancho Cucamonga CA 91730 909-987-4213
Web: www.trinityracing.com

Umicore Technical Materials North America Inc
9 Pruyn's Island Dr .... Glens Falls NY 12801 518-792-7700
Web: www.umicore.com

Unico Inc 3725 Nicholson Rd. .... Franksville WI 53126 262-886-5678 504-7396
Web: www.unicous.com

Unitron LP 10925 Miller Rd PO Box 38902 .... Dallas TX 75238 214-340-8600 341-2099
TF: 800-527-1279 ■ *Web:* www.unitronlp.com

UQM Technologies Inc 4120 Specialty Pl .... Longmont CO 80504 303-682-4900 682-4901
NYSE: UQM ■ *Web:* www.uqm.com

Vicor Corp 25 Frontage Rd. .... Andover MA 01810 978-470-2900 475-6715
NASDAQ: VICR ■ *TF:* 800-869-5300 ■ *Web:* www.vicorpower.com

VLSI Standards Inc 5 Technology Dr .... Milpitas CA 95035 408-428-1800
Web: www.vlsistandards.com

Wabtec Railway Electronics
21200 Dorsey Mill Rd. .... Germantown MD 20876 301-515-2000 515-2100
Web: www.wabtec.com

Ward Leonard Electric Company Inc
401 Watertown Rd .... Thomaston CT 06787 860-283-5801 283-5777
Web: www.wardleonard.com

Wenthe-Davidson Engineering Co
16300 W Rogers Dr PO Box 510286 .... New Berlin WI 53151 262-782-1550 782-2020
Web: www.wenthe-davidson.com

Wolverine Power Systems Inc 3229 80th Ave. .... Zeeland MI 49464 616-879-0040
TF: 800-485-8068 ■ *Web:* www.wolverinepower.com

Yamaha Motor Corp USA 6555 Katella Ave. .... Cypress CA 90630 800-656-7695
TF Cust Svc: 800-656-7695 ■ *Web:* www.yamaha-motor.com

Yaskawa America Inc 2121 Norman Dr S .... Waukegan IL 60085 847-887-7000 887-7310*
**Fax:* Mktg ■ *TF:* 800-927-5292 ■ *Web:* www.yaskawa.com

519 MOVING COMPANIES

See Also Trucking Companies p. 3271

Companies that have the moving of household belongings as their primary business.

Phone Fax

A Colonial Moving & Storage Co
17 Mercer St. .... Hackensack NJ 07601 201-343-5777 343-1934
TF: 877-549-7783 ■ *Web:* www.colonialmoving.com

Ace World Wide Moving 1900 E College Ave .... Cudahy WI 53110 414-764-1000 764-1650
TF: 800-558-3980 ■ *Web:* www.aceworldwide.com

Air Van Moving Group
2340 130th Ave NE Ste 201 .... Bellevue WA 98005 425-629-4101 629-4120
TF: 800-989-8905 ■ *Web:* www.airvanmoving.com

Allied International NA Inc 700 Oakmont Ln .... Westmont IL 60559 630-570-3500 570-3496
TF: 800-444-6787 ■ *Web:* www.allied.com

American Red Ball International
9750 Third Ave NE Ste 200. .... Seattle WA 98115 206-526-1730 526-2967
TF: 800-669-6424 ■ *Web:* americanredball.com

American Red Ball Transit Company Inc
PO Box 1127 .... Indianapolis IN 46206 800-733-8139
TF: 800-733-8139 ■ *Web:* www.redball.com

Andrews Van Lines Inc 310 S Seventh St .... Norfolk NE 68701 402-371-5440
TF Cust Svc: 800-228-8146 ■ *Web:* www.andrewsvanlines.com

Arnoff Moving & Storage Inc
1282 Dutchess Tpke. .... Poughkeepsie NY 12603 845-471-1504 452-3606
TF: 800-633-6683 ■ *Web:* www.arnoff.com

Atlantic Relocation Systems Inc
1314 Chattahoochee Ave NW .... Atlanta GA 30318 404-351-5311 350-6530
TF Cust Svc: 800-241-1140 ■ *Web:* www.atlanticrelocation.com

Atlas Van Lines Inc 1212 St George Rd. .... Evansville IN 47711 812-424-2222 421-7129*
**Fax:* Cust Svc ■ *TF:* 800-638-9797 ■ *Web:* www.atlasvanlines.com

Bekins Van Lines LLC 8010 Castleton Rd .... Indianapolis IN 46250 800-456-8092 570-4635*
**Fax Area Code:* 317 ■ *TF:* 800-456-8092 ■ *Web:* www.bekins.com

Berger Transfer & Storage Inc
2950 Long Lk Rd .... Saint Paul MN 55113 877-268-2101 639-2277*
**Fax Area Code:* 651 ■ *TF:* 877-268-2101 ■ *Web:* www.bergerallied.com

Beverly Hills Transfer & Storage Co
15500 S Main St. .... Gardena CA 90248 800-999-7114
TF: 800-999-7114 ■ *Web:* www.beverlyhillstransfer.com

Bohrens Moving & Storage Inc
3 Applegate Dr .... Robbinsville NJ 08691 609-208-1470 208-1471
TF: 800-326-4736 ■ *Web:* www.bohrensmoving.com

Buehler Moving & Storage 3899 Jackson St .... Denver CO 80205 303-388-4000 388-0296
TF: 800-234-6683 ■ *Web:* www.buehlercompanies.com

Callan & Woodworth Moving & Storage
900 Hwy 212 .... Michigan City IN 46360 269-447-1578
TF: 800-584-0551 ■ *Web:* www.callanmoving.com

Cartwright Cos, The 11901 Cartwright Ave .... Grandview MO 64030 800-821-2334 442-6360*
**Fax Area Code:* 816 ■ *TF:* 800-821-2334 ■ *Web:* www.cartwrightcompanies.com

Castine Moving & Storage 1235 Chestnut St. .... Athol MA 01331 978-249-9105 249-5337
TF: 800-225-8068 ■ *Web:* www.castinemovers.com

Coast to Coast Moving & Storage Co
136 41st St. .... Brooklyn NY 11232 718-443-5800
TF: 800-872-6683 ■ *Web:* www.ctcvanlines.com

Cook Moving Systems Inc 1845 Dale Rd .... Buffalo NY 14225 800-828-7144
TF: 800-828-7144 ■ *Web:* www.cookmoving.com

Corrigan Moving Systems
23923 Research Dr .... Farmington Hills MI 48335 800-267-7442
TF: 800-267-7442 ■ *Web:* www.corriganmoving.com

Davidson Transfer & Storage Co
1701 Florida Ave NW .... Washington DC 20009 202-234-5600
Web: www.secor-group.com

East Side Moving & Storage
4836 SE Powell Blvd .... Portland OR 97206 503-777-4181 775-8443
TF: 800-547-4600 ■ *Web:* www.move-northwest.com

Graebel Van Lines Inc 16346 Airport Cir. .... Aurora CO 80011 303-214-6683
TF: 800-568-0031 ■ *Web:* www.graebel.com

Hartford Despatch Moving & Storage Inc
225 Prospect St .... East Hartford CT 06108 860-528-9551

Hilford Moving & Storage 1595 Arundell Ave. .... Ventura CA 93003 805-642-0221
TF: 800-739-6683 ■ *Web:* www.hilford.com

Hollister Moving & Storage 1650 Lana Way .... Hollister CA 95023 831-637-6250 636-5029
TF: 800-767-8580 ■ *Web:* hollistermovers.com

I-Go Van & Storage 9820 S 142nd St. .... Omaha NE 68138 402-891-1222
TF: 800-228-9276 ■ *Web:* www.igovanandstorage.com

Johnson Storage & Moving Co 221 Broadway. .... Denver CO 80202 303-778-6683
TF: 800-289-6683 ■ *Web:* www.johnsonstorage.com

King Relocation Services
13535 Larwin Cir .... Santa Fe Springs CA 90670 800-854-3679
TF: 800-854-3679 ■ *Web:* www.kingcompaniesusa.com

Lido Van & Storage Co Inc
2152 Alton Pkwy Ste N. .... Irvine CA 92606 949-863-9000 221-3479*
**Fax Area Code:* 323 ■ *TF:* 800-339-5436

Mayflower Transit LLC 1 Mayflower Dr. .... Fenton MO 63026 636-305-4000
TF: 800-325-3924 ■ *Web:* www.mayflower.com/moving

McCollister's Transportation Group Inc
1800 Rt 130 N PO Box 9. .... Burlington NJ 08016 609-386-0600 386-5608
TF: 800-257-9595 ■ *Web:* www.mccollisters.com

National Van Lines Inc 2800 W Roosevelt Rd .... Broadview IL 60155 708-450-2900 450-9320*
**Fax:* Cust Svc ■ *TF:* 877-590-2810 ■ *Web:* www.nationalvanlines.com

Nationwide Van Lines Inc 1421 NW 65th Ave .... Plantation FL 33313 954-585-3945 585-3970
TF: 800-310-0056 ■ *Web:* www.nationwidevanlines.com

Nelson Westerberg Inc
1500 Arthur Ave .... Elk Grove Village IL 60007 847-437-2080
TF: 800-245-2080 ■ *Web:* www.nelsonwesterberg.com

NorthStar Moving Corp 9120 Mason Ave .... Chatsworth CA 91311 818-727-0128
TF: 800-275-7767 ■ *Web:* www.northstarmoving.com

Palmer Moving & Storage 24660 Dequindre Rd. .... Warren MI 48091 586-436-3804 834-3414
TF: 800-521-3954 ■ *Web:* www.palmermoving.com

Paxton Van Lines Inc 5300 Port Royal Rd .... Springfield VA 22151 703-321-7600
TF: 800-336-4536 ■ *Web:* www.paxton.com

Pickens-Kane Moving Co 410 N Milwaukee Ave .... Chicago IL 60610 312-942-0330
TF: 888-871-9998 ■ *Web:* www.pickenskane.com

S & M Moving Systems Inc
12128 Burke St. .... Santa Fe Springs CA 90670 562-567-2100
TF: 800-528-4561 ■ *Web:* www.smmoving.com

Security Storage Co 1701 Florida Ave NW .... Washington DC 20009 202-234-5600 234-3513
TF: 888-903-7695 ■ *Web:* www.secor-group.com

Smith Dray Line 320 Frontage Rd .... Greenville SC 29611 866-642-6389
TF: 866-642-6389 ■ *Web:* www.smithdray.com

Starving Students Moving & Storage Co
1850 Sawtelle Blvd Ste 300 .... Los Angeles CA 90025 888-931-6683 825-1145*
**Fax Area Code:* 800 ■ *TF:* 888-931-6683 ■ *Web:* www.ssmovers.com

Stevens Worldwide Van Lines 527 W Morley Dr. .... Saginaw MI 48601 800-678-3836 755-3000*
**Fax Area Code:* 989 ■ *TF:* 888-860-4566 ■ *Web:* www.stevensworldwide.com

Suddath Cos 815 S Main St. .... Jacksonville FL 32207 904-352-2577 858-1208*
**Fax:* Hum Res ■ *TF:* 800-395-7100 ■ *Web:* www.suddath.com

Truckin Movers Corp 1031 Harvest St. .... Durham NC 27704 919-682-2300 688-2264
TF: 800-334-1651 ■ *Web:* www.truckinmovers.com

Two Guys Relocation Systems Inc
3571 Pacific Hwy .... San Diego CA 92101 619-296-7995
TF: 800-896-4897 ■ *Web:* www.twomenwillmoveyou.com

Two Men & A Truck International Inc
3400 Belle Chase Way .... Lansing MI 48911 517-394-7210 394-7432
TF: 800-345-1070 ■ *Web:* www.twomenandatruck.com

	City	State	ZIP	Phone	Fax
United Van Lines Inc 1 United Dr. TF: 877-740-3040 ■ Web: www.unitedvanlines.com	St. Louis	MO	63026	636-343-3900	349-8794
Von Paris Enterprises Inc 8691 Larkin Rd TF: 800-866-6355 ■ Web: www.vonparis.com	Savage	MD	20763	410-888-8500	888-9062
Wald Relocation Services Ltd 8708 W Little York Rd Ste 190 TF: 800-527-1408 ■ Web: www.waldrelocation.com	Houston	TX	77040	713-512-4800	512-4881
Wheaton Van Lines Inc 8010 Castleton Rd *Fax: Cust Svc ■ TF: 800-932-7799 ■ Web: www.wheatonworldwide.com	Indianapolis	IN	46250	317-849-7900	570-4635*

520 MUSEUMS

See Also Museums - Children's p. 2812; Museums & Halls of Fame - Sports p. 2814
Listings for museums are organized alphabetically within state and province groupings. (Canadian provinces are interfiled among the US states, in alphabetical order.)

Alabama

	City	State	ZIP	Phone	Fax
Alabama Constitution Village 109 Gates Ave. TF: 800-678-1819 ■ Web: earlyworks.com	Huntsville	AL	35801	256-564-8100	
Alabama Dept of Archives & History 624 Washington Ave PO Box 300100 Web: www.archives.state.al.us	Montgomery	AL	36104	334-242-4435	240-3433
Alabama Jazz Hall of Fame 1631 Fourth Ave Web: www.jazzhall.com	Birmingham	AL	35203	205-254-2731	254-2785
Alabama Museum of Natural History PO Box 870340 Web: almnh.ua.edu	Tuscaloosa	AL	35487	205-348-7550	348-9292
American Sport Art Museum & Archives 1 Academy Dr Web: www.asama.org	Daphne	AL	36526	251-626-3303	
Barber Vintage Motorsports Museum 6030 Barber Motorsports Pkwy Web: www.barbermuseum.org	Leeds	AL	35094	205-699-7275	
Bessemer Hall of History 1905 Alabama Ave Web: www.bhamrails.info	Bessemer	AL	35020	205-426-1633	
Birmingham Civil Rights Institute 520 16th St N TF: 866-328-9696 ■ Web: www.bcri.org	Birmingham	AL	35203	205-328-9696	323-5219
Birmingham Museum of Art 2000 Eigth Ave N Web: www.artsbma.org	Birmingham	AL	35203	205-254-2565	
Bragg-Mitchell Mansion 1906 Springhill Ave. Web: www.braggmitchellmansion.com	Mobile	AL	36607	251-471-6364	478-3800
Burritt on the Mountain 3101 Burritt Dr Web: www.burrittonthemountain.com	Huntsville	AL	35801	256-536-2882	532-1784
City of Birmingham, Alabama 331 Cotton Ave SW Web: www.informationbirmingham.com	Birmingham	AL	35211	205-780-5656	
Huntsville Museum of Art 300 Church St SW. TF: 800-786-9095 ■ Web: www.hsvmuseum.org	Huntsville	AL	35801	256-535-4350	532-1743
Jasmine Hill Gardens & Outdoor Museum 3001 Jasmine Hill Rd Web: www.jasminehill.org	Wetumpka	AL	36093	334-567-6463	
Kentuck Museum 503 Main Ave. Web: kentuck.org	Northport	AL	35476	205-758-1257	758-1258
McWane Science Center 200 19th St N Web: www.mcwane.org	Birmingham	AL	35203	205-714-8300	714-8400
Mobile Museum of Art 4850 Museum Dr Web: www.mobilemuseumofart.com	Mobile	AL	36608	251-208-5200	
Montgomery Museum of Fine Arts 1 Museum Dr PO Box 230819 Web: www.mmfa.org	Montgomery	AL	36117	334-240-4333	240-4384
North Alabama Railroad Museum 694 Chase Rd Web: www.northalabamarailroadmuseum.com	Huntsville	AL	35815	256-851-6276	
Phoenix Fire Museum 203 S Claiborne St. Web: www.museumofmobile.com	Mobile	AL	36602	251-208-7569	
Richards-DAR House Museum 256 N Joachim St Web: www.richardsdarhouse.com	Mobile	AL	36603	251-208-7320	
Sloss Furnaces National Historic Landmark 20 32nd St N Web: www.slossfurnaces.com	Birmingham	AL	35222	205-324-1911	324-6758
Southern Museum of Flight 4343 73rd St N. Web: www.southernmuseumofflight.org	Birmingham	AL	35206	205-833-8226	836-2439
Weeden House Museum 300 Gates Ave SE. Web: www.weedenhousemuseum.com	Huntsville	AL	35801	256-536-7718	
White House of the Confederacy 644 Washington St. Web: firstwhitehouse.org	Montgomery	AL	36130	334-242-1861	

Alaska

	City	State	ZIP	Phone	Fax
Alaska Aviation Heritage Museum 4721 Aircraft Dr Web: alaskaairmuseum.org	Anchorage	AK	99502	907-248-5325	
Alaska Native Heritage Ctr 8800 Heritage Ctr Dr. TF: 800-315-6608 ■ Web: www.alaskanative.net	Anchorage	AK	99504	907-330-8000	330-8030
Alaska State Museum 395 Whittier St. TF: 800-440-2919 ■ Web: museums.alaska.gov	Juneau	AK	99801	907-465-2901	465-2976
Anchorage Museum of History & Art 625 C St. Web: www.anchoragemuseum.org	Anchorage	AK	99501	907-929-9200	929-9290
Baranov Museum, The 101 Marine Way Web: www.baranovmuseum.org	Kodiak	AK	99615	907-486-5920	486-3166
Fraternal Order of Alaska State Troopers Museum 245 W Fifth Ave TF: 800-770-5050 ■ Web: www.alaskatroopermuseum.com	Anchorage	AK	99501	907-279-5050	279-5054
Imaginarium Science Discovery Ctr 625 C St Web: www.visit-ketchikan.com	Anchorage	AK	99501	907-225-6166	
Juneau-Douglas City Museum 114 W Fourth St Web: www.juneau.lib.ak.us	Juneau	AK	99801	907-586-3572	586-3203
Oscar Anderson House Museum 420 M St PO Box 102205	Anchorage	AK	99510	907-274-2336	
Sheldon Jackson Museum 104 College Dr. TF: 800-587-0430 ■ Web: museums.alaska.gov	Sitka	AK	99835	907-747-8981	747-3004
Tongass Historical Museum 629 Dock St Web: www.ktn-ak.us/museums	Ketchikan	AK	99901	907-225-5900	225-5602
University of Alaska Museum of the North 907 Yukon Dr TF: 866-478-2721 ■ Web: www.uaf.edu/museum	Fairbanks	AK	99775	907-474-7505	474-5469

Alberta

	City	Prov	Postal Code	Phone	Fax
Aero Space Museum of Calgary 4629 McCall Way NE Web: www.asmac.ab.ca	Calgary	AB	T2E8A5	403-250-3752	250-8399
Alberta Aviation Museum 11410 Kingsway Ave Web: www.albertaaviationmuseum.com	Edmonton	AB	T5G0X4	780-451-1175	451-1607
Glenbow Museum 130-9 Ave SE. Web: www.glenbow.org	Calgary	AB	T2G0P3	403-268-4100	265-9769
Reynolds-Alberta Museum 6426 40 Ave PO Box 6360 TF: 800-661-4726 ■ Web: www.history.alberta.ca/reynolds	Wetaskiwin	AB	T9A2G1	780-361-1351	361-1239
Royal Alberta Museum 102nd Ave Ste 12845 Web: www.royalalbertamuseum.ca	Edmonton	AB	T5N0M6	780-453-9100	454-6629
Royal Tyrrell Museum of Palaeontology Hwy 838 Midland Provincial Pk TF: 888-440-4240 ■ Web: www.tyrrellmuseum.com	Drumheller	AB	T0J0Y0	403-823-7707	823-7131
TELUS World of Science 11211 142nd St Web: telusworldofscienceedmonton.ca	Edmonton	AB	T5M4A1	780-451-3344	455-5882

Arizona

	City	State	ZIP	Phone	Fax
390th Memorial Museum 6000 E Valencia Rd TF: 800-639-4992 ■ Web: 390th.org	Tucson	AZ	85706	520-574-0287	574-3030
Arizona Doll & Toy Museum 5847 W Myrtle Ave	Glendalemaricopa	AZ	85301	623-939-6186	
Arizona Historical Society Museum 1300 N College Ave Web: www.arizonahistoricalsociety.org	Tempe	AZ	85281	480-929-0292	967-5450
Arizona Historical Society Pioneer Museum 2340 N Ft Valley Rd Web: www.arizonahistoricalsociety.org	Flagstaff	AZ	86001	928-774-6272	774-1596
Arizona Science Ctr 600 E Washington St. Web: www.azscience.org	Phoenix	AZ	85004	602-716-2000	716-2099
Arizona State Capitol Museum 1700 W Washington St. TF: 800-228-4710 ■ Web: azlibrary.gov/azcm	Phoenix	AZ	85007	602-542-4675	256-7985
Arizona State Museum 1013 E University Blvd University of Arizona Web: www.statemuseum.arizona.edu	Tucson	AZ	85721	520-621-6302	626-6761
Arizona State University Art Museum 10th St & Mill Ave Nelson Fine Arts Ctr Arizona State University TF: 855-278-5080 ■ Web: www.asuartmuseum.asu.edu	Tempe	AZ	85287	480-965-2787	965-5254
Arizona Wing Commemorative Air Force Museum 2017 N Greenfield Rd Falcon Field Web: azcaf.org	Mesa	AZ	85215	480-924-1940	981-1954
Center for Creative Photography 1030 N Olive Rd TF: 888-472-4732 ■ Web: www.creativephotography.org	Tucson	AZ	85721	520-621-7968	621-9444
DeGrazia Gallery in the Sun 6300 N Swan Rd TF: 800-545-2185 ■ Web: www.degrazia.org	Tucson	AZ	85718	520-299-9191	299-1381
Flandrau Science Ctr & Planetarium 1601 E University Blvd Web: www.flandrau.org	Tucson	AZ	85719	520-621-4516	621-8451
Fort Lowell Museum 2900 N Craycroft Rd Web: arizonahistoricalsociety.org	Tucson	AZ	85712	520-885-3832	
Grand Canyon National Park Museum Collection Grand Canyon National Pk 2C Albright Ave Web: www.nps.gov	Grand Canyon	AZ	86023	928-638-7769	
Hall of Flame Museum of Firefighting 6101 E Van Buren St. Web: www.hallofflame.org	Phoenix	AZ	85008	602-275-3473	275-0896
Heard Museum 2301 N Central Ave. Web: www.heard.org	Phoenix	AZ	85004	602-252-8840	252-9757
International Wildlife Museum 4800 W Gates Pass Rd Web: www.thewildlifemuseum.org	Tucson	AZ	85745	520-629-0100	
Mesa Historical Museum 51 E Main St PO Box 582 Web: www.valleyhistoryinc.com	Mesa	AZ	85201	480-835-7358	
Meteor Crater & Museum of Astrogeology Exit 233 Off I-40 Meteor Crater Rd *Fax Area Code: 928 ■ TF: 800-289-5898 ■ Web: www.meteorcrater.com	Winslow	AZ	86047	800-289-5898	289-2598*
Museum of Northern Arizona 3101 N Ft Valley Rd TF: 800-423-1069 ■ Web: www.musnaz.org	Flagstaff	AZ	86001	928-774-5211	774-1229
Old Pueblo Archaeology Ctr 2201 W 44th St. Web: www.oldpueblo.org	Tucson	AZ	85713	520-798-1201	798-1966
Petersen House Museum 1414 W Southern Ave. Web: www.tempe.gov/museum	Tempe	AZ	85282	480-350-5100	350-5150
Phoenix Art Museum 1625 N Central Ave Web: www.phxart.org	Phoenix	AZ	85004	602-257-1222	253-8662
Phoenix Police Museum 17 S Second Ave Web: phoenixpolicemuseum.org	Phoenix	AZ	85003	602-534-7278	
Pima Air & Space Museum 6000 E Valencia Rd Web: www.pimaair.org	Tucson	AZ	85706	520-574-0462	574-9238

Phone | Fax

Pioneer Arizona Living History Museum
3901 W Pioneer Rd ... Phoenix AZ 85086 623-465-1052 465-0683
Web: www.pioneeraz.org

Pueblo Grande Museum & Archaeological Park
4619 E Washington St ... Phoenix AZ 85034 602-495-0901
TF: 877-706-4408 ■ *Web:* www.phoenix.gov/recreation/arts/museums/pueblo

Rosson House Historic Museum 113 N Sixth St ... Phoenix AZ 85004 602-262-5070
Web: heritagesquarephx.org

Scottsdale Historical Museum
7333 E Scottsdale Mall ... Scottsdale AZ 85251 480-945-4499
Web: www.scottsdalemuseum.com

Scottsdale Museum of Contemporary Art (SMOCA)
7374 E Second St ... Scottsdale AZ 85251 480-874-4666
Web: www.smoca.org

Shemer Arts Ctr & Museum Assn Inc (SACAMA)
5005 E Camelback Rd ... Phoenix AZ 85018 602-262-4727
Web: www.shemerartcenter.org

Tempe Historical Museum 809 E Southern Ave ... Tempe AZ 85282 480-350-5100 350-5150
Web: www.tempe.gov/museum

University of Arizona Museum of Art
1031 N Olive Rd University of Arizona ... Tucson AZ 85721 520-621-7567 621-8770
Web: artmuseum.arizona.edu

Arkansas

Phone | Fax

Arkansas Arts Ctr 501 E Ninth St ... Little Rock AR 72202 501-372-4000 375-8053
TF: 800-264-2787 ■ *Web:* www.arkarts.com

Arkansas Museum of Science & History
Museum of Discovery
500 President Clinton Ave Ste 150 ... Little Rock AR 72201 501-396-7050 396-7054
Web: museumofdiscovery.org

Arkansas State University Museum
PO Box 490 ... State University AR 72467 870-972-2074 972-2793
TF: 800-342-2923 ■ *Web:* www.astate.edu/museum

Fort Smith Museum of History
320 Rogers Ave ... Fort Smith AR 72901 479-783-7841
Web: www.fortsmithmuseum.org

Fort Smith Trolley Museum 100 S Fourth St ... Fort Smith AR 72901 479-783-0205
Web: www.fstm.org

Historic Arkansas Museum 200 E Third St ... Little Rock AR 72201 501-324-9351
Web: www.historicarkansas.org

Josephine Tussaud Wax Museum
250 Central Ave ... Hot Springs AR 71901 501-623-5836
Web: www.rideaduck.com

MacArthur Museum of Arkansas Military History
503 E Ninth St ... Little Rock AR 72202 501-376-4602 376-4593
Web: www.littlerock.org/parksrecreation/arkmilitaryheritage

Mid-America Science Museum
500 Mid-America Blvd ... Hot Springs AR 71913 501-767-3461
Web: www.midamericamuseum.org

Museum of Discovery
500 President Clinton Ave Ste 150 ... Little Rock AR 72201 501-396-7050 396-7054
Web: museumofdiscovery.org

Old State House Museum 300 W Markham St ... Little Rock AR 72201 501-324-9685
Web: www.oldstatehouse.com

British Columbia

Phone | Fax

Canadian Museum of Flight
5333 216th St Hngr 3 ... Langley BC V2Y2N3 604-532-0035 532-0056
Web: www.canadianflight.org

Canadian Museum of Rail Travel
57 Van Horne St S PO Box 400 ... Cranbrook BC V1C4H9 250-489-3918 489-5744
Web: www.crowsnest.bc.ca/cmrt

Comox Air Force Museum 19 Wing Military Row ... Comex BC V0R2K0 250-339-8162 339-8162
Web: www.comoxairforcemuseum.ca

Museum of Vancouver
1100 Chestnut St Vanier Pk ... Vancouver BC V6J3J9 604-736-4431 736-5417
Web: www.museumofvancouver.ca

Royal British Columbia Museum (RBCM)
675 Belleville St ... Victoria BC V8W9W2 250-356-7226 387-5674
TF: 888-447-7977 ■ *Web:* www.royalbcmuseum.bc.ca

University of British Columbia Museum of Anthropology
6393 NW Marine Dr ... Vancouver BC V6T1Z2 604-822-5087 822-2974
Web: www.moa.ubc.ca

California

Phone | Fax

African American Historical & Cultural Museum of San Joaquin Valley
1857 Fulton St ... Fresno CA 93721 559-268-7102
Web: aahcmsjv.org

African American Museum & Library in Oakland
659 14th St ... Oakland CA 94612 510-637-0200
Web: oaklandlibrary.org/locations/african-american-museum-library-oakland

Agua Caliente Cultural Museum
219 S Palm Canyon Dr ... Palm Springs CA 92262 760-778-1079
Web: www.accmuseum.org

Ainsley House 300 Grant St ... Campbell CA 95008 408-866-2119
Web: www.campbellmuseums.org

Alice Arts Ctr 1428 Alice St ... Oakland CA 94612 510-238-7526
Web: mccatheater.com

Ardenwood Historic Farm 34600 Ardenwood Blvd ... Fremont CA 94555 510-544-2797 796-0231
TF: 888-327-2757 ■ *Web:* www.ebparks.org

Asian Art Museum
200 Larkin St Civic Ctr Plz ... San Francisco CA 94102 415-581-3500 581-4700
Web: www.asianart.org

Autry National Ctr Museum of the American West
4700 Western Heritage Way ... Los Angeles CA 90027 323-667-2000 660-5721
Web: theautry.org

Phone | Fax

Bakersfield Museum of Art 1930 R St ... Bakersfield CA 93301 661-323-7219 323-7266
Web: www.bmoa.org

Banning Museum, The 401 E 'M' St ... Wilmington CA 90744 310-548-7777
Web: banningmuseum.org

Berkeley Art Museum & Pacific Film Archive
2626 Bancroft Way Ste 2250 ... Berkeley CA 94720 510-642-0808 642-4889
Web: www.bampfa.berkeley.edu

Bowers Museum of Cultural Art
2002 N Main St ... Santa Ana CA 92706 714-567-3600 567-3603
Web: www.bowers.org

Brand Library & Art Ctr 1601 W Mountain St ... Glendale CA 91201 818-548-2051
Web: www.glendaleca.gov/government/departments/library-arts-culture/brand-library-art-center

Buena Vista Museum of Natural History
2018 Chester Ave ... Bakersfield CA 93301 661-324-6350 324-7522
Web: www.sharktoothhill.org

Burning Man 1900 Third St ... San Francisco CA 94158 415-865-3800
Web: burningman.org

Cabot's Pueblo Museum
67-616 E Desert View Ave ... Desert Hot Springs CA 92240 760-329-7610
Web: www.cabotsmuseum.org

California Academy of Sciences
55 Music Concourse Dr Golden Gate Pk ... San Francisco CA 94103 415-321-8000
Web: www.calacademy.org

California African American Museum
600 State Dr Exposition Pk ... Los Angeles CA 90037 213-744-7432 744-2050
Web: www.caamuseum.org

California Living Museum (CALM)
10500 Alfred Harrell Hwy ... Bakersfield CA 93306 661-872-2256 872-2205
Web: www.calmzoo.org

California Military Museum 1119 Second St ... Sacramento CA 95814 916-442-2883
Web: www.militarymuseum.org

California Museum for History Women & the Arts
1020 'O' St ... Sacramento CA 95814 916-653-7524 653-0314
Web: www.californiamuseum.org

California Museum of Photography
3824 Main St ... Riverside CA 92501 951-827-4787 827-4797
Web: artsblock.ucr.edu

California Science Ctr
700 Exposition Park Dr ... Los Angeles CA 90037 213-744-7400
Web: californiasciencecenter.org

California State Archives 1020 'O' St ... Sacramento CA 95814 916-653-7715 653-7134
TF: 800-633-5155 ■ *Web:* www.sos.ca.gov

California State Railroad Museum
125 "I" St 111 'I' St ... Sacramento CA 95814 916-323-9280 327-5655
TF: 866-240-4655 ■ *Web:* www.csrmf.org

Campbell Historical Museum 51 N Central Ave ... Campbell CA 95008 408-866-2757
Web: www.ci.campbell.ca.us

Carnegie Art Museum 424 S 'C' St ... Oxnard CA 93030 805-385-8158 483-3654
Web: www.carnegieam.org

Cartoon Art Museum 655 Mission St ... San Francisco CA 94105 415-227-8666 243-8666
Web: www.cartoonart.org

Center for Beethoven Studies & Museum
150 E San Fernando St
Dr MLK Jr Library 5th Fl ... San Jose CA 95112 408-808-2058 808-2060
Web: www.sjsu.edu

Chabot Space & Science Ctr
10000 Skyline Blvd ... Oakland CA 94619 510-336-7300 336-7491
TF: 800-704-9804 ■ *Web:* www.chabotspace.org

Chula Vista Heritage Museum
360 Third Ave ... Chula Vista CA 91910 619-427-8092
Web: www.chulavistaca.gov

Clarke Historical Museum 240 E St ... Eureka CA 95501 707-443-1947
Web: www.clarkemuseum.org

Coachella Valley History Museum
82616 Miles Ave ... Indio CA 92201 760-342-6651 863-5232
Web: www.cvhm.org

Colton Hall Museum
570 Pacific St Monterey City Hall ... Monterey CA 93940 831-646-5648 646-3917
Web: www.monterey.org/museum

Computer History Museum, The
1401 N Shoreline Blvd ... Mountain View CA 94043 650-810-1010
Web: www.computerhistory.org

County of San Bernardino
2024 Orange Tree Ln ... Redlands CA 92374 909-307-2669 307-0539
Web: sbcounty.gov

Crocker Art Museum 216 'O' St ... Sacramento CA 95814 916-808-7000
Web: www.crockerartmuseum.org

Crown Point Press 20 Hawthorne St ... San Francisco CA 94105 415-974-6273 495-4220
Web: www.crownpoint.com

de Saisset Museum at Santa Clara University
500 El Camino Real ... Santa Clara CA 95053 408-554-4528 554-7840
TF: 866-554-6800 ■ *Web:* www.scu.edu/deSaisset

Death Valley Museum
Death Vly National Pk PO Box 579 ... Death Valley CA 92328 760-786-2331 786-3283
Web: www.nps.gov/deva

Discovery Science Ctr 2500 N Main St ... Santa Ana CA 92705 714-542-2823
Web: www.discoverycube.org

Dr Willella Howe-Waffle House & Medical Museum
120 Civic Ctr Dr ... Santa Ana CA 92701 714-547-9645
Web: www.santaanahistory.com

Euphrat Museum of Art
21250 Stevens Creek Blvd ... Cupertino CA 95014 408-864-5464
Web: www.deanza.edu

Exploratorium, The 3601 Lyon St ... San Francisco CA 94123 415-561-0360 561-0370
TF: 800-232-9698 ■ *Web:* www.exploratorium.edu

Firehouse Museum 1572 Columbia St ... San Diego CA 92101 619-232-3473
Web: sandiegofirehousemuseum.com

Flying Leatherneck Aviation Museum
Anderson Ave MCAS Miramar ... San Diego CA 92145 858-693-1723 693-0037
TF: 877-359-8762 ■ *Web:* www.flyingleathernecks.org

Fort MacArthur Museum 3601 S Gaffey St ... San Pedro CA 90731 310-548-2631 241-0847
Web: www.ftmac.org

Fresno Art Museum (FAM) 2233 N First St ... Fresno CA 93703 559-441-4221 441-4227
Web: www.fresnoartmuseum.org

Name	City	State	Zip	Phone	Fax
George C Page Museum at La Brea Tar Pits 5801 Wilshire Blvd *Web:* www.tarpits.org	Los Angeles	CA	90036	323-857-6300	
Grier-Musser Museum 403 S Bonnie Brae St *Web:* griermussermuseum.org	Los Angeles	CA	90057	213-413-1814	
Haggin Museum, The 1201 N Pershing Ave *Web:* www.hagginmuseum.org	Stockton	CA	95203	209-940-6300	462-1404
Hellenic Heritage Museum 1650 Senter Rd *Web:* hhisj.org	San Jose	CA	95112	408-247-4685	
Heritage Museum of Orange County, The 3101 W Harvard St *Web:* heritagemuseumoc.org	Santa Ana	CA	92704	714-540-0404	
Heritage of the Americas Museum 12110 Cuyamaca College Dr W *TF:* 800-234-1597 ■ *Web:* www.cuyamaca.net	El Cajon	CA	92019	619-670-5194	670-5198
Heritage Square Museum 3800 Homer St *TF:* 800-375-1771 ■ *Web:* www.heritagesquare.org	Los Angeles	CA	90031	323-225-2700	225-2725
Hiller Aviation Museum 601 Skyway Rd *TF:* 888-500-1555 ■ *Web:* hiller.org	San Carlos	CA	94070	650-654-0200	
Historical Glass Museum 1157 Orange St *Web:* historicalglassmuseum.com	Redlands	CA	92374	909-798-0868	
Hobby City Doll & Toy Museum 1238 S Beach Blvd	Anaheim	CA	92804	714-527-2323	236-9762
Hollywood Museum 1660 N Highland Ave *Web:* www.thehollywoodmuseum.com	Hollywood	CA	90028	323-464-7776	
Hollywood Wax Museum 6767 Hollywood Blvd *TF:* 800-214-3661 ■ *Web:* www.hollywoodwaxmuseum.com	Hollywood	CA	90028	323-462-5991	462-3953
Intel Museum 2200 Mission College Blvd. *TF:* 800-628-8686 ■ *Web:* www.intel.in	Santa Clara	CA	95052	408-765-0503	
International Surfing Museum 411 Olive Ave *Web:* www.surfingmuseum.org	Huntington Beach	CA	92648	714-960-3483	
J Paul Getty Museum 1200 Getty Ctr Dr **Fax:* Hum Res ■ *Web:* www.getty.edu	Los Angeles	CA	90049	310-440-7300	440-7720*
Japanese American National Museum 369 E First St *TF:* 800-461-5266 ■ *Web:* www.janm.org	Los Angeles	CA	90012	213-625-0414	625-0414
Japanese-American Museum 535 N Fifth St *Web:* www.jamsj.org	San Jose	CA	95112	408-294-3138	294-1657
Jensen-Alvarado Historic Ranch & Museum 4307 Briggs St *Web:* rivcoparks.org	Riverside	CA	92509	951-369-6055	
Judah L Magnes Museum 2911 Russell St *Web:* www.magnes.org	Berkeley	CA	94705	510-549-6950	
Junipero Serra Museum 2727 Presidio Dr *Web:* www.sandiegohistory.org	San Diego	CA	92103	619-232-6203	
Kearney Mansion Museum 7160 W Kearney Blvd *Web:* www.valleyhistory.org	Fresno	CA	93706	559-441-0862	441-1372
Kern County Museum 3801 Chester Ave *Web:* www.kcmuseum.org	Bakersfield	CA	93301	661-437-3330	
Kern Valley Museum 49 Big Blue Rd PO Box 651 *Web:* kernvalleymuseum.org	Kernville	CA	93238	760-376-6683	
Legion of Honor Museum 100 34th Ave Lincoln Pk *Web:* legionofhonor.famsf.org	San Francisco	CA	94121	415-750-3600	
Legion of Valor Museum 2425 Fresno St at O St *Web:* legionofvalor.org/museum	Fresno	CA	93721	559-498-0510	
Lindsay Wildlife Museum 1931 First Ave *Web:* lindsaywildlife.org	Walnut Creek	CA	94597	925-627-2920	
Long Beach Museum of Art 2300 E Ocean Blvd *Web:* www.lbma.org	Long Beach	CA	90803	562-439-2119	439-3587
Los Angeles County Museum of Art 5905 Wilshire Blvd *Web:* www.lacma.org	Los Angeles	CA	90036	323-857-6000	857-6212
Lux Art Institute 1550 S El Camino Real *Web:* www.luxartinstitute.org	Encinitas	CA	92024	760-436-6611	
March Field Air Museum 22550 Van Buren Blvd *Web:* www.marchfield.org	Riverside	CA	92518	951-902-5949	
Maritime Museum of San Diego 1492 N Harbor Dr *Web:* www.sdmaritime.org	San Diego	CA	92101	619-234-9153	234-8345
McClellan Aviation Museum 3200 Freedom Pk Dr. *Web:* www.aerospaceca.org	McClellan	CA	95652	916-643-3192	
McHenry Museum 1402 'I' St *Web:* www.mchenrymuseum.org	Modesto	CA	95354	209-577-5235	
Merritt Museum of Anthropology 12500 Campus Dr *Web:* merritt.edu	Oakland	CA	94619	510-531-4911	
Meux Home Museum 1007 R St *Web:* www.meux.mus.ca.us	Fresno	CA	93721	559-233-8007	233-2331
Mexican Museum Fort Mason Ctr 2 Marina Blvd Bldg D *Web:* www.mexicanmuseum.org	San Francisco	CA	94123	415-202-9700	
Mingei International Museum of Folk Art 1439 El Prado *Web:* www.mingei.org	San Diego	CA	92101	619-239-0003	239-0605
Minter Field Air Museum 401 Vultee St PO Box 445 *Web:* www.minterfieldairmuseum.com	Shafter	CA	93263	661-393-0291	393-3296
Mission Basilica San Diego de Alcala 10818 San Diego Mission Rd *Web:* www.missionsandiego.com	San Diego	CA	92108	619-283-7319	283-7762
Mission Inn Museum 3696 Main St *Web:* missioninnmuseum.org	Riverside	CA	92501	951-788-9556	341-6574
Monterey Maritime & History Museum 5 Custom House Plz *Web:* museumofmonterey.org	Monterey	CA	93940	831-372-2608	
Monterey Museum of Art 559 Pacific St *Web:* www.montereyart.org	Monterey	CA	93940	831-372-5477	372-5680
Museo Italo-Americano Fort Mason Ctr Bldg C *Web:* www.museoitaloamericano.org	San Francisco	CA	94123	415-673-2200	673-2292
Museum of Contemporary Art 250 S Grand Ave *Web:* www.moca.org	Los Angeles	CA	90012	213-621-2766	620-8674
Museum of Contemporary Art San Diego 700 Prospect St *Web:* www.mcasd.org	La Jolla	CA	92037	858-454-3541	
Museum of History & Art 1100 Orange Ave *TF:* 866-599-7242 ■ *Web:* www.coronadohistory.org	Coronado	CA	92118	619-435-7242	435-8504
Museum of Jurassic Technology 9341 Venice Blvd *Web:* www.mjt.org	Culver City	CA	90232	310-836-6131	287-2267
Museum of Latin American Art 628 Alamitos Ave *Web:* molaa.org	Long Beach	CA	90802	562-437-1689	
Museum of Local History 190 Anza St *Web:* www.museumoflocalhistory.org	Fremont	CA	94539	510-623-7907	
Museum of Making Music 5790 Armada Dr *TF:* 877-551-9976 ■ *Web:* www.museumofmakingmusic.org	Carlsbad	CA	92008	760-438-5996	438-8964
Museum of Neon Art 501 W Olympic Blvd Ste 101 *Web:* www.neonmona.org	Los Angeles	CA	90015	213-489-9918	
Museum of Photographic Arts 1649 El Prado *Web:* www.mopa.org	San Diego	CA	92101	619-238-7559	238-8777
Museum of San Diego History 1649 El Prado Balboa Pk *Web:* www.sandiegohistory.org	San Diego	CA	92101	619-232-6203	232-6297
Museum of Tolerance 9786 W Pico Blvd *TF:* 800-900-9036 ■ *Web:* www.wiesenthal.com	Los Angeles	CA	90035	310-553-8403	
National Steinbeck Ctr 1 Main St *Web:* www.steinbeck.org	Salinas	CA	93901	831-796-3833	796-3828
Natural History Museum of Los Angeles County 900 Exposition Blvd *Web:* www.nhm.org	Los Angeles	CA	90007	213-763-3466	746-2999
Newland House Museum 19820 Beach Blvd *Web:* www.hbsurfcity.com/history/newland.htm	Huntington Beach	CA	92648	714-962-5777	
Norton Simon Museum 411 W Colorado Blvd *Web:* nortonsimon.org	Pasadena	CA	91105	626-449-6840	796-4978
Oakland Aviation Museum 8252 Earhart Rd *Web:* www.oaklandaviationmuseum.org	Oakland	CA	94621	510-638-7100	
Oakland Museum of California 1000 Oak St *TF General:* 888-625-6873 ■ *Web:* www.museumca.org	Oakland	CA	94607	510-238-2200	238-2258
Orange County Museum of Art South Coast Plaza 850 San Clemente Dr 3rd Fl *Web:* www.ocma.net	Newport Beach	CA	92660	949-759-1122	759-5623
Pacific Asia Museum 46 N Los Robles Ave *Web:* www.pacificasiamuseum.org	Pasadena	CA	91101	626-449-2742	449-2754
Pacific Grove Museum of Natural History 165 Forest Ave *Web:* www.pgmuseum.org	Pacific Grove	CA	93950	831-648-5716	
Pacific Southwest Railway Museum 4695 Nebo Dr *Web:* www.psrm.org	La Mesa	CA	91941	619-465-7776	
Paley Ctr for Media, The 465 N Beverly Dr *Web:* www.paleycenter.org	Beverly Hills	CA	90210	310-786-1000	786-1086
Palm Springs Air Museum 745 N Gene Autry Trl *Web:* palmspringsairmuseum.org	Palm Springs	CA	92262	760-778-6262	320-2548
Palm Springs Art Museum 101 Museum Dr *Web:* www.psmuseum.org	Palm Springs	CA	92262	760-322-4800	327-5069
Pardee Home Museum 672 11th St *Web:* www.pardeehome.org	Oakland	CA	94607	510-444-2187	
Petersen Automotive Museum 6060 Wilshire Blvd *Web:* www.petersen.org	Los Angeles	CA	90036	323-930-2277	
Planes of Fame Air Museum 7000 Merrill Ave #17 *Web:* www.planesoffame.org	Chino	CA	91710	909-597-3722	597-4755
Rancho Los Alamitos Historic Ranch & Gardens 6400 E Bixby Hill Rd *Web:* www.rancholosalamitos.com	Long Beach	CA	90815	562-431-3541	430-9694
Rancho Los Cerritos Historic Ranch 4600 Virginia Rd *Web:* www.rancholoscerritos.org	Long Beach	CA	90807	562-570-1755	570-1893
Randall Museum 199 Museum Way *TF:* 866-807-7148 ■ *Web:* www.randallmuseum.org	San Francisco	CA	94114	415-554-9600	554-9609
Reuben H Fleet Science Ctr 1875 El Prado *Web:* www.rhfleet.org	San Diego	CA	92101	619-238-1233	685-5771
Richard Nixon Foundation, The 18001 Yorba Linda Blvd *Web:* www.nixonfoundation.org	Yorba Linda	CA	92886	714-993-5075	528-0544
Ripley's Believe It or Not! Museum 6780 Hollywood Blvd *Web:* www.ripleys.com/hollywood	Hollywood	CA	90028	323-466-6335	
Riverside Art Museum 3425 Mission Inn Ave *Web:* www.riversideartmuseum.org	Riverside	CA	92501	951-684-7111	
Riverside Metropolitan Museum 3580 Mission Inn Ave *Web:* www.riversideca.gov/museum	Riverside	CA	92501	951-826-5273	369-4970
Robert V Fullerton Art Museum 5500 University Pkwy California State University *Web:* raffma.csusb.edu	San Bernardino	CA	92407	909-537-7373	537-7068
Ronald Reagan Presidential Library & Museum 40 Presidential Dr *TF:* 800-410-8354	Simi Valley	CA	93065	805-522-2977	577-4074
Rosicrucian Egyptian Museum & Planetarium 1342 Naglee Ave Rosicrucian Pk *Web:* www.rosicrucian.org	San Jose	CA	95191	408-947-3600	
San Diego Air & Space Museum 2001 Pan American Plz Balboa Pk *Web:* sandiegoairandspace.org	San Diego	CA	92101	619-234-8291	233-4526

				Phone	Fax
San Diego Aircraft Carrier Museum 910 N Harbor Dr Navy Pier *Web:* www.midway.org	San Diego	CA	92101	619-544-9600	544-9188
San Diego Archaeological Ctr 16666 San Pasqual Vly Rd *Web:* www.sandiegoarchaeology.org	Escondido	CA	92027	760-291-0370	291-0371
San Diego Automotive Museum 2080 Pan American Plz Balboa Pk *Web:* www.sdautomuseum.org	San Diego	CA	92101	619-231-2886	231-9869
San Diego Hall of Champions Sports Museum 2131 Pan American Plz Balboa Pk *Web:* www.sdhoc.com	San Diego	CA	92101	619-234-2544	234-4543
San Diego Model Railroad Museum 1649 El Prado Balboa Pk *Web:* www.sdmodelrailroadm.com	San Diego	CA	92101	619-696-0199	
San Diego Museum of Art 1450 El Prado Balboa Pk PO Box 122107 *Web:* www.sdmart.org	San Diego	CA	92101	619-232-7931	232-9367
San Diego Museum of Man 1350 El Prado Balboa Pk *Web:* www.museumofman.org	San Diego	CA	92101	619-239-2001	239-2749
San Diego Natural History Museum 1788 El Prado PO Box 121390 *TF:* 877-946-7797 ■ *Web:* www.sdnhm.org	San Diego	CA	92101	619-232-3821	232-0248
San Francisco Fire Dept Museum 655 Presidio Ave *Web:* guardiansofthecity.org	San Francisco	CA	94115	415-563-4630	
San Francisco Museum of Modern Art 151 Third St *Web:* www.sfmoma.org	San Francisco	CA	94103	415-357-4000	357-4037
San Joaquin County Historical Society & Museum 11793 N Micke Grove Rd *Web:* www.sanjoaquinhistory.org	Lodi	CA	95240	209-331-2055	331-2057
San Jose Museum of Art 110 S Market St *Web:* www.sjmusart.org	San Jose	CA	95113	408-271-6840	294-2977
San Jose Museum of Quilts & Textiles 520 S First St *Web:* www.sjquiltmuseum.org	San Jose	CA	95113	408-971-0323	971-7226
Santa Barbara Museum of Art 1130 State St *Web:* www.sbma.net/	Santa Barbara	CA	93101	805-963-4364	966-6840
Santa Barbara Museum of Natural History 2559 Puesta Del Sol Rd *Web:* www.sbnature.org	Santa Barbara	CA	93105	805-682-4711	569-3170
Santa Monica Museum of Art 2525 Michigan Ave Ste G1 *Web:* www.smmoa.org	Santa Monica	CA	90404	310-586-6488	
Seabee Museum 99 23rd Ave *Web:* www.seabeehf.org	Port Hueneme	CA	93043	805-982-5167	
Seymour Pioneer Museum Society of California Pioneers 300 Fourth St *Web:* www.californiapioneers.org	San Francisco	CA	94107	415-957-1849	957-9858
Southwest Museum 234 Museum Dr *Web:* theautry.org	Los Angeles	CA	90065	323-221-2164	
Stanley Ranch Museum 12174 S Euclid St PO Box 4297 *Web:* www.ci.garden-grove.ca.us	Garden Grove	CA	92840	714-530-8871	534-2611
Tech Museum of Innovation 201 S Market St *TF:* 800-660-4287 ■ *Web:* www.thetech.org	San Jose	CA	95113	408-294-8324	279-7167
Timken Museum of Art 1500 El Prado Balboa Pk *Web:* www.timkenmuseum.org	San Diego	CA	92101	619-239-5548	531-9640
Triton Museum of Art 1505 Warburton Ave *Web:* www.tritonmuseum.org	Santa Clara	CA	95050	408-247-3754	247-3796
Turtle Bay Exploration Park 840 Auditorium Dr *TF:* 800-887-8532 ■ *Web:* www.turtlebay.org	Redding	CA	96001	530-243-8850	243-8898
UCLA Fowler Museum of Cultural History University of California 308 Charles E Young Dr *Web:* www.fowler.ucla.edu	Los Angeles	CA	90095	310-825-4361	206-7007
UCLA Hammer Museum 10899 Wilshire Blvd *Web:* www.hammer.ucla.edu	Los Angeles	CA	90024	310-443-7000	443-7099
University Art Museum 1250 N Bellflower Blvd *Web:* www.csulb.edu	Long Beach	CA	90840	562-985-5761	985-7602
USC Fisher Museum of Art 823 Exposition Blvd University Pk *Web:* www.usc.edu	Los Angeles	CA	90089	213-740-4561	740-7676
USS Hornet Museum 707 W Hornet Ave Pier 3 *TF:* 800-555-8355 ■ *Web:* www.uss-hornet.org	Alameda	CA	94501	510-521-8448	749-3699
Ventura County Museum of History & Art 100 E Main St *Web:* www.venturamuseum.org	Ventura	CA	93001	805-653-0323	653-5267
Veterans Museum & Memorial Ctr 2115 Pk Blvd *Web:* www.veteranmuseum.org	San Diego	CA	92101	619-239-2300	239-7445
Walt Disney Family Museum LLC, The 104 Montgomery St *Web:* www.waltdisney.org	San Francisco	CA	94129	415-345-6800	
Wells Fargo History Museum 333 S Grand Ave *Web:* www.wellsfargohistory.com	Los Angeles	CA	90071	213-253-7166	
Wells Fargo History Museum 420 Montgomery St *Web:* www.wellsfargohistory.com	San Francisco	CA	94163	415-396-2619	
Wells Fargo History Museum 400 Capitol Mall *Web:* www.wellsfargohistory.com	Sacramento	CA	95814	916-440-4161	
Whaley House Museum 2476 San Diego Ave *Web:* www.whaleyhouse.org	San Diego	CA	92110	619-297-7511	291-3576
William S Hart Museum 24151 Newhall Ave *Web:* www.hartmuseum.org	Newhall	CA	91321	661-254-4584	
Wings of History Air Museum 12777 Murphy Ave PO Box 495 *Web:* www.wingsofhistory.org	San Martin	CA	95046	408-683-2290	
Yerba Buena Ctr for the Arts (YBCA) 701 Mission St *Web:* www.ybca.org	San Francisco	CA	94103	415-978-2787	978-9635

Colorado

				Phone	Fax
Aspen Art Museum 590 N Mill St *Web:* aspenartmuseum.org	Aspen	CO	81611	970-925-8050	925-8054
Aurora History Museum 15051 E Alameda Pkwy *Web:* www.auroragov.org	Aurora	CO	80012	303-739-6660	739-6657
Boulder History Museum 1206 Euclid Ave *Web:* www.boulderhistory.org	Boulder	CO	80302	303-449-3464	938-8322
Boulder Museum of Contemporary Art 1750 13th St *Web:* www.bmoca.org	Boulder	CO	80302	303-443-2122	
Buffalo Bill Memorial Museum 987 1/2 Lookout Mtn Rd *Web:* www.buffalobill.org	Golden	CO	80401	303-526-0744	526-0197
Byers-Evans House Museum 1310 Bannock St *Web:* www.historycolorado.org	Denver	CO	80204	303-620-4933	
Center of Southwest Studies 1000 Rim Dr *Web:* swcenter.fortlewis.edu	Durango	CO	81301	970-247-7456	247-7422
Colorado Railroad Museum 17155 W 44th Ave *TF:* 800-365-6263 ■ *Web:* coloradorailroadmuseum.org	Golden	CO	80403	303-279-4591	279-4229
Colorado Springs Fine Arts Ctr 30 W Dale St *Web:* colorado.com	Colorado Springs	CO	80903	719-634-5581	
Colorado Springs Pioneers Museum 215 S Tejon St *Web:* www.springsgov.com	Colorado Springs	CO	80903	719-385-5990	385-5645
Denver Art Museum 100 W 14th Ave Pkwy *Web:* www.denverartmuseum.org	Denver	CO	80204	720-865-5000	913-0001
Denver Firefighters Museum 1326 Tremont Pl *Web:* www.denverfirefightersmuseum.org	Denver	CO	80204	303-892-1436	892-1436
Denver Museum of Miniatures Dolls & Toys 1880 Gaylord St *Web:* dmmdt.org	Denver	CO	80206	303-322-1053	
Denver Museum of Nature & Science 2001 Colorado Blvd *Web:* www.dmns.org	Denver	CO	80205	303-370-6000	331-6492
Forney Museum of Transportation 4303 Brighton Blvd *Web:* www.forneymuseum.org	Denver	CO	80216	303-297-1113	287-3113
Fort Collins Museum 200 Matthews St *Web:* www.fcgov.com	Fort Collins	CO	80524	970-221-6738	416-2236
Fort Collins Museum of Contemporary Art 201 S College Ave *Web:* ftcma.org	Fort Collins	CO	80524	970-482-2787	
Fort Collins Museum of Discovery 408 Mason Ct *Web:* www.fcmdsc.org	Fort Collins	CO	80524	970-221-6738	
Ghost Town Museum 400 S 21st St *Web:* www.ghosttownmuseum.com	Colorado Springs	CO	80904	719-634-0696	
History Colorado Ctr 1200 Broadway *Web:* www.historycolorado.org/adult-visitors/museums-and-historic-sites	Denver	CO	80203	303-447-8679	
Leanin' Tree Museum of Western Art 6055 Longbow Dr *TF:* 800-525-0656 ■ *Web:* www.leanintree.com	Boulder	CO	80301	303-530-1442	530-5124
Manitou Cliff Dwellings Museum 10 Cliff Rd *TF:* 800-354-9971 ■ *Web:* www.cliffdwellingsmuseum.com	Manitou Springs	CO	80829	719-685-5242	
McAllister House Museum 423 N Cascade Ave *Web:* www.mcallisterhouse.org	Colorado Springs	CO	80903	719-635-7925	
Miramont Castle Museum 9 Capitol Hill Ave *TF:* 888-685-1011 ■ *Web:* www.miramontcastle.org	Manitou Springs	CO	80829	719-685-1011	685-1985
Mizel Museum of Judaica 400 S Kearney St *Web:* www.mizelmuseum.org	Denver	CO	80224	303-394-9993	394-1119
Molly Brown House 1340 Pennsylvania St *Web:* www.mollybrown.org	Denver	CO	80203	303-832-4092	832-2340
Museo de las Americas 861 Santa Fe Dr *Web:* www.museo.org	Denver	CO	80204	303-571-4401	607-9761
Museum of Contemporary Art Denver 1485 Delgany *Web:* mcadenver.org	Denver	CO	80202	303-298-7554	
Museum of Outdoor Arts 1000 Englewood Pkwy Ste 2-230 *Web:* www.artcom.com/museums/nv/mr/80111.htm	Englewood	CO	80110	303-806-0444	
Rocky Mountain Motorcycle Museum & Hall of Fame 5867 N Nevada Ave *Web:* www.themotorcyclemuseum.com	Colorado Springs	CO	80918	719-487-8005	487-8005
Rocky Mountain Quilt Museum 1213 Washington Ave *Web:* www.rmqm.org	Golden	CO	80401	303-277-0377	
State Historical Society of Colorado 1560 Broadway Ste 400 *Web:* www.historycolorado.org	Denver	CO	80202	303-447-8679	
University of Colorado Museum of Natural History 1030 Broadway St *Web:* cumuseum.colorado.edu	Boulder	CO	80309	303-492-6892	492-4195
Vance Kirkland Museum 1311 Pearl St *Web:* www.kirklandmuseum.org	Denver	CO	80203	303-832-8576	832-8404
Western Museum of Mining & Industry 225 N Gate Blvd *TF:* 800-752-6558 ■ *Web:* www.wmmi.org	Colorado Springs	CO	80921	719-488-0880	488-9261
Wings Over the Rockies Air & Space Museum 7711 E Academy Blvd *Web:* www.wingsmuseum.org	Denver	CO	80230	303-360-5360	360-5328

Connecticut

Museum	City	State	Zip	Phone	Fax
American Clock & Watch Museum 100 Maple St. *Web:* www.clockmuseum.org	Bristol	CT	06010	860-583-6070	
Barnum Museum 820 Main St. *Web:* www.barnum-museum.org	Bridgeport	CT	06604	203-331-1104	331-0079
Bruce Museum of Arts & Science 1 Museum Dr *Web:* www.brucemuseum.org	Greenwich	CT	06830	203-869-0376	869-0963
Connecticut Audubon Society Birdcraft Museum & Sanctuary 314 Unquowa Rd *Web:* www.ctaudubon.org	Fairfield	CT	06824	203-259-0416	
Connecticut Historical Society Museum 1 Elizabeth St *Web:* www.chs.org	Hartford	CT	06105	860-236-5621	236-2664
Connecticut Science Center Inc 250 Columbus Blvd *Web:* www.ctsciencecenter.org	Hartford	CT	06103	860-724-3623	
Connecticut State Museum of Natural History 2019 Hillside Rd. *Web:* www.mnh.uconn.edu	Storrs	CT	06268	860-486-4460	486-0827
Discovery Museum & Planetarium 4450 Pk Ave *Web:* www.discoverymuseum.org	Bridgeport	CT	06604	203-372-3521	374-1929
Eli Whitney Museum 915 Whitney Ave *Web:* www.eliwhitney.org	Hamden	CT	06517	203-777-1833	777-1229
Ethnic Heritage Ctr 270 Fitch St Southern Connecticut State University *Web:* www.southernct.edu	New Haven	CT	06515	203-392-6126	392-5140
Fairfield Museum & History Ctr 370 Beach Rd *Web:* www.fairfieldhistoricalsociety.org	Fairfield	CT	06824	203-259-1598	255-2716
Henry Whitfield State Museum 248 Old Whitfield St *Web:* www.cultureandtourism.org	Guilford	CT	06437	203-453-2457	453-7544
Hill-Stead Museum 35 Mountain Rd *Web:* www.hillstead.org	Farmington	CT	06032	860-677-4787	677-0174
Housatonic Museum of Art Housatonic Community College 900 Lafayette Blvd *Web:* www.hcc.commnet.edu	Bridgeport	CT	06604	203-332-5000	332-5123
Institute for American Indian Studies, The 38 Curtis Rd PO Box 1260 *Web:* www.iaismuseum.org	Washington	CT	06793	860-868-0518	868-1649
Lock Museum of America 230 Main St Rt 6 PO Box 104 *Web:* lockmuseumofamerica.org	Terryville	CT	06786	860-589-6359	
Lockwood-Mathews Mansion Museum 295 W Ave *Web:* www.ohwy.com	Norwalk	CT	06850	203-838-9799	
Lyman Allyn Art Museum 625 Williams St *Web:* www.lymanallyn.org	New London	CT	06320	860-443-2545	442-1280
Mark Twain House & Museum 351 Farmington Ave *Web:* www.marktwainhouse.org	Hartford	CT	06105	860-247-0998	
Mattatuck Museum of the Mattatuck Historical Society 144 W Main St *Web:* www.mattatuckmuseum.org	Waterbury	CT	06702	203-753-0381	756-6283
Mike's Famous Harley-Davidson of Groton 951 Bank St *Web:* www.mikesfamous.com	New London	CT	06320	860-574-9200	
Mystic Seaport -- The Museum of America & the Sea 75 Greenmanville Ave PO Box 6000 *TF:* 888-973-2767 ■ *Web:* www.mysticseaport.org	Mystic	CT	06355	860-572-0711	572-5395
New Britain Museum of American Art 56 Lexington St *Web:* www.nbmaa.org	New Britain	CT	06052	860-229-0257	229-3445
Noah Webster House 227 S Main St *Web:* www.noahwebsterhouse.org	West Hartford	CT	06107	860-521-5362	521-4036
Shore Line Trolley Museum 17 River St *Web:* www.bera.org	East Haven	CT	06512	203-467-6927	467-7635
Slater Memorial Museum 108 Crescent St *Web:* slatermuseum.org	Norwich	CT	06360	860-887-2506	
Stamford Historical Society Museum 1508 High Ridge Rd *Web:* www.stamfordhistory.org	Stamford	CT	06903	203-329-1183	322-1607
Stamford Museum & Nature Ctr 39 Scofieldtown Rd. *Web:* www.stamfordmuseum.org	Stamford	CT	06903	203-322-1646	322-0408
Wadsworth Atheneum Museum of Art 600 Main St *Web:* thewadsworth.org	Hartford	CT	06103	860-278-2670	
Yale Ctr for British Art 1080 Chapel St PO Box 208280 *TF:* 877-274-8278 ■ *Web:* britishart.yale.edu	New Haven	CT	06510	203-432-2800	432-9695
Yale Peabody Museum of Natural History 170 Whitney Ave Yale University *Web:* www.peabody.yale.edu	New Haven	CT	06511	203-432-3759	432-9816
Yale University Art Gallery 1111 Chapel St *Web:* www.yale.edu	New Haven	CT	06520	203-432-0600	
Yale University Collection of Musical Instruments 15 Hillhouse Ave *Web:* www.yale.edu	New Haven	CT	06511	203-432-0822	432-8342

Delaware

Museum	City	State	Zip	Phone	Fax
Barratt's Chapel & Museum 6362 Bay Rd *Web:* www.barrattschapel.org	Frederica	DE	19946	302-335-5544	
Delaware Agricultural Museum & Village 866 N DuPont Hwy *Web:* www.agriculturalmuseum.org	Dover	DE	19901	302-734-1618	734-0457
Delaware Art Museum 2301 Kentmere Pkwy *TF:* 866-232-3714 ■ *Web:* www.delart.org	Wilmington	DE	19806	302-571-9590	571-0220
Delaware History Museum 504 N Market St *Web:* dehistory.org	Wilmington	DE	19801	302-656-0637	655-7844
Delaware Museum of Natural History 4840 Kennett Pk *Web:* www.delmnh.org	Wilmington	DE	19807	302-658-9111	658-2610
Hagley Museum & Library 298 Buck Rd E *Web:* www.hagley.org	Greenville	DE	19807	302-658-2400	658-0568
Harrington Museum 108 Fleming St	Harrington	DE	19952	302-398-3698	
Indian River Lifesaving Station Museum 25039 Costal Hwy *TF:* 877-987-2757 ■ *Web:* www.destateparks.com	Rehoboth Beach	DE	19971	302-227-6991	227-6438
Johnson Victrola Museum 375 S New St *Web:* history.delaware.gov	Dover	DE	19901	302-744-5055	
Kalmar Nyckel Foundation 1124 E Seventh St *Web:* www.kalmarnyckel.org	Wilmington	DE	19801	302-429-7447	429-0350
Lewes Historical Society 110 Shipcarpenter St *Web:* www.historiclewes.org	Lewes	DE	19958	302-645-7670	645-2375
Old Swedes Church & Hendrickson House Museum 606 Church St *Web:* www.oldswedes.org	Wilmington	DE	19801	302-652-5629	652-8615
Sewell C Biggs Museum of American Art 406 Federal St *Web:* www.biggsmuseum.org	Dover	DE	19901	302-674-2111	674-5133
Taylor & Messick Inc 325 Walt Messick Rd *TF:* 800-237-1272 ■ *Web:* taylormessick.com	Harrington	DE	19952	302-398-3729	398-4732
Winterthur Museum & Country Estate 5105 Kennett Pk *TF:* 800-448-3883 ■ *Web:* www.winterthur.org	Winterthur	DE	19735	302-888-4600	

District of Columbia

Museum	City	State	Zip	Phone	Fax
African-American Civil War Memorial & Museum 1200 U St NW *Web:* www.afroamcivilwar.org	Washington	DC	20001	202-667-2667	667-6771
B'nai B'rith Klutznick National Jewish Museum 1120 20th St NW *TF:* 888-388-4224 ■ *Web:* www.bnaibrith.org	Washington	DC	20036	202-857-6600	
DAR Museum 1776 D St NW *Web:* www.dar.org/museum	Washington	DC	20006	202-879-3241	628-0820
Decatur House Museum 1610 H St NW *Web:* www.whitehousehistory.org	Washington	DC	20006	202-842-0917	
Dumbarton Oaks 1703 32nd St NW *Web:* www.doaks.org	Washington	DC	20007	202-339-6400	
Frederick Douglass Museum & Hall of Fame for Caring Americans 320 A St NE *Web:* www.caringinstitute.org	Washington	DC	20002	202-547-4273	
Freer and Sackler Galleries (Smithsonian Institution) 1050 Independence Ave SW PO Box 37012 *Web:* www.asia.si.edu	Washington	DC	20013	202-633-1000	357-4911
Freer Gallery of Art / Arthur M. Sackler Gallery 1050 Independence Ave SW PO Box 37012 *Web:* www.asia.si.edu	Washington	DC	20013	202-633-1000	357-4911
Hillwood Estate Museum & Gardens 4155 Linnean Ave NW *Web:* www.hillwoodmuseum.org	Washington	DC	20008	202-686-5807	966-7846
Hirshhorn Museum & Sculpture Garden (Smithsonian Institution) 700 Independence Ave *Web:* www.hirshhorn.si.edu	Washington	DC	20560	202-633-1000	786-2682
Historical Society of Washington DC 801 K St NW Historical Society of Washington DC *Web:* www.dchistory.org	Washington	DC	20001	202-249-3955	417-3823
International Spy Museum 800 F St NW *Web:* www.spymuseum.org	Washington	DC	20004	202-393-7798	393-7797
Kreeger Museum, The 2401 Foxhall Rd NW *Web:* www.kreegermuseum.org	Washington	DC	20007	202-338-3552	337-3051
Lillian & Albert Small Jewish Museum 701 Third St NW *Web:* www.loc.gov/rr/main/religion/jhw.html	Washington	DC	20001	202-789-0900	789-0485
Marian Koshland Science Museum 6th & E Sts NW *TF:* 888-567-4526 ■ *Web:* www.koshland-science-museum.org	Washington	DC	20001	202-334-1201	334-1548
National Air & Space Museum (Smithsonian Institution) Independence Ave & Sixth St SW *Web:* airandspace.si.edu	Washington	DC	20560	202-633-1000	
National Bldg Museum 401 F St NW *Web:* www.nbm.org	Washington	DC	20001	202-272-2448	272-2564
National Gallery of Art 6th St & Constitution Ave NW *Web:* www.nga.gov	Washington	DC	20565	202-737-4215	
National Geographic Society Explorers Hall 1145 17th St NW **Fax Area Code: 202* ■ *TF:* 800-647-5463 ■ *Web:* www.nationalgeographic.com	Washington	DC	20036	800-647-5463	429-5709*
National Ladies Auxiliary Jewish War Veterans of USA Inc 1811 R St Nw *Web:* www.jwv.org	Washington	DC	20009	202-667-9061	
National Museum of African Art (Smithsonian Institution) 950 Independence Ave SW MRC 708 *Web:* africa.si.edu	Washington	DC	20560	202-633-4600	357-4879
National Museum of American History (Smithsonian Institution) (NMAH) 14th St & Constitution Ave NW *Web:* americanhistory.si.edu	Washington	DC	20560	202-633-1000	
National Museum of American Jewish Military History (JWV-NMI) 1811 R St NW *Web:* www.nmajmh.org	Washington	DC	20009	202-265-6280	462-3192
National Museum of Natural History (Smithsonian Institution) 10th St & Constitution Ave NW *TF:* 866-868-7774 ■ *Web:* naturalhistory.si.edu	Washington	DC	20560	202-633-1000	357-4779

Phone Fax

National Museum of the American Indian (Smithsonian Institution)
4th St & Independence Ave SW .... Washington DC 20560 202-633-1000
Web: www.nmai.si.edu

National Museum of Women in the Arts
1250 New York Ave NW .... Washington DC 20005 202-783-5000 393-3234
TF: 866-875-4627 ■ *Web:* www.nmwa.org

National Postal Museum (Smithsonian Institution)
2 Massachusetts Ave NE.................. Washington DC 20002 202-633-5555 633-9393
Web: www.postalmuseum.si.edu

Navy Museum
805 Kidder Breese St SE
Washington Navy Yard .... Washington DC 20374 202-433-4882 433-8200
Web: www.history.navy.mil

Newseum Inc 555 Pennsylvania Ave Nw .... Washington DC 20001 202-292-6100
Web: www.newseum.org

Phillips Collection 1600 21st St NW .... Washington DC 20009 202-387-2151 387-2436
Web: www.phillipscollection.org

Renwick Gallery of the Smithsonian American Art Museum
1661 Pennsylvania Ave NW .... Washington DC 20006 202-633-7970 786-2810
Web: americanart.si.edu/renwick

Smithsonian Institution
SI Bldg Rm 153 MRC 010 PO Box 37012.......... Washington DC 20013 202-633-1000
Web: www.si.edu

Textile Museum, The 2320 S St NW .... Washington DC 20008 202-667-0441 483-0994
Web: museum.gwu.edu

US Holocaust Memorial Museum
100 Raoul Wallenburg Pl SW .... Washington DC 20024 202-488-0400
Web: www.ushmm.org

Woodrow Wilson House Museum 2340 S St NW .... Washington DC 20008 202-387-4062 483-1466
Web: www.woodrowwilsonhouse.org

Florida

Phone Fax

African American Museum of the Arts
325 S Clara Ave .... DeLand FL 32721 386-736-4004 736-4088
Web: www.africanmuseumdeland.org

Amelia Island Museum of History
233 S Third St .... Fernandina Beach FL 32034 904-261-7378 261-9701
Web: ameliamuseum.org

American Police Hall of Fame & Museum
6350 Horizon Dr.................. Titusville FL 32780 321-264-0911 264-0033
Web: www.aphf.org

Audubon House & Tropical Garden
250 Whitehead St.................. Key West FL 33040 305-294-2116
Web: www.audubonhouse.com

Bailey Matthews Shell Museum
3075 Sanibel-Captiva Rd PO Box 1580 .... Sanibel FL 33957 239-395-2233 395-6706
TF: 888-679-6450 ■ *Web:* www.shellmuseum.org

Black Archives Research Ctr & Museum
445 Gamble St Rm 207.................. Tallahassee FL 32307 850-599-3020
Web: cis.famu.edu

Boca Raton Museum of Art
501 Plaza Real Mizner Pk .... Boca Raton FL 33432 561-392-2500 391-6410
TF: 866-481-1689 ■ *Web:* www.bocamuseum.org

Bonnet House Museum & Garden
900 N Birch Rd.................. Fort Lauderdale FL 33304 954-563-5393 561-4174
Web: www.bonnethouse.org

Broward County Historical Commission
151 SW Second St.................. Fort Lauderdale FL 33301 954-765-4670 765-4437
TF: 866-682-2258 ■ *Web:* www.broward.org

Charles Hosmer Morse Museum of American Art
445 N Pk Ave .... Winter Park FL 32789 407-645-5311 647-1284
Web: www.morsemuseum.org

Collier County Museum 3331 Tamiami Trl E.......... Naples FL 34112 239-252-8476
Web: www.colliermuseums.com

Colonial Spanish Quarter Museum
33 St George St .... Saint Augustine FL 32084 904-825-6830
Web: colonialquarter.com

Cornell Fine Arts Museum 1000 Holt Ave.......... Winter Park FL 32789 407-646-2526
Web: www.rollins.edu/cfam

Crowley Museum & Nature Ctr 16405 Myakka Rd...... Sarasota FL 34240 941-322-1000 322-1000
Web: www.crowleymuseumnaturectr.org

Cummer Museum of Art & Gardens
829 Riverside Ave.................. Jacksonville FL 32204 904-356-6857 353-4101
Web: www.cummermuseum.org

Florida Agricultural Museum
7900 Old Kings Rd .... Palm Coast FL 32137 386-446-7630 446-7631
Web: www.myagmuseum.com

Florida Heritage Museum
167 San Marco Ave .... Saint Augustine FL 32084 904-829-9729
TF: 800-268-7252 ■ *Web:* www.amtrakvacations.com

Florida Holocaust Museum
55 Fifth St S .... Saint Petersburg FL 33701 727-820-0100 821-8435
TF: 800-388-4069 ■ *Web:* www.flholocaustmuseum.org

Florida International Museum
244 Second Ave N
St Petersburg College Downtown Ctr .... Saint Petersburg FL 33701 727-341-7900 341-7908
Web: www.floridamuseum.org

Florida Museum of Natural History
3215 Hull Rd .... Gainesville FL 32611 352-392-1721 392-8783
Web: www.flmnh.ufl.edu

Florida State University Museum of Fine Arts
530 W Call St Fine Arts Bldg .... Tallahassee FL 32306 850-644-6836 644-7229
Web: www.mofa.fsu.edu

Fort East Martello Museum
3501 S Roosevelt Blvd .... Key West FL 33040 305-296-3913
Web: kwahs.com

Fort Lauderdale Antique Car Museum
1527 SW First Ave .... Fort Lauderdale FL 33315 954-779-7300
Web: www.antiquecarmuseum.org

Fort Lauderdale Historical Society
219 SW Second Ave .... Fort Lauderdale FL 33301 954-463-4431 523-6228
Web: www.fortlauderdalehistoricalsociety.org

Phone Fax

Fort Lauderdale Museum of Art
1 E Las Olas Blvd .... Fort Lauderdale FL 33301 954-525-5500
Web: www.moafl.org

Frost Art Museum at Florida International University
10975 SW 17th St .... Miami FL 33199 305-348-2890 348-2762
Web: frost.fiu.edu

Gillespie Museum of Minerals
421 N Woodland Blvd Unit 8403 .... DeLand FL 32723 386-822-7330 822-7328
TF: 800-688-0101 ■ *Web:* www.stetson.edu

Goodwood Museum & Gardens
1600 Miccosukee Rd .... Tallahassee FL 32308 850-877-4202 877-3090
Web: www.goodwoodmuseum.org

Gulf Beaches Historical Museum
115 Tenth Ave.................. Saint Pete Beach FL 33706 727-552-1610
Web: gulfbeachesmuseum.com

Halifax Historical Museum
252 S Beach St.................. Daytona Beach FL 32114 386-255-6976 255-7605
Web: www.halifaxhistorical.org

Harry S Truman's Little White House Museum
111 Front St .... Key West FL 33040 305-294-9911 294-9988
TF: 800-435-7352 ■ *Web:* www.trumanlittlewhitehouse.com

Henry B Plant Museum 401 W Kennedy Blvd .... Tampa FL 33606 813-254-1891 258-7272
Web: www.plantmuseum.com

Henry Morrison Flagler Museum
1 Whitehall Way .... Palm Beach FL 33480 561-655-2833 655-2826
Web: www.flaglermuseum.us

Historical Museum of Southern Florida
101 W Flagler St.................. Miami FL 33130 305-375-1492
Web: www.historical-museum.org

Historical Society of Palm Beach County, The
300 N Dixie Hwy Ste 471 .... West Palm Beach FL 33401 561-832-4164
Web: www.historicalsocietypbc.org

Indian Temple Mound Museum
107 Miracle Strip Pkwy SW .... Fort Walton Beach FL 32548 850-833-9500 833-9640
TF: 866-847-1301 ■ *Web:* www.fwb.org

Jacksonville Museum of Modern Art
333 N Laura St .... Jacksonville FL 32202 904-366-6911 366-6901
Web: www.mocajacksonville.org

Jewish Museum of Florida
301 Washington Ave.................. Miami Beach FL 33139 305-672-5044 672-5933
Web: jmof.fiu.edu

John & Mable Ringling Museum of Art
5401 Bay Shore Rd.................. Sarasota FL 34243 941-359-5700
Web: www.ringling.org

John G Riley Ctr/Museum of African American History & Culture
419 E Jefferson St.................. Tallahassee FL 32301 850-681-7881 681-7000
Web: www.rileymuseum.org

Karpeles Manuscript Library Museum
101 W First St.................. Jacksonville FL 32206 904-356-2992
Web: www.rain.org

Key West Art & Historical Society
281 Front St .... Key West FL 33040 305-295-6616
Web: www.kwahs.com

Key West Lighthouse & Keepers Quarters Museum
938 Whitehead St .... Key West FL 33040 305-294-0012 294-0012
Web: www.kwahs.org

Kingsley Plantation 11676 Palmetto Ave.......... Jacksonville FL 32226 904-251-3537 251-3577
TF: 877-874-2478 ■ *Web:* www.nps.gov/timu

Knott House Museum 301 E Pk Ave.......... Tallahassee FL 32301 850-922-2459
Web: museumoffloridahistory.com

Lightner Museum, The 75 King St.......... Saint Augustine FL 32084 904-824-2874
Web: www.lightnermuseum.org

Lowe Art Museum University of Miami
1301 Stanford Dr .... Coral Gables FL 33124 305-284-3535 284-2024
Web: www6.miami.edu/lowe

Mel Fisher Maritime Museum 200 Greene St .... Key West FL 33040 305-294-2633
Web: www.melfisher.org

Mennello Museum of American Folk Art
900 E Princeton St .... Orlando FL 32803 407-246-4278 246-4329
Web: www.mennellomuseum.com

Miami Museum of Science & Planetarium
3280 S Miami Ave .... Miami FL 33129 305-646-4200 646-4300
Web: www.miamisci.org

Morikami Museum & Japanese Gardens
4000 Morikami Pk Rd.................. Delray Beach FL 33446 561-495-0233
Web: www.morikami.org

Museum of Arts & Sciences
352 S Nova Rd .... Daytona Beach FL 32114 386-255-0285
TF: 866-439-4769 ■ *Web:* www.moas.org

Museum of Contemporary Art Inc
770 NE 125th St Joan Lehman Bldg.......... North Miami FL 33161 305-893-6211
Web: www.mocanomi.org

Museum of Fine Arts 255 Beach Dr NE .... Saint Petersburg FL 33701 727-896-2667 894-4638
Web: mfastpete.org

Museum of Florida History
500 S Bronough St RA Gray Bldg.................. Tallahassee FL 32399 850-245-6400 245-6433
Web: www.museumoffloridahistory.com

Museum of Science & History of Jacksonville
1025 Museum Cir.................. Jacksonville FL 32207 904-396-6674
Web: www.themosh.org

Museum of Science & Industry 4801 E Fowler Ave....... Tampa FL 33617 813-987-6000 987-6310
TF: 800-995-6674 ■ *Web:* www.mosi.org

Museum of Southern History
4304 Herschel St .... Jacksonville FL 32210 904-388-3574
Web: www.scv-kirby-smith.org

Museum of the Americas (MoA)
2500 NW 79th Ave Ste 104.................. Doral FL 33122 305-599-8089
Web: www.museumamericas.org

Museum of the Everglades
105 W Broadway.................. Everglades City FL 34139 239-695-0008
Web: colliermuseums.com

My Jewish Discovery Place Children's Museum
6501 W Sunrise Blvd .... Plantation FL 33313 954-792-6700 792-4839
Web: www.sorefjcc.org

Phone | Fax

Naples Museum of Art 5833 Pelican Bay Blvd. . . . . Naples FL 34108 239-597-1111
TF: 800-597-1900 ■ *Web:* artisnaples.org

National Museum of Naval Aviation
1750 Radford Blvd Ste C . . . . Pensacola FL 32508 850-452-3604 452-3296
TF General: 800-247-6289 ■ *Web:* www.navalaviationmuseum.org

Norton Museum of Art
1451 S Olive Ave . . . . West Palm Beach FL 33401 561-832-5196
Web: www.norton.org

Old Dillard Museum 1009 NW Fourth St . . . . Fort Lauderdale FL 33311 754-322-8828
Web: www.browardschools.com

Old Florida Museum 259 San Marco Ave. . . . . Saint Augustine FL 32084 904-824-8874
TF: 800-813-3208 ■ *Web:* www.oldfloridamuseum.com

Orange County Regional History Ctr
65 E Central Blvd . . . . Orlando FL 32801 407-836-8500
TF: 800-965-2030 ■ *Web:* www.thehistorycenter.org

Orlando Museum of Art 2416 N Mills Ave. . . . . Orlando FL 32803 407-896-4231 896-9920
TF: 800-435-7352 ■ *Web:* www.omart.org

Orlando Science Ctr 777 E Princeton St . . . . Orlando FL 32803 407-514-2000
TF: 888-672-4386 ■ *Web:* www.osc.org

Ormond Memorial Art Museum & Gardens
78 E Granada Blvd . . . . Ormond Beach FL 32176 386-676-3347 676-3244
Web: www.ormondartmuseum.org

Palm Beach Photographic Centre
415 Clematis St . . . . West Palm Beach FL 33401 561-253-2600
Web: www.workshop.org

Pensacola Museum of Art 407 S Jefferson St . . . . Pensacola FL 32502 850-432-6247 469-1532
Web: www.pensacolamuseum.org

Perez Art Museum Miami 1103 Biscayne Blvd. . . . . Miami FL 33130 305-375-3000 375-1725
Web: www.pamm.org

Pinellas County Heritage Village
11909 125th St N . . . . Largo FL 33774 727-582-2123
Web: www.pinellascounty.org

Pro Clear Aquatic Systems Inc
2959 Mercury Rd . . . . Jacksonville FL 32207 904-448-6800
Web: www.pro-clear.com

Ripley's Believe It or Not! Museum
19 San Marco Ave . . . . Saint Augustine FL 32084 904-824-1606 829-1790
TF: 800-226-6545 ■ *Web:* www.ripleys.com

Ripley's Believe It or Not! Orlando Odditorium
8201 International Dr . . . . Orlando FL 32819 407-345-0501
Web: www.ripleys.com

Ritz Theatre & La Villa Museum
829 N Davis St . . . . Jacksonville FL 32202 904-632-5555 632-5553
Web: www.ritzjacksonville.com

Saint Augustine Lighthouse & Museum
81 Lighthouse Ave . . . . Saint Augustine FL 32080 904-829-0745 808-1248
Web: www.staugustinelighthouse.com

Saint Petersburg Museum of History (SPMOH)
335 Second Ave NE . . . . Saint Petersburg FL 33701 727-894-1052 525-8689

South Florida Museum 201 Tenth St W. . . . . Bradenton FL 34205 941-746-4131 747-2556
Web: www.southfloridamuseum.org

South Florida Science Museum
4801 Dreher Trail N . . . . West Palm Beach FL 33405 561-832-1988 833-0551
Web: www.sfsciencecenter.org

Southeast Museum of Photography
1200 W International Speedway Blvd Bldg 100
Daytona Beach Community College . . . . Daytona Beach FL 32114 386-506-4475
Web: www.smponline.org

Stranahan House Museum Inc
335 SE Sixth Ave . . . . Fort Lauderdale FL 33301 954-524-4736 525-2838
TF: 800-435-7352 ■ *Web:* www.stranahanhouse.org

Tallahassee Antique Car Museum
6800 Mahan Dr. . . . . Tallahassee FL 32308 850-942-0137 576-8500
Web: www.tacm.com

Tallahassee Museum of History & Natural Science
3945 Museum Dr . . . . Tallahassee FL 32310 850-575-8684 574-8243
Web: www.tallahasseemuseum.org

Tampa Bay History Ctr 801 Old Water St. . . . . Tampa FL 33602 813-228-0097 223-7021
Web: www.tampabayhistorycenter.org

Tampa Museum of Art 120 W Gasparilla Plaza . . . . Tampa FL 33602 813-274-8131
TF: 866-790-4111 ■ *Web:* www.tampagov.net

University Galleries
400 SW 13th St Fine Arts Bldg B
PO Box 115803 . . . . Gainesville FL 32611 352-273-3000 846-0266
TF: 800-745-3000 ■ *Web:* www.arts.ufl.edu

Vizcaya Museum & Gardens 3251 S Miami Ave . . . . Miami FL 33129 305-250-9133 285-2004
Web: vizcaya.org

Wolfsonian Museum 1001 Washington Ave. . . . . Miami Beach FL 33139 305-531-1001 531-2133

Ximenez-Fatio House Museum
20 Aviles St . . . . Saint Augustine FL 32084 904-829-3575 829-3445
Web: www.ximenezfatiohouse.org

Ybor City Museum State Park 1818 Ninth Ave . . . . Tampa FL 33605 813-247-6323
Web: www.floridastateparks.org

Georgia

Phone | Fax

African-American Panoramic Experience Museum
135 Auburn Ave NE . . . . Atlanta GA 30303 404-523-2739 523-3248
Web: www.apexmuseum.org

Atlanta History Ctr 130 W Paces Ferry Rd . . . . Atlanta GA 30305 404-814-4000
Web: www.atlantahistorycenter.com

Augusta Museum of History 560 Reynolds St . . . . Augusta GA 30901 706-722-8454 724-5192
Web: www.augustamuseum.org

Challenger Learning Ctr
701 Front Ave Coca-Cola Space Science Ctr . . . . Columbus GA 31901 706-649-1470 649-1478
Web: www.ccssc.org

Coca-Cola Space Science Ctr 701 Front Ave. . . . . Columbus GA 31901 706-649-1470 649-1478
Web: www.ccssc.org

Columbus Museum 1251 Wynnton Rd . . . . Columbus GA 31906 706-748-2562 748-2570
Web: www.columbusmuseum.com

Davenport House Museum 324 E State St. . . . . Savannah GA 31401 912-236-8097 233-7938
Web: www.davenporthousemuseum.org

Fernbank Science Ctr 156 Heaton Pk Dr NE . . . . Atlanta GA 30307 678-874-7102 874-7110
Web: fernbank.edu

Georgia Museum of Art
90 Carlton St University of Georgia . . . . Athens GA 30602 706-542-4662
Web: www.uga.edu

Gertrude Herbert Institute of Art
506 Telfair St . . . . Augusta GA 30901 706-722-5495 722-3670
Web: www.ghia.org

Goethe Institut Atlanta/German Cultural Ctr
1197 Peachtree St NE . . . . Atlanta GA 30361 404-892-2388 892-3832
TF: 888-446-3843 ■ *Web:* www.goethe.de

High Museum of Art 1280 Peachtree St NE . . . . Atlanta GA 30309 404-733-4400 733-4502
Web: www.high.org

Jimmy Carter Library & Museum
441 Freedom Pkwy . . . . Atlanta GA 30307 404-865-7100 865-7102
Web: www.jimmycarterlibrary.gov

Lucy Craft Laney Museum 1116 Phillips St . . . . Augusta GA 30901 706-724-3576 724-3576
Web: www.lucycraftlaneymuseum.com

Michael C Carlos Museum 571 S Kilgo St . . . . Atlanta GA 30322 404-727-4282 727-4292
Web: www.carlos.emory.edu

Mighty Eighth Air Force Museum 175 Bourne Ave . . . . Pooler GA 31322 912-748-8888 748-0209
Web: www.mightyeighth.org

Morris Museum of Art 1 Tenth St . . . . Augusta GA 30901 706-724-7501 724-7612
Web: www.themorris.org

Museum of Arts & Sciences 4182 Forsyth Rd . . . . Macon GA 31210 478-477-3232 477-3251
Web: www.masmacon.org

Museum of Aviation PO Box 2469. . . . . Warner Robins GA 31099 478-926-2791
Web: www.museumofaviation.org

Museum of Design Atlanta
285 Peachtree Ctr Ave . . . . Atlanta GA 30303 404-979-6455 521-9311
Web: www.museumofdesign.org

National Infantry Museum 1775 Legacy Way. . . . . Columbus GA 31903 706-685-5800 545-5158
Web: www.nationalinfantrymuseum.org

National Museum of Patriotism
1927 Piedmont Cir . . . . Atlanta GA 30324 404-875-0691
Web: foundationofpatriotism.org

Oak Hill & Martha Berry Museum
2277 Martha Berry Hwy NW PO Box 490189 . . . . Mount Berry GA 30149 706-291-1883
Web: www.berry.edu

Oglethorpe University Museum of Art
4484 Peachtree Rd NE . . . . Atlanta GA 30319 404-364-8555 364-8556
Web: museum.oglethorpe.edu

Port Columbus National Civil War Naval Museum
1002 Victory Dr . . . . Port Columbus GA 31901 706-327-9798
Web: www.portcolumbus.org

Savannah History Museum 303 ML King Jr Blvd . . . . Savannah GA 31401 912-651-6840
Web: www.chsgeorgia.org

Ships of the Sea Maritime Museum
41 Martin Luther King Junior Blvd . . . . Savannah GA 31401 912-232-1511
Web: www.shipsofthesea.org

Telfair Museum of Art 121 Barnard St. . . . . Savannah GA 31401 912-790-8800
Web: telfair.org

Tubman African American Museum 310 Cherry St . . . . . . Macon GA 31201 478-743-8544 743-9063
Web: www.tubmanmuseum.com

Tybee Island Lighthouse & Museum
30 Meddin Dr . . . . Tybee Island GA 31328 912-786-5801 786-6538
Web: www.tybeelighthouse.org

William Breman Jewish Heritage Museum
1440 Spring St NW. . . . . Atlanta GA 30309 678-222-3700
Web: www.thebreman.org

World of Coca-Cola Atlanta 121 Baker St NW. . . . . Atlanta GA 30313 404-676-5151 586-6299
TF: 888-855-5701 ■ *Web:* www.worldofcoca-cola.com

Wren's Nest, The
1050 Ralph David Abernathy Blvd SW . . . . Atlanta GA 30310 404-753-7735 753-8535
Web: wrensnest.org

Hawaii

Phone | Fax

Bishop Museum 1525 Bernice St . . . . Honolulu HI 96817 808-847-3511
Web: www.bishopmuseum.org

Hawaii's Plantation Village (HPV)
94-695 Waipahu St. . . . . Waipahu HI 96797 808-677-0110 676-6727
Web: www.hawaiiplantationvillage.org

Honolulu Academy of Arts 900 S Beretania St . . . . Honolulu HI 96814 808-532-8700 532-8787
TF: 866-385-3849 ■ *Web:* honolulumuseum.org

Japanese Cultural Ctr of Hawaii
2454 S Beretania St . . . . Honolulu HI 96826 808-945-7633 944-1123
Web: www.jcch.com

King Kamehameha V - Judiciary History Ctr
417 S King St . . . . Honolulu HI 96813 808-539-4999
Web: jhchawaii.net

Lyman Museum & Mission House 276 Haili St. . . . . Hilo HI 96720 808-935-5021 969-7685
Web: www.lymanmuseum.org

Mission Houses Museum 553 S King St. . . . . Honolulu HI 96813 808-447-3910 545-2280
Web: www.missionhouses.org

Pacific Aviation Museum Pearl Harbor
319 Lexington Blvd. . . . . Honolulu HI 96818 808-441-1017
Web: www.pacificaviationmuseum.org

Polynesian Cultural Ctr 55-370 Kamehameha Hwy . . . . Laie HI 96762 808-293-3005 293-3027
TF: 800-367-7060 ■ *Web:* www.polynesia.com

Tropic Lightning Museum
Waianae Ave Bldg 361 . . . . Honolulu HI 96857 808-655-0438 655-8301

US Army Museum of Hawaii PO Box 8064 . . . . Honolulu HI 96830 808-438-2821 941-3617
Web: www.hiarmymuseumsoc.org

USS Bowfin Submarine Museum & Park
11 Arizona Memorial Dr . . . . Honolulu HI 96818 808-423-1341 422-5201
Web: www.bowfin.org

Idaho

				Phone	Fax
Basque Museum & Cultural Ctr 611 W Grove St *Web:* www.basquemuseum.com	Boise	ID	83702	208-343-2671	
Boise Art Museum 670 Julia Davis Dr *Web:* www.boiseartmuseum.org	Boise	ID	83702	208-345-8330	345-2247
Discovery Ctr of Idaho (DCI) 131 Myrtle St *Web:* www.dcidaho.com	Boise	ID	83702	208-343-9895	
Idaho Black History Museum 508 Julia Davis Dr *Web:* www.ibhm.org	Boise	ID	83702	208-433-0017	
Idaho Historical Museum 610 N Julia Davis Dr *Web:* history.idaho.gov	Boise	ID	83702	208-334-2120	334-4059
Idaho Military History Museum 4692 W Harvard St *Web:* museum.mil.idaho.gov	Boise	ID	83705	208-272-4841	
Museum of North Idaho 115 NW Blvd PO Box 812 *Web:* www.museumni.org	Coeur d'Alene	ID	83816	208-664-3448	664-3448
Nez Perce County Historical Society & Museum 0306 Third St *Web:* npchistsoc.org	Lewiston	ID	83501	208-743-2535	
Warhawk Air Museum 201 Municipal Dr *Web:* www.warhawkairmuseum.org	Nampa	ID	83687	208-465-6446	465-6232

Illinois

				Phone	Fax
Abraham Lincoln Presidential Library & Museum 112 N Sixth St *TF:* 800-610-2094 ■ *Web:* www.alplm.org	Springfield	IL	62701	217-557-6250	
African American Museum Hall of Fame 309 Du Sable St *Web:* aahfmpeoria.org	Peoria	IL	61605	309-673-2206	
Art Institute of Chicago 111 S Michigan Ave *Web:* www.artic.edu	Chicago	IL	60603	312-443-3600	
Balzekas Museum of Lithuanian Culture 6500 S Pulaski Rd *Web:* www.balzekasmuseum.org	Chicago	IL	60629	773-582-6500	582-5133
Burpee Museum of Natural History 737 N Main St *Web:* www.burpee.org	Rockford	IL	61103	815-965-3433	965-2703
Chanute Air Museum 1011 Pacesetter Dr	Rantoul	IL	61866	217-893-1613	892-5774
Chicago History Museum 1601 N Clark St *Web:* www.chicagohs.org	Chicago	IL	60614	312-642-4600	266-2077
Clarke House Museum 1827 S Indiana Ave *Web:* www.cityofchicago.org	Chicago	IL	60616	312-326-1480	
Daughters of Union Veterans of the Civil War 503 S Walnut St PO Box 211 *Web:* www.duvcw.org	Springfield	IL	62704	217-544-0616	
DuSable Museum of African American History 740 E 56th Pl *Web:* www.dusablemuseum.org	Chicago	IL	60637	773-947-0600	947-0716
Erlander Home Museum 404 S Third St *Web:* www.swedishhistorical.org	Rockford	IL	61104	815-963-5559	963-5559
Ernest Hemingway Museum 200 N Oak Pk Ave *Web:* www.ehfop.org	Oak Park	IL	60302	708-524-5383	
Ethnic Heritage Museum 1129 S Main St *Web:* ethnicheritagemuseum.org	Rockford	IL	61101	815-962-7402	
Field Museum, The 1400 S Lk Shore Dr *Web:* www.fieldmuseum.org	Chicago	IL	60605	312-922-9410	
Frank Lloyd Wright Home & Studio 951 Chicago Ave *Web:* flwright.org	Oak Park	IL	60302	708-848-1976	848-1248
Glessner House Museum 1800 S Prairie Ave *TF:* 800-657-0687 ■ *Web:* www.glessnerhouse.org	Chicago	IL	60616	312-326-1480	
Hellenic Museum & Cultural Ctr 333 S Halsted Ave *Web:* www.nationalhellenicmuseum.org	Chicago	IL	60661	312-655-1234	655-1221
Illinois State Military Museum 1301 N MacArthur Blvd *TF:* 800-732-8868	Springfield	IL	62702	217-761-3910	761-3709
Illinois State Museum 502 S Spring St *Web:* www.museum.state.il.us	Springfield	IL	62706	217-782-7386	782-1254
International Museum of Surgical Science 1524 N Lk Shore Dr *Web:* www.imss.org	Chicago	IL	60610	312-642-6502	642-9516
Intuit The Center for Intuitive & Outsider 756 N Milwaukee Ave *Web:* www.art.org	Chicago	IL	60642	312-243-9088	
ISM Dickson Mounds Museum 10956 N Dickson Mounds Rd *Web:* www.museum.state.il.us/ismsites/dickson	Lewistown	IL	61542	309-547-3721	547-3189
Krannert Art Museum & Kinkead Pavilion 500 E Peabody Dr *Web:* www.kam.uiuc.edu	Champaign	IL	61820	217-333-1861	333-0883
Lincoln's New Salem State Historic Site 15588 History Ln *Web:* www.lincolnsnewsalem.com	Petersburg	IL	62675	217-632-4000	632-4010
Lizzadro Museum of Lapidary Art 220 Cottage Hill Ave Wilder Pk *Web:* www.lizzadromuseum.org	Elmhurst	IL	60126	630-833-1616	833-1225
Midway Village Museum 6799 Guilford Rd *Web:* www.midwayvillage.com	Rockford	IL	61107	815-397-9112	397-9156
Museum of Contemporary Art 220 E Chicago Ave *Web:* www.mcachicago.org	Chicago	IL	60611	312-280-2660	
Museum of Contemporary Photography 600 S Michigan Ave Columbia College *Web:* www.mocp.org	Chicago	IL	60605	312-663-5554	
Museum of Science & Industry 5700 S Lk Shore Dr *TF:* 800-468-6674 ■ *Web:* www.msichicago.org	Chicago	IL	60637	773-684-1414	
Museum of the Grand Prairie 600 N Lombard St PO Box 1040 *Web:* www.museumofthegrandprairie.org	Mahomet	IL	61853	217-586-3360	586-5724
National Museum of Mexican Art 1852 W 19th St *Web:* www.nationalmuseumofmexicanart.org	Chicago	IL	60608	312-738-1503	738-9740
Oriental Institute Museum 1155 E 58th St University of Chicago *TF:* 800-791-9354 ■ *Web:* www.oi.uchicago.edu	Chicago	IL	60637	773-702-9514	702-9853
Peggy Notebaert Nature Museum 2430 N Cannon Dr *Web:* www.naturemuseum.org	Chicago	IL	60614	773-755-5100	
Peoria Riverfront Museum 222 SW Washington St *Web:* www.peoriariverfrontmuseum.org	Peoria	IL	61602	309-686-7000	
Polish Museum of America (PMA) 984 N Milwaukee Ave *Web:* www.polishmuseumofamerica.org	Chicago	IL	60642	773-384-3352	384-3799
Rockford Art Museum 711 N Main St *TF:* 800-521-0849 ■ *Web:* www.rockfordartmuseum.org	Rockford	IL	61103	815-968-2787	316-2179
Sousa Archives & Ctr for American Music (SACAM) 1103 S Sixth St 236 Harding Band Bldg *Web:* www.library.illinois.edu	Champaign	IL	61820	217-244-9309	244-8695
Spertus Museum 610 S Michigan Ave *Web:* www.spertus.edu	Chicago	IL	60605	312-322-1700	922-6406
Spurlock Museum *University of Illinois at Urbana* 600 S Gregory St *Web:* www.spurlock.illinois.edu	Urbana	IL	61801	217-333-2360	244-9419
Swedish American Museum 5211 N Clark St *Web:* www.swedishamericanmuseum.org	Chicago	IL	60640	773-728-8111	728-8870
Tinker Swiss Cottage Museum 411 Kent St *Web:* www.tinkercottage.com	Rockford	IL	61102	815-964-2424	
Ukrainian National Museum 2249 W Superior St *Web:* www.ukrainiannationalmuseum.org	Chicago	IL	60612	312-421-8020	
University Museum Southern Illinois University Faner Hall Rm 2469 *Web:* www.museum.siu.edu	Carbondale	IL	62901	618-453-5388	453-7409

Indiana

				Phone	Fax
Auburn Cord Duesenberg Museum 1600 S Wayne St *Web:* www.automobilemuseum.org	Auburn	IN	46706	260-925-1444	925-6266
Children's Museum of Indianapolis 3000 N Meridian St *TF:* 800-820-6214 ■ *Web:* www.childrensmuseum.org	Indianapolis	IN	46208	317-334-3322	920-2001
Conner Prairie Living History Museum 13400 Allisonville Rd *TF:* 800-966-1836 ■ *Web:* www.connerprairie.org	Fishers	IN	46038	317-776-6000	776-6014
Eiteljorg Museum of American Indians & Western Art 500 W Washington St *Web:* www.eiteljorg.org	Indianapolis	IN	46204	317-636-9378	275-1400
Evansville Museum of Arts History & Science 411 SE Riverside Dr *Web:* www.emuseum.org	Evansville	IN	47713	812-425-2406	421-7509
Firefighters' Museum 226 W Washington Blvd *Web:* fortwaynefiremuseum.com	Fort Wayne	IN	46802	260-426-0051	
Fort Wayne Museum of Art 311 E Main St *Web:* www.fwmoa.org	Fort Wayne	IN	46802	260-422-6467	422-1374
Freetown Village Living History Museum PO Box 1041 *Web:* www.freetown.org	Indianapolis	IN	46206	317-631-1870	631-0224
History Ctr 302 E Berry St *Web:* www.fwhistorycenter.com	Fort Wayne	IN	46802	260-426-2882	424-4419
Indiana Medical History Museum 3045 W Vermont St *Web:* imhm.org	Indianapolis	IN	46222	317-635-7329	635-7349
Indiana State Museum 650 W Washington St *Web:* www.in.gov	Indianapolis	IN	46204	317-232-1637	
Indiana University Art Museum 1133 E Seventh St *Web:* www.indiana.edu	Bloomington	IN	47405	812-855-5445	855-1023
Indianapolis Motor Speedway & Hall of Fame Museum 4790 W 16th St *Web:* www.indianapolismotorspeedway.com	Indianapolis	IN	46222	317-492-6747	492-6571
Indianapolis Museum of Art 4000 Michigan Rd *Web:* www.imamuseum.org	Indianapolis	IN	46208	317-923-1331	931-1978
James Whitcomb Riley Museum Home 528 Lockerbie St *Web:* www.rileykids.org	Indianapolis	IN	46202	317-631-5885	
Macedonian Tribune Museum 124 W Wayne St Ste 204 *Web:* www.macedonian.org	Fort Wayne	IN	46802	260-422-5900	422-1348
Mathers Museum of World Cultures 416 N Indiana Ave *Web:* indiana.edu	Bloomington	IN	47408	812-855-6873	855-0205
Monroe County History Ctr 202 E Sixth St *Web:* monroehistory.org	Bloomington	IN	47408	812-332-2517	355-5593
Reitz Home Museum 224 SE First St *Web:* reitzhome.com	Evansville	IN	47706	812-426-1871	426-2179
Science Central 1950 N Clinton St *TF:* 888-240-7268 ■ *Web:* www.sciencecentral.org	Fort Wayne	IN	46805	260-424-2400	422-2899
Snite Museum of Art University of Notre Dame *Web:* www.nd.edu/~sniteart	Notre Dame	IN	46556	574-631-5466	631-8501
South Bend Museum of Art (SBM) 120 S St Joseph St *Web:* www.southbendart.org	South Bend	IN	46601	574-235-9102	235-5782
Studebaker National Museum 201 Chapin St *TF:* 888-391-5600 ■ *Web:* www.studebakermuseum.org	South Bend	IN	46601	574-235-9714	235-5522

				Phone	Fax
Swope Art Museum 25 S Seventh St *Web:* www.swope.org	Terre Haute	IN	47807	812-238-1676	238-1677
Wylie House Museum 307 E Second St *Web:* www.indiana.edu	Bloomington	IN	47401	812-855-6224	

Iowa

				Phone	Fax
African American Historical Museum & Cultural Ctr of Iowa 55 12th Ave SE *Web:* www.blackiowa.org	Cedar Rapids	IA	52406	319-862-2101	862-2105
Cedar Rapids Museum of Art 410 Third Ave SE *Web:* www.crma.org	Cedar Rapids	IA	52401	319-366-7503	366-4111
Des Moines Art Ctr 4700 Grand Ave *Web:* www.desmoinesartcenter.org	Des Moines	IA	50312	515-277-4405	271-0357
Dubuque Museum of Art 701 Locust St *Web:* www.dbqart.com	Dubuque	IA	52001	563-557-1851	
Duffy's Collectible Cars 1195 Boyson Rd *Web:* www.duffys.com	Hiawatha	IA	52233	319-849-1400	
Figge Art Museum 225 W Second St *Web:* www.figgeartmuseum.org	Davenport	IA	52801	563-326-7804	326-7876
Granger House Museum 970 Tenth St *Web:* grangerhousemuseum.org	Marion	IA	52302	319-377-6672	
Herbert Hoover Presidential Library & Museum 210 Parkside Dr *Web:* www.hoover.archives.gov	West Branch	IA	52358	319-643-5301	643-6045
Hoyt Sherman Place 1501 Woodland Ave *Web:* www.hoytsherman.org	Des Moines	IA	50309	515-244-0507	
Iowa Gold Star Military Museum 7105 NW 70th Ave *TF:* 800-294-6607 ■ *Web:* www.iowanationalguard.com	Johnston	IA	50131	515-252-4531	
Iowa Masonic Library & Museum 813 First Ave SE *Web:* www.gl-iowa.org	Cedar Rapids	IA	52402	319-365-1438	
John Wayne Birthplace 216 S Second St *Web:* johnwaynebirthplace.museum	Winterset	IA	50273	515-462-1044	
Living History Farms 2600 111th St *Web:* www.lhf.org	Urbandale	IA	50322	515-278-5286	278-9808
National Balloon Museum 1601 N Jefferson Way PO Box 149 *Web:* www.nationalballoonmuseum.com	Indianola	IA	50125	515-961-3714	
National Czech & Slovak Museum & Library 87 16th Ave SW *Web:* www.ncsml.org	Cedar Rapids	IA	52404	319-362-8500	363-2209
National Farm Toy Museum 1110 16th Ave SE *TF:* 877-475-2727 ■ *Web:* www.nationalfarmtoymuseum.com	Dyersville	IA	52040	563-875-2727	
National Mississippi River Museum & Aquarium 350 E Third St *TF:* 800-226-3369 ■ *Web:* www.mississippirivermuseum.com	Dubuque	IA	52001	563-557-9545	
Pella Historical Village 507 Franklin St *Web:* pellahistorical.org	Pella	IA	50219	641-628-4311	
Science Ctr of Iowa 401 W Martin Luther King Jr Pkwy *Web:* www.sciowa.org	Des Moines	IA	50309	515-274-6868	274-3404
Sioux City Art Ctr 225 Nebraska St *Web:* siouxcityartcenter.org	Sioux City	IA	51101	712-279-6272	255-2921
Sioux City Public Museum 2901 Jackson St *Web:* www.sioux-city.org	Sioux City	IA	51104	712-279-6174	
State Historical Society of Iowa 600 E Locust St *Web:* iowaculture.gov/history	Des Moines	IA	50319	515-281-5111	242-6498
University Museum 3219 Hudson Rd University of Northern Iowa *TF:* 800-772-2736 ■ *Web:* www.uni.edu/museum	Cedar Falls	IA	50614	319-273-2188	273-6924
University of Iowa Museum of Art 1375 Hwy 1 W 1840 Studio Arts Bldg *Web:* uima.uiowa.edu	Iowa City	IA	52242	319-335-1727	335-3677

Kansas

				Phone	Fax
Boot Hill Museum 500 W Wyatt Earp Blvd *Web:* www.boothill.org	Dodge City	KS	67801	620-227-8188	
Combat Air Museum 7016 SE Forbes Ave Forbes Field *Web:* www.combatairmuseum.org	Topeka	KS	66619	785-862-3303	862-3304
Dwight D Eisenhower Presidential Library & Museum 200 SE Fourth St *TF:* 877-746-4453 ■ *Web:* www.eisenhower.utexas.edu	Abilene	KS	67410	785-263-6700	263-6715
Great Plains Transportation Museum 700 E Douglas St *Web:* www.gptm.us	Wichita	KS	67202	316-263-0944	
Indian Ctr Museum *Mid America All Indian Ctr* 650 N Seneca St *Web:* theindiancenter.org	Wichita	KS	67203	316-350-3340	
Kansas African American Museum 601 N Water St *Web:* tkaamuseum.org	Wichita	KS	67203	316-262-7651	265-6953
Kansas Aviation Museum 3350 S George Washington Blvd *Web:* www.kansasaviationmuseum.org	Wichita	KS	67210	316-683-9242	683-0573
Kansas Museum of History 6425 SW Sixth St *TF:* 800-279-3730 ■ *Web:* www.kshs.org	Topeka	KS	66615	785-272-8681	272-8682
Lowell D Holmes Museum of Anthropology 114 Neff Hall Wichita State University *Web:* webs.wichita.edu/anthropology	Wichita	KS	67260	316-978-3195	978-3351
Mulvane Art Museum 1700 SW Jewell Ave *Web:* www.washburn.edu	Topeka	KS	66621	785-670-1124	
Museum of World Treasures 835 E First St *TF:* 888-700-1311 ■ *Web:* www.worldtreasures.org	Wichita	KS	67202	316-263-1311	
National Agricultural Ctr & Hall of Fame 630 N 126th St *Web:* www.aghalloffame.com	Bonner Springs	KS	66012	913-721-1075	
Old Cowtown Museum 1865 W Museum Blvd *Web:* www.oldcowtown.org	Wichita	KS	67203	316-219-1871	
Santa Fe Trail Ctr 1349 K-156 Hwy *Web:* www.santafetrailcenter.org	Larned	KS	67550	620-285-2054	285-7491
Spencer Museum of Art 1301 Mississippi St University of Kansas *Web:* www.spencerart.ku.edu	Lawrence	KS	66045	785-864-4710	864-3112
Strawberry Hill Museum & Cultural Ctr 720 N Fourth St *Web:* www.strawberryhillmuseum.org	Kansas City	KS	66101	913-371-3264	
Ulrich Museum of Art 1845 Fairmount St Wichita State University *Web:* wichita.edu	Wichita	KS	67260	316-978-3664	978-3898
Wichita Art Museum 1400 W Museum Blvd *Web:* www.wichitaartmuseum.org	Wichita	KS	67203	316-268-4921	268-4980
Wichita-Sedgwick County Historical Museum 204 S Main St *Web:* www.wichitahistory.org	Wichita	KS	67202	316-265-9314	265-9319

Kentucky

				Phone	Fax
American Saddlebred Museum 4083 Iron Works Pkwy *TF:* 800-829-4438 ■ *Web:* www.asbmuseum.org	Lexington	KY	40511	859-259-2746	255-4909
Aviation Museum of Kentucky 4020 Airport Rd *Web:* www.aviationky.org	Lexington	KY	40510	859-231-1219	
Bluegrass Scenic Railroad & Museum 175 Beasley Rd Woodford County Pk *Web:* www.bgrm.org	Versailles	KY	40383	859-873-2476	873-0408
Conrad Caldwell House Museum, The 1402 St James Ct *Web:* www.conrad-caldwell.org	Louisville	KY	40208	502-636-5023	
Farmington Historic Plantation 3033 BaRdstown Rd	Louisville	KY	40205	502-452-9920	456-1976
Filson Historical Society Museum 1310 S Third St *Web:* www.filsonhistorical.org	Louisville	KY	40208	502-635-5083	635-5086
Frazier International History Museum 829 W Main St *Web:* www.fraziermsmuseum.org	Louisville	KY	40202	502-753-5663	
Headley-Whitney Museum 4435 Old Frankfort Pike *Web:* www.headley-whitney.org	Lexington	KY	40510	859-255-6653	255-8375
International Museum of the Horse 4089 Iron Works Pkwy *TF:* 800-678-8813 ■ *Web:* www.imh.org	Lexington	KY	40511	859-259-4232	
John James Audubon Museum 3100 Hwy 41 N	Henderson	KY	42419	270-826-2247	
Kentucky Derby Museum 704 Central Ave *TF:* 800-273-3729 ■ *Web:* www.derbymuseum.org	Louisville	KY	40208	502-637-1111	636-5855
Kentucky Historical Society 100 W Broadway *Web:* history.ky.gov	Frankfort	KY	40601	502-564-1792	
Kentucky Military History Museum 125 E Main St *Web:* www.history.ky.gov	Frankfort	KY	40601	502-564-3265	
Louisville Science Ctr 727 W Main St *TF:* 800-591-2203 ■ *Web:* www.kysciencecenter.org	Louisville	KY	40202	502-561-6100	561-6145
Muhammad Ali Ctr 144 N Sixth St *Web:* www.alicenter.org	Louisville	KY	40202	502-584-9254	589-4905
Museum of The American Quilters Society Inc 215 Jefferson St *Web:* www.quiltmuseum.org	Paducah	KY	42001	270-442-8856	
National Corvette Museum 350 Corvette Dr *TF:* 800-538-3883 ■ *Web:* www.corvettemuseum.org	Bowling Green	KY	42101	270-781-7973	781-5286
Old State Capitol Museum 300 W Broadway St *Web:* history.ky.gov	Frankfort	KY	40601	502-564-2301	564-4701
Shaker Village of Pleasant Hill 3501 Lexington Rd *TF:* 800-734-5611 ■ *Web:* www.shakervillageky.org	Harrodsburg	KY	40330	859-734-5411	734-5411
Speed Art Museum, The 2035 S Third St *Web:* changingspeed.org	Louisville	KY	40208	502-634-2700	
Thomas Edison House 729-731 E Washington St	Louisville	KY	40202	502-585-5247	585-5231
University of Kentucky Art Museum Rose St & Euclid Ave *Web:* www.uky.edu/artmuseum	Lexington	KY	40506	859-257-5716	323-1994
University of Kentucky Museum of Anthropology 211 Lafferty Hall *Web:* anthropology.as.uky.edu	Lexington	KY	40506	859-257-2710	323-1968

Louisiana

				Phone	Fax
8th Air Force Museum 88 Shreveport Rd *Web:* barksdaleglobalpowermuseum.com	Bossier City	LA	71110	318-752-0055	
Alexandre Mouton House/Lafayette Museum 1122 Lafayette St	Lafayette	LA	70501	337-234-2208	234-2208
Cathedral of Saint John the Evangelist Museum 515 Cathedral St *Web:* www.saintjohncathedral.org/welcome.html	Lafayette	LA	70501	337-232-1322	232-1379
Confederate Museum 929 Camp St *Web:* www.confederatemuseum.com	New Orleans	LA	70130	504-523-4522	
Enchanted Mansion Doll Museum 190 Lee Dr *Web:* www.enchantedmansion.org	Baton Rouge	LA	70808	225-769-0005	
Gallier House Museum 1132 Royal St PO Box 56836 *Web:* www.hgghh.org	New Orleans	LA	70156	504-525-5661	568-9735

Phone | Fax

Grandmother's Buttons Museum
9814 Royal St .... Saint Francisville LA 70775 225-635-4107 635-6067
TF: 800-580-6941 ■ *Web:* www.grandmothersbuttons.com

Historic New Orleans Collection
533 Royal St .... New Orleans LA 70130 504-523-4662 598-7108
Web: www.hnoc.org

House of Broel's Historic Mansion & Dollhouse Museum
2220 St Charles Ave .... New Orleans LA 70130 504-522-2220
Web: www.houseofbroel.com

Imperial Calcasieu Museum
204 W Sallier St .... Lake Charles LA 70601 337-439-3797
Web: www.imperialcalcasieumuseum.org

Lafayette Museum 1122 Lafayette St .... Lafayette LA 70501 337-234-2208 234-2208
TF: 800-346-1958 ■ *Web:* lafayettetravel.com

Longue Vue House & Gardens 7 Bamboo Rd .... New Orleans LA 70124 504-488-5488 486-7015
Web: www.longuevue.com

Louisiana Art & Science Museum
100 S River Rd .... Baton Rouge LA 70802 225-344-5272 344-9477
Web: www.lasm.org

Louisiana Naval War Memorial
305 S River Rd .... Baton Rouge LA 70802 225-342-1942 342-2039
Web: www.usskidd.com

Louisiana State Museum 751 Chartres St .... New Orleans LA 70116 504-568-6968 568-4995
TF: 800-568-6968 ■ *Web:* www.crt.state.la.us

Louisiana State University Museum of Art
100 Lafayette St .... Baton Rouge LA 70801 225-389-7200 389-7219
Web: www.lsumoa.org

Magnolia Mound Plantation
2161 Nicholson Dr .... Baton Rouge LA 70802 225-343-4955 343-6739
Web: brec.org

Meadows Museum of Art at Centenary College
2911 Centenary Blvd .... Shreveport LA 71104 318-869-5169 869-5730
TF: 800-234-4448 ■ *Web:* www.centenary.edu/meadows

Musee Conti Historical Wax Museum of New Orleans
917 Rue Conti .... New Orleans LA 70112 504-525-2605

New Orleans Museum of Art
1 Collins Diboll Cir .... New Orleans LA 70124 504-658-4100 658-4199
Web: www.noma.org

New Orleans Pharmacy Museum
514 Chartres St .... New Orleans LA 70130 504-565-8027
Web: www.pharmacymuseum.org

Nottoway Plantation
31025 Louisiana Hwy 1 .... White Castle LA 70788 225-545-2730 545-8632
TF: 866-527-6884 ■ *Web:* www.nottoway.com

Ogden Museum of Southern Art 925 Camp St .... New Orleans LA 70130 504-539-9650
Web: www.ogdenmuseum.org

Old Arsenal Museum 900 State Capitol dr .... Baton Rouge LA 70802 225-342-0401
Web: www.sos.la.gov

Pitot House Museum 1440 Moss St .... New Orleans LA 70119 504-482-0312
Web: www.pitothouse.org

Plaquemine Lock State Historic Site
57730 Main St .... Plaquemine LA 70764 225-687-7158
TF: 877-987-7158 ■ *Web:* crt.state.la.us

RW Norton Art Gallery 4747 Creswell Ave .... Shreveport LA 71106 318-865-4201 869-0435
Web: www.rwnaf.org

Sci-Port Discovery Ctr
820 Clyde Fant Pkwy .... Shreveport LA 71101 318-424-3466 222-5592
TF: 877-724-7678 ■ *Web:* www.sciport.org

Southern University Museum of Art
801 Harding Blvd .... Baton Rouge LA 70807 225-771-4500
Web: www.sus.edu/pagedisplay.asp?p1=4371

Southern University Museum of Art (SUSLA)
3050 Martin Luther King Jr Dr .... Shreveport LA 71107 318-670-6000 670-6457
TF: 800-458-1472 ■ *Web:* www.susla.edu

Spring Street Historical Museum
525 Spring St .... Shreveport LA 71101 318-424-0964
Web: www.springstreetmuseum.com

Touchstone Wildlife & Art Museum
3386 Highway 80 .... Haughton LA 71037 318-949-2323
Web: touchstonemuseum.com

University Art Museum
710 E St Mary Blvd PO Box 42571 .... Lafayette LA 70503 337-482-2278 262-1268
Web: museum.louisiana.edu

West Baton Rouge Museum
845 N Jefferson Ave .... Port Allen LA 70767 225-336-2422 336-2448
TF: 888-881-6811 ■ *Web:* www.westbatonrougemuseum.com

West Feliciana Historical Society Museum
11757 Ferdinand St .... Saint Francisville LA 70775 225-635-4224 635-4626

Maine

Phone | Fax

Abbe Museum 26 Mt Desert St .... Bar Harbor ME 04609 207-288-3519 288-8979
Web: www.abbemuseum.org

Bangor Museum & History Ctr 159 Union St .... Bangor ME 04401 207-942-1900 942-1910
Web: www.bangorhistoricalsociety.org

Bowdoin College Museum of Art
9400 College Stn .... Brunswick ME 04011 207-725-3275
Web: www.bowdoin.edu

Brick Store Museum 117 Main St .... Kennebunk ME 04043 207-985-4802
Web: www.brickstoremuseum.org

Colby College Museum of Art
5600 Mayflower Hill .... Waterville ME 04901 207-859-5600 859-5606
Web: www.colby.edu

Cole Land Transportation Museum 405 Perry Rd .... Bangor ME 04401 207-990-3600 990-2653
Web: www.colemuseum.org

Farnsworth Art Museum 16 Museum St .... Rockland ME 04841 207-596-6457 596-0509
Web: www.farnsworthmuseum.org

Hudson Museum 5746 Collins Ctr for the Arts .... Orono ME 04469 207-581-1901 581-1950
Web: www.umaine.edu/hudsonmuseum

Maine Historical Society
489 Congress St Maine Historical Society .... Portland ME 04101 207-774-1822 775-4301
Web: mainehistory.org

Phone | Fax

Maine Maritime Museum 243 Washington St .... Bath ME 04530 207-443-1316 443-1665
Web: mainemaritimemuseum.org

Maine Narrow Gauge Railroad Museum
58 Fore St .... Portland ME 04101 207-828-0814
Web: www.mainenarrowgauge.org

Maine State Museum 83 State House Stn .... Augusta ME 04333 207-287-2301 287-6633
Web: www.mainestatemuseum.org

Museum at Portland Head Light
1000 Shore Rd .... Cape Elizabeth ME 04107 207-799-2661 799-2800
Web: www.portlandheadlight.com/museum.html

Old Fort Western 16 Cony St .... Augusta ME 04330 207-626-2385 626-2304
Web: www.oldfortwestern.org

Old Town Museum 353 Main St .... Old Town ME 04468 207-827-7256
Web: www.old-town.org

Penobscot Marine Museum
5 Church St PO Box 498 .... Searsport ME 04974 207-548-2529 548-2520
TF: 800-268-8030 ■ *Web:* www.penobscotmarinemuseum.org

Portland Fire Museum 157 Spring St .... Portland ME 04101 207-772-2040
Web: www.portlandfiremuseum.com

Portland Museum of Art 7 Congress Sq .... Portland ME 04101 207-775-6148 773-7324
Web: www.portlandmuseum.org

State House 1 State House Stn .... Augusta ME 04333 207-287-3531 287-6548
Web: www.maine.gov

Tate House Museum 1267 Westbrook St .... Portland ME 04102 207-774-6177 774-6198
Web: www.tatehouse.org

University of Maine Museum of Art
40 Harlow St Norumbega Hall .... Bangor ME 04401 207-561-3350 561-3351
Web: www.umma.umaine.edu

Manitoba

Phone | Fax

Ivan Franko Museum
1040 - 555 Main St 595 Pritchard Ave .... Winnipeg MB R3B1C3 204-947-1782 942-3749
TF: 866-747-9323 ■ *Web:* www.museumsmanitoba.com

Living Prairie Museum 2795 Ness Ave .... Winnipeg MB R3J3S4 204-832-0167
Web: www.livingprairie.ca

Manitoba Museum 190 Rupert Ave .... Winnipeg MB R3B0N2 204-956-2830 942-3679
Web: www.manitobamuseum.ca/main

Maryland

Phone | Fax

Accokeek Foundation 3400 Bryan Pt Rd .... Accokeek MD 20607 301-283-2113
Web: www.accokeekfoundation.org

American Visionary Art Museum 800 Key Hwy .... Baltimore MD 21230 410-244-1900 244-5858
Web: www.avam.org

Annapolis Maritime Museum
723 Second St PO Box 3088 .... Annapolis MD 21403 410-295-0104
Web: www.amaritime.org

B & O Railroad Museum 901 W Pratt St .... Baltimore MD 21223 410-752-2490 752-2499
TF: 866-468-7630 ■ *Web:* www.borail.org

Baltimore Museum of Art 10 Art Museum Dr .... Baltimore MD 21218 443-573-1700 573-1582
TF: 800-735-2964 ■ *Web:* www.artbma.org

Baltimore Museum of Industry 1415 Key Hwy .... Baltimore MD 21230 410-727-4808 727-4869
Web: www.thebmi.org

Baltimore Streetcar Museum 1901 Falls Rd .... Baltimore MD 21211 410-547-0264 547-0264
Web: www.baltimoremd.com

Banneker-Douglas Museum 84 Franklin St .... Annapolis MD 21401 410-216-6180 974-2553
TF: 877-634-6361 ■ *Web:* bdmuseum.maryland.gov

Calvert Marine Museum
14200 Solomons Island Rd PO Box 97 .... Solomons MD 20688 410-326-2042 326-6691
TF: 800-735-2258 ■ *Web:* www.calvertmarinemuseum.com

Calvin B Taylor House Museum 208 N Main St .... Berlin MD 21811 410-641-1019
Web: www.taylorhousemuseum.org

Chesapeake Bay Maritime Museum
213 N Talbot St .... Saint Michaels MD 21663 410-745-2916 745-6088
Web: www.cbmm.org

Fire Museum of Maryland 1301 York Rd .... Lutherville MD 21093 410-321-7500
Web: www.firemuseummd.org

Fort McHenry National Monument & Historic Shrine
2400 E Fort Ave .... Baltimore MD 21230 410-962-4290 962-2500
TF: 866-945-7920 ■ *Web:* www.nps.gov

Hammond-Harwood House 19 Maryland Ave .... Annapolis MD 21401 410-263-4683
Web: www.hammondharwoodhouse.org

Historic Annapolis Foundation Museum
77 Main St .... Annapolis MD 21401 410-267-7619
Web: www.annapolis.org

Homewood Museum
3400 N Charles St Johns Hopkins University .... Baltimore MD 21218 410-516-5589 516-7859
Web: www.museums.jhu.edu

Jewish Museum of Maryland 15 Lloyd St .... Baltimore MD 21202 410-732-6400 732-6451
TF All: 800-235-4045 ■ *Web:* jewishmuseummd.org

Lacrosse Hall of Fame & Museum
113 W University Pkwy .... Baltimore MD 21210 410-235-6882 366-6735
TF: 866-877-7550 ■ *Web:* www.uslacrosse.org

Lovely Lane Museum 2200 St Paul St .... Baltimore MD 21218 410-889-4458
Web: www.lovelylanemuseum.org

Maryland Historical Society Museum & Library
201 W Monument St .... Baltimore MD 21201 410-685-3750 385-2105
TF: 800-537-5487 ■ *Web:* www.mdhs.org

Maryland Science Ctr 601 Light St .... Baltimore MD 21230 410-685-2370 545-5974
Web: www.mdsci.org

Mount Clare Museum House
1500 Washington Blvd Carroll Pk .... Baltimore MD 21230 410-837-3262 837-0251
Web: www.mountclare.org

National Children's Museum
145 Fleet St Ste 202 .... National Harbor MD 20745 301-392-2400
Web: www.ccm.org

National Great Blacks in Wax Museum
1601-03 E N Ave .... Baltimore MD 21213 410-563-3404
Web: www.ngbiwm.com

				Phone	Fax
National Museum of Dentistry 31 S Greene St *TF:* 866-787-8637 ■ *Web:* www.dental.umaryland.edu	Baltimore	MD	21201	410-706-0600	706-8313
National Museum of Health & Medicine 2500 Linden Ln *Web:* www.medicalmuseum.mil	Silver Spring	MD	20910	202-782-2200	
Ocean City Life-Saving Station Museum 813 S Atlantic Ave *Web:* www.ocmuseum.org	Ocean City	MD	21842	410-289-4991	289-4991
Reginald F Lewis Museum of Maryland African American History & Culture 830 E Pratt St **Fax Area Code:* 410 ■ *Web:* www.lewismuseum.org	Baltimore	MD	21202	443-263-1800	333-1138*
Star-Spangled Banner Flag House, The 844 E Pratt St *Web:* www.flaghouse.org	Baltimore	MD	21202	410-837-1793	
US Naval Academy Museum 118 Maryland Ave *Web:* www.usna.edu	Annapolis	MD	21402	410-293-2108	
Walters Art Museum 600 N Charles St *Web:* www.thewalters.org	Baltimore	MD	21201	410-547-9000	783-7969
Ward Museum of Wildfowl Art 909 S Schumaker Dr *Web:* www.wardmuseum.org	Salisbury	MD	21804	410-742-4988	742-3107
Washington County Museum of Fine Arts 401 Museum Dr PO Box 423 *Web:* www.wcmfa.org	Hagerstown	MD	21741	301-739-5727	745-3741
Wheels of Yesterday Antique & Classic Cars Museum 12708 Ocean Gateway	Ocean City	MD	21842	410-213-7329	

Massachusetts

				Phone	Fax
American Jewish Historical Society 101 Newbury St *Web:* www.ajhs.org	Boston	MA	02116	617-226-1245	
American Textile History Museum 491 Dutton St *Web:* www.athm.org	Lowell	MA	01854	978-441-0400	441-1412
Cape Cod Maritime Museum 135 S St PO Box 443 *Web:* www.capecodmaritimemuseum.org	Hyannis	MA	02601	508-775-1723	775-1706
Cape Cod Museum of Natural History 869 Main St *Web:* www.ccmnh.org	Brewster	MA	02631	508-896-3867	896-8844
Childrens Discovery Museum, The 177 Main St *Web:* www.discoverymuseums.org	Acton	MA	01720	978-264-4200	
Fogg Art Museum 32 Quincy St Harvard University *Web:* www.harvardartmuseums.org	Cambridge	MA	02138	617-495-9400	
Fuller Craft Museum 455 Oak St *Web:* fullercraft.org	Brockton	MA	02301	508-588-6000	587-6191
Gibson House Museum 137 Beacon St *Web:* www.thegibsonhouse.org	Boston	MA	02116	617-267-6338	267-6338
Harvard Museum of Natural History 26 Oxford St Harvard University *Web:* www.mcz.harvard.edu	Cambridge	MA	02138	617-495-5891	496-8308
Higgins Armory Museum 100 Barber Ave *Web:* www.higgins.org	Worcester	MA	01606	508-853-6015	
Historic Deerfield PO Box 321 *Web:* www.historic-deerfield.org	Deerfield	MA	01342	413-774-5581	775-7220
Isabella Stewart Gardner Museum 25 Evans Way *Web:* www.gardnermuseum.org	Boston	MA	02115	617-566-1401	
John F Kennedy Hyannis Museum 397 Main St *Web:* jfkhyannismuseum.org	Hyannis	MA	02601	508-790-3077	
John F Kennedy Presidential Library & Museum Columbia Pt *TF:* 866-535-1960 ■ *Web:* www.jfklibrary.org	Boston	MA	02125	617-514-1600	514-1652
Martha's Vineyard Museum 59 School St PO Box 1310 *Web:* www.mvmuseum.org	Edgartown	MA	02539	508-627-4441	627-4436
Massachusetts Historical Society, The 1154 Boylston St *Web:* www.masshist.org	Boston	MA	02215	617-646-0500	
MIT Museum 265 Massachusetts Ave *TF:* 800-228-9000 ■ *Web:* www.web.mit.edu	Cambridge	MA	02139	617-253-4444	253-8994
Museum of African American History 46 Joy St *Web:* www.afroammuseum.org	Boston	MA	02114	617-725-0022	720-5225
Museum of Fine Arts Boston 465 Huntington Ave *Web:* www.mfa.org	Boston	MA	02115	617-267-9300	
Museum of Science Science Pk *Web:* www.mos.org	Boston	MA	02114	617-723-2500	589-0454
Museum of the National Ctr of Afro-American Artists (NCAAA) 300 Walnut Ave *Web:* www.ncaaa.org/museum.html	Roxbury	MA	02119	617-442-8614	
New Bedford Whaling Museum 18 Johnny Cake Hill *Web:* www.whalingmuseum.org	New Bedford	MA	02740	508-997-0046	
Nichols House Museum 55 Mt Vernon St *Web:* www.nicholshousemuseum.org	Boston	MA	02108	617-227-6993	
Old Sturbridge Village 1 Old Sturbridge Village Rd *Web:* www.osv.org	Sturbridge	MA	01566	508-347-3362	347-0375
Peabody Essex Museum 161 Essex St *TF:* 866-745-1876 ■ *Web:* www.pem.org	Salem	MA	01970	978-745-1876	744-6776
Peabody Museum of Archaeology & Ethnology 11 Divinity Ave *Web:* www.peabody.harvard.edu	Cambridge	MA	02138	617-496-1027	495-7535
Pilgrim Hall Museum 75 Ct St *Web:* www.pilgrimhallmuseum.org	Plymouth	MA	02360	508-746-1620	
Plimoth Plantation 137 Warren Ave *Web:* www.plimoth.org	Plymouth	MA	02360	508-746-1622	
Revere Paul House 19 N Sq *Web:* www.paulreverehouse.org	Boston	MA	02113	617-523-2338	523-1775
Salem Witch Museum 19 1/2 Washington Sq N *TF:* 800-392-6100 ■ *Web:* www.salemwitchmuseum.com	Salem	MA	01970	978-744-1692	
Sandwich Glass Museum 129 Main St PO Box 103 *Web:* www.sandwichglassmuseum.org	Sandwich	MA	02563	508-888-0251	888-4941
Springfield Museums 21 Edwards St *TF:* 800-625-7738 ■ *Web:* www.springfieldmuseums.org	Springfield	MA	01103	413-263-6800	263-6807
Sterling & Francine Clark Art Institute 225 S St **Fax:* PR ■ *Web:* www.clarkart.edu	Williamstown	MA	01267	413-458-2303	458-5902*
Storrowton Village Museum 1305 Memorial Ave Eastern States Exposition *Web:* www.thebige.com	West Springfield	MA	01089	413-205-5051	205-5054
Titanic Museum 208 Main St *Web:* www.titanic1.org	Indian Orchard	MA	01151	413-543-4770	583-3633
USS Constitution Museum PO Box 291812 *Web:* www.ussconstitutionmuseum.org	Boston	MA	02129	617-426-1812	242-0496
Whaling Museum 13 Broad St *Web:* nha.org	Nantucket	MA	02554	508-228-1894	228-5618
Willard House & Clock Museum 11 Willard St *Web:* www.willardhouse.org	North Grafton	MA	01536	508-839-3500	
Worcester Art Museum 55 Salisbury St *Web:* www.worcesterart.org	Worcester	MA	01609	508-799-4406	798-5646
Worcester Historical Museum 30 Elm St *Web:* www.worcesterhistory.org	Worcester	MA	01609	508-753-8278	753-9070

Michigan

				Phone	Fax
Air Zoo, The 6151 Portage Rd *TF:* 866-524-7966 ■ *Web:* www.airzoo.org	Portage	MI	49002	269-382-6555	
Art Center Kalamazoo Inst 314 S Park St *Web:* www.kiarts.org	Kalamazoo	MI	49007	269-349-7775	
Automotive Hall of Fame 21400 Oakwood Blvd *Web:* www.automotivehalloffame.org	Dearborn	MI	48124	313-240-4000	240-8641
Charles H Wright Museum of African American History 315 E Warren Ave *Web:* thewright.org	Detroit	MI	48201	313-494-5800	494-5855
Cranbrook Art Museum 39221 Woodward Ave *Web:* www.cranbrookart.edu/museum	Bloomfield Hills	MI	48303	248-645-3323	645-3324
Cranbrook Institute of Science 39221 Woodward Ave PO Box 801 *Web:* www.cranbrook.edu	Bloomfield Hills	MI	48303	248-645-3000	645-3050
Detroit Historical Museum 5401 Woodward Ave *Web:* www.detroithistorical.org	Detroit	MI	48202	313-833-1805	833-5342
Detroit Institute of Arts 5200 Woodward Ave *Web:* www.dia.org	Detroit	MI	48202	313-833-7900	
Dossin Great Lakes Museum 100 Strand Dr Belle Isle *Web:* www.detroithistorical.org	Detroit	MI	48207	313-833-5538	833-5342
Exhibit Museum of Natural History 1109 Geddes Ave *Web:* www.lsa.umich.edu	Ann Arbor	MI	48109	734-764-0478	647-2767
Flint Institute of Arts 1120 E Kearsley St *Web:* www.flintarts.org	Flint	MI	48503	810-234-1695	234-1692
Gallerie 454 15105 Kercheval Ave *Web:* www.gallerie454.com	Grosse Pointe Park	MI	48230	313-822-4454	822-3768
Gerald R Ford Museum 303 Pearl St NW *TF:* 800-888-9487 ■ *Web:* fordlibrarymuseum.gov	Grand Rapids	MI	49504	616-254-0400	254-0386
Grand Rapids Art Museum 101 Monroe Ctr *TF:* 800-272-8258 ■ *Web:* www.artmuseumgr.org	Grand Rapids	MI	49503	616-831-1000	831-1001
Greenfield Village 20900 Oakwood Blvd **Fax:* Cust Svc ■ *TF:* 800-835-5237 ■ *Web:* thehenryford.org/village	Dearborn	MI	48124	313-271-1620	982-6225*
Henry Ford Museum 20900 Oakwood Blvd *TF:* 800-835-5237 ■ *Web:* thehenryford.org	Dearborn	MI	48124	313-271-1620	982-6225
Historic Hack House Museum 775 County St *Web:* www.michigan.org	Milan	MI	48160	734-439-7522	
Holocaust Memorial Ctr 28123 OrchaRd Lake Rd *TF:* 800-875-5275 ■ *Web:* www.holocaustcenter.org	Farmington Hills	MI	48334	248-553-2400	553-2433
Impression 5 Science Ctr 200 Museum Dr *Web:* www.impression5.org	Lansing	MI	48933	517-485-8116	485-8125
International Institute of Metropolitan Detroit 111 E Kirby St *Web:* www.iimd.org	Detroit	MI	48202	313-871-8600	871-1651
Kelsey Museum of Archaeology 434 S State St University of Michigan *TF:* 800-562-3559 ■ *Web:* www.lsa.umich.edu/kelsey	Ann Arbor	MI	48109	734-763-3559	763-8976
Kempf House Museum 312 S Div St *Web:* www.kempfhousemuseum.org	Ann Arbor	MI	48104	734-994-4898	
Kingman Museum 175 Limit St *Web:* www.kingmanmuseum.org	Battle Creek	MI	49037	269-965-5117	
Leslie Science & Nature Ctr 1831 Traver Rd *Web:* lesliesnc.org	Ann Arbor	MI	48105	734-997-1553	997-1072
Manistee County Historical Museum 425 River St *Web:* www.manisteemuseum.org	Manistee	MI	49660	231-723-5531	
Michigan Historical Museum 702 W Kalamazoo St *Web:* michigan.gov	Lansing	MI	48915	517-373-3559	241-3647
Michigan State University Museum W Cir Dr *Web:* museum.msu.edu	East Lansing	MI	48824	517-355-2370	432-2846
Michigan Women's Historical Ctr & Hall of Fame 213 W Main St *Web:* www.michiganwomenshalloffame.org	Lansing	MI	48933	517-484-1880	372-0170
Midland Ctr for the Arts Inc 1801 W St Andrews Rd *Web:* www.mcfta.org	Midland	MI	48640	989-631-5930	631-7890
Milford Historical Society 124 E Commerce St Ste 2 *Web:* www.milfordhistory.org	Milford	MI	48381	248-685-7308	
Monroe County Historical Museum 126 S Monroe St *Web:* co.monroe.mi.us	Monroe	MI	48161	734-240-7780	240-7788

Phone Fax

Montrose Historical & Telephone Pioneer Museum
144 E Hickory St. . . . . Montrose MI 48457 810-639-6644
Web: montrosemuseum.com

Motown Museum 2648 W Grand Blvd . . . . . Detroit MI 48208 313-875-2264 875-2267
Web: www.motownmuseum.org

Public Museum of Grand Rapids
272 Pearl St NW Van Andel Museum Ctr . . . . . Grand Rapids MI 49504 616-456-3977
Web: grpm.org

RE Olds Transportation Museum 240 Museum Dr . . . . . Lansing MI 48933 517-372-0529 372-2901
Web: www.reoldsmuseum.org

Rosedale Products Inc
3730 W Liberty Rd PO Box 1085 . . . . . Ann Arbor MI 48106 734-665-8201
Web: www.rosedaleproducts.com

Sloan Museum 1221 E Kearsley St . . . . . Flint MI 48503 810-237-3450 237-3451
Web: 'www.sloanlongway.org

Tuskegee Airman Natl Historical Museum
6325 W Jefferson . . . . . Detroit MI 48209 313-843-8849 595-6576*
**Fax Area Code:* 800 ■ *Web:* www.tuskegeemuseum.org

University of Michigan Museum of Art
525 S State St. . . . . Ann Arbor MI 48109 734-764-0395 764-3731
Web: www.umma.umich.edu

Voigt House Victorian Museum
115 College Ave SE . . . . . Grand Rapids MI 49504 616-929-1700
Web: grpm.org

Ypsilanti Historical Museum 220 N Huron St . . . . . Ypsilanti MI 48197 734-482-4990
Web: www.ypsilantihistoricalsociety.org

Minnesota

Phone Fax

American Swedish Institute, The (ASI)
2600 Pk Ave . . . . . Minneapolis MN 55407 612-871-4907 871-8682
Web: www.asimn.org

Bakken, The 3537 Zenith Ave S. . . . . . Minneapolis MN 55416 612-926-3878 927-7265
Web: www.thebakken.org

Bell Museum of Natural History
10 Church St SE. . . . . Minneapolis MN 55455 612-624-7083 626-7704
Web: www.bellmuseum.umn.edu

Depot, The
Saint Louis County Heritage & Arts Ctr
506 W Michigan St . . . . . Duluth MN 55802 218-727-8025
Web: www.duluthdepot.org

Fitger's Brewery Museum 600 E Superior St . . . . . Duluth MN 55802 218-722-8826 722-8826
TF: 888-348-4377 ■ *Web:* www.fitgers.com

Gibbs Museum of Pioneer & Dakotah Life
2097 W Larpenteur Ave . . . . . Saint Paul MN 55113 651-646-8629 659-0345
Web: www.rchs.com

Hennepin History Museum 2303 Third Ave S. . . . . . Minneapolis MN 55404 612-870-1329
Web: www.hennepinhistory.org

Juxtaposition Arts Inc
2007 Emerson Ave N . . . . . Minneapolis MN 55411 612-588-1148
Web: www.juxtaposition.org

Karpeles Manuscript Library Museum
902 E First St . . . . . Duluth MN 55805 218-728-0630
Web: www.rain.org

Lake Superior Maritime Visitors Ctr
600 Lake Ave S. . . . . Duluth MN 55802 218-727-2497
Web: www.lsmma.com

Lake Superior Railroad Museum
506 W Michigan St. . . . . Duluth MN 55802 218-727-8025
Web: www.lsrm.org

Mill City Museum 704 S Second St . . . . . Minneapolis MN 55401 612-341-7555
TF: 800-657-3773 ■ *Web:* www.millcitymuseum.org

Minneapolis Institute of Arts
2400 Third Ave S . . . . . Minneapolis MN 55404 612-870-3000 870-3004
TF: 888-642-2787 ■ *Web:* new.artsmia.org

Minnesota Discovery Ctr 1005 Discovery Dr . . . . . Chisholm MN 55719 218-254-7959 254-7971
TF: 800-372-6437 ■ *Web:* www.mndiscoverycenter.com

Minnesota Historical Society History Ctr Museum
345 Kellogg Blvd W . . . . . Saint Paul MN 55102 651-259-3001 296-1004
TF: 800-657-3773 ■ *Web:* www.mnhs.org

Minnesota State University Moorhead Regional Science Ctr
1104 Seventh Ave S . . . . . Moorhead MN 56563 218-477-2920 477-4372
TF: 800-593-7246 ■ *Web:* www.mnstate.edu/regsci

Minnesota Transportation Museum
193 E Pennsylvania Ave . . . . . Saint Paul MN 55130 651-228-0263 293-0857
Web: transportationmuseum.org

Minnesota Wing Commemorative Air Force Museum
310 Airport Rd
Hanger 3 Fleming Field . . . . . South Saint Paul MN 55075 651-455-6942
Web: www.cafmn.org

Museum of Russian Art 5500 Stevens Ave S. . . . . . Minneapolis MN 55419 612-821-9045 821-4392
Web: www.tmora.org

Pavek Museum of Broadcasting
3517 Raleigh Ave . . . . . Saint Louis Park MN 55416 952-926-8198 929-6105
Web: www.pavekmuseum.org

Schubert Club Museum, The
75 W Fifth St 302 Landmark Ctr . . . . . Saint Paul MN 55102 651-292-3267 292-4317
Web: www.schubert.org

Science Museum of Minnesota
120 W Kellogg Blvd . . . . . Saint Paul MN 55102 651-221-9444 221-4777
TF: 800-221-9444 ■ *Web:* www.smm.org

Tweed Museum of Art 1201 ordean Ct . . . . . Duluth MN 55812 218-726-8222 726-8503
TF: 866-999-6995 ■ *Web:* www.d.umn.edu/tma

Twin Cities Model Railroad Museum
1021 Bandana Blvd E Ste 222. . . . . Saint Paul MN 55108 651-647-9628
Web: www.tcmrm.org

Walker Art Ctr 1750 Hennepin Ave. . . . . . Minneapolis MN 55403 612-375-7600 375-7618
TF: 888-339-4496 ■ *Web:* www.walkerart.org

Weisman Art Museum 333 E River Pkwy. . . . . . Minneapolis MN 55455 612-625-9494
Web: www.weisman.umn.edu

Mississippi

Phone Fax

Elvis Presley Birthplace & Museum
306 Elvis Presley Dr . . . . . Tupelo MS 38804 662-841-1245
Web: www.elvispresleybirthplace.com

International Checker Hall of Fame
220 Lynn Ray Rd . . . . . Petal MS 39465 601-582-7090
Web: nccheckers.org

International Museum of Muslim Cultures
201 E Pascagoula St Ste 102 . . . . . Jackson MS 39201 601-960-0440
Web: www.muslimmuseum.org

Landrum's Homestead & Village 1356 Hwy 15 S . . . . . Laurel MS 39443 601-649-2546
Web: landrums.com

Lauren Rogers Museum of Art 565 N Fifth Ave . . . . . Laurel MS 39440 601-649-6374 649-6379
Web: www.lrma.org

Manship House Museum 420 E Fortification St. . . . . . Jackson MS 39202 601-961-4724
Web: mdah.state.ms.us

Mississippi Agriculture & Forestry Museum/National Agricultural Aviation Museum
1150 Lakeland Dr . . . . . Jackson MS 39216 601-359-1100 982-4292
TF: 800-844-8687 ■ *Web:* www.mdac.ms.gov

Mississippi Dept of Archives & History (MDAH)
200 N St . . . . . Jackson MS 39201 601-576-6876 576-6964
Web: mdah.state.ms.us

Mississippi Museum of Art 380 S Lamar St. . . . . . Jackson MS 39201 601-960-1515 960-1505
TF: 866-843-9278 ■ *Web:* www.msmuseumart.org

Mississippi Museum of Natural Science
2148 Riverside Dr. . . . . . Jackson MS 39202 601-576-6000 354-7227
TF: 800-467-2757 ■ *Web:* www.mdwfp.com

Museum of the Southern Jewish Experience
PO Box 16528 . . . . . Jackson MS 39236 601-362-6357 366-6293
Web: isjl.org

Ohr-O'Keefe Museum of Art 386 Beach Blvd . . . . . Biloxi MS 39530 228-374-5547 436-3641
Web: www.georgeohr.org

Old Capitol Museum 100 S State St. . . . . . Jackson MS 39201 601-576-6920 576-6981
Web: www.mdah.state.ms.us

Oren Dunn City Museum
689 Rutherford Rd PO Box 2674. . . . . . Tupelo MS 38801 662-841-6438

Smith Robertson Museum & Cultural Ctr
528 Bloom St . . . . . Jackson MS 39202 601-960-1457
TF: 800-354-7695

Missouri

Phone Fax

Alexander Majors Historic House & Museum
8201 State Line Rd . . . . . Kansas City MO 64114 816-333-5556
Web: wornallmajors.org

American Jazz Museum 1616 E 18th St . . . . . Kansas City MO 64108 816-474-8463 474-0074
TF: 800-734-3447 ■ *Web:* americanjazzmuseum.org

American Kennel Club Museum of the Dog
1721 S Mason Rd. . . . . . Saint Louis MO 63131 314-821-3647
Web: www.akc.org

Arabia Steamboat Museum 400 Grand Blvd . . . . . Kansas City MO 64106 816-471-1856
Web: www.1856.com

Boone County Historical Society Museum
3801 Ponderosa St. . . . . . Columbia MO 65201 573-443-8936
Web: boonehistory.org

Chatillon-DeMenil Mansion & Museum
3352 DeMenil Pl. . . . . . Saint Louis MO 63118 314-771-5828
Web: www.demenil.org

Cole County Historical Museum
109 Madison St . . . . . Jefferson City MO 65101 573-635-1850
Web: www.colecohistsoc.org

Concordia Historical Institute
804 Seminary Pl . . . . . Saint Louis MO 63105 314-505-7900 505-7901
Web: www.lutheranhistory.org

Contemporary Art Museum Saint Louis
3750 Washington Blvd . . . . . Saint Louis MO 63108 314-535-4660 535-1226
Web: camstl.org

Dutton Family Theatre 3454 W 76 Country Blvd. . . . . . Branson MO 65616 417-332-2772 339-4900
Web: www.theduttons.com

Eugene Field House & Saint Louis Toy Museum
634 S Broadway . . . . . Saint Louis MO 63102 314-421-4689
Web: www.eugenefieldhouse.org

Harry S Truman Presidential Library & Museum
500 W Hwy 24 . . . . . Independence MO 64050 816-268-8200 268-8295
TF: 800-833-1225 ■ *Web:* www.trumanlibrary.org

Historic Aircraft Restoration Museum
3127 Creve Coeur Mill Rd . . . . . Saint Louis MO 63146 314-434-3368 878-6453
Web: www.historicaircraftrestorationmuseum.org

History Museum On The Square
157 central park square 4th Fl . . . . . Springfield MO 65806 417-864-1976
Web: historymuseumonthesquare.org

Hollywood Wax Museum 3030 W Hwy 76. . . . . . Branson MO 65616 417-337-8277 334-8202
TF: 800-214-3661 ■ *Web:* www.hollywoodwaxmuseum.com

International Photography Hall of Fame & Museum
3415 Olive St . . . . . St Louis MO 63103 405-424-4055
Web: www.iphf.org

John Wornall House Museum
6115 Wornall Rd. . . . . . Kansas City MO 64113 816-444-1858
Web: wornallhouse.org

Kemper Museum of Contemporary Art
4420 Warwick Blvd. . . . . . Kansas City MO 64111 816-753-5784 753-5806
Web: www.kemperart.org

Laumeier Sculpture Park & Museum
12580 Rott Rd. . . . . . Saint Louis MO 63127 314-615-5278
Web: laumeiersculpturepark.org

Laura Ingalls Wilder Museum & Home
3068 Hwy A . . . . . Mansfield MO 65704 877-924-7126
TF: 877-924-7126 ■ *Web:* www.lauraingallswilderhome.com

Liberty Memorial Museum 100 W 26th St . . . . . Kansas City MO 64108 816-784-1918
Web: www.theworldwar.org

	City	State	ZIP	Phone	Fax
Margaret Harwell Art Museum 421 N Main St *Web:* www.mham.org	Poplar Bluff	MO	63901	573-686-8002	
Miniature Museum of Greater Saint Louis 4746 Gravois Ave *Web:* www.miniaturemuseum.org	Saint Louis	MO	63116	314-832-7790	
Missouri History Museum 5700 Lindell Blvd PO Box 11940 *Web:* www.mohistory.org	Saint Louis	MO	63112	314-746-4599	454-3162
Missouri State Museum 201 W Capitol *Web:* mostateparks.com	Jefferson City	MO	65101	573-751-2854	
Museum of Anthropology 104 Swallow Hall University of Missouri *Web:* anthromuseum.missouri.edu	Columbia	MO	65211	573-882-3573	884-3627
Museum of Art & Archaeology 1 Pickard Hall *TF:* 866-447-9821 ■ *Web:* maa.missouri.edu	Columbia	MO	65211	573-882-3591	884-4039
Museum of Contemporary Religious Art 221 N Grand Blvd *TF:* 800-442-1142 ■ *Web:* www.slu.edu	Saint Louis	MO	63103	314-977-7170	977-2999
Museum of Missouri Military History 2302 Militia Dr *TF:* 888-526-6664 ■ *Web:* www.moguard.com	Jefferson City	MO	65101	573-638-9603	638-9676
Museums at 18th & Vine 1616 E 18th St *TF:* 800-734-3447 ■ *Web:* americanjazzmuseum.org	Kansas City	MO	64108	816-474-8463	474-0074
National Airline History Museum 201 Lou Holland Dr *Web:* www.airlinehistory.org	Kansas City	MO	64116	816-421-3401	421-3421
National World War I Museum 100 W 26th St *Web:* www.libertymemorialmuseum.org	Kansas City	MO	64108	816-784-1918	
Nelson-Atkins Museum of Art 4525 Oak St *Web:* www.nelson-atkins.org	Kansas City	MO	64111	816-751-1278	
Pony Express National Museum 914 Penn St *TF:* 800-530-5930 ■ *Web:* www.ponyexpress.org	Saint Joseph	MO	64503	816-279-5059	233-9370
Ralph Foster Museum College of the Ozarks PO Box 17 *Web:* www.rfostermuseum.com	Point Lookout	MO	65726	417-690-3407	
Ripley's Believe It or Not! Museum 3326 W Hwy 76 *Web:* www.ripleys.com	Branson	MO	65616	417-337-5300	
Roy Rogers-Dale Evans Museum 3950 Green Mtn Dr *Web:* www.royrogers.com	Branson	MO	65616	417-339-1900	
Saint Louis Art Museum 1 Fine Arts Dr *Web:* www.slam.org	Saint Louis	MO	63110	314-721-0072	721-6172
Saint Louis Science Ctr 5050 Oakland Ave *TF:* 800-456-7572 ■ *Web:* www.slsc.org	Saint Louis	MO	63110	314-289-4400	535-0104
Saint Louis University Museum of Art 3663 Lindell Blvd O'Donnell Hall *Web:* sluma.slu.edu	Saint Louis	MO	63103	314-977-3399	
Sappington House Museum 1015 S Sappington Rd *Web:* sappingtonhouse.org	Crestwood	MO	63126	314-822-8171	
Shoal Creek Living History Museum 7000 NE Barry Rd Hodge Pk *Web:* www.shoalcreeklivinghistorymuseum.com	Kansas City	MO	64156	816-792-2655	
Soldiers Memorial Military Museum 1315 Chestnut St *Web:* mohistory.org/soldiersmemorial	Saint Louis	MO	63103	314-622-4550	
Springfield Art Museum 1111 E Brookside Dr *Web:* sgfmuseum.org	Springfield	MO	65807	417-837-5700	837-5704
State Historical Society of Missouri, The 1020 Lowry St *TF:* 800-747-6366 ■ *Web:* shsmo.org	Columbia	MO	65201	573-882-1187	884-4950

Montana

	City	State	ZIP	Phone	Fax
Children's Museum of Montana 22 Railroad Sq	Great Falls	MT	59401	406-452-6661	
CM Russell Museum 400 13th St N *Web:* www.cmrussell.org	Great Falls	MT	59401	406-727-8787	727-2402
Holter Museum of Art 12 E Lawrence St *Web:* www.holtermuseum.org	Helena	MT	59601	406-442-6400	442-2404
Malmstrom Air Force Base Museum & Air Park 341 Missile Wing/MU 21 77th St N Ste 144 *Web:* www.malmstrom.af.mil	Malmstrom AFB	MT	59402	406-731-2705	731-2769
Montana Historical Society Museum 225 N Roberts St *TF:* 800-243-9900 ■ *Web:* mhs.mt.gov	Helena	MT	59620	406-444-2694	444-2696
Museum of the Rockies 600 W Kagy Blvd Montana State University *Web:* www.museumoftherockies.org	Bozeman	MT	59717	406-994-1998	994-2682
Paris Gibson Square Museum of Art 1400 First Ave N *Web:* www.the-square.org	Great Falls	MT	59401	406-727-8255	727-8256
Peter Yegen Jr Yellowstone County Museum 1950 Terminal Cir *Web:* www.pyjrycm.org	Billings	MT	59105	406-256-6811	254-6031
World Museum of Mining 155 Museum Way PO Box 33 *Web:* www.miningmuseum.org	Butte	MT	59703	406-723-7211	723-7211
Yellowstone Art Museum 401 N 27th St *Web:* www.yellowstone.artmuseum.org	Billings	MT	59101	406-256-6804	256-6817
Yellowstone Western Heritage Ctr 2822 Montana Ave *Web:* www.ywhc.org	Billings	MT	59101	406-256-6809	256-6850

Nebraska

	City	State	ZIP	Phone	Fax
Bank of Florence Museum 8502 N 30th St *Web:* www.historicflorence.org/attractions.php	Omaha	NE	68112	402-496-9923	
Durham Museum 801 S Tenth St *Web:* www.durhammuseum.org	Omaha	NE	68108	402-444-5071	444-5397
El Museo Latino 4701 S 25th St *Web:* www.elmuseolatino.org	Omaha	NE	68107	402-731-1137	733-7012
Great Plains Art Museum 1155 Q St PO Box 880250 *Web:* www.unl.edu	Lincoln	NE	68588	402-472-6220	472-0463
Joslyn Art Museum 2200 Dodge St *Web:* www.joslyn.org	Omaha	NE	68102	402-342-3300	342-2376
Museum of Nebraska History 15th & P St PO Box 82554 *TF:* 800-833-6747 ■ *Web:* www.nebraskahistory.org/sites/mnh	Lincoln	NE	68508	402-471-4754	471-3314
National Museum of Roller Skating 4730 S St *Web:* www.rollerskatingmuseum.com	Lincoln	NE	68506	402-483-7551	483-1465
Nebraska Jewish Historical Museum 333 S 132nd St	Omaha	NE	68154	402-334-6441	
Sheldon Museum of Art PO Box 880300 *Web:* www.sheldonartmuseum.org	Lincoln	NE	68588	402-472-2461	
Strategic Air & Space Museum 28210 W Pk Hwy *Web:* sacmuseum.org	Ashland	NE	68003	402-944-3100	944-3160
Stuhr Museum of the Prairie Pioneer 3133 W Hwy 34 *Web:* stuhrmuseum.org	Grand Island	NE	68801	308-385-5316	385-5028
University of Nebraska State Museum 14Th & U *Web:* museum.unl.edu	Lincoln	NE	68588	402-472-2642	472-8899
University of Nebraska-Lincoln 1155 Q St Hewit Pl *Web:* www.unl.edu	Lincoln	NE	68588	402-472-5841	472-0463

Nevada

	City	State	ZIP	Phone	Fax
Atomic Testing Museum 755 E Flamingo Rd *Web:* www.nationalatomictestingmuseum.org	Las Vegas	NV	89119	702-794-5151	794-5155
Boulder City/Hoover Dam Museum 1305 Arizona St *Web:* www.bcmha.org	Boulder City	NV	89005	702-294-1988	
Carson Valley Museum & Cultural Ctr 1477 old US Hwy 395 S	Gardnerville	NV	89410	775-782-2555	783-8802
Churchill County Museum & Archives 1050 S Maine St *Web:* www.ccmuseum.org	Fallon	NV	89406	775-423-3677	423-3662
Clark County Museum 1830 S Boulder Hwy *Web:* clarkcountynv.gov	Henderson	NV	89002	702-455-7955	455-7948
Guggenheim Hermitage Museum 3355 Las Vegas Blvd S Venetian Resort Hotel & Casino *TF:* 800-329-6109 ■ *Web:* guggenheim.org	Las Vegas	NV	89109	212-423-3575	
Las Vegas Natural History Museum 900 Las Vegas Blvd N *Web:* www.lvnhm.org	Las Vegas	NV	89101	702-384-3466	
Lost City Museum of Archeology PO Box 807 *Web:* museums.nevadaculture.org	Overton	NV	89040	702-397-2193	397-8987
Marjorie Barrick Museum 4505 S Maryland Pkwy *TF:* 877-895-0334 ■ *Web:* www.unlv.edu/barrickmuseum	Las Vegas	NV	89154	702-895-3381	895-5737
National Automobile Museum 10 S Lake St *Web:* www.automuseum.org	Reno	NV	89501	775-333-9300	333-9309
Nevada Museum of Art 160 W Liberty St *Web:* www.nevadaart.org	Reno	NV	89501	775-329-3333	329-1541
Nevada State Museum 600 N Carson St *Web:* museums.nevadaculture.org	Carson City	NV	89701	775-687-4810	687-4168
Nevada State Railroad Museum 2180 S Carson St *Web:* www.nsrm-friends.org	Carson City	NV	89701	775-687-6953	
Northeastern Nevada Museum 1515 Idaho St *Web:* www.museumelko.org	Elko	NV	89801	775-738-3418	
Roberts House Museum 1207 N Carson St	Carson City	NV	89701	775-887-2174	
Sparks Heritage Museum 814 Victorian Ave *Web:* www.sparksmuseum.org	Sparks	NV	89431	775-355-1144	
Way It Was Museum 113 N St	Virginia City	NV	89440	775-847-0766	
Wilbur D May Museum 1595 N Sierra St *Web:* www.washoecounty.us	Reno	NV	89503	775-785-5961	785-4707

New Brunswick

	City	State	ZIP	Phone	Fax
New Brunswick Museum 1 Market Sq *TF:* 888-268-9595 ■ *Web:* www.nbm-mnb.ca/index.php?option=com_content&view=article&id=121&itemid=316	Saint John	NB	E2L4Z6	506-643-2300	643-6081
University of Moncton 18 Ave Antonine-Maillet *Web:* www.umoncton.ca	Moncton	NB	E1A3E9	506-858-4088	858-4043

New Hampshire

	City	State	ZIP	Phone	Fax
Canterbury Shaker Village 288 Shaker Rd *Web:* www.shakers.org	Canterbury	NH	03224	603-783-9511	
Currier Museum of Art 150 Ash St *Web:* www.currier.org	Manchester	NH	03104	603-669-6144	669-7194
Lawrence L Lee Scouting Museum 571 Holt Ave *Web:* www.scoutingmuseum.org	Manchester	NH	03109	603-669-8919	625-2467

	City	State	ZIP	Phone	Fax
Mount Kearsarge Indian Museum 18 Highlawn Rd PO Box 142 *Web:* indianmuseum.org	Warner	NH	03278	603-456-2600	456-3092
Museum of New Hampshire History 30 Park St *Web:* www.nhhistory.org	Concord	NH	03301	603-228-6688	
New Hampshire Historical Society 30 Pk St. *Web:* www.nhhistory.org	Concord	NH	03301	603-228-6688	
New Hampshire Institute of Art 148 Concord St *TF:* 866-241-4918 ■ *Web:* www.nhia.edu	Manchester	NH	03104	603-623-0313	647-0658
Seacoast Science Center Inc 570 Ocean Blvd. *Web:* www.seacoastsciencecenter.org	Rye	NH	03870	603-436-8043	
SEE Science Ctr 200 Bedford St *Web:* www.see-sciencecenter.org	Manchester	NH	03101	603-669-0400	669-0400
Strawbery Banke Museum 14 Hancock St *Web:* www.strawberybanke.org	Portsmouth	NH	03801	603-433-1100	433-1129

New Jersey

	City	State	ZIP	Phone	Fax
Afro-American Historical Society Museum 1841 Kennedy Blvd. *Web:* www.cityofjerseycity.org	Jersey City	NJ	07305	201-547-5262	547-5392
Aljira Ctr for Contemporary Arts 591 Broad St *TF:* 800-852-7699 ■ *Web:* www.aljira.org	Newark	NJ	07102	973-622-1600	622-6526
American Labor Museum/Botto House National Landmark 83 Norwood St *Web:* www.labormuseum.net	Haledon	NJ	07508	973-595-7953	595-7291
Atlantic County Historical Society Museum 907 Shore Rd *Web:* www.aclink.org	Somers Point	NJ	08244	609-927-5218	927-5218
Creative Glass Center of America 1501 Glasstown Rd. *Web:* www.wheatonarts.org	Millville	NJ	08332	856-825-6800	
Jersey City Museum 350 Montgomery St *Web:* jerseycityonline.com	Jersey City	NJ	07302	201-413-0303	413-9922
Liberty Science Ctr Liberty State Pk 222 Jersey City Blvd *Web:* www.lsc.org	Jersey City	NJ	07305	201-200-1000	
Marine Mammal Stranding Ctr 3625 Brigantine Blvd *Web:* www.mmsc.org	Brigantine	NJ	08203	609-266-0538	
Mid Atlantic Center for The Arts 1048 Washington St *TF:* 800-275-4278 ■ *Web:* www.capemaymac.org	Cape May	NJ	08204	609-884-5404	
Montclair Art Museum 3 S Mtn Ave *Web:* montclairartmuseum.org	Montclair	NJ	07042	973-746-5555	746-0536
Morris Museum 6 Normandy Heights Rd *Web:* www.morrismuseum.org	Morristown	NJ	07960	973-971-3700	
New Jersey Historical Society Museum 52 Pk Pl *Web:* www.jerseyhistory.org	Newark	NJ	07102	973-596-8500	596-6957
New Jersey State Museum 205 W State St. *Web:* www.state.nj.us/state/museum	Trenton	NJ	08625	609-292-6300	292-7636
Newark Museum 49 Washington St *TF:* 888-370-6765 ■ *Web:* www.newarkmuseum.org	Newark	NJ	07102	973-596-6550	642-0459
Noyes Museum of Art 733 Lily Lake Rd *Web:* www.noyesmuseum.org	Oceanville	NJ	08231	609-652-8848	652-6166
Old Barracks Museum 101 Barrack St *Web:* www.barracks.org	Trenton	NJ	08608	609-396-1776	777-4000
Paterson Museum 2 Market St Ste 1 *Web:* www.thepatersonmuseum.com	Paterson	NJ	07501	973-321-1260	
Ripley's Believe It or Not! Museum 1441 Boardwalk *Web:* ripleys.com	Atlantic City	NJ	08401	609-347-2001	
Trenton City Museum at Ellarslie Mansion PO Box 1034 *Web:* www.ellarslie.org	Trenton	NJ	08606	609-989-1191	989-3624

New Mexico

	City	State	ZIP	Phone	Fax
American International Rattlesnake Museum 202 San Felipe NW Ste A *Web:* www.rattlesnakes.com	Albuquerque	NM	87104	505-242-6569	242-6569
Bataan Memorial Museum 1050 Old Pecos Trl *Web:* bataanmuseum.com	Santa Fe	NM	87505	505-474-1670	474-1670
Bradbury Science Museum 1350 Central PO Box 1663 *Web:* www.lanl.gov	Los Alamos	NM	87545	505-667-4444	665-6932
El Rancho de las Golondrinas Museum 334 Los Pinos Rd *Web:* www.golondrinas.org	Santa Fe	NM	87507	505-471-2261	471-5623
Explora 1701 Mtn Rd NW *Web:* explora.us	Albuquerque	NM	87104	505-224-8300	224-8325
Georgia O'Keeffe Museum 217 Johnson St *Web:* www.okeeffemuseum.org	Santa Fe	NM	87501	505-946-1000	
Historical Lawmen Museum 845 Motel Blvd *TF:* 800-332-2121 ■ *Web:* donaanacounty.org	Las Cruces	NM	88007	575-525-1911	647-7800
Hubbard Museum of the American West 26301 Hwy 70 W PO Box 40 *Web:* hubbardmuseum.org	Ruidoso Downs	NM	88346	575-378-4142	378-4166
Indian Pueblo Cultural Ctr 2401 12th St NW *TF:* 866-855-7902 ■ *Web:* www.indianpueblo.org	Albuquerque	NM	87104	505-843-7270	
Institute of American Indian Arts Museum 108 Cathedral Pl *Web:* www.iaia.edu	Santa Fe	NM	87501	505-983-8900	
Las Cruces Museum of Natural History PO Box 20000 *Web:* www.las-cruces.org	Las Cruces	NM	88004	575-532-3372	
Los Alamos Historical Museum 1050 Bathtub Row PO Box 43 *Web:* www.losalamoshistory.org	Los Alamos	NM	87544	505-662-6272	662-6312
Maxwell Museum of Anthropology University of New Mexico *Web:* www.unm.edu	Albuquerque	NM	87131	505-277-4405	277-1547
Museum of Indian Arts & Culture 710 Camino Lejo PO Box 2087 *Web:* www.miaclab.org	Santa Fe	NM	87501	505-476-1250	476-1330
Museum of International Folk Art 706 Camino Lejo *Web:* www.internationalfolkart.org	Santa Fe	NM	87505	505-476-1200	476-1300
Museum of Spanish Colonial Arts 750 Camino Lejo *Web:* spanishcolonial.org	Santa Fe	NM	87502	505-982-2226	982-4585
New Mexico Farm & Ranch Heritage Museum 4100 Dripping Springs Rd *Web:* www.nmfarmandranchmuseum.org	Las Cruces	NM	88011	575-522-4100	522-3085
New Mexico Holocaust & Intolerance Museum & Study Ctr 616 Central Ave SW *Web:* www.nmholocaustmuseum.org	Albuquerque	NM	87102	505-247-0606	
New Mexico Museum of Art 107 W Palace Ave *TF:* 877-567-7380 ■ *Web:* www.nmartmuseum.org	Santa Fe	NM	87501	505-476-5072	476-5076
New Mexico Museum of Natural History & Science 1801 Mtn Rd NW *Web:* www.nmnaturalhistory.org	Albuquerque	NM	87104	505-841-2800	841-2866
New Mexico Museum of Space History Top of Hwy 2001 *TF:* 877-333-6589 ■ *Web:* www.nmspacemuseum.org	Alamogordo	NM	88311	575-437-2840	434-2245
New Mexico State University Museum University Ave & Solano Dr Kent Hall PO Box 30001 MSC 3564 *Web:* univmuseum.nmsu.edu	Las Cruces	NM	88001	575-646-3739	646-1419
Roswell Museum & Art Ctr 100 W 11th St *Web:* www.roswellmuseum.org	Roswell	NM	88201	575-624-6744	
Space Murals Museum 12450 Hwy 70 E	Las Cruces	NM	88011	575-382-0977	
Telephone Pioneer Museum of New Mexico 110 Fourth St NW *Web:* www.museumsusa.org	Albuquerque	NM	87102	505-842-2937	
Tinkertown Museum PO Box 303 *Web:* www.tinkertown.com	Sandia Park	NM	87047	505-281-5233	
University of New Mexico Art Museum 1 University of New Mexico *Web:* unmartmuseum.org	Albuquerque	NM	87131	505-277-4001	277-7315
Wheelwright Museum of the American Indian 704 Camino Lejo *TF:* 800-607-4636 ■ *Web:* www.wheelwright.org	Santa Fe	NM	87505	505-982-4636	989-7386
White Sands Missile Range Museum & Missile Park US Hwy 70 *Web:* www.wsmr-history.org	White Sands	NM	88002	575-678-8824	678-2199

New York

	City	State	ZIP	Phone	Fax
Albany Institute of History & Art 125 Washington Ave. *Web:* www.albanyinstitute.org	Albany	NY	12210	518-463-4478	462-1522
Albright-Knox Art Gallery 1285 Elmwood Ave *Web:* www.albrightknox.org	Buffalo	NY	14222	716-882-8700	882-1958
Alice Austen House Museum & Garden 2 Hylan Blvd *Web:* www.aliceausten.8m.com	Staten Island	NY	10305	718-816-4506	815-3959
American Folk Art Museum 2 Lincoln Sq. *Web:* www.folkartmuseum.org	New York	NY	10019	212-265-1040	
American Numismatic Society 75 Varick St 11th Fl *Web:* www.numismatics.org	New York	NY	10013	212-571-4470	571-4479
Amherst Museum 3755 Tonawanda Creek Rd. *Web:* www.bnhv.org	Amherst	NY	14228	716-689-1440	689-1409
Bartow-Pell Mansion Museum 895 Shore Rd Pelham Bay Pk *Web:* www.bartowpellmansionmuseum.org	Bronx	NY	10464	718-885-1461	885-9164
Bear Mountain Trailside Museums & Zoo Bear Mtn State Pk Rt 9 W *Web:* www.trailsidezoo.org	Bear Mountain	NY	10911	845-786-2701	
Bronx County Historical Society 3309 Bainbridge Ave *Web:* www.bronxhistoricalsociety.org	Bronx	NY	10467	718-881-8900	881-4827
Bronx Museum of the Arts 1040 Grand Concourse *Web:* www.bronxmuseum.org	Bronx	NY	10456	718-681-6000	681-6181
Brooklyn Historical Society 128 Pierrepont St *Web:* www.brooklynhistory.org	Brooklyn	NY	11201	718-222-4111	
Brooklyn Museum of Art 200 Eastern Pkwy *Web:* www.brooklynmuseum.org	Brooklyn	NY	11238	718-638-5000	501-6136
Buffalo Fire Historical Museum 1850 William St *Web:* bfhsmuseum.com	Buffalo	NY	14206	716-892-8400	
Buffalo Museum of Science 1020 Humboldt Pkwy *TF:* 866-291-6660 ■ *Web:* www.sciencebuff.org	Buffalo	NY	14211	716-896-5200	897-6723
Children's Museum of Science & Technology 250 Jordan Rd *Web:* www.cmost.org	Troy	NY	12180	518-235-2120	235-6836
Cloisters Museum Fort Tryon Pk *TF:* 800-662-3397 ■ *Web:* www.metmuseum.org	New York	NY	10040	212-923-3700	795-3640
Cooper-Hewitt National Design Museum (Smithsonian Institution) 2 E 91st St *Web:* www.cooperhewitt.org	New York	NY	10128	212-849-8400	849-8401
Corning Museum of Glass 1 Museum Way *TF Cust Svc:* 800-732-6845 ■ *Web:* www.cmog.org	Corning	NY	14830	607-937-5371	438-5410
Doyle New York 175 E 87th St *Web:* doyle.com	New York	NY	10128	212-427-2730	369-0892
Dyckman Farmhouse Museum 4881 Broadway at 204th St *Web:* www.dyckmanfarmhouse.org	New York	NY	10034	212-304-9422	

	City	State	ZIP	Phone	Fax
Empire State Aerosciences Museum 250 Rudy Chase Dr. *Web:* www.esam.org	Glenville	NY	12302	518-377-2191	377-1959
Erie Canal Museum 318 Erie Blvd E. *Web:* www.eriecanalmuseum.org	Syracuse	NY	13202	315-471-0593	471-7220
Everson Museum of Art 401 Harrison St. *Web:* www.everson.org	Syracuse	NY	13202	315-474-6064	474-6943
Fasny Museum of Firefighting 117 Harry Howard Ave *Web:* www.fasnyfiremuseum.com	Hudson	NY	12534	518-822-1875	
Franklin D Roosevelt Presidential Library & Museum 4079 Albany Post Rd *TF:* 800-337-8474 ■ *Web:* www.fdrlibrary.marist.edu	Hyde Park	NY	12538	845-486-7770	486-1147
Frick Collection 1 E 70th St *Web:* www.frick.org	New York	NY	10021	212-288-0700	628-4417
Genesee Country Village & Museum 1410 Flint Hill Rd *Web:* www.gcv.org	Mumford	NY	14511	585-538-6822	538-6927
Harbor Defense Museum 230 Sheridan Loop *Web:* harbordefensemuseum.com	Brooklyn	NY	11252	718-630-4349	
Herbert F Johnson Museum of Art 114 Central Ave *Web:* www.museum.cornell.edu	Ithaca	NY	14853	607-255-6464	
Hudson River Museum 511 Warburton Ave *Web:* www.hrm.org	Yonkers	NY	10701	914-963-4550	963-8558
Hyde Collection 161 Warren St. *Web:* www.hydecollection.org	Glens Falls	NY	12801	518-792-1761	792-9197
International Ctr of Photography 1133 Ave of the Americas *Web:* www.icp.org	New York	NY	10036	212-857-0000	
International Museum of Photography & Film at George Eastman House 900 E Ave *Web:* www.eastman.org	Rochester	NY	14607	585-271-3361	271-3970
Intrepid Sea-Air-Space Museum W 46th St & 12th Ave Pier 86 *TF:* 877-957-7447 ■ *Web:* www.intrepidmuseum.org	New York	NY	10036	212-245-0072	
Iron Island Museum 998 E Lovejoy St *Web:* www.ironislandmuseum.com	Buffalo	NY	14206	716-892-3084	
Iroquois Indian Museum 324 Caverns Rd *Web:* www.iroquoismuseum.org	Howes Cave	NY	12092	518-296-8949	
Jacques Marchais Museum of Tibetan Art 338 Lighthouse Ave *Web:* www.tibetanmuseum.org	Staten Island	NY	10306	718-987-3500	
Jefferson County Historical Society 228 Washington St *Web:* jeffersoncountyhistory.org	Watertown	NY	13601	315-782-3491	782-2913
Jewish Museum 1109 Fifth Ave *Web:* www.thejewishmuseum.org	New York	NY	10128	212-423-3200	423-3232
Karpeles Manuscript Library 453 Porter Ave. *Web:* www.rain.org/~karpeles	Buffalo	NY	14201	716-885-4139	
Katonah Museum of Art Inc 134 Jay St *Web:* www.katonahmuseum.org	Katonah	NY	10536	914-232-9555	
Long Island Museum of American Art History & Carriages 1200 Rt 25A *Web:* www.longislandmuseum.org	Stony Brook	NY	11790	631-751-0066	751-0353
Lower East Side Tenement Museum National Historic Site 108 Orchard St *Web:* www.tenement.org	New York	NY	10002	212-431-0233	431-0402
Madame Tussauds New York Inc 234 W 42nd St Times Sq *Web:* www.madametussauds.com	New York	NY	10036	212-512-9600	
Memorial Art Gallery of the University of Rochester 500 University Ave *Web:* www.mag.rochester.edu	Rochester	NY	14607	585-276-8900	
Metropolitan Museum of Art 1000 Fifth Ave *TF:* 800-468-7386 ■ *Web:* www.metmuseum.org	New York	NY	10028	212-879-5500	
Morris-Jumel Mansion 65 Jumel Terr at 160th St *Web:* www.morrisjumel.org	New York	NY	10032	212-923-8008	
Mount Vernon Hotel Museum & Garden 421 E 61st St *Web:* www.mvhm.org	New York	NY	10065	212-838-6878	838-7390
Munson-Williams-Proctor Arts Institute 310 Genesee St. *Web:* www.mwpai.org	Utica	NY	13502	315-797-0000	797-5608
Museo del Barrio 1230 Fifth Ave *Web:* www.elmuseo.org	New York	NY	10029	212-831-7272	
Museum of American Financial History 48 Wall St. *Web:* www.moaf.org	New York	NY	10005	212-908-4110	908-4601
Museum of American Illustration 128 E 63rd St *Web:* www.societyillustrators.org	New York	NY	10065	212-838-2560	838-2561
Museum of Arts & Design 2 Columbus Cir. *Web:* madmuseum.org	New York	NY	10019	212-299-7777	
Museum of Jewish Heritage 36 Battery Pl Battery Pk City *Web:* www.mjhnyc.org	New York	NY	10280	212-968-1800	
Museum of Modern Art 11 W 53rd St *Web:* www.moma.org	New York	NY	10019	212-708-9400	
Museum of Science & Technology 500 S Franklin St *Web:* www.most.org	Syracuse	NY	13202	315-425-9068	
Museum of Sex 233 Fifth Ave Rm 3b *Web:* museumofsex.com	New York	NY	10016	212-689-6337	
Museum of the City of New York 1220 Fifth Ave *Web:* www.mcny.org	New York	NY	10029	212-534-1672	423-0758
Museum of the Moving Image 3601 35th Ave	New York	NY	11106	718-777-6800	784-4681
National Academy Museum of Art 1083 Fifth Ave *Web:* www.nationalacademy.org	New York	NY	10128	212-369-4880	360-6795
National Museum of the American Indian (Smithsonian Institution) 1 Bowling Green *TF:* 800-242-6624 ■ *Web:* www.nmai.si.edu	New York	NY	10004	212-514-3700	
National Women's Hall of Fame 76 Fall St PO Box 335 *Web:* www.womenofthehall.org	Seneca Falls	NY	13148	315-568-8060	568-2976
Neuberger Museum of Art 735 Anderson Hill Rd Purchase College SUNY *Web:* www.neuberger.org	Purchase	NY	10577	914-251-6100	251-6101
New Museum of Contemporary Art 235 Bowery *Web:* www.newmuseum.org	New York	NY	10002	212-219-1222	
New York City Fire Museum 278 Spring St *Web:* www.nycfiremuseum.org	New York	NY	10013	212-691-1303	352-3117
New York City Police Museum 100 Old Slip *Web:* www.nycpm.org/gift-shop	New York	NY	10005	212-480-3100	480-9757
New York Hall of Science 47-01 111th St *Web:* www.nysci.org	Queens	NY	11368	718-699-0005	
New York Historical Society 170 Central Pk W *Web:* www.nyhistory.org	New York	NY	10024	212-873-3400	874-8706
New York State Museum 260 Madison Ave *Web:* www.nysm.nysed.gov	Albany	NY	12210	518-474-5877	486-3696
New York Transit Museum Boerum Pl & Schermerhorn St Fl 10 *Web:* mta.info/mta/museum	Brooklyn	NY	11201	718-694-1600	
Pedaling History Bicycle Museum 3943 N Buffalo Rd *Web:* www.pedalinghistory.com	Orchard Park	NY	14127	716-662-3853	
Pierpont Morgan Library 225 Madison Ave *Web:* www.themorgan.org	New York	NY	10016	212-685-0008	481-3484
Queens County Farm Museum 73-50 Little Neck Pkwy *Web:* www.queensfarm.org	Floral Park	NY	11004	718-347-3276	
Queens Museum of Art New York City Bldg *TF:* 866-867-9665 ■ *Web:* www.queensmuseum.org	Queens	NY	11368	718-592-9700	592-5778
Roberson Museum & Science Ctr 30 Front St *TF:* 888-269-5325 ■ *Web:* www.roberson.org	Binghamton	NY	13905	607-772-0660	771-8905
Rochester Museum & Science Ctr 657 E Ave. *Web:* www.rmsc.org	Rochester	NY	14607	585-271-4320	271-0492
Sainte Marie among the Iroquois Museum 6680 Onondaga Lk Pkwy *Web:* ongov.net	Liverpool	NY	13088	315-453-6768	
Schenectady Museum & Suits-Bueche Planetarium 15 Nott Terr Heights *Web:* www.schenectadymuseum.org	Schenectady	NY	12308	518-382-7890	382-7893
Solomon R Guggenheim Museum 1071 Fifth Ave *TF:* 800-329-6109 ■ *Web:* www.guggenheim.org	New York	NY	10128	212-423-3500	
South Street Seaport Museum 12 Fulton St *Web:* www.southstreetseaportmuseum.org	New York	NY	10038	212-748-8600	
Staten Island Institute of Arts & Sciences 75 Stuyvesant Pl. *Web:* statenislandmuseum.org	Staten Island	NY	10301	718-727-1135	273-5683
Steel Plant Museum 100 Lee St Heritage Discovery Ctr *Web:* steelplantmuseumwny.org	Buffalo	NY	14210	716-821-9361	
Strong - National Museum of Play 1 Manhattan Sq *Web:* www.museumofplay.org	Rochester	NY	14607	585-263-2700	263-2493
Studio Museum in Harlem 144 W 125th St. *Web:* www.studiomuseuminharlem.org	New York	NY	10027	212-864-4500	864-4800
Suffolk County Historical Society 300 W Main St *Web:* suffolkcountyhistoricalsociety.org	Riverhead	NY	11901	631-727-2881	727-3467
Ten Broeck Mansion 9 Ten Broeck Pl *Web:* tenbroeckmansion.org	Albany	NY	12201	518-436-9826	436-1489
Theodore Roosevelt Inaugural National Historic Site 641 Delaware Ave *Web:* www.nps.gov/thri	Buffalo	NY	14202	716-884-0095	884-0330
Ukrainian Museum 222 E Sixth St *Web:* www.ukrainianmuseum.org	New York	NY	10003	212-228-0110	228-1947
University Art Museum 1400 Washington Ave SUNY Albany *Web:* www.albany.edu/museum	Albany	NY	12222	518-442-4035	442-5075
Victorian Doll Museum 4332 Buffalo Rd *Web:* chilidollhospital.com	North Chili	NY	14514	585-247-0130	
Whitney Museum of American Art 945 Madison Ave *TF:* 800-944-8639 ■ *Web:* www.whitney.org	New York	NY	10021	212-570-3600	
Wildenstein & Co 19 E 64th St *Web:* www.wildenstein.com	New York	NY	10021	212-879-0500	
Yager Museum of Art & Culture, The Hartwick College PO Box 4020 *Web:* www.hartwick.edu/academics/museum	Oneonta	NY	13820	607-431-4000	
Yeshiva University Museum 15 W 16th St *Web:* www.yu.edu	New York	NY	10011	212-294-8330	

North Carolina

	City	State	ZIP	Phone	Fax
Antique Car Museum/Grovewood Gallery 111 Grovewood Rd *TF:* 877-622-7238 ■ *Web:* www.grovewood.com	Asheville	NC	28804	828-253-7651	
Artspace Inc 201 E Davie St *Web:* www.artspacenc.org	Raleigh	NC	27601	919-821-2787	
Asheville Art Museum 2 S Pack Sq PO Box 1717 *Web:* ashevilleart.org	Asheville	NC	28801	828-253-3227	257-4503
Backing Up Classics Auto Museum 4545 Concord Pkwy S *Web:* www.backingupclassics.com	Concord	NC	28027	704-788-9500	
CAM Raleigh (CAM) 409 W Martin St. *Web:* camraleigh.org	Raleigh	NC	27603	919-261-5920	
Charlotte Hawkins Brown Museum 6136 Burlington Rd PO Box B *Web:* www.nchistoricsites.org	Sedalia	NC	27342	336-449-4846	449-0176

Phone Fax

Charlotte Museum of History & Hezekiah Alexander Homesite
3500 Shamrock Dr .... Charlotte NC 28215 704-568-1774 566-1817
Web: www.charlottemuseum.org

Charlotte Nature Museum 1658 Sterling Rd. .... Charlotte NC 28209 704-372-6261
TF: 800-935-0553 ■ *Web:* www.charlottenaturemuseum.org

Charlotte Trolley Inc 2104 S Blvd .... Charlotte NC 28203 704-375-0850
Web: charlottetrolley.org

Colburn Earth Science Museum 2 S Pack Sq .... Asheville NC 28801 828-254-7162 257-4505
Web: colburnmuseum.org

EnergyExplorium 13339 Hagers Ferry Rd ....Huntersville NC 28078 980-875-5600 875-5602*
**Fax Area Code:* 704 ■ *TF:* 800-777-0003 ■ *Web:* m.duke-energy.com

Estes-Winn Memorial Automobile Museum
111 Grovewood Rd .... Asheville NC 28804 828-253-7651
TF: 877-622-7238 ■
Web: www.grovewood.com/about-us/estes-winn-antique-car-museum

Folk Art Ctr PO Box 9545 .... Asheville NC 28815 828-298-7928 298-7962
TF: 888-672-7717 ■ *Web:* www.southernhighlandguild.org

Greensboro Science Center
4301 Lawndale Dr. .... Greensboro NC 27455 336-288-3769 288-2531
Web: www.greensboroscience.org

Greenville Museum of Art 802 S Evans St .... Greenville NC 27834 252-758-1946 758-7989
Web: www.gmoa.org

International Civil Rights Ctr & Museum
134 S Elm St. .... Greensboro NC 27401 336-274-9199 274-6244
TF: 800-748-7116 ■ *Web:* www.sitinmovement.org

Joel Lane House Museum & Gardens
728 W Hargett St .... Raleigh NC 27603 919-833-3431
Web: www.joellane.org

Levine Museum of the New South
200 E Seventh St .... Charlotte NC 28202 704-333-1887 333-1896
Web: www.museumofthenewsouth.org

Marbles Kids Museum 201 E Hargett St .... Raleigh NC 27601 919-834-4040 834-3516
TF: 800-745-3000 ■ *Web:* www.marbleskidsmuseum.org

Mint Museum of Art 2730 Randolph Rd. .... Charlotte NC 28207 704-337-2000 337-2101
Web: www.mintmuseum.org

Museum of Anthropology
Wake Forest University Wingate Rd
PO Box 7267 .... Winston-Salem NC 27109 336-758-5282 758-5116
TF: 888-925-3622 ■ *Web:* www.wfu.edu

Museum of Early Southern Decorative Arts (MESDA)
924 S Main St. .... Winston-Salem NC 27101 336-721-7360 721-7367
TF: 800-441-5303 ■ *Web:* www.mesda.org

Nasher Museum of Art at Duke University
2001 Campus Dr Duke University. .... Durham NC 27701 919-684-5135 681-8624
Web: www.duke.edu

North Carolina Museum of Art
2110 Blue Ridge Rd .... Raleigh NC 27607 919-839-6262 733-8034
Web: www.ncartmuseum.org

North Carolina Museum of History
5 E Edenton St .... Raleigh NC 27601 919-807-7900 733-8655
Web: www.ncdcr.gov

North Carolina Museum of Life & Science
433 Murray Ave .... Durham NC 27704 919-220-5429 220-5575
Web: lifeandscience.org

North Carolina Museum of Natural Sciences
11 W Jones St .... Raleigh NC 27601 919-733-7450 733-1573
TF: 877-462-8724 ■ *Web:* www.naturalsciences.org

Old Salem 600 S Main St .... Winston-Salem NC 27101 336-721-7300 721-7335
TF: 800-441-5305 ■ *Web:* www.oldsalem.org

Raleigh City Museum 220 Fayetteville St. .... Raleigh NC 27601 919-996-2220
Web: www.cityofraleighmuseum.org

Reynolda House Museum of American Art
2250 Reynolda Rd .... Winston-Salem NC 27106 336-758-5150 758-5704
TF: 888-663-1149 ■ *Web:* www.reynoldahouse.org

Richard Petty Museum 142 W Academy St. .... Randleman NC 27317 336-495-1143
Web: www.richardpettymotorsports.com

Schiele Museum of Natural History & James H Lynn Planetarium
1500 E Garrison Blvd .... Gastonia NC 28054 704-866-6908 866-6041
Web: www.schielemuseum.org/planetarium.php

SciWorks Science Ctr & Environmental Park of Forsyth County
400 Hanes-Mill Rd .... Winston-Salem NC 27105 336-767-6730 661-1777
Web: www.sciworks.org

Smith McDowell House Museum
283 Victoria Rd. .... Asheville NC 28801 828-253-9231
Web: www.wnchistory.org

Weatherspoon Art Museum 500 Tate St. .... Greensboro NC 27402 336-334-5770 334-5907
TF: 877-862-4123 ■ *Web:* www.uncg.edu

North Dakota

Phone Fax

Bonanzaville USA 1351 Main Ave W. .... West Fargo ND 58078 701-282-2822 282-7606
Web: www.bonanzaville.org

Fargo Air Museum 1609 19th Ave N. ....Fargo ND 58102 701-293-8043 293-8103
Web: www.fargoairmuseum.org

Myra Museum 2405 Belmont Rd ....Grand Forks ND 58201 701-775-2216
Web: www.grandforkshistory.com

North Dakota Game & Fish Dept
100 N Bismarck Expy ....Bismarck ND 58501 701-328-6300 328-6352
TF: 800-406-6409 ■ *Web:* www.gf.nd.gov

North Dakota Museum of Art
261Centennial Dr S-7305. ....Grand Forks ND 58202 701-777-4195 777-4425
Web: www.ndmoa.com

Nova Scotia

Phone Fax

Anne Murray Centre 36 Main St .... Springhill NS B0M1X0 902-597-8614 597-2001
Web: www.annemurraycentre.com

Black Cultural Centre for Nova Scotia
10 Cherry Brook Rd ....Cherry Brook NS B2Z1A8 902-434-6223 434-2306
TF: 800-465-0767 ■ *Web:* web1.bccnsweb.com

Fisheries Museum of the Atlantic
68 Bluenose Dr PO Box 1363. ....Lunenburg NS B0J2C0 902-634-4794 634-8990
TF: 866-579-4909 ■ *Web:* museum.novascotia.ca

Maritime Museum of the Atlantic
1675 Lower Water St .... Halifax NS B3J1S3 902-424-7490 424-0612
Web: maritime.museum.gov.ns.ca

Nova Scotia Museum of Industry
147 N Foord St. ....Stellarton NS B0K1S0 902-755-5425 755-7045
Web: museumofindustry.novascotia.ca

Nova Scotia Museum of Natural History
1747 Summer St. .... Halifax NS B3H3A6 902-424-7353 424-0560
Web: naturalhistory.novascotia.ca

Ohio

Phone Fax

Akron Art Museum 1 S High St ....Akron OH 44308 330-376-9185 376-1180
Web: www.akronartmuseum.org

Akron Police - Community Relations
217 S High St Rm 402 ....Akron OH 44308 330-375-2390 375-2412
Web: akronohio.gov

Arms Family Museum of Local History
648 Wick Ave .... Youngstown OH 44502 330-743-2589 743-7210
Web: www.mahoninghistory.org

Blair Museum of Lithopanes
5403 Elmer Dr 5403 Elmer Dr. ....Toledo OH 43615 419-245-1356
Web: www.lithophanemuseum.org

Boonshoft Museum of Discovery
2600 DeWeese Pkwy ....Dayton OH 45414 937-275-7431 275-5811
Web: www.boonshoftmuseum.org

Butler Institute of American Art
524 Wick Ave .... Youngstown OH 44502 330-743-1711 743-9567
Web: www.butlerart.com

Carillon Historical Park 1000 Carillon Blvd ....Dayton OH 45409 937-293-2841 293-5798
Web: www.daytonhistory.org

Century Village 14653 E Pk St ....Burton OH 44021 440-834-1492
Web: centuryvillagemuseum.org

Cincinnati Art Museum 953 Eden Pk Dr .... Cincinnati OH 45202 513-721-2787
TF: 877-472-4226 ■ *Web:* www.cincinnatiartmuseum.org

Cincinnati History Museum
1301 Western Ave Cincinnati Museum Ctr. .... Cincinnati OH 45203 513-287-7000
TF: 800-733-2077 ■ *Web:* www.cincymuseum.org

Citizens Motorcar Company America's Packard Museum, The
420 S Ludlow St ....Dayton OH 45402 937-226-1710 224-1918
Web: www.americaspackardmuseum.org

Cleveland Museum of Art 11150 E Blvd. .... Cleveland OH 44106 216-421-7340 707-6679
TF Sales: 800-469-4449 ■ *Web:* www.clevelandart.org

Cleveland Museum of Natural History
1 Wade Oval Dr. .... Cleveland OH 44106 216-231-4600 231-5919
TF: 800-317-9155 ■ *Web:* www.cmnh.org

Columbus Museum of Art 480 E Broad St. .... Columbus OH 43215 614-221-6801 221-0226
Web: www.columbusmuseum.org

COSI Columbus 333 W Broad St .... Columbus OH 43215 614-228-2674 228-6363
TF: 888-819-2674 ■ *Web:* www.cosi.org

COSI Toledo 1 Discovery Way ....Toledo OH 43604 419-244-2674 255-2674
Web: imaginationstationtoledo.org

Crawford Auto-Aviation Museum 10825 E Blvd ...... Cleveland OH 44106 216-721-5722 721-0891
Web: wrhs.org

Dayton Art Institute 456 Belmonte Pk N ....Dayton OH 45405 937-223-5277 223-3140
TF: 800-272-8258 ■ *Web:* www.daytonartinstitute.org

Dittrick Museum of Medical History
11000 Euclid Ave .... Cleveland OH 44106 216-368-3648 368-0165
TF: 800-368-4723 ■ *Web:* www.cwru.edu

Dunham Tavern Museum 6709 Euclid Ave .... Cleveland OH 44103 216-431-1060
Web: www.dunhamtavern.org

Great Lakes Science Ctr 601 Erieside Ave .... Cleveland OH 44114 216-694-2000 696-2140
Web: www.greatscience.com

Hale Farm & Village 2686 Oakhill Rd PO Box 296 ....Bath OH 44210 330-666-3711
TF: 800-589-9703 ■ *Web:* www.wrhs.org

Harriet Beecher Stowe House
2950 Gilbert Ave. .... Cincinnati OH 45206 513-751-0651
Web: www.ohiohistory.org

Heritage Village Museum 11450 Lebanon Pk .... Cincinnati OH 45241 513-563-9484 563-0914
Web: www.heritagevillagecincinnati.org

Hower House 60 Fir Hill University of Akron ....Akron OH 44325 330-972-6909 384-2635
Web: www3.uakron.edu/howerhse

International Women's Air & Space Museum
1501 N Marginal Rd Burke Lakefront Airport .... Cleveland OH 44114 216-623-1111 623-1113
TF: 877-287-4752 ■ *Web:* www.iwasm.org

Invent Now, Inc 3701 Highland Park NW ....North Canton OH 44720 800-968-4332
TF: 800-968-4332 ■ *Web:* www.invent.org

Kelton House Museum & Garden 586 E Town St ..... Columbus OH 43215 614-464-2022
Web: www.keltonhouse.com

Kent State University Museum PO Box 5190 ....Kent OH 44242 330-672-3450 672-3218
TF: 800-988-5368 ■ *Web:* www.kent.edu

Krohn Conservatory 1501 Eden Pk Dr .... Cincinnati OH 45202 513-421-5707
Web: www.cincinnatiparks.com

Lake View Cemetery 12316 Euclid Ave. .... Cleveland OH 44106 216-421-2665 421-2415
Web: lakeviewcemetery.com

McDonough Museum of Art 525 Wick Ave. .... Youngstown OH 44502 330-941-1400 941-1492
Web: web.ysu.edu

Museum of Contemporary Art Cleveland
11400 Euclid Ave .... Cleveland OH 44106 216-421-8671 421-0737
Web: www.mocacleveland.org

Museum of Natural History & Science
1301 Western Ave Cincinnati Museum Ctr. .... Cincinnati OH 45203 513-287-7000
TF: 800-733-2077 ■ *Web:* www.cincymuseum.org

National Afro-American Museum & Cultural Ctr
1350 Brush Row Rd PO Box 578 .... Wilberforce OH 45384 937-376-4944 376-2007
TF: 800-752-2603 ■ *Web:* www.ohiohistory.org

National Inventors Hall of Fame
3701 Highland Park NW. .... North Canton OH 44720 800-968-4332
TF: 800-968-4332 ■ *Web:* www.invent.org

	City	State	ZIP	Phone	Fax
National Museum of the United States Air Force 1100 Spaatz St Wright-Patterson Air Force Base *Web:* www.nationalmuseum.af.mil	Dayton	OH	45433	937-255-3284	255-3286
National Underground Railroad Freedom Ctr 50 E Freedom Way *Web:* www.freedomcenter.org	Cincinnati	OH	45202	513-333-7739	
Ohio Craft Museum 1665 W Fifth Ave *Web:* www.ohiocraft.org	Columbus	OH	43212	614-486-4402	486-7110
Ohio Historical Society 1982 Velma Ave *TF:* 800-686-6124 ■ *Web:* www.ohiohistory.org	Columbus	OH	43211	614-297-2300	
Patterson Homestead Historic House Museum Rental Facility 1815 Brown St *Web:* www.daytonhistory.org	Dayton	OH	45409	937-222-9724	
Rock & Roll Hall of Fame & Museum 1100 Rock & Roll Blvd *Web:* www.rockhall.com	Cleveland	OH	44114	216-781-7625	515-1283
Roscoe Village 600 N Whitewoman St *TF:* 800-877-1830 ■ *Web:* www.roscoevillage.com	Coshocton	OH	43812	740-622-7644	623-6555
Sauder Village 22611 SR 2 *TF:* 800-590-9755 ■ *Web:* www.saudervillage.org	Archbold	OH	43502	419-446-2541	445-5251
Stan Hywet Hall & Gardens 714 N Portage Path *TF:* 888-836-5533 ■ *Web:* www.stanhywet.org	Akron	OH	44303	330-836-5533	
Taft Museum of Art, The 316 Pike St *Web:* www.taftmuseum.org	Cincinnati	OH	45202	513-241-0343	241-7762
Thurber House 77 Jefferson Ave *Web:* www.thurberhouse.org	Columbus	OH	43215	614-464-1032	280-3645
Toledo Firefighters Museum 918 Sylvania Ave *Web:* www.toledofiremuseum.com	Toledo	OH	43612	419-478-3473	
Toledo Museum of Art 2445 Monroe St *TF:* 800-644-6862 ■ *Web:* www.toledomuseum.org	Toledo	OH	43620	419-255-8000	255-5638
War Vet Museum 23 E Main St *Web:* warvetmuseum.org	Canfield	OH	44406	330-533-6311	533-6311
Western Reserve Historical Society Museum 10825 E Blvd *Web:* www.wrhs.org	Cleveland	OH	44106	216-721-5722	
Wexner Ctr for the Arts 1871 N High St Ohio State University *Web:* www.wexarts.org	Columbus	OH	43210	614-292-0330	292-3369
Works, The 55 S First St *Web:* www.attheworks.org	Newark	OH	43055	740-349-9277	

Oklahoma

	City	State	ZIP	Phone	Fax
45th Infantry Div Museum 2145 NE 36th St *Web:* www.45thdivisionmuseum.com	Oklahoma City	OK	73111	405-424-5313	
Cherokee Heritage Ctr & National Museum 21192 S Keeler Dr *TF:* 888-999-6007 ■ *Web:* www.cherokeeheritage.org	Park Hill	OK	74451	918-456-6007	
Elsing Museum 7777 S Lewis Ave *Web:* www.oru.edu	Tulsa	OK	74171	918-495-6262	
Five Civilized Tribes Museum 1101 Honor Heights Dr *Web:* www.fivetribes.org	Muskogee	OK	74401	918-683-1701	683-3070
Fred Jones Jr Museum of Art 555 Elm Ave University of Oklahoma *Web:* www.ou.edu	Norman	OK	73019	405-325-3272	325-7696
Gilcrease Museum 1400 N Gilcrease Museum Rd *TF:* 888-655-2278 ■ *Web:* gilcrease.org	Tulsa	OK	74127	918-596-2700	596-2770
Harn Homestead & 1889er Museum 1721 N Lincoln Blvd *Web:* www.harnhomestead.com	Oklahoma City	OK	73105	405-235-4058	235-4041
JM Davis Arms & Historical Museum PO Box 966 *Web:* www.thegunmuseum.com	Claremore	OK	74018	918-341-5707	341-5771
National Cowboy & Western Heritage Museum 1700 NE 63rd St *Web:* www.nationalcowboymuseum.org	Oklahoma City	OK	73111	405-478-2250	478-4714
Oklahoma City Museum of Art 415 Couch Dr *TF:* 800-579-9278 ■ *Web:* www.okcmoa.com	Oklahoma City	OK	73102	405-236-3100	236-3122
Oklahoma City National Memorial & Memorial Ctr Museum 620 N Harvey Ave *TF:* 888-542-4673 ■ *Web:* www.oklahomacitynationalmemorial.org	Oklahoma City	OK	73102	405-235-3313	235-3315
Oklahoma Jazz Hall of Fame 111 E First St Upper Level *Web:* www.okjazz.org	Tulsa	OK	74103	918-281-8600	948-7737
Oklahoma Museum of History 800 Nazih Zuhdi Dr *Web:* www.okhistory.org	Oklahoma City	OK	73105	405-522-5248	522-5402
Oklahoma Museum of Natural History 2401 Chautaugua Ave *Web:* samnoblemuseum.ou.edu	Norman	OK	73072	405-325-4712	
Oklahoma Territorial Museum 406 E Oklahoma Ave *Web:* www.okterritorialmuseum.org	Guthrie	OK	73044	405-282-1889	
Philbrook Museum of Art & Gardens 2727 S Rockford Rd *Web:* www.philbrook.org	Tulsa	OK	74114	918-749-7941	
Science Museum Oklahoma 2100 NE 52nd St *TF:* 800-532-7652 ■ *Web:* sciencemuseumok.org	Oklahoma City	OK	73111	405-602-6664	
Sherwin Miller Museum of Jewish Art 2021 E 71st St *Web:* www.jewishmuseum.net	Tulsa	OK	74136	918-492-1818	492-1888
Tulsa Air & Space Museum 3624 N 74 E Ave *Web:* www.tulsaairandspacemuseum.org	Tulsa	OK	74115	918-834-9900	834-6723
Will Rogers Memorial Museum 1720 W Will Rogers Blvd *TF:* 800-324-9455 ■ *Web:* willrogers.com	Claremore	OK	74017	918-341-0719	
Woolaroc Ranch Museum & Wildlife Preserve 1925 Woolaroc Ranch Rd *TF:* 888-966-5276 ■ *Web:* www.woolaroc.org	Bartlesville	OK	74003	918-336-0307	336-0084
World Organization of China Painters Museum 2641 NW Tenth St *Web:* wocporg.com	Oklahoma City	OK	73107	405-521-1234	521-1265

Ontario

	City	Prov	Postal Code	Phone	Fax
ARTspace 165 King St W *Web:* www.artspacechathamkent.com	Chatham	ON	N7M1E4	519-352-1064	
Bytown Museum 1 Canal Ln PO Box 523 Stn B *Web:* www.bytownmuseum.com	Ottawa	ON	K1P5P6	613-234-4570	234-4846
Canada Agriculture Museum Prince of Wales Dr PO Box 9724 Stn T *TF:* 866-442-4416 ■ *Web:* cafmuseum.techno-science.ca	Ottawa	ON	K1G5A3	613-991-3044	993-7923
Canada Aviation Museum & Space Museum 11 Aviation Pkwy *Web:* casmuseum.techno-science.ca	Ottawa	ON	K1K2X5	613-993-2010	990-3655
Canada Science & Technology Museum 1867 St Laurent Blvd PO Box 9724 *TF:* 866-442-4416 ■ *Web:* cstmuseum.techno-science.ca/en	Ottawa	ON	K1G5A3	613-991-3044	990-3654
Canadian Museum of Contemporary Photography 380 Sussex Dr PO Box 427 Stn A *TF:* 800-319-2787 ■ *Web:* www.gallery.ca	Ottawa	ON	K1N9N4	613-990-1985	993-4385
Canadian Museum of Nature 240 McLeod St **Fax:* Mktg ■ *TF:* 800-263-4433 ■ *Web:* www.nature.ca	Ottawa	ON	K2P2R1	613-566-4700	364-4021*
Fort Henry National Historic Site PO Box 213 *TF Cust Svc:* 800-437-2233 ■ *Web:* www.forthenry.com	Kingston	ON	K7L4V8	613-542-7388	542-3054
Gardiner Museum 111 Queen's Pk *Web:* www.gardinermuseum.on.ca	Toronto	ON	M5S2C7	416-586-8080	586-8085
Guinness World Records Museum 4943 Clifton Hill *TF:* 866-656-0310 ■ *Web:* falls.com	Niagara Falls	ON	L2G3N5	905-357-4330	
Lithuanian Museum/Archives of Canada 2185 Stavebank Rd *Web:* www.klb.org	Mississauga	ON	L5C1T3	416-533-3292	
Mackenzie House Museum 82 Bond St *Web:* www.toronto.ca	Toronto	ON	M5B1X2	416-392-6915	392-0114
Movieland Wax Museum of the Stars 4848 Clifton Hill *Web:* www.cliftonhill.com/attractions/movieland-wax-museum-stars	Niagara Falls	ON	L2G3N4	905-358-3061	
Ontario Science Centre 770 Don Mills Rd *TF:* 888-696-1110 ■ *Web:* www.ontariosciencecentre.ca	Toronto	ON	M3C1T3	416-696-1000	696-3166
Presqu'ile Provincial Park 328 Presqu Pkwy *Web:* ontarioparks.com	Brighton	ON	K0K1H0	613-475-4324	
Ripley's Believe It or Not! Museum 4960 Clifton Hill *Web:* ripleys.com/niagarafalls	Niagara Falls	ON	L2G3N4	905-356-2238	
Royal Canadian Military Institute 426 University Ave *TF:* 800-585-1072 ■ *Web:* www.rcmi.org	Toronto	ON	M5G1S9	416-597-0286	597-6919
Royal Ontario Museum 100 Queen's Pk *Web:* www.rom.on.ca	Toronto	ON	M5S2C6	416-586-8000	586-5504
Scarborough Historical Museum 1007 Brimley Rd *Web:* toronto.ca	Toronto	ON	M1P3E8	416-338-8807	
Toronto Aerospace Museum RPO Evans Brown Ln PO Box 60005 *Web:* www.casmuseum.org	Etobicoke	ON	M8W4Z8	416-638-6078	638-5509
Toronto's First Post Office 260 Adelaide St E *Web:* www.townofyork.com	Toronto	ON	M5A1N1	416-865-1833	
York Museum 2694 Eglinton Ave W *Web:* www.toronto.ca	Toronto	ON	M6M1T9	416-394-2759	

Oregon

	City	State	ZIP	Phone	Fax
Antique Powerland Museum 3995 Brooklake Rd NE *Web:* www.antiquepowerland.com	Brooks	OR	97303	503-393-2424	393-2424
Bush House Museum 600 Mission St SE *Web:* www.oregonlink.com/bush_house	Salem	OR	97302	503-363-4714	
Columbia River Maritime Museum 1792 Marine Dr *Web:* www.crmm.org	Astoria	OR	97103	503-325-2323	325-2331
Hallie Ford Museum of Art 700 State St *TF:* 844-232-7228 ■ *Web:* willamette.edu/arts/hfma	Salem	OR	97301	503-370-6855	375-5458
High Desert Museum 59800 S Hwy 97 *TF:* 866-632-9992 ■ *Web:* www.highdesertmuseum.org	Bend	OR	97702	541-382-4754	382-5256
Jensen Arctic Museum 590 Church St W *Web:* wou.edu/president/advancement/jensen	Monmouth	OR	97361	503-838-8468	838-8289
Jordan Schnitzer Museum of Art 1430 Johnson Ln *Web:* jsma.uoregon.edu	Eugene	OR	97403	541-346-3027	346-0976
Keizer Heritage Museum 980 Chemawa Rd NE *Web:* www.keizerheritage.org	Keizer	OR	97303	503-393-9660	393-0209
Klamath County 1451 Main St *Web:* co.klamath.or.us	Klamath Falls	OR	97601	541-883-4208	883-5170
Marion County Historical Society Museum (MCHS) 260 12th St SE *Web:* www.marionhistory.org	Salem	OR	97301	503-364-2128	
Oregon Air & Space Museum 90377 Boeing Dr *Web:* oasm.info	Eugene	OR	97402	541-461-1101	461-1101
Oregon Historical Society 1200 SW Pk Ave *Web:* www.ohs.org	Portland	OR	97205	503-222-1741	221-2035
Oregon Maritime Ctr & Museum 115 SW Ash St Ste 400-C *Web:* www.oregonmaritimemuseum.org	Portland	OR	97204	503-224-7724	

Name / Address	City	State	Zip	Phone	Fax
Oregon Museum of Science & Industry 1945 SE Water Ave	Portland	OR	97214	503-797-4000	797-4500
TF: 800-955-6674 ■ *Web:* www.omsi.edu					
Portland Art Museum 1219 SW Pk Ave	Portland	OR	97205	503-226-2811	226-4842
Web: www.portlandartmuseum.org					
Springfield Museum 590 Main St	Springfield	OR	97477	541-726-2300	
Tillamook County Pioneer Museum 2106 Second St	Tillamook	OR	97141	503-842-4553	842-4553
Web: www.tcpm.org					
University of Oregon Museum of Natural & Cultural History 1680 E 15th Ave	Eugene	OR	97401	541-346-3024	346-5334

Pennsylvania

Name / Address	City	State	Zip	Phone	Fax
Academy of Natural Sciences Museum 1900 Benjamin Franklin Pkwy	Philadelphia	PA	19103	215-299-1000	299-1028
Web: www.ansp.org					
African-American Museum in Philadelphia 701 Arch St	Philadelphia	PA	19106	215-574-0380	574-3110
Web: www.aampmuseum.org					
Allentown Art Museum 31 N Fifth St	Allentown	PA	18101	610-432-4333	434-7409
Web: www.allentownartmuseum.org					
American Helicopter Museum & Education Ctr 1220 American Blvd W	West Chester	PA	19380	610-436-9600	436-8642
Web: www.americanhelicopter.museum					
American Swedish Historical Museum 1900 Pattison Ave	Philadelphia	PA	19145	215-389-1776	389-7701
Web: www.americanswedish.org					
Andy Warhol Museum 117 Sandusky St	Pittsburgh	PA	15212	412-237-8300	237-8340
Web: www.warhol.org					
Atwater Kent Museum 15 S Seventh St	Philadelphia	PA	19106	215-685-4830	685-4837
Web: www.philadelphiahistory.org					
Barnes Foundation 300 N Latch's Ln	Merion	PA	19066	610-667-0290	664-4026
Web: www.barnesfoundation.org					
Brandywine Conservancy Inc US Rt 1	Chadds Ford	PA	19317	610-388-2700	
Web: www.brandywine.org/conservancy					
Brandywine River Museum 1 Hoffman's Mill Rd	Chadds Ford	PA	19317	610-388-2700	388-1197
Web: www.brandywine.org/museum					
Carnegie Museum of Art 4400 Forbes Ave	Pittsburgh	PA	15213	412-622-3131	622-3112
Web: www.cmoa.org					
Carnegie Science Ctr 1 Allegheny Ave	Pittsburgh	PA	15212	412-237-3400	237-3375
Web: www.carnegiesciencecenter.org					
Chester County Historical Society General Info Lin 225 N High St	West Chester	PA	19380	610-692-4800	
Web: www.chestercohistorical.org					
Da Vinci Discovery Ctr of Science & Technology 3145 Hamilton Blvd Bypass	Allentown	PA	18103	484-664-1002	
Web: www.davincisciencecenter.org					
Electric City Trolley Station & Museum 300 Cliff St	Scranton	PA	18503	570-963-6590	963-6447
TF: 800-732-0999 ■ *Web:* www.ectma.org					
Elfreth's Alley Museum 126 Elfreth's Alley	Philadelphia	PA	19106	215-574-0560	
Web: www.elfrethsalley.org					
Erie Art Museum 411 State St	Erie	PA	16501	814-459-5477	452-1744
Web: www.erieartmuseum.org					
Everhart Museum 1901 Mulberry St	Scranton	PA	18510	570-346-7186	346-0652
Web: everhart-museum.org					
Fabric Workshop & Museum 1214 Arch St	Philadelphia	PA	19107	215-561-8888	561-8887
Web: www.fabricworkshopandmuseum.org					
Fort Pitt Museum 601 Commonwealth Pl,Bldg C	Pittsburgh	PA	15222	412-471-1764	
Web: fortpittblockhouse.com					
Franklin Institute Science Museum 222 N 20th St	Philadelphia	PA	19103	215-448-1200	448-1235
TF: 800-732-0999 ■ *Web:* www.fi.edu					
Frick Art & Historical Ctr 7227 Reynolds St	Pittsburgh	PA	15208	412-371-0600	
Web: thefrickpittsburgh.org					
Gettysburg Battle Theatre 571 Steinwehr Ave	Gettysburg	PA	17325	717-334-6100	
Web: www.gettysburgbattlefieldtours.com					
Gettysburg Heritage Center 297 Steinwehr Ave	Gettysburg	PA	17325	717-334-6245	
Web: www.gettysburgmuseum.com					
Historical Society of Erie County, The 356 W sixth St Erie County Historical Society	Erie	PA	16507	814-454-1813	454-6890
Web: eriehistory.com					
Holocaust Museum & Resource Ctr 601 Jefferson Ave	Scranton	PA	18510	570-961-2300	346-6147
Web: www.jewishnepa.org					
Houdini Museum 1433 N Main Ave	Scranton	PA	18508	570-342-5555	
Web: www.houdini.org					
Independence Seaport Museum 211 S Columbus Blvd	Philadelphia	PA	19106	215-413-8655	925-6713
Web: www.phillyseaport.org					
Institute of Contemporary Art 118 S 36th St University of Pennsylvania	Philadelphia	PA	19104	215-898-7108	898-5050
Web: www.icaphila.org					
Kemerer Museum of Decorative Arts 427 N New St	Bethlehem	PA	18018	610-868-6868	
Web: historicbethlehem.org					
Lake Shore Railway Museum 31 Wall St Lake Shore Historical Society	North East	PA	16428	814-725-1911	725-1911
TF: 800-945-0340 ■ *Web:* lakeshorerailway.com					
Lehigh County Museum 432 W Walnut St	Allentown	PA	18102	610-435-1074	
Web: www.lchs.museum					
Mercer Museums 84 S Pine St	Doylestown	PA	18901	215-345-0210	
Web: www.mercermuseum.org					
Mummers Museum 1100 S Second St	Philadelphia	PA	19147	215-336-3050	389-5630
Web: www.mummersmuseum.com					
National Constitution Ctr 525 Arch St Independence Mall	Philadelphia	PA	19106	215-409-6600	409-6650
Web: www.constitutioncenter.org					
National Liberty Museum 321 Chestnut St	Philadelphia	PA	19106	215-925-2800	925-3800
Web: libertymuseum.org					
National Museum of American Jewish History 101 S Independence Mall E	Philadelphia	PA	19106	215-923-3811	923-0763
Web: www.nmajh.org					
National Watch & Clock Museum 514 Poplar St	Columbia	PA	17512	717-684-8261	684-0878
TF: 800-368-6511 ■ *Web:* www.nawcc.org					
North Museum of Natural History & Science 400 College Ave	Lancaster	PA	17603	717-291-3941	358-4504
TF: 800-732-0999 ■ *Web:* www.northmuseum.org					
Old Economy Village 270 16th St	Ambridge	PA	15003	724-266-4500	266-7506
Web: www.oldeconomyvillage.org					
Pennsylvania Academy of the Fine Arts Museum (PAFA) 118 N Broad St	Philadelphia	PA	19102	215-972-7600	569-0153
TF: 800-799-7233 ■ *Web:* pafa.org/1					
Pennsylvania Anthracite Heritage Museum Bald Mountain Rd Ste 1	Scranton	PA	18504	570-963-4804	963-4194
TF: 800-732-0999 ■ *Web:* anthracitemuseum.org					
Philadelphia Museum of Art 2600 Benjamin Franklin Pkwy	Philadelphia	PA	19130	215-763-8100	236-4465
TF: 800-732-0999 ■ *Web:* www.philamuseum.org					
Photo Antiquities-Museum of Photographic History 531 E Ohio St	Pittsburgh	PA	15212	412-231-7881	231-1217
Web: www.photoantiquities.org					
Polish American Cultural Ctr Museum 308 Walnut St	Philadelphia	PA	19106	215-922-1700	922-1518
Web: www.polishamericancenter.org					
Reading Public Museum & Art Gallery 500 Museum Rd	Reading	PA	19611	610-371-5850	371-5632
Web: readingpublicmuseum.org					
Rosenbach Museum & Library 2008-2010 Delancey St	Philadelphia	PA	19103	215-732-1600	545-7529
Web: www.rosenbach.org					
Senator John Heinz Pittsburgh Regional History Ctr 1212 Smallman St	Pittsburgh	PA	15222	412-454-6000	
Web: www.heinzhistorycenter.org					
Shriver House Museum 309 Baltimore St	Gettysburg	PA	17325	717-337-2800	
Web: www.shriverhouse.org					
Soldier's National Museum 777 Baltimore St	Gettysburg	PA	17325	717-334-4890	
Web: gettysburgbattlefieldtours.com					
Soldiers & Sailors National Military Museum & Memorial 4141 Fifth Ave	Pittsburgh	PA	15213	412-621-4253	683-9339
Web: www.soldiersandsailorshall.org					
State Museum of Pennsylvania, The 300 N St	Harrisburg	PA	17120	717-787-4980	783-4558
Web: www.statemuseumpa.org					
Stenton Museum 4601 N 18th St	Philadelphia	PA	19140	215-329-7312	329-7312
Web: www.stenton.org					
University of Pennsylvania Museum of Archaeology & Anthropology 3260 S St	Philadelphia	PA	19104	215-898-4000	898-0657
Web: www.penn.museum					
Wagner Free Institute of Science 1700 W Montgomery Ave	Philadelphia	PA	19121	215-763-6529	763-1299
Web: www.pacscl.org					
Westmoreland Museum of American Art 221 N Main St	Greensburg	PA	15601	724-837-1500	
Web: thewestmoreland.org					
Whitaker Center for Science & Arts 225 Market St	Harrisburg	PA	17101	717-214-2787	
Web: www.whitakercenter.org					
Woodmere Art Museum 9201 Germantown Ave	Philadelphia	PA	19118	215-247-0476	247-2387
Web: www.woodmereartmuseum.org					

Prince Edward Island

Name / Address	City	Prov	Postal Code	Phone	Fax
Prince Edward Island Museum & Heritage Foundation 2 Kent St	Charlottetown	PE	C1A1M6	902-368-6600	831-7944

Quebec

Name / Address	City	Prov	Postal Code	Phone	Fax
Canadian Centre for Architecture 1920 Baile St	Montreal	QC	H3H2S6	514-939-7000	939-7020
Web: cca.qc.ca					
Canadian Museum of Civilization 100 Laurier St	Gatineau	QC	K1A0M8	819-776-7000	776-8300
TF: 800-555-5621 ■ *Web:* historymuseum.ca					
Jules Saint-Michel Luthier - Economuseum of Violin-Making 57 Ontario St W	Montreal	QC	H2X1Y8	514-288-4343	288-9296
Web: www.luthiersaintmichel.com					
McCord Museum of Canadian History 690 Sherbrooke St W	Montreal	QC	H3A1E9	514-398-7100	398-5045
Web: www.mccord-museum.qc.ca/en					
Montreal Holocaust Memorial Centre 5151 Ch de la C(te-Sainte-Catherine	Montreal	QC	H3W1M6	514-345-2605	344-2651
Web: www.mhmc.ca					
Musee de la Civilisation 85 Rue Dalhousie St	Quebec	QC	G1K8R2	418-643-2158	
Musee Des Beaux-Arts De Montreal 1380 Rue Sherbrooke O	Montreal	QC	H3G1J5	514-285-1600	
Web: www.mbam.qc.ca					
Pointe-a-Calliere - The Montreal Museum of Archaeology & History 350 Royale Pl Angle Joint	Old Montreal	QC	H2Y3Y5	514-872-9150	872-9151
Web: www.pacmusee.qc.ca					
Richard Robitaille Fourrures 329 St Paul St	Quebec	QC	G1K3W8	418-692-9699	692-3646

Rhode Island

Phone | Fax

Artillery Company of Newport Military Museum
23 Clark St. Newport RI 02840 401-846-8488
Web: www.newportartillery.org

Culinary Arts Museum at Johnson & Wales University
315 Harborside Blvd. Providence RI 02905 401-598-2805
Web: www.culinary.org

Governor Henry Lippitt House Museum
199 Hope St. Providence RI 02906 401-453-0688 453-8221
Web: preserveri.org

Haffenreffer Museum of Anthropology
300 Tower St. Bristol RI 02809 401-253-8388 253-1198
Web: www.brown.edu

Museum of Newport History at the Brick Market
127 Thames St. Newport RI 02840 401-841-8770 846-1853
Web: newporthistory.org

Museum of Yachting Fort Adams State Pk. Newport RI 02840 401-848-5777
Web: www.iyrs.edu

National Museum of American Illustration
492 Bellevue Ave. Newport RI 02840 401-851-8949 851-8974
Web: www.americanillustration.org

Naval War College Museum 686 Cushing Rd. Newport RI 02841 401-841-4052 841-7074
Web: www.usnwc.edu

Newport Art Museum 76 Bellevue Ave. Newport RI 02840 401-848-8200 848-8205
Web: www.newportartmuseum.org

Newport Historical Society 82 Touro St. Newport RI 02840 401-846-0813 846-1853
Web: newporthistory.org

Providence Athenaeum 251 Benefit St. Providence RI 02903 401-421-6970
Web: www.providenceathenaeum.org

Providence Jewelry Museum 4 Edward St. Providence RI 02904 401-274-0999
Web: www.providencejewelrymuseum.com

Rhode Island Historical Society
110 Benevolent St. Providence RI 02906 401-331-8575 351-0127
Web: www.rihs.org

Rhode Island School of Design - Museum of Art
224 Benefit St. Providence RI 02903 401-454-6502 454-6556
Web: www.risdmuseum.org

Thames & Kosmos LLC 301 Friendship St. Providence RI 02903 401-459-6787
Web: www.thamesandkosmos.com

Warwick Museum of Art 3259 Post Rd. Warwick RI 02886 401-737-0010
Web: www.warwickmuseum.org

Saskatchewan

Phone | Fax

Moose Jaw Museum & Art Gallery
461 Langdon Crescent Pk. Moose Jaw SK S6H0X6 306-692-4471 694-8016
Web: www.mjmag.ca

Prince Albert Historical Museum
10 River St E. Prince Albert SK S6V8A9 306-764-2992
Web: www.historypa.com

RCMP Heritage Ctr 5907 Dewdney Ave. Regina SK S4T0P4 306-522-7333
TF: 866-567-7267 ■ *Web:* www.rcmpheritagecentre.com

Royal Saskatchewan Museum 2445 Albert St. Regina SK S4P4W7 306-787-2815 787-2820
TF: 866-984-4964 ■ *Web:* www.royalsaskmuseum.ca

Western Development Museum
2610 Lorne Ave S. Saskatoon SK S7J0S6 306-931-1910 934-0525
Web: www.wdm.ca

South Carolina

Phone | Fax

Avery Research Ctr for African-American History & Culture
125 Bull St. Charleston SC 29424 843-953-7609 953-7607
Web: www.cofc.edu

Bob Jones University Museum & Gallery
Bob Jones University
1700 Wade Hampton Blvd. Greenville SC 29614 864-770-1331
Web: www.bjumg.org

Cayce Historical Museum 1800 12th St. Cayce SC 29033 803-796-9020 796-9072
Web: www.caycesc.net

Challenger Learning Ctr
2600-A Barhamville Rd. Columbia SC 29204 803-929-3951 929-3959
Web: www.richlandone.org

Charleston Museum 360 Meeting St. Charleston SC 29403 843-722-2996 722-1784
Web: www.charlestonmuseum.org

Columbia Museum of Art 1515 Main St. Columbia SC 29201 803-799-2810
Web: columbiamuseum.org

Franklin G Burroughs-Simeon B Chapin Art Museum
3100 S Ocean Blvd. Myrtle Beach SC 29577 843-238-2510 238-2910
Web: www.myrtlebeachartmuseum.org

Gibbes Museum of Art 135 Meeting St. Charleston SC 29401 843-722-2706 720-1682
Web: www.gibbesmuseum.org

Greenville County Museum of Art
420 College St. Greenville SC 29601 864-271-7570
Web: www.gcma.org

Karpeles Manuscript Library Museum
68 Spring St. Charleston SC 29403 843-853-4651 853-4651
Web: www.rain.org

Patriots Point Naval & Maritime Museum
40 Patriots Pt Rd. Mount Pleasant SC 29464 803-771-0131 881-4232*
**Fax Area Code: 843* ■ *TF:* 800-248-3508 ■ *Web:* www.state.sc.us

Ripley's Believe It or Not! Museum
901 N Ocean Blvd. Myrtle Beach SC 29577 843-448-2331
Web: www.ripleys.com

Roper Mountain Science Ctr
402 Roper Mtn Rd. Greenville SC 29615 864-355-8900
Web: www.ropermountain.org

Phone | Fax

South Carolina Civil War Museum
4857 Hwy 17 Bypass S. Myrtle Beach SC 29577 843-293-3377
Web: mbisr.com

South Carolina Museum & Library of Confederate History
15 Boyce Ave. Greenville SC 29601 864-421-9039
Web: confederatemuseumandlibrary.org

South Carolina State Museum 301 Gervais St. Columbia SC 29201 803-898-4921 898-4969
Web: www.museum.state.sc.us

University of South Carolina McKissick Museum
University of S Carolina 816 Bull St. Columbia SC 29208 803-777-7251 777-2829
TF: 888-825-9711 ■ *Web:* artsandsciences.sc.edu

US Army Basic Combat Training Museum
4442 Ft Jackson Blvd. Columbia SC 29209 803-751-7419
Web: goarmy.com

South Dakota

Phone | Fax

1881 Custer CountyCourthouse Museum
411 Mt Rushmore Rd PO Box 826. Custer SD 57730 605-673-2443 673-2443
Web: www.1881courthousemuseum.com

Adams Museum 54 Sherman St. Deadwood SD 57732 605-578-1714
Web: deadwoodhistory.org

Center for Western Studies
2101 S Summit Ave Augustana College. Sioux Falls SD 57197 605-274-4007 274-4999
TF: 800-727-2844 ■ *Web:* www.augie.edu

Delbridge Museum of Natural History
805 S Kiwanis Ave. Sioux Falls SD 57104 605-367-7003 367-8340
Web: www.greatzoo.org

Fort Meade Museum PO Box 164 PO Box 164. Fort Meade SD 57741 605-347-9822
Web: www.fortmeademuseum.org

Journey Museum 222 New York St. Rapid City SD 57701 605-394-6923 394-6940
TF: 877-343-8220 ■ *Web:* www.journeymuseum.org

Museum of Geology
501 E St Joseph St
S Dakota School of Mines & Technology. Rapid City SD 57701 605-394-2467 394-6131
TF: 800-544-8162 ■ *Web:* www.sdsmt.edu

Museum of South Dakota State Historical Society
900 Governors Dr Cultural Heritage Ctr. Pierre SD 57501 605-773-3458 773-6041
Web: www.history.sd.gov

National Museum of Woodcarving
Hwy 16 W PO Box 747. Custer SD 57730 605-673-4404
Web: woodcarving.blackhills.com

National Music Museum 414 E Clark St. Vermillion SD 57069 605-677-5306 677-6995
TF: 877-225-0027 ■ *Web:* orgs.usd.edu

National Presidential Wax Museum
609 Hwy 16A. Keystone SD 57751 605-666-4455
Web: www.blackhillsbadlands.com

Old Courthouse Museum 200 W Sixth St. Sioux Falls SD 57104 605-367-4210 367-6004
Web: siouxlandmuseums.com

Pettigrew Home & Museum 131 N Duluth Ave. Sioux Falls SD 57104 605-367-7097
Web: siouxlandmuseums.com

Sioux Empire Medical Museum
1305 W 18th St. Sioux Falls SD 57105 605-333-6397
Web: www.sdmuseums.org

South Dakota Discovery Ctr & Aquarium
805 W Sioux Ave. Pierre SD 57501 605-224-8295
Web: sd-discovery.org

South Dakota National Guard Museum
425 E Capitol Ave. Pierre SD 57501 605-773-3269
Web: military.sd.gov/default.html

Washington Pavilion of Arts & Science
301 S Main PO Box 984. Sioux Falls SD 57104 605-367-6000 367-7399
TF: 877-927-4728 ■ *Web:* www.washingtonpavilion.org

Tennessee

Phone | Fax

Adventure Science Ctr 800 Ft Negley Blvd. Nashville TN 37203 615-862-5160 862-5178
Web: www.adventuresci.org

American Museum of Science & Energy
300 S Tulane Ave. Oak Ridge TN 37830 865-576-3200 576-6024
Web: amse.org

Art Museum of the University of Memphis
142 Communication & Fine Arts Bldg
The University of Memphis. Memphis TN 38152 901-678-2224 678-5118
Web: www.memphis.edu

B Carroll Reece Museum PO Box 70660. Johnson City TN 37614 423-439-4392 439-4283
TF: 855-590-3878 ■ *Web:* www.etsu.edu/reece

Belle Meade Plantation 5025 Harding Pk. Nashville TN 37205 615-356-0501 356-0501
TF: 800-270-3991 ■ *Web:* www.bellemeadeplantation.com

Bessie Smith Cultural Ctr
200 E Martin Luther King Blvd. Chattanooga TN 37403 423-266-8658 267-1076
Web: www.bessiesmithcc.org

Center for Southern Folklore 119 S Main St. Memphis TN 38103 901-525-3655
Web: www.southernfolklore.com

Chattanooga History Ctr
2 W Acquarium Way. Chattanooga TN 37402 423-265-3247
Web: chattanoogahistory.com

Country Music Hall of Fame & Museum
222 Fifth Ave S. Nashville TN 37203 615-416-2001 255-2245
TF: 800-852-6437 ■ *Web:* countrymusichalloffame.org

Dixon Gallery & Gardens 4339 Pk Ave. Memphis TN 38117 901-761-5250 682-0943
Web: www.dixon.org

Doak House Museum 690 Erwin Hwy. Greeneville TN 37745 423-636-8554

East Tennessee Historical Society
601 S Gay St PO Box 1629. Knoxville TN 37901 865-215-8824 215-8819
Web: www.easttnhistory.org

Farragut Folklife Museum
11408 Municipal Ctr Dr. Farragut TN 37934 865-966-7057 675-2096
Web: www.townoffarragut.org

Fire Museum of Memphis 118 Adams Ave. Memphis TN 38103 901-320-5650 529-8422
Web: www.firemuseum.com

Phone | Fax

Frank H McClung Museum
1327 Cir Pk Dr University of Tennessee .... Knoxville TN 37996 865-974-2144 974-3827
Web: mcclungmuseum.utk.edu

Graceland (Elvis Presley Mansion)
3734 Elvis Presley Blvd .... Memphis TN 38116 901-332-3322
TF: 800-238-2000 ■ *Web:* www.graceland.com

Hermitage The (Home of Andrew Jackson)
4580 Rachel's Ln .... Hermitage TN 37076 615-889-2941 889-9289
Web: www.thehermitage.com

Historic Jonesborough Visitors Ctr & Museum
117 Boone St .... Jonesborough TN 37659 423-753-1010 753-1020
TF: 866-401-4223 ■ *Web:* jonesborough.com

Houston Museum of Decorative Arts
201 High St .... Chattanooga TN 37403 423-267-7176
Web: thehoustonmuseum.com

Hunter Museum of American Art
10 Bluff View St .... Chattanooga TN 37403 423-267-0968 267-9844
Web: www.huntermuseum.org

International Board of Jewish Missions Inc
5106 Genesis Lane .... Hixson TN 37343 423-876-8150
Web: tnguy.com

International Towing & Recovery Hall of Fame & Museum
3315 Broad St .... Chattanooga TN 37408 423-267-3132 267-0867
Web: www.internationaltowingmuseum.org

James White's Fort 205 E Hill Ave .... Knoxville TN 37915 865-525-6514
Web: jameswhitesfort.org

Knoxville Museum of Art
1050 World Fair Pk Dr .... Knoxville TN 37916 865-525-6101 546-3635
Web: www.knoxart.org

Memphis Brooks Museum of Art
1934 Poplar Ave Overton Pk .... Memphis TN 38104 901-544-6200 725-4071
Web: www.brooksmuseum.org

Memphis Cotton Exchange, The
65 Union Ave Mezzanine .... Memphis TN 38103 901-531-7826
Web: www.memphiscottonmuseum.org

Memphis Pink Palace Museum 3050 Central Ave .... Memphis TN 38111 901-636-2362 320-6391
Web: www.memphismuseums.org

Memphis Rock 'n' Soul Museum 191 Beale St .... Memphis TN 38103 901-205-2533 205-2534
Web: www.memphisrocknsoul.org

Mississippi River Museum 125 N Front St .... Memphis TN 38103 901-576-7241 576-6666
TF: 800-507-6507 ■ *Web:* www.mudisland.com

Museum of Appalachia 2819 Andersonville Hwy .... Clinton TN 37716 865-494-7680 494-8957
Web: museumofappalachia.org

National Civil Rights Museum 450 Mulberry St .... Memphis TN 38103 901-521-9699
Web: www.civilrightsmuseum.org

National Medal of Honor Museum of Military History
PO Box 11467 .... Chattanooga TN 37401 423-877-2525
Web: www.mohm.org

National Ornamental Metal Museum
374 Metal Museum Dr .... Memphis TN 38106 901-774-6380 774-6382
TF: 877-881-2326 ■ *Web:* www.metalmuseum.org

Parthenon, The
2600 W End Ave Centennial Pk PO Box 196340 .... Nashville TN 37203 615-862-8431
Web: nashville.gov/parks-and-recreation/parthenon.aspx

Rocky Mount Museum
200 Hyder Hill Rd PO Box 160 .... Piney Flats TN 37686 423-538-7396 538-1086
TF: 888-538-1791 ■ *Web:* www.rockymountmuseum.com

Slave Haven Underground Railroad Museum
826 N Second St .... Memphis TN 38173 901-527-3427
Web: www.slavehavenundergroundrailroadmuseum.org

Tennessee Agricultural Museum 440 Hogan Rd .... Nashville TN 37204 615-837-5197 837-5194
Web: www.picktnproducts.org

Tennessee Sports Hall of Fame Museum
501 Broadway .... Nashville TN 37203 615-242-4750
Web: www.tshf.net

Tennessee State Museum 505 Deaderick St .... Nashville TN 37243 615-741-2692
TF: 800-407-4324 ■ *Web:* www.tnmuseum.org

Tennessee Valley Railroad Museum
4119 Cromwell Rd .... Chattanooga TN 37421 423-894-8028 894-8029
Web: www.tvrail.com

Upper Room Chapel & Museum 1908 Grand Ave .... Nashville TN 37212 615-340-7200
TF: 800-972-0433 ■ *Web:* www.upperroom.org

Texas

Phone | Fax

12th Armored Div Memorial Museum
1289 N Second St .... Abilene TX 79601 325-677-6515
Web: www.12tharmoredmuseum.com

African American Museum 3536 Grand Ave .... Dallas TX 75210 214-565-9026 421-8204
Web: www.aamdallas.org

Alamo, The 300 Alamo Plz .... San Antonio TX 78205 210-225-1391
Web: www.thealamo.org

Amarillo Museum of Art 2200 S Van Buren St .... Amarillo TX 79109 806-371-5050
Web: www.amarilloart.org

American Airlines CR Smith Museum
4601 Hwy 360 at FAA Rd .... Fort Worth TX 76155 817-967-1560 967-5737
TF: 877-277-6484 ■ *Web:* www.crsmithmuseum.org

American Wind Power Ctr 1701 Canyon Lk Dr .... Lubbock TX 79403 806-747-8734 740-0668
Web: www.windmill.com

Amon Carter Museum 3501 Camp Bowie Blvd .... Fort Worth TX 76107 817-738-1933
TF: 800-573-1933 ■ *Web:* www.cartermuseum.org

Arlington Museum of Art 201 W Main St .... Arlington TX 76010 817-275-4600
Web: www.arlingtonmuseum.org

Asian Cultures Museum
1809 N Chaparral St .... Corpus Christi TX 78401 361-881-8827
Web: www.asianculturesmuseum.org

Austin Museum of Art Downtown
700 Congress Ave .... Austin TX 78701 512-453-5312
Web: thecontemporaryaustin.org

Austin Museum of Art Laguna Gloria
3809 W 35th St .... Austin TX 78703 512-458-8191
Web: thecontemporaryaustin.org

Phone | Fax

Battleship Texas SHS
San Jacinto Battleground State Historic Site
3523 Independence Pkwy .... La Porte TX 77571 281-479-2431 479-5618
Web: tpwd.texas.gov

Bayou Bend Collection & Gardens
6003 Memorial Dr at Westcott St PO Box 6826 .... Houston TX 77007 713-639-7750
Web: www.mfah.org/bayoubend

Blanton Museum of Art
200 E. Martin Luther King Jr. Blvd
University of Texas at Austin .... Austin TX 78701 512-471-7324 471-7023
Web: blantonmuseum.org

Bob Bullock Texas State History Museum
1800 N Congress Ave .... Austin TX 78701 512-936-8746 936-4699
Web: www.thestoryoftexas.com

Buckhorn Saloon & Museum
318 E Houston St .... San Antonio TX 78205 210-247-4000 247-4020
Web: www.buckhornmuseum.com

Buddy Holly Ctr 1801 Crickets Ave .... Lubbock TX 79401 806-775-3560 767-0732
Web: www.mylubbock.us/departmental-websites/departments/buddy-holly-center/home

Cattle Raisers Museum 1600 Gendy St .... Fort Worth TX 76107 817-332-8551 336-2470
Web: www.cattleraisersmuseum.org

Cavanaugh Flight Museum
4572 Claire Chennault Addison Airport .... Addison TX 75001 972-380-8800
Web: www.cavanaughflightmuseum.com

Center for Women & Their Work 1710 Lavaca St .... Austin TX 78701 512-477-1064
Web: www.womenandtheirwork.org

Contemporary Arts Museum 5216 Montrose Blvd .... Houston TX 77006 713-284-8250 284-8275
Web: www.camh.org

Corpus Christi Museum of Science & History
1900 N Chaparral St .... Corpus Christi TX 78401 361-826-4667
Web: ccmuseum.com

Dallas Firefighters Museum 3801 Parry Ave .... Dallas TX 75226 214-821-1500 821-1500
Web: dallasfiremuseum.com

Dallas Heritage Village 1515 S Harwood .... Dallas TX 75215 214-421-5141 428-6351
Web: www.dallasheritagevillage.org

Dallas Holocaust Museum
211 N Record St Ste 100 .... Dallas TX 75202 214-741-7500 747-2270
Web: www.dallasholocaustmuseum.org

Dallas Museum of Art 1717 N Harwood St .... Dallas TX 75201 214-922-1200 736-6767*
**Fax Area Code: 212* ■ *Web:* dma.org

El Paso Centennial Museum
University & Wiggins University of Texas .... El Paso TX 79968 915-747-5565 747-5411
Web: admin.utep.edu

El Paso Museum of Art 1 Art Festival Plz .... El Paso TX 79901 915-532-1707 532-1010
Web: www.elpasoartmuseum.org

El Paso Museum of History 510 Santa Fe St .... El Paso TX 79901 915-351-3588 351-4345
Web: elpasotexas.gov

Elisabet Ney Museum 304 E 44th St .... Austin TX 78751 512-458-2255 453-0638
TF: 800-680-7289 ■ *Web:* www.ci.austin.tx.us

Fielder House Museum 1616 W Abram St .... Arlington TX 76013 817-460-4001
Web: historicalarlington.org

Fort Bend Museum 500 Houston St .... Richmond TX 77469 281-342-6478
Web: www.fortbendmuseum.org

Fort Worth Museum of Science & History
1600 Gendy St .... Fort Worth TX 76107 817-255-9300 732-7635
TF: 888-255-9300 ■ *Web:* www.fortworthmuseum.org

French Legation Museum 802 San Marcos St .... Austin TX 78702 512-472-8180
Web: www.frenchlegationmuseum.org

Frontiers of Flight Museum 6911 Lemon Ave .... Dallas TX 75209 214-350-1651
Web: www.flightmuseum.com

Garland Landmark Museum 200 Museum Plz Dr .... Garland TX 75040 972-205-2749
Web: garlandhistorical.org

George Bush Library & Museum
1000 George Bush Dr W .... College Station TX 77845 979-691-4000 346-1699*
**Fax Area Code: 214*

George Ranch Historical Park 10215 FM 762 .... Richmond TX 77469 281-343-0218 343-9316
Web: www.georgeranch.org

George Washington Carver Museum & Cultural Ctr
1165 Angelina St .... Austin TX 78702 512-974-4926 974-3699
Web: austintexas.gov/search404

Grace Museum 102 Cypress St .... Abilene TX 79601 325-673-4587 675-5993
Web: www.thegracemuseum.org

Heard Natural Science Museum & Wildlife Sanctuary
1 Nature Pl .... McKinney TX 75069 972-562-5566 548-9119
Web: www.heardmuseum.org

Heritage Farmstead Museum 1900 W 15th St .... Plano TX 75075 972-881-0140 422-6481
Web: heritagefarmstead.org

Historic Brownsville Museum
641 E Madison St .... Brownsville TX 78520 956-548-1313
Web: mitteculturaldistrict.org

Historic Fort Worth Inc 1110 Penn St .... Fort Worth TX 76102 817-332-5875 336-2346
Web: www.historicfortworth.org

Holocaust Museum Houston 5401 Caroline St .... Houston TX 77004 713-942-8000 942-7953
Web: www.hmh.org

Houston Fire Museum 2403 Milam St .... Houston TX 77006 713-524-2526 520-7566
Web: www.houstonfiremuseum.org

Houston Maritime Museum 2204 Dorrington St .... Houston TX 77030 713-666-1910
Web: houstonmaritime.org

Houston Museum of Natural Science
5555 Hermann Pk Dr .... Houston TX 77030 713-639-4629
Web: www.hmns.org

Institute of Texan Cultures
801 E Durango Blvd .... San Antonio TX 78205 210-458-2300 458-2205
TF: 800-447-3372 ■ *Web:* www.texancultures.com

International Museum of Cultures
411 U.S. Hwy 67 Southbound Frontage Rd .... Duncanville TX 75137 972-572-0462
Web: www.internationalmuseumofcultures.org

Interurban Railway Museum 901 E 15th St .... Plano TX 75074 972-941-2117
Web: www.plano.gov

John E Conner Museum
905 W Santa Gertrudis Ave
700 University Blvd .... Kingsville TX 78363 361-593-2810 593-2112
TF: 800-726-8192 ■ *Web:* www.tamuk.edu/artsci/museum

Phone Fax

Kimbell Art Museum 3333 Camp Bowie Blvd ....Fort Worth TX 76107 817-332-8451 877-1264
Web: www.kimbellart.org

Lawndale Art & Performance Ctr 4912 Main St........Houston TX 77002 713-528-5858 528-4140
Web: lawndaleartcenter.org

LBJ Library & Museum 2313 Red River St............. Austin TX 78705 512-721-0216 721-0170
TF: 800-874-6451 ■ Web: www.lbjlib.utexas.edu

Log Cabin Village
2100 Log Cabin Village Ln.......................Fort Worth TX 76109 817-392-5881
Web: www.logcabinvillage.org

Lone Star Flight Museum 2002 Terminal Dr.......... Galveston TX 77554 409-740-7722 740-7612
TF: 888-359-5736 ■ Web: www.lsfm.org

Louis Tussaud's Plaza Wax Museum & Ripley's Believe It or Not! Museum
301 Alamo Plz ....San Antonio TX 78205 210-224-9299
Web: www.ripleys.com

Meadows Museum
5900 Bishop Blvd
Southern Methodist University .... Dallas TX 75205 214-768-2516 768-1688
Web: www.meadowsmuseumdallas.org

Menil Collection 1515 Sul Ross St...................Houston TX 77006 713-525-9400 525-9444
Web: www.menil.org

Mexic-Arte Museum 419 Congress Ave................ Austin TX 78701 512-480-9373
Web: www.mexic-artemuseum.org

Modern Art Museum of Fort Worth
3200 Darnell St...............................Fort Worth TX 76107 817-738-9215
TF: 866-824-5566 ■ Web: themodern.org

Museum of Fine Arts 1001 Bissonnet St..............Houston TX 77005 713-639-7300
Web: www.mfah.org

Museum of Health & Medical Science
1515 Hermann Dr................................Houston TX 77004 713-521-1515 526-1434
Web: www.mhms.org

Museum of Nature & Science 2201 N Field St .... Dallas TX 75201 214-428-5555
Web: www.perotmuseum.org

Museum of Texas Tech University
3301 Fourth St .... Lubbock TX 79409 806-742-2442 742-1136
Web: www.depts.ttu.edu/museumttu

Museum of the American Railroad
1105 Washington St.............................. Frisco TX 75034 214-428-0101 426-1937
Web: www.museumoftheamericanrailroad.org

National Border Patrol Museum
4315 Woodrow Bean TransMtn Rd....................... El Paso TX 79924 915-759-6060 759-0992
TF: 877-276-8738 ■ Web: www.borderpatrolmuseum.com

National Cowgirl Museum & Hall of Fame
1720 Gendy St ....Fort Worth TX 76107 817-336-4475 336-2470
TF: 800-476-3263 ■ Web: www.cowgirl.net

National Ctr for Children's Illustrated Literature Museum
102 Cedar St.................................... Abilene TX 79601 325-673-4586 673-0085
Web: www.nccil.org

National Museum of Funeral History
415 Barren Springs Dr ....Houston TX 77090 281-876-3063
Web: www.nmfh.org

National Ranching Heritage Ctr
3121 Fourth St .... Lubbock TX 79409 806-742-0498 742-0616
Web: www.depts.ttu.edu

National Scouting Museum
1329 W Walnut Hill Ln.............................Irving TX 75038 972-580-2100
TF: 800-303-3047 ■ Web: www.bsamuseum.org

O Henry Home & Museum 409 E Fifth St................ Austin TX 78701 512-472-1903
Web: www.ci.austin.tx.us

Panhandle-Plains Historical Museum
2503 Fourth Ave................................. Canyon TX 79015 806-651-2244 651-2250
Web: www.panhandleplains.org

Ripley Entertainment Inc
601 E Palace Pkwy ....Grand Prairie TX 75050 972-263-2391
Web: www.ripleys.com

River Legacy Park 701 NW Green Oaks Blvd...........Arlington TX 76006 817-860-6752 860-1595
Web: www.riverlegacy.org

San Antonio Museum of Art
200 W Jones Ave ....San Antonio TX 78215 210-978-8100 978-8134
Web: samuseum.org

San Jacinto Museum of History
1 Monument Cir ....La Porte TX 77571 281-479-2421
Web: www.sanjacinto-museum.org

Science Spectrum-Omni Theater
2579 S Loop 289 .... Lubbock TX 79423 806-745-2525
Web: sciencespectrum.org

Sixth Floor Museum
411 Elm St Ste 120 Dealey Plz .... Dallas TX 75202 214-747-6660
TF: 888-485-4854 ■ Web: www.jfk.org

South Texas Institute for the Arts
1902 N Shoreline Blvd.........................Corpus Christi TX 78401 361-825-3500 825-3520
Web: www.artmuseumofsouthtexas.org

Space Ctr Houston 1601 Nasa Rd 1..................Houston TX 77058 281-244-2100 283-7724
Web: www.spacecenter.org

Steves Homestead Museum
509 King William St ....San Antonio TX 78204 210-225-5924 223-9014
Web: saconservation.org

Stillman House & Museum
1325 E Washington St .... Brownsville TX 78520 956-541-5560
Web: www.brownsvillehistory.org

Stockyards Museum
131 E Exchange Ave Ste 113 ....Fort Worth TX 76164 817-625-5082
Web: stockyardsmuseum.org

Texas Memorial Museum 2400 Trinity St.............. Austin TX 78705 512-471-1604 471-4794
TF: 800-687-4132 ■ Web: www.utexas.edu

Texas Military Forces Museum PO Box 5218.......... Austin TX 78763 512-782-5659 782-6750
Web: www.texasmilitaryforcesmuseum.org

Texas Transportation Museum
11731 Wetmore Rd..............................San Antonio TX 78247 210-490-3554
Web: www.txtransportationmuseum.org

Tyler Museum of Art 1300 S Mahon Ave................. Tyler TX 75701 903-595-1001 595-1055
Web: www.tylermuseum.org

Umlauf Sculpture Garden & Museum
605 Robert E Lee Rd.............................. Austin TX 78704 512-445-5582
Web: www.umlaufsculpture.org

Phone Fax

USS Lexington Museum on the Bay
2914 N Shoreline Blvd ....Corpus Christi TX 78402 361-888-4873
TF: 800-523-9539 ■ Web: www.usslexington.com

Vintage Flying Museum
505 NW 38th St Hanger 33 S Meacham Field.........Fort Worth TX 76106 817-624-1935
Web: www.vintageflyingmuseum.org

Witte Museum 3801 Broadway St.................San Antonio TX 78209 210-357-1900 357-1882
Web: www.wittemuseum.org

Utah

Phone Fax

Brigham Young University Museum of Peoples & Cultures
100 East 700 North 105 Allen Hall ....Provo UT 84602 801-422-0020 422-0026
Web: mpc.byu.edu

Chase Home Museum of Utah Folk Art
617 East South Temple....................... Salt Lake City UT 84102 801-533-5760 533-4202
Web: heritage.utah.gov

Crandall Historical Printing Museum
275 E Ctr St ....Provo UT 84606 801-377-7777
Web: crandallmuseum.org

Daughters of Utah Pioneers Museum
300 N Main St .... Salt Lake City UT 84103 801-532-6479 532-4436
Web: www.dupinternational.org

Fort Douglas Military Museum
32 Potter St Ft Douglas...................... Salt Lake City UT 84113 801-581-1251
Web: www.fortdouglas.org

Hill Aerospace Museum
7961 WaRdleigh Rd Bldg 1955.......................Hill AFB UT 84056 801-777-6818 775-3034
Web: hill.af.mil

John Hutchings Museum of Natural History
55 N Ctr St ....Lehi UT 84043 801-768-7180
Web: www.hutchingsmuseum.org

John M Browning Firearms Museum 2501 Wall Ave ..... Ogden UT 84401 801-393-9886
Web: theunionstation.org/museums-2/john-m-browning-firearms-museum

Monte L Bean Life Science Museum
Brigham Young University 645 E 1430 N..............Provo UT 84602 801-422-5051 422-0093
Web: mlbean.byu.edu

Museum of Church History & Art
45 NW Temple St .... Salt Lake City UT 84150 801-240-3310 240-5342
Web: history.lds.org

Museum of Utah Art & History
825 North 300 West Ste W109................. Salt Lake City UT 84103 801-364-4080 364-3468
Web: www.muahnet.org

Ogden Eccles Dinosaur Park 1544 E Pk Blvd........... Ogden UT 84401 801-393-3466
Web: www.dinosaurpark.org

Pioneer Memorial Museum 300 N Main St .... Salt Lake City UT 84103 801-532-6479 532-4436
Web: www.dupinternational.org

Springville Museum of Art
126 East 400 South ....Springville UT 84663 801-489-2727
Web: www.springville.org

Union Station 2501 Wall Ave.......................... Ogden UT 84401 801-393-9886
Web: theunionstation.org

Utah Museum of Fine Arts
410 Campus Ctr Dr University of Utah .... Salt Lake City UT 84112 801-581-7332 585-5198
Web: www.umfa.utah.edu

Utah Museum of Natural History, The
301 Wakara Way........................... Salt Lake City UT 84108 801-581-4303 585-3684
Web: nhmu.utah.edu

Utah State Railroad Museum 2501 Wall Ave............ Ogden UT 84401 801-393-9886
Web: theunionstation.org

Wattis-Dumke Model Railroad Museum
2501 Wall Ave .... Ogden UT 84401 801-393-9886

Wheeler Historic Farm
6351 South 900 East .... Salt Lake City UT 84121 385-468-1755 264-2213*
*Fax Area Code: 801 ■ Web: www.wheelerfarm.com

Vermont

Phone Fax

Bennington Museum 75 Main St .... Bennington VT 05201 802-447-1571 442-8305
Web: www.bennington.com

Fairbanks Museum & Planetarium
1302 Main St .... Saint Johnsbury VT 05819 802-748-2372 748-1893
Web: www.fairbanksmuseum.org

Lake Champlain Maritime Museum
4472 Basin Harbor Rd .... Vergennes VT 05491 802-475-2022 475-2953
Web: www.lcmm.org

Robert Hull Fleming Museum
61 Colchester Ave University of Vermont .... Burlington VT 05405 802-656-0750 656-8059
TF: 888-382-1222 ■ Web: www.uvm.edu

Rokeby Museum 4334 Rt 7........................ Ferrisburgh VT 05456 802-877-3406 877-3406
Web: www.rokeby.org

Shelburne Museum 5555 Shelburne Rd.............. Shelburne VT 05482 802-985-3346 985-2331
Web: www.shelburnemuseum.org

Virginia

Phone Fax

Agecroft Hall 4305 Sulgrave Rd .... Richmond VA 23221 804-353-4241
Web: www.agecrofthall.com

Alexandria Archaeology Museum
105 N Union St Ste 327 ....Alexandria VA 22314 703-746-4399 838-6491
TF: 800-367-7623 ■ Web: www.alexandriava.gov/historic/archaeology

Alexandria Black History Museum
902 Wythe St ....Alexandria VA 22314 703-838-4356 706-3999
TF: 800-367-7623 ■ Web: www.alexandriava.gov/historic/blackhistory

Anderson Gallery 907 W Franklin St .... Richmond VA 23284 804-828-1522
Web: arts.vcu.edu/andersongallery

Arlington Historical Museum
1805 S Arlington Ridge Rd.......................... Arlington VA 22202 703-942-9247
Web: www.arlingtonhistoricalsociety.org

Phone | Fax

Atlantic Wildfowl Heritage Museum
1113 Atlantic Ave ... Virginia Beach VA 23451 757-437-8432
Web: www.awhm.org

Beth Ahabah Museum & Archives
1109 W Franklin St ... Richmond VA 23220 804-353-2668
Web: www.bethahabah.org

Black History Museum & Cultural Ctr of Virginia
00 Clay St ... Richmond VA 23220 804-780-9093
Web: www.blackhistorymuseum.org

Carlyle House Historic Park
121 N Fairfax St ... Alexandria VA 22314 703-549-2997 549-5738
Web: www.novaparks.com

Chrysler Museum of Art 245 W Olney Rd ... Norfolk VA 23510 757-664-6200 664-6201
Web: www.chrysler.org

DeWitt Wallace Decorative Arts Museum
326 Francis St W ... Williamsburg VA 23185 800-447-8679
TF: 800-447-8679 ■ *Web:* www.colonialwilliamsburg.com

Drug Enforcement Administration Museum & Visitors Ctr
700 Army Navy Dr ... Arlington VA 22202 202-307-3463 307-8956
Web: www.deamuseum.org

Edgar Allan Poe Museum 1914 E Main St ... Richmond VA 23223 804-648-5523 648-8729
TF: 888-213-2763 ■ *Web:* www.poemuseum.org

Endview Plantation 362 Yorktown Rd ... Newport News VA 23603 757-887-1862 888-3369
Web: www.endview.org

Federal Reserve Money Museum 701 E Byrd St ... Richmond VA 23219 804-697-8000
Web: www.richmondfed.org

Fort Ward Museum & Historic Site
4301 W Braddock Rd ... Alexandria VA 22304 703-838-4848 671-7350
Web: www.alexandriava.gov/FortWard

Gadsby's Tavern Museum Society
134 N Royal St ... Alexandria VA 22314 703-746-4242
Web: www.gadsbystavernmuseum.us

George C Marshall Foundation VMI Parade ... Lexington VA 24450 540-463-7103
Web: www.marshallfoundation.org

Hampton Roads Naval Museum
1 Waterside Dr Ste 248 ... Norfolk VA 23510 757-322-2987 445-1867
Web: www.history.navy.mil/museums/hrnm/index.html

Henricus Historical Park Henricus Pk Rd ... Chester VA 23836 804-748-1613
TF: 800-514-3849 ■ *Web:* www.henricus.org

Hermitage Foundation Museum 7637 N Shore Rd ... Norfolk VA 23505 757-423-2052 423-2410
Web: www.thehermitagemuseum.org

History Museum & Historical Society of Western Virginia
1 Market Sq ... Roanoke VA 24011 540-342-5770
Web: vahistorymuseum.org

Hunter House Victorian Museum
240 W Freemason St ... Norfolk VA 23510 757-623-9814
Web: www.hunterhousemuseum.org

Lee-Fendall House Museum 614 Oronoco St ... Alexandria VA 22314 703-548-1789
Web: www.leefendallhouse.org

Lyceum History Museum 201 S Washington St ... Alexandria VA 22314 703-838-4994 838-4997
Web: www.alexandriava.gov/lyceum

MacArthur Memorial Museum, The 198 Bank St ... Norfolk VA 23510 757-441-2965 441-5389
Web: macarthurmemorial.org

Magnolia Grange & Museum
10201 Iron Bridge Rd PO Box 40 ... Chesterfield VA 23832 804-796-7121 777-9643
Web: www.chesterfieldhistory.com

Mariners' Museum 100 Museum Dr ... Newport News VA 23606 757-596-2222 591-7320
TF: 800-581-7245 ■ *Web:* marinersmuseum.org

Maymont 2201 Shields Dr ... Richmond VA 23220 804-358-7166 358-9994
Web: www.maymont.org

Muscarelle Museum of Art PO Box 8795 ... Williamsburg VA 23187 757-221-2700 221-2711
Web: wm.edu/index.php

National Firearms Museum
11250 Waples Mill Rd ... Fairfax VA 22030 703-267-1000 267-3913
Web: explore.nra.org

National Museum of the Marine Corps
18900 Jefferson Davis Hwy ... Triangle VA 22172 703-221-1581
Web: www.usmcmuseum.org

NAUTICUS the National Maritime Ctr
1 Waterside Dr ... Norfolk VA 23510 757-664-1000 623-1287
TF: 800-664-1080 ■ *Web:* www.nauticus.org

Newsome House Museum & Cultural Ctr
2803 Oak Ave ... Newport News VA 23607 757-247-2360 926-6754
TF: 888-493-7386 ■ *Web:* www.newsomehouse.org

Old City Cemetery Museums & Arboretum
401 Taylor St ... Lynchburg VA 24501 434-847-1465 856-2004
Web: www.gravegarden.org

Old Coast Guard Station
2401 Atlantic Ave ... Virginia Beach VA 23451 757-422-1587 491-8609
Web: www.oldcoastguardstation.com

Old Guard Museum 201 Lee Ave Ft Myer ... Fort Myer VA 22211 703-696-6670
Web: www.army.mil

Richmond National Battlefield Park
3215 E Broad St ... Richmond VA 23223 804-226-1981 771-8522
TF: 866-733-7768 ■ *Web:* www.nps.gov

Salem Museum 801 E Main St ... Salem VA 24153 540-389-6760 389-6760
Web: www.salemmuseum.org

Science Museum of Western Virginia
1 Market Sq ... Roanoke VA 24011 540-342-5710 224-1240
Web: www.smwv.org

Sherwood Forest Plantation
14501 John Tyler Memorial Hwy ... Charles City VA 23030 804-829-5377
Web: www.sherwoodforest.org

Taubman Museum of Art 110 Salem Ave Se ... Roanoke VA 24011 540-342-5760 342-5798
Web: taubmanmuseum.org

US Army Transportation Museum
300 Washington Blvd ... Fort Eustis VA 23604 757-878-1115
Web: www.transchool.lee.army.mil/museum/transportation%20museum/museum.htm

Valentine, The 1015 E Clay St ... Richmond VA 23219 804-649-0711 643-3510
Web: thevalentine.org

Virginia Aquarium & Marine Science Ctr
717 General Booth Blvd ... Virginia Beach VA 23451 757-385-3474
Web: www.virginiaaquarium.com/pages/default.aspx

Phone | Fax

Virginia Aviation Museum 5701 Huntsman Rd ... Richmond VA 23250 804-236-3622 236-3623
Web: www.vam.smv.org

Virginia Historical Society Museum of Virginia History
428 N Blvd ... Richmond VA 23220 804-358-4901 355-2399
Web: www.vahistorical.org

Virginia Holocaust Museum 2000 E Cary St ... Richmond VA 23223 804-257-5400 257-4314
Web: www.va-holocaust.com

Virginia Living Museum
524 J Clyde Morris Blvd ... Newport News VA 23601 757-595-1900 599-4897
Web: www.thevlm.org

Virginia Museum of Fine Arts 200 N Blvd ... Richmond VA 23220 804-340-1400 340-1548
Web: vmfa.museum

Virginia Museum of Transportation
303 Norfolk Ave ... Roanoke VA 24016 540-342-5670 342-6898
Web: www.vmt.org

Virginia War Museum 9285 Warwick Blvd ... Newport News VA 23607 757-247-8523 247-8627
TF: 888-493-7386 ■ *Web:* www.warmuseum.org

Watermen's Museum 309 Water St ... Yorktown VA 23690 757-887-2641
Web: www.watermens.org

Wilton House Museum 215 S Wilton Rd ... Richmond VA 23226 804-282-5936 288-9805
Web: www.wiltonhousemuseum.org

Washington

Phone | Fax

Bellevue Arts Museum 510 Bellevue Way NE ... Bellevue WA 98004 425-519-0770 637-1799
TF: 800-367-2648 ■ *Web:* www.bellevuearts.org

Burke Museum of Natural History & Culture
University of Washington
17th Ave NE & NE 45th St ... Seattle WA 98195 206-543-5590 685-3039
Web: www.burkemuseum.org

Center for Wooden Boats 1010 Valley St ... Seattle WA 98109 206-382-2628 382-2699
Web: www.cwb.org

Charles & Emma Frye Free Public Art Museum
704 Terry Ave ... Seattle WA 98104 206-622-9250
Web: www.fryemuseum.org

Clark County Historical Museum
1511 Main St ... Vancouver WA 98660 360-993-5679 993-5683
Web: cchmuseum.org

DuPont Historical Museum 207 Barksdale Ave ... Dupont WA 98327 253-964-2399
Web: www.dupontmuseum.com

Fireworks Fine Crafts Gallery
3307 Utah Ave S ... Seattle WA 98134 206-682-8707 467-6366
TF: 800-505-8882 ■ *Web:* www.fireworksgallery.net

Fort Lewis Military Museum PO Box 331001 ... Fort Lewis WA 98433 253-967-7206
Web: fortlewismuseum.com

Foss Waterway Seaport 705 Dock St ... Tacoma WA 98402 253-272-2750
Web: www.fosswaterwayseaport.org

Frye Art Museum 704 Terry Ave ... Seattle WA 98104 206-622-9250 223-1701
Web: smoking.vapingguide.org

Henderson House Museum 602 Deschutes Way ... Tumwater WA 98501 360-754-4217
Web: www.ci.tumwater.wa.us

Henry Art Gallery
University of Washington
15th Ave NE & NE 41st St ... Seattle WA 98195 206-543-2281
Web: www.henryart.org

Jundt Art Museum 202 E Cataldo Ave ... Spokane WA 99258 509-313-6611
Web: www.gonzaga.edu

Karpeles Manuscript Library Museum
407 S 'G' St ... Tacoma WA 98405 253-383-2575
Web: www.rain.org

Lacey Museum 829 1/2 Lacey St SE ... Lacey WA 98503 360-438-0209
Web: ci.lacey.wa.us

Meeker Mansion 312 Spring St ... Puyallup WA 98372 253-848-1770
Web: www.meekermansion.org

Museum of Flight 9404 E Marginal Way S ... Seattle WA 98108 206-764-5700 764-5707
Web: www.museumofflight.org

Museum of Glass 1801 Dock St ... Tacoma WA 98402 253-284-4750
TF General: 866-468-7386 ■ *Web:* www.museumofglass.org

Museum of History & Industry 2700 24th Ave E ... Seattle WA 98112 206-324-1126 324-1346
Web: www.mohai.org

Nordic Heritage Museum 3014 NW 67th St ... Seattle WA 98117 206-789-5707
Web: www.nordicmuseum.com

Northwest Museum of Arts & Culture
2316 W First Ave ... Spokane WA 99201 509-456-3931 363-5303
Web: www.northwestmuseum.org

Olympic Flight Museum 7637A Old Hwy 99 SE ... Olympia WA 98501 360-705-3925 236-9839
Web: www.olympicflightmuseum.com

Pacific Science Ctr 200 Second Ave N ... Seattle WA 98109 206-443-2001 443-3631
TF: 800-664-8775 ■ *Web:* www.pacificsciencecenter.org

Port Townsend Marine Science Ctr
532 Battery Way ... Port Townsend WA 98368 360-385-5582 385-7248
TF: 800-566-3932 ■ *Web:* www.ptmsc.org

Seattle Art Museum 1300 First Ave ... Seattle WA 98101 206-654-3100
Web: www.seattleartmuseum.org

Seattle Asian Art Museum
1400 E Prospect St Volunteer Pk ... Seattle WA 98112 206-654-3210
Web: www.seattleartmuseum.org

Tacoma Art Museum 1701 Pacific Ave ... Tacoma WA 98402 253-272-4258 627-1898
Web: www.tacomaartmuseum.org

Tenino Depot Museum 399 Pk Ave W ... Tenino WA 98589 360-956-7575
Web: ci.tenino.wa.us

Two Rivers Heritage Museum
001 Durgan St PO Box 204 ... Washougal WA 98671 360-835-8742
Web: 2rhm.com

Washington State Capital Museum
211 21st Ave SW ... Olympia WA 98501 360-753-2580 586-8322
Web: www.washingtonhistory.org

Wing Luke Asian Museum 719 S King St ... Seattle WA 98104 206-623-5124 623-4559
Web: www.wingluke.org

World Kite Museum & Hall of Fame
303 Sid Snyder Dr ... Long Beach WA 98631 360-642-4020 642-4020
Web: kitefestival.com

West Virginia

Museum	City	State	Zip	Phone	Fax
Challenger Learning Ctr (CLC) 316 Washington Ave Wheeling Jesuit University *TF:* 800-624-6992 ■ *Web:* www.wju.edu/clc	Wheeling	WV	26003	304-243-2279	243-4397
Huntington Museum of Art Inc 2033 McCoy Rd *Web:* www.hmoa.org	Huntington	WV	25701	304-529-2701	529-7447
Kruger Street Toy & Train Museum 144 Kruger St *TF:* 877-242-8133 ■ *Web:* www.toyandtrain.com	Wheeling	WV	26003	304-242-8133	242-1925
Marks Toy Museum 915 Second St *Web:* www.marxtoymuseum.com	Moundsville	WV	26041	304-845-6022	
Museums of Oglebay Institute 1330 National Rd *TF:* 800-624-6988 ■ *Web:* www.oionline.com	Wheeling	WV	26003	304-242-7272	
West Virginia State Museum 1900 Kanawha Blvd E The Cultural Ctr *TF:* 800-946-9471 ■ *Web:* www.wvculture.org/museum	Charleston	WV	25305	304-558-0220	558-2779

Wisconsin

Museum	City	State	Zip	Phone	Fax
Cedarburg Cultural Center W62 N546 Washington Ave *Web:* www.cedarburgculturalcenter.org	Cedarburg	WI	53012	262-375-3676	
Charles Allis Art Museum 1801 N Prospect Ave *Web:* www.cavtmuseums.org	Milwaukee	WI	53202	414-278-8295	
Chazen Museum of Art 800 University Ave University of Wisconsin *Web:* www.chazen.wisc.edu	Madison	WI	53706	608-263-2246	263-8188
Circus World Museum 550 Water St *TF:* 866-693-1500 ■ *Web:* circusworldbaraboo.org	Baraboo	WI	53913	608-356-8341	356-1800
Discovery World 500 N Harbor Dr *Web:* www.discoveryworld.org	Milwaukee	WI	53202	414-765-9966	765-0311
EAA AirVenture Museum 3000 Poberezny Rd *TF:* 888-322-3229 ■ *Web:* eaa.org/en/eaa-museum	Oshkosh	WI	54902	920-426-4800	426-6560
Greene Memorial Museum 3209 N Maryland Ave Lapham Hall UWM Campus *Web:* www.uwm.edu	Milwaukee	WI	53211	414-229-4561	229-5452
Hazelwood Historic Home Museum 1008 S Monroe Ave *Web:* www.browncohistoricalsoc.org	Green Bay	WI	54301	920-437-1840	455-4518
John Michael Kohler Arts Center 608 New York Ave *Web:* www.jmkac.org	Sheboygan	WI	53081	920-458-6144	
Kenosha Public Museum 5500 First Ave *TF:* 888-258-9966 ■ *Web:* www.kenosha.org	Kenosha	WI	53140	262-653-4140	653-4437
Madison Geology Museum 1215 W Dayton St *Web:* www.geologymuseum.org	Madison	WI	53706	608-262-2399	
Milwaukee Art Museum 700 N Art Museum Dr *TF:* 888-322-3326 ■ *Web:* www.mam.org	Milwaukee	WI	53202	414-224-3200	271-7588
Milwaukee Public Museum 800 W Wells St *Web:* www.mpm.edu	Milwaukee	WI	53233	414-278-2728	
Mitchell Gallery of Flight 5300 S Howell Ave General Mitchell International Airport *Web:* www.mitchellgallery.org	Milwaukee	WI	53207	414-747-5300	747-4525
National Railroad Museum 2285 S Broadway St *TF:* 866-468-7630 ■ *Web:* www.nationalrrmuseum.org	Green Bay	WI	54304	920-437-7623	437-1291
Neville Public Museum of Brown County 210 Museum Pl *Web:* www.nevillepublicmuseum.org	Green Bay	WI	54303	920-448-4460	448-4458
Old World Wisconsin W372 S9727 Hwy 67 PO Box 69 *Web:* oldworldwisconsin.wisconsinhistory.org	Eagle	WI	53119	262-594-6301	594-6342
Oshkosh Public Museum 1331 Algoma Blvd *Web:* www.oshkoshmuseum.org	Oshkosh	WI	54901	920-236-5799	424-4738
Patrick & Beatrice Haggerty Museum of Art 13th & Clybourn Sts Marquette University *Web:* www.marquette.edu/haggerty	Milwaukee	WI	53201	414-288-7290	288-5415
Villa Terrace Decorative Arts Museum & Gardens 2220 N Terr Ave *Web:* www.villaterracemuseum.org	Milwaukee	WI	53202	414-271-3656	271-3986
Wisconsin Black Historical Society Museum 2620 W Ctr St *Web:* www.wbhsm.org	Milwaukee	WI	53206	414-372-7677	372-4888
Wisconsin Historical Museum 30 N Carroll St *TF:* 888-748-7479 ■ *Web:* historicalmuseum.wisconsinhistory.org	Madison	WI	53703	608-264-6555	264-6575
Wisconsin Maritime Museum 75 Maritime Dr *TF:* 866-724-2356 ■ *Web:* www.wisconsinmaritime.org	Manitowoc	WI	54220	920-684-0218	684-0219
Wisconsin State Fair Park 640 S 84th St *TF:* 800-884-3247 ■ *Web:* www.wistatefair.com	West Allis	WI	53214	414-266-7033	266-7007
Wisconsin Veterans Museum 30 W Mifflin St *Web:* www.wisvetsmuseum.com	Madison	WI	53703	608-264-6086	264-7615

Wyoming

Museum	City	State	Zip	Phone	Fax
Buffalo Bill Historical Ctr 720 Sheridan Ave *Web:* centerofthewest.org	Cody	WY	82414	307-587-4771	
Cheyenne Depot Museum 121 W 15th St Ste 300 *TF:* 800-544-2151 ■ *Web:* www.cheyennedepotmuseum.org	Cheyenne	WY	82001	307-632-3905	632-0614
Cheyenne Frontier Days Old West Museum 4610 N Carey Ave PO Box 2720 *Web:* www.oldwestmuseum.org	Cheyenne	WY	82001	307-778-7290	778-7288
Fort Caspar Museum 4001 Fort Caspar Rd *TF:* 800-877-7353 ■ *Web:* www.casperwy.gov	Casper	WY	82604	307-235-8462	
Geological Museum 1000 E University Ave *TF:* 800-842-2776 ■ *Web:* www.uwyo.edu/geomuseum	Laramie	WY	82071	307-766-2646	766-6679
Jackson Hole Historical Society & Museum 105 Mercill *Web:* www.jacksonholehistory.org	Jackson	WY	83001	307-733-9605	739-9019
Laramie Plains Museum 603 E Ivinson St *Web:* www.laramiemuseum.org	Laramie	WY	82070	307-742-4448	
Museum of the Mountain Man 700 E Hennick St *TF:* 877-686-6266 ■ *Web:* www.pinedaleonline.com	Pinedale	WY	82941	307-367-4101	367-6768
National Museum of Wildlife Art 2820 Rungius Rd PO Box 6825 *TF:* 800-313-9553 ■ *Web:* www.wildlifeart.org	Jackson	WY	83002	307-733-5771	733-5787
Nelson Museum of the West 1714 Carey Ave *Web:* www.nelsonmuseum.com	Cheyenne	WY	82001	307-635-7670	
Nicolaysen Art Museum 400 E Collins Dr *Web:* www.thenic.org	Casper	WY	82601	307-235-5247	235-0923
Ripley's Believe It or Not! Museum 140 N Cache St *Web:* www.ripleys.com	Jackson Hole	WY	83001	407-345-8010	
Sweetwater County Historical Museum 3 E Flaming Gorge Way *Web:* www.sweetwatermuseum.org	Green River	WY	82935	307-872-6435	872-3234
Werner Wildlife Museum 405 E 15th St *Web:* caspercollege.edu	Casper	WY	82601	307-235-2108	
Wyoming Dinosaur Ctr 110 Carter Ranch Rd *Web:* www.wyodino.org	Thermopolis	WY	82443	307-864-2997	
Wyoming State Museum 2301 Central Ave *Web:* wyomuseum.state.wy.us	Cheyenne	WY	82002	307-777-7022	777-5375

Yukon

Museum	City	Prov	Postal Code	Phone	Fax
MacBride Museum 1124 First Ave *Web:* www.macbridemuseum.com	Whitehorse	YT	Y1A1A4	867-667-2709	633-6607

521 MUSEUMS - CHILDREN'S

Children's museums are organized alphabetically by states.

Museum	City	State	Zip	Phone	Fax
Children's Hands-On Museum 2213 University Blvd *Web:* www.chomonline.org	Tuscaloosa	AL	35401	205-349-4235	349-4276
EarlyWorks Children's Museum 404 Madison St *Web:* earlyworks.com	Huntsville	AL	35801	256-564-8100	
Gulf Coast Exploreum Science Ctr 65 Government St *Web:* www.exploreum.com	Mobile	AL	36602	251-208-6873	208-6889
Tucson Children's Museum 200 S Sixth Ave *Web:* childrensmuseumtucson.org	Tucson	AZ	85702	520-792-9985	792-0639
Bay Area Discovery Museum 557 McReynolds Rd *Web:* www.baykidsmuseum.org	Sausalito	CA	94965	415-339-3900	
Bowers Kidseum, The 1802 N Main St *Web:* bowers.org/index.php/visit/kidseum/about-kidseum	Santa Ana	CA	92706	714-480-1520	
Children's Discovery Museum of San Jose 180 Woz Way *Web:* www.cdm.org	San Jose	CA	95110	408-298-5437	298-6826
Children's Discovery Museum of the Desert 71701 Gerald Ford Dr *Web:* www.cdmod.org	Rancho Mirage	CA	92270	760-321-0602	321-1605
Children's Museum of Stockton 402 W Weber Ave *Web:* www.stocktongov.com	Stockton	CA	95202	209-465-4386	
Discovery Ctr (TDC) 1944 N Winery Ave *Web:* www.thediscoverycenter.net	Fresno	CA	93703	559-251-5533	
Gull Wings Children's Museum 418 W Fourth St *Web:* www.gullwings.org	Oxnard	CA	93030	805-483-3005	
Lori Brock Children's Discovery Ctr 3801 Chester Ave *Web:* www.mocha.org	Bakersfield	CA	93301	661-437-3330	633-9829
Museum of Children's Art 1625 Clay Ste 100	Oakland	CA	94612	510-465-8770	
My Museum 425 Washington St *Web:* www.mymuseum.org	Monterey	CA	93940	831-649-6444	649-1304
Sacramento History Museum 101 'I' St *Web:* www.historicoldsac.org/museum/default.asp	Sacramento	CA	95814	916-808-7059	
Youth Science Institute 296 Garden Hill Dr *Web:* www.ysi-ca.org	Los Gatos	CA	95032	408-356-4945	
Children's Museum of Denver 2121 Children's Museum Dr *Web:* www.mychildsmuseum.org	Denver	CO	80211	303-433-7444	433-9520
Durango Discovery Museum 1333 Camino Del Rio *Web:* powsci.org	Durango	CO	81301	970-259-9234	
Connecticut Children's Museum 22 Wall St *Web:* www.childrensbuilding.org	New Haven	CT	06511	203-562-5437	787-9414
Living Classrooms Foundation 515 M St SE Ste 222 *Web:* livingclassrooms.org	Washington	DC	20003	202-488-0627	
Children's Museum 498 Crawford Blvd *Web:* www.cmboca.org	Boca Raton	FL	33432	561-368-6875	
Children's Science Explorium 300 S Military Trl *Web:* www.scienceexplorium.org	Boca Raton	FL	33486	561-347-3912	347-3910
G Wiz Hands on Science Museum 1001 Blvd of the Arts	Sarasota	FL	34236	941-309-4949	906-7292
Great Explorations Children's Museum 1925 Fourth St N *Web:* greatex.org	Saint Petersburg	FL	33704	727-821-8992	823-7287
Miami Children's Museum 980 MacArthur Cswy *Web:* www.miamichildrensmuseum.org	Miami	FL	33132	305-373-5437	373-5431

Name / Address	City	State	Zip	Phone	Fax
Young at Art Children's Museum 751 SW 121st Ave *TF:* 800-435-7352 ■ *Web:* www.youngatartmuseum.org	Davie	FL	33325	954-424-0085	473-8798
Imagine It! Children's Museum of Atlanta 275 Centennial Olympic Pk Dr NW *Web:* www.childrensmuseumatlanta.org	Atlanta	GA	30313	404-659-5437	223-3675
Hawaii Children's Discovery Ctr 111 Ohe St *Web:* www.discoverycenterhawaii.org	Honolulu	HI	96813	808-524-5437	524-5400
Chicago Children's Museum 700 E Grand Ave *Web:* chicagochildrensmuseum.org	Chicago	IL	60611	312-527-1000	527-9082
Discovery Ctr Museum 711 N Main St *Web:* www.discoverycentermuseum.org	Rockford	IL	61103	815-963-6769	968-0164
Orpheum Children's Science Museum 346 N Neil St *Web:* orpheumkids.net	Champaign	IL	61820	217-352-5895	
Hannah Lindahl Children's Museum 1402 S Main St *Web:* www.hlcm.org	Mishawaka	IN	46544	574-254-4540	254-4585
HealthWorks! Kids' Museum 111 W Jefferson Blvd Ste 200 *Web:* www.healthworkskids.org	South Bend	IN	46601	574-647-5437	
Koch Family Children's Museum of Evansville 22 SE Fifth St *Web:* www.cmoekids.org	Evansville	IN	47708	812-464-2663	477-4339
Muncie Children's Museum 515 S High St *Web:* munciemuseum.com	Muncie	IN	47305	765-286-1660	
Exploration Place 300 N McLean Blvd *TF:* 877-904-1444 ■ *Web:* www.exploration.org	Wichita	KS	67203	316-660-0600	660-0670
Kansas Cosmosphere & Space Ctr 1100 N Plum St *TF:* 800-397-0330 ■ *Web:* www.cosmo.org	Hutchinson	KS	67501	620-662-2305	662-3693
Explorium of Lexington 440 W Short St *Web:* www.explorium.com	Lexington	KY	40507	859-258-3253	258-3255
Children's Museum of Acadiana 201 E Congress St *Web:* www.childrensmuseumofacadiana.com/home	Lafayette	LA	70501	337-232-8500	232-8167
Children's Museum of Lake Charles 327 Broad St *Web:* www.swlakids.org	Lake Charles	LA	70601	337-433-9420	
Louisiana Children's Museum 420 Julia St *Web:* www.lcm.org	New Orleans	LA	70130	504-586-0725	529-3666
Children's Museum of Maine 142 Free St PO Box 4041 *Web:* www.kitetails.org	Portland	ME	04101	207-828-1234	828-5726
Chesapeake Children's Museum 25 Silopanna Rd *Web:* www.theccm.org	Annapolis	MD	21403	410-990-1993	
Port Discovery Children's Museum in Baltimore 35 Market Pl *Web:* www.portdiscovery.org	Baltimore	MD	21202	410-727-8120	727-3042
Boston Children's Museum 308 Congress St *Web:* www.bostonchildrensmuseum.org	Boston	MA	02210	617-426-6500	426-1944
Cape Cod Children's Museum 577 Great Neck Rd S *Web:* www.capecodchildrensmuseum.org	Mashpee	MA	02649	508-539-8788	539-3285
EcoTarium 222 Harrington Way *Web:* www.ecotarium.org	Worcester	MA	01604	508-929-2700	929-2701
Flint Children's Museum 1602 W University Ave *Web:* thefcm.org	Flint	MI	48504	810-767-5437	767-4936
Grand Rapids Children's Museum 11 Sheldon Ave NE *Web:* www.grcm.org	Grand Rapids	MI	49503	616-235-4726	235-4728
Minnesota Children's Museum 10 W Seventh St *Web:* www.mcm.org	Saint Paul	MN	55102	651-225-6000	225-6006
Lynn Meadows Discovery Ctr 246 Dolan Ave *Web:* www.lmdc.org	Gulfport	MS	39507	228-897-6039	248-0071
Discovery Ctr of Springfield 438 E St Louis St *TF:* 888-636-4395 ■ *Web:* www.discoverycenter.org	Springfield	MO	65806	417-862-9910	862-6898
Kaleidoscope 2500 Grand Blvd PO Box 419580 *Web:* hallmarkkaleidoscope.com	Kansas City	MO	64108	816-274-8301	
Magic House Saint Louis Children's Museum 516 S Kirkwood Rd *Web:* www.magichouse.org	Saint Louis	MO	63122	314-822-8900	822-8930
Lincoln Children's Museum 1420 P St *Web:* www.lincolnchildrensmuseum.org	Lincoln	NE	68508	402-477-4000	477-2004
Omaha Children's Museum 500 S 20th St *Web:* www.ocm.org	Omaha	NE	68102	402-342-6164	342-6165
Children's Museum of Northern Nevada 813 N Carson St *Web:* www.cmnn.org	Carson City	NV	89701	775-884-2226	884-2179
Lied Discovery Children's Museum 360 Promenade Pl *Web:* www.discoverykidslv.org	Las Vegas	NV	89106	702-382-3445	382-0592
Children's Museum of New Hampshire 6 Washington St *Web:* www.childrens-museum.org	Dover	NH	03820	603-742-2002	
Santa Fe Children's Museum 1050 Old Pecos Trl *Web:* www.santafechildrensmuseum.org	Santa Fe	NM	87505	505-989-8359	989-7506
Children's Museum of History Natural History Science & Technology 311 Main St *Web:* www.museum4kids.net	Utica	NY	13501	315-724-6129	724-6120
Children's Museum of Manhattan 212 W 83rd St *Web:* www.cmom.org	New York	NY	10024	212-721-1223	721-1127
Children's Museum of the Arts 103 Charlton St *Web:* www.cmany.org	New York	NY	10014	212-274-0986	274-1776
Discovery Ctr of the Southern Tier 60 Morgan Rd *Web:* www.thediscoverycenter.org	Binghamton	NY	13903	607-773-8661	773-8019
Explore & More-A Children's Museum 300 Gleed Ave *Web:* www.exploreandmore.org	East Aurora	NY	14052	716-655-5131	
Long Island Children's Museum 11 Davis Ave *Web:* www.licm.org	Garden City	NY	11530	516-224-5800	302-8188
Staten Island Children's Museum 1000 Richmond Terr at Snug Harbor *Web:* sichildrensmuseum.org	Staten Island	NY	10301	718-273-2060	273-2836
Discovery Place 301 N Tryon St *TF:* 800-935-0553 ■ *Web:* www.discoveryplace.org	Charlotte	NC	28202	704-372-6261	337-2670
Greensboro Children's Museum 220 N Church St *Web:* www.gcmuseum.com	Greensboro	NC	27401	336-574-2898	574-3810
Rocky Mount Children's Museum 270 Gay St *Web:* museum.imperialcentre.org	Rocky Mount	NC	27804	252-972-1167	
Yunker Farm Children's Museum 1201 28th Ave N *Web:* www.childrensmuseum-yunker.org	Fargo	ND	58102	701-232-6102	
Children's Museum of Cleveland 3813 Euclid Ave *Web:* www.clevelandchildrensmuseum.org	Cleveland	OH	44115	216-791-7114	791-8838
Cincinnati Fire Museum 315 W Court St Ste 1 *Web:* www.cincyfiremuseum.com	Cincinnati	OH	45202	513-621-5553	
Cinergy Children's Museum 1301 Western Ave Cincinnati Museum Ctr *TF:* 800-733-2077 ■ *Web:* www.cincymuseum.org	Cincinnati	OH	45203	513-287-7000	
AC Gilbert's Discovery Village 116 Marion St NE *Web:* www.acgilbert.org	Salem	OR	97301	503-371-3631	316-3485
Portland Children's Museum 4015 SW Canyon Rd *Web:* www.portlandcm.org	Portland	OR	97221	503-223-6500	223-6600
Science Factory Children's Museum & Planetarium 2300 Leo Harris Pkwy *Web:* www.sciencefactory.org	Eugene	OR	97401	541-682-7888	484-9027
Children's Museum of Pittsburgh 10 Children's Way *Web:* www.pittsburghkids.org	Pittsburgh	PA	15212	412-322-5058	
ExpERIEnce Children's Museum 420 French St *Web:* www.eriechildrensmuseum.org	Erie	PA	16507	814-453-3743	459-9735
Explore & More Hands-On Children's Museum 20 E High St *Web:* www.exploreandmore.com	Gettysburg	PA	17325	717-337-9151	
Hands-On House Children's Museum of Lancaster 721 Landis Vly Rd *Web:* www.handsonhouse.org	Lancaster	PA	17601	717-569-5437	
Please Touch Museum Memorial Hall Fairmount Pk 4231 Ave of the Republic *TF:* 800-732-0999 ■ *Web:* www.pleasetouchmuseum.org	Philadelphia	PA	19131	215-963-0667	581-3183
Providence Children's Museum 100 S St *Web:* www.childrenmuseum.org	Providence	RI	02903	401-273-5437	273-1004
Children's Museum of South Carolina 2204 N Oak St *Web:* www.cmsckids.org	Myrtle Beach	SC	29577	843-946-9469	946-7011
Children's Museum of the Lowcountry 25 Ann St *Web:* www.explorecml.org	Charleston	SC	29403	843-853-8962	853-1042
EdVenture Children's Museum 211 Gervais St *TF:* 888-236-2427 ■ *Web:* www.edventure.org	Columbia	SC	29201	803-779-3100	779-3144
Children's Museum of Memphis 2525 Central Ave *Web:* www.cmom.com	Memphis	TN	38104	901-458-2678	458-4033
Children's Museum of Oak Ridge 461 W Outer Dr *TF:* 877-524-1223 ■ *Web:* www.childrensmuseumofoakridge.org	Oak Ridge	TN	37830	865-482-1074	481-4889
Creative Discovery Museum 321 Chestnut St *Web:* www.cdmfun.org	Chattanooga	TN	37402	423-756-2738	267-9344
East Tennessee Discovery Ctr 516 N Beaman St Chilhowee Pk *Web:* themuseknoxville.com	Knoxville	TN	37914	865-594-1494	
Hands On! Regional Museum 315 E Main St *Web:* www.handsonmuseum.org	Johnson City	TN	37601	423-434-4263	928-6915
Austin Children's Museum 201 Colorado St *Web:* thinkeryaustin.org	Austin	TX	78701	512-472-2499	
Children's Museum of Houston 1500 Binz St *Web:* www.cmhouston.org	Houston	TX	77004	713-522-1138	522-5747
Don Harrington Discovery Ctr 1200 Streit Dr *Web:* www.dhdc.org	Amarillo	TX	79106	806-355-9547	
Grace Museum 102 Cypress St *Web:* www.thegracemuseum.org	Abilene	TX	79601	325-673-4587	675-5993
Imaginarium of South Texas 5300 San Dario Ste 505 *Web:* www.imaginariumstx.org	Laredo	TX	78041	956-728-0404	725-7776
San Antonio Children's Museum 2800 Broadway *Web:* www.sakids.org	San Antonio	TX	78209	210-212-4453	
Science Place, The 2201 N Field St *Web:* www.perotmuseum.org	Dallas	TX	75201	214-428-5555	756-5916
Discovery Gateway 444 West 100 South *Web:* www.discoverygateway.org	Salt Lake City	UT	84101	801-456-5437	456-5440
Treehouse Museum 347 22nd St *Web:* www.treehousemuseum.org	Ogden	UT	84401	801-394-9663	
Children's Museum of Richmond 2626 W Broad St *TF:* 866-737-5965 ■ *Web:* c-mor.org	Richmond	VA	23220	804-474-7000	474-7099
Children's Museum of Virginia 221 High St *Web:* childrensmuseumvirginia.com	Portsmouth	VA	23704	757-393-5258	393-8083
Virginia Discovery Museum 524 E Main St PO Box 1128 *Web:* www.vadm.org	Charlottesville	VA	22902	434-977-1025	977-9681
Children's Museum of Tacoma 936 Broadway *Web:* www.playtacoma.org	Tacoma	WA	98402	253-627-6031	627-2436

	City	State	Zip	Phone	Fax
Children's Museum Seattle 305 Harrison St *Web:* www.thechildrensmuseum.org	Seattle	WA	98109	206-441-1768	448-0910
Hands On Children's Museum 414 Jefferson St NE *Web:* www.hocm.org	Olympia	WA	98501	360-956-0818	754-8626
Betty Brinn Children's Museum 929 E Wisconsin Ave *Web:* www.bbcmkids.org	Milwaukee	WI	53202	414-390-5437	291-0906
Madison Children's Museum 100 N Hamilton St *Web:* www.madisonchildrensmuseum.org	Madison	WI	53703	608-256-6445	

522 MUSEUMS & HALLS OF FAME - SPORTS

	City	State	Zip	Phone	Fax
1932 & 1980 Lake Placid Winter Olympic Museum Olympic Ctr 2634 Main St *TF:* 800-462-6236 ■ *Web:* www.orda.org	Lake Placid	NY	12946	518-523-1655	523-9275
Alabama Sports Hall of Fame 2150 Richard Arrington Junior Blvd *Web:* www.ashof.org	Birmingham	AL	35203	205-323-6665	252-2212
Alberta Sports Hall of Fame & Museum 4200 Hwy 2 Ste 102 *Web:* ashfm.ca	Red Deer	AB	T4N1E3	403-341-8614	341-8619
American Museum of Fly Fishing 4104 Main Rd *TF:* 800-333-1550 ■ *Web:* www.amff.com	Manchester	VT	05254	802-362-3300	362-3308
American Water Ski Hall of Fame & Museum 1251 Holy Cow Rd *Web:* usawaterskifoundation.org	Polk City	FL	33868	863-324-2472	324-3996
Ansel Adams Gallery, The 9031 Village Dr *Web:* www.anseladams.com	Yosemite National Park	CA	95389	209-372-4413	
Arizona-Sonora Desert Museum Inc 2021 N Kinney Rd *Web:* www.desertmuseum.org	Tucson	AZ	85743	520-883-1380	
Arthaus Foundation 3840 S Ridgewood Ave *Web:* arthaus.org	Port Orange	FL	32129	386-767-0076	
Artonomy 544 W Liberty St Ste A *Web:* www.artonomyinc.com	Cincinnati	OH	45214	513-651-2787	
Arts Center of Cannon County Inc, The 1424 John Bragg Hwy *Web:* www.artscenterofcc.com	Woodbury	TN	37190	615-536-2791	
Arts Club of Chicago, The 201 E Ontario St *Web:* artsclubchicago.org	Chicago	IL	60611	312-787-3997	
Babe Ruth Birthplace Museum 216 Emory St *Web:* baberuthmuseum.org	Baltimore	MD	21230	410-727-1539	727-1652
Baseball Hall of Fame 910 S 3rd St *TF:* 888-375-9707 ■ *Web:* www.domeplus.com	Minneapolis	MN	55415	612-375-9707	
Baseball Reliquary PO Box 1850 *Web:* www.baseballreliquary.org	Monrovia	CA	91017	626-791-7647	
Billingsley House Museum 6900 Green Landing Rd *Web:* pgparks.com	Upper Marlboro	MD	20772	301-627-0730	
Blazing Editions 75 Pheasant Dr *Web:* www.blazing.com	East Greenwich	RI	02818	401-885-4329	
Bob Feller Museum 310 Mill St PO Box 95 *Web:* www.bobfellermuseum.org	Van Meter	IA	50261	515-996-2806	
Bobby Riggs Tennis Museum 875 Santa Fe Dr *Web:* bobbyriggs.net	Encinitas	CA	92024	760-473-2672	
Boca Raton Historical Society & Museum 71 N Federal Hwy *Web:* www.bocahistory.org	Boca Raton	FL	33432	561-395-6766	
British Columbia Sports Hall of Fame & Museum 777 Pacific Blvd S *Web:* www.bcsportshalloffame.com	Vancouver	BC	V6B4Y8	604-687-5520	687-5510
Britto Central Inc 818 Lincoln Rd *Web:* www.britto.com	Miami	FL	33139	305-531-8821	
Brunswick Historical Society 605 Brunswick Rd *Web:* townofbrunswick.org	Troy	NY	12180	518-279-4024	
Canada Olympic Hall of Fame & Museum 88 Canada Olympic Rd SW *Web:* www.winsport.ca	Calgary	AB	T3B5R5	403-247-5452	286-7213
Canada's Sports Hall of Fame 169 Canada Olympic Rd SW *Web:* www.sportshall.ca	Calgary	AB	T3B6B7	403-776-1040	
Canadian Football Hall of Fame & Museum 58 Jackson St W	Hamilton	ON	L8P1L4	905-528-7566	528-9781
Canadian Golf Hall of Fame & Museum Glen Abbey Golf Course 1333 Dorval Dr Ste 1 *TF:* 800-263-0009 ■ *Web:* golfcanada.ca	Oakville	ON	L6M4X7	905-849-9700	845-7040
Canadian Warplane Heritage Museum 9280 Airport Rd *Web:* www.warplane.com	Mount Hope	ON	L0R1W0	905-679-4183	
Canton Twp Historical Museum 1022 N Canton Ctr Rd *Web:* www.cantonhistoricalsociety.org	Canton	MI	48187	734-397-0088	
Caramoor Center for Music and The Arts Inc 149 Girdle Ridge Rd *Web:* www.caramoor.org	Katonah	NY	10536	914-232-5035	
Carolina Raptor Center 6000 Sample Rd *Web:* carolinaraptorcenter.org	Huntersville	NC	28078	704-875-6521	
Cheap Joe's Art Stuff Inc 374 Industrial Park Dr *TF:* 800-227-2788 ■ *Web:* www.cheapjoes.com	Boone	NC	28607	828-263-5472	
Clyfford Still Museum 1250 Bannock St *Web:* www.clyffordstillmuseum.org	Denver	CO	80204	720-354-4880	
Colorado Sports Hall of Fame 1701 Mile High Stadium *Fax Area Code:* 303 ■ *Web:* www.coloradosports.org	Denver	CO	80204	720-258-3888	244-1003*
Craft Emergency Relief Fund 24 Elm St *Web:* www.craftemergency.org	Montpelier	VT	05602	802-229-2306	
Delaware Sports Museum & Hall of Fame 801 Shipyard Dr *Web:* www.desports.org	Wilmington	DE	19801	302-425-3263	425-3713
Don Garlits Museums 13700 SW 16th Ave *TF:* 877-271-3278 ■ *Web:* www.garlits.com	Ocala	FL	34473	352-245-8661	
Dr Pepper Museum & Free Enterprise Institute, The 300 S Fifth St *Web:* www.drpeppermuseum.com	Waco	TX	76701	254-757-1025	
Eastern Museum of Motor Racing 100 Baltimore Rd *Web:* www.emmr.org	York Springs	PA	17372	717-528-8279	
Edward Tyler Nahem Fine Art Llc 37 W 57th St Frnt 2 *Web:* www.edwardtylernahemfineart.com	New York	NY	10019	212-517-2453	
Elmhurst Art Museum 150 S Cottage Hill Ave *Web:* elmhurstartmuseum.org	Elmhurst	IL	60126	630-834-0202	
Fernbank Museum of Natural History 767 Clifton Rd NE *Web:* www.fernbankmuseum.org	Atlanta	GA	30307	404-929-6300	
Florida Air Museum at Sun 'n Fun 4175 Medulla Rd *Web:* www.sun-n-fun.org	Lakeland	FL	33811	863-644-2431	648-9264
Fox Cities Performing Arts Center 400 W College Ave *Web:* foxcitiespac.com	Appleton	WI	54911	920-730-3782	
Georgia Sports Hall of Fame 301 Cherry St PO Box 4644 *Web:* georgiasportshalloffame.com/site	Macon	GA	31201	478-752-1585	752-1587
Grammy Museum Foundation Inc 800 W Olympic Blvd Ste 305 *Web:* www.grammymuseum.org	Los Angeles	CA	90015	213-765-6800	
Greyhound Hall of Fame 407 S Buckeye Ave *TF:* 800-932-7881 ■ *Web:* www.greyhoundhalloffame.com	Abilene	KS	67410	785-263-3000	
Harness Racing Museum & Hall of Fame 240 Main St *Web:* www.harnessmuseum.com	Goshen	NY	10924	845-294-6330	294-3463
Hendrick Motorsports Museum 4400 Papa Joe Hendrick Blvd *Fax Area Code:* 704 ■ *TF:* 877-467-4890 ■ *Web:* www.hendrickmotorsports.com	Charlotte	NC	28262	877-467-4890	455-0346*
Hockey Hall of Fame 30 Yonge St *Web:* www.hhof.com	Toronto	ON	M5E1X8	416-360-7735	360-1316
Hyde Park Art Center 5020 S Cornell Ave *Web:* hydeparkart.org	Chicago	IL	60615	773-324-5520	
IGFA Fishing Hall of Fame & Museum 300 Gulf Stream Way *Web:* www.igfa.org	Dania Beach	FL	33004	954-922-4212	924-4220
Improv Asylum 216 Hanover St *TF:* 888-396-6887 ■ *Web:* www.improvasylum.com	Boston	MA	02113	617-263-6887	
Indiana Basketball Hall of Fame 408 Trojan Ln *Web:* www.hoopshall.com	New Castle	IN	47362	765-529-1891	529-0273
Indiana Football Hall of Fame 815 N A St PO Box 40 *Web:* www.indiana-football.org	Richmond	IN	47374	765-966-2235	966-5700
International Bowling Museum & Hall of Fame 621 Six Flags Dr *TF:* 800-514-2695 ■ *Web:* www.bowlingmuseum.com	Arlington	TX	76011	817-385-8215	385-8210
International Boxing Hall of Fame Museum 1 Hall of Fame Dr *Web:* www.ibhof.com	Canastota	NY	13032	315-697-7095	697-5356
International Gymnastics Hall of Fame & Museum 2100 NE 52nd St *Web:* www.ighof.com	Oklahoma City	OK	73111	405-602-6664	
International Jewish Sports Hall of Fame 7922 Turncrest Dr *Web:* www.jewishsports.net	Potomac	MD	20854	301-602-9953	765-9865
International Motorsports Hall of Fame & Museum 3198 Speedway Blvd *Web:* www.motorsportshalloffame.com	Talladega	AL	35160	256-362-5002	
International Snowmobile Hall of Fame 1521 N Railroad St *TF:* 800-746-8963 ■ *Web:* www.ishof.com	Eagle River	WI	54521	715-479-2186	
International Swimming Hall of Fame 1 Hall of Fame Dr *Web:* www.ishof.org	Fort Lauderdale	FL	33316	954-462-6536	525-4031
International Tennis Hall of Fame & Museum 194 Bellevue Ave *TF:* 800-745-3000 ■ *Web:* www.tennisfame.com	Newport	RI	02840	401-849-3990	
International Wrestling Institute & Museum 303 Jefferson St *Web:* www.nwhof.org	Waterloo	IA	50701	319-233-0745	233-3477
Ivan Allen Jr Braves Museum & Hall of Fame 755 Hank Aaron Dr SE *Web:* atlanta.braves.mlb.com	Atlanta	GA	30315	404-614-2310	
Jack Nicklaus Museum 2355 Olentangy River Rd *Web:* www.nicklausmuseum.org	Columbus	OH	43210	614-247-5959	247-5906
Kansas Sports Hall of Fame 515 S Wichita *Web:* www.kshof.org	Wichita	KS	67202	316-262-2038	
Krasl Art Center 707 Lake Blvd *Web:* krasl.org	Saint Joseph	MI	49085	269-983-0271	
Legends of the Game Baseball Museum 1000 Ballpark Way *Fax Area Code:* 817 ■ *TF:* 866-274-9053 ■ *Web:* texas.rangers.mlb.com	Arlington	TX	76011	866-274-9053	273-5093*
Louisiana Sports Hall of Fame 500 Front St *Web:* www.lasportshall.com	Natchitoches	LA	71457	318-238-4255	238-4258
Louisville Slugger Museum 800 W Main St *TF:* 877-775-8443 ■ *Web:* www.sluggermuseum.com	Louisville	KY	40202	502-585-5226	585-1179
Mackinac Island Butterfly 6750 Mcgulpin St *Web:* www.originalbutterflyhouse.com	Mackinac Island	MI	49757	906-847-3972	
Manitoba Sports Hall of Fame & Museum 145 Pacific Ave *Web:* www.halloffame.mb.ca	Winnipeg	MB	R3B2Z6	204-925-5600	

Phone / Fax

Mexican Heritage Plaza 1700 Alum Rock Ave San Jose CA 95116 408-928-5563
Web: mhcviva.org

Milwaukee Jewish Federation Inc
1360 N Prospect Ave Milwaukee WI 53202 414-390-5700
Web: milwaukeejewish.org

Mississippi Sports Hall of Fame & Museum
1152 Lakeland Dr Jackson MS 39216 601-982-8264
TF: 800-280-3263 ■ *Web:* www.msfame.com

Missouri Sports Hall of Fame
3861 E Stan Musial Dr Springfield MO 65809 417-889-3100 889-2761
TF: 800-498-5678 ■ *Web:* www.mosportshalloffame.com

Moncton Museum 20 Mountain Rd Moncton NB E1C2J8 506-856-4383
Web: www.moncton.ca

Motorcycle Hall of Fame Museum
13515 Yarmouth Dr Pickerington OH 43147 614-856-2222 856-2221
TF: 800-262-5646 ■ *Web:* www.americanmotorcyclist.com

Motorsports Hall of Fame of America (MSHFA)
1801 W International Speedway Blvd Daytona Beach FL 32114 248-349-7223
Web: www.mshf.com

Museum Store Products Inc
430 Sandshore Rd Ste 4 5 Hackettstown NJ 07840 908-852-2078
Web: www.museumstoreproducts.com

Naismith Memorial Basketball Hall of Fame
1000 W Columbus Ave Springfield MA 01105 413-781-6500
TF: 877-446-6752 ■ *Web:* www.hoophall.com

NASCAR Hall of Fame
400 E Martin Luther King Jr Blvd Charlotte NC 28202 704-654-4400
Web: www.nascarhall.com

National Baseball Hall of Fame & Museum
25 Main St Cooperstown NY 13326 607-547-7200 547-2044
TF: 888-425-5633 ■ *Web:* baseballhall.org

National Fresh Water Fishing Hall of Fame
10360 Hall of Fame Dr PO Box 690 Hayward WI 54843 715-634-4440 634-4440
TF: 866-268-4333 ■ *Web:* www.freshwater-fishing.org

National Italian American Sports Hall of Fame
1431 W Taylor St Chicago IL 60607 312-226-5566 226-5678
Web: www.niashf.org

National Museum of Polo & Hall of Fame
9011 Lk Worth Rd Lake Worth FL 33467 561-969-3210 964-8299
Web: www.polomuseum.com

National Museum of Racing & Hall of Fame
191 Union Ave Saratoga Springs NY 12866 518-584-0400 584-4574
TF: 800-562-5394 ■ *Web:* www.racingmuseum.org

National Polish-American Sports Hall of Fame
11727 Gallagher St Hamtramck MI 48212 313-407-3300
Web: www.polishsportshof.com

National Soaring Museum 51 Soaring Hill Dr. Elmira NY 14903 607-734-3128 732-6745
Web: www.soaringmuseum.org

National Soccer Hall of Fame
1801 S. Prairie Ave. Chicago IL 60616 312-808-1300 808-1301
Web: www.ussoccer.com

National Softball Hall of Fame & Museum
2801 NE 50th St Oklahoma City OK 73111 405-424-5266 424-3855
TF: 800-654-8337 ■ *Web:* www.teamusa.org/usa-softball.aspx

National Sprint Car Hall of Fame & Museum
1 Sprint Capital Pl Knoxville IA 50138 641-842-6176 842-6177
TF: 800-874-4488 ■ *Web:* www.sprintcarhof.com

National Wrestling Hall of Fame (NWHOF)
405 W Hall of Fame Ave Stillwater OK 74075 405-377-5243 377-5244
Web: nwhof.org

Negro Leagues Baseball Museum
1616 E 18th St Kansas City MO 64108 816-221-1920 221-8424
Web: www.nlbm.com

New Brunswick Sports Hall of Fame
503 Queen St PO Box 6000 Fredericton NB E3B5H1 506-453-3747 459-0481
Web: nbsportshalloffame.com/sports/default.aspx

Nolan Ryan Exhibit Ctr 2925 S Bypass 35 Alvin TX 77511 281-388-1134
Web: www.nolanryanfoundation.org

North Carolina Auto Racing Hall of Fame
119 Knob Hill Rd Lakeside Pk Mooresville NC 28117 704-663-5331 663-6949
Web: www.ncarhof.com

North Carolina Sports Hall of Fame
5 E Edenton St NC Museum of History Raleigh NC 27601 919-807-7900 733-8655
TF: 877-627-6724 ■ *Web:* www.ncdcr.gov

North Carolina Tennis Hall of Fame
2709 Henry St. Greensboro NC 27405 336-852-8577 852-7334
Web: www.nctennis.com

Northwestern Ontario Sports Hall of Fame
219 May St S Thunder Bay ON P7E1B5 807-622-2852 622-2736
Web: www.nwosportshalloffame.com

Nu Promo International
11697 Chesterdale Rd Ste Cincinnati OH 45246 513-782-0168
Web: 74585.asisupplier.com

Oceanside Museum of Art 704 Pier View Way Oceanside CA 92054 760-435-3720
Web: www.oma-online.org

Oklahoma Sports Hall of Fame & Jim Thorpe Museum
4040 N Lincoln Blvd. Oklahoma City OK 73105 405-427-1400
Web: www.jimthorpeassoc.org

Pat Croce & Co 402 W Lancaster Ave Ste Haverford PA 19003 610-658-5270
Web: www.patcroce.com

Paul W Bryant Museum 300 Paul W Bryant Dr Tuscaloosa AL 35487 205-348-4668 348-8883
TF General: 866-772-2327 ■ *Web:* bryantmuseum.com

Peter J McGovern Little League Baseball Museum
539 US Rt 15 Hwy PO Box 3485 Williamsport PA 17701 570-326-1921 326-1074
Web: littleleague.org/learn/museum.htm

Philadelphia Sports Hall of Fame Foundation
2701 Grant Ave. Philadelphia PA 19114 215-254-5049
Web: www.phillyhall.org

Pretend City, The Childrens Museum of Orange County
17752 Sky Park Cir Ste 280 Irvine CA 92614 949-428-3900
Web: pretendcity.org

Pro Football Hall of Fame
2121 George Halas Dr NW Canton OH 44708 330-456-8207 456-8175
Web: www.profootballhof.com

Phone / Fax

ProRodeo Hall of Fame & Museum of the American Cowboy
101 ProRodeo Dr Colorado Springs CO 80919 719-528-4703
Web: www.prorodeo.org

Putnam Museum of History & Natural Science
1717 W 12th St. Davenport IA 52804 563-324-1933
Web: putnam.org

Rose Bowl Hall of Fame
391 S Orange Grove Blvd Pasadena CA 91184 626-449-4100
Web: www.tournamentofroses.com

Rowland Institute for Science Inc, The
100 Edwin H Land Blvd Cambridge MA 02142 617-497-4600
Web: www2.rowland.harvard.edu

Rubin Museum, The 150 W 17th St New York NY 10011 212-620-5000
Web: www.rubinmuseum.org

Santa Maria Museum of Flight Inc
3015 Airpark Dr Santa Maria CA 93455 805-922-8758
Web: www.smmof.org

Saskatchewan Sports Hall of Fame & Museum
2205 Victoria Ave Regina SK S4P0S4 306-780-9232
Web: www.sshfm.com

Shanaman Sports Museum of Tacoma
2727 E 'D' St Tacoma WA 98421 206-627-5857
Web: www.tacomasportsmuseum.com

Sports Immortals Museum
6830 N Federal Hwy Boca Raton FL 33487 561-997-2575 997-6949
Web: www.sportsimmortals.com

Sports Legends at Camden Yards
301 W Camden St. Baltimore MD 21201 410-727-1539 727-1652
Web: baberuthmuseum.org

Sports Museum, The 100 Legends Way Boston MA 02114 617-624-1234
Web: www.sportsmuseum.org

Stepping Stones Museum For Children Inc
303 W Ave Norwalk CT 06850 203-899-0606
Web: www.steppingstonesmuseum.org

Texas Sports Hall of Fame
1108 S University Parks Dr. Waco TX 76706 254-756-1633 756-2384
TF: 800-567-9561 ■ *Web:* www.tshof.org

Trapshooting Hall of Fame & Museum
601 W National Rd Vandalia OH 45377 937-660-5663
Web: www.traphof.org

U.S. National Ski Hall of Fame
610 Palms Ave Ishpeming MI 49849 906-485-6323 486-4570
TF: 800-648-0720 ■ *Web:* www.skihall.com

University of Iowa Athletics Hall of Fame
2425 Prairie Meadow Dr. Iowa City IA 52242 319-384-1031 335-9726
TF: 877-462-6342 ■ *Web:* hof.hawkeyesports.com

Us Art Company Inc 66 Pacella Park Dr Randolph MA 02368 781-986-6500
TF: 800-872-7826 ■ *Web:* www.usart.com

Vancouver Art Gallery 750 Hornby St Vancouver BC V6Z2H7 604-662-4700
Web: vanartgallery.bc.ca

Ventura County Arts Council
646 County Sq Dr Ste 154 Ventura CA 93003 805-658-2213
Web: vcartscouncil.org

Virginia Sports Hall of Fame (VSHFM)
206 High St Portsmouth VA 23704 757-393-8031 393-8288
Web: www.vshfm.com

Volleyball Hall of Fame 444 Dwight St Holyoke MA 01040 413-536-0926
Web: www.volleyhall.org

Washoe Tribe 919 Us Hwy 395 N Gardnerville NV 89410 775-265-4191
Web: www.washoetribe.us

Waterloo Regional Childrens Museum Studio
10 King St W Kitchener ON N2G1A3 519-749-9387
Web: kitchener-ontario.cylex.ca

Whale Museum, The 62 1st St. Friday Harbor WA 98250 360-378-4710
Web: whale-museum.org

Women's Basketball Hall of Fame
700 Hall of Fame Dr Knoxville TN 37915 865-633-9000 633-9294
Web: www.wbhof.com

World Figure Skating Museum & Hall of Fame
20 First St. Colorado Springs CO 80906 719-635-5200 635-9548
Web: www.worldskatingmuseum.org

523 MUSIC DISTRIBUTORS

Phone / Fax

A-r Editions Inc 1600 Aspen Cmns Ste 100 Middleton WI 53562 608-836-9000 831-8200
TF: 800-736-0070 ■ *Web:* www.areditions.com

Allegro Corp 20048 NE San Rafael St Portland OR 97230 503-491-8480 491-8488*
**Fax:* Orders ■ *TF:* 800-288-2007 ■ *Web:* www.allegro-music.com

Baker & Taylor Inc 2550 W Tyvola Rd Ste 300 Charlotte NC 28217 800-775-1800 998-3316*
**Fax Area Code:* 704 ■ *TF:* 800-775-1800 ■ *Web:* www.btol.com

Caroline Distribution 150 Fifth Ave New York NY 10011 212-786-8100
Web: www.caroline.com

EMI Christian Music Group 101 Winners Cir Brentwood TN 37027 615-371-4300 371-4305
Web: www.capitolchristianmusicgroup.com.

Gotham Distributing Corp 60 Portland Rd Conshohocken PA 19428 610-649-7650 649-0315
TF: 800-446-8426 ■ *Web:* oldies.com

Inspired Studios
9920 Royal Cardigan Way West Palm Beach FL 33411 561-333-9142
Web: www.inspired-studios.com

Malaco Music Group Inc 3023 W Northside Dr Jackson MS 39213 601-982-4522 982-4528
TF Cust Svc: 800-272-7936 ■ *Web:* www.malaco.com

Orchard Enterprises Inc 23 E 4th St 3rd Fl New York NY 10003 212-201-9280 201-9203
Web: www.theorchard.com

RED Distribution 345 Hudson St 6th Fl. New York NY 10014 917-421-7601
Web: www.redmusic.com

Select-O-Hits Inc 1981 Fletcher Creek Dr. Memphis TN 38133 901-388-1190
TF: 800-346-0723 ■ *Web:* www.selectohits.com

524 MUSIC PROGRAMMING SERVICES

Phone *Fax*

Music Choice 110 Gibraltar Rd Ste 200 Horsham PA 19044 646-459-3357 784-5870*
**Fax Area Code:* 215 ■ *Web:* www.musicchoice.com

Muzak LLC 3318 Lakemont Blvd. Fort Mill SC 29708 770-246-3941 396-3136*
**Fax Area Code:* 803 ■ *TF:* 888-689-2559 ■ *Web:* us.moodmedia.com

PlayNetwork Inc 8727 148th Ave NE Redmond WA 98052 425-497-8100 497-8181
Web: www.playnetwork.com

525 MUSIC STORES

See Also Book, Music, Video Clubs p. 1867

Phone *Fax*

A D Vision Inc 5750 Bintliff Dr Ste 210 Houston TX 77036 713-341-7100
Web: www.advfilms.com

Amazon.com Inc 1200 12th Ave S Ste 1200 Seattle WA 98144 206-266-1000
NASDAQ: AMZN ■ *TF Cust Svc:* 800-201-7575 ■ *Web:* www.amazon.com

Anonymizer Inc
6755 Mira Mesa Blvd Ste 123-164 San Diego CA 92121 888-270-0141
TF: 888-270-0141 ■ *Web:* www.anonymizer.com

Apex Software Solutions LLC
5039 Beckwith Blvd Ste 109 San Antonio TX 78249 210-699-6666
Web: www.apexwin.com

AptSoft Corp 20 Mall Rd Burlington MA 01803 781-270-4900
Web: aptsoft-corporation.software.informer.com

apyEdge Inc, The 2505 Meridian Pkwy Ste 350 Durham NC 27713 919-572-6709
Web: www.ablsa.com

Arial Software LLC 1501 Stampede Ave Ste 9005 Cody WY 82414 949-218-3852
Web: www.arialsoftware.com

Bay-Pointe Technology Ltd
2662 Brecksville Rd Richfield OH 44286 330-659-6400
Web: www.baypointetech.com

Bellamy Software Ltd
13220 St Albert Trail Ste 310 Edmonton AB T5L4W1 780-489-5756
Web: www.bellamysoftware.com

Best Buy Company Inc 7601 Penn Ave S. Minneapolis MN 55423 612-291-1000 292-2323*
NYSE: BBY ■ **Fax:* Cust Svc ■ *TF:* 888-237-8289 ■ *Web:* www.bestbuy.com

Bexel Corp 2701 N Ontario St Burbank CA 91504 818-565-4322
Web: www.bexel.com

Cal Coast Telecom 886 Faulstich Ct San Jose CA 95112 408-275-8888
Web: www.cctcom.net

Candlewest Systems Group Ltd
4400 Dominion St Unit 100 Burnaby BC V5G4G3 604-737-8570
Web: www.encorebusiness.com

CD Universe 101 N Plains Industrial Rd Wallingford CT 06492 203-294-1648 294-0391
TF: 800-231-7937 ■ *Web:* www.cduniverse.com

CD Warehouse 900 N Broadway Oklahoma City OK 73102 919-577-6000 949-2566*
**Fax Area Code:* 405 ■ *TF:* 800-641-9394 ■ *Web:* cdwarehouse.com

Clear Technologies Inc
1199 S Beltline Rd Ste 120 Coppell TX 75019 972-906-7500
Web: www.cleartechnologies.net

Clocktower Technology Services Inc
308 W Central St Ste B Franklin MA 02038 508-541-6143
Web: www.clocktowertech.com

Commerce Solutions Inc 7 4th St Ste 46 Petaluma CA 94952 707-773-1198
Web: www.commercesolutions.com

Conexnet Corp 1020 S Wabash Ave Apt 5d Chicago IL 60605 312-692-0898
Web: conexnet.com

Contigo Systems Inc 2700 Production Way Vancouver BC V5A4X1 604-683-3106
Web: www.contigo.com

Cord Camera Centers Inc 2030 Dividend Dr Columbus OH 43228 614-343-5000
Web: www.cordcamera.com

Delta Solutions Inc 4 Parkway N. Deerfield IL 60015 847-317-9544
Web: www.delta-pharma.com

Dryden Municipal Telephone System
65 Princess St Dryden ON P8N1C8 807-223-1100
Web: dmts.biz

DS-IQ Inc 15831 NE 8th St Ste E-220 Bellevue WA 98008 425-213-1400
Web: ds-iq.com

DSN Group Inc 152 Lorraine Dr. Lake Zurich IL 60047 888-445-2919
TF: 888-445-2919 ■ *Web:* www.dsngroup.net

eMusic.com Inc 511 Avenue of the Americas New York NY 10011 212-201-9240
Web: www.emusic.com

Express Technologies 117 Vip Dr Ste 110 Wexford PA 15090 724-940-5000
Web: www.xpresstech.com

First Piedmont Corp 108 S Main St. Chatham VA 24531 434-432-0211
Web: www.fpcwaste.com

FirstCom Music 1325 Capital Pkwy Ste 109 Carrollton TX 75006 972-446-8742 242-6526
TF Cust Svc: 800-858-8880 ■ *Web:* www.firstcom.com

Flying Hippo Investments L L C
130 E Third St. Des Moines IA 50309 515-288-5316
Web: www.flyinghippo.com

Foliage Inc 20 N Ave Burlington MA 01803 781-993-5500
Web: www.foliage.com

Foresite Software LLC 133 Third Ave Baraboo WI 53913 608-356-0286
Web: www.foresitesoftware.com

Global Electronic Music Marketplace
PO Box 4062 Palm Springs CA 92263 800-207-4366
TF: 800-207-4366

Grabar Voice and Data Inc
921 S 9th St Ste 108 Bismarck ND 58504 701-258-3528
Web: www.grabarvoice.com

Hansen Software Corp
1855 Kirschner Rd Ste 380 Kelowna BC V1Y4N7 250-861-9166
Web: www.hansensoftware.com

Hastings Entertainment Inc 3601 Plains Blvd Amarillo TX 79102 877-427-8464
NASDAQ: HAST ■ *TF Cust Svc:* 877-427-8464 ■ *Web:* www.gohastings.com

Idilia Inc 1470 Peel St Twr B Ste 810 Montreal QC H3A1T1 514-843-6897
Web: www.idilia.com

Phone *Fax*

Impact Marketing Inc
7696 Golden Triangle Dr Eden Prairie MN 55344 952-562-6000
Web: www.impactmn.com

Ita Inc 2162 Dana Ave. Cincinnati OH 45207 513-631-8877
Web: www.ita.com

Knaster Technology Group, The
7955 E Arapahoe Ct Ste 1000 Englewood CO 80112 303-796-7626
Web: www.theknastergroup.com

Leader Business Systems
35436 Mound Rd Sterling Heights MI 48310 586-264-4908
Web: www.leaderbusiness.com

Med-Tech Resource Inc 29485 Airport Rd. Eugene OR 97402 888-627-7779
TF: 888-627-7779 ■ *Web:* www.gomed-tech.com

Midwest Office Automations Inc
3200 Line Dr. Sioux City IA 51106 712-277-4555
Web: www.moasolutions.com

Mississippi Music Inc 222 N Main St Hattiesburg MS 39401 601-544-5821 544-5841
TF: 800-844-5821 ■ *Web:* mississippimusic.net

Mncl Inc 9810 E 42nd St Ste 223 Tulsa OK 74146 918-728-6032
Web: mncl.net

Monticello Corp, The
4060 Peachtree Rd Ste D-339 Atlanta GA 30319 770-446-9000
Web: www.thepapertiger.com

Newbury Comics Inc 5 Guest St. Brighton MA 02135 617-254-1666 254-1085
Web: www.newbury.com

NotePage Inc 86 Ring Rd Plympton MA 02367 781-829-0500
Web: www.notepage.net

Nova Networks Inc 1700 Woodward Dr Ste 100 Ottawa ON K2C3R8 613-563-6682
Web: novanetworks.com

Numetrics Management Systems Inc
20863 Stevens Creek Blvd Ste 510 Cupertino CA 95014 408-351-5800
Web: www.numetrics.com

Officeware Inc 11401 Bluegrass Pkwy. Louisville KY 40299 502-491-2722
Web: www.officeware.com

OneName Corp 18 W Mercer Ste 300 Seattle WA 98119 206-812-6000
Web: onename.com

Paradigm Design Associates Inc
142 Ferry Rd Ste 8 Old Saybrook CT 06475 860-510-0750
Web: m.pda4.com

Patrick Solutions Inc 955 W 3rd Ave Columbus OH 43212 614-257-0300
Web: patricksolutions.com

Profound Logic Software Inc
396 Congress Park Dr Dayton OH 45459 937-439-7925
Web: www.profoundlogic.com

Proviatek Inc 80 Broad St Fl 5 New York NY 10004 212-500-6037
Web: proviatek.com

Quantrum Llc 2371 Lkview Dr Beavercreek OH 45431 937-281-6272
Web: quantrum-llc.com

RD Data Solutions LLC 2608 Avalon Dr Lewisville TX 75056 214-594-9080
Web: www.rddatasolutions.com

Record Exchange, The 1105 W Idaho St. Boise ID 83702 208-344-8010
Web: www.therecordexchange.com

Record Town Inc 38 Corporate Cir Albany NY 12203 518-452-1242
Web: www.twec.com

Retail Computer Group LLC, The
8194 Traphagen St NW. Massillon OH 44646 330-830-5363
Web: www.trcgllc.com

RiverOne Inc 121 Innovation Dr Ste 150 Irvine CA 92617 949-856-1500
Web: www.riverone.com

Satellite Records 259 Bowery New York NY 10012 212-995-1744
Web: www.satelliterecords.com

SEAS Education 971 Coley Dr. Mountain Home AR 72653 870-425-6933
Web: www.computerautomation.com

Shunra Software Ltd 1800 JFK Blvd. Philadelphia PA 19103 215-564-4046
Web: www.shunra.com

SightSound Technologies Inc
311 S Craig St Ste 205 Pittsburgh PA 15213 412-621-6100
Web: www.sightsound.com

Signix Inc 1203 Carter St Chattanooga TN 37402 423-648-2012
Web: www.signix.net

Simon & Arrington Inc 6215 Brookshire Ter. Fort Myers FL 33912 305-718-0630
Web: www.s-a.us

SkyTECH Solutions LLC
953 Plum Grove Rd Ste D Schaumburg IL 60173 847-995-8450
Web: www.skytechsolutions.com

Softek Solutions Inc
4500 W. 89th St Ste 100 Prairie Village KS 66207 913-649-1024
Web: www.softekinc.com

Software Business Systems Inc
7401 Metro Blvd Ste 550 Minneapolis MN 55439 952-835-0100
Web: sbsweb.com

Solatech Inc 1560 N Main St Ste 102 High Point NC 27262 336-889-2455
Web: www.solatech.com

Sperry Software Inc 833 Pheasant Ct Jacksonville FL 32259 503-973-5054
Web: www.SperrySoftware.com

SpikeSource Inc
2000 Seaport Blvd 2nd Fl Redwood City CA 94063 650-249-4140
Web: www.blackducksoftware.com

Starthis Inc 1460 W Dundee Rd Arlington Heights IL 60004 847-255-9330
Web: www.starthis.com

Suncoast Solutions Inc
19337 US Hwy 19 N Ste 450 Clearwater FL 33764 727-599-2500
Web: www.sncoast.com

Sundial Software Corp 5325 Wall St Ste 2900 Madison WI 53718 608-663-8100
Web: www.sundialsc.com

Synectic Systems Inc 4180 Via Real Ste A Carpenteria CA 93013 805-745-1920
Web: www.synecticsusa.com

Syrasoft Llc 307 Kasson Rd. Camillus NY 13031 315-708-0341
Web: syrasoft.com

Tabula Rosa Systems LLC 17 Cedar Ln. Titusville NJ 08560 609-818-1802
Web: www.tabularosa.net

Tek Data Systems 31 Crestview Dr Unit 2 Westerly RI 02891 401-596-5175
Web: tekdata.com

Company	City	State	ZIP	Phone	Fax
Telsoft Solutions Inc 100 N Brand Blvd Ste 400 *Web:* www.telsoft-solutions.com	Glendale	CA	91203	818-545-8680	
Test com Inc 1501 Euclid Ave Ste 407 *TF:* 877-502-8600 ■ *Web:* www.test.com	Cleveland	OH	44115	877-502-8600	
Threewide Corp 453 Suncrest Towne Centre 2nd Fl Ste 200 *Web:* www.threewide.com	Morgantown	WV	26505	304-296-9595	
Total Control Software Corp 12010 Watson Rd *Web:* www.tcsoft.com	Sherwood	AR	72120	501-833-3281	
TranSenda International LLC 2700 156th Ave NE Ste 250 *Web:* www.bioclinica.com	Bellevue	WA	98007	425-895-1300	
Trillion Communications Corp 3871 Pine Ln *Web:* www.trillionusa.com	Bessemer	AL	35022	205-481-1678	
TriStar Inc 3740 E La Salle St *Web:* www.tristar.com	Phoenix	AZ	85040	602-333-1600	
Tuscany Design Automation Inc 3030 S College Ave Ste 102 *Web:* tuscanyda.com	Fort Collins	CO	80525	970-377-0717	
V-Technologies LLC 675 W Johnson Ave *TF:* 800-462-4016 ■ *Web:* www.vtechnologies.com	Cheshire	CT	06705	800-462-4016	
VelQuest Corp 25 S St *Web:* www.velquest.com	Hopkinton	MA	01748	508-497-9911	
Voice & Data Networks Inc 6981 Washington Ave S *Web:* www.voicedata.com	Minneapolis	MN	55439	952-946-5353	
Vortaloptics Inc 7251 W Lk Mead Blvd Ste 300 *Web:* www.vortaloptics.com	Las Vegas	NV	89128	702-369-2500	
WebVision Inc 19950 Mariner Ave *Web:* www.webvisioninc.com	Torrance	CA	90503	310-793-4500	
Workplace Technology Center Inc 2101 W 41st St Ste 39 *Web:* workplace-it.com	Sioux Falls	SD	57105	605-367-3767	
Workspace com Inc 10451 Mill Run Cir Ste 400 *Web:* www.workspace.com	Owings Mills	MD	21117	410-872-9110	
Xavient Information Systems Inc 2125 Madera Rd Ste B *Web:* www.xavient.com	Simi Valley	CA	93065	805-955-4111	
ZAMBA Corp 3033 Excelsior Blvd Ste 200 *Web:* www.zambasolutions.com	Minneapolis	MN	55416	952-832-9800	

526 MUSICAL INSTRUMENT STORES

Company	City	State	ZIP	Phone	Fax
Al C Rinaldi Inc 1718 Chestnut St *Web:* www.chopinpiano.com	Philadelphia	PA	19103	215-568-7800	
Alamo Music Ctr 425 N Main Ave *TF:* 800-822-5010 ■ *Web:* www.alamomusic.com	San Antonio	TX	78205	210-224-1010	226-8742
American Musical Supply PO Box 152 *TF:* 800-458-4076 ■ *Web:* www.americanmusical.com	Spicer	MN	56288	320-796-2088	
Amro Music Stores 2918 Poplar Ave *TF General:* 800-626-2676 ■ *Web:* www.amromusic.com	Memphis	TN	38111	901-323-8888	325-6407
Annex Pro Inc 49 Dunlevy Ave Ste 220 *TF:* 800-682-6639 ■ *Web:* www.annexpro.com	Vancouver	BC	V6A3A3	604-682-6639	
Ardsley Musical Instrument Service Ltd 219 Sprain Rd *Web:* www.ardsleymusic.com	Scarsdale	NY	10583	914-693-6639	693-6974
Armadillo Enterprises Inc 4924 W Waters Ave *Web:* www.armadilloent.com	Tampa	FL	33634	813-600-3920	
Bananas at Large 1504 Fourth St *Web:* www.bananas.com	San Rafael	CA	94901	415-457-7600	457-9148
Beatport LLC 2399 Blake St Ste 170 *Web:* www.beatport.com	Denver	CO	80205	720-974-9500	
Bodine's Pianos 9361 Penn Ave S	Bloomington	MN	55431	612-866-2025	866-0463
Brook Mays Music Co 8605 John Carpenter Fwy *TF Cust Svc:* 800-637-8966 ■ *Web:* www.brookmays.com	Dallas	TX	75247	214-631-0928	905-4964
Buddy Rogers Music Inc 6891 Simpson Ave *TF:* 800-536-2263 ■ *Web:* www.buddyrogers.com	Cincinnati	OH	45239	513-729-1950	728-6010
Casavant Freres Inc 900 rue Girouard est *Web:* www.casavant.ca	St. Hyacinthe	QC	J2S2Y2	450-773-5001	
Cascio Interstate Music 13819 W National Ave *TF:* 800-462-2263 ■ *Web:* www.interstatemusic.com	New Berlin	WI	53151	262-789-7600	786-6840
Chaney's Music Exchange 1501 N Main St *Web:* www.listentocds.com	Walnut Creek	CA	94596	925-933-6310	
Corner Music Inc 2705 12th Ave S *Web:* cornermusicnashville.com	Nashville	TN	37204	615-297-9559	
Cream City Music 12505 W Bluemound Rd *TF:* 800-800-0087 ■ *Web:* www.warpdrivemusic.com	Brookfield	WI	53005	262-860-1800	
Creative Allies Inc 9 W Walnut St Ste 3B *Web:* www.creativeallies.com	Asheville	NC	28801	828-252-6300	
Elderly Instruments 1100 N Washington Ave *TF:* 888-473-5810 ■ *Web:* www.elderly.com	Lansing	MI	48906	517-372-7890	372-5155
Evola Music Center Inc 12745 23 Mile Rd *Web:* www.evola.com	Shelby Township	MI	48315	586-726-6570	
First Act Inc 745 Boylston St *TF:* 888-551-1115 ■ *Web:* www.firstact.com	Boston	MA	02116	617-226-7888	226-7890
Fletcher Music Centers Inc 3966 Airway Cir *TF:* 800-258-1088 ■ *Web:* www.fletchermusic.com	Clearwater	FL	33762	727-571-1088	
Fodera Guitars Inc 68 34th St Ste 3 *Web:* www.fodera.com	Brooklyn	NY	11232	718-832-3455	
Foster Family Music Center LLC 2967 State St	Bettendorf	IA	52722	563-355-0647	
Foxes Music Co 416 S Washington St *TF:* 800-446-4414 ■ *Web:* www.foxesmusic.com	Falls Church	VA	22046	703-533-7393	536-2171
Front End Audio 130 Hunter Village Dr Ste D *TF:* 888-228-4530 ■ *Web:* www.frontendaudio.com	Irmo	SC	29063	803-748-0914	
Georges Music Inc 912 Third St S *Web:* www.georgesmusic.com	Jacksonville Beach	FL	32250	904-270-2220	
Gigasonic 260 E Gish Rd *TF:* 888-246-4442 ■ *Web:* www.gigasonic.com	San Jose	CA	95112	408-573-1400	
Graves Piano & Organ Company Inc 5798 Karl Rd *TF:* 800-686-4322 ■ *Web:* gravespianos.com	Columbus	OH	43229	614-847-4322	847-0808
Gruhn Guitars 2120 Eight Ave S *Web:* guitars.com	Nashville	TN	37204	615-256-2033	255-2021
Guitar Center Inc 5795 Lindero Canyon Rd *Web:* www.guitarcenter.com	Westlake Village	CA	91362	818-735-8800	
Heid Music Company Inc 308 East College Ave *Web:* www.heidmusic.com	Appleton	WI	54911	920-734-1969	
Hermes Trading Company Inc 830 N Cage Blvd *Web:* www.hermes-music.com	Pharr	TX	78577	956-781-8472	
International Violin Co Ltd 1421 Clarkview Rd *TF:* 800-542-3538 ■ *Web:* www.internationalviolin.com	Baltimore	MD	21209	410-832-2525	832-2528
John Keal Music Company Inc 819 Livingston Ave *Web:* www.myjohnkeal.com	Albany	NY	12206	518-482-4405	
JW Pepper & Son Inc 2480 Industrial Blvd *TF:* 800-345-6296 ■ *Web:* www.jwpepper.com	Paoli	PA	19301	610-648-0500	993-0563
Kanstul Musical Instruments Inc 1332 S Claudina St *Web:* www.kanstul.com	Anaheim	CA	92805	714-563-1000	
Leitz Music Company Inc 508 Harrison Ave *Web:* www.leitzmusic.com	Panama City	FL	32401	850-769-0111	
Lone Star Percussion 10611 Control Pl *TF:* 866-792-0143 ■ *Web:* www.lonestarpercussion.com	Dallas	TX	75238	214-340-0835	
Long & McQuade Musical Instruments 722 Rosebank Rd *Web:* www.long-mcquade.com	Pickering	ON	L1W4B2	905-837-9785	837-9786
Lpd Music International Corp 32575 Industrial Dr *Web:* www.lpdmusic.com	Madison Heights	MI	48071	248-585-9630	
Lynx Studio Technology Inc 1048 Irvine Ave *Web:* www.lynxstudio.com	Newport Beach	CA	92660	949-515-8265	
M Steinert & Sons Co 162 Boylston St *Web:* www.msteinert.com	Boston	MA	02116	617-426-1900	
Malmark Inc 5712 Easton Rd *Web:* www.malmark.com	Plumsteadville	PA	18949	215-766-7200	
Marshall Music Co 4555 Wilson Ave SW Ste 1 *Web:* www.marshallmusic.com	Grandville	MI	49418	616-530-7700	
Moog Music Inc 160 Broadway St *Web:* www.moogmusic.com	Asheville	NC	28801	828-251-0090	
Mullen Guitar Company Inc 11906 County Rd Mm *Web:* www.mullenguitars.com	Flagler	CO	80815	970-664-2518	
Music & Arts Centers Inc 4626 Wedgewood Blvd *TF:* 888-731-5396 ■ *Web:* www.musicarts.com	Frederick	MD	21703	888-731-5396	
Musician's Friend Inc PO Box 7479 *TF:* 800-391-8762 ■ *Web:* www.musiciansfriend.com	Westlake Village	CA	91359	801-501-8110	
Musiciansbuy.com Inc 7830 Byron Dr Ste 1 *TF:* 877-778-7845 ■ *Web:* www.musiciansbuy.com	West Palm Beach	FL	33404	561-842-7451	840-9032
Princeton University Store 36 University Pl *Web:* www.pustore.com	Princeton	NJ	08540	609-921-8500	
Quantum Audio Designs Inc 6408 State Hwy 77 *TF:* 888-545-4404 ■ *Web:* www.quantumaudiodesigns.com	Benton	MO	63736	573-545-4404	
Quinlan & Fabish Music Co 166 Shore Dr *Web:* www.qandf.com	Burr Ridge	IL	60527	630-654-4111	
Railroad Bazaar LLC 1207 Eidson St *Web:* www.railroadbazaar.com	Athens	AL	35611	256-232-5800	
Reverb Music LLC 3316 N Lincoln Ave *Web:* www.chicagomusicexchange.com	Chicago	IL	60657	773-525-7773	
Saga Musical Instruments Inc 137 Utah Ave *Web:* www.sagamusic.com	South San Francisco	CA	94080	650-588-5558	
Schmitt Music Co 2400 Fwy Blvd *Web:* www.schmittmusic.com	Brooklyn Center	MN	55430	763-566-4560	
Seattle Sport Sciences Inc 24066 NE 53rd Pl *Web:* www.seattlesportsciences.com	Redmond	WA	98053	425-939-0015	
Seymour Duncan Inc 5427 Hollister Ave *Web:* www.seymourduncan.com	Santa Barbara	CA	93111	805-964-9610	
Sherman Clay & Company Inc 1111 Bayhill Dr Ste 450 *Web:* www.shermanclay.com	San Bruno	CA	94066	650-952-2300	
Stanton's Sheet Music 330 S Fourth St *TF:* 800-426-8742 ■ *Web:* www.stantons.com	Columbus	OH	43215	614-224-4257	224-5929
Steve's Music 51 Rue Saint-antoine O *Web:* www.stevesmusic.com	Montreal	QC	H2Z1G9	514-878-2216	
Strait Music Co 2428 W Ben White Blvd *TF:* 800-725-8877 ■ *Web:* www.straitmusic.com	Austin	TX	78704	512-476-6927	
Stringworks 327 Franklin St *Web:* www.stringworks.com	Geneva	IL	60134	920-830-0928	
Sweetwater Sound Inc 5501 US Hwy 30 W *TF:* 800-222-4700 ■ *Web:* www.sweetwater.com	Fort Wayne	IN	46818	260-432-8176	432-1758
Tacoma Guitar Company Inc 4615 E 192nd St *Web:* www.tacomaguitars.com	Tacoma	WA	98446	253-847-6508	
Tom Lee Music Ltd 929 Granville St *TF:* 888-886-6533 ■ *Web:* www.tomleemusic.ca	Vancouver	BC	V6Z1L3	604-685-8471	
Washington Music Ctr 11151 Veirs Mill Rd *Web:* chucklevins.com	Wheaton	MD	20902	301-946-8808	946-0487
West Music Inc 1212 Fifth St PO Box 5521 *TF:* 800-373-2000 ■ *Web:* www.westmusic.com	Coralville	IA	52241	319-351-2000	
Woodwind & Brasswind 4004 Technology Dr *TF:* 800-348-5003 ■ *Web:* www.wwbw.com	South Bend	IN	46628	574-251-3500	

	City	State	Zip	Phone	Fax
World Music Supply 2414 W Seventh St *TF:* 800-867-4611 ■ *Web:* www.worldmusicsupply.com	Muncie	IN	47302	765-213-6085	

527 MUSICAL INSTRUMENTS

	City	State	Zip	Phone	Fax
Alembic Inc 3005 Wiljan Ct *TF:* 800-322-5893 ■ *Web:* www.alembic.com	Santa Rosa	CA	95407	707-523-2611	523-2935
Allen Organ Co 150 Locust St *Web:* www.allenorgan.com	Macungie	PA	18062	610-966-2202	965-3098
ALLParts Music Corp 13027 Brittmoore Park Dr *Web:* www.allparts.com	Houston	TX	77041	713-466-6414	
AP International Enterprise Inc 3301 SR- 66 *Web:* www.apintl.com	Neptune	NJ	07753	732-918-7001	
Austin Organs Inc 156 Woodland St *Web:* www.austinorgans.com	Hartford	CT	06105	860-522-8293	524-9828
Avedis Zildjian Co 22 Longwater Dr *TF:* 800-229-8672 ■ *Web:* www.zildjian.com	Norwell	MA	02061	781-871-2200	871-3984
Beamz Interactive Inc 15354 N 83rd Way Ste 101 **Fax Area Code:* 877 ■ *Web:* thebeamz.com	Scottsdale	AZ	85260	480-424-2053	591-8899*
Bevin Bros 10 Bevin Rd *Web:* www.bevinbells.com	East Hampton	CT	06424	860-267-4431	
Brannen Brothers-flutemakers Inc 58 Dragon Ct *Web:* brannenflutes.com	Woburn	MA	01801	781-935-9522	
Burkart-Phelan Inc 2 Shaker Rd *Web:* www.burkart.com	Shirley	MA	01464	978-425-4500	425-9800
Carvin Corp 12340 World Trade Dr *TF:* 800-854-2235 ■ *Web:* www.carvin.com	San Diego	CA	92128	858-487-8700	521-6034
CF Martin & Company Inc 510 Sycamore St PO Box 329 *TF:* 888-433-9177 ■ *Web:* www.martinguitar.com	Nazareth	PA	18064	610-759-2837	759-5757
Chesbro Music Company Inc 327 Broadway St *Web:* www.chesbromusic.com	Idaho Falls	ID	83402	208-522-8691	
Chime Master Systems PO Box 936 **Fax Area Code:* 740 ■ *TF:* 800-344-7464 ■ *Web:* www.chimemaster.com	Lancaster	OH	43130	800-344-7464	746-9566*
Conn-Selmer Inc 600 Industrial Pkwy *Web:* www.bachbrass.com	Elkhart	IN	46516	574-522-1675	
Daisy Rock Guitars 16320 Roscoe Blvd Ste 100 *TF:* 877-693-2479 ■ *Web:* www.daisyrock.com	Van Nuys	CA	91410	877-693-2479	
Davitt & Hanser Music Co 3015 Kustom Dr *TF:* 800-999-5558 ■ *Web:* www.hansermusicgroup.com	Hebron	KY	41048	859-817-7100	817-7150
Dean Markley Strings Inc 3350 Scott Blvd Bldg 45 *Web:* www.deanmarkley.com	Santa Clara	CA	95054	408-988-2456	
Deering Banjo Co 3733 Kenora Dr *TF:* 800-845-7791 ■ *Web:* www.deeringbanjos.com	Spring Valley	CA	91977	619-464-8252	
Dunlop Manufacturing Inc 150 Industrial Way *Web:* www.jimdunlop.com	Benicia	CA	94510	707-745-2722	
E & O Mari Inc 256 Broadway *Web:* www.labella.com	Newburgh	NY	12550	845-562-4400	
Edwards Instrument Co 530 S Hwy H *TF:* 800-562-6838 ■ *Web:* www.edwards-instruments.com	Elkhorn	WI	53121	262-723-4221	723-4245
Ernie Ball 151 Suburban Rd *TF:* 866-823-2255 ■ *Web:* www.ernieball.com	San Luis Obispo	CA	93401	805-544-7726	
Fender Musical Instruments Corp 17600 N Perimeter Dr Ste 100 *TF Cust Svc:* 800-488-1818 ■ *Web:* www.fender.com	Scottsdale	AZ	85255	480-596-9690	596-1384
Gemeinhardt Company LLC 57882 State Rd 19 S *Web:* www.gemeinhardt.com	Elkhart	IN	46517	574-295-5280	
General Music Corp 605 Country Club Dr	Bensenville	IL	60106	630-766-8230	
George Heinl & Co 201 Church St *TF:* 800-387-7858 ■ *Web:* www.georgeheinl.com	Toronto	ON	M5B1Y7	416-363-0093	
Getzen Company Inc 530 S Cty Hwy H PO Box 440 *TF:* 800-366-5584 ■ *Web:* www.getzen.com	Elkhorn	WI	53121	262-723-4221	723-4245
GHS Corp 2813 Wilber Ave *TF:* 800-388-4447 ■ *Web:* www.ghsstrings.com	Battle Creek	MI	49037	800-388-4447	860-6913
Gibson Guitar Corp 309 Plus Pk Blvd *TF:* 800-444-2766 ■ *Web:* www2.gibson.com	Nashville	TN	37217	615-871-4500	
Gibson Piano Ventures Inc 309 Plus Pk Blvd *TF:* 800-444-2766 ■ *Web:* www.gibson.com	Nashville	TN	37217	615-871-4500	889-5509
Hammond Suzuki USA Inc 743 Annoreno Dr *TF:* 888-765-2900 ■ *Web:* www.hammondorganco.com	Addison	IL	60101	630-543-0277	
Hohner Inc 1000 Technology Pk Dr *TF:* 800-446-6010 ■ *Web:* www.hohnerusa.com	Glen Allen	VA	23059	804-515-1900	515-0189
Hoshino USA Inc 1726 Winchester Rd *Web:* www.ibanez.com	Bensalem	PA	19020	215-638-8670	245-8583
J D'Addario & Company Inc 595 Smith St *TF:* 800-323-2746 ■ *Web:* www.daddario.com	Farmingdale	NY	11735	631-439-3300	439-3333
JD Calato Mfg Company Inc 4501 Hyde Pk Blvd *TF Cust Svc:* 800-358-4590 ■ *Web:* www.regaltip.com	Niagara Falls	NY	14305	716-285-3546	285-2710
Kawai America Corp PO Box 9045 *Web:* www.kawaius.com	Rancho Dominguez	CA	90224	310-631-1771	
Korg USA Inc 316 S Service Rd *Web:* www.korg.com	Melville	NY	11747	631-390-6500	390-6501
La Bella Strings 256 Broadway *Web:* www.labella.com	Newburgh	NY	12550	845-562-4400	
Lindeblad Piano Restoration 101 Us 46 *TF:* 888-587-4266 ■ *Web:* www.lindebladpiano.com	Pine Brook	NJ	07058	888-587-4266	
Lowrey Organ Co 989 AEC Dr *TF:* 800-451-5939 ■ *Web:* www.lowrey.com	Wood Dale	IL	60191	800-451-5939	
Lyon & Healy Harps Inc 168 N Ogden Ave *TF:* 800-621-3881 ■ *Web:* www.lyonhealy.com	Chicago	IL	60607	312-786-1881	226-1502
Maas-Rowe Carillons Inc 2255 Meyers Ave **Fax Area Code:* 760 ■ *TF:* 800-854-2023 ■ *Web:* www.maasrowe.com	Escondido	CA	92029	800-854-2023	747-2677*
Manhasset Specialty Co 3505 Fruitvale Blvd *TF:* 800-795-0965 ■ *Web:* www.manhasset-specialty.com	Yakima	WA	98902	509-248-3810	248-3834
Marimba One Inc 901 O St Ste D *TF:* 888-990-6663 ■ *Web:* www.marimbaone.com	Arcata	CA	95521	707-822-9570	
Mason & Hamlin Piano Co 35 Duncan St *Web:* www.masonhamlin.com	Haverhill	MA	01830	978-374-8888	374-8080
Morley Pedals 325 Cary Pt Dr *TF:* 800-284-5172 ■ *Web:* www.morleypedals.com	Cary	IL	60013	847-639-4646	639-4723
Musicorp 2456 Remount Rd	North Charleston	SC	29406	843-745-8501	
NATIVE INSTRUMENTS North America Inc 5631 A Hollywood Blvd *Web:* www.native-instruments.com	Los Angeles	CA	90028	323-467-5260	
Noble & Cooley Co 42 Water St *Web:* www.noblecooley.com	Granville	MA	01034	413-357-6321	357-6314
Nothing Shocking LLC 513 S Dudley St *Web:* www.mojotone.com	Burgaw	NC	28425	910-259-7291	
Organ Supply Industries Inc 2320 W 50th St *TF:* 800-458-0289 ■ *Web:* www.organsupply.com	Erie	PA	16506	814-835-2244	838-0349
OS Kelly Co 318 E N St	Springfield	OH	45503	937-322-4921	322-1322
Paul Reed Smith Guitars (PRS) 380 Log Canoe Cir *Web:* www.prsguitars.com	Stevensville	MD	21666	410-643-9970	643-9980
PianoDisc 4111 N Fwy Blvd *TF:* 800-566-3472 ■ *Web:* www.pianodisc.com	Sacramento	CA	95834	916-567-9999	567-1941
Prestini Musical Instruments Inc 2020 N Aurora Dr *TF General:* 800-528-6569 ■ *Web:* www.prestiniusa.com	Nogales	AZ	85628	520-287-4931	287-4931
QRS Music Technologies 2011 Seward Ave *Web:* www.qrsmusic.com	Naples	FL	34109	239-597-5888	
Remo Inc 28101 Industry Dr *TF:* 800-525-5134 ■ *Web:* www.remo.com	Valencia	CA	91355	661-294-5600	294-5700
Reuter Organ Co 1220 Timberedge Rd *Web:* www.reuterorgan.com	Lawrence	KS	66049	785-843-2622	843-3302
Rhythm Tech 29 Beechwood Ave *TF:* 800-726-2279 ■ *Web:* rhythmtech.com	New Rochelle	NY	10801	914-636-6900	
Rickenbacker International Corp 3895 S Main St *Web:* www.rickenbacker.com	Santa Ana	CA	92707	714-545-5574	
Rodgers Instruments LLC 1300 NE 25th Ave *Web:* www.rodgersinstruments.com	Hillsboro	OR	97124	503-648-4181	681-0444
Roland Corp US 5100 S Eastern Ave *Web:* www.rolandus.com	Los Angeles	CA	90040	323-890-3700	890-3701
Sabian Ltd 219 Main St *TF:* 800-817-2242 ■ *Web:* www.sabian.com	Meductic	NB	E6H2L5	506-272-2019	272-2040
Saint Louis Music Inc 1400 Ferguson Ave *TF:* 800-727-4512 ■ *Web:* www.stlouismusic.com	Saint Louis	MO	63133	314-727-4512	727-8929
Samick Music Corp 1329 Gateway Dr *Web:* www.smcmusic.com	Gallatin	TN	37066	615-206-0077	
Schaff Piano Supply Co 451 Oakwood Rd *TF:* 800-747-4266 ■ *Web:* www.schaffpiano.com	Lake Zurich	IL	60047	847-438-4556	438-4615
Schecter Guitar Research Inc 10953 Pendleton St *TF:* 800-660-6621 ■ *Web:* www.schecterguitars.com	Sun Valley	CA	91352	800-660-6621	
Schulmerich Carillons Inc Carillon Hill *TF:* 800-772-3557 ■ *Web:* www.schulmerichbells.com	Sellersville	PA	18960	215-257-2771	257-1910
Source Audio LLC 120 Cummings Park *Web:* www.sourceaudio.net	Woburn	MA	01801	781-932-8080	
Steinway & Sons 1 Steinway Pl *TF:* 800-783-4692 ■ *Web:* www.steinway.com	Long Island	NY	11105	718-721-2600	932-4332
Steinway Musical Instruments Inc 800 S St Ste 305 *NYSE:* LVB ■ *Web:* steinway.com/steinway-musical-instruments	Waltham	MA	02453	781-894-9770	894-9803
Suzuki Musical Instrument Corp PO Box 710459 *TF Cust Svc:* 800-854-1594 ■ *Web:* www.suzukimusic.com	Santee	CA	92072	619-258-1896	873-1997
Taylor-Listug Inc 1980 Gillespie Way *Web:* www.taylorguitars.com	El Cajon	CA	92020	619-258-1207	258-1623
TC Electronic Inc 5706 Corsa Ave Ste 107 *Web:* www.tcelectronic.com	Westlake Village	CA	91362	818-665-4900	
Tonepros Sound Lab Intl 1449 E F St Ste 101en205 *Web:* www.tonepros.com	Oakdale	CA	95361	209-848-4966	
Ultimate Support Systems Inc 5836 Wright Dr **Fax Area Code:* 970 ■ *TF:* 800-525-5628 ■ *Web:* www.ultimatesupport.com	Loveland	CO	80538	800-525-5628	776-1941*
Verne Q Powell Flutes Inc 1 Clock Tower Pl Ste 300 *Web:* www.powellflutes.com	Maynard	MA	01754	978-461-6111	461-6155
Wenger Corp 555 Pk Dr PO Box 448 *TF:* 800-493-6437 ■ *Web:* www.wengercorp.com	Owatonna	MN	55060	507-455-4100	455-4258
Wicks Pipe Organ Co 1100 Fifth St *TF Cust Svc:* 877-654-2191 ■ *Web:* www.organ.wicks.com	Highland	IL	62249	618-654-2191	654-3770
Wm S Haynes Company Inc 68 Nonset Path *Web:* wmshaynes.com	Acton	MA	01720	978-268-0600	268-0601
Woodstock Percussion Inc 167 DuBois Rd *Web:* www.chimes.com	Shokan	NY	12481	845-657-6000	
Yamaha Corp of America 6600 Orangethorpe Ave **Fax:* Hum Res ■ *Web:* www.yamaha.com	Buena Park	CA	90620	714-522-9011	522-9235*

528 MUTUAL FUNDS

	City	State	Zip	Phone	Fax
32 Degrees Capital 650 635-8th Ave S W *TF:* 866-695-1069 ■ *Web:* www.32degrees.ca	Calgary	AB	T2P3M3	403-695-1074	
Abacus Private Equity Brookfield Pl Pl - TD-Canada Trust Tower 161 Bay St Ste 2430 *Web:* www.abacuspe.com	Toronto	ON	M5J2S1	416-861-8711	
Academy Capital Management 500 N Vly Mills Dr Ste 200 *Web:* www.academycapitalmgmt.com	Waco	TX	76710	254-751-0555	
ACG Advisory Services Inc 1640 Huguenot Rd *TF:* 800-231-6409 ■ *Web:* www.acgworldwide.com	Midlothian	VA	23113	804-323-1886	

Phone | Fax

Advanced Pension Solutions Inc
6830 Commerce Court Dr. Blacklick OH 43004 614-501-7790
Web: www.advpen.com

Aether Investment Partners LLC
1900 Sixteenth St Ste 825 Denver CO 80202 720-961-4190
Web: www.aetherip.com

Agilith Capital Inc
Victory Bldg 80 Richmond St W Ste 203 Toronto ON M5H2A4 416-915-0284
TF: 866-345-1231 ■ *Web:* www.agilith.com

Alberta Enterprise Corp
10830 Jasper Ave Ste 1100 Edmonton AB T5J2B3 780-392-3901
Web: www.alberta-enterprise.ca

Albright Capital Management LLC
1101 New York Ave NW Ste 900 Washington DC 20005 202-370-3500
Web: www.albrightcapital.com

Alerus Retirement Solutions
2 Pine Tree Dr Ste 400 Arden Hills MN 55112 800-795-2697
TF: 800-795-2697 ■ *Web:* www.alerusretirementsolutions.com

Alger Family of Funds PO Box 8480 Boston MA 02266 800-992-3863
TF: 800-992-3863 ■ *Web:* www.alger.com

Alta Capital Management LLC
6440 South Wasatch Blvd Ste 260 Salt Lake City UT 84121 801-274-6010
Web: www.atlacapital.net

Altavista Wealth Management Inc
4 Vanderbilt Park Dr Ste 310 Asheville NC 28803 828-684-2600
Web: www.altavistawealth.com

American Century Proprietary Holdings Inc
PO Box 419200 Kansas City MO 64141 816-531-5575 340-7962*
**Fax:* Cust Svc ■ *TF:* 800-345-2021 ■ *Web:* www.americancentury.com

Annapolis Capital Limited 9 Avenue SW Calgary AB T2P0T1 403-231-4430
Web: www.annapoliscapital.ca

Aquila Group of Funds
380 Madison Ave Ste 2300 New York NY 10017 212-697-6666
TF: 800-437-1020 ■ *Web:* www.aquilafunds.com

Arizona State Retirement System
3300 N Central Ave Phoenix AZ 85012 602-240-2000
Web: www.azasrs.gov

Artisan Funds PO Box 8412 Boston MA 02266 800-344-1770
TF Cust Svc: 800-344-1770 ■
Web: www.artisanpartners.com/individual-investors.html

Artisan Partners Limited Partnership
875 E Wisconsin Ave Ste 800 Milwaukee WI 53202 414-390-6100
Web: www.artisanpartners.com

Ascendant Advisors LLC
4 Oaks Pl 1330 Post Oak Blvd Ste 1550 Houston TX 77056 800-552-6010
TF: 800-552-6010 ■ *Web:* www.ascendantadvisors.com

Ashkenazy Acquisition Corp
150 E 58th St 39th Fl New York NY 10155 212-213-4444
Web: www.aacrealty.com

Asia Pacific Capital
345 S Figueroa St Ste 100 Los Angeles CA 90071 213-680-8811
Web: www.apccusa.com

Asset Preservation Advisors Inc
3344 Peachtree Rd Ste 2050 Atlanta GA 30326 404-261-1333
Web: assetpreservationadvisors.com

Aston Funds PO Box 9765 Providence RI 02940 312-268-1400
TF: 800-992-8151 ■ *Web:* www.astonfunds.com

Auda Private Equity LLC
888 Seventh Ave 41st Fl New York NY 10106 212-863-2300
Web: www.auda.net

Augenblick & Company Pc 368 W Bridge St New Hope PA 18938 215-862-9153
Web: augenblickpc.com

Aurelius Capital Management LP
535 Madison Ave 22nd Fl New York NY 10022 646-445-6500
Web: www.aurelius-capital.com

Auven Therapeutics Management L.L.L.P
6501 Redhook Plz Ste 201 Saint Thomas VI 00802 340-779-6908
Web: www.auventx.com

Avrio Capital Inc
Crowfoot W Business Centre #235 600 Crowfoot Crescent NW
Calgary AB T3G0B4 403-215-5492
Web: www.avriocapital.com

B.C. Advantage (VCC) Funds Ltd
Ste 410 221 W Esplanade Ste 410 North Vancouver BC V7M3J3 604-688-6877
Web: www.bcadvantagefunds.com

Barnes Investment Advisory Inc
7250 N 16th St Ste 412 Phoenix AZ 85020 602-248-9099
Web: www.barnesinvest.com

Baron Funds 767 Fifth Ave 49th Fl New York NY 10153 212-583-2000 583-2150
TF: 800-992-2766 ■ *Web:* www.baronfunds.com

Barrantagh Investment Management Inc
100 Yonge St Ste 1700 Toronto ON M5C2W1 416-868-6295
Web: www.barrantagh.com

Bastion Infrastructure Group
801 - 1 Richmond St W Toronto ON M5H3W4 416-583-2600
Web: www.bastionfunds.com

BC Investment Management Corp
2940 Jutland Rd Sawmill Point Victoria BC V8T5K6 250-356-0263
Web: www.bcimc.com

Billings Capital Management LLC
1001 Nineteenth St N 19th Fl Arlington VA 22209 703-962-1871
Web: www.billingscap.com

Bowen, Hanes & Company Inc
The Forum 3290 Northside Pkwy Ste 880 Atlanta GA 30327 404-995-0507
Web: www.bowenhanes.com

Bridges Investment Counsel Inc
256 Durham Plz 8401 W Dodge Rd Ste 256 Omaha NE 68114 402-397-4700
Web: www.bridgesfund.com

Brookdale Group, The
3455 Peachtree Rd NE Ste 700 Atlanta GA 30326 404-364-8080
Web: www.brookdalegroup.com

Brotman Financial Group Inc
16 Greenmeadow Dr Ste 201 Timonium MD 21093 410-252-4555
Web: www.brotmanfinancial.com

Phone | Fax

Brownfields Capital LLC 1125 17th St Ste 2350 Denver CO 80202 303-534-2100
Web: brownfieldscapital.com

BTR Capital Management Inc
550 Kearny St Ste 510 San Francisco CA 94108 415-989-0100
Web: www.btrcap.com

C.A. Delaney Capital Management Ltd
66 Wellington St W
Ste 4410 TD Bank Tower Toronto Dominion Ctr Toronto ON M5K1H1 416-361-0688
Web: www.delaneycapital.com

C.S. McKee LP 1 Gateway Ctr 8th Fl Pittsburgh PA 15222 412-566-1234
Web: www.csmckee.com

Cabot Wealth Management Inc 216 Essex St Salem MA 01970 978-745-9233
Web: www.ecabot.com

Callisto Capital LP 333 Bay St Ste 640 Toronto ON M5H2R2 416-868-4900
Web: www.callistocapital.ca

Calvert Investments Inc
4550 Montgomery Ave Ste 1000N Bethesda MD 20814 301-951-4800
TF: 800-368-2748 ■ *Web:* www.calvert.com

Castletop Capital
3600 N Capital of Texas Hwy Bldg B Ste 320 Austin TX 78746 512-329-6600
Web: www.castletopcapital.com

Celtic House Venture Partners Inc
80 Aberdeen St Ste 300 Ottawa ON K1S5R5 613-569-7200
Web: www.celtic-house.com

Center Coast Capital Advisors LP
1600 Smith Ste 3800 Houston TX 77002 713-759-1400
Web: www.centercoastcap.com

Centre Lane Partners LLC
1 Grand Central Pl 60 E 42nd St Ste 1250 New York NY 10165 646-843-0710
Web: www.centrelanepartners.com

CGM Funds 38 Newbury St Ste 8 Boston MA 02116 617-859-7714
TF: 800-345-4048 ■ *Web:* www.cgmfunds.com

Chandler Asset Management Inc
6225 Lusk Blvd San Diego CA 92121 858-546-3737
TF: 800-317-4747 ■ *Web:* www.chandlerasset.com

Chicago Equity Partners LLC
180 N LaSalle St Ste 3800 Chicago IL 60601 312-629-8200
Web: www.chicagoequity.com

CIBC Mellon Global Securities Services Co
320 Bay St PO Box 1 Toronto ON M5H4A6 416-643-5000
TF: 888-439-2457 ■ *Web:* www.cibcmellon.com

City of Austin Employees' Retirement System
418 E Highland Mall Blvd Austin TX 78752 512-458-2551
Web: www.coaers.org

Claremont Companies Inc
1 Lakeshore Center Bridgewater MA 02324 508-279-4300
TF: 800-848-9077 ■ *Web:* www.claremontcorp.com

Clark Dodge Asset Management
2 Gannett Dr, 2nd Fl White Plains NY 10604 914-694-2390
Web: www.clarkdodgewealth.com

Clipper Fund 2949 E Elvira Rd Ste 101 Tucson AZ 85756 800-432-2504
TF: 800-432-2504 ■ *Web:* www.clipperfund.com

Cobb Planning Group 1206 N Broadway Santa Ana CA 92701 714-550-7242
Web: www.cobbplanninggroup.com

Coe Capital Management LLC 9 Pkwy N Ste 325 Deerfield IL 60015 847-597-1700
Web: www.coecapital.com

Compass Capital Management Inc
400 Baker Bldg 706 Second Ave South Minneapolis MN 55402 612-338-4051
Web: www.compasscap.com

Congruent Investment Partners LLC
3400 Carlisle Sẗ Ste 430 Dallas TX 75204 214-760-7411
Web: www.congruentinv.com

Connective Capital Management LLC
385 Homer Ave Palo Alto CA 94301 650-321-4826
Web: www.connectivecapital.com

Cordiant Capital Inc
1002 Sherbrooke St W Ste 2800 Montreal QC H3A2R7 514-286-1142
Web: cordiantcap.com

CornerCap Investment Counsel Inc
1355 Peachtree St NE The Peachtree Ste 1700 Atlanta GA 30309 404-870-0700
TF: 800-728-0670 ■ *Web:* www.cornercap.com

Covalent Partners LLC
Reservoir Woods 930 Winter St Ste 2800 Waltham MA 02451 617-658-5500
Web: www.covalentpartnersllc.com

Cozad Asset Management Inc 2501 Galen Dr Champaign IL 61821 217-356-8363
TF: 800-437-1686 ■ *Web:* www.cozadassetmgmt.com

Creststreet Asset Management Ltd
70 University Ave Ste 1450 Toronto ON M5J2M4 416-864-6330 862-8950

Crow Holdings Capital Partners LLC
3819 Maple Ave Dallas TX 75219 214-661-8000
Web: www.crowholdingscapital.com

Curian Capital LLC 7601 Technology Way Denver CO 80237 303-846-3800
Web: www.curian.com

Dalfen America Corp
Westmount 4444 rue Sainte-Catherine W
Ste 100 Montreal QC H3Z1R2 514-938-1050
Web: www.dalfen.com

Dancap Private Equity Inc 197 Sheppard Ave W Toronto ON M2N1M9 416-590-9444
Web: www.dancap.ca

Davis Capital Partners LLC
3 Harbor Dr Ste 301 Sausalito CA 94965 415-362-3600
Web: www.daviscapitalpartners.com

Davis Funds 2949 E Elvira Rd Ste 101 Tucson AR 85756 800-279-0279
TF: 800-279-0279 ■ *Web:* www.davisfunds.com

del Rey Global Investors LLC
6701 Ctr Dr W Ste 655 Los Angeles CA 90045 310-649-1233

Delafield Hambrecht Inc
1301 Second Ave Ste 2850 Seattle WA 98101 206-254-4100
Web: www.delafieldhambrecht.com

Diamond Creek Capital
28 N Vista De Catalina Laguna Beach CA 92651 949-429-7707
Web: www.diamondcreekcap.com

Dixon Mitchell Investment Counsel Inc
Ste 1680 1055 W Hastings St Vancouver BC V6E2E9 604-669-3136
Web: www.dixonmitchell.com

Phone | Fax

Dodge & Cox Funds 30 Dan Rd PO Box 8422 Canton MA 02021 800-621-3979
TF: 800-621-3979 ■ *Web:* www.dodgeandcox.com

Domini Social Investments PO Box 9785 Providence RI 02940 800-582-6757
TF: 800-582-6757 ■ *Web:* www.domini.com

Dos Rios Partners
205 Wild Basin Rd S Bldg 3 Ste 100 Austin TX 78746 512-298-0801
Web: www.dosriospartners.com

Double Eagle Capital Management LP
909 Lk Carolyn Pkwy Ste 1825 Irving TX 75039 972-869-6880
Web: www.doubleeaglecapital.com

Dreyfus Family of Funds PO Box 55299 Boston MA 02205 800-843-5466
TF: 800-843-5466 ■ *Web:* public.dreyfus.com

Dts Financial Group 5401 Tech Cir Moorpark CA 93021 805-532-9000

Eaton Vance Mutual Funds 2 International Pl Boston MA 02110 617-482-8260
TF: 800-225-6265 ■ *Web:* www.eatonvance.com

Elmhurst Group, The 1 Bigelow Sq Ste 630 Pittsburgh PA 15219 412-281-8731
Web: www.elmhurstgroup.com

Equity Investment Corp
3007 Piedmont Rd Ste 200 Atlanta GA 30305 404-239-0111
TF: 877-342-0111 ■ *Web:* www.eicatlanta.com

Essex Financial Services Inc 176 Westbrook Rd Essex CT 06426 860-767-4300
TF: 800-900-5972 ■ *Web:* www.essexfinancialservices.com

Ewing Morris & Company Investment Partners
1407 Yonge St Ste 500 Toronto ON M4T1Y7 416-640-2791
Web: www.ewingmorris.com

Fascet LLC 224 W 30 St Ste 203 New York NY 10001 212-448-9830
Web: fascet.com

Fengate Capital Management Ltd
5000 Yonge St Ste 1805 Toronto ON M2N7E9 416-488-4184
Web: fengate.com

Ferguson Wellman Capital Management Inc
888 S W Fifth Ave Portland OR 97204 503-226-1444
TF: 800-327-5765 ■ *Web:* www.fergusonwellman.com

Fidelity Advisor Funds PO Box 770002 Cincinnati OH 45277 800-522-7297 321-7349*
**Fax Area Code:* 888 ■ **Fax:* Mktg ■ *TF:* 800-522-7297 ■ *Web:* www.advisor.fidelity.com

Fidelity Investment Funds PO Box 770001 Cincinnati OH 45277 800-343-3548
TF: 800-343-3548 ■ *Web:* www.fidelity.com

Fidelity Investments Institutional Operations Company Inc
PO Box 770002 Cincinnati OH 45277 877-208-0098
TF: 877-208-0098 ■ *Web:* www.fidelity.com

Fidelity Partnership 1995 483 Bay St Ste 200 Toronto ON M5G2N7 416-307-5200
TF: 800-263-4077 ■ *Web:* www.fidelity.ca

First American Funds PO Box 701 Milwaukee WI 53201 800-677-3863
TF: 800-677-3863 ■ *Web:* www.firstamericanfunds.com

First Green Partners
1550 Utica Ave S Ste 450 Minneapolis MN 55416 952-288-2760
Web: www.firstgreenpartners.com

Fondaction
Bureau 103 2175 Blvd de Maisonneuve Est Montreal QC H2K4S3 514-525-5505
TF: 800-253-6665 ■ *Web:* www.fondaction.com

Fonds de solidarit? FTQ
545 Cremazie Blvd E Ofc 200 Montreal QC H2M2W4 514-383-8383
Web: www.fondsftq.com

Fort Pitt Capital Group Inc
680 Andersen Dr Foster Plz Ten Pittsburgh PA 15220 412-921-1822
TF: 800-471-5827 ■ *Web:* www.fortpittcapital.com

Fulham & Company Inc 593 Washington St Wellesley MA 02482 781-235-2266
Web: www.fulhamco.com

Galecki Financial Management Inc
7743 W Jefferson Blvd Fort Wayne IN 46804 260-436-8525
TF: 800-838-6441 ■ *Web:* www.galecki.com

GAMCO Investors Inc 1 Corporate Ctr Rye NY 10580 914-921-5100 921-5118
NYSE: GBL ■ *TF:* 800-422-3554 ■ *Web:* www.gabelli.com

Garrett Nagle & Company Inc
300 Unicorn Park Dr 19th Fl Woburn MA 01801 617-737-9090
Web: www.garrettnagle.com

GeneChem 1 Westmount Sq Ste 800 Montreal QC H3Z2P9 514-849-7696
Web: www.genechem.com

Geolo Capital
Pier 5 The Embarcadero Ste 102 San Francisco CA 94111 415-694-5802
Web: www.geolo.com

Gestion Fonds Capital Culture Quebec Inc
485 McGill St Ste 900 Montreal QC H2Y2H4 514-940-6820
Web: capitalculture.ca

Glenmede Funds 1650 Market St Ste 1200 Philadelphia PA 19103 215-419-6000 419-6199
TF: 800-966-3200 ■ *Web:* www.glenmede.com

GMO Trust Funds 40 Rowes Wharf Boston MA 02110 617-330-7500 261-0134
Web: www.gmo.com

Goldman Sachs 200 W St New York NY 10282 212-902-1000
NYSE: GS ■ *TF:* 800-526-7384 ■ *Web:* www.goldmansachs.com

Greybrook Capital Inc 890 Yonge St 7th Fl Toronto ON M4W3P4 416-322-9700
Web: www.greybrook.com

Greystone Investment Management LLC
3805 Edwards Rd Ste 180 Cincinnati OH 45209 513-731-8444
TF: 877-293-0908 ■ *Web:* www.greystoneinvestment.com

GroundSwell 1776 Park Ave Ste 4-175 Park City UT 84060 858-345-2637
Web: www.groundswellinc.com

Gryphon Investment Counsel Inc
20 Bay St Ste 1905 Toronto ON M5J2N8 416-364-2299
Web: www.gryphon.ca

Guild Investment Management Inc
12400 Wilshire Blvd Ste 1080 Los Angeles CA 90025 310-826-8600
Web: www.guildinvestment.com

Hadley Capital
1200 Central Ave Ste 300 Chase Bank Bldg Wilmette IL 60091 847-906-5300
Web: www.hadleycapital.com

Harbor Capital Management Inc
831 E Morehead St Ste 350 Charlotte NC 28202 704-377-6945
Web: harborcapitalmgmt.com

Hartford Mutual Funds 30 Dan Rd Ste 55022 Canton MA 02021 888-843-7824
TF: 888-843-7824 ■ *Web:* www.hartfordfunds.com

Harvest Capital Management Inc
114 N Main St Ste 301 Concord NH 03301 603-224-6994
Web: www.harvestcap.com

Health Technology Exchange, The
439 University Ave 5th Fl Toronto ON M5G1Y8 437-836-3101
Web: www.htx.ca

HealthCap Partners LLC
5910 N Central Expy Ste 1000 Dallas TX 75206 214-953-1722
Web: healthcap.com

Heartland Funds 789 N Water St Ste 500 Milwaukee WI 53202 414-347-7777 347-1339
TF: 800-432-7856 ■ *Web:* www.heartlandadvisors.com/heartland-advisors

Hotaling Investment Management LLC
100 W Lancaster Ave Ste 105 Wayne PA 19087 610-688-0616
Web: www.hotalingllc.com

Huron Valley Financial Inc
2395 Oak Vly Dr Ste 200 Ann Arbor MI 48103 734-669-8000
Web: www.huronvalleyfinancial.com

ICMARC 777 N Capitol St NE Ste 600 Washington DC 20002 202-962-4600 962-4601
TF General: 800-669-7471 ■ *Web:* www.icmarc.org

iGan Partners Rowanwood Centre 1067 Yonge St Toronto ON M4W2L2 416-925-2433
Web: www.iganpartners.com

Illumina Partners Inc 67 Yonge St Ste 600 Toronto ON M5E1J8 416-861-1717
Web: www.illuminapartners.com

ING Funds 7337 E Doubletree Ranch Rd Scottsdale AZ 85258 800-992-0180 477-2700*
**Fax Area Code:* 480 ■ *TF:* 800-992-0180 ■ *Web:* investments.voya.com

Invenshure LLC 227 Colfax Ave N Ste 148 Minneapolis MN 55405 612-520-7361
Web: invenshure.com

Invesco 11 Greenway Plaza Ste 100 Houston TX 77046 713-626-1919
TF: 800-959-4246 ■ *Web:* invesco.com/us

Invesco Trimark Ltd 5140 Yonge St Ste 800 Toronto ON M2N6X7 416-590-9855
TF: 800-874-6275 ■ *Web:* www.invesco.ca

Iron Yard LLC, The 101 N Main St Ste 400 Greenville SC 29601 864-605-3976
Web: theironyard.com

JAG Advisors 9841 Clayton Rd Saint Louis MO 63124 314-997-1277
Web: www.jaglynn.com

JMT Consulting Group Inc
2200-2202 Route 22 Patterson NY 12563 845-278-9262
Web: www.jmtconsulting.com

John Hancock Funds 601 Congress St Boston MA 02210 617-375-1500
TF: 800-338-8080 ■ *Web:* www.jhinvestments.com

Ken Fowler Enterprises Ltd
110 Hannover Dr Ste 203B St. Catharines ON L2W1A4 905-688-9740
Web: www.kfe.on.ca

Klitzberg Associates Inc 600 Alexander Rd Princeton NJ 08540 609-452-2888
Web: klitzbergfundsolutions.com

Kopp Funds 7701 France Ave S Minneapolis MN 55435 952-841-0480

Laborers National Pension Fund
14140 Midway Rd Ste 105 Dallas TX 75244 972-233-4458
Web: www.lnpf.org

Lazard Funds 30 Rockefeller Plz 57th Fl New York NY 10112 800-823-6300
TF: 800-823-6300 ■ *Web:* lazardnet.com/us/mutual-funds/open-end-funds

Leonis Partners 1 W Court Sq Ste 210 Atlanta GA 30030 404-347-3992
Web: www.leonispartners.com

Levy Affiliated Holdings LLC
201 Wilshire Blvd 2nd Fl Santa Monica CA 90401 310-395-5200
Web: www.levyaffiliated.com

Liberty Funds Group Inc 4711 Lakeside Dr Colleyville TX 76034 214-369-0500

Lincluden Investment Management
1275 N Service Rd W Ste 607 Oakville ON L6M3G4 905-825-9000
TF: 800-532-7071 ■ *Web:* www.lincluden.com

Loomis Sayles Funds 1 Financial Ctr Boston MA 02111 617-482-2450
TF: 800-633-3330 ■ *Web:* www.loomissayles.com

Louisbourg Investments 770 Main St 10th Fl Moncton NB E1C8L1 506-853-5410
Web: www.louisbourg.net

Lubitz Financial Group, The
9130 S Dadeland Blvd Ste 1625 Miami FL 33156 305-670-4440
Web: www.lubitzfinancial.com

Lynx Equity Ltd 692 Queen St E Ste 205 Toronto ON M4M1G9 416-323-3512
Web: www.lynxequity.com

Mairs & Power Funds
332 Minnesota St Ste W-1520 Saint Paul MN 55101 651-222-8478
TF: 800-304-7404 ■ *Web:* mairsandpower.com

Market Street Trust Co 80 E Market St Ste 300 Corning NY 14830 607-962-6876
Web: www.marketstreettrust.com

Market Traders Institute
400 Colonial Ctr Pkwy Ste 350 Lake Mary FL 32746 407-740-0900
TF: 800-866-7431 ■ *Web:* www.markettraders.com

MASTER Teacher Inc, The 2600 Leadership Ln Manhattan KS 66505 800-669-9633
TF: 800-669-9633 ■ *Web:* www.masterteacher.com

Matan Companies LLLP
4600 Wedgewood Blvd Ste A Frederick MD 21703 301-694-9200
Web: www.mataninc.com

Mather Group LLC, The
Oakbrook Ter Tower One Tower Ln
Ste 1820 Oakbrook Terrace IL 60181 630-537-1080
Web: www.themathergroup.com

Mawer Investment Management Ltd
517 - 10th Ave S W Ste 600 Calgary AB T2R0A8 403-262-4673
Web: www.mawer.com

Maxim Partners LLC 105 E First St Ste 203 Hinsdale IL 60521 630-206-4040
Web: www.maximpartnersllc.com

MBG Technologies Inc 1105 Pittsburgh St Cheswick PA 15204 724-274-7741
Web: mbgtech.com

McElvaine Investment Management Ltd
Ste 219 2187 Oak Bay Ave Ste 219 Victoria BC V8R1G1 250-708-8345
Web: mcelvaine.com

McLean & Partners Wealth Management Ltd
801 Tenth Ave S W Calgary AB T2R0B4 403-234-0005
Web: www.mcleanpartners.com

MD Physician Services Inc 1870 Alta Vista Dr Ottawa ON K1G6R7 613-731-4552
TF: 800-267-4022 ■ *Web:* mdm.ca

MFC Global Investment Management (U S A) Limited
200 Bloor St E N Tower Toronto ON M4W1E5 852-251-3180
Web: www.manulifeam.com

Missouri State Employees' Retirement System
907 Wildwood Dr Jefferson City MO 65109 573-632-6100
TF: 800-827-1063 ■ *Web:* www.mosers.org

Phone | Fax

MITIMCo Private Equity 238 Main St Ste 200 ... Cambridge MA 02142 617-253-4900
Web: www.mitimco.org

Monetta Family of Mutual Funds
1776A S Naperville Rd Ste 100 ... Wheaton IL 60189 630-462-9800
TF: 800-241-9772 ■ *Web:* www.monetta.com

Montrusco Bolton Investments Inc
1501 McGill College Ave Ste 1200 ... Montreal QC H3A3M8 514-842-6464
Web: www.montruscobolton.com

Morgan Meighen & Associates Ltd
10 Toronto St ... Toronto ON M5C2B7 416-366-2931
TF: 866-443-6097 ■ *Web:* www.mmainvestments.com

Mraz, Amerine & Associates Inc
1120 13th St Ste K ... Modesto CA 95354 209-593-5870
Web: www.mrazamerine.com

Mutual Benefit Group
409 Penn St PO Box 577 ... Huntingdon PA 16652 814-643-3000 643-7210
TF: 800-283-3531 ■ *Web:* www.mutualbenefitgroup.com

NDI Capital Inc 736 Granville St Ste 210 ... Vancouver BC V6Z1G3 604-620-8424
Web: ndicapital.com

Neuberger Berman Funds PO Box 8403 ... Boston MA 02266 212-476-8800
TF: 800-877-9700 ■ *Web:* www.nb.com

New Mexico Educational Retirement Board
701 Camino de Los Marquez PO Box 26129 ... Santa Fe NM 87502 505-827-8030
TF: 866-691-2345 ■ *Web:* www.nmerb.org

Nicholas Family of Funds
700 N Water St Ste 1010 ... Milwaukee WI 53202 414-272-6133
TF: 800-227-5987 ■ *Web:* www.nicholasfunds.com

Nicola-Crosby Real Estate Asset Management Ltd
420-1508 W Broadway ... Vancouver BC V6J1W8 778-383-6940
Web: www.nicolacrosby.com

Norris, Perne & French LLP
40 Pearl St N W Ste 300 ... Grand Rapids MI 49503 616-459-3421
TF: 800-748-0544 ■ *Web:* www.norrisperne.com

Norstone Financial Corp
130 King St W The Exchange Twr Ste 1800 ... Toronto ON M5XIE3 416-860-6245
Web: www.norstonecorp.com

North Growth Management Ltd
Ste 830 One Bentall Centre 505 Burrard St ... Vancouver BC V7X1M4 604-688-5440
Web: www.northgrowth.com

North Sky Capital 33 S Sixth St Ste 4646 ... Minneapolis MN 55402 612-435-7150
Web: www.northskycapital.com

Northern Funds PO Box 75986 ... Chicago IL 60675 800-595-9111 557-0411*
**Fax Area Code:* 312 ■ *TF:* 800-595-9111 ■ *Web:* www.northerntrust.com/wealth-management

Northern Institutional Funds
801 S Canal St C5S ... Chicago IL 60607 800-637-1380 557-0411*
**Fax Area Code:* 312 ■ *TF:* 800-637-1380 ■ *Web:* www.northerntrust.com/asset-management

NorthSpring Capital Partners
100 Pinebush Rd ... Cambridge ON N1R8J8 519-721-7144
Web: www.northspringcapitalpartners.com

Northstar Investment Advisors LLC
700 17th St Ste 2350 ... Denver CO 80202 303-832-2300
TF: 800-204-6199 ■ *Web:* www.northstarinvest.com

Nova Scotia Pension Agency
Ste 400 Fourth Fl 1949 Upper Water St ... Halifax NS B3J3N3 902-424-5070
Web: www.novascotiapension.ca

Novare Capital Management
521 E Morehead St The Morehead Bldg
Ste 510 ... Charlotte NC 28202 704-334-3698
TF: 877-334-3698 ■ *Web:* www.novarecapital.com

Oak Assoc Funds PO Box 8233 ... Denver CO 80201 888-462-5386
TF: 888-462-5386 ■ *Web:* www.oakfunds.com

OakBrook Investments LLC 2300 Cabot Dr Ste 300 ... Lisle IL 60532 630-271-0100
Web: www.oakbrookinvest.com

Oakmark Family of Funds 330 W nineth St ... Kansas City MO 64105 617-483-8327
TF: 800-625-6275 ■ *Web:* www.oakmark.com

Old Dominion Capital Management Inc
815 E Jefferson St ... Charlottesville VA 22902 434-977-1550
TF: 800-446-2029 ■ *Web:* odcm.com

OppenheimerFunds Inc 225 Liberty St ... New York NY 10281 800-525-7048
TF: 800-525-7048 ■ *Web:* www.oppenheimerfunds.com

Optimum Asset Management Inc
425 De Maisonneuve Blvd W Ste 1620 ... Montreal QC H3A3G5 514-288-7545
Web: www.optimumgestion.com

Orinda Asset Management LLC
4 Orinda Way Ste 150-A ... Orinda CA 94563 925-253-1300
Web: orindamanagement.com

Pasadena Capital Partners LLC PO Box 60786 ... Pasadena CA 91116 626-432-7070
Web: www.pasadenacapitalpartners.com

Pax World Fund Family
30 Penhallow St Ste 400 ... Portsmouth NH 03801 603-431-8022
TF: 800-767-1729 ■ *Web:* www.paxworld.com

Penfund
Bay Adelaide Centre 333 Bay St Ste 610 ... Toronto ON M5H2R2 416-865-0707
Web: www.penfund.com

Pension Corp Stn Prov Govt Po Box 9460 ... Victoria BC V8W9V8 250-387-1002
Web: www.pensionsbc.ca

PFM Capital Inc 1925 Victoria Ave 2nd Fl ... Regina SK S4P0R3 306-791-4855
Web: www.pfm.ca

Phillips, Hager & North Investment Management Ltd
200 Burrard St 20th Fl ... Vancouver BC V6C3N5 604-408-6100
TF: 800-661-6141 ■ *Web:* www.phn.com

PIMCO Institutional Funds PO Box 219024 ... Kansas City MO 64121 800-927-4648 421-2861*
**Fax Area Code:* 816 ■ *TF:* 800-927-4648 ■ *Web:* www.investments.pimco.com

Pioneer Funds 60 State St ... Boston MA 02109 617-742-7825
TF: 800-225-6292 ■ *Web:* pioneerfunds.com

Polar Securities Inc
401 Bay St Ste 1900 PO Box 19 ... Toronto ON M5H2Y4 416-367-4364
Web: polaramp.com

Poplar Forest Capital LLC
70 S Lk Ave Ste 930 ... Pasadena CA 91101 626-304-6000
Web: www.poplarforestllc.com

Prado Group Inc, The
150 Post St Ste 320 ... San Francisco CA 94108 415-395-0880
Web: www.pradogroup.com

Phone | Fax

Presima Inc
1000 Jean-Paul-Riopelle Pl Montreal
Herald Bldg 4th Fl ... Montreal QC H2Z2B6 514-673-1375
Web: www.presima.com

Primevest Capital Corp
400 Burrard St Ste 1730 ... Vancouver BC V6C3A6 604-630-7011
Web: www.primevestcapital.ca

Priviti Capital Corp 850 444 Fifth Ave S W ... Calgary AB T2P2T8 403-263-9943
TF: 855-333-9943 ■ *Web:* www.priviticapital.com

Pro-Financial Asset Management Inc
5090 Oribtor Dr Unit 3 ... Mississauga ON L4W5B5 905-815-6900

Punch & Associates Inc 3601 W 76th St Ste 225 ... Edina MN 55435 952-224-4350
TF: 800-241-5552 ■ *Web:* punchinvest.com

Putnam Family of Funds PO Box 41203 ... Providence RI 02940 800-225-1581
TF: 800-225-1581 ■ *Web:* www.putnam.com

QV Investors Inc
222 - Third Ave SW Livingston Pl S Tower
Ste 1008 ... Calgary AB T2P0B4 403-265-7007
Web: www.qvinvestors.com

Qwest Investment Management Corp
750 West Pender St Ste 802 ... Vancouver BC V6C2T8 604-601-5804
Web: www.qwestfunds.com

R. G. Niederhoffer Capital Management Inc
1700 Broadway 39th Fl ... New York NY 10019 212-245-0400
Web: www.niederhoffer.com

Rainier Investment Management Mutual Funds
601 Union St Ste 2801 ... Seattle WA 98101 800-536-4640
TF: 800-536-4640 ■ *Web:* www.rainierfunds.com

Raven Capital Management LLC
110 Greene St Ste 9G ... New York NY 10012 212-966-7926
Web: ravencm.com

Raymond Martin Co
4709 Bluebonnet Blvd Ste A ... Baton Rouge LA 70809 225-291-9300
Web: www.raymondmartin.com

Redwood Asset Management Inc
Richmond Adelaide Centre 120 Adelaide St W
Ste 2400 ... Toronto ON M5H1T1 416-368-8898
TF: 877-313-7011 ■ *Web:* www.redwoodasset.com

RidgeWorth Funds 50 Hurt Plaza Ste 1400 ... Atlanta GA 30305 866-595-2470
TF: 866-595-2470 ■ *Web:* www.ridgeworth.com

Ross Smith Asset Management Inc
407 - 8th Avenue S.W Ste 305 ... Calgary AB T2P1E5 888-494-6893
TF: 888-494-6893 ■ *Web:* www.rsam.ca

Roxbury Capital Management LLC
6001 Shady Oak Rd Ste 200 ... Minnetonka MN 55343 952-230-6140
Web: www.roxcap.com

Rydex Funds 805 King Farm Blvd Ste 600 ... Rockville MD 20850 301-296-5100 296-5107*
**Fax:* Admin ■ *TF Cust Svc:* 800-820-0888 ■ *Web:* guggenheiminvestments.com

Sandstone Asset Management Inc
115 101 - Sixth St SW ... Calgary AB T2P5K7 403-218-6125
TF: 866-318-6140 ■ *Web:* www.sandstoneam.com

Sayer Energy Advisors
1620 540 - Fifth Ave SW ... Calgary AB T2P0M2 403-266-6133
Web: www.sayeradvisors.com

Scholtz & Company LLC
107 Elm St 4 Stamford Plz 5th Fl ... Norwalk CT 06902 203-714-9900
Web: www.scholtzandco.com

School Employees Retirement System of Ohio
300 E Broad St Ste 100 ... Columbus OH 43215 614-222-5853
TF: 800-878-5853 ■ *Web:* www.ohsers.org

Schwartz Investment Counsel Inc
801 W Ann Arbor Trl Ste 244 ... Plymouth MI 48170 734-455-7777
Web: www.schwartzinvest.com

Seabury Venture Partners PO Box 2249 ... Redwood City CA 94064 650-373-1030
Web: seaburypartners.com

SEAMARK Asset Management Ltd
1801 Hollis St Ste 810 ... Halifax NS B3J3N4 902-423-9367
TF: 888-303-5055 ■ *Web:* www.seamark.ca

Security Funds 1 Security Benefit Pl ... Topeka KS 66636 785-438-3000 438-5177
TF: 800-888-2461 ■ *Web:* www.securitybenefit.com

SEI 1 Freedom Vly Dr ... Oaks PA 19456 610-676-1000
NASDAQ: SEIC ■ *TF:* 800-342-5734 ■ *Web:* www.seic.com

Selected Funds PO Box 8243 ... Boston MA 02266 800-243-1575
TF: 800-243-1575 ■ *Web:* www.selectedfunds.com

Sensato Investors LLC
1 Sansome St Ste 3430 ... San Francisco CA 94104 415-391-4600
Web: www.sensatoinvestors.com

Sentry Investments Inc
Commerce Court W 199 Bay St Ste 2700
PO Box 108 ... Toronto ON M5L1E2 416-861-8729
Web: www.sentry.ca

Sequoia Fund Inc 767 Fifth Ave Ste 4701 ... New York NY 10153 212-832-5280 832-5298
TF: 800-686-6884 ■ *Web:* www.sequoiafund.com

Sheridan Legacy Group
400 N Michigan Ave Ste 900 ... Chicago IL 60611 312-324-0879
Web: sheridancp.com

Shore Capital Partners LLC
1 E Wacker Dr Ste 400 ... Chicago IL 60601 312-348-7580
Web: www.shorecp.com

Signal Hill Equity Partners
2 Carlton St Ste 1700 ... Toronto ON M5B1J3 416-847-1502
Web: www.signalhillequity.com

Silver Companies 1001 E Telecom Dr ... Boca Raton FL 33431 561-981-5252
Web: www.silvercompanies.com

Silver Heights Capital Management Inc
90 Adelaide St W Ste 400 ... Toronto ON M5H3V9 416-342-5626
Web: www.silverheights.com

Skyline Asset Management LP
120 S Lasalle St Ste 1320 ... Chicago IL 60603 312-913-0900
Web: www.skylinelp.com

Slate Properties Inc 200 Front St W Ste 2400 ... Toronto ON M5V3K2 416-644-4264

Solowave Investments Limited
103 Bauer Pl Ste 5 ... Waterloo ON N2L6B5 519-725-5379
Web: www.solowave.com

Phone Fax

Sound Shore Fund 3 Canal Plz........................Portland ME 04101 800-754-8758
TF: 800-754-8758 ■ *Web:* www.soundshorefund.com

Southpaw Asset Management LP
2 W Greenwich Office Park........................Greenwich CT 06831 203-862-6200
Web: www.southpawassetmanagement.com

Southridge LLC 90 Grove St Ste 206................Ridgefield CT 06877 203-431-8300
Web: www.southridge.com

SpringBank TechVentures
160 MacLaurin Dr Ste #1........................Calgary AB T3Z3S4 403-685-8001

Sprott Inc
200 Bay St Ste 2700 Royal Bank Plz S Twr..............Toronto ON M5J2J1 416-362-7172
Web: www.sprottinc.com

SSgA Funds 1 Lincoln St........................Boston MA 02111 617-786-3000
TF: 800-997-7327 ■ *Web:* www.ssgafunds.com

State Farm Mutual Funds PO Box 219548.........Kansas City MO 64121 800-447-4930
TF: 800-447-4930 ■ *Web:* www.statefarm.com/mutual/mutual.htm

State Teachers Retirement System of Ohio
275 E Broad St........................Columbus OH 43215 888-227-7877
TF: 888-227-7877 ■ *Web:* www.strsoh.org

Steadyhand Investment Funds Limited Partnership
1747 W Third Ave........................Vancouver BC V6J1K7 888-888-3147
TF: 888-888-3147 ■ *Web:* www.steadyhand.com

Steele Capital Management Inc
788 Main St #200........................Dubuque IA 52001 563-588-2097
TF: 800-397-2097 ■ *Web:* www.steelecapital.com

Sterling Bay Companies LLC
1040 W Randolph St........................Chicago IL 60607 312-466-4100
Web: www.sterlingbay.com

Stewart & Patten Company LLC
1 Post St Ste 850........................San Francisco CA 94104 415-421-4932
Web: www.stewartandpatten.com

Strategic Global Advisors LLC
100 Bayview Cir Ste 650........................Newport Beach CA 92660 949-706-2640
Web: www.sgadvisors.com

SW Capital Partners
Ste 1800 Scotia Centre 700 - Second St SW............Calgary AB T2P2W1 403-261-4239
Web: www.swenergycap.com

Tandem 1250 Rene Levesque Blvd W 38th Fl...........Montreal QC H3B4W8 514-510-8900
Web: www.tandemexpansion.com

Tannor Capital Management LLC
150 Grand St Ste 401........................White Plains NY 10601 914-509-5000
Web: www.tannorpartners.com

TCW Group Inc 865 S Figueroa St Ste 1800..........Los Angeles CA 90017 213-244-0000
TF: 800-386-3829 ■ *Web:* www.tcw.com

Tepper Holdings Inc
225 E Beaver Creek Rd Ste 201................Richmond Hill ON L4B3P4 905-889-0663
Web: www.tepperholdings.com

Teralys Capital
999, boul. de Maisonneuve O. Ste 1700..............Montreal QC H3A3L4 514-509-2080
Web: www.teralyscapital.com

Terracap Group 100 Sheppard Ave E Ste 502...........Toronto ON M2N6N5 416-222-9345
TF: 800-363-3207 ■ *Web:* www.terracap.ca

Tetrem Capital Management Ltd
1910-201 Portage Ave........................Winnipeg MB R3B3K6 204-975-2865
Web: www.tetrem.com

Teucrium Trading LLC 232 Hidden Lk Rd............Brattleboro VT 05301 802-257-1617
Web: www.teucrium.com

TFS Capital LLC 10 N High St Ste 500............West Chester PA 19380 888-837-4446
TF: 888-837-4446 ■ *Web:* www.tfscapital.com

TGV Partners 23 Corporate Plz Ste 215...........Newport Beach CA 92660 949-284-1114
Web: www.tgvpartners.com

Third Avenue Funds 622 Third Ave 32nd Fl............New York NY 10017 212-888-5222
Web: thirdave.com

Thornburg Investment Management Funds
2300 N Ridgetop Rd........................Santa Fe NM 87506 505-984-0200 984-8973
TF: 800-533-9337 ■ *Web:* www.thornburginvestments.com

Tillar-Wenstrup Advisors LLC
1065 E Centerville Sta Rd........................Centerville OH 45459 937-428-9700
Web: twadvisors.com

Torray Fund 7501 Wisconsin Ave Ste 750 W............Bethesda MD 20814 301-493-4600
TF: 800-443-3036 ■ *Web:* www.torray.com

TransLink Capital 228 Hamilton Ave Ste 210...........Palo Alto CA 94301 650-330-7353
Web: www.translinkcapital.com

Trez Capital Limited Partnership
1550 - 1185 W Georgia St........................Vancouver BC V6E4E6 416-350-1299
Web: www.trezcapital.com

Triasima Portfolio Management Inc
1555 Peel St Ste 1205........................Montreal QC H3A3L8 514-906-0667
Web: www.triasima.com

TriLinc Global LLC
1230 Rosecrans Ave Ste 605................Manhattan Beach CA 90266 310-997-0580
Web: www.trilincglobal.com

Trillium Asset Management LLC
2 Financial Ctr 60 S St Ste 1100........................Boston MA 02111 617-423-6655
TF: 800-548-5684 ■ *Web:* www.trilliuminvest.com

Trinity Fiduciary Partners LLC
106 Decker Court Ste 226........................Irving TX 75062 877-334-1283
TF: 877-334-1283 ■ *Web:* www.trinityfiduciary.com

Turtle Creek Asset Management
4 King St W Ste 1300........................Toronto ON M5H1B6 416-363-7400
Web: www.turtlecreek.ca

TVV Capital 201 Fourth Ave N Ste 1250..............Nashville TN 37219 615-256-8061
Web: tvvcapital.com

TWIN Capital Management Inc
3244 Washington Rd Ste 202........................Mcmurray PA 15317 724-942-2000
Web: www.twincapital.com

Ulland Investment Advisors
4550 IDS Ctr Eighty S Eighth St..................Minneapolis MN 55402 612-312-1400
Web: www.ullandinvestment.com

Upton Financial Group Inc
131 Stony Cir Ste 500........................Santa Rosa CA 95401 707-523-9651
Web: www.uptonco.com

Valiant Trust Co 310 - 606 Fourth St SW..............Calgary AB T2P1T1 403-233-2801
Web: www.valianttrust.com

Vaughan Nelson Investment Management LP
600 Travis St Ste 6300........................Houston TX 77002 713-224-2545
TF: 888-888-8676 ■ *Web:* www.vaughannelson.com

Vested Business Brokers Inc
50 Karl Ave # 102........................Smithtown NY 11787 631-265-7300
TF: 877-735-5224 ■ *Web:* www.vestedbb.com

Victory Funds 4900 Tiedeman Rd PO Box 182593.......Brooklyn OH 44144 800-539-3863
TF: 800-539-3863 ■ *Web:* www.vcm.com

Vigilant Capital Management LLC
2 City Ctr 4th Fl........................Portland ME 04101 207-523-1110
Web: www.vigilantcap.com

Vision Capital Management Inc
1 SW Columbia Ste 915........................Portland OR 97258 503-221-5656
Web: www.vcmi.net

Wealthsimple Financial Inc
372 Richmond St W Ste 120........................Toronto ON M5V1X6 647-350-7675
Web: www.wealthsimple.com

Weaver C. Barksdale & Associates Inc
1 Burton Hills Blvd Ste 100........................Nashville TN 37215 615-665-1085
Web: www.wcbarksdale.com

Welch & Forbes LLC
45 School St Fifth Fl Old City Hall....................Boston MA 02108 617-523-1635
Web: www.welchforbes.com

Welch Group LLC, The
3940 Montclair Rd 5th Fl........................Birmingham AL 35213 205-879-5001
TF: 800-709-7100 ■ *Web:* www.welchgroup.com

Wesley Clover Corp 390 March Rd Ste 110..............Ottawa ON K2K0G7 613-271-6305
Web: www.wesleyclover.com

Westcap Management Ltd 830 410 22nd St E........Saskatoon SK S7K5T6 306-652-5557
Web: www.westcapmgt.ca

Westwood Trust 1125 S 103rd St Ste 580..............Dallas TX 75201 214-756-6900
Web: www.mccarthyadvisors.com

Wharton Equity Partners LLC
505 Park Ave 18th Fl........................New York NY 10022 212-570-5959
Web: www.whartonequity.com

Wheelock Partners LLC 213 School St Ste 301.........Gardner MA 01440 978-632-9800
Web: www.wheelockpartners.com

White Elm Capital LLC
537 Steamboat Rd Ste 300........................Greenwich CT 06830 203-742-6000
Web: www.whiteelmcapital.com

White Oak Partners LLC
5150 E Dublin Granville Rd Ste One................Westerville OH 43081 614-855-1155
Web: www.whiteoakpartners.com

Whitecap Venture Partners
22 St Clair Ave E Ste 1010........................Toronto ON M4T2S3 416-961-5355
Web: whitecastle.ca

Wilkins Investment Counsel Inc
160 Federal St 17th Fl........................Boston MA 02110 617-951-9969
Web: www.wilkinsinvest.com

Wilshire Mutual Funds Inc PO Box 219512.........Kansas City MO 64121 888-200-6796
TF: 888-200-6796 ■ *Web:* advisor.wilshire.com

XPV Capital Corp 266 King St W Ste 403..............Toronto ON M5V1H8 416-864-0475
Web: www.xpvwaterpartners.com

Yaletown Venture Partners Inc
1122 Mainland St Ste 510........................Vancouver BC V6B5L1 604-688-7807
Web: www.yaletown.com

Zynik Capital Corp
1040 W Georgia St Grosvenor Bldg Ste 950..........Vancouver BC V6E4H1 604-654-2555
Web: www.zynik.com

529 NAVIGATION & GUIDANCE INSTRUMENTS & SYSTEMS

Phone Fax

AAI Corp 124 Industry Ln........................Hunt Valley MD 21030 410-666-1400
Web: textronsystems.com/company-overview/rebrand

Acutronic USA Inc 700 Waterfront Dr................Pittsburgh PA 15222 412-926-1200
Web: www.acutronic.com

Adducent Technology Inc
230 Parque Margarita........................Rohnert Park CA 94928 707-478-8136
TF: 800-648-0656 ■ *Web:* www.adducenttechnology.com

Aeroprobe Corp 2200 Kraft Dr Ste 1475.............Blacksburg VA 24060 540-443-9215
Web: www.aeroprobe.com

Allen Aircraft Products Inc
6168 Woodbine Ave........................Ravenna OH 44266 330-296-9621
Web: www.allenaircraft.com

Alpine Electronics of America
19145 Gramercy Pl........................Torrance CA 90501 310-326-8000 320-5089*
*Fax: Hum Res ■ *TF:* 800-257-4631 ■ *Web:* www.alpine-usa.com

American Reliance Inc (AMREL)
3445 Fletcher Ave........................El Monte CA 91731 626-443-6818 443-8600
Web: www.amrel.com

American Seal & Engineering Company Inc
295 Indian River Rd........................Orange CT 06477 203-789-8819
Web: www.ameriseal.com

AMRO Fabrication Corp 1430 Adelia Ave........South El Monte CA 91733 626-579-2200
Web: www.amrofab.com

Apex Machine Tool Co 1790 New Britain Ave........Farmington CT 06032 860-677-2884
Web: www.apexmachinetool.com

Archangel Systems Inc 1635 Pumphrey Ave............Auburn AL 36832 334-826-8008
Web: www.archangel.com

Astronautics Corp of America
4115 N Teutonia Ave PO Box 523....................Milwaukee WI 53201 414-449-4000 447-8231
Web: www.astronautics.com

Aviat Aircraft Inc 672 S Washington....................Afton WY 83110 307-885-3151
Web: www.aviataircraft.com

Aviation Materials Management Inc
2581 Rulon White Blvd........................Ogden UT 84404 801-782-8450
Web: www.avmat.com

Aviation Partners Inc 7213 Perimeter Rd S..............Seattle WA 98108 206-762-1171
Web: www.aviationpartners.com

Avionics & Systems Integration Group LLC
10 Collins Industrial Pl Ste 3b..............North Little Rock AR 72113 501-771-9388
Web: asigllc.com

Company	City	State	ZIP	Phone	Fax
Ball Aerospace & Technologies Corp 1600 Commerce St; **Fax: Mail Rm* ■ *Web:* www.ball.com/aerospace	Boulder	CO	80301	303-939-4000	460-2315*
Ballard Technology Inc 11400 Airport Rd Ste 201; *Web:* www.ballardtech.com	Everett	WA	98204	425-339-0281	
Baron Services Inc 4930 Research Dr; *Web:* www.baronweather.com	Huntsville	AL	35805	256-881-8811	
Bell Aerospace Services Inc 1305 Airport Fwy Ste 123	Bedford	TX	76021	817-278-0750	
Blue Ridge Optics LLC 1617 Longwood Ave; *Web:* www.blueridgeoptics.com	Bedford	VA	24523	540-586-8526	
Boeing Phantom Works PO Box 2515; *Web:* www.boeing.com	Seal Beach	CA	90740	562-797-2020	
Brek Manufacturing Co 1513 W 132nd St; *Web:* www.brek.aero	Gardena	CA	90249	310-329-7638	
Bright Lights USA Inc 145 Shreve Ave; *Web:* www.brightlightsusa.com	Barrington	NJ	08007	856-546-5656	
Butler National Corp 19920 W 161st St; *OTC: BUKS* ■ *TF:* 800-690-6903 ■ *Web:* www.butlernational.com	Olathe	KS	66062	913-780-9595	780-5088
C & D Zodiac Inc 5701 Bolsa Ave	Huntington Beach	CA	92647	714-934-0000	
Cicon Engineering 6633 Odessa Ave; *Web:* www.cicon.com	Van Nuys	CA	91406	818-909-6060	
CLC Networks 2275 Northwest Pkwy SE Ste 110; *Web:* www.clcnetworks.com	Marietta	GA	30067	678-564-0522	
Cloud Cap Technology Inc 205 N Wasco Loop Ste 103; *Web:* www.cloudcaptech.com	Hood River	OR	97031	541-387-2120	387-2030
CMI Inc 316 E Ninth St; *TF:* 866-835-0690 ■ *Web:* www.alcoholtest.com	Owensboro	KY	42303	270-685-6545	685-6678
Contract Fabrication & Design LLC 5427 Fm 546; *Web:* cfdintl.com	Princeton	TX	75407	972-736-2260	
Cubic Corp 9333 Balboa Ave PO Box 85587; *NYSE: CUB* ■ *TF:* 800-937-5449 ■ *Web:* www.cubic.com	San Diego	CA	92186	858-277-6780	505-1523
Cubic Defense Systems 9333 Balboa Ave; *TF:* 800-937-5449 ■ *Web:* www.cubic.com	San Diego	CA	92123	858-277-6780	505-1524
Cummins Aerospace 2200 E Orangethorpe Ave; *Web:* www.cumminsaerospace.com	Anaheim	CA	92806	714-879-2800	
Dean Baldwin Painting LP 2395 Bulverde Rd Ste 105; *Web:* www.deanbaldwinpainting.com	Bulverde	TX	78163	830-438-5340	
Del Mar Avionics 1601 Alton Pkwy Ste C; *TF:* 800-854-0481 ■ *Web:* www.dma.com	Irvine	CA	92606	949-250-3200	261-0529
DRS C3 Systems LLC 400 Professional Dr; *TF:* 800-694-5005 ■ *Web:* www.drs.com	Gaithersburg	MD	20879	301-921-8100	921-8010
DRS Technologies Inc 5 Sylvan Way; *TF:* 800-694-5005 ■ *Web:* www.drs.com	Parsippany	NJ	07054	973-898-1500	
DRS Training & Control Systems 645 Anchors St NW; *TF:* 800-694-5005 ■ *Web:* www.drs.com	Fort Walton Beach	FL	32548	850-302-3000	302-3371
Dynalec Corp 87 W Main St; *Web:* www.dynalec.com	Sodus	NY	14551	315-483-6923	483-6656
Eaton Corp 1111 Superior Ave Eaton Ctr; *Web:* www.eaton.com	Cleveland	OH	44114	216-523-5000	
Esterline Technologies Corp 500 108th Ave NE Ste 1500; *NYSE: ESL* ■ *Web:* www.esterline.com	Bellevue	WA	98004	425-453-9400	453-2916
EWR Weather Radar 336 Leffingwell Ave; *Web:* www.ewradar.com	Saint Louis	MO	63122	314-821-1022	
First Class Air Repair 15380 County Rd 565A Ste G; *Web:* firstclassairrepair.com	Groveland	FL	34736	352-241-7684	
Flash Technology Corp 332 Nichol Mill Ln; *TF:* 888-313-5274 ■ *Web:* www.spx.com	Franklin	TN	37067	615-503-2000	261-2000
FLIR Systems Inc 27700-A SW Pkwy Ave; *NASDAQ: FLIR* ■ **Fax: Sales* ■ *TF:* 877-773-3547 ■ *Web:* www.flir.com	Wilsonville	OR	97070	503-498-3547	498-3904*
Forrest Machining Inc 27756 Ave Mentry; *Web:* www.forrestmachining.com	Valencia	CA	91355	661-257-0231	
Fortner Aerospace Manufacturing Inc 401 N Pleasant St; *Web:* syncaero.com	Prescott	AZ	86301	928-771-2434	
Frontier Electronic Systems Corp 4500 W Sixth Ave; **Fax: Hum Res* ■ *TF:* 800-677-1769 ■ *Web:* www.fescorp.com	Stillwater	OK	74074	405-624-1769	624-7898*
Gables Engineering Inc 247 Greco Ave; *Web:* www.gableseng.com	Coral Gables	FL	33146	305-774-4400	774-4465
Garmin Ltd 1200 E 151st St; *NASDAQ: GRMN* ■ *TF:* 888-442-7646 ■ *Web:* www.garmin.com	Olathe	KS	66062	913-397-8200	397-8282
GCE Industries Inc 1891 Nirvana Ave; *Web:* www.gceindustries.com	Chula Vista	CA	91911	619-421-1151	
GCM North American Aerospace LLC 21719 84th Ave S	Kent	WA	98032	253-872-7488	
GE Aviation Systems Div 3290 Patterson Ave SE; *Web:* www.geaviation.com	Grand Rapids	MI	49512	616-241-8274	
General Dynamics Advanced Information Systems 12450 Fair Lakes Cir Ste 600	Fairfax	VA	22033	703-263-2800	
General Dynamics C4 Systems 400 John Quincy Adams Rd Bldg 80; *TF:* 877-449-0600 ■ *Web:* www.gdc4s.com	Taunton	MA	02780	877-449-0600	
Goodrich Corp 2730 W Tyvola Rd 4 Coliseum Ctr; *NYSE: GR* ■ *TF:* 800-735-7899 ■ *Web:* utcaerospacesystems.com	Charlotte	NC	28217	704-423-7000	423-7002
Hampson Aerospace Inc 2700 112th St Ste 300	Grand Prairie	TX	75050	214-988-0630	
Honeywell Aerospace 1944 E Sky Harbor Cir; **Fax Area Code: 602* ■ *TF:* 800-601-3099 ■ *Web:* www.honeywell.com	Phoenix	AZ	85034	800-601-3099	365-3343*
Innovative Configuration Inc 712 Via Palo Alto	Aptos	CA	95003	831-688-6917	
Innovative Solutions & Support Inc 720 Pennsylvania Dr; *NASDAQ: ISSC* ■ *TF:* 866-359-7876 ■ *Web:* www.innovative-ss.com	Exton	PA	19341	610-646-9800	646-0149
Interface Displays & Controls Inc 4630 N Ave; *Web:* www.interfacedisplays.com	Oceanside	CA	92056	760-945-0230	
Interstate Electronics Corp 602 E Vermont Ave PO Box 3117; *TF:* 800-854-6979 ■ *Web:* www.l-3com.com	Anaheim	CA	92803	714-758-0500	758-4148
ITT Industries Inc 1133 Westchester Ave; *NYSE: ITT* ■ *TF:* 800-254-2823 ■ *Web:* www.itt.com	White Plains	NY	10604	914-641-2000	696-2950
Jewell Instruments LLC 850 Perimeter Rd; *TF:* 800-227-5955 ■ *Web:* jewellinstruments.com	Manchester	NH	03103	603-669-6400	669-5962
Kearfott Guidance & Navigation Corp 1150 McBride Ave; *Web:* www.kearfott.com	Little Falls	NJ	07424	973-785-6000	785-6025
Kelly Manufacturing Co 555 S Topeka St; *Web:* www.kellymfg.com	Wichita	KS	67202	316-265-6868	265-6687
Kollsman Inc 220 Daniel Webster Hwy; *TF:* 800-772-9603 ■ *Web:* www.elbitsystems-us.com	Merrimack	NH	03054	603-889-2500	
Kor Electronics 10855 Business Ctr Dr; *Web:* www.mrcy.com	Cypress	CA	90630	714-898-8200	
KVH Industries Inc 50 Enterprise Ctr; *NASDAQ: KVHI* ■ *Web:* www.kvh.com	Middletown	RI	02842	401-847-3327	849-0045
L-3 Avionics Systems 5353 52nd St SE; *TF:* 800-253-9525 ■ *Web:* www.l-3avionics.com	Grand Rapids	MI	49512	616-949-6600	
L-3 Communications Corp Aviation Recorders Div 6000 Fruitville Rd; *TF:* 877-726-2228 ■ *Web:* www.l-3ar.com	Sarasota	FL	34232	941-371-0811	377-5598
L-3 Communications Corp Communication Systems East Div 1 Federal St; *TF:* 800-339-6197 ■ *Web:* www.l-3com.com/CS-East	Camden	NJ	08103	856-338-3000	338-6014
L-3 Communications Corp Randtron Antenna Systems Div 130 Constitution Dr; *TF Sales:* 866-900-7270 ■ *Web:* www.l-3com.com/randtron	Menlo Park	CA	94025	650-326-9500	326-1033
L-3 Communications Holdings Inc 640 North 2200 West PO Box 16850; *Web:* www.l-3com.com/csw	Salt Lake City	UT	84116	801-594-2000	594-3572
L-3 Ocean Systems 15825 Roxford St; *Web:* www2.l3com.com	Sylmar	CA	91342	818-367-0111	
Laitram LLC 200 Laitram Ln; *TF:* 800-535-7631 ■ *Web:* www.laitram.com	Harahan	LA	70123	504-733-6000	733-2143
Liquid Measurement Systems 141 Morse Dr PO Box 2070; *Web:* www.liquidmeasurement.com	Georgia	VT	05468	802-528-8100	528-8131
Lockheed Martin Canada 3001 Solandt Rd; *Web:* www.lockheedmartin.com/canada	Kanata	ON	K2K2M8	613-599-3270	599-3282
Lockheed Martin Corp 6801 Rockledge Dr; *NYSE: LMT* ■ *TF:* 866-562-2363 ■ *Web:* www.lockheedmartin.com	Bethesda	MD	20817	301-897-6000	
Lockheed Martin MS2 199 Borton Landing Rd; *Web:* lockheedmartin.com	Moorestown	NJ	08057	856-722-4100	
Lockheed Martin Sippican 7 Barnabas Rd; *Web:* www.sippican.com	Marion	MA	02738	508-748-1160	748-3626
Loral Space & Communications Ltd 600 Third Ave; *NASDAQ: LORL* ■ *Web:* www.loral.com	New York	NY	10016	212-697-1105	
Lowrance Electronics Inc 12000 E Skelly Dr; **Fax: Hum Res* ■ *TF:* 800-628-4487 ■ *Web:* www.lowrance.com	Tulsa	OK	74128	918-437-6881	234-1705*
Lycoming Engines 652 Oliver St; *TF:* 800-258-3279 ■ *Web:* www.lycoming.com	Williamsport	PA	17701	570-323-6181	
Mackay Communications Inc 3691 Trust Dr; **Fax Area Code: 919* ■ *TF:* 888-798-7979 ■ *Web:* www.mackaycomm.com	Raleigh	NC	27616	281-478-6245	954-1707*
Martin-Baker America Inc 423 Walters Ave; *Web:* www.martin-baker.com	Johnstown	PA	15904	814-262-9325	
Maven Engineering Corp 15946 Derwood Rd; *Web:* www.mavencorporation.com	Rockville	MD	20855	301-519-3400	
Mikros Systems Corp 707 Alexander Rd Ste 208 PO Box 7189; *Web:* www.mikrossystems.com	Princeton	NJ	08540	609-987-1513	
Nabtesco Aerospace Inc 17770 NE 78th Pl; *Web:* www.nabtescoaero.com	Redmond	WA	98052	425-602-8400	
NavCom Defense Electronics Inc 9129 Stellar Ct; *Web:* www.navcom.com	Corona	CA	92883	951-268-9230	
Navigation Solutions LLC 3314 N Central Expy Ste 210; *Web:* www.navigationsolutions.com	Plano	TX	75074	972-633-2301	
NephroGenex Inc 79 Tw Alexander Dr 4401 Research Commons Bldg Ste 290 PO Box 14188; *Web:* www.nephrogenex.com	Research Triangle Park	NC	27709	609-986-1780	
Newcon Optik 105 Sparks Ave; *TF:* 877-368-6666 ■ *Web:* www.newcon-optik.com	North York	ON	M2H2S5	416-663-6963	663-9065
Northrop Grumman Corp 2980 Fairview Park Dr; *NYSE: NOC* ■ *Web:* www.northropgrumman.com	Falls Church	VA	22042	703-280-2900	
Onboard Systems International 13915 NW Third Ct; *TF:* 800-275-0883 ■ *Web:* www.onboardsystems.com	Vancouver	WA	98685	360-546-3072	
Orbit International Corp 80 Cabot Ct; *NASDAQ: ORBT* ■ *Web:* www.orbitintl.com	Hauppauge	NY	11788	631-435-8300	435-8458
Oregon Aero Inc 34020 Skyway Dr; *TF:* 800-888-6910 ■ *Web:* www.oregonaero.com	Scappoose	OR	97056	503-543-7399	
Parker Electronic Systems 300 Marcus Blvd; *Web:* www.parker.com	Smithtown	NY	11787	631-231-3737	434-8152
Pixel Velocity Inc 3917 Research Park Dr Ste B-1; *Web:* www.pixel-velocity.com	Ann Arbor	MI	48108	734-213-3715	
Plures Technologies Inc 5297 Parkside Dr Ste 400	Canandaigua	NY	14424	585-905-0554	
Pratt & Whitney AutoAir Inc 5640 Enterprise Dr; *Web:* www.autoair.com	Lansing	MI	48911	517-393-4040	
Precision Aircraft Components Inc 2787 Armstrong Ln	Dayton	OH	45414	937-278-0265	278-4466

	City	State	Zip	Phone	Fax
Professional Aircraft Accessories Inc 7035 Ctr Ln *Web:* www.gopaa.com	Titusville	FL	32780	321-267-1040	
Proxy Technologies Inc 1840 Michael Faraday Dr Ste 220 *Web:* www.proxyaviation.com	Reston	VA	20190	703-485-1035	
Q Holdings Inc 615 Arapeen Dr Ste 102 *Web:* www.qthera.com	Salt Lake City	UT	84108	801-582-5400	
Radio Holland USA Inc 8943 Gulf Fwy *Web:* imtech.com/en/imtechmarine-usa	Houston	TX	77017	713-378-2100	378-2101
Raymarine Inc 21 Manchester St *TF:* 800-539-5539 ■ *Web:* www.raymarine.com	Merrimack	NH	03054	603-881-5200	
Raytheon Air Traffic Management Systems 870 Winter St *Web:* raytheon.com/capabilities/products/cnsatm	Waltham	MA	02451	781-522-3000	522-5200
Raytheon Canada Ltd 360 Albert St Ste 1640 *Web:* www.raytheon.com	Ottawa	ON	K1R7X7	613-233-4121	233-1099
Raytheon Integrated Defense Systems 50 Apple Hill Dr *Web:* raytheon.com/ourcompany/businesses	Tewksbury	MA	01876	978-858-5000	
Raytheon Network Centric Systems (NCS) 2501 W University Dr *Web:* www.raytheon.com	McKinney	TX	75071	781-522-3000	
Rockwell Collins Inc 400 Collins Rd NE *NYSE: COL* ■ **Fax: PR* ■ *TF:* 888-721-3094 ■ *Web:* www.rockwellcollins.com	Cedar Rapids	IA	52498	319-295-1000	295-1542*
Rodale Electronics Inc 20 Oser Ave *Web:* www.rodaleelectronics.com	Hauppauge	NY	11788	631-231-0044	231-1345
Ross Laboratories Inc 3138 Fairview Ave E *Web:* www.rosslaboratories.com	Seattle	WA	98102	206-324-3950	
Rostra Precision Controls Inc 2519 Dana Dr *TF Cust Svc:* 800-782-3379 ■ *Web:* www.rostra.com	Laurinburg	NC	28352	910-276-4853	276-1354
Safe Flight Instrument Corp 20 New King St *Web:* www.safeflight.com	White Plains	NY	10604	914-946-9500	946-7882
SELEX Inc 11300 W 89th St *TF:* 800-765-0861 ■ *Web:* us.selex-es.com	Overland Park	KS	66214	913-495-2600	492-0870
Shadin LP 6831 Oxford St *TF:* 800-328-0584 ■ *Web:* www.shadin.com	St Louis Park	MN	55426	952-927-6500	
Solacom Technologies Inc 84 Jean-Proulx *Web:* www.solacom.com	Gatineau	QC	J8Z1W1	613-693-0641	693-0642
Sonatech Inc 879 Ward Dr *Web:* channeltechgroup.com/products-and-services/systems	Santa Barbara	CA	93111	805-683-1431	690-5388
Spectralux Corp 12335 134th Ct Ne *Web:* www.spectralux.com	Redmond	WA	98052	425-285-3000	
Sperry Marine Northrop Grumman 1070 Seminole Trl *Web:* www.sperrymarine.com	Charlottesville	VA	22901	434-974-2000	974-2259
SSR Engineering 950 Fee Ana Ste A106 *Web:* www.ssreng.com	Placentia	CA	92870	714-229-9020	
Stark Aerospace Inc 319 Charleigh D Ford Jr Dr *Web:* www.starkaerospace.com	Columbus	MS	39701	662-798-4075	
Stewart Warner South Wind Corp 2495 Directors Row Ste F *Web:* www.stewart-warner.com	Indianapolis	IN	46241	317-486-2600	
Superior Air Parts Inc 621 S Royal Ln Ste 100 *TF:* 800-420-4727 ■ *Web:* www.superiorairparts.com	Coppell	TX	75019	972-829-4600	829-4648
Systron Donner Inertial 355 Lennon Ln *TF:* 866-234-4976 ■ *Web:* www.systron.com	Walnut Creek	CA	94598	925-979-4400	979-9827
Teledyne Benthos Inc 49 Edgerton Dr *Web:* www.benthos.com	North Falmouth	MA	02556	508-563-1000	563-6444
Teledyne Odom Hydrographic Systems Inc 1450 Seaboard Ave *Web:* www.odomhydrographic.com	Baton Rouge	LA	70810	225-769-3051	
Teledyne RD Instruments Inc 14020 Stowe Dr *Web:* www.rdinstruments.com	Poway	CA	92064	858-842-2600	
Textron Systems Corp 201 Lowell St *Web:* textron.com	Wilmington	MA	01887	978-657-5111	657-6644
Thales ATM 23501 W 84th St *Web:* www.thalesgroup.com	Shawnee	KS	66227	913-422-2600	422-2917
Thales USA Inc 2733 S Crystal Dr Ste 1200 *Web:* www.thalesgroup.com	Arlington	VA	22202	703-838-9685	838-1688
Tideland Signal Corp 4310 Directors Row *Web:* www.tidelandsignal.com	Houston	TX	77092	713-681-6101	
Transbotics Corp 3400 Latrobe Dr *OTC: TNSB* ■ *Web:* www.transbotics.com	Charlotte	NC	28211	704-362-1115	364-4039
Trimble Navigation Ltd 935 Stewart Dr *NASDAQ: TRMB* ■ *TF:* 800-538-7800 ■ *Web:* www.trimble.com	Sunnyvale	CA	94085	408-481-8000	
Trutrak Flight Systems Inc 1500 S Old Missouri Rd *TF:* 866-878-8725 ■ *Web:* www.trutrakap.com	Springdale	AR	72764	479-751-0250	
Tyonek Mfg Group Inc 229 Palmer Rd *TF:* 877-258-6200 ■ *Web:* www.tyonek.com	Madison	AL	35758	256-258-6200	
Ultra Electronics 3Phoenix Inc 14585 Avion Pkwy Ste 200 *Web:* ultra-3pi.com	Chantilly	VA	20151	703-956-6480	
Union Machine Company of Lynn Inc 6 Federal Way *Web:* www.unionmachine.com	Groveland	MA	01834	978-521-5100	
United Paradyne Corp 2415 Professional Pkwy *Web:* www.unitedparadyne.com	Santa Maria	CA	93455	805-348-3155	
Van's Aircraft Inc 14401 Keil Rd Ne *Web:* www.vansaircraft.com	Aurora	OR	97002	503-678-6545	
Vumii Inc 1100 Abernathy Rd 500 Northpark Town Ctr Ste 1100 *Web:* www.vumii.com	Atlanta	GA	30328	678-578-4700	
Wellbore Navigation Inc 15032 Red Hill Ave Ste D *Web:* www.welnavinc.com	Tustin	CA	92780	714-259-7760	259-9257
Western Methods Machinery Corp 2344 Pullman St	Santa Ana	CA	92705	949-252-6600	
Whistler Group Inc 13016 N Walton Blvd *TF Cust Svc:* 800-531-0004 ■ *Web:* www.whistlergroup.com	Bentonville	AR	72712	479-273-6012	
Wipaire Inc 1700 Henry Ave *TF:* 888-947-2473 ■ *Web:* www.wipaire.com	South St. Paul	MN	55075	651-451-1205	
XRS Corporation 12900 Whitewater Dr Ste 300 *TF:* 800-348-7227 ■ *Web:* xrscorp.com	Hopkins	MN	55343	800-348-7227	
Zonar Systems LLC 18200 Cascade Ave S *TF:* 877-843-3847 ■ *Web:* www.zonarsystems.com	Seattle	WA	98188	206-878-2459	878-3082

530 NEWS SYNDICATES, SERVICES, BUREAUS

	City	State	Zip	Phone	Fax
AccountingWEB Inc PO Box 2252 *TF:* 866-688-1678 ■ *Web:* www.accountingweb.com	Westerville	OH	43086	866-688-1678	
AccuWeather Inc 385 Science Pk Rd *TF Sales:* 800-566-6606 ■ *Web:* www.accuweather.com	State College	PA	16803	814-235-8650	238-1339
Aero-News PO Box 9132 *Web:* www.aero-news.net	Winter Haven	FL	33883	863-299-8680	
Africa News Service Inc 922 M St Se *Web:* www.allafrica.com	Washington	DC	20003	202-546-0777	
Agence France-Presse (AFP) 1500 K St NW Ste 600 *Web:* www.afp.com	Washington	DC	20005	202-414-0600	
Al-Wali Corp 401 Thornton Rd *Web:* www.newleaf-dist.com	Lithia Springs	GA	30122	770-948-7845	
American Baptist News Service PO Box 851 *TF:* 800-222-3872 ■ *Web:* www.abc-usa.org	Valley Forge	PA	19482	610-768-2000	
American Chiropractor, The 8619 NW 68Th St *TF:* 888-369-1396 ■ *Web:* www.theamericanchiropractor.com	Miami	FL	33166	888-369-1396	
Anderson Merchandisers LP 421 SE 34th Ave *Web:* www.amerch.com	Amarillo	TX	79103	806-376-6251	
Andrews McMeel Universal 1130 Walnut *Web:* www.amuniversal.com	Kansas City	MO	64106	816-581-7500	932-6684
Argus Interactive Agency Inc 217 N Main St Ste 200 *TF:* 866-595-9597 ■ *Web:* www.argusinteractive.com	Santa Ana	CA	92701	866-595-9597	
Associated Press (AP) 450 W 33rd St *Web:* www.ap.org	New York	NY	10001	212-621-1500	621-1679
Baptist Press 901 Commerce St *Web:* www.sbc.net	Nashville	TN	37203	615-244-2355	
Bay News 1624 N Meadowcrest Blvd *Web:* www.baynews9.com	Crystal River	FL	34429	352-563-2052	
Bloomberg LP 731 Lexington Ave *Web:* www.bloomberg.com	New York	NY	10022	212-318-2000	893-5000
Brickyard VFX 2054 Broadway *Web:* www.brickyardvfx.com	Santa Monica	CA	90404	310-453-5722	
Business Wire 44 Montgomery St 39th Fl *Web:* www.businesswire.com	San Francisco	CA	94104	415-986-4422	788-5335
California Newspaper Service Bureau 915 E First St *Web:* dailyjournal.com	Los Angeles	CA	90012	213-229-5500	229-5481
Creators Syndicate Inc 5777 W Century Blvd Ste 700 *Web:* www.creators.com	Los Angeles	CA	90045	310-337-7003	337-7625
Csrwire LLC 250 Albany St *Web:* csrwire.com	Springfield	MA	01105	802-251-0110	
Disaster News Network (DNN) PO Box 1746 *TF:* 888-384-3028 ■ *Web:* www.disasternews.net	Ellicott City	MD	21041	443-393-3330	420-0085
EcoMedia LLC 919 Manhattan Ave Ste 100 *Web:* ecomedia.cbs.com	Manhattan Beach	CA	90266	310-374-8212	
eDirectory 7004 Little River Tpke Ste O *Web:* www.edirectory.com	Annandale	VA	22003	703-914-0770	
Elias Sports Bureau Inc 500 Fifth Ave *Web:* www.esb.com	New York	NY	10110	212-869-1530	354-0980
FADER Inc, The 71 W 23 St Fl 13 *Web:* www.thefader.com	New York	NY	10010	212-741-7100	
Federal Network Inc (FedNet) 122 C St NW Ste 520 *Web:* www.fednet.net	Washington	DC	20001	202-393-7300	
Federal News Services 77 K St *Web:* www.fednews.com	Washington	DC	20002	202-650-6500	
FurnitureDealer.net Inc PO Box 22251 *TF:* 866-387-6357 ■ *Web:* www.furnituredealer.net	Eagan	MN	55122	866-387-6357	
Gantec Publishing Solutions LLC 1111 N Plz Dr Ste 652 *Web:* www.gantecpublishing.com	Schaumburg	IL	60173	847-598-1144	
Gateway Newstands 240 Chrislea Rd *TF:* 800-942-5351 ■ *Web:* www.gatewaynewstands.com	Woodbridge	ON	L4L8V1	905-851-9652	
German Press Agency 529 14th St Nw Ste 1112 *Web:* www.dpa.com	Washington	DC	20045	202-662-1220	
Hearst News Service 700 12th St NW Ste 1000 *Web:* www.hearst.com	Washington	DC	20005	202-263-6400	
Hispanic Link Inc 1420 N St NW	Washington	DC	20005	202-234-0280	
Hudson Group 1 Meadowlands Plz Ste 902 *Web:* www.hudsongroup.com	East Rutherford	NJ	07073	201-939-5050	
Inman News 1100 Marina Village Pkwy Ste 102 *TF:* 800-775-4662 ■ *Web:* www.inman.com	Alameda	CA	94501	510-658-9252	
Jewish Telegraphic Agency Inc 330 Seventh Ave 17th Fl *Web:* www.jta.org	New York	NY	10001	212-643-1890	643-8498
JM DigitalWorks 2460 Impala Dr	Carlsbad	CA	92010	760-476-1783	
JUGGLE Magazine 3315 E Russell Rd #A4 203 *Web:* www.juggle.org	Las Vegas	NV	89120	702-798-0099	
Kagan 981 Calle Amanecer *TF:* 800-933-2667 ■ *Web:* www.kaganonline.com	San Clemente	CA	92673	949-369-6310	
Kansas Press Assn Inc 5423 SW Seventh St *TF:* 855-572-1863 ■ *Web:* www.kspress.com	Topeka	KS	66606	785-271-5304	271-7341

				Phone	Fax
Kearney Hub 13 E 22Nd PO Box 1988 *Web:* www.kearneyhub.com	Kearney	NE	68847	308-237-2152	
King Features Syndicate Inc 300 W 57th St 15th Fl **Fax Area Code:* 646 ■ *TF:* 800-708-7311 ■ *Web:* www.kingfeatures.com	New York	NY	10019	212-969-7550	280-1550*
Lester Catalog Co 9850 Hillview Rd	Newcastle	CA	95658	530-823-0963	
Levy Home Entertainment LLC 1420 Kensington Rd Ste 300 *TF:* 800-549-5389 ■ *Web:* www.readerlink.com	Oak Brook	IL	60523	708-547-4400	
Los Angeles Times-Washington Post News Service Inc 1150 15th St NW *TF:* 800-627-1150 ■ *Web:* www.washingtonpost.com	Washington	DC	20071	202-334-6000	
Mainebiz 48 Free St 3rd Fl *Web:* www.mainebiz.biz	Portland	ME	04101	207-761-8379	
Majon International PO Box 6059 *Web:* www.majon.com	Los Osos	CA	93412	805-528-2100	
Market Wire Inc 100 N Sepulveda Blvd Ste 325 *TF General:* 800-774-9473 ■ *Web:* www.marketwired.com	El Segundo	CA	90245	310-765-3200	765-3297
Metro News Services 150 Dalton Dr	Desoto	TX	75115	972-230-4277	
Microfinance Information Exchange Inc 2020 Pennsylvania Ave NW Ste 353 *Web:* www.mixmarket.org	Washington	DC	20006	202-659-9094	
New York Times News Service Div 620 Eigth Ave 9th Fl *TF:* 800-698-4637 ■ *Web:* www.nytimes.com	New York	NY	10018	212-556-7652	
NewRetirement LLC 100 Pine St Ste 590 *TF:* 866-441-0246 ■ *Web:* www.newretirement.com	San Francisco	CA	94111	415-738-2435	
NY1 75 Ninth Ave *Web:* www.ny1.com	New York	NY	10011	212-379-3311	
Oversee.net 515 S Flower St Ste 4400 *Web:* www.oversee.net	Los Angeles	CA	90071	213-408-0080	
Pacific News Service 275 Ninth St *Web:* newamericamedia.org	San Francisco	CA	94103	415-503-4170	503-0970
Postmedia Network Inc 365 Bloor St E *Web:* www.postmedia.com	Toronto	ON	M4W3L4	416-383-2300	
PR Photos 4521 Pga Blvd *TF:* 866-551-7827 ■ *Web:* www.prphotos.com	Palm Beach Gardens	FL	33418	866-551-7827	
ProductionHUB 1806 Hammerlin Ave *Web:* www.productionhub.com	Winter Park	FL	32789	407-629-4122	
Religion News Service (RNS) 529 14th St NW Ste 425 *TF:* 800-767-6781 ■ *Web:* www.religionnews.com	Washington	DC	20045	202-463-8777	463-0033
SCB Marketing 5131 Industry Dr *Web:* scbmarketing.com	Melbourne	FL	32940	321-622-5986	
Scripps Howard News Service (SHNS) 1090 Vermont Ave NW Ste 1000	Washington	DC	20005	202-408-1484	408-2062
Shalom TV PO Box 1989 *Web:* shalomtv.tv/live	Fort Lee	NJ	07024	201-242-9460	
Sofizar Inc 7845 Bellakaren pl *Web:* www.sofizar.com	La jolla	CA	92037	760-494-0692	
Softomate LLC 901 N Pitt St Ste 325 *TF:* 877-243-8735 ■ *Web:* www.softomate.com	Alexandria	VA	22314	877-243-8735	
Sports Network 2200 Byberry Rd Ste 200	Hatboro	PA	19040	215-441-8444	441-5767
Stargate Digital 1001 El Centro St *Web:* www.stargatestudios.net	South Pasadena	CA	91030	626-403-8403	
Sticks 809 Central Ave Ste 315 *Web:* www.ssoutdooradventures.com	Fort Dodge	IA	50501	515-573-8898	
Strategic News Service 38 Yew Ln *Web:* www.tapsns.com	Friday Harbor	WA	98250	360-378-1023	
Streetwise Reports LLC 101 Second St Ste 110 *Web:* www.theaureport.com	Petaluma	CA	94952	707-981-8999	
Talk Radio News Service 236 Massachusetts Ave NE Ste 306 *Web:* www.talkradionews.com	Washington	DC	20002	202-337-5322	
Tass News Agency 780 Third Ave Rm 1900	New York	NY	10017	212-245-4250	
Texas Fish & Game Magazine 1745 Greens Rd *Web:* www.fishgame.com	Houston	TX	77032	281-227-3001	
United Methodist News Service 810 12th Ave S *TF:* 800-251-8140 ■ *Web:* www.umcom.org	Nashville	TN	37203	615-742-5470	
United Press International (UPI) 1133 19th St NW *Web:* www.upi.com	Washington	DC	20036	202-898-8000	
Washington Post Writers Group 1150 15th St NW *TF:* 800-879-9794 ■ *Web:* syndication.washingtonpost.com	Washington	DC	20071	202-334-6375	334-5669
Website Magazine Inc 999 E Touhy Ave *TF:* 800-817-1518 ■ *Web:* www.websitemagazine.com	Des Plaines	IL	60018	773-628-2779	
Wireless Flash News Service PO Box 633030 *Web:* www.flashnews.com	San Diego	CA	92163	619-220-7191	
World Property Journal 1221 Brickell Ave Ste 900 *Web:* www.worldpropertyjournal.com	Miami	FL	33131	305-375-9292	

531 NEWSLETTERS

531-1 Banking & Finance Newsletters

				Phone	Fax
Banking Daily 1801 S Bell St *TF:* 800-372-1033	Arlington	VA	22202	800-372-1033	
Bankruptcy Court Decisions 360 Hiatt Dr *TF:* 800-621-5463 ■ *Web:* www.lrp.com	Palm Beach Gardens	FL	33418	561-622-6520	622-2423
Best's Underwriting Newsletter Ambest Rd *Web:* www3.ambest.com/buglcem	Oldwick	NJ	08858	908-439-2200	
BestWeek Life/Health Newsletter Ambest Rd *Web:* www.ambest.com	Oldwick	NJ	08858	908-439-2200	439-3363
Commercial Lending Litigation News 360 Hiatt Dr *TF:* 800-621-5463 ■ *Web:* www.lrp.com	Palm Beach Gardens	FL	33418	561-622-6520	622-2423
Consumer Bankruptcy News 360 Hiatt Dr *TF:* 800-621-5463 ■ *Web:* www.lrp.com	Palm Beach Gardens	FL	33418	561-622-6520	622-2423
Credit Union Directors Newsletter 5710 Mineral Pt Rd **Fax:* Cust Svc ■ *TF:* 800-356-9655 ■ *Web:* www.cuna.org	Madison	WI	53705	608-231-4000	231-1869*
Electronic Commerce & Law Report 1801 S Bell St *TF:* 800-372-1033 ■ *Web:* www.bna.com/electronic-commerce-law-p6796	Arlington	VA	22202	800-372-1033	
Forecaster Newsletter 19623 Ventura Blvd	Tarzana	CA	91356	818-345-4421	
International Business & Finance Daily 1801 S Bell St *TF:* 800-372-1033	Arlington	VA	22202	800-372-1033	
International Tax Monitor 1801 S Bell St *TF:* 800-372-1033	Arlington	VA	22202	800-372-1033	
Louisiana Banker PO Box 2871 *TF:* 888-249-3050 ■ *Web:* www.lba.org	Baton Rouge	LA	70821	225-387-3282	343-3159
Money Management Letter 225 Pk Ave S 7th Fl *Web:* www.moneymanagementintelligence.com	New York	NY	10003	212-224-3300	
New York Banker 99 Pk Ave 4th Fl **Fax:* PR ■ *Web:* www.nyba.com	New York	NY	10016	212-297-1600	297-1683*
Security Letter 166 E 96th St	New York	NY	10128	212-348-1553	
Specialty Finance 212 Seventh St NE *Web:* www.snl.com	Charlottesville	VA	22902	434-977-1600	977-4466

531-2 Business & Professional Newsletters

				Phone	Fax
Antitrust & Trade Regulation Daily 1801 S Bell St *TF:* 800-372-1033 ■ *Web:* www.bna.com/atrc	Arlington	VA	22202	800-372-1033	
Authors Guild Bulletin 31 E 32nd St 7th Fl *Web:* www.authorsguild.org	New York	NY	10016	212-563-5904	564-5363
CD Publications 8204 Fenton St *TF:* 800-666-6380 ■ *Web:* cdpublications.com/pcodeprocess/pcodes.php?pc=pubs	Silver Spring	MD	20910	301-588-6380	588-6385
Corporate Writer & Editor 111 E Wacker Dr Ste 500 *TF:* 800-878-5331 ■ *Web:* www.ragan.com/main/home.aspx	Chicago	IL	60601	312-960-4140	
Customer Communicator, The (TCC) 712 Main St Ste 187B *TF:* 800-232-4317 ■ *Web:* www.customerservicegroup.com/the_customer_communicator.php	Boonton	NJ	07005	973-265-2300	402-6056
Daily Report for Executives 1801 S Bell St *TF:* 800-372-1033 ■ *Web:* www.bna.com/daily-report-executives-p6093	Arlington	VA	22202	800-372-1033	
Daily Tax Report 1801 S Bell St *TF:* 800-372-1033 ■ *Web:* www.bna.com/daily-tax-report-p7889	Arlington	VA	22202	800-372-1033	
Distribution Ctr Management (DCM) 712 Main St Ste 187B *TF:* 800-232-4317 ■ *Web:* www.distributiongroup.com/distribution_center_management.php	Boonton	NJ	07005	973-265-2300	402-6056
Downtown Idea Exchange (DIX) 712 Main St Ste 187B *TF:* 800-232-4317 ■ *Web:* www.downtowndevelopment.com/downtown_idea_exchange.php	Boonton	NJ	07005	973-265-2300	402-6056
Federal EEO Advisor 360 Hiatt Dr *TF:* 800-341-7874 ■ *Web:* www.lrp.com	Palm Beach Gardens	FL	33418	561-622-6520	622-2423
Government Employee Relations Report 1801 S Bell St *TF:* 800-372-1033 ■ *Web:* www.bna.com/government-employee-relations-p5468	Arlington	VA	22202	800-372-1033	
Journal of Employee Communication Management 316 N Michigan Ave Ste 400 *TF:* 800-878-5331 ■ *Web:* www.ragan.com/main/home.aspx	Chicago	IL	60601	312-960-4100	960-4106
Law Officer's Bulletin 610 Opperman Dr *TF:* 800-344-5008 ■ *Web:* legalsolutions.thomsonreuters.com	Eagan	MN	55123	651-687-7000	
Manager's Intelligence Report (MIR) 316 N Michigan Ave Ste 400 **Fax Area Code:* 312 ■ *TF:* 800-878-5331 ■ *Web:* www.managersintelligencereport.biz	Chicago	IL	60601	800-878-5331	861-3592*
Payroll Practitioner's Monthly 3 Bethesda Metro Ctr Ste 250 *TF:* 800-372-1033 ■ *Web:* bna.com/ioma-site-m17179881473	Bethesda	MD	20814	800-372-1033	253-0332
Ragan Communications Inc 316 N Michigan Ave Ste 400 *TF:* 800-878-5331 ■ *Web:* www.ragan.com/main/home.aspx	Chicago	IL	60601	312-960-4100	960-4106
Teamwork Newsletter 2222 Sedwick Dr *TF:* 800-223-8720 ■ *Web:* www.dartnellcorp.com	Durham	NC	27713	800-223-8720	508-2592
Working Together 360 Hiatt Dr *TF:* 800-621-5463 ■ *Web:* www.lrp.com	Palm Beach Gardens	FL	33418	561-622-6520	622-2423

531-3 Computer & Internet Newsletters

				Phone	Fax
Biotechnology Software 140 Huguenot St 3rd Fl *TF:* 800-654-3237 ■ *Web:* www.liebertpub.com	New Rochelle	NY	10801	914-740-2100	740-2109
Business Intelligence Advisor 37 Broadway Ste 1 *TF:* 800-964-5118 ■ *Web:* www.cutter.com	Arlington	MA	02474	781-648-8700	648-8707
Computer Economics Report, The 2082 Business Ctr Dr Ste 240 *TF:* 800-326-8100 ■ *Web:* www.computereconomics.com	Irvine	CA	92612	949-831-8700	442-7688
Cutter Consortium 37 Broadway Ste 1 *TF:* 800-964-5118 ■ *Web:* www.cutter.com	Arlington	MA	02474	781-648-8700	648-8707
Electronic Information Report 60 Longridge Rd Ste 300 *Web:* simbainformation.com	Stamford	CT	06902	203-325-8193	325-8915

Phone | Fax

Lawrence Ragan Communications Inc
316 N Michigan Ave Ste 400 .... Chicago IL 60601 312-960-4100 960-4106
TF: 800-878-5331 ■ *Web:* www.ragan.com
Microprocessor Report 355 Chesley Ave .... Mountain View CA 94040 408-270-3772 745-1490*
**Fax Area Code:* 650 ■ *TF:* 800-413-2881 ■ *Web:* www.linleygroup.com
Technology News of America 123 Seventh Ave........ Brooklyn NY 11215 718-369-7682 965-3039
Web: www.tech-news.com
Washington Internet Daily 2115 Ward Ct NW .... Washington DC 20037 202-872-9200
TF: 800-771-9202 ■ *Web:* www.warren-news.com

531-4 Education Newsletters

Phone | Fax

Early Childhood Report
360 Hiatt Dr .... Palm Beach Gardens FL 33418 561-622-6520 622-2423
TF: 800-621-5463 ■ *Web:* www.lrp.com
Education Grants Alert
360 Hiatt Dr .... Palm Beach Gardens FL 33418 561-622-6520 622-2423
TF: 800-621-5463 ■ *Web:* www.lrp.com
Educational Research Newsletter
PO Box 2347 .... South Portland ME 04116 207-632-1954 461-5647*
**Fax Area Code:* 815 ■ *TF:* 800-321-7471 ■ *Web:* www.ernweb.com
Electronic Education Report
60 Longridge Rd Ste 300 .... Stamford CT 06902 203-325-8193 325-8915*
**Fax:* Sales ■ *Web:* simbainformation.com
New Jersey Law Journal 238 Mulberry St............. Newark NJ 07102 973-642-0075
Web: www.law.com
New York Education Law Report
360 Hiatt Dr .... Palm Beach FL 33418 561-622-6520 622-1375*
**Fax:* Edit ■ *TF:* 800-341-7874 ■ *Web:* www.lrp.com
School Law News 360 Hiatt Dr............ Palm Beach Gardens FL 33418 800-341-7874 622-2423*
**Fax Area Code:* 561 ■ *TF:* 800-341-7874 ■ *Web:* www.lrp.com
Special Education Report
360 Hiatt Dr .... Palm Beach Gardens FL 33418 561-622-6520 622-2423
TF Sales: 800-621-5463 ■ *Web:* www.lrp.com

531-5 Energy & Environmental Newsletters

Phone | Fax

Chemical Regulation Reporter
1801 S Bell St. .... Arlington VA 22202 800-372-1033
TF: 800-372-1033
Clean Air Report 1919 S Eads St Ste 201.............. Arlington VA 22202 703-416-8505 416-8543
TF: 800-424-9068 ■ *Web:* www.insideepa.com
Coal Outlook 1200 G St NW Ste 1100.............. Washington DC 20005 212-904-3070 904-4209
TF: 800-752-8878 ■ *Web:* www.platts.com
Daily Environment Report 1801 S Bell St.............. Arlington VA 22202 800-372-1033
TF: 800-372-1033 ■ *Web:* www.bna.com/daily-environment-report-p4751
Electric Utility Week 2 Penn Plz 25th Fl............. New York NY 10121 212-904-3070
TF: 800-752-8878 ■ *Web:* www.platts.com
Environment Reporter 1801 S Bell St.............. Arlington VA 22202 800-372-1033
TF: 800-372-1033 ■ *Web:* www.bna.com/environment-reporter-p4885
Gas Daily 1200 G St NW Ste 1000.................. Washington DC 20005 202-383-2000 383-2024
TF: 800-752-8878 ■ *Web:* www.platts.com/products/gasdaily
Global Power Report 2 Penn Plz 25th Fl............. New York NY 10121 800-752-8878
TF: 800-752-8878 ■ *Web:* www.platts.com
Inside FERC 2 Penn Plz 25th Fl.................. New York NY 10121 800-752-8878
TF: 800-752-8878 ■ *Web:* www.platts.com
Inside NRC 2 Penn Plz 25th Fl.................. New York NY 10121 800-752-8878
TF: 800-752-8878 ■ *Web:* www.platts.com
Megawatt Daily 2 Penn Plz 25th Fl.................. New York NY 10121 212-904-3070 752-8878*
**Fax Area Code:* 800 ■ *TF:* 800-752-8878 ■ *Web:* platts.com/products/megawatt-daily
Northeast Power Report 2 Penn Plz 25th Fl........... New York NY 10121 800-752-8878
TF: 800-752-8878 ■ *Web:* www.platts.com
NuclearFuel 1200 G St NW Ste 1000............... Washington DC 20005 202-383-2000 383-2024
TF: 800-228-9290 ■ *Web:* platts.com/products/nuclear-fuel
Nucleonics Week 2 Penn Plaza 25th Fl.............. New York NY 10121 212-904-3070
TF: 800-752-8878 ■ *Web:* platts.com/products/nucleonics-week
Oil Price Information Service
3349 Hwy 138 Bldg D Ste D.......................... Wall NJ 07719 732-901-8800
TF Cust Svc: 888-301-2645 ■ *Web:* www.opisnet.com
OPIS 9737 Washingtonian Blvd Ste 200 .... Gaithersburg MD 20878 301-287-2645 287-2820
TF: 888-301-2645 ■ *Web:* www.opisnet.com
Solid Waste Assn of North America (SWANA)
1100 Wayne Ave Ste 700.......................... Silver Spring MD 20910 301-585-2898 589-7068
TF: 800-467-9262 ■ *Web:* swana.org
State Environment Daily 1801 S Bell St.............. Arlington VA 22202 800-372-1033
TF: 800-372-1033
Toxics Law Reporter 1801 S Bell St.................. Arlington VA 22202 800-372-1033
TF: 800-372-1033 ■ *Web:* www.bna.com/toxics-law-reporter-p5947
Utility Environment Report
2 Penn Plz 25th Fl.......................... New York NY 10121 800-752-8878
TF: 800-752-8878 ■ *Web:* www.platts.com
Water Tech Online 19 British American Blvd W.......... Latham NY 12110 888-431-2877
TF: 888-431-2877 ■ *Web:* www.watertechonline.com

531-6 General Interest Newsletters

Phone | Fax

Bottom Line/Personal 281 Tresser Blvd 8th Fl .... Stamford CT 06901 800-274-5611 967-3621*
**Fax Area Code:* 203 ■ **Fax:* Edit ■ *TF Cust Svc:* 800-678-5835 ■ *Web:* blinepubs.com
FRM Weekly 54 Adams St.......................... Garden City NY 11530 516-746-6700 294-8141
NRTA/AARP Bulletin 601 E St NW.................. Washington DC 20049 202-434-2277
TF: 888-867-2277 ■ *Web:* aarp.org/about-aarp/nrta
Preferred Traveler 4501 Forbes Blvd.................. Lanham MD 20706 866-679-8655
TF: 866-679-8655 ■ *Web:* www.preferredtraveller.com

531-7 Government & Law Newsletters

Phone | Fax

Alcoholic Beverage Control PO Box 27491.......... Richmond VA 23261 804-213-4565 213-4574
TF: 800-552-3200 ■ *Web:* www.abc.virginia.gov/enforce/offices.html
American Association for Justice
777 6th St NW Ste 200.......................... Washington DC 20001 202-965-3500 625-7084
TF: 800-424-2727 ■ *Web:* www.justice.org
Bankruptcy Law Letter 610 Opperman Dr............... Eagan MN 55123 651-687-7000 687-8722
TF: 800-937-8529 ■ *Web:* legalsolutions.thomsonreuters.com
BD Week 9737 Washingtonian Blvd Ste 100 .... Gaithersburg MD 20878 646-223-6771
TF: 866-777-8567 ■ *Web:* iawatch.com
Bioethics Legal Review
1617 JFK Blvd Ste 1750.......................... Philadelphia PA 19103 215-557-2300
TF: 877-256-2472 ■ *Web:* www.lawjournalnewsletters.com
Class Action Litigation Report
1801 S Bell St.......................... Arlington VA 22202 800-372-1033
TF: 800-372-1033 ■ *Web:* www.bna.com/class-action-litigation-p5442
Community Development Digest
8204 Fenton St.......................... Silver Spring MD 20910 301-588-6380 588-6385
TF: 800-666-6380 ■ *Web:* www.cdpublications.com
Community Health Funding Week
8204 Fenton St.......................... Silver Spring MD 20910 301-588-6380 588-0519
TF: 800-666-6380 ■ *Web:* www.cdpublications.com
Computer Technology Law Report
1801 S Bell St.......................... Arlington VA 22202 800-372-1033
TF: 800-372-1033 ■ *Web:* www.bna.com/computer-technology-law-p6795
Congress Daily
600 New Hampshire Ave The Watergate............. Washington DC 20037 202-266-7000
Web: nationaljournal.com
Congressional Quarterly House Action Reports
77 K St NE .... Washington DC 20002 202-650-6500 380-3810*
**Fax Area Code:* 800 ■ *Web:* cqrollcall.com
Consumer Financial Services Law Report
360 Hiatt Dr .... Palm Beach Gardens FL 33418 561-622-6520 622-2423
TF: 800-621-5463 ■ *Web:* www.lrp.com
Corporate Compliance & Regulatory
1617 JFK Blvd Ste 1750.......................... Philadelphia PA 19103 215-557-2300
TF: 877-256-2472 ■ *Web:* www.lawjournalnewsletters.com
Criminal Law Reporter 1801 S Bell St............... Arlington VA 22202 800-372-1033
TF: 800-372-1033 ■ *Web:* www.bna.com/criminal-law-reporter-p5446
Daily Labor Report 1801 S Bell St.................. Arlington VA 22202 800-372-1033
TF: 800-372-1033 ■ *Web:* www.bna.com/daily-labor-report-p5449
Development Director's Letter
8204 Fenton St.......................... Silver Spring MD 20910 301-588-6380 588-6385
TF: 800-666-6380 ■
Web: cdpublications.com/pcodeprocess/pcodes.php?pc=pubs
Disability Law Compliance Report
610 Opperman Dr.......................... Eagan MN 55123 651-687-7000 687-8722
TF Cust Svc: 800-328-4880 ■ *Web:* legalsolutions.thomsonreuters.com
e-Commerce Law & Strategy
1617 JFK Blvd Ste 1750.......................... Philadelphia PA 19103 215-557-2300
TF: 877-256-2472 ■ *Web:* www.lawjournalnewsletters.com
e-Discovery Law & Strategy
1617 JFK Blvd Ste 1750.......................... Philadelphia PA 19103 215-557-2300
TF: 877-256-2472 ■ *Web:* www.lawjournalnewsletters.com
Employment Discrimination Report
1801 S Bell St.......................... Arlington VA 22202 800-372-1033
TF: 800-372-1033 ■
Web: www.bna.com/employment-discrimination-report-p5458
Expert Evidence Report 1801 S Bell St.............. Arlington VA 22202 800-372-1033
TF: 800-372-1033 ■ *Web:* www.bna.com/expert-evidence-report-p5463
Family Law Reporter 1801 S Bell St .... Arlington VA 22202 800-372-1033
TF: 800-372-1033 ■ *Web:* www.bna.com/family-law-reporter-p6014
Federal Assistance Monitor
8204 Fenton St.......................... Silver Spring MD 20910 301-588-6380 588-6385
TF: 800-666-6380 ■ *Web:* www.cdpublications.com
Federal Contracts Report 1801 S Bell St............ Arlington VA 22202 800-372-1033
TF: 800-372-1033 ■ *Web:* www.bna.com/federal-contracts-report-p6016
Franchising Business & Law Alert
1617 JFK Blvd Ste 1750.......................... Philadelphia PA 19103 215-557-2300
TF: 877-256-2472 ■ *Web:* www.lawjournalnewsletters.com
Health Law Reporter 1801 S Bell St .... Arlington VA 22202 800-372-1033
TF: 800-372-1033 ■ *Web:* www.bna.com/health-law-reporter-p6785
Homeland Security Funding Week
8204 Fenton St.......................... Silver Spring MD 20910 301-588-6380 588-6385
TF: 800-666-6380 ■ *Web:* www.cdpublications.com
Hospital Litigation Reporter
590 Dutch Vly Rd NE .... Atlanta GA 30324 404-881-1141 881-0074
TF: 800-926-7926 ■ *Web:* www.straffordpub.com
Hospitality Law 360 Hiatt Dr.............. Palm Beach Gardens FL 33418 561-622-6520 622-2423
TF: 800-621-5463 ■ *Web:* www.lrp.com
Insurance Coverage Law Bulletin, The
1617 JFK Blvd Ste 1750.......................... Philadelphia PA 19103 215-557-2300
TF: 877-256-2472 ■ *Web:* www.lawjournalnewsletters.com
Internet Law & Strategy
1617 JFK Blvd Ste 1750.......................... Philadelphia PA 19103 215-557-2300
TF: 877-256-2472 ■ *Web:* www.lawjournalnewsletters.com
IRS Practice Adviser 1801 S Bell St .... Arlington VA 22202 800-372-1033
TF: 800-372-1033 ■ *Web:* www.bna.com/contact-us-form-p17179924216
Medical Research Law & Policy Report
1801 S Bell St.......................... Arlington VA 22202 800-372-1033
TF: 800-372-1033 ■ *Web:* www.bna.com/medical-research-law-p6788
Medicare Compliance Alert
11300 Rockville Pk Ste 1100.......................... Rockville MD 20852 301-287-2700 816-8945
TF: 800-929-4824 ■ *Web:* store.decisionhealth.com
Mergers & Acquisitions Law Report
1801 S Bell St.......................... Arlington VA 22202 800-372-1033
TF: 800-372-1033 ■ *Web:* www.bna.com/mergers-acquisitions-law-p5940
Money & Politics Report 1801 S Bell St............. Arlington VA 22202 800-372-1033
TF: 800-372-1033 ■ *Web:* www.bna.com/money-politics-report-p6103

Newsletter	City	State	Zip	Phone	Fax
Municipal Litigation Reporter 590 Dutch Vly Rd NE *TF:* 800-926-7926 ■ *Web:* www.straffordpub.com	Atlanta	GA	30324	404-881-1141	881-0074
Patent Trademark & Copyright Law Daily 1801 S Bell St *TF:* 800-372-1033 ■ *Web:* www.bna.com/patent-trademark-copyright-daily-p5943	Arlington	VA	22202	800-372-1033	
Pharmaceutical Law & Industry Report 1801 S Bell St *TF:* 800-372-1033 ■ *Web:* www.bna.com/pharmaceutical-law-industry-p6790	Arlington	VA	22202	800-372-1033	
Privacy & Data Security Law Resource Center 1801 S Bell St *TF:* 800-372-1033	Arlington	VA	22202	800-372-1033	
Real Estate Law Report 610 Opperman Dr **Fax Area Code:* 800 ■ **Fax:* Sales ■ *TF Cust Svc:* 800-328-4880 ■ *Web:* legalsolutions.thomsonreuters.com	Eagan	MN	55123	651-687-7000	741-1414*
Roll Call 77 K St NE *TF:* 800-432-2250 ■ *Web:* www.rollcall.com	Washington	DC	20002	202-650-6500	824-0475
Securities Law Daily 1801 S Bell St *TF:* 800-372-1033 ■ *Web:* www.bna.com/securities-law-daily-p5944	Arlington	VA	22202	800-372-1033	
UCG Holdings 11300 Rockville Pike Ste 1100 *TF:* 800-929-4824 ■ *Web:* www.ucg.com	Rockville	MD	20852	301-287-2700	816-8945
Virginia Dept of Taxation 1957 Westmoreland St PO Box 1115 *TF:* 800-828-1120 ■ *Web:* www.tax.virginia.gov	Richmond	VA	23230	804-367-8037	254-6111
Washington International Business Report 818 Connecticut Ave NW 12th Fl *Web:* www.ibgc.com	Washington	DC	20006	202-872-8181	872-8696
Workplace Law Report 1801 S Bell St *TF:* 800-372-1033 ■ *Web:* www.bna.com/workplace-law-report-p5953	Arlington	VA	22202	800-372-1033	
World Securities Law Report 1801 S Bell St *TF:* 800-372-1033 ■ *Web:* www.bna.com	Arlington	VA	22202	800-372-1033	

531-8 Health & Social Issues Newsletters

Newsletter	City	State	Zip	Phone	Fax
Affordable Housing Update 8204 Fenton St *TF:* 800-666-6380 ■ *Web:* www.cdpublications.com	Silver Spring	MD	20910	301-588-6380	588-6385
Aging News Alert 8204 Fenton St *TF:* 800-666-6380 ■ *Web:* cdpublications.com/pcodeprocess/pcodes.php?pc=pubs	Silver Spring	MD	20910	301-588-6385	588-6385
AICR Newsletter 1759 R St NW *TF:* 800-843-8114 ■ *Web:* www.aicr.org	Washington	DC	20009	202-328-7744	328-7226
APCO Bulletin 351 N Williamson Blvd *TF:* 888-272-6911 ■ *Web:* www.apcointl.org	Daytona Beach	FL	32114	386-322-2500	322-2501
Cancer Letter PO Box 9905 *TF:* 800-513-7042 ■ *Web:* www.cancerletter.com	Washington	DC	20016	202-362-1809	379-1787
Children & Youth Funding Report 8204 Fenton St *TF:* 800-666-6380 ■ *Web:* www.cdpublications.com/cyf	Silver Spring	MD	20910	301-588-6380	588-6385
Consumer Reports On Health 101 Truman Ave *TF:* 800-234-1645 ■ *Web:* www.consumerreports.org	Yonkers	NY	10703	914-378-2000	378-2900
Dairy Council Digest 10255 W Higgins Rd Ste 900 *Web:* www.nationaldairycouncil.org	Rosemont	IL	60018	847-627-3790	
Disability Funding Week 8204 Fenton St **Fax Area Code:* 301 ■ *TF:* 800-666-6380 ■ *Web:* cdpublications.com/pcodeprocess/pcodes.php?pc=pubs	Silver Spring	MD	20910	800-666-6380	588-6385*
Dr. Sinatra 95 Old Shoals Rd *TF:* 800-304-1708 ■ *Web:* www.drsinatra.com	Arden	NC	28704	800-304-1708	
Environment of Care Leader 9737 Washintonian Blvd Ste 100 *TF Cust Svc:* 800-929-4824 ■ *Web:* www.ucg.com	Gaithersburg	MD	20878	301-287-2700	287-2039
Harvard Men's Health Watch 10 Shattuck St *Web:* www.health.harvard.edu	Boston	MA	02115	617-432-1370	
Harvard Women's Health Watch PO Box 9308 *TF:* 877-649-9457 ■ *Web:* www.health.harvard.edu	Big Sandy	TX	75755	877-649-9457	
Health After 50 750 Third Ave Fl 6 *TF:* 800-829-0422 ■ *Web:* www.healthafter50.com	New York	NY	10017	800-829-0422	
Health Care Daily Report 1801 S Bell St *TF:* 800-372-1033 ■ *Web:* www.bna.com/health-care-daily-p6781	Arlington	VA	22202	800-372-1033	
Health Law Week 590 Dutch Vly Rd NE *TF:* 800-926-7926 ■ *Web:* www.straffordpub.com	Atlanta	GA	30324	404-881-1141	881-0074
Healthcare Disparities Report 8204 Fenton St *TF:* 800-666-6380 ■ *Web:* www.cdpublications.com	Silver Spring	MD	20910	301-588-6385	588-6380
Home Health Line 11300 Rockville Pk Ste 1100 *TF:* 800-929-4824 ■ *Web:* www.ucg.com	Rockville	MD	20852	301-287-2700	816-8945
International Medical Device Regulatory Monitor 300 N Washington St Ste 200 *TF:* 888-838-5578 ■ *Web:* fdanews.com/publications/18	Falls Church	VA	22046	703-538-7600	538-7676
Mayo Clinic Health Letter 200 First St NW **Fax Area Code:* 507 ■ *TF:* 800-291-1128 ■ *Web:* store.mayoclinic.com	Rochester	MN	55905	800-291-1128	284-0252*
Medicare Compliance Alert 11300 Rockville Pk Ste 1100 *TF:* 800-929-4824 ■ *Web:* store.decisionhealth.com	Rockville	MD	20852	301-287-2700	816-8945
Nutrition Action 1875 Connecticut Way NW Ste 300 *Web:* www.cspinet.org	Washington	DC	20009	202-332-9110	265-4954
OSHA Up-to-Date Newsletter 1121 Spring Lk Dr *TF Cust Svc:* 800-621-7615 ■ *Web:* www.nsc.org	Itasca	IL	60143	630-285-1121	285-1315

531-9 Investment Newsletters

Newsletter	City	State	Zip	Phone	Fax
Bert Dohmen's Wellington Letter 1100 Glendon Ave Ste 1130 Westwood Ctr *Web:* dohmencapital.com	Los Angeles	CA	90024	310-208-6622	208-1038
Cabot Market Letter 176 N St PO Box 2049 *TF Orders:* 800-326-8826 ■ *Web:* www.cabot.net	Salem	MA	01970	978-745-5532	745-1283
Chartist Newsletter PO Box 758 *TF:* 800-942-4278 ■ *Web:* thechartist.com	Seal Beach	CA	90740	562-596-2385	
Commodity Research Bureau 330 S Wells St Ste 612 *TF:* 800-621-5271 ■ *Web:* www.crbtrader.com	Chicago	IL	60606	312-554-8456	939-4135
Dow Theory Forecasts 7412 Calumet Ave *TF:* 800-233-5922 ■ *Web:* www.dowtheory.com	Hammond	IN	46324	800-233-5922	
DRIP Investor 7412 Calumet Ave *TF:* 800-233-5922 ■ *Web:* www.dripinvestor.com	Hammond	IN	46324	219-852-3200	931-6487
Elliott Wave Theorist PO Box 1618 *TF:* 800-336-1618 ■ *Web:* www.elliottwave.com	Gainesville	GA	30503	770-536-0309	536-2514
Fabian's Investment Resources 300 New Jersey Ave NW Ste 500 *TF:* 800-950-8765 ■ *Web:* www.fabian.com	Washington	DC	20001	267-295-8713	
Global Market Perspective PO Box 1618 *TF:* 800-336-1618 ■ *Web:* www.elliottwave.com/products/gmp	Gainesville	GA	30503	770-536-0309	536-2514
Gold Newsletter PO Box 84900 *TF:* 800-877-8847 ■ *Web:* jeffersoncompanies.com	Phoenix	AZ	85071	800-877-8847	
Growth Fund Guide 4020 Jackson Blvd *Web:* marketwatch.com	Rapid City	SD	57702	605-341-1971	
Investment Quality Trends (IQT) 2888 Loker Ave E Ste 116 **Fax Area Code:* 866 ■ *Web:* www.iqtrends.com	Carlsbad	CA	92010	858-459-3818	927-5251*
Option Advisor 5151 Pfeiffer Rd Ste 250 *TF:* 800-448-2080 ■ *Web:* www.schaeffersresearch.com	Cincinnati	OH	45242	513-589-3800	589-3810
Personal Finance Newsletter 7600A Leesburg Pk W Bldg Ste 300 *TF:* 800-832-2330 ■ *Web:* www.investingdaily.com	Falls Church	VA	22043	703-394-4931	905-8100
Peter Dag Portfolio Strategy & Management, The 65 Lk Front Dr *TF:* 800-833-2782 ■ *Web:* www.peterdag.com	Akron	OH	44319	330-644-2782	
Profitable Investing 9201 Corporate Blvd *TF:* 800-219-8592 ■ *Web:* www.profitableinvesting.investorplace.com	Rockville	MD	20850	301-250-2200	
Richard Young's Intelligence Report 700 Indian Springs Dr *TF Cust Svc:* 800-219-8592 ■ *Web:* intelligencereport.investorplace.com	Lancaster	PA	17601	800-219-8592	
Systems & Forecasts 150 Great Neck Rd Ste 301 *TF:* 800-982-4372 ■ *Web:* www.systemsandforecasts.com	Great Neck	NY	11021	516-829-6444	466-4676
Utility Forecaster 7600A Leesburg Pk W Bldg Ste 300 *TF:* 800-832-2330 ■ *Web:* www.investingdaily.com	Falls Church	VA	22043	703-394-4931	905-8100

531-10 Marketing & Sales Newsletters

Newsletter	City	State	Zip	Phone	Fax
Book Marketing Update PO Box 2887 *TF:* 888-468-7386 ■ *Web:* www.bookmarket.com	Taos	NM	87571	575-751-3398	751-3398
CD Publications 2222 Sedwick Dr **Fax Area Code:* 301 ■ *TF:* 800-666-6380 ■ *Web:* www.cdpublications.com/products.php	Durham	NC	27713	855-237-1396	588-6385*
Educational Marketer 60 Long Ridge Rd Ste 300 *Web:* educationalmarketer.net	Stamford	CT	06902	203-325-8193	
Marketing Library Services 143 Old Marlton Pk *TF:* 800-300-9868 ■ *Web:* www.infotoday.com/mls	Medford	NJ	08055	609-654-6266	654-4309
Sales Leader 2222 Sedwick Dr *TF:* 800-223-8720 ■ *Web:* www.dartnellcorp.com	Durham	NC	27713	800-223-8720	508-2592

531-11 Media & Communications Newsletters

Newsletter	City	State	Zip	Phone	Fax
Book Publishing Report 60 Long Ridge Rd Ste 300 *Web:* www.bookpublishingreport.com	Stamford	CT	06902	203-325-8193	325-8915
Broadcasters Letter 1400 Independence Ave SW *Web:* www.usda.gov	Washington	DC	20250	202-720-4623	720-5773
Children's Book Insider 901 Columbia Rd *Web:* cbiclubhouse.com/clubhouse	Fort Collins	CO	80525	970-495-0056	493-1810
Communications Daily 2115 Ward Ct NW *TF:* 800-771-9202 ■ *Web:* www.warren-news.com	Washington	DC	20037	202-872-9200	
First Draft 316 N Michigan Ave Ste 400 **Fax Area Code:* 312 ■ *TF:* 800-878-5331 ■ *Web:* www.ragan.com/main/home.aspx	Chicago	IL	60601	800-493-4867	960-4106*
Jack O'Dwyer's PR Newsletter 271 Madison Ave Ste 600 *TF:* 866-395-7710 ■ *Web:* www.odwyerpr.com	New York	NY	10016	212-679-2471	683-2750
Media Industry Newsletter (MIN) 110 William St 11th Fl *TF:* 888-707-5814 ■ *Web:* www.minonline.com	New York	NY	10038	212-621-4880	621-4879
Media Law Reporter 1801 S Bell St *TF:* 800-372-1033 ■ *Web:* www.bna.com/media-law-reporter-p5934	Arlington	VA	22202	800-372-1033	
Media Relations Report 316 N Michigan Ave Ste 400 *TF:* 800-878-5331 ■ *Web:* www.ragan.com	Chicago	IL	60601	312-960-4100	960-4106
Professional Publishing Report 60 Long Ridge Rd Ste 300 *Web:* simbainformation.com	Stamford	CT	06902	203-325-8193	325-8915
Speechwriter's Newsletter 316 N Michigan Ave Ste 400 *TF:* 800-878-5331 ■ *Web:* www.ragan.com/main/home.aspx	Chicago	IL	60601	312-960-4100	960-4106
State Telephone Regulation Report 2115 Ward Ct NW *TF:* 800-771-9202 ■ *Web:* www.warren-news.com	Washington	DC	20037	202-872-9200	
Telecom AM 2115 Ward Ct NW *TF:* 800-771-9202 ■ *Web:* www.warren-news.com	Washington	DC	20037	202-872-9200	

531-12 Science & Technology Newsletters

Phone *Fax*

Flame Retardancy News 49 Walnut Pk Bldg 2 .... Wellesley MA 02481 781-489-7301 253-3933
TF: 866-285-7215 ■ *Web:* www.bccresearch.com

Food Ingredient News 49 Walnut Pk Bldg 2 .... Wellesley MA 02481 781-489-7301 253-3933
TF: 866-285-7215 ■ *Web:* www.bccresearch.com

Frost & Sullivan 7550 IH 10 W Ste 400 ....San Antonio TX 78229 210-348-1000 690-3329*
**Fax Area Code:* 888 ■ *TF:* 877-463-7678 ■ *Web:* www.frost.com

Genetic Engineering News
140 Huguenot St 3rd Fl .... New Rochelle NY 10801 914-740-2100 740-2101
TF: 888-211-4235 ■ *Web:* www.genengnews.com

Geophysical Research Letter
2000 Florida Ave NW .... Washington DC 20009 202-462-6900 328-0566
TF: 800-966-2481 ■ *Web:* onlinelibrary.wiley.com

Physical Review Letters 1 Research Rd .... Ridge NY 11961 631-591-4000
Web: aps.org

531-13 Trade & Industry Newsletters

Phone *Fax*

AviationWeek 1200 G St NW Ste 900 .... Washington DC 20005 800-525-5003 383-2438*
**Fax Area Code:* 202 ■ *TF:* 800-525-5003 ■ *Web:* www.aviationweek.com/businessaviation.aspx

Construction Claims Monthly 2222 Sedwick Rd .... Durham NC 27713 800-223-8720 508-2592
TF: 800-223-8720 ■ *Web:* www.constructionclaimsmonthly.org

Construction Labor Report 1801 S Bell St .... Arlington VA 22202 800-372-1033
TF: 800-372-1033 ■ *Web:* www.bna.com/construction-labor-report-p6002

Cotton's Week 7193 Goodlett Farms Pkwy .... Cordova TN 38016 901-274-9030 725-0510
TF: 888-232-1738 ■ *Web:* www.cotton.org/news/cweek

Cruise Industry News
441 Lexington Ave Ste 809 .... New York NY 10017 212-986-1025 986-1033
Web: www.cruiseindustrynews.com

DealersEdge PO Box 606 .... Barnegat Light NJ 08006 609-879-4456
TF: 800-321-5312 ■ *Web:* www.dealersedge.com

Engineering Outlook
1308 W Green St 306 Engineering Hall .... Urbana IL 61801 217-333-2151 244-7705
Web: engineering.illinois.edu

Funeral Service Insider
3349 Hwy 138 Bldg D Ste D .... Wall NJ 07719 800-500-4585
TF: 800-500-4585 ■ *Web:* www.kates-boylston.com

Kiplinger Agriculture Letter 1729 H St NW .... Washington DC 20006 202-887-6400 778-8976
TF: 800-544-0155 ■ *Web:* www.kiplinger.com

Metals Week 2 Penn Plaza .... New York NY 10121 800-752-8878
TF: 800-752-8878 ■ *Web:* www.platts.com

National Farmers Union News (NFU)
20 F St NW Ste 300 .... Washington DC 20001 202-554-1600 554-1654
Web: www.nfu.org

PhotoSource 5106 Louetta Rd .... Spring TX 77379 281-370-2220
TF: 800-786-6277 ■ *Web:* www.photosource.com/cart/pl.php

Pro Farmer 6612 Chancellor Dr Ste 300 .... Cedar Falls IA 50613 319-277-1278 277-7982
TF Cust Svc: 800-772-0023 ■ *Web:* www.agweb.com

Questex LLC 275 Grove St Ste 2-130 .... Newton MA 02466 617-219-8300 219-8310
TF: 888-552-4346 ■ *Web:* www.questex.com

Shopping Centers Today
1221 Ave of the Americas .... New York NY 10020 646-728-3800 589-5555*
**Fax Area Code:* 212 ■ *TF:* 888-427-2885 ■ *Web:* www.icsc.org

Uniform Commercial Code Law Letter
610 Opperman Dr .... Eagan MN 55123 651-687-7000
TF Cust Svc: 800-328-4880 ■ *Web:* legalsolutions.thomsonreuters.com

Union Labor Report 1801 S Bell St .... Arlington VA 22202 800-372-1033
TF: 800-372-1033 ■ *Web:* www.bna.com/union-labor-report-p6722

Urban Transport News 65 E Wacker Pl Ste 400 .... Chicago IL 60601 312-782-3900 782-3901
Web: www.highbeam.com

US Rail News 65 E Wacker Pl Ste 400 .... Chicago IL 60601 312-782-3900 782-3901
Web: www.highbeam.com

Whitaker Newsletters Inc
14305 Shoreham Dr .... Silver Spring MD 20905 301-384-1573 879-8803
Web: www.bevnewsonline.com

532 NEWSPAPERS

See Also Newspaper Publishers p. 3002

532-1 Daily Newspapers - Canada

Phone *Fax*

Calgary Herald
215-16th St SE PO Box 2400 Stn M .... Calgary AB T2E7P5 403-235-7100 235-7379
TF: 800-372-9219 ■ *Web:* www.calgaryherald.com

Calgary Sun 2615 12th St NE .... Calgary AB T2E7W9 403-410-1010
TF: 877-624-1463 ■ *Web:* www.calgarysun.com

Cape Breton Post 255 George St PO Box 1500 .... Sydney NS B1P6K6 902-564-5451 564-6280
Web: www.capebretonpost.com

Chatham Daily News 138 King St W .... Chatham ON N7M1E3 519-354-2000 436-0949
Web: www.chathamdailynews.ca

Chronicle Herald, The PO Box 610 .... Halifax NS B3J2T2 902-426-2811 426-1158
TF: 800-563-1187 ■ *Web:* thechronicleherald.ca

Chronicle-Journal, The
75 S Cumberland St .... Thunder Bay ON P7B1A3 807-343-6200
Web: www.chroniclejournal.com

Cornwall Standard Freeholder, The
1150 Montreal Rd .... Cornwall ON K6H1E2 613-933-3160
Web: www.standard-freeholder.com

Daily Courier 550 Doyle Ave .... Kelowna BC V1Y7V1 250-762-4445 762-3866
Web: www.kelownadailycourier.ca

Edmonton Journal 10006 - 101 St .... Edmonton AB T5J2S6 780-429-5100 498-5696
TF: 800-232-9486 ■ *Web:* www.edmontonjournal.com

Edmonton Sun 4990 92nd Ave Ste 250 .... Edmonton AB T6B3A1 780-468-0100
TF: 877-468-2401 ■ *Web:* www.edmontonsun.com

Phone *Fax*

Expositor, The 195 Henry St Bldg 4 .... Brantford ON N3S5C9 519-756-2020 756-3285
Web: www.brantfordexpositor.ca

Globe & Mail Inc, The 444 Front St W .... Toronto ON M5V2S9 416-585-5000 585-5085
Web: www.theglobeandmail.com

Guardian, The 165 Prince St .... Charlottetown PE C1A4R7 902-629-6000 566-3808
Web: www.theguardian.pe.ca

Journal Le Droit 47 Clarence St .... Ottawa ON K1N9K1 613-562-0555
TF: 800-267-6961 ■ *Web:* www.lapresse.ca

Kamloops Daily News 393 Seymour St .... Kamloops BC V2C6P6 250-372-2331 372-0823
Web: www.kamloopsnews.ca

Kenora Daily Miner & News
33 Main St S PO Box 1620 .... Kenora ON P9N3X7 807-468-5555 468-4318
Web: www.kenoradailyminerandnews.com

Kingston Whig-Standard, The 6 Cataraqui St .... Kingston ON K7L4Z7 613-544-5000 530-4122
Web: www.thewhig.com

L'Acadie-Nouvelle 476 St-Pierre W .... Caraquet NB E1W1B7 506-727-4444 727-7620
TF: 800-561-2255 ■ *Web:* www.acadienouvelle.com

La Tribune 1950 Rue Roy .... Sherbrooke QC J1K2X8 819-564-5450
Web: www.lapresse.ca

Le Devoir 2050 Bleury St 9th Fl .... Montreal QC H3A3M9 514-985-3333 985-3360
TF: 800-463-7559 ■ *Web:* www.ledevoir.com

Le Quotidien & Progres Dimanche
1051 boul Talbot .... Chicoutimi QC G7H5C1 418-545-4474
Web: www.lapresse.ca

Le Soleil 410 Charest Blvd E PO Box 1547 .... Quebec QC G1K8G3 418-686-3233
Web: www.lapresse.ca

Lethbridge Herald
504 - Seventh St S PO Box 670 .... Lethbridge AB T1J3Z7 403-328-4411 328-4536
Web: lethbridgeherald.com

London Free Press 369 York St PO Box 2280 .... London ON N6A4G1 519-679-1111 667-4528
TF: 866-541-6757 ■ *Web:* www.lfpress.com

National Post 1450 Don Mills Rd Ste 300 .... Toronto ON M3B3R5 416-383-2300 383-2305
TF: 800-267-6568 ■ *Web:* www.nationalpost.com

Niagara Falls Review 4424 Queen St .... Niagara Falls ON L2R2L3 905-358-5711 356-0785
Web: www.niagarafallsreview.ca

Northern News 8 Duncan Ave PO Box 1030 .... Kirkland Lake ON P2N3L4 705-567-5321 567-5377
Web: www.northernnews.ca

Nugget, The 259 Worthington St W .... North Bay ON P1B3B5 705-472-3200 472-1438
Web: www.nugget.ca

Observer, The 140 S Front St .... Sarnia ON N7T7M8 519-344-3641 332-2951
TF: 866-541-6757 ■ *Web:* www.theobserver.ca

Ottawa Citizen 1101 Baxter Rd PO Box 5020 .... Ottawa ON K2C3M4 613-829-9100 726-1198
TF: 800-267-6100 ■ *Web:* www.ottawacitizen.com

Ottawa Sun PO Box 9729 .... Ottawa ON K1G5H7 613-739-7000 739-8041
TF: 877-624-1463 ■ *Web:* www.ottawasun.com

Owen Sound Sun Times 290 Ninth St E .... Owen Sound ON N4K5P2 519-376-2250 376-7190
Web: www.owensoundsuntimes.com

Prince George Citizen 150 Brunswick St .... Prince George BC V2L2B3 250-562-2441
Web: www.princegeorgecitizen.com

Record, The 160 King St E .... Kitchener ON N2G4E5 519-894-2231 894-3829
TF: 800-265-8261 ■ *Web:* www.therecord.com

Record, The 1195 Galt St E .... Sherbrooke QC J1G1Y7 819-569-9525 821-3179
Web: www.sherbrookerecord.com

Red Deer Advocate 2950 Bremner Ave .... Red Deer AB T4R1M9 403-343-2400 341-6560
Web: www.reddeeradvocate.com

Regina Leader Post 1964 Pk St .... Regina SK S4P3G4 306-781-5211 565-2588
TF: 800-667-9999 ■ *Web:* www.leaderpost.com

Sault Star, The
145 Old Garden River Rd .... Sault Sainte Marie ON P6A5M5 705-759-3030
Web: www.saultstar.com

Spectator, The 44 Frid St .... Hamilton ON L8N3G3 905-526-3333 526-1395
TF: 800-263-6902 ■ *Web:* www.thespec.com

Sudbury Star, The 128 Pine St Ste 201 .... Sudbury ON P3C1X3 705-674-5271 674-0624
Web: www.thesudburystar.com

Telegraph-Journal 210 Crown St PO Box 2350 .... Saint John NB E2L3V8 888-295-8665
TF: 888-295-8665 ■
Web: telegraphjournal.com/csp/cms/sites/tjonline/greatersj/index.csp

Thompson Citizen 141 Commercial Pl .... Thompson MB R8N1T1 204-677-4534 677-3681
Web: www.thompsoncitizen.net

Times Colonist 2621 Douglas St .... Victoria BC V8T4M2 250-380-5211 380-5353
Web: www.timescolonist.com

Times-Transcript 939 Main St .... Moncton NB E1C8P3 506-859-4909
Web: www.telegraphjournal.com/times-transcript

Toronto Star 1 Yonge St .... Toronto ON M5E1E6 416-869-4949 869-4328*
**Fax:* News Rm ■ *TF:* 800-268-9756 ■ *Web:* www.thestar.com

Toronto Sun 333 King St E .... Toronto ON M5A3X5 416-947-2222 947-1664
TF: 888-786-7821 ■ *Web:* www.torontosun.com

Tribune, The 228 E Main St .... Welland ON L3B5P5 905-732-2411
Web: www.wellandtribune.ca

Vancouver Province 200 Granville St Ste 1 .... Vancouver BC V6C3N3 604-605-2000
Web: www.theprovince.com

Vancouver Sun 200 Granville St Ste 1 .... Vancouver BC V6C3N3 604-605-2000 605-2323*
**Fax:* News Rm ■ *TF:* 866-372-3707 ■ *Web:* www.vancouversun.com

Windsor Star, The 167 Ferry St .... Windsor ON N9A4M5 519-255-5711 255-5515
TF: 800-265-5647 ■ *Web:* www.windsorstar.com

Winnipeg Free Press 1355 Mountain Ave .... Winnipeg MB R2X3B6 204-697-7000 697-7412*
**Fax:* News Rm ■ *TF:* 800-542-8900 ■ *Web:* www.winnipegfreepress.com

Winnipeg Sun 1700 Church Ave .... Winnipeg MB R2X3A2 204-694-2022
Web: www.winnipegsun.com

World Journal 2288 Clark Dr .... Vancouver BC V5N3G8 604-876-1338
Web: worldjournal.com

532-2 Daily Newspapers - US

Listings here are organized by city names within state groupings. Most of the fax numbers given connect directly to the newsroom.

Alabama

Phone *Fax*

Anniston Star 4305 McClellan Blvd PO Box 189 .... Anniston AL 36202 256-236-1551 241-1991
TF: 866-814-9253 ■ *Web:* www.annistonstar.com

				Phone	Fax
Birmingham News 2201 Fourth Ave N *TF:* 800-283-4001 ■ *Web:* www.alabamamediagroup.com	Birmingham	AL	35203	205-325-4444	
Decatur Daily 201 First Ave SE *TF:* 888-353-4612 ■ *Web:* www.decaturdaily.com	Decatur	AL	35601	256-353-4612	340-2392
Dothan Eagle PO Box 1968 *TF:* 800-811-1771 ■ *Web:* www.dothaneagle.com	Dothan	AL	36302	334-792-3141	712-7979
Times Daily PO Box 797 *Web:* www.timesdaily.com	Florence	AL	35631	256-766-3434	740-4717
Gadsden Times 401 Locust St *TF:* 800-762-2464 ■ *Web:* www.gadsdentimes.com	Gadsden	AL	35901	256-549-2000	549-2105
Huntsville Times 2317 S Memorial Pkwy *TF:* 800-239-5271 ■ *Web:* www.alabamamediagroup.com	Huntsville	AL	35801	256-532-4000	
Montgomery Advertiser 425 Molton St *TF:* 877-424-0007 ■ *Web:* www.montgomeryadvertiser.com	Montgomery	AL	36104	334-262-1611	
Daily Sentinel 701 Veterans Dr *TF:* 877-985-9212 ■ *Web:* www.thedailysentinel.com	Scottsboro	AL	35768	256-259-1020	259-2709
Messenger, The PO Box 727 *Web:* www.troymessenger.com	Troy	AL	36081	334-566-4270	566-4281
Tuscaloosa News 315 28th Ave *TF:* 800-888-8639 ■ *Web:* www.tuscaloosanews.com	Tuscaloosa	AL	35401	205-345-0505	722-0187

Alaska

				Phone	Fax
Anchorage Daily News 1001 Northway Dr **Fax:* Edit ■ *TF:* 800-478-4200 ■ *Web:* www.adn.com	Anchorage	AK	99508	907-257-4200	258-2157*
Fairbanks Daily News Miner 200 N Cushman St *Web:* www.newsminer.com	Fairbanks	AK	99707	907-456-6661	452-7917
Juneau Empire 3100 Ch Dr *Web:* juneauempire.com	Juneau	AK	99801	907-586-3740	586-9097

Arizona

				Phone	Fax
Arizona Daily Sun 1751 S Thompson St *Web:* www.azdailysun.com	Flagstaff	AZ	86001	928-774-4545	774-4790
East Valley Tribune 120 W First Ave *TF:* 877-728-5414 ■ *Web:* www.eastvalleytribune.com	Mesa	AZ	85210	480-898-6500	898-6362
Arizona Republic 200 E Van Buren St **Fax:* News Rm ■ *TF:* 800-331-9303 ■ *Web:* www.azcentral.com/arizonarepublic	Phoenix	AZ	85004	602-444-8000	444-8044*
Daily Courier 1958 Commerce Ctr Cir *Web:* dcourier.com	Prescott	AZ	86301	928-445-3333	
Scottsdale Tribune 6991 Camelback Rd *Web:* www.eastvalleytribune.com	Scottsdale	AZ	85251	480-970-2330	970-2360
Daily News-Sun 10102 Santa Fe Dr *Web:* www.yourwestvalley.com	Sun City	AZ	85351	623-977-8351	876-3698
Arizona Daily Star 4850 S Pk Ave *TF:* 800-695-4492 ■ *Web:* tucson.com	Tucson	AZ	85714	520-573-4343	573-4107
Yuma Daily Sun 2055 Arizona Ave *Web:* www.yumasun.com	Yuma	AZ	85364	928-783-3333	

Arkansas

				Phone	Fax
Times Record 3600 Wheeler Ave *TF:* 888-274-4051 ■ *Web:* www.swtimes.com	Fort Smith	AR	72901	479-785-7700	784-0413
Sentinel-Record 300 Spring St *Web:* www.hotsr.com	Hot Springs National Park	AR	71902	501-623-7711	
Jonesboro Sun 518 Carson St *TF:* 800-237-5341 ■ *Web:* www.jonesborosun.com	Jonesboro	AR	72401	870-935-5525	935-5823
Arkansas Democrat-Gazette 121 E Capital St *TF Cust Svc:* 800-482-1121 ■ *Web:* www.arkansasonline.com	Little Rock	AR	72203	501-378-3400	372-4765
Newport Daily Independent 2408 Hwy 367 N *Web:* www.newportindependent.com	Newport	AR	72112	870-523-5855	
Pine Bluff Commercial 300 S Beech St *Web:* www.pbcommercial.com	Pine Bluff	AR	71601	870-534-3400	534-0113
Morning News of Northwest Arkansas 2560 N Lowell Rd *Web:* www.nwaonline.com	Springdale	AR	72764	479-751-6200	872-5055

California

				Phone	Fax
China Daily Press 2121 W Mission Rd *Web:* usqiaobao.com	Alhambra	CA	91803	626-281-8500	
Record-Gazette 218 N Murray St *Web:* www.recordgazette.net	Banning	CA	92220	951-849-4586	849-2437
Ventura County Star 550 Camarillo Ctr Dr *TF:* 800-221-7827 ■ *Web:* www.vcstar.com	Camarillo	CA	93010	805-437-0000	482-6167
Chico Enterprise Record 400 E Pk Ave PO Box 9 *TF:* 877-229-8655 ■ *Web:* www.chicoer.com	Chico	CA	95927	530-891-1234	342-3617
Daily Pilot 1375 Sunflower Ave *Web:* www.latimes.com/socal/daily-pilot	Costa Mesa	CA	92626	714-966-4600	966-4679
Los Angeles Times Orange County 1375 W Sunflower Ave *Web:* www.reptiland.com	Costa Mesa	CA	92626	714-966-5600	
Davis Enterprise 315 G St *Web:* www.davisenterprise.com	Davis	CA	95616	530-756-0800	756-6707
Imperial Valley Press 205 N Eigth St *Web:* www.ivpressonline.com	El Centro	CA	92243	760-337-3400	353-3003
Times-Standard 930 Sixth St *TF:* 800-514-0301 ■ *Web:* www.times-standard.com	Eureka	CA	95501	707-498-1817	441-0501
Daily Republic 1250 Texas St *Web:* www.dailyrepublic.com	Fairfield	CA	94533	707-425-4646	425-5924
Fresno Bee 1626 E St *TF:* 800-877-3400 ■ *Web:* www.fresnobee.com	Fresno	CA	93786	559-441-6111	441-6436
Asbarez Armenian Daily 419 W Colorado St *Web:* www.asbarez.com	Glendale	CA	91204	818-500-9363	
Union, The 464 Sutton Way *Web:* www.theunion.com	Grass Valley	CA	95945	530-273-9561	477-4292
Sentinel, The 300 W Sixth St *TF:* 800-582-0471	Hanford	CA	93230	559-582-0471	587-1876
Lodi News-Sentinel 125 N Church St *TF:* 877-333-4507 ■ *Web:* www.lodinews.com	Lodi	CA	95240	209-369-2761	369-6706
Press-Telegram 300 Oceangate *Web:* www.presstelegram.com	Long Beach	CA	90844	562-435-1161	437-7892
Daily Commerce 915 E First St *Web:* www.dailyjournal.com	Los Angeles	CA	90012	213-229-5300	229-5481
Investor's Business Daily 12655 Beatrice St **Fax:* Cust Svc ■ *TF:* 800-831-2525 ■ *Web:* www.investors.com	Los Angeles	CA	90066	310-448-6000	577-7303*
La Opinion 700 S Flower St Ste 3000 *Web:* www.laopinion.com	Los Angeles	CA	90017	213-622-8332	896-2144
Los Angeles Times 202 W First St *TF:* 800-528-4637 ■ *Web:* www.latimes.com	Los Angeles	CA	90012	213-237-5000	237-4712
Appeal-Democrat 1530 Ellis Lk Dr PO Box 431 **Fax:* News Rm ■ *TF:* 800-831-2345 ■ *Web:* www.appeal-democrat.com	Marysville	CA	95901	530-741-2345	749-8390*
Merced Sun-Star 3033 N G St *Web:* www.mercedsunstar.com	Merced	CA	95340	209-722-1511	
Modesto Bee 1325 H St *TF:* 800-776-4233 ■ *Web:* www.modbee.com	Modesto	CA	95354	209-578-2000	578-2207
Monterey County Herald 2200 Garden Rd *TF:* 800-688-1808 ■ *Web:* www.montereyherald.com	Monterey	CA	93940	831-372-3311	372-8401
Napa Valley Register 1615 Second St *Web:* www.napanews.com	Napa	CA	94559	707-226-3711	
Marin Independent Journal 150 Alameda Del Prado *TF:* 877-229-8655 ■ *Web:* www.marinij.com	Novato	CA	94949	415-883-8600	883-5458
Inland Valley Daily Bulletin 2041 E Fourth St *Web:* www.dailybulletin.com	Ontario	CA	91764	909-987-6397	
Desert Sun 750 N Gene Autry Trl *TF:* 800-233-3741 ■ *Web:* desertsun.com	Palm Springs	CA	92263	760-322-8889	
Antelope Valley Press 37404 Sierra Hwy *TF:* 888-874-2527 ■ *Web:* www.avpress.com	Palmdale	CA	93550	661-273-2700	947-4870
Pasadena Star-News 911 E Colorado Blvd *TF:* 800-788-1200 ■ *Web:* www.pasadenastarnews.com	Pasadena	CA	91106	626-578-6300	
Tri-Valley Herald 127 Spring St *Web:* www.eastbaytimes.com	Pleasanton	CA	94566	925-935-2525	
Record Searchlight PO Box 492397 *TF:* 800-666-1331 ■ *Web:* www.redding.com	Redding	CA	96049	530-243-2424	
Press-Enterprise 3450 14th St *TF:* 877-473-6397 ■ *Web:* www.pe.com	Riverside	CA	92501	951-684-1200	368-9023
Sacramento Bee PO Box 15779 *TF Cust Svc:* 800-284-3233 ■ *Web:* www.sacbee.com	Sacramento	CA	95852	916-321-1000	321-1109
Californian, The 123 W Alisal St *Web:* www.thecalifornian.com	Salinas	CA	93901	831-424-2221	754-4293
Sun, The 4030 N Georgia Blvd *TF:* 800-922-0922 ■ *Web:* www.sbsun.com	San Bernardino	CA	92407	909-889-9666	
San Diego Daily Transcript 2131 Third Ave **Fax:* Edit ■ *TF:* 800-697-6397 ■ *Web:* www.sddt.com	San Diego	CA	92101	619-232-4381	236-8126*
San Diego Union-Tribune 350 Camino De La Reina *TF:* 800-244-6397 ■ *Web:* www.sandiegouniontribune.com	San Diego	CA	92108	619-299-3131	293-1896
San Francisco Chronicle 901 Mission St *TF:* 866-732-4766 ■ *Web:* www.sfgate.com	San Francisco	CA	94103	415-777-1111	896-1107
San Francisco Examiner 835 Market St Ste 550 *Web:* www.sfexaminer.com	San Francisco	CA	94103	415-359-2868	359-2766
Press-Enterprise, The 474 W Esplanade Ave *Web:* www.pe.com	San Jacinto	CA	92583	951-763-3452	763-3450
El Mexicano 5801 Rue Ferrari *Web:* elmexicano.net/mexicano_wordpress	San Jose	CA	95138	619-267-6010	
San Jose Mercury News 750 Ridder Pk Dr *Web:* www.mercurynews.com	San Jose	CA	95190	408-920-5000	288-8060
Tribune, The 3825 S Higuera St *TF:* 800-477-8799 ■ *Web:* www.sanluisobispo.com	San Luis Obispo	CA	93401	805-781-7800	781-7905
San Mateo County Times 477 Ninth Ave Ste 110 *TF:* 800-870-6397 ■ *Web:* www.mercurynews.com/san-mateo-county	San Mateo	CA	94402	650-348-4321	348-4446
Orange County Register 625 N Grand Ave *TF:* 877-469-7344 ■ *Web:* www.ocregister.com	Santa Ana	CA	92701	714-796-7000	796-5052
Santa Maria Times PO Box 400 *Web:* www.santamariatimes.com	Santa Maria	CA	93456	805-925-2691	928-5657
Press Democrat 427 Mendocino Ave *TF:* 800-675-5056 ■ *Web:* www.pressdemocrat.com	Santa Rosa	CA	95401	707-546-2020	521-5330
Tahoe Daily Tribune 3079 Harrison Ave *Web:* www.tahoedailytribune.com	South Lake Tahoe	CA	96150	530-541-3880	
Record, The PO Box 900 *TF:* 800-606-9741 ■ *Web:* www.recordnet.com	Stockton	CA	95201	209-943-6397	547-8186
Daily Breeze 5215 Torrance Blvd **Fax:* Edit ■ *TF:* 800-253-2687 ■ *Web:* www.dailybreeze.com	Torrance	CA	90503	310-540-5511	540-6272*
Turlock Journal 138 S Center St *Web:* www.turlockjournal.com	Turlock	CA	95380	209-634-9141	632-8813
Reporter, The 916 Cotting Ln *Web:* www.thereporter.com	Vacaville	CA	95688	707-448-6401	447-8411
Vallejo Times Herald 440 Curtola Pkwy *TF:* 800-600-1141 ■ *Web:* www.timesheraldonline.com	Vallejo	CA	94590	707-644-1141	643-0128
Daily Press 13891 Pk Ave PO Box 1389 *TF:* 844-287-3897 ■ *Web:* www.vvdailypress.com	Victorville	CA	92393	760-241-7744	241-1860
Visalia Times-Delta 330 NW St *Web:* www.visaliatimesdelta.com	Visalia	CA	93279	559-735-3200	735-3399
Nguoi Viet News 14771 Moran St *Web:* www.nguoi-viet.com	Westminster	CA	92683	714-892-9414	894-1381
Daily News of Los Angeles 21221 Oxnard St *Web:* www.dailynews.com	Woodland Hills	CA	91367	818-713-3000	713-0058

Colorado

				Phone	Fax
Aspen Times 310 E Main St *Web:* www.aspentimes.com	Aspen	CO	81611	970-925-3414	
Boulder Daily Camera 1048 Pearl St *Web:* www.dailycamera.com	Boulder	CO	80302	303-442-1202	449-9358
Colorado Daily 5450 Western Ave *Web:* www.coloradodaily.com	Boulder	CO	80301	303-473-1111	
Durango Herald 1275 Main Ave *TF:* 800-530-8318 ■ *Web:* www.durangoherald.com	Durango	CO	81301	970-247-3504	259-5011
Coloradoan, The 1300 Riverside Ave *TF:* 877-424-0063 ■ *Web:* www.coloradoan.com	Fort Collins	CO	80524	970-493-6397	
Daily Sentinel PO Box 668 *TF:* 800-332-5832 ■ *Web:* www.gjsentinel.com	Grand Junction	CO	81502	970-242-5050	244-8578
Greeley Tribune 501 Eigth Ave *Web:* www.greeleytribune.com	Greeley	CO	80631	970-352-0211	356-5780
Gunnison Country Times 218 N Wisconsin St *Web:* www.gunnisontimes.com	Gunnison	CO	81230	970-641-1414	641-6515
Daily Times-Call 350 Terry St *Web:* www.timescall.com	Longmont	CO	80501	303-776-2244	
Loveland Daily Reporter-Herald 201 E Fifth St *TF:* 800-244-5613 ■ *Web:* www.reporterherald.com	Loveland	CO	80537	970-669-5050	667-1111
Pueblo Chieftain 825 W Sixth St PO Box 440 *TF:* 800-279-6397 ■ *Web:* www.chieftain.com	Pueblo	CO	81003	719-544-3520	

Connecticut

				Phone	Fax
Connecticut Post 410 State St *Web:* www.ctpost.com	Bridgeport	CT	06604	203-333-0161	367-8158
News-Times 333 Main St *TF:* 877-542-6057 ■ *Web:* www.newstimes.com	Danbury	CT	06810	203-744-5100	792-8730
Hartford Courant 285 Broad St *TF:* 800-524-4242 ■ *Web:* www.courant.com	Hartford	CT	06115	860-241-6200	520-6941
Journal Inquirer 306 Progress Dr PO Box 510 *TF:* 800-237-3606 ■ *Web:* www.journalinquirer.com	Manchester	CT	06045	860-646-0500	646-9867
Record-Journal 11 Crown St *TF:* 800-228-6915 ■ *Web:* myrecordjournal.com	Meriden	CT	06450	203-235-1661	639-0210
Citizens News 71 Weid Dr *Web:* mycitizensnews.com	Naugatuck	CT	06770	203-729-2228	729-9099
New Britain Herald, The 1 Ct St 4th Fl *Web:* www.centralctcommunications.com/newbritainherald	New Britain	CT	06051	860-225-4601	225-2611
New Haven Register 40 Sargent Dr *TF:* 800-925-2509 ■ *Web:* www.nhregister.com	New Haven	CT	06511	203-789-5200	
Hour, The 1 Selleck St *Web:* www.thehour.com	Norwalk	CT	06851	203-846-3281	
Norwich Bulletin 66 Franklin St *Web:* www.norwichbulletin.com	Norwich	CT	06360	860-887-9211	

Delaware

				Phone	Fax
Delaware State News 110 Galaxy Dr PO Box 737 *TF:* 800-282-8586 ■ *Web:* www.newszap.com	Dover	DE	19903	302-674-3600	
News Journal 950 W Basin Rd *TF:* 800-235-9100 ■ *Web:* www.delawareonline.com	New Castle	DE	19720	302-324-2500	324-5509

District of Columbia

				Phone	Fax
Washington Examiner 1015 15th St NW Ste 500 *Web:* www.examiner.com	Washington	DC	20005	202-903-2000	
Washington Post 1301 K St NW *TF:* 800-627-1150 ■ *Web:* www.washingtonpost.com	Washington	DC	20071	202-334-6000	
Washington Times, The 3600 New York Ave NE *Web:* www.washingtontimes.com	Washington	DC	20002	202-636-3000	636-8906

Florida

				Phone	Fax
Herald, The 102 Manatee Ave W *Web:* www.bradenton.com	Bradenton	FL	34205	941-748-0411	745-7097
Citrus County Chronicle 1624 N Meadowcrest Blvd *Web:* www.chronicleonline.com	Crystal River	FL	34429	352-563-6363	563-3280
Daytona Beach News-Journal 901 Sixth St *Web:* www.news-journalonline.com	Daytona Beach	FL	32117	386-252-1511	258-8465
El Nuevo Herald 3511 NW 91st Ave *TF:* 866-949-6722 ■ *Web:* www.elnuevoherald.com	Doral	FL	33172	305-376-3535	
South Florida Sun-Sentinel 200 E Las Olas Blvd *TF Cust Svc:* 800-548-6397 ■ *Web:* www.sun-sentinel.com	Fort Lauderdale	FL	33301	954-356-4000	
Northwest Florida Daily News PO Box 2949 *TF:* 800-755-1185 ■ *Web:* www.nwfdailynews.com	Fort Walton Beach	FL	32549	850-863-1111	863-7834
Florida Times-Union 1 Riverside Ave *TF:* 800-472-6397 ■ *Web:* jacksonville.com	Jacksonville	FL	32202	904-359-4111	359-4478
Key West Citizen 3420 Northside Dr *Web:* www.keysnews.com	Key West	FL	33040	305-292-7777	292-3008
Ledger, The 300 W Lime St *TF:* 888-431-7323 ■ *Web:* www.theledger.com	Lakeland	FL	33815	863-802-7000	802-7809
Daily Commercial 212 E Main St *TF:* 877-688-3028 ■ *Web:* www.dailycommercial.com	Leesburg	FL	34748	352-365-8200	365-1951
Diario Las Americas 888 Brickell Ave 5th Fl *Web:* www.diariolasamericas.com	Miami	FL	33131	305-633-3341	
Naples Daily News 1100 Immokalee Rd *TF:* 800-404-7343 ■ *Web:* www.naplesnews.com	Naples	FL	34102	239-213-6000	263-4816
Orlando Sentinel 633 N Orange Ave *TF:* 800-974-7488 ■ *Web:* www.orlandosentinel.com	Orlando	FL	32801	407-420-5000	420-5350
News-Herald 501 W 11th St *Web:* www.newsherald.com	Panama City	FL	32401	850-747-5000	
Port Saint Lucie News 760 NW Enterprise Dr *Web:* www.tcpalm.com	Port Saint Lucie	FL	34986	772-408-5300	
Seminole Herald PO Box 1667 *TF:* 800-955-8770 ■ *Web:* www.mysanfordherald.com	Sanford	FL	32772	407-322-2611	323-9408
Sarasota Herald-Tribune 1741 Main St *TF:* 866-284-7102 ■ *Web:* www.heraldtribune.com	Sarasota	FL	34236	941-953-7755	361-4800
Highlands Today 315 US Hwy 27 N *TF General:* 866-607-2187 ■ *Web:* www.highlandstoday.com	Sebring	FL	33870	863-386-5800	
Vero Beach Press-Journal PO Box 1268 *TF:* 866-894-9851 ■ *Web:* www.tcpalm.com	Vero Beach	FL	32961	772-562-2315	
Palm Beach Post 2751 S Dixie Hwy *TF:* 800-432-7595 ■ *Web:* www.palmbeachpost.com	West Palm Beach	FL	33405	561-820-4100	

Georgia

				Phone	Fax
Athens Banner-Herald 1 Press Pl *TF:* 800-533-4252 ■ *Web:* onlineathens.com	Athens	GA	30601	706-549-0123	208-2246
Atlanta Journal-Constitution 223 Perimeter Ctr Pkwy NE *Web:* www.ajc.com	Atlanta	GA	30346	404-526-5151	526-5746
Augusta Chronicle 725 Broad St **Fax:* News Rm ■ *TF:* 866-249-8223 ■ *Web:* chronicle.augusta.com	Augusta	GA	30901	706-724-0851	722-7403*
Brunswick News PO Box 1557 *Web:* www.thebrunswicknews.com	Brunswick	GA	31521	912-265-8320	280-0926
Columbus Ledger-Enquirer 17 W 12th St *TF:* 800-282-7859 ■ *Web:* www.ledger-enquirer.com	Columbus	GA	31901	706-324-5526	576-6290
Rockdale Citizen 969 S Main St NE *Web:* www.rockdalecitizen.com	Conyers	GA	30012	770-483-7108	483-5797
Gainesville Times 345 Green St NW *TF:* 800-395-5005 ■ *Web:* www.gainesvilletimes.com	Gainesville	GA	30501	770-532-1234	532-0457
Gwinnett Daily Post 725 Old Norcross Rd *Web:* www.gwinnettdailypost.com	Lawrenceville	GA	30045	770-963-9205	339-8081
Macon Telegraph 120 Broadway *TF:* 800-679-6397 ■ *Web:* www.macon.com	Macon	GA	31201	478-744-4200	744-4385
Telegraph, The 1675 Montpelier Ave Ste B *TF:* 800-342-5845 ■ *Web:* macon.com	Macon	GA	31201	800-342-5845	
Marietta Daily Journal 580 Fairground St *Web:* www.mdjonline.com	Marietta	GA	30060	770-428-9411	428-7945
La Vision 2200 Norcross Pkwy *Web:* www.lavisionnewspaper.com	Norcross	GA	30071	770-963-7521	963-7218
Rome News-Tribune 305 E Sixth Ave PO Box 1633 *Web:* northwestgeorgianews.com/rome	Rome	GA	30161	706-290-5252	
Savannah Morning News 1375 Chatham Pkwy *Web:* savannahnow.com	Savannah	GA	31405	912-236-9511	525-0795
Valdosta Daily Times PO Box 968 *TF:* 800-600-4838 ■ *Web:* www.valdostadailytimes.com	Valdosta	GA	31603	229-244-1880	244-2560

Hawaii

				Phone	Fax
Hawaii Tribune-Herald 355 Kinoole St *Web:* www.hawaiitribune-herald.com	Hilo	HI	96720	808-935-6621	
Honolulu Advertiser 500 Ala Moana Blvd *TF:* 800-801-5999 ■ *Web:* www.staradvertiser.com	Honolulu	HI	96813	808-529-4747	
Maui News 100 Mahalani St **Fax:* Edit ■ *TF:* 888-683-1115 ■ *Web:* www.mauinews.com	Wailuku	HI	96793	808-244-3981	242-9087*

Idaho

				Phone	Fax
Idaho Statesman PO Box 40 *TF:* 800-635-8934 ■ *Web:* www.idahostatesman.com	Boise	ID	83707	208-377-6400	377-6449
Coeur d'Alene Press 201 N Second St *Web:* www.cdapress.com	Coeur d'Alene	ID	83814	208-664-8176	664-0212
Post-Register PO Box 1800 *TF:* 800-574-6397 ■ *Web:* www.postregister.com	Idaho Falls	ID	83403	208-522-1800	
Lewiston Morning Tribune PO Box 957 *Web:* www.lmtribune.com	Lewiston	ID	83501	208-743-9411	746-1185
Idaho Press-Tribune 1618 N Midland Blvd *Web:* www.idahopress.com	Nampa	ID	83651	208-467-9251	467-9562
Idaho State Journal 305 S Arthur Ave *TF:* 800-669-9777 ■ *Web:* www.idahostatejournal.com	Pocatello	ID	83204	208-232-4161	233-8007
Times-News PO Box 548 *TF:* 800-658-3883 ■ *Web:* www.magicvalley.com	Twin Falls	ID	83303	208-733-0931	734-5538

Illinois

				Phone	Fax
Telegraph, The PO Box 278 *TF:* 866-299-9256 ■ *Web:* www.thetelegraph.com	Alton	IL	62002	618-463-2500	
Daily Herald 155 E Algonquin Rd *TF:* 888-903-4070 ■ *Web:* www.dailyherald.com	Arlington Heights	IL	60005	847-427-4300	427-1301
Belleville News-Democrat 120 S Illinois St *TF:* 800-642-3878 ■ *Web:* www.bnd.com	Belleville	IL	62220	618-234-1000	236-9773
Pantagraph PO Box 2907 *TF:* 800-747-7323 ■ *Web:* www.pantagraph.com	Bloomington	IL	61702	309-829-9000	829-7000
Southern Illinoisan 710 N Illinois Ave PO Box 2108 *TF:* 800-228-0429 ■ *Web:* www.thesouthern.com	Carbondale	IL	62902	618-529-5454	457-2935

				Phone	Fax
Centralia Sentinel 232 E Broadway *Web:* www.morningsentinel.com	Centralia	IL	62801	618-532-5604	532-1212
News Gazette 15 Main St *Web:* www.news-gazette.com	Champaign	IL	61820	217-351-5252	351-5374
Chicago Defender 4445 S King Dr *Web:* www.chicagodefender.com	Chicago	IL	60653	312-225-2400	
Chicago Sun-Times 350 N Orleans St *Web:* www.suntimes.com	Chicago	IL	60654	312-321-3000	321-3084
Chicago Tribune 435 N Michigan Ave *TF:* 800-874-2863 ■ *Web:* www.chicagotribune.com	Chicago	IL	60611	312-222-3232	222-2598
ViveloHoy 435 N Michigan Ave 12th Fl *Web:* www.vivelohoy.com	Chicago	IL	60611	312-527-8400	
Commercial-News 17 W N St **Fax:* News Rm ■ *TF:* 877-732-8258 ■ *Web:* www.commercial-news.com	Danville	IL	61832	217-446-1000	446-6648*
Herald & Review 601 E Williams St *TF:* 800-437-2533 ■ *Web:* www.herald-review.com	Decatur	IL	62523	217-429-5151	421-6913
Telegraph 113 S Peoria Ave *Web:* www.saukvalley.com	Dixon	IL	61021	815-284-2224	284-2078
Journal-Standard 27 S State Ave *TF:* 800-325-6397 ■ *Web:* www.journalstandard.com	Freeport	IL	61032	815-232-1171	232-0105
Daily Journal 8 Dearborn Sq *NASDAQ:* DJCO ■ *TF:* 866-299-9256 ■ *Web:* www.daily-journal.com	Kankakee	IL	60901	815-937-3300	937-3876
News-Tribune 426 Second St *TF:* 800-892-6452 ■ *Web:* www.newstrib.com	La Salle	IL	61301	815-223-3200	224-6443
Macomb Journal 203 N Randolph St *TF:* 800-747-5401 ■ *Web:* www.mcdonoughvoice.com	Macomb	IL	61455	309-833-2114	
Dispatch, The 1720 Fifth Ave *Web:* www.qconline.com	Moline	IL	61265	309-764-4344	797-0317
My Web Times 110 W Jefferson St *Web:* www.mywebtimes.com	Ottawa	IL	61350	815-433-2000	433-1639
Reporter 12247 S Harlem Ave *TF:* 800-633-4227 ■ *Web:* thereporteronline.net	Palos Heights	IL	60463	708-448-6161	448-4012
Pekin Daily Times PO Box 430 *Web:* www.pekintimes.com	Pekin	IL	61555	309-346-1111	
Peoria Journal Star 1 News Plz **Fax:* News Rm ■ *TF:* 800-225-5757 ■ *Web:* www.pjstar.com	Peoria	IL	61643	309-686-3000	686-3296*
Quincy Herald-Whig 130 S Fifth St *TF:* 800-373-9444 ■ *Web:* www.whig.com	Quincy	IL	62301	217-223-5100	221-3395
Rock Island Argus 1724 Fourth Ave *TF:* 800-660-2472 ■ *Web:* qconline.com	Rock Island	IL	61201	309-786-6441	786-7639
Rockford Register Star 99 E State St **Fax:* News Rm ■ *Web:* www.rrstar.com	Rockford	IL	61104	815-987-1200	987-1365*
Shelbyville Daily Union 100 W Main St *TF:* 800-772-1213 ■ *Web:* www.shelbyvilledailyunion.com	Shelbyville	IL	62565	217-774-2161	774-5732
State Journal-Register PO Box 219 *TF:* 800-397-6397 ■ *Web:* www.sj-r.com	Springfield	IL	62705	217-788-1300	788-1551
Daily Southtown 6901 W 159th St **Fax Area Code:* 312 ■ *Web:* www.chicagotribune.com/suburbs/daily-southtown	Tinley Park	IL	60477	708-633-6700	222-4674*

Indiana

				Phone	Fax
Herald Bulletin 1133 Jackson St *TF:* 800-750-5049 ■ *Web:* www.heraldbulletin.com	Anderson	IN	46016	765-622-1212	640-4815
Herald-Republican 45 S Public Sq *Web:* www.kpcnews.com	Angola	IN	46703	260-665-3117	665-2322
Times-Mail 813 16th St PO Box 849 *TF:* 800-333-2451 ■ *Web:* www.tmnews.com	Bedford	IN	47421	812-275-3355	
Republic, The 333 Second St *TF:* 800-876-7811 ■ *Web:* www.therepublic.com	Columbus	IN	47201	812-372-7811	379-5711
Truth, The PO Box 487 *TF:* 800-585-5416 ■ *Web:* www.elkharttruth.com	Elkhart	IN	46515	574-294-1661	294-3895
Evansville Courier & Press 300 E Walnut St *TF:* 800-288-3200 ■ *Web:* www.courierpress.com	Evansville	IN	47713	812-424-7711	422-8196
Journal Gazette 600 W Main St *TF:* 888-966-4532 ■ *Web:* www.journalgazette.net	Fort Wayne	IN	46802	260-461-8773	461-8648
News-Sentinel 600 W Main St	Fort Wayne	IN	46802	260-461-8439	461-8817
Daily Journal 2575 N Morton St PO Box 699 *TF:* 888-736-7101 ■ *Web:* www.dailyjournal.net	Franklin	IN	46131	317-736-2777	
Goshen News 114 S Main St PO Box 569 *TF:* 800-487-2151 ■ *Web:* www.goshennews.com	Goshen	IN	46527	574-533-2151	534-8830
Indianapolis Star 307 N Pennsylvania St *TF:* 800-669-7827 ■ *Web:* www.indystar.com	Indianapolis	IN	46204	317-444-4000	444-6600
Kokomo Tribune (KT) 300 N Union St PO Box 9014 *TF:* 800-382-0696 ■ *Web:* www.kokomotribune.com	Kokomo	IN	46901	765-459-3121	854-6733
Journal & Courier 217 N Sixth St *TF News Rm:* 800-407-5813 ■ *Web:* www.jconline.com	Lafayette	IN	47901	765-423-5511	
Chronicle-Tribune 610 S Adams St *TF:* 800-955-7888 ■ *Web:* www.chronicle-tribune.com	Marion	IN	46953	765-664-5111	668-4256
Muncie Star-Press 345 S High St *TF:* 800-783-7827 ■ *Web:* www.thestarpress.com	Muncie	IN	47305	765-747-5700	213-5858
Times, The 601 W 45th Ave *TF:* 800-837-3232 ■ *Web:* www.nwitimes.com	Munster	IN	46321	219-933-3200	933-3249
Palladium-Item 1175 N a St *Web:* www.pal-item.com	Richmond	IN	47374	765-962-1575	973-4570
South Bend Tribune 225 W Colfax Ave *TF:* 800-220-7378 ■ *Web:* www.southbendtribune.com	South Bend	IN	46626	574-235-6464	
Tribune-Star PO Box 149 *TF:* 800-783-8742 ■ *Web:* www.tribstar.com	Terre Haute	IN	47808	812-231-4200	231-4321

Iowa

				Phone	Fax
Hawk Eye, The 800 S Main St PO Box 10 *TF:* 800-397-1708 ■ *Web:* www.thehawkeye.com	Burlington	IA	52601	319-754-8461	754-6824
Gazette, The 501 Second Ave SE *TF:* 800-397-8333 ■ *Web:* www.thegazette.com	Cedar Rapids	IA	52401	319-398-8333	
Daily Nonpareil 535 W Broadway Ste 300 *TF:* 800-283-1882 ■ *Web:* www.nonpareilonline.com	Council Bluffs	IA	51503	712-328-1811	325-5776
Quad-City Times 500 E Third St *TF:* 800-437-4641 ■ *Web:* www.qctimes.com	Davenport	IA	52801	563-383-2200	383-2370
Des Moines Register 715 Locust St *TF:* 800-247-5346 ■ *Web:* www.desmoinesregister.com	Des Moines	IA	50309	515-284-8000	
Telegraph Herald 801 Bluff St **Fax:* Edit ■ *TF:* 800-553-4801 ■ *Web:* www.thonline.com	Dubuque	IA	52001	563-588-5611	588-5745*
Messenger, The 713 Central Ave *TF:* 800-622-6613 ■ *Web:* www.messengernews.net	Fort Dodge	IA	50501	515-573-2141	574-4529
Globe-Gazette 300 N Washington St PO Box 271 *TF:* 800-421-0546 ■ *Web:* www.globegazette.com	Mason City	IA	50402	641-421-0500	421-7108
Ottumwa Courier 213 E Second St **Fax:* News Rm ■ *TF:* 800-532-1504 ■ *Web:* www.ottumwacourier.com	Ottumwa	IA	52501	641-684-4611	684-7326*
Sioux City Journal 515 Pavonia St *TF:* 800-397-3530 ■ *Web:* www.siouxcityjournal.com	Sioux City	IA	51101	712-293-4300	279-5059
Pilot Tribune PO Box 1187 *TF:* 800-447-1985 ■ *Web:* www.stormlakepilottribune.com	Storm Lake	IA	50588	712-732-3130	732-3152
Waterloo Cedar Falls Courier PO Box 540 *TF:* 800-798-1730 ■ *Web:* www.wcfcourier.com	Waterloo	IA	50701	319-291-1421	291-2069

Kansas

				Phone	Fax
Goodland Star-News 1205 Main St *Web:* www.nwkansas.com	Goodland	KS	67735	785-899-2338	899-6186
Hiawatha World 607 Utah St *Web:* cityofhiawatha.org	Hiawatha	KS	66434	785-742-2111	742-2276
Hutchinson News 300 W Second St *TF:* 800-766-3311 ■ *Web:* www.hutchnews.com	Hutchinson	KS	67504	620-694-5700	662-4186
Norton Telegram 215 S Kansas St	Norton	KS	67654	785-877-3361	877-3732
Russell County News 958 Wichita Ave	Russell	KS	67665	785-483-2116	483-4012*
Salina Journal PO Box 740 *TF:* 800-827-6363 ■ *Web:* www.salina.com	Salina	KS	67402	785-823-6363	827-6363
Topeka Capital-Journal 616 SE Jefferson St *TF:* 800-777-7171 ■ *Web:* cjonline.com	Topeka	KS	66607	785-295-1111	295-1230
Wichita Eagle, The 825 E Douglas Ave *TF:* 800-200-8906 ■ *Web:* kansas.com	Wichita	KS	67202	316-268-6000	268-6627
Winfield Daily Courier PO Box 543 *Web:* www.winfieldcourier.com	Winfield	KS	67156	620-221-1050	221-1101

Kentucky

				Phone	Fax
Daily News 813 College St PO Box 90012 *Web:* www.bgdailynews.com	Bowling Green	KY	42102	270-781-1700	
Times-Tribune, The 201 N Kentucky Ave *TF:* 877-629-9722 ■ *Web:* thetimestribune.com	Corbin	KY	40701	606-528-2464	528-1335
Kentucky Enquirer 226 Grandview Dr *Web:* www.kentucky.gov	Covington	KY	41017	859-578-5500	
News-Enterprise 408 W Dixie Ave *TF:* 877-246-2322 ■ *Web:* www.thenewsenterprise.com	Elizabethtown	KY	42701	270-769-1200	769-6965
State Journal, The 1216 Wilkinson Blvd *TF:* 800-621-3362	Frankfort	KY	40601	502-227-4556	227-2831
Lexington Herald-Leader 100 Midland Ave *TF:* 800-999-8881 ■ *Web:* www.kentucky.com	Lexington	KY	40508	859-231-3100	231-3224
Courier-Journal 525 W Broadway PO Box 740031 *TF:* 800-765-4011 ■ *Web:* www.courier-journal.com	Louisville	KY	40201	502-582-4011	582-4200
Messenger-Inquirer 1401 Fredrica St *Web:* www.messenger-inquirer.com	Owensboro	KY	42301	270-926-0123	686-7868
Paducah Sun 408 Kentucky Ave *Web:* www.paducahsun.com	Paducah	KY	42003	270-575-8600	

Louisiana

				Phone	Fax
Alexandria Daily Town Talk PO Box 7558 *TF:* 800-523-8391 ■ *Web:* www.thetowntalk.com	Alexandria	LA	71306	318-487-6397	487-6488
Advocate, The 7290 Blue Bonnet Blvd *TF:* 800-960-6397 ■ *Web:* theadvocate.com	Baton Rouge	LA	70810	225-383-1111	388-0371
Courier, The 3030 Barrow St *Web:* www.houmatoday.com	Houma	LA	70360	985-879-1557	857-2244
Daily Advertiser, The 1100 Bertrand Dr *TF:* 800-526-8720 ■ *Web:* www.theadvertiser.com	Lafayette	LA	70506	337-289-6300	
American Press 4900 Hwy 90 E *TF News Rm:* 800-442-2511 ■ *Web:* www.americanpress.com	Lake Charles	LA	70615	337-494-4080	494-4070
News-Star 411 N Fourth St *TF:* 888-677-2524 ■ *Web:* www.thenewsstar.com	Monroe	LA	71201	318-322-5161	
Times-Picayune 3800 Howard Ave **Fax:* News Rm ■ *TF:* 800-925-0000 ■ *Web:* www.nola.com	New Orleans	LA	70125	504-826-3279	826-3007*
Times 222 Lake St *TF:* 800-551-8892 ■ *Web:* www.shreveporttimes.com	Shreveport	LA	71101	318-459-3200	459-3301

Maine

				Phone	Fax
Bangor Daily News 491 Main St PO Box 1329 *TF:* 800-432-7964 ■ *Web:* www.bangordailynews.com	Bangor	ME	04402	207-990-8000	
Sun-Journal PO Box 4400 *TF:* 800-482-0759 ■ *Web:* www.sunjournal.com	Lewiston	ME	04243	207-784-5411	777-3436
Morning Sentinel 31 Front St *TF:* 800-287-1945 ■ *Web:* centralmaine.com	Waterville	ME	04901	207-873-3341	861-9191

Maryland

				Phone	Fax
Capital, The 2000 Capital Dr *Web:* www.capitalgazette.com	Annapolis	MD	21401	410-268-5000	268-4643
Baltimore Sun 501 N Calvert St *TF:* 800-829-8000 ■ *Web:* www.baltimoresun.com	Baltimore	MD	21278	410-332-6000	332-6455

				Phone	Fax
Cumberland Times-News 19 Baltimore St. Cumberland *TF:* 800-742-8149 ■ *Web:* www.times-news.com	Cumberland	MD	21502	301-722-4600	722-5270
Star Democrat 29088 Airpark Dr PO Box 600 *TF:* 888-634-4002 ■ *Web:* www.stardem.com	Easton	MD	21601	410-822-1500	770-4019
Frederick News Post 200 E Patrick St *TF:* 800-486-1177 ■ *Web:* www.fredericknewspost.com	Frederick	MD	21701	301-662-1177	
Daily Times 618 Beam St *TF:* 877-335-6278 ■ *Web:* www.delmarvanow.com	Salisbury	MD	21801	410-749-7171	
Carroll County Times 201 Railroad Ave *Web:* www.carrollcountytimes.com	Westminster	MD	21157	410-848-4400	

Massachusetts

				Phone	Fax
Sun Chronicle PO Box 600 *Web:* www.thesunchronicle.com	Attleboro	MA	02703	508-222-7000	236-0462
Boston Globe 135 Morrissey Blvd *Web:* www.boston.com	Boston	MA	02125	617-929-2000	
Herald News 207 Pocasset St Ste 8 **Fax:* Edit ■ *Web:* www.northjersey.com	Fall River	MA	02722	973-569-7000	569-7268*
Herald-News 207 Pocasset St *Web:* www.heraldnews.com	Fall River	MA	02722	508-676-8211	676-2566
Sentinel & Enterprise PO Box 730 *Web:* www.sentinelandenterprise.com	Fitchburg	MA	01420	978-343-6911	342-1158
MetroWest Daily News 33 New York Ave **Fax:* News Rm ■ *Web:* www.metrowestdailynews.com	Framingham	MA	01701	508-626-4412	626-4400*
Cape Cod Times 319 Main St **Fax:* Edit ■ *TF:* 800-451-7887 ■ *Web:* www.capecodonline.com	Hyannis	MA	02601	508-775-1200	771-3292*
Daily Item, The 38 Exchange St PO Box 951 *Web:* www.itemlive.com	Lynn	MA	01903	781-593-7700	
Malden Evening News 277 Commercial St *Web:* maldennews.com	Malden	MA	02148	781-321-8000	321-8008
Haverhill Gazette 100 Turnpike St *TF:* 888-411-3245 ■ *Web:* www.hgazette.com	N Andover	MA	01831	978-946-2000	556-3703
Eagle-Tribune 100 Tpke St *Web:* www.eagletribune.com	North Andover	MA	01845	978-946-2000	687-6045
Daily Hampshire Gazette 115 Conz St *Web:* www.gazettenet.com	NorthHampton	MA	01060	413-584-5000	585-5299
Berkshire Eagle 75 S Church St PO Box 1171 *TF:* 800-234-7404 ■ *Web:* www.berkshireeagle.com	Pittsfield	MA	01202	413-447-7311	499-3419
Patriot Ledger 400 Crown Colony Dr PO Box 699159 *TF:* 888-782-2267 ■ *Web:* www.patriotledger.com	Quincy	MA	02269	617-786-7000	786-7025

Michigan

				Phone	Fax
Daily Telegram 133 N Winter St *TF:* 800-968-5111 ■ *Web:* www.lenconnect.com	Adrian	MI	49221	517-265-5111	
Huron Daily Tribune 211 N Heisterman St *Web:* www.michiganthumb.com	Bad Axe	MI	48413	989-269-6461	269-9435
Battle Creek Enquirer 155 W Van Buren St *TF:* 800-333-4139 ■ *Web:* www.battlecreekenquirer.com	Battle Creek	MI	49017	269-964-7161	
Bay City Times 311 Fifth St **Fax:* Edit ■ *TF:* 800-727-7661 ■ *Web:* www.mlive.com	Bay City	MI	48708	989-895-8551	893-0649*
Detroit Free Press 615 W Lafayette Blvd **Fax:* News Rm ■ *TF:* 800-395-3300 ■ *Web:* www.freep.com	Detroit	MI	48226	313-222-6400	222-5981*
Detroit News 615 W Lafayette Blvd **Fax:* News Rm ■ *TF General:* 800-395-3300 ■ *Web:* www.detroitnews.com	Detroit	MI	48226	313-222-2300	222-2335*
Flint Journal 200 E First St *TF Circ:* 800-875-6200 ■ *Web:* www.mlive.com	Flint	MI	48502	810-766-6100	
Holland Sentinel 54 W Eigth St *TF:* 800-633-4227 ■ *Web:* www.hollandsentinel.com	Holland	MI	49423	616-392-2311	392-3526
Jackson Citizen Patriot 100 E Michigan Ave Ste 100 *TF:* 877-213-3754 ■ *Web:* experiencejackson.com	Jackson	MI	49201	877-213-3754	
Kalamazoo Gazette 401 S Burdick St *TF:* 800-466-6397 ■ *Web:* www.mlive.com	Kalamazoo	MI	49007	269-345-3511	
Lansing State Journal 120 E Lenawee St *TF:* 800-234-1719 ■ *Web:* www.lansingstatejournal.com	Lansing	MI	48919	517-377-1000	
Mining Journal PO Box 430 *Web:* www.miningjournal.net	Marquette	MI	49855	906-228-2500	228-2617
Midland Daily News 124 McDonald St *TF:* 877-411-2762 ■ *Web:* www.ourmidland.com	Midland	MI	48640	989-835-7171	835-6991
Monroe Evening News 20 W First St *Web:* www.monroenews.com	Monroe	MI	48161	734-242-1100	242-0937
Macomb Daily 100 Macomb Daily Dr *Web:* www.macombdaily.com	Mount Clemens	MI	48043	586-469-4510	
Muskegon Chronicle 981 Third St *TF:* 800-783-3161 ■ *Web:* www.mlive.com	Muskegon	MI	49440	231-722-3161	722-2552
Times Herald 911 Military St **Fax:* Edit ■ *TF:* 800-462-4057 ■ *Web:* www.thetimesherald.com	Port Huron	MI	48060	810-985-7171	989-6294*
Saginaw News 203 S Washington Ave *TF:* 877-611-6397 ■ *Web:* www.mlive.com	Saginaw	MI	48607	989-752-7171	
Herald-Palladium 3450 Hollywood Rd *TF:* 800-356-4262 ■ *Web:* www.heraldpalladium.com	Saint Joseph	MI	49085	269-429-2400	429-4398
Traverse City Record-Eagle 120 W Front St *Web:* www.record-eagle.com	Traverse City	MI	49684	231-946-2000	946-8632

Minnesota

				Phone	Fax
Duluth News-Tribune 424 W First St *TF Circ:* 800-456-8080 ■ *Web:* www.duluthnewstribune.com	Duluth	MN	55802	218-723-5281	720-4120
Free Press 418 S Second St *TF:* 800-657-4662 ■ *Web:* www.mankatofreepress.com	Mankato	MN	56001	507-625-4451	388-4355
Star Tribune 425 Portland Ave *TF:* 800-827-8742 ■ *Web:* www.startribune.com	Minneapolis	MN	55488	612-673-4000	673-4359
Saint Cloud Times 3000 Seventh St N PO Box 768 *TF:* 855-336-0360 ■ *Web:* www.sctimes.com	Saint Cloud	MN	56303	320-255-8700	255-8773
West Central Tribune PO Box 839 *TF:* 800-450-1150 ■ *Web:* www.wctrib.com	Willmar	MN	56201	320-235-1150	235-6769

Mississippi

				Phone	Fax
Delta Democrat Times 988 N Broadway St *Web:* www.ddtonline.com	Greenville	MS	38701	662-335-1155	335-2860
Hattiesburg American 825 N Main St **Fax:* News Rm ■ *TF:* 800-844-2637 ■ *Web:* www.hattiesburgamerican.com	Hattiesburg	MS	39401	601-582-4321	584-3130*
Clarion-Ledger, The 201 S Congress St *TF:* 877-850-5343 ■ *Web:* www.clarionledger.com	Jackson	MS	39201	601-961-7000	961-7211
Meridian Star, The PO Box 1591 *TF:* 800-232-2525 ■ *Web:* www.meridianstar.com	Meridian	MS	39302	601-693-1551	485-1275
Northeast Mississippi Daily Journal 1242 S Green St *TF:* 800-264-6397 ■ *Web:* www.djournal.com	Tupelo	MS	38804	662-842-2611	842-2233
Vicksburg Post 1601 N Frontage Rd Ste F *Web:* www.vicksburgpost.com	Vicksburg	MS	39180	601-636-4545	634-0897

Missouri

				Phone	Fax
Linn County Leader 107 N Main St PO Box 40 *Web:* www.linncountyleader.com	Brookfield	MO	64628	660-258-7237	
Southeast Missourian 301 Broadway St *TF:* 800-879-1210 ■ *Web:* www.semissourian.com	Cape Girardeau	MO	63701	573-335-6611	334-7288
Columbia Daily Tribune 101 N Fourth St *TF:* 800-333-6799 ■ *Web:* www.columbiatribune.com	Columbia	MO	65201	573-815-1700	815-1701
Columbia Missourian 221 S Eigth St **Fax:* News Rm ■ *TF:* 855-270-6572 ■ *Web:* columbiamissourian.com	Columbia	MO	65201	573-882-5700	882-5702*
Excelsior Springs Standard 417 S Thompson Ave *Web:* www.excelsiorspringsstandard.com	Excelsior Springs	MO	64024	816-637-6155	637-8411
Branson Daily News 200 Industrial Pk Dr *Web:* bransontrilakesnews.com	Hollister	MO	65672	417-334-3161	335-3933
Jefferson City News Tribune 210 Monroe St *TF:* 888-892-6333 ■ *Web:* www.newstribune.com	Jefferson City	MO	65101	573-636-3131	
Joplin Globe 117 E Fourth St *TF:* 800-444-8514 ■ *Web:* www.joplinglobe.com	Joplin	MO	64801	417-623-3480	623-8598
Kansas City Star 1729 Grand Ave *TF:* 877-962-7827 ■ *Web:* www.kansascity.com	Kansas City	MO	64108	877-962-7827	
Daily Journal 1513 St Joe Dr PO Box A *Web:* dailyjournalonline.com	Park Hills	MO	63601	573-431-2010	431-7640
Daily American Republic 208 Poplar St PO Box 7 *TF:* 888-276-2242 ■ *Web:* darnews.com	Poplar Bluff	MO	63901	573-785-1414	785-2706
Springfield News Leader 651 N Boonville Ave *TF:* 800-445-1059 ■ *Web:* www.news-leader.com	Springfield	MO	65806	417-836-1100	837-1381

Montana

				Phone	Fax
Billings Gazette 401 N 28th St *TF:* 800-543-2505 ■ *Web:* www.billingsgazette.com	Billings	MT	59101	406-657-1200	657-1208
Montana Standard 25 W Granite St *TF:* 800-877-1074 ■ *Web:* www.mtstandard.com	Butte	MT	59701	406-496-5500	496-5551
Great Falls Tribune 205 River Dr S **Fax:* News Rm ■ *TF:* 800-438-6600 ■ *Web:* www.greatfallstribune.com	Great Falls	MT	59405	406-791-1444	791-1431*
Independent Record 317 Cruse Ave *TF:* 800-523-2272 ■ *Web:* www.helenair.com	Helena	MT	59601	406-447-4000	447-4052
Daily Inter Lake 727 E Idaho St *Web:* www.dailyinterlake.com	Kalispell	MT	59901	406-755-7000	752-6114
Missoulian PO Box 8029 *TF:* 800-366-7102 ■ *Web:* www.missoulian.com	Missoula	MT	59807	406-523-5200	523-5294

Nebraska

				Phone	Fax
Grand Island Independent 422 W First St *TF:* 800-658-3160 ■ *Web:* www.theindependent.com	Grand Island	NE	68801	308-382-1000	382-8129
Holdrege Daily Citizen 418 Garfield St PO Box 344	Holdrege	NE	68949	308-995-4441	995-5992
Lincoln Journal-Star 926 P St **Fax:* News Rm ■ *TF:* 800-742-7315 ■ *Web:* www.journalstar.com	Lincoln	NE	68508	402-475-4200	473-7291*
Norfolk Daily News PO Box 977 *TF:* 877-371-1020 ■ *Web:* www.norfolkdailynews.com	Norfolk	NE	68702	402-371-1020	371-5802
Omaha World-Herald 1314 Douglas St *TF:* 800-284-6397 ■ *Web:* www.omaha.com	Omaha	NE	68102	402-444-1000	345-0183

Nevada

				Phone	Fax
Nevada Appeal 580 Mallory Way *TF General:* 877-689-3249 ■ *Web:* www.nevadaappeal.com	Carson City	NV	89701	775-882-2111	423-9696
Las Vegas Sun 2360 Corporate Cir *Web:* www.lasvegassun.com	Henderson	NV	89074	702-385-3111	383-7264
Las Vegas Review-Journal 1111 W Bonanza Rd PO Box 70 *Web:* www.reviewjournal.com	Las Vegas	NV	89106	702-383-0211	383-4676
Reno Gazette-Journal PO Box 22000 *TF:* 800-648-5048 ■ *Web:* www.rgj.com	Reno	NV	89520	775-788-6200	788-6458
Reno Gazette-Journal 955 Kuenzli St *TF:* 800-970-7366 ■ *Web:* www.rgj.com	Reno	NV	89502	775-788-6397	788-6458

New Hampshire

				Phone	Fax
Concord Monitor 1 Monitor Dr PO Box 1177 *Web:* www.concordmonitor.com	Concord	NH	03302	603-224-5301	224-8120
Foster's Daily Democrat 150 Venture Dr *TF:* 800-660-8310 ■ *Web:* www.fosters.com	Dover	NH	03820	603-742-4455	749-7079
Union Leader 100 William Loeb Dr **Fax:* Edit ■ *TF:* 800-562-8218 ■ *Web:* www.unionleader.com	Manchester	NH	03109	603-668-4321	668-0382*
Telegraph, The PO Box 1008 *Web:* www.nashuatelegraph.com	Nashua	NH	03061	603-882-2741	882-2681
Valley News 24 Interchange Dr *TF:* 800-874-2226 ■ *Web:* www.vnews.com	West Lebanon	NH	03784	603-298-8711	298-0212

New Jersey

				Phone	Fax
Millville/Bridgeton News 100 E Commerce St *Web:* www.nj.com	Bridgeton	NJ	08302	856-451-1000	455-3098
Courier-Post 301 Cuthbert Blvd. *TF:* 800-677-6289 ■ *Web:* www.courierpostonline.com	Cherry Hill	NJ	08002	856-663-6000	
Asbury Park Press 3601 Hwy 66 PO Box 1550 **Fax:* News Rm ■ *TF:* 800-883-7737 ■ *Web:* www.app.com	Neptune	NJ	07754	732-922-6000	643-4014*
Star-Ledger, The 1 Star Ledger Plz. *TF:* 800-501-2100 ■ *Web:* www.nj.com	Newark	NJ	07102	973-877-4141	392-5845
New Jersey Herald 2 Spring St. *TF:* 800-423-3725 ■ *Web:* www.njherald.com	Newton	NJ	07860	973-383-1500	383-8477
Press of Atlantic City 11 Devins Ln *Web:* www.pressofatlanticcity.com	Pleasantville	NJ	08232	609-272-7000	272-7224
Jersey Journal 1 Harmon Plz Ste 1010 *Web:* www.jjournal.com	Secaucus	NJ	07094	201-653-1000	
Home News Tribune 92 E Main St Ste 202 *TF:* 800-627-4663 ■ *Web:* www.mycentraljersey.com	Somerville	NJ	08876	732-246-5500	
Times of Trenton 500 Perry St *Web:* www.nj.com	Trenton	NJ	08618	609-989-7870	396-6563
Times, The 500 Perry St. *Web:* www.nj.com/times	Trenton	NJ	08618	609-989-5454	
Trentonian 600 Perry St. *TF:* 855-549-6525 ■ *Web:* www.trentonian.com	Trenton	NJ	08618	609-989-7800	393-6072
Daily Journal 891 E Oak Rd. *TF:* 800-222-0104 ■ *Web:* www.thedailyjournal.com	Vineland	NJ	08360	856-691-5000	563-5308
Burlington County Times 4284 US-130 *Web:* www.phillyburbs.com	Willingboro	NJ	08046	609-871-8000	
Gloucester County Times 309 S Broad St. *Web:* www.nj.com	Woodbury	NJ	08096	856-845-3300	845-5480

New Mexico

				Phone	Fax
Albuquerque Journal 7777 Jefferson St NE *TF:* 800-990-5765 ■ *Web:* www.abqjournal.com	Albuquerque	NM	87109	505-823-7777	823-3994
Carlsbad Current-Argus 620 S Main St PO Box 1629 *Web:* www.currentargus.com	Carlsbad	NM	88221	575-887-5501	
Daily Times 201 N Allen Ave *TF:* 877-599-3331 ■ *Web:* www.daily-times.com	Farmington	NM	87401	505-325-4545	564-4630
Gallup Independent 500 N Ninth St *Web:* www.gallupindependent.com	Gallup	NM	87301	505-863-6811	722-5750
Las Cruces Sun-News 256 W Las Cruces Ave *TF:* 877-827-7200 ■ *Web:* www.lcsun-news.com	Las Cruces	NM	88005	575-541-5400	541-5498
Observer, The 1594 Sara Rd SE Ste D. *Web:* www.rrobserver.com	Rio Rancho	NM	87124	505-892-8080	892-5719
Santa Fe New Mexican, The 202 E Marcy St PO Box 2048 *Web:* www.santafenewmexican.com	Santa Fe	NM	87504	505-983-3303	

New York

				Phone	Fax
Times Union 645 Albany Shaker Rd PO Box 15000 *TF:* 877-263-7995 ■ *Web:* www.timesunion.com	Albany	NY	12212	518-454-5420	454-5628
Daily Challenge 1195 Atlantic Ave *Web:* www.challenge-group.com	Brooklyn	NY	11216	718-636-9500	
Buffalo News 1 News Plz PO Box 100 *TF:* 800-777-8640 ■ *Web:* buffalonews.com	Buffalo	NY	14240	716-849-4444	856-5150
Evening Observer 8-10 E Second St PO Box 391 *TF:* 800-836-0931 ■ *Web:* www.observertoday.com	Dunkirk	NY	14048	716-366-3000	366-3005
Star-Gazette 201 Baldwin St *TF:* 800-836-8970 ■ *Web:* www.stargazette.com	Elmira	NY	14902	607-734-5151	
Post-Star 76 Lawrence St *TF:* 800-724-2543 ■ *Web:* www.poststar.com	Glens Falls	NY	12801	518-792-3131	761-1255
Register-Star 364 Warren St *TF:* 800-836-4069 ■ *Web:* www.registerstar.com	Hudson	NY	12534	518-828-1616	828-9437
Ithaca Journal 123 W State St. *Web:* www.ithacajournal.com	Ithaca	NY	14850	607-272-2321	
Post-Journal 15 W Second St *TF:* 866-756-9600 ■ *Web:* www.post-journal.com	Jamestown	NY	14701	716-487-1111	
Daily Freeman 79 Hurley Ave *Web:* www.dailyfreeman.com	Kingston	NY	12401	845-331-5000	331-3557
Newsday Inc 235 Pinelawn Rd. **Fax:* News Rm ■ *TF:* 888-280-4719 ■ *Web:* www.newsday.com	Melville	NY	11747	631-843-2700	843-5459*
Times Herald-Record 40 Mulberry St PO Box 2046 *TF:* 800-295-2181 ■ *Web:* www.recordonline.com	Middletown	NY	10940	845-341-1100	343-2170
AM New York 330 W 34th St 17th Fl *Web:* www.amny.com	New York	NY	10001	212-239-5555	239-2828
Financial Times 1330 Ave of the Americas *TF:* 800-628-8088 ■ *Web:* www.ft.com	New York	NY	10019	212-641-6500	
International Herald Tribune 229 W 43rd St *Web:* international.nytimes.com	New York	NY	10036	212-556-7777	
New York Daily News 450 W 33rd St 3rd Fl. *TF:* 800-692-6397 ■ *Web:* www.nydailynews.com	New York	NY	10001	212-210-2100	643-7831
New York Post 1211 Ave of the Americas *TF:* 800-552-7678 ■ *Web:* www.nypost.com	New York	NY	10036	212-930-8000	930-8542
New York Times 620 Eigth Ave *Web:* www.nytco.com	New York	NY	10018	212-556-1234	921-0385
Niagara Gazette 310 Niagara St PO Box 549 *Web:* www.niagara-gazette.com	Niagara Falls	NY	14302	716-282-2311	286-3895
Olean Times-Herald 639 Norton Dr **Fax:* News Rm ■ *TF:* 800-722-8812 ■ *Web:* www.oleantimesherald.com	Olean	NY	14760	716-372-3121	373-6397*
Daily Star 102 Chestnut St PO Box 250 *TF:* 800-721-1000 ■ *Web:* www.thedailystar.com	Oneonta	NY	13820	607-432-1000	432-5707
Press-Republican 170 Margaret St PO Box 459 *TF:* 800-288-7323 ■ *Web:* www.pressrepublican.com	Plattsburgh	NY	12901	518-561-2300	561-3362
Poughkeepsie Journal 85 Civic Ctr Plz. *TF:* 800-765-1120 ■ *Web:* www.poughkeepsiejournal.com	Poughkeepsie	NY	12601	845-437-4800	437-4921
Daily Record 16 W Main St *TF:* 800-451-9998 ■ *Web:* www.nydailyrecord.com	Rochester	NY	14614	585-232-6920	232-2740
Democrat & Chronicle 55 Exchange Blvd **Fax:* News Rm ■ *TF:* 800-790-9565 ■ *Web:* www.democratandchronicle.com	Rochester	NY	14614	585-232-7100	258-2237*
Daily Gazette 2345 Maxon Rd Ext PO Box 1090. *TF:* 800-262-2211 ■ *Web:* www.dailygazette.com	Schenectady	NY	12301	518-374-4141	395-3072
Staten Island Advance 950 W FingerboaRd Rd. *Web:* www.silive.com	Staten Island	NY	10305	718-981-1234	
Post-Standard PO Box 4915 *TF:* 866-447-3787 ■ *Web:* www.syracuse.com	Syracuse	NY	13221	315-470-0011	
Record, The 501 Broadway *Web:* www.troyrecord.com	Troy	NY	12180	518-270-1200	
Watertown Daily Times 260 Washington St *TF:* 800-642-6222 ■ *Web:* www.watertowndailytimes.com	Watertown	NY	13601	315-782-1000	661-2523

North Carolina

				Phone	Fax
Courier-Tribune 500 Sunset Ave. *TF:* 800-488-0444 ■ *Web:* www.courier-tribune.com	Asheboro	NC	27203	336-625-2101	626-7074
Asheville Citizen Times 14 O'Henry Ave *TF:* 800-800-4204 ■ *Web:* www.citizen-times.com	Asheville	NC	28801	828-252-5622	251-0585
Times-News PO Box 481 *TF:* 800-488-0085 ■ *Web:* www.thetimesnews.com	Burlington	NC	27216	336-227-0131	
Charlotte Observer, The 600 S Tryon St. *TF:* 800-332-0686 ■ *Web:* www.charlotteobserver.com	Charlotte	NC	28202	704-358-5000	358-5036
Herald-Sun, The 2828 Pickett Rd *TF:* 866-348-6479 ■ *Web:* www.heraldsun.com	Durham	NC	27705	919-419-6500	
Fayetteville Observer 458 Whitfield St *TF:* 800-345-9895 ■ *Web:* fayobserver.com	Fayetteville	NC	28306	910-323-4848	486-3545
Gaston Gazette 1893 Remount Rd *TF:* 800-527-5226 ■ *Web:* www.gastongazette.com	Gastonia	NC	28054	704-869-1700	867-5751
Goldsboro News-Argus PO Box 10629 **Fax:* News Rm ■ *Web:* www.newsargus.com	Goldsboro	NC	27532	919-778-2211	778-5408*
News & Record 200 E Market St *TF:* 800-553-6880 ■ *Web:* www.greensboro.com	Greensboro	NC	27401	336-373-7000	373-7382
Times-News PO Box 490 *TF:* 800-849-8050 ■ *Web:* www.blueridgenow.com	Hendersonville	NC	28793	828-692-0505	693-5581
Hickory Daily Record 1100 Pk Pl. *TF:* 800-849-8586 ■ *Web:* www.hickoryrecord.com	Hickory	NC	28602	828-322-4510	
High Point Enterprise 210 Church Ave *Web:* www.hpenews.com	High Point	NC	27262	336-888-3500	
Daily News 724 Bell Fork Rd PO Box 196 *TF:* 877-878-2120 ■ *Web:* www.jdnews.com	Jacksonville	NC	28541	910-353-1171	
Mount Airy News 319 N Renfro St *Web:* www.mtairynews.com	Mount Airy	NC	27030	336-786-4141	789-2816
Sun Journal 3200 Wellons Blvd *Web:* www.newbernsj.com	New Bern	NC	28562	252-638-8101	
News & Observer 215 S McDowell St. *TF:* 800-522-4205 ■ *Web:* www.newsobserver.com	Raleigh	NC	27602	919-829-4500	829-4529
Wilson Daily Times 2001 Downing St *Web:* www.wilsontimes.com	Wilson	NC	27893	252-243-5151	243-2999
Winston-Salem Journal 418 N Marshall St. *TF:* 800-642-0925 ■ *Web:* www.journalnow.com	Winston-Salem	NC	27101	336-727-7211	727-7315

North Dakota

				Phone	Fax
Bismarck Tribune 707 E Front Ave **Fax:* Edit ■ *TF:* 866-476-5348 ■ *Web:* www.bismarcktribune.com	Bismarck	ND	58504	701-223-2500	223-2063*
Forum, The 101 N Fifth St *TF:* 800-274-5445 ■ *Web:* www.inforum.com	Fargo	ND	58102	701-235-7311	241-5487
Grand Forks Herald 375 Second Ave N *Web:* www.grandforksherald.com	Grand Forks	ND	58203	701-780-1100	780-1123
Minot Daily News 301 Fourth St SE *Web:* www.minotdailynews.com	Mohall	ND	58761	701-857-1900	857-1907

Ohio

				Phone	Fax
Star Beacon PO Box 2100 *TF:* 800-554-6768 ■ *Web:* www.starbeacon.com	Ashtabula	OH	44005	440-998-2323	998-7938
Repository 500 Market Ave S **Fax:* News Rm ■ *Web:* www.cantonrep.com	Canton	OH	44702	330-580-8300	454-5745*
Chillicothe Gazette 50 W Main St *TF:* 877-424-0215 ■ *Web:* www.chillicothegazette.com	Chillicothe	OH	45601	740-773-2111	772-9505
Cincinnati Enquirer 312 Elm St *TF:* 800-876-4500 ■ *Web:* www.cincinnati.com/?from=global&sessionkey=&autologin=	Cincinnati	OH	45202	513-721-2700	768-8340

	City	State	Zip	Phone	Fax
Kentucky Post 1720 Gilbert Ave *TF:* 877-667-4265 ■ *Web:* www.wcpo.com	Cincinnati	OH	45202	513-721-9900	
Plain Dealer 1801 Superior Ave. *TF:* 800-362-0727 ■ *Web:* www.cleveland.com	Cleveland	OH	44114	216-999-5000	
Columbus Dispatch 34 S Third St *TF:* 800-942-2745 ■ *Web:* www.dispatch.com	Columbus	OH	43215	614-461-5000	
Dayton Daily News 1611 S Main St *TF:* 888-397-6397 ■ *Web:* www.daytondailynews.com	Dayton	OH	45409	937-225-2000	225-2489
Crescent-News 624 W Second St PO Box 249 *Web:* www.crescent-news.com	Defiance	OH	43512	419-784-5441	784-1492
Chronicle-Telegram 225 E Ave *TF:* 800-848-6397 ■ *Web:* chronicle.northcoastnow.com	Elyria	OH	44035	440-329-7000	329-7282
Courier, The 701 W Sandusky St PO Box 609 *Web:* www.thecourier.com	Findlay	OH	45839	419-422-5151	422-2937
Journal News 228 Ct St *Web:* www.journal-news.com	Hamilton	OH	45011	513-863-8200	896-9489
Record-Courier 1050 W Main St PO Box 5199 *TF:* 800-560-9657 ■ *Web:* www.recordpub.com	Kent	OH	44240	330-541-9400	296-2698
Lancaster Eagle-Gazette 138 W Chestnut St *TF:* 877-513-7355 ■ *Web:* www.lancastereaglegazette.com	Lancaster	OH	43130	740-654-1321	
Lima News 3515 Elida Rd *TF:* 800-686-9924 ■ *Web:* www.limaohio.com	Lima	OH	45807	419-223-1010	229-2926
Morning Journal 1657 Broadway Ave *TF:* 888-757-0727 ■ *Web:* www.morningjournal.com	Lorain	OH	44052	440-245-6901	245-6912
News Journal 70 W Fourth St *TF:* 800-472-5547 ■ *Web:* www.mansfieldnewsjournal.com	Mansfield	OH	44903	419-522-3311	521-7415
Marion Star, The 163 E Center St *TF:* 877-987-2782 ■ *Web:* www.marionstar.com	Marion	OH	43302	740-387-0400	
Times Leader 200 S Fourth St *TF:* 800-244-5671 ■ *Web:* www.timesleaderonline.com	Martins Ferry	OH	43935	740-633-1131	633-1122
Medina Gazette 885 W Liberty St *TF:* 800-633-4623 ■ *Web:* medinagazette.northcoastnow.com	Medina	OH	44256	330-725-4166	
Times Reporter 629 Wabash Ave NW *TF:* 800-686-5577 ■ *Web:* www.timesreporter.com	New Philadelphia	OH	44663	330-364-5577	364-8416
Advocate, The 22 N First St *TF:* 877-424-0208 ■ *Web:* www.newarkadvocate.com	Newark	OH	43055	740-345-4053	328-8581
Kroner Publications Inc 1123a W Pk Ave	Niles	OH	44446	330-544-5500	544-5511
Daily Sentinel 111 Ct St *Web:* www.mydailysentinel.com	Pomeroy	OH	45769	740-992-2155	992-2157
Portsmouth Daily Times 637 Sixth St *TF:* 800-582-7277 ■ *Web:* www.portsmouth-dailytimes.com	Portsmouth	OH	45662	740-353-3101	
Sandusky Register 314 W Market St *TF:* 800-466-1243 ■ *Web:* www.sanduskyregister.com	Sandusky	OH	44870	419-625-5500	625-3007
Daily Globe 37 W Main St *Web:* www.sdgnewsgroup.com	Shelby	OH	44875	419-342-3261	
Springfield News-Sun 202 N Limestone St *TF:* 800-441-6397 ■ *Web:* www.springfieldnewssun.com	Springfield	OH	45503	937-328-0300	328-0328
Blade 541 N Superior St *TF:* 800-245-3317 ■ *Web:* www.toledoblade.com	Toledo	OH	43660	419-724-6000	724-6439
Tribune Chronicle 240 Franklin St SE *TF:* 888-550-8742 ■ *Web:* tribtoday.com	Warren	OH	44482	330-841-1600	841-1717
News-Herald 7085 Mentor Ave *Fax:* News Rm ■ *TF:* 800-947-2737 ■ *Web:* www.news-herald.com	Willoughby	OH	44094	440-951-0000	975-2293*
Daily Record 212 E Liberty St PO Box 918 *TF:* 800-686-2958 ■ *Web:* www.the-daily-record.com	Wooster	OH	44691	330-264-1125	
Vindicator, The 107 Vindicator Sq PO Box 780 *TF:* 877-700-4647 ■ *Web:* www.vindy.com	Youngstown	OH	44501	330-747-1471	747-6712
Times Recorder 34 S Fourth St *TF:* 888-217-2614 ■ *Web:* www.zanesvilletimesrecorder.com	Zanesville	OH	43701	740-452-4561	

Oklahoma

	City	State	Zip	Phone	Fax
Edmond Sun PO Box 2470 *Web:* www.edmondsun.com	Edmond	OK	73083	405-341-2121	340-7363
Enid News & Eagle 227 W Broadway PO Box 3451 *TF:* 800-299-6397 ■ *Web:* www.enidnews.com	Enid	OK	73701	580-548-8186	233-7645
Lawton Constitution 102 SW Third St PO Box 2069 *Web:* www.swoknews.com	Lawton	OK	73502	580-353-0620	
Muskogee Daily Phoenix 214 Wall St *Web:* www.muskogeephoenix.com	Muskogee	OK	74401	918-684-2828	684-2865
Norman Transcript 215 E Comanche St PO Box 1058 *Web:* www.normantranscript.com	Norman	OK	73069	405-321-1800	366-3516
Journal Record Oklahoma City 101 N Robinson St Ste 101 *Web:* www.journalrecord.com	Oklahoma City	OK	73102	405-235-3100	
Oklahoman, The 9000 N Broadway *TF:* 800-375-6397 ■ *Web:* www.newsok.com	Oklahoma City	OK	73114	405-475-3311	
Tulsa World 315 S Boulder Ave *TF:* 800-897-3557 ■ *Web:* www.tulsaworld.com	Tulsa	OK	74103	918-583-2161	581-8353
Wewoka Times PO Box 61 *Web:* www.wewokatimes.com	Wewoka	OK	74884	405-257-3341	

Oregon

	City	State	Zip	Phone	Fax
Albany Democrat-Herald 600 Lyons St SW PO Box 130 *TF:* 877-634-2867 ■ *Web:* www.democratherald.com	Albany	OR	97321	541-926-2211	926-4799
Bulletin, The 1777 SW Chandler Ave *TF:* 800-503-3933 ■ *Web:* www.bendbulletin.com	Bend	OR	97702	541-382-1811	385-5804
Register-Guard 3500 Chad Dr *Web:* www.registerguard.com	Eugene	OR	97408	541-485-1234	683-7631
Daily Courier 409 SE Seventh St *TF:* 800-228-0457 ■ *Web:* www.thedailycourier.com	Grants Pass	OR	97526	541-474-3700	474-3824
Medford Mail Tribune PO Box 1108 *TF:* 800-452-4011 ■ *Web:* www.mailtribune.com	Medford	OR	97501	541-776-4411	858-5126
Daily Journal of Commerce 921 SW Washington St Ste 210 *Fax:* News Rm ■ *Web:* djcoregon.com	Portland	OR	97205	503-226-1311	802-7239*
Oregonian 1320 SW Broadway *TF News Rm:* 800-723-3638 ■ *Web:* www.oregonlive.com	Portland	OR	97201	503-221-8100	
News-Review 345 NE Winchester St *Fax:* Edit ■ *TF:* 800-863-3321 ■ *Web:* www.nrtoday.com	Roseburg	OR	97470	541-672-3321	673-5994*
Statesman Journal 280 Church St NE *Fax:* News Rm ■ *Web:* www.statesmanjournal.com	Salem	OR	97301	503-399-6611	399-6706*

Pennsylvania

	City	State	Zip	Phone	Fax
Morning Call PO Box 1260 *TF:* 800-666-5492 ■ *Web:* www.mcall.com	Allentown	PA	18105	610-820-6500	820-6693
Altoona Mirror 301 Cayuga Ave *TF:* 800-222-1962 ■ *Web:* www.altoonamirror.com	Altoona	PA	16602	814-946-7411	946-7540
Beaver County Times 400 Fair Ave *Fax:* Edit ■ *Web:* www.timesonline.com	Beaver	PA	15009	724-775-3200	775-4180*
Dispatch, The 116 E Market St *TF:* 800-221-9282 ■ *Web:* triblive.com	Blairsville	PA	15717	724-459-6100	459-7366
Butler Eagle 114 W Diamond St *TF:* 800-842-8098 ■ *Web:* www.butlereagle.com	Butler	PA	16001	724-282-8000	282-4180
Sentinel, The 457 E N St *TF:* 800-829-5570 ■ *Web:* www.cumberlink.com	Carlisle	PA	17013	717-243-2611	243-3121
Public Opinion 77 N Third St *Fax:* News Rm ■ *Web:* www.publicopiniononline.com	Chambersburg	PA	17201	717-264-6161	264-0377*
Intelligencer, The 333 N Broad St *Web:* www.phillyburbs.com	Doylestown	PA	18901	215-345-3000	
Express-Times 30 N Fourth St *TF:* 800-360-3601 ■ *Web:* www.lehighvalleylive.com	Easton	PA	18042	610-258-7171	258-7130
Erie Times-News 205 W 12th St *TF:* 800-352-0043 ■ *Web:* www.goerie.com	Erie	PA	16534	814-870-1600	870-1808
Gettysburg Times, The 1570 Fairfield Rd *Web:* www.gettysburgtimes.com	Gettysburg	PA	17325	717-334-1131	334-4243
Evening Sun 135 Baltimore St PO Box 514 *TF:* 800-877-3786 ■ *Web:* www.eveningsun.com	Hanover	PA	17331	717-637-3736	637-7730
Patriot-News 812 Market St *TF:* 800-692-7207 ■ *Web:* www.pennlive.com	Harrisburg	PA	17101	717-255-8100	
Hazleton Standard Speaker 21 N Wyoming St *TF Cust Svc:* 800-843-6680 ■ *Web:* www.standardspeaker.com	Hazleton	PA	18201	570-455-3636	455-4244
Wayne Independent 220 Eigth St *Web:* www.wayneindependent.com	Honesdale	PA	18431	570-253-3055	
Indiana Gazette 899 Water St *Web:* indianagazette.com	Indiana	PA	15701	724-465-5555	465-8267
Tribune-Democrat 425 Locust St *TF:* 855-255-5975 ■ *Web:* tribdem.com	Johnstown	PA	15907	814-532-5050	539-1409
Intelligencer Journal 8 W King St PO Box 1328 *TF:* 800-809-4666 ■ *Web:* www.lancasteronline.com	Lancaster	PA	17603	717-291-8622	
Lancaster New Era 8 W King St PO Box 1328 *TF:* 800-809-4666 ■ *Web:* www.lancasteronline.com	Lancaster	PA	17603	717-291-8811	
Reporter, The 307 Derstine Ave *Web:* www.thereporteronline.com	Lansdale	PA	19446	215-855-8440	
Lebanon Daily News 718 Poplar St *TF:* 800-457-5929 ■ *Web:* www.ldnews.com	Lebanon	PA	17042	717-272-5611	274-1608
Meadville Tribune 947 Federal Ct *TF:* 800-879-0006 ■ *Web:* www.meadvilletribune.com	Meadville	PA	16335	814-724-6370	724-8755
Valley Independent Eastgate 19 *Web:* triblive.com	Monessen	PA	15062	724-684-5200	684-2602
Valley Mirror 3910 Main St	Munhall	PA	15120	412-462-0626	
New Castle News PO Box 60 *Web:* www.ncnewsonline.com	New Castle	PA	16103	724-654-6651	654-5976
Times Herald PO Box 591 *Web:* www.timesherald.com	Norristown	PA	19404	610-272-2500	
Philadelphia Daily News PO Box 8263 *Web:* www.philly.com	Philadelphia	PA	19101	215-854-2000	854-5910
Philadelphia Inquirer 801 Market St Ste 300 PO Box 8263 *TF:* 800-341-3413 ■ *Web:* philly.com/subscribe	Philadelphia	PA	19107	215-854-2000	
Pittsburgh Post-Gazette 34 Blvd of the Allies *Web:* www.post-gazette.com	Pittsburgh	PA	15222	412-263-1100	391-8452
Pittsburgh Tribune-Review 503 Martindale St 3rd Fl *TF:* 800-909-8742 ■ *Web:* triblive.com	Pittsburgh	PA	15212	412-321-6460	
Mercury, The 24 N Hanover St *Web:* www.pottsmerc.com	Pottstown	PA	19464	610-323-3000	
Pottsville Republican 111 Mahantongo St *Web:* www.pottsville.com	Pottsville	PA	17901	570-622-3456	
Delaware County Daily Times 500 Mildred Ave *TF:* 888-799-6299 ■ *Web:* www.delcotimes.com	Primos	PA	19018	610-622-8800	
Scranton Times-Tribune 149 Penn Ave *TF:* 800-228-4637 ■ *Web:* thetimes-tribune.com	Scranton	PA	18503	570-348-9100	348-9135
Herald, The 52 S Dock St *TF:* 800-981-1692 ■ *Web:* www.sharonherald.com	Sharon	PA	16146	724-981-6100	981-5116
Centre Daily Times 3400 E College Ave *TF:* 800-327-5500 ■ *Web:* www.centredaily.com	State College	PA	16801	814-238-5000	
Pocono Record 511 Lenox St *Fax:* News Rm ■ *TF:* 800-530-6310 ■ *Web:* www.poconorecord.com	Stroudsburg	PA	18360	570-421-3000	421-6284*
Valley News Dispatch 210 Fourth Ave *Fax Area Code:* 724 ■ *TF:* 877-698-2553 ■ *Web:* triblive.com	Tarentum	PA	15084	800-909-8742	226-4677*
Herald-Standard 8 E Church St *TF:* 800-342-8254 ■ *Web:* www.heraldstandard.com	Uniontown	PA	15401	724-439-7500	439-7559
Observer-Reporter 122 S Main St *Fax:* News Rm ■ *TF:* 800-222-6397 ■ *Web:* www.observer-reporter.com	Washington	PA	15301	724-222-2200	225-2077*
Daily Local News 250 N Bradford Ave *TF:* 800-568-7355 ■ *Web:* www.dailylocal.com	West Chester	PA	19382	610-696-1775	
Citizens' Voice 75 N Washington St *Fax:* News Rm ■ *Web:* www.citizensvoice.com	Wilkes-Barre	PA	18711	570-821-2000	821-2247*
Times Leader, The 15 N Main St *Fax:* News Rm ■ *TF:* 800-427-8649 ■ *Web:* www.timesleader.com	Wilkes-Barre	PA	18711	570-829-7100	829-5537*

	City	State	ZIP	Phone	Fax
Williamsport Sun-Gazette 252 W Fourth St *TF:* 800-339-0289 ■ *Web:* www.sungazette.com	Williamsport	PA	17701	570-326-1551	326-0314
York Daily Record (YDR) 1891 Loucks Rd *Web:* www.ydr.com	York	PA	17408	717-771-2000	
York Dispatch 205 N George St *Web:* www.yorkdispatch.com	York	PA	17401	717-854-1575	

Rhode Island

	City	State	ZIP	Phone	Fax
Newport Daily News 101 Malbone Rd *Web:* www.newportri.com	Newport	RI	02840	401-849-3300	849-3306
Times, The 23 Exchange St *Web:* www.pawtuckettimes.com	Pawtucket	RI	02860	401-722-4000	727-9280
Providence Journal 75 Fountain St *TF:* 888-697-7656 ■ *Web:* www.providencejournal.com	Providence	RI	02902	401-277-7303	277-8175
Evening Call Publishing Co, The 75 Main St *Web:* www.woonsocketcall.com	Woonsocket	RI	02895	401-762-3000	765-2834

South Carolina

	City	State	ZIP	Phone	Fax
Anderson Independent-Mail PO Box 2507 *TF:* 800-859-6397 ■ *Web:* www.independentmail.com	Anderson	SC	29622	864-224-4321	260-1276
Island Packet 10 Buck Island Rd *TF:* 877-706-8100 ■ *Web:* www.islandpacket.com	Bluffton	SC	29910	843-706-8100	706-3070
Post & Courier 134 Columbus St **Fax:* News Rm ■ *Web:* www.postandcourier.com	Charleston	SC	29403	843-577-7111	937-5579*
State, The 1401 Shop Rd *TF:* 800-888-5353 ■ *Web:* www.thestate.com	Columbia	SC	29201	803-771-6161	771-8430
Morning News 310 S Dargan St *Web:* www.scnow.com	Florence	SC	29506	843-317-6397	317-7292
Greenville News 305 S Main St *TF:* 800-800-5116 ■ *Web:* www.greenvilleonline.com	Greenville	SC	29601	864-298-4100	298-4395
Index Journal 610 Phoenix St *Web:* www.indexjournal.com	Greenwood	SC	29648	864-223-1411	223-7331
Sun News 914 Frontage Rd E *TF:* 800-568-1800 ■ *Web:* www.myrtlebeachonline.com	Myrtle Beach	SC	29578	843-626-8555	626-0356
Spartanburg Herald-Journal 189 W Main St *TF:* 800-922-4158 ■ *Web:* www.goupstate.com	Spartanburg	SC	29306	864-582-4511	594-6350
Item, The 20 N Magnolia St PO Box 1677 *Web:* www.theitem.com	Sumter	SC	29151	803-774-1200	774-1210

South Dakota

	City	State	ZIP	Phone	Fax
Aberdeen American News 124 S Second St *TF:* 800-925-4100 ■ *Web:* www.aberdeennews.com/mld/americannews	Aberdeen	SD	57402	605-225-4100	229-7532
Capital Journal 333 W Dakota Ave *TF:* 800-537-0025 ■ *Web:* www.capjournal.com	Pierre	SD	57501	605-224-7301	224-9210
Rapid City Journal 507 Main St *TF:* 800-843-2300 ■ *Web:* www.rapidcityjournal.com	Rapid City	SD	57701	605-394-8300	394-8463
Argus Leader 200 S Minnesota Ave **Fax:* Edit ■ *TF:* 800-530-6397 ■ *Web:* www.argusleader.com	Sioux Falls	SD	57104	605-331-2200	331-2294*
Black Hills Pioneer 315 Seaton Cir *Web:* bhpioneer.com	Spearfish	SD	57783	605-642-2761	

Tennessee

	City	State	ZIP	Phone	Fax
Chattanooga Times Free Press 400 E 11th St *Web:* www.timesfreepress.com	Chattanooga	TN	37403	423-756-6900	757-6383
Leaf-Chronicle PO Box 31029 *Web:* www.theleafchronicle.com	Clarksville	TN	37040	931-552-1808	
Greeneville Sun 121 W Summer St *Web:* www.greenevillesun.com	Greeneville	TN	37743	423-638-4181	638-7348
Jackson Sun 245 W LaFayette St *TF:* 800-372-3922 ■ *Web:* www.jacksonsun.com	Jackson	TN	38301	731-427-3333	425-9639
Johnson City Press 204 W Main St *Web:* www.johnsoncitypress.com	Johnson City	TN	37604	423-929-3111	929-7484
Kingsport Times-News 701 Lynn Garden Dr *TF:* 800-251-0328 ■ *Web:* www.timesnews.net	Kingsport	TN	37660	423-246-8121	392-1385
Knoxville News-Sentinel 2332 News Sentinel Dr **Fax:* Edit ■ *TF:* 800-237-5821 ■ *Web:* www.knoxnews.com	Knoxville	TN	37921	865-521-8181	342-8635*
Daily Times 307 E Harper St *Web:* www.thedailytimes.com	Maryville	TN	37804	865-981-1100	981-1175
Commercial Appeal 495 Union Ave *TF:* 800-444-6397 ■ *Web:* www.commercialappeal.com	Memphis	TN	38103	901-529-2345	
Citizen Tribune 1609 W First N St PO Box 625 *TF:* 800-624-0281 ■ *Web:* www.citizentribune.com	Morristown	TN	37815	423-581-5630	581-8863
Daily News Journal 224 N Walnut St *Web:* www.dnj.com	Murfreesboro	TN	37130	615-893-5860	
City Paper, The 210 12th Ave S Ste 100 *Web:* www.nashvillecitypaper.com	Nashville	TN	37203	615-244-7989	244-8578
Tennessean 1100 Broadway *TF:* 800-342-8237 ■ *Web:* www.tennessean.com	Nashville	TN	37203	615-257-0928	

Texas

	City	State	ZIP	Phone	Fax
Abilene Reporter-News 101 Cypress St **Fax:* Edit ■ *TF:* 866-604-2020 ■ *Web:* www.reporternews.com	Abilene	TX	79601	325-673-4271	670-5242*
Amarillo Globe News PO Box 2091 *Web:* amarillo.com	Amarillo	TX	79166	806-376-4488	373-0810
Austin American-Statesman 305 S Congress Ave *TF:* 800-445-9898 ■ *Web:* www.statesman.com	Austin	TX	78704	512-445-4040	445-3679
Bay City Tribune 2901 16th St *Web:* www.baycitytribune.com	Bay City	TX	77414	979-245-5555	245-1537
Beaumont Enterprise 380 Main St *Web:* www.beaumontenterprise.com	Beaumont	TX	77701	409-838-2888	880-0757
Banner-Press PO Box 585 *Web:* www.brenhambanner.com	Brenham	TX	77834	979-836-7956	830-8577
Adpro International Advertising Co 1144 Lincoln St	Brownsville	TX	78521	956-542-5800	542-6023
Brownsville Herald, The 1135 E Van Buren St *TF:* 800-488-4301 ■ *Web:* www.brownsvilleherald.com	Brownsville	TX	78520	956-542-4301	542-0840
Bryan-College Station Eagle 1729 Briarcrest Dr *Web:* theeagle.com	Bryan	TX	77802	979-776-4444	776-8923
Brazosport Facts 720 S Main St *TF:* 800-864-8340 ■ *Web:* www.thefacts.com	Clute	TX	77531	979-265-7411	265-9052
Caller-Times 820 N Lower Broadway **Fax:* Edit ■ *TF:* 800-827-2011 ■ *Web:* www.caller.com	Corpus Christi	TX	78401	361-884-2011	886-3732*
Dallas Morning News 508 Young St *TF:* 800-431-0010 ■ *Web:* www.dallasnews.com	Dallas	TX	75202	214-977-8222	977-8319
Focus Daily News 1337 Marilyn Ave *Web:* www.focus-news.com	De Soto	TX	75115	972-223-9175	
Herald Democrat 331 W Woodard *Web:* www.heralddemocrat.com	Denison	TX	75020	903-465-7171	465-7188
Denton Record-Chronicle 314 E Hickory St *TF:* 800-275-1722 ■ *Web:* www.dentonrc.com	Denton	TX	76201	940-387-3811	566-6888
El Paso Times 300 N Campbell St Times Plz **Fax:* News Rm ■ *Web:* www.elpasotimes.com	El Paso	TX	79901	915-546-6100	546-6415*
Fort Worth Star-Telegram 808 Throckmorton St *Web:* www.dfw.com	Fort Worth	TX	76102	817-390-7761	
Galveston County Daily News 8522 Teichman Rd PO Box 628 *TF:* 800-561-3611 ■ *Web:* www.galvnews.com	Galveston	TX	77553	409-683-5200	740-3421
Valley Morning Star PO Box 511 *TF:* 877-786-7612 ■ *Web:* www.valleymorningstar.com	Harlingen	TX	78551	956-430-6200	430-6233
Houston Chronicle 801 Texas Ave *TF:* 800-735-3800 ■ *Web:* www.chron.com	Houston	TX	77002	713-362-7171	362-6806
Killeen Daily Herald 1809 Florence Rd PO Box 1300 *Web:* www.kdhnews.com	Killeen	TX	76540	254-634-2125	200-7640
Laredo Morning Times 111 Esperanza Dr **Fax:* Edit ■ *TF:* 800-232-7907 ■ *Web:* www.lmtonline.com	Laredo	TX	78041	956-728-2500	724-3036*
Longview News-Journal 320 E Methvin St **Fax:* News Rm ■ *TF:* 800-825-9799 ■ *Web:* www.news-journal.com	Longview	TX	75601	903-757-3311	757-3742*
Lubbock Avalanche-Journal 710 Ave J *TF:* 800-692-4021 ■ *Web:* lubbockonline.com	Lubbock	TX	79401	806-762-8844	744-9603
Lufkin Daily News 300 Ellis Ave *TF:* 888-664-8792 ■ *Web:* www.lufkindailynews.com	Lufkin	TX	75904	936-632-6631	632-6655
Monitor, The 1400 E Nolana Loop *TF:* 800-366-4343 ■ *Web:* www.themonitor.com	McAllen	TX	78504	956-683-4000	683-4401
Midland Reporter-Telegram PO Box 1650 *TF:* 800-542-3952 ■ *Web:* mrt.com	Midland	TX	79702	432-682-5311	570-7650
Odessa American PO Box 2952 *TF:* 800-592-4433 ■ *Web:* www.oaoa.com	Odessa	TX	79760	432-337-4661	333-7742
Pecos Enterprise PO Box 2057 *Web:* www.pecos.net	Pecos	TX	79772	432-445-5475	445-4321
Plano Star Courier 624 Crona Dr Ste 170 *Web:* starlocalmedia.com	Plano	TX	75074	972-398-4200	398-4270
Port Arthur News 3501 Turtle Creek Dr # 105 *Web:* www.panews.com	Port Arthur	TX	77642	409-729-6397	724-6840
Fort Bend Herald 1902 S Fourth St *Web:* www.fbherald.com	Rosenberg	TX	77471	281-342-4474	342-3219
San Angelo Standard-Times 34 W Harris Ave *TF:* 800-588-1884 ■ *Web:* www.gosanangelo.com	San Angelo	TX	76903	325-659-8200	659-8173
Metrocom Herald 17400 Judson Rd *Web:* www.primetimenewspapers.com	San Antonio	TX	78247	210-453-3300	
San Antonio Express-News Ave E & Third St *TF:* 800-555-1551 ■ *Web:* www.mysanantonio.com	San Antonio	TX	78205	210-250-3000	250-3105
Herald Democrat 603 S Sam Rayburn Fwy *TF:* 800-827-7183 ■ *Web:* www.heralddemocrat.com	Sherman	TX	75090	903-893-8181	868-1930
Texarkana Gazette 315 Pine St *TF General:* 888-784-4747 ■ *Web:* www.texarkanagazette.com	Texarkana	TX	75501	903-794-3311	794-3315
Tyler Morning Telegraph PO Box 2030 **Fax:* News Rm ■ *TF:* 800-772-1213 ■ *Web:* www.tylerpaper.com	Tyler	TX	75710	903-597-8111	595-0335*
Victoria Advocate PO Box 1518 **Fax:* News Rm ■ *TF:* 800-234-8108 ■ *Web:* www.victoriaadvocate.com	Victoria	TX	77902	361-575-1451	574-1220*
Waco Tribune-Herald 900 Franklin Ave *TF:* 800-678-8742 ■ *Web:* www.wacotrib.com	Waco	TX	76701	254-757-5757	757-0302
Times Record News PO Box 120 *TF:* 800-627-1646 ■ *Web:* www.timesrecordnews.com	Wichita Falls	TX	76307	940-767-8341	767-1741

Utah

	City	State	ZIP	Phone	Fax
Herald Journal 75 W 300 N *TF:* 800-275-0423 ■ *Web:* www.hjnews.com	Logan	UT	84321	435-752-2121	753-6642
Standard-Examiner 332 Standard Way *TF:* 888-221-7070 ■ *Web:* www.standard.net	Ogden	UT	84404	801-625-4200	
Daily Herald 1555 N Freedom Blvd *TF:* 800-880-8075 ■ *Web:* www.heraldextra.com	Provo	UT	84604	801-373-5050	344-2985
Spectrum, The 275 E St George Blvd *Web:* www.thespectrum.com	Saint George	UT	84770	435-674-6200	674-6265
Deseret News 30 E 100 S Suite 400 PO Box 1257 *TF:* 800-999-7511 ■ *Web:* www.deseretnews.com	Salt Lake City	UT	84110	801-236-6000	237-2121
Salt Lake Tribune 90 South 400 West Ste 700 *Web:* www.sltrib.com	Salt Lake City	UT	84101	801-257-8742	257-8525

Vermont

				Phone	Fax
Burlington Free Press 100 Bank St ... Burlington *TF:* 800-427-3124 ■ *Web:* www.burlingtonfreepress.com		VT	05401	802-863-3441	660-1802
Rutland Herald PO Box 668 ... Rutland *TF:* 800-498-4296 ■ *Web:* www.rutlandherald.com		VT	05702	800-498-4296	

Virginia

				Phone	Fax
Bristol Herald-Courier 320 Bob Morrison Blvd ... Bristol *TF:* 888-228-2098 ■ *Web:* www.heraldcourier.com		VA	24201	276-669-2181	669-3696
Free Lance Star 616 Amelia St ... Fredericksburg **Fax:* News Rm ■ *TF:* 800-877-0500 ■ *Web:* www.fredericksburg.com		VA	22401	540-374-5000	373-8455*
Daily News-Record 231 S Liberty St ... Harrisonburg *Web:* www.dnronline.com		VA	22801	540-574-6200	
News & Advance PO Box 10129 ... Lynchburg *TF:* 800-275-8830 ■ *Web:* www.newsadvance.com		VA	24506	434-385-5555	385-5538
Martinsville Bulletin PO Box 3711 ... Martinsville *TF:* 800-234-6575 ■ *Web:* www.martinsvillebulletin.com		VA	24115	276-638-8801	
Daily Press 7505 Warwick Blvd ... Newport News *Web:* www.dailypress.com		VA	23607	757-247-4600	245-8618
Virginian-Pilot 150 W Bramelton Ave ... Norfolk *TF:* 800-446-2004 ■ *Web:* www.hamptonroads.com		VA	23510	757-446-2000	446-2414
Progress-Index 15 Franklin St ... Petersburg *Web:* www.progress-index.com		VA	23803	804-732-3456	732-8417
Roanoke Times 201 W Campbell Ave SW ... Roanoke *TF:* 800-346-1234 ■ *Web:* www.roanoke.com		VA	24011	540-981-3340	981-3346
News Leader 11 N Central Ave ... Staunton *TF:* 800-793-2459 ■ *Web:* www.newsleader.com		VA	24401	540-885-7281	
Winchester Star 2 N Kent St ... Winchester *TF:* 800-296-8639 ■ *Web:* www.winchesterstar.com		VA	22601	540-667-3200	667-1649

Washington

				Phone	Fax
Daily World 315 S Michigan St ... Aberdeen *TF:* 800-829-7880 ■ *Web:* www.thedailyworld.com		WA	98520	360-532-4000	533-6039
Bellingham Herald 1155 N State St ... Bellingham **Fax:* News Rm ■ *Web:* www.bellinghamherald.com		WA	98225	360-676-2600	756-2826*
Kitsap Sun PO Box 259 ... Bremerton *TF:* 888-377-3711 ■ *Web:* www.kitsapsun.com		WA	98337	360-377-3711	
Tri-City Herald 333 W Canal Dr ... Kennewick *TF:* 800-874-0445 ■ *Web:* www.tri-cityherald.com		WA	99336	509-582-1500	582-1510
Daily News 770 11th Ave PO Box 189 ... Longview **Fax:* News Rm ■ *TF:* 800-341-4745 ■ *Web:* www.tdn.com		WA	98632	360-577-2500	577-2538*
Skagit Valley Herald 1000 E College Way PO Box 578 ... Mount Vernon **Fax:* News Rm ■ *TF:* 800-683-3300 ■ *Web:* www.goskagit.com		WA	98273	360-424-3251	424-5300*
Olympian, The PO Box 407 ... Olympia **Fax:* News Rm ■ *Web:* www.theolympian.com		WA	98507	360-754-5400	357-0202*
Peninsula Daily News 305 W First St PO Box 1330 ... Port Angeles *TF:* 800-826-7714 ■ *Web:* www.peninsuladailynews.com		WA	98362	360-452-2345	417-3521
Seattle Daily Journal of Commerce PO Box 11050 ... Seattle *Web:* www.djc.com		WA	98111	206-622-8272	622-8416
Seattle Post-Intelligencer 101 Elliott Ave W 2nd Fl ... Seattle *TF:* 800-542-0820 ■ *Web:* www.seattlepi.com		WA	98119	206-448-8000	448-8166
Seattle Times 1120 John St ... Seattle *Web:* seattletimes.com		WA	98109	206-464-2111	464-2261
News Tribune 1950 S State St ... Tacoma *TF:* 800-388-8742 ■ *Web:* www.thenewstribune.com		WA	98405	253-597-8742	597-8274
Columbian 701 W Eigth St PO Box 180 ... Vancouver *TF:* 800-743-3391 ■ *Web:* www.columbian.com		WA	98660	360-694-3391	699-6033
Wenatchee World 14 N Mission St ... Wenatchee *TF:* 800-572-4433 ■ *Web:* wenatcheeworld.com		WA	98801	509-663-5161	665-1183
Yakima Herald-Republic PO Box 9668 ... Yakima *TF:* 800-343-2799 ■ *Web:* www.yakimaherald.com		WA	98909	509-248-1251	577-7767

West Virginia

				Phone	Fax
Register-Herald 801 N Kanawha St ... Beckley *TF:* 800-950-0250 ■ *Web:* www.register-herald.com		WV	25801	304-255-4400	255-4427
Charleston Gazette 1001 Virginia St E ... Charleston *TF:* 800-982-6397 ■ *Web:* www.wvgazettemail.com		WV	25301	304-348-5140	348-1233
Clarksburg Exponent Telegram 324 Hewes Ave ... Clarksburg *TF:* 800-982-6034 ■ *Web:* theet.com		WV	26301	304-626-1400	624-4188
Exponent Telegram 324 Hewes Ave ... Clarksburg **Fax Area Code:* 304 ■ *TF:* 800-982-6034 ■ *Web:* theet.com		WV	26301	800-982-6034	624-4188*
Herald-Dispatch 946 Fifth Ave ... Huntington *TF:* 800-444-2446 ■ *Web:* www.herald-dispatch.com		WV	25701	304-526-4000	526-2857
Journal, The 207 W King St ... Martinsburg **Fax:* PR ■ *TF:* 800-448-1895 ■ *Web:* www.journal-news.net		WV	25402	304-263-8931	267-2903*
Daily Athenaeum 284 Prospect St ... Morgantown *Web:* www.thedaonline.com		WV	26505	304-293-4141	293-6857
Parkersburg News 519 Juliana St ... Parkersburg *Web:* www.newsandsentinel.com		WV	26101	304-485-1891	485-5122
Intelligencer, The 1500 Main St ... Wheeling *Web:* www.theintelligencer.net		WV	26003	304-233-0100	232-1399
Wheeling News-Register 1500 Main St ... Wheeling **Fax:* Edit ■ *Web:* theintelligencer.net		WV	26003	304-233-0100	232-1399*

Wisconsin

				Phone	Fax
Beloit Daily News 149 State St ... Beloit *TF:* 800-356-3411 ■ *Web:* www.beloitdailynews.com		WI	53511	608-365-8811	365-1420
Leader-Telegram 701 S Farwell St ... Eau Claire **Fax:* Edit ■ *TF:* 800-236-8808 ■ *Web:* www.leadertelegram.com		WI	54701	715-833-9200	858-7308*
Action Reporter Media N6637 Rolling Meadows Dr PO Box 1955 ... Fond du Lac *Web:* www.fdlreporter.com		WI	54936	920-922-4600	
Green Bay Press-Gazette PO Box 23430 ... Green Bay *TF:* 800-422-7128 ■ *Web:* www.greenbaypressgazette.com		WI	54305	920-431-8400	431-8379
Janesville Gazette 1 S Parker Dr PO Box 5001 ... Janesville **Fax:* Edit ■ *TF:* 800-362-6712 ■ *Web:* www.gazettextra.com		WI	53547	608-754-3311	755-8349*
Kenosha News 5800 Seventh Ave ... Kenosha *TF:* 800-292-2700 ■ *Web:* www.kenoshanews.com		WI	53140	262-657-1000	657-8455
La Crosse Tribune 401 N Third St ... La Crosse **Fax:* Edit ■ *TF:* 800-262-0420 ■ *Web:* www.lacrossetribune.com		WI	54601	608-782-9710	782-9723*
Capital Times 1901 Fish Hatchery Rd ... Madison *TF:* 800-362-8333 ■ *Web:* host.madison.com		WI	53713	608-252-6400	
Wisconsin State Journal 1901 Fish Hatchery Rd ... Madison *TF:* 800-362-8333 ■ *Web:* host.madison.com		WI	53713	608-252-6200	252-6445
Herald Times Reporter 902 Franklin St ... Manitowoc *TF:* 800-783-7323 ■ *Web:* www.htrnews.com		WI	54221	920-684-4433	
Milwaukee Journal Sentinel 333 W State St ... Milwaukee *TF:* 800-456-5943 ■ *Web:* www.jsonline.com		WI	53201	414-224-2000	224-2047
Journal Times 212 Fourth St ... Racine *Web:* www.journaltimes.com		WI	53403	262-634-3322	631-1780
Sheboygan Press 632 Center Ave PO Box 358 ... Sheboygan *TF:* 800-686-3900 ■ *Web:* www.sheboyganpress.com		WI	53081	920-457-7711	457-3573
Waukesha County Freeman 801 N Barstow St PO Box 7 ... Waukesha *TF:* 800-762-6219 ■ *Web:* www.gmtoday.com		WI	53187	262-542-2501	542-8259
Wausau Daily Herald 800 Scott St ... Wausau *TF:* 800-477-4838 ■ *Web:* www.wausaudailyherald.com		WI	54403	715-842-2101	

Wyoming

				Phone	Fax
Star-Tribune 170 Star Ln ... Casper *Web:* www.trib.com		WY	82604	307-266-0500	266-0568
Wyoming Tribune-Eagle 702 W Lincolnway ... Cheyenne *TF:* 800-561-6268 ■ *Web:* www.wyomingnews.com		WY	82001	307-634-3361	633-3189

532-3 National Newspapers

				Phone	Fax
Advertising Age 685 Third Ave ... New York *Web:* www.adage.com		NY	10017	212-210-0100	
Alameda Sun 3215 Encinal Ave Ste J ... Alameda *Web:* www.alamedasun.com		CA	94501	510-263-1470	
Alberta Newsprint Company Ltd Whitecourt Plant Postal Bag 9000 10km W Hwy 43 ... Whitecourt *Web:* www.albertanewsprint.com		AB	T7S1P9	780-778-7000	
All Island Media Inc 1 Rodeo Dr ... Edgewood *Web:* www.lipennysaver.com		NY	11717	631-698-8400	
Alliance Publishing Company Inc 40 S Linden Ave ... Alliance *Web:* www.the-review.com		OH	44601	330-821-1200	
American Town Network LLC 43 Ruane St ... Fairfield *Web:* www.americantowns.com		CT	06824	203-256-3390	
American Waste Digest Corp 226 King St ... Pottstown *Web:* www.americanwastedigest.com		PA	19464	610-326-9480	
Apologetics Press Inc Publshr 230 Landmark Dr ... Montgomery *Web:* www.apologeticspress.org		AL	36117	334-272-8558	
Arizona Jewish Post 3822 E River Rd Ste 300 ... Tucson *Web:* www.jewishtucson.org		AZ	85718	520-319-1112	
Atlanta Daily World Inc 3485 N Desert Dr Ste 2109 ... Atlanta *Web:* www.atlantadailyworld.com		GA	30344	404-761-1114	761-1164
Auburn Journal Inc 1030 High St ... Auburn *Web:* www.auburnjournal.com		CA	95603	530-885-5656	
Bay Area Reporter 395 Ninth St ... San Francisco *Web:* www.ebar.com		CA	94103	415-861-5019	
Bay Citizen, The 126 Post St Ste 500 ... San Francisco		CA	94108	415-821-8520	
Bedford Gazette 424 W Penn St ... Bedford *TF:* 800-242-4250 ■ *Web:* www.bedfordgazette.com		PA	15522	814-623-1151	
BH Media Group Inc 1314 Douglas St Ste 1500 ... Omaha *Web:* bhmginc.com		NE	68102	402-444-1493	
BlackBook Media Corp 29 E 19th St ... New York *Web:* bbook.com		NY	10003	212-334-1800	
Broadcaster Press Inc, The 201 W Cherry St ... Vermillion *Web:* www.broadcasteronline.com		SD	57069	605-624-4429	
Bulletin Daily 211 N Main St ... Colfax *Web:* www.colfax.com		WA	99111	509-397-3332	
BZ Media LLC 225 BroadHollow Rd Ste 211 E ... Melville *Web:* www.bzmedia.com		NY	11747	631-421-4158	
Cabinet Press Inc, The 17 Executive Dr ... Hudson *Web:* www.cabinet.com		NH	03051	603-673-3100	
Canadian Press Ltd, The 36 King St E ... Toronto *Web:* www.thecanadianpress.com		ON	M5C2L9	416-364-0321	
Capitol Hill Publishing Corp 1625 K St NW Ste 900 ... Washington *Web:* www.thehill.com		DC	20006	202-628-8500	

Name / Address	City	State	ZIP	Phone	Fax
Central Ohio Printing Co 55 W High St *Web:* www.madison-press.com	London	OH	43140	740-852-1616	
Challenge Graphics Corp 16611 Roscoe Pl *Web:* www.challenge-graphics.com	North Hills	CA	91343	818-892-0123	
Charleston Newspapers Ltd 1001 Virginia St E *TF:* 800-982-6397 ■ *Web:* www.cnpapers.com	Charleston	WV	25301	304-348-4848	
Cherokee Ledger News, The 521 E Main St *Web:* www.ledgernews.com	Canton	GA	30114	770-479-1441	
Chesterton Tribune 193 S Calumet Rd *Web:* www.chestertontribune.com	Chesterton	IN	46304	219-926-1131	
Christian Science Monitor 210 Massachusetts Ave *TF:* 800-453-3432 ■ *Web:* www.csmonitor.com	Boston	MA	02115	617-450-2000	
Circle Media Inc 5817 Old Leeds Rd *TF:* 800-356-9916 ■ *Web:* www.ncregister.com	Irondale	AL	35210	800-356-9916	
Clipper Magazine LLC 3708 Hempland Rd *Web:* www.clippermagazine.com	Mountville	PA	17554	717-569-5100	
Conway Daily Sun 64 Seavey St *Web:* badgerrealty.com	North Conway	NH	03860	603-356-3456	
Cookeville Newspapers Inc 1300 Neal St *Web:* www.herald-citizen.com	Cookeville	TN	38501	931-526-9715	
Covington Leader, The 2001 Hwy 51 S *Web:* www.covingtonleader.com	Covington	TN	38019	901-476-7116	
Cowles Publishing Co 999 W Riverside Ave *Web:* www.spokesman.com	Spokane	WA	99201	509-459-5000	
Crittenden Publishing Company Inc 1010 State Hwy 77 *Web:* www.theeveningtimes.com	Marion	AR	72364	870-735-2383	
CrossRoadsNews Inc 2346 Candler Rd *Web:* www.crossroadsnews.com	Decatur	GA	30032	404-284-1888	
Current Newspaper 6930 Carroll Ave Ste 350 *Web:* www.current.org	Takoma Park	MD	20912	301-270-7240	
Daily Californian 600 Eshleman Hall *Web:* www.dailycal.org	Berkeley	CA	94720	510-548-8300	
Daily Herald Co, The 1213 California St *Web:* www.heraldnet.com	Everett	WA	98201	425-339-3433	
Daily Item, The 200 Market St *Web:* www.dailyitem.com	Sunbury	PA	17801	570-286-5671	
Daily News Publishing Co 193 Jefferson Ave *Web:* www.memphisdailynews.com	Memphis	TN	38103	901-523-1561	
Daily Texan-student Newspaper 2500 Whitis Ave *Web:* www.dailytexanonline.com	Austin	TX	78712	512-471-4591	
Davis County Clipper Today 1370 South 500 West *Web:* www.spectrumpress.us	Woods Cross	UT	84010	801-295-2251	
Dispatch Publishing Company Inc, The 30 E First Ave *Web:* www.the-dispatch.com	Lexington	NC	27293	336-249-3981	
Dix Communications LLC 212 E Liberty St *Web:* www.dixcom.com	Wooster	OH	44691	330-264-1125	
Dover Publications Inc 31 E Second St *Web:* www.doverpublications.com	Mineola	NY	11501	516-294-7000	
Dowagiac 217 N Fourth St *Web:* www.leaderpub.com	Niles	MI	49120	269-683-2101	
Drummer & Wright Cnty Journal 108 Central Ave *TF:* 800-880-5047 ■ *Web:* www.thedrummer.com	Buffalo	MN	55313	763-682-1221	
Eagle Herald Publishing LLC 1809 Dunlap Ave *Web:* www.eagleherald.com	Marinette	WI	54143	715-735-6611	
Eagle Newspapers Inc 4901 Indian School Rd NE PO Box 12008 *Web:* www.eaglenewspapers.com	Salem	OR	97305	503-393-1774	
Easy-ad Inc 155 S Harvard St *Web:* www.easyadlive.com	Hemet	CA	92543	951-658-2244	
Edwards Publications Inc 125 Eagles Nest Dr St A *Web:* www.edwgroupinc.com	Seneca	SC	29678	864-882-3272	
El Observador Publications Inc 99 N First St Ste 100 *Web:* www.el-observador.com	San Jose	CA	95113	408-938-1700	
El Periodico u s a Inc 801 E Fir Ave *Web:* www.elperiodicousa.com	Mcallen	TX	78501	956-631-5628	
EO Media Group 211 SE Byers Ave *Web:* www.eastoregonian.com	Pendleton	OR	97801	541-276-2211	
Epoch Times Atlanta PO Box 2041 *Web:* www.epochtimes.com	Suwanee	GA	30024	678-485-0136	
Fayette Daily News 210 Jeff Davis Pl *Web:* www.fayettedailynews.com	Fayetteville	GA	30214	770-461-6317	
Free Press Standard, The 43 E Main St *Web:* www.freepressstandard.com	Carrollton	OH	44615	330-627-5591	
Garavi Gujarat Publications 2020 Beaver Ruin Rd *Web:* www.amg.biz	Norcross	GA	30071	770-263-7728	
Genesee Valley Penny Saver Inc 1471 W Henrietta Rd *Web:* www.gvpennysaver.com	Avon	NY	14414	585-226-8111	
Gleim Publications Inc 4201 Nw 95th Blvd *Web:* www.gleim.com	Gainesville	FL	32606	352-375-0772	
Glendale Star 7122 N 59th Ave *Web:* www.glendalestar.com	Glendale	AZ	85301	623-842-6000	
Glennville Sentinel Inc, The 105 W Barnard St *Web:* www.glennvillesentinel.net	Glennville	GA	30427	912-654-2515	
Greenspun Media Group LLC, The 2360 Corporate Cir 3rd Fl *Web:* www.gmgvegas.com	Henderson	NV	89074	702-990-2550	
Hatchet Publications Inc 2140 G St Nw *Web:* www.gwhatchet.com	Washington	DC	20052	202-847-0400	
Havre Daily News 119 Second St *Web:* www.havredailynews.com	Havre	MT	59501	406-265-6795	
Heppner Gazette Times 188 Willow St PO Box 337 *Web:* www.heppner.net	Heppner	OR	97836	541-676-9228	
High Country News 119 Grand Ave *TF:* 800-311-5852 ■ *Web:* www.hcn.org	Paonia	CO	81428	970-527-4898	
Highland Lakes Newspapers Inc 304 Gateway Loop *Web:* www.highlandernews.com	Marble Falls	TX	78654	830-693-4367	
Hill Times 69 Sparks St *Web:* www.hilltimes.com	Ottawa	ON	K1P5A5	613-232-5952	
Hood County News 1501 S Morgan St *Web:* www.hcnews.com	Granbury	TX	76048	817-573-7066	279-8371
Horizon Publications Inc 1120 N Carbon St Ste 100 *Web:* horizonpublicationsinc.com	Marion	IL	62959	618-993-1711	
Houston Newspapers- Herald & The Messenger 113 N Grand Ave *Web:* www.houstonherald.com	Houston	MO	65483	417-967-2000	
Improper Bostonian 142 Berkeley St 3rd Fl *Web:* www.improper.com	Boston	MA	02116	617-859-1400	
Indeco North America Inc 135 Research Dr *Web:* www.indeco-breakers.com	Milford	CT	06460	203-713-1030	
Jewish Press Inc 338 Third Ave *Web:* www.jewishpress.com	Brooklyn	NY	11215	718-330-1100	
Joongang Daily News California Inc 690 Wilshire Pl *Web:* www.koreadaily.com	Los Angeles	CA	90005	213-368-2500	
Kentucky New Era Inc PO Box 729 *Web:* www.kentuckynewera.com	Hopkinsville	KY	42241	270-886-4444	
Korea Times Los Angeles Inc, The 4525 Wilshire Blvd *Web:* www.koreatimes.com	Los Angeles	CA	90010	323-692-2000	
La Jolla Light Newspaper 565 Pearl St Ste 300 *Web:* www.lajollalight.com	La Jolla	CA	92037	858-459-4201	
Lafromboise Communications Inc 321 N Pearl St *Web:* www.chronline.com	Centralia	WA	98531	360-736-3311	
Lakeview Publishing of Elbow Lake Inc 35 Central Ave N *TF:* 877-852-2796 ■ *Web:* www.grantherald.com	Elbow Lake	MN	56531	218-685-5326	
Lawyers Weekly Inc 10 Milk St Ste 1000 *TF:* 800-444-5297 ■ *Web:* www.masslawyersweekly.com	Boston	MA	02108	617-451-7300	
Lebanon Publishing Company Inc 402 N Cumberland St *Web:* www.lebanondemocrat.com	Lebanon	TN	37087	615-444-3952	
Lewistown News-argus 521 W Main St *TF:* 800-879-5627 ■ *Web:* www.lewistownnews.com	Lewistown	MT	59457	406-535-3401	
Lompoc Record, The 115 N H St *Web:* www.lompocrecord.com	Lompoc	CA	93436	805-736-2313	
Long Island Business News Inc 2150 Smithtown Ave Ste 7 *Web:* www.libn.com	Ronkonkoma	NY	11779	631-737-1700	
Luso Americano Company Inc 66 Union St *Web:* www.lusoamericano.com	Newark	NJ	07105	973-344-3200	
Mader News Inc 913 Ruberta Ave *Web:* www.madernews.com	Glendale	CA	91201	818-551-5000	
Main Street Media Group LLC 6400 Monterey St *Web:* www.mainstreetmediagroup.com	Gilroy	CA	95020	408-842-6400	
Manufacturers' News Inc 1633 Central St *Web:* www.manufacturersnews.com	Evanston	IL	60201	847-864-7000	
MD Buyline Inc 5910 N Central Expy Ste 1800 *Web:* www.mdbuyline.com	Dallas	TX	75206	214-891-6700	
Metroland Media Group Ltd 3125 Wolfedale Rd *Web:* www.metroland.com	Mississauga	ON	L5C1W1	905-281-5656	281-5630
Mid Atlantic Printers Ltd 503 Third St *Web:* www.mapl.net	Altavista	VA	24517	434-369-6633	
Minnesota Womens Press Inc 771 Raymond Ave *Web:* www.womenspress.com	Saint Paul	MN	55114	651-646-3968	
Missouri Valley Times-enterprise Inc 501 E Erie St *Web:* www.dcpostgazette.com	Missouri Valley	IA	51555	712-642-2791	
Mobridge Tribune 1413 E Grand Xing *Web:* www.mobridgetribune.com	Mobridge	SD	57601	605-845-3646	
Montgomery Communications Inc 222 W Sixth St *Web:* www.dailyu.com	Junction City	KS	66441	785-762-5000	
Morris Herald-News 1804 N Division St *Web:* www.morrisherald-news.com	Morris	IL	60450	815-942-3221	
Mountain Democrat 1360 Broadway *Web:* www.mtdemocrat.com	Placerville	CA	95667	530-622-1255	
N'digo Profiles 1006 S Michigan Ave Ste 200 *Web:* ndigo.com	Chicago	IL	60605	312-822-0202	
New Century Press Inc 310 First Ave *Web:* www.ncppub.com	Rock Rapids	IA	51246	712-472-2525	
News Examiner, The 847 Washington St *Web:* www.news-examiner.net	Montpelier	ID	83254	208-847-0552	
News-banner Publications Inc 125 N Johnson St *TF:* 800-579-7476 ■ *Web:* www.news-banner.com	Bluffton	IN	46714	260-824-0224	
Newspaper Services of America Inc 3025 Highland Pkwy Ste 700 *Web:* nsamedia.com	Downers Grove	IL	60515	630-729-7500	
Newsvine Inc 101 Elliott Ave W Ste 120 *Web:* www.newsvine.com	Seattle	WA	98119	206-529-4444	
Next Year's News 1 S Saint Clair St Ste 1b	Toledo	OH	43604	419-241-3698	
Nittany Valley Offset Nittany Vly Offset 1015 Benner Pk *Web:* www.nittanyvalley.com	State College	PA	16801	814-238-3071	
Northern Michigan Review Inc 319 State St *Web:* www.petoskeynews.com	Petoskey	MI	49770	231-347-2544	

Phone Fax

Oahu Publications Inc
500 Ala Moana Blvd Ste 7-500 ... Honolulu HI 96813 808-529-4700
Web: www.oahupublications.com

Ottawa Herald Inc 104 S Cedar St ... Ottawa KS 66067 785-242-4700
TF: 800-467-8383 ■ *Web:* www.ottawaherald.com

Outlook Publishing Inc 415 E Main PO Box 278 ... Laurel MT 59044 406-628-4412
Web: www.laureloutlook.com

Overton County News 415 W Main St ... Livingston TN 38570 931-823-6485
Web: www.overtoncountynews.com

Park Record PO Box 3688 ... Park City UT 84060 435-649-9014
Web: www.parkrecord.com

Pars International Corp 253 W 35th St Fl 7 ... New York NY 10001 212-221-9595
Web: www.magreprints.com

Payson Roundup Newspaper 708 N Beeline Hwy ... Payson AZ 85541 928-474-5251
Web: www.paysonroundup.com

Philadelphia Gay News 505 S Fourth St ... Philadelphia PA 19147 215-625-8501
Web: www.epgn.com

Pleasanton Weekly 5506 Sunol Blvd Ste 100 ... Pleasanton CA 94566 925-600-0840
Web: www.pleasantonweekly.com

Port Lavaca Wave 107 E Austin St ... Port Lavaca TX 77979 361-552-9788
Web: www.portlavacawave.com

Record Herald Publishing 30 Walnut St ... Waynesboro PA 17268 717-762-2151
Web: www.therecordherald.com

Richner Communications Inc 2 Endo Blvd ... Garden City NY 11530 516-569-4000
Web: www.liherald.com

River Falls Journal 2815 Prairie Dr ... River Falls WI 54022 715-425-1561
Web: www.rivertowns.net

Robesonian, The 2175 N Roberts Ave ... Lumberton NC 28358 910-739-4322
Web: www.robesonian.com

Rubber & Plastics News 1725 Merriman Rd ... Akron OH 44313 330-836-9180
Web: www.rubbernews.com

San Diego Community Newspaper
4645 Cass St Fl 2 ... San Diego CA 92109 858-270-3103
Web: www.sdnews.com

Sand Mountain Reporter 1603 Progress Dr ... Albertville AL 35950 256-840-2987
Web: www.sandmountainreporter.com

Santa Cruz Sentinel Inc 207 Church St ... Santa Cruz CA 95060 831-423-4242
Web: www.santacruzsentinel.com

Santa Rosa Press Democrat Inc, The
427 Mendocino Ave PO Box 569 ... Santa Rosa CA 95402 707-526-8570
Web: www.pressdemocrat.com

Schurz Communications Inc
1301 E Douglas Rd ... Mishawaka IN 46545 574-247-7237
Web: www.schurz.com

Sentinel Power Services Inc 7517 E Pine St ... Tulsa OK 74115 918-359-0350
TF: 800-831-9550 ■ *Web:* www.sentinelpowerservices.com

Sentinel Systems Corp 1620 Kipling St ... Lakewood CO 80215 303-242-2000
TF: 800-456-9955 ■ *Web:* www.sentinelsystems.com

Sentinel Transportation LLC
3521 Silverside Rd Ste 2A ... Wilmington DE 19810 302-477-1640
Web: www.sentineltrans.com

Show-me Publishing Inc 2049 Wyandotte St ... Kansas City MO 64108 816-842-9994
Web: ingrams.com

Small Business Times
126 N Jefferson St Ste 403 ... Milwaukee WI 53202 414-277-8181
Web: biztimes.com

Smart Business Network Inc
835 Sharon Dr Ste 200 ... Cleveland OH 44145 440-250-7000
Web: www.sbnonline.com

Specht Newspapers Inc 203 Gleason St ... Minden LA 71055 318-377-1866
Web: www.nwlanews.com

Stanwood Camano News 9005 271st St Nw ... Stanwood WA 98292 360-629-2155
Web: www.scnews.com

State News 435 E Grand River Ave ... East Lansing MI 48823 517-432-3000
Web: statenews.com

Staunton Star Times 108 W Main St ... Staunton IL 62088 618-635-2000
Web: www.stauntonstartimes.com

Stockpickr LLC 14 Wall St Fl 15 ... New York NY 10005 212-321-5000
Web: www.stockpickr.com

Stone County Publishing Company Inc
104 W Main St ... Mountain View AR 72560 870-269-3841
Web: www.stonecountyleader.com

Straus News Inc 20 W Ave ... Chester NY 10918 845-469-9000
Web: www.strausnews.com

Swift Communications Inc 580 Mallory Way ... Carson City NV 89701 775-283-5500
Web: www.swiftcom.com

Synthesis 210 W Sixth St ... Chico CA 95928 530-899-7708
Web: synthesisweekly.com

Target Media Partners Inc
1800 N Highland Ave Ste 400 ... Los Angeles CA 90028 323-930-3123
Web: www.targetmediapartners.com

Times Record, The 3 Business Pkwy ... Brunswick ME 04011 207-729-3311
Web: www.timesrecord.com

TimesLedger Newspapers, The
41-02 Bell Blvd 2nd Fl ... Bayside NY 11361 718-260-4545
Web: www.timesledger.com

Tomahawk Leader 315 W Wisconsin Ave ... Tomahawk WI 54487 715-453-2151
Web: www.tomahawkleader.com

Tribune Inc 2012 Forest Ave ... Great Bend KS 67530 620-792-1211
Web: www.gbtribune.com

Tucson Shopper LLC 1861 W Grant Rd ... Tucson AZ 85745 520-622-0101

Tukwila Reporter, The 19426 68th Ave S Ste A ... Kent WA 98032 253-872-6600
Web: www.pnwlocalnews.com

Turley Publications Inc 24 Water St ... Palmer MA 01069 413-283-8393
Web: www.turley.com

USA Today 7950 Jones Branch Dr ... McLean VA 22108 703-854-3400
TF Cust Svc: 800-872-0001 ■ *Web:* www.usatoday.com

Vineyard Gazette Inc 34 S Summer St ... Edgartown MA 02539 508-627-4311
Web: vineyardgazette.com

Wall Street Journal, The
1211 Ave of the Americas ... New York NY 10036 212-416-2000
TF General: 800-568-7625 ■ *Web:* www.wsj.com/india

Phone Fax

Washington Daily News, The
217 N Market St ... Washington NC 27889 252-946-2144
Web: www.wdnweb.com

Watertown Public Opinion 120 Third Ave Nw ... Watertown SD 57201 605-886-6901
Web: www.coteaushopper.com

Webster-Kirkwood Times Inc
122 W Lockwood Ave ... St. Louis MO 63119 314-968-2699
Web: www.websterkirkwoodtimes.com

Wednesday Journal 141 S Oak Park Ave ... Oak Park IL 60302 708-524-8300
Web: www.chicagoparent.com

Wehco Newspapers Inc 115 E Capitol Ave ... Little Rock AR 72201 501-378-3400
Web: www.arkansasonline.com

Western Producer Publications
2310 Millar Ave ... Saskatoon SK S7K2Y2 306-665-3500 665-4961
Web: www.producer.com

Wilson Post, The 216 Hartmann Dr ... Lebanon TN 37087 615-444-6008
Web: www.wilsonpost.com

Winneconne News 908 E Main St ... Winneconne WI 54986 920-582-4541
TF: 800-545-5026 ■ *Web:* www.rogerspublishing.com

World Publishing Co 14 N Mission St ... Wenatchee WA 98801 509-663-5161
Web: www.wenatcheeworld.com

532-4 Weekly Newspapers

Listings here are organized by city names within state groupings.

Alabama

Phone Fax

Birmingham Times 115 Third Ave W ... Birmingham AL 35204 205-251-5158 323-2294
TF: 866-456-4995 ■ *Web:* birminghamtimes.com

Over The Mountain Journal
2016 Columbiana Rd ... Birmingham AL 35216 205-823-9646 824-1246
Web: www.otmj.com

Shelby County Reporter 115 N Main St ... Columbiana AL 35051 205-669-3131 669-4217
Web: www.shelbycountyreporter.com

Courier Journal 1828 Darby Dr ... Florence AL 35630 256-764-4268 760-9618
Web: www.courierjournal.net

Greenville Advocate, The PO Box 507 ... Greenville AL 36037 334-382-3111 382-7104
Web: www.greenvilleadvocate.com

Hartselle Enquirer PO Box 929 ... Hartselle AL 35640 256-773-6566 773-1953
Web: www.hartselleenquirer.com

Montgomery Independent 141 Market Pl ... Montgomery AL 36117 334-265-7323
Web: www.al.com

Alaska

Phone Fax

Anchorage Press 540 E Fifth Ave ... Anchorage AK 99501 907-561-7737 561-7777
Web: www.anchoragepress.com

Arizona

Phone Fax

Apache Junction Independent
850 S Ironwood Dr Ste 112 ... Apache Junction AZ 85120 480-982-7799
Web: ajnews.com

West Valley View 200 W Wigwam Blvd ... Litchfield Park AZ 85323 623-535-8439 935-2103
Web: www.westvalleyview.com

Ahwatukee Foothills News
10631 S 51st St Ste 1 ... Phoenix AZ 85044 480-898-7900 893-1684*
**Fax:* News Rm ■ *Web:* www.ahwatukee.com

Sun Cities Independent
17220 N Boswell Blvd Ste 101 ... Sun City AZ 85373 623-972-6101
Web: www.newszap.com

California

Phone Fax

Bakersfield News Observer 1219 20th St ... Bakersfield CA 93301 661-324-9466 324-9472

Beverly Hills Courier
8840 W Olympic Blvd ... Beverly Hills CA 90211 310-278-1322 271-5118
Web: www.bhcourier.com

Chino Champion PO Box 607 ... Chino CA 91708 909-628-5501 590-1217
Web: www.championnewspapers.com

Rialto Record PO Box 110 ... Colton CA 92324 909-381-9898
Web: www.iecn.com

Huntington Beach Independent
1375 Sunflower Ave ... Costa Mesa CA 92626 714-966-4600
Web: www.latimes.com/socal/hb-independent

Elk Grove Citizen 8970 Elk Grove Blvd ... Elk Grove CA 95624 916-685-3945
Web: www.egcitizen.com

Gardena Valley News 15005 S Vermont Ave ... Gardena CA 90247 310-329-6351 329-7501
TF: 800-329-6351 ■ *Web:* gvnoffset.com

Burbank Leader 111 W Wilson Ave ... Glendale CA 91203 818-637-3200 241-1975
Web: www.latimes.com/socal/burbank-leader

Hesperia Resorter PO Box 400937 ... Hesperia CA 92345 760-244-0021 244-6609
Web: www.valleywidenewspaper.com

Independent, The 2250 First St ... Livermore CA 94550 925-447-8700 447-0212
TF: 877-952-3588 ■ *Web:* www.independentnews.com

Los Altos Town Crier 138 Main St ... Los Altos CA 94022 650-948-9000 948-6647
Web: losaltosonline.com

Los Angeles Downtown News
1264 W First St ... Los Angeles CA 90026 213-481-1448 250-4617
TF: 877-338-1010 ■ *Web:* www.ladowntownnews.com

Mammoth Times, The PO Box 3929 ... Mammoth Lakes CA 93546 760-934-3929 934-3951
TF: 800-427-7623 ■ *Web:* www.mammothtimes.com

Argonaut, The PO Box 11209 ... Marina del Rey CA 90295 310-822-1629
Web: argonautnews.com

Almanac, The 3525 Alameda De Las Pulgas ... Menlo Park CA 94025 650-854-2626 854-0677
Web: www.almanacnews.com

	City	State	ZIP	Phone	Fax
Milpitas Post 59 Marylinn Dr TF: 800-870-6397 ■ Web: www.mercurynews.com	Milpitas	CA	95035	408-262-2454	263-9710
Bay Area Press 1520 Broadway Web: www.bayarearapidpress.com	Oakland	CA	94612	510-835-2731	
Paradise Post 5399 Clark Rd Web: www.paradisepost.com	Paradise	CA	95969	530-877-4413	877-1326
Paso Robles Press 829 10th St Ste B Web: www.pasoroblespress.com	Paso Robles	CA	93446	805-237-6060	237-6066
Riverside County Record 4080 Lemon St Web: www.countyofriverside.us	Riverside	CA	92501	951-955-1000	
Community Voice PO Box 2038 Web: www.thecommunityvoice.com	Rohnert Park	CA	94927	707-584-2222	
Palos Verdes Peninsula News 609 Deep Valley Dr Ste 200 Web: www.pvnews.com	Rolling Hills Estates	CA	90274	310-372-0388	
Cupertino Courier 1095 The Alameda Web: www.mercurynews.com	San Jose	CA	95126	408-200-1000	200-1013
Sunnyvale Sun 1095 The Alameda Web: www.mercurynews.com	San Jose	CA	95126	408-200-1000	200-1013
Sonoma Index-Tribune PO Box C Web: www.sonomanews.com	Sonoma	CA	95476	707-938-2111	938-1600
Ceres Courier 138 S Center St Web: cerescourier.com	Turlock	CA	95380	209-537-5032	537-0543
Glendora Highlander Press 1210 N Azusa Canyon Rd TF: 800-788-1200 ■ Web: sgvtribune.com/highlanders	West Covina	CA	91790	626-962-8811	

Colorado

	City	State	ZIP	Phone	Fax
Aurora Sentinel 14305 E Alameda Ave Ste 200 TF: 855-269-4484 ■ Web: www.aurorasentinel.com	Aurora	CO	80012	303-750-7555	750-7699
Eagle Valley Enterprise 108 W Second St Web: www.vaildaily.com	Eagle	CO	81631	970-328-6656	328-6393

Connecticut

	City	State	ZIP	Phone	Fax
Hartford News 563 Franklin Ave	Hartford	CT	06114	860-296-6128	296-3350
Bridgeport News 1000 Bridgeport Ave TF Advestisement: 855-247-8573 ■ Web: thebridgeportnews.com	Shelton	CT	06484	203-926-2080	
Milford Mirror 1000 Bridgeport Ave TF Advestisement: 800-372-2790 ■ Web: www.milfordmirror.com	Shelton	CT	06484	203-402-2315	
Stratford Star 1000 Bridgeport Ave TF Advestisement: 800-372-2790 ■ Web: www.stratfordstar.com	Shelton	CT	06484	203-402-2319	926-2091
Voices PO Box 383 Web: www.voicesnews.com	Southbury	CT	06488	203-262-6631	262-6665
Reminder, The PO Box 210 TF: 888-456-2211 ■ Web: courant.com/reminder-news	Vernon	CT	06066	860-875-3366	
Westport Minuteman 1775 Post Rd E Web: minutemannewscenter.com	Westport	CT	06880	203-752-2711	

Delaware

	City	State	ZIP	Phone	Fax
Dover Post 1196 S Little Creek Rd TF: 800-942-1616 ■ Web: www.doverpost.com	Dover	DE	19901	302-678-3616	
Cape Gazette 17585 Nassau Commons Blvd PO Box 213 Web: capegazette.villagesoup.com	Lewes	DE	19958	302-645-7700	645-1664
Dialog, The 1925 Delaware Ave TF: 877-225-7870 ■ Web: www.cdow.org	Wilmington	DE	19806	302-573-3109	573-6948

Florida

	City	State	ZIP	Phone	Fax
Bonita Banner PO Box 40 Web: www.naplesnews.com	Bonita Springs	FL	34133	239-213-6000	
Hernando Today 15299 Cortez Blvd Web: www.hernandotoday.com	Brooksville	FL	34613	352-544-5200	799-5246
Observer Newspaper 201 N Federal Hwy Ste 103 Web: observernewspaperonline.com	Deerfield Beach	FL	33441	954-428-9045	428-9096
Clay Today 3513 US Hwy 17 TF: 888-434-9844 ■ Web: www.claytodayonline.com	Fleming Island	FL	32003	904-264-3200	
Osceola News-Gazette 108 Church St *Fax Area Code: 321 ■ TF: 866-354-2637 ■ Web: www.aroundosceola.com	Kissimmee	FL	34741	407-846-7600	402-2946*
Lake Worth Herald/Coastal Observer 130 S 'H' St Web: www.lwherald.com	Lake Worth	FL	33460	561-585-9387	
Longboat Observer 5570 Gulf of Mexico Dr Web: www.yourobserver.com	Longboat Key	FL	34228	941-383-5509	
Miami Today 710 Brickell Ave TF: 800-283-2707 ■ Web: www.miamitodaynews.com	Miami	FL	33131	305-358-2663	358-4811
Pelican Press 5011 Ocean Blvd Ste 206 Web: www.yourobserver.com	Sarasota	FL	34242	941-349-4949	
News-Sun 2227 US 27 S Web: www.newssun.com	Sebring	FL	33870	863-385-6155	385-1954
Kendall News Gazette 6796 SW 62nd Ave Web: www.communitynewspapers.com	South Miami	FL	33143	305-669-7355	
Carrollwood News 1000 N Ashley Drive, 7th Fl	Tampa	FL	33602	813-259-8295	249-5316
Daily Sun 1100 Main St Web: www.thevillagesdailysun.com	The Villages	FL	32159	352-753-1119	
Venice Gondolier Sun 200 E Venice Ave Web: www.venicegondoliersun.com	Venice	FL	34285	941-207-1000	

Georgia

	City	State	ZIP	Phone	Fax
Revue & News, The 319 N Main St TF: 800-342-9819 ■ Web: www.northfulton.com	Alpharetta	GA	30004	770-442-3278	475-1216
Northside Neighbor & Sandy Springs Neighbor 5290 Roswell Rd NW Ste M Web: www.mdjonline.com/neighbor_newspapers	Atlanta	GA	30342	404-256-3100	256-3292
Crier Newspapers LLC 5064 Nandina Ln Ste C Web: www.thecrier.net	Dunwoody	GA	30338	770-451-4147	451-4223
Clayton Neighbor 5442 Frontage Rd Ste 130 Web: www.mdjonline.com/neighbor_newspapers	Forest Park	GA	30297	404-363-8484	363-0212
Barrow County News 189 W Athens St Ste 22 Web: www.barrowcountynews.com	Winder	GA	30680	770-867-7557	867-1034

Illinois

	City	State	ZIP	Phone	Fax
Times Record 219 S College Ave TF: 800-784-6776 ■ Web: www.aledotimesrecord.com	Aledo	IL	61231	309-582-5112	
Herald/Country Market 500 Brown Blvd Web: www.bbherald.com	Bourbonnais	IL	60914	815-933-1131	933-3785
Bridgeport News 3506 S Halsted st TF: 877-828-3838 ■ Web: www.bridgeportnews.net	Chicago	IL	60609	773-927-0025	
Inside Publications 6221 N Clark St 2nd Fl Web: www.insideonline.com	Chicago	IL	60618	773-465-9700	465-9800
Des Plaines Journal 622 Graceland Ave Web: www.journal-topics.com	Des Plaines	IL	60016	847-299-5511	298-8549
MySuburbanLife.com 1101 W 31st St Ste 100 Web: www.mysuburbanlife.com	Downers Grove	IL	60515	630-368-1100	969-0228
Galena Gazette 716 S Bench St TF: 800-373-6397 ■ Web: www.galenagazette.com	Galena	IL	61036	815-777-0019	777-3809
Lombardian 116 S Main St Web: lombardian.info	Lombard	IL	60148	630-627-7010	627-7027
Regional Publishing Corp, The 12243 S Harlem Ave Web: regionalpublishing.com	Palos Heights	IL	60463	708-448-4000	
Chicago Tribune 6901 W 159th St TF: 800-874-2863 ■ Web: www.chicagotribune.com	Tinley Park	IL	60477	312-222-3232	
Washington Courier 100 Ford Ln Web: www.courierpapers.com	Washington	IL	61571	309-444-3139	

Indiana

	City	State	ZIP	Phone	Fax
Hendricks County Flyer 8109 Kingston St Ste 500 TF: 800-359-3747 ■ Web: www.flyergroup.com	Avon	IN	46123	317-272-5800	272-5887
Westside Community News 608 S Vine St	Indianapolis	IN	46241	317-241-7363	240-6397*
Papers, The 206 S Main St PO Box 188 TF: 800-733-4111 ■ Web: www.the-papers.com	Milford	IN	46542	574-658-4111	658-4701
Banner-Gazette 490 E State Rd 60 PO Box 38 TF: 800-889-3390 ■ Web: www.gbpnews.com	Pekin	IN	47165	812-967-3176	967-3194
Giveaway, The 183 E McClain St Web: www.gbpnews.com	Scottsburg	IN	47170	812-752-3171	

Kentucky

	City	State	ZIP	Phone	Fax
West Kentucky News 1540 McCracken Blvd Web: www.ky-news.com	Paducah	KY	42001	270-442-7389	442-5220

Louisiana

	City	State	ZIP	Phone	Fax
Bossier Press Tribune 4250 Viking Dr Web: www.bossierpress.com	Bossier City	LA	71111	318-747-7900	747-5298
Times of Acadiana 1100 Bertrand Dr TF: 877-289-2216 ■ Web: www.theadvertiser.com	Lafayette	LA	70506	337-289-6300	
Avoyelles Journal 105 N Main St TF: 800-565-4321 ■ Web: avoyellestoday.com	Marksville	LA	71351	318-253-5413	253-7223
Ouachita Citizen 4423 Cypress St Web: hannapub.com/ouachitacitizen	West Monroe	LA	71291	318-322-3161	

Maine

	City	State	ZIP	Phone	Fax
Coastal Journal 97 Commercial St TF: 800-649-6241 ■ Web: www.coastaljournal.com	Bath	ME	04530	207-443-6241	
Biddeford-Saco-OOB Courier 180 Main St Web: www.biddefordsacooobcourier.com	Biddeford	ME	04005	207-282-4337	
Forecaster, The 5 Fundy Rd Web: www.theforecaster.net	Falmouth	ME	04105	207-781-3661	781-2060

Maryland

	City	State	ZIP	Phone	Fax
Maryland Gazette 2000 Capital Dr Web: www.capitalgazette.com	Annapolis	MD	21401	410-268-5000	268-4643
Baltimore Times 2513 N Charles St TF: 800-944-7403 ■ Web: baltimoretimes-online.com	Baltimore	MD	21218	410-366-3900	243-1627
Dundalk Eagle PO Box 8936 Web: www.dundalkeagle.com	Dundalk	MD	21222	410-288-6060	288-6963
Maryland Beachcomber 12417 Ocean Gateway Ste A-7 Web: www.mddcpress.com	Ocean City	MD	21842	410-213-9442	

Michigan

	City	State	ZIP	Phone	Fax
Camden Publications 331 E Bell St TF: 800-222-6336 ■ Web: www.farmersadvance.com	Camden	MI	49232	517-368-0365	368-5131
Cedar Springs Post 36 E Maple PO Box 370 TF: 888-937-4514 ■ Web: www.cedarspringspost.com	Cedar Springs	MI	49319	616-696-3655	696-9010

				Phone	Fax
Dearborn Times-Herald 13730 Michigan Ave *TF:* 866-468-7630 ■ *Web:* downriversundaytimes.com	Dearborn	MI	48126	313-584-4000	584-1357
Grosse Pointe News 96 Kercheval Ave *Web:* www.grossepointenews.com	Grosse Pointe Farms	MI	48236	313-882-6900	882-1585
Ada/Cascade/Forest Hills Advance PO Box 9 *TF:* 800-439-0960 ■ *Web:* www.advancenewspapers.com	Jenison	MI	49429	616-669-2700	
Advance Newspaper PO Box 9 *Web:* www.advancenewspapers.com	Jenison	MI	49429	616-669-2700	
Grand Valley Advance PO Box 9 *Web:* www.advancenewspapers.com	Jenison	MI	49428	616-669-2700	
Walker/Westside Advance PO Box 9 *Web:* www.advancenewspapers.com	Jenison	MI	49429	616-669-2700	
Wyoming Advance PO Box 9 *Web:* www.advancenewspapers.com	Jenison	MI	49429	616-669-2700	
County Press PO Box 220 *Web:* thecountypress.mihomepaper.com	Lapeer	MI	48446	810-664-0811	664-5852
Voice, The 51180 Bedford St *TF:* 800-561-2248 ■ *Web:* www.voicenews.com	New Baltimore	MI	48047	586-716-8100	716-8533
Advisor & Source Newspapers 48075 Van Dyke Ave *TF:* 800-252-7345 ■ *Web:* www.sourcenewspapers.com	Shelby Township	MI	48317	586-731-1000	
News-Herald 1 Heritage Dr Ste 100 *Web:* www.thenewsherald.com	Southgate	MI	48195	734-246-0800	246-2727

Minnesota

				Phone	Fax
Proctor Journal 215 E Fifth St *Web:* www.proctorjournal.com	Duluth	MN	55805	218-624-3344	
Morrison County Record 216 SE First St *TF:* 888-637-2345 ■ *Web:* www.mcrecord.com	Little Falls	MN	56345	320-632-2345	632-2348
Southwest Journal 1115 Hennepin Ave S *Web:* southwestjournal.com	Minneapolis	MN	55403	612-825-9205	
Plainview News 409 W Broadway	Plainview	MN	55964	507-534-3121	534-3920
Northern Watch 324 Main Ave N *Web:* www.trftimes.com	Thief River Falls	MN	56701	218-681-4450	

Missouri

				Phone	Fax
Bethany Republican-Clipper 202 N 16 St *Web:* www.bethanyclipper.com	Bethany	MO	64424	660-425-6325	425-3441
News Democrat Journal 14522 S Outer 40 Rd *Web:* www.stltoday.com	Chesterfield	MO	63017	636-296-1800	
Press Journal 14522 S Outer 40 Dr	Chesterfield	MO	63017	314-821-1110	
Farmington Press 218 N Washington St *TF:* 800-455-0206 ■ *Web:* dailyjournalonline.com	Farmington	MO	63640	573-756-8927	756-9160
Jefferson County Journal 1405 N Truman Blvd *TF:* 800-365-0820 ■ *Web:* www.stltoday.com	Festus	MO	63028	636-937-9811	931-2638
Liberty Tribune 104 N Main St *Web:* www.libertytribune.com	Liberty	MO	64068	816-781-4941	781-0909
Washington Missourian 14 W Main St PO Box 336 *TF:* 888-239-7701 ■ *Web:* www.emissourian.com	Washington	MO	63090	636-239-7701	239-0915

Montana

				Phone	Fax
Billings Times 2919 Montana Ave *Web:* billingstimes.net	Billings	MT	59101	406-245-4994	245-5115

Nebraska

				Phone	Fax
Bellevue Leader 604 Fort Crook Rd N *TF:* 800-284-6397 ■ *Web:* www.omaha.com	Bellevue	NE	68005	402-733-7300	733-9116
West Nebraska Register PO Box 608 *TF:* 800-652-2229 ■ *Web:* www.gidiocese.org	Grand Island	NE	68802	308-382-4660	382-6569

Nevada

				Phone	Fax
Ely Times 515 Murry St PO Box 150820 *Web:* www.elynews.com	Ely	NV	89315	775-289-4491	289-4566

New Jersey

				Phone	Fax
Suburbanite 210 Knickerbocker Rd 2nd Fl	Cresskill	NJ	07626	201-894-6700	568-4360
Twin-Boro News 210 Knickerbocker Rd *TF:* 888-473-2673	Cresskill	NJ	07626	201-894-6715	457-2520
Hunterdon County Democrat 8 Minneakoning Rd *TF:* 888-782-7533 ■ *Web:* www.nj.com	Flemington	NJ	08822	908-782-4747	782-6572
Sentinel, The 198 Rte 9 N Ste 100 *Web:* www.gmnews.com	Manalapan	NJ	07726	732-358-5200	780-4192
Central Record PO Box 1027 *Web:* southjerseylocalnews.com	Medford	NJ	08055	609-654-5000	
Reminder Newspaper 2 W Vine St PO Box 1600 *Web:* reminderusa.net	Millville	NJ	08332	856-825-8811	825-0011
Town Topics 305 Witherspoon St *Web:* www.towntopics.com	Princeton	NJ	08542	609-924-2200	924-8818
Two River Times 46 Newman Springs Rd E *Web:* tworivertimes.com	Red Bank	NJ	07701	732-219-5788	747-7213
Cape May County Herald 1508 Rt 47	Rio Grande	NJ	08242	609-886-8600	886-1879
Community Life 372 Kinderkamack Rd	Westwood	NJ	07675	201-664-2501	664-1332

New Mexico

				Phone	Fax
Las Cruces Bulletin 840 N Telshor Blvd Ste E *Web:* www.lascrucesbulletin.com	Las Cruces	NM	88011	575-524-8061	526-4621

New York

				Phone	Fax
Queens Courier 38-15 Bell Blvd *TF:* 800-275-8777 ■ *Web:* qns.com	Bayside	NY	11361	718-224-5863	224-5441
Chronicle, The 15 Ridge St *Web:* glensfallschronicle.com	Glens Falls	NY	12801	518-792-1126	793-1587
Forum South 155-19 Lahn St *Web:* www.theforumnewsgroup.com	Howard Beach	NY	11414	718-845-3221	
New York Observer 915 Broadway 9th Fl *Web:* www.observer.com	New York	NY	10010	212-755-2400	
People's Weekly World 235 W 23rd St *Web:* www.peoplesworld.org	New York	NY	10011	212-924-2523	229-1713
Queens Tribune 150-50 14th Rd *Web:* www.queenstribune.com	New York	NY	11357	718-357-7400	357-9417
Villager, The 145 Sixth Ave 1st Fl *Web:* www.thevillager.com	New York	NY	10013	212-229-1890	229-2790
Our Town 36 Ridge St *Web:* ourtownnews.com	Pearl River	NY	10965	845-735-1342	620-9533
Times Newsweekly PO Box 860299 *Web:* www.timesnewsweekly.com	Ridgewood	NY	11386	718-821-7500	456-0120
Suburban News 1776 Hilton Palmar Corners Rd	Spencerport	NY	14559	585-352-3411	352-4811
Southern Duchess News 84 E Main St *Web:* sdutchessnews.com	Wappingers Falls	NY	12590	845-297-3723	297-6810

North Carolina

				Phone	Fax
Mountain Times PO Box 1815 *Web:* www.wataugademocrat.com/mountaintimes	Boone	NC	28607	828-264-6397	262-0282
Journal-Patriot PO Box 70 *Web:* journalpatriot.com	North Wilkesboro	NC	28659	336-838-4117	838-9864
Pilot, The PO Box 58 *Web:* www.thepilot.com	Southern Pines	NC	28388	910-692-7271	692-9382

North Dakota

				Phone	Fax
West Fargo Pioneer 101 5th St N *TF:* 888-382-1222 ■ *Web:* www.westfargopioneer.com	West Fargo	ND	58078	701-451-5718	282-9248
Plains Reporter PO Box 1447 *TF:* 800-950-2165 ■ *Web:* www.willistonherald.com	Williston	ND	58802	701-572-2165	572-9563

Ohio

				Phone	Fax
Sun Messenger 5510 Cloverleaf Pkwy *Web:* www.cleveland.com/sunmessenger	Cleveland	OH	44125	216-986-2600	
Sun Press 5510 Cloverleaf Pkwy *Web:* www.cleveland.com/sunpress	Cleveland	OH	44125	216-986-2600	
Rural-Urban Record 24487 Squire Rd	Columbia Station	OH	44028	440-236-8982	236-9198
Early Bird, The 5312 Sebring Warner Rd *TF:* 866-627-4557 ■ *Web:* earlybirdpaper.com	Greenville	OH	45331	937-548-3330	547-2292
Cuyahoga Falls News-Press 1050 W Main St PO Box 5199 *TF:* 800-560-9657 ■ *Web:* www.recordpub.com	Kent	OH	44240	330-541-9421	
Gateway News 1050 West Main St *TF:* 800-560-9657 ■ *Web:* www.recordpub.com	Kent	OH	44240	330-541-9400	296-2698
Today's Pulse 200 Harmon Ave *Web:* www.todayspulse.com	Lebanon	OH	45036	513-696-4520	932-6056
Delaware This Week 7801 N Central Dr *Web:* www.thisweeknews.com	Lewis Center	OH	43035	740-888-6100	888-6006
Dublin Villager 7801 N Central Dr *TF:* 866-790-4502 ■ *Web:* www.thisweeknews.com	Lewis Center	OH	43035	740-888-6100	888-6006
Hilliard This Week 7801 N Central Dr *TF:* 888-837-4342 ■ *Web:* www.thisweeknews.com	Lewis Center	OH	43035	740-888-6100	888-6006
Reynoldsburg This Week 7801 N Central Dr *TF:* 888-837-4342 ■ *Web:* www.thisweeknews.com	Lewis Center	OH	43035	740-888-6100	888-6006
Southside This Week 7801 N Central Dr *Web:* www.thisweeknews.com	Lewis Center	OH	43035	740-888-6100	888-6006
This Week in Upper Arlington 7801 N Central Dr *Web:* www.thisweeknews.com	Lewis Center	OH	43035	740-888-6100	888-6006
Upper Arlington News 7801 N Central Dr **Fax:* Edit ■ *TF:* 800-860-1267 ■ *Web:* www.thisweeknews.com	Lewis Center	OH	43035	740-888-6000	888-6001*
Westerville This Week 7801 N Central Dr *TF:* 888-837-4342 ■ *Web:* www.thisweeknews.com	Lewis Center	OH	43035	740-888-6100	888-6006
Worthington This Week 7801 N Central Dr *Web:* www.thisweeknews.com	Lewis Center	OH	43035	740-888-6100	888-6006
Fairfield Echo 7320 Yankee Rd *Web:* www.todayspulse.com	Liberty Township	OH	45044	513-755-5060	
Pulse-Journal 7320 Yankee Rd *Web:* www.todayspulse.com	Liberty Township	OH	45044	513-755-5060	
Forest Hills Journal 394 WaRds Corner Rd Ste 170 **Fax Area Code:* 212 ■ *TF:* 888-894-2113	Loveland	OH	45140	513-248-8600	688-7444*
Suburban Press & Metro Press 1550 Woodville Rd *TF:* 800-300-6158 ■ *Web:* www.presspublications.com	Millbury	OH	43447	419-836-2221	836-1319
Beacon, The 205 SE Catawba Rd Ste G *Web:* www.thebeacon.net	Port Clinton	OH	43452	419-732-2154	734-5382

	City	State	ZIP	Phone	Fax
Budget, The 134 N Factory St PO Box 249 *Web:* www.thebudgetnewspaper.com	Sugarcreek	OH	44681	330-852-4634	852-4421
Boardman Town Crier 240 Franklin St SE *Web:* www.towncrieronline.com	Warren	OH	44483	330-629-6200	629-6210
Star-Republican 47 S S St	Wilmington	OH	45177	937-382-7796	382-4392

Oregon

	City	State	ZIP	Phone	Fax
Hillsboro Argus 1500 SW First Ave *Web:* www.oregonlive.com	Portland	OR	97201	503-648-1131	648-9191
Woodburn Independent 650 N First St *Web:* www.pamplinmedia.com	Woodburn	OR	97071	503-981-3441	

Pennsylvania

	City	State	ZIP	Phone	Fax
Lancaster Farming PO Box 609 *Web:* www.lancasterfarming.com	Ephrata	PA	17522	717-626-1164	733-6058
Progress of Montgomery County PO Box 311 *Web:* www.montcopa.org	Norristown	PA	19044	610-278-3061	
Almanac, The 2600 Boyce Plz Rd Ste 142 **Fax:* Edit ■ *TF:* 800-222-6397 ■ *Web:* www.thealmanac.net	Pittsburgh	PA	15241	724-941-7725	941-8685*
Northeast Times 2512 Metropolitan Dr *Web:* www.northeasttimes.com	Trevose	PA	19053	215-354-3040	
York Sunday News 1891 Loucks Rd *TF:* 888-629-4095 ■ *Web:* www.ydr.com	York	PA	17408	717-767-6397	771-2009

Rhode Island

	City	State	ZIP	Phone	Fax
Newport Mercury 101 Malbone Rd *Web:* www.newportri.com	Newport	RI	02840	401-380-2371	
Newport This Week 86 Broadway *Web:* www.newportchamber.com	Newport	RI	02840	401-847-7766	846-4974

South Carolina

	City	State	ZIP	Phone	Fax
Bluffton Today 52 Persimmon St *TF:* 855-665-8549 ■ *Web:* blufftontoday.com	Bluffton	SC	29910	843-815-0800	815-0898
Chronicle Independent 909 W Dekalb St *TF General:* 800-922-5431 ■ *Web:* www.chronicle-independent.com	Camden	SC	29020	803-432-6157	432-7609
Moultrie News 134 Columbus St *Web:* www.moultrienews.com	Charleston	SC	29403	843-958-7489	
Georgetown Times 615 Front St *TF:* 800-772-1213 ■ *Web:* www.southstrandnews.com	Georgetown	SC	29440	843-546-4148	264-5511
Myrtle Beach Herald 4761 US 501	Myrtle Beach	SC	29579	843-626-3131	
Star, The 404 E Martintown Rd Ste 2 *TF:* 888-397-3742 ■ *Web:* www.northaugustastar.com	North Augusta	SC	29841	803-279-2793	278-4070

Tennessee

	City	State	ZIP	Phone	Fax
Dickson Herald PO Box 387 *Web:* www.tennessean.com	Ashland City	TN	37015	615-446-2811	
Farragutpress 11863 Kingston Pike *Web:* www.farragutpress.com	Knoxville	TN	37934	865-675-6397	675-1675

Texas

	City	State	ZIP	Phone	Fax
Preston Hollow People 750 N St Paul St Ste 2100 *Web:* www.prestonhollowpeople.com	Dallas	TX	75201	214-739-2244	
Houston Forward Times 4411 ALMEDA	Houston	TX	77004	713-526-4727	526-3170
Leader Newspapers 3500 T C Jester Blvd PO Box 924487 *Web:* theleadernews.com	Houston	TX	77292	713-686-8494	686-0970
Pearland Journal 650 FM 1959 *Web:* www.yourhoustonnews.com/pearland	Houston	TX	77034	281-674-1340	922-4499
Humble Observer 907 E Main St Ste B *Web:* www.yourhoustonnews.com	Humble	TX	77338	281-446-4438	964-4423
Hardin County News PO Box 8240 *Web:* www.beaumontenterprise.com	Lumberton	TX	77657	409-755-4912	755-7731
Valley Town Crier 1811 N 23rd St *TF:* 800-621-3362 ■ *Web:* www.yourvalleyvoice.com	McAllen	TX	78501	956-682-2423	

Utah

	City	State	ZIP	Phone	Fax
Millard County Chronicle Progress 40 North 300 West *Web:* millardccp.com	Delta	UT	84624	435-864-2400	

Vermont

	City	State	ZIP	Phone	Fax
World, The 403 US Rt 302-Berlin *TF:* 800-639-9753 ■ *Web:* www.vt-world.com	Barre	VT	05641	802-479-2582	

Virginia

	City	State	ZIP	Phone	Fax
Arlington Connection 1606 King St *Web:* www.connectionnewspapers.com	Alexandria	VA	22314	703-778-9410	
Loudoun Times-Mirror PO Box 359 *TF:* 888-351-1660 ■ *Web:* www.northernvatimes.com	Leesburg	VA	20178	703-777-1111	771-0036
Mechanicsville Local 6400 Mechanicsville Tpke *TF:* 800-468-3382 ■ *Web:* www.richmond.com	Mechanicsville	VA	23111	804-746-1235	730-0476
Fairfax County Times 1920 Association Dr Ste 500 *Web:* www.fairfaxtimes.com	Reston	VA	20191	703-437-5400	
Fauquier Times-Democrat 39 Culpeper St *TF:* 888-351-1660 ■ *Web:* www.fauquier.com	Warrenton	VA	20186	540-347-4222	349-8676
Virginia Gazette 216 Ironbound Rd *Web:* www.vagazette.com	Williamsburg	VA	23188	757-220-1736	220-1665

Washington

	City	State	ZIP	Phone	Fax
Reflector, The PO Box 2020 *Web:* www.thereflector.com	Battle Ground	WA	98604	360-687-5151	687-5162
Dispatch, The PO Box 248 *Web:* www.dispatchnews.com	Eatonville	WA	98328	360-832-4411	
Journal of the San Juan Islands PO Box 519 *Web:* www.sanjuanjournal.com	Friday Harbor	WA	98250	360-378-5696	
Issaquah Press PO Box 1328 *Web:* www.theeastside.news/issaquah	Issaquah	WA	98027	425-392-6434	391-1541
Bothell/Kenmore Reporter 11630 Slater Ave NE Stes 8-9 *Web:* www.bothell-reporter.com	Kirkland	WA	98034	425-483-3732	
Port Orchard Independent PO Box 27 *Web:* www.portorchardindependent.com	Port Orchard	WA	98366	360-876-4414	876-4458
Capitol Hill Times 4000 Aurora Ave N Ste 100 *Web:* www.pacificpublishingcompany.com	Seattle	WA	98103	206-461-1300	
Tribune Newspapers of Snohomish County 127 Ave C Ste B PO Box 499 *TF:* 877-894-4663 ■ *Web:* www.snoho.com	Snohomish	WA	98291	360-568-4121	568-1484

West Virginia

	City	State	ZIP	Phone	Fax
Coal Valley News 475 Main St *Web:* www.coalvalleynews.com	Madison	WV	25130	304-369-1165	369-1166

Wisconsin

	City	State	ZIP	Phone	Fax
Country Today 701 S Farwell St *Web:* www.thecountrytoday.com	Eau Claire	WI	54701	715-833-9270	
Foto News 807 E First St *Web:* www.merrillfotonews.com	Merrill	WI	54452	715-536-7121	
Milwaukee Courier 6310 N Port Washington Rd *Web:* milwaukeecourieronline.com	Milwaukee	WI	53217	414-449-4860	906-5383

Wyoming

	City	State	ZIP	Phone	Fax
Jackson Hole News & Guide 1225 Maple Way *Web:* jhnewsandguide.com	Jackson	WY	83001	307-733-2047	733-2138

532-5 Weekly Newspapers - Alternative

	City	State	ZIP	Phone	Fax
Ace Weekly 185 Jefferson *Web:* www.aceweekly.com	Lexington	KY	40508	859-225-4889	
Alabama Rivers Alliance 2014 Sixth Ave N Ste 200 *Web:* alabamarivers.org	Birmingham	AL	35203	205-322-6395	
Arkansas Times 201 E Markham Ste 200 *Web:* www.arktimes.com	Little Rock	AR	72201	501-375-2985	375-3623
ArtVoice 810 Main St *Web:* www.artvoice.com	Buffalo	NY	14202	716-881-6604	881-6682
Austin Chronicle PO Box 49066 *TF:* 866-271-4900 ■ *Web:* www.austinchronicle.com	Austin	TX	78765	512-454-5766	458-6910
Baltimore City Paper 812 Pk Ave *Web:* citypaper.com	Baltimore	MD	21201	410-523-2300	523-2222
Boise Weekly 523 Broad St *Web:* www.boiseweekly.com	Boise	ID	83702	208-344-2055	342-4733
Boston Phoenix, The 126 Brookline Ave **Fax:* Advertising ■ *Web:* thephoenix.com	Boston	MA	02215	617-536-5390	536-1463*
Bostons Weekly Dig 242 E Berkeley St 5th Fl *Web:* digboston.com	Boston	MA	02118	617-426-8942	426-8942
Boulder Weekly 690 S Lashley Ln *Web:* boulderweekly.com	Boulder	CO	80305	303-494-5511	494-2585
C-Ville Weekly 106 E Main St *Web:* www.c-ville.com	Charlottesville	VA	22902	434-817-2749	817-2758
Charleston City Paper 1049 Morrison Dr # B *Web:* www.charlestoncitypaper.com	Charleston	SC	29403	843-577-5304	576-0380
Chicago Reader 11 E Illinois St *TF:* 888-473-5362 ■ *Web:* www.chicagoreader.com	Chicago	IL	60611	312-828-0350	828-9926
Chico News & Review 353 E Second St *TF:* 866-703-3873 ■ *Web:* www.newsreview.com	Chico	CA	95928	530-894-2300	894-0143
Cincinnati CityBeat 811 Race St	Cincinnati	OH	45202	513-665-4700	665-4368
City Newspaper 250 N Goodman St *Web:* www.rochestercitynewspaper.com	Rochester	NY	14607	585-244-3329	244-1126
City Pages 300 Third St PO Box 942 *Web:* www.thecitypages.com	Wausau	WI	54402	715-845-5171	848-5887
Cityview 414 61st St *Web:* www.dmcityview.com	Des Moines	IA	50312	515-953-4822	953-1394
Colorado Springs Independent 235 S Nevada Ave *Web:* www.csindy.com	Colorado Springs	CO	80903	719-577-4545	577-4107

				Phone	Fax
Columbus Alive 34 S Third St *Web:* www.columbusalive.com	Columbus	OH	43215	614-221-2449	461-8746
Creative Loafing Atlanta 384 Northyards Blvd Ste 600 *TF:* 888-242-0208 ■ *Web:* clatl.com	Atlanta	GA	30313	404-688-5623	614-3599
Creative Loafing Tampa 1911 N 13th St Ste W200 *Web:* www.cltampa.com	Tampa	FL	33605	813-739-4800	739-4801
Dallas Observer 2501 Oak Lawn Ave Ste 700 PO Box 190289 *Web:* www.dallasobserver.com	Dallas	TX	75219	214-757-9000	757-8590
Dayton City Paper 126 N Main St Ste 240 *TF:* 888-228-3630 ■ *Web:* www.daytoncitypaper.com	Dayton	OH	45402	937-222-8855	222-6113
East Bay Express 1335 Stanford Ave Ste 100 *Web:* www.eastbayexpress.com	Emeryville	CA	94608	510-879-3700	879-3794
Eugene Weekly 1251 Lincoln St *Web:* www.eugeneweekly.com	Eugene	OR	97401	541-484-0519	484-4044
Flagpole PO Box 1027 *Web:* www.flagpole.com	Athens	GA	30603	706-549-9523	548-8981
Folio Weekly 45 W Bay St Ste 103 *Web:* www.folioweekly.com	Jacksonville	FL	32202	904-260-9770	260-9773
Fort Worth Weekly 3311 Hamilton Ave *Web:* www.fwweekly.com	Fort Worth	TX	76107	817-321-9700	335-9575
Gambit Weekly 3923 Bienville St *Web:* www.bestofneworleans.com	New Orleans	LA	70119	504-486-5900	483-3116
Georgia Straight 1701 W Broadway *Web:* www.straight.com	Vancouver	BC	V6J1Y3	604-730-7000	730-7010
Honolulu Weekly 1111 Ford St Mall *Web:* www.honoluluweekly.com	Honolulu	HI	96813	808-528-1475	
Houston Press 1621 Milam St Ste 100 *TF:* 877-926-8300 ■ *Web:* www.houstonpress.com	Houston	TX	77002	713-280-2400	280-2444
Independent Weekly PO Box 2690 *Web:* www.indyweek.com	Durham	NC	27715	919-286-1972	286-4274
Isthmus Publishing Company Inc 101 King St *Web:* isthmus.com	Madison	WI	53703	608-251-5627	251-2165
Ithaca Times 109 N Cayuga St *Web:* www.ithaca.com	Ithaca	NY	14850	607-277-7000	277-1012
LA Weekly 6715 Sunset Blvd *Fax Area Code: 323 ■ *TF:* 866-789-6188 ■ *Web:* www.laweekly.com	Los Angeles	CA	90028	866-789-6188	465-3220*
Long Island Press 575 Underhill Blvd Ste 210 *TF:* 800-545-6683 ■ *Web:* www.longislandpress.com	Syosset	NY	11791	516-284-3300	284-3310
Louisville Eccentric Observer 607 W. Main St Ste 001 *Web:* www.leoweekly.com	Louisville	KY	40202	502-895-9770	895-9779
Maui Time Weekly 33 N Market St Ste 201 *Web:* www.mauitime.com	Wailuku	HI	96793	808-244-0777	244-0446
Memphis Flyer 460 Tennessee St *TF:* 877-292-3804 ■ *Web:* www.memphisflyer.com	Memphis	TN	38103	901-521-9000	521-0129
Metro Pulse 602 S Gay St Ste Mezzanine *TF:* 800-686-4208	Knoxville	TN	37902	865-522-5399	522-2955
Metro Santa Cruz 550 S First St *Web:* www.metroactive.com	San Jose	CA	95113	408-298-8500	
Metro Silicon Valley 550 S First St *Web:* www.metroactive.com	San Jose	CA	95113	408-298-8000	298-0602
Metro Times 733 St Antoine St *TF:* 866-501-3627 ■ *Web:* www.metrotimes.com	Detroit	MI	48226	313-961-4060	961-6598
Metroland 523 Western Ave Ste 1	Albany	NY	12203	518-463-2500	463-3712
Miami New Times 2800 Biscayne Blvd *Web:* www.miaminewtimes.com	Miami	FL	33137	305-576-8000	571-7677
Minneapolis/St. Paul City Pages 401 N Third St Ste 550 *TF:* 844-387-6962 ■ *Web:* www.citypages.com	Minneapolis	MN	55401	612-375-1015	372-3737
Missoula Independent 317 S Orange St *Web:* missoulanews.bigskypress.com	Missoula	MT	59801	406-543-6609	543-4367
Monday Magazine 818 Broughton St *Web:* www.mondaymag.com	Victoria	BC	V8W1E4	250-382-6188	
Monterey County Weekly 668 Williams Ave *Web:* www.montereycountyweekly.com	Seaside	CA	93955	831-394-5656	394-2909
Mountain Xpress 2 Wall St Ste 211 *Web:* www.mountainx.com	Asheville	NC	28801	828-251-1333	251-1311
Nashville Scene 210 12th Ave S Ste 100 *Web:* www.nashvillescene.com	Nashville	TN	37203	615-244-7989	244-8578
New City Communications 770 N Halsted St Ste 303 *Web:* newcity.com	Chicago	IL	60642	312-243-8786	
New Haven Advocate 900 Chapel St Ste 1100 *Web:* www.ct.com	New Haven	CT	06510	203-789-0010	
New Times Broward Palm Beach 16 NE Fourth St *Web:* www.browardpalmbeach.com	Fort Lauderdale	FL	33301	954-233-1600	233-1521
New York Press 333 Seventh Ave 14th Fl *Web:* www.nypress.com	New York	NY	10001	212-244-2282	244-9864
North Bay Bohemian 847 Fifth St *Web:* www.bohemian.com	Santa Rosa	CA	95404	707-527-1200	527-1288
NOW Magazine 189 Church St *Web:* www.nowtoronto.com	Toronto	ON	M5B1Y7	416-364-1300	364-1166
NUVO Newsweekly 3951 N Meridian St Ste 200 *Web:* www.nuvo.net	Indianapolis	IN	46208	317-254-2400	254-2405
OC Weekly 2975 Red Hill Ave Ste 150 *Web:* www.ocweekly.com	Costa Mesa	CA	92626	714-550-5900	550-5908
Oklahoma Gazette 3701 N Shartel Ave *Web:* okgazette.com	Oklahoma City	OK	73118	405-528-6000	528-4600
Orlando Weekly 1505 E Colonial Dr St Ste 200 *TF:* 800-474-7576 ■ *Web:* www.orlandoweekly.com	Orlando	FL	32803	407-377-0400	377-0420
Pacific Northwest Inlander 9 S Washington St *TF:* 888-431-9911 ■ *Web:* www.inlander.com	Spokane	WA	99201	509-325-0634	325-0638
Pacific Sun 1200 Fifth Ave Ste 200 *Web:* www.pacificsun.com	San Rafael	CA	94901	415-485-6700	485-6226
Palo Alto Weekly 450 Cambridge Ave *Web:* www.paloaltoonline.com/weekly	Palo Alto	CA	94306	650-326-8210	326-3928
Pasadena Weekly 50 S Delacey Ave Ste 200 *Web:* www.pasadenaweekly.com	Pasadena	CA	91105	626-584-1500	795-0149
Philadelphia City Paper 123 Chestnut St 3rd Fl *Web:* mycitypaper.com	Philadelphia	PA	19106	215-735-8444	
Phoenix New Times 1201 E Jefferson *Web:* www.phoenixnewtimes.com	Phoenix	AZ	85034	602-271-0040	340-8806
Pitch, The 1701 Main St *Web:* www.pitch.com	Kansas City	MO	64108	816-561-6061	756-0502
Pittsburgh City Paper 650 Smithfield St Ste 2200 *Web:* www.pghcitypaper.com	Pittsburgh	PA	15222	412-316-3342	316-3388
Portland Phoenix 16 York St Ste 102 *Web:* portland.thephoenix.com	Portland	ME	04101	207-773-8900	773-8905
Providence Phoenix 150 Chestnut St *Web:* providence.thephoenix.com	Providence	RI	02903	401-273-6397	273-0920
PW-Philadelphia Weekly 1500 Sansom St 3rd Fl *Web:* www.philadelphiaweekly.com	Philadelphia	PA	19102	215-563-7400	563-0620
Random Lengths News 1300 S Pacific Ave *Web:* www.randomlengthsnews.com	San Pedro	CA	90731	310-519-1442	832-1000
Reader, The 2314 M St PO Box 7360 *Web:* www.thereader.com	Omaha	NE	68107	402-341-7323	341-6967
Reno News & Review 708 N Ctr St *TF:* 866-703-3873 ■ *Web:* www.newsreview.com	Reno	NV	89501	916-498-1234	498-7910
Riverfront Times 6358 Delmar Blvd Ste 200 *Web:* www.riverfronttimes.com	Saint Louis	MO	63130	314-754-5966	754-5955
Sacramento News & Review 1124 Del Paso Blvd *Web:* www.newsreview.com	Sacramento	CA	95815	916-498-1234	498-7920
Salt Lake City Weekly 248 S Main St *Web:* cityweekly.net	Salt Lake City	UT	84101	801-575-7003	575-6106
San Antonio Current 915 Dallas St *Web:* sacurrent.com	San Antonio	TX	78215	210-227-0044	227-6611
San Francisco Bay Guardian 135 Mississippi St *Web:* www.sfbg.com	San Francisco	CA	94107	415-255-3100	
San Luis Obispo New Times 505 Higuera St *TF:* 800-546-4219 ■ *Web:* www.newtimesslo.com	San Luis Obispo	CA	93401	805-546-8208	546-8641
Santa Barbara Independent 122 W Figueroa St *Web:* www.independent.com	Santa Barbara	CA	93101	805-965-5205	965-5518
Santa Fe Reporter 132 E Marcy St *Web:* sfreporter.com	Santa Fe	NM	87501	505-988-5541	988-5348
Scene 1468 W Ninth St Ste 805 *TF:* 877-598-8703 ■ *Web:* www.clevescene.com	Cleveland	OH	44113	216-241-7550	802-7212
Seattle Weekly 1008 Western Ave Ste 300 *Web:* www.seattleweekly.com	Seattle	WA	98104	206-623-0500	467-4338
Seven Days 255 S Champlain St Ste 5 PO Box 1164 *Web:* www.7dvt.com	Burlington	VT	05401	802-864-5684	
SF Weekly 185 Berry St Lbby 4 Ste 3800 *Web:* www.sfweekly.com	San Francisco	CA	94107	415-536-8100	777-1839
Shepherd Express 207 E Buffalo St Ste 410 *Web:* shepherdexpress.com	Milwaukee	WI	53202	414-276-2222	276-3312
Stranger, The 1535 11th Ave 3rd Fl *Web:* www.thestranger.com	Seattle	WA	98122	206-323-7101	323-7203
Style Weekly 1707 Summit Ave Ste 201 *Web:* www.styleweekly.com	Richmond	VA	23230	804-358-0825	358-9089
Syracuse New Times 1415 W Genesee St *Web:* syracusenewtimes.com	Syracuse	NY	13204	315-422-7011	422-1721
Tucson Weekly 3280 E Hemisphere Loop Ste 180 PO Box 27087 *Web:* www.tucsonweekly.com	Tucson	AZ	85706	520-294-1200	792-2096
Ventura County Reporter 700 E Main St *Web:* www.vcreporter.com	Ventura	CA	93001	805-648-2244	648-7801
Washington City Paper 2390 Champlain St NW *Web:* www.washingtoncitypaper.com	Washington	DC	20009	202-332-2100	332-8500
Weekly Alibi 2118 Central Ave SE PO Box 151 *Web:* www.alibi.com	Albuquerque	NM	87106	505-346-0660	256-9651
Westword 969 Broadway *Web:* www.westword.com	Denver	CO	80203	303-296-7744	296-5416
Willamette Week 2220 NW Quimby St *Web:* wweek.com	Portland	OR	97210	503-243-2122	243-1115

533 NURSES ASSOCIATIONS - STATE

See Also Health & Medical Professionals Associations p. 1789

				Phone	Fax
Alabama State Nurses Assn (ASNA) 360 N Hull St *TF:* 800-270-2762 ■ *Web:* www.alabamanurses.org	Montgomery	AL	36104	334-262-8321	262-8578
Alaska Humanities Forum 161 E First Ave *Web:* www.akhf.org	Anchorage	AK	99501	907-272-3979	
Alaska Municipal League Joint Insurance Association 807 G St Ste 356 *TF:* 800-337-3682 ■ *Web:* www.amljia.org	Anchorage	AK	99501	907-258-2625	
Alaska Nurses Assn (AaNA) 3701 E Tudor Rd Ste 208 *Web:* www.aknurse.org	Anchorage	AK	99507	907-274-0827	272-0292
American Nurses Assn California (ANA\C) 1121 L St Ste 409 *Web:* www.anacalifornia.org	Sacramento	CA	95814	916-447-0225	
Arizona Nurses Assn (AzNA) 1850 E Southern Ave Ste 1 *Web:* www.aznurse.org	Tempe	AZ	85282	480-831-0404	839-4780
Arizona Osteopathic Medical Association 5150 N 16th St Ste A122 *TF:* 888-266-6699 ■ *Web:* az-osteo.org	Phoenix	AZ	85016	602-266-6699	
Arkansas Nurses Assn (ARNA) 1123 S University Ste 800 *Web:* www.arna.org	Little Rock	AR	72204	501-244-2363	244-9903

Name / Address	City	State	Zip	Phone	Fax
Art Directors Club Inc 106 W 29th St *Web:* adcglobal.org	New York	NY	10001	212-643-1440	
B Oma Suburban Chicago 1515 E Woodfield Rd Ste 110 *Web:* www.bomasuburbanchicago.com	Schaumburg	IL	60173	847-995-0970	
CAI-CLAC 1809 S St Ste 101-245 *Web:* www.caiclac.com	Sacramento	CA	95811	916-791-4750	
California Nurses Assn (CNA) 2000 Franklin St *Web:* www.nationalnursesunited.org	Oakland	CA	94612	510-273-2200	663-1625
Chester County Bar Association, The 15 W Gay St 2nd Fl *Web:* chescobar.org	West Chester	PA	19380	610-692-1889	
Colorado Nurses Assn (CNA) 2851 S. Parker Rd Ste 1210 *Web:* coloradonurses.org	Aurora	CO	80014	303-597-0128	
Connecticut Nurses Assn (CNA) 377 Research Pkwy Ste 2D *Web:* www.ctnurses.org	Meriden	CT	06450	203-238-1207	238-3437
Council of Ethical Organizations 214 S Payne St *Web:* councilofethicalorganizations.com	Alexandria	VA	22314	703-683-7916	
Dallas County Medical Society 140 E 12th St *Web:* www.dallas-cms.org	Dallas	TX	75203	214-948-3622	
Delaware Nurses Assn (DNA) 4765 Ogletown-Stanton Rd Ste L10 *TF:* 800-626-4081 ■ *Web:* www.denurses.org	Newark	DE	19713	302-733-5880	
Diesel Technology Forum Inc 5291 Corporate Dr Ste 102 *Web:* dieselforum.org	Frederick	MD	21703	301-668-7230	
District of Columbia Nurses Assn (DCNA) 5100 Wisconsin Ave NW Ste 306 *Web:* www.dcna.org	Washington	DC	20016	202-244-2705	362-8285
Employers Group 1150 S Olive St Ste 2300 *Web:* www.employersgroup.com	Los Angeles	CA	90015	213-748-0421	
Federal Hearings & Appeals Services Inc 117 W Main St *TF:* 800-664-7177 ■ *Web:* fhas.com	Plymouth	PA	18651	570-779-5122	
Fine Book Club of Claifornia 312 Sutter St Ste 500 *Web:* www.bccbooks.org	San Francisco	CA	94108	415-781-7532	
Florida Nurses Assn (FNA) 1235 E Concord St PO Box 536985 *Web:* www.floridanurse.org	Orlando	FL	32853	407-896-3261	896-9042
Florida Osteopathic Medical Association District 3 Inc 7855 Argyle Forest Blvd Ste 601 *Web:* www.fomadistrict2.com	Jacksonville	FL	32301	850-878-7364	
Georgia Avenue Rock Creek East Family Support Collaborative 1104 Allison St Nw *Web:* gafsc-dc.org	Washington	DC	20011	202-722-1815	
Georgia Municipal Association 201 Pryor St SW *TF:* 888-488-4462 ■ *Web:* www.gmanet.com	Atlanta	GA	30303	404-688-0472	
Georgia Nurses Assn (GNA) 3032 Briarcliff Rd NE *TF:* 800-324-0462 ■ *Web:* www.georgianurses.org	Atlanta	GA	30329	404-325-5536	325-0407
Girls Inc of Alameda County 13666 E 14th St *Web:* www.girlsinc-alameda.org	San Leandro	CA	94578	510-357-5515	
Hawaii Nurses Assn (HNA) 949 Kapiolani Blvd Ste 107 *TF:* 800-617-2677 ■ *Web:* www.hawaiinurses.org	Honolulu	HI	96814	808-531-1628	524-2760
Hydrocephalus Association 870 Market St Ste 705 *Web:* www.hydroassoc.org	San Francisco	CA	94102	415-732-7040	
Iapp 170 Cider Hill Rd *Web:* iapp.org	York	ME	03909	207-351-1500	
Ichp Building Company LLC 4055 N Perryville Rd *Web:* ichpnet.org	Loves Park	IL	61111	815-227-9292	
Idaho Nurses Assn (INA) 1850 E Southern Ave Ste 1 *Fax Area Code: 404 ■ *TF:* 888-721-8904 ■ *Web:* www.idahonurses.org	Tempe	AZ	85224	888-721-8904	240-0998*
Idaho Primary Care Association Inc 1087 W River St Ste 160 *Web:* www.idahopca.org	Boise	ID	83702	208-345-2335	
Illinois Alcoholism & Drug Dependence Assn 937 S Second St *Web:* iadda.org	Springfield	IL	62704	217-528-7335	
Illinois Health Care Association 1029 S Fourth St *TF:* 800-252-8988 ■ *Web:* www.ihca.com	Springfield	IL	62703	217-528-6455	
Illinois Nurses Assn (INA) 105 W Adams St Ste 2101 *TF:* 800-262-2500 ■ *Web:* www.illinoisnurses.com	Chicago	IL	60603	312-419-2900	419-2920
Illinois Principals Association 2940 Baker Dr *Web:* www.ilprincipals.org	Springfield	IL	62703	217-525-1383	
Indiana Association of School Principals Inc 11025 E 25th St *TF:* 800-285-2188 ■ *Web:* www.iasp.org	Indianapolis	IN	46229	317-891-9900	
Indiana State Nurses Assn (ISNA) 2915 N High School Rd *Web:* www.indiananurses.org	Indianapolis	IN	46224	317-299-4575	297-3525
Iowa Mortgage Association 8800 Nw 62nd Ave *TF:* 800-800-2353 ■ *Web:* www.iowama.org	Johnston	IA	50131	515-286-4352	
Iowa Nurses Assn (INA) 2400 86th St Ste 32 *Web:* www.iowanurses.org	Urbandale	IA	50322	515-225-0495	
Kansas Action for Children Inc 720 Sw Jackson St Ste 201 *Web:* www.kac.org	Topeka	KS	66603	785-232-0550	
Kansas State Nurses Assn (KSNA) 1109 SW Topeka Blvd *Web:* www.ksnurses.com	Topeka	KS	66612	785-233-8638	233-5222
Kentucky Bankers Association 600 W Main St Ste 400 *TF:* 800-392-4045 ■ *Web:* www.kybanks.com	Louisville	KY	40202	502-582-2453	
Kentucky Hospital Association 2501 Nelson Miller Pkwy Ste 200 *TF:* 800-945-4542 ■ *Web:* www.kyha.com	Louisville	KY	40223	502-426-6220	
Lake Mission Viejo Association 22555 Olympiad Rd *Web:* lakemissionviejo.org	Mission Viejo	CA	92692	949-770-1327	
League of Kansas Municipalities 300 Sw Eighth Ave Ste 100 *Web:* lkm.org	Topeka	KS	66603	785-354-9565	
Louisiana State Nurses Assn, The (LSNA) 5713 Superior Dr Ste A-6 *TF:* 800-457-6378 ■ *Web:* www.lsna.org	Baton Rouge	LA	70816	225-201-0993	201-0971
Maine Nurse Practitioners Association 11 Columbia St *Web:* www.mnpa.us	Augusta	ME	04330	207-621-0313	
Maine State Nurses Assn (MSNA) 160 Capitol St Ste 1 *Web:* www.nationalnursesunited.org	Augusta	ME	04330	207-622-1057	623-4072
Managed Funds Association 600 14th St NW Ste 900 *Web:* www.managedfunds.org	Washington	DC	20005	202-367-1140	
Maryland Municipal League Insurance Agency Inc 1212 W St Ste 100 *TF:* 800-492-7121 ■ *Web:* www.mdmunicipal.org	Annapolis	MD	21401	410-268-5514	
Maryland Nurses Assn (MNA) 21 Governor's Ct Ste 195 *Web:* www.marylandrn.org	Baltimore	MD	21244	410-944-5800	944-5802
Massachusetts Assn of Registered Nurses (MARN) PO Box 285 *Web:* anamass.org/?	Milton	MA	02186	617-990-2856	
Massachusetts Nurses Assn (MNA) 340 Tpke St *TF:* 800-882-2056 ■ *Web:* www.massnurses.org	Canton	MA	02021	781-821-4625	821-4445
MedReview Inc 1 Seaport Plz 199 Water St 27th Fl *Web:* www.medreview.us	New York	NY	10038	212-897-6000	
Mha an Association of Montana Health Care Providers 1720 Ninth Ave *TF:* 800-351-3551 ■ *Web:* mtha.org	Helena	MT	59601	406-442-1911	
Michigan Boating Industries Association 32398 5 Mile Rd *Web:* www.mbia.org	Livonia	MI	48154	734-261-0123	
Michigan Nurses Assn (MNA) 2310 Jolly Oak Rd *TF:* 888-646-8773 ■ *Web:* www.minurses.org	Okemos	MI	48864	517-349-5640	349-5818
Michigan Society of Association Executives 1350 Haslett Rd *Web:* www.msae.org	East Lansing	MI	48823	517-332-6723	
Microcredit Summit 440 First St Nw Ste 460 *Web:* www.microcreditsummit.org	Washington	DC	20001	202-637-9600	
Midwest Reliability Organization 380 Saint Peter St Ste 800 *Web:* www.midwestreliability.org	Saint Paul	MN	55102	651-855-1760	
Minnesota Nurses Assn (MNA) 345 Randolph Ave Ste 200 *TF:* 800-536-4662 ■ *Web:* www.mnnurses.org	Saint Paul	MN	55102	651-646-4807	
Mississippi Nurses Assn (MNA) 31 Woodgreen Pl *Web:* www.msnurses.org	Madison	MS	39110	601-898-0670	898-0190
Missouri Municipal League 1727 Southridge Dr *Web:* www.mocities.com	Jefferson City	MO	65109	573-635-9134	
Missouri Nurses Assn (MONA) 1904 Bubba Ln PO Box 105228 *Web:* www.missourinurses.org	Jefferson City	MO	65110	573-636-4623	636-9576
Montana Nurses Assn (MNA) 20 Old Montana State Hwy *Web:* www.mtnurses.org	Montana City	MT	59634	406-442-6710	442-1841
Multnomah Bar Association 620 Sw Fifth Ave Ste 1220 *Web:* mbabar.org	Portland	OR	97204	503-222-3275	
N J Coalition of Automotive Retailers 856 River Rd *Web:* www.njcar.org	Ewing	NJ	08628	609-883-5056	
Napaba 1612 K St Nw Ste 1400 *Web:* www.napaba.org	Washington	DC	20006	202-775-9555	
National Latino Education Institute 2011 W Pershing Rd *Web:* www.nlei.org	Chicago	IL	60609	773-247-0707	
Nebraska Nurses Assn (NNA) PO Box 3107 *TF:* 800-582-3014 ■ *Web:* www.nebraskanurses.org	Kearney	NE	68848	402-475-3859	
New Hampshire Nurses Assn (NHNA) 210 N State St Ste 1A *Web:* www.nhnurses.org	Concord	NH	03301	603-225-3783	228-6672
New Jersey State Nurses Assn (NJSNA) 1479 Pennington Rd *TF:* 800-662-0108 ■ *Web:* www.njsna.org	Trenton	NJ	08618	609-883-5335	883-5343
New York County Lawyers Association 14 Vesey St *Web:* www.nycla.org	New York	NY	10007	212-267-6646	
New York Professional Nurses Union (NYPNU) 241 E 75th St *Web:* www.nypnu.org	New York	NY	10021	212-988-5565	
New York State Nurses Assn (NYSNA) 11 Cornell Rd *TF:* 800-724-6976 ■ *Web:* www.nysna.org	Latham	NY	12110	518-782-9400	782-9530
North Carolina Nurses Assn (NCNA) 103 Enterprise St PO Box 12025 *TF:* 800-626-2153 ■ *Web:* www.ncnurses.org	Raleigh	NC	27605	919-821-4250	829-5807
Ohio a C e p 3510 Snouffer Rd Ste 100 *TF:* 888-642-2374 ■ *Web:* www.ohacep.org	Columbus	OH	43235	614-792-6506	
Ohio Grantmakers Forum 37 W Broad St Ste 800 *Web:* www.philanthropyohio.org	Columbus	OH	43215	614-224-1344	
Ohio Nurses Assn (ONA) 4000 E Main St *TF:* 800-735-0056 ■ *Web:* www.ohnurses.org	Columbus	OH	43213	614-237-5414	237-6074
Ohio Poultry Association 5930 Sharon Woods Blvd *Web:* www.ohiopoultry.org	Columbus	OH	43229	614-882-6111	

				Phone	Fax
Ohio Quarter Horse 101 Tawa Rd *Web:* oqha.com	Richwood	OH	43344	740-943-2346	
Oklahoma Nurses Assn (ONA) 1111 N Lee Ste 243 *Web:* www.oklahomanurses.org	Oklahoma City	OK	73103	405-840-3476	840-3013
Oregon Nurses Assn (ONA) 18765 SW Boones Ferry Rd *TF:* 800-634-3552 ■ *Web:* www.oregonrn.org	Tualatin	OR	97062	503-293-0011	293-0013
Oregon Society of CPAs 10206 SW Laurel St *Web:* www.orcpa.org	Beaverton	OR	97005	503-641-7200	
Pasadena Heritage 651 S Saint John Ave *Web:* pasadenaheritage.org	Pasadena	CA	91105	626-441-6333	
Pennsylvania Assn of Staff Nurses & Allied Professionals (PASNAP) 1 Fayette St Ste 475 *TF:* 800-500-7850 ■ *Web:* www.pennanurses.org	Conshohocken	PA	19428	610-567-2907	567-2915
Planetree Inc 130 Division St *Web:* planetree.org	Derby	CT	06418	203-732-1365	
Polaris Project PO Box 77892 *Web:* polarisproject.org	Washington	DC	20013	202-745-1001	
Public Company Accounting Oversight Board (PCAOB) 1666 K St NW *Web:* www.pcaobus.org	Washington	DC	20006	202-207-9100	
Red Hat Society Store 431 S Acacia Ave *TF:* 866-386-2850 ■ *Web:* www.redhatsociety.com	Fullerton	CA	92831	714-738-0001	
Rhode Island State Nurses Assn (RISNA) 150 Washington St Ste 415 *Web:* www.risna.org	Providence	RI	02903	401-331-5644	331-5646
San Jose Downtown Association 28 N First St Ste 1000 *Web:* www.sjdowntown.com	San Jose	CA	95113	408-279-1775	
Soaring Society of America Jack Gomez Blvd *Web:* www.ssa.org	Hobbs	NM	88240	575-392-1177	
South Carolina Education Association, The 421 Zimalcrest Dr *TF:* 800-422-7232 ■ *Web:* www.thescea.org	Columbia	SC	29210	803-772-6553	
South Carolina Nurses Assn (SCNA) 1821 Gadsden St *Web:* www.scnurses.org	Columbia	SC	29201	803-252-4781	779-3870
South Dakota Nurses Assn (SDNA) PO Box 1015 **Fax Area Code:* 888 ■ *TF:* 888-425-3032 ■ *Web:* www.sdnursesassociation.org	Pierre	SD	57501	605-945-4265	425-3032*
Southeast Valley Regional Association of Realtors 1363 S Vineyard *Web:* www.sevrar.com	Mesa	AZ	85210	480-833-7510	
Tennessee Nurses Assn (TNA) 545 Mainstream Dr Ste 405 *Web:* www.tnaonline.org	Nashville	TN	37228	615-254-0350	254-0303
Tennessee State Employees Association 627 Woodland St *TF:* 800-251-8732 ■ *Web:* www.tseaonline.org	Nashville	TN	37206	615-256-4533	
Texas Beef Council 8708 N Fm 620 *Web:* www.beeflovingtexans.com	Austin	TX	78726	512-335-2333	
United Nurses & Allied Professionals 375 Branch Ave *Web:* www.unap.org	Providence	RI	02904	401-831-3647	
Utah Nurses Assn (UNA) 4505 S Wastch Blvd Ste 330B *TF:* 800-338-7657 ■ *Web:* www.utnurse.org/?	Salt Lake City	UT	84124	801-272-4510	
Van Alen Institute 30 W 22nd St Fl 6 *Web:* www.vanalen.org	New York	NY	10010	212-924-7000	
Vermont State Nurses Assn (VSNA) 100 Dorset St Ste 13 *TF:* 800-540-9390 ■ *Web:* www.vsna-inc.org	South Burlington	VT	05403	802-651-8886	651-8998
Virginia Nurses Assn (VNA) 7113 Three Chopt Rd Ste 204 *Web:* www.virginianurses.com	Richmond	VA	23226	804-282-1808	282-4916
Washington State Nurses Assn (WSNA) 575 Andover Pk W Ste 101 *TF:* 800-231-8482 ■ *Web:* www.wsna.org	Seattle	WA	98188	206-575-7979	575-1908
West Coast Conference 1111 Bayhill Dr Ste 405 *Web:* wccsports.com	San Bruno	CA	94066	650-873-8622	
West Virginia Nurses Assn (WVNA) 1007 Bigley Ave Ste 308 *TF:* 800-400-1226 ■ *Web:* www.wvnurses.org	Charleston	WV	25302	304-342-1169	
Western Institutional Review Board Inc 1019 39th Ave SE Ste 120 *Web:* www.wirb.com	Puyallup	WA	98374	360-252-2500	
Wisconsin Nurses Assn (WNA) 6117 Monona Dr *Web:* www.wisconsinnurses.org	Madison	WI	53716	608-221-0383	221-2788

534 OFFICE & SCHOOL SUPPLIES

See Also Office Supply Stores p. 2844; Writing Paper p. 2866; Pens, Pencils, Parts p. 2911; Printing & Photocopying Supplies p. 2987

				Phone	Fax
A & W Products Company Inc 14 Gardner St *Web:* www.awproducts.com	Port Jervis	NY	12771	845-856-5156	
Aakron Rule Corp 8 Indianola Ave *Web:* www.aakronline.com	Akron	NY	14001	585-542-5483	
Acroprint Time Recorder Co 5640 Departure Dr *TF:* 800-334-7190 ■ *Web:* acroprint.com	Raleigh	NC	27616	919-872-5800	850-0720
American Product Distributors Inc (APD) 8350 Arrowridge Blvd *TF:* 800-849-5842 ■ *Web:* www.americanproduct.com	Charlotte	NC	28273	704-522-9411	
American Solutions for Business 31 E Minnesota Ave PO Box 218 **Fax Area Code:* 320 ■ *TF:* 800-862-3690 ■ *Web:* home.americanbus.com	Glenwood	MN	56334	800-862-3690	634-5265*
Arlington Industries Inc 1616 Lakeside Dr *TF:* 800-323-4147 ■ *Web:* www.arli.com	Waukegan	IL	60085	847-689-2754	689-1616
Aurora Corp of America 3500 Challenger St *TF:* 800-327-8508 ■ *Web:* www.auroracorp.com	Torrance	CA	90503	310-793-5650	793-5658
Avery Dennison Corp 207 Goode Ave *NYSE: AVY* ■ *TF Cust Svc:* 888-567-4387 ■ *Web:* www.averydennison.com	Glendale	CA	91203	626-304-2000	
Avery Dennison Worldwide Office Products Div 207 Goode Ave **Fax Area Code:* 800 ■ *TF:* 800-462-8379 ■ *Web:* www.averydennison.com	Glendale	CA	91203	626-304-2000	848-2169*
Bartizan Corp 217 Riverdale Ave *TF:* 800-899-2278 ■ *Web:* www.bartizan.com	Yonkers	NY	10705	914-965-7977	965-7746
Baumgarten's 144 Ottley Dr **Fax Area Code:* 480 ■ *TF:* 800-247-5547 ■ *Web:* www.b3.net	Atlanta	GA	30324	404-874-7675	964-1279*
Business Stationery LLC 4944 Commerce Pkwy *TF:* 800-234-9954 ■ *Web:* www.identitygroup.com/bps/business-stationery	Cleveland	OH	44128	216-514-1277	
C & S Sales Inc 12947 Chadron Ave *Web:* www.cssales.com	Hawthorne	CA	90250	310-538-1219	538-2814
C-Line Products Inc 1100 E Business Ctr Dr *TF:* 800-323-6084 ■ *Web:* www.c-lineproducts.com	Mount Prospect	IL	60056	847-827-6661	827-3329
Cardinal Office Products Inc 576 E Main St **Fax Area Code:* 800 ■ *TF:* 800-589-5886 ■ *Web:* cardinaloffice.com	Frankfort	KY	40601	502-875-3300	539-4325*
Case Logic Inc 6303 Dry Creek Pkwy *TF:* 800-925-8111 ■ *Web:* www.caselogic.com	Longmont	CO	80503	303-652-1000	
Champion Industries Inc PO Box 2968 PO Box 2968 *OTC: CHMP* ■ *TF:* 800-624-3431 ■ *Web:* champion-industries.com	Huntington	WV	25728	304-528-2791	528-2746
Dahle North America Inc 49 Vose Farm Rd Ste 110 *TF:* 800-243-8145 ■ *Web:* www.dahle.com	Peterborough	NH	03458	603-924-0003	924-1616
Dart Manufacturing Co 3860 La Reunion Pkwy *Web:* www.dartpromo.com	Dallas	TX	75212	214-631-8024	
Deflect-O Corp 7035 E 86th St **Fax Area Code:* 317 ■ *TF:* 800-428-4328 ■ *Web:* www.deflecto.com	Indianapolis	IN	46250	800-428-4328	915-4456*
Douglas Stewart Co, The 2402 Advance Rd *TF:* 800-279-2795 ■ *Web:* www.dstewart.com	Madison	WI	53718	608-221-1155	221-5217
Eaton Office Supply Company Inc 180 John Glenn Dr *TF:* 800-365-3237 ■ *Web:* www.eatonofficesupply.com	Buffalo	NY	14228	716-691-6100	691-0074
GBS Corp 7233 Freedom Ave NW *TF:* 800-552-2427 ■ *Web:* www.gbscorp.com	North Canton	OH	44720	330-494-5330	494-7075
International Imaging Materials Inc 310 Commerce Dr *TF:* 888-464-4625 ■ *Web:* www.iimak.com	Amherst	NY	14228	716-691-6333	691-3395
Lakeshore Learning Materials 2695 E Dominguez St *TF:* 800-778-4456 ■ *Web:* www.lakeshorelearning.com	Carson	CA	90895	800-778-4456	537-5403
Lee Products Co 800 E 80th St *TF:* 800-989-3544 ■ *Web:* www.leeproducts.com	Bloomington	MN	55420	952-854-3544	854-7177
Magna Visual Inc 9400 Watson Rd **Fax Area Code:* 314 ■ *TF:* 800-843-3399 ■ *Web:* www.magnavisual.com	Sappington	MO	63126	800-843-3399	843-0000*
McGill Inc 131 E Prairie St *Web:* www.mcgillinc.com	Marengo	IL	60152	815-568-7244	
Millennium Marking Co 2600 Greenleaf Ave *Web:* www.millmarking.com	Elk Grove Village	IL	60007	847-806-1750	806-1751
PBS Supply Company Inc 7013 S 216th St *TF:* 877-727-7515 ■ *Web:* www.pbssupply.com	Kent	WA	98032	253-395-5550	395-5575
PerfectData Corp 1323 Conshohocken Rd *TF:* 800-973-7332 ■ *Web:* www.perfectdata.com	Plymouth Meeting	PA	19462	800-973-7332	
Staples Business Advantage 500 Staples Dr *TF:* 877-826-7755 ■ *Web:* www.staplesadvantage.com	Framingham	MA	01702	877-826-7755	
TAB Products Co 605 Fourth St **Fax Area Code:* 800 ■ *TF:* 888-466-8228 ■ *Web:* www.tab.com	Mayville	WI	53050	888-466-8228	304-4947*
United Stationers Inc 1 PkwyN Blvd Ste 100 *TF:* 855-275-6947 ■ *Web:* www.unitedstationers.com	Deerfield	IL	60015	847-627-7000	
United Stationers Supply Co (USSCO) 1 Pkwy N Blvd Ste 100 Ste 100 *Web:* www.essendant.com	Deerfield	IL	60015	847-627-7000	
Van Ausdall & Farrar Inc 6430 E 75th St *TF:* 800-467-7474 ■ *Web:* www.vanausdall.com	Indianapolis	IN	46250	317-634-2913	638-1843
Weeks-Lerman Group 58-38 Page Pl *TF:* 800-544-5959 ■ *Web:* www.weekslerman.com	Maspeth	NY	11378	718-803-5000	821-1515

535 OFFICE SUPPLY STORES

				Phone	Fax
AJ Stationers Inc 6675 Business Pkwy	Elkridge	MD	21075	410-360-4900	360-4291
Artlite Office Supply Co 1860 Chshire Bridge Rd NE *Web:* www.artlite.net	Atlanta	GA	30324	404-875-7271	875-2623
Audit & Adjustment Company Inc 20700 44th Ave W Ste 100 *TF:* 800-526-1074 ■ *Web:* www.audit-adjustment.com	Lynnwood	WA	98036	425-776-9797	
B J Bindery 833 S Grand Ave *Web:* www.bjbindery.com	Santa Ana	CA	92705	714-835-7342	
Barker Business Systems Inc 600 S Rock Blvd Ste 17 *Web:* www.e-totalprint.com	Reno	NV	89502	775-856-1771	
Belitec Inc 3320 boul Gene-H-Kruger *Web:* www.belitec.ca	Trois-Rivieres	QC	G9A4M3	819-373-3880	
BenefitHelp Solutions Inc 10505 SE 17th Ave *TF:* 888-398-8057 ■ *Web:* www.benefithelpsolutions.com	Milwaukie	OR	97222	503-219-3679	
Benjamin Office Supply & Services Inc 760 E Gude Dr *Web:* www.benjaminofficesupply.com	Rockville	MD	20850	301-340-1384	
BNBS Inc 11600 Otter Creek S Rd *Web:* bnbsolutionsinc.com	Mabelvale	AR	72103	501-224-1992	
Brilliance Educator Supplies & Resources Inc 8679 Sudley Rd	Manassas	VA	20110	571-292-2331	
Burkett's Office Supplies Inc 8520 Younger Creek Dr *Web:* www.burkettsoffice.com	Sacramento	CA	95828	916-387-8900	

Name	City	State	Zip	Phone	Fax
Business Cards Tomorrow Inc 3000 NE 30th Pl 5th Fl *Web:* www.bctonline.net	Fort Lauderdale	FL	33306	954-563-1224	
C M School Supply Inc 940 N Central Ave. *TF:* 800-464-6681 ■ *Web:* www.cmschoolsupply.com	Upland	CA	91786	909-982-9695	
Cambridge Lasers Inc 853 Brown Rd *Web:* www.cambridgelasers.com	Fremont	CA	94539	510-651-0110	
Cash Control Business Systems 9101 Lackland Rd. *Web:* www.cashcontrolbiz.com	Overland	MO	63114	314-427-6143	
Center Municipal Revenue Collection PO Box 195387 *Web:* www.crimpr.net	San Juan	PR	00926	787-625-2746	
Church & Stagg Office Supply Company Inc 3421 Sixth Ave	Birmingham	AL	35222	205-251-2951	324-6874
Columbia Omnicorp 14 W 33rd St *Web:* columbiaomni.com	New York	NY	10001	212-279-6161	
Computer Designs Inc 5235 W Coplay Rd. *Web:* www.computer-designs.com	Whitehall	PA	18052	610-261-2100	
Conney Safety Products LLC 3202 Latham Dr *Web:* www.conney.com	Madison	WI	53744	608-271-3300	
Copy Products Inc 2103 W Vista St *Web:* copyproductsinc.com	Springfield	MO	65807	417-889-5665	
Create-a-card Inc 16 Brasswood Rd *TF:* 800-753-6867 ■ *Web:* www.createacardinc.com	Saint James	NY	11780	631-584-2273	
Danby Group LLP, The 3060-A Business Park Dr *TF:* 800-262-2629 ■ *Web:* www.danbygroup.com	Norcross	GA	30071	770-416-9844	
DBI Inc 912 E Michigan Ave *TF:* 800-968-1324 ■ *Web:* www.dbiyes.com	Lansing	MI	48912	517-485-3200	485-3202
Ddl Business Systems 5321 Mulberry St. *Web:* www.ddlbusiness.com	Stephens City	VA	22655	540-869-7855	
Dick Blick Holdings Inc 1849 Green Bay Rd Ste 310 *Web:* dickblick.com	Highland Park	IL	60035	847-681-6800	
Discover Group Inc 2741 W 23rd St. *TF:* 866-456-6555 ■ *Web:* www.discovergroup.net	Brooklyn	NY	11224	718-456-4500	
Dynetics Technical Services Inc 1002 Explorer Blvd. *Web:* www.dts-dynetics.com	Huntsville	AL	35806	256-544-0764	
Eakes Office Plus 617 W Third St *TF:* 800-652-9396 ■ *Web:* www.eakes.com	Grand Island	NE	68801	308-382-8026	382-7401
Econ-o-copy Inc 4437 Trenton St Ste A *TF:* 877-256-0310 ■ *Web:* www.econ-o-copy.com	Metairie	LA	70006	504-457-0032	457-0114
Economy Office Supply Co 1725 Gardena Ave *Web:* www.economyofficesupply.com	Glendale	CA	91204	818-548-1525	
Egyptian Stationers Inc 129 W Main St *TF Cust Svc:* 800-642-3949 ■ *Web:* www.egyptian-stationers.com	Belleville	IL	62220	618-234-2323	234-0693
EIS Electro Imaging Systems 6553 Las Positas Rd. *TF:* 800-207-4757 ■ *Web:* www.eisonline.net	Livermore	CA	94551	800-207-4757	
Envelopes Only Inc 2000 S Park Ave *Web:* envelopesonly.net	Streamwood	IL	60107	630-213-2500	
Envoy Plan Services Inc 901 Calle Amanecer Ste 200. *TF:* 800-248-8858 ■ *Web:* www.envoyplanservices.com	San Clemente	CA	92673	949-366-5070	
FASCore LLC 8515 E Orchard Rd *TF:* 800-232-0859 ■ *Web:* www.fascore.com	Greenwood Village	CO	80111	800-537-2033	
Firstline Business Systems Inc 211 E 11th St Ste 101. *Web:* firstline-online.com	Vancouver	WA	98660	360-695-3138	
Fisher Hawaii 450 Cooke St *Web:* www.fisherhawaii.net	Honolulu	HI	96813	808-524-8770	524-8785
Friend's Professional Stationery Inc 1535 Lewis Ave *TF:* 800-323-4394 ■ *Web:* www.friendsstationery.com	Zion	IL	60099	800-323-4394	323-1535
GEMGroup LP 1200 Three Gateway Ctr *Web:* www.gemgrouplp.com	Pittsburgh	PA	15222	412-471-2885	
Gobin's Inc 615 N Santa Fe Ave. *TF:* 800-425-2324 ■ *Web:* www.gobins.com	Pueblo	CO	81003	719-544-2324	544-2378
Guernsey Office Products 45070 Old Ox Rd. *Web:* www.buyguernsey.com/thm103home.aspx	Dulles	VA	20166	703-968-8200	
Gulfland Office Supplies Inc 801 Brashear Ave *Web:* gulfoffice.com	Morgan City	LA	70380	985-384-3250	
Halsey & Griffith Inc 1983 Tenth Ave N. *Web:* www.halseygriffith.com	Lake Worth	FL	33461	561-820-8000	
High Technology Inc 109 Production Rd. *Web:* www.htmed.com	Walpole	MA	02081	508-660-2221	
Hurst Group 257 E Short St *TF:* 800-926-4423 ■ *Web:* www.hurstgroup.net	Lexington	KY	40507	859-255-4422	
Infomax Office Systems Inc 1010 Illinois St *Web:* infomaxoffice.com	Des Moines	IA	50314	515-244-5203	
JL Darling LLC 2614 Pacific Hwy E *Web:* www.riteintherain.com	Tacoma	WA	98424	253-922-5000	
Keeton's Office & Art Supply Co 817 Manatee Ave W *Web:* www.keetonsonline.com	Bradenton	FL	34205	941-747-2995	
Kennedy Office Supply 4211-A Atlantic Ave *TF:* 800-733-9401 ■ *Web:* kennedyoffice.com	Raleigh	NC	27604	919-878-5400	790-9649
Kinloch Consulting Group Inc 25 Melville Park Rd Ste 260 *Web:* www.kinlochcg.com	Melville	NY	11747	631-773-6600	
Koch Bros 325 Grand Ave. *Web:* www.kochbros.com	Des Moines	IA	50309	515-283-2451	
Kore Inc 355 Madison Ave *Web:* www.korecorp.com	Morristown	NJ	07960	973-883-0308	
Lafayette Copier Service & Sales 310 Farabee Dr. *Web:* lafayettecopier.com	Lafayette	IN	47905	765-446-2230	
Lamination Depot Inc 1505 E McFadden Ave *TF:* 800-925-0054 ■ *Web:* www.laminationdepot.com	Santa Ana	CA	92705	714-954-0632	
Latta's School Supply 1502 Fourth Ave. *TF:* 800-624-3501 ■ *Web:* www.lattas.com	Huntington	WV	25701	304-523-8400	525-5038
Louisiana Office Supply Co 7643 Florida Blvd *Web:* losco.com	Baton Rouge	LA	70806	225-927-1110	927-3085
Madden Communications Inc 901 Mittel Dr *Web:* www.madden.com	Wood Dale	IL	60191	630-787-2200	
Mallory Safety & Supply Inc 1040 Industrial Way PO Box 2068 *Web:* www.malloryco.com	Longview	WA	98632	360-636-5750	
Marimon Business Systems Inc 7300 N Gessner *Web:* www.marimoninc.com	Houston	TX	77040	713-856-2000	856-2001
Match Eyewear LLC 82 Union St *Web:* www.matcheyewear.com	Mineola	NY	11501	516-877-0170	
Matik Inc 33 Brook St *TF:* 800-245-1628 ■ *Web:* www.matik.com	West Hartford	CT	06110	860-232-2323	
McCowan Design & Mfg Ltd 1760 Birchmount Rd. *TF:* 888-782-5189 ■ *Web:* www.mccowan.ca	Toronto	ON	M1P2H7	416-291-7111	
MCR Technologies 6 Greenwood St. *Web:* www.mcrtechnologies.com	Wakefield	MA	01880	781-245-6644	
Metro Business Systems 2950 Kaverton Rd *Web:* www.mbs-copiers.com	District Heights	MD	20747	301-967-8758	
Mg Scientific Inc 8500 107th St. *TF:* 800-343-8338 ■ *Web:* www.mgscientific.com	Pleasant Prairie	WI	53158	262-947-7000	
New World Imports Inc 160 Athens Way *Web:* www.newworldimports.com	Nashville	TN	37228	615-329-1906	
Newport Stationers Inc 17681 Mitchell N. *Web:* www.newportstationers.com	Irvine	CA	92614	949-863-1200	852-8970
Nexus Office Systems Inc 898 Featherstone Rd. *Web:* nexusofficesystems.com	Rockford	IL	61107	815-227-0170	
Northern Business Products Inc PO Box 16127 *TF:* 800-647-8775 ■ *Web:* www.nbpoffice.com	Duluth	MN	55816	218-726-0167	726-1023
NOVA Scientific Inc 10 Picker Rd. *Web:* www.novascientific.com	Sturbridge	MA	01566	508-347-7679	
Novacopy Inc 7251 Appling Farms Pkwy. *TF:* 800-264-0637 ■ *Web:* www.novacopy.net	Memphis	TN	38133	901-388-3399	432-2682
Oak Cliff Office Supply 1876 Lone Star Dr	Dallas	TX	75212	214-943-7421	
Office Depot Inc 2200 Old Germantown Rd *NASDAQ: ODP* ■ *TF:* 800-937-3600 ■ *Web:* www.officedepot.com	Delray Beach	FL	33445	561-438-4800	
Office Resources Inc 374 Congress St *Web:* www.ori.com	Boston	MA	02210	617-423-9100	423-5590
Office Suppliers Inc 13621 Crayton Blvd. *Web:* www.hyperspacellc.com	Hagerstown	MD	21742	301-797-3120	797-1504
Opus Framing Ltd 3445 Cornett Rd. *TF:* 800-663-6953 ■ *Web:* opusartsupplies.com	Vancouver	BC	V5M2H3	604-435-9991	
Paper Pigeon Inc 14701 SW 94 Ave. *Web:* paperpigeonmiami.com	Miami	FL	33176	305-235-7887	
Patrick & Co 560 Market St. *Web:* patrickandco.com	San Francisco	CA	94104	415-392-2640	591-0773
Perma Pom LLC 9611 Hwy 60 S *Web:* www.pepcopoms.com	Lane City	TX	77453	979-532-3106	
Phillips Group 501 Fulling Mill Rd *TF:* 800-538-7500 ■ *Web:* www.buyphillips.com	Middletown	PA	17057	717-944-0400	948-5297
Polack Corp, The 1400 Keystone Ave. *Web:* www.polackcorp.com	Lansing	MI	48911	517-393-3440	
Prestige Graphics Inc 9630 Ridgehaven Ct Ste B *TF:* 800-383-9361 ■ *Web:* www.pgisd.com	San Diego	CA	92123	858-560-8213	
Printers & Stationers Inc 113 N Ct St *TF:* 800-624-5334 ■ *Web:* www.psi-online.net	Florence	AL	35630	256-764-8061	764-5024
Questa Engineering Corp 1010 Tenth St.	Golden	CO	80401	303-277-1629	
ShurTech Brands 32150 Just Imagine Dr *TF:* 800-321-0253 ■ *Web:* shurtech.com	Avon	OH	44011	440-937-7000	
Smith & Butterfield Co Inc 2800 Lynch Rd *TF:* 800-321-6543 ■ *Web:* www.smithbutterfield.com	Evansville	IN	47711	812-422-3261	429-0532
SpecialCare Hospital Management Corp 1551 Wall St Ste 210 *Web:* www.specialcarecorp.com	St. Charles	MO	63303	314-770-2212	
Stationers Inc 1945 Fifth Ave *TF:* 800-862-7200 ■ *Web:* www.stationers-wv.com	Huntington	WV	25703	304-528-2780	528-2795
Supply Room Cos Inc 14140 N Washington Hwy *TF:* 800-849-7239 ■ *Web:* tsrcinc.net	Ashland	VA	23005	804-412-1200	412-1313
Tamarack Products Inc 1071 N Old Rand Rd *Web:* www.tamarackproducts.com	Wauconda	IL	60084	847-526-9333	
Techneal Inc 2100 S Reservoir St. *TF:* 800-545-6325 ■ *Web:* www.techneal.com	Pomona	CA	91766	909-465-6325	
Thomas Lee Printing & Mailing Inc 3721 W 12th St.	Erie	PA	16505	814-833-3233	
Total Merchant Concepts Inc 12300 NE Fourth Plain Rd A *TF:* 888-249-9919 ■ *Web:* www.totalmerchantconcepts.com	Vancouver	WA	98682	360-253-5934	
Triplett Office Essentials Corp 3553 109th St. *TF:* 800-437-5034 ■ *Web:* www.tripletts.com	Urbandale	IA	50322	515-270-9150	270-9683
Unisource Canada Inc 50 E Wilmot St. *Web:* www.unisource.ca	Richmond Hill	ON	L4B3Z3	905-771-4000	771-4219
Universal Bookbindery Inc 1200 N Colorado St *Web:* universalbookbindery.com	San Antonio	TX	78207	210-734-9502	
Valley Business Machines Inc 5825 Mayflower Ct *Web:* www.vbmalaska.com	Wasilla	AK	99654	907-376-5077	
Variant Microsystems 4128 Business Ctr Dr *TF:* 800-827-4268 ■ *Web:* www.variantusa.com	Fremont	CA	94538	510-440-2870	
Veritas Press 1250 Belle Meade Dr. *TF:* 800-922-5082 ■ *Web:* www.veritaspress.com	Lancaster	PA	17601	717-519-1974	
WALZ Label & Mailing Systems 624 High Point Ln *TF:* 877-971-1500 ■ *Web:* walzeq.com	East Peoria	IL	61611	309-698-1500	
Wist Office Products Co 107 W Julie Dr. *TF:* 800-999-9478 ■ *Web:* www.wist.com	Tempe	AZ	85283	480-921-2900	921-2121

Phone | Fax

Wrapmail Inc
305 S Andrews Ave Ste 601 .... Fort Lauderdale FL 33301 954-376-4750
Web: www.wrapmail.com

Xpedx 3351 W Addison St .... Chicago IL 60618 773-442-6200
Web: www.xpedx.com

Xpedx Paper & Graphics 6285 Tri-Ridge Blvd .... Loveland OH 45140 513-965-2900
Web: www.xpedx.com

Zymo Research Corp 17062 Murphy Ave .... Irvine CA 92614 949-679-1190
Web: www.zymoresearch.com

536 OIL & GAS EXTRACTION

Phone | Fax

1st NRG Corp 10184 Park Meadows Dr .... Lone Tree CO 80124 720-484-5706
Web: 1stnrg-corp.com

5J Oilfield Services LLC 4090 N Hwy 79 .... Palestine TX 75801 903-723-0253
Web: www.5joilfield.net

A H Belo Corp 508 Young St PO Box 224866 .... Dallas TX 75202 214-977-8200 977-8201
NYSE: AHC ■ *TF:* 800-230-1074 ■ *Web:* www.ahbelo.com

ABARTA Oil & Gas Company Inc 200 Alpha Dr .... Pittsburgh PA 15238 412-963-6443
Web: www.abartaenergy.com

Abraxas Petroleum Corp 18803 Meisner Dr .... San Antonio TX 78258 210-490-4788 490-8816*
NASDAQ: AXAS ■ **Fax:* Acctg ■ *Web:* www.abraxaspetroleum.com

Adams Resources & Energy Inc
17 S. Briar Hollow Ln Ste 100 .... Houston TX 77027 713-881-3600
NYSE: AE ■ *Web:* www.adamsresources.com

AES Safety Services 8588 Katy Fwy Ste 430 .... Houston TX 77024 979-505-0052

Africa Fortesa Corp
7880 San Felipe St Ste 105 .... Houston TX 77063 713-278-2727
Web: www.fortesa.com

Africa Oil Corp 885 W Georgia St Ste 2000 .... Vancouver BC V6C3E8 604-689-7842
Web: www.africaoilcorp.com

Alberta Oilsands Inc 815-8th Ave S.W Ste 600 .... Calgary AB T2P3P2 403-263-6700
Web: www.aboilsands.ca

Allied-Horizontal Wireline Services LLC
15995 N Barker's Landing Ste 140 .... Houston TX 77079 713-343-7280
TF: 888-494-9580 ■ *Web:* alliedhorizontal.com

Alvopetro Energy Ltd 332 - 6 Ave SW Ste 1175 .... Calgary AB T2P0B2 587-794-4224
Web: www.alvopetro.com

Aly Centrifuge Inc 6126 Private Rd 902 .... Celina TX 75009 972-382-4400
Web: www.alycentrifuge.com

America's Natural Gas Alliance
701 Eighth St NW Ste 800 .... Washington DC 20001 202-789-2642
Web: www.anga.us

American Eagle Energy Corp
2549 W Main St Ste 202 .... Littleton CO 80120 303-385-1230
Web: www.americaneagleenergy.com

AMERIgreen Energy Inc
1862 Charter Ln Ste 101 .... Lancaster PA 17601 717-945-1392
Web: www.amerigreen.com

Amerril Energy LLC 3721 Briarpark Dr Ste 155 .... Houston TX 77042 713-660-1620

Anadarko Petroleum Corp 1201 Lk Robbins Dr .... Spring TX 77380 832-636-1000
NYSE: APC ■ *TF:* 800-800-1101 ■ *Web:* www.anadarko.com

Antrim Energy Inc 610-301 8 Ave SW .... Calgary AB T2P1C5 403-264-5111
Web: www.antrimenergy.com

Apache Corp 2000 Post Oak Blvd Ste 100 .... Houston TX 77056 713-296-6000
NYSE: APA ■ *TF:* 800-272-2434 ■ *Web:* www.apachecorp.com

Apollo Industries Inc 105 N End Dr .... North Clarendon VT 05759 802-446-3466
Web: www.apollo-systems.com

Applied LNG 31111 Agoura Rd Ste 208 .... Westlake Village CA 91361 818-450-3650
Web: www.appliedlng.com

Aramco Services Co 9009 W Loop S .... Houston TX 77096 713-432-4000 432-4146
TF: 866-287-3592 ■ *Web:* www.aramcoservices.com

Arctic Hunter Energy Inc
1610 675 W Hastings St .... Vancouver BC V6B1N2 604-681-3131
Web: www.arctichunter.com

Arete Industries Inc 7260 Osceola St .... Westminster CO 80030 303-427-8688
Web: www.areteindustries.com

Arkanova Energy Corp
305 Camp Craft Rd Ste 525 .... West Lake Hills TX 78746 512-222-0975
Web: www.arkanovaenergy.com

Aruba Petroleum Inc 555 Republic Dr Ste 505 .... Plano TX 75074 972-312-9366
Web: www.arubapetroleum.com

ATP Oil & Gas Corp 4600 Post Oak Pl Ste 200 .... Houston TX 77027 713-622-3311 622-5101
OTC: ATPAQ

Bakerwell Inc 6295 Maxtown Rd Ste 300 .... Westerville OH 43082 614-898-7590
Web: www.bakerwell.com

Ballard Petroleum LLC 845 12th St W .... Billings MT 59102 406-259-8790
Web: www.ballardpetroleum.com

Barnwell Industries Inc
1100 Alakea St Ste 2900 .... Honolulu HI 96813 808-531-8400 531-7181
NYSE: BRN ■ *Web:* www.brninc.com

Bayou State Oil Corp 1115 Hawn Ave .... Shreveport LA 71107 318-222-0737 222-0730

Baytex Energy Corp 2800 520 - Third Ave SW .... Calgary AB T2P0R3 587-952-3000
TF: 800-524-5521 ■ *Web:* www.baytexenergy.com

Bently Nevada Inc 1631 Bently Pkwy South .... Minden NV 89423 775-782-3611

Beredco Inc 2020 N Bramblewood St .... Wichita KS 67208 316-265-2856
Web: www.beredco.com

Berry Petroleum Co 1999 Broadway Ste 3700 .... Denver CO 80202 303-825-3344 999-4401
NYSE: BRY

Beusa Energy Inc
4 Waterway Sq Pl Ste 900 .... The Woodlands TX 77380 281-296-1500
Web: www.beusaenergy.com

BHP Billiton Petroleum (Americas) Inc
1360 Post Oak Blvd Ste 150 .... Houston TX 77056 713-961-8500 961-8400
Web: www.bhpbilliton.com

Big Cat Energy Corp
121 Merino Stree, PO Box 500 .... Upton WY 82730 307-468-9369
Web: www.bigcatenergy.com

Big Horn Energy Services II LLC
4321 Greenville Cir .... Midland TX 79707 432-312-4071
Web: www.bighornenergyservices.com

Phone | Fax

Black Ridge Oil & Gas Inc
110 North fifth St Ste 410 .... Minnetonka MN 55305 952-426-1241
Web: www.blackridgeoil.com

Black Swan Energy Ltd
Ste 1200 Bow Vly Sq III 255 - Fifth Ave SW
Ste 1200 .... Calgary AB T2P3G6 403-930-4400
Web: www.blackswanenergy.com

BlackBrush Oil & Gas LP
18615 Tuscany Stone Ste 300 .... San Antonio TX 78258 210-495-5577
Web: www.blackbrushenergy.com

Blacksands Petroleum Inc
Ste 410 25025 I-45 N .... The Woodlands TX 77380 713-554-4491

Blaser Swisslube Inc 31 Hatfield Ln .... Goshen NY 10924 845-294-3200
Web: www.blaser.com

Blaze Energy Ltd 900 - Sixth Ave SW Ste 1010 .... Calgary AB T2P3K2 403-264-0877
Web: www.blazeenergy.com

Blue Dolphin Energy Co 801 Travis St Ste 2100 .... Houston TX 77002 713-568-4725 227-7626
OTC: BDCO

Bonterra Energy Corp
1015 - Fourth St SW Ste 901 .... Calgary AB T2R1J4 403-262-5307
Web: www.bonterraenergy.com

BP Canada Energy Co 240 Fourth Ave SW .... Calgary AB T2P2H8 403-233-1359 233-1476*
**Fax:* Mail Rm ■ *TF:* 877-833-1359 ■ *Web:* www.bp.com

BP Canada Energy Resources Co
240- Fourth Ave SW .... Calgary AB T2P2H8 403-233-1313
TF: 800-255-4268

BP PLC 28100 Torch Pkwy .... Warrenville IL 60555 800-333-3991
NYSE: BP ■ *TF:* 800-333-3991 ■ *Web:* www.bp.com

BPZ Resources Inc
580 Westlake Park Blvd Ste 525 .... Houston TX 77079 281-556-6200
Web: www.bpzenergy.com

Breitling Energy Corp
Ste 12000 1910 PACIFIC Ave Ste 12000 .... Dallas TX 75201 214-716-2600
TF: 866-884-0224 ■ *Web:* www.breitlingenergy.com

Brenham Oil & Gas Corp 601 Cien Rd Ste 235 .... Kemah TX 77565 281-334-9479
Web: www.brenhamoil.com

Brigham Exploration Co
6300 Bridge Pt Pkwy Bldg 2 Ste 500 .... Austin TX 78730 512-427-3300 427-3400
NASDAQ: BEXP ■ *Web:* www.statoil.com

Bright Horizon Resources LLC
6120 S Yale Ave Ste 900 .... Tulsa OK 74136 918-879-3200
Web: www.bhrep.com

BTA Oil Producers LLC 104 S Pecos .... Midland TX 79701 432-682-3753
Web: www.btaoil.com

Bukit Energy Inc
2310, 700 - 2nd St SW Scotia Tower .... Calgary AB T2P2W2 403-930-2250
Web: www.bukitenergy.com

Cabot Oil & Gas Corp 840 Gessner Rd Ste 1200 .... Houston TX 77024 281-848-2799
NYSE: COG ■ *TF:* 800-434-3985 ■ *Web:* cabotog.com

Caiterra International Energy Corp
900 Hastings St W .... Vancouver BC V6C1E5 778-330-1270
Web: www.caiterra.com

Caldera Corp 8290 W Sahara Ave Ste 186 .... Las Vegas NV 89117 702-838-0716
Web: ww2.calderacorp.com

Callon Petroleum Co 200 N Canal St .... Natchez MS 39120 601-442-1601 446-1410
NYSE: CPE ■ *TF:* 800-451-1294 ■ *Web:* www.callon.com

Canadian Natural Resources Ltd (CNRL)
855 Second St SW Ste 2500 .... Calgary AB T2P4J8 403-517-6700 517-7350
NYSE: CNQ ■ *TF:* 888-878-3700 ■ *Web:* www.cnrl.com

Canamax Energy Ltd Eighth Ave SW Ste 610 .... Calgary AB T2P2Z2 587-779-4259
Web: www.canamaxenergy.ca

Cano Petroleum Inc 6500 N Belt Line Rd Ste 200 .... Irving TX 75063 214-687-0030
OTC: CANOQ

Canyon Exploration Co 600 S Tyler St .... Amarillo TX 79101 806-374-0071
Web: www.canyonexplorations.com

Capital Well Service LLC 1437 E St .... Jourdanton TX 78026 830-767-2036
Web: www.capitalwellservice.com

Capstone Natural Resources LLC 2250 E 73rd St .... Tulsa OK 74136 918-236-3800
Web: capstonenr.com

Carrizo Oil & Gas Inc 1000 Louisiana Ste 1500 .... Houston TX 77002 713-328-1000 328-1035
NASDAQ: CRZO ■ *Web:* carrizo.com

CASA Exploration LLC
1800 Post Oak Blvd Ste 380 .... Houston TX 77056 832-325-2300
Web: www.casaexploration.com

Case Pomeroy & Co Inc 529 Fifth Ave .... New York NY 10017 212-867-2211 682-2353

Caspian Energy Inc
649 Varsity Estates Crescent NW .... Calgary AB T2R0C5 403-252-2462
Web: www.caspianenergyinc.com

Catalyst Energy Inc 424 S 27th St Ste 304 .... Pittsburgh PA 15203 412-325-4350
Web: www.catalystenergyinc.com

Caza Oil & Gas Inc
Ste 200 10077 Grogan's Mill Rd .... The Woodlands TX 77380 281-363-4442
Web: www.cazapetro.com

Cenovus Energy Inc (USA)
2600 500 Centre St SE PO Box 766 .... Calgary AB T2P0M5 403-766-2000
Web: www.cenovus.com

Century Wireline Services 1223 S 71st E Ave .... Tulsa OK 74112 918-838-9811
Web: www.centurywirelineservices.com

Cequence Energy Ltd 525 8h Ave SW Ste 3100 .... Calgary AB T2P1G1 403-229-3050
Web: www.cequence-energy.com

CGX Energy Inc 333 Bay St Ste 1100 .... Toronto ON M5H2R2 416-364-5569
Web: www.cgxenergy.com

Changfeng Energy Inc
25 Adelaide St E Ste 1612 .... Toronto ON M5H2G4 416-362-5032
Web: www.changfengenergy.com

Chesapeake Energy Corp
6100 N Western Ave .... Oklahoma City OK 73118 405-848-3000
NYSE: CHK ■ *Web:* chk.com

Chevron Corp 6001 Bollinger Canyon Rd .... San Ramon CA 94583 925-842-1000
NYSE: CVX ■ *TF Cust Svc:* 800-368-8357 ■ *Web:* www.chevron.com

Chuma Holdings Inc
350 N Glendale Ave Ste B 212 .... Glendale CA 91206 702-751-8455

Company / Address	City	State	Zip	Phone	Fax
Cimmaron Field Services Inc 303 W Wall St Bank of America Tower Ste 600. TF: 877-944-2705 ■ Web: www.cimmaron.com	Midland	TX	79701	877-944-2705	
Circle Star Energy Corp 7065 Confederate Park Rd Ste 102	Fort Worth	TX	76108	817-744-8502	
Citation Oil & Gas Corp 14077 Cutten Rd Web: www.cogc.com	Houston	TX	77069	281-891-1000	
Citizens Gas Fuel Co 127 N Main St Web: www.citizensgasfuel.com	Adrian	MI	49221	517-265-2144	
Clayton Williams Energy Inc 6 Desta Dr NASDAQ: CWEI ■ Web: www.claytonwilliams.com	Midland	TX	79705	432-682-6324	
ClearStream Energy Services LP 2112 Premier Way TF: 855-410-9835 ■ Web: www.clearstreamenergy.ca	Sherwood Park	AB	T8H2G4	780-410-9835	
Coastal Mountain Fuels 501 Industrial Pk Pl Web: www.cmfuels.ca	Gold River	BC	V0P2G0	250-283-2514	
Cobra Oil & Gas Corp 2201 Kell Blvd PO Box 8206 Web: www.cobraogc.com	Wichita Falls	TX	76308	940-716-5100	716-5190
Comstock Resources Inc 5300 Town & Country Blvd Ste 500 NYSE: CRK ■ TF: 800-929-4884 ■ Web: crkfrisco.com	Frisco	TX	75034	972-668-8800	668-8812
Connacher Oil & Gas Ltd Ste 900 332-6 Ave SW Web: www.connacheroil.com	Calgary	AB	T2P0B2	403-538-6201	
ConocoPhillips 600 N Dairy Ashford Rd NYSE: COP ■ Web: www.conocophillips.com	Houston	TX	77079	281-293-1000	
ConocoPhillips Canada 401 Ninth Ave SW Ste 1600 Web: www.conocophillips.ca	Calgary	AB	T2P3C5	403-233-4000	
Contango Oil & Gas Co 3700 Buffalo Speedway Ste 960 NYSE: MCF ■ Web: www.contango.com	Houston	TX	77098	713-960-1901	960-1065
Cordillera Energy Partners III LLC 8450 E Crescent Pkwy Ste 400 Web: www.cordilleraep.com	Greenwood Village	CO	80111	303-290-0990	
Corridor Resources Inc 5475 Spring Garden Rd TF: 888-429-4511 ■ Web: www.corridor.ca	Halifax	NS	B3J3T2	902-429-4511	
Cortech Engineering Inc 22785 Savi Ranch Pkwy Web: cortecheng.com	Yorba Linda	CA	92887	714-779-0911	
Crawford Energy Inc 770 S Post Oak Ln Ste 520 Web: www.crawfordenergy.com	Houston	TX	77056	713-626-2637	
Crawley Petroleum Corp 105 N Hudson Ste 800 Web: www.crawleypetroleum.com	Oklahoma City	OK	73102	405-232-9700	
Crescent Point Energy Corp 585 Eighth Ave Sw Ste 2000 Web: www.crescentpointenergy.com	Calgary	AB	T2P1G1	403-693-0020	
Crew Energy Inc 250 5 St SW Ste 800 Web: www.crewenergy.com	Calgary	AB	T2P0R4	403-266-2088	
Crimson Resource Management Corp 410 17th St Ste 1010 Web: www.crimsonrm.com	Denver	CO	80202	303-892-9333	
Crown Central Petroleum Corp 1 N Charles St Web: www.crowncentral.com	Baltimore	MD	21201	410-539-7400	
Crown Energy Co 333 N Portland Web: www.crownec.com	Oklahoma City	OK	73107	405-526-0111	
CUB Energy Inc 5120 Woodway Dr Ste 10010 Web: www.cubenergyinc.com	Houston	TX	77056	713-677-0439	
Cubic Energy Inc 9870 PLANO Rd Web: www.cubicenergyinc.com	Dallas	TX	75238	972-686-0369	
Culberson Construction Inc 4500 Colony Rd Web: www.ccincservices.com	Granbury	TX	76048	817-573-3079	
Curlew Lake Resources Inc 595 Howe St Ste 303 Web: www.curlew-lake.com	Vancouver	BC	V6C2T5	604-336-8613	
Cypress Hills Resource Corp 602-11th Ave SW Ste 416 Web: www.cypresshillsresource.com	Calgary	AB	V7X1J1	403-265-7663	
D d Dunlap Companies Inc 16897 Algonquin St Ste A Web: dddunlap.com	Huntington Beach	CA	92649	714-840-6460	
D&L Energy Inc 2761 Salt Springs Rd Web: www.dandlenergy.com	Youngstown	OH	44509	330-792-9524	
D.F. Industries (DFI) Inc 2404 - 51 Ave Web: www.dfi.ca	Edmonton	AB	T6B3B8	780-466-5237	
D.J. Simmons Inc 1009 Ridgeway Pl Ste 200 Web: www.djsimmons.com	Farmington	NM	87401	505-326-3753	
Daleco Resources Corp 17 Wilmont Mews 5th Fl. Web: www.dalecoresources.com	West Chester	PA	19382	610-429-0181	
Danmark Energy L P 1907 E Old Hwy 80 Web: danmarkenergy.com	White Oak	TX	75693	903-297-5136	
DCOR LLC 290 Maple Court Ste 290 Web: www.dcorusa.com	Ventura	CA	93003	805-535-2000	
DCP Midstream Partners LP 370 17th St Ste 2775 NYSE: DPM ■ Web: dcppartners.com	Denver	CO	80202	303-633-2900	605-2225
Dejour Energy Inc 598-999 Canada Pl Web: www.dxienergy.com	Vancouver	BC	V6C3E1	604-638-5050	
Delmar Systems Inc 8114 W Hwy 90 Web: www.delmarus.com	Broussard	LA	70518	337-365-0180	
Delphi Energy Corp 500 - Fourth Ave SW Ste 300 Web: www.delphienergy.ca	Calgary	AB	T2P2V6	403-265-6171	
Delta Oil & Gas Inc 700 W Pender St Ste 604 TF: 866-355-3644 ■ Web: www.deltaoilandgas.com	Vancouver	BC	V6C1G8	604-602-1500	
Denbury Resources Inc 5320 Legacy Dr NYSE: DNR ■ TF General: 800-348-9030 ■ Web: www.denbury.com	Plano	TX	75024	972-673-2000	673-2430
Devon Energy Corp 20 N Broadway NYSE: DVN ■ TF: 877-860-5820 ■ Web: www.devonenergy.com	Oklahoma City	OK	73102	405-235-3611	
DHI Services Inc 33502 State Hwy 249 Web: www.dhiservices.com	Pinehurst	TX	77362	281-201-4141	

Company / Address	City	State	Zip	Phone	Fax
Diamondback Energy Services LLC 14301 Caliber Dr Ste 200 Web: www.diamondbackenergy.com	Oklahoma City	OK	73134	405-242-4080	
DKRW Advanced Fuels LLC 5444 Westheimer Ste 1560 TF: 855-876-4595 ■ Web: www.dkrwaf.com	Houston	TX	77056	855-876-4595	
Dorchester Minerals LP 3838 Oak Lawn Ave Ste 300 NASDAQ: DMLP ■ Web: www.dmlp.net	Dallas	TX	75219	214-559-0300	559-0301
Doxa Energy Ltd 777 Hornby St Ste 2080 Web: www.doxaenergy.com	Vancouver	BC	V6Z1S4	604-662-3692	
Doyon Ltd 1 Doyon Pl Ste 300 TF: 888-478-4755 ■ Web: www.doyon.com	Fairbanks	AK	99701	907-459-2000	
Dugan Production Corp 709 E Murray Dr Web: daily-times.com	Farmington	NM	87401	505-325-1821	327-4613
Dynamic Energy Services International LLC 600 Jefferson St Ste 1400 Web: www.morenogroupllc.com	Lafayette	LA	70501	337-237-1898	
E&B Natural Resources Management Corp 1600 Norris Rd Web: www.ebresources.com	Bakersfield	CA	93308	661-679-1700	
Eagle Energy Trust 500 4 Ave SW Ste 2710 TF: 855-531-1575 ■ Web: www.eagleenergytrust.com	Calgary	AB	T2P2V6	403-531-1575	
Eagle Ford Oil & Gas Corp 1110 Nasa Pkwy Ste 311	Houston	TX	77058	281-383-9648	
Earthstone Energy Inc 633 17th St Ste 2320 Web: www.earthstoneenergy.com	Denver	CO	80202	303-296-3076	
EDCON-PRJ Inc 171 S Van Gordon St Ste E Web: edcon-prj.com	Denver	CO	80228	303-980-6556	
EFT Energy 251 W 30th St Ste 15E Web: www.eft-energy.com	Garden City	NY	10001	212-290-2300	
Elbow River Marketing Ltd 1500 335 Eighth Ave SW Web: www.elbowriver.com	Calgary	AB	T2P1C9	403-232-6868	
Elevation Resources LLC 200 N Loraine Ste 1010 Web: www.elevationres.com	Midland	TX	79701	432-686-7500	
Emerald Bay Energy Inc 4015 - First St SE Ste 3A Web: www.emeraldbayenergy.com	Calgary	AB	T2G4X7	403-262-6000	
Empire Energy Corporation International Level 3 65 Murray St Hobart Tasmania Web: www.empireenergy.com	Leawood	KS	66211	913-663-2310	
EnCana Corp 500 Ctr St SE Po Box 2850 NYSE: ECA ■ TF: 888-568-6322 ■ Web: www.encana.com	Calgary	AB	T2G1A6	403-645-2000	645-3400
Endurance Resources Holdings LLC 15455 Dallas Pkwy Ste 600 Web: www.enduranceresourcesllc.com	Addison	TX	75001	972-764-3131	
Energy & Exploration Partners Inc 100 Throckmorton Ste 1700 Web: www.enxp.com	Fort Worth	TX	76102	817-789-6712	
Energy Water Solutions LLC 9595 Six Pines Dr Ste 8210 Web: www.energywatersolutions.com	The Woodlands	TX	77380	713-722-0408	
Enertopia Corp Suite 950, 1130 W Pender St Web: www.enertopia.com	Vancouver	BC	V6E4A4	604-602-1675	
Enhance Energy Inc 333 5 Ave SW Ste 900 Web: www.enhanceenergy.com	Calgary	AB	T2P3B6	403-984-0202	
Enhanced Oil Resources Inc 1 Riverway Ste 610 Web: www.enhancedoilres.com	Houston	TX	77056	832-485-8500	
Eni Petroleum Co 1200 Louisiana St Ste 1707 Web: eni.com	Houston	TX	77002	713-393-6100	
Enpro Services Of Vermont Inc 19 National Dr Web: enpro.com	Franklin	MA	02038	802-860-1200	
EOR Energy Services Inc 3950 Braxton Ste 100 Web: www.eorenergy.com	Houston	TX	77063	713-914-9300	
EQT Corp 625 Liberty Ave Ste 1700 NYSE: EQT ■ TF: 800-242-1776 ■ Web: www.eqt.com	Pittsburgh	PA	15222	412-553-5700	
ERHC Energy Inc Ste 1440 5444 Westheimer Rd Web: erhc.com	Houston	TX	77056	713-626-4700	
EVOenergy LLC 10211 219th St, S.E. Web: www.evonrg.com	Snohomish	WA	98296	415-533-0998	
Extreme Plastics Plus Inc 148 Roush Cir. TF: 866-408-2837 ■ Web: www.extremeplasticsplus.com	Fairmont	WV	26554	866-408-2837	
Exxon Mobil Corp 5959 Las Colinas Blvd NYSE: XOM ■ TF: 800-252-1800 ■ Web: www.exxonmobil.com	Irving	TX	75039	972-444-1000	444-1433
Fairborne Energy Ltd 450 1 St SW	Calgary	AB	T2P5H1	403-290-7750	
Famcor Oil Inc 7887 San Felipe Ste 250 Web: www.famcor.com	Houston	TX	77063	713-974-0002	
Far East Energy Corp SUITE 380, 363 N SAM HOUSTON PKWY Web: www.fareastenergy.com	Houston	TX	77060	832-598-0470	
FHG Inc 6809 Orchard Ridge Dr Web: www.fhg-inc.com	Charlotte	NC	28227	704-567-9548	
FieldPoint Petroleum Corp 609 Castle Ridge Rd Ste 335 NYSE: FPP ■ Web: www.fppcorp.com	Cedar Park	TX	78746	512-250-8692	
First Titan Energy LLC 495 Grand Blvd Ste 206 Web: www.firsttitanenergy.com	Miramar Beach	FL	32550	850-269-7267	
FLS Energy Inc 130 Roberts St Web: www.flsenergy.com	Asheville	NC	28801	828-350-3993	
Forbes Energy Services LLC 3000 S Business Hwy 28 Web: www.forbesenergyservices.com	Alice	TX	78333	361-664-0549	
Forge Energy LLC 10999 W Interstate 10 Web: www.forgenergy.com	San Antonio	TX	78230	210-478-5950	
Fusion Geophysical LLC 103 W Boyd St Web: www.fusiongeo.com	Norman	OK	73069	405-364-8663	
Future Acquisition Company LLC 1455 W Loop South Web: www.futureacq.com	Houston	TX	77027	832-831-3700	

Company	City	State	Zip	Phone	Fax
FX Energy Inc 3006 Highland Dr Ste 206 *Web:* www.fxenergy.com	Salt Lake City	UT	84106	801-486-5555	
Gasco Energy Inc 7979 E. Tufts Ave Ste 1150 *OTC: GSXN* ■ *Web:* www.gascoenergy.com	Denver	CO	80237	303-483-0044	483-0011
Gastar Exploration Ltd 1331 Lamar St Ste 1080 *NYSE: GST* ■ *Web:* www.gastar.com	Houston	TX	77010	713-739-1800	739-0458
Gear Energy Ltd 2600 500 - Fourth Ave SW *TF:* 877-494-3430 ■ *Web:* www.gearenergy.com	Calgary	AB	T2P2V6	403-538-8435	
Geoforce Inc 750 Canyon Dr Ste 140 *TF:* 888-574-3878 ■ *Web:* www.geoforce.com	Coppell	TX	75019	972-546-3878	
Geologic Data Systems Inc 2145 S Clermont St *Web:* www.geologicdata.com	Denver	CO	80222	303-837-1699	
GeoMark Research Ltd 218 Higgins St *Web:* www.geomarkresearch.com	Humble	TX	77338	832-644-1184	
GeoResources Inc 110 Cypress Stn Dr Ste 220 *NASDAQ: GEOI* ■ *TF:* 855-538-0599 ■ *Web:* www.halconresources.com	Williston	ND	58802	281-537-9920	537-8324
Gibson Energy Inc 440 - Second Ave SW Ste 1700 *Web:* www.gibsons.com	Calgary	AB	T2P5E9	403-206-4000	
GMX Resources Inc 9400 Bdwy Extension Hwy *NYSE: GMXRQ* ■ *Web:* www.gmxresources.com	Oklahoma City	OK	73114	405-600-0711	
Gold Hill Corp 2233 W Lindsey Ste 117 *Web:* www.goldhill-inc.com	Norman	OK	73069	405-321-8371	
Gran Tierra Energy Inc 200 150 13th Ave SW *Web:* www.grantierra.com	Calgary	AB	T2R0V2	403-265-3221	
Great Western Drilling Co Inc 700 W Louisiana St *Web:* www.gwdc.com	Midland	TX	79701	432-682-5241	684-3702
Grizzly Oil Sands ULC 605 - 5 Ave SW Ste 2600 *Web:* www.grizzlyoilsands.com	Calgary	AB	T2P3H5	403-930-6450	
Gulfport Energy Corp 14313 N May Ave Ste 100 *Web:* www.gulfportenergy.com	Oklahoma City	OK	73134	405-848-8807	
GulfSlope Energy Inc Ste 800 2500 City W Blvd. *Web:* www.gulfslope.com	Houston	TX	77042	281-918-4100	
Gullett & Associates Inc 7705 S Loop E *Web:* www.gulonline.com	Houston	TX	77012	713-644-3219	
Gunnison Energy Corp 1801 Broadway Ste 1200 *Web:* www.oxbow.com	Denver	CO	80202	303-296-4222	296-4555
H2 Plains LLC North Hwy 283 *Web:* www.hartmanoil.com	Ness City	KS	67560	785-798-3995	
Harken Energy Corp 180 State St Ste 200 *OTC: HKNI* ■ *Web:* www.hkninc.com	Southlake	TX	76092	817-424-2424	
Harvest Natural Resources Inc 1177 Enclave Pkwy Ste 300 *NYSE: HNR* ■ *Web:* www.harvestnr.com	Houston	TX	77077	281-899-5700	899-5702
Headington Oil Co 2711 N Haskell Ave Ste 2800 *Web:* www.headington.com	Dallas	TX	75204	214-696-0606	696-7746
Heavy Earth Resources Inc 625 2nd St Ste 280	San Francisco	CA	94107	415-813-5079	
HG Energy LLC 5260 Dupont Rd *Web:* hgenergyllc.com	Parkersburg	WV	26101	304-420-1100	
Hibernia Management & Development Company Ltd 100 New Gower St Ste 1000 *Web:* www.hibernia.ca	St. John's	NL	A1C6K3	709-778-7000	
Hillwood International Energy L P 3090 Olive St Ste 420 *Web:* www.hillwood.com	Dallas	TX	75219	214-754-2316	
HLI Energy Services Inc 3600 W Hwy 67 *Web:* www.hlienergy.com	Cleburne	TX	76033	817-558-1018	
Hunt Oil Co 1900 N Akard St *Web:* www.huntoil.com	Dallas	TX	75201	214-978-8000	978-8888
Husky Energy Inc 707 Eighth Ave SW PO Box 6525 *TSE: HSE* ■ *TF:* 877-262-2111 ■ *Web:* www.huskyenergy.com	Calgary	AB	T2P3G7	403-298-6111	298-7464
Hyperdynamics Corp 12012 Wickchester Ln Ste 475 *OTC: HDYN* ■ *Web:* www.hyperdynamics.com	Houston	TX	77079	713-353-9400	353-9421
Imperium Renewables Inc 568 First Ave S Ste 600 *Web:* www.imperiumrenewables.com	Seattle	WA	98104	206-254-0203	
Iona Energy Inc The Grain Exchange Bldg Ste 310 815-1st St SW *Web:* www.ionaenergy.com	Calgary	AB	T2P1N3	203-757-4980	
J-W Operating Company Inc 15505 Wright Brothers Dr. *Web:* www.jwenergy.com	Addison	TX	75001	972-233-8191	
Japan Canada Oil Sands Ltd 639-5th Ave SW Standard Life Bldg Ste 2300 *Web:* www.jacos.ca	Calgary	AB	T2P0M9	403-264-9046	
JBL Energy Partners LLC 23902 FM 2978 Ste B *Web:* www.jblenergypartners.com	Tomball	TX	77375	281-516-3137	
JM Huber Corp 499 Thornall St 8th Fl **Fax:* Hum Res ■ *TF:* 877-418-0038 ■ *Web:* www.huber.com	Edison	NJ	08837	732-549-8600	549-2239*
JMA Energy Company LLC 1021 NW Grand Blvd *Web:* www.jmaenergy.com	Oklahoma City	OK	73118	405-947-4322	
Jonah Energy LLC 755 Mulberry Ave Ste 450 *Web:* jonahenergy.com	San Antonio	TX	78212	210-375-3060	
JP Oil Company LLC 1604 W Pinhook Rd Ste 300 *Web:* www.jpoil.com	Lafayette	LA	70508	337-234-1170	
JPW Riggers Inc 6376 Thompson Rd *Web:* www.jpwriggers.com	Syracuse	NY	13206	315-432-1111	
Junex Inc 2795 Laurier Blvd Ste 200 *Web:* www.junex.ca	Quebec	QC	G1V4M7	418-654-9661	
Kerr Energy Companies LLC 3400 Louisiana St *Web:* www.kerrenergycompanies.com	Houston	TX	77002	281-216-5089	
Kings Oil Tools Inc P.O. Box 441 *Web:* www.kingsoiltools.com	San Ardo	CA	93450	831-627-2581	
Kosmos Energy LLC 8176 Park Ln Ste 500 *Web:* www.kosmosenergy.com	Dallas	TX	75231	214-445-9600	

Company	City	State	Zip	Phone	Fax
Kraken Oil & Gas LLC 9821 Katy Fwy Ste 460 *Web:* www.krakenoil.com	Houston	TX	77024	713-360-7705	
Lario Oil & Gas Co 301 S Market St *Web:* lariooil.com	Wichita	KS	67202	316-265-5611	265-5610
Legend Energy Services LLC 510 E Memorial Rd Bldg D *Web:* www.legendenergyservices.com	Oklahoma City	OK	73114	405-600-1264	
Lenape Resources Inc 9489 Alexander Rd *Web:* www.lenaperesources.com	Alexander	NY	14005	585-344-1200	344-3283
Lightning Energy Services LLC 415 Benedum Dr. *Web:* lightningenergyservices.com	Bridgeport	WV	26330	724-731-0370	
Limestone Exploration II LLC 1100 W Wall St *Web:* www.limestone2.com	Midland	TX	79701	432-687-4220	
Loftin Equipment Company Inc 12 N 45th Ave *TF:* 800-437-4376 ■ *Web:* www.loftinequip.com	Phoenix	AZ	85043	602-272-9466	
Lonestar Resources Inc 509 Pecan Ste 200 *Web:* lonestarresources.com	Fort Worth	TX	76102	817-921-1889	
Loon Energy Corp 1500-700 4 Ave SW *Web:* www.loonenergy.com	Calgary	AB	T2P3J4	403-264-8877	
LPC Crude Oil Marketing LLC 408 W Wall *Web:* lpccrude.com	Midland	TX	79701	432-682-8555	
Luca International Group LLC 39650 Liberty St Ste 410 *TF:* 877-988-6688 ■ *Web:* www.luca88.com	Fremont	CA	94538	510-498-8829	
Lucas Energy Inc 450 Gears Rd Ste 860 *Web:* www.lucasenergy.com	Houston	TX	77067	713-528-1881	
Mack Energy Co 1202 N Tenth St *Web:* www.mackenergy.com	Duncan	OK	73533	580-252-5580	
Macpherson Oil Co 2716 Ocean Park Blvd Ste 3080 *Web:* www.macphersonenergy.com	Santa Monica	CA	90405	310-452-3880	
Magellan Petroleum Corp 1775 Sherman St Ste 1950 *NASDAQ: MPET* ■ *Web:* www.magellanpetroleum.com	Denver	CO	80203	720-484-2400	
Magnum Hunter Resources 120 Prosperous Pl Ste 201 *Web:* www.magnumhunterresources.com	Lexington	KY	40509	859-263-3948	
Manitok Energy Inc 639 5 Ave SW Ste 2500 *Web:* www.manitokenergy.com	Calgary	AB	T2P0M9	403-984-1750	
Manx Energy Inc 7400 W 132nd St Ste 160 *Web:* www.kinleyexploration.com	Overland Park	KS	66213	913-851-0433	
Marathon Oil Corp 5555 San Felipe St *Web:* www.marathonoil.com	Houston	TX	77056	713-629-6600	296-2952
Maritech Resources Inc 24955 Interstate 45 N *Web:* www.maritechresources.com	The Woodlands	TX	77380	281-364-4343	
Matador Resources Co 5400 Lyndon B Johnson Fwy Ste 1500 *Web:* www.matadorresources.com	Dallas	TX	75240	972-371-5200	
McCombs Energy Ltd 5599 San Felipe Ste 1200 *Web:* www.mccombsenergy.com	Houston	TX	77056	713-621-0033	
MCW Energy Group Ltd 344 Mira Loma Ave *TF:* 800-979-1897 ■ *Web:* www.mcwenergygroup.com	Glendale	CA	91204	800-979-1897	
MEG Energy Corp 1500 520 - 3 Ave SW *Web:* www.megenergy.com	Calgary	AB	T2P0R3	403-770-0446	
Merrion Oil & Gas 610 Reilly Ave *Web:* www.merrion.bz	Farmington	NM	87401	505-324-5300	
Mewbourne Oil Company Inc 3901 S Broadway Ave. *Web:* mewbourne.net	Tyler	TX	75701	903-561-2900	
Mexco Energy Corp 214 W Texas Ave Ste 1101 PO Box 10502 *NYSE: MXC* ■ *Web:* www.mexcoenergy.com	Midland	TX	79701	432-682-1119	682-1123
Mid-Con Energy Partners LP 2501 N Harwood St Ste 2410 *Web:* www.midconenergypartners.com	Dallas	TX	75201	918-743-7575	
Modern Exploration Inc 4900 Texoma Pkwy *Web:* www.modernexploration.com	Sherman	TX	75090	903-893-1129	
Momentum Oil and Gas LLC 20445 Texas 249 *Web:* www.momentumog.com	Houston	TX	77070	713-419-8198	
Moncla Marine LLC 2107 Carmel Dr *Web:* www.moncla.com	Lafayette	LA	70501	337-456-8799	
Montana Exploration Corp 144 4 Ave SW Ste 2300 *Web:* www.montanaexplorationcorp.com	Calgary	AB	T2P3N4	403-265-9091	
Mountain V Oil & Gas Inc 712 Masonic Dr *Web:* mountainvoilandgas.com	Bridgeport	WV	26330	304-842-6320	
MPX Geophysics Ltd Unit 14 25 Valleywood Dr. *Web:* www.mpxgeophysics.com	Markham	ON	L3R5L9	905-947-1782	
Navajo Nation Oil and Gas Company Inc 50 Narbono Cir W Seconf Fl *Web:* www.nnogc.net	St. Michaels	AZ	86511	928-871-4880	
Nerd Gas Company LLC 1701 East St. *Web:* www.nerdgas.com	Casper	WY	82601	307-234-0583	
New Dominion LLC 1307 S Boulder Ave Ste 400 *Web:* www.newdominion.net	Tulsa	OK	74119	918-587-6242	
New Era Petroleum LLC 251 S Thurmond St. *Web:* www.new-era-petroleum.com	Sheridan	WY	82801	307-673-4812	
New Source Energy Partners LP 914 N Broadway Ste 230 *Web:* www.newsource.com	Oklahoma City	OK	73102	405-272-3028	
Newfield Exploration Co 363 N Sam Houston Pkwy E Ste 100 *NYSE: NFX* ■ *TF:* 866-902-0562 ■ *Web:* newfield.com	Houston	TX	77060	281-847-6000	405-4242
Nexen Inc 801 Seventh Ave SW *NYSE: NXY* ■ *Web:* nexencnoocltd.com	Calgary	AB	T2P3P7	403-699-4000	699-5800
Nexen Petroleum USA Inc 945 Bunker Hill Ste 1400 *Web:* nexencnoocltd.com	Houston	TX	77024	832-714-5000	
Niko Resources Ltd 400 Third Ave SW *TSE: NKO* ■ *Web:* www.nikoresources.com	Calgary	AB	T2P4H2	403-262-1020	263-2686
Nine Energy Service Inc 16945 Northchase Dr Ste 1600 *Web:* nineenergyservice.com	Houston	TX	77060	281-730-5100	

				Phone	Fax
Noble Energy Inc 100 Glenborough Dr Ste 100 .... Houston *NYSE: NBL* ■ *TF:* 800-220-5824 ■ *Web:* www.nobleenergyinc.com	TX	77067		281-872-3100	872-3111
Nomad Energy Inc 22762 Westheimer Pkwy Ste 515 .... Houston *TF:* 866-387-0287 ■ *Web:* www.nomadenergy.com	TX	77450		866-387-0287	
North Atlantic Refining Ltd 29 Pippy Pl PO Box 40 .... St. John's *TF:* 877-635-3645 ■ *Web:* www.northatlantic.ca	NL	A1B3X2		709-463-8811	
Noveda Technologies Inc 1200 US Hwy 22 East Ste 2000 .... Bridgewater *Web:* www.noveda.com	NJ	08807		908-534-8855	
NuVista Energy Ltd 3500 700 - Second St SW .... Calgary *Web:* www.nuvistaenergy.com	AB	T2P2W2		403-538-8500	
NW Natural 220 NW Second Ave PO Box 6017 .... Portland **Fax:* Cust Svc ■ *TF:* 800-422-4012 ■ *Web:* www.nwnatural.com	OR	97209		503-226-4211	273-4824*
O'Brien Energy Co 425 Ashley Ridge Blvd Ste 300 .... Shreveport *Web:* www.obrienenergyco.com	LA	71106		318-865-8568	
Occidental Oil & Gas Corp 5 Greenway Plaza Ste 110 .... Houston *Web:* www.oxy.com	TX	77046		713-215-7000	215-7399
Ohio Gas Co PO Box 528 .... Bryan *TF:* 800-331-7396 ■ *Web:* www.ohiogas.com	OH	43506		419-636-1117	636-9837
Oil Producers Inc of Kansas 1710 N WaterFrnt Pkwy .... Wichita *Web:* www.oilprod.com	KS	67206		316-681-0231	
Okland Oil Co 110 N Robinson Ave .... Oklahoma City *Web:* www.oklandoil.com	OK	73102		405-236-3046	
Omimex Resources Inc 7950 John T White Rd .... Fort Worth *Web:* www.omimex.com	TX	76120		817-460-7777	
Omni Valve Company LLC 4520 Chandler Rd .... Muskogee *Web:* www.omnivalve.com	OK	74403		918-687-6100	
OriginClear Inc 5645 W Adams Blvd .... Los Angeles *TF:* 877-999-6645 ■ *Web:* www.originoil.com	CA	90016		323-939-6645	
Oryx Midstream Services LLC 4000 N Big Spring Ste 210 .... Midland *Web:* www.oryxmidstream.com	TX	79705		432-684-4272	
Oryx Petroleum Corporation Ltd 350 7 Ave SW .... Calgary *Web:* www.oryxpetroleum.com	AB	T2P3N9		415-872-0932	
Oxbow Carbon & Minerals Inc 1601 Forum Pl Ste 1400 .... West Palm Beach *Web:* www.oxbow.com	FL	33401		561-697-4300	697-1876
Pantera Energy Co 817 S Polk St Ste 201 .... Amarillo *Web:* www.panteraenergy.com	TX	79101		806-376-6625	
Park Energy Services LLC 514 Colcord Dr .... Oklahoma City *Web:* www.parkenergyservices.com	OK	73102		405-896-3169	
Parsley Energy Inc 303 Colorado St Ste 3000 .... Austin *Web:* www.parsleyenergy.com	TX	78701		432-818-2100	
Pasadena Refining System Inc 111 Red Bluff Rd .... Pasadena *Web:* www.pasadenarefining.com	TX	77506		713-472-2461	
Pegasi Energy Resources Corp 218 N Broadway Ave Ste 204 .... Tyler *Web:* www.pegasienergy.com	TX	75702		903-595-4139	
Pemex Procurement International Inc 10344 sam houston park dr .... Houston *TF:* 888-254-1487 ■ *Web:* www.pemexprocurement.com	TX	77064		713-430-3100	
Penn Virginia Corp 100 Matsonford Rd Ste 200 .... Radnor *NYSE: PVA* ■ *TF:* 877-316-5288 ■ *Web:* www.pennvirginia.com	PA	19087		610-687-8900	687-3688
Penn West Petroleum Ltd Ninth Ave SW Ste 200 .... Calgary *TSE: PWT* ■ *TF:* 866-693-2707 ■ *Web:* www.pennwest.com	AB	T2P1K3		403-777-2500	777-2699
Perf-O-Log Inc 101 Bolton St .... Lafayette *TF:* 888-892-8276 ■ *Web:* www.perfolog.com	LA	70508		888-892-8276	
Perpetual Energy Inc 605 5 Ave SW Ste 3200 .... Calgary *Web:* www.perpetualenergyinc.com	AB	T2P3H5		403-269-4400	
Petro Lucrum Inc 3525 Sage .... Houston *Web:* www.petrolucrum.com	TX	77056		832-993-5426	
Petro Vista Energy Corp 789 W Pender St Ste 800 .... Vancouver *Web:* www.pvecorp.com	BC	V6C1H2		604-638-8067	
Petrobras USA 10350 Richmond Ave Ste 1400 .... Houston *Web:* www.petrobras.com	TX	77042		713-808-2000	
Petrodorado Energy Ltd 850 - 2nd St SW Ste 1500 .... Calgary *Web:* www.petrodorado.com	AB	T2P0R8		403-800-9240	
Petroglyph Energy Inc 960 Broadway Ave Ste 500 .... Boise *Web:* www.intermountainindustries.com	ID	83706		208-685-7600	
Petroleum Development Corp (PDC) 120 Genesis Blvd PO Box 26 .... Bridgeport *NASDAQ: PDCE* ■ *TF:* 800-624-3821 ■ *Web:* www.petd.com	WV	26330		303-860-5800	
Petrolia Inc 305 Charest Blvd E 10th Fl .... Quebec *Web:* petrolia-inc.com	QC	G1K3H3		418-657-1966	
Petroplex Energy Inc 110 N Marienfeld St Ste 290 .... Midland *Web:* www.petroplex.net	TX	79701		432-570-7030	
PHX Energy Services Corp 1400-250 2 St SW .... Calgary *Web:* www.phxtech.com	AB	T2P0C1		403-543-4466	
Pioneer Exploration LLC 15603 Kuykendahl Ste 200 .... Houston *Web:* www.pecogas.com	TX	77090		281-893-9400	
Pioneer Natural Resources Co 5205 N O'Connor Blvd Ste 200 .... Irving *NYSE: PXD* ■ *TF:* 888-234-6372 ■ *Web:* www.pxd.com	TX	75039		972-444-9001	
Pioneer Oil & Gas Unit B 1206 W S Jordan Pkwy .... South Jordan *Web:* www.piol.com	UT	84095		801-566-3000	
Pioneer Petrotech Services Inc Ste 1 1431-40 Ave NE .... Calgary *Web:* www.pioneerps.com	AB	T2E8N6		403-282-7669	
Primexx Energy Partners Ltd 4849 Greenville Ave Two Energy Sq Ste 1600 .... Dallas *TF:* 800-754-5908 ■ *Web:* primexx.com	TX	75206		214-369-5909	
Pro-Stim Services LLC 22503 Katy Fwy .... Katy *Web:* www.prostimservices.com	TX	77450		281-769-5727	
Questerre Energy Corp 1650 AMEC Place 801 Sixth Ave SW .... Calgary *Web:* www.questerre.com	AB	T2P3W2		403-777-1185	
RAAM Global Energy Co 1537 Bull Lea Rd Ste 200 .... Lexington	KY	40511		859-253-1300	
Raging River Exploration Inc 605 - 5th Ave SW 17th Fl .... Calgary *Web:* www.rrexploration.com	AB	T2P3H5		403-387-2950	
Range Resources Corp 100 Throckmorton St Ste 1200 .... Fort Worth *NYSE: RRC* ■ *Web:* www.rangeresources.com	TX	76102		817-870-2601	869-9100
Ranken Energy Corp 417 W 18th St Ste 101 .... Edmond *Web:* www.ranken-energy.com	OK	73013		405-340-2363	
RCW Energy Services LLC 4125 Fairway Dr Ste 150 .... Carrollton *Web:* www.rcwenergyservices.com	TX	75010		972-394-1000	
Redbud E&P Inc 16000 Stuebner Airline Ste 320 .... Spring *Web:* www.redbudinc.com	TX	77379		832-698-4234	
Regent Resources Ltd 1000 605 - Fifth Ave SW .... Calgary *Web:* www.regentresources.com	AB	T2P3H5		403-264-0018	
Reserve Petroleum Co 6801 Broadway Ext Ste 300 .... Oklahoma City *Web:* www.reserve-petro.com	OK	73116		405-848-7551	
Resolute Energy Corp 1700 N Lincoln St Ste 2800 .... Denver *Web:* www.resoluteenergy.com	CO	80203		303-573-4886	
Rex Energy Corp 366 Walker Dr .... State College *Web:* www.rexenergycorp.com	PA	16801		814-278-7267	
Rice Energy Inc 400 Woodcliff Dr .... Canonsburg *Web:* www.riceenergy.com	PA	15317		724-746-6720	
Rife Resources Ltd 400 144 - Fourth Ave SW .... Calgary *TF:* 888-257-1873 ■ *Web:* www.rife.com	AB	T2P3N4		403-221-0800	
Ring Energy Inc 901 West Wall St 3rd Fl .... Midland *Web:* ringenergy.com	TX	79701		918-499-3880	
Rio Bravo Oil Inc 5858 Westheimer Rd Ste 669 .... Houston	TX	77057		713-787-9060	
RMP Energy Inc 1200-500 4 Ave SW .... Calgary *Web:* www.rmpenergyinc.com	AB	T2P2V6		403-930-6300	
Rockdale Resources Corp 710 N Post Oak Rd Ste 512 .... Houston *Web:* www.rockdaleresources.com	TX	77024		832-941-0011	
Rooster Energy Ltd 16285 Park Ten Pl Ste 120 .... Houston *Web:* www.roosterenergyltd.com	TX	77084		832-772-6313	
Royale Energy Inc 3777 WILLOW GLEN Dr .... El Cajon *Web:* www.royl.com	CA	92019		619-881-2800	
RSP Permian Inc 3141 Hood St Ste 500 .... Dallas *Web:* www.rsppermian.com	TX	75219		214-252-2700	
Sage Petroleum 2148 S Jefferson St .... Casper *Web:* sagepetroleum.com	WY	82601		307-265-6992	
Saguaro Resources Ltd 3000 500 - Fourth Ave SW .... Calgary *TF:* 855-835-4434 ■ *Web:* saguaroresources.com	AB	T2P2V6		403-453-3040	
Samson Oil and Gas USA Inc 1726 Cole Blvd Ste 210 .... Lakewood *Web:* www.samsonoilandgas.com	CO	80401		303-295-0344	
Sandridge Midstream Inc 1601 Northwest Expy Ste 1600 .... Oklahoma City *Web:* www.sandridgeenergy.com	OK	73118		405-429-5500	
SeaBird Exploration Americas Inc 1155 N Dairy Ashford Ste 206 .... Houston *Web:* www.sbexp.com	TX	77079		281-556-1666	
Seamar Holdings LLC 13715 N Promenade Blvd .... Stafford *Web:* www.seamardivers.com	TX	77477		281-208-2522	
Sefton Resources Inc 2050 S Oneida St Ste 102 .... Denver *Web:* www.seftonresources.com	CO	80224		303-759-2700	
Seismic Ventures LLC 4805 Westway Park Bouvelard Ste 100 .... Houston *Web:* www.seismicventures.com	TX	77041		281-240-1234	
Seneca Resources Corp 1201 Louisiana St Ste 400 .... Houston *TF:* 800-365-3234 ■ *Web:* natfuel.com	TX	77002		713-654-2600	
Sequel Energy LLC 1600 Stout St Ste 1900 .... Denver *Web:* www.sequelenergy.com	CO	80202		303-468-2106	
Shell Canada Ltd 400 Fourth Ave SW .... Calgary *TF:* 877-656-3111 ■ *Web:* www.shell.ca	AB	T2P0J4		403-691-3111	
Shell Oil Co 910 Louisanna St .... Houston *TF:* 888-467-4355 ■ *Web:* www.shell.us	TX	77002		713-241-6161	
Shoal Point Energy Ltd 1060-1090 Georgia St W .... Vancouver *Web:* www.shoalpointenergy.com	BC	V6E3V7		416-637-2181	
Sinopec Daylight Energy Ltd 112-4th Ave SW Sun Life Plz E Tower Ste 2700 .... Calgary *TF:* 877-266-6901 ■ *Web:* www.sinopecdaylight.com	AB	T2P0H3		403-266-6900	
Slawson Cos Inc 727 N Waco St Ste 400 .... Wichita *Web:* www.slawsoncompanies.com	KS	67203		316-263-3201	268-0702
Snyder Brothers Inc 1 Glade Park Dr .... Kittanning *Web:* www.snyderbrothersinc.com	PA	16201		724-548-8101	
Southwestern Energy Co 2350 N Sam Houston Pkwy E Ste 300 .... Houston *NYSE: SWN* ■ *TF:* 866-322-0801 ■ *Web:* www.swn.com	TX	77032		832-796-1000	796-4818
Spartan Energy Corp 850 - Second St SW Ste 500 .... Calgary *Web:* www.spartanenergy.ca	AB	T2P0R8		403-355-8920	
Spartan Offshore Drilling LLC 516 JF Smith Ave .... Slidell *Web:* www.spartanoffshore.com	LA	70460		504-885-7449	
Special Energy Corp 4815 Perkins Rd .... Stillwater *Web:* www.specialenergycorp.com	OK	74076		405-377-1177	
Speedy Heavy Hauling Inc 610 25 Rd .... Grand Junction *Web:* www.speedyhh.com	CO	81505		970-241-3420	
Spinnaker Exploration Co 1200 Smith St Ste 800 .... Houston *Web:* www.subsea.org	TX	77002		713-759-1770	

Phone / Fax

Spyglass Resources Corp
Livingston Place 250 2 St SW Tower 1700 Calgary AB T2P0C1 403-303-8500
Web: www.spyglassresources.com

SR2020 Inc 3 Pointe Dr Ste 212 Brea CA 92821 714-482-1922
Web: www.sr2020inc.com

Starboard Resources Inc
300 E Sonterra Blvd Ste 1220 San Antonio TX 78258 210-999-5400
Web: www.starboardresources.com

Steelhead LNG Corp 650 - 669 Howe St. Vancouver BC V6C0B4 604-235-3800
Web: www.steelheadlng.com

Stelbar Oil Corp Inc
1625 N Waterfront Pkwy Ste 200 Wichita KS 67206 316-264-8378

Stone Energy Corp 625 E Kaliste Saloom Rd Lafayette LA 70508 337-237-0410 521-2072
NYSE: SGY ■ *Web:* www.stoneenergy.com

Stonegate Production Company LLC
952 Echo Ln Ste 400 Houston TX 77024 713-600-8000
Web: www.stone-gate.net

Storm Resources Ltd 640 5 Ave SW Ste 200 Calgary AB T2P3G4 403-817-6145
Web: www.stormresourcesltd.com

Strad Energy Services Ltd
440 - Second Ave SW Ste 1200 Calgary AB T2P5E9 403-232-6900
Web: www.stradenergy.com

Strat Land Exploration Co
15 E Fifth St Ste 2020 Tulsa OK 74103 918-584-3844
Web: stratland.com

Strata Oil & Gas Inc
10010 - 98 St PO Box 7770 Peace River AB T8S1T3 403-237-5443
TF: 877-237-5443 ■ *Web:* www.strataoil.com

Strike Energy Services Inc
1300 505 - Third St SW Calgary AB T2P3E6 403-232-8448
Web: www.strikegroup.ca

Suemaur Exploration & Production LLC
802 N Carancahua Frost Bank Plz
Ste 1000 Corpus Christi TX 78470 361-884-8824
Web: www.suemaur.com

Summit Midstream Partners LP
1790 Hughes Landing Blvd Ste 500 The Woodlands TX 77380 832-413-4770
Web: www.summitmidstream.com

Suncor Energy Inc 150 - 6 Ave SW PO Box 2844 Calgary AB T2P3E3 403-296-8000 296-3030
NYSE: SU ■ *TF:* 800-558-9071 ■ *Web:* www.suncor.com

Sunoco Inc 1735 Market St Ste LL Philadelphia PA 19103 215-977-3000 977-3409
NYSE: SUN ■ *TF:* 800-786-6261 ■ *Web:* sunoco.com

Sunshine Oilsands Ltd 8h Ave SW Ste 903 Calgary AB T2P0P7 403-984-1450
Web: www.sunshineoilsands.com

Surge Energy Inc 2100 635 Eighth Ave SW Calgary AB T2P3M3 403-930-1010
Web: www.surgeenergy.ca

Swift Energy Co 16825 Northchase Dr Ste 400 Houston TX 77060 281-874-2700
NYSE: SFY ■ *TF:* 800-777-2412 ■ *Web:* www.swiftenergy.com

Sylios Corp
735 Arlington Ave N Ste 308 St. Petersburg FL 33701 727-821-6200
Web: www.sylios.com

Syntroleum Corp 5416 S Yale Ave Ste 400 Tulsa OK 74135 918-592-7900 592-7979
NASDAQ: SYNM

Tammany Oil & Gas LLC
20445 State Hwy 249 Ste 200 Houston TX 77070 281-517-0770
Web: www.tammanyoil.com

Tangle Creek Energy Ltd
715 Fifth Ave SW Ste 1400 Calgary AB T2P2X6 403-648-4900
Web: www.tanglecreekenergy.com

TanMar Companies LLC 711 S Chestnut Tomball TX 77375 281-591-6480
Web: www.tanmarcompanies.com

Tanos Exploration LLC
110 N College Ave Ste 1001 Tyler TX 75702 903-597-7667
Web: www.tanosexp.com

Taylor Energy Company LLC 1 Lee Cir New Orleans LA 70130 504-581-5491
Web: www.taylorenergy.com

TCE LLC 1015 Grant Ave Coon Rapids IA 50058 712-684-5102
Web: tcellc.net

Teine Energy Ltd 2300 520 - Third Ave SW Calgary AB T2P0R3 403-698-8300
TF: 866-900-2711 ■ *Web:* www.teine-energy.com

Tellus Operating Group LLC
602 Crescent Pl Ste 100 Ridgeland MS 39157 601-898-7444
Web: www.tellusoperating.com

Tengasco Inc 11121 Kingston Pk Ste E Knoxville TN 37934 865-675-1554 675-1621
NYSE: TGC ■ *TF:* 888-669-0684 ■ *Web:* www.tengasco.com

Termo Co, The 3275 Cherry Ave Long Beach CA 90807 888-260-4715
TF: 888-260-4715 ■ *Web:* www.termoco.com

TerraSond Ltd 1617 S Industrial Way Ste 3 Palmer AK 99645 907-745-7215
Web: www.terrasond.com

Tervita Corp 500 140 - 10 Ave SE Calgary AB T2G0R1 403-233-7565
Web: www.tervita.com

Tesla Exploration Ltd 4500 8A St NE Calgary AB T2E4J7 403-216-0999
Web: www.teslaexploration.com

THUMS Long Beach Co 5 Greenway Plz Ste 110 Houston TX 77046 713-215-7000
Web: www.oxy.com

Titan Oil & Gas Services Inc
6809 King Ave W Bldg E Billings MT 59106 406-945-5036
TF: 800-406-5209 ■ *Web:* www.titanoilgas.com

Topaz Resources Inc 1012 N Masch Branch Rd Denton TX 76207 940-243-1122
Web: www.topazresourcesinc.com

Torchlight Energy Resources Inc
5700 W Plano Pkwy Ste 3600 Plano TX 75093 214-432-8002
Web: www.torchlightenergy.com

Tourmaline Oil Corp
Suite 3700, 250 6th Ave S.W Calgary AB T2P3H7 403-767-3593
Web: www.tourmalineoil.com

Trans Energy Inc 210 Second St PO Box 393 St. Marys WV 26170 304-684-7053
Web: transenergyinc.com

Tri-Star Protector Service Co
19233 FM 1485 Rd. New Caney TX 77357 281-399-2600
Web: www.tristarprotector.com

Trilogy Energy Corp 1400-332 6 Ave SW Calgary AB T2P0B2 403-290-2900
Web: www.trilogyenergy.com

TriPower Resources LLC 16 E St Ardmore OK 73401 580-226-6700
Web: www.tripowerresources.com

Tundra Oil & Gas Limited
1700 One Lombard Pl Winnipeg MB R3B0X3 204-934-5850
Web: www.tundraoilandgas.com

TXCO Resources Inc
777 E.Sonterra Blvd.,Suite 350; San Antonio TX 78258 210-496-5300
Web: www.txco.com

Ultra Petroleum Corp
400 N Sam Houston Pkwy E Ste 1200 Houston TX 77060 281-876-0120 876-2831
NYSE: UPL ■ *Web:* www.ultrapetroleum.com

Unconventional Gas Resources Canada Operating Inc
736 - 8 Ave SW Ste 700 Calgary AB T2P1H4 403-269-1690
Web: www.ugresources.com

Unit Corp 7130 S Lewis Ave Ste 1000 Tulsa OK 74136 918-493-7700 493-7711
NYSE: UNT ■ *TF:* 800-722-3612 ■ *Web:* www.unitcorp.com

United Hydrocarbon International Corp
308 - Fourth Ave SW Ste 2500 Calgary AB T2P0H7 403-774-9900
Web: www.unitedhydrocarbon.com

Unitex Oil & Gas LLC 310 W Wall Ste 503 Midland TX 79701 432-685-0014
Web: unitexoilandgas.com

Valence Operating Co
1 Kingwood Pl 600 Rockmead Dr Ste 200 Kingwood TX 77339 281-359-3659
Web: www.valenceoperating.com

Valeura Energy Inc 1200-202 6 Ave SW Calgary AB T2P2R9 403-237-7102
Web: www.valeuraenergy.com

Value Creation Inc 1100 635 - Eighth Ave SW Calgary AB T2P3M3 403-539-4500
TF: 855-908-8800 ■ *Web:* www.vctek.com

Vangold Resources Ltd
7681 Prince Edward St Vancouver BC V5X3R4 604-684-1974
TF: 866-684-1974 ■ *Web:* www.vangold.ca

Vanguard Energy Corp
Suite 1600, 1330 Post Oak Blvd. Houston TX 77056 713-627-2500
Web: www.vanguardenergycorp.com

Venado Oil & Gas LLC
12600 Hill Country Blvd Bldg R Ste 250 Austin TX 78738 512-735-9000
Web: www.vogllc.com

Venture Oil & Gas Inc
3575 N Belt Line Rd Ste 346 Irving TX 75062 214-912-7017
Web: ventureoil.net

Vernon E. Faulconer Inc
1001 ESE Loop 323 Ste 160 Tyler TX 75701 903-581-4382
Web: www.vefinc.com

Vess Oil Corp 1700 WaterFrnt Pkwy Bldg 500 Wichita KS 67206 316-682-1537
Web: www.vessoil.com

W & T Offshore Inc 9 Greenway Plz Ste 300 Houston TX 77046 713-626-8525 626-8527
Web: www.wtoffshore.com

Wagner & Brown Ltd 300 N Marienfeld St Midland TX 79701 432-682-7936 686-5928
Web: wbltd.com

Wagner Oil Co 500 Commerce St Ste 600 Fort Worth TX 76102 817-335-2222 334-0053
TF: 800-457-5332 ■ *Web:* www.wagneroil.com

Walden Energy LLC 8908 S Yale Ste 402 Tulsa OK 74137 918-645-7409
Web: www.waldenenergy.com

Waldron Energy Corp 600-510 5 St SW Calgary AB T2P3S2 403-532-6700
Web: www.waldronenergy.ca

Ward Petroleum Corp 502 S Fillmore PO Box 1187 Enid OK 73702 580-234-3229 242-4334*
**Fax Area Code:* 405 ■ *Web:* www.wardpetroleum.com

Warpaint Resources LLC
1925 Cedar Springs Ste 103 Dallas TX 75201 469-250-7555
Web: www.warpaintresources.com

Warren Resources Inc
1114 Ave of the Americas 34th Fl New York NY 10036 212-697-9660 697-9466
NASDAQ: WRES ■ *TF:* 877-587-9494 ■ *Web:* www.warrenresources.com

Washakie Renewable Energy LLC
670 E 3900 S Ste 300 Salt Lake City UT 84107 801-327-8695
Web: wrebiofuels.com

Wayne Oil Company Inc
1301 Wayne Memorial Dr Goldsboro NC 27534 919-735-2021
Web: www.ballparkstores.com

Well Testing Inc 415 W Wall Ste 1600 Midland TX 79701 432-620-0600
Web: www.welltesting.net

Wenzlau Engineering Inc
1517 Fair Oaks Ave South Pasadena CA 91030 310-604-3400
Web: www.wenzlau.com

West Penn Energy Services LLC
4257 Gibsonia Rd Gibsonia PA 15044 724-444-0875
Web: www.wpes-pa.com

Western Land Services Inc
1100 Conrad Industrial Dr Ludington MI 49431 231-843-8878
Web: westernls.com

Wexpro Co 333 S State St Salt Lake City UT 84145 801-324-2534 324-2637
Web: www.questar.com

Whitecap Resources Inc 3800 525 - 8th Ave SW Calgary AB T2P1G1 403-266-0767
TF: 866-590-5289 ■ *Web:* www.wcap.ca

Whiting Petroleum Corp 1700 Broadway Ste 2300 Denver CO 80290 303-837-1661 861-4023
NYSE: WLL ■ *Web:* www.whiting.com

Wildcat Development Corp
230 Spring Hill Dr Ste 300 Spring TX 77386 281-863-9370
Web: wildcatdev.com

Wilshire Enterprises Inc
100 Eagle Rock Ave Ste 100 East Hanover NJ 07936 973-585-7770 585-7771
OTC: WLSE ■ *TF:* 888-697-3962 ■ *Web:* www.wilshireenterprisesinc.com

Wood Group 17325 Park Row Ste 500 Houston TX 77084 281-828-3500
Web: www.woodgroup.com

Wynn - Crosby Energy Inc
5500 W Plano Pkwy Ste 200 Plano TX 75093 972-380-5500
Web: www.wynncrosby.com

XTO Energy Inc 810 Houston St Fort Worth TX 76102 817-870-2800 870-1671
TF: 800-299-2800 ■ *Web:* www.xtoenergy.com

Yangarra Resources Ltd
715 - 5 Ave SW Ste 1530 Calgary AB T2P2X6 403-262-9558
Web: www.yangarra.ca

Yates Petroleum Corp 105 S Fourth St Artesia NM 88210 575-748-1471 748-4570*
**Fax:* Hum Res ■ *Web:* www.yatespetroleum.com

Phone Fax

Zargon Oil & Gas Ltd
333 - Fifth Ave SW Ste 700 .... Calgary AB T2P3B6 403-264-9992
Web: www.zargon.ca

ZaZa Energy Corp 1301 McKinney St Ste 2800........ Houston TX 77010 713-595-1900 595-1919
NASDAQ: ZAZA ■ *TF:* 866-202-3048

Zone Energy LLC
Greenway Plz 3800 Buffalo Speedway Ste 125........ Houston TX 77098 713-877-9920
Web: www.zoneoilandgas.com

537 OIL & GAS FIELD EQUIPMENT

Phone Fax

Abanaki Corp 17387 Munn Rd .... Chagrin Falls OH 44023 440-543-7400
Web: www.abanaki.com

Accumulators Inc 1175 Brittmoore Rd........ Houston TX 77043 713-465-0202
Web: www.accumulators.com

Alberta Oil Tool 9530 60th Ave........ Edmonton AB T6E0C1 780-434-8566 436-4329
TF: 877-432-3404 ■ *Web:* www.albertaoiltool.com

Alloy Carbide Co 7827 Ave H........ Houston TX 77012 713-923-2700 923-4652
Web: www.alloycarbide.com

Baker Hughes Inc (BHI) 2929 Allen Pkwy Ste 1200........ Houston TX 77019 713-439-8600
NYSE: BHI ■ *TF:* 800-229-7447 ■ *Web:* www.bakerhughes.com

Bolt Technology Corp 4 Duke Pl........ Norwalk CT 06854 203-853-0700 854-9601
NASDAQ: BOLT ■ *Web:* www.bolt-technology.com

BVM Corp 430 S Navajo St........ Denver CO 80223 303-975-1402
Web: www.bvmcorp.com

Cameron 1333 W Loop S Ste 1700........ Houston TX 77027 713-513-3300 513-3456
NYSE: CAM ■ *Web:* cameron.slb.com

Carbo Ceramics Inc
575 N. Dairy Ashford Rd. Ste 300........ Houston TX 77079 281-921-6400
NYSE: CRR ■ *TF:* 800-551-3247 ■ *Web:* www.carboceramics.com

Cuming Corp 225 Bodwell St........ Avon MA 02322 508-580-2660 580-0960
TF: 800-432-6464 ■ *Web:* www.cumingcorp.com

Dril-Quip Inc 13550 Hempstead Hwy........ Houston TX 77040 713-939-7711 939-8063
NYSE: DRQ ■ *TF:* 877-316-2631 ■ *Web:* www.dril-quip.com

Drillers Service Inc 1792 Highland Ave NE........ Hickory NC 28601 828-322-1100 322-7436
TF: 800-334-2308 ■ *Web:* www.dsidsi.com

En-fab Inc 3905 Jensen Dr........ Houston TX 77026 713-225-4913 224-7937
Web: www.en-fabinc.com

FMC Technologies Inc 1803 Gears Rd........ Houston TX 77067 281-591-4000 591-4102
NYSE: FTI ■ *TF:* 800-356-4898 ■ *Web:* www.fmctechnologies.com

Gearench Inc 4450 S Hwy 6 PO Box 192........ Clifton TX 76634 254-675-8651 675-6100
Web: www.gearench.com

GEFCO Inc (GEFCO) 2215 S Van Buren........ Enid OK 73703 580-234-4141 233-6807
TF: 800-759-7441 ■ *Web:* www.gefco.com

Gulf Coast Manufacturing LLC 3622 W Main St........ Gray LA 70359 985-872-0187
Web: gulfcoastmfg.com

Gulf Island Fabrication Inc
567 Thompson Rd PO Box 310........ Houma LA 70361 985-872-2100
NASDAQ: GIFI ■ *Web:* www.gulfisland.com

Halliburton Energy Services
10200 Bellaire Blvd........ Houston TX 77072 281-871-4000
Web: www.halliburton.com

Harbison-Fischer 901 N Crowley Rd........ Crowley TX 76036 817-297-2211 297-4248
TF: 800-364-7867 ■ *Web:* doverals.com

Kimray Inc 52 NW 42nd St........ Oklahoma City OK 73118 405-525-6601 525-7520
Web: www.kimray.com

LDI Industries Inc
1864 Nage Ave PO Box 1810........ Manitowoc WI 54221 920-682-6877 684-7210
Web: www.ldi-industries.com

M & M Supply Co 909 W Peach Ave PO Box 548........ Duncan OK 73534 580-252-7879 252-7708
TF: 800-424-9300 ■ *Web:* www.mmsupply.com

Midwestern Manufacturing Company Inc
2119 S Union Ave........ Tulsa OK 74107 918-446-1587
Web: www.sidebooms.com

Morris Industries Inc 777 Rt 23........ Pompton Plains NJ 07444 973-835-6600 835-1245
TF: 800-835-0777 ■ *Web:* www.morrispipe.com

Morrison Bros Co 570 E Seventh St........ Dubuque IA 52001 563-583-5701 583-5028
TF: 800-553-4840 ■ *Web:* www.morbros.com

Natural Gas Services Group Inc (NGSG)
508 W Wall Ste 550........ Midland TX 79701 432-262-2700 262-2701
NYSE: NGS ■ *Web:* www.ngsgi.com

Norriseal 11122 W Little York Rd........ Houston TX 77041 713-466-3552 896-7386*
*Fax: Sales ■ *Web:* www.norriseal.com

NXT Energy Solutions Inc
3320 17th Ave SW Ste 302........ Calgary AB T3E0B4 403-264-7020
Web: www.nxtenergy.com

OTS International Inc 2615 Industrial Ln........ Conroe TX 77301 936-539-0099
Web: otsintl.com

Plant Process Equipment Inc
280 Reynolds Ave........ League City TX 77573 281-333-7850 332-6280
Web: www.plant-process.com

Ruhrpumpen Inc 4501 S 86th E Ave........ Tulsa OK 74145 918-627-8400
Web: www.ruhrpumpen.com

Sandvik Mining & Construction USA LLC
13500 NW CR 235........ Alachua FL 32615 386-462-4100 462-5996
Web: www.miningandconstruction.sandvik.com

Schramm Inc 800 E Virginia Ave........ West Chester PA 19380 610-696-2500 696-6950
TF: 888-737-9438 ■ *Web:* www.schramminc.com

ShawCor Ltd 25 Bethridge Rd........ Toronto ON M9W1M7 416-743-7111 743-7199
TSE: SCL/A ■ *TF:* 855-744-5789 ■ *Web:* www.shawcor.com

Southern Company Inc 3101 Carrier St........ Memphis TN 38116 901-345-2531
TF: 800-264-7626 ■ *Web:* www.socomemphis.com

Southtex Treaters LP 13405 Hwy 191........ Odessa TX 79765 432-563-2766 563-1729
Web: www.southtex.com

Southwest Oilfield Products Inc
10340 Wallisville Rd........ Houston TX 77013 713-675-7541
Web: www.swoil.com

Stewart & Stevenson LLC 1000 Louisiana St........ Houston TX 77002 713-613-0633
Web: www.stewartandstevenson.com

Stratco Inc 14821 N 73rd St........ Scottsdale AZ 85260 480-991-0450 991-0314
Web: www.stratco.com

Phone Fax

Stream-Flo Industries Ltd 4505 - 74 Ave........ Edmonton AB T6B2H5 780-468-6789 469-7724
Web: www.streamflo.com

Surface Equipment Corp 337 Cargill Rd........ Kilgore TX 75662 903-984-0400 983-0018
TF: 800-256-7732 ■ *Web:* www.surfaceequip.com

Tam International Inc 4620 Southerland Rd........ Houston TX 77092 713-462-7617 462-1536
TF: 800-462-7617 ■ *Web:* www.tamintl.com

Taylor Rigs LLC 6015 N Xanthus........ Tulsa OK 74130 918-266-7301
Web: www.taylorindustries.net

Titan Specialties Inc 11785 Hwy 152........ Pampa TX 79065 806-665-3781 669-6674
TF Sales: 800-692-4486 ■ *Web:* hunting-intl.com/hunting-titan

TIW Corp 12300 S Main St PO Box 35729........ Houston TX 77035 713-729-2110 728-4767
Web: www.tiwoiltools.com

Trendsetter Engineering Inc 10430 Rodgers Rd........ Houston TX 77070 281-465-8858
Web: www.trendsetterengineering.com

Weatherford Artificial Lift Systems
918 Hodgkins St........ Houston TX 77032 281-449-1383 449-6235
Web: www.weatherford.com

Weatherford International Inc
515 Post Oak Blvd Ste 600........ Houston TX 77027 713-693-4000 693-4270*
NYSE: WFT ■ *Fax: Hum Res ■ *TF:* 866-398-0010 ■ *Web:* www.weatherford.com

Winston F2S Corp 1604 Cherokee Trace........ White Oak TX 75693 903-757-7341 759-6986
TF: 800-527-8465 ■ *Web:* www.winstonf2s.com

538 OIL & GAS FIELD EXPLORATION SERVICES

Phone Fax

3S Services LLC
2535 Loop 517 PO Box 248........ Carrizo Springs TX 78834 830-876-4155
Web: 3sservices.com

Acadian Contractors Inc
17102 West La Hwy 330........ Abbeville LA 70510 337-893-6397
Web: www.acadiancontractors.com

Adler Hot Oil Services Inc
5035 South 4630 East........ Vernal UT 84078 435-828-0900
Web: www.adlerhotoil.com

Allied Cementing Co LLC 24 S Lincoln St........ Russell KS 67665 785-483-2627
Web: alliedcementing.com

Allied Oilfield Machine and Pump LLC
202 Hulon Moreland Rd........ Levelland TX 79336 855-378-4787
TF: 855-378-4787 ■ *Web:* www.alliedoilfield.com

Allied Well Service Inc 2681 W Frnt St........ Alice TX 78332 361-664-6122
Web: www.alliedwells.com

Ankor Energy LLC 1615 Poydras St Ste 1100........ New Orleans LA 70112 504-596-3737
Web: www.ankorenergy.com

Arctic Slope Regional Corp
1230 Agvik St PO Box 129........ Barrow AK 99723 907-852-8633 852-5733
TF: 800-770-2772 ■ *Web:* www.asrc.com

Arena Energy 4200 RES Forest Dr Ste 500........ The Woodlands TX 77381 281-681-9500 681-9503
Web: www.arenaenergy.com

Arkos Field Services LP 919 Milam Ste 825........ Houston TX 77002 832-783-5400
Web: www.arkos.com

Armstrong Oil and Gas Inc 1421 BLk St........ Denver CO 80202 303-623-1821
Web: www.armstrongoilandgas.com

B & B Petroleum LLC 19153 HAEIDD Dr........ Hammond LA 70401 985-230-9959
Web: www.bbpetroleum.com

Baker Hughes INTEQ 17015 Aldine Westfield Rd........ Houston TX 77073 713-625-4200
Web: www.bakerhughes.com

Bankers Petroleum Ltd
Suite, 800,-777 8 Ave SW........ Calgary AB T2P3R5 403-513-2699
Web: www.bankerspetroleum.com

Belvedere Terminals Inc
138 107th Ave Ste 313........ Treasure Island FL 33706 800-716-8515
TF: 800-716-8515 ■ *Web:* www.belvedereterminals.com

Bill Barrett Corp 1099 18th St Ste 2300........ Denver CO 80202 303-293-9100 291-0420
NYSE: BBG ■ *TF:* 800-826-6762 ■ *Web:* www.billbarrettcorp.com

BP Prudhoe Bay Royalty Trust 101 Barclay St........ New York NY 10007 212-815-6908
NYSE: BPT

Breitburn Energy Partners LP
515 S Flower St Ste 4800........ Los Angeles CA 90071 213-225-5900 225-5916
NASDAQ: BBEP ■ *TF:* 800-732-0330 ■ *Web:* www.breitburn.com

Brenner Oil Co 12948 Quincy St........ Holland MI 49424 616-399-9742
Web: www.brenneroil.com

Cad Control Systems 1017 Frenchman Dr........ Broussard LA 70518 337-369-3737
Web: cadoil.com

CAMAC Inc 1330 Post Oak Blvd Ste 2200........ Houston TX 77056 713-965-5100 965-5128
Web: www.camacholdings.com

Care Industries Inc 27312-68 Twp. Rd. 394........ Blackfalds AB T0M0J0 403-347-7337
Web: www.careindustries.ca

Cascade Earth Sciences ?Ltd
4900 California Blvd Tower B-210........ Bakersfield CA 93309 661-324-2668
Web: www.cascade-earth.com

CBG Corp 4616 W Howard Ln Ste 900........ Austin TX 78758 512-491-7541
Web: www.cbgcorp.com

Central Resources Inc 1775 Sherman St Ste 2600........ Denver CO 80203 303-830-0100 830-9297
Web: www.centralresources.com

CETCO Energy Services Company LLC
1001 Ochsner Blvd Ste 425........ Covington LA 70433 985-871-4700
Web: cetcoenergyservices.com

Chaparral Energy Inc
701 Cedar Lake Blvd........ Oklahoma City OK 73114 405-478-8770
TF: 866-478-8770 ■ *Web:* www.chaparralenergy.com

Cold Bore Technology Inc
5970 Centre St SE Ste 200........ Calgary AB T2H0C1 403-806-1670
Web: coldboretechnology.com

Concho Resources Inc 600 W Illinois Ave........ Midland TX 79701 432-683-7443 683-7441
NYSE: CXO ■ *Web:* www.concho.com

ConocoPhillips 600 N Dairy Ashford Rd........ Houston TX 77079 281-293-1000
NYSE: COP ■ *Web:* www.conocophillips.com

CYGAM Energy Inc 706-340 12 Ave SW........ Calgary AB T2R1L5 403-802-6983
Web: www.cygamenergy.com

Phone Fax

Cypress E&P Corp
8601 Ranch Rd 2222 Bldg III Ste 200 Austin TX 78730 512-342-6300
Web: www.cypressep.com

Cypress Operating Inc
330 Marshall St Ste 930 Shreveport LA 71101 318-424-2031
Web: www.cypressop.com

Dawson Geophysical Co 508 W Wall St Ste 800 Midland TX 79701 432-684-3000 684-3030
NASDAQ: DWSN ■ *TF:* 800-332-9766 ■ *Web:* www.dawson3d.com

Driessen Water Inc 1690 Hwy 3 S Northfield MN 55057 507-645-6621
Web: www.culliganiswater.com

Electro-Petroleum Inc 8 Wistar Rd Villanova PA 19085 484-380-3456
Web: electropetroleum.com

Elexco Land Service Inc 505 W Henley St Olean NY 14760 716-372-0788
Web: www.elexco.com

Emera Energy Services Inc
One Cumberland Pl Ste 102 Bangor ME 04401 207-945-4735
Web: www.emeraenergy.com

Enbase LLC 3303 Louisiana St Ste 210 Houston TX 77006 888-400-2719
TF: 888-400-2719 ■ *Web:* www.enbasesolutions.com

Endeavour international corp
811 Main St Ste 2100 Houston TX 77002 713-307-8700
OTC: ENDRQ ■ *Web:* www.endeavourcorp.com

Energy Operators L P 1431 Graham Dr Ste 203 Tomball TX 77375 281-351-1780
Web: energyoperators.com

Energy XXI 1021 Main Ste 2626 Houston TX 77002 713-351-3000
NASDAQ: EXXI ■ *Web:* www.eplweb.com

EOG Resources Inc 1111 Bagby Sky Lobby 2 Houston TX 77002 713-651-7000 651-6995
NYSE: EOG ■ *TF:* 877-363-3647 ■ *Web:* www.eogresources.com

Esrey Energy Ltd 1075 Georgia St W Ste 250 Vancouver BC V6E3C9 778-373-0103
Web: www.esreyenergy.com

EXCO Resources Inc 12377 Merit Dr Ste 1700 Dallas TX 75251 214-368-2084 368-2087
NYSE: XCO ■ *TF:* 888-788-9449 ■ *Web:* www.excoresources.com

Falcon Natural Gas Corp
Westchase Ctr2500 City W Blvd.Suite 300 Houston TX 77042 713-267-2240
Web: www.falcongas.com

Fidelity Exploration & Production Co
1801 California St Ste 2500 Denver CO 80202 303-893-3133 893-1964
TF: 800-986-3133

Flamingo Seismic Solutions
4815 S Harvard Ste 401 Tulsa OK 74135 918-492-3773
Web: www.flamingoseismic.com

GeoGlobal Resources Inc (GGR) 625 Fourth Ave SW Calgary AB T2P0K2 403-777-9250
OTC: GGLR ■ *Web:* www.geoglobal.com

Global Energy Services USA Inc
Unit A3, 3220 FM 1960W Houston TX 77068 281-866-8544
Web: www.global-energyusa.com

Global Flow Inc 5796 - 40th St SE Calgary AB T2E2A1 403-219-7373
Web: globalflowinc.com

Goodrich Petroleum Corp
333 Texas St Ste 1375 Shreveport LA 71101 318-429-1375
Web: www.goodrichpetroleum.com

Great White Energy Services
14201 Caliber Dr Ste 300 Oklahoma City OK 73134 405-285-5812

Greenlite Ventures Inc
810 Peace Portal Dr Ste 201 Blaine WA 98230 360-220-5218
Web: www.greenlitecarboncredits.com

GulfMark Energy Inc
17 S Briar Hollow Ln Ste 100 Houston TX 77027 713-881-3603
Web: gulfmarkenergy.com

Halliburton Energy Services
10200 Bellaire Blvd Houston TX 77072 281-871-4000
Web: www.halliburton.com

Heat USA Inc 32 Ave of the Americas 23rd Fl New York NY 10013 212-254-4328
Web: www.heatusa.com

Hernco Fabrication & Service
2047 S Loop 250 W Midland TX 79703 432-522-1444
Web: www.herncofabrication.com

Horizon Mud Co 4417 N Lovington Hwy Hobbs NM 88240 575-393-8641
Web: www.horizonmud.com

Hydril Company LP 3300 N Sam Houston Pkwy Houston TX 77032 281-449-2000
Web: www.hydril.com

Intercept Energy Services Inc
11464 - 149 St Edmonton AB T5M1W7 877-975-0558
TF: 877-975-0558 ■ *Web:* interceptenergy.ca

Jankovich Co, The Berth 74 San Pedro CA 90731 800-836-5355
TF: 800-836-5355 ■ *Web:* www.jankovichcompany.com

Jet Specialty Inc 211 Market Ave Boerne TX 78006 830-331-9457
Web: www.jetspecialty.com

KFG Resources Ltd
118 Lwr Woodville Rd Unit 2 Natchez MS 39120 601-446-5219
Web: www.kfgresources.com

Killam Oil Co Ltd 4320 University Blvd Laredo TX 78042 956-724-7141
Web: www.killamco.com

Lamamco Drilling Co 4444 E 146th St N M Skiatook OK 74070 918-396-3020
Web: www.lamamco.net

Lary Archer & Associates Inc
681 Maddux Rd Weatherford TX 76088 940-682-4069
Web: www.archerassoc.com

Latigo Petroleum Inc 15 W 6th St Ste 1100 Tulsa OK 74119 918-582-7770
Web: www.laredopetro.com

Lavigne Oil Company LLC 310 NW Railroad Ave Hammond LA 70401 985-542-5111
Web: www.lavigneoil.com

Lean Horizons Consulting LLC
79 Kingswood Dr South Glastonbury CT 06073 860-430-1174
Web: www.leanhorizons.com

LEED Tool Corp
P.O. Box 329 1352 Factory Dr Fort Lupton CO 80621 303-857-0876
Web: www.ces-wellsrvs.com

LineStar Services Inc 4203 Montrose Blvd Houston TX 77006 713-338-3433
Web: www.linestar.com

Maverick Oilfield Services Ltd
PO Box 597 3808 - 52 Ave Provost AB T0B3S0 780-753-2992
Web: mavoil.com

Merchant Energy Partners
10901 W Toller Dr Ste 200 Littleton CO 80127 720-351-4000
Web: mehllc.com

Murex Petroleum Corp
363 N. Sam Houston Pkwy E Ste 200 Houston TX 77060 281-590-3313
Web: www.murexpetroleum.com

Mustang Fuel Corp 9800 N Oklahoma Ave Oklahoma City OK 73114 405-748-9400
TF: 800-332-9400 ■ *Web:* www.mustangfuel.com

Mustang Gas Compression LLC
14825 St. Mary?s Ln Ste 200 Houston TX 77079 281-973-6201
Web: mustangcompression.com

N L Fisher Supervision & Engineering Ltd
522 - 11th Ave SW 2nd FL Calgary AB T2R0C8 403-266-7478
Web: nlfisher.com

Navigator Energy Services LLC
2626 Cole Ave Ste 850 Dallas TX 75204 214-520-0700
Web: www.navigatorenergyservices.com

NCS Multistage LLC 702 Spring Cypress Rd Spring TX 77373 281-528-6553
Web: www.ncsfrac.com

New Jersey Natural Gas Co 1415 Wyckoff Rd Wall NJ 07719 732-938-1480 938-3154
TF: 800-221-0051 ■ *Web:* www.njresources.com

Noble Royalties Inc
15601 N Dallas Pkwy Ste 900 Addison TX 75001 972-720-1888
Web: www.nobleroyalties.com

Northern Oil & Gas Inc
315 Manitoba Ave Ste 200 Wayzata MN 55391 952-476-9800 476-9801
NYSE: NOG ■ *Web:* www.northernoil.com

Occidental International Corp
1717 Pennsylvania Ave NW Ste 400 Washington DC 20006 202-857-3000
Web: www.oxy.com

One Nation Energy Solutions LLC
401 Studewood St Ste 204 Houston TX 77007 713-861-0600
Web: www.onenationenergy.com

Pacific Process Systems Inc
5055 California Ave Ste 220 Bakersfield CA 93309 661-321-9681
Web: www.pps-equipment.com

Panhandle Royalty Co
5400 N Grand Blvd
Grand Ctr Bldg Ste 300 Oklahoma City OK 73112 405-948-1560 948-2038
TF: 800-884-4225 ■ *Web:* www.panhandleoilandgas.com

Paragon Geophysical Services Inc
3500 N Rock Rd Bldg 800 Ste B Wichita KS 67226 316-636-5552
Web: www.paragongeo.com

Patterson-UTI Energy Inc 450 Gears Rd Ste 500 Houston TX 77067 281-765-7100 765-7175
NASDAQ: PTEN ■ *TF:* 866-387-1933 ■ *Web:* www.patenergy.com

PetroQuest Energy Inc
400 E Kaliste Saloom Rd Ste 6000 Lafayette LA 70508 337-232-7028 232-0044
NYSE: PQ ■ *Web:* www.petroquest.com

Plains Midstream Canada
Suite 1400, 607 Eighth Ave S.W. Calgary AB T2P0A7 403-298-2100
Web: www.pmclp.com

Platinum Energy Solutions Inc
2100 W Loop S Suite 1601 Houston TX 77027 713-622-7731
Web: www.platinumenergysolutions.com

PML Exploration Services LLC
5208 W Reno Ste 325 Oklahoma City OK 73127 405-606-2701
Web: www.pmles.com

Power Service Products Inc PO Box 1089 Weatherford TX 76086 817-599-9486 599-4893
TF: 800-643-9089 ■ *Web:* www.powerservice.com

Principle Environmental LLC
1925 Ft Worth Hwy Ste 101 Weatherford TX 76086 817-599-5332
Web: www.principleenergyservices.com

Proserv Offshore Inc
13105 Northwest Fwy Ste 250 Houston TX 77040 713-462-9990
Web: www.proserv-offshore.com

Purestream Technology LLC
510 South 600 East Salt Lake City UT 84102 801-433-2526
Web: purestreamtechnology.com

QOREX LLC
101 Hammer Mill Rd Millbrook Business Ctr
Rocky Hill CT 06067 860-727-1031
Web: www.petrospec.com

Quicksilver Resources Inc
777 W Rosedale St Ste 300 Fort Worth TX 76104 817-665-5000 665-5014
OTC: KWKAQ ■ *TF:* 877-665-8600 ■ *Web:* www.qrinc.com

R M Roach & Sons Inc
333 E John St P.O. Box 2899 Martinsburg WV 25401 304-263-3329
Web: www.roachenergy.com

Radius Professional HDD Tools
1614 N Main St Weatherford TX 76086 800-892-9114
TF: 800-892-9114 ■ *Web:* www.radiushdd.com

RedHawk Energy Corp 1118 Jefferson St. Lafayette LA 70501 337-269-5933
Web: www.redhawkenergycorp.com

Rosemore Inc
One N Charles St 22nd Fl Ste 2300 Baltimore MD 21201 410-347-7080
Web: www.rosemoreinc.com

Rosetta Resources Inc 717 Texas Ste 2800 Houston TX 77002 713-335-4000 335-4197
NASDAQ: ROSE ■ *Web:* www.rosettaresources.com

Royalty Exploration LLC
3222 S Vance St Ste 100 Lakewood CO 80227 303-217-5151
Web: royaltyexploration.com

Roywell Services Inc
4545 Bissonnet St Ste 104 Bellaire TX 77401 713-661-4747
Web: roywellservices.com

RSX Energy Inc 407?2nd St SW Ste 1030 Calgary AB T2P2Y3 403-266-0600
Web: www.rsxenergy.com

Sanjel Usa Inc 511 22nd St E Williston ND 58801 403-269-1420
Web: www.sanjel.com

Schlumberger Ltd 5599 San Felipe Ste 100 Houston TX 77056 713-513-2000 513-2006
NYSE: SLB ■ *Web:* www.slb.com

Scott Safety Supply Services Inc
5012 Caxton St W PO Box 1983 Whitecourt AB T7S1P7 780-778-3389
Web: www.scottsafety.ca

Company / Address	City	State	ZIP	Phone	Fax
Seitel Inc 10811 S Westview Cir Dr Bldg C Ste 100 — *Web:* www.seitel.com	Houston	TX	77043	832-295-8300	295-8301
Serva Group LLC 1045 Keystone Ave. — *Web:* www.servagroup.com	Catoosa	OK	74015	918-266-2888	
Simulis LLC 6450 Louetta Rd Ste 140 — *Web:* www.simulis.com	Spring	TX	77379	713-956-9000	
Slawson Cos Inc 727 N Waco St Ste 400 — *Web:* www.slawsoncompanies.com	Wichita	KS	67203	316-263-3201	268-0702
SPIRIT Global Energy Solutions Inc 3406 S State HW 349 — *Web:* www.spiritenergysolutions.com	Midland	TX	79706	432-522-2288	
Statoil Marketing & Trading 120 Long Ridge Rd Ste 3E01 — *Web:* www.statoil.com	Stamford	CT	06902	203-978-6900	978-6952
STEP Energy Services Ltd 505 - 3rd St SW Ste 300 — *Web:* www.stepenergyservices.com	Calgary	AB	T2P3E6	403-457-1772	
STRATA Energy Services Inc 39207 Range Rd 271 Blindman Industrial Park Ste 8 — *Web:* www.strataenergy.net	Red Deer County	AB	T4S2M4	403-358-3442	
Stratagraph Inc 125 Raggio Rd — *Web:* www.stratagraph.com	Scott	LA	70583	337-232-5510	
Stuart Petroleum Testers Inc 1910 E Tom Green St — *Web:* www.stuartpetroleumtesters.com	Brenham	TX	77833	979-836-3799	
Sun Well Service Inc 201 26th St East — *Web:* www.sunwellservice.com	Williston	ND	58801	701-774-3001	
Superior Energy Services Inc 601 Poydras St Ste 2400 — *NYSE:* SPN ■ *TF:* 800-259-7774 ■ *Web:* www.superiorenergy.com	New Orleans	LA	70130	504-587-7374	362-1818
Supreme Vacuum Services Inc 1200 Bensdale Rd — *Web:* www.supremevsinc.com	Pleasanton	TX	78064	830-281-8008	
Surepoint Technologies Group Inc 744 - 4th Ave SW Ste 1000 — *TF:* 855-777-7873 ■ *Web:* www.surepoint.ca	Calgary	AB	T2P3T4	855-777-7873	
Tech-Seal International Inc 5656 Wheatley St — *Web:* www.tech-seal.net	Houston	TX	77091	713-691-0668	
TGC Industries Inc 101 E Pk Blvd Ste 955 — *NASDAQ:* TGE ■ *TF:* 800-223-7470	Plano	TX	75074	972-881-1099	424-3943
Total E & P USA Inc 1201 Louisiana St Total Plaza Ste 1800 — *Web:* www.total.com	Houston	TX	77002	713-647-4000	647-4030
Total Wellhead & Rental Tools LLC 401 S Juniper St — *Web:* www.totalwellhead.com	Perryton	TX	79070	806-435-3800	
Trans Tech Energy Inc 2417 Winstead Rd Ste — *Web:* www.transtechenergy.com	Rocky Mount	NC	27804	252-446-4357	
TransGlobe Energy Corp 250 Fifth St SW Ste 2300 — *TSE:* TGL ■ *Web:* www.trans-globe.com	Calgary	AB	T2P0R6	403-264-9888	770-8855
Triad Energy Corp 1616 Voss, Ste 650 — *Web:* www.triad-energy.com	Houston	TX	77057	713-337-1440	
Tribute Resources Inc(NDA) 309 Commissioners Rd W Unit D — *Web:* www.tributeresources.com	London	ON	N6J1Y4	519-657-7624	
Turbo-Chem International Inc 106 W Saul — *Web:* www.turbochem.com	Scott	LA	70583	337-235-3098	
Tuscany Energy Ltd Suite 1800, 633 - 6th Ave S.W. — *Web:* www.tuscanyenergy.com	Calgary	AB	T2P2Y5	403-269-9889	
Twin Eagle Resource Management LLC 8847 W Sam Houston Pkwy N — *Web:* www.termna.com	Houston	TX	77040	713-341-7300	
VAALCO Energy Inc 9800 Richmond Ste 700 — *NYSE:* EGY ■ *Web:* www.vaalco.com	Houston	TX	77042	713-623-0801	623-0982
Veritas DGC Inc 10300 Townpark Dr. — *TF:* 800-028-1299 ■ *Web:* cgg.com	Houston	TX	77072	832-351-8300	351-8300
VetcoGray Inc 4424 W Sam Houston Pkwy N Ste 100 — *Web:* www.vetco.com	Houston	TX	77041	713-683-2400	
Vulcan Minerals Inc 333 Duckworth St — *Web:* www.vulcanminerals.ca	St. Johns	NL	A1C1G9	709-754-3186	
Walter Oil & Gas Corp 1100 Louisiana St Ste 200 — *TF:* 888-756-7880 ■ *Web:* www.walteroil.com	Houston	TX	77002	713-659-1221	756-1155
Welder Exploration & Production Inc 115 E Travis St, Ste 900 The Milam Bldg — *Web:* www.weldergroup.com	San Antonio	TX	78205	210-354-1515	
West Bay Exploration Co 13685 S W Bay Shore Ste 200 — *Web:* www.westbayexploration.com	Traverse City	MI	49684	231-946-0200	
WesternGeco 10001 Richmond Ave — *Web:* www.slb.com	Houston	TX	77042	713-789-9600	789-0172
Zion Oil & Gas Inc 6510 Abrams Rd Ste 300 — *Web:* www.zionoil.com	Dallas	TX	75231	214-221-4610	221-6510

539 OIL & GAS FIELD SERVICES

See Also Oil & Gas Field Exploration Services p. 2851

Company / Address	City	State	ZIP	Phone	Fax
3es Innovation Inc Ste 400 227 - 11th Ave SW — *Web:* 3esi-enersight.com	Calgary	AB	T2R1R9	403-270-3270	
4Refuel Canada Ltd 9440-202 St Ste 215 — *Web:* 4refuel.com	Langley	BC	V1M4A6	604-513-0386	
Absolute Energy LLC 1372 State Line Rd — *Web:* www.absenergy.org	St. Ansgar	IA	50472	641-326-2220	
AccessESP LLC 3656 Westchase Dr Ste 421 — *Web:* www.accessesp.com	Houston	TX	77042	713-589-2599	
ACT Clean Technologies Inc 5412 Bolsa Ave Ste a	Huntington Beach	CA	92649	210-691-3335	
Advocate Media Inc 181 Brown's Point Rd — *Web:* www.advocatemediainc.com	Pictou	NS	B0K1H0	902-485-1990	
AGI Industries Inc 2110 S W Evangeline Thruway — *Web:* www.agiindustries.com	Lafayette	LA	70508	337-233-0626	
AKS Technologies Inc 1416 N Sam Houston Pkwy E Ste 140 — *Web:* www.aks-technologies.com	Houston	TX	77032	281-987-2244	
Alaska Clean Seas Inc 4720 Business Park Blvd Ste 42 — *Web:* www.alaskacleanseas.org	Anchorage	AK	99503	907-743-8989	
Alaska Interstate Construction LLC 301 W Northern Lights Blvd Ste 600 — *Web:* www.aicllc.com	Anchorage	AK	99503	907-562-2792	
Alco Gas & Oil Production Equipment Ltd 5203 - 75th St — *Web:* www.alcogasoil.com	Edmonton	AB	T6E5S5	780-465-9061	
Allamon Tool Company Inc 18935 Freeport Dr — *TF:* 877-449-5433 ■ *Web:* www.allamontool.com	Montgomery	TX	77356	877-449-5433	
Americas Petrogas Inc 3911 Trasimene Cres SW — *Web:* www.americaspetrogas.com	Calgary	AB	T3E7J6	403-685-1888	
Amplified Geochemical Imaging LLC 100 Chesapeake Blvd	Elkton	MD	21921	410-392-7600	
Apex Resources Inc 549 Stonegate Dr. — *Web:* apexr.com	Katy	TX	77494	832-786-7492	
Aqueos Corp 101 Millstone Rd — *Web:* www.aqueossubsea.com	Broussard	LA	70518	337-714-0033	
ARC Pressure Data Inc 3718 Warschun Rd. — *Web:* www.arcpressure.com	Aubrey	TX	76277	940-565-8090	
Argus Machine Company Ltd 5820 97th St NW — *TF:* 888-434-9451 ■ *Web:* www.argusmachine.com	Edmonton	AB	T6E3J1	780-434-9451	
ASRC Energy Services Inc 3900 C St — *Web:* www.asrcenergy.com	Anchorage	AK	99503	907-339-6200	
Atchafalaya Measurement Inc 124 Credit Dr — *Web:* atchafalayameasurement.com	Scott	LA	70583	337-237-7675	
Atlanta Petroleum Equipment Co 4732 N Royal Atlanta Dr — *TF:* 800-562-4060 ■ *Web:* www.atlantapetroleum.com	Tucker	GA	30084	770-491-6644	
AXH air-coolers LLC 2230 E 49th St — *Web:* www.axh.com	Tulsa	OK	74105	918-712-8268	
Axon Pressure Products Inc 8909 Jackrabbit Rd — *Web:* www.axonep.com	Houston	TX	77095	281-855-3200	
B & R Eckel's Transport Ltd 5514B - 50 Ave. — *TF:* 800-661-3290 ■ *Web:* www.breckels.com	Bonnyville	AB	T9N2K8	780-826-3889	
Badger Daylighting Corp 1300 E US Hwy 136 Ste E — *Web:* badgerinc.com	Pittsboro	IN	46167	317-892-2666	
Baker Hughes Inc (BHI) 2929 Allen Pkwy Ste 1200 — *NYSE:* BHI ■ *TF:* 800-229-7447 ■ *Web:* www.bakerhughes.com	Houston	TX	77019	713-439-8600	
Basic Energy Services Inc 500 W Illinois Ste 800 Ste 800 — *NYSE:* BAS ■ *Web:* www.basicenergyservices.com	Midland	TX	79701	432-620-5500	
Bayou Companies LLC, The 5200 Curtis Ln — *Web:* www.bayoucompanies.com	New Iberia	LA	70560	337-369-3761	
Beckman Production Services Inc 3786 Beebe Rd — *Web:* www.beckmanproduction.com	Kalkaska	MI	49646	231-258-9524	
Bell Geospace Inc 400 N Sam Houston Pkwy E Ste 325 — *Web:* bellgeo.com	Houston	TX	77060	281-591-6900	
Bellatrix Exploration Ltd 1920 800 Fifth Ave Sw — *Web:* www.bellatrixexploration.com	Calgary	AB	T2P3T6	403-266-8670	
Black Elk Energy LLC 11451 Katy Fwy Ste 500 — *Web:* www.blackelkenergy.com	Houston	TX	77079	281-598-8600	
Blake International USA Rigs LLC 410 S Van Ave. — *Web:* www.blakeinternationalrigs.com	Houma	LA	70363	985-274-2200	
Blakely Construction Company Inc 2830 W Interstate 20 — *Web:* www.blakelycc.com	Odessa	TX	79763	432-381-3540	
Blarney Castle Oil Co 12218 W St PO Box 246 — *Web:* www.blarneycastleoil.com	Bear Lake	MI	49614	231-864-3111	
BlueStone Natural Resources LLC 2100 S Utica Ste 200 — *Web:* www.bluestone-nr.com	Tulsa	OK	74114	918-392-9200	
Brady Oilfield Services LP Box 271 — *Web:* www.brady.sk.ca	Midale	SK	S0C1S0	306-458-2344	
Brammer Engineering Inc 400 Texas St Bank One Bldg Ste 600 — *Web:* www.brammer.com	Shreveport	LA	71101	318-429-2345	
Bronco Mfg LLC 4953 S 48th W Ave — *Web:* www.broncomfg.com	Tulsa	OK	74107	918-446-7196	
Burbank Water & Power 164 W Magnolia Blvd — *Web:* www.burbankwaterandpower.com	Burbank	CA	91502	818-238-3700	
C E Oil Tools & Supply Inc 104 Ridona St. — *Web:* www.ceoiltool.com	Lafayette	LA	70508	337-237-4941	
Cal Dive International Inc Ste 2200 2500 CityWest Blvd	Houston	TX	77042	713-361-2600	
Calfrac Well Services Ltd 411 8 Ave SW — *TF:* 866-770-3722 ■ *Web:* www.calfrac.com	Calgary	AB	T2P1E3	403-266-6000	
Camex Equipment Sales & Rental Inc 1806 Second St — *TF:* 877-955-2770 ■ *Web:* www.camex.ca	Nisku	AB	T9E0W8	780-955-2770	
Camino Agave Inc RT3 Box 77A — *Web:* www.caminoagave.com	Laredo	TX	78043	956-723-1701	
Canada Energy Partners Inc 595 Burrard St Ste 3123 — *Web:* www.canadaenergypartners.com	Vancouver	BC	V6C3L6	604-909-1154	

Company / Address	City	State	Zip	Phone	Fax
Capitol Petroleum Equipment Inc 11319 Old Baltimore Pk *Web:* www.cpe123.com	Beltsville	MD	20705	301-931-9090	
Carbon Sciences Inc 5511C Ekwill St *Web:* www.carbonsciences.com	Santa Barbara	CA	93111	805-456-7000	
CarbonWrap Solutions LLC 2820 E Ft Lowell Rd *TF:* 866-380-1269 ■ *Web:* www.carbonwrapsolutions.com	Tucson	AZ	85716	520-292-3109	
Cel Oil Products Corp 5402 Dutton Ave *Web:* www.beequik.com	Charleston	SC	29406	843-744-2525	
Central Industries Inc 11438 Cronridge Dr Ste W *TF:* 800-304-8484 ■ *Web:* www.centralindustriesusa.com	Owings Mills	MD	21117	800-304-8484	932-1222
Chinn Exploration Co 4601 Mccann Rd *Web:* www.chinnexploration.com	Longview	TX	75605	903-663-4260	
Choice Exploration Inc 2221 Ave J *Web:* www.choiceexploration.com	Arlington	TX	76006	817-633-7777	
Cimarron Energy Inc 1012 24th Ave NW Ste 100 PO Box 722110 *Web:* www.cimarronenergy.com	Norman	OK	73070	405-928-7373	
Cirm Corp 109 Long Hill Ter *Web:* www.cirmcorp.com	New Haven	CT	06515	203-387-2068	
City Water, Light & Power 401 N 11th St 4th Fl *Web:* www.cwlp.com	Springfield	IL	62757	217-789-2116	
Coil Tubing Technology Holding Inc 19511 Wied Rd Ste E *Web:* www.coiltubingtechnology.com	Spring	TX	77388	281-651-0200	
Collarini Corp 11111 Richmond Ave Ste 126 *Web:* www.collarini.com	Houston	TX	77082	504-887-7127	
Colloid Environmental Technologies Co (CETCO) 2870 Forbs Ave **Fax Area Code:* 800 ■ *TF:* 800-527-9948 ■ *Web:* www.cetco.com	Hoffman Estates	IL	60192	847-851-1899	527-9948*
Computer Modelling Group Ltd 200 1824 Crowchild Trl NW *Web:* www.cmgl.ca	Calgary	AB	T2M3Y7	403-531-1300	
Cordy Oilfield Services Inc 5366 55 St SE *Web:* www.cordy.ca	Calgary	AB	T2C3G9	403-266-2067	
Core Laboratories 6316 Windfern Rd *NYSE: CLB* ■ *Web:* www.corelab.com	Houston	TX	77040	713-328-2673	328-2150
Cougar Drilling Solutions Inc 7319 - 17 St *Web:* www.cougards.com	Edmonton	AB	T6P1P1	780-440-2400	
Cps Building Company Ltd 4327 Red Bank Rd *TF:* 877-295-9876 ■ *Web:* www.cpsconsult.com	Cincinnati	OH	45227	513-271-9026	
Crain Bros Inc 300 Rita Dr *Web:* www.crainbrothers.com	Bell City	LA	70630	337-905-2411	905-2700
Cross Group Inc, The 1950 S Van Ave *Web:* www.thecrossgroup.com	Houma	LA	70363	985-868-3906	
CSV Midstream Solutions Corp 521 - Third Ave SW Eau Claire Pl II Ste 800 *Web:* www.csvmidstream.com	Calgary	AB	T2P3T3	587-316-6900	
CWC Energy Services Corp 205 - Fifth Ave SW Bow Vly Sq II Ste 610 *Web:* www.cwcenergyservices.com	Calgary	AB	T2P2V7	403-264-2177	
Cypress Energy Partners LP 5727 S Lewis Ave Ste 500 *Web:* www.cypressenergy.com	Tulsa	OK	74105	918-748-3900	
D & J Oil Company Inc 4720 W Garriott *Web:* www.djoil.com	Enid	OK	73706	580-242-3636	
Dalmac Oilfield Services Inc 4934 - 89 St *TF:* 888-632-5622 ■ *Web:* www.dalmacenergy.com	Edmonton	AB	T6E5K1	780-988-8510	
Danos & Curole Marine Contractors Inc 13083 Louisiana 308 *TF:* 800-487-5971 ■ *Web:* www.danos.com	Larose	LA	70373	985-693-3313	
Datalog Technology Inc 10707 - 50th St SE *Web:* www.datalogtechnology.com	Calgary	AB	T2C3E5	403-243-2024	
Daybreak Oil & Gas Inc(NDA) 601 W Main Ave Ste 1012 *Web:* www.daybreakoilandgas.com	Spokane	WA	99201	509-232-7674	
Deep Down Inc 8827 W Sam Houston Pkwy N Ste 100 *Web:* www.deepdowninc.com	Houston	TX	77040	281-517-5000	
Delta Compression & Equipment LLC 160 James Ln *Web:* www.deltacompression.com	Krotz Springs	LA	70750	337-566-8888	
Delta SubSea LLC 550 Club Dr Ste 345 *Web:* www.deltasubsea-rov.com	Montgomery	TX	77316	936-582-7237	
Derrick Equipment Co 15630 Export Plz Dr *Web:* derrick.com	Houston	TX	77032	281-590-3003	
Desmarais Energy Corp 751-815 8 Ave SW *Web:* www.desmaraisenergy.com	Calgary	AB	T2P3P2	403-265-8007	
DEVIN International Inc 2545 SE Evangeline Thruway *Web:* www.devindevin.com	Lafayette	LA	70508	337-233-3846	
Dialog Wireline Services LLC 3100 Maverick Dr *Web:* www.dialogwireline.com	Kilgore	TX	75662	903-988-2311	
Diamond Oil Well Drilling Company Inc 2003 Commerce Dr *Web:* www.diamondoffshore.com	Midland	TX	79703	281-492-5300	
Diamond Services Co 4220 Oklahoma Ave *Web:* diamond-services.com	Woodward	OK	73801	580-256-3385	256-9873
Diamond Services Corp 503 S DeGravelle Rd *TF:* 800-879-1162 ■ *Web:* www.dscgom.com	Amelia	LA	70340	985-631-2187	631-2442
Divergent Energy Services Corp 1170 800 - Sixth Ave SW *Web:* www.divergentenergyservices.com	Calgary	AB	T2P3G3	403-543-0060	
Downing Wellhead Equipment Inc 8528 S W Second St *Web:* www.downingwell.com	Oklahoma City	OK	73128	405-789-8182	
Drilltec Technologies Inc 10875 Kempwood Ste 2 *Web:* www.drilltec.com	Houston	TX	77043	713-895-9852	
Duoline Technologies LP 250 W Bluebird Rd *Web:* www.duoline.com	Gilmer	TX	75645	903-734-1371	
Dwfritz Automation Inc 12100 SW Tualatin Rd *TF:* 800-763-4161 ■ *Web:* dwfritz.com	Wilsonville	OR	97070	503-598-9393	
E. L. Farmer & Co 3800 E 42nd St Ste 417 *Web:* www.elfarmer.com	Odessa	TX	79762	432-366-2010	
EagleClaw Midstream Services LLC 414 W Texas Ave Ste 315 *Web:* www.eagleclawmidstream.com	Midland	TX	79701	432-789-1333	
Eaton Oil Tools Inc 118 Rue DuPain *Web:* www.eatonoiltools.com	Broussard	LA	70518	337-856-8820	
EFC Valve & Controls LLC 230 Progress Rd *Web:* www.efcvalve.com	Longview	TX	75604	903-759-0126	
Elastec Inc 1309 W Main *Web:* www.elastec.com	Carmi	IL	62821	618-382-2525	
Emerge Energy Services LP 1400 Civic Pl Ste 250 *Web:* www.emergelp.com	Southlake	TX	76092	817-488-7775	
Emmart & Son Inc W H 305 Brick Kiln Rd	Winchester	VA	22601	540-662-3848	
EN Bisso & Son Inc 3939 N Causeway Blvd Ste 401 *Web:* www.enbisso.com	Metairie	LA	70002	504-828-3296	
Epic Lift Systems LLC 14485 Hwy 377 South *Web:* www.epiclift.com	Fort Worth	TX	76126	817-443-3500	
ERG Resources LLC 3 Allen Ctr 333 Clay St Ste 4400 *Web:* www.energy-reserves.com	Houston	TX	77002	713-812-1800	
ExPert E&P Consultants LLC 101 Ashland Way *Web:* www.expertep.com	Madisonville	LA	70447	985-801-4040	
Exterran Water Solutions Ltd 1721 27th Ave Noth E *Web:* www.exterran.com/products/produced-water-treatment	Calgary	AB	T2E7E1	403-219-2210	
Failsafe Controls LLC 2712 Southwest Dr *Web:* failsafecontrols.com	New Iberia	LA	70560	337-365-2493	
Fairweather LLC 9525 King St *TF:* 800-319-8802 ■ *Web:* www.fairweather.com	Anchorage	AK	99515	907-346-3247	349-1920
Faith Mfg Company Inc 406 Atascocita Rd *Web:* www.faithmfg.com	Humble	TX	77396	281-441-9595	
FESCO Ltd 1000 Fesco Ave *TF:* 800-375-3479 ■ *Web:* www.fescoinc.com	Alice	TX	78332	361-661-7000	661-7000
Fire Creek Resources Ltd 206-11th Ave *Web:* www.fcrl.ca	Calgary	AB	T2G0X8	403-234-9309	
Flow Petroleum Services Inc 209 Marcon Dr *Web:* www.flowps.com	Lafayette	LA	70507	337-593-9987	
Fluid Delivery Solutions LLC 6795 Corporation Pkwy Ste 200 *Web:* www.fdsllc.com	Fort Worth	TX	76126	817-730-9761	
Fluid Systems Inc 16619 Aldine Westfield Rd *Web:* www.fluidsystems.com	Houston	TX	77032	832-467-9898	467-9897
Forent Energy Ltd 12th Ave SW *Web:* www.forentenergy.com	Calgary	AB	T2R1L5	403-262-9444	
Fossil Creek Resources LLC 1521 N Cooper St Ste 650 *Web:* www.fossilcreekres.com	Arlington	TX	76011	817-701-4970	
Freestone Resources Inc 325 N St Paul St Republic Ctr Ste 1350 *Web:* www.freestoneresourcesinc.com	Dallas	TX	75201	214-880-4870	
Gas Field Specialists Inc 2107 SR- 44 S *Web:* www.gfsinc.net	Shinglehouse	PA	16748	814-698-2122	698-2124
Gas Liquids Engineering Ltd 2749-39th Ave NE Ste 300 *Web:* www.gasliquids.com	Calgary	AB	T1Y4T8	403-250-2950	
Genco Energy Services Inc 1701 W Hwy 107 *Web:* www.genco.us	Mcallen	TX	78504	956-380-3710	
Geophysical Pursuit Inc 3501 Allen Pkwy *Web:* www.geopursuit.com	Houston	TX	77019	713-529-3000	
Gilliam and Sons Inc 9831 Rosedale Hwy *Web:* www.gilliamandsons.com	Bakersfield	CA	93312	661-589-0913	
Global Industries Ltd 8000 Global Dr **Fax Area Code:* 337 ■ *Web:* lake-charles.gopickle.com	Sulphur	LA	70665	208-992-9226	583-5100*
Globe Energy Services LLC 3204 W Hwy 180 *Web:* globeenergyservices.com	Snyder	TX	79549	325-573-1310	
Gly-Tech Services Inc 2054 Paxton St *Web:* www.glytech.com	Harvey	LA	70058	504-348-8566	
Goldston Oil Corp 1819 Saint James Pl *Web:* goldstonoil.com	Houston	TX	77056	713-355-3408	
Goodrich Petroleum Corp 801 Louisiana Ste 700 *NYSE: GDP* ■ *Web:* www.goodrichpetroleum.com	Houston	TX	77002	713-780-9494	780-9254
Gordon Petroleum Inc 950 Holmdel Rd *Web:* www.gordonpetroleum.com	Holmdel	NJ	07733	732-946-6000	
GOTCO International Inc 11410 Spring Cypress Rd *TF:* 800-683-7746 ■ *Web:* www.gotco-usa.com	Tomball	TX	77375	281-376-3784	
Grit Industries Inc 5508 59 Ave *Web:* www.gritindustries.com	Lloydminster	AB	T9V3A8	780-875-5577	
Gulf Offshore Logistics LLC 120 White Rose Dr *TF:* 866-532-1060 ■ *Web:* www.gulf-log.com	Raceland	LA	70394	866-532-1060	
Gulfmark Offshore Inc 842 W Sam Houston Pkwy N Ste 400 *NYSE: GLF* ■ *Web:* www.gulfmark.com	Houston	TX	77024	713-963-9522	
Guttman Group LLC, The 200 Speers St *Web:* www.guttmangroup.com	Belle Vernon	PA	15012	724-483-3533	
Guttmann & Blaevoet 2351 Powell St *Web:* www.gb-eng.com	San Francisco	CA	94133	415-655-4000	
Halliburton Energy Services 10200 Bellaire Blvd *Web:* www.halliburton.com	Houston	TX	77072	281-871-4000	
Hawk Rope Access Inc 124 Parker Ave	Rodeo	CA	94572	510-245-8728	
Hawkeye LLC 100 Marcus Blvd Ste 1	Hauppauge	NY	11788	631-447-3100	
Helix Energy Solutions Inc 400 N Sam Houston Pkwy E Ste 400 *NYSE: HLX* ■ *TF:* 888-345-2347 ■ *Web:* www.helixesg.com	Houston	TX	77060	281-618-0400	618-0500

Phone Fax

HII Technologies Inc 8588 Katy Fwy Ste 430 .... Houston TX 77024 713-821-3157
Web: www.hiitinc.com

Hilliard Energy Inc
3001 W Loop 250 N Ste E103 .... Midland TX 79705 432-683-9100
Web: www.hilliardenergy.com

HSE Integrated Ltd 630-6th Ave SW Ste 1000 .... Calgary AB T2P0S8 403-266-1833
Web: www.hseintegrated.com

HTC Purenergy Inc 002 2305 Victoria Ave .... Regina SK S4P0S7 306-352-6132
Web: www.htcenergy.com

I Reservoir Com Corp
1490 W Canal Court Ste 2000 .... Littleton CO 80120 303-713-1112
Web: ireservoir.com

Indel-Davis Inc 4401 S Jackson Ave .... Tulsa OK 74107 918-587-2151 446-1583
TF: 800-331-6300 ■ *Web:* www.indel-davis.com

INOVA Geophysical Equipment Ltd
12200 Parc Crest Dr .... Stafford TX 77477 281-568-2000
Web: www.inovageo.com

Integrated Service Company LLC
1900 N 161st E Ave .... Tulsa OK 74116 918-234-4150
Web: www.inservusa.com

InterAct PMTI 4567 Telephone Rd Ste 203 .... Ventura CA 93003 805-658-5600
Web: www.pacificmti.com

JEBCO Seismic LP 2450 Fondren Rd Ste 112 .... Houston TX 77063 713-975-0202
Web: www.jebcoseis.com

Jetta Operating Company Inc
777 Taylor St Ft Worth Club Tower Ste P1 .... Fort Worth TX 76102 817-335-1179
Web: www.jettaoperating.com

Joining Technologies Inc
17 Connecticut S Dr .... East Granby CT 06026 860-653-0111
Web: www.joiningtech.com

Jones & Frank Corp 1330 St Mary's St Ste 210 .... Raleigh NC 27605 919-838-7555
Web: www.jones-frank.com

JW Williams Inc 2180 Renauna Ave .... Casper WY 82601 307-237-8345

Kaiser-Francis Oil Co 6733 S Yale Ave .... Tulsa OK 74136 918-494-0000
Web: www.kfoc.net

Katalyst Data Management LLC
10311 Westpark Dr .... Houston TX 77042 281-529-3200
Web: www.katalystdm.com

Ketek Industries Ltd 20204 - 110 Ave NW .... Edmonton AB T5S1X8 780-447-5050
Web: www.ketek.ca

Keystone Clearwater Solutions LLC
34 Northeast Dr .... Hershey PA 17033 717-508-0550
Web: www.keystoneclear.com

Klinge Corp 4075 E Market St .... York PA 17402 717-840-4500
Web: www.klingecorp.com

Koch Specialty Plant Services
12221 E Sam Houston Pkwy N .... Houston TX 77044 713-427-7700 427-7747
TF: 800-765-9177 ■ *Web:* www.kochservices.com

LaBarge Coating LLC 211 N Bdwy Ste 3050 .... Saint Louis MO 63102 314-646-3400
TF: 866-992-4191 ■ *Web:* www.labargecoating.com

Lauren Concise 300 736-6 Ave SW .... Calgary AB T2P3T7 403-237-7160
Web: laurenec.com

Leam Drilling Systems Inc 2027a Airport Rd .... Conroe TX 77301 800-426-5349
TF: 800-426-5349 ■ *Web:* leam.net

LH Gault & Son Inc 11 Ferry Ln W .... Westport CT 06880 203-227-5181
Web: www.gaultenergy.com

Lincoln Manufacturing Inc 31209 FM 2978 Rd .... Magnolia TX 77354 281-252-9494
Web: www.lincolnmanufacturing.com

Little Red Services Inc
3700 Centerpoint Dr Ste 1300 .... Anchorage AK 99503 907-349-2931
Web: www.littleredservices.com

Loadmaster Derrick & Equipment Inc
1084 Cruse Ave .... Broussard LA 70518 337-837-5429
Web: www.loadmasterderrick.com

Logan Industries International Corp
Blasingame Rd .... Hempstead TX 77445 713-849-2979
Web: www.loganindustries.net

LoneStar West Inc RR 1 Box 1, Site 5 .... Sylvan Lake AB T4S1X6 403-887-2074
Web: www.lonestarwest.com

M & M Pipeline Services LLC
274 Mount Moriah Rd .... Eupora MS 39744 662-258-7101
Web: www.mmpipeline.com

Mansfield Oil Co 1025 Airport Pkwy SW .... Gainesville GA 30501 800-695-6626
TF: 800-695-6626 ■ *Web:* mansfield.energy

Marksmen Energy Inc 368 Sunmills Dr SE .... Calgary AB T2X3H6 403-265-7270
Web: www.marksmenenergy.com/s/home.asp

Marmik Oil Co 200 N Jefferson Ave .... El Dorado AR 71730 870-862-8546
Web: www.marmikoil.com

Marquee Energy Ltd 500 Fourth Ave SW Ste 1700 .... Calgary AB T2P2V6 403-384-0000
Web: www.marquee-energy.com

Matrix Service Co 5100 E Skelly Dr 74135 .... Tulsa OK 74135 866-367-6879 838-8810*
NASDAQ: MTRX ■ **Fax Area Code:* 918 ■ *TF:* 866-367-6879 ■ *Web:* www.matrixservice.com

MENA Hydrocarbons Inc
Bow Vly Sq 205 - Fifth Ave SW Ste 1000 .... Calgary AB T2P2V7 403-930-7500

Meritage Midstream Services LLC
1331 Seventeenth St Ste 1100 .... Denver CO 80202 303-551-8150
Web: www.meritagemidstream.com

Merlin Petroleum Company Inc 235 Post Rd W .... Westport CT 06880 203-227-3200
Web: www.merlinpetroleum.com

Metro Fuel Oil Corp 500 Kingsland Ave .... Brooklyn NY 11222 718-383-1400
Web: metroenergy.com

MGS Services LLC
18775 N Frederick Ave Ste E .... Gaithersburg MD 20879 301-330-9793
TF: 877-647-4255 ■ *Web:* www.mgsservices.com

MIDCON Data Services Inc 401 W 33rd St .... Edmond OK 73013 405-478-1234
Web: www.midcondata.com

Milbar Hydro-Test Inc 651 Aero Dr .... Shreveport LA 71107 318-227-8210 222-2558
TF: 800-259-8210 ■ *Web:* www.milbarhydro-test.com

MK Tech Solutions Inc 12843 Covey Ln .... Houston TX 77099 281-564-8851
Web: www.mktechsolutions.com

Mmi Services Inc 4042 Patton Way .... Bakersfield CA 93308 661-589-9366
Web: www.mmi-services.com

Mosaic Energy Ltd 606-4th St SW Ste 900 .... Calgary AB T2P1T1 403-699-7650
Web: mosaicenergy.ca

Multi-Shot LLC 3335 Pollok Dr .... Conroe TX 77303 936-442-2500
Web: msenergyservices.com

Nabors Industries Ltd
515 W Greens Rd Ste 1200 .... Houston TX 77067 281-874-0035 872-5205
NYSE: NBR ■ *Web:* www.nabors.com

Nabors Offshore Corp 515 W Greens Rd Ste 500 .... Houston TX 77067 281-874-0406 872-5205
Web: www.nabors.com

NANA Regional Corporation Inc
1001 E Benson Blvd .... Kotzebue AK 99752 907-442-3301
TF: 800-478-3301 ■ *Web:* www.nana.com

Narragansett Bay Commission 1 Service Rd .... Providence RI 02905 401-461-8848
Web: www.narrabay.com

New Jersey Water Supply Authority Inc
1851 State Rt 31 .... Clinton NJ 08809 908-638-6121
Web: www.njwsa.org

New West Energy Services Inc
Ste 500 435 - Fourth Ave SW .... Calgary AB T2P3A8 403-984-9798
Web: www.newwestenergyservices.com

Newcomb Oil Co LLC 1360 E John Rowan Blvd .... Bardstown KY 40004 502-348-3961 348-6346
Web: www.newcomboil.com

Newpark Mats & Integrated Services LLC
2700 Research Forest Dr Ste 100 .... The Woodlands TX 77381 281-362-6800 984-4445*
**Fax Area Code:* 337 ■ *TF:* 877-628-7623 ■ *Web:* www.newpark.com

Northern Gulf Trading Group
164 St Francis St Ste 205 .... Mobile AL 36602 251-432-0757
Web: www.ngtg.net

NOW Inc 7402 N Eldridge Pkwy .... Houston TX 77041 281-823-4700
TF: 800-228-2893 ■ *Web:* www.distributionnow.com

Oceaneering International Inc 11911 FM 529 .... Houston TX 77041 713-329-4500 329-4951
NYSE: OII ■ *TF:* 877-680-5478 ■ *Web:* www.oceaneering.com

Offshore Energy Services Inc
5900 US Hwy 90 E .... Broussard LA 70518 337-837-1024
Web: www.offshoreenergyservices.com

Offshore Specialty Fabricators LLC
115 Menard Rd .... Houma LA 70363 985-868-1438
Web: www.osf-llc.com

Oil States International Inc
333 Clay St Three Allen Ctr Ste 4620 .... Houston TX 77002 713-652-0582 652-0499
NYSE: OIS ■ *Web:* www.oilstatesintl.com

Oil States Skagit SMATCO LLC 1180 Mulberry Rd .... Houma LA 70363 985-868-0630
Web: oilstates.com

One Earth Oil & Gas Inc
600-6th Ave SW Ste 320 .... Calgary AB T2P0S5 403-984-3151

OneSubsea LLC 4646 W Sam Houston Pkwy N .... Houston TX 77041 713-939-2211
Web: cameron.slb.com/onesubsea

OPPORTUNE 711 Louisiana Ste 3100 .... Houston TX 77002 713-622-8955
Web: opportune.com/practice-areas/reserve-engineering-geosciences

Pacific Paradym Energy Inc
1518-1030 Georgia St W .... Vancouver BC V6E2Y3 604-689-2646
Web: www.pacificparadym.com

Painted Pony Petroleum Ltd
736 Sixth Ave SW Ste 1800 .... Calgary AB T2P3T7 403-475-0440
Web: www.paintedpony.ca

Pajak Engineering Ltd 300-707 Seventh Ave SW .... Calgary AB T2P3H6 403-264-1197
Web: www.pajakeng.com

Palo Petroleum Inc 5944 Luther Ln Ste 900 .... Dallas TX 75225 214-691-3676
Web: www.palopetro.com

PanGeo Subsea Inc 277 Water St .... St John's NL A1C6L3 709-739-8032
Web: www.pangeosubsea.com

Paragon Offshore PLC
3151 Briarpark Dr Ste 700 .... Houston TX 77042 832-783-4000
Web: www.paragonoffshore.com

Paramount Resources Ltd
4700 Bankers Hall W 888 Third St SW .... Calgary AB T2P5C5 403-290-3600
Web: www.paramountres.com

Peak Completion Technologies Inc
7710 W Hwy 80 .... Midland TX 79706 432-684-4155
Web: peakcompletions.com

Peak Oilfield Services Co 2525 C St Ste 201 .... Anchorage AK 99503 907-263-7000 263-7070
Web: www.peakalaska.com

Pentagon Optimization Services Inc
220 7700 - 76 St Close .... Red Deer AB T4P4G6 403-347-6277

Petro-Techna International Ltd
28 Village Centre Pl .... Mississauga ON L4Z1V9 905-277-5423
Web: www.petro-techna.com

Petroleum Strategies Inc 303 W Wall St .... Midland TX 79701 432-682-0292
Web: www.petroleumstrategies.com

PetroMax Operating Company Inc
603 Main St Ste 201 .... Garland TX 75040 972-271-0999
Web: www.petromaxoperating.com

PetroSkills LLC 2930 S Yale Ave .... Tulsa OK 74114 918-828-2500
Web: www.petroskills.com

Pine Cliff Energy Ltd
1015 Fourth St SW Ste 850 .... Calgary AB T2R1J4 403-269-2289
Web: www.pinecliffenergy.com

Pinnergy Ltd 111 Congress Ave Ste 2020 .... Austin TX 78701 512-343-8880 343-8885
Web: www.pinnergy.com

Piper Valve Systems Inc
1020 E Grand Blvd .... Oklahoma City OK 73129 405-671-2000
Web: piper-oilfield.com

Platinum Control Technologies Corp
2822 W Fifth St .... Fort Worth TX 76107 817-529-6485
TF: 877-374-1115 ■ *Web:* platinumcontrol.com

Plump Engineering Inc 914 E Katella Ave .... Anaheim CA 92805 714-385-1835
Web: www.peica.com

PPV Inc 4927 NW Front Ave .... Portland OR 97210 503-261-9800
Web: www.ppvnw.com

Premier Oilfield Equipment Co
2550 E Bijou .... Fort Morgan CO 80701 970-542-1975
Web: poequipment.com

Presco Inc
10200 Grogan's Mill Rd Ste 520 .... The Woodlands TX 77380 281-292-7792
Web: www.prescocorp.com

			Phone	Fax
Pride International Inc 5847 San Felipe St Ste 3300 ... Houston	TX	77057	713-789-1400	789-1430
TF: 877-736-3772 ■ *Web:* rigzone.com				
Prime Marine Services Inc 312 S Bernard Rd ... Broussard	LA	70518	337-837-6500	
Web: www.primemarineinc.com				
Producers Service Corp 109 Graham St ... Zanesville	OH	43701	740-454-6253	
Web: www.producersservicecorp.com				
Production Management Industries LLC 9761 Hwy 90 E ... Morgan City	LA	70380	985-631-3837	631-0729
TF: 888-229-3837 ■ *Web:* www.pmi.net				
ProSep (USA) Inc 5353 W Sam Houston Pkwy N Ste 150 ... Houston	TX	77041	281-504-2040	
Web: prosep.com				
Pumpco Energy Services Inc 117 Elm Grove Rd ... Valley View	TX	76272	940-726-1800	
Web: www.pumpcoservices.com				
Pyramid Tubular Products LP 2 Northpoint Dr Ste 610 ... Houston	TX	77060	281-405-8090	
Web: www.pyramidtubular.com				
Questor Technology Inc 1121 940 - Sixth Ave SW ... Calgary	AB	T2P3T1	403-571-1530	
TF: 844-477-8669 ■ *Web:* www.questortech.com				
Real Time Measurements Inc Bay 18 4750 106th Ave SE ... Calgary	AB	T2C3G5	403-720-3444	
Web: www.rty.ca				
Reaveley Engineers & Associates Inc 675 East 500 South ... Salt Lake City	UT	84102	801-486-3883	
Web: www.reaveley.com				
Reef Oil & Gas Partners LP 1901 N Central Expy Ste 300 ... Richardson	TX	75080	972-437-6792	
Web: www.reefogc.com				
Regent Energy Group Ltd 3735 - 8 St ... Nisku	AB	T9E8J8	780-769-4100	
Web: www.rglrm.com/combined				
RGL Reservoir Management Inc 734 - 7th Ave SW Ste 1600 ... Calgary	AB	T2P3P8	403-269-8088	
Web: www.rglrm.com/combined				
Rig-Chem Inc 132 Thompson Rd ... Houma	LA	70363	985-873-7208	
TF: 800-375-7208 ■ *Web:* www.rigchem.com				
Rising Star Services Inc 6106 Cargo Rd ... Odessa	TX	79762	432-617-0114	
Web: www.risingstarservices.com				
Roberson Wireline Inc 314 SE Ninth Ave ... Perryton	TX	79070	806-435-3087	
Web: robersonwireline.com				
Robert L. Bayless, Producer LLC 621 17th St Ste 2300 ... Denver	CO	80293	303-296-9900	
Web: www.rlbayless.com				
RPC Inc 2801 Buford Hwy Ste 520 ... Atlanta	GA	30324	404-321-2140	321-5483
NYSE: RES ■ *Web:* www.rpc.net				
S.S. Papadopulos & Associates Inc 7944 Wisconsin Ave ... Bethesda	MD	20814	301-718-8900	
Web: www.sspa.com				
Saddle Butte Pipeline LLC 858 Main Ave Ste 301 ... Durango	CO	81301	970-375-3150	
Web: www.sbpipeline.com				
SageRider Inc 3330 F County Rd 56 Ste 160 ... Stafford	TX	77477	281-271-7095	
Web: www.sageriderinc.com				
Sahara Energy Ltd 700 4 Ave SW Ste 610 ... Calgary	AB	T2P3J4	403-232-1359	
Web: www.saharaenergyltd.com				
Salazar Service & Trucking Corp 1360 S US 385 ... Andrews	TX	79714	432-523-9658	
Web: www.salazarservice.com				
Samson Resources Corp Samson Plz Two W Second St Ste 1500 ... Tulsa	OK	74103	918-591-1791	
Web: www.samson.com				
Schlumberger Wireline & Testing 210 Schlumberger Dr ... Sugar Land	TX	77478	281-285-4551	
TF: 800-272-7328 ■ *Web:* www.slb.com				
Schoeller-Bleckmann Energy Services LLC 712 Saint Etienne Rd ... Broussard	LA	70518	337-837-2030	
Web: www.sbesllc.com				
SEC Energy Products & Services LP 9523 Fairbanks N ... Houston	TX	77064	281-890-9977	
Web: www.sec-ep.com				
Seismic Source Co 9425 E Tower Rd ... Ponca City	OK	74604	580-362-3402	
Web: seismicsource.com				
Shaw Pipeline Services Inc 4250 N Sam Houston Pkwy E Ste 180 ... Houston	TX	77032	832-601-0850	
TF: 866-912-5314 ■ *Web:* www.shawpipeline.com				
Sklar Exploration Company LLC 401 Edwards St Ste 1601 ... Shreveport	LA	71101	318-227-8668	
Web: www.sklarexploration.com				
Sound & Cellular Inc 824 W Yellowstone Hwy ... Casper	WY	82601	307-234-7256	
TF: 800-689-7256 ■ *Web:* www.soundandcellular.com				
Southern Concrete Products Inc 266 E Church St ... Lexington	TN	38351	731-968-8394	
Web: www.southernconcrete.com				
Spartek Systems Inc 1 Thevenaz Industrial Trl ... Sylvan Lake	AB	T4S2J6	403-887-2443	
Web: www.sparteksystems.com				
Spatial Insights Inc 4938 Hampden Ln ... Bethesda	MD	20814	301-229-4413	
Web: www.spatialinsights.com				
Stabil Drill Specialties LLC 110 Consolidate Dr ... Lafayette	LA	70508	337-837-3001	
Web: www.stabildrill.com				
Stewart & Stevenson LLC 1000 Louisiana St ... Houston	TX	77002	713-613-0633	
Web: www.stewartandstevenson.com				
Stokes & Spiehler Inc 110 Rue Jean Lafitte ... Lafayette	LA	70508	337-233-6871	
Web: www.stokesandspiehler.com				
Stric-Lan Companies LLC 104 Sable St ... Duson	LA	70529	337-984-7850	
Web: www.striclan.com				
Sub-Surface Tools LLC 1767 W Hwy 380 ... Bridgeport	TX	76426	940-683-8283	
Web: www.subsurfacetools.com				
Superior Derrick Services LLC 4506 S Lewis St ... New Iberia	LA	70560	337-359-1955	
Web: www.superiorderrick.com				
Supreme Oil Co 2109 W Monte Vista Rd ... Phoenix	AZ	85009	800-752-7888	258-8801*
**Fax Area Code:* 602 ■ *TF:* 800-752-7888 ■ *Web:* www.supremeoil.com				
Surefire Industries LLC 1400 Brittmoore ... Houston	TX	77043	713-481-9600	
Web: www.surefireindustries.com				
T-3 Energy Services Inc 140 Cypress Stn Dr Ste 225 ... Houston	TX	77090	713-996-4110	943-2042*
**Fax Area Code:* 281				
T-Rex Engineering & Construction LC 16425 Jacintoport Blvd ... Houston	TX	77015	281-833-9200	
Web: www.trexec.com				
Talisman Energy USA Inc 337 Daniel Zenker Dr ... Horseheads	NY	14845	607-562-4000	
Web: www.talismanusa.com				
Tana Exploration Company LLC 25025 I-45 N Ste 600 ... The Woodlands	TX	77380	832-325-6000	
Web: www.tanaexp.com				
Team Inc 200 Hermann Dr ... Alvin	TX	77511	281-331-6154	
NYSE: TISI ■ *TF:* 800-662-8326 ■ *Web:* www.teamindustrialservices.com				
Team Trident LLC 16300 Katy Fwy Ste 180 ... Houston	TX	77094	281-600-1412	
Web: www.teamtrident.com				
TEC Well Service Inc 851 W Harrison Rd ... Longview	TX	75604	903-759-0082	
Web: www.tecwell.com				
Terroco Industries Ltd Site 14 RR Ste 1 Box 10 ... Red Deer	AB	T4N5E1	403-346-1171	
TF: 800-670-1100 ■ *Web:* www.terroco.com				
Testco 3445 Executive Center Dr Ste 117 ... Austin	TX	78731	432-683-2951	
Web: www.testco.com				
Teton Buildings LLC 2701 Magnet St ... Houston	TX	77054	713-351-6300	
Web: tetonbuildings.com				
Texas Electric Utility Construction Ltd 4613 Hwy 1417 N ... Sherman	TX	75092	903-893-0949	
Web: www.texaselectric.com				
Thru Tubing Solutions Inc 11515 S Portland ... Oklahoma City	OK	73170	405-692-1900	
Web: www.thrutubing.com				
TK Stanley Inc 6739 Hwy 184 ... Waynesboro	MS	39367	800-477-2855	735-2857*
**Fax Area Code:* 601 ■ *TF:* 800-477-2855 ■ *Web:* dwservices.com				
Tri-C Resources Inc 909 Wirt Rd ... Houston	TX	77024	713-685-3600	
Web: www.tricresources.com				
Trican Well Service Ltd 645 Seventh Ave SW Ste 2900 ... Calgary	AB	T2P4G8	403-266-0202	237-7716
TSE: TCW ■ *TF:* 877-473-2008 ■ *Web:* www.tricanwellservice.com				
United Hunter Oil & Gas Corp 700 W Pender St Ste 615 ... Vancouver	BC	V6C1G8	832-487-0813	
Web: www.unitedhunteroil.com				
Upham Oil & Gas Company LP 999 Energy Ave ... Mineral Wells	TX	76067	940-325-4491	
Web: www.uphamoilandgas.com				
Valiant Corp 6555 Hawthorne Dr ... Windsor	ON	N8T3G6	519-974-5200	
TF: 888-825-4268 ■ *Web:* www.valiantcorp.com				
Vector Seismic Data Processing Inc 1801 Broadway Ste 1150 ... Denver	CO	80202	303-571-1515	
Web: www.slb.com/services/seismic/vector-seismic.aspx				
Vidler Water Company Inc 3480 GS Richards Blvd Ste 101 ... Carson City	NV	89703	775-885-5000	
Web: www.vidlerwater.com				
Viking Drilling LLC 3720 S Co Rd 1309 ... Odessa	TX	79765	432-550-0100	
Web: www.viking-drilling.com				
Viking Oil Tools 25211 Grogans Mill Rd Ste 460 ... The Woodlands	TX	77380	281-907-9676	
Ward Williston Oil Company Inc 36700 Woodward Ave Ste 101 ... Bloomfield Hills	MI	48304	248-594-6622	
Web: www.wardwilliston.com				
Waschuk Pipe Line Construction Ltd #127-39015 Hwy 2A ... Red Deer	AB	T4N2A3	403-346-1114	
Web: www.waschukpipeline.com				
Weatherford Completion Systems 11420 W Hwy 80 E ... Midland	TX	79711	432-563-7957	
Web: www.weatherford.com				
Welker Inc 13839 W Bellfort ... Sugar Land	TX	77498	281-491-2331	
Web: www.welker.com				
Well Power Inc 11111 Katy Fwy Ste 9-110 ... Houston	TX	77079	713-973-5738	
Web: www.wellpowerinc.com				
Wet Tech Energy Inc 4598 Woodlawn Rd ... Maurice	LA	70555	337-893-9992	
Web: www.wettechenergy.com				
White Oak Operating Company LLC 12941 N Fwy Ste 550 ... Houston	TX	77060	281-876-2025	
Web: www.whiteoakenergy.com				
Wilbanks Energy Logistics 11246 Lovington Hwy Lovington Hwy PO Box 1390 ... Artesia	NM	88211	575-746-6318	
Web: www.wilbanksel.com				
Wood Group PSN Inc 182 Equity Blvd ... Houma	LA	70360	985-868-4116	
Web: www.wgps.com				
Woodside Energy (USA) Inc Sage Plz 5151 San Felipe St Ste 1200 ... Houston	TX	77056	713-401-0000	
Web: www.woodside.com.au				
Yoho Resources Inc 521-3rd Ave SW Ste 500 ... Calgary	AB	T2P3T3	403-537-1771	
Web: www.yohoresources.ca				
Yuba City Water Treatment Plant 701 Northgate Dr ... Yuba City	CA	95991	530-822-4636	
Web: www.yubacity.net				
Zedi Inc 902 11th Ave SW ... Calgary	AB	T2R0E7	403-444-1100	
Web: www.zedi.ca				

540 OIL & GAS WELL DRILLING

			Phone	Fax
Aera Energy LLC 10000 Ming Ave ... Bakersfield	CA	93311	661-665-5000	
Web: www.aeraenergy.com				
AKITA Drilling Ltd 333 Seventh Ave SW Ste 900 ... Calgary	AB	T2P3H2	403-292-7979	
Web: www.akita-drilling.com				

Phone Fax

Apex Distribution Inc 407 - 2 St SW Ste 550 .... Calgary AB T2P2Y3 403-268-7333
Web: www.apexdistribution.com

Aquila Drilling Co LP
2525 Kell Blvd Ste 405 .... Wichita Falls TX 76308 940-761-3153
Web: aquiladrilling.com

Arrow Energy Services Inc 4030 Columbus Dr .... Kalkaska MI 49646 231-258-4596
Web: www.arrowenergyservices.com

Atwood Oceanics Inc 15011 Katy Fwy Ste 800 .... Houston TX 77094 281-749-7800
NYSE: ATW ■ *Web:* www.atwd.com

Aztec Well Servicing Company Inc
300 Legion Rd PO Box 100 .... Aztec NM 87410 505-334-6194
Web: www.aztecwell.com

BCM Energy Partners Inc 5005 Riverway Ste 350 .... Houston TX 77056 713-623-2003
Web: www.bcmenergy.com

Bengal Energy Ltd 801 6 Ave SW Ste 1810 .... Calgary AB T2P3W2 403-205-2526
Web: bengalenergy.ca

Berenergy Corp 1888 Sherman St .... Denver CO 80203 303-295-2323

BICO Drilling Tools Inc 1604 Greens Rd .... Houston TX 77032 281-590-6966
Web: www.bicodrilling.com

Big 6 Drilling Co 7500 San Felipe St .... Houston TX 77063 713-783-2300
Web: www.big6drilling.com

Cabo Drilling (Ontario) Corp
20 Sixth St .... New Westminster BC V3L2Y8 705-567-9311
Web: www.cabo.ca

Callon Petroleum Co 200 N Canal St .... Natchez MS 39120 601-442-1601 446-1410
NYSE: CPE ■ *TF:* 800-451-1294 ■ *Web:* www.callon.com

Cambrian Management 2398 W 44th St .... Odessa TX 79764 432-550-5245

Cathedral Energy Services Ltd 6030 3 St SE .... Calgary AB T2H1K2 403-265-2560
Web: www.cathedralenergyservices.com

Childress Directional Drilling
6429 cunningham rd .... Houston TX 77041 713-466-7979
Web: www.childressdrilling.com

Coast Oil Co 4250 Williams Rd .... San Jose CA 95129 408-252-7720
Web: www.coastoil.com

Crescent Directional Drilling LP
2040 Aldine Western Rd .... Houston TX 77038 281-668-9535
Web: crescentdirectional.com

Crescent Energy Services LLC
1304 Engineers Rd .... Belle Chasse LA 70037 504-433-4188
Web: crescentes.com

CrownQuest Operating LLC
18 Desta Dr PO Box 53310 .... Midland TX 79710 432-818-0300
Web: www.crownquest.com

Cyclone Drilling Inc PO Box 908 .... Gillette WY 82717 307-682-4161 682-3158
TF: 800-318-3724 ■ *Web:* www.cyclonedrilling.com

DHS Drilling Co 1813 Coleman Cir .... Casper WY 82601 307-473-5377
Web: www.dhsdrilling.com

Diamond Offshore Drilling Inc 15415 Katy Fwy .... Houston TX 77094 281-492-5300 492-5316
NYSE: DO ■ *TF:* 800-848-1980 ■ *Web:* www.diamondoffshore.com

Doyon Drilling Inc 11500 C St Ste 200 .... Anchorage AK 99515 907-563-5530
TF: 800-478-9675 ■ *Web:* www.doyondrilling.com

Eagle Well Servicing Corp 8113-49 Ave Close .... Red Deer AB T4P2V5 403-346-7789
Web: www.wesc.ca

Eastham Drilling Inc
4710 Bellaire Blvd Ste 350 .... Bellaire TX 77401 713-661-6890
Web: www.bigedrilling.com

EGL Resources Inc 508 W Wall St Ste 1250 .... Midland TX 79701 432-687-6560
Web: www.egloilshale.com

Ensign Energy Services Inc
400 Fifth Ave SW Ste 1000 .... Calgary AB T2P0L6 403-262-1361 262-8215
TSE: ESI ■ *Web:* www.ensignenergy.com

Falcon Seaboard Resources Inc
109 N Post Oak Ln Ste 540 .... Houston TX 77024 713-622-0055
Web: www.falconseaboard.com

GEO Drilling Fluids Inc 1431 Union Ave .... Bakersfield CA 93305 661-325-5919 325-5648
TF: 800-438-7436 ■ *Web:* www.geodf.com

Great White Pressure Control LLC
4500 SE 59th St .... Oklahoma City OK 73135 405-605-2700
Web: www.greatwhitepressurecontrol.com

Halliburton Energy Services
10200 Bellaire Blvd .... Houston TX 77072 281-871-4000
Web: www.halliburton.com

Helmerich & Payne Inc 1437 S Boulder Ave .... Tulsa OK 74119 918-742-5531
NYSE: HP ■ *TF:* 800-205-4913 ■ *Web:* www.hpinc.com

Hercules Offshore Inc
9 Greenway Plaza Ste 2200 .... Houston TX 77046 713-350-5100 350-5105
NASDAQ: HERO ■ *TF:* 888-647-1715 ■ *Web:* www.herculesoffshore.com

High Arctic Energy Services Inc
444 , 5th Ave, S.W. Ste 2010 .... Calgary AB T2P2T8 403-340-9825
Web: www.haes.ca

Iron Horse Energy Services Inc
1901 Dirkson Dr NE .... Redcliff AB T0J2P0 403-526-4600
TF: 877-526-4666 ■ *Web:* www.ihes.ca

Jomax Drilling (1988) Ltd
140 - 4 Ave SW Ste 1750 .... Calgary AB T2P3N3 403-265-5312
Web: www.jomax.ca

Justiss Oil Company Inc 1120 E Oak St .... Jena LA 71342 318-992-4111 992-7201
TF: 800-256-2501 ■ *Web:* www.justissoil.com

Kenai Drilling Ltd 6430 Cat Canyon Rd .... Santa Maria CA 93454 805-937-7871
Web: www.kenaidrilling.com

Kicking Horse Energy Inc 1520-700 6 Ave SW .... Calgary AB T2P0T8 403-234-8663
TF: 877-672-2121

Liberty Pioneer Energy Source Inc
1411 East 840 North .... Orem UT 84097 801-224-4771
Web: www.libertypioneer.com

MATRRIX Energy Technologies
808 - Fourth Ave SW Ste 350 .... Calgary AB T2P3E8 403-984-5042
Web: www.matrrix.com

Maverick Directional Services
25615 Oakhurst Dr .... Spring TX 77386 281-364-1212
TF: 866-459-0233 ■ *Web:* www.maverickdirectional.com

McClelland Oilfield Rentals Limited Patnership
8720-110 St .... Grande Prairie AB T8V8K1 780-539-3656
TF: 866-539-3656 ■ *Web:* www.mcclellandoilfieldrentals.com

Murfin Drilling Company Inc
250 N Water St Ste 300 .... Wichita KS 67202 316-267-3241
Web: www.murfininc.com

Nabors Alaska Drilling Inc
2525 C St Ste 200 .... Anchorage AK 99503 907-263-6000 563-3734
Web: www.nabors.com

Nabors Drilling International Ltd
515 W Greens Rd Ste 1000 .... Houston TX 77067 281-874-0035 872-5205
TF: 877-344-7529 ■ *Web:* nabors.com

Nabors Drilling USA Inc
515 W Greens Rd Ste 1000 .... Houston TX 77067 281-874-0035 872-5205
Web: nabors.com

Nabors Industries Ltd
515 W Greens Rd Ste 1200 .... Houston TX 77067 281-874-0035 872-5205
NYSE: NBR ■ *Web:* www.nabors.com

Nicklos Drilling Co 2229 San Felipe Ste 1401 .... Houston TX 77019 713-224-5959
Web: www.nicklosdrilling.com

Noble Corp
13135 S Dairy Ashford Rd Ste 800 .... Sugar Land TX 77478 281-276-6100 491-2092
NYSE: NE ■ *TF:* 877-285-4162 ■ *Web:* www.noblecorp.com

Omron Oilfield & Marine Inc
9510 N Houston Rosslyn Rd .... Houston TX 77088 713-849-1700
Web: www.oilfield.omron.com

Orchard Petroleum Inc 3585 Maple St Ste 284 .... Ventura CA 93003 805-644-8555
Web: www.orchardpetroleum.com

Orion Drilling Company LLC
674 Flato Rd .... Corpus Christi TX 78405 361-299-9800
Web: www.oriondrilling.com

Parker Drilling Co 1401 Enclave Pkwy Ste 600 .... Houston TX 77077 281-406-2000 406-2001
NYSE: PKD ■ *TF:* 800-468-9716 ■ *Web:* www.parkerdrilling.com

Patterson-UTI Energy Inc 450 Gears Rd Ste 500 .... Houston TX 77067 281-765-7100 765-7175
NASDAQ: PTEN ■ *TF:* 866-387-1933 ■ *Web:* www.patenergy.com

Pioneer Drilling Co
1250 NE Loop 410 Ste 1000 .... San Antonio TX 78209 210-828-7689 447-6080
NASDAQ: PDCE ■ *Web:* www.pioneeres.com

ProPetro Services Inc
1706 S Midkiff Rd Bldg B PO Box 873 .... Midland TX 79701 432-688-0012
Web: www.propetroservices.com

Pure Energy Services (USA) Inc
9635 Maroon Cir Ste 420 .... Englewood CO 80112 303-708-0200
Web: www.pure-energy.ca

Quail Tools LP 3713 Hwy 14 .... New Iberia LA 70560 337-364-0407
Web: www.quailtools.com

Radial Drilling Services Inc
4921 Spring Cypress .... Spring TX 77379 281-374-7507
Web: radialdrilling.com

Range Resources Corp
100 Throckmorton St Ste 1200 .... Fort Worth TX 76102 817-870-2601 869-9100
NYSE: RRC ■ *Web:* www.rangeresources.com

Reliance Well Service Inc 237 Hwy 79 S .... Magnolia AR 71753 870-234-2700

Ringo Drilling I LP 104 Spinks Rd .... Tye TX 79563 325-695-5600
Web: www.ringodrilling.com

Roll'n Oilfield Industries Ltd
305, 5208 ? 53 Ave .... Red Deer AB T4N5K2 403-343-1710
Web: www.rolln.com

Scandrill Inc 11777 Katy Fwy Ste 470 .... Houston TX 77079 281-496-5571
Web: www.scandrill.com

Scientific Drilling Controls Inc
16701 Greenspoint Pk Dr Ste 200 .... Houston TX 77060 281-443-3300
TF: 800-514-8949 ■ *Web:* www.scientificdrilling.com

Seadrill Americas Inc 11210 Equity Dr Ste 150 .... Houston TX 77041 713-329-1150
Web: www.seadrill.com

Seventy Seven Energy Inc
777 NW 63rd St .... Oklahoma City OK 73116 405-608-7777
Web: www.77nrg.com

SITE Ltd 120 Pembina Rd Ste 170 .... Sherwood Park AB T8H0M2 780-400-7483
Web: www.siteenergy.com

Sorensen Craig F Construction Inc
918 South 2000 West .... Syracuse UT 84075 801-773-4390
Web: www.gosci.com

SST Energy Corp 8901 W Yellowstone Hwy .... Casper WY 82604 307-235-3529 473-1650
Web: www.sstenergy.com

Steinberger Drilling Co
10063 State Hwy 25 E .... Windthorst TX 76389 940-423-6900
Web: www.steinbergerdrilling.com

Target Drilling Inc 1112 Glacier Dr .... Smithton PA 15479 724-633-3927
Web: www.targetdrilling.com

Texas Keystone Inc 560 Epsilon Dr .... Pittsburgh PA 15238 412-434-5616
Web: www.texaskeystone.com

Topco Oilsite Products Ltd
Bay 7 3401 - 19 St NE .... Calgary AB T2E6S8 403-219-0255
Web: www.topcooilsite.com

Total Energy Services Ltd
2550 300-5th Ave SW Ste 2550 .... Calgary AB T2P3C4 403-216-3939 234-8731
NYSE: TOT ■ *TF:* 877-818-6825 ■ *Web:* www.totalenergy.ca

Transocean Inc 4 Greenway Plaza .... Houston TX 77046 713-232-7500
NYSE: RIG ■ *TF:* 877-440-0173 ■ *Web:* www.deepwater.com

Trinidad Drilling Ltd 2500-700 9 Ave SW .... Calgary AB T2P3V4 403-265-6525
Web: www.trinidaddrilling.com

True Drilling LLC 455 N Poplar PO Box 2360 .... Casper WY 82602 307-237-9301 266-0373
Web: truecos.com

U.S. Energy Development Corp
2350 N Forest Rd .... Getzville NY 14068 716-636-0401
TF: 800-636-7606 ■ *Web:* usedc.com

Union Drilling Inc
4055 International Plz Ste 610 .... Fort Worth TX 76109 817-735-8793 546-4368
NASDAQ: UDRL ■ *Web:* sidewinderdrilling.com

Unit Corp 7130 S Lewis Ave Ste 1000 .... Tulsa OK 74136 918-493-7700 493-7711
NYSE: UNT ■ *TF:* 800-722-3612 ■ *Web:* www.unitcorp.com

Vantage Drilling Co 777 Post Oak Blvd Ste 800 .... Houston TX 77056 281-404-4700 404-4749
NYSE: VTG ■ *Web:* www.vantagedrilling.com

Veracity Energy Services Ltd
200 744 - Fourth Ave SW .... Calgary AB T2P3T4 403-537-1300
Web: www.veracityenergy.com

				Phone	Fax
Vermilion Energy Trust 3500 520 Third Ave SW *TSE:* VET ■ *TF:* 866-895-8101 ■ *Web:* www.vermilionenergy.com	Calgary	AB	T2P0R3	403-269-4884	476-8100
Victory Energy Corp 220 Airport Rd *Web:* www.victoryenergycorp.com	Indiana	PA	15701	724-349-6366	
Xtreme Drilling & Coil Services Corp 9805 Katy Freeway Ste 650 *TF:* 800-564-6253 ■ *Web:* www.xtremecoildrilling.com	Houston	TX	77024	403-262-9500	

541 OILS & GREASES - LUBRICATING

See Also Chemicals - Specialty p. 1934; Petroleum Refineries p. 2932

				Phone	Fax
Ackerman Oil Company Inc 2060 S Lube Way *Web:* www.ackoil.com	Jasper	IN	47546	812-482-6666	
Allied Sales Co 5005 E Seventh St *Web:* www.alliedsales.com	Austin	TX	78702	512-385-2167	
American Lubrication Equipment Corp 11212A McCormick Rd PO Box 1350 **Fax Area Code:* 800 ■ *TF:* 888-252-9300 ■ *Web:* americanlube.com	Hunt Valley	MD	21030	888-252-9300	759-2637*
Amsoil Inc 925 Tower Ave *TF Sales:* 800-777-7094 ■ *Web:* www.amsoil.com	Superior	WI	54880	715-392-7101	392-5225
Anderol Inc 215 Merry Ln *TF:* 888-263-3765 ■ *Web:* www.anderol.com	East Hanover	NJ	07936	973-887-7410	887-8404
Axel Plastics Research Laboratories Inc 5820 Broadway *TF:* 800-332-2935 ■ *Web:* www.axelplastics.com	Woodside	NY	11377	718-672-8300	
Battenfeld Grease & Oil Corp of New York 1174 Erie Ave PO Box 728 *Web:* www.battenfeld-grease.com	North Tonawanda	NY	14120	716-695-2100	695-0367
Bel Ray Company Inc PO Box 526 *Web:* www.belray.com	Farmingdale	NJ	07727	732-938-2421	938-4232
Benz Oil Inc 2724 W Hampton Ave *Web:* www.benzoil.com	Milwaukee	WI	53209	414-442-2900	442-8388
BG Products Inc 740 S Wichita St *TF:* 800-961-6228 ■ *Web:* www.bgprod.com	Wichita	KS	67213	316-265-2686	265-1082
Blachford Corp 401 Ctr Rd **Fax Area Code:* 630 ■ *Web:* www.blachford.com	Frankfort	IL	60423	905-823-3200	231-8321*
Bolton Oil Company Ltd 1316 54th St PO Box 3176 *Web:* www.boltonoil.com	Lubbock	TX	79412	806-747-1629	
BP Lubricants USA Inc 1500 Valley Rd *TF:* 800-333-3991 ■ *Web:* www.bp.com	Wayne	NJ	07470	973-633-2200	
Canada Forgings Inc 130 Hagar St *TF:* 800-263-0440 ■ *Web:* www.canforge.com	Welland	ON	L3B5P8	905-735-1220	
Castrol Industrial North America Inc 150 W Warrenville Rd *TF:* 877-641-1600 ■ *Web:* www.castrol.com	Naperville	IL	60563	877-641-1600	648-9801
Chem-Trend LP 1445 McPherson Pk Dr *TF:* 800-727-7730 ■ *Web:* www.chemtrend.com	Howell	MI	48843	517-546-4520	
Colorado Petroleum Products Co 4080 Globeville Rd *Web:* www.colopetro.com	Denver	CO	80216	303-294-0302	
CRC Industries Inc 885 Louis Dr *TF Cust Svc:* 800-556-5074 ■ *Web:* www.crcindustries.com	Warminster	PA	18974	215-674-4300	674-2196
D-A Lubricant Co 1340 W 29th St **Fax:* Cust Svc ■ *TF:* 800-645-5823 ■ *Web:* www.dalube.com	Indianapolis	IN	46208	317-923-5321	923-3884*
Delta Petroleum Co 10352 River Rd *Web:* ww1.deltapetro.com	Saint Rose	LA	70087	504-467-1399	467-1398
Elco Corp 1000 Belt Line St *TF:* 800-321-0467 ■ *Web:* www.elcocorp.com	Cleveland	OH	44109	216-749-2605	749-7462
Fiske Bros Refining Co 129 Lockwood St *TF:* 800-733-4755 ■ *Web:* www.lubriplate.com	Newark	NJ	07105	973-589-9150	589-4432
Fuchs Lubricants Canada Ltd Eastern Canada Div 405 Dobbie Dr PO Box 909 *Web:* www.fuchs.com	Cambridge	ON	N1R5X9	519-622-2040	
Fuchs Lubricants Co 17050 Lathrop Ave *Web:* www.fuchs.com	Harvey	IL	60426	708-333-8900	333-9180
Hangsterfer's Laboratories Inc 175 Ogden Rd *TF:* 800-433-5823 ■ *Web:* www.hangsterfers.com	Mantua	NJ	08051	856-468-0216	468-0200
Hercules Chemical Company Inc 111 S St *TF:* 800-221-9330 ■ *Web:* www.oatey.com	Passaic	NJ	07055	973-778-5000	777-4115
Honstein Oil Co 11 Paseo Real *Web:* www.honsteinoil.com	Santa Fe	NM	87507	505-471-1800	
Houghton International Inc 945 Madison Ave PO Box 930 *TF:* 888-459-9844 ■ *Web:* www.houghtonintl.com	Valley Forge	PA	19482	610-666-4000	666-0174
Hydrotex Inc 12920 Senlac D Ste 190 *TF:* 800-527-9439 ■ *Web:* www.hydrotexlube.com	Farmers Branch	TX	75234	800-527-9439	
ITW Rocol North America 3650 W Lake Ave *TF:* 800-452-5823 ■ *Web:* itwfluidsna.com	Glenview	IL	60026	847-657-5278	
Jackson Oil & Solvents Inc 1970 Kentucky Ave *TF:* 800-221-4603 ■ *Web:* www.jacksonoilsolvents.com	Indianapolis	IN	46221	317-636-4421	685-2403
JD Streett & Company Inc 144 Weldon Pkwy *Web:* www.jdstreett.com	Maryland Heights	MO	63043	314-432-6600	432-4248
Jet-Lube Inc 4849 Homestead Rd Ste 232 *TF:* 800-538-5823 ■ *Web:* www.jetlube.com	Houston	TX	77226	713-670-5700	678-4604
Kluber Lubrication North America LP 32 Industrial Dr *TF:* 800-447-2238 ■ *Web:* www.klueber.com	Londonderry	NH	03053	603-647-4104	647-4106
Leadership Performance Sustainability Laboratories 4647 Hugh Howell Rd **Fax Area Code:* 770 ■ *TF:* 800-241-8334 ■ *Web:* www.lpslabs.com	Tucker	GA	30084	800-241-8334	243-8899*
LiQuifix LLC 110 Lenox Ave *Web:* www.liquifix.com	Stamford	CT	06906	203-653-4689	
Lubri-Lab Inc 1540 de Coulomb *Web:* www.lubrilab.com	Boucherville	QC	J4B8A3	450-449-1626	449-9174
Lubricating Specialties Co 8015 Paramount Blvd *Web:* www.lsc-online.com	Pico Rivera	CA	90660	562-776-4000	776-4004
Lubrication Engineers Inc 300 Bailey Ave **Fax Area Code:* 800 ■ **Fax:* Sales ■ *TF:* 800-537-7683 ■ *Web:* www.lelubricants.com	Fort Worth	TX	76107	817-834-6321	228-1142*
Lubrication Technologies Inc 900 Mendelssohn Ave N *TF:* 800-328-5573 ■ *Web:* www.lubetech.com	Golden Valley	MN	55427	763-545-0707	545-9256
Lubrizol Corp 29400 Lakeland Blvd *NYSE:* LZ ■ *TF:* 800-380-5397 ■ *Web:* www.lubrizol.com	Wickliffe	OH	44092	440-943-4200	943-5337
Master Chemical Corp 501 W Boundry St *Web:* www.masterchemical.com	Perrysburg	OH	43551	419-874-7902	874-0684
Metalworking Lubricants Co 25 Silverdome Industrial Park *TF:* 800-394-5494 ■ *Web:* www.metalworkinglubricants.com	Pontiac	MI	48342	248-332-3500	332-4959
Northland Products Co 1000 Rainbow Dr	Waterloo	IA	50701	319-234-5585	234-5580
Northtown Products Inc 5202 Argosy Ave *TF:* 800-972-7274 ■ *Web:* www.northtowncompany.com	Huntington Beach	CA	92649	714-897-0700	
Nye Lubricants Inc 12 Howland Rd *Web:* www.nyelubricants.com	Fairhaven	MA	02719	508-996-6721	997-5285
Oil Chem Inc 711 W 12th St *Web:* www.oilcheminc.com	Flint	MI	48503	810-235-3040	238-5260
Oil Ctr Research LLC 106 Montrose Ave *TF:* 800-256-8977 ■ *Web:* www.oilcenter.com	Lafayette	LA	70503	337-993-3559	993-3149
Orelube Corp, The 20 Sawgrass Dr *TF:* 800-645-9124 ■ *Web:* www.orelube.com	Bellport	NY	11713	631-205-9700	205-9797
Perkins Oil Company Inc 4707 Pflaum Rd *TF:* 800-634-9937 ■ *Web:* perkinsoil.com	Madison	WI	53718	608-221-4736	
Primrose Oil Company Inc 11444 Denton Dr *TF:* 800-275-2772 ■ *Web:* www.primrose.com	Dallas	TX	75229	972-241-1100	241-4188
Richards-Apex Inc 4202-24 Main St *Web:* www.richardsapex.com	Philadelphia	PA	19127	215-487-1100	487-3090
Schaeffer Mfg Company Inc 102 Barton St *TF Cust Svc:* 800-325-9962 ■ *Web:* www.schaefferoil.com	Saint Louis	MO	63104	314-865-4100	865-4107
Schultz Lubricants Inc 164 Shrewsbury St *TF:* 800-262-3962 ■ *Web:* www.schultzlubricants.com	West Boylston	MA	01583	508-835-4446	
Shell Lubricants 1000 Main 12th Fl *TF Cust Svc:* 888-743-5586 ■ *Web:* www.shell.us	Houston	TX	77002	713-241-6161	
Smitty's Supply Inc 63399 Hwy 51 N PO Box 530 *TF:* 800-256-7575 ■ *Web:* www.smittysinc.net	Roseland	LA	70456	985-748-9687	748-3004
Southwestern Petroleum Corp PO Box 961005 *TF:* 800-877-9372 ■ *Web:* www.swepcousa.com	Fort Worth	TX	76161	817-332-2336	877-4047
Sun Drilling Products Corp 503 Main St *TF:* 800-962-6490 ■ *Web:* www.sundrilling.com	Belle Chasse	LA	70037	504-393-2778	391-1383
Texas Refinery Corp 840 N Main St *TF:* 800-827-0711 ■ *Web:* www.texasrefinery.com	Fort Worth	TX	76164	817-332-1161	332-6110
Total Lubricants USA 5 N Stiles St *TF:* 800-323-3198 ■ *Web:* www.totalspecialties.com	Linden	NJ	07036	908-862-9300	862-5374
Tri Star Energy LLC 1740 Ed Temple Blvd *Web:* dailys.com	Nashville	TN	37208	615-313-3600	
Valvoline Co 3499 Blazer Pkwy PO Box 14000 *TF:* 800-832-6825 ■ *Web:* www.valvoline.com	Lexington	KY	40512	859-357-7777	
WD-40 Co 1061 Cudahy Pl *NASDAQ:* WDFC ■ *TF:* 800-448-9340 ■ *Web:* www.wd40company.com	San Diego	CA	92110	619-275-1400	275-5823
Westpower Equipment Ltd 4451-54 Ave S.E. *Web:* www.westpower.ca	Calgary	AB	T2C2A2	403-720-3300	236-9812

542 OPHTHALMIC GOODS

See Also Personal Protective Equipment & Clothing p. 2926

				Phone	Fax
Aearo Co 5457 W 79th St *TF:* 877-327-4332 ■ *Web:* earsc.com	Indianapolis	IN	46268	317-692-6666	692-6772
Art Optical Contact Lens Inc PO Box 1848 *Web:* www.artoptical.com	Grand Rapids	MI	49501	616-453-1888	453-8702
Art-Craft Optical Company Inc 57 Goodway Dr S *TF:* 800-828-8288 ■ *Web:* www.artcraftoptical.com	Rochester	NY	14623	585-546-6640	546-5133
Bausch & Lomb Inc 1400 N Goodman St *TF:* 800-553-5340 ■ *Web:* www.bausch.com	Rochester	NY	14609	585-338-6000	338-6896
Beitler-Mckee Optical Co 160 S 22nd St *TF:* 800-989-4700 ■ *Web:* beitlermckee.com	Pittsburgh	PA	15203	412-481-4700	
Bolle Inc 9200 Cody St *TF:* 800-423-3537 ■ *Web:* www.bolle.com	Overland Park	KS	66214	913-752-3400	752-3550
Carskadden Optical Co 1525 Highpoint Ct	Zanesville	OH	43701	740-452-9306	
CIBA Vision Corp 11460 Johns Creek Pkwy *TF:* 800-875-3001 ■ *Web:* www.alcon.com/about-us/who-we-are/business-focus/alcon-cibavision	Duluth	GA	30097	678-415-3937	415-4260
Conforma Laboratories Inc 4705 Colley Ave *TF:* 800-426-1700 ■ *Web:* www.conforma.com	Norfolk	VA	23508	757-321-0200	321-0201
Cooper Cos Inc 6140 Stoneridge Mall Rd Ste 590 *NYSE:* COO ■ *TF:* 888-822-2660 ■ *Web:* www.coopercos.com	Pleasanton	CA	94588	925-460-3600	
CooperVision Inc 209 High Point Dr Ste 200 *TF:* 800-538-7850 ■ *Web:* www.coopercos.com	Victor	NY	14564	585-385-6810	
Costa Del Mar 2361 Mason Ave Ste 100 *TF:* 800-447-3700 ■ *Web:* www.costadelmar.com	Daytona Beach	FL	32117	386-274-4000	274-4001
Cumberland Optical Laboratory 806 Olympic St	Nashville	TN	37203	615-254-5868	254-5868
DAC Vision 3630 W Miller Ste 350 *TF:* 800-800-1550 ■ *Web:* www.dacvision.com	Garland	TX	75041	972-677-2700	677-2800
De'Vons Optics Inc 10823 Bell Ct *Web:* coppermax.com	Rancho Cucamonga	CA	91730	909-466-4700	
Dispensers Optical Service Corp 1815 Plantside Dr Bluegrass Industrial Park	Louisville	KY	40299	502-491-3440	491-3446
ER Precision Optical Corp 805 W Central Blvd *Web:* www.eroptics.com	Orlando	FL	32805	407-292-5395	
Essilor of America Inc 13515 N Stemmons Fwy *Web:* www.essilorusa.com	Dallas	TX	75234	214-496-1000	

Phone | Fax

Eye-Kraft Optical Inc 8 McLeland Rd .... Saint Cloud MN 56303 888-455-2022 950-7070*
**Fax Area Code:* 800 ■ *TF:* 888-455-2022 ■ *Web:* www.eyekraft.com

Gargoyles Inc 500 George Washington Hwy .... Smithfield RI 02917 401-231-3800 356-4248*
**Fax Area Code:* 800 ■ *TF:* 866-807-0195 ■ *Web:* gargoyleseyewear.com

Gentex Optics Inc 324 Main St. .... Simpson PA 18407 570-282-3550 282-8555
TF: 800-736-0554 ■ *Web:* www.gentexcorp.com

Homer Optical Company Inc
2401 Linden Ln .... Silver Spring MD 20910 301-585-9060 585-5934
TF: 800-627-2710 ■ *Web:* www.homeroptical.com

Hoya Holdings Inc 3285 Scott Blvd .... Santa Clara CA 95054 408-654-2300
Web: www.hoya.co.jp

Icare Industries Inc 4399 35th St N. .... Saint Petersburg FL 33714 727-526-0501 522-1408
TF: 877-422-7352 ■ *Web:* www.icarelabs.com

IcareLabs 4399 35th St N. .... Saint Petersburg FL 33714 877-422-7352 522-1408*
**Fax Area Code:* 727 ■ *TF:* 877-422-7352 ■ *Web:* www.icarelabs.com

Instrument Technology Inc 33 Airport Rd .... Westfield MA 01085 413-562-3606
Web: www.scopes.com

Johnson & Johnson Vision Care Inc
7500 Centurion Pkwy .... Jacksonville FL 32256 800-874-5278
TF: 800-843-2020 ■ *Web:* www.acuvueprofessional.com

LBI Eyewear 20801 Nordhoff St. .... Chatsworth CA 91311 818-407-1890 407-1895
TF Cust Svc: 800-423-5175 ■ *Web:* www.lbieyewear.com

LensVector Inc 677 Palomar Ave .... Sunnyvale CA 94085 408-542-0300
Web: www.lensvector.com

Maui Jim Inc 721 Wainee St .... Lahaina HI 96761 808-661-8841 661-0351
TF: 888-352-2001 ■ *Web:* www.mauijim.com

MEMS Optical Inc 205 Import Cir. .... Huntsville AL 35806 256-859-1886
Web: www.memsoptical.com

Night Optics USA Inc
15182 Triton Ln Ste 101 .... Huntington Beach CA 92649 714-899-4475
TF: 800-306-4448 ■ *Web:* www.nightoptics.com

Oakley Inc 1 Icon .... Foothill Ranch CA 92610 949-951-0991 368-2443*
**Fax Area Code:* 502 ■ **Fax:* Cust Svc ■ *TF Cust Svc:* 800-403-7449 ■ *Web:* www.oakley.com

Rosin Eyecare Ctr 6233 W Cermak Rd .... Berwyn IL 60402 708-749-2020
Web: www.rosineyecare.com

Serengeti Eyewear Inc 9200 Cody St .... Overland Park KS 66214 913-752-3400 752-3550
TF Cust Svc: 800-423-3537 ■ *Web:* www.serengeti-eyewear.com

Sigma Corp of America 15 Fleetwood Ct. .... Ronkonkoma NY 11779 631-585-1144
TF: 800-896-6858 ■ *Web:* www.sigmaphoto.com

Signature Eyewear Inc 498 N Oak St .... Inglewood CA 90302 310-330-2700
OTC: SEYE ■ *TF:* 800-765-3937 ■ *Web:* www.signatureeyewear.com

STAAR Surgical Co 1911 Walker Ave .... Monrovia CA 91016 626-303-7902 303-2962*
NASDAQ: STAA ■ **Fax:* Mktg ■ *TF:* 800-352-7842 ■ *Web:* www.staar.com

Telops Inc 100-2600 St-Jean-Baptiste Ave .... Quebec QC G2E6J5 418-864-7808 864-7843
Web: www.telops.com

Transitions Optical Inc
9251 Belcher Rd .... Pinellas Park FL 33782 727-545-0400 546-4732
TF: 800-533-2081 ■ *Web:* www.transitions.com

US Vision Inc
1 Harmon Dr Glen Oaks Industrial Pk .... Glendora NJ 08029 856-228-1000 228-3339
TF: 866-435-7111 ■ *Web:* www.usvision.com

Vision-Ease Lens Inc 7000 Sunwood Dr NW. .... Ramsey MN 55303 320-251-8140 251-4312
TF Cust Svc: 800-328-3449 ■ *Web:* www.visionease.com

Walman Optical Company Inc
801 12th Ave N. .... Minneapolis MN 55411 612-520-6000 520-6069
TF: 800-873-9256 ■ *Web:* www.walman.com

X-Cel Optical Company Inc
806 S Benton Dr .... Sauk Rapids MN 56379 320-251-8404 232-9235*
**Fax Area Code:* 800 ■ *TF General:* 800-747-9235 ■ *Web:* www.x-celoptical.com

X-Ray Optical Systems Inc
15 Tech Valley Dr .... East Greenbush NY 12061 518-880-1500
Web: www.xos.com

Younger Optics 2925 California St .... Torrance CA 90503 310-783-1533 783-6477
TF: 800-366-5367 ■ *Web:* www.youngeroptics.com

543 OPTICAL GOODS STORES

Phone | Fax

Allegany Optical LLC 17301 Vly Mall Rd. .... Hagerstown MD 21740 301-582-1771
Web: www.alleganyoptical.com

Art Partners LLC 284 S Sharon Amity Rd .... Charlotte NC 28211 888-472-6866
TF: 888-472-6866 ■ *Web:* www.bindersart.com

Aspen Optical Inc 1050 W Main St Ste 102. .... Mesa AZ 85201 480-894-8770
Web: www.aspenoptical.com

Atlantic Optical Company Inc
20801 Nordhoff St .... Chatsworth CA 91311 818-407-1890
Web: www.ce-tru.com

Barnett & Ramel Optical Co 7154 N 16th St .... Omaha NE 68112 800-228-9732
TF: 800-228-9732 ■ *Web:* www.broptical.com

BARSKA Optics 1721 Wright Ave. .... La Verne CA 91750 909-445-8168
Web: www.barska.com/index.html

Beacon Advanced Eye Care Center
1320 Shelfer St. .... Leesburg FL 34748 352-728-8318
Web: www.beaconvisioncenter.com

Carolina Eyecare Physicians
2060 Charlie Hall Blvd Ste 201 .... Charleston SC 29414 843-722-2010
Web: www.carolinaeyecare.com

CCHC Southern Gastroenterology Associates
3100 Wellons Blvd .... New Bern NC 28562 252-634-9000
Web: www.cchchealthcare.com

Center for Behavioral Health Inc, The
175 Cedar Ln Ste A. .... Teaneck NJ 07666 201-692-9500
Web: www.njpsychologist.com

Cliff Weil Inc 8043 Industrial Pk Rd .... Mechanicsville VA 23116 804-746-1321 746-2595
TF: 800-446-9345 ■ *Web:* www.cliffweil.com

Co/op Optical Vision Designs
2424 E Eight-Mile. .... Detroit MI 48234 313-366-5100 366-7313
Web: www.coopoptical.com

Colonial Opticians 4942 St Elmo Ave. .... Bethesda MD 20814 301-657-3332
Web: colonialopticians.com

Crown Vision Ctr 211 E Broadway .... Alton IL 62002 618-462-9818
Web: www.crownvisioncenter.com

Phone | Fax

Dakota Vision Center LLC
5012 S Bur Oak Pl .... Sioux Falls SD 57108 605-361-1680
Web: dakotavisioncenter.com

Designs for Vision Inc 760 Koehler Ave .... Ronkonkoma NY 11779 631-585-3300
Web: www.designsforvision.com

Doctors Vision Ctr
413 Mill St PO Box 7396 .... Rocky Mount NC 27804 252-442-0802 442-2820
Web: www.doctorsvisioncenter.com

Dr Tavel Optical Group
2839 Lafayette Rd .... Indianapolis IN 46222 317-924-1300
Web: www.drtavel.com

Emerging Vision Inc 520 Eigth Ave Ste 2300. .... New York NY 10018 646-737-1500
Web: www.emergingvision.com

Empire Optical Inc 3238 E 21st St .... Tulsa OK 74114 918-744-8005
Web: empireoptical.com

Empire Vision Centers 2921 Erie Blvd E .... Syracuse NY 13224 315-446-5120
TF: 877-959-4160

Epic Labs Inc 95 Third St NE. .... Waite Park MN 56387 320-656-1473
Web: www.epiclabs.com

Exact Eye Care 431 Pierce St .... Sioux City IA 51101 712-252-4691
Web: www.exacteyecare.com

Eye Glass World Inc
2435 Commerce Ave Bldg 2200. .... Duluth GA 30096 800-637-3597
TF: 800-637-3597 ■ *Web:* www.eyeglassworld.com

Eye To Eye Vision Ctr
2255 Sewell Mill Rd Ste 310 .... Marietta GA 30062 770-578-1900
Web: www.eyetoeyevisioncenter.com

Eye-Mart Express Inc
13800 Senlac Dr Ste 200 .... Farmers Branch TX 75234 972-488-2002 206-5194*
**Fax Area Code:* 469 ■ *TF:* 888-372-2763 ■ *Web:* www.eyemartexpress.com

Eye-Mate Inc 77 N Centre Ave. .... Rockville Centre NY 11570 516-678-9613

Eyetique Corp 2242 Murray Ave .... Pittsburgh PA 15217 412-422-5300
Web: www.eyetique.com

For Eyes/Insight Optical 285 W 74th Pl .... Hialeah FL 33014 305-557-9004
TF: 877-688-9891 ■ *Web:* www.foreyes.com

General Vision Services LLC
520 Eigth Ave 9th Fl .... New York NY 10018 212-729-5300 967-4781
TF: 855-653-0586 ■ *Web:* www.generalvision.com

Glasses Ltd 50 E Oak St Apt Bsmt .... Chicago IL 60611 312-944-6876
Web: www.glasses.com

H Rubin Vision Centers
7539 Garners Sperry Rd .... Columbia SC 29209 803-779-9313 779-9551*
**Fax:* Cust Svc ■ *Web:* www.hrubinvision.com

Hakim Optical Laboratory Limited
128 Hazelton Ave .... Toronto ON M5R2E5 416-924-5600
Web: www.hakimoptical.ca

Hart Specialties Inc
5000 New Horizons Blvd .... Amityville NY 11701 631-226-5600
Web: www.newyorkeye.net

Henry Ford OptimEyes
655 W 13-Mile Rd .... Madison Heights MI 48071 248-588-9300
TF: 800-393-2273 ■ *Web:* henryford.com/homepage_optimeyes.cfm?id=51936

Heritage Optical Center Inc
19010 Livernois Ave. .... Detroit MI 48221 313-863-9581
Web: www.heritageoptical.com

Hi-tech Optical Inc 3139 Christy Way S .... Saginaw MI 48603 989-799-9390
Web: www.hi-techoptical.com

Horner Rausch Optical Super Store
968 Main St .... Nashville TN 37206 615-226-0251
Web: hornerrauschoptical.com

HOYA Optical Laboratories Inc
651 E Corporate Dr. .... Lewisville TX 75057 972-221-4141
Web: www.hoyavision.com

I-MED Pharma Inc
1601 St. Regis Blvd .... Dollard-des-Ormeaux QC H9B3H7 514-685-8118 685-8998
Web: www.imedpharma.com

INNOVA Medical Ophthalmics Inc
48 Carnforth Rd .... Toronto ON M4A2K7 416-615-0185
Web: www.innovamed.com

JAK Enterprises Inc 8309 N Knoxville Ave. .... Peoria IL 61615 309-692-8222
TF: 800-752-3295 ■ *Web:* www.bardoptical.com

JC Penney Optical Co 821 N Central Expressway .... Plano TX 75075 972-516-1393
TF: 866-435-7111 ■ *Web:* www.jcpenneyoptical.com

KBco The Polarized Lens Co
7328 S Revere Pkwy Unit 208. .... Centennial CO 80112 303-253-6600
Web: www.kbco.net

LensCrafters Inc 4000 Luxottica Pl. .... Mason OH 45040 513-765-4321
TF: 877-753-6727 ■ *Web:* www.lenscrafters.com

Live Eyewear Inc 3490 Broad St. .... San Luis Obispo CA 93401 805-782-5070
Web: www.liveeyewear.com

Lobob Laboratories Inc 1440 Atteberry Ln .... San Jose CA 95131 408-432-0580
Web: loboblabs.com

Lockport Optical 36 E Ave .... Lockport NY 14094 716-434-6900 434-8461

Magnifying Ctr 10086 W McNab Rd. .... Tamarac FL 33321 954-722-1580
TF: 800-364-1612 ■ *Web:* www.magnifyingcenter.com

Malbar Vision Ctr 409 N 78th St .... Omaha NE 68114 402-391-6600 493-4041
Web: www.malbar.com

Marco Ophthalmic Inc 11825 Central Pkwy .... Jacksonville FL 32224 904-642-9330
Web: www.marco.com

McLeod Optical Company Inc
50 Jefferson Park Rd. .... Warwick RI 02888 401-467-3000
Web: www.mcleodoptical.com

Medical Associates Healthcare
911 Carter St Nw .... Elkader IA 52043 563-245-1717
Web: www.mahealthcare.com

Moscot Mobileyes Foundation Inc
118 Orchard St .... New York NY 10002 212-477-3796
Web: www.moscot.com

National Vision Inc 296 Grayson Hwy .... Lawrenceville GA 30045 770-822-3600
TF Cust Svc: 800-637-3597 ■ *Web:* www.nationalvision.com

Native Eyewear Inc 1444 Wazee St Ste 215. .... Denver CO 80202 888-776-2848
TF: 888-776-2848 ■ *Web:* www.nativeyewear.com

Nea Optical LLC 1426 E Washington. .... Jonesboro AR 72401 870-935-2179
Web: neaoptical.com

Company / Address	City	State	ZIP	Phone	Fax
Omni Optical Lab 3255 Executive Blvd Ste 100 *TF:* 800-364-6664 ■ *Web:* www.omnioptical.com	Beaumont	TX	77705	800-364-6664	
Ophthalmic Consultants of Boston Inc 50 Staniford St Ste 600 *Web:* www.eyeboston.com	Boston	MA	02114	617-367-4800	
Opti Care Eye Health Center 87 Grandview Ave *TF:* 800-334-3937	Waterbury	CT	06708	203-574-2020	596-2230
Optical Distributor Group LLC 12301 NW 39th St *TF:* 800-852-8089 ■ *Web:* www.opticaldg.com	Coral Springs	FL	33065	914-347-7400	
Optical Options 4620 J C Nichols Pkwy Ste 427 *Web:* www.cibiseyecare.com	Kansas City	MO	64112	816-561-4907	
Optovue Inc 2800 Bayview Dr *Web:* www.optovue.com	Fremont	CA	94538	510-623-8868	
Pacific Eyecare 20696 Bond Rd Ne *Web:* www.pacificsurgerycenter.com	Poulsbo	WA	98370	360-779-2020	
Paris Miki Usa Inc 2863 152nd Ave Ne *Web:* parismikiusa.com	Redmond	WA	98052	425-883-2464	
Partec Inc 9301 Belmont Ave *Web:* partec-inc.com	Franklin Park	IL	60131	847-678-9520	
Pearle Vision Inc 4000 Luxottica Pl *Web:* www.pearlevision.com	Mason	OH	45040	513-765-4321	765-6388
Polyvision Inc 10700 Abbotts Bridge Rd Ste 100 *Web:* www.polycore-usa.com	Johns Creek	GA	90670	562-944-3924	
Precision Tool Technologies Inc 309 13th Ave Nw *Web:* www.precisiontooltech.com	Little Falls	MN	56345	320-632-5320	
Premier Eyecare Group Inc 1524 Cedar Cliff Dr *Web:* www.premiereyes.com	Camp Hill	PA	17011	717-761-3077	
ProCare Vision Ctr Inc 1955 Newark-Granville Rd *Web:* www.procarevisioncenters.com	Granville	OH	43023	740-587-3937	587-3589
Retina Consultants of Oklahoma 9913 S May Ave Ste C *Web:* retinaconsultantsoklahoma.com	Oklahoma City	OK	73159	405-691-0505	
Revision Military Ltd 7 Corporate Dr *Web:* www.revisionmilitary.com	Essex Junction	VT	05452	802-879-7002	
Rite-Style Optical Co 12240 Emmet St *TF:* 800-373-3200 ■ *Web:* ritestyle.com	Omaha	NE	68164	612-520-6058	
RJ Rippey Od Pa Dba Vision Vision Source 1635A S Voss Rd	Houston	TX	77057	713-954-2020	
Rockwell Laser Industries Inc 7754 Camargo Rd Ste 3 *Web:* www.rli.com	Cincinnati	OH	45243	513-271-1568	
Rosin Eyecare Ctr 6233 W Cermak Rd *Web:* www.rosineyecare.com	Berwyn	IL	60402	708-749-2020	
Rx Optical 1700 S Pk St *TF:* 800-792-2737 ■ *Web:* www.rxoptical.com	Kalamazoo	MI	49001	269-342-0003	342-4284
Saint Charles Vision 8040 St Charles Ave *Web:* www.stcharlesvision.com	New Orleans	LA	70118	504-866-6311	
Singer Specs 211 W Lincoln Hwy *Web:* singerspecs.net	Exton	PA	19341	610-524-8886	
Solar Bat Enterprises Inc 3628 E County Rd 600 N *Web:* www.solarbat.com	Brazil	IN	47834	812-986-3551	
SPY Inc 2070 Las Palmas Dr *Web:* www.spyoptic.com	Carlsbad	CA	92011	760-804-8420	
Sterling Optical 520 Eigth Ave 23rd Fl *TF:* 800-393-7789 ■ *Web:* www.sterlingoptical.com	New York	NY	10018	516-390-2117	390-2183
Style Eyes Optics 824 W 18th St *Web:* www.styleeyes.com	Costa Mesa	CA	92627	949-548-5355	
SVS Vision 140 Macomb Pl *TF:* 800-787-4600 ■ *Web:* www.svsvision.com	Mount Clemens	MI	48043	586-468-7612	468-7682
TearLab Corp 7360 Carroll Rd Ste 200 *Web:* www.tearlab.com	San Diego	CA	92121	858-455-6006	
Today's Vision 6970 FM 1960 W Ste A *Web:* www.todaysvision.com	Houston	TX	77069	281-469-2020	469-7531
Tryiton Eyewear LLC 147 Post Rd E *TF:* 888-896-3885 ■ *Web:* www.eyeglasses.com	Westport	CT	06880	203-544-0770	
Union Eyecare Centers 4750 Beidler Rd *TF:* 800-443-9699 ■ *Web:* www.unioneyecare.com	Willoughby	OH	44094	216-986-9700	986-1996
US Vision Inc 1 Harmon Dr Glen Oaks Industrial Pk *TF:* 866-435-7111 ■ *Web:* www.usvision.com	Glendora	NJ	08029	856-228-1000	228-3339
Vision Care Associates 1120 E Washington St *Web:* www.visioncareclinic.com	Grayslake	IL	60030	847-223-2000	
VisionAid Inc 11 Kendrick Rd *Web:* visionaidinc.com	Wareham	MA	02571	508-295-3300	
Visionworks 854 Plaza Blvd *Web:* total-visioncare.com	Lancaster	PA	17601	717-295-3111	
Visionworks of America Inc 175 E Houston St *TF:* 800-669-1183 ■ *Web:* www.visionworks.com	San Antonio	TX	78205	210-340-3531	524-6996
Vistar Eye Center Inc 707 S Jefferson St *TF:* 866-615-5454 ■ *Web:* www.vistareye.com	Roanoke	VA	24016	540-855-5100	
Vogue Optical Inc 20 Great George St *TF:* 866-594-3937 ■ *Web:* www.vogueoptical.com	Charlottetown	PE	C1A4J6	902-566-3326	
Volk Optical Inc 7893 Enterprise Dr *Web:* www.volk.com	Mentor	OH	44060	440-942-6161	
Vuzix Corp 2166 Brighton Henrietta Town Line Rd *Web:* www.vuzix.com	Rochester	NY	14623	585-359-5900	
Wiley X Inc 7800 Patterson Pass Rd *Web:* www.wileyx.com	Livermore	CA	94550	925-243-9810	
Winchester Optical Company Inc 1935 Lake St *Web:* www.winoptical.com	Elmira	NY	14901	607-734-4251	
Wing Eyecare Inc 5305 Glenway Ave *Web:* www.wingeyecare.com	Cincinnati	OH	45238	513-791-2222	

544 OPTICAL INSTRUMENTS & LENSES

See Also Laboratory Analytical Instruments p. 2623

Company / Address	City	State	ZIP	Phone	Fax
4D Technology Corp 3280 E Hemisphere Loop Ste 146 *Web:* www.4dtechnology.com	Tucson	AZ	85706	520-294-5600	
A C Tool Supply 5456 E Mcdowell Rd Ste 123 *Web:* www.aikencolon.com	Mesa	AZ	85215	480-968-6698	
Access Optics LLC 2001 N Willow Ave *Web:* www.accessoptics.com	Broken Arrow	OK	74012	918-294-1234	
Alcon Canada Inc 2665 Meadowpine Blvd *Web:* www.alcon.ca	Mississauga	ON	L5N8C7	905-826-6700	
Allergan Inc 2525 Dupont Dr *NYSE:* AGN ■ **Fax:* Mail Rm ■ *TF:* 800-347-4500 ■ *Web:* www.allergan.com	Irvine	CA	92612	714-246-4500	246-6987*
Altarum Institute 3520 Green Ct Ste 300 *Web:* www.altarum.org	Ann Arbor	MI	48105	734-302-4600	
American Polarizers Inc 141 S Seventh St *TF:* 800-736-9031 ■ *Web:* www.apioptics.com	Reading	PA	19602	610-373-5177	373-2229
American Technology Network Corp 1341 San Mateo Ave *TF:* 800-910-2862 ■ *Web:* www.atncorp.com	South San Francisco	CA	94080	650-875-0130	
Applied Fiber Inc PO Box 1339 *TF:* 800-226-5394 ■ *Web:* www.appliedfiber.com	Leesburg	GA	31763	229-759-8301	
Awareness Technology Inc PO Box 1679 *Web:* www.awaretech.com	Palm City	FL	34991	772-283-6540	283-8020
B E Meyers & Co Inc 9461 Willows Rd NE *TF:* 800-327-5648 ■ *Web:* www.bemeyers.com	Redmond	WA	98052	425-881-6648	867-1759
BAE Systems OASYS LLC 645 Harvey Rd Ste 9	Manchester	NH	03103	603-232-8221	
Beena Vision Systems Inc 600 Pinnacle Ct *Web:* www.beenavision.com	Norcross	GA	30071	678-597-3156	
Benz Research & Development Corp 6447 Parkland Dr *Web:* www.benzrd.com	Sarasota	FL	34243	941-758-8256	
Bond Optics LLC 76 Etna Rd PO Box 422 *Web:* www.bondoptics.com	Lebanon	NH	03766	603-448-2300	448-5489
Bristol Instruments Inc 50 Victor Heights Pkwy *Web:* www.bristol-inst.com	Victor	NY	14564	585-924-2620	
Burris Company Inc 331 E Eigth St *TF:* 888-228-7747 ■ *Web:* www.burrisoptics.com	Greeley	CO	80631	970-356-1670	356-8702
Bushnell Corp 9200 Cody St *TF:* 800-423-3537 ■ *Web:* www.bushnell.com	Overland Park	KS	66214	913-752-3400	752-3550
Carl Zeiss Inc 1 Zeiss Dr *Web:* www.zeiss.com	Thornwood	NY	10594	914-747-1800	681-7446
ChromaGen Vision LLC 326 W Cedar St Ste 1 *TF:* 855-473-2323 ■ *Web:* www.ireadbetternow.com	Kennett Square	PA	19348	855-473-2323	
Conoptics International Sales Corp 19 Eagle Rd *TF:* 800-748-3349 ■ *Web:* www.conoptics.com	Danbury	CT	06810	203-743-3349	790-6145
CSC Laboratories Inc 180 Westgate Dr *Web:* www.csclabs.com	Watsonville	CA	95076	831-763-6931	
CST/Berger Corp 255 W Fleming St **Fax Area Code:* 800 ■ *TF:* 800-435-1859 ■ *Web:* www.cstberger.us	Watseka	IL	60970	815-432-5237	913-0049*
Deltronic Corp 3900 W Segerstrom Ave *TF:* 800-451-6922 ■ *Web:* www.deltronic.com	Santa Ana	CA	92704	714-545-5800	545-9548
Deltronic Crystal Industries Inc 64 Harding Ave *Web:* www.deltroniccrystal.com	Dover	NJ	07801	973-328-7000	
Direct Optical Research Co 8725 115th Ave *Web:* www.dorc.com	Largo	FL	33773	727-319-9000	
Directed Energy Solutions (DES) 890 Elkton Dr Ste 101 *Web:* www.denergysolutions.com	Colorado Springs	CO	80907	719-593-7848	593-7846
Edmund Optics Inc 101 E Gloucester Pk *TF:* 800-363-1992 ■ *Web:* edmundoptics.com	Barrington	NJ	08007	856-547-3488	573-6295
Electro-optical Imaging Inc 4300 Fortune Pl Ste C *Web:* www.eoimaging.com	West Melbourne	FL	32904	321-435-8722	
Epilog Corp 16371 Table Mtn Pkwy *TF:* 888-437-4564 ■ *Web:* www.epiloglaser.com	Golden	CO	80403	303-277-1188	
Eschenbach Optik of America Inc 904 Ethan Allen Hwy *Web:* www.eschenbach.com	Ridgefield	CT	06877	203-438-7471	
Fosta-Tek Optics Inc 320 Hamilton St *TF:* 866-221-9157 ■ *Web:* www.fosta-tek.com	Leominster	MA	01453	978-534-6511	537-2168
Fraser-Volpe Corp Warminster Industrial Pk 1025 Thomas Dr	Warminster	PA	18974	215-675-5062	
G-S Supplies 408 St Paul St *TF:* 800-295-3050 ■ *Web:* www.gssupplies.com	Rochester	NY	14605	585-295-0250	232-3866
General Scientific Corp 1201 M St SE Ste 120 *Web:* www.genscicorp.com	Washington	DC	20003	202-547-4299	547-7550
Gooch & Housego (Ohio) LLC 676 Alpha Dr *Web:* www.goochandhousego.com	Cleveland	OH	44143	216-486-6100	
Gould Technology LLC 1121 Benfield Blvd Stes J-P *TF:* 800-544-6853 ■ *Web:* www.gouldfo.com	Millersville	MD	21108	410-987-5600	
Hamilton Associates Inc 11403 Cronridge Dr *Web:* www.atitest.com	Owings Mills	MD	21117	410-363-9696	
Hitachi High Technologies America Inc 10 N Martingale Rd Ste 500 *Web:* www.hitachi-hightech.com/us	Schaumburg	IL	60173	847-273-4141	273-4407
II-VI Inc 375 Saxonburg Blvd *NASDAQ:* IIVI ■ *Web:* www.ii-vi.com	Saxonburg	PA	16056	724-352-4455	360-5848
Intevac Inc 3560 Bassett St *NASDAQ:* IVAC ■ *Web:* www.intevac.com	Santa Clara	CA	95054	408-986-9888	
ISP Optics Corp 50 S Buckhout St *Web:* www.ispoptics.com	Irvington	NY	10533	914-591-3070	

Phone Fax

ITT Night Vision & Imaging
7635 Plantation Rd .... Roanoke VA 24019 540-563-0371 362-4979
TF: 800-448-8678 ■ *Web:* www.nightvision.com

Janos Technology LLC 55 Black Brook Rd. .... Keene NH 03431 603-757-0070 365-4596*
**Fax Area Code:* 802 ■ *Web:* www.janostech.com

JML Optical Industries Inc 820 Linden Ave .... Rochester NY 14625 585-248-8900 248-8924
Web: www.jmloptical.com

Karl Storz Imaging Inc 175 Cremona Dr .... Goleta CA 93117 805-968-3568
Web: www.optronics.com

Kollmorgen Corp Electro-Optical Div
50 Prince St .... NorthHampton MA 01060 413-586-2330 586-1324*
**Fax:* Sales ■ *TF:* 877-282-1168 ■ *Web:* www2.l-3com.com

LaCroix Optical Company Inc 50 LaCroix Dr .... Batesville AR 72501 870-698-1881
Web: www.lacroixoptical.com

LaserMax Corp 3495 Winton Pl. .... Rochester NY 14623 585-272-5420
TF: 800-527-3703 ■ *Web:* www.lasermax.com

Latham & Phillips Ophthalmic Products Inc
2300 Southwest Blvd .... Grove City OH 43123 614-871-6200
Web: lpoproducts.com

Leica Camera Inc 1 Pearl Ct. .... Allendale NJ 07401 201-995-0051
Web: www.leica-camera.com

Lenstec Inc 1765 Commerce Ave N. .... St. Petersburg FL 33716 727-571-2272
Web: www.lenstec.com

Lighthouse Imaging Corp 477 Congress St .... Portland ME 04101 207-253-5350
Web: www.lighthouseoptics.com

LightPath Technologies Inc
2603 Challenger Tech Ct Ste 100 .... Orlando FL 32826 407-382-4003 382-4007
NASDAQ: LPTH ■ *Web:* lightpath.com

Lincoln Laser Co 234 E Mohave St .... Phoenix AZ 85004 602-257-0407 257-0728
Web: www.lincolnlaser.com

Luxury Optical Holdings Inc
2651 N Crimson Canyon Dr Ste 200 .... Las Vegas NV 89128 702-798-8638
Web: www.loholdings.com

Lyric Optical Company Wholsle
3533 Cardiff Ave .... Cincinnati OH 45209 513-321-2456
TF: 800-543-7376 ■ *Web:* www.superoptical.com

Meade Instruments Corp 27 Hubble .... Irvine CA 92618 949-451-1450 451-1460
NASDAQ: MEAD ■ *TF:* 800-626-3233 ■ *Web:* www.meade.com

Microvision Inc 6222 185th Ave NE .... Redmond WA 98052 425-936-6847 882-6600
NASDAQ: MVIS ■ *Web:* www.microvision.com

Mirrotek International LLC 90 Dayton Ave .... Passaic NJ 07055 973-472-1400
TF: 888-659-3030 ■ *Web:* www.mirrotek.com

MyEyeDr Inc 401 Maple Ave W .... Vienna VA 22180 703-938-5544
Web: www.myeyedr.com

MZA Associates Corp
2021 Girard Blvd SE Ste 150 .... Albuquerque NM 87106 505-245-9970
Web: www.mza.com

Neoptix Inc 1415 Frank-Carrel Ste 220 .... Quebec QC G1N4N7 418-687-2500
Web: www.neoptix.com

Newport Corp 1791 Deere Ave .... Irvine CA 92606 949-863-3144 253-1680*
NASDAQ: NEWP ■ **Fax:* Sales ■ *TF Sales:* 800-222-6440 ■ *Web:* www.newport.com

Nightforce Optics 336 Hazen Ln. .... Orofino ID 83544 208-476-9814
Web: www.nightforceoptics.com

Obzerv Technologies Inc
400 Jean-Lesage Ste 201 .... Quebec QC G1K8W1 418-524-3522 524-6745
Web: www.obzerv.com

Ocean Optics Inc 830 Douglas Ave .... Dunedin FL 34698 727-733-2447 733-3962
Web: www.oceanoptics.com

Opotek Inc 2233 Faraday Ave Ste E .... Carlsbad CA 92008 760-929-0770
Web: www.opotek.com

OPT-Sciences Corp 1912 Bannard St .... Cinnaminson NJ 08077 856-829-2800
Web: www.optsciences.com

Optek Systems Inc 12 Pilgrim Rd .... Greenville SC 29607 864-272-2640
Web: www.opteksystems.com

Optical Gaging Products Inc 850 Hudson Ave .... Rochester NY 14621 585-544-0450 544-4998
TF: 800-647-4243 ■ *Web:* www.ogpnet.com

Optim LLC 64 Technology Park Rd .... Sturbridge MA 01566 508-347-5100
Web: www.optimnet.com

Optometrics Corp
8 Nemco Way Stony Brook Industrial Pk .... Ayer MA 01432 978-772-1700
Web: www.optometrics.com

Parker Hannifin Corp Daedal Div
1140 Sandy Hill Rd .... Irwin PA 15642 724-861-8200
TF: 800-245-6903 ■ *Web:* parker.com

PerkinElmer Inc 940 Winter St .... Waltham MA 02451 203-925-4602 944-4904
NYSE: PKI ■ *Web:* www.perkinelmer.com

Photon Technology International Inc
300 Birmingham Rd PO Box 272 .... Birmingham NJ 08011 609-894-4420
TF: 877-784-4349 ■ *Web:* www.pti-nj.com

ProPhotonix Inc 32 Hampshire Rd .... Salem NH 03079 603-893-8778 575-2420*
OTC: STKR ■ **Fax Area Code:* 781 ■ *TF:* 877-941-8631 ■ *Web:* www.prophotonix.com

Quality Vision International Inc
850 Hudson Ave .... Rochester NY 14621 585-544-0450
Web: www.qvii.com

Rancocas Nature Ctr 794 Rancocas Rd .... Westampton NJ 08060 609-261-2495
Web: www.njaudubon.org

Raytheon Canada Ltd 360 Albert St Ste 1640 .... Ottawa ON K1R7X7 613-233-4121 233-1099
Web: www.raytheon.com

Raytheon Network Centric Systems (NCS)
2501 W University Dr .... McKinney TX 75071 781-522-3000
Web: www.raytheon.com

Reflex Photonics Inc
1250 Oakmead Pkwy Ste 210 .... Sunnyvale CA 94085 408-501-8886
Web: www.reflexphotonics.com

Reichert Inc 3362 Walden Ave .... Depew NY 14043 716-686-4500
Web: www.reichert.com

Research Electro-optics Inc
5505 Airport Blvd .... Boulder CO 80301 303-938-1960 245-4396
Web: www.reoinc.com

Research Frontiers Inc
240 Crossways Park Dr .... Woodbury NY 11797 516-364-1902
Web: www.smartglass.com

Phone Fax

Ross Optical Industries Inc
1410 Gail Borden Pl .... El Paso TX 79935 915-595-5417 595-5466
TF: 800-880-5417 ■ *Web:* www.rossoptical.com

RPC Photonics Inc 330 Clay Rd .... Rochester NY 14623 585-272-2840
Web: www.rpcphotonics.com

Science & Engineering Services (SESI)
6992 Columbia Gateway Dr .... Columbia MD 21046 443-539-0139 539-1757
Web: www.sesi-md.com

Seiko Optical Products of America Inc
575 Corporate Dr .... Mahwah NJ 07430 201-529-9099
Web: www.seikoeyewear.com

Seiler Instrument & Mfg Company Inc
3433 Tree Court Industrial Blvd .... Saint Louis MO 63122 314-968-2282 968-2637
TF: 800-489-2282 ■ *Web:* www.seilerinst.com

Sellmark Corp 2201 Heritage Pkwy .... Mansfield TX 76063 817-225-0310
Web: www.sellmark.net

Servo Corp of America 123 Frost St .... Westbury NY 11590 516-938-9700 938-9644
Web: www.servo.com

SheerVision Inc(NDA)
4030 Palos Verdes Dr N Ste 104 .... Rolling Hills Estates CA 90274 310-265-8918
TF: 877-678-4274 ■ *Web:* www.sheervision.com

Sorenson Media Inc 13961 Minuteman Dr Ste 100 .... Draper UT 84020 801-501-8650
TF: 888-767-3676 ■ *Web:* www.sorensonmedia.com

Stevens Water Monitoring Systems
12067 NE Glenn Widing Dr Ste 106 .... Portland OR 97220 503-469-8000 469-8100
TF: 800-452-5272 ■ *Web:* www.stevenswater.com

Suzo-Happ Group Inc 1743 Linneman Rd .... Mount Prospect IL 60056 847-593-6130
Web: www.suzohapp.com

Synergy International Optronics LLC
101 Comac St .... Ronkonkoma NY 11779 631-277-0500
Web: www.siollc.com

Unilens Corp USA 10431 72nd St N .... Largo FL 33777 727-544-2531
Web: www.unilens.com

Vectronix Inc
19775 Belmont Executive Plz Ste 550 .... Ashburn VA 20147 703-777-3900
Web: www.vectronix.us

Veeco Instruments Inc 1 Terminal Dr .... Plainview NY 11803 516-677-0200
NASDAQ: VECO ■ *TF:* 888-724-9511 ■ *Web:* www.veeco.com

Voxis Inc
1160 Brickyard Cove Rd Ste 202 .... Point Richmond CA 94801 510-232-8333

Western Ophthalmics Corp
19019 36th Ave W Ste G .... Lynnwood WA 98036 425-672-9332
TF: 800-426-9938 ■ *Web:* www.west-op.com

Xenonics Holdings Inc 3186 Lionshead Ave .... Carlsbad CA 92010 760-477-8900 477-8897
OTC: XNNH

Zygo Corp Laurel Brook Rd .... Middlefield CT 06455 860-347-8506 347-3968
NASDAQ: ZIGO ■ *TF:* 800-994-6669 ■ *Web:* www.zygo.com

545 ORGAN & TISSUE BANKS

See Also Eye Banks p. 2276

Phone Fax

Alamo Tissue Service Ltd
5844 Rocky Point Dr .... San Antonio TX 78249 210-738-2663 732-4263
TF: 800-226-9091 ■ *Web:* www.alamotissueservice.com

AlloSource 6278 S Troy Cir .... Centennial CO 80111 720-873-0213 873-0212
TF: 888-873-8330 ■ *Web:* www.allosource.org

Bio-Tissue 7000 SW 97th Ave Ste 211 .... Miami FL 33173 305-412-4430 412-4429
TF: 888-296-8858 ■ *Web:* www.biotissue.com

Blood & Tissue Ctr of Central Texas
4300 N Lamar Blvd .... Austin TX 78756 512-206-1266
Web: www.bloodandtissue.org

Bone Bank Allografts 4808 Research Dr .... San Antonio TX 78240 210-696-7616 696-7609
TF Sales: 800-397-0088 ■ *Web:* www.bonebank.com

California Cryobank Inc
11915 La Grange Ave .... Los Angeles CA 90025 310-443-5244 826-1605
TF: 866-927-9622 ■ *Web:* www.cryobank.com

California Cryobank Inc
950 Massachusetts Ave .... Cambridge MA 02139 617-497-8646 497-6531
TF: 888-810-2796 ■ *Web:* www.cryobank.com

California Cryobank Inc
700 Welch Rd Ste 103 .... Palo Alto CA 94304 650-324-1900 324-1946
Web: www.cryobank.com

Community Tissue Services 2900 College Dr .... Kettering OH 45420 800-684-7783 461-4237*
**Fax Area Code:* 937 ■ *TF:* 800-684-7783 ■ *Web:* www.communitytissue.org

Community Tissue Services
3573 Bristol Pike Ste 201 .... Bensalem PA 19020 215-245-4506
TF: 800-684-7783 ■ *Web:* www.communitytissue.org

Comprehensive Tissue Ctr
11402 University Ave Rm 7415 .... Edmonton AB T6G2J3 780-407-7510
TF: 866-407-1970 ■ *Web:* albertahealthservices.ca/pagenotfound.htm

Cryobiology Inc 4830D Knightsbridge Blvd .... Columbus OH 43214 614-451-4375 451-5284
TF: 800-359-4375 ■ *Web:* www.cryobio.com

Cryogenic Laboratories Inc
1944 Lexington Ave N .... Roseville MN 55113 651-489-8000 489-8989
TF: 800-466-2796 ■ *Web:* www.cryolab.com

Donor Alliance Inc
720 S Colorado Blvd Ste 800-N .... Denver CO 80246 303-329-4747 321-1183
TF: 888-868-4747 ■ *Web:* www.donoralliance.org

Donor Awareness Coalition
5323 Harry Hines Blvd MC 9074 .... Dallas TX 75390 214-648-2609 648-2086

Donor Network West 12667 Alcosta Blvd Ste 600 .... Oakland CA 94607 925-480-3101
TF: 888-570-9400 ■ *Web:* www.donornetworkwest.org

Gift of Hope Organ & Tissue Donor Network
425 Spring Lake Dr .... Itasca IL 60143 630-758-2600
TF: 877-577-3747 ■ *Web:* www.giftofhope.org

Gift of Life Donor Program
401 N Third St .... Philadelphia PA 19123 215-557-8090
TF: 800-543-6391 ■ *Web:* www.donors1.org

Idant Laboratories 350 Fifth Ave Ste 7120 .... New York NY 10118 212-330-8500 330-8536
Web: www.idant.com

Indiana Donor Network 3760 Guion Rd .... Indianapolis IN 46222 317-685-0389
TF: 888-275-4676 ■ *Web:* indianadonornetwork.org

	City	State	ZIP	Phone	Fax
Kentucky Organ Donor Affiliates (KODA) 10160 Linn Station Rd *TF:* 800-525-3456 ■ *Web:* www.kyorgandonor.org	Louisville	KY	40223	502-581-9511	589-5157
LifeBanc 4775 Richmond Rd *TF:* 888-558-5433 ■ *Web:* www.lifebanc.org	Cleveland	OH	44128	216-752-5433	751-4204
LifeCell Corp 1 Millennium Way **Fax Area Code:* 908 ■ *TF:* 800-226-2714 ■ *Web:* www.lifecell.com	Branchburg	NJ	08876	800-226-2714	947-1089*
Lifeline of Ohio 770 Kinnear Rd Ste 200 *TF:* 800-525-5667 ■ *Web:* www.lifelineofohio.org	Columbus	OH	43212	614-291-5667	291-0660
LifeLink Tissue Bank 8510 Sunstate St *TF:* 800-683-2400 ■ *Web:* www.lifelinktissuebank.org	Tampa	FL	33634	813-886-8111	888-9419
LifeNet 1864 Concert Dr *TF:* 800-847-7831 ■ *Web:* www.lifenethealth.org	Virginia Beach	VA	23453	757-464-4761	301-6582
LifeNet Health Northwest 501 SW 39th St *TF:* 800-858-2282	Renton	WA	98057	425-981-8900	
LifeShare Transplant Donor Services of Oklahoma 4705 NW Expy *TF:* 888-580-5680 ■ *Web:* www.lifeshareoklahoma.org	Oklahoma City	OK	73132	405-840-5551	840-9748
Lifesharing Community Organ & Tissue Donation 3465 Camino del Rio S Ste 410 *TF:* 866-797-2366 ■ *Web:* www.lifesharing.org	San Diego	CA	92108	619-521-1983	521-2833
Louisiana Organ Procurement Agency (LOPA) 3545 N I-10 Service Rd Ste 300 *TF:* 800-521-4483 ■ *Web:* www.lopa.org	Metairie	LA	70002	800-521-4483	
Mid-America Transplant Services (MTS) 1110 Highlands Plz Dr E Ste 100 *TF:* 888-376-4854 ■ *Web:* www.midamericatransplant.org	Saint Louis	MO	63110	314-735-8200	
Musculoskeletal Transplant Foundation 125 May St Ste 300 *TF:* 800-946-9008 ■ *Web:* www.mtf.org	Edison	NJ	08837	732-661-0202	661-2298
Nevada Donor Network Inc 2061 E Sahara Ave *TF:* 855-683-6667 ■ *Web:* www.nvdonor.org	Las Vegas	NV	89104	702-796-9600	796-4225
New England Organ Bank 60 First Ave *TF:* 800-446-6362 ■ *Web:* www.neob.org	Waltham	MA	02451	617-244-8000	
New York Cryo 900 Northern Blvd Ste 230 *TF:* 877-769-2796 ■ *Web:* www.newyorkcryo.com	Great Neck	NY	11021	516-487-2700	487-2007
OneLegacy Transplant Donor Network 221 S Figueroa St Ste 500 *TF:* 800-786-4077 ■ *Web:* www.onelegacy.org	Los Angeles	CA	90012	213-229-5600	229-5601
Regional Tissue Bank QEII Health Sciences Centre 5788 University Ave Rm 431 MacKenzie Bldg *TF:* 800-314-6515 ■ *Web:* www.cdha.nshealth.ca/regional-tissue-bank	Halifax	NS	B3H1V7	902-473-4171	473-2170
Rocky Mountain Tissue Bank 2993 S Peoria St Ste 390 *TF:* 800-424-5169 ■ *Web:* www.rmtb.org	Aurora	CO	80014	303-337-3330	337-9383
ScienceCare Inc 21410 N 19th Ave Ste 126 *TF:* 800-417-3747 ■ *Web:* www.sciencecare.com	Phoenix	AZ	85027	602-331-3641	331-4344
Sierra Donor Services 1760 Creekside Oak Dr Ste 220 *TF:* 877-401-2546 ■ *Web:* sierradonor.org	Sacramento	CA	95833	916-567-1600	
South Texas Blood & Tissue Ctr 6211 IH-10 W *TF:* 800-292-5534 ■ *Web:* southtexasblood.org	San Antonio	TX	78201	210-731-5555	731-5501
Southeast Tissue Alliance (SETA) 6241 NW 23rd St Ste 400 *TF:* 866-432-1164 ■ *Web:* www.donorcare.org	Gainesville	FL	32653	352-248-2114	
Tennessee/DCI Donor Services 1600 Hayes St *Web:* www.donatelifetn.org	Nashville	TN	37203	615-234-5251	
Wright Medical Technology Inc 5677 Airline Rd **Fax:* Cust Svc ■ *TF:* 800-238-7188 ■ *Web:* www.wmt.com	Arlington	TN	38002	901-867-9971	867-9534*

546 PACKAGE DELIVERY SERVICES

	City	State	ZIP	Phone	Fax
Air T Inc 3524 Airport Rd *NASDAQ: AIRT* ■ *Web:* www.airt.net/mac	Maiden	NC	28650	828-464-8741	465-5281
AirNet Systems Inc 7250 Star Check Dr *Web:* www.airnet.com	Columbus	OH	43217	614-409-4900	
Careful Courier Service Inc 2444 Old Middlefield Way *Web:* www.carefulcourier.com	Mountain View	CA	94043	650-903-9393	
Columbia Fruit Packers Inc 2575 Euclid Ave PO Box 920 *Web:* www.columbiafruit.com	Wenatchee	WA	98801	509-662-7153	662-0933
Crosscountry Courier Inc PO Box 4030 *TF:* 800-521-0287 ■ *Web:* www.crosscountrycourier.com	Bismarck	ND	58502	701-222-8498	223-5963
CS Logistics Inc 11001 W Mitchell St *Web:* cslog.com	Milwaukee	WI	53214	414-774-6322	
DHL Global Mail 2700 S Commerce Pkwy Ste 400 *TF:* 800-805-9306	Weston	FL	33331	954-903-6300	
Dynamex Inc 5429 LBJ Fwy Ste 1000 *TF Cust Svc:* 888-478-1660 ■ *Web:* www.dynamex.com	Dallas	TX	75240	214-560-9000	560-9349
Federal Express Europe Inc 3610 Hacks Cross Rd *TF:* 800-463-3339 ■ *Web:* www.fedex.com	Memphis	TN	38125	901-369-3600	
FedEx Custom Critical Inc 1475 Boettler Rd *TF Cust Svc:* 800-463-3339 ■ *Web:* www.customcritical.fedex.com	Uniontown	OH	44685	234-310-4090	
Financial Courier Service Inc 6099 Mt Moriah Ext Ste 13	Memphis	TN	38115	901-761-4555	366-6165
Hot Shot Delivery Inc 747 N Shepherd Dr Ste 100 PO Box 701189 *TF:* 866-261-3184 ■ *Web:* www.hotshot-delivery.com	Houston	TX	77007	713-869-5525	862-6354
Howard Ternes Packaging Co 12285 Dixie *Web:* www.ternespackaging.com	Redford	MI	48239	313-531-5867	531-5868
Mass Bay Commuter Railroad Co 89 S St	Boston	MA	02111	617-222-8001	
National Delivery Systems Inc 8700 Robert Fulton Dr *Web:* www.national-delivery.com	Columbia	MD	21046	410-312-4770	
Network Global Logistics (NGL) 320 Interlocken Pkwy Ste 100 *TF:* 866-938-1870 ■ *Web:* www.nglog.com	Broomfield	CO	80021	866-938-1870	
Newgistics Inc 2700 Via Fortuna Ste 300 *Web:* newgistics.com	Austin	TX	78746	512-225-6000	225-6001
One Source Industries LLC 185 Technology Dr *TF:* 800-899-4990 ■ *Web:* www.osicreative.com	Irvine	CA	92618	800-899-4990	
Priority Express Courier 5 Chelsea Pkwy *TF:* 800-526-4646 ■ *Web:* www.priorityexpress.com	Boothwyn	PA	19061	610-364-3300	364-3310
Purolator Inc 5995 Avebury Rd *TF:* 888-744-7123 ■ *Web:* www.purolator.com	Mississauga	ON	L5R3T8	905-712-8101	
Titan Trucks 306 Austin St *Web:* www.titanco.com	Levelland	TX	79336	806-894-4852	
TNT USA Inc 68 S Service Rd *Web:* tnt.com	Melville	NY	11747	631-712-6700	
Tricor America Inc 717 Airport Blvd *Web:* www.tricor.com	South San Francisco	CA	94080	650-877-3650	583-3197
Tyburn Railroad LLC 505 S Broad St *Web:* www.tyburnrr.com	Kennett Square	PA	19348	610-925-0131	
Unishippers Assn Inc 746 E Winchester Ste 200 **Fax Area Code:* 801 ■ *TF:* 800-999-8721 ■ *Web:* www.unishippers.com	Salt Lake City	UT	84107	800-999-8721	487-7468*
United Parcel Service Inc (UPS) 55 Glenlake Pkwy NE *NYSE: UPS* ■ *TF Cust Svc:* 800-742-5877 ■ *Web:* www.ups.com	Atlanta	GA	30328	404-828-6000	828-6440
United Shipping Solutions 6985 Union Pk Ctr Ste 565 *Web:* www.usshipit.com	Midvale	UT	84047	801-352-0012	352-0339
Universal Travel 1425C SE 17th St **Fax Area Code:* 561	Ft. Lauderdale	FL	33316	954-525-5000	367-6124*
Washington Express Service LLC 12240 Indian Creek Ct Ste 100 *TF:* 800-939-5463 ■ *Web:* www.washingtonexpress.net	Beltsville	MD	20705	301-210-0899	419-7075
World Courier Inc 1313 Fourth Ave **Fax:* Cust Svc ■ *TF:* 800-221-6600 ■ *Web:* www.worldcourier.com	New Hyde Park	NY	11040	516-354-2600	354-2637*
Worldwide Express 2602 McKinney Ave Ste 400 *TF:* 800-758-7447 ■ *Web:* www.wwex.com	Dallas	TX	75204	214-720-2400	720-2446
WPX Delivery Solutions 3320 W Valley Hwy N Ste 111 *TF:* 800-562-1091 ■ *Web:* www.wpx.com	Auburn	WA	98001	253-876-2760	876-2799
Yamato Transport USA Inc 80 Seaview Dr *Web:* www.yamatoamerica.com	Secaucus	NJ	07094	201-583-9706	583-9703

547 PACKAGING MACHINERY & EQUIPMENT

	City	State	ZIP	Phone	Fax
A-B-C Packaging Machine Corp 811 Live Oak St *TF:* 800-237-5975 ■ *Web:* www.abcpackaging.com	Tarpon Springs	FL	34689	727-937-5144	938-1239
Accuplace 1800 Nw 69th Ave Ste 102 *Web:* www.accuplace.com	Plantation	FL	33313	954-791-1500	
Acraloc Corp 113 Flint Rd *Web:* www.acraloc.com	Oak Ridge	TN	37830	865-483-1368	483-3500
ALine Systems Corp 13844 Struikman Rd *Web:* www.alinesys.com	Cerritos	CA	90703	562-229-9727	
AMS Filling Systems 2500 Chestnut Tree Rd *TF:* 800-647-5390 ■ *Web:* www.amsfilling.com	Honey Brook	PA	19344	610-942-4200	
ARPAC Group 9511 W River St *TF:* 800-496-7210 ■ *Web:* www.arpac.com	Schiller Park	IL	60176	847-678-9034	671-7006
Automated Packaging Systems Inc 10175 Phillip Pkwy *TF Sales:* 800-527-0733 ■ *Web:* www.autobag.com	Streetsboro	OH	44241	330-528-2000	342-2400
B & H Manufacturing Co 3461 Roeding Rd *TF:* 888-643-0444 ■ *Web:* www.bhlabeling.com	Ceres	CA	95307	209-556-6160	537-6854
Barry-Wehmiller Cos Inc 8020 Forsyth Blvd **Fax:* Sales ■ *TF:* 800-862-8020 ■ *Web:* www.barrywehmiller.com	Saint Louis	MO	63105	314-862-8000	862-2744*
Barry-Wehmiller Cos Inc Accraply Div 3580 Holly Ln N *TF:* 800-328-3997 ■ *Web:* www.accraply.com	Plymouth	MN	55447	763-557-1313	519-9656
Belco Packaging Systems Inc 910 S Mountain Ave *TF:* 800-833-1833 ■ *Web:* www.belcopackaging.com	Monrovia	CA	91016	626-357-9566	359-3440
Bell-Mark Corp 331 Changebridge Rd *Web:* www.bell-mark.com	Pine Brook	NJ	07058	973-882-0202	808-4616
Brenton LLC 4750 County Rd 13 NE *TF:* 800-535-2730 ■ *Web:* www.brentonengineering.com	Alexandria	MN	56308	320-852-7705	852-7621
Butler Automatic Inc 41 Leona Dr *Web:* www.butlerautomatic.com	Middleboro	MA	02346	508-923-0544	923-0886
Campbell Wrapper Corp 1415 Fortune Ave **Fax:* Sales ■ *TF:* 800-727-4210 ■ *Web:* www.campbellwrapper.com	De Pere	WI	54115	920-983-7100	983-7300*
Corrugated Gear & Services Inc 100 Anderson Rd *Web:* www.corrugatedgear.com	Alpharetta	GA	30004	770-475-8929	442-3371
Data Technology Inc 14225 Dayton Cir Ste 4 *TF General:* 888-334-9300 ■ *Web:* drtinc.com	Omaha	NE	68137	402-891-0711	
Delkor Systems Inc 8700 Rendova St NE *TF:* 800-328-5558 ■ *Web:* www.delkorsystems.com	Circle Pines	MN	55014	763-783-0855	783-0875
Dynaric Inc 5740 Bayside Rd *TF:* 800-526-0827 ■ *Web:* www.dynaric.com	Virginia Beach	VA	23455	800-526-0827	
E-pak Machinery Inc 1535 S State Rd 39 *TF:* 800-328-0466 ■ *Web:* www.epakmachinery.com	La Porte	IN	46350	219-393-5541	324-2884
EDL Packaging Systems 1260 Parkview Rd *Web:* www.edlpackaging.com	Green Bay	WI	54304	920-336-7744	
Elliott Mfg Company Inc 2664 Cherry Ave PO Box 11277 *Web:* www.elliott-mfg.com	Fresno	CA	93772	559-233-6235	233-6235
Elmar Worldwide Inc 200 Gould Ave PO Box 245 *Web:* www.elmarworldwide.com	Depew	NY	14043	716-681-5650	681-5650
Exact Packaging Inc 1145 E Wellspring Rd *Web:* www.epilabelers.com	New Freedom	PA	17349	717-235-8345	
Fischbein Co 151 Walker Rd *Web:* www.fischbein.com	Statesville	NC	28625	704-871-1159	872-3303

Phone Fax

Flexicon Corp 2400 Emrick Blvd . . . Bethlehem PA 18020 610-814-2400 814-0600
TF: 888-353-9426 ■ *Web:* www.flexicon.com

Fowler Products Co
150 Collins Industrial Blvd . . . Athens GA 30601 706-549-3300 548-1278
Web: www.fowlerproducts.com

Fox IV Technologies 6011 Enterprise Dr . . . Export PA 15632 724-387-3500
Web: www.foxiv.com

Gottscho Printing Systems Inc
740 Veterans Cir . . . Warminster PA 18974 267-387-3005 387-3015
Web: www.gottscho.com

Hartness International Inc
1200 Garlington Rd PO Box 26509 . . . Greenville SC 29616 864-297-1200 288-5390
TF: 800-845-8791 ■ *Web:* www.hartness.com

Heat Seal LLC 4580 E 71st St . . . Cleveland OH 44125 216-341-2022 341-2163
TF: 800-342-6329 ■ *Web:* www.heatsealco.com

Heisler Industries Inc 224 Passaic Ave . . . Fairfield NJ 07004 973-227-6300 227-7627
Web: www.heislerind.com

Hibar Systems Ltd 35 Pollard St . . . Richmond Hill ON L4B1A8 905-731-2400 731-6035
Web: www.hibar.com

John R Nalbach Engineering Co
621 E Plainfield Rd . . . Countryside IL 60525 708-579-9100 579-0122
Web: www.nalbach.com

Kirk Rudy Inc 125 Lorraine Pkwy . . . Woodstock GA 30188 770-427-4203 427-4036
TF: 800-897-1910 ■ *Web:* www.kirkrudy.com

Kliklok-Woodman USA 5224 Snapfinger Woods Dr . . . Decatur GA 30035 770-981-5200 987-7160
Web: www.kliklokwoodman.com

Klikwood Corp 5224 Snapfinger Woods Dr . . . Decatur GA 30035 770-981-5200
Web: www.kliklokwoodman.com

Krones Inc 9600 S 58th St PO Box 321801 . . . Franklin WI 53132 414-409-4000 409-4100*
**Fax:* Cust Svc ■ *TF:* 800-752-3787 ■ *Web:* www.krones.com

Label-Aire Inc 550 Burning Tree Rd . . . Fullerton CA 92833 714-449-5155 526-0300
Web: www.label-aire.com

Lantech Inc 11000 Bluegrass Pkwy . . . Louisville KY 40299 502-815-9109 266-5031
TF: 800-866-0322 ■ *Web:* www.lantech.com

Liquid Packaging Solutions
3999 E Hupp Rd Bldg R43 . . . La Porte IN 46350 219-393-3600
Web: www.liquidpackagingsolution.com

Loveshaw Corp 2206 Easton Tpke . . . South Canaan PA 18459 570-937-4921
TF Cust Svc: 800-747-1586 ■ *Web:* www.loveshaw.com

Metro Machine & Engineering Corp
8001 Wallace Rd . . . Eden Prairie MN 55344 952-937-2800 937-2374
Web: www.metromachine.com

Mid-States Packaging Inc
12163 State Rte 274 . . . Lewistown OH 43333 937-843-3243 843-4378
Web: www.midstatespackaging.com

Mooney General Paper Co
1451 Chestnut Ave PO Box 3800 . . . Hillside NJ 07205 973-926-3800 926-0425
TF: 800-882-8846 ■ *Web:* www.mooneygeneral.com

MTS Medication Technologies Inc
2003 Gandy Blvd N Ste 800 . . . Saint Petersburg FL 33702 800-845-0053
TF General: 800-845-0053 ■ *Web:* www.mts-mt.com

Muller Martini Mailroom Systems Inc
40 Rabro Dr . . . Hauppauge NY 11788 631-582-4343 348-1961
Web: www.mullermartini.com/ms

National Instrument LLC 4119 Fordleigh Rd . . . Baltimore MD 21215 410-764-0900 764-7719
TF: 866-258-1914 ■ *Web:* www.filamatic.com

New England Machinery Inc 2820 62nd Ave E . . . Bradenton FL 34203 941-755-5550 751-6281
Web: www.neminc.com

New Jersey Machine Inc 56 Etna Rd . . . Lebanon NH 03766 603-448-0300 448-4810
TF Sales: 800-432-2990 ■ *Web:* www.njmpackaging.com

New Way Packaging Machinery Inc
210 Blettner Ave . . . Hanover PA 17331 717-637-2133
TF: 844-801-3711

Omega Design Corp 211 Philips Rd . . . Exton PA 19341 610-363-6555
Web: www.omegadesign.com

Ossid Corp 4000 College Rd . . . Battleboro NC 27809 252-446-6177 442-7694
TF: 800-334-8369 ■ *Web:* www.ossid.com

Package Machinery Co
380 Union St Ste 58 . . . West Springfield MA 01089 413-732-4000 732-1163
Web: www.packagemachinery.com

Packaging Systems International Inc
4990 Acoma St . . . Denver CO 80216 303-296-4445 298-1016
TF: 800-525-6110 ■ *Web:* www.pkgsys.com

Pearson Packaging Systems 8120 W Sunset Hwy . . . Spokane WA 99224 509-838-6226 747-8532
TF: 800-732-7766 ■ *Web:* www.pearsonpkg.com

PMC Industries 275 Hudson St . . . Hackensack NJ 07601 201-342-3684 342-3568
Web: www.pmc-industries.com

PMI Cartoning Inc 850 Pratt Blvd . . . Elk Grove Village IL 60007 847-437-1427
Web: www.pmicartoning.com

Pneumatic Scale Angelus 4485 Allen Rd . . . Stow OH 44224 330-247-1800 928-7077
Web: www.psangelus.com

Prodo-Pak Corp 77 Commerce St . . . Garfield NJ 07026 973-777-7770 772-0471
Web: www.prodo-pak.com

Qed Systems Inc 4646 N Witchduck Rd . . . Virginia Beach VA 23455 757-490-5000 490-5027
Web: www.qedsysinc.com

Quadrel Labeling Systems 7670 Jenther Dr . . . Mentor OH 44060 440-602-4700
TF: 800-321-8509 ■ *Web:* www.quadrel.com

Raque Food Systems LLC PO Box 99594 . . . Louisville KY 40269 502-267-9641 267-2352
Web: www.raque.com

Robert Bosch Corp Packaging Technology Div
2440 Summer Blvd . . . Raleigh NC 27616 919-877-0886 877-0976
Web: www.boschpackaging.com

Rollstock Inc 5720 Brighton Ave . . . Kansas City MO 64130 616-570-0430 455-8469*
**Fax Area Code:* 816 ■ *TF:* 800-295-2949 ■ *Web:* www.rollstock.com

Satake USA Inc 10905 Cash Rd . . . Stafford TX 77477 281-276-3600 494-1427
Web: www.satake-usa.com

Scandia Packaging Machinery Co
15 Industrial Rd . . . Fairfield NJ 07004 973-473-6100 473-7226
Web: www.scandiapack.com

Schneider Packaging Equipment Company Inc
5370 Guy Young Rd . . . Brewerton NY 13029 315-676-3035 676-2875
Web: www.schneiderpackaging.com

Phone Fax

Shibuya Hoppmann Corp
13129 Airpark Dr Ste 120 . . . Elkwood VA 22718 540-829-2564 829-1726
TF Cust Svc: 800-368-3582 ■ *Web:* www.shibuyahoppmann.com

Sidel Inc 5600 Sun Ct . . . Norcross GA 30092 770-449-8058 447-0084
Web: www.sidel.com

Speedline Technologies 16 Forge Pk . . . Franklin MA 02038 508-520-0083 520-2288
Web: www.speedlinetech.com

Standard Knapp Inc 63 Pickering St . . . Portland CT 06480 860-342-1100 342-0782
TF Cust Svc: 800-628-9565 ■ *Web:* www.standard-knapp.com

Stock America Inc 900 Cheyenne Ave Ste 700 . . . Grafton WI 53024 262-375-4100
Web: www.stockamerica.com

Stolle Machinery Co LLC 6949 S Potomac St . . . Centennial CO 80112 303-708-9044 708-9045
Web: www.stollemachinery.com

Summit Packaging Systems Inc 400 Gay St . . . Manchester NH 03103 603-669-5410 644-2594
Web: summitpackagingsystems.com

SWF Cos 1949 E Manning Ave . . . Reedley CA 93654 559-638-8484 638-7478
TF: 800-344-8951 ■ *Web:* www.swfcompanies.com

Taylor Products Company Inc 2205 Jothi Ave . . . Parsons KS 67357 620-421-5550
Web: www.taylorproducts.com

Thiele Technologies 315 27th Ave NE . . . Minneapolis MN 55418 612-782-1200 782-1203
TF: 800-932-3647 ■ *Web:* www.thieletech.com

Tri-Pak Machinery Inc 1102 N Commerce St . . . Harlingen TX 78550 956-423-5140 423-9362
Web: www.tri-pakmachinery.com

Triangle Package Machinery Co
6655 W Diversey Ave . . . Chicago IL 60707 773-889-0200 889-4221
TF: 800-621-4170 ■ *Web:* www.trianglepackage.com

U S Bottlers Machinery Co
11911 Steele Creek Rd . . . Charlotte NC 28273 704-588-4750 588-3808
Web: www.usbottlers.com

Universal Labeling Systems Inc
3501 Eigth Ave S . . . Saint Petersburg FL 33711 727-327-2123
TF: 877-236-0266 ■ *Web:* www.universal1.com

US Digital Media Inc 1929 W Lone Cactus Dr . . . Phoenix AZ 85027 623-587-4900 587-4920
TF: 877-992-3766 ■ *Web:* www.usdigitalmedia.com

Weiler Engineering Inc 1395 Gateway Dr . . . Elgin IL 60123 847-697-4900 697-4915
Web: www.weilerengineering.com

Wulftec International Inc
209 Wulftec St . . . Ayer's Cliff QC J0B1C0 819-838-4232 838-5539
TF: 877-985-3832 ■ *Web:* www.wulftec.com

548 PACKAGING MATERIALS & PRODUCTS - PAPER OR PLASTICS

See Also Bags - Paper p. 1837; Bags - Plastics p. 1837; Blister Packaging p. 1862; Coated & Laminated Paper p. 2866; Paper Converters p. 2867; Plastics Foam Products p. 2945

Phone Fax

Acme Paper & Supply Company Inc
8229 Sandy Ct PO Box 422 . . . Savage MD 20763 410-792-2333 792-2137
TF: 800-462-5812 ■ *Web:* www.acmepaper.com

Adhesive Packaging Specialties Inc PO Box 31 . . . Peabody MA 01960 978-531-3300 532-8901
TF: 800-222-1117 ■ *Web:* www.adhesivepackaging.com

Admiral Packaging Inc 10 Admiral St . . . Providence RI 02908 401-274-7000 331-1910
TF: 800-556-6454 ■ *Web:* www.admiralpkg.com

Advance Bag & Packaging Technologies
5720 Williams Lk Rd . . . Waterford MI 48329 248-674-3126 674-2630
TF: 800-475-2247 ■ *Web:* www.advancepac.com

Advanced Paper Forming 541 W Rincon St . . . Corona CA 92878 951-738-1800
Web: www.advancedpaper.com

Alliance Rubber Co 210 Carpenter Dam Rd . . . Hot Springs AR 71901 800-626-5940 262-3948*
**Fax Area Code:* 501 ■ *TF:* 800-626-5940 ■ *Web:* www.rubberband.com

American Packaging Corp 777 Driving Pk Ave . . . Rochester NY 14613 585-254-9500 254-5801
TF: 800-551-8801 ■ *Web:* www.ampkcorp.com

American Packaging Corp Extrusion Div
777 Driving Pk Ave . . . Rochester NY 14613 585-254-9500 254-5801
TF: 800-551-8801 ■ *Web:* www.ampkcorp.com

Apco Extruders Inc 180 National Rd . . . Edison NJ 08817 732-287-3000 287-1421
TF Orders: 800-942-8725

Automated Packaging Systems Inc
10175 Phillip Pkwy . . . Streetsboro OH 44241 330-528-2000 342-2400
TF Sales: 800-527-0733 ■ *Web:* www.autobag.com

BagcraftPapercon 3900 W 43rd St . . . Chicago IL 60632 773-254-8000 254-8204
TF: 800-621-8468 ■ *Web:* www.bagcraft.com

Beaver Mfg Company Inc 12 Ed Needham Dr . . . Mansfield GA 30055 770-786-1622
Web: www.beaverloc.com

Bedford Industries Inc 1659 Rowe Ave . . . Worthington MN 56187 507-376-4136 376-6742
TF Cust Svc: 877-233-3673 ■ *Web:* bedford.com

Bemis Co Inc Bemis Clysar Div
2451 Badger Ave . . . Oshkosh WI 54903 920-303-7800 303-7820
TF: 888-425-9727 ■ *Web:* www.clysar.com

Bemis Company Inc
1 Neenah Ctr Fourth Fl PO Box 669 . . . Neenah WI 54957 920-727-4100
NYSE: BMS ■ *Web:* www.bemis.com

Bemis Company Inc Paper Packaging Div
2445 Deer Pk Blvd . . . Omaha NE 68105 800-541-4303
TF: 800-541-4303 ■ *Web:* www.bemispaper.com

Bomarko Inc 1955 N Oak Rd . . . Plymouth IN 46563 574-936-9901 936-5314
Web: www.bomarko.com

BPM Inc 200 W Front St . . . Peshtigo WI 54157 715-582-4551 582-4853
TF: 800-826-0494 ■ *Web:* www.bpmpaper.com

Bryce Corp 4505 Old Lamar Ave . . . Memphis TN 38118 901-369-4400 369-4419*
**Fax:* Sales ■ *TF:* 800-238-7277 ■ *Web:* www.brycecorp.com

Burrows Paper Corp Packaging Group
2000 Commerce Ctr Dr . . . Franklin OH 45005 937-746-1933 746-0344
TF: 800-732-1933 ■ *Web:* www.burrowspaper.com

Carton Service Inc First Quality Dr PO Box 702 . . . Shelby OH 44875 419-342-5010 342-4804
TF General: 800-533-7744 ■ *Web:* www.cartonservice.com

Catty Corp 6111 White Oaks Rd . . . Harvard IL 60033 815-943-2288 943-4473
Web: www.cattycorp.com

CCL Industries Inc
105 Gordon Baker Rd Ste 500 . . . Toronto ON M2H3P8 416-756-8500 756-8555
TSE: CCL/B ■ *Web:* www.cclind.com

Phone / Fax

Charter Films Inc 1901 Winter St PO Box 277 .... Superior WI 54880 715-395-8258 395-8259
TF: 877-411-3456 ■ *Web:* www.charternex.com

Clear Lam Packaging Inc
1950 Pratt Blvd............................Elk Grove Village IL 60007 847-439-8570 439-8589
Web: www.clearlam.com

Command Plastic Corp 124 W Ave .... Tallmadge OH 44278 330-434-3497 434-8316
TF: 800-321-8001 ■ *Web:* www.commandplastic.com

Consolidated Container Co (CCC)
3101 Towercreek Pkwy Ste 300.....................Atlanta GA 30339 678-742-4600 742-4750
TF Sales: 888-831-2184 ■ *Web:* www.ccclic.com

Crawford Industries LLC
1414 Crawford Dr..........................Crawfordsville IN 47933 800-428-0840 962-3343
TF: 800-428-0840 ■ *Web:* www.crawford-industries.com

Crown Packaging Corp
17854 Chesterfld Airport Rd...................Chesterfield MO 63005 636-681-8000 681-9600
TF: 800-883-9400 ■ *Web:* www.crownpack.com

Cryovac Food Packaging & Food Solutions
100 Rogers Bridge Rd................................Duncan SC 29334 800-391-5645
TF: 800-391-5645 ■ *Web:* www.cryovac.com/en/default.aspx

Dade Paper & Bag Co 9601 NW 112th Ave .... Miami FL 33178 305-805-2600 883-9363
Web: www.dadepaper.com

DuPont Packaging & Industrial Polymers
Barley Mill Plaza 26-2122 PO Box 80026............ Wilmington DE 19880 703-305-7666 892-7390*
**Fax Area Code:* 302 ■ *TF:* 800-438-7225 ■ *Web:* www.dupont.com

Exopack LLC 23810 China Lake Ct PO Box 5687 .... Katy TX 77494 864-596-7140 596-7150
TF: 877-447-3539

Fibercel Packaging LLC
46 Brooklyn St PO Box 610 ....Portville NY 14770 716-933-8703
Web: www.fibercel.com

Fibre Converters Inc PO Box 130 ....Constantine MI 49042 269-279-1700
Web: www.fibreconverters.com

Fisher Container Corp 1111 Busch Pkwy ....Buffalo Grove IL 60089 847-541-0000 541-0075
TF: 800-837-2247 ■ *Web:* www.fishercontainer.com

Flextron Industries Inc 720 Mt Rd ....Aston PA 19014 610-459-4600 459-5379
TF: 800-633-2181 ■ *Web:* www.flextronindustries.com

Flower City Tissue Mills Inc
700 Driving Pk Ave............................. Rochester NY 14613 585-458-9200
TF: 800-595-2030 ■ *Web:* www.flowercitytissue.com

FPC Flexible Packaging Corp
1891 Eglinton Ave E ....Toronto ON M1L2L7 416-288-3060 288-0808
TF: 888-288-7386 ■ *Web:* www.fpcflexible.com

Gateway Packaging Co 100 S Fourth St Ste 600 ....St Louis MO 63102 618-451-0010
Web: www.gatewaypackaging.com

General Plastic Extrusions Inc
1238 Kasson Dr ....Prescott WI 54021 715-262-3806 262-3836
TF: 800-532-3888 ■ *Web:* www.generalplastic.com

Genpak Corp 68 Warren St.......................... Glens Falls NY 12801 518-798-9511
TF: 800-626-6695 ■ *Web:* www.genpak.com

Gift Wrap Co 338 Industrial Blvd............................ Midway GA 31320 800-443-4429
TF General: 800-443-4429 ■ *Web:* www.giftwrapcompany.com

Grayling Industries 1008 Branch Dr................. Alpharetta GA 30004 770-751-9095 751-3710
TF: 800-635-1551 ■ *Web:* www.graylingindustries.com

Green Bay Packaging Inc 1700 Webster Ct .... Green Bay WI 54302 920-433-5111
TF: 800-236-8400 ■ *Web:* www.gbp.com

HCP Packaging USA Inc 370 Monument Rd .... Hinsdale NH 03451 603-256-3141 256-6979
Web: www.hcpackaging.com

Huhtamaki Inc North America 9201 Packaging Dr ...... DeSoto KS 66018 913-583-3025 583-8756*
**Fax:* Hum Res ■ *TF:* 800-255-4243 ■ *Web:* www2.huhtamaki.com

Indiana Ribbon Inc 106 N Second St.................. Wolcott IN 47995 219-279-2112
TF: 800-531-3100 ■ *Web:* www.giftwrapgifts.com

Innovative Enterprises Inc
25 Town & Country Dr.........................Washington MO 63090 636-390-0300 390-4004
TF: 800-280-0300 ■ *Web:* www.innovative-1.com

International Paper Co 6400 Poplar Ave.............Memphis TN 38197 901-419-9000
NYSE: IP ■ *TF Prod Info:* 800-223-1268 ■ *Web:* www.internationalpaper.com

ITW Hi-Cone 1140 W Bryn Mawr Ave.....................Itasca IL 60143 630-438-5300 438-5315
Web: www.itwhicone.com

Joshen Paper & Packaging Company Inc
5808 Grant Ave................................ Cleveland OH 44105 216-441-5600 441-7647
Web: www.joshen.com

LallyPak Inc 1209 Central Ave.......................... Hillside NJ 07205 908-351-4141 351-4411
TF: 800-523-8484 ■ *Web:* www.lallypak.com

Laminations 3010 E Venture Dr....................... Appleton WI 54911 920-831-0596
TF: 800-925-2626 ■ *Web:* www.laminationsonline.com

Letica Corp 52585 Dequindre Rd.................... Rochester MI 48307 248-652-0557 608-2153
Web: www.letica.com

LPS Industries Inc 10 Caesar Pl................... Moonachie NJ 07074 201-438-3515 643-0180*
**Fax Area Code:* 732 ■ *TF Sales:* 800-275-6577 ■ *Web:* www.lpsind.com

Multifilm Packaging Corp 1040 N McLean Blvd .... Elgin IL 60123 847-695-7600 695-7645
Web: www.multifilm.com

Novacel 21 Third St ....Palmer MA 01069 413-283-3468 283-3964
TF: 877-668-2235 ■ *Web:* www.novacelinc.com

Oracle Packaging 220 E Polo Rd................Winston-Salem NC 27105 336-777-5000 777-5440
Web: www.oraclepackaging.com

Overwraps Packaging LP 3950 La Reunion Pkwy......... Dallas TX 75212 214-634-0427
Web: www.overwraps.com

Packaging Concepts Inc
9832 Evergreen Indus Dr .... Saint Louis MO 63123 314-329-9700 487-2666
Web: www.packagingconceptsinc.com

Pactiv Corp 1900 W Field Ct........................ Lake Forest IL 60045 847-482-2000 482-4738
TF: 888-828-2850 ■ *Web:* www.pactiv.com

Pak West Paper & Packaging
4042 W Garry Ave.............................. Santa Ana CA 92704 714-557-7420
TF: 800-927-7299 ■ *Web:* www.pakwest.com

Pratt Industries USA 1800C Sarasota Pkwy.............Conyers GA 30013 770-918-5678 918-5679
TF: 800-835-2088 ■ *Web:* www.prattindustries.com

Printpack Inc 2800 Overlook PkwyNE....................Atlanta GA 30339 404-460-7000 460-7165
TF: 800-669-6820 ■ *Web:* www.printpack.com

Robert Family Holdings Inc (RFH)
12430 Tesson Ferry Rd Ste 313................... Saint Louis MO 63128 636-305-2830 965-0309*
**Fax Area Code:* 314 ■ *Web:* www.rf-holdings.com

Robinson Industries Inc 3051 W Curtis Rd............. Coleman MI 48618 989-465-6111 465-1217
TF: 877-465-4055 ■ *Web:* www.robinsonind.com

Phone / Fax

Rollprint Packaging Products Inc
320 S Stewart Ave.................................Addison IL 60101 630-628-1700 628-8510
TF: 800-276-7629 ■ *Web:* www.rollprint.com

Sabert Corp 2288 Main St Ext ....Sayreville NJ 08872 800-722-3781 721-0622*
**Fax Area Code:* 732 ■ *TF:* 800-722-3781 ■ *Web:* www.sabert.com

Scholle Packaging Corporation 200 W N Ave.........Northlake IL 60164 708-562-7290 723-6014*
**Fax Area Code:* 231 ■ *Web:* www.scholleipn.com

Sealed Air Corp Packaging Products Div
301 Mayhill St ....Saddle Brook NJ 07663 201-712-7000 712-7070
TF: 800-648-9093 ■ *Web:* sealedair.com

SI Jacobson Mfg Co 1414 Jacobson Dr.............. Waukegan IL 60085 847-623-1414 623-2556
Web: www.sij.com

Silgan Holdings Inc 4 Landmark Sq Ste 400 .... Stamford CT 06901 203-975-7110 975-7902
NASDAQ: SLGN ■ *Web:* www.silganholdings.com

Southern Container Ltd
10410 Papalote St Ste 130.........................Houston TX 77041 713-466-5661 466-4223
Web: www.southerncontainer.com

Technimark Inc 180 Commerce Pl...................Asheboro NC 27203 336-498-4171 498-5042
Web: www.technimark.com

Technipaq Inc 975 Lutter Dr ....Crystal Lake IL 60014 815-477-1800 477-0777
Web: www.technipaq.com

Trinity Packaging Corp 84 Business Pk Dr............ Armonk NY 10504 914-273-4111 273-4715
Web: www.trinitypackaging.com

UFP Technologies Inc 172 E Main St ....Georgetown MA 01833 978-352-2200
NASDAQ: UFPT ■ *TF:* 800-372-3172 ■ *Web:* www.ufpt.com

Unger Co 12401 Berea Rd.......................... Cleveland OH 44111 216-252-1400 252-1427
TF: 800-321-1418 ■ *Web:* www.ungerco.com

Unicorr 455 Sackett Pt Rd...................... North Haven CT 06473 203-248-2161 248-0241
Web: www.unicorr.com

Vision Plastics Inc 26000 SW Pkwy Ctr Dr.......... Wilsonville OR 97070 503-685-9000 685-9254
Web: www.visionplastics.com

Viskase Cos Inc 8205 S Cass Ste 115 .... Darien IL 60561 630-874-0700 874-0176
TF: 800-323-8562 ■ *Web:* www.viskase.com

Walter G. Anderson Inc 4535 Willow Dr................ Hamel MN 55340 763-478-2133 478-6572
Web: www.wgacarton.com

Warp Bros Flex-O-Glass Inc
4647 W Augusta Blvd................................Chicago IL 60651 773-261-5200 261-5204
TF: 800-621-3345 ■ *Web:* www.warpbros.com

Wausau Paper Corp 100 Paper Pl .... Mosinee WI 54455 715-693-4470 692-2082
NYSE: WPP ■ *TF:* 800-723-0008 ■ *Web:* www.wausaupaper.com

Weyerhaeuser Co 33663 Weyerhaeuser Way S ....Federal Way WA 98003 253-924-2345
NYSE: WY ■ *TF:* 800-525-5440 ■ *Web:* www.weyerhaeuser.com

Winpak Ltd 100 Saltеaux Crescent.....................Winnipeg MB R3J3T3 204-889-1015 888-7806
TSE: WPK ■ *TF:* 800-841-2600 ■ *Web:* www.winpak.com

WS Packaging Group Inc 2571 S. Hemlock Rd........ Green Bay WI 54229 800-818-5481 866-6485*
**Fax Area Code:* 920 ■ *TF:* 800-236-3424 ■ *Web:* www.wspackaging.com

Wynalda Packaging 8221 Graphic Dr NE...............Belmont MI 49306 616-866-1561 866-4316
Web: www.wynalda.com

549 PACKING & CRATING

Phone / Fax

Allied Container Systems Inc
201 N Civic Dr Ste 180........................Walnut Creek CA 94596 800-943-6510
TF: 800-943-6510 ■ *Web:* www.alliedcontainer.com

American Copak Corp 9175 Eton Ave .... Chatsworth CA 91311 818-576-1000 882-1637
Web: www.americancopak.com

Bentley World Packaging Ltd
4080 N Port Washington Rd.......................Milwaukee WI 53212 414-967-8000 967-8001
Web: www.bentleywp.com

Cooke's Crating Inc 3124 E 11th St...............Los Angeles CA 90023 323-268-5101 262-2001
Web: www.cookescrating.com

Craters & Freighters 331 Corporate Cir Ste J ....Golden CO 80401 800-736-3335 399-9964*
**Fax Area Code:* 303 ■ *TF:* 800-736-3335 ■ *Web:* www.cratersandfreighters.com

ECI Technology Inc 60 Gordon Dr......................Totowa NJ 07512 973-890-1114
Web: www.cvstechnology.com

Export Corp 6060 Whitmore Lk Rd................... Brighton MI 48116 810-227-6153
Web: www.exportcorporation.com

Fapco Inc 216 Post Rd........................... Buchanan MI 49107 269-695-6889 695-5145
TF: 800-782-0167 ■ *Web:* www.fapcoinc.com

GJ Nikolas & Company Inc
2800 Washington Blvd ....Bellwood IL 60104 708-544-0320
Web: www.finish1.com

Government Contracting Resources Inc
315 Page Rd # 7...................................Pinehurst NC 28374 910-215-1900
Web: www.gcrinc.net

Houston Crating Inc 18941 Aldine Westfield............Houston TX 77073 281-443-3222 443-3234
Web: www.houstoncrating.com

Icepak Inc 909 S E Everett Mall Way Ste B220 .... Everett WA 98208 425-293-0310
Web: www.goicepak.com

Independent Packing Services Inc
7600-32nd Ave N.................................Crystal MN 55427 763-425-7155
Web: www.ipsipack.com

Macmillan Piper Inc 1509 Taylor Way................. Tacoma WA 98421 253-627-3767
Web: www.macpiper.com

Navis Logistics Network
6551 S Revere Pkwy Ste 250 ....Centennial CO 80111 800-344-3528 741-6653*
**Fax Area Code:* 303 ■ *TF:* 800-344-3528 ■ *Web:* www.gonavis.com

Navis Pack & Ship Centers
6551 S Revere Pkwy Ste 250 ....Centennial CO 80111 800-344-3528 741-6653*
**Fax Area Code:* 303 ■ *TF:* 800-344-3528 ■ *Web:* www.gonavis.com

Packaging Services of Maryland Inc
16461 Elliott Pkwy .... Williamsport MD 21795 301-223-6200 223-8247
TF: 800-223-6255 ■ *Web:* www.psimd.com

Rollins Moving & Storage Inc
1900 E Leffel Ln ....Springfield OH 45505 937-325-2484
Web: www.rollins3pl.com

Southern States Packaging Co PO Box 650 ....Spartanburg SC 29304 800-621-2051 579-3932*
**Fax Area Code:* 864 ■ *TF:* 800-621-2051 ■ *Web:* www.sspc.biz

Suntreat Packing & Shipping Co
391 Oxford Ave.................................. Lindsay CA 93247 559-562-4991
Web: suntreat.com

Phone Fax

Tech Packaging Inc
13241 Bartram Pk Blvd Ste 601 .... Jacksonville FL 32258 904-288-6403
TF: 866-453-8324 ■ *Web:* www.techpackaging.net

Trans-Pak Inc 520 Marburg Way.................... San Jose CA 95133 408-254-0500 254-0551
Web: www.transpak.com

Trans.NET Inc 710 NW Juniper St Ste 100 .... Issaquah WA 98027 425-557-0558
Web: www.transnetinc.com

Transaction Packing Inc
2928 Greens Rd Ste 100............................ Houston TX 77032 281-443-0476
Web: www.transactionpacking.com

Trident Crating & Services Inc
14320 InterDr E .... Houston TX 77032 281-227-3999
Web: www.tridentcrating.com

Trisept Solutions 777 W Glencoe Pl.................. Milwaukee WI 53217 414-934-3900 934-3950
Web: www.triseptsolutions.com

Tucson Container Corp 6601 S Palo Verde............. Tucson AZ 85756 520-746-3171
Web: www.tucsoncontainer.com

Unicep Packaging Inc 1702 Industrial Dr............ Sandpoint ID 83864 208-265-9696 265-4726
TF: 800-354-9396 ■ *Web:* www.unicep.com

Venchurs Packaging 800 Liberty St.................... Adrian MI 49221 517-263-8937 265-7468
Web: www.venchurs.com

Walnut Industries Inc 1356 Adams Rd .... Bensalem PA 19020 215-638-7847
Web: www.ty-gard2000.com

Warren Industries Inc 3100 Mt Pleasant St............ Racine WI 53404 262-639-7800 639-0920
Web: www.wrnind.com

550 PAINTS, VARNISHES, RELATED PRODUCTS

Phone Fax

Accurate Dispersions Inc
192 W 155th St.............................. South Holland IL 60478 708-333-1337
Web: www.accurate-dispersions.com

Aervoe Industries Inc PO Box 485 .... Gardnerville NV 89410 775-783-3100 782-5687
TF: 800-227-0196 ■ *Web:* www.aervoe.com

Aexcel Corp 7373 Production Dr....................... Mentor OH 44060 440-974-3800 974-3808
TF: 800-854-0782 ■ *Web:* www.aexcelcorp.com

Akron Paint & Varnish Inc 1390 Firestone Pkwy .... Akron OH 44301 330-773-8911 773-1028
TF: 800-772-3452 ■ *Web:* arcat.com

AkzoNobel Wood Finishes & Adhesives
2031 Nelson Miller Pkwy.......................... Louisville KY 40223 502-254-0470
Web: www.akzonobel.com

American Safety Technologies Inc
565 Eagle Rock Ave .... Roseland NJ 07068 973-403-2600 403-1108
TF: 800-631-7841 ■ *Web:* www.astantislip.com

AP Nonweiler Co 3321 County Rd A PO Box 1007....... Oshkosh WI 54903 920-231-0850
Web: apnonweiler.com

Behr Process Corp 3400 W Segerstrom Ave .... Santa Ana CA 92704 714-545-7101 241-1002
TF: 800-854-0133 ■ *Web:* www.behr.com

Benjamin Moore & Co 101 Paragon Dr................. Montvale NJ 07645 201-573-9600 573-9046
TF: 800-344-0400 ■ *Web:* www.benjaminmoore.com

Brewer Science Inc 2401 Brewer Dr .... Rolla MO 65401 573-364-0300
Web: www.brewerscience.com

Brewster WaLLPaper Corp 67 Pacella Park Dr .... Randolph MA 02368 781-963-4800
Web: www.brewsterwallcovering.com

BryCoat Inc 207 Vollmer Ave......................... Oldsmar FL 34677 727-490-1000
TF: 800-989-8788 ■ *Web:* www.brycoat.com

C. E. Bradley Laboratories Inc
PO Box 8238 .... Brattleboro VT 05304 802-257-7971 257-7070
Web: www.cebradley.com

California Products Corp 150 Dascomb Rd .... Andover MA 01810 978-623-9980 533-6788*
**Fax Area Code:* 800 ■ *TF:* 800-225-1141 ■ *Web:* www.californiapaints.com

Carboline Co 350 Hanley Industrial Ct............... Saint Louis MO 63144 314-644-1000 644-4617
TF: 800-848-4645 ■ *Web:* www.carboline.com

Coating & Adhesive Corp (CAC)
1901 Popular St PO Box 1080 .... Leland NC 28451 910-371-3184 371-5580
TF: 800-410-2999 ■ *Web:* www.cacoatings.com

Coatings Resource Corp
15541 Commerce Ln .... Huntington Beach CA 92649 714-894-5252 893-2322
Web: www.coatingsresource.com

Color Putty Company Inc PO Box 738 .... Monroe WI 53566 608-325-6033 325-6397
Web: www.colorputty.com

Color Wheel Paint Mfg Co Inc
2814 Silver Star Rd.............................. Orlando FL 32808 407-293-6810 293-0945
TF: 855-862-6639 ■ *Web:* brands.sherwin-williams.com

DAP Products Inc 2400 Boston St Ste 200............ Baltimore MD 21224 410-675-2100 558-1068*
**Fax:* Cust Svc ■ *TF Cust Svc:* 800-543-3840 ■ *Web:* www.dap.com

Davis Paint Company Inc
1311 Iron St PO Box 7589 .... North Kansas City MO 64116 816-471-4447 471-1460
TF: 800-821-2029 ■ *Web:* www.davispaint.com

Day-Glo Color Corp 4515 St Clair Ave .... Cleveland OH 44103 216-391-7070 391-7751
TF: 800-424-9300 ■ *Web:* www.dayglo.com

Diamond Vogel Paints
1110 Albany Pl SE PO Box 380 .... Orange City IA 51041 712-737-8880 737-4998
TF: 800-728-6435 ■ *Web:* www.vogelpaint.com

Duckback Products 2644 Hegan Ln PO Box 980.............Chico CA 95927 800-825-5382 343-3283*
**Fax Area Code:* 530 ■ *TF:* 800-825-5382 ■ *Web:* www.superdeck.com

Dunn-Edwards Corp 4885 E 52nd Pl .... Los Angeles CA 90058 323-771-3330 771-4440
TF: 800-537-4098 ■ *Web:* www.dunnedwards.com

DuPont Automotive 950 Stephenson Hwy PO Box 7013 ...... Troy MI 48007 248-583-8000
TF: 800-533-1313 ■ *Web:* www.dupont.com

DuPont Performance Coatings
1007 Market St................................ Wilmington DE 19898 302-774-1000
TF: 800-441-7515 ■ *Web:* www.dupont.com

EPKO Industries Inc
1200 Arthur Ave .... Elk Grove Village IL 60007 847-437-4000
Web: www.epko.com

Farrell-Calhoun Inc 221 E Carolina Ave............... Memphis TN 38126 901-526-2211 774-4213
TF: 888-832-7735 ■ *Web:* www.farrellcalhoun.com

Ferro Corp 6060 Parkland Blvd .... Mayfield Heights IN 44124 216-875-5600 688-3201*
**Fax Area Code:* 513 ■ *TF:* 800-321-3314 ■ *Web:* compositesworld.com

Ferro Corp 1000 Lakeside Ave..................... Cleveland OH 44114 216-641-8580
NYSE: FOE ■ *Web:* www.ferro.com

Phone Fax

Ferro Corp Plastics Colorants Div
6060 Parkland Blvd Ste 250.................. Mayfield Heights OH 44124 419-682-3311 682-4924
TF: 800-521-9094 ■ *Web:* www.ferro.com

FinishMaster Inc
115 W Washington St 700 S..................... Indianapolis IN 46204 317-237-3678 237-2150
TF: 888-311-3678 ■ *Web:* www.finishmaster.com

Gallagher-Kaiser Corp 13710 Mt Elliott St .... Detroit MI 48212 313-368-3100 368-3109
Web: www.gkcorp.com

Gemini Coatings Inc 421 SE 27th St .... El Reno OK 73036 405-262-5710
TF: 800-262-5710 ■ *Web:* www.gemini-coatings.com

Great Lake Woods Inc 3303 John F Donnelly Dr......... Holland MI 49424 616-399-3300
Web: www.greatlakewoods.com

Hallman Lindsay Paints Inc
1717 N Bristol St .... Sun Prairie WI 53590 608-834-8844 837-1064
Web: www.hallmanlindsay.com

Harrison Paint Co 1329 Harrison Ave SW .... Canton OH 44706 330-455-5125 454-1750
TF: 800-321-0680 ■ *Web:* www.harrisonpaint.com

HB Fuller Co
1200 Willow Lk Blvd PO Box 64683................. Saint Paul MN 55164 651-236-5900 236-5898
NYSE: FUL ■ *TF:* 888-423-8553 ■ *Web:* www.hbfuller.com

Hempel (USA) Inc 600 Conroe Park N Dr .... Conroe TX 77303 936-523-6000
Web: www.hempel.com

Hentzen Coatings Inc 6937 W Mill Rd............... Milwaukee WI 53218 414-353-4200 353-0286
TF: 800-236-6589 ■ *Web:* www.hentzen.com

Hirshfield's Inc 725 Second Ave N .... Minneapolis MN 55405 612-377-3910 436-3384
Web: www.hirshfields.com

Hudson Color Concentrates Inc
50 Francis St .... Leominster MA 01453 978-537-3538
TF: 888-858-9065 ■ *Web:* www.hudsoncolor.com

Insl-X Products Corp 101 Paragon Dr.............. Montvale NJ 07645 800-225-5554 248-2143*
**Fax Area Code:* 888 ■ *TF Cust Svc:* 800-225-5554 ■ *Web:* www.insl-x.com

Kalcor Coatings Company Inc
37721 Stevens Blvd .... Willoughby OH 44094 440-946-4700
Web: www.kalcor.com

Kelley Technical Coatings Inc
1445 S 15th St PO Box 3726 .... Louisville KY 40201 502-636-2561
Web: www.smartsealco.com

Kelly-Moore Paint Company Inc
987 Commercial St.............................. San Carlos CA 94070 650-592-8337 508-8563*
**Fax:* Hum Res ■ *TF:* 800-874-4436 ■ *Web:* www.kellymoore.com

Kenyon Plastering Inc
4001 W Indian School Rd.......................... Phoenix AZ 85019 602-233-1191 278-6801
TF: 800-949-4319 ■ *Web:* www.kenyonweb.com

KJ Quinn & Co Inc 34 Folly Mill Rd .... Seabrook NH 03874 603-474-5753 474-7122

Kop-Coat Inc
436 Seventh Ave 1850 Koppers Bldg .... Pittsburgh PA 15219 412-227-2426 227-2618
TF: 800-221-4466 ■ *Web:* www.kop-coat.com

Lancaster Distributing Co 1310 Union St.......... Spartanburg SC 29302 864-583-3011 542-1315
TF General: 800-845-8287 ■ *Web:* www.lancasterco.com

Lansco Colors
1 Blue Hill Plaza 11th Fl PO Box 1685 .... Pearl River NY 10965 845-507-5942 735-2787
TF: 800-526-2783 ■ *Web:* www.pigments.com

Magni Group Inc 390 Pk St......................... Birmingham MI 48009 248-647-4500 647-7506
Web: Www.magnicoatings.com

Magni-Industries Inc 2771 Hammond St................ Detroit MI 48209 313-843-7855 842-6730
Web: magnicoatings.com

Mantros-Haeuser & Company Inc
1175 Post Rd E.................................. Westport CT 06880 203-454-1800 227-0558
TF General: 800-344-4229 ■ *Web:* www.mantrose.com

Masterchem Industries LLC 3135 Old Hwy M .... Imperial MO 63052 866-774-6371 942-3663*
**Fax Area Code:* 636 ■ *TF:* 866-774-6371 ■ *Web:* www.kilz.com

Michelman Inc 9080 Shell Rd..................... Cincinnati OH 45236 513-793-7766 793-2504
Web: www.michelman.com

Miller Paint Company Inc
12812 NE Whitaker Way............................ Portland OR 97230 503-255-0190 255-0192
Web: www.millerpaint.com

Minwax Co 10 Mountainview Rd .... Upper Saddle River NJ 07458 800-523-9299 818-7605*
**Fax Area Code:* 201 ■ *TF:* 800-523-9299 ■ *Web:* www.minwax.com

Mobile Paint Manufacturing Co
4775 Hamilton Blvd .... Theodore AL 36582 251-443-6110 408-0410
TF: 800-621-6952 ■ *Web:* www.blpmobilepaint.com

Morwear Manufacturing Inc 620 Lamar St .... Los Angeles CA 90031 323-222-7000
Web: www.morwear.com

Muralo Company Inc 148 E Fifth St.................. Bayonne NJ 07002 201-437-0770 437-0664
TF: 800-631-3440 ■ *Web:* www.muralo.com

Neogard Div Jones-blair Co
2728 Empire Central St............................. Dallas TX 75235 214-353-1600
TF: 800-492-9400 ■ *Web:* www.jones-blair.com

O'Leary Paint 300 E Oakland Ave .... Lansing MI 48906 517-487-2066 487-1680
TF: 800-477-2066 ■ *Web:* www.olearypaint.com

Old Master Products Inc
7751 Hayvenhurst Ave .... Van Nuys CA 91406 818-785-8886

Painters Supply & Equipment Co 25195 Brest Rd........ Taylor MI 48180 734-946-8119
TF: 800-589-8100 ■ *Web:* www.painters-supply.com

Parker Paint Mfg Co Inc 3003 S Tacoma Way .... Tacoma WA 98409 855-862-6639 473-0448*
**Fax Area Code:* 253 ■ *TF:* 855-862-6639 ■ *Web:* brands.sherwin-williams.com

Penn Color Inc 400 Old Dublin Pk .... Doylestown PA 18901 215-345-6550 345-0270
TF: 866-617-7366 ■ *Web:* www.penncolor.com

Pioneer Mfg 4529 Industrial Pkwy................... Cleveland OH 44135 216-671-5500 671-5502
TF: 800-877-1500 ■ *Web:* www.pioneerathletics.com

PPG Industries Inc 17451 Von Karman Ave............. Irvine CA 92614 949-474-0400 474-7269
TF: 800-544-3338 ■ *Web:* www.ppgaerospace.com

PPG Industries Inc 1 PPG Pl .... Pittsburgh PA 15272 412-434-3131 434-4291*
NYSE: PPG ■ **Fax:* Hum Res ■ *Web:* www.ppg.com

Red Spot Paint & Varnish Co Inc
1107 E Louisiana St .... Evansville IN 47711 812-428-9100
TF: 877-777-4778 ■ *Web:* www.redspot.com

Republic Powdered Metals Inc 2628 Pearl Rd .... Medina OH 44256 800-382-1218 273-5061*
**Fax Area Code:* 330 ■ *TF:* 800-382-1218 ■
Web: www.tremcoroofing.com/roofing-systems/roof-restoration/republic-restoration-systems

Rhino Linings Corp 9151 Rehco Rd .... San Diego CA 92121 858-450-0441
Web: www.rhinolatino.com

Rodda Paint Co 6107 N Marine Dr .... Portland OR 97203 503-521-4300 521-4400
TF: 800-452-2315 ■ *Web:* www.roddapaint.com

Company	City	State	ZIP	Phone	Fax
Roymal Inc 3 Roymal Ln *Web:* www.roymalinc.com	Newport	NH	03773	603-863-2410	
RPM International Inc 2628 Pearl Rd *NYSE:* RPM ■ *TF:* 800-776-4488 ■ *Web:* www.rpminc.com	Medina	OH	44256	330-273-5090	225-8743
Rust-Oleum Corp 11 E Hawthorn Pkwy *TF:* 800-323-3584 ■ *Web:* www.rustoleum.com	Vernon Hills	IL	60061	847-367-7700	
Samuel Cabot Inc 100 Hale St *TF:* 800-877-8246 ■ *Web:* www.cabotstain.com	Newburyport	MA	01950	978-465-1900	
Seymour of Sycamore Inc 917 Crosby Ave *TF:* 800-435-4482 ■ *Web:* www.seymourpaint.com	Sycamore	IL	60178	815-895-9101	895-8475
Sheboygan Paint Company Inc 1439 N 25th St PO Box 417 *TF:* 800-773-7801 ■ *Web:* www.shebpaint.com	Sheboygan	WI	53082	920-458-2157	458-5620
Sherwin-Williams Automotive Finishes 4440 Warrensville Ctr Rd *TF:* 800-798-5872 ■ *Web:* sherwin-automotive.com	Warrensville Heights	OH	44128	216-332-8330	
SP Kish Industries Inc 600 W Seminary St *Web:* www.kishindustries.com	Charlotte	MI	48813	517-543-2650	
Sterling-Clark-Lurton Corp PO Box 130 *TF:* 800-225-9872 ■ *Web:* www.savogran.com	Norwood	MA	02062	781-762-5400	762-1095
Talbot Industries Inc 5725 Howard Bush Dr	Neosho	MO	64850	417-451-7440	451-7830
Textured Coatings Of America 2422 E 15th St *TF:* 800-454-0340 ■ *Web:* www.texcote.com	Panama City	FL	32405	850-769-0347	913-8619
Tnemec Company Inc 6800 Corporate Dr *TF:* 800-863-6321 ■ *Web:* www.tnemec.com	Kansas City	MO	64120	816-483-3400	483-3969
Troy Corp 8 Vreeland Rd PO Box 955 *TF:* 800-448-2843 ■ *Web:* www.troycorp.com	Florham Park	NJ	07932	973-443-4200	443-0258
United Gilsonite Laboratories Inc 1396 Jefferson Ave *Web:* www.ugl.com	Scranton	PA	18509	570-344-1202	
Valspar Refinish Inc 210 Crosby St *TF Cust Svc:* 800-844-3691 ■ *Web:* www.valsparrefinish.com	Picayune	MS	39466	800-845-2500	
Vista Paint Corp 2020 E Orangethorpe Ave *Web:* www.vistapaint.com	Fullerton	CA	92831	714-680-3810	459-4708
Whitmore Manufacturing Co PO Box 9300 *TF:* 800-699-6318 ■ *Web:* www.whitmores.com	Rockwall	TX	75087	972-771-1000	722-2108
Willamette Valley Co 1075 Arrowsmith St *TF:* 800-333-9826 ■ *Web:* www.wilvaco.com	Eugene	OR	97402	541-484-9621	345-7480
WM Barr & Company Inc 2105 Ch Ave **Fax Area Code:* 800 ■ *TF:* 800-238-2672 ■ *Web:* www.wmbarr.com	Memphis	TN	38109	901-775-0100	621-9508*
Wolf Gordon Inc 33-00 47th Ave **Fax Area Code:* 718 ■ *TF:* 800-347-0550 ■ *Web:* www.wolfgordon.com	Long Island	NY	11101	800-347-0550	361-1090*
Yenkin-Majestic Paint Corp 1920 Leonard Ave *TF:* 800-848-1898 ■ *Web:* www.yenkin-majestic.com	Columbus	OH	43219	614-253-8511	253-6327
ZC&R Coatings for Optics Inc 1401 Abalone Ave *Web:* abrisatechnologies.com/redirect	Torrance	CA	90501	310-381-3060	

551 PALLETS & SKIDS

Company	City	State	ZIP	Phone	Fax
American Pallet Inc 1001 Knox Rd *Web:* www.americanpallet.com	Oakdale	CA	95361	209-847-6122	847-6154
Anderson Forest Products Inc 1267 Old Edmonton Rd *TF:* 800-489-6778 ■ *Web:* www.afp-usa.com	Tompkinsville	KY	42167	270-487-6778	487-8953
Brunswick Box Company Inc 852 Planters Rd PO Box 7	Lawrenceville	VA	23868	434-848-2222	848-3647
Clinch-Tite Corp 5264 Lake St PO Box 456 *TF General:* 800-241-0900 ■ *Web:* www.clinchtite.com	Sandy Lake	PA	16145	724-376-7315	376-2785
Cutter Lumber Products (CLP) 10 Rickenbacker Cir *Web:* cutterlumber.com	Livermore	CA	94551	925-443-5959	443-0648
Day Lumber Co 34 S Broad St *Web:* www.daylumber.com	Westfield	MA	01085	413-568-3511	568-6668
Delisa Pallet Corp 91-97 Blanchard St *Web:* www.delisapallet.com	Newark	NJ	07105	973-344-8600	
Eastern Wood Products Inc 2020 Mill Ln	Williamsport	PA	17701	570-326-1946	
Edwards Wood Products Inc 2215 Old Lawyers Rd PO Box 219 *Web:* www.ewpi.com	Marshville	NC	28103	704-624-5098	624-6812
Hill Wood Products Inc 9483 Ashawa Rd *TF:* 800-788-9689 ■ *Web:* www.hillwoodproducts.com	Cook	MN	55723	218-666-5933	666-5726
Hinchcliff Products Co 13550 Falling Water Rd *Web:* www.hinchcliffproducts.com	Strongsville	OH	44136	440-238-5200	238-5202
Hunter Woodworks Inc 21038 S Wilmington Ave PO Box 4937 *TF:* 800-966-4751 ■ *Web:* www.hunterpallets.com	Carson	CA	90749	323-775-2544	775-2540
Ifco Systems 3030 N Rocky Point Dr Ste 300 *Web:* www.ifco.com	Tampa	FL	33607	813-463-4100	286-2070
Litco International Inc 1 Litco Dr PO Box 150 *Web:* www.litco.com	Vienna	OH	44473	330-539-5433	539-5388
Mountain Valley Farms & Lumber Inc 1240 Nawakwa Rd *Web:* www.mtvalleyfarms.com	Biglerville	PA	17307	717-677-6166	677-9283
Nelson Co 2116 Sparrows Pt Rd *Web:* www.nelsoncompany.com	Baltimore	MD	21219	410-477-3000	388-0246
Pallet Consultants Corp PO Box 1692 *TF:* 888-782-2909 ■ *Web:* www.palletconsultants.com	Pompano Beach	FL	33061	954-946-2212	
Pallet Masters Inc 655 E Florence Ave *TF:* 800-675-2579	Los Angeles	CA	90001	323-758-6559	758-9600
PalletOne Inc 1470 US Hwy 17 S *TF:* 800-771-1148 ■ *Web:* www.palletone.com	Bartow	FL	33830	863-533-1147	533-3065
Potomac Supply Corp 1398 Kinsale Rd *TF Sales:* 800-365-3900 ■ *Web:* www.potomacsupply.com	Kinsale	VA	22488	804-472-2527	472-5058
Precision Wood Products Inc 2456 Aukerman Crk Rd *Web:* www.precisionwoodproducts.com	Camden	OH	45311	503-285-0393	252-6046
Savanna Pallets Co 41496 State Hwy 65 *Web:* www.savannapallets.com	McGregor	MN	55760	218-768-2077	
Tasler Inc 1804 Tasler Dr *TF:* 800-482-7537 ■ *Web:* www.tasler.com	Webster City	IA	50595	515-832-5200	832-2721
United Wholesale Lumber Co 8009 Doe Ave *Web:* www.uwlco.com	Visalia	CA	93291	559-651-2037	651-0742
WNC Pallet & Forest Products Co Inc 1414 Smokey Pk Hwy *Web:* www.wncpallet.com	Candler	NC	28715	828-667-5426	665-4759
Wooden Pallets Gp LLC PO Box 555 *Web:* www.woodenpalletsltd.com	Silsbee	TX	77656	409-385-1234	385-6203
Yoder Lumber Company Inc 4515 TR 367 *Web:* www.yoderlumber.com	Millersburg	OH	44654	330-893-3131	893-3031

552 PAPER - MFR

See Also Packaging Materials & Products - Paper or Plastics p. 2863

552-1 Coated & Laminated Paper

Company	City	State	ZIP	Phone	Fax
Appleton Papers Inc 825 E Wisconsin Ave PO Box 359 *TF:* 888-593-9546 ■ *Web:* www.appletonideas.com	Appleton	WI	54912	920-734-9841	
Avery Dennison Worldwide Graphics Div 207 Goode Ave Bldg 8 *TF:* 800-443-9380 ■ *Web:* www.averygraphics.com	Glendale	CA	44077	440-358-3700	
BPM Inc 200 W Front St *TF:* 800-826-0494 ■ *Web:* www.bpmpaper.com	Peshtigo	WI	54157	715-582-4551	582-4853
Diversified Labeling Solutions 1285 Hamilton Pkwy *TF:* 800-397-3013 ■ *Web:* teamdls.com	Itasca	IL	60143	630-625-1225	
Exopack Advanced Coatings 700 Crestdale St *Web:* coverisadvancedcoatings.com	Matthews	NC	28105	704-847-9171	845-4307
Felix Schoeller North America Inc 179 County Route 2A Ste 2A *Web:* www.schoeller.com	Pulaski	NY	13142	315-298-5133	298-3664
Fortifiber Building Systems Group 300 Industrial Dr *TF:* 800-773-4777 ■ *Web:* www.fortifiber.com	Fernley	NV	89408	775-333-6400	333-6411
French Paper Co 100 French St *Web:* www.frenchpaper.com	Niles	MI	49120	269-683-1100	683-3025
Horizon Paper Co Inc 1010 Washington Blvd *TF:* 866-358-0855 ■ *Web:* www.horizonpaper.com	Stamford	CT	06901	203-358-0855	358-0828
Lofton Label Inc 6290 Claude Way *TF:* 877-447-8118 ■ *Web:* www.loftonlabel.com	Inver Grove Heights	MN	55076	651-552-6257	457-3709
Nashua Corp 11 Trafalgar Sq 2nd Fl **Fax Area Code:* 417 ■ *TF:* 800-430-7488 ■ *Web:* www.nashua.com	Nashua	NH	03063	603-880-2323	626-8415*
National/AZON 1148 Rochester Rd **Fax Area Code:* 866 ■ *TF:* 800-325-5939 ■ *Web:* www.azon.com	Troy	MI	48083	800-325-5939	318-7323*
Onyx Specialty Papers Inc 40 Willow St *Web:* onyxpapers.com	South Lee	MA	01260	413-243-1231	243-4602
Sappi Fine Paper North America 255 State St **Fax:* Mail Rm ■ *Web:* www.na.sappi.com	Boston	MA	02109	617-423-7300	423-5494*
Shawsheen Rubber Company Inc PO Box 4296 *Web:* www.shawsheencc.com	Andover	MA	01810	978-475-1710	475-8603
Technicote Westfield Inc 222 Mound Ave *TF:* 800-358-4448 ■ *Web:* www.technicote.com	Miamisburg	OH	45342	937-859-4448	859-9096
TST/Impreso Inc 652 Southwestern Blvd **Fax Area Code:* 800 ■ **Fax:* Cust Svc ■ *TF:* 800-527-2878 ■ *Web:* www.tstimpreso.com	Coppell	TX	75019	972-462-0100	562-5359*
Verso Corp 8540 Gander Creek Dr **Fax Area Code:* 937 ■ *TF:* 877-855-7243 ■ *Web:* www.versoco.com	Miamisburg	OH	45342	877-855-7243	242-9329*
Wausau Paper Corp 100 Paper Pl *NYSE:* WPP ■ *TF:* 800-723-0008 ■ *Web:* www.wausaupaper.com	Mosinee	WI	54455	715-693-4470	692-2082
Wausau Paper Corp Specialty Paper Div 100 Paper Pl *TF:* 800-723-0008 ■ *Web:* www.wausaupaper.com	Mosinee	WI	54455	715-693-4470	692-2082
Wcp Solutions 6703 S 234th St Ste 120 **Fax Area Code:* 253 ■ *TF:* 877-398-3030 ■ *Web:* wcpsolutions.com/index.php	Kent	WA	98032	877-398-3030	852-9272*

552-2 Writing Paper

Company	City	State	ZIP	Phone	Fax
Anna Griffin Inc 99 Armour Dr *TF:* 888-817-8170 ■ *Web:* www.annagriffin.com	Atlanta	GA	30324	404-817-8170	817-0590
Crane & Co Inc 30 S St *TF Cust Svc:* 800-268-2281 ■ *Web:* www.crane.com	Dalton	MA	01226	800-268-2281	
Geographics 108 Main St 3rd Fl **Fax Area Code:* 866 ■ *TF:* 800-436-4919 ■ *Web:* www.geographics.com	Norwalk	CT	06851	800-436-4919	520-1955*
Gordon Paper Company Inc PO Box 1806 *TF:* 800-457-7366 ■ *Web:* www.gordonpaper.com	Norfolk	VA	23501	757-464-3581	363-9355
Louisiana Assn For, The Blind, The 1750 Claiborne Ave *TF:* 877-913-6471 ■ *Web:* www.lablind.com	Shreveport	LA	71103	318-635-6471	635-8902
Mafcote Industries Inc 108 Main St *Web:* www.mafcote.com	Norwalk	CT	06851	203-847-8500	849-9177
Mohawk Fine Papers Inc 465 Saratoga St *TF:* 800-843-6455 ■ *Web:* www.mohawkconnects.com	Cohoes	NY	12047	518-237-1740	237-7394
Neenah Paper Inc 3460 Preston Ridge Rd Ste 600 *NYSE:* NP ■ *Web:* www.neenah.com	Alpharetta	GA	30005	678-566-6500	
Performance Office Papers 21565 Hamburg Ave *TF:* 800-458-7189 ■ *Web:* www.perfpapers.com	Lakeville	MN	55044	800-458-7189	488-5058
Schurman Fine Papers 500 Chadbourne Rd **Fax Area Code:* 707 ■ *TF Sales:* 800-789-1649 ■ *Web:* www.papyrusonline.com	Fairfield	CA	94533	800-789-1649	428-0641*
Southworth Co 265 Main St *TF:* 800-225-1839 ■ *Web:* www.southworth.com	Agawam	MA	01001	413-789-1200	
Specialty Loose Leaf Inc 1 Cabot St *TF:* 800-227-3623 ■ *Web:* www.specialtyll.com	Holyoke	MA	01040	413-532-0106	
Top Flight Inc 1300 Central Ave *TF:* 800-777-3740 ■ *Web:* www.topflightpaper.com	Chattanooga	TN	37408	423-266-8171	266-6857

Company	City	State	ZIP	Phone	Fax
Wausau Paper Corp 100 Paper Pl *NYSE:* WPP ■ *TF:* 800-723-0008 ■ *Web:* www.wausaupaper.com	Mosinee	WI	54455	715-693-4470	692-2082
Wausau Paper Corp Printing & Writing Paper Div 1 Clark's Island *TF:* 800-723-0008 ■ *Web:* www.wausaupaper.com	Wausau	WI	54403	715-693-4470	

553 PAPER - WHOL

Company	City	State	ZIP	Phone	Fax
2072906 Ontario Ltd 177 Crosby Ave *Web:* plasticap.com	Richmond Hill	ON	L4C2R3	905-883-4343	
America Chung Nam Inc 1163 Fairway Dr *Web:* www.acni.net	City of Industry	CA	91789	909-839-8383	869-6310
Anchor Paper Company Inc 480 Broadway St *TF:* 800-652-9755 ■ *Web:* www.anchorpaper.com	Saint Paul	MN	55101	651-298-1311	298-0060
AT Clayton & Co Inc 300 Atlantic St *TF:* 800-282-5298 ■ *Web:* www.atclayton.com	Stamford	CT	06901	203-658-1200	658-1201
Atlantic Packaging Co 806 N 23rd St *TF:* 800-722-5841 ■ *Web:* www.atlanticpkg.com	Wilmington	NC	28405	910-343-0624	763-5421
Atlus USA Inc 199 Technology Dr *Web:* www.atlus.com	Irvine	CA	92618	949-788-0455	
Brawner Paper Company Inc 5702 Armour Dr *Web:* www.brawnerpaper.com	Houston	TX	77020	713-675-6584	
C&K Industrial Services Inc 5617 Schaaf Rd *Web:* www.ckindustrial.com	Independence	OH	44131	216-642-0055	
Central Lewmar Paper Co 261 River Rd	Clifton	NJ	07014	609-518-9700	518-9736
Clampitt Paper Company of Dallas 9207 Ambassador Row *Web:* www.clampitt.com	Dallas	TX	75247	214-638-3300	634-7837
Clifford Paper Inc 600 E Crescent Ave *Web:* www.cliffordpaper.com	Upper Saddle River	NJ	07458	201-934-5115	934-5188
Cole Papers Inc 1300 N 38th St *TF:* 800-800-8090 ■ *Web:* www.colepapers.com	Fargo	ND	58102	701-282-5311	282-5513
Com-Pac International Inc 800 W Industrial Park Rd *Web:* com-pac.com	Carbondale	IL	62901	618-529-2421	
Dennis Paper Co 910 Acorn Dr *TF:* 800-441-5684 ■ *Web:* www.dennispaper.com	Nashville	TN	37210	615-883-9010	885-2969
Elof Hansson Pulp Inc 565 Taxter Rd *Web:* www.elofhansson.com	Elmsford	NY	10523	914-345-8380	345-8112
Field Paper Co 3950 D St *TF:* 800-969-3435 ■ *Web:* www.fieldpaper.com	Omaha	NE	68107	402-733-3600	731-7113
Gpa Specialty Printable Sbstrt 8740 W 50th St **Fax Area Code:* 800 ■ *TF:* 800-395-9000 ■ *Web:* www.askgpa.com	McCook	IL	60525	773-650-2020	395-3581*
GreenLine Paper Company Inc 631 S Pine St *TF:* 800-641-1117 ■ *Web:* www.greenlinepaper.com	York	PA	17403	717-845-8697	846-3806
Hearn Paper Co 556 N Meridian Rd *TF:* 800-225-2989 ■ *Web:* www.hearnpaper.com	Youngstown	OH	44509	330-792-6533	792-4762
Kelly Paper Co 288 Brea Canyon Rd **Fax Area Code:* 909 ■ *TF:* 800-675-3559 ■ *Web:* www.kellypaper.com	Walnut	CA	91789	800-675-3559	859-8903*
Lindenmeyr Book Publishing Papers 521 Fifth Ave *TF:* 800-842-8480 ■ *Web:* www.lindenmeyr.com	New York	NY	10175	800-842-8480	
Lindenmeyr Munroe 14 Research Pkwy *TF:* 800-842-8480 ■ *Web:* lindenmeyrmunroe.com	Wallingford	CT	06492	800-842-8480	890-3115
Lindenmeyr Munroe Central Central National-Gottesman Inc 3 Manhattanville Rd **Fax Area Code:* 914 ■ *TF:* 800-221-3042 ■ *Web:* www.cng-inc.com	Purchase	NY	10577	800-221-3042	696-9333*
Lindenmeyr Munroe Paper Corp 115 Moonachie Ave *TF:* 800-221-3042 ■ *Web:* www.lindenmeyr.com	Moonachie	NJ	07074	201-440-6491	440-6492
Mac Papers 3300 Phillips Hwy PO Box 5369 *TF:* 800-622-2968 ■ *Web:* www.macpapers.com	Jacksonville	FL	32207	904-348-3300	348-3340
Marquardt & Co 161 Ave of the Americas	New York	NY	10013	212-645-7200	536-0282
Midland Paper 101 E Palatine Rd *TF:* 800-323-8522 ■ *Web:* www.midlandpaper.com	Wheeling	IL	60090	847-777-2700	777-2552
Millcraft Paper Co 6800 Grant Ave *TF:* 800-860-2482 ■ *Web:* www.millcraft.com	Cleveland	OH	44105	216-441-5500	641-2610
Miller Supply Inc 29902 Avenida de las Banderas *Web:* www.millersupplyinc.com	Rancho Santa Margarita	CA	92688	949-589-6033	
Morrisette Paper Company Inc 5925 Summit Ave PO Box 20768 *TF:* 800-822-8882 ■ *Web:* morrisette.com	Browns Summit	NC	27214	336-375-1515	621-0751
Murnane Paper Corp 345 W Fischer Farm Rd *TF:* 855-632-8191 ■ *Web:* www.murnanepaper.com	Elmhurst	IL	60126	630-530-8222	530-8325
Newell Paper Co 1212 Grand Ave **Fax Area Code:* 601 ■ *TF:* 800-844-8894 ■ *Web:* www.newellpaper.com	Meridian	MS	39301	800-844-8894	483-4900*
PaperDirect Inc 1005 E Woodmen Rd **Fax Area Code:* 719 ■ *TF:* 800-272-7377 ■ *Web:* www.paperdirect.com	Colorado Springs	CO	80920	800-272-7377	534-1741*
Paterson Card & Paper Co PO Box 2286 *Web:* www.patersonpapers.com	Paterson	NJ	07501	973-278-2410	278-0677
Perez Trading Company Inc 3490 NW 125th St *Web:* www.pereztrading.com	Miami	FL	33167	305-769-0761	681-7963
Redd Paper Co 3851 Ctr Loop *TF:* 800-961-6656 ■ *Web:* www.reddpaper.com	Orlando	FL	32808	407-299-6656	299-8142
Rohn Industries Inc 862 Hersey St *TF:* 800-289-8580 ■ *Web:* rohnind.com	St. Paul	MN	55114	651-647-1300	
Roosevelt Paper Co 1 Roosevelt Dr **Fax:* Sales ■ *TF:* 800-523-3470 ■ *Web:* www.rooseveltpaper.com	Mount Laurel	NJ	08054	856-303-4100	642-1949*
Spicers Paper Inc 12310 Slauson Ave *TF:* 800-774-2377 ■ *Web:* www.spicers.com	Santa Fe Springs	CA	90670	562-698-1199	945-2597
Unisource Worldwide Inc 6600 Governors Lake Pkwy *TF:* 800-864-7687 ■ *Web:* www.unisourceworldwide.com	Norcross	GA	30071	770-447-9000	734-2000
White Paper Co 9990 River Way *TF:* 888-840-7300 ■ *Web:* www.whitepaper.com	Delta	BC	V4G1M9	604-951-3900	951-3944

Company	City	State	ZIP	Phone	Fax
Wilcox Paper LLC 11100 Jefferson HWY N. *Web:* www.wilcoxpaper.com	Champlin	MN	55316	763-404-8400	

554 PAPER CONVERTERS

Company	City	State	ZIP	Phone	Fax
Ameri-Fax Corp 6520 W 20th Ave Unit 2 **Fax Area Code:* 305 ■ *TF:* 800-262-8214 ■ *Web:* www.faxpaper.com	Hialeah	FL	33016	800-262-8214	824-1604*
Artistry in Motion Inc 15101 Keswick St *Web:* www.artistryinmotion.com	Van Nuys	CA	91405	818-994-7388	994-7688
Asian American Civic Association Inc 87 Tyler St Fl 5 *Web:* www.aaca-boston.org	Boston	MA	02111	617-426-9492	
B & B Paper Converters Inc 12500 Elmwood Ave *Web:* bbpaper.com	Cleveland	OH	44111	216-941-8100	941-8174
BagcraftPapercon 3900 W 43rd St *TF:* 800-621-8468 ■ *Web:* www.bagcraft.com	Chicago	IL	60632	773-254-8000	254-8204
C-P Flexible Packaging 15 Grumbacher Rd *TF:* 800-815-0667 ■ *Web:* www.cpconverters.com	York	PA	17406	717-764-1193	764-2039
Caraustar Industries Inc 5000 Austell-Powder Springs Rd Ste 300 *TF:* 800-858-1438 ■ *Web:* www.caraustar.com	Austell	GA	30106	770-948-3100	
Case Paper Company Inc 500 Mamaroneck Ave *TF:* 800-222-2922 ■ *Web:* www.casepaper.com	Harrison	NY	10528	914-899-3500	777-1028
Cindus Corp 515 Stn Ave **Fax Area Code:* 513 ■ *TF:* 800-543-4691 ■ *Web:* www.cindus.com	Cincinnati	OH	45215	800-543-4691	948-8805*
Commercial Cutting & Graphics LLC 208 Central Ave *Web:* www.commercialcutting.com	Mansfield	OH	44905	419-526-4800	
Crusader Paper Company Inc 350 Holt Rd **Fax Area Code:* 978 ■ *TF:* 800-421-0007 ■ *Web:* www.crusaderpaper.com	North Andover	MA	01845	800-421-0007	794-1625*
Damsky Paper Co 3501 First Ave N *Web:* www.damskypaper.com	Birmingham	AL	35222	205-521-9840	521-9840
Fabricon Products 1721 W Pleasant Ave *Web:* www.fabriconproducts.com	River Rouge	MI	48218	313-841-8200	841-4819
Gleason Industrial Products Inc 8575 Forest Home Ave Ste 100 *Web:* www.milwaukeehandtrucks.com	Greenfield	WI	53228	414-529-8357	
Graphic Converting LLC 877 N Larch Ave *Web:* www.graphicconverting.com	Elmhurst	IL	60126	630-758-4100	833-1058
Great Southwest Paper Co 5707 Harvey Wilson Dr *Web:* www.gswpaper.com	Houston	TX	77020	713-223-5050	223-3030
Hampden Papers Inc 100 Water St PO Box 149 *Web:* www.hampdenpapers.com	Holyoke	MA	01040	413-536-1000	532-9161
Hazen Paper Co 240 S Water St PO Box 189 *Web:* www.hazen.com	Holyoke	MA	01041	413-538-8204	533-1420
International Converter Inc 17153 Industrial Hwy *TF:* 800-848-6623 ■ *Web:* www.i-convert.com	Caldwell	OH	43724	740-732-5665	732-7515
Interstate Paper Supply Co Inc (IPSCO) 103 Good St PO Box 670 *Web:* www.ipscoinc.com	Roscoe	PA	15477	724-938-2218	938-3415
Kanzaki Specialty Papers 1 Monarch Pl Ste 800 *TF:* 888-526-9254 ■ *Web:* www.kanzakiusa.com	Springfield	MA	01144	888-526-9254	
Lauterbach Group Inc W222 N5710 Miller Way *TF Sales:* 800-841-7301 ■ *Web:* www.lauterbachgroup.com	Sussex	WI	53089	262-820-8130	820-1806
Loyola Paper Co 951 W Lunt Ave	Elk Grove Village	IL	60007	847-956-7770	956-6897
Mafcote Industries Inc 108 Main St *Web:* www.mafcote.com	Norwalk	CT	06851	203-847-8500	849-9177
Maritime Paper Products Ltd 25 Borden Ave PO Box 668 *Web:* www.maritimepaper.com	Dartmouth	NS	B2Y3Y9	902-468-5353	
Max International Converters Inc 2360 Dairy Rd *TF:* 800-233-0222 ■ *Web:* www.maxintl.com	Lancaster	PA	17601	800-233-0222	
New Leaf Paper LLC 510 16th St Ste 520 *Web:* www.newleafpaper.com	Oakland	CA	94612	415-291-9210	
Northeastern PA Carton & Finishing Co Inc 4820 Birney Ave US Rt 11 *Web:* www.nepacartons.com	Moosic	PA	18507	570-457-7711	457-3801
Pacon Corp 2525 N Casaloma Dr **Fax Area Code:* 920 ■ *TF:* 800-333-2545 ■ *Web:* www.pacon.com	Appleton	WI	54912	800-333-2545	830-5099*
Paper Systems Inc 185 S Pioneer Blvd *TF:* 888-564-6774 ■ *Web:* www.papersystems.com	Springboro	OH	45066	937-746-6841	746-1089
PM Co 9220 Glades Dr *TF:* 800-327-4359 ■ *Web:* www.pmcompany.com	Fairfield	OH	45011	513-825-7626	825-2877
Port Townsend Paper Corp 100 Mill Rd *Web:* www.ptpc.com	Port Townsend	WA	98368	360-385-3170	
Protect-All Inc 109 Badger Pkwy *TF:* 888-432-8526 ■ *Web:* www.protect-all.com	Darien	WI	53114	888-432-8526	
Southeastern Paperboard Inc 100 S Harris Rd *Web:* www.southeasternpaperboard.com	Piedmont	SC	29673	864-277-7353	
Spectra-Kote Corp 301 E Water St *TF:* 800-241-4626 ■ *Web:* www.spectra-kote.com	Gettysburg	PA	17325	717-334-3177	
Spinnaker Coating Inc 518 E Water St *TF:* 800-543-9452 ■ *Web:* spinnakercoating.com	Troy	OH	45373	937-332-6500	332-6518
SureVoid Products Inc 1895 W Dartmouth Ave *Web:* www.surevoid.com	Englewood	CO	80110	303-762-0324	
Texpack Inc 1001 Brickell Bay Dr *Web:* www.texpack.com	Miami	FL	33131	305-358-9696	
TimeMed Labeling Systems Inc 144 Tower Dr **Fax Area Code:* 800 ■ *TF Cust Svc:* 800-323-4840 ■ *Web:* www.pdchealthcare.com	Burr Ridge	IL	60527	630-986-1800	548-5359*
Tramont Corp 3701 N Humboldt Blvd *Web:* www.tramont.com	Milwaukee	WI	53212	414-967-8800	
Tufco Technologies Inc PO Box 23500 *NASDAQ:* TFCO ■ *TF:* 800-558-8145 ■ *Web:* www.tufco.com	Green Bay	WI	54305	920-336-0054	
Viking Paper Corp 5148 Stickney Ave *Web:* www.packpros.net	Toledo	OH	43612	419-729-4951	

Phone Fax

Wedlock Paper Converters Ltd
2327 Stanfield Rd .... Mississauga ON L4Y1R6 905-277-9461 272-1108
Web: www.wedlockpaper.com

Western Robidoux Inc 4006 S 40th St .... Saint Joseph MO 64503 816-279-1617
Web: www.eyecandygraphicarts.com

Woodland Paper Inc 50785 Pontiac Trl .... Wixom MI 48393 248-926-5550
Web: www.woodlandpaper.com

555 PAPER FINISHERS (EMBOSSING, COATING, GILDING, STAMPING)

Phone Fax

Colad Group 801 Exchange St .... Buffalo NY 14210 716-961-1776 961-1753
TF: 800-950-1755 ■ *Web:* www.colad.com

Complemar Partners 500 Lee Rd Ste 200 .... Rochester NY 14606 585-647-5800 647-5800
TF: 800-388-7254 ■ *Web:* www.complemar.com

Diecrafters Inc 1349 55th Ct .... Cicero IL 60804 708-656-3336 656-3386
Web: www.diecrafters.com

Graphic Arts Finishers Inc
32 Cambridge St .... Charlestown MA 02129 617-241-9292
Web: graphicartsfinishers.com

Jen-Coat Inc 132 N Elm St PO Box 274 .... Westfield MA 01085 413-562-2315
Web: www.jencoat.com

Loroco Industries Inc 5000 Creek Rd .... Cincinnati OH 45242 513-891-9544 891-9549
TF: 800-215-9474 ■ *Web:* www.lorocoindustries.com

Madison Cutting Die Inc 2547 Progress Rd .... Madison WI 53716 608-221-3422 223-6850
TF: 800-395-9405 ■ *Web:* www.mcd.net

Markal Finishing Corp 400 Bostwick Ave .... Bridgeport CT 06605 203-384-8219 336-1231
Web: markalfinishing.com

McGraphics Inc 601 Hagan St .... Nashville TN 37203 615-242-8779

Unifoil Corp 12 Daniel Rd .... Fairfield NJ 07004 973-244-9900 244-5555
Web: www.unifoil.com

Walton Press (WP) 402 Mayfield Dr .... Monroe GA 30655 770-267-2596 267-9463
TF: 800-354-0235 ■ *Web:* www.waltonpress.com

556 PAPER INDUSTRIES MACHINERY

Phone Fax

Baumfolder Corp 1660 Campbell Rd .... Sidney OH 45365 937-492-1281 492-7280
TF: 800-543-6107 ■ *Web:* www.baumfolder.com

Black Clawson Converting Machinery Inc
46 N First St .... Fulton NY 13069 315-598-7121 593-0396
Web: www.davis-standard.com

Cranston Machinery Company Inc
2251 SE Oak Grove Blvd .... Oak Grove OR 97267 503-654-7751 654-7751
TF: 800-547-1012 ■ *Web:* www.cranston-machinery.com

Curt G Joa Inc
100 Crocker Ave PO Box 903 .... Sheboygan Falls WI 53085 920-467-6136 467-2924
Web: www.joa.com

Double E Co 319 Manley St .... West Bridgewater MA 02379 508-588-8099 580-2915
Web: ee-co.com

Entwistle Co Dietzco Div 6 Bigelow St .... Hudson MA 01749 508-481-4000 481-4004
TF: 800-445-8909 ■ *Web:* www.entwistleco.com

Faustel Inc W 194 N 11301 McCormick Dr .... Germantown WI 53022 262-253-3333 253-3334
Web: www.faustel.com

HG Weber & Company Inc 725 Fremont St .... Kiel WI 53042 920-894-2221
Web: www.holwegweber.com

Holyoke Machine Co 514 Main St PO Box 988 .... Holyoke MA 01040 413-534-5612 532-9244
Web: www.holyokemachine.com

Kadant Black Clawson Inc 7312 Central Pk Blvd .... Mason OH 45040 513-229-8100
Web: www.kadant.com

Kadant Inc 1 Technology Pk Dr .... Westford MA 01886 978-776-2000 635-1593
NYSE: KAI ■ *Web:* www.kadant.com

Kempsmith Machine Co 1819 S 71st St .... Milwaukee WI 53214 414-256-8160 476-0564
Web: www.kempsmith-dl.com

Magna Machine Co 11180 Southland Rd .... Cincinnati OH 45240 513-851-6900 851-6904
Web: www.magna-machine.com

MarquipWardUnited 1300 N Airport Rd .... Phillips wi 54555 715-339-2191 339-4469
Web: www.marquipwardunited.com

Maxson Automatic Machinery Co 70 Airport Rd .... Westerly RI 02891 401-596-0162 596-1050
Web: www.maxsonautomatic.com

Metso Paper USA Inc 25 Beloit St .... Aiken SC 29805 803-293-2100
Web: www.metso.com

Paco Winders Manufacturing Inc
2040 Bennett Rd .... Philadelphia PA 19116 215-673-6265 673-2027
Web: www.pacowinders.com

Paper Machinery Corp
8900 W Bradley Rd PO Box 240100 .... Milwaukee WI 53224 414-354-8050 354-8614
Web: www.papermc.com

Pemco Inc 3333 Crocker Ave .... Sheboygan WI 53082 920-458-2500 458-1265
TF: 888-310-1898 ■ *Web:* www.pemco-solutions.com

Sandusky International Inc 615 W Market St .... Sandusky OH 44870 419-626-5340 626-8674

Voith Paper Inc 2200 N Roemer Rd PO Box 2337 .... Appleton WI 54912 920-731-7724 997-9625
Web: voith.com

Zerand Corp 15800 W Overland Dr .... New Berlin WI 53151 262-827-3800
Web: cerutti.it

557 PAPER MILLS

See Also Paperboard Mills p. 2870; Pulp Mills p. 3007

Phone Fax

AbitibiBowater Inc 1155 Metcalfe St Ste 800 .... Montreal QC H3B5H2 514-875-2160
Web: www.resolutefp.com

Acupac Packaging Inc 55 Ramapo Vly Rd .... Mahwah NJ 07430 201-529-3434
Web: www.acupac.com

Advanced Poly Packaging Inc 1331 Emmitt Rd .... Akron OH 44306 330-785-4000
TF: 800-754-4403 ■ *Web:* www.advancedpoly.com

Phone Fax

Ahlstrom Filtration LLC
122 W Butler St Mount Holly Springs plant
.... Mount Holly Springs PA 17065 717-486-3438
Web: www.ahlstrom.com

Allen Packaging Co 1150 Valencia Ave .... Tustin CA 92780 714-259-0100
Web: www.allenpkg.com

Arjobex America Mill 10901 Westlake Dr .... Charlotte NC 28273 800-765-9278
TF: 800-765-9278 ■ *Web:* www.polyart.com

Armor Protective Packaging 951 Jones St .... Howell MI 48843 517-546-1117
TF: 800-365-1117 ■ *Web:* www.armorvci.com

Atlantic Tape Company Inc
611 Hwy 74 S Ste 300 .... Peachtree City GA 30269 770-461-3557
Web: www.atlantictape.com

Bag to Earth Inc 201 Richmond Blvd .... Napanee ON K7R3Z9 613-354-1330 354-1923
Web: bagtoearth.com

Bear Island Paper Company LLC
10026 Old Ridge Rd .... Ashland VA 23005 804-227-3394
Web: www.paperage.com

Boise Cascade LLC 1111 W Jefferson St Ste 300 .... Boise ID 83702 208-384-6161 384-7189
Web: www.bc.com

BPM Inc 200 W Front St .... Peshtigo WI 54157 715-582-4551 582-4853
TF: 800-826-0494 ■ *Web:* www.bpmpaper.com

Burrows Paper Corp 501 W Main St .... Little Falls NY 13365 315-823-2300 823-3892
TF: 800-272-7122 ■ *Web:* www.burrowspaper.com

Buschman Corp 4100 Payne Ave Ste 1 .... Cleveland OH 44103 216-431-6633
Web: buschmancorp.com

Cad Store Inc, The 15353 N 91st Ave .... Peoria AZ 85381 623-931-7936
TF: 800-576-6789 ■ *Web:* thecadstore.com

Cases By Source Inc 215 Island Rd .... Mahwah NJ 07430 201-831-0005
Web: www.casesbysource.com

Catalyst Paper Corp 3600 Lysander Ln 2nd Fl .... Richmond BC V7B1C3 604-247-4400 247-0512
TSE: CTL ■ *Web:* www.catalystpaper.com

Cauthorne Paper Co 12124 S Washington Hwy .... Ashland VA 23005 804-798-6999 798-6466
TF: 800-552-3011 ■ *Web:* www.cauthornepaper.com

Climax Manufacturing Co 7840 SR 26 .... Lowville NY 13367 315-376-8000 376-2034
TF: 800-225-4629 ■ *Web:* www.climaxpkg.com

Conder Flag Co 4705 Dwight Evans Rd .... Charlotte NC 28217 800-868-3524
TF: 800-868-3524 ■ *Web:* www.conderflags.com

Ecological Fibers Inc 40 Pioneer Dr .... Lunenburg MA 01462 978-537-0003 537-2238
Web: www.ecofibers.com

Economy Paper Company of Rochester Inc
1175 E Main St .... Rochester NY 14609 585-482-5340
Web: www.economypaper.com

FF Soucy Inc 191 Delage .... Riviere-du-Loup QC G5R3Z1 418-862-6941 867-1134
Web: www.ffsoucy.com

FiberMark North America, Inc.
161 Wellington Rd .... Brattleboro VT 05302 802-257-0365
TF Cust Svc: 800-784-8558 ■ *Web:* www.fibermark.com

Finch Paper LLC 1 Glen St .... Glens Falls NY 12801 518-793-2541
TF: 800-833-9983 ■ *Web:* www.finchpaper.com

Frankston Packaging 699 N Frankston Hwy .... Frankston TX 75763 903-876-2550
TF: 800-881-1495 ■ *Web:* frankstonpackaging.com

FutureMark Paper Co 13101 S Pulaski Rd .... Alsip IL 60803 708-272-8700

Gabriel Container Co
8844 S Millergrove Dr .... Santa Fe Springs CA 90670 562-699-1051 699-3284
Web: www.gabrielcontainer.com

Glatfelter 96 S George St Ste 500 .... York PA 17401 717-225-4711 846-7208
Web: www.glatfelter.com

Grays Harbor Paper LP 801 23rd St .... Hoquiam WA 98550 360-532-9600
Web: www.ghpaper.com

Green Field Paper Co
7196 Clairemont Mesa Blvd .... San Diego CA 92111 858-565-2585
TF: 888-402-9979 ■ *Web:* www.greenfieldpaper.com

Harvard Crimson Inc, The 14 Plympton St .... Cambridge MA 02138 617-576-6600
Web: thecrimson.com

Hollingsworth & Vose Co
112 Washington St .... East Walpole MA 02032 508-850-2000 668-3557
Web: www.hollingsworth-vose.com

Inland Empire Paper Co 3320 N Argonne .... Millwood WA 99212 509-924-1911 927-8461
TF: 866-437-7711 ■ *Web:* www.iepco.com

International Paper Co 6400 Poplar Ave .... Memphis TN 38197 901-419-9000
NYSE: IP ■ *TF Prod Info:* 800-223-1268 ■ *Web:* www.internationalpaper.com

Interstate Paper LLC 2366 Interstate Rd .... Riceboro GA 31323 912-884-3371
Web: www.interstatepaper.com

Interstate Resources Inc
1300 Wilson Blvd Ste 1075 .... Arlington VA 22209 703-243-3355 243-4681
Web: www.interstateresources.com

Just Packaging
450 Oak Tree Ave Ste 1 .... South Plainfield NJ 07080 908-753-6700
Web: www.justpackaging.com

K D M Enterprise LLC
820 Commerce Pkwy .... Carpentersville IL 60110 847-783-0333
TF: 877-591-9768 ■ *Web:* www.gokdm.com

KAPS-ALL Packaging Systems Inc 200 Mill Rd .... Riverhead NY 11901 631-727-0300
Web: www.kapsall.com

Kapstone 5600 Virginia Ave PO Box 118005 .... Charleston SC 29423 843-745-3000 745-3067
Web: kapstonepaper.com

KapStone Paper & Packaging Corp
1101 Skokie Blvd Ste 300 .... Northbrook IL 60062 847-239-8800 205-7551
NYSE: KS ■ *Web:* www.kapstonepaper.com

KapStone Paper and Packaging Corp
300 Fibre Way PO Box 639 .... Longview WA 98632 360-425-1550
Web: www.kapstonepaper.com

Katahdin Paper Co 50 Main St .... East Millinocket ME 04430 207-723-5131 723-2200

Keystone Adjustable Cap Co 1591 Hylton Rd .... Pennsauken NJ 08110 856-663-5740
Web: www.beringer.net

Kimberly-Clark Corp 351 Phelps Dr .... Irving TX 75038 972-281-1200
NYSE: KMB ■ *TF:* 888-525-8388 ■ *Web:* www.kimberly-clark.com

Kruger Inc 3285 Ch Bedford .... Montreal QC H3S1G5 514-737-1131 343-3124
Web: www.kruger.com

LBP Manufacturing Inc 1325 S Cicero Ave .... Cicero IL 60804 708-652-5600
Web: www.lbpmfg.com

				Phone	Fax

M&A Advisor LLC, The
108-18 Queens Blvd 2nd Fl ... Forest Hills NY 11375 718-997-7900
TF: 877-996-3743 ■ *Web:* www.maadvisor.com

Marq Packaging Systems Inc
3801 W Washington Ave ... Yakima WA 98903 509-966-4300
TF: 800-998-4301 ■ *Web:* www.marq.net

Maryland Paper Company LP
16144 Elliott Pkwy ... Williamsport MD 21795 301-223-6550 223-7730
Web: www.marylandpaper.com

Menshen Packaging USA Inc 21 Industrial Pk ... Waldwick NJ 07463 201-445-7436
Web: www.menshenusa.com

Merchants Paper Co 4625 SE 24th Ave ... Portland OR 97202 503-235-2171
TF: 800-605-6301 ■ *Web:* merchantspaper.com

Mercury Paper Inc 495 Radio Sta Rd ... Strasburg VA 22657 540-773-5355
Web: www.mercurypaper.com

Metro Packaging & Imaging Inc 5 Haul Rd ... Wayne NJ 07470 973-709-9100 709-9477
Web: metro-pi.com

Minas Basin Pulp & Power Co Ltd
53 Prince St PO Box 401 ... Hantsport NS B0P1P0 902-835-7100
Web: www.minas.ns.ca

Monadnock Paper Mills Inc 117 Antrim Rd ... Bennington NH 03442 603-588-3311 588-3158*
**Fax:* Sales ■ *TF Orders:* 800-221-2159 ■ *Web:* www.mpm.com

Nelson Jit Packaging Supplies Inc
4022 W Turney Ave Ste 3 ... Phoenix AZ 85019 623-939-3365
TF: 800-939-3647 ■ *Web:* www.nelsonjit.com

Newton Falls Fine Paper Company LLC
875 County Rt 60 ... Newton Falls NY 13666 315-848-3321

Norkol Inc & Converting 11650 W Grand Ave ... Northlake IL 60164 708-531-1000 531-0030
Web: www.norkol.com

Oakland Packaging & Supply
3200 Regatta Blvd Ste F ... Richmond CA 94804 510-307-4242
Web: www.oakpackaging.com

One Source Document Management Inc
905 Marconi Ave ... Ronkonkoma NY 11779 631-205-1200
Web: www.onesourcedoc.com

Pac Tech USA - Packaging Technologies Inc
328 Martin Ave ... Santa Clara CA 95050 408-588-1925
Web: www.pactech-usa.com

Palmetto Infusion Services LLC
172 Mcswain Dr Ste A ... West Columbia SC 29169 803-771-7740
Web: www.palmettoinfusion.com

Plastiform Packaging Inc 114 Beach St ... Rockaway NJ 07866 973-983-8900
Web: www.plastiformpkg.com

Potlatch Corp 601 W First Ave Ste 1600 ... Spokane WA 99201 509-835-1500
NASDAQ: PCH ■ *Web:* www.potlatchcorp.com

Pratt Industries USA 1800C Sarasota Pkwy ... Conyers GA 30013 770-918-5678 918-5679
TF: 800-835-2088 ■ *Web:* www.prattindustries.com

Roll Bond Converting 12855 Vly Branch Ln ... Dallas TX 75234 972-866-0880
Web: www.rbconverting.com

Sabin Robbins Paper Co 9365 Allen Rd ... West Chester OH 45069 513-874-5270 874-0667

Sandusky Packaging Corp 2016 George St ... Sandusky OH 44870 419-626-8520
Web: www.sanduskypackaging.com

Schweitzer-Mauduit International Inc
100 N Pt Ctr E Ste 600 ... Alpharetta GA 30022 770-569-4271
NYSE: SWM ■ *TF:* 800-514-0186 ■ *Web:* www.swmintl.com

Seaman Paper Co of Massachusetts
51 Main St ... Otter River MA 01436 978-632-1513 632-6319
Web: www.seamanpaper.com

Sierra Converting Corp 1400 Kleppe Ln ... Sparks NV 89431 775-331-8221
Web: www.sierraconverting.com

SP Newsprint Co 709 Papermill Rd ... Dublin GA 31027 478-272-1600 979-6615*
**Fax Area Code:* 404

Spicers Canada Ltd 200 Galcat Dr ... Vaughan ON L4L0B9 905-265-5000
Web: www.spicers.ca

Technocell Inc 3075 rue Bernier ... Drummondville QC J2C6Y4 819-475-0066
Web: www.felix-schoeller.com

Telmark Packaging Corp 30 Freneau Ave ... Matawan NJ 07747 732-739-9100
Web: www.telmarkpkg.com

Twin Rivers Paper Company Inc
707 Sable Oaks Dr Ste 010 ... South Portland ME 04106 207-523-2350
Web: www.twinriverspaper.com

Verso Corp 8540 Gander Creek Dr ... Miamisburg OH 45342 877-855-7243 242-9329*
**Fax Area Code:* 937 ■ *TF:* 877-855-7243 ■ *Web:* www.versoco.com

Verso Corp 6775 Lenox Ctr Ct Ste 400 ... Memphis TN 38115 877-837-7606 369-4174*
NYSE: VRS ■ **Fax Area Code:* 901 ■ *TF:* 877-837-7606 ■ *Web:* www.versoco.com

West Linn Paper Co 4800 Mill St ... West Linn OR 97068 503-557-6500 557-6616
TF: 800-989-3608 ■ *Web:* www.wlinpco.com

Western Pulp Products Co 5025 SW Hout St ... Corvallis OR 97333 541-757-1151
Web: www.westernpulp.com

Willard Packaging Company Inc
18940 Woodfield Rd ... Gaithersburg MD 20879 301-948-7700
Web: www.willardpackaging.com

Woodland Pulp LLC 144 Main St ... Baileyville ME 04694 207-427-3311

WR Rayson Company Inc 720 S Dickerson St ... Burgaw NC 28425 910-259-8100
Web: www.wrrayson.com

Xamax Industries Inc 63 Silvermine Rd ... Seymour CT 06483 203-888-7200 888-1002
TF: 888-926-2988 ■ *Web:* www.xamax.com

558 PAPER PRODUCTS - SANITARY

				Phone	Fax

Aspen Products Inc 4231 Clary Blvd ... Kansas City MO 64130 816-921-0234 924-1488
Web: www.aspenpro.com

Associated Hygienic Products LLC
3400 River Green Ct Ste 600 ... Duluth GA 30096 770-497-9800 623-8887
TF General: 800-757-0927 ■ *Web:* www.ahp-dsg.com

Atlas Paper Mills LLC 3301 NW 107th St ... Miami FL 33167 305-636-5740
TF: 800-562-2860 ■ *Web:* www.atlaspapermills.com

Bright of America Inc 300 Greenbrier Rd ... Summersville WV 26651 304-872-3000 872-3033

Erving Paper Mills 97 E Main St ... Erving MA 01344 413-422-2700
Web: ervingpaper.com

				Phone	Fax

Ferris Manufacturing Corp 16W300 83rd St ... Burr Ridge IL 60527 630-887-9797
Web: www.polymem.com

Georgia-Pacific Corp 133 Peachtree St NE ... Atlanta GA 30303 404-652-4000
Web: www.gp.com

Hoffmaster 2920 N Main St ... Oshkosh WI 54901 920-235-9330 235-1642
TF: 800-327-9774 ■ *Web:* www.hoffmaster.com

Kimberly-Clark Corp 351 Phelps Dr ... Irving TX 75038 972-281-1200
NYSE: KMB ■ *TF:* 888-525-8388 ■ *Web:* www.kimberly-clark.com

Kleen Test Products Inc
1611 Sunset Rd ... Port Washington WI 53074 262-284-6600 284-6623
Web: www.kleentest.com

Nice-Pak Products Inc 2 Nice-Pak Pk ... Orangeburg NY 10962 845-365-1700 365-1717
TF: 800-444-6725 ■ *Web:* www.nicepak.com

Orchids Paper Products Co 4826 Hunt St ... Pryor OK 74361 918-825-0616
NYSE: TIS ■ *Web:* www.orchidspaper.com

Personal Products Co
1 Johnson & Johnson Plaza ... New Brunswick NJ 08933 732-524-0400
Web: www.jnj.com/our_company/family_of_companies

Potlatch Corp 601 W First Ave Ste 1600 ... Spokane WA 99201 509-835-1500
NASDAQ: PCH ■ *Web:* www.potlatchcorp.com

Precision Paper Converters LLC
2600 Northridge Dr ... Kaukauna WI 54130 920-462-0050
Web: www.cornerstone-business.com

Principle Business Enterprises Inc
PO Box 129 ... Dunbridge OH 43414 419-352-1551 352-8340
TF: 800-467-3224 ■ *Web:* www.tranquilityproducts.com

Roses Southwest Papers Inc
1701 Second St SW ... Albuquerque NM 87102 505-842-0134 242-0342
Web: www.rosessouthwestpapers.com

SCA Americas 2929 Arch St Ste 2600 ... Philadelphia PA 19104 610-499-3700 499-3391
TF Cust Svc: 800-328-9043 ■ *Web:* www.sca.com

Tranzonic Cos
26301 Curtiss Wright Pkwy Ste 200 ... Cleveland OH 44143 216-535-4300 831-5647
Web: www.tranzonic.com

Wausau Paper Corp 100 Paper Pl ... Mosinee WI 54455 715-693-4470 692-2082
NYSE: WPP ■ *TF:* 800-723-0008 ■ *Web:* www.wausaupaper.com

559 PAPER PRODUCTS - WHOL

				Phone	Fax

American Hotel Register Co
100 S Milwaukee Ave ... Vernon Hills IL 60061 847-743-3000 688-9108*
**Fax Area Code:* 800 ■ **Fax:* Sales ■ *TF:* 800-323-5686 ■ *Web:* www.americanhotel.com

American Paper & Twine Co
7400 Cockrill Bend Blvd ... Nashville TN 37209 615-350-9000 413-5055*
**Fax Area Code:* 877 ■ *TF:* 800-251-2437 ■ *Web:* shopapt.com

Atlantic Paper & Twine Co Inc 85 York Ave ... Pawtucket RI 02904 401-725-0950
TF: 800-613-0950 ■ *Web:* www.atlanticpaper.com

BGR Inc 6392 Gano Rd ... West Chester OH 45069 513-755-7100 755-7855
TF: 800-628-9195 ■ *Web:* bgr.us

Brame Specialty Company Inc PO Box 27 ... Durham NC 27702 919-683-1331 682-6034
TF: 800-533-2041 ■ *Web:* www.brameco.com

Butler-Dearden Paper Service Inc
PO Box 1069 ... Boylston MA 01505 508-869-9000 869-0211
TF: 800-634-7070 ■ *Web:* www.butlerdearden.com

Central Paper Products Co Inc
350 Gay St Brown Ave Industrial Pk ... Manchester NH 03103 603-624-4065 624-8795
TF: 800-339-4065 ■ *Web:* www.centralpaper.com

D-K Trading Corp PO Box E ... Clarks Summit PA 18411 570-586-9662
Web: www.dk-t.com

Dacotah Paper Co 3940 15th Ave NW ... Fargo ND 58102 701-281-1734 281-9799
TF: 800-270-6352 ■ *Web:* www.dacotahpaper.com

Ernest Paper Products 5777 Smithway St ... Commerce CA 90040 800-233-7788
TF: 800-233-7788 ■ *Web:* www.ernestpackaging.com

Fleetwood-Signode 3624 W Lake Ave ... Glenview IL 60026 630-268-9999
TF: 800-862-7997 ■ *Web:* www.fleetsig.com

Garland C Norris Co 1101 Terry Rd ... Apex NC 27502 919-387-1059 387-1325
TF: 800-331-8920 ■ *Web:* www.gcnorris.com

Gem State Paper & Supply Co
1801 Highland Ave E ... Twin Falls ID 83303 208-733-6081 734-9870
TF: 800-727-2737 ■ *Web:* www.gemstatepaper.com

George H Swatek Inc 1095 Edgewater Ave ... Ridgefield NJ 07657 201-941-2400 941-8681
Web: www.ghswatek.com

H. T. Berry Co Inc PO Box B ... Canton MA 02021 781-828-6000 828-9788
TF: 800-736-2206 ■ *Web:* www.htberry.com

Harder Corp 7029 Raywood Rd ... Monona WI 53713 608-271-5127 271-4677
Web: www.hardercorp.com

Hathaway Inc PO Box 1618 ... Waynesboro VA 22980 540-949-8285 943-7619
Web: www.hathawaypaper.com

Heartland Paper Co 808 W Cherokee St ... Sioux Falls SD 57104 605-336-1190 332-8378
TF Cust Svc: 800-843-7922 ■ *Web:* www.heartland-paper.com

Johnston Paper Co 2 Eagle Dr ... Auburn NY 13021 315-253-8435 253-8744
TF: 800-800-7123 ■ *Web:* www.johnstonpaper.com

Landsberg Orora 1640 S Greenwood Ave ... Montebello CA 90640 323-832-2000
TF Cust Svc: 888-526-3723 ■ *Web:* www.landsberg.com

Leonard Paper Co 725 N Haven St ... Baltimore MD 21205 800-327-5547 563-0249*
**Fax Area Code:* 410 ■ *TF Cust Svc:* 800-327-5547 ■ *Web:* www.leonardpaper.com

M Conley Co 1312 Fourth St SE ... Canton OH 44707 330-456-8243 588-2572*
**Fax:* Cust Svc ■ *TF:* 800-362-6001 ■ *Web:* www.mconley.com

Mainland preparatory Academy 319 Newman Rd ... La Marque TX 77568 409-934-9100 934-9130
Web: www.mainpaperparty.com

Max-Pak LLC 2808 New Tampa Hwy ... Lakeland FL 33815 863-682-0123 683-7895
Web: www.maxpak.cc

Mayfield Paper Co 1115 S Hill St ... San Angelo TX 76903 325-653-1444 653-7031
TF: 800-725-1441 ■ *Web:* www.mayfieldpaper.com

NAPCO 2400 Cantrell Rd Ste 116 ... Little Rock AR 72202 501-374-5884 374-5129

National Paper & Sanitary Supply
2511 S 156th Cir ... Omaha NE 68130 402-330-5507 330-4109
TF: 800-647-2737 ■ *Web:* catalog.nationalew.com/catalog

Nichols Paper & Supply Company Inc
PO Box 291 ... Muskegon MI 49443 231-799-2120
TF: 800-442-0213 ■ *Web:* www.enichols.com

Phone | Fax

Pacific Packaging Products Inc
24 Industrial Way, Wilmington MA 01887 978-657-9100 658-4933
TF: 800-777-0300 ■ *Web:* www.pacificpkg.com

Packaging Distribution Services Inc (PDS)
2308 Sunset Rd, Des Moines IA 50321 515-243-3156 243-1741
TF: 800-747-2699 ■ *Web:* www.pdspack.com

Paper Products Company Inc
36 Terminal Way, Pittsburgh PA 15219 412-481-6200 481-4787
Web: www.paperproducts-pgh.com

Paterson Pacific Parchment Co 625 Greg St, Sparks NV 89431 775-353-3000 456-8104*
**Fax Area Code:* 800 ■ *TF:* 800-678-8104 ■ *Web:* www.patersonpaper.com

Perez Trading Company Inc 3490 NW 125th St, Miami FL 33167 305-769-0761 681-7963
Web: www.pereztrading.com

Phillips Distribution Inc
3000 E Houston St, San Antonio TX 78220 210-227-2397 222-0790*
**Fax Area Code:* 361 ■ *TF:* 800-580-2397 ■ *Web:* www.phillipsdistribution.com

Pollock Paper & Packaging 1 Pollock Pl, Grand Prairie TX 75050 972-263-2126 262-4737
TF Cust Svc: 800-843-7320 ■ *Web:* www.pollockpaper.com

S. Freedman & Sons Inc 3322 Pennsy Dr, Landover MD 20785 301-322-5000 772-7563
TF: 800-545-7277 ■ *Web:* www.sfreedman.com

Saint Louis Paper & Box Co
3843 Garfield Ave, Saint Louis MO 63113 314-531-7900 531-0968
TF: 800-779-7901 ■ *Web:* www.stlpaper.com

Schwarz 8338 Austin Ave, Morton Grove IL 60053 800-323-4903 966-1271*
**Fax Area Code:* 847 ■ *TF:* 800-323-4903 ■ *Web:* www.schwarz.com

Shorr Packaging Inc 800 N Commerce St, Aurora IL 60504 630-978-1000
TF: 888-885-0055 ■ *Web:* www.shorr.com

Snyder Paper Corp
250 26th St Dr SE PO Box 758, Hickory NC 28603 828-328-2501 222-8562*
**Fax Area Code:* 800 ■ *TF:* 800-222-8562

TSN Inc 4001 Salazar Way PO Box 679, Frederick CO 80530 303-530-0600 530-1919
TF General: 888-997-5959 ■ *Web:* bunzldistribution.com

Unisource Worldwide Inc
6600 Governors Lake Pkwy, Norcross GA 30071 770-447-9000 734-2000
TF: 800-864-7687 ■ *Web:* www.unisourceworldwide.com

Western Paper Distributors Inc
11551 E 45th Ave Ste A, Denver CO 80239 303-371-6000 371-6111
Web: www.western-paper.com

Xpedx 6285 Tri-Ridge Blvd, Loveland OH 45140 513-965-2900 965-2849
Web: www.xpedx.com

560 PAPERBOARD & CARDBOARD - DIE-CUT

Phone | Fax

Alvah Bushnell Co 519 E Chelten Ave, Philadelphia PA 19144 215-842-9520 843-7725
TF: 800-255-7434 ■ *Web:* www.bushnellco.com

Blanks/USA Inc 7700 68th Ave N #7, Minneapolis MN 55428 800-328-7311
TF: 800-328-7311 ■ *Web:* www.laserblanks.com

Crescent Cardboard Company LLC
100 W Willow Rd, Wheeling IL 60090 847-537-3400 537-7153
TF: 888-293-3956 ■ *Web:* www.crescentcardboard.com

Demco Inc 4810 Forest Run Rd, Madison WI 53704 608-241-1201 241-1799
TF Orders: 800-356-1200 ■ *Web:* www.demco.com

GBS Filing Solutions 224 Morges Rd, Malvern OH 44644 330-494-5330
TF: 800-873-4427 ■ *Web:* www.gbscorp.com

Tap Packaging Solutions 2160 Superior Ave, Cleveland OH 44114 216-781-6000
TF: 800-827-5679 ■ *Web:* www.tap-usa.com

Topps Company Inc 1 Whitehall St, New York NY 10004 212-376-0300 376-0573
TF: 800-489-9149 ■ *Web:* www.topps.com

University Products Inc 517 Main St, Holyoke MA 01040 413-532-3372 532-9281*
**Fax Area Code:* 800 ■ *TF:* 800-628-1912 ■ *Web:* www.universityproducts.com

Warren Industries Inc 3100 Mt Pleasant St, Racine WI 53404 262-639-7800 639-0920
Web: www.wrnind.com

Westcott Displays Inc 450 Amsterdam St, Detroit MI 48202 313-872-1200 875-3295
Web: www.westcottdisplays.com

Xertrex International Inc Tabbies Div
1530 W Glenlake Ave, Itasca IL 60143 630-773-4160
Web: www.tabbies.com

561 PAPERBOARD MILLS

See Also Paper Mills p. 2868; Pulp Mills p. 3007

Phone | Fax

Cascades Inc 404 Marie-Victorin Blvd, Kingsey Falls QC J0A1B0 819-363-5100 363-5155
TSE: CAS ■ *TF:* 800-361-4070 ■ *Web:* www.cascades.com

Century Packaging Inc 42 Edgeboro Rd, East Brunswick NJ 08816 732-249-6600
Web: www.centurypackaginginc.com

Combined Technologies Inc
13970 W Polo Trl Dr, Lake Forest IL 60045 847-968-4855
TF: 877-968-4855 ■ *Web:* ctipack.com

DEX Products Inc
2019 E Monte Vista Ave Ste 500, Vacaville CA 95688 707-451-7864
Web: www.dexbaby.com

Dorn Color Inc 11555 Berea Rd, Cleveland OH 44102 216-634-2252
Web: dorncolor.com

FiberMark Inc 161 Wellington Rd, Brattleboro VT 05301 802-257-0365
Web: www.fibermark.com

FiberMark North America, Inc.
161 Wellington Rd, Brattleboro VT 05302 802-257-0365
TF Cust Svc: 800-784-8558 ■ *Web:* www.fibermark.com

Globe Die-Cutting Products Inc
76 Liberty St, Metuchen NJ 08840 732-494-7744
Web: www.globediecutting.com

International Paper Co 6400 Poplar Ave, Memphis TN 38197 901-419-9000
NYSE: IP ■ *TF Prod Info:* 800-223-1268 ■ *Web:* www.internationalpaper.com

Interpress Technologies Inc
1120 Del Paso Rd, Sacramento CA 95834 916-929-9771
Web: www.iptec.com

KapStone Paper and Packaging Corp
300 Fibre Way PO Box 639, Longview WA 98632 360-425-1550
Web: www.kapstonepaper.com

Phone | Fax

Los Angeles Paper Box 6027 S Eastern Ave, Commerce CA 90040 323-685-8900
Web: www.lapb.com

Lydall Inc 1 Colonial Rd, Manchester CT 06042 860-646-1233 646-4917
NYSE: LDL ■ *Web:* www.lydall.com

Newark Group 20 Jackson Dr, Cranford NJ 07016 908-276-4000 276-9126
Web: www.newarkgroup.com

Newman & Company Inc 6101 Tacony St, Philadelphia PA 19135 215-333-8700 332-8586
TF: 800-523-3256 ■ *Web:* newmanpaperboard.com

Norampac Industries Inc
4001 Packard Rd, Niagara Falls NY 14303 716-285-3681

Oji Intertech Inc 906 W Hanley Rd, North Manchester IN 46962 260-982-1544
Web: www.ojiintertech.com

Packaging Corp of America
1955 W Field Ct, Lake Forest IL 60045 800-456-4725
NYSE: PKG ■ *TF:* 800-456-4725 ■ *Web:* www.packagingcorp.com

Pactiv Corp 1900 W Field Ct, Lake Forest IL 60045 847-482-2000 482-4738
TF: 888-828-2850 ■ *Web:* www.pactiv.com

Paper Cut Inc, The 234 W Northland Ave, Appleton WI 54911 920-954-6210
Web: www.thepapercut.com

PaperWorks Industries Inc
5000 Flat Rock Rd, Philadelphia PA 19127 215-984-7000
Web: www.paperworksindustries.com

Potlatch Corp 601 W First Ave Ste 1600, Spokane WA 99201 509-835-1500
NASDAQ: PCH ■ *Web:* www.potlatchcorp.com

Rock-Tenn Alliance Division
5950 Grassy Creek Blvd, Winston-salem NC 27105 336-661-1700
Web: gallery.alliancerocktenn.com

Specialty Roll Products Inc 601 25th Ave, Meridian MS 39302 601-693-1771
Web: www.specialtyroll.com

Superior Packaging Solutions
26858 Almond Ave, Redlands CA 92374 800-680-2393
TF: 844-792-2626 ■ *Web:* www.sps4pkg.com

United States Box Corp 1296 Mccarter Hwy, Newark NJ 07104 973-481-2000
Web: www.usbox.com

WinterBell Co 2018 Brevard Rd, High Point NC 27263 336-887-2651
TF: 800-685-2957 ■ *Web:* www.winterbell.com

562 PARKING SERVICE

Phone | Fax

717 Parking Svc Inc 1523 N Franklin St, Tampa FL 33602 813-228-7722
Web: 717parking.com

Ace Parking Management Inc 645 Ash St, San Diego CA 92101 619-233-6624 233-0741
TF General: 855-223-7275 ■ *Web:* www.aceparking.com

Alco Parking Corp 501 Martindale St, Pittsburgh PA 15212 412-323-4455

Allpro Parking LLC
465 Main St Lafayette Court Bldg
Ste 200Annex, Buffalo NY 14203 716-849-7275
Web: www.allproparking.com

B & J Parking Lot Maintenance
12207 Inkster Rd, Taylor MI 48180 734-941-7570
Web: www.bandjmaint.com

Baltimore County Revenue Authority
115 Towsontown Blvd E, Baltimore MD 21286 410-887-3127 296-7459
TF: 888-246-5384 ■ *Web:* www.baltimoregolfing.com

City Center Parking Inc
920 S.W. Sixth Ave Ste 223, Portland OR 97204 503-221-1666
Web: www.citycenterparking.com

Classic Parking Inc 3208 Royal St, Los Angeles CA 90007 213-742-1238
Web: classicparking.com

Colonial Parking Inc
1050 Thomas Jefferson St NW Ste 100, Washington DC 20007 202-295-8100 295-8111
TF: 877-777-4778 ■ *Web:* www.ecolonial.com

Denison Parking
36 S Pennsylvania St Ste 200, Indianapolis IN 46204 317-633-4003 655-3101
Web: www.denisonparking.com

Diamond Parking Inc 605 First Ave Ste 6000, Seattle WA 98104 206-284-3100
Web: www.diamondparking.com

Douglas Parking LLC 1721 Webster St, Oakland CA 94612 510-444-7412
Web: www.douglasparking.com

Edison Properties LLC 100 Washington St, Newark NJ 07102 973-643-0895 643-2169
TF: 888-727-5327 ■ *Web:* www.parkfast.com

GGMC Parking LLC 1651 Third Ave, New York NY 10128 212-996-6363
Web: www.ggmcparking.com

Imperial Parking Corp
601 W Cordova St Ste 300, Vancouver BC V6B1G1 604-681-7311
Web: www.impark.com

Integrity Parking Systems LLC
9828 E Washington St, Chagrin Falls OH 44023 440-543-4123
Web: integrityparking.com

InterPark 200 N LaSalle St Ste 1400, Chicago IL 60601 312-935-2800 935-2999
Web: www.interparkholdings.com

Landmark Parking Inc 33 S Gay St, Baltimore MD 21202 410-837-5600
Web: landmarkparking.com

Lanier Parking Solutions 233 Peachtree St NE, Atlanta GA 30303 404-881-6076 881-6077
Web: www.lanierparking.com

LAZ Parking Ltd 15 Lewis St, Hartford CT 06103 860-522-7641
Web: www.lazparking.com

Loop Parking 1430 W Lake St, Minneapolis MN 55408 612-333-2293
Web: www.loopparking.com

Miami Parking System 190 Ne Third St, Miami FL 33132 305-373-6789
Web: miamiparking.com

Modern Parking Inc
1200 Wilshire Blvd Ste 300, Los Angeles CA 90017 213-482-8400
Web: www.modernparking.com

Park 'N Fly 2060 Mt Paran Rd Ste 207, Atlanta GA 30327 800-325-4863 264-1115*
**Fax Area Code:* 404 ■ **Fax:* Hum Res ■ *TF Cust Svc:* 800-325-4863 ■ *Web:* www.pnf.com

Park To Fly Inc 7800 Narcoossee Rd, Orlando FL 32822 407-851-8875 851-8011
TF: 888-851-8875 ■ *Web:* www.parktofly.com

Parking Auth City of Rahway 67 Lewis St, Rahway NJ 07065 732-381-8778
Web: www.rahwayparking.org

Phone Fax

Parking Company of America (PCA)
11101 Lakewood Blvd .... Downey CA 90241 562-862-2118 862-4409
Web: www.parkpca.com

Parking Company of America Inc
250 W Court St Ste 200E .... Cincinnati OH 45202 513-241-0415
Web: www.pca-star.com

Parking Concepts Inc 12 Mauchly Bldg I .... Irvine CA 92618 949-753-7525
Web: parkingconcepts.com

Parking Management Inc
1725 Desales St NW Ste 300 .... Washington DC 20036 202-785-9191
Web: www.pmi-parking.com

Parking Panda Corp 3422 Fait Ave .... Baltimore MD 21224 800-232-6415
TF: 800-232-6415 ■ *Web:* www.parkingpanda.com

Parking Solutions Inc 850 Michigan Ave .... Columbus OH 43215 614-469-7000
Web: www.parkingsolutionsinc.com

Parkway Corp 150 N Broad St .... Philadelphia PA 19102 215-575-4000
Web: www.parkwaycorp.com

Penn Parking Inc 7257 Pkwy Dr Ste 100 .... Hanover MD 21076 410-782-9110
Web: pennparking.com

PPS Parking Inc 1800 E Garry Ave Ste 107 .... Santa Ana CA 92705 949-223-8707
Web: www.occruiser.com

Quality IP LLC 145 S River St .... Kent OH 44240 330-931-4141
Web: www.qualityip.com

Republic Parking System
633 Chestnut St Ste 2000 .... Chattanooga TN 37450 423-756-2771 265-5728
Web: republicparking.com

Robbins Parking Service Ltd 1102 Fort St .... Victoria BC V8V3K8 250-382-4411
Web: www.robbinsparking.com

Southern Parking Inc
420 S Dixie Hwy .... Hallandale Beach FL 33309 305-866-3409
Web: southernparkinginc.com

St. Louis Parking Company Inc
505 N Seventh St Ste 2405 .... Saint Louis MO 63101 314-241-7777
Web: stlouisparking.com

Standard Parking Corp
900 N Michigan Ave Ste 1600 .... Chicago IL 60611 312-274-2000 640-6169*
**Fax: Hum Res* ■ *TF:* 888-700-7275 ■ *Web:* spplus.com/?ref=standard

Sunset Parking Service Inc
2151 Newcastle Ave .... Cardiff CA 92007 760-753-4004
Web: www.sunsetparking.com

Us Airport Parking 18000 E 81st Ave .... Commerce City CO 80022 303-371-7575
Web: www.usairportparking.com

USA Parking Systems Inc
1330 SE Fourth Ave Ste D .... Fort Lauderdale FL 33316 954-524-6500
Web: www.usaparking.net

Valet Park of America 185 Spring St .... Springfield MA 01105 413-827-8916
Web: www.valetparkofamerica.com

Valet Parking Service 1335 S Flower St .... Los Angeles CA 90015 213-342-3388 222-0981
TF: 800-794-7275 ■ *Web:* www.valetparkingservice.com

PARKS - AMUSEMENT

See Amusement Park Companies p. 1734; Amusement Parks p. 1735

563 PARKS - NATIONAL - CANADA

Phone Fax

Parks Canada 25-7-N Eddy St. .... Gatineau QC K1A0M5 613-860-1251
TF: 888-773-8888 ■ *Web:* www.pc.gc.ca/eng/index.aspx

Auyuittuq National Park PO Box 353 .... Pangnirtung NU X0A0R0 867-473-2500 473-8612
Web: www.pc.gc.ca

Banff National Park PO Box 900 .... Banff AB T1L1K2 403-762-1550 762-1551
TF: 877-737-3783 ■ *Web:* www.pc.gc.ca

Battle of the Windmill National Historic Site
370 Vankoughnet St .... Prescott ON K0E1T0 613-925-2896 925-1536
Web: www.pc.gc.ca/eng/lhn-nhs/on/windmill/index.aspx

Bellevue House National Historic Site
35 Centre St .... Kingston ON K7L4E5 613-545-8666 545-8721
Web: www.pc.gc.ca/eng/lhn-nhs/on/bellevue/index.aspx

Bethune Memorial House National Historic Site
235 John St N .... Gravenhurst ON P1P1G4 705-687-4261 687-4935
Web: www.pc.gc.ca/eng/lhn-nhs/on/bethune/index.aspx

Bois Blanc Island Lighthouse National Historic Site
C/O Ft Malden Nhsc .... Amherstburg ON N9V2Z2 519-736-5416 736-6603
Web: www.pc.gc.ca/eng/lhn-nhs/on/boisblanc/index.aspx

Canso Islands National Historic Site
1465 Union St .... Canso NS B0E1B0 902-366-3136 295-3496
Web: www.pc.gc.ca/eng/lhn-nhs/ns/canso/index.aspx

Carleton Martello Tower National Historic Site
454 Whipple St .... Saint John NB E2M2R3 506-636-4011 636-4574
Web: www.pc.gc.ca/eng/lhn-nhs/nb/carleton/index.aspx

Fathom Five National Marine Park
PO Box 189 .... Tobermory ON N0H2R0 519-596-2233 596-2298
Web: www.pc.gc.ca

Fort Langley National Historic Site
23433 Mavis Ave .... Fort Langley BC V1M2R5 604-513-4777 513-4798
Web: www.pc.gc.ca/eng/lhn-nhs/bc/langley/index.aspx

Fort Malden National Historic Site
100 Laird Ave .... Amherstburg ON N9V2Z2 519-736-5416 736-6603
Web: www.pc.gc.ca/eng/lhn-nhs/on/malden/index.aspx

Fort McNab National Historic Site
C/O Halifax Citadel National Historic Site .... Halifax NS B3K5M7 902-426-5080 426-4228
Web: www.pc.gc.ca/eng/lhn-nhs/ns/mcnab/contact.aspx

Fort Rodd Hill National Historic Site
603 Ft Rodd Hill Rd .... Victoria BC V9C2W8 250-478-5849 478-2816
Web: www.pc.gc.ca/eng/lhn-nhs/bc/fortroddhill/index.aspx

Fort Wellington National Historic Site
370 Vankoughnet St .... Prescott ON K0E1T0 613-925-2896 925-1536
Web: www.pc.gc.ca/eng/lhn-nhs/on/wellington/index.aspx

Glacier National Park PO Box 350 .... Revelstoke BC V0E2S0 250-837-7500 837-7536
TF: 866-787-6221 ■ *Web:* www.pc.gc.ca

Gwaii Haanas National Park Reserve &Haida Heritage Site
PO Box 37 .... Queen Charlotte BC V0T1S0 250-559-8818 559-8366
Web: www.pc.gc.ca

HMCS Haida National Historic Site
57 Discovery Dr .... Hamilton ON L8L8K4 905-526-6742 526-9734
Web: www.pc.gc.ca/eng/lhn-nhs/on/haida/index.aspx

Inverarden House National Historic Site
370 Vankoughnet St .... Prescott ON K0E1T0 613-925-2896 925-1536
Web: www.pc.gc.ca/eng/lhn-nhs/on/inverarden/index.aspx

Kluane National Park & Reserve of Canada
PO Box 5495 .... Haines Junction YT Y0B1L0 867-634-7250 634-7208
TF: 877-852-3100 ■ *Web:* www.pc.gc.ca

Laurier House National Historic Site
335 Laurier Ave E .... Ottawa ON K1N6R4 613-992-8142 947-4851
Web: www.pc.gc.ca/eng/lhn-nhs/on/laurier/index.aspx

Lower Fort Garry National Historic Site
5925 Hwy 9 .... Saint Andrews MB R1A4A8 204-785-6050 482-5887
Web: www.pc.gc.ca/eng/lhn-nhs/mb/fortgarry/index.aspx

Manoir-Papineau National Historic Site
500 Notre-Dame .... Montebello QC J0V1L0 819-423-6965 423-6455
Web: www.pc.gc.ca/eng/lhn-nhs/qc/manoirpapineau/index.aspx

Mingan Archipelago National Park Reserve of Canada
1340 de la Digue St .... Havre-Saint-Pierre QC G0G1P0 418-538-3331 538-3595
TF: 877-737-3783 ■ *Web:* www.pc.gc.ca/pn-np/qc/mingan/index.aspx

Mount Revelstoke National Park of Canada
PO Box 350 .... Revelstoke BC V0E2S0 250-837-7500 837-7536
TF: 866-787-6221 ■ *Web:* www.pc.gc.ca

Point Pelee National Park of Canada
407 Monarch Ln RR 1 .... Leamington ON N8H3V4 519-322-2365 322-1277
TF: 888-773-8888 ■ *Web:* www.pc.gc.ca/pn-np/on/pelee/index.aspx

Prince Albert National Park of Canada
Northern Prairies Field Unit
PO Box 100 .... Waskesiu Lake SK S0J2Y0 306-663-4522
TF Campground Resv: 877-737-3783 ■ *Web:* www.pc.gc.ca/pn-np/sk/princealbert/index.aspx

Prince Edward Island National Park of Canada
2 Palmers Ln .... Charlottetown PE C1A5V8 902-672-6350 672-6370
TF Campground Resv: 800-663-7192 ■
Web: www.pc.gc.ca/pn-np/pe/pei-ipe/natcul/natcul3.aspx

Pukaskwa National Park of Canada
PO Box 212 .... Heron Bay ON P0T1R0 807-229-0801 229-2097
Web: www.pc.gc.ca

Queenston Heights National Historic Site of Canada
26 Queen St .... Niagara-On-The-Lake ON L0S1J0 905-468-4257 468-4638
Web: www.pc.gc.ca/eng/lhn-nhs/on/queenston/index.aspx

Quttinirpaaq National Park PO Box 278 .... Iqaluit NU X0A0H0 867-975-4673 975-4674
Web: www.pc.gc.ca/pn-np/nu/quttinirpaaq/contact.aspx

Riding Mountain Park East Gate Registration Complex National Historic Site of Canada
1 Wasagaming Dr .... Wasagaming MB R0J2H0 204-848-7275 848-2596
Web: www.pc.gc.ca/eng/lhn-nhs/mb/eastgate/index.aspx

Riel House National Historic Site of Canada
330 River Rd .... Winnipeg MB R2M3Z8 204-257-1783 252-3766*
**Fax Area Code:* 867 ■ *TF:* 877-852-3100

Saguenay-Saint Lawrence Marine Park
182 Rue de l'Eglise PO Box 220 .... Tadoussac QC G0T2A0 418-235-4703 235-4686
Web: pc.gc.ca/amnc%2dnmca/qc/saguenay

Sault Ste Marie Canal National Historic Site of Canada
1 Canal Dr .... Sault Sainte Marie ON P6A6W4 705-941-6262 941-6206
Web: www.pc.gc.ca/eng/lhn-nhs/on/ssmarie/index.aspx

Sirmilik National Park PO Box 300 .... Pond Inlet NU X0A0S0 867-899-8092 899-8104
Web: www.pc.gc.ca

St. Andrews Blockhouse National Historic Site of Canada
454 Whipple St .... Saint John NB E2M2R3 506-636-4011 636-4574
Web: www.pc.gc.ca/eng/lhn-nhs/nb/standrews/index.aspx

Thousand Islands National Park of Canada
2 County Rd 5 .... Mallorytown ON K0E1R0 613-923-5261 923-1021
Web: www.pc.gc.ca

Tuktut Nogait National Park of Canada
PO Box 91 .... Paulatuk NT X0E1N0 867-580-3233 580-3234
Web: www.pc.gc.ca

Wapusk National Park of Canada PO Box 127 .... Churchill MB R0B0E0 204-675-8863 675-2026
TF: 888-773-8888 ■ *Web:* www.pc.gc.ca/pn-np/mb/wapusk/index.aspx

Wood Buffalo National Park of Canada
PO Box 750 .... Fort Smith NT X0E0P0 867-872-7900 872-3910
Web: www.pc.gc.ca

564 PARKS - NATIONAL - US

See Also Nature Centers, Parks, Other Natural Areas p. 1813; Cemeteries - National p. 1897; Parks - State p. 2878

Alabama

Phone Fax

Horseshoe Bend National Military Park
11288 Horseshoe Bend Rd .... Daviston AL 36256 256-234-7111 329-9905
Web: www.nps.gov

Little River Canyon National Preserve
2141 Gault Ave N .... Fort Payne AL 35967 256-845-9605 997-9129
Web: www.nps.gov

Russell Cave National Monument
3729 County Rd 98 .... Bridgeport AL 35740 256-495-2672 495-9220
TF: 866-705-5711 ■ *Web:* www.nps.gov/ruca

Tuskegee Airmen National Historic Site
1616 Chappie James Ave .... Tuskegee AL 36083 334-724-0922 724-0952
Web: www.nps.gov

Tuskegee Institute National Historic Site
1212 W Montgomery Rd .... Tuskegee Institute AL 36088 334-727-3200 727-1448
Web: www.nps.gov/tuin

Alaska

Phone Fax

Alagnak Wild River PO Box 245 .... King Salmon AK 99613 907-246-3305 246-2116
Web: www.nps.gov/alag

	City	State	Zip	Phone	Fax
Aniakchak National Monument & Preserve PO Box 245 *Web:* www.nps.gov/ania	King Salmon	AK	99613	907-246-3305	246-2116
Cape Krusenstern National Monument PO Box 1029 *Web:* www.nps.gov/cakr	Kotzebue	AK	99752	907-442-3890	442-8316
Denali National Park & Preserve PO Box 9 *Web:* www.nps.gov	Denali Park	AK	99755	907-733-9119	683-9617
Gates of the Arctic National Park & Preserve 4175 Geist Rd *TF:* 866-869-6887 ■ *Web:* www.nps.gov/gaar	Fairbanks	AK	99709	907-457-5752	455-0601
Katmai National Park & Preserve King Salmon Mall PO Box 7 *Web:* www.nps.gov/katm	King Salmon	AK	99613	907-246-3305	246-2116
Klondike Gold Rush National Historical Park Second St & Broadway PO Box 517 *Web:* www.nps.gov/klgo	Skagway	AK	99840	907-983-2921	983-9249
Kobuk Valley National Park PO Box 1029 *Web:* www.nps.gov/kova	Kotzebue	AK	99752	907-442-3890	442-8316
Lake Clark National Park & Preserve 240 W Fifth Ave Ste 236 *Web:* www.nps.gov	Anchorage	AK	99501	907-644-3626	644-3810
National Park Service Regional Offices *Alaska Region* 240 W Fifth Ave Ste 114 *Web:* nps.gov	Anchorage	AK	99501	907-644-3510	644-3816
Noatak National Preserve PO Box 1029 *Web:* www.nps.gov/noat	Kotzebue	AK	99752	907-442-3890	442-8316
Sitka National Historical Park 106 Metlakatla St *Web:* www.nps.gov	Sitka	AK	99835	907-747-6281	747-5938
Wrangell-Saint Elias National Park & Preserve Mile 1068 Richardson Hwy PO Box 439 *TF:* 866-705-5711 ■ *Web:* www.nps.gov/wrst	Copper Center	AK	99573	907-822-5234	822-7216
Yukon-Charley Rivers National Preserve 4175 Geist Rd *Web:* www.nps.gov/yuch	Fairbanks	AK	99709	907-457-5752	455-0601

Arizona

	City	State	Zip	Phone	Fax
Canyon de Chelly National Monument PO Box 588 *Web:* www.nps.gov	Chinle	AZ	86503	928-674-5500	674-5507
Casa Grande Ruins National Monument 1100 W Ruins Dr *TF:* 877-642-4743 ■ *Web:* www.nps.gov	Coolidge	AZ	85128	520-723-3172	723-7209
Chiricahua National Monument 12856 E Rhyolite Creek Rd *TF:* 877-444-6777 ■ *Web:* www.nps.gov/chir	Willcox	AZ	85643	520-824-3560	824-3421
Coronado National Memorial 4101 E Montezuma Canyon Rd *Web:* www.nps.gov/coro	Hereford	AZ	85615	520-366-5515	366-5705
Fort Bowie National Historic Site 3203 S Old Ft Bowie Rd *Web:* www.nps.gov/fobo	Bowie	AZ	85605	520-847-2500	847-2221
Glen Canyon National Recreation Area 691 Scenic View Dr PO Box 1507 *Web:* www.nps.gov/glca	Page	AZ	86040	928-608-6200	608-6259
Grand Canyon National Park PO Box 129 **Fax:* Mail Rm ■ *Web:* www.nps.gov	Grand Canyon	AZ	86023	928-638-7888	638-7797*
Hohokam Pima National Monument c/o Casa Grande Ruins National Monument 1100 W Ruins Dr *TF:* 866-705-5711 ■ *Web:* www.nps.gov/pima	Coolidge	AZ	85228	520-723-3172	723-7209
Hubbell Trading Post National Historic Site 1/2 Mile W Hwy 191 on Hwy 264 PO Box 150 *Web:* www.nps.gov	Ganado	AZ	86505	928-755-3475	755-3405
Montezuma Castle National Monument 527 S Main St *Web:* www.nps.gov/moca	Camp Verde	AZ	86322	928-567-5276	567-3597
Navajo National Monument HC 71 PO Box 3 *Web:* www.nps.gov	Tonalea	AZ	86044	928-672-2700	672-2703
Petrified Forest National Park PO Box 2217 *Web:* www.nps.gov	Petrified Forest	AZ	86028	928-524-6228	524-3567
Pipe Spring National Monument 406 N Pipe Spring Rd HC 65 PO Box 5 *Web:* www.nps.gov/pisp	Fredonia	AZ	86022	928-643-7105	643-7583
Saguaro National Park 3693 S Old Spanish Trl *Web:* www.nps.gov	Tucson	AZ	85730	520-733-5100	733-5183
Tonto National Monument 26260 N Az Hwy 188 2 *Web:* www.nps.gov/tont	Roosevelt	AZ	85545	928-467-2241	467-2225
Tumacacori National Historical Park 1891 E Frontage Rd PO Box 8067 *Web:* www.nps.gov/tuma	Tumacacori	AZ	85640	520-377-5060	398-9271
Tuzigoot National Monument 527 S Main St *Web:* www.nps.gov/tuzi	Camp Verde	AZ	86322	928-634-5564	567-3597
Wupatki National Monument Flagstaff Area National Monuments 6400 N Hwy 89 *Web:* www.nps.gov/wupa	Flagstaff	AZ	86004	928-679-2365	679-2349

Arkansas

	City	State	Zip	Phone	Fax
Arkansas Post National Memorial 1741 Old Post Rd *Web:* www.nps.gov	Gillett	AR	72055	870-548-2207	548-2431
Buffalo National River 402 N Walnut St Ste 136 *Web:* www.nps.gov	Harrison	AR	72601	870-741-5443	741-7286
Fort Smith National Historic Site 301 Parker Ave *Web:* www.nps.gov	Fort Smith	AR	72901	479-783-3961	783-5307
Hot Springs National Park 101 Reserve St *Web:* www.nps.gov	Hot Springs	AR	71901	501-620-6715	620-6778
Little Rock Central High School National Historic Site 2120 W Daisy L Gatson Bates Dr *Web:* www.nps.gov	Little Rock	AR	72202	501-374-1957	376-4728
Pea Ridge National Military Park 15930 Hwy 62 E *Web:* www.nps.gov	Garfield	AR	72732	479-451-8122	451-0219
President William Jefferson Clinton Birthplace Home National Historic Site 117 S Hervey St *Web:* www.nps.gov/wicl/index.htm	Hope	AR	71801	870-777-4455	777-4935

British Columbia

	City	State	Zip	Phone	Fax
Wildplay Element Parks 485 Garbally Rd *Web:* www.wildplay.com	Victoria	BC	V8T2J9	250-595-2251	

California

	City	State	Zip	Phone	Fax
Cabrillo National Monument 1800 Cabrillo Memorial Dr *TF:* 800-236-7916 ■ *Web:* www.nps.gov	San Diego	CA	92106	619-557-5450	226-6311
Channel Islands National Park 1901 Spinnaker Dr *Web:* www.nps.gov	Ventura	CA	93001	805-658-5730	658-5799
City of Piedmont Recreation Department 358 Hillside Ave *Web:* ci.piedmont.ca.us	Piedmont	CA	94611	510-420-3078	
Death Valley National Park PO Box 579 *TF:* 866-713-9688 ■ *Web:* www.nps.gov/deva	Death Valley	CA	92328	760-786-3200	786-3283
Devils Postpile National Monument PO Box 3999 *Web:* www.nps.gov/depo	Mammoth Lakes	CA	93546	760-934-2289	934-2289
Eugene O'Neill National Historic Site 1000 Kuss Rd **Fax Area Code:* 410 ■ *TF:* 866-945-7920 ■ *Web:* www.nps.gov	Danville	CA	94526	925-838-0249	396-3393*
Fort Point National Historic Site Fort Mason Bldg 201 *Web:* www.nps.gov/fopo	San Francisco	CA	94123	415-556-1693	561-4390
Golden Gate National Recreation Area Fort Mason Bldg 201 **Fax:* Hum Res ■ *Web:* www.nps.gov/goga	San Francisco	CA	94123	415-561-4700	561-4750*
John Muir National Historic Site 4202 Alhambra Ave *Web:* www.nps.gov	Martinez	CA	94553	925-228-8860	228-8192
Joshua Tree National Park 74485 National Pk Dr *Web:* www.nps.gov	Twentynine Palms	CA	92277	760-367-5500	367-6392
Lassen Volcanic National Park 38050 Hwy 36 E PO Box 100 *Web:* www.nps.gov/lavo	Mineral	CA	96063	530-595-4480	595-3262
Lava Beds National Monument 1 Indian Well Headquarters *TF:* 866-705-5711 ■ *Web:* www.nps.gov/labe	Tulelake	CA	96134	530-260-0537	
Manzanar National Historic Site 5001 Hwy 395 PO Box 426 *Web:* www.nps.gov/manz	Independence	CA	93526	760-878-2194	878-2949
Mojave National Preserve 2701 Barstow Rd *Web:* www.nps.gov/moja	Barstow	CA	92311	760-252-6100	252-6174
Muir Woods National Monument 1 Muir Woods Rd *Web:* www.nps.gov/muwo	Mill Valley	CA	94941	415-388-2596	389-6957
Park Maintenance 20500 Madrona Ave *Web:* www.torrnet.com	Torrance	CA	90503	310-781-6901	
Pinnacles National Monument 5000 Hwy 146 *TF:* 877-444-6777 ■ *Web:* www.nps.gov/pinn	Paicines	CA	95043	831-389-4485	389-4489
Point Reyes National Seashore 1 Bear Valley Rd *TF:* 877-874-2478 ■ *Web:* www.nps.gov	Point Reyes Station	CA	94956	415-464-5100	663-8132
Redwood National & State Parks 1111 Second St *Web:* www.nps.gov/redw	Crescent City	CA	95531	707-465-7335	464-1812
Roar Foundation 6867 Soledad Canyon Rd *Web:* www.shambala.org	Acton	CA	93510	661-268-0380	
Rosie the Riveter/World War II Home Front National Historical Park 1401 Marina Way S *Web:* www.nps.gov	Richmond	CA	94804	510-232-5050	
San Francisco Maritime National Historical Park 2 Marina Blvd Bldg E *Web:* www.nps.gov/safr	San Francisco	CA	94123	415-561-7000	556-1624
Santa Monica Mountains National Recreation Area 401 W Hillcrest Dr *TF:* 888-275-8747 ■ *Web:* www.nps.gov/samo	Thousand Oaks	CA	91360	805-370-2300	370-1851
Sequoia & Kings Canyon National Parks 47050 Generals Hwy *Web:* www.nps.gov/seki	Three Rivers	CA	93271	559-565-3341	565-3730
Whiskeytown-Shasta-Trinity National Recreation Area PO Box 188 *Web:* www.nps.gov	Whiskeytown	CA	96095	530-246-1225	246-5154
Yosemite National Park 9039 Village Dr PO Box 577 *Web:* www.nps.gov/yose	Yosemite	CA	95389	209-372-0200	

Colorado

	City	State	Zip	Phone	Fax
Bent's Old Fort National Historic Site 35110 Hwy 194 E *Web:* www.nps.gov/beol	La Junta	CO	81050	719-383-5010	383-2129
Black Canyon of the Gunnison National Park 102 Elk Creek *Web:* www.nps.gov/blca	Gunnison	CO	81230	970-641-2337	641-3127

				Phone	Fax
Colorado National Monument 1750 Rim Rock Dr *TF:* 866-945-7920 ■ *Web:* www.nps.gov	Fruita	CO	81521	970-858-3617	858-0372
Curecanti National Recreation Area 102 Elk Creek *TF:* 866-713-9688 ■ *Web:* www.nps.gov/cure	Gunnison	CO	81230	970-641-2337	641-3127
Dinosaur National Monument 4545 E Hwy 40 *Web:* www.nps.gov/dino	Dinosaur	CO	81610	970-374-3000	374-3003
Florissant Fossil Beds National Monument PO Box 185 *Web:* www.nps.gov	Florissant	CO	80816	719-748-3253	748-3164
Great Sand Dunes National Park & Preserve 11500 Hwy 150 *Web:* www.nps.gov/grsa	Mosca	CO	81146	719-378-6300	378-6310
Hovenweep National Monument McElmo Rt *Web:* www.nps.gov/hove	Cortez	CO	81321	970-562-4282	562-4283
National Park Service Regional Offices Intermountain Region 12795 W Alameda Pkwy *Web:* www.nps.gov	Denver	CO	80225	303-969-2500	
Rocky Mountain National Park 1000 Hwy 36 *Web:* www.nps.gov	Estes Park	CO	80517	970-586-1206	586-1256
Sand Creek Massacre National Historic Site 910 Wansted *Web:* www.nps.gov/sand	Eads	CO	81036	719-729-3003	438-5410
Yucca House National Monument c/o Mesa Verde National Pk PO Box 8 *Web:* www.nps.gov/yuho	Mesa Verde	CO	81330	970-529-4465	529-4637

Connecticut

				Phone	Fax
Weir Farm National Historic Site 735 Nod Hill Rd *Web:* www.nps.gov/wefa	Wilton	CT	06897	203-834-1896	834-2421

District of Columbia

				Phone	Fax
National Park Service (NPS) 1849 C St NW Rm 1013 *Web:* www.nps.gov	Washington	DC	20240	202-208-6843	219-0910
Constitution Gardens 900 Ohio Dr SW *Web:* www.nps.gov/coga	Washington	DC	20024	202-426-6841	724-0764
Ford's Theatre National Historic Site 511 Tenth St NW *Web:* www.nps.gov/foth	Washington	DC	20004	202-233-0701	233-0706
Frederick Douglass National Historic Site 1900 Anacostia Dr SE *Web:* www.nps.gov/frdo	Washington	DC	20020	202-426-5961	426-0880
Korean War Veterans Memorial c/o National Capital Parks - Central 900 Ohio Dr SW *Web:* www.nps.gov/kowa	Washington	DC	20004	202-426-6841	
Mary McLeod Bethune Council House National Historic Site 1318 Vermont Ave NW *Web:* www.nps.gov/mamc	Washington	DC	20005	202-673-2402	673-2414
National Mall c/o National Capitol Parks - Central 900 Ohio Dr SW *Web:* www.nps.gov/nama	Washington	DC	20024	202-426-6841	426-1835
National Park Service Regional Offices National Capital Region 1100 Ohio Dr SW *Web:* www.nps.gov/ncro	Washington	DC	20242	202-619-7000	619-7220
Pennsylvania Avenue National Historic Site 900 Ohio Dr SW 900 Ohio Dr SW *Web:* www.nps.gov/paav	Washington	DC	20024	202-606-9686	
Rock Creek Park 5200 Glover Rd NW *Web:* www.nps.gov	Washington	DC	20015	202-895-6000	895-6015
Thomas Jefferson Memorial c/o National Capital Parks - Central 900 Ohio Dr SW *TF:* 866-705-5711 ■ *Web:* www.nps.gov/thje	Washington	DC	20024	202-426-6841	426-1835

Florida

				Phone	Fax
Big Cypress National Preserve 33100 Tamiami Trl E *Web:* www.nps.gov	Ochopee	FL	34141	239-695-2000	695-3901
Biscayne National Park 9700 SW 328th St *Web:* www.nps.gov/bisc	Homestead	FL	33033	305-230-1144	230-1190
Canaveral National Seashore 212 S Washington Ave *Web:* www.nps.gov/cana	Titusville	FL	32796	321-267-1110	264-2906
Castillo de San Marcos National Monument 1 S Castillo Dr *Web:* www.nps.gov/casa	Saint Augustine	FL	32084	904-829-6506	823-9388
De Soto National Memorial 8300 Desoto Memorial Hwy *TF:* 888-831-7526 ■ *Web:* www.nps.gov	Bradenton	FL	34209	941-792-0458	792-5094
Dry Tortugas National Park PO Box 6208 *Web:* www.nps.gov/drto	Key West	FL	33041	305-242-7700	242-7711
Everglades National Park 40001 SR-9336 *Web:* www.nps.gov/ever	Homestead	FL	33034	305-242-7700	242-7728
Fort Caroline National Memorial 12713 Ft Caroline Rd *Web:* www.nps.gov/foca	Jacksonville	FL	32225	904-641-7155	641-3798
Fort Matanzas National Monument 8635 A1A S *Web:* www.nps.gov/foma	Saint Augustine	FL	32080	904-471-0116	471-7605
Gulf Islands National Seashore (Florida) 1801 Gulf Breeze Pkwy *Web:* www.nps.gov	Gulf Breeze	FL	32563	850-934-2600	932-9654
Reeves Park 600 Nw 10th St *Web:* www.ci.norman.ok.us	Miami	FL	33136	305-579-6970	
Timucuan Ecological & Historic Preserve 12713 Ft Caroline Rd *Web:* www.nps.gov/timu	Jacksonville	FL	32225	904-641-7155	
William J Rish Park 6773 Hwy C 30 E *Web:* apdcares.org	Port St Joe	FL	32456	850-227-1876	

Georgia

				Phone	Fax
Andersonville National Historic Site 496 Cemetery Rd *Web:* www.nps.gov/ande	Andersonville	GA	31711	229-924-0343	924-1086
Chattahoochee River National Recreation Area 1978 Island Ford Pkwy *Fax Area Code: 770 ■ *TF:* 877-874-2478 ■ *Web:* www.nps.gov/chat	Atlanta	GA	30350	678-538-1200	399-8087*
Chickamauga & Chattanooga National Military Park 3370 Lafayette Rd PO Box 2128 *Fax Area Code: 423 ■ *Web:* www.nps.gov/chch	Fort Oglethorpe	GA	30742	706-866-9241	752-5215*
Cumberland Island National Seashore 101 Wheeler St *TF:* 877-860-6787 ■ *Web:* www.nps.gov	Saint Marys	GA	31558	912-882-4336	673-7747
Fort Frederica National Monument 6515 Frederica Rd *Web:* www.nps.gov	Saint Simons Island	GA	31522	912-638-3639	634-5357
Fort Pulaski National Monument US Hwy 80 E *TF:* 800-228-5150 ■ *Web:* www.nps.gov	Savannah	GA	31410	912-786-5787	786-6023
Jimmy Carter National Historic Site 300 N Bond St *Web:* www.nps.gov/jica	Plains	GA	31780	229-824-4104	824-3441
Kennesaw Mountain National Battlefield Park 900 Kennesaw Mtn Dr *Web:* www.nps.gov	Kennesaw	GA	30152	770-427-4686	528-8398
Martin Luther King Jr National Historic Site 450 Auburn Ave NE *Web:* www.nps.gov/malu	Atlanta	GA	30312	404-331-5190	730-3112
Ocmulgee National Monument 1207 Emery Hwy *Web:* www.nps.gov/ocmu	Macon	GA	31217	478-752-8257	752-8259

Guam

				Phone	Fax
War in the Pacific National Historical Park 135 Murray Blvd Ste 100 *Web:* www.nps.gov/wapa	Hagatna	GU	96910	671-477-7278	

Hawaii

				Phone	Fax
Haleakala National Park PO Box 369 *Web:* www.nps.gov	Makawao	HI	96768	808-572-4400	572-1304
Hawaii Volcanoes National Park PO Box 52 *Web:* www.nps.gov	Hawaii National Park	HI	96718	808-985-6000	985-6004
Kalaupapa National Historical Park PO Box 2222 *Web:* www.nps.gov	Kalaupapa	HI	96742	808-567-6802	567-6729
Kaloko-Honokohau National Historical Park 73-4786 Kanalani St Ste 14 *Web:* www.nps.gov	Kailua-Kona	HI	96740	808-329-6881	
Puukohola Heiau National Historic Site 62-3601 Kawaihae Rd *Web:* www.nps.gov	Kawaihae	HI	96743	808-882-7218	882-1215
USS Arizona Memorial 1 Arizona Memorial Pl *Web:* www.nps.gov/usar	Honolulu	HI	96818	808-422-0561	483-8608

Idaho

				Phone	Fax
City of Rocks National Reserve PO Box 169 *Web:* www.nps.gov/ciro	Almo	ID	83312	208-824-5910	824-5563
Craters of the Moon National Monument & Preserve PO Box 29 *Web:* www.nps.gov/crmo	Arco	ID	83213	208-527-1335	527-3073
Hagerman Fossil Beds National Monument 221 N State St PO Box 570 *Web:* www.nps.gov	Hagerman	ID	83332	208-933-4100	837-4857
Minidoka National Historic Site PO Box 570 *Web:* www.nps.gov/miin	Hagerman	ID	83332	208-933-4127	837-4857
Nez Perce National Historical Park 39063 US Hwy 95 *Web:* www.nps.gov/nepe	Spalding	ID	83540	208-843-2261	843-7003

Illinois

				Phone	Fax
Lincoln Home National Historic Site 413 S Eigth St *Web:* www.nps.gov	Springfield	IL	62701	217-492-4241	492-4673

Indiana

				Phone	Fax
George Rogers Clark National Historical Park 401 S Second St *Web:* www.nps.gov	Vincennes	IN	47591	812-882-1776	882-7270
Indiana Dunes National Lakeshore 1100 N Mineral Springs Rd *Web:* www.nps.gov/indu	Porter	IN	46304	219-395-1772	926-7561
Lincoln Boyhood National Memorial 2916 E S St PO Box 1816 *Web:* www.nps.gov/libo	Lincoln City	IN	47552	812-937-4541	937-9929

Iowa

Phone Fax

Effigy Mounds National Monument
151 Hwy 76 Harpers Ferry IA 52146 563-873-3491
Web: www.nps.gov/efmo

Herbert Hoover National Historic Site
110 Parkside Dr PO Box 607 West Branch IA 52358 319-643-2541 643-7864
Web: www.nps.gov/heho

Kansas

Phone Fax

Brown Vs Board of Education National Historic Site
1515 SE Monroe St Topeka KS 66612 785-354-4273 354-7213
Web: www.nps.gov

Fort Larned National Historic Site
1767 Kansas Hwy 156 Larned KS 67550 620-285-6911 285-3571
Web: www.nps.gov

Fort Scott National Historic Site
PO Box 918 Fort Scott KS 66701 620-223-0310 223-0188
Web: www.nps.gov

Nicodemus National Historic Site
510 Washington Ave B1 Bogue KS 67625 785-839-4233 839-4325
Web: www.nps.gov

Tallgrass Prairie National Preserve
226 Broadway PO Box 585 Cottonwood Falls KS 66845 620-273-6034 273-6099
Web: www.nps.gov

Kentucky

Phone Fax

Abraham Lincoln Birthplace National Historic Site
2995 Lincoln Farm Rd Hodgenville KY 42748 270-358-3137 358-3874
Web: www.nps.gov

Cumberland Gap National Historical Park
91 Bartlett Pk Rd PO Box 1848 Middlesboro KY 40965 606-248-2817 248-7276
TF: 888-831-7526 ■ *Web:* www.nps.gov/cuga

Mammoth Cave National Park
1 Mammoth Cave Pkwy PO Box 7 Mammoth Cave KY 42259 270-758-2180 758-2349
Web: www.nps.gov/maca

Louisiana

Phone Fax

Cane River Creole National Historical Park
400 Rapides Dr Natchitoches LA 71457 318-356-8441 352-4549
Web: www.nps.gov/cari

Jean Lafitte National Historical Park & Preserve
419 Decatur St New Orleans LA 70130 504-589-3882 589-3851
Web: www.nps.gov

New Orleans Jazz National Historical Park
419 Decatur St New Orleans LA 70130 504-589-4806 589-3865
TF: 877-520-0677 ■ *Web:* www.nps.gov

Poverty Point National Monument
c/o Poverty Pt State Historic Site PO Box 276 Epps LA 71237 318-926-5492
TF: 888-926-5492 ■ *Web:* www.nps.gov

Maine

Phone Fax

Acadia National Park 20 McFarland Hill Dr Bar Harbor ME 04609 207-288-3338 288-8813
Web: www.nps.gov

Saint Croix Island International Historic Site
PO Box 247 Calais ME 04619 207-454-3871 288-8813
Web: www.nps.gov/sacr

Maryland

Phone Fax

Antietam National Battlefield
5831 Dunker Church Rd PO Box 158 Sharpsburg MD 21782 301-432-5124 432-4590
Web: www.nps.gov/anti

Assateague Island National Seashore
7206 National Seashore Ln PO Box 38 Berlin MD 21811 410-641-1441
Web: www.nps.gov/asis

Catoctin Mountain Park 6602 Foxville Rd Thurmont MD 21788 301-663-9330
Web: www.nps.gov

Chesapeake & Ohio Canal National Historical Park
1850 Dual Hwy Ste 100 Hagerstown MD 21740 301-739-4200 739-5275
Web: www.nps.gov/choh

Clara Barton National Historic Site
5801 Oxford Rd Glen Echo MD 20812 301-320-1410
Web: www.nps.gov/clba

Fort McHenry National Monument & Historic Shrine
2400 E Fort Ave Baltimore MD 21230 410-962-4290 962-2500
TF: 866-945-7920 ■ *Web:* www.nps.gov

Fort Washington Park
13551 Ft Washington Rd Fort Washington MD 20744 301-763-4600 763-1389
Web: www.nps.gov

Greenbelt Park 6565 Greenbelt Rd Greenbelt MD 20770 301-344-3948
Web: www.nps.gov/gree

Hampton National Historic Site 535 Hampton Ln Towson MD 21286 410-823-1309 823-8394
Web: www.nps.gov

Monocacy National Battlefield
5201 Urbana Pk Frederick MD 21704 301-662-3515 662-3420
Web: www.nps.gov

Piscataway Park
c/o Ft Washington Pk
13551 Ft Washington Rd Fort Washington MD 20744 301-763-4600 763-1389
TF: 866-705-5711 ■ *Web:* www.nps.gov/pisc

Thomas Stone National Historic Site
6655 Rose Hill Rd Port Tobacco MD 20677 301-392-1776 934-8793
Web: www.nps.gov

Massachusetts

Phone Fax

Adams National Historical Park 135 Adams St Quincy MA 02169 617-773-1177
Web: www.nps.gov

Boston African-American National Historic Site
14 Beacon St Ste 401 Boston MA 02108 617-742-5415 720-0848
Web: www.nps.gov

Boston Harbor Islands National Recreation Area
408 Atlantic Ave Ste 228 Boston MA 02110 617-223-8666 223-8671
TF: 877-874-2478 ■ *Web:* www.nps.gov

Boston National Historical Park
Charlestown Navy Yard Boston MA 02129 617-242-5601 242-6006
Web: www.nps.gov/bost

Frederick Law Olmsted National Historic Site
99 Warren St Brookline MA 02445 617-566-1689 232-4073
Web: www.nps.gov/frla

John F Kennedy National Historic Site
83 Beals St Brookline MA 02446 617-566-7937 730-9884
Web: www.nps.gov/jofi

Longfellow National Historic Site
105 Brattle St Cambridge MA 02138 617-876-4491 497-8718
Web: www.nps.gov/long

Lowell National Historical Park 67 Kirk St Lowell MA 01852 978-970-5000
Web: www.nps.gov

Minute Man National Historical Park
174 Liberty St Concord MA 01742 978-369-6993 318-7800
Web: www.nps.gov

New Bedford Whaling National Historical Park
33 William St New Bedford MA 02740 508-996-4095 984-1250
Web: www.nps.gov/nebe

Salem Maritime National Historic Site
160 Derby St Salem MA 01970 978-740-1650 740-1654
Web: www.nps.gov/sama

Saugus Iron Works National Historic Site
244 Central St Saugus MA 01906 781-233-0050 231-7345
Web: www.nps.gov

Springfield Armory National Historic Site
1 Armory Sq Ste 2 Springfield MA 01105 413-734-8551 747-8062
Web: www.nps.gov/spar

Michigan

Phone Fax

Isle Royale National Park
800 E Lakeshore Dr Houghton MI 49931 906-482-0984 482-8753
Web: www.nps.gov

Keweenaw National Historical Park
25970 Red Jacket Rd PO Box 471 Calumet MI 49913 906-337-3168 337-3169
Web: www.nps.gov

Pictured Rocks National Lakeshore
N8391 Sandpoint Rd PO Box 40 Munising MI 49862 906-387-2607 387-4025
Web: www.nps.gov

Sleeping Bear Dunes National Lakeshore
9922 Front St Empire MI 49630 231-326-5134 326-5382
Web: www.nps.gov/slbe

Minnesota

Phone Fax

Grand Portage National Monument
PO Box 668 Grand Marais MN 55604 218-387-2788 387-2790
Web: www.nps.gov

Mississippi National River & Recreation Area
111 E Kellogg Blvd Ste 105 Saint Paul MN 55101 651-290-4160 290-3214
Web: www.nps.gov/miss

Sauk Rapids Recreation Program
901 First St S Sauk Rapids MN 56379 320-253-6631
Web: www.isd47.org

Voyageurs National Park
360 Hwy 11 E International Falls MN 56649 218-283-6600 285-7407
TF: 888-381-2873 ■ *Web:* www.nps.gov/voya

Mississippi

Phone Fax

Brice's Crossroads National Battlefield Site
2680 Natchez Trace Pkwy Tupelo MS 38804 662-680-4025 680-4033
TF: 800-305-7417 ■ *Web:* www.nps.gov/brcr

Gulf Islands National Seashore (Mississippi)
3500 Pk Rd Ocean Springs MS 39564 850-934-2600
Web: www.nps.gov/guis

Natchez National Historical Park
1 Melrose Montebello Pkwy Natchez MS 39120 601-446-5790 442-9516
Web: www.nps.gov/natc

Natchez Trace National Scenic Trail
2680 Natchez Trace Pkwy Tupelo MS 38804 662-680-4025
TF: 800-305-7417 ■ *Web:* www.nps.gov/natt

Tupelo National Battlefield
2680 Natchez Trace Pkwy Tupelo MS 38804 662-680-4025 680-4033
TF: 800-305-7417 ■ *Web:* www.nps.gov

Vicksburg National Military Park
3201 Clay St Vicksburg MS 39183 601-636-0583 636-9497
Web: www.nps.gov/vick

Missouri

Phone Fax

George Washington Carver National Monument
5646 Carver Rd Diamond MO 64840 417-325-4151 325-4231
Web: www.nps.gov

Phone | Fax

Harry S Truman National Historic Site
223 N Main St .... Independence MO 64050 816-254-2720 254-4491
TF: 877-642-4743 ■ *Web:* www.nps.gov

Jefferson National Expansion Memorial
11 N Fourth St .... Saint Louis MO 63102 314-655-1700 655-1641
TF: 855-733-4522 ■ *Web:* www.nps.gov/jeff

Ozark National Scenic Riverways
404 Watercress Dr PO Box 490 .... Van Buren MO 63965 573-323-4236 323-4140
TF: 877-444-6777 ■ *Web:* www.nps.gov/ozar

Ulysses S Grant National Historic Site
7400 Grant Rd .... Saint Louis MO 63123 314-842-3298 842-1659
Web: www.nps.gov/ulsg

Wilson's Creek National Battlefield
6424 W Farm Rd 182 .... Republic MO 65738 417-732-2662 732-1167
Web: www.nps.gov

Montana

Phone | Fax

Big Hole National Battlefield 16425 Hwy 43 W .... Wisdom MT 59761 406-689-3155 689-3151
Web: www.nps.gov

Bighorn Canyon National Recreation Area
5 Ave B PO Box 7458 .... Fort Smith MT 59035 406-666-2412 666-2415
Web: www.nps.gov/bica

Glacier National Park PO Box 128 .... West Glacier MT 59936 406-888-7800 888-7808
Web: www.nps.gov/glac

Grant-Kohrs Ranch National Historic Site
266 Warren Ln .... Deer Lodge MT 59722 406-846-2070 846-3962
Web: www.nps.gov

Little Bighorn Battlefield National Monument
PO Box 39 .... Crow Agency MT 59022 406-638-3214 638-2623
Web: www.nps.gov/libi

Nebraska

Phone | Fax

Agate Fossil Beds National Monument
301 River Rd .... Harrison NE 69346 308-668-2211 668-2318
Web: www.nps.gov

Homestead National Monument of America
8523 W State Hwy 4 .... Beatrice NE 68310 402-223-3514 228-4231
Web: www.nps.gov

Niobrara National Scenic River
146 S Hall St PO Box 319 .... Valentine NE 69201 402-376-1901 376-1949
Web: www.nps.gov/niob

Nevada

Phone | Fax

Great Basin National Park
100 Great Basin National Pk .... Baker NV 89311 775-234-7331 234-7269
Web: www.nps.gov/grba

Lake Mead National Recreation Area
601 Nevada Hwy .... Boulder City NV 89005 702-293-8990 293-8936
Web: www.nps.gov

New Hampshire

Phone | Fax

Saint-Gaudens National Historic Site
139 St Gaudens Rd .... Cornish NH 03745 603-675-2175 675-2701
Web: www.nps.gov/saga

New Jersey

Phone | Fax

Morristown National Historical Park
30 Washington Pl .... Morristown NJ 07960 973-543-4030 451-9212
Web: www.nps.gov/morr

Pinelands National Reserve
15 Springfield Rd .... New Lisbon NJ 08064 609-894-7300 894-7330
Web: www.nps.gov/pine

Thomas Edison National Historic Site
211 Main St .... West Orange NJ 07052 973-736-0550 736-6567
Web: www.nps.gov/edis

New Mexico

Phone | Fax

Aztec Ruins National Monument 84 Ruins Rd 2900 .... Aztec NM 87410 505-334-6174 334-6372
Web: www.nps.gov

Capulin Volcano National Monument
46 Volcano Rd .... Capulin NM 88414 505-278-2201 278-2211
Web: www.nps.gov/cavo

Chaco Culture National Historical Park
PO Box 220 .... Nageezi NM 87037 505-786-7014 786-7061
TF: 877-642-4743 ■ *Web:* www.nps.gov/chcu

El Malpais National Monument
123 E Roosevelt Ave .... Grants NM 87020 505-285-4641 285-5661
Web: www.nps.gov

El Morro National Monument HC 61 PO Box 43 .... Ramah NM 87321 505-783-4226 783-4689
Web: www.nps.gov

Fort Union National Monument PO Box 127 .... Watrous NM 87753 505-425-8025 454-1155
Web: www.nps.gov

Gila Cliff Dwellings National Monument
HC 68 PO Box 100 .... Silver City NM 88061 505-536-9461 536-9344
Web: www.nps.gov/gicl

Pecos National Historical Park PO Box 418 .... Pecos NM 87552 505-757-7200 757-7207
Web: www.nps.gov/peco

White Sands National Monument
PO Box 1086 .... Holloman AFB NM 88330 575-479-6124
Web: www.nps.gov/whsa

New York

Phone | Fax

African Burial Ground National Monument
290 Broadway 1st Fl .... New York NY 10007 212-637-2019
Web: www.nps.gov/afbg

Cortlandt Recreation Dept 1 Heady St .... Cortlandt Manor NY 10567 914-734-1050
Web: www.townofcortlandt.com

Eleanor Roosevelt National Historic Site
4097 Albany Post Rd .... Hyde Park NY 12538 845-229-9115 229-0739
TF: 800-337-8474 ■ *Web:* www.nps.gov/elro

Federal Hall National Memorial 26 Wall St .... New York NY 10005 212-825-6990 668-2899
Web: www.nps.gov/feha/index.htm

Fire Island National Seashore
120 Laurel St .... Patchogue NY 11772 631-687-4750 289-4898
Web: www.nps.gov/fiis

Gateway National Recreation Area
210 New York Ave .... Staten Island NY 10305 718-354-4606 354-4605
Web: www.nps.gov/gate

General Grant National Memorial
Riverside Dr & W 122nd St .... New York NY 10027 212-666-1640 932-9631
Web: www.nps.gov/gegr

Hamilton Grange National Memorial (HAGR)
122 St Riverside Dr .... New York NY 10027 212-666-1640
Web: www.nps.gov/hagr

Home of Franklin D Roosevelt National Historic Site
4097 Albany Post Rd .... Hyde Park NY 12538 845-229-9115 229-0739
Web: www.nps.gov/hofr

Martin Van Buren National Historic Site
1013 Old Post Rd .... Kinderhook NY 12106 518-758-9689 758-6986
Web: www.nps.gov

Sagamore Hill National Historic Site
20 Sagamore Hill Rd .... Oyster Bay NY 11771 516-922-4788 922-4792
Web: www.nps.gov/sahi

Saint Paul's Church National Historic Site
897 S Columbus Ave .... Mount Vernon NY 10550 914-667-4116 667-3024
TF: 866-705-5711 ■ *Web:* www.nps.gov

Saratoga National Historical Park
648 Rt 32 .... Stillwater NY 12170 518-664-9821
Web: www.nps.gov/sara

Statue of Liberty National Monument & Ellis Island
Liberty Island .... New York NY 10004 212-363-3200
Web: www.nps.gov/stli

Theodore Roosevelt Birthplace National Historic Site
28 E 20th St .... New York NY 10003 212-260-1616
Web: www.nps.gov/thrb

Thomas Cole National Historic Site
218 Spring St .... Catskill NY 12414 518-943-7465 943-0652
Web: www.thomascole.org

Vanderbilt Mansion National Historic Site
4097 Albany Post Rd .... Hyde Park NY 12538 845-229-9115 229-0739
Web: www.nps.gov/vama

Women's Rights National Historical Park
136 Fall St .... Seneca Falls NY 13148 315-568-2991 568-2141
Web: www.nps.gov/wori

North Carolina

Phone | Fax

Cape Hatteras National Seashore
1401 National Pk Dr .... Manteo NC 27954 252-473-2111 473-2595
Web: www.nps.gov/caha

Cape Lookout National Seashore
131 Charles St .... Harkers Island NC 28531 252-728-2250 728-2160
Web: www.nps.gov

Carl Sandburg Home National Historic Site
81 Carl Sadburg Ln .... Flat Rock NC 28731 828-693-4178 693-4179
TF: 877-642-4743 ■ *Web:* www.nps.gov

Fort Raleigh National Historic Site
1401 National Pk Dr .... Manteo NC 27954 252-473-5772 473-2595
Web: www.nps.gov

Guilford Courthouse National Military Park
2332 New Garden Rd .... Greensboro NC 27410 336-288-1776 282-2296
Web: www.nps.gov/guco

Moores Creek National Battlefield
40 Patriots Hall Dr .... Currie NC 28435 910-283-5591 283-5351
Web: www.nps.gov

Reidsville Recreation Dept
200 N Franklin St .... Reidsville NC 27320 336-349-1090
Web: ci.reidsville.nc.us

North Dakota

Phone | Fax

Fort Union Trading Post National Historic Site
15550 Hwy 1804 .... Williston ND 58801 701-572-9083 572-7321
Web: www.nps.gov

Knife River Indian Villages National Historic Site
564 County Rd 37 PO Box 9 .... Stanton ND 58571 701-745-3300 745-3708
TF: 866-705-5711 ■ *Web:* www.nps.gov

Theodore Roosevelt National Park
315 Second Ave PO Box 7 .... Medora ND 58645 701-623-4466 623-4840
Web: www.nps.gov/thro

Northern Mariana Islands

Phone | Fax

American Memorial Park PO Box 5198-Chrb. .... Saipan MP 96950 670-234-7207 234-6698
Web: www.nps.gov/amme

Ohio

				Phone	Fax
Cuyahoga Valley National Park 15610 Vaughn Rd **Fax Area Code: 440* ■ *TF:* 800-445-9667 ■ *Web:* www.nps.gov	Brecksville	OH	44141	216-524-1497	546-5989*
Dayton Aviation Heritage National Historical Park 16 S Williams St *Web:* www.nps.gov	Dayton	OH	45402	937-225-7705	222-4512
First Ladies National Historic Site 205 Market Ave S *Web:* www.nps.gov	Canton	OH	44702	330-452-0876	456-3414
Hopewell Culture National Historical Park 16062 SR-104 *Web:* www.nps.gov/hocu	Chillicothe	OH	45601	740-774-1126	774-1140
James A Garfield National Historic Site 8095 Mentor Ave *Web:* www.nps.gov/jaga	Mentor	OH	44060	440-255-8722	255-8545
Metro Parks 1069 W Main St Unit A *Web:* www.metroparks.net	Westerville	OH	43081	614-891-0700	
Oxford Recreation Dept 6025 Fairfield Rd *Web:* www.cityofoxford.org	Oxford	OH	45056	513-523-6314	
Perry's Victory & International Peace Memorial 93 Delaware Ave PO Box 549 *Web:* www.nps.gov/pevi	Put-in-Bay	OH	43456	419-285-2184	285-2516
Whitehall Community Park 402 N Hamilton Rd *Web:* cityofwhitehall.com	Whitehall	OH	43213	614-863-0121	
William Howard Taft National Historic Site 2038 Auburn Ave *Web:* www.nps.gov/wiho	Cincinnati	OH	45219	513-684-3262	684-3627

Oklahoma

				Phone	Fax
Chickasaw National Recreation Area 1008 W Second St *Web:* www.nps.gov	Sulphur	OK	73086	580-622-7234	622-6931
Washita Battlefield National Historic Site 18555 HWY 47A *Web:* www.nps.gov/waba	Cheyenne	OK	73628	580-497-2742	497-2712

Oregon

				Phone	Fax
Alton Baker Park 1820 Roosevelt Blvd *Web:* www.ci.eugene.or.us	Eugene	OR	97402	541-682-4800	
Crater Lake National Park PO Box 7 *Web:* www.nps.gov	Crater Lake	OR	97604	541-594-3000	594-3010
John Day Fossil Beds National Monument 32651 Hwy 19 *Web:* www.nps.gov/joda	Kimberly	OR	97848	541-987-2333	987-2336
Oregon Caves National Monument 19000 Caves Hwy *TF:* 877-245-9022 ■ *Web:* www.nps.gov/orca	Cave Junction	OR	97523	541-592-2100	592-3981
Tualatin Hills Aquatic Ctr 15707 Sw Walker Rd *Web:* www.thprd.org/facilities/aquatics/aquatic-center	Beaverton	OR	97006	503-645-6433	

Pennsylvania

				Phone	Fax
Allegheny Portage Railroad National Historic Site 110 Federal Pk Rd *Web:* www.nps.gov	Gallitzin	PA	16641	814-886-6150	884-0206
Delaware National Scenic River Delaware Water Gap National Recreation Area 1978 River Rd *Web:* www.nps.gov/dewa	Bushkill	PA	18324	570-426-2435	
Edgar Allan Poe National Historic Site 532 N Seventh St *Web:* www.nps.gov/edal	Philadelphia	PA	19123	215-597-8780	597-1901
Eisenhower National Historic Site 1195 Baltimore Pk Ste 100 *Web:* www.nps.gov	Gettysburg	PA	17325	717-338-9114	338-0821
Flight 93 National Memorial *National Park Service* PO Box 911 *Web:* www.nps.gov/flni/index.htm	Shanksville	PA	15560	814-893-6322	443-2180
Fort Necessity National Battlefield 1 Washington Pkwy *Web:* www.nps.gov	Farmington	PA	15437	724-329-5512	329-8682
Friendship Hill National Historic Site 223 New Geneva Rd *Web:* www.nps.gov/frhi	Point Marion	PA	15474	724-725-9190	725-1999
Gettysburg National Military Park 97 Taneytown Rd *Web:* www.nps.gov/gett	Gettysburg	PA	17325	717-334-1124	334-1891
Hopewell Furnace National Historic Site 2 Mark Bird Ln *TF:* 866-705-5711 ■ *Web:* www.nps.gov	Elverson	PA	19520	610-582-8773	582-2768
Independence National Historical Park 143 S Third St *Web:* www.nps.gov/inde	Philadelphia	PA	19106	215-597-8787	861-4950
Johnstown Flood National Memorial 733 Lake Rd *Web:* www.nps.gov/jofl	South Fork	PA	15956	814-495-4643	495-7463
National Park Service Regional Offices NortheastRegion 200 Chestnut St Ste 3 *Web:* www.nps.gov	Philadelphia	PA	19106	215-597-7013	597-0815
Natural Lands Trust Inc 1031 Palmers Mill Rd *Web:* www.natlands.org	Media	PA	19063	610-353-5587	
Steamtown National Historic Site 150 S Washington Ave *TF:* 888-693-9391 ■ *Web:* www.nps.gov	Scranton	PA	18503	570-340-5200	
Upper Delaware Scenic & Recreation River 274 River Rd *Web:* www.nps.gov/upde	Beach Lake	PA	18405	570-729-7134	
Valley Forge National Historical Park 1400 N Outer Line Dr *Web:* www.nps.gov/vafo	King of Prussia	PA	19406	610-783-1077	783-1060

Puerto Rico

				Phone	Fax
San Juan National Historic Site 501 Norzagaray St *Web:* www.nps.gov/saju	San Juan	PR	00901	787-729-6960	289-7972

Rhode Island

				Phone	Fax
Roger Williams National Memorial 282 N Main St *Web:* www.nps.gov/rowi	Providence	RI	02903	401-521-7266	521-7239

Saskatchewan

				Phone	Fax
City of Saskatoon Parks Branch 1101 Ave P N *Web:* www.city.saskatoon.sk.ca	Saskatoon	SK	S7K0J5	306-975-3300	

South Carolina

				Phone	Fax
Charles Pinckney National Historic Site 1214 Middle St *Web:* www.nps.gov/chpi	Sullivans Island	SC	29482	843-881-5516	881-7070
Congaree National Park 100 National Pk Rd *Web:* www.nps.gov	Hopkins	SC	29061	803-776-4396	783-4241
Cowpens National Battlefield 4001 Chesnee Hwy PO Box 308 *Web:* www.nps.gov/cowp	Gaffney	SC	29341	864-461-2828	461-7795
Fort Sumter National Monument 1214 Middle St *Web:* www.nps.gov/fosu	Sullivans Island	SC	29482	843-883-3123	883-3910
Historic Camden Revolutionary War Site 222 Broad St *Web:* historiccamden.org	Camden	SC	29021	803-432-9841	432-3815
Kings Mountain National Military Park 2625 Pk Rd *Web:* www.nps.gov	Blacksburg	SC	29702	864-936-7921	936-9897
Ninety Six National Historic Site 1103 Hwy 248 PO Box 418 *Web:* www.nps.gov/nisi	Ninety Six	SC	29666	864-543-4068	543-2058

South Dakota

				Phone	Fax
Badlands National Park 25216 Ben Reifel Rd PO Box 6 *Web:* www.nps.gov/badl	Interior	SD	57750	605-433-5361	433-5404
Jewel Cave National Monument 11149 US Hwy 16 Bldg B-12 *Web:* www.nps.gov	Custer	SD	57730	605-673-2288	673-3294
Minuteman Missile National Historic Site 21280 SD Hwy 240 *Web:* www.nps.gov	Philip	SD	57567	605-433-5552	433-5558
Missouri National Recreational River 508 E Second St *Web:* www.nps.gov/mnrr	Yankton	SD	57078	605-665-0209	665-4183
Mount Rushmore National Memorial 13000 Hwy 244 Bldg 31 Ste 1 *Web:* www.nps.gov	Keystone	SD	57751	605-574-2523	574-2307
Wind Cave National Park 26611 US Hwy 385 *Web:* www.nps.gov	Hot Springs	SD	57747	605-745-4600	745-4207

Tennessee

				Phone	Fax
Big South Fork National River & Recreation Area 4564 Leatherwood Rd *Web:* www.nps.gov	Oneida	TN	37841	423-569-9778	569-5505
Fort Donelson National Battlefield PO Box 434 *Web:* www.nps.gov	Dover	TN	37058	931-232-5706	232-4085
Great Smoky Mountains National Park 107 Pk Headquarters Rd *Web:* www.nps.gov	Gatlinburg	TN	37738	865-436-1200	436-1220
Obed Wild & Scenic River 208 N Maiden St *Web:* www.nps.gov	Wartburg	TN	37887	423-346-6294	346-3362
Rotary Park 1030-B Cumberland Heights Rd	Clarksville	TN	37040	931-648-5732	
Shiloh National Military Park 1055 Pittsburg Landing Rd *Web:* www.nps.gov/shil	Shiloh	TN	38376	731-689-5696	689-5450

Texas

				Phone	Fax
Alibates Flint Quarries National Monument PO Box 1460 *Web:* www.nps.gov/alfl	Fritch	TX	79036	806-857-3151	857-2319

				Phone	Fax
Amistad National Recreation Area 4121 Hwy 90 W *Web:* www.nps.gov	Del Rio	TX	78840	830-775-7491	778-9248
Big Bend National Park PO Box 129 *Web:* www.nps.gov/bibe	Big Bend National Park	TX	79834	432-477-2251	477-1175
Big Thicket National Preserve 6044 FM 420 *Web:* www.nps.gov/bith	Kountze	TX	77625	409-951-6700	951-6714
Chamizal National Memorial 800 S San Marcial St *TF:* 877-642-4743 ■ *Web:* www.nps.gov	El Paso	TX	79905	915-532-7273	532-7240
Fort Davis National Historic Site PO Box 1379 *Web:* www.nps.gov/foda	Fort Davis	TX	79734	432-426-3224	426-3122
Guadalupe Mountains National Park 400 Pine Canyon Rd *Web:* www.nps.gov	Salt Flat	TX	79847	915-828-3251	828-3269
Lake Meredith National Recreation Area 419 E Broadway *Web:* www.nps.gov/lamr	Fritch	TX	79036	806-857-3151	857-2319
Lyndon B. Johnson National Historical Park 100 Lady Bird Ln *Web:* www.nps.gov/lyjo	Johnson City	TX	78636	830-868-7128	868-7863
Padre Island National Seashore PO Box 181300 *Web:* www.nps.gov/pais	Corpus Christi	TX	78480	361-949-8068	949-8023
Rio Grande Wild & Scenic River PO Box 129 *Web:* www.nps.gov/rigr	Big Bend National Park	TX	79834	432-477-2251	477-1175
San Antonio Missions National Historical Park 2202 Roosevelt Ave *TF:* 866-945-7920 ■ *Web:* www.nps.gov/saan	San Antonio	TX	78210	210-534-8833	534-1106

Utah

				Phone	Fax
Bryce Canyon National Park PO Box 640201 *Web:* www.nps.gov	Bryce Canyon	UT	84764	435-834-5322	834-4102
Canyonlands National Park 2282 SW Resource Blvd. *Web:* www.nps.gov/cany	Moab	UT	84532	435-719-2313	719-2300
Capitol Reef National Park 16 Scenic Dr. *Web:* www.nps.gov	Torrey	UT	84775	435-425-3791	425-3026
Cedar Breaks National Monument 2390 W Hwy 56 Ste 11 *TF:* 877-642-4743 ■ *Web:* www.nps.gov	Cedar City	UT	84720	435-586-9451	586-3813
City of Logan Recreation Center 195 South 100 West *Web:* loganutah.org	Logan	UT	84321	435-716-9250	
Golden Spike National Historic Site PO Box 897 *Web:* www.nps.gov/gosp	Brigham City	UT	84302	435-471-2209	471-2341
Natural Bridges National Monument HC 60 PO Box 1 *Web:* www.nps.gov/nabr	Lake Powell	UT	84533	435-692-1234	692-1111
Timpanogos Cave National Monument RR 3 PO Box 200 *Web:* www.nps.gov	American Fork	UT	84003	801-756-5239	756-5661
Zion National Park SR 9 *Web:* www.nps.gov/zion	Springdale	UT	84767	435-772-3256	772-3426

Vermont

				Phone	Fax
Marsh-Billings-Rockefeller National Historical Park 54 Elm St *Web:* www.nps.gov	Woodstock	VT	05091	802-457-3368	457-3405

Virgin Islands

				Phone	Fax
Buck Island Reef National Monument 2100 Church St Ste 100 *Web:* www.nps.gov/buis	Christiansted	VI	00820	340-773-1460	773-5995
Salt River Bay National Historical Park & Ecological Preserve c/o Christiansted National Historic Site 2100 Church St Ste 100 *TF:* 866-705-5711 ■ *Web:* www.nps.gov/sari	Christiansted	VI	00820	340-773-1460	773-5995

Virginia

				Phone	Fax
Appomattox Court House National Historical Park Hwy 24 PO Box 218 *Web:* www.nps.gov/apco	Appomattox	VA	24522	434-352-8987	352-8330
Arlington House-Robert E Lee Memorial George Washington Memorial Pkwy Turkey Run Pk *Web:* www.nps.gov/arho	McLean	VA	22101	703-235-1530	235-1546
Booker T. Washington National Monument 12130 Booker T Washington Hwy *Web:* www.nps.gov/bowa	Hardy	VA	24101	540-721-2094	721-8311
Cedar Creek & Belle Grove National Historical Park 7718 1/2 Main St *Web:* www.nps.gov	Middletown	VA	22645	540-868-9176	869-4527
Colonial National Historical Park PO Box 210 *TF:* 866-945-7920 ■ *Web:* www.nps.gov/colo	Yorktown	VA	23690	757-898-3400	898-6346
Fredericksburg & Spotsylvania National Military Park 120 Chatham Ln *Web:* www.nps.gov/frsp	Fredericksburg	VA	22405	540-371-0802	371-1907
George Washington Birthplace National Monument 1732 Popes Creek Rd *Web:* www.nps.gov/gewa	Washington's Birthplace	VA	22443	804-224-1732	224-2142
George Washington Memorial Parkway Turkey Run Pk *Web:* www.nps.gov/gwmp	McLean	VA	22101	703-289-2500	289-2598
Locust Shade Park 4701 Locust Shade Dr. *Web:* www.pwcparks.org	Triangle	VA	22172	703-221-8579	
Lyndon Baines Johnson Memorial Grove on the Potomac Turkey Run Pk George Washington Memorial Pkwy *Web:* www.nps.gov/lyba	McLean	VA	22101	703-289-2500	289-2598
Maggie L Walker National Historic Site 600 N Second St. *Web:* www.nps.gov/malw	Richmond	VA	23223	804-771-2017	771-2226
Petersburg National Battlefield 1539 Hickory Hill Rd *Web:* www.nps.gov/pete	Petersburg	VA	23803	804-732-3531	732-0835
Prince William Forest Park 18100 Pk Headquarters Rd *Web:* www.nps.gov	Triangle	VA	22172	703-221-7181	221-3258
Red Hill Patrick Henry National Memorial 1250 Red Hill Rd *TF:* 800-514-7463 ■ *Web:* www.redhill.org	Brookneal	VA	24528	434-376-2044	376-2647
Richmond National Battlefield Park 3215 E Broad St *TF:* 866-733-7768 ■ *Web:* www.nps.gov	Richmond	VA	23223	804-226-1981	771-8522
Shenandoah National Park 3655 US Hwy 211E *TF:* 800-732-0911 ■ *Web:* www.nps.gov/shen	Luray	VA	22835	540-999-3500	999-3601
Theodore Roosevelt Island Park c/o Turkey Run Pk George Washington Memorial Pkwy *Web:* www.nps.gov/this	McLean	VA	22101	703-289-2500	289-2598
Wolf Trap National Park for the Performing Arts 1551 Trap Rd *Web:* www.nps.gov/wotr	Vienna	VA	22182	703-255-1800	255-1971

Washington

				Phone	Fax
Ebey's Landing National Historical Reserve 162 Cemetery Rd *Web:* www.nps.gov	Coupeville	WA	98239	360-678-6084	678-2246
Fort Vancouver National Historic Site 612 E Reserve St. *TF:* 800-832-3599 ■ *Web:* www.nps.gov	Vancouver	WA	98661	360-816-6230	
Klondike Gold Rush National Historical Park - Seattle Unit 319 Second Ave S *Web:* www.nps.gov	Seattle	WA	98104	206-220-4240	
Lake Chelan National Recreation Area 810 State Rt 20 *Web:* www.nps.gov/lach	Sedro Woolley	WA	98284	360-854-7200	856-1934
Lake Roosevelt National Recreation Area 1008 Crest Dr *Web:* www.nps.gov	Coulee Dam	WA	99116	509-633-9441	633-9332
Mount Rainier National Park 55210 238th Ave E *Web:* www.nps.gov/mora	Ashford	WA	98304	360-569-2211	569-6519
North Cascades National Park 810 SR 20 *Web:* www.nps.gov/noca	Sedro Woolley	WA	98284	360-856-5700	856-1934
Ross Lake National Recreation Area 810 State Rt 20 *TF:* 866-705-5711 ■ *Web:* www.nps.gov/rola	Sedro Woolley	WA	98284	360-854-7200	856-1934
San Juan Island National Historical Park 4668 Cattle Pt Rd PO Box 429 *Web:* www.nps.gov/sajh	Friday Harbor	WA	98250	360-378-2240	378-2615
Whitman Mission National Historic Site 328 Whitman Mission Rd *Web:* www.nps.gov	Walla Walla	WA	99362	509-522-6360	522-6355

West Virginia

				Phone	Fax
Appalachian National Scenic Trail PO Box 807 *Web:* www.nps.gov/appa	Harpers Ferry	WV	25425	304-535-6331	535-2667
Bluestone National Scenic River PO Box 246 PO Box 246 *Web:* www.nps.gov/blue	Glen Jean	WV	25846	304-465-0508	465-0591
Gauley River National Recreation Area 104 Main St PO Box 246 *Web:* www.nps.gov/gari	Glen Jean	WV	25846	304-465-0508	465-0591
Harpers Ferry National Historic Park PO Box 65 *Web:* www.nps.gov/hafe	Harpers Ferry	WV	25425	304-535-6029	535-6244
New River Gorge National River 104 Main St PO Box 246 *Web:* www.nps.gov/neri	Glen Jean	WV	25846	304-465-0508	465-0591
Potomac Heritage National Scenic Trail PO Box B *Web:* www.nps.gov/pohe	Harpers Ferry	WV	25425	304-535-4014	

Wisconsin

				Phone	Fax
Saint Croix National Scenic Riverway 401 N Hamilton St *Web:* www.nps.gov	Saint Croix Falls	WI	54024	715-483-3284	483-3288

Wyoming

				Phone	Fax
Devils Tower National Monument Hwy 110 Bldg 170 PO Box 10 *Web:* www.nps.gov/deto	Devils Tower	WY	82714	307-467-5283	467-5350

Phone *Fax*

Fort Laramie National Historic Site
965 Grey Rocks Rd . . . . Fort Laramie WY 82212 307-837-2221 837-2120
Web: www.nps.gov/fola

Fossil Butte National Monument PO Box 592 . . . . Kemmerer WY 83101 307-877-4455 877-4457
Web: www.nps.gov

Grand Teton National Park
Teton Pk Rd PO Box 170 . . . . Moose WY 83012 307-739-3300 739-3438
Web: www.nps.gov/grte

John D. Rockefeller Jr Memorial Parkway
PO Box 170 . . . . Moose WY 83012 307-739-3300 739-3438
Web: www.nps.gov/jodr

Yellowstone National Park
PO Box 168 . . . . Yellowstone National Park WY 82190 307-344-7381 344-2323*
**Fax:* Mail Rm ■ *Web:* www.nps.gov

565 PARKS - STATE

See Also Nature Centers, Parks, Other Natural Areas p. 1813; Parks - National - Canada p. 2871; Parks - National - US p. 2871

Alabama

Phone *Fax*

Bladon Springs State Park
3921 Bladon Rd . . . . Bladon Springs AL 36919 251-754-9207 754-9207
TF: 800-252-7275 ■ *Web:* www.alapark.com/parks

Blue Springs State Park 2595 Alabama 10 . . . . Clio AL 36017 334-397-4875 397-4875
Web: www.alapark.com

Buck's Pocket State Park 393 County Rd 174 . . . . Grove Oak AL 35975 256-659-2000 659-2000
TF: 800-760-4089 ■ *Web:* www.alapark.com

Cathedral Caverns State Park 637 Cave Rd . . . . Woodville AL 35776 256-728-8193 728-8193
TF: 800-252-7275 ■ *Web:* www.alapark.com

Cheaha Resort State Park 19644 Hwy 281 . . . . Delta AL 36258 256-488-5111 488-5885
TF: 800-610-5801 ■ *Web:* www.alapark.com

Chewacla State Park 124 Shell Toomer Pkwy . . . . Auburn AL 36830 334-887-5621 821-2439
TF: 800-252-7275 ■ *Web:* www.alapark.com

Chickasaw State Park 26955 US Hwy 43 . . . . Gallion AL 36742 334-295-8230 295-8230
TF: 800-760-4089 ■ *Web:* www.alapark.com

Frank Jackson State Park 100 Jerry Adams Dr . . . . Opp AL 36467 334-493-6988 493-2478
TF: 800-760-4089 ■ *Web:* www.alapark.com

Gulf State Park 20115 Alabama 135 . . . . Gulf Shores AL 36542 251-948-7275 948-7726
Web: www.alapark.com

Lake Lurleen State Park 13226 Lake Lurleen Rd . . . . Coker AL 35452 205-339-1558 339-8885
TF: 800-760-4089 ■ *Web:* www.alapark.com

Lakepoint Resort State Park 104 Lakepoint Dr . . . . Eufaula AL 36027 334-687-8011 687-3273
TF: 800-544-5253 ■ *Web:* www.alapark.com

Meaher State Park 5200 Battleship Pkwy . . . . Spanish Fort AL 36577 251-626-5529 626-5529
TF: 800-252-7275 ■ *Web:* www.alapark.com

Monte Sano State Park 5105 Nolen Ave . . . . Huntsville AL 35801 256-534-3757 539-7069
TF: 800-252-7275 ■ *Web:* www.alapark.com

Oak Mountain State Park 200 Terr Dr PO Box 278 . . . . . . Pelham AL 35124 205-620-2520 620-2531
TF: 800-252-7275 ■ *Web:* www.alapark.com

Paul M. Grist State Park 1546 Grist Rd . . . . Selma AL 36701 334-872-5846 872-5846
TF: 800-252-7275 ■ *Web:* www.alapark.com

Rickwood Caverns State Park
370 Rickwood Pk Rd . . . . Warrior AL 35180 205-647-9692 647-9692
TF: 800-252-7275 ■ *Web:* www.alapark.com

Roland Cooper State Park 285 Deer Run Dr . . . . Camden AL 36726 334-682-4838 682-4050
TF: 800-252-7275 ■ *Web:* www.alapark.com

Wind Creek State Park 4325 Al Hwy 128 . . . . Alexander City AL 35010 256-329-0845 234-4870
TF: 800-252-7275 ■ *Web:* www.alapark.com

Alaska

Phone *Fax*

Big Delta State Historical Park
c/o Northern Area Office 3700 Airport Way . . . . Fairbanks AK 99709 907-451-2695
Web: www.dnr.alaska.gov/parks/units/deltajct/bigdelta.htm

Birch Lake State Recreation Area
c/o Northern Area Office 3700 Airport Way . . . . Fairbanks AK 99709 907-451-2695
Web: www.dnr.alaska.gov/parks/units/birch.htm

Blueberry Lake State Recreation Site
23 Richardson Hwy . . . . Valdez AK 99686 907-269-8400
Web: dnr.alaska.gov/parks/aspunits/kenai/blueberrylksrs.htm

Boswell Bay State Marine Park PO Box 1247 . . . . Soldotna AK 99669 907-262-5581
Web: dnr.alaska.gov/parks/units/pwssmp/smpcord.htm

Chena River State Recreation Area
c/o Northern Area Office 3700 Airport Way . . . . Fairbanks AK 99709 907-451-2705
Web: www.dnr.alaska.gov/parks/units/chena

Chilkat Islands State Marine Park
550 W Seventh Ave Ste 1260 . . . . Anchorage AK 99501 907-269-8400
Web: dnr.alaska.gov/parks/units/haines.htm

Chilkoot Lake State Recreation Site
1069 Haines Hwy . . . . Haines AK 99827 907-465-4563
Web: www.dnr.alaska.gov/parks/aspunits/southeast/chilkootlksrs.htm

Chugach State Park 18620 Seward Highway . . . . Anchorage AK 99516 907-345-5014 345-6982
TF: 800-478-6196 ■ *Web:* dnr.alaska.gov

Clam Gulch State Recreation Area
PO Box 1247 . . . . Soldotna AK 99669 907-262-5581
Web: dnr.alaska.gov/parks/units/clamglch.htm

Clearwater State Recreation Site
3700 Airport Way . . . . Fairbanks AK 99709 907-451-2695
Web: www.dnr.alaska.gov/parks/units/deltajct/clearwtr.htm

Crooked Creek State Recreation Site
PO Box 1247 . . . . Soldotna AK 99669 907-262-5581
Web: dnr.alaska.gov/parks/units/kasilof.htm

Dall Bay State Marine Park
400 Willoughby Ave PO Box 111071 . . . . Juneau AK 99811 907-465-4563
Web: www.dnr.alaska.gov/parks/aspunits/marinepark/dallbay.htm

Decision Point State Marine Park
550 W Seventh Ave PO Box 1247 . . . . Anchorage AK 99501 907-269-8400 269-8901
Web: dnr.alaska.gov/parks/units/pwssmp/smpwhit1.htm

Phone *Fax*

Deep Creek State Recreation Area
PO Box 1247 . . . . Soldotna AK 99669 907-262-5581
Web: dnr.alaska.gov/parks/units/deepck.htm

Delta State Recreation Site
3700 Airport Wy 3700 Airport Way . . . . Fairbanks AK 99709 907-451-2695
Web: www.dnr.alaska.gov/parks/units/deltajct/deltasrs.htm

Denali State Park 7278 E Bogard Rd . . . . Wasilla AK 99654 907-745-3975 745-0938
TF: 800-478-6196 ■ *Web:* dnr.alaska.gov/parks/units/denali1.htm

Department of Natural Resources
550 W Seventh Ave Ste 1260 . . . . Anchorage AK 99501 907-269-8400
Web: dnr.alaska.gov/parks/units/haines.htm

Donnelly Creek State Recreation Site
3700 Airport Way . . . . Fairbanks AK 99709 907-451-2695
Web: www.dnr.alaska.gov/parks/units/deltajct/donnelly.htm

Driftwood Bay State Marine Park PO Box 1247 . . . . Soldotna AK 99669 907-262-5581
Web: dnr.alaska.gov/parks/units/pwssmp/smpsewd.htm

Eagle Beach State Recreation Area
400 Willoughby Ave 4th Fl . . . . Juneau AK 99811 907-465-4563
Web: www.dnr.alaska.gov/parks/aspunits/southeast/eaglebeachsra.htm

Eagle Trail State Recreation Site
c/o Northern Area Office 3700 Airport Way . . . . Fairbanks AK 99709 907-883-3686
Web: www.dnr.alaska.gov/parks/aspunits/northern/eagletrailsrs.htm

Entry Cove State Marine Park PO Box 1247 . . . . Soldotna AK 99669 907-262-5581
Web: dnr.alaska.gov/parks/units/pwssmp/smpwhit1.htm

Fielding Lake State Recreation Site
3700 Airport Way . . . . Fairbanks AK 99709 907-451-2695
Web: www.dnr.alaska.gov/parks/units/deltajct/fielding.htm

Finger Lake State Recreation Area
7278 E Bogard Rd . . . . Wasilla AK 99654 907-745-3975
Web: dnr.alaska.gov/parks/aspunits/matsu/fingerlksrs.htm

Funter Bay State Marine Park
400 Willoughby Ave PO Box 111071 . . . . Juneau AK 99811 907-465-3400 586-2954

Granite Bay State Marine Park PO Box 1247 . . . . Soldotna AK 99669 907-262-5581
Web: dnr.alaska.gov/parks/units/pwssmp/smpwhit2.htm

Grindall Island State Marine Park
400 Willoughby Ave PO Box 111071 . . . . Juneau AK 99811 907-465-4563
Web: www.dnr.alaska.gov/parks/aspunits/southeast/grindallimp.htm

Harding Lake State Recreation Area
c/o Northern Area Office 3700 Airport Way . . . . Fairbanks AK 99709 907-451-2695
Web: www.dnr.alaska.gov/parks/units/harding.htm

Horseshoe Bay State Marine Park PO Box 1247 . . . . . . Soldotna AK 99669 907-262-5581
Web: dnr.alaska.gov/parks/units/pwssmp/smpwhit2.htm

King Mountain State Recreation Site
Mile 76 Glenn Hwy 33915 N Glenn Hwy . . . . Palmer AK 99645 907-240-9797
Web: dnr.alaska.gov/parks/aspunits/matsu/kingmtnsrs.htm

Lake Aleknagik State Recreation Site
550 W Seventh Ave Ste 1380 . . . . Anchorage AK 99501 907-842-2641
Web: www.dnr.alaska.gov/parks/aspunits/woodtik/lkaleknsrs.htm

Liberty Falls State Recreation Site
Mile 23.5 Edgerton Hwy . . . . Glennallen AK 99588 907-823-2223
Web: dnr.alaska.gov/parks/aspunits/matsu/libertyflsrs.htm

Lower Chatanika River State Recreation Area
c/o Northern Area Office 3700 Airport Way . . . . Fairbanks AK 99709 907-269-8400
Web: www.dnr.alaska.gov/parks/aspunits/northern/lrchatrivsra.htm

Matanuska Glacier State Recreation Site
c/o Mat-Su/Copper Basin Area Office
7278 E Bogard Rd . . . . Wasilla AK 99654 907-745-3975
Web: dnr.alaska.gov/parks/aspunits/matsu/matsuglsrs.htm

Moon Lake State Recreation Site
c/o Northern Area Office 3700 Airport Way . . . . Fairbanks AK 99709 907-883-3686
Web: www.dnr.alaska.gov/parks/aspunits/northern/moonlksrs.htm

Nancy Lake State Recreation Area
7278 E Bogard Rd HC 32 PO Box 6706 . . . . Wasilla AK 99654 907-745-3975
Web: dnr.alaska.gov/parks/units/nancylk/nancylk.htm

Ninilchik State Recreation Area PO Box 1247 . . . . Soldotna AK 99669 907-262-5581
Web: dnr.alaska.gov/parks/units/nilchik.htm

Old Sitka State Historic Site
7.5 Halibut Point Rd . . . . Sitka AK 99835 907-465-4563

Oliver Inlet State Marine Park
400 Willoughby Ave PO Box 111071 . . . . Juneau AK 99801 907-465-4563 586-3113
TF: 855-277-4491 ■ *Web:* www.dnr.alaska.gov/parks

Petroglyph Beach State Historic Site
400 Willoughby Ave PO Box 111071 . . . . Juneau AK 11071 907-465-4563
Web: www.dnr.alaska.gov/parks/aspunits/southeast/wrangpetroshs.htm

Portage Cove State Recreation Site
400 Willoughby Ave Fourth Fl PO Box 111010 . . . . Juneau AK 99811 907-465-4563
Web: www.dnr.alaska.gov/parks/aspunits/southeast/portcovesrs.htm

Quartz Lake State Recreation Area
c/o Northern Area Office 3700 Airport Way . . . . Fairbanks AK 99709 907-451-2695
Web: www.dnr.alaska.gov/parks/units/deltajct/quartz.htm

Saint James Bay State Marine Park
400 Willoughby Ave Ste 500 . . . . Juneau AK 99811 907-465-4563 586-3113
Web: dnr.alaska.gov

Salcha River State Recreation Site
c/o Northern Area Office 3700 Airport Way . . . . Fairbanks AK 99709 907-451-2695
Web: www.dnr.alaska.gov/parks/units/salcha.htm

Shelter Island State Marine Park
PO Box 111071 . . . . Juneau AK 99811 907-465-4563
Web: dnr.alaska.gov/parks/cabins/south.htm

Summit Lake State Recreation Area
550 W 7th Ave Ste 160 . . . . Anchorage AK 99501 402-374-1727
Web: dnr.alaska.gov/parks/index

Summit Lake State Recreation Site
c/o Mat-Su/CB Area Office 7278 E Bogard Rd . . . . Wasilla AK 99654 907-745-3975
Web: dnr.alaska.gov/parks/units/summit.htm

Tok River State Recreation Site
c/o Northern Area Office 3700 Airport Way . . . . Fairbanks AK 99709 907-883-3686
Web: www.dnr.alaska.gov/parks/aspunits/northern/tokrvsrs.htm

Totem Bight State Historical Park
400 Willoughby Ave PO Box 111071 . . . . Juneau AK 99811 907-465-4563
Web: www.dnr.alaska.gov/parks/units/totembgh.htm

Wickersham State Historic Site
400 Willoughby Ave Ste 500 PO Box 111071 . . . . Juneau AK 99811 907-465-4563
Web: www.dnr.alaska.gov/parks/units/wickrshm.htm

Phone | Fax

Willow Creek State Recreation Area
7278 E Bogard Rd. Wasilla AK 99654 907-745-3975
Web: dnr.alaska.gov/parks/aspunits/matsu/willowcksra.htm

Wood-Tikchik State Park
PO Box 1822 Ste 1390 Dillingham AK 99576 907-269-8698
Web: dnr.alaska.gov

Worthington Glacier State Recreation Site
287 Richardson Hwy. Soldotna AK 99669 907-262-5581
Web: dnr.alaska.gov/parks/aspunits/kenai/worthglsrs.htm

Arizona

Phone | Fax

Buckskin Mountain State Park 5476 Hwy 95 Parker AZ 85344 928-667-3231

Catalina State Park 11570 N Oracle Rd. Tucson AZ 85737 520-628-5798 628-5797

Dead Horse Ranch State Park
675 Dead Horse Ranch Rd Cottonwood AZ 86326 928-634-5283

Fool Hollow Lake Recreation Area
1500 N Fool Hollow Lk Rd Show Low AZ 85901 928-537-3680

Homolovi Ruins State Park 87 N Rd. Winslow AZ 86047 928-289-4106 289-2021
Web: www.azstateparks.com

Jerome State Historic Park PO Box D Jerome AZ 86331 928-634-5381
Web: www.azstateparks.com

Kartchner Caverns State Park 2980 Arizona 90 Benson AZ 85602 520-586-2283
Web: www.azstateparks.com

Lake Havasu State Park
699 London Bridge Rd Lake Havasu City AZ 86403 928-855-2784
Web: golakehavasu.com

Lost Dutchman State Park
6109 N Apache Tr. Apache Junction AZ 85219 480-982-4485
Web: azstateparks.com

Lyman Lake State Park 11 US 180 Saint Johns AZ 85936 928-337-4441
Web: www.azstateparks.com

Oracle State Park 3820 Wildlife Dr Oracle AZ 85623 520-896-2425
Web: azstateparks.com

Patagonia Lake State Park
400 Patagonia Lk Rd. Patagonia AZ 85624 520-287-6965
Web: azstateparks.com

Picacho Peak State Park
15520 Picacho Peak Rd Picacho AZ 85241 520-466-3183
Web: www.azstateparks.com

Red Rock State Park 4050 Red Rock Loop Rd. Sedona AZ 86336 928-282-6907 282-5972
Web: azstateparks.com

Riordan Mansion State Historic Park
409 W Riordan Rd Flagstaff AZ 86001 928-779-4395 556-0253

Roper Lake State Park 101 E Roper Lk Rd Safford AZ 85546 928-428-6760 428-7879
Web: azstateparks.itinio.com

San Rafael Ranch State Park
2036 Duquesne Rd. Patagonia AZ 85624 520-394-2447
Web: azstateparks.com

Slide Rock State Park 6871 N Hwy 89A Sedona AZ 86336 928-282-3034
Web: azpra.org

Tombstone Courthouse State Historic Park
223 E Toughnut St Tombstone AZ 85638 520-457-3311
Web: azstateparks.com

Tonto Natural Bridge State Park Hwy 87 N Payson AZ 85547 928-476-4202 476-2264
Web: www.azstateparks.com

Tubac Presidio State Historic Park
1 Burruel St Tubac AZ 85646 520-398-2252
Web: azstateparks.com

Yuma Territorial Prison State Historic Park
1 Prison Hill Rd PO Box 10792 Yuma AZ 85364 928-783-4771

Arkansas

Phone | Fax

Arkansas Museum of Natural Resources
3853 Smackover Hwy. Smackover AR 71762 870-725-2877 725-2161
TF: 888-287-2757 ■ *Web:* www.arkansasstateparks.com

Arkansas Post Museum 5530 Hwy 165 S Gillett AR 72055 870-548-2634
Web: www.arkansasstateparks.com

Bull Shoals-White River State Park
140 Boat Dock Cove Rd Bull Shoals AR 72169 870-431-5521
Web: www.arkansasstateparks.com

Cane Creek State Park 50 State Pk Rd Star City AR 71667 870-628-4714 628-3611
TF: 888-287-2757 ■ *Web:* www.arkansasstateparks.com

Conway Cemetery State Park
140 Boat Dock Cove Rd 1 Capitol Mall. Bull Shoals AR 72169 888-287-2757
TF: 888-287-2757 ■ *Web:* www.arkansasstateparks.com/conwaycemetery

Cossatot River State Park-Natural Area
1980 Hwy 278 W Wickes AR 71973 870-385-2201 385-7858
TF: 877-665-6343 ■ *Web:* www.arkansasstateparks.com

Crater of Diamonds State Park
209 State Pk Rd Murfreesboro AR 71958 870-285-3113
Web: www.craterofdiamondsstatepark.com

Crowley's Ridge State Park 2092 Hwy 168 N Paragould AR 72450 870-573-6751
Web: www.arkansasstateparks.com

Daisy State Park 103 E Pk Kirby AR 71950 870-398-4487
Web: www.arkansasstateparks.com/daisy

DeGray Lake Resort State Park
2027 State Pk Entrance Rd Bismarck AR 71929 501-865-2801
TF: 800-737-8355 ■ *Web:* www.degray.com

Delta Heritage Trail State Park PO Box 193. Watson AR 71674 870-644-3474
Web: www.arkansasstateparks.com

Devil's Den State Park
11333 W Arkansas Hwy 74. West Fork AR 72774 479-761-3325
TF: 888-742-8701 ■ *Web:* www.arkansasstateparks.com

Hampson Archeological Museum State Park
PO Box 156 Wilson AR 72395 870-655-8622
TF: 888-742-8701 ■ *Web:* www.arkansasstateparks.com

Herman Davis State Park
Corner of Ark 18 Baltimore St. Manila AR 72201 888-287-2757
TF: 888-287-2757 ■ *Web:* www.arkansasstateparks.com/hermandavis

Phone | Fax

Hobbs State Park-Conservation Area
21392 E Hwy 12 Rogers AR 72756 479-789-2380
Web: www.arkansasstateparks.com

Jacksonport State Park 1 Capitol Mall. Newport AR 72112 870-523-2143
TF: 888-287-2757 ■ *Web:* www.arkansasstateparks.com

Lake Catherine State Park
1200 Catherine Pk Rd. Hot Springs AR 71913 501-844-4176
Web: www.arkansasstateparks.com

Lake Charles State Park 3705 Hwy 25 Powhatan AR 72458 870-878-6595
Web: www.arkansasstateparks.com/lakecharles

Lake Chicot State Park 2542 Hwy 257 Lake Village AR 71653 870-265-5480
TF: 800-264-2430 ■ *Web:* www.arkansasstateparks.com

Lake Dardanelle State Park
100 State Pk Dr. Russellville AR 72802 479-967-5516
Web: www.arkansasstateparks.com

Lake Fort Smith State Park PO Box 4 Mountainburg AR 72946 479-369-2469
Web: www.arkansasstateparks.com

Lake Frierson State Park 7904 Hwy. Jonesboro AR 72401 870-932-2615
Web: www.arkansasstateparks.com

Lake Ouachita State Park
5451 Mtn Pine Rd. Mountain Pine AR 71956 501-767-9366
Web: www.arkansasstateparks.com

Lake Poinsett State Park 5752 State Pk Ln Harrisburg AR 72432 870-578-2064
Web: www.arkansasstateparks.com

Logoly State Park PO Box 245 McNeil AR 71752 870-695-3561
Web: www.arkansasstateparks.com

Lower White River Museum State Park
2009 Main St Des Arc AR 72040 870-256-3711 256-9202
Web: www.arkansasstateparks.com

Mammoth Spring State Park PO Box 36 Mammoth Spring AR 72554 870-625-7364
Web: www.arkansasstateparks.com

Millwood State Park 1564 Hwy 32 E. Ashdown AR 71822 870-898-2800
Web: www.arkansasstateparks.com

Moro Bay State Park 6071 US Hwy 600 Jersey AR 71651 870-463-8555
TF: 888-742-8701 ■ *Web:* www.arkansasstateparks.com

Mount Magazine State Park 16878 Hwy 309 S. Paris AR 72855 479-963-8502 963-1031
Web: www.arkansasstateparks.com

Mount Nebo State Park
16728 W State Hwy 155 Dardanelle AR 72834 479-229-3655
Web: www.arkansasstateparks.com

Old Davidsonville State Park
7953 Hwy 166 S. Pocahontas AR 72455 870-892-4708
Web: www.arkansasstateparks.com

Old Washington Historic State Park
PO Box 129 Washington AR 71862 870-983-2684 983-2736
Web: www.historicwashingtonstatepark.com

Ozark Folk Ctr State Park 1032 Pk Ave Mountain View AR 72560 870-269-3851 269-2909
TF: 800-264-3655 ■ *Web:* www.ozarkfolkcenter.com

Parkin Archeological State Park PO Box 1110 Parkin AR 72373 870-755-2500
Web: www.arkansasstateparks.com

Petit Jean State Park
1285 Petit Jean Mtn Rd Morrilton AR 72110 501-727-5441
Web: www.petitjeanstatepark.com

Pinnacle Mountain State Park
11901 Pinnacle Vly Rd Little Rock AR 72223 501-868-5806 868-5018
Web: www.arkansasstateparks.com

Plantation Agriculture Museum PO Box 87 Scott AR 72142 501-961-1409
Web: www.arkansasstateparks.com

Prairie Grove Battlefield State Park
506 E Douglas St Prairie Grove AR 72753 479-846-2990
Web: www.arkansasstateparks.com

Queen Wilhelmina State Park 3877 Arkansas 88 Mena AR 71953 479-394-2863
TF: 888-287-2757 ■ *Web:* www.arkansasstateparks.com

South Arkansas Arboretum PO Box 7010. El Dorado AR 71731 888-287-2757
TF: 888-287-2757 ■
Web: www.arkansasstateparks.com/southarkansasarboretum

Toltec Mounds Archeological State Park
490 Toltec Mounds Rd Scott AR 72142 501-961-9442 961-9221
Web: www.arkansasstateparks.com

Village Creek State Park 201 County Rd 754. Wynne AR 72396 870-238-9406
Web: www.arkansasstateparks.com

White Oak Lake State Park 563 Hwy 387 Bluff City AR 71722 870-685-2748
Web: www.arkansasstateparks.com

Withrow Springs State Park 33424 Spur 23 Huntsville AR 72740 479-559-2593
Web: www.arkansasstateparks.com

Woolly Hollow State Park
82 Woolly Hollow Rd Greenbrier AR 72058 501-679-2098
Web: www.arkansasstateparks.com

California

Phone | Fax

Ahjumawi Lava Springs State Park
c/o Northern Buttes District Office
400 Glen Dr Oroville CA 95966 530-538-2200
Web: www.parks.ca.gov/?page_id=464

Antelope Valley Indian Museum State Historic Park
Antelope Vly Fwy Ave M. Perris CA 92571 661-946-3055
Web: www.avim.parks.ca.gov

Anza-Borrego Desert State Park
200 Palm Canyon Dr Borrego Springs CA 92004 760-767-5311 767-3427
Web: www.parks.ca.gov/?page_id=638

Armstrong Redwoods State Reserve
17000 Armstrong Woods Rd Guerneville CA 95446 707-869-2015 869-5629
Web: www.parks.ca.gov/default.asp?page_id=450

Asilomar State Beach & Conference Grounds
804 Crocker Ave 2211 Garden Rd. Pacific Grove CA 93950 831-646-6440
Web: www.parks.ca.gov/default.asp?page_id=566

Auburn State Recreation Area
501 El Dorado St 7806 Folsom-Auburn Rd Auburn CA 95603 530-885-4527
Web: www.parks.ca.gov/default.asp?page_id=502

Austin Creek State Recreation Area
17000 Armstrong Woods Rd Guerneville CA 95446 707-869-2015
Web: www.parks.ca.gov/default.asp?page_id=452

				Phone	Fax
Azalea State Reserve c/o N Coast Redwoods District Office PO Box 2006 *Web:* www.parks.ca.gov/default.asp?page_id=420	Eureka	CA	95502	707-677-3132	
Benbow Lake State Recreation Area 1600 Hwy 101 *Web:* www.parks.ca.gov/default.asp?page_id=426	Garberville	CA	95542	707-923-3238	
Benicia Capitol State Historic Park 115 W G St 845 Casa Grande Rd *Web:* www.parks.ca.gov/default.asp?page_id=475	Benicia	CA	94510	707-745-3385	
Benicia State Recreation Area 1 State Park Rd 845 Casa Grande Rd *Web:* www.parks.ca.gov/default.asp?page_id=476	Benicia	CA	94510	707-648-1911	
Bidwell-Sacramento River State Park 1416 Ninth St 400 Glen Dr *Web:* www.parks.ca.gov/default.asp?page_id=463	Sacramento	CA	95814	530-342-5185	
Big Basin Redwoods State Park 21600 Big Basin Way *Web:* www.parks.ca.gov	Boulder Creek	CA	95006	831-338-8860	
Bodie State Historic Park PO Box 515 *Web:* www.parks.ca.gov	Bridgeport	CA	93517	760-647-6445	
Border Field State Park 301 Caspian Way 4477 Pacific Hwy *Web:* www.parks.ca.gov/default.asp?page_id=664	Imperial Beach	CA	91932	619-575-3613	
Bothe-Napa Valley State Park 3801 St Helena Hwy 845 Casa Grande Rd *Web:* www.parks.ca.gov/default.asp?page_id=477	Calistoga	CA	94515	707-942-4575	
Brannan Island State Recreation Area 17645 California 160 7806 Folsom-Auburn Rd *Web:* www.parks.ca.gov/default.asp?page_id=487	Rio Vista	CA	94571	916-777-7701	
Butano State Park 1500 Cloverdale Rd 303 Big Trees Pk Rd *Web:* www.parks.ca.gov/default.asp?page_id=536	Pescadero	CA	94060	650-879-2040	
Calaveras Big Trees State Park 1170 California 4 22708 Broadway St *Web:* www.parks.ca.gov/default.asp?page_id=551	Arnold	CA	95223	209-795-2334	
California State Mining & Mineral Museum 5005 Fairgrounds Rd *Web:* www.parks.ca.gov/default.asp?page_id=588	Mariposa	CA	95338	209-742-7625	966-3597
California State Railroad Museum 125 "I" St 111 'I' St *TF:* 866-240-4655 ■ *Web:* www.csrmf.org	Sacramento	CA	95814	916-323-9280	327-5655
Carlsbad State Beach c/o San Diego Coast District Office 4477 Pacific Hwy *TF:* 800-777-0369 ■ *Web:* www.parks.ca.gov/default.asp?page_id=653	San Diego	CA	92110	760-438-3143	
China Camp State Park 101 Peacock Gap Trl *Web:* www.parks.ca.gov/default.asp?page_id=466	San Rafael	CA	94901	415-456-0766	
Clay Pit State Vehicular Recreation Area 400 Glen Dr *Web:* www.parks.ca.gov	Oroville	CA	95966	530-538-2200	
Columbia State Historic Park 11255 Jackson St *Web:* www.parks.ca.gov	Columbia	CA	95310	209-588-9128	
Corona del Mar State Beach 3001 Ocean Blvd *Web:* www.parks.ca.gov/default.asp?page_id=652	Corona Del Mar	CA	92625	949-644-3151	
Crystal Cove State Park 8471 N Coast Hwy *Web:* www.parks.ca.gov/default.asp?page_id=644	Laguna Beach	CA	92651	949-494-3539	
Cuyamaca Rancho State Park 13652 Hwy 79 *TF:* 800-444-7275 ■ *Web:* www.parks.ca.gov/default.asp?page_id=667	Julian	CA	92036	760-765-0755	765-3021
Del Norte Coast Redwoods State Park 1111 Second St *Web:* www.parks.ca.gov/default.asp?page_id=414	Crescent City	CA	95531	707-465-7335	
Delta Meadows 17645 State Hwy 160 *Web:* www.parks.ca.gov/default.asp?page_id=492	Rio Vista	CA	94571	916-777-7701	
DL Bliss State Park c/o Sierra District Office PO Box 266 *Web:* www.parks.ca.gov/?page_id=505	Tahoma	CA	96142	530-525-7277	
Dockweiler State Beach c/o Los Angeles County Dept of Beaches & Harbors 13837 Fiji Way *Web:* www.parks.ca.gov	Marina del Rey	CA	90292	310-305-9503	
Doheny State Beach 25300 Dana Pt Harbor Dr *Web:* www.parks.ca.gov	Dana Point	CA	92629	949-496-6172	
Donner Memorial State Park c/o Sierra District Office PO Box 266 *Web:* www.parks.ca.gov/default.asp?page_id=503	Tahoma	CA	96142	530-582-7892	
Emerald Bay State Park c/o Sierra District Office PO Box 266 *Web:* www.parks.ca.gov/default.asp?page_id=506	Tahoma	CA	96142	530-525-7277	
Empire Mine State Historic Park c/o Sierra District Office PO Box 266 *Web:* www.parks.ca.gov/default.asp?page_id=499	Tahoma	CA	96142	530-273-8522	
Folsom Powerhouse State Historic Park 9980 Greenback Ln 7806 Folsom-Auburn Rd *Web:* www.parks.ca.gov	Folsom	CA	95630	916-985-4843	
Forest of Nisene Marks State Park c/o Santa Cruz District Office 303 Big Trees Pk Rd *Web:* www.parks.ca.gov/?page_id=666	Felton	CA	95018	831-763-7062	
Fort Humboldt State Historic Park c/o N Coast Redwoods District Office PO Box 2006 *Web:* www.parks.ca.gov/default.asp?page_id=665	Eureka	CA	95502	707-445-6567	
Fort Ross State Historic Park 19005 Coast Hwy 1 *Web:* www.parks.ca.gov/default.asp?page_id=449	Jenner	CA	95450	707-847-3286	
Fort Tejon State Historic Park c/o Central Valley District Office 22708 Broadway St. **Fax Area Code:* 661 ■ *Web:* www.parks.ca.gov/default.asp?page_id=585	Columbia	CA	95310	209-536-5930	248-8373*
Governor's Mansion State Historic Park 1526 H St *Web:* www.parks.ca.gov	Sacramento	CA	95814	916-323-3047	
Half Moon Bay State Beach c/o San Mateo Coast Sector Office 95 Kelly Ave *TF:* 800-444-7275 ■ *Web:* www.parks.ca.gov	Half Moon Bay	CA	94019	650-726-8819	726-8816
Hearst San Simeon State Historical Monument 750 Hearst Castle Rd *TF:* 800-444-4445 ■ *Web:* www.parks.ca.gov/default.asp?page_id=591	San Simeon	CA	93452	805-927-2020	
Hendy Woods State Park c/o Mendocino District Office PO Box 440 *Web:* www.parks.ca.gov/default.asp?page_id=438	Mendocino	CA	95460	707-895-3141	
Henry Cowell Redwoods State Park c/o Santa Cruz District Office 303 Big Trees Pk Rd *Web:* www.parks.ca.gov/default.asp?page_id=546	Felton	CA	95018	831-335-4598	
Henry W. Coe State Park c/o Monterey District Office 2211 Garden Rd *Web:* www.parks.ca.gov/default.asp?page_id=561	Monterey	CA	93940	408-779-2728	
Hollister Hills State Vehicular Recreation Area 7800 Cienega Rd *Web:* www.parks.ca.gov	Hollister	CA	95023	831-637-8186	
Humboldt Lagoons State Park c/o N Coast Redwoods District Office PO Box 2006 *Web:* www.parks.ca.gov/default.asp?page_id=416	Eureka	CA	95502	707-677-3132	
Humboldt Redwoods State Park PO Box 100 PO Box 2006. *Web:* www.parks.ca.gov/default.asp?page_id=425	Weott	CA	95571	707-946-2409	
Hungry Valley State Vehicular Recreation Area 46001 Orwin Way *Web:* www.parks.ca.gov	Gorman	CA	93243	661-248-7007	
Huntington State Beach 21601 Pacific Coast Hwy 3030 Avenida del Presidente *Web:* www.parks.ca.gov/?page_id=643	Huntington Beach	CA	92646	714-536-1454	
Indian Grinding Rock State Historic Park 14881 Pine Grove-Volcano Rd *Web:* www.parks.ca.gov/default.asp?page_id=553	Pine Grove	CA	95665	209-296-7488	
Jack London State Historic Park 2400 London Ranch Rd *Web:* www.parks.ca.gov/default.asp?page_id=478	Glen Ellen	CA	95442	707-938-5216	
Julia Pfeiffer Burns State Park Hwy 1 2211 Garden Rd *Web:* www.parks.ca.gov/default.asp?page_id=578	Big Sur	CA	93920	831-667-2315	
Kenneth Hahn State Recreation Area c/o Angeles District Office 1925 Las Virgenes *Web:* www.parks.ca.gov/default.asp?page_id=612	Calabasas	CA	91302	323-298-3660	
Kings Beach State Recreation Area c/o Sierra District Office PO Box 266 *Web:* www.parks.ca.gov/default.asp?page_id=511	Tahoma	CA	96142	530-546-4212	
Lake Oroville State Recreation Area 917 Kelly Ridge Rd *Web:* www.parks.ca.gov/default.asp?page_id=462	Oroville	CA	95966	530-538-2219	
Lake Perris State Recreation Area 17801 Lk Perris Dr *Web:* www.parks.ca.gov	Perris	CA	92571	951-657-0676	
Leland Stanford Mansion State Historic Park 800 N St	Sacramento	CA	95814	916-324-0575	324-5885
Leucadia State Beach 948 Neptune Ave *Web:* www.parks.ca.gov/default.asp?page_id=661	Encinitas	CA	92024	760-633-2740	
Lighthouse Field State Beach West Cliff Dr *Web:* www.parks.ca.gov/default.asp?page_id=550	Santa Cruz	CA	95060	831-429-2850	
Limekiln State Park 1416 Ninth St *Web:* www.parks.ca.gov/default.asp?page_id=577	Sacramento	CA	94296	916-653-6995	
MacKerricher State Park 24100 MacKerricher Park Rd *Web:* www.parks.ca.gov/default.asp?page_id=436	Fort Bragg	CA	95437	707-964-9112	
Maillard Redwoods State Reserve PO Box 440 *Web:* www.parks.ca.gov/default.asp?page_id=439	Mendocino	CA	95460	707-937-5804	
Malibu Creek State Park 1925 Las Virgenes Rd *Web:* www.parks.ca.gov/default.asp?page_id=614	Calabasas	CA	91302	818-880-0367	
Malibu Lagoon State Beach 23200 Pacific Coast Hwy *Web:* www.parks.ca.gov/default.asp?page_id=835	Malibu	CA	90265	310-457-8143	
Manchester State Park 44500 Kinney Rd *Web:* www.parks.ca.gov/default.asp?page_id=437	Manchester	CA	95459	707-882-2463	
Marina State Beach c/o Monterey District 2211 Garden Rd *Web:* www.parks.ca.gov	Monterey	CA	93940	831-384-7695	
Marshall Gold Discovery State Historic Park 310 Back St PO Box 265 *Web:* www.parks.ca.gov/default.asp?page_id=484	Coloma	CA	95613	530-622-3470	
McArthur-Burney Falls Memorial State Park c/o Northern Buttes District Office 400 Glen Dr *Web:* www.parks.ca.gov/?page_id=455	Oroville	CA	95966	530-538-2200	
McConnell State Recreation Area 8810 McConnell Rd *Web:* www.parks.ca.gov/default.asp?page_id=554	Ballico	CA	95303	209-394-7755	
Mendocino Headlands State Park 8001 N Hwy 1 *Web:* www.parks.ca.gov/default.asp?page_id=442	Little River	CA	95456	707-937-5804	
Mendocino Woodlands State Park 39350 Little Lk Rd *Web:* www.parks.ca.gov	Mendocino	CA	95460	707-937-5755	
Millerton Lake State Recreation Area 5290 Millerton Rd. *Web:* www.parks.ca.gov/default.asp?page_id=587	Friant	CA	93626	559-822-2332	
Mono Lake Tufa State Reserve PO Box 99 *Web:* www.parks.ca.gov	Lee Vining	CA	93541	760-647-6331	

				Phone	Fax
Montara State Beach c/o Santa Cruz District Office 303 Big Trees Pk Rd *Web:* www.parks.ca.gov/?page_id=532	Felton	CA	94018	650-726-8819	
Monterey State Beach c/o Monterey District Office 2211 Garden Rd *Web:* www.parks.ca.gov/default.asp?page_id=576	Monterey	CA	93940	831-649-2836	
Monterey State Historic Park 20 Custom House Plz *Web:* www.parks.ca.gov	Monterey	CA	93940	831-649-7118	
Montgomery Woods State Reserve c/o Mendocino District Office PO Box 440 *Web:* www.parks.ca.gov/default.asp?page_id=434	Mendocino	CA	95460	707-937-5804	
Morro Bay State Park 60 State Pk Rd Morro Bay State Pk Rd *TF:* 800-777-0369 ■ *Web:* www.parks.ca.gov/?page_id=23793	Morro Bay	CA	93442	800-777-0369	
Morro Strand State Beach 60 State Pk Rd Morro Bay State Pk Rd *Web:* www.parks.ca.gov/?page_id=23793	Morro Bay	CA	93442	805-772-2560	
Moss Landing State Beach c/o Monterey District Office 2211 Garden Rd *Web:* www.parks.ca.gov/default.asp?page_id=574	Monterey	CA	93940	831-384-7695	
Natural Bridges State Beach 2531 W Cliff Dr *Web:* www.parks.ca.gov/default.asp?page_id=541	Santa Cruz	CA	95060	831-423-4609	
Ocotillo Wells State Vehicular Recreation Area 5172 Hwy 78 # 10 *Web:* www.parks.ca.gov	Borrego Springs	CA	92004	760-767-1302	
Old Town San Diego State Historic Park 4002 Wallace St *TF:* 800-777-0369 ■ *Web:* www.parks.ca.gov	San Diego	CA	92110	619-220-5422	688-3229
Olompali State Historic Park PO Box 1016 *Web:* www.parks.ca.gov	Novato	CA	94948	415-892-3383	
Pacheco State Park 38787 Dinosaur Point Rd 22708 Broadway St *Web:* www.parks.ca.gov/default.asp?page_id=560	Hollister	CA	95023	209-826-6283	
Pacifica State Beach 1416 Ninth St *Web:* www.parks.ca.gov/default.asp?page_id=524	Sacramento	CA	95814	650-738-7381	
Palomar Mountain State Park 200 Palm Canyon Dr *Web:* www.parks.ca.gov/default.asp?page_id=637	Borrego Springs	CA	92004	760-742-3462	
Patrick's Point State Park 4150 Patrick's Pt Dr *Web:* www.parks.ca.gov	Trinidad	CA	95570	707-677-3570	
Pescadero State Beach 1416 Ninth St 303 Big Trees Pk Rd *Web:* www.parks.ca.gov/?page_id=522	Sacramento	CA	95814	916-653-6995	
Petaluma Adobe State Historic Park 3325 Old Adobe Rd *Web:* www.parks.ca.gov	Petaluma	CA	94954	707-762-4871	
Pfeiffer Big Sur State Park c/o Monterey District Office 2211 Garden Rd *Web:* parks.ca.gov/?page_id=570	Monterey	CA	93940	831-667-2315	
Picacho State Recreation Area 1416 Ninth St PO Box 942896 *TF:* 800-777-0369 ■ *Web:* www.parks.ca.gov	Sacramento	CA	95814	916-653-6995	654-6374
Pigeon Point Light Station State Historic Park 210 Pigeon Pt Rd *Web:* www.parks.ca.gov	Pescadero	CA	94060	650-879-0633	
Plumas-Eureka State Park 310 Johnsville Rd *Web:* www.parks.ca.gov	Blairsden	CA	96103	530-836-2380	
Point Dume State Beach c/o Angeles District Office 1925 Las Virgenes *Web:* www.parks.ca.gov/default.asp?page_id=623	Calabasas	CA	91302	310-457-8143	
Point Sur State Historic Park c/o Monterey District Office 2211 Garden Rd *Web:* www.parks.ca.gov/default.asp?page_id=565	Monterey	CA	93940	831-625-4419	
Pomponio State Beach c/o Santa Cruz District Office 303 Big Trees Pk Rd *Web:* www.parks.ca.gov/?page_id=521	Felton	CA	95018	831-335-6318	
Portola Redwoods State Park c/o Santa Cruz District Office 303 Big Trees Pk Rd *Web:* www.parks.ca.gov/default.asp?page_id=539	Felton	CA	95018	916-988-0205	
Prairie City State Vehicular Recreation Area 13300 White Rock Rd *Web:* www.parks.ca.gov	Rancho Cordova	CA	95742	916-985-7378	
Providence Mountains State Recreation Area 1416 Ninth St *TF:* 800-777-0369 ■ *Web:* www.parks.ca.gov/default.asp?page_id=615	Sacramento	CA	95814	800-777-0369	
Railtown 1897 State Historic Park PO Box 1250 *Web:* www.railtown1897.org	Jamestown	CA	95327	209-984-3953	
Richardson Grove State Park c/o N Coast Redwoods District Office PO Box 2006 *Web:* www.parks.ca.gov/default.asp?page_id=422	Eureka	CA	95502	707-445-6547	
Robert H. Meyer Memorial State Beach c/o Angeles District Office 1925 Las Virgenes Rd *Web:* www.parks.ca.gov/default.asp?page_id=633	Calabasas	CA	91302	310-457-8143	
Salt Point State Park 25050 Hwy 1 *Web:* www.parks.ca.gov/default.asp?page_id=453	Jenner	CA	95450	707-847-3221	
Salton Sea State Recreation Area 100-225 State Pk Rd *Web:* www.parks.ca.gov/?page_id=639	North Shore	CA	92254	760-393-3052	
Samuel P. Taylor State Park PO Box 251 *Web:* www.parks.ca.gov	Lagunitas	CA	94938	415-488-9897	
San Clemente State Beach c/o Orange Coast District Office 3030 Avenida del Presidente *Web:* www.parks.ca.gov/default.asp?page_id=646	San Clemente	CA	92672	949-492-3156	
San Pasqual Battlefield State Historic Park 15808 San Pasqual Vly Rd *Web:* www.parks.ca.gov	Escondido	CA	92027	760-737-2201	
Santa Cruz Mission State Historic Park c/o Santa Cruz District Office 303 Big Trees Pk Rd *Web:* www.parks.ca.gov/default.asp?page_id=548	Felton	CA	95060	831-425-5849	429-2870
Santa Monica State Beach c/o Angeles District Office 1925 Las Virgenes Rd *Web:* www.parks.ca.gov/default.asp?page_id=624	Calabasas	CA	91302	818-880-0363	
Santa Susana Pass State Historic Park c/o Angeles District Office 1925 Las Virgenes Rd *Web:* www.parks.ca.gov/default.asp?page_id=611	Calabasas	CA	91302	213-620-6152	
Shasta State Historic Park c/o Northern Buttes District Office 400 Glen Dr *Web:* www.parks.ca.gov/default.asp?page_id=456	Oroville	CA	95966	530-243-8194	
Silver Strand State Beach 5000 California 75 4477 Pacific Hwy *Web:* www.parks.ca.gov/default.asp?page_id=654	Coronado	CA	92118	619-435-5184	
Sinkyone Wilderness State Park PO Box 245 *Web:* www.parks.ca.gov	Whitethorn	CA	95489	707-986-7711	
Sonoma State Historic Park c/o Diablo Vista District Office 845 Casa Grande Rd *Web:* www.parks.ca.gov	Petaluma	CA	94954	707-938-9560	
South Yuba River State Park 17660 Pleasant Vly Rd *Web:* www.parks.ca.gov	Penn Valley	CA	95946	530-432-2546	
Sutter's Fort State Historic Park 2701 L St *Web:* www.parks.ca.gov	Sacramento	CA	95816	916-445-4422	447-9318
Tolowa Dunes State Park 1375 Elk Vly Rd *Web:* www.parks.ca.gov	Crescent City	CA	95531	707-465-2145	
Tomales Bay State Park 1208 Pierce Pt Rd *Web:* www.parks.ca.gov/default.asp?page_id=470	Inverness	CA	94937	415-669-1140	
Topanga State Park 1925 Las Virgenes *Web:* www.parks.ca.gov/default.asp?page_id=629	Calabasas	CA	91302	818-880-0367	
Torrey Pines State Beach 4477 Pacific Hwy *Web:* www.parks.ca.gov/default.asp?page_id=658	San Diego	CA	92110	858-755-2063	
Torrey Pines State Reserve c/o San Diego Coast District 4477 Pacific Hwy *TF:* 866-240-4655 ■ *Web:* www.parks.ca.gov/?page_id=657	San Diego	CA	92110	858-755-2063	
Trinidad State Beach 4150 Patrick's Point Dr PO Box 2006 *Web:* www.parks.ca.gov/default.asp?page_id=418	Trinidad	CA	95570	707-677-3570	
Tule Elk State Reserve 8653 Station Rd *Web:* www.parks.ca.gov/default.asp?page_id=584	Buttonwillow	CA	93206	661-764-6881	
Turlock Lake State Recreation Area 22600 Lake Rd *Web:* www.parks.ca.gov/default.asp?page_id=555	Columbia	CA	95310	209-874-2056	
Van Damme State Park 12301 N Hwy 1 PO Box 440 *Web:* www.parks.ca.gov/default.asp?page_id=433	Mendocino	CA	95460	707-937-5804	
Verdugo Mountains c/o Angeles District Office 1925 Las Virgenes *Web:* www.parks.ca.gov/default.asp?page_id=635	Calabasas	CA	91302	213-620-6152	
Watts Towers of Simon Rodia State Historic Park 1765 E 107th St 1925 Las Virgenes *TF:* 866-240-4655 ■ *Web:* www.parks.ca.gov/default.asp?page_id=613	Calabasas	CA	91302	213-847-4646	
Will Rogers State Beach 1925 Las Virgenes *Web:* www.parks.ca.gov/default.asp?page_id=625	Calabasas	CA	91302	310-305-9503	
Will Rogers State Historic Park 1925 Las Virgenes *Web:* www.parks.ca.gov/default.asp?page_id=626	Calabasas	CA	91302	310-454-8212	

Colorado

				Phone	Fax
Arkansas Headwaters Recreation Area 307 W Sackett Ave *Web:* cpw.state.co.us	Salida	CO	81201	719-539-7289	
Barr Lake State Park 13401 Picadilly Rd *Web:* cpw.state.co.us	Brighton	CO	80603	303-659-6005	
Boyd Lake State Park 3720 N County Rd Ste 11-C *Web:* cpw.state.co.us	Loveland	CO	80539	970-669-1739	
Castlewood Canyon State Park 2989 S Hwy 83 *Web:* cpw.state.co.us	Franktown	CO	80116	303-688-5242	
Chatfield State Park 11500 N Roxborough Pk Rd *Web:* cpw.state.co.us	Littleton	CO	80125	303-791-7275	
Cherry Creek State Park 4201 S Parker Rd *TF:* 866-265-6447 ■ *Web:* cpw.state.co.us	Aurora	CO	80014	303-699-3860	699-3864
Cheyenne Mountain State Park 4255 Sinton Rd *Web:* cpw.state.co.us	Colorado Springs	CO	80907	719-227-5256	
Crawford State Park PO Box 147 *Web:* cpw.state.co.us	Crawford	CO	81415	970-921-5721	
Crawford State Park 40468 Hwy 92 *Web:* cpw.state.co.us/placestogo/parks/crawford	Crawford	CO	81415	970-921-5721	
Eldorado Canyon State Park 9 Kneale Rd PO Box B *TF:* 866-265-6447 ■ *Web:* cpw.state.co.us	Eldorado Springs	CO	80025	303-494-3943	499-2729
Eleven Mile State Park 4229 County Rd 92 *Web:* cpw.state.co.us	Lake George	CO	80827	719-748-3401	
Eleven Mile State Park c/o Eleven Mile State Pk 4229 County Rd 92 *Web:* cpw.state.co.us	Lake George	CO	80827	719-748-3401	

	City	State	Zip	Phone	Fax
Golden Gate Canyon State Park 92 Crawford Gulch Rd *TF:* 866-265-6447 ■ *Web:* cpw.state.co.us	Golden	CO	80403	303-582-3707	582-3712
Harvey Gap State Park c/o Rifle Gap State Pk 5775 Hwy 325 *Web:* cpw.state.co.us	Rifle	CO	81650	970-625-1607	
Highline Lake State Park 1800 118 Rd *Web:* cpw.state.co.us	Loma	CO	81524	970-858-7208	
Jackson Lake State Park 26363 County Rd 3 *Web:* cpw.state.co.us	Orchard	CO	80649	970-645-2551	
James M. Robb - Colorado River State Park PO Box 700 *Web:* cpw.state.co.us	Clifton	CO	81520	970-434-3388	
Lake Pueblo State Park 640 Pueblo Reservoir Rd *Web:* cpw.state.co.us	Pueblo	CO	81005	719-561-9320	
Lathrop State Park 70 County Rd 502 *Web:* cpw.state.co.us	Walsenburg	CO	81089	719-738-2376	
Lory State Park 708 Lodgepole Dr *Web:* cpw.state.co.us	Bellvue	CO	80512	970-493-1623	
Mancos State Park 42545 County Rd N *Web:* cpw.state.co.us	Mancos	CO	81328	970-533-7065	
Mueller State Park PO Box 39 *Web:* cpw.state.co.us	Divide	CO	80814	719-687-2366	
Navajo State Park PO Box 1697 *Web:* cpw.state.co.us	Arboles	CO	81121	970-883-2208	
North Sterling State Park 24005 County Rd 330 *Web:* cpw.state.co.us	Sterling	CO	80751	970-522-3657	
Paonia State Park PO Box 147 *Web:* cpw.state.co.us	Crawford	CO	81415	970-921-5721	
Pearl Lake State Park PO Box 750 *Web:* cpw.state.co.us	Clark	CO	80428	970-879-3922	
Ridgway State Park 28555 Hwy 550 *Web:* cpw.state.co.us	Ridgway	CO	81432	970-626-5822	
Rifle Falls State Park 5775 Hwy 325 *Web:* cpw.state.co.us	Rifle	CO	81650	970-625-1607	
Rifle Gap State Park 5775 Hwy 325 *Web:* cpw.state.co.us	Rifle	CO	81650	970-625-1607	
Roxborough State Park 4751 Roxborough Dr *Web:* cpw.state.co.us	Littleton	CO	80125	303-973-3959	
Saint Vrain State Park 3525 State Hwy 119 *Web:* cpw.state.co.us	Firestone	CO	80504	303-678-9402	
San Luis State Park & Wildlife Area PO Box 150 *Web:* cpw.state.co.us	Mosca	CO	81146	719-378-2020	
Stagecoach State Park 25500 County Rd 14 *Web:* cpw.state.co.us	Oak Creek	CO	80467	970-736-2436	
State Forest State Park 56750 Hwy 14 *TF:* 866-265-6447 ■ *Web:* cpw.state.co.us	Walden	CO	80480	970-723-8366	723-8325
Steamboat Lake State Park PO Box 750 *Web:* cpw.state.co.us	Clark	CO	80428	970-879-3922	
Sweitzer Lake State Park 1735 E Rd PO Box 173 *Web:* cpw.state.co.us	Delta	CO	81416	970-874-4258	
Sylvan Lake State Park 10200 Brush Creek Rd PO Box 1475 *Web:* cpw.state.co.us	Eagle	CO	81631	970-328-2021	
Trinidad Lake State Park 32610 State Hwy 12 *Web:* cpw.state.co.us	Trinidad	CO	81082	719-846-6951	
Vega State Park PO Box 186 *Web:* cpw.state.co.us	Collbran	CO	81624	970-487-3407	
Yampa River State Park 6185 W US Hwy 40 *Web:* cpw.state.co.us	Hayden	CO	81639	970-276-2061	

Connecticut

	City	State	Zip	Phone	Fax
Bigelow Hollow State Park & Nipmuck State Forest c/o Shenipsit State Forest 166 Chestnut Hill Rd *Web:* www.ct.gov	Stafford Springs	CT	06076	860-684-3430	
Black Rock State Park c/o Topsmead State Forest PO Box 1081 *Web:* www.ct.gov	Litchfield	CT	06759	860-567-5694	
Bluff Point State Park c/o Ft Trumbull State Pk 90 Walbach St *Web:* www.ct.gov	New London	CT	06320	860-444-7591	
Burr Pond State Park 384 Burr Mtn Rd *Web:* www.ct.gov	Torrington	CT	06790	860-482-1817	
Chatfield Hollow State Park 381 Rt 80 *Web:* www.ct.gov	Killingworth	CT	06419	860-663-2030	
Cockaponset State Forest c/o Chatfield Hollow State Pk 18 Ranger Rd *Web:* www.ct.gov	Haddam	CT	06438	860-663-2030	
Connecticut Valley Railroad State Park 1 Railroad Ave PO Box 452 *TF:* 866-526-2014 ■ *Web:* www.essexsteamtrain.com	Essex	CT	06426	860-767-0103	767-0104
Day Pond State Park c/o Eastern District HQ 209 Hebron Rd *Web:* www.ct.gov	Marlborough	CT	06447	860-295-9523	
Dennis Hill State Park c/o Burr Pond State Pk 385 Burr Mtn Rd *Web:* www.ct.gov	Torrington	CT	06790	860-482-1817	
Devil's Hopyard State Park 366 HopyaRd Rd *Web:* www.ct.gov	East Haddam	CT	06423	860-526-2336	
Dinosaur State Park 400 W St *Web:* www.ct.gov	Rocky Hill	CT	06067	860-529-5816	257-1405
Fort Griswold Battlefield State Park c/o Ft Trumbull State Pk 90 Walbach St *Web:* www.ct.gov	New London	CT	06320	860-444-7591	
Fort Trumbull State Park 90 Walbach St *Web:* www.ct.gov/dep/cwp/view.asp?a=2716&q=325200	New London	CT	06320	860-444-7591	
Gay City State Park c/o Eastern District HQ 209 Hebron Rd *Web:* www.ct.gov	Marlborough	CT	06447	860-424-3000	
Gillette Castle State Park 67 River Rd *Web:* www.ct.gov	East Haddam	CT	06423	860-526-2336	
Haley Farm State Park c/o Ft Trumbull State Pk 90 Walbach St *Web:* www.ct.gov	New London	CT	06320	860-444-7591	
Hammonasset Beach State Park 1288 Boston Post Rd PO Box 271 *Web:* www.ct.gov	Madison	CT	06443	203-245-2785	245-9201
Haystack Mountain State Park c/o Burr Pond State Pk 385 Burr Mtn Rd *Web:* www.ct.gov	Torrington	CT	06790	860-482-1817	
Hopeville Pond State Park 193 Roode Rd *Web:* www.ct.gov	Jewett City	CT	06351	860-376-2920	
Housatonic Meadows State Park c/o Macedonia Brook State Pk 159 Macedonia Brook Rd *Web:* www.ct.gov	Kent	CT	06757	860-927-3238	
Hurd State Park c/o Gillette Castle State Pk 67 River Rd *Web:* www.ct.gov	East Haddam	CT	06423	860-526-2336	
Indian Well State Park c/o Osbornedale State Pk PO Box 113 *Web:* www.ct.gov	Derby	CT	06418	203-735-4311	
James L. Goodwin State Forest Goodwin Forest Conservation Education Ctr 23 Potter Rd *Web:* www.ct.gov	Hampton	CT	06226	860-455-9534	455-9857
John A. Minetto State Park c/o Burr Pond State Pk 385 Burr Mtn Rd *Web:* www.ct.gov	Torrington	CT	06790	860-482-1817	
Kent Falls State Park c/o Macedonia Brook State Pk 159 Macedonia Brook Rd *Web:* www.ct.gov	Kent	CT	06757	860-927-3238	
Kettletown State Park 1400 Georges Hill Rd *Web:* www.ct.gov	Southbury	CT	06488	203-264-5678	
Lake Waramaug State Park 30 Lk Waramaug Rd *Web:* www.ct.gov	New Preston	CT	06777	860-868-2592	
Macedonia Brook State Park 159 Macedonia Brook Rd *Web:* www.ct.gov	Kent	CT	06757	860-927-3238	
Mansfield Hollow State Park c/o Mashamoquet Brook State Pk RFD Wolf Den Rd Ste 1 *Web:* www.ct.gov	Pomfret Center	CT	06259	860-928-6121	
Mashamoquet Brook State Park 147 Wolf Den Dr *Web:* www.ct.gov	Pomfret Center	CT	06259	860-928-6121	
Mohawk State Forest 20 Mohawk Mtn Rd *Web:* www.ct.gov	Goshen	CT	06756	860-491-3620	
Mount Tom State Park c/o Lk Waramaug State Pk 30 Lk Waramaug Rd *Web:* www.ct.gov	New Preston	CT	06777	860-868-2592	
Natchaug State Forest c/o Mashamoquet Brook State Pk RFD 1 Wolf Den Rd *Web:* www.ct.gov	Pomfret Center	CT	06259	860-928-6121	
Osbornedale State Park 555 Roosevelt Dr *Web:* www.ct.gov	Derby	CT	06418	203-735-4311	
Pachaug State Forest Rt 49 PO Box 5	Voluntown	CT	06384	860-376-4075	
Penwood State Park 57 Gunn Mill Rd *Web:* www.ct.gov	Bloomfield	CT	06002	860-242-1158	
Putnam Memorial State Park 429 Black Rock Tpke *Web:* www.ct.gov	Redding	CT	06896	203-938-2285	
Quaddick State Park c/o Mashamoquet Brook State Pk 147 Wolf Den Dr *Web:* www.ct.gov	Pomfret Center	CT	06259	860-928-6121	
Rocky Neck State Park PO Box 676 *Web:* www.ct.gov	Niantic	CT	06357	860-739-5471	
Salmon River State Forest c/o Eastern District HQ 209 Hebron Rd *Web:* www.ct.gov	Marlborough	CT	06447	860-295-9523	
Selden Neck State Park c/o Gillette Castle State Pk 67 River Rd *Web:* www.ct.gov	East Haddam	CT	06423	860-526-2336	
Shenipsit State Forest 166 Chestnut Hill Rd Rt 190 *Web:* www.ct.gov/dep/cwp/view.asp?a=2716&q=332506	Stafford Springs	CT	06076	860-684-3430	684-4130
Sherwood Island State Park PO Box 188 *Web:* www.ct.gov	Greens Farms	CT	06838	203-226-6983	
Silver Sands State Park c/o Osbornedale State Pk PO Box 113 *Web:* www.ct.gov/dep/cwp/view.asp?a=2716&q=325262	Derby	CT	06418	203-735-4311	
Sleeping Giant State Park 200 Mt Carmel Ave *Web:* www.ct.gov	Hamden	CT	06518	203-789-7498	
Southford Falls State Park Quaker Farms Rd Rt 188 *Web:* www.ct.gov	Southbury	CT	06488	203-264-5169	
Squantz Pond State Park 178 Shortwoods Rd *Web:* www.ct.gov	New Fairfield	CT	06812	203-797-4165	
Stratton Brook State Park 57 Gun Mill Rd *Web:* www.ct.gov	Bloomfield	CT	06002	860-566-4840	
Talcott Mountain State Park c/o Penwood State Pk 57 Gunn Mill Rd *Web:* www.ct.gov	Bloomfield	CT	06002	860-242-1158	

Phone Fax

Topsmead State Forest PO Box 1081 Litchfield CT 06759 860-567-5694
Web: www.ct.gov

Wadsworth Falls State Park
727 Wadsworth St Middletown CT 06457 860-663-2030
Web: www.ct.gov

West Rock Ridge State Park
200 Mt Carmel Ave c/o Sleeping Giant State Pk Hamden CT 06518 203-789-7498
Web: www.ct.gov

Wharton Brook State Park
200 Mt Carmel Ave c/o Sleeping Giant State Pk Hamden CT 06518 203-789-7498
Web: www.ct.gov

Delaware

Phone Fax

Bellevue State Park 800 Carr Rd Wilmington DE 19809 302-761-6963 761-6951
Web: www.destateparks.com

Brandywine Creek State Park PO Box 3782 Greenville DE 19807 302-577-3534
Web: www.destateparks.com

Cape Henlopen State Park 42 Cape Henlopen Dr Lewes DE 19958 302-645-8983
Web: www.destateparks.com

Delaware Seashore State Park
130 Coastal Hwy Rehoboth Beach DE 19971 302-227-2800
Web: destateparks.com/park/delaware-seashore

Fenwick Island State Park
39415 Inlet Rd Rehoboth Beach DE 19971 302-227-2800 227-7400
Web: www.destateparks.com/park/fenwick-island/index.asp

First State Heritage Park 102 S State St Dover DE 19901 302-739-9194 739-6264
Web: www.destateparks.com/heritagepark

Fort Delaware State Park PO Box 170 Delaware City DE 19706 302-834-7941 836-2539
Web: www.destateparks.com

Fort DuPont State Park 45 Clinton St Delaware City DE 19706 302-834-7941
Web: www.destateparks.com

Fox Point State Park
c/o Bellevue State Pk 800 Carr Rd Wilmington DE 19809 302-761-6963
Web: www.destateparks.com/foxpt/foxpt.htm

Holts Landing State Park 89 Kings Hwy Dover DE 19901 302-227-2800
Web: www.destateparks.com

Killens Pond State Park 5025 Killens Pond Rd Felton DE 19943 302-284-4526 284-4694
Web: www.destateparks.com

Lums Pond State Park 1068 Howell School Rd Bear DE 19701 302-368-6989
Web: www.destateparks.com

Trap Pond State Park 33587 Baldcypress Ln Laurel DE 19956 302-875-5153
Web: www.destateparks.com

White Clay Creek State Park 89 Kings Hwy Dover DE 19901 302-368-6900
Web: www.destateparks.com

Wilmington State Parks 1021 W 18th St Wilmington DE 19802 302-656-3665 577-7084
Web: www.destateparks.com/wilmsp/wilmsp.htm

Florida

Phone Fax

Alafia River State Park 14326 S County Rd 39 Lithia FL 33547 813-672-5320
Web: www.floridastateparks.org

Alfred B. Maclay Gardens State Park
14326 S County Rd 39 Lithia FL 33547 813-672-5320
Web: www.floridastateparks.org

Amelia Island State Park
12157 Heckscher Dr Jacksonville FL 32226 904-251-2320
Web: www.floridastateparks.org/ameliaisland

Bahia Honda State Park
36850 Overseas Hwy Big Pine Key FL 33043 305-872-2353
Web: www.floridastateparks.org

Bald Point State Park 146 PO Box Cut Alligator Point FL 32346 850-349-9146
Web: www.floridastateparks.org

Barnacle Historic State Park, The
3485 Main Hwy Coconut Grove FL 33133 305-442-6866 442-6872
Web: www.floridastateparks.org

Big Lagoon State Park 12301 Gulf Beach Hwy Pensacola FL 32507 850-492-1595
Web: www.floridastateparks.org/biglagoon

Big Shoals State Park PO Box G White Springs FL 32096 386-397-4331
TF: 877-635-3655 ■ *Web:* www.floridastateparks.org

Big Talbot Island State Park
12157 Heckscher Dr Jacksonville FL 32226 904-251-2320
Web: www.floridastateparks.org/bigtalbotisland

Bill Baggs Cape Florida State Park
1200 S Crandon Blvd Key Biscayne FL 33149 305-361-5811
Web: www.floridastateparks.org

Blackwater River State Park
7720 Deaton Bridge Rd Holt FL 32564 850-983-5363
Web: www.floridastateparks.org

Blue Spring State Park 2100 W French Ave Orange City FL 32763 386-775-3663
Web: www.floridastateparks.org

Bulow Creek State Park
3351 Old Dixie Hwy Ormond Beach FL 32174 386-676-4050
Web: www.floridastateparks.org/bulowcreek

Bulow Plantation Ruins Historic State Park
3501 Old Kings Rd Flagler Beach FL 32136 386-517-2084
Web: www.floridastateparks.org

Caladesi Island State Park 1 Cswy Blvd Dunedin FL 34698 727-469-5918
Web: www.floridastateparks.org/caladesiisland

Camp Helen State Park
23937 Panama City Beach Pkwy Panama City Beach FL 32413 850-233-5059 236-3204
Web: www.floridastateparks.org

Cayo Costa State Park PO Box 1150 Boca Grande FL 33921 941-964-0375
Web: www.floridastateparks.org/cayocosta

Cedar Key Museum State Park
12231 SW 166 Ct Cedar Key FL 32625 352-543-5350
Web: www.floridastateparks.org

Collier-Seminole State Park
20200 E Tamiami Trl Naples FL 34114 239-394-3397 394-5113
Web: www.floridastateparks.org/collierseminole

Phone Fax

Constitution Convention Museum State Park
200 Allen Memorial Way Port Saint Joe FL 32456 850-229-8029
Web: www.floridastateparks.org

Crystal River Archaeological State Park
3400 N Museum Pointe Crystal River FL 34428 352-795-3817

Crystal River Preserve State Park
3266 N Sailboat Ave Crystal River FL 34428 352-563-0450
TF: 800-326-3521 ■ *Web:* www.floridastateparks.org/crystalriverpreserve

Dade Battlefield Historic State Park
3900 Commonwealth Blvd Tallahassee FL 32399 352-793-4781
Web: www.floridastateparks.org

Dagny Johnson Key Largo Hammock Botanical State Park
905 County Rd Key Largo FL 33037 305-451-1202
Web: www.floridastateparks.org/keylargohammock

De Leon Springs State Park
601 Ponce De Leon Blvd De Leon Springs FL 32130 386-985-4212
Web: www.floridastateparks.org

Deer Lake State Park 357 Main Pk Rd Santa Rosa Beach FL 32459 850-267-8300
Web: www.floridastateparks.org/deerlake

Delnor-Wiggins Pass State Park
11135 Gulfshore Dr Naples FL 34108 239-597-6196
Web: www.floridastateparks.org/delnorwiggins/default.cfm

Devil's Millhopper Geological State Park
4732 Millhopper Rd Gainesville FL 32653 352-955-2008
Web: www.floridastateparks.org/devilsmillhopper

Don Pedro Island State Park
8450 Placida Rd PO Box 1150 Boca Grande FL 33921 941-964-0375
Web: www.floridastateparks.org/donpedroisland

Dudley Farm Historic State Park
18730 W Newberry Rd Newberry FL 32669 352-472-1142
Web: www.floridastateparks.org

Econfina River State Park
4741 Econfina River Rd Lamont FL 32336 850-922-6007
Web: www.floridastateparks.org

Eden Gardens State Park
181 Eden Gardens Rd Santa Rosa Beach FL 32459 850-267-8320
Web: www.floridastateparks.org

Edward Ball Wakulla Springs State Park
465 Wakulla Park Dr Wakulla Springs FL 32327 850-561-7276
Web: www.floridastateparks.org

Egmont Key State Park
3900 Commonwealth Blvd Tallahassee FL 32399 727-893-2627
Web: www.floridastateparks.org

Fakahatchee Strand Preserve State Park
137 Coastland Dr Copeland FL 34137 239-695-4593
Web: www.floridastateparks.org

Falling Waters State Park 1130 State Pk Rd Chipley FL 32428 850-638-6130
Web: www.floridastateparks.org

Fanning Springs State Park
18020 NW Hwy 19 Fanning Springs FL 32693 352-463-3420 463-3420
Web: www.floridastateparks.org

Faver-Dykes State Park
1000 Faver Dykes Rd Saint Augustine FL 32086 904-794-0997 446-6781*
*Fax Area Code: 386 ■ *Web:* www.floridastateparks.org

Florida Caverns State Park 3345 Caverns Rd Marianna FL 32446 850-482-9598
Web: www.floridastateparks.org

Forest Capital Museum State Park
204 Forest Pk Dr Perry FL 32348 850-584-3227
Web: www.floridastateparks.org

Fort Clinch State Park
2601 Atlantic Ave Fernandina Beach FL 32034 904-277-7274 277-7225
Web: www.floridastateparks.org

Fort Cooper State Park
3100 S Old Floral City Rd Inverness FL 34450 352-726-0315
Web: www.floridastateparks.org

Fort George Island Cultural State Park
12157 Heckscher Dr Jacksonville FL 32226 904-251-2320
Web: www.floridastateparks.org/fortgeorgeisland

Fort Mose Historic State Park
15 Ft Mose Trl Saint Augustine FL 32084 904-823-2232
Web: www.floridastateparks.org/fortmose

Fort Pierce Inlet State Park
905 Shorewinds Dr Fort Pierce FL 34949 772-468-3985
Web: www.floridastateparks.org

Fred Gannon Rocky Bayou State Park
4281 E Hwy 20 Niceville FL 32578 850-833-9144
Web: www.floridastateparks.org

Gamble Plantation Historic State Park
3708 Patten Ave Ellenton FL 34222 941-723-4536
Web: www.floridastateparks.org

Gasparilla Island State Park
880 Belche Rd Boca Grande FL 33921 941-964-0375
Web: www.floridastateparks.org/gasparillaisland

Grayton Beach State Park
357 Main Pk Rd Santa Rosa Beach FL 32459 850-267-8300
Web: www.floridastateparks.org/graytonbeach

Henderson Beach State Park
17000 Emerald Coast Pkwy Destin FL 32541 850-837-7550
Web: www.floridastateparks.org

Highlands Hammock State Park 5931 Hammock Rd Sebring FL 33872 863-386-6094 386-6095
Web: www.floridastateparks.org/highlandshammock

Hillsborough River State Park
15402 US 301 N Thonotosassa FL 33592 813-987-6771
Web: www.floridastateparks.org

Homosassa Springs Wildlife State Park
4150 S Suncoast Blvd Homosassa FL 34446 352-628-5343 628-4243
Web: www.floridastateparks.org

Hontoon Island State Park 2309 River Ridge Rd DeLand FL 32720 386-736-5309
Web: www.floridastateparks.org

Hugh Taylor Birch State Park
3109 E Sunrise Blvd Fort Lauderdale FL 33304 954-564-4521
Web: www.floridastateparks.org

Ichetucknee Springs State Park
12087 SW US Hwy 27 Fort White FL 32038 850-245-2157
Web: www.floridastateparks.org

Name / Address	City	State	Zip	Phone	Fax
Indian Key Historic State Park 77200 Overseas Hwy *Web:* www.floridastateparks.org/indiankey	Islamorada	FL	33036	305-664-2540	
John D. MacArthur Beach State Park 10900 SR 703 (A1A) *Web:* www.floridastateparks.org	North Palm Beach	FL	33408	561-624-6950	
John Gorrie Museum State Park PO Box 267 *Web:* www.floridastateparks.org	Apalachicola	FL	32320	850-653-9347	
John U. Lloyd Beach State Park 6503 N Ocean Dr *Web:* www.floridastateparks.org	Dania	FL	33004	954-923-2833	
Kissimmee Prairie Preserve State Park 33104 NW 192 Ave *Web:* www.floridastateparks.org	Okeechobee	FL	34972	863-462-5360	
Koreshan State Historic Site 3800 Corkscrew Rd *Web:* www.floridastateparks.org	Estero	FL	33928	239-992-0311	992-1607
Lake Griffin State Park 3089 US 441-27 *Web:* www.floridastateparks.org	Fruitland Park	FL	34731	352-360-6760	
Lake Kissimmee State Park 14248 Camp Mack Rd *Web:* www.floridastateparks.org	Lake Wales	FL	33898	863-696-1112	
Lake Louisa State Park 7305 US Hwy 27 *Web:* www.floridastateparks.org	Clermont	FL	34714	352-394-3969	
Lake Manatee State Park 20007 Hwy 64 E *Web:* www.floridastateparks.org	Bradenton	FL	34212	941-741-3028	
Lignumvitae Key Botanical State Park Offshore Island *Web:* www.floridastateparks.org/lignumvitaekey	Islamorada	FL	33036	305-664-2540	
Little Manatee River State Park 215 Lightfoot Rd *Web:* www.floridastateparks.org	Wimauma	FL	33598	813-671-5005	
Little Talbot Island State Park 12157 Heckscher Dr *TF:* 800-326-3521 ■ *Web:* www.floridastateparks.org/littletalbotisland	Jacksonville	FL	32226	904-251-2320	251-2325
Long Key State Park PO Box 776 *Web:* www.floridastateparks.org	Long Key	FL	33001	305-664-4815	
Lovers Key State Park 8700 Estero Blvd *TF:* 800-326-3521 ■ *Web:* www.floridastateparks.org	Fort Myers Beach	FL	33931	239-463-4588	463-8851
Lower Wekiva River Preserve State Park 1800 Wekiwa Cir *TF:* 800-326-3521 ■ *Web:* www.floridastateparks.org	Apopka	FL	32712	407-884-2008	884-2039
Manatee Springs State Park 11650 NW 115th St *Web:* www.floridastateparks.org	Chiefland	FL	32626	352-493-6072	
Marjorie Kinnan Rawlings Historic State Park 18700 S County Rd 325 *Web:* www.floridastateparks.org	Cross Creek	FL	32640	352-466-3672	
Mike Roess Gold Head Branch State Park 6239 SR 21 *Web:* www.floridastateparks.org	Keystone Heights	FL	32656	352-473-4701	
Myakka River State Park 13208 SR 72 *TF:* 800-326-3521 ■ *Web:* www.floridastateparks.org	Sarasota	FL	34241	941-361-6511	361-6501
Natural Bridge Battlefield Historic State Park 7502 Natural Bridge Rd *TF:* 800-326-3521 ■ *Web:* www.floridastateparks.org/naturalbridge	Tallahassee	FL	32305	850-922-6007	488-0366
O'Leno State Park 410 SE Oleno Pk Rd *Web:* www.floridastateparks.org	High Springs	FL	32643	386-454-1853	
Ochlockonee River State Park 429 State Pk Rd *Web:* www.floridastateparks.org	Sopchoppy	FL	32358	850-962-2771	
Oleta River State Park 3400 NE 163rd St *TF:* 800-326-3521 ■ *Web:* www.floridastateparks.org	North Miami Beach	FL	33160	305-919-1846	919-1845
Orman House 177 Fifth St *Web:* www.floridastateparks.org/ormanhouse	Apalachicola	FL	32320	850-653-1209	
Oscar Scherer State Park 1843 S Tamiami Trail *TF:* 800-326-3521 ■ *Web:* www.floridastateparks.org	Osprey	FL	34229	941-483-5956	480-3007
Paynes Creek Historic State Park 888 Lake Branch Rd *TF:* 800-326-3521 ■ *Web:* www.floridastateparks.org	Bowling Green	FL	33834	863-375-4717	375-4510
Paynes Prairie Preserve State Park 100 Savannah Blvd *Web:* www.floridastateparks.org	Micanopy	FL	32667	352-466-3397	
Perdido Key State Park 15301 Perdido Key Dr *Web:* www.floridastateparks.org/perdidokey	Pensacola	FL	32507	850-492-1595	
Ponce de Leon Springs State Park 2860 Ponce de Leon Springs Rd *Web:* www.floridastateparks.org	Ponce de Leon	FL	32455	850-836-4281	
Rainbow Springs State Park 19158 SW 81st Pl Rd *Web:* www.floridastateparks.org	Dunnellon	FL	34432	352-465-8555	
Ravine Gardens State Park 1600 Twigg St *TF:* 800-326-3521 ■ *Web:* www.floridastateparks.org	Palatka	FL	32177	386-329-3721	329-3718
Rock Springs Run State Reserve 30601 CR 433 *TF:* 800-326-3521 ■ *Web:* www.floridastateparks.org/rockspringsrun	Sorrento	FL	32776	407-884-2008	884-2039
Saint Andrews State Park 4607 State Pk Ln *Web:* www.floridastateparks.org	Panama City	FL	32408	850-233-5140	
San Felasco Hammock Preserve State Park 12720 NW 109 Ln *Web:* www.floridastateparks.org	Alachua	FL	32615	386-462-7905	
San Marcos de Apalache Historic State Park 148 Old Ft Rd *Web:* www.floridastateparks.org	Saint Marks	FL	32327	850-925-6216	
San Pedro Underwater Archaeological Preserve State Park US 1 *Web:* www.floridastateparks.org/sanpedro	Islamorada	FL	33036	305-664-2540	
Sebastian Inlet State Park 9700 S A1A *Web:* www.floridastateparks.org	Melbourne Beach	FL	32951	321-984-4852	
Silver River State Park 1425 NE 58th Ave *Web:* www.floridastateparks.org	Ocala	FL	34470	352-236-7148	
Stephen Foster Folk Culture Ctr State Park 11016 Lillian Saunders Dr *Web:* www.floridastateparks.org	White Springs	FL	32096	386-397-2733	
Stump Pass Beach State Park Barrier Islands State Parks PO Box 1150 *Web:* www.floridastateparks.org	Boca Grande	FL	33921	941-964-0375	964-1154
Suwannee River State Park 3631 201st Path *Web:* www.floridastateparks.org	Live Oak	FL	32060	386-362-2746	
TH Stone Memorial Saint Joseph Peninsula State Park 8899 Cape San Blas Rd *Web:* www.floridastateparks.org	Port Saint Joe	FL	32456	850-227-1327	227-1488
Three Rivers State Park 7908 Three Rivers Pk Rd *Web:* www.floridastateparks.org	Sneads	FL	32460	850-482-9006	
Tomoka State Park 2099 N Beach St *Web:* www.floridastateparks.org/tomoka	Ormond Beach	FL	32174	386-676-4050	676-4050
Topsail Hill Preserve State Park 7525 W Scenic Hwy 30A *Web:* www.floridastateparks.org	Santa Rosa Beach	FL	32459	850-245-2157	
Torreya State Park 2576 NW Torreya Pk Rd *Web:* www.floridastateparks.org	Bristol	FL	32321	850-643-2674	
Troy Springs State Park 674 NE Troy Springs Rd *Web:* www.floridastateparks.org/troyspring	Branford	FL	32008	386-935-4835	
Washington Oaks Gardens State Park 6400 N Oceanshore Blvd *Web:* www.floridastateparks.org	Palm Coast	FL	32137	386-446-6780	446-6781
Wekiwa Springs State Park 1800 Wekiwa Cir *Web:* www.floridastateparks.org/wekiwasprings	Apopka	FL	32712	407-884-2008	884-2039
Ybor City Museum State Park 1818 Ninth Ave *Web:* www.floridastateparks.org	Tampa	FL	33605	813-247-6323	

Georgia

Name / Address	City	State	Zip	Phone	Fax
AH Stephens State Historic Park 456 Alexander St NW *Web:* www.gastateparks.org	Crawfordville	GA	30631	706-456-2602	
Amicalola Falls State Park & Lodge 418 Amicalola Falls State Pk Rd *Web:* www.gastateparks.org	Dawsonville	GA	30534	706-265-4703	
Black Rock Mountain State Park 3085 Black Rock Mtn Pkwy *Web:* www.gastateparks.org	Mountain City	GA	30562	706-746-2141	
Bobby Brown State Park 2509 Bobby Brown State Pk Rd *Web:* www.gastateparks.org/info/bobbybrown	Elberton	GA	30635	706-213-2046	
Chief Vann House State Historic Site 82 Georgia 225 *Web:* www.gastateparks.org	Chatsworth	GA	30705	706-695-2598	
Cloudland Canyon State Park 122 Cloudland Canyon Pk *Web:* www.gastateparks.org	Rising Fawn	GA	30738	706-657-4050	
Crooked River State Park 6222 Charlie Smith Sr Hwy *Web:* www.gastateparks.org	Saint Marys	GA	31558	912-882-5256	
Dahlonega Gold Museum State Historic Site 1 Public Sq *Web:* www.gastateparks.org	Dahlonega	GA	30533	706-864-2257	
Elijah Clark State Park 2959 McCormick Hwy *Web:* www.gastateparks.org	Lincolnton	GA	30817	706-359-3458	
Etowah Indian Mounds State Historic Site 813 Indian Mounds Rd SW *Web:* www.gastateparks.org	Cartersville	GA	30120	770-387-3747	
FD Roosevelt State Park 2970 GA Hwy 190 *TF:* 800-864-7275 ■ *Web:* www.gastateparks.org	Pine Mountain	GA	31822	706-663-4858	663-8906
Fort King George State Historic Site 1600 Wayne St *Web:* www.gastateparks.org	Darien	GA	31305	912-437-4770	
Fort McAllister State Historic Park 3894 Ft McAllister Rd *TF:* 800-864-7275 ■ *Web:* www.gastateparks.org	Richmond Hill	GA	31324	912-727-2339	727-3614
Fort Morris State Historic Site 2559 Ft Morris Rd *Web:* www.gastateparks.org	Midway	GA	31320	912-884-5999	
Fort Mountain State Park 181 Ft Mtn Pk Rd *Web:* www.gastateparks.org	Chatsworth	GA	30705	706-695-2621	
Fort Yargo State Park 210 S Broad St *Web:* www.gastateparks.org	Winder	GA	30680	770-867-3489	
General Coffee State Park 46 John Coffee Rd *Web:* www.gastateparks.org	Nicholls	GA	31554	912-384-7082	
George L. Smith State Park 371 Geo L Smith St Pk Rd *Web:* www.gastateparks.org	Twin City	GA	30471	478-763-2759	
George T. Bagby State Park & Lodge 330 Bagby Pkwy *TF:* 877-591-5575 ■ *Web:* www.gastateparks.org	Fort Gaines	GA	39851	229-768-2571	
Georgia Veterans State Park 2459 US 280 W *Web:* www.gastateparks.org	Cordele	GA	31015	229-276-2371	
Hamburg State Park 6071 Hamburg State Pk Rd *Web:* www.gastateparks.org	Mitchell	GA	30820	478-552-2393	
Hard Labor Creek State Park Knox Chapel Rd *Web:* www.gastateparks.org	Rutledge	GA	30663	706-557-3001	
Hart State Park 330 Hart Pk Rd *Web:* www.gastateparks.org	Hartwell	GA	30643	706-376-8756	
High Falls State Park 76 High Falls Pk Dr *Web:* www.gastateparks.org	Jackson	GA	30233	478-993-3053	
Hofwyl-Broadfield Plantation State Historic Site 5556 US Hwy 17 N *Web:* www.gastateparks.org	Brunswick	GA	31525	912-264-7333	

Phone Fax

Indian Springs State Park 678 Lk Clark Rd .... Flovilla GA 30216 770-504-2277
Web: www.gastateparks.org

James H. Sloppy Floyd State Park
2800 Sloppy Floyd Lk Rd .... Summerville GA 30747 706-857-0826
Web: www.gastateparks.org

Jarrell Plantation State Historic Site
711 Jarrell Plantation Rd .... Juliette GA 31046 478-986-5172
Web: www.gastateparks.org

Jefferson Davis Memorial State Historic Site
338 Jeff Davis Pk Rd .... Fitzgerald GA 31750 229-831-2335
Web: www.gastateparks.org

John Tanner State Park
354 Tanner's Beach Rd .... Carrollton GA 30117 770-830-2222
Web: www.gastateparks.org

Kolomoki Mounds State Historic Park
205 Indian Mounds Rd .... Blakely GA 39823 229-724-2150
Web: www.gastateparks.org

Lapham-Patterson House State Historic Site
626 N Dawson St .... Thomasville GA 31792 229-225-4004
Web: www.gastateparks.org

Laura S. Walker State Park
5653 Laura Walker Rd .... Waycross GA 31503 912-287-4900
Web: www.gastateparks.org

Little Ocmulgee State Park & Lodge PO Box 149 .... McRae GA 31055 229-868-7474
Web: www.gastateparks.org

Little White House State Historic Site
401 Little White House Rd .... Warm Springs GA 31830 706-655-5870 655-5872
TF: 800-864-7275 ■ *Web:* gastateparks.org/info/littlewhite

Magnolia Springs State Park
1053 Magnolia Springs Dr .... Millen GA 30442 478-982-1660
Web: www.gastateparks.org

Mistletoe State Park 3723 Mistletoe Rd .... Appling GA 30802 706-541-0321
Web: www.gastateparks.org

Moccasin Creek State Park 3655 Hwy 197 .... Clarkesville GA 30523 706-947-3194
Web: www.gastateparks.org

New Echota State Historic Site
1211 Chatsworth Hwy NE .... Calhoun GA 30701 706-624-1321
Web: www.gastateparks.org

Panola Mountain State Park
2600 Georgia 155 .... Stockbridge GA 30281 770-389-7801
Web: www.gastateparks.org

Pickett's Mill Battlefield State Historic Site
4432 Mt Tabor Church Rd .... Dallas GA 30157 770-443-7850
Web: www.gastateparks.org

Reed Bingham State Park 542 Reed Bingham Rd .... Adel GA 31620 229-896-3551
Web: www.gastateparks.org

Richard B. Russell State Park
2650 Russell State Pk Rd .... Elberton GA 30635 706-213-2045
Web: www.gastateparks.org

Robert Toombs House State Historic Site
216 E Robert Toombs Ave .... Washington GA 30673 706-678-2226
Web: www.gastateparks.org

Seminole State Park 7870 State Pk Dr .... Donalsonville GA 39845 229-861-3137
Web: www.gastateparks.org

Skidaway Island State Park 52 Diamond Cswy .... Savannah GA 31411 912-598-2300 598-2365
Web: www.gastateparks.org/info/skidaway

Smithgall Woods Conservation Area & Lodge
61 Tsalaki Trl .... Helen GA 30545 706-878-3087
TF: 800-864-7275 ■ *Web:* www.gastateparks.org/info/smithgall

Sprewell Bluff State Park
740 Sprewell Bluff Rd .... Thomaston GA 30286 706-646-6026
Web: www.gastateparks.org

Stephen C. Foster State Park 17515 Hwy 177 .... Fargo GA 31631 912-637-5274
Web: www.gastateparks.org

Sweetwater Creek State Park
1750 Mt Vernon Rd PO Box 816 .... Lithia Springs GA 30122 770-732-5871
Web: www.gastateparks.org/sweetwatercreek

Tallulah Gorge State Park
338 Jane Hurt Yarn Dr .... Tallulah Falls GA 30573 706-754-7970
Web: www.gastateparks.org

Traveler's Rest State Historic Site
4339 Riverdale Rd .... Toccoa GA 30577 706-886-2256
Web: www.gastateparks.org

Tugaloo State Park 1763 Tugaloo State Pk Rd .... Lavonia GA 30553 706-356-4362
Web: www.gastateparks.org

Unicoi State Park & Lodge 1788 Hwy 356 Rd .... Helen GA 30545 800-573-9659
TF: 800-573-9659 ■ *Web:* www.gastateparks.org/info/unicoi

Vogel State Park 7485 Vogel State Pk Rd .... Blairsville GA 30512 706-745-2628
Web: www.gastateparks.org

Watson Mill Bridge State Park
650 Watson Mill Rd .... Comer GA 30629 706-783-5349
Web: www.gastateparks.org

Wormsloe State Historic Site
7601 Skidaway Rd .... Savannah GA 31406 912-353-3023
Web: www.gastateparks.org/info/wormsloe

Hawaii

Phone Fax

Diamond Head State Monument PO Box 621 .... Honolulu HI 96809 808-587-0404 587-0390
Web: www.hawaii.gov

Haena State Park 3060 Eiwa St Ste 306 .... Lihue HI 96766 808-274-3444 274-3448
Web: dlnr.hawaii.gov/dsp/parks/kauai/haena-state-park

Halekii-Pihana Heiau State Monument
54 S High St Rm 101 .... Wailuku HI 96793 808-984-8109 984-8111
Web: dlnr.hawaii.gov/dsp

Hanauma Bay State Underwater Park
3949 Diamond Head Rd .... Honolulu HI 96816 808-587-0300
Web: www.hawaii.gov

Hapuna Beach State Recreation Area
75 Aupuni St Rm 204 PO Box 936 .... Hilo HI 96721 808-882-6206 961-9599
Web: dlnr.hawaii.gov/dsp

Hawaii Information Consortium (HIC)
201 Merchant St Ste 1805 .... Honolulu HI 96813 808-695-4620 695-4618
TF: 800-295-0089 ■ *Web:* www.hawaii.gov

Hawaii State Parks
Kalanimoku Bldg 1151 Punchbowl St Rm 310 .... Honolulu HI 96813 808-587-0300 587-0311
Web: dlnr.hawaii.gov/dsp

Heeia State Park 46-465 Kamehameha Hwy .... Kaneohe HI 96744 808-235-6509 235-6519
Web: www.heeiastatepark.org

Iao Valley State Monument 54 S High St Rm 101 .... Wailuku HI 96793 808-984-8109 984-8111
Web: dlnr.hawaii.gov/dsp

Iolani Palace State Monument PO Box 621 .... Honolulu HI 96809 808-587-0300
Web: dlnr.hawaii.gov/dsp

Kaena Point State Park
1151 Punchbowl St Rm 310 .... Honolulu HI 96813 808-587-0300
Web: dlnr.hawaii.gov/dsp

Kahana Valley State Park
52-222 Kamehameha Hwy .... Honolulu HI 96809 808-587-0300
Web: dlnr.hawaii.gov/dsp

Kalopa State Recreation Area
75 Aupuni St Rm 204 PO Box 936 .... Hilo HI 96721 808-961-9540 961-9599
Web: www.hawaii.gov

Kaumahina State Wayside 54 S High St Rm 101 .... Wailuku HI 96793 808-984-8109 984-8111
Web: dlnr.hawaii.gov/dsp

Keaiwa Heiau State Recreation Area
1151 Punchbowl St Rm 310 PO Box 621 .... Honolulu HI 96813 808-483-2511
Web: www.hawaii.gov

Kealakekua Bay State Historical Park PO Box 936 .... Hilo HI 96721 808-974-6200
Web: www.hawaii.gov

Kohala Historical Sites State Monument
PO Box 936 .... Hilo HI 96721 808-974-6200
Web: dlnr.hawaii.gov/dsp

Kokee State Park 3060 Eiwa St Rm 306 .... Lihue HI 96766 808-274-3444
Web: dlnr.hawaii.gov/dsp/parks/kauai/kokee-state-park

Laie Point State Wayside
55-001 Naupaka St PO Box 621 .... Laie HI 96809 808-587-0300
Web: www.hawaiistateparks.org/parks/oahu/index.cfm?park_id=25

Lapakahi State Historical Park
75 Aupuni St Rm 204 Rm 204 .... Hilo HI 96721 808-327-4958
Web: dlnr.hawaii.gov/dsp/parks/hawaii/lapakahi-state-historical-park

Malaekahana State Recreation Area
PO Box 621 .... Honolulu HI 96809 808-587-0300
Web: dlnr.hawaii.gov/dsp/parks/oahu/malaekahana-state-recreation-area

Polihale State Park 3060 Eiwa St Ste 306 .... Lihue HI 96766 808-274-3444 274-3448
Web: dlnr.hawaii.gov/dsp/parks/kauai/polihale-state-park

Polipoli Spring State Recreation Area
54 S High St Rm 101 .... Wailuku HI 96793 808-984-8109 984-8111
Web: www.hawaii.gov

Puaa Kaa State Wayside 54 S High St Rm 101 .... Wailuku HI 96793 808-984-8109 984-8111
Web: dlnr.hawaii.gov/dsp/parks/maui/puaa-kaa-state-wayside

Puu o Mahuka Heiau State Monument
1151 Punchbowl St Rm 310 PO Box 621 .... Honolulu HI 96809 808-587-0300 587-0311
Web: www.hawaii.gov

Puu Ualakaa State Wayside PO Box 621 .... Honolulu HI 96809 808-587-0300
Web: dlnr.hawaii.gov/dsp/parks/oahu/puu-ualakaa-state-wayside

Royal Mausoleum State Monument
2261 Nuuanu Ave .... Honolulu HI 96817 808-587-0300
Web: dlnr.hawaii.gov/dsp/parks/oahu/royal-mausoleum-state-monument

Russian Fort Elizabeth State Historical Park
3060 Eiwa St Ste 306 .... Lihue HI 96766 808-274-3444 274-3448
Web: dlnr.hawaii.gov/dsp/parks/kauai/russian-fort-elizabeth-state-historical-park

Sand Island State Recreation Area
PO Box 621 .... Honolulu HI 96809 808-832-3781
Web: dlnr.hawaii.gov/dsp/parks/oahu/sand-island-state-recreation-area

Ulupo Heiau State Monument
1151 Punchbowl St Rm 310 .... Honolulu HI 96813 808-587-0300 587-0311
Web: dlnr.hawaii.gov/dsp/parks/oahu/ulupo-heiau-state-historic-site

Waahila Ridge State Recreation Area
1151 Punchbowl St PO Box 621 .... Honolulu HI 96809 808-587-0300 587-0311
Web: www.hawaii.gov

Wahiawa Freshwater State Recreation Area
PO Box 621 .... Honolulu HI 96809 808-622-6316
Web: dlnr.hawaii.gov/dsp/parks/oahu/wahiawa-freshwater-state-recreation-area

Waianapanapa State Park 54 S High St Rm 101 .... Wailuku HI 96793 808-984-8109 984-8111
Web: dlnr.hawaii.gov/dsp/parks/maui/waianapanapa-state-park

Wailoa River State Recreation Area PO Box 936 .... Hilo HI 96721 808-933-0416
Web: dlnr.hawaii.gov/dsp/parks/hawaii/wailoa-river-state-recreation-area

Wailua River State Park 3060 Eiwa St .... Lihue HI 96766 808-274-3444
Web: www.hawaii.gov

Wailua Valley State Wayside
54 S High St Rm 101 .... Wailuku HI 96793 808-984-8109 984-8111
Web: dlnr.hawaii.gov/dsp/parks/maui/wailua-valley-state-wayside

Waimea Canyon State Park 3060 Eiwa St Ste 306 .... Lihue HI 96766 808-274-3444 274-3448
Web: www.hawaii.gov

Idaho

Phone Fax

Bruneau Dunes State Park
27608 Sand Dunes Rd .... Mountain Home ID 83647 208-366-7919 366-2844
Web: www.parksandrecreation.idaho.gov

Dworshak State Park PO Box 115 .... Ahsahka ID 83520 208-476-5994
Web: www.visitidaho.org

Eagle Island State Park 4000 W Hatchery Rd .... Eagle ID 83616 208-939-0696 939-0696
Web: www.visitidaho.org

Farragut State Park 13550 E Hwy 54 .... Athol ID 83801 208-683-2425
Web: www.visitidaho.org

Harriman State Park 3489 Green Canyon Rd .... Island Park ID 83429 208-558-7368
TF: 866-634-3246 ■
Web: www.stateparks.com/harriman_state_park_in_idaho.html

Hells Gate State Park 5100 Hells Gate Rd .... Lewiston ID 83501 208-799-5015
Web: www.idahoparks.org

Henrys Lake State Park 3917 E 5100 N .... Island Park ID 83429 208-558-7532
Web: idahostateparks.reserveamerica.com

				Phone	Fax
Heyburn State Park 57 Chatcolet Rd	Plummer	ID	83851	208-686-1308	
TF: 866-634-3246 ■ *Web:* www.parksandrecreation.idaho.gov					
Lake Cascade State Park 970 Dam Rd	Cascade	ID	83611	208-382-6544	382-4071
TF: 866-634-3246 ■ *Web:* www.parksandrecreation.idaho.gov					
Lake Walcott State Park 959 E Minidoka Dam	Rupert	ID	83350	208-436-1258	436-1268
Web: www.parksandrecreation.idaho.gov					
Land of the Yankee Fork State Park PO Box 1086	Challis	ID	83226	208-879-5244	879-5243
Web: www.parksandrecreation.idaho.gov					
Massacre Rocks State Park 3592 N Pk Ln	American Falls	ID	83211	208-548-2672	
Web: parksandrecreation.idaho.gov					
McCroskey State Park 57 Chatcolet Rd	Plummer	ID	83851	208-686-1308	
Web: www.visitidaho.org/attraction/parks/mccroskey-state-park					
Old Mission State Park 31732 S Mission Rd	Cataldo	ID	83810	208-682-3814	682-4032
Web: parksandrecreation.idaho.gov					
Ponderosa State Park 1920 N Davis Ave	McCall	ID	83638	208-634-2164	
Web: parksandrecreation.idaho.gov/parks/ponderosa					
Priest Lake State Park 314 Indian Creek Pk Rd	Coolin	ID	83821	208-443-2200	
TF Resv: 888-922-6743 ■ *Web:* www.visitidaho.org					
Round Lake State Park PO Box 170	Sagle	ID	83860	208-263-3489	
Web: idahostateparks.reserveamerica.com					
Three Island Crossing State Park 1083 S Three Island Pk Dr	Glenns Ferry	ID	83623	208-366-2394	
TF: 888-922-6743 ■ *Web:* www.visitidaho.org/attraction/visitor-centers/three-island-crossing-state-park					
Winchester Lake State Park (IDPR) PO Box 186	Winchester	ID	83555	208-924-7563	924-5941
Web: idahostateparks.reserveamerica.com					

Illinois

				Phone	Fax
Anderson Lake Conservation Area 647 N State Hwy 100	Astoria	IL	61501	309-759-4484	
Web: www.dnr.state.il.us					
Apple River Canyon State Park 8763 E Canyon Rd	Apple River	IL	61001	815-745-3302	
Web: www.dnr.state.il.us					
Argyle Lake State Park 640 Argyle Pk Rd	Colchester	IL	62326	309-776-3422	
Web: www.dnr.state.il.us					
Banner Marsh State Fish & Wildlife Area 19721 N US 24	Canton	IL	61520	309-647-9184	
Web: www.dnr.state.il.us/lands/landmgt/parks/r1/banner.htm					
Beall Woods State Park 9285 Beall Woods Ave	Mount Carmel	IL	62863	618-298-2442	
Web: www.dnr.state.il.us					
Beaver Dam State Park 14548 Beaver Dam Ln	Plainview	IL	62685	217-854-8020	
Web: www.dnr.state.il.us					
Big Bend State Fish & Wildlife Area PO Box 181	Prophetstown	IL	61277	815-537-2270	
Web: www.dnr.state.il.us/lands/landmgt/parks/r1/bigbend.htm					
Big River State Forest RR 1 PO Box 118	Keithsburg	IL	61442	309-374-2496	
Web: www.dnr.state.il.us/lands/landmgt/parks/r1/bigriver.htm					
Buffalo Rock State Park & Effigy Tumuli 1300 N 27th Rd PO Box 2034	Ottawa	IL	61350	815-433-2220	
Web: www.dnr.state.il.us					
Cache River State Natural Area 930 Sunflower Ln	Belknap	IL	62908	618-634-9678	
Web: www.dnr.state.il.us					
Cahokia Mounds State Historic Site 30 Ramey St	Collinsville	IL	62234	618-346-5160	346-5162
Web: cahokiamounds.org					
Carlyle Lake State Fish & Wildlife Area RR 2	Vandalia	IL	62471	618-425-3533	
Web: www.dnr.state.il.us					
Castle Rock State Park 1365 W Castle Rd	Oregon	IL	61061	815-732-7329	
Web: www.dnr.state.il.us/lands/landmgt/parks/r1/castle.htm					
Cave-In-Rock State Park 1 New State Pk Rd PO Box 338	Cave-In-Rock	IL	62919	618-289-4325	
Web: www.dnr.state.il.us					
Chain O'Lakes State Park 8916 Wilmot Rd	Spring Grove	IL	60081	847-587-5512	
Web: www.dnr.state.il.us					
Channahon State Park PO Box 54	Channahon	IL	60410	815-467-4271	
Web: www.dnr.state.il.us					
Clinton Lake State Recreation Area RR 1 PO Box 4	DeWitt	IL	61735	217-935-8722	
Web: www.dnr.state.il.us					
Coffeen Lake State Fish & Wildlife Area 15084 N Fourth Ave	Coffeen	IL	62017	217-537-3351	
Web: www.dnr.state.il.us					
Crawford County State Fish & Wildlife Area 12609 E 1700th Ave	Hutsonville	IL	62433	618-563-4405	
Web: www.dnr.state.il.us					
Des Plaines State Fish & Wildlife Area 24621 N River Rd	Wilmington	IL	60481	815-423-5326	
Web: www.dnr.state.il.us					
Donnelley/DePue State Fish & Wildlife Areas 1001 W Fourth St PO Box 52	DePue	IL	61322	815-447-2353	
Web: www.dnr.state.il.us					
Eagle Creek State Recreation Area PO Box 16	Findlay	IL	62534	217-756-8260	
Web: www.dnr.state.il.us					
Edward R. Madigan State Fish & Wildlife Area 1366 1010th Ave	Lincoln	IL	62656	217-735-2424	
Web: www.dnr.state.il.us					
Eldon Hazlet State Recreation Area 20100 Hazlet Pk Rd	Carlyle	IL	62231	618-594-3015	
Web: www.dnr.state.il.us/lands/landmgt/parks/r4/eldon.htm					
Ferne Clyffe State Park PO Box 10	Goreville	IL	62939	618-995-2411	
Web: www.dnr.state.il.us					
Fort Massac State Park 1308 E Fifth St	Metropolis	IL	62960	618-524-4712	
Web: www.dnr.state.il.us					
Fox Ridge State Park 18175 State Pk Rd	Charleston	IL	61920	217-345-6416	
Web: www.dnr.state.il.us					
Frank Holten State Recreation Area 4500 Pocket Rd	East Saint Louis	IL	62205	618-874-7920	
Web: www.dnr.state.il.us					
Franklin Creek State Natural Area 1872 Twist Rd	Franklin Grove	IL	61031	815-456-2878	
Web: www.dnr.state.il.us					
Fults Hill Prairie & Kidd Lake State Natural Areas c/o Randolph County State Recreation Area 4301 S Lk Dr	Chester	IL	62233	618-826-2706	
Web: dnr.state.il.us/lands/landmgt/parks/r4/fhp.htm					
Gebhard Woods State Park 401 Ottawa St PO Box 272	Morris	IL	60450	815-942-0796	
Web: www.dnr.state.il.us/lands/landmgt/parks/i&m/east/gebhard/park.htm					
Giant City State Park 235 Giant City Rd	Makanda	IL	62958	618-457-4836	
Web: www.dnr.state.il.us					
Goose Lake Prairie State Natural Area 5010 N Jugtown Rd	Morris	IL	60450	815-942-2899	
Web: www.dnr.state.il.us/lands/landmgt/parks/i&m/east/goose/home.htm					
Green River State Wildlife Area 375 Game Rd	Harmon	IL	61042	815-379-2324	
Web: www.dnr.state.il.us					
Hamilton County State Fish & Wildlife Area RR 4 PO Box 242	McLeansboro	IL	62859	618-773-4340	
Web: www.dnr.state.il.us					
Harry "Babe" Woodyard State Natural Area 19284 E 670 N	Georgetown	IL	61846	217-442-4915	
Web: www.dnr.state.il.us					
Heidecke Lake State Fish & Wildlife Area 5010 N Jugtown Rd	Morris	IL	60450	815-942-6352	
Web: www.dnr.state.il.us					
Henderson County Conservation Area PO Box 118	Keithsburg	IL	61442	309-374-2496	
Web: www.dnr.state.il.us/lands/landmgt/parks/r1/henderso.htm					
Hennepin Canal Parkway State Park 16006 875 E St	Sheffield	IL	61361	815-454-2328	
Web: www.dnr.state.il.us/lands/landmgt/parks/r1/hennpin.htm					
Hidden Springs State Forest RR 1 PO Box 200	Strasburg	IL	62465	217-644-3091	
Web: www.dnr.state.il.us					
Horseshoe Lake State Fish & Wildlife Area (Alexander County) 21204 Promised Land Rd	Miller City	IL	62962	618-776-5689	
Web: www.dnr.state.il.us					
Horseshoe Lake State Park (Madison County) 3321 Hwy 111	Granite City	IL	62040	618-931-0270	
Web: www.dnr.state.il.us					
Illini State Park 2660 E 2350th Rd	Marseilles	IL	61341	815-795-2448	
Web: www.dnr.state.il.us/lands/landmgt/parks/i&m/east/illini/park.htm					
Illinois & Michigan Canal State Trail PO Box 272	Morris	IL	60450	815-942-0796	942-9690
Web: www.dnr.state.il.us/lands/landmgt/parks/i&m/main.htm					
Illinois Beach State Park Lake Front	Zion	IL	60099	847-662-4811	662-6433
Web: www.dnr.state.il.us					
Illinois Caverns State Natural Area 10981 Conservation Rd	Baldwin	IL	62217	618-458-6699	
Web: www.dnr.state.il.us					
Iroquois County State Wildlife Area RR 1 2803 E 3300 N Rd	Beaverville	IL	60912	815-435-2218	
Web: www.dnr.state.il.us					
James Pate Philip State Park 2050 W Stearns Rd	Bartlett	IL	60103	847-608-3100	
Web: www.dnr.state.il.us/lands/landmgt/parks/r2/jpatephillip.htm					
Jim Edgar Panther Creek State Fish & Wildlife Area (JEPC) 10149 County Hwy 11	Chandlerville	IL	62627	217-452-7741	
Web: www.dnr.state.il.us/lands/landmgt/parks/r4/jepc.htm					
Johnson-Sauk Trail State Park 28616 Sauk Trl Rd	Kewanee	IL	61443	309-853-5589	
Web: www.dnr.state.il.us					
Jubilee College State Park 13921 W Rt 150	Brimfield	IL	61517	309-446-3758	446-3183
Web: www.dnr.state.il.us					
Kankakee River State Park 5314 W Rt 102 PO Box 37	Bourbonnais	IL	60914	815-933-1383	
Web: www.dnr.state.il.us					
Kaskaskia River State Fish & Wildlife Area 10981 Conservation Rd	Baldwin	IL	62217	618-785-2555	
Web: www.dnr.state.il.us/lands/landmgt/parks/r4/kaskas.htm					
Kickapoo State Recreation Area 10906 Kickapoo Pk Rd	Oakwood	IL	61858	217-442-4915	
Web: www.dnr.state.il.us/lands/landmgt/parks/r3/kickapoo.htm					
Kinkaid Lake State Fish & Wildlife Area 52 Cinder Hill Dr	Murphysboro	IL	62966	618-684-2867	
Web: www.dnr.state.il.us/lands/landmgt/parks/r5/kinkaid.htm					
Lake Le-Aqua-Na State Recreation Area 8542 N Lk Rd	Lena	IL	61048	815-369-4282	
Web: www.dnr.state.il.us					
Lake Murphysboro State Park 52 Cinder Hill Dr	Murphysboro	IL	62966	618-684-2867	
Web: www.dnr.state.il.us/lands/landmgt/parks/r5/murphysb.htm					
LaSalle Lake State Fish & Wildlife Area 2660 E 2350th Rd	Marseilles	IL	61341	815-357-1608	
Web: www.dnr.state.il.us					
Lincoln Trail State Park 16985 E 1350th Rd	Marshall	IL	62441	217-826-2222	
Web: www.dnr.state.il.us					
Lowden State Park 1411 N River Rd	Oregon	IL	61061	815-732-6828	
Web: www.dnr.state.il.us/lands/landmgt/parks/r1/lowdensp.htm					
Lowden-Miller State Forest 1365 W Castle Rock Rd	Oregon	IL	61061	815-732-7329	
Web: www.dnr.state.il.us/lands/landmgt/parks/r1/lowdenmi.htm					
Mackinaw River State Fish & Wildlife Area 15470 Nelson Rd	Mackinaw	IL	61755	309-963-4969	
Web: www.dnr.state.il.us					
Marshall State Fish & Wildlife Area 236 State Rt 26	Lacon	IL	61540	309-246-8351	
Web: www.dnr.state.il.us					
Matthiessen State Park PO Box 509	Utica	IL	61373	815-667-4868	
Web: www.dnr.state.il.us/lands/landmgt/parks/r1/mttindex.htm					

Phone Fax

Mautino State Fish & Wildlife Area
16006-875 E St ... Sheffield IL 61361 815-454-2328
Web: www.dnr.state.il.us/lands/landmgt/parks/r1/mautino.htm

Mazonia-Braidwood State Fish & Wildlife Areas
PO Box 126 ... Braceville IL 60407 815-237-0063
Web: www.dnr.state.il.us

Mermet Lake State Fish & Wildlife Area
1812 Grinnell Rd ... Belknap IL 62908 618-524-5577
Web: www.dnr.state.il.us

Middle Fork State Fish & Wildlife Area
10906 Kickapoo Pk Rd ... Oakwood IL 61858 217-442-4915
Web: www.dnr.state.il.us/lands/landmgt/parks/r3/middle.htm

Mississippi Palisades State Park
16327A IL Rt 84 ... Savanna IL 61074 815-273-2731
Web: www.dnr.state.il.us

Mississippi River State Fish & Wildlife Area
17836 State Hwy 100 N ... Grafton IL 62037 618-376-3303
Web: www.dnr.state.il.us/lands/landmgt/parks/r4/miss.htm

Moraine Hills State Park 1510 S River Rd ... McHenry IL 60051 815-385-1624
Web: www.dnr.state.il.us

Moraine View State Recreation Area
27374 Moraine View Pk Rd ... Le Roy IL 61752 309-724-8032
Web: www.dnr.state.il.us

Morrison-Rockwood State Park 18750 Lake Rd ... Morrison IL 61270 815-772-4708
Web: www.dnr.state.il.us

Nauvoo State Park PO Box 426 ... Nauvoo IL 62354 217-453-2512
Web: www.dnr.state.il.us

Newton Lake State Fish & Wildlife Area
3490 E 500th Ave ... Newton IL 62448 618-783-3478
Web: www.dnr.state.il.us

Peabody River King State Fish & Wildlife Area
8900 Darmstadt Rd ... New Athens IL 62264 618-475-9339
Web: www.dnr.state.il.us/lands/landmgt/parks/r4/peabody.htm

Pere Marquette State Park
13112 Visitor Ctr Ln ... Grafton IL 62037 618-786-3323
Web: www.dnr.state.il.us/lands/landmgt/parks/r4/peremarq.htm

Piney Creek Ravine State Natural Area
4301 N Lake Dr ... Chester IL 62233 618-826-2706
Web: www.dnr.state.il.us

Powerton Lake State Fish & Wildlife Area
7982 S Pk Rd ... Manito IL 61546 309-968-7135
Web: www.dnr.state.il.us/lands/landmgt/parks/r1/powerton.htm

Prophetstown State Recreation Area
Riverside Dr PO Box 181 ... Prophetstown IL 61277 815-537-2926
Web: www.dnr.state.il.us/lands/landmgt/parks/r1/prophet.htm

Pyramid State Recreation Area
1562 Pyramid Pk Rd ... Pinckneyville IL 62274 618-357-2574
Web: www.dnr.state.il.us

Ramsey Lake State Recreation Area
Ramsey Lk Rd PO Box 97 ... Ramsey IL 62080 618-423-2215
Web: www.dnr.state.il.us

Randolph County State Recreation Area
4301 S Lake Dr ... Chester IL 62233 618-826-2706
Web: www.dnr.state.il.us/lands/landmgt/parks/r4/rand.htm

Ray Norbut State Fish & Wildlife Area
46816 290th Ave ... Griggsville IL 62340 217-833-2811
Web: www.dnr.state.il.us

Red Hills State Park RR 2 3571 Ranger Ln ... Sumner IL 62466 618-936-2469
Web: www.dnr.state.il.us

Rend Lake State Fish & Wildlife Area
10885 E Jefferson Rd ... Bonnie IL 62816 618-279-3110
Web: www.dnr.state.il.us

Rice Lake State Fish & Wildlife Area
19721 N US Hwy 24 ... Canton IL 61520 309-647-9184
Web: www.dnr.state.il.us/lands/landmgt/parks/r1/rice.htm

Rock Cut State Park 7318 Harlem Rd ... Loves Park IL 61111 815-885-3311
Web: www.dnr.state.il.us

Rock Island Trail State Park
311 E Williams St PO Box 64 ... Wyoming IL 61491 309-695-2228
Web: www.dnr.state.il.us

Saline County State Fish & Wildlife Area
85 Glen O Jones Rd ... Equality IL 62934 618-276-4405
Web: www.dnr.state.il.us

Sam Parr State Fish & Wildlife Area
13225 E State Hwy 33 ... Newton IL 62448 618-783-2661
Web: www.dnr.state.il.us

Sand Ridge State Forest PO Box 111 ... Forest City IL 61532 309-597-2212
Web: www.dnr.state.il.us

Sanganois State Fish & Wildlife Area
3594 County Rd 200 N ... Chandlerville IL 62627 309-546-2628
Web: www.dnr.state.il.us/lands/landmgt/parks/r4/sangill.htm

Sangchris Lake State Park 9898 Cascade Rd ... Rochester IL 62563 217-498-9208
Web: www.dnr.state.il.us

Shabbona Lake State Park
4201 Shabbona Grove Rd ... Shabbona IL 60550 815-824-2106
Web: www.dnr.state.il.us

Shelbyville State Fish & Wildlife Area
562 State Hwy 121 PO Box 42A ... Bethany IL 61914 217-665-3112
Web: www.dnr.state.il.us

Siloam Springs State Park 938 E 3003rd Ln ... Clayton IL 62324 217-894-6205
Web: www.dnr.state.il.us

Silver Springs State Fish & Wildlife Area
13608 Fox Rd ... Yorkville IL 60560 630-553-6297
Web: www.dnr.state.il.us

South Shore State Park
c/o Eldon Hazlet State Recreation Area
20100 Hazlet Pk Rd ... Carlyle IL 62231 618-594-3015
Web: www.dnr.state.il.us/lands/landmgt/parks/r4/sts.htm

Spitler Woods State Natural Area
705 Spitler Pk Dr ... Mount Zion IL 62549 217-864-3121
Web: www.dnr.state.il.us/lands/landmgt/parks/r3/spitler.htm

Spring Lake State Fish & Wildlife Area
7982 S Pk Rd ... Manito IL 61546 309-968-7135
Web: www.dnr.state.il.us/lands/landmgt/parks/r1/spl.htm

Phone Fax

Starved Rock State Park PO Box 509 ... Utica IL 61373 815-667-4726
Web: www.dnr.state.il.us/lands/landmgt/parks/i&m/east/starve/park.htm

Stephen A. Forbes State Park 6924 Omega Rd ... Kinmundy IL 62854 618-547-3381
Web: www.dnr.state.il.us

Ten Mile Creek State Fish & Wildlife Area
RR 1 PO Box 179 ... McLeansboro IL 62859 618-643-2862
Web: www.dnr.state.il.us

Trail of Tears State Forest
3240 State Forest Rd ... Jonesboro IL 62952 618-833-4910
Web: www.dnr.state.il.us

Tunnel Hill State Trail 302 E Vine St ... Vienna IL 62995 618-658-2168
Web: www.dnr.state.il.us

Turkey Bluffs State Fish & Wildlife Area
4301 S Lakeside Dr ... Chester IL 62233 618-826-2706
Web: dnr.state.il.us

Union County State Fish & Wildlife Area
2755 Refuge Rd ... Jonesboro IL 62952 618-833-5175
Web: www.dnr.state.il.us

Volo Bog State Natural Area
28478 W Brandenburg Rd ... Ingleside IL 60041 815-344-1294
Web: www.dnr.state.il.us

Walnut Point State Park
2331 E County Rd 370 N ... Oakland IL 61943 217-346-3336
Web: www.dnr.state.il.us

Washington County State Recreation Area
18500 Conservation Dr ... Nashville IL 62263 618-327-3137
Web: www.dnr.state.il.us

Wayne Fitzgerrell State Recreation Area
11094 Ranger Rd ... Whittington IL 62897 618-629-2320
Web: www.dnr.state.il.us

Weinberg-King State Park PO Box 203 ... Augusta IL 62311 217-392-2345
Web: www.dnr.state.il.us

Weldon Springs State Park
4734 Weldon Springs Rd RR 2 PO Box 87 ... Clinton IL 61727 217-935-2644
Web: www.dnr.state.il.us

White Pines Forest State Park
6712 W Pines Rd ... Mount Morris IL 61054 815-946-3717
Web: www.dnr.state.il.us

William W. Powers State Recreation Area
12949 S Ave O ... Chicago IL 60633 773-646-3270
Web: www.dnr.state.il.us

Wolf Creek State Park RR 1 PO Box 99 ... Windsor IL 61957 217-459-2831
Web: www.dnr.state.il.us

Indiana

Phone Fax

Brookville Lake PO Box 100 ... Brookville IN 47012 765-647-2657
Web: www.in.gov

Brown County State Park
1405 State Rd 46 W PO Box 608 ... Nashville IN 47448 812-988-6406
Web: www.in.gov

Cagles Mill Lake 1317 W Lieber Rd Ste 1 ... Cloverdale IN 46120 765-795-4576
Web: www.in.gov

Cecil M. Harden Lake 1588 S Raccoon Pkwy ... Rockville IN 47872 765-344-1412
Web: www.in.gov

Chain O'Lakes State Park 2355 E 75 S ... Albion IN 46701 260-636-2654
Web: www.in.gov

Charlestown State Park 12500 Indiana 62 ... Charlestown IN 47111 812-256-5600
Web: www.in.gov

Clifty Falls State Park 1501 Green Rd ... Madison IN 47250 812-273-8885
Web: www.in.gov

Deam Lake State Recreation Area
1217 Deam Lk Rd ... Borden IN 47106 812-246-5421
Web: www.in.gov

Falls of the Ohio State Park
201 W Riverside Dr ... Clarksville IN 47129 812-280-9970 280-7110
Web: www.in.gov

Fort Harrison State Park 5753 Glenn Rd ... Indianapolis IN 46216 317-591-0904
Web: www.in.gov

Hardy Lake 4171 E Harrod Rd ... Scottsburg IN 47170 812-794-3800
Web: www.in.gov

Harmonie State Park
3451 Harmonie State Pk Rd ... New Harmony IN 47631 812-682-4821
TF: 866-622-6746 ■ *Web:* www.in.gov

Indiana Dunes State Park 1600 N 25 E ... Chesterton IN 46304 219-926-1952
Web: www.in.gov

J. Edward Roush Lake 517 N Warren Rd ... Huntington IN 46750 260-468-2165
Web: www.in.gov

Lincoln State Park Hwy 162 PO Box 216 ... Lincoln City IN 47552 812-937-4710
TF: 877-478-3657 ■ *Web:* www.in.gov

McCormick's Creek State Park
250 McCormick's Creek Rd ... Spencer IN 47460 812-829-2235
Web: www.in.gov

Mississinewa Lake 4673 S 625 E ... Peru IN 46970 765-473-6528
Web: www.in.gov

Monroe Lake 4850 S State Rd 446 ... Bloomington IN 47401 812-837-9546
Web: www.in.gov

Mounds State Park 4306 Mounds Rd ... Anderson IN 46017 765-642-6627
Web: www.in.gov

O'Bannon Woods State Park
7234 Old Forest Rd SW ... Corydon IN 47112 812-738-8232
Web: www.in.gov

Ouabache State Park 4930 E State Rd 201 ... Bluffton IN 46714 260-824-0926
Web: www.in.gov

Patoka Lake 3084 N DillaRd Rd ... Birdseye IN 47513 812-685-2464
Web: www.in.gov

Pokagon State Park 450 Ln 100 Lk James ... Angola IN 46703 260-833-2012
Web: in.gov/ai/errors/dnr_404.html

Potato Creek State Park
25601 State Rd 4 PO Box 908 ... North Liberty IN 46554 574-656-8186
Web: www.in.gov

Salamonie Lake 9214 Lost Bridge Rd W ... Andrews IN 46702 260-468-2125
Web: www.in.gov

Park	City	State	ZIP	Phone	Fax
Shakamak State Park 6265 W State Rd 48 *Web:* www.in.gov	Jasonville	IN	47438	812-665-2158	
Spring Mill State Park PO Box 376 *Web:* www.in.gov	Mitchell	IN	47446	812-849-4129	
Starve Hollow State Recreation Area 4345 S County Rd 275 W *Web:* www.in.gov	Vallonia	IN	47281	812-358-3464	
Summit Lake State Park 5993 N Messick Rd *Web:* www.in.gov	New Castle	IN	47362	765-766-5873	
Tippecanoe River State Park 4200 N US Hwy 35 *Web:* www.in.gov	Winamac	IN	46996	574-946-3213	
Turkey Run State Park 8121 Pk Rd *Web:* www.in.gov	Marshall	IN	47859	765-597-2635	
Versailles State Park US Hwy 50 PO Box 205 *Web:* www.in.gov	Versailles	IN	47042	812-689-6424	
White River State Park 801 W Washington St *TF:* 800-665-9056 ■ *Web:* www.in.gov	Indianapolis	IN	46204	317-233-2434	
Whitewater Memorial State Park 1418 S State Rd 101 *Web:* www.in.gov	Liberty	IN	47353	765-458-5565	

Iowa

Park	City	State	ZIP	Phone	Fax
Backbone State Park 1282 120th St *Web:* www.iowadnr.gov	Strawberry Point	IA	52076	563-924-2000	
Beed's Lake State Park 1422 165th St Pk *Web:* www.iowadnr.gov	Hampton	IA	50441	641-456-2047	
Big Creek State Park 8794 NW 125th Ave *Web:* www.iowadnr.gov	Polk City	IA	50226	515-984-6473	984-9320
Black Hawk State Park 228 S Blossom *Web:* www.iowadnr.gov	Lake View	IA	51450	712-657-8712	657-2289
Brushy Creek State Recreation Area 2802 Brushy Creek Rd *Web:* www.iowadnr.gov	Lehigh	IA	50557	515-543-8298	843-8395
Cedar Rock 2611 Quasqueton Diagonal Blvd Buch Co Hwy W-35 *Web:* www.iowadnr.gov	Independence	IA	50644	319-934-3572	
Clear Lake State Park 2730 S Lakeview Dr *Web:* www.iowadnr.gov	Clear Lake	IA	50428	641-357-4212	357-4242
Dolliver Memorial State Park 2757 Dolliver Pk Ave *Web:* www.iowadnr.gov	Lehigh	IA	50557	515-359-2539	359-2542
Elinor Bedell State Park c/o Gull Pt State Pk 1500 Harpen St *Web:* www.iowabeautiful.com	Milford	IA	51351	712-330-5192	
Elk Rock State Park 811 146th Ave *Web:* www.iowadnr.gov	Knoxville	IA	50138	641-842-6008	
Fort Atkinson State Preserve c/o Volga River State Recreation Area 10225 Ivy Rd *Web:* www.iowadnr.gov	Fayette	IA	52142	563-425-4161	
Fort Defiance State Park c/o Gull Pt State Pk 1500 Harpen St *Web:* www.iowadnr.gov	Milford	IA	51351	712-337-3211	
Geode State Park 3333 Racine Ave *Web:* www.iowadnr.gov	Danville	IA	52623	319-392-4601	
George Wyth State Park 3659 Wyth Rd *Web:* www.iowadnr.gov	Waterloo	IA	50703	319-232-5505	
Green Valley State Park 1480 130th St *Web:* www.iowadnr.gov	Creston	IA	50801	641-782-5131	
Gull Point State Park 1500 Harpen St *Web:* www.iowadnr.gov	Milford	IA	51351	712-337-3211	
Honey Creek State Park 12194 Honey Creek Pl *Web:* www.iowadnr.gov	Moravia	IA	52571	641-724-3739	724-9846
Lake Ahquabi State Park 1650 118th Ave *Web:* www.iowadnr.gov	Indianola	IA	50125	515-961-7101	
Lake Anita State Park 55111 750th St *Web:* www.iowadnr.gov	Anita	IA	50020	712-762-3564	
Lake Darling State Park 111 Lk Darling Rd *Web:* www.iowadnr.gov	Brighton	IA	52540	319-694-2323	
Lake Keomah State Park 2720 Keomah Ln *Web:* www.iowadnr.gov	Oskaloosa	IA	52577	641-673-6975	673-0647
Lake Macbride State Park 3525 Hwy 382 NE *Web:* www.iowadnr.gov	Solon	IA	52333	319-624-2200	624-2188
Lake Manawa State Park 1100 S Shore Dr *Web:* www.iowadnr.gov	Council Bluffs	IA	51501	712-366-0220	366-0474
Lake of Three Fires State Park 2303 Lake Rd *Web:* www.iowadnr.gov	Bedford	IA	50833	712-523-2700	523-3104
Lake Wapello State Park 15248 Campground Rd *TF:* 866-495-4868 ■ *Web:* www.iowadnr.gov	Drakesville	IA	52552	641-722-3371	
Ledges State Park 1515 P Ave *Web:* www.iowadnr.gov	Madrid	IA	50156	515-432-1852	
Lewis & Clark State Park 21914 Pk Loop *Web:* www.lewisandclarktrail.com	Onawa	IA	51040	712-423-2829	
Maquoketa Caves State Park 10970 98th St *Web:* www.iowadnr.gov	Maquoketa	IA	52060	563-652-5833	652-0061
McIntosh Woods State Park 1200 E Lake St *Web:* www.iowadnr.gov	Ventura	IA	50482	641-829-3847	
Mines of Spain State Recreation Area 8991 Bellevue Heights *Web:* www.iowadnr.gov	Dubuque	IA	52003	563-556-0620	556-8474
Nine Eagles State Park RR 1 *Web:* www.iowadnr.gov	Davis City	IA	50065	641-442-2855	442-2856
Palisades-Kepler State Park 700 Kepler Dr *Web:* www.iowadnr.gov	Mount Vernon	IA	52314	319-895-6039	
Pikes Peak State Park 15316 Great River Rd *Web:* www.iowadnr.gov	McGregor	IA	52157	563-873-2341	873-3167
Pilot Knob State Park 2148 340th St *Web:* www.iowadnr.gov	Forest City	IA	50436	641-581-4835	
Pine Lake State Park 22620 County Hwy S56 *Web:* www.iowadnr.gov	Eldora	IA	50627	641-858-5832	858-5641
Pleasant Creek State Recreation Area 4530 McClintock Rd *Web:* www.iowadnr.gov	Palo	IA	52324	319-436-7716	
Prairie Rose State Park 680 Rd M47 *Web:* www.iowadnr.gov	Harlan	IA	51537	712-773-2701	773-2702
Preparation Canyon State Park 206 Polk St PO Box 158 *Web:* www.iowadnr.gov	Pisgah	IA	51564	712-423-2829	
Red Haw State Park 24550 US Hwy 34 *Web:* www.iowadnr.gov	Chariton	IA	50049	641-774-5632	774-8821
Rock Creek State Park 5627 Rock Creek E *Web:* www.iowadnr.gov	Kellogg	IA	50135	641-236-3722	236-5599
Shimek State Forest 33653 Rt J56 *Web:* www.iowadnr.gov	Farmington	IA	52626	319-878-3811	
Springbrook State Park 2437 160th Rd *Web:* www.iowadnr.gov	Guthrie Center	IA	50115	641-747-3591	747-8401
Stephens State Forest 1111 N Eigth St *Web:* www.iowadnr.gov	Chariton	IA	50049	641-774-4559	
Stone State Park 5001 Talbot Rd *Web:* www.iowadnr.gov	Sioux City	IA	51103	712-255-4698	
Twin Lakes State Park c/o Black Hawk Lk State Pk 228 S Blossom St *Web:* www.iowadnr.gov	Lake View	IA	51450	712-657-8712	657-2289
Union Grove State Park 1215 220th St *Web:* www.iowadnr.gov	Gladbrook	IA	50635	641-473-2556	473-3059
Viking Lake State Park 2780 Viking Lk Rd *Web:* www.iowadnr.gov	Stanton	IA	51573	712-829-2235	829-2842
Volga River State Recreation Area 10225 Ivy Rd *Web:* www.iowadnr.gov	Fayette	IA	52142	563-425-4161	425-3272
Walnut Woods State Park 3155 Walnut Woods Dr *Web:* www.iowadnr.gov	West Des Moines	IA	50265	515-285-4502	285-7476
Wapsipinicon State Park 21301 County Rd E34 *Web:* www.iowadnr.gov	Anamosa	IA	52205	319-462-2761	462-4878
Waubonsie State Park 2585 Waubonsie Pk Rd *Web:* www.iowadnr.gov	Hamburg	IA	51640	712-382-2786	
Wildcat Den State Park 1884 Wildcat Den Rd *Web:* www.iowadnr.gov	Muscatine	IA	52761	563-263-4337	
Wilson Island State Recreation Area 32801 Campground Ln *Web:* www.iowadnr.gov	Missouri Valley	IA	51555	712-642-2069	
Yellow River State Forest 729 State Forest Rd YRSF *Web:* www.iowadnr.gov	Harpers Ferry	IA	52146	563-586-2254	

Kansas

Park	City	State	ZIP	Phone	Fax
Cedar Bluff State Park 32001 147 Hwy *Web:* ksoutdoors.com	Ellis	KS	67637	785-726-3212	
Cheney State Park 16000 NE 50th St *Web:* ksoutdoors.com	Cheney	KS	67025	316-542-3664	
Clinton State Park 798 N 1415 Rd *Web:* ksoutdoors.com	Lawrence	KS	66049	785-842-8562	
Crawford State Park 1 Lake Rd *Web:* ksoutdoors.com	Farlington	KS	66734	620-362-3671	
Cross Timbers State Park 144 Hwy 105 *Web:* ksoutdoors.com/State-Parks/Locations/Cross-Timbers	Toronto	KS	66777	620-637-2213	
Eisenhower State Park 29810 S Fairlawn Rd *Web:* ksoutdoors.com	Osage City	KS	66523	785-528-4102	
El Dorado State Park 618 NE Bluestem Rd *Web:* ksoutdoors.com/state-parks/locations/el-dorado	El Dorado	KS	67042	316-321-7180	
Elk City State Park 4825 Squaw Creek Rd *Web:* ksoutdoors.com/state-parks/locations/elk-city	Independence	KS	67301	620-331-6295	
Glen Elder State Park 2131 180 Rd *Web:* ksoutdoors.com/state-parks/locations/glen-elder	Glen Elder	KS	67446	785-545-3345	
Hillsdale State Park 26001 W 255th St *Web:* ksoutdoors.com/state-parks/locations/hillsdale	Paola	KS	66071	913-783-4507	
Kanopolis State Park 200 Horsethief Rd *Web:* ksoutdoors.com/state-parks/locations/kanopolis	Marquette	KS	67464	785-546-2565	
Lake Scott State Park 520 W Scott Lk Dr *Web:* www.kansastravel.org	Scott City	KS	67871	620-872-2061	
Lovewell State Park 2446 250 Rd *Web:* ksoutdoors.com/State-Parks/Locations/Lovewell	Webber	KS	66970	785-753-4971	
Meade State Park 13051 V Rd *Web:* www.stateparks.com"«	Meade	KS	67864	620-873-2572	
Milford State Park 3612 State Pk Rd *Web:* ksoutdoors.com/State-Parks/Locations/Milford	Milford	KS	66514	785-238-3014	
Mushroom Rock State Park 200 Horsethief Rd *Web:* ksoutdoors.com/State-Parks/Locations/Mushroom-Rock	Marquette	KS	67464	785-546-2565	
Perry State Park 5441 Westlake Rd *Web:* ksoutdoors.com/State-Parks/Locations/Perry	Ozawkie	KS	66070	785-246-3449	246-0224
Pomona State Park 22900 S Hwy 368 *Web:* ksoutdoors.com/State-Parks/Locations/Pomona	Vassar	KS	66543	785-828-4933	
Prairie Spirit Trail 419 S Oak St *Web:* bikeprairiespirit.com	Garnett	KS	66032	785-448-6767	
Tuttle Creek State Park 5800-A River Pond Rd *Web:* ksoutdoors.com/State-Parks/Locations/Tuttle-Creek	Manhattan	KS	66502	785-539-7941	
Webster State Park 1210 Nine Rd *Web:* ksoutdoors.com/State-Parks/Locations/Webster	Stockton	KS	67669	785-425-6775	

Kentucky

Phone Fax

Ben Hawes State Park 400 Boothfield Rd .... Owensboro KY 42301 270-687-7137 687-7138
Web: www.kentuckytourism.com/outdoor_adventure/attraction/ben-hawes-park/19

Big Bone Lick State Park 3380 Beaver Rd .... Union KY 41091 859-384-3522
Web: www.parks.ky.gov

Blue Licks Battlefield State Resort Park
Hwy 68.. Mount Olivet KY 41064 800-443-7008
TF: 800-443-7008 ■ *Web:* www.parks.ky.gov

Boone Station State Historic Site
240 Gentry Rd.................................. Lexington KY 40502 859-527-3131
Web: www.parks.ky.gov

Buckhorn Lake State Resort Park
4441 Kentucky Hwy 1833.......................... Buckhorn KY 41721 800-325-0058
TF: 800-325-0058 ■ *Web:* www.parks.ky.gov

Carr Creek State Park Hwy 15...................... Sassafras KY 41759 606-642-4050
Web: www.parks.ky.gov

Columbus-Belmont State Park 350 Pk Rd........... Columbus KY 42032 270-677-2327
Web: www.parks.ky.gov

Constitution Square State Historic Site
134 S Second St.................................. Danville KY 40422 859-239-7089
Web: www.parks.ky.gov

Cumberland Falls State Resort Park
7351 Hwy 90 .... Corbin KY 40701 800-325-0063
TF: 800-325-0063 ■ *Web:* www.parks.ky.gov

Dr Thomas Walker State Historic Site
4929 KY 459....................................... Barbourville KY 40906 606-546-4400
Web: www.parks.ky.gov

EP "Tom" Sawyer State Park
3000 Freys Hill Rd .... Louisville KY 40241 502-429-7270 429-7273
Web: www.parks.ky.gov

Fishtrap Lake State Park 2204 Fishtrap Rd .... Shelbiana KY 41562 502-564-2172
Web: www.stateparks.com/fishtrap_lake_state_park_in_kentucky.html

Fort Boonesborough State Park
4375 Boonesborough Rd .... Richmond KY 40475 859-527-3131
Web: www.parks.ky.gov

General Burnside Island State Park
8801 S Hwy 27..................................... Burnside KY 42519 606-561-4104
Web: www.parks.ky.gov

Grayson Lake State Park
314 Grayson Lk Pk Rd .... Olive Hill KY 41164 606-474-9727
Web: www.parks.ky.gov

Green River Lake State Park
179 Pk Office Rd............................ Campbellsville KY 42718 270-465-8255
Web: www.parks.ky.gov

Jenny Wiley State Resort Park
75 Theatre Ct .... Prestonsburg KY 41653 800-325-0142
TF: 800-325-0142 ■ *Web:* www.parks.ky.gov

John James Audubon State Park
3100 US Hwy 41 N............................... Henderson KY 42419 270-826-2247
Web: www.parks.ky.gov

Kenlake State Resort Park 542 Kenlake Rd .... Hardin KY 42048 270-474-2211
TF: 800-325-0143 ■ *Web:* www.parks.ky.gov/findparks/resortparks/kl

Kincaid Lake State Park 565 Kincaid Pk Rd........... Falmouth KY 41040 859-654-3531
Web: www.parks.ky.gov

Kingdom Come State Park 502 Pk Rd .... Cumberland KY 40823 606-589-2479
Web: www.parks.ky.gov

Lake Barkley State Resort Park
3500 State Pk Rd.................................. Cadiz KY 42211 800-325-1708
TF: 800-325-1708 ■ *Web:* parks.ky.gov/findparks/resortparks/lb

Levi Jackson State Park
998 Levi Jackson Mill Rd.......................... London KY 40744 606-330-2130
Web: www.parks.ky.gov

Lincoln Homestead State Park
5079 Lincoln Pk Rd .... Springfield KY 40069 859-336-7461
Web: www.parks.ky.gov

Mineral Mound State Park 48 Finch Ln.............. Eddyville KY 42038 270-388-3673
Web: www.parks.ky.gov

My Old Kentucky Home State Park
501 E Stephen Foster Ave........................ Bardstown KY 40004 502-348-3502
Web: www.parks.ky.gov

Natural Bridge State Resort Park
2135 Natural Bridge Rd .... Slade KY 40376 800-325-1710
TF: 800-325-1710 ■ *Web:* www.parks.ky.gov

Nolin Lake State Park PO Box 340 .... Bee Spring KY 42207 270-286-4240
Web: www.parks.ky.gov

Old Fort Harrod State Park
100 S College St............................... Harrodsburg KY 40330 859-734-3314
Web: www.parks.ky.gov

Old Mulkey Meetinghouse State Historic Site
38 Old Mulkey Pk Rd .... Tompkinsville KY 42167 270-487-8481 487-8481
Web: www.parks.ky.gov

Pennyrile Forest State Resort Park
20781 Pennyrile Lodge Rd .... Dawson Springs KY 42408 800-325-1711
TF: 800-325-1711 ■ *Web:* www.parks.ky.gov

Pine Mountain State Resort Park
1050 State Pk Rd .... Pineville KY 40977 800-325-1712
TF: 800-325-1712 ■ *Web:* www.parks.ky.gov

Rough River Dam State Resort Park
450 Lodge Rd.............................. Falls of Rough KY 40119 800-325-1713
TF: 800-325-1713 ■ *Web:* www.parks.ky.gov

Taylorsville Lake State Park 1320 Pk Rd .... Taylorsville KY 40071 502-477-8713
Web: www.parks.ky.gov

Waveland Museum State Historic Site
225 Waveland Museum Ln........................ Lexington KY 40514 859-272-3611
Web: www.parks.ky.gov

White Hall State Historic Site
500 White Hall Shrine Rd......................... Richmond KY 40475 859-623-9178
Web: www.parks.ky.gov

Wickliffe Mounds State Historic Site
94 Green St...................................... Wickliffe KY 42087 270-335-3681
Web: www.parks.ky.gov/parks/historicsites/wickliffe-mounds/default.aspx

Phone Fax

William Whitley House State Historic Site
625 William Whitley Rd .... Stanford KY 40484 606-355-2881
Web: www.parks.ky.gov

Yatesville Lake State Park PO Box 767................ Louisa KY 41230 606-673-1492
Web: www.parks.ky.gov

Louisiana

Phone Fax

Bayou Segnette State Park
7777 Westbank Expy .... Westwego LA 70094 504-736-7140 436-4788
TF: 888-677-2296 ■ *Web:* www.crt.state.la.us

Centenary State Historic Site
3522 College St .... Jackson LA 70748 225-634-7925
TF: 888-677-2364 ■ *Web:* www.crt.state.la.us

Chemin-A-Haut State Park 14656 State Pk Rd.......... Bastrop LA 71220 318-283-0812
TF: 888-677-2436 ■ *Web:* www.crt.state.la.us

Chicot State Park 3469 Chicot Pk Rd .... Ville Platte LA 70586 337-363-2403
TF: 888-677-2442 ■ *Web:* www.crt.state.la.us

Cypremort Point State Park
306 Beach Ln .... Cypremort Point LA 70538 337-867-4510
TF: 888-867-4510 ■ *Web:* www.crt.state.la.us

Fairview-Riverside State Park
119 Fairview Dr .... Madisonville LA 70447 985-845-3318
TF: 888-677-3247 ■ *Web:* www.crt.state.la.us

Fontainebleau State Park 67825 US Hwy 190........ Mandeville LA 70448 985-624-4443
TF: 888-677-3668 ■ *Web:* www.crt.state.la.us

Fort Jesup State Historic Site 32 Geoghagan Rd .... Many LA 71449 318-256-4117
TF: 888-677-5378 ■ *Web:* www.crt.state.la.us

Fort Saint Jean Baptiste State Historic Site
155 Jefferson St .... Natchitoches LA 71457 318-357-3101
TF: 888-677-7853 ■ *Web:* www.crt.state.la.us

Grand Isle State Park Admiral Craik Dr............. Grand Isle LA 70358 985-787-2559
TF: 888-787-2559 ■ *Web:* www.crt.state.la.us

Jimmie Davis State Park 1209 State Pk Rd............ Chatham LA 71226 318-249-2595
TF: 888-677-2263 ■ *Web:* www.crt.state.la.us

Lake Bistineau State Park 103 State Pk Rd .... Doyline LA 71023 318-745-3503
TF: 888-677-2478 ■ *Web:* www.crt.state.la.us

Lake Bruin State Park 201 State Pk Rd .... Saint Joseph LA 71366 318-766-3530
TF: 888-677-2784 ■ *Web:* www.crt.state.la.us

Lake Claiborne State Park 225 State Pk Rd............ Homer LA 71040 318-927-2976
TF: 888-677-2524 ■ *Web:* www.crt.state.la.us

Lake D'Arbonne State Park
3628 Evergreen Rd .... Farmerville LA 71241 318-368-2086
TF: 888-677-5200 ■ *Web:* www.crt.state.la.us

Longfellow-Evangeline State Historic Site
1200 N Main St .... Saint Martinville LA 70582 337-394-3754
TF: 888-677-2900 ■ *Web:* www.crt.state.la.us

Los Adaes State Historic Site 6354 Hwy 485 .... Robeline LA 71469 318-472-9449
TF: 888-677-5378 ■ *Web:* www.crt.state.la.us

Louisiana State Arboretum
4213 Chicot Pk Rd .... Ville Platte LA 70586 337-363-6289
TF: 888-677-6100 ■ *Web:* www.crt.state.la.us

Mansfield State Historic Site
15149 Hwy 175 .... Mansfield LA 71052 318-872-1474
TF: 888-677-6267 ■ *Web:* www.crt.state.la.us

Marksville State Historic Site
837 ML King Dr .... Marksville LA 71351 318-253-8954
TF: 888-253-8954 ■ *Web:* www.crt.state.la.us

North Toledo Bend State Park
2907 N Toledo Pk Rd .... Zwolle LA 71486 318-645-4715
TF: 888-677-6400 ■ *Web:* www.crt.state.la.us

Palmetto Island State Park
19501 Pleasant Rd .... Abbeville LA 70510 337-893-3930
TF: 888-677-3668

Port Hudson State Historic Site 236 Hwy 61 .... Jackson LA 70748 225-654-3775 654-4413
TF: 888-677-3400 ■ *Web:* www.crt.state.la.us

Poverty Point Reservoir State Park
1500 Poverty Pt Pkwy................................ Delhi LA 71232 318-878-7536
TF: 800-474-0392 ■ *Web:* www.crt.state.la.us

Poverty Point State Historic Site
6859 Hwy 577 .... Pioneer LA 71266 318-926-5492
TF: 888-926-5492 ■ *Web:* www.crt.state.la.us

Rebel State Historic Site 1260 Hwy 1221 .... Marthaville LA 71450 318-472-6255
TF: 888-677-3600 ■ *Web:* www.crt.state.la.us

Saint Bernard State Park
501 St Bernard Pkwy .... Braithwaite LA 70040 504-682-2101
TF: 888-677-7823 ■ *Web:* www.crt.state.la.us

Sam Houston Jones State Park
107 Sutherland Rd .... Lake Charles LA 70611 337-855-2665
TF: 888-677-7264 ■ *Web:* www.crt.state.la.us

South Toledo Bend State Park
120 Bald Eaglel Rd................................ Anacoco LA 71403 337-286-9075
TF: 888-398-4770 ■ *Web:* www.crt.state.la.us

Tickfaw State Park 27225 Patterson Rd .... Springfield LA 70462 225-294-5020
TF: 888-981-2020 ■ *Web:* www.crt.state.la.us

Winter Quarters State Historic Site
4929 Hwy 608 .... Newellton LA 71357 888-677-2784
TF: 888-677-9468 ■ *Web:* www.crt.state.la.us

Maine

Phone Fax

Allagash Wilderness Waterway
106 Hogan Rd Ste 7 .... Bangor ME 04401 207-941-4014
Web: www.maine.gov

Aroostook State Park 87 State Pk Rd .... Presque Isle ME 04769 207-768-8341
Web: www.maine.gov

Baxter State Park 64 Balsam Dr.................. Millinocket ME 04462 207-723-5140
Web: www.baxterstateparkauthority.com

Birch Point Beach State Park
c/o Bureau of Parks & Lands 106 Hogan Rd............. Bangor ME 04401 207-941-4014
Web: maine.gov/dacf/mgs/index.shtml

Phone | Fax

Bradbury Mountain State Park 528 Hallowell Rd .... Pownal ME 04069 207-688-4712
Web: www.maine.gov

Camden Hills State Park 280 Belfast Rd............... Camden ME 04843 207-236-3109
Web: www.maine.gov

Cobscook Bay State Park 40 S Edmunds Rd .... Dennysville ME 04628 207-726-4412
Web: www.maine.gov

Colonial Pemaquid State Historic Site
PO Box 304 .... New Harbor ME 04554 207-677-2423
Web: www.maine.gov

Damariscotta Lake State Park 8 State Pk Rd .... Jefferson ME 04348 207-549-7600
Web: www.maine.gov

Ferry Beach State Park 95 Bayview Rd.................. Saco ME 04072 207-283-0067
Web: www.maine.gov

Fort Edgecomb State Historic Site 66 Ft Rd......... Edgecomb ME 04556 207-882-7777
Web: www.maine.gov

Fort Halifax State on the Kennebec
c/o Bureau of Parks & Lands 106 Hogan Rd............. Bangor ME 04401 207-941-4014
Web: maine.gov/dacf/parks/index.shtml

Fort Kent State Historic Site 106 Hogan Rd .... Bangor ME 04401 207-941-4014
Web: www.maine.gov/cgi-bin/online/doc/parksearch/index.pl

Fort Knox State Historic Site
711 Ft Knox Rd.................................. Prospect ME 04981 207-469-7719
Web: maine.gov/dacf/parks/index.shtml

Fort McClary State Historic Site Rt 103............. Kittery Pt ME 03905 207-384-5160
Web: maine.gov/dacf/parks/index.shtml

Fort O'Brien State Historic Site 106 Hogan Rd......... Bangor ME 04401 207-941-4014
Web: www.maine.gov/cgi-bin/online/doc/parksearch/index.pl

Fort Point State Park
c/o Bureau of Parks & Lands 106 Hogan Rd............. Bangor ME 04401 207-941-4014
Web: maine.gov/dacf/parks/index.shtml

Fort Popham State Historic Site
10 Perkins Farm Ln .... Phippsburg ME 04562 207-389-1335
Web: www.maine.gov

Grafton Notch State Park 1941 Bear River Rd .... Newry ME 04261 207-824-2912
Web: www.maine.gov

Holbrook Island Sanctuary PO Box 35............ Brooksville ME 04617 207-326-4012
Web: www.maine.gov

John Paul Jones State Historic Site
c/o Bureau of Parks & Lands .... Bangor ME 04401 207-941-4014 941-4222
TF: 800-452-1942 ■ *Web:* maine.gov/dacf/parks/index.shtml

Katahdin Iron Works State Historic Site
c/o Bureau of Parks & Lands 106 Hogan Rd............. Bangor ME 04401 207-941-4014
Web: maine.gov/dacf/mgs/index.shtml

Lake Saint George State Park
278 Belfast Augusta Rd................................ Liberty ME 04949 207-589-4255
Web: www.maine.gov

Lamoine State Park 23 State Pk Rd................. Lamoine ME 04605 207-667-4778
Web: www.maine.gov

Lily Bay State Park 13 Myrle's Way................. Greenville ME 04441 207-695-2700
Web: www.maine.gov

Moose Point State Park 310 W Main St............. Searsport ME 04974 207-548-2882
Web: www.maine.gov

Mount Blue State Park Ctr Hill RR1 PO Box 610 .... Weld ME 04285 207-585-2261
Web: www.maine.gov

Peaks-Kenny State Park
401 State Pk Rd .... Dover-Foxcroft ME 04426 207-564-2003
Web: www.maine.gov

Popham Beach State Park
10 Perkins Farm Ln .... Phippsburg ME 04562 207-389-1335
Web: www.maine.gov

Quoddy Head State Park 973 S Lubec Rd.............. Lubec ME 04652 207-733-0911
Web: www.maine.gov

Range Ponds State Park PO Box 475............ Poland Spring ME 04274 207-998-4104
Web: www.maine.gov

Rangeley Lake State Park HC 32 PO Box 5000......... Rangeley ME 04970 207-864-3858
Web: www.maine.gov

Reid State Park 375 Seguinland Rd............... Georgetown ME 04548 207-371-2303
Web: www.maine.gov

Roque Bluffs State Park
145 Schoppee Pt Rd.............................. Roque Bluffs ME 04654 207-255-3475
Web: www.maine.gov

Sebago Lake State Park 11 Pk Access Rd .... Casco ME 04055 207-693-6613
Web: www.maine.gov

Shackford Head State Park 106 Hogan Ave............ Bangor ME 04401 207-941-4014
TF: 800-400-6856 ■
Web: www.maine.gov/cgi-bin/online/doc/parksearch/search_name.pl?state_park=68

Swan Lake State Park 100 W Pk Ln .... Swanville ME 04915 207-525-4404
Web: www.maine.gov

Two Lights State Park 7 Tower Dr.............. Cape Elizabeth ME 04107 207-799-5871
Web: www.maine.gov

Vaughan Woods State Park
28 Oldfields Rd.............................. South Berwick ME 03908 207-287-3200
Web: www.maine.gov/cgi-bin/online/doc/parksearch/index.pl

Warren Island State Park PO Box 105............ Lincolnville ME 04849 207-446-7090
Web: www.maine.gov

Whaleback Shell Midden State Historic Site
PO Box 333 .... Damariscotta ME 04543 207-563-1393
Web: www.maine.gov

Wolfe's Neck Woods State Park
426 Wolfe's Neck Rd................................ Freeport ME 04032 207-865-4465
Web: www.maine.gov

Maryland

Phone | Fax

Assateague State Park
7307 Stephen Decatur Hwy............................ Berlin MD 21811 410-641-2120 641-3615
TF: 888-432-2267 ■ *Web:* dnr2.maryland.gov

Big Run State Park
c/o New Germany State Pk
10368 Savage River Rd.............................. Swanton MD 21561 301-895-5453
Web: dnr2.maryland.gov/publiclands/pages/western/bigrun.aspx

Calvert Cliffs State Park
10540 H. G. Trueman Rd PO Box 1042 .... Lusby MD 20657 301-743-7613
Web: dnr2.maryland.gov/publiclands/pages/southern/calvertcliffs.aspx

Casselman River Bridge State Park
580 Taylor Ave Tawes State Ofc Bldg .... Annapolis MD 21401 877-620-8367
TF: 877-620-8367 ■ *Web:* dnr2.maryland.gov

Cedarville State Forest 10201 Bee Oak Rd.......... Brandywine MD 20613 301-888-1410
Web: dnr2.maryland.gov

Choptank River Fishing Piers
29761 Bolingbroke Pt Dr .... Trappe MD 21673 410-820-1668
Web: dnr2.maryland.gov

Cunningham Falls State Park
14039 Catoctin Hollow Rd .... Thurmont MD 21788 301-271-7574
Web: www.dnr.state.md.us/publiclands/western/cunningham.asp

Elk Neck State Park 4395 Turkey Pt Rd............. North East MD 21901 410-287-5333
Web: dnr2.maryland.gov

Fair Hill Natural Resources Management Area
300 Tawes Dr .... Elkton MD 21921 410-398-1246
Web: dnr2.maryland.gov

Fort Frederick State Park
11100 Ft Frederick Rd .... Big Pool MD 21711 301-842-2155
Web: dnr2.maryland.gov

Gambrill State Park 8602 Gambrill Pk Rd .... Frederick MD 21702 301-271-7574
TF: 800-830-3974 ■
Web: www.dnr.state.md.us/publiclands/western/gambrill.asp

Garrett State Forest 1431 Potomac Camp Rd........... Oakland MD 21550 301-334-2038
Web: www.dnr.state.md.us/publiclands/western/garrettforest.asp

Green Ridge State Forest
28700 Headquarters Dr NE.......................... Flintstone MD 21530 301-478-3124
Web: dnr2.maryland.gov

Greenbrier State Park 21843 National Pk........... Boonsboro MD 21713 301-791-4767
Web: dnr2.maryland.gov

Greenwell State Park
25450 Rosedale Manor Ln PO Box 198 .... Hollywood MD 20636 301-373-9775
Web: www.greenwellfoundation.org

Gunpowder Falls State Park
2813 Jerusalem Rd PO Box 480.................... Kingsville MD 21087 410-592-2897
Web: dnr2.maryland.gov

Hart-Miller Island State Park
c/o Gunpowder Falls State Pk 2813 Jerusalem Rd
PO Box 480 .... Kingsville MD 21087 410-592-2897
Web: dnr2.maryland.gov

Herrington Manor State Park
222 Herrington Ln .... Oakland MD 21550 301-334-9180
Web: dnr2.maryland.gov/publiclands/pages/western/herrington.aspx

Janes Island State Park
26280 Alfred Lawson Dr............................... Crisfield MD 21817 410-968-1565 968-2515
TF: 877-620-8367 ■ *Web:* dnr2.maryland.gov

Martinak State Park 137 Deep Shore Rd................ Denton MD 21629 410-820-1668
Web: dnr2.maryland.gov

Merkle Wildlife Sanctuary 580 Taylor Ave.......... Annapolis MD 21401 877-620-8367
TF: 877-620-8367 ■ *Web:* dnr2.maryland.gov

Monocacy River Natural Resources Management Area
c/o Seneca Creek State Pk
11950 Clopper Rd .... Gaithersburg MD 20878 301-924-2127
Web: dnr2.maryland.gov

Morgan Run Natural Environment Area
Benros Ln.. Eldersburg MD 21784 410-461-5005
TF: 800-830-3974 ■
Web: www.dnr.state.md.us/publiclands/central/morganrun.asp

New Germany State Park
349 Headquarters Ln .... Grantsville MD 21536 301-895-5453
TF: 800-830-3974 ■
Web: www.dnr.state.md.us/publiclands/western/newgermany.asp

Patapsco Valley State Park
8020 Baltimore National Pk .... Ellicott City MD 21043 410-461-5005
Web: dnr2.maryland.gov

Patuxent River State Park
c/o Seneca Creek State Pk
11950 Clopper Rd .... Gaithersburg MD 20878 301-924-2127
Web: www.dnr.state.md.us/publiclands/central/patuxentriver.asp

Pocomoke River State Park
3461 Worcester Hwy.................................. Snow Hill MD 21863 410-632-2566 632-2914
TF: 877-620-8367 ■ *Web:* dnr2.maryland.gov

Pocomoke State Forest 580 Taylor Ave .... Annapolis MD 21401 877-620-8367
TF: 877-620-8367 ■ *Web:* dnr2.maryland.gov

Point Lookout State Park
11175 Pt Lookout Rd .... Scotland MD 20687 301-872-5688 872-5084
Web: dnr2.maryland.gov

Potomac-Garrett State Forest
1431 Potomac Camp Rd................................. Oakland MD 21550 301-334-2038
Web: dnr2.maryland.gov

Rocks State Park
3318 Rocks Chrome Hill Rd .... Jarrettsville MD 21084 410-557-7994
Web: dnr2.maryland.gov/publiclands/pages/central/rocks.aspx

Rocky Gap State Park
12500 Pleasant Vly Rd .... Flintstone MD 21530 301-722-1480
Web: www.dnr.state.md.us/publiclands/western/rockygap.asp

Rosaryville State Park
7805 W Marlton Ave......................... Upper Marlboro MD 20735 301-856-9656
Web: www.dnr.state.md.us/publiclands/southern/rosaryville.asp

Saint Mary's River State Park
c/o Pt Lookout State Pk 11175 Pt Lookout Rd .... Scotland MD 20687 301-872-5688
TF: 800-830-3974 ■
Web: www.dnr.state.md.us/publiclands/southern/stmarysriver.asp

Sandy Point State Park 1100 E College Pkwy......... Annapolis MD 21409 410-974-2149 974-2647
TF: 877-620-8836 ■ *Web:* dnr2.maryland.gov

Sassafras Natural Resources Management Area
13070 Crouse Mill Rd .... Queen Anne MD 21657 410-820-1668
Web: www.dnr.state.md.us/publiclands/eastern/sassafras.asp

Seneca Creek State Park
11950 Clopper Rd .... Gaithersburg MD 20878 301-924-2127
Web: dnr2.maryland.gov

Smallwood State Park 2750 Sweden Pt Rd............. Marbury MD 20658 301-743-7613
Web: dnr2.maryland.gov/pages/default.aspx

				Phone	Fax
Soldiers Delight Natural Environment Area 5100 Deer Park Rd	Owings Mills	MD	21117	410-461-5005	
TF: 800-830-3974 ■ *Web:* www.dnr.state.md.us/publiclands/central/soldiersdelight.asp					
Somers Cove Marina 715 Broadway PO Box 67	Crisfield	MD	21817	410-968-0925	968-1408
TF: 800-967-3474 ■ *Web:* dnr2.maryland.gov					
South Mountain State Park c/o S Mtn Recreation Area 21843 National Pk	Boonsboro	MD	21713	301-791-4767	
Web: www.dnr.state.md.us/publiclands/western/southmountain.asp					
Swallow Falls State Park c/o Herrington Manor State Pk 222 Herrington Ln	Oakland	MD	21550	301-387-6938	
Web: www.dnr.state.md.us/publiclands/western/swallowfalls.asp					
Tuckahoe State Park 13070 Crouse Mill Rd	Queen Anne	MD	21657	410-820-1668	
Web: dnr2.maryland.gov					
Washington Monument State Park c/o Greenbrier State Pk 6620 Zittlestown Rd	Middletown	MD	21769	301-791-4767	
Web: www.dnr.state.md.us/publiclands/western/washington.asp					
Wye Island Natural Resources Management Area 632 Wye Island Rd	Queenstown	MD	21658	410-827-7577	
Web: dnr2.maryland.gov					
Wye Oak State Park c/o Tuckahoe State Pk 13070 Crouse Mill Rd	Queen Anne	MD	21657	410-820-1668	
Web: www.dnr.state.md.us/publiclands/eastern/wyeoak.asp					
Youghiogheny River Natural Resources Management Area c/o Deep Creek Lake State Pk 898 State Pk Rd	Swanton	MD	21561	301-387-5563	387-4462
TF: 877-620-8367 ■ *Web:* dnr2.maryland.gov					

Massachusetts

				Phone	Fax
Ames Nowell State Park Linwood St	Abington	MA	02351	781-857-1336	
Web: www.mass.gov					
Beartown State Forest 69 Blue Hill Rd	Monterey	MA	01245	413-528-0904	
Web: www.mass.gov/eea/agencies/dcr/massparks/region-west/beartown-state-forest.html					
Blackstone River & Canal Heritage State Park 287 Oak St	Uxbridge	MA	01569	508-278-7604	
Web: www.mass.gov					
Blue Hills Reservation 695 Hillside St	Milton	MA	02186	617-698-1802	
Web: www.mass.gov/dcr/parks/metroboston/blue.htm					
Borderland State Park Massapoag Ave	North Easton	MA	02356	508-238-6566	
Web: www.mass.gov					
Brimfield State Forest 86 Dearth Hill Rd	Brimfield	MA	01010	413-267-9687	
Web: www.mass.gov					
Chicopee Memorial State Park 570 Burnett Rd	Chicopee Falls	MA	01020	413-594-9416	
Web: www.mass.gov					
Clarksburg State Park 1199 Middle Rd	Clarksburg	MA	01247	413-664-8345	
Web: www.mass.gov					
Connecticut River Greenway State Park 136 Damon Rd	NorthHampton	MA	01060	413-586-8706	
Web: mass.gov					
DAR State Forest 78 Cape St Rt 112	Goshen	MA	01032	413-268-7098	
Demarest Lloyd State Park 115 Barneys Joy Rd	Dartmouth	MA	02748	508-636-3298	
Web: www.mass.gov					
Dighton Rock State Park Bay View Ave	Berkley	MA	02779	508-822-7537	
Web: www.mass.gov					
Douglas State Forest 107 Wallum Lk Rd	Douglas	MA	01516	508-476-7872	
Web: www.mass.gov					
Dunn State Park Rt 101	Gardner	MA	01440	978-632-7897	
Web: www.mass.gov/eea/agencies/dcr/massparks/region-central/dunn-state-park.html					
Ellisville Harbor State Park 198 Purgatory Rd	Sutton	MA	01590	508-234-3733	
Web: www.mass.gov					
Erving State Forest 200 E Main St Rt 2A	Erving	MA	01344	978-544-3939	
Web: www.mass.gov					
F. Gilbert Hills State Forest 45 Mill St	Foxboro	MA	02035	508-543-5850	
Web: www.mass.gov					
Fall River Heritage State Park Davol St	Fall River	MA	02720	508-675-5759	
Web: www.mass.gov					
Fort Phoenix State Reservation Green St	Fairhaven	MA	02719	508-992-4524	
Freetown-Fall River State Forest 110 Slab Bridge Rd	Assonet	MA	02702	508-644-5522	
Web: www.mass.gov					
Gardner Heritage State Park (GHSP) 26 Lake St	Gardner	MA	01440	978-632-7897	
Web: www.mass.gov/dcr/parks/central/ghsp.htm					
Granville State Forest 323 W Hartland Rd	Granville	MA	01034	413-357-6611	
Web: www.mass.gov					
Great Brook Farm State Park 165 N Rd	Carlisle	MA	01741	978-369-6312	
Web: www.mass.gov					
Halibut Point State Park Gott Ave	Rockport	MA	01966	978-546-2997	
Web: www.mass.gov					
Hampton Ponds State Park 1048 N Rd	Westfield	MA	01085	413-532-3985	533-1837
Web: www.mass.gov					
Harold Parker State Forest 305 Middleton Rd	North Andover	MA	01845	978-686-3391	
Web: www.mass.gov					
Holyoke Heritage State Park 221 Appleton St	Holyoke	MA	01040	413-534-1723	
Web: mass.gov					
Hopkinton State Park 71 Cedar St	Hopkinton	MA	01748	508-435-4303	
Web: www.mass.gov					
Horseneck Beach State Reservation 5 John Reed Rd	Westport	MA	02791	508-636-8816	
Web: www.mass.gov					
JA Skinner State Park PO Box 91	Hadley	MA	01035	413-586-0350	
Web: www.mass.gov					
Lake Wyola State Park 94 Lk View Rd	Shutesbury	MA	01072	413-367-0317	
Web: www.mass.gov					
Lawrence Heritage State Park 1 Jackson St	Lawrence	MA	01840	978-794-1655	
Web: www.mass.gov					
Leominster State Forest 90 Fitchburg Rd Rt 31	Westminster	MA	01473	978-874-2303	
Web: www.mass.gov					
Lowell Heritage State Park 160 Pawtucket Blvd	Lowell	MA	01854	978-458-8750	
Massasoit State Park Middleboro Ave	East Taunton	MA	02718	508-822-7405	
Web: www.mass.gov					
Maudslay State Park 74 Curzon Mill Rd	Newburyport	MA	01950	978-465-7223	
Web: www.mass.gov					
Mohawk Trail State Forest 175 Mohawk Trl/ Rt 2	Charlemont	MA	01339	413-339-5504	
Moore State Park Mill St	Paxton	MA	01612	508-792-3969	
TF: 800-437-5922 ■ *Web:* www.mass.gov					
Mount Everett State Reservation c/o Rd 3 E St	Mount Washington	MA	01258	413-528-0330	
Mount Grace State Forest Winchester Rd	Warwick	MA	01378	978-544-3939	
Web: www.mass.gov					
Mount Greylock State Reservation 30 Rockwell Rd	Lanesborough	MA	01237	413-499-4262	
Web: www.mass.gov					
Mount Sugarloaf State Reservation 300 Sugarloaf St	South Deerfield	MA	01373	413-665-2928	
Web: www.mass.gov					
Mount Tom State Reservation 125 Resv Rd	Holyoke	MA	01040	413-534-1186	
Web: mass.gov					
Mount Washington State Forest Rd 3 E St	Mount Washington	MA	01258	413-528-0330	
Myles Standish Monument State Reservation Crescent St Duxbury	Duxbury	MA	02332	508-747-5360	
Web: www.mass.gov					
Myles Standish State Forest Cranberry Rd	South Carver	MA	02366	508-866-2526	
Web: www.mass.gov					
Natural Bridge State Park McCauley Rd off Rte 8 PO Box 1757	North Adams	MA	01247	413-663-6392	
Web: www.mass.gov					
Nickerson State Park 3488 Main St	Brewster	MA	02631	508-896-3491	
Web: mass.gov					
October Mountain State Forest 317 Woodland Rd	Lee	MA	01238	413-243-1778	
Web: www.mass.gov					
Pittsfield State Forest 1041 Cascade St	Pittsfield	MA	01201	413-442-8992	
Web: www.mass.gov/dcr/parks/western/pitt.htm					
Purgatory Chasm State Reservation Purgatory Rd	Sutton	MA	01590	508-234-3733	
Web: www.mass.gov					
Quinsigamond State Park 10 Lake Ave N	Worcester	MA	01612	508-755-6880	
Web: www.mass.gov					
Robinson State Park 428 N St PO Box 42	Feeding Hills	MA	01030	413-786-2877	
Web: www.mass.gov					
Roland C. Nickerson State Park c/o Nickerson State Pk 3488 Main St	Brewster	MA	02631	508-896-3491	
Rutland State Park 2 Crawford Rd	Rutland	MA	01543	508-886-6333	
Web: www.mass.gov					
Salisbury Beach State Reservation Beach Rd Rt 1A	Salisbury	MA	01952	978-462-4481	
Savoy Mountain State Forest 260 Central Shaft Rd	Florida	MA	01247	413-663-8469	
Web: www.mass.gov					
Schooner Ernestina New Bedford State Pier	New Bedford	MA	02741	508-992-4900	
Web: ernestina.org					
Scusset Beach State Reservation 20 Scusset Beach Rd	Sandwich	MA	02563	508-888-0859	
Web: www.mass.gov					
South Cape Beach State Park Great Oak Rd	Mashpee	MA	02649	508-457-0495	
Web: www.mass.gov					
Spencer State Forest Howe Pond Rd	Spencer	MA	01562	508-886-6333	
Web: www.mass.gov					
Streeter Point Recreation Area 6 Ster Pt Ave	Sturbridge	MA	01566	508-347-9316	
Web: www.mass.gov/eea/agencies/dcr/massparks/region-central/streeter-point-recreation-area.html					
Tolland State Forest 410 Tolland Rd PO Box 342	East Otis	MA	01029	413-269-6002	
Web: www.mass.gov					
Upton State Forest 205 Westboro Rd	Upton	MA	01568	508-278-6486	
Web: www.mass.gov					
Wachusett Mountain State Reservation 345 Mountain Rd	Princeton	MA	01541	978-464-2987	
Web: www.mass.gov					
Walden Pond State Reservation 915 Walden St	Concord	MA	01742	978-369-3254	
Web: www.mass.gov					
Watson Pond State Park Bay Rd	Taunton	MA	02780	508-884-8280	
Web: www.mass.gov					
Wells State Park 159 Walker Pond Rd	Sturbridge	MA	01566	508-347-9257	
Web: www.mass.gov/dcr/parks/central/well.htm					
Wendell State Forest Montague Rd	Wendell	MA	01379	413-659-3797	
Web: www.mass.gov					
Western Gateway Heritage State Park 115 State St Ste 4	North Adams	MA	01247	413-663-6312	
Web: www.mass.gov					
Willard Brook State Forest 595 Main St	Townsend	MA	01474	978-597-8802	
Web: www.mass.gov					
Wompatuck State Park 204 Union St	Hingham	MA	02043	781-749-7160	
Web: www.mass.gov					

Michigan

				Phone	Fax
Albert E. Sleeper State Park 6573 State Pk Rd	Caseville	MI	48725	989-856-4411	
TF: 800-447-2757 ■ *Web:* www.michigan.org/property/albert-e-sleeper-state-park					
Algonac State Park 8732 River Rd	Marine City	MI	48039	810-765-5605	
Web: www.michigandnr.com					

Phone *Fax*

Bald Mountain Recreation Area
1330 E Greenshield Rd....Lake Orion MI 48360 248-693-6767
Web: www.michigandnr.com

Baraga State Park 1300 US Hwy 41 S....Baraga MI 49908 906-353-6558
Web: www.michigandnr.com

Bay City Recreation Area 3582 State Pk Dr....Bay City MI 48706 989-684-3020
Web: www.michigandnr.com

Bewabic State Park 720 Idlewild Rd....Crystal Falls MI 49920 906-875-3324
Web: www.michigandnr.com

Brighton Recreation Area 6360 Chilson Rd....Howell MI 48843 810-229-6566
Web: www.michigandnr.com

Brimley State Park 9200 W 6-Mile Rd....Brimley MI 49715 906-248-3422
Web: www.michigandnr.com

Burt Lake State Park 6635 State Pk Dr....Indian River MI 49749 231-238-9392
Web: www.michigandnr.com

Charles Mears State Park 400 W Lowell St....Pentwater MI 49449 231-869-2051
Web: www.michigandnr.com

Cheboygan State Park 4490 Beach Rd....Cheboygan MI 49721 231-627-2811
Web: www.michigandnr.com

Clear Lake State Park 20500 M-33 N....Atlanta MI 49709 989-785-4388
Web: www.michigandnr.com

Coldwater Lake State Park Copeland Rd....Coldwater MI 49036 517-780-7866
Web: www.michigandnr.com

Craig Lake State Park 851 County Rd AKE....Champion MI 49814 906-339-4461
Web: michigandnr.com

Dodge #4 State Park 4250 Pkwy Dr....Waterford MI 48327 248-682-7323
Web: www.michigandnr.com

Duck Lake State Park 3560 Memorial Dr....North Muskegon MI 49445 231-744-3480
Web: www.michigandnr.com/parksandtrails/details.aspx?type=sprk&id=446

Fisherman's Island State Park
Bells Bay Rd PO Box 456....Charlevoix MI 49720 231-547-6641
Web: www.michigandnr.com

FJ McLain State Park 18350 Hwy M-203....Hancock MI 49930 906-482-0278
Web: www.michigandnr.com

Fort Custer Recreation Area
5163 Ft Custer Dr....Augusta MI 49012 269-731-4200
Web: www.michigandnr.com

Fort Wilkins State Park
15223 US Hwy 41....Copper Harbor MI 49918 906-289-4215
Web: www.michigandnr.com

Grand Haven State Park 1001 S Harbor Ave....Grand Haven MI 49417 616-847-1309
Web: www.michigandnr.com

Harrisville State Park
248 State Pk Rd PO Box 326....Harrisville MI 48740 989-724-5126

Hartwick Pines State Park 4216 Ranger Rd....Grayling MI 49738 989-348-7068
Web: www.michigandnr.com

Highland Recreation Area
5200 E Highland Rd....White Lake MI 48383 248-889-3750
Web: www.michigandnr.com

Historic Mill Creek Discovery Park
9001 US-23 PO Box 370....Mackinac Island MI 49701 231-436-4100 847-3815*
*Fax Area Code: 906 ■ *Web:* mackinacparks.com/parks-and-attractions

Holland State Park 2215 Ottawa Beach Rd....Holland MI 49424 616-399-9390
Web: www.michigandnr.com

Holly Recreation Area 8100 Grange Hall Rd....Holly MI 48442 248-634-8811
Web: www.michigandnr.com

Indian Lake State Park
8970W County Rd 442....Manistique MI 49854 906-341-2355
Web: www.michigandnr.com

Interlochen State Park M-137....Interlochen MI 49643 231-276-9511
Web: www.michigandnr.com

Ionia Recreation Area 2880 W David Hwy....Ionia MI 48846 616-527-3750
Web: www.michigandnr.com

Island Lake Recreation Area
12950 E Grand River Rd....Brighton MI 48116 810-229-7067
Web: www.michigandnr.com

JW Wells State Park N7670 Hwy M-35....Cedar River MI 49887 906-863-9747
Web: www.michigandnr.com

Kal-Haven Trail State Park
219 E Paw Paw St Ste 303 PO Box 156....Paw Paw MI 49079 269-674-8011
Web: www.michigandnr.com/parksandtrails/Details.aspx?type=SPRK&id=463

Lake Gogebic State Park
N9995 State Hwy M-64....Marenisco MI 49947 906-842-3341
Web: www.michigandnr.com

Lake Hudson Recreation Area 5505 Morey Hwy....Clayton MI 49235 517-445-2265
Web: www.michigandnr.com

Lakelands Trail State Park
8555 Silver Hill Rd 8555 Silver Hill Rt 1....Pinckney MI 48169 734-426-4913
Web: www.michigan.gov

Lakeport State Park 7605 Lakeshore Rd....Saint Clair MI 48059 810-327-6224
Web: www.michigandnr.com

Leelanau State Park
15310 N Lighthouse Pt Rd....Northport MI 49670 231-386-5422
Web: www.michigandnr.com

Ludington State Park PO Box 709....Ludington MI 49431 231-843-2423
Web: www.michigandnr.com

Maybury State Park 20145 Beck Rd....Northville MI 48167 248-349-8390
Web: www.michigandnr.com

Meridian-Baseline State Park
16345 McClure Rd....Chelsea MI 48118 734-475-8307
Web: www.michigandnr.com/parksandtrails/details.aspx?type=sprk&id=471

Metamora-Hadley Recreation Area
3871 Herd Rd....Metamora MI 48455 810-797-4439
Web: www.michigandnr.com

Muskallonge Lake State Park
30042 County Rd 407....Newberry MI 49868 906-658-3338
Web: www.michigandnr.com

Muskegon State Park 3560 Memorial Dr....North Muskegon MI 49445 231-744-3480
Web: www.michigandnr.com/parksandtrails/details.aspx?type=sprk&id=475

Newaygo State Park 2793 Beech St....Newaygo MI 49337 231-856-4452
Web: www.michigandnr.com

North Higgins Lake State Park
11747 N Higgins Lk Dr....Roscommon MI 48653 989-821-6125
Web: www.michigandnr.com/parksandtrails/details.aspx?id=478&type=sprk

Orchard Beach State Park
2064 N Lakeshore Rd....Manistee MI 49660 231-723-7422
Web: www.michigandnr.com

Ortonville Recreation Area 5779 Hadley Rd....Ortonville MI 48462 810-797-4439
Web: www.michigandnr.com

Otsego Lake State Park 7136 Old 27 S....Gaylord MI 49735 989-732-5485
Web: michigandnr.com

Petoskey State Park 2475 M-119 Hwy....Petoskey MI 49712 231-347-2311
Web: www.michigandnr.com

PH Hoeft State Park 5001 US Hwy 23 N....Rogers City MI 49779 989-734-2543
Web: www.michigandnr.com

Pinckney Recreation Area 8555 Silver Hill....Pinckney MI 48169 734-426-4913
Web: michigandnr.com

PJ Hoffmaster State Park 6585 Lk Harbor Rd....Muskegon MI 49441 231-798-3711
Web: www.michigandnr.com

Pontiac Lake Recreation Area 7800 Gale Rd....Waterford MI 48327 248-666-1020
Web: www.michigandnr.com/parksandtrails/details.aspx?id=485&type=sprk

Porcupine Mountains Wilderness State Park
33303 Headquarters Rd....Ontonagon MI 49953 906-885-5275
Web: www.michigandnr.com

Port Crescent State Park
1775 Port Austin Rd....Port Austin MI 48467 989-738-8663
Web: www.michigandnr.com

Rifle River Recreation Area 2550 Rose City Rd....Lupton MI 48635 989-473-2258
Web: www.michigandnr.com

Seven Lakes State Park 14390 Fish Lk Rd....Holly MI 48442 248-634-7271
Web: www.michigandnr.com

Silver Lake State Park 9679 W State Pk Rd....Mears MI 49436 231-873-3083
Web: michigandnr.com

Sleepy Hollow State Park 7835 E Price Rd....Laingsburg MI 48848 517-651-6217
Web: www.michigandnr.com

South Higgins Lake State Park
106 State Pk Dr....Roscommon MI 48653 989-821-6374
Web: www.michigandnr.com

Sterling State Park 2800 State Pk Rd....Monroe MI 48162 734-289-2715
Web: www.michigandnr.com

Straits State Park 720 Church St....Saint Ignace MI 49781 906-643-8620
Web: www.michigandnr.com

Tahquamenon Falls State Park 41382 W M-123....Paradise MI 49768 906-492-3415
Web: www.michigandnr.com

Tawas Point State Park 686 Tawas Beach Rd....East Tawas MI 48730 989-362-5041
Web: www.michigandnr.com

Thompson's Harbor State Park
c/o Cheboygan Field Office
120 A St PO Box 117....Cheboygan MI 49721 231-627-9011
Web: www.michigan.gov

Traverse City State Park 1132 US-31 N....Traverse City MI 49686 231-922-5270
Web: www.michigandnr.com

Tri-Centennial State Park & Harbor
1900 Atwater St....Detroit MI 48207 313-396-0217
Web: www.michigandnr.com

Twin Lakes State Park 6204 E Poyhonen Rd....Toivola MI 49965 906-288-3321
Web: www.michigandnr.com

Van Buren Trail State Park
23960 Ruggles Rd....South Haven MI 49090 269-637-2788
Web: www.michigandnr.com

Van Riper State Park 851 County Rd AKE....Champion MI 49814 906-339-4461
Web: www.michigandnr.com

Warren Dunes State Park 12032 Red Arrow Hwy....Sawyer MI 49125 269-426-4013
Web: www.michigandnr.com

Waterloo Recreation Area 16345 McClure Rd....Chelsea MI 48118 734-475-8307
Web: www.michigandnr.com

Wilderness State Park 903 Wilderness Pk Dr....Carp Lake MI 49718 231-436-5381
Web: www.michigandnr.com

William Michell State Park Camp Grounds
6093 E M-115....Cadillac MI 49601 231-775-7911

William Mitchell State Park 6093 E M-115....Cadillac MI 49601 231-775-7911

Wilson State Park 910 N First St PO Box 333....Harrison MI 48625 989-539-3021
Web: www.michigandnr.com

WJ Hayes State Park 1220 Wampler's Lk Rd....Onsted MI 49265 517-467-7401
Web: www.michigandnr.com

Yankee Springs Recreation Area
2104 S Briggs Rd....Middleville MI 49333 269-795-9081
Web: www.michigandnr.com

Young State Park 02280 Boyne City Rd....Boyne City MI 49712 231-582-7523
Web: www.michigandnr.com

Minnesota

Phone *Fax*

Afton State Park 6959 Peller Ave S....Hastings MN 55033 651-436-5391 436-6912
TF: 800-366-8917 ■ *Web:* www.dnr.state.mn.us

Banning State Park
61101 Banning Pk Rd PO Box 643....Sandstone MN 55072 320-245-2668 245-0251
Web: www.dnr.state.mn.us

Bear Head Lake State Park
9301 Bear Head State Pk Rd....Ely MN 55731 218-365-7229 365-7204
Web: www.dnr.state.mn.us

Beaver Creek Valley State Park
15954 County Rd 1....Caledonia MN 55921 507-724-2107 724-2107
Web: www.dnr.state.mn.us

Big Bog State Recreation Area
55716 Hwy 72 NE....Waskish MN 56685 218-647-8592 647-8730
Web: www.dnr.state.mn.us

Big Stone Lake State Park
35889 Meadowbrook State Pk Rd....Ortonville MN 56278 320-839-3663 839-3676
TF: 888-646-6367 ■ *Web:* www.dnr.state.mn.us

Blue Mounds State Park 1410 161st St....Luverne MN 56156 507-283-1307 283-1306
TF: 888-646-6367 ■ *Web:* www.dnr.state.mn.us

Buffalo River State Park
155 S St Hwy 10 PO Box 352....Glyndon MN 56547 218-498-2124 498-2583
Web: www.dnr.state.mn.us

Name / Address	City	State	ZIP	Phone	Fax
Camden State Park 1897 County Rd *Web:* www.dnr.state.mn.us	Lynd	MN	56157	507-865-4530	865-4608
Carley State Park 19041 Hwy 74 *TF:* 888-646-6367 ■ *Web:* www.stateparks.com/carley.html	Altura	MN	55910	507-932-3007	
Cascade River State Park 3481 W Hwy 61 *Web:* www.dnr.state.mn.us	Lutsen	MN	55612	218-387-3053	387-3054
Charles A. Lindbergh State Park 1615 Lindbergh Dr S PO Box 364 *TF:* 888-646-6367 ■ *Web:* www.dnr.state.mn.us	Little Falls	MN	56345	320-616-2525	616-2526
Crow Wing State Park 3124 State Pk Rd *TF:* 888-646-6367 ■ *Web:* www.dnr.state.mn.us	Brainerd	MN	56401	218-825-3075	825-3077
Cuyuna Country State Recreation Area 307 Third St PO Box 404 *Web:* www.dnr.state.mn.us	Ironton	MN	56455	218-546-5926	546-7369
Father Hennepin State Park 41294 Father Hennepin Pk Rd PO Box 397 *TF:* 888-646-6367 ■ *Web:* www.dnr.state.mn.us	Isle	MN	56342	320-676-8763	676-3748
Flandrau State Park 1300 Summit Ave *Web:* www.dnr.state.mn.us	New Ulm	MN	56073	507-233-9800	
Forestville/Mystery Cave State Park 21071 County 118 *TF:* 888-646-6367 ■ *Web:* www.dnr.state.mn.us	Preston	MN	55965	507-352-5111	352-5113
Fort Ridgely State Park 72158 County Rd 30 *TF:* 888-646-6367 ■ *Web:* www.dnr.state.mn.us	Fairfax	MN	55332	507-426-7840	426-7112
Fort Snelling State Park 101 Snelling Lake Rd *TF:* 888-646-6367 ■ *Web:* www.dnr.state.mn.us	Saint Paul	MN	55111	612-725-2389	725-2391
Franz Jevne State Park State Hwy 11 3684 54th Ave NW *Web:* www.dnr.state.mn.us/state_parks/franz_jevne	Birchdale	MN	56629	218-783-6252	783-6253
Frontenac State Park 29223 County 28 Blvd *TF:* 888-646-6367 ■ *Web:* www.dnr.state.mn.us	Frontenac	MN	55026	651-345-3401	345-3694
Garden Island State Recreation Area c/o Zippel Bay State Pk 3684 54th Ave NW *Web:* www.dnr.state.mn.us/state_parks/garden_island	Williams	MN	56686	218-783-6252	783-6253
George H. Crosby Manitou State Park c/o Tettegouche State Pk 5702 Hwy 61 *TF:* 888-646-6367 ■ *Web:* www.dnr.state.mn.us/state_parks/george_crosby_manitou	Silver Bay	MN	55614	218-226-6365	226-6366
Glacial Lakes State Park 25022 County Rd 41 *TF:* 888-646-6367 ■ *Web:* www.dnr.state.mn.us	Starbuck	MN	56381	320-239-2860	239-4605
Glendalough State Park 25287 Whitetail Ln *Web:* www.dnr.state.mn.us/state_parks/glendalough/index.html	Battle Lake	MN	56515	218-864-0110	864-0587
Gooseberry Falls State Park 3206 Hwy 61 *TF:* 888-646-6367 ■ *Web:* www.dnr.state.mn.us/state_parks/gooseberry_falls	Two Harbors	MN	55616	218-834-3855	834-3787
Grand Portage State Park 9393 E Hwy 61 *TF:* 888-646-6367 ■ *Web:* www.dnr.state.mn.us	Grand Portage	MN	55605	218-475-2360	475-2365
Great River Bluffs State Park 43605 Kipp Dr *TF:* 888-646-6367 ■ *Web:* www.dnr.state.mn.us	Winona	MN	55987	507-643-6849	643-6849
Hayes Lake State Park 48990 County Rd 4 *Web:* www.dnr.state.mn.us/state_parks/hayes_lake	Roseau	MN	56751	218-425-7504	
Interstate State Park 307 Milltown Rd PO Box 254 *Web:* www.dnr.state.mn.us	Taylors Falls	MN	55084	651-465-5711	465-0517
Itasca State Park 36750 Main Pk Dr *Web:* www.dnr.state.mn.us	Park Rapids	MN	56470	218-266-2100	266-3942
Jay Cooke State Park 780 Hwy 210 *Web:* www.dnr.state.mn.us	Carlton	MN	55718	218-384-4610	384-4851
Judge CR Magney State Park 4051 E Hwy 61 *Web:* www.dnr.state.mn.us	Grand Marais	MN	55604	218-387-3039	
Kilen Woods State Park 50200 860th St *Web:* www.dnr.state.mn.us	Lakefield	MN	56150	507-831-2900	
Lac Qui Parle State Park 14047 20th St NW **Fax Area Code:* 320 ■ *Web:* www.dnr.state.mn.us	St. Paul	MN	55155	651-296-6157	734-4452*
Lake Bemidji State Park 500 Lafayette Rd **Fax Area Code:* 218 ■ *Web:* www.dnr.state.mn.us	St. Paul	MN	55155	651-296-6157	755-4073*
Lake Bronson State Park County Hwy 28 *Web:* www.dnr.state.mn.us	Lake Bronson	MN	56734	218-754-2200	754-6141
Lake Carlos State Park 2601 County Rd 38 NE *Web:* www.dnr.state.mn.us	Carlos	MN	56319	320-852-7200	852-7349
Lake Louise State Park c/o Forestville/Mystery Cave State Pk 21071 County Rd 118 *Web:* www.dnr.state.mn.us	Preston	MN	55965	507-352-5111	352-5113
Lake Maria State Park 11411 Clementa Ave NW *Web:* www.dnr.state.mn.us	Monticello	MN	55362	763-878-2325	878-2620
Lake Shetek State Park 163 State Pk Rd *Web:* www.dnr.state.mn.us	Currie	MN	56123	507-763-3256	763-3330
Maplewood State Park 39721 Pk Entrance Rd *Web:* www.dnr.state.mn.us	Pelican Rapids	MN	56572	218-863-8383	
McCarthy Beach State Park 7622 McCarthy Beach Rd *Web:* www.dnr.state.mn.us	Side Lake	MN	55781	218-254-7979	254-7980
Mille Lacs Kathio State Park 15066 Kathio State Pk Rd *Web:* www.dnr.state.mn.us	Onamia	MN	56359	320-532-3523	532-3529
Minneopa State Park 54497 Gadwall Rd *Web:* www.dnr.state.mn.us	Mankato	MN	56001	507-389-5464	389-5174
Minnesota Valley State Recreation Area 19825 Park Blvd 101 Snelling Lk Rd *Web:* www.dnr.state.mn.us	Jordan	MN	55352	651-259-5774	
Monson Lake State Park 1690 15th St NE *Web:* www.dnr.state.mn.us	Sunburg	MN	56289	320-366-3797	
Moose Lake State Park 4252 County Rd 137 *Web:* www.dnr.state.mn.us	Moose Lake	MN	55767	218-485-5420	485-5422
Myre-Big Island State Park 19499 780th Ave *TF:* 888-646-6367 ■ *Web:* www.dnr.state.mn.us	Albert Lea	MN	56007	507-379-3403	379-3405
Nerstrand-Big Woods State Park 9700 170th St E *Web:* www.dnr.state.mn.us	Nerstrand	MN	55053	507-333-4840	333-4852
Old Mill State Park 33489 240th Ave NW *Web:* www.dnr.state.mn.us	Argyle	MN	56713	218-437-8174	437-8104
Red River State Recreation Area 515 Second St NW *Web:* www.dnr.state.mn.us	East Grand Forks	MN	56721	218-773-4950	773-4951
Rice Lake State Park 8485 Rose St *Web:* www.dnr.state.mn.us	Owatonna	MN	55060	507-455-5871	446-2326
Saint Croix State Park 30065 St Croix Pk Rd *TF:* 888-646-6367 ■ *Web:* www.dnr.state.mn.us	Hinckley	MN	55037	320-384-6591	384-7070
Sakatah Lake State Park 50499 Sakatah Lake State Pk Rd *TF:* 888-646-6367 ■ *Web:* www.dnr.state.mn.us	Waterville	MN	56096	507-362-4438	362-4558
Savanna Portage State Park 55626 Lake Pl *TF:* 888-646-6367 ■ *Web:* www.dnr.state.mn.us	McGregor	MN	55760	218-426-3271	426-4437
Scenic State Park 56956 Scenic Hwy 7 *Web:* www.dnr.state.mn.us	Bigfork	MN	56628	218-743-3362	743-1362
Sibley State Park 800 Sibley Pk Rd *TF:* 888-646-6367 ■ *Web:* www.dnr.state.mn.us	New London	MN	56273	320-354-2055	354-2372
Soudan Underground Mine State Park 1302 McKinley Park Rd *TF:* 888-646-6367 ■ *Web:* www.dnr.state.mn.us	Soudan	MN	55782	218-753-2245	753-2246
Split Rock Creek State Park 50th Ave *TF:* 888-646-6367 ■ *Web:* www.dnr.state.mn.us	Jasper	MN	56144	507-348-7908	348-8940
Split Rock Lighthouse State Park 3755 Split Rock Lighthouse Rd *TF:* 800-366-8917 ■ *Web:* www.dnr.state.mn.us/state_parks/split_rock_lighthouse	Two Harbors	MN	55616	218-595-7625	226-6378
Temperance River State Park 5702 Hwy 61 *Web:* www.dnr.state.mn.us	Silver Bay	MN	55613	218-663-7476	
Tettegouche State Park 5702 Hwy 61 *TF:* 800-366-8917 ■ *Web:* www.dnr.state.mn.us/state_parks/tettegouche	Silver Bay	MN	55614	218-226-6365	226-6366
Upper Sioux Agency State Park 5908 Hwy 67 *TF:* 800-366-8917 ■ *Web:* www.dnr.state.mn.us	Granite Falls	MN	56241	320-564-4777	564-4838
Whitewater State Park 19041 Hwy 74 *TF:* 800-366-8917 ■ *Web:* www.dnr.state.mn.us	Altura	MN	55910	507-932-3007	932-5938
Wild River State Park 39797 Pk Trl	Center City	MN	55012	651-583-2125	583-3101
William O'Brien State Park 16821 O'Brien Trl N *Web:* www.dnr.state.mn.us	Marine-on-Saint Croix	MN	55047	651-433-0500	
Zippel Bay State Park 3684 54th Ave NW *Web:* www.dnr.state.mn.us/state_parks/zippel_bay	Williams	MN	56686	218-783-6252	783-6253

Mississippi

Name / Address	City	State	ZIP	Phone	Fax
Buccaneer State Park 1150 S Beach Blvd *Web:* www.mdwfp.com	Waveland	MS	39576	228-467-3822	
Clarkco State Park 386 Clarkco Rd *Web:* www.mdwfp.com/parkview/parks.asp?id=4842	Quitman	MS	39355	601-776-6651	
Golden Memorial State Park 2104 Damascus Rd *Web:* www.mdwfp.com/parkview/parks.asp?id=4843	Walnut Grove	MS	39189	601-253-2237	
Holmes County State Park 5369 State Pk Rd *Web:* www.mdwfp.com/parkview/parks.asp?id=3824	Durant	MS	39063	662-653-3351	
John W. Kyle State Park 4235 State Pk Rd *Web:* www.mdwfp.com	Sardis	MS	38666	662-487-1345	
JP Coleman State Park 613 County Rd 321 *Web:* www.mdwfp.com/parkview/parks.asp?id=1814	Iuka	MS	38852	662-423-6515	
Lake Lincoln State Park 2573 Sunset Dr *Web:* reserveamerica.com	Wesson	MS	39191	601-643-9044	
Lake Lowndes State Park 3319 Lk Lowndes Rd *Web:* www.mdwfp.com	Columbus	MS	39702	662-328-2110	
LeFleur's Bluff State Park 2140 Riverside Dr *TF:* 800-237-6278 ■ *Web:* www.mdwfp.com	Jackson	MS	39202	601-987-3923	354-6930
Legion State Park 635 Legion State Pk Rd *Web:* www.mdwfp.com	Louisville	MS	39339	662-773-8323	
Leroy Percy State Park PO Box 176 *Web:* www.mdwfp.com	Hollandale	MS	38748	662-827-5436	
Natchez State Park 230-B Wickcliff Rd *Web:* www.mdwfp.com	Natchez	MS	39120	601-442-2658	
Percy Quin State Park 2036 Percy Quin Dr *Web:* www.mdwfp.com/parkview/parks.asp?id=5847	McComb	MS	39648	601-684-3938	
Roosevelt State Park 2149 Hwy 13 S *Web:* www.mdwfp.com	Morton	MS	39117	601-732-6316	
Shepard State Park 1034 Graveline Rd *Web:* www.mdwfp.com	Gautier	MS	39553	228-497-2244	
Tombigbee State Park 264 Cabin Dr *TF:* 800-467-2757 ■ *Web:* www.mdwfp.com	Tupelo	MS	38804	662-842-7669	
Wall Doxey State Park 3946 Hwy 7 S *Web:* www.mdwfp.com	Holly Springs	MS	38635	662-252-4231	

Missouri

Name / Address	City	State	ZIP	Phone	Fax
Arrow Rock State Historic Site PO Box 1 *Web:* www.mostateparks.com	Arrow Rock	MO	65320	660-837-3330	
Battle of Lexington State Historic Site 1101 Deleware *Web:* www.mostateparks.com	Lexington	MO	64067	660-259-4654	
Bennett Spring State Park 26250 Hwy 64A *Web:* www.mostateparks.com	Lebanon	MO	65536	417-532-4338	
Big Lake State Park 204 Lk Shore Dr *Web:* www.mostateparks.com	Craig	MO	64437	660-442-3770	
Big Oak Tree State Park 13640 S Hwy 102 *Web:* www.mostateparks.com	East Prairie	MO	63845	573-649-3149	

Phone | Fax

Bollinger Mill State Historic Site
113 Bollinger Mill Rd . . . . . Burfordville MO 63739 573-243-4591
Web: www.mostateparks.com

Bothwell Lodge State Historic Site
19349 Bothwell State Pk Rd . . . . . Sedalia MO 65301 660-827-0510
Web: www.mostateparks.com

Castlewood State Park 1401 Kiefer Creek Rd . . . . . Ballwin MO 63021 636-227-4433
Web: www.mostateparks.com

Confederate Memorial State Historic Site
211 W First St . . . . . Higginsville MO 64037 660-584-2853
Web: www.mostateparks.com

Crowder State Park 76 Hwy 128 . . . . . Trenton MO 64683 660-359-6473
Web: www.mostateparks.com

Cuivre River State Park 678 State Rt 147 . . . . . Troy MO 63379 636-528-7247
Web: www.mostateparks.com

Dillard Mill State Historic Site
142 DillaRd Mill Rd . . . . . Davisville MO 65456 573-244-3120
Web: www.mostateparks.com

Dr. Edmund A Babler Memorial State Park
800 Guy Pk Dr . . . . . Wildwood MO 63005 636-458-3813
Web: www.mostateparks.com

Edward Ted & Pat Jones- Confluence Point State Park
1000 Riverlands Way . . . . . West Alton MO 63386 636-899-1135
Web: www.mostateparks.com/park/edward-ted-and-pat-jones-confluence-point-state-park

Felix Valle House State Historic Site
198 Merchant St . . . . . Sainte Genevieve MO 63670 573-883-7102
Web: mostateparks.com/park/felixvallehousestatehistoricsite

Finger Lakes State Park 1505 E Peabody Rd . . . . . Columbia MO 65202 573-443-5315
Web: www.mostateparks.com

Fort Davidson State Historic Site
118 E Maple . . . . . Pilot Knob MO 63663 573-546-3454
Web: www.mostateparks.com/ftdavidson.htm

General John J. Pershing Boyhood Home State Historic Site
1100 Pershing Dr . . . . . Laclede MO 64651 660-963-2525
Web: www.mostateparks.com

Governor Daniel Dunklin's Grave State Historic Site
104 Dunklin Dr 2901 Hwy 61 . . . . . Herculaneum MO 65102 800-334-6946
TF: 800-334-6946 ■ *Web:* www.mostateparks.com

Ha Ha Tonka State Park 1491 State Rd D . . . . . Camdenton MO 65020 573-346-2986
Web: www.mostateparks.com

Harry S Truman Birthplace State Historic Site
1009 Truman St . . . . . Lamar MO 64759 417-682-2279
Web: www.mostateparks.com

Harry S Truman State Park 28761 State Pk Rd . . . . . Warsaw MO 65355 660-438-7711
Web: www.mostateparks.com

Hawn State Park 12096 Pk Dr . . . . . Sainte Genevieve MO 63670 573-883-3603
Web: www.mostateparks.com

Hunter-Dawson State Historic Site
PO Box 308 . . . . . New Madrid MO 63869 573-748-5340
Web: www.mostateparks.com

Iliniwek Village State Historic Site
c/o Battle of Athens State Historic Site Rt 1
PO Box 26 . . . . . Revere MO 63465 660-877-3871
Web: www.mostateparks.com

Jefferson Landing State Historic Site & Missouri State Museum
201 W Capitol 1st Fl State Capitol . . . . . Jefferson City MO 65101 573-751-2854
Web: mostateparks.com/park/missouri-state-museum

Jewell Cemetery State Historic Site
c/o Rock Bridge Memorial State Pk
5901 S Hwy 163 . . . . . Columbia MO 65203 573-449-7402
Web: www.mostateparks.com/jewellcem.htm

Johnson's Shut-Ins State Park
148 Taum Sauk Trl . . . . . Middlebrook MO 63656 573-546-2450
Web: mostateparks.com/park/johnsons-shut-ins-state-park

Knob Noster State Park 873 SE 10th . . . . . Knob Noster MO 65336 660-563-2463
Web: www.mostateparks.com

Lake of the Ozarks State Park PO Box 170 . . . . . Kaiser MO 65047 573-348-2694
Web: www.mostateparks.com

Lake Wappapello State Park Hwy 172 . . . . . Williamsville MO 63967 573-297-3232
Web: www.mostateparks.com

Lewis & Clark State Park 801 Lk Crest Blvd . . . . . Rushville MO 64484 816-579-5564
Web: www.mostateparks.com

Long Branch State Park 28615 Visitor Ctr Rd . . . . . Macon MO 63552 660-773-5229
Web: www.mostateparks.com

Mark Twain Birthplace State Historic Site
37352 Shrine Rd . . . . . Florida MO 65283 573-565-3449
Web: mostateparks.com/park/mark-twain-birthplace-state-historic-site

Mark Twain State Park 20057 State Pk Rd . . . . . Stoutsville MO 65283 573-565-3440
Web: www.mostateparks.com

Mastodon State Historic Site
1050 Charles J Becker Dr . . . . . Imperial MO 63052 636-464-2976
TF: 800-334-6946 ■ *Web:* www.mostateparks.com

Meramec State Park 115 Meramec Pk Dr . . . . . Sullivan MO 63080 573-468-6072
Web: www.mostateparks.com

Missouri Mines State Historic Site
4000 Missouri 32 . . . . . Park Hills MO 63601 573-431-6226
Web: www.mostateparks.com

Missouri State Parks PO Box 176 . . . . . Jefferson City MO 65102 800-334-6946
TF: 800-334-6946 ■ *Web:* www.mostateparks.com

Montauk State Park 345 County Rd 6670 . . . . . Salem MO 65560 573-548-2201
Web: www.mostateparks.com

Nathan Boone Homestead State Historic Site
7850 N State Hwy V . . . . . Ash Grove MO 65604 417-751-3266
Web: www.mostateparks.com

Onondaga Cave State Park 7556 Hwy H . . . . . Leasburg MO 65535 573-245-6576
TF: 877-422-6766 ■ *Web:* www.mostateparks.com

Pershing State Park 29277 Hwy 130 . . . . . Laclede MO 64651 660-963-2299
Web: www.mostateparks.com

Pomme de Terre State Park Hwy 64B . . . . . Pittsburg MO 65724 417-852-4291
Web: www.mostateparks.com/park/pomme-de-terre-state-park

Prairie State Park 128 NW 150th Ln . . . . . Mindenmines MO 64769 417-843-6711
Web: www.mostateparks.com

Roaring River State Park
12716 Farm Rd 2239 . . . . . Cassville MO 65625 417-847-2539
Web: mostateparks.com

Robertsville State Park 900 State Pk Dr . . . . . Robertsville MO 63077 636-257-3788
Web: www.mostateparks.com

Rock Bridge Memorial State Park
5901 S Hwy 163 . . . . . Columbia MO 65203 573-449-7402 442-2249
TF: 800-334-6946 ■ *Web:* www.mostateparks.com

Route 66 State Park 97 N Outer Rd Ste 1 . . . . . Eureka MO 63025 636-938-7198
Web: www.mostateparks.com

Saint Francois State Park
8920 US Hwy 67 N . . . . . Bonne Terre MO 63628 573-358-2173
Web: www.mostateparks.com

Saint Joe State Park 2800 Pimville Rd . . . . . Park Hills MO 63601 573-431-1069
Web: www.mostateparks.com

Sam A. Baker State Park Rt 1 PO Box 18150 . . . . . Patterson MO 63956 573-856-4411
Web: www.mostateparks.com

Sandy Creek Covered Bridge State Historic Site
c/o Mastodon State Historic Site
1050 Museum Dr . . . . . Imperial MO 63052 636-464-2976
Web: www.mostateparks.com

Scott Joplin House State Historic Site
2658 Delmar Blvd . . . . . Saint Louis MO 63103 314-340-5790
Web: www.mostateparks.com

Stockton State Park 19100 S Hwy 215 . . . . . Dadeville MO 65635 417-276-4259
Web: www.mostateparks.com

Table Rock State Park 5272 State Hwy 165 . . . . . Branson MO 65616 417-334-4704
Web: www.mostateparks.com

Taum Sauk Mountain State Park
148 Taum Sauk Trl . . . . . Middlebrook MO 63656 573-546-2450
Web: mostateparks.com/park/taum-sauk-mountain-state-park

Thomas Hart Benton Home & Studio State Historic Site
3616 Belleview . . . . . Kansas City MO 64111 816-931-5722
Web: www.mostateparks.com

Thousand Hills State Park
20431 State Hwy 157 . . . . . Kirksville MO 63501 660-665-6995
Web: www.mostateparks.com

Trail of Tears State Park
429 Moccasin Springs . . . . . Jackson MO 63755 573-290-5268
Web: www.mostateparks.com

Van Meter State Park 32146 N Hwy 122 . . . . . Miami MO 65344 660-886-7537
Web: www.mostateparks.com

Wakonda State Park 32836 State Pk Rd . . . . . LaGrange MO 63448 573-655-2280
Web: www.mostateparks.com

Wallace State Park 10621 NE Hwy 121 . . . . . Cameron MO 64429 816-632-3745
Web: www.mostateparks.com

Washington State Park 13041 State Hwy 104 . . . . . DeSoto MO 63020 636-586-2995
Web: www.mostateparks.com

Watkins Woolen Mill State Park & State Historic Site
26600 Pk Rd N . . . . . Lawson MO 64062 816-580-3387
Web: www.mostateparks.com

Weston Bend State Park 16600 Hwy 45 N . . . . . Weston Bend MO 64098 816-640-5443
Web: www.mostateparks.com

Montana

Phone | Fax

Ackley Lake State Park
4600 Giant Springs Rd . . . . . Great Falls MT 59405 406-454-5840
Web: www.fwp.mt.gov

Anaconda Smoke Stack State Park
3201 Spurgin Rd FWP Reg 2 Ofc . . . . . Missoula MT 59804 406-542-5500
Web: stateparks.mt.gov

Bannack State Park 4200 Bannack Rd . . . . . Dillon MT 59725 406-834-3413 834-3548
TF: 855-922-6768

Beaverhead Rock State Park
c/o Bannack State Pk 4200 Bannack Rd . . . . . Dillon MT 59725 406-834-3413
Web: stateparks.mt.gov

Beavertail Hill State Park
3201 Spurgin Rd FWP Reg 2 Ofc . . . . . Missoula MT 59804 406-542-5500
Web: stateparks.mt.gov

Big Arm State Park 490 N Meridian Rd . . . . . Kalispell MT 59901 406-752-5501
Web: www.fwp.mt.gov

Black Sandy State Park
1420 E 6thAve PO Box 200701 . . . . . Helena MT 59620 406-444-2535
Web: stateparks.mt.gov

Chief Plenty Coups State Park PO Box 100 . . . . . Pryor MT 59066 406-252-1289
Web: www.fwp.mt.gov

Clark's Lookout State Park
c/o Bannack State Pk 4200 Bannack Rd . . . . . Dillon MT 59725 406-834-3413
Web: stateparks.mt.gov

Cooney State Park PO Box 254 . . . . . Joliet MT 59041 406-445-2326
Web: www.fwp.mt.gov

Council Grove State Park
3201 Spurgin Rd FWP Reg 2 Ofc . . . . . Missoula MT 59804 406-542-5500
Web: stateparks.mt.gov

Elkhorn State Park 1420 E 6thAve PO Box 200701 . . . . . Helena MT 59620 406-444-2535
Web: stateparks.mt.gov

Finley Point State Park 490 N Meridian Rd . . . . . Kalispell MT 59901 406-752-5501
Web: www.fwp.mt.gov

First Peoples Buffalo Jump State Park
342 Ulm Vaughn Rd . . . . . Ulm MT 59485 406-866-2217
Web: www.fwp.mt.gov

Fort Owen State Park PO Box 995 . . . . . Lolo MT 59847 406-273-4253
Web: stateparks.mt.gov

Frenchtown Pond State Park
3201 Spurgin Rd FWP Reg 2 Ofc . . . . . Missoula MT 59804 406-542-5500
Web: stateparks.mt.gov

Giant Springs State Park
4600 Giant Springs Rd . . . . . Great Falls MT 59405 406-454-5840 761-8477
TF: 855-922-6768 ■ *Web:* www.fwp.mt.gov

Granite Ghost Town State Park
3201 Spurgin Rd . . . . . Missoula MT 59804 406-542-5500
Web: stateparks.mt.gov

Phone Fax

Greycliff Prairie Dog Town State Park
2300 Lk Elmo Dr. Billings MT 59105 406-247-2940
Web: stateparks.mt.gov

Hell Creek State Park PO Box 1630 Miles City MT 59301 406-557-2362
Web: fwp.mt.gov

Lake Elmo State Park 2300 Lk Elmo Dr. Billings MT 59105 406-247-2955
Web: stateparks.mt.gov

Lake Mary Ronan State Park
490 N Meridian Rd Kalispell MT 59901 406-752-5501
Web: www.fwp.mt.gov

Lewis & Clark Caverns State Park
PO Box 489 Whitehall MT 59759 406-287-3541
Web: stateparks.mt.gov

Lone Pine State Park 490 N Meridian Kalispell MT 59901 406-752-5501
Web: www.fwp.mt.gov

Lost Creek State Park 3201 Spurgin Rd Missoula MT 59804 406-542-5500
Web: stateparks.mt.gov

Madison Buffalo Jump State Park
1400 S 19th St Bozeman MT 59715 406-994-4042
Web: www.fwp.mt.gov

Makoshika State Park PO Box 1242 Glendive MT 59330 406-377-6256
Web: www.fwp.mt.gov

Medicine Rocks State Park PO Box 1630 Miles City MT 59301 406-234-0926
Web: fwp.mt.gov

Missouri Headwaters State Park
1400 S 19th Ave Bozeman MT 59715 406-994-4042
Web: www.stateparks.mt.gov

Painted Rocks State Park 3201 Spurgin Rd. Missoula MT 59804 406-542-5500
Web: stateparks.mt.gov

Pirogue Island State Park PO Box 1630 Miles City MT 59301 406-234-0926
Web: fwp.mt.gov

Placid Lake State Park PO Box 136 Seeley Lake MT 59868 406-677-6804
Web: stateparks.mt.gov

Rosebud Battlefield State Park
PO Box 1630 Miles City MT 59301 406-757-2219
Web: fwp.mt.gov

Salmon Lake State Park PO Box 136 Seeley Lake MT 59868 406-677-6804
Web: stateparks.mt.gov

Sluice Boxes State Park
4600 Giant Springs Rd Great Falls MT 59406 406-454-5840
Web: www.fwp.mt.gov

Smith River State Park
4600 Giant Springs Rd Great Falls MT 59405 406-454-5840
Web: www.fwp.mt.gov

Spring Meadow Lake State Park
1420 E 6thAve PO Box 200701 Helena MT 59620 406-444-2535
Web: stateparks.mt.gov

Thompson Falls State Park
375 Blue Slide Rd Thompson Falls MT 59873 406-752-5501
Web: montanastateparks.reserveamerica.com/camping/thompson-falls/r/campgroundDetails.do?contractCode=MT&parkId=630117

Tongue River Reservoir State Park
PO Box 1630 Miles City MT 59301 406-757-2298
Web: fwp.mt.gov

Wayfarers State Park 490 N Meridian Rd Kalispell MT 59901 406-752-5501
Web: www.fwp.mt.gov

West Shore State Park 490 N Meridian Rd Kalispell MT 59901 406-752-5501
Web: www.fwp.mt.gov

Wild Horse Island State Park
490 N Meridian Rd Kalispell MT 59901 406-752-5501
Web: www.fwp.mt.gov

Yellow Bay State Park 490 N Meridian Rd Kalispell MT 59901 406-752-5501
Web: www.fwp.mt.gov

Nebraska

Phone Fax

Alexandria State Recreation Area
57426 710th Rd Fairbury NE 68352 402-729-5777
Web: outdoornebraska.gov/alexandria

Arbor Lodge State Historical Park
PO Box 15 Nebraska City NE 68410 402-873-7222
Web: www.arbordayfarm.org/attractions/arbor-lodge.cfm

Arnold State Recreation Area
HC 69 PO Box 117 Anselmo NE 68813 308-749-2235
Web: www.outdoornebraska.ne.gov/parks

Ash Hollow State Historical Park PO Box 70 Lewellen NE 69147 308-778-5651
Web: outdoornebraska.gov/ashhollow

Ashfall Fossil Beds State Historical Park
86930 517th Ave Royal NE 68773 402-893-2000
Web: ashfall.unl.edu

Atkinson Lake State Recreation Area
PO Box 508 Bassett NE 68714 402-684-2921
Web: www.travelnebraska.com/atkinson-lake-state-recreation-area

Blue River State Recreation Area
3019 Apple St. Lincoln NE 68503 402-471-0641
Web: outdoornebraska.gov/blueriver

Bowring Ranch State Historical Park Hwy 61 Merriman NE 69218 402-684-3428

Branched Oak State Recreation Area
12000 W Branched Oak Rd Raymond NE 68428 402-783-3400
Web: outdoornebraska.gov

Buffalo Bill Ranch State Historical Park
2921 Scouts Rest Ranch Rd North Platte NE 69101 308-535-8035
Web: outdoornebraska.gov

Chadron State Park 15951 Hwy 385 Chadron NE 69337 308-432-6167
Web: outdoornebraska.gov

Champion Mill State Historical Park
73122 338 Ave Enders NE 69027 308-737-6577
Web: outdoornebraska.gov

Cheyenne State Recreation Area
PO Box 944 Grand Island NE 68832 308-385-6210
Web: outdoornebraska.gov

Phone Fax

Conestoga State Recreation Area
3800 NW 105th St Lincoln NE 68524 402-796-2362
Web: outdoornebraska.gov

Cottonwood Lake State Recreation Area
PO Box 38 Merriman NE 69218 308-684-3428
Web: outdoornebraska.gov

Crystal Lake State Recreation Area
7425 S US Hwy 281 Doniphan NE 68832 308-385-6210
Web: outdoornebraska.gov

Dead Timber State Recreation Area
227 County Rd & 12 Blvd Scribner NE 68057 402-727-2922
Web: outdoornebraska.gov/deadtimber

DLD State Recreation Area 7425 S US Hwy 281 Doniphan NE 68832 308-385-6211
Web: outdoornebraska.gov

Enders Reservoir State Recreation Area
73122 338th Ave Enders NE 69027 308-394-5118
Web: outdoornebraska.gov/endersreservoir

Eugene T Mahoney State Park 28500 W Pk Hwy Ashland NE 68003 402-944-2523
Web: nebraskastateparks.reserveamerica.com

Fort Atkinson State Historical Park
201 S 7th St Fort Calhoun NE 68023 402-468-5611 468-5066
Web: www.fortatkinsononline.org

Fort Hartsuff State Historical Park
82034 Fort Ave Burwell NE 68823 308-346-4715
Web: outdoornebraska.gov/forthartsuff

Fort Kearny State Recreation Area
1020 V Rd 1020 'V' Rd Kearney NE 68845 308-865-5305
Web: www.nps.gov/index.htm

Fort Robinson State Park PO Box 392 Crawford NE 69339 308-665-2900
Web: www.stateparks.com/fort_robinson_state_park_in_nebraska.html

Fremont Lakes State Recreation Area
9677 County Rd 3 Nickerson NE 68025 402-727-3290
Web: www.visitfremontne.org

Game & Parks Commission
301 E State Farm Rd North Platte NE 69101 308-535-8025

Indian Cave State Park 65296 720 Rd Shubert NE 68437 402-883-2575
Web: gonebraskacity.com

Lake McConaughy State Recreation Area
1450 Hwy 61N Ogallala NE 69153 308-284-8800
Web: outdoornebraska.gov

Lake Minatare State Recreation Area
PO Box 188 Minatare NE 69356 308-783-2911
Web: outdoornebraska.gov

Lake Ogallala State Recreation Area
1450 Hwy 61N Ogallala NE 69153 308-284-8800
Web: outdoornebraska.gov/lakeogallala

Lewis & Clark State Recreation Area
54731 897 Rd Crofton NE 68730 402-388-4169
Web: outdoornebraska.gov/lewisandclark

Long Lake State Recreation Area
524 Panzer St PO Box 508 Bassett NE 68714 402-684-2921
Web: outdoornebraska.gov/longlake

Long Pine State Recreation Area
524 Panzer St PO Box 508 Bassett NE 68714 402-684-2921
Web: outdoornebraska.gov/longpine

Louisville State Recreation Area
15810 Hwy 50 Louisville NE 68037 402-234-6855
Web: outdoornebraska.gov/louisville

Medicine Creek State Recreation Area
40611 Rd 728 Cambridge NE 69022 308-697-4667
Web: outdoornebraska.gov/medicinecreek

Merritt Reservoir State Recreation Area
420 E First St Valentine NE 69201 402-376-3320
Web: outdoornebraska.gov/merrittreservoir

Mormon Island State Recreation Area
7425 S Hwy 281 Doniphan NE 68832 308-385-6211
Web: outdoornebraska.gov/mormonisland

Niobrara State Park 89261 522 Ave Niobrara NE 68760 402-857-3373
Web: www.stateparks.com/niobrara_state_park_in_nebraska.html

North Loup State Recreation Area
7425 S US Hwy 281 Doniphan NE 68832 308-385-6211
Web: outdoornebraska.gov/northloup

Oliver Reservoir State Recreation Area
210615 Hwy 71 Gering NE 69341 308-436-3777
Web: visitnebraska.com/see_and_dos/oliver-reservoir-state-recreation-area

Pawnee State Recreation Area 3900 NW 105th Lincoln NE 68524 402-796-2362
Web: outdoornebraska.gov/pawnee

Pibel Lake State Recreation Area
301 Centennial Mall S PO Box 98907 Lincoln NE 68509 308-346-5666
Web: visitnebraska.com/see_and_dos/pibel-lake-recreation-area

Platte River State Park 14421 346th St Louisville NE 68037 402-234-2217
Web: outdoornebraska.gov/platteriver

Ponca State Park 88090 Spur 26 E Ponca NE 68770 402-755-2284
Web: www.outdoornebraska.ne.gov/parks

Riverview Marina State Recreation Area
N Fourth St Nebraska City NE 68410 402-873-7222
Web: gonebraskacity.com/member/riverview-marina-state-recreation-area

Rock Creek Lake State Recreation Area
73122 338 Ave Enders NE 69027 308-394-5118
Web: outdoornebraska.gov/rockcreeklake

Rock Creek Station State Historical Park
57426 710th Rd Fairbury NE 68352 402-729-5777
Web: outdoornebraska.gov/rockcreekstation

Rock Creek Station State Recreation Area
57426 710th Rd Fairbury NE 68352 402-729-5777
Web: www.outdoornebraska.ne.gov/parks

Schramm Park State Recreation Area
15810 Hwy 50 Louisville NE 68037 402-234-6855
Web: www.outdoornebraska.ne.gov/parks

Sherman Reservoir State Recreation Area
RR 2 PO Box 117 Loup City NE 68853 308-745-0230
Web: outdoornebraska.gov

Smith Falls State Park HC 13 PO Box 25 Valentine NE 69201 402-376-1306 376-3558
Web: outdoornebraska.gov

Phone Fax

Swanson Reservoir State Recreation Area
36166 Rd 44B .... Trenton NE 69044 308-334-5493

Two Rivers State Recreation Area
27702 'F' St .... Waterloo NE 68069 402-359-5165
Web: outdoornebraska.gov

Wagon Train State Recreation Area
3019 Apple St .... Lincoln NE 68503 402-471-5566
Web: outdoornebraska.gov

Walgren Lake State Recreation Area
15951 Hwy 385 .... Chadron NE 69337 308-432-6167 432-6102
Web: outdoornebraska.gov

War Axe State Recreation Area PO Box 427 .... Gibbon NE 68840 308-468-5700
Web: outdoornebraska.gov

Wildcat Hills State Recreation Area
210615 Hwy 71 .... Gering NE 69341 308-436-3777
Web: outdoornebraska.gov

Willow Creek State Recreation Area
54876 852 Rd .... Pierce NE 68767 402-329-4053
Web: outdoornebraska.gov

Windmill State Recreation Area PO Box 427 .... Gibbon NE 68840 308-468-5700
Web: outdoornebraska.gov

Nevada

Phone Fax

Beaver Dam State Park PO Box 985 .... Caliente NV 89008 775-728-4460
Web: www.parks.nv.gov

Belmont Courthouse State Historic Site
c/o Fallon Region Headquarters
16799 Lahontan Dam .... Fallon NV 89406 775-867-3001
Web: parks.nv.gov/wp-content/uploads/2009/10/nevada-state-parks-brochure.pdf

Berlin-Ichthyosaur State Park
HC 61 PO Box 61200 .... Austin NV 89310 775-964-2440 964-2012
Web: www.parks.nv.gov

Big Bend of the Colorado State Recreation Area
PO Box 32850 .... Laughlin NV 89028 702-298-1859
Web: www.parks.nv.gov

Cathedral Gorge State Park PO Box 176 .... Panaca NV 89042 775-728-4460
Web: www.parks.nv.gov

Cave Lake State Park PO Box 151761 .... Ely NV 89315 775-867-3001
Web: parks.nv.gov/parks/cave-lake-state-park

Dayton State Park PO Box 1478 .... Dayton NV 89403 775-687-5678
Web: www.parks.nv.gov

Echo Canyon State Park HC 74 PO Box 295 .... Pioche NV 89043 775-962-5103
Web: www.parks.nv.gov

Fort Churchill State Historic Park
10000 Hwy 95A .... Silver Springs NV 89429 775-577-2345
Web: www.parks.nv.gov

Kershaw-Ryan State Park PO Box 985 .... Caliente NV 89008 775-726-3564 726-3557
Web: parks.nv.gov/parks/kershaw-ryan-state-park

Lahontan State Recreation Area
16799 Lahontan Dam .... Fallon NV 89406 775-577-2226
Web: www.parks.nv.gov

Lake Tahoe Nevada State Park
PO Box 8867 .... Incline Village NV 89452 775-831-0494 831-2514
Web: www.parks.nv.gov

Mormon Station State Historic Park PO Box 302 .... Genoa NV 89411 775-782-2590
Web: parks.nv.gov/parks/mormon-station-state-historic-park

Old Las Vegas Mormon Fort State Historic Park
500 E Washington Ave .... Las Vegas NV 89101 702-486-3511 486-3734
Web: www.parks.nv.gov

Rye Patch State Recreation Area
2505 Rye Patch Reservoir Rd .... Lovelock NV 89419 775-538-7321
Web: www.parks.nv.gov

South Fork State Recreation Area
353 Lower S Fork Unit 8 .... Spring Creek NV 89815 775-744-4346
Web: www.parks.nv.gov

Spring Mountain Ranch State Park
PO Box 124 .... Blue Diamond NV 89004 702-875-4141
Web: www.parks.nv.gov

Spring Valley State Park HC 74 PO Box 201 .... Pioche NV 89043 775-962-5102
Web: www.parks.nv.gov

Ward Charcoal Ovens State Historic Park
PO Box 151761 .... Ely NV 89315 775-867-3001
Web: parks.nv.gov/parks/ward-charcoal-ovens-state-historic-park

Washoe Lake State Park 4855 E Lk Blvd .... Carson City NV 89704 775-687-4319
Web: www.parks.nv.gov

Wild Horse State Recreation Area State Rte 225 .... Elko NV 89801 775-385-5939
Web: www.parks.nv.gov

New Hampshire

Phone Fax

Ahern State Park Right Way Path .... Laconia NH 03246 603-485-2034
Web: www.nhstateparks.org/explore/state-parks/ahern-state-park.aspx

Androscoggin Wayside Park 1607 Berlin Rd .... Errol NH 03579 603-538-6707
Web: www.nhstateparks.org/explore/state-parks/androscoggin-wayside-park.aspx

Annett Wayside Park Cathedral Rd .... Rindge NH 03461 603-485-2034
Web: www.nhstateparks.org

Bear Brook State Park 157 Deerfield Rd .... Allenstown NH 03275 603-271-3556 271-3553
Web: www.nhstateparks.org

Cardigan State Park 658 Cardigan Mtn Rd .... Orange NH 03741 603-227-8745
Web: www.nhstateparks.org/explore/state-parks/cardigan-state-park.aspx

Chesterfield Gorge Natural Area
1823 Route 9 .... Chesterfield NH 03443 603-363-8373
Web: www.nhstateparks.org

Clough State Park 455 Clough Pk Rd .... Weare NH 03281 603-529-7112
Web: www.nhstateparks.org/explore/state-parks/clough-state-park.aspx

Coleman State Park 1155 Diamond Pond Rd .... Stewartstown NH 03597 603-237-5382
Web: www.nhstateparks.org

Crawford Notch State Park
1464 US Rt 302 .... Harts Location NH 03812 603-374-2272
Web: www.nhstateparks.org

Phone Fax

Daniel Webster Birthplace 131 N Rd .... Franklin NH 03235 603-934-5057
Web: www.nhstateparks.org

Deer Mountain Campground 5309 N Main St .... Pittsburg NH 03592 603-538-6965
Web: www.nhstateparks.org/explore/state-parks/deer-mountain-campground.aspx

Dixville Notch State Park Rt 26 .... Dixville NH 03576 603-538-6707
Web: www.nhstateparks.org

Echo Lake State Park 60 Echo Lk Rd .... Conway NH 03818 603-356-2672
Web: www.nhstateparks.org/explore/state-parks/echo-lake-state-park.aspx

Endicott Rock State Historic Site
17 Endicott St .... Laconia NH 03246 603-271-3556

Forest Lake State Park 397 Forest Lk Rd .... Dalton NH 03598 603-466-3860
Web: www.nhstateparks.org/explore/state-parks/forest-lake-state-park.aspx

Fort Stark Historic Site Wildrose Ln .... New Castle NH 03854 603-436-1552
Web: www.nhstateparks.org

Franconia Notch State Park
9 Franconia Notch Pkwy .... Franconia NH 03580 603-745-8391
Web: www.nhstateparks.org/explore/state-parks/franconia-notch-state-park.aspx

Governor Wentworth Historic Site Rt 109 .... Wolfeboro NH 03894 603-823-7722
Web: www.nhstateparks.org

Hampton Beach State Park Rt 1A .... Hampton NH 03842 603-926-3784
Web: www.nhstateparks.org

Hannah Duston Memorial Exit 17 Off I-93 .... Boscawen NH 03303 603-271-3556
Web: www.nhstateparks.org

Jenness State Beach 2280 Ocean Blvd .... Rye NH 03870 603-436-1552
Web: www.nhstateparks.org/explore/state-parks/jenness-state-beach.aspx

John Wingate Weeks Historic Site
200 Weeks State Park Rd .... Lancaster NH 03584 603-788-4004
Web: www.nhstateparks.org/explore/state-parks/weeks-state-park.aspx

Kingston State Park 124 Main St .... Kingston NH 03848 603-642-5471
Web: www.nhstateparks.org

Lake Francis State Park 439 River Rd .... Pittsburg NH 03592 603-538-6965
Web: www.nhstateparks.org/parkspages/lakefrancis/lakefrancis.html

Lake Tarleton State Park 949 Rt 25C .... Piermont NH 03779 603-823-7722
Web: www.nhstateparks.org

Madison Boulder Natural Area 473 Boulder Rd .... Madison NH 03849 603-227-8745
Web: www.nhstateparks.org/explore/state-parks/madison-boulder-natural-area.aspx

Milan Hill State Park 427 Milan Hill Rd .... Milan NH 03588 603-449-2429
Web: www.nhstateparks.org/parkspages/milanhill/milanhill.html

Miller State Park 13 Miller Park Rd .... Peterborough NH 03458 603-924-3672
Web: www.nhstateparks.org

Mollidgewock State Park 1437 Berlin Rd .... Errol NH 03579 603-482-3373
Web: www.nhstateparks.org/explore/state-parks/mollidgewock-state-park.aspx

Monadnock State Park 116 Poole Rd .... Jaffrey NH 03452 603-532-8862
Web: www.nhstateparks.org

Mount Sunapee State Park 1460 Rt 103 .... Newbury NH 03255 603-763-5561
Web: www.nhstateparks.org/explore/state-parks/mount-sunapee-state-park.aspx

North Beach Rt 1A .... Hampton NH 03842 603-436-1552
Web: www.nhstateparks.org

North Hampton State Beach
27 Ocean Blvd .... North Hampton NH 03862 603-227-8722
Web: www.nhstateparks.org/explore/state-parks/north-hampton-state-beach.aspx

Northwood Meadows State Park
755 First NH Tpke .... Northwood NH 03261 603-485-1031
Web: www.nhstateparks.org/explore/state-parks/northwood-meadows-state-park.aspx

Odiorne Point State Park 570 Ocean Blvd .... Rye NH 03870 603-436-7406
Web: www.nhstateparks.org/explore/state-parks/odiorne-point-state-park.aspx

Pawtuckaway State Park 128 Mountain Rd .... Nottingham NH 03290 603-895-3031
Web: www.nhstateparks.org

Pillsbury State Park
100 Pillsbury State Park Rd .... Washington NH 03280 603-863-2860
Web: www.nhstateparks.org/explore/state-parks/pillsbury-state-park.aspx

Rhododendron State Park
424 Rockwood Pond Rd .... Fitzwilliam NH 03447 603-532-8862
Web: www.nhstateparks.org

Robert Frost Farm Historic Site
122 Rockingham Rd .... Derry NH 03038 603-432-3091
Web: www.nhstateparks.org

Rollins State Park 1066 Kearsarge Mtn Rd .... Warner NH 03278 603-456-3808
Web: www.nhstateparks.org

Rye Harbor State Park 1730 Ocean Blvd .... Rye NH 03870 603-227-8722
Web: www.nhstateparks.org/explore/state-parks/rye-harbor-state-park.aspx

Silver Lake State Park 138 Silver Lk Rd .... Hollis NH 03049 603-465-2342
Web: www.nhstateparks.org

Taylor Mill Historic Site Island Pond Rd .... Derry NH 03038 603-431-6774
Web: www.nhstateparks.org/explore/state-parks/taylor-mill-state-historic-site.aspx

Umbagog Lake State Park 172 Pembroke Rd .... Concord NH 03301 603-482-7795
Web: www.nhstateparks.org

Wallis Sands State Beach 1050 Ocean Blvd .... Rye NH 03870 603-436-9404
Web: www.nhstateparks.org/explore/state-parks/wallis-sands-state-beach.aspx

Wellington State Park 614 W Shore Rd .... Bristol NH 03222 603-744-2197
Web: www.nhstateparks.org/explore/state-parks/wellington-state-park.aspx

Wentworth State Park
297 Governor Wentworth Hwy .... Wolfeboro NH 03894 603-569-3699
Web: www.nhstateparks.org

Wentworth-Coolidge Mansion Historic Site
375 Little Harbor Rd .... Portsmouth NH 03801 603-436-6607
Web: www.nhstateparks.org

White Lake State Park Rt 16 .... Tamworth NH 03886 603-323-7350
Web: www.nhstateparks.org

Winslow State Park Kearsarge Mtn Rd .... Wilmot NH 03287 603-526-6168
Web: www.nhstateparks.org/explore/state-parks/winslow-state-park.aspx

New Jersey

Phone Fax

Abram S. Hewitt State Forest
c/o Wawayanda State Pk 885 Warwick Tpke .... Hewitt NJ 07421 973-853-4462
Web: www.njparksandforests.org/parks/abram.html

Allaire State Park PO Box 220 .... Farmingdale NJ 07727 732-938-2371
Web: www.njparksandforests.org

				Phone	Fax
Allamuchy Mountain State Park c/o Stephens State Pk 800 Willow Grove St. *Web:* www.njparksandforests.org	Hackettstown	NJ	07840	908-852-3790	
Barnegat Lighthouse State Park PO Box 167 *Web:* www.njparksandforests.org	Barnegat Light	NJ	08006	609-494-2016	
Bass River State Forest 762 Stage Rd *Web:* www.njparksandforests.org	Tuckerton	NJ	08087	609-296-1114	
Batsto Village State Historic Site Rd 9 *Web:* www.njparksandforests.org/historic/index.html	Hammonton	NJ	08037	609-561-0024	
Belleplain State Forest County Rt 50 PO Box 450 *Web:* www.njparksandforests.org/parks/belle.html	Woodbine	NJ	08270	609-861-2404	
Boxwood Hall State Historic Site 1073 E Jersey St *Web:* www.state.nj.us/dep/parksandforests/historic	Elizabeth	NJ	07201	908-282-7617	
Brendan T. Byrne State Forest PO Box 215 *Web:* www.njparksandforests.org/parks/byrne.html	New Lisbon	NJ	08064	609-726-1191	
Bull's Island Recreation Area 2185 Daniel Bray Hwy *Web:* www.njparksandforests.org	Stockton	NJ	08559	609-397-2949	
Cape May Point State Park PO Box 107 *Web:* www.njparksandforests.org	Cape May Point	NJ	08212	609-884-2159	
Cheesequake State Park 300 Gordon Rd *Web:* www.njparksandforests.org	Matawan	NJ	07747	732-566-2161	
Corson's Inlet State Park 1304 Sloatsburg Rd County Rt 550 PO Box 450 *Web:* www.njparksandforests.org/parks/corsons.html	Ringwood	NJ	07456	609-861-2404	
Craig House State Historic Site 347 Freehold-Englishtown Rd *Web:* www.njparksandforests.org/historic/index.html	Manalapan	NJ	07726	732-462-9616	
Delaware & Raritan Canal State Park 145 Mapleton Rd *Web:* www.njparksandforests.org	Princeton	NJ	08540	609-924-5705	
Double Trouble State Park 581 Pinewald Keswick Rd *Web:* www.state.nj.us	Bayville	NJ	08721	732-341-6662	
Farny State Park c/o Ringwood State Pk 1304 Sloatsburg Rd *Web:* www.njparksandforests.org/parks/farny.html	Ringwood	NJ	07456	973-962-7031	
Fort Mott State Park 454 Ft Mott Rd *Web:* www.njparksandforests.org	Pennsville	NJ	08070	856-935-3218	
Grover Cleveland Birthplace State Historic Site 207 Bloomfield Ave *Web:* www.njparksandforests.org	Caldwell	NJ	07006	973-226-0001	
Hacklebarney State Park 119 Hacklebarney Rd 119 Hacklebarney Rd *TF:* 800-659-4044 ■ *Web:* www.njparksandforests.org	Long Valley	NJ	07853	908-638-6969	
Hancock House State Historic Site 3 Front St PO Box 139 *Web:* www.njparksandforests.org	Hancock's Bridge	NJ	08038	856-935-4373	
Hermitage State Historic Site, The 335 N Franklin Tpke *Web:* www.thehermitage.org	Ho-Ho-Kus	NJ	07423	201-445-8311	445-0437
High Point State Park 1480 Rt 23 *Web:* www.njparksandforests.org	Sussex	NJ	07461	973-875-4800	
Hopatcong State Park PO Box 8519 *Web:* www.njparksandforests.org	Landing	NJ	07850	973-398-7010	
Indian King Tavern State Historic Site 233 Kings Hwy *Web:* www.njparksandforests.org	Haddonfield	NJ	08033	856-429-6792	
Island Beach State Park PO Box 37 *Web:* www.njparksandforests.org	Seaside Park	NJ	08752	732-793-0506	
Jenny Jump State Forest 330 State Pk Rd *Web:* www.njparksandforests.org	Hope	NJ	07844	908-459-4366	
Kittatinny Valley State Park PO Box 621 *Web:* www.njparksandforests.org	Andover	NJ	07821	973-786-6445	
Leonardo State Marina 102 Concord Ave *Web:* www.state.nj.us/dep/parksandforests/parks/marinas.html	Leonardo	NJ	07737	732-291-1333	
Liberty State Park 200Morris Pesin Dr *Web:* www.njparksandforests.org/parks/liberty.html	Jersey City	NJ	07305	201-915-3440	915-3408
Long Pond Ironworks State Park c/o Ringwood State Pk 1304 Sloatsburg Rd *Web:* www.njparksandforests.org/parks/longpond.html	Ringwood	NJ	07456	973-962-7031	
Monmouth Battlefield State Park 347 Freehold-Englishtown Rd *Web:* www.njparksandforests.org/parks/monbat.html	Manalapan	NJ	07726	732-462-9616	
Norvin Green State Forest c/o Ringwood State Pk 1304 Sloatsburg Rd *Web:* www.njparksandforests.org/parks/norvin.html	Ringwood	NJ	07456	973-962-7031	
Parvin State Park 701 Almond Rd *Web:* www.njparksandforests.org	Pittsgrove	NJ	08318	856-358-8616	
Penn State Forest c/o Bass River State Forest 762 Stage Rd *Web:* www.njparksandforests.org	Tuckerton	NJ	08087	609-296-1114	
Princeton Battlefield State Park 500 Mercer Rd *Web:* www.njparksandforests.org	Princeton	NJ	08540	609-921-0074	
Ramapo Mountain State Forest c/o Ringwood State Pk 1304 Sloatsburg Rd *Web:* www.njparksandforests.org/parks/ramapo.html	Ringwood	NJ	07456	973-962-7031	
Rancocas State Park c/o Brendan T Byrne State Forest PO Box 215 *Web:* www.njparksandforests.org/parks/rancocas.html	New Lisbon	NJ	08064	609-726-1191	
Ringwood State Park 1304 Sloatsburg Rd *Web:* www.njparksandforests.org	Ringwood	NJ	07456	973-962-7031	
Rockingham State Historic Site 84 Laurel Ave *Web:* www.rockingham.net	Kingston	NJ	08528	609-683-7132	
Round Valley Recreation Area 1220 Lebanon-Stanton Rd *Web:* www.njparksandforests.org	Lebanon	NJ	08833	908-236-6355	
Senator Frank S Farley State Marina 600 Huron Ave *Web:* www.njparksandforests.org/parks/marinas.html#senator	Atlantic City	NJ	08401	609-441-8482	
Somers Mansion State Historic Site 1000 Shore Rd *Web:* www.njparksandforests.org	Somers Point	NJ	08244	609-927-2212	
Spruce Run Recreation Area 68 Van Syckel's Rd *Web:* www.njparksandforests.org	Clinton	NJ	08809	908-638-8572	
Stephens State Park 800 Willow Grove St *Web:* www.njparksandforests.org	Hackettstown	NJ	07840	908-852-3790	
Steuben House State Historic Site 1209 Main St *Web:* www.njparksandforests.org	River Edge	NJ	07661	201-487-1739	
Stokes State Forest 1 Coursen Rd *Web:* www.njparksandforests.org	Branchville	NJ	07826	973-948-3820	
Swartswood State Park PO Box 123 *Web:* www.njparksandforests.org	Swartswood	NJ	07877	973-383-5230	
Twin Lights State Historic Site Lighthouse Rd *Web:* www.twinlightslighthouse.com	Highlands	NJ	07732	732-872-1814	
Voorhees State Park 251 County Rd 513 *Web:* www.njparksandforests.org	Glen Gardner	NJ	08826	908-638-6969	
Wallace House State Historic Site 71 Somerset St *Web:* www.njparksandforests.org	Somerville	NJ	08876	908-725-1015	
Walt Whitman House State Historic Site 330 Mickle Blvd *TF:* 800-843-6420 ■ *Web:* www.njparksandforests.org	Camden	NJ	08103	800-843-6420	
Washington Crossing State Park 355 Washington Crossing-Pennington Rd *Web:* www.njparksandforests.org	Titusville	NJ	08560	609-737-0623	
Washington Rock State Park 355 Milltown Rd *Web:* www.njparksandforests.org/parks/washrock.html	Bridgewater	NJ	08807	908-722-1200	
Wawayanda State Park 885 Warwick Tpke *Web:* www.njparksandforests.org/parks/wawayanda.html	Hewitt	NJ	07421	973-853-4462	
Wharton State Forest 31 Batsto Rd *Web:* www.njparksandforests.org/parks/wharton.html	Hammonton	NJ	08037	609-561-0024	
Worthington State Forest HC 62 PO Box 2 *Web:* www.njparksandforests.org	Columbia	NJ	07832	908-841-9575	

New Mexico

				Phone	Fax
Coyote Creek State Park Hwy 434 Mile Marker 17 *Web:* www.emnrd.state.nm.us	Guadalupita	NM	87722	575-387-2328	
Fenton Lake State Park 455 Fenton Lake	Jemez Springs	NM	87025	575-829-3630	
Hyde Memorial State Park 740 Hyde Pk Rd	Santa Fe	NM	87501	505-983-7175	
Oasis State Park 1891 Oasis Rd *Web:* www.emnrd.state.nm.us	Portales	NM	88130	575-356-5331	
Oliver Lee Memorial State Park 409 Dog Canyon Rd **Fax Area Code:* 505 ■ *Web:* emnrd.state.nm.us	Alamogordo	NM	88310	575-437-8284	439-1290*
Rio Grande Nature Ctr State Park 2901 Candelaria Rd NW *Web:* emnrd.state.nm.us	Albuquerque	NM	87107	505-344-7240	344-4505

New York

				Phone	Fax
Allan H. Treman State Marine Park c/o Robert H Tremin State Pk 105 Enfield Falls Rd *Web:* www.nysparks.com	Ithaca	NY	14850	607-273-3440	
Allegany State Park 2373 ASP Rt 1 Ste 3 *Web:* nysparks.com	Salamanca	NY	14779	716-354-9121	
Battle Island State Park 2150 State Rt 48 *Web:* nysparks.com	Fulton	NY	13069	315-593-3408	
Bayswater Point State Park 1479 Point Breeze Pl *Web:* nysparks.com	Far Rockaway	NY	11691	718-786-6385	
Bear Mountain State Park Palisades Pkwy Rt 9W N *Web:* www.nysparks.com/parks/13/details.aspx	Bear Mountain	NY	10911	845-786-2701	
Beaver Island State Park 2136 W Oakfield Rd *Web:* nysparks.com	Grand Island	NY	14072	716-773-3271	
Belmont Lake State Park PO Box 247 *Web:* nysparks.com	Babylon	NY	11702	631-667-5055	
Bethpage State Park Bethpage Pkwy *TF:* 800-456-2267 ■ *Web:* nysparks.com	Farmingdale	NY	11735	516-249-0701	753-0413
Blauvelt State Park Palisades Interstate Park Commission Adminstration Bldg Rt 9 W *Web:* www.nysparks.com/parks/49/details.aspx	Bear Mountain	NY	10911	845-359-0544	
Bowman Lake State Park 745 Bliven Sherman Rd *Web:* nysparks.com	Oxford	NY	13830	607-334-2718	
Burnham Point State Park 340765 NYS Rt 12E *Web:* www.nysparks.com	Cape Vincent	NY	13618	315-654-2522	
Buttermilk Falls State Park c/o Robert H Tremin State Pk 105 Enfield Falls Rd *Web:* nysparks.com	Ithaca	NY	14850	607-273-5761	
Caleb Smith State Park Preserve 581 W Jericho Tpke PO Box 963 *Web:* nysparks.com	Smithtown	NY	11787	631-265-1054	
Canandaigua Lake State Marine Park 620 S Main St *Web:* www.nysparks.com/parks/3/details.aspx	Canandaigua	NY	14424	315-789-2331	

				Phone	Fax
Canoe-Picnic Point State Park 36661 Cedar Pt State Pk Dr *Fax Area Code: 518 ■ *Web:* nysparks.com	Clayton	NY	13624	315-686-3048	408-1032*
Captree State Park PO Box 247 *Web:* nysparks.com	Babylon	NY	11702	631-669-0449	
Caumsett State Historic Park 25 Lloyd Harbor Rd *Web:* www.nysparks.com	Huntington	NY	11743	631-423-1770	
Cayuga Lake State Park 2678 Lower Lk Rd *Web:* nysparks.com/parks/123/details.aspx	Seneca Falls	NY	13148	315-568-5163	568-5336
Cedar Island State Park County Rt 93 *Web:* nysparks.com	Hammond	NY	13646	315-482-3331	
Cedar Point State Park 36661 Cedar Pt State Pk Dr *Web:* nysparks.com	Clayton	NY	13624	315-654-2522	
Chenango Valley State Park 153 State Pk Rd *Web:* nysparks.com	Chenango Forks	NY	13746	607-648-5251	
Cherry Plain State Park 10 State Park Rd	Petersburg	NY	12138	518-733-5400	
Chittenango Falls State Park 2300 Rathbun Rd *Web:* nysparks.com	Cazenovia	NY	13035	315-655-9620	
Clarence Fahnestock State Park 1498 Rt 301 *Web:* nysparks.com	Carmel	NY	10512	845-225-7207	
Clark Reservation State Park 6105 E Seneca Tpke *Web:* nysparks.com	Jamesville	NY	13078	315-492-1590	
Clay Pit Ponds State Park Preserve 83 Nielsen Ave *Web:* nysparks.com	Staten Island	NY	10309	718-967-1976	966-5294
Clermont State Historic Site 1 Clermont Ave. *TF:* 800-456-2267 ■ *Web:* www.nysparks.com	Germantown	NY	12526	518-537-4240	537-6240
Clinton House State Historic Site 549 Main St PO Box 88 *Web:* nysparks.com	Poughkeepsie	NY	12602	845-471-1630	
Cold Spring Harbor State Park 25 Lloyd Harbor Rd *Web:* www.nysparks.com	Huntington	NY	11743	631-423-1770	
Coles Creek State Park 13003 NY-37	Waddington	NY	13694	315-388-5636	
Connetquot River State Park Preserve PO Box 505 *Web:* www.nysparks.com	Oakdale	NY	11769	631-581-1005	
Crailo State Historic Site 9 1/2 Riverside Ave.	Rensselaer	NY	12144	518-463-8738	
Crown Point State Historic Site 21 Grandview Dr. *TF:* 800-456-2267 ■ *Web:* www.nysparks.com	Crown Point	NY	12928	518-597-4666	597-3666
Cumberland Bay State Park 152 Cumberland Head Rd. *Web:* nysparks.com	Plattsburgh	NY	12901	518-563-5240	
Darien Lakes State Park 10289 Harlow Rd *Web:* nysparks.com	Darien Center	NY	14040	585-547-9242	
Darwin Martin House State Historic Site 125 Jewett Pkwy *Web:* nysparks.com	Buffalo	NY	14214	716-856-3858	
Delta Lake State Park 8797 SR- 46 *Web:* nysparks.com	Rome	NY	13440	315-337-4670	
Devil's Hole State Park c/o Niagara Frontier Region PO Box 1132 *Web:* nysparks.com	Niagara Falls	NY	14303	716-284-5778	
Dewolf Point State Park 45920 County Rt 191 *Web:* nysparks.com	Fineview	NY	13640	315-482-2012	
Earl W. Brydges Artpark State Park 450 S Fourth St *Web:* nysparks.com	Lewiston	NY	14092	716-754-7766	
Empire-Fulton Ferry State Park 1 Water St.	Brooklyn	NY	11201	718-222-9939	
Evangola State Park 10191 Old Lk Shore Rd *Web:* nysparks.com	Irving	NY	14081	716-549-1802	
Fair Haven Beach State Park 14985 State Park Rd. *TF General:* 800-456-2267	Sterling	NY	13156	315-947-5205	
Fillmore Glen State Park 1686 St Rt 38 *TF:* 800-456-2267 ■ *Web:* nysparks.com	Moravia	NY	13118	315-497-0130	
Fort Montgomery State Historic Site 690 Route 9W PO Box 213 *Web:* www.nysparks.com/sites/info.asp?siteid=36	Fort Montgomery	NY	10922	845-446-2134	
Fort Niagara State Park 1 Scott Ave. *Web:* www.nysparks.com/parks/175/details.aspx	Youngstown	NY	14174	716-745-7273	
Fort Ontario State Historic Site 1 E Fourth St. *Web:* www.nysparks.com	Oswego	NY	13126	315-343-4711	
Four Mile Creek State Park 1055 Lake Rd. *Web:* www.nysparks.com/parks/info.asp?parkid=110	Youngstown	NY	14174	716-745-3802	
Franklin D. Roosevelt State Park 2957 Crompond Rd *Web:* www.nysparks.com	Yorktown Heights	NY	10598	914-245-4434	
Ganondagan State Historic Site 1488 SR 444 *Web:* www.nysparks.com	Victor	NY	14564	585-924-5848	
Gantry Plaza State Park 4-09 47th Rd *Web:* www.nysparks.com	Long Island	NY	11101	718-786-6385	
Gilbert Lake State Park 18 CCC Rd *Web:* www.nysparks.com	Laurens	NY	13796	607-432-2114	
Glimmerglass State Park 1527 County Hwy 31 *Web:* www.nysparks.com/parks/info.asp?parkid=22	Cooperstown	NY	13326	607-547-8662	
Golden Hill State Park 9691 Lower Lake Rd *Web:* www.nysparks.com	Barker	NY	14012	716-795-3885	
Goosepond Mountain State Park 1198 New York 17M Adminstration Bldg Rt 9 W *Web:* www.nysparks.com/parks/55/details.aspx	Chester	NY	10918	845-786-2701	
Grant Cottage State Historic Site PO Box 2294 *Web:* www.nysparks.com	Wilton	NY	12831	518-587-8277	
Grass Point State Park 42247 Grassy Pt Rd *Web:* nysparks.com	Alexandria Bay	NY	13607	315-686-4472	
Green Lakes State Park 7900 Green Lakes Rd *Web:* www.nysparks.com	Fayetteville	NY	13066	315-637-6111	
Hamlin Beach State Park 1 Hamlin Beach Blvd W *TF:* 800-456-2267	Hamlin	NY	14464	585-964-2462	
Harriman State Park Palisades Pkwy Exit 17 *Web:* www.nysparks.com/parks/145/details.aspx	Bear Mountain	NY	10911	845-942-2560	
Heckscher State Park 1 Heckscher State Pkwy *Web:* www.nysparks.com	East Islip	NY	11730	631-581-2100	
Hempstead Lake State Park Lakeside Dr. *Web:* www.nysparks.com	West Hempstead	NY	11552	516-766-1029	
Herkimer Home State Historic Site 200 SR- 169 *Web:* www.nysparks.com	Little Falls	NY	13365	315-823-0398	
High Tor State Park 417 S Mountain Rd	New City	NY	10956	845-634-8074	
Highland Lakes State Park 55-223 Tamms Rd. *Web:* www.nysparks.com/parks/5/details.aspx	Middletown	NY	10911	845-786-2701	
Higley Flow State Park 442 Cold Brook Dr. *Web:* www.nysparks.com	Colton	NY	13625	315-262-2880	
Hither Hills State Park 164 Old Montauk Hwy *Web:* www.nysparks.com	Montauk	NY	11954	631-668-2554	
Hudson Highlands State Park Rt 9D *Web:* www.nynjtc.org	Cold Spring	NY	10516	845-225-7207	
Hudson River Islands State Park Schodack Island State Pk *TF:* 800-456-2267 ■ *Web:* www.nysparks.com	Schodack Landing	NY	12156	518-732-0187	
Hyde Hall State Historic Site PO Box 721 *Web:* www.nysparks.com/sites/info.asp?siteid=13	Cooperstown	NY	13326	518-486-1868	
James Baird State Park 280 Club House Rd Ste 1 *Web:* www.nysparks.com	Pleasant Valley	NY	12569	845-452-1489	
John Boyd Thacher State Park 1 Hailes Cave Rd *TF:* 800-456-2267 ■ *Web:* www.nysparks.com	Voorheesville	NY	12186	518-872-1237	872-9133
John Brown Farm State Historic Site 115 John Brown Rd *Web:* www.nysparks.com	Lake Placid	NY	12946	518-523-3900	
John Jay Homestead State Historic Site PO Box 832 *TF:* 800-456-2267 ■ *Web:* www.nysparks.com	Katonah	NY	10536	914-232-5651	
Johnson Hall State Historic Site 139 Hall Ave *Web:* www.nysparks.com	Johnstown	NY	12095	518-762-8712	
Jones Beach State Park PO Box 1000 *Web:* www.nysparks.com	Wantagh	NY	11793	516-785-1600	
Joseph Davis State Park 4143 Lower River Rd. *Web:* www.nysparks.com	Lewiston	NY	14092	716-754-4596	
Keewaydin State Park 46165 NYS Rt 12 PO Box 247 *Web:* www.nysparks.com	Alexandria Bay	NY	13607	315-482-3331	
Keuka Lake State Park 3560 Pepper Rd. *Web:* www.nysparks.com	Keuka Park	NY	14478	315-536-3666	
Knox's Headquarters State Historic Site PO Box 207 *Web:* www.nysparks.com	Vails Gate	NY	12584	845-561-5498	
Kring Point State Park 25950 Kring Pt Rd *Web:* www.nysparks.com	Redwood City	NY	13679	315-482-2444	
Lake Erie State Park 5838 Route 5 *Web:* www.nysparks.com	Brocton	NY	14716	716-792-9214	
Lake Taghkanic State Park 1528 Rt 82 *Web:* www.nysparks.com	Ancram	NY	12502	518-851-3631	851-3633
Lakeside Beach State Park Rt 18. *Web:* www.nysparks.com/parks/info.asp?parkid=8	Waterport	NY	14571	585-682-4888	
Letchworth State Park 1 Letchworth State Pk. *Web:* www.nysparks.com	Castile	NY	14427	585-493-3600	
Lodi Point State Marine Park c/o Sampson State Pk 6096 Rt 96A *Web:* www.nysparks.com/parks/info.asp?parkid=38	Romulus	NY	14541	315-585-6392	
Long Point State Park - Finger Lakes 2063 Lake Rd *Web:* www.nysparks.com	Aurora	NY	13026	315-497-0130	
Long Point State Park - Thousand Islands 7495 State Pk Rd *Web:* www.nysparks.com	Three Mile Bay	NY	13693	315-649-5258	
Long Point State Park on Lake Chautauqua 4459 Rt 430 *Web:* www.nysparks.com	Bemus Point	NY	14712	716-386-2722	
Lorenzo State Historic Site 17 Rippleton Rd *Web:* www.nysparks.com	Cazenovia	NY	13035	315-655-3200	
Macomb Reservation State Park 201 Campsite Rd *Web:* www.nysparks.com	Schuyler Falls	NY	12985	518-643-9952	
Margaret Lewis Norrie State Park 9 Old Post Rd PO Box 308 *Web:* nysparks.com	Staatsburg	NY	12580	845-889-4646	889-8321
Mark Twain State Park & Soaring Eagles Golf Course 201 Middle Rd *Web:* www.nysparks.com	Horseheads	NY	14845	607-739-0034	
Mine Kill State Park PO Box 923 Rt 30 *Web:* www.nysparks.com/parks/info.asp?parkid=117	North Blenheim	NY	12131	518-827-6111	827-6782
Montauk Downs State Park 50 S Fairview Ave *Web:* www.nysparks.com/parks/info.asp?parkid=165	Montauk	NY	11954	631-668-3781	
Montauk Point State Park 2000 Montauk Hwy *Web:* www.nysparks.com/parks/info.asp?parkId=136	Montauk	NY	11954	631-668-3781	

				Phone	Fax
Moreau Lake State Park 605 Old Saratoga Rd *Web:* www.nysparks.com	Gansevoort	NY	12831	518-793-0511	
New Windsor Cantonment State Historic Site 374 Temple Hill Rd Rt 300 *Web:* www.nysparks.com	Vails Gate	NY	12584	845-561-1765	
Niagara Falls State Park PO Box 1132 *Web:* www.nysparks.com/parks/info.asp?parkid=113	Niagara Falls	NY	14303	716-278-1796	
Nissequogue River State Park 799 St Johnland Rd PO Box 639 *Web:* wwwdecnygov	Kings Park	NY	11754	631-269-4927	
Nyack Beach State Park 698 N Broadway *Web:* www.nysparks.com/parks/info.asp?parkid=62	Upper Nyack	NY	10960	845-358-1316	
Oak Orchard State Marine Park c/o Lakeside Beach State Pk Rt 18	Carlton	NY	14571	585-682-4888	
Ogden Mills & Ruth Livingston Mills State Park Mills Mansion 1 Rd *Web:* www.nysparks.com/parks/info.asp?parkid=133	Staatsburg	NY	12580	845-889-4646	
Olana State Historic Site 5720 State Rt 9G *Web:* www.olana.org	Hudson	NY	12534	518-828-0135	828-6742
Old Croton Aqueduct State Historic Park 15 Walnut St *Web:* www.nysparks.com	Dobbs Ferry	NY	10522	914-693-5259	
Old Fort Niagara State Historic Site PO Box 169 *Web:* www.oldfortniagara.org	Youngstown	NY	14174	716-745-7611	745-9141
Oquaga Creek State Park 5995 County Rt 20 *Web:* www.nysparks.com	Bainbridge	NY	13733	607-467-4160	
Oriskany Battlefield State Historic Site 7801 State Rt 69 *Web:* www.nysparks.com/sites/info.asp?siteid=23	Oriskany	NY	13424	315-768-7224	377-3081
Peebles Island State Park 1 Delaware Ave PO Box 295 *Web:* www.nysparks.com/parks/111/details.aspx	Waterford	NY	12047	518-237-8643	
Philipse Manor Hall State Historic Site 29 Warburton Ave *Web:* philipsemanorhall.blogspot.in	Yonkers	NY	10701	914-965-4027	
Pinnacle State Park & Golf Course 1904 Pinnacle Rd *Web:* nysparks.com	Addison	NY	14801	607-359-2767	
Point Au Roche State Park 19 Camp Red Cloud Rd *Web:* www.nysparks.com	Plattsburgh	NY	12901	518-563-0369	
Reservoir State Park c/o Niagara Frontier Region PO Box 1132 *Web:* www.nysparks.com/parks/info.asp?parkid=112	Niagara Falls	NY	14303	716-284-4691	
Riverbank State Park 679 Riverside Dr *Web:* www.nysparks.com	New York	NY	10031	212-694-3600	
Robert H. Treman State Park 105 Enfield Falls Rd *Web:* www.nysparks.com	Ithaca	NY	14850	607-273-3440	
Robert Moses State Park - Long Island Robert Moses State Pkwy PO Box 247 *Web:* www.nysparks.com/parks/info.asp?parkid=45	Babylon	NY	11702	631-669-0449	
Robert Moses State Park - Thousand Islands 19 Robinson Bay Rd *Web:* www.nysparks.com	Massena	NY	13662	315-769-8663	
Roberto Clemente State Park 301 W Tremont Ave *Web:* nysparks.com	Bronx	NY	10453	718-299-8750	
Rockefeller State Park Preserve 125 Phelps Way *Web:* www.nysparks.com	Pleasantville	NY	10570	914-631-1470	
Rockland Lake State Park PO Box 217 *Web:* nysparks.com	Congers	NY	10920	845-268-3020	
Saint Lawrence State Park Golf Course 4955 State Hwy 37 *Web:* www.nysparks.com	Ogdensburg	NY	13669	315-393-2286	
Sampson State Park 6096 Rt 96A *Web:* www.nysparks.com/parks/info.asp?parkid=100	Romulus	NY	14541	315-585-6392	
Saratoga Spa State Park 19 Roosevelt Dr *Web:* nysparks.com/parks/saratogaspa/details.aspx	Saratoga Springs	NY	12866	518-584-2535	
Schodack Island State Park 1 Schodack Way PO Box 7 *Web:* newyorkstateparksreserveamericacom	Schodack Landing	NY	12156	518-732-0187	
Schoharie Crossing State Historic Site 129 Schoharie St PO Box 140 *TF:* 800-456-2267 ■ *Web:* www.nysparks.com	Fort Hunter	NY	12069	518-829-7516	
Schuyler Mansion State Historic Site 32 Catherine St *TF:* 800-456-2267 ■ *Web:* nysparks.com	Albany	NY	12202	518-434-0834	
Selkirk Shores State Park 7101 State Rt 3 *Web:* www.nysparks.com	Pulaski	NY	13142	315-298-5737	
Senate House State Historic Site 296 Fair St *TF:* 800-456-2267 ■ *Web:* www.nysparks.com	Kingston	NY	12401	845-338-2786	
Seneca Lake State Park 100 Waterloo Geneva Rd	Geneva	NY	14456	315-789-2331	
Shadmoor State Park 900 Montauk Hwy *Web:* nysparks.com	Montauk	NY	11954	631-668-3781	
Silver Lake State Park 156 Lakeshore Dr *Web:* www.nysparks.com	Castile	NY	14427	585-237-6629	
Southwick Beach State Park 8119 Southwicks Pl *Web:* www.nysparks.com	Henderson	NY	13650	315-846-5338	
Staatsburgh State Historic Site 75 Mills Mansion Rd	Staatsburg	NY	12580	845-889-8851	889-8321
Sterling Forest State Park 116 Old Forge Rd *Web:* www.nysparks.com	Tuxedo	NY	10987	845-351-5907	
Steuben Memorial State Historic Site c/o Ft Stanwix National Monument 100 N James St *Web:* www.nysparks.com	Rome	NY	13440	315-338-7730	
Stony Brook State Park 10820 Rt 36 S *Web:* www.nysparks.com/parks/118/details.aspx	Dansville	NY	14437	585-335-8111	
Stony Point Battlefield State Historic Site PO Box 182 *Web:* nysparks.com	Stony Point	NY	10980	845-786-2521	
Storm King State Park Palisades Interstate Park Commission *Web:* www.nysparks.com/parks/152/details.aspx	Bear Mountain	NY	10911	845-786-2701	
Sunken Meadow State Park Sunken Meadow Pkwy *Web:* www.nysparks.com/parks/37/details.aspx	Kings Park	NY	11754	631-269-4333	
Taconic State Park - Copake Falls Area Route 344 *Web:* www.nysparks.com	Copake Falls	NY	12517	518-329-3993	
Taconic State Park - Rudd Pond Area 59 Rudd Pond Dr *Web:* www.nysparks.com	Millerton	NY	12546	518-789-3059	
Tallman Mountain State Park Rt 9 W	Sparkill	NY	10976	845-359-0544	
Taughannock Falls State Park 2221 Taughannock Rd *Web:* www.nysparks.com	Trumansburg	NY	14886	607-387-6739	
Thompson's Lake State Park 68 Thompson's Lk Rd *Web:* www.nysparks.com	East Berne	NY	12059	518-872-1674	872-9133
Valley Stream State Park PO Box 670 *Web:* www.nysparks.com	Valley Stream	NY	11580	516-825-4128	
Verona Beach State Park PO Box 245 *Web:* www.nysparks.com	Verona Beach	NY	13162	315-762-4463	
Walt Whitman Birthplace State Historic Site 246 Old Walt Whitman Rd *Web:* www.nysparks.com	Huntington Station	NY	11746	631-427-5240	427-5247
Washington's Headquarters State Historic Site PO Box 1783 *Web:* nysparks.com	Newburgh	NY	12551	845-562-1195	
Waterson Point State Park 44927 Cross Island Rd *Web:* www.nysparks.com	Fineview	NY	13640	315-482-2722	
Watkins Glen State Park PO Box 304 *Web:* www.nysparks.com	Watkins Glen	NY	14891	607-535-4511	
Wellesley Island State Park 44927 Cross Island Rd *Web:* www.nysparks.com	Fineview	NY	13640	315-482-2722	
Westcott Beach State Park Rt 3 *Web:* www.nysparks.com	Henderson	NY	13650	315-938-5083	
Whetstone Gulf State Park 6065 W Rd *Web:* www.nysparks.com	Lowville	NY	13367	315-376-6630	
Whirlpool State Park 3180 De Veaux Woods Dr PO Box 1132 *Web:* www.nysparks.com/parks/info.asp?parkid=29	Niagara Falls	NY	14303	716-284-5778	
Wildwood State Park N Wading River Rd PO Box 518	Wading River	NY	11792	631-929-4314	
Wilson-Tuscarora State Park 3371 Lake Rd *Web:* www.nysparks.com	Wilson	NY	14172	716-751-6361	
Woodlawn Beach State Park 3580 Lk Shore Rd *Web:* www.nysparks.com	Blasdell	NY	14219	716-826-1930	

North Carolina

				Phone	Fax
Carolina Beach State Park 1010 State Pk Rd PO Box 475 *Web:* www.ncparks.gov	Carolina Beach	NC	28428	910-458-8206	
Cliffs of the Neuse State Park 240 Park Entrance Rd *Web:* www.ncparks.gov/visit/parks/clne/main.php	Seven Springs	NC	28578	919-778-6234	
Crowders Mountain State Park 522 Pk Office Ln *Web:* www.ncparks.gov	Kings Mountain	NC	28086	704-853-5375	
Eno River State Park 6101 Cole Mill Rd *Web:* www.ncparks.gov	Durham	NC	27705	919-383-1686	
Falls Lake State Recreation Area 13304 Creedmoor Rd *Web:* www.ncparks.gov	Wake Forest	NC	27587	919-676-1027	
Fort Fisher State Recreation Area 1000 Loggerhead Rd *Web:* www.ncparks.gov	Kure Beach	NC	28449	910-458-5798	
Goose Creek State Park 2190 Camp Leach Rd *TF:* 877-722-6762 ■ *Web:* www.ncparks.gov	Washington	NC	27889	252-923-2191	
Gorges State Park 976 Grassy Ridge Rd *Web:* www.ncparks.gov	Sapphire	NC	28774	828-966-9099	
Hammocks Beach State Park 1572 Hammock Beach Rd *Web:* www.ncparks.gov	Swansboro	NC	28584	910-326-4881	326-2060
Jockey's Ridge State Park PO Box 592 *Web:* www.jockeysridgestatepark.com	Nags Head	NC	27959	252-441-7132	
Jones Lake State Park 4117 NC 242 Hwy *Web:* www.ncparks.gov	Elizabethtown	NC	28337	910-588-4550	
Jordan Lake State Recreation Area 280 State Pk Rd *TF:* 877-722-6762 ■ *Web:* www.ncparks.gov	Apex	NC	27523	919-362-0586	
Kerr Lake State Recreation Area 6254 Satterwhite Pt Rd *Web:* www.ncparks.gov	Henderson	NC	27537	252-456-2328	
Lake James State Park 6883 NC Hwy 126 PO Box 340 *Web:* www.ncparks.gov/lake-james-state-park	Nebo	NC	28761	828-584-7728	
Lake Norman State Park 159 Inland Sea Ln *Web:* ncparks.gov	Troutman	NC	28166	704-528-6350	
Lake Waccamaw State Park 1866 State Pk Dr *Web:* www.ncparks.gov	Lake Waccamaw	NC	28450	910-646-4748	
Lumber River State Park 2819 Princess Ann Rd *Web:* www.ncparks.gov/visit/parks/luri/main.php	Orrum	NC	28369	910-628-4564	
Medoc Mountain State Park 1541 Medoc State Pk Rd *Web:* www.ncparks.gov	Hollister	NC	27844	252-586-6588	

Phone | Fax

Morrow Mountain State Park
49104 Morrow Mtn Rd .... Albemarle NC 28001 704-982-4402
Web: www.ncparks.gov

Mount Jefferson State Natural Area
1481 Mt Jefferson State Park Rd .... West Jefferson NC 28694 336-246-9653
Web: ncparks.gov

Mount Mitchell State Park
2388 State Hwy 128 .... Burnsville NC 28714 828-675-4611 675-9655
Web: www.ncparks.gov

New River State Park
358 New River State Park Rd .... Laurel Springs NC 28644 336-982-2587
Web: www.ncparks.gov/visit/parks/neri/main.php

Pettigrew State Park 2252 Lk Shore Rd .... Creswell NC 27928 252-797-4475
Web: www.ncparks.gov/visit/parks/pett/main.php

Pilot Mountain State Park
1792 Pilot Knob Pk Rd .... Pinnacle NC 27043 336-325-2355
Web: www.ncparks.gov

Raven Rock State Park 3009 Raven Rock Rd .... Lillington NC 27546 910-893-4888
Web: www.ncparks.gov

Singletary Lake State Park 6707 NC 53 Hwy E .... Kelly NC 28448 910-669-2928
Web: www.ncparks.gov

South Mountains State Park (SOMO)
3001 S Mtns State Pk Ave .... Connelly Springs NC 28612 828-433-4772
Web: www.ncparks.gov

Stone Mountain State Park
3042 Frank Pkwy .... Roaring Gap NC 28668 336-957-8185
TF: 877-722-6762 ■ *Web:* ncparks.gov

Weymouth Woods Sandhills Nature Preserve
1024 Ft Bragg Rd .... Southern Pines NC 28387 910-692-2167
Web: www.ncparks.gov

William B Umstead State Park
8801 Glenwood Ave .... Raleigh NC 27617 919-571-4170
Web: ncparks.gov

North Dakota

Phone | Fax

Beaver Lake State Park 3850 70th St SE .... Wishek ND 58495 701-452-2752
Web: www.ndparks.com

De Mores State Historic Site PO Box 106 .... Medora ND 58645 701-623-4355
Web: www.nd.gov

Double Ditch State Historic Site
N Dakota 1804 .... Bismarck ND 58503 701-328-2666 328-3710
Web: www.history.nd.gov/historicsites/doubleditch/index.html

Doyle Memorial State Park
5981 Walt Hjelle Pkwy .... Wishek ND 58495 701-452-2351
Web: www.ndparks.com/parks/doyle-memorial-state-park

Former Governors' Mansion State Historic Site
612 E Blvd Ave .... Bismarck ND 58505 701-328-2666 328-3710
TF: 866-243-5352 ■ *Web:* www.nd.gov

Fort Abercrombie State Historic Site
PO Box 148 .... Abercrombie ND 58001 701-553-8513
Web: www.nd.gov

Fort Abraham Lincoln State Park
4480 Ft Lincoln Rd .... Mandan ND 58554 701-667-6340
Web: ndparks.com/parks/fort-abraham-lincoln-state-park

Fort Buford State Historic Site
15349 39th Ln NW .... Williston ND 58801 701-572-9034
Web: www.nd.gov

Fort Ransom State Park
5981 Walt Hjelle Pkwy .... Fort Ransom ND 58033 701-973-4331
Web: www.ndparks.com

Fort Stevenson State Park 1252A 41st St NW .... Garrison ND 58540 701-337-5576
Web: www.ndparks.com

Fort Totten State Historic Site
PO Box 224 .... Fort Totten ND 58335 701-766-4441
Web: www.nd.gov

Icelandic State Park 13571 Hwy 5 .... Cavalier ND 58220 701-265-4561
Web: www.ndparks.com

Indian Hills State Recreation Area & Resort
7302 14th St NW .... Garrison ND 58763 701-743-4122
Web: www.ndparks.com

Lake Metigoshe State Park
2 Lk Metigoshe State Pk .... Bottineau ND 58318 701-263-4651
Web: www.ndparks.com

Mouse River State Forest 307 - First St E .... Bottineau ND 58318 701-228-5422 228-5448
Web: www.ndsu.edu

Sully Creek State Recreation Area
c/o Ft Abraham Lincoln State Pk
4480 Ft Lincoln Rd .... Mandan ND 58554 701-667-6340
Web: www.parkrec.nd.gov

Tetrault Woods State Forest
1037 Forestry Dr .... Bottineau ND 58318 701-228-3700 228-5111
Web: www.ndsu.edu

Turtle River State Park 3084 Pk Ave .... Arvilla ND 58214 701-591-4445
Web: www.ndparks.com

Whitestone Hill State Historic Site
C/O Dorene Brandeburger 8692 98th Ave .... Monango ND 58436 701-349-4103
Web: history.nd.gov/historicsites/whitestone/index.html

Ohio

Phone | Fax

Adams Lake State Park
c/o Shawnee State Pk 4404 State Rt 125 .... Portsmouth OH 45663 740-858-6652
Web: parks.ohiodnr.gov/adamslake

Alum Creek State Park 3615 S Old State Rd .... Delaware OH 43015 740-548-4631
Web: alum-creek-state-park.org

Barkcamp State Park 65330 Barkcamp Rd .... Belmont OH 43718 740-484-4064
Web: www.ohiodnr.com

Beaver Creek State Park
12021 Echo Dell Rd .... East Liverpool OH 43920 330-385-3091
Web: www.ohiodnr.com

Blue Rock State Park 7924 Cutler Lk Rd .... Blue Rock OH 43720 740-674-4794
Web: www.ohiodnr.com/default.aspx?alias=www.ohiodnr.com/parks

Buck Creek State Park 1901 Buck Creek Ln .... Springfield OH 45502 937-322-5284
Web: www.ohiodnr.com

Buckeye Lake State Park
2905 Liebs Island Rd .... Millersport OH 43046 740-467-2690
Web: www.ohiodnr.com

Burr Oak State Park 10220 Burr Oak Lodge Rd .... Glouster OH 45732 740-767-3570
Web: www.ohiodnr.com

Caesar Creek State Park
8570 E State Rt 73 .... Waynesville OH 45068 513-897-1092
Web: www.caesarcreekstatepark.com

Catawba Island State Park
4049 E Moores Dock Rd .... Port Clinton OH 43452 419-797-4530
Web: www.ohiodnr.com

Cowan Lake State Park 1750 Osborn Rd .... Wilmington OH 45177 937-382-1096
Web: www.ohiodnr.com

Crane Creek State Park 2045 Morse Rd .... Columbus OH 43229 614-265-6561
Web: www.ohiodnr.com

Deer Creek State Park
20635 State Park Rd 20 .... Mount Sterling OH 43143 740-869-3124
Web: www.ohiodnr.com

Delaware State Park 5202 US Rt 23 N .... Delaware OH 43015 740-548-4631
TF: 866-644-6727 ■ *Web:* www.dnr.state.oh.us

Dillon State Park 5265 Dillon Hills Dr .... Nashport OH 43830 740-453-4377
Web: www.ohiodnr.com

East Fork State Park 3294 Elklick Rd .... Bethel OH 45106 513-734-4323
Web: www.ohiodnr.com

East Harbor State Park
1169 N Buck Rd .... Lakeside-Marblehead OH 43440 419-734-4424
Web: eastharborstatepark.org

Findley State Park 25381 State Rt 58 .... Wellington OH 44090 440-647-4490
Web: www.ohiodnr.com

Forked Run State Park
63300 SR- 124 PO Box 127 .... Reedsville OH 45772 740-378-6206
Web: www.ohiodnr.com

Geneva State Park
4499 Pandanarum Rd PO Box 429 .... Geneva OH 44041 440-466-8400
Web: www.ohiodnr.com

Great Seal State Park 4908 Marietta Rd .... Chillicothe OH 45601 740-663-2125
Web: www.ohiodnr.com

Guilford Lake State Park 6835 E Lake Rd .... Lisbon OH 44432 330-222-1712
Web: www.ohiodnr.com

Harrison Lake State Park
26246 Harrison Lk Rd .... Fayette OH 43521 419-237-2593
Web: www.ohiodnr.com

Headlands Beach State Park
c/o Cleveland Lakefront State Pk
8701 Lakeshore Blvd NE .... Cleveland OH 44108 216-881-8141
Web: www.dnr.state.oh.us

Hocking Hills State Park 19852 State Rt 664 S .... Logan OH 43138 740-385-6842
Web: thehockinghills.org

Hueston Woods State Park
6301 Pk Office Rd .... College Corner OH 45003 513-523-6347
Web: www.ohiodnr.com

Indian Lake State Park 12774 State Rt 235 N .... Lakeview OH 43331 937-843-2717
Web: www.ohiodnr.com

Jackson Lake State Park
35 Tommy Been Rd PO Box 174 .... Oak Hill OH 45656 740-596-5253
Web: www.ohiodnr.com

Jefferson Lake State Park
501 Township Rd 261A .... Richmond OH 43944 740-765-4459
Web: www.ohiodnr.com

John Bryan State Park 3790 SR- 370 .... Yellow Springs OH 45387 937-767-1274
Web: www.ohiodnr.com

Kelleys Island State Park
c/o Catawba Island State Pk
920 Division St .... Kelleys Island OH 43452 419-734-4424
Web: www.dnr.state.oh.us

Lake Hope State Park 27331 State Rt 278 .... McArthur OH 45651 740-596-4938
Web: parks.ohiodnr.gov/lakehope

Lake Logan State Park
20160 State Rd 664 20160 State Rd 664 .... Logan OH 43138 740-385-6842
Web: www.dnr.state.oh.us

Lake Loramie State Park
4401 Ft Loramie Swanders Rd .... Minster OH 45865 937-295-2011
Web: www.ohiodnr.com

Lake Milton State Park
16801 Mahoning Ave .... Lake Milton OH 44429 330-654-4989
Web: www.ohiodnr.com

Lake White State Park 2767 SR- 551 .... Waverly OH 45690 740-493-2212
Web: www.ohiodnr.com

Malabar Farm State Park 4050 Bromfield Rd .... Lucas OH 44843 419-892-2784 892-3988
Web: www.ohiodnr.com

Marblehead Lighthouse State Park
110 Lighthouse Dr .... Marblehead OH 43440 419-734-4424
Web: www.dnr.state.oh.us

Mary Jane Thurston State Park
1466 State Rt 65 .... McClure OH 43534 419-832-7662
TF: 866-644-6727 ■ *Web:* www.dnr.state.oh.us

Maumee Bay State Park 1400 State Pk Rd .... Oregon OH 43618 419-836-7758 836-8711
Web: www.ohiodnr.com

Middle Bass Island State Park
1719 Fox Rd .... Middle Bass Island OH 43446 419-285-0311
TF: 866-644-6727 ■ *Web:* parks.ohiodnr.gov

Mohican State Park 3116 SR- 3 .... Loudonville OH 44842 419-938-6222
Web: www.ohiodnr.com

Mosquito Lake State Park 1439 State Rt 305 .... Cortland OH 44410 330-637-2856
Web: www.ohiodnr.com

Mosquito Lake State Recreation Site
1439 State Rt 305 .... Cortland OH 44410 330-637-2856

Mount Gilead State Park
4119 State Rt 95 .... Mount Gilead OH 43338 419-946-1961
Web: www.ohiodnr.com

Phone | Fax

Muskingum River State Park
1390 Ellis Dam Rd .... Zanesville OH 43701 740-453-4377
Web: www.ohiodnr.com

ODNR Oil & Gas Resources Management
2045 Morse Rd Bldg C-3 .... Columbus OH 43229 740-869-3124

Ohio DNR 422 Lake Alma Rd.......................... Wellston OH 45692 740-384-4474
Web: oilandgas.ohiodnr.gov/well-information/oil-gas-well-database

Ohio DNR 4860 E Pk Dr............................. London OH 43140 937-322-5284
Web: parks.ohiodnr.gov/lakehope

Paint Creek State Park 280 Taylor Rd .... Bainbridge OH 45612 937-981-7061
TF: 866-644-6727 ■ *Web:* parks.ohiodnr.gov/paintcreek

Pike Lake State Park 1847 Pike Lk Rd .... Bainbridge OH 45612 740-493-2212
Web: www.pikelakestatepark.com/pikelake.html

Portage Lakes State Park 5031 Manchester Rd........... Akron OH 44319 330-644-2220 644-7550
Web: www.ohiodnr.com

Punderson State Park 11755 Kinsman Rd .... Newbury OH 44065 440-564-5465
Web: parks.ohiodnr.gov/punderson

Pymatuning State Park PO Box 1000 .... Andover OH 44003 440-293-6030
Web: www.ohiodnr.com

Rocky Fork State Park 9800 N Shore Dr............. Hillsboro OH 45133 937-393-4284
Web: www.ohiodnr.com

Salt Fork State Park 14755 Cadiz Rd .... Lore City OH 43755 740-439-3521
Web: www.ohiodnr.com

Scioto Trail State Park 144 Lake Rd................ Chillicothe OH 45601 866-644-6727
TF: 866-644-6727 ■ *Web:* parks.ohiodnr.gov

Shawnee State Park 4404 SR- 125............ West Portsmouth OH 45663 740-858-6652
Web: www.ohiodnr.com

Stonelick State Park 2895 Lake Dr.............. Pleasant Plain OH 45162 513-734-4323
Web: www.ohiodnr.com

Strouds Run State Park 2045 Morse Rd............ Columbus OH 43229 740-592-2302
TF: 800-945-3543 ■ *Web:* www.ohiodnr.com

Sycamore State Park 4675 N Diamond Mill Rd......... Trotwood OH 45426 513-523-6347
Web: www.ohiodnr.com

Tar Hollow State Park
16396 Tar Hollow Rd .... Laurelville OH 43135 740-887-4818
Web: www.ohiodnr.com

Tinkers Creek State Park
2045 Morse Rd 10303 Aurora Hudson Rd .... Columbus OH 43229 440-564-2279
Web: www.dnr.state.oh.us

Van Buren State Park 12259 Township Rd 218........ Van Buren OH 45889 419-832-7662
TF: 866-644-6727 ■ *Web:* www.dnr.state.oh.us

West Branch State Park 5708 Esworthy Rd .... Ravenna OH 44266 330-296-3239
Web: www.ohiodnr.com

Wolf Run State Park 16170 Wolf Run Rd............. Caldwell OH 43724 740-732-5035
Web: www.ohiodnr.com

Oklahoma

Phone | Fax

Adair State Park Hwy 51 & Hwy 59 .... Stilwell OK 74960 918-696-6613
Web: www.oklahomacampers.com

Alabaster Caverns State Park 217036 SH 50A......... Freedom OK 73842 580-621-3381 621-3572
Web: www.travelok.com

Arrowhead State Park 3995 Main Pk Rd............. Canadian OK 74425 918-339-2204 339-7236
Web: www.travelok.com

Beaver Dunes State Park Hwy 270 N .... Beaver OK 73932 580-625-3373
TF: 800-654-8240 ■ *Web:* www.travelok.com

Beavers Bend Resort Park PO Box 10 .... Broken Bow OK 74728 580-494-6300
TF: 800-435-5514 ■ *Web:* www.beaversbend.com

Bernice State Park 901 State Pk Rd.................. Grove OK 74344 918-786-9447 787-5634
Web: www.travelok.com

Black Mesa State Park & Nature Preserve
County Rd 325 .... Kenton OK 73946 580-426-2222 426-2405
Web: www.travelok.com

Boggy Depot State Park 475 S Pk Ln .... Atoka OK 74525 580-889-5625 889-7868
Web: www.travelok.com

Boiling Springs State Park
207697 Boiling Springs Rd .... Woodward OK 73801 580-256-7664 256-4338
Web: www.travelok.com

Cherokee Landing State Park 28610 Pk 20........... Park Hill OK 74451 918-457-5716 457-4871
Web: www.travelok.com

Cherokee State Park N 4475 Rd .... Langley OK 74350 918-435-8066
TF: 866-602-4653 ■ *Web:* www.travelok.com

Clayton Lake State Park Hwy 271 .... Clayton OK 74536 918-569-7981
Web: www.travelok.com

Disney/Little Blue State Park Hwy 28 E.............. Disney OK 74340 918-435-8066 435-2101
TF: 800-622-6317 ■ *Web:* www.travelok.com

Dripping Springs State Park
16830 Dripping Springs Rd .... Okmulgee OK 74447 918-756-5971 759-9933
TF: 800-622-6317 ■ *Web:* www.travelok.com/listings/view.profile/id.2368

Fort Cobb Lake State Park
27022 Copperhead Rd .... Fort Cobb OK 73038 405-643-2249 643-5167
TF: 800-622-6317 ■ *Web:* www.travelok.com

Foss State Park 10252 Hwy 44.......................... Foss OK 73647 580-592-4433 592-4701
TF: 800-622-6317 ■ *Web:* www.travelok.com

Gloss Mountain State Park Hwy 412 .... Fairview OK 73737 580-227-2512 227-2513
Web: www.travelok.com/listings/view.profile/id.3030

Great Plains State Park
22487 E 1566 Rd .... Mountain Park OK 73559 580-569-2032 569-2375
TF: 800-622-6317 ■ *Web:* www.travelok.com

Great Salt Plains State Park Rt 1 PO Box 28............... Jet OK 73749 580-626-4731
Web: www.travelok.com

Greenleaf State Park Hwy 10 S........................ Braggs OK 74423 918-487-5196 487-5406
Web: www.travelok.com

Heavener Runestone State Park
18365 Runestone Rd .... Heavener OK 74937 918-653-2241
Web: travelok.com

Honey Creek State Park 901 State Pk Rd .... Grove OK 74344 918-786-9447 787-5634
TF: 800-622-6317 ■ *Web:* www.travelok.com

Keystone State Park 1926 S Hwy 151............ Sand Springs OK 74063 918-865-4991 865-2083
TF: 800-654-8240 ■ *Web:* www.travelok.com/listings/view.profile/id.4163

Lake Eufaula State Park HC 60 PO .... Checotah OK 74426 918-689-7337
Web: www.travelok.com

Phone | Fax

Lake Murray State Park
120 N Robinson Ave 6th Fl.................. Oklahoma City OK 73152 800-652-6552
TF: 800-652-6552 ■ *Web:* www.travelok.com

Lake Thunderbird State Park 13101 Alameda Dr........ Norman OK 73026 405-360-3572 366-8150
Web: www.travelok.com

Lake Wister State Park 25567 US Hwy 270 .... Wister OK 74966 918-655-7212 655-7274
TF: 800-622-6317 ■ *Web:* www.travelok.com

Little Sahara State Park 101 Main St................ Waynoka OK 73860 580-824-1471 824-1472
Web: www.travelok.com

McGee Creek State Park
576-A S McGee Creek Dam Rd......................... Atoka OK 74525 580-889-5822 889-7868
Web: www.travelok.com

Okmulgee State Park
16830 Dripping Springs Rd .... Okmulgee OK 74447 918-756-5971 759-9933
Web: www.travelok.com/listings/view.profile/id.5520

Osage Hills State Park
2131 Osage Hills State Pk Rd .... Pawhuska OK 74056 918-336-4141 337-2176
TF: 800-622-6317 ■ *Web:* www.travelok.com

Raymond Gary State Park Hwy 70 .... Fort Towson OK 74735 580-873-2307 326-2305
TF: 800-622-6317 ■ *Web:* www.travelok.com

Red Rock Canyon State Park Hwy 281 S............... Hinton OK 73047 405-542-6344
Web: www.travelok.com

Robbers Cave State Park Hwy 2 N .... Wilburton OK 74578 918-465-2565 465-5763
TF: 800-654-8240 ■ *Web:* travelok.com

Sequoyah Bay State Park 6237 E 100th St N .... Wagoner OK 74467 918-683-0878 687-6797
TF: 800-622-6317 ■ *Web:* www.travelok.com

Sequoyah State Park & Western Hills Guest Ranch
17131 Pk 10... Hulbert OK 74441 918-772-2046 772-3042
Web: www.travelok.com

Snowdale State Park 501 S 439 .... Salina OK 74361 918-434-2651 435-2101
TF: 800-622-6317 ■ *Web:* www.travelok.com

Southwestern Oklahoma State University (SWOSU)
100 Campus Dr .... Weatherford OK 73096 580-772-6611
Web: www.swosu.edu

Spavinaw State Park 555 S Main .... Spavinaw OK 74366 918-589-2651 435-2101
TF: 800-622-6317 ■ *Web:* www.travelok.com

Talimena State Park 50884 US Hwy 271 .... Talihina OK 74571 918-567-2052 567-2052
Web: www.travelok.com

Twin Bridges State Park 14801 Hwy 137 S .... Fairland OK 74343 918-540-2545 540-2545
TF: 800-622-6317 ■ *Web:* www.travelok.com

Wah-Sha-She State Park HC 75 Hwy 60.............. Copan OK 74022 918-532-4334 337-2176
TF: 800-622-6317 ■ *Web:* www.travelok.com

Walnut Creek State Park PO Box 26 .... Prue OK 74060 918-242-3362 865-2050

Oregon

Phone | Fax

Alfred A. Loeb State Park
725 Summer St NE Ste C .... Salem OR 97301 503-986-0707
TF: 800-551-6949 ■
Web: oregonstateparks.org/index.cfm?do=parkpage.dsp_parkpage&parkid=51

Alsea Bay Historic Interpretive Ctr
725 Summer St NE Ste C .... Salem OR 97301 800-551-6949
TF: 800-551-6949 ■ *Web:* www.oregonstateparks.org

Beverly Beach State Park 198 NE 123rd St .... Newport OR 97365 800-452-5687
TF: 800-452-5687 ■ *Web:* www.oregonstateparks.org

Bob Straub State Park US 101 .... Pacific City OR 97112 800-551-6949
TF: 800-551-6949 ■ *Web:* www.oregonstateparks.org

Bonnie Lure State Recreation Area
11321 SW Terwilliger Blvd.......................... Portland OR 97219 800-551-6949
TF: 800-551-6949 ■ *Web:* www.oregonstateparks.org

Bridal Veil Falls State Scenic Viewpoint
E Bridal Veil Rd PO Box 100...................... Bridal Veil OR 97010 800-551-6949
TF: 800-551-6949 ■ *Web:* www.oregonstateparks.org

Bullards Beach State Park PO Box 569............... Bandon OR 97411 541-347-2209
TF: 800-551-6949 ■
Web: oregonstateparks.org/index.cfm?do=parkpage.dsp_parkpage&parkid=50

Cape Arago State Park Cape Arago Hwy.............. Coos Bay OR 97420 541-888-3778
TF: 800-551-6949 ■ *Web:* www.oregonstateparks.org

Cape Blanco State Park 39745 S Hwy 101......... Port Orford OR 97465 541-332-6774
Web: www.oregonstateparks.org

Cape Lookout State Park
13000 Whiskey Creek Rd W .... Tillamook OR 97141 503-842-4981
Web: oregonstateparks.org/index.cfm?do=parkpage.dsp_parkpage&parkid=134

Cascadia State Park 725 Summer St NE Ste C........... Salem OR 97301 503-986-0707
Web: www.oregonstateparks.org

Cline Falls State Scenic Viewpoint
62976 OB Riley Rd.................................. Redmond OR 97756 800-551-6949
TF: 800-551-6949 ■ *Web:* www.oregonstateparks.org

Collier Memorial State Park 46000 Hwy 97 N......... Chiloquin OR 97624 541-783-2471
Web: www.oregonstateparks.org

Coquille Myrtle Grove State Natural Site
PO Box 569 .... Myrtle Point OR 97458 800-551-6949
TF: 800-551-6949 ■ *Web:* www.oregonstateparks.org

Cove Palisades State Park 7300 Jordan Rd............. Culver OR 97734 541-546-3412
Web: www.oregonstateparks.org

Crissey Field State Recreation Site
1655 Hwy 101 N................................... Brookings OR 97415 541-469-2021
TF: 800-551-6949 ■ *Web:* www.oregonstateparks.org

D River State Recreation Site
725 Summer St NE Ste C .... Salem OR 97301 541-994-7341
TF: 800-551-6949 ■ *Web:* www.oregonstateparks.org

Dabney State Recreation Area
725 Summer St NE Ste C .... Salem OR 97301 503-695-2261
TF: 800-551-6949 ■ *Web:* www.oregonstateparks.org

Darlingtonia State Natural Site
84505 Hwy 101 S .... Florence OR 97439 541-997-3851
TF: 800-551-6949 ■ *Web:* www.oregonstateparks.org

Del Rey Beach State Recreation Site
100 Peter Iredale Rd .... Hammond OR 97121 800-551-6949
TF: 800-551-6949 ■ *Web:* www.oregonstateparks.org

				Phone	Fax
Depoe Bay Whale Center *Oregon Parks and Recreation Department* 58 US-101 198 NE 123rd St *TF:* 800-551-6949 ■ *Web:* www.oregonstateparks.org	Depoe Bay	OR	97341	541-765-3304	
Deschutes River State Recreation Area 89600 Biggs-Rufus Hwy *Web:* oregonstateparks.org/index.cfm?do=parkpage.dsp_parkpage&parkid=29	Wasco	OR	97065	541-739-2322	
Detroit Lake State Recreation Area PO Box 549 *Web:* www.oregonstateparks.org	Detroit	OR	97342	503-854-3346	
Devil's Lake State Recreation Area 198 NE 123rd St *TF:* 800-551-6949 ■ *Web:* www.oregonstateparks.org	Lincoln City	OR	97367	800-551-6949	
Dexter State Recreation Site 725 Summer St NE Ste C *Web:* www.oregonstateparks.org	Salem	OR	97301	541-937-1173	
Driftwood Beach State Recreation Site 5580 S Coast Hwy *TF:* 800-551-6949 ■ *Web:* www.oregonstateparks.org	Newport	OR	97366	800-551-6949	
Ecola State Park 84318 Ecola State Park Rd *Web:* www.oregonstateparks.org	Cannon Beach	OR	97110	503-436-2844	
Ellmaker State Wayside 198 NE 123rd St. *TF:* 800-551-6949 ■ *Web:* www.oregonstateparks.org	Newport	OR	97365	800-551-6949	
Fall Creek State Recreation Area 84610 Peninsula Rd PO Box 511 *Web:* oregonstateparks.org/index.cfm?do=parkpage.dsp_parkpage&parkid=176	Fall Creek	OR	97438	541-937-1173	
Farewell Bend State Recreation Area 23751 Old Hwy 30 *Web:* www.oregonstateparks.org	Huntington	OR	97907	541-869-2365	
Fogarty Creek State Recreation Area 725 Summer St NE Ste C *TF:* 800-551-6949 ■ *Web:* www.oregonstateparks.org	Salem	OR	97341	800-551-6949	
Fort Rock State Natural Area 725 Summer St NE Ste C *TF:* 800-551-6949 ■ *Web:* www.oregonstateparks.org	Salem	OR	97739	800-551-6949	
Fort Stevens State Park 100 Peter Iredale Rd *Web:* www.oregonstateparks.org	Hammond	OR	97121	503-861-1671	
Gleneden Beach State Recreation Site 198 NE 123rd St *TF:* 800-551-6949 ■ *Web:* www.oregonstateparks.org	Newport	OR	97365	800-551-6949	
Golden & Silver Falls State Natural Area 89814 Cape Arago Hwy *Web:* www.oregonstateparks.org	Coos Bay	OR	97420	541-888-3778	
Government Island State Recreation Area 725 Summer St NE Ste C *TF:* 800-551-6949 ■ *Web:* www.oregonstateparks.org/park_250.php	Salem	OR	97301	800-551-6949	
Governor Patterson Memorial State Recreation Site 5580 S Coast Hwy 5580 S Coast Hwy *TF:* 800-551-6949 ■ *Web:* www.oregonstateparks.org	Waldport	OR	97394	800-551-6949	
H. B. Van Duzer Forest State Scenic Corridor 198 NE 123rd St *TF:* 800-551-6949 ■ *Web:* www.oregonstateparks.org	Otis	OR	97368	800-551-6949	
Harris Beach State Park 1655 Hwy 101 N *Web:* oregonstateparks.org/index.cfm?do=parkpage.dsp_parkpage&parkid=58	Brookings	OR	97415	541-469-2021	
Heceta Head Lighthouse State Scenic Viewpoint 93111 Hwy 101 N *TF:* 800-551-6949 ■ *Web:* www.oregonstateparks.org	Florence	OR	97439	800-551-6949	
Hoffman Memorial State Wayside PO Box 569 *TF:* 800-551-6949 ■ *Web:* www.oregonstateparks.org	Myrtle Point	OR	97458	800-551-6949	
Humbug Mountain State Park PO Box 1345 *Web:* www.oregonstateparks.org	Port Orford	OR	97465	541-332-6774	
Jasper State Recreation Site 725 Summer St NE Ste C *Web:* www.oregonstateparks.org	Salem	OR	97301	541-937-1173	
Joseph H. Stewart State Recreation Area 35251 Hwy 62 *TF:* 800-452-5687 ■ *Web:* www.oregonstateparks.org	Prospect	OR	97536	541-560-3334	
Kam Wah Chung State Heritage Site (KWC) 725 Summer St NE Ste C *TF:* 800-551-6949 ■ *Web:* oregonstateparks.org/index.cfm?do=parkpage.dsp_parkpage&parkid=5	Salem	OR	97301	503-986-0707	
Koberg Beach State Recreation Site 725 Summer St NE Ste C *TF:* 800-551-6949 ■ *Web:* oregonstateparks.org/index.cfm?do=parkpage.dsp_parkpage&parkid=115	Salem	OR	97301	503-986-0707	
Lake Owyhee State Park 725 Summer St NE Ste C *TF:* 800-551-6949 ■ *Web:* oregonstateparks.org/index.cfm?do=parkpage.dsp_parkpage&parkid=10	Salem	OR	97301	503-986-0707	
LaPine State Park 15800 State Recreation Rd *TF:* 800-551-6949 ■ *Web:* oregonstateparks.org/index.cfm?do=parkpage.dsp_parkpage&parkid=32	La Pine	OR	97739	800-551-6949	
Lewis & Clark State Recreation Site 725 Summer St NE Ste C *TF:* 800-551-6949 ■ *Web:* oregonstateparks.org/index.cfm?do=parkpage.dsp_parkpage&parkid=116	Salem	OR	97301	503-986-0707	
Manhattan Beach State Recreation Site 725 Summer St NE Ste C *TF:* 800-551-6949 ■ *Web:* oregonstateparks.org/index.cfm?do=parkpage.dsp_parkpage&parkid=138	Salem	OR	97301	503-986-0707	
Milo McIver State Park 24101 SE Entrance Rd *Web:* www.oregonstateparks.org	Estacada	OR	97023	503-630-7150	
Nehalem Bay State Park 9500 Sandpiper Ln PO Box 366 *Web:* www.oregonstateparks.org	Nehalem	OR	97131	503-368-5154	
Neskowin Beach State Recreation Site 198 NE 123rd St *TF:* 800-551-6949 ■ *Web:* www.oregonstateparks.org	Neskowin	OR	97149	800-551-6949	
North Santiam State Recreation Area PO Box 549 *TF:* 800-551-6949 ■ *Web:* www.oregonstateparks.org	Detroit	OR	97342	800-551-6949	
OC&E Woods Line State Trail 46000 Hwy 97 N 46000 Hwy 97 N *TF:* 800-551-6949 ■ *Web:* oregonstateparks.org/index.cfm?do=parkpage.dsp_parkpage&parkid=167	Chiloquin	OR	97624	541-883-5558	
Oceanside Beach State Recreation Site 13000 Whiskey Creek Rd W *TF:* 800-551-6949 ■ *Web:* www.oregonstateparks.org	Tillamook	OR	97141	800-551-6949	
Ona Beach State Park 5580 S Coast Hwy *TF:* 800-551-6949 ■ *Web:* www.oregonstateparks.org	Newport	OR	97366	800-551-6949	
Ontario State Recreation Site 23751 Old Hwy 30 *TF:* 800-551-6949 ■ *Web:* www.oregonstateparks.org	Huntington	OR	97907	800-551-6949	
Otter Point State Recreation Site PO Box 1345 *TF:* 800-551-6949 ■ *Web:* www.oregonstateparks.org	Gold Beach	OR	97444	800-551-6949	
Paradise Point State Recreation Site PO Box 1345 *TF:* 800-551-6949 ■ *Web:* www.oregonstateparks.org	Port Orford	OR	97465	800-551-6949	
Prineville Reservoir State Park 725 Summer St NE Ste C *Web:* www.oregonstateparks.org	Salem	OR	97301	541-447-4363	
Seneca Fouts Memorial State Natural Area Wygant Trail *TF:* 800-551-6949 ■ *Web:* www.oregonstateparks.org	Hood River	OR	97014	800-551-6949	
Shore Acres State Park 89039 Cape Arago Hwy *Web:* www.oregonstateparks.org	Coos Bay	OR	97420	541-888-3732	
Silver Falls State Park 20024 Silver Falls Hwy SE *Web:* www.oregonstateparks.org	Sublimity	OR	97385	503-873-8681	
Smith Rock State Park 9241 NE Crooked River Dr *Web:* www.oregonstateparks.org	Terrebonne	OR	97760	541-548-7501	
South Beach State Park 5580 S Coast Hwy *TF:* 800-452-5687 ■ *Web:* oregonstateparks.org/index.cfm?do=parkpage.dsp_parkpage&parkid=149	Newport	OR	97366	541-867-4715	
Starvation Creek State Park Historic Columbia River Highway State Trail *Web:* www.oregonstateparks.org	Cascade Locks	OR	97014	503-695-2261	
Stonefield Beach State Recreation Site 725 Summer St NE 84505 Hwy 101 S *TF:* 800-551-6949 ■ *Web:* www.oregonstateparks.org	Salem	OR	97301	800-551-6949	
Succor Creek State Natural Area 1298 Lk Owyhee Dam Rd *TF:* 800-551-6949 ■ *Web:* www.oregonstateparks.org	Adrian	OR	97901	800-551-6949	
Sunset Bay State Park 89814 Cape Arago Hwy *Web:* www.oregonstateparks.org	Coos Bay	OR	97420	541-888-3778	
Tokatee Klootchman State Natural Site 93111 Hwy 101 N *TF:* 800-551-6949 ■ *Web:* www.oregonstateparks.org	Florence	OR	97439	800-551-6949	
Touvelle State Recreation Site Table Rock Rd 3792 N River Rd *TF:* 800-551-6949 ■ *Web:* www.oregonstateparks.org	Central Point	OR	97502	541-983-2277	
Tryon Creek State Natural Area 11321 SW Terwilliger Blvd *Web:* www.oregonstateparks.org	Portland	OR	97219	503-636-9886	
Tub Springs State Wayside 12845 Green Springs Hwy 3792 N River Rd *TF:* 800-551-6949 ■ *Web:* www.oregonstateparks.org	Ashland	OR	97520	800-551-6949	
Tumalo State Park 64120 OB Riley Rd *Web:* www.oregonstateparks.org	Bend	OR	97701	541-382-3586	
Umpqua Lighthouse State Park 84505 Hwy 101 S *TF:* 800-551-6949 ■ *Web:* www.oregonstateparks.org	Florence	OR	97439	800-551-6949	
Unity Lake State Recreation Site 725 Summer St NE Ste C *TF:* 800-551-6949 ■ *Web:* www.oregonstateparks.org	Salem	OR	97301	541-932-4453	
W.B. Nelson State Recreation Site 5580 S Coast Hwy *TF:* 800-551-6949 ■ *Web:* www.oregonstateparks.org	Newport	OR	97366	800-551-6949	
Wallowa Lake State Park 72214 Marina Ln *Web:* www.oregonstateparks.org	Joseph	OR	97846	541-388-6055	
Willamette Stone State Heritage Site 11321 SW Terwilliger Blvd *TF:* 800-551-6949 ■ *Web:* www.oregonstateparks.org	Portland	OR	97219	800-551-6949	
William M. Tugman State Park 72549 Hwy 101 *TF:* 800-551-6949 ■ *Web:* oregonstateparks.org/index.cfm?do=parkpage.dsp_parkpage&parkid=69	Lakeside	OR	97449	800-551-6949	
Winchuck State Recreation Site 1655 Hwy 101 N *TF:* 800-551-6949 ■ *Web:* www.oregonstateparks.org	Brookings	OR	97415	800-551-6949	
Wolf Creek Inn State Heritage Site PO Box 6 *Web:* www.oregonstateparks.org	Wolf Creek	OR	97497	541-866-2474	
Yachats Ocean Road State Natural Site 5580 S Coast Hwy *TF:* 800-551-6949 ■ *Web:* www.oregonstateparks.org	Newport	OR	97366	800-551-6949	

Pennsylvania

				Phone	Fax
Allegheny Islands State Park c/o Point State Park 601 Commonwealth Pl Bldg A *Web:* www.dcnr.state.pa.us/stateparks/parks/alleghenyislands.aspx	Pittsburgh	PA	15222	412-565-2850	
Bald Eagle State Park 149 Main Pk Rd *Web:* www.dcnr.state.pa.us	Howard	PA	16841	814-625-2775	
Beltzville State Park 2950 Pohopoco Dr *Web:* www.dcnr.state.pa.us	Lehighton	PA	18235	610-377-0045	
Bendigo State Park 533 State Pk Rd *Web:* www.dcnr.state.pa.us	Johnsonburg	PA	15845	814-965-2646	
Benjamin Rush State Park c/o Ft Washington State Pk *Web:* www.dcnr.state.pa.us	Fort Washington	PA	19034	215-591-5250	

Name / Address	City	State	Zip	Phone	Fax
Big Pocono State Park c/o Tobyhanna State Pk PO Box 387 *Web:* www.dcnr.state.pa.us/stateparks/parks/bigpocono.aspx	Tobyhanna	PA	18466	570-894-8336	
Big Spring State Park c/o Colonel Denning State Pk 1599 Doubling Gap Rd *Web:* www.dcnr.state.pa.us/stateparks/parks/bigspring.aspx	Newville	PA	17241	717-776-5272	
Black Moshannon State Park 4216 Beaver Rd *Web:* www.dcnr.state.pa.us	Philipsburg	PA	16866	814-342-5960	
Blue Knob State Park 124 Pk Rd *Web:* www.dcnr.state.pa.us	Imler	PA	16655	814-276-3576	
Buchanan's Birthplace State Park c/o Cowans Gap State Pk 6235 Aughwick Rd *Web:* www.dcnr.state.pa.us/stateparks/parks/buchanansbirthplace.aspx	Fort Loudon	PA	17224	717-485-3948	
Bucktail State Park c/o Region 1 Office *Web:* www.dcnr.state.pa.us	Emporium	PA	15834	814-486-3365	
Caledonia State Park 101 Pine Grove Rd *Web:* www.dcnr.state.pa.us/stateparks/parks/caledonia.aspx	Fayetteville	PA	17222	717-352-2161	352-7026
Canoe Creek State Park 205 Canoe Creek Rd *Web:* www.dcnr.state.pa.us	Hollidaysburg	PA	16648	814-695-6807	
Chapman State Park 4790 Chapman Dam Rd *Web:* www.dcnr.state.pa.us	Clarendon	PA	16313	814-723-0250	
Cherry Springs State Park c/o Lyman Run State Pk 454 Lyman Run Rd *Web:* www.dcnr.state.pa.us/stateparks/parks/cherrysprings.aspx	Galeton	PA	16922	814-435-5010	
Clear Creek State Park 38 Clear Creek State Pk Rd *Web:* www.dcnr.state.pa.us	Sigel	PA	15860	814-752-2368	
Codorus State Park 2600 Smith Stn Rd *Web:* www.dcnr.state.pa.us	Hanover	PA	17331	717-637-2816	637-4720
Colonel Denning State Park 1599 Doubling Gap Rd *Web:* www.dcnr.state.pa.us	Newville	PA	17241	717-776-5272	
Colton Point State Park c/o Leonard Harrison State Pk 4797 Rt 660 *Web:* www.dcnr.state.pa.us/stateparks/parks/coltonpoint.aspx	Wellsboro	PA	16901	570-724-3061	
Cook Forest State Park PO Box 120 *Web:* www.dcnr.state.pa.us	Cooksburg	PA	16217	814-744-8407	
Cowans Gap State Park 6235 Aughwick Rd *Web:* www.dcnr.state.pa.us/stateparks/parks/cowansgap.aspx	Fort Loudon	PA	17224	717-485-3948	
Delaware Canal State Park 11 Lodi Hill Rd *Web:* www.dcnr.state.pa.us	Upper Black Eddy	PA	18972	610-982-5560	
Denton Hill State Park c/o Lyman Run 454 Lyman Run Rd *Web:* www.dcnr.state.pa.us/stateparks/parks/dentonhill.aspx	Galeton	PA	16922	814-435-2115	
Elk State Park c/o Bendigo State Pk 533 State Pk Rd *Web:* www.dcnr.state.pa.us/stateparks/parks/elk.aspx	Johnsonburg	PA	15845	814-965-2646	
Evansburg State Park 851 May Hall Rd *Web:* www.dcnr.state.pa.us	Collegeville	PA	19426	610-409-1150	
Fort Washington State Park 500 Bethlehem Pk *Web:* www.dcnr.state.pa.us	Fort Washington	PA	19034	215-591-5250	
Fowlers Hollow State Park c/o Colonel Denning State Pk 1599 Doubling Gap Rd *Web:* www.dcnr.state.pa.us/stateparks/parks/fowlershollow.aspx	Newville	PA	17241	717-776-5272	
Frances Slocum State Park 565 Mt Olivet Rd *Web:* www.dcnr.state.pa.us/stateparks/parks/francesslocum.aspx	Wyoming	PA	18644	570-696-3525	
French Creek State Park 843 Pk Rd *Web:* www.dcnr.state.pa.us	Elverson	PA	19520	610-582-9680	
Gifford Pinchot State Park 2200 Rosstown Rd *Web:* www.dcnr.state.pa.us	Lewisberry	PA	17339	717-432-5011	
Gouldsboro State Park c/o Tobyhanna State Pk PO Box 387 *Web:* www.dcnr.state.pa.us/stateparks/parks/gouldsboro.aspx	Tobyhanna	PA	18466	570-894-8336	
Greenwood Furnace State Park 15795 Greenwood Rd *Web:* www.dcnr.state.pa.us	Huntingdon	PA	16652	814-667-1800	
Hickory Run State Park PO Box 81 *Web:* www.dcnr.state.pa.us/stateparks/parks/hickoryrun.aspx	White Haven	PA	18661	570-443-0400	
Hills Creek State Park 111 Spillway Rd *Web:* www.dcnr.state.pa.us	Wellsboro	PA	16901	570-724-4246	
Hyner Run State Park 86 Hyner Pk Rd *Web:* www.dcnr.state.pa.us/stateparks/parks/hynerrun.aspx	Hyner	PA	17738	570-923-6000	
Hyner View State Park c/o Hyner Run State Pk 86 Hyner Pk Rd *Web:* www.dcnr.state.pa.us/stateparks/parks/hynerview.aspx	Hyner	PA	17738	570-923-6000	
Jacobsburg Environmental Education Ctr 835 Jacobsburg Rd *Web:* www.dcnr.state.pa.us	Wind Gap	PA	18091	610-746-2801	
Jennings Environmental Education Ctr 2951 Prospect Rd *Web:* www.dcnr.state.pa.us	Slippery Rock	PA	16057	724-794-6011	
Joseph E. Ibberson Conservation Area c/o Little Buffalo State Pk 1579 State Pk Rd *Web:* www.dcnr.state.pa.us/stateparks/parks/josepheibberson.aspx	Newport	PA	17074	717-567-9255	
Kettle Creek State Park 97 Kettle Creek Pk Ln *Web:* www.dcnr.state.pa.us	Renovo	PA	17764	570-923-6004	
Keystone State Park 1150 Keystone Pk Rd *Web:* www.dcnr.state.pa.us	Derry	PA	15627	724-668-2939	
Kings Gap Environmental Education & Training Ctr 500 Kings Gap Rd *Web:* www.dcnr.state.pa.us	Carlisle	PA	17015	717-486-5031	
Kinzua Bridge State Park c/o Bendigo State Pk 533 State Pk Rd *Web:* www.dcnr.state.pa.us/stateparks/parks/kinzuabridge.aspx	Johnsonburg	PA	15845	814-965-2646	
Kooser State Park 943 Glades Pk *Web:* www.dcnr.state.pa.us	Somerset	PA	15501	814-445-8673	
Lackawanna State Park 1839 Abington Rd *Web:* www.dcnr.state.pa.us/stateparks/parks/lackawanna.aspx	North Abington Township	PA	18414	570-945-3239	
Laurel Hill State Park 1454 Laurel Hill Pk Rd *Web:* www.dcnr.state.pa.us	Somerset	PA	15501	814-445-7725	
Laurel Mountain State Park c/o Linn Run *Web:* www.dcnr.state.pa.us/stateparks/parks/laurelmountain.aspx	Rector	PA	15677	724-238-6623	
Laurel Ridge State Park 1117 Jim Mtn Rd *Web:* www.dcnr.state.pa.us	Rockwood	PA	15557	724-455-3744	
Laurel Summit State Park PO Box 50 *Web:* www.dcnr.state.pa.us/stateparks/parks/laurelsummit.aspx	Rector	PA	15677	724-238-6623	
Lehigh Gorge State Park RR 1 PO Box 81 *Web:* www.dcnr.state.pa.us/stateparks/parks/lehighgorge.aspx	White Haven	PA	18661	570-443-0400	
Leonard Harrison State Park 4797 Rt 660 *Web:* www.dcnr.state.pa.us/stateparks/parks/leonardharrison.aspx	Wellsboro	PA	16901	570-724-3061	
Linn Run State Park PO Box 50 *Web:* www.dcnr.state.pa.us	Rector	PA	15677	724-238-6623	
Little Buffalo State Park 1579 State Pk Rd *Web:* www.dcnr.state.pa.us	Newport	PA	17074	717-567-9255	
Little Pine State Park 4205 Little Pine Creek Rd *Web:* www.dcnr.state.pa.us/stateparks/parks/littlepine.aspx	Waterville	PA	17776	570-753-6000	
Little Pine State Park c/o Little Pine State Pk 4205 Little Pine Creek Rd *Web:* www.dcnr.state.pa.us/stateparks/parks/upperpinebottom.aspx	Waterville	PA	17776	570-753-6000	
Locust Lake State Park 687 Tuscarora Pk Rd *Web:* www.dcnr.state.pa.us/stateparks/parks/locustlake.aspx	Barnesville	PA	18214	570-467-2404	
Lyman Run State Park 454 Lyman Run Rd *Web:* www.dcnr.state.pa.us/stateparks/parks/lymanrun.aspx	Galeton	PA	16922	814-435-5010	
Marsh Creek State Park 675 Pk Rd *Web:* www.dcnr.state.pa.us	Downingtown	PA	19335	610-458-5119	
Maurice K. Goddard State Park 684 Lk Wilhelm Rd *Web:* www.dcnr.state.pa.us	Sandy Lake	PA	16145	724-253-4833	
McCalls Dam State Park 17215 Buffalo Rd *Web:* www.dcnr.state.pa.us/stateparks/parks/mccallsdam.aspx	Mifflinburg	PA	17844	570-966-1455	
Memorial Lake State Park 18 Boundary Rd *Web:* www.dcnr.state.pa.us/stateparks/parks/memoriallake.aspx	Grantville	PA	17028	717-865-6470	
Milton State Park Bridge Ave *Web:* www.dcnr.state.pa.us/stateparks/parks/milton.aspx	Sunbury	PA	17801	570-988-5557	
Mont Alto State Park 101 Pine Grove Rd *Web:* www.dcnr.state.pa.us/stateparks/parks/montalto.aspx	Fayetteville	PA	17222	717-352-2161	352-7026
Moraine State Park 225 Pleasant Vly Rd *Web:* www.dcnr.state.pa.us/stateparks/parks/moraine.aspx	Portersville	PA	16051	724-368-8811	
Mount Pisgah State Park 28 Entrance Rd *Web:* www.dcnr.state.pa.us/stateparks/parks/mtpisgah.aspx	Troy	PA	16947	570-297-2734	
Nescopeck State Park 1137 Honey Hole Rd *Web:* www.dcnr.state.pa.us/stateparks/parks/nescopeck.aspx	Drums	PA	18222	570-403-2006	
Neshaminy State Park 3401 State Rd *Web:* www.dcnr.state.pa.us	Bensalem	PA	19020	215-639-4538	
Nockamixon State Park 1542 Mtn View Dr *Web:* www.dcnr.state.pa.us	Quakertown	PA	18951	215-529-7300	
Nolde Forest Environmental Education Ctr 2910 New Holland Rd *Web:* www.dcnr.state.pa.us	Reading	PA	19607	610-796-3699	
Norristown Farm Park 2500 Upper Farm Rd *Web:* www.dcnr.state.pa.us	Norristown	PA	19403	610-270-0215	
Oil Creek State Park 305 State Pk Rd *Web:* www.dcnr.state.pa.us	Oil City	PA	16301	814-676-5915	
Ole Bull State Park 31 Valhella VW *Web:* www.dcnr.state.pa.us	Cross Fork	PA	17729	814-435-5000	
Parker Dam State Park 28 Fairview Rd *Web:* www.dcnr.state.pa.us/stateparks/parks/parkerdam.aspx	Penfield	PA	15849	814-765-0630	
Patterson State Park c/o Lyman Run 454 Lyman Run Rd *Web:* www.dcnr.state.pa.us/stateparks/parks/patterson.aspx	Galeton	PA	16922	814-435-5010	
Penn-Roosevelt State Park c/o Greenwood Furnace PO Box 118 *Web:* www.dcnr.state.pa.us/stateparks/parks/pennroosevelt.aspx	Huntingdon	PA	16652	814-667-1800	
Pine Grove Furnace State Park 1100 Pine Grove Rd *TF:* 888-727-2757 ■ *Web:* www.dcnr.state.pa.us	Gardners	PA	17324	717-486-7174	486-4961
Poe Paddy State Park c/o Reeds Gap *Web:* www.dcnr.state.pa.us/stateparks/parks/poepaddy.aspx	Milroy	PA	17063	717-667-3622	
Point State Park 101 Commonwealth Pl *Web:* www.dcnr.state.pa.us	Pittsburgh	PA	15222	412-471-0235	
Presque Isle State Park 301 Peninsula Dr Ste 1 *TF:* 888-727-2757 ■ *Web:* www.dcnr.state.pa.us	Erie	PA	16505	814-833-7424	833-0266
Prince Gallitzin State Park 966 Marina Rd *Web:* www.dcnr.state.pa.us	Patton	PA	16668	814-674-1000	
Promised Land State Park PO Box 96 *Web:* www.dcnr.state.pa.us	Greentown	PA	18426	570-676-3428	
Prompton State Park c/o Lackawanna *TF:* 888-727-2757 ■ *Web:* www.dcnr.state.pa.us/stateparks/parks/prompton.aspx	North Abington Township	PA	18414	570-945-3239	
Prouty Place State Park c/o Lyman Run State Pk 454 Lyman Run Rd *Web:* www.dcnr.state.pa.us/stateparks/parks/proutyplace.aspx	Galeton	PA	16922	814-435-5010	
Pymatuning State Park 2660 Williamsfield Rd *Web:* www.dcnr.state.pa.us	Jamestown	PA	16134	724-932-3141	
R. B. Winter State Park 17215 Buffalo Rd *Web:* www.dcnr.state.pa.us/stateparks/parks/rbwinter.aspx	Mifflinburg	PA	17844	570-966-1455	
Raccoon Creek State Park 3000 State Rt 18 *Web:* www.dcnr.state.pa.us/stateparks/parks/raccooncreek.aspx	Hookstown	PA	15050	724-899-2200	
Ralph Stover State Park c/o Delaware Canal State Pk 11 Lodi Hill Rd *Web:* www.dcnr.state.pa.us	Upper Black Eddy	PA	18972	610-982-5560	

				Phone	Fax
Ravensburg State Park c/o R B Winter State Pk 17215 Buffalo Rd *Web:* www.dcnr.state.pa.us/stateparks/parks/ravensburg.aspx	Mifflinburg	PA	17844	570-966-1455	
Reeds Gap State Park 1405 New Lancaster Vly Rd *Web:* www.dcnr.state.pa.us	Milroy	PA	17063	717-667-3622	
Ricketts Glen State Park 695 State Rt 487 *Web:* www.dcnr.state.pa.us/stateparks/parks/rickettsglen.aspx	Benton	PA	17814	570-477-5675	
Ridley Creek State Park 1023 Sycamore Mills Rd *Web:* www.dcnr.state.pa.us	Media	PA	19063	610-892-3900	
Ryerson Station State Park 361 Bristoria Rd *Web:* www.dcnr.state.pa.us	Wind Ridge	PA	15380	724-428-4254	
S. B. Elliott State Park c/o Parker Dam State Pk 28 Fairview Rd *Web:* www.dcnr.state.pa.us/stateparks/parks/sbelliott.aspx	Penfield	PA	15849	814-765-0630	
Salt Springs State Park c/o Lackawanna *TF:* 888-727-2757 ■ *Web:* www.dcnr.state.pa.us/stateparks/parks/saltsprings.aspx	North Abington Township	PA	18414	570-945-3239	
Samuel S. Lewis State Park c/o Gifford Pinchot State Pk 2200 Rosstown Rd *Web:* www.dcnr.state.pa.us	Lewisberry	PA	17339	717-432-5011	
Sand Bridge State Park c/o R B Winter State Pk 13180 Buffalo Rd *Web:* www.dcnr.state.pa.us/stateparks/parks/sandbridge.aspx	Mifflinburg	PA	17844	570-966-1455	
Shawnee State Park 132 State Pk Rd *Web:* www.dcnr.state.pa.us	Schellsburg	PA	15559	814-733-4218	
Shikellamy State Park Bridge Ave. *Web:* www.dcnr.state.pa.us	Sunbury	PA	17801	570-988-5557	
Sinnemahoning State Park 8288 First Fork Rd *Web:* www.dcnr.state.pa.us	Austin	PA	16720	814-647-8401	
Sizerville State Park 199 E Cowley Run Rd *Web:* www.dcnr.state.pa.us	Emporium	PA	15834	814-486-5605	
Susquehannock State Park 1880 Pk Dr *Web:* www.dcnr.state.pa.us	Drumore	PA	17518	717-432-5011	
Tobyhanna State Park PO Box 387 *Web:* www.dcnr.state.pa.us	Tobyhanna	PA	18466	570-894-8336	
Tuscarora State Park 687 Tuscarora Pk Rd *Web:* www.dcnr.state.pa.us/stateparks/parks/tuscarora.aspx	Barnesville	PA	18214	570-467-2404	
Tyler State Park 101 Swamp Rd *Web:* www.dcnr.state.pa.us	Newtown	PA	18940	215-968-2021	
White Clay Creek Preserve PO Box 172 *Web:* www.dcnr.state.pa.us	Landenberg	PA	19350	610-274-2900	
Worlds End State Park 82 Cabin Bridge Rd *Web:* www.dcnr.state.pa.us/stateparks/parks/worldsend.aspx	Forksville	PA	18616	570-924-3287	
Yellow Creek State Park 170 Rt 259 Hwy *Web:* www.dcnr.state.pa.us	Penn Run	PA	15765	724-357-7913	

Rhode Island

				Phone	Fax
Charlestown Breachway Charlestown Beach Rd *Web:* riparks.com	Charlestown	RI	02813	401-364-7000	322-3083
Colt State Park Hope St *Web:* www.riparks.com	Bristol	RI	02809	401-253-7482	253-6766
East Beach 1 Burlingame State Pk *Web:* www.riparks.com	Charlestown	RI	02813	401-322-0450	322-3083
East Matunuck State Beach 950 Succotash Rd *Web:* www.riparks.com	South Kingstown	RI	02881	401-789-8585	
Fishermen's Memorial State Park 1011 Pt Judith Rd *Web:* www.riparks.com	Narragansett	RI	02882	401-789-8374	
Fort Adams State Park Harrison Ave *Web:* www.riparks.com	Newport	RI	02840	401-847-2400	841-9821
Goddard Memorial State Park 1095 Ives Rd *Web:* riparks.com	Warwick	RI	02818	401-884-2010	885-7720
Lincoln Woods State Park 2 Manchester Print Works Rd *Web:* www.riparks.com	Lincoln	RI	02865	401-723-7892	724-7951
Roger W. Wheeler State Beach 100 Sand Hill Cove Rd *Web:* www.riparks.com	Narragansett	RI	02882	401-789-3563	
Snake Den State Park 2321 Hartford Ave *Web:* www.riparks.com	Johnston	RI	02919	401-222-2632	
World War II Memorial State Park c/o Lincoln Woods State Pk 2 Manchester Print Works Rd *Web:* www.riparks.com	Lincoln	RI	02865	401-762-9717	

South Carolina

				Phone	Fax
Aiken State Natural Area 1145 State Pk Rd *TF:* 866-345-7275 ■ *Web:* www.southcarolinaparks.com	Windsor	SC	29856	803-649-2857	
Andrew Jackson State Park 196 Andrew Jackson Pk Rd *Web:* www.southcarolinaparks.com	Lancaster	SC	29720	803-285-3344	
Baker Creek State Park 863 Baker Creek Rd *Web:* southcarolinaparks.com/bakercreek/default.aspx	McCormick	SC	29835	864-443-2457	
Barnwell State Park 223 State Pk Rd *Web:* www.southcarolinaparks.com	Blackville	SC	29817	803-284-2212	
Caesars Head State Park 8155 Geer Hwy *TF:* 866-345-7275 ■ *Web:* www.southcarolinaparks.com	Cleveland	SC	29635	864-836-6115	836-3081
Calhoun Falls State Recreation Area 46 Maintenance Shop Rd *TF:* 866-345-7275 ■ *Web:* www.southcarolinaparks.com	Calhoun Falls	SC	29628	864-447-8267	447-8638
Charles Towne Landing State Historic Site 1500 Old Towne Rd *TF:* 866-345-7275 ■ *Web:* www.southcarolinaparks.com	Charleston	SC	29407	843-852-4200	852-4205
Cheraw State Park 100 State Pk Rd *TF:* 800-868-9630 ■ *Web:* www.southcarolinaparks.com	Cheraw	SC	29520	843-537-9656	
Chester State Park 759 State Pk Dr *TF:* 866-345-7275 ■ *Web:* www.southcarolinaparks.com	Chester	SC	29706	803-385-2680	
Colleton State Park 147 Wayside Ln *Web:* www.southcarolinaparks.com	Canadys	SC	29433	843-538-8206	
Colonial Dorchester State Historic Site 300 State Pk Rd *Web:* www.southcarolinaparks.com	Summerville	SC	29485	843-873-1740	
Croft State Natural Area 450 Croft State Pk Rd *Web:* www.southcarolinaparks.com	Spartanburg	SC	29302	864-585-1283	
Devils Fork State Park 161 Holcombe Cir *TF:* 866-345-7275 ■ *Web:* www.southcarolinaparks.com	Salem	SC	29676	864-944-2639	
Dreher Island State Recreation Area 3677 State Pk Rd *TF:* 866-345-7275 ■ *Web:* www.southcarolinaparks.com	Prosperity	SC	29127	803-364-4152	364-0756
Edisto Beach State Park 8377 State Cabin Rd *TF:* 800-315-3087 ■ *Web:* www.southcarolinaparks.com	Edisto Island	SC	29438	843-869-2756	869-4428
Givhans Ferry State Park 746 Givhans Ferry Rd *Web:* www.southcarolinaparks.com	Ridgeville	SC	29472	843-873-0692	
Goodale State Park 650 Pk Rd *Web:* www.southcarolinaparks.com	Camden	SC	29020	803-432-2772	
Hamilton Branch State Recreation Area 111 Campground Rd *Web:* www.southcarolinaparks.com	Plum Branch	SC	29845	864-333-2223	
Hampton Plantation State Historic Site 1950 Rutledge Rd *TF:* 800-315-3087 ■ *Web:* www.southcarolinaparks.com	McClellanville	SC	29458	843-546-9361	527-4995
Hickory Knob State Resort Park 1591 Resort Dr *TF:* 800-491-1764 ■ *Web:* www.southcarolinaparks.com	McCormick	SC	29835	864-391-2450	391-5390
Hunting Island State Park 2555 Sea Island Pkwy *TF:* 800-315-3087 ■ *Web:* www.southcarolinaparks.com	Hunting Island	SC	29920	843-838-2011	838-4263
Huntington Beach State Park 16148 Ocean Hwy *TF:* 800-491-1764 ■ *Web:* www.southcarolinaparks.com	Murrells Inlet	SC	29576	843-237-4440	
Jones Gap State Park 303 Jones Gap Rd *Web:* www.southcarolinaparks.com	Marietta	SC	29661	864-836-3647	
Keowee-Toxaway State Natural Area 108 Residence Dr *Web:* www.southcarolinaparks.com	Sunset	SC	29685	864-868-2605	
Kings Mountain State Park 1277 Pk Rd *Web:* www.southcarolinaparks.com	Blacksburg	SC	29702	803-222-3209	222-6948
Lake Greenwood State Recreation Area 302 State Pk Rd *TF:* 866-345-7275 ■ *Web:* www.southcarolinaparks.com	Ninety Six	SC	29666	864-543-3535	
Lake Hartwell State Recreation Area 19138 S Hwy 11 Ste A *Web:* www.southcarolinaparks.com	Fair Play	SC	29643	864-972-3352	
Lake Warren State Park 1079 Lk Warren Rd *Web:* www.southcarolinaparks.com	Hampton	SC	29924	803-943-5051	
Lake Wateree State Recreation Area 881 State Pk Rd *Web:* www.southcarolinaparks.com	Winnsboro	SC	29180	803-482-6401	482-6126
Landsford Canal State Park 2051 Pk Dr *Web:* www.southcarolinaparks.com	Catawba	SC	29704	803-789-5800	
Lee State Natural Area 487 Loop Rd *Web:* www.southcarolinaparks.com	Bishopville	SC	29010	803-428-5307	
Little Pee Dee State Park 1298 State Pk Rd *TF:* 800-491-1764 ■ *Web:* www.southcarolinaparks.com	Dillon	SC	29536	843-774-8872	
Musgrove Mill State Historic Site 398 State Pk Rd *Web:* www.southcarolinaparks.com	Clinton	SC	29325	864-938-0100	
Myrtle Beach State Park 4401 S Kings Hwy *Web:* www.southcarolinaparks.com	Myrtle Beach	SC	29575	843-238-5325	
Oconee State Park 624 State Pk Rd *TF:* 888-803-0844 ■ *Web:* www.southcarolinaparks.com	Mountain Rest	SC	29664	864-638-5353	638-8776
Oconee Station State Historic Site 500 Oconee Stn Rd *Web:* www.southcarolinaparks.com	Walhalla	SC	29691	864-638-0079	
Paris Mountain State Park 2401 State Pk Rd *TF:* 866-345-7275 ■ *Web:* www.southcarolinaparks.com	Greenville	SC	29609	864-244-5565	
Poinsett State Park 6660 Poinsett Pk Rd *Web:* www.southcarolinaparks.com	Wedgefield	SC	29168	803-494-8177	
Redcliffe Plantation State Historic Site 181 Redcliffe Rd *Web:* www.southcarolinaparks.com	Beech Island	SC	29842	803-827-1473	
Rivers Bridge State Historic Site 325 State Pk Rd *Web:* www.southcarolinaparks.com	Ehrhardt	SC	29081	803-267-3675	
Rose Hill Plantation State Historic Site 2677 SaRdis Rd *Web:* www.southcarolinaparks.com	Union	SC	29379	864-427-5966	
Sadlers Creek State Park 940 Sadlers Creek Rd *Web:* www.southcarolinaparks.com	Anderson	SC	29626	864-226-8950	
Santee State Park 251 State Pk Rd *Web:* www.southcarolinaparks.com	Santee	SC	29142	803-854-2408	854-4834
Sesquicentennial State Park 9564 Two Notch Rd *TF:* 888-245-9300 ■ *Web:* www.southcarolinaparks.com	Columbia	SC	29223	803-788-2706	788-4414
Table Rock State Park 158 E Ellison Ln *Web:* www.southcarolinaparks.com	Pickens	SC	29671	864-878-9813	878-9077
Woods Bay State Natural Area 11020 Woods Bay Rd *Web:* www.southcarolinaparks.com	Olanta	SC	29114	843-659-4445	

South Dakota

Phone Fax

Adams Homestead & Nature Preserve
272 Westshore Dr McCook Lake SD 57049 605-232-0873
Web: gfp.sd.gov

Bear Butte State Park 20250 Hwy 79 PO Box 688 Sturgis SD 57785 605-347-5240
Web: gfp.sd.gov/state-parks/directory/bear-butte

Beaver Creek Nature Area
20641 SD Hwy 1806 25495 485th Ave. Fort Pierre SD 57532 605-223-7660 773-6245
TF: 800-710-2267 ■ *Web:* gfp.sd.gov

Big Sioux Recreation Area 410 Pk Ave. Brandon SD 57005 605-582-7243
Web: gfp.sd.gov/state-parks/directory/big-sioux

Big Stone Island Nature Area
c/o Hartford Beach State Pk
13672 Hartford Beach Rd Corona SD 57227 605-432-6374
Web: gfp.sd.gov/state-parks/directory/big-stone

Burke Lake Recreation Area
523 E Capitol Ave 35316 SD Hwy 44 Pierre SD 57501 605-223-7660
Web: www.gfp.sd.gov

Buryanek Recreation Area 27450 Buryanek Rd Burke SD 57523 605-337-2587
Web: www.gfp.sd.gov/state-parks/directory/buryanek

Chief White Crane Recreation Area
31323 Toe Rd Yankton SD 57078 605-668-2985
Web: www.gfp.sd.gov/state-parks/directory/chief-white-crane

Custer State Park 13329 US Hwy 16A Custer SD 57730 605-255-4515 255-4460
Web: gfp.sd.gov

Farm Island Recreation Area
1301 Farm Island Rd Pierre SD 57501 605-773-2885
Web: gfp.sd.gov

Fisher Grove State Park 17290 Fishers Ln Frankfort SD 57440 605-472-1336
Web: gfp.sd.gov

Fort Sisseton State Historical Park
11907 434th Ave Lake City SD 57247 605-448-5474
Web: gfp.sd.gov/state-parks/directory/fort-sisseton

George S. Mickelson Trail 11361 Nevada Gulch Rd Lead SD 57754 605-584-3896
Web: gfp.sd.gov/state-parks/directory/mickelson-trail

Hartford Beach State Park
13672 Hartford Beach Rd Corona SD 57227 605-432-6374
Web: gfp.sd.gov/state-parks/directory/hartford-beach

Indian Creek Recreation Area
12905 288th Ave Mobridge SD 57601 605-845-7112
Web: www.gfp.sd.gov/state-parks/directory/indian-creek

Lake Alvin Recreation Area
c/o Newton Hills State Pk 27225 480th Ave Harrisburg SD 57032 605-987-2263
Web: gfp.sd.gov

Lake Cochrane Recreation Area 3454 Edgewater Dr Gary SD 57237 605-882-5200
Web: gfp.sd.gov/state-parks/directory/lake-cochrane

Lake Herman State Park 23409 State Pk Dr Madison SD 57042 605-256-5003
Web: gfp.sd.gov

Lake Hiddenwood Recreation Area
c/o W Whitlock Recreation Area
16157A W Whitlock Rd Gettysburg SD 57442 605-765-9410
Web: www.gfp.sd.gov

Lake Poinsett Recreation Area 46109 202nd St. Bruce SD 57220 605-627-5441
Web: sd.gov

Lake Thompson Recreation Area
21176 Flood Club Rd Lake Preston SD 57249 605-847-4893
Web: gfp.sd.gov

Lake Vermillion Recreation Area
26140 451st Ave. Canistota SD 57012 605-296-3643

Lewis & Clark Recreation Area
43349 SD Hwy 52 Yankton SD 57078 605-668-2985
Web: lewisandclarkpark.com

Little Moreau Recreation Area
c/o Shadehill Recreation Area
19150 Summerville Rd Shadehill SD 57653 605-374-5114
Web: gfp.sd.gov/state-parks/directory/little-moreau

Llewellyn Johns Recreation Area
c/o Shadehill Recreation Area
19150 Summerville Rd Shadehill SD 57653 605-374-5114
Web: gfp.sd.gov

Mina Lake Recreation Area
c/o Richmond Lk Recreation Area 402 Park Ave. Mina SD 57451 605-626-3488
Web: www.gfp.sd.gov

Newton Hills State Park 28767 482nd Ave Canton SD 57013 605-987-2263
Web: gfp.sd.gov

North Point Recreation Area
38180 297th St. Lake Andes SD 57356 605-487-7046
Web: www.gfp.sd.gov/state-parks/directory/north-point

North Wheeler Recreation Area
29084 N Wheeler Rd. Geddes SD 57342 605-487-7046
Web: www.gfp.sd.gov/state-parks/directory/north-wheeler

Oahe Downstream Recreation Area
20439 Marina Loop Rd Fort Pierre SD 57532 605-223-7722
Web: www.gfp.sd.gov/state-parks/directory/oahe-downstream

Oakwood Lakes State Park 46109 202nd St Bruce SD 57220 605-627-5441
Web: sd.gov

Okobojo Point Recreation Area
19425 Okobojo Pt Dr Fort Pierre SD 57532 605-223-7722
Web: www.gfp.sd.gov/state-parks/directory/okobojo-point

Pease Creek Recreation Area 37270 293rd St Geddes SD 57342 605-487-7046
Web: www.gfp.sd.gov/state-parks/directory/pease-creek

Pickerel Lake Recreation Area
12980 446th Ave Grenville SD 57239 605-486-4753
Web: gfp.sd.gov

Pierson Ranch Recreation Area 31144 Toe Rd. Yankton SD 57078 605-668-2985
Web: www.gfp.sd.gov/state-parks/directory/pierson-ranch

Platte Creek Recreation Area
c/o Snake Creek Recreation Area
35910 282nd St Platte SD 57369 605-337-2587
Web: gfp.sd.gov

Roy Lake State Park 11545 Northside Dr Lake City SD 57247 605-448-5701
Web: gfp.sd.gov

Sica Hollow State Park
44950 Park Rd 44950 Park Rd Sisseton SD 57247 605-448-5701
Web: gfp.sd.gov

Snake Creek Recreation Area 35316 SD Hwy 44 Platte SD 57369 605-337-2587
Web: gfp.sd.gov

Spirit Mound Historic Prairie
31148 SD Hwy 19 Vermillion SD 57069 605-987-2263
Web: www.gfp.sd.gov/state-parks/directory/spirit-mound

Spring Creek Recreation Area
c/o Oahe Downstream Recreation Area
20439 Marina Loop Rd Fort Pierre SD 57532 605-223-7722
Web: www.gfp.sd.gov/state-parks/directory/spring-creek

Swan Creek Recreation Area
c/o W Whitlock Recreation Area
16157A W Whitlock Rd Gettysburg SD 57442 605-765-9410
Web: www.gfp.sd.gov

Union Grove State Park
c/o Newton Hills State Pk 30828 471st Ave Beresford SD 57004 605-987-2263
Web: gfp.sd.gov

West Bend Recreation Area 22154 Wt Bend Rd Harrold SD 57536 605-773-2885
Web: gfp.sd.gov

West Whitlock Recreation Area
16157A W Whitlock Rd. Gettysburg SD 57442 605-765-9410
Web: gfp.sd.gov

Tennessee

Phone Fax

Bicentennial Capitol Mall State Park
600 James Robertson Pkwy Nashville TN 37243 615-741-5280
Web: www.state.tn.us

Big Cypress Tree State Park
295 Big Cypress Rd Greenfield TN 38230 731-235-2700
Web: www.state.tn.us

Big Hill Pond State Park
1435 John Howell Rd Pocahontas TN 38061 731-645-7967
Web: www.state.tn.us

Big Ridge State Park 1015 Big Ridge Rd. Maynardville TN 37807 865-992-5523
TF: 800-471-5305 ■ *Web:* www.state.tn.us

Bledsoe Creek State Park 400 Zieglers Ft Rd. Gallatin TN 37066 615-452-3706
Web: www.state.tn.us

Booker T. Washington State Park
5801 Champion Rd. Chattanooga TN 37416 423-894-4955
Web: www.state.tn.us

Burgess Falls State Natural Area
4000 Burgess Falls Dr Sparta TN 38583 931-432-5312
Web: www.state.tn.us

Cedars of Lebanon State Park
328 Cedar Forest Rd Lebanon TN 37090 615-443-2769
TF: 800-250-8615 ■ *Web:* www.state.tn.us

Chickasaw State Park 20 Cabin Ln. Henderson TN 38340 731-989-5141
Web: www.state.tn.us

Cordell Hull Birthplace State Park
1300 Cordell Hull Memorial Dr Byrdstown TN 38549 931-864-3247
Web: www.state.tn.us

Cove Lake State Park 110 Cove Lake Ln. Caryville TN 37714 423-566-9701
TF: 800-250-8615

Cumberland Mountain State Park
24 Office Dr Crossville TN 38555 931-484-6138
Web: www.state.tn.us

David Crockett State Park
1400 W Gaines PO Box 398 Lawrenceburg TN 38464 931-762-9408
Web: www.state.tn.us

Davy Crockett Birthplace State Park
1245 Davy Crockett Pk Rd Limestone TN 37681 423-257-2167
TF: 800-250-8615 ■ *Web:* www.state.tn.us

Dunbar Cave State Natural Area
401 Dunbar Cave Rd. Clarksville TN 37043 931-648-5526

Edgar Evins State Park
1630 Edgar Evins State Pk Rd. Silver Point TN 38582 931-858-2446
TF: 800-250-8619 ■ *Web:* www.state.tn.us

Fall Creek Falls State Resort Park
2009 Village Camp Rd Spencer TN 38585 423-881-5298
Web: www.state.tn.us

Fort Loudoun State Historic Park
338 Ft Loudoun Rd. Vonore TN 37885 423-884-6217
Web: www.state.tn.us

Fort Pillow State Historic Park 3122 Pk Rd Henning TN 38041 731-738-5581
TF: 800-250-8615 ■ *Web:* www.state.tn.us

Frozen Head State Natural Area
964 Flat Fork Rd. Wartburg TN 37887 423-346-3318
TF: 800-250-8615 ■ *Web:* www.state.tn.us

Harrison Bay State Park
8411 Harrison Bay Rd. Harrison TN 37341 423-344-6214
Web: www.state.tn.us

Henry Horton State Resort Park
4358 Nashville Hwy Chapel Hill TN 37034 931-364-2222
Web: tnstateparks.com/parks/about/henry-horton

Indian Mountain State Park 143 State Pk Cir Jellico TN 37762 423-784-7958
Web: www.state.tn.us

Johnsonville State Historic Park
900 Nell Beard Rd. New Johnsonville TN 37134 931-535-2789
Web: tnstateparks.com

Justin P. Wilson Cumberland Trail State Park
220 Pk Rd. Caryville TN 38555 423-566-2229 566-2290
TF: 800-342-3145 ■
Web: tnstateparks.com/parks/contact/cumberland-trail

Meeman-Shelby Forest State Park
910 Riddick Rd. Millington TN 38053 901-876-5215
Web: www.state.tn.us

Montgomery Bell State Resort Park
1020 Jackson Hill Rd Burns TN 37029 615-797-9052
TF: 800-250-8613 ■ *Web:* www.state.tn.us

Phone Fax

Mousetail Landing State Park 3 Campground Rd........Linden TN 37096 731-847-0841
Web: www.state.tn.us
Natchez Trace State Park
24845 Natchez Trace Rd........................Wildersville TN 38388 731-968-3742
Web: www.state.tn.us
Nathan Bedford Forrest State Park
1825 Pilot Knob Rd.................................Eva TN 38333 731-584-6356
Web: www.state.tn.us
Norris Dam State Resort Park
125 Village Green Cir............................Lake City TN 37769 865-426-7461
Web: www.state.tn.us
Old Stone Fort State Archaeological Park
732 Stone Ft Dr................................Manchester TN 37355 931-723-5073
Web: www.state.tn.us
Panther Creek State Park
2010 Panther Creek Pk Rd.......................Morristown TN 37814 423-587-7046 587-7047
Web: www.state.tn.us
Paris Landing State Park 16055 Hwy 79N..........Buchanan TN 38222 731-641-4465
Web: www.state.tn.us
Pickett State Park 4605 Pickett Pk Hwy...........Jamestown TN 38556 931-879-5821
TF: 877-260-0010 ■ Web: www.state.tn.us
Pickwick Landing State Resort Park
PO Box 15.................................Pickwick Dam TN 38365 731-689-3129
Web: tnstateparks.com/parks/about/pickwick-landing
Pinson Mounds State Archaeological Park
460 Ozier Rd...Pinson TN 38366 731-988-5614
Web: www.state.tn.us
Port Royal State Historic Park
3300 Old Clarksville Hwy...........................Adams TN 37010 931-648-5526
Web: www.state.tn.us
Radnor Lake State Park 1160 Otter Creek Rd.........Nashville TN 37220 615-373-3467
Web: tnstateparks.com
Red Clay State Historic Park
1140 Red Clay Pk Rd...........................Cleveland TN 37311 423-478-0339
Web: www.state.tn.us
Roan Mountain State Park 1015 Hwy 143.......Roan Mountain TN 37687 423-772-0190
Web: tnstateparks.com
Rock Island State Park 82 Beach Rd..............Rock Island TN 38581 931-686-2471
TF: 800-250-8614 ■ Web: www.state.tn.us
Sergeant Alvin C. York State Historic Park
2609 N York Hwy...................................Pall Mall TN 38577 931-879-6456
Web: www.state.tn.us
South Cumberland Recreation Area
11745 US 41......................................Monteagle TN 37356 931-692-3887
Web: www.state.tn.us
Standing Stone State Park
1674 Standing Stone Pk Hwy........................Hilham TN 38568 931-823-6347
Web: www.state.tn.us
Sycamore Shoals State Historic Park
1651 W Elk Ave..................................Elizabethton TN 37643 423-543-5808
Web: www.state.tn.us
T. O. Fuller State Park 1500 Mitchell Rd............Memphis TN 38109 901-543-7581
Web: www.state.tn.us
Tims Ford State Park 570 Tims Ford Dr...........Winchester TN 37398 931-962-1183
TF: 800-471-5295 ■ Web: www.state.tn.us
Warriors' Path State Park
312 Rosa L Parks Ave.............................Nashville TN 37243 423-239-8531 239-4982
Web: tnstateparks.com/parks/about/warriors-path

Texas

Phone Fax

Abilene State Park 150 Pk Rd 32.....................Tuscola TX 79562 325-572-3204 572-3008
Web: tpwd.texas.gov/state-parks/abilene
Admiral Nimitz State Historic Site
328 E Main St...............................Fredericksburg TX 78624 830-997-4379
Web: www.thc.state.tx.us
Atlanta State Park 927 Pk Rd 42.......................Atlanta TX 75551 903-796-6476
Web: tpwd.texas.gov/state-parks/atlanta
Balmorhea State Park PO Box 15..................Toyahvale TX 79786 432-375-2370
Web: tpwd.texas.gov/state-parks/balmorhea
Barton Warnock Environmental Education Ctr
PO Box 375 HC 70...............................Terlingua TX 79852 432-424-3327
Web: tpwd.texas.gov
Bastrop State Park 3005 Hwy 21 E....................Bastrop TX 78602 512-321-2101
Web: tpwd.texas.gov
Bentsen-Rio Grande Valley State Park
2800 S Bensen Palm Dr...........................Mission TX 78572 956-585-1107
TF: 800-792-1112 ■ Web: www.theworldbirdingcenter.com
Big Bend Ranch State Park PO Box 2319...........Presidio TX 79845 432-229-3416
Web: tpwd.texas.gov/state-parks/big-bend-ranch
Big Spring State Park 1 Scenic Dr................Big Spring TX 79720 432-263-4931
Web: tpwd.texas.gov/state-parks/big-spring
Blanco State Park PO Box 493........................Blanco TX 78606 830-833-4333
Web: tpwd.texas.gov/state-parks/blanco
Bonham State Park 1363 State Pk 24................Bonham TX 75418 903-583-5022
Web: tpwd.texas.gov/state-parks/bonham
Brazos Bend State Park 21901 FM 762..............Needville TX 77461 409-553-5101
Web: tpwd.texas.gov/state-parks/brazos-bend
Buescher State Park PO Box 75....................Smithville TX 78957 512-237-2241
Web: tpwd.texas.gov/state-parks/buescher
Caddo Lake State Park 245 Pk Rd 2..................Karnack TX 75661 903-679-3351
Web: tpwd.texas.gov/state-parks/caddo-lake
Caddoan Mounds State Historic Site
1649 Texas 21..Alto TX 75925 936-858-3218
Web: www.thc.texas.gov/historic-sites/caddo-mounds-state-historic-site
Caprock Canyons State Park & Trailway
850 Caprock Canyon Pk Rd.........................Quitaque TX 79255 806-455-1492
Web: tpwd.texas.gov/state-parks/caprock-canyons
Casa Navarro State Historic Site
228 S Laredo St...............................San Antonio TX 78207 210-226-4801 226-4801
Web: www.thc.texas.gov/historic-sites/casa-navarro-state-historic-site
Cedar Hill State Park 1570 W FM 1382.............Cedar Hill TX 75104 972-291-3900
Web: tpwd.texas.gov/state-parks/cedar-hill
Choke Canyon State Park PO Box 2.................Calliham TX 78007 361-786-3868
Web: tpwd.texas.gov/state-parks/choke-canyon
Cleburne State Park 5800 Pk Rd 21.................Cleburne TX 76031 817-645-4215
Web: tpwd.texas.gov/state-parks/cleburne
Colorado Bend State Park 6031 Colorado Pk Rd.........Bend TX 76824 325-628-3240
Web: tpwd.texas.gov/state-parks/colorado-bend
Confederate Reunion Grounds State Historic Site
c/o Ft Parker State Pk 194 Pk Rd 28..................Mexia TX 76667 254-562-5751
Web: www.thc.texas.gov/historic-sites/confederate-reunion-grounds-state-historic-site
Cooper Lake State Park 1664 Farm Rd 1529 S..........Cooper TX 75432 903-395-3100
Web: tpwd.texas.gov/state-parks/cooper-lake
Copper Breaks State Park 777 Pk Rd 62.............Quanah TX 79252 940-839-4331
Web: tpwd.texas.gov/state-parks/copper-breaks
Daingerfield State Park 455 Pk Rd 17.............Daingerfield TX 75638 903-645-2921
Web: tpwd.texas.gov/state-parks/daingerfield
Davis Mountains State Park PO Box 1458..........Fort Davis TX 79734 432-426-3337
Web: tpwd.texas.gov/state-parks/davis-mountains
Devil's Sinkhole State Natural Area
101 N Sweeten St.............................Rocksprings TX 78880 830-683-3762
Web: tpwd.texas.gov
Devils River State Natural Area
HC 01 PO Box 513...................................Del Rio TX 78840 830-395-2133
Web: tpwd.texas.gov/state-parks/devils-river
Eisenhower Birthplace State Historic Site
609 S Lamar Ave....................................Denison TX 75021 903-465-8908
Web: www.thc.texas.gov/historic-sites/eisenhower-birthplace/eisenhower-birthplace-history
Eisenhower State Park 50 Pk Rd 20................Denison TX 75020 903-465-1956
Web: tpwd.texas.gov/state-parks/eisenhower
Enchanted Rock State Natural Area
16710 Ranch Rd 965..........................Fredericksburg TX 78624 325-247-3903
Web: tpwd.texas.gov/state-parks/enchanted-rock
exas Parks and Wildlife Departmentÿ
1331 McKelligon Canyon Rd...........................El Paso TX 79930 915-566-6441
Web: tpwd.texas.gov
exas Parks and Wildlife Departmentÿ
PO Box 1859...Fulton TX 78358 361-729-0386
Web: tpwd.texas.gov
Fairfield Lake State Park
123 State Pk Rd 64................................Fairfield TX 75840 903-389-4514
Web: tpwd.texas.gov/state-parks/fairfield-lake
Falcon State Park PO Box 2..................Falcon Heights TX 78545 956-848-5327
Web: tpwd.texas.gov/state-parks/falcon
Fannin Battleground State Historic Site
c/o Goliad State Pk 108 Pk Rd 6.......................Goliad TX 77963 361-645-3405
Web: www.thc.texas.gov/historic-sites/fannin-battleground-state-historic-site
Fanthorp Inn State Historic Site
579 Main St.......................................Anderson TX 77830 936-873-2633
Web: tpwd.texas.gov/state-parks/fanthorp-inn
Fort Griffin State Park & Historic Site
1701 N US Hwy 283..................................Albany TX 76430 325-762-3592
Web: www.thc.texas.gov/historic-sites/fort-griffin-state-historic-site
Fort Lancaster State Historic Site
PO Box 306.......................................Sheffield TX 79781 432-836-4391
Web: www.thc.texas.gov/historic-sites/fort-lancaster-state-historic-site
Fort Leaton State Historic Site PO Box 2319..........Presidio TX 79845 432-229-3613
Web: tpwd.texas.gov/state-parks/fort-leaton
Fort McKavett State Historic Site
7066 FM 864 Rd...............................Fort McKavett TX 76841 325-396-2358
Web: www.thc.state.tx.us/historic-sites/fort-mckavett-state-historic-site?page=9
Fort Parker State Park 194 Pk Rd 28...................Mexia TX 76667 254-562-5751
Web: tpwd.texas.gov/state-parks/fort-parker
Fort Richardson State Park Historic Site & Lost Creek Reservoir State Trailway
228 State Pk Rd 61................................Jacksboro TX 76458 940-567-3506
Web: tpwd.texas.gov
Galveston Island State Park
14901 Termini San Luis Pass Rd....................Galveston TX 77554 409-737-1222
Web: tpwd.texas.gov/state-parks/galveston-island
Goliad State Park 108 Pk Rd 6........................Goliad TX 77963 361-645-3405
Web: tpwd.texas.gov/state-parks/goliad
Goose Island State Park 202 S Palmetto St...........Rockport TX 78382 361-729-2858
Web: tpwd.texas.gov/state-parks/goose-island
Government Canyon State Natural Area
12861 Galm Rd.................................San Antonio TX 78254 210-688-9055
Web: tpwd.texas.gov
Guadalupe River State Park
3350 Pk Rd 31..................................Spring Branch TX 78070 830-438-2656
Web: tpwd.texas.gov/state-parks/guadalupe-river
Hill Country State Natural Area
10600 Bandera Creek Rd............................Bandera TX 78003 830-796-4413
Web: tpwd.texas.gov/state-parks/hill-country
Honey Creek State Natural Area
c/o Guadalupe River State Pk
3350 Pk Rd 31..................................Spring Branch TX 78070 830-438-2656
Web: tpwd.texas.gov/state-parks/honey-creek
Hueco Tanks State Historic Site
6900 Hueco Tanks Rd Ste 1...........................El Paso TX 79938 915-857-1135 845-1794*
*Fax Area Code: 979 ■ TF: 800-792-1112 ■ Web: tpwd.texas.gov/state-parks/hueco-tanks
Huntsville State Park PO Box 508.................Huntsville TX 77342 936-295-5644
Web: tpwd.texas.gov/state-parks/huntsville
Inks Lake State Park 3630 Pk Rd 4.....................Burnet TX 78611 512-793-2223
Web: tpwd.texas.gov/state-parks/inks-lake
Kickapoo Cavern State Park PO Box 705..........Brackettville TX 78832 830-563-2342
Web: tpwd.texas.gov/state-parks/kickapoo-cavern
Lake Arrowhead State Park 229 Pk Rd 63.........Wichita Falls TX 76310 940-528-2211
Web: tpwd.texas.gov/state-parks/lake-arrowhead
Lake Bob Sandlin State Park
341 State Pk Rd 2117...............................Pittsburg TX 75686 903-572-5531
Web: tpwd.texas.gov/state-parks/lake-bob-sandlin
Lake Brownwood State Park
200 Hwy Pk Rd 15...............................Lake Brownwood TX 76801 325-784-5223
Web: tpwd.texas.gov/state-parks/lake-brownwood
Lake Colorado City State Park
4582 FM 2836...................................Colorado City TX 79512 325-728-3931
Web: tpwd.texas.gov/state-parks/lake-colorado-city

				Phone	Fax
Lake Corpus Christi State Park 23194 Pk Rd 25 *Web:* tpwd.texas.gov/state-parks/lake-corpus-christi	Mathis	TX	78368	361-547-2635	
Lake Mineral Wells State Park & Trailway 100 Pk Rd 71 *Web:* tpwd.texas.gov/state-parks/lake-mineral-wells	Mineral Wells	TX	76067	940-328-1171	
Lake Somerville State Park 14222 Pk Rd 57 *Web:* tpwd.texas.gov/state-parks/lake-somerville	Somerville	TX	77879	979-535-7763	
Lake Tawakoni State Park 10822 Fm 2475 *Web:* tpwd.texas.gov/state-parks/lake-tawakoni	Wills Point	TX	75169	903-560-7123	
Lake Texana State Park 46 Pk Rd 1 *Web:* tpwd.texas.gov	Edna	TX	77957	361-782-5718	
Lake Whitney State Park PO Box 1175 *Web:* tpwd.texas.gov/state-parks/lake-whitney	Whitney	TX	76692	254-694-3793	
Landmark Inn State Historic Site 402 E Florence St *Web:* www.thc.texas.gov/historic-sites/landmark-inn-state-historic-site	Castroville	TX	78009	830-931-2133	
Lipantitlan State Historic Site c/o Lk Corpus Christi State Pk PO Box 1167 *Web:* tpwd.texas.gov/state-parks/lipantitlan	Mathis	TX	78368	361-547-2635	
Lockhart State Park 4179 State Pk Rd *Web:* tpwd.texas.gov/state-parks/lockhart	Lockhart	TX	78644	512-398-3479	
Longhorn Cavern State Park PO Box 732 *Web:* www.longhorncaverns.com	Burnet	TX	78611	830-598-2283	
Lyndon B. Johnson State Park & Historic Site PO Box 238 *Web:* tpwd.texas.gov	Stonewall	TX	78671	830-644-2252	
Magoffin Home State Historic Site 1120 Magoffin Ave *Web:* www.thc.texas.gov/historic-sites/magoffin-home-state-historic-site	El Paso	TX	79901	915-533-5147	
Martin Creek Lake State Park 9515 CR 2181D *Web:* tpwd.texas.gov	Tatum	TX	75691	903-836-4336	
Martin Dies Jr State Park 634 Private Rd 5025 *Web:* tpwd.texas.gov	Jasper	TX	75951	409-384-5231	
Matagorda Island Wildlife Management Area 1700 Seventh St *Web:* tpwd.texas.gov	Bay City	TX	77414	979-244-7670	
McKinney Falls State Park 5808 McKinney Falls Pkwy *Web:* tpwd.texas.gov	Austin	TX	78744	512-243-1643	243-0536
Meridian State Park 173 Pk Rd 7 *Web:* tpwd.texas.gov	Meridian	TX	76665	254-435-2536	
Mission Tejas State Park 120 State Pk Rd 44 *Web:* tpwd.texas.gov	Grapeland	TX	75844	936-687-2394	
Monahans Sandhills State Park PO Box 1738 *Web:* tpwd.texas.gov/state-parks/monahans-sandhills	Monahans	TX	79756	432-943-2092	
Monument Hill & Kreische Brewery State Historic Sites 414 State Loop 92 *Web:* tpwd.texas.gov/state-parks/monument-hill-kreische-brewery	La Grange	TX	78945	979-968-5658	
Mother Neff State Park 1680 Texas 236 Hwy *Web:* tpwd.texas.gov/state-parks/mother-neff	Moody	TX	76557	254-853-2389	
Mustang Island State Park 17047 State Hwy 361 *Web:* tpwd.texas.gov/state-parks/mustang-island	Port Aransas	TX	78373	361-749-5246	749-6455
Palmetto State Park 78 Pk Rd 11 S. *Web:* tpwd.texas.gov/state-parks/palmetto	Gonzales	TX	78629	830-672-3266	
Palo Duro Canyon State Park 11450 Pk Rd 5 *Web:* tpwd.texas.gov/state-parks/palo-duro-canyon	Canyon	TX	79015	806-488-2227	488-2556
Pedernales Falls State Park 2585 Pk Rd 6026 *Web:* tpwd.texas.gov/state-parks/pedernales-falls	Johnson City	TX	78636	830-868-7304	
Port Isabel Lighthouse State Historic Site 421 E Queen Isabella Blvd *Web:* tpwd.texas.gov/state-parks/port-isabel-lighthouse	Port Isabel	TX	78578	956-943-2262	
Possum Kingdom State Park PO Box 70 *Web:* tpwd.texas.gov/state-parks/possum-kingdom	Caddo	TX	76429	940-549-1803	
Purtis Creek State Park 14225 FM 316 *Web:* tpwd.texas.gov/state-parks/purtis-creek	Eustace	TX	75124	903-425-2332	
Ray Roberts Lake State Park 100 PW 4137 *Web:* tpwd.texas.gov/state-parks/ray-roberts-lake	Pilot Point	TX	76258	940-686-2148	
Rusk/Palestine State Park 1 Hwy 84 W *Web:* www.texasstaterr.com/parks-campgrounds	Rusk	TX	75785	903-683-3098	
Sabine Pass Battleground State Park & Historic Site c/o Sea Rim State Pk PO Box 1066 *Web:* tpwd.texas.gov/spdest/parkinfo/former_tpwd_parks	Sabine Pass	TX	77655	409-971-2559	
Sam Bell Maxey House State Historic Site 812 S Church St *Web:* www.thc.texas.gov/historic-sites/sam-bell-maxey-house-state-historic-site	Paris	TX	75460	903-785-5716	
San Jacinto Battleground State Historic Site 3523 Battleground Rd *Web:* tpwd.texas.gov/state-parks/san-jacinto-battleground	La Porte	TX	77571	281-479-2431	479-5618
Sea Rim State Park PO Box 356 *Web:* tpwd.texas.gov/state-parks/sea-rim	Sabine Pass	TX	77655	409-971-2559	
Sebastopol State Historic Site PO Box 900 *Web:* www.seguintexas.gov/parks_recreation/detail/sebastopol_house	Seguin	TX	78156	830-379-4833	
Seminole Canyon State Park & Historic Site PO Box 820 *Web:* tpwd.texas.gov/state-parks/seminole-canyon	Comstock	TX	78837	432-292-4464	
Sheldon Lake State Park & Environmental Learning Ctr 15315 Beaumont Hwy at Pk Rd 138 *Web:* tpwd.texas.gov/state-parks/sheldon-lake	Houston	TX	77049	281-456-2800	
South Llano River State Park 1927 Park Rd 73 *Web:* tpwd.texas.gov	Junction	TX	76849	325-446-3994	
Stephen F. Austin State Park & San Felipe State Historic Site 120 Main St *Web:* tpwd.texas.gov	San Felipe	TX	77473	979-885-3613	
Texas State Railroad State Park PO Box 39 *Web:* tpwd.texas.gov	Rusk	TX	75785	903-683-2561	
Tyler State Park 789 Pk Rd 16 *Web:* tpwd.texas.gov	Tyler	TX	75706	903-597-5338	
Varner-Hogg Plantation State Historic Site 1702 N 13th St *Web:* tpwd.texas.gov	West Columbia	TX	77486	979-345-4656	
Village Creek State Park 8854 Pk Rd 74 *Web:* tpwd.texas.gov	Lumberton	TX	77657	409-755-7322	
Washington-on-the-Brazos State Historic Site PO Box 305 *Web:* tpwd.texas.gov/state-parks/washington-on-the-brazos	Washington	TX	77880	936-878-2214	

Utah

				Phone	Fax
Anasazi State Park Museum 460 North Hwy 12 *Web:* www.stateparks.utah.gov	Boulder	UT	84716	435-335-7308	
Antelope Island State Park 4528 West 1700 South *Web:* www.stateparks.utah.gov	Syracuse	UT	84075	801-773-2941	
Bear Lake State Park 1030 N Bear Lk Blvd *Web:* www.stateparks.utah.gov	Garden City	UT	84028	435-946-3343	
Camp Floyd/Stagecoach Inn State Park & Museum 18035 West 1540 North *Web:* www.stateparks.utah.gov	Fairfield	UT	84013	801-768-8932	
Coral Pink Sand Dunes State Park PO Box 95 *Web:* www.stateparks.utah.gov	Kanab	UT	84741	435-648-2800	
Dead Horse Point State Park State Route 313 *Web:* www.stateparks.utah.gov	Moab	UT	84532	435-259-2614	
Deer Creek State Park PO Box 257 *Web:* www.stateparks.utah.gov	Midway	UT	84049	435-654-0171	
East Canyon State Park 5535 South Hwy 66 *Web:* www.stateparks.utah.gov	Morgan	UT	84050	801-829-6866	
Edge of the Cedars State Park Museum 660 West 400 North *Web:* stateparks.utah.gov	Blanding	UT	84511	435-678-2238	
Escalante State Park 710 N Reservoir Rd *Web:* www.stateparks.utah.gov	Escalante	UT	84726	435-826-4466	
Fremont Indian State Park & Museum 3820 W Clear Creek Canyon Rd *Web:* www.stateparks.utah.gov	Sevier	UT	84766	435-527-4631	
Goblin Valley State Park PO Box 637 *Web:* www.utah.com	Green River	UT	84525	435-275-4584	
Goosenecks State Park PO Box 788 660 W 400 N *Web:* stateparks.utah.gov	Blanding	UT	84511	435-678-2238	
Green River State Park PO Box 637 *Web:* www.utah.com	Green River	UT	84525	435-564-3633	
Gunlock State Park 4405 West 3600 South *Web:* www.stateparks.utah.gov	Hurricane	UT	84737	435-680-0715	
Historic Union Pacific Rail Trail State Park PO Box 754 *Web:* www.stateparks.utah.gov	Park City	UT	84060	435-649-6839	
Huntington State Park PO Box 1343 *TF:* 800-322-3770 ■ *Web:* stateparks.utah.gov	Huntington	UT	84528	435-687-2491	
Huntington State Park 1343 Huntington *Web:* www.stateparks.utah.gov	Price	UT	84528	435-687-2491	
Hyrum State Park 405 West 300 South *Web:* www.stateparks.utah.gov	Hyrum	UT	84319	435-245-6866	
Iron Mission State Park 635 N Main St *Web:* www.stateparks.utah.gov	Cedar City	UT	84720	435-586-9290	
Jordanelle State Park SR 319 515 PO Box 4 *Web:* www.stateparks.utah.gov	Heber City	UT	84032	435-649-9540	
Millsite State Park Ferron Canyon Rd PO Box 1343 *TF:* 800-322-3770 ■ *Web:* stateparks.utah.gov	Huntington	UT	84528	435-384-2552	
Otter Creek State Park 400 East SR 22 *Web:* www.stateparks.utah.gov	Antimony	UT	84712	435-624-3268	
Palisade State Park 2200 E Palisade Rd *Web:* www.stateparks.utah.gov	Sterling	UT	84665	435-835-7275	
Piute State Park PO Box 43 *Web:* www.stateparks.utah.gov	Antimony	UT	84712	435-624-3268	
Quail Creek State Park 472 North 5300 West *Web:* www.stateparks.utah.gov	Hurricane	UT	84737	435-879-2378	
Red Fleet State Park 8750 North Hwy 191 *TF:* 800-322-3770 ■ *Web:* stateparks.utah.gov	Vernal	UT	84078	435-789-4432	
Sand Hollow State Park 4405 West 3600 South *Web:* www.stateparks.utah.gov	Hurricane	UT	84737	435-680-0715	
Snow Canyon State Park 1002 Snow Canyon Dr *Web:* www.stateparks.utah.gov	Ivins	UT	84738	435-628-2255	
Starvation State Park 24220 W 7655 S State Park Rd *Web:* www.stateparks.utah.gov	Duchesne	UT	84021	435-738-2326	
Steinaker State Park 4335 N Hwy 191 *TF:* 800-322-3770 ■ *Web:* stateparks.utah.gov	Vernal	UT	84078	435-789-4432	789-4475
Territorial Statehouse State Park 50 W Capitol Ave *Web:* www.stateparks.utah.gov	Fillmore	UT	84631	435-743-5316	
Utah Field House of Natural History State Park 496 E Main St *Web:* stateparks.utah.gov	Vernal	UT	84078	435-789-3799	
Utah Lake State Park 4400 W Ctr St	Provo	UT	84601	801-375-0731	373-4215
Wasatch Mountain State Park 1281 Warm Springs Rd *Web:* www.stateparks.utah.gov	Midway	UT	84049	435-654-1791	
Willard Bay State Park 900 West 650 North Ste A *TF:* 800-322-3770 ■ *Web:* www.stateparks.utah.gov	Willard	UT	84340	435-734-9494	734-2659
Yuba State Park 12225 S Yuba Dam Rd *Web:* www.stateparks.utah.gov	Levan	UT	84639	435-758-2611	

Vermont

				Phone	Fax
Alburg Dunes State Park 151 Coon Pt Rd *Web:* www.vtstateparks.com	Alburg	VT	05440	802-796-4170	
Allis State Park 284 Allis State Pk Rd *Web:* www.vtstateparks.com	Randolph	VT	05060	802-276-3175	

Phone *Fax*

Ascutney State Park 1826 Black Mtn Rd . . . . Windsor VT 05089 802-674-2060
Web: www.vtstateparks.com

Big Deer State Park 1467 Boulder Beach Rd . . . . Groton VT 05046 802-584-3822
Web: www.vtstateparks.com/htm/bigdeer.cfm

Bomoseen State Park 22 Cedar Mtn Rd . . . . Fair Haven VT 05743 802-265-4242
Web: www.vtstateparks.com

Boulder Beach State Park 44 Stillwater Rd . . . . Groton VT 05046 802-584-3823
Web: www.vtstateparks.com

Branbury State Park 3570 Lk Dunmore Rd Rt 53 . . . . Brandon VT 05733 802-247-5925
Web: www.vtstateparks.com

Brighton State Park 102 State Pk Rd . . . . Island Pond VT 05846 802-723-4360
Web: www.vtstateparks.com

Button Bay State Park
5 Button Bay State Pk Rd . . . . Vergennes VT 05491 802-475-2377
Web: www.vtstateparks.com

Camp Plymouth State Park 2008 Scout Camp Rd . . . . Ludlow VT 05149 802-228-2025
Web: www.vtstateparks.com

Coolidge State Park
855 Coolidge State Pk Rd . . . . Plymouth VT 05056 802-672-3612
Web: www.vtstateparks.com

Crystal Lake State Park 96 Bellwater Ave . . . . Barton VT 05822 802-525-6205
TF: 888-409-7579 ■ *Web:* www.vtstateparks.com

D.A.R. State Park 6750 VT Rt 17 W . . . . Addison VT 05491 802-759-2354
Web: www.vtstateparks.com

Elmore State Park 856 VT Rt 12 . . . . Lake Elmore VT 05657 802-888-2982
Web: www.vtstateparks.com

Emerald Lake State Park 65 Emerald Lk Ln . . . . East Dorset VT 05253 802-362-1655
Web: www.vtstateparks.com

Fort Dummer State Park
517 Old Guilford Rd . . . . Brattleboro VT 05301 802-254-2610
Web: www.vtstateparks.com

Gifford Woods State Park 34 Gifford Woods . . . . Killington VT 05751 802-775-5354
Web: www.vtstateparks.com

Grand Isle State Park 36 E Shore S . . . . Grand Isle VT 05458 802-372-4300
Web: www.vtstateparks.com

Green River Reservoir State Park
1393 Green River Dam Rd . . . . Hyde Park VT 05655 802-888-1349
Web: www.vtstateparks.com

Half Moon Pond State Park
1621 Black Pond Rd . . . . Fair Haven VT 05743 802-273-2848
Web: www.vtstateparks.com/htm/halfmoon.cfm

Jamaica State Park 48 Salmon Hole Ln . . . . Jamaica VT 05343 802-874-4600
Web: www.vtstateparks.com

Kill Kare State Park
2714 Hathaway Point Rd PO Box 123 . . . . Saint Albans Bay VT 05481 802-524-6021
Web: www.vtstateparks.com/htm/killkare.htm

Kingsland Bay State Park
787 Kingsland Bay State Pk Rd . . . . Ferrisburgh VT 05456 802-877-3445
Web: www.vtstateparks.com

Knight Island State Park
1 Knight Island PO Box 123 . . . . North Hero VT 05474 802-524-6353
Web: www.vtstateparks.com/htm/knightisland.htm

Lake Carmi State Park
460 Marsh Farm Rd . . . . Enosburg Falls VT 05450 802-933-8383
TF Resv: 888-409-7579 ■ *Web:* www.vtstateparks.com

Lake Saint Catherine State Park
3034 VT Rt 30 S . . . . Poultney VT 05764 802-287-9158
Web: www.vtstateparks.com

Lake Shaftsbury State Park
262 Shaftsbury State Pk Rd . . . . Shaftsbury VT 05262 802-375-9978
Web: www.vtstateparks.com

Little River State Park
3444 Little River Rd . . . . Waterbury VT 05676 802-244-7103
Web: www.vtstateparks.com

Maidstone State Park 4858 Maidstone Lk Rd . . . . Maidstone VT 05905 802-676-3930
Web: www.vtstateparks.com

Molly Stark State Park 705 Rt 9 E . . . . Wilmington VT 05363 802-464-5460
Web: www.vtstateparks.com

Mount Philo State Park 5425 Mt Philo Rd . . . . Charlotte VT 05445 802-425-2390
Web: www.vtstateparks.com

North Hero State Park 3803 Lakeview Dr . . . . North Hero VT 05474 802-372-8727
Web: www.vtstateparks.com

Quechee State Park
1 National Life Dr Davis 2 . . . . Montpelier VT 05620 802-295-2990
Web: www.vtstateparks.com

Ricker Pond State Park
18 Ricker Pond Camp Ground Rd . . . . Groton VT 05046 802-584-3821
Web: www.vtstateparks.com

Sand Bar State Park 1215 US Rt 2 . . . . Milton VT 05468 802-893-2825
Web: www.vtstateparks.com

Seyon Lodge State Park 1 National Life Dr . . . . Vermont VT 05620 802-584-3829
TF: 888-409-7579 ■ *Web:* www.vtstateparks.com/htm/seyon.htm

Smugglers Notch State Park 6443 Mountain Rd . . . . Stowe VT 05672 802-253-4014
Web: www.vtstateparks.com

Stillwater State Park 44 Stillwater Rd . . . . Groton VT 05046 802-584-3822
Web: www.vtstateparks.com

Thetford Hill State Park 622 Academy Rd . . . . Thetford VT 05075 802-785-2266
Web: www.vtstateparks.com

Townshend State Park 2755 State Forest Rd . . . . Townshend VT 05353 802-365-7500
Web: www.vtstateparks.com

Underhill State Park PO Box 249 . . . . Underhill Center VT 05490 802-899-3022
Web: www.vtstateparks.com

Waterbury Ctr State Park
177 Reservoir Rd . . . . Waterbury Center VT 05677 802-244-1226
Web: www.vtstateparks.com

Wilgus State Park PO Box 196 . . . . Ascutney VT 05030 802-674-5422
Web: www.vtstateparks.com

Woodford State Park 142 State Pk Rd . . . . Bennington VT 05201 802-447-7169
Web: www.vtstateparks.com

Virginia

Phone *Fax*

Bear Creek Lake State Park
22 Bear Creek Lk Rd . . . . Cumberland VA 23040 804-492-4410
TF: 800-933-7275 ■
Web: dcr.virginia.gov/state-parks/bear-creek-lake.shtml

Belle Isle State Park 1632 Belle Isle Rd . . . . Lancaster VA 22503 804-462-5030
Web: www.dcr.state.va.us

Bethel Beach Natural Area Preserve
600 E Main St 24th Fl . . . . Richmond VA 23219 804-786-7951
Web: www.dcr.virginia.gov/natural_heritage/natural_area_preserves/bethel.shtml

Breaks Interstate Park
627 Commission Cir PO Box 100 . . . . Breaks VA 24607 276-865-4413
Web: www.breakspark.com

Caledon State Park 11617 Caledon Rd . . . . King George VA 22485 540-663-3861
TF: 800-933-7275 ■ *Web:* www.dcr.virginia.gov

Chippokes Plantation State Park
695 Chippokes Pk Rd . . . . Surry VA 23883 757-294-3728
Web: www.dcr.state.va.us

Claytor Lake State Park 6620 Ben H Boden Dr . . . . Dublin VA 24084 540-643-2500
Web: www.dcr.virginia.gov

Douthat State Park
14239 Douthat State Pk Rd . . . . Millboro VA 24460 540-862-8100 862-8104
TF General: 800-933-7275 ■ *Web:* www.dcr.state.va.us

Fairy Stone State Park 967 Fairystone Lk Dr . . . . Stuart VA 24171 276-930-2424
Web: www.dcr.state.va.us

False Cape State Park
4001 Sandpiper Rd . . . . Virginia Beach VA 23456 757-426-7128 426-0055
TF General: 800-933-7275 ■ *Web:* www.dcr.state.va.us

George Washington's Grist Mill
5513 Mt Vernon Memorial Hwy . . . . Mount Vernon VA 22309 703-780-3383
Web: mountvernon.org

Holliday Lake State Park 2759 State Pk Rd . . . . Appomattox VA 24522 434-248-6308
TF: 800-933-7275 ■ *Web:* www.dcr.state.va.us

Hungry Mother State Park 2854 Pk Blvd . . . . Marion VA 24354 276-781-7400
Web: www.dcr.state.va.us

Kiptopeke State Park 3540 Kiptopeke Dr . . . . Cape Charles VA 23310 757-331-2267
Web: www.dcr.state.va.us

Lake Anna State Park 6800 Lawyers Rd . . . . Spotsylvania VA 22553 540-854-5503
Web: www.dcr.state.va.us

Leesylvania State Park
2001 Daniel K Ludwig Dr . . . . Woodbridge VA 22191 703-730-8205
Web: www.dcr.state.va.us

Mason Neck State Park 7301 High Pt Rd . . . . Lorton VA 22079 703-490-4979
Web: www.dcr.virginia.gov/state-parks/mason-neck

Natural Tunnel State Park
1420 Natural Tunnel Pkwy . . . . Duffield VA 24244 276-940-2674
Web: www.dcr.state.va.us

New River Trail State Park
116 Orphanage Dr . . . . Max Meadows VA 24360 276-699-6778

Occoneechee State Park
1192 Occoneechee Pk Rd . . . . Clarksville VA 23927 434-374-2210 374-9243
TF: 800-933-7275 ■ *Web:* dcr.virginia.gov

Pocahontas State Park 10301 State Pk Rd . . . . Chesterfield VA 23832 804-796-4255 796-4004
TF: 800-933-7275 ■ *Web:* www.dcr.virginia.gov

Raymond R Andy Guest Jr Shenandoah River State Park
350 Daughter of Stars Dr . . . . Bentonville VA 22610 540-622-6840 622-6841
TF: 800-933-7275 ■ *Web:* www.dcr.virginia.gov

Sailor's Creek Battlefield State Park
6541 Saylers Creek Rd . . . . Rice VA 23966 804-561-7510
Web: www.dcr.virginia.gov

Shot Tower Historical State Park
176 Orphanage Dr . . . . Foster Falls VA 24360 276-699-6778
Web: www.dcr.virginia.gov

Sky Meadows State Park 11012 Edmonds Ln . . . . Delaplane VA 20144 540-592-3556
Web: www.dcr.state.va.us

Staunton River State Park
1170 Staunton Tr . . . . Scottsburg VA 24589 434-572-4623
Web: www.dcr.state.va.us

Twin Lakes State Park 788 Twin Lakes Rd . . . . Green Bay VA 23942 434-392-3435
TF: 800-933-7275 ■ *Web:* www.dcr.virginia.gov

Wilderness Road State Park 8051 Wilderness Rd . . . . Ewing VA 24248 276-445-3065
Web: www.friendsofwildernessroad.org

Washington

Phone *Fax*

Battle Ground Lake State Park
18002 NE 249th St . . . . Battle Ground WA 98604 360-687-4621
TF: 888-226-7688 ■ *Web:* www.parks.wa.gov

Bay View State Park
10901 Bay View-Edison Rd . . . . Mount Vernon WA 98273 360-757-0227
Web: www.parks.wa.gov

Beacon Rock State Park 34841 State Rd 14 . . . . Skamania WA 98648 509-427-8265 427-8265
TF: 888-226-7688 ■ *Web:* parks.state.wa.us/474/Beacon-Rock

Belfair State Park 3151 NE State Rt 300 . . . . Belfair WA 98528 360-275-0668 275-8734
Web: www.parks.wa.gov

Birch Bay State Park 5105 Helwig Rd . . . . Blaine WA 98230 360-371-2800 371-0455
Web: www.parks.wa.gov

Bogachiel State Park 185983 Hwy 101 . . . . Forks WA 98331 360-374-6356
Web: www.parks.wa.gov

Bridle Trails State Park
5300 116th Ave. N.W 20606 SE 56th St . . . . Issaquah WA 98027 425-455-7010
Web: www.parks.wa.gov

Brooks Memorial State Park 2465 Hwy 97 . . . . Goldendale WA 98620 509-773-4611
Web: www.parks.wa.gov

Camano Island State Park
2269 S Lowell Pt Rd . . . . Camano Island WA 98282 360-387-3031
Web: parks.wa.gov

Cape Disappointment State Park PO Box 488 . . . . Ilwaco WA 98624 360-642-3078
Web: capedisappointment.org

				Phone	Fax
Columbia Hills State Park PO Box 426	Dallesport	WA	98617	509-767-1159	
Web: www.parks.wa.gov					
Conconully State Park 119 W Broadway Ave	Conconully	WA	98819	509-826-7408	
Web: www.parks.wa.gov					
Curlew Lake State Park 62 State Pk Rd	Republic	WA	99166	509-775-3592	
Web: www.parks.wa.gov					
Daroga State Park 1 S Daroga Pk Rd	Orondo	WA	98843	509-664-6380	
Web: www.parks.wa.gov					
Dash Point State Park 5700 SW Dash Pt Rd	Federal Way	WA	98023	253-661-4955	
TF: 888-226-7688 ■ *Web:* www.parks.wa.gov					
Deception Pass State Park 41229 Washington 20	Oak Harbor	WA	98277	360-675-2417	675-8991
Web: www.parks.wa.gov					
Fay Bainbridge State Park 15446 Sunrise Dr NE	Bainbridge Island	WA	98110	206-842-3931	
Web: www.parks.wa.gov					
Federation Forest State Park 49201 SE Enumclaw Chinook Pass Rd	Enumclaw	WA	98022	360-663-2207	
Web: www.parks.wa.gov					
Fields Spring State Park 992 Pk Rd	Anatone	WA	99401	509-256-3332	
Web: www.parks.wa.gov					
Fort Casey State Park 1280 S Engle Rd	Coupeville	WA	98239	360-678-4519	
Web: www.parks.wa.gov					
Fort Columbia State Park PO Box 488	Chinook	WA	98614	360-642-3078	
Web: www.parks.wa.gov					
Fort Ebey State Park 400 Hill Vly Dr	Coupeville	WA	98239	360-678-4636	
Web: www.parks.wa.gov					
Fort Flagler State Park 10541 Flagler Rd	Nordland	WA	98358	360-385-1259	
Web: www.parks.wa.gov					
Fort Simcoe State Park 5150 Ft Simcoe Rd	White Swan	WA	98952	509-874-2372	
Web: www.parks.wa.gov					
Fort Worden State Park 200 Battery Way	Port Townsend	WA	98368	360-344-4400	
Web: www.parks.wa.gov/fortworden					
Ginkgo Petrified Forest State Park 4511 Huntzinger Rd	Vantage	WA	98950	509-856-2700	
Web: www.parks.wa.gov					
Goldendale Observatory State Park 1602 Observatory Dr.	Goldendale	WA	98620	509-773-3141	
Web: www.parks.wa.gov					
Hope Island State Park E 391 Wingert Rd.	Shelton	WA	98584	360-426-9226	
Web: www.parks.wa.gov					
Ike Kinswa State Park 873 SR 122	Silver Creek	WA	98585	360-983-3402	
Web: www.parks.wa.gov					
Illahee State Park 3540 NE Bahia Vista Dr	Bremerton	WA	98310	360-478-6460	
Web: www.parks.wa.gov					
Jarrell Cove State Park 391 E Wingert Rd	Shelton	WA	98584	360-426-9226	
Web: www.parks.wa.gov					
Kanaskat-Palmer State Park 32101 Kanaskat-Cumberland Rd	Ravensdale	WA	98051	360-886-0148	
Web: www.parks.wa.gov					
Kitsap Memorial State Park 202 NE Pk St.	Poulsbo	WA	98370	360-779-3205	
Web: www.parks.wa.gov					
Kopachuck State Park 11101 56th St NW	Gig Harbor	WA	98335	253-265-3606	
Web: www.parks.wa.gov					
Lake Chelan State Park 7544 S Lakeshore Dr	Chelan	WA	98816	509-687-3710	
Web: www.parks.wa.gov					
Lake Easton State Park 150 Lk Easton State Pk Rd	Easton	WA	98925	509-656-2230	
Web: www.parks.wa.gov					
Lake Sammamish State Park 1111 Israel Rd SW	Tumwater	WA	98504	425-455-7010	
Web: www.parks.wa.gov					
Lake Sylvia State Park PO Box 701	Montesano	WA	98563	360-249-3621	
Web: www.parks.wa.gov					
Lake Wenatchee State Park 21588 A Hwy 207	Leavenworth	WA	98826	509-763-3101	
Web: www.parks.wa.gov					
Larrabee State Park 245 Chuckanut Dr	Bellingham	WA	98226	360-676-2093	
Web: www.parks.wa.gov					
Lewis & Clark State Park 4583 Jackson Hwy	Winlock	WA	98596	360-864-2643	
Web: www.parks.wa.gov					
Lewis & Clark Trail State Park 36149 Hwy 12	Dayton	WA	99328	509-337-6457	
Web: www.parks.wa.gov					
Lime Kiln Point State Park 1567 Westside Rd.	Friday Harbor	WA	98250	360-378-2044	
Web: www.parks.wa.gov					
Lincoln Rock State Park 13253 State Rt 2	East Wenatchee	WA	98802	509-884-8702	
Web: www.parks.wa.gov					
Manchester State Park 7767 E Hilldale	Port Orchard	WA	98366	360-871-4065	
Maryhill State Park 50 Hwy 97	Goldendale	WA	98620	509-773-5007	
Millersylvania State Park 12245 Tilley Rd S	Olympia	WA	98512	360-753-1519	664-2180
Web: www.parks.wa.gov					
Moran State Park 3572 Olga Rd.	Eastsound	WA	98245	360-376-2326	
Web: www.parks.wa.gov					
Nolte State Park 36921 Veazie Cumberland Rd	Enumclaw	WA	98022	360-825-4646	
Web: www.parks.wa.gov					
Ocean City State Park 148 State Rt 115	Hoquiam	WA	98550	360-289-3553	
Web: www.parks.wa.gov					
Old Fort Townsend State Park 1370 Old Ft Townsend Rd	Port Townsend	WA	98368	360-385-3595	
Web: parks.state.wa.us					
Olmstead Place State Park 921 N Ferguson Rd.	Ellensburg	WA	98926	509-925-1943	
Web: www.parks.wa.gov					
Osoyoos Lake State Park 2207 Juniper	Oroville	WA	98844	509-476-2926	
Web: www.oroville-wa.com					
Pacific Pines State Park 25904 R St	Ocean Park	WA	98640	360-902-8844	
Web: www.stateparks.com					
Palouse Falls State Park 100 SW Main St PO Box 541	Washtucna	WA	99371	360-902-8844	
Web: www.parks.wa.gov					
Paradise Point State Park 33914 NW Paradise Pk Rd	Ridgefield	WA	98642	360-263-2350	
Web: www.parks.wa.gov					
Peace Arch State Park PO Box 87	Blaine	WA	98230	360-332-8221	
Web: www.parks.wa.gov					
Pearrygin Lake State Park 561 Bear Creek Rd	Winthrop	WA	98862	509-996-2370	
Web: www.parks.wa.gov					
Penrose Point State Park 321 158th KPS	Lakebay	WA	98349	253-884-2514	
Potholes State Park 6762 Hwy 262 SE	Othello	WA	99344	509-346-2759	
Web: parks.state.wa.us					
Potlatch State Park 21020 N US Hwy 101	Shelton	WA	98584	360-877-5361	
Web: www.parks.wa.gov					
Rainbow Falls State Park 4008 Washington 6	Chehalis	WA	98532	360-291-3767	291-3377
Web: www.parks.wa.gov					
Rasar State Park 38730 Cape Horn Rd	Concrete	WA	98237	360-826-3942	
Web: parks.state.wa.us					
Rockport State Park 51905 WA-20	Rockport	WA	98283	360-853-8461	
Web: www.parks.wa.gov					
Sacajawea State Park 2503 Sacajawea Pk Rd	Pasco	WA	99301	509-545-2361	
Web: www.parks.wa.gov					
Saint Edward State Park 14445 Juanita Dr NE	Kenmore	WA	98028	425-823-2992	
Web: www.parks.wa.gov					
Saltwater State Park 25205 Eigth Pl S	Des Moines	WA	98198	253-661-4956	
Web: www.parks.wa.gov					
Scenic Beach State Park PO Box 7	Seabeck	WA	98380	360-830-5079	
Web: www.parks.wa.gov					
Schafer State Park W 1365 Schafer Pk Rd	Elma	WA	98541	360-482-3852	
Web: parks.state.wa.us					
Seaquest State Park 3030 Spirit Lk Hwy.	Castle Rock	WA	98611	360-274-8633	
Web: www.parks.wa.gov					
Sequim Bay State Park 269035 Hwy 101	Sequim	WA	98382	360-683-4235	
Web: www.parks.wa.gov					
Shine Tidelands State Park 202 NE Pk St	Poulsbo	WA	98370	360-902-8844	
Web: parks.state.wa.us					
South Whidbey Island State Park 4128 Smugglers Cove Rd	Freeland	WA	98249	360-331-4559	
Web: parks.state.wa.us					
Steamboat Rock State Park 51052 Washington 155	Electric City	WA	99123	509-633-1304	
Web: www.parks.wa.gov					
Sun Lakes State Park 34875 Pk Ln Rd NE.	Coulee City	WA	99115	509-632-5583	
Web: www.parks.wa.gov					
Tolmie State Park 7730 61st Ave NE	Olympia	WA	98506	360-456-6464	459-0104
Web: www.parks.wa.gov					
Twanoh State Park 12190 E Hwy 106	Union	WA	98592	360-275-2222	
Web: www.parks.wa.gov					
Twenty-Five Mile Creek State Park 20530 S Lakeshore Rd	Chelan	WA	98816	509-687-3710	
Web: www.parks.wa.gov					
Twin Harbors Beach State Park Hwy 105	Westport	WA	98595	360-268-9717	
Wallace Falls State Park 14503 Wallace Lk Rd	Gold Bar	WA	98251	360-793-0420	
Web: parks.state.wa.us					
Wenatchee Confluence State Park 333 Olds Stn Rd	Wenatchee	WA	98801	509-664-6373	
Web: www.parks.wa.gov					
Wenberg State Park 15430 E Lk Goodwin Rd	Stanwood	WA	98292	360-652-7417	
Yakima Sportsman State Park 904 Keys Rd	Yakima	WA	98901	509-665-4319	
Web: parks.state.wa.us					

West Virginia

				Phone	Fax
Babcock State Park 486 Babcock Rd	Clifftop	WV	25831	304-438-3004	
TF: 800-225-5982 ■ *Web:* www.babcocksp.com					
Beartown State Park HC 64 PO Box 189	Hillsboro	WV	24946	304-653-4254	653-4254
TF General: 800-225-5982 ■ *Web:* www.beartownstatepark.com					
Beech Fork State Park 5601 Long Branch Rd.	Barboursville	WV	25504	304-528-5794	
Web: www.beechforksp.com					
Blackwater Falls State Park PO Box 490	Davis	WV	26260	304-259-5216	
Web: www.blackwaterfalls.com					
Blennerhassett Island Historical State Park 137 Juliana St.	Parkersburg	WV	26101	304-420-4800	
Web: www.blennerhassettislandstatepark.com					
Bluestone State Park HC 78	Hinton	WV	25951	304-466-2805	
Web: www.bluestonesp.com					
Cabwaylingo State Forest 4279 Cabwaylingo Pk Rd	Dunlow	WV	25511	304-385-4255	
Web: www.cabwaylingo.com					
Cacapon Resort State Park 818 Cacapon Lodge Dr.	Berkeley Springs	WV	25411	304-258-1022	
Web: www.cacaponresort.com					
Camp Creek State Park PO Box 119	Camp Creek	WV	25820	304-425-9481	
Web: www.campcreekstatepark.com					
Carnifex Ferry Battlefield State Park 1194 Carnifex Ferry Rd.	Summersville	WV	26651	304-872-0825	
Web: www.carnifexferrybattlefieldstatepark.com					
Cass Scenic Railroad State Park 242 Main St	Cass	WV	24927	304-456-4300	
Web: www.cassrailroad.com					
Cathedral State Park Rt 1 12 Cathedral Way	Aurora	WV	26705	304-735-3771	
TF: 800-225-5982 ■ *Web:* www.cathedralstatepark.com					
Cedar Creek State Park 2947 Cedar Creek Rd	Glenville	WV	26351	304-462-7158	
Web: www.cedarcreeksp.com					
Chief Logan State Park General Delivery	Logan	WV	25601	304-792-7125	
Web: www.chiefloganstatepark.com					
Coopers Rock State Forest 61 County Line Dr	Bruceton Mills	WV	26525	304-594-1561	
TF: 800-225-5982 ■ *Web:* www.coopersrockstateforest.com					
Droop Mountain Battlefield State Park 683 Droop Park Rd.	Hillsboro	WV	24946	304-653-4254	653-4254
Web: www.droopmountainbattlefield.com					

	City	State	Zip	Phone	Fax
Hawks Nest State Park PO Box 857 *Web:* www.hawksnestsp.com	Ansted	WV	25812	304-658-5212	658-4549
Holly River State Park PO Box 70 *Web:* www.hollyriver.com	Hacker Valley	WV	26222	304-493-6353	
Kanawha State Forest 7500 Kanawha State Forest Dr *Web:* www.kanawhastateforest.com	Charleston	WV	25314	304-558-3500	558-3508
Kumbrabow State Forest PO Box 65 *Web:* kumbrabow.com	Huttonsville	WV	26273	304-335-2219	
Little Beaver State Park 1402 Grandview Rd *Web:* www.littlebeaverstatepark.com	Beaver	WV	25813	304-763-2494	
Lost River State Park 321 Pk Dr *Web:* www.lostriversp.com	Mathias	WV	26812	304-897-5372	
Moncove Lake State Park Rt-4 PO Box 73-A *Web:* www.moncovelakestatepark.com	Gap Mills	WV	24941	304-772-3450	772-3450
North Bend State Park 202 N Bend Pk Rd *Web:* www.northbendsp.com	Cairo	WV	26337	304-643-2931	
Panther State Forest HC 63 PO Box Box 923 *TF:* 800-225-5982 ■ *Web:* www.pantherstateforest.com	Panther	WV	24872	304-938-2252	
Pinnacle Rock State Park 6407 Coal Heritage Rd *Web:* www.pinnaclerockstatepark.com	Bluefield	WV	24701	304-248-8565	
Pipestem Resort State Park PO Box 150 *TF:* 800-225-5982 ■ *Web:* www.pipestemresort.com	Pipestem	WV	25979	304-466-1800	
Pricketts Fort State Park 106 Overfort Ln *Web:* www.prickettsfortstatepark.com	Fairmont	WV	26554	304-363-3030	
Seneca State Forest 10135 Browns Creek Rd *Web:* www.senecastateforest.com	Dunmore	WV	24934	304-799-6213	799-6213
Tomlinson Run State Park PO Box 97 *Web:* www.tomlinsonrunsp.com	New Manchester	WV	26056	304-564-3651	
Tu-Endie-Wei State Park PO Box 486 *Web:* www.tu-endie-weistatepark.com	Point Pleasant	WV	25550	304-675-0869	
Twin Falls Resort State Park PO Box 667 Rt 97 *Web:* www.twinfallsresort.com	Mullens	WV	25882	304-294-4000	294-4000
Watters Smith Memorial State Park PO Box 296 *Web:* www.watterssmithstatepark.com	Lost Creek	WV	26385	304-745-3081	

Wisconsin

	City	State	Zip	Phone	Fax
Amnicon Falls State Park 4279 County Hwy U *Web:* dnr.wi.gov/topic/parks/name/amnicon	South Range	WI	54874	715-398-3000	
Aztalan State Park 1213 S Main St *Web:* dnr.wi.gov	Lake Mills	WI	53551	920-648-8774	648-5166
Big Foot Beach State Park 1452 Wells St *TF:* 888-936-7463 ■ *Web:* www.dnr.wi.gov	Lake Geneva	WI	53147	262-248-2528	
Black River State Forest 101 S Webster St PO Box 7921 *TF:* 888-936-7463 ■ *Web:* dnr.wi.gov	Madison	WI	53707	608-266-2621	275-3338
Blue Mound State Park 4350 Mounds Pk Rd *Web:* dnr.wi.gov	Blue Mounds	WI	53517	608-437-5711	
Browntown-Cadiz Springs State Recreation Area PO Box 36 *Web:* www.cadizsprings.com	Browntown	WI	53522	608-966-3777	
Brule River State Forest 6250 S Ranger Rd *Web:* www.dnr.wi.gov	Brule	WI	54820	715-372-5678	372-4836
Brunet Island State Park 23125 255th St *Web:* dnr.wi.gov/newurl.html	Cornell	WI	54732	715-239-6888	
Buckhorn State Park W8450 Buckhorn Pk Ave *Web:* dnr.wi.gov/newurl.html	Necedah	WI	54646	608-565-2789	
Capital Springs 3101 Lk Farm Rd *Web:* friendsofcapitalsprings.org	Madison	WI	53711	608-224-3606	
Chippewa Moraine Ice Age State Recreation Area 13394 County Hwy M *Web:* dnr.wi.gov	New Auburn	WI	54757	715-967-2800	967-2801
Copper Falls State Park 36764 Copper Falls Rd *Web:* dnr.wi.gov	Mellen	WI	54546	715-274-5123	
Council Grounds State Park N1895 Council Grounds Dr *Web:* reserveamerica.com	Merrill	WI	54452	715-536-8773	
Devil's Lake State Park S5975 Pk Rd *Web:* dnr.wi.gov	Baraboo	WI	53913	608-356-8301	356-4281
Flambeau River State Forest W1613 County Rd *Web:* dnr.wi.gov	Winter	WI	54896	715-332-5271	
Governor Dodge State Park 4175 State Hwy 23 N *Web:* dnr.wi.gov	Dodgeville	WI	53533	608-935-2315	
Governor Knowles State Forest 325 SR 70 *Web:* dnr.wi.gov/newurl.html	Grantsburg	WI	54840	715-463-2898	
Governor Nelson State Park 5140 County Hwy M *Web:* www.dnr.wi.gov	Waunakee	WI	53597	608-831-3005	
Governor Thompson State Park N10008 Paust Ln *Web:* www.dnr.wi.gov	Crivitz	WI	54114	715-757-3979	
Harrington Beach State Park 531 County Rd D *Web:* dnr.wi.gov	Belgium	WI	53004	262-285-3015	
Hartman Creek State Park N2480 Hartman Creek Rd *Web:* dnr.wi.gov	Waupaca	WI	54981	715-258-2372	
Havenwoods State Forest 6141 N Hopkins St *TF:* 888-936-7463 ■ *Web:* dnr.wi.gov	Milwaukee	WI	53209	414-527-0232	527-0761
Heritage Hill State Historical Park 2640 S Webster Ave *TF:* 800-721-5150 ■ *Web:* heritagehillgb.org	Green Bay	WI	54301	920-448-5150	
High Cliff State Park N7630 State Pk Rd *Web:* dnr.wi.gov/newurl.html	Sherwood	WI	54169	920-989-1106	
Hoffman Hills State Recreation Area 921 BrickyaRd Rd *Web:* www.dnr.wi.gov	Menomonie	WI	54751	715-232-1242	
Interstate State Park PO Box 703 *Web:* dnr.wi.gov	Saint Croix Falls	WI	54024	715-483-3747	
Kettle Moraine State Forest - Northern Unit N1765 Hwy G *Web:* www.dnr.wi.gov	Campbellsport	WI	53010	262-626-2116	
Kettle Moraine State Forest - Pike Lake Unit 3544 Kettle Moraine Rd *Web:* dnr.wi.gov	Hartford	WI	53027	262-670-3400	670-3411
Kettle Moraine State Forest Southern Unit S91 W39091 Hwy 59 *Web:* dnr.wi.gov/newurl.html	Eagle	WI	53119	262-594-6200	
Kettle Moraine State Forest-Lapham Peak Unit W329 N846 County Hwy C *Web:* dnr.wi.gov	Delafield	WI	53018	262-646-4421	
Kinnickinnic State Park W11983 820th Ave. *Web:* dnr.wi.gov	River Falls	WI	54022	715-425-1129	425-0010
Kohler-Andrae State Park 1020 Beach Pk Ln *Web:* dnr.wi.gov/topic/parks/name/kohlerandrae	Sheboygan	WI	53081	920-451-4080	451-4086
Lake Kegonsa State Park 2405 Door Creek Rd *TF General:* 888-947-2757 ■ *Web:* dnr.wi.gov	Stoughton	WI	53589	608-873-9695	873-0674
Lake Wissota State Park 18127 County Hwy O *TF:* 800-847-9367 ■ *Web:* dnr.wi.gov	Chippewa Falls	WI	54729	715-382-4574	382-5187
Lakeshore State Park 2300 N Martin Luther King Jr Dr *Web:* dnr.wi.gov	Milwaukee	WI	53212	414-263-8500	
Merrick State Park S2965 Sr 35 *Web:* dnr.wi.gov	Fountain City	WI	54629	608-687-4936	
Mirror Lake State Park E10320 Fern Dell Rd *Web:* dnr.wi.gov	Baraboo	WI	53913	608-254-2333	
Nelson Dewey State Park PO Box 658 *TF:* 888-936-7463 ■ *Web:* dnr.wi.gov/topic/parks/name/nelsondewey	Cassville	WI	53806	608-725-5374	
New Glarus Woods State Park (NGWSP) W5446 County Hwy NN *Web:* dnr.wi.gov	New Glarus	WI	53574	608-527-2335	527-6435
Newport State Park 475 County Rd NP *TF:* 800-847-9367 ■ *Web:* dnr.wi.gov	Ellison Bay	WI	54210	920-854-2500	854-1914
Northern Highland - American Legion State Forest 4125 County Hwy M *TF:* 800-847-9367 ■ *Web:* dnr.wi.gov	Boulder Junction	WI	54512	715-385-2727	385-2752
Pattison State Park 6294 S State Rd 35 *Web:* dnr.wi.gov/newurl.html	Superior	WI	54880	715-399-3111	
Peninsula State Park 9462 Shore Rd *Web:* www.dnr.wi.gov	Fish Creek	WI	54212	920-868-3258	
Perrot State Park W26247 Sullivan Rd *Web:* dnr.wi.gov	Trempealeau	WI	54661	608-534-6409	
Peshtigo River State Forest N10008 Paust Ln. *Web:* dnr.wi.gov/newurl.html	Crivitz	WI	54114	715-757-3965	
Point Beach State Forest 9400 County Hwy O *Web:* dnr.wi.gov/newurl.html	Two Rivers	WI	54241	920-794-7480	
Potawatomi State Park 3740 County Rd PD *TF:* 800-847-9367 ■ *Web:* www.dnr.wi.gov	Sturgeon Bay	WI	54235	920-746-2890	746-2896
Richard Bong State Recreation Area 26313 Burlington Rd *Web:* dnr.wi.gov/newurl.html	Kansasville	WI	53139	262-878-5600	878-5615
Rock Island State Park 1924 Indian Pt Rd *Web:* dnr.wi.gov/newurl.html	Washington Island	WI	54246	920-847-2235	
Tower Hill State Park 5808 County Rd C *Web:* dnr.wi.gov	Spring Green	WI	53588	608-588-2116	
Whitefish Dunes State Park 3275 County Hwy WD *Web:* dnr.wi.gov	Sturgeon Bay	WI	54235	920-823-2400	823-2640
Wildcat Mountain State Park E13660 State Hwy 33 PO Box 99 *Web:* www.dnr.wi.gov	Ontario	WI	54651	608-337-4775	
Willow River State Park 1034 County Hwy A *TF:* 800-847-9367 ■ *Web:* dnr.wi.gov	Hudson	WI	54016	715-386-5931	386-0431
Wyalusing State Park 13081 State Pk Ln *Web:* www.wyalusing.org	Bagley	WI	53801	608-996-2261	
Yellowstone Lake State Park 8495 Lake Rd *Web:* www.dnr.wi.gov	Blanchardville	WI	53516	608-523-4427	

Wyoming

	City	State	Zip	Phone	Fax
Bear River State Park 601 Bear River Dr	Evanston	WY	82930	307-789-6547	
Boysen State Park 15 Ash St	Shoshoni	WY	82649	307-876-2796	
Buffalo Bill State Park 47 Lakeside Rd	Cody	WY	82414	307-587-9227	
Connor Battlefield State Historic Site Hwy 14 *Web:* wyoparks.state.wy.us/site/siteinfo.aspx?siteid=15	Ranchester	WY	82842	307-684-7629	
Fort Bridger State Historic Site PO Box 35 *Web:* www.wyomingtourism.org	Fort Bridger	WY	82933	307-782-3842	
Fort Fetterman State Historic Site 752 Hwy 93	Douglas	WY	82633	307-358-2864	
Fort Fred Steele State Historic Site I-80 Exit 228 *Web:* wyoparks.state.wy.us	Sinclair	WY	82334	307-320-3013	
Fort Phil Kearny State Historic Site 528 Wagon Box Rd *Web:* wyoparks.state.wy.us	Story	WY	82842	307-684-7629	684-7967
Glendo State Park 397 Glendo Pk Rd *Web:* wyoparks.state.wy.us	Glendo	WY	82213	307-735-4433	
Guernsey State Park PO Box 429 *Web:* wyoparks.state.wy.us/site/siteinfo.aspx?siteid=7	Guernsey	WY	82214	307-836-2334	
Hawk Springs State Recreation Area 2301 Central Ave *Web:* wyoparks.state.wy.us/permits/index.aspx	Cheyenne	WY	82002	307-777-6323	
Historic Governors' Mansion 300 E 21st St	Cheyenne	WY	82001	307-777-7878	
Independence Rock State Historic Site State Rt 220	Alcova	WY	82620	307-577-5150	

Phone Fax

Keyhole State Park 22 Marina Rd .... Moorcroft WY 82721 307-756-3596
Web: wyoparks.state.wy.us

Medicine Lodge State Archaeological Site
Hwy 31 .... Hyattville WY 82428 307-469-2234
Web: wyoparks.state.wy.us

Seminoe State Park Seminoe Dam Rt .... Sinclair WY 82334 307-320-3013
Web: wyoparks.state.wy.us

Trail End State Historic Site
400 Clarendon Ave .... Sheridan WY 82801 307-674-4589 672-1720
Web: www.trailend.co

566 PARTY GOODS

Phone Fax

Alin Party Supplies Co 4139 Woodruff Ave .... Lakewood CA 90713 562-420-2489
Web: www.alinpartysupply.com

Amscan Inc 80 Grasslands Rd .... Elmsford NY 10523 914-345-2020 345-3884
TF: 800-444-8887 ■ *Web:* www.amscan.com

Balloons Everywhere Inc 16474 Greeno Rd .... Fairhope AL 36532 800-239-2000 210-2105*
**Fax Area Code:* 251 ■ *TF:* 800-239-2000 ■ *Web:* www.balloons.com

Beistle Co 1 Beistle Plz .... Shippensburg PA 17257 717-532-2131 532-7789
Web: www.beistle.com

Designware Inc 54 Fieldstone-Bashan Dr .... East Haddam CT 06423 860-873-8938 873-9993
Web: www.designwareinc.com

iParty Corp 270 Bridge St Ste 301 .... Dedham MA 02026 781-329-3952
NYSE: IPT ■ *Web:* partycity.com

Paper Shack & Party Store Inc, The
2430 E Texas St .... Bossier City LA 71111 318-746-4108
Web: www.papershackpartystore.com

Paper Store Inc 20 Main St .... Acton MA 01720 844-480-7100 263-2466*
**Fax Area Code:* 978 ■ *TF:* 844-480-7100 ■ *Web:* www.thepaperstore.com

Party City Corp 25 Green Pond Rd Ste 1 .... Rockaway NJ 07866 973-453-8600
TF: 800-727-8924 ■ *Web:* www.partycity.com

Party Fair Inc 4345 US Hwy 9 .... Freehold NJ 07728 732-780-1110
Web: www.partyfair.com

567 PATTERNS - INDUSTRIAL

Phone Fax

Allen Pattern of Michigan
202 McGrath Pl .... Battle Creek MI 49014 269-963-4131 963-4327

Anderson Global Inc
500 W Sherman Blvd .... Muskegon Heights MI 49444 231-733-2164 733-1288
Web: www.andersonglobal.com

Central Pattern Co 8830 Pershall Rd .... Hazelwood MO 63042 314-524-3626 522-8399
Web: www.centralpattern.com

Cunningham Pattern & Engineering Inc
4399 US 31 N PO Box 854 .... Columbus IN 47201 812-379-9571 379-9574
Web: www.cpepattern.com

D & F Corp 42455 Merrill Rd .... Sterling Heights MI 48314 586-254-5300 254-5610
Web: clientinfo.com/d-f

Foley Pattern Company Inc
500 W 11th St PO Box 150 .... Auburn IN 46706 260-925-4113 925-4115

Freeman Mfg & Supply Co 1101 Moore Rd .... Avon OH 44011 440-934-1902 934-7200
TF: 800-321-8511 ■ *Web:* www.freemansupply.com

General Pattern Company Inc 3075 84th Ln NE .... Blaine MN 55449 763-780-3518
Web: www.generalpattern.com

Gopher Pattern Works Inc
422 Roosevelt St NE .... Minneapolis MN 55413 612-331-5512 331-6513

Hub Pattern Corp 2113 Salem Ave .... Roanoke VA 24016 540-342-3505 343-5337
TF: 800-482-3505 ■ *Web:* www.hubcorp.net

Kakivik Asset Management LLC
560 E 34th Ave Ste 200 .... Anchorage AK 99503 907-770-9400 770-9450
Web: www.kakivik.com

Production Pattern Co 560 Solon Rd .... Bedford OH 44146 440-439-3243
Web: www.prodpatt.com

United Industries Inc 1901 Revere Beach Pkwy .... Everett MA 02149 617-387-9500 387-6331
Web: www.united-ind.com

568 PATTERNS - SEWING

Phone Fax

Bonfit America Inc
5741 Buckingham Pkwy Unit A .... Culver City CA 90232 310-204-7880
TF: 800-526-6348 ■ *Web:* www.bonfit.com

Kwik-Sew Pattern Co Inc
3000 N Washington Ave .... Minneapolis MN 55411 612-521-7651
Web: kwiksew.mccall.com

McCall Pattern Co 615 McCall Rd .... Manhattan KS 66502 800-255-2762
TF: 800-255-2762 ■ *Web:* www.mccall.com

569 PAWN SHOPS

Phone Fax

EZCORP Inc 1901 Capital Pkwy .... Austin TX 78746 512-314-3400
NASDAQ: EZPW ■ *TF:* 800-873-7296 ■ *Web:* www.ezcorp.com

Facekey Corp 900 NE Loop 410 Ste D401 .... San Antonio TX 78209 210-826-8811
Web: www.facekey.com

First Cash Financial Services Inc
690 E Lamar Blvd Ste 400 .... Arlington TX 76011 817-460-3947 461-7019
NASDAQ: FCFS ■ *TF:* 800-290-4598 ■ *Web:* ww2.firstcash.com

Go Apply Inc 27081 Aliso Creek Rd Ste 200 .... Aliso Viejo CA 92656 949-681-4884
Web: www.eleadz.com

Intuition Systems Inc
9428 Baymeadows Rd Ste 600 .... Jacksonville FL 32256 904-421-7115
Web: www.intuitionsystems.com

Phone Fax

Maxium Financial Services Inc
30 Vogell Rd Ste 1 .... Richmond Hill ON L4B3K6 905-780-6150
TF: 800-379-5888 ■ *Web:* www.maxium.net

Resurgent Capital Services L P
15 S Main St Ste 600 .... Greenville SC 29601 888-665-0374
TF: 888-665-0374 ■ *Web:* www.rcap.com

Us Pawn & Auto Inc 821 N US Hwy 17-92 .... Longwood FL 32750 407-699-5885
Web: www.uspawnandauto.com

570 PAYROLL SERVICES

See Also Data Processing & Related Services p. 2181; Professional Employer Organizations (PEOs) p. 2989

Phone Fax

Advantage Payroll Services Inc
126 Merrow Rd PO Box 1330 .... Auburn ME 04211 207-784-0178 786-0490
TF Cust Svc: 800-876-0178 ■ *Web:* www.advantagepayroll.com

Automatic Data Processing Inc (ADP) 1 ADP Blvd .... Roseland NJ 07068 800-225-5237
NASDAQ: ADP ■ *TF:* 800-225-5237 ■ *Web:* www.adp.com

Basic Pay LLC 231 W 29th St Ste 1207 .... New York NY 10001 212-684-8827 684-6036
Web: www.basicpay.biz

Celergo LLC 750 Estate Dr Ste 110 .... Deerfield IL 60015 847-512-2600
Web: www.celergo.com

CheckPoint HR 2035 Lincoln Hwy Ste 1080 .... Edison NJ 08817 732-287-8270 287-2297
TF: 800-385-0331 ■ *Web:* www.checkpointhr.com

Corporate Business Solutions LLC
600 S Tower 225 Peachtree St NE .... Atlanta GA 30303 404-521-6030
TF: 800-239-8182 ■ *Web:* www.cbshro.com

DLH Holdings Corp
1776 Peachtree St NW Ste 300S .... Atlanta GA 30309 770-554-3545
NASDAQ: DLHC ■ *Web:* www.dlhcorp.com

DSI Payroll Services 300 Atrium Dr .... Somerset NJ 08873 732-748-3200
Web: businessfinder.lehighvalleylive.com

Employers Resource Management Co
1301 S Vista Ave Ste 200 .... Boise ID 83705 208-376-3000 363-7356
TF: 800-574-4668 ■ *Web:* www.employersresource.com

Hiregenics 47742 Van Dyke Ave .... Shelby Township MI 48317 866-315-5489
TF: 866-315-5489 ■ *Web:* hiregenics.acsicorp.com

Media Services
500 S Sepulveda Blvd 4th Fl .... Los Angeles CA 90049 310-440-9600 472-9979
TF: 800-738-0409 ■ *Web:* www.media-services.com

Mosaic Business Solutions LLC
3262 Superior Ln Ste 217 .... Bowie MD 20715 301-464-2665
Web: www.mosaicbusiness.net

Nexpay 5121 N Mccoll Rd .... Mcallen TX 78504 956-994-1800
Web: www.nexpay.us

Patriot Staffing & Services Llc
47 Eggert Ave .... Metuchen NJ 08840 888-412-6999
TF: 888-412-6999 ■ *Web:* www.patstaffing.com

Paychex Inc 911 Panorama Trl S .... Rochester NY 14625 585-385-6666
NASDAQ: PAYX ■ *TF:* 800-828-4411 ■ *Web:* www.paychex.com

Paychex Major Market Services
12647 Alcosta Blvd Ste 200 .... San Ramon CA 94583 925-242-0700
TF: 888-243-9329 ■ *Web:* www.paychex.com

PayData Payroll Services Inc
PO Box 706 .... Essex Junction VT 05453 802-655-6160
Web: www.paydata.com

Payday Payroll Services
6465 College Park Sq Ste 200 .... Virginia Beach VA 23464 757-523-0605
Web: www.paydaypayroll.com

Paypro Corp 450 Wireless Blvd .... Hauppauge NY 11788 631-777-1100
Web: www.payprocorp.com

Payroll Factory, The 18 E Lancaster Ave .... Malvern PA 19355 610-644-4569
Web: www.thepayrollfactory.com

Payroll Management Inc
348 Miracle Strip Pkwy Ste 39 .... Fort Walton Beach FL 32548 850-243-5604 243-5640
Web: www.pmipeo.com

SurePayroll 2350 Ravine Way Ste 100 .... Glenview IL 60025 847-676-8420
TF: 877-954-7873 ■ *Web:* www.surepayroll.com

571 PENS, PENCILS, PARTS

See Also Art Materials & Supplies - Mfr p. 1745; Office & School Supplies p. 2844

Phone Fax

Alvin & Company Inc 1335 Blue Hills Ave .... Bloomfield CT 06002 860-243-8991 777-2896*
**Fax Area Code:* 800 ■ *TF:* 800-444-2584 ■ *Web:* www.alvinco.com

Avery Dennison Corp 207 Goode Ave .... Glendale CA 91203 626-304-2000
NYSE: AVY ■ *TF Cust Svc:* 888-567-4387 ■ *Web:* www.averydennison.com

BIC Corp 1 BIC Way Ste 1 .... Shelton CT 06484 203-783-2000 783-2081*
**Fax:* Hum Res ■ *Web:* www.bicworld.com

California Cedar Products Co
1340 N Washingtron St .... Stockton CA 95203 209-944-5800
Web: www.calcedar.com

Dixon Ticonderoga Co 195 International Pkwy .... Heathrow FL 32746 407-829-9000 232-9396*
**Fax Area Code:* 800 ■ **Fax:* Cust Svc ■ *TF:* 800-824-9430 ■ *Web:* www.dixonticonderoga.com

Dri Mark Products Inc
999 S Oyster Bay Rd Ste 312 .... Bethpage NY 11714 516-484-6200 484-6279
TF: 800-645-9118 ■ *Web:* www.drimark.com

Fisher Space Pen Co 711 Yucca St .... Boulder City NV 89005 702-293-3011 293-6616
Web: www.spacepen.com

General Pencil Co Inc 3160 Bay Rd .... Redwood City CA 94063 650-369-4889 369-7169
Web: www.generalpencil.com

Harcourt Pencil Co 7765 S 175 W .... Milroy IN 46156 800-428-6584 629-2218*
**Fax Area Code:* 765 ■ *TF:* 800-428-6584 ■ *Web:* www.harcourtoutlinesstore.com

Hartley-Racon 1987 Placentia Ave .... Costa Mesa CA 92627 201-703-0663
Web: www.hartleyraconusa.com

Jensen's Inc 715 W Jackson St .... Shelbyville TN 37160 931-684-5021 685-9229
Web: jensensincorporated.com

Listo Pencil Corp 1925 Union St .... Alameda CA 94501 510-522-2910
TF: 800-547-8648 ■ *Web:* www.listo.com

Name / Address	City	State	Zip	Phone	Fax
Mercury Pen Company Inc 245 Eastline Rd *Web:* www.mercurypen.com	Ballston	NY	12019	518-899-9653	899-9657
Musgrave Pencil Company Inc 701 W Ln St *TF:* 800-736-2450 ■ *Web:* pencils.net	Shelbyville	TN	37160	931-684-3611	685-1049
National Pen Corp (NPC) 12121 Scripps Summit Dr Ste 200 *TF:* 800-854-1000 ■ *Web:* www.pens.com	San Diego	CA	92131	858-675-3000	675-0890
Pentel of America Ltd 2715 Columbia St *Web:* www.pentel.com	Torrance	CA	90503	760-200-0547	200-0586

572 PERFORMING ARTS FACILITIES

See Also Convention Centers p. 2148; Stadiums & Arenas p. 3204; Theaters - Broadway p. 3245; Theaters - Resident p. 3246
Most of the fax numbers provided for these facilities are for the box office.

Alabama

Name / Address	City	State	Zip	Phone	Fax
Alabama Theatre 1817 Third Ave N *Web:* www.alabamatheatre.com	Birmingham	AL	35203	205-252-2262	251-3155
Bama Theatre 600 Greensboro Ave *Web:* www.tuscarts.org	Tuscaloosa	AL	35401	205-758-5195	345-2787
Birmingham Festival Theater 1901 1/2 11th Ave S PO Box 55321 *Web:* www.bftonline.org	Birmingham	AL	35205	205-933-2383	
Birmingham-Jefferson Convention Complex 2100 Richard Arrington Jr Blvd N *Web:* www.bjcc.org	Birmingham	AL	35203	205-458-8400	328-8523
Davis Theatre for the Performing Arts 251 Montgomery St *Web:* trojan.troy.edu	Montgomery	AL	36104	334-241-9567	241-9756
Library Theatre 200 Municipal Dr *Web:* www.thelibrarytheatre.com	Hoover	AL	35216	205-444-7888	
Renaissance Theatre Inc 1214 Meridian St *Web:* www.renaissancetheatre.net	Huntsville	AL	35801	256-536-3117	
Saenger Theatre 6 S Joachim St *Web:* www.mobilesaenger.com	Mobile	AL	36602	251-208-5600	
Von Braun Ctr 700 Monroe St *Web:* www.vonbrauncenter.com	Huntsville	AL	35801	256-533-1953	551-2203

Alaska

Name / Address	City	State	Zip	Phone	Fax
Alaska Ctr for the Performing Arts 621 W Sixth Ave *Web:* www.myalaskacenter.com	Anchorage	AK	99501	907-263-2900	263-2927

Arizona

Name / Address	City	State	Zip	Phone	Fax
Arizona State University's Kerr Cultural Ctr 6110 N Scottsdale Rd *Web:* www.asukerr.com	Scottsdale	AZ	85253	480-596-2660	
Celebrity Theatre 440 N 32nd St *Web:* celebritytheatre.com	Phoenix	AZ	85008	602-267-1600	
Chandler Ctr for the Arts 250 N Arizona Ave *Web:* www.chandlercenter.org	Chandler	AZ	85225	480-782-2680	782-2684
Comerica Theatre 400 W Washington St *Web:* www.comericatheatre.com	Phoenix	AZ	85003	602-379-2800	
Grady Gammage Memorial Auditorium 1200 S Forest Ave *Web:* www.asugammage.com	Tempe	AZ	85281	480-965-3434	965-3583
Herberger Theater Ctr 222 E Monroe St *Web:* www.herbergertheater.org	Phoenix	AZ	85004	602-254-7399	258-9521
Orpheum Theatre 203 W Adams St *Web:* www.phoenix.gov	Phoenix	AZ	85003	602-262-6011	
Rialto, The 318 E Congress St *Web:* www.rialtotheatre.com	Tucson	AZ	85701	520-740-1000	
Scottsdale Ctr for the Performing Arts 7380 E Second St *TF:* 800-309-8532 ■ *Web:* www.scottsdaleperformingarts.org	Scottsdale	AZ	85251	480-994-2787	874-4699
Tucson Convention Ctr 260 S Church Ave *Web:* tucsonaz.gov	Tucson	AZ	85701	520-791-4101	791-5572

Arkansas

Name / Address	City	State	Zip	Phone	Fax
Fort Smith Convention Ctr 55 S Seventh St *Web:* www.fortsmith.org	Fort Smith	AR	72901	479-788-8932	
Robinson Ctr 101 S. Spring St PO Box 3232 *TF:* 800-844-4781 ■ *Web:* www.littlerockmeetings.com	Little Rock	AR	72201	501-376-4781	376-7833

British Columbia

Name / Address	City	State	Zip	Phone	Fax
Orpheum Theatre 865 Seymour St *Web:* www.vancouver.ca	Vancouver	BC	V6B3L4	604-665-3050	665-2149

California

Name / Address	City	State	Zip	Phone	Fax
Alex Theatre 216 N Brand Blvd *Web:* www.alextheatre.org	Glendale	CA	91203	818-243-7700	241-2089
Annenberg Theater 101 Museum Dr Palm Springs Art Museum *Web:* www.psmuseum.org	Palm Springs	CA	92262	760-325-4490	
B Street Theatre 2711 B St *Web:* www.bstreettheatre.org	Sacramento	CA	95816	916-443-5300	
Bayview Opera House 4705 Third St *Web:* www.bvoh.org	San Francisco	CA	94124	415-824-0386	824-7124
Bill Graham Civic Auditorium 99 Grove St *Web:* billgrahamcivicauditorium.com	San Francisco	CA	94102	510-548-3010	
Bren Events Ctr 100 Bren Events Ctr *Web:* www.ucirvinesports.com/bren/index	Irvine	CA	92697	949-824-5050	824-5097
California Ctr for the Arts 340 N Escondido Blvd *TF:* 800-988-4253 ■ *Web:* www.artcenter.org	Escondido	CA	92025	760-839-4138	
California Theatre of Performing Arts 562 W Fourth St *TF:* 800-745-3000 ■ *Web:* www.californiatheatre.net	San Bernardino	CA	92401	909-885-5152	885-8948
Cerritos Ctr for the Performing Arts 12700 Ctr Ct Dr *TF:* 800-300-4345 ■ *Web:* www.cerritoscenter.com	Cerritos	CA	90703	562-916-8501	916-8514
EXIT Theatre 156 Eddy St *Web:* www.theexit.org	San Francisco	CA	94102	415-931-1094	931-2699
Fresno Convention Ctr 848 M St *Web:* www.fresnoconventioncenter.com	Fresno	CA	93721	559-445-8100	445-8110
Gary Soren Smith Ctr for the Fine & Performing Arts *Ohlone College* 43600 Mission Blvd *TF:* 800-309-2131 ■ *Web:* www.ohlone.edu/org/smithcenter	Fremont	CA	94539	510-659-6031	659-6188
Glendale Centre Theatre 324 N Orange St *Web:* www.glendalecentretheatre.com	Glendale	CA	91203	818-244-8481	244-5042
Good Company Players 928 E Olive Ave *Web:* gcplayers.com	Fresno	CA	93728	559-266-0660	266-1342
Greek, Theatre, The 2700 N Vermont Ave *Web:* www.greektheatrela.com	Los Angeles	CA	90027	323-665-5857	666-8202
Hollywood Bowl 2301 N Highland Ave *TF:* 800-745-3000 ■ *Web:* www.hollywoodbowl.com	Hollywood	CA	90068	323-850-2000	850-2155
Irvine Barclay Theatre 4242 Campus Dr *Web:* www.thebarclay.org	Irvine	CA	92612	949-854-4646	
John Anson Ford Theatres 2580 Cahuenga Blvd E *TF:* 800-352-0050 ■ *Web:* www.fordamphitheatre.org	Hollywood	CA	90068	323-461-3673	871-5904
Long Beach Playhouse 5021 E Anaheim St *Web:* www.lbplayhouse.org	Long Beach	CA	90804	562-494-1014	
Luckman Fine Arts Complex 5151 State University Dr *Web:* www.luckmanarts.org	Los Angeles	CA	90032	323-343-6611	343-6423
Marines Memorial Theatre 609 Sutter St *Web:* marinesmemorialtheatre.com	San Francisco	CA	94102	415-447-0188	
McCallum Theatre 73000 Fred Waring Dr *TF:* 866-889-2787 ■ *Web:* www.mccallumtheatre.com	Palm Desert	CA	92260	760-340-2787	779-9445
Monterey Peninsula College Theatre 980 Fremont St *Web:* www.mpctheatreco.com	Monterey	CA	93940	831-646-4213	
Music Ctr of Los Angeles County 135 N Grand Ave *Web:* www.musiccenter.org	Los Angeles	CA	90012	213-972-7211	
New Conservatory Theatre Centre 25 Van Ness Ave *Web:* www.nctcsf.org	San Francisco	CA	94102	415-861-4914	861-6988
Palace of Fine Arts Theatre 3301 Lyon St *Web:* www.palaceoffinearts.org	San Francisco	CA	94123	415-563-6504	
Palm Canyon Theatre 538 N Palm Canyon Dr *Web:* www.palmcanyontheatre.org	Palm Springs	CA	92262	760-323-5123	
Pantages Theatre 6233 Hollywood Blvd *TF:* 800-430-8903 ■ *Web:* www.pantages-theater.com	Los Angeles	CA	90028	800-430-8903	
Paramount Theatre 2025 Broadway *TF:* 800-745-3000 ■ *Web:* www.paramounttheatre.com	Oakland	CA	94612	510-465-6400	893-5098
Pasadena Convention Center 300 E Green St *Web:* pasadenacenter.visitpasadena.com	Pasadena	CA	91101	626-793-2122	
Redding Civic Auditorium 700 Auditorium Dr *Web:* www.reddingcivic.com	Redding	CA	96001	530-229-0036	229-0062
Redlands Bowl 25 Grant St *Web:* www.redlandsbowl.org	Redlands	CA	92373	909-793-7316	
Richard & Karen Carpenter Performing Arts Ctr (CPAC) 6200 Atherton St *Web:* www.carpenterarts.org	Long Beach	CA	90815	562-985-7000	985-7023
San Francisco War Memorial & Performing Arts Ctr (SFWMPAC) 401 Van Ness Ave Rm 110 *Web:* www.sfwmpac.org	San Francisco	CA	94102	415-621-6600	621-5091
San Jose Convention Center (SJC) 150 W San Carlos St *TF:* 800-726-5673 ■ *Web:* www.sanjose.org/plan-a-meeting-event/venues/convention-center	San Jose	CA	95110	408-792-4194	277-3535
San Jose Ctr for the Performing Arts 255 Almaden Blvd *TF:* 800-726-5673 ■ *Web:* www.sanjose.org	San Jose	CA	95113	408-792-4111	277-3535
San Manuel Amphitheater 2575 Glen Helen Pkwy *Web:* www.livenation.com	San Bernardino	CA	92407	909-880-6500	
Santa Cruz Civic Auditorium 307 Church St *Web:* www.cityofsantacruz.com	Santa Cruz	CA	95060	831-420-5240	420-5261
Segerstrom Center for the Arts (SCFTA) 600 Town Ctr Dr *Web:* www.scfta.org/home/default.aspx	Costa Mesa	CA	92626	714-556-2121	556-8984
Shoreline Amphitheatre 1 Amphitheatre Pkwy *Web:* www.mountainviewamphitheater.com	Mountain View	CA	94043	650-967-4040	967-4994
Shrine Auditorium & Exposition Ctr 665 W Jefferson Blvd *Web:* www.shrineauditorium.com	Los Angeles	CA	90007	213-748-5116	
Sleep Train Amphitheatre 2050 Entertainment Cir *Web:* www.chulavistaamphitheatre.com	Chula Vista	CA	91911	530-743-5200	634-0157
Sleep Train Pavilion at Concord 2000 Kirker Pass Rd *Web:* www.livenation.com	Concord	CA	94521	925-676-8742	

Phone Fax

State Theatre 1307 J St PO Box 1492 ... Modesto CA 95354 209-527-4697
Web: www.thestate.org

Sturges Ctr for the Fine Arts
780 NE St ... San Bernardino CA 92410 909-384-5415 384-5449
Web: www.sturgescenter.org

Thousand Oaks Civic Arts Plaza
2100 Thousand Oaks Blvd ... Thousand Oaks CA 91362 805-449-2787
Web: www.toaks.org/theatre

Tower Theatre for the Performing Arts
815 E Olive Ave ... Fresno CA 93728 559-485-9050
Web: www.towertheatrefresno.com

Walt Disney Concert Hall 111 S Grand Ave ... Los Angeles CA 90012 323-850-2000
Web: laphil.com

Warnors Ctr for the Performing Arts
1400 Fulton St ... Fresno CA 93721 559-650-1154
Web: warnors.publishpath.com

Wiltern Theatre 3790 Wilshire Blvd ... Los Angeles CA 90010 213-388-1400
TF: 800-348-8499 ■ *Web:* www.wilterntheatertickets.com

Colorado

Phone Fax

Arvada Ctr for the Arts & Humanities
6901 Wadsworth Blvd. ... Arvada CO 80003 720-898-7200 898-7204
Web: www.arvadacenter.org

Aurora Fox Arts Ctr 9900 E Colfax Ave. ... Aurora CO 80010 303-739-1970 739-1975
Web: www.aurorafoxartscenter.org

Denver Ctr for the Performing Arts
1101 13th St. ... Denver CO 80204 303-893-4000 595-9634
TF: 800-641-1222 ■ *Web:* www.denvercenter.org

Denver Performing Arts Complex
1400 Curtis St 1St Fl ... Denver CO 80204 720-865-4220 865-4247
TF: 800-745-3000 ■ *Web:* www.artscomplex.com

Macky Auditorium Concert Hall
285 UCB University Ave ... Boulder CO 80309 303-492-8423 492-1651
Web: www.colorado.edu

Newman Ctr for the Performing Arts
2344 E Iliff Ave ... Denver CO 80208 303-871-7720 871-6507
Web: www.newmancenterpresents.com

Pikes Peak Ctr 190 S Cascade Ave. ... Colorado Springs CO 80903 719-477-2100 477-2199
TF: 866-464-2626 ■ *Web:* www.pikespeakcenter.com

Red Rocks Amphitheater 18300 W Alameda Pkwy ... Morrison CO 80465 720-865-2494 865-2467
Web: www.redrocksonline.com

Sangre de Cristo Arts & Conference Ctr
210 N Santa Fe Ave ... Pueblo CO 81003 719-295-7200 295-7230
Web: www.sdc-arts.org

Wheeler Opera House 320 E Hyman St ... Aspen CO 81611 970-920-5770
TF: 866-449-0464 ■ *Web:* www.wheeleroperahouse.com

Connecticut

Phone Fax

Bushnell Ctr for the Performing Arts
166 Capitol Ave ... Hartford CT 06106 860-987-6000 987-6070
TF: 888-824-2874 ■ *Web:* www.bushnell.org

Fairfield University
Fairfield University 1073 N Benson Rd ... Fairfield CT 06824 203-254-4010 254-4113
TF: 877-278-7396 ■ *Web:* www.fairfield.edu

Fairmount Theatre 33 Main St Annex ... New Haven CT 06512 203-467-3832 467-3832

Garde Arts Ctr 325 State St ... New London CT 06320 860-444-7373 701-0189
Web: www.gardearts.org

John Lyman Ctr for the Performing Arts
501 Crescent St ... New Haven CT 06515 203-392-6154 392-6158
Web: tickets.southernct.edu

Long Wharf Theatre 222 Sargent Dr ... New Haven CT 06511 203-787-4282 776-2287
TF: 800-782-8497 ■ *Web:* www.longwharf.org

Norwalk Concert Hall 125 E Ave ... Norwalk CT 06851 203-854-7900 854-7939
TF: 800-357-9577 ■ *Web:* www.norwalkct.org

Oakdale Theatre 95 S Tpke Rd ... Wallingford CT 06492 203-269-8721
Web: www.oakdale.com

Sacred Heart University Edgerton Ctr for Performing Arts
5151 Pk Ave ... Fairfield CT 06825 203-371-7908 365-4858
Web: www.edgertoncenter.org

Shubert Theater 247 College St ... New Haven CT 06510 203-624-1825 789-2286
Web: www.shubert.com

Stamford Ctr for the Arts 61 Atlantic St ... Stamford CT 06901 203-325-4466 358-2313
Web: palacestamford.org

Sterling Farms Theatre Complex
1349 Newfield Ave ... Stamford CT 06905 203-329-8207 322-3656
Web: www.curtaincallinc.com

TheaterWorks 233 Pearl St ... Hartford CT 06103 860-527-7838
Web: www.theaterworkshartford.org

Westport Country Playhouse 25 Powers Ct ... Westport CT 06880 203-227-4177 221-7482
TF: 888-927-7529 ■ *Web:* www.westportplayhouse.org

XFINITY Theatreÿ 61 Savitt Way ... Hartford CT 06120 203-204-8892

Delaware

Phone Fax

Christina Cultural Arts Ctr
705 N Market St ... Wilmington DE 19801 302-652-0101 652-7480
Web: ccacde.org

DuPont Theatre 1007 N Market St ... Wilmington DE 19801 302-656-4401
TF: 800-338-0881 ■ *Web:* www.duponttheatre.com

Grand, The 818 N Market St. ... Wilmington DE 19801 302-658-7897
TF: 800-374-7263 ■ *Web:* www.thegrandwilmington.org

Schwartz Ctr for the Arts 226 S State St. ... Dover DE 19901 302-678-5152 678-1267
Web: www.schwartzcenter.com

District of Columbia

Phone Fax

Arena Stage 1101 Sixth St SW ... Washington DC 20024 202-554-9066 488-4056
Web: www.arenastage.org

Carter Barron Amphitheatre
4850 Colorado Ave NW ... Washington DC 20008 202-426-0486
Web: www.nps.gov/rocr/planyourvisit/cbarron.htm

DAR Constitution Hall 1776 D St NW ... Washington DC 20006 202-628-1776
Web: dar.org/constitution-hall

Discovery Theater 1100 Jefferson Dr SW. ... Washington DC 20560 202-633-8700 343-1073
Web: www.discoverytheater.org

John F Kennedy Ctr for the Performing Arts
2700 F St NW ... Washington DC 20566 202-416-8000 416-8205
TF: 800-444-1324 ■ *Web:* www.kennedy-center.org

National Theatre 1321 Pennsylvania Ave NW ... Washington DC 20004 202-628-6161
Web: thenationaldc.org

Warner Theatre 513 13th St NW. ... Washington DC 20004 202-783-4000 783-0204
Web: warnertheatredc.com

Florida

Phone Fax

Adrienne Arsht Ctr for the Performing Arts of Miami-Dade County Inc
1300 Biscayne Blvd ... Miami FL 33132 786-468-2000 468-2001
TF: 877-949-6722 ■ *Web:* www.arshtcenter.org

American Stage 163 Third St N ... Saint Petersburg FL 33731 727-823-1600 821-2444
TF: 800-435-7352 ■ *Web:* www.americanstage.org

Barbara B Mann Performing Arts Hall
13350 FSW Pkwy ... Fort Myers FL 33919 239-489-3033 481-4620
TF: 800-440-7469 ■ *Web:* www.bbmannpah.com

Broward Ctr for the Performing Arts
201 SW Fifth Ave ... Fort Lauderdale FL 33312 954-462-0222
TF: 877-311-7469 ■ *Web:* www.browardcenter.org

Coral Springs Ctr for the Arts
2855 Coral Springs Dr ... Coral Springs FL 33065 954-344-5990 344-5980
Web: www.coralspringscenterforthearts.com

Curtis M Phillips Ctr for the Performing Arts
315 Hull Rd PO Box 112750. ... Gainesville FL 32611 352-392-1900 392-3775
TF: 800-905-2787 ■ *Web:* www.performingarts.ufl.edu

David A. Straz Jr Ctr for, The Performing Arts, The
1010 N WC MacInnes Pl ... Tampa FL 33602 813-222-1000 222-1057
TF: 800-955-1045 ■ *Web:* www.strazcenter.org

Florida Theatre 128 E Forsyth St Ste 300. ... Jacksonville FL 32202 904-355-5661 358-1874
Web: www.floridatheatre.com

GableStage
1200 Anastasia Ave Biltmore Hotel. ... Coral Gables FL 33134 305-446-1116 445-8645
Web: www.gablestage.org

Jackie Gleason Theater of the Performing Arts
1700 Washington Ave. ... Miami Beach FL 33139 305-673-7300
Web: fillmoremb.com

James L Knight International Ctr
400 SE Second Ave ... Miami FL 33131 305-416-5970 350-7910
Web: www.jlkc.com

Lakeland Ctr 701 W Lime St ... Lakeland FL 33815 863-834-8100 834-8101
Web: www.thelakelandcenter.com

Limelight Theatre 11 Old Mission Ave. ... Saint Augustine FL 32084 904-825-1164
Web: www.limelight-theatre.org

Mahaffey Theater for the Performing Arts
400 First St S ... Saint Petersburg FL 33701 727-892-5798 892-5897
TF: 800-435-7352 ■ *Web:* www.themahaffey.com

Marina Civic Ctr 8 Harrison Ave. ... Panama City FL 32401 850-763-4696
Web: www.marinaciviccenter.com

Miami-Dade County Auditorium 2901 W Flagler St. ... Miami FL 33135 305-547-5414 541-7782

North Miami Beach/Julius Littman Performing Arts Theater
17011 NE 19th Ave. ... North Miami Beach FL 33162 305-948-2957 787-6040
Web: www.littmantheater.com

Ocean Ctr 101 N Atlantic Ave. ... Daytona Beach FL 32118 386-254-4500 254-4512
TF: 800-858-6444 ■ *Web:* www.oceancenter.com

Old School Square Cultural Arts Ctr
51 N Swinton Ave. ... Delray Beach FL 33444 561-243-7922 243-7018
Web: oldschoolsquare.org

Olympia Theaterÿÿÿ 174 E Flagler St. ... Miami FL 33131 305-374-2444
Web: www.gusmancenter.org

Orlando Repertory Theatre
1001 E Princeton St ... Orlando FL 32803 407-896-7365 897-3284
Web: www.orlandorep.com

Parker Playhouse 707 NE Eigth St. ... Fort Lauderdale FL 33304 954-462-0222 524-9952*
**Fax:* Administration ■ *Web:* www.parkerplayhouse.com

Peabody Auditorium 600 Auditorium Blvd. ... Daytona Beach FL 32118 386-671-3460 239-6435
Web: www.peabodyauditorium.org

Pensacola Civic Ctr 201 E Gregory St. ... Pensacola FL 32502 850-432-0800 432-1707
Web: www.pensacolabaycenter.com

Pensacola Cultural Ctr (PCC)
400 S Jefferson St ... Pensacola FL 32502 850-432-2042
Web: www.pensacolalittletheatre.com/pcc

Philharmonic Ctr for the Arts
5833 Pelican Bay Blvd ... Naples FL 34108 239-597-1111
TF: 800-597-1900 ■ *Web:* artisnaples.org

Plaza Live, The 425 N Bumby Ave ... Orlando FL 32803 407-228-1220
TF: 877-435-9849 ■ *Web:* www.plazaliveorlando.com

Pompano Beach Amphitheater
1801 NE Sixth St ... Pompano Beach FL 33060 954-519-5500
Web: Www.theamppompano.org

Raymond F Kravis Ctr for the Performing Arts
701 Okeechobee Blvd ... West Palm Beach FL 33401 561-832-7469 833-0691*
**Fax:* Mktg ■ *TF:* 800-572-8471 ■ *Web:* www.kravis.org

Red Barn Theatre 319 Duval St Rear ... Key West FL 33040 305-296-9911
Web: redbarntheatre.com

Ritz Theatre & La Villa Museum
829 N Davis St ... Jacksonville FL 32202 904-632-5555 632-5553
Web: www.ritzjacksonville.com

Ruth Eckerd Hall 1111 McMullen Booth Rd ... Clearwater FL 33759 727-791-7060 724-5976
TF: 800-875-8682 ■ *Web:* www.rutheckerdhall.com

Saenger Theatre 118 S Palafox Pl ... Pensacola FL 32502 850-595-3880 595-3886
Web: www.pensacolasaenger.com

Sugden Community Theatre 701 Fifth Ave S ... Naples FL 34102 239-263-7990 434-7772
Web: www.naplesplayers.org

Phone Fax

Tampa Theater 711 N Franklin St PO Box 172188 Tampa FL 33602 813-274-8286
Web: www.tampatheatre.org

Tennessee Williams Theatre
5901 W College Rd. Key West FL 33040 305-296-1520 292-3725

Theatre Tallahassee (TLT)
1861 Thomasville Rd Tallahassee FL 32303 850-224-4597
Web: theatretallahassee.org

University of West Florida Ctr for Fine & Performing Arts
11000 University Pkwy Bldg 82 Pensacola FL 32514 850-474-2000 857-6176
TF: 800-263-1074 ■ *Web:* uwf.edu/cfpa

Van Wezel Performing Arts Ctr
777 N Tamiami Trl Sarasota FL 34236 941-953-3368 951-1449
TF: 800-826-9303 ■ *Web:* www.vanwezel.org

Waterfront Playhouse 312 Wall St Key West FL 33040 305-294-5015

Georgia

Phone Fax

14th Street Playhouse 1280 Peachtree St NE Atlanta GA 30309 404-733-4738 733-5356

Boisfeuillet Jones Atlanta Civic Ctr
395 Piedmont Ave Atlanta GA 30308 404-523-6275
TF: 877-430-7596

Douglass Theatre 355 ML King Jr Blvd Macon GA 31201 478-742-2000
Web: www.douglasstheatre.org

Fox Theatre 660 Peachtree St NE Atlanta GA 30308 404-881-2100 872-2972
TF: 855-285-8499 ■ *Web:* www.foxtheatre.org

Georgia Mountains Ctr
301 Main St SW PO Box 2496 Gainesville GA 30501 770-534-8420
Web: www.gainesville.org

Grand Opera House 651 Mulberry St Macon GA 31201 478-301-5470
Web: www.thegrandmacon.com

Imperial Theatre 749 Broad St Augusta GA 30901 706-722-8293 312-1202
Web: www.imperialtheatre.com

Macon City Auditorium 415 First St Macon GA 31201 478-751-9152 751-9154
TF: 877-532-6144 ■ *Web:* www.maconcentreplex.org

Macon Little Theater 4220 Forsyth Rd Macon GA 31210 478-477-3342 471-8711
Web: www.maconlittletheatre.org

Rialto Ctr for the Arts
80 Forsyth St NW PO Box 2627 Atlanta GA 30303 404-413-9800 413-9801
Web: rialto.gsu.edu

Savannah Civic Ctr 301 W Oglethorp Ave Savannah GA 31401 912-651-6550 651-6552
TF: 800-337-1101 ■ *Web:* www.savannahga.gov

Spivey Hall
Clayton College & State University
2000 Clayton State Blvd Morrow GA 30260 678-466-4200 466-4494
Web: www.spiveyhall.org

Springer Opera House 103 Tenth St. Columbus GA 31901 706-327-3688 324-4461
Web: www.springeroperahouse.org

Townsend Ctr for the Performing Arts
1601 Maple St Carrollton GA 30118 678-839-4722 839-4805
Web: westga.edu/~tcpa

Woodruff Arts Ctr 1280 Peachtree St NE Atlanta GA 30309 404-733-4200
Web: www.woodruffcenter.org

Illinois

Phone Fax

Apollo Theater 2540 N Lincoln Ave Chicago IL 60614 773-935-6100
Web: www.apollochicago.com

Auditorium Theatre 50 E Congress Pkwy. Chicago IL 60605 312-341-2310
TF: 800-982-2787 ■ *Web:* www.auditoriumtheatre.org

Broadway In Chicago 24 W Randolph St. Chicago IL 60601 312-977-1700 977-0519
Web: www.broadwayinchicago.com

Chicago Shakespeare Theater
800 E Grand Ave Navy Pier Chicago IL 60611 312-595-5600 595-5644
Web: www.chicagoshakes.com

Civic Opera House 20 N Wacker Dr Chicago IL 60606 312-332-2244 332-8120
Web: www.lyricopera.org

Coronado Theatre 314 N Main St. Rockford IL 61101 815-968-2722 968-1318
Web: www.coronadopac.org

Goodman Theatre 170 N Dearborn St. Chicago IL 60601 312-443-3811 443-3821
Web: www.goodmantheatre.org

Krannert Ctr for the Performing Arts
500 S Goodwin Ave Urbana IL 61801 217-333-6700 244-0810
TF: 800-527-2849 ■ *Web:* www.krannertcenter.com

Lifeline Theatre 6912 N Glenwood Ave Chicago IL 60626 773-761-4477 761-4582
Web: www.lifelinetheatre.com

Marriott Theatre in Lincolnshire
10 Marriott Dr. Lincolnshire IL 60069 847-634-0200
Web: www.marriotttheatre.com

North Shore Ctr for the Performing Arts in Skokie
9501 N Skokie Blvd Skokie IL 60077 847-673-6300 679-3704
Web: www.northshorecenter.org

Paramount Theatre 23 East Galena Blvd Ste 230 Aurora IL 60506 630-896-7676 892-1084
Web: paramountaurora.com

Parkland College Theatre
2400 W Bradley Ave Champaign IL 61821 217-351-2528 373-3899
TF: 800-346-8089 ■ *Web:* www.parkland.edu/theatre

Peoria Civic Ctr 201 SW Jefferson Ave. Peoria IL 61602 309-673-8900 673-9223
Web: peoriaciviccenter.com

Rosemont Theatre 5400 N River Rd. Rosemont IL 60018 847-671-5100 671-6405
Web: rosemont.com/theatre

Royal George Theatre Ctr 1641 N Halsted St Chicago IL 60614 312-988-9105
Web: www.theroyalgeorgetheatre.com

Springfield Theatre Centre
420 S Sixth St. Springfield IL 62701 217-523-0878
Web: springfieldtheatrecentre.com

Station Theatre 223 N Broadway Ave. Urbana IL 61801 217-384-4000
Web: www.stationtheatre.com

Steppenwolf Theatre 1650 N Halsted St Chicago IL 60614 312-335-1650 335-0440
Web: www.steppenwolf.org

Symphony Ctr 220 S Michigan Ave Chicago IL 60604 312-294-3000 294-3035*
**Fax:* Mktg ■ *TF Cust Svc:* 800-223-7114 ■ *Web:* www.cso.org

Phone Fax

Virginia Theatre 203 W Pk Ave. Champaign IL 61820 217-356-9053
Web: www.thevirginia.org

Indiana

Phone Fax

American Cabaret Theatre
121 Monument Cir Ste 516 Indianapolis IN 46204 317-275-1169
Web: www.thecabaret.org

Christel DeHaan Fine Arts Ctr
1400 E Hanna Ave
University of Indianapolis Indianapolis IN 46227 317-788-3566 788-3383
TF: 800-232-8634 ■ *Web:* www.uindy.edu/arts

Embassy Theatre 125 W Jefferson Blvd Fort Wayne IN 46802 260-424-6287
Web: fwembassytheatre.org

Evansville Civic Theatre 717 N Fulton St. Evansville IN 47710 812-425-2800 423-2636
Web: www.evansvillecivictheatre.org

Indiana University Auditorium
1211 E Seventh St Bloomington IN 47405 812-855-1103 855-4244
Web: www.iuauditorium.com

Indianapolis Artsgarden
Above the Intersection of Washington
Illinois St Indianapolis IN 46204 317-624-2563
Web: www.indyarts.org

Madame Walker Theatre Ctr
617 Indiana Ave Indianapolis IN 46202 317-236-2099 236-2097
Web: thewalkertheatre.org

Morris Performing Arts Ctr
211 N Michigan St South Bend IN 46601 574-235-9190 235-5945
TF: 800-537-6415 ■ *Web:* www.morriscenter.org

Warren Performing Arts Ctr
9500 E 16th St Indianapolis IN 46229 317-532-6280
Web: www.warrenpac.org

Iowa

Phone Fax

Civic Ctr of Greater Des Moines
221 Walnut St. Des Moines IA 50309 515-246-2300 246-2305
Web: www.desmoinesperformingarts.org

Paramount Theatre 123 Third Ave SE Cedar Rapids IA 52401 319-398-5226
TF: 800-369-8863 ■ *Web:* www.paramounttheatrecr.com

RiverCenter Adler Theatre 136 E Third St Davenport IA 52801 563-326-8500 326-8505
Web: www.riverctr.com

Kansas

Phone Fax

Century II Performing Arts & Convention Ctr
225 W Douglas Ave Wichita KS 67202 316-264-9121
Web: www.century2.org

Orpheum Performing Arts Centre
200 N Broadway Wichita KS 67202 316-263-0884
Web: www.wichitaorpheum.com

Topeka Performing Arts Ctr 214 SE Eigth Ave. Topeka KS 66603 785-234-2787 234-2307
Web: www.topekaperformingarts.org

Wichita Community Theatre 258 N Fountain st. Wichita KS 67208 316-686-1282
Web: wichitact.org

Wichita Ctr for the Arts 9112 E Central Ave. Wichita KS 67206 316-634-2787 634-0593
Web: www.wcfta.com

Kentucky

Phone Fax

Kentucky Ctr for, The Performing Arts, The
501 W Main St Louisville KY 40202 502-562-0100
Web: www.kentuckycenter.org

Kentucky Theater 214 E Main St Lexington KY 40507 859-231-7924
Web: www.kentuckytheater.com

Lexington Opera House 401 W Short St Lexington KY 40507 859-233-4567 253-2718
Web: www.lexingtonoperahouse.com

Louisville Palace Theatre 625 S Fourth St. Louisville KY 40202 502-583-4555
Web: www.louisvillepalace.com

Louisiana

Phone Fax

Baton Rouge Little Theater
7155 Florida Blvd. Baton Rouge LA 70806 225-924-6496
Web: theatrebr.org

Baton Rouge River Ctr 275 S River Rd Baton Rouge LA 70802 225-389-3030 389-4954
Web: www.brrivercenter.com

Contemporary Arts Ctr 900 Camp St. New Orleans LA 70130 504-528-3805 528-3828
TF: 800-568-6968 ■ *Web:* www.cacno.org

East Bank Community Theatre
630 Barksdale Blvd. Bossier City LA 71111 318-741-8310
Web: bossierarts.org

Heymann Performing Arts Ctr
1373 S College Rd Lafayette LA 70503 337-291-5540 291-5580
TF: 800-745-3000 ■ *Web:* heymanncenter.com

Lake Charles Civic Ctr 900 Lakeshore Dr Lake Charles LA 70601 337-491-1256 491-1534
TF: 888-620-1749 ■ *Web:* www.cityoflakecharles.com

Monroe Civic Ctr 401 Lea Joyner Expy Monroe LA 71201 318-329-2225 329-2548
Web: ci.monroe.la.us

Preservation Hall 726 St Peter St. New Orleans LA 70116 504-522-2841
Web: www.preservationhall.com

Phone | Fax

Strand Theatre 619 Louisiana Ave Shreveport LA 71101 318-226-1481 424-5434
TF: 800-313-6373 ■ *Web:* www.thestrandtheatre.com

Maine

Phone | Fax

Merrill Auditorium 20 Myrtle St Portland ME 04101 207-842-0800 842-0810
Web: tickets.porttix.com

Manitoba

Phone | Fax

Burton Cummings Theatre 364 Smith St Winnipeg MB R3B2H2 204-956-5656
Web: burtoncummingstheatre.ca

Maryland

Phone | Fax

Annapolis Summer Garden Theatre
143 Compromise St Annapolis MD 21401 410-268-9212
Web: www.summergarden.com
Chesapeake Arts Ctr 194 Hammonds Ln Brooklyn Park MD 21225 410-636-6597 636-9653
Web: www.chesapeakearts.org
Everyman Theatre 1727 N Charles St Baltimore MD 21201 410-752-2208 752-5891
Web: www.everymantheatre.org
Gordon Ctr for Performing Arts
3506 Gwynnbrook Ave Owings Mills MD 21117 410-356-7469 356-7605
Web: www.jcc.org
Joseph Meyerhoff Symphony Hall
1212 Cathedral St Baltimore MD 21201 410-783-8100
TF: 877-276-1444 ■ *Web:* www.bsomusic.org
Lyric Opera House 110 W Mt Royal Ave Baltimore MD 21201 410-685-5086 332-8234
TF: 800-872-7245 ■ *Web:* lyricbaltimore.com
Maryland Hall for the Creative Arts
801 Chase St Annapolis MD 21401 410-263-5544 263-5114
TF: 866-438-3808 ■ *Web:* www.marylandhall.org
Maryland Theatre 21 S Potomac St Hagerstown MD 21740 301-790-3500 791-6114
Web: www.mdtheatre.org
Merriweather Post Pavilion (MPP)
10475 Little Patuxent Pkwy Columbia MD 21044 410-715-5550 715-5560
TF: 877-435-9849 ■ *Web:* www.merriweathermusic.com
Recher, Theatre, The 512 York Rd Towson MD 21204 410-337-7178
Web: torrentnightclub.com

Massachusetts

Phone | Fax

Bank of America Pavilion 290 Northern Ave Boston MA 02210 617-728-1600
Web: www.bostonpavilion.net
Berklee Performance Ctr 136 Massachusetts Ave Boston MA 02115 617-747-2261 375-9228
TF: 877-237-5533 ■ *Web:* www.berklee.edu
Boston Ctr for the Arts 539 Tremont St Boston MA 02116 617-426-5000 426-5336
Web: www.bcaonline.org
Boston Symphony Hall 301 Massachusetts Ave Boston MA 02115 617-266-1492
TF: 888-266-1200 ■ *Web:* www.bso.org
Charles Playhouse 74 Warrenton St Boston MA 02116 617-426-6912
Web: www.blueman.com
Citi Performing Arts Ctr Wang Theatre
270 Tremont St Boston MA 02116 800-982-2787
TF: 800-982-2787 ■ *Web:* citicenter.org
Colonial Theatre 106 Boylston St Boston MA 02116 212-307-2166 880-2449*
**Fax Area Code:* 617 ■ *Web:* boston.broadway.com
Cutler Majestic Theatre at Emerson College
219 Tremont St Boston MA 02116 617-824-8000 824-3209
TF: 888-627-7115 ■ *Web:* www.emerson.edu
Mechanics Hall 321 Main St Worcester MA 01608 508-752-5608 754-8442
Web: www.mechanicshall.org
South Shore Music Circus 130 Sohier St Cohasset MA 02025 781-383-9850 383-9804
Web: www.themusiccircus.org
Stuart Street Playhouse 200 Stuart St Boston MA 02116 617-457-2623
Wang Theatre 270 Tremont St Boston MA 02116 800-982-2787
TF: 800-982-2787 ■ *Web:* citicenter.org
Wilbur Theatre 246 Tremont St Boston MA 02116 617-248-9700
Web: thewilbur.com
Xfinity Center 885 S Main St Mansfield MA 02048 508-339-2331 339-0550

Michigan

Phone | Fax

Ann Arbor Civic Theatre 322 W Ann St Ann Arbor MI 48104 734-971-0605 971-2769
Web: www.a2ct.org
Circle Theatre 1607 Robinson Rd SE Grand Rapids MI 49506 616-632-1980 456-8540
Web: www.circletheatre.org
Detroit Opera House 1526 Broadway Detroit MI 48226 313-961-3500 237-3412
Web: www.michiganopera.org
Dow Event Ctr 303 Johnson St Saginaw MI 48607 989-759-1320 759-1322
Web: www.doweventcenter.com
Fillmore Detroit, The 2115 Woodward Ave Detroit MI 48201 313-961-5451
Web: thefillmoredetroit.com
Fisher Theatre 3011 W Grand Blvd Detroit MI 48202 313-872-1000
Web: www.broadwayindetroit.com
Fox Theatre 2211 Woodward Ave Detroit MI 48201 313-471-3200
Web: www.olympiaentertainment.com
Gem Theatre & Century Grille 333 Madison Ave Detroit MI 48226 313-963-9800 963-0873
Web: gemcolonyevents.com
Grand Rapids Civic Theatre 30 N Div Ave Grand Rapids MI 49503 616-222-6650
TF: 888-823-6837 ■ *Web:* www.grct.org
Interlochen Ctr for the Arts
4000 Michigan 137 Interlochen MI 49643 231-276-7200 276-7444
Web: www.interlochen.org

Phone | Fax

Kerrytown Concert House 415 N Fourth Ave Ann Arbor MI 48104 734-769-2999
Web: www.kerrytownconcerthouse.com
Majestic Theatre 4120 Woodward Ave Detroit MI 48201 313-833-9700
Web: www.majesticdetroit.com
Masonic Temple Theatre 500 Temple St Detroit MI 48201 313-832-7100
Web: www.themasonic.com
Michigan Theater 603 E Liberty St Ann Arbor MI 48104 734-668-8397 668-7136
TF: 800-745-3000 ■ *Web:* www.michtheater.org
Midland Ctr for the Arts Inc
1801 W St Andrews Rd Midland MI 48640 989-631-5930 631-7890
Web: www.mcfta.org
Music Hall Ctr for the Performing Arts
350 Madison Detroit MI 48226 313-887-8500 887-8502
Web: www.musichall.org
Riverside Arts Ctr 76 N Huron St Ypsilanti MI 48197 734-480-2787
Web: www.riversidearts.org
Riverwalk Theatre 228 Museum Dr Lansing MI 48933 517-482-5700 482-9812
Web: www.riverwalktheatre.com
University of Michigan - Flint Theater
303 E Kearsley St Flint MI 48502 810-762-3300
Web: www.umflint.edu/theatredance
Wharton Ctr for the Performing Arts
Michigan State University East Lansing MI 48824 517-432-2000 353-5329
TF: 800-942-7866 ■ *Web:* www.whartoncenter.com
Whiting Auditorium 1241 E Kearsley St Flint MI 48503 810-237-7333 237-7335
Web: www.thewhiting.com

Minnesota

Phone | Fax

Duluth Playhouse 506 W Michigan St Duluth MN 55802 218-733-7555
Web: www.duluthplayhouse.org
Fitzgerald Theater 10 E Exchange St Saint Paul MN 55101 651-290-1200 290-1195
Web: fitzgeraldtheater.publicradio.org
Great American History Theatre
30 E Tenth St Saint Paul MN 55101 651-292-4323 292-4322
Web: www.historytheatre.com
Guthrie Theater 818 S Second St Minneapolis MN 55415 612-377-2224 225-6004
TF Resv: 877-447-8243 ■ *Web:* www.guthrietheater.org
Hennepin State Theatre
615 Hennepin Ave Ste 140 Minneapolis MN 55403 612-455-9500 455-9502
Web: hennepintheatretrust.org
Historic Orpheum Theatre
910 Hennepin Ave Minneapolis MN 55403 612-339-7007
Web: www.hennepintheatretrust.org/our-theatres/orpheum-theatre
Historic Pantages Theatre
710 Hennepin Ave Minneapolis MN 55403 612-339-7007 339-4146
Web: www.hennepintheatretrust.org
Jungle Theater 2951 Lindale Ave S Minneapolis MN 55408 612-822-4002
Web: www.jungletheater.com
Macphail Center For Music - Minneapolis
501 S Second St Minneapolis MN 55401 612-321-0100 321-9740
Web: www.macphail.org
Music Box Theatre 1407 Nicollet Ave Minneapolis MN 55403 612-874-1100
Web: musicboxtheatre.org
Orchestra Hall 1111 Nicollet Mall Minneapolis MN 55403 612-371-5600
TF: 800-292-4141 ■ *Web:* www.minnesotaorchestra.org
Ordway Ctr for the Performing Arts
345 Washington St Saint Paul MN 55102 651-282-3000
Web: www.ordway.org
Penumbra Theatre 270 Kent St Saint Paul MN 55102 651-224-3180 288-6789
Web: www.penumbratheatre.org
Reif Ctr 720 NW Conifer Dr Grand Rapids MN 55744 218-327-5780
Web: www.reifcenter.org
Renegade Theatre Co 222 E Superior St Duluth MN 55802 218-722-6775
Web: www.renegadetheatercompany.org
Rochester Civic Theatre 20 Civic Ctr Dr SE Rochester MN 55904 507-282-8481
Web: www.rochestercivictheatre.org

Mississippi

Phone | Fax

Thalia Mara Hall 255 E Pascagoula St Jackson MS 39201 601-960-1537
Web: www.thaliamara.org
Tupelo Community Theatre
201 N Broadway PO Box 1094 Tupelo MS 38802 662-844-1935 844-2990
Web: www.tctwebstage.com/lyric.htm

Missouri

Phone | Fax

Andy Williams Moon River Theatre 2500 Hwy 76 Branson MO 65616 417-334-1800 334-3200
TF: 800-666-6094 ■ *Web:* www.andywilliamspac.com
Coterie, Theatre, The
2450 Grand Blvd Ste 144 Kansas City MO 64108 816-474-6785 474-7112
Web: thecoterie.org
Fabulous Fox, The 527 N Grand Blvd Saint Louis MO 63103 314-534-1678 534-1678
TF: 800-293-5949 ■ *Web:* www.fabulousfox.com
Folly Theater
300 West 12th St PO Box 26505 Kansas City MO 64105 816-474-4444 842-8709
Web: follytheater.org
Gem Theater Cultural & Performing Arts Ctr
1615 E 18th St Kansas City MO 64108 816-474-6262
Web: americanjazzmuseum.com
Juanita K Hammons Hall for the Performing Arts
901 S National Ave Springfield MO 65897 417-836-6776 836-6891
TF: 888-476-7849 ■ *Web:* www.hammonshall.com
Legends Theater 1600 W Hwy 76 Branson MO 65616 417-339-3003
TF: 800-374-7469 ■ *Web:* www.legendsinconcert.com
Maplewood Barn Community Theatre
Maplewood Barn Community Theatre
PO Box 1704 Columbia MO 65205 573-227-2276
Web: www.maplewoodbarn.com

Facility	City	State	ZIP	Phone	Fax
Midland by AMC, The 1228 Main St *Web:* www.midlandkc.com	Kansas City	MO	64105	816-283-9900	
Missouri Theatre Ctr for the Arts 203 S Ninth St *Web:* www.motheatre.org	Columbia	MO	65201	573-875-0600	
Quality Hill Playhouse 303 W Tenth St *Web:* www.qualityhillplayhouse.com	Kansas City	MO	64105	816-421-1700	
Shepherd of the Hills Homestead & Outdoor Theatre 5586 W Hwy 76 *TF:* 800-653-6288 ■ *Web:* theshepherdofthehills.com	Branson	MO	65616	417-334-4191	
Stained Glass Theatre 1996 W Evangel *Web:* www.sgtheatre.com	Ozark	MO	65721	417-581-9192	
Starlight Theatre 4600 Starlight Rd Swope Pk *TF:* 800-776-1730 ■ *Web:* www.kcstarlight.com	Kansas City	MO	64132	816-363-7827	361-6398
Unicorn Theatre 3828 Main St *Web:* www.unicorntheatre.org	Kansas City	MO	64111	816-531-7529	531-0421
University of Missouri 129 Fine Arts Bldg. *Web:* theatre.missouri.edu	Columbia	MO	65211	573-882-2021	
Verizon Wireless Amphitheater 14141 Riverport Dr *Web:* www.livenation.com	Maryland Heights	MO	63043	314-298-9944	291-4719

Montana

Facility	City	State	ZIP	Phone	Fax
Alberta Bair Theater for the Performing Arts 2722 Third Ave N Ste 200 PO Box 1556 *TF:* 877-321-2074 ■ *Web:* www.albertabairtheater.org	Billings	MT	59103	406-256-8915	256-5060
Billings Studio Theatre (BST) 1500 Rimrock Rd *Web:* www.billingsstudiotheatre.com	Billings	MT	59102	406-248-1141	
Grand Street Theater 325 N Pk Ave. *Web:* www.grandstreettheatre.com	Helena	MT	59601	406-442-4270	447-1573
Helena Civic Ctr 340 Neill Ave *Web:* www.helenaciviccenter.com	Helena	MT	59601	406-447-8481	447-8480

Nebraska

Facility	City	State	ZIP	Phone	Fax
Blue Barn Theatre 614 S 11th St *Web:* www.bluebarn.org	Omaha	NE	68102	402-345-1576	
Lied Ctr for Performing Arts 301 N 12th St *TF:* 800-432-3231 ■ *Web:* www.unl.edu	Lincoln	NE	68588	402-472-4700	
Lincoln Community Playhouse 2500 S 56th St *Web:* www.lincolnplayhouse.com	Lincoln	NE	68506	402-489-7529	489-1035
Omaha Community Playhouse 6915 Cass St. *TF:* 888-782-4338 ■ *Web:* www.omahaplayhouse.com	Omaha	NE	68132	402-553-0800	553-6288
Orpheum Theatre 409 S 16th St *TF:* 866-434-8587 ■ *Web:* www.omahaperformingarts.org	Omaha	NE	68102	402-345-0202	345-0222
Pershing Ctr 226 Centennial Mall S.	Lincoln	NE	68508	402-441-8744	441-7913

Nevada

Facility	City	State	ZIP	Phone	Fax
Artemus W Ham Concert Hall 4505 Maryland Pkwy *Web:* www.unlv.edu/pac	Las Vegas	NV	89154	702-895-2787	895-4714
Brewery Arts Ctr 449 W King St *Web:* www.breweryarts.org	Carson City	NV	89703	775-883-1976	

New Hampshire

Facility	City	State	ZIP	Phone	Fax
Capitol Ctr for the Arts 44 S Main St *Web:* www.ccanh.com	Concord	NH	03301	603-225-1111	224-3408
Hopkins Ctr for the Arts 6041 Wilson Hall *TF:* 800-451-4067 ■ *Web:* dartmouth.edu	Hanover	NH	03755	603-646-2422	646-1375
Palace Theatre 80 Hanover St *Web:* www.palacetheatre.org	Manchester	NH	03101	603-668-5588	668-5804

New Jersey

Facility	City	State	ZIP	Phone	Fax
Count Basie Theatre 99 Monmouth St *Web:* www.countbasietheatre.org	Red Bank	NJ	07701	732-842-9000	842-9323
McCarter Theatre 91 University Pl. *Web:* www.mccarter.org	Princeton	NJ	08540	609-258-6500	497-0369
New Jersey Performing Arts Ctr 1 Ctr St. *TF:* 888-466-5722 ■ *Web:* www.njpac.org	Newark	NJ	07102	973-642-8989	648-6724
Newark Symphony Hall 1030 Broad St *Web:* www.newarksymphonyhall.org	Newark	NJ	07102	973-643-8014	
Patriots Theater Memorial Dr. *TF:* 866-847-7682 ■ *Web:* www.state.nj.us	Trenton	NJ	08608	609-984-8484	777-0581
PNC Bank Art Ctr Exit 116 Garden State Pkwy *Web:* livenation.com/venues/16839?from_tm=true	Holmdel	NJ	07733	732-203-2500	
State Theatre 15 Livingston Ave. *Web:* www.statetheatrenj.org	New Brunswick	NJ	08901	732-247-7200	247-4005
Stockton Performing Arts Ctr 101 Vera King Farris Dr *Web:* stocktonpac.org	Galloway	NJ	08205	609-652-9000	626-5523

New Mexico

Facility	City	State	ZIP	Phone	Fax
Adobe Theater Inc 9813 Fourth St NW PO Box 276 *Web:* www.adobetheater.org	Albuquerque	NM	87114	505-898-9222	
Albuquerque Little Theatre 224 San Pasquale SW *Web:* www.albuquerquelittletheatre.org	Albuquerque	NM	87104	505-242-4750	
Flickinger Ctr for Performing Arts 1110 New York Ave *Web:* www.flickingercenter.com	Alamogordo	NM	88310	575-437-2202	434-0067
Greer Garson Theatre Ctr 1600 St Michael's Dr College of Santa Fe. *TF:* 800-456-2673 ■ *Web:* www.santafeuniversity.edu	Santa Fe	NM	87505	505-473-6011	
KiMo Theater 423 Central Ave NW *Web:* kimotickets.com	Albuquerque	NM	87102	505-768-3522	
Las Cruces Community Theatre 313 N Downtown Mall *Web:* www.lcctnm.org	Las Cruces	NM	88001	575-523-1200	
Lensic Performing Arts Ctr 211 W San Francisco St *Web:* www.lensic.org	Santa Fe	NM	87501	505-988-7050	988-4370
Popejoy Hall UNM Public Events Popejoy Hall UNM Ctr for the Arts MSC 04 2580 *Web:* www.popejoypresents.com	Albuquerque	NM	87131	505-277-3824	277-7353
Santa Fe Performing Arts 1050 Old Pecos Trail *Web:* www.sfperformingarts.org	Santa Fe	NM	87502	505-982-7992	
Santa Fe Playhouse 142 E DeVargas St. *Web:* www.santafeplayhouse.org	Santa Fe	NM	87501	505-988-4262	

New York

Facility	City	State	ZIP	Phone	Fax
Alleyway Theatre 1 Curtain Up Alley *Web:* www.alleyway.com	Buffalo	NY	14202	716-852-2600	
Apollo Theatre 253 W 125th St. *Web:* www.apollotheater.org	New York	NY	10027	212-531-5300	749-2743
Artpark 450 S Fourth St *TF:* 877-325-5787 ■ *Web:* www.artpark.net	Lewiston	NY	14092	716-754-9000	754-2741
Brooklyn Academy of Music (BAM) 30 Lafayette Ave *Web:* www.bam.org	Brooklyn	NY	11217	718-636-4100	636-4121
Brooklyn Ctr for the Performing Arts PO Box 100843 *Web:* www.brooklyncenter.com	Brooklyn	NY	11210	718-951-4600	
Capitol Theatre 149 Westchester Ave. *Web:* www.thecapitoltheatre.com	Port Chester	NY	10573	914-937-4126	
Carnegie Hall 881 Seventh Ave *TF:* 800-728-3843 ■ *Web:* www.carnegiehall.org	New York	NY	10019	212-247-7800	581-6539
Center for the Arts 103 Ctr for the Arts *TF:* 800-745-3000 ■ *Web:* www.ubcfa.org	Buffalo	NY	14260	716-645-2787	645-6973
Eastman Theatre 26 Gibbs St. *Web:* www.esm.rochester.edu	Rochester	NY	14604	585-274-1110	274-1067
Egg, The Empire State Plz Concourse Level Performing Arts Ctr. *Web:* www.theegg.org	Albany	NY	12220	518-473-1845	473-1848
Emelin Theater 153 Library Ln *Web:* www.emelin.org	Mamaroneck	NY	10543	914-698-0098	698-1404
Geva Theatre Ctr 75 Woodbury Blvd *Web:* www.gevatheatre.org	Rochester	NY	14607	585-232-1366	232-4031
Kavinoky Theatre 320 Porter Ave. *Web:* www.kavinokytheatre.com	Buffalo	NY	14201	716-829-7668	829-7790
Kleinhans Music Hall 3 Symphony Cir *Web:* www.kleinhansbuffalo.org	Buffalo	NY	14201	716-883-3560	
Landmark Theatre 362 S Salina St. *Web:* www.landmarktheatre.org	Syracuse	NY	13202	315-475-7980	
Lucille Lortel Theatre 121 Christopher St. *Web:* www.lortel.org	New York	NY	10014	212-924-2817	
Manhattan Ctr Studios 311 W 34th St *Web:* www.mcstudios.com	New York	NY	10001	212-279-7740	564-1072
Mid-Hudson Civic Ctr 14 Civic Ctr Plz. *Web:* www.midhudsonciviccenter.org	Poughkeepsie	NY	12601	845-454-5800	
New York City Ctr 130 W 56th St *Web:* www.nycitycenter.org	New York	NY	10019	212-247-0430	246-9778
Palace Theatre 19 Clinton Ave. *Web:* www.palacealbany.com	Albany	NY	12207	518-465-3334	
Paul Robeson Theatre *Theatre Alliance of Buffalo* 350 Masten Ave *Web:* www.theatreallianceofbuffalo.com	Buffalo	NY	14209	716-884-2013	
Performing Arts Ctr 735 Anderson Hill Rd. *Web:* www.artscenter.org	Purchase	NY	10577	914-251-6200	251-6171
Performing Arts Ctr at Rockwell Hall 1300 Elmwood Ave Rockwell Hall Rm 210 *Web:* www.buffalostate.edu	Buffalo	NY	14222	716-878-3005	878-4234
Proctor's Theatre 432 State St. *Web:* www.proctors.org	Schenectady	NY	12305	518-382-3884	346-2468
Public, Theater, The 425 Lafayette St *Web:* www.publictheater.org	New York	NY	10003	212-539-8500	539-8505
Radio City Music Hall 1260 Ave of the Americas *Web:* www.radiocity.com	New York	NY	10020	212-247-4777	
Saratoga Performing Arts Ctr (SPAC) 108 Ave of the Pines *Web:* www.spac.org	Saratoga Springs	NY	12866	518-584-9330	584-0809
Shea's Performing Arts Ctr 646 Main St *TF:* 866-341-5945 ■ *Web:* www.sheas.org	Buffalo	NY	14202	716-847-1410	847-1644
Snug Harbor Cultural Ctr 1000 Richmond Terr. *Web:* www.snug-harbor.org	Staten Island	NY	10301	718-448-2500	
Stanley Ctr for the Arts 259 Genesee St *Web:* www.thestanley.org	Utica	NY	13501	315-724-1113	624-2926
Tarrytown Music Hall 13 Main St PO Box 686 *TF:* 877-840-0457 ■ *Web:* www.tarrytownmusichall.org	Tarrytown	NY	10591	914-631-3390	
TRIBECA Performing Arts Ctr 199 Chambers St *Web:* tickets.tribecapac.org	New York	NY	10007	212-220-1459	732-2482

North Carolina

Facility	City	State	ZIP	Phone	Fax
Actor's Theatre of Charlotte 650 E Stonewall St *Web:* www.atcharlotte.org	Charlotte	NC	28202	704-342-2251	
Asheville Community Theatre 35 E Walnut St *Web:* www.ashevilletheatre.org	Asheville	NC	28801	828-254-1320	252-4723
Carolina Theatre 310 S Greene St *Web:* www.carolinatheatre.com	Greensboro	NC	27401	336-333-2600	
Carolina, Theatre of Durham, The 309 W Morgan St *Web:* www.carolinatheatre.org	Durham	NC	27701	919-560-3040	560-3065
Diana Wortham Theatre at Pack Place 2 S Pack Sq *TF:* 800-999-2160 ■ *Web:* www.dwtheatre.com	Asheville	NC	28801	828-257-4530	251-5652
Flat Rock Playhouse 2661 Greenville Hwy *TF:* 866-732-8008 ■ *Web:* www.flatrockplayhouse.org	Flat Rock	NC	28731	828-693-0731	
Greensboro Coliseum Complex 1921 W Lee St *Web:* www.greensborocoliseum.com	Greensboro	NC	27403	336-373-7400	373-2170
Theatre in the Park 107 Pullen Rd *Web:* www.theatreinthepark.com	Raleigh	NC	27607	919-831-6936	831-9475

North Dakota

Facility	City	State	ZIP	Phone	Fax
Chester Fritz Auditorium 3475 University Ave *TF:* 800-375-4068 ■ *Web:* und.edu	Grand Forks	ND	58202	701-777-3076	777-4710
Empire Arts Ctr 415 DeMers Ave *Web:* www.empireartscenter.com	Grand Forks	ND	58201	701-746-5500	746-0500
Fargo Theatre 314 Broadway N *Web:* www.fargotheatre.org	Fargo	ND	58102	701-239-8385	
Festival Concert Hall *North Dakota State University* PO Box 5691 *TF:* 800-726-1724 ■ *Web:* www.ndsu.edu	Fargo	ND	58105	701-231-7932	231-2085
Fire Hall Theatre 412 Second Ave N *Web:* ggfct.com	Grand Forks	ND	58203	701-746-0847	

Ohio

Facility	City	State	ZIP	Phone	Fax
Akron Civic Theatre 182 S Main St *Web:* www.akroncivic.com	Akron	OH	44308	330-535-3179	535-9828
Aronoff Ctr for the Arts 650 Walnut St *Web:* www.cincinnatiarts.org	Cincinnati	OH	45202	513-721-3344	977-4150
Blossom Music Ctr Tickets 1145 W Steels Corners Rd *TF:* 800-745-3000 ■ *Web:* www.livenation.com	Cuyahoga Falls	OH	44223	330-920-8040	
Cain Park Theatre 40 Severance Cir *Web:* cainpark.com	Cleveland Heights	OH	44118	216-371-3000	371-6995
Canton Palace Theatre 605 Market Ave N *Web:* www.cantonpalacetheatre.org	Canton	OH	44702	330-454-8172	454-8171
Cincinnati Music Hall 650 Walnut St *Web:* www.cincinnatiarts.org	Cincinnati	OH	45202	513-744-3344	744-3345
Cincinnati Playhouse in the Park 962 Mt Adams Cir *TF:* 800-582-3208 ■ *Web:* www.cincyplay.com	Cincinnati	OH	45202	513-345-2242	345-2250
Coach House Theatre 732 W Exchange St *Web:* www.coachhousetheatre.org	Akron	OH	44302	330-434-7741	
Dobama Theater 2340 Lee Rd *Web:* www.dobama.org	Cleveland Heights	OH	44118	216-932-6838	932-6838
Edward W Powers Auditorium 260 Federal Plz W *Web:* www.youngstownsymphony.com/symphony_center.html	Youngstown	OH	44503	330-744-4269	
EJ Thomas Performing Arts Hall 198 Hill St University of Akron *TF:* 800-745-3000 ■ *Web:* www.uaevents.com	Akron	OH	44325	330-972-7570	
Fraze Pavilion 695 Lincoln Pk Blvd *Web:* www.fraze.com	Dayton	OH	45429	937-296-3300	296-3302
Ohio Theatre 55 E State St *Web:* www.capa.com/venues/ohio-theatre	Columbus	OH	43215	614-469-1045	461-0429
Palace Theatre 34 W Broad St *Web:* www.capa.com	Columbus	OH	43215	614-469-9850	
Playhouse Square 1501 Euclid Ave Ste 200 *TF:* 866-546-1353 ■ *Web:* www.playhousesquare.org	Cleveland	OH	44115	216-771-4444	771-0217
Riverbend Music Ctr 6295 Kellogg Ave *Web:* www.riverbend.org	Cincinnati	OH	45230	513-232-6220	
Severance Hall 11001 Euclid Ave *TF:* 800-686-1141 ■ *Web:* www.clevelandorchestra.com	Cleveland	OH	44106	216-231-7300	
Stambaugh Auditorium 1000 Fifth Ave *TF:* 866-516-2269 ■ *Web:* www.stambaughauditorium.com	Youngstown	OH	44504	330-747-5175	747-1981
Stranahan Theater 4645 Heatherdowns Blvd *TF:* 866-381-7469 ■ *Web:* www.stranahantheater.org	Toledo	OH	43614	419-381-8851	
Taft, Theatre, The 317 E Fifth St *Web:* www.tafttheatre.org	Cincinnati	OH	45202	513-232-6220	
Valentine, Theatre, The 410 Adams St *Web:* www.valentinetheatre.com	Toledo	OH	43604	419-242-3490	242-2791
Victoria Theatre 138 N Main St *TF:* 888-228-3630 ■ *Web:* www.victoriatheatre.com	Dayton	OH	45402	937-228-3630	449-5068
Weathervane Community Playhouse 1301 Weathervane Ln *Web:* www.weathervaneplayhouse.com	Akron	OH	44313	330-836-2626	873-2150
Youngstown Playhouse 600 Playhouse Ln PO Box 11108 *Web:* www.theyoungstownplayhouse.com	Youngstown	OH	44511	330-788-8739	

Oklahoma

Facility	City	State	ZIP	Phone	Fax
Civic Ctr Music Hall 201 N Walker St *Web:* www.okcciviccenter.org	Oklahoma City	OK	73102	405-297-2584	
Jewel Box Theatre 3700 N Walker Ave *Web:* www.jewelboxtheatre.org	Oklahoma City	OK	73118	405-521-1786	
Tulsa Performing Arts Ctr 110 E Second St *Web:* www.tulsapac.com	Tulsa	OK	74103	918-596-7122	596-7144

Ontario

				Phone	Fax
Centre in the Square 101 Queen St N *TF:* 800-265-8977 ■ *Web:* centreinthesquare.com	Kitchener	ON	N2H6P7	519-578-1570	
Massey Hall 178 Victoria St *Web:* www.masseyhall.com	Toronto	ON	M5B1T7	416-872-4255	

Oregon

Facility	City	State	ZIP	Phone	Fax
Florence Events Ctr 715 Quince St *TF:* 888-968-4086 ■ *Web:* www.ci.florence.or.us	Florence	OR	97439	541-997-1994	902-0991
Historic Elsinore Theatre (HET) 170 High St SE *Web:* www.elsinoretheatre.com	Salem	OR	97301	503-375-3574	375-0284
Hult Ctr for the Performing Arts 1 Eugene Ctr *Web:* www.hultcenter.org	Eugene	OR	97401	541-682-5087	682-5426
McDonald Theatre 1010 Willamette St *Web:* www.mcdonaldtheatre.com	Eugene	OR	97401	541-345-4442	
Pentacle Theater 324 52nd Ave NW *Web:* www.pentacletheatre.org	Salem	OR	97304	503-364-7200	
Portland Ctr for the Performing Arts 1111 SW Broadway *Web:* www.portland5.com	Portland	OR	97205	503-248-4335	274-7490
Woodmen of the World Hall 291 W Eigth Ave *Web:* www.wowhall.org	Eugene	OR	97401	541-687-2746	687-1664

Pennsylvania

Facility	City	State	ZIP	Phone	Fax
Academy of Music 1500 Walnut St *Web:* www.kimmelcenter.org	Philadelphia	PA	19102	215-790-5800	
Annenberg Ctr for the Performing Arts 3680 Walnut St *Web:* www.annenbergcenter.org	Philadelphia	PA	19104	215-898-3900	
Civic Theatre of Allentown 527 N 19th St *Web:* www.civictheatre.com	Allentown	PA	18104	610-432-8943	432-7381
Eichelberger Performing Arts Ctr 195 Stock St Ste 203 *Web:* theeich.org	Hanover	PA	17331	717-632-9356	637-4504
Erie Playhouse 13 W Tenth St *Web:* www.erieplayhouse.org	Erie	PA	16501	814-454-2852	454-0601
Fulton Opera House Foundation 12 N Prince St PO Box 1865 *TF:* 888-480-1265 ■ *Web:* www.thefulton.org	Lancaster	PA	17603	717-397-7425	397-3780
Heinz Hall for the Performing Arts 600 Penn Ave *TF:* 800-743-8560 ■ *Web:* www.pittsburghsymphony.org	Pittsburgh	PA	15222	412-392-4900	392-3328
Kimmel Ctr for the Performing Arts 1500 Walnut St Fl 17 *Web:* www.kimmelcenter.org	Philadelphia	PA	19102	215-790-5800	790-5801
Liacouras Ctr 1776 N Broad St *TF:* 800-298-4200 ■ *Web:* www.liacourascenter.com	Philadelphia	PA	19121	215-204-2400	
Mann Ctr for the Performing Arts 5201 Parkside Ave *Web:* www.manncenter.org	Philadelphia	PA	19131	215-546-7900	546-9524
Music Box Dinner Playhouse 196 Hughes St *TF:* 800-698-7529 ■ *Web:* www.musicbox.org	Swoyersville	PA	18704	570-283-2195	
Providence Playhouse 1256 Providence Rd *Web:* actorscircle.org	Scranton	PA	18508	570-342-9707	
Scranton Cultural Ctr 420 N Washington Ave *Web:* www.scrantonculturalcenter.org	Scranton	PA	18503	570-346-7369	346-7365
Society Hill Playhouse 507 S Eigth St *Web:* www.societyhillplayhouse.org	Philadelphia	PA	19147	215-923-0210	
Sovereign Performing Arts Ctr 136 N Sixth St *Web:* santander-arena.com	Reading	PA	19601	610-898-7299	
Walnut Street Theatre 825 Walnut St *Web:* www.walnutstreettheatre.org	Philadelphia	PA	19107	215-574-3550	
Warner Theatre 811 State St *Web:* www.erieevents.com	Erie	PA	16501	814-452-4857	455-9931
Wilma Theater 265 S Broad St *TF:* 800-732-0999 ■ *Web:* www.wilmatheater.org	Philadelphia	PA	19107	215-893-9456	893-0895

Rhode Island

Facility	City	State	ZIP	Phone	Fax
AS220 115 Empire St *Web:* www.as220.org	Providence	RI	02903	401-831-9327	454-7445
Providence Performing Arts Ctr 220 Weybosset St *Web:* www.ppacri.org	Providence	RI	02903	401-421-2997	351-7827
Veterans Memorial Auditorium 1 Ave of the Arts *Web:* thevetsri.com	Providence	RI	02903	401-222-1467	

South Carolina

Facility	City	State	ZIP	Phone	Fax
Alabama Theatre 4750 Hwy 17 S *TF:* 800-342-2262 ■ *Web:* www.alabama-theatre.com	North Myrtle Beach	SC	29582	843-272-1111	
Arts Ctr of Coastal Carolina 14 Shelter Cove Ln *TF:* 888-860-2787 ■ *Web:* www.artshhi.com	Hilton Head Island	SC	29928	843-686-3945	842-7877
Carolina Opry 8901 Hwy 17 N *TF:* 800-843-6779 ■ *Web:* thecarolinaopry.com	Myrtle Beach	SC	29572	800-843-6779	

Name / Address	City	State	ZIP	Phone	Fax
Gaillard Municipal Auditorium 77 Calhoun St	Charleston	SC	29401	843-577-7400	
Greenville Little Theatre 444 College St *Web:* www.greenvillelittletheatre.org	Greenville	SC	29601	864-233-6238	
Koger Ctr for the Arts 1051 Greene St *Web:* www.kogercenterforthearts.com	Columbia	SC	29201	803-777-7500	777-9774
Palace, Theatre, The 1420 Celebrity Cir Broadway at the Beach *TF:* 888-841-2787 ■ *Web:* www.palacetheatremyrtlebeach.com	Myrtle Beach	SC	29577	843-448-9224	
Town Theatre 1012 Sumter St *Web:* www.towntheatre.com	Columbia	SC	29201	803-799-4764	799-6463
Township Auditorium 1703 Taylor St *Web:* www.thetownship.org	Columbia	SC	29201	803-576-2350	576-2359
Trustus Theatre 520 Lady St *Web:* www.trustus.org	Columbia	SC	29201	803-254-9732	
Warehouse Theatre 37 Augusta St *Web:* www.warehousetheatre.com	Greenville	SC	29601	864-235-6948	
Workshop Theatre 1136 Bull St *Web:* www.workshoptheatre.com	Columbia	SC	29211	803-799-4876	799-0227

South Dakota

Name / Address	City	State	ZIP	Phone	Fax
Matthews Opera House 612 Main St *Web:* www.matthewsopera.com	Spearfish	SD	57783	605-642-7973	

Tennessee

Name / Address	City	State	ZIP	Phone	Fax
Chattanooga Theatre Centre 400 River St *Web:* www.theatrecentre.com	Chattanooga	TN	37405	423-267-8534	664-1211
Circuit Playhouse, The 51 S Cooper St *TF:* 888-648-8154 ■ *Web:* www.playhouseonthesquare.org	Memphis	TN	38104	901-725-0776	726-5521
Clarence Brown Theatre *University of Tennessee* 206 McClung Tower *Web:* www.clarencebrowntheatre.com	Knoxville	TN	37996	865-974-5161	974-4867
Darkhorse Theater Ltd 4610 Charlotte Ave *Web:* darkhorsetheater.com	Nashville-Davidson	TN	37209	615-297-7113	
Germantown Performing Arts Centre (GPAC) 1801 Exeter Rd *Web:* www.gpacweb.com	Germantown	TN	38138	901-751-7500	
Grand Ole Opry 2804 Opryland Dr *TF:* 800-733-6779 ■ *Web:* www.opry.com	Nashville	TN	37214	615-871-6779	871-5719
Knoxville Civic Auditorium/Coliseum 500 Howard Baker Jr Ave *TF:* 877-995-9961 ■ *Web:* www.knoxvillecoliseum.com	Knoxville	TN	37915	865-215-8900	215-8989
Laurel Theatre 1538 Laurel Ave *Web:* www.jubileearts.org	Knoxville	TN	37916	865-522-5851	
Memphis Cook Convention Ctr 3205 Elvis Presley Blvd *Web:* www.memphistravel.com	Memphis	TN	38116	901-543-5333	
Nashville Municipal Auditorium 417 Fourth Ave N *Web:* www.nashville.gov	Nashville	TN	37201	615-862-6390	862-6394
Orpheum Theatre 203 S Main St *Web:* www.orpheum-memphis.com	Memphis	TN	38103	901-525-3000	
Ryman Auditorium 116 Fifth Ave N *TF:* 800-733-6779 ■ *Web:* www.ryman.com	Nashville	TN	37219	615-458-8700	458-8701
Soldiers & Sailors Memorial Auditorium 399 McCallie Ave *Web:* www.chattanooga.gov	Chattanooga	TN	37402	423-757-5156	
Tennessee Performing Arts Ctr 505 Deaderick St *TF:* 866-455-2823 ■ *Web:* www.tpac.org	Nashville	TN	37219	615-782-4000	782-4001
Texas Troubadour Theatre 2416 Music Valley Dr *Web:* etrecordshop.com	Nashville	TN	37214	615-889-2474	
Theatre Memphis 630 Perkins Ext *Web:* www.theatrememphis.org	Memphis	TN	38117	901-682-8323	
University of Tennessee Music Hall 1741 Volunteer Blvd *Web:* www.music.utk.edu	Knoxville	TN	37996	865-974-3241	974-1941

Texas

Name / Address	City	State	ZIP	Phone	Fax
Abilene Civic Ctr 1100 N Sixth St *Web:* www.abilenetx.com	Abilene	TX	79601	325-676-6211	676-6343
Abilene Community Theatre (ACT) 809 Barrow *Web:* www.abilenecommunitytheatre.org	Abilene	TX	79605	325-673-6271	
Alley Theatre 615 Texas Ave *Web:* www.alleytheatre.org	Houston	TX	77002	713-220-5700	222-6542
Amarillo Civic Ctr 401 S Buchanan St *Web:* amarillociviccenter.com	Amarillo	TX	79101	806-378-4297	378-4234
American Bank Ctr 1901 N Shoreline Blvd *Web:* www.americanbankcenter.com	Corpus Christi	TX	78401	361-826-4700	826-4905
Arneson River Theatre 418 Villita St La Villita	San Antonio	TX	78205	210-207-8614	207-4390
Bass Performance Hall 4th & Calhoun Sts *TF:* 877-212-4280 ■ *Web:* www.basshall.com	Fort Worth	TX	76102	817-212-4300	810-9294
Camille Lightner Playhouse 1 Dean Porter Pk *Web:* camilleplayhouse.org	Brownsville	TX	78520	956-542-8900	
Casa Manana Theatre 3101 W Lancaster Ave *Web:* www.casamanana.org	Fort Worth	TX	76107	817-332-2272	332-5711
Circle Theatre 230 W Fourth St *Web:* www.circletheatre.com	Fort Worth	TX	76102	817-877-3040	877-3536
Creative Arts Theatre & School 602 E S St *Web:* www.creativearts.org	Arlington	TX	76010	817-861-2287	274-0793
Cynthia Woods Mitchell Pavilion 2005 Lk Robbins Dr *Web:* www.woodlandscenter.org	The Woodlands	TX	77380	281-363-3300	364-3011
El Paso Convention & Performing Arts Ctr 1 Civic Ctr Plz *TF:* 800-351-6024 ■ *Web:* www.visitelpaso.com	El Paso	TX	79901	915-534-0600	534-0687
Ensemble Theatre 3535 Main St *Web:* www.ensemblehouston.com	Houston	TX	77002	713-520-0055	520-1269
Grand 1894 Opera House 2020 Postoffice St *TF:* 800-821-1894 ■ *Web:* www.thegrand.com	Galveston	TX	77550	409-765-1894	763-1068
Harbor Playhouse 1802 N Chaparral Bldg Ste 2 *Web:* www.harborplayhouse.com	Corpus Christi	TX	78401	361-882-5500	
Hobby Ctr for the Performing Arts 800 Bagby St Ste 300 *Web:* www.thehobbycenter.org	Houston	TX	77002	713-315-2400	315-2402
Irving Arts Center 3333 N MacArthur Blvd *Web:* www.irvingartscenter.com	Irving	TX	75062	972-252-7558	
Irving Arts Center 3333 N MacArthur Blvd *Web:* www.irvingartscenter.com	Irving	TX	75062	972-252-7558	
Irving Arts Ctr 3333 N MacArthur Blvd *Web:* www.irvingartscenter.com	Irving	TX	75062	972-252-7558	
Jesse H Jones Hall for the Performing Arts 615 Louisiana St Ste 101 *Web:* www.houstontx.gov	Houston	TX	77002	713-227-3974	
Jubilee Theatre 506 Main St *Web:* www.jubileetheatre.org	Fort Worth	TX	76102	817-338-4204	338-4206
Lila Cockrell Theatre 200 E Market St *TF General:* 877-504-8895	San Antonio	TX	78205	210-207-8500	
Majestic Theatre 1925 Elm St Ste 500 *Web:* www.dallasculture.org/majestictheatre	Dallas	TX	75201	214-670-3687	670-1404
Miller Outdoor Theatre 6000 Hermann Pk Dr **Fax Area Code:* 713 ■ *Web:* www.milleroutdoortheatre.com	Houston	TX	77030	281-823-9103	942-0863*
Morton H Meyerson Symphony Ctr 2301 Flora St *Web:* www.dallasculture.org	Dallas	TX	75201	214-670-3600	670-4334
Music Hall at Fair Park 909 First Ave *Web:* www.liveatthemusichall.com	Dallas	TX	75210	214-565-1116	565-0071
One World Theatre 7701 Bee Caves Rd *TF:* 888-616-0522 ■ *Web:* www.oneworldtheatre.org	Austin	TX	78746	512-330-9500	330-9600
Palace Arts Ctr 300 S Main St *Web:* www.grapevinetexasusa.com/Heritage/PalaceArtsCenter	Grapevine	TX	76051	817-410-3100	
Paramount Theatre 352 Cypress St *Web:* www.paramount-abilene.org	Abilene	TX	79601	325-676-9620	676-0642
Paramount, Theatre, The 713 Congress Ave *Web:* www.austintheatre.org	Austin	TX	78701	512-472-5470	472-5824
Patty Granville Performing Arts Ctr 300 N Fifth St *Web:* www.garlandarts.com	Garland	TX	75040	972-205-2000	
Perot Theatre 219 Main St *Web:* www.trahc.org	Texarkana	TX	75501	903-792-4992	793-8511
Rockport Ctr for the Arts 902 Navigation Cir *Web:* www.rockportartcenter.com	Rockport	TX	78382	361-729-5519	729-3551
Sammons Ctr for the Arts 3630 Harry Hines Blvd *Web:* www.sammonsartcenter.org	Dallas	TX	75219	214-520-7789	522-9174
San Antonio Municipal Auditorium 200 E Market St PO Box 1809 *TF:* 877-504-8895 ■ *Web:* www.sahbgcc.com	San Antonio	TX	78205	210-207-8500	223-1495
San Pedro Playhouse 800 W Ashby Pl PO Box 12356 *Web:* www.theplayhousesa.org	San Antonio	TX	78212	210-733-7258	734-2651
Theatre Three 2800 Routh St Ste 168 *Web:* www.theatre3dallas.com	Dallas	TX	75201	214-871-3300	
University of Texas at Austin Performing Arts Ctr E 23rd St & E Robert Dedman Dr *TF:* 800-687-6010 ■ *Web:* www.texasperformingarts.org	Austin	TX	78713	512-471-1444	471-4783
Wichita Falls CVB 1000 Fifth St **Fax Area Code:* 940 ■ *TF:* 800-799-6732 ■ *Web:* wichitafalls.org	Wichita Falls	TX	76301	800-799-6732	716-5509*
Williams Performing Arts Ctr *Abilene Christian University* 1600 Campus Ct *TF:* 800-460-6228 ■ *Web:* www.acu.edu	Abilene	TX	79601	325-674-2199	674-2369
Zachary Scott Theatre Ctr 1510 Toomey Rd *Web:* www.zachtheatre.org	Austin	TX	78704	512-476-0541	476-0314

Utah

Name / Address	City	State	ZIP	Phone	Fax
Capitol Theatre 50 W 200 S *Web:* artsaltlake.org	Salt Lake City	UT	84101	801-355-2787	
Hale Centre Theater 3333 S Decker Lake Dr *TF:* 877-829-5500 ■ *Web:* www.hct.org	West Valley City	UT	84119	801-984-9000	984-9009
Hale Ctr Theater Orem 225 West 400 North *Web:* www.haletheater.org	Orem	UT	84057	801-226-8600	852-3189
Off Broadway Theatre 272 S Main St *Web:* www.theobt.org	Salt Lake City	UT	84101	801-355-4628	
Salt Lake Community College Grand Theatre 1575 S State St *Web:* www.slcc.edu/the-grand	Salt Lake City	UT	84115	801-957-3322	
Terrace Plaza Playhouse 99 E 4700 S *Web:* www.terraceplayhouse.com	Ogden	UT	84405	801-393-0070	
Tuacahn Amphitheatre & Ctr for the Arts 1100 Tuacahn Dr *Web:* www.tuacahn.org	Ivins	UT	84738	435-652-3300	652-3227

Vermont

Name / Address	City	State	ZIP	Phone	Fax
Barre Opera House 6 N Main St PO Box 583 *Web:* www.barreoperahouse.org	Barre	VT	05641	802-476-8188	476-5648

Phone | Fax

Flynn Ctr for the Performing Arts
153 Main St .... Burlington VT 05401 802-863-5966 863-8788
Web: www.flynncenter.org

Virginia

Phone | Fax

Generic Theater 215 St Paul's Blvd .... Norfolk VA 23510 757-441-2160
Web: www.generictheater.org
George Mason University's Ctr for the Arts
George Mason University
4400 University Dr MS 2F5 .... Fairfax VA 22030 703-993-8888 993-8650
Web: cfa.gmu.edu
Jefferson Ctr 541 Luck Ave Ste 221 .... Roanoke VA 24016 540-343-2624 343-3744
TF: 866-345-2550 ■ *Web:* www.jeffcenter.org
Little Theatre of Alexandria 600 Wolfe St .... Alexandria VA 22314 703-683-5778 683-1378
Web: www.thelittletheatre.com
Little Theatre of Norfolk 801 Claremont Ave .... Norfolk VA 23507 757-627-8551
Web: www.ltnonline.org
MetroStage 1201 N Royal St .... Alexandria VA 22314 703-548-9044 548-9089
Web: www.metrostage.org
Mill Mountain Theatre 1 Market Sq 2nd Fl .... Roanoke VA 24011 540-342-5740
Web: www.millmountain.org
Peninsula Community Theatre
10251 Warwick Blvd PO Box 11056 .... Newport News VA 23601 757-595-5728
Web: www.pctlive.org
Roper Performing Arts Ctr 340 Granby St .... Norfolk VA 23510 757-822-1450 822-1451
Web: www.tccropercenter.org
Willett Hall 3701 Willett Dr .... Portsmouth VA 23707 757-393-5144 393-7324
Web: www.willett-hall-portsmouth.com
Wolf Trap Foundation for the Performing Arts
1645 Trap Rd .... Vienna VA 22182 703-255-1900 255-4077
TF: 877-965-3872 ■ *Web:* www.wolftrap.org
WSC Avant Bard 3700 S Four Mile Run .... Arlington VA 22206 703-418-4808
Web: wscavantbard.org

Washington

Phone | Fax

A Contemporary Theatre (ACT)
700 Union St Kreielsheimer Pl .... Seattle WA 98101 206-292-7660 292-7670
TF: 888-584-4849 ■ *Web:* www.acttheatre.org
Behnke Ctr for Contemporary Performance
100 W Roy St PO Box 19515 .... Seattle WA 98119 206-217-9886 217-9887
Web: www.ontheboards.org
Broadway Ctr for the Performing Arts
901 Broadway .... Tacoma WA 98402 253-591-5890 591-2013
TF: 800-291-7593 ■ *Web:* www.broadwaycenter.org
Pantages Theater 901 Broadway .... Tacoma WA 98402 253-591-5890 591-2013
TF: 800-291-7593 ■ *Web:* www.broadwaycenter.org
Rialto Theater 310 S Ninth St .... Tacoma WA 98402 253-591-5890 591-2013
TF: 800-291-7593 ■ *Web:* www.broadwaycenter.org
Seattle Ctr 305 Harrison St .... Seattle WA 98109 206-684-7200
Web: www.seattlecenter.com
Spokane Civic Theatre 1020 N Howard St .... Spokane WA 99201 509-325-1413 325-9287
TF: 800-325-7328 ■ *Web:* www.spokanecivictheatre.com
Spokane Ctr 720 W Mallon Ave .... Spokane WA 99201 509-279-7000 279-7050
Web: www.spokanecenter.com
Tacoma Little Theatre 210 N 'I' St .... Tacoma WA 98403 253-272-2281
Web: www.tacomalittletheatre.com
Washington Ctr for the Performing Arts
512 Washington St SE .... Olympia WA 98501 360-753-8586 754-1177
Web: www.washingtoncenter.org

West Virginia

Phone | Fax

Charleston Civic Ctr & Coliseum
200 Civic Ctr Dr .... Charleston WV 25301 304-345-1500 345-3492
Web: www.charlestonwvciviccenter.com
Clay Ctr for the Arts & Sciences
1 Clay Sq .... Charleston WV 25301 304-561-3570 561-3598
Web: www.theclaycenter.org
Oglebay Institute's Towngate Theatre
2118 Market St .... Wheeling WV 26003 304-233-0820
Web: www.oionline.com
Victoria Vaudeville Theater 1228 Market St .... Wheeling WV 26003 304-233-7464
TF: 800-505-7464 ■ *Web:* www.victoria-theater.com

Wisconsin

Phone | Fax

American Players Theater
5950 Golf Course Rd PO Box 819 .... Spring Green WI 53588 608-588-7401 588-7085
Web: www.americanplayers.org
Barrymore Theatre 2090 Atwood Ave .... Madison WI 53704 608-241-8633
Web: www.barrymorelive.com
Broom Street Theatre 1119 Williamson St .... Madison WI 53703 608-244-8338
Web: bstonline.org
Marcus Ctr for the Performing Arts
929 N Water St .... Milwaukee WI 53202 414-273-7206
TF: 888-612-3500 ■ *Web:* www.marcuscenter.org
Milwaukee Chamber Theatre
158 N Broadway Broadway Theatre Ctr .... Milwaukee WI 53202 414-276-8842 277-4477
Web: www.chamber-theatre.com
Overture Ctr for the Arts 201 State St .... Madison WI 53703 608-258-4177 258-4971
Web: www.overturecenter.org
Pabst Theater 144 E Wells St .... Milwaukee WI 53202 414-286-3205
TF: 866-948-6483 ■ *Web:* www.pabsttheater.org
Rave, The 2401 W Wisconsin Ave .... Milwaukee WI 53233 414-342-7283
Web: www.therave.com

Phone | Fax

Riverside Theatre 116 W Wisconsin Ave .... Milwaukee WI 53203 414-286-3663
Web: www.pabsttheater.org
Weidner Ctr for the Performing Arts
2420 Nicolet Dr
University of Wisconsin at Green Bay .... Green Bay WI 54311 920-465-2726 465-2619
TF: 800-895-0071 ■ *Web:* www.weidnercenter.com

Wyoming

Phone | Fax

Cheyenne Civic Ctr 510 W 20th St .... Cheyenne WY 82001 307-637-6364 637-6365
TF: 877-691-2787 ■ *Web:* www.cheyennecity.org
Cheyenne Little Theatre Players
PO Box 20087 .... Cheyenne WY 82003 307-638-6543
Web: www.cheyennelittletheatre.org
Jackson Hole Playhouse 145 W Deloney Ave .... Jackson WY 83001 307-733-6994
Web: jacksonholeplayhouse.com
Stage III Community Theatre 900 N Ctr St .... Casper WY 82601 307-234-0946
Web: www.stageiiitheatre.org

573 PERFORMING ARTS ORGANIZATIONS

See Also Arts & Artists Organizations p. 1753

573-1 Dance Companies

Phone | Fax

Abilene Ballet Theatre 1265 N Second St .... Abilene TX 79601 325-675-0303
Web: www.abileneballettheatre.org
Alabama Ballet 2726 First Ave S .... Birmingham AL 35233 205-322-4300 322-4444
Web: www.alabamaballet.org
Alabama Dance Theatre 1018 Madison Ave .... Montgomery AL 36104 334-241-2590
Web: www.alabamadancetheatre.com
Alonzo King's LINES Contemporary Ballet
26 Seventh St .... San Francisco CA 94102 415-863-3040 863-1180
Web: www.linesballet.org
Alvin Ailey American Dance Theater
405 W 55th St .... New York NY 10019 212-405-9000 405-9001
Web: www.alvinailey.org
American Ballet Theatre (ABT)
890 Broadway 3rd Fl .... New York NY 10003 212-477-3030 254-5938
Web: www.abt.org
American Repertory Ballet
7 Livingston Ave .... New Brunswick NJ 08901 732-249-1254 249-8475
Web: www.americanrepertoryballet.org
Ann Arbor Civic Ballet 3900 E Jackson .... Ann Arbor MI 48103 734-668-8066
Aspen Santa Fe Ballet 0245 Sage Way .... Aspen CO 81611 970-925-7175 925-1127
TF: 866-449-0464 ■ *Web:* www.aspensantafeballet.com
Atlanta Ballet 1695 Marietta Blvd NW .... Atlanta GA 30318 404-873-5811 874-7905
Web: www.atlantaballet.com
Augusta Ballet Inc 1301 Greene St .... Augusta GA 30901 706-261-0555
Web: www.augustaballet.org
Axis Dance Co 1428 Alice St Ste 200 .... Oakland CA 94612 510-625-0110 625-0321
TF: 800-838-3006 ■ *Web:* www.axisdance.org
Ballet Arizona 2835 E Washington St .... Phoenix AZ 85034 602-381-0184 381-0189
Web: www.balletaz.org
Ballet Arkansas 1521 Merrill Dr .... Little Rock AR 72211 501-223-5150
Web: www.balletarkansas.org
Ballet Austin 501 W Third St .... Austin TX 78701 512-476-9051 472-3073
Web: www.balletaustin.org
Ballet British Columbia 677 Davie St 6th Fl .... Vancouver BC V6B2G6 604-732-5003 732-4417
Web: www.balletbc.com
Ballet Chicago 17 N State St Ste 1900 .... Chicago IL 60602 312-251-8838 251-8840
Web: www.balletchicago.org
Ballet Hispanico of New York 167 W 89th St .... New York NY 10024 212-362-6710 362-7809
Web: www.ballethispanico.org
Ballet Idaho 501 S Eigth St .... Boise ID 83702 208-343-0556 424-3129
Web: www.balletidaho.org
Ballet Lubbock 5702 Genoa Ave Ste A9 .... Lubbock TX 79424 806-785-3090 785-3309
Web: www.balletlubbock.org
Ballet Magnificat 5406 I-55 N .... Jackson MS 39211 601-977-1001 977-8948
TF: 866-617-3257 ■ *Web:* www.balletmagnificat.com
Ballet Mississippi
201 E Pascagoula St Ste 106 PO Box 1787 .... Jackson MS 39215 601-960-1560 960-2135
Web: www.balletms.com
Ballet Quad Cities 613 17th St .... Rock Island IL 61201 309-786-3779 786-2677
Web: www.balletquadcities.com
Ballet Tech 890 Broadway .... New York NY 10003 212-777-7710 353-0936
Web: ballettechschool.org
Ballet Tennessee 3202 Kelly's Ferry Rd .... Chattanooga TN 37419 423-821-2055
Web: www.ballettennessee.org
Ballet Theatre of Maryland
801 Chase St
Maryland Hall for the Creative Arts .... Annapolis MD 21401 410-263-8289 626-1835
Web: www.balletmaryland.org
Ballet Theatre of New Mexico
6913 Natalie NE .... Albuquerque NM 87110 505-888-1054
Web: www.btnm.org
Ballet West 50 West 200 South .... Salt Lake City UT 84101 801-323-6900 359-3504
Web: www.balletwest.org
Ballet Western Reserve
218 W Boardman St PO Box 1684 .... Youngstown OH 44501 330-744-1934 744-2631
Web: www.balletwesternreserve.org
BalletMet Columbus 322 Mt Vernon Ave .... Columbus OH 43215 614-229-4860
Web: www.balletmet.org
Baton Rouge Ballet Theatre
10745 Linkwood Ct PO Box 82288 .... Baton Rouge LA 70884 225-766-8379
Web: www.batonrougeballet.org
Bill T Jones/Arnie Zane Dance Co
219 W 19th St .... New York NY 10011 212-691-6500 633-1974
Web: www.newyorklivearts.org

Organization	City	State	ZIP	Phone	Fax
Boston Ballet 19 Clarendon St *Web:* www.bostonballet.org	Boston	MA	02116	617-695-6950	695-6995
Boulder Ballet 2590 Walnut St Ste 10 *Web:* www.boulderballet.org	Boulder	CO	80302	303-443-0028	
Buglisi Dance Theatre 229 W 42nd St Ste 502 *TF:* 800-754-0797 ■ *Web:* www.buglisi-foreman.org	New York	NY	10036	212-719-3301	719-3302
California Ballet Co (CBC) 4819 Ronson Ct *Web:* www.californiaballet.org	San Diego	CA	92111	858-560-5676	560-0072
Canyon Concert Ballet 1031 Conifer St *Web:* www.ccballet.org	Fort Collins	CO	80524	970-472-4156	
Carolina Ballet Inc 3401-131 Atlantic Ave *Web:* www.carolinaballet.com	Raleigh	NC	27604	919-719-0800	719-0910
Carolyn Dorfman Dance Co (CDDC) 2780 Morris Ave Ste 1-A *Web:* carolyndorfman.dance	Union	NJ	07083	908-687-8855	686-5245
Cassandra Ballet of Toledo 3157 Sylvania Ave *Web:* cassandraballet.com	Toledo	OH	43613	419-475-0458	
Central West Ballet Co (CWB) 5039 Pendecost Dr Ste B2 *Web:* cwballet.org	Modesto	CA	95356	209-576-8957	576-1308
Charleston Ballet 100 Capitol St Ste 302 *Web:* www.thecharlestonballet.com	Charleston	WV	25301	304-342-6541	
Chitresh Das Dance Co 2325 Third St Ste 320 *Web:* www.kathak.org	San Francisco	CA	94107	415-333-9000	333-9029
Cincinnati Ballet 1555 Central Pkwy *Web:* www.cballet.org	Cincinnati	OH	45214	513-621-5219	621-4844
Cleo Parker Robinson Dance 119 Pk Ave W *Web:* www.cleoparkerdance.org	Denver	CO	80205	303-295-1759	
Collage Dance Theatre 2934 1/2 Beverly Glen Cir **Fax Area Code: 604* ■ *TF:* 866-300-4287	Los Angeles	CA	90077	818-784-8669	682-1715*
Colorado Ballet 1278 Lincoln St *Web:* www.coloradoballet.org	Denver	CO	80203	303-837-8888	861-7174
Columbia City Ballet 1545 Main St *Web:* www.columbiacityballet.com	Columbia	SC	29201	803-799-7605	
Connecticut Ballet 20 Acosta St *Web:* connecticutballet.org	Stamford	CT	06902	203-964-1211	961-1928
Contemporary Dance Theatre 1805 Larch Ave *Web:* www.cdt-dance.org	Cincinnati	OH	45224	513-591-1222	
Corpus Christi Ballet 1621 N Mesquite St *Web:* www.corpuschristiballet.com	Corpus Christi	TX	78401	361-882-4588	881-9291
Dallas Black Dance Theatre 2700 Flora St *Web:* www.dbdt.com	Dallas	TX	75201	214-871-2376	871-2842
Dance Theatre of Harlem Inc 466 W 152nd St *TF:* 800-538-2538 ■ *Web:* www.dancetheatreofharlem.org	New York	NY	10031	212-690-2800	690-8736
Dayton Ballet 140 N Main St *TF:* 800-745-3000 ■ *Web:* daytonperformingarts.org	Dayton	OH	45402	937-449-5060	223-9189
Dayton Contemporary Dance Co 840 Germantown St *TF:* 888-228-3630 ■ *Web:* www.dcdc.org	Dayton	OH	45402	937-228-3232	223-6156
Doug Varone & Dancers 37 W 32nd St *TF:* 800-366-2100 ■ *Web:* www.dougvaroneanddancers.org	New York	NY	10001	212-279-3344	279-3344
Ethnic Dance Theatre 3507 Clinton Ave S *Web:* www.ethnicdancetheatre.com	Minneapolis	MN	55408	763-545-1333	
First State Ballet Theatre 818 N Market St *Web:* www.firststateballet.com	Wilmington	DE	19801	302-658-7897	
Flamenco Vivo Carlota Santana 4 W 43rd St Ste 608 *Web:* flamenco-vivo.org	New York	NY	10036	212-736-4499	
Fort Wayne Ballet Inc 300 E Main St *Web:* www.fortwayneballet.org	Fort Wayne	IN	46802	260-484-9646	484-9647
Fort Wayne Dance Collective 437 E Berry St *Web:* www.fwdc.org	Fort Wayne	IN	46802	260-424-6574	
Garth Fagan Dance 50 Chestnut St *Web:* www.garthfagandance.org	Rochester	NY	14604	585-454-3260	
Georgia Ballet 1255 Field Pkwy *Web:* www.georgiaballet.org	Marietta	GA	30066	770-528-0881	
Grand Rapids Ballet Co 341 Ellsworth Ave SW *Web:* www.grballet.com	Grand Rapids	MI	49503	616-454-4771	454-0672
Greater Lansing Ballet Co 2225 E Grand River Ave *Web:* greaterlansingballet.com	Lansing	MI	48912	517-372-9887	372-9887
Hawaii State Ballet 1418 Kapiolani Blvd *Web:* www.hawaiistateballet.com	Honolulu	HI	96814	808-947-2755	
Houston Ballet 601 Preston St *TF:* 800-828-2787 ■ *Web:* www.houstonballet.org	Houston	TX	77002	713-523-6300	523-4038
HT Chen & Dancers 70 Mulberry St 2nd Fl *Web:* www.chendancecenter.org	New York	NY	10013	212-349-0126	349-0494
Hubbard Street Dance Chicago 1147 W Jackson Blvd *Web:* www.hubbardstreetdance.com	Chicago	IL	60607	312-850-9744	455-8240
Huntsville Ballet 800 Regal Dr SW *Web:* www.communityballet.org	Huntsville	AL	35801	256-539-0961	
Inland Pacific Ballet 5050 Arrow Hwy *Web:* www.ipballet.org	Montclair	CA	91763	909-482-1590	482-1589
James Sewell Ballet 528 Hennepin Ave Ste 215 *Web:* www.jsballet.org	Minneapolis	MN	55403	612-672-0480	
Joe Goode Performance Group (JGPG) 499 Alabama St Ste 150 *Web:* www.joegoode.org	San Francisco	CA	94110	415-561-6565	561-6562
Joffrey Ballet of Chicago 10 E Randolph St *Web:* joffrey.org	Chicago	IL	60601	312-739-0120	739-0119
John Jasperse Co 140 Second Ave Ste 501 *Web:* www.johnjasperse.org	New York	NY	10003	212-375-8283	
Jose Matteo's Ballet Theatre 400 Harvard St *Web:* www.ballettheatre.org	Cambridge	MA	02138	617-354-7467	354-7856

Organization	City	State	ZIP	Phone	Fax
Kelly-Strayhorn Theater 5941 Penn Ave *Web:* www.kelly-strayhorn.org	Pittsburgh	PA	15206	412-363-3000	
Lar Lubovitch Dance Co 229 W 42nd St 8th Fl *Web:* www.lubovitch.org	New York	NY	10036	212-221-7909	221-7938
Lexington Ballet Co (LBC) 161 N Mill St *Web:* www.lexingtonballet.org	Lexington	KY	40507	859-233-3925	
Limon Dance Co 466 West 152nd St Fl 2 *Web:* www.limon.org	New York	NY	10031	212-777-3353	777-4764
Liz Lerman Dance Exchange 7117 Maple Ave *Web:* www.danceexchange.org	Takoma Park	MD	20912	301-270-6700	
Louisville Ballet 315 E Main St *Web:* www.louisvilleballet.org	Louisville	KY	40202	502-583-3150	583-0006
Madison Ballet 160 Westgate Mall *Web:* www.madisonballet.org	Madison	WI	53711	608-278-7990	278-7992
Maine State Ballet 348 US Rt 1 *Web:* www.mainestateballet.org	Falmouth	ME	04105	207-781-7672	781-3663
Mark Morris Dance Group 3 Lafayette Ave *TF:* 800-957-1046 ■ *Web:* www.markmorrisdancegroup.org	Brooklyn	NY	11217	718-624-8400	624-8900
Merce Cunningham Dance Co 130 W 56TH St Ste 707 *Web:* www.mercecunningham.org	New York	NY	10019	212-255-8240	
Miami City Ballet 2200 Liberty Ave *TF:* 877-929-7010 ■ *Web:* www.miamicityballet.org	Miami Beach	FL	33139	305-929-7000	
Milwaukee Ballet 504 W National Ave *TF:* 888-612-3500 ■ *Web:* www.milwaukeeballet.org	Milwaukee	WI	53204	414-643-7677	649-4066
Minnesota Ballet 301 W First St Ste 800 *TF:* 800-627-3529 ■ *Web:* www.minnesotaballet.org	Duluth	MN	55802	218-529-3742	529-3744
Minnesota Dance Theatre 528 Hennepin Ave 6th Fl *Web:* www.mndance.org	Minneapolis	MN	55403	612-338-0627	
Montgomery Ballet 2101 E Blvd Ste 223 *Web:* www.montgomeryballet.org	Montgomery	AL	36117	334-409-0522	
Mordine & Company Dance Theatre 1016 N Dearborn Pkwy *Web:* www.mordine.org	Chicago	IL	60610	312-654-9540	
Nashville Ballet 3630 Redmon St *Web:* www.nashvilleballet.com	Nashville	TN	37209	615-297-2966	297-9972
National Ballet 1816 Margaret Ave *Web:* www.nationalballet.com	Annapolis	MD	21401	301-218-9822	686-7040
National Ballet of Canada Walter Carsen Centre for the National Ballet of Canada 470 Queens Quay W *Web:* national.ballet.ca	Toronto	ON	M5V3K4	416-345-9686	345-8323
Nevada Ballet Theatre 1651 Inner Cir *Web:* nevadaballet.org	Las Vegas	NV	89134	702-243-2623	804-0365
New Haven Ballet 70 Audubon St *Web:* www.newhavenballet.org	New Haven	CT	06510	203-782-9038	
New Jersey Ballet Co 15 Microlab Rd *Web:* www.njballet.org	Livingston	NJ	07039	973-597-9600	597-9442
New York City Ballet Inc 20 Lincoln Ctr New York State Theatre *Web:* www.nycballet.com	New York	NY	10023	212-870-5656	870-7791
New York Theatre Ballet 30 E 31st St *Web:* www.nytb.org	New York	NY	10016	212-679-0401	679-8171
Northern Ballet Theatre 36 Arlington St *Web:* nbtdc.com	Nashua	NH	03060	603-889-8406	
Northwest Florida Ballet 310 Perry Ave SE *Web:* www.nfballet.org	Fort Walton Beach	FL	32548	850-664-7787	664-0130
Oakland Ballet Co 2201 Broadway Ste 206 *TF:* 866-711-6037 ■ *Web:* www.oaklandballet.org	Oakland	CA	94612	510-893-3132	
ODC/San Francisco 3153 17th St *Web:* www.odcdance.org	San Francisco	CA	94110	415-863-6606	863-9833
Ohio Ballet 354 E Market St	Akron	OH	44325	330-972-7900	972-7902
Oklahoma City Ballet 7421 N Classen Blvd *Web:* www.okcballet.com	Oklahoma City	OK	73116	405-843-9898	843-9894
Oregon Ballet Theatre 818 SE Sixth Ave *Web:* www.obt.org	Portland	OR	97214	503-227-0977	227-4186
Pacific Northwest Ballet 301 Mercer St *Web:* www.pnb.org	Seattle	WA	98109	206-441-2424	441-2420
Parsons Dance Co 229 W 42nd St 8th Fl *Web:* www.parsonsdance.org	New York	NY	10036	212-869-9275	944-7417
Paul Taylor Dance Co 551 Grand St *Web:* ptamd.org/ptdc-promo	New York	NY	10002	212-431-5562	966-5673
Peninsula Ballet Theatre 1880 S Grant St *Web:* www.peninsulaballet.org	San Mateo	CA	94402	650-342-3262	
Pennsylvania Ballet 1819 John F Kennedy Blvd *TF:* 800-732-0999 ■ *Web:* www.paballet.org	Philadelphia	PA	19103	215-551-7000	551-7224
Pennsylvania Youth Ballet (PYB) 556 Main St *Web:* www.bglv.org	Bethlehem	PA	18018	610-865-0353	
Peoria Ballet 809 W Detweiller Dr *Web:* www.peoriaballet.org	Peoria	IL	61615	309-690-7990	690-7991
Philadelphia Dance Co 9 N Preston St Philadanco Way *Web:* www.philadanco.org	Philadelphia	PA	19104	215-387-8200	387-8203
Pittsburgh Ballet Theatre 2900 Liberty Ave *TF:* 800-441-1414 ■ *Web:* www.pbt.org	Pittsburgh	PA	15201	412-281-0360	281-9901
Repertory Dance Theatre 138 West 300 South *Web:* www.xmission.com/~rdt	Salt Lake City	UT	84101	801-534-1000	534-1110
Richmond Ballet 407 E Canal St 1st Fl *Web:* richmondballet.com	Richmond	VA	23219	804-344-0906	344-0901
Ririe-Woodbury Dance Co 138 West Broadway *Web:* www.ririewoodbury.com	Salt Lake City	UT	84101	801-297-4241	297-4235
Robinson Ballet 107 Union St *Web:* www.robinsonballet.org	Bangor	ME	04401	207-990-3140	
Rochester City Ballet 1326 University Ave *Web:* www.rochestercityballet.org	Rochester	NY	14607	585-461-5850	473-8847

Phone Fax

Sacramento Ballet 1631 K St. Sacramento CA 95814 916-552-5800 552-5815
TF: 800-925-9989 ■ *Web:* sacballet.org
San Diego Ballet 2650 Truxtun Rd San Diego CA 92106 619-294-7378
Web: sandiegoballetdancecompany.org
San Francisco Ballet 455 Franklin St San Francisco CA 94102 415-865-2000 861-2684
TF: 888-622-2108 ■ *Web:* www.sfballet.org
Sarasota Ballet of Florida
5555 N Tamiami Trail Sarasota FL 34243 941-359-0099 358-1504
Web: www.sarasotaballet.org
Southland Ballet Academy
Fountain Valley 9527 Garfield Ave Fountain Valley CA 92708 714-962-5440 962-9383
State Ballet of Rhode Island, The
52 Sherman Ave PO Box 155 Lincoln RI 02865 401-334-2560 334-0412
Web: www.stateballet.com
Stuart Pimsler Dance & Theater
528 Hennepin Ave S Ste 707 Minneapolis MN 55403 763-521-7738
Web: www.stuartpimsler.com
Texas Ballet Theater 1540 Mall Cir Fort Worth TX 76116 817-763-0207 763-0624
Web: www.texasballettheater.org
Texas International Theatrical Arts Society (TITAS)
2100 Ross Ave Ste 650 Dallas TX 75201 214-528-6112
Web: www.titas.org
Trisha Brown Dance Co 341 W 38th St Ste 801 New York NY 10018 212-977-5365
Web: www.trishabrowncompany.org
Tulsa Ballet 1212 E 45th Pl Tulsa OK 74105 918-749-6030 749-0532
Web: www.tulsaballet.org
Tupelo Ballet Co 775 Poplarville Dr Tupelo MS 38801 662-844-1928
Web: www.tupeloballet.com
Urban Bush Women 138 S Oxford St Ste 4B Brooklyn NY 11217 718-398-4537 398-4783
Web: www.urbanbushwomen.org
Virginia Ballet Theatre 134 W Olney Rd Norfolk VA 23510 757-622-4822 622-7904
Washington Ballet 3515 Wisconsin Ave NW Washington DC 20016 202-362-3606 362-1311
Web: www.washingtonballet.org
Zenon Dance Company & School
528 Hennepin Ave Minneapolis MN 55403 612-338-1101 338-2479
Web: www.zenondance.org

573-2 Opera Companies

Phone Fax

Academy of Vocal Arts (AVA) 1920 Spruce St Philadelphia PA 19103 215-735-1685 732-2189
Web: www.avaopera.org
Amarillo Opera 2223 S Van Buren St Amarillo TX 79109 806-372-7464
Web: www.amarilloopera.org
Anchorage Opera 1507 Spar Ave Anchorage AK 99501 907-279-2557 279-7798
Web: www.anchorageopera.org
Annapolis Opera Inc
801 Chase St
Maryland Hall for the Creative Arts Annapolis MD 21401 410-267-8135 267-6440
Web: www.annapolisopera.org
Aspen Opera Theater 225 Music School Rd Aspen CO 81611 970-925-3254 925-3802
Web: www.aspenmusicfestival.com
Augusta Opera 1215 Troupe St Augusta GA 30904 706-364-9114
Austin Opera 3009 Industrial Terrace Ste 100 Austin TX 78758 512-472-5927
Web: austinopera.org
Central City Opera 400 S Colorado Blvd Ste 530 Denver CO 80246 303-292-6500 292-4958
Web: www.centralcityopera.org
Charleston Light Opera Guild
411 Tennessee Ave Charleston WV 25302 304-343-2287
Web: charlestonwv.com
Chicago Opera Theater 70 E Lake St Ste 815 Chicago IL 60601 312-704-8420
Web: www.chicagooperatheater.org
Cincinnati Opera 1243 Elm St Cincinnati OH 45202 513-768-5500 768-5553
Web: www.cincinnatiopera.org
Dallas Opera 8350 N Central Expy Ste 210 Dallas TX 75206 214-443-1000 443-1060
TF: 888-353-4537 ■ *Web:* www.dallasopera.org
Dayton Opera 126 N Main St Ste 210 Dayton OH 45402 937-224-3521 223-9189
Web: www.daytonperformingarts.org
Des Moines Metro Opera 106 W Boston Ave Indianola IA 50125 515-961-6221 961-6221
Web: www.desmoinesmetroopera.org
Fargo-Moorhead Opera Co 114 Broadway Ste S-1 Fargo ND 58102 701-239-4558
Web: www.fmopera.org
Florentine Opera Co 700 N Water St Ste 950 Milwaukee WI 53202 414-291-5700 291-5706
TF: 800-326-7372 ■ *Web:* www.florentineopera.org
Florida Grand Opera 8390 NW 25th St Miami FL 33122 305-854-1643 856-1042
TF: 800-741-1010 ■ *Web:* www.fgo.org
Fort Worth Opera 1300 Gendy St Fort Worth TX 76107 817-731-0833 731-0835
TF: 877-396-7372 ■ *Web:* www.fwopera.org
Fresno Grand Opera 2405 Capitol St Ste 103 Fresno CA 93721 559-442-5699 442-5649
Web: www.fresnograndopera.org
Glimmerglass Festival
7300 State Hwy 80 PO Box 191 Cooperstown NY 13326 607-547-0700 547-6030
TF: 866-568-2388 ■ *Web:* www.glimmerglass.org
Hawaii Opera Theatre
848 S Beretania St Ste 301 Honolulu HI 96813 808-596-7372 596-0379
Web: www.hawaiiopera.org
Houston Grand Opera 510 Preston St Houston TX 77002 713-546-0200
TF: 800-626-7372 ■ *Web:* www.houstongrandopera.org
Indianapolis Opera 250 E 38th St Indianapolis IN 46205 317-283-3531 923-5611
Web: www.indyopera.org
Kentucky Opera Assn 323 W Broadway Ste 601 Louisville KY 40202 502-584-4500
TF: 800-690-9236 ■ *Web:* www.kyopera.org
Knoxville Opera Co 612 E Depot Ave Knoxville TN 37917 865-524-0795 524-7384
Web: www.knoxvilleopera.com
Long Beach Opera 507 Pacific Ave Long Beach CA 90802 562-432-5934 683-2109
Web: www.longbeachopera.org
Los Angeles Opera 135 N Grand Ave Ste 327 Los Angeles CA 90012 213-972-7219 687-3490
Web: laopera.org
Lyric Opera of Chicago
20 N Wacker Dr Civic Opera House Ste 860 Chicago IL 60606 312-332-2244 332-8120
Web: www.lyricopera.org

Phone Fax

Metropolitan Opera 65th St & Broadway New York NY 10023 212-799-3100
Web: metopera.org
Michigan Opera Theatre 1526 Broadway Detroit MI 48226 313-961-3500 237-3412
Web: michiganopera.org
Minnesota Opera 620 N First St Minneapolis MN 55401 612-333-2700 333-0869
TF: 800-676-6737 ■ *Web:* www.mnopera.org
Mississippi Opera PO Box 1551 Jackson MS 39215 601-960-2300
Web: www.msopera.org
Mobile Opera Inc 257 Dauphin St Mobile AL 36602 251-432-6772 431-7613
Web: mobileopera.org
Musical Theatre Southwest (MTS)
6320 Domingo Rd NE Ste B Albuquerque NM 87108 505-265-9119
Web: www.musicaltheatresw.com
Ohio Light Opera, The 1189 Beall Ave Wooster OH 44691 330-263-2345 263-2272
Web: www.ohiolightopera.org
Opera Birmingham 3601 Sixth Ave S Birmingham AL 35222 205-322-6737 322-6206
Web: www.operabirmingham.org
Opera Carolina 345 N College St Ste 409 Charlotte NC 28202 704-332-7177 332-6448
Web: www.operacarolina.org
Opera Colorado 695 S Colorado Blvd Ste 20 Denver CO 80246 303-778-1500 778-0479
Web: www.operacolorado.org
Opera Company of Brooklyn
33 Indian Rd Ste 1G New York NY 10034 212-567-3283
Web: www.operabrooklyn.org
Opera Company of North Carolina
612 Wade Ave Ste 100 Raleigh NC 27605 919-792-3850
Web: www.ncopera.org
Opera Company of Philadelphia
1420 Locust St Ste 210 Philadelphia PA 19102 215-893-3600 893-7801
Web: www.operaphila.org
Opera Memphis 6745 Wolf River Pkwy Memphis TN 38120 901-257-3100
Web: www.operamemphis.org
Opera Omaha 1625 Farnam St Ste 100 Omaha NE 68102 402-346-4398 346-7323
TF: 877-346-7372 ■ *Web:* www.operaomaha.org
Opera Roanoke 541 Luck Ave Roanoke VA 24016 540-982-2742
Web: www.operaroanoke.org
Opera San Jose 2149 Paragon Dr San Jose CA 95131 408-437-4450 437-4455
TF: 800-745-3000 ■ *Web:* operasj.org
Opera Santa Barbara 1330 State St Santa Barbara CA 93101 805-898-3890 898-3892
Web: www.operasb.com
Opera Theatre at Wildwood 20919 Denny Rd Little Rock AR 72223 501-821-7275
Web: www.wildwoodpark.org
OperaDelaware 4 S Poplar St Wilmington DE 19801 302-658-8063
Web: www.operade.org
Palm Beach Opera 415 S Olive Ave West Palm Beach FL 33401 561-833-7888
TF: 800-435-7352 ■ *Web:* pbopera.org
Pensacola Opera 75 S Tarragona St Pensacola FL 32502 850-433-6737
Web: www.pensacolaopera.com
Pittsburgh Civic Light Opera
719 Liberty Ave Pittsburgh PA 15222 412-281-3973 281-5339
Web: www.pittsburghclo.org
Pittsburgh Opera 2425 Liberty Ave Pittsburgh PA 15222 412-281-0912 281-4324
Web: www.pittsburghopera.org
Pocket Opera 469 Bryant St San Francisco CA 94107 415-972-8930
Web: www.pocketopera.org
Portland Opera 211 SE Caruthers St Portland OR 97214 503-241-1407 241-4212
TF: 866-739-6737 ■ *Web:* www.portlandopera.org
San Diego Opera 233 A St Ste 500 San Diego CA 92101 619-232-7636 231-6915
Web: www.sdopera.org
San Francisco Opera 301 Van Ness Ave San Francisco CA 94102 415-861-4008
Web: www.sfopera.com
Santa Fe Opera, The 301 Opera Dr Santa Fe NM 87506 505-986-5900 986-5999
TF: 800-280-4654 ■ *Web:* www.santafeopera.org
Sarasota Opera 61 N Pineapple Ave Sarasota FL 34236 941-366-8450 955-5571
TF: 866-951-0111 ■ *Web:* www.sarasotaopera.org
Seattle Musical Theatre
7400 Sand Pt Way NE Ste 101-N Seattle WA 98103 206-363-2809
Web: www.seattlemusicaltheatre.org
Seattle Opera PO Box 9248 Seattle WA 98109 206-389-7600 389-7651
TF Sales: 800-426-1619 ■ *Web:* www.seattleopera.org
Shreveport Opera 212 Texas St Ste 101 Shreveport LA 71101 318-227-9503 227-9518
Web: www.shreveportopera.org
Skylight Opera Theatre 158 N Broadway Milwaukee WI 53202 414-291-7811 291-7815
Web: www.skylightmusictheatre.org
Syracuse Opera 411 Montgomery St Ste 60 Syracuse NY 13202 315-475-5915 475-6319
Web: www.syracuseopera.com
Tacoma Opera 1119 Pacific Ave Tacoma WA 98402 253-627-7789
Web: www.tacomaopera.com
Toledo Opera 425 Jefferson Ave Ste 601 Toledo OH 43604 419-255-7464 255-6344
TF: 866-860-9048 ■ *Web:* www.toledoopera.org
Tri-Cities Opera 315 Clinton St Binghamton NY 13905 607-729-3444 797-6344
Web: www.tricitiesopera.com
Tulsa Opera 1610 S Boulder Ave Tulsa OK 74119 918-582-4035 592-0380
TF: 866-298-2530 ■ *Web:* www.tulsaopera.com
Wichita Grand Opera
225 W Douglas Ave
Century II Performing Arts Ctr Wichita KS 67202 316-683-3444 263-2126
TF: 855-755-7328 ■ *Web:* www.wichitagrandopera.org

573-3 Orchestras

Phone Fax

Abilene Philharmonic Orchestra
401 Cypress St Ste 520 Abilene TX 79601 325-677-6710
Web: www.abilenephilharmonic.org
Acadiana Symphony Orchestra 412 Travis St Lafayette LA 70503 337-232-4277 237-4712
TF: 800-826-4919 ■ *Web:* www.acadianasymphony.org
Alabama Symphony Orchestra
3621 Sixth Ave S Birmingham AL 35222 205-975-2787 251-6840
Web: www.alabamasymphony.org

Organization	City	State	ZIP	Phone	Fax
Albany Symphony Orchestra 19 Clinton Ave PO Box 70065 *Web:* www.albanysymphony.org	Albany	GA	31707	229-430-8933	
Alexandria Symphony Orchestra 2121 Eisenhower Ave Ste 608 *Web:* www.alexsym.org	Alexandria	VA	22314	703-548-0885	
Allentown Symphony Orchestra 23 N Sixth St *Web:* www.millersymphonyhall.org	Allentown	PA	18101	610-432-6715	432-6735
American Composers Orchestra 240 W 35th St Ste 405 *Web:* www.americancomposers.org	New York	NY	10001	212-977-8495	977-8995
American Symphony Orchestra 263 W 38 St 10th Fl *Web:* www.americansymphony.org	New York	NY	10018	212-868-9276	868-9277
Anchorage Symphony Orchestra 400 D St Ste 230 *Web:* www.anchoragesymphony.org	Anchorage	AK	99501	907-274-8668	272-7916
Anderson Symphony Orchestra (ASO) 1124 Meridian Plz *Web:* www.andersonsymphony.org	Anderson	IN	46016	765-644-2111	
Ann Arbor Symphony Orchestra 220 E Huron St Ste 470 *Web:* www.a2so.com	Ann Arbor	MI	48104	734-994-4801	994-3949
Annapolis Symphony Orchestra 801 Chase St Maryland Hall *Web:* www.annapolissymphony.org	Annapolis	MD	21401	410-269-1132	263-0616
Arapahoe Philharmonic 2100 W Littleton Blvd Ste 250 *Web:* www.arapahoe-phil.org	Littleton	CO	80120	303-781-1892	
Arkansas Symphony Orchestra 2417 N Tyler St PO Box 7328 *Web:* www.arkansassymphony.org	Little Rock	AR	72217	501-666-1761	666-3193
Asheville Symphony Orchestra 87 Haywood St PO Box 2852 *Web:* www.ashevillesymphony.org	Asheville	NC	28802	828-254-7046	254-1761
Aspen Chamber Symphony 225 Music School Rd *Web:* www.aspenmusicfestival.com	Aspen	CO	81611	970-925-3254	925-3802
Atlanta Pops 1830 Briarcliff Cir NE *Web:* www.altieriandassociates.com	Atlanta	GA	30329	404-636-0020	636-0020
Atlanta Symphony Orchestra 1280 Peachtree St NE Ste 4074 *Web:* www.atlantasymphony.org	Atlanta	GA	30309	404-733-4900	733-4901
Aurora Symphony Orchestra PO Box 441481 *Web:* www.aurorasymphony.org	Aurora	CO	80044	303-873-6622	
Austin Chamber Music Ctr 3814 Medical Pkwy *Web:* www.austinchambermusic.org	Austin	TX	78756	512-454-7562	454-0029
Austin Civic Orchestra PO Box 27132 *Web:* www.austincivicorchestra.org	Austin	TX	78755	512-200-2261	
Austin Symphony Orchestra 1101 Red River St *TF:* 888-462-3787 ■ *Web:* www.austinsymphony.org	Austin	TX	78701	512-476-6064	476-6242
Bakersfield Symphony Orchestra 1328 34th St Ste A *Web:* www.bsonow.org	Bakersfield	CA	93301	661-323-7928	323-7331
Baltimore Symphony Orchestra 1212 Cathedral St *TF:* 877-276-1444 ■ *Web:* www.bsomusic.org	Baltimore	MD	21201	410-783-8100	783-8004
Bangor Symphony Orchestra PO Box 1441 *TF General:* 800-639-3221 ■ *Web:* www.bangorsymphony.org	Bangor	ME	04402	207-942-5555	990-1272
Berkeley Symphony Orchestra 1942 University Ave Ste 207 *Web:* www.berkeleysymphony.org	Berkeley	CA	94704	510-841-2800	841-5422
Billings Symphony 2721 Second Ave N *Web:* www.billingssymphony.org	Billings	MT	59101	406-252-3610	252-3353
Bismarck-Mandan Symphony Orchestra 215 N Sixth St *Web:* www.bismarckmandansymphony.org	Bismarck	ND	58501	701-258-8345	258-8345
Boise Philharmonic Assn Inc 516 S Ninth St *Web:* boisephil.org	Boise	ID	83702	208-344-7849	336-9078
Boston Modern Orchestra Project 376 Washington St *Web:* www.bmop.org	Malden	MA	02148	781-324-0397	
Boston Philharmonic Orchestra 295 Huntington Ave Ste 210 *Web:* www.bostonphil.org	Boston	MA	02115	617-236-0999	236-8613
Boston Pops 301 Massachusetts Ave Symphony Hall *TF:* 888-266-1200 ■ *Web:* www.bso.org	Boston	MA	02115	617-266-1492	
Boston Symphony Orchestra 301 Massachusetts Ave Symphony Hall *TF:* 888-266-1200 ■ *Web:* www.bso.org	Boston	MA	02115	617-266-1492	638-9367
Boulder Philharmonic Orchestra 2590 Walnut St *Web:* www.boulderphil.org	Boulder	CO	80302	303-449-1343	443-9203
Brockton Symphony Orchestra PO Box 1407 *Web:* www.brocktonsymphony.org	Brockton	MA	02303	508-588-3841	
Buffalo Philharmonic Orchestra 499 Franklin St *Web:* www.bpo.org	Buffalo	NY	14202	716-885-0331	885-9372
Calgary Philharmonic Orchestra 205 Eigth Ave SE *Web:* calgaryphil.com	Calgary	AB	T2G0K9	403-571-0270	294-7424
California Philharmonic Orchestra 600 Playhouse Alley *Web:* calphil.com/home	Pasadena	CA	91101	626-300-8200	
Camellia Symphony Orchestra 1731 Howe Ave Ste 499 *Web:* www.camelliasymphony.org	Sacramento	CA	95825	916-929-6655	
Canton Symphony Orchestra 1001 Market Ave N *Web:* www.cantonsymphony.org	Canton	OH	44702	330-452-3434	452-4429
Carson City Symphony PO Box 2001 PO Box 2001 *Web:* www.ccsymphony.com	Carson City	NV	89702	775-883-4154	883-4371
Chamber Orchestra of Philadelphia 1520 Locust St Ste 500 *TF:* 800-732-0999 ■ *Web:* www.chamberorchestra.org	Philadelphia	PA	19102	215-545-5451	545-3868
Champaign-Urbana Symphony Orchestra (CUSO) 701 Devonshire Dr Ste C-24 *Web:* www.cusymphony.org	Champaign	IL	61820	217-351-9139	
Charleston Symphony Orchestra 756 St Andrews Blvd *Web:* www.charlestonsymphony.com	Charleston	SC	29407	843-723-7528	
Chattanooga Symphony & Opera (CSO) 701 Broad St *Web:* chattanoogasymphony.org	Chattanooga	TN	37402	423-267-8583	265-6520
Cheyenne Symphony Orchestra (CSO) 1904 Thomes Ave *Web:* www.cheyennesymphony.org	Cheyenne	WY	82001	307-778-8561	634-7512
Chicago Sinfonietta 70 E Lake St Ste 226 *Web:* www.chicagosinfonietta.org	Chicago	IL	60601	312-236-3681	236-5429
Chicago Symphony Orchestra 220 S Michigan Ave *TF:* 800-223-7114 ■ *Web:* www.cso.org	Chicago	IL	60604	312-294-3000	294-3035
Cincinnati Symphony Orchestra 1241 Elm St Music Hall *Web:* www.cincinnatisymphony.org	Cincinnati	OH	45202	513-621-1919	744-3535
Civic Orchestra of Tucson (COT) PO Box 42764 *Web:* www.cotmusic.org	Tucson	AZ	85733	520-730-3371	
Cleveland Chamber Symphony, The (CCS) 11125 Magnolia Dr The Music School Settlement *Web:* www.clevelandchambersymphony.org	Cleveland	OH	44106	216-202-4227	
Cleveland Orchestra, The 11001 Euclid Ave Severance Hall *TF:* 800-686-1141 ■ *Web:* www.clevelandorchestra.com	Cleveland	OH	44106	216-231-1111	231-4029
Cleveland Pops Orchestra 24000 Mercantile Rd Ste 11 *Web:* www.clevelandpops.com	Cleveland	OH	44122	216-765-7677	765-1931
Colorado Springs Philharmonic PO Box 1266 *Web:* www.csphilharmonic.org	Colorado Springs	CO	80901	719-575-9632	575-9656
Colorado Symphony Orchestra 1000 14th St Unit 15 *TF:* 877-292-7979 ■ *Web:* www.coloradosymphony.org	Denver	CO	80202	303-623-7876	293-2649
Columbus Symphony Orchestra 935 First Ave *Web:* www.csoga.org	Columbus	GA	31901	706-323-5059	323-7051
Columbus Symphony Orchestra 55 E State St *TF:* 800-745-3000 ■ *Web:* www.columbussymphony.com	Columbus	OH	43215	614-228-9600	224-7273
Corpus Christi Symphony Orchestra 555 N Carancahua St Tower II Ste 410 Ste 410 *TF:* 877-286-6683 ■ *Web:* www.ccsymphony.org	Corpus Christi	TX	78401	361-883-6683	882-4132
Da Camera of Houston 1427 Branard St *Web:* www.dacamera.com	Houston	TX	77006	713-524-7601	524-4148
Dallas Symphony Orchestra 2301 Flora St *Web:* mydso.com	Dallas	TX	75201	214-849-4376	
Dayton Philharmonic Orchestra 126 N Main St Ste 210 *TF:* 888-228-3630 ■ *Web:* daytonperformingarts.org	Dayton	OH	45402	937-224-3521	223-9189
Daytona Beach Symphony Society PO Box 2 *Web:* new.dbss.org	Daytona Beach	FL	32115	386-253-2901	253-5774
DeKalb Symphony Orchestra (DSO) PO Box 1313 *Web:* www.dekalbsymphony.org	Tucker	GA	30085	678-891-3565	891-3575
Delaware Symphony Orchestra 818 N Market St *Web:* www.desymphony.org	Wilmington	DE	19801	302-656-7442	
Des Moines Symphony 221 Walnut St *Web:* www.dmsymphony.org	Des Moines	IA	50309	515-280-4000	280-4005
Detroit Symphony Orchestra 3711 Woodward Ave *TF:* 800-434-6340 ■ *Web:* dso.org	Detroit	MI	48201	313-576-5111	576-5109
Dubuque Symphony Orchestra 2728 Asbury Rd Ste 900 *TF:* 866-803-9280 ■ *Web:* www.dubuquesymphony.org	Dubuque	IA	52001	563-557-1677	557-9841
Durham Symphony Orchestra PO Box 1993 *Web:* www.durhamsymphony.org	Durham	NC	27702	919-560-2736	
Eastern Connecticut Symphony Orchestra 289 State St *Web:* www.ectsymphony.com	New London	CT	06320	860-443-2876	
Edmonton Symphony Orchestra 9720 102nd Ave *TF:* 800-563-5081 ■ *Web:* www.edmontonsymphony.com	Edmonton	AB	T5J4B2	780-428-1108	
El Paso Symphony Orchestra 1 Civic Ctr Plz *Web:* www.epso.org	El Paso	TX	79901	915-532-3776	533-8162
Erie Philharmonic 609 Walnut St *Web:* www.eriephil.org	Erie	PA	16502	814-455-1375	455-1377
Eugene Symphony 115 W Eigth Ave Ste 115 *Web:* www.eugenesymphony.org	Eugene	OR	97401	541-687-9487	687-0527
Evansville Philharmonic Orchestra 401 SE Sixth St *Web:* evansvillephilharmonic.org	Evansville	IN	47708	812-425-5050	426-7008
Fairbanks Symphony Orchestra 312 Tanana Dr *Web:* www.fairbankssymphony.org	Fairbanks	AK	99775	907-474-5733	
Fairfax Symphony Orchestra 2667 Prosperity Ave *Web:* www.fairfaxsymphony.org	Fairfax	VA	22031	703-563-1990	
Flagstaff Symphony Orchestra 113 E Aspen Ave # A *TF:* 888-520-7214 ■ *Web:* www.flagstaffsymphony.org	Flagstaff	AZ	86001	928-774-5107	774-5109
Fort Collins Symphony 214 S College Ave *Web:* www.fcsymphony.org	Fort Collins	CO	80524	970-482-4823	482-4858
Fort Worth Symphony Orchestra Assn 330 E Fourth St Ste 200 *Web:* www.fwsymphony.org	Fort Worth	TX	76102	817-665-6500	665-6600
Fresno Philharmonic 7170 N. Financial Dr Ste 135 *Web:* www.fresnophil.org	Fresno	CA	93711	559-261-0600	261-0700
Grand Rapids Symphony 300 Ottawa Ave NW Ste 100 *Web:* www.grsymphony.org	Grand Rapids	MI	49503	616-454-9451	454-7477
Grant Park Orchestra 205 E Randolph St *Web:* www.grantparkmusicfestival.com	Chicago	IL	60601	312-742-7638	742-7662

Phone Fax

Greater Bridgeport Symphony (GBS)
446 University Ave .... Bridgeport CT 06604 203-576-0263 367-0064
Web: www.bptsym.org

Greater Trenton Symphony Orchestra
28 W State St Ste 202 .... Trenton NJ 08608 609-394-1338
Web: www.trentonsymphony.org

Greensboro Symphony Orchestra
200 N Davie St Ste 301 .... Greensboro NC 27401 336-335-5456 335-5580
Web: www.greensborosymphony.org

Greenville Symphony Orchestra
200 S Main St .... Greenville SC 29601 864-232-0344 467-3113
Web: www.greenvillesymphony.org

Greenwich Symphony Orchestra PO Box 35 .... Greenwich CT 06836 203-869-2664
Web: www.greenwichsymphony.org

Handel & Haydn Society 300 Massachusetts Ave .... Boston MA 02115 617-262-1815 266-4217
Web: www.handelandhaydn.org

Harrisburg Symphony Orchestra
800 Corporate Cir Ste 101 .... Harrisburg PA 17110 717-545-5527 545-6501
Web: www.harrisburgsymphony.org

Houston Symphony Orchestra
615 Louisiana St Ste 102 .... Houston TX 77002 713-224-4240
Web: www.houstonsymphony.org

Huntsville Symphony Orchestra
700 Monroe St PO Box 2400 .... Huntsville AL 35801 256-539-4818 539-4819
Web: www.hso.org

Idaho State Civic Symphony
921 S Eigth Ave S- 8099 .... Pocatello ID 83209 208-234-1587
Web: www.thesymphony.us

Illinois Symphony Orchestera
524 E Capitol Ave .... Springfield IL 62701 217-522-2838 522-7374
TF: 800-401-7222 ■ *Web:* www.ilsymphony.org

Indianapolis Symphony Orchestra
45 Monument Cir .... Indianapolis IN 46204 317-262-1100
TF: 800-366-8457 ■ *Web:* www.indianapolissymphony.org

Jacksonville Symphony Orchestra (JSO)
300 W Water St Ste 200 .... Jacksonville FL 32202 904-354-5479 354-9238
Web: www.jaxsymphony.org

Johnson City Symphony Orchestra
PO Box 533 .... Johnson City TN 37605 423-926-8742 926-8979
Web: www.jcsymphony.com

Juneau Symphony Orchestra
522 W Tenth St PO Box 21236 .... Juneau AK 99802 907-586-4676 463-2555
Web: www.juneausymphony.org

Kalamazoo Symphony Orchestra
359 S Kalamazoo Mall Ste 100 .... Kalamazoo MI 49007 269-349-7759 349-9229
Web: www.kalamazoosymphony.com

Kansas City Symphony
1703 Wyandotte Ste 200 .... Kansas City MO 64108 816-471-1100 471-0976
TF: 877-829-5590 ■ *Web:* www.kcsymphony.org

Kennedy Ctr Opera House Orchestra
John F Kennedy Ctr for the Performing Arts
2700 F St NW .... Washington DC 20566 800-444-1324 416-8205*
**Fax Area Code:* 202 ■ *TF:* 800-444-1324 ■ *Web:* www.kennedy-center.org

Kentucky Symphony Orchestra
540 Linden Ave PO Box 72810 .... Newport KY 41072 859-431-6216 431-3097
Web: www.kyso.org

Knoxville Symphony Orchestra
100 S Gay St Ste 302 .... Knoxville TN 37902 865-523-1178 546-3766
Web: www.knoxvillesymphony.com

Lansing Symphony Orchestra (LSO)
501 S Capitol Ave Ste 400 .... Lansing MI 48933 517-487-5001 487-0210
Web: www.lansingsymphony.org

Las Cruces Symphony Orchestra
1075 N Horseshoe Cir .... Las Cruces NM 88003 575-646-3709 646-1086
Web: www.lascrucessymphony.com

Lexington Philharmonic 161 N Mill St .... Lexington KY 40507 859-233-4226 233-7896
TF: 888-494-4226 ■ *Web:* www.lexphil.org

Lincoln Symphony Orchestra
233 S 13th St Ste 1702 .... Lincoln NE 68508 402-476-2211
Web: lincolnsymphony.org

Long Beach Symphony Orchestra (LBSO)
249 E Ocean Blvd Ste 200 .... Long Beach CA 90802 562-436-3203 491-3599
Web: longbeachsymphony.org

Long Island Baroque Ensemble
154 West 123rd St .... New York NY 10027 212-222-5795
Web: www.libaroque.org

Long Island Philharmonic (LIP)
1 Huntington Quadrangle Ste 2C21 .... Melville NY 11747 631-293-2223 293-2655

Los Angeles Philharmonic Assn
151 S Grand Ave .... Los Angeles CA 90012 323-850-2000
Web: www.laphil.com

Louisiana Philharmonic Orchestra
1010 Common St Ste 2120 .... New Orleans LA 70112 504-523-6530
Web: www.lpomusic.com

Louisville Orchestra
323 W Broadway Ste 700 .... Louisville KY 40202 502-587-8681 589-7870
Web: www.louisvilleorchestra.org

Macon Symphony Orchestra 400 Poplar St .... Macon GA 31201 478-301-5300
Web: www.maconsymphony.com

Madison Symphony Orchestra 201 State St .... Madison WI 53703 608-257-3734 280-6192
Web: www.madisonsymphony.org

Manitoba Chamber Orchestra
393 Portage Ave Portage Pl Ste Y300 .... Winnipeg MB R3B3H6 204-783-7377 783-7383
Web: www.themco.ca

Marin Symphony 4340 Redwood Hwy Ste 409C .... San Rafael CA 94903 415-479-8100 479-8110
Web: www.marinsymphony.org

Maryland Symphony Orchestra, The
30 W Washington St .... Hagerstown MD 21740 301-797-4000 797-2314
Web: www.marylandsymphony.org

Massachusetts Symphony Orchestra
Po Box 20070 Po Box 20070 .... Worcester MA 01609 508-754-1234 752-3671
Web: www.tuckermanhall.org/pops.html

Memphis Symphony Orchestra
585 S Mendenhall Rd .... Memphis TN 38117 901-537-2525 537-2550
Web: www.memphissymphony.org

Phone Fax

Miami Symphony Orchestra, The (MISO)
10689 N Kendall Dr Ste 307 .... Miami FL 33176 305-275-5666 275-4363
Web: www.miamisymphony.org

Milwaukee Symphony Orchestra
1101 N Market St STE 100 .... Milwaukee WI 53202 414-273-7121
TF: 888-367-8101 ■ *Web:* milwaukee.broadway.com

Minnesota Orchestra
1111 Nicollet Mall Orchestra Hall .... Minneapolis MN 55403 612-371-5600 371-7170
TF: 800-292-4141 ■ *Web:* www.minnesotaorchestra.org

Mississippi Symphony Orchestra
201 E Pascagoula St .... Jackson MS 39201 601-960-1565 960-1564
Web: www.msorchestra.com

Mobile Symphony PO Box 3127 .... Mobile AL 36652 251-432-2010 432-6618
Web: www.mobilesymphony.org

Modesto Symphony Orchestra 911 13th St .... Modesto CA 95354 209-523-4156 523-0201
TF: 877-488-3380 ■ *Web:* www.modestosymphony.org

Muncie Symphony Orchestra
2000 W University Ave # Ac112 .... Muncie IN 47306 765-285-5531 285-9128
Web: www.munciesymphony.org

Music of the Baroque 111 N Wabash Ave Ste 810 .... Chicago IL 60602 312-551-1414 551-1444
Web: www.baroque.org

National Philharmonic
5301 Tuckerman Ln .... North Bethesda MD 20852 301-493-9283 493-9284
Web: www.nationalphilharmonic.org

National Symphony Orchestra 2700 F St NW .... Washington DC 20566 202-416-8000 416-8105
TF: 800-444-1324 ■ *Web:* www.kennedy-center.org/nso

New Hampshire Music Festival Orchestra
52 Symphony Ln .... Center Harbor NH 03226 603-279-3300
Web: www.nhmf.org

New Haven Symphony Orchestra
105 Ct St # 302 .... New Haven CT 06511 203-865-0831 865-0845
Web: www.newhavensymphony.org

New Jersey Symphony Orchestra 60 Pk Pl .... Newark NJ 07102 973-624-3713 624-2115
Web: www.njsymphony.org

New West Symphony
2100 E Thousand Oaks Blvd Ste D .... Thousand Oaks CA 91362 805-497-5800 497-5839
Web: www.newwestsymphony.org

New World Symphony 500 17th St .... Miami Beach FL 33139 305-673-3330 673-6749
TF: 800-597-3331 ■ *Web:* www.nws.edu

New York Philharmonic
10 Lincoln Ctr Plaza Avery Fisher Hall .... New York NY 10023 212-875-5900 875-5717*
**Fax:* Mktg ■ *Web:* www.nyphil.org

New York Pops 333 W 52nd St Ste 600 .... New York NY 10019 212-765-7677 315-3199
Web: www.newyorkpops.org

North Arkansas Symphony 605 W Dixon St .... Fayetteville AR 72701 479-521-4166
Web: sonamusic.org

North Carolina Symphony
3700 Glenwood Ave Ste 130 .... Raleigh NC 27612 919-733-2750 733-9920
Web: www.ncsymphony.org

Northeastern Pennsylvania Philharmonic
4101 Birney Ave .... Moosic PA 18507 570-341-1568
Web: www.nepaphil.org

Oklahoma City Philharmonic
424 Colcord Dr Ste B .... Oklahoma City OK 73102 405-232-7575 232-4353
Web: okcphil.org

Omaha Symphony 1605 Howard St .... Omaha NE 68102 402-342-3836 342-3819
Web: www.omahasymphony.org

Opera Orchestra of New York, The
344 E 63rd St Ste B-1 .... New York NY 10065 212-906-9137
Web: www.operaorchestrany.org

Orchestra Iowa 119 Third Ave SE .... Cedar Rapids IA 52401 319-366-8206
Web: artsiowa.com/orchestra

Orchestra New England PO Box 200123 .... New Haven CT 06520 203-777-4690
TF: 800-595-4849 ■ *Web:* orchestranewengland.org

Orchestre Metropolitain du Grand Montreal
486 St Catherine St W Ste 401 .... Montreal QC H3B1A6 514-598-0870 840-9195
Web: www.orchestremetropolitain.com

Orchestre Symphonique de Montreal
260 de Maisonneuve Blvd W 2nd Fl .... Montreal QC H2X1Y9 514-842-9951 842-0728
TF: 888-842-9951 ■ *Web:* www.osm.ca

Oregon Symphony Orchestra
921 SW Washington St Ste 200 .... Portland OR 97205 503-228-4294 228-4150
TF: 800-228-7343 ■ *Web:* www.orsymphony.org

Orlando Philharmonic Orchestra
812 E Rollins St Ste 300 .... Orlando FL 32803 407-896-6700 896-5512
Web: www.orlandophil.org

Orpheus Chamber Orchestra
490 Riverside Dr 11th Fl .... New York NY 10027 212-896-1700 896-1717
Web: orpheusnyc.org

Ottawa Symphony Orchestra (OSO)
2 Daly Ave Ste 250 .... Ottawa ON K1N6E2 613-231-7802 231-3610
Web: www.ottawasymphony.com

Owensboro Symphony Orchestra
211 E Second St .... Owensboro KY 42303 270-684-0661 683-0740
Web: theoso.com

Paducah Symphony Orchestra 760 Broadway .... Paducah KY 42001 270-444-0065 444-0456
Web: paducahsymphony.org

Pensacola Symphony Orchestra
205 E Zaragossa St PO Box 1752 .... Pensacola FL 32502 850-435-2533 444-9910
Web: www.pensacolasymphony.com

Peoria Symphony Orchestra 101 State St .... Peoria IL 61602 309-671-1096
Web: www.peoriasymphony.org

Peter Nero & the Philly Pops
1518 Walnut St Ste 1706 .... Philadelphia PA 19102 215-875-8004
Web: www.phillypops.com

Philadelphia Orchestra
260 S Broad St Ste 1600 .... Philadelphia PA 19102 215-893-1955
Web: www.philorch.org

Philharmonia Baroque Orchestra
180 Redwood St Ste 200 .... San Francisco CA 94102 415-252-1288 252-1488
Web: www.philharmonia.org

Phoenix Symphony 1 N First St Ste 200 .... Phoenix AZ 85004 602-495-1117 253-1772
TF: 800-776-9080 ■ *Web:* www.phoenixsymphony.org

				Phone	Fax
Pittsburgh Symphony Orchestra 600 Penn Ave Heinz Hall for the Performing Arts	Pittsburgh	PA	15222	412-566-7366	392-3311
TF: 800-743-8560 ■ *Web:* www.pittsburghsymphony.org					
Plano Symphony Orchestra 5236 Tennyson Pkwy Ste 200	Plano	TX	75024	972-473-7262	473-4639
Web: www.planosymphony.org					
Portland Baroque Orchestra 1020 SW Taylor St Ste 200	Portland	OR	97205	503-222-6000	226-6635
Web: www.pbo.org					
Portland Symphony Orchestra 50 Monument Sq 2nd Fl	Portland	ME	04101	207-773-6128	773-6089
Web: www.portlandsymphony.org					
ProMusica Chamber Orchestra 620 E Broad St Ste 300	Columbus	OH	43215	614-464-0066	464-4141
Web: www.promusicacolumbus.org					
Raleigh Symphony Orchestra PO Box 25878	Raleigh	NC	27611	919-546-9755	
Web: raleighsymphony.org					
Redlands Symphony 1200 E Colton Ave	Redlands	CA	92373	909-748-8018	335-5213
Web: www.redlandssymphony.com					
Reno Chamber Orchestra 925 Riverside Dr Ste 5	Reno	NV	89503	775-348-9413	348-0643
Web: www.renochamberorchestra.org					
Reno Philharmonic Orchestra 925 Riverside Dr Ste 3	Reno	NV	89503	775-323-6393	323-6711
Web: www.renophil.com					
Rhode Island Philharmonic Orchestra 667 Waterman Ave	East Providence	RI	02914	401-248-7070	248-7071
Web: www.ri-philharmonic.org					
Richmond Symphony Orchestra 380 Hubelchison Pkwy PO Box 982	Richmond	IN	47375	765-966-5181	962-8447
Web: www.richmondsymphony.org					
Ridgefield Symphony Orchestra 90 E Ridge	Ridgefield	CT	06877	203-438-3889	
Web: www.ridgefieldsymphony.org					
River City Brass Band Inc 500 Grant St Ste 2720	Pittsburgh	PA	15219	412-434-7222	235-9015
TF: 800-292-7222 ■ *Web:* www.rivercitybrass.org					
Roanoke Symphony Orchestra 541 Luck Ave Ste 200	Roanoke	VA	24016	540-343-6221	343-0065
Web: www.rso.com					
Rochester Orchestra & Chorale 400 S Broadway	Rochester	MN	55904	507-286-8742	
Web: www.rochestersymphony.org					
Rochester Philharmonic Orchestra 108 E Ave	Rochester	NY	14604	585-454-7311	325-4905
Web: www.rpo.org					
Rockford Symphony Orchestra 711 N Main St	Rockford	IL	61103	815-965-0049	965-0642
Web: www.rockfordsymphony.com					
Saint Louis Symphony Orchestra 718 N Grand Blvd	Saint Louis	MO	63103	314-533-2500	286-4111
TF: 800-232-1880 ■ *Web:* www.stlsymphony.org					
Saint Paul Chamber Orchestra 408 St Peter St 3rd Fl	Saint Paul	MN	55102	651-291-1144	292-3281
Web: www.thespco.org					
San Antonio Symphony 711 Navarro St Ste235	San Antonio	TX	78205	210-554-1000	554-1008
Web: sasymphony.org					
San Diego Symphony Orchestra 1245 Seventh Ave	San Diego	CA	92101	619-235-0804	
Web: www.sandiegosymphony.org					
San Francisco Symphony 201 Van Ness Ave	San Francisco	CA	94102	415-864-6000	
Web: www.sfsymphony.org					
Santa Barbara Symphony 1330 State St Ste 102	Santa Barbara	CA	93101	805-898-9386	
Web: www.thesymphony.org					
Santa Cruz Symphony 307 Church St	Santa Cruz	CA	95060	831-462-0553	426-1193
Web: www.santacruzsymphony.org					
Santa Fe Symphony Orchestra & Chorus Inc 551 W Cordova Rd Ste D Ste D	Santa Fe	NM	87505	505-983-3530	982-3888
TF: 800-480-1319 ■ *Web:* www.santafesymphony.org					
Santa Rosa Symphony (SRS) 50 Santa Rosa Ave Ste 410	Santa Rosa	CA	95404	707-546-8742	546-7284
Web: srsymphony.org					
Sarasota Orchestra 709 N Tamiami Trl	Sarasota	FL	34236	941-953-4252	953-3059
TF: 866-508-0611 ■ *Web:* www.sarasotaorchestra.org					
Scottsdale Symphony Orchestra 3127 N 81st Pl	Scottsdale	AZ	85251	480-945-8071	
Seattle Symphony 200 University St	Seattle	WA	98101	206-215-4700	215-4701
TF: 866-833-4747 ■ *Web:* www.seattlesymphony.org					
Shreveport Symphony Orchestra 619 Louisiana Ave	Shreveport	LA	71101	318-222-7496	222-7490
Web: www.shreveportsymphony.com					
Sioux City Symphony Orchestra 518 Pierce St PO Box 754	Sioux City	IA	51101	712-277-2111	252-0224
Web: www.siouxcitysymphony.org					
South Bend Symphony Orchestra (SBSO) 127 N Michigan St	South Bend	IN	46601	574-232-6343	232-6627
TF: 800-537-6415 ■ *Web:* www.southbendsymphony.com					
South Carolina Philharmonic 721 Lady St	Columbia	SC	29201	803-771-7937	771-0268
Web: www.scphilharmonic.com					
South Dakota Symphony Orchestra 301 S Main Ave	Sioux Falls	SD	57104	605-335-7933	
Web: www.sdsymphony.org					
Spokane Symphony PO Box 365	Spokane	WA	99210	509-624-1200	252-2637
TF: 800-899-1482 ■ *Web:* www.spokanesymphony.org					
Springfield Symphony Orchestra 1350 Main St	Springfield	MA	01103	413-733-0636	781-4129
Web: www.springfieldsymphony.org					
Springfield Symphony Orchestra 411 N Sherman Pkwy	Springfield	MO	65802	417-864-6683	864-8967
Web: www.springfieldmosymphony.org					
Symphony Nova Scotia 6101 University Ave Dalhousie Arts Ctr	Halifax	NS	B3H4R2	902-494-3820	494-2883
TF: 800-874-1669 ■ *Web:* www.symphonynovascotia.ca					
Symphony of the Mountains 1200 E Ctr St	Kingsport	TN	37660	423-392-8423	392-8428
Web: www.symphonyofthemountains.org					
Symphony Orchestra Augusta 1301 Greene St Ste 200	Augusta	GA	30901	706-826-4705	826-4735
Web: soaugusta.org					
Symphony Silicon Valley 345 S First St	San Jose	CA	95113	408-286-2600	286-2600
Web: www.symphonysiliconvalley.org					
Tacoma Symphony 901 Broadway Ste 600	Tacoma	WA	98402	253-272-7264	
TF: 800-291-7593 ■ *Web:* www.tacomasymphony.org					
Tallahassee Symphony Orchestra 1020 E Lafayette St	Tallahassee	FL	32301	850-224-0461	
Thayer Symphony Orchestra 14 Monument Sq # 406	Leominster	MA	01453	978-466-1800	840-1000
Web: www.thayersymphony.org					
Toledo Symphony 1838 Parkwood Ave	Toledo	OH	43604	419-246-8000	321-6890
TF: 800-348-1253 ■ *Web:* www.toledosymphony.com					
Topeka Symphony 2100 SE 29th St PO Box 2206	Topeka	KS	66601	785-232-2032	232-6204
Web: www.topekasymphony.org					
Traverse Symphony Orchestra (TSO) 300 E Front St Ste 230	Traverse City	MI	49684	231-947-7120	
Web: www.traversesymphony.org					
Tucson Symphony Orchestra 2175 N Sixth Ave	Tucson	AZ	85705	520-792-9155	
Web: www.tucsonsymphony.org					
Tupelo Symphony Orchestra 1800 W Main St PO Box 474	Tupelo	MS	38801	662-842-8433	
Web: nmsymphony.com					
Tuscaloosa Symphony Orchestra PO Box 20001	Tuscaloosa	AL	35402	205-752-5515	
Web: www.tsoonline.org					
Union League Club 65 W Jackson Blvd Ste 133	Chicago	IL	60604	312-427-7800	
Utah Symphony & Opera 123 W S Temple	Salt Lake City	UT	84101	801-533-6683	
Web: www.utahsymphony.org					
Vermont Symphony Orchestra 2 Church St Ste 3B	Burlington	VT	05401	802-864-5741	864-5109
TF: 800-876-9293 ■ *Web:* www.vso.org					
Virginia Symphony Orchestra 861 Glenrock Rd Ste 200	Norfolk	VA	23502	757-466-3060	466-3046
TF: 855-876-7677 ■ *Web:* www.virginiasymphony.org					
Wallingford Symphony Orchestra PO Box 6023	Wallingford	CT	06492	203-697-2261	
Web: www.wallingfordsymphony.org					
Washington Metropolitan Philharmonic Assn (WMPA) PO Box 120	Mount Vernon	VA	22121	703-799-8229	360-7391
Web: www.wmpamusic.org					
Washington Symphony Orchestra (WSO) PO Box 178	Washington	PA	15301	724-223-9796	
Web: www.washsym.org					
Waterbury Symphony Orchestra 110 Bank St	Waterbury	CT	06702	203-574-4283	
Web: www.waterburysymphony.org					
Waterloo-Cedar Falls Symphony Orchestra Gallagher-Bluedorn Performing Arts Ctr Ste 17	Cedar Falls	IA	50614	319-273-3373	
Web: wcfsymphony.org					
Westchester Philharmonic 123 Main St Lobby Level	White Plains	NY	10601	914-682-3707	682-3716
TF: 800-553-0031 ■ *Web:* www.westchesterphil.org					
Western Piedmont Symphony 243 Third Ave NE Ste 1-N	Hickory	NC	28601	828-324-8603	324-1301
Web: www.wpsymphony.org					
Wheeling Symphony Orchestra 1025 Main St Ste 811	Wheeling	WV	26003	304-232-6191	232-6192
Web: wheelingsymphony.com					
Wichita Symphony Orchestra (WSO) 225 W Douglas St Ste 207	Wichita	KS	67202	316-267-5259	267-1937
Web: wichitasymphony.org					
Windsor Symphony Orchestra 487 Oullette Ave	Windsor	ON	N9A4J2	519-973-1238	973-0764
TF: 888-327-8327 ■ *Web:* www.windsorsymphony.com					
Winston-Salem Symphony 201 N Broad St Ste 200	Winston-Salem	NC	27101	336-725-1035	725-3924
Web: www.wssymphony.org					
Wyoming Symphony Orchestra 225 S David Ste B	Casper	WY	82601	307-266-1478	266-4522
Web: www.wyomingsymphony.org					
Youngstown Symphony Orchestra 260 Federal Plz W	Youngstown	OH	44503	330-744-4269	
Web: www.youngstownsymphony.com					

573-4 Theater Companies

				Phone	Fax
A Contemporary Theatre (ACT) 700 Union St Kreielsheimer Pl	Seattle	WA	98101	206-292-7660	292-7670
TF: 888-584-4849 ■ *Web:* www.acttheatre.org					
Actors Theatre of Louisville 316 W Main St	Louisville	KY	40202	502-584-1205	561-3300
TF: 800-428-5849 ■ *Web:* www.actorstheatre.org					
Alabama Shakespeare Festival 1 Festival Dr	Montgomery	AL	36117	334-271-5300	271-5348
TF: 800-841-4273 ■ *Web:* www.asf.net					
Alaska Junior Theater 430 W Seventh Ave Ste 30	Anchorage	AK	99501	907-272-7546	272-3035
Web: www.akjt.org					
Alley Theatre 615 Texas Ave	Houston	TX	77002	713-220-5700	222-6542
Web: www.alleytheatre.org					
Alliance Theatre Co 1280 Peachtree St NE Woodruff Arts Ctr	Atlanta	GA	30309	404-733-4650	733-4625
Web: www.alliancetheatre.org					
American Conservatory Theater (ACT) 30 Grant Ave 6th Fl	San Francisco	CA	94108	415-834-3200	749-2291
Web: www.act-sf.org					
American Stage 163 Third St N	Saint Petersburg	FL	33731	727-823-1600	821-2444
TF: 800-435-7352 ■ *Web:* www.americanstage.org					
Arden Theatre Co 40 N Second St	Philadelphia	PA	19106	215-922-8900	922-7011
Web: www.ardentheatre.org					
Arena Stage 1101 Sixth St SW	Washington	DC	20024	202-554-9066	488-4056
Web: www.arenastage.org					

Organization	City	State	ZIP	Phone	Fax
Arkansas Repertory Theatre 601 Main St PO Box 110 *TF:* 866-684-3737 ■ *Web:* www.therep.org	Little Rock	AR	72201	501-378-0445	378-0012
Artists Repertory Theatre 1516 SW Alder St *Web:* www.artistsrep.org	Portland	OR	97205	503-241-9807	241-8268
Augusta Players, The 1301 Greene St Ste 304 PO Box 2352 *Web:* augustaplayers.org	Augusta	GA	30901	706-826-4707	
Barter Theatre 127 W Main St *Web:* www.bartertheatre.com	Abingdon	VA	24210	276-628-3991	619-3335
Baton Rouge Little Theater 7155 Florida Blvd *Web:* theatrebr.org	Baton Rouge	LA	70806	225-924-6496	
Berkshire Theatre Festival 83 E Main St *Web:* www.berkshiretheatregroup.org	Stockbridge	MA	01262	413-298-5576	298-3368
Biloxi Little Theatre 220 Lee St *Web:* www.4blt.org	Biloxi	MS	39530	228-432-8543	392-7639
Birmingham Festival Theater 1901 1/2 11th Ave S PO Box 55321 *Web:* www.bftonline.org	Birmingham	AL	35205	205-933-2383	
Capital Repertory Theatre 432 State St *Web:* www.capitalrep.org	Schenectady	NY	12305	518-462-4531	881-1823
Casa Manana Theatre 3101 W Lancaster Ave *Web:* www.casamanana.org	Fort Worth	TX	76107	817-332-2272	332-5711
Center Stage 700 N Calvert St *Web:* www.centerstage.org	Baltimore	MD	21202	410-986-4000	539-3912
Center Theatre Group 601 W Temple St *Web:* centertheatregroup.org	Los Angeles	CA	90012	213-628-2772	
Children's Musical Theater San Jose (CMTS) 1401 Parkmoor Ave Ste 100 *Web:* www.cmtsj.org	San Jose	CA	95126	408-288-5437	
Circle Theatre 1607 Robinson Rd SE *Web:* www.circletheatre.org	Grand Rapids	MI	49506	616-632-1980	456-8540
City Lights Theatre 529 S Second St *Web:* www.cltc.org	San Jose	CA	95112	408-295-4200	295-8318
City Theatre Co 1300 Bingham St *Web:* www.citytheatrecompany.org	Pittsburgh	PA	15203	412-431-4400	431-5535
Clarence Brown Theatre *University of Tennessee* 206 McClung Tower *Web:* www.clarencebrowntheatre.com	Knoxville	TN	37996	865-974-5161	974-4867
Cleveland Public Theatre 6415 Detroit Ave *Web:* www.cptonline.org	Cleveland	OH	44102	216-631-2727	631-2575
Corn Stock Theatre 1700 Pk Rd *TF:* 800-220-1185 ■ *Web:* www.cornstocktheatre.com	Peoria	IL	61604	309-676-2196	
Court Theatre 5535 S Ellis Ave *Web:* www.courttheatre.org	Chicago	IL	60637	773-702-7005	834-1897
Dallas Theater Ctr 3636 Turtle Creek Blvd *Web:* www.dallastheatercenter.org	Dallas	TX	75219	214-526-8210	521-7666
Downtown Cabaret Theatre 263 Golden Hill St *Web:* www.dtcab.com	Bridgeport	CT	06604	203-576-1636	576-1444
Ensemble Theatre of Cincinnati 1127 Vine St *Web:* www.cincyetc.com	Cincinnati	OH	45202	513-421-3555	
Erie Playhouse 13 W Tenth St *Web:* www.erieplayhouse.org	Erie	PA	16501	814-454-2852	454-0601
Evansville Civic Theatre 717 N Fulton St *Web:* www.evansvillecivictheatre.org	Evansville	IN	47710	812-425-2800	423-2636
Fairbanks Shakespeare Theatre PO Box 73447 *Web:* www.fstalaska.org	Fairbanks	AK	99707	907-457-7638	457-4511
Fargo-Moorhead Community Theatre 333 Fourth St S *Web:* www.fmct.org	Fargo	ND	58103	701-235-1901	
Fort Smith Little Theatre 401 N Sixth St *Web:* www.fslt.org	Fort Smith	AR	72913	479-783-2966	
Fort Wayne Civic Theater 303 E Main St *Web:* www.fwcivic.org	Fort Wayne	IN	46802	260-422-8641	
GableStage 1200 Anastasia Ave Biltmore Hotel *Web:* www.gablestage.org	Coral Gables	FL	33134	305-446-1116	445-8645
Garland Civic Theatre 108 N Sixth St *Web:* www.garlandcivictheatre.org	Garland	TX	75040	972-485-8884	
Geffen Playhouse 10886 Le Conte Ave *Web:* www.geffenplayhouse.org	Los Angeles	CA	90024	310-208-5454	208-8383
Generic Theater 215 St Paul's Blvd *Web:* www.generictheater.org	Norfolk	VA	23510	757-441-2160	
Geva Theatre Ctr 75 Woodbury Blvd *Web:* www.gevatheatre.org	Rochester	NY	14607	585-232-1366	232-4031
Goodman Theatre 170 N Dearborn St *Web:* www.goodmantheatre.org	Chicago	IL	60601	312-443-3811	443-3821
Goodspeed Musicals PO Box A *Web:* www.goodspeed.org	East Haddam	CT	06423	860-873-8664	873-2329
Great Lakes Theater Festival 1501 Euclid Ave Ste 300 *Web:* www.greatlakestheater.org	Cleveland	OH	44115	216-241-5490	241-6315
Guthrie Theater 818 S Second St *TF Resv:* 877-447-8243 ■ *Web:* www.guthrietheater.org	Minneapolis	MN	55415	612-377-2224	225-6004
Huntington Beach Playhouse (HBPH) 7111 Talbert Ave *Web:* www.hbplayhouse.com	Huntington Beach	CA	92648	714-375-0696	
Huntington Theatre Co 264 Huntington Ave Boston University Theatre *Web:* www.huntingtontheatre.org	Boston	MA	02115	617-266-7900	353-8300
Indiana Repertory Theatre Inc 140 W Washington St *Web:* www.irtlive.com	Indianapolis	IN	46204	317-635-5277	236-0767
International City Theatre 110 Pine Ave Ste 820 Ste 820 *Web:* www.ictlongbeach.org	Long Beach	CA	90802	562-495-4595	436-7895
Invisible Theatre 1400 N First Ave *Web:* www.invisibletheatre.com	Tucson	AZ	85719	520-882-9721	884-5410
Irish Classical Theatre 625 Main St *Web:* www.irishclassicaltheatre.com	Buffalo	NY	14203	716-853-4282	853-0592
Jubilee Theatre 506 Main St *Web:* www.jubileetheatre.org	Fort Worth	TX	76102	817-338-4204	338-4206
La Jolla Playhouse PO Box 12039 *Web:* www.lajollaplayhouse.org	La Jolla	CA	92039	858-550-1070	550-1075
Laguna Playhouse, The 606 Laguna Canyon Rd PO Box 1747 *Web:* www.lagunaplayhouse.com	Laguna Beach	CA	92651	949-497-2787	497-6948
Lincoln Ctr Theater 150 W 65th St **Fax Area Code:* 212 ■ *TF:* 800-432-7250 ■ *Web:* www.lct.org	New York	NY	10023	800-432-7250	873-0761*
Little Theatre of Alexandria 600 Wolfe St *Web:* www.thelittletheatre.com	Alexandria	VA	22314	703-683-5778	683-1378
Lost Nation Theater 39 Main St *Web:* www.lostnationtheater.org	Montpelier	VT	05602	802-229-0492	
Lyric Theatre of Oklahoma 1727 NW 16th St *Web:* www.lyrictheatreokc.com	Oklahoma City	OK	73106	405-524-9312	524-9316
Maltz Jupiter Theatre 1001 E Indiantown Rd *TF:* 800-445-1666 ■ *Web:* www.jupitertheatre.org	Jupiter	FL	33477	561-743-2666	743-0107
Manhattan Theatre Club Inc 311 W 43rd St 8th Fl *Web:* www.manhattantheatreclub.com	New York	NY	10036	212-399-3000	
McCarter Theatre 91 University Pl *Web:* www.mccarter.org	Princeton	NJ	08540	609-258-6500	497-0369
Merrimack Repertory Theatre 132 Warren St *Web:* www.mrt.org	Lowell	MA	01852	978-654-7550	654-7575
Milwaukee Repertory Theater 108 E Wells St *Web:* www.milwaukeerep.com	Milwaukee	WI	53202	414-224-1761	224-9097
Music Theatre of Wichita 225 W Douglas Ste 202 *Web:* www.mtwichita.org	Wichita	KS	67202	316-265-3253	265-8708
Nashville Repertory Theatre 161 Rains Ave *Web:* nashvillerep.org	Nashville	TN	37203	615-244-4878	349-3222
National Theatre of the Deaf (NTD) 139 N Main St *Web:* www.ntd.org	West Hartford	CT	06107	860-236-4193	
Nebraska Repertory Theatre PO Box 880201 *TF:* 800-432-3231 ■ *Web:* www.unl.edu	Lincoln	NE	68588	402-472-2072	472-9055
New Stage Theatre 1100 Carlisle St *Web:* www.newstagetheatre.com	Jackson	MS	39202	601-948-3531	948-3538
North Carolina Theatre 1 E S St Memorial Auditorium *Web:* www.nctheatre.com	Raleigh	NC	27601	919-831-6941	831-6951
Northlight Theatre 9501 Skokie Blvd *Web:* www.northlight.org	Skokie	IL	60077	847-673-6300	679-1879
Old Globe Theatre 1363 Old Globe Way *Web:* www.oldglobe.org	San Diego	CA	92101	619-231-1941	231-5879
Omaha Community Playhouse 6915 Cass St *TF:* 888-782-4338 ■ *Web:* www.omahaplayhouse.com	Omaha	NE	68132	402-553-0800	553-6288
Pacific Repertory Theater PO Box 222035 *TF:* 866-622-0709 ■ *Web:* www.pacrep.org	Carmel	CA	93922	831-622-0700	622-0703
Pasadena Playhouse, The 39 S El Molino Ave *TF:* 800-733-2767 ■ *Web:* www.pasadenaplayhouse.org	Pasadena	CA	91101	626-356-7529	204-7399
Penobscot Theatre Co 131 Main St *Web:* www.penobscottheatre.org	Bangor	ME	04401	207-942-3333	
Pensacola Little Theatre (PLT) 400 S Jefferson St Pensacola Cultural Ctr *Web:* www.pensacolalittletheatre.com	Pensacola	FL	32502	850-432-2042	
People's Light & Theatre Co 39 Conestoga Rd *TF:* 800-732-0999 ■ *Web:* www.peopleslight.org	Malvern	PA	19355	610-647-1900	640-9521
Perseverance Theatre 914 Third St *TF:* 855-462-8497 ■ *Web:* www.ptalaska.org	Douglas	AK	99824	907-364-2421	364-2603
Pittsburgh Public Theater 621 Penn Ave *TF:* 800-732-0999 ■ *Web:* www.ppt.org	Pittsburgh	PA	15222	412-316-8200	316-8219
PlayMakers Repertory Co 150 Country Club Rd *Web:* www.playmakersrep.org	Chapel Hill	NC	27599	919-962-7529	
Portland Ctr Stage (PCS) 128 NW Eleventh Ave *Web:* www.pcs.org	Portland	OR	97209	503-445-3700	445-3701
Portland Stage Co PO Box 1458 *Web:* www.portlandstage.org	Portland	ME	04104	207-774-1043	774-0576
Prince Music Theater 1412 Chestnut St *Web:* www.princetheater.org	Philadelphia	PA	19102	267-239-2941	
Public, Theater, The 425 Lafayette St *Web:* www.publictheater.org	New York	NY	10003	212-539-8500	539-8505
Repertory Theatre of Saint Louis 130 Edgar Rd PO Box 191730 *Web:* www.repstl.org	Saint Louis	MO	63119	314-968-7340	968-9638
Rochester Repertory Theatre Co 103 Seventh St NE *Web:* www.rochesterrep.org	Rochester	MN	55906	507-289-1737	
Roundabout Theatre Co 231 W 39th St Ste 1200 *Web:* www.roundabouttheatre.org	New York	NY	10018	212-719-9393	869-8817
Sacramento Theatre Co 1419 H St *Web:* www.sactheatre.org	Sacramento	CA	95814	916-443-6722	446-4066
San Diego Repertory Theatre 79 Horton Plz *Web:* www.sdrep.org	San Diego	CA	92101	619-231-3586	
San Jose Repertory Theatre 101 Paseo de San Antonio	San Jose	CA	95113	408-367-7255	367-7236
San Jose Stage Co 490 S First St *Web:* www.sanjose-stage.com	San Jose	CA	95113	408-283-7142	
San Pedro Playhouse 800 W Ashby Pl PO Box 12356 *Web:* www.theplayhousesa.org	San Antonio	TX	78212	210-733-7258	734-2651
Sandra Feinstein-Gamm Theatre 172 Exchange St *Web:* www.gammtheatre.org	Pawtucket	RI	02860	401-723-4266	
Seattle Repertory Theatre (SRT) 155 Mercer St PO Box 900923 *TF:* 877-900-9285 ■ *Web:* www.seattlerep.org	Seattle	WA	98109	206-443-2210	443-2379
Second City Chicago 1608 N Wells St *Web:* www.secondcity.com	Chicago	IL	60614	312-664-4032	664-9837
Shakespeare Theatre 516 Eigth St SE *TF:* 877-487-8849 ■ *Web:* www.shakespearetheatre.org	Washington	DC	20003	202-547-3230	547-0226

	City	State	Zip	Phone	Fax
Signature Theatre 4200 Campbell Ave. *Web:* www.sigtheatre.org	Arlington	VA	22206	703-820-9771	820-7790
South Carolina Children's Theatre 153 Augusta St *Web:* www.scchildrenstheatre.org	Greenville	SC	29601	864-235-2885	235-0208
South Coast Repertory 655 Town Ctr Dr *Web:* www.scr.org	Costa Mesa	CA	92626	714-708-5500	708-5576
Springfield Little Theatre 311 E Walnut Ave *Web:* www.springfieldlittletheatre.org	Springfield	MO	65806	417-869-1334	869-4047
Stage Coach Theatre 4802 W Emerald *Web:* www.stagecoachtheatre.com	Boise	ID	83706	208-342-2000	
Stages Repertory Theatre 3201 Allen Pkwy Ste 101 *Web:* www.stagestheatre.com	Houston	TX	77019	713-527-0220	527-8669
Stockton Civic Theatre (SCT) 2312 Rose Marie Ln *Web:* www.sctlivetheatre.com	Stockton	CA	95207	209-473-2400	473-1502
Swine Palace Productions 105 Music & Dramatic Arts Bldg Dalrymple Dr LSU *Web:* swinepalace.wix.com/sp-test#!__find	Baton Rouge	LA	70803	225-578-3533	
Syracuse Stage 820 E Genesee St *Web:* www.syracusestage.org	Syracuse	NY	13210	315-443-4008	443-9846
Tacoma Musical Playhouse 7116 Sixth Ave *Web:* www.tmp.org	Tacoma	WA	98406	253-565-6867	564-7863
Tempe Little Theatre 132 E Sixth St	Tempe	AZ	85281	480-350-8388	
Theater of the Stars 2970 Clairmont Rd NE Ste 645	Atlanta	GA	30309	404-252-8960	252-1460
THEATERWORK PO Box 842 *Web:* theaterwork.org	Santa Fe	NM	87504	505-471-1799	
Theatre Arlington 305 W Main St *Web:* www.theatrearlington.org	Arlington	TX	76010	817-275-7661	
Theatre Cedar Rapids 102 Third St SE *Web:* www.theatrecr.org	Cedar Rapids	IA	52401	319-366-8592	
Theatre Charlotte 501 Queens Rd *Web:* www.theatrecharlotte.org	Charlotte	NC	28207	704-376-3777	
Theatre For A New Audience 154 Christopher St Ste 3D *TF:* 866-811-4111 ■ *Web:* www.tfana.org	New York	NY	10014	212-229-2819	229-2911
Theatre Harrisburg 513 Hurlock St *Web:* www.theatreharrisburg.com	Harrisburg	PA	17110	717-232-5501	
Theatre of Youth (TOY) 203 Allen St *Web:* www.theatreofyouth.org	Buffalo	NY	14201	716-884-4400	819-9653
Theatre Tulsa 412 N Boston Ave *Web:* www.theatretulsa.org	Tulsa	OK	74103	918-587-8402	
Theatre Tuscaloosa 9500 Old Greensboro Rd Ste 135 *Web:* www.theatretusc.com	Tuscaloosa	AL	35405	205-391-2277	391-2329
Theatre Under the Stars 800 Bagby St Ste 200 *Web:* www.tuts.com	Houston	TX	77002	713-558-2600	558-2650
TheatreWorks 350 Twin Dolphin Dr *Web:* www.theatreworks.org	Redwood City	CA	94065	650-463-1950	463-1963
Tihati Productions Ltd 3615 Harding Ave Ste 507 *TF:* 877-846-5554 ■ *Web:* www.tihati.com	Honolulu	HI	96816	808-735-0292	735-9479
Toledo Repertoire Theatre 16 Tenth St *Web:* www.toledorep.org	Toledo	OH	43604	419-243-9277	
Trinity Repertory Co 201 Washington St *Web:* www.trinityrep.com	Providence	RI	02903	401-521-1100	751-5577
Tuscaloosa Children's Theatre 10889 Magnolia Ln	Coaling	AL	35453	205-462-0100	
Unicorn Theatre 3828 Main St *Web:* www.unicorntheatre.org	Kansas City	MO	64111	816-531-7529	531-0421
Warehouse Theatre 37 Augusta St *Web:* www.warehousetheatre.com	Greenville	SC	29601	864-235-6948	
West Virginia Public Theatre 111 High St *Web:* www.wvpublictheatre.org	Morgantown	WV	26505	304-291-4117	
Western Nevada Musical Theater Co *Western Nevada College* 2201 W College Pkwy Cedar Bldg 113 *Web:* www.wnc.edu	Carson City	NV	89703	775-445-4249	445-3154
Westport Community Theatre 110 Myrtle Ave *Web:* www.westportcommunitytheatre.com	Westport	CT	06880	203-226-1983	
Wild Swan Theater 6175 Jackson Rd Ste B *Web:* www.wildswantheater.org	Ann Arbor	MI	48103	734-995-0530	
Wilma Theater 265 S Broad St *TF:* 800-732-0999 ■ *Web:* www.wilmatheater.org	Philadelphia	PA	19107	215-893-9456	893-0895
Wilmington Drama League (WDL) 10 W Lea Blvd *Web:* www.wilmingtondramaleague.org	Wilmington	DE	19802	302-764-1172	
Yale Repertory Theatre 1120 Chapel St PO Box 1257 *TF:* 800-973-2837 ■ *Web:* www.yalerep.org	New Haven	CT	06505	203-432-1234	432-6423

574 PERFUMES

See Also Cosmetics, Skin Care, and Other Personal Care Products p. 2170

	City	State	Zip	Phone	Fax
Avon Products Inc 1345 Ave of the Americas *NYSE: AVP* ■ *TF Cust Svc:* 800-367-2866 ■ *Web:* www.avon.com	New York	NY	10017	212-282-7000	
Bijan Boutique 420 N Rodeo Dr *Web:* www.bijan.com	Beverly Hills	CA	90210	310-273-6544	273-6535
Chanel Inc 15 E 57th St *TF:* 800-550-0005 ■ *Web:* www.chanel.com	New York	NY	10022	212-355-5050	
Coty & Lancaster Inc 350 Fifth Ave 17th Fl *Web:* www.coty.com	New York	NY	10118	212-389-7300	
Crabtree & Evelyn Ltd 102 Peake Brook Rd *TF:* 800-272-2873 ■ *Web:* www.crabtree-evelyn.com	Woodstock	CT	06281	860-928-2761	928-1296
Eagle Marketing Inc Perfume Originals Products Div 2412 Sequoia Pk **Fax Area Code:* 405 ■ *TF:* 800-233-7424 ■ *Web:* www.eimi.com	Yukon	OK	73099	800-233-7424	354-7882*
Elizabeth Arden Inc 2400 NE 145th Ave 2nd Fl *NASDAQ: RDEN* ■ *TF:* 800-326-7337 ■ *Web:* www.elizabetharden.com	Miramar	FL	33027	954-364-6900	364-6910
Inter Parfums Inc 551 Fifth Ave Ste 1500 *NASDAQ: IPAR* ■ *Web:* www.interparfumsinc.com	New York	NY	10176	212-983-2640	983-4197
Key West Aloe 13095 N Telecom Pkwy *TF:* 800-445-2563 ■ *Web:* www.keywestaloe.com	Tampa	FL	33637	800-445-2563	
Parfums Givenchy LLC 19 E 57th St *Web:* www.givenchybeauty.com	New York	NY	10022	212-931-2600	
ULTA Beauty 1000 Remington Blvd Ste 120 *TF:* 866-983-8582 ■ *Web:* www.ulta.com	Bolingbrook	IL	60440	630-410-4800	226-8210

575 PERSONAL EMERGENCY RESPONSE SYSTEMS

	City	State	Zip	Phone	Fax
AlertOne Services Inc 1000 Commerce Park Dr Ste 300 *TF Cust Svc:* 866-581-4540 ■ *Web:* www.alert-1.com	Williamsport	PA	17701	866-581-4540	
Life Alert 16027 Ventura Blvd *TF:* 800-920-3410 ■ *Web:* www.lifealert.com	Encino	CA	91436	818-700-7000	
LifeFone 16 Yellowstone Ave *TF:* 888-687-0451 ■ *Web:* www.lifefone.com	White Plains	NY	10607	888-687-0451	

576 PERSONAL PROTECTIVE EQUIPMENT & CLOTHING

See Also Medical Supplies - Mfr p. 2745; Safety Equipment - Mfr p. 3142; Safety Equipment - Whol p. 3143; Sporting Goods p. 3193

	City	State	Zip	Phone	Fax
Aearo Co 5457 W 79th St *TF:* 877-327-4332 ■ *Web:* earsc.com	Indianapolis	IN	46268	317-692-6666	692-6772
AGO Industries Inc 500 Sovereign Rd PO Box 7132 *Web:* www.ago1.com	London	ON	N6M1A4	519-452-3780	452-3053
Airborne Systems Group 5800 Magnolia Ave *Web:* www.airborne-sys.com	Pennsauken	NJ	08109	856-663-1275	663-3028
Allen-Vanguard Corp 2400 St Laurent Blvd *TF:* 800-644-9078 ■ *Web:* www.allenvanguard.com	Ottawa	ON	K1G5B4	613-739-9646	
Ansell Healthcare Inc 111 S Wood Ave Ste 210 *TF:* 800-365-2282 ■ *Web:* www.ansell.com	Iselin	NJ	08830	732-345-5400	219-5114
Bell Sports Corp 6225 N St Hwy 161 Ste 300 *TF:* 866-525-2357 ■ *Web:* www.bellhelmets.com/en_eu	Irving	TX	75038	469-417-6600	492-1639
Biomarine Inc 456 Creamery Way *TF:* 800-378-2287 ■ *Web:* www.neutronicsinc.com	Exton	PA	19341	610-524-8800	524-8807
Bullard Co 1898 Safety Way *TF:* 800-227-0423 ■ *Web:* www.bullard.com	Cynthiana	KY	41031	859-234-6611	234-4352
Carleton Technologies Inc 10 Cobham Dr *Web:* resources.carltech.com	Orchard Park	NY	14127	716-662-0006	662-0747
Choctaw-Kaul Distribution Co 3540 Vinewood Ave *Web:* www.choctawkaul.com	Detroit	MI	48208	313-894-9494	894-7977
David Clark Company Inc 360 Franklin St **Fax:* Sales ■ *TF Cust Svc:* 800-298-6235 ■ *Web:* www.davidclark.com	Worcester	MA	01615	508-751-5800	753-5827*
Desco Industries Inc 3651 Walnut Ave *Web:* desco.descoindustries.com	Chino	CA	91710	909-627-8178	627-7449
Encon Safety Products Co 6825 W Sam Houston Pkwy N PO Box 3826 *TF:* 800-283-6266 ■ *Web:* www.enconsafety.com	Houston	TX	77041	713-466-1449	466-1703
Essex PB&R Corp 8007 Chivvis Dr	Saint Louis	MO	63123	314-351-6116	
Fibre-Metal 2000 Plainfield Pk *TF:* 800-430-4110 ■ *Web:* www.honeywellsafety.com	Cranston	RI	02921	800-430-4110	572-6346
Fire-End & Croker Corp 7 Westchester Plz *TF:* 800-759-3473 ■ *Web:* www.fire-end.com	Elmsford	NY	10523	914-592-3640	592-3892
Galls Inc 2680 Palumbo Dr *TF:* 800-477-7766 ■ *Web:* www.galls.com	Lexington	KY	40509	859-266-7227	
General Econopak Inc 1725 N Sixth St *TF:* 888-871-8568 ■ *Web:* www.generaleconopak.com	Philadelphia	PA	19122	215-763-8200	763-8118
Gexco 3460 Vine St *Web:* gexcoenterprises.com	Norco	CA	92860	951-735-4951	
Globe Mfg Co 37 Loudon Rd *TF:* 800-232-8323 ■ *Web:* www.globeturnoutgear.com	Pittsfield	NH	03263	603-435-8323	435-6388
Graham Medical Products 2273 Larsen Rd *TF Cust Svc:* 800-558-6765 ■ *Web:* www.grahammedical.com	Green Bay	WI	54303	920-494-8701	
Handgards Inc 901 Hawkins Blvd **Fax Area Code:* 915 ■ *TF:* 800-351-8161 ■ *Web:* www.handgards.com	El Paso	TX	79915	800-351-8161	779-1312*
HeatMax Inc 505 Hill Rd PO Box 1191 *TF:* 800-432-8629 ■ *Web:* www.heatmax.com	Dalton	GA	30721	706-226-1800	
Helmet House Inc 26855 Malibu Hill Rd *Web:* www.helmethouse.com	Calabasas Hills	CA	91301	818-880-0000	
Honeywell Safety Products 2000 Plainfield Pike **Fax Area Code:* 800 ■ *TF Cust Svc:* 800-430-4110 ■ *Web:* honeywellsafety.com	Cranston	RI	02921	401-943-4400	572-6346*
ILC Dover Inc 1 Moonwalker Rd *TF:* 800-631-9567 ■ *Web:* www.ilcdover.com	Frederica	DE	19946	302-335-3911	335-0762
Indiana Mills & Manufacturing Inc 18881 US 31 N *Web:* www.imminet.com	Westfield	IN	46074	317-896-9531	896-2142
International Sew-Right Co 6190 Don Murie St *Web:* www.safetyclothing.com	Niagara Falls	ON	L2G0B4	905-374-3600	374-6121
Kappler Inc 115 Grimes Dr PO Box 490 *TF:* 800-600-4019 ■ *Web:* www.kappler.com	Guntersville	AL	35976	256-505-4005	505-4151
Lakeland Industries Inc 701-7 Koehler Ave *NASDAQ: LAKE* ■ *TF:* 800-645-9291 ■ *Web:* www.lakeland.com	Ronkonkoma	NY	11779	631-981-9700	981-9751
Landauer Inc 2 Science Rd *NYSE: LDR* ■ *TF:* 800-323-8830 ■ *Web:* www.landauer.com	Glenwood	IL	60425	708-755-7000	755-7016
Little Rapids Corp 2273 Larsen Rd *Web:* www.littlerapids.com	Green Bay	WI	54303	920-496-3040	494-5340

Phone Fax

Louis M Gerson Company Inc
16 Commerce Blvd . . . . . Middleboro MA 02346 508-947-4000 947-5442
TF: 800-225-8623 ■ *Web:* www.gersonco.com

MCR Safety 5321 E Shelby Dr . . . . . Memphis TN 38118 901-795-5810 999-3908*
*Fax Area Code: 800 ■ *Fax: Sales ■ *TF:* 800-955-6887 ■ *Web:* www.mcrsafety.com

Medline Industries Inc 1 Medline Pl . . . . . Mundelein IL 60060 847-949-5500 643-3295
TF Cust Svc: 800-351-1512 ■ *Web:* www.medline.com

Miller Products Company Inc
2511 S Tricenter Blvd . . . . . Durham NC 27713 919-313-2100 313-2101
TF: 800-782-7437 ■ *Web:* www.millerproducts.com

Moldex Metric Inc 10111 W Jefferson Blvd . . . . . Culver City CA 90232 310-837-6500 837-9563*
*Fax: Sales ■ *TF:* 800-421-0668 ■ *Web:* www.moldex.com

MTS Safety Products Inc (MTS) PO Box 204 . . . . . Golden MS 38847 800-647-8168 329-9687
TF General: 800-647-8168 ■ *Web:* www.mts-safety.com

National Safety Apparel Inc (NSA)
15825 Industrial Pkwy . . . . . Cleveland OH 44135 800-553-0672 941-1130*
*Fax Area Code: 216 ■ *TF:* 800-553-0672 ■ *Web:* www.thinknsa.com

Newtex Industries Inc 8050 Victor Mendon Rd . . . . . Victor NY 14564 585-924-9135 924-4645
TF: 800-836-1001 ■ *Web:* www.newtex.com

Performance Designs Inc
1300 E International Speedway Blvd . . . . . DeLand FL 32724 386-738-2224 734-8297
Web: www.performancedesigns.com

Plastic Safety Systems Inc 2444 Baldwin Rd . . . . . Cleveland OH 44104 800-662-6338 231-2702*
*Fax Area Code: 216 ■ *TF:* 800-662-6338 ■ *Web:* pss-innovations.com

PolyConversions Inc 505 Condit Dr . . . . . Rantoul IL 61866 217-893-3330 893-3003
TF: 888-893-3330 ■ *Web:* www.polyconversions.com

Precept Medical Products Inc
370 Airport Rd PO Box 2400 . . . . . Arden NC 28704 828-681-0209 681-8626
TF: 800-851-4431 ■ *Web:* www.preceptmed.com

Protech Armored Products
13386 International Pkwy . . . . . Jacksonville FL 32218 904-741-5400
Web: protecharmored.com

Right-Gard Corp 531 N Fourth St . . . . . Denver PA 17517 717-336-7594

Saf-T-Gard International Inc 205 Huehl Rd . . . . . Northbrook IL 60062 847-291-1600 291-1610
TF: 800-548-4273 ■ *Web:* www.saftgard.com

Safariland LLC 13386 International Pkwy . . . . . Jacksonville FL 32218 904-741-5400
TF: 800-347-1200 ■ *Web:* www.safariland.com/our-brands/aba

Safe-T-Gard Corp 12105 W Cedar Dr . . . . . Lakewood CO 80228 303-763-8900 763-8071
TF Cust Svc: 800-356-9026 ■ *Web:* www.safetgard.com

Scott Health & Safety
4320 Goldmine Rd PO Box 569 . . . . . Monroe NC 28110 704-291-8300 291-8340
TF: 800-247-7257 ■ *Web:* www.scottsafety.com

Seattle Manufacturing Corp
6930 Salashan Pkwy . . . . . Ferndale WA 98248 360-366-5534 366-5723
TF: 800-426-6251 ■ *Web:* smcgear.com

Sellstrom Manufacturing Co
2050 Hammond Dr . . . . . Schaumburg IL 60173 847-358-2000 358-8564
TF: 800-323-7402 ■ *Web:* www.sellstrom.com

Standard Textile Company Inc
1 Knollcrest Dr . . . . . Cincinnati OH 45237 513-761-9255 761-0467
TF: 800-999-0400 ■ *Web:* www.standardtextile.com

Steel Grip Inc 1501 E Voorhees St . . . . . Danville IL 61832 217-442-6240 442-9370
TF: 800-223-1595 ■ *Web:* www.steelgripinc.com

Steiner Industries 5801 N Tripp Ave . . . . . Chicago IL 60646 773-588-3444 588-3450
TF: 800-621-4515 ■ *Web:* www.steinerindustries.com

Stemaco Products Inc 2211 Ogden Rd . . . . . Rock Hill SC 29730 803-328-2191 328-2808

Strong Enterprises Inc 11236 Satellite Blvd . . . . . Orlando FL 32837 407-859-9317 850-6978
TF: 800-344-6319 ■ *Web:* www.strongparachutes.com

Tingley Rubber Corp
1551 S Washington Ave Ste 403 Ste 403 . . . . . Piscataway NJ 08854 800-631-5498
TF Cust Svc: 800-631-5498 ■ *Web:* www.tingleyrubber.com

United Pioneer Co 2777 Summer St Ste 206 . . . . . Stamford CT 06905 800-466-9823 466-9828
TF: 800-466-9823 ■ *Web:* www.b340.com

Uvex Safety Inc 900 Douglas Pk . . . . . Smithfield RI 02917 800-682-0839 322-1330
TF General: 800-682-0839 ■ *Web:* www.uvex.us

White Knight Engineered Products
9525 Monroe Rd Ste 100 . . . . . Charlotte NC 28270 704-542-6876
TF: 888-743-4700 ■ *Web:* www.wkep.com

Wolf X-Ray Corp 100 W Industry Ct . . . . . Deer Park NY 11729 631-242-9729 925-5003
TF Cust Svc: 800-356-9729 ■ *Web:* www.wolfxray.com

577 PEST CONTROL SERVICES

Phone Fax

A 1 Termite & Pest Control Inc
2686 Morganton Blvd Sw . . . . . Lenoir NC 28645 828-758-4312
TF: 800-532-7378 ■ *Web:* www.a1termitepc.com

ABC Home & Commercial Services 9475 Hwy 290 E . . . . . Austin TX 78724 512-837-9500
Web: www.abchomeandcommercial.com

Action Pest Control Inc
2301 S Green River Rd . . . . . Evansville IN 47715 812-477-5546
Web: www.actionpest.com

Al Hoffer's Pest Protection Inc
12329 NW 35 St . . . . . Coral Springs FL 33065 866-549-7987
TF: 866-549-7987 ■ *Web:* www.hofferpest.com

Allgood Services Inc 106 Roosevelt St . . . . . Dublin GA 31021 478-272-6271
Web: www.allgoodpestsolutions.com

Antimite Associates Inc 5867 Pine Ave . . . . . Chino Hills CA 91709 909-606-2300
Web: www.antimitepestcontrol.com

Arrow Environmental Services Inc
6225 Tower Ln . . . . . Sarasota FL 34240 941-531-9108
Web: www.arrowservices.com

Bain Pest Control Service Inc
1320 Middlesex St . . . . . Lowell MA 01851 978-452-9621
TF: 800-272-3661 ■ *Web:* bainpestcontrol.com

Banks Pest Control Inc
215 Golden State Ave . . . . . Bakersfield CA 93301 661-323-7858
Web: bankspest.com

Bird Solutions International
1338 N Melrose Dr Ste H . . . . . Vista CA 92083 760-758-9747
TF: 800-210-9514 ■ *Web:* www.birdsolutions.com

Phone Fax

Black Pest Prevention Inc
605 Springbrook Rd . . . . . Charlotte NC 28217 704-522-9222
Web: www.blackpest.com

Blue Sky Pest Control
3050 S Country Club Dr Ste 7 . . . . . Mesa AZ 85210 480-635-8492
Web: blueskypest.com

Bright Pest Control Co 4340 Sanita Ct . . . . . Louisville KY 40213 502-452-9600
Web: brightpest.com

Bug Off Exterminators Inc
1064 NW 54th St . . . . . Fort Lauderdale FL 33309 954-772-8338
Web: bugoffexterminatorsflorida.com

Bug-Out Service Inc
5951 Arlington Expwy . . . . . Jacksonville FL 32211 904-743-8272
Web: bugoutservice.com

Burns Pest Elimination Inc
2620 W Grovers Ave . . . . . Phoenix AZ 85053 602-971-4782
TF: 877-971-4782 ■ *Web:* burnspestelimination.com

Clean Master 2201 Park Ave . . . . . Chico CA 95928 530-343-0123
Web: www.onlyforpc.com

Clegg's Termite and Pest Control LLC
2401 Reichard St . . . . . Durham NC 27705 919-968-8304
Web: www.cleggs.com

Cook's Pest Control Inc 1741 Fifth Ave SE . . . . . Decatur AL 35601 256-355-3285
Web: www.cookspest.com

Copesan Services Inc
W175 N5711 Technology Dr . . . . . Menomonee Falls WI 53051 800-267-3726 783-6267*
*Fax Area Code: 262 ■ *TF:* 800-267-3726 ■ *Web:* www.copesan.com

Craig Thomas Pest Control Inc
1186 Route 9G . . . . . Hyde Park NY 12538 845-229-6833
Web: callcraig.com

Crane Pest Control Inc 2700 Geary Blvd . . . . . San Francisco CA 94118 415-922-1666
Web: www.cranepestcontrol.com

Dewey Services Inc 939 E Union St . . . . . Pasadena CA 91106 626-568-9248
TF: 877-339-3973 ■ *Web:* deweypest.com

Dodson Bros Exterminating Company Inc
3712 Campbell Ave . . . . . Lynchburg VA 24501 434-847-9051 847-2034
Web: www.dodsonbros.com

Fischer Environmental Service Inc
1980 Surgi Dr . . . . . Mandeville LA 70448 800-391-2565
TF: 800-391-2565 ■ *Web:* www.fischerenv.com

Florida Pest Control & Chemical Company Inc
116 NW 16th Ave . . . . . Gainesville FL 32601 352-376-2661 376-2791
Web: www.flapest.com

Gilbert Industries Inc 5611 Krueger Dr . . . . . Jonesboro AR 72401 870-932-6070
TF: 800-643-0400 ■ *Web:* www.gilbertinc.com

Green Lawn Fertilizing Inc
1004 Saunders Ln . . . . . West Chester PA 19380 888-581-5296
TF: 888-581-5296 ■ *Web:* www.greenlawnfertilizing.com

Havasu Pest Control Inc
2716 Maricopa Ave . . . . . Lake Havasu City AZ 86406 928-855-1054 855-3329

Home Paramount Pest Control Cos Inc
PO Box 850 . . . . . Forest Hill MD 21050 410-510-0700
TF: 888-888-4663 ■ *Web:* www.homeparamount.com

Horizon Termite & Pest Control Corp
45 Cross Ave . . . . . Midland Park NJ 07432 201-447-2530
TF: 888-612-2847 ■ *Web:* www.horizonpestcontrol.com

Isotech Pest Management Inc
12881 Ramona Blvd . . . . . Baldwin Park CA 91706 909-594-8939
Web: www.isotechpest.com

Jp Mchale Pest Management Inc
241 Bleakley Ave . . . . . Buchanan NY 10511 800-479-2284
TF: 800-479-2284 ■ *Web:* nopests.com

Knockout Pest Control Inc 1009 Front St . . . . . Uniondale NY 11553 516-489-7817 489-4348
TF: 800-244-7378 ■ *Web:* www.knockoutpest.com

Lawn Doctor Inc 142 SR 34 . . . . . Holmdel NJ 07733 800-631-5660
TF: 800-845-0580 ■ *Web:* www.lawndoctor.com

Lewis Pest Control Inc 25 West Frnt St S . . . . . Thomasville AL 36784 334-636-4530
Web: www.lewispestcontrol.net

Light Brigade Inc, The 837 Industry Dr . . . . . Tukwila WA 98188 206-575-0404
Web: www.lightbrigade.com

Lloyd Pest Control Co Inc, The
935 Sherman St . . . . . San Diego CA 92110 619-298-9865
Web: www.lloydpest.com

Loyal Termite & Pest Control Company Inc
2610 E Parham Rd . . . . . Richmond VA 23228 804-737-7777
Web: www.loyalpest.com

Massey Services Inc 315 Groveland St E . . . . . Orlando FL 32804 407-645-2500 802-3736*
*Fax: Cust Svc ■ *TF:* 888-262-7739 ■ *Web:* www.masseyservices.com

McCall Service Inc 2861 College St . . . . . Jacksonville FL 32205 904-389-5561 389-3212
TF: 800-342-6948 ■ *Web:* www.mccallservice.com

NaturaLawn of America Inc 1 E Church St . . . . . Frederick MD 21701 301-694-5440 846-0320
TF: 800-989-5444 ■ *Web:* www.naturalawn.com

Nutrilawn Inc 25-1040 Martin Grove Rd . . . . . Toronto ON M9W4W1 416-620-7100
Web: www.nutrilawn.com

Ohio Exterminating Company Inc
1347 N High St . . . . . Columbus OH 43201 614-294-6311
Web: ohioexterminating.com

Oliver Exterminating Corp 658 NW 99th St . . . . . Miami FL 33150 305-758-1811
Web: guaranteepest.com

Orkin Exterminating Co Inc
2170 Piedmont Rd NE . . . . . Atlanta GA 30324 877-250-1652 265-0238*
*Fax Area Code: 510 ■ *Fax: Cust Svc ■ *TF:* 844-499-3453 ■ *Web:* www.orkin.com

PCO Services Corp 5840 Falbourne St . . . . . Mississauga ON L5R4B5 905-502-9700
Web: www.orkincanada.ca

Pest Shield Pest Control Inc
15329 Tradesman . . . . . San Antonio TX 78249 210-525-8823
TF: 888-728-8237 ■ *Web:* www.sanantonio-pestcontrol.com

Pestmaster Services Inc 137 East S St . . . . . Bishop CA 93514 760-873-8100
Web: www.pestmaster.com

Plunkett's Pest Control 40 NE 52nd Way . . . . . Fridley MN 55421 218-723-8464
TF: 866-906-1780 ■ *Web:* www.plunketts.net

Presto-X Co 1221 S Saddle Creek Rd Ste 101 . . . . . Omaha NE 68106 800-759-1942
TF: 800-759-1942 ■ *Web:* www.prestox.com

Phone | Fax

Railinc Corp 7001 Weston Pkwy Ste 200 .... Cary NC 27513 919-651-5193
Web: www.railinc.com

Rollins Inc 2170 Piedmont Rd NE .... Atlanta GA 30324 404-888-2000
NYSE: ROL ■ *Web:* www.rollins.com

Rottler Pest & Lawn Solutions
8625 St Charles Rock Rd .... Saint Louis MO 63114 314-426-6100
Web: www.rottler.com

Sandwich Isle Pest Solutions Inc
96-1368 Waihona St. .... Pearl City HI 96782 808-456-7716
Web: www.sandwichisle.com

Schendel Pest Services 1035 SE Quincy St .... Topeka KS 66612 785-232-9357 232-4165
TF: 800-591-7378 ■ *Web:* www.schendelpest.com

Senske Lawn & Tree Care Inc 400 N Quay St. .... Kennewick WA 99336 509-586-5296
Web: www.senske.com

Serfco Termite & Pest Control Inc
1701 S Walton Blvd .... Bentonville AR 72712 479-273-2220

Skyline Pest Solutions Inc
1745 Pennsylvania Ave. .... Mcdonough GA 30253 678-432-5464
Web: www.skylinepest.com

Smithereen Exterminators Inc
7400 N Melvina Ave .... Niles IL 60714 847-647-0010 647-0606
TF: 800-336-3500 ■ *Web:* smithereen.com

Sprague Pest Solutions Inc
2725 Pacific Ave Ste 200 .... Tacoma WA 98402 253-272-4400
Web: www.spraguepest.com

Spring-Green Lawn Care Corp
11909 Spaulding School Dr .... Plainfield IL 60585 815-436-8777 436-9056
TF: 800-435-4051 ■ *Web:* www.spring-green.com

Steritech Group Inc, The 7600 Little Ave .... Charlotte NC 28226 704-544-1900
Web: www.steritech.com

Sure Thing Pest Control
11541 Goldcoast Dr .... Cincinnati OH 45249 513-247-0030
Web: www.surethingpc.com

Terminix International Company LP
860 Ridge Lk Blvd .... Memphis TN 38120 866-399-0453 363-8541*
**Fax Area Code:* 901 ■ **Fax:* Mktg ■ *TF:* 855-212-6399 ■ *Web:* www.terminix.com

Terminix Service Inc 3618 Fernandina Rd. .... Columbia SC 29202 803-772-1783

Tomlinson Bomberger Lawn Care & Landscaping Inc
3055 Yellow Goose Rd .... Lancaster PA 17601 717-399-1991
Web: tomlinsonbomberger.com

TruGreen ChemLawn 860 Ridge Lk Blvd .... Memphis TN 38120 866-369-9539
TF: 866-369-9539 ■ *Web:* www.trugreen.com

Truly Nolen of America Inc
3636 E Speedway Blvd .... Tucson AZ 85716 800-528-3442 322-4002*
**Fax Area Code:* 520 ■ *TF:* 800-468-7859 ■ *Web:* www.trulynolen.com

TruTech LLC PO Box 6849 .... Marietta GA 30065 770-977-2034
TF: 800-842-7296 ■ *Web:* www.trutechinc.com

Turf Management Systems LLC PO Box 26389 .... Birmingham AL 35260 205-979-8604 979-6063
Web: www.turfmanagementsystems.com

Waltham Services Inc 817 Moody St .... Waltham MA 02453 781-893-1810 893-7921
TF: 866-974-7378 ■ *Web:* www.walthamservices.com

Weed Man 2399 Royal Windsor Dr .... Mississauga ON L5J1K9 905-823-8300
Web: www.weedmancanada.com

Western Exterminator Co 305 N Crescent Way .... Anaheim CA 92801 714-517-9000
TF: 800-698-2440 ■ *Web:* www.westernexterminator.com

Western Pest Services Inc 800 Lanidex Plz .... Parsippany NJ 07054 973-515-0100
Web: www.westernpest.com

Zelenka Nursery LLC 16127 Winans St .... Grand Haven MI 49417 616-842-1367
Web: www.zelenkanursery.com

PESTICIDES

578 PET PRODUCTS

See Also Leather Goods - Personal p. 2645; Livestock & Poultry Feeds - Prepared p. 2680

Phone | Fax

Ainsworth Pet Nutrition 18746 Mill St .... Meadville PA 16335 814-724-7710 337-2743
Web: www.ainsworthpets.com

Amalgamated Dairies Ltd 79 Water St .... Summerside PE C1N1A6 902-888-5088
Web: www.adl.ca

American Nutrition Inc 2813 Wall Ave .... Ogden UT 84401 801-394-3477
Web: www.anibrands.com

Arctic Glacier Holdings Inc 625 Henry Ave .... Winnipeg MB R3A0V1 204-772-2473
TF: 888-573-9237 ■ *Web:* www.arcticglacier.com

Bailey Farms LLC 549 Karem Dr .... Marshall WI 53559 800-655-1705
TF: 800-655-1705 ■ *Web:* www.baileyfarmspets.com

Baker Boy Bake Shop Inc 170 Gta Dr .... Dickinson ND 58601 701-225-4444
Web: www.bakerboy.com

BioZyme Inc 6010 Stockyards Expy .... Saint Joseph MO 64504 816-238-3326 238-7549
TF: 800-821-3070 ■ *Web:* www.biozymeinc.com

Church & Dwight Company Inc
469 N Harrison St. .... Princeton NJ 08543 609-683-5900
NYSE: CHD ■ *Web:* www.churchdwight.com

Clorox Co 1221 Broadway .... Oakland CA 94612 510-271-7000 832-1463
NYSE: CLX ■ *TF Cust Svc:* 800-424-9300 ■ *Web:* www.thecloroxcompany.com

Companion Pets Inc (CPI)
2001 N Black Canyon Hwy .... Phoenix AZ 85009 602-255-0166 255-0841
TF: 800-646-3611 ■ *Web:* www.cpipets.com

Doctors Foster & Smith Inc
2253 Air Pk Rd PO Box 100 .... Rhinelander WI 54501 715-369-3305 562-7169*
**Fax Area Code:* 800 ■ **Fax:* Cust Svc ■ *TF:* 800-826-7206 ■ *Web:* www.drsfostersmith.com

Doskocil Mfg Company Inc PO Box 1246 .... Arlington TX 76004 877-738-6283
TF: 877-738-6283 ■ *Web:* www.petmate.com

Eagle Pack Pet Foods Inc 200 Ames Pond Dr .... Tewksbury MA 01876 574-259-7834
TF: 800-255-5959 ■ *Web:* www.eaglepack.com

Efficas Inc 7007 Winchester Cir Ste 120 .... Boulder CO 80301 303-381-2070
TF: 866-446-0388 ■ *Web:* www.efficas.com

FL Emmert Co Inc 2007 Dunlap St .... Cincinnati OH 45214 513-721-5808 721-6087
TF: 800-441-3343 ■ *Web:* www.emmert.com

Phone | Fax

Hartz Mountain Corp, The 400 Plz Dr .... Secaucus NJ 07094 800-275-1414
TF: 800-275-1414 ■ *Web:* www.hartz.com

Healthy Pet 6960 Salashan Pkwy. .... Ferndale WA 98248 360-734-7415 671-1588
TF: 800-242-2287 ■ *Web:* www.healthy-pet.com

Heath Manufacturing Co 140 Mill St .... Coopersville MI 49404 616-997-8181 997-9491
Web: heathoutdoorproducts.com

Hill's Pet Nutrition Inc 400 SW Eigth St .... Topeka KS 66603 785-354-8523 368-5786
Web: www.hillspet.com

IAMS Co 3700 Ohio 65 .... Leipsic OH 45856 419-943-4267
TF Cust Svc: 800-675-3849 ■ *Web:* www.iams.com

Jeffers Inc 310 W Saunders Rd PO Box 100 .... Dothan AL 36301 334-793-6257 793-5179
TF: 800-533-3377 ■ *Web:* www.jefferspet.com

John A Van Den Bosch Co 4511 Holland Ave .... Holland MI 49424 800-968-6477
TF: 800-968-6477 ■ *Web:* www.vbosch.com

Joy Dog Food PO Box 305 .... Pinckneyville IL 62274 800-245-4125 357-3651*
**Fax Area Code:* 618 ■ *TF:* 800-245-4125 ■ *Web:* www.joypetfood.com

Kaytee Products Inc 521 Clay St. .... Chilton WI 53014 920-849-2321 849-7044
TF: 800-669-9580 ■ *Web:* www.kaytee.com

Lake Country Foods Inc 132 S Concord Rd .... Oconomowoc WI 53066 262-567-5521
Web: www.lcfoods.com

Manna Pro Corp
707 Spirit 40 Pk Dr Ste 150 .... Chesterfield MO 63005 800-690-9908
TF: 800-690-9908 ■ *Web:* www.mannapro.com

Mark Hershey Farms Inc 479 Horseshoe Pk .... Lebanon PA 17042 717-867-4624 867-4313
TF: 888-801-3301 ■ *Web:* www.markhersheyfarms.com

Mars Snack Food 800 High St .... Hackettstown NJ 07840 908-852-1000 850-2734
Web: www.mars.com

MIDWEST Homes for Pets
3142 S Cowan Rd PO Box 1031 .... Muncie IN 47302 765-289-3355 289-6524
TF: 800-428-8560 ■ *Web:* www.midwesthomes4pets.com

Moyer & Son Inc 113 E Reliance Rd .... Souderton PA 18964 215-799-2000
TF: 866-669-3747 ■ *Web:* www.emoyer.com

Multipet International Inc
265 W Commercial Ave .... Moonachie NJ 07074 201-438-6600 438-2990
TF: 800-900-6738 ■ *Web:* www.multipet.com

Natural Life Pet Products Inc
205 E 29th St .... Pittsburg KS 66762 620-230-0888 230-0403
TF: 800-367-2391 ■ *Web:* www.nlpp.com

Nestle Purina PetCare Co
801 Chouteau Ave .... Saint Louis MO 63102 314-982-1000
TF: 800-778-7462 ■ *Web:* www.purina.com

North States Industries Inc 1507 92nd Ln NE .... Blaine MN 55449 763-486-1756 486-1763
TF: 800-848-8421 ■ *Web:* www.northstatesind.com

Orrco Inc 515 Collins Blvd PO Box 147 .... Orrville OH 44667 330-683-5015 683-0738
TF: 800-321-3085 ■ *Web:* www.orrvillepet.com

Penn-Plax Inc 35 Marcus Blvd .... Hauppauge NY 11788 631-273-3787 273-2196
Web: www.pennplax.com

Pet Food Express 500 85th Ave .... oakland CA 94621 510-924-3300 346-7788
Web: www.petfoodexpress.com

Pet Safe International 10427 Electric Ave .... Knoxville TN 37932 865-777-5404
TF Cust Svc: 800-732-2677 ■ *Web:* petsafe.net/home

Pet Supermarket Inc 1100 International Pkwy. .... Sunrise FL 33323 954-351-0834 351-0897
TF: 866-434-1990 ■ *Web:* www.petsupermarket.com

Pet Supplies "Plus" Inc
17197 N Laurel Prk Dre Ste 402 .... Livonia MI 48152 734-793-6600
Web: www.petsuppliesplus.com

Pet Valu Canada Inc 225 Royal Crest Crt .... Markham ON L3R9X6 905-946-1200
TF: 800-845-4759 ■ *Web:* www.petvalu.com

PETCO Animal Supplies Inc 9125 Rehco Rd. .... San Diego CA 92121 858-453-7845 784-3489
TF: 877-738-6742 ■ *Web:* www.petco.com

PetFoodDirect.com 189 Main St .... Harleysville PA 19438 215-513-1999 894-5034*
**Fax Area Code:* 877 ■ *TF Cust Svc:* 877-738-3663 ■ *Web:* www.petfooddirect.com

Petland Discounts Inc 355 Crooked Hill Rd .... Brentwood NY 11717 631-273-6363 273-6513
Web: www.petlanddiscounts.com

Petland Inc 250 Riverside St .... Chillicothe OH 45601 740-775-2464 775-2575
TF: 800-221-5935 ■ *Web:* petland.com

PetMed Express Inc 1441 SW 29th Ave. .... Pompano Beach FL 33069 954-979-5995 971-0544
NASDAQ: PETS ■ *TF:* 800-738-6337 ■ *Web:* www.1800petmeds.com

PETsMART Inc 19601 N 27th Ave .... Phoenix AZ 85027 623-580-6100
NASDAQ: PETM ■ *TF Cust Svc:* 800-738-1385 ■ *Web:* www.petsmart.com

Pied Piper Mills Inc 423 E Lake Dr .... Hamlin TX 79520 325-576-3684 576-3460

Prevue Pet Products Inc 224 N Maplewood Ave .... Chicago IL 60612 312-243-3624 243-3624
TF: 800-243-3624 ■ *Web:* prevuepet.com

Prince Corp 8351 County Rd H .... Marshfield WI 54449 715-384-3105 387-6924
TF: 800-777-2486 ■ *Web:* www.prince-corp.com

Ralco Nutrition Inc 1600 Hahn Rd .... Marshall MN 56258 800-533-5306 532-5740*
**Fax Area Code:* 507 ■ *TF:* 800-533-5306 ■ *Web:* www.ralconutrition.com

Rich Products Corp 1 Robert Rich Way .... Buffalo NY 14213 716-878-8000
Web: www.byronsbbq.com

Rolf C. Hagen Corp 305 Forbes Blvd .... Mansfield MA 02048 508-339-9531 339-6973
TF Cust Svc: 800-724-2436 ■ *Web:* www.hagen.com

Simmons Pet Foods Inc 316 N Hico .... Siloam Springs AR 72761 479-524-8151
Web: simmonspetfood.com

Star Milling Co 24067 Water St. .... Perris CA 92570 951-657-3143 657-3114
TF: 800-733-6455 ■ *Web:* www.starmilling.com

Sunshine Mills Inc 500 Sixth St SW .... Red Bay AL 35582 256-356-9541 356-8287*
**Fax:* Sales ■ *TF:* 800-633-3349 ■ *Web:* www.sunshinemills.com

Texas Farm Products Co 915 S Fredonia St .... Nacogdoches TX 75964 936-564-3711 560-8200
TF: 800-392-3110 ■ *Web:* www.texasfarm.com

Triumph Pet Industries Inc 500 Sixth St SW .... Red Bay AL 35582 256-356-9541 331-5140*
**Fax Area Code:* 800 ■ *TF:* 800-633-3349 ■ *Web:* triumphpetfood.com

United Pacific Pet 12060 Cabernet Dr .... Fontana CA 92337 951-360-8550 360-8540
TF: 800-979-3333 ■ *Web:* www.uppet.com

United Pharmacal Company of Missouri Inc
3705 Pear St. .... Saint Joseph MO 64503 816-233-8800 233-9696
TF: 800-254-8726 ■ *Web:* www.upco.com

Virbac Corp 3200 Meacham Blvd. .... Fort Worth TX 76137 817-831-5030 831-8327
Web: www.virbac.com

Wild Birds Unlimited Inc
11711 N College Ave Ste 146 .... Carmel IN 46032 317-571-7100 571-7110
TF: 800-326-4928 ■ *Web:* www.wbu.com

579 PETROLEUM & PETROLEUM PRODUCTS - WHOL

Phone Fax

A & W Oil Company Inc 1101 N Liberty St. Waynesboro GA 30830 706-554-2121
Web: www.awoil.com

A.R. Sandri Inc 400 Chapman St Greenfield MA 01301 413-772-2121
TF: 800-628-1900 ■ *Web:* www.sandri.com

Abercrombie Oil Company Inc PO Box 1422 Danville VA 24543 434-792-8022
Web: www.abercrombieoil.com

Adams Resources Inc 17 S Briar Hollow Ln Houston TX 77001 713-881-3600
Web: www.adamsresources.com

Adium Oil Company Inc 310 Blattner Dr Avon MN 56310 320-356-7350

Advance Petroleum Distributing Company Inc
2451 Great SW Pkwy Fort Worth TX 76106 817-626-5458 624-3102
Web: www.advancefuel.com

Allen Oil Co 1215 Old Birmingham Hwy Sylacauga AL 35150 256-245-5478
Web: www.allenoil.com

Allied Oil & Supply Inc 2209 S 24th St Omaha NE 68108 402-344-4343 344-4360
TF: 800-333-3717 ■ *Web:* www.alliedoil.com

Allied Propane Service Inc 5000 Seaport Ave Richmond CA 94804 510-237-7077
Web: www.alliedpropaneservice.com

Allied Washoe Petroleum 2500 E 4th St Reno NV 89512 775-323-3146
Web: www.alliedwashoe.com

Amber Resources LLC 1543 W 16th St Long Beach CA 90813 562-432-3946
Web: www.sawyerpetroleum.com

American Biodiesel Inc
171 Saxony Rd Ste 202 Encinitas CA 92023 760-942-9306
Web: www.communityfuels.com

AmeriGas Propane Inc PO Box 965 Valley Forge PA 19482 610-337-7000
Web: www.amerigas.com

Aos Thermal Compounds LLC
22 Meridian Rd Ste 6 Eatontown NJ 07724 732-389-5514
TF: 888-662-7337 ■ *Web:* www.aosco.com

Apex Oil Company Inc
8235 Forsyth Blvd Ste 400 Clayton MO 63105 314-889-9600 854-8539
Web: www.apexoil.com

Apex-Petroleum Corp
9500 Arena Dr Ste 360 Upper Marlboro MD 20744 301-773-9009
Web: www.apexpetroleum.com

Arkansas Valley Petroleum Inc
8336 E 73rd St Ste 100 Tulsa OK 74133 918-252-0508 250-4921
Web: arkvalprop.com

Armada Oil & Gas Company Inc
13530 Michigan Ave Ste 400 Dearborn MI 48126 313-582-1777
Web: www.armadaoil.com

Arr-maz Custom Chemicals Inc
9189 stevedoring rd Convent LA 70723 863-578-1206
Web: m.arrmaz.com

Ascent Aviation Group Inc 1 Mill St Parish NY 13131 315-625-7299
Web: www.ascent1.com

Atlas Oil Co 24501 Ecorse Rd Taylor MI 48180 313-292-5500 731-0264
TF: 800-878-2000 ■ *Web:* www.atlasoil.com

Axeon Specialty Products LLC
750 Washington Blvd Ste 600 Stamford CT 06901 855-378-4958
TF: 855-378-4958 ■ *Web:* www.axeonsp.com

Beach Oil Company Inc
631 US Hwy 76 PO Box 3010 Clarksville TN 37041 931-358-9303 358-9331
Web: www.beachoil.com

Behnke Lubricants Inc
W134N5373 Campbell Dr. Menomonee Falls WI 53051 262-781-8850
Web: www.jax.com

Bell Gas Inc 1811 SE Main St Roswell NM 88203 575-622-1733

Berry Oil 3193 Leigh Ave Tetonia ID 83452 208-456-2271 456-2091
Web: www.berryoil.net

Best Line Oil Co Inc 219 N 20th St Tampa FL 33605 813-248-1044
Web: www.bestlineoil.com

Big Bear Oil Company Inc
11685 Pebble Hills Blvd El Paso TX 79936 915-921-1905
Web: www.ysletadelsurpueblo.org

Big River Oil Company Inc 1920 Orchard Ave. Hannibal MO 63401 573-221-0226
Web: www.bigriveroil.com

Blue Sun Biodiesel LLC
1687 Cole Blvd Ste 100 Lakewood CO 80401 303-865-7700
Web: www.gobluesun.com

Blueox Corp 38 N Canal St Oxford NY 13830 607-843-2583
Web: www.blueoxenergy.com

Blythewood Oil Company Inc 4118 Us Hwy 21 S Ridgeway SC 29130 803-754-3319

Boler Pump Co 4611 Andrews Hwy Midland TX 79703 432-694-3461
Web: boler-pump-co.hub.biz

Boyett Petroleum 601 McHenry Ave Modesto CA 95350 209-577-6000 577-6040
TF: 800-545-9212 ■ *Web:* www.boyett.net

BP Lubricants USA Inc 1500 Valley Rd Wayne NJ 07470 973-633-2200
TF: 800-333-3991 ■ *Web:* www.bp.com

Bradco Inc 107-11th Ave PO Box 997 Holbrook AZ 86025 928-524-3976
Web: www.bradcoinc.com

Bretthauer Oil Co 453 SW Washington St Hillsboro OR 97123 503-648-2531
TF: 800-359-3113 ■ *Web:* www.bretthauer.com

Brewer Oil Co 2701 Candelaria NE Albuquerque NM 87107 505-884-2040
Web: www.breweroil.com

Brewer-Hendley Oil Co
207 N Forest Hills School Rd Marshville NC 28103 704-233-2600
Web: brewerhendley.com

Broadus Oil Corp of Illinois
201 Dannys Dr Ste 5 Streator IL 61364 815-673-5515
Web: www.broadusoil.com

Burkett Oil Company Inc 6788 Best Friend Rd Norcross GA 30071 770-447-8030
Web: www.burkettoil.com

Byron Originals Fuel Sales
119 E State Hwy 175 Ida Grove IA 51445 712-364-2009
Web: byronfuels.com

Phone Fax

C & R Distributing Inc 8528 Alameda Ave El Paso TX 79907 915-860-4205
Web: www.candrdistributing.com

Campbell Oil Company Inc 611 Erie St S Massillon OH 44646 330-833-8555
TF: 800-589-8555 ■ *Web:* campbelloil.com

Canyon State Oil Company Inc 2640 N 31st Ave Phoenix AZ 85009 602-269-7981
Web: www.canyonstateoil.com

Cardwell Distributing Inc 8137 S State St Midvale UT 84047 801-561-4251
Web: www.cardwelldist.com

Cargill Energy PO Box 9300 Minneapolis MN 55440 952-742-7575
TF: 800-227-4455 ■ *Web:* www.cargill.com

Carson 3125 NW 35th Ave Portland OR 97210 503-224-8500 222-0186
TF: 800-998-7767 ■ *Web:* www.carsonoil.com

Cavalier Energy Inc 5 Ave SW Ste 2500-255 Calgary AB T2P3G6 403-268-3940
Web: cavalierenergy.com

Center Oil Co
600 Mason Ridge Ctr Dr 2nd Fl Saint Louis MO 63141 314-682-3500
Web: www.centeroil.com

Champlain Oil Company Inc
45 San Remo Dr South Burlington VT 05403 802-864-5380
Web: www.champlainoil.com

Chemoil Corp 4 Embarcadero Ctr 34thFl San Francisco CA 94111 656-880-8200
Web: www.chemoil.com

Chronister Oil Co 2026 N Republic St Springfield IL 62702 217-523-5050

Citation Crude Marketing Inc
8223 Willow Pl Dr Houston TX 77070 281-955-8954
Web: cogc.com

Coen Oil Co 1045 W Chestnut St Washington PA 15301 724-223-5515
Web: www.coenoil.com

Colonial Group Inc 101 N Lathrop Ave Savannah GA 31415 912-236-1331 235-3881
Web: colonialgroupinc.com

Concord Oil Company Inc 147 Lowell Rd Concord MA 01760 978-369-3333
Web: www.concordoilcompany.com

Condon Oil Co 126 E Jackson St Ripon WI 54971 920-748-3186 748-3201
TF: 800-452-1212 ■ *Web:* www.condoncompanies.com

Conservancy Oil Company of Grand Junction Inc
825 1st Ave. Grand Junction CO 81501 970-243-6934
Web: www.conservancyoil.com

Consolidated Energy Co 910 Main St Jesup IA 50648 319-827-1211 827-3154
TF: 800-338-3021 ■ *Web:* www.cecgas.com

Consumers Petroleum of Ct
204 Spring Hill Rd Trumbull CT 06611 203-261-3123
Web: www.cameca.com

Crestwood Energy Partners LP
700 Louisiana St Ste 2550 Houston TX 77002 832-519-2200
Web: www.crestwoodlp.com

Crossamerica Partners LP
515 Hamilton St Ste 200 Allentown PA 18101 610-625-8000
Web: www.crossamericapartners.com

Crossroads Fuel Service Inc
1441 Fentress Rd Chesapeake VA 23322 757-482-2179 482-7849
Web: www.crossroadsfuel.com

CRS Reprocessing LLC
13551 Triton Park Blvd One Triton Office Park
Ste 1200 Louisville KY 40223 502-778-3600
Web: www.crs-reprocessing.com

Crystal Flash Limited Partnership
1754 Alpine Ave NW Grand Rapids MI 49504 616-363-4851
Web: www.crystalflash.com

Davison Fuels Inc 8450 Tanner Williams Rd Mobile AL 36608 251-633-4444
Web: www.davisonoil.com

Dickey Transport 401 E Fourth St Packwood IA 52580 319-695-3601
TF: 800-247-1081 ■ *Web:* dickeytransport.com

Dion & Sons Inc 1543 W 16th St Long Beach CA 90813 562-432-3946
Web: www.dionandsons.com

District Petroleum Products Inc
1814 River Rd Ste 100 Huron OH 44839 419-433-8373 433-9646
Web: hymiler.com

Dominion Aviation Services Inc
7511 Airfield Dr Richmond VA 23237 804-271-7793
TF: 800-366-7793 ■ *Web:* dominionaviation.com

Doss Aviation Inc 3670 Rebecca Ln Colorado Springs CO 80917 719-570-9804
TF: 888-803-4415 ■ *Web:* www.dossaviation.com

Drake Petroleum Co Inc
221 Quinebaug Rd North Grosvenordale CT 06255 800-243-6366
TF: 800-243-6366 ■ *Web:* www.drakepetro.com

Duncan Oil Company Inc 849 Factory Rd Beavercreek OH 45434 937-426-5945
Web: www.duncan-oil.com

Dutch Oil Company Inc 730 Alabama St Columbus MS 39702 662-327-5202
Web: www.dutchoil-victory.com

Earhart Petroleum Inc 1494 Lytle Rd Troy OH 45373 937-335-2928
TF: 800-686-2928 ■ *Web:* www.earhartpetroleum.com

East River Energy Inc 401 Soundview Rd Guilford CT 06437 203-453-1200
Web: www.eastriverenergy.com

Eastern Oil Co 590 S Paddock St Pontiac MI 48341 248-333-1333
Web: www.easternoil.com

EEL River Fuels Inc 3371 N State St Ukiah CA 95482 707-462-5554
Web: www.erenergy.com

Englefield Oil Co 447 James Pkwy Heath OH 43056 740-928-8215 928-1531
TF Cust Svc: 800-837-4458 ■ *Web:* www.englefieldoil.com

Evans Oil Company LLC 8450 Millhaven Rd Monroe LA 71203 318-345-1502

Falcon Fuels Inc 7300 Alondra Blvd Ste 204 Paramount CA 90723 562-272-4226
Web: www.falconfuelsinc.com

Fannon Petroleum Services Inc
7755 Progress Ct Gainesville VA 20155 703-468-2060 754-2590
Web: www.fannonpetroleum.com

Farm & Home Oil Co 3115 State Rd Telford PA 18969 800-776-7263
TF: 800-776-7263 ■ *Web:* www.suburbanpropane.com

Farmers Ranchers Coop 224 S Main St Ainsworth NE 69210 402-387-2811
Web: www.farmersrancherscoop.com

Fauser Energy Resources 106 Center St Elgin IA 52141 563-426-5811
Web: www.fauserenergy.com

Federated Co-ops Inc 502 S Second St Princeton MN 55371 763-389-2582
TF: 800-638-8228 ■ *Web:* www.federatedcoops.com

				Phone	Fax
Flash Market Inc 105 West Harrison St. *Web:* flashmarketinc.com	West Memphis	AR	72301	870-732-2242	
Fleet Card Fuels Inc 4200 Buck Owens Blvd *Web:* fleetcardfuels.com	Bakersfield	CA	93380	661-321-9961	321-9125
Fleetwing Corp 742 S Combee Rd *Web:* www.fleetwingoil.com	Lakeland	FL	33801	863-665-7557	
Flint Hills Resources LP 4111 E 37th St N *Web:* www.fhr.com	Wichita	KS	67220	316-828-3477	828-4228
Foster Blue Water Oil LLC 36065 Water St. *Web:* www.fosteroil.com	Richmond	MI	48062	586-727-3996	
Foster Fuels Inc 16720 Brookneal Hwy *Web:* www.fosterfuels.com	Brookneal	VA	24528	434-376-2322	
Fraley & Company Inc 6723 Hwy 160-491	Cortez	CO	81321	970-565-8538	565-8743
Fred Garrison Oil Co 1107 Walter Griffin St PO Box 100 *Web:* www.allstarfuel.com	Plainview	TX	79073	806-296-6353	
Fronk Oil Co Inc 900 E Industrial Ave *Web:* www.fronkoil.com	Booker	TX	79005	806-658-4565	
Fuel Masters LLC 1049 N 3rd St Ste 200 *Web:* www.fuelmasters.com	Abilene	TX	79601	325-676-3835	
G & G Oil Company of Indiana Inc 220 E Centennial Ave *Web:* www.ggoil.com	Muncie	IN	47303	765-288-7795	
Galen e Wilson Petroleum Co 3057 Davenport Ave *Web:* gewilsonpetroleum.com	Saginaw	MI	48602	989-793-2181	
Gassco 7515 Lindsay Rd. *TF:* 800-390-7837 ■ *Web:* gasscoinc.com	Bakersfield	CA	93313	661-832-7406	832-9795
Gate Petroleum Co 9540 San Jose Blvd PO Box 23627 *TF:* 866-571-1982 ■ *Web:* www.gatepetro.com	Jacksonville	FL	32241	904-737-7220	732-7660
Geer Tank Trucks Inc 1136 S Main St.	Jacksboro	TX	76458	940-567-2677	
General Petroleum Inc 7404 Disalle Blvd *Web:* www.genpet.com	Fort Wayne	IN	46825	260-489-8504	
George E Warren Corp 3001 Ocean Dr Ste 203 *Web:* www.gewarren.com	Vero Beach	FL	32963	772-778-7100	778-7171
Giant Oil Inc 1806 N Franklin St *Web:* www.giantoil.com	Tampa	FL	33602	813-740-0422	
Glacial Lakes Energy LLC 301 20th Ave SE PO Box 933 *TF:* 866-934-2676 ■ *Web:* www.glaciallakesenergy.com	Watertown	SD	57201	605-882-8480	
Global Partners LP 800 S St Ste 200 *NYSE: GLP* ■ *TF:* 800-685-7222 ■ *Web:* www.globalp.com	Waltham	MA	02454	781-894-8800	
Goetz Energy Corp 344 Vulcan St. *Web:* www.goetzenergy.com	Buffalo	NY	14207	716-876-4324	
Graham C- Stores Co 33978 N US Hwy 45. *Web:* www.grahamcstores.com	Grayslake	IL	60030	847-726-8188	
Great Plains Ethanol LLC 27716-462nd Ave. *Web:* www.poetenergy.com	Chancellor	SD	57015	605-647-0040	
Gulf Oil LP 100 Crossing Blvd	Framingham	MA	01702	508-270-8300	
Gull Industries 3404 Fourth Ave S	Seattle	WA	98134	206-624-5900	
H.N. Funkhouser & Company Inc 2150 S Loudoun St. *Web:* www.hnfunkhouser.com	Winchester	VA	22601	540-662-9000	
H.R. Lewis Petroleum Co 1432 Cleveland St *Web:* www.lewispetroleum.com	Jacksonville	FL	32209	904-356-0731	
Hagan Kennington Oil 9250 S Carolina 9	Nichols	SC	29581	843-392-1300	
HALCO Industries LLC 1015 Norcross Industrial Ct *Web:* www.halcolubricants.com	Norcross	GA	30071	770-840-3480	
Halron Lubricants Inc 1618 State St *Web:* www.halron.com	Green Bay	WI	54304	920-436-4000	
Harnois Groupe Petrolier Inc 80 Rt 158. *Web:* www.harnoisgroupepetrolier.com	Saint Thomas	QC	J0K3L0	450-759-7979	
Hasco Oil Company Inc 2800 Temple Ave. *TF:* 800-456-8491 ■ *Web:* www.hascooil.com	Long Beach	CA	90806	562-595-8491	
Hawaii Petroleum Inc 16 Railroad Ave Ste 202 *Web:* www.hawaiipetroleum.com	Hilo	HI	96720	808-969-1405	
Heartland Petroleum LLC 4001 E Fifth Ave. *TF:* 800-889-7831 ■ *Web:* www.heartland-petroleum.com	Columbus	OH	43219	614-441-4001	
Herdrich Petroleum 210 E US 52. *Web:* herdrich.com	Rushville	IN	46173	765-932-3224	932-4622
Heritage Petroleum LLC 516 N Seventh Ave *Web:* www.heritageoil.com	Evansville	IN	47719	812-422-3251	
Highlands Fuel Delivery LLC 190 Commerce Way *Web:* www.irvingenergy.com	Portsmouth	NH	03801	603-559-8759	
Hightowers Petroleum Co 3577 Commerce Dr. *Web:* hpc1952.businesscatalyst.com	Franklin	OH	45005	513-423-4272	
Hill City Oil Company Inc 1409 Dunn St. *Web:* www.hillcityoil.com	Houma	LA	70360	985-851-4000	
Hocon Gas of Guilford LLC 736 Boston Post Rd *Web:* www.hocongas.com	Guilford	CT	06437	203-458-2790	
Holiday Oil Co 3115 West 2100 South. *Web:* www.holidayoil.com	West Valley City	UT	84119	801-973-7002	
Inlet Petroleum Co 459 W Bluff Dr. *Web:* inletpetroleum.com	Anchorage	AK	99501	907-274-3835	
Inter City Oil Company Inc (ICO) 1921 S St. *Web:* www.icofuel.com	Duluth	MN	55812	218-728-3641	
Intercontinental Fuels 17617 Aldine Westfield Rd	Houston	TX	77073	281-821-2225	821-8225
Isgett Distributors Inc 51 Highland Ctr Blvd *Web:* www.isgettdistributors.com	Asheville	NC	28806	828-667-9846	
Isobunkers LLC 5353 E Princess Anne Rd Ste F *Web:* www.isoindustries.com	Norfolk	VA	23502	757-855-0900	855-6200
Jat Oil Inc 600 W Main St. *Web:* www.jatoil.com	Chattanooga	TN	37402	423-629-6611	
Jenkins Oil Company Inc 1100 W Industrial Rd *Web:* www.jenkins-oil.com	Cedar City	UT	84720	435-586-6931	
Jerry Brown Company Inc, The 2690 Prairie Rd *Web:* www.jbco.com	Eugene	OR	97402	541-688-8211	
JH Williams Oil Company Inc 1237 E Twiggs St *Web:* www.jhwoil.com	Tampa	FL	33602	813-228-7776	224-9413
JJ Powell Inc 109 W Presqueisle St *Web:* www.jjpowell.com	Philipsburg	PA	16866	814-342-3190	
John W Stone Oil Distributor LLC 87 First St. *Web:* www.stoneoil.com	Gretna	LA	70053	504-366-3401	
Johnson Oil Co (JOC) 1113 E Sara DeWitt Dr *TF:* 800-284-2432 ■ *Web:* www.johnsonoilcompany.com	Gonzales	TX	78629	800-284-2432	
JP Energy Partners LP 600 Las Colinas Blvd E Ste 2000 *Web:* www.jpenergypartners.com	Irving	TX	75039	972-444-0300	
Keller Equipment Supply Ltd 1228 26 Ave Se *Web:* www.keller.ca	Calgary	AB	T2G5S2	403-243-8666	
Kern Oil & Refining Co 7724 E Panama Ln *Web:* www.kernoil.com	Bakersfield	CA	93307	661-845-0761	
Kildair Service Ltee 92 Delangis Rd *Web:* www.kildair.com	St-paul De Joliette	QC	J0K3E0	450-756-8091	
Kimbro Oil Company Inc 2200 Clifton Ave *Web:* www.kimbrooil.com	Nashville	TN	37203	615-320-7484	
King Fuels Inc 14825 Willis St *Web:* www.king fuels.com	Houston	TX	77039	281-449-9975	
L. G. Jordan Oil Company Inc 314 N Hughes St. *Web:* www.lgjordanoil.com	Apex	NC	27502	919-362-8388	
Laguna Development Corp Interstate 40 W Exit 140 14500 Central Ave SW *Web:* www.lagunadevcorp.com	Albuquerque	NM	87121	505-352-7866	
Lakeside Oil Company Inc 555 W Brown Deer Rd Ste 200 *Web:* lakesideoil.com	Milwaukee	WI	53217	414-540-4000	540-4100
Lane Supply Inc 120 Fairview *Web:* www.lanesupplyinc.com	Arlington	TX	76010	817-261-9116	275-1660
Lank Oil Co 420 W McNab Rd *Web:* lankoil.com	Ft. Lauderdale	FL	33309	954-979-4070	
Lanman Oil Co Inc PO Box 108. *TF:* 800-677-2819 ■ *Web:* www.lanmanoil.com	Charleston	IL	61920	800-677-2819	
Lard Oil Company Inc 914 Florida Blvd SW. *TF:* 800-738-7738 ■ *Web:* www.lardoil.com	Denham Springs	LA	70726	225-664-3311	
Leffler Energy Inc 15 Mt Joy St *TF:* 800-984-1411 ■ *Web:* www.lefflerenergy.com	Mount Joy	PA	17552	800-984-1411	
Licking Valley Oil Inc PO Box 246. *TF:* 800-899-9449 ■ *Web:* www.lvoinc.com	Butler	KY	41006	859-472-7111	472-7112
Littlefield Oil Co 3403 Cavanaugh Rd. *Web:* www.littlefieldcompanies.com	Fort Smith	AR	72908	479-646-0595	
LQM Petroleum Services Inc 80 Broadway *Web:* www.lqm.com	Cresskill	NJ	07626	201-871-9010	
Lyden Oil Company Inc 30692 Tracy Rd. *Web:* www.lydenoilcompany.com	Walbridge	OH	43465	419-666-1948	
MacEwen Petroleum Inc 18 Adelaide St PO Box 100. *Web:* www.macewen.ca	Maxville	ON	K0C1T0	613-527-2100	
Main-Care Energy PO Box 11029. **Fax Area Code: 518* ■ *TF:* 800-542-5552 ■ *Web:* www.maincareenergy.com	Albany	NY	12211	800-542-5552	438-5991*
Maritime Energy Inc 234 Pk St PO Box 485 *TF:* 800-333-4489 ■ *Web:* www.maritimeenergy.com	Rockland	ME	04841	207-594-4487	
Martin Eagle Oil Company Inc 2700 James St. *TF:* 800-316-6148 ■ *Web:* www.martineagle.com	Denton	TX	76205	940-383-2351	
Martin Midstream Partners LP 4200 Stone Rd *NASDAQ: MMLP* ■ *TF:* 800-256-6644 ■ *Web:* martinmidstream.com	Kilgore	TX	75662	903-983-6200	983-6215
Maxum Petroleum Inc 20 Horseneck Ln. *Web:* www.maxumpetroleum.com	Greenwich	CT	06830	203-861-1200	
Mc Glaughlin Oil Co, The 3750 E Livingston Ave *Web:* www.mcglaughlinoil.com	Columbus	OH	43227	614-231-2518	
McCall Oil & Chemical Corp 5480 NW Front Ave *TF:* 800-622-2558 ■ *Web:* www.mccalloil.com	Portland	OR	97210	503-221-6400	
McClure Oil Corp Junction of Hwys 35 and 37 PO Box 1750 *Web:* in.mcclureoil.net	Marion	IN	46952	765-674-9771	
McNeece Brothers Oil Company Inc 691 E Heil Ave *TF:* 877-782-6543 ■ *Web:* www.mcneecebros.com	El Centro	CA	92243	760-352-4721	
Merle Boes Inc 11372 E Lakewood Blvd. *Web:* www.merleboes.com	Holland	MI	49424	616-392-7036	
Metalloid Southwest 1829 Norman Dr *Web:* metalloidcorp.com	Jacksonville	TX	75766	903-589-3933	
MG Oil Inc 1002 W Main St. *Web:* www.mgoil.com	Rapid City	SD	57701	605-342-0527	
Mid South Sales Inc 243 County Rd 414 *Web:* midsouthsales.com/index.php	Jonesboro	AR	72404	870-933-6457	933-0446
Mid-Atlantic Petroleum Properties LLC (MAPP) 12311 Middlebrook Rd.	Germantown	MD	20874	301-972-4116	972-3137
Miller Oil Co 1000 E City Hall Ave. *Web:* www.milleroil.com	Norfolk	VA	23504	757-695-3143	625-0528
Miller Oil Company Inc 4504 Bells Ln *Web:* www.mocgas.com	Louisville	KY	40211	502-772-1722	
Mitsubishi International Corp 655 Third Ave *Web:* www.mitsubishicorp.com	New York	NY	10017	212-605-2000	
Monroe Energy LLC 4101 Post Rd Trainer *Web:* www.monroe-energy.com	Trainer	PA	19061	610-364-8000	
Morgan Distributing Inc 3425 N 22nd St *Web:* www.mdilubes.com	Decatur	IL	62526	217-877-3570	
Mountain Empire Oil Co 282 Christian Church Rd *Web:* www.roadrunnermarkets.com	Johnson City	TN	37616	423-928-7241	

Company	City	State	ZIP	Phone	Fax
Mutual Oil Inc 863 Crescent St PO Box 250 *Web:* www.mutualoil.com	Brockton	MA	02303	508-583-5777	
MW Sewall & Co 259 Front St	Bath	ME	04530	207-442-7994	
National Oil & Gas Inc 409 N Main St *TF:* 800-322-8454 ■ *Web:* natloil.com	Bluffton	IN	46714	260-824-2220	824-2223
Newport Capital Group LLC 12 Broad St 5th Fl *Web:* www.newportcapitalgroup.com	Red Bank	NJ	07701	732-741-8400	
Nisbet Oil Co PO Box 35367 *Web:* www.nisbetoil.com	Charlotte	NC	28235	704-332-7755	377-1607
NOCO Energy Corp 2440 Sheridan Dr *TF:* 800-500-6626 ■ *Web:* www.noco.com	Tonawanda	NY	14150	716-833-6626	832-1312
Northwest Fuel Systems Inc 115 Industry Ct *Web:* nwestco.com	Kalispell	MT	59901	406-755-4343	
Nuvera Fuel Cells 129 Concord Rd Bldg 1 *Web:* www.nuvera.com	Billerica	MA	01821	617-245-7500	245-7511
Ocean Petroleum LLC 7167 Worcester Hwy Ste *Web:* www.oceanpetroleum.com	Newark	MD	21841	410-632-0400	
Offen Petroleum Inc 5100 E 78th Ave *TF:* 866-657-3835 ■ *Web:* www.offenpet.com	Commerce	CO	80022	303-297-3835	
Oilmen's Equipment Corp 140 Cedar Springs Rd *Web:* www.oilmens.com	Spartanburg	SC	29302	864-573-9311	
On Site Gas Systems Inc 35 Budney Rd Budney Industrial Park *Web:* www.onsitegas.com	Newington	CT	06111	860-667-8888	
Orange Line Oil Company Inc 404 E Commercial St *TF:* 800-492-6864 ■ *Web:* www.orangelineoil.com	Pomona	CA	91767	909-623-0533	
Oscar W Larson Co 10100 Dixie Hwy *Web:* www.larsonco.com	Clarkston	MI	48348	248-620-0070	
Palmdale Oil Company Inc 911 N 2nd St *Web:* www.palmdaleoil.com	Fort Pierce	FL	34950	772-461-2300	
Panef Inc 5700 W Douglas Ave *Web:* www.panef.com	Milwaukee	WI	53218	414-464-7200	
Papco Inc 4920 Southern Blvd *Web:* www.papco.com	Virginia Beach	VA	23462	757-499-5977	
Parent Petroleum Inc 37 W 370 Rt 38 *Web:* www.parentpetroleum.com	Saint Charles	IL	60175	630-584-2505	
Parker Oil Company Inc PO Box 120 *Web:* www.parkeroilcompany.com	South Hill	VA	23970	434-447-3146	447-2646
Parker Oil Products Inc 508 California Parker *Web:* www.parkeroilproducts.com	Parker	AZ	85344	928-669-2617	
Patten Energy Enterprises Inc 3437 S Main St *Web:* pattenenergy.com	Los Angeles	CA	90007	323-235-3500	
Peerless Distributing Co 21700 NW Hwy Ste 1160	Southfield	MI	48075	248-559-1800	559-1861
Petro Lock Inc 45315 N Trevor Ave *Web:* petrolock.com	Lancaster	CA	93534	661-948-6044	948-9524
Petro Service Inc 1880 State Rt 35 2nd Fl *Web:* www.petroserviceinc.com	South Amboy	NJ	08879	732-721-8000	
PetroCard Systems Inc 730 Central Ave S *Web:* www.petrocard.com	Kent	WA	98032	253-852-2777	
Petroleum Traders Corp 7120 Pointe Inverness Way *Web:* www.petroleumtraders.com	Fort Wayne	IN	46804	260-432-6622	
Petroleum Wholesale LP 8550 Technology Forest Pl *Web:* petroleumwholesale.com	The Woodlands	TX	77381	281-681-1000	
PetroLiance LLC 739 N State St **Fax Area Code:* 847 ■ *TF:* 800-628-7231 ■ *Web:* www.petroliance.com	Elgin	IL	60123	877-738-7699	741-2590*
Petrosouth Inc 234 N Hill St *Web:* www.petrosouth.com	Griffin	GA	30224	770-227-8804	
Pfau Industrial Animal Oils 800 Wall St *Web:* pfauoil.com	Jeffersonville	IN	47130	812-283-6697	
Pioneer Oil LLC 1728 Lampman Dr Ste A *Web:* www.pioneeroil-co.com	Billings	MT	59102	406-254-7071	254-2560
Port Consolidated Inc 3141 SE 14th Ave *Web:* www.portconsolidated.com	Fort Lauderdale	FL	33316	954-522-1182	
Pro Petroleum Inc 4985 N Sloan Ln *TF:* 877-791-4900 ■ *Web:* www.propetroleum.com	Las Vegas	NV	89115	877-791-4900	
Pugh Oil Company Inc 701 McDowell Rd PO Box 4006 *Web:* www.pughoil.com	Asheboro	NC	27203	336-629-2061	
Pure Energy Corp 61 S Paramus Rd *Web:* www.pure-energy.com	Paramus	NJ	07652	201-843-8100	
Quality Petroleum Inc 11610 Maybelline Dr *Web:* www.qualitypetroleuminc.com	North Little Rock	AR	72117	501-955-2166	
R K Allen Oil Inc 36002 AL Hwy 21 *TF:* 800-445-5823 ■ *Web:* www.rkallenoil.com	Talladega	AL	35161	256-362-4261	362-6792
R Kidd Fuels Corp 1172 Twinney Dr *TF:* 866-274-2315 ■ *Web:* www.kiddfuels.com	Newmarket	ON	L3Y9E2	866-274-2315	
R L Vallee Inc 280 S Main St *Web:* www.rlvallee.com	Saint Albans	VT	05478	802-524-8710	
R W Hays Co Inc 1890 S Pacific Hwy *Web:* www.haysoil.com	Medford	OR	97501	541-772-2053	
Ramos Oil Company Inc 1515 S River Rd *TF Cust Svc:* 800-477-7266 ■ *Web:* www.ramosoil.com	West Sacramento	CA	95691	916-371-2570	371-0635
RE Carroll Inc 1570 N Olden Ave *Web:* www.recarroll.com	Trenton	NJ	08638	609-695-6211	
Red Triangle Oil Co 2809 S Chestnut Ave *Web:* redtrianglepropane.com	Fresno	CA	93725	559-485-4320	
Reeder Distributors Inc 5450 Wilbarger St *TF:* 800-722-3103 ■ *Web:* www.reederdistributors.com	Fort Worth	TX	76119	817-429-5957	429-9052
Renkert Oil Inc 3817 Main St PO Box 246 *Web:* www.renkertoil.com	Morgantown	PA	19543	610-286-8012	
Rentech Inc 10877 Wilshire Blvd 10th Fl *NASDAQ:* RTK ■ *Web:* www.rentechinc.com	Los Angeles	CA	90024	310-571-9800	571-9799
Retif Oil & Fuel Inc 527 Destrehan Ave *TF:* 800-349-9000 ■ *Web:* www.retif.com	Harvey	LA	70058	504-349-9000	
Rex Oil Co Inc 814 & 1000 Lexington Ave **Fax Area Code:* 800 ■ *TF:* 800-843-0572 ■ *Web:* www.rexoil.com	Thomasville	NC	27360	336-472-3368	843-0572*
Rhinehart Oil Company Inc 585 E State Rd *TF:* 801-756-5233 ■ *Web:* www.rhinehartoil.com	American Fork	UT	84003	801-756-9681	
Rinehart Oil Inc 2401 N State St *Web:* www.rinehartoil.com	Ukiah	CA	95482	707-462-8811	
Risser Oil Corp 2865 Executive Dr *Web:* www.therissercompanies.com	Clearwater	FL	33762	727-573-4000	572-9075
Rite Way Oil & Gas Company Inc PO Box 27049 **Fax Area Code:* 800	Omaha	NE	68127	402-331-6400	279-6401*
RKA Petroleum Companies Inc 28340 Wick Rd *Web:* www.rkapetroleum.com	Romulus	MI	48174	734-946-2199	
Robert V. Jensen Inc 4029 S Maple Ave *Web:* www.rvjensen.com	Fresno	CA	93725	559-485-8210	
Running Foxes Petroleum Inc 6855 S Havana St Ste 400 *Web:* www.runningfoxes.com	Centennial	CO	80112	303-617-7242	
S.A. White Oil Company Inc 590 Atlanta St SE *Web:* www.sawhite.com	Marietta	GA	30060	770-427-1387	
San Luis Butane Distributors Inc PO Box 3068 *Web:* www.deltaliquidenergy.com	Paso Robles	CA	93447	805-239-0616	239-2607
Sapp Bros. Petroleum Inc 9915 S 148th St *Web:* www.sappbros.net	Omaha	NE	68138	402-895-2202	
Saracen Energy Partners LP 3033 W Alabama *Web:* www.saracenenergy.com	Houston	TX	77098	713-285-2900	
Seay Oil Company Inc 700 West 15th St *Web:* www.seayoil.com	Hopkinsville	KY	42240	270-885-5488	
Senergy Petroleum LLC 622 S 56th Ave *TF:* 800-964-0076 ■ *Web:* www.brownevans.com	Phoenix	AZ	85043	602-272-6795	
Shoco Oil Inc 5135 E 74th Ave *Web:* www.shocooil.com	Commerce	CO	80037	303-289-1677	
Sierra Energy 1020 Winding Creek Rd Ste 100 *TF:* 800-576-2264 ■ *Web:* www.sierraenergy.net	Roseville	CA	95678	916-218-1600	
Silco Oil Company Inc 181 E 56th Ave Ste 600	Denver	CO	80216	303-292-0500	293-8069
Silvas Oil Company Inc 3217 E Lorena Ave *Web:* www.silvasoil.com	Fresno	CA	93725	559-233-5171	
SNC-Lavalin Constructors Inc 19015 N Creek Pkwy Ste 300 *Web:* www.slthermal.com	Bothell	WA	98011	425-489-8000	
SoCo Group Inc, The 5962 Priestly Dr *Web:* www.thesocogroup.com	Carlsbad	CA	92008	760-804-8460	
South Central Oil Company Inc 2121 W Main St *Web:* www.southcentraloil.com	Albemarle	NC	28001	704-982-2173	982-6434
Southern Maryland Oil Co Inc (SMO) 109 N Maple Ave **Fax Area Code:* 301 ■ **Fax:* Cust Svc ■ *TF:* 888-222-3720 ■ *Web:* www.smoenergy.com	La Plata	MD	20646	888-222-3720	932-3718*
Spencer Cos Inc 120 Woodson St *TF:* 800-633-2910 ■ *Web:* www.spencercos.com	Huntsville	AL	35801	256-533-1150	535-2910
Sprague Energy 185 International Dr Ste 200 **Fax:* Hum Res ■ *TF:* 800-225-1560 ■ *Web:* www.spragueenergy.com	Portsmouth	NH	03801	603-431-1000	430-5320*
Stern Oil Company Inc PO Box 218 *TF:* 800-477-2744 ■ *Web:* www.sternoil.com	Freeman	SD	57029	605-925-7999	925-4367
Sturdy Oil Company Inc 1511 Abbott St *Web:* www.sturdyoil.com	Salinas	CA	93901	831-422-8801	
Sun Coast Resources Inc 6405 Cavalcade St Bldg 1 *TF:* 800-677-3835 ■ *Web:* www.suncoastresources.com	Houston	TX	77028	713-844-9600	
Sundays Energy Inc 2637 27th Ave S *Web:* www.sundaysenergy.com	Minneapolis	MN	55406	612-605-1788	
Super-Lube Inc 1311 N Paul Russell Rd *Web:* www.superlube.com	Tallahassee	FL	32301	850-222-5823	
Tauber Oil Co 55 Waugh Dr # 700 *Web:* www.tauberoil.com	Houston	TX	77007	713-869-8700	869-8069
Taylor Enterprises Inc (TEI) 2586 Southport Rd *TF:* 800-922-3149 ■ *Web:* taylorlubricants.com	Spartanburg	SC	29302	864-573-9518	583-4150
Taylor Oil Company Inc 77 Second St 77 Second St *Web:* www.tayloroilco.com	Somerville	NJ	08876	908-725-7737	
Technical Gas Products Inc 66 Leonardo Dr *TF:* 800-847-0745 ■ *Web:* www.tgpoxygen.com	North Haven	CT	06473	800-847-0745	
Tesoro Corp 1225 17th St *TF:* 800-299-0570 ■ *Web:* www.tsocorp.com	Denver	CO	80202	800-299-0570	
Tetco Inc 1100 NE Loop 410 Ste 900 *Web:* www.tetco.com	San Antonio	TX	78209	210-821-5900	826-3003
Tex Con Oil Co 1701 Grand Ave Pkwy *Web:* www.texconoil.com	Pflugerville	TX	78660	512-670-7401	
Texas Enterprises Inc 5005 E Seventh St *TF:* 800-545-4412 ■ *Web:* www.alliedsalesco.com	Austin	TX	78702	512-385-2167	
Texor Petroleum Company Inc 3340 S Harlem Ave *Web:* www.texor.com	Riverside	IL	60546	708-447-1999	
Time Oil Co 2737 W Commodore Way	Seattle	WA	98199	206-285-2400	286-4479
Titan Laboratories 1380 Zuni St PO Box 40567 *TF:* 800-848-4826 ■ *Web:* www.titanlab.com	Denver	CO	80204	800-848-4826	
Total Airport Services Inc 6501 W. Imperial Hwy Ste 230 *Web:* www.totalairportservices.com	Los Angeles	CA	90045	805-522-3565	
Tower Oil & Technology Co 4300 S Tripp Ave *Web:* www.toweroil.com	Chicago	IL	60632	773-927-6161	
Transglobal Gas & Oil Co 10904A Mcbride Ln	Knoxville	TN	37932	865-777-2162	
Trego Dugan Aviation Inc Lee Bird Fld *Web:* www.trego-dugan.com	North Platte	NE	69101	308-532-5864	

Company / Address	City	State	Zip	Phone	Fax
Tri-Con Inc 7076 W Port Arthur Rd PO Box 20555 — *Web:* www.triconinc.org	Beaumont	TX	77705	409-835-2237	
Tropic Oil Company Inc 10002 NW 89th Ave — *TF:* 866-645-3835 ■ *Web:* www.tropicoil.com	Miami	FL	33178	305-888-4611	
Truman Arnold Cos 701 S Robison Rd — **Fax Area Code:* 806 ■ *Web:* www.tacair.com	Texarkana	TX	75501	903-794-3835	335-2612*
Tucker Oil Company Inc 910 Industrial Dr — *Web:* www.tuckeroilcompany.com	Slaton	TX	79364	806-828-6277	
Tulco Oils Inc 5240 E Pine — *TF:* 800-375-2347 ■ *Web:* www.tulco.com	Tulsa	OK	74115	918-838-3354	834-1263
Turner Gas Company Inc PO Box 26554 — *TF:* 800-932-4277 ■ *Web:* www.turnergas.com	Salt Lake City	UT	84126	801-973-6886	973-6882
Tyree Oil Inc 1355 W First Ave — *Web:* www.tyreeoil.com	Eugene	OR	97402	541-687-0076	
Ullman Oil Inc PO Box 23399 — *TF:* 800-543-5195 ■ *Web:* www.ullmanoil.com	Chagrin Falls	OH	44023	440-543-5195	543-6549
Union Distributing Company of Tucson 4000 E Michigan St — *Web:* www.uniondistributing.connekt2.com	Tucson	AZ	85714	520-571-7600	
United Petroleum Co 8040 NE Sandy Blvd Ste 300 — *Web:* www.unitedpetroleum.com	Portland	OR	97213	503-287-4000	
US Oil Co Inc 425 Better Way — **Fax:* Acctg ■ *Web:* www.usventure.com	Appleton	WI	54915	920-739-6101	788-0531*
Valor Oil 1200 Alsop Ln — **Fax Area Code:* 270 ■ *TF:* 800-544-5823 ■ *Web:* www.valoroil.com	Owensboro	KY	42303	844-468-2567	684-6654*
Van Manen Petroleum Group 0-305 Lk Michigan Dr NW — *Web:* www.vanmanen.com	Grand Rapids	MI	49534	616-453-6344	
Varouh Oil Inc 970 Griswold Rd — *TF:* 866-482-7684 ■ *Web:* www.varouhoil.com	Elyria	OH	44035	440-324-5025	
Venture Fuels LLC 3819 Creekside St — *Web:* venturefuels.com	Holman	WI	54636	608-783-9516	
Vesco Oil Corp 16055 W 12-Mile Rd — **Fax Area Code:* 248 ■ *TF:* 800-527-5358 ■ *Web:* www.vesco-oil.com	Southfield	MI	48076	800-527-5358	557-2236*
Veterans Oil Delivery 2070 Hwy 150 — *Web:* www.veteransoilinc.com	Bessemer	AL	35022	205-424-4400	424-4448
Waguespack Oil Company Inc 1818 HWY 3185 PO Box 326 — *Web:* www.wagoil.com	Thibodaux	LA	70302	985-447-3668	447-5730
Walthall Oil Company Inc 2510 Allen Rd — *TF:* 800-633-5685 ■ *Web:* www.walthall-oil.com	Macon	GA	31216	478-781-1234	
Warex Terminals Corp 1 S Water St PO Box 488 — *TF:* 800-724-0818 ■ *Web:* www.warex-terminals.com	Newburgh	NY	12550	845-561-4000	
Waring Oil Company LLC 431 Port Terminal Cir — *Web:* www.waringoil.com	Vicksburg	MS	39183	601-636-1065	
Warren Oil Company Inc PO Box 1507 — *TF:* 800-779-6456 ■ *Web:* www.warrenoil.com	Dunn	NC	28335	910-892-6456	892-4245
Wesson Inc PO Box 2127 — *Web:* www.wessonenergy.com	Waterbury	CT	06722	203-756-7041	754-6664
West Penn Oil Company Inc 2305 Market St — *Web:* www.westpenn.com	Warren	PA	16365	814-723-9000	
Western Marketing Inc 1010 S Access Rd — *Web:* www.westmktg.com	Tye	TX	79563	325-692-4662	
Western Petroleum Co 9531 W 78th St — *TF:* 800-972-3835 ■ *Web:* www.westernpetro.com	Eden Prairie	MN	55344	952-941-9090	941-7470
Western States Petroleum Inc 450 S 15th Ave — *TF:* 800-220-1353 ■ *Web:* www.westernstatespetroleum.com	Phoenix	AZ	85007	602-252-4011	
Williams Oil Company Inc 44 Reuter Blvd — *Web:* www.williamsoil.com	Towanda	PA	18848	570-265-6673	
Willis Oil Company Inc 1403 N Expy Ste B — *Web:* www.mikam.com	Griffin	GA	30223	770-227-5724	
Windward Petroleum Inc 1064 Goffs Falls Rd — *Web:* www.ghberlinwindward.com	Manchester	NH	03103	603-222-2900	622-0834
Woodfin Co 8180 Mechanicsville Turnpike — *Web:* www.askwoodfin.com	Mechanicsville	VA	23111	804-730-5000	
Workman Oil Co 14680 Forest Rd	Forest	VA	24551	434-525-1615	
World Fuel Services Corp 9800 NW 41st St Ste 400 — *NYSE:* INT ■ *TF:* 800-345-3818 ■ *Web:* www.wfscorp.com	Miami	FL	33178	305-428-8000	392-5600
Yocum Oil Company Inc 2719 Stillwater Rd — *Web:* www.yocumoil.com	St. Paul	MN	55119	651-739-9141	
Yorkston Oil Company Inc 2801 Roeder Ave — *TF:* 800-401-2201 ■ *Web:* www.yorkstonoil.com	Bellingham	WA	98225	360-734-2201	

580 PETROLEUM REFINERIES

Company / Address	City	State	Zip	Phone	Fax
A H Belo Corp 508 Young St PO Box 224866 — *NYSE:* AHC ■ *TF:* 800-230-1074 ■ *Web:* www.ahbelo.com	Dallas	TX	75202	214-977-8200	977-8201
Allegheny Petroleum Products Co 999 Airbrake Ave — *TF:* 800-600-2900 ■ *Web:* www.oils.com	Wilmerding	PA	15148	412-829-1990	
Alon USA Energy Inc 7616 LBJ Fwy Ste 300 — *NYSE:* ALJ ■ *Web:* www.alonusa.com	Dallas	TX	75251	972-367-3600	367-3728
Alpha Oil Inc 490 Garyray Dr — *Web:* www.alphaoil.ca	Weston	ON	M9L1P8	416-745-6131	
Arco Products Co 4 Ctr Point Dr — *Web:* arco.com	Los Angeles	CA	90063	213-670-5136	
Balch Petroleum Contractors & Builders Inc 930 Ames Ave — *Web:* www.balchpetroleum.com	Milpitas	CA	95035	408-942-8686	
Beroth Oil Co 20 W 32nd St — *Web:* www.berothoil.com	Winston-Salem	NC	27105	336-757-7600	
BioProcess Algae LLC 45 High Point Ave — *Web:* www.bioprocessalgae.com	Portsmouth	RI	02871	401-683-5400	
BioUrja Trading LLC 1080 Eldridge Pkwy Ste 1175 — *Web:* www.biourja.com	Houston	TX	77077	832-775-9000	
Bootheel Petroleum Company Inc 623 N SR- 25 PO Box 187 — *Web:* www.bootheelpetroleum.com	Dexter	MO	63841	573-624-4160	
Boyer Petroleum Co 1817 Hull Ave — *Web:* www.boyerpetroleum.com	Des Moines	IA	50313	515-243-4450	
BP Pipelines (North America) Inc 150 W Warrenville Rd — *Web:* www.bp.com/en_us/bp-us/what-we-do/bp-pipelines.html	Naperville	IL	60563	630-536-2532	
BP PLC 28100 Torch Pkwy — *NYSE:* BP ■ *TF:* 800-333-3991 ■ *Web:* www.bp.com	Warrenville	IL	60555	800-333-3991	
Bradley Petroleum Inc 7268 S Tucson Way — *Web:* www.bradleygas.com	Centennial	CO	80112	303-792-3444	
Caballo Energy LLC 2007 E 15th St — *Web:* www.caballoenergy.com	Tulsa	OK	74104	918-794-8800	
Calcasieu Refining Co 4359 W Tank Farm Rd — *Web:* www.calcasieurefining.com	Lake Charles	LA	70605	337-478-2130	
Calumet Specialty Products Partners LP 2780 Waterfront Pkwy E Dr Ste 200 — *NASDAQ:* CLMT ■ *TF:* 800-437-3188 ■ *Web:* www.calumetspecialty.com	Indianapolis	IN	46214	317-328-5660	328-5668
Canwest Propane Ltd 1700 440 - Second Ave SW — *Web:* www.canwestpropane.com	Calgary	AB	T2P5E9	403-206-4100	
Chalmette Refining LLC 500 W Saint Bernard Hwy — *Web:* www.chalmetterefining.com	Chalmette	LA	70043	504-281-1212	
Chevron Canada Ltd 1200 - 1050 W Pender St — *TF:* 800-663-1650 ■ *Web:* www.chevron.ca	Vancouver	BC	V6E3T4	604-668-5300	
Chevron Corp 6001 Bollinger Canyon Rd — *NYSE:* CVX ■ *TF Cust Svc:* 800-368-8357 ■ *Web:* www.chevron.com	San Ramon	CA	94583	925-842-1000	
Chevron Global Marine Products LLC 1500 Louisiana 4th Fl — *Web:* www.chevronmarineproducts.com	Houston	TX	77002	914-285-7390	
CITGO Petroleum Corp 1293 Eldridge Pkwy — *TF:* 800-424-9300 ■ *Web:* www.citgo.com	Houston	TX	77077	832-486-4700	
Clean Fuels Ohio 530 W Spring St Ste 250 — *Web:* cleanfuelsohio.org	Columbus	OH	43215	614-884-7336	
Clipper Oil Co 2040 Harbor Island Dr Ste 203 — *Web:* www.clipperoil.com	San Diego	CA	92101	619-692-9701	
ConocoPhillips 600 N Dairy Ashford Rd — *NYSE:* COP ■ *Web:* www.conocophillips.com	Houston	TX	77079	281-293-1000	
Cross Oil Refining & Marketing Inc 484 E Sixth St — *TF:* 800-725-3066 ■ *Web:* www.crossoil.com	Smackover	AR	71762	870-881-8700	864-8656
Crown Central Petroleum Corp 1 N Charles St — *Web:* www.crowncentral.com	Baltimore	MD	21201	410-539-7400	
Custom Carbon Processing Inc 17310-106 Ave NW — *Web:* www.customcarbonprocessing.com	Edmonton	AB	T5S1H9	780-443-4237	
Delaware City Refining Company LLC 4550 Wrangle Hill Rd — *Web:* www.pbfenergy.com	Delaware City	DE	19720	302-834-6000	
Delek Refining Ltd 425 McMurrey Dr — *Web:* www.delekus.com	Tyler	TX	75702	903-579-3400	
East Kansas Agri-Energy LLC 1304 S Main — *Web:* www.ekaellc.com	Garnett	KS	66032	785-448-2888	
Edwards-Etherton Oil Company Inc 411 N Fair St — *Web:* www.edcospecialtyproducts.com	Marion	IL	62959	618-993-6935	
Elementa Group Inc 509 Glendale Ave E Ste 302	Niagara-on-the-lake	ON	L0S1J0	905-687-1900	
Elkton Gas Co 125 E High St — *Web:* www.elktongas.com	Elkton	MD	21921	410-398-4626	
Enjet Inc 5373 W Alabama Ste 502 — *Web:* www.enjet.com	Houston	TX	77056	713-552-1559	
Ergon Refining 2611 Haining Rd — *Web:* www.ergon.com	Vicksburg	MS	39183	601-933-3000	630-8311
Exxon Mobil Corp 5959 Las Colinas Blvd — *NYSE:* XOM ■ *TF:* 800-252-1800 ■ *Web:* www.exxonmobil.com	Irving	TX	75039	972-444-1000	444-1433
Farstad Oil Inc 100 NE 27th St — *Web:* www.farstadoil.com	Minot	ND	58703	701-852-1194	
Flint Hills Resources LP 4111 E 37th St N — *Web:* www.fhr.com	Wichita	KS	67220	316-828-3477	828-4228
General Utilities Inc 100 Fairchild Ave — *Web:* www.generalutilities.com	Plainview	NY	11803	516-414-2700	
Greenline Industries Inc 2425 Larkspur Landing Cir — *Web:* www.greenlineindustries.com	Larkspur	CA	94939	415-526-7600	
Guardian Energy LLC 4745 380th Ave — *Web:* www.guardiannrg.com	Janesville	MN	56048	507-234-5000	
Guardian Lima LLC 2485 Houx Pkwy — *Web:* www.guardianlima.com	Lima	OH	45804	567-940-9500	
Harbert Management Corp 2100 Third Ave N Ste 600 — *Web:* www.harbert.net	Birmingham	AL	35203	205-987-5500	
Harms Oil Co 337 22nd Ave S — *Web:* www.harmsoil.net	Brookings	SD	57006	605-696-5000	
Hart Petroleum 323 Skidmores Rd — *TF:* 800-796-3342 ■ *Web:* www.harthomecomfort.com	Deer Park	NY	11729	631-667-3200	
Haycock Petroleum Co 715 W Bonanza Rd — *Web:* www.haycockpetroleum.com	Las Vegas	NV	89106	702-382-1620	
Heritage Gas Ltd Park Pl 1 Brownlow Ave Ste 200 - 238 — *Web:* www.heritagegas.com	Dartmouth	NS	B3B1Y2	902-466-2003	
Hough Petroleum Corp 340 Fourth St — *Web:* houghpetroleum.com	Ewing	NJ	08638	609-771-1022	
Hunt Oil Co 1900 N Akard St — *Web:* www.huntoil.com	Dallas	TX	75201	214-978-8000	978-8888

Company	City	State	ZIP	Phone	Fax
Hunt Refining Co 100 Towncenter Blvd Ste 300 *Web:* www.huntrefining.com	Tuscaloosa	AL	35406	205-391-3300	752-6480
Hutchens Petroleum Corp 22 Performance Dr *Web:* www.hutchenspetro.com	Stuart	VA	24171	276-694-7000	
Hythane Company LLC 12420 N Dumont Way *Web:* www.hythane.com	Littleton	CO	80125	303-486-1705	
Imperial Oil Resources Ltd 237 Fourth Ave SW PO Box 2480 Stn M *TF:* 800-567-3776 ■ *Web:* www.imperialoil.ca	Calgary	AB	T2P3M9	800-567-3776	
INEOS Bio USA LLC 3030 Warrenville Rd Ste 650 *Web:* www.ineos.com	Lisle	IL	60532	630-857-7146	
Inspection Oilfield Services 2809 Youngsville Hwy 89 *Web:* www.iospci.com	Youngsville	LA	70592	337-856-9001	
Integro Earth Fuels Inc 6 Celtic Dr Ste A2 *Web:* www.integrofuels.com	Arden	NC	28704	828-651-8988	
International Group Inc 85 Old Eagle School Rd *TF:* 800-852-6537 ■ *Web:* www.igiwax.com	Wayne	PA	19087	610-687-9030	687-2792
Kinney Electrical Manufacturing Co 678 Buckeye St *Web:* www.kinneyelectric.com	Elgin	IL	60123	847-742-9600	
Laredo Energy LP 840 W Sam Houston Pkwy N Ste 400 *Web:* www.laredoenergy.com	Houston	TX	77024	713-600-6000	
Lipton Inc 458 S St *Web:* www.liptonenergy.com	Pittsfield	MA	01201	413-443-9191	
Marquis Energy LLC 11953 Prairie Industrial Pkwy *Web:* www.marquisgrain.com	Hennepin	IL	61327	815-925-7300	
Maxi Volt Corporation Inc 800 S Rusk St *Web:* www.maxivolt.com	Amarillo	TX	79106	806-371-0722	
Millsap Fuel Distributors Ltd 905 Ave P S *Web:* millsapfuels.ca	Saskatoon	SK	S7M2X3	306-244-7916	
Montana Refining Co 1900 Tenth St NE *Web:* calumetspecialty.com	Great Falls	MT	59404	317-328-5660	328-2359
Motiva Enterprises LLC 700 Milam St *TF:* 877-668-4825 ■ *Web:* www.motivaenterprises.com	Houston	TX	77002	713-277-8000	
Murphy Oil Corp 200 Peach St *TF:* 888-289-9314 ■ *Web:* www.murphyoilcorp.com	El Dorado	AR	71730	870-862-6411	875-7675
National Co-op Refinery Assn 2000 S Main St *Web:* www.ncrarefinery.com	McPherson	KS	67460	620-241-2340	
Neslo Petroleum Products Inc 950 King George Rd *Web:* www.neslopetroleum.com	Fords	NJ	08863	732-738-0700	
NextFuels LLC 86 Third St *Web:* www.nextfuels.com	Los Altos	CA	94022	650-490-4500	
Outrigger Energy LLC 1200 Seventeenth St Ste 900 *Web:* outriggerenergy.com	Denver	CO	80202	720-638-7312	
Paramount Petroleum Corp 14700 Downey Ave **Fax:* Hum Res ■ *Web:* www.ppcla.com	Paramount	CA	90723	562-531-2060	634-7057*
Placid Refining Company LLC 1940 Louisiana Hwy 1 N *Web:* www.placidrefining.com	Port Allen	LA	70767	225-387-0278	346-7403
Poet 4615 N Lewis Ave *Web:* poet.com	Sioux Falls	SD	57104	605-965-2200	
Poma Holding Company Inc 571 W Slover Ave *Web:* www.pomacos.com	Bloomington	CA	92316	909-877-2441	
Pri Mar Petroleum Inc 1207 Broad St *Web:* www.primarpetro.com	Saint Joseph	MI	49085	269-983-7314	
Proton PRC Ltd 4805 S Colony Blvd *Web:* www.protonprc.com	The Colony	TX	75056	972-931-8200	
Raincii 1330 Greengate Dr Ste 300 *Web:* www.raincii.com	Covington	LA	77339	281-318-2400	
RPMG Inc 1157 Vly Park Dr Ste 100 *Web:* www.rpmgllc.com	Shakopee	MN	55379	952-465-3220	
San Joaquin Refining Company Inc 3129 Standard St *Web:* www.sjr.com	Bakersfield	CA	93308	661-327-4257	327-3236
SEMCO ENERGY Gas Co 1411 Third St Ste A *TF:* 800-624-2019 ■ *Web:* www.semcoenergygas.com	Port Huron	MI	48060	800-624-2019	
Siluria Technologies Inc 409 Illinois St Ste 100 *Web:* siluria.com	San Francisco	CA	94158	415-978-2170	
Sinclair Oil Corp PO Box 30825 *Web:* www.sinclairoil.com	Salt Lake City	UT	84130	801-524-2700	524-2880
Source North America Corp 510 S Westgate *Web:* www.sourcena.com	Addison	IL	60101	847-364-9000	
Southland Oil Co 5170 Galaxie Dr *Web:* petroleum-oil-wholesalers.cmac.ws	Jackson	MS	39206	601-981-4151	
Star Tex Distributors Inc 12705 S Kirkwood Ste 218 *Web:* www.startexoil.com	Stafford	TX	77477	281-277-0077	
Star-Seal 6596 New Peachtree Rd *TF:* 800-779-6066 ■ *Web:* www.herculessealcoat.com	Atlanta	GA	30340	770-455-6551	
Sunoco Inc 1735 Market St Ste LL *NYSE:* SUN ■ *TF:* 800-786-6261 ■ *Web:* sunoco.com	Philadelphia	PA	19103	215-977-3000	977-3409
Supreme Petroleum Inc 1001 S Church St *Web:* www.supremepetro.com	Smithfield	VA	23430	757-357-9652	
Tesoro Corp 19100 Ridgewood Pkwy *NYSE:* TSO ■ *TF:* 800-299-0570 ■ *Web:* www.tsocorp.com	San Antonio	TX	78259	210-626-6000	
Texas Oil & Chemical Co 7752 FM 418	Silsbee	TX	77656	409-385-1400	385-2453
Tower Energy Group 1983 W 190th St *Web:* www.towerenergy.com	Torrance	CA	90504	310-538-8000	
Tristate Midstream LP 3311 N Interstate 35 Ste 120 *Web:* www.tsmidstream.com	Denton	TX	76207	940-387-4955	
United Refining Company Inc 15 Bradley St *Web:* www.urc.com	Warren	PA	16365	814-723-1500	726-4709
US Energy Markets Inc 700 Louisiana St 39th Fl *Web:* www.usenergymarkets.com	Houston	TX	77002	813-438-3837	
US Oil & Refining Co 3001 Marshall Ave *Web:* www.usor.com	Tacoma	WA	98421	253-383-1651	383-9970
Vp Racing Fuels Inc 7124 Richter Rd *Web:* www.vpracingfuels.com	Elmendorf	TX	78112	210-635-7744	
Western Dubuque Biodiesel LLC 904 Jamesmeier Rd PO Box 82 *Web:* www.wdbiodiesel.net	Farley	IA	52046	563-744-3554	
Western Refining Inc 123 W Mills Ave *NYSE:* WNR ■ *Web:* www.wnr.com	El Paso	TX	79905	915-534-1400	
WMPI Pty LLC 10 Gilberton Rd	Gilberton	PA	17934	570-874-1602	
World Oil Co 9302 Garfield Ave	South Gate	CA	90280	562-928-0100	928-3234
Wynnewood Refining Co 906 S Powell Ave *Web:* cvrenergy.com	Wynnewood	OK	73098	405-665-6565	

581 PETROLEUM STORAGE TERMINALS

Company	City	State	ZIP	Phone	Fax
Acorn Petroleum Inc 529 Sahwatch St *Web:* www.acornpetroleuminc.com	Colorado Springs	CO	80903	719-634-8874	
Allied Energy Company LLC 2700 Ishkooda Wenonah Rd *Web:* alliedenergycorp.com	Birmingham	AL	35211	205-925-6600	
Bayside Fuel Oil Depot Corp 1776 Shore Pkwy *Web:* www.baysidedepot.com	Brooklyn	NY	11214	718-372-9800	
Beck Suppliers Inc 1000 N Frnt St *Web:* www.beckoil.com	Fremont	OH	43420	419-332-5527	
Bennett Oil Co 810 E Sheldon St *Web:* www.bennettoil.com	Prescott	AZ	86301	928-445-1181	
Best-Wade Petroleum Inc 201 Dodge Dr *Web:* www.bestwade.com	Ripley	TN	38063	731-635-9661	
Bi-Petro Inc 3150 Executive Park Dr *Web:* www.bipetro.com	Springfield	IL	62794	217-535-0181	
Blaylock Oil Company Inc 724 S Flagler Ave *Web:* www.blaylockoil.com	Homestead	FL	33030	305-247-7249	
Bountyland Petroleum Inc 1510 Blue Ridge Blvd Ste 202 *Web:* mybountyland.com	Seneca	SC	29672	864-647-7282	
Brabham Oil Company Inc 525 Midway St *Web:* www.brabhamoil.com	Bamberg	SC	29003	803-245-2471	
Buckley Oil Company Inc 1809 Rock Island St *TF:* 800-721-4147 ■ *Web:* www.buckleyoil.com	Dallas	TX	75207	214-421-4147	
Busch Distributors Inc 7603 State Rt 270 *Web:* www.buschdist.com	Pullman	WA	99163	208-882-3021	
C Steinweg Inc 1201 Wallace St *Web:* www.steinweg.com	Baltimore	MD	21230	410-752-8254	
C.K. Smith & Company Inc 99 Crescent St *Web:* www.cksmithsuperior.com	Worcester	MA	01605	508-753-1475	
CarterEnergy Corp 6000 Metcalf Ave *Web:* www.carterenergy.com	Overland Park	KS	66202	913-643-2300	
Cary Oil Company Inc 110 Mackenan Dr *TF:* 800-227-9645 ■ *Web:* www.caryoil.com	Cary	NC	27511	919-462-1100	481-6862
Central Crude Inc 4187 Hwy 3059 PO Box 1863 *TF:* 800-245-8408 ■ *Web:* www.centralcrude.com	Lake Charles	LA	70602	337-436-1000	436-9602
Central Oil & Supply Corp 2300 Booth St *Web:* www.central-oil.com	Monroe	LA	71201	318-388-2602	
Childers Oil Co 51 Hwy 2034 *Web:* www.doublekwik.com	Whitesburg	KY	41858	606-633-2525	
CHS Inc 3520 E River Rd PO Box 6878 *TF:* 888-254-0632 ■ *Web:* www.chsrochester.com	Rochester	MN	55903	507-289-4086	289-7653
Coleman Oil Co 335 Mill Rd *Web:* www.colemanoil.com	Lewiston	ID	83501	208-799-2000	
Connell Oil Inc 1015 N Oregon Ave PO Box 3998 *Web:* www.connelloil.com	Pasco	WA	99302	509-547-3326	
Conrad & Bischoff Inc 2251 N Holmes Ave *Web:* www.conradbischoff.com	Idaho Falls	ID	83401	208-522-4217	
Cross Petroleum Inc 6920 Lockheed Dr *Web:* www.crosspetroleum.com	Redding	CA	96002	530-221-2588	
Don Small & Sons Oil Distributing Co Inc 112 3rd St NW *Web:* www.smallandsonsoil.com	Auburn	WA	98002	253-833-0430	
Dooley's Petroleum Inc 304 Main Ave *Web:* www.dooleypetro.com	Murdock	MN	56271	320-875-2641	
Douglass Distributing Co 325 E Forest Ave *Web:* www.douglassdist.com	Sherman	TX	75090	903-893-1181	
E & V Energy Corp 5700 State Rt 34 *Web:* www.eandvenergy.com	Auburn	NY	13021	315-253-6522	
Eastern Fuels Inc 386 NC Hwy 42 W *Web:* www.easternfuels.com	Ahoskie	NC	27910	252-332-5021	
Finley Resources Inc 1308 Lake St *Web:* www.finleyresources.com	Fort Worth	TX	76102	817-336-1924	
G&B Oil Company Inc 667 N Bridge St *Web:* www.gbenergy.com	Elkin	NC	28621	336-835-3607	
Gresham Petroleum Co 415 Pershing Ave P O Box 690 *TF:* 800-748-8934 ■ *Web:* www.greshampetroleum.com	Indianola	MS	38751	662-884-5000	
Hampel Oil Distributors Inc 3727 S W St *Web:* www.hampeloil.com	Wichita	KS	67217	316-529-1162	
Harpel Oil Company Inc 5480 Brighton Blvd *Web:* www.harpeloil.com	Commerce	CO	80022	303-294-0767	
Hicks Oils & Hicksgas Inc 204 Hwy 54 E *Web:* www.hicksoils.com	Roberts	IL	60962	217-395-2281	
HOC Industries Inc 3511 N Ohio St *Web:* www.hocindustries.com	Wichita	KS	67219	316-838-4663	
Houston Fuel Oil Terminal Co 16642 Jacintoport Blvd *Web:* www.hfotco.com	Houston	TX	77015	281-452-3390	452-6306

Phone *Fax*

Houston-Pasadena Apache Oil Company LP
5136 Spencer Hwy ... Pasadena TX 77505 281-487-5400
Web: www.apacheoilcompany.com

Jack Becker Distributors Inc
6800 Suemac Pl ... Jacksonville FL 32254 800-488-8411
TF: 800-488-8411 ■ *Web:* www.jackbecker.com

JBC Inc 1414 E 20th St Ste 6 ... Scottsbluff NE 69361 308-635-0455
Web: www.jbc1.com

Jernigan Oil Company Inc
415 E Main St PO Box 688 ... Ahoskie NC 27910 252-332-2131
Web: www.jerniganoil.com

Johnson Oil Company of Gaylord
507 S Otsego Ave ... Gaylord MI 49734 989-732-2451
Web: www.johnsonspropane.com

Jones Petroleum Company Inc 407 E Second St ... Jackson GA 30233 770-775-2386
Web: www.jonespetroleum.com

Kellerstrass Oil Co 1500 West 2550 South ... Ogden UT 84401 801-392-9516 392-9589
Web: kellerstrassoil.com

Ken Bettridge Distributing Inc
386 North 100 West ... Cedar City UT 84721 435-586-2411
Web: www.kboil.net

Kentucky Oil & Refining Co
156 Kentucky Oil Village ... Betsy Layne KY 41605 606-478-9501
Web: www.teamkore.com

LBC Houston 11666 Port Rd ... Seabrook TX 77586 281-474-4433 291-3428
Web: www.lbchouston.com

Lee Oil Company Inc 1655 Bypass 35 ... Alvin TX 77511 281-331-3445
Web: www.leeoilalvin.com

Link Energy LLC 39 Rivalda Rd 2nd Fl ... Toronto ON M9M2M4 855-444-5465
TF: 855-444-5465 ■ *Web:* www.linkenergy.com

Lott Oil Company Inc 1855 Hwy 1 ... Natchitoches LA 71457 318-352-2055
Web: www.lottoil.com

Magellan Midstream Partners LP 1 Williams Ctr ... Tulsa OK 74172 918-574-7000
NYSE: MMP ■ *TF:* 800-574-6671 ■ *Web:* www.magellanlp.com

Magness Oil Co 167 Tucker Cemetary Rd ... Gassville AR 72635 870-425-4353
Web: www.magnessoil.com

Maples Gas Company Inc 101-65th Ave ... Meridian MS 39301 601-693-5115
Web: www.maplesgas.com

Max Arnold & Sons LLC 702 N Main St ... Hopkinsville KY 42240 270-885-8488
Web: www.maxfuel.net

Mccraw Oil Company Inc 2207 N Ctr St ... Bonham TX 75418 903-583-7481
Web: www.mccrawoil.com

McPherson Companies Inc, The
5051 Cardinal St ... Trussville AL 35173 205-661-4400
Web: www.mcphersonoil.com

MFA Oil Co 1 Ray Young Dr ... Columbia MO 65205 573-442-0171
TF: 800-366-0200 ■ *Web:* www.mfaoil.com

Mid-State Petroleum Inc
4192 Mendenhall Oaks Pkwy ... High Point NC 27265 336-841-3000
Web: www.mid-statepetroleum.com

Molo Oil Company Inc 123 Southern Ave ... Dubuque IA 52003 563-557-7540
TF: 877-983-3761 ■ *Web:* www.molocompanies.com

Nickey Petroleum Company Inc
925 S Lkview Ave ... Placentia CA 92870 714-547-4123
Web: nickeypetroleum.com

Nittany Oil Company Inc 1540 Martin St ... State College PA 16803 814-237-4859
Web: www.nittanyoil.com

NuStar Terminal Canada Partnership
4090 Port Malcolm Rd ... Point Tupper NS B9A1Z5 902-625-1711 625-3098

Oiltanking Houston LP
15602 Jacinto Port Blvd ... Houston TX 77015 281-457-7900 457-7991
Web: www.oiltanking.com

Pumpelly Oil Company LLC
1890 Swisco Rd PO Box 2059 ... Sulphur LA 70664 337-625-1117
Web: www.reladyne.com

Quarles Petroleum Inc
1701 Fall Hill Ave ... Fredericksburg VA 22401 540-371-2400
Web: www.quarlesinc.com

R.H. Smith Distributing Co
315 E Wine Country Rd PO Box 6 ... Grandview WA 98930 509-882-3377
Web: www.rhsmith.com

Reed Oil Co Inc 106 Washington St ... Doniphan MO 63935 573-996-2321
Web: m.reedoil.com

Richard Oil and Fuel LLC 2330 Hwy 70 ... Donaldsonville LA 70346 225-473-8389
Web: www.popingos.com

Scott Petroleum Corporation Inc
102 Main St ... Itta Bena MS 38941 662-254-9024
Web: www.scottpetroleuminc.com

Sweetwater Valley Oil Company Inc
1236 New Hwy 68 ... Sweetwater TN 37874 423-337-6671
TF: 800-362-4519 ■ *Web:* www.sweetwatervalleyoil.com

Team Schierl Companies 2201 Madison St ... Stevens Point WI 54481 715-345-5060
Web: www.teamschierl.com

TexPar Energy LLC 920 10th Ave North ... Onalaska WI 54650 608-779-6601
Web: www.texpar.com

Thomas Petroleum LLC 9701 US Hwy 59 N ... Victoria TX 77905 361-573-7662
Web: www.thomaspetro.com

Victron Energy Inc 105 YMCA Dr ... Waxahachie TX 75165 469-517-2000
Web: victrongroup.com

Vital Records Inc PO Box 688 ... Flagtown NJ 08821 908-369-6900
Web: www.vitalrecords.com

W.H. Breshears Inc 720 B St ... Modesto CA 95354 209-522-7291
TF: 800-637-4427 ■ *Web:* www.whbreshears.com

Yoder Oil Co Inc 2204 California Rd ... Elkhart IN 46514 574-264-2107
Web: www.yoderoil.com

582 PHARMACEUTICAL COMPANIES

See Also Biotechnology Companies p. 1859; Diagnostic Products p. 2192; Medicinal Chemicals & Botanical Products p. 2748; Pharmaceutical Companies - Generic Drugs p. 2936; Pharmaceutical & Diagnostic Products - Veterinary p. 2937; Vitamins & Nutritional Supplements p. 3296

Phone *Fax*

Abbott Laboratories Pharmaceutical Products Div
100 Research Dr Bioresearch Ctr ... Worcester MA 01605 224-667-6100
TF: 866-427-8477 ■ *Web:* www.abbott.com

Accentia BioPharmaceuticals Inc
324 S Hyde Pk Ave Ste 350 ... Tampa FL 33606 813-864-2554 258-6912
OTC: ABPI

Accucaps Industries Ltd 2125 Ambassador Dr ... Windsor ON N9C3R5 519-969-5404
TF: 800-665-7210 ■ *Web:* www.accucaps.com

Advanced Life Sciences Inc 1440 Davey Rd ... Woodridge IL 60517 630-739-6744 739-6754
OTC: ADLS ■ *Web:* www.advancedlifesciences.com

Allergan Inc 2525 Dupont Dr ... Irvine CA 92612 714-246-4500 246-6987*
NYSE: AGN ■ **Fax:* Mail Rm ■ *TF:* 800-347-4500 ■ *Web:* www.allergan.com

Alva-Amco Pharmacal Cos Inc 7711 Merrimac Ave ... Niles IL 60714 847-663-0700 663-1400
TF: 800-792-2582 ■ *Web:* www.alva-amco.com

Aminex Therapeutics Inc
11335 NE 122nd Ste 105 ... Kirkland WA 98034 425-286-4222
Web: www.aminextherapeutics.com

Amneal Pharmaceuticals LLC 75 Adams Ave ... Hauppauge NY 11788 631-952-0214 947-4146*
NYSE: IPAH ■ **Fax Area Code:* 908 ■ *TF:* 866-525-7270

Amphastar Pharmaceuticals Inc
11570 Sixth St ... Rancho Cucamonga CA 91730 909-980-9484
TF: 800-423-4136 ■ *Web:* www.amphastar.com

Amylin Pharmaceuticals Inc
9360 Towne Ctr Dr ... San Diego CA 92121 858-552-2200 552-2212
NASDAQ: AMLN ■ *Web:* www.bms.com

Apotex Inc 150 Signet Dr ... Toronto ON M9L1T9 416-749-9300 401-3849
TF: 800-268-4623 ■ *Web:* www.apotex.com

Apothecus Pharmaceutical Corp
220 Townsend Sq ... Oyster Bay NY 11771 516-624-8200
Web: www.apothecus.com

AROG Pharmaceuticals LLC 12400 Coit Rd ... Dallas TX 75251 214-593-0500
Web: www.arogpharma.com

AstraZeneca Canada Inc
1004 Middlegate Rd ... Mississauga ON L4Y1M4 905-277-7111 270-3248
TF: 800-565-5877 ■ *Web:* www.astrazeneca.ca

AstraZeneca Pharmaceuticals LP
1800 Concord Pk PO Box 15437 ... Wilmington DE 19850 800-236-9933
TF: 800-236-9933 ■ *Web:* www.astrazeneca-us.com

Atossa Genetics Inc
2345 Eastlake Ave E Ste 201 ... Seattle WA 98102 206-588-0256
Web: www.atossagenetics.com

AustarPharma LLC 300 Columbus Cir Unit F ... Edison NJ 08837 732-225-8850
Web: www.austarpharma.com

AutoImmune Inc 1199 Madia St ... Pasadena CA 91103 626-792-1235
OTC: AIMM ■ *Web:* www.autoimmuneinc.com

Banner Pharmacaps Inc
4100 Mendenhall Oaks Pkwy ... High Point NC 27265 336-812-3442
Web: www.patheon.com

Bausch & Lomb Inc 1400 N Goodman St ... Rochester NY 14609 585-338-6000 338-6896
TF: 800-553-5340 ■ *Web:* www.bausch.com

Bausch & Lomb Pharmaceuticals Inc
8500 Hidden River Pkwy ... Tampa FL 33637 800-553-5340
TF Cust Svc: 800-323-0000 ■ *Web:* www.bausch.com

Baxter International Inc 1 Baxter Pkwy ... Deerfield IL 60015 847-948-2000 948-3948
NYSE: BAX ■ *TF:* 800-422-9837 ■ *Web:* www.baxter.com

Bayer Corp 100 Bayer Blvd ... Whippany NJ 07981 973-254-5000
Web: www.bayer.us

Bayer Corp 100 Bayer Rd ... Pittsburgh PA 15205 862-404-3000 777-3899*
**Fax Area Code:* 412 ■ *Web:* www.bayer.us

Bayer Inc 77 Belfield Rd ... Toronto ON M9W1G6 416-248-0771
TF: 800-622-2937 ■ *Web:* www.bayer.ca

Beluga Composites Corp
6830 du Parc Ave Ste 572 ... Montreal QC H3N1W7 514-278-7856
Web: www.belugacorporation.com.

Biocare Medical LLC 4040 Pike Ln ... Concord CA 94520 925-603-8000
Web: biocare.net

BioSante Pharmaceuticals Inc
111 Barclay Blvd ... Lincolnshire IL 60069 847-478-0500 478-9152
NASDAQ: BPAX ■ *Web:* www.biospace.com

BioSpecifics Technologies Corp 35 Wilbur St ... Lynbrook NY 11563 516-593-7000 593-7039
NASDAQ: BSTC ■ *Web:* www.biospecifics.com

Blistex Inc 1800 Swift Dr ... Oak Brook IL 60523 800-837-1800 571-3437*
**Fax Area Code:* 630 ■ *TF Cust Svc:* 800-837-1800 ■ *Web:* www.blistex.com

Boehringer Ingelheim Ltd
5180 S Service Rd ... Burlington ON L7L5H4 905-639-0333
Web: www.boehringer-ingelheim.com

Boehringer Ingelheim Pharmaceuticals Inc
900 Ridgebury Rd ... Ridgefield CT 06877 203-798-9988 791-6234*
**Fax:* Cust Svc ■ *TF:* 800-243-0127 ■ *Web:* www.boehringer-ingelheim.com

Botanical Laboratories Inc 1441 W Smith Rd ... Ferndale WA 98248 360-384-5656 384-1140
TF: 800-232-4005 ■ *Web:* www.wellesse.com

Bracco Diagnostics Inc
259 Prospect Plns Rd Bldg H ... Monroe Township NJ 08831 609-514-2200
Web: corporate.bracco.com

Brioschi Inc 19-01 Pollitt Dr ... Fair Lawn NJ 07410 201-796-4226

Bristol-Myers Squibb Canada Inc
2344 Alfred-Nobel Blvd Ste 300 ... Montreal QC H4S0A4 514-333-3200
TF Cust Svc: 800-267-0005 ■ *Web:* www.bmscanada.ca

Bristol-Myers Squibb Co 345 Pk Ave ... New York NY 10154 212-546-4000
NYSE: BMY ■ *TF:* 800-332-2056 ■ *Web:* www.bms.com

Cardiovascular Consultants Pc
4330 Wornall Rd Ste 2000 ... Kansas City MO 64111 816-931-1883
Web: saintlukeshealthsystem.org

Company	City	State	Zip	Phone	Fax
Care-Tech Laboratories Inc 3224 S KingsHwy Blvd *TF:* 800-325-9681 ■ *Web:* www.caretechlabs.com	Saint Louis	MO	63139	314-772-4610	772-4613
Cary Pharmaceuticals Inc 9903 Windy Hollow Rd *Web:* www.carypharma.com	Great Falls	VA	22066	703-759-7460	
CB Fleet Co Inc 4615 Murray Pl *TF:* 866-255-6960 ■ *Web:* www.cbfleet.com	Lynchburg	VA	24502	434-528-4000	
Chattem Inc 1715 W 38th St PO Box 2219 *Web:* www.chattem.com	Chattanooga	TN	37409	423-821-4571	821-0395
Chembio Diagnostics Inc 3661 Horseblock Rd *NASDAQ: CEMI* ■ *TF:* 844-243-6246 ■ *Web:* www.chembio.com	Medford	NY	11763	631-924-1135	
Cirrus Healthcare Products LLC 60 Main St PO Box 220 *Web:* www.cirrushealthcare.com	Cold Spring Harbor	NY	11724	631-692-7600	692-9844
Coating Place Inc 200 Paoli St *Web:* www.coatingplace.com	Verona	WI	53593	608-845-9521	845-9526
Combe Inc 1101 Westchester Ave *TF:* 800-431-2610 ■ *Web:* www.combe.com	White Plains	NY	10604	914-694-5454	
Contract Packaging Resources Inc 8009 Industrial Village Rd *Web:* www.cprwebsite.com	Greensboro	NC	27409	336-665-1300	
Corium International Inc 4558 50th St SE *Web:* www.coriumgroup.com	Grand Rapids	MI	49512	616-656-4563	
Coty Inc 2 Pk Ave 17th Fl *Web:* www.coty.com	New York	NY	10016	212-389-7300	
Covalon Technologies Ltd 405 Britannia Rd E Ste 106 *TF:* 877-711-6055 ■ *Web:* www.covalon.com	Mississauga	ON	L4Z3E6	905-568-8400	
Daiichi Sankyo Inc 2 Hilton Ct *Web:* www.dsi.com	Parsippany	NJ	07054	973-359-2600	944-2645
Darby Group Cos Inc 300 Jericho Quad	Jericho	NY	11753	516-683-1800	688-2880
Delavau LLC 10101 Roosevelt Blvd *Web:* www.delavau.com	Philadelphia	PA	19154	215-671-1400	671-1401
Dickinson Brands Inc 31 E High St *Web:* dickinsonbrands.com	East Hampton	CT	06424	860-267-2279	
Discharge Resource Group 400 Oyster Point Blvd Ste 440 *Web:* drgstaffing.com	South San Francisco	CA	94080	650-877-8111	
DPT Laboratories Ltd 318 McCullough *TF:* 866-225-5378 ■ *Web:* www.dptlabs.com	San Antonio	TX	78215	210-476-8150	224-6505
Dr Reddy's Laboratories Inc 200 Summerset Corporate Blvd *NYSE: RDY* ■ *Web:* www.drreddys.com	Bridgewater	NJ	08807	908-203-4900	203-4940
DxNA LLC 180 North 300 East *Web:* www.dxna.com	Saint George	UT	84770	435-628-0324	
Dynavax Technologies Corp 2929 Seventh St Ste 100 *NASDAQ: DVAX* ■ *TF:* 877-848-5100 ■ *Web:* www.dynavax.com	Berkeley	CA	94710	510-848-5100	848-1327
Eco-Med Pharmaceuticals Inc 7050B Bramalea Rd Unit 58 *Web:* www.eco-med.com	Mississauga	ON	L5S1S9	905-405-1050	405-0775
Edwards Lifesciences Corp 1 Edwards Way *NYSE: EW* ■ **Fax:* Cust Svc ■ *TF:* 800-424-3278 ■ *Web:* www.edwards.com	Irvine	CA	92614	949-250-2500	250-2525*
Eisai Inc 100 Tice Blvd *TF:* 866-613-4724 ■ *Web:* www.eisai.com	Woodcliff Lake	NJ	07677	201-692-1100	692-1804
Eli Lilly & Co Lilly Corporate Ctr *NYSE: LLY* ■ *TF Prod Info:* 800-545-5979 ■ *Web:* www.lilly.com	Indianapolis	IN	46285	317-276-2000	
Eli Lilly Canada Inc 3650 Danforth Ave **Fax:* Hum Res ■ *TF:* 888-545-5972 ■ *Web:* www.lilly.ca	Toronto	ON	M1N2E8	416-694-3221	699-7252*
Elona Bio Technologies Inc 1040 Sierra Dr Ste 1000 *Web:* elonabiotech.wordpress.com	Greenwood	IN	46143	317-513-3138	
Endo Pharmaceuticals Holdings Inc 100 Endo Blvd *TF Cust Svc:* 800-462-3636 ■ *Web:* www.endo.com	Chadds Ford	PA	19317	610-558-9800	558-8979
First Check Diagnostics Corp 13 Spectrum Pointe Dr *Web:* www.firstcheckfamily.com	Lake Forest	CA	92630	949-598-8378	
First Priority Inc 1590 Todd Farm Dr *TF:* 800-650-4899 ■ *Web:* www.prioritycare.com	Elgin	IL	60123	847-289-1600	
Forest Pharmaceutical Inc 13600 Shoreline Dr *TF:* 800-678-1605 ■ *Web:* www.frx.com	Earth City	MO	63045	314-493-7000	
G & W Laboratories Inc 111 Coolidge St **Fax:* Sales ■ *TF:* 800-922-1038 ■ *Web:* www.gwlabs.com	South Plainfield	NJ	07080	908-753-2000	753-5174*
Galderma Laboratories Inc 14501 N Fwy *TF:* 866-735-4137 ■ *Web:* www.galderma.com	Fort Worth	TX	76177	817-961-5000	
Germiphene Corp 1379 Colborne St E PO Box 1748 *TF:* 800-265-9931 ■ *Web:* www.germiphene.com	Brantford	ON	N3T5M1	519-759-7100	759-1625
GlaxoSmithKline Inc 7333 Mississauga Rd N *TF:* 800-387-7374 ■ *Web:* ca.gsk.com	Mississauga	ON	L5N6L4	905-819-3000	819-3099
GMP Laboratories of America Inc 2931 E La Jolla St *Web:* www.gmplabs.com	Anaheim	CA	92806	714-630-2467	237-1374
Halocarbon Products Corp PO Box 661 *TF:* 800-338-5803 ■ *Web:* www.halocarbon.com	River Edge	NJ	07661	201-262-8899	262-0019
Halozyme Therapeutics Inc 11388 Sorrento Vly Rd *NASDAQ: HALO* ■ *Web:* www.halozyme.com	San Diego	CA	92121	858-794-8889	704-8311
Heron Therapeutics Inc 123 Saginaw Dr *OTC: HRTX* ■ *Web:* www.herontx.com	Redwood City	CA	94063	650-366-2626	365-6490
Hoffmann-LaRoche Inc 340 Kingsland St *TF:* 800-526-6367 ■ *Web:* www.roche.com	Nutley	NJ	07110	973-235-5000	
Hope Pharmaceuticals Inc 16416 N 92nd St Ste 125 **Fax Area Code:* 480 ■ *TF:* 800-755-9595 ■ *Web:* www.hopepharm.com	Scottsdale	AZ	85260	800-755-9595	607-1971*
Hospira Inc 275 N Field Dr *NYSE: HSP* ■ *TF:* 877-946-7747 ■ *Web:* www.hospira.com	Lake Forest	IL	60045	224-212-2000	
Humco Holding Group Inc 7400 Alumax Dr *TF:* 800-662-3435 ■ *Web:* www.humco.com	Texarkana	TX	75501	903-334-6200	334-6300
Immtech Pharmaceuticals Inc 1 N End Ave *TF:* 877-898-8038 ■ *Web:* www.immtechpharma.com	New York	NY	10282	212-791-2911	791-2917
Infinity Pharmaceuticals Inc 780 Memorial Dr *NASDAQ: INFI* ■ *Web:* www.infi.com	Cambridge	MA	02139	617-453-1000	453-1001
Jaapharm Canada Inc 510 Rowntree Dairy Rd Bldg B *TF:* 800-465-9587 ■ *Web:* www.jaapharm.com	Woodbridge	ON	L4L8H2	905-851-7885	856-5838
Janssen Pharmaceutica Inc 1125 Trenton-Harbourton Rd *TF:* 800-526-7736 ■ *Web:* www.janssen.com	Titusville	NJ	08560	609-730-2000	730-2323
Jazz Pharmaceuticals Inc 3180 Porter Dr *TF:* 866-997-3688 ■ *Web:* www.jazzpharma.com	Palo Alto	CA	94304	650-496-3777	
Juniper Pharmaceuticals Inc 33 Arch St *NASDAQ: CBRX* ■ *TF:* 866-566-5636	Boston	MA	02110	973-994-3999	994-3001
K P Pharmaceutical Technology Inc 1212 W Rappel Ave *Web:* www.kppt.com	Bloomington	IN	47404	812-330-8121	330-8363
Keryx Biopharmaceuticals Inc 750 Lexington Ave 20th Fl *NASDAQ: KERX* ■ *TF:* 800-903-0247 ■ *Web:* www.keryx.com	New York	NY	10022	212-531-5965	531-5961
King Bio Pharmaceuticals Inc 3 Westside Dr *TF:* 800-543-3245 ■ *Web:* www.kingbio.com	Asheville	NC	28806	828-255-0201	255-0940
Konsyl Pharmaceuticals Inc 8050 Industrial Pk Rd *TF:* 800-356-6795 ■ *Web:* www.konsyl.com	Easton	MD	21601	410-822-5192	
Kramer Laboratories Inc 8778 SW Eigth St *TF:* 800-824-4894 ■ *Web:* www.kramerlabs.com	Miami	FL	33174	305-223-1287	223-5510
LED Medical Diagnostics Inc 2 Ravinia Dr Unit 900 *Web:* www.leddental.com	Atlanta	GA	30346	604-434-4614	
Ligand Pharmaceuticals Inc 11085 N Torrey Pines Rd Ste 300 *NASDAQ: LGND* ■ *Web:* www.ligand.com	La Jolla	CA	92037	858-550-7500	550-7506
Major Pharmaceutical Co 31778 Enterprise Dr *TF:* 800-875-0123 ■ *Web:* www.majorpharmaceuticals.com	Livonia	MI	48150	734-743-6161	
McNeil Consumer & Specialty Pharmaceuticals 7050 Camp Hill Rd **Fax:* Cust Svc ■ *Web:* www.mcneil-consumer.com	Fort Washington	PA	19034	215-273-7000	273-7000*
MedAvante Inc 100 American Metro Blvd Ste 106 *Web:* www.medavante.net	Hamilton	NJ	08619	609-528-9400	
Medical Devices Inc 4600 140th Ave N Ste 200 *Web:* www.mdevicesinc.com	Clearwater	FL	33762	727-451-7160	
Medical Products Laboratories Inc 9990 Global Rd *TF:* 800-523-0191 ■ *Web:* www.mplusa.com	Philadelphia	PA	19115	215-677-2700	677-7736
Medicis Pharmaceutical Corp 7720 N Dobson Rd *TF Cust Svc:* 866-246-8245 ■ *Web:* valeant.com/operational-expertise/valeant-united-states	Scottsdale	AZ	85256	800-321-4576	
Medivation Inc 201 Spear St 3rd Fl *NASDAQ: MDVN* ■ *Web:* www.medivation.com	San Francisco	CA	94105	415-543-3470	543-3411
MedPointe Pharmaceuticals 265 Davidson Ave Ste 300 *Web:* meda.us	Somerset	NJ	08873	732-564-2200	
Melaleuca Inc 3910 S Yellowstone Hwy **Fax Area Code:* 888 ■ *TF Sales:* 800-282-3000 ■ *Web:* www.melaleuca.com	Idaho Falls	ID	83402	208-522-0700	528-2090*
Mentholatum Company Inc 707 Sterling Dr *TF:* 800-688-7660 ■ *Web:* www.mentholatum.com	Orchard Park	NY	14127	716-677-2500	677-9528
Merck & Company Inc 1 Merck Dr PO Box 100 *NYSE: MRK* ■ *TF Cust Svc:* 800-672-6372 ■ *Web:* www.merck.com	Whitehouse Station	NJ	08889	908-423-1000	
Merial Canada Inc 20000 Clark Graham *Web:* ca.merial.com	Baie-d'urfe	QC	H9X4B6	514-457-1555	
Mikart Inc 1750 Chattahoochee Ave NW *TF:* 888-464-5278 ■ *Web:* www.mikart.com	Atlanta	GA	30318	404-351-4510	350-0432
Mission Pharmacal PO Box 786099 *TF:* 800-531-3333 ■ *Web:* missionpharmacal.com	San Antonio	TX	78278	210-696-8400	696-6010
MIT Holding Inc 37 W Fairmont Ave Ste 202 *Web:* www.mitholdingsinc.com	Savannah	GA	31406	912-925-1905	
Mueller Sports Medicine Inc 1 Quench Dr *Web:* www.muellersportsmed.com	Prairie Du Sac	WI	53578	608-643-8530	
Murty Pharmaceuticals Inc 518 Codell Dr *Web:* www.mpirx.com	Lexington	KY	40509	859-266-2446	
Mylan 1000 Mylan Blvd *TF:* 800-527-4278 ■ *Web:* www.mylan.com/en/businesses/rx-products	Canonsburg	PA	15317	724-514-1800	
Mylan Pharmaceuticals Inc 781 Chestnut Ridge Rd *TF:* 800-796-9526 ■ *Web:* mylan.com/products	Morgantown	WV	26505	800-796-9526	
NanoScreen LLC 917 Commerce Cir *Web:* www.nanoscreen.com	Hanahan	SC	29410	843-881-8841	
Nature's Value Inc 468 Mill Rd *Web:* www.naturesvalue.com	Coram	NY	11727	631-846-2500	846-2527
Navinta LLC 1499 Lower Ferry Rd *Web:* navinta.com	Ewing	NJ	08618	609-883-1135	
NBTY Manufacturing 901 E 233rd St *Web:* www.nbty.com	Carson	CA	90745	310-835-8400	
Neos Therapeutics 2940 N Hwy 360 Ste 100 *TF:* 844-375-8324 ■ *Web:* www.neostx.com	Grand Prairie	TX	75050	972-408-1300	408-1143
NextPharma Technologies Inc 5340 Eastgate Mall *Web:* www.nextpharma.com	San Diego	CA	92121	858-450-3123	450-0785
Noramco Inc 1440 Olympic Dr *Web:* www.noramco.com	Athens	GA	30601	706-353-4400	353-3205
NovaDel Pharma Inc 1200 Rt 22 E Ste 2000	Bridgewater	NJ	08807	908-203-4640	203-4744
Novartis Pharmaceuticals Canada Inc 385 boul Bouchard **Fax:* Cust Svc ■ *TF:* 800-465-2244 ■ *Web:* www.novartis.ca	Dorval	QC	H9S1A9	514-631-6775	631-1867*

	City	State	ZIP	Phone	Fax
Novartis Pharmaceuticals Co					
10401 Cornhusker Hwy	Waverly	NE	68462	862-778-2100	
TF: 888-669-6682 ■ *Web:* www.us.novartis.com					
Noven Pharmaceuticals Inc 11960 SW 144th St	Miami	FL	33186	305-253-5099	251-1887
Web: www.noven.com					
Novo Nordisk of North America Inc					
100 College Rd W	Princeton	NJ	08540	609-987-5800	987-5394
TF: 800-727-6500 ■ *Web:* www.novonordisk-us.com					
Novo Nordisk Pharmaceuticals Inc					
800 Scudders Mill Rd	Princeton	NJ	08536	609-987-5800	
TF Cust Svc: 800-727-6500 ■ *Web:* www.novonordisk-us.com					
Numark Laboratories Inc 164 Northfield Ave	Edison	NJ	08837	800-338-8079	225-0066*
**Fax Area Code:* 732 ■ *TF:* 800-338-8079 ■ *Web:* www.numarkbrands.com					
NutriCology Inc 2300 N Loop Rd	Alameda	CA	94502	510-263-2000	263-2100
Web: www.nutricology.com					
Odor Management Inc					
18-6 E Dundee Rd Ste 101	Barrington	IL	60010	847-304-9111	304-0989
TF: 800-662-6367 ■ *Web:* www.odormanagement.com					
Ono Pharma USA Inc 2000 Lenox Dr	Trenton	NJ	08648	609-219-1010	219-9229
Web: www.ono.co.jp					
Otsuka America Pharmaceutical Inc					
2440 Research Blvd	Rockville	MD	20850	301-990-0030	
Web: www.otsuka-us.com					
Pain Therapeutics Inc					
7801 N Capital of Texas Hwy Ste 260	Austin	TX	78731	512-501-2444	614-0414
NASDAQ: PTIE ■ *Web:* www.paintrials.com					
Particle Dynamics International LLC					
2629 S Hanley Rd	Saint Louis	MO	63144	314-968-2376	781-3354
TF: 800-452-4682 ■ *Web:* pdhllc.com					
Pegasus Laboratories Inc 8809 Ely Rd	Pensacola	FL	32514	850-478-2770	478-5639
Web: www.pegasuslabs.com					
Pfizer Animal Health 5 Giralda Farms	Madison	NJ	07940	888-963-8471	
TF: 888-963-8471 ■ *Web:* www.zoetisus.com					
Pfizer Canada Inc 17300 TransCanada Hwy	Kirkland	QC	H9J2M5	514-695-0500	
TF: 800-463-6001 ■ *Web:* www.pfizer.ca					
Pfizer Inc 235 E 42nd St	New York	NY	10017	212-733-2323	573-7851
NYSE: PFE ■ *TF:* 800-879-3477 ■ *Web:* www.pfizer.com					
PharmAthene Inc 1 Pk Pl Ste 450	Annapolis	MD	21401	410-269-2600	269-2601
Web: www.pharmathene.com					
Pharmos Corp 99 Wood Ave S Ste 302	Iselin	NJ	08830	732-452-9556	
PINK: PARS ■ *Web:* www.pharmoscorp.com					
Procter & Gamble Pharmaceuticals Canada Inc					
PO Box 355 Stn A	Toronto	ON	M5W1C5	416-730-4711	
TF: 800-668-0150					
Prometheus Laboratories Inc					
9410 Carroll Pk Dr	San Diego	CA	92121	888-892-8391	816-4019*
**Fax Area Code:* 877 ■ *TF:* 888-892-8391 ■ *Web:* www.prometheuslabs.com					
ProPhase Labs Inc 621 Shady Retreat Rd	Doylestown	PA	18901	215-345-0919	
NASDAQ: PRPH ■ *TF:* 800-505-2653 ■ *Web:* www.prophaselabs.com					
Protide Pharmaceuticals Inc					
505 Oakwood Rd Ste 200	Lake Zurich	IL	60047	847-726-3100	726-3110
TF: 800-552-3569 ■ *Web:* www.protidepharma.com					
Qal-Tek Associates LLC 3998 Commerce Cir	Idaho Falls	ID	83401	208-523-5557	
Web: www.qaltek.com					
QLT USA Inc 887 Great Northern Way Ste 250	Vancouver	CO	80525	970-482-5868	707-7001*
**Fax Area Code:* 604 ■ *TF:* 877-764-3131 ■ *Web:* www.qltinc.com					
Qualicaps Inc 6505 Franz Warner Pkwy	Whitsett	NC	27377	336-449-3900	449-3333
TF: 800-227-7853 ■ *Web:* www.qualicaps.com					
Qualitest Pharmaceuticals 130 Vintage Dr	Huntsville	AL	35811	800-444-4011	
TF: 800-444-4011					
Quatrx Pharmaceuticals Co					
777 E Eisenhower Pkwy Ste 100	Ann Arbor	MI	48108	734-913-9900	913-0743
Web: www.quatrx.com					
Quintiles Canada Inc					
18 Rue Elderidge	Dollard-des-Ormeaux	QC	H9A2P4	514-855-0888	
TF General: 866-267-4479 ■ *Web:* www.quintiles.com					
Quintiles Transnational Corp					
4820 Emperor Blvd	Durham	NC	27703	919-998-2000	998-2003
TF: 866-267-4479 ■ *Web:* www.quintiles.com					
RegeneRx Biopharmaceuticals Inc					
15245 Shady Grove Rd Ste 470	Rockville	MD	20850	301-208-9191	
OTC: RGRX ■ *Web:* www.regenerx.com					
Regenesis Biomedical Inc 5301 N Pima Rd	Scottsdale	AZ	85250	480-970-4970	
Web: www.regenesisbio.com					
Regis Technologies Inc 8210 Austin Ave	Morton Grove	IL	60053	847-967-6000	967-5876
TF: 800-323-8144 ■ *Web:* www.registech.com					
Roche Carolina Inc 6173 E Old Marion Hwy	Florence	SC	29506	843-629-4300	
Web: www.rochecarolina.com					
Roche Molecular Systems Inc					
4300 Hacienda Dr	Pleasanton	CA	94588	925-730-8200	
Web: www.roche-diagnostics.com					
Rules-based Medicine Inc 3300 Duval Rd	Austin	TX	78759	512-835-8026	835-4687
TF: 866-726-6277 ■ *Web:* rbm.myriad.com					
Sagent Pharmaceuticals Inc					
1901 N Roselle Rd	Schaumburg	IL	60195	847-908-1600	908-1601
NASDAQ: SGNT ■ *Web:* www.sagentpharma.com					
Salix Pharmaceuticals Inc					
8510 Colonnade Ctr Dr	Raleigh	NC	27615	919-862-1000	862-1095
NASDAQ: SLXP ■ *TF:* 800-508-0024 ■ *Web:* www.salix.com					
SciClone Pharmaceuticals Inc					
950 Tower Ln Ste 900	Foster City	CA	94404	650-358-3456	358-3469
NASDAQ: SCLN ■ *TF:* 800-724-2566 ■ *Web:* www.sciclone.com					
Sigma-Tau Pharmaceutical Inc					
9841 Washingtonian Blvd Ste 500	Gaithersburg	MD	20878	301-948-1041	948-1862
TF: 800-447-0169 ■ *Web:* www.sigmatau.com					
Silipos Inc 7049 Williams Rd	Niagara Falls	NY	14304	716-283-0700	
TF: 800-229-4404 ■ *Web:* www.silipos.com					
SISU Inc 7635 N Fraser Way Ste 102	Burnaby	BC	V5J0B8	604-420-6610	
TF: 800-663-4163 ■ *Web:* www.sisu.com					
Solvay America Inc 3333 Richmond Ave	Houston	TX	77098	713-525-6000	525-7887
TF General: 800-365-6565 ■ *Web:* www.solvay.com					
Somerset Pharmaceuticals Inc					
2202 N.W. Shore Blvd Ste 450	Tampa	FL	33607	813-288-0040	
Web: www.somersetpharm.com					

	City	State	ZIP	Phone	Fax
Sovereign Pharmaceuticals Ltd					
7590 Sand St	Fort Worth	TX	76118	817-284-0429	284-0531
TF: 877-248-0228 ■ *Web:* www.sovpharm.com					
SSS Co 71 University Ave	Atlanta	GA	30315	404-521-0857	880-0383
TF: 800-237-3843 ■ *Web:* www.ssspharmaceuticals.com					
Standing Stone Inc					
49 Richmondville Ave The Mill Ste 306	Westport	CT	06880	203-227-8710	
Web: www.standingstoneinc.com					
Sucampo Pharmaceuticals Inc					
805 King Farm Blvd Ste 550	Rockville	MD	20850	301-961-3400	961-3440
NASDAQ: SCMP ■ *TF:* 877-825-3327 ■ *Web:* www.sucampo.com					
Summa Information Systems Inc					
111 E Fire Tower Rd	Winterville	NC	28590	252-756-6110	
Synta Pharmaceuticals Corp 45 Hartwell Ave	Lexington	MA	02421	781-274-8200	274-8228
NASDAQ: SNTA ■ *Web:* www.syntapharma.com					
Taisho Pharmaceutical California Inc					
3878 W Carson St Ste 216	Torrance	CA	90503	310-543-2035	
Web: lipovitan.com					
Tamir Biotechnology Inc					
12625 High Bluff Dr Ste 113	San Diego	CA	92130	732-823-1003	652-4575
OTC: ACEL ■ *Web:* www.alfacell.com					
Taro Pharmaceuticals Inc 130 E Dr	Brampton	ON	L6T1C1	905-791-8276	791-5008
TF: 800-268-1975 ■ *Web:* www.taro.ca					
Tethys Bioscience Inc					
5858 Horton St Ste 280	Emeryville	CA	94608	510-420-6700	
Web: www.tethysbio.com					
Tower Laboratories Ltd PO Box 306	Centerbrook	CT	06409	860-767-2127	767-2129
Web: www.towerlabs.com					
UCB Pharma Inc 1950 Lake Pk Dr	Smyrna	GA	30080	770-970-7500	970-8857*
**Fax:* Hum Res ■ *TF:* 800-477-7877 ■ *Web:* www.ucb.com					
Unipack Inc 3253 Old Frankstown Rd	Pittsburgh	PA	15239	724-733-7381	327-6265
Web: www.unipackinc.com					
Unipharm Inc 350 Fifth Ave Ste 6701	New York	NY	10118	212-594-3260	594-3261
Web: www.unipharmus.com					
United Therapeutics Corp					
1040 Spring St	Silver Spring	MD	20910	301-608-9292	608-9291
NASDAQ: UTHR ■ *TF:* 877-864-8437 ■ *Web:* www.unither.com					
Upsher-Smith Laboratories Inc					
6701 Evenstad Dr	Maple Grove	MN	55369	763-315-2000	315-2001
TF: 800-654-2299 ■ *Web:* www.upsher-smith.com					
Vanda Pharmaceuticals Inc					
2200 Pennsylvania Ave NW Ste 300E	Washington	DC	20037	202-734-3400	296-1450
NASDAQ: VNDA ■ *Web:* www.vandapharmaceuticals.com					
Vivus Inc 1172 Castro St	Mountain View	CA	94040	650-934-5200	934-5389
NASDAQ: VVUS ■ *TF:* 800-607-0088 ■ *Web:* www.vivus.com					
WF Young Inc 302 Benton Dr	East Longmeadow	MA	01028	413-526-9999	526-8990
TF: 800-628-9653 ■ *Web:* www.absorbine.com					
Wright Group, The 6428 Airport Rd	Crowley	LA	70526	337-783-3096	
TF: 800-201-3096 ■ *Web:* www.thewrightgroup.net					
Zalicus Inc 245 First St 3rd Fl	Cambridge	MA	02142	617-301-7000	425-7010
NASDAQ: ZLCS					
ZLB Behring LLC					
1020 First Ave PO Box 61501	King of Prussia	PA	19406	610-878-4000	878-4009
TF: 800-683-1288 ■ *Web:* www.cslbehring.com					
Zogenix Inc 12400 High Bluff Dr Ste 650	San Diego	CA	92130	858-259-1165	259-1166
TF: 866-964-3649 ■ *Web:* www.zogenix.com					

583 PHARMACEUTICAL COMPANIES - GENERIC DRUGS

See Also Biotechnology Companies p. 1859; Diagnostic Products p. 2192; Medicinal Chemicals & Botanical Products p. 2748; Pharmaceutical Companies p. 2934; Pharmaceutical & Diagnostic Products - Veterinary p. 2937; Vitamins & Nutritional Supplements p. 3296

	City	State	ZIP	Phone	Fax
Apotex Corp 2400 N Commerce Pkwy Ste 400	Weston	FL	33326	877-427-6839	706-5576*
**Fax Area Code:* 800 ■ *TF:* 877-427-6839 ■ *Web:* www.apotex.com					
Biocept Inc 5810 Nancy Ridge Dr Ste 150	San Diego	CA	92121	858-320-8200	
Web: www.biocept.com					
Biotools Inc 17546 Bee Line Hwy	Jupiter	FL	33458	561-625-0133	
TF: 866-286-6571 ■ *Web:* www.btools.com					
Capricorn Pharma Inc					
6900 English Muffin Way	Frederick	MD	21703	301-696-8520	696-1424
Church & Dwight Canada Corp					
635 Secretariat Ct	Mississauga	ON	L5S2A5	905-696-6570	
Web: www.churchdwight.ca					
Difusion Technologies Inc					
111 Cooperative Way Ste 250	Georgetown	TX	78626	512-863-7777	
Web: www.difusiontech.com					
E Fougera & Co 60 Baylis Rd	Melville	NY	11747	631-454-6996	756-7017
TF: 800-645-9833 ■ *Web:* www.fougera.com					
Ethex Corp 1 Corporate Woods Dr	Bridgeton	MO	63044	314-646-3750	
Glenwood LLC 111 Cedar Ln	Englewood	NJ	07631	201-569-0050	569-0250
TF: 800-542-0772 ■ *Web:* www.glenwood-llc.com					
Healthpoint 3909 Hulen St	Fort Worth	TX	76107	817-900-4000	900-4100
TF Cust Svc: 800-441-8227 ■ *Web:* www.smith-nephew.com					
Impax Laboratories Inc 30831 Hun2od Ave	Hayward	CA	94544	510-240-6450	
NASDAQ: IPXL ■ *TF:* 877-994-6729 ■ *Web:* www.impaxlabs.com					
Legacy Pharmaceutical Packaging LLC					
13480 Lakefront Dr	St. Louis	MO	63045	314-813-1555	
Web: legacypackaging.com					
Letco Medical Inc 1316 Commerce Dr NW	Decatur	AL	35601	256-350-1297	
Web: www.letcomedical.com					
Martec USA LLC 1800 N Topping Ave	Kansas City	MO	64120	816-241-4144	
Merical Inc 233 E Bristol Ln	Orange	CA	92865	714-283-9551	238-7249
Web: www.merical.com					
Mericon Industries Inc 8819 N Pioneer Rd	Peoria	IL	61615	309-693-2150	
TF: 800-242-6464 ■ *Web:* www.mericon-industries.com					
Meta Pharmaceutical Services LLC					
482 Norristown Rd Ste 200	Blue Bell	PA	19422	610-834-9988	
Web: www.metapharm.net					

	Phone	Fax
Morton Grove Pharmaceuticals Inc 6451 Main St . . . . . Morton Grove IL 60053 **Fax Area Code:* 973 ■ *TF:* 800-346-6854 ■ *Web:* www.wockhardtusa.com	847-967-5600	257-4978*
Mylan Pharmaceuticals ULC 85 Advance Rd . . . . . Etobicoke ON M8Z2S6 *TF:* 800-575-1379 ■ *Web:* www.mylan.ca	416-236-2631	236-2940
Nephron Pharmaceuticals Corp 4121 SW 34th St . . . . . Orlando FL 32811 *TF:* 800-443-4313 ■ *Web:* www.nephronpharm.com	407-999-2225	872-1733
Nexgen Pharma Inc 46 Corporate Pk Ste 100 . . . . . Irvine CA 92606 *Web:* www.nexgenpharma.com	949-863-0340	261-2928
Norman Noble Inc 5507 Avion Park Dr . . . . . Highland Heights OH 44143 *Web:* www.normannoble.net	216-761-5387	
NuCare Pharmaceuticals Inc 622 W Katella Ave . . . . . Orange CA 92867 *TF:* 888-482-9545 ■ *Web:* www.nucarerx.com	888-482-9545	
Osteohealth Co 1 Luitpold Dr . . . . . Shirley NY 11967 *Web:* www.osteohealth.com	631-924-4000	
Par Pharmaceutical Cos Inc 6 Ram Ridge Rd . . . . . Chestnut Ridge NY 10977 *NYSE: PRX* ■ *TF:* 800-828-9393 ■ *Web:* www.parpharm.com	201-802-4000	
Par Pharmaceutical Inc 1 Ram Ridge Rd . . . . . Spring Valley NY 10977 *TF:* 800-828-9393 ■ *Web:* www.parpharm.com	201-802-4000	802-4600
Payless Drug Stores Inc 16100 SW 72nd Ave PO Box 230969 . . . . . Portland OR 97224 *TF:* 800-330-3665 ■ *Web:* www.paylessdrug.com	503-626-9436	372-1792
Perrigo Co 515 Eastern Ave . . . . . Allegan MI 49010 *NYSE: PRGO* ■ *TF:* 800-719-9260 ■ *Web:* www.perrigo.com	269-673-8451	673-9128
Pharmaceutical Calibrations & Instrumentation LLC 8100 Brownleigh Dr Ste 100-A . . . . . Raleigh NC 27617 *TF:* 877-724-2257 ■ *Web:* www.pci-llc.com	877-724-2257	
Pharmanet Development Group Inc 504 Carnegie Ctr . . . . . Princeton NJ 08540 *Web:* www.inventivhealthclinical.com	609-951-6800	514-0390
Ranbaxy Pharmaceuticals Inc 600 College Rd E Ste 2100 . . . . . Princeton NJ 08540	609-720-9200	720-1155
Rowpar Pharmaceuticals Inc 16100 N Greenway Hayden Loop Ste 400 . . . . . Scottsdale AZ 85260 *Web:* www.closys.com	480-948-6997	
Sandoz Inc 506 Carnegie Ctr Ste 400 . . . . . Princeton NJ 08540 *Web:* www.us.sandoz.com	609-627-8500	627-8659
Sentry BioPharma Services Inc 4605 Decatur Blvd Ameriplex Park . . . . . Indianapolis IN 46241 *Web:* www.sentrybps.com	317-856-5889	
Skilled Care Pharmacy Inc 6175 Hi Tek Ct . . . . . Mason OH 45040 *TF:* 800-334-1624 ■ *Web:* www.skilledcare.com	513-459-7455	459-8278
Taro Pharmaceuticals USA Inc 3 Skyline Dr . . . . . Hawthorne NY 10532 *TF:* 800-544-1449 ■ *Web:* www.taro.com/usa	914-345-9001	345-8727
Teva Animal Health Inc 3915 S 48th St Ter . . . . . St. Joseph MO 64503	816-364-3777	
Teva Pharmaceutical USA 1090 Horsham Rd . . . . . North Wales PA 19454 *NYSE: TEVA* ■ *TF:* 800-545-8800 ■ *Web:* www.tevagenerics.com	215-591-3000	591-8600
Triumph Pharmaceuticals Inc 1918 Innerbelt Business Ctr Dr . . . . . St. Louis MO 63114 *Web:* www.smartmouth.com	314-995-3090	
TruTouch Technologies Inc 73 Carriage Way . . . . . Sudbury MA 01776 *TF:* 866-721-6221 ■ *Web:* www.trutouchtechnologies.com	866-721-6221	
UDL Laboratories Inc 1718 Northrock Ct . . . . . Rockford IL 61103 **Fax Area Code:* 815 ■ *TF:* 800-435-5272 ■ *Web:* mylan.com/products	800-848-0462	282-9391*
USL Pharma 301 S Cherokee St . . . . . Denver CO 80223 *TF:* 800-654-2299 ■ *Web:* www.upsher-smith.com	303-607-4500	
Vectech Pharmaceutical Consultants International Inc 5640 W Maple Rd Ste 312 . . . . . West Bloomfield MI 48322 *Web:* www.vpcint.com	248-538-5150	
West-Ward Pharmaceutical Corp 401 Industrial Way W . . . . . Eatontown NJ 07724 *TF Cust Svc:* 800-631-2174	732-542-1191	542-0940
X-Gen Pharmaceuticals Inc 300 Daniels Zenker Dr . . . . . Horseheads NY 14845 *TF:* 866-390-4411 ■ *Web:* www.x-gen.us	866-390-4411	
Xanodyne Pharmaceuticals Inc 1 Riverfront Pl . . . . . Newport KY 41071	859-371-6383	371-6391

584 PHARMACEUTICAL & DIAGNOSTIC PRODUCTS - VETERINARY

	Phone	Fax
Abbott Laboratories Animal Health Div 1401 Sheridan Rd . . . . . North Chicago IL 60064 *TF:* 888-299-7416	847-937-6100	938-0659
ABS Corp 7031 N 16th St . . . . . Omaha NE 68112 *Web:* www.abs-corporation.com	402-453-6970	
Addison Biological Laboratory Inc 507 N Cleveland Ave . . . . . Fayette MO 65248 *TF:* 800-331-2530 ■ *Web:* www.addisonlabs.com	660-248-2215	248-2554
Alltech Inc 3031 Catnip Hill Pike . . . . . Nicholasville KY 40356 *TF:* 800-289-8324 ■ *Web:* www.alltech.com	859-885-9613	887-3256
Bimeda-MTC Animal Health Inc 420 Beaverdale Rd . . . . . Cambridge ON N3C2W4 *TF:* 888-524-6332 ■ *Web:* www.bimedamtc.com	519-654-8000	654-8001
Bio-Serv 3 Foster Lane Ste 201 . . . . . Flemington NJ 08822 *TF:* 800-996-9908 ■ *Web:* www.bio-serv.com	908-284-2155	284-4753
Biomune Co 8906 Rosehill Rd . . . . . Lenexa KS 66215 *Web:* ceva.us	913-894-0230	894-0236
Bioniche Life Sciences Inc. 231 Dundas St E . . . . . Belleville ON K8N1E2 *TSE: BNC* ■ *TF:* 800-265-5464 ■ *Web:* www.bionicheanimalhealth.com	613-966-8058	
Biovet Inc 4375 Ave Beaudry . . . . . Saint-Hyacinthe QC J2S8W2 *TF:* 888-824-6838 ■ *Web:* biovet.ca	450-771-7291	771-4158
Biovet USA Inc 9025 Penn Ave S . . . . . Bloomington MN 55431 *TF:* 877-824-6838 ■ *Web:* biovet.ca	952-884-3113	
Boehringer Ingelheim Vetmedica Inc 2621 N Belt Hwy . . . . . Saint Joseph MO 64506 *TF:* 800-821-7467 ■ *Web:* www.bi-vetmedica.com	816-233-2571	
Central Coast Pharmacy 590 Main St Ste B . . . . . Templeton CA 93465	805-434-5999	
Cut-Heal Animal Care Products Inc 923 S Cedar Hill Rd . . . . . Cedar Hill TX 75104 **Fax Area Code:* 240 ■ *TF:* 800-288-4325	972-293-9700	597-2157*
Darby Group Cos Inc 300 Jericho Quad . . . . . Jericho NY 11753	516-683-1800	688-2880
Dawe's Laboratories 3355 N Arlington Heights Rd . . . . . Arlington Heights IL 60004 *Web:* dawesnutrition.com	847-577-2020	577-1898
Delmont Laboratories Inc 715 Harvard Ave PO Box 269 . . . . . Swarthmore PA 19081 *TF:* 800-562-5541 ■ *Web:* www.delmontlabs.com	610-543-2747	543-6298
DMS Laboratories Inc 2 Darts Mill Rd . . . . . Flemington NJ 08822 *TF:* 800-567-4367 ■ *Web:* www.rapidvet.com	908-782-3353	782-0832
Dominion Veterinary Laboratories Inc 1199 Sanford St . . . . . Winnipeg MB R3E3A1 *TF:* 800-465-7122 ■ *Web:* www.domvet.com	204-589-7361	943-9612
Elanco Animal Health 2500 Innovation Way . . . . . Greenfield IN 46140 *TF:* 877-352-6261 ■ *Web:* www.elanco.com	317-276-2000	
Heska Corp 3760 Rocky Mtn Ave . . . . . Loveland CO 80538 *NASDAQ: HSKA* ■ *TF:* 800-464-3752 ■ *Web:* www.heska.com	970-493-7272	619-3005
IMMVAC Inc 6080 Bass Ln . . . . . Columbia MO 65201 *TF:* 800-944-7563 ■ *Web:* www.immvac.com	573-443-5363	874-7108
K & K Veterinary Supply Inc 675 E Laura Ln . . . . . Tontitown AR 72770 **Fax Area Code:* 470 ■ *Web:* www.kkvet.com	479-361-1516	361-1744*
King Bio Pharmaceuticals Inc 3 Westside Dr . . . . . Asheville NC 28806 *TF:* 800-543-3245 ■ *Web:* www.kingbio.com	828-255-0201	255-0940
Lake Immunogenics Inc 348 Berg Rd . . . . . Ontario NY 14519 **Fax Area Code:* 585 ■ *TF:* 800-648-9990 ■ *Web:* www.lakeimmunogenics.com	800-648-9990	265-2306*
Lloyd Inc 604 W Thomas Ave PO Box 130 . . . . . Shenandoah IA 51601 *TF:* 800-831-0004 ■ *Web:* www.lloydinc.com	712-246-4000	246-5245
Luitpold Pharmaceuticals Inc 1 Luitpold Dr PO Box 9001 . . . . . Shirley NY 11967 *TF:* 800-645-1706 ■ *Web:* www.luitpold.com	631-924-4000	924-1731
Merial Ltd 3239 Satellite Blvd Bldg 500 . . . . . Duluth GA 30096 *TF:* 888-637-4251 ■ *Web:* www.merial.com	678-638-3000	
MVP Laboratories Inc 4805 G St . . . . . Omaha NE 68117 *TF:* 800-856-4648 ■ *Web:* www.mvplabs.com	402-331-5106	331-8776
MWI Veterinary Supply Inc 3041 W Pasadena Dr . . . . . Boise ID 83705 *NASDAQ: MWIV* ■ *Web:* www.mwivet.com	208-955-8930	
Novartis Animal Health US Inc 1447 140th St . . . . . Larchwood IA 51241	712-477-2811	
Nutra-Blend Inc 3200 Second St . . . . . Neosho MO 64850 **Fax Area Code:* 417 ■ *TF:* 800-657-5657 ■ *Web:* www.nutrablend.net	800-657-5657	451-4515*
Pfizer Inc Animal Health Group 235 E 42nd St . . . . . New York NY 10017 *TF:* 800-879-3477 ■ *Web:* www.pfizer.com	212-733-2323	
ProtaTek International Inc 2635 University Ave W Ste 140 . . . . . Saint Paul MN 55114 *Web:* www.protatek.com	651-644-5391	644-6831
Renco Corp 116 Third Ave N . . . . . Minneapolis MN 55401 *TF:* 800-359-8181 ■ *Web:* www.rencocorp.com	612-338-6124	333-9026
Texas Vet Lab Inc 1702 N Bell St . . . . . San Angelo TX 76903 *TF:* 800-284-8403 ■ *Web:* www.texasvetlab.com	800-284-8403	
Veterinary Pharmacies of America Inc 2854 Antoine Dr . . . . . Houston TX 77092 *TF:* 877-838-7979 ■ *Web:* www.vetrxrx.com	877-838-7979	329-7979
Vetoquinol Canada Inc 2000 Ch Georges . . . . . Lavaltrie QC J5T3S5 *TF:* 800-363-1700 ■ *Web:* www.vetoquinol.ca	450-586-2252	586-4649
XF Enterprises Inc 500 S Taylor Ste 301 PO Box 229 . . . . . Amarillo TX 79101 **Fax Area Code:* 620 ■ *Web:* www.xfent.com	806-367-5810	672-5564*

585 PHARMACY ASSOCIATIONS - STATE

See Also Health & Medical Professionals Associations p. 1789

	Phone	Fax
Alabama Pharmacy Assn 1211 Carmichael Way . . . . . Montgomery AL 36106 *TF General:* 877-877-3962 ■ *Web:* www.aparx.org	334-271-4222	271-5423
Alaska Pharmacist's Assn 203 W 15th Ave Ste 100 . . . . . Anchorage AK 99501 *TF:* 800-228-9290 ■ *Web:* www.alaskapharmacy.org	907-563-8880	563-7880
Arizona Pharmacy Assn 1845 E Southern Ave . . . . . Tempe AZ 85282 *Web:* www.azpharmacy.org	480-838-3385	838-3557
Arkansas Pharmacists Assn 417 S Victory St . . . . . Little Rock AR 72201 *Web:* www.arpharmacists.org	501-372-5250	372-0546
California Pharmacists Assn (CPhA) 4030 Lennane Dr . . . . . Sacramento CA 95834 *TF:* 866-365-7472 ■ *Web:* www.cpha.com	916-779-1400	779-1401
Colorado Pharmacists Society 6825 E Tennessee Ave Ste 440 . . . . . Denver CO 80224 *Web:* www.copharm.org	303-756-3069	756-3649
Connecticut Pharmacists Assn 35 Cold Spring Rd Ste 121 . . . . . Rocky Hill CT 06067 *Web:* www.ctpharmacists.org	860-563-4619	257-8241
Delaware Pharmacists Society 27 N Main St . . . . . Smyrna DE 19977 *Web:* www.dpsrx.org	302-659-3088	
Florida Pharmacy Assn 610 N Adams St . . . . . Tallahassee FL 32301 *Web:* www.pharmview.com	850-222-2400	561-6758
Georgia Pharmacy Assn (GPhA) 50 Lenox Pointe NE . . . . . Atlanta GA 30324 *TF:* 888-871-5590 ■ *Web:* www.gpha.org	404-231-5074	237-8435
Idaho State Pharmacy Assn (ISPA) 816 W Bannock St Ste 105 . . . . . Boise ID 83702 *Web:* www.idahopharmacists.com	208-870-8312	
Illinois Pharmacists Assn (IPhA) 204 W Cook St . . . . . Springfield IL 62704 *Web:* www.ipha.org	217-522-7300	522-7349
Indiana Pharmacists Alliance 729 N Pennsylvania St . . . . . Indianapolis IN 46204 *TF:* 800-516-0313 ■ *Web:* netforum.avectra.com	317-634-4968	632-1219
Iowa Pharmacy Assn 8515 Douglas Ave Ste 16 . . . . . Des Moines IA 50322 *TF:* 866-512-1800 ■ *Web:* www.iarx.org	515-270-0713	270-2979
Kansas Pharmacists Assn 1020 SW Fairlawn Rd . . . . . Topeka KS 66604 *TF:* 888-792-6273 ■ *Web:* kansaspharmacistsassociation.wildapricot.org	785-228-2327	
Kentucky Pharmacists Assn 1228 US 127 S . . . . . Frankfort KY 40601 *TF:* 800-922-1557 ■ *Web:* kphanet.org	502-227-2303	227-2258

Phone Fax

Louisiana Pharmacists Assn
450 Laurel St Ste 1400 . . . . Baton Rouge LA 70801 225-346-6883 344-1132
TF: 877-252-5100 ■ *Web:* www.louisianapharmacists.com

Maine Pharmacy Assn 127 Pleasant Hill Rd . . . . Scarborough ME 04074 207-396-5340 396-5341
Web: www.mparx.com

Maryland Pharmacists Assn
9115 Guilford Rd Ste 200 . . . . Columbia MD 21046 410-727-0746 727-2253
TF: 877-463-3464 ■ *Web:* www.marylandpharmacist.org

Massachusetts Pharmacists Assn
500 W Cummings Pk Ste 3475 . . . . Woburn MA 01801 781-933-1107 933-1109
TF: 888-772-7227 ■ *Web:* netforum.avectra.com

Michigan Pharmacists Assn 408 Kalamazoo Plz . . . . Lansing MI 48933 517-484-1466 484-4893
TF: 800-227-2345 ■ *Web:* www.michiganpharmacists.org

Minnesota Pharmacists Assn (MPhA)
1935 W County Rd B2 . . . . Roseville MN 55113 651-697-1771 697-1776
TF: 800-451-8349 ■ *Web:* www.mpha.org

Mississippi Pharmacists Assn
341 Edgewood Terr Dr . . . . Jackson MS 39206 601-981-0416 981-0451
TF: 800-421-2408 ■ *Web:* www.mspharm.org

Missouri Pharmacy Assn
211 E Capitol Ave . . . . Jefferson City MO 65101 573-636-7522 636-7485
TF: 800-468-4672 ■ *Web:* www.morx.com

Nebraska Pharmacists Assn
6221 S 58th St Ste A . . . . Lincoln NE 68516 402-420-1500 420-1406
TF: 866-365-7472 ■ *Web:* www.npharm.org

New Jersey Pharmacists Assn
760 Alexander Rd PO Box 1 . . . . Princeton NJ 08543 609-275-4246 275-4066
Web: njpharmacists.org

New Mexico Pharmacists Assn (NMPhA)
2716 San Pedro Dr NE # C . . . . Albuquerque NM 87110 505-265-8729
Web: www.nm-pharmacy.com

North Carolina Assn of Pharmacists
109 Church St . . . . Chapel Hill NC 27516 919-967-2237 968-9430
Web: www.ncpharmacists.org

North Dakota Pharmacists Assn (NDPhA)
1641 Capitol Way . . . . Bismarck ND 58501 701-258-4968 258-9312
Web: www.nodakpharmacy.net

Ohio Pharmacists Assn 2674 Federated Blvd . . . . Columbus OH 43235 614-389-3236 389-4582
Web: www.associationdatabase.com

Oklahoma Pharmacists Assn
45 NE 52nd St . . . . Oklahoma City OK 73105 405-528-3338 528-1417
Web: www.opha.com

Oregon State Pharmacy Assn (OSPA)
147 SE 102nd Ave . . . . Portland OR 97216 503-582-9055 253-9172
Web: www.oregonpharmacy.org

Pennsylvania Pharmacists Assn
508 N Third St . . . . Harrisburg PA 17101 717-234-6151 236-1618
Web: www.papharmacists.com

Pharmacists Society of the State of New York
210 Washington Ave Ext . . . . Albany NY 12203 518-869-6595 464-0618
TF: 800-632-8822 ■ *Web:* www.pssny.org

Pharmacy Society of Wisconsin
701 Heartland Trl . . . . Madison WI 53717 608-827-9200 827-9292
Web: www.pswi.org

South Carolina Pharmacy Assn
1350 Browning Rd . . . . Columbia SC 29210 803-354-9977 354-9207
Web: www.scrx.org

South Dakota Pharmacists Assn PO Box 518 . . . . Pierre SD 57501 605-224-2338 224-1280
Web: www.sdpha.org

Tennessee Pharmacists Assn
500 Church St Ste 650 . . . . Nashville TN 37219 615-256-3023 255-3528
Web: www.tnpharm.org

Texas Pharmacy Assn
12007 Research Blvd Ste 201 . . . . Austin TX 78759 512-836-8350 836-0308
TF: 800-505-5463 ■ *Web:* www.texaspharmacy.org

Washington State Pharmacy Assn
411 Williams Ave S . . . . Renton WA 98057 425-228-7171 277-3897
TF: 800-562-6000 ■ *Web:* www.wsparx.org

West Virginia Pharmacists Assn
2016 1/2 Kanawha Blvd E . . . . Charleston WV 25311 304-344-5302 344-5316
Web: wvpharmacy.org

Wyoming Pharmacists Assn 150 Powell St . . . . Green River WY 82935 307-272-3361
Web: www.wpha.net

586 PHARMACY BENEFITS MANAGEMENT SERVICES

A pharmacy benefits management service (PBM) is a company that manages various pharmacy-related aspects of a health insurance plan, such as the assignment of pharmacy cards, claims filing and processing, formulary management, etc. For the most part, PBM clients are insurance companies, HMOs, or PPOs rather than individuals or pharmacies.

Phone Fax

Abtex Corp 89 Main St PO Box 188 . . . . Dresden NY 14441 315-536-7403
Web: www.abtex.com

BioScrip 1600 Bdwy Ste 950 . . . . Denver CO 80202 720-697-5200
NASDAQ: BIOS ■ *TF:* 877-409-2301 ■ *Web:* www.bioscrip.com

Caremark Rx Inc PO Box 832407 . . . . Richardson TX 75083 877-460-7766
TF: 877-460-7766 ■ *Web:* www.caremark.com

CoreSource Inc 400 Field Dr. . . . . Lake Forest IL 60045 847-604-9200 615-3900
TF: 800-832-3332 ■ *Web:* www.coresource.com

Cvs Caremark 695 George Washington Hwy . . . . Lincoln RI 02865 401-334-0069
Web: www.cvs.com

Health Smart Rx 1301 E Ninth St . . . . Cleveland OH 44114 800-681-6912 479-2015*
**Fax Area Code:* 216 ■ *TF:* 800-681-6912 ■ *Web:* www.healthsmart.com

Maxor National Pharmacy Services Corp
320 S Polk St Ste 100 . . . . Amarillo TX 79101 806-324-5400 324-5495
TF: 800-658-6146 ■ *Web:* www.maxor.com

Medco Health Solutions Inc
100 Parsons Pond Dr . . . . Franklin Lakes NJ 07417 201-269-3400
NYSE: MHS ■ *Web:* www.express-scripts.com

MedImpact Healthcare Systems Inc
10680 Treena St Ste 500 . . . . San Diego CA 92131 858-566-2727 790-6454
TF: 800-788-2949 ■ *Web:* www.medimpact.com

Phone Fax

Old Dominion Brush Co 5118 Glen Alden Dr . . . . Richmond VA 23231 804-226-4433
Web: www.odbco.com

Premier Paint Roller LLC
131-11 Atlantic Ave . . . . Richmond Hill NY 11418 718-441-7700
Web: www.premierpaintroller.com

Prescription Solutions 3515 Harbor Blvd . . . . Costa Mesa CA 92626 800-788-4863
TF: 800-788-4863 ■ *Web:* www.optumrx.com

Prime Therapeutics Inc 1305 Corporate Ctr Dr . . . . Eagan MN 55121 612-777-4000 286-4263*
**Fax Area Code:* 651 ■ *TF:* 800-858-0723 ■ *Web:* www.primetherapeutics.com

San Antonio Lighthouse for The Blind
2305 Roosevelt Ave . . . . San Antonio TX 78210 210-533-5195
Web: www.idworld.net

Schaefer Brush Manufacturing Company Inc
1101 S Prairie Ave . . . . Waukesha WI 53186 262-547-3500
Web: schaeferbrush.com

ScripNet 10050 Banburry Cross Dr Ste 290 . . . . Las Vegas NV 89144 702-248-2692 245-1745*
**Fax Area Code:* 888 ■ *TF:* 888-880-8562 ■ *Web:* www.scripnet.com

Script Care Inc 6380 Folsom Dr . . . . Beaumont TX 77706 800-880-9988 833-7435*
**Fax Area Code:* 409 ■ *TF:* 800-880-9988 ■ *Web:* www.scriptcare.com

ScriptSave 4911 E Broadway Blvd Ste 200 . . . . Tucson AZ 85711 800-347-5985
TF: 800-347-5985 ■ *Web:* www.scriptsave.com

Serve You Custom Prescription Management
10201 Innovation Dr Ste 600 . . . . Milwaukee WI 53226 414-410-8100 410-8181
TF: 888-243-6890 ■ *Web:* www.serve-you-rx.com

Walgreens Health Services
1411 Lake Cook Rd . . . . Deerfield IL 60015 800-207-2568
TF: 800-207-2568 ■ *Web:* www.walgreenshealth.com

587 PHARMACY MANAGEMENT SERVICES

Companies that provide long-term care pharmacy services to individuals with special needs (e.g., chronic disease or advanced age); and those that provide pharmacy management services to hospitals or other institutions.

Phone Fax

Accredo Health Group Inc
1640 Century Ctr Pkwy . . . . Memphis TN 38134 901-385-3600
TF: 877-222-7336 ■ *Web:* www.accredo.com

Catalyst Pharmaceutical Research LLC
1111 S Arroyo Pkwy Ste 200 . . . . Pasadena CA 91105 626-568-8645
Web: www.catalystpharm.com

Fisher Bio Svc Inc 14665 Rothgeb Dr. . . . . Rockville MD 20850 301-315-8460 838-9320
Web: www.fisherbioservices.com

JAF Consulting Inc 6 Washington Ave . . . . Mullica Hill NJ 08062 856-241-1900
Web: www.jafconsulting.com

McKesson Pharmaceutical 1 Post St. . . . . San Francisco CA 94104 415-983-8300
TF: 800-571-2889 ■ *Web:* www.mckesson.com

Monster Medic Inc 909 Perkins Dr. . . . . Mukwonago WI 53149 262-363-3066
Web: www.monstermedic.com

Omnicare Inc 201 E 4th St. . . . . Cincinnati OH 45202 800-990-6664 392-3333*
NYSE: OCR ■ **Fax Area Code:* 859 ■ *TF:* 800-342-5627 ■ *Web:* omnicare.com

Pharmacy Systems Inc
5050 Bradenton Ave PO Box 130 . . . . Dublin OH 43017 614-766-0101 766-4448
Web: www.pharmacysystems.com

Tech Pharmacy Services Inc
900 S Loop W Ste 100 . . . . Houston TX 77054 713-391-2200
Web: www.advancedpharmacy.com

588 PHOTO PROCESSING & STORAGE

Phone Fax

Advanced Photographic Solutions
1525 Hardeman Ln . . . . Cleveland TN 37312 423-479-5481
TF: 800-241-9234 ■ *Web:* www.advancedphoto.com

BCP International Ltd
1800 N Beauregard St Ste 350 . . . . Alexandria VA 22311 703-575-7300

Burrell Imaging 1311 Merrillville Rd. . . . . Crown Point IN 46307 219-663-3210 662-0915
TF: 800-348-8732 ■ *Web:* www.burrellprolabs.com

Candid Color Systems Inc
1300 Metropolitan Ave . . . . Oklahoma City OK 73108 405-947-8747 951-7353
TF: 800-336-4550 ■ *Web:* www.candid.com

Dale Laboratories 2960 Simms St . . . . Hollywood FL 33020 954-925-0103 922-3008
TF: 800-327-1776 ■ *Web:* www.dalelabs.com

District Photo Inc 10501 Rhode Island Ave . . . . Beltsville MD 20705 301-937-5300 937-5627
Web: www.districtphoto.com

dotPhoto Inc PO Box 92 2nd Fl. . . . . Titusville NJ 08560 609-434-0340 434-0344
Web: www.dotphoto.com

Dreamstime LLC 1616 Wgate Cir . . . . Brentwood TN 37027 615-771-5611
Web: www.dreamstime.com

FLM Graphics 123 Lehigh Dr. . . . . Fairfield NJ 07004 973-575-9450 575-6424
Web: www.flmgraphics.com

Graphic Systems Inc 2632 26th Ave S. . . . . Minneapolis MN 55406 612-721-6100
Web: www.graphicsystems.com

H & H Color Lab Inc 8906 E 67th St . . . . Raytown MO 64133 816-358-6677 313-1480
TF: 800-821-1305 ■ *Web:* www.hhcolorlab.com

iMemories 9181 E Bell Rd . . . . Scottsdale AZ 85260 800-845-7986 767-2511*
**Fax Area Code:* 480 ■ *TF:* 800-845-7986 ■ *Web:* www.imemories.com

McKenna Pro Imaging 2800 Falls Ave. . . . . Waterloo IA 50701 319-235-6265 235-1121
TF General: 800-238-3456 ■ *Web:* www.mckennapro.com

Meisel Visual Imaging 2019 McKenzie Dr . . . . Carrollton TX 75006 214-688-4950 688-4950
TF: 800-527-5186 ■ *Web:* www.meisel.com

Photo USA 2140 Colonial Ave . . . . Roanoke VA 24015 540-344-0961
TF: 888-234-6320 ■ *Web:* www.photousa.com

PNI Digital Media Inc
425 Carrall St Ste 590 . . . . Vancouver BC V6B6E3 604-893-8955
TSE: PN ■ *Web:* www.pnidigitalmedia.com

Shutterfly.com 2800 Bridge Pkwy Ste 101 . . . . Redwood City CA 94065 650-610-5200 654-1299
Web: www.shutterfly.com

Yahoo! Photos 701 First Ave. . . . . Sunnyvale CA 94089 408-349-3300 349-3301
TF: 888-267-7574 ■ *Web:* www.flickr.com

589 PHOTOCOPYING EQUIPMENT & SUPPLIES

See Also Business Machines - Whol p. 1884

				Phone	Fax
Coast to Coast Business Equipment Inc 8 Vanderbilt *TF:* 877-382-4357 ■ *Web:* www.ctcbe.com	Irvine	CA	92619	949-457-7300	457-7365
Eastman Kodak Co 343 State St *OTC: EKDKQ* ■ *Web:* www.kodak.com	Rochester	NY	14650	585-724-4000	
FlexPrint Inc 2845 N Omaha St *Web:* www.flexprintinc.com	Mesa	AZ	85215	480-368-0011	
Imaging Supplies Company Inc 804 Woodland Ave *TF:* 800-518-1152 ■ *Web:* www.imagingsuppliesco.com	Sanford	NC	27330	919-776-1152	
Konica Minolta Business Solutions USA Inc 100 Williams Dr *Web:* www.kmbs.konicaminolta.us	Ramsey	NJ	07446	201-825-4000	
Kyocera Mita Corp 225 Sand Rd PO Box 40008 *Web:* www.kyoceradocumentsolutions.com	Fairfield	NJ	07004	973-808-8444	
Lasercycle USA Inc 528 S Taylor Ave *Web:* www.lasercycleusa.com	Louisville	CO	80027	303-666-7776	
Masterfile Corp 3 Concorde Gate 4th Fl *TF:* 800-387-9010 ■ *Web:* www.masterfile.com	Toronto	ON	M3C3N7	416-929-3000	
Northwest Print Strategies Inc 8175 Sw Nimbus Ave *TF:* 800-648-5156 ■ *Web:* www.nwpsi.com	Beaverton	OR	97008	503-641-5156	
Oce-USA Inc 5450 N Cumberland Ave *TF:* 800-877-6232 ■ *Web:* csa.canon.com	Chicago	IL	60656	773-714-8500	693-7634
Precision Printer Services Inc 9185 Portage Industrial Dr *Web:* www.precisionprinterservices.com	Portage	MI	49024	269-384-5725	
R & D Computers 6767 Peachtree Industrial Blvd Ste B *TF:* 800-350-3071 ■ *Web:* www.randdcomp.com	Atlanta	GA	30092	770-416-0103	
Sharp Electronics Corp 1 Sharp Plz *TF:* 800-237-4277 ■ *Web:* www.sharpusa.com	Mahwah	NJ	07430	201-529-8200	529-8413
Toshiba America Inc 1251 Ave of the Americas Ste 4100 *TF:* 800-457-7777 ■ *Web:* www.toshiba.com	New York	NY	10020	212-596-0600	593-3875
Virtual Backgrounds Llc 101 Uhland Rd Ste 201 *Web:* www.virtualbackgrounds.net	San Marcos	TX	78666	512-805-4844	
Xerox Canada Ltd 5650 Yonge St *TF:* 800-939-3769 ■ *Web:* www.xerox.ca	North York	ON	M2M4G7	800-939-3769	
Xerox Corp 45 Glover Ave PO Box 4505 *NYSE: XRX* ■ *TF:* 800-327-9753 ■ *Web:* www.xerox.com	Norwalk	CT	06856	203-968-3000	

590 PHOTOGRAPH STUDIOS - PORTRAIT

				Phone	Fax
Alderman Studios 325 Model Farm Rd *Web:* aldermancompany.com	High Point	NC	27263	336-889-6121	889-7717
All-League Sports Photos & Lab Inc 27062 Burbank *Web:* www.allleaguesportsphotos.com	Foothill Ranch	CA	92610	949-598-9297	
Andy Rice Photography 7226 Rue De Roark *Web:* www.andyricephoto.com	La Jolla	CA	92037	858-459-8458	
Artech Photography Studio 3404 Bath Rd	Perry	MI	48872	517-625-5177	
Bell Photographers 341 Garfield St *Web:* www.bellphoto.com	Idaho Falls	ID	83401	208-524-4601	
Berliner Photography LLC 314 N La Brea Ave	Los Angeles	CA	90036	323-857-1282	
Bryn-Alan Studios Inc 502 W Grand Central Ave *Web:* lifetouch.com	Tampa	FL	33606	813-253-2693	
Cherry Hill Photo Enterprises Inc 4 East Stow Rd *TF:* 800-969-2440 ■ *Web:* www.cherryhillphoto.com	Marlton	NJ	08053	800-969-2440	
CPI Corp 1706 Washington Ave *OTC: CPIC* ■ *Web:* www.cpicorp.com	Saint Louis	MO	63103	314-231-1575	
CPI Daylighting Inc 28662 N Ballard Dr *Web:* www.cpidaylighting.com	Lake Forest	IL	60045	847-816-1060	
Forster Daniel Marine Photography 57 High St *Web:* www.yachtphoto.com	Jamestown	RI	02835	401-423-1900	
Fox Edward Photography 4900 N Milwaukee Ave *Web:* www.edwardfox.com	Chicago	IL	60630	773-736-0200	
Freed Photography Inc 4931 Cordell Ave Ste 101 *Web:* www.freedphoto.com	Bethesda	MD	20814	301-652-5452	
Freestyle Photo Biz 5124 Sunset Blvd *TF:* 800-292-6137 ■ *Web:* www.freestylephoto.biz	Hollywood	CA	90027	800-292-6137	
Freeze Frame LLC 4205 Vineland Rd *Web:* www.freezeframe.com	Orlando	FL	32811	407-648-2111	
Gartner Studios Inc 220 Myrtle St E *Web:* www.gartnerstudios.com	Stillwater	MN	55082	651-351-7700	351-1408
George STREET Photo & Video LLC 230 W Huron St Ste 3W *TF:* 866-831-4103 ■ *Web:* www.georgestreetphoto.com	Chicago	IL	60654	866-831-4103	
Hallmark Institute of Photography 241 Millers Falls Rd *Web:* www.hallmark.edu	Turners Falls	MA	01376	413-863-2478	
Imaging Associates Inc 11110 Westlake Dr *Web:* www.imaginga.com	Charlotte	NC	28273	704-522-8094	
Jostens Inc 3601 Minnesota Ave Ste 400 **Fax:* Hum Res ■ *TF:* 800-235-4774 ■ *Web:* www.jostens.com	Minneapolis	MN	55435	952-830-3300	830-3293*
Lafayette Frame Shop 651 Germantown Pk *Web:* www.lafayette.com	Lafayette Hill	PA	19444	610-629-0704	
Lumedyne Technologies Inc 9275 Sky Park Ct Ste 100 *Web:* www.omegasensors.com	San Diego	CA	92123	858-560-5208	
MarathonFoto 3490 Martin Hurst Rd *TF:* 800-424-3686 ■ *Web:* www.marathonfoto.com	Tallahassee	FL	32312	972-330-7656	
New England School of Photography 537 Commonwealth Ave *Web:* www.nesop.edu	Boston	MA	02215	617-437-1868	
Olan Mills Inc 4325 Amnicola Hwy *Web:* www.olanmills.com	Chattanooga	TN	37406	423-622-5141	
Peters Main Street Photography 314 N Main St *Web:* www.petersphotography.com	London	OH	43140	740-852-2731	
Portrait Express 441 N Water St *TF:* 800-228-3759 ■ *Web:* www.portraitexpress.com	Silverton	OR	97381	503-873-6365	
Portrait Innovations Inc 2016 Ayrsley Town Blvd Ste 200 *Web:* www.portraitinnovations.com	Charlotte	NC	28273	704-499-9300	
Portraits International 10835 Rockley Rd *TF:* 888-838-1495 ■ *Web:* www.portraitsinternational.com	Houston	TX	77099	281-879-8444	
Ripcho Studio 7630 Lorain Ave *TF:* 800-686-7427 ■ *Web:* www.ripchostudio.com	Cleveland	OH	44102	216-631-0664	
Shugart Studios Inc 812 College Ave	Levelland	TX	79336	806-897-1754	
Spark Studios LLC 10811 Washington Blvd 4th Fl *Web:* www.sparkstudios.com	Culver City	CA	90232	424-298-8950	
Visual Image Photography W63 N582 Hanover Ave *Web:* www.vipis.com	Cedarburg	WI	53012	262-375-4457	
Walters Photography 1013 Suffolk Dr *Web:* portalmedia.com	Janesville	WI	53546	608-752-8808	

591 PHOTOGRAPHIC EQUIPMENT & SUPPLIES

See Also Cameras & Related Supplies - Retail p. 1889

				Phone	Fax
Advance Reproductions Corp 100 Flagship Dr *Web:* www.advancerepro.com	North Andover	MA	01845	978-685-2911	685-1771
Agfa Corp 611 River Dr *TF:* 888-274-8626 ■ *Web:* www.agfagraphics.com/gs/usa/en/internet/maings	Elmwood Park	NJ	07407	201-440-2500	
Alan Gordon Enterprises Inc 5625 Melrose Ave *Web:* www.alangordon.com	Hollywood	CA	90038	323-466-3561	871-2193
Anton/Bauer Inc 14 Progress Dr *TF:* 800-422-3473 ■ *Web:* www.antonbauer.com	Shelton	CT	06484	203-929-1100	929-9935
Ballantyne Strong Inc 13710 FNB Pkwy *NYSE: BTN* ■ *TF General:* 800-424-1215 ■ *Web:* ballantynestrong.com	Omaha	NE	68154	800-424-1215	
Beta Screen Corp 707 Commercial Ave *TF:* 800-272-7336 ■ *Web:* www.betascreen.com	Carlstadt	NJ	07072	201-939-2400	939-7656
Carr Corp 1547 11th St *TF:* 800-952-2398 ■ *Web:* www.carrcorporation.com	Santa Monica	CA	90401	310-587-1113	395-9751
Casio Inc 570 Mt Pleasant Ave **Fax:* Hum Res ■ *TF Cust Svc:* 800-634-1895 ■ *Web:* www.casio.com	Dover	NJ	07801	973-361-5400	537-8964*
Ceiva Logic Inc 214 E Magnolia Blvd *TF Tech Supp:* 877-693-7263 ■ *Web:* www.ceiva.com	Burbank	CA	91502	818-562-1495	562-1491
Champion Photochemistry 7895 Tranmere Dr *TF:* 800-387-3430 ■ *Web:* www.championphotochemistry.com	Mississauga	ON	L5S1V9	905-670-7900	670-2581
Da-Lite Screen Company Inc 3100 N Detroit St *TF:* 800-622-3737 ■ *Web:* www.da-lite.com	Warsaw	IN	46581	574-267-8101	267-7804
Douthitt Corp 245 Adair St *TF:* 800-368-8448 ■ *Web:* www.douthittcorp.com	Detroit	MI	48207	313-259-1565	259-6806
Draper Shade & Screen Co 411 S Pearl St *TF:* 800-238-7999 ■ *Web:* www.draperinc.com	Spiceland	IN	47385	765-987-7999	987-7999
DRS Technologies Inc 2345 Crystal Dr Ste 1000 *Web:* www.drs.com	Arlington	VA	22202	201-337-3800	
Dukane Communication Systems 2900 Dukane Dr *Web:* www.dukane.com	Saint Charles	IL	60174	630-584-2300	584-2300
Eastman Kodak Co 343 State St *OTC: EKDKQ* ■ *Web:* www.kodak.com	Rochester	NY	14650	585-724-4000	
Fuji Photo Film USA Inc 200 Summit Lake Dr **Fax Area Code:* 914 ■ *Web:* www.fujifilm.com	Valhalla	NY	10595	936-520-2720	789-8664*
Geosystems Inc 210 S Washington Ave *Web:* zippermast.com	Titusville	FL	32796	321-383-9585	747-0601
Identatronics Inc 165 N Lively Blvd *TF Cust Svc:* 800-323-5403 ■ *Web:* www.identatronics.com	Elk Grove Village	IL	60007	847-437-2654	
InFocus Corp 13190 SW 68th Pkwy Ste 200 *TF:* 877-388-8385 ■ *Web:* www.infocus.com	Portland	OR	97223	503-207-4700	207-1937
Integrated Design Tools Inc 1202 E Pk Ave *Web:* www.idtvision.com	Tallahassee	FL	32301	850-222-5939	222-4591
Matthews Studio Equipment Group 2405 W Empire Ave **Fax Area Code:* 323 ■ *TF:* 800-237-8263 ■ *Web:* www.msegrip.com	Burbank	CA	91504	818-843-6715	849-1525*
Mogg QuickSet 3650 Woodhead Dr *Web:* www.tripods.com	Northbrook	IL	60062	847-498-0700	498-1258
MVM Products LLC 940 Calle Amanecer Ste K *TF:* 888-246-5832 ■ *Web:* www.ink-jet.com	San Clemente	CA	92673	949-366-1470	
Navitar Inc 200 Commerce Dr *TF Cust Svc:* 800-828-6778 ■ *Web:* www.navitar.com	Rochester	NY	14623	585-359-4000	359-4999
Neumade Products Corp 30 Pecks Ln Ste 40	Newtown	CT	06470	203-270-1100	270-7778
Nikon Inc 1300 Walt Whitman Rd *TF Cust Svc:* 800-645-6687 ■ *Web:* www.nikonusa.com	Melville	NY	11747	631-547-4200	547-0299
OConnor Engineering 2701 N Ontario St *Web:* www.ocon.com	Burbank	CA	91504	818-847-8666	847-1205
Panavision Inc 6219 DeSoto Ave *TF:* 800-260-1846 ■ *Web:* www.panavision.com	Woodland Hills	CA	91367	818-316-1000	316-1111
Peter Pepper Products Inc 17929 S Susana Rd *TF:* 800-496-0204 ■ *Web:* www.peterpepper.com	Compton	CA	90221	310-639-0390	639-6013

	City	State	ZIP	Phone	Fax
Phase One Inc 200 Broadhollow Rd Ste 312	Melville	NY	11747	631-757-0400	547-9898
TF: 888-742-7366 ■ *Web:* www.phaseone.com					
Research Technology International Inc 4700 W Chase Ave	Lincolnwood	IL	60712	847-677-3000	677-1311
TF Sales: 800-323-7520 ■ *Web:* www.rti-us.com					
Sanyo Fisher Co 21605 Plummer St	Chatsworth	CA	91311	818-998-7322	717-2759
Schneider Optics Century Div 7701 Haskell Ave	Van Nuys	CA	91406	818-766-3715	505-9865
TF: 800-228-1254 ■ *Web:* www.schneideroptics.com					
Sharp Electronics Corp 1 Sharp Plz	Mahwah	NJ	07430	201-529-8200	529-8413
TF: 800-237-4277 ■ *Web:* www.sharpusa.com					
Sony Corp of America 550 Madison Ave	New York	NY	10022	212-833-6800	
TF: 800-282-2848 ■ *Web:* www.sony.com					
Stewart Filmscreen Corp 1161 W Sepulveda Blvd	Torrance	CA	90502	310-784-5300	326-6870
TF: 800-762-4999 ■ *Web:* stewartfilmscreen.com					
Tamron USA Inc 10 Austin Blvd	Commack	NY	11725	631-858-8400	543-5666
Web: www.tamron.com/en					
Tiffen Company LLC 90 Oser Ave	Hauppauge	NY	11788	631-273-2500	273-2557
TF: 800-645-2522 ■ *Web:* www.tiffen.com					
Toshiba America Inc 1251 Ave of the Americas Ste 4100	New York	NY	10020	212-596-0600	593-3875
TF: 800-457-7777 ■ *Web:* www.toshiba.com					
Visual Departures Ltd 48 Sheffield Business Park Ste 195	Ashley Falls	MA	01222	800-628-2003	
TF: 800-628-2003 ■ *Web:* www.visualdepartures.com					
Vivitar Corp 195 Carter Dr	Edison	NJ	08817	732-248-1306	
TF: 800-592-9541 ■ *Web:* www.vivitar.com					
Vutec Corp 11711 W Sample Rd	Coral Springs	FL	33065	954-545-9000	545-9011
TF: 800-770-4700 ■ *Web:* www.vutec.com					
Waterhouse Inc 670 Queen St Ste 200	Honolulu	HI	96813	808-592-4800	
Wein Products Inc 115 W 25th St	Los Angeles	CA	90007	213-749-6049	749-6250
Web: www.weinproducts.com					

592 PHOTOGRAPHY - COMMERCIAL

	City	State	ZIP	Phone	Fax
A M C Colorgrafix Inc 2085 Peck Rd	El Monte	CA	91733	626-575-1788	
Web: www.amc-color.com					
Aero Graphics Inc 40 W Oakland Ave	Salt Lake City	UT	84115	801-487-3273	
Web: www.aero-graphics.com					
Albion Associates Inc 622 Southwest St	High Point	NC	27260	336-883-8028	
Web: www.albionassociates.net					
G f Studio Inc 540 Ravine Ct	Wyckoff	NJ	07481	201-445-1002	
Web: www.gfstudio.net					
Holland Litho Printing Service Inc 10972 Chicago Dr	Zeeland	MI	49464	616-392-4644	
Web: www.hollandlitho.com					
Image Craft LLC 3401 E Broadway Rd	Phoenix	AZ	85040	602-276-2082	
Web: www.imagecraft.com					
Image Inc 1100 S Lynndale Dr	Appleton	WI	54914	920-738-4080	
Web: www.imagestudios.com					
Irvin Simon Photographers Inc 146 Meacham Ave	Elmont	NY	11003	516-437-4700	
Web: www.irvinsimon.com					
Kinetic The Technology Agency 200 Distillery Commons Ste 200	Louisville	KY	40206	502-719-9500	
Web: kinetic.thetechnologyagency.com/default.aspx					
Magnum Photos Inc 151 W 25th St Fl 5	New York	NY	10001	212-929-6000	
Web: www.magnumphotos.com					
Photocrazy Inc 509 Raindance St	Thousand Oaks	CA	91360	805-492-0562	
Web: www.photocrazy.com					
Scenic Prints Landscape Photos 536 Sweetwater St	Lander	WY	82520	307-332-1532	
Web: www.scenicprints.com					
Sharp Shooter Spectrum Ventures LLC 11901 W 48th Ave	Wheat Ridge	CO	80033	303-962-2345	
Web: www.sharpshots.com					
Showtime Pictures LLC 5722 S Flamingo Rd Ste 309	Fort Lauderdale	FL	33330	954-252-9591	
Web: www.showtimepictures.com					
Shutterstock Inc 350 Fifth Ave Fl 21	New York	NY	10118	646-419-4452	
Web: www.shutterstock.com					
Sport Graphics PO Box 95	Shrewsbury	MA	01545	508-925-0406	330-7774*
**Fax Area Code:* 877 ■ *Web:* www.sportgraphics.com					
Sprint Multimedia Inc 15619 Premiere Dr Ste 204	Tampa	FL	33624	813-971-0531	
Web: sprintmultimedia.com					
Studio 3 Inc 1316 Se 12th Ave	Portland	OR	97214	503-238-1748	
Web: studio3.com					
Universal Image PO Box 77090	Winter Garden	FL	34787	407-352-5302	
TF: 800-553-5499 ■ *Web:* www.universalphoto.com					
Van Gogh School Photographers 401 Cornell Ave	Barrington	IL	60010	847-382-2282	
Web: vangoghschoolphotographers.com					
Visible Productions Inc 1300 Riverside Ave Ste 101	Fort Collins	CO	80524	970-407-7240	
Web: www.visibleproductions.com					
Wasatch Photonics 1305 North 1000 West Ste 120	Logan	UT	84321	435-752-4301	
Web: www.wasatchphotonics.com					
Zaio Corp 6940 Fisher Rd Se, Ste 200	Calgary	AB	T2HOW3	403-984-9246	
Web: www.zaio.com					

593 PHOTOGRAPHY - STOCK

	City	State	ZIP	Phone	Fax
Alaska Stock Images 2505 Fairbanks St	Anchorage	AK	99503	907-276-1343	258-7848
TF: 800-487-4285 ■ *Web:* www.alaskastock.com					
Bygone Designs PO Box 229	Newport	MN	55055	651-451-6737	
Web: www.bygones.com					
Corbis Corp 710 Second Ave Ste 200	Seattle	WA	98104	646-613-4000	373-6100*
**Fax Area Code:* 206 ■ *TF:* 800-260-0444 ■ *Web:* www.gettyimages.com?corbis					
Custom Medical Stock Photo Inc 3660 W Irving Pk Rd	Chicago	IL	60618	773-267-3100	267-6071
TF: 800-373-2677					
Image Works PO Box 443	Woodstock	NY	12498	845-679-8500	679-0606
TF: 800-475-8801 ■ *Web:* www.theimageworks.com					
ImageState New York 29 E 19th St 4th Fl	New York	NY	10003	212-982-1915	
Mountain Light Photography Inc 106 S Main St	Bishop	CA	93514	760-873-7700	873-3980
Web: www.mountainlight.com					
Photo Researchers Inc 307 Fifth Ave 3rd Fl	New York	NY	10016	212-758-3420	
TF: 800-833-9033 ■ *Web:* www.sciencesource.com					
Photo Resource Hawaii PO Box 1082 Ste 241	Honoka'a	HI	96727	808-599-7773	

594 PIECE GOODS & NOTIONS

See Also Fabric Stores p. 2277

	City	State	ZIP	Phone	Fax
A Meyers & Sons Corp 325 W 38th St	New York	NY	10018	212-279-6632	594-4093
Advanced Probing Systems Inc 2300 Central Ave	Boulder	CO	80301	303-939-9384	
TF: 800-631-0005 ■ *Web:* www.advancedprobing.com					
American Process Lettering Inc 30 Bunting Ln	Primos	PA	19018	610-623-9000	
Web: amprosports.com					
Aplix Inc 12300 Steele Creek Rd	Charlotte	NC	28273	704-588-1920	588-1941
Web: www.aplix.com					
Associated Fabrics Corp 15-01 Pollitt Dr Unit 7	Fair Lawn	NJ	07410	800-232-4077	710-3850*
**Fax Area Code:* 866 ■ *TF:* 800-232-4077 ■ *Web:* www.afc-fabrics.com					
B Berger Co 1380 Highland Rd	Macedonia	OH	44056	330-425-3838	
TF Cust Svc: 800-288-8400 ■ *Web:* duralee.com					
Baum Textile Mills Inc 812 Jersey Ave	Jersey City	NJ	07310	201-659-0444	659-9719
TF: 866-842-7631 ■ *Web:* www.baumtextile.com					
Bay Island Sportswear Inc 225 By Pass 72 NW	Greenwood	SC	29649	864-229-1298	
Web: www.bayislandsportswear.com					
Blank Quilting Corp *Blank Quilting* 49 West 37th St 14th fl	New York	NY	10018	800-294-9495	679-4578*
**Fax Area Code:* 212 ■ *TF:* 800-294-9495 ■ *Web:* blankquilting.net					
Blumenthal Lansing Co 30 Two Bridges Rd Ste 110	Fairfield	NJ	07004	201-935-6220	935-0055
TF: 800-448-9749 ■ *Web:* www.buttons.com					
Bob Barker Company Inc PO Box 429	Fuquay Varina	NC	27526	800-334-9880	
TF: 800-334-9880 ■ *Web:* www.bobbarker.com					
Brookwood Cos Inc 25 W 45th St 11th Fl	New York	NY	10036	212-551-0100	472-0294*
**Fax Area Code:* 646 ■ *TF:* 800-426-5468 ■ *Web:* www.brookwoodcos.net					
Burch Fabrics Group 4200 Brockton Dr SE	Grand Rapids	MI	49512	616-698-2800	698-0011
TF: 800-841-8111 ■ *Web:* www.burchfabrics.com					
Criterion Thread Company Inc 21744 98th Ave	Queens Village	NY	11429	718-464-4200	464-3594
TF General: 800-695-0080 ■ *Web:* www.cthread.com					
Custom Metal Crafters Inc 815 N Mountain Rd	Newington	CT	06111	860-953-4210	953-1746
Web: www.custom-metal.com					
Design/Craft Fabrics Corp 2230 Ridge Dr	Glenview	IL	60025	847-904-7000	904-7102
Web: www.design-craft.com					
Douglass Industries Inc 412 Boston Ave	Egg Harbor City	NJ	08215	609-965-6030	
Web: www.dougind.com					
Dunlap Industries Inc 297 Industrial Park Rd	Dunlap	TN	37327	800-251-7214	949-3648*
**Fax Area Code:* 423 ■ *TF:* 800-251-7214 ■ *Web:* www.dunlapworld.com					
Duralee Fabrics Ltd Inc 1775 Fifth Ave	Bay Shore	NY	11706	631-273-8800	275-3297*
**Fax Area Code:* 800 ■ **Fax:* Cust Svc ■ *TF Cust Svc:* 800-275-3872 ■ *Web:* www.duralee.com					
Eagle Button Co Inc 700 Broadway	Westwood	NJ	07675	201-652-4063	
Web: www.eaglebutton.com					
Edgar Fabrics Inc 50 Commerce Dr	Hauppauge	NY	11788	631-435-9116	435-9151
EE Schenck Co 6000 N Cutter Cir	Portland	OR	97217	503-284-4124	288-4475
TF: 800-433-0722 ■ *Web:* www.eeschenck.com					
Hanes Cos Inc 500 N McLin Creek Rd	Conover	NC	28613	828-464-4673	269-7787*
**Fax Area Code:* 602 ■ *TF:* 877-252-3052 ■ *Web:* www.hanescompanies.com					
Hoffman California Fabrics Inc 25792 Obrero Dr	Mission Viejo	CA	92691	800-547-0100	770-4022*
**Fax Area Code:* 949 ■ *TF:* 800-547-0100 ■ *Web:* www.hoffmanfabrics.com					
Ideal Fastener Corp 603 W Industry Dr	Oxford	NC	27565	919-693-3115	693-3118
Web: www.idealfastener.com					
Jaftex Corp 49 W 37th St	New York	NY	10018	212-686-5194	545-0058
Janlynn Corp 2070 Westover Rd	Chicopee	MA	01022	413-206-0002	206-0060
TF: 800-445-5565 ■ *Web:* www.janlynn.com					
Keyston Bros 2801 Academy Way Ste A	Sacramento	CA	95815	916-927-5851	
TF: 800-453-1112 ■ *Web:* www.keystonbros.com					
Lew Jan Textile Corp 366 Veterans Memorial Hwy	Commack	NY	11725	800-899-0531	543-0561*
**Fax Area Code:* 631 ■ *TF:* 800-899-0531 ■ *Web:* www.lewjan.com					
Majilite Corp 1530 Broadway Rd	Dracut	MA	01826	978-441-6800	441-0835
Web: www.majilite.com					
Marcus Bros Textiles Inc 980 Ave of the Americas	New York	NY	10018	212-354-8700	768-0799
TF: 800-548-8295 ■ *Web:* marcusfabrics.com					
McKee Surfaces PO Box 230	Muscatine	IA	52761	563-263-2421	264-5365
TF Cust Svc: 800-553-9662 ■ *Web:* www.mckeesurfaces.com					
Meow Inc 307 W 36th St 16th Fl	New York	NY	10018	888-485-6738	
TF: 888-485-6738 ■ *Web:* www.rebeccataylor.com					
Miami Corp, The 720 Anderson Ferry Rd	Cincinnati	OH	45238	513-451-6700	
TF: 800-543-0448 ■ *Web:* www.miamicorp.com					
Mon Cheri Bridals LLC 1018 Whitehead Rd Extn	Trenton	NJ	08638	609-530-1900	
Web: www.moncheribridals.com					
Pine Cone Hill Inc 125 Pecks Rd	Pittsfield	MA	01201	877-586-4771	629-2400*
**Fax Area Code:* 413 ■ *TF:* 877-586-4771 ■ *Web:* pineconehill.annieselke.com					
Prym-Dritz Corp 950 Brisack Rd	Spartanburg	SC	29303	864-576-5050	
TF Cust Svc: 800-255-7796 ■ *Web:* www.dritz.com					
Raytex Fabrics Inc 130 Crossways Pk Dr	Woodbury	NY	11797	516-584-1111	
Web: www.raytexindustries.com					
Richloom Fabrics Group 261 Fifth Ave	New York	NY	10016	212-685-5400	689-0230
Web: richloom.com					

Phone Fax

Robert Allen Fabrics Inc 225 Foxboro Blvd ....Foxboro MA 02035 800-333-3777 332-8256*
*Fax: Sales ■ TF: 800-333-3777 ■ Web: www.robertallendesign.com

Robert Kaufman Company Inc PO Box 59266.........Los Angeles CA 90059 310-538-3482 538-9235
TF: 800-877-2066 ■ Web: www.robertkaufman.com

Rockville Fabrics Corp
99 W Hawthorne Ave ....Valley Stream NY 11580 516-561-9810

Rome Fastener Corp 257 Depot Rd ....Milford CT 06460 203-874-6719 877-0201
Web: www.romefast.com

Scher Fabrics Inc 450 Fashion Ave ....New York NY 10123 212-382-2266

Schott International Inc 2850 Gilchrist Rd.............Akron OH 44305 330-794-2121 794-2122
TF: 877-661-2121 ■ Web: www.schotttextiles.com

Scovill Fasteners Inc 1802 Scovill Dr.............Clarkesville GA 30523 706-754-1000 754-4000*
*Fax: Cust Svc ■ TF Cust Svc: 888-726-8455 ■ Web: www.scovill.com

Spradling International Inc
200 Cahaba Vly Pkwy PO Box 1668 ....Pelham AL 35124 205-985-4206 985-9176
TF: 800-333-0955 ■ Web: www.spradlingvinyl.com

Sumersault ltd 17 Overlook Rd.......................Scarsdale NY 10583 914-472-5778
Web: www.sumersault.com

Swimwear Anywhere Inc 85 Sherwood Ave .... Farmingdale NY 11735 631-420-1400
Web: www.swimwearanywhere.com

Tiger Button Company Inc 307 W 38th St ....New York NY 10018 212-594-0570 695-0265
TF: 800-223-2754 ■ Web: www.tigerbutton.com

Tingue 535 N Midland Ave ....Saddle Brook NJ 07663 201-796-5233
Web: www.tinguebrownco.com

Transhield Inc 2932 Thorne Dr.........................Elkhart IN 46514 574-266-4118
Web: www.transhield-usa.com

Twin Dragon Marketing Inc
14600 S Broadway St.............................Gardena CA 90248 310-715-7070
Web: www.twindragonmarketing.com

United Notions Inc 13800 Hutton St.....................Dallas TX 75234 972-484-8901
TF: 800-527-9447 ■ Web: storefront.unitednotions.com

US Button Corp 328 Kennedy Dr.........................Putnam CT 06260 860-928-2707 928-2847
TF: 800-243-1842 ■ Web: www.usbutton.com

Valley Forge Fabrics Inc
2981 Gateway Dr ....Pompano Beach FL 33069 954-971-1776 968-1775
Web: www.valleyforge.com

Velcro USA Inc 406 Brown Ave ....Manchester NH 03103 603-669-4880 669-9271
TF: 800-225-0180 ■ Web: www.velcro.com

Waterbury Button Co 1855 Peck Ln..................Cheshire CT 06410 800-928-1812
TF: 800-928-1812 ■ Web: www.waterburybutton.com

Weber & Sons Button Company Inc
1009 E Sixth St.................................Muscatine IA 52761 563-263-9451

World Emblem International Inc 1500 NE 131 St........ Miami FL 33161 305-772-0362
Web: www.worldemblem.com

YKK USA Inc 1251 Vly Brook Ave....................Lyndhurst NJ 07071 201-935-4200 964-0123
Web: www.ykkfastening.com

Young Fashions Inc 10300 Perkins Rd ....Baton Rouge LA 70810 225-766-1010
TF: 800-824-4154 ■ Web: www.youngfashions.com

Zabin Industries Inc 3957 S Hill St ....Los Angeles CA 90037 213-749-1215
Web: www.zabin.com

595 PIPE & PIPE FITTINGS - METAL (FABRICATED)

See Also Metal Tube & Pipe p. 2760

Phone Fax

Ace Tube Bending 14 Journey ....Aliso Viejo CA 92656 949-362-2220
Web: www.acetubebending.com

Acme Manufacturing Co 7601 State Rd ....Philadelphia PA 19136 215-268-1700 335-1905

Advanced Tubing Technology Inc
150 Intercraft Dr ....Statesville NC 28625 704-924-7020
Web: www.tubularproducts.com

Airdrome Precision Components
3251 E Airport Way.............................Long Beach CA 90806 562-426-9411 492-6909
Web: airdrome.com

Allegan Tubular Products Inc 1276 Lincoln Rd......... Allegan MI 49010 269-673-6636 673-2477
Web: www.allegantube.com

Allied Chucker & Engineering Co
3529 Scheele Dr...................................Jackson MI 49202 517-787-1370 787-2878
Web: alliedchucker.com

Alloy Stainless Products Co 611 Union Blvd............Totowa NJ 07512 973-256-1616 256-5256
TF: 800-631-8372 ■ Web: www.alloystainless.com

AY McDonald Manufacturing Co
4800 Chavenelle Rd PO Box 508 ....Dubuque IA 52002 563-583-7311 588-0720
TF Cust Svc: 800-292-2737 ■ Web: www.aymcdonald.com

Beck Mfg 330 E Ninth St ....Waynesboro PA 17268 717-762-9141 762-9153
Web: www.beckmfg.com

Bendco Inc 801 Houston Ave.........................Pasadena TX 77502 713-473-1557 473-1882
Web: www.bendco.com

BendTec Inc 366 Garfield Ave ....Duluth MN 55802 218-722-0205
TF: 800-236-3832 ■ Web: www.bendtec.com

Berkley Industries 9938 Pigeon Rd......................Bay Port MI 48720 989-656-2171
Web: www.avci.net

Betts Industries Inc 1800 Pennsylvania Ave W...........Warren PA 16365 814-723-1250 723-7030
Web: www.bettsind.com

Campbell Manufacturing Inc
127 E Spring St ....Bechtelsville PA 19505 610-367-2107 369-3580
TF: 800-523-0224 ■ Web: www.bakerwatersystems.com

Carpenter Powder Products 600 Mayer St...........Bridgeville PA 15017 412-257-5102 257-5058
TF: 866-790-9092 ■ Web: www.cartech.com

Cascade Waterworks Manufacturing
1213 Badger St...................................Yorkville IL 60560 630-553-0840
Web: www.cascademfg.com

Central Pipe Supply Inc 101 Ware Rd PO Box 5470........ Pearl MS 39288 601-939-3322 932-8944
TF: 800-844-7700 ■ Web: www.centralpipe.com

Champion Mfg Industries Inc 6021 N Galena Rd......... Peoria IL 61614 309-685-1031 685-1088
TF: 800-452-7473

Classic Tube 80 Rotech Dr ....Lancaster NY 14086 716-759-1800
TF: 800-882-3711 ■ Web: www.classictube.com

Colonial Engineering Inc 6400 Corporate Ave .... Portage MI 49002 269-323-2495 323-0630
TF: 800-374-0234 ■ Web: www.colonialengineering.com

Controls Southeast Inc PO Box 7500 .... Charlotte NC 28241 704-588-3030 644-5100
TF: 877-788-3030 ■ Web: www.csiheat.com

Phone Fax

Core Pipe 170 Tubeway Dr........................Carol Stream IL 60188 630-690-7000 690-9701
Web: www.gerlin.com

Custom Fab Inc 109 Fifth St ....Orlando FL 32824 407-859-3954
Web: www.customfab.com

Custom Pipe & Coupling Inc
10560 Fern St PO Box 978...........................Stanton CA 90680 714-761-8801
Web: www.custompipe.com

Douglas Bros 423 Riverside Industrial Pkwy ....Portland ME 04103 207-797-6771 797-8385
TF: 800-341-0926 ■ Web: www.douglasbrothers.com

Elkhart Products Corp 1255 Oak St.......................Elkhart IN 46514 574-264-3181 264-4835
TF: 800-284-4851 ■ Web: www.elkhartproducts.com

Empire Industries Inc 180 Olcott St................ Manchester CT 06040 860-647-1431 647-1160
TF: 800-243-4844 ■ Web: www.empireindustries.com

Ever Roll Specialties Co
3988 Lawrenceville Dr ....Springfield OH 45504 937-964-1302
Web: www.ever-roll.com

FabCorp Inc 6951 W Little York.........................Houston TX 77040 713-466-3962 466-3470
Web: www.fabcorp.com

Flotech Inc 3330 Evergreen Ave ....Jacksonville FL 32206 904-358-1849
Web: www.flotechinc.com

Fuller Industrial 65 Nelson Rd ....Lively ON P3Y1P4 705-682-2777 682-4777
TF: 888-524-3777 ■ Web: www.fullerindustrial.com

Future Pipe Industries Inc
11811-11812 Proctor Rd ....Houston TX 77038 281-847-2987
Web: www.futurepipe.com

General Plug & Mfg Co Inc 455 Main St .... Grafton OH 44044 440-926-2411 926-3305
TF: 800-289-7584 ■ Web: www.generalplug.com

Griffin Pipe Products Co
1011 Warrenville Rd Ste 200 .... Lisle IL 60532 630-719-6500 719-2252
Web: uspipe.com

H & H Tube & Manufacturing Co
579 Garfield Ave...............................Vanderbilt MI 49795 989-983-2800
Web: www.h-htube.com

H-P Products Inc 512 W Gorgas St...................Louisville OH 44641 330-875-5556 875-7584
TF: 800-822-8356 ■ Web: www.h-pproducts.com

Highfield Manufacturing Co
380 Mtn Grove St..............................Bridgeport CT 06605 203-384-2281 368-3906
Web: www.highfield-mfg.com

Houston Pipe Benders 14500 E Hardy Rd ....Houston TX 77039 281-449-8241
Web: www.hpbenders.com

Hydro Tube Enterprises Inc 137 Artino St .... Oberlin OH 44074 440-774-1022 774-1482
Web: www.hydrotube.com

Ideal Welders Ltd 660 Caldew St .... Delta BC V3M5S2 604-525-5558 525-5313
Web: www.idealwelders.com

Industrial Manufacturing & Machining
5495 E 69th Ave ....Commerce CO 80022 303-287-2125
Web: www.dualdraw.com

JB Smith Manufacturing Co
6618 Navigation Blvd ....Houston TX 77011 713-928-5711 928-5219
Web: www.jbsmith.com

JD Squared Inc 2244 Eddie Williams Rd...........Johnson City TN 37601 423-979-0309
Web: www.jd2.com

Kelly Pipe Company LLC
11680 Bloomfield Ave ....Santa Fe Springs CA 90670 562-868-0456 863-4695
TF: 800-305-3559 ■ Web: www.kellypipe.com

Kraftube Inc 925 E Church Ave.......................Reed City MI 49677 231-832-5562 832-2937
Web: www.kraftube.com

Long Island Pipe Supply Inc
586 Commercial Ave ....Garden City NY 11530 516-222-8008
Web: www.lipipe.com

McWane Inc 2900 Hwy 280 Ste 300 ....Birmingham AL 35223 205-414-3100 414-3170
Web: www.mcwane.com

Merit Brass Co 1 Merit Dr.......................... Cleveland OH 44143 216-261-9800
Web: www.meritbrass.com

MicroGroup Inc 7 Industrial Pk Rd ....Medway MA 02053 508-533-4925 533-5691
TF: 800-255-8823 ■ Web: www.microgroup.com

Mills Iron Works Inc 14834 Maple Ave ....Gardena CA 90248 323-321-6520 532-0476*
*Fax Area Code: 310 ■ TF: 800-421-2281 ■ Web: www.millsiron.com

Milwaukee Valve Company Inc
16550 W Stratton Dr............................New Berlin WI 53151 262-432-2800 432-2801
TF: 800-348-6544 ■ Web: www.milwaukeevalve.com

Morton Industries LLC 70 Commerce Dr.............. Morton IL 61550 309-263-2590 263-0862
Web: www.mortonwelding.com

National Excelsior Co 1999 N Ruby St ....Melrose Park IL 60160 708-343-4225 681-0041
TF: 855-373-9235 ■ Web: www.excelsiorhvac.com

National Tube Form Inc 3405 Engle Rd............ Fort Wayne IN 46809 260-478-2363
Web: www.nationaltubeform.com

NIBCO Inc 1516 Middlebury St........................Elkhart IN 46515 574-295-3000 295-3307
TF: 800-234-0227 ■ Web: www.nibco.com

Nor-Cal Products Inc 1967 S Oregon St ....Yreka CA 96097 530-842-4457 842-9130*
*Fax: Sales ■ TF: 800-824-4166 ■ Web: www.n-c.com

Parker Hannifin Corp Brass Products Div
100 Parker Dr ....Otsego MI 49078 269-694-9411 694-4614
TF: 800-272-7537 ■ Web: www.parker.com

Parker Hannifin Corp Instrumentation Products Div
1005 A Cleaner Way .... Huntsville AL 35805 256-885-3800 885-3853
Web: www.parker.com

Penn Machine Co 106 Stn St ....Johnstown PA 15905 814-288-1547 497-3325*
*Fax Area Code: 610 ■ TF: 800-736-6872 ■ Web: www.pennusa.com

Perma-Pipe Inc 7720 N Lehigh Ave .... Niles IL 60714 847-966-2235 470-1204
Web: www.permapipe.com

Pevco Sys Intl Inc 1401 Tangier Dr ....Baltimore MD 21220 410-931-8800
TF: 800-296-7382 ■ Web: www.pevco.com

Pioneer Pipe Inc 2021 Hanna Rd ....Marietta OH 45750 740-376-2400 373-8964
Web: www.pioneerpipeinc.com

Piping Technology & Products Inc
3701 Holmes Rd PO Box 34506.......................Houston TX 77051 713-422-2271 731-8640
TF: 866-746-9172 ■ Web: www.pipingtech.com

Propipe Technologies Inc 1800 Clayton Ave .... Middletown OH 45042 513-424-5311 424-5095

R & B Wagner Inc PO Box 423 ....Butler WI 53007 414-214-0444 214-0450
TF: 888-243-6914 ■ Web: www.wagnercompanies.com

Rado Enterprises 20 Industrial Dr..................Bloomsburg PA 17815 570-759-0303
Web: www.radoenterprises.com

Phone Fax

Richards Industries Inc 3170 Wasson Rd .... Cincinnati OH 45209 513-533-5600 871-0105*
*Fax: Sales ■ TF Cust Svc: 800-543-7311 ■ Web: www.richardsind.com

Robert Mitchell Inc
350 Decarie Blvd via St-Louis and Crevier St .... St-laurent QC H4L3K5 514-747-2471
Web: www.robertmitchell.com

Romac Industries Inc 21919 20th Ave SE .... Bothell WA 98021 425-951-6200 951-6201
TF: 800-426-9341 ■ Web: www.romac.com

Roscoe Moss Co 4360 Worth St .... Los Angeles CA 90063 323-263-4111 263-4497
Web: www.roscoemoss.com

Rovanco Piping Systems Inc
20535 SE Frontage Rd .... Joliet IL 60431 815-741-6700 741-4229
Web: www.rovanco.com

Shaw Group Inc, The 4171 Essen Ln .... Baton Rouge LA 70809 832-513-1000
NYSE: SHAW

Smart Pipe Company Inc
1319 West Sam Houston Pkwy Ste 100 .... Houston TX 77043 281-945-5700
Web: www.smart-pipe.com

Snap-Tite Inc 8325 Hessinger Dr .... Erie PA 16509 814-838-5700
Web: www.snap-tite.com

Spitzer Industries Inc 11250 Tanner Rd .... Houston TX 77041 713-466-1518
Web: www.spitzerind.com

Star Pipe LLC 4018 Westhollow Pkwy .... Houston TX 77082 281-558-3000
TF: 800-999-3009 ■ Web: www.starpipeproducts.com

Steico Industries Inc 1814 Ord Way .... Oceanside CA 92056 760-438-8015
Web: www.steicoindustries.com

Swagelok Co 29500 Solon Rd .... Solon OH 44139 440-248-4600 349-5970
Web: www.swagelok.com

Synalloy Corp
775 Spartan Blvd Ste 102 PO Box 5627 .... Spartanburg SC 29304 864-585-3605 596-1501
NASDAQ: SYNL ■ TF Orders: 800-937-5449 ■ Web: www.synalloy.com

Tate Andale Inc 1941 Lansdowne Rd .... Baltimore MD 21227 410-247-8700 247-9672
TF: 800-296-8283 ■ Web: www.tateandale.com

Tennessee Tubebending Inc
5112 N National Dr .... Knoxville TN 37914 865-546-6511
Web: www.evertite.com

Texas Steel Conversion Inc 3101 Holmes Rd .... Houston TX 77051 713-733-6013
Web: www.texassteelconversion.com

Thermacor Process LP
1670 Hicks Field Rd E .... Fort Worth TX 76179 817-847-7300 847-7222
Web: www.thermacor.com

Triangle Engineering Inc 6 Industrial Way .... Hanover MA 02339 781-878-1500
Web: www.trieng.com

Triple d Bending 4707 Glenmore Trail Se .... Calgary AB T2C2R9 403-255-2944 253-3261
Web: www.pipebending.com

Troy Tube & Manufacturing Co
50100 E Russell Schmidt Blvd .... Chesterfield MI 48051 586-949-8700
Web: www.troytube.com

Tru Line Manufacturing Inc
3510 Central Pkwy Sw .... Decatur AL 35603 256-350-1002
Web: www.trulinemfg.com

Tru-Flex Metal Hose Corp
2391 S State Rd 263 PO Box 247 .... West Lebanon IN 47991 765-893-4403 893-4114
TF: 800-255-6291 ■ Web: www.tru-flex.com

Tube Forgings of America Inc
5200 NW Front Ave .... Portland OR 97210 503-241-0716
Web: www.tubeforgings.com

Tube Processing Corp
604 E Le Grande Ave .... Indianapolis IN 46203 317-787-1321 786-3074
TF: 800-295-4119 ■ Web: www.tubeproc.com

Tubular Fabricators Industry Inc
600 W Wythe St .... Petersburg VA 23803 804-733-4000
Web: www.tfihealthcare.com

Tylok International Inc 1061 E 260th St .... Euclid OH 44132 216-261-7310
TF: 800-321-0466 ■ Web: www.tylok.com

United Spiral Pipe LLC 900 E Third St .... Pittsburg CA 94565 925-526-3100
Web: www.unitedspiralpipe.com

Universal Tube Inc 2607 Bond St .... Rochester Hills MI 48309 248-853-5100 853-7365
TF: 800-394-8823 ■ Web: www.universaltube.com

US Pipe & Foundry Co
2 Chase Corporate Drive Ste 200 .... Birmingham AL 35244 866-347-7473 417-8411*
*Fax Area Code: 205 ■ TF: 866-347-7473 ■ Web: www.uspipe.com

Vacco Industries Inc 10350 Vacco St .... South El Monte CA 91733 626-443-7121 442-6943
Web: www.vacco.com

Victaulic Co 4901 Kesslersville Rd .... Easton PA 18040 610-559-3300 250-8817
TF Sales: 800-742-5842 ■ Web: www.victaulic.com

Vulcan Industries Corp
N113 W18830 Carnegie Dr .... Germantown WI 53022 262-253-5420
Web: www.vulcancorp.com

Watson McDaniel Co
428 Jones Blvd
Limerick Airport Business Ctr .... Pottstown PA 19464 610-495-5131 495-5134
Web: www.watsonmcdaniel.com

Webster Valve Co 583 S Main St .... Franklin NH 03235 603-934-5110 934-1390

Whitley Products Inc 493 S Circle Dr W .... Warsaw IN 46580 574-267-7114

Woolf Aircraft Products Inc 6401 Cogswell Rd .... Romulus MI 48174 734-721-5330 721-3490
Web: www.woolfaircraft.com

World Wide Fittings Inc 7501 N Natchez Ave .... Niles IL 60714 847-588-2200 588-2212
TF: 800-393-9894 ■ Web: www.worldwidefittings.com

596 PIPE & PIPE FITTINGS - PLASTICS

Phone Fax

Advanced Drainage Systems Inc
4640 Trueman Blvd .... Hilliard OH 43026 800-821-6710 658-0204*
*Fax Area Code: 614 ■ TF: 800-821-6710 ■ Web: www.ads-pipe.com

Ameron International Corp
245 S Los Robles Ave .... Pasadena CA 91101 626-683-4000 683-4060
Web: www.nov.com

Bakersfield Pipe & Supply Inc
3301 Zachary Ave .... Shafter CA 93263 661-589-9141 589-3739
Web: www.bakersfieldpipe.com

CANTEX Inc 202 Progress Rd .... Auburndale FL 33823 817-215-7000 215-7001
Web: www.cantexinc.com

CertainTeed Corp 750 E Swedesford Rd .... Valley Forge PA 19482 610-341-7000 341-7777
TF Prod Info: 800-782-8777 ■ Web: www.certainteed.com

Charlotte Pipe & Foundry Company Plastics Div
PO Box 35430 .... Charlotte NC 28235 704-289-2531
Web: unioncountycoc.com

Chemtrol Div NIBCO Inc 1516 Middlebury St .... Elkhart IN 46516 574-295-3000 295-3307
TF: 800-234-0227 ■ Web: nibco.com/industrial-plastics/chemtrol

Chevron Phillips Chemical Company Performance Pipe Div
5085 W Pk Blvd Ste 500 .... Plano TX 75093 972-599-6600
TF: 800-527-0662 ■ Web: www.performancepipe.com

Crane ChemPharma Resistoflex 1 Quality Way .... Marion NC 28752 828-724-4000
Web: www.resistoflex.com

Cresline-West Inc 600 Crosspointe Blvd .... Evansville IN 47715 812-428-9300 428-9353
Web: www.cresline.com

Diamond Plastics Corp
1212 Johnstown Rd PO Box 1608 .... Grand Island NE 68802 308-384-4400 384-9345
TF: 800-782-7473 ■ Web: www.dpcpipe.com

Dura Plastics Products Inc 533 E Third St .... Beaumont CA 92223 951-845-3161 845-7644
Web: www.duraplastics.com

Endot Industries Inc 60 Green Pond Rd .... Rockaway NJ 07866 973-625-8500 625-4087
TF: 800-443-6368 ■ Web: www.endot.com

Excalibur Extrusions Inc
110 E Crowther Ave .... Placentia CA 92870 714-528-8834 524-7453
TF: 800-648-6804 ■ Web: www.excaliburextrusions.com

Fernco Inc 300 S Dayton St .... Davison MI 48423 810-653-9626 653-8714
TF: 800-521-1283 ■ Web: www.fernco.com

Fusibond Piping Systems Inc
2615 Curtiss St .... Downers Grove IL 60515 630-969-4488 969-2355
Web: www.fusibond.com

Hancor Inc PO Box 1047 .... Findlay OH 45839 419-422-6521
TF: 888-892-2694 ■ Web: www.hancor.com

Hobas Pipe USA LP 1413 E Richey Rd .... Houston TX 77073 281-821-2200 821-7715
TF: 800-856-7473 ■ Web: www.hobaspipe.com

Isco Industries 926 Baxter Ave PO Box 4545 .... Louisville KY 40204 502-583-6591 238-8165
TF: 800-345-4726 ■ Web: www.isco-pipe.com

JM Manufacturing Company Inc
5200 West Century Blvd .... Los Angeles CA 90045 800-621-4404
TF: 800-621-4404 ■ Web: www.jmeagle.com

Lasco Fittings Inc
414 Morgan St PO Box 116 .... Brownsville TN 38012 731-772-3180 772-0835
TF: 800-776-2756 ■ Web: www.lascofittings.com

Maloney Technical Products
1300 E Berry St .... Fort Worth TX 76119 817-923-3344 923-1339
TF: 800-231-7236 ■ Web: www.maloneytech.com

Mueller Plastics Corp 3070 E Cedar .... Ontario CA 91761 909-930-2060 930-2070
TF: 800-348-8464 ■ Web: www.muellerindustries.com

National Pipe & Plastics Inc
3421 Old Vestal Rd .... Vestal NY 13850 800-836-4350 729-6130*
*Fax Area Code: 607 ■ TF: 800-836-4350 ■ Web: www.nationalpipe.com

Nebraska Plastics Inc PO Box 45 .... Cozad NE 69130 308-784-2500
TF: 800-445-2887 ■ Web: www.countryestate.com

North American Pipe Corp
2801 Post Oak Blvd Ste 600 .... Houston TX 77056 713-840-7473 552-0087
TF: 855-624-7473 ■ Web: www.northamericanpipe.com

Oil Creek Plastics Inc
45619 State Hwy 27 PO Box 385 .... Titusville PA 16354 814-827-3661 827-9599
TF: 800-537-3661 ■ Web: oilcreekplastics.com

Silver-Line Plastics 900 Riverside Dr .... Asheville NC 28804 828-252-8755 285-8901
Web: www.slpipe.com

Teel Plastics Inc 1060 Teel Ct .... Baraboo WI 53913 608-355-3080 355-3088
Web: www.teel.com

Texas United Pipe Inc
11627 N Houston Rosslyn Rd .... Houston TX 77086 281-448-3276 448-6983
TF Sales: 800-966-8741 ■ Web: www.texasunitedpipe.com

Vinylplex Inc 1800 Atkinson Ave .... Pittsburg KS 66762 620-231-8290 232-8547
TF: 877-779-7473 ■ Web: www.vinylplex.com/main.html

Vinyltech Corp 201 S 61st Ave .... Phoenix AZ 85043 602-233-0071 272-4847
TF: 800-255-3924 ■ Web: www.vtpipe.com

Winrock Enterprises
1501 N University Ave Ste 360 .... Little Rock AR 72207 501-663-5340 663-4456

597 PIPELINES (EXCEPT NATURAL GAS)

Phone Fax

Alyeska Pipeline Service Co
Alaska Corp, The
3700 Centerpoint Dr PO Box 196660 .... Anchorage AK 99503 907-787-8870 787-8330

Belle Fourche Pipeline 455 N Poplar St .... Casper WY 82601 307-237-9301 266-0252
Web: truecos.com

BP Exploration (Alaska) Inc (BPXA)
PO Box 196612 .... Anchorage AK 99519 907-561-5111
Web: www.bp.com

BP PLC 28100 Torch Pkwy .... Warrenville IL 60555 800-333-3991
NYSE: BP ■ TF: 800-333-3991 ■ Web: www.bp.com

Buckeye Partners LP
5 Radnor Corporate Ctr
100 Matsonford Rd Ste 500 .... Radnor PA 19087 484-232-4000
NYSE: BPL ■ Web: www.buckeye.com

Buckeye Partners LP 1 Greenway Plz Ste 600 .... Houston TX 77046 832-615-8600
Web: www.buckeye.com

Chevron Pipe Line Co 4800 Fournace Pl .... Bellaire TX 77401 713-432-6000
TF: 877-596-2800 ■ Web: www.chevron.com/prodserv/cpl

CITGO Pipeline Co 1293 Eldridge Pkwy .... Houston TX 77077 832-486-4000
Web: www.citgo.com

Collins Pipeline Co 355 Mississippi 588 .... Collins MS 39428 601-765-6593

Colonial Pipeline Co
1185 Sanctuary Pkwy Ste 100 .... Alpharetta GA 30009 678-762-2200 762-2883
TF: 800-275-3004 ■ Web: www.colpipe.com

Country Mark Co-op 1200 Refinery Rd .... Mount Vernon IN 47620 800-832-5490 838-8196*
*Fax Area Code: 812 ■ TF: 800-832-5490 ■ Web: www.countrymark.com

	Phone	Fax
Enbridge Energy Partners LP 1100 Louisiana Ste 3300 ... Houston TX 77002	713-821-2000	834-8133*
NYSE: EEP ■ **Fax Area Code: 646* ■ *TF:* 800-481-2804 ■ *Web:* www.enbridgepartners.com		
ExxonMobil Pipeline Co 800 Bell St Rm 653A ... Houston TX 77002	713-656-6885	656-9586
Web: www.exxonmobilpipeline.com		
Genesis Energy LP 919 Milam Ste 2100 ... Houston TX 77002	713-860-2500	860-2640
NYSE: GEL ■ *TF:* 800-284-3365 ■ *Web:* www.genesisenergy.com		
Hess Co 420 Hook Rd ... Bayonne NJ 07002	201-437-1017	
Web: hess.com		
Imperial Oil Resources Ltd 237 Fourth Ave SW PO Box 2480 Stn M ... Calgary AB T2P3M9	800-567-3776	
TF: 800-567-3776 ■ *Web:* www.imperialoil.ca		
Jayhawk Pipeline LLC 2000 S Main St ... McPherson KS 67460	620-241-9270	241-9215
Web: www.jayhawkpl.com		
Kinder Morgan Energy Partners LP 500 Dallas St Ste 1000 ... Houston TX 77002	713-369-9000	514-6401*
NYSE: KMI ■ **Fax Area Code: 403* ■ **Fax:* Hum Res ■ *TF:* 866-208-3372 ■ *Web:* www.kindermorgan.com		
Kinder Morgan Management LLC 500 Dallas St 1 Allen Ctr Ste 1000 ... Houston TX 77002	713-369-9000	
NYSE: KMI ■ *TF:* 800-781-4152 ■ *Web:* www.kindermorgan.com		
Magellan Midstream Partners LP 1 Williams Ctr ... Tulsa OK 74172	918-574-7000	
NYSE: MMP ■ *TF:* 800-574-6671 ■ *Web:* www.magellanlp.com		
Marathon Pipe Line LLC (MPL) 539 S Main St ... Findlay OH 45840	419-422-2121	425-7040
Web: www.marathonpipeline.com		
MarkWest Energy Partners LP 1515 Arapahoe St Tower 1 Ste 1600 ... Denver CO 80202	303-925-9200	290-8769
NYSE: MWE ■ *TF:* 800-730-8388 ■ *Web:* www.markwest.com		
Pioneer Pipe Line Company Inc 245 East 1100 North ... North Salt Lake UT 84054	801-295-2325	
Web: conocophillips.com		
Plains All American Pipeline LP 333 Clay St Ste 1600 ... Houston TX 77002	713-646-4100	
NYSE: PAA ■ *TF Mktg:* 866-753-3619 ■ *Web:* www.plainsallamerican.com		
Plantation Pipe Line Co 1100 Alderman Dr Ste 200 ... Alpharetta GA 30005	770-751-4000	751-4133
Web: www.kindermorgan.com		
Precision Pipeline Solutions LLC 617 Little Britain Rd Ste 200 ... New Windsor NY 12553	845-566-8332	
Web: www.precisionpipelinesolutions.com		
Sunoco Inc 1735 Market St Ste LL ... Philadelphia PA 19103	215-977-3000	977-3409
NYSE: SUN ■ *TF:* 800-786-6261 ■ *Web:* sunoco.com		
Sunoco Logistics Partners LP 525 Fritztown Rd ... Sinking Spring PA 19608	610-670-3200	
NYSE: SXL ■ *Web:* www.sunocologistics.com		
Teppco Crude Oil LP 210 Pk Ave ... Oklahoma City OK 73102	405-239-7191	
Valero LP PO Box 696000 ... San Antonio TX 78269	210-345-2233	
TF: 800-333-3377 ■ *Web:* www.valero.com		

598 PLANETARIUMS

	Phone	Fax
Abrams Planetarium Michigan State University ... East Lansing MI 48824	517-355-4676	432-3838
Web: www.pa.msu.edu/abrams		
Adler Planetarium & Astronomy Museum 1300 S Lk Shore Dr ... Chicago IL 60605	312-922-7827	
Web: www.adlerplanetarium.org		
Andrus Planetarium 511 Warburton Ave Hudson River Museum ... Yonkers NY 10701	914-963-4550	963-8558
Web: www.hrm.org/planetarium.html		
Arizona State University 550 E Tyler Mall PO Box 871404 ... Tempe AZ 85287	480-965-6891	965-8102
Web: asu.edu		
Arnim D Hummel Planetarium Eastern Kentucky University ... Richmond KY 40475	859-622-1547	622-6666
Web: www.planetarium.eku.edu		
Bays Mountain Planetarium & Observatory 853 Bays Mtn Pk Rd ... Kingsport TN 37660	423-229-9447	224-2589
Web: baysmountain.com		
BCC Planetarium & Obersvatory 1519 Clearlake Rd ... Cocoa FL 32922	321-433-7373	
Web: www.easternflorida.edu		
Buehler Planetarium & Observatory (BC) 3501 SW Davie Rd ... Davie FL 33314	954-201-6681	
Web: www.broward.edu/locations/central/buehler.jsp		
Casper Planetarium 904 N Poplar St ... Casper WY 82601	307-577-0310	
Web: casperplanetarium.com		
Cernan Earth & Space Ctr 2000 N Fifth Ave Triton College ... River Grove IL 60171	708-456-0300	583-3153
TF: 800-972-7000 ■ *Web:* www.triton.edu		
Charles Hayden Planetarium 1 Science Pk ... Boston MA 02114	617-723-2500	589-0362
Web: www.mos.org		
Chesapeake Planetarium 312 Cedar Rd ... Chesapeake VA 23322	757-547-0153	
Web: virginia.org		
Christa McAuliffe Planetarium 2 Institute Dr ... Concord NH 03301	603-271-7827	271-7832
Web: www.starhop.com		
Clark Planetarium 110 S 400 W ... Salt Lake City UT 84101	385-468-7827	
Web: www.clarkplanetarium.net		
Community College of Southern Nevada Planetarium & Observatory 3200 E Cheyenne Ave ... North Las Vegas NV 89030	702-651-4759	651-4825
TF: 800-630-7563 ■ *Web:* www.csn.edu/planetarium		
Discovery Museum & Planetarium 4450 Pk Ave ... Bridgeport CT 06604	203-372-3521	374-1929
Web: www.discoverymuseum.org		
Downing Planetarium 5320 N Maple Ave MS DP132 California State University Fresno ... Fresno CA 93740	559-278-4121	278-4070
Web: www.fresnostate.edu/csm/downing-planetarium/index.html		
Dreyfuss Planetarium 49 Washington St ... Newark NJ 07102	973-596-6529	642-0459
TF: 888-370-6765 ■ *Web:* www.newarkmuseum.org		
Fiske Planetarium 2414 Regent Dr ... Boulder CO 80309	303-492-5002	492-1725
Web: www.colorado.edu		
Flandrau Science Ctr & Planetarium 1601 E University Blvd ... Tucson AZ 85719	520-621-4516	621-8451
Web: www.flandrau.org		
Fleischmann Planetarium & Science Ctr University of Nevada ... Reno NV 89557	775-784-4811	784-4822
Web: planetarium.unr.nevada.edu		
Gheens Science Hall & Rauch Planetarium Rauch Planetarium University of Louisville ... Louisville KY 40292	502-852-6664	852-0831
TF: 800-996-7566 ■ *Web:* louisville.edu/planetarium		
Hayden Planetarium 81st St & Central Pk W ... New York NY 10024	212-769-5606	769-5427
Web: www.amnh.org		
Hopkins Planetarium 1 Market Square SE ... Roanoke VA 24011	540-342-5710	224-1240
Web: www.smwv.org		
JI Holcomb Observatory & Planetarium 4600 Sunset Ave ... Indianapolis IN 46208	317-940-8333	
Web: www.butler.edu/holcomb-observatory		
John Deere Planetarium 820 38th St Augustana College ... Rock Island IL 61201	309-794-7327	794-7564
TF: 800-798-8100 ■ *Web:* augustana.edu		
Kenner Planetarium & MegaDome Cinema 2020 Fourth St Rivertown ... Kenner LA 70062	504-468-7231	
Web: www.kenner.la.us		
Kitt Peak National Observatory 950 N Cherry Ave ... Tucson AZ 85719	520-318-8600	318-8724
TF: 888-809-4012 ■ *Web:* www.noao.edu/kpno		
Lafayette Natural History Museum & Planetarium 433 Jefferson St ... Lafayette LA 70501	337-291-5544	
Web: www.lafayettesciencemuseum.org		
Lake Afton Public Observatory 1845 Fairmount ... Wichita KS 67260	316-978-7827	978-3350
Web: www.webs.wichita.edu/lapo		
Lick Observatory 7281 Mt Hamilton Rd ... Mt Hamilton CA 95140	408-274-5061	
Web: www.ucolick.org		
Lodestar Astronomy Ctr 1801 Mtn Rd NW ... Albuquerque NM 87104	505-841-2800	
Web: www.nmnaturalhistory.org		
Longway Planetarium 1310 E Kearsley St ... Flint MI 48503	810-237-3400	237-3417
Web: www.sloanlongway.org		
Lowell Observatory 1400 W Mars Hill Rd ... Flagstaff AZ 86001	928-774-3358	774-6296
Web: www.lowell.edu		
Maria Mitchell Assn 4 Vestal St ... Nantucket MA 02554	508-228-9273	
Web: www.mmo.org		
Montgomery City Planetarium 1010 Forest Ave ... Montgomery AL 36106	334-241-4799	241-2301
Moody Planetarium 3301 Fourth St Museum of Texas Tech University ... Lubbock TX 79409	806-742-2432	742-1136
Web: www.depts.ttu.edu/museumttu		
Morehead Planetarium 250 E Franklin St UNC Chapel Hill CB 3480 ... Chapel Hill NC 27599	919-962-1236	962-1238
Web: www.moreheadplanetarium.org		
Mueller Planetarium University of Nebraska 210 Morrill Hall ... Lincoln NE 68588	402-472-2641	
Web: www.spacelaser.com		
Ott Planetarium 1551 Edvalson St ... Ogden UT 84408	801-626-6871	
Web: www.ottplanetarium.org		
Portland Observatory 138 Congress St ... Portland ME 04101	207-774-5561	774-2509
Web: www.portlandlandmarks.org/observatory.htm		
Roger B Chaffee Planetarium 272 Pearl St NW ... Grand Rapids MI 49504	616-456-3977	
Web: grpm.org/planetarium		
Rosicrucian Egyptian Museum & Planetarium 1342 Naglee Ave Rosicrucian Pk ... San Jose CA 95191	408-947-3600	
Web: www.rosicrucian.org		
Russell C Davis Planetarium 201 E Pascagoula St ... Jackson MS 39201	601-960-1550	
Web: www.jacksonms.gov/index.aspx?nid=142		
Saint Petersburg College (SPC) PO Box 13489 ... Saint Petersburg FL 33733	727-341-4772	
Web: www.spcollege.edu		
Sanford Museum & Planetarium 117 E Willow St ... Cherokee IA 51012	712-225-3922	
Web: www.sanfordmuseum.org		
Science Factory Children's Museum & Planetarium 2300 Leo Harris Pkwy ... Eugene OR 97401	541-682-7888	484-9027
Web: www.sciencefactory.org		
Science Museum of Virginia 2500 W Broad St ... Richmond VA 23220	804-864-1400	
Web: www.smv.org		
Science Place, The 2201 N Field St ... Dallas TX 75201	214-428-5555	756-5916
Web: www.perotmuseum.org		
Sharpe Planetarium 3050 Central Ave ... Memphis TN 38111	901-636-2362	320-6391
Web: www.memphismuseums.org		
Southworth Planetarium 96 Falmouth St ... Portland ME 04104	207-780-4249	780-4055
Web: www.usm.maine.edu		
Space Transit Planetarium 3280 S Miami Ave ... Miami FL 33129	305-646-4200	646-4200
TF: 866-268-0250 ■ *Web:* www.miamisci.org		
Strasenburgh Planetarium 657 E Ave Rochester Museum & Science Ctr ... Rochester NY 14607	585-271-4320	271-0492
Web: www.rmsc.org		
Tomchin Planetarium & Observatory 425 Hodges Hall ... Morgantown WV 26506	304-293-4961	
Web: planetarium.wvu.edu		
University of Toledo, The 2801 W Bancroft MS 218 ... Toledo OH 43606	419-530-2650	530-5167
Web: www.utoledo.edu		
William M Staerkel Planetarium 2400 W Bradley Ave Parkland College ... Champaign IL 61821	217-351-2568	
Web: www.parkland.edu		

599 PLASTICS - LAMINATED - PLATE, SHEET, PROFILE SHAPES

Company	City	State	Zip	Phone	Fax
AccuTrex Products Inc 112 Southpointe Blvd *Web:* www.accutrex.com	Canonsburg	PA	15317	724-746-4300	
American Renolit Corp 1207 E Lincolnway *Web:* laminatefinder.com	LaPorte	IN	46350	219-324-6886	324-5332
American Thermoplastic Extrusion Co 4851 NW 128th St Rd	Opa Locka	FL	33054	305-769-9566	769-1998
AMETEK Inc Westchester Plastics Div 42 Mountain Ave *Web:* www.ametek-westchesterplas.com	Nesquehoning	PA	18240	570-645-6900	645-6959
Applied Plastics Company Inc 7320 S Sixth St *Web:* www.appliedplasticsinc.com	Oak Creek	WI	53154	414-764-2900	764-8606
Bourne Industries Inc 491 S Comstock St *Web:* www.bourneindustries.com	Corunna	MI	48817	989-743-3461	
C-K Composites Inc 361 Bridgeport Rd *Web:* www.ckcomposites.com	Mount Pleasant	PA	15666	724-547-4581	547-2890
California Combining Corp 5607 S Santa Fe Ave *Web:* www.californiacombining.com	Los Angeles	CA	90058	323-589-5727	585-8078
Commodore Plastics LLC 26 Maple Ave *Web:* www.commodoresolutions.com	Bloomfield	NY	14469	585-657-7777	
Connecticut Laminating Company Inc 162 James St *TF:* 800-753-9119 ■ *Web:* www.ctlaminating.com	New Haven	CT	06513	203-787-2184	787-4073
Current Inc 30 Tyler St PO Box 120183 *TF:* 877-436-6542 ■ *Web:* www.currentcomposites.com	East Haven	CT	06512	203-469-1337	467-8435
Custom Pultrusions Inc 1331 S Chillicothe Rd	Aurora	OH	44202	330-562-5201	
DuPont Surfaces 4417 Lancaster Pk CRP 728/3105 *TF:* 800-448-9835 ■ *Web:* www.dupont.com	Wilmington	DE	19805	302-774-1000	
Fiberesin Industries Inc 37031 E Wisconsin Ave PO Box 88 *Web:* www.fiberesin.com	Oconomowoc	WI	53066	262-567-4427	567-4814
Flexsystems USA Inc 727 W Main St *Web:* www.flexsystems.com	El Cajon	CA	92020	619-401-1858	
Formica Corp 10155 Reading Rd *TF:* 800-367-6422 ■ *Web:* www.formica.com	Cincinnati	OH	45241	513-786-3400	
Franklin Fibre-Lamitex Corp 903 E 13th St *TF:* 800-233-9739 ■ *Web:* www.franklinfibre.com	Wilmington	DE	19802	302-652-3621	571-9754
Hartson-kennedy Cabinet Top Company Inc 522 W 22nd St PO Box 3095 *TF:* 800-388-8144 ■ *Web:* www.hartson-kennedy.com	Marion	IN	46953	765-668-8144	662-3452
Insulfab Plastics Inc 834 Hayne St *TF:* 800-845-7599 ■ *Web:* www.insulfab.com	Spartanburg	SC	29301	864-582-7506	582-5215
Insultab Inc 45 Industrial Pkwy *TF Cust Svc:* 800-468-4822 ■ *Web:* www.insultab.com	Woburn	MA	01801	781-935-0800	935-0879
Iten Industries 4602 Benefit Ave *TF Orders:* 800-227-4836 ■ *Web:* www.itenindustries.com	Ashtabula	OH	44004	440-997-6134	992-4966
Klockner Pentaplast of America Inc 3585 Klockner Rd PO Box 500 **Fax Area Code:* 540 ■ *Web:* www.kpfilms.com	Gordonsville	VA	22942	492-602-9150	832-1405*
Lakeland Plastics Inc (LP) 1550 McCormick Blvd *TF:* 800-454-4006 ■ *Web:* www.lakelandplastics.com	Mundelein	IL	60060	847-680-1550	680-1595
Lamart Corp 16 Richmond St *Web:* www.lamartcorp.com	Clifton	NJ	07015	973-772-6262	772-3673
Laminating Company of America 20322 Windrow Dr *Web:* www.lcoa.com	Lake Forest	CA	92630	949-587-3300	454-0066
Lamsco West Inc 24823 Anza Dr *Web:* www.shimtechgroup.com	Santa Clarita	CA	91355	661-295-8620	295-8626
LSI Corp of America Inc 704 W Main St *Web:* www.lsi-casework.com	Teutopolis	IL	62467	763-559-4664	559-4395
Madico Inc 64 Industrial Pkwy *TF:* 800-456-4331 ■ *Web:* www.madico.com	Woburn	MA	01801	781-935-7850	935-6841
Mantec Services Inc 4400 24th Ave W *Web:* www.mantecservicesinc.com	Seattle	WA	98199	206-285-5656	
Mar-Bal Inc 16930 Munn Rd *Web:* www.mar-bal.com	Chagrin Falls	OH	44023	440-543-7526	543-4374
Miniature Precision Components Inc 820 Wisconsin St *Web:* www.mpc-inc.com	Walworth	WI	53184	262-275-5791	275-6346
Olon Industries Inc 42 Armstrong Ave *TF:* 800-387-2319 ■ *Web:* www.olon.ca	Georgetown	ON	L7G4R9	905-877-7300	877-7383
Optical Filters 13447 S Mosiertown Rd Ste A *Web:* www.opticalfiltersusa.com	Meadville	PA	16335	814-333-2222	
Petro Plastics Company Inc 450 S Ave *TF:* 800-486-4738 ■ *Web:* www.petroplastics.com	Garwood	NJ	07027	908-789-1200	789-1381
Reef Industries Inc 9209 Almeda Genoa Rd *TF:* 800-231-6074 ■ *Web:* www.reefindustries.com	Houston	TX	77075	713-507-4200	507-4295
Rotuba Extruders Inc 1401 S Pk Ave *Web:* www.rotuba.com	Linden	NJ	07036	908-486-1000	486-0874
Rowmark Inc 2040 Industrial Dr *TF:* 800-243-3339 ■ *Web:* www.rowmark.com	Findlay	OH	45840	419-425-2407	425-2927
Sabin Corp 3800 Constitution Ave PO Box 788 **Fax Area Code:* 800 ■ *TF:* 800-457-4500 ■ *Web:* www.cookgroup.com	Bloomington	IN	47403	812-339-2235	554-8335*
Schneller Inc 6019 Powdermille Rd *Web:* www.schneller.com	Kent	OH	44240	330-673-1400	676-7122
Spaulding Composites Co 55 Nadeau Dr *TF:* 800-801-0560 ■ *Web:* www.spauldingcom.com	Rochester	NH	03867	603-332-0555	332-5357
Techniform Industries Inc 2107 Hayes Ave *TF:* 800-691-2816 ■ *Web:* www.techniform-plastics.com	Fremont	OH	43420	419-332-8484	334-5222
V-T Industries Inc 1000 Industrial Pk *TF:* 800-827-1615 ■ *Web:* www.vtindustries.com	Holstein	IA	51025	712-368-4381	368-4111
Wilmington Fibre Specialty Co 700 Washington St *TF:* 800-220-5132 ■ *Web:* www.wilmfibre.com	New Castle	DE	19720	302-328-7525	328-6630
Wilsonart International Inc 2400 Wilson Pl *TF Cust Svc:* 800-433-3222 ■ *Web:* www.wilsonart.com	Temple	TX	76504	254-207-7000	207-2545

600 PLASTICS - UNSUPPORTED - FILM, SHEET, PROFILE SHAPES

See Also Blister Packaging p. 1862

Company	City	State	Zip	Phone	Fax
Advance Bag & Packaging Technologies 5720 Williams Lk Rd *TF:* 800-475-2247 ■ *Web:* www.advancepac.com	Waterford	MI	48329	248-674-3126	674-2630
AEP Industries Inc 125 Phillips Ave *NASDAQ: AEPI* ■ *TF:* 800-999-2374 ■ *Web:* www.aepinc.com	South Hackensack	NJ	07606	201-641-6600	
Alte-Rego Corp 36 Tidemore Ave *Web:* www.alte-rego.com	Toronto	ON	M9W5H4	416-740-3397	
Anaheim Custom Extruders 4640 E La Palma Ave *TF Cust Svc:* 800-229-2760 ■ *Web:* acextrusions.com	Anaheim	CA	92807	714-693-8508	693-9531
Arlon Graphics 2811 S Harbor Blvd **Fax Area Code:* 800 ■ *TF:* 800-232-7161 ■ *Web:* www.arlon.com	Santa Ana	CA	92704	714-540-2811	329-2756*
Atlas Roofing Falcon Foam Div 8240 Byron Ctr Rd SW **Fax Area Code:* 616 ■ *TF:* 800-917-9138 ■ *Web:* atlaseps.com	Byron Center	MI	49315	800-917-9138	878-9942*
Avery Dennison Worldwide Graphics Div 207 Goode Ave Bldg 8 *TF:* 800-443-9380 ■ *Web:* www.averygraphics.com	Glendale	CA	44077	440-358-3700	
Bemis Company Inc 1 Neenah Ctr Fourth Fl PO Box 669 *NYSE: BMS* ■ *Web:* www.bemis.com	Neenah	WI	54957	920-727-4100	
Bi-ax Intl Inc 596 Cedar Ave *Web:* www.biaxinc.com	Wingham	ON	N0G2W0	519-357-1818	
Bixby International Corp 1 Preble Rd *Web:* www.bixbyintl.com	Newburyport	MA	01950	978-462-4100	465-5184
Brandywine Investment Group Homalite Div 11 Brookside Dr *TF:* 800-346-7802 ■ *Web:* www.homalite.com	Wilmington	DE	19804	302-652-3686	652-4578
Catalina Graphic Films Inc 27001 Agoura Rd Ste 100 *TF:* 800-333-3136 ■ *Web:* www.catalinagraphicfilms.com	Calabasas Hills	CA	91301	818-880-8060	880-1144
Celgard LLC 13800 S Lakes Dr *Web:* www.celgard.com	Charlotte	NC	28273	704-588-5310	
Clopay Plastic Products Co 8585 Duke Blvd *TF:* 800-282-2260 ■ *Web:* www.clopayplastics.com	Mason	OH	45040	513-770-4800	
Coburn Co, The 834 E Milwaukee St *TF:* 800-776-7042 ■ *Web:* coburn.com	Whitewater	WI	53190	262-473-2822	473-3522
Crown Plastics Co 116 May Dr *TF:* 800-368-0238 ■ *Web:* www.crownplastics.com	Harrison	OH	45030	513-367-0238	
CUE Inc 11 Leonberg Rd *TF:* 800-283-4621 ■ *Web:* www.cue-inc.com	Cranberry Township	PA	16066	724-772-5225	772-5280
Daliah Plastics Corp 134 W Wainman Ave *Web:* www.daliahplastics.com	Asheboro	NC	27203	336-629-0551	
Dielectrics Industries Inc 300 Burnett Rd *TF:* 800-472-7286 ■ *Web:* www.dielectrics.com	Chicopee	MA	01020	413-594-8111	594-2343
Dunmore Corp 145 Wharton Rd *TF:* 800-444-0242 ■ *Web:* www.dunmore.com	Bristol	PA	19007	215-781-8895	781-9293
E S Robbins Corp 2802 Avalon Ave *TF:* 866-934-6018 ■ *Web:* www.esrobbins.com	Muscle Shoals	AL	35661	256-248-2400	248-2410
Enflo Corp 315 Lake Ave *TF:* 888-887-4093 ■ *Web:* www.enflo.com	Bristol	CT	06010	860-589-0014	589-7179
FLEXcon Company Inc 1 Flexcon Industrial Pk *Web:* www.flexcon.com	Spencer	MA	01562	508-885-8200	885-8400
Gary Plastic Packaging Corp 1340 Viele Ave *TF:* 800-221-8150 ■ *Web:* www.plasticboxes.com	Bronx	NY	10474	718-893-2200	378-2141
General Formulations Inc 309 S Union St *TF:* 800-253-3664 ■ *Web:* www.generalformulations.com	Sparta	MI	49345	616-887-7387	887-0537
GSE Lining Technology Inc 19103 Gundle Rd *TF:* 800-435-2008 ■ *Web:* www.gseworld.com	Houston	TX	77073	281-443-8564	875-6010
i2M Inc 755 Oak Hill Rd Crestwood Industrial Park *Web:* www.hpg-intl.com	Mountain Top	PA	18707	570-474-6741	
ILPEA Industries Inc 745 S Gardner St *Web:* www.ilpeaindustries.com	Scottsburg	IN	47170	812-752-2526	752-3563
Kayline Processing Inc 31 Coates St *TF Sales:* 800-367-5546 ■ *Web:* www.kayline.com	Trenton	NJ	08611	609-695-1449	989-1094
Kendall Packaging Corp 10200 N Port Washington Rd *TF:* 800-237-0951 ■ *Web:* www.kendallpkg.com	Mequon	WI	53092	262-404-1200	404-1221
Kepner Plastics Fabricators Inc 3131 Lomita Blvd *Web:* www.kepnerplastics.com	Torrance	CA	90505	310-325-3162	326-8560
Kimoto Tech Inc PO Box 1783 *TF:* 888-546-6861 ■ *Web:* www.kimototech.com	Cedartown	GA	30125	770-748-2643	748-2648
Lavanture Products Co 22825 Gallatin Way *TF:* 800-348-7625 ■ *Web:* www.lavanture.com	Elkhart	IN	46514	574-264-0658	264-6601
Louisiana Plastic Industries Inc 501 Downing Pines Rd *Web:* laplastic.com	West Monroe	LA	71292	318-388-4562	387-5642
Major Prime Plastics Inc 649 N Ardmore Ave *Web:* majorprime.com	Villa Park	IL	60181	630-834-9400	
McNeel International Corp 5401 W Kennedy Blvd	Tampa	FL	33609	813-286-8680	286-1535
Mississippi Polymers Inc 2733 S Harper Rd *Web:* www.mississippipolymers.com	Corinth	MS	38834	662-287-1401	
Mitsubishi Polyester Film LLC 2001 Hood Rd **Fax:* Mktg ■ *TF:* 800-334-1934 ■ *Web:* www.m-petfilm.com	Greer	SC	29650	864-879-5000	879-5006*
MPI Technologies 37 E St *TF:* 888-674-8088 ■ *Web:* www.mpirelease.com	Winchester	MA	01890	781-729-8300	729-9093
Natvar 8720 US Hwy 70 W **Fax Area Code:* 919 ■ *TF:* 800-395-6288 ■ *Web:* natvar.tekni-plex.com	Clayton	NC	27520	909-594-3660	553-4156*

Phone | Fax

New Hampshire Plastics Inc 1 Bouchard St. Manchester NH 03103 603-669-8523 622-4888
TF: 800-258-3036 ■ *Web:* www.nhplastics.com

Northland Plastics Inc
1420 S 16th St PO Box 290 Sheboygan WI 53081 800-776-7163 458-4881*
**Fax Area Code:* 920 ■ *TF:* 800-776-7163 ■ *Web:* www.northlandplastics.com

O'Sullivan Films Inc 1944 Valley Ave. Winchester VA 22601 540-667-6666
Web: www.osul.com

Orcon Corp 1570 Atlantic St. Union City CA 94587 510-489-8100 489-6436
TF General: 800-227-0505 ■ *Web:* www.orcon-aerospace.com

Pacur LLC 3555 Moser St. Oshkosh WI 54901 920-236-2888
Web: www.pacur.com

Paragon Films Inc 3500 W Tacoma Broken Arrow OK 74012 918-250-3456 355-3456
Web: www.paragon-films.com

Penn Fibre Plastics 2434 Bristol Rd Bensalem PA 19020 800-662-7366 702-9552*
**Fax Area Code:* 215 ■ *TF Cust Svc:* 800-662-7366 ■ *Web:* www.pennfibre.com

Performance Coating International
600 Murray St. Bangor PA 18013 610-588-7900 588-7901
Web: pcoatingsintl.com

Performance Materials Corp
1150 Calle Suerte Camarillo CA 93012 805-482-1722 482-8776
Web: tencate.com/amer/industrial-composites/default.aspx

Petoskey Plastics Inc 1 Petoskey St. Petoskey MI 49770 231-347-2602
Web: www.petoskeyplastics.com

Pexco LLC 2500 Northwinds Pkwy Ste 472 Alpharetta GA 30009 404-564-8560 564-8579
Web: www.pexco.com

Phoenix Films Inc PO Box 3816. Clearwater FL 33767 727-446-0300
Web: www.phoenixfilms.com

Pinnacle Films Inc 10701-A S Commerce Blvd. Charlotte NC 28273 704-504-3200
Web: www.pinnaclefilms.com

Plaskolite Inc 1770 Joyce Ave Columbus OH 43219 614-294-3281 297-7287
TF: 800-848-9124 ■ *Web:* www.plaskolite.com

Polyethics Industries Inc 301 Forest Ave N Orillia ON L3V6H9 705-329-2266
Web: polyethics.com

Polyfil 74 Green Pond Rd Rockaway NJ 07866 973-627-4070
TF: 866-765-9345 ■ *Web:* www.polyfilcorp.com

Polyvinyl Films Inc PO Box 753. Sutton MA 01590 508-865-3558 865-1562
TF: 800-343-6134 ■ *Web:* www.stretchtite.com

Primex Plastics Corp 1235 N 'F' St Richmond IN 47374 765-966-7774 935-1083
TF: 800-222-5116 ■ *Web:* www.primexplastics.com

Prinsco Inc 108 W Hwy 7 PO Box 265. Prinsburg MN 56281 320-222-6800 978-8602
TF: 800-992-1725 ■ *Web:* www.prinsco.com

Raven Industries Inc 205 E Sixth St Sioux Falls SD 57104 605-336-2750 335-0268
NASDAQ: RAVN ■ *TF:* 800-243-5435 ■ *Web:* www.ravenind.com

Republic Plastics 355 SCHUMANN Rd McQueeney TX 78123 830-557-5574
Web: www.republicplastics.com

Ross & Roberts Inc 1299 W Broad St. Stratford CT 06615 203-378-9363 377-8841

Sancap Liner Technology Inc
16125 Armour St NE. Alliance OH 44601 330-821-1166
Web: www.sancapliner.com

Shepherd CE Company Inc 2221 Canada Dry St. Houston TX 77023 713-924-4300 928-2324
TF: 800-324-6733 ■ *Web:* www.ceshepherd.com

Shield Pack LLC 411 Downing Pines Rd. West Monroe LA 71292 318-387-4743 325-4800
TF: 800-551-5185 ■ *Web:* www.shieldpack.com

Sigma Plastics Group
Page & Schuyler Aves Bldg 5 Lyndhurst NJ 07071 201-507-9100 507-0447
Web: www.sigmaplastics.com

Sinclair & Rush Inc 123 Manufacturers Dr. Arnold MO 63010 636-282-6800 282-6888
Web: www.sinclair-rush.com

SLM Manufacturing Corp 215 Davidson Ave Somerset NJ 08873 732-469-7500 469-5546
TF: 800-526-3708 ■ *Web:* www.slmcorp.com

Soliant LLC 1872 Hwy 9 Bypass. Lancaster SC 29720 803-285-9401 313-8227
TF: 800-288-9401 ■ *Web:* www.paintfilm.com

Southern Film Extruders Inc
2319 English Rd. High Point NC 27262 336-885-8091 885-1221
TF: 800-334-6101 ■ *Web:* www.southernfilm.com

Summit Plastics Inc 107 S Laurel St Summit MS 39666 601-276-7500 276-2400
TF: 800-790-7117 ■ *Web:* www.summitplasticsus.com

Sunlite Plastics Inc
W 194 N 11340 McCormick Dr Germantown WI 53022 262-253-0600 253-0601
Web: www.sunliteplastics.com

Tee Group Films 605 N Main St Ladd IL 61329 815-894-2331 894-3387
Web: www.tee-group.com

Thermoplastic Processes Inc 1268 Valley Rd. Stirling NJ 07980 908-561-3000 753-6749
TF: 888-554-6400 ■ *Web:* www.thermoplasticprocesses.com

Valley Decorating Co 2829 E Hamilton Ave. Fresno CA 93721 559-495-1100
Web: www.pomponcentral.com

VCF Films Inc 1100 Sutton Ave. Howell MI 48843 888-905-7680 546-2984*
**Fax Area Code:* 517 ■ *TF:* 888-905-7680 ■ *Web:* vcffilms.com

Vinylex Corp 2636 Byington Rd. Knoxville TN 37931 865-690-2211 691-6273*
**Fax:* Cust Svc ■ *Web:* www.omegaplastics.com

VPI Corp 3123 S Ninth St Sheboygan WI 53081 920-458-4664 458-1368
TF Orders: 800-874-4240 ■ *Web:* www.vpicorp.com

Watersaver Company Inc 5870 E 56th Ave. Commerce CO 80022 303-289-1818 287-3136
TF: 800-525-2424 ■ *Web:* www.watersaver.com

Zippertubing Co 7150 W Erie St Chandler AZ 85226 480-285-3990 285-3997
TF: 855-289-1874 ■ *Web:* www.zippertubing.com

601 PLASTICS FOAM PRODUCTS

Phone | Fax

A-Z Sponge & Foam Products Ltd
811 Cundy Ave Annacis Island Delta BC V3M5P6 604-525-1665 525-1081
TF: 800-665-3990 ■ *Web:* www.a-zfoam.com

ACH Foam Technologies LLC 5250 Sherman St. Denver CO 80216 303-297-3844
TF: 800-525-8697 ■ *Web:* www.achfoam.com

Advanced Polymer Technology Corp
109 Conica Ln Harmony PA 16037 724-452-1330
Web: www.advpolytech.com

Aero Plastics Inc 91 Citation Dr. Concord ON L4K2Y8 905-738-9010 738-9175
TF: 877-660-2376 ■ *Web:* www.aeroplastics.ca

Phone | Fax

AGC Chemicals Americas Inc
55 E Uwchlan Ave Ste 201 Exton PA 19341 610-423-4300
Web: www.agcchem.com

Airdex International Inc
8975 S Pecos Rd Ste 7A. Henderson NV 89074 702-270-6004
Web: www.airdex.com

Allied Aerofoam Products LLC 216 Kelsey Ln Tampa FL 33619 813-626-0090 569-0629
TF: 800-338-9140 ■ *Web:* www.alliedaerofoam.com

Alpla Inc 289 Hwy 155 S Mcdonough GA 30253 770-914-1407
Web: www.alpla.com

Amatech Inc 1460 Grimm Dr. Erie PA 16501 814-452-0010
Web: www.amatechinc.com

Amcor Ltd 935 Technology Dr Ste 100. Ann Arbor MI 48108 734-428-9741
Web: www.amcor.com

American Excelsior Co 850 Ave H E Arlington TX 76011 800-777-7645 649-7816*
**Fax Area Code:* 817 ■ *TF:* 800-777-7645 ■ *Web:* www.americanexcelsior.com

American Gilsonite Co
29950 South Bonanza Hwy Bonanza UT 84008 435-789-1921
Web: www.americangilsonite.com

Anchor Packaging Inc
13515 Barrett Pkwy Dr Saint Louis MO 63021 314-822-7800
Web: www.anchorpackaging.com

Aragon Elastomers LLC 740 S Pierce Ave Louisville CO 80027 303-666-9519
Web: www.aragonelastomers.com

Astrofoam Molding Company Inc
4117 Calle Tesoro Camarillo CA 93012 805-482-7276 482-6599
Web: www.astrofoam.com

Balcan Plastics Ltd 9340 Meaux St. Saint Leonard QC H1R3H2 514-326-0200 326-4565
TF: 877-422-5226 ■ *Web:* www.balcan.com

Barger Packaging Inc 2901 Oakland Ave Elkhart IN 46517 888-525-2845
TF: 888-525-2845 ■ *Web:* www.bargerpkg.com

Belle-Pak Packaging Inc 7465 Birchmount Rd Markham ON L3R5X9 905-475-5151 475-9295
TF: 800-565-2137 ■ *Web:* www.belle-pak.com

Big 3 Packaging LLC 4201 Torresdale Ave. Philadelphia PA 19124 215-743-4201
Web: big3packaging.com

Boltaron Performance Products LLC
1 General St Newcomerstown OH 43832 740-498-5900
Web: www.boltaron.com

Bontex Inc 12918 Whitehorse Ln. St. Louis MO 63131 314-965-8059
OTC: BOTX ■ *Web:* www.bontex.com

Brushfoil LLC 1 Shoreline Dr Unit 6. Guilford CT 06437 203-453-7403
Web: www.brushfoil.com

Bulldog Bag Ltd 13631 Vulcan Way Richmond BC V6V1K4 604-273-8021 273-9927
TF: 800-665-1944 ■ *Web:* www.bulldogbag.com

Carpenter Co 5016 Monument Ave Richmond VA 23230 804-359-0800 353-0694
TF: 800-288-3830 ■ *Web:* www.carpenter.com

CDF Corp 77 Industrial Park Rd. Plymouth MA 02360 508-747-5858
Web: www.cdf1.com

Cellofoam North America Inc
1917 Rockdale Industrial Blvd Conyers GA 30012 770-929-3688 929-3608
TF: 800-241-3634 ■ *Web:* www.cellofoam.com

Cellox Corp 1200 Industrial St. Reedsburg WI 53959 608-524-2316 524-2362
Web: www.cellox.com

Chestnut Ridge Foam Inc PO Box 781 Latrobe PA 15650 724-537-9000
Web: www.chestnutridgefoam.com

CKS Packaging Inc 445 Great SW Pkwy. Atlanta GA 30336 404-691-8900
Web: www.ckspackaging.com

Clark Foam Products Corp
655 Remington Blvd. Bolingbrook IL 60440 630-226-5900 226-5959
TF: 888-284-2290 ■ *Web:* www.clarkfoam.net

Classic Packaging Co 5570 Bethania Rd. Pfafftown NC 27040 336-922-4224
Web: www.classicpackaging.com

Clayton Corp 866 Horan Dr Fenton MO 63026 636-349-5333 349-5335
TF Cust Svc: 800-729-8220 ■ *Web:* www.claytoncorp.com

Clear-Vu Products Inc 29 New York Ave. Westbury NY 11590 516-333-8880
Web: www.clear-vu.com

ClingZ Inc 541 Laser Rd NE Rio Rancho NM 87124 505-892-2500
Web: www.clingz.com

Conglom Inc 2600 Marie-Curie Ave. Saint-Laurent QC H4S2C3 514-333-6666
TF: 877-333-0098 ■ *Web:* www.conglom.com

Creative Foam Corp 300 N Alloy Dr. Fenton MI 48430 810-629-4149 629-7368
TF: 800-529-4149 ■ *Web:* www.creativefoam.com

Crest Foam Industries Inc 100 Carol Pl. Moonachie NJ 07074 201-807-0809 807-1113
Web: www.inoacusa.com

CSP Technologies 960 W Veterans Blvd. Auburn AL 36832 334-887-8300
Web: www.csptechnologies.com

Custom Pack Inc 662 Exton Cmns Exton PA 19341 610-321-2525 321-2526
TF: 800-722-7005 ■ *Web:* www.custompackinc.com

Cyclics Corp 2135 Technology Dr Schenectady NY 12308 518-881-1440 881-1439
Web: www.cyclics.com

Dart Container Corp 500 Hogsback Rd Mason MI 48854 800-248-5960 676-3883*
**Fax Area Code:* 517 ■ *TF:* 800-248-5960 ■ *Web:* www.dartcontainer.com

Deltapac Packaging Inc 8200 de l'Industrie St. Anjou QC H1J1S7 514-352-5546 352-5703
Web: www.deltapac.ca

Diversified Plastics Corp 120 W Mount Vernon St. Nixa MO 65714 417-725-2622
Web: www.dpcap.com

Dow Chemical Company, The 1881 W Oak Pkwy Marietta GA 30062 770-428-2684 428-9431
TF: 800-331-6451 ■ *Web:* www.dow.com

Edge-Sweets Co 2887 Three-Mile Rd NW. Grand Rapids MI 49534 616-453-5458 453-5458
Web: www.edge-sweets.com

Eldon James Corp 10325 E 47th Ave Denver CO 80238 970-667-2728
Web: www.eldonjames.com

Elliott Company of Indianapolis Inc
9200 Zionsville Rd Indianapolis IN 46268 317-291-1213 291-1213
TF Orders: 800-545-1213 ■ *Web:* www.elliottfoam.com

Enduro Composites Inc
16602 Central Green Blvd. Houston TX 77032 713-358-4000 358-4100
TF: 800-231-7271 ■ *Web:* www.endurocomposites.com

Evergreen Plastics Inc 202 Watertower Dr Clyde OH 43410 419-547-1400
Web: www.evergreenplastics.com

Federal Foam Technologies Inc
600 Wisconsin Dr. New Richmond WI 54017 715-246-9500 246-9500
TF: 800-898-9559 ■ *Web:* www.federalfoam.com

Company	City	State	Zip	Phone	Fax
Federal Plastics Manufacturing Ltd 5100 Fisher St *Web:* www.fedplast.com	St-laurent	QC	H4T1J5	514-342-5411	342-3744
Filmtech Corp 2121 31st St SW *Web:* www.filmtech-corp.com	Allentown	PA	18103	610-709-9999	
Flexible Packaging Company Inc PO Box 4321 *Web:* www.flepak.com	Bayamon	PR	00958	787-622-7225	
Flexpak Corp 3720 W Washington St *Web:* www.nelipak.com	Phoenix	AZ	85009	602-269-7648	269-7640
FLEXSTAR Packaging Inc 13320 River Rd *TF:* 800-663-1177 ■ *Web:* www.flexstar.ca	Richmond	BC	V6V1W7	604-273-9277	
Flextron Industries Inc 720 Mt Rd *TF:* 800-633-2181 ■ *Web:* www.flextronindustries.com	Aston	PA	19014	610-459-4600	459-5379
FM Corp 3535 Hudson Rd *Web:* www.fmcorp.com	Rogers	AR	72756	479-636-3540	
Foam Fabricators Inc 950 Progress Blvd *Web:* www.foamfabricatorsinc.com	New Albany	IN	47150	812-948-1696	948-2450
Foam Molders & Specialty Corp 20004 State Rd *TF:* 800-378-8987 ■ *Web:* www.foammolders.com	Cerritos	CA	90703	800-378-8987	
Foam Products Corp 350 Beamer Rd *Web:* www.foamproducts.com	Calhoun	GA	30701	706-629-1256	
Foam Rubber Products Inc 2000 Troy Ave *Web:* www.foamrubberllc.com	New Castle	IN	47362	765-521-2000	521-2759
Fomo Products Inc 2775 Barber Rd **Fax:* Cust Svc ■ *TF:* 800-321-5585 ■ *Web:* www.fomo.com	Norton	OH	44203	330-753-4585	753-9566*
Free Flow Packaging International Inc 1090 Mills Way *TF:* 800-866-9946 ■ *Web:* www.fpintl.com	Redwood City	CA	94063	650-261-5300	361-1713
FRX Polymers Inc 200 Turnpike Rd *Web:* www.frxpolymers.com	Chelmsford	MA	01824	978-244-9500	
Future Foam Inc 1610 Ave N Council Bluffs *TF:* 800-733-8061 ■ *Web:* www.futurefoam.com	Council Bluffs	IA	51501	712-323-9122	
FXI 1400 N Providence Rd *TF:* 800-355-3626 ■ *Web:* fxi.com	Media	PA	19063	610-744-2300	
G & T Industries Inc 1001 76th St SW **Fax Area Code:* 616 ■ *TF:* 800-968-6035 ■ *Web:* www.gtindustries.com	Byron Center	MI	49315	800-968-6035	583-1524*
Gaco Western Inc 200 W Mercer St Ste 202 *TF:* 800-456-4226 ■ *Web:* www.gaco.com	Seattle	WA	98119	206-575-0450	575-0587
General Foam Plastics Corp 3321 E Princess Anne Rd *Web:* www.genfoam.com	Norfolk	VA	23502	757-857-0153	857-0033
General Plastics Mfg Co 4910 S Burlington Way *TF:* 800-806-6051 ■ *Web:* www.generalplastics.com	Tacoma	WA	98409	253-473-5000	473-5104
Gracious Living Innovations Inc 151 Courtney Park Drive W *Web:* www.glinnov.com	Mississauga	ON	L5W1Y5	905-795-5505	795-5523
Green-Tek Inc 3708 Enterprise Dr *Web:* www.green-tek.com	Janesville	WI	53546	608-754-7336	
Guardian Packaging Inc 3615 Security St *TF:* 800-259-1502 ■ *Web:* www.guardianpackaging.com	Garland	TX	75042	214-349-1500	349-1584
Gunther Mele Ltd 30 Craig St *TF:* 888-486-8437 ■ *Web:* www.gunthermele.com	Brantford	ON	N3R7J1	519-756-4330	
Hermann Companies Inc 7701 Forsyth Blvd Ste 1000 *Web:* www.hermanncompanies.com	St. Louis	MO	63105	314-863-9200	
Hibco Plastics Inc 1820 Us 601 Hwy *TF:* 800-849-8683 ■ *Web:* www.hibco.com	Yadkinville	NC	27055	336-463-2391	463-5591
Houston Foam Plastics Inc 2019 Brooks St *Web:* www.houstonfoam.com	Houston	TX	77026	713-224-3484	224-5511
Inland Plastics Inc 201 Center St *Web:* www.inlandplastics.com	Rosedale	AB	T0J0Y0	403-823-6252	
Innovative Plastics Corp 400 Rt 303 *Web:* innovative-plastics.com	Orangeburg	NY	10962	845-359-7500	359-0237
Intertrade Industries Ltd 14600 Commerce Ln *TF:* 800-944-9277 ■ *Web:* www.intertradeindustries.com	Huntington Beach	CA	92649	714-894-5566	894-3927
ISO Poly Films Inc 101 ISO Pkwy *Web:* www.isopoly.com	Gray Court	SC	29645	864-876-4300	
ITW Minigrip Inc 8125 Cobb Ctr Dr *Web:* www.minigrip.com	Kennesaw	GA	30152	770-422-4187	
Jif-Pak Manufacturing Inc 1451 Engineer St *Web:* www.jifpak.com	Vista	CA	92081	760-597-2665	
Keyes Packaging Group Inc 3715 State Hwy *Web:* www.keyespackaging.com	Wenatchee	WA	98807	509-663-8537	
KNF Flexpak Corp 734 W Penn Pk *Web:* www.knfcorporation.com	Tamaqua	PA	18252	570-386-3550	
Lantec Products Inc 5302 Derry Ave Ste G *Web:* www.lantecp.com	Agoura Hills	CA	91301	818-707-2285	
Lomont Molding Imt 1516 E Mapleleaf Dr *Web:* www.lomontimt.com	Mount Pleasant	IA	52641	319-385-1528	
Lucent Polymers Inc 1700 Lynch Rd *Web:* www.lucentpolymers.com	Evansville	IN	47711	812-421-2216	
MBA Polymers Inc 500 W Ohio Ave *Web:* www.mbapolymers.com	Richmond	CA	94804	510-231-9031	
MDL Doors Inc 42918-B Cranbrook Rd *Web:* www.mdldoors.com	Brussels	ON	N0G1H0	519-887-6974	
MedPlast Inc 405 W Geneva Dr *Web:* medplastgroup.com	Tempe	AZ	85282	480-553-6400	
Mg International Inc 90 International Pkwy	Dallas	GA	30157	770-505-0004	443-2154
Minnesota Diversified Products Inc 9091 County Rd 50 *Web:* www.diversifoam.com	Rockford	MN	55373	763-477-5854	477-5863
Modern Plastics Inc 88 Long Hill Cross Rd *Web:* www.modernplastics.com	Shelton	CT	06484	203-333-3128	
Monarch Plastics Inc 1205 65th St *Web:* www.monarch-plastics.com	Kenosha	WI	53143	262-652-4444	
MonoSol LLC 707 E 80th Pl Ste 301 *Web:* www.monosol.com	Merrillville	IN	46410	219-762-3165	
Mossberg Industries Inc 204 N Second St *Web:* mossbergind.com	Garrett	IN	46738	260-357-5141	357-5144
Munot Plastics Inc 2935 W 17th St *Web:* www.munotplastics.com	Erie	PA	16505	814-838-7721	833-2095
NACO Industries Inc 395 West 1400 North *Web:* www.herndon-assoc.com	Logan	UT	84341	435-753-8020	
Nan Ya Plastics Corporation America 9 Peach Tree Hill Rd *Web:* www.npcam.com	Livingston	NJ	07039	973-992-2090	
NAP Windows & Doors Ltd 2150 Enterprise Way *TF:* 888-762-5311 ■ *Web:* www.napwindows.com	Kelowna	BC	V1Y6H7	250-762-5343	
Newmar Window Manufacturing Inc 7630 Airport Rd *Web:* www.newmar.com	Mississauga	ON	L4T4G6	905-672-1233	
Noltex LLC 3930 Ventura Dr Ste 355 *Web:* www.soarus.com	Arlington Heights	IL	60004	847-255-1211	
North Carolina Foam Industries Inc 1515 Carter St *TF:* 800-346-8229 ■ *Web:* www.ncfi.com	Mount Airy	NC	27030	336-789-9161	789-9586
Northern Pipe Products Inc 1302 39th St N *Web:* www.northernpipe.com	Fargo	ND	58102	701-282-7655	
Pacific Packaging Products Inc 24 Industrial Way *TF:* 800-777-0300 ■ *Web:* www.pacificpkg.com	Wilmington	MA	01887	978-657-9100	658-4933
Pacon Inc 4249 N Puente Ave *Web:* www.paconinc.com	Baldwin Park	CA	91706	626-814-4654	
Palmetto Industries International Inc 6001 Horizon W Pkwy *Web:* www.palmetto-industries.com	Grovetown	GA	30813	706-737-7999	
Peel Plastic Products Ltd 49 Rutherford Rd S *Web:* www.peelplastics.com	Brampton	ON	L6W3J3	905-456-3660	456-0870
Peninsula Packaging Company LLC 1030 N Anderson Rd *Web:* peninsulapackaging.com	Exeter	CA	93221	559-594-6813	
Perfect Turf Inc 622 Sandpebble Dr *TF:* 888-796-8873 ■ *Web:* www.perfectturfinc.com	Schaumburg	IL	60193	888-796-8873	
Pinova Holdings Inc 2801 Cook St *TF:* 888-807-2958 ■ *Web:* www.pinovaholdings.com	Brunswick	GA	31520	888-807-2958	
Plastic & Steel Supply Company Inc 50 Tannery Rd Readington Industrial Ctr Bldg 3 *TF:* 800-407-3726 ■ *Web:* www.pep-plastic.com	Branchburg	NJ	08876	908-534-6111	
Plastic Container Corp 2508 N Oak St *Web:* www.netpcc.com	Urbana	IL	61802	217-352-2722	
Plastipak Industries Inc 150 Industriel Blvd *TF:* 800-387-7452 ■ *Web:* www.plastipak.ca	Boucherville	QC	J4B2X3	450-650-2200	650-2201
Plastomer Corp 37819 Schoolcraft Rd *Web:* www.plastomer.com	Livonia	MI	48150	734-464-0700	464-4792
Plastube Inc 590 Simonds S *Web:* www.plastube.com	Granby	QC	J2J1E1	450-378-2633	
PMC Biogenix Inc 1231 Pope St *Web:* www.pmcbiogenix.com	Memphis	TN	38108	901-325-4930	
PMC Global Inc 12243 Branford St *Web:* www.pmcglobalinc.com	Sun Valley	CA	91352	818-896-1101	686-2531
Poly Molding LLC 96 Fourth Ave *TF:* 800-229-7161 ■ *Web:* polymoldingllc.com	Haskell	NJ	07420	973-835-7161	835-2438
Polycel Structural Foam Inc 68 County Line Rd *Web:* www.polycel.com	Somerville	NJ	08876	908-722-5254	722-7457
Polymer Industries LLC 10526 Alabama Hwy 40 PO Box 32 *TF:* 877-489-0039 ■ *Web:* www.polymerindustries.com	Henagar	AL	35978	256-657-5197	
Precision Products Group Inc 9207 51st Ave *Web:* www.ppgintl.com	College Park	MD	20740	301-474-3100	
Prestige Fabricators Inc 2206 Dumont St *Web:* www.prestigefab.com	Asheboro	NC	27204	336-672-3383	
Pretium Packaging LLC 15450 S Outer Forty Dr Ste 120 *Web:* www.pretiumpkg.com	Chesterfield	MO	63017	314-727-8200	
Professional Plastics Inc 1810 E Valencia Dr *Web:* www.professionalplastics.com	Fullerton	CA	92831	714-446-6500	
Prolamina Corp 840 S Waukegan Rd Ste 208 *TF:* 877-536-2628 ■ *Web:* www.prolamina.com	Lake Forest	IL	60045	877-536-2628	
Radva Corp 604 17th St PO Box 2900 *NYSE: RDVA* ■ *Web:* www.radva.com	Radford	VA	24143	540-731-3731	
Republic Packaging Corp 9160 S Green St *Web:* www.repco.com	Chicago	IL	60620	773-233-6530	233-6005
Resilux America LLC 265 John Brooks Rd *Web:* www.uniqueplastics.com	Pendergrass	GA	30567	706-693-7110	
Retail Resource Group International LLC 226 New Gate Loop *Web:* www.rrgtravelmugs.com	Lake Mary	FL	32746	407-878-6650	
Richards Packaging Inc 2321 NE Argyle St Ste D *Web:* www.richardspackaging.com	Portland	OR	97211	503-290-0000	
RL Adams Plastics Inc 5955 Crossroads Commerce *TF:* 800-968-2241 ■ *Web:* www.goadams.com	Wyoming	MI	49519	616-261-4400	249-8955
Robbie Manufacturing Inc 10810 Mid America Ave *TF:* 800-255-6328 ■ *Web:* www.robbieflexibles.com	Lenexa	KS	66219	913-492-3400	492-1543
Roberts PolyPro Inc 5416 Wyoming Ave *Web:* www.robertspolypro.com	Charlotte	NC	28273	704-588-1794	
Rogers Foam Corp 20 Vernon St *Web:* rogersfoam.com	Somerville	MA	02145	617-623-3010	629-2585
Rubberlite Inc 2501 Guyan Ave *Web:* www.rubberlite.com	Huntington	WV	25703	304-525-3116	523-4316
Safas Corp 2 Ackerman Ave *Web:* www.safascorp.com	Clifton	NJ	07011	973-772-5252	
SBA Materials Inc 9430-H San Mateo Blvd NE *Web:* www.sbamaterials.com	Albuquerque	NM	87113	505-924-2807	

Phone | Fax

Sekisui Voltek LLC 100 Shepard St ... Lawrence MA 01843 978-685-2557 685-9861
TF: 800-225-0668 ■ *Web:* www.sekisuivoltek.com

Sertapak Packaging Corp 1039 Dundas St ... Woodstock ON N4S0B1 519-539-3330
Web: www.sertapak.com

Shawnee Chemical Company Inc
136 Main St Ste 300 ... Princeton NJ 08540 609-799-3930
Web: www.shawchem.com

Sigma Stretch Film Corp
Page & Schuyler Aves Bldg 8 ... Lyndhurst NJ 07071 201-507-9100
Web: www.sigmastretchtools.com

SimPak International LLC
2107 Production Dr ... Louisville KY 40299 502-671-8250
Web: www.simpakinternational.com

Sonoco 1 N Second St ... Hartsville SC 29550 800-377-2692
NYSE: SON ■ *TF:* 800-377-2692 ■ *Web:* www.sonoco.com

Sonoma Graphic Products Inc
961 Stockton Ave ... San Jose CA 95110 408-294-2072
Web: www.sgpweb.com

Spectratek Technologies Inc
5405 Jandy Pl ... Los Angeles CA 90066 310-822-2400 822-2660
Web: www.spectratek.net

Spectrum Bags Inc 12850 Midway Pl ... Cerritos CA 90703 562-623-2555
Web: www.spectrumbags.com

Stone Plastics & Manufacturing Inc
8245 Riley St ... Zeeland MI 49464 616-748-9740
Web: www.stoneplasticsmfg.com

Storopack Inc 12007 S Woodruff Ave ... Downey CA 90241 562-803-5582 803-4462
TF: 800-829-1491 ■ *Web:* www.storopack.us

StyroChem Canada Ltee 19250 Clark Graham ... Baie-D'Urfe QC H9X3R8 514-457-3226 457-4390
Web: www.styrochem.com

Styrotek Inc 545 Rd 176 ... Delano CA 93215 661-725-4957 725-7064
Web: www.styrotek.com

Sufix USA Inc 651 Brigham Rd Ste D ... Greensboro NC 27409 336-605-1950
Web: www.sufix.com

SupplyOne Corp 20 N Waterloo Rd Ste 200 ... Devon PA 19333 484-582-5005
Web: supplyone.com

Syfan USA Corp 1522 Twin Bridges Rd ... Everetts NC 27825 252-792-2547
Web: www.syfanusa.com

T-H Marine Supplies Inc 200 Finney Dr ... Huntsville AL 35824 256-772-0164
Web: www.thmarine.com

Therma Foam Inc 8910 Oak Grove Rd ... Fort Worth TX 76140 817-624-7204
Web: www.thermafoam.com

ThermoSafe Brands
3930 N Ventura Dr Ste 450 ... Arlington Heights IL 60004 847-398-0110 398-0653
TF: 800-323-7442 ■ *Web:* www.thermosafe.com

ThermoServ 3901 Pipestone Rd ... Dallas TX 75212 214-631-0307 631-0566
TF: 800-635-5559 ■ *Web:* www.thermoserv.com

TMP Technologies Inc 1200 Northland Ave ... Buffalo NY 14215 716-895-6100
Web: www.tmptech.com

TO Plastics Inc 830 County Rd 75 PO Box 37 ... Clearwater MN 55320 320-558-2407
Web: www.toplastics.com

Topp Industries Inc
420 N State Rd 25 PO Box 420 ... Rochester IN 46975 574-223-3681 223-6106
TF: 800-354-4534 ■ *Web:* www.toppindustries.com

UFP Technologies Inc 172 E Main St ... Georgetown MA 01833 978-352-2200
NASDAQ: UFPT ■ *TF:* 800-372-3172 ■ *Web:* www.ufpt.com

Unique Fabricating Inc
800 Standard Pkwy ... Auburn Hills MI 48326 248-853-2333 853-7720
Web: www.uniquefab.com

Universal Protective Packaging Inc
61 Texaco Rd ... Mechanicsburg PA 17050 717-766-1578
Web: www.uppi.com

Wellman Plastics Recycling LLC
520 Kingsburg Hwy ... Johnsonville SC 29555 843-386-2011
Web: www.wellmanplastics.com

Western Concord Manufacturing Ltd
880 Cliveden Ave ... Vancouver BC V3M5R5 604-525-1061
Web: www.westernconcord.com

WinCup 4640 Lewis Rd ... Stone Mountain GA 30083 770-938-5281
TF: 800-292-2877 ■ *Web:* www.wincup.com

Woodbridge Foam Corp
4240 Sherwoodtowne Blvd ... Mississauga ON L4Z2G6 905-896-3626 896-9262
Web: www.woodbridgegroup.com

Zurn Pex Inc 1900 W Hively Ave ... Elkhart IN 46517 574-294-7541
Web: www.zurnpex.com

602 PLASTICS MACHINING & FORMING

See Also Plastics Molding - Custom p. 2948

Phone | Fax

Akra Plastic Products Inc 1504 E Cedar St ... Ontario CA 91761 909-930-1999
Web: akraplastics.com

Bardes Plastics Inc 5225 W Clinton Ave ... Milwaukee WI 53223 800-558-5161 354-6331*
**Fax Area Code:* 414 ■ *TF Cust Svc:* 800-558-5161 ■ *Web:* www.bardesplastics.com

Comco Plastics Inc 98-31 Jamaica Ave ... Woodhaven NY 11421 718-849-9000
Web: www.comcoplastics.com

Conroy & Knowlton Inc
320 S Montebello Blvd ... Montebello CA 90640 323-665-5288 722-4670
Web: www.conroyknowlton.com

East Jordan Plastics Inc PO Box 575 ... East Jordan MI 49727 800-353-1190 536-7090*
**Fax Area Code:* 231 ■ *TF:* 800-353-1190 ■ *Web:* www.eastjordanplastics.com

Empire West Inc 9270 Graton Rd PO Box 511 ... Graton CA 95444 707-823-1190 823-8531
TF: 800-521-4261 ■ *Web:* www.empirewest.com

Engineered Plastics Inc 211 Chase St ... Gibsonville NC 27249 336-449-4121 449-6352
TF: 800-711-1740 ■ *Web:* www.engplas.com

Fabri-Form Co 200 S Friendship Dr ... New Concord OH 43762 740-826-5000 826-5001
TF: 800-837-2574 ■ *Web:* portal.pendaform.com

Fabri-Kal Corp 600 Plastics Pl ... Kalamazoo MI 49001 269-385-5050 385-0197
TF: 800-888-5054 ■ *Web:* www.fabri-kal.com

FNW Industrial Plastics Inc
12500 Jefferson Ave PO Box 2778 ... Newport News VA 23602 757-874-7795 989-2501
TF: 800-721-2590 ■ *Web:* www.ferguson.com

Phone | Fax

Formall Inc 3908 Fountain Vly Dr ... Knoxville TN 37918 865-922-7514 922-3941
TF: 800-643-3676 ■ *Web:* www.formall.com

Gage Industries Inc 6710 McEwan Rd ... Lake Oswego OR 97035 503-639-2177

Gregstrom Corp 64 Holton St ... Woburn MA 01801 781-935-6600 935-4905
Web: www.gregstrom.com

Inline Plastics Corp 42 Canal St ... Shelton CT 06484 203-924-2015 924-0370
TF: 800-826-5567 ■ *Web:* www.inlineplastics.com

Innovize Inc 500 Oak Grove Pkwy ... Saint Paul MN 55127 877-605-6580
TF: 877-605-6580 ■ *Web:* www.innovize.com

Jamestown Plastics Inc 8806 Highland Ave ... Brocton NY 14716 716-792-4144 792-4154
Web: www.jamestownplastics.com

Kal Plastics 2050 E 48th St ... Los Angeles CA 90058 323-581-6194 581-1805
Web: www.kal-plastics.com

Lamar Plastic Packaging Ltd 216 N Main St ... Freeport NY 11520 516-378-2500 378-6192
Web: lamarplastics.net

Mack Prototype Inc 424 Main St ... Gardner MA 01440 978-632-3700 632-3777
Web: www.mackprototype.com

McNeal Enterprises Inc 2031 Ringwood Ave ... San Jose CA 95131 408-922-7290 922-7299
TF: 800-562-6325 ■ *Web:* www.mcnealplasticmachining.com

Meyer Plastics Inc 5167 E 65th St ... Indianapolis IN 46220 317-259-4131 252-4687
TF: 800-968-4131 ■ *Web:* www.meyerplastics.com

Morgan Hill Plastics Inc 640 E Dunne Ave ... Morgan Hill CA 95037 408-779-2118 779-0322
Web: morganhillplastics.net

New Concept Mfg LLC
320 Busser Rd PO Box 297 ... Emigsville PA 17318 717-741-0840 741-4301
Web: www.newconcepttech.com

Paradise Plastics
1200 W Dr Martin Luther King Jr Blvd ... Plant City FL 33563 813-752-1155 754-3168
Web: www.paradiseplastics.com

Perkasie Industries Corp PO Box 179 ... Perkasie PA 18944 215-257-6581 453-1703
TF Sales: 800-523-6747 ■ *Web:* perkasie.cylex-usa.com

Placon Corp 6096 McKee Rd ... Madison WI 53719 608-271-5634 271-3162
TF: 800-541-1535 ■ *Web:* www.placon.com

Polygon Co 103 Industrial Pk Dr PO Box 176 ... Walkerton IN 46574 574-586-3145 586-7336
TF: 800-918-9261 ■ *Web:* www.polygoncomposites.com

Precision Molding Inc
5500 Roberts Matthews Hwy ... Sparta TN 38583 931-738-8376 738-8429
Web: www.precision-molding.com

Prent Corp 2225 Kennedy Rd ... Janesville WI 53545 608-754-0276 754-2410
Web: www.prent.com

Productive Plastics Inc 103 W Pk Dr ... Mount Laurel NJ 08054 856-778-4300 234-3310
Web: www.productiveplastics.com

PSC Manufacturinf Inc 312 Brokaw Rd ... Santa Clara CA 95050 408-988-5115

Quadrant Engineering Plastic Products USA
2120 Fairmont Ave PO Box 14235 ... Reading PA 19612 610-320-6600 320-6638
TF: 800-366-0300 ■ *Web:* www.quadrantplastics.com

Ray Products Company Inc 1700 Chablis Ave ... Ontario CA 91761 909-390-9906 390-9984
TF: 800-423-7859 ■ *Web:* rayplastics.com

Ronningen Research & Development Co
6700 E 'YZ' Ave ... Vicksburg MI 49097 269-649-0520 649-0526
Web: www.ronningenresearch.com

Soroc Products Inc Plastics Div
4349 S Dort Hwy ... Burton MI 48529 810-743-2660 743-5922
Web: www.sorocproducts.com

Speck Plastics Inc PO Box 421 ... Nazareth PA 18064 610-759-1807 759-3916

Stewart Industries Inc 16 S Idaho St ... Seattle WA 98134 206-652-9110 660-0421*
**Fax Area Code:* 269

Sur-Flo Plastics & Engineering Inc
24358 Groesbeck Hwy ... Warren MI 48089 586-773-0400 773-8946
Web: www.sur-flo.com

Teak Isle Manufacturing Inc
401 Capitol Ct PO Box 417 ... Ocoee FL 34761 407-656-8885 656-2344
Web: www.teakisle.com

Thermo-Fab Corp 76 Walker Rd ... Shirley MA 01464 978-425-2311 425-2305
TF: 888-494-9777 ■ *Web:* www.thermofab.com

Total Plastics Inc 3316 Pagosa Ct ... Indianapolis IN 46226 317-543-3540 543-3553
TF: 800-382-4635 ■ *Web:* www.totalplastics.com

Tri-Town Precision Plastics Inc
12 Bridge St ... Deep River CT 06417 860-526-3200 526-4848

Underwood Mold Co Inc 104 Dixie Dr ... Woodstock GA 30189 770-926-2465 926-6565
Web: www.underwoodmoldco.com

Western Fibre Products Inc
10924 Vulcan St ... South Gate CA 90280 562-861-6665 862-9692

603 PLASTICS MATERIALS - WHOL

Phone | Fax

A Daigger & Company Inc
620 Lakeview Pkwy ... Vernon Hills IL 60061 847-816-5060 320-7200*
**Fax Area Code:* 800 ■ *TF:* 800-621-7193 ■ *Web:* www.daigger.com

ABC Polymers Inc
5682 E Ponce De Leon Ave ... Stone Mountain GA 30083 770-938-8336
Web: www.abcpolymers.com

Aetna Plastics Corp 1702 St Clair Ave ... Cleveland OH 44114 216-781-4421 781-4474
TF: 800-634-3074 ■ *Web:* www.aetnaplastics.com

AIN Plastics Inc 1750 E Heights Dr ... Madison Heights MI 48071 248-356-4000 542-3920
TF Cust Svc: 877-246-7700 ■ *Web:* www.tkmna.com

All American Containers Inc 9330 NW 110th Ave ... Miami FL 33178 305-887-0797 888-4133
Web: www.americancontainers.com

Allpak Co 1010 Lake St ... Oak Park IL 60301 708-383-7200

Aztec Supply 954 N Batavia St ... Orange CA 92867 714-771-6580 771-3013
TF: 800-836-3210 ■ *Web:* www.mezzaninesandmore.com

B. Schoenberg & Company Inc 345 Kear St ... Yorktown NY 10598 914-962-1200
Web: www.bschoenberg.info

Bamberger Polymers Inc 2 Jericho Plz Ste 109 ... Jericho NY 11753 516-622-3600 622-3610
TF: 800-888-8959 ■ *Web:* www.bambergerpolymers.com

Buckley Industries Inc 1850 E 53rd St N ... Wichita KS 67219 316-744-7587 744-8463
TF: 800-835-2779 ■ *Web:* www.buckleyind.com

Calsak Corp 1411 West 190th St Ste 400 ... Gardena CA 90248 310-719-9500 719-1300
TF: 888-663-6005 ■ *Web:* www.calsak.com

Cope Plastics Inc 4441 Industrial Dr ... Godfrey IL 62002 618-466-0221 466-7975*
**Fax:* Acctg ■ *TF:* 800-851-5510 ■ *Web:* www.copeplastics.com

				Phone	Fax
Delta Polymers Midwest Inc 6685 Sterling Dr N	Sterling Heights	MI	48312	586-795-2900	
TF: 800-860-6848 ■ *Web:* www.deltapoly.com					
E Hofmann Plastics 51 Centennial Rd	Orangeville	ON	L9W3R1	855-452-4014	
TF: 855-452-4014 ■ *Web:* www.hofmannplastics.com					
El Mar Plastics Inc 109 W 134th St	Los Angeles	CA	90061	310-436-6444	436-6445
TF: 800-255-5210 ■ *Web:* www.elmarplastics.com					
Faith Group Company Inc 195 Route 9 Ste 205	Manalapan	NJ	07726	732-431-1326	
Web: www.faith-group.com					
Golden Eagle Extrusions Inc 1762 State Rt 131	Milford	OH	45150	513-248-8292	
Web: www.goldeneagleextrusions.com					
Gvd Corp 45 Spinelli Pl	Cambridge	MA	02138	617-661-0060	
Web: www.gvdcorp.com					
H Muehlstein & Company Inc 10 Westport Rd	Wilton	CT	06897	203-855-6000	
TF: 800-257-3746 ■ *Web:* www.muehlstein.com					
H Sattler Plastics Co Inc 5410 W Roosevelt Rd	Chicago	IL	60644	773-287-3600	
Laird Plastics Inc 6800 Broken Sound Pkwy Ste 150	Boca Raton	FL	33487	561-443-9100	443-9108
TF: 800-243-9696 ■ *Web:* www.lairdplastics.com					
M Holland Co 400 Skokie Blvd Ste 600	Northbrook	IL	60062	847-272-7370	
TF: 877-578-4000 ■ *Web:* www.m-holland.com					
Maine Plastics Inc 1817 Kenosha Rd	Zion	IL	60099	847-379-9100	
Web: www.maineplastics.com					
Momentum Technologies Inc (MTI) 1507 Boettler Rd	Uniontown	OH	44685	330-896-5900	896-9943
TF: 800-720-0261 ■ *Web:* www.momentumtech.net					
Multi-Plastics Inc 7770 N Central Dr	Lewis Center	OH	43035	740-548-4894	548-5177
Web: www.multi-plastics.com					
Nytef Plastics Ltd Inc 6643 42nd Terr N	West Palm Beach	FL	33407	561-840-9499	638-7674*
**Fax Area Code:* 215 ■ *TF:* 800-646-9833 ■ *Web:* www.nytefplastics.com					
Orange County Industrial Plastics Inc 4811 E La Palma Ave	Anaheim	CA	92807	714-632-9450	630-6489
TF: 800-974-6247 ■ *Web:* www.ocip.com					
Pilcher Hamilton Corp 6845 Kingery Hwy	Willowbrook	IL	60527	630-655-8100	655-9948
Web: www.pilcherhamilton.com					
Plastic Film Corporation of America Inc 1287 Naperville Dr	Romeoville	IL	60446	630-887-0800	
TF: 800-654-6589 ■ *Web:* www.plasticfilmcorporation.com					
Plastics International Inc 7600 Anagram Dr	Eden Prairie	MN	55344	952-934-2303	
TF: 800-776-7769 ■ *Web:* www.plasticsintl.com					
Port Plastics Inc 15325 Fairfield Ranch Rd Ste 150	Chino Hills	CA	91709	480-813-6118	597-0116*
**Fax Area Code:* 909 ■ *TF:* 800-800-0039 ■ *Web:* www.portplastics.com					
Primepak Co 133 Cedar Ln	Teaneck	NJ	07666	201-836-5060	
Web: www.primepakcompany.com					
Regal Plastic Supply Co 111 E Tenth Ave	North Kansas City	MO	64116	816-421-6290	421-8206
TF: 800-627-2102 ■ *Web:* www.regalplastic.com					
Ryan Herco Products Corp 3010 N San Fernando Blvd	Burbank	CA	91504	818-841-1141	973-2600
TF: 800-848-1141 ■ *Web:* www.ryanherco.com					
San Diego Plastics Inc 2220 Mckinley Ave	National City	CA	91950	619-477-4855	
TF: 800-925-4855 ■ *Web:* www.sdplastics.com					
Seelye Plastics Inc 9700 Newton Ave S	Bloomington	MN	55431	800-328-2728	881-3503*
**Fax Area Code:* 952 ■ **Fax:* Sales ■ *TF:* 800-328-2728 ■ *Web:* seelyeplastics.com					
Sekisui America Corp 333 Meadowlands Pkwy	Secaucus	NJ	07094	201-423-7960	423-7979
TF General: 866-260-5851 ■ *Web:* www.sekisui-corp.com					
Superior Oil Co Inc 1402 N Capitol Ave Ste 100	Indianapolis	IN	46202	317-781-4400	781-4401
TF: 800-553-5480 ■ *Web:* www.superioroil.com					
Targun Plastics Co 899 Skokie Blvd	Northbrook	IL	60062	847-509-9355	509-9359
Web: targun.com					
Tekra Corp 16700 W Lincoln Ave	New Berlin	WI	53151	262-784-5533	797-3276
TF: 800-448-3572 ■ *Web:* www.tekra.com					

604 PLASTICS MOLDING - CUSTOM

				Phone	Fax
Akron Porcelain & Plastics Co 2739 Cory Ave PO Box 15157	Akron	OH	44314	330-745-2159	745-6688
TF: 800-737-9664 ■ *Web:* www.akronporcelain.com					
Aline Components Inc 1830 Tomlinson Rd PO Box 263	Kulpsville	PA	19443	215-368-0300	361-1400
Web: www.alinecomponents.com					
Alladin Plastics Inc 140 Industrial Dr	Surgoinsville	TN	37873	423-345-2351	
TF: 877-536-4693 ■ *Web:* www.alladinplasticsline.com					
AMA Plastics Inc 1100 Citrus St	Riverside	CA	92507	951-734-5600	734-5666
Web: amaplastics.com					
American Metal & Plastics Inc 450 32nd St SW	Grand Rapids	MI	49548	616-452-6061	452-3835
TF: 800-382-0067 ■ *Web:* www.ampi-gr.com					
American Plastic Molding Corp 965 S Elm St	Scottsburg	IN	47170	812-752-7000	752-5155
Web: www.apmc.com					
American Plastics Group Inc 715 W Pk Rd	Union	MO	63084	636-583-2583	
Web: www.americanplasticsgroup.com					
American Urethane Inc 1905 Betson Ct	Odenton	MD	21113	410-672-2100	672-2191
Web: www.americanurethane.com					
AMS Plastics Inc 1530 Hilton Head Rd Ste 205	El Cajon	CA	92019	619-713-2000	713-2975
Web: www.amsplastics.com					
Apollo Plastics Corp 5333 N Elston Ave	Chicago	IL	60630	773-282-9222	282-2763
Web: spcmfg.com					
Arrowhead Plastic Engineering Inc 2909 S Hoyt Ave	Muncie	IN	47302	765-286-0533	286-1681
Web: www.arrowheadinc.com					
ASK Plastics Inc 9750 Ashton Rd	Philadelphia	PA	19114	215-969-0800	969-2164
Web: www.askplastics.com					
Bekum America Corp 1140 W Grand River Ave PO Box 567	Williamston	MI	48895	517-655-4331	655-4121
Web: www.bekumamerica.com					
Berry Plastics 44 Oneil St	EastHampton	MA	01027	413-527-1250	
Berry Plastics Corp 101 Oakley St	Evansville	IN	47710	812-424-2904	424-0128
TF: 877-662-3779 ■ *Web:* www.berryplastics.com					
C & J Industries 760 Water St	Meadville	PA	16335	814-724-4950	724-4959
Web: www.cjindustries.com					
C Brewer Co 3630 E Miraloma Ave	Anaheim	CA	92806	714-630-6810	630-5527
Web: www.cbrewer.com					
Capsonic Group 460 Second St	Elgin	IL	60123	847-888-7300	
Web: www.capsonic.com					
Centro Inc 950 N Bend Dr	North Liberty	IA	52317	319-626-3200	626-3203
Web: www.centroinc.com					
Commercial Plastics Co (CPC) 800 Allanson Rd	Mundelein	IL	60060	847-566-1700	566-4737
Web: www.ecommercialplastics.com					
Confer Plastics Inc (CPI) 97 Witmer Rd	North Tonawanda	NY	14120	716-693-2056	694-3102
TF: 800-635-3213 ■ *Web:* www.conferplastics.com					
Connor Corp 10633 Coldwater Rd Ste 200	Fort Wayne	IN	46845	260-424-1601	
Web: www.connorcorp.com					
Core Molding Technologies Inc (CMT) 800 Manor Pk Dr	Columbus	OH	43228	614-870-5000	
NYSE: CMT ■ *Web:* www.coremt.com					
Cosmo Corp 30201 Aurora Rd	Cleveland	OH	44139	440-498-7500	498-7515
Web: www.cosmocorp.com					
Curtil 12 Betnr Industrial Dr	Pittsfield	MA	01201	413-443-4481	
Web: www.curtil.com					
Cuyahoga Molded Plastics Corp 1265 Babbitt Rd	Cleveland	OH	44132	216-261-2744	261-3537
TF: 800-805-9549 ■ *Web:* www.cuyahogaplastics.com					
D & M Plastic Corp 150 French Rd PO Box 158	Burlington	IL	60109	847-683-2054	
Web: www.dmplastics.com					
D-M-E Co 29111 Stephenson Hwy	Madison Heights	MI	48071	248-398-6000	544-5705
TF: 800-626-6653 ■ *Web:* www.dme.net					
Design & Molding Services Inc 25 Howard St	Piscataway	NJ	08854	732-752-0300	752-9672
Dickten Masch Plastics LLC N44 W33341 Watertown Plank Rd	Nashotah	WI	53058	262-369-5555	367-5630
Web: www.dicktenplastics.com					
Diemolding Corp 125 Rasbach St	Canastota	NY	13032	315-697-2221	697-2221
Web: www.diemolding.com					
Double H Plastics Inc 50 W St Rd	Warminster	PA	18974	215-674-4100	674-5469
TF: 800-523-3932 ■ *Web:* www.doublehplastics.com					
EFP Corp 223 Middleton Run Rd	Elkhart	IN	46516	574-295-4690	295-6512
TF: 800-205-8537 ■ *Web:* www.efpcorp.com					
Eifel Mold & Engineering 31071 Fraser Dr	Fraser	MI	48026	586-296-9640	
Web: eifelmoldandengineering.com					
Elgin Molded Plastics 909 Grace St	Elgin	IL	60120	847-931-2455	524-0087*
**Fax Area Code:* 800 ■ *TF:* 800-548-5483 ■ *Web:* www.elginmolded.com					
Ensinger Putnam Precision Molding 11 Danco Rd	Putnam	CT	06260	860-928-7911	928-2229
TF: 800-752-7865 ■ *Web:* www.ensinger-pc.com					
Evco Plastics 100 W N St PO Box 497	DeForest	WI	53532	800-507-6000	251-0822
TF: 800-507-6000 ■ *Web:* www.evcoplastics.com					
Falcon Plastics Inc 1313 Western Ave	Brookings	SD	57006	605-696-2500	696-2585
Web: falconplastics.com					
Fawn Industries Inc 1920 Greenspring Dr Ste 140	Timonium	MD	21093	410-308-9200	308-9202
Web: fawnplastics.com					
Filtertek Inc 11411 Price Rd	Hebron	IL	60034	815-648-1001	648-2929
TF: 800-248-2461 ■ *Web:* www.filtertek.com					
Flambeau Inc 15981 Valplast Rd	Middlefield	OH	44062	440-632-1631	632-1581
TF: 800-457-5252 ■ *Web:* www.flambeau.com					
FPI Thermoplastic Technologies 520 Speedwell Ave Ste 116	Morris Plains	NJ	07950	973-998-9801	
Web: www.njmep.org					
Green Tokai Company Ltd 55 Robert Wright Dr	Brookville	OH	45309	937-833-5444	833-2087
Gruber Systems Inc 25636 Ave Stanford	Valencia	CA	91355	661-257-4060	257-4791
TF: 800-257-4070 ■ *Web:* www.gruber-systems.com					
GW Plastics Inc 239 Pleasant St	Bethel	VT	05032	802-234-9941	234-9940
Web: www.gwplastics.com					
Hoffer Plastics Corp 500 N Collins St	South Elgin	IL	60177	847-741-5740	741-3086
Web: www.hofferplastics.com					
Industrial Molding Corp 616 E Slaton Rd	Lubbock	TX	79404	806-474-1000	474-1168
Web: www.nninc.com					
Innovative Injection Technologies Inc 2360 Grand Ave	West Des Moines	IA	50265	515-225-6707	225-9673
Web: www.i2-tech.com					
Intec Group Inc 666 S Vermont St	Palatine	IL	60067	847-358-0088	358-4391
Web: www.intecgrp.com					
Ironwood Industries Inc 115 S Bradley Rd	Libertyville	IL	60048	847-362-8681	362-9190
Web: www.ironind.com					
Jones & Vining Inc 1115 W Chestnut St	Brockton	MA	02301	508-232-7470	232-7477
Web: www.jonesandvining.com					
Jordan Specialty Plastics Inc 1751 Lake Cook Rd	Deerfield	IL	60015	847-945-5591	945-5698
Juno Inc 1100 McKinley St	Anoka	MN	55303	763-553-1312	553-1360
Web: www.junoinc.com					
Kennerley Spratling Inc 2116 Farallon Dr	San Leandro	CA	94577	510-351-8230	352-9240
Web: ksplastic.com					
KI Industries Inc 5540 McDermott Dr	Berkeley	IL	60163	708-449-1990	449-1997
Web: www.kiindustries.com					
Lacks Enterprises 5460 Cascade Rd SE	Grand Rapids	MI	49546	616-949-6570	285-2367
Web: www.lacksenterprises.com					
Lakeland Tool & Engineering Inc 2939 Sixth Ave	Anoka	MN	55303	763-422-8866	422-8867
Lehigh Valley Plastics Inc 187 N Commerce Way	Bethlehem	PA	18017	484-893-5500	893-5511
TF: 800-354-5344 ■ *Web:* www.lehighvalleyplastics.com					
Lenco Inc - PMC 10240 Deer Pk Rd	Waverly	NE	68462	402-786-2000	786-2096
Web: www.lencopmc.com					

Phone Fax

Leon Plastics Inc 4901 Clay Ave SW.............Grand Rapids MI 49548 616-531-7970 531-3393
Web: www.leonplastics.com

LMC Industries Inc 100 Manufacturers Dr..............Arnold MO 63010 636-282-8080 282-7114
Web: www.lmcindustries.com

M & Q Plastic Products Inc
542 N Lewis Rd Ste 206...........................Limerick PA 19468 267-498-4000 385-4954*
**Fax Area Code:* 570 ■ *Web:* www.mqplastics.com

Mack Molding Company Inc 608 Warm Brook Rd......Arlington VT 05250 802-375-2511 375-0792*
**Fax:* Hum Res ■ *Web:* www.mack.com

Makray Manufacturing Co 4400 N Harlem Ave........Norridge IL 60706 708-456-7100
Web: www.makray.com

Mar-Lee Cos 55 Marshall St.....................Leominster MA 01453 978-534-8305 534-0472
Web: www.mar-leecompanies.com

Master Molded Products Corp 1000 Davis Rd...........Elgin IL 60123 847-695-9700 695-9707
Web: www.mastermolded.com

Midwest Plastic Components
7309 W 27th St..................................Minneapolis MN 55426 952-929-3312 929-8404
Web: spectrumplasticsgroup.com

Miner Elastomer Products Corp 1200 E State St........Geneva IL 60134 630-232-3000 232-3172
Web: www.minerelastomer.com

Minnesota Rubber & Plastics
1100 Xenium Ln N...........................Minneapolis MN 55441 952-927-1400 927-1470
Web: www.mnrubber.com

Molded Fiber Glass Cos
2925 MFG Pl PO Box 675.......................Ashtabula OH 44005 440-997-5851 994-5162
TF: 800-860-0196 ■ *Web:* www.moldedfiberglass.com

Molding Corp of America 10349 Norris Ave...........Pacoima CA 91331 818-890-7877 890-7885
TF: 800-423-2747 ■ *Web:* www.moldingcorp.com

Mullinix Packages Inc 3511 Engle Rd............Fort Wayne IN 46809 260-747-3149 747-1598
Web: www.mullinixpackages.com

MXL Industries Inc 1764 Rohrerstown Rd.............Lancaster PA 17601 717-569-8711 569-8716
TF: 800-233-0159 ■ *Web:* www.mxl-industries.com

Nyloncraft Inc 616 W McKinley Ave................Mishawaka IN 46545 574-256-1521 255-3278
Web: www.nyloncraft.com

NYX Inc 36111 Schoolcraft Rd.......................Livonia MI 48150 734-462-2385 464-4830
Web: www.nyxinc.com

Plaspros Inc 1143 Ridgeview Dr....................McHenry IL 60050 815-430-2300 430-2260
TF: 800-752-7776 ■ *Web:* www.plaspros.com

Plastech Corp 920 S Field Ave......................Rush City MN 55069 651-407-5700 407-5495
Web: www.plastechcorporation.com

Plastek Group 2425 W 23rd St............................Erie PA 16506 814-878-4400 878-4529
Web: www.plastekgroup.com

Plastic Components Inc
N 116 W 18271 Morse Dr.......................Germantown WI 53022 877-253-1496 253-1497
TF: 877-253-1496 ■ *Web:* www.plasticcomponents.com

Plastic Design International Inc
111 Industrial Pk Rd..........................Middletown CT 06457 860-632-2001 632-1776
Web: www.plasticdesign.com

Plastic Molded Concepts Inc PO Box 490...............Eagle WI 53119 262-594-5050 594-5075
Web: www.pmcplastics.com

Plastic Moldings Company LLC
9825 Kenwood Rd Ste 302.......................Cincinnati OH 45242 513-921-5040
Web: www.pmcsmartsolutions.com

Plastic Products Company Inc
30355 Akerson St..............................Lindstrom MN 55045 651-257-5980 257-9774
Web: www.plasticproductsco.com

Plastic-Plate Inc 5460 Cascade Rd SE............Grand Rapids MI 49546 616-949-6570
Web: www.lacksenterprises.com

Plastics Group Inc 7409 S Quincy St.............Willowbrook IL 60527 630-325-1210 325-1393
Web: www.theplasticsgroup.net

Plastics Molding Company Inc
4211 N Broadway..............................Saint Louis MO 63147 314-241-2479 241-3757
Web: plasticsmoldingco.com

Polymer Corp 180 Pleasant St......................Rockland MA 02370 781-871-4606 871-5460
Web: www.polymerdesign.com

Port Erie Plastics Inc 909 Troupe Rd.............Harborcreek PA 16421 814-899-7602 899-7854
Web: www.porterie.com

Precision Plastics Inc
900 W Connexion Way.......................Columbia City IN 46725 260-244-6114 244-5995
Web: www.pplastic.com

Premix Inc
6151 Wilson Mills Rd Ste 310...............Highland Heights OH 44143 440-224-2181 224-2766
Web: www.premix.com

Product Miniature Co 627 Capitol Dr..............Pewaukee WI 53072 262-691-1700 691-4405
Web: www.pmplastic.com

Proper Mold & Engineering Inc
13870 E 11-Mile Rd..............................Warren MI 48089 586-779-8787 779-4530
Web: propertooling.com

PTA Corp 148 Christian St...........................Oxford CT 06478 203-888-0585 888-1757
Web: www.ptaplastics.com

Quality Mold Inc 2200 Massillon Rd...................Akron OH 44312 330-645-6653 645-2493
Web: www.qualitymold.com

R & R Technologies LLC
7560 E County Line Rd..........................Edinburgh IN 46124 812-526-2655 526-9294
Web: www.rrtech.com

Recto Molded Products Inc (RMP)
4425 Appleton St...............................Cincinnati OH 45209 513-871-5544
Web: www.rectomolded.com

REO Plastics Inc 11850 93rd Ave N..............Maple Grove MN 55369 763-425-4171 425-0735
Web: www.reoplastics.com

Rodgard 92 Msgr Valente Dr..........................Buffalo NY 14206 716-823-1411 852-7690
Web: www.rodgard.com

Royal Plastics Inc 9410 Pineneedle Dr.................Mentor OH 44060 440-352-1357 352-6681
Web: www.royalplastics.com

Sabin Corp
3800 Constitution Ave PO Box 788..............Bloomington IN 47403 812-339-2235 554-8335*
**Fax Area Code:* 800 ■ *TF:* 800-457-4500 ■ *Web:* www.cookgroup.com

Sajar Plastics Inc
15285 S State Ave PO Box 37....................Middlefield OH 44062 440-632-5203 632-1848
Web: www.sajarplastics.com

Seitz LLC 212 Industrial Ln.........................Torrington CT 06790 860-489-0476 482-6616
TF: 800-261-2011 ■ *Web:* www.seitzllc.com

Steere Enterprises Inc 285 Commerce St............Tallmadge OH 44278 330-633-4926
TF: 800-875-4926 ■ *Web:* www.steere.com

Phone Fax

Sturgis Molded Products Co 1950 Clark St............Sturgis MI 49091 269-651-9381 651-4072
Web: www.smpco.com

Tech Group Inc, The 14677 N 74th St..............Scottsdale AZ 85260 480-281-4500
Web: westpharma.com/en/techgroup/pages/tech-group.aspx

Tech II Inc 1765 W County Line Rd...................Urbana OH 45502 937-969-7000
Web: www.techii.com

Thermotech Co 1302 S Fifth St......................Hopkins MN 55343 952-933-9400 933-9412
Web: www.thermotech.com

Tigerpoly Manufacturing Inc
6231 Enterprise Pkwy..........................Grove City OH 43123 614-871-0045 871-2576
Web: www.tigerpoly.com

Toledo Molding & Die Inc 4 E Laskey Rd..............Toledo OH 43612 419-476-0581 476-6053
Web: www.tmdinc.com

Tri-Star Plastics Inc 1915 E Via Burton..............Anaheim CA 92806 714-533-7360 533-4383
Web: www.tri-starplastics.com

Tricon Industries Inc Electromechanical Div
2325 Wisconsin Ave........................Downers Grove IL 60515 630-964-2330 964-5179
Web: industrialinterface.com

Trimold LLC 200 Pittsburgh Rd....................Circleville OH 43113 740-474-7591

Tuthill Corp Plastics Group
2050 Sunnydale Blvd...........................Clearwater FL 33765 727-446-8593 446-8595
TF: 800-634-2695 ■ *Web:* www.tuthill.com

United Plastics Group Inc (UPG)
7865 Northcourt Rd..............................Houston TX 77040 713-466-5563
Web: www.upgintl.com

Universal Plastic Mold Inc
13245 Los Angeles St.........................Baldwin Park CA 91706 888-893-1587 960-7166*
**Fax Area Code:* 626 ■ *TF:* 888-893-1587 ■ *Web:* www.upminc.com

ValTech LLC 1667 Emerson St......................Rochester NY 14606 585-647-2300 647-6123
Web: www.thevaltechgroup.com

Vaupell Inc 1144 NW 53rd St.........................Seattle WA 98107 206-784-9050 784-9708
Web: www.vaupell.com

Venture Plastics Inc
4000 Warren Rd PO Box 249...................Newton Falls OH 44444 330-872-5774 872-3597
Web: www.ventureplastics.com

W-L Molding Co, The 8212 Shaver Rd.................Portage MI 49024 269-327-3075 323-8416
Web: www.wlmolding.com

Westlake Plastics Co PO Box 127......................Lenni PA 19052 610-459-1000 459-1084
TF: 800-999-1700 ■ *Web:* www.westlakeplastics.com

Williams Industries Inc
2201 E Michigan Rd............................Shelbyville IN 46176 317-392-4701 398-3561
Web: www.williamsindustries.com

Winzeler Gear Inc 7355 W Wilson Ave..........Harwood Heights IL 60706 708-867-7971 867-7974
Web: www.winzelergear.com

WM Plastics Inc 5151 Bolger Ct.....................McHenry IL 60050 815-578-8888
Web: www.wmplastics.com

605 PLASTICS & OTHER SYNTHETIC MATERIALS

605-1 Synthetic Fibers & Filaments

Phone Fax

Buckeye Technologies Inc 1001 Tillman St...........Memphis TN 38112 901-320-8100 320-8836
NYSE: BKI

Color-Fi Inc 320 Neeley St..........................Sumter SC 29150 803-436-4200 436-4220
Web: www.colorfi.com

Consolidated Fibers 8100 S Blvd..................Charlotte NC 28273 800-243-8621
TF: 800-243-8621 ■ *Web:* www.consolidatedfibers.com

Deltech Corp 11911 Scenic Hwy..................Baton Rouge LA 70807 225-775-0150 358-3149
TF: 800-424-9300 ■ *Web:* www.deltechcorp.com

DuPont Advanced Fibers Systems
5401 Jefferson Davis Hwy........................Richmond VA 23234 804-383-3845
TF: 800-441-7515 ■ *Web:* www.dupont.com

Fairfield Processing Corp 88 Rose Hill Ave............Danbury CT 06810 203-744-2090 792-9710
TF: 800-980-8000 ■ *Web:* www.fairfieldworld.com

Hexcel Corp 281 Tresser Blvd 16th Fl................Stamford CT 06901 800-688-7734
NYSE: HXL ■ *TF:* 800-444-3923 ■ *Web:* www.hexcel.com

Honeywell Specialty Materials
101 Columbia Rd..............................Morristown NJ 07962 973-455-2145 455-6154
TF: 800-222-0094 ■ *Web:* www.honeywell-additives.com

International Fiber Corp
50 Bridge St..............................North Tonawanda NY 14120 716-693-4040 693-3528
TF: 888-698-1936 ■ *Web:* www.ifcfiber.com

InterTech Group Inc
4838 Jenkins Ave.........................North Charleston SC 29405 843-744-5174 747-4092
Web: www.theintertechgroup.com

INVISTA 4123 E 37th St N..........................Wichita KS 67220 316-828-1000
TF: 877-446-8478 ■ *Web:* www.invista.com

Nylon Corp of America 333 Sundial Ave............Manchester NH 03103 603-627-5150 627-5154
TF: 800-851-2001 ■ *Web:* www.nycoa.net

RadiciSpandex Corp 3145 NW Blvd..................Gastonia NC 28052 704-864-5495
Web: www.radicigroup.com

Stein Fibers Ltd 4 Computer Dr W.....................Albany NY 12205 518-489-5700 489-5713
Web: www.steinfibers.com

TenCate Grass North America 1131 Broadway St........Dayton TN 37321 423-775-0792 775-4460
TF: 800-251-1033 ■ *Web:* www.tencate.com

Toray Industries America Inc
461 Fifth Ave 9th Fl...........................New York NY 10017 212-697-8150 972-4279
Web: www.toray.com

United Plastic Fabricating Inc
165 Flagship Dr..........................North Andover MA 01845 800-638-8265
TF: 800-638-8265 ■ *Web:* www.unitedplastic.com

Waltrich Plastic Corp 3005 Airport Rd............Walthourville GA 31333 912-368-9341
Web: www.waltrich.com

605-2 Synthetic Resins & Plastics Materials

Phone Fax

A Schulman Inc 3550 W Market St......................Akron OH 44333 330-666-3751 668-7204
NASDAQ: SHLM ■ *TF:* 800-547-3746 ■ *Web:* www.aschulman.com

	City	State	ZIP	Phone	Fax
Acton Technologies Inc 100 Thompson St. *Web:* www.actontech.com	Pittston	PA	18640	570-654-0612	
Advanced Laser Materials LLC 3115 Lucius Mccelvey *Web:* www.alm-llc.com	Temple	TX	76504	254-773-3080	
Akcros Chemicals America 500 Jersey Ave *TF Cust Svc:* 800-500-7890 ■ *Web:* www.akcros.com	New Brunswick	NJ	08901	732-220-6882	247-2287
Alloy Polymers Inc (AP) 3310 Deepwater Terminal Rd *Web:* www.alloypolymers.com	Richmond	VA	23234	804-232-8000	230-0386
American Stainless & Supply LLC 815 State Rd *Web:* americanstainlessandsupply.com	Cheraw	SC	29520	843-537-5231	
AOC LLC 955 Tennessee 57 *Web:* www.aoc-resins.com	Collierville	TN	38017	901-854-2800	854-1183
Asahi Kasei America Inc 800 Third Ave 30rd Fl *Web:* www.ak-america.com	New York	NY	10022	212-371-9900	371-9050
Asahi Kasei Plastics North America Inc 900 E Van Riper Rd *TF Cust Svc:* 800-993-5382 ■ *Web:* akplastics.com	Fowlerville	MI	48836	517-223-2000	223-2002
Bayer Corp 100 Bayer Rd **Fax Area Code:* 412 ■ *Web:* www.bayer.us	Pittsburgh	PA	15205	862-404-3000	777-3899*
Bayer Inc 77 Belfield Rd *TF:* 800-622-2937 ■ *Web:* www.bayer.ca	Toronto	ON	M9W1G6	416-248-0771	
Bayer MaterialScience LLC 100 Bayer Rd *TF:* 800-662-2927	Pittsburgh	PA	15205	412-777-2000	777-3899
Cambridge Resources Corp 960 Alabama Ave *Web:* www.cambridgeresources.com	Brooklyn	NY	11207	718-927-0009	
Canplas Industries Ltd 500 Veterans Dr *TF:* 800-461-1771 ■ *Web:* www.canplas.com	Barrie	ON	L4M4V3	705-726-3361	
Capital Resin Corp 324 Dering Ave *Web:* www.capitalresin.com	Columbus	OH	43207	614-445-7177	445-7290
Cartec International Inc 106 Powder Mill Rd *TF:* 800-821-4434 ■ *Web:* www.cartec.com	Canton	CT	06019	860-693-9395	
CL Hauthaway & Sons Corp 638 Summer St *Web:* www.hauthaway.com	Lynn	MA	01905	781-592-6444	599-9565
ConsumerMetrics Inc 2299 Perimeter Park Dr *Web:* www.cmiresearch.com	Atlanta	GA	30341	678-805-4000	
Crossfield Products Corp 3000 E Harcourt St *Web:* www.crossfieldproducts.com	Rancho Dominguez	CA	90221	310-886-9100	886-9119
Cytec Engineered Materials 2085 E Technology Cir Ste 300 *Web:* www.cytec.com	Tempe	AZ	85284	480-730-2000	730-2088
Daikin America Inc 20 Olympic Dr *TF Cust Svc:* 800-365-9570 ■ *Web:* www.daikin-america.com	Orangeburg	NY	10962	845-365-9500	365-9515
Dow Chemical Co 2030 Dow Ctr *NYSE:* DOW ■ *TF Cust Svc:* 800-422-8193 ■ *Web:* www.dow.com	Midland	MI	48674	989-636-1463	636-1830
Dow Chemical Co, The 100 Independence Mall W *Web:* www.dow.com	Philadelphia	PA	19106	215-592-3000	
DSM Engineering Plastics Inc 2267 W Mill Rd **Fax:* Cust Svc ■ *TF:* 800-333-4237 ■ *Web:* www.dsm.com	Evansville	IN	47720	812-435-7500	435-7702*
DSM NeoResins Inc 730 Main St *Web:* dsm.com	Wilmington	MA	01887	978-658-6600	
DuPont Engineering Polymers Lancaster Pike Rt 141 Barley Mill Plz Bldg 22 *TF:* 800-441-7515 ■ *Web:* www.dupont.com	Wilmington	DE	19805	302-999-4592	
Eastman Chemical Co 200 S Wilcox Dr *NYSE:* EMN ■ *TF Cust Svc:* 800-327-8626 ■ *Web:* www.eastman.com	Kingsport	TN	37660	423-229-2000	
Elster Perfection Corp 436 N Eagle St *Web:* www.elster-perfection.com	Geneva	OH	44041	440-415-1600	
Engineered Polymer Solutions Inc 1400 N State St **Fax Area Code:* 815 ■ *TF:* 800-654-4242 ■ *Web:* www.epscca.com/en/index.html	Marengo	IL	60152	800-654-4242	568-4145*
Essco Inc 1933 Highland Rd *TF:* 800-321-2664 ■ *Web:* www.essco.net	Twinsburg	OH	44087	216-524-4141	
Esterline Technologies Corp 500 108th Ave NE Ste 1500 *NYSE:* ESL ■ *Web:* www.esterline.com	Bellevue	WA	98004	425-453-9400	453-2916
ExxonMobil Chemical Co 13501 Katy Fwy *Web:* www.exxonmobilchemical.com	Houston	TX	77079	281-870-6000	
Fabick Inc 4118 Robertson Rd *Web:* www.fabick.com	Madison	WI	53714	608-242-1100	
Ferro Corp Filled & Reinforced Plastics Div 5001 O'Hara Dr *Web:* www.ferro.com	Evansville	IN	47711	812-423-5218	423-5218
Formosa Plastics Corp USA 9 Peach Tree Hill Rd *Web:* www.fpcusa.com	Livingston	NJ	07039	973-992-2090	
Gallagher Corp 3908 Morrison Dr *TF:* 800-524-8597 ■ *Web:* www.gallaghercorp.com	Gurnee	IL	60031	847-249-3440	249-3473
Goldsmith & Eggleton Inc 300 First St *TF:* 800-321-0954 ■ *Web:* www.goldsmith-eggleton.com	Wadsworth	OH	44281	330-336-6616	334-4709
Heritage Plastics Inc 1002 Hunt St *TF:* 800-245-4623 ■ *Web:* www.heritage-plastics.com	Picayune	MS	39466	601-798-8663	
Hexion Specialty Chemicals Inc 180 E Broad St *Web:* www.momentive.com	Columbus	OH	43215	614-225-4000	
Huntsman Corp 500 Huntsman Way *NYSE:* HUN ■ *TF:* 888-490-8484 ■ *Web:* www.huntsman.com	Salt Lake City	UT	84108	801-584-5700	584-5781
Indelco Plastics Corp 6530 Cambridge St *TF:* 800-486-6456 ■ *Web:* www.indelco.com	Minneapolis	MN	55426	952-925-5075	
Industrial Dielectrics Inc 407 S Seventh St PO Box 357 *Web:* www.idicomposites.com	Noblesville	IN	46061	317-773-1766	773-3877
Interplastic Corp 1225 Wolters Blvd *TF:* 800-736-5497 ■ *Web:* www.interplastic.com	Saint Paul	MN	55110	651-481-6860	481-9836
Isotron Corp 1443 N Northlake Way Ste 101 *Web:* www.isotron.net	Seattle	WA	98103	206-547-1196	
Kraton Performance Polymers Inc 15710 John F Kennedy Blvd Ste 300 *NYSE:* KRA ■ *TF:* 800-457-2866 ■ *Web:* www.kraton.com	Houston	TX	77032	281-504-4950	504-4743
Landec Corp 3603 Haven Ave *NASDAQ:* LNDC ■ *Web:* www.landec.com	Menlo Park	CA	94025	650-306-1650	
Lewcott Corp 86 Providence Rd *TF Sales:* 800-225-7725 ■ *Web:* barrday.com	Millbury	MA	01527	508-865-1791	865-0302
Lord Corp 111 Lord Dr *TF:* 877-275-5673 ■ *Web:* www.lord.com	Cary	NC	27511	919-468-5979	
Markel Corp 435 School Ln **Fax:* Sales ■ *Web:* www.markelcorporation.com	Plymouth Meeting	PA	19462	610-272-8960	270-3138*
Marval Industries Inc 315 Hoyt Ave *Web:* www.marvalindustries.com	Mamaroneck	NY	10543	914-381-2400	381-2259
Michael Day Enterprises Inc 960 Seville Rd	Wadsworth	OH	44282	330-336-7611	
Minova USA Inc 150 Carley Ct *TF:* 800-626-2948 ■ *Web:* www.minovaglobal.com	Georgetown	KY	40324	502-863-6800	863-6805
Mitsui Chemicals America Inc 800 Westchester Ave **Fax:* PR ■ *TF:* 800-972-7252 ■ *Web:* www.mitsuichemicals.com	Rye Brook	NY	10573	914-253-0777	253-0790*
Modern Dispersions Inc 78 Marguerite Ave *Web:* www.moderndispersions.com	Leominster	MA	01453	978-534-3370	537-6065
MRC Polymers Inc 3307 S Lawndale Ave *Web:* www.mrcpolymers.com	Chicago	IL	60623	773-890-9000	890-9007
Neville Chemical Co 2800 Neville Rd *TF Cust Svc:* 877-704-4200 ■ *Web:* www.nevchem.com	Pittsburgh	PA	15225	412-331-4200	771-0226
NOVA Chemicals Corp 1000 Seventh Ave SW PO Box 2518 *TF:* 866-289-6682 ■ *Web:* www.novachem.com	Calgary	AB	T2P5C6	403-750-3600	269-7410
Orion Enterprises Inc 2850 Fairfax Trafficway *Web:* www.orionfittings.com	Kansas City	KS	66115	913-342-1653	
Osterman & Company Inc 726 S Main St *TF:* 800-914-4437 ■ *Web:* www.osterman-co.com	Cheshire	CT	06410	203-272-2233	
Parker Hannifin Corp Chomerics Div 77 Dragon Ct *Web:* www.parker.com	Woburn	MA	01801	781-935-4850	933-4318
Perstorp Polyols Inc 600 Matzinger Rd *TF Cust Svc:* 800-537-0280 ■ *Web:* www.perstorp.com	Toledo	OH	43612	419-729-5448	729-3291
Plastics Color & Compounding Inc 14201 Paxton Ave *TF:* 800-922-9936 ■ *Web:* www.plasticscolor.com	Calumet City	IL	60409	800-922-9936	
Plastics Engineering Company Inc 3518 Lk Shore Rd *Web:* www.plenco.com	Sheboygan	WI	53083	920-458-2121	458-1923
Plextronics Inc 2180 William Pitt Way *Web:* www.plextronics.com	Pittsburgh	PA	15238	412-423-2030	
PolyOne Corp 33587 Walker Rd *NYSE:* POL ■ *TF:* 866-765-9663 ■ *Web:* www.polyone.com	Avon Lake	OH	44012	440-930-1000	930-3064
PSC Fabricating Co 1100 W Market St *Web:* pscindustries.com	Louisville	KY	40203	502-625-7700	625-7837
Reichhold Inc 2400 Ellis Rd *TF:* 800-448-3482 ■ *Web:* www.reichhold.com	Durham	NC	27703	919-990-7500	990-7711
Resinall Corp PO Box 195 *TF:* 800-421-0561 ■ *Web:* www.resinall.com	Severn	NC	27877	800-421-0561	
Revstone Industries LLC 2250 Thunderstick Dr Ste 1203	Lexington	KY	40505	859-294-5590	
RheTech Inc 1500 E N Territorial Rd *TF:* 800-869-1230 ■ *Web:* www.rhetech.com	Whitmore Lake	MI	48189	734-769-0585	769-3565
Rimtec Corp 1702 Beverly Rd *Web:* www.rimtec.com	Burlington	NJ	08016	609-387-0011	387-1436
Rogers Corp 1 Technology Dr *TF:* 800-237-2267 ■ *Web:* www.rogerscorp.com	Rogers	CT	06263	860-774-9605	779-5509
RTP Co 580 E Front St **Fax:* Hum Res ■ *TF:* 800-433-4787 ■ *Web:* www.rtpcompany.com	Winona	MN	55987	507-454-6900	454-2041*
Rubicon Inc 9156 Hwy 75 PO Box 517 *Web:* www.huntsman.com	Geismar	LA	70734	225-673-6141	673-6442
Rutland Plastic Technologies 10021 Rodney St *TF:* 800-438-5134 ■ *Web:* www.rutlandinc.com	Pineville	NC	28134	704-553-0046	552-6589
S & E Specialty Polymers LLC 140 Leominster-Shirley Rd *Web:* sespoly.com	Lunenburg	MA	01462	978-537-8261	537-5310
Sartomer Co 502 Thomas Jones Way *TF:* 800-345-8247 ■ *Web:* www.sartomer.com	Exton	PA	19341	610-363-4100	363-4140
Scientific Polymer Products Inc 6265 Dean Pkwy *Web:* www.scientificpolymer.com	Ontario	NY	14519	585-265-0413	265-1390
Shintech Inc 3 Greenway Plz Ste 1150 *Web:* www.shintechinc.com	Houston	TX	77046	713-965-0713	965-0629
Shuman Plastics Inc 35 Neoga St *Web:* www.shuman-plastics.com	Depew	NY	14043	716-685-2121	685-3236
SI Group Inc 2750 Balltown Rd *Web:* www.siigroup.com	Schenectady	NY	12301	518-347-4200	346-6908
Sterling Fibers Inc 5005 Sterling Way *TF Cust Svc:* 800-342-3779 ■ *Web:* www.sterlingfibers.com	Pace	FL	32571	850-994-5311	994-2579
Tahoma Rubber & Plastics Inc 255 Wooster Rd N *Web:* www.tahomarubberplastics.com	Barberton	OH	44203	330-745-9016	745-4886
Talco Plastics Inc 1000 W Rincon St *Web:* www.talcoplastics.com	Corona	CA	92880	951-531-2000	531-2058
Teijin Kasei America Inc 5555 Triangle Pkwy Ste 275 *Web:* www.teijinkasei.com	Norcross	GA	30092	770-346-8949	346-7610
Texon USA Inc 1190 Huntington Rd *Web:* www.texon.com	Russell	MA	01071	413-862-3652	
Thermoclad Co 361 W 11th St *Web:* www.protechpowder.com	Erie	PA	16501	814-456-1243	459-2853
Ticona LLC 8040 Dixie Hwy **Fax:* Sales ■ *TF:* 800-833-4882 ■ *Web:* www.celanese.com	Florence	KY	41042	859-372-3244	372-3125*
Tube-Mac Industries Ltd 853 Arvin Ave *TF:* 877-643-8823 ■ *Web:* www.tube-mac.com	Stoney Creek	ON	L8E5N8	905-643-8823	
Vi-Chem Corp 55 Cottage Grove St SW *TF:* 800-477-8501 ■ *Web:* www.vichem.com	Grand Rapids	MI	49507	616-247-8501	247-8703

Company	City	State	Zip	Phone	Fax
Westlake Chemical Corp 2801 Post Oak Blvd Ste 600 *NYSE: WLK* ■ *TF:* 888-953-3623 ■ *Web:* www.westlakechemical.com	Houston	TX	77056	713-960-9111	963-1562
WTE Corp 7 Alfred Cir *Web:* www.wte.com	Bedford	MA	01730	781-275-6400	275-8612

605-3 Synthetic Rubber

Company	City	State	Zip	Phone	Fax
AirBoss of America Corp Rubber Compounding 101 Glasgow St *TF:* 800-294-5723 ■ *Web:* www.airbossrubbercompounding.com	Kitchener	ON	N2G4X8	519-576-5565	576-1315
Akrochem Corp 255 Fountain St *TF:* 800-321-2260 ■ *Web:* www.akrochem.com	Akron	OH	44304	330-535-2100	535-8947
Bryant Rubber Corp 1112 Lomita Blvd *Web:* www.bryantrubber.com	Harbor City	CA	90710	310-530-2530	530-9143
Goodyear Tire & Rubber Co 200 Innovation Way *NASDAQ: GT* ■ **Fax:* Cust Svc ■ *TF Cust Svc:* 800-321-2136 ■ *Web:* www.goodyear.com	Akron	OH	44316	330-796-2121	796-2222*
Lanxess Corp 111 RIDC Pk W Dr *TF:* 800-526-9377 ■ *Web:* www.lanxess.com	Pittsburgh	PA	15275	412-809-1000	
Midwest Elastomers Inc 700 Industrial Dr PO Box 412 *TF:* 800-786-3539 ■ *Web:* www.midwestelastomers.com	Wapakoneta	OH	45895	419-738-8844	
Preferred Rubber Compounding Corp 1020 Lambert St *Web:* preferredperforms.com	Barberton	OH	44203	330-798-4790	
R & S Processing Company Inc 15712 Illinois Ave PO Box 2037 *Web:* rsprocessing.com	Paramount	CA	90723	562-531-1403	531-4318
Teknor Apex Co 505 Central Ave *TF:* 800-556-3864 ■ *Web:* www.teknorapex.com	Pawtucket	RI	02861	401-725-8000	725-8095
Textile Rubber & Chemical Company Inc 1300 Tiarco Dr SW *TF:* 800-727-8453 ■ *Web:* www.trcc.com	Dalton	GA	30721	706-277-1300	277-3738

606 PLASTICS PRODUCTS - FIBERGLASS REINFORCED

Company	City	State	Zip	Phone	Fax
Crane Composites Inc 23525 W Eames St **Fax:* Hum Res ■ *TF:* 800-435-0080 ■ *Web:* www.cranecomposites.com	Channahon	IL	60410	815-467-8600	467-8666*
Ershigs Inc 742 Marine Dr *Web:* www.ershigs.com	Bellingham	WA	98225	360-733-2620	733-2628
Fibergrate Composite Structures Inc 5151 Beltline Rd Ste 700 *TF:* 800-527-4043 ■ *Web:* www.fibergrate.com	Dallas	TX	75254	972-250-1633	250-1530
Formed Fiber Technologies Inc 125 Allied Rd PO Box 1300 *Web:* www.formedfiber.com	Auburn	ME	04211	207-784-1118	784-1137
Glastic Corp 4321 Glenridge Rd *TF:* 800-360-1319 ■ *Web:* www.glastic.com	Cleveland	OH	44121	216-486-0100	486-1091
GMI Composites Inc 1355 W Sherman Blvd *TF:* 800-330-4045 ■ *Web:* www.gmicomposites.com	Muskegon	MI	49441	231-755-1611	755-1613
Haysite Reinforced Plastics 5599 Perry Hwy *Web:* www.haysite.com	Erie	PA	16509	814-868-3691	864-7803
McClarin Plastics Inc 15 Industrial Dr *TF:* 800-233-3189 ■ *Web:* www.mcclarinplastics.com	Hanover	PA	17331	717-637-2241	637-2091
Peterson Products Inc 10 Airpark Vista Blvd *Web:* www.petersonproducts.com	Dayton	NV	89403	650-591-7311	
Red Ewald Inc 2669 US 181 *TF:* 800-242-3524 ■ *Web:* www.redewald.com	Karnes City	TX	78118	830-780-3304	
Strongwell 400 Commonwealth Ave *Web:* www.strongwell.com	Bristol	VA	24201	276-645-8000	645-8132

607 PLASTICS PRODUCTS - HOUSEHOLD

Company	City	State	Zip	Phone	Fax
Ayanna Plastics & Engineering 4701 110th Ave N *Web:* www.ayannaplastics.com	Clearwater	FL	33762	727-561-4329	
Bow Plastics Ltd 5700 Cote de Liesse *TF:* 800-852-8527 ■ *Web:* www.bow-group.com	Montreal	QC	H4T1B1	514-735-5671	
Eagle Affiliates Inc 1000 S Second St *TF:* 800-237-9255	Plainfield	NJ	07063	908-757-4464	
GT Water Products Inc 5239 N Commerce Ave *TF:* 800-862-5647 ■ *Web:* www.gtwaterproducts.com	Moorpark	CA	93021	805-529-2900	529-4558
Home Products International Inc 4501 W 47th St *TF:* 800-327-3534 ■ *Web:* www.homzproducts.com	Chicago	IL	60632	773-890-1010	890-0523
Igloo Products Corp 777 Igloo Rd *TF:* 866-509-3503 ■ *Web:* www.igloocoolers.com	Katy	TX	77494	713-584-6800	
Iris USA Inc 11111 80th Ave *TF:* 800-320-4747 ■ *Web:* www.irisusainc.com	Pleasant Prairie	WI	53158	262-612-1000	612-1010
King Plastics Inc 840 N Elm St *Web:* www.kingplastics.com	Orange	CA	92867	714-997-7540	997-0491
Kraftware Corp 270 Cox St *TF Cust Svc:* 800-221-1728 ■ *Web:* www.kraftwarecorp.com	Roselle	NJ	07203	800-221-1728	
Mainetti USA 300 Mac Ln **Fax Area Code:* 732 ■ *Web:* www.mainetti.com	Keasbey	NJ	08832	201-215-2900	738-7210*
Maryland Plastics Inc 251 E Central Ave *TF Cust Svc:* 800-544-5582 ■ *Web:* www.marylandplastics.com	Federalsburg	MD	21632	410-754-5566	754-8882
Prolon Inc 305 Industrial Ave **Fax Area Code:* 888 ■ *TF:* 800-628-7749 ■ *Web:* www.prolon.biz	Port Gibson	MS	39150	601-437-4211	480-9828*
Silestone 2245 Texas Dr Ste 600 *Web:* www.silestoneusa.com	Sugar Land	TX	77479	281-494-7277	
Sterilite Corp PO Box 524 *TF:* 800-225-1046 ■ *Web:* www.sterilite.com	Townsend	MA	01469	800-225-1046	
TAP Plastics Inc 6475 Sierra Ln *TF:* 800-894-0827 ■ *Web:* www.tapplastics.com	Dublin	CA	94568	925-829-4889	
Thermos Co 475 N Martingale Rd Ste 1100 *TF:* 800-243-0745 ■ *Web:* www.thermos.com	Schaumburg	IL	60173	847-439-7821	593-5570
Tupperware Corp 14901 S Orange Blossom Trail *NYSE: TUP* ■ *TF Cust Svc:* 800-468-9716 ■ *Web:* ir.tupperwarebrands.com	Orlando	FL	32837	407-826-5050	847-1897
US Acrylic Inc 1320 Harris Rd *Web:* www.usacrylic.com	Libertyville	IL	60048	847-837-4800	837-1955

608 PLASTICS PRODUCTS (MISC)

Company	City	State	Zip	Phone	Fax
7-sigma Inc 2843 26th Ave S *TF:* 888-722-8396 ■ *Web:* www.7-sigma.com	Minneapolis	MN	55406	612-722-5358	
Accent Plastics Inc 1925 Elise Cir *Web:* www.accentplastics.com	Corona	CA	92879	951-273-7777	
ACCS Enterprises Inc 539 Sawgrass Corporate Pkwy *Web:* www.headsuponline.com	Sunrise	FL	33325	954-472-3300	
Accudyn Products Inc 2400 Yoder Dr *Web:* www.accudyn.com	Erie	PA	16506	814-833-7615	
Aco Polymer Products Inc 12080 Ravenna Rd *Web:* acousa.com	Chardon	OH	44024	440-285-7000	
Acry Fab Inc 584 Progress Way *Web:* vollrath.com	Sun Prairie	WI	53590	608-837-0045	
Acrylic Plastic Products Company Inc 4815 Hwy 80 W *TF:* 800-331-8819 ■ *Web:* acrylic1plasticproducts.com	Jackson	MS	39209	601-922-2651	
Adapt Plastics Inc 7949 Forest Hills Rd *Web:* adaptplastics.com	Loves Park	IL	61111	815-633-9263	
Advanced Fiberglass Technologies Inc 4400 Commerce Dr *Web:* www.ecccorrosion.com	Wisconsin Rapids	WI	54494	715-421-2060	
Agape Plastics Inc 11474 First Ave NW *Web:* www.agapeplastics.com	Grand Rapids	MI	49534	616-735-4091	735-4392
Aigner Index Inc 23 Mac Arthur Ave *TF:* 800-242-3919 ■ *Web:* www.aignerlabelholder.com	New Windsor	NY	12553	845-562-4510	562-2638
Ajax United Patterns & Molds Inc 34585 Seventh St *Web:* www.ajaxmfg.com	Union City	CA	94587	510-476-8000	476-8001
Albar Industries Inc 780 Whitney Dr *Web:* www.albar.com	Lapeer	MI	48446	810-667-0150	
Alco Plastics Inc 160 E Pond Dr *Web:* www.alcoplastics.com	Romeo	MI	48065	586-752-4527	
Alfred Manufacturing Co 4398 Elati St *Web:* alfredmfg.com	Denver	CO	80216	303-433-6385	
All Plastics Molding Inc 15700 Midway Rd *Web:* www.all-plastics.com	Addison	TX	75001	972-239-2686	
All States Inc 602 N 12th St *TF Cust Svc:* 800-621-5837 ■ *Web:* cable-ties.com	Saint Charles	IL	60174	773-728-0525	
Allied Plastic Supply LLC 1544 Valwood Pkwy *Web:* www.alliedplastic.org	Carrollton	TX	75006	972-241-0762	
ALP Lighting Components Inc 6333 Gross Point Rd *Web:* alplighting.com	Niles	IL	60714	773-774-9550	774-9331
American Window & Glass Inc 2715 Lynch Rd *TF:* 877-671-6943 ■ *Web:* www.americanwindowandglass.com	Evansville	IN	47711	812-464-9400	464-3131
Amerimade Technology Inc 449 Mtn Vista Pkwy *TF:* 800-938-3824 ■ *Web:* www.amerimade.com	Livermore	CA	94551	925-243-9090	243-9266
Armstrong Systems & Consulting 5101 Tremont Ave Ste A	Davenport	IA	52807	563-386-9090	391-2237
Ashland Hardware Systems 790 W Commercial Ave *Web:* www.ashlandhardware.com	Lowell	IN	46356	219-696-5950	
Automation Plastics Corp 150 Lena Dr *Web:* www.automationplastics.com	Aurora	OH	44202	330-562-5148	
Avery Dennison Fastener Div 224 Industrial Rd *TF:* 800-225-5913 ■ *Web:* www.fastener.averydennison.com	Fitchburg	MA	01420	800-225-5913	848-2169
Axion International Holdings Inc 4005 All American Way *Web:* www.axionintl.com	Zanesville	OH	43701	740-452-2500	452-5488
AXYS Technologies Inc 2045 Mills Rd *TF:* 877-792-7878 ■ *Web:* www.axystechnologies.com	Sidney	BC	V8L5X2	250-655-5850	655-5856
Bay Polymer Corp 44530 S Grimmer Blvd *Web:* www.baypolymer.com	Fremont	CA	94538	510-490-1791	490-5914
Bemis Manufacturing Co 300 Mill St *TF:* 800-558-7651 ■ *Web:* www.bemismfg.com	Sheboygan Falls	WI	53085	920-467-4621	467-8573
Bentonville Plastics Inc 607 SW A St *Web:* www.bentonvilleplastics.com	Bentonville	AR	72712	479-273-7272	
Blackmore Company Inc 10800 Blackmore Ave *TF:* 800-874-8660 ■ *Web:* www.blackmoreco.com	Belleville	MI	48111	734-483-8661	483-5454
Blow Molded Products Inc 4720 Felspar St *Web:* www.blowmoldedproducts.com	Riverside	CA	92509	951-360-6055	
Blue Star Plastics Inc 801 Nandino Blvd *Web:* www.bluestarplastics.com	Lexington	KY	40511	859-255-0714	
Bowman Mfg Company Inc 17301 51st Ave Ne *TF:* 800-962-4660 ■ *Web:* www.bowmandispensers.com	Arlington	WA	98223	360-435-5005	
Burco Molding Inc 15015 Herriman Blvd *TF:* 888-883-6656	Noblesville	IN	46060	317-773-5699	
C. L. Smith Co 1311 S 39th St *TF:* 800-264-1202 ■ *Web:* www.clsmith.com	Saint Louis	MO	63110	314-771-1202	771-3351
Cashmere Molding 20004 144th Ave Ne	Woodinville	WA	98072	425-485-6515	
Century Manufacturing Inc 3351 N Webb Rd *Web:* www.centurymfg.com	Wichita	KS	67226	316-636-5423	
Charter Plastics 221 S Perry St *Web:* www.charterplastics.com	Titusville	PA	16354	814-827-9665	
CMI Plastics Inc 222 Pepsi Way *TF:* 877-395-1920 ■ *Web:* www.cmiplastics.com	Ayden	NC	28513	252-746-2171	
Coeur Inc 209 Creekside Dr *Web:* coeurinc.com	Washington	NC	27889	252-946-1963	
Concept Plastics Inc (CPI) PO Box 847 *Web:* www.cpico.com	High Point	NC	27261	336-889-2001	889-5752

Company	City	State	ZIP	Phone	Fax
Cool Polymers Inc 51 Circuit Dr *TF:* 888-811-3787 ■ *Web:* www.coolpolymers.com	North Kingstown	RI	02852	401-739-7602	
Coverbind Corp 3200 Corporate Dr *TF:* 800-366-6060 ■ *Web:* www.coverbind.com	Wilmington	NC	28405	910-799-4116	799-3935
Craftech EDM Corp 2941 E La Jolla St *Web:* www.craftechcorp.com	Anaheim	CA	92806	714-630-8117	630-7959
Criterion Technologies Inc 101 Mcintosh Pkwy *Web:* criteriondomes.com	Thomaston	GA	30286	706-647-5082	
Crystal-Like Plastics 21701 Plummer St *Fax Area Code: 818 ■ *TF:* 800-554-6091 ■ *Web:* www.crystal-likeplastics.com	Chatsworth	CA	91311	323-849-1735	846-0877*
Curbell Inc 7 Cobham Dr *Web:* www.curbell.com	Orchard Park	NY	14127	716-667-3377	
Custom Accents 1940 Lunt Ave *TF:* 888-553-6789 ■ *Web:* www.customaccents.com	Elk Grove Village	IL	60007	847-640-4725	
Danner Manufacturing Inc 160 Oval Dr *Web:* www.dannermfg.com	Islandia	NY	11749	631-234-5261	
Daramic Inc 5525 US Hwy 60 E *Web:* www.daramic.com	Owensboro	KY	42303	270-683-1561	686-9226
Dealernet Inc 608 Matthews Mint Hill Rd Ste E *Web:* www.dealernetinc.com	Matthews	NC	28105	704-321-3215	
DelStar Technologies Inc 220 E St Elmo Rd *TF:* 800-521-6713 ■ *Web:* www.delstarinc.com	Austin	TX	78745	512-447-7000	447-7444
Delta Pacific Products Inc 33170 Central Ave *Web:* www.deltapacificinc.com	Union City	CA	94587	510-487-4411	
Den Hartog Industries Inc 4010 Hospers Dr S PO Box 425 *TF:* 800-342-3408 ■ *Web:* www.denhartogindustries.com	Hospers	IA	51238	712-752-8432	752-8222
DK Manufacturing Lancaster Inc 2118 Commerce St *Web:* dkmanufacturing.com	Lancaster	OH	43130	740-654-5566	
Dreco Inc 7887 Root Rd *Web:* www.drecoinc.com	North Ridgeville	OH	44039	440-327-6021	
Durabac Inc 22 ch Milton *Web:* www.durabac.ca	Granby	QC	J2J0P2	450-378-1723	
Duron Plastics Ltd 965 Wilson Ave	Kitchener	ON	N2C1J1	519-884-8011	
Dutchland Plastics Corp 54 Enterprise Ct *Web:* www.dutchlandplastics.com	Oostburg	WI	53070	920-564-3633	564-3337
Dynamic Plastics Inc 29831 Commerce Blvd *Web:* www.dynamicplastics.com	Chesterfield	MI	48051	586-749-6100	
E & O Tool & Plastics Inc 19178 Industrial Blvd NW *Web:* www.eoplastics.com	Elk River	MN	55330	763-441-6100	441-6452
Easyturf 2750 La Mirada Dr *TF:* 866-353-3518 ■ *Web:* www.easyturf.com	Vista	CA	92081	760-789-7772	
Egli Machine Company Inc 240 State Hwy 7 *Web:* www.eglimachine.com	Sidney	NY	13838	607-563-3021	
Eimo Americas 14320 Portage Rd *Web:* www.eimo.com	Vicksburg	MI	49097	269-649-0545	
Engineered Polymers Corp (EPC) 1020 Maple Ave E *TF:* 800-388-2155 ■ *Web:* www.epcmolding.com	Mora	MN	55051	320-679-3232	679-2323
Enor Corp 245 Livingston St *TF:* 800-977-6427 ■ *Web:* www.enor.com	Northvale	NJ	07647	201-750-1680	
Exotic Automation & Supply Inc 34700 Grand River Ave *Web:* www.exoticautomation.com	Farmington Hills	MI	48335	248-477-2122	477-0427
Fabricated Extrusion Company LLC 2331 Hoover Ave *Web:* www.fabexco.com	Modesto	CA	95354	209-529-9200	
Fiber Pad Inc 17260 E Young St *Web:* www.fiberpad.com	Tulsa	OK	74116	918-438-7430	
Fiberglass Specialties Inc PO Box 1340 *TF:* 800-527-1459 ■ *Web:* www.fsiweb.com	Henderson	TX	75653	903-657-6522	657-2318
First American Plastic Molding Enterprise 2 Choctaw Trl *Web:* www.firstamericanplastic.com	Ocean Springs	MS	39564	228-872-4635	
Flagship Converters Inc 205 Shelter Rock Rd *Web:* www.flagshipconverters.com	Danbury	CT	06810	203-792-0034	797-0410
Form Plastics Co 3825 Stern Ave *Web:* www.formplastics.com	Saint Charles	IL	60174	630-443-1400	
Fox Lite Inc 8300 Dayton Rd *Web:* www.foxlite.com	Fairborn	OH	45324	937-864-1966	864-7010
Freetech Plastics Inc 2211 Warm Springs Ct *Web:* freetechplastics.com	Fremont	CA	94539	510-651-9996	
Fusion Optix Inc 19 Wheeling Ave *TF:* 866-506-8300 ■ *Web:* www.fusionoptix.com	Woburn	MA	01801	781-995-0805	
Garner Industries Inc 7201 N 98th St PO Box 29709 *TF:* 800-228-0275 ■ *Web:* www.garnerindustries.com	Lincoln	NE	68507	402-434-9100	434-9133
Gavco Plastics 9840 S 219th E Ave *Web:* www.gavcoplastics.com	Broken Arrow	OK	74014	918-455-7888	
Genova Products Inc 7034 E Court St *TF:* 800-521-7488 ■ *Web:* www.genovaproducts.com	Davison	MI	48423	810-744-4500	
GenPore 1136 Morgantown Rd PO Box 380 *TF:* 800-654-4391 ■ *Web:* www.genpore.com	Reading	PA	19607	610-374-5171	374-4990
Geonautics Manufacturing Inc 506 Merrimac St *Web:* www.geonauticsmfg.com	Newburyport	MA	01950	978-462-7161	
Gessner Products Company Inc 241 N Main St *TF:* 800-874-7808 ■ *Web:* gessnerproducts.com	Ambler	PA	19002	215-646-7667	
Glasteel-stabilit America Inc 285 Industrial Dr *TF:* 800-238-5546 ■ *Web:* www.glasteel.com	Moscow	TN	38057	901-877-3010	
GPK Products Inc 1601 43rd St NW *TF:* 800-437-4670 ■ *Web:* www.gpk-fargo.com	Fargo	ND	58102	701-277-3225	277-9286
GWI Inc 8 Pomerleau St *TF:* 866-494-2020 ■ *Web:* www.gwi.net	Biddeford	ME	04005	207-286-8686	
H.Q.C Inc 230 Kendall Pt Dr *Web:* www.hqcinc.com	Oswego	IL	60543	630-820-5550	820-5549
Habasit America 805 Satellite Blvd *Fax Area Code: 678 ■ *TF:* 800-458-6431 ■ *Web:* www.habasit.com	Suwanee	GA	30024	800-458-6431	288-3651*
Hackney Ladish Inc 400 E Willow *Web:* www.hackney.com	Enid	OK	73701	580-237-4212	
Hanscom Inc 331 Market St *TF:* 877-725-6788 ■ *Web:* www.hanscominc.com	Warren	RI	02885	401-247-1999	247-4575
Hansen Plastic Corp 2758 Alft Ln *Web:* www.hansenplastics.com	Elgin	IL	60124	847-741-4510	
Harbec Plastics Inc 369 SR- 104 *TF:* 888-521-4416 ■ *Web:* www.harbec.com	Ontario	NY	14519	585-265-0010	265-1306
Henry Plastic Molding Inc 41703 Albrae St *Web:* www.henryplastic.com	Fremont	CA	94538	510-490-7993	490-3548
Hicks Plastics Company Inc 51308 Industrial Dr *Web:* www.hicksplastics.com	Macomb	MI	48042	586-786-5640	
Hilco Technologies Inc 4172 Danvers Ct SE *Web:* www.hilcotech.com	Grand Rapids	MI	49512	616-957-1081	
Hycomp Inc 17960 Englewood Dr *Web:* hycompinc.com	Cleveland	OH	44130	440-234-2002	
Hygolet Inc 349 SE Second Ave *TF:* 800-494-6538 ■ *Web:* www.hygolet.com	Deerfield Beach	FL	33441	954-481-8601	481-8669
Ideal Pet Products Inc 24735 Ave Rockefeller *TF:* 800-378-4385 ■ *Web:* www.idealpetproducts.com	Valencia	CA	91355	661-294-2266	
Imark Molding Inc 104 Park Ave *Web:* www.imarkmolding.com	Woodville	WI	54028	715-698-3144	
Integrity Rotational Molding LLC 701 Carr Rd *Web:* www.integrityrotational.com	Plainfield	IN	46168	317-837-1101	
Ironwood Plastics Inc 1235 Wall St *Web:* www.ironwood.com	Ironwood	MI	49938	906-932-5025	
Jacobson Plastics 1401 Freeman Ave *Web:* www.jacobsonplastics.com	Long Beach	CA	90804	562-433-4911	
Jatco Inc 725 Zwissig Way *Web:* www.jatco.com	Union City	CA	94587	510-487-0888	487-1880
Jentec Engineering Co 2820 E Coronado St	Anaheim	CA	92806	714-632-6762	
Kalwall Corp 1111 Candia Rd PO Box 237 *TF:* 800-258-9777 ■ *Web:* www.kalwall.com	Manchester	NH	03105	603-627-3861	627-7905
Kelcourt Plastics Inc 1000 Calle Recodo *Web:* www.kelcourt.com	San Clemente	CA	92673	949-361-0774	
King Plastic Corp 1100 N Toledo Blade Blvd *TF:* 800-780-5502 ■ *Web:* www.kingplastic.com	North Port	FL	34288	941-493-5502	497-3274
Kleiss Gears 390 Industrial Ave *Web:* www.kleissgears.com	Grantsburg	WI	54840	715-463-5995	
Lakeside Plastics Inc 450 W 33rd Ave PO Box 2384 *Web:* www.lakesideplastics.net	Oshkosh	WI	54903	920-235-3620	235-6545
Lamcraft Partition Company Inc 1231 County Rd 4781	Boyd	TX	76023	940-433-5857	
Lamvin Inc 4675 N Ave *TF:* 800-446-6329 ■ *Web:* www.lamvin.com	Oceanside	CA	92056	760-806-6400	806-3200
Landmark Plastic Corp 1331 Kelly Ave *TF:* 800-242-1183 ■ *Web:* www.landmarkplastic.com	Akron	OH	44306	330-785-2200	785-9200
LCS Precision Molding Inc 119 S Second St *Web:* www.lcsplastics.com	Waterville	MN	56096	507-362-8685	
Leaktite Corp 40 Francis St *TF:* 800-392-0039 ■ *Web:* www.leaktite.com	Leominster	MA	01453	978-537-8000	534-3539
LHR Services & Equipment Inc Ic-disc 4200 Fm 1128 Rd *TF:* 800-943-2324 ■ *Web:* lhrservices.com	Pearland	TX	77584	713-943-2324	
Little Kids Inc 225 Chapman St Ste 202 *TF:* 800-545-5437 ■ *Web:* www.littlekidsinc.com	Providence	RI	02905	401-454-7600	
LSP Products Group Inc 3689 Arrowhead Dr *TF:* 800-854-3215 ■ *Web:* www.lspproducts.com	Carson City	NV	89706	800-854-3215	243-1777
Magic Plastics Inc 25215 Ave Stanford *TF:* 800-369-0303 ■ *Web:* www.magicplastics.com	Valencia	CA	91355	661-257-4485	
Majors Plastics Inc 10117 I St *Web:* www.majorsplastics.com	Omaha	NE	68127	402-331-1660	331-9041
Mariplast North America Inc 365 Business Pkwy *Web:* mariplast.com	Greer	SC	29651	864-989-0560	989-0561
Masonry Technology Inc 24235 Electric St *Web:* iqpowertools.com/product-category/tec-connect	Cresco	IA	52136	563-547-1122	
Matlab Inc 1112 Nc Hwy 49 S *Web:* www.matlabinc.com	Asheboro	NC	27205	336-629-4161	
Matrix Iv Inc 610 E Judd St *Web:* www.matrixiv.com	Woodstock	IL	60098	815-338-4500	
Mauser USA LLC 35 Cotters Ln *Web:* mausergroup.com	Brunswick	IL	60440	732-353-7100	651-9777
Mc Pherson Plastics Inc PO Box 58 *Web:* www.mcpherson-plastics.com	Otsego	MI	49078	269-694-9487	694-6662
MedGyn Products Inc 100 W Industrial Rd *TF:* 800-451-9667 ■ *Web:* www.medgyn.com	Addison	IL	60101	630-627-4105	
Merrick Engineering Inc 1275 Quarry St *Web:* www.merrickengineering.com	Corona	CA	92879	951-737-6040	
Micro Plastics Inc 11 Industry Ln Hwy 178 N PO Box 149 *TF:* 800-466-1467 ■ *Web:* secure.microplastics.com	Flippin	AR	72634	870-453-2261	453-8676
Microdyne Plastics Inc 1901 E Cooley Dr *Web:* www.microdyneplastics.com	Colton	CA	92324	909-503-4010	503-4011
Middlefield Plastics Inc PO Box 708 *Web:* www.middlefieldplastics.com	Middlefield	OH	44062	440-834-4638	
MOCAP Inc 409 Parkway Dr *TF:* 800-633-6775 ■ *Web:* www.mocap.com	Park Hills	MO	63601	314-543-4000	543-4111
Mold-masters Ltd 41 Todd Rd *Web:* moldmasters.com	Georgetown	ON	L7G4R8	905-702-8955	
Mold-Rite Plastics LLC 1 Plant St *TF:* 800-432-5277 ■ *Web:* www.mrpcap.com	Plattsburgh	NY	12901	518-561-1812	561-0017
Moldamatic LLC 29 Noeland Ave *Web:* www.moldamatic.com	Penndel	PA	19047	215-757-4819	
Molded Devices Inc 6918 Ed Perkic St *Web:* moldeddevices.com	Riverside	CA	92504	951-509-6918	

Company	City	State	Zip	Phone	Fax
Mylan Technologies Inc 1000 Mylan Blvd *TF:* 800-294-1322 ■ *Web:* mylan.com/products/packaging-and-delivery-systems	Canonsburg	PA	15317	724-514-1800	
N-K Manufacturing Technologies 1134 Freeman Ave SW *Web:* www.nkmfgtech.com	Grand Rapids	MI	49503	616-248-3200	
Neil Enterprises Inc 450 E Bunker Ct. *TF:* 800-621-5584 ■ *Web:* www.neilenterprises.com	Vernon Hills	IL	60061	847-549-7627	
New Boston Rtm Inc 19155 Shook Rd *Web:* www.newbostonrtm.com	New Boston	MI	48164	734-753-9956	753-9221
Nishiba Industries Corp 2360 Marconi Ct. *Web:* www.nishiba.com	San Diego	CA	92154	619-482-9900	482-1585
Nissen Chemitec America 350 E High St *Web:* nissenchemitec.com	London	OH	43140	740-852-3200	852-4547
Nordson MEDICAL 3325 S Timberline Rd *TF:* 888-404-5837 ■ *Web:* www.nordsonmedical.com/default.aspx	Fort Collins	CO	80525	970-267-5200	223-0953
Octex Corp 901 Sarasota Ctr Blvd *Web:* www.octex360.com	Sarasota	FL	34240	941-371-6767	
Pac Tec 12365 Haynes St. *TF:* 877-554-2544 ■ *Web:* www.pactecinc.com	Clinton	LA	70722	877-554-2544	
Paktech 1680 Irving Rd *Web:* www.paktech-opi.com	Eugene	OR	97402	541-461-5000	
Pelham Plastics Inc 42 Dick Tracy Dr *Web:* www.pelhamplastics.com	Pelham	NH	03076	603-886-7226	
PI Inc 213 Dennis St *Web:* www.pi-inc.com	Athens	TN	37303	423-745-6213	745-7852
Pinnacle Plastic Products 513 Napoleon Rd *Web:* pinnacleplasticproducts.com	Bowling Green	OH	43402	419-352-8688	
Piolax Corp 139 Etowah Industrial Ct. *Web:* www.piolaxusa.com	Canton	GA	30114	770-479-2227	479-2399
Plastics Plus Technology Inc 1495 Research Dr *Web:* www.plasticsplus.com	Redlands	CA	92374	909-747-0555	
Plastikon Industries Inc 688 Sandoval Way *TF:* 800-370-0858 ■ *Web:* www.plastikon.com	Hayward	CA	94544	510-400-1010	400-1133
Plastiques Milsi Inc Les 2412 Rue De La Province *Web:* plastiquesmilsi.com	Longueuil	QC	J4G1G1	450-463-4568	
Plastpro Inc 5200 W Century Blvd 9F *TF:* 800-779-0561 ■ *Web:* www.plastproinc.com	Los Angeles	CA	90045	310-693-8600	693-8620
Pleiger Plastics Co PO Box 1271 *TF:* 800-753-4437 ■ *Web:* www.pleiger.com	Washington	PA	15301	724-228-2244	228-2253
Plitek LLC 69 Rawls Rd *TF:* 800-966-1250 ■ *Web:* www.plitek.com	Des Plaines	IL	60018	800-966-1250	
Ply Gem Holdings Inc 5020 Weston Pkwy Ste 400 *Web:* www.plygem.com	Cary	NC	27513	919-677-4019	
PMC Group Inc 1288 Rt 73 S Pmc Group Bldg Ste 401 *Web:* www.pmc-group.com	Mount Laurel	NJ	08054	856-533-1866	
Polymer Conversions Inc 5732 Big Tree Rd	Orchard Park	NY	14127	716-662-8550	
Polymos Inc 3333 Rue F-X-Tessier	Vaudreuil-Dorion	QC	J7V5V5	450-424-5333	
Polytec Products Corp 1190 Obrien Dr. *Web:* polytecproducts.com	Menlo Park	CA	94025	650-322-7555	
Polyvel Inc 100 Ninth St *Web:* www.polyvel.com	Hammonton	NJ	08037	609-567-0080	
Porex Technologies Corp 500 Bohannon Rd *TF Cust Svc:* 800-241-0195 ■ *Web:* www.porex.com	Fairburn	GA	30213	770-964-1421	969-0954
Precision Southeast Inc 4900 Hwy 501 PO Box 50610 *Web:* www.precisionsoutheast.com	Myrtle Beach	SC	29579	843-347-4218	
Precision Thermoplastic Components Inc PO Box 1296 *TF:* 800-860-4505 ■ *Web:* www.ptclima.com	Lima	OH	45802	419-227-4500	
Preferred Plastics Inc 800 E Bridge St *Web:* www.preferredplastics.net	Plainwell	MI	49080	269-685-5873	685-1148
Preproduction Plastics Inc 210 Teller St *Web:* ppiplastics.com	Corona	CA	92879	951-340-9680	
Prism Plastics Inc 1544 Hwy 65 *TF:* 877-246-7535 ■ *Web:* www.prismplasticsinc.com	New Richmond	WI	54017	715-246-7535	246-5661
Pure-logic Industries Inc 1730 W Sunrise Blvd Ste A102 *Web:* www.purelogicind.com	Gilbert	AZ	85233	480-892-9395	
Questech Corp 92 Park St *Web:* www.questech.com	Rutland	VT	05701	802-773-1228	
Randall Mfg LLC 722 Church Rd *TF:* 800-323-7424 ■ *Web:* www.randallmfg.com	Elmhurst	IL	60126	630-782-0001	
Rayner Covering Systems Inc 665 Schneider Dr *TF:* 800-648-0757 ■ *Web:* www.raynercovering.com	South Elgin	IL	60177	847-695-2264	695-2363
Regency Plastics Company Ltd 50 Brisbane Rd *Web:* www.regencyplastics.com	North York	ON	M3J2K2	416-661-3000	
Rest-a-Phone Corp 2801 NW Lower River Rd Ste A *Web:* www.abcplas.com	Vancouver	WA	98660	503-235-6778	
RGE USA Inc 365 Oliver Cromwell Dr *Web:* www.rgegroup.com	Newport	TN	37821	423-625-4909	
Richards & Richards 1741 Elm Hill Pk *Web:* www.richardsandrichards.com	Nashville	TN	37210	615-242-9600	
Rieke Corp 500 W Seventh St *Web:* www.riekepackaging.com	Auburn	IN	46706	260-925-3700	
Riverdale Color Manufacturing Inc 1 Walnut St *Web:* www.riverdalecolor.com	Perth Amboy	NJ	08861	732-376-9300	
RL Hudson & Co 2000 W Tacoma *Web:* www.rlhudson.com	Broken Arrow	OK	74012	918-259-6600	
Ro Mai Industries 1605 Enterprise Pkwy *Web:* www.rmihardware.com	Twinsburg	OH	44087	330-425-9090	
Rogan Corp 3455 Woodhead Dr *TF:* 800-584-5662 ■ *Web:* www.rogancorp.com	Northbrook	IL	60062	847-498-2300	498-2334
Rohrer Corp 717 Seville Rd PO Box 1009 *TF:* 800-243-6640 ■ *Web:* www.rohrer.com	Wadsworth	OH	44282	330-335-1541	336-5147
Rolco Inc 336 E Industrial St *Web:* www.rolcoinc.com	Kasota	MN	56050	507-931-4525	
Rolenn Mfg 2065 Roberta St *Web:* www.rolenn.com	Riverside	CA	92507	951-682-1185	
Roncelli Plastics Inc 330 W Duarte Rd *Web:* www.roncelli.com	Monrovia	CA	91016	626-359-2551	
Rubbermaid Commercial Products (RCP) 3124 Valley Ave *TF:* 800-347-9800 ■ *Web:* www.rubbermaidcommercial.com	Winchester	VA	22601	540-667-8700	542-8770
Safety Technology International Inc 2306 Airport Rd *TF:* 800-888-4784 ■ *Web:* www.sti-usa.com	Waterford	MI	48327	248-673-9898	
Sare Plastics 14600 Commerce St Ne. *Web:* www.sareplastics.com	Alliance	OH	44601	330-821-4299	
Semco Plastic Co 5301 Old Baumgartner Rd *Web:* www.semcoplastics.com	Saint Louis	MO	63129	314-487-4557	487-4724
Seville Flexpack Corp 9905 S Ridgeview Dr *Web:* sevilleflexpack.com	Oak Creek	WI	53154	414-761-2751	761-3140
Shakespeare Monofilaments & Specialty Polymers 6111 Shakespeare Rd *TF:* 800-845-2110 ■ *Web:* www.shakespearemonofilaments.com	Columbia	SC	29223	803-754-7011	786-2568
Simonton Windows Inc 5300 Briscoe Rd PO Box 1646 *Web:* www.simonton.com	Parkersburg	WV	26102	304-428-8261	
Smith McDonald Corp 1270 Niagara St *TF:* 800-753-8548 ■ *Web:* www.smithmcdonald.com	Buffalo	NY	14213	800-753-8548	
Spears Manufacturing Co PO Box 9203 *TF:* 800-862-1499 ■ *Web:* www.spearsmfg.com	Sylmar	CA	91392	818-364-1611	
Spencer Plastics Inc 4811 Industrial Dr *Web:* www.spencerplastics.com	Mesick	MI	49668	231-885-1443	
Spilltech Environmental Inc 1627 Odonoghue St *TF:* 800-228-3877 ■ *Web:* www.spilltech.com	Mobile	AL	36615	800-228-3877	
Spiratex Company Inc 1916 Frenchtown Ctr Dr. *Web:* www.spiratex.com	Monroe	MI	48162	734-289-4800	
Stack Plastics 3525 Haven Ave *Web:* www.stackplastics.com	Menlo Park	CA	94025	650-361-8600	
Stanridge Color Corp PO Box 1086 *Web:* www.standridgecolor.com	Social Circle	GA	30025	770-464-3362	464-2202
Stant Corp 1620 Columbia Ave *TF:* 800-822-3121 ■ *Web:* www.stant.com	Connersville	IN	47331	765-825-3121	825-2875
Star Die Molding Inc 2741 Katherine Way *Web:* www.stardie.com	Elk Grove Village	IL	60007	847-766-7952	
Steinwall Inc 1759 116th Ave NW. *TF:* 800-229-9199 ■ *Web:* www.steinwall.com	Coon Rapids	MN	55448	763-767-7060	767-7061
Sueba USA 8235 El Rio St *Web:* www.s-h-m.com	Houston	TX	77054	713-747-7333	
Sunrise Windows Ltd. LLC 200 Enterprise Dr *Web:* www.sunrisewindows.com	Temperance	MI	48182	734-847-8778	847-7758
Syndicate Sales Inc PO Box 756 *TF:* 800-428-0515 ■ *Web:* www.syndicatesales.com	Kokomo	IN	46903	765-457-7277	
Syracuse Plastics LLC 7400 Morgan Rd *Web:* www.syracuseplastics.com	Liverpool	NY	13090	315-637-9881	637-9260
Tearepair Inc 2200 Knight Rd *Web:* tear-aid.com	Land O Lakes	FL	34639	813-948-6898	
Tech Nh Inc 8 Continental Blvd *Web:* www.technh.com	Merrimack	NH	03054	603-424-4404	
Techmer PM LLC 1 Quality Cir *Web:* www.techmerpm.com	Clinton	TN	37716	865-457-6700	
Technetics Group 3125 Damon Way *TF:* 800-618-4701 ■ *Web:* technetics.com	Burbank	CA	91505	818-841-9667	841-8057
Tecstar Manufacturing Co W190N11701 Moldmakers Way *Web:* www.mgstech.com	Germantown	WI	53022	262-250-2950	
Tessy Plastics Corp 488 Rt 5 W. *Web:* www.tessy.com	Elbridge	NY	13060	315-689-3924	689-2027
Thermal Plastic Design Inc 1116 E Pine St *Web:* www.tdimolding.com	St Croix Falls	WI	54024	715-483-1841	
Thermo-tech Plastics Ltd 2299 Drew Rd *Web:* thermotechplastics.com	Mississauga	ON	L5S1A3	905-678-9448	
Thombert Inc 316 E Seventh St N *TF:* 800-433-3572 ■ *Web:* www.thombert.com	Newton	IA	50208	800-433-3572	433-3517
TMI LLC 5350 Campbells Run Rd *TF:* 800-888-9750 ■ *Web:* www.tmi-pvc.com	Pittsburgh	PA	15205	412-787-9750	
Totex Manufacturing Inc 2927 Lomita Blvd *Web:* www.batterytechnologies.com	Torrance	CA	90505	310-326-2028	
Transparent Container Company Inc 625 Thomas Dr. **Fax Area Code:* 630 ■ *Web:* www.transparentcontainer.com	Bensenville	IL	60106	708-449-8520	860-3651*
Triad Products Co 1801 W 'B' St *TF General:* 888-253-4227 ■ *Web:* www.triadproducts.net	Hastings	NE	68901	402-462-2181	462-2246
Trippnt Inc 8830 NE 108th St. *TF:* 800-874-7768 ■ *Web:* www.trippnt.com	Kansas City	MO	64157	816-792-2604	
Triwood Corp of Georgia Inc 124 Austin Rd. *Web:* triwood.com	Americus	GA	31719	229-928-2233	
TSE Industries Inc 4370 112th Terr N *TF:* 800-237-7634 ■ *Web:* www.tse-industries.com	Clearwater	FL	33762	727-573-7676	572-0487
U S Farathane Corp 38000 Mound Rd *Web:* www.usfarathane.com	Sterling Heights	MI	48310	586-978-2800	
Ultra-Poly Corp 102 Demi Rd PO Box 330 *TF:* 800-932-0619 ■ *Web:* www.ultra-poly.com	Portland	PA	18351	570-897-7500	
Unette Corp 1578 Sussex Tpke Bldg Ste 5 *Web:* www.unette.com	Randolph	NJ	07871	973-328-6800	584-4794
Univenture Inc 13311 Industrial Pkwy. **Fax Area Code:* 937 ■ *TF:* 800-992-8262 ■ *Web:* www.univenture.com	Marysville	OH	43040	800-992-8262	645-4700*
Vantage Plastics 1415 W Cedar St *Web:* www.vantageplastics.com	Standish	MI	48658	989-846-1029	846-0939
Ven-Tel Plastics Corp 11311 74th St N. *Web:* www.ventelplastics.com	Largo	FL	33773	727-546-7470	

Phone | Fax

Ventana USA 6001 Enterprise Dr .... Export PA 15632 724-325-3400
Web: www.ventana-usa.com
Ventra Plastics - Russellville
140 Progress Dr .... Russellville KY 42276 270-726-4767
Viking Plastics Inc 1 Viking St .... Corry PA 16407 814-664-8671
Web: www.vikingplastics.com
Vinyl Window Technologies Inc PO Box 588 .... Paducah KY 42002 270-442-7870
Web: www.viwintech.com
Vitec LLC 2627 Clark St .... Detroit MI 48210 313-297-6676 843-1298
Web: www.vitec-usa.com
Viwinco Inc PO Box 499 .... Morgantown PA 19543 610-286-8884
Web: www.viwinco.com
Viziflex Seels Inc 406 N Midland Ave .... Saddle Brook NJ 07663 800-627-7752 487-3266*
**Fax Area Code:* 201 ■ *TF:* 800-627-7752 ■ *Web:* www.viziflex.com
Watertown Plastics 830 Echo Lk Rd .... Watertown CT 06795 860-274-7535
Web: www.watertownplastics.com
Wausaukee Composites Inc 837 Cedar St .... Wausaukee WI 54177 715-856-6321 856-5567
Web: www.wauscomp.com
Weener Plastics Inc 2201 Stantonsburg Rd SE .... Wilson NC 27893 252-206-1400
Westec Plastics Corp 6757 A Las Positas Rd .... Livermore CA 94551 925-454-3400
Web: www.westecplastics.com
Williamston Products Inc (WPI)
845 Progress Ct .... Williamston MI 48895 517-655-2131 655-2607
Web: www.wpius.com
WinDoor Inc 7500 Amsterdam Dr .... Orlando FL 32832 407-481-8400
Web: www.windoorinc.com
Window Factory Inc, The 7550 Miramar Rd .... San Diego CA 92126 858-905-5908
Web: www.windowfactory.com
World Class Plastics Inc 7695 SR- 708 .... Russells Point OH 43348 937-843-4927 843-4934
TF: 800-954-3140 ■ *Web:* www.worldclassplastics.com
Worldwide Dispensers USA 78 2nd Ave S .... Lester Prairie MN 55354 320-395-2553
Web: dssmith.com
Wren Assoc Ltd 124 Wren Pkwy .... Jefferson City MO 65109 573-893-2249
TF: 800-881-2249 ■ *Web:* www.wrensolutions.com
Yeti Coolers 3411 Hidalgo St .... Austin TX 78702 512-394-9384
TF: 888-872-0227 ■ *Web:* www.yeticoolers.com
Zadro Products Inc 5422 Argosy Ave .... Huntington Beach CA 92649 714-892-9200
TF: 800-468-4348 ■ *Web:* www.zadroinc.com
ZAGG Inc 3855 South 500 West Ste J .... Salt Lake City UT 84115 801-263-0699
TF: 800-700-9244 ■ *Web:* www.zagg.com

609 PLUMBING FIXTURES & FITTINGS - METAL

Phone | Fax

Accurate Partitions Corp
8000 Joliet Rd PO Box 287 .... McCook IL 60525 708-442-6800 442-7439
Web: www.accuratepartitions.com
Acorn Engineering Co
15125 Proctor Ave PO Box 3527 .... City of Industry CA 91744 626-336-4561 961-2200
TF: 800-488-8999 ■ *Web:* www.acorneng.com
American Brass Manufacturing Co
5000 Superior Ave .... Cleveland OH 44103 216-431-6565 431-9420
TF: 800-431-6440 ■ *Web:* www.americanbrass.com
American Specialties Inc (ASI)
441 Saw Mill River Rd .... Yonkers NY 10701 914-476-9000 476-0688
Web: www.americanspecialties.com
Ames Fire & Waterworks
1427 N Market Blvd Ste 9 .... Sacramento CA 95834 916-928-0123 928-9333
Web: www.amesfirewater.com
Anderson Copper & Brass Co
7231 W Laraway Rd .... Frankfort IL 60423 708-535-9030 535-9038
TF: 800-323-5284 ■ *Web:* andersonfittings.com
Barclay Products Ltd 4000 Porett Dr Ste B .... Gurnee IL 60031 847-244-1234
TF: 800-446-9700 ■ *Web:* www.barclayproducts.com
Bathcraft Inc 1610 James P Rodgers Dr .... Valdosta GA 31601 229-333-0805
Web: www.bathcraft.com
Bootz Industries PO Box 18010 .... Evansville IN 47719 812-423-5401 429-2254
Web: www.bootz.com
Bradley Corp
W 142 N 9101 Fountain Blvd .... Menomonee Falls WI 53051 262-251-6000 251-5817
TF: 800-272-3539 ■ *Web:* www.bradleycorp.com
Brass-Craft Manufacturing Co
39600 Orchard Hill Pl .... Novi MI 48375 248-305-6000 305-6012*
**Fax:* Sales ■ *Web:* www.brasscraft.com
Brasstech Inc 2001 Carnegie Ave .... Santa Ana CA 92705 949-417-5207 417-5208
Web: www.brasstech.com
Central Brass Mfg Company Inc
2950 E 55th St .... Cleveland OH 44127 216-883-0220
TF: 800-321-8630 ■ *Web:* www.centralbrass.com
Champion-Arrowhead LLC 5147 Alhambra Ave .... Los Angeles CA 90032 323-221-9137 221-2579
TF: 800-332-4267 ■ *Web:* www.arrowheadbrass.com
Chicago Faucets A Geberit Co
2100 S Clearwater Dr .... Des Plaines IL 60018 847-803-5000 298-3101*
**Fax:* Sales ■ *TF:* 800-323-5060 ■ *Web:* www.chicagofaucets.com
Elias Industries Inc 605 Epsilon Dr .... Pittsburgh PA 15238 412-782-4300
Web: tapcogenuinepartscenter.com
Eljer Inc 1 Centennial Ave .... Piscataway NJ 08855 800-442-1902
TF: 800-442-1902 ■ *Web:* www.eljer.com
Elkay Manufacturing Co 2222 Camden Ct .... Oak Brook IL 60523 630-574-8484 574-5012
Web: www.elkay.com
Fisher Manufacturing Co PO Box 60 .... Tulare CA 93275 800-421-6162 832-8238
TF: 800-421-6162 ■ *Web:* www.fisher-mfg.com
Fluidmaster Inc
30800 Rancho Viejo Rd .... San Juan Capistrano CA 92675 949-728-2000 728-2205
TF: 800-631-2011 ■ *Web:* www.fluidmaster.com
Fortune Brands Home & Hardware Inc
520 Lk Cook Rd .... Deerfield IL 60015 847-484-4400
Web: www.fbhs.com
Gerber Plumbing Fixtures LLC
2500 International Pkwy .... Woodridge IL 60517 888-648-6466 636-2021*
**Fax Area Code:* 514 ■ *TF:* 888-648-6466 ■ *Web:* www.gerberonline.com

Phone | Fax

Global Partitions 2171 Liberty Hill Rd .... Eastanollee GA 30538 706-827-2700 827-2710
Web: www.globalpartitions.com
Grohe America Inc 241 Covington Dr .... Bloomingdale IL 60108 630-582-7711 582-7722
TF: 800-444-7643 ■ *Web:* www.grohe.com
Hansgrohe Inc 1490 Bluegrass Lakes Pkwy .... Alpharetta GA 30004 770-360-9880 360-9887
TF: 800-334-0455 ■ *Web:* www.hansgrohe-usa.com
In-Sink-Erator 4700 21st St .... Racine WI 53406 262-554-5432
TF: 800-558-5712 ■ *Web:* www.insinkerator.com
Josam Co 525 W US Hwy 20 .... Michigan City IN 46360 219-872-5531 627-0008*
**Fax Area Code:* 800 ■ *TF:* 800-365-6726 ■ *Web:* www.josam.com
Keeney Manufacturing Co 1170 Main St .... Newington CT 06111 860-666-3342 665-0374*
**Fax:* Cust Svc ■ *TF Cust Svc:* 800-243-0526 ■ *Web:* www.keeneymfg.com
Kohler Plumbing North America 444 Highland Dr .... Kohler WI 53044 920-457-4441 459-1826*
**Fax:* Sales ■ *TF:* 800-456-4537 ■ *Web:* www.us.kohler.com
LDR Industries Inc 600 N Kilbourn Ave .... Chicago IL 60624 773-265-3000 265-3130
TF: 800-545-5230 ■ *Web:* www.ldrind.com
Masco Corp 21001 Van Born Rd .... Taylor MI 48180 313-274-7400 792-4177
NYSE: MAS ■ *TF:* 888-627-6397 ■ *Web:* www.masco.com
Microphor Inc 452 E Hill Rd .... Willits CA 95490 707-459-5563 459-6617
TF Orders: 800-358-8280 ■ *Web:* www.wabtec.com/business-units/microphor
Moen Inc 25300 Al Moen Dr .... North Olmsted OH 44070 440-962-2000 848-6636*
**Fax Area Code:* 800 ■ **Fax:* Hum Res ■ *TF Cust Svc:* 800-289-6636 ■ *Web:* www.moen.com
Moen Inc CSI Bath Accessories Div
25300 Al Moen Dr .... North Olmsted OH 44070 440-962-2000 962-2145
TF: 800-289-6636 ■ *Web:* www.moen.com
NAPAC Inc 229 Southbridge St .... Worcester MA 01608 508-363-4411
Web: www.napacinc.com
Norman Supply Co 825 SW Fifth St .... Oklahoma City OK 73109 405-235-9511
Web: www.morsco.com
Oatey Co 4700 W 160th St .... Cleveland OH 44135 216-267-7100 321-9535*
**Fax Area Code:* 800 ■ *TF Cust Svc:* 800-321-9532 ■ *Web:* www.oatey.com
Pan-Pacific Plumbing Co
18250 Euclid St .... Fountain Valley CA 92708 949-474-9170 474-9180
Web: ppmechanical.com
Price Pfister Inc 19701 Da Vinci St .... Lake Forest CA 92610 949-672-4000 672-4000
TF: 800-732-8238 ■ *Web:* www.pfisterfaucets.com
Quality Metal Finishing Company Inc
421 N Walnut St .... Byron IL 61010 815-234-2711 234-2243
Web: www.qmfco.com
SH Leggitt Co 1000 Civic Ctr Loop .... San Marcos TX 78666 512-396-2257
Web: shleggitt.com
Sloan Valve Co 10500 Seymour Ave .... Franklin Park IL 60131 847-671-4300 671-6944
TF: 800-982-5839 ■ *Web:* www.sloan.com
Speakman Co 400 Anchor Mill Rd .... New Castle DE 19720 800-537-2107 977-2747
TF: 800-537-2107 ■ *Web:* speakman.com
Starline Manufacturing Company Inc
6060 W Douglas Ave .... Milwaukee WI 53218 414-358-4060
Sterling Plumbing 444 Highland Dr .... Kohler WI 53044 920-457-4441
TF Cust Svc: 888-783-7546 ■ *Web:* www.sterlingplumbing.com
Symmons Industries Inc 31 Brooks Dr .... Braintree MA 02184 781-848-2250 843-3849
TF: 800-796-6667 ■ *Web:* www.symmons.com
T & S Brass & Bronze Works Inc
PO Box 1088 .... Travelers Rest SC 29690 864-834-4102 834-3518
TF Cust Svc: 800-476-4103 ■ *Web:* www.tsbrass.com
Water Pik Inc 1730 E Prospect Rd .... Fort Collins CO 80553 800-525-2774
TF: 800-525-2774 ■ *Web:* www.waterpik.com
Water Saver Faucet Co 701 W Erie St .... Chicago IL 60654 312-666-5500 666-5501
TF Parts: 800-973-7278 ■ *Web:* www.wsflab.com
Waterworks Operating Company LLC
60 Backus Ave .... Danbury CT 06810 203-546-6000
TF: 800-899-6757 ■ *Web:* www.waterworks.com
William Steinen Manufacturing Co
29 E Halsey Rd .... Parsippany NJ 07054 973-887-6400 887-4632
Web: www.steinen.com
Woodford Manufacturing Co
2121 Waynoka Rd .... Colorado Springs CO 80915 800-621-6032 574-7699*
**Fax Area Code:* 719 ■ *TF Sales:* 800-621-6032 ■ *Web:* www.woodfordmfg.com

610 PLUMBING FIXTURES & FITTINGS - PLASTICS

Phone | Fax

1st Mechanical 1295 Bluegrass Lakes Pkwy .... Alpharetta GA 30004 770-346-0792
TF: 888-346-0792 ■ *Web:* www.1stmech.com
A & A Industrial Piping Inc 6 Gardner Rd .... Fairfield NJ 07004 973-882-2622
Web: www.a-agroup.com
A & R Mechanical Contractors Inc
11244 E 55th Pl .... Tulsa OK 74146 918-250-6500
Web: www.aandrmechanical.com
A T Klemens & Son Inc 814 12th St N .... Great Falls MT 59401 406-452-9541
Web: www.atklemens.com
A-account Plumbing & Drain Cleaning LLC
5128 S Eastern Ave .... Oklahoma City OK 73129 405-672-5754
AAA Refrigeration Service Inc 1804 Nereid Ave .... Bronx NY 10466 718-324-2231
Web: www.aaarefrig.com
Able Plumbing Inc 2336 Bob Boozer Dr .... Omaha NE 68130 402-334-8887
Absocold Corp PO Box 1545 .... Richmond IN 47375 765-935-7501 935-3450
TF: 800-843-3714 ■ *Web:* www.absocold.com
Accurate Heating & Cooling 3001 River Rd .... Chillicothe OH 45601 740-775-5005
Web: accuratehvac.com
Accurate Plumbing 7595 Fishel Dr S .... Dublin OH 43016 614-526-0131
Web: plumbingrepairandservices.com
Accutrans Inc 2740 Indiana Ave .... Kenner LA 70062 504-469-0500
Web: accutransinc.com
ACE Duraflo Pipe Restoration Inc
3122 W Alpine Ave .... Santa Ana CA 92704 714-564-7600
Web: www.restoremypipes.com
Ace-Atlas Corp 5214 Flushing Ave .... Maspeth NY 11378 718-497-3003
Web: www.ace-atlas.com
Acker & Sons Inc 10516 Summit Ave .... Kensington MD 20895 301-897-0700
Web: ackerandsonsinc.com
Acorn Industrial Inc 7311 Acc Blvd .... Raleigh NC 27617 919-256-6500
Web: www.acornindustrial.com

Company	City	State	ZIP	Phone	Fax
Action Air Conditioning & Htg 3506 Ave S	Galveston	TX	77550	409-765-8026	
Adams Electric & Plumbing LLC 606 N Main St *Web:* adamsep.com	Pratt	KS	67124	620-672-7279	
Aero Automatic Sprinkler Co 21605 N Central Ave *Web:* www.aerofire.com	Phoenix	AZ	85024	623-580-7800	
Aero Energy 230 Lincoln Way E *Web:* www.aeroenergy.com	New Oxford	PA	17350	717-624-4311	
Afrl Hea 6030 S Kent Bldg 570	Mesa	AZ	85212	480-988-2040	
Agco Inc 2782 Simpson Cir	Norcross	GA	30071	770-447-6990	
Aiello Home Services Inc 600 Old County Cir *Web:* www.aiellohomeservices.com	Windsor Locks	CT	06096	860-292-2600	
AJ Demor & Sons Inc 2150 Eldo Rd *Web:* www.ajdemor.com	Monroeville	PA	15146	412-242-6125	
Ajax Santa Barbara Refrigeration & Heating 401 E Montecito St *Web:* ajaxrefrigerationandac.com	Santa Barbara	CA	93101	805-963-1322	
Alex Mccoy Plumbing 160 Binnington Crt. *Web:* amph.ca	Kingston	ON	K7M8N1	613-546-6846	
All-Temp Refrigeration Services Inc 271 Hwy 1085 *TF:* 888-626-1277 ■ *Web:* www.alltempinc.com	Madisonville	LA	70447	888-626-1277	
All-Tex Pipe & Supply Inc 9743 Brockbank *Web:* www.alltexsupply.com	Dallas	TX	75220	214-350-5886	
Allan Automatic Sprinkler Corp of so Cal 3233 Enterprise St *Web:* www.allansocal.com	Brea	CA	92821	714-993-9500	
Allied Blower & Sheet Metal 1350 Polson Dr *Web:* www.alliedblower.com	Vernon	BC	V1T8H2	250-503-2533	
Alpha Energy Solutions Inc 7200 Distribution Dr *TF:* 888-212-6324 ■ *Web:* www.alphamechanicalservice.com	Louisville	KY	40258	502-968-0121	
Alpha Mechanical Heating & Air Condi 4885 Greencraig Ln *Web:* alphamech.com	San Diego	CA	92123	858-278-3500	
Alpine Plumbing Inc 14580 W Greenfield Ave *Web:* www.alpineplumbinginc.com	Brookfield	WI	53005	262-797-4120	
Amason & Assoc Inc 1820 Rice Mine Rd N Ste 100 *Web:* www.amason-associates.com	Tuscaloosa	AL	35406	205-345-9626	
American Air Distributing Inc 830 S Bolmar St *Web:* aa.com	West Chester	PA	19382	610-918-7090	
American Fire Protection 4019 E Summit Ln. *Web:* www.firesafetyboise.com	Nampa	ID	83687	208-463-0209	
American Moistening Company Inc 10402 Rodney St *TF:* 800-948-5540 ■ *Web:* www.amco.com	Pineville	NC	28134	704-889-7281	
AMI Mechanical Inc 12141 Pennsylvania St *Web:* www.amimechanical.com	Thornton	CO	80241	303-280-1401	
Ampam Ldi Mechanical Inc 10920 Pump House Rd	Annapolis Junction	MD	20701	301-497-6500	
Answer Heating & Cooling Inc 8490 Midland Rd *Web:* www.answerheating.com	Freeland	MI	48623	989-695-9461	
Apex Mechanical Systems Inc 7440 Trade St *Web:* www.apexmech.com	San Diego	CA	92121	858-536-8700	
Apex Piping Systems Inc 302 Falco Dr *TF:* 888-995-2739 ■ *Web:* www.apexpiping.com	Wilmington	DE	19804	302-995-6136	
Applied Mechanical Systems Inc 5598 Wolf Creek Pk *TF:* 888-854-3073 ■ *Web:* www.appliedmechanicalsys.com	Dayton	OH	45426	937-854-3073	
Aqua Bath Company Inc 921 Cherokee Ave *TF:* 800-232-2284 ■ *Web:* www.aquabath.com	Nashville	TN	37207	615-227-0017	
Aqua-Chem Inc 3001 E Governor John Sevier Hwy *Web:* www.aqua-chem.com	Knoxville	TN	37914	865-544-2065	
Arete Development Inc 20 Industrial Rd	Fairfield	NJ	07004	973-244-0037	
Arneg Canada Inc 18 Rue Richelieu *TF:* 800-363-3439 ■ *Web:* arneg.ca	Lacolle	QC	J0J1J0	450-246-3837	246-2368
Arneg LLC 750 Old Hargrave Rd *TF:* 800-276-3487 ■ *Web:* www.arnegusa.com	Lexington	NC	27295	336-956-5300	
Astro Mechanical Contractors Inc 603 S Marshall Ave *Web:* astro-mech.com	El Cajon	CA	92020	619-442-9686	
Atlas Butler Heating & Cooling 619 Reynolds Ave *Web:* www.atlasbutler.com	Columbus	OH	43201	614-294-8600	
Atlas Sheet Metal Inc 19 Musick *Web:* atlassheetmetal.com	Irvine	CA	92618	949-600-8787	
Aurora Contractors Inc 100 Raynor Ave *TF:* 866-423-2197 ■ *Web:* www.auroracontractors.com	Ronkonkoma	NY	11779	631-981-3785	
Automatic Fire Protection Inc 4582 Old Christoval Rd *Web:* www.automaticfireprotection.com	San Angelo	TX	76904	325-651-9000	651-9003
Automatic Fire Sprinkler Inc 7272 Mars Dr *TF:* 800-436-2066	Huntington Beach	CA	92647	714-841-2066	
Automatic Sprinkler of Texas Inc 1147 S Cedar Ridge Dr *Web:* www.autosprinkleroftx.com	Duncanville	TX	75137	972-298-2772	
B & B Trade Distribution Centre 1950 Oxford St E *TF:* 800-265-0382 ■ *Web:* bbtrade.ca	London	ON	N5V2Z8	519-679-1770	
B Z Plumbing Company Inc 1901 Aviation Blvd	Lincoln	CA	95648	916-645-1600	
Baker Septic Installations 7740 S George Blvd *Web:* bakersepticfl.net	Sebring	FL	33875	863-385-0917	
Ball Heating & Air 8332 W Oaklawn Rd *Web:* www.callballthatsall.com	Biloxi	MS	39532	228-392-5432	
Basic Plumbing Inc 1409 Mechanical Blvd *Web:* www.basicplumbinginc.com	Garner	NC	27529	919-662-1082	
Beaudin Le Prohon Inc 6171 Boul Bourque *Web:* www.leprohon.com	Sherbrooke	QC	J1N1H2	819-563-2454	
Bel-Aire Mechanical Inc 4201 N 47th Ave *Web:* belairemechanical.com	Phoenix	AZ	85031	623-846-8600	
Belding Tank Technologies Inc 200 N Gooding St PO Box 160 *TF:* 800-253-4252 ■ *Web:* www.beldingtank.com	Belding	MI	48809	616-794-1130	794-3666
Bell Pipe & Supply 215 E Ball Rd *Web:* www.bellpipe.com	Anaheim	CA	92805	714-772-3200	
Bell Products Inc 722 Soscol Ave *Web:* www.bellproducts.com	Napa	CA	94559	707-255-1811	
Benjamin Manufacturing 3215 S Sweetwater Rd *Web:* www.benjaminmfg.com	Lithia Springs	GA	30122	770-941-1433	
BERG Chilling Systems Inc 51 Nantucket Blvd *Web:* www.berg-group.com	Toronto	ON	M1P2N5	416-755-2221	
Bernsohn & Fetner LLC 625 W 51st St *Web:* bfbuilding.com	New York	NY	10019	212-315-4330	
Best Plumbing Tile & Stone 49 Rt 138 *Web:* www.bestplg.com	Somers	NY	10589	914-232-2020	
BG National Plumbing & Heating 200 Montrose Rd *Web:* www.bgnational.com	Westbury	NY	11590	516-334-8282	
BIOgroupUSA Inc 1059 Broadwy Ste F *Web:* www.biobagusa.com	Dunedin	FL	34698	727-789-1646	
Blauch Bros Inc 911 Chicago Ave *TF:* 888-881-3939 ■ *Web:* blauchbrothers.com	Harrisonburg	VA	22802	540-434-2589	
Blue Mountain Air Inc 707 Aldridge Rd *TF:* 800-889-2085 ■ *Web:* www.bluemountainair.net	Vacaville	CA	95688	800-889-2085	
Blue Sky Energy Inc 2598 Fortune Way Ste K *TF:* 800-493-7877 ■ *Web:* www.blueskyenergyinc.com	Vista	CA	92081	760-597-1642	
Boda Plumbing Inc 1909 Tower Industrial Dr *Web:* www.bodaplumbing.com	Monroe	NC	28110	704-291-9097	
Boland 30 W Watkins Mill Rd *TF:* 800-552-6526 ■ *Web:* www.boland.com	Gaithersburg	MD	20878	240-306-3000	
Boykin Contracting Inc 167 Lott Ct	West Columbia	SC	29169	803-926-4930	
Brennan J m Inc 2101 W Saint Paul Ave *Web:* www.jmbrennan.com	Milwaukee	WI	53201	414-342-3829	
Broadway Mechanical 873 81st Ave *TF:* 800-862-4930 ■ *Web:* www.broadwaymechanical.com	Oakland	CA	94621	510-746-4000	
Brower Mechanical Inc 4060 Alvis Ct *TF:* 877-816-6649 ■ *Web:* www.browermechanical.com	Rocklin	CA	95677	916-624-0808	
C & C Boiler Sales & Service Inc 3401 Rotary Dr *Web:* www.ccboiler.com	Charlotte	NC	28269	704-597-0003	
C H Garmong & Son Inc 3050 Poplar St *TF:* 800-894-2962 ■ *Web:* www.garmong.net	Terre Haute	IN	47803	812-234-3714	
Cambridgeport Air Systems 8 Fanaras Dr *TF:* 877-648-2872 ■ *Web:* www.cambridgeport.net	Salisbury	MA	01952	978-465-8481	
Can-am Plumbing Inc 151 Wyoming St *TF:* 800-786-9797 ■ *Web:* www.canamplumbing.com	Pleasanton	CA	94566	925-846-1833	
Can-Eng Furnaces International Ltd 6800 Montrose Rd PO Box 628 *Web:* www.can-eng.com	Niagara Falls	ON	L2E6V5	905-356-1327	
Canyon Air Service Inc 416 S Vermont Ave *Web:* canyonair.com	Glendora	CA	91741	626-339-3777	
Carlo Doria Plbg & Htg Plumbr 23 Waterhouse Rd	Cape Elizabeth	ME	04107	207-799-0066	
Carrier Interamerica 3450 NW 115th Ave *Web:* www.carriercca.com	Miami	FL	33178	305-590-1000	
Casto Technical Services Inc 540 Leon Sullivan Way *TF:* 800-232-2221 ■ *Web:* castotech.com	Charleston	WV	25301	304-346-0549	
Catalina Mechanical Contracting Inc 2702 S Alvernon Way *Web:* www.btucson.com	Tucson	AZ	85713	520-745-3000	
Cecchin Plumbing & Heating Inc 4N275 Cavalry Dr *Web:* cecchin-inc.com	Bloomingdale	IL	60108	630-529-4046	
Century Mechanical Contractors Inc 3008 Wichita Ct *Web:* www.centurymech.com	Fort Worth	TX	76140	817-293-3803	
Certified Plumbing of Brevard 1401 Pennykamp St Ne *Web:* www.certpah.com	Palm Bay	FL	32907	321-676-0812	
Cfi Mechanical Inc 6109 Brittmoore Rd *Web:* cfimechanical.com	Houston	TX	77041	832-467-8200	467-8203
CJ Erickson Plumbing Co 4141 W 124th Pl *Web:* www.cjerickson.com	Alsip	IL	60803	708-371-4900	
Clarke & Rush Mechanical Inc 4411 Auburn Blvd *Web:* clarke-rush.com	Sacramento	CA	95841	916-609-2665	
Claybar Constracting Inc 424 Macnab St *TF:* 866-801-9305 ■ *Web:* www.claybar.ca	Dundas	ON	L9H2L3	905-627-8000	
ClimateCraft Inc 518 N Indiana Ave *Web:* www.climatecraft.com	Oklahoma City	OK	73106	405-415-9230	
CMS Mechanical Services Inc 609 Technology Cir Ste A *Web:* mechanicalservicesco.com	Windsor	CO	80550	970-686-6800	
Cole Industrial Inc 5924 203rd St SW *TF:* 800-627-2653 ■ *Web:* www.coleindust.com	Lynnwood	WA	98036	425-774-6602	
Colite International Ltd 5 Technology Cir *TF:* 800-760-7926 ■ *Web:* www.colite.com	Columbia	SC	29203	803-926-7926	
Combined Refrigeration Resources Inc 1118 First St *Web:* www.combinedrefrigeration.com	Humble	TX	77338	281-540-7552	
Comprehensive Energy Services Inc 777 Bennett Dr *Web:* www.cesmechanical.com	Longwood	FL	32750	407-682-1313	
Computerworks Technologies 711 S Victory Blvd *Web:* www.computerworkstech.com	Burbank	CA	91502	818-244-4484	
Concepts Av Integration 3712 S 132nd St *TF:* 877-422-3933 ■ *Web:* www.conceptsav.com	Omaha	NE	68144	402-298-5011	

Company	City	State	Zip	Phone	Fax
Continental Fire Sprinkler Co 4518 S 133rd St *TF:* 800-543-5170 ■ *Web:* www.continental-fire.com	Omaha	NE	68137	402-330-5170	
Convoy Servicing Company Inc 3323 Jane Ln *Web:* www.convoyservicing.com	Dallas	TX	75247	214-638-3050	
Conway Services LLC 6426 Summer Gale *Web:* www.conwayservices.net	Memphis	TN	38134	901-384-3511	
Cool Check Air Conditioning 4-25 Coronet Rd *Web:* coolcheck.ca	Etobicoke	ON	M8Z2L8	416-236-1000	
Couts Heating & Cooling Inc 1693 Rimpau Ave *Web:* www.couts.com	Corona	CA	92881	951-278-5560	
Cregger Company Inc 629 12th St Extn *Web:* www.creggercompany.com	West Columbia	SC	29169	803-791-5195	
Crosby-brownlie Inc 100 Nassau St *Web:* crosbybrownlie.com	Rochester	NY	14605	585-325-1290	
Crossland Mechanical Inc 237 W 37th St Rm 400 *Web:* www.crosslandmech.com	New York	NY	10018	212-719-5330	
Custom Air 6384 Tower Ln *Web:* www.customairinc.com	Sarasota	FL	34240	941-371-0833	
D V Brown & Assoc Inc 567 Vickers St *Web:* www.dvbrown.com	Tonawanda	NY	14150	716-695-5533	
D'Onofrio General Contractors Corp 202 28th St *Web:* donofrio.biz	Brooklyn	NY	11232	718-832-5700	
D'vontz 7208 E 38th St *TF:* 877-322-3600 ■ *Web:* www.dvontz.com	Tulsa	OK	74145	918-622-3600	
Dacon Corp 16 Huron Dr *Web:* www.dacon1.com	Natick	MA	01760	508-651-3600	
Dallago Corp 2411 E Aztec Ave	Gallup	NM	87301	505-722-6638	863-9433
Danamark Watercare Ltd 2-90 Walker Dr *TF:* 888-326-2627 ■ *Web:* danamark.com	Brampton	ON	L6T4H6	888-326-2627	
David Boland Inc 219 Indian River Ave Ste 201 *Web:* www.dboland.com	Titusville	FL	32796	321-269-1345	
DCM Manufacturing Inc 4540 W 160th St *Web:* www.dcm-mfg.com	Cleveland	OH	44135	216-265-8006	
Delhur Industries Inc 4333 Tumwater Truck Rte *Web:* delhur.com	Port Angeles	WA	98363	360-457-1133	
DeVincenzi Metal Products Inc 1655 Rollins Rd *Web:* www.devmetal.com	Burlingame	CA	94010	650-692-5800	
Devore & Johnson Inc 176 Forest Pkwy *Web:* devoreandjohnson.com	Forest Park	GA	30297	404-366-4243	
Dispensing Dynamics International 1020 Bixby Dr *TF:* 800-888-3698 ■ *Web:* www.dispensingdynamics.com	City of Industry	CA	91745	626-961-3691	330-5266
Dominion Energy Management 11250 Hopson Rd *Web:* www.demiva.com	Ashland	VA	23005	804-798-3189	
Dominion Mechanical Contractors Inc 12329 Braddock Rd *Web:* dominion-mechanical.com	Fairfax	VA	22030	703-992-9588	
Donner Plumbing & Heating Inc 107 Candelaria Rd NW *Web:* donnerplumbing.com	Albuquerque	NM	87107	505-884-1017	
Dornbracht Americas Inc 1700 Executive Dr S Ste 600 *TF:* 800-774-1181 ■ *Web:* www.dornbracht.com	Duluth	GA	30096	800-774-1181	
Douglas Orr Plumbing Inc 301 Flagler Dr *Web:* www.orrplumbing.com	Miami Springs	FL	33166	305-887-1687	
dPoint Technologies Inc 1275 Venables St Ste 330 *Web:* www.dpoint.ca	Vancouver	BC	V6A2E4	604-488-1132	
DRM LLC 520 Crews St *Web:* www.drmcontrols.com	Lawrenceburg	TN	38464	931-766-4500	
Duffey Southeast Inc 7716 England St Ste A *Web:* duffeyse.com	Charlotte	NC	28273	704-527-3612	
Eastway Supplies Inc 1561 Alum Creek Dr *Web:* www.eastwaysupplies.com	Columbus	OH	43209	614-252-0974	
ECSM Utility Contractors Inc 1200 Walnut Bottom Rd Ste 101 *Web:* ecsminc.com	Carlisle	PA	17015	717-258-8001	
Eddie Johnson Private Contractor 5005 Creston St	Hyattsville	MD	20781	301-772-0466	
Edward B O'reilly & Assoc Inc 30 W Highland Ave *Web:* www.eboreilly.com	Philadelphia	PA	19118	215-242-8100	
Effective Solar Products LLC 601 Crescent Ave *TF:* 888-824-0090 ■ *Web:* www.effectivesolar.com	Lockport	LA	70374	985-532-0800	
Elmbrook Management Co 1908 12th Ave NW Ste E *Web:* www.elmbrookhomes.com	Ardmore	OK	73401	580-226-3055	
Enagic USA Inc 4115 Spencer St *Web:* www.enagic.com	Torrance	CA	90503	310-542-7700	
Enerco 750 Third Ave 9th Fl *Web:* www.ener.co	New York	NY	10017	212-572-0783	
Energy Air Inc 5401 Energy Air Ct *Web:* www.energyair.com	Orlando	FL	32810	407-886-3729	
Energy Inspectors 8515 Edna Ave *Web:* www.energyinspectors.com	Las Vegas	NV	89117	702-365-8080	
Equiptec Mechanical Inc 523 Capitola Ave	Capitola	CA	95010	831-462-9511	
Ez-flo International Inc 2750 E Mission Blvd **Fax Area Code:* 866 ■ *Web:* www.ez-flo.net	Ontario	CA	91761	909-947-5256	827-3012*
F & G Mechanical Corp 348 New County Rd *Web:* www.fgmech.com	Secaucus	NJ	07094	201-864-3580	
Falasca Mechanical Inc 3329 N Mill Rd *Web:* www.falascamechanical.com	Vineland	NJ	08360	856-794-2010	
Federal Heating & Engineering Company Inc 160 Cross St	Winchester	MA	01890	781-721-2468	
Ferguson Enterprises Inc 57-22 49th St *Web:* ferguson.com/davis-and-warshow	Maspeth	NY	11378	718-937-9500	
Ferrandino & Son Inc 71 Carolyn Blvd *TF:* 866-571-4609 ■ *Web:* www.ferrandinoandson.com	Farmingdale	NY	11735	516-735-0097	
Finken Plumbing Heating & Cooling 628 19th Ave NE *TF:* 877-346-5367 ■ *Web:* www.finkens.com	Saint Joseph	MN	56374	320-258-2005	258-2006
Fire Fighter Sales & Service Co 791 Commonwealth Dr *TF:* 888-412-3473 ■ *Web:* www.firefighter-pgh.com	Warrendale	PA	15086	724-720-6000	
Fitzgerald Electro-mechanical Company Inc 6 S Linden Ave Ste 4 *Web:* www.fitzgeraldemco.com	South San Francisco	CA	94080	650-589-9935	
Florestone Products Company Inc 2851 Falcon Dr *TF:* 800-446-8827 ■ *Web:* www.florestone.com	Madera	CA	93637	559-661-4171	661-2070
Florida Cooling Supply Inc 1954 Carroll St *Web:* www.flcoolingsupply.com	Clearwater	FL	33765	727-449-1230	
Florida Industrial Products Inc 1602 N 39th St *Web:* www.fiponline.com	Tampa	FL	33605	813-247-5356	
Florida Mechanical LLC 3615 Fiscal Ct *Web:* www.flamech.com	Riviera Beach	FL	33404	561-863-3606	
Fluid Conditioning Products Inc Kleine & Warwick Sts *Web:* www.fcp-filters.com	Lititz	PA	17543	717-627-1550	
Food Service Technologies Inc 5256 Eisenhower Ave *Web:* www.mytech24.com	Alexandria	VA	22304	703-354-3835	
Ford Meter Box Company Inc, The 775 Manchester Ave PO Box 443 *Web:* www.fordmeterbox.com	Wabash	IN	46992	260-563-3171	
Freedom Fire Pro LLC 811 Lester Ln *Web:* www.freefirepro.com	Rogers	AR	72756	479-631-6363	
Freeland Contracting 11350 OH-335 *Web:* freelandcontracting.com	Lucasville	OH	45648	614-443-2718	
Freitag Weinhardt Inc 5900 N 13th St *Web:* www.freitaginc.com	Terre Haute	IN	47805	812-466-9861	
Fresh Meadow Mechanical Corp 65-01 Fresh Meadow Ln *Web:* www.fmmcorp.com	Fresh Meadows	NY	11365	718-961-6634	
Frigel North America Inc 150 Prairie Lk Rd *Web:* www.frigel.com	East Dundee	IL	60118	847-540-0160	
Frontier Mechanical Inc 2771 W Mansfield Ave *Web:* www.frontiermech.net	Englewood	CO	80110	303-806-5400	
Fujitsu General America Inc 353 Rt 46 W *TF:* 888-888-3424 ■ *Web:* www.fujitsugeneral.com	Fairfield	NJ	07004	973-575-0380	
Galapagos Partners LP 55 Waugh Dr Ste 1130 *Web:* www.gplp.com	Houston	TX	77007	713-803-4326	
Garden City Plumbing & Heating Inc 4025 Flynn Ln *Web:* www.gardencityplumbing.com	Missoula	MT	59808	406-728-5550	
Gateway Pacific Contractors Inc 8055 Freeport Blvd *Web:* www.chinachef.com	Sacramento	CA	95832	916-665-4100	
GEM Technologies Inc 2033 Castaic Ln *Web:* www.gemtech.biz/default.asp	Knoxville	TN	37932	865-560-9434	
Gemini Industries Inc 200 Wheeler Rd N Tower *Web:* www.gemini-ind.com	Burlington	MA	01803	781-203-0100	
Gilbert Plumbing Co PO BOX 8 *Web:* gilbertplumbingllc.com	West Simsbury	CT	06092	860-658-4653	
Gill Mike Pluming & Heating 46 Temi Rd *Web:* mikegillplumbing.com	Hudson	MA	01749	978-568-8086	
Greenberry Industrial 2273 NW Professional Dr *Web:* www.greenberry.com	Corvallis	OR	97330	541-757-8458	
Groeniger & Company Inc 27750 Industrial Blvd *Web:* www.groeniger.com	Hayward	CA	94545	510-786-3333	
Groth Gates Heating & Sheet Metal Inc 2614 SE Hwy 101 *Web:* www.grothgates.com	Lincoln City	OR	97367	541-994-2631	
Guaranteed Industries Ltd 5420 Rue Pare *Web:* www.guaranteedindustries.com	Montreal	QC	H4P1R3	514-342-3400	
Gulf Breeze News Inc 913 Gulf Breeze Pkwy Ste 35 *Web:* www.gulfbreezenews.com	Gulf Breeze	FL	32561	850-932-8986	
Haller Enterprises Inc 212 Bucky Dr *Web:* www.hallerent.com	Lititz	PA	17543	717-207-9813	
Halvorson Trane 2220 Nw 108Th St *Web:* www.halvorsontrane.com	Clive	IA	50325	515-270-0004	
Hansen Mechanical Contractors Inc 4580 W Post Rd *Web:* www.hansenmechanical.com	Las Vegas	NV	89118	702-361-5111	
Harrison Orr Air Conditioning LLC 4100 N Walnut *Web:* www.harrisonorr.com	Oklahoma City	OK	73105	405-528-3333	
HBD Industries Inc 5200 Upper Metro Pl Ste 110 *Web:* www.hbdindustries.com	Dublin	OH	43017	614-526-7000	
Healy Systems Inc 3760 Marsh Rd *Web:* www.franklinfueling.com	Madison	WI	53718	608-838-8786	
Heat Transfer Products Group LLC 201 Thomas French Dr *Web:* www.htpgusa.com	Scottsboro	AL	35769	256-259-7400	
HelioPower Inc 25767 Jefferson Ave *Web:* www.heliopower.com	Murrieta	CA	92562	951-677-7755	
Herrman & Goetz Inc 225 S Lafayette Blvd	South Bend	IN	46601	574-282-2596	
High Tech Fire Protection Company Inc 84 Hackett Mills Rd	Poland	ME	04274	207-998-2551	
Hospitality Investments LP 16114 E Indiana Ave Ste 200 *Web:* www.hospitalityassociates.com	Spokane Valley	WA	99216	509-928-3736	

Company	City	State	Zip	Phone	Fax
Housh-the Home Energy Experts 18 South Main St *TF:* 866-611-5752 ■ *Web:* www.houshhomeenergy.com	Monroe	OH	45050	513-793-6374	
HPI LLC 15503 W Hardy Rd *Web:* www.hpi-llc.com	Houston	TX	77060	713-457-7500	
Hussung Mechanical Contractors 6913 Enterprise Dr *TF:* 800-446-2738 ■ *Web:* www.hussung.com	Louisville	KY	40214	502-375-3500	
Illingworth Engineering Co 6855 Phillips Pkwy Dr S *Web:* boiler.publishpath.com	Jacksonville	FL	32256	904-262-4700	
IMA LIFE North America Inc 2175 Military Rd *Web:* www.ima.it	Tonawanda	NY	14150	716-695-6354	
Imperial Manufacturing Group Inc 40 Industrial Park St *TF:* 800-561-3100 ■ *Web:* www.imperialgroup.ca	Richibucto	NB	E4W4A4	506-523-9117	
Imperial Mechanical Inc 30685 Solon Industrial Pkwy *Web:* imperialhvac.com	Solon	OH	44139	440-498-1788	
Industrial Ventilation Inc W6395 Speciality Dr *Web:* www.ivinc.com	Greenville	WI	54942	920-757-6001	
Infinity Contractors International Ltd 2563 E Loop 820 N *Web:* www.infinitycontractors.com	Fort Worth	TX	76118	817-838-8700	
Ingenuity Ieq 3600 Centennial Dr *TF:* 800-669-9726 ■ *Web:* www.ingenuityieq.com	Midland	MI	48642	989-496-2233	
IO Environmental & Infrastructure Inc 2840 Adams Ave Ste 301 *Web:* ioenvironmental.com	San Diego	CA	92116	619-280-3278	
Iron City Pipe & Supply 330 E Broadway St *TF:* 877-286-7447 ■ *Web:* ironcitypipe.com	Jackson	OH	45640	740-286-8080	
J C Wilkins Plumbing Company Inc 840 Massengill Pond Rd	Angier	NC	27501	919-639-6201	
J Lorber Company Inc 2659 Bristol Pk *Web:* www.jlorber.com	Bensalem	PA	19020	215-638-2300	
James Lane Air Conditioning Company Inc 5024 Old Jacksboro Hwy *TF:* 800-460-2204 ■ *Web:* www.jameslane.com	Wichita Falls	TX	76302	940-766-0244	
Jem Group LLC 509 N Second St *Web:* www.jemgroup.net	Harrisburg	PA	17101	717-238-7709	
Jestar Plumbing & Heating 23130 Ridge Rd	Germantown	MD	20876	301-353-1841	
Jet Industries Inc 1935 Silverton Rd NE PO Box 7362 *TF:* 800-659-0620 ■ *Web:* jet.industries	Salem	OR	97303	503-363-2334	
Johnson & Jordan Inc 18 Mussey Rd *Web:* johnsonandjordan.net	Scarborough	ME	04074	207-883-8345	
Johnson March Systems Inc 220 Railroad Dr *Web:* www.johnsonmarch.com	Ivyland	PA	18974	215-364-2500	
Jones Stephens Corp 3249 Moody Pkwy *Web:* www.jonesstephens.com	Moody	AL	35004	205-640-7200	
K & s Air Conditioning Inc 143 E Meats Ave *Web:* www.kandsair.com	Orange	CA	92865	714-685-0077	
K Bell Plumbing & Heating Inc 3476 West 4600 South *Web:* kbellplumbingandfire.com	West Haven	UT	84401	801-731-6886	
Kansas Building Systems Inc 1701 SW 41st St *Web:* kbsci.com	Topeka	KS	66609	785-266-4222	
Kazal Fire Protection Inc 3499 E 34th St *Web:* kazalfire.com	Tucson	AZ	85713	520-323-1518	
Kbaer Design Center 1020 Michigan Ave	Sheboygan	WI	53081	920-452-9666	
Kiewit Energy Co 10740 N Gessner Rd Ste 400 *Web:* kiewit.com	Houston	TX	77064	281-517-8900	
Kinetics Mechanical Service Inc 6691 Brisa St *TF:* 866-567-7378 ■ *Web:* www.kms-inc.com	Livermore	CA	94550	925-245-6200	
KITCO Fiber Optics Inc 5269 Cleveland St *TF:* 866-643-5220 ■ *Web:* www.kitcofo.com	Virginia Beach	VA	23462	757-518-8100	
Kliemann Bros Heating & Air Conditioning Inc 4703 116th St E *Web:* kliemannbros.com	Tacoma	WA	98446	253-537-0655	
Kohler Canada Company Hytec Plumbing Products Div 4150 Spallumcheen Dr *TF:* 800-871-8311 ■ *Web:* www.hytec.ca	Armstrong	BC	V0E1B6	250-546-3067	546-3170
Konarka Technologies Inc 116 John St Third Fl Ste 12	Lowell	MA	01852	978-569-1400	
Krystal Klear Water Systems 10502 W 150th St *Web:* krystalklearh2o.com	Overland Park	KS	66221	913-897-6571	
Kuck Mechanical Contractors Inc 395 W 67th St PO Box 388 *Web:* www.kuckmechanical.com	Loveland	CO	80538	970-461-3553	
Kysor Warren Corp 5201 Transport Blvd *Web:* www.kysorwarren.com	Columbus	GA	31907	706-568-1514	
L B Plastics Inc PO Box 907 *TF:* 800-752-7739 ■ *Web:* www.lbplastics.com	Mooresville	NC	28115	704-663-1543	664-2989
Lawrence Green Fire Protection 18323 Weaver St	Detroit	MI	48228	313-835-5800	
Leduc & Dexter Inc 2833A Dowd Dr PO Box 11157 *Web:* www.leducanddexterplumbing.com	Santa Rosa	CA	95406	707-575-1500	
Lescure Company Inc 3667 Mt Diablo Blvd PO Box 968 *Web:* www.lescurecompany.com	Lafayette	CA	94549	925-283-2528	
Little Caesars Pizza 2524 Third Line *Web:* littlecaesars.ca	Oakville	ON	L6M4Y7	905-825-0199	
Lochard Inc 903 Wapakoneta Ave *Web:* www.lochard-inc.com	Sidney	OH	45365	937-492-8811	
Louden Tunneling Company Inc 103 Shaw Rd	Sterling	VA	20166	703-450-5656	
Love Heating & Air Conditioning Inc 4115 E 10th St *Web:* love-hvac.com	Indianapolis	IN	46201	317-353-2141	
Luminalt Energy Corp 1320 Potrero Ave *Web:* www.luminalt.com	San Francisco	CA	94110	415-641-4000	
Lunseth Plumbing & Heating Co 1710 N Washington St *Web:* www.dakotafire.com	Grand Forks	ND	58203	701-772-6631	
Luppen & Hawley Inc 7400 14th Ave *Web:* www.luppenandhawleyinc.com	Sacramento	CA	95820	916-456-7831	
Lute Plumbing Supply Inc 3920 US Hwy 23 *Web:* www.lutesupply.com	Portsmouth	OH	45662	740-353-7638	
M Davis & Sons Inc 19 Germay Dr *TF:* 800-913-2847 ■ *Web:* www.mdavisinc.com	Wilmington	DE	19804	302-998-3385	
M&M Refrigeration Inc 412 Railroad Ave *Web:* www.mmrefrigeration.com	Federalsburg	MD	21632	410-754-8005	
Maax Corp 160 St Joseph Blvd *TF:* 888-957-7816 ■ *Web:* www.maax.com	Lachine	QC	H8S2L3	877-438-6229	
Maax Spas (Arizona) Inc 25605 S Arizona Ave *Web:* www.colemanspas.com	Chandler	AZ	85248	480-895-0598	
Madison Mechanical Inc 1539 Fannie Dorsey Rd *Web:* www.madisonmechanical.net	Sykesville	MD	21784	410-461-7301	
Maintenx 2202 N Howard Ave **Fax Area Code: 813* ■ *TF:* 855-751-0075 ■ *Web:* maintenx.com	Tampa	FL	33607	855-751-0075	915-5582*
Mallick Plumbing & Heating 8010 Cessna Ave *Web:* www.mallickplumbing.com	Gaithersburg	MD	20879	301-840-5860	
Mark Harris Plumbing Company Inc 1830 Gillespie Way Ste 104 *Web:* mhp-co.com	El Cajon	CA	92020	619-596-9470	
Marquee Fire Protection 710 W Stadium Ln *Web:* www.marqueefire.com	Sacramento	CA	95834	916-641-7997	
Marvin Groves Electric Company Inc 506 Seventh St *Web:* www.marvingroveselectric.com	Wichita Falls	TX	76301	940-767-2711	
Matco-Norca Inc Rt 22 *TF:* 800-431-2082 ■ *Web:* www.matco-norca.com	Brewster	NY	10509	845-278-7570	
Matherly Mechanical Contractors LLC 1520 Ocama Blvd PO Box 30889 *Web:* www.matherlymech.com	Midwest City	OK	73140	405-737-3488	
Matthews Mfg 41 Branch St	Saint Louis	MO	63147	314-231-4900	
Mckenneys Air Conditioning Inc 2323 R St *Web:* mckenneysair.com	Bakersfield	CA	93301	661-327-4037	
McLain Plumbing & Electrical Service Inc 107 Magnolia St *Web:* www.mclaininc.com	Philadelphia	MS	39350	601-656-6333	
Mechanical Design Systems Inc 6302 Aaron Ln *TF:* 877-960-0301 ■ *Web:* www.mds-hvac.com	Clinton	MD	20735	301-877-9600	
Mechanical Services Inc 400 Presumpscot St *Web:* www.mechanicalservices.com	Portland	ME	04103	207-774-1531	
Mechanical Systems of Dayton 4401 Springfield St *TF:* 800-254-9455 ■ *Web:* www.msdinc.net	Dayton	OH	45431	937-254-3235	
Meckley Services Inc 5701 General Washington Dr Ste O *TF:* 877-632-5539 ■ *Web:* www.meckleyservices.com	Alexandria	VA	22312	703-333-2040	
Meier Supply Company Inc 530 Bloomingburg Rd *TF:* 800-418-3216 ■ *Web:* www.meiersupply.com	Middletown	NY	10940	845-733-5666	
Mesa Mechanical Inc 3514 Pinemont Dr *Web:* www.mesamechanical.com	Houston	TX	77018	713-681-5300	681-6675
Metro Hvac Mechanical Contractor Inc 7802 Norris Fwy	Knoxville	TN	37938	865-922-5912	
Metro Mechanical Contractors Inc 1200 SW 24th St	Newcastle	OK	73065	405-387-3930	
MG Mechanical Contracting Inc 1513 Lamb Rd *Web:* www.mgmechanical.com	Woodstock	IL	60098	815-334-9450	
Michels Plumbing & Heating 36352 Priestap St	Richmond	MI	48062	586-727-4636	
Miller Bonded Inc 4538 Mcleod Rd Ne *Web:* millerbonded.com	Albuquerque	NM	87109	505-881-0220	
Modern Controls Inc 7 Bellecor Dr *Web:* www.moderncontrols.com	New Castle	DE	19720	302-325-6800	
Mohr Power Solar Inc 1452 Pomona Rd *TF:* 800-637-6527 ■ *Web:* www.mohrpower.com	Corona	CA	92882	951-736-2000	
Monona Plumbing & Fire Protection Inc 3126 Watford Way *Web:* www.mononapfp.com	Madison	WI	53713	608-273-4556	
Monroe Energy Complex 208 Cherry Hill Rd	Monroe	GA	30656	770-207-5456	
Moss & Assoc 3019 SW 27th Ave Ste 202 *Web:* mosscm.com	Ocala	FL	34471	352-291-2940	
Mtech Mechanical Technologies Group Inc 12300 Pecos St *Web:* www.mtechg.com	Westminster	CO	80234	303-650-4000	
Nading Mechanical Inc 11673 N County Rd 775 E *Web:* nadingmechanicalinc.com	Hope	IN	47246	812-546-6111	
Nailor Industries Inc 98 Toryork Rd *Web:* www.map-hvac.com	Toronto	ON	M9L1X6	416-744-3300	744-3360
National Meter & Automation 7220 S Fraser St *TF:* 877-212-8340 ■ *Web:* www.nmaai.com	Centennial	CO	80112	303-339-9100	649-1017
National Office Systems Inc 7621 Rickenbacker Dr Ste 400 *Web:* nosinc.com	Gaithersburg	MD	20879	301-840-6264	
Nelson's Plumbing & Electric Inc 25269 Us Hwy 12 *Web:* nelsonsplumbingandelectric.com	Tomah	WI	54660	608-372-5469	
New Generation Mechanical 1133 Empire Central Dr *Web:* www.newgenm.com	Dallas	TX	75247	972-830-9900	830-9993
NextEnergy Inc 35 Earl Martin Dr **Fax Area Code: 877*	Elmira	ON	N3B3L4	519-669-1015	684-3112*
North South Supply Inc 686 Third Pl *Web:* www.northsouth.net	Vero Beach	FL	32962	772-569-3810	
Noveo Technologies Inc 9655 A Ignace St *TF:* 877-314-2044 ■ *Web:* www.noveo.ca	Brossard	QC	J4Y2P3	450-444-2044	

Company / Address	City	State	Zip	Phone	Fax
Nupla Corp 11912 Sheldon St	Sun Valley	CA	91352	818-768-6800	546-8752*
**Fax Area Code: 800* ■ *TF:* 800-872-7661 ■ *Web:* www.nuplacorp.com					
O&M Industries Inc 5901 Ericson Way	Arcata	CA	95521	707-822-8800	
Web: www.omindustries.com					
Ontario Refrigeration Service 635 S Mountain Ave	Ontario	CA	91762	909-984-2771	
Web: www.ontariorefrigeration.com					
Oswald Company Inc 308 E Eigth St Ste 500	Cincinnati	OH	45202	513-793-8080	
Web: www.oswaldco.com					
OZZ Corp 20 Floral Pkwy	Concord	ON	L4K4R1	905-669-6223	
Web: www.ozzcorp.com					
Padgett Business Services LLC 140 Mtn Brook Dr	Canton	GA	30115	770-345-6100	
Web: www.padgettservices.com					
Palmer-christiansen Company Inc 2510 South West Temple	Salt Lake City	UT	84115	801-466-1679	
Web: palmerchris.com					
Parris & Assoc Inc 480 Turnpike St Ste 1	South Easton	MA	02375	508-230-0255	
Web: www.parrisandassociates.com					
Patriot Fire Protection Inc 2707 70th Ave E	Fife	WA	98424	253-926-2290	
Web: www.patriotfire.com					
Pedal Valves Inc 13625 River Rd	Luling	LA	70070	985-785-9997	
TF: 800-431-3668 ■ *Web:* pedalvalve.com					
Perfection Group Inc 2649 Commerce Blvd	Cincinnati	OH	45241	513-772-7545	
Web: perfectiongroup.com					
Performance Pulsation Control Inc 3309 Essex Dr Ste 200	Richardson	TX	75082	972-699-8600	
Web: www.pulsationcontrol.com					
Performance Water Products Inc 6902 Aragon Cir	Buena Park	CA	90620	714-736-0137	
Web: www.pwqa.org					
Phybridge Inc 3495 Laird Rd Ste 12	Mississauga	ON	L5L5S5	905-901-3633	
TF: 888-901-3633 ■ *Web:* www.phybridge.com					
Pilot Contracting Corp 1452 Donaldson Hwy	Erlanger	KY	41018	859-525-8585	
Web: www.pilotbuilds.com					
Plumbing Concepts Inc 2445 Railroad St	Corona	CA	92880	951-520-8590	
Web: www.plumbingconcepts.com					
Pmc Mechanical Contractors Inc 15 S Ridge Ave	Ambler	PA	19002	215-628-3806	
Web: mcaepa.org					
PolyJohn Enterprises Corp 2500 Gaspar Ave	Whiting	IN	46394	219-659-1152	
Web: www.polyjohn.com					
Prier Products Inc 4515 E 139th St	Grandview	MO	64030	816-763-4100	
TF: 800-362-1463 ■ *Web:* www.prier.com					
Progressive Plumbing Inc 1064 W Hwy 50	Clermont	FL	34711	352-394-7171	
Web: progressiveplumbing.com					
PSF Mechanical Inc 9322 14th Ave S	Seattle	WA	98108	206-764-9663	
Web: www.psfmechanical.com					
Pumping Solutions Inc 1906 S Quaker Ridge Pl	Ontario	CA	91761	708-272-1800	
Web: www.pump.ws					
Pyron Solar Inc 1216 Liberty Way Ste A	Vista	CA	92081	760-599-5100	
Web: www.pyronsolar.com					
Quality Sprinkler Company Inc 10301 Old Concord Rd	Charlotte	NC	28213	704-549-8220	
Web: www.qualitysprinkler.com					
R J Lanthier Company Inc 485 Corporate Dr	Escondido	CA	92029	760-738-9798	
Web: www.rjlincco.com					
Rabe Environmental Systems Inc 2300 W 23 St	Erie	PA	16506	814-456-5374	
Web: www.rabehvac.com					
RASIRC Inc 7815 Silverton Ave	San Diego	CA	92126	858-259-1220	
Web: www.rasirc.com					
RCR Plumbing & Mechanical Inc 12620 Magnolia Ave	Riverside	CA	92503	951-371-5000	
Web: www.ampam.com					
Regency Fire Protection Inc 7651 Densmore Ave	Van Nuys	CA	91406	818-982-0126	
Web: www.regencyfire.com					
Reliance Heating & Air Conditioning Inc 1694 Hwy 138 Ne	Conyers	GA	30013	770-483-3850	
Web: www.reliance-hvac.com					
Remtec International 1100 Haskins Rd	Bowling Green	OH	43402	419-867-8990	
Web: www.remtec.net					
Resin Systems Corp 62 Rt 101a	Amherst	NH	03031	603-673-1234	673-4512
Web: www.resinsystems.com					
Rex Pipe & Supply Co 10311 Berea Rd	Cleveland	OH	44102	216-651-1900	
Web: www.rexpipe.com					
RF Macdonald Co 25920 Eden Landing Rd	Hayward	CA	94545	510-784-0110	
Web: www.rfmacdonald.com					
Richter & Ratner Contracting Corp 5505 Flushing Ave	Maspeth	NY	11378	718-497-1600	
Web: www.richterratner.com					
Rim Country Mechanical Inc 261 N Eighth St	Show Low	AZ	85901	928-537-1803	
Web: rimcountrymechanical.com					
RoboVent Products Group Inc 37900 Mound Rd	Sterling Heights	MI	48310	586-698-1800	
Web: www.robovent.com					
Rock City Mechanical Company LLC 2715 Grandview Ave	Nashville	TN	37211	615-251-3045	
Web: www.rcm-nashville.com					
Rohde Bros Inc W5745 Woodchuck Ln	Plymouth	WI	53073	920-893-5905	
Web: rohdebros.com					
Rolac Contracting Inc 1800 Valley St	Minot	ND	58701	701-839-6525	
Web: www.rolac-nd.com					
Rose Leonard & Sons Inc 212 Decatur St	Doylestown	PA	18901	215-345-9263	
Rowland Constructors 14811 N Kierland Blvd Ste 800	Scottsdale	AZ	85254	480-477-8300	
Web: www.rowlandconstructioncompany.com					
RS Harritan & Company Inc 3280 Formex Rd	Richmond	VA	23224	804-275-7821	
Web: www.rsharritan.com					
Ryan FireProtection Inc 9740 E 148th St	Noblesville	IN	46060	317-770-7100	
Web: www.indianasubcontractors.org					
S R C Refrigeration 6615 19 Mile Rd	Sterling Heights	MI	48314	586-254-0610	
TF: 800-521-0398 ■ *Web:* www.srcrefrigeration.com					
Salof Refrigeration Company Inc 1150 Schwab Rd	New Braunfels	TX	78132	830-625-1613	
Samuel t Wood Co 2704 Cedar Dr	Riva	MD	21140	410-798-7440	
Schuylerville Central School District 14-18 Spring St	Schuylerville	NY	12871	518-695-3255	
Web: www.schuylervilleschools.org					
SCI Infrastructure LLC 2825 S 154th St	SeaTac	WA	98188	206-242-0633	
Web: www.sciinfrastructure.com					
Service Roundtable 131 W Main St	Lewisville	TX	75057	817-416-0978	
Web: www.serviceroundtable.com					
Shank Constructors Inc 3501 85Th Ave N	Brooklyn Park	MN	55443	763-424-8300	
Web: www.shankconstructors.com					
Shoffner Mechanical Industrial & Service Company Inc 3600 Papermill Dr	Knoxville	TN	37909	865-523-1129	
Web: skmes.com					
Solar Electric Systems 742 Hampshire Rd Ste A	Westlake Village	CA	91361	805-497-9808	
Web: www.solarelectricalsystems.com					
Solar Light Co Inc 100 E Glenside Ave	Glenside	PA	19038	215-517-8700	517-8747
Web: www.solarlight.com					
Solar Store LLC, The 2833 N Country Club Rd	Tucson	AZ	85716	520-322-5180	
TF: 877-264-6374 ■ *Web:* www.solarstore.com					
Spangler & Boyer Mechanical 5175 Commerce Dr	York	PA	17408	717-792-8854	
Web: www.spanglerboyer.com					
SSW Mechanical Inc Air Cond 670 S Oleander Rd	Palm Springs	CA	92264	760-325-6007	
Web: www.sswmechanical.com					
Standard Heating & Air Conditioning 1082 Payne Ave	Saint Paul	MN	55130	651-772-2449	
Web: www.standardheating.com					
Star Services 4663 Halls Mill Rd	Mobile	AL	36693	251-661-4050	
TF: 800-661-9050 ■ *Web:* www.star-service.com					
State Supply Co 597 Seventh St E	Saint Paul	MN	55130	651-774-5985	
TF: 877-775-7705 ■ *Web:* www.statesupply.com					
Stillwell Hansen Inc 3 Fernwood Ave	Edison	NJ	08837	732-225-7474	
Web: www.stillwell-hansen.com					
Stouffer Mechanical Contractor LLC 2185 Carbaugh Ave	Chambersburg	PA	17201	717-262-0078	
Web: stouffermechanical.com					
Stutman Contracting Inc 22 Sutton Ave	Oxford	MA	01540	508-987-9472	
Web: stutmancontracting.com					
Summitt Energy 4370 Dominion St	Burnaby	BC	V5G4L7	604-451-4466	
Sunforce Products Inc 9015 Ch Avon	Montreal-Ouest	QC	H4X2G8	514-989-2100	
Web: sunforceproducts.com					
Sunland Fire Protection Inc 1218 Elon Pl	High Point	NC	27263	336-886-7027	
Web: www.sunlandfire.com					
Sunstore Solar Energy Solutions 3090 S Hwy 14	Greer	SC	29650	864-297-6776	
Web: www.sunstoresolar.com					
Superior Alarms 600 Ash Ave	Mcallen	TX	78501	956-682-6005	
Web: www.superioralarms.com					
Superior Group Inc, The 8861 Elim St	Anchorage	AK	99507	907-349-6572	
Web: www.superiorpnh.com					
Suttles Plumbing & Mechanical Corp 21541 Nordhoff St Ste C	Chatsworth	CA	91311	818-718-9779	
Web: www.suttlesplumbing.com					
Syntrol Plumbing Heating Adn Air Inc 2120 March Rd	Roseville	CA	95747	916-772-5813	
Web: syntrol.net					
Tekmar Control Systems Ltd 5100 Silver Star Rd	Vernon	BC	V1B3K4	250-545-7749	545-0650
Web: www.tekmarcontrols.com					
Tezel & Cotter Air Conditioning Co 2730 Castroville Rd	San Antonio	TX	78237	210-734-5156	
Web: www.tezelandcotter.com					
Therma-Stor LLC 4201 Lien Rd	Madison	WI	53704	608-237-8400	
Web: www.thermastor.com					
Thermal Services Inc 13330 I St	Omaha	NE	68137	402-397-8100	
Web: www.thermalservices.com					
Thetford Corp 7101 Jackson Ave PO Box 1285	Ann Arbor	MI	48106	734-769-6000	769-2023
TF: 800-521-3032 ■ *Web:* www.thetford.com					
Thetford Corp Recreational Vehicle Group 2901 E Bristol St Ste B	Elkhart	IN	46514	574-266-7980	266-7984
TF: 800-831-1076 ■ *Web:* www.rvbusiness.com					
Thomas Partitions & Specialties Inc 4031 Verdugo Rd	Los Angeles	CA	90065	323-256-8666	
Thompson Industrial Services LLC 104 N Main	Sumter	SC	29150	803-773-8005	
TF: 800-849-8040 ■ *Web:* www.thompsonindustrialservices.com					
Tidewater Heating & Air Conditioning 150 Southern Blvd	Wilmington	NC	28401	910-343-1234	
Web: tidewaterac.com					
Tolin Mechanical Systems Co 12005 E 45th Ave	Denver	CO	80239	303-455-2825	
Web: www.tolin.com					
Total Energy Control Systems Inc 47-25 34th St Ste 4	Long Island	NY	11101	718-247-2100	
Web: tecsystemsnyc.com					
Total Maintenance Solutions 3540 Rutherford Rd	Taylors	SC	29687	864-268-2891	
Web: www.tmssouth.com					
Total Plumbing Inc 12300 Pecos St	Westminster	CO	80234	303-393-7271	
Web: www.totalplbg.com					
Tri-state Fabricators Inc 1146 Ferris Rd	Amelia	OH	45102	513-752-5005	
TF: 888-523-1488 ■ *Web:* www.tristatefabricators.com					
Tri-state Home Services 82A Wormans Mill Ct	Frederick	MD	21701	301-624-5970	
Web: tristatehomeservices.com					
Trilogy Plumbing Inc 184 E Liberty Ave	Anaheim	CA	92801	714-888-8575	
Web: www.cadlot.com					
Tru Flow Plumbing & Mechanical Inc 27893 Lenox Ave	Madison Heights	MI	48071	248-398-3560	
Tudi Mechanical Systems of Tampa Inc 343 Munson Ave	Mc Kees Rocks	PA	15136	412-771-4100	
TF: 877-367-8834 ■ *Web:* www.tudi.com					

Phone Fax

Tustin Mechanical Services Lehigh Valley LLC
2555 Industry Ln ... Norristown PA 19403 610-539-8200
Web: www.thetustingroup.com

TWC Services Inc 2601 Bell Ave ... Des Moines IA 50321 515-284-1911
Web: www.twcservices.com

Tweet-Garot Mechanical Inc 2545 Larsen Rd ... Green Bay WI 54307 920-498-0400
Web: www.tweetgarot.com

Universal Air Conditioner Inc
1441 Heritage Pkwy ... Mansfield TX 76063 817-740-3900
Web: www.uacparts.com

Upchurch Plumbing Inc 2606 Baldwin Rd ... Greenwood MS 38930 662-453-6860
Web: www.upchurchplumbing.com

Velocity Futures LLC
5373 W Alabama St Ste 600 ... Houston TX 77056 713-490-7600
Web: www.velocityfutures.com

Ventrol Air Handling Systems Inc
9100 Rue Du Parcours ... Montreal QC H1J2Z1 514-354-7776
Web: www.ventrol.com

Venture Mechanical Inc 2222 Century Cir ... Irving TX 75062 972-871-1300 871-1301
Web: www.venturemech.com

Verigent LLC
149 Plantation Ridge Dr Ste 100 ... Mooresville NC 28117 704-658-3271
TF: 877-637-6422 ■ *Web:* www.verigent.com

Victory Energy Operations LLC
10701 E 126th St N ... Collinsville OK 74021 918-274-0023
Web: www.victoryenergyinc.com

Victory Heating & Air Conditioning Company Inc
115 Mendon St ... Bellingham MA 02019 508-966-9858
Web: www.victoryhvac.com

Vinotemp International Corp
16782 Von Karman Ave Ste 15 ... Irvine CA 92606 310-886-3332
Web: www.vinotemp.com

W O Blackstone & Company Inc 1841 Shop Rd ... Columbia SC 29202 803-252-8222
Web: www.woblackstone.com

Weldon Mechanical Corp 3428 W Pioneer Pkwy ... Arlington TX 76013 817-460-1111 460-3111
Web: www.weldon-contractors.com

Westbrook Service Corp
1411 S Orange Blossom Trl ... Orlando FL 32805 407-841-3310
Web: www.westbrookfl.com

William Gotelli Plumbing Inc
21 Lovell Ave ... San Rafael CA 94901 415-457-1145
Web: www.gotelliplumbing.com

Winger Contracting Co 918 Hayne St ... Ottumwa IA 52501 641-682-3407
Web: www.wingermechanical.com

Wisco Supply Inc 815 S Saint Vrain St ... El Paso TX 79901 915-544-8294 533-1804
TF: 800-947-2689 ■ *Web:* www.wiscosupply.com

Worly Plumbing Supply Inc 54 E Harrison St ... Delaware OH 43015 740-363-1151
TF: 800-365-1175 ■ *Web:* worly.com

WW Gay Fire & Integrated Systems Inc
522 Stockton St ... Jacksonville FL 32204 904-387-7973
Web: www.wwgfp.com

York Mahoning Mechanical Contrs Inc
724 Canfield Rd ... Youngstown OH 44511 330-788-7011
Web: yorkmahoning.com

Zampell Cos 9 Stanley Tucker Dr ... Newburyport MA 01950 978-465-0055
TF: 877-926-7355 ■ *Web:* www.zampell.com

Zehnder America Inc
6 Merrill Industrial Dr Ste 7 ... Hampton NH 03842 603-601-8544
TF: 888-778-6701 ■ *Web:* www.zehnderamerica.com

Zone Mechanical Inc 12539 Holiday Dr Ste A ... Alsip IL 60803 708-388-1370
Web: www.zonemechanical.com

611 PLUMBING FIXTURES & FITTINGS - VITREOUS CHINA & EARTHENWARE

Phone Fax

American Standard Cos Inc Bath & Kitchen Products Div
1 Centennial Ave PO Box 6820 ... Piscataway NJ 08855 800-442-1902
TF: 800-442-1902 ■ *Web:* www.americanstandard-us.com

Briggs Plumbing Products 300 Eagle Rd ... Goose Creek SC 29445 800-888-4458 627-4449
TF: 800-888-4458 ■ *Web:* www.briggsplumbing.com

Eljer Inc 1 Centennial Ave ... Piscataway NJ 08855 800-442-1902
TF: 800-442-1902 ■ *Web:* www.eljer.com

Gerber Plumbing Fixtures LLC
2500 International Pkwy ... Woodridge IL 60517 888-648-6466 636-2021*
**Fax Area Code:* 514 ■ *TF:* 888-648-6466 ■ *Web:* www.gerberonline.com

Kohler Plumbing North America 444 Highland Dr ... Kohler WI 53044 920-457-4441 459-1826*
**Fax:* Sales ■ *TF:* 800-456-4537 ■ *Web:* www.us.kohler.com

Mansfield Plumbing Products Inc
150 E First St ... Perrysville OH 44864 419-938-5211 938-6234
TF: 877-850-3060 ■ *Web:* www.mansfieldplumbing.com

Microphor Inc 452 E Hill Rd ... Willits CA 95490 707-459-5563 459-6617
TF Orders: 800-358-8280 ■ *Web:* www.wabtec.com/business-units/microphor

Norman Supply Co 825 SW Fifth St ... Oklahoma City OK 73109 405-235-9511
Web: www.morsco.com

Peerless Pottery Inc 319 S Fifth St ... Rockport IN 47635 800-457-5785 649-6429*
**Fax Area Code:* 812 ■ *TF:* 866-457-5785 ■ *Web:* www.peerlesspottery.com

Sterling Plumbing 444 Highland Dr ... Kohler WI 53044 920-457-4441
TF Cust Svc: 888-783-7546 ■ *Web:* www.sterlingplumbing.com

Sunrise Specialty Co 930 98th Ave ... Oakland CA 94603 510-729-7277 729-7270
TF: 800-444-4280 ■ *Web:* www.sunrisespecialty.com

Toto USA Inc 1155 Southern Rd ... Morrow GA 30260 770-282-8686 282-8701*
**Fax:* Cust Svc ■ *TF:* 888-295-8134 ■ *Web:* www.totousa.com

612 PLUMBING, HEATING, AIR CONDITIONING EQUIPMENT & SUPPLIES - WHOL

See Also Refrigeration Equipment - Whol p. 3058

Phone Fax

A & B Pipe & Supply Inc 6500 Nw 37th Ave ... Miami FL 33147 305-691-5000

Phone Fax

Aaron & Company Inc PO Box 8310 ... Piscataway NJ 08855 732-752-8200
TF: 800-734-4822 ■ *Web:* www.aaronco.com

AB Young Cos Inc 15305 Stony Creek Way ... Noblesville IN 46060 317-565-5000
TF: 800-886-7001 ■ *Web:* www.abyoung.com

ACR Group Inc 3200 Wilcrest Dr Ste 440 ... Houston TX 77042 713-780-8532 780-4067
Web: www.acrgroup.com

Active Plumbing Supply Co
216 Richmond St ... Painesville OH 44077 440-352-4411 352-0096
Web: www.activeplumbing.com

ADCO Companies LTD 3657 Pine Ln ... Bessemer AL 35022 205-428-2326
Web: www.adcoboiler.com

Advanced Modern Technologies Corp
6409 Independence Ave ... Woodland Hills CA 91367 818-883-2682
Web: www.amtcorporation.com

Advanced Solar Products Inc
270 S Main St Ste 203 ... Flemington NJ 08822 908-751-5818
Web: www.advancedsolarproducts.com

Agile Sourcing Partners Inc 2385 Railroad St ... Corona CA 92880 951-279-4154
Web: www.agilesp.com

Air Monitor Corp 1050 Hopper Ave ... Santa Rosa CA 95403 707-544-2706 526-9970
TF: 800-247-3569 ■ *Web:* www.airmonitor.com

Air Purchases Inc 24 Blanchard Rd ... Burlington MA 01803 781-273-2050
Web: www.airpurchases.com

Alltek Energy Systems 58 Hudson River Rd ... Waterford NY 12188 518-238-2600
Web: www.alltekenergy.com

Altmas Products 1201 Francisco St ... Torrance CA 90502 310-559-4093
TF: 800-678-6463 ■ *Web:* www.altmansproducts.com

American Backflow Specialties
3940 Home Ave ... San Diego CA 92105 619-527-2525
TF: 800-662-5356 ■ *Web:* www.americanbackflow.com

American Faucet & Coating Corp
3280 Corporate Vw ... Vista CA 92081 760-598-5895
TF: 800-621-8383 ■ *Web:* www.sigmafaucet.com

American Granby Inc 7652 Morgan Rd ... Liverpool NY 13090 315-451-1100 451-1876*
**Fax:* Acctg ■ *TF:* 800-776-2266 ■ *Web:* www.americangranby.com

American Pipe & Supply Company Inc
4100 Eastlake Blvd ... Birmingham AL 35217 205-252-9460
Web: www.americanpipe-mt.com

Anderson Tube Company Inc
1400 Fairgrounds Rd ... Hatfield PA 19440 215-855-0118
TF: 800-523-2258 ■ *Web:* www.atube.com

Applied Membranes Inc 2325 Cousteau Ct ... Vista CA 92081 760-727-3711 727-4427
TF: 800-321-9321 ■ *Web:* www.appliedmembranes.com

Applied Thermal Systems
8401 73rd Ave N Ste 74 ... Brooklyn Park MN 55428 763-535-5545
TF: 800-479-4783 ■ *Web:* www.apptherm.com

Arctic Combustion Ltd
2283 Argentia Rd Unit 25 ... Mississauga ON L5N5Z2 905-858-4604
Web: www.arctic-combustion.com

Arizona Partsmaster Inc
7125 W Sherman St PO Box 23169 ... Phoenix AZ 85043 602-233-3580 233-3607
TF: 888-924-7278 ■ *Web:* www.azpartsmaster.com

Arizona Wholesale Supply Co
2020 E University Dr ... Phoenix AZ 85034 602-258-7901 258-8335
TF: 866-977-6849 ■ *Web:* www.arizonawholesalesupply.com

Atlas Heating & Vent Company Ltd
340 Roebling Rd ... South San Francisco CA 94080 650-873-7000
Web: www.atlasheat.com

Auburn Supply Co 3850 W 167th St ... Markham IL 60428 708-596-9800 596-0981
Web: www.auburnsupply.com

BA Robinson Company Ltd 619 Berry St ... Winnipeg MB R3H0S2 204-784-0150
TF: 866-903-6275 ■ *Web:* www.barobinson.com

Badger Plug Company Inc
N1045 Technical Dr PO Box 199 ... Greenville WI 54942 920-757-7300
Web: www.badgerplug.com

Baker Distributing Co
14610 Breakers Dr Ste 100 ... Jacksonville FL 32258 800-217-4698
TF: 844-289-0033 ■ *Web:* www.bakerdist.com

Bardon Supplies Ltd
405 College St East PO Box 1023 ... Belleville ON K8N4Z6 613-966-5643
Web: www.bardonsupplies.com

Barnett Inc 801 W Bay St ... Jacksonville FL 32204 904-384-6530
TF: 888-803-4467 ■ *Web:* www.e-barnett.com

Bartle & Gibson Company Ltd 13475 Ft Rd NW ... Edmonton AB T5A1C6 780-472-2850
TF: 800-661-5615 ■ *Web:* www.bartlegibson.com

Barton Supply Inc
1260 Marlkress Rd PO Box 2240 ... Cherry Hill NJ 08034 856-429-6500
Web: bartonsupply.com

Bascom-Turner Instrument 111 Downey St ... Norwood MA 02062 781-769-9660
TF: 800-225-3298 ■ *Web:* www.bascomturner.com

Bay Associates Group Inc 1432 Front Ave ... Lutherville MD 21093 410-825-6616
Web: www.bayassociates.com

Be-Cool Inc 310 Woodside Ave ... Essexville MI 48732 989-895-9699
TF: 800-691-2667 ■ *Web:* www.becool.com

Behler-Young Co 4900 Clyde Pk SW ... Grand Rapids MI 49509 616-531-3400 531-1453
Web: www.behler-young.com

Bender Plumbing Supplies Inc 550 Grand Ave ... New Haven CT 06511 203-787-4288
Web: www.benderplumbing.com

Best Plumbing Specialties 3039 Ventrie Ct ... Myersville MD 21773 800-448-6710
TF: 800-448-6710 ■ *Web:* www.bestplumbingonline.com

Bestwill Corp 439 Wald ... Irvine CA 92618 949-502-5700
Web: www.bestwill.com

Biolonix Inc 4603 Triangle St ... Mcfarland WI 53558 608-838-0300
Web: www.biolonix.com

BJW Berghorst & Sons 11430 James St ... Holland MI 49424 616-772-2114
Web: www.berghorst.com

Blackman Plumbing Supply Company Inc
3480 Sunrise Hwy ... Wantagh NY 11793 516-785-6000
Web: www.blackman.com

Bob J Johnson & Associates Inc
16420 W Hardy Rd Ste 100 ... Houston TX 77060 281-873-5555
Web: www.bjja.com

Brock-McVey Co 1100 Brock-McVey Dr ... Lexington KY 40509 859-255-1412
Web: www.brockmcvey.com

Company	City	State	ZIP	Phone	Fax
Broedell Plumbing Supply Inc 1601 Commerce Ln *TF:* 888-328-2383 ■ *Web:* www.broedell.com	Jupiter	FL	33458	561-743-6663	743-4644
Bruce Supply Corp 8805 18th Ave *Web:* www.brucesupplyplumbing.com	Brooklyn	NY	11214	718-259-4900	256-5082
Buss Mechanical Services Inc 4471 Henry St. *Web:* bussmechanical.com	Boise	ID	83709	208-562-0600	
Butcher Distributors Inc 101 Boyce Rd *TF:* 800-960-0008 ■ *Web:* www.butcherdistributors.com	Broussard	LA	70518	337-837-2088	837-2069
Caroplast Inc PO Box 668405 *TF:* 800-327-5797 ■ *Web:* www.caroplast.com	Charlotte	NC	28266	704-394-4191	
Caylor Industrial Sales Inc PO Box 4659 *Web:* www.caylorindustrial.com	Dalton	GA	30721	706-226-3198	278-4104
Central Arizona Supply 208 S Country Club Dr. *TF:* 800-416-6490 ■ *Web:* www.centralazsupply.com	Mesa	AZ	85210	480-834-5817	
Century Plumbing Inc 901 SouthWest 69th Ave. *Web:* www.centuryplumbing.com	Miami	FL	33144	305-261-4731	
Champions Pipe & Supply Inc 2 NorthPoint Dr Ste 800 *Web:* www.championspipe.com	Houston	TX	77060	713-468-6555	468-7936
City Plumbing & Electric Supply Co 730 EE Butler Pkwy. *TF:* 800-260-2024 ■ *Web:* www.cpesupply.com	Gainesville	GA	30501	770-532-4123	
City Supply Corp 2326 Bell Ave *TF:* 800-400-2377 ■ *Web:* www.citysupplycorp.com	Des Moines	IA	50321	515-288-3211	
Clement Support Services Inc 480 Vandell Way. *Web:* www.clementsupport.com	Campbell	CA	95008	408-227-1171	
Cleveland Plumbing Supply Company Inc 143 E Washington St *TF:* 800-331-1078 ■ *Web:* www.clevelandplumbing.com	Chagrin Falls	OH	44022	440-247-2555	247-2116
Coastal Plumbing Supply Company Inc 480 Bay St *Web:* www.coastalsupplygroup.com.	Staten Island	NY	10304	718-447-2692	
Coburn Supply Company Inc 390 Pk St Ste 100. *TF:* 800-832-8492 ■ *Web:* www.coburns.com	Beaumont	TX	77701	409-838-6363	838-1920
Comfort Products Distributing LLC 13202 I St. *Web:* www.comfortproducts.com	Omaha	NE	68137	402-334-7777	
Connor Co 2800 N E Adams *Web:* www.connorco.com	Peoria	IL	61603	309-688-1068	
Consolidated Supply Co 7337 SW Kable Ln *TF:* 800-929-5810 ■ *Web:* www.consolidatedsupply.com	Tigard	OR	97224	503-620-7050	684-3254
Corr Tech Inc 4545 Homestead Rd *Web:* www.corr-tech.com	Houston	TX	77028	713-674-7887	674-0840
Crawford Supply Co 8150 Lehigh Ave *Web:* www.crawfordsupply.com	Morton Grove	IL	60053	847-967-1414	
Cunningham Supply Inc 674 Oakwood Ave. *Web:* www.cunninghamsupply.com	West Hartford	CT	06110	860-953-2101	
D-S Pipe & Supply Company Inc 1301 Wicomico St Ste 3. *TF:* 800-368-8880 ■ *Web:* www.dspipe.com	Baltimore	MD	21230	410-539-8000	
Dana Kepner Company Inc 700 Alcott St *Web:* www.danakepner.com	Denver	CO	80204	303-623-6161	623-1667
Dawson Co 1681 W Second St. *Web:* www.dawsonco.com	Pomona	CA	91766	626-797-9710	
Delta T Inc 8323 Loch Lomond Dr. *TF:* 800-928-5828 ■ *Web:* www.deltat.com	Pico Rivera	CA	90660	800-928-5828	
Desco Plumbing & Heating Supply Inc 65 Worcester Rd. *TF:* 800-564-5146 ■ *Web:* www.desco.ca	Etobicoke	ON	M9W5N7	416-213-1555	
Desert Pipe & Supply 75200 Merle Dr. *Web:* www.desertpipe.com	Palm Desert	CA	92211	760-340-6322	
Downeast Energy Corp 18 Spring St *Web:* www.downeastenergy.com	Brunswick	ME	04011	207-729-9921	
Duncan Supply Company Inc 910 N Illinois St. *TF:* 800-382-5528 ■ *Web:* www.duncansupply.com	Indianapolis	IN	46204	317-634-1335	264-6689
Duravit USA Inc 2205 Northmont Pkwy Ste 200 *TF:* 888-387-2848 ■ *Web:* www.duravit.com	Duluth	GA	30096	770-931-3575	
Dutton-Lainson Co 451 W Second St. *Web:* www.dutton-lainson.com	Hastings	NE	68901	402-462-4141	
East Coast Metal Distributors, Inc 1313 South Briggs Ave. **Fax Area Code:* 919 ■ *TF:* 844-227-9531 ■ *Web:* www.ecmdi.com	Durham	NC	27703	844-227-9531	598-1404*
Eastern Pennsylvania Supply Co 700 Scott St *TF:* 800-432-8075 ■ *Web:* www.easternpenn.com	Wilkes-Barre	PA	18705	570-823-1181	824-2514
El Mustee & Sons Inc 5431 W 164th St. *Web:* www.mustee.com	Brook Park	OH	44142	216-267-3100	
EMCO Corp 1108 Dundas St. *Web:* www.emcoltd.com	London	ON	N5W3A7	519-453-9600	645-2465
Emerson-Swan Inc 300 Pond St. *TF:* 800-346-9219 ■ *Web:* www.emersonswan.com	Randolph	MA	02368	781-986-2000	986-2028
Engineering & Equipment Company Inc 910 N Washington St *Web:* www.engineeringandequipmentcoalbany.com	Albany	GA	31701	229-435-5601	
EPSCO International & Companies Inc 717 Georgia Ave. *Web:* www.epscointl.com	Deer Park	TX	77536	281-476-8100	
ETNA Supply Company Inc 529 32nd St *Web:* www.etnasupply.com	Grand Rapids	MI	49548	616-241-5414	
Everett J Prescott Inc 32 Prescott St *TF:* 800-357-2447 ■ *Web:* www.ejprescott.com	Gardiner	ME	04345	207-582-1851	582-5637
Ferguson Enterprises Inc 12500 Jefferson Ave. *TF:* 800-721-2590 ■ *Web:* www.ferguson.com	Newport News	VA	23602	757-874-7795	989-2501
First Supply LLC 6800 Gisholt Dr *TF:* 800-236-9795 ■ *Web:* www.1supply.com	Madison	WI	53713	608-222-7799	223-6621
Flynn Burner Corp 425 Fifth Ave. *Web:* www.flynnburner.com	New Rochelle	NY	10801	914-636-1320	
Four Seasons Inc 1801 Waters Ridge Dr *TF:* 888-505-4567 ■ *Web:* www.4s.com	Lewisville	TX	75057	972-316-8100	316-8213

Company	City	State	ZIP	Phone	Fax
Fresno Distributing Company Inc 2055 E McKinley Ave *TF:* 800-655-2542 ■ *Web:* www.fresnod.com	Fresno	CA	93703	559-442-8800	264-3809
Frontier Supply Inc 981 Van Horn Rd *Web:* www.frontierplumbing.com	Fairbanks	AK	99701	907-374-3500	374-3570
Fujikin of America Inc 4677 Old Ironsides Dr *Web:* www.fujikin.com	Santa Clara	CA	95054	408-980-8269	980-0572
Gateway Supply Company Inc 1312 Hamrick St *TF:* 800-922-5312 ■ *Web:* www.gatewaysupply.net	Columbia	SC	29202	803-771-7160	376-5600
General Plumbing Supply Company Inc 1530 San Luis Rd PO Box 4666 *Web:* www.generalplumbingsupply.com	Walnut Creek	CA	94597	925-939-4622	939-1548
Gensco Inc 4402 20th St E *TF:* 877-620-8203 ■ *Web:* www.gensco.com	Tacoma	WA	98424	253-620-8203	926-2073
Goodin Co 2700 N Second St *TF:* 800-328-8433 ■ *Web:* www.goodinco.com	Minneapolis	MN	55411	612-588-7811	588-7820
Granite Group Wholesalers LLC 6 Storrs St. *TF:* 800-258-3690 ■ *Web:* www.thegranitegroup.com	Concord	NH	03301	603-224-1901	224-4125
Great Western Supply Inc 2626 Industrial Dr *Web:* www.gwsupply.com	Ogden	UT	84401	801-621-5412	
Greengate Power Corp 407 - Second St SW *Web:* www.greengatepower.com	Calgary	AB	T2P2Y3	403-514-0556	
Greenscape Pump Services Inc 1425 Whitlock Ln Ste 108 *TF:* 877-401-4774 ■ *Web:* www.greenscapepump.com	Carrollton	TX	75006	972-446-0037	
Groupe Deschenes Inc 3901 Jarry St E Ste 250 *Web:* www.groupedeschenes.com	Montreal	QC	H1Z2G1	514-253-3110	
Gulf Coast Paper Company Inc 3705 Houston Hwy *Web:* www.gulfcoastpaper.com	Victoria	TX	77901	361-576-1237	
GW Berkheimer Company Inc 6000 Southport Rd *Web:* www.gwberkheimer.com	Portage	IN	46368	219-764-5200	764-5203
Habegger Corp 4995 Winton Rd **Fax Area Code:* 513 ■ *Web:* www.habeggercorp.com	Cincinnati	OH	45232	309-793-4328	681-9892*
Hahn Supply Inc 2101 Main St *Web:* www.hahnsupply.com	Lewiston	ID	83501	208-743-1577	
Hajoca Corp 127 Coulter Ave. **Fax Area Code:* 505 ■ *TF:* 888-328-2383 ■ *Web:* www.hajoca.com	Ardmore	PA	19003	610-649-1430	884-2455*
Hajoca Corp Keenan Supply Div 1341 Philadelphia St *Web:* www.hajoca.com	Pomona	CA	91766	909-613-1363	
Harri Plumbing & Heating Inc 809 W 12th St *TF:* 800-478-3190 ■ *Web:* www.harriplumbing.com	Juneau	AK	99801	907-586-3190	
Harry Cooper Supply Company Inc 605 N Sherman Pkwy *TF:* 800-426-6737 ■ *Web:* www.harrycooper.com	Springfield	MO	65802	417-865-8392	873-9146
Heat Transfer Sales of the Carolinas Inc 4101 Beechwood Dr *Web:* www.heattransfersales.com	Greensboro	NC	27410	336-294-3838	
Henry Quentzel Plumbing Supply Co 379 Throop Ave *TF:* 800-889-2294 ■ *Web:* www.quentzel.com	Brooklyn	NY	11221	718-455-6600	
Hercules Industries Inc 1310 W Evans Ave *TF:* 800-356-5350 ■ *Web:* www.herculesindustries.com	Denver	CO	80223	303-937-1000	937-0903
Hinkle Metals & Supply Company Inc 3300 11th Ave N. *Web:* hinklemetals.com	Birmingham	AL	35234	205-326-3300	
Hot Water Products Inc 7254 N Teutonia Ave. *Web:* www.hotwaterproducts.com	Milwaukee	WI	53209	414-434-1371	
Hubbard Pipe & Supply Inc 463 Robeson St *Web:* www.hubbardkitchenandbath.com	Fayetteville	NC	28301	910-484-9015	
Hugh M Cunningham Inc 13755 Benchmark Dr *Web:* hughcunningham.com	Dallas	TX	75234	972-888-3800	
Hughes Supply Inc 600 Ferguson Dr *Web:* www.hughessupply.com	Orlando	FL	32805	407-843-9100	
Hydro-flo Products Inc 3655 N 124th St *TF:* 800-843-3569 ■ *Web:* www.hydro-flo.com	Brookfield	WI	53005	262-781-2810	
I D Booth Inc PO Box 579 *TF:* 888-432-6684 ■ *Web:* www.idbooth.com	Elmira	NY	14902	607-733-9121	733-9111
Ideal Supply Company Inc 2935 S Highland Dr *Web:* www.idealsupplylv.com	Las Vegas	NV	89109	702-731-3445	
ILLCO Inc 535 S River St. *Web:* www.illco.com	Aurora	IL	60506	630-892-7904	892-0318
Indeck Keystone Energy LLC 5340 Fryling Rd Ste 200. *Web:* www.indeck-keystone.com	Erie	PA	16510	814-452-6421	
Independent Pipe & Supply Corp Whitman Rd *Web:* www.indpipe.com	Canton	MA	02021	781-828-8500	
Industrial Pipe & Supply Company Inc 1779 Martin Luther King Junior Blvd *Web:* www.industrialpipega.com	Gainesville	GA	30501	770-536-0517	
Irr Supply Centers Inc 908 Niagara Falls Blvd *Web:* www.irrsupply.com	North Tonawanda	NY	14120	716-692-1600	692-1611
J & B Supply Inc 4915 S Zero St. *Web:* www.jandbsupply.com	Fort Smith	AR	72903	479-649-4915	649-4911
JE Sawyer & Company Inc 64 Glen St *TF:* 800-724-3983 ■ *Web:* www.jesawyer.com	Glens Falls	NY	12801	800-724-3983	
JH Larson Co 10200 51st Ave N. *TF:* 800-292-7970 ■ *Web:* www.jhlarson.com	Plymouth	MN	55442	763-545-1717	545-1144
John M Frey Co Inc 2735 62nd St Ct *TF:* 800-397-3739 ■ *Web:* www.jmfcompany.com	Bettendorf	IA	52722	563-332-9200	332-9880
Johnson Supply Inc 10151 Stella Link Rd *TF:* 800-833-5455 ■ *Web:* www.johnsonsupply.com	Houston	TX	77025	713-830-2499	662-5519
Johnson's Boiler & Control Inc 2440 S Gearhart Ave. *Web:* www.johnsonsboiler.com	Fresno	CA	93725	559-237-7772	
Just Manufacturing Company Inc 9233 King St. *Web:* www.justmfg.com	Franklin Park	IL	60131	847-678-5151	

Company	City	State	ZIP	Phone	Fax
Keeling Co PO Box 15310 *Web:* www.keelingcompany.com	North Little Rock	AR	72231	501-945-4511	
Keidel Supply Co 1150 Tennessee Ave *Web:* www.keidel.com	Cincinnati	OH	45229	513-351-1600	351-9649
Keller Supply Company Inc 3209 17th Ave W *Fax: Acctg ■ *TF:* 800-285-3302 ■ *Web:* www.kellersupply.com	Seattle	WA	98119	206-285-3300	283-8668*
Kelly's Pipe & Supply Co Inc 2124 Industrial Rd *TF:* 888-382-4957 ■ *Web:* www.kellyspipe.com	Las Vegas	NV	89102	888-382-4957	382-4879
Kent Supply Co 50 Jon Barrett Rd *Web:* www.kentsupply.com	Patterson	NY	12563	845-878-6940	
Kleen Air Service Corp 5354 N Northwest Hwy *Web:* www.kleenair.com	Chicago	IL	60630	773-631-0007	
Koch Air LLC 1900 W Lloyd Expy *Web:* www.kochair.com	Evansville	IN	47744	812-962-5200	962-5306
Larsen Supply Company Inc 12055 E Slauson Ave PO Box 4388 *Web:* www.lasco.net	Santa Fe Springs	CA	90670	562-698-0731	
LDK Solar Tech USA Inc 1290 Oakmead Pkwy Ste 306 *Web:* www.ldksolar.com	Sunnyvale	CA	94085	408-245-0858	
Lee Supply Corp 6610 Guion Rd *TF:* 800-873-1103 ■ *Web:* leesupplycorp.com	Indianapolis	IN	46268	317-290-2500	290-2512
Lemna Corporation Inc 2445 Park Ave *Web:* www.lemnatechnologies.com	Minneapolis	MN	55404	612-253-2000	
Longley Supply Company Inc 2018 Oleander Dr *Web:* longleysupplycompany.com	Wilmington	NC	28403	910-762-7793	762-9178
M & A Supply Company Inc 1540 Amherst Rd *Web:* www.masupplycompany.com	Knoxville	TN	37909	865-584-0510	
Mark's Plumbing Parts 3312 Ramona Dr *Web:* www.markspp.com	Fort Worth	TX	76116	817-731-6211	
Martz Supply Co 5330 Pecos St *Web:* www.martzsupply.com	Denver	CO	80221	303-421-6665	
Masters' Supply Inc 4505 Bishop Ln *TF:* 800-388-6353 ■ *Web:* www.masterssupply.net	Louisville	KY	40218	800-388-6353	
May Supply Company Inc 1775 Erickson Ave *TF:* 800-296-9997 ■ *Web:* www.maysupply.com	Harrisonburg	VA	22801	540-433-2611	
McCain Engineering Inc 2002 Mccain Pkwy *Web:* www.mccainengineering.com	Pelham	AL	35124	205-663-0123	
McGuire Manufacturing 60 Grandview Ct *TF:* 800-676-1832 ■ *Web:* www.mcguiremfg.com	Cheshire	CT	06410	203-699-1801	
Mid-Lakes Distributing Inc 1029 W Adams St *TF:* 888-733-2700 ■ *Web:* www.mid-lakes.com	Chicago	IL	60607	312-733-1033	733-1721
Mid-States Supply Co 1716 Guinotte Ave *TF:* 800-825-1410 ■ *Web:* www.midcoonline.com	Kansas City	MO	64120	816-842-4290	842-3630
Minvalco Inc 3340 Gorham Ave *TF:* 800-642-9090 ■ *Web:* minvalco.com	Minneapolis	MN	55426	952-920-0131	
Mirixa Corp 11600 Sunrise Vly Dr Ste 100 *Web:* www.mirixa.com	Reston	VA	20191	703-683-1955	
Moore Supply Co 200 N Loop 336 W *Web:* www.mooresupply.com	Conroe	TX	77301	936-756-4445	441-8468
Morley-Murphy Co 200 S Washington St Ste 305 *TF:* 877-499-3171 ■ *Web:* www.morley-murphycompany.com	Green Bay	WI	54301	920-499-3171	499-9409
Morrison Supply Company Inc 311 E Vickery Blvd *TF:* 800-451-9343 ■ *Web:* www.morsco.com	Fort Worth	TX	76104	817-870-2227	
Morrow Control & Supply Co 810 Marion Motley Ave Ne *TF:* 800-362-9830 ■ *Web:* www.morrowcontrol.com	Canton	OH	44705	330-452-9791	
Mountain States Pipe & Supply Co 111 W Las Vegas St *TF:* 800-777-7173 ■ *Web:* www.msps.com	Colorado Springs	CO	80903	719-634-5555	634-5551
Mountain States Supply Inc 184 West 3300 South *Web:* www.mountainlandsupply.com	Salt Lake City	UT	84115	801-484-8885	
Mountain Supply Co 2101 Mullan Rd *TF:* 800-821-1646 ■ *Web:* www.mountainsupply.com	Missoula	MT	59808	406-543-8255	
Mountainland Supply Co 1505 West 130 South *Web:* www.mtncom.net	Orem	UT	84058	801-224-6050	
Murray Supply Co (MSC) 102 W Third St *Web:* www.murraysupply.com	Winston-Salem	NC	27101	336-765-9480	245-0686
N & S Supply of Fishkill Inc 205 Old Rt 9 *Web:* www.nssupply.com	Fishkill	NY	12524	845-896-6291	
NanOasis Technologies Inc 4677 Meade St Ste 210 *Web:* www.nanoasisinc.com	Richmond	CA	94804	510-215-0186	
New Wave Enviro Products Inc 6595 S Dayton St Ste 1000 *Web:* www.newwaveenviro.com	Englewood	CO	80155	303-221-3232	
New York Replacement Parts Corp 19 School St *TF:* 800-228-4718 ■ *Web:* www.nyrpcorp.com	Yonkers	NY	10701	914-965-0122	
Newton Distributing Company Inc 966 Watertown St *TF:* 877-837-7745 ■ *Web:* newtondistributing.com	Newton	MA	02465	617-969-4002	
Next Generation Energy LLC 75 Waneka Pkwy *Web:* www.ngeus.com	Lafayette	CO	80026	303-665-2000	
Nexus Valve Inc 9982 E 121st St *Web:* www.nexusvalve.com	Fishers	IN	46037	317-257-6050	
Niagara Conservation Corp 45 Horsehill Rd *TF:* 800-831-8383 ■ *Web:* www.niagaraconservation.com	Cedar Knolls	NJ	07927	973-829-0800	
Northeastern Supply Co Inc 8323 Pulaski Hwy *Fax: Sales ■ *Web:* northeastern.com	Baltimore	MD	21237	410-574-0010	574-3315*
Northwest Pipe Fittings Inc 33 S Eigth St W *TF:* 800-937-4737 ■ *Web:* www.northwestpipe.net	Billings	MT	59101	406-252-0142	248-8072
O'Connor Sales Inc 16107 Piuma Ave *Web:* www.oconnorsales.net	Cerritos	CA	90703	562-403-3848	403-3858
Pasco Specialty & Manufacturing Inc 11156 Wright Rd *Web:* www.pascospecialty.com	Lynwood	CA	90262	310-537-7782	
Pbbs Equipment Corp N59W16500 Greenway Cir *Web:* www.pbbs.com	Menomonee Falls	WI	53051	262-252-7575	
Peabody Supply Co Inc PO Box 669 *TF:* 800-445-5816 ■ *Web:* www.peabodysupply.com	Peabody	MA	01960	978-532-2200	532-1463
Pepco Sales of Dallas Inc 11310 Gemini Ln *TF:* 877-737-2699 ■ *Web:* www.pepcosales.com	Dallas	TX	75229	972-823-8700	
Performance Engineering Group Inc 32995 Industrial Rd *Web:* www.performanceengineering.com	Livonia	MI	48150	734-266-5300	
Perry Supply Company Inc 2625 Vassar NE *Web:* www.perrysupply.net	Albuquerque	NM	87107	505-884-6972	
PHD Manufacturing Inc 44018 Columbiana-Waterford Rd *Web:* www.phd-mfg.com	Columbiana	OH	44408	330-482-9256	
Pipeline Supply Inc 620-16th Ave S *Web:* www.pipeline-supply.com	Hopkins	MN	55343	952-935-0445	
Platsky Company Inc 298 Montrose Rd *Web:* www.platsky.com	Westbury	NY	11590	516-333-9292	
Plumb Supply Co 1622 NE 51st Ave *TF:* 800-483-9511 ■ *Web:* www.plumbsupply.com	Des Moines	IA	50313	515-262-9511	262-9790
Plumbers Supply Co 1000 E Main St *TF:* 800-626-5133 ■ *Web:* www.plumbers-supply-co.com	Louisville	KY	40206	502-582-2261	585-5521
Plumbing Distributors Inc 1025 Old Norcross Rd *TF:* 800-262-9231 ■ *Web:* relyonpdi.com	Lawrenceville	GA	30046	770-963-9231	
Plymouth Technology Inc 2925 Waterview Dr *Web:* www.plymouthtechnology.com	Rochester Hills	MI	48309	248-537-0081	
Porter Pipe & Supply Co 303 S Rohlwing Rd *Web:* www.porterpipe.com	Addison	IL	60101	630-543-8145	543-6830
PrairieCoast Equipment 15102 101 St *Web:* www.prairiecoastequipment.com	Grande Prairie	AB	T8V0P7	780-532-8402	
Prima Supply Inc 4603 Poplar Level Rd Ste 1 *TF:* 888-810-5043 ■ *Web:* primasupply.com	Louisville	KY	40213	502-966-4578	
Proctor Sales Inc 20715 50th Ave W *Web:* www.proctorsales.com	Lynnwood	WA	98036	425-774-1441	
Ramapo Wholesalers Inc 54B Kennedy Dr *Web:* ramapowholesalers.com	Spring Valley	NY	10977	845-425-8400	
Rampart Supply Inc 1801 N Union Blvd *TF:* 800-748-1837 ■ *Web:* www.rampartsupply.com	Colorado Springs	CO	80909	719-482-7333	
Reeves-Wiedeman Co Inc 14861 W 100th St *TF:* 800-365-0024 ■ *Web:* rwco.com	Lenexa	KS	66215	913-492-7100	492-6962
Refrigeration Sales Corp 9450 Allen Dr Ste A *TF:* 866-894-8200 ■ *Web:* www.refrigerationsales.net	Valley View	OH	44125	216-881-7800	
Republic Plumbing Supply Company Inc 890 Providence Hwy *Fax Area Code: 781 ■ *TF:* 800-696-3900 ■ *Web:* www.republicsupplyco.com	Norwood	MA	02062	800-696-3900	769-7842*
Roberts-Hamilton 6601 Pkwy Cir Ste A *TF:* 800-888-2222 ■ *Web:* www.robertshamilton.com	Brooklyn Center	MN	55430	763-315-0100	315-0199
Robertson Heating Supply Co 2155 W Main St *TF:* 800-433-9532 ■ *Web:* www.robertsonheatingsupply.com	Alliance	OH	44601	330-821-9180	821-8251
Robertson Supply Inc PO Box 1366 *Web:* www.robertsonsupply.com	Nampa	ID	83653	208-466-8907	466-8900
ROHL LLC 3 Parker *Web:* www.rohlhome.com	Irvine	CA	92618	714-557-1933	
Ruehlen Supply Company Inc 491 Corban Ave Se *Web:* www.ruehlensupply.com	Concord	NC	28025	704-788-2180	
Rundle-Spence Manufacturing Co PO Box 510008 *TF:* 800-783-6060 ■ *Web:* www.rundle-spence.com	New Berlin	WI	53151	262-782-3000	782-5078
Samon's Tiger Stores Inc 2511 Monroe NE *Web:* www.samons.biz	Albuquerque	NM	87110	505-884-4615	
San Jose Boiler Works Inc 1585 Schallenberger Rd *Web:* www.sanjoseboiler.com	San Jose	CA	95131	408-295-5235	
Schumacher & Seiler Inc 10 W Aylesbury Rd *TF:* 800-992-9356 ■ *Web:* www.schumacherseiler.com	Timonium	MD	21093	410-465-7000	
Security Supply Corp 196 Maple Ave *TF:* 800-333-2226 ■ *Web:* www.secsupply.com	Selkirk	NY	12158	518-767-2226	767-2065
Sexauer Ltd 3-6990 Creditview Rd	Mississauga	ON	L5N8R9	905-821-8292	
Shore Distributors Inc 807 Brown St *Web:* www.shoredist.com	Salisbury	MD	21804	410-749-3121	
Sid Harvey Industries Inc 605 Locust St *Web:* www.sidharvey.com	Garden City	NY	11530	516-745-9200	222-9027
Sioux Chief Manufacturing Company Inc 24110 S Peculiar Dr *Web:* www.siouxchief.com	Peculiar	MO	64078	816-779-6104	
Smardan-Hatcher Company Inc 810 East Mason St *Web:* www.smardan.com	Santa Barbara	CA	93103	805-963-8991	
Solar Energy Systems LLC 1205 Manhattan Ave Ste 1210 *Web:* www.solaresystems.com	Brooklyn	NY	11222	718-389-1545	
SPS Cos Inc 6363 Minnesota 7 *Web:* www.spscompanies.com	Minneapolis	MN	55416	952-929-1377	929-1862
Standard Air & Lite Corp 2406 Woodmere Dr *TF:* 800-472-2458 ■ *Web:* www.stdair.com	Pittsburgh	PA	15205	412-920-6505	
Sunbelt Marketing Investment Corp 3255 S Sweetwater Rd *TF:* 800-257-5566 ■ *Web:* www.sunbeltmarketing.com	Lithia Springs	GA	30122	770-739-3740	
Superlon Plastic Pipe Co 2116 Taylor Way *Web:* www.superlon.com	Tacoma	WA	98421	253-383-4000	
Swan Corp, The 515 Olive St Ste 900 *TF:* 800-325-7008 ■ *Web:* www.swanstone.com	St. Louis	MO	63101	314-231-8148	
TBA LLC 6700 Enterprise Dr *TF:* 800-626-3525 ■ *Web:* www.cmiproduct.com	Louisville	KY	40214	502-367-0222	361-0715
Temperature Equipment Corp 17725 Volbrecht Rd *Web:* www.tecmungo.com	Lansing	IL	60438	708-418-0900	418-5100

	City	State	Zip	Phone	Fax
Temperature Systems Inc 5001 Voges Rd *TF:* 800-366-0930 ■ *Web:* www.tsihvac.com	Madison	WI	53718	608-271-7500	274-1609
Therm Air Sales Corp 1413 41st Stn *TF:* 800-726-7520 ■ *Web:* www.thermairsales.com	Fargo	ND	58102	701-282-9500	
Thermal Corp 1264 Slaughter Rd. *TF:* 800-633-2962 ■ *Web:* www.thermalcorporation.com	Madison	AL	35758	256-837-1122	837-0265
Trident Technologies Inc 7425 Mission Valley Rd Ste 207 *Web:* www.tridenttech.com	San Diego	CA	92108	619-688-9600	
Upturn Solutions Inc 1396 Riverside Rd *TF:* 866-891-4363 ■ *Web:* www.sprocketcmms.com	Bigfork	MT	59911	866-891-4363	
US Airconditioning Distributors 16900 Chestnut St **Fax:* Sales ■ *TF:* 800-937-7222 ■ *Web:* www.us-ac.com	City of Industry	CA	91748	626-854-4500	854-4690*
US Supply Company Inc 50 Portland Rd *Web:* www.ussupply.com	West Conshohocken	PA	19428	610-828-5600	
V P Supply Corp PO Box 23868 *Web:* www.vpsupply.com	Rochester	NY	14692	585-272-0110	272-0547
Vamac Inc 4201 Jacque St *TF:* 800-768-2622 ■ *Web:* www.vamac.com	Richmond	VA	23230	804-353-7811	358-7855
W C Rouse & Son Inc 110 Longale Rd *Web:* www.wcrouse.com	Greensboro	NC	27409	336-299-3035	
WA Roosevelt Co 2727 Commerce St *TF:* 800-279-2726 ■ *Web:* www.waroosevelt.com	La Crosse	WI	54603	608-781-2000	781-8372
Ward Manufacturing LLC 117 Gulick St *TF:* 800-248-1027 ■ *Web:* www.wardmfg.com	Blossburg	PA	16912	570-638-2131	
Waxman Industries Inc 24460 Aurora Rd *OTC:* WXMN ■ **Fax:* Cust Svc ■ *TF:* 800-201-7298 ■ *Web:* www.waxman.com	Bedford Heights	OH	44146	440-439-1830	439-8678*
Wayne Pipe & Supply Inc 6040 Innovation Blvd *TF:* 800-552-3697 ■ *Web:* www.waynepipe.com	Fort Wayne	IN	46818	260-423-9577	
Webber Supply Inc 32 Thatcher St *Web:* www.webbersupply.com	Bangor	ME	04401	207-942-7361	
Webstone Company Inc 1 Appian Way *Web:* www.webstonevalves.com	Worcester	MA	01610	508-438-0131	
Wellness Enterprises LLC 418 SW 140th Terrace *Web:* www.naturallyfiltered.com	Newberry	FL	32669	352-333-0480	
Western Nevada Supply Co 950 S Rock Blvd *TF:* 800-648-1230 ■ *Web:* www.wns1.com	Sparks	NV	89431	775-359-5800	359-4649
Wholesale Specialties Inc 4800 E 48th Ave *Web:* www.wholesalespecialties.com	Denver	CO	80216	303-296-2212	
Wholesale Supply Group Inc 885 Keith St NW *Web:* www.wsgwww.com	Cleveland	TN	37311	423-478-1191	478-5120
Wilkinson Supply Co 3300 Bush St *Web:* www.wilkinsonsupplyco.com	Raleigh	NC	27609	919-834-0395	
Willoughby Industries Inc 2210 W Morris St *Web:* www.willoughby-ind.com	Indianapolis	IN	46221	317-638-2381	
Windland Inc 7669 W Riverside Dr Ste 102 *Web:* www.windland.com	Boise	ID	83714	208-377-7777	
WinWholesale Inc 3110 Kettering Blvd *Web:* winwholesale.com	Dayton	OH	45439	937-294-5331	293-9591
Wolff Bros Supply Inc 6078 Wolff Rd *Web:* www.wolffbros.com	Medina	OH	44256	330-725-3451	
Wolverine Brass Inc 2951 Hwy 501 East **Fax Area Code:* 800 ■ *Web:* www.wolverinebrass.com	Conway	SC	29526	843-347-3121	945-9292*
Woodhill Supply Inc 4665 Beidler Rd *TF:* 800-362-6111 ■ *Web:* www.woodhillsupply.com	Willoughby	OH	44094	440-269-1100	269-1027
Yorkshire Supply Inc 8205 Centreville Rd *Web:* www.yorkshiresupply.com	Manassas	VA	20111	703-368-9226	
Zurier Company of San Francisco Inc 6147 Industrial Way Ste A *Web:* zurier.com	Livermore	CA	94551	925-449-5858	

613 PLYWOOD & VENEERS

See Also Lumber & Building Supplies p. 2095; Home Improvement Centers p. 2479

	City	State	Zip	Phone	Fax
Aetna Plywood Inc 1401 St Charles Rd *Web:* www.aetnaplywood.com	Maywood	IL	60153	708-343-1515	343-1616
Amos-Hill Assoc Inc 112 Shelby Ave *Web:* www.amoshill.com	Edinburgh	IN	46124	812-526-2671	526-5865
Anderson Hardwood Floors PO Box 1155 *Web:* www.andersonfloors.com	Clinton	SC	29325	864-833-6250	
Atlantic Veneer Corp 2457 Lennoxville Rd PO Box 660 *Web:* www.moehringgroup.com	Beaufort	NC	28516	252-728-3169	728-4906
Bacon Veneer Co 6951 High Grove Blvd *TF:* 800-443-7995 ■ *Web:* www.baconveneer.com	Burr Ridge	IL	60527	630-323-1414	323-1499
Barmon Door & Plywood Inc 2508 Hartford Dr	Lake Stevens	WA	98258	425-334-1222	335-0404
Buffalo Veneer & Plywood Company Inc 501 Sixth Ave NE *Web:* www.buffaloveneerandplywood.com	Buffalo	MN	55313	763-682-1822	682-9769
California Panel & Veneer Co 14055 Artesia Blvd *TF:* 800-451-1745 ■ *Web:* www.calpanel.com	Cerritos	CA	90703	562-926-5834	926-3139
Capital Veneer Works Inc 2550 Jackson Ferry Rd *Web:* capitalmat.com	Montgomery	AL	36104	334-264-1401	264-6923
Capitol Plywood Inc 160 Commerce Cir *TF:* 800-326-1505 ■ *Web:* www.capitolplywood.com	Sacramento	CA	95815	916-922-8861	922-0775
Columbia Forest Products Inc Columbia Plywood Div 7900 Triad Ctr Dr Ste 200 *TF:* 800-637-1609 ■ *Web:* columbiaforestproducts.com	Greensboro	NC	27409	800-637-1609	
Columbia Panel Manufacturing Co 100 Giles St	High Point	NC	27263	336-861-4100	
Constantine's Wood Ctr 1040 E Oakland Pk Blvd *TF:* 800-443-9667 ■ *Web:* www.constantines.com	Fort Lauderdale	FL	33334	954-561-1716	565-8149
Cummings Veneers Inc 601 E Fourth St	New Albany	IN	47150	812-944-2269	944-0212
Darlington Veneer Company Inc 225 Fourth St *TF:* 800-845-2388 ■ *Web:* www.darlingtonveneer.com	Darlington	SC	29532	843-393-3861	393-8243
Davis Wood Products Inc PO Box 604 *Web:* www.daviswoodproducts.com	Hudson	NC	28638	828-728-8444	728-4601
Eggers Industries Inc 1 Eggers Dr *Web:* www.eggersindustries.com	Two Rivers	WI	54241	920-793-1351	793-2958
Fiber-Tech Industries Inc 2000 Kenskill Ave *TF:* 800-879-4377 ■ *Web:* fiber-tech.net	Washington Court House	OH	43160	740-335-9400	335-4843
Flexible Materials Inc 1202 Port Rd *TF:* 800-244-6492 ■ *Web:* www.flexwood.com	Jeffersonville	IN	47130	812-280-7000	280-7001
Freeman Corp, The 415 Magnolia St PO Box 96 *Web:* www.freemancorp.com	Winchester	KY	40392	859-744-4311	744-4363
Freres Lumber Company Inc PO Box 276 *Web:* www.frereslumber.com	Lyons	OR	97358	503-859-2121	
G-L Veneer Co Inc 2224 E Slauson Ave *TF:* 800-588-5003 ■ *Web:* www.glveneer.com	Huntington Park	CA	90255	323-582-5203	582-9681
Hambro Forest Products Inc 445 Elk Valley Rd	Crescent City	CA	95531	707-464-6131	464-9375
Harbor Sales 1000 Harbor Ct *TF:* 800-345-1712 ■ *Web:* www.harborsales.net	Sudlersville	MD	21668	800-345-1712	868-9257
Hasty Plywood Co 100 N Austin St *Web:* www.hasply.com	Maxton	NC	28364	910-844-5267	
Hood Cos Inc 623 N Main St Ste 300 *Web:* www.hoodcompanies.com	Hattiesburg	MS	39401	601-582-4486	
Hood Industries Inc 15 Professional Pkwy # 8 *Web:* www.hoodindustries.com	Hattiesburg	MS	39402	601-264-2559	296-4755
Hoquiam Plywood Company Inc 1000 Woodlawn Rd	Hoquiam	WA	98550	360-533-3060	532-6980
Inland Plywood Co 375 N Cass Ave *TF:* 800-521-4355 ■ *Web:* www.inlandplywood.com	Pontiac	MI	48342	248-334-4706	338-7407
Louisiana-Pacific Corp 414 Union St Ste 2000 *NYSE:* LPX ■ *TF:* 888-820-0325 ■ *Web:* www.lpcorp.com	Nashville	TN	37219	615-986-5600	986-5666
Marion Plywood Corp 222 S Parkview Ave PO Box 497 *Web:* www.marionplywood.com	Marion	WI	54950	715-754-5231	754-2582
Murphy Hardwood Plywood 2350 Prairie Rd *TF:* 888-461-4545 ■ *Web:* www.murphyplywood.com	Eugene	OR	97402	541-461-4545	461-4547
Murphy Plywood Co 2350 Prairie Rd *TF:* 888-461-4545 ■ *Web:* www.murphyplywood.com	Eugene	OR	97402	541-461-4545	461-4547
Norbord Inc 1 Toronto St Ste 600 *TSE:* NBD ■ *TF:* 888-667-2673 ■ *Web:* www.norbord.com	Toronto	ON	M5C2W4	416-365-0705	365-3292
North American Plywood Corp 12343 Hawkins St *TF Sales:* 800-421-1372 ■ *Web:* naply.com	Santa Fe Springs	CA	90670	562-941-7575	
Pasquier Panel Products Inc 1510 Puyallup St PO Box 1170 *Web:* www.pasquierpanel.com	Sumner	WA	98390	253-863-6323	891-7993
Pavco Industries Inc PO Box 612 *Web:* www.pavcoind.com	Pascagoula	MS	39568	228-762-3172	762-3170
Phillips Plywood Company Inc 13599 Desmond St *TF Cust Svc:* 800-649-6410 ■ *Web:* www.phillipsplywood.com	Pacoima	CA	91331	818-897-7736	897-6571
Plywood Supply Inc 7036 NE 175th St *TF:* 888-774-9663 ■ *Web:* www.plywoodsupply.com	Kenmore	WA	98028	425-485-8585	485-6195
Potlatch Corp 601 W First Ave Ste 1600 *NASDAQ:* PCH ■ *Web:* www.potlatchcorp.com	Spokane	WA	99201	509-835-1500	
Potlatch Corp Wood Products Div 805 Mill Rd PO Box 1388 *Web:* www.potlatchcorp.com	Lewiston	ID	83501	509-835-1500	
Robert Weed Plywood Corp 705 Maple St PO Box 487 *Web:* www.robertweedplywood.com	Bristol	IN	46507	574-848-4408	848-5679
Roseburg Forest Products Co PO Box 1088 *TF:* 800-245-1115 ■ *Web:* www.roseburg.com	Roseburg	OR	97470	541-679-3311	
SDS Lumber Co PO Box 266 *Web:* sdslumber.com	Bingen	WA	98605	509-493-2155	493-2535
South Coast Lumber Co 885 Railroad Ave PO Box 670 *Web:* www.socomi.com	Brookings	OR	97415	541-469-2136	469-3487
States Industries Inc 29495 W Enid Rd *TF:* 800-626-1981 ■ *Web:* www.statesind.com	Eugene	OR	97402	541-688-7871	
StemWood Corp 2710 Grant Line Rd *Web:* www.stemwood.com	New Albany	IN	47150	812-945-6646	945-7549
Stimson Lumber Co 520 SW Yamhill St Ste 700 *TF:* 800-445-9758 ■ *Web:* www.stimsonlumber.com	Portland	OR	97204	503-222-1676	222-2682
Stoll Brother True Value Lumber 509 S E St *Web:* truevalue.com	Odon	IN	47562	812-636-4053	
Texas Plywood & Lumber Co Inc 1001 E Ave K *Web:* www.texasplywood.com	Grand Prairie	TX	75050	972-262-1331	642-2225
Trimac Panel Products 5201 SW Westgate Dr Ste 200 *Web:* www.trimacpanel.com	Portland	OR	97221	503-297-1826	
United Plywood & Lumber Inc 1640 Mims Ave SW *TF:* 800-272-6486 ■ *Web:* www.unitedplywoods.com	Birmingham	AL	35211	205-925-7601	923-9511
Wavell-Huber Wood Products Inc 180 North 170 West *Web:* www.wavell-huber.com	North Salt Lake	UT	84054	801-936-6080	936-6078
Wisconsin Veneer & Plywood Inc Railroad St PO Box 140 *Web:* www.bessegroup.com/public/companies/wi_veneer.php	Mattoon	WI	54450	715-489-3611	489-3268

614 POINT-OF-SALE (POS) & POINT-OF-INFORMATION (POI) SYSTEMS

Company / Address	City	State	Zip	Phone	Fax
3M Digital Signage 600 Ericksen Ave NE Ste 200 *TF:* 888-464-7239 ■ *Web:* www.3mdigitalsignage.com	Bainbridge Island	WA	98110	206-855-2000	855-4930
Checkpoint Systems Inc 101 Wolf Dr *NYSE: CKP* ■ *TF:* 800-257-5540 ■ *Web:* www.checkpointsystems.com	Thorofare	NJ	08086	856-848-1800	848-0937
Comtrex Systems Corp 1827 Powers Ferry Rd SE Ste 200 *Web:* comtrex.co.uk	Atlanta	GA	30339	856-778-0090	778-9322
Datalogic Scanning 959 Terry St *TF:* 800-695-5700 ■ *Web:* www.datalogic.com	Eugene	OR	97402	541-683-5700	345-7140
Kiosk Information Systems Inc (KIS) 346 S Arthur Ave *TF General:* 800-509-5471 ■ *Web:* www.kis-kiosk.com	Louisville	CO	80027	303-466-5471	466-6730
Micros Systems Inc 7031 Columbia Gateway Dr *NASDAQ: MCRS* ■ *TF:* 800-937-2211 ■ *Web:* www.micros.com	Columbia	MD	21046	443-285-6000	
MTI Inc 1050 NW 229th Ave *TF:* 800-426-6844 ■ *Web:* www.mti-interactive.com	Hillsboro	OR	97124	503-648-6500	648-7500
NextG Networks Inc 890 Tasman Dr *TF:* 877-486-9377 ■ *Web:* www.crowncastle.com	Milpitas	CA	95035	877-486-9377	
PAR Technology Corp 8383 Seneca Tpke *NYSE: PAR* ■ *TF:* 800-448-6505 ■ *Web:* www.partech.com	New Hartford	NY	13413	315-738-0600	738-0562
SeePoint Technology LLC 2619 Manhattan Beach Blvd *TF:* 888-587-1777 ■ *Web:* www.seepoint.com	Redondo Beach	CA	90278	310-725-9660	535-9234
TouchSystems Corp 220 Tradesmen Dr *TF:* 800-320-5944 ■ *Web:* www.touchsystems.com	Hutto	TX	78634	512-846-2424	846-2425
UTC RETAIL Inc 100 Rawson Rd **Fax Area Code:* 585 ■ *TF:* 800-349-0546 ■ *Web:* www.utcretail.com	Victor	NY	14564	800-349-0546	924-1434*
VeriFone Inc 2099 Gateway Pl Ste 600 *NYSE: PAY* ■ *TF:* 800-837-4366 ■ *Web:* www.verifone.asia	San Jose	CA	95110	408-232-7800	232-7811
VeriFone Systems Inc 88 W Plumeria Dr Ste 600 *NYSE: PAY* ■ *TF:* 800-837-4366 ■ *Web:* www.verifone.asia	San Jose	CA	95134	408-232-7800	232-7811

615 POLITICAL ACTION COMMITTEES

See Also Civic & Political Organizations p. 1758

Organization / Address	City	State	Zip	Phone	Fax
A Jewish Voice for Peace Inc 1611 Telegraph Ave Ste 550 *Web:* jewishvoiceforpeace.org	Oakland	CA	94612	510-465-1777	
Action Committee for Rural Electrification (ACRE) 4301 Wilson Blvd *Web:* www.nreca.coop	Arlington	VA	22203	703-907-5500	
AFL-CIO Committee on Political Education 815 16th St NW **Fax Area Code:* 202 ■ *TF:* 855-712-8441 ■ *Web:* www.aflcio.org	Washington	DC	20006	855-712-8441	637-5058*
American Academy of Ophthalmology PAC Governmental Affairs Div 20 F St NW Ste 400 *TF:* 866-561-8558 ■ *Web:* www.aao.org	Washington	DC	20001	202-737-6662	737-7061
American Academy of Physician Assistants (AAPA) 2318 Mill Rd Ste 1300 *Web:* www.aapa.org	Alexandria	VA	22314	703-836-2272	684-1924
American Apparel & Footwear Assn PAC 1601 N Kent St Ste 1200 *TF:* 800-520-2262 ■ *Web:* www.wewear.org	Arlington	VA	22209	703-524-1864	522-6741
American Assn for Justice PAC 777 Sixth St NW Ste 200 *Web:* www.justice.org	Washington	DC	20001	202-965-3500	
American Assn of Nurse Anesthetists PAC (AANAPAC) 222 S Prospect Ave *TF:* 855-526-2262	Park Ridge	IL	60068	847-692-7050	692-7082
American Assn of Orthodontists PAC 401 N Lindbergh Blvd *TF:* 800-424-2841 ■ *Web:* www.aaoinfo.org	Saint Louis	MO	63141	314-993-1700	997-1745
American Bakers Assn PAC 601 Pennsylvania Ave NW Ste 230 *Web:* americanbakers.org	Washington	DC	20004	202-789-0300	898-1164
American Bankers Assn PAC (ABAPAC) 1120 Connecticut Ave NW **Fax Area Code:* 202 ■ *TF:* 800-226-5377 ■ *Web:* www.aba.com/default.htm	Washington	DC	20036	800-226-5377	663-7544*
American Beverage Assn PAC 1101 16th St NW *Web:* www.ameribev.org	Washington	DC	20036	202-463-6732	
American Chiropractic Assn PAC (ACA-PAC) 1701 Clarendon Blvd *TF:* 800-986-4636 ■ *Web:* www.acatoday.org	Arlington	VA	22209	703-276-8800	243-2593
American Dental Assn 1111 14th St NW Ste 1100 *TF:* 800-353-2237 ■ *Web:* www.ada.org	Washington	DC	20005	202-898-2424	898-2437
American Family Life Assurance Co PAC (AFLAC PAC) 1932 Wynnton Rd Ste 300 *NYSE: AFL* ■ **Fax Area Code:* 877 ■ *TF Cust Svc:* 800-992-3522 ■ *Web:* www.aflac.com	Columbus	GA	31999	706-323-3431	442-3522*
American Frozen Food Institute (AFFI) 2000 Corporate Ridge Blvd Ste 1000 *Web:* www.affi.org	McLean	VA	22102	703-821-0770	821-1350
American Health Care Assn PAC 1201 L St NW *Web:* ahcancal.org	Washington	DC	20005	202-842-4444	842-3860
American Hospital Assn PAC (AHAPAC) 325 Seventh St NW *TF:* 800-424-4301 ■ *Web:* aha.org	Washington	DC	20004	202-638-1100	626-2345
American Insurance Assn PAC 2101 L St Nw Ste 400 *Web:* www.aiadc.org	Washington	DC	20037	202-828-7100	293-1219
American Iron & Steel Institute PAC 1140 Connecticut Ave NW Ste 705 *Web:* www.steel.org	Washington	DC	20036	202-452-7100	463-6573
American Medical Assn PAC 25 Massachusetts Ave NW # 600 *Web:* ama-assn.org	Washington	DC	20001	312-464-4430	
American Motorcyclist Assn 101 Constitution Ave NW Ste 800W *TF:* 888-985-6090 ■ *Web:* www.americanmotorcyclist.com	Washington	DC	20001	202-742-4301	742-4304
American Moving & Storage Assn PAC 1611 Duke St *TF:* 888-849-2672 ■ *Web:* www.promover.org	Alexandria	VA	22314	703-683-7410	683-7527
American Nurses Assn PAC (ANA PAC) 8515 Georgia Ave Ste 400 *TF:* 800-274-4262 ■ *Web:* www.nursingworld.org	Silver Spring	MD	20910	301-628-5000	628-5001
American Pharmacists Assn PAC 2215 Constitution Ave NW *TF:* 800-237-2742 ■ *Web:* www.pharmacist.com	Washington	DC	20037	202-628-4410	783-2351
American Postal Workers Union PAC (COPA) 1300 L St NW *Web:* apwu.org	Washington	DC	20005	202-842-4200	
American Society of Travel Agents PAC 1101 King St Ste 490 *TF:* 800-275-2782 ■ *Web:* www.asta.org	Alexandria	VA	22314	703-739-2782	838-8467
American Sportfishing Assnn PAC (ASA PAC) 225 Reinekers Ln Ste 420 *Web:* www.asafishing.org	Alexandria	VA	22314	703-519-9691	519-1872
American Supply Assn PAC (ASA PAC) 1200 N Arlington Heights Rd Ste 150 *Web:* www.asa.net	Itasca	IL	60143	630-467-0000	
American Veterinary Medical Assn PAC (AVMA) 1910 Sunderland Pl NW *TF:* 800-321-1473 ■ *Web:* www.avma.org	Washington	DC	20036	202-789-0007	842-4360
ArchiPAC 1735 New York Ave NW	Washington	DC	20006	202-626-7300	626-7426
Associated General Contractors PAC 2300 Wilson Blvd Ste 400 *TF:* 800-242-1767 ■ *Web:* www.agc.org/cs/about_agc/recognition_programs/agc_pac_donor_recognition	Arlington	VA	22201	703-548-3118	548-3119
Association of Home Appliance Manufacturers PAC (AHAM PAC) 1111 19th St NW Ste 402 *Web:* aham.org	Washington	DC	20036	202-872-5955	872-9354
Benenson Strategy Group LLC 14 E 60th St Ste 1002 *Web:* www.bsgco.com	New York	NY	10022	212-702-8777	
Burlington Northern Santa Fe Corp (BNSF) 500 New Jersey Ave NW Ste 550 *TF:* 800-964-9386 ■ *Web:* www.bnsf.com	Washington	DC	20001	202-347-8662	347-8675
Business-Industry Political Action Committee (BIPAC) 888 16th St NW Ste 305 *Web:* www.bipac.org	Washington	DC	20006	202-833-1880	833-2338
BUSPAC 700 13th St NW Ste 575 *TF:* 800-283-2877 ■ *Web:* buses.org	Washington	DC	20005	202-842-1645	842-0850
Campaign for Working Families (CWF) PO Box 1222 *Web:* www.cwfpac.com	Arlington	VA	22206	703-671-8800	
Caterpillar Inc Employees PAC 100 NE Adams St *Web:* caterpillar.com	Peoria	IL	61629	309-675-2337	
Coca-Cola Nonpartisan Committee for Good Government PO Box 1734 *TF:* 800-438-2653 ■ *Web:* www.coca-colacompany.com	Atlanta	GA	30301	800-438-2653	
College of American Pathologists PAC 1350 I St NW Ste 590 *TF:* 800-392-9994 ■ *Web:* www.cap.org	Washington	DC	20005	202-354-7100	354-7155
Consumer Specialty Products Assn PAC 1667 K St NW Ste 300 *Web:* www.cspa.org	Washington	DC	20006	202-872-8110	223-2636
Cosmetic Toiletry & Fragrance Assn PAC (CTFA PAC) 1101 17th St NW Ste 300 *Web:* cir-safety.org	Washington	DC	20036	202-331-1770	331-1969
Credit Union Legislative Action Council of CUNA (CULCAC) 601 Pennsylvania Ave NW S Bldg Ste 600 *Web:* cuna.org	Washington	DC	20004	202-638-5777	638-7734
DGA-PAC 7920 W Sunset Blvd *TF:* 800-421-4173 ■ *Web:* www.dga.org	Los Angeles	CA	90046	310-289-2000	289-2029
ESOP Assn PAC 1726 M St NW Ste 501 *TF:* 866-366-3832 ■ *Web:* www.esopassociation.org	Washington	DC	20036	202-293-2971	293-7568
FedEx Corp Government Affairs 942 S Shady Grove Rd *Web:* www.fedex.com	Memphis	TN	38120	901-818-7500	
FRAN-PAC 1501 K St Ste 350 *TF:* 800-543-1038 ■ *Web:* www.franchise.org	Washington	DC	20005	202-628-8000	628-0812
Freedom Alliance 22570 Markey Ct Ste 240 *Web:* freedomalliance.org	Sterling	VA	20166	703-444-7940	
Friends Committee on National Legislation (FCNL) 245 Second St NE *TF:* 800-630-1330 ■ *Web:* www.fcnl.org	Washington	DC	20002	202-547-6000	547-6019
GASPAC 400 N Capitol St NW *Web:* www.aga.org	Washington	DC	20001	202-824-7000	
General Electric Company PAC 1299 Pennsylvania Ave NW Ste 900	Washington	DC	20004	202-637-4000	637-4006
GOPAC 1101 16th St NW *Web:* www.gopac.org	Washington	DC	20036	202-464-5170	
HotelPAC 1201 New York Ave NW Ste 600 *Web:* www.ahla.com/default.aspx	Washington	DC	20005	202-289-3100	289-3185
IAFF 1750 New York Ave NW Ste 300 *Web:* www.iaff.org	Washington	DC	20006	202-737-8484	737-8418
IATSE PAC 1430 Broadway 20th Fl *TF:* 844-422-9273 ■ *Web:* iatse.net	New York	NY	10018	212-730-1770	730-7809
Ice Cream Milk & Cheese PAC 1250 H St NW Ste 900 *Web:* www.idfa.org	Washington	DC	20005	202-737-4332	331-7820
Independent Insurance Agents & Brokers of America PAC (INSURPAC) 412 First St SE Ste 300 *Web:* independentagent.com	Washington	DC	20003	202-863-7000	863-7015

	City	State	Zip	Phone	Fax
Iowa State Association of Counties 5500 Westown Pkwy 5500 Westown Pkwy *Web:* www.iowacounties.org	West Des Moines	IA	50266	515-244-7181	
Ironworkers Political Action League 1750 New York Ave NW Ste 400 *TF:* 800-368-0105 ■ *Web:* ironworkers.org/get-organized/politicalaction.aspx	Washington	DC	20006	202-383-4800	638-4856
Liberal Party of Canada 81 Metcalfe St *TF:* 888-542-3725 ■ *Web:* www.liberal.ca	Ottawa	ON	K1P6M8	888-542-3725	
Magazine Publishers of AmNAerica PAC 1211 Connecticut Ave NW Ste 610 *Web:* magazine.org	Washington	DC	20036	202-296-7277	296-0343
Maine People's Alliance 27 State St Ste 44 *Web:* mainepeoplesalliance.org	Bangor	ME	04401	207-990-0672	
Manufactured Housing Institute PAC (MHI PAC) 1655 N Ft Myer Dr Ste 104 *TF:* 800-505-5500 ■ *Web:* www.manufacturedhousing.org	Arlington	VA	22209	703-558-0400	558-0401
MassMutual PAC 1295 State St *TF:* 800-272-2216 ■ *Web:* www.massmutual.com/pac	Springfield	MA	01111	413-788-8411	744-6005
MinePAC 101 Constitution Ave NW Ste 500 E *Web:* nma.org	Washington	DC	20001	202-463-2625	463-2666
Mortgage Bankers Assn PAC (MORPAC) 1717 Rhode Island Ave NW 5th Fl *Web:* www.mba.org/get-involved/mbas-political-action-committee	Washington	DC	20036	202-557-2700	721-0249
Motorola PAC 600 N US Hwy 45 **Fax Area Code:* 202 ■ *TF:* 800-102-2344 ■ *Web:* motorola-mobility-en-in.custhelp.com	Libertyville	IL	60048	800-102-2344	842-3578*
NA of Home Builders PAC 1201 15th St NW *TF:* 800-368-5242 ■ *Web:* www.nahb.org	Washington	DC	20005	202-266-8200	266-8400
NA of Retired Federal Employees 606 N Washington St *TF:* 800-627-3394 ■ *Web:* www.narfe.org	Alexandria	VA	22314	703-838-7760	838-7785
NAADAC PAC 44 Canal Center Plz Ste 301 *TF:* 800-377-1136 ■ *Web:* www.naadac.org	Alexandria	VA	22314	703-741-7686	741-7698
NASBIC PAC 1100 H St NW Ste 610 *TF:* 800-471-6153 ■ *Web:* www.sbia.org	Washington	DC	20005	202-628-5055	628-5080
National Cattlemen's Beef Assn PAC 1301 Pennsylvania Ave NW Ste 300 *Web:* beef.org	Washington	DC	20004	202-347-0228	
National Confectioners Assn PAC (NCA) 8320 Old Courthouse Rd Ste 300 *TF:* 800-433-1200 ■ *Web:* www.candyusa.com	Vienna	VA	22182	202-534-1440	
National Milk Producers Federation PAC (NMPF PAC) 2101 Wilson Blvd Ste 400 *Web:* nmpf.org	Arlington	VA	22201	703-243-6111	841-9328
National Multi Housing Council PAC 1850 M St NW Ste 540 *TF:* 866-987-7367 ■ *Web:* www.nmhc.org	Washington	DC	20036	202-974-2300	775-0112
National Pork Producers Council PAC 122 C St NW Ste 875 *TF:* 866-844-9416 ■ *Web:* www.nppc.org	Washington	DC	20001	202-347-3600	347-5265
National Roofing Contractors Assn PAC (NRCAPAC) 324 Fourth St NE *Web:* nrca.net	Washington	DC	20002	202-546-7584	546-9289
National Sunflower Assn PAC 2401 46th Ave SE Ste 206 *TF:* 888-718-7033 ■ *Web:* www.sunflowernsa.com	Mandan	ND	58554	701-328-5100	328-5101
National Venture Capital Assn (NVCA) 25 Massachusetts Ave NW Ste 730 *Web:* www.nvca.org	Washington	DC	20001	703-524-2549	524-3940
NATSO PAC 1737 King St Ste 200 *Web:* natso.com	Alexandria	VA	22314	703-549-2100	684-4525
NCFC Co-op PAC 50 F St NW Ste 900 *Web:* www.ncfc.org	Washington	DC	20001	202-626-8700	626-8722
NEA Fund for Children & Public Education 1201 16th St NW *Web:* www.neafund.org	Washington	DC	20036	202-833-4000	822-7974
North American Meat Institute (AMIPAC) 1150 Connecticut Ave NW *Web:* www.meatinstitute.org	Washington	DC	20036	202-587-4200	587-4300
NRA Institute for Legislative Action 11250 Waples Mill Rd **Fax Area Code:* 703 ■ *TF:* 800-392-8683 ■ *Web:* www.nraila.org	Fairfax	VA	22030	800-392-8683	267-3918*
Ontario Pc Party 19 Duncan St *TF:* 800-903-6453 ■ *Web:* www.ontariopc.com	Toronto	ON	M5H3H1	416-861-9593	
Outdoor Adv Assn of America Inc (OAAA) 1850 M St NW Ste 1040 *TF:* 800-325-3694 ■ *Web:* www.oaaa.org	Washington	DC	20036	202-833-5566	833-1522
Outdoor Amusement Business Assn PAC (OABA-PAC) 1035 S Semoran Blvd Ste 1045A *TF:* 800-517-6222 ■ *Web:* www.oaba.org	Winter Park	FL	32792	407-681-9444	681-9445
Petroleum Marketers Assn of America's Small Business Community 1901 N Fort Myer Dr Ste 500 *TF:* 888-372-7341 ■ *Web:* epa.gov	Arlington	VA	22209	703-351-8000	351-9160
Planned Parenthood Action Fund Inc 1110 Vermont Ave NW *TF:* 800-430-4907 ■ *Web:* www.plannedparenthoodaction.org	Washington	DC	20005	202-973-4800	296-3242
Print PAC 2800 Overlook Pkwy *Web:* www.printpaconline.org	Atlanta	GA	30339	202-730-7970	730-7987
REITPAC 1875 'I' St NW Ste 600 *TF:* 800-362-7348 ■ *Web:* www.reit.com	Washington	DC	20006	202-739-9400	739-9401
Title Industry PAC (TIPAC) 1828 L St NW Ste 705 *TF:* 800-787-2582 ■ *Web:* www.alta.org	Washington	DC	20036	202-296-3671	223-5843
Truck PAC 430 First St SE Ste 100 *Web:* www.trucking.org	Washington	DC	20003	202-544-6245	675-6568

POLITICAL LEADERS

See Governors - State p. 2441; US Senators, Representatives, Delegates p. 2433

616 POLITICAL PARTIES (MAJOR)

See Also Civic & Political Organizations p. 1758

	City	State	Zip	Phone	Fax
Communist Party USA 235 W 23rd St 8th Fl *Web:* www.cpusa.org	New York	NY	10011	212-989-4994	229-1713
Democratic National Committee 430 S Capitol St SE *Web:* www.democrats.org	Washington	DC	20003	202-863-8000	
Democratic Socialists of America 75 Maiden Ln Ste 505 *Web:* www.dsausa.org	New York	NY	10038	212-727-8610	
Libertarian Party 2600 Virginia Ave NW Ste 200 *TF:* 800-353-2887 ■ *Web:* www.lp.org	Washington	DC	20037	202-333-0008	333-0072
Republican National Committee (RNC) 310 First St SE *TF:* 800-445-5768 ■ *Web:* www.gop.com	Washington	DC	20003	202-863-8500	
Socialist Labor Party of America PO Box 218 *Web:* www.slp.org	Mountain View	CA	94042	408-280-7266	280-6964

616-1 Democratic State Committees

	City	State	Zip	Phone	Fax
Alabama Democratic Party 501 Adams Ave *Web:* aladems.org	Montgomery	AL	36104	334-262-2221	
Alaska Democratic Party 2602 Fairbanks St *Web:* www.alaskademocrats.org	Anchorage	AK	99503	907-258-3050	258-1626
Arkansas Democratic Party 1300 W Capitol Ave *Web:* www.arkdems.org	Little Rock	AR	72201	501-374-2361	
California Democratic Party 1401 21st St Ste 200 *Web:* www.cadem.org	Sacramento	CA	95811	916-442-5707	
Colorado Democratic Party 789 Sherman St *Web:* www.coloradodems.org	Denver	CO	80204	303-623-4762	623-2443
Connecticut Democratic Party 30 Arbor St *Web:* www.ctdems.org	Hartford	CT	06106	860-560-1775	387-0147
Delaware Democratic Party 19 E Commons Blvd 2nd Fl *Web:* www.deldems.org	New Castle	DE	19720	302-328-9036	328-9386
Florida Democratic Party 214 S Bronough St *TF:* 855-352-7233 ■ *Web:* www.floridadems.org	Tallahassee	FL	32301	850-222-3411	222-0916
Hawaii Democratic Party 1050 Ala Moana Blvd Ste D-26 *TF:* 844-596-2980 ■ *Web:* www.hawaiidemocrats.org	Honolulu	HI	96814	808-596-2980	
Idaho Democratic Party 943 W Overland Rd *TF:* 800-626-0471 ■ *Web:* idahodems.org	Meridian	ID	83642	208-336-1815	
Indiana Democratic Party 115 W Washington St Ste 1165 *TF:* 800-223-3387 ■ *Web:* www.indems.org	Indianapolis	IN	46204	317-231-7100	231-7129
Iowa Democratic Party 5661 Fleur Dr *Web:* www.iowademocrats.org	Des Moines	IA	50321	515-244-7292	244-5051
Kansas Democratic Party 501 JEFFERSON St Ste 30 *Web:* www.ksdp.org	Topeka	KS	66607	785-234-0425	234-8420
Kentucky Democratic Party 190 Democrat Dr *Web:* www.kydemocrat.com	Frankfort	KY	40601	502-695-4828	695-7629
Louisiana Democratic Party 701 Government St *Web:* louisianademocrats.org	Baton Rouge	LA	70802	225-336-4155	336-0046
Maine Democratic Party PO Box 5258 *Web:* www.mainedems.org	Augusta	ME	04332	207-622-6233	622-2657
Massachusetts Democratic Party 77 Summer St 10th Fl *Web:* www.massdems.org	Boston	MA	02110	617-939-0800	426-5126
Michigan Democratic Party 606 Townsend St *Web:* www.michigandems.com	Lansing	MI	48933	517-371-5410	371-2056
Missouri Democratic Party PO Box 719 *Web:* missouridemocrats.org	Jefferson City	MO	65102	573-636-5241	634-4259
Montana Democratic Party PO Box 802 *Web:* www.montanademocrats.org	Helena	MT	59624	406-442-9520	442-9534
New Hampshire Democratic Party 105 N State St *Web:* nhdp.org	Concord	NH	03301	603-225-6899	
New Jersey Democratic State Committee 196 W State St *Web:* www.njdems.org	Trenton	NJ	08608	609-392-3367	396-4778
New Mexico Democratic Party (DPNM) 8214 Second St NW ste A *TF:* 800-624-2457 ■ *Web:* www.dpnm.net	Albuquerque	NM	87114	505-830-3650	830-3645
North Carolina Democratic Party 220 Hillsborough St *Web:* www.ncdp.org	Raleigh	NC	27603	919-821-2777	821-4778
North Dakota Democratic Party 1902 E Divide Ave *Web:* www.demnpl.com	Bismarck	ND	58501	701-255-0460	255-7823
Ohio Democratic Party 340 E Fulton St *Web:* www.ohiodems.org	Columbus	OH	43215	614-221-6563	221-0721
Oklahoma Democratic Party 4100 N Lincoln Blvd *TF:* 800-547-5600 ■ *Web:* www.okdemocrats.org	Oklahoma City	OK	73105	405-427-3366	
Oregon Democratic Party 232 NE Ninth Ave *Web:* www.dpo.org	Portland	OR	97232	503-224-8200	224-5335
Pennsylvania Democratic Party 229 State St *Web:* www.padems.com	Harrisburg	PA	17101	717-920-8470	901-7829

	City	State	Zip	Phone	Fax
Rhode Island Democratic Party 151 Broadway Ste 310 *Web:* www.ridemocrats.org	Providence	RI	02903	401-272-3367	272-3368
South Carolina Democratic Party 915 Lady St Ste 111 *TF:* 800-841-1817 ■ *Web:* www.scdp.org	Columbia	SC	29250	803-799-7798	765-1692
South Dakota Democratic Party 335 N Main Ave Ste 200 *Web:* www.sddp.org	Sioux Falls	SD	57104	605-271-5405	
Tennessee Democratic Party 1900 Church St Ste 203 *Web:* www.tndp.org	Nashville	TN	37203	615-327-9779	327-9759
Texas Democratic Party 1106 Lavaca St Ste 100 *Web:* www.txdemocrats.org	Austin	TX	78701	512-478-9800	480-2500
Virginia Democratic Party 1710 E Franklin St 2nd Fl *TF:* 800-322-1144 ■ *Web:* www.vademocrats.org	Richmond	VA	23223	804-644-1966	343-3642
Washington Democratic Party PO Box 4027 *Web:* www.wa-democrats.org	Seattle	WA	98194	206-583-0664	583-0301
West Virginia Democratic Party 717 Lee St Ste 214	Charleston	WV	25301	304-342-8121	342-8122
Wisconsin Democratic Party 110 King St Ste 203 *Web:* www.wisdems.org	Madison	WI	53703	608-255-5172	255-8919

616-2 Republican State Committees

	City	State	Zip	Phone	Fax
Alabama Republican Party 3505 Lorna Rd Ste 219 *TF:* 800-274-8683 ■ *Web:* www.algop.org	Birmingham	AL	35216	205-212-5900	212-5910
Alaska Republican Party 1001 W Fireweed Ln *Web:* www.alaskagop.org	Anchorage	AK	99503	907-276-4467	276-0425
Arizona Republican Party 3501 N 24th St *Web:* arizonagop.org	Phoenix	AZ	85016	602-957-7770	224-0932
California Republican Party 1903 W Magnolia Blvd *Web:* www.cagop.org	Burbank	CA	91506	818-841-5210	
Colorado Republican Party 5950 S Willow Dr Ste 210 *Web:* www.cologop.org	Greenwood Village	CO	80111	303-758-3333	
Connecticut Republican Party 31 Pratt St 4th Fl *Web:* ct.gop	Hartford	CT	06103	860-422-8211	422-8175
Georgia Republican Party 3110 Maple Dr Ste 200-E *Web:* www.gagop.org	Atlanta	GA	30305	404-257-5559	257-0779
Hawaii Republican Party 725 Kapiolani Blvd Ste C105 *Web:* www.gophawaii.com	Honolulu	HI	96813	808-593-8180	593-7742
Idaho Republican State Committee 802 W Bannock Lowr Plz 103 PO Box 2267 *Web:* www.idgop.org	Boise	ID	83702	208-343-6405	343-6414
Indiana Republican Party 47 S Meridian St 2nd fl *Web:* indiana.gop/	Indianapolis	IN	46204	317-635-7561	632-8510
Iowa Republican Party 621 E Ninth St *Web:* www.iowagop.org	Des Moines	IA	50309	515-282-8105	
Kansas Republican Party 2605 SW 21st St PO Box 4157 *Web:* www.ksgop.org	Topeka	KS	66604	785-234-3456	228-0353
Kentucky Republican Party PO Box 1068 *Web:* www.rpk.org	Frankfort	KY	40602	502-875-5130	223-5625
Louisiana Republican Party 530 Lk Land Rd *Web:* www.lagop.com	Baton Rouge	LA	70802	225-389-4495	389-4493
Maine Republican Party 9 Higgins St *Web:* www.mainegop.com	Augusta	ME	04330	207-622-6247	623-5322
Maryland Republican Party 95 Cathedral St *Web:* www.mdgop.org	Annapolis	MD	21401	410-263-2125	
Massachusetts Republican State Committee 85 Merrimac St Ste 400 *Web:* www.massgop.com	Boston	MA	02114	617-523-5005	
Michigan Republican State Committee 520 Seymour Ave *Web:* www.migop.org	Lansing	MI	48933	517-487-5413	487-0090
Minnesota Republican Party 2200 E Franklin Ave Ste 201 *Web:* www.mngop.com	Minneapolis	MN	55404	651-222-0022	224-4122
Mississippi Republican Party 415 Yazoo St PO Box 60 *Web:* www.msgop.org	Jackson	MS	39201	601-948-5191	354-0972
Montana Republican Party PO Box 935 *Web:* www.mtgop.org	Helena	MT	59624	406-442-6469	
Nebraska Republican Party 1610 N St *Web:* nadc.nebraska.gov	Lincoln	NE	68508	402-475-2122	475-3541
Nevada Republican Party 6330 McLeod Dr Ste 1 *Web:* www.nevadagop.org	Las Vegas	NV	89120	702-258-9182	258-9186
New Hampshire Republican State Committee 10 Water St *Web:* nh.gop	Concord	NH	03301	603-225-9341	225-7498
New Mexico Republican Party (RPNM) 5150-A San Francisco Rd NE PO Box 94083 *Web:* newmexico.gop	Albuquerque	NM	87109	505-298-3662	292-0755
New York Republican State Committee 315 State St *Web:* newyork.gop	Albany	NY	12210	518-462-2601	449-7443
North Carolina Republican Party PO Box 12905 *Web:* www.ncgop.org	Raleigh	NC	27605	919-828-6423	899-3815
Ohio Republican Party 211 S Fifth St *Web:* www.ohiogop.org	Columbus	OH	43215	614-228-2481	
Oklahoma Republican State Committee 4031 N Lincoln Blvd *Web:* ok.gop	Oklahoma City	OK	73105	405-528-3501	521-9531
Pennsylvania Republican State Committee 112 State St *Web:* www.pagop.org	Harrisburg	PA	17101	717-234-4901	231-3828
South Carolina Republican Party, The 1913 Marion St *Web:* www.scgop.com	Columbia	SC	29201	803-988-8440	988-8444
South Dakota Republican State Central Committee PO Box 1099 *Web:* www.southdakotagop.com	Pierre	SD	57501	605-224-7347	224-7349
Tennessee Republican Party 2424 21st Ave Ste 200 *Web:* www.tngop.org	Nashville	TN	37212	615-269-4260	
Texas Republican Party 1108 Lavaca Ste 500 *TF:* 800-525-5555 ■ *Web:* www.texasgop.org	Austin	TX	78701	512-477-9821	480-0709
Utah Republican Party 117 E S Temple St *Web:* utah.gop	Salt Lake City	UT	84111	801-533-9777	533-0327
Virginia Republican Party 115 E Grace St *Web:* www.virginia.gop	Richmond	VA	23219	804-780-0111	343-1060
West Virginia Republican State Committee PO Box 2711 *Web:* www.wvgop.org	Charleston	WV	25330	304-768-0493	768-6083
Wisconsin Republican Party 148 E Johnson St *Web:* www.wisgop.org	Madison	WI	53703	608-257-4765	
Wyoming Republican Party 1821 Carey Ave PO Box 984 *Web:* wyoming.gop	Casper	WY	82003	307-234-9166	

617 PORTALS - VOICE

Voice portals permit users to access web-based messaging as well as various types of Internet information (e.g., weather, stock quotes, driving directions, etc.) via the telephone (wired or wireless).

	City	State	Zip	Phone	Fax
GoSolo Technologies Inc 5410 Mariner St Ste 175 *TF:* 866-246-7656 ■ *Web:* www.teamgosolo.com	Tampa	FL	33609	866-246-7656	
InternetSpeech.com 6980 Santa Teresa Blvd Ste 201 *Web:* www.internetspeech.com	San Jose	CA	95119	408-360-7730	
Tellme Networks Inc 1310 Villa St *Web:* www.bing.com	Mountain View	CA	94041	650-930-9000	930-9101

618 PORTS & PORT AUTHORITIES

See Also Airports p. 1730; Cruise Lines p. 2177

	City	State	Zip	Phone	Fax
Alabama State Port Authority PO Box 1588 *Web:* www.asdd.com	Mobile	AL	36633	251-441-7234	441-7216
Bradford Licensing Associates 7 Oak Pl Ste 1 *Web:* www.bradfordlicensing.com	Montclair	NJ	07042	973-509-0200	
Cleveland-Cuyahoga County Port Authority 1375 E Ninth St Ste 2300 *Web:* portofcleveland.com	Cleveland	OH	44114	216-241-8004	
Delaware River Port Authority 1 Port Center 2 Riverside Dr PO Box 1949 *Fax: Hum Res ■ *Web:* www.drpa.org	Camden	NJ	08101	856-968-2000	968-2242*
Detroit-Wayne County Port Authority 130 E Atwater St *Web:* www.portdetroit.com	Detroit	MI	48226	313-259-5091	259-5093
Eastport Port Authority 3 Madison St *Web:* www.portofeastport.org	Eastport	ME	04631	207-853-4614	853-9584
Erie-Western Pennsylvania Port Authority 208 E Bayfront Pkwy Ste 201 *Web:* www.porterie.org	Erie	PA	16507	814-455-7557	455-8070
Georgia Ports Authority PO Box 2406 *TF:* 800-342-8012 ■ *Web:* www.gaports.com	Savannah	GA	31402	912-964-3811	964-3921
Greater Lafourche Port Commission PO Box 490 *Web:* www.portfourchon.com	Galliano	LA	70354	985-632-6701	632-6703
Halifax Port Authority 1215 Marginal Rd PO Box 336 *Web:* www.portofhalifax.ca	Halifax	NS	B3J2P6	902-426-8222	426-7335
Hamilton Port Authority 605 James St N 6th Fl *TF:* 800-263-2131 ■ *Web:* www.hamiltonport.ca	Hamilton	ON	L8L1K1	905-525-4330	
Hawaii Dept of Transportation Harbors Div 79 S Nimitz Hwy *Web:* www.hawaii.gov	Honolulu	HI	96813	808-587-1927	587-1928
Humboldt Bay Harbor District 601 Startare Dr *Web:* www.portofhumboldtbay.org	Eureka	CA	95501	707-443-0801	443-0800
Illinois International Port District 3600 E 95th St *TF:* 800-843-7678 ■ *Web:* iipd.com	Chicago	IL	60617	773-646-4400	221-7678
Indiana Port Commission 150 W Market St Ste 100 *TF:* 800-232-7678 ■ *Web:* www.portsofindiana.com	Indianapolis	IN	46204	317-232-9200	232-0137
International Port of Dutch Harbor PO Box 610 *TF:* 800-526-6731 ■ *Web:* ci.unalaska.ak.us	Unalaska	AK	99685	907-581-1251	
Juneau Harbor 155 S Seward St *Web:* www.juneau.org/harbors	Juneau	AK	99801	907-586-5255	586-2507
Ketchikan Ports & Harbors Dept 2933 Tongass Ave *Web:* www.ktn-ak.us	Ketchikan	AK	99901	907-228-5632	247-3610
Kodiak Port & Harbor 403 Marine Way *TF:* 800-563-4254 ■ *Web:* city.kodiak.ak.us	Kodiak	AK	99615	907-486-8080	486-8090

Phone | Fax

Manatee County Port Authority
300 Tampa Bay Way ... Palmetto FL 34221 941-722-6621 729-1463
Web: www.portmanatee.com

Massachusetts Port Authority
1 Harborside Dr Ste 200S ... East Boston MA 02128 617-568-7300
Web: www.massport.com

Mississippi State Port Authority at Gulfport
2510 14th St Ste 1450 ... Gulfport MS 39501 228-865-4300 865-4335
TF: 877-881-4367 ■ *Web:* www.shipmspa.com

Montreal Port Authority
Port of Montreal Bldg
2100 Pierre-Dupuy Ave Wing 1 ... Montreal QC H3C3R5 514-283-7011 283-0829
Web: www.port-montreal.com

Nanaimo Port Authority
104 Front St PO Box 131 ... Nanaimo BC V9R5H7 250-753-4146 753-4899
Web: www.npa.ca

New Bedford Harbor Development Commission
52 Fisherman S Wharf PO Box 50899 ... New Bedford MA 02745 508-961-3000 979-1517
Web: www.portofnewbedford.org

New Hampshire State Port Authority
555 Market St ... Portsmouth NH 03801 603-436-8500
Web: www.portsmouthnh.com

North Carolina State Ports Authority
2202 Burnett Blvd PO Box 9002 ... Wilmington NC 28402 910-763-1621
TF: 800-334-0682 ■ *Web:* www.ncports.com

Ogdensburg Bridge & Port Authority
1 Bridge Plaza ... Ogdensburg NY 13669 315-393-4080 393-7068
Web: www.ogdensport.com

Oregon International Port of Coos Bay
125 Central Ave Ste 300 PO Box 1215 ... Coos Bay OR 97420 541-267-7678 269-1475
TF: 800-463-3339 ■ *Web:* www.portofcoosbay.com

Oshawa Harbour Commission 1050 Farewell Ave ... Oshawa ON L1H6N6 905-576-0400 576-5701
Web: portofoshawa.ca

Philadelphia Regional Port Authority
3460 N Delaware Ave 2nd Fl ... Philadelphia PA 19134 215-426-2600 426-6800
Web: www.philaport.com

Port Alberni Port Authority
2750 Harbour Rd ... Port Alberni BC V9Y7X2 250-723-5312 723-1114
Web: portalberniportauthority.ca

Port Authority of New York/New Jersey
225 Pk Ave S 15th Fl ... New York NY 10003 212-435-7000
Web: www.panynj.gov

Port Canaveral 445 Challanger Rd ... Cape Canaveral FL 32920 321-783-7831 784-6223
TF: 888-767-8226 ■ *Web:* www.portcanaveral.com

Port Everglades 1850 Eller Dr ... Fort Lauderdale FL 33316 954-523-3404 525-1910
TF: 800-421-0188 ■ *Web:* www.porteverglades.org

Port Freeport 1001 N Gulf Blvd ... Freeport TX 77541 979-233-2667 233-5625
TF: 800-362-5743 ■ *Web:* www.portfreeport.com

Port Metro Vancouver
100 The Pt 999 Canada Pl ... Vancouver BC V6C3T4 604-665-9000 284-4271*
*Fax Area Code: 866 ■ *Web:* www.portvancouver.com

Port Metro Vancouver 999 Canada Pl ... Vancouver BC V6C3T4 604-665-9000 284-4271*
*Fax Area Code: 866 ■ *TF:* 888-767-8826 ■ *Web:* www.portvancouver.com

Port of Albany
Albany Port District Commission
106 Smith Blvd ... Albany NY 12202 518-463-8763 463-8767
Web: www.portofalbany.us

Port of Anacortes 100 Commercial Ave ... Anacortes WA 98221 360-293-3134 293-9608
Web: www.portofanacortes.com

Port of Anchorage 2000 Anchorage Port Rd ... Anchorage AK 99501 907-343-6200
TF: 877-650-8400 ■ *Web:* www.muni.org

Port of Astoria 422 Gateway Ave ... Astoria OR 97103 503-325-4521 325-4525
TF: 800-860-4093 ■ *Web:* www.portofastoria.com

Port of Baltimore
Maryland Port Administration
401 E Pratt St ... Baltimore MD 21202 800-638-7519
TF General: 800-638-7519 ■ *Web:* www.mpa.maryland.gov

Port of Beaumont 1225 Main St ... Beaumont TX 77701 409-835-5367 832-9592
Web: www.portofbeaumont.com

Port of Bellingham 1801 Roeder Ave ... Bellingham WA 98225 360-676-2500 671-6411
Web: www.portofbellingham.com

Port of Brownsville 1000 Foust Rd ... Brownsville TX 78521 956-831-4592 831-5006
TF: 800-378-5395 ■ *Web:* www.portofbrownsville.com

Port of Burns Harbor 6625 S Boundary Dr ... Portage IN 46368 219-787-8636
Web: www.portsofindiana.com

Port of Corpus Christi 222 Power St ... Corpus Christi TX 78401 361-882-5633 882-7110
TF: 800-580-7110 ■ *Web:* www.portofcc.com

Port of Duluth
Duluth Seaway Port Authority
1200 Port Terminal Dr ... Duluth MN 55802 218-727-8525 727-6888
TF: 800-232-0703 ■ *Web:* www.duluthport.com

Port of Everett 2911 Bond St Ste 202 ... Everett WA 98201 425-259-3164 252-7366
TF: 800-729-7678 ■ *Web:* www.portofeverett.com

Port of Galveston 123 25th St ... Galveston TX 77550 409-765-9321 766-6107
Web: www.portofgalveston.com

Port of Grays Harbor 111 S Wooding St ... Aberdeen WA 98520 360-533-9528 533-9505
Web: www.portofgraysharbor.com

Port of Greater Baton Rouge
Greater Baton Rouge Port Commission
2425 Ernest Wilson Dr PO Box 380 ... Port Allen LA 70767 225-342-1660 342-1666
Web: www.portgbr.com

Port of Homer 4350 Homer Spit Rd ... Homer AK 99603 907-235-3160 235-3152
Web: www.cityofhomer-ak.gov

Port of Houston 111 E Loop N ... Houston TX 77029 713-670-2400 671-0359
Web: www.portofhouston.com

Port of Iberia 4611 S Lewis St PO Box 9986 ... New Iberia LA 70560 337-364-1065 364-3136
Web: www.portofiberia.com

Port of Jacksonville
Jacksonville Port Authority
2831 Talleyrand Ave PO Box 3005 ... Jacksonville FL 32206 904-357-3000 357-3060
Web: www.jaxport.com

Port of Lake Charles 150 Marine St ... Lake Charles LA 70601 337-439-3661 493-3523
Web: www.portlc.com

Port of Long Beach 925 Harbor Plz ... Long Beach CA 90801 562-437-0041 901-1725
Web: www.polb.com

Port of Longview 10 Port Way ... Longview WA 98632 360-425-3305 425-8650
Web: www.portoflongview.com

Port of Los Angeles 425 S Palos Verdes St ... San Pedro CA 90731 310-732-7678
Web: www.portoflosangeles.org

Port of Miami
Dante B. Fascell 1015 N America Way ... Miami FL 33132 305-371-7678 347-4843
Web: www.miamidade.gov

Port of Milwaukee
2323 S Lincoln Memorial Dr ... Milwaukee WI 53207 414-286-3511 286-8506
TF: 800-367-5690 ■ *Web:* city.milwaukee.gov/port

Port of Mobile
Alabama State Docks Dept 250 N Water St ... Mobile AL 36602 251-441-7203 441-7216
Web: www.asdd.com

Port of Monroe
Monroe Port Commission
2929 E Front St PO Box 585 ... Monroe MI 48161 734-241-6480 241-0813
Web: www.portofmonroe.com

Port of New London
Connecticut Bureau of Aviation & Ports
State Pier ... New London CT 06320 860-443-3856
Web: www.ct.gov

Port of New Orleans
1350 Port of New Orleans Pl ... New Orleans LA 70130 504-522-2551 524-4156
TF: 800-776-6652 ■ *Web:* www.portno.com

Port of Newport 600 SE Bay Blvd ... Newport OR 97365 541-265-7758 265-4235
Web: www.portofnewport.com

Port of Nome 307 Belmont St ... Nome AK 99762 907-443-6619 443-5473
Web: www.nomealaska.org

Port of Oakland 530 Water St ... Oakland CA 94607 510-627-1100
Web: www.portoakland.com

Port of Olympia 915 Washington St NE ... Olympia WA 98501 360-528-8000 528-8090
Web: www.portolympia.com

Port of Orange
Orange County Navigation Port District
1201 Childers Rd ... Orange TX 77630 409-883-4363 883-5607
TF: 800-368-3749 ■ *Web:* www.portoforange.com

Port of Oswego Authority 1 E Second St ... Oswego NY 13126 315-343-4503 343-5498
Web: www.portoswego.com

Port of Palm Beach 1 E 11th St Ste 600 ... Riviera Beach FL 33404 561-842-4201 842-4240
TF: 877-377-1737 ■ *Web:* www.portofpalmbeach.com

Port of Pascagoula
Jackson County Port Authority
3033 Pascagoula St ... Pascagoula MS 39567 228-762-4041 762-7476
Web: www.portofpascagoula.com

Port of Pensacola 700 S Barracks St ... Pensacola FL 32502 850-436-5070 436-5076
TF: 800-711-1712 ■ *Web:* www.portofpensacola.com

Port of Pittsburgh 425 Sixth Ave Ste 2990 ... Pittsburgh PA 15219 412-201-7330 201-7337
Web: www.port.pittsburgh.pa.us

Port of Port Angeles
338 W First St PO Box 1350 ... Port Angeles WA 98362 360-457-8527 452-3959
Web: www.portofpa.com

Port of Port Arthur 221 Houston Ave ... Port Arthur TX 77640 409-983-2011 983-7572
Web: www.portofportarthur.com

Port of Port Lavaca-Point Comfort
Calhoun Port Authority PO Box 397 ... Point Comfort TX 77978 361-987-2813 987-2189
TF: 800-933-3643 ■ *Web:* www.calhounport.com

Port of Portland 7200 NE Airport Way ... Portland OR 97218 503-415-6000
TF: 800-547-8411 ■ *Web:* www.portofportland.com

Port of Portland 389 Congress St ... Portland ME 04101 207-874-8892 874-8473
Web: portlandmaine.gov

Port of Redwood City 675 Seaport Blvd ... Redwood City CA 94063 650-306-4150 369-7636
Web: www.redwoodcityport.com

Port of Richmond Commission 900 E Broad St ... Richmond VA 23219 804-646-6335 646-5789
TF: 800-467-4943 ■ *Web:* richmondgov.com

Port of Sacramento
1110 W Capitol Ave ... West Sacramento CA 95691 916-371-8000 372-4802
Web: www.cityofwestsacramento.org

Port of Saint Helens 100 E St ... Columbia City OR 97018 503-397-2888 397-6924
Web: www.portsh.org

Port of San Diego 3165 Pacific Hwy ... San Diego CA 92101 619-686-6200
TF: 800-854-2757 ■ *Web:* www.portofsandiego.org

Port of San Francisco
Pier 1 The Embarcadero ... San Francisco CA 94111 415-274-0400 732-0400
TF: 800-479-5314 ■ *Web:* www.sfport.com

Port of Seattle PO Box 1209 ... Seattle WA 98111 206-728-3000 728-3280
TF: 800-426-7817 ■ *Web:* www.portseattle.org

Port of Sept-Iles
1 Rue Monseigneur Blanche ... Sept-Iles QC G4R5P3 418-968-1231 962-4445
Web: www.portsi.com

Port of Seward PO Box 167 ... Seward AK 99664 907-224-3138 224-7187
TF: 855-445-7131 ■ *Web:* www.cityofseward.net

Port of South Louisiana
171 Belle Terre Blvd PO Box 909 ... LaPlace LA 70068 985-652-9278 568-6270*
*Fax Area Code: 504 ■ *TF:* 866-536-8300 ■ *Web:* www.portsl.com

Port of Stockton 2201 W Washington St ... Stockton CA 95203 209-946-0246 465-7244
TF: 800-344-3213 ■ *Web:* www.portofstockton.com

Port of Tacoma 1 Sitcum Way ... Tacoma WA 98421 253-383-5841 593-4570
Web: www.portoftacoma.com

Port of Valdez 412 Ferry Terminal Way ... Valdez AK 99686 907-835-4564 835-4479
Web: www.ci.valdez.ak.us

Port of Vancouver 3103 NW Lower River Rd ... Vancouver WA 98660 360-693-3611 735-1565
TF: 800-475-8012 ■ *Web:* www.portvanusa.com

Port of Wilmington 1 Hausel Rd ... Wilmington DE 19801 302-472-7678 472-7740
Web: www.portofwilmington.com

Port Panama City 5321 W Hwy 98 ... Panama City FL 32401 850-767-3220 767-3235
Web: www.panamacityportauthority.com

Prince Rupert Port Authority
200-215 Cow Bay Rd ... Prince Rupert BC V8J1A2 250-627-8899 627-8980
Web: www.rupertport.com

Quebec Port Authority
150 Dalhousie St PO Box 80 Stn Haute-Ville ... Quebec QC G1R4M8 418-648-3640 648-4160
Web: www.portquebec.ca

				Phone	Fax
Saguenay Port Authority 6600 Quai-Marcel-Dionne Rd. *Web:* www.portsaguenay.ca	La Baie	QC	G7B3N9	418-697-0250	697-0243
Saint John Port Authority 111 Water St *Web:* www.sjport.com	Saint John	NB	E2L0B1	506-636-4869	636-4443
Sitka Harbor 617 Katlian St *TF:* 866-948-8683 ■ *Web:* cityofsitka.com	Sitka	AK	99835	907-747-3439	747-6278
South Carolina State Ports Authority 176 Concord St *TF:* 800-845-7106 ■ *Web:* www.scspa.com	Charleston	SC	29401	843-723-8651	577-8710
South Jersey Port Corp Second & Beckett St *Web:* www.southjerseyport.com	Camden	NJ	08103	856-757-4969	757-4903
Tampa Port Authority 1101 Channelside Dr *TF:* 800-741-2297 ■ *Web:* www.tampaport.com	Tampa	FL	33602	813-905-7678	905-5109
Thunder Bay Port Authority 100 Main St *Web:* www.portofthunderbay.com	Thunder Bay	ON	P7B6R9	807-345-6400	345-9058
Toledo-Lucas County Port Authority 1 Maritime Plaza *TF:* 800-969-4700 ■ *Web:* www.toledoport.org	Toledo	OH	43604	419-243-8251	243-1835
Toronto Port Authority 60 Harbour St *Web:* www.portstoronto.com/home.aspx	Toronto	ON	M5J1B7	416-863-2000	863-0495
Trois-Rivieres Port Authority 1545 Du Fleuve St Ste 300 *Web:* www.porttr.com	Trois-Rivieres	QC	G9A6K4	819-378-2887	378-2487
Virginia Port Authority 101 W Main St *Web:* www.portofvirginia.com	Norfolk	VA	23510	757-683-8000	683-8500
Waukegan Port District 55 S Harbor Pl PO Box 620 *Web:* www.waukeganport.com	Waukegan	IL	60085	847-244-3133	244-1348
Windsor Port Authority 3190 Sandwich St Ste 502 *Web:* www.portwindsor.com	Windsor	ON	N9C1A6	519-258-5741	258-5905
Wrangell Harbor PO Box 531 *TF:* 800-347-4462 ■ *Web:* www.wrangell.com	Wrangell	AK	99929	907-874-3736	874-3197

619 POULTRY PROCESSING

See Also Meat Packing Plants p. 2735

				Phone	Fax
Allen Family Foods Inc 126 N Shipley St *Web:* allenharimllc.com/index.cfm	Seaford	DE	19973	302-629-9163	629-0514
American Dehydrated Foods Inc 3801 E Sunshine *TF:* 800-456-3447 ■ *Web:* www.adf.com	Springfield	MO	65809	417-881-7755	881-4963
Amick Farms Inc 2079 Batesburg Hwy *TF:* 800-926-4257 ■ *Web:* www.amickfarms.com	Batesburg	SC	29006	803-532-1400	
Barber's Poultry Inc 810 E 50th Ave *Web:* www.barberspoultry.com	Denver	CO	80216	303-466-7338	466-6960
Bell & Evans 154 W Main St PO Box 39 *Web:* www.bellandevans.com	Fredericksburg	PA	17026	717-865-6626	865-7046
Brakebush Bros Inc N4993 Sixth Dr *TF:* 800-933-2121 ■ *Web:* www.brakebush.com	Westfield	WI	53964	608-296-2121	296-3192
Brown Produce Co IL 37	Farina	IL	62838	618-245-3301	
Butterfield Foods Co 225 Hubbard Ave	Butterfield	MN	56120	507-956-5103	956-5751
Case Farms Inc 121 Rand St *Web:* casefarms.com	Morganton	NC	28655	828-438-6900	
Claxton Poultry Farms 8816 Hway 301 PO Box 428 *TF:* 888-739-3181 ■ *Web:* www.claxtonpoultry.com	Claxton	GA	30417	912-739-3181	
Culver Duck Farms Inc PO Box 910 *TF:* 800-825-9225 ■ *Web:* www.culverduck.com	Middlebury	IN	46540	574-825-9537	825-2613
Echo Lake Farm Produce Co PO Box 279 *TF:* 800-888-3447 ■ *Web:* www.echolakefoods.com	Burlington	WI	53105	800-888-3447	
Empire Kosher Poultry Inc 247 Empire Dr *Web:* www.empirekosher.com	Mifflintown	PA	17059	717-436-7055	
Far Best Foods Inc 4689 S 400 W PO Box 480 *Web:* www.farbestfoods.com	Huntingburg	IN	47542	812-683-4200	683-4226
Fieldale Farms Corp 555 Broiler Blvd *TF:* 800-241-5400 ■ *Web:* www.fieldale.com	Baldwin	GA	30511	706-778-5100	778-3767
Foster Farms Inc PO Box 306 PO Box 457 *TF:* 800-255-7227 ■ *Web:* www.fosterfarms.com	Livingston	CA	95334	800-255-7227	
Georges Inc 402 W Robinson Ave *Web:* georgesinc.com	Springdale	AR	72764	479-927-7000	
Henningsen Foods Inc 14334 Industrial Rd *Web:* www.henningsenfoods.com	Omaha	NE	68144	402-330-2500	330-0875
Holmes Foods Inc 101 S Liberty Ave *Web:* holmesfoods.com	Nixon	TX	78140	830-582-1551	582-1090
House of Raeford Farms Inc 520 E Central Ave *TF:* 800-888-7539 ■ *Web:* www.houseofraeford.com	Raeford	NC	28376	910-875-5161	
ISE America Inc PO Box 267 *Web:* www.iseamerica.com	Galena	MD	21635	410-755-6300	755-6367
Jennie-O Turkey Store 2505 Willmar Ave SW *TF:* 800-621-3505 ■ *Web:* www.jennieo.com	Willmar	MN	56201	320-235-2622	
Keystone Foods LLC 300 Bar Harbor Dr Ste 600 5 Tower Bridge *Web:* www.keystonefoods.com	West Conshohocken	PA	19428	610-668-6700	
Koch Foods Inc 1300 Higgins Rd Ste 100 *TF:* 800-837-2778 ■ *Web:* www.kochfoods.com	Park Ridge	IL	60068	847-384-5940	384-5961
Mar-Jac Poultry Inc 1020 Aviation Blvd PO Box 1017 *Web:* www.marjacpoultry.com	Gainesville	GA	30501	770-531-5007	
Marshall Durbin Co 2830 Commerce Blvd *TF Sales:* 800-245-8204 ■ *Web:* www.marshalldurbin.com	Birmingham	AL	35210	205-380-3251	
Michael Foods Inc 301 Carlson Pkwy Ste 400 *TF:* 800-328-5474 ■ *Web:* www.michaelfoods.com	Minnetonka	MN	55305	952-258-4000	258-4911
Mid-valley Distributors Inc 3886 E Jensen Ave *Web:* www.mvdinc.com	Fresno	CA	93725	559-485-2660	
Mountaire Farms 17269 NC Hwy 71 N **Fax Area Code:* 302 ■ **Fax:* Hum Res ■ *TF:* 877-887-1490 ■ *Web:* www.mountaire.com	Lumber Bridge	NC	28357	910-843-5942	732-6723*
OK Foods Inc PO Box 1787 *TF:* 800-635-9441 ■ *Web:* www.tenderbird.com	Fort Smith	AR	72902	800-635-9441	
Olymel LP 2200 Pratte Ave Pratte *TF:* 800-361-7990 ■ *Web:* www.olymel.com	Saint-Hyacinthe	QC	J2S4B6	450-771-0400	645-2869
PECO Foods Inc 3701 Kauloosa Ave *Web:* www.pecofoods.com	Tuscaloosa	AL	35401	205-345-3955	343-2401
Pennfield Corp 2260 Erin Ct PO Box 4366	Lancaster	PA	17601	717-299-2561	295-8766
Perdue Farms Inc 31149 Old Ocean City Rd *TF:* 800-473-7383 ■ *Web:* www.perdue.com	Salisbury	MD	21804	410-543-3000	543-3532
Pilgrim's Corp 1770 Promontory Cir *NASDAQ: PPC* ■ *TF:* 800-321-1470 ■ *Web:* www.pilgrimspride.com	Greeley	CO	80634	800-321-1470	
Randall Foods Inc PO Box 2669 *Web:* randallfoods.com	Huntington Park	CA	90255	323-261-6565	
Simmons Foods Inc 601 N Hico St *Web:* simmonsfoods.com	Siloam Springs	AR	72761	479-524-8151	
Sonstegard Foods Co 5005 S Bur Oak Pl Ste 102 *TF:* 800-533-3184 ■ *Web:* www.sonstegard.com	Sioux Falls	SD	57108	800-533-3184	
Stevens Sausage Company Inc 3411 Stevens Sausage Rd *Web:* www.stevens-sausage.com	Smithfield	NC	27577	919-934-3159	
Tip Top Poultry Inc 327 Wallace Rd *TF:* 800-241-5230 ■ *Web:* tiptoppoultry.com	Marietta	GA	30062	770-973-8070	973-6897
Turkey Valley Farms 112 S Sixth St PO Box 200 *Web:* www.turkeyvalleyfarms.com	Marshall	MN	56258	507-337-3100	337-3009
Tyson Foods Inc 2210 W Oaklawn Dr PO Box 2020 *NYSE: TSN* ■ *TF:* 800-643-3410 ■ *Web:* www.tyson.com	Springdale	AR	72762	479-290-4000	
Valley Fresh Inc 3600 E Linwood Ave *TF:* 800-523-4635	Turlock	CA	95380	209-669-5600	
Wayne Farms Enterprises LLC 1020 County Rd 114 *Web:* waynefarms.com	Jack	AL	36346	334-897-3435	897-1000
West Liberty Foods LLC 228 W Second St *TF:* 888-511-4500 ■ *Web:* www.wlfoods.com	West Liberty	IA	52776	319-627-6000	627-6334

620 POWER TRANSMISSION EQUIPMENT - MECHANICAL

See Also Bearings - Ball & Roller p. 1850

				Phone	Fax
Adams Co 8040 Chavenelle Rd *Web:* www.theadamscompany.com	Dubuque	IA	52002	563-583-3591	583-8048
Allied-Locke Industries 1088 Corregidor Rd *TF:* 800-435-7752 ■ *Web:* www.alliedlocke.com	Dixon	IL	61021	815-288-1471	288-7945
American Metal Bearing Co 7191 Acacia Ave *TF:* 800-888-3048 ■ *Web:* www.ambco.net	Garden Grove	CA	92841	714-892-5527	898-3217
Ameridrives Couplings 1802 Pittsburgh Ave PO Box 4000 *TF:* 800-352-0141 ■ *Web:* www.ameridrives.com	Erie	PA	16502	814-480-5000	453-5891
AmeriDrives International 1802 Pittsburgh Ave *TF:* 800-352-0141 ■ *Web:* www.ameridrives.com	Erie	PA	16502	814-480-5000	453-5891
Barden Corp 200 Pk Ave *TF:* 800-243-1060 ■ *Web:* www.bardenbearings.com	Danbury	CT	06810	203-744-2211	744-3756
Beemer Precision Inc 230 New York Dr PO Box 3080 *TF:* 800-836-2340 ■ *Web:* www.oilite.com	Fort Washington	PA	19034	215-646-8440	283-3397
Bird Precision 1 Spruce St PO Box 540569 *TF Cust Svc:* 800-454-7369 ■ *Web:* www.birdprecision.com	Waltham	MA	02454	781-894-0160	894-6308
Bishop-Wisecarver Corp 2104 Martin Way *TF:* 888-580-8272 ■ *Web:* www.bwc.com	Pittsburg	CA	94565	925-439-8272	439-5931
Buckeye Power Sales Company Inc 6850 Commerce Ct Dr PO Box 489 *TF:* 800-523-3587 ■ *Web:* www.buckeyepowersales.com	Blacklick	OH	43004	614-861-6000	861-2291
Cablecraft Motion Controls LLC 2110 Summit St *Web:* www.cablecraft.com	New Haven	IN	46774	260-749-5105	493-2387
Cangro Industries Long Island Transmission Co 495 Smith St *TF:* 800-422-9210 ■ *Web:* www.cangroindustries.com	Farmingdale	NY	11735	631-454-9000	454-9155
Capitol Stampings Corp 2700 W N Ave *Web:* www.capitolstampings.com	Milwaukee	WI	53208	414-372-3500	372-3535
Carlyle Johnson Machine Co (CJM) 291 Boston Tpke *TF:* 888-629-4867 ■ *Web:* www.cjmco.com	Bolton	CT	06043	860-643-1531	646-2645
Certified Power Inc 970 Campus Dr *TF:* 888-905-7411 ■ *Web:* www.certifiedpower.com	Mundelein	IL	60060	847-573-3800	573-3832
Deublin Co 2050 Norman Dr W *Web:* www.deublin.com	Waukegan	IL	60085	847-689-8600	689-8690
Diamond Chain Co 402 Kentucky Ave *TF Cust Svc:* 800-872-4246 ■ *Web:* www.diamondchain.com	Indianapolis	IN	46225	317-638-6431	638-6431
Don Dye Company Inc 524 NW 20th Ave PO Box 107 *Web:* dondyeco.com	Kingman	KS	67068	620-532-3131	532-2141
Eaton Corp 1111 Superior Ave Eaton Ctr *Web:* www.eaton.com	Cleveland	OH	44114	216-523-5000	
EC Styberg Engineering Company Inc 1600 Gold St PO Box 788 *Web:* www.styberg.com	Racine	WI	53401	262-637-9301	637-1319
Elliott Manufacturing Inc 11 Beckwith Ave *Web:* www.elliottmfg.com	Binghamton	NY	13901	607-772-0404	772-0431
Entek International LLC 250 N Hansard Ave PO Box 127 *Web:* entek.com/lead-acid	Lebanon	OR	97355	541-259-3901	259-3932
Force Control Industries Inc 3660 Dixie Hwy *TF:* 800-829-3244 ■ *Web:* www.forcecontrol.com	Fairfield	OH	45014	513-868-0900	868-2105
General Bearing Corp 44 High St *TF Sales:* 800-431-1766 ■ *Web:* www.generalbearing.com	West Nyack	NY	10994	845-358-6000	358-6277
GGB North America 700 Mid Atlantic Pkwy PO Box 189 **Fax:* Sales ■ *TF:* 888-840-2349 ■ *Web:* www.ggbearings.com	Thorofare	NJ	08086	856-848-3200	848-5115*

	City	State	Zip	Phone	Fax
GKN Rockford Inc 1200 Windsor Rd. *Web:* www.gkn.com	Loves Park	IL	61111	815-633-7460	633-1311
Hebeler Corp 2000 Military Rd *TF:* 800-486-4709 ■ *Web:* www.hebeler.com	Tonawanda	NY	14150	716-873-9300	873-7538
Helical Products Co Inc 901 W McCoy Ln *TF:* 877-353-9873 ■ *Web:* www.heli-cal.com	Santa Maria	CA	93455	805-928-3851	928-2369
Hilliard Corp 100 W Fourth St *Web:* www.hilliardcorp.com	Elmira	NY	14902	607-733-7121	733-3009
Horton Inc 2565 Walnut St *TF:* 800-621-1320 ■ *Web:* www.hortonww.com	Saint Paul	MN	55113	651-361-6400	
Iberdrola Renewables Inc 1125 NW Couch Ste 700 *Web:* www.iberdrolarenewables.us	Portland	OR	97209	503-796-7000	796-6901
Industrial Clutch 1701-3 Pearl St *Web:* www.indclutch.com	Waukesha	WI	53186	262-547-3357	547-2949
John Deere Coffeyville Works Inc 2624 N US Hwy **Fax Area Code: 620* ■ *TF:* 800-844-1337 ■ *Web:* www.deere.com	Coffeyville	KS	67337	800-844-1337	251-3262*
Kamatics Corp 1330 Blue Hills Ave *TF:* 866-540-5760 ■ *Web:* www.kaman.com	Bloomfield	CT	06002	860-243-9704	243-7993
Kingsbury Inc 10385 Drummond Rd *TF Sales:* 866-581-5464 ■ *Web:* www.kingsbury.com	Philadelphia	PA	19154	215-824-4000	824-4999
Linn Gear Co 100 N Eigth St PO Box 397 *TF:* 800-547-2471 ■ *Web:* www.linngear.com	Lebanon	OR	97355	541-259-1211	259-1299
Lovejoy Inc 2655 Wisconsin Ave *Web:* www.lovejoy-inc.com	Downers Grove	IL	60515	630-852-0500	
Magtrol Inc 70 Gardenville Pkwy W *TF:* 800-828-7844 ■ *Web:* www.magtrol.com	Buffalo	NY	14224	716-668-5555	668-8705
Marland Clutch 2032 VALLEYDALE Rd **Fax Area Code: 877* ■ *TF:* 800-216-3515 ■ *Web:* www.marland.com	Birmingham	AL	35244	800-216-3515	216-3001*
Martin Sprocket & Gear Inc 3100 Sprocket Dr PO Box 91588 *Web:* www.martinsprocket.com	Arlington	TX	76015	817-258-3000	258-3333
Maurey Manufacturing Corp 410 Industrial Pk Rd **Fax Area Code: 662* ■ *TF:* 800-284-2161 ■ *Web:* www.maurey.biz	Holly Springs	MS	38635	800-284-2161	252-6364*
Metallized Carbon Corp 19 S Water St *Web:* www.metcar.com	Ossining	NY	10562	914-941-3738	941-4050
Midwest Control Products Corp 590 E Main St *Web:* www.midwestcontrol.com	Bushnell	IL	61422	309-772-3163	772-2266
Nook Industries 4950 E 49th St *TF:* 800-321-7800 ■ *Web:* www.nookindustries.com	Cleveland	OH	44125	216-271-7900	271-7020
North American Clutch Corp 4360 N Green Bay Ave *Web:* www.noramclutch.com	Milwaukee	WI	53209	414-267-4000	267-4024
NSK Corp 4200 Goss Rd **Fax Area Code: 734* ■ *TF:* 888-446-5675 ■ *Web:* www.nskamericas.com	Ann Arbor	MI	48105	800-675-9930	913-7102*
NTN Bearing Corp of America 1600 E Bishop Ct *TF:* 800-323-2358 ■ *Web:* www.ntnamericas.com	Mount Prospect	IL	60056	847-298-7500	699-9744
OPW Engineered Systems 2726 Henkle Dr **Fax:* Cust Svc ■ *TF Cust Svc:* 800-547-9393 ■ *Web:* www.opwglobal.com/opw-es	Lebanon	OH	45036	513-932-9114	932-9845*
Ormat Technologies Inc 6225 Neil Rd Ste 300 *NYSE: ORA* ■ *Web:* www.ormat.com	Reno	NV	89511	775-356-9029	356-9039
Peer Bearing Co 2200 Norman Dr S **Fax:* Orders ■ *TF:* 800-433-7337 ■ *Web:* www.peerbearing.com	Waukegan	IL	60085	847-578-1000	578-1200*
Pic Design Corp 86 Benson Rd PO Box 1004 *TF:* 800-243-6125 ■ *Web:* www.pic-design.com	Middlebury	CT	06762	203-758-8272	758-8271
Ramsey Products Corp 3701 Performance Rd PO Box 668827 *Web:* www.ramseychain.com	Charlotte	NC	28266	704-394-0322	394-9134
RBC Bearings Inc 3131 W Segerstrom Ave PO Box 1953 *TF:* 866-722-2376 ■ *Web:* www.rbcbearings.com	Santa Ana	CA	92704	714-546-3131	545-9885
Real Goods Solar 833 W S Boulder Rd *NASDAQ: RSGE* ■ *TF:* 888-567-6527 ■ *Web:* rgsenergy.com	Louisville	CO	80027	888-567-6527	
Reell Precision Manufacturing Corp 1259 Willow Lk Blvd *Web:* www.reell.com	Saint Paul	MN	55110	651-484-2447	484-3867
Regal-Beloit Corp 200 State St *NYSE: RBC* ■ *TF:* 800-672-6495 ■ *Web:* www.regalbeloit.com	Beloit	WI	53511	608-364-8800	364-8818
Renold Ajax Inc 100 Bourne St *TF:* 800-251-9012 ■ *Web:* www.renold.com	Westfield	NY	14787	716-326-3121	326-6121
Rollease Inc 200 Harvard Ave *Web:* www.rollease.com	Stamford	CT	06902	203-964-1573	358-5865
Schaeffler Group USA Inc 308 Springhill Farm Rd *TF:* 800-361-5841 ■ *Web:* www.schaeffler.us	Fort Mill	SC	29715	803-548-8500	548-8599
Siemens Power Transmission & Distribution Inc 7000 Siemens Rd *Web:* siemens.com	Wendell	NC	27591	919-365-2200	
Solaria Corp 6200 Paseo Padre Pkwy *Web:* www.solaria.com	Fremont	CA	94555	510-270-2500	793-8388
Solomon Corp 103 W Main *TF:* 800-234-2867 ■ *Web:* www.solomoncorp.com	Solomon	KS	67480	785-655-2191	655-2502
Speed Selector Inc 17050 Munn Rd *Web:* speedselector.com	Chagrin Falls	OH	44023	440-543-8233	543-8527
SS White Technologies Inc 151 Old New Brunswick Rd *Web:* www.sswt.com	Piscataway	NJ	08854	732-752-8300	752-8315
Stock Drive Products/Sterling Instrument 2101 Jericho Tpke *TF:* 800-737-7436 ■ *Web:* www.sdp-si.com	New Hyde Park	NY	11040	516-328-3300	326-8827
TB Wood's Inc 440 N Fifth Ave *TF:* 888-829-6637 ■ *Web:* www.tbwoods.com	Chambersburg	PA	17201	717-264-7161	264-6420
Twin Disc Inc 1328 Racine St *NASDAQ: TWIN* ■ *Web:* www.twindisc.com	Racine	WI	53403	262-638-4000	
Universal Bearings Inc 431 N Birkey St *Web:* www.univbrg.com	Bremen	IN	46506	574-546-2261	546-5085
US Tsubaki Inc 301 E Marquardt Dr *TF:* 800-323-7790 ■ *Web:* www.ustsubaki.com	Wheeling	IL	60090	847-459-9500	459-9515
Warner Electric 449 Gardner St *TF:* 800-825-6544 ■ *Web:* www.warnernet.com	South Beloit	IL	61080	815-389-3771	
Waukesha Bearings Corp W 231 N 2811 Roundy Cir E Ste 200 *TF:* 888-832-3517 ■ *Web:* www.waukbearing.com	Pewaukee	WI	53072	262-506-3000	506-3001
Wheeler Industries 7261 Investment Dr *Web:* www.wheelerfluidfilmbearings.com	North Charleston	SC	29418	843-552-1251	552-4790
Whittet-Higgins Co 33 Higginson Ave PO Box 8 *Web:* www.whittet-higgins.com	Central Falls	RI	02863	401-728-0700	728-0703
Zero-Max Inc 13200 Sixth Ave N *TF:* 800-533-1731 ■ *Web:* www.zero-max.com	Plymouth	MN	55441	763-546-4300	546-8260

621 PRECISION MACHINED PRODUCTS

See Also Aircraft Parts & Auxiliary Equipment p. 1726; Machine Shops p. 2688

	City	State	Zip	Phone	Fax
A-1 Production Inc 5809 E Leighty Rd *Web:* www.a1production.com	Kendallville	IN	46755	260-347-0960	347-4727
Abbott Interfast Corp 190 Abbott Dr *TF:* 800-877-0789 ■ *Web:* www.abbott-interfast.com	Wheeling	IL	60090	847-459-6200	459-4076
Accellent Inc 200 W Seventh Ave *Web:* www.accellent.com/aboutus	Collegeville	PA	19426	610-489-0300	489-1150
Adept Fasteners Inc 28709 Industry Dr *Web:* www.adeptfasteners.com	Valencia	CA	91355	661-257-6600	
Afco Products Inc 2074 S Mannheim Rd *Web:* www.afco-products.com	Des Plaines	IL	60018	847-299-1055	299-8455
Air-Matic Products Company Inc 22218 Telegraph Rd *Web:* www.air-matic.com	Southfield	MI	48033	248-356-4200	
Alco Manufacturing Corp 10584 Middle Ave *Web:* www.alcomfgcorp.com	Elyria	OH	44035	440-458-5165	458-6821
Alger Mfg Company Inc 724 S Bon View Ave *TF:* 800-854-9833 ■ *Web:* www.alger1.com	Ontario	CA	91761	909-986-4591	983-3351
Allan Tool & Machine Company Inc 1822 E Maple Rd *Web:* allantool.com	Troy	MI	48083	248-585-2910	585-7728
Allied Screw Products Inc 815 E Lowell Ave *Web:* www.aspi-nc.com	Mishawaka	IN	46546	574-255-4718	255-4173
Allmetal Screw Products Corp 94 E Jefryn Blvd Ste A *Web:* www.allmetalcorp.com	Deer Park	NY	11729	631-243-5200	243-5307
Alpha Grainger Manufacturing Inc 20 Discovery Way *Web:* www.agmi.com	Franklin	MA	02038	508-520-4005	520-4185
American Products Company Inc 610 Rahway Ave *Web:* www.amerprod.com	Union	NJ	07083	908-687-4100	687-0037
American Turned Products Inc 7626 Klier Dr *Web:* www.atpteam.com	Fairview	PA	16415	814-474-4200	474-4718
Amsco-Wire Products Co 610 Grand Ave	Ridgefield	NJ	07657	201-945-5618	
Amtec Precision Products Inc 1355 Holmes Rd *Web:* www.amtecprecision.com	Elgin	IL	60123	847-695-8030	
Anchor Coupling Inc 5520 13th St *Web:* www.anchorcoupling.com	Menominee	MI	49858	906-863-2671	863-3242
Anderson Automatics Inc 6401 Welcome Ave N *Web:* www.andersonautomatics.com	Minneapolis	MN	55429	763-533-2206	533-0320
Anderson Precision Inc 20 Livingston Ave *Web:* www.andersonprecision.com	Jamestown	NY	14701	716-484-1148	484-7779
Anoplate Inc 459 Pulaski St 475 *Web:* anoplate.com	Syracuse	NY	13204	315-471-6143	471-7132
Ashley Ward Inc 7490 Easy St *Web:* www.ashleyward.com	Mason	OH	45040	513-398-1414	398-1125
Astro Seal Inc 827 Palmyrita Ave # B *Web:* www.astroseal.com	Riverside	CA	92507	951-787-6670	787-6677
ATEC Inc 12600 Executive Dr *Web:* www.atec.com	Stafford	TX	77477	281-276-2700	240-2682
Athanor Group Inc 921 E California Ave	Ontario	CA	91761	909-467-1205	467-1208
Auer Precision Inc 1050 W Birchwood Ave *Web:* www.auerprecision.com	Mesa	AZ	85210	480-834-4637	964-8237
Automatic Machine Products Co (AMP) 400 Constitution Dr *Web:* www.ampcomp.com	Taunton	MA	02780	508-822-4226	822-4476
Automatic Products Corp 2735 Forest Ln *Web:* www.ap-corp.com	Garland	TX	75042	972-272-6422	494-0533
Avanti Engineering Inc 200 W Lake Dr *Web:* www.avantiengineering.com	Glendale Heights	IL	60139	630-260-1333	260-1762
Barber-Nichols Inc 6325 W 55th Ave *Web:* www.barber-nichols.com	Arvada	CO	80002	303-421-8111	420-4679
Bay Swiss Mfg Company Inc 5 Airpark Vista Blvd *TF:* 800-247-3207 ■ *Web:* www.bayswiss.com	Dayton	NV	89403	775-246-7100	246-7104
Berkley Screw Machine Products Inc 2100 Royce Haley Dr *Web:* berkleyscrew.com	Rochester Hills	MI	48309	248-853-0044	853-1532
Berkshire Industries Inc 109 Apremont Way *Web:* www.berkshireindustries.com	Westfield	MA	01085	413-568-8676	562-0061
Betar Inc 1524 Millstone River Rd *Web:* www.betar.net	Hillsborough	NJ	08844	908-359-4200	359-1010
Betty Machine Co 324 Freehill Rd *Web:* www.bettymachine.com	Hendersonville	TN	37075	615-826-6004	826-6262
Biddle Precision Components Inc 701 S Main St *TF:* 800-428-4387 ■ *Web:* www.emcprecision.com	Sheridan	IN	46069	317-758-4451	758-5260
Birken Manufacturing Co 3 Old Windsor Rd *Web:* www.birken.net	Bloomfield	CT	06002	860-242-2211	242-2749
Blackhawk Machine Products Inc 6 Industrial Dr *Web:* www.blackhawk-machine.com	Smithfield	RI	02917	401-232-7563	232-0770
Boker's Inc 3104 Snelling Ave *TF:* 800-927-4377 ■ *Web:* www.bokers.com	Minneapolis	MN	55406	612-729-9365	

Phone Fax

Bracalente Mfg Group
20 W Creamery Rd .... Trumbauersville PA 18970 215-536-3077 536-4844
Web: www.bracalente.com
Burgess-Norton Manufacturing Co 737 Peyton St ...... Geneva IL 60134 630-232-4100 232-3700*
**Fax:* Hum Res ■ *Web:* www.burgessnorton.com
Camcraft Inc 1080 Muirfield Dr. .... Hanover Park IL 60133 630-582-6000 582-6019
Web: www.camcraft.com
Cass Screw Machine Products Co
4800 N Lilac Dr .... Brooklyn Center MN 55429 763-535-0501 535-9238
Web: www.csmp.com
CE Holden Inc 938 Rt 910 .... Cheswick PA 15024 412-767-5050 767-9922
Web: www.ceholden.com
Celina Aluminum Precision Technology Inc (CAPT)
7059 Staeger Rd. .... Celina OH 45822 419-586-2278 586-6474
Web: www.capt-celina.com
Charleston Metal Products Inc 350 Grant St .... Waterloo IN 46793 260-837-8211 837-8101
Web: www.charlestonmetal.com
Cherry Aerospace LLC 1224 E Warner Ave .... Santa Ana CA 92705 714-545-5511
Web: www.cherryaerospace.com
CNW Inc 4710 Madison Rd. .... Cincinnati OH 45227 513-321-2775 321-2618
Cole Screw Machine Products Inc
36 Nettleton Ave PO Box 1007 .... North Haven CT 06473 203-772-6675
Web: colescrew.com
Contour Tool Inc 38830 Taylor Pkwy .... North Ridgeville OH 44039 440-365-7333 365-7335
Web: contourprecisionmilling.com
Corlett-Turner Co 2500 104th Ave .... Zeeland MI 49464 616-772-9082
Web: www.corlett.com
Cox Manufacturing Co 5500 N Loop 1604 E. .... San Antonio TX 78247 210-657-7731 657-2345
TF: 800-900-7981 ■ *Web:* www.coxmanufacturing.com
CPI Aerostructures Inc 91 Heartland Blvd. .... Edgewood NY 11717 631-586-5200 586-5840
NYSE: CVU ■ *Web:* www.cpiaero.com
Curtis Screw Company Inc 50 Thielman Dr .... Buffalo NY 14206 716-898-7800
Dabko Industries Inc 50 Emmett St. .... Bristol CT 06010 860-589-0756 585-0874
Web: www.rgdtech.com
Davies Molding LLC 350 Kehoe Blvd .... Carol Stream IL 60188 630-510-8188 510-9944
TF: 800-554-9208 ■ *Web:* www.daviesmolding.com
DCG Precision Mfg 9 Trowbridge Dr .... Bethel CT 06801 203-743-5525 791-1737
Web: www.dcgprecision.com
Delo Screw Products Co 700 London Rd .... Delaware OH 43015 740-363-1971 363-0042
Web: www.deloscrew.com
Devon Precision Industries Inc 251 Munson Rd. .... Wolcott CT 06716 203-879-1437 879-5556
Web: www.devonprecision.com
Dirksen Screw Products Co
14490 23-Mile Rd .... Shelby Township MI 48315 586-247-5400 247-9507
Web: www.dirksenscrew.com
Diversified Machine Inc 28059 Ctr Oaks Ct .... Wixom MI 48393 248-277-4400 277-4399
Dow Screw Products 3810 Paule Ave .... Saint Louis MO 63125 314-638-5100 638-4838
Ducommun Inc 268 E Gardena Blvd .... Gardena CA 90248 310-380-5390 380-5238
Web: www.ducommun.com
Duffin Manufacturing Co
316 Warden Ave PO Box 4036 .... Elyria OH 44036 440-323-4681 323-7389
Web: www.duffinmfg.com
DuPage Machine Products Inc
311 Longview Dr .... Bloomingdale IL 60108 630-690-5400 690-5504
Efficient Machine Products
12133 Alameda Dr .... Strongsville OH 44149 440-268-0205 268-0215
Web: www.efficientm.com
EJ Basler Co 9511 Ainslie St .... Schiller Park IL 60176 847-678-8880 678-8896
Web: www.ejbasler.com
Elyria Mfg Corp 145 Northrup St PO Box 479. .... Elyria OH 44035 440-365-4171 365-4000
TF: 866-365-4171 ■ *Web:* www.emcprecision.com
Enoch Manufacturing Co 14242 SE 82nd Dr .... Clackamas OR 97015 503-659-2660 659-4439
TF: 888-659-2660 ■ *Web:* enochmachining.com
Fairchild Auto-mated Parts Inc 10 White St. .... Winsted CT 06098 860-379-2725 379-5340
TF: 800-927-2545 ■ *Web:* www.fairchildparts.com
Farrar Corp 142 W Burns St. .... Norwich KS 67118 620-478-2212 478-2200
TF: 800-536-2215 ■ *Web:* www.farrarusa.com
FC Phillips Inc 471 Washington St .... Stoughton MA 02072 781-344-9400 344-3440
Web: www.fcphillips.com
FCI Inc 4661 Giles Rd .... Cleveland OH 44135 216-251-5200 251-5206
TF: 800-321-1032 ■ *Web:* www.fci-usa.com
Federal Screw Works 34846 Goddard Rd .... Romulus MI 48174 586-443-4200
OTC: FSCR ■ *Web:* www.federalscrew.com
Fischer Special Manufacturing Co
1188 Industrial Rd .... Cold Spring KY 41076 859-781-1400 781-4702
Web: www.fischerspecial.com
Form Cut Industries Inc 197 Mt Pleasant Ave. .... Newark NJ 07104 973-483-5154 483-4512
Web: www.formcut.com
Fraen Machining Corp 324 New Boston St .... Woburn MA 01801 781-205-5400 205-5472
Web: www.fraen.com
Gates Albert Inc 3434 Union St .... North Chili NY 14514 585-594-9401 594-4305
TF: 800-937-9311 ■ *Web:* www.gatesalbert.com
General Automotive Mfg LLC
5215 W Airways Ave. .... Franklin WI 53132 414-423-6400
Web: www.gamfg.com
General Engineering Works
1515 W Wrightwood Ct .... Addison IL 60101 630-543-8000 543-8005
Web: www.gewinc.com
Grand Traverse Machine (GTM) 1247 Boon St ..... Traverse City MI 49686 231-946-8006
Web: www.gtmachine.com
Greystone of Lincoln Inc 7 Wellington Rd .... Lincoln RI 02865 401-333-0444 334-5745
TF: 800-446-1761 ■ *Web:* greyst.com
Griner Engineering Inc 2500 N Curry Pk. .... Bloomington IN 47404 812-332-2220 332-2229
Web: www.griner.com
H & H Swiss Screw Machine Products Company Inc
1478 Chestnut Ave .... Hillside NJ 07205 800-826-9985 688-3503*
**Fax Area Code:* 908 ■ *TF:* 800-826-9985 ■ *Web:* www.hhswiss.com
H & L Tool Company Inc
32701 Dequindre Rd. .... Madison Heights MI 48071 248-585-7474 585-5774
Web: www.hltool.com
Hadady Corp 510 W 172nd St .... South Holland IL 60473 708-596-5168 596-7563
Web: hadady.wpengine.com

Phone Fax

Hall Industries Inc 514 Mecklem Ln .... Ellwood City PA 16117 724-752-2000 758-1558
Web: hallindustries.com
Herker Industries Inc
N57 W13760 Carmen Ave .... Menomonee Falls WI 53051 262-781-8270 781-0931
Web: www.herker.com
High Precision Inc 375 Morse St .... Hamden CT 06517 203-777-5395 773-1976
Web: www.highprecisioninc.com
Highland Machine 700 Fifth St. .... Highland IL 62249 618-654-2103 654-8016
Web: www.highlandmachine.com
Horizon Mfg Industries Inc
11417 Cyrus Way Ste 1 .... Mukilteo WA 98275 425-493-1220 493-0042
Web: www.horizonman.com
Horspool & Romine Manufacturing Inc
5850 Marshall St .... Oakland CA 94608 800-446-2263 652-3455*
**Fax Area Code:* 510 ■ *TF:* 800-446-2263 ■ *Web:* www.horspool.com
Huron Automatic Screw Co PO Box 610068. .... Port Huron MI 48061 810-364-6636 364-6639
Web: www.huronauto.com
Huron Inc 6554 Lakeshore Rd. .... Lexington MI 48450 810-359-5344 359-7521
Web: huroninc.com
Hyland Screw Machine Products 1900 Kuntz Rd .... Dayton OH 45404 937-233-8600 233-7067
Web: www.hylandmach.com
Insaco Inc 1365 Canary Rd .... Quakertown PA 18951 215-536-3500 536-7750
Web: www.insaco.com
Intat Precision Inc
2148 N State Rd 3 PO Box 488. .... Rushville IN 46173 765-932-5323 932-3032
Web: www.intat.com
Iseli Co 402 N Main St .... Walworth WI 53184 262-275-2108 275-6094
Web: iseli.com
J T M Technologies Inc 204 Industrial Ct. .... Wylie TX 75098 972-429-6575 635-6905
Web: www.jtmtechnologies.com
Jay Sons Screw Machine Products Inc
197 Burritt St .... Milldale CT 06467 860-621-0141 621-0142
Web: www.jaysons.com
Jessen Mfg Company Inc
1409 W Beardsley Ave PO Box 1729 .... Elkhart IN 46515 574-295-3836 522-2962
Web: www.jessenmfg.com
Kaddis Mfg Corp 293 Patriot Wy PO Box 92985. .... Rochester NY 14692 585-464-9000 464-0008
Web: www.kaddis.com
Kenlee Precision Corp 1701 Inverness Ave. .... Baltimore MD 21230 410-525-3800 646-3278
TF: 800-969-5278 ■ *Web:* www.kenlee.com
Kerr Lakeside Inc 26841 Tungsten Rd .... Euclid OH 44132 216-261-2100 261-9798
TF: 800-487-5377 ■ *Web:* www.kerrlakeside.com
Keystone Engineering 6310 Sidney St .... Houston TX 77021 713-747-1478
Web: www.keystoneeng.com
Komet Of America Inc 2050 Mitchell Blvd. .... Schaumburg IL 60193 847-923-8400 865-6638*
**Fax Area Code:* 800 ■ *TF:* 800-865-6638 ■ *Web:* www.komet.com
Liberty Brass Turning Company Inc
38-01 Queens Blvd. .... Long Island NY 11101 718-784-2911 784-2038
TF: 800-345-5939 ■ *Web:* www.libertybrass.com
Machine Specialties Inc (MSI)
6511 Franz Warner Pkwy .... Whitsett NC 27377 336-603-1919
Web: www.machspec.com
Maddox Foundry & Machine Works Inc
13370 SW 170th St .... Archer FL 32618 352-495-2121 495-3962
Web: www.maddoxfoundry.com
Mantel Machine Products Inc
W141 N9350 Fountain Blvd .... Menomonee Falls WI 53051 262-255-6780 255-9724
Web: www.mantelmachine.com
Manth-Brownell Inc 1120 Fyler Rd .... Kirkville NY 13082 315-687-7263 687-6856
Web: www.manth.com
MarathonNorco Aerospace Inc 8301 Imperial Dr .... Waco TX 76712 254-776-0650 776-6558
Web: www.mnaerospace.com
Marox Corp 373 Whitney Ave. .... Holyoke MA 01040 413-536-1300 534-1829
Web: www.marox.com
Meaden Precision Machined Products Co
16W210 83rd St .... Burr Ridge IL 60527 630-655-0888 655-3012
Web: www.meaden.com
Mennie's Machine Co (MMC)
Rt 71 & Mennie Dr PO Box 110 .... Mark IL 61340 815-339-2226 339-6550
Web: www.mennies.com
Metric Machining Co 1425 S Vineyard Ave. .... Ontario CA 91761 909-947-9222 923-1796
TF: 800-937-9311 ■ *Web:* www.metricorp.com
Micor Industries Inc 1314 A State Docks Rd. .... Decatur AL 35601 256-560-0770
Web: www.micorind.com
Micro-Matics Corp 8050 Ranchers Rd. .... Fridley MN 55432 763-780-2700 780-2706
Web: www.micro-matics.com
Microbest Inc 670 Captain Neville Dr .... Waterbury CT 06705 203-597-0355 597-0655
Web: www.microbest.com
Midwest Screw Products Inc
34700 Lakeland Blvd .... Eastlake OH 44095 440-951-2333 951-2336
Web: www.midwestllc.com
Mitchel & Scott Machine Co
1841 Ludlow Ave .... Indianapolis IN 46201 317-639-5331 684-8245
Web: www.mitsco.com
Modern Machine & Engineering Corp
9380 Winnetka Ave N .... Brooklyn Park MN 55445 612-781-3347 781-0030
Web: www.mmeincmn.com
Mold-Masters Injectioneering LLC
103 Peyerk Ct Ste E .... Romeo MI 48065 586-752-6551 752-6552
TF: 800-387-2483 ■ *Web:* www.moldmasters.com
MSK Precision Products Inc 10101 NW 67th St .... Tamarac FL 33321 954-776-0770 776-3780
TF: 800-992-5018 ■ *Web:* www.mskprecision.com
Multimatic Products Inc 390 Oser Ave. .... Hauppauge NY 11788 631-231-1515 231-1625
TF: 800-767-7633 ■ *Web:* www.multimaticproducts.com
National Technologies Inc 7641 S Tenth St. .... Oak Creek WI 53154 414-571-1000 571-1010
Web: www.nationaltechnologies.com
New Castle Industries Inc
1399 Countyline Rd .... New Castle PA 16101 724-656-5620 656-5620
TF: 800-897-2830
Northern Screw Machine Company Inc
300 Atwater St .... Saint Paul MN 55117 651-488-2568
Northwest Swiss-Matic Inc
8400 89th Ave N. .... Minneapolis MN 55445 763-544-4222 544-6873
Web: www.nwswissmatic.com

Company	City	State	Zip	Phone	Fax
NTN-Bower Corp 707 Bower Rd. *Web:* www.ntnbower.com	Macomb	IL	61455	309-837-0440	
Ohio Screw Products Inc 818 Lowell St *Web:* www.ohioscrew.com	Elyria	OH	44035	440-322-6341	322-0750
Omni-Lite Industries Canada Inc 17210 Edwards Rd *TF:* 800-577-6664 ■ *Web:* www.omni-lite.com	Cerritos	CA	90703	562-404-8510	
P&R Fasteners Inc 325 Pierce St *Web:* www.prfasteners.com	Somerset	NJ	08873	732-302-3600	
Pacific Aerospace & Electronics Inc 434 Olds Stn Rd *TF:* 855-285-5200 ■ *Web:* www.pacaero.com	Wenatchee	WA	98801	509-667-9600	
Pacific Rim Manufacturing Inc 5456 SE International Way *Web:* www.pacificrimmfg.com	Milwaukie	OR	97222	503-654-9543	654-8050
Palladin Precision Products Inc 57 Bristol St *Web:* www.palladin.com	Waterbury	CT	06708	203-574-0246	756-9478
Paul R Briles Inc 1700 W 132nd St *Web:* www.pbfasteners.com	Gardena	CA	90249	310-323-6222	
Peerless Screw Products Corp 286 Sandbank Rd	Cheshire	CT	06410	203-272-6413	271-2269
Peterson Tool Company Inc 739 Fesslers Ln PO Box 100830 *Web:* www.petersontool.com	Nashville	TN	37224	615-242-7341	242-7362
Pohlman Inc 140 Long Rd *Web:* www.pohlman.com	Chesterfield	MO	63005	636-537-1909	537-1930
Powin Corp 20550 SW 115th Ave *Web:* www.powin.com	Tualatin	OR	97062	503-598-6659	598-3941
Precision Machine Works Inc 2024 Puyallup Ave. *Web:* www.cadenceaerospace.com	Tacoma	WA	98421	253-272-5119	272-6921
Precision Metal Products Co 353 Garden Ave PO Box 1047 *Web:* www.pmpc1.com	Holland	MI	49422	616-392-3109	392-3100
Precision Plus Inc 840 Kootman Ln PO Box 168 *Web:* www.preplus.com	Elkhorn	WI	53121	262-743-1700	743-1701
Precision Screw Machine Products Inc 20 Gooch St *Web:* www.psmp.com	Biddeford	ME	04005	207-283-0121	283-4824
Precisionform Inc 148 W Airport Rd *TF:* 800-233-3821 ■ *Web:* www.precisionform.com	Lititz	PA	17543	717-560-7610	
Prime Engineered Components 1012 Buckingham St PO Box 359 *Web:* www.primeeci.com	Watertown	CT	06795	860-274-6773	274-7939
Production Products Co 6176 E Molloy Rd *TF:* 800-800-6652 ■ *Web:* www.ppc-online.com	East Syracuse	NY	13057	315-431-7200	431-7201
Quality Control Corp (QCC) 7315 W Wilson Ave *Web:* www.qccorp.com	Howard Heights	IL	60706	708-867-5400	887-5009
Rable Machine Inc 30 Paragon Pkwy PO Box 1583 *Web:* www.rablemachineinc.com	Mansfield	OH	44901	419-525-2255	525-2371
RB Royal Industries Inc 1350 S Hickory St PO Box 1168 *TF:* 800-892-1550 ■ *Web:* www.rbroyal.com	Fond du Lac	WI	54936	920-921-1550	921-4713
Rima Mfg Co 3850 Munson Hwy *Web:* www.rimamfg.com	Hudson	MI	49247	517-448-8921	448-7142
Robert A Main & Sons Inc 555 Goffle Rd *Web:* www.ramsco-inc.com	Wyckoff	NJ	07481	201-447-3700	447-0302
Roberts Automatic Products Inc 880 Lake Dr *TF:* 800-879-9837 ■ *Web:* www.robertsautomatic.com	Chanhassen	MN	55317	952-949-1000	949-9240
Rollin J Lobaugh Inc 240 Ryan Way *Web:* www.rjlobaugh.com	South San Francisco	CA	94080	650-583-9682	
Royal Screw Machine Products Co 409 LAKE AVENUE	Bristol	CT	06010	860-845-8567	845-8789
RW Screw Products Inc 999 Oberlin Rd SW *TF:* 866-797-2739 ■ *Web:* rwscrew.com	Massillon	OH	44647	330-837-9211	837-9223
Selflock Screw Products Co Inc 461 E Brighton Ave *Web:* www.selflockscrew.com	Syracuse	NY	13210	315-541-4464	475-1093
Senior Aerospace Jet Products 9106 Balboa Ave *Web:* www.seniorplc.com/aerospace/company.cfm/9	San Diego	CA	92123	858-430-2203	278-8768
SFS intec Inc Spring St & Van Reed Rd *TF:* 800-234-4533 ■ *Web:* www.sfsintecusa.com	Wyomissing	PA	19610	610-376-5751	
Skyway Precision Inc 41225 Plymouth Rd *Web:* www.skywayprecision.com	Plymouth	MI	48170	734-454-3550	455-9659
Smith & Richardson Manufacturing Co PO Box 589 *TF:* 800-426-0876 ■ *Web:* www.smithandrichardson.com	Geneva	IL	60134	630-232-2581	232-2610
Smithfield Manufacturing Inc 237 Kraft St	Clarksville	TN	37040	931-552-4327	648-4460
Sorenson Engineering Inc 32032 Dunlap Blvd *Web:* www.sorensoneng.com	Yucaipa	CA	92399	909-795-2434	795-7190
Specialty Screw Machine Products Inc 1028 Dillerville Rd PO Box 4185 *Web:* www.ssmp-online.com	Lancaster	PA	17604	717-397-2867	397-5912
Sperry Automatics Company Inc 1372 New Haven Rd PO Box 717 *TF:* 800-923-3709 ■ *Web:* www.sperryautomatics.com	Naugatuck	CT	06770	203-729-4589	729-7787
Stadco Corp 1931 N Broadway *Web:* www.stadco.com	Los Angeles	CA	90031	323-227-8888	222-0053
Standby Screw Machine Products Company Inc 1122 W Bagley Rd *Web:* standbyscrew.com	Berea	OH	44017	440-243-8200	243-8310
Superior Products Inc 3786 Ridge Rd *TF:* 800-651-9490 ■ *Web:* www.superiorprod.com	Cleveland	OH	44144	216-651-9400	651-4071
Supreme Machined Products Company Inc 18686 172nd Ave *Web:* www.supreme1.com	Spring Lake	MI	49456	616-842-6550	842-4481
Supreme-Lake Manufacturing Inc 455 Atwater St PO Box 19 *Web:* www.supremelake.com	Plantsville	CT	06479	860-621-8911	628-9746
T & L Automatics Inc 770 Emerson St *Web:* www.tandlautomatics.com	Rochester	NY	14613	585-647-3717	
Talladega Machinery & Supply Co Inc 301 N Johnson Ave PO Box 736 *TF Cust Svc:* 800-289-8672 ■ *Web:* www.tmsco.com	Talladega	AL	35161	256-362-4124	761-2579
Tamer Industries 185 Riverside Ave *Web:* www.tamerind.com	Somerset	MA	02725	508-677-0900	677-3037
Tanko Screw Products Corp 515 Thomas Dr *Web:* ldredmer.com	Bensenville	IL	60106	630-787-0504	
Taylor Metalworks Inc 3925 California Rd *Web:* www.taylorcnc.com	Orchard Park	NY	14127	716-662-3113	662-1096
Thorrez Industries Inc 4909 W Michigan Ave *Web:* www.thorrez.com	Jackson	MI	49201	517-750-3160	750-1792
Tompkins Products Inc 1040 W Grand Blvd *Web:* www.tompkinsproducts.com	Detroit	MI	48208	313-894-2222	894-2901
Torco Inc 1330 Old 41 Hwy NW *TF:* 800-876-5228 ■ *Web:* www.torcoinc.com	Marietta	GA	30060	770-427-3704	426-9369
Trace-A-Matic Inc (T-A-M) 1570 Commerce Ave *TF:* 877-375-0217 ■ *Web:* www.traceamatic.com	Brookfield	WI	53045	262-797-7300	797-9434
Tri Tool Inc 3041 Sunrise Blvd *TF:* 800-345-5015 ■ *Web:* www.tritool.com	Rancho Cordova	CA	95742	916-288-6100	288-6160
Triumph Components 203 N Johnson Ave *Web:* www.triumphgroup.com	El Cajon	CA	92020	619-440-2504	440-2509
Triumph Corp 2130 S Industrial Pk Ave *Web:* www.triumphcorp.com	Tempe	AZ	85282	480-967-3337	921-0446
V-S Industries Inc 900 Chaddick Dr	Wheeling	IL	60090	847-520-1800	520-0269
Vallorbs Jewel Co 2599 Old Philadelphia Pk *Web:* vallorbs.com	Bird-in-Hand	PA	17505	717-392-3978	392-8947
Vanamatic Co 701 Ambrose Dr *Web:* www.vanamatic.com	Delphos	OH	45833	419-692-6085	692-3260
Willie Washer Manufacturing Corp 2101 Greenleaf Ave *Web:* www.williewasher.com	Elk Grove Village	IL	60007	847-956-1344	
Winslow Automatic Inc 23 St Clair Ave *Web:* winslowautomatics.com	New Britain	CT	06051	860-225-6321	
Xaloy Inc 1399 Countyline Rd **Fax Area Code:* 724 ■ *TF:* 800-897-2830 ■ *Web:* www.xaloy.com	New Castle	PA	16101	800-897-2830	656-5620*

622 PREPARATORY SCHOOLS - BOARDING

See Also Preparatory Schools - Non-boarding p. 2973

Schools listed here are independent, college-preparatory schools that provide housing facilities for students and teachers. All are members of The Association of Boarding Schools (TABS), and many are considered to be among the top prep schools in the United States.

School	City	State	Zip	Phone	Fax
Academie Ste Cecile International School (ASCIS) 925 Cousineau Rd *Web:* stececile.ca	Windsor	ON	N9G1V8	519-969-1291	969-7953
Admiral Farragut Academy 501 Pk St N *Web:* www.farragut.org	Saint Petersburg	FL	33710	727-384-5500	347-5160
Albert College 160 Dundas St W *TF:* 800-952-5237 ■ *Web:* www.albertcollege.ca	Belleville	ON	K8P1A6	613-968-5726	968-9651
American Boychoir School 19 Lambert Dr *TF:* 800-627-7468 ■ *Web:* www.americanboychoir.org	Princeton	NJ	08540	609-924-5858	924-5812
Andrews Osborne Academy 38588 Mentor Ave *Web:* www.andrewsosborne.org	Willoughby	OH	44094	440-942-3600	
Annie Wright School 827 N Tacoma Ave *Web:* aw.org	Tacoma	WA	98403	253-272-2216	572-3616
Appleby College 540 Lakeshore Rd W *Web:* www.appleby.on.ca	Oakville	ON	L6K3P1	905-845-4681	845-9505
Army & Navy Academy 2605 Carlsbad Blvd PO Box 3000 *TF:* 888-762-2338 ■ *Web:* www.armyandnavyacademy.org	Carlsbad	CA	92018	760-729-2385	434-5948
Asheville School 360 Asheville School Rd *Web:* www.ashevilleschool.org	Asheville	NC	28806	828-254-6345	
Athenian School 2100 Mt Diablo Scenic Blvd *Web:* www.athenian.org	Danville	CA	94506	925-837-5375	
Avon Old Farms School 500 Old Farms Rd *TF:* 800-464-2866 ■ *Web:* www.avonoldfarms.com	Avon	CT	06001	860-404-4100	675-6051
Balmoral Hall School 630 Westminster Ave *Web:* www.balmoralhall.com	Winnipeg	MB	R3C3S1	204-784-1600	774-5534
Bement School 94 Main St PO Box 8 *TF:* 877-405-3949 ■ *Web:* www.bement.org	Deerfield	MA	01342	413-774-7061	774-7863
Ben Lippen School 7401 Monticello Rd *TF:* 800-777-2227 ■ *Web:* www.benlippen.com	Columbia	SC	29203	803-786-7200	744-1387
Berkshire School 245 N Undermountain Rd *TF:* 866-738-5500 ■ *Web:* www.berkshireschool.org	Sheffield	MA	01257	413-229-8511	229-1016
Bishop Strachan School 298 Lonsdale Rd *Web:* www.bss.on.ca	Toronto	ON	M4V1X2	416-483-4325	481-5632
Bishop's College School 80 Moulton Hill Rd PO Box 5001 *Web:* www.bishopscollegeschool.com	Lennoxville	QC	J1M1Z8	819-566-0227	
Blair Academy 2 Pk St PO Box 600 *Web:* www.blair.edu	Blairstown	NJ	07825	908-362-6121	362-7975
Blue Ridge School 273 Mayo Dr *Web:* blueridgeschool.com	Saint George	VA	22935	434-985-2811	
Boarding Schools Start Class 154 S Mountain Rd *Web:* boarding-schools.startclass.com	Northfield	MA	01360	413-498-2906	
Bolles School 7400 San Jose Blvd *Web:* www.bolles.org	Jacksonville	FL	32217	904-733-9292	739-9929
Brandon Hall School 1701 Brandon Hall Dr *Web:* www.brandonhall.org	Atlanta	GA	30350	770-394-8177	
Branksome Hall 10 Elm Ave *Web:* www.branksome.on.ca	Toronto	ON	M4W1N4	416-920-9741	920-5390

School	City	State	ZIP	Phone	Fax
Brehm Preparatory School 950 S Brehm Ln. *Web:* www.brehm.org	Carbondale	IL	62901	618-457-0371	529-1248
Brentwood College School 2735 Mt Baker Rd *Web:* www.brentwood.bc.ca	Mill Bay	BC	V0R2P1	250-743-5521	743-2911
Brewster Academy 80 Academy Dr *TF:* 800-842-9961 ■ *Web:* www.brewsteracademy.org	Wolfeboro	NH	03894	603-569-7200	569-7272
Bridgton Academy PO Box 292 *Web:* www.bridgtonacademy.org	North Bridgton	ME	04057	207-647-3322	647-8513
Brooks School 1160 Great Pond Rd *Web:* www.brooksschool.org	North Andover	MA	01845	978-725-6300	
Cambridge School of Weston 45 Georgian Rd. *Web:* www.csw.org	Weston	MA	02493	781-642-8650	
Canterbury School 101 Aspetuck Ave. *Web:* www.cbury.org	New Milford	CT	06776	860-210-3800	350-1120
Canyonville Christian Academy 250 E First St *Web:* www.canyonville.net	Canyonville	OR	97417	541-839-4401	839-6228
Cardigan Mountain School 62 Alumni Dr. *Web:* www.cardigan.org	Canaan	NH	03741	603-523-4321	
Carson Long Military Institute 200 N Carlisle St *Web:* www.carsonlong.org	New Bloomfield	PA	17068	717-582-2121	
Cate School 1960 Cate Mesa Rd *Web:* www.cate.org	Carpinteria	CA	93013	805-684-4127	
CFS the School at Church Farm PO Box 2000. *TF:* 800-439-4745 ■ *Web:* www.gocfs.net	Paoli	PA	19301	610-363-7500	280-6746
Chaminade College Preparatory School 425 S Lindbergh Blvd. *TF:* 877-378-6847 ■ *Web:* chaminade-stl.org	Saint Louis	MO	63131	314-993-4400	993-5732
Chatham Hall 800 Chatham Hall Cir *TF:* 877-644-2941 ■ *Web:* www.chathamhall.org	Chatham	VA	24531	434-432-2941	432-2405
Cheshire Academy 10 Main St. *Web:* www.cheshireacademy.org	Cheshire	CT	06410	203-272-5396	250-7209
Choate Rosemary Hall 333 Christian St *Web:* www.choate.edu	Wallingford	CT	06492	203-697-2239	697-2629
Christ School 500 Christ School Rd *TF:* 800-422-3212 ■ *Web:* www.christschool.org	Arden	NC	28704	828-684-6232	684-4869
Christchurch School 49 Seahorse Ln. *TF:* 800-296-2306 ■ *Web:* www.christchurchschool.org	Christchurch	VA	23031	804-758-2306	758-0721
Colorado Rocky Mountain School 1493 County Rd 106. *Web:* www.crms.org	Carbondale	CO	81623	970-963-2562	963-9865
Concord Academy 166 Main St *TF:* 800-768-2983 ■ *Web:* www.concordacademy.org	Concord	MA	01742	978-402-2200	402-2210
Cotter High School 1115 W Broadway *Web:* www.cotterschools.org	Winona	MN	55987	507-453-5000	
Cranbrook Schools 39221 Woodward Ave. *Web:* www.schools.cranbrook.edu	Bloomfield Hills	MI	48304	248-645-3610	645-3025
Culver Academies 1300 Academy Rd. *TF:* 800-528-5837 ■ *Web:* www.culver.org	Culver	IN	46511	574-842-7000	
Cushing Academy 39 School St PO Box 8000 *Web:* www.cushing.org	Ashburnham	MA	01430	978-827-7000	827-6253
Dana Hall School 45 Dana Rd PO Box 9010. *Web:* www.danahall.org	Wellesley	MA	02482	781-235-3010	
Darlington School 1014 Cave Spring Rd *TF:* 800-368-4437 ■ *Web:* www.darlingtonschool.org	Rome	GA	30161	706-235-6051	232-3600
Darrow School 110 Darrow Rd *TF:* 877-432-7769 ■ *Web:* www.darrowschool.org	New Lebanon	NY	12125	518-794-6000	794-7065
Deerfield Academy 7 Boyden Ln *Web:* www.deerfield.edu	Deerfield	MA	01342	413-772-0241	772-1100
Devereux Glenholme School 81 Sabbaday Ln *Web:* www.theglenholmeschool.org	Washington	CT	06793	860-868-7377	868-7894
Dublin School 18 Lehmann Way PO Box 522 *Web:* www.dublinschool.org	Dublin	NH	03444	603-563-8584	563-8671
Dunn School 2555 Hwy 154 PO Box 98. *TF:* 800-287-9197 ■ *Web:* www.dunnschool.org	Los Olivos	CA	93441	805-688-6471	686-9715
Eagle Hill School 242 Old Petersham Rd PO Box 116 *Web:* www.eaglehill.school/page	Hardwick	MA	01037	413-477-6000	477-6837
Eaglebrook School 271 Pine Nook Rd. *Web:* www.eaglebrook.org	Deerfield	MA	01342	413-774-9111	774-9119
Emma Willard School 285 Pawling Ave. *Web:* www.emmawillard.org	Troy	NY	12180	518-833-1300	833-1805
Episcopal High School 1200 N Quaker Ln. *TF:* 877-933-4347 ■ *Web:* www.episcopalhighschool.org	Alexandria	VA	22302	703-933-4062	933-3016
Ethel Walker School 230 Bushy Hill Rd. *Web:* www.ethelwalker.org	Simsbury	CT	06070	860-408-4200	
Fay School 48 Main St. *TF:* 800-933-2925 ■ *Web:* www.fayschool.org	Southborough	MA	01772	508-485-0100	481-7872
Fessenden School 250 Waltham St *Web:* www.fessenden.org	West Newton	MA	02465	617-630-2300	630-2303
Flintridge Sacred Heart Academy 440 St Katherine Dr **Fax:* Admissions ■ *Web:* www.fsha.org	La Canada	CA	91011	626-685-8333	685-8520*
Forman School 12 Norfolk Rd PO Box 80 *Web:* www.formanschool.org	Litchfield	CT	06759	860-567-1802	567-3501
Fountain Valley School of Colorado 6155 Fountain Vly School Rd. *Web:* www.fvs.edu	Colorado Springs	CO	80911	719-390-7035	390-7762
Foxcroft School 22407 Foxhound Ln *TF:* 800-858-2364 ■ *Web:* www.foxcroft.org	Middleburg	VA	20117	540-687-5555	687-3627
Fryeburg Academy 745 Main St. *Web:* www.fryeburgacademy.org	Fryeburg	ME	04037	207-935-2013	935-5013
Garrison Forest School 300 Garrison Forest Rd. *Web:* www.gfs.org	Owings Mills	MD	21117	410-363-1500	
George School 1690 Newtown-Langhorne Rd. *TF:* 888-804-1300 ■ *Web:* www.georgeschool.org	Newtown	PA	18940	215-579-6547	579-6549
Georgetown Preparatory School 10900 Rockville Pk. *Web:* www.gprep.org	North Bethesda	MD	20852	301-493-5000	493-6128
Gilmour Academy 34001 Cedar Rd. *TF:* 800-533-5140 ■ *Web:* www.gilmour.org	Gates Mills	OH	44040	440-442-1104	473-8010
Girard College 2101 S College Ave. *Web:* www.girardcollege.com	Philadelphia	PA	19121	215-787-2600	
Gould Academy PO Box 860 *Web:* www.gouldacademy.org	Bethel	ME	04217	207-824-7777	824-2926
Governor Dummer Academy 1 Elm St. *Web:* www.thegovernorsacademy.org	Byfield	MA	01922	978-499-3120	462-1278
Gow School 2491 Emery Rd PO Box 85 *Web:* www.gow.org	South Wales	NY	14139	716-652-3450	652-3457
Grand River Academy 3042 College St PO Box 222 *Web:* www.grandriver.org	Austinburg	OH	44010	440-275-2811	275-1825
Greenwood School 14 Greenwood Ln. *TF:* 800-380-9218 ■ *Web:* greenwood.org	Putney	VT	05346	802-387-4545	387-5396
Grier School 2522 Grier Rd PO Box 308 *Web:* www.grier.org	Tyrone	PA	16686	814-684-3000	684-2177
Groton School 282 Farmers Row PO Box 991 *Web:* www.groton.org	Groton	MA	01450	978-448-3363	448-3100
Gunnery, The 99 Green Hill Rd *Web:* www.gunnery.org/page	Washington	CT	06793	860-868-7334	868-1614
Hackley School 293 Benedict Ave. *Web:* www.hackleyschool.org	Tarrytown	NY	10591	914-631-0128	
Hampshire Country School 28 Patey Cir. *Web:* www.hampshirecountryschool.org	Rindge	NH	03461	603-899-3325	899-6521
Hargrave Military Academy (HMA) 200 Military Dr *TF:* 800-432-2480 ■ *Web:* www.hargrave.edu	Chatham	VA	24531	434-432-2481	432-3129
Harvey School 260 Jay St *Web:* www.harveyschool.org	Katonah	NY	10536	914-232-3161	232-6034
Havergal College 1451 Ave Rd *Web:* www.havergal.on.ca	Toronto	ON	M5N2H9	416-483-3519	483-6796
Hawaii Preparatory Academy 65-1692 Kohala Mountain Rd. *TF:* 800-644-4481 ■ *Web:* www.hpa.edu	Kamuela	HI	96743	808-885-7321	881-4045
Hebron Academy 339 Rd PO Box 309 *TF:* 888-432-7664 ■ *Web:* www.hebronacademy.org	Hebron	ME	04238	207-966-2100	
High Mowing School 222 Isaac Frye Hwy *Web:* www.highmowing.org	Wilton	NH	03086	603-654-2391	654-6588
Hill School 717 E High St. *TF:* 877-651-2800 ■ *Web:* www.thehill.org	Pottstown	PA	19464	610-326-1000	705-1753
Hillside School 404 Robin Hill Rd. *TF:* 800-344-8328 ■ *Web:* www.hillsideschool.net	Marlborough	MA	01752	508-485-2824	485-4420
Hockaday School 11600 Welch Rd. *Web:* www.hockaday100.org	Dallas	TX	75229	214-363-6311	
Holderness School Chapel Ln PO Box 1879 *TF:* 877-262-1492 ■ *Web:* www.holderness.org	Plymouth	NH	03264	603-536-1747	536-2125
Hoosac School 14 Pine Vly Rd *Web:* www.hoosac.com	Hoosick	NY	12089	518-686-7331	686-3370
Hotchkiss School 11 Interlaken Rd PO Box 800 *Web:* www.hotchkiss.org	Lakeville	CT	06039	860-435-3102	435-0042
Houghton Academy 9790 Thayer St. *Web:* www.houghtonacademy.org	Houghton	NY	14744	585-567-8115	567-8048
Howe Military School PO Box 240 *TF:* 888-462-4693 ■ *Web:* howemilitary.org	Howe	IN	46746	260-562-2131	562-3678
Hun School of Princeton 176 Edgerstoune Rd *Web:* www.hunschool.org	Princeton	NJ	08540	609-921-7600	
Hyde School 150 Rt 169 PO Box 237. *Web:* www.hyde.edu	Woodstock	CT	06281	860-963-4736	
Hyde School 616 High St. *Web:* www.hyde.edu	Bath	ME	04530	207-443-5584	
Idyllwild Arts Academy 52500 Temecula Rd PO Box 38 *Web:* www.idyllwildarts.org	Idyllwild	CA	92549	951-659-2171	659-2058
Incarnate Word High School 727 E Hildebrand Ave. *Web:* www.incarnatewordhs.org	San Antonio	TX	78212	210-829-3100	829-3101
Indian Mountain School 211 Indian Mtn Rd *Web:* www.indianmountain.org	Lakeville	CT	06039	860-435-0871	435-0641
Indian Springs School 190 Woodward Dr *TF General:* 888-843-9477 ■ *Web:* www.indiansprings.org	Pelham	AL	35124	205-988-3350	988-3797
Kent School PO Box 2006 *TF:* 800-538-5368 ■ *Web:* www.kent-school.edu	Kent	CT	06757	860-927-6111	927-6109
Kents Hill School 1614 Main St *Web:* www.kentshill.org	Kents Hill	ME	04349	207-685-4914	685-9529
Kildonan School 425 Morse Hill Rd *Web:* www.kildonan.org	Amenia	NY	12501	845-373-8111	373-2004
Kimball Union Academy 7 Campus Ctr Dr *Web:* www.kua.org	Meriden	NH	03770	603-469-2000	469-2040
Kiski School 1888 Brett Ln *TF:* 877-547-5448 ■ *Web:* www.kiski.org	Saltsburg	PA	15681	724-639-3586	639-8596
Knox School 541 E Long Beach Rd *Web:* www.knoxschool.org	Saint James	NY	11780	631-686-1600	686-1650
La Lumiere School 6801 N Wilhelm Rd *Web:* www.lalumiere.org	La Porte	IN	46350	219-326-7450	325-3185
Lake Forest Academy 1500 W Kennedy Rd. *Web:* www.lfanet.org	Lake Forest	IL	60045	847-234-3210	
Lakefield College School 4391 County Rd 29	Lakefield	ON	K0L2H0	705-652-3324	652-6320
Landmark School 429 Hale St PO Box 227 *TF:* 866-333-0859 ■ *Web:* www.landmarkschool.org	Prides Crossing	MA	01965	978-236-3010	927-7268
Lawrence Academy Powderhouse Rd PO Box 992 *TF:* 800-977-4698 ■ *Web:* www.lacademy.edu	Groton	MA	01450	978-448-6535	448-9208
Lawrenceville School 2500 Main St PO Box 6008 *TF:* 800-735-2030 ■ *Web:* www.lawrenceville.org	Lawrenceville	NJ	08648	609-896-0400	895-2217
Leelanau School 1 Old Homestead Rd *Web:* www.leelanau.org	Glen Arbor	MI	49636	231-334-5800	334-5898
Linden Hall School for Girls 212 E Main St *TF:* 800-258-5778 ■ *Web:* www.lindenhall.org	Lititz	PA	17543	717-626-8512	627-1384
Linsly School 60 Knox Ln *TF:* 866-648-1893 ■ *Web:* www.linsly.org	Wheeling	WV	26003	304-233-3260	234-4614

School	City	State	Zip	Phone	Fax
Loomis Chaffee School 4 Batchelder Rd *Web:* www.loomischaffee.org	Windsor	CT	06095	860-687-6400	298-8756
MacDuffie School 66 School St *Web:* macduffie.org	Granby	MA	01033	413-255-0000	467-1607
Madeira School 8328 Georgetown Pk *Web:* www.madeira.org	McLean	VA	22102	703-556-8200	
Maine Central Institute 295 MAIN ST *Web:* www.mci-school.org	Pittsfield	ME	04967	207-487-3355	487-3512
Marianapolis Preparatory School 26 Chase Rd PO Box 304 *Web:* www.marianapolis.org	Thompson	CT	06277	860-923-9565	923-3730
Marvelwood School 476 Skiff Mountain Rd *Web:* marvelwood.org	Kent	CT	06757	860-927-0047	
Massanutten Military Academy 614 S Main St *TF:* 877-466-6222 ■ *Web:* www.militaryschool.com	Woodstock	VA	22664	540-459-2167	459-5421
Masters School, The 49 Clinton Ave *Web:* www.mastersny.org	Dobbs Ferry	NY	10522	914-479-6400	693-1230
Maur Hill-Mount Academy 1000 Green St *Web:* www.maurhillmountacademy.com	Atchison	KS	66002	913-367-5482	367-5096
McCallie School 500 Dodds Ave *TF:* 800-234-2163 ■ *Web:* www.mccallie.org	Chattanooga	TN	37404	423-624-8300	493-5426
Mercersburg Academy 300 E Seminary St *TF:* 800-588-2550 ■ *Web:* www.mercersburg.edu	Mercersburg	PA	17236	717-328-6173	328-6319
Mid-Pacific Institute 2445 Kaala St *Web:* www.midpac.edu	Honolulu	HI	96822	808-973-5000	973-5099
Middlesex School 1400 Lowell Rd *Web:* www.mxschool.edu	Concord	MA	01742	978-369-2550	287-4759
Midland School 5100 Figueroa Mtn Rd PO Box 8 *Web:* www.midland-school.org	Los Olivos	CA	93441	805-688-5114	686-2470
Millbrook School 131 Millbrook School Rd *Web:* www.millbrook.org	Millbrook	NY	12545	845-677-8261	677-1265
Miller School 1000 Samuel Miller Loop *Web:* millerschoolofalbemarle.org	Charlottesville	VA	22903	434-823-4805	823-6617
Milton Academy 170 Centre St *Web:* www.milton.edu	Milton	MA	02186	617-898-1798	
Milton Hershey School PO Box 830 *TF:* 800-322-3248 ■ *Web:* www.mhskids.org	Hershey	PA	17033	717-520-2100	520-2117
Miss Hall's School 492 Holmes Rd *Web:* www.misshalls.org	Pittsfield	MA	01201	413-443-6401	448-2994
Miss Porter's School 60 Main St *Web:* www.porters.org/page	Farmington	CT	06032	860-409-3530	409-3531
Monte Vista Christian School 2 School Way *Web:* www.mvcs.org	Watsonville	CA	95076	831-722-8178	722-6003
Montverde Academy 17235 Seventh St *Web:* www.montverde.org	Montverde	FL	34756	407-469-2561	469-3711
National Sports Academy 821 Mirror Lk Dr *Web:* www.nationalsportsacademy.com	Lake Placid	NY	12946	518-523-3460	523-3488
New Hampton School 70 Main St *Web:* www.newhampton.org	New Hampton	NH	03256	603-677-3400	
New York Military Academy 78 Academy Ave *TF:* 888-275-6962 ■ *Web:* www.nyma.org	Cornwall On Hudson	NY	12520	845-534-3710	534-7699
North Country School 4382 Cascade Rd *Web:* www.nct.org	Lake Placid	NY	12946	518-523-9329	
Northfield Mount Hermon School 1 Lamplighter Way *TF:* 866-664-4483 ■ *Web:* www.nmhschool.org	Gill	MA	01354	413-498-3227	498-3152
Northwest School 1415 Summit Ave *Web:* www.northwestschool.org	Seattle	WA	98122	206-682-7309	328-1776
Northwood School PO Box 1070 *Web:* www.northwoodschool.com	Lake Placid	NY	12946	518-523-3382	
Oak Grove School 220 W Lomita Ave *Web:* oakgroveschool.org	Ojai	CA	93023	805-646-8236	646-6509
Oak Hill Academy 2635 Oak Hill Rd *Web:* www.oak-hill.net	Mouth of Wilson	VA	24363	276-579-2619	579-4722
Oakwood Friends School 22 Spackenkill Rd *Web:* www.oakwoodfriends.org	Poughkeepsie	NY	12603	845-462-4200	462-4251
Ojai Valley School 723 El Paseo Rd *Web:* www.ovs.org	Ojai	CA	93023	805-646-1423	646-0362
Oldfields School 1500 Glencoe Rd *Web:* www.oldfieldsschool.org	Glencoe	MD	21152	410-472-4800	472-6839
Olney Friends School 61830 Sandy Ridge Rd *TF:* 800-303-4291 ■ *Web:* www.olneyfriends.org	Barnesville	OH	43713	740-425-3655	425-3202
Oregon Episcopal School 6300 SW Nicol Rd *Web:* www.oes.edu	Portland	OR	97223	503-246-7771	768-3140
Orme School HC 63 PO Box 3040 *Web:* www.ormeschool.org	Mayer	AZ	86333	928-632-7601	632-7601
Oxford Academy 1393 Boston Post Rd *Web:* www.oxfordacademy.net	Westbrook	CT	06498	860-399-6247	
Peddie School 201 S Main St *Web:* www.peddie.org	Hightstown	NJ	08520	609-944-7500	944-7901
Pennington School 112 W Delaware Ave *Web:* www.pennington.org	Pennington	NJ	08534	609-737-1838	730-1405
Perkiomen School 200 Seminary St PO Box 130 *TF:* 866-966-9998 ■ *Web:* www.perkiomen.org	Pennsburg	PA	18073	215-679-9511	679-1146
Phelps School 583 Sugartown Rd *TF:* 800-344-8328 ■ *Web:* www.thephelpsschool.org	Malvern	PA	19355	610-644-1754	644-6679
Phillips Academy 180 Main St *TF:* 877-445-5477 ■ *Web:* www.andover.edu	Andover	MA	01810	978-749-4000	749-4068
Phillips Exeter Academy 20 Main St *TF:* 800-245-2525 ■ *Web:* www.exeter.edu	Exeter	NH	03833	603-772-4311	777-4399
Pickering College 16945 Bayview Ave *Web:* www.pickeringcollege.on.ca	Newmarket	ON	L3Y4X2	905-895-1700	895-9076
Piney Woods School 5096 Hwy 49 S PO Box 69 *Web:* www.pineywoods.org	Piney Woods	MS	39148	601-845-2214	845-2604
Pomfret School 398 Pomfret St PO Box 128 *Web:* www.pomfretschool.org	Pomfret	CT	06258	860-963-6100	963-2042
Portsmouth Abbey School 285 Cory's Ln *Web:* www.portsmouthabbey.org	Portsmouth	RI	02871	401-683-2000	
Proctor Academy 204 Main St PO Box 500 *TF:* 800-626-4907 ■ *Web:* www.proctoracademy.org	Andover	NH	03216	603-735-6000	
Purnell School 51 Pottersville Rd PO Box 500 *TF:* 800-228-9290 ■ *Web:* www.purnell.org	Pottersville	NJ	07979	908-439-2154	439-4088
Putney School 418 Houghton Brook Rd *TF:* 800-999-9080 ■ *Web:* www.putneyschool.org	Putney	VT	05346	802-387-5566	387-6278
Rabun Gap-Nacoochee School 339 Nacoochee Dr *TF:* 800-543-7467 ■ *Web:* www.rabungap.org	Rabun Gap	GA	30568	706-746-7467	746-2594
Randolph-Macon Academy 200 Academy Dr *TF:* 800-272-1172 ■ *Web:* www.rma.edu	Front Royal	VA	22630	540-636-5200	636-5419
Rectory School 528 Pomfret St PO Box 68 *Web:* www.rectoryschool.org	Pomfret	CT	06258	860-928-7759	928-4961
Ridley College 2 Ridley Rd PO Box 3013 *Web:* www.ridley.on.ca	Saint Catharines	ON	L2R7C3	905-684-1889	684-8875
Riverside Military Academy 2001 Riverside Dr **Fax Area Code: 678* ■ *TF:* 800-462-2338 ■ *Web:* www.riversidemilitary.com	Gainesville	GA	30501	770-532-6251	291-3364*
Rock Point School 1 Rock Pt Rd *Web:* www.rockpointschool.org	Burlington	VT	05408	802-863-1104	863-6628
Rosseau Lake College 1967 Bright St *Web:* www.rosseaulakecollege.com	Rosseau	ON	P0C1J0	705-732-4351	732-6319
Rumsey Hall School 201 Romford Rd *Web:* www.rumseyhall.org	Washington Depot	CT	06794	860-868-0535	868-7907
Saint Andrew's College 15800 Yonge St *TF:* 877-378-1899 ■ *Web:* www.sac.on.ca	Aurora	ON	L4G3H7	905-727-3178	727-9032
Saint Andrew's School 3900 Jog Rd *TF:* 888-357-7332	Boca Raton	FL	33434	561-210-2000	
Saint Andrew's School 63 Federal Rd *Web:* www.standrews-ri.org	Barrington	RI	02806	401-246-1230	246-0510
Saint Andrew's-Sewanee School 290 QuintaRd Rd *Web:* www.sasweb.org	Sewanee	TN	37375	931-598-5651	
Saint Anne's-Belfield School 2132 Ivy Rd *Web:* www.stab.org	Charlottesville	VA	22903	434-296-5106	
Saint Anthony's Catholic High School 3200 McCullough Ave *Web:* www.sachs.org	San Antonio	TX	78212	210-832-5600	832-5633
Saint Bernard Preparatory School 1600 St Bernard Dr SE *TF:* 800-722-0999 ■ *Web:* www.stbernardprep.com	Cullman	AL	35055	256-739-6682	734-2925
Saint Catherine's School 6001 Grove Ave *TF:* 800-648-4982 ■ *Web:* www.st.catherines.org	Richmond	VA	23226	804-288-2804	285-8169
Saint James School 17641 College Rd *Web:* www.stjames.edu	Saint James	MD	21740	301-733-9330	739-1310
Saint John's Northwestern Military Academy 1101 N Genesee St *TF:* 800-752-2338 ■ *Web:* www.sjnma.org	Delafield	WI	53018	262-646-7115	646-7128
Saint John's Preparatory School 1857 Watertower Rd PO Box 4000 *TF:* 800-525-7737 ■ *Web:* www.sjprep.net	Collegeville	MN	56321	320-363-3321	363-3322
Saint John's-Ravenscourt School 400 S Dr *TF:* 800-437-0040 ■ *Web:* www.sjr.mb.ca	Winnipeg	MB	R3T3K5	204-477-2400	477-2429
Saint Mark's School 25 Marlborough Rd *Web:* www.stmarksschool.org	Southborough	MA	01772	508-786-6000	786-6120
Saint Mary's School 900 Hillsborough St *TF:* 800-948-2557 ■ *Web:* www.sms.edu	Raleigh	NC	27603	919-424-4000	424-4122
Saint Michael's University School 3400 Richmond Rd *TF:* 800-661-5199 ■ *Web:* www.smus.ca	Victoria	BC	V8P4P5	250-592-2411	592-2812
Saint Paul's School 325 Pleasant St *Web:* www.sps.edu	Concord	NH	03301	603-229-4600	
Saint Stanislaus College 304 S Beach Blvd *Web:* www.ststan.com	Bay Saint Louis	MS	39520	228-467-9057	466-2972
Saint Stephen's Episcopal School 6500 St Stephen's Dr *Web:* www.sstx.org	Austin	TX	78746	512-327-1213	327-6771
Saint Thomas Choir School 202 W 58th St *Web:* www.choirschool.org	New York	NY	10019	212-247-3311	247-3393
Saint Timothy's School 8400 Greenspring Ave *Web:* www.stt.org	Stevenson	MD	21153	410-486-7400	
Salem Academy (SA) 942 Lancaster Dr NE *Web:* www.salemacademy.org	Salem	OR	97301	503-378-1219	
Salisbury School 251 Canaan Rd *Web:* www.salisburyschool.org	Salisbury	CT	06068	860-435-5732	435-5750
San Domenico School 1500 Butterfield Rd *Web:* www.sandomenico.org	San Anselmo	CA	94960	415-258-1905	258-1906
San Marcos Academy 2801 Ranch to Market 12 *TF Admissions:* 800-428-5120 ■ *Web:* www.smabears.org	San Marcos	TX	78666	512-353-2400	753-8031
Sandy Spring Friends School 16923 Norwood Rd *Web:* www.ssfs.org	Sandy Spring	MD	20860	301-774-7455	924-1115
Santa Catalina School 1500 Mark Thomas Dr *Web:* www.santacatalina.org	Monterey	CA	93940	831-655-9300	655-7535
Scattergood Friends School 1951 Delta Ave *TF:* 888-737-4636 ■ *Web:* www.scattergood.org	West Branch	IA	52358	319-643-7628	643-7638
Shady Side Academy 423 Fox Chapel Rd *Web:* www.shadysideacademy.org	Pittsburgh	PA	15238	412-968-3000	968-3213
Shattuck-Saint Mary's School 1000 Shumway Ave PO Box 218 *TF:* 800-421-2724 ■ *Web:* www.s-sm.org	Faribault	MN	55021	507-333-1616	333-1661
Shawnigan Lake School (SLS) 1975 Renfrew Rd *Web:* www.shawnigan.ca	Shawnigan Lake	BC	V0R2W1	250-743-5516	743-6200

Phone Fax

Solebury School 6832 Phillips Mill Rd New Hope PA 18938 215-862-5261 862-3366
TF: 800-675-6900 ■ *Web:* www.solebury.org
South Kent School 40 Bulls Bridge Rd South Kent CT 06785 860-927-3539 803-0040*
**Fax Area Code:* 888 ■ *Web:* www.southkentschool.org
Southwestern Academy 2800 Monterey Rd San Marino CA 91108 626-799-5010 799-0407
Web: www.southwesternacademy.edu
Stanstead College 450 Dufferin St Stanstead QC J0B3E0 819-876-2223 876-5891
Web: www.stansteadcollege.com
Stevenson School 3152 Forest Lk Rd Pebble Beach CA 93953 831-625-8300 625-5208
Web: www.stevensonschool.org
Stoneleigh-Burnham School
574 BernaRdston Rd Greenfield MA 01301 413-774-2711 772-2602
Web: www.sbschool.org
Stony Brook School 1 Chapman Pkway Stony Brook NY 11790 631-751-1800 751-4211
Web: www.stonybrookschool.org
Storm King School 314 Mountain Rd Cornwall On Hudson NY 12520 845-534-7892
TF: 800-225-9144 ■ *Web:* www.sks.org
Stuart Hall School
235 W Frederick St PO Box 210 Staunton VA 24402 540-885-0356 886-2275
TF: 888-306-8926 ■ *Web:* www.stuarthallschool.org
Subiaco Academy 405 N Subiaco Ave Subiaco AR 72865 479-934-1000 934-1033
Web: www.subi.org
Suffield Academy 185 N Main St Suffield CT 06078 860-668-7315 668-2966
Web: www.suffieldacademy.org
Tabor Academy 66 Spring St Marion MA 02738 508-748-2000
Web: www.taboracademy.org
Taft School 110 Woodbury Rd Watertown CT 06795 860-945-7777 945-7808
Web: www.taftschool.org
Tallulah Falls School
201 Campus Dr PO Box 10 Tallulah Falls GA 30573 706-754-0400 754-3595
Web: www.tallulahfalls.org
Texas Military Institute (TMI)
20955 W Tejas Trail San Antonio TX 78257 210-698-7171 698-0715
Web: www.tmi-sa.org
Thacher School 5025 Thacher Rd Ojai CA 93023 805-640-3210 640-1033
Web: www.thacher.org
Thomas Jefferson School
4100 S Lindbergh Blvd Saint Louis MO 63127 314-843-4151 843-3527
Web: www.tjs.org
Thomas More Prep-Marian 1701 Hall St Hays KS 67601 785-625-6577 625-3912
Web: www.tmp-m.org
Tilton School 30 School St Tilton NH 03276 603-286-4342
Web: www.tiltonschool.org
Trafalgar Castle School 401 Reynolds St Whitby ON L1N3W9 905-668-3358 668-4136
Web: www.trafalgarcastle.ca
Trinity College School 55 Deblaquire St N Port Hope ON L1A4K7 905-885-4565 885-7444
Web: www.tcs.on.ca
Trinity-Pawling School 700 Rt 22 Pawling NY 12564 845-855-3100 855-3816
Web: www.trinitypawling.org
Universal Ballet Academy
4301 Harewood Rd NE Washington DC 20017 202-832-1087 526-4274
Web: universalballet.com
Upper Canada College 200 Lonsdale Rd Toronto ON M4V1W6 416-488-1125 484-8611
Web: www.ucc.on.ca
Valley Forge Military Academy & College
1001 Eagle Rd Wayne PA 19087 610-989-1300 688-1545*
**Fax:* Admissions ■ *TF:* 800-234-8362 ■ *Web:* www.vfmac.edu
Vanguard School 22000 US Hwy 27 Lake Wales FL 33859 863-676-6091 676-8297
Web: www.vanguardschool.org
Verde Valley School 3511 Verde Vly School Rd Sedona AZ 86351 928-284-2272 284-0432
Web: www.vvsaz.org
Vermont Academy PO Box 500 Saxtons River VT 05154 802-869-6229 869-6242
TF: 800-698-8867 ■ *Web:* www.vermontacademy.org
Villanova Preparatory School
12096 N Ventura Ave Ojai CA 93023 805-646-1464 646-4430
Web: www.villanovaprep.org
Virginia Episcopal School 400 VES Rd Lynchburg VA 24503 434-385-3607 385-3603
TF: 800-937-3582 ■ *Web:* www.ves.org
Wasatch Academy 120 South 100 West Mount Pleasant UT 84647 435-462-1400 462-3380
TF: 800-634-4690 ■ *Web:* www.wasatchacademy.org
Washington Academy 66 High St East Machias ME 04630 207-255-8301 255-8303
Web: www.washingtonacademy.org
Wayland Academy 101 N University Ave Beaver Dam WI 53916 920-885-3373 887-3373
TF: 800-860-7725 ■ *Web:* www.wayland.org
Webb School PO Box 488 Bell Buckle TN 37020 931-389-9322 389-6657
TF: 888-733-9322 ■ *Web:* www.thewebbschool.com
Webb Schools 1175 W Baseline Rd Claremont CA 91711 909-482-5214 621-4582
Web: www.webb.org
West Nottingham Academy 1079 Firetower Rd Colora MD 21917 410-658-5556 658-9264
TF: 866-381-3684 ■ *Web:* www.wna.org
Western Reserve Academy 115 College St Hudson OH 44236 330-650-9717
TF: 877-486-2048 ■ *Web:* www.wra.net
Westminster School 995 Hopmeadow St Simsbury CT 06070 860-408-3060 408-3042
Web: www.westminster-school.org
Westover School PO Box 847 Middlebury CT 06762 203-758-2423 577-4588
Web: www.westoverschool.org
Westtown School PO Box 1799 Westtown PA 19395 610-399-0123 399-3760
Web: www.westtown.edu
White Mountain School 371 W Farm Rd Bethlehem NH 03574 603-444-2928 444-5568
Web: www.whitemountain.org
Wilbraham & Monson Academy 423 Main St Wilbraham MA 01095 413-596-6811 596-2448
TF: 800-616-3659 ■ *Web:* wma.us
Williston Northampton School
19 Payson Ave EastHampton MA 01027 413-529-3241 527-9494
Web: www.williston.com
Winchendon School 172 Ash St Winchendon MA 01475 978-297-4476 297-0911
Web: winchendon.org
Wolfeboro Camp School 93 Camp School Rd Wolfeboro NH 03894 603-569-3451
Web: www.wolfeboro.org
Woodhall School 58 Harrison Ln PO Box 550 Bethlehem CT 06751 203-266-7788 266-5896
Web: www.woodhallschool.org

Phone Fax

Woodlands Academy of the Sacred Heart
760 E Westleigh Rd Lake Forest IL 60045 847-234-4300 234-4348
TF: 888-234-3080 ■ *Web:* www.woodlandsacademy.org
Woodside Priory School 302 Portola Rd Portola Valley CA 94028 650-851-8221 851-2839
Web: www.prioryca.org
Worcester Academy 81 Providence St Worcester MA 01604 508-754-5302 752-2382
TF: 800-235-6426 ■ *Web:* www.worcesteracademy.org
Wyoming Seminary 201 N Sprague Ave Kingston PA 18704 570-270-2160 270-2191
TF: 877-996-7361 ■ *Web:* www.wyomingseminary.org

623 PREPARATORY SCHOOLS - NON-BOARDING

See Also Preparatory Schools - Boarding p. 2970
The schools listed here are among the leading private elementary and secondary schools in the U.S. None of these schools are boarding schools.

Phone Fax

Academica Corp 6340 Sunset Dr Miami FL 33143 305-669-2906
Web: www.academica.org
Albuquerque Academy 6400 Wyoming Blvd NE Albuquerque NM 87109 505-828-3200 828-3320
Web: www.aa.edu
Blake School 110 Blake Rd S Hopkins MN 55343 952-988-3405 988-3455
Web: www.blakeschool.org
Blyth Academy 300 John St Ste 276 Thornhill ON L3T5W4 905-889-8081
Web: blytheducation.com
Brearley School 610 E 83rd St New York NY 10028 212-744-8582 472-8020
Web: www.brearley.org
Canada School of Public Service 373 Sussex Dr Ottawa ON K1N6Z2 819-953-5400
Web: www.csps-efpc.gc.ca/
Chapin School 100 E End Ave New York NY 10028 212-744-2335
Web: www.chapin.edu
Coeur d Alene 810 Coeur D Alene Ave Venice CA 90291 310-821-7813
Web: coeurdalene.org
Colchester Christian Academy 15 Elm St Truro NS B2N3H5 902-895-6520
Web: colchesterchristianacademy.ca
College Jacques-prevert 12349 Rue De Serres Montreal QC H4J2H1 514-336-2330
Web: collegejacquesprevert.ca
Ecole Secondaire Chavigny
365 Rue Chavigny Trois-RiviŠres QC G9B1A7 819-377-4391
Web: www.chavigny.qc.ca
Glen Mills Schools PO Box 5001 Concordville PA 19331 610-459-8100 558-1493
TF: 800-441-2064 ■ *Web:* www.glenmillsschool.org
Hillfield Strathallan College
299 Fennell Ave W Hamilton ON L9C1G3 905-389-1367
Web: www.hsc.on.ca
Iolani School 563 Kamoku St Honolulu HI 96826 808-949-5355 943-2297
TF: 888-879-8970 ■ *Web:* www.iolani.org
Kingsway Christian School
7979 E County Rd 100 N Avon IN 46123 317-272-2227
Web: www.kingswaychurch.org
Kinkaid School, The 201 Kinkaid School Dr Houston TX 77024 713-782-1640 782-3543
Web: www.kinkaid.org
Latin School of Chicago 59 W N Blvd Chicago IL 60610 312-582-6000
Web: www.latinschool.org
Lost River Career Cooperative 600 Elm St Ste 1 Paoli IN 47454 812-723-4818
Web: lostrivercareercoop.com
Mary Institute & Saint Louis Country Day School
101 N Warson Rd Saint Louis MO 63124 314-993-5100
Web: www.micds.org
National Cathedral School
3609 Woodley Rd NW Washington DC 20016 202-537-6300 537-5743
Web: www.ncs.cathedral.org
North Shore Country Day School
310 Green Bay Rd Winnetka IL 60093 847-446-0674 446-0675
Web: www.nscds.org
Orchard School 615 W 64th St Indianapolis IN 46260 317-251-9253 254-8454
Web: www.orchard.org
Prairie Valley School Division No 208 Gd Indian Head SK S0G2K0 306-695-3939
Web: www.pvsd.ca
Punahou School 1601 Punahou St Honolulu HI 96822 808-944-5711 944-5779
Web: www.punahou.edu
Redeemer Catholic Schools
1 McRae St PO Box 1318 Okotoks AB T1S1B3 403-938-2659
Web: www.redeemer.ab.ca
RenWeb School Management Software
101 E Renfro St Ste A Burleson TX 76028 866-800-6593
TF: 866-800-6593 ■ *Web:* www.renweb.com
Roxbury Latin School 101 St Theresa Ave West Roxbury MA 02132 617-325-4920 325-3585
Web: www.roxburylatin.org
Saint Albans School 3001 Wisconsin Ave NW Washington DC 20016 202-537-6435 537-5613
Saint Stephen's & Saint Agnes School
1000 St Stephen's Rd Alexandria VA 22304 703-751-2700 683-5930
Web: www.sssas.org
Sidwell Friends School
3825 Wisconsin Ave NW Washington DC 20016 202-537-8100 537-8138
Web: www.sidwell.edu
St. Mary's Elementary School
422 - 20 St S Lethbridge AB T1J2V5 403-327-3098
Web: www.holyspirit.ab.ca
St. Marys Area Senior High School
977 S Saint Marys St Saint Marys PA 15857 814-834-7831
Web: smasd.org
University School
Hunting Vly Campus 2785 SOM Ctr Rd Hunting Valley OH 44022 216-831-2200 292-7810
Web: www.us.edu
University School of Milwaukee
2100 W Fairy Chasm Rd Milwaukee WI 53217 414-352-6000 352-8076
Web: www.usm.k12.wi.us
Westminster Schools 1424 W Paces Ferry Rd NW Atlanta GA 30327 404-355-8673 355-6606
Web: www.westminster.net
Youth Opportunities Unlimited
422 E S St Ste A Kalamazoo MI 49007 269-349-9676
Web: kresa.org

624 PRESS CLIPPING SERVICES

Phone | Fax

3i People Inc 5755 N Point Pkwy Ste 9 ... Alpharetta GA 30022 404-636-2397
Web: www.3ipeople.com
ActioNet Inc 2600 Park Tower Dr Ste 1000 ... Vienna VA 22180 703-204-0090
Web: www.actionet.com
Acumera Inc 3112 Windsor Rd Ste A-130 ... Austin TX 78703 512-473-2290
Web: www.acumera.net
Alta Associates Inc 8 Bartles Corner Rd ... Flemington NJ 08822 908-806-8442
Web: www.altaassociates.com
Antiok Holdings Inc
34 Shining Willow Way # 132 ... La Plata MD 20646 301-743-2100
Web: www.antiok.com
Appian Analytics Inc
2000 Crow Canyon Pl Ste 300 ... San Ramon CA 94583 877-757-7646
TF: 877-757-7646 ■ *Web:* www.appiananalytics.com
Aria Solutions Inc 110 - 12th Ave SW Ste 600 ... Calgary AB T2A0G7 403-235-0227
Web: www.ariasolutions.com
Art Resource Inc 536 Broadway 5th Fl ... New York NY 10012 212-505-8700
TF: 888-505-8666 ■ *Web:* www.artres.com
Attendee Management Inc
15572 Ranch Rd 12 Ste 1 ... Wimberley TX 78676 512-847-5174
TF: 877-947-5174 ■ *Web:* attendeenet.com
BC Public School Employers' Association
106-1525 W Eighth Ave ... Vancouver BC V6J1T5 604-730-4507
Web: www.bcpsea.bc.ca
BurrellesLuce
30 B Vreeland Rd PO Box 674 ... Florham Park NJ 07932 973-992-6600 992-7675
TF: 800-631-1160 ■ *Web:* www.burrellesluce.com
C Rrg Inc 5331 Lemons Rd ... Fort Worth TX 76140 817-561-9100
Web: www.crrginc.com
Cherry Systems Inc
2270 Northwest Pkwy Ste 125 ... Marietta GA 30067 770-955-2395
Web: www.cherrysystems.com
Cision US Inc 130 East Randolph St 7th Fl ... Chicago IL 60601 312-922-2400
Web: www.cision.com
Colorado Press Clipping Service
1336 Glenarm Pl ... Denver CO 80204 303-571-5117 571-1803
Web: www.coloradopressassociation.com
CompetitivEdge 196 S Main St ... Colchester CT 06415 860-537-6731
Datatech Labs 8000 e quincy ave ... Denver CO 80237 303-770-3282
TF: 888-288-3282 ■ *Web:* www.datatechlab.com
Daticon LLC 11 Stott Ave ... Norwich CT 06360 860-823-4400
Web: www.daticon.com
DocuData Solutions LLC
7777 John Carpenter Fwy ... Dallas TX 75247 214-678-9898
Web: www.docudatasolutions.com
Enginuity PLM LLC
Merritt Crossing Bldg 440 Wheelers Farms Rd ... Milford CT 06461 203-876-9400
Web: www.enginuityplm.com
Excet 8001 Braddock Rd Ste 360 ... Springfield VA 22151 703-635-7089
Web: www.excetinc.com
Florida Newsclips LLC PO Box 2190 ... Palm Harbor FL 34682 800-442-0332 736-5005*
**Fax Area Code:* 727 ■ *TF:* 800-442-0332 ■ *Web:* www.newsclipsonweb.com
FlyData Inc
1043 N Shoreline Blvd Ste 200 ... Mountain View CA 94043 855-427-9787
TF: 855-427-9787 ■ *Web:* www.flydata.com
Identifix Inc 2714 Patton Rd ... Saint Paul MN 55113 651-633-8007
Web: www.identifix.com
IG2 Data Security Inc P.O. Box 59034 ... Schaumburg IL 60159 847-839-0300
Web: ig2data.com
Imagewerks Marketing 3758 Dunlap St N ... Arden Hills MN 55112 651-770-1319
Web: www.iwmarketing.com
INFINITT North America Inc
755 Memorial Pkwy Hillcrest Professional Plz
Ste 304 ... Phillipsburg NJ 08865 908-387-6960
Web: www.infinittna.com
InfySource Ltd 8345 NW 66th St ... Miami FL 33166 800-275-7503
TF: 800-275-7503 ■ *Web:* www.infy-source.com
Insight Investments Corp
611 Anton Blvd Ste 700 ... Costa Mesa CA 92626 714-939-2300
TF: 888-442-1441 ■ *Web:* www.insightinvestments.com
IT Direct LLC 67 Prospect Ave Ste 202 ... West Hartford CT 06106 860-656-9110
Web: www.gettingyouconnected.com
Itm Marketing Inc 470 Downtowner Plz ... Coshocton OH 43812 740-295-3575
Web: www.itmmarketing.com
Kentucky Press Assn 101 Consumer Ln ... Frankfort KY 40601 502-223-8821 226-3867
TF Cust Svc: 800-264-5721 ■ *Web:* www.kypress.com
Landis Computer 1120 Division Hwy ... Ephrata PA 17522 717-733-0793
Web: landiscomputer.com
LCS Technologies Inc
11230 Gold Express Dr Ste 310-140 ... Gold River CA 95670 855-277-5527
TF: 855-277-5527 ■ *Web:* www.lcs-technologies-inc.com
Link Solutions Inc
12007 Sunrise Vly Dr Ste 280 ... Reston VA 20191 703-707-6256
Web: www.linksol-inc.com
Magnolia Clipping Service
298 Commerce Pk Dr Ste A ... Ridgeland MS 39157 601-856-0911 856-3340
Web: www.magnoliaclips.com
MedValue Offshore Solutions Inc
1415 W 22nd St Tower Fl Regency Towers ... Oak Brook IL 60523 630-299-7370
Web: www.medvaluebpo.com
Michiana Health Information Network Llc
220 W Colfax Ave, Ste 300 ... South Bend IN 46601 574-968-1001
Web: www.mhin.org
Michigan Suburbs Alliance 300 E 9 Mile Rd ... Ferndale MI 48220 248-591-7022
Web: www.michigansuburbsalliance.org
Mindgruve Inc 1018 Eight Ave ... San Diego CA 92101 619-757-1325
Web: mindgruve.com
New York State Clipping Service
200 Central Pk Ave N ... Hartsdale NY 10530 914-948-2525 948-3534

Phone | Fax

OCZ Storage Solutions Inc
6373 San Ignacio Ave ... San Jose CA 95119 408-733-8400
Web: ocz.com
Oklahoma Press Service Inc
3601 N Lincoln Blvd ... Oklahoma City OK 73105 405-524-4421 524-2201
TF: 888-815-2672 ■ *Web:* www.okpress.com
Pro Computer Service LLC, The
180 Tuckerton Rd Ste 11 ... Medford NJ 08055 856-596-4446
Web: www.helpmepcs.com
Pulse Seismic Inc Ste 2400 639 Fifth Ave SW ... Calgary AB T2P0M9 403-237-5559
Web: www.pulseseismic.com
Rf Connect LLC
37735 Enterprise Ct Ste 200 ... Farmington Hills MI 48331 248-489-5800
Web: www.rfconnect.com
Roytman Info Svc Inc 504 Old Harbor Ct ... Dayton OH 45458 937-885-0821
Web: www.roytmanis.com
Sainergy 284 Digital Dr ... Morgan Hill CA 95037 408-532-9800
Web: www.sainergy.net
SearchAmerica Inc 6450 Wedgwood Rd ... Maple Grove MN 55311 763-416-1000
Web: www.searchamerica.com
Senture LLC 460 Industrial Blvd ... London KY 40741 606-877-6670
Web: www.senture.com
SightLine Systems Corp
4035 Ridge Top Rd Ste 510 ... Fairfax VA 22030 703-563-3000
Web: sightline.com
SIX Financial Information USA Inc
1 Omega Dr River Bend Centre Bldg 3 ... Stamford CT 06907 203-353-8100
Web: www.six-group.com
Slk Global Bpo Services 4032 Aladdin Dr ... Plano TX 75093 972-758-5497
Web: www.slkglobalbpo.com
SMS proTECH 1089 Fairington Dr ... Sidney OH 45365 937-498-7080
Web: perryprotech.com
South Carolina Press Services Inc
106 Outlet Pointe Blvd PO Box 11429 ... Columbia SC 29210 803-750-9561 551-0903
TF: 888-727-7377 ■ *Web:* www.scpress.org
South Dakota Newspaper Services
1125 32nd Ave ... Brookings SD 57006 605-692-4300 692-6388
TF: 800-658-3697 ■ *Web:* www.sdna.com
Ssf Conference Catering LLC
255 S Airport Blvd ... South San Francisco CA 94080 650-877-8787
Web: ssfconf.com
Synteractive Corp 1100 H St NW Ste 900 ... Washington DC 20005 703-286-0913
Web: www.synteractive.com
Talton Communications Inc 910 Ravenwood Dr ... Selma AL 36701 334-877-0704
Web: talton.com
Thrive Networks Inc
836 North St Bldg 300 Ste 3201 ... Tewksbury MA 01876 978-461-3999
TF: 866-205-2810 ■ *Web:* www.thrivenetworks.com
United Data Technologies Inc
8825 NW 21st Terrace ... Doral FL 33172 305-882-0435
Web: udtonline.com
Vigilant Technologies LLC
1050 Wilshire Dr Ste 307 ... Troy MI 48084 248-614-2500
Web: www.vigt.com
Virginia Press Services Inc
11529 Nuckols Rd ... Glen Allen VA 23059 804-521-7570 521-7590
TF: 800-849-8717 ■ *Web:* www.vpa.net
West Virginia Press Associationÿ
3422 Pennsylvania Ave ... Charleston WV 25302 304-342-6908 343-5879
TF: 800-235-6881 ■ *Web:* www.wvpress.org
WorkSmart Inc 100 Meredith Dr Ste 200 ... Durham NC 27713 919-484-1010
Web: www.worksmart.com
XCEL Solutions Corp
254 Rt 34 Oakdale Plz Second Fl Ste 3 ... Matawan NJ 07747 732-765-9235
Web: www.xcelcorp.com
Xylo Technologies Inc
2434 Superior Dr NW Ste 105 ... Rochester MN 55901 507-289-9956
Web: www.xylotechnologies.com

625 PRINTED CIRCUIT BOARDS

See Also Electronic Components & Accessories - Mfr p. 2226; Semiconductors & Related Devices p. 3177

Phone | Fax

3Dlabs Inc Ltd 1901 McCarthy Blvd ... Milpitas CA 95035 408-530-4700
TF: 800-464-3348 ■ *Web:* www.3dlabs.com
A Star Electric Co 200 Seegers Ave ... Elk Grove Village IL 60007 847-439-4122
Web: www.astareg.com
Abelconn LLC 9210 Science Ctr Dr ... New Hope MN 55428 763-533-3533 536-0349
Web: www.abelconn.com
Acromag Inc 30765 S Wixom Rd ... Wixom MI 48393 248-624-1541 624-9234
TF: 877-295-7092 ■ *Web:* www.acromag.com
Advanced Circuits Inc 21101 E 32nd Pkwy ... Aurora CO 80011 303-576-6610 224-3291*
**Fax Area Code:* 888 ■ *TF:* 800-979-4722 ■ *Web:* www.4pcb.com
Aimtron Corp 555 S Vermont St ... Palatine IL 60107 630-372-7500
Web: www.aimtroncorporation.com
AMDTechnologies Inc 1 Commerce Vly Dr E ... Markham ON L3T7X6 905-882-2600 882-2620
Web: www.amd.com
American Board Assembly Inc
5456 Endeavour Ct ... Moorpark CA 93021 805-523-0274 523-1185
Web: www.americanboard.com
Amitron Inc 2001 Landmeier Rd ... Elk Grove Village IL 60007 847-290-9800 290-9823
Web: www.amitroncorp.com
Ansen Corp 100 Chimney Pt Dr ... Ogdensburg NY 13669 315-393-3573 393-7638
Web: www.ansencorp.com
Antex Electronics Corp 19160 Van Ness Ave ... Torrance CA 90501 310-532-3092
Web: www.antex.com
Arc-tronics Inc 1150 Pagni Dr ... Elk Grove Village IL 60007 847-437-0211 437-0181
Web: www.arc-tronics.com
ASUSTeK Computer International
800 Corporate Way ... Fremont CA 94539 510-739-3777 608-4555
Web: www.asus.com

Phone Fax

Benchmark Electronics Inc
3000 Technology Dr .... Angleton TX 77515 979-849-6550
NYSE: BHE ■ *Web:* www.bench.com

Bicom Inc 755 Main St .... Monroe CT 06468 203-268-4484
Web: www.bicominc.com

Bourns Inc 1200 Columbia Ave .... Riverside CA 92507 951-781-5690 781-5006
TF: 877-426-8767 ■ *Web:* www.bourns.com

Cal Quality Electronics 2700 S Fairview St .... Santa Ana CA 92704 714-545-8886 545-4975
Web: www.calquality.com

Centon Electronics Inc
27412 Aliso Viejo Pkwy .... Aliso Viejo CA 92656 949-855-9111
TF: 800-234-9292 ■ *Web:* www.centon.com

Circuit Express Inc 229 S Clark Dr .... Tempe AZ 85281 800-979-4722 966-5896*
**Fax Area Code: 480* ■ *TF:* 800-979-4722 ■ *Web:* www.4pcb.com

CM Solutions Inc 2674 S Harper Rd .... Corinth MS 38834 662-287-8810
Web: www.cm-solutions.biz

Compunetics Inc 700 Seco Rd .... Monroeville PA 15146 412-373-8110 373-8060
Web: www.compunetics.com

Computer Modules Inc 11409 W Bernardo Ct .... San Diego CA 92127 858-613-1818 613-1815
Web: www.dveo.com

Creative Labs Inc 1901 McCarthy Blvd .... Milpitas CA 95035 408-428-6600 428-6611
TF Cust Svc: 800-998-1000 ■ *Web:* www.us.creative.com

Crucial Technology 3475 E Commercial Ct .... Meridian ID 83642 208-363-5790 363-5501
TF: 800-336-8915 ■ *Web:* www.crucial.com

Data Translation Inc 100 Locke Dr .... Marlborough MA 01752 508-481-3700 481-3700
OTC: DATX ■ *TF:* 800-525-8528 ■ *Web:* www.datatranslation.com

Dataram Corp 777 Alexander Rd Ste 100 .... Princeton NJ 08540 609-799-0071 799-6734
NASDAQ: DRAM ■ *TF:* 800-328-2726 ■ *Web:* www.dataram.com

DCX-CHOL Enterprises Inc
12831 S Figueroa St .... Los Angeles CA 90061 310-516-1692
Web: www.dcxchol.com

Diversified Technology Inc
476 Highland Colony Pkwy .... Ridgeland MS 39157 601-856-4121
Web: www.dtims.com

DIVSYS International LLC
8110 Zionsville Rd .... Indianapolis IN 46268 317-405-9427
Web: www.divsys.com

DRS Laurel Technologies 246 Airport Rd .... Johnstown PA 15904 814-534-8900
Web: www.drs.com

Dynaco Corp 3020 S Pk Dr .... Tempe AZ 85282 602-437-8003 437-8015

Dynatem Inc 23263 Madero Ste C .... Mission Viejo CA 92691 949-855-3235 770-3481
TF: 800-543-3830 ■ *Web:* www.dynatem.com

EDGE Tech Corp 655 Leffingwell Ave .... Saint Louis MO 63122 314-856-4042
Web: www.edgetechcorp.com

El Microcircuits Inc 1651 Pohl Rd .... Mankato MN 56001 507-345-5786 345-7559
Web: www.eimicro.com

Electropac Company Inc 252 Willow St .... Manchester NH 03103 603-622-3711
Web: www.electropac.com

Epec LLC 174 Duchaine Blvd .... New Bedford MA 02745 508-995-5171
Web: www.epectec.com

Federal Electronics Inc 75 Stamp Farm Rd .... Cranston RI 02921 401-944-6200 946-6280
Web: www.federalelec.com

Flex Technologies 5479 Gundy Dr PO Box 400 .... Midvale OH 44653 740-922-5992 922-4416
Web: www.flextechnologies.com

GE Fanuc Embedded Systems Inc
7401 Snaproll NE .... Albuquerque NM 87109 505-875-0600
TF: 888-790-1820 ■ *Web:* www.geautomation.com

Gigabyte Technology Inc
17358 Railroad St .... City of Industry CA 91748 626-854-9338
Web: gigabyte.com

GoldenRAM Computer Products 13 Whatney .... Irvine CA 92618 949-460-9000 460-7600
TF: 800-222-8861 ■ *Web:* www.goldenram.com

Hauppauge Computer Works Inc 91 Cabot Ct .... Hauppauge NY 11788 631-434-1600 434-3198
TF: 800-443-6284 ■ *Web:* www.hauppauge.com

Hauppauge Digital Inc 91 Cabot Ct .... Hauppauge NY 11788 631-434-1600 434-3198
OTC: HAUP ■ *TF:* 800-443-6284 ■ *Web:* www.hauppauge.com

Holaday Circuits Inc 11126 Bren Rd W .... Minnetonka MN 55343 952-933-3303
TF: 800-362-3303 ■ *Web:* www.holaday.com

I-Bus Corp 3350 Scott Blvd Bldg 54 .... Santa Clara CA 95054 408-450-7880 450-7881
Web: www.ibus.com

IEC Electronics Corp 105 Norton St .... Newark NY 14513 315-331-7742 331-3547
NYSE: IEC ■ *Web:* www.iec-electronics.com

Intel Corp 2200 Mission College Blvd .... Santa Clara CA 95052 408-765-8080
NASDAQ: INTC ■ *TF Cust Svc:* 800-628-8686 ■ *Web:* www.intel.in

IXI Technology 23231 La Palma Ave .... Yorba Linda CA 92887 714-692-3800 692-3838
Web: ixitech.com

Jabil Circuit Inc
10560 ML King St N .... Saint Petersburg FL 33716 727-577-9749
NYSE: JBL ■ *TF:* 877-217-6328 ■ *Web:* www.jabil.com

Joule Technologies Inc 4167 W Orleans St .... Mchenry IL 60050 815-759-0600
Web: www.jouletechnologies.com

KCA Electronics Inc 223 N Crescent Way .... Anaheim CA 92801 714-239-2433
Web: www.kcamerica.com

Killdeer Mountain Manufacturing Inc (KMM)
233 Rodeo Dr PO Box 450 .... Killdeer ND 58640 701-764-5651 764-5427
Web: www.kmmnet.com

Kimball Electronics 13700 Reptron Blvd .... Tampa FL 33626 813-814-5000
TF: 800-903-8328

Kimball Electronics Group 1038 E 15th St .... Jasper IN 47549 812-634-4200 634-4330*
**Fax: Sales* ■ *TF:* 800-482-1616 ■ *Web:* www.kimballelectronics.com

Leadtek Research Inc 910 Auburn Ct .... Fremont CA 94538 510-490-8076 490-7759
Web: www.leadtek.com

Leda Corp 7080 Kearny Dr .... Huntington Beach CA 92648 714-841-7821 842-3683
Web: www.ledacorp.net

Libra Industries Inc 7770 Div Dr .... Mentor OH 44060 440-974-7770 974-7779
TF: 800-825-1674 ■ *Web:* www.libraindustries.com

Lone Star Circuits 901 Hensley Ln .... Wylie TX 75098 214-291-1427
TF: 800-303-9266 ■ *Web:* lscpcbs.com

M-Wave Inc 1300 Norwood Ave .... Itasca IL 60143 630-562-5550
Web: www.mwav.com

Macrolink Inc 1500 N Kellogg Dr .... Anaheim CA 92807 714-777-8800 777-8807
Web: www.macrolink.com

Phone Fax

Masterwork Electronics Inc
630 Martin Ave .... Rohnert Park CA 94928 707-588-9906 588-9908
Web: www.masterworkelectronics.com

McDonald Technologies International Inc
2310 McDaniel Dr .... Carrollton TX 75006 972-421-4100
Web: www.mcdonald-tech.com

Micro-Star Int'l Co.,Ltd
901 Canada Ct .... City of Industry CA 91748 626-913-0828 913-0818
Web: msicomputer.com

Microboard Processing Inc 36 Cogwheel Ln .... Seymour CT 06483 203-881-4300 881-4302
Web: www.microboard.com

Micron Technology Inc 8000 S Federal Way .... Boise ID 83707 208-368-4000 368-4617
NASDAQ: MU ■ *TF:* 888-363-2589 ■ *Web:* www.micron.com

Micron Technology Inc SpecTek Div
8000 S Federal Way PO Box 6 .... Boise ID 83707 208-363-5716
Web: www.spectek.com

MIKTAM Technologies Americas Inc
2362 Qume Dr Ste B .... San Jose CA 95131 408-392-0668
Web: www.miktamusa.com

Modular Components National Inc
105 E Jarrettsville Rd PO Box 453 .... Forest Hill MD 21050 410-879-6553 838-7629
Web: www.modularcomp.com

Mti Electronics Inc
W133 N5139 Campbell Dr .... Menomonee Falls WI 53051 262-783-6080 783-4959
Web: www.mtielectronics.com

Natel Engineering Co Inc
9340 Owensmouth Ave .... Chatsworth CA 91311 818-734-6500 734-6530
TF: 800-590-5774 ■ *Web:* www.natelems.com

National Semiconductor Corp
2900 Semiconductor Dr .... Santa Clara CA 95051 408-721-5000 739-9803
Web: www.ti.com

National Technology Inc
1101 Carnegie St .... Rolling Meadows IL 60008 847-506-1300 506-1340
Web: www.nationaltech.com

NVIDIA Corp 2701 San Tomas Expy .... Santa Clara CA 95050 408-486-2000 486-2200
NASDAQ: NVDA ■ *Web:* www.nvidia.com

Oncore Mfg Services LLC 225 Carando Dr .... Springfield MA 01104 413-736-2121 736-6373

Osi Electronics Inc
2385 Pleasant Valley Rd .... Camarillo CA 93012 805-499-6877
Web: www.osielectronics.com

Parallax Inc 599 Menlo Dr Ste 100 .... Rocklin CA 95765 916-624-8333 624-8003
TF: 888-512-1024 ■ *Web:* www.parallax.com

Park Electrochemical Corp
48 S Service Rd Ste 300 .... Melville NY 11747 631-465-3600 465-3100
NYSE: PKE ■ *Web:* www.parkelectro.com

Pentek Inc 1 Pk Way .... Upper Saddle River NJ 07458 201-818-5900 818-5692*
**Fax: Acctg* ■ *Web:* www.pentek.com

Pioneer Circuits Inc (PCI) 3000 S Shannon St .... Santa Ana CA 92704 714-641-3132 641-3120
Web: www.pioneercircuits.com

Plexus Corp 1 Plexus Way PO Box 156 .... Neenah WI 54957 920-722-3451 751-5395
NASDAQ: PLXS ■ *TF:* 877-733-7260 ■ *Web:* www.plexus.com

PNC Inc 115 E Centre St .... Nutley NJ 07110 973-284-1600 284-1925
Web: www.pnconline.com

Printed Circuits Assembly Corp
13221 SE 26th St Ste E .... Bellevue WA 98005 425-644-7754 644-6430
Web: www.pcacorporation.com

Progress Instruments Inc
807 NW Commerce Dr .... Lees Summit MO 64086 816-524-4442
TF: 800-580-9881 ■ *Web:* www.progressthermal.com

Projects Unlimited Inc 6300 Sand Lk Rd .... Dayton OH 45414 937-918-2200
Web: www.pui.com

Promise Technology Inc 580 Cottonwood Dr .... Milpitas CA 95035 408-228-1400 228-1100
TF Sales: 800-888-0245 ■ *Web:* www.promise.com

Q-flex Inc 1301 E Hunter Ave .... Santa Ana CA 92705 714-664-0101
Web: qflexinc.com

Qual-pro Corp 18510 S Figueroa St .... Gardena CA 90248 310-329-7535
Web: www.qual-pro.com

Quality Circuits Inc 1102 Progress Dr .... Fergus Falls MN 56537 218-739-9707 739-9705
Web: www.qciusa.com

Quality Systems Integrated Corp
6720 Cobra Way .... San Diego CA 92121 858-587-9797
Web: www.qsic.com

Quatech Inc 5675 Hudson Industrial Pkwy .... Hudson OH 44236 330-655-9000 655-9010
TF: 800-553-1170 ■ *Web:* bb-elec.com

RadiSys Corp 5445 NE Dawson Creek Dr .... Hillsboro OR 97124 503-615-1100
NASDAQ: RSYS ■ *TF:* 800-950-0044 ■ *Web:* www.radisys.com

Riverside Electronics Ltd 1 Riverside Dr .... Lewiston MN 55952 507-523-3220 523-2831
Web: riversideelectronics.com

SAE Circuits Colorado Inc 4820 N 63rd St .... Boulder CO 80301 303-530-1900 530-0210
TF: 800-234-9001 ■ *Web:* www.saecircuits.com

Sanmina-SCI Corp 2700 N First St .... San Jose CA 95134 408-964-3500 964-3440
NASDAQ: SANM ■ *Web:* www.sanmina-sci.com

Saturn Electronics & Engineering Inc
2120 Austin Ave .... Rochester Hills MI 48309 248-853-5724 299-8514
Web: www.elmanalytics.com/profile/4c4a7/saturn-electronics-engineering-inc-corporate-headquarters

Saturn Electronics Corp 28450 Northline Rd .... Romulus MI 48174 734-941-8100 941-3707
Web: www.saturnelectronics.com

Siemens Mfg Company Inc 410 W Washington St .... Freeburg IL 62243 618-539-3000 539-6172
Web: www.siemensmfg.com

Sigma Designs Inc 1778 Mcarthy Blvd .... Milpitas CA 95035 408-262-9003
NASDAQ: SIGM ■ *Web:* www.sigmadesigns.com

SigmaTron International Inc
2201 Landmeier Rd .... Elk Grove Village IL 60007 847-956-8000
NASDAQ: SGMA ■ *TF:* 800-700-9095 ■ *Web:* www.sigmatronintl.com

SIIG Inc 6078 Stewart Ave .... Fremont CA 94538 510-657-8688 657-5962
Web: www.siig.com

Sopark Corp 3300 S Pk Ave .... Buffalo NY 14218 716-822-0434 822-5062
TF: 866-576-7275 ■ *Web:* www.sopark.com

Spectrum Signal Processing by Vecima
2700 Production Way Ste 300 .... Burnaby BC V5A4X1 604-676-6700 421-1764
TF: 800-663-8986 ■ *Web:* www.spectrumsignal.com

Supermicro Computer Inc (SMCI) 980 Rock Ave .... San Jose CA 95131 408-503-8000 503-8008
NASDAQ: SMCI ■ *Web:* www.supermicro.com/index.cfm

	City	State	Zip	Phone	Fax
TechWorks 4030 W Braker Ln *Web:* techwrks.com	Austin	TX	78759	512-794-8533	794-8520
Tekram USA 14228 Albers Way Ste B *Web:* www.tekram.com	Chino	CA	91710	909-606-1111	597-3713
TTM Technologies Inc 1665 Scenic Ave Ste 250 *Web:* www.ttmtechnologies.com	Costa Mesa	CA	92626	714-327-3000	
TYAN Computer Corp USA 3288 Laurelview Ct *Web:* www.tyan.com	Fremont	CA	94538	510-651-8868	651-7688
Unicircuit Inc 8192 Southpark Ln *TF:* 800-648-6449 ■ *Web:* www.anaren.com	Littleton	CO	80120	303-730-0505	730-0606
Unigen Corp 45388 Warm Springs Blvd. *TF:* 800-826-0808 ■ *Web:* www.unigen.com	Fremont	CA	94539	510-668-2088	668-4889
Universal Scientific of Illinois Inc 2101 Arthur Ave *Web:* www.usipcb.com	Elk Grove Village	IL	60007	847-228-6464	228-0523
VM Services Inc 6701 Mowry Ave	Newark	CA	94560	510-744-3720	744-3730
Voyetra Turtle Beach Inc 150 Clearbrook Rd Ste 162 *Web:* www.turtlebeach.com	Elmsford	NY	10523	914-345-2255	345-2266
Westak Inc 1225 Elko Dr *TF:* 800-387-3766 ■ *Web:* www.westak.com	Sunnyvale	CA	94089	408-734-8686	734-3592
Western Electronics LLC 1550 S Tech Ln. **Fax Area Code:* 303 ■ *Web:* www.westernelectronics.com	Meridian	ID	83642	208-955-9700	465-9798*
Wintec Industries Inc 675 Sycamore Dr *TF:* 866-989-4683 ■ *Web:* www.wintecindustries.com	Milpitas	CA	95035	408-856-0500	856-0501
Yun Industrial Company Ltd 161 Selandia Ln *Web:* www.yic-assm.com	Carson	CA	90746	310-715-1898	
ZTEST Electronics Inc 523 Mcnicoll Ave. *TF:* 866-393-4891 ■ *Web:* www.ztest.com	North York	ON	M2H2C9	416-297-5155	

626 PRINTING COMPANIES - BOOK PRINTERS

	City	State	Zip	Phone	Fax
Ace Group Inc, The 149 W 27th St.	New York	NY	10001	212-255-7846	
Adair Printing Technologies 7850 Second St *TF:* 800-637-5025 ■ *Web:* adairgraphic.com	Dexter	MI	48130	734-426-2822	426-4360
B Squared Inc 104 W 29th St 7th Fl *Web:* www.bsqu.com	New York	NY	10001	212-777-2044	
Bang Printing Inc 3323 Oak St. *TF:* 800-328-0450 ■ *Web:* www.bangprinting.com	Brainerd	MN	56401	218-829-2877	829-7145
Berryville Graphics 25 Jack Enders Blvd *Web:* www.beprintersamerica.com	Berryville	VA	22611	540-955-2750	955-2633
BOLT Solutions Inc 90 Park Ave Ste 1700 *Web:* boltinc.com	New York	NY	10016	212-608-4646	
Bradford & Bigelow Inc 3 Perkins Way *Web:* www.bradford-bigelow.com	Newburyport	MA	01950	978-904-3100	
Calendar Holdings LLC 6411 Burleson Rd. *Web:* calendarholdings.com/index.asp	Austin	TX	78744	512-386-7220	369-6192
CJK 3962 Virginia Ave *TF:* 800-598-7808 ■ *Web:* www.cjkusa.com	Cincinnati	OH	45227	513-271-6035	271-6082
Claitor's Law Books & Publishing PO Box 261333 *TF:* 800-274-1403 ■ *Web:* www.claitors.com	Baton Rouge	LA	70826	225-344-0476	344-0480
Command Financial Press Corp 345 Hudson St *Web:* www.commandfinancial.com	New York	NY	10014	212-274-0070	
Command Web Offset Inc 100 Castle Rd *Web:* www.commandweb.com	Secaucus	NJ	07094	201-863-8100	863-5443
Consolidated Printers Inc 2630 Eigth St *Web:* www.consoprinters.com	Berkeley	CA	94710	510-843-8524	486-0580
Cookbook Publishers Inc 9825 Widmer Rd *TF:* 800-227-7282 ■ *Web:* www.cookbookpublishers.com	Lenexa	KS	66215	913-492-5900	492-5947
CRW Graphics Inc 9100 Pennsauken Hwy *Web:* www.crwgraphics.com	Pennsauken	NJ	08110	856-662-9111	
Cushing-Malloy Inc 1350 N Main St *TF:* 888-295-7244 ■ *Web:* www.cushing-malloy.com	Ann Arbor	MI	48104	734-663-8554	663-5731
Darby Printing Co 6215 Purdue Dr	Atlanta	GA	30336	404-344-2665	346-3332
E & M Bindery Inc 11 Peekay Dr. *TF:* 800-736-2463 ■ *Web:* www.embindery.com	Clifton	NJ	07014	973-777-9300	
Edwards Bros Inc 2500 S State St **Fax:* Cust Svc ■ *Web:* www.edwardsbrothersmalloy.com	Ann Arbor	MI	48104	734-769-1000	913-1338*
Friesens Corp 1 Printers Way *Web:* www.friesens.com	Altona	MB	R0G0B0	204-324-6401	324-1333
Garlich Printing Co 525 Rudder Rd *TF:* 800-276-2622 ■ *Web:* www.garlich.com	Fenton	MO	63026	636-349-8000	
Geyer Printing Company Inc 55 38th St. *Web:* www.geyerprinting.com	Pittsburgh	PA	15201	412-682-3633	
Gospel Publishing House 1445 N Boonville Ave *TF Orders:* 800-641-4310 ■ *Web:* www.gospelpublishing.com	Springfield	MO	65802	417-862-2781	
Griffin Publishing Group 18022 Cowan.	Irvine	CA	92614	949-263-3733	
Hagadone Printing Company Inc 274 Puuhale Rd *Web:* www.hagadoneprinting.com	Honolulu	HI	96819	808-847-5310	
Hamilton Printing Co Inc 22 Hamilton Way	CastletononHudson	NY	12033	518-732-4491	
Heritage Auctions Inc 3500 Maple Ave 17th Fl. *Web:* www.ha.com	Dallas	TX	75219	214-528-3500	443-8407
Houchen Bindery Ltd 340 First St *TF:* 800-869-0420 ■ *Web:* www.houchenbindery.com	Utica	NE	68456	402-534-2261	
ICS Corp 2225 Richmond St *Web:* ics-corporation.com	Philadelphia	PA	19125	215-427-3278	
Joe Christensen Inc 1540 Adams St *Web:* www.jcitest.com/public	Lincoln	NE	68521	402-476-7535	476-3094
John Henry Co 5800 W Grand River Ave **Fax Area Code:* 800 ■ *TF:* 800-748-0517 ■ *Web:* www.jhc.com	Lansing	MI	48906	517-323-9000	968-5646*
Jostens Inc 3601 Minnesota Ave Ste 400 **Fax:* Hum Res ■ *TF:* 800-235-4774 ■ *Web:* www.jostens.com	Minneapolis	MN	55435	952-830-3300	830-3293*
Lehigh Phoenix 18249 Phoenix Dr *Web:* www.phoenixcolor.com	Hagerstown	MD	21742	301-733-0018	
Library Reproduction Service 14214 S Figueroa St. *TF:* 800-255-5002 ■ *Web:* www.largeprintschoolbooks.com	Los Angeles	CA	90061	800-255-5002	
Maple-Vail Book Mfg Group 480 Willow Springs Ln *Web:* www.maple-vail.com	York	PA	17406	717-764-5911	764-4702
McAdams Graphics Inc 7200 S First St. *Web:* www.mcadamsgraphics.com	Oak Creek	WI	53154	414-768-8080	768-8099
MCB Printing Inc 230 Walnut Hill Ln *Web:* www.mcbprinting.com	Havertown	PA	19083	610-446-6011	446-6013
McNaughton & Gunn Inc 960 Woodland Dr **Fax Area Code:* 800 ■ *Web:* www.mcnaughton-gunn.com	Saline	MI	48176	734-429-5411	677-2665*
Moran Printing Inc 5425 Florida Blvd *TF:* 800-211-8335 ■ *Web:* www.moranprinting.com	Baton Rouge	LA	70806	225-923-2550	
Mossberg & Company Inc 301 E Sample St *TF:* 800-428-3340 ■ *Web:* www.mossbergco.com	South Bend	IN	46601	574-289-9253	
New Video Group Inc 902 Broadway 9th Fl *Web:* newvideo.com	New York	NY	10010	212-206-8600	
Offset Paperback Manufacturers Inc 101 Memorial Hwy *Web:* www.beprintersamerica.com	Dallas	PA	18612	570-675-5261	
Omaha Printing Co 4700 F St. *Web:* www.omahaprint.com	Omaha	NE	68117	402-734-4400	
Packaging Printing Specialists Inc 3915 Stern Ave *Web:* www.ppsofil.com	St Charles	IL	60174	630-513-8060	
Page Litho Inc 6445 E Vernor Hwy	Detroit	MI	48207	313-921-6880	921-6771
Plunkett Research Ltd PO Box 541737 *Web:* www.plunkettresearch.com	Houston	TX	77254	713-932-0000	
Print Communications Inc 2457 E Washington St	Indianapolis	IN	46201	317-266-8208	266-9395
Publishers Press Inc 100 Frank E Simon Ave *TF:* 800-627-5801 ■ *Web:* www.pubpress.com	Shepherdsville	KY	40165	502-955-6526	543-8808
Rose Printing Company Inc 2503 Jackson Bluff Rd *TF:* 800-227-3725 ■ *Web:* www.roseprinting.com	Tallahassee	FL	32304	850-576-4151	
RR Donnelley 111 S Wacker Dr **Fax Area Code:* 925 ■ *TF:* 800-742-4455 ■ *Web:* www.rrdonnelley.com	Chicago	IL	60606	800-742-4455	951-1355*
Sheridan Group 11311 McCormick Rd Ste 260 *TF:* 800-352-2210 ■ *Web:* www.sheridan.com	Hunt Valley	MD	21031	410-785-7277	785-7217
Smith-Edwards-Dunlap Co 2867 E Allegheny Ave *TF:* 800-829-0020 ■ *Web:* www.sed.com	Philadelphia	PA	19134	215-425-8800	425-9110
Southwest Publishing & Mailing Corp 2600 NW Topeka Blvd *Web:* www.swpks.com	Topeka	KS	66617	785-233-5662	
Thomson-Shore Inc 7300 W Joy Rd **Fax Area Code:* 800 ■ *Web:* www.thomsonshore.com	Dexter	MI	48130	734-426-3939	706-4545*
Tweddle Litho Co 24700 Maplehurst Dr *Web:* www.tweddle.com	Clinton Township	MI	48036	586-307-3700	307-3708
Typecraft Wood & Jones Inc 2040 E Walnut St *Web:* www.typecraft.com	Pasadena	CA	91107	626-795-8093	795-2423
United Graphics Inc 2916 Marshall Ave. *Web:* www.unitedgraphicsinc.com	Mattoon	IL	61938	217-235-7161	234-6274
United Record Pressing LLC 453 Chestnut St *TF:* 866-407-3165 ■ *Web:* www.urpressing.com	Nashville	TN	37203	615-259-9396	
Versa Press Inc 1465 Springbay Rd **Fax Area Code:* 309 ■ *TF:* 800-447-7829 ■ *Web:* www.versapress.com	East Peoria	IL	61611	800-447-7829	822-8141*
Vicks Lithograph & Printing Co 5166 Commercial Dr *Web:* www.vicks.biz	Yorkville	NY	13495	315-736-9344	
Victor Graphics Inc 1211 Bernard Dr. *Web:* www.victorgraphics.com	Baltimore	MD	21223	410-233-8300	233-8304
Webcrafters Inc 2211 Fordem Ave *Web:* www.webcrafters-inc.com	Madison	WI	53704	608-244-3561	244-5120
Whitehall Printing Co 4244 Corporate Sq **Fax Area Code:* 239 ■ *TF:* 800-321-9290 ■ *Web:* www.whitehallprinting.com	Naples	FL	34104	800-321-9290	643-6439*
Worzalla Publishing Co 3535 Jefferson St PO Box 307 *Web:* www.worzalla.com	Stevens Point	WI	54481	715-344-9600	344-2578
Wright Color Graphics 9051 Sunland Blvd *TF:* 877-246-8877	Sun Valley	CA	91352	818-246-8877	246-8984

627 PRINTING COMPANIES - COMMERCIAL PRINTERS

	City	State	Zip	Phone	Fax
1 to 1 Printers LLC 15031 Woodham Dr Ste 370 *Web:* www.1to1printers.com	Houston	TX	77073	281-821-4400	
1-800 Postcards Inc 121 Varick St *TF:* 800-767-8227 ■ *Web:* www.1800postcards.com	New York	NY	10013	800-767-8227	
11 X 17 Inc 2034 N *Web:* www.11x17.com	Jacksonville	TX	75766	903-541-0100	
3e Marketing Communications 3933 N Ventura Dr *Web:* www.3elitho.com	Arlington Heights	IL	60004	847-398-8677	
4over Inc 5900 San Fernando Rd *TF:* 877-782-2737 ■ *Web:* www.4over.com	Glendale	CA	91202	877-782-2737	
518 Prints LLC 1548 Burden Lk Rd Ste 4 *Web:* www.518prints.com	Averill Park	NY	12018	518-674-5346	
A & a Printing Inc 320 Queen Anne Ave N *Web:* aaprinting.com	Seattle	WA	98109	206-285-1700	
A & M Printing 3589 Nevada St. *Web:* www.anmprinting.com	Pleasanton	CA	94566	925-484-3690	
A Better Image Printing 4310 Garrett Rd *Web:* www.abetterimageprinting.com	Durham	NC	27707	919-967-0319	
A&B Printing & Mailing 2908 S Highland Dr Ste B. *Web:* www.abprint.com	Las Vegas	NV	89109	702-731-5888	
A&h Lithoprint Inc 2540 S 27th Ave. *TF:* 855-305-7628 ■ *Web:* www.ahlithoprint.com	Broadview	IL	60155	708-345-1196	

	City	State	Zip	Phone	Fax
A-Plus Printing & Graphic Center Inc 6561 NW 18th Ct *Web:* www.a-plusprinting.com	Plantation	FL	33313	954-327-7315	
A. Carlisle & Company of Nevada Inc 1080 Bible Way *Web:* www.acarlisleprinting.com	Reno	NV	89502	775-323-5163	
A.E. Litho Offset Printers Inc 450 Broad St. *Web:* aelitho.com	Beverly	NJ	08010	609-239-0700	
AAA Mailing Services Inc 5224 Hwy 50 W *Web:* www.aaamailing.com	Jefferson City	MO	65109	573-893-7679	
Abb Enterprise Inc 1010 E 18th St. *Web:* www.abblabels.com	Los Angeles	CA	90021	213-748-7480	
Abbott Printing Company Inc 110 Atlantic Dr *Web:* www.abbottcg.com	Maitland	FL	32751	407-831-2999	
ABG Marketing & Business Communications 3810 Wabash Dr. *Web:* www.abgraphics.com	Jurupa Valley	CA	91752	951-361-7100	
Abigal Press Inc 9735 133rd Ave *Web:* abigal.com	Ozone Park	NY	11417	718-641-5350	
Ability Building Center Inc 1911 14th St NW *Web:* www.abcinc.org	Rochester	MN	55903	507-281-6262	
Accent InterMedia LLC 300 Missouri Ave Ste 300 *Web:* www.accentintermedia.com	Jeffersonville	IN	47130	812-206-2475	
Accu-Label Inc 2021 Research Dr. *TF:* 888-482-5223 ■ *Web:* www.acculabel.com	Fort Wayne	IN	46808	260-482-5223	
Acculink 1055 Greenville Blvd Sw *TF:* 800-948-4110 ■ *Web:* www.acculink.com	Greenville	NC	27834	252-321-5805	
Accuprint Inc 2414 Palumbo Dr *Web:* www.accuprint.us	Lexington	KY	40509	859-268-8844	
Ace Reprographic Service Inc 74 E 30th St. *Web:* www.acereprographics.com	Paterson	NJ	07514	973-684-5945	
Acorn Press Inc 500 E Oregon Rd *Web:* www.acornpress.com	Lancaster	PA	17606	717-569-3264	
Adams McClure LP 1245 S Inca St. *Web:* www.adamsmcclure.com	Denver	CO	80223	303-777-1984	
Adcraft Products Company Inc 1230 S Sherman St. *Web:* www.adcraftproducts.com	Anaheim	CA	92805	714-776-1230	
Adera Corp 4545 W Diablo Dr Ste A *Web:* www.adera.com	Las Vegas	NV	89118	702-257-2810	
Adidas Printing Inc 264 Salem St. *Web:* adidasprinting.com	Medford	MA	02155	781-391-8850	
AdMail Express Inc 31640 Hayman St *TF:* 800-273-6245 ■ *Web:* www.admail.com	Hayward	CA	94544	800-273-6245	
Adp Media Group LLC 7700 Camp Bowie W Blvd Ste B. *TF:* 800-925-5700 ■ *Web:* www.adpmediagroup.com	Fort Worth	TX	76116	817-244-2740	
Advance Printing & Graphics 1349 Delashmut Ave. *Web:* www.advancecolumbus.com	Columbus	OH	43212	614-299-9770	
AGS Custom Graphics Inc 8107 Bavaria Rd *Web:* www.agscustomgraphics.com	Macedonia	OH	44056	330-963-7770	
Air Waves Inc 7750 Green Meadows Dr N. *Web:* www.airwavesinc.com	Lewis Center	OH	43035	740-548-1200	
Aj Images Inc 259 E First Ave *Web:* ajimages.com	Roselle	NJ	07203	908-241-6900	
Aka Printing & Mailing Inc 44 Joseph Mills Dr. *TF:* 800-232-1515 ■ *Web:* akaprintingandmailing.com	Fredericksburg	VA	22408	540-373-1111	
Alabama Small Business Development Consortium 1732 5th Ave N. *Web:* www.asbdc.org	Birmingham	AL	35203	205-324-5231	
Alcom Printing Group Inc 140 Christopher Ln. *Web:* www.alcomprinting.com	Harleysville	PA	19438	215-513-1600	
Alden Hauk Inc 68 Vine St. *Web:* www.aldenhauk.com	Everett	MA	02149	617-394-0302	
Aldine Inc 150 Varick St Fl 6 *Web:* aldine.com	New York	NY	10013	212-226-2870	
All About Packaging Inc 2200 W Everett St *Web:* www.aapack.com	Appleton	WI	54912	920-830-2700	
All-Pro Printing 11626 Prosperous Dr *Web:* www.allproprinting.com	Odessa	FL	33556	727-375-1502	
Allegra Digital Imaging 1302 Anderson Rd. *Web:* www.allegratroywest.com	Clawson	MI	48017	248-655-0444	
Allen Printing Inc 415-A Spence Ln *Web:* www.allenprinting.com	Nashville	TN	37210	615-255-2078	
Allied Photocopy Inc 1821 University Dr NW. *TF:* 877-539-2973 ■ *Web:* alliedphotocopy.com	Huntsville	AL	35801	256-539-2973	
Allied Printing Services Inc 1 Allied Way *TF:* 800-225-8777 ■ *Web:* www.alliedprinting.com	Manchester	CT	06045	860-643-1101	
Alpha Beta Press Inc 8301 183rd St *Web:* www.visionps.com	Tinley Park	IL	60487	708-429-2000	
AlphaGraphics Inc 215 S State St Ste 320 *TF:* 800-955-6246 ■ *Web:* www.alphagraphics.com	Salt Lake City	UT	84111	801-595-7270	595-7271
Alpine Packaging Inc 4000 Crooked Run Rd *Web:* www.alpinepackaging.com	North Versailles	PA	15137	412-664-4000	
ALTA Systems Inc 6825 NW 18th Dr *Web:* altainc.com	Gainesville	FL	32653	352-372-2534	
Alwan Printing 7825 S. Roberts Rd. *Web:* alwanprinting.com	Bridgeview	IL	60455	708-598-9600	
Ambrose Printing Co 210 Cumberland Bend *Web:* www.ambroseprint.com	Nashville	TN	37228	615-256-1151	
American Banknote Corp 2200 Fletcher Ave *Web:* www.abnote.com	Fort Lee	NJ	07024	201-592-3400	224-2762
American Spirit Graphics Corp 801 SE Ninth St *Web:* www.asgc.com	Minneapolis	MN	55414	612-623-3333	623-9314
Americor Press 880 Louis Dr *Web:* www.americorpress.com	Warminster	PA	18974	215-259-1600	
Amidon Graphics 1966 Benson Ave *TF:* 800-328-6502 ■ *Web:* www.amidongraphics.com	Saint Paul	MN	55116	651-690-2401	690-4009
Ampco Manufacturers Inc 9 Burbidge St Ste 101. *TF:* 800-663-5482 ■ *Web:* www.ampcomfg.com	Coquitlam	BC	V3K7B2	604-472-3800	
Anderson Printing & Mailing 139 S Mechanic St *Web:* www.printanderson.com	Jackson	MI	49201	517-787-4562	
Angel Printing & Reproduction Inc 1400 W 57th St. *Web:* www.angelprinting.com	Cleveland	OH	44102	216-631-5225	
Angstrom Graphics 2025 McKinley St *TF:* 800-634-1262 ■ *Web:* www.angstromgraphics.com	Hollywood	FL	33020	954-920-7300	
Angstrom Graphics Inc 4437 E 49th St *TF:* 800-634-1262 ■ *Web:* www.angstromgraphics.com	Cleveland	OH	44125	216-271-5300	271-7650
Annan & Bird Lithographers Ltd 1060 Tristar Dr *TF:* 800-565-5618 ■ *Web:* www.annan-bird.com	Mississauga	ON	L5T1H9	905-670-0604	
Another Printer Inc 10 Bush River Ct. *Web:* anotherprinterinc.com	Columbia	SC	29210	803-798-1380	
ANRO Inc 931 S Matlack St. *Web:* www.anro.com	West Chester	PA	19382	610-687-1200	
Any Budget Printing & Mailing 8170 Ronson Rd Ste L *Web:* www.anybudget.com	San Diego	CA	92111	858-278-3151	
Apollo Graphics 6501 SW Macadam Ave *Web:* www.apollographicsprinting.com	Portland	OR	97239	503-288-9191	
Arandell Inc N 82 W 13118 Leon Rd *TF:* 800-558-8724 ■ *Web:* www.arandell.com	Menomonee Falls	WI	53051	262-255-4400	
Arbor Press LLC 4303 Normandy Ct *Web:* www.arboroakland.com	Royal Oak	MI	48073	248-549-0150	
Ares Printing & Packaging Corp 63 Flushing Ave Unit 224. *Web:* www.aresny.com	Brooklyn	NY	11205	718-858-8760	
Argosy Publishing Inc 109 Oak St. *Web:* www.argosypublishing.com	Newton	MA	02464	617-527-9999	
Arkansas Graphics Inc 800 S Gaines St *TF:* 877-918-4847 ■ *Web:* www.arkansasgraphics.com	Little Rock	AR	72201	501-376-8436	
Asap Printing Corp 643 Billinis Rd. *Web:* www.asapprintingcorp.com	Salt Lake City	UT	84119	801-263-2727	
Ashton-Potter (USA) Ltd 2855 Broadway St. *Web:* www.ashtonpotter.com	Buffalo	NY	14227	716-633-2000	
Aspen Graphics Inc 4795 Oakland St.	Denver	CO	80239	303-371-2345	
Astley Gilbert Ltd 42 Carnforth Rd *Web:* www.astleygilbert.com	Toronto	ON	M4A2K7	416-288-8666	
Aus-Tex Printing & Mailing 2431 Forbes Dr *TF:* 800-472-7581 ■ *Web:* www.austex.com	Austin	TX	78754	512-476-7581	
Austin Business Printing 404 W Powell Ln *Web:* www.abpcreative.com	Austin	TX	78753	512-836-6902	
Autumn Press Inc 945 Camelia St *Web:* www.autumnpress.com	Berkeley	CA	94710	510-654-4545	
B & B Express Printing Inc 7519 W Kennewick Ave A. *Web:* www.bbprinting.com	Kennewick	WA	99336	509-783-7383	
B & b Printing Company Inc 521 Research Rd. *Web:* www.bbprintnet.com	Richmond	VA	23236	804-794-8273	
B & D Litho of Arizona 3820 N 38th Ave *TF:* 800-735-0375 ■ *Web:* www.bndlithoaz.com	Phoenix	AZ	85019	602-269-2526	
B & G House of Printing Inc 1825 W 169th St Ste A. *Web:* bgprinting.com	Gardena	CA	90247	310-532-1533	
B H G Inc PO Box 309. *TF:* 800-658-3485 ■ *Web:* www.bhgnews.com	Garrison	ND	58540	701-463-2201	
B-W Graphics Inc 101 Westview St. *Web:* www.bwgraphics.com	Versailles	MO	65084	573-378-6363	
Badger Press Inc 100 E Blackhawk Dr *Web:* badgergroup.com	Fort Atkinson	WI	53538	920-563-5144	
Balmar Inc 2818 Fallfax Dr. *Web:* www.balmar.com	Falls Church	VA	22042	703-289-9000	
Barker Blue Digital Imaging Inc 363 N Amphlett Blvd. *Web:* www.barkerblue.com	San Mateo	CA	94401	650-696-2100	
Basin Printing 1437 E Second Ave *Web:* www.basinprinting.com	Durango	CO	81301	970-247-5212	
Bassett Printing Corp 3321 Fairystone Park Hwy *TF:* 800-336-5102 ■ *Web:* www.bassettprinting.com	Bassett	VA	24055	800-336-5102	
Bay State Envelope Inc 440 Chauncy St. *Web:* www.baystateenvelope.com	Mansfield	MA	02048	508-337-8900	
BCW Diversified 514 E 31st St *TF:* 800-433-4229 ■ *Web:* www.bcwpages.com	Anderson	IN	46016	765-644-2033	
Beckmanxmo 376 Morrison Rd *TF:* 800-864-2232 ■ *Web:* beckmanxmo.com	Columbus	OH	43213	614-864-2232	864-3305
Bel Aire Displays 506 W Ohio Ave *TF:* 877-439-4320 ■ *Web:* www.belairedisplays.com	Richmond	CA	94804	510-439-4300	
Berlin Industries Inc 175 Mercedes Dr. *Web:* www.berlinindustries.com	Carol Stream	IL	60188	630-682-0600	
Berney Office Solutions LLC 10690 John Knight Close *Web:* www.berney.com	Montgomery	AL	36117	334-271-4750	
Bertek Systems Inc 133 Bryce Blvd *TF:* 800-367-0210 ■ *Web:* www.berteksystems.com	Fairfax	VT	05454	802-752-3170	
Best Press Inc 4201 Airborn Dr *Web:* www.bestpress.com	Addison	TX	75001	972-930-1000	
Better Label & Products Inc 3333 Empire Blvd SW. *TF:* 800-448-1813 ■ *Web:* www.betterlabel.com	Atlanta	GA	30354	404-763-8440	
BFC Forms Service Inc 1051 N Kirk Rd. *TF:* 800-774-6840 ■ *Web:* www.bfcprint.com	Batavia	IL	60510	630-879-9240	

Phone Fax

Bfi Print Communications Holding Co
602 Bedford St ... Whitman MA 02382 781-447-1199
Web: www.bfiprint.com

BFS Business Printing Inc 76 South St ... Boston MA 02111 617-482-7770
Web: www.bfsprinters.com

Bibbero Systems Inc 1300 N McDowell Blvd ... Petaluma CA 94954 707-778-3131 778-0824
TF: 800-242-2376 ■ *Web:* www.bibbero.com

Biz Print 600 W Front St ... Boise ID 83702 208-338-9746
Web: bizprint.com

Blue Dog Printing & Design
1039 Andrew Dr ... West Chester PA 19380 610-430-7992
Web: getbluedog.com

Blue Ocean Press Inc
6299 NW 27th Way ... Fort Lauderdale FL 33309 954-973-1819
Web: www.blueoceanpress.com

Blue Tape Inc 16101 College Oak ... San Antonio TX 78249 210-222-0580
Web: www.blue-tape.com

Boelte-Hall Litho Inc 4710 Roe Pkwy ... Roeland Park KS 66205 905-389-1367
Web: boelte.com

Bolder Graphics 5375 50 St Se ... Calgary AB T2C3W1 403-299-9400
Web: www.boldergraphics.com

Bolger LLC 3301 Como Ave SE ... Minneapolis MN 55414 651-645-6311 645-1750
TF: 866-264-3287 ■ *Web:* www.bolgerinc.com

Bonanza Press Inc 19860 141st Pl NE ... Woodinville WA 98072 425-486-3399
TF: 800-233-0008 ■ *Web:* www.bonanzapress.com

Bond Printing Company Inc 104 Plain St ... Hanover MA 02339 781-871-3990
Web: www.bondprinting.com

Boone Printing & Graphics Inc
70 S Kellogg Ave ... Goleta CA 93117 805-683-2349
Web: boonegraphics.net

BOPI 1705 S Veterans Pkwy ... Bloomington IL 61701 309-662-3395
Web: www.bopi.com

Bounty Print Ltd 6359 Bayne St ... Halifax NS B3K2V6 902-453-0300
Web: www.bountyprint.com

Bourne Brothers Printing Company Inc
5276 Hwy 42 ... Hattiesburg MS 39401 601-582-1808
Web: www.bournebrothers.com

Br Printers Inc 10154 toebben dr ... Independence KY 41051 859-292-1700
Web: www.brprinters.com

Bradley Graphic Solutions Inc 941 Mill Rd ... Bensalem PA 19020 215-638-8771
TF: 800-638-8223 ■ *Web:* bradleygraphics.net

Brady Palmer Label Corp
1791 Rt 6 Carmel PO Box 490 ... New York NY 10512 800-783-3097
TF: 800-783-3097 ■ *Web:* www.bradypalmer.com

Breakaway Press Inc
9620 Topanga Canyon Pl ... Chatsworth CA 91311 818-727-7388
Web: www.breakawaypress.com

Brenneman Printing Inc
1909 Olde Homestead Ln ... Lancaster PA 17601 717-299-2847
Web: www.brennemaninc.com

Brenner Printing Inc 1234 Triplett St ... San Antonio TX 78216 210-349-4024
TF: 877-349-4024 ■ *Web:* www.brennerprinting.com

Briabe Mobile
200 Corporate Pointe Ste 490 ... Culver City CA 90230 310-694-3283
Web: www.briabemobile.com

Bridgetown Printing Co 5300 N Channel Ave ... Portland OR 97217 503-863-5300
Web: www.bridgetownprinting.com

Brimar Industries Inc 64 Outwater Ln ... Garfield NJ 07026 800-274-6271
TF: 800-274-6271 ■ *Web:* www.brimar.com

Brodock Press Inc 502 Court St ... Utica NY 13502 315-735-9577
Web: www.brodock.com

Brown Industries Inc 205 W Industrial Blvd ... Dalton GA 30720 706-277-1977
Web: www.brownind.com

Buffalo Printing Co 2620/30 Elmwood Ave ... Kenmore NY 14217 716-877-9444
Web: www.buffaloprinting.com

Burns Printing Inc
6131 Industrial Heights Dr ... Knoxville TN 37909 865-584-2265
TF: 866-288-5618 ■ *Web:* www.burnsmp.com

Burton & Mayer Inc
W140 N9000 Lilly Rd ... Menomonee Falls WI 53051 262-781-0770 781-9598
TF: 800-236-1770 ■ *Web:* www.burtonmayer.com

Business Card Service Inc 3200 143rd Cir ... Burnsville MN 55306 952-895-6750
Web: www.bcsinet.com

Business Wise Inc 6190 Powers Ferry Rd Nw ... Atlanta GA 30339 770-956-1955
Web: www.businesswise.com

Butler Color Press Inc 119 Bonnie Dr ... Butler PA 16002 724-283-9132
Web: www.butlercp.com

C & E Specialities 2530 Laude Dr ... Rockford IL 61109 815-229-9230
Web: www.cespecialties.com

C Commerce Register in 190 Godwin Ave ... Midland Park NJ 07432 201-857-1267
Web: www.cridps.com

C r & a Custom Inc 312 W Pico Blvd ... Los Angeles CA 90015 213-749-4440
Web: www.cracustom.com

Cab Signs 38 Livonia Ave ... Brooklyn NY 11212 718-385-1600
Web: www.cab-signs.com

Caddy Printing & Graphics Inc
13701 Neutron Rd ... Dallas TX 75244 972-991-1770
Web: www.caddyprinting.com

Calev Print Media LLC 333 S Miami Ave ... Miami FL 33130 305-672-2900
Web: www.cpmprint.com

Campbell Printing Co 2017 Cleveland Hwy ... Dalton GA 30721 706-259-3344
TF: 866-828-5240 ■ *Web:* www.campbellprintingco.com

Canaan Printing Inc
4820 Jefferson Davis Hwy ... Richmond VA 23234 804-271-4820
Web: www.canaanprinting.net

Canada Economic Development
Tour de la Bourse 800 Sq Victoria Bureau 3800 C.P. 247
... Montreal QC H4Z1E8 514-283-6412
Web: www.dec-ced.gc.ca

Canadian Bank Note Company Ltd (CBNC)
145 Richmond Rd ... Ottawa ON K1Z1A1 613-722-3421 722-2548
Web: www.cbnco.com

Canfield & Tack Inc 925 Exchange St ... Rochester NY 14608 585-235-7710 235-4166
TF General: 800-836-0861 ■ *Web:* www.canfieldtack.com

Phone Fax

Capital Imaging Inc 2521 E Michigan Ave ... Lansing MI 48912 517-482-2292
Web: www.capital-imaging.com

Capital Printing Corp 420 South Ave ... Middlesex NJ 08846 732-560-1515
Web: www.capitalprintingcorp.com

Capitol Press 5306 Beethoven St ... Los Angeles CA 90066 310-577-6606
Web: www.capitolpress.com

Card Personalization Solutions Inc
999 Postal Rd ... Allentown PA 18109 610-231-1860
Web: www.crdpersol.com

Cardwell Printing & Advertising
15470 Warwick Blvd ... Newport News VA 23608 757-888-0993
Web: cardwellprinting.com

Carlith LLC 250 Carpenter Blvd ... Carpentersville IL 60110 847-426-3488
Web: www.carlith.com

Carlson Craft Inc 1750 Tower Blvd ... North Mankato MN 56003 800-774-6848
TF: 800-774-6848 ■ *Web:* www.carlsoncraft.com

Carter Composition Corp 2007 N Hamilton St ... Richmond VA 23230 804-359-9206
Web: www.carterprinting.com

Carter Printing Company Inc
1739 E Grand Ave ... Des Moines IA 50316 515-265-6139
Web: carterprinting.net

Casey Printing Inc 398 E San Antonio Dr ... King City CA 93930 831-385-3222
Web: www.caseyprinting.com

Castle-Pierce Printing Co 2247 Ryf Rd ... Oshkosh WI 54903 920-235-2020
Web: www.castlepierce.com

Cathedral Corp
632 Ellsworth Rd Griffis Technology Park ... Rome NY 13441 315-338-0021
TF: 800-698-0299 ■ *Web:* www.cathedralcorporation.com

Cavanaugh Press Inc 8960 Yellow Brick Rd ... Baltimore MD 21237 410-391-1900
Web: www.cavanaughpress.com

Cayuga Press of Ithaca Inc 215 S Main St ... Cortland NY 13045 607-257-2811
Web: cayugapress.com

Ceci New York 130 W 23rd St Fl 2 ... New York NY 10011 212-989-0695
Web: cecinewyork.com

Century Marketing Solutions LLC
3000 Cameron St ... Monroe LA 71201 800-256-6000
TF: 800-256-6000 ■ *Web:* www.centurymarketingsolutions.com

Cenveo Inc 201 Broad St 1 Canterberry Green ... Stamford CT 06901 203-595-3000
NYSE: CVO ■ *Web:* www.cenveo.com

Cereus Graphics Printing Co
2950-2 E Broadway Rd ... Phoenix AZ 85040 602-445-0681
Web: cereusgraphics.com

Chakra Communications Inc 644 Ellicott St ... Buffalo NY 14203 716-505-7300
Web: www.chakracentral.com

Challenge Printing Co, The 2 Bridewell Pl ... Clifton NJ 07014 973-471-4700
TF: 800-654-1234 ■ *Web:* www.challengeprintingco.com

Chameleon Like Inc 345 Kishimura Dr ... Gilroy CA 95020 408-847-3661
Web: www.chameleonlike.com

Champion Graphics 3901 Virginia Ave ... Cincinnati OH 45227 513-271-3800 271-5963
Web: champion-graphics.com

Champion Industries Inc
PO Box 2968 PO Box 2968 ... Huntington WV 25728 304-528-2791 528-2746
OTC: CHMP ■ *TF:* 800-624-3431 ■ *Web:* champion-industries.com

Chippewa Graphics Inc 8801 Bass Lk Rd ... Minneapolis MN 55428 763-536-9889

Circle Graphics LLC 120 Ninth Ave ... Longmont CO 80501 303-532-2370
Web: www.circlegraphicsonline.com

City Printing Company Inc
122 Oak Hill Ave ... Youngstown OH 44502 330-747-5691
Web: www.cityprinting.com

Claxton Printing Co Inc 1835 MacArthur Blvd ... Atlanta GA 30318 404-521-0933
Web: www.claxtonprinting.com

Clear Image Printing Inc 731 W Wilson Ave ... Glendale CA 91203 818-547-4684
Web: clearimageprinting.com

Clearpath Capital Partners
222 Front St 3rd Fl ... San Francisco CA 94111 415-682-6900
Web: clearpathcapital.com

Click2mail 3103 10th St N Ste 201 ... Arlington VA 22201 703-521-9029
TF: 866-665-2787 ■ *Web:* click2mail.com

Clintrak Clinical Labeling Services LLC
2800 Veterans Hwy ... Bohemia NY 11716 631-467-3900
Web: www.clintrak.com

CM Reprographics Inc
4445 S Valley View Ste #1 ... Las Vegas NV 89103 702-222-1757
Web: www.cmrepro.com

Cme Printing Inc 8181 Commerce Park Dr ... Houston TX 77036 713-271-7700
Web: cmeprinting.com

Coastal Printing Inc of Sarasota
1730 Independence Blvd Ste 34234 ... Sarasota FL 34234 941-351-1515
Web: www.coastalprint.com

Coastal Tag & Label Inc
13233 Barton Cir ... Santa Fe Springs CA 90670 562-946-4318
Web: www.coastaltag.com

Cober Evolving Solutions 1351 Strasburg Rd ... Kitchener ON N2R1H2 519-745-7136
TF: 800-263-7136 ■ *Web:* www.cobersolutions.com

Colonial Press Inc, The 10607 Harrison St ... Omaha NE 68128 402-593-0580
Web: www.thecolonialpress.net

Color Ad Inc 19627 S Santa Fe Ave ... Rancho Dominguez CA 90221 888-264-6991
TF: 888-264-6991 ■ *Web:* www.gocolorad.com

Color Ink Inc W250 N6681 Hwy 164 PO Box 360 ... Sussex WI 53089 262-246-5000
Web: www.colorink.com

Color Place, The 1330 Conant St ... Dallas TX 75207 214-631-7174
Web: www.thecolorplace.com

Color Web Printers Inc
4700 Bowling St S.W. ... Cedar Rapids IA 52404 319-265-6894
Web: www.colorwebprinters.com

Color West Inc 2228 N Hollywood Way ... Burbank CA 91505 818-840-8881

ColorCentric Corp 100 Carlson Rd ... Rochester NY 14610 585-288-1240
Web: www.colorcentriccorp.com

ColorDynamics 200 E Bethany Dr ... Allen TX 75002 972-390-6500
Web: www.colordynamics.com

ColorGraphics Inc 150 N Myers St ... Los Angeles CA 90033 323-261-7171 261-7077
Web: www.colorgraphics.com

Company	City	State	ZIP	Phone	Fax
Colormark LC 1840 Hutton Dr Bldg 208 *Web:* www.colormark-lc.com	Carrollton	TX	75006	972-243-1919	
Colortech Graphics Inc 28700 Hayes Rd *Web:* www.colortechgraphics.com	Roseville	MI	48066	586-779-7800	
Colwell North America 2605 Marian Dr *Web:* www.colwellcolour.com	Kendallville	IN	46755	260-347-1981	
Commerce Printing Service 322 N 12th St *Web:* www.commerceprinting.com	Sacramento	CA	95811	916-442-8100	
Communicorp Inc 1001 Lockwood Ave *Web:* www.communicorp-inc.com	Columbus	GA	31999	706-324-1182	
Compucolor Associates Inc 2200 Marcus Ave *Web:* www.compucolor.com	New Hyde Park	NY	11042	516-358-0000	
Computype Inc 2285 W County Rd C *Web:* www.computype.com	St. Paul	MN	55113	651-633-0633	
Concord Litho Group 92 Old Tpke Rd *TF:* 800-258-3662 ■ *Web:* www.concordlitho.com	Concord	NH	03301	603-225-3328	225-6120
Conley Publishing Group Ltd 119 Monroe St	Beaver Dam	WI	53916	920-885-7800	887-0439
Consolidated Graphics Group Inc 1614 E 40th St *Web:* csinc.com	Cleveland	OH	44103	216-881-9191	881-3442
Consolidated Graphics Inc 5858 Westheimer Rd Ste 200 *NYSE:* CGX	Houston	TX	77057	713-787-0977	787-5013
Content Management Corp 37900 Central Ct *TF:* 877-495-3720 ■ *Web:* www.cmcondemand.com	Newark	CA	94560	510-505-1100	
Continental Web Press Inc 1430 Industrial Dr *Web:* www.continentalweb.com	Itasca	IL	60143	630-773-1903	773-1903
Control Printing Group Inc 4212 S Hocker Dr Ste 150 *Web:* www.controlprinting.com	Independence	MO	64055	816-350-8100	
COP Communications Inc 620 W Elk Ave *Web:* www.copprints.com	Glendale	CA	91204	818-291-1100	291-1190
Copy Cat Printing 365 N Broadwell Ave *TF:* 800-400-8520 ■ *Web:* www.copycatprinting.com	Grand Island	NE	68803	308-384-8520	
Copy Super Center 128 W Market St *Web:* www.totallypromotional.com	Celina	OH	45822	419-586-6620	
Copy Systems Southwest 3201 Mercantile Ct *Web:* www.southwestcopy.com	Santa Fe	NM	87507	505-216-0124	
Copy World 1728 Warwick Ave *Web:* copyworldri.com	Warwick	RI	02889	401-739-7400	
CopyPage Inc 5418 McConnell Ave *Web:* www.copypage.com	Los Angeles	CA	90066	310-822-1620	
Coral Color Process Ltd 50 Mall Dr *TF:* 800-564-7303 ■ *Web:* www.coralcolor.com	Commack	NY	11725	631-543-5200	
Corporate Graphics International Inc 1885 Northway Dr *Web:* www.cgintl.com	North Mankato	MN	56003	507-625-4400	
Cosmos Communications Inc 11-05 44th Dr *TF:* 800-223-5751 ■ *Web:* www.cosmoscommunications.com	Long Island	NY	11101	718-482-1800	482-1968
Courier Graphics Corp 2621 S 37th St *TF:* 800-454-6381 ■ *Web:* www.couriergraphics.com	Phoenix	AZ	85034	602-437-9700	
Courier Printing 1 Courier Pl *TF:* 800-467-0444 ■ *Web:* www.courierprinting.com	Smyrna	TN	37167	615-355-4000	
Cowan Graphics Inc 9253 48 St Nw *Web:* www.cowan.ca	Edmonton	AB	T6B2R9	780-577-5700	
Coyle Reproductions Inc 14949 Firestone Blvd *TF:* 866-269-5373 ■ *Web:* www.coylerepro.com	La Mirada	CA	90638	714-690-8200	690-8219
CP Direct Inc 4600 Boston Way A *Web:* www.cpdirect.org	Lanham	MD	20706	301-918-4084	
CP Graphics Inc 3915 San Fernando Rd *Web:* cpgraphics.net	Glendale	CA	91204	818-241-0861	
CPS Printing Inc 2304 Faraday Ave *Web:* www.cpsprinting.com	Carlsbad	CA	92008	760-438-9411	
Craftsman Printing Inc 120 Citation Ct *TF:* 800-543-1051 ■ *Web:* craftsmanprintinginc.com	Birmingham	AL	35209	205-942-3939	
Creative Imaging Group 64 Mussey Rd *Web:* creative-ig.com	Scarborough	ME	04074	207-883-2999	
Creel Printing LLC 6330 W Sunset Rd *Web:* www.creelprint.com	Las Vegas	NV	89118	702-735-8161	
Creps United Publications 1163 Water St *Web:* www.crepsunited.com	Indiana	PA	15701	724-463-8522	
Crest Craft Co 3860 Virginia Ave *Web:* www.crestcraft.com	Cincinnati	OH	45227	513-271-4858	
Crestec USA Inc 1010 Knox St *Web:* www.crestecusa.com	Torrance	CA	90803	310-327-9000	
Crossmark Graphics Inc 16100 W Overland Dr *TF:* 800-236-1994 ■ *Web:* www.crossmarkgraphicsinc.com	New Berlin	WI	53151	262-821-1343	
Cushing & Company Inc 420 W Huron St *Web:* www.cushingco.com	Chicago	IL	60654	312-266-8228	
Cyber Press 3380 Viso Ct	Santa Clara	CA	95054	408-970-9200	
Cyril Scott Company Inc, The 3950 State Rt 37 E	Lancaster	OH	43130	740-654-2112	
Dahlstrom Display Inc 2875 S 25th Ave *Web:* dahlstromdisplay.com	Broadview	IL	60155	708-410-4500	
Daily Printing Inc 2333 Niagara Ln *Web:* www.dailyprinting.com	Plymouth	MN	55447	763-475-2333	
DALB Inc 73 Industrial Blvd *Web:* www.dalb.com	Kearneysville	WV	25430	304-725-0300	
Dan Dolan Printing Inc 2301 E Hennepin Ave *Web:* www.dolanprinting.com	Minneapolis	MN	55413	612-379-2311	
Darwill Inc 11900 Roosevelt Rd *Web:* www.darwill.com	Hillside	IL	60162	708-236-4900	236-5820
Datamark Graphics Inc 603 W Bailey St *TF:* 888-629-6300 ■ *Web:* www.datamarkgraphics.com	Asheboro	NC	27203	888-629-6300	
David A Smith Printing Inc 742 S 22nd St *TF:* 800-564-3117 ■ *Web:* www.dasprint.com	Harrisburg	PA	17104	717-564-3719	
Davis Direct Inc 1241 Newell Pkwy *TF:* 877-277-0878 ■ *Web:* davisdirect.net	Montgomery	AL	36110	334-277-0878	
Deluxe Check Printing 1600 E Touhy Ave *Web:* www.deluxe.com	Des Plaines	IL	60018	651-483-7111	
Delzer Lithograph Co 510 S W Ave *Web:* www.delzer.com	Waukesha	WI	53186	262-522-2600	
Demand Printing Solutions Inc 3900 Rutledge Rd NE *Web:* www.dpsnm.com	Albuquerque	NM	87109	505-881-2927	
DESIGNASHIRT.COM 905 N Scottsdale Rd *Web:* www.designashirt.com	Tempe	AZ	85281	480-966-3500	
Designers' Press Inc 6305 Chancellor Dr *Web:* www.designerspressinc.com	Orlando	FL	32809	407-843-3141	
Devlinhair Productions Inc 120 Wooster St 3 Ste *Web:* www.devlinhair.com	New York	NY	10012	212-941-9009	
Df Grafix Inc 5131 Santa Fe St Ste C *Web:* www.dfgrafix.com	San Diego	CA	92109	858-866-0858	
DG3 North America Inc 100 Burma Rd *Web:* www.dg3.com	Jersey City	NJ	07305	201-793-5000	
Di Graphics Inc 4850 Ward Rd *TF:* 800-433-2257 ■ *Web:* www.digraphics.com	Wheat Ridge	CO	80033	303-425-0510	
Diagraph of Northern Ohio Inc 15400 Industrial Pkwy *Web:* www.diagraphohio.com	Cleveland	OH	44135	216-267-8734	
Diamond Graphics Inc 14350 Azurite St NW *Web:* www.dgiusa.net	Ramsey	MN	55303	763-235-4141	
Diego & Son Printing Inc 2104 National Ave *Web:* www.diegoandson.com	San Diego	CA	92113	619-233-5373	
Digital Evolution Inc 139 Fulton St *Web:* www.digitalevolution.com	New York	NY	10038	212-732-2722	
Digital Room Inc 8000 Haskell Ave *TF:* 866-266-5047 ■ *Web:* www.digitalroom.com	Van Nuys	CA	91406	866-266-5047	
Direct Connection Printing & Mailing 1968 Yeager Ave *TF:* 800-420-9937 ■ *Web:* www.directconnectionmail.com	La Verne	CA	91750	909-392-2334	
Disc Graphics Inc 10 Gilpin Ave *Web:* www.discgraphics.com	Hauppauge	NY	11788	631-234-1400	234-1460
District Creative Printing Inc 6350 Fallard Dr *Web:* www.dcpprint.com	Upper Marlboro	MD	20772	301-868-8610	
Docu Legal Llc 1650 Main Pl Tower *Web:* www.doculegal.com	Buffalo	NY	14202	716-847-1500	
Document Automation and Production Service 5450 Carlisle Pk *Web:* www.daps.dla.mil	Mechanicsburg	PA	17050	717-605-2362	
Document Security Systems Inc 200 Canal View Blvd Ste 300 *NYSE:* DSS ■ *TF:* 877-407-8031 ■ *Web:* www.dsssecure.com	Rochester	NY	14623	585-325-3610	325-2977
Docuplex Inc 725 E Bayley *Web:* www.docuplex.com	Wichita	KS	67214	316-262-2662	
DocuSource of North Carolina LLC 2800 Slater Rd *Web:* www.docusourceofnc.com	Morrisville	NC	27560	919-459-5900	
Dolce Printing Inc 29 Brook Ave *Web:* www.dolceprint.com	Maywood	NJ	07607	201-843-0400	
Dolphin Shirt Co 757 Buckley Rd *TF:* 800-377-3256 ■ *Web:* www.dolphinshirt.com	San Luis Obispo	CA	93401	805-541-2566	
Dome Printing 340 Commerce Cir *TF:* 800-343-3139 ■ *Web:* www.domeprinting.com	Sacramento	CA	95815	800-343-3139	
Dominion Blue Digital Reprographics 99 Sixth Ave W *Web:* dominionblue.com	Vancouver	BC	V5Y1K2	604-681-7504	
Doodad Printing LLC 7990 Second Flags Dr *Web:* www.doodad.com	Austell	GA	30168	770-732-0321	
Doremus Financial Printing 228 E 45th St 5th Fl *Web:* www.doremusfp.com	New York	NY	10014	212-366-3800	
Dot Generation Inc 16 Dyke Ln *Web:* www.dotgeneration.com	Stamford	CT	06902	203-967-8112	
Double Quick Printing Services Inc 2180 S Colorado Blvd *Web:* www.dqprint.com	Denver	CO	80222	303-759-9999	
Dowling Graphics Inc 12920 Automobile Blvd *TF:* 800-749-6933 ■ *Web:* www.dowlinggraphics.com	Clearwater	FL	33762	727-573-5997	
Downeast Graphics & Printing Inc 477 Washington Jct Rd *TF:* 800-427-5582 ■ *Web:* www.downeastgraphics.com	Ellsworth	ME	04605	207-667-5582	
DPS Printing Service Inc 3500 S Blvd St 38c *Web:* www.dpsprinting.com	Edmond	OK	73013	405-340-0004	
Drew & Rogers Inc 30 Plymouth St *Web:* www.drewandrogers.com	Fairfield	NJ	07004	973-575-6210	
Drug Package Inc 901 Drug Package Ln *TF:* 800-325-6137 ■ *Web:* www.drugpackage.com	O'Fallon	MO	63366	800-325-6137	
Drummond Press Inc, The 2472 Dennis St	Jacksonville	FL	32204	904-354-2818	
Drummond Printing Inc 2114 S Main St *Web:* www.drum-line.com	Stuttgart	AR	72160	870-673-2726	
DS Graphics Inc 120 Stedman St *Web:* www.dsgraphics.com	Lowell	MA	01851	978-970-1359	
Dsj Printing Inc 3103 Pico Blvd *Web:* www.dsjprinting.com	Santa Monica	CA	90405	310-828-8051	
Dual Printing Inc 340 Nagel Dr *Web:* www.dualprinting.com	Cheektowaga	NY	14225	716-684-3825	
Duncan Printing Co 619 S Fremont Ave Ste A *Web:* www.duncanprinting.com	Alhambra	CA	91803	626-281-2016	
Dupli Graphics Corp 6761 Thompson Rd N *TF:* 800-724-2477 ■ *Web:* www.duplionline.com	Syracuse	NY	13211	800-724-2477	
DuraColor 1840 Oakdale Ave *TF:* 877-899-7900 ■ *Web:* www.duracolor.net	Racine	WI	53406	877-899-7900	
Eagle Flexible Packaging 1100 Kingsland Dr *Web:* www.eagleflexible.com	Batavia	IL	60510	630-406-1760	
Eagle:XM LLC 5105 E 41st Ave *Web:* www.eaglexm.com	Denver	CO	80216	303-320-5411	

Phone Fax

Earl d Arnold Printing Co
630 Lunken Park Dr .... Cincinnati OH 45226 513-533-6900
Web: www.arnoldprinting.com

East Ridge Printing 1249 Ridgeway Ave Ste Y......... Rochester NY 14615 585-266-4911
Web: www.eastridgeprint.com

Eclipse Colour & Imaging Corp
875 Laurentian Dr.............................. Burlington ON L7N3W7 905-634-1900
Web: www.eclipseimaging.ca

Economy Advertising Co, The 2800 Hwy 6 E.......... Iowa City IA 52240 319-354-1020
Web: www.bankersadvertising.com

Edison Lithograph & Printing Corp
3725 tonnelle ave .... North bergen NJ 07047 201-902-9191
Web: www.edisonlitho.com

eDOC Communications
555 E Business Ctr Dr .... Mount Prospect IL 60056 847-824-5610
Web: www.edoccommunications.com

Edwards Graphic Arts Inc 2700 Bell Ave .... Des Moines IA 50321 515-280-9765
Web: www.ega.com

Edwards Label 2277 Knoll Dr .... Ventura CA 93003 805-658-2626
Web: www.edwardslabel.com

Egan Printing, Co 1245 Elati St .... Denver CO 80204 303-534-0171
Web: eganprinting.com

EGT Printing Solutions LLC
32031 Townley St.......................... Madison Heights MI 48071 248-583-2500
Web: www.egprint.com

Electric City Printing Co 730 Hampton Rd.......... Williamston SC 29697 864-224-6331
Web: www.ecprint.com

Elite Reprographics 363 Sixth St................ San Francisco CA 94103 415-957-1234
Web: www.eliterepro.com

Elk Grove Graphics Inc
1200 Chase Ave .... Elk Grove Village IL 60007 847-439-7834
Web: elkgrovegraphics.com

Elm Press 16 Tremco Dr............................ Terryville CT 06786 860-583-3600
Web: www.elmpress.com

Embossed Graphics 1175 S Frontenac Rd.............. Aurora IL 60504 630-236-4000
Web: embossedgraphics.com

Embossing Printers Inc 5404 Wayne Rd .... Battle Creek MI 49037 269-968-2221
Web: www.epiinc.com

Emerald City Graphics 23328 66th Ave S .... Kent WA 98032 253-520-2600 520-2607
TF General: 877-631-5178 ■ *Web:* www.emeraldcg.com

Ennis Inc 2441 Presidential Pkwy........................ Midlothian TX 76065 972-775-9801
TF: 800-972-1069 ■ *Web:* www.ennis.com

Envelopes & Forms Inc 2505 Meadowbrook Pkwy .... Duluth GA 30096 770-623-5140
Web: efsurebill.com/envelopes-forms

Envelopes Etcetera Inc
69-71 Townsend St .... Port Chester NY 10573 914-937-6162
Web: envetc.com

Essence Printing Inc
270 Oyster Point Blvd Ste................ South San Francisco CA 94080 650-952-5072
Web: www.essenceprinting.com

EU Services 649 N Horners Ln........................ Rockville MD 20850 301-424-3300 424-3696
Web: www.euservices.com

Eveready Printing Inc 5729 Fleet Ave............... Cleveland OH 44105 216-429-2389
Web: www.evereadyprint.com

Excel Printing and Mailing
924 E 162nd St............................ South Holland IL 60473 708-333-0773
Web: www.excelprintmail.com

Excelsior Printing Company Inc
123 MASS MoCA Way .... North Adams MA 01247 413-663-3771
Web: www.excelsiorprinting.com

Express Envelopes Unlimited 3799 N Alvin St......... Appleton WI 54913 920-997-0182
Web: expressenvelopesunlimited.com

Express Printing & Graphics Inc
1205 Alderwood Ave.......................... Sunnyvale CA 94089 408-400-0223
Web: expressprintingusa.com

Expresscopy.com 6623 NE 59th Pl .... Portland OR 97218 503-234-4880
Web: www.expresscopy.com

F&M Expressions Inc 211 Island Rd .... Mahwah NJ 07430 201-512-3338
Web: www.fmexpressions.com

Falcon Printing Inc 6360 Fulton St E.................... Ada MI 49301 616-676-3737
Web: falconprintinginc.com

Fallbrook Printing Corp 504 E Alvarado St............ Fallbrook CA 92028 760-731-2020
Web: www.fallbrookprinting.com

Farley Printing Co Inc 96 Vandever Ave .... Wilmington DE 19802 302-656-4466
Web: www.farleyprinting.com

FB Johnston Graphics Inc 300 E Boundary Rd .... Chapin SC 29036 803-345-7993
Web: www.fbjohnston.com

FCL Graphics Inc 4600 N Olcott Ave........... Harwood Heights IL 60706 708-867-5500 867-7768
TF: 800-274-3380 ■ *Web:* www.fclgraphics.com

FEY Printing Co 910 29th Ave N.............. Wisconsin Rapids WI 54495 715-423-2400
Web: feyprinting.com

Filogix Limited Partnership
276 King St W Ste 400.............................. Toronto ON M5V1J2 416-360-1777
Web: www.filogix.com

Fineline Printing Group
8081 Zionsville Rd.............................. Indianapolis IN 46268 317-872-4490
TF: 877-334-7687 ■ *Web:* finelineprintinggroup.com

Finlay Printing LLC 44 Tobey Rd .... Bloomfield CT 06002 860-242-2800
Web: www.finlay.com

Firehouse Image Center
2000 N Illinois St .... Indianapolis IN 46202 317-236-1747
Web: onyx.fire-house.net

Fittje Bros Printing Co
804 Garden of the Gods Rd.................. Colorado Springs CO 80907 719-392-4286
Web: www.fittje.com

Flagship Press Inc 150 Flagship Dr............... North Andover MA 01845 978-975-3100 975-0635
TF: 800-733-1520 ■ *Web:* www.flagshippress.com

Flexo Impressions 8647 Eagle Creek Pkwy .... Savage MN 55378 952-884-9442
TF: 800-752-2357 ■ *Web:* www.flexoimpressions.com

Foley's Graphic Center Inc
60 Triangle Ctr......................... Yorktown Heights NY 10598 914-245-3625
Web: foleygraphics.com

Fort Dearborn Co 6035 W Gross Pt Rd........................ Niles IL 60714 773-774-4321 774-9105
Web: www.fortdearborn.com

Phone Fax

Fort Orange Press Inc 11 Sand Creek Rd .... Albany NY 12205 518-489-3233
TF: 800-777-3233 ■ *Web:* www.fortorangepress.com

Foster Printing Service Inc
4295 Ohio St .... Michigan City IN 46360 219-879-8366
Web: www.fosterprinting.com

Fotoprint 975 Pandora Ave........................... Victoria BC V8V3P4 250-382-8218
TF: 888-382-8211 ■ *Web:* www.fotoprint.ca

Fotorecord Print Center
45 E Pittsburgh St............................... Greensburg PA 15601 724-837-0530
Web: www.fotorecord.com

Four Colour Print Group
2410 Frankfort Ave .... Louisville KY 40206 502-896-9644
Web: www.fourcolour.com

Foxfire Printing & Packaging Inc
750 Dawson Dr.................................. Newark DE 19713 302-368-9466

FP Horak Co 401 Saginaw St.......................... Bay City MI 48708 989-892-6505
Web: www.fphorak.com

Fracture LLC 112 SW Sixth St...................... Gainesville FL 32601 352-234-3722
Web: www.fractureme.com

Franklin Imaging LLC 500 Schrock Rd............... Columbus OH 43229 614-885-6894
TF: 877-885-6894 ■ *Web:* www.franklinimaging.com

Franzen Graphics Inc 5300 State Hwy 42 .... Sheboygan WI 53083 920-565-4656
Web: www.franzenlitho.com

Frederic Printing Co 14701 E 38th Ave................. Aurora CO 80011 303-371-7990
Web: www.fredericprinting.com

Freeport Press Inc 121 Main St...................... Freeport OH 43973 740-658-4000
Web: www.freeportpress.com

Fricke-Parks Press Inc 33250 Transit Ave .... Union City CA 94587 510-489-6543
Web: www.fricke-parks.com

Frontend Graphics Inc
1951 Old Cuthbert Rd Ste 404 .... Cherry Hill NJ 08034 856-547-1600
Web: www.frontendgraphics.com

Fruitridge Printing & Lithograph Inc
3258 Stockton Blvd .... Sacramento CA 95820 916-452-9213
TF: 800-835-4846 ■ *Web:* www.fruitridgeprinting.com

Fry Communications Inc 800 W Church Rd ...... Mechanicsburg PA 17055 717-766-0211
Web: www.frycomm.com

Fundcraft Publishing Inc 410 Hwy 72 W .... Collierville TN 38027 901-853-7070 853-6196
TF: 800-964-5715 ■
Web: www.fundcraft.com/fundraising-cookbooks/index.asp

G & a Label Inc 1601 Wyoming Ave .... El Paso TX 79902 915-544-1766
Web: www.ganda-printandlabel.com

Gallus Inc 2800 Black Lk Pl .... Philadelphia PA 19154 215-677-9600
Web: www.gallus.org

Gannett Offset 7950 Jones Branch Dr.................. McLean VA 22107 703-750-8673
Web: www.gannett.com

Garlock Printing & Converting Corp
164 Fredette St .... Gardner MA 01440 978-630-1028
Web: garlockprinting.com

Garner Printing Co 1697 NE 53rd Ave .... Des Moines IA 50313 515-266-2171
Web: www.garnerprint.com

Garrett Printing & Graphics Inc
331 Riverside Ave.................................. Bristol CT 06010 860-589-6710
Web: www.garrettprinting.us

Garrity Print Solutions 109 Research Dr.............. Harahan LA 70123 504-733-9654
TF: 877-568-1555 ■ *Web:* www.garritysolutions.com

Gasch Printing LLC 1780 Crossroads Dr .... Odenton MD 21113 301-362-0700
Web: www.gaschprinting.com

Gator Media Group LLC 40 Fairfield Pl .... West Caldwell NJ 07006 973-244-5900
Web: www.gatormediagroup.com

Gazette Publishing Inc 1114 Broadway................ Wheaton MN 56296 320-563-8146 563-8147
TF: 800-567-8303 ■ *Web:* www.mnnews.com

GBF Inc 2427 Penny Rd .... High Point NC 27265 336-665-0205
Web: www.gbf-inc.com

General Financial Supply Inc 1235 N Ave............. Nevada IA 50201 515-382-3549
Web: www.generalfinancialsupply.com

General Press Corp 110 Allegheny Dr .... Natrona Heights PA 15065 724-224-3500
Web: www.generalpress.com

Genie Repros Inc 2211 Hamilton Ave................ Cleveland OH 44114 216-696-6677
TF: 877-496-6611 ■ *Web:* www.genierepros.com

George Schmitt & Company Inc
251 Boston Post Rd .... Guilford CT 06437 203-453-4334
Web: www.georgeschmitt.com

Georgia Printco 90 S Oak St......................... Lakeland GA 31635 866-572-0146
TF: 866-572-0146 ■ *Web:* www.georgiaprintco.com

Gerald Printing Service Inc
105 Hunter Ct............................. Bowling Green KY 42103 270-781-4770
Web: www.geraldprinting.com

Ginny's Printing 8410-B Tuscany Way .... Austin TX 78754 512-454-6874 453-2178
Web: www.ginnysprinting.com

Global Trim Sales Inc
22835 Savi Ranch Pkwy Ste A .... Yorba Linda CA 92887 714-998-4400
Web: www.globaltrim.com

Globe Ticket & Label Co 11 Eisenhower Ln S.......... Lombard IL 60148 800-523-5968
TF: 800-523-5968 ■ *Web:* globeticket.mybigcommerce.com

Goetz Printing Co, The 7939 Angus Ct .... Springfield VA 22153 703-569-8232
TF: 866-245-0977 ■ *Web:* www.goetzprinting.com

Golden Ink Litho & Design 7602 Vickers St .... San Diego CA 92111 858-541-2259
Web: www.goldeninklitho.com

Gooding Company Inc 5568 Davison Rd .... Lockport NY 14094 716-434-5501
TF: 800-769-7768 ■ *Web:* www.theinsertoutsertexperts.com

Goodway Print & Copy Inc
15121 Ventura Blvd .... Sherman Oaks CA 91403 818-783-5172
Web: www.goodwayprintcopy.com

Grafico Inc 15320 Cornet Ave .... Santa Fe Springs CA 90670 562-921-6731
Web: www.grafico.com

Grafika Commercial Printing Inc
710 Johnston St.......................... Sinking Spring PA 19608 610-678-8630
Web: www.grafikaprint.com

Grand Central Graphics Inc 272 N 12th St........... Milwaukee WI 53233 414-273-7446
Web: grandcentralgraphics.com

Company / Address	City	State	ZIP	Phone	Fax
Grandville Printing Company Inc 4719 Ivanrest Ave SW *Web:* www.gpco.com	Grandville	MI	49418	616-534-8647	
Graphcom Inc 1219 Chambersburg Rd *Web:* www.graphcom.com	Gettysburg	PA	17325	717-334-3107	
Graphic Design Inc 315 Second St E PO Box 307 *Web:* www.gd-inc.com	Hastings	MN	55033	651-437-6459	
Graphic Resource Group Inc 1380 Hamel Rd *Web:* www.grg-inc.com	Medina	MN	55340	763-746-0400	
Graphic Technology of Maryland Inc 8620 Old Dorsey Run Rd *Web:* www.graphtec.com	Jessup	MD	20794	301-317-0100	
Graphics Plus Inc 1808 Ogden Ave *Web:* www.gpdelivers.com	Lisle	IL	60532	630-968-9073	
Graphics Type & Color Enterprises Inc 2300 NW Seventh Ave *TF:* 800-433-9298 ■ *Web:* www.clubflyers.com	Miami	FL	33127	305-591-7600	
Graphicworks 5611 Silverado Way # D *Web:* www.graphicworks.net	Anchorage	AK	99518	907-272-7400	
Graphiques m & H 87 Rue Prince *Web:* mh.ca	Montreal	QC	H3C2M7	514-866-6736	
Graphtech 1310 Crooked Hill Rd *Web:* www.thinkgraphtech.com	Harrisburg	PA	17110	717-238-5751	
Graytor Printing Company Inc 149 Park Ave *Web:* www.graytor.com	Lyndhurst	NJ	07071	201-933-0100	
Greenway Print Solutions 5425 E Bell Rd #120 *Web:* www.greenwayprintsolutions.com	Scottsdale	AZ	85254	602-482-1100	
Greenwell Chisholm Printing Co 420 E Parrish Ave *Web:* www.gc1919.com	Owensboro	KY	42303	270-684-3267	
Greystone Graphics Inc 101 Greystone Ave *Web:* www.greystonegraphics.com	Kansas City	KS	66103	913-342-1393	
Grigg Graphic Services Inc 20982 Bridge St *Web:* www.grigg.com	Southfield	MI	48033	248-356-5005	
Grit Commercial Printing Inc 80 Choate Cir *TF:* 800-872-0409 ■ *Web:* www.gritprinting.com	Montoursville	PA	17754	570-368-8021	
Groupe Lelys Inc 3275 Ave Francis Hughes *Web:* www.lelys.com	Laval	QC	H7L5A5	450-662-7161	
Grove Printing Corp 4225 Howard Ave *TF:* 877-290-5793 ■ *Web:* www.groveprinting.com	Kensington	MD	20895	301-571-1024	
GSL Fine Lithographers 8386 Rovana Cir *Web:* www.gslitho.com	Sacramento	CA	95828	916-231-1410	
Guide, The 24904 Sussex Hwy *Web:* www.theguide.com	Seaford	DE	19973	302-629-5060	
Guynes Printing Company of Texas Inc 927 Tony Lama *Web:* www.guynesprinting.com	El Paso	TX	79915	915-772-2211	
H&N Printing & Graphics Inc 1913 Greenspring Dr *Web:* www.hnprinting.com	Timonium	MD	21093	410-252-5300	
H&W Printing Inc 1724 Sands Pl *Web:* www.hwprinting.com	Marietta	GA	30067	770-951-9800	
H.O.T. Printing & Graphics Inc 2595 Tracy Ct *Web:* www.h-o-tgraphics.com	Northwood	OH	43619	419-242-7000	242-3299
Haig's Quality Printing 6360 Sunset Corporate Dr *Web:* www.haigsprinting.com	Las Vegas	NV	89120	702-966-1000	
Hall Letter Shop Inc 5200 Rosedale Hwy *Web:* www.hallprintmail.com	Bakersfield	CA	93308	661-327-3228	
Hammer Packaging Corp 200 Lucius Gordon Dr *Web:* www.hammerpackaging.com	Rochester	NY	14692	585-424-3880	
Hampton Paper & Transfer Printing Inc 2230 Eddie Williams Rd *Web:* www.hamptonprints.com	Johnson City	TN	37601	423-928-7247	
Handbill Printers Inc 820 E Parkridge Ave *Web:* www.handbillprinters.com	Corona	CA	92879	951-547-5910	
Hanes Erie Inc 7601 Klier Dr S *Web:* www.haneserie.com	Fairview	PA	16415	814-474-1999	
Harman Press Inc, The 6840 Vineland Ave *Web:* www.harmanpress.com	North Hollywood	CA	91605	818-432-0570	
Harmony Press 717 W Berwick St *Web:* www.harmonypress.com	Easton	PA	18042	610-559-9800	
Harper Engraving & Printing Co 2626 Fisher Rd *TF:* 800-848-5196 ■ *Web:* www.harperengraving.com	Columbus	OH	43204	614-276-0700	
Hart Industries Inc 11412 Cronridge Dr *TF:* 800-638-2700 ■ *Web:* hartind.com	Owings Mills	MD	21117	410-581-1900	
Harty Press Inc, The PO Box 324 *TF:* 800-654-0562 ■ *Web:* www.hartynet.com	New Haven	CT	06513	203-562-5112	782-9168
Hatteras Press Inc 56 Park Rd *Web:* www.hatteraspress.com	Tinton Falls	NJ	07724	732-223-9888	
Hazard Communication Systems LLC 190 Old Milford Rd *Web:* www.clarionsafety.com	Milford	PA	18337	570-296-5686	
HBP Inc 952 Frederick St *Web:* www.hbp.com	Hagerstown	MD	21740	301-733-2000	
Hennegan Co 7455 Empire Dr *Web:* www.hennegan.com	Florence	KY	41042	859-282-3600	
Henry Wurst Inc 1331 Saline St *Web:* www.henrywurst.com	North Kansas City	MO	64116	816-842-3113	
Heuss Printing Inc 903 N Second St *Web:* www.heuss.com	Ames	IA	50010	515-232-6710	
Heyrman Printing LLC 2083 Holmgren Way *TF:* 800-236-4815 ■ *Web:* heyrman.com	Green Bay	WI	54304	920-499-4815	
Hickory Printing Group Inc 725 Reese Dr SW *TF:* 800-442-5679 ■ *Web:* www.hickoryprinting.com	Conover	NC	28613	828-465-3431	465-2517
Highroad Press LLC 220 Anderson Ave *Web:* www.highroadpress.com	Moonachie	NJ	07074	212-675-6500	
Hooven-Dayton Corp 511 Byers Rd *Web:* www.hoovendayton.com	Miamisburg	OH	45342	937-233-4473	
Hopkins Printing Inc 2246 CityGate Dr *Web:* www.hopkinsprinting.com	Columbus	OH	43219	614-509-1080	
Horseheads Printing 2077 Grand Central Ave *Web:* horseheadsprinting.com	Horseheads	NY	14845	607-796-2681	
Horton & Horton Printing Co 12412 Sardis Rd *Web:* hortonandhorton.com	Mabelvale	AR	72103	501-455-3168	
I C Group 3985 Pinedale Ct *Web:* www.ic-group.net	Highlands Ranch	CO	80126	303-972-2111	
Ideal Jacobs Corp 515 Valley St *TF:* 877-873-4332 ■ *Web:* idealjacobs.com	Maplewood	NJ	07040	973-275-5100	
Image Press Inc, The 2221 Erie Blvd E *Web:* www.theimagepress.com	Syracuse	NY	13224	315-449-3474	
ImageMark Business Services Inc 141 Robins St *Web:* www.imagemarkonline.com	Lowell	NC	28098	704-478-8988	
imageMEDIA Inc 425 E Spruce *TF:* 866-885-4468 ■ *Web:* www.imagemedia.com	St Tarpon Springs	FL	34689	727-772-8889	
Imagine! Print Solutions Inc 1000 Vly Park Dr *Web:* www.imagineps.com	Minneapolis	MN	55379	952-903-4400	
Immedia Inc 3311 Broadway St NE *TF:* 866-832-2734 ■ *Web:* www.immediaretail.com	Minneapolis	MN	55413	612-524-3400	
Indexx Inc 303 Haywood Rd *Web:* www.indexx.com	Greenville	SC	29607	864-234-1024	
Infinite Media Inc 583 Chestnut St Ste 13 *Web:* www.infinitemediainc.com	Lynn	MA	01904	781-599-5175	
Infovine Inc 1100 W 23rd St Ste 100 *Web:* www.infovine.com	Houston	TX	77008	713-223-9994	
Ink Spot Inc, The 40 Oval Rd Ste 1 *Web:* theinkspot.com	Quincy	MA	02170	617-773-7605	
Inkjet International Ltd 4443 Simonton Rd *Web:* www.inkjetintl.com	Dallas	TX	75244	972-991-4577	
Inkstone Printing Inc 129 Liberty St *Web:* www.inkstone.com	Brockton	MA	02301	508-587-5200	
Inland Arts & Graphics Inc 14440 Edison Dr *TF:* 800-437-6003	New Lenox	IL	60451	800-437-6003	
Inland Printing Co 2009 W Ave South *Web:* www.inlandpackaging.com	La Crosse	WI	54601	608-788-5800	
Inovar Packaging Group LLC 602 Magic Mile *Web:* www.inovarpkg.com	Arlington	TX	76011	817-277-6666	
Instant Sign Center 1400 Providence Hwy Ste 2500 *Web:* www.instantsigncenter.com	Norwood	AL	02062	251-666-9567	
Integra Graphix 160 Koser Rd *Web:* www.yourvisitorguide.com	Lititz	PA	17543	717-626-7895	
Integra Printing Inc 2000 Oak Industrial Dr NE *Web:* integraprinting.com	Grand Rapids	MI	49505	616-459-4142	
IntegraColor 3210 Innovative Way *TF:* 800-933-9511 ■ *Web:* www.integracolor.com	Mesquite	TX	75149	972-289-0705	285-4881
Intelligencer Printing Co 330 Eden Rd **Fax Area Code:* 877 ■ *TF:* 800-233-0107 ■ *Web:* www.intellprinting.com	Lancaster	PA	17601	800-233-0107	834-1443*
Interprint Inc 12350 US Hwy 19 N *TF:* 800-749-5152 ■ *Web:* www.printerusa.com	Clearwater	FL	33764	727-531-8957	
Interprint LLC 7111 Hayvenhurst Ave *TF:* 800-926-9873 ■ *Web:* www.interprintusa.com	Van Nuys	CA	91406	818-989-3600	
IPC Print Services Inc 2180 Maiden Ln *Web:* www.ipcprintservices.com	St. Joseph	MI	49085	269-983-9121	
Ironmark Inc 9040 Jct Dr *Web:* www.ironmarkusa.com	Annapolis Junction	MD	20701	410-280-6633	
Ironwood Lithographers Inc 455 S 52nd St *Web:* www.ironwoodlitho.com	Tempe	AZ	85281	480-829-7700	
Island Litho Plate Service Inc 35 Davids Dr *Web:* www.islandprodigital.com	Hauppauge	NY	11788	631-293-4217	
Issgr Inc 6611 Portwest Dr Ste 190 *Web:* www.imageset.com	Houston	TX	77024	713-869-7700	
Itp of Usa Inc 520 E Bainbridge St *Web:* www.itpofusa.com	Elizabethtown	PA	17022	717-367-3670	
J & A Printing Inc PO Box 457 *TF:* 800-793-1781 ■ *Web:* www.japrinting.com	Hiawatha	IA	52233	319-393-1781	
J. J. Collins' Sons Inc 7125 Janes Ave Ste 200 *Web:* www.jjcollins.com	Woodridge	IL	60517	630-960-2525	
J.B. Kenehan LLC W238 N1700 Rockwood Dr *Web:* www.jbkenehan.com	Waukesha	WI	53188	262-523-8400	
J.S. McCarthy Printers Inc 15 Darin Dr *Web:* www.jsmccarthy.com	Augusta	ME	04330	207-622-6241	
Jaco-Bryant Printing LLC 4783 Hickory Hill Rd *Web:* www.jaco-bryant.com	Memphis	TN	38141	901-546-9600	
Jacob North Companies 3721 W Mathis St *Web:* www.jacobnorth.com	Lincoln	NE	68524	402-470-5335	
Jakprints Inc 3133 Chester Ave *Web:* www.jakprints.com	Cleveland	OH	44114	216-622-6360	
James Allyn Printing Inc 6575 Trinity Ct Ste B *Web:* www.jamesallyn.com	Dublin	CA	94568	925-828-5530	
James Mulligan Printing Corp 1808 Washington Ave *Web:* mobile.weprint.com	St. Louis	MO	63103	314-621-0875	
Jarvis Press Inc, The 9112 Viscount Row *Web:* www.jarvispress.com	Dallas	TX	75247	214-637-2340	
Jena Communications 125 Stokes Ave *TF:* 800-367-5362 ■ *Web:* www.downtownstroud.com	Stroudsburg	PA	18360	570-476-6900	
Jessen Press Inc 3982 Alabama Ave S *Web:* www.jessenpress.com	Minneapolis	MN	55416	952-929-0346	
JK Creative Printers & Mailing 2029 Hollister Whitney Pkwy Ste *Web:* www.jkcreative.com	Quincy	IL	62305	217-222-5145	

Company	City	State	Zip	Phone	Fax
Joat Screen Printing 3601 W Parmer Ln *Web:* joatscreenprinting.com	Austin	TX	78727	512-836-1300	
John Manlove Marketing & Communications 5125 Preston Ave *Web:* johnmanlove.com	Pasadena	TX	77505	281-668-9826	
John Roberts Co 9687 E River Rd *TF:* 800-551-1534 ■ *Web:* www.johnroberts.com	Coon Rapids	MN	55433	763-755-5500	754-4400
JohnsByrne Co 6701 W Oakton St *Web:* www.johnsbyrne.com	Niles	IL	60714	847-583-3100	
Johnson Litho Graphics of Eau Claire Ltd 2219 Galloway St *Web:* www.johnsonlitho.com	Eau Claire	WI	54703	715-832-3211	
Johnson Press of America Inc 800 N Court St *Web:* jpapontiac.com	Pontiac	IL	61764	815-844-5161	
Jondo Ltd 8030 E Crystal Dr *Web:* jondo-usa.com	Anaheim	CA	92807	714-279-2300	
Jones Printing Service Inc 931 Ventures Way *Web:* www.jones-printing.com	Chesapeake	VA	23320	757-436-3331	
JP Graphics Inc 3001 E Venture Dr *Web:* www.jpinc.com	Appleton	WI	54911	920-788-5295	
JTS Direct LLC 1180 Walnut Ridge Dr *Web:* www.jtsdirect.com	Hartland	WI	53029	262-369-9500	
Just-Us Printers Inc 555 N Old Missouri Rd *Web:* www.just-usprinters.com	Springdale	AR	72764	479-751-0385	
K & H Printers-Lithographers Inc 7720 Hardeson Rd *Web:* www.khprint.com	Everett	WA	98203	425-252-2145	
K&M Printing Company Inc 1410 N Meacham Rd *Web:* www.kmprinting.com	Schaumburg	IL	60173	847-884-1100	
Karol Media Hanover Industrial Estates 375 Stewart Rd	Wilkes-barre	PA	18706	570-822-8899	
Kay Toledo Tag Inc PO Box 5038 *TF:* 800-822-8247 ■ *Web:* www.kaytag.com	Toledo	OH	43612	419-729-5479	729-0315
KDM Signs Inc 10450 N Medallion Dr *Web:* www.kdmpop.com	Cincinnati	OH	45241	513-769-3500	
Keiger Printing Co 3735 Kimwell Dr *Web:* keiger.com	Winston-Salem	NC	27103	336-760-0099	
Kellmark Corp 2501 Ada Dr *Web:* www.kellmark.net	Elkhart	IN	46514	574-264-9695	
Kelly Press Inc 1701 Cabin Branch Dr *TF:* 888-535-5940 ■ *Web:* www.thekellycompanies.com	Cheverly	MD	20785	301-386-2800	
Kennickell Printing Co 1700 E President St *TF:* 800-673-6455 ■ *Web:* www.kennickell.com	Savannah	GA	31404	800-673-6455	
Kenny The Printer 17931 Sky Park Cir *Web:* www.kennytheprinter.com	Irvine	CA	92614	949-250-3212	
Kenwel Printers Inc 4272 Indianola Ave *Web:* kenwelprinters.com	Columbus	OH	43214	614-261-1011	
Kenyon Press Inc 1 Kenyon Press Dr PO Box 710 *Web:* www.kenyonpress.net	Sherburne	NY	13460	607-674-9066	
Keys Printing Co 1004 Keys Dr *Web:* www.keysprinting.com	Greenville	SC	29615	864-288-6560	
Kingery Printing Co 3012 S Banker PO Box 727 *Web:* www.kingeryprinting.com	Effingham	IL	62401	217-347-5151	
Kingsbury Printing Co Mount Royal Plz State Rte 9 *Web:* www.kingsburyprinting.com	Queensbury	NY	12804	518-747-6606	
Kirkwood Printing Company Inc 904 Main St *Web:* www.kirkwoodprinting.com	Wilmington	MA	01887	978-658-4200	658-5547
Kiwi Coders Corp 265 E Messner Dr *Web:* www.kiwicoders.com	Wheeling	IL	60090	847-541-4511	
Knepper Press Corp 2251 Sweeney Dr *Web:* www.knepperpress.com	Clinton	PA	15026	724-899-4200	899-1331
Knight Printing LLC 16 South 16th St *Web:* www.knightprinting.com	Fargo	ND	58103	701-235-1121	
Knight-Abbey Commercial Prntrs 315 Caillavet St	Biloxi	MS	39530	228-374-3298	
Knox Services 2250 Fourth Ave *TF:* 800-995-6694 ■ *Web:* www.knoxservices.com	San Diego	CA	92101	619-233-9700	
Kolossos Printing Inc 2055 W Stadium Blvd *Web:* kolossosprinting.com	Ann Arbor	MI	48103	734-994-5400	
Kornit Digital North America Inc 10541 n commerce st *Web:* www.kornit.com	Mequon	WI	53092	262-518-0336	
Koza Inc 2910 S Main St *TF:* 800-594-5555 ■ *Web:* www.kozas.com	Pearland	TX	77581	281-485-1462	
Kreate & Print Inc 14 Central St *Web:* www.kreateandprint.com	Norwood	MA	02062	781-255-0505	
Kristal Graphics 6029 Reseda Blvd *Web:* www.kristalgraphics.net	Tarzana	CA	91356	818-342-7822	
Kwik Kopy Corp 12715 Telge Rd *Web:* www.iced.net	Cypress	TX	77429	281-256-4100	
Kwik Kopy Printing Canada Corp 1550-16th Ave Bldg D *Web:* www.kkpcanada.ca	Richmond Hill	ON	L4B3K9	416-798-7007	
l'Usine Tactic Inc 127e rue E Ste 2030 *Web:* www.samplingproduct.com	Saint George	QC	G5Y2W8	418-227-4279	
La Crosse Graphics Inc 3025 East Ave S *TF:* 800-832-2503 ■ *Web:* www.lacrossegraphics.com	La Crosse	WI	54601	608-788-2500	
Label Impression Inc 1831 W Sequoia Ave *Web:* www.labelimpressions.com	Orange	CA	92868	714-634-3466	
Label Printers Lp, The 1710 N Landmark Rd *Web:* www.thelabelprinters.com	Aurora	IL	60506	630-897-6970	
Label Systems Inc 4111 Lindbergh Dr *TF:* 800-220-9552 ■ *Web:* www.labelsystemsinc.com	Addison	TX	75001	972-387-4512	
Label Technology Inc 2050 Wardrobe Ave *Web:* www.labeltech.com	Merced	CA	95341	209-384-1000	

Company	City	State	Zip	Phone	Fax
Label Works 2025 Lookout Dr *TF:* 800-522-3558 ■ *Web:* www.labelworks.com	North Mankato	MN	56003	800-522-3558	553-8698
Lake County Press Inc 98 Noll St *Web:* www.lakecountypress.com	Waukegan	IL	60085	847-336-4333	336-5846
Lake Erie Graphics Inc 5372 W 130th St *TF:* 888-293-7397 ■ *Web:* www.lakeeriegraphics.com	Brook Park	OH	44142	216-265-7575	
Lake Printing Company Inc 6815 Hwy 54 *Web:* www.lakeprinting.com	Osage Beach	MO	65065	573-346-0600	
Lamcom Technologies inc 2330 Rue Masson *Web:* www.lamcom.ca	Montreal	QC	H2G2A6	514-271-2891	
Laminex Inc 4211 Pleasant Rd *Web:* www.laminex.com	Fort Mill	SC	29708	704-679-4170	
Lane Press Inc 87 Meadowland Dr PO Box 130 *TF:* 800-733-3740 ■ *Web:* www.lanepress.com	Burlington	VT	05402	802-863-5555	264-1485
Lange Graphics Inc 1360 S Lipan St *Web:* www.langegraphics.com	Denver	CO	80223	303-777-1737	
Laser Image Inc 2451 N Stemmons Fwy *TF:* 866-812-3491 ■ *Web:* www.laserimagedallas.com	Dallas	TX	75207	866-812-3491	
Laser Imaging Systems Inc 120 N St	York	PA	17403	717-718-1300	
Laser Print Plus Inc 1261 First St S Ext Ste A *Web:* www.laserprintplus.com	Columbia	SC	29209	803-695-7090	
Laser Reproductions Inc 950E Taylor Sta Rd	Gahanna	OH	43230	614-552-6905	
Lasting Impressions Inc 7406 43rd Ave NE *TF:* 866-859-7625 ■ *Web:* www.lastingimp.com	Marysville	WA	98270	360-659-1255	
Lawrence Printing Co 400 Stribling Ave PO Box 886 *Web:* www.laprico.com	Greenwood	MS	38935	662-453-6301	
LCI Graphics Inc 2400 Main St Extension Ste 8 *Web:* www.lcigraphics.com	Sayreville	NJ	08872	973-893-2913	
Lebon Press Inc 73 Homestead Ave Ste *Web:* www.lebonpress.com	Hartford	CT	06112	860-278-6355	
Lee Printing Company Inc 3904 Leeland St *Web:* www.leeprintingco.com	Houston	TX	77003	713-227-5566	
Lellyett & Rogers Services Company LLC 1717 Lebanon Pk *Web:* www.lrprint.com	Nashville	TN	37210	615-316-0780	
Lester Lithograph Inc 1128 N Gilbert St *Web:* www.lesterlitho.com	Anaheim	CA	92801	714-491-3981	
Lew A. Cummings Company Inc 4 Peters Brook Dr *TF:* 800-647-0035 ■ *Web:* www.cummingsprinting.com	Hooksett	NH	03106	800-647-0035	
Lewisburg Printing Inc 135 Legion Ave *Web:* www.lewisburgprinting.com	Lewisburg	TN	37091	931-359-1526	
Linemark Printing Inc 501 Prince Georges Blvd *Web:* www.linemark.com	Upper Marlboro	MD	20774	301-925-9000	
Litho-Krome Co 5700 Old Brim Dr *TF:* 800-572-8028 ■ *Web:* www.lithokrome.com	Midland	GA	31820	706-562-7900	
LithoFlexo Grafics Inc 2400 South 600 West *Web:* lithoflexo.com	Salt Lake City	UT	84115	801-484-8503	
Lithographix Inc 12250 Crenshaw Blvd **Fax Area Code:* 310 ■ *Web:* www.lithographix.com	Hawthorne	CA	90250	323-770-1000	706-6574*
Lithotone Inc 1313 W Hively Ave *Web:* www.lithotone.com	Elkhart	IN	46517	574-294-5521	
Lithtex Northwest LLC 2000 Kentucky St Ste 6 *Web:* www.lithtexnw.com	Bellingham	WA	98225	360-676-1977	
Lithtex Printing Solutions Inc 6770 NW Century Blvd *Web:* www.lithtex.com	Hillsboro	OR	97124	503-641-5367	
Litigation Solution Inc, The 901 Main St Ste C121 *Web:* www.lsilegal.com	Dallas	TX	75202	303-820-2000	
Little Mountain Printing 234 E Rosebud Rd *Web:* littlemountainprinting.com	Myerstown	PA	17067	717-933-8091	
Livewire Printing Co 310 Second St PO Box 208 *Web:* www.livewireprinting.com	Jackson	MN	56143	507-847-3771	
LMI Packaging Solutions Inc 8911 102nd St *Web:* www.lmipackaging.com	Pleasant Prairie	WI	53158	262-947-3300	
Logmatix Labels & Tags Inc 1235 C Kennestone Cir *Web:* www.logmatix.com	Marietta	GA	30066	770-792-3777	
LogoNation Inc PO Box 3847 Ste 102 *TF:* 800-955-7375 ■ *Web:* www.logonation.com	Mooresville	NC	28117	704-799-0612	
Logoworks 333 South 520 West Ste 360 *Web:* www.logoworks.com	Lindon	UT	84042	747-666-5646	
Lone Peak Labeling Systems Inc 1272 West 2240 South Ste B *Web:* www.lonepeaklabeling.com	Salt Lake City	UT	84119	801-975-1818	
Lowen Corp PO Box 1528 *TF:* 800-835-2365 ■ *Web:* www.lowen.com	Hutchinson	KS	67504	620-663-2161	
Lti Printing Inc 518 N Centerville Rd *TF:* 800-592-6990 ■ *Web:* www.ltiprinting.com	Sturgis	MI	49091	269-651-7574	
Lynn Blueprint & Supply Company Inc 328 Old Vine St *Web:* www.lynnimaging.com	Lexington	KY	40507	859-255-1021	
Lynx Group Inc 2746 Front St NE *Web:* www.lynxgroup.com	Salem	OR	97301	503-588-9339	
M & G Graphics 3500 W 38th St *Web:* m-g-graphics.com	Chicago	IL	60632	773-247-1596	
M & R Sales & Service Inc 1n 372 Main St *TF:* 800-736-6431 ■ *Web:* www.mrprint.com	Glen Ellyn	IL	60137	630-858-6101	858-6134
M&D Printing 515 University Ave *TF:* 888-242-7552 ■ *Web:* www.mdprint.com	Henry	IL	61537	309-364-3957	
M. Lee Smith Publishers LLC PO Box 5094 *TF:* 800-274-6774 ■ *Web:* www.mleesmith.com	Brentwood	TN	37024	615-373-7517	373-5183
Magna IV 2401 Commercial Ln *TF:* 800-946-2462 ■ *Web:* www.magna4.com	Little Rock	AR	72206	501-376-2397	

Phone | Fax

Mahaffey's Quality Printing Inc
355 W Pearl St . . . Jackson MS 39203 601-353-9663
Web: quality-printing.com

Mail Communications Group LLC
4100 121st St . . . Des Moines IA 50323 515-727-7700
Web: www.mailcommunicationsgroup.com

Mail Handling Inc 7550 Corporate Way . . . Eden Prairie MN 55344 952-975-5000
Web: mailhandling.com

Mail Stream Inc 125 Mason Cir Ste K . . . Concord CA 94520 925-676-6711
Web: mail-stream.net

Mainline Printing Inc 3500 SW Topeka Blvd . . . Topeka KS 66611 785-233-2338
Web: www.mainlineprinting.com

Mandel Co 727 W Glendale Ave Ste 100 . . . Milwaukee WI 53209 414-271-6970
Web: www.mandelcompany.com

Marathon Press Inc 1500 Sq Turn Blvd . . . Norfolk NE 68701 402-371-5040
Web: www.marathonpress.com

Marfield Corporate Stationery
1225 E Crosby Rd Ste B1 . . . Carrollton TX 75006 972-245-9122
Web: www.marfield.com

Marina Graphic Center 12901 Cerise Ave . . . Hawthorne CA 90250 310-970-1777
TF: 800-974-5777 ■ *Web:* marinagraphics.com

Marrakech Express Inc
720 Wesley Ave Ste 10 . . . Tarpon Springs FL 34689 727-942-2218
Web: www.marrak.com

Martino-White Printing 543 N Central Ave . . . Atlanta GA 30354 404-768-8708
Web: www.martinowhite.com

Master Graphics LLC 1100 S Main St . . . Rochelle IL 61068 815-562-5800 562-6600
Web: www.mg-printing.com

Master Print Inc 8401 Terminal Rd . . . Newington VA 22122 703-550-9555 550-9673
Web: www.master-print.com

MATLET Group LLC 60 Delta Dr . . . Pawtucket RI 02860 401-834-3007
Web: www.thematletgroup.com

Matrix Imaging Solutions Inc 6341 Inducon Dr . . . Sanborn NY 14132 716-504-9700
Web: www.matriximaging.com

Mc Carty Printing Corp 246 E Seventh St . . . Erie PA 16503 814-454-6337
Web: www.mccartyprinting.com

McCallum Printing Group Inc
11755 108 Ave Northwest . . . Edmonton AB T5H1B8 780-455-8885
Web: www.mcprint.ca

Mccarthy Print Inc 1804 Chicon St Ste 106 . . . Austin TX 78702 512-479-8938
Web: www.mccarthyprint.com

Mccormick Armstrong Company Inc
1501 E Douglas . . . Wichita KS 67211 316-264-1363
Web: www.mcaprint.com

McKay Press Inc 7600 W Wackerly Rd . . . Midland MI 48642 989-631-2360
Web: mckaypress.com

Mcnerney & Associates Inc
440 Northland Blvd . . . Cincinnati OH 45240 513-825-5547
Web: www.pjmcnerney.com

Media Lithographics Inc 6080 Triangle Dr . . . Commerce CA 90040 323-888-8997
Web: www.medialitho.com

Media Sciences International Inc 203 Ridge Rd . . . Goshen NY 10924 201-677-9311
Web: www.mediasciences.com

Mello Smello LLC 3440 Winnetka Ave N . . . Minneapolis MN 55427 763-504-5400
Web: www.mellosmellollc.com

Mercersburg Printing 9964 Buchanan Trl W . . . Mercersburg PA 17236 717-328-3902
TF: 800-955-3902 ■ *Web:* www.mercersburg.net

Mercury Press Inc 1910 S Nicklas St . . . Oklahoma City OK 73128 405-682-3468
TF: 800-423-5984 ■ *Web:* www.mercurypressinc.com

Meredith-Webb Printing Company Inc
334 N Main St . . . Burlington NC 27217 336-228-8378
Web: www.meredithwebb.com

Meridian Graphics Inc 2652 Dow Ave . . . Tustin CA 92780 949-833-3500
Web: www.mglitho.com

Merrill Corp 1 Merrill Cir . . . Saint Paul MN 55108 651-646-4501 646-5332
TF: 800-688-4400 ■ *Web:* www.merrillcorp.com

Metro Web Corp 5901 Tonnelle Ave . . . North Bergen NJ 07047 201-553-0700
Web: www.metrowebnj.com

Meyercord Revenue Inc 475 Village Dr . . . Carol Stream IL 60188 630-682-6200
Web: meyercord.com

Meyers Printing Cos Inc, The
7277 Boone Ave N . . . Minneapolis MN 55428 763-533-9730 531-5771
Web: www.meyers.com

MicroPRINT 335 Bear Hill Rd . . . Waltham MA 02451 781-890-7500
Web: www.mprint.com

Midland Information Resources Co
5440 Corporate Pk Dr . . . Davenport IA 52807 563-359-3696 359-1333
TF: 800-232-3696 ■ *Web:* elandersamericas.com/pages/redirect.aspx

Midtown Printing LLC 2115 59th St . . . St. Louis MO 63110 314-781-6505
Web: www.modernlitho.com

Migu Press Inc 260 Ivyland Rd . . . Warminster PA 18974 215-957-9763
Web: www.migupress.com

Millbrook Printing Co 3540 Jefferson Hwy . . . Grand Ledge MI 48837 517-627-4078
Web: millbrookprinting.com

Millet the Printer Inc 1000 S Ervay St . . . Dallas TX 75201 214-741-3602
Web: www.milletttheprinter.com

Mines Press Inc, The 231 Croton Ave . . . Cortlandt Manor NY 10567 914-788-1698
TF: 800-447-6788 ■ *Web:* www.minespress.com

Minuteman Press International Inc
61 Executive Blvd . . . Farmingdale NY 11735 631-249-1370 249-5618
TF: 800-645-3006 ■ *Web:* www.minutemanpress.com

MM&T Packaging Co 5485 Tomken Rd . . . Mississauga ON L4W3Y3 905-625-1010
Web: www.mmt.ca

Modern Press Inc 1 Colonie St . . . Albany NY 12207 518-434-2921
Web: www.modernpress.com

Modern Print Shop 508 Cortlandt St . . . Houston TX 77007 713-861-7262
Web: modernprintshop.com

Modern Way Printing & Fulfillment
8817 Production Ln . . . Ooltewah TN 37363 423-238-4500
TF: 800-603-5135 ■ *Web:* www.modernwayco.com

Mojave Copy & Printing Inc
12402 Industrial Blvd . . . Victorville CA 92395 760-241-7898
Web: www.mojavecopy.com

Mold in Graphic Systems 999 Hwy 89 . . . Clarkdale AZ 86324 928-634-8838
Web: www.moldingraphics.com

Monarch Litho Inc 1501 Date St . . . Montebello CA 90640 323-727-0300 720-1169
Web: www.monarchlitho.com

Monroe Litho Inc 39 Delevan St . . . Rochester NY 14605 585-454-3290
Web: www.monroelitho.com

Moore Langen Printing Company Inc
200 Hulman St . . . Terre Haute IN 47802 812-238-1551
Web: www.moorelangen.com

Moquin Press Inc 555 Harbor Blvd . . . Belmont CA 94002 650-592-0575
Web: www.moquinpress.com

Morgan Printing Inc 402 Hill Ave . . . Grafton ND 58237 701-352-0640
Web: www.morganprinting.com

Morgantown Printing & Binding LLC
915 Greenbag Rd . . . Morgantown WV 26508 304-292-3368
Web: www.morgantownprinting.com

Morris Printing Group 3212 Hwy 30 E . . . Kearney NE 68847 308-236-7888
TF: 800-445-6621 ■ *Web:* www.morriscookbooks.com

Motivating Graphics Inc 3100 Eagle Pkwy . . . Fort Worth TX 76177 817-491-4788
Web: www.motivatingraphics.com

Mound Printing Company Inc 2455 Belvo Rd . . . Miamisburg OH 45342 937-866-2872
Web: www.moundprinting.com

Mount Royal Printing Company Inc
6310 Blair Hill Ln . . . Baltimore MD 21209 410-296-1117
Web: mtroyalprinting.com

Mr Button Products Inc
7840 Rockville Rd . . . Indianapolis IN 46214 317-273-4333
Web: www.mrbutton.com

MR Label Inc 5018 Gray Rd . . . Cincinnati OH 45232 513-681-2088
TF: 888-522-3526 ■ *Web:* www.mrlabelco.com

MRI Flexible Packaging Co 122 Penns Trl . . . Newtown PA 18940 215-860-7676
Web: www.mriflex.com

MT&L Card Products & Fulfillment Services
2911 Kraft Dr . . . Nashville TN 37204 615-254-9471
Web: www.mtlcard.com

Multi-Craft Litho Inc
131 E Sixth St PO Box 72960 . . . Newport KY 41072 859-581-2754
Web: www.multi-craft.com

Mutual Engraving Company Inc
511 Hempstead Ave Ste . . . West Hempstead NY 11552 516-486-2996
Web: www.mutualengraving.com

Mv Printing Solutions Inc
23531 Ridge Rt Dr Ste A . . . Laguna Hills CA 92653 949-598-9610
Web: mvprintsolutions.com

MWM Dexter Inc 107 Washington Ave . . . Aurora MO 65605 417-841-1040
Web: www.mwmdexter.com

Nahan Printing Inc
7000 Saukview Dr PO Box 697 . . . Saint Cloud MN 56302 320-251-7611 259-1378
Web: www.nahan.com

Nameplate & Panel Technology
387 Gundersen Dr . . . Carol Stream IL 60188 630-690-9360
TF: 800-833-8397 ■ *Web:* www.nptec.com

Napa Printing & Graphics Center Inc
630 Airpark Rd Ste D . . . Napa CA 94558 707-257-6555
Web: www.napaprinting.com

National Graphics Inc 248 Branford Rd . . . North Branford CT 06471 203-481-2351
Web: natgraphics.com

National Mail Graphics Corp 300 Old Mill Ln . . . Exton PA 19341 610-524-1600 524-7638
Web: www.nmgcorp.com

Nationwide Graphics Inc 2500 W Loop S Ste 500 . . . Houston TX 77027 713-961-4700 961-4701
Web: www.nwas-llc.com

NCL Graphic Specialties Inc
N29 W 22960 Marjean Ln . . . Waukesha WI 53186 262-832-6100
Web: nclgs.com

ND Graphic Product Ltd
55 Interchange Way Unit 1 . . . Concord ON L4K5W3 416-663-6416
TF: 800-811-0194 ■ *Web:* www.ndgraphics.com

Nebraska Printing Company Inc
4411 W Tampa Bay Blvd . . . Tampa FL 33614 813-873-7117 873-1193

Network Communications Inc
2 Sun Ct NW Ste 300 . . . Norcross GA 30092 678-346-9300
Web: www.nci.com

New Era Portfolio 2101 E St Elmo Rd Ste 110 . . . Austin TX 78744 512-928-3200
Web: www.newerahd.com

New World Group Inc 500 County Ave . . . Secaucus NJ 07094 201-770-1404
Web: www.newworldgroup.com

Newark Trade Digital Graphics 177 Oakwood Ave . . . Orange NJ 07050 973-674-3727
Web: www.newarktrade.com

Neyenesch Printers Inc 2750 Kettner Blvd . . . San Diego CA 92101 415-566-1599
Web: www.neyenesch.com

Nieman Printing Inc 10615 Newkirk St Ste 100 . . . Dallas TX 75220 972-506-7400
Web: niemanprinting.com

Nightowl Document Management Services
724 N First St Ste 500 . . . Minneapolis MN 55401 612-337-0448
Web: www.nightowldms.com

North Toledo Graphics LLC 5225 Telegraph Rd . . . Toledo OH 43612 419-476-8808
Web: www.northtoledographics.com

Northern Ohio Printing Inc
4721 Hinckley Indus Pkwy . . . Cleveland OH 44109 216-398-0000
TF: 800-407-7284 ■ *Web:* www.nohioprint.com

Nowata Printing Co Po Box 472 . . . Nowata OK 74048 918-273-1950
Web: www.nowataprinting.com

NPC Inc 13710 Dunnings Hwy . . . Claysburg PA 16625 814-239-8787
Web: www.npcweb.com

Nta Graphics South Inc 501 Republic Cir . . . Birmingham AL 35214 205-798-2123
TF: 888-798-2123 ■ *Web:* www.ntagraphics.com

Nutis Press Inc 3540 E Fulton St . . . Columbus OH 43227 614-237-8626
Web: nutis.com

O'Neil Printing Inc 366 N Second Ave . . . Phoenix AZ 85003 602-258-7789
Web: www.oneilprint.com

Oatmeal Studios Inc PO Box 138 . . . Rochester VT 05767 802-767-3171
Web: www.oatmealstudios.com

Odyssey Digital Printing Inc
5301 S 125th E Ave . . . Tulsa OK 74146 918-660-0492

				Phone	Fax
Old Trail Printing Company Inc, The 100 Fornoff Rd *Web:* www.oldtrailprinting.com	Columbus	OH	43207	614-443-4852	
Oliver Printing Company Inc 1760 Enterprise Pkwy *Web:* www.oliverprinting.com	Twinsburg	OH	44087	330-425-7890	
Olympus Press Inc 3400 S 150th St *Web:* www.olympuspress.com	Seattle	WA	98188	206-242-2700	
Omega Printing Inc 201-207 Williams St *Web:* omegaprinting.com	Bensenville	IL	60106	630-595-6344	
Origen Partners Inc 2260 Defoor Hills Rd *Web:* www.origenpartners.com	Atlanta	GA	30318	404-355-8910	
Original Impressions LLC 12900 SW 89th Ct *Web:* www.originalimpressions.com	Miami	FL	33176	305-233-1322	
Outlook Group Corp 1180 American Dr *Web:* www.outlookgroup.com	Neenah	WI	54956	920-722-2333	727-8529
Output Services Inc 6410 O'Dell Pl *Web:* www.outputservices.com	Boulder	CO	80301	303-530-3403	
OvernightPrints Inc 1800 E Garry Ave *Web:* www.overnightprints.com	Santa Ana	CA	92705	949-231-5632	
Oxley Enterprises Inc 85 Cranston Ln *Web:* www.oxleyenterprises.com	Stafford	VA	22555	540-752-8822	
P & P Press Inc 6513 N Galena Rd *Web:* pppress.com	Peoria	IL	61614	309-691-8511	
Pacific Color Graphics 440 Boulder Ct 100d *TF:* 888-551-1482 ■ *Web:* www.pacificcolor.com	Pleasanton	CA	94566	925-600-3006	
Packaging Products Corporation LLC 6820 Squibb Rd *Web:* www.packagingproductscorp.com	Mission	KS	66202	913-262-3033	
Page International Communications 2748 Bingle Rd *TF:* 888-464-8484 ■ *Web:* www.page-intl.com	Houston	TX	77055	713-464-8484	
Palm Printing 6001 Business Blvd *Web:* palmprinting.com	Sarasota	FL	34240	941-907-0090	
Palmas Printing Inc 200 East Dr *Web:* www.palmasprinting.com	Melbourne	FL	32904	321-984-4451	
Palmer Printing Company Inc 2902 3rd St S *Web:* www.palmerprinting.com	Waite Park	MN	56387	320-252-0033	
Palmetto Cooperative Services LLC 7440 Broad River Rd *Web:* www.palmettocoop.com	Irmo	SC	29063	803-781-0091	
Panoramic Press Inc 2920 N 35th St *Web:* panoramicpress.com	Phoenix	AZ	85018	602-955-2001	
Paradigm Imaging Group 1590 Metro Dr Ste 116 *TF:* 888-221-7226 ■ *Web:* www.paradigmimaging.com	Costa Mesa	CA	92626	714-432-7226	
Paragon Press Inc 2532 South 3270 West *Web:* www.paragonpress.com	Salt Lake City	UT	84119	801-978-3500	
Paramount Graphics Inc 11000 SW 11th Ste 400 *Web:* www.paramountgraphics.com	Beaverton	OR	97005	503-641-7771	
Paravista Inc 1055 Centennial Ave *Web:* www.paravistainc.com	Piscataway	NJ	08854	732-752-1222	
Paris Art Label Company Inc 217 River Ave *Web:* www.parisartlabel.com	Patchogue	NY	11772	631-648-6200	
Park Printing Inc 2801 California St NE *Web:* www.parkprint.com	Minneapolis	MN	55418	612-789-4333	
Parris Printing 211 Whitsett Rd *Web:* www.parrisprinting.com	Nashville	TN	37210	615-832-7170	
Party Cat Inc 2727 Exposition Blvd Ste 119 *Web:* partycat.com	Austin	TX	78703	512-472-8250	
Pauler Communications Inc 7271 Engle Rd Ste 309 *Web:* townplanner.com	Cleveland	OH	44130	440-243-1229	
Pavsner Press Inc 9008 Yellow Brick Rd *Web:* www.pavsnerpress.com	Baltimore	MD	21237	410-687-7550	
Payne Printery Inc 3235 Memorial Hwy *Web:* www.payneinc.net	Dallas	PA	18612	570-675-1147	
Pazazz Printing Inc 5584 Cote-de-Liesse *TF:* 866-449-4417 ■ *Web:* www.pazazz.com	Montreal	QC	H4P1A9	514-856-3330	
PBM Graphics Inc 3700 S Miami Blvd *TF:* 800-849-8100 ■ *Web:* www.pbmgraphics.com	Durham	NC	27703	919-544-6222	544-6695
PCA LLC 15 W Aylesbury Rd *Web:* www.printpca.com	Timonium	MD	21093	410-561-5533	
PCH Litho Inc 1497 Poinsettia Ave 159 *Web:* pchlitho.com	Vista	CA	92081	760-798-1190	
PCI Group Inc 11632 Harrisburg Rd *Web:* www.pcigroup.com	Fort Mill	SC	29707	803-578-7700	
PDQ Print Center Inc 27 Stauffer Industrial Pky *Web:* www.pdqprint.com	Taylor	PA	18517	570-343-0414	
PDQ Printing Inc 3820 S Vly View Blvd *Web:* www.pdqvegas.com	Las Vegas	NV	89103	702-876-3235	
Peake DeLancey Printers LLC 2500 Schuster Dr *TF:* 800-521-7325 ■ *Web:* www.peakedelancey.com	Cheverly	MD	20781	301-341-4600	
Pel Hughes Printing Inc 3801 Toulouse St *Web:* www.pelhughes.com	New Orleans	LA	70119	504-486-8646	
Pemcor LLC 2100 State Rd *Web:* www.pemcor.com	Lancaster	PA	17601	717-898-1555	
Penmor Lithographers Inc 8 Lexington St PO Box 2003 *Web:* penmor.com	Lewiston	ME	04241	207-784-1341	
Perfect Image Inc 8505 Crown Crescent Ct *Web:* www.perfectimageprint.com	Charlotte	NC	28227	704-841-2464	
Perkinson Reprographics Inc 735 E Brill St *TF:* 888-330-8782 ■ *Web:* www.prigraphics.com	Phoenix	AZ	85006	602-393-3131	
Philipp Lithographing Co 1960 Wisconsin Ave PO Box 4 *Web:* www.philipplitho.com	Grafton	WI	53024	262-377-1100	
Phoenix Innovate Inc 1775 Bellingham *Web:* www.phoenixinnovate.com	Troy	MI	48083	248-457-9000	
Phoenix Lithographing Corp 11631 Caroline Rd *Web:* www.phoenixlitho.com	Philadelphia	PA	19154	215-698-9000	
Photocraft Inc 4468 NW Yeon Ave *Web:* www.photocraft.com	Portland	OR	97210	503-225-0515	
Piccadilly Printing Co 1000 Valley Ave *Web:* www.picprinting.com	Winchester	VA	22601	540-662-3804	
Pictorial Offset Corp 111 Amor Ave	Carlstadt	NJ	07072	201-935-7100	935-3254
Piedmont Graphics Inc 6903 International Dr *Web:* www.piedmontgraphics.com	Greensboro	NC	27409	336-230-0040	
Pioneer Printing & Stationery Co Inc 514 W 19th St *Web:* wypioneer.com	Cheyenne	WY	82001	307-635-4114	
PIP Printing & Document Services Inc 26722 Plaza Dr Ste 200 *Web:* www.pip.com	Mission Viejo	CA	92691	949-348-5000	348-5066
Platon Digital Graphics 136 Oregon St *TF:* 800-499-0292 ■ *Web:* platongraphics.com	El Segundo	CA	90245	800-499-0292	
Plum Grove Inc 2160 Stoningtone Ave *Web:* www.plumgroveprinters.com	Hoffman Estates	IL	60169	847-882-4020	
Plymouth Printing Co Inc 450 North Ave E *Web:* www.plymouthprinting.com	Cranford	NJ	07016	908-276-8100	
Pma Inc 17128 Edwards Rd *Web:* www.printmgt.com	Cerritos	CA	90703	562-407-9977	
Pollock Printing Company Inc 928 Sixth Ave South *TF:* 800-349-1205 ■ *Web:* www.pollockprinting.com	Nashville	TN	37203	615-255-0526	
Polytype America Corp 10 Industrial Ave *Web:* www.wifag-polytype.com	Mahwah	NJ	07430	201-995-1000	995-1080
Premier Graphics LLC 1248 W Fourth St *TF:* 800-511-4881 ■ *Web:* www.premiergraphicsinc.com	Mansfield	OH	44906	203-378-6200	
Premium Color Group LLC 95-B Industrial *Web:* www.premiumcolor.com	Clifton	NJ	07012	973-472-7007	
Prentice Products 4236 W Ferguson Rd *Web:* www.prenticeproducts.com	Fort Wayne	IN	46809	260-747-3195	
Press Room Inc, The 100 Youngs Rd Ste 2 *Web:* thepressroominc.com	Mercerville	NJ	08619	609-689-3817	
Pressnet Express Inc 7283 Engineer Rd Ste A/B *Web:* pressnetexpress.com	San Diego	CA	92111	858-694-0070	
Prestone Printing Company Inc 47-50 30th St *Web:* www.prestoneprinting.com	New York	NY	11101	347-468-7900	
Print Basics Inc 1059 Sw 30th Ave *Web:* www.printbasics.com	Deerfield Beach	FL	33442	954-354-0700	
Print Direction Inc 1600 Indian Brook Way *TF:* 877-435-1672 ■ *Web:* www.printdirection.com	Norcross	GA	30093	770-446-6446	
Print Fulfillment Services LLC 2929 Magazine St *Web:* www.printfulfillmentservices.com	Louisville	KY	40211	502-776-7704	
Print House, The 200 Maplewood St *Web:* www.printhouse.com	Malden	MA	02148	781-324-4455	
Print NW LLC 9914 32nd Ave S *Web:* printnw.rocks	Tacoma	WA	98499	253-284-2300	
Print Papa 1920 Lafayette St Ste L *TF:* 800-657-7181 ■ *Web:* www.printpapa.com	Santa Clara	CA	95050	408-567-9553	
Print Tech LLC 49 Fadem Rd *Web:* www.print-tech.com	Springfield	NJ	07081	908-232-2287	
Print Time Inc 1105 W 24th Ste 111 *Web:* www.printtime.com	Kansas City	MO	64108	816-756-3900	
Print Works 3850 98 St Nw *TF:* 888-452-8921 ■ *Web:* www.printworksprint.com	Edmonton	AB	T6E3L2	780-452-8921	
Printed Image, The 41 S Grant Ave *Web:* www.printedimage.com	Columbus	OH	43215	614-221-1412	
Printer Inc, The 1220 Thomas Beck Rd *Web:* www.the-printer.com	Des Moines	IA	50315	515-288-7241	288-9234
PrintFleet Inc 275 Ontario St Ste 301 *Web:* www.printfleet.com	Kingston	ON	K7K2X5	613-549-3221	
Printing Arts Press 8028 Newark Rd *Web:* www.printingartspress.com	Mount Vernon	OH	43050	740-397-6106	
Printing Control Services Inc 1011 Andover Park E *Web:* printingcontrol.com	Tukwila	WA	98188	206-575-4114	
Printing Images Inc 12266 Wilkins Ave A *TF:* 866-685-4356 ■ *Web:* www.printingimages.com	Rockville	MD	20852	301-984-1140	
Printing Methods Inc 1525 Emerson St *Web:* www.printingmethods.com	Rochester	NY	14606	585-458-2133	
Printing Partners Inc 929 W 16th St *Web:* www.printingpartners.net	Indianapolis	IN	46202	317-635-2282	
Printing Source Inc, The 2373 Ball Dr *Web:* www.theprintingsource.com	St. Louis	MO	63146	314-373-7200	
PrintingForLess.com Inc 100 PFL Way *TF:* 800-930-6040 ■ *Web:* www.printingforless.com	Livingston	MT	59047	800-930-6040	
PrintPlace.com 1130 Ave H E *TF:* 877-405-3949 ■ *Web:* www.printplace.com	Arlington	TX	76011	817-701-3555	
Printpoint Printing Inc 150 S Patterson Blvd *Web:* www.printpointprinting.com	Dayton	OH	45402	937-223-9041	
Printscape Inc 700 Vista Park Dr Ste 7 *Web:* www.myprintscape.com	Pittsburgh	PA	15205	412-788-0640	
Printsouth Printing Inc 1114 Silstar Rd *Web:* www.myprintsouth.com	West Columbia	SC	29170	803-796-2619	
Printswell Inc 135 Cahaba Valley Pkwy *Web:* www.printswell.com	Pelham	AL	35124	205-985-9690	
Prisma Graphic Corp 2937 E Broadway Rd *TF:* 800-379-5777 ■ *Web:* www.prismagraphic.com	Phoenix	AZ	85040	602-243-5777	268-4804
Pro Copy 5219 E Fowler Ave *Web:* www.pro-copy.com	Tampa	FL	33617	813-988-5900	
Pro-Graphics Communications Inc 5664 New Peachtree Rd *Web:* www.prographinc.com	Atlanta	GA	30341	678-597-1050	

				Phone	Fax
Process Displays Co 7108 31st Ave N Web: www.processdisplays.com	Minneapolis	MN	55427	763-546-1133	
Production Press Inc 307 E Morgan St TF: 800-231-3880 ■ Web: www.productionpress.com	Jacksonville	IL	62650	217-243-3353	245-0400
Profile Digital Printing LLC 5449 Marina Dr Web: www.profiledpi.com	Dayton	OH	45449	937-866-4241	
ProForma 8800 E Pleasant Vly Rd TF: 800-825-1525 ■ Web: www.proforma.com	Independence	OH	44131	216-520-8400	
Progress Printing Co 2677 Waterlick Rd *Fax Area Code: 434 ■ TF: 800-572-7804 ■ Web: www.progressprintplus.com	Lynchburg	VA	24502	800-572-7804	237-1618*
Prosource Fitness Equipment 6503 Hilburn Dr TF: 877-781-8077 ■ Web: prosourcefitness.com	Raleigh	NC	27613	919-781-8077	
PSPrint LLC 2861 Mandela Pkwy Web: www.psprint.com	Oakland	CA	94608	510-444-3933	
Pub Cite 191 Rue Theberge Web: pubcite.com	Delson	QC	J5B2J9	450-635-0635	
Publication Printers Corp 2001 S Platte River Dr TF: 888-824-0303 ■ Web: www.publicationprinters.com	Denver	CO	80223	303-936-0303	934-6712
PXP Inc 2485 Merritt Dr Web: www.pxpsolutions.com	Garland	TX	75041	214-221-7669	
Pyramid Checks & Printing Inc 208 Riverside Indus Pkwy Web: www.pyramidchecks-printing.com	Portland	ME	04103	207-878-9832	
Quad/Graphics Inc N63 W23075 Main St NYSE: QUAD ■ Web: www.qg.com	Sussex	WI	53089	414-566-6000	
Quadriscan Inc 6600 Rue Saint-urbain Web: quadriscan.com	Montreal	QC	H2S3G6	514-277-6022	
Quartier Printing Company Inc 5795 Bridge St E Syracuse Web: www.quartierprinting.com	Syracuse	NY	13057	315-449-0900	
Queen City Printers Inc 701 Pine St Web: www.qcpinc.com	Burlington	VT	05401	802-864-4566	
Questmark Information Management Inc 9440 Kirby Dr Web: questmark.net	Houston	TX	77054	713-662-9022	
Quick Color Solutions Inc 829 Knox Rd TF: 877-698-0951 ■ Web: www.quickcolorsolutions.com	Mc Leansville	NC	27301	336-698-0951	
Quick Tab Ii Inc 241 Heritage Dr TF: 800-332-5081 ■ Web: www.qt2.com	Tiffin	OH	44883	419-448-6622	
R I Bryan Co, The 301 Greystone Blvd Web: www.rlbryan.com	Columbia	SC	29210	803-779-3560	
R.C. Brayshaw & Company Inc 45 Waterloo St Web: www.rcbrayshaw.com	Warner	NH	03278	603-456-3101	
R.R. Donnelley Seymour Inc 709 A Ave E Web: www.rrdonnelley.com	Seymour	IN	47274	812-523-1800	
Raff Printing Inc PO Box 42365 Web: www.raffprinting.com	Pittsburgh	PA	15203	412-431-4044	
Rainbow Graphics Inc 933 Tower Rd Web: www.rainbowgraphics.com	Mundelein	IL	60060	847-824-9600	
Raintree Graphics Inc 5921 Richard St Web: www.raintreegraphics.com	Jacksonville	FL	32216	904-396-1653	
Ramallo Bros Printing Inc Carr. 1 Km. 25.5 Bo Quebrad Web: www.ramallo.com	Rio Piedras	PR	00926	787-287-0303	
Ramsbottom Printing Inc 135 Waldron Rd Web: www.rpiprinting.net	Fall River	MA	02720	508-730-2220	
Rand Graphics Inc 500 S Florence St TF: 800-435-7263 ■ Web: www.randgraphics.com	Wichita	KS	67209	316-942-1218	
Range Inc 1022 Madison St Web: www.rangeprinting.com	Brainerd	MN	56401	218-824-1800	
Rapid Press Printing & Copy Center Inc 608 Lake St S Web: www.rapidpressprinting.com	Forest Lake	MN	55025	651-464-6200	
Rapid Printers of Monterey 201 Foam St Web: www.rapidprinters.com	Monterey	CA	93940	831-373-1822	
Rapid Pump & Meter Service Co Inc 285 Straight St Web: www.rapidservice.com	Paterson	NJ	07509	201-933-3569	
Rapid Rater Co Po Box 13055 Web: www.rapidpress.com	Tallahassee	FL	32317	850-893-7346	
Rapit Printing Inc 1415 1st Ave NW Web: www.rapit.com	New Brighton	MN	55112	651-633-8108	
Raven Printing 325 S Union Web: www.ravenprinting.com	Lakewood	CO	80228	303-989-9888	
Rayment & Collins Ltd 119 Ferrier St Web: www.raymentcollins.com	Markham	ON	L3R3K6	905-940-4030	
Regal Press Inc, The 129 Guild St TF: 800-447-3425 ■ Web: www.regalpress.com	Norwood	MA	02062	781-769-3900	769-7361
Reindl Printing Inc 1300 Johnson St TF: 800-236-9637 ■ Web: www.reindlprinting.com	Merrill	WI	54452	715-536-9537	
Reischling Press Inc 3325 S 116th St Ste 161 Web: www.rpiprint.com	Seattle	WA	98168	206-905-5999	
Reni Publishing Inc 150 Third St SW TF: 800-274-2812 ■ Web: www.reni.net	Winter Haven	FL	33880	800-274-2812	
Richmond Printing LLC 5825 Schumacher Web: www.richmondprinting.com	Houston	TX	77057	713-952-0800	
Rider Dickerson Inc 815 Twenty-Fifth Ave Web: www.riderdickerson.com	Bellwood	IL	60104	312-427-2926	
Ridge Printing Corp 8900 Yellow Brick Rd Web: www.ridgeprinting.com	Rosedale	MD	21237	410-668-4780	
Riegel Printing Company Inc 1 Graphics Dr Web: www.riegelprintinginc.com	Ewing	NJ	08628	609-771-0555	
Ries Graphics Ltd 12727 W Custer Ave Web: www.riesgraphics.com	Butler	WI	53007	262-781-5720	
Rinaldi Printing Co 4514 E Adamo Dr TF: 800-766-3224 ■ Web: www.rinaldiprinting.com	Tampa	FL	33605	813-247-3921	
Rink Printing Company Inc 814 S Main St Web: www.rinkprinting.com	South Bend	IN	46601	574-232-7935	
RMF Printing Technologies Inc 50 Pearl St TF: 800-828-7999 ■ Web: www.rmfprinting.com	Lancaster	NY	14086	716-683-7500	
Ro-Ark Printing Inc 1600 N 35th St Web: www.roarkgroup.com	Rogers	AR	72756	479-636-1686	

				Phone	Fax
Roberts Co Inc 180 Franklin St Web: www.firecatalog.com	Framingham	MA	01702	508-875-8877	
Roberts Printing Co 2049 Calumet St Web: www.robpri.com	Clearwater	FL	33765	727-442-4011	
Robyn Inc 7717 W Britton Rd TF: 877-211-9711 ■ Web: www.robynpromo.com	Oklahoma City	OK	73132	877-211-9711	
Rocket Imaging Inc 12365 Rhea Dr	Plainfield	IL	60585	815-577-6315	
Rogers Printing Inc PO Box 215 TF: 800-622-5591 ■ Web: www.rogersprinting.net	Ravenna	MI	49451	231-853-2244	853-6558
Rotary Multiforms Inc 1340 E 11 Mile Rd TF: 800-762-5644 ■ Web: www.rmi-printing.com	Madison Heights	MI	48071	586-558-7960	
Rotary Offset Press Inc 6600 S 231st St Web: www.rotaryoffsetpress.com	Kent	WA	98032	253-813-9900	
Royal Conservatory of Music The 273 Bloor St W Web: www.rcmusic.ca	Toronto	ON	M5S1W2	416-408-2824	
Royle Printing Co 745 S Bird St Web: www.royle.com	Sun Prairie	WI	53590	608-837-5161	
RP Graphics Group Inc 5990 Falbourne St Web: rpgraphics.com	Mississauga	ON	L5R3S7	905-507-8782	
Salt Lake Mailing & Printing Inc 1841 S Pioneer Rd Web: www.saltlakemailing.com	Salt Lake City	UT	84104	801-923-4800	
San Diego Printers 9190 Camino Santa Fe Web: www.sdprinters.com	San Diego	CA	92121	858-684-5200	
Sandy Alexander Inc 200 Entin Rd Web: www.sandyinc.com	Clifton	NJ	07014	973-470-8100	470-9269
Santa Fe Professional Duplicating Inc 1248 San Felipe Ave Web: www.ptig.com	Santa Fe	NM	87505	505-983-3101	
Sauers Group Inc, The 1585 Roadhaven Dr Web: www.sauersgroup.com	Stone Mountain	GA	30083	770-621-8888	
Schawk Inc 1695 S River Rd NYSE: SGK ■ Web: www.schawk.com	Des Plaines	IL	60018	847-827-9494	827-1264
Schmidt Printing Inc 1101 Frontage Rd NW Web: www.schmidt.com	Byron	MN	55920	507-775-6400	775-6655
Schumann Printers Inc 701 S Main St Web: www.spiweb.com	Fall River	WI	53932	920-484-3348	484-3661
Scott Advertising & Publishing 30595 8 Mile Rd Web: www.scottpublications.com	Livonia	MI	48152	248-477-6650	
Screenco Enterprises 9 Bell Rd Web: www.screenco.biz	Selma	AL	36701	334-872-0051	
Seagull Printing Services Inc 6969 High Tech Dr Web: seagullprinting.com	Midvale	UT	84047	801-565-1393	
Seaway Printing Company Inc 1609 Western Ave Ste Web: www.seawayprinting.com	Green Bay	WI	54303	920-468-1500	
Sekuworks LLC 9487 Dry Fork Rd	Harrison	OH	45030	513-202-1210	
Sennett Security Products 4212A Technology Ct Web: banknote.com	Chantilly	VA	20151	703-803-8880	
Senton Printing & Packaging Inc 1669 Oxford St E TF: 800-445-9808 ■ Web: www.senton.com	London	ON	N5V2Z5	519-455-5500	
SEP Communications LLC 1100 Holland Dr Web: sepcommunications.com	Boca Raton	FL	33487	561-998-0870	
Service Litho-Print Inc 50 W Fernau Ave Web: www.service-litho.com	Oshkosh	WI	54901	920-231-3060	
Sewell Printing Service Inc 2697 Apple Vly Rd NE Web: www.sewellprinting.com	Atlanta	GA	30319	404-237-2553	
Sexton Printing Inc 250 Lothenbach Ave Web: www.sextonprinting.com	St. Paul	MN	55118	651-457-9255	
SG360 Inc 1351 S Wheeling Rd Web: www.segerdahl.com	Wheeling	IL	60090	847-541-1080	
Sharprint Silkscreen & Graphics Inc 4200 W Wrightwood Ave TF: 888-800-5646 ■ Web: www.sharprint.com	Chicago	IL	60639	773-862-9300	
Shawnee Systems Inc 3616 Church St Web: www.shawneesystems.com	Cincinnati	OH	45244	513-561-4803	
Shea Brothers Inc 65 Innerbelt Rd Web: www.sheabrothers.com	Somerville	MA	02143	617-623-2001	
Shelton-Turnbull Printers Inc 3403 W Seventh Ave Web: www.stprint.com	Eugene	OR	97402	541-687-1214	
Sheridan Group 11311 McCormick Rd Ste 260 TF: 800-352-2210 ■ Web: www.sheridan.com	Hunt Valley	MD	21031	410-785-7277	785-7217
Sigler Companies Inc 3100 S Riverside Dr PO Box 887 Web: www.sigler.com	Ames	IA	50010	515-232-6997	
Sign-ups & Banners Corp 2764 W T C Jester Blvd TF: 877-682-7979 ■ Web: www.signupsandbanners.com	Houston	TX	77018	713-682-7979	
Signature Printing Inc 5 Almeida Ave Web: www.signatureprinters.com	East Providence	RI	02914	401-438-1200	
Sinclair Printing Co 4005 Whiteside St Web: www.sinclairprinting.com	Los Angeles	CA	90063	323-264-4000	
Sing Tao Newspapers San Francisco Ltd 5000 Marina Blvd Ste 300 Web: www.stgloballink.com	Brisbane	CA	94005	650-808-8800	
Sir Speedy Inc 26722 Plaza Dr TF: 800-854-8297 ■ Web: www.sirspeedy.com	Mission Viejo	CA	92691	949-348-5000	348-5066
Skinner & Kennedy Co 9451 Natural Bridge Rd Web: www.skinnerkennedy.com	Saint Louis	MO	63134	314-426-2800	
SMS Productions Inc 10555 Guilford Rd Ste 114 TF: 800-289-7671 ■ Web: www.smsproductions.com	Jessup	MD	20794	301-953-0011	
Solar Communications Inc 1150 Frontenac Rd Web: www.solarcommunications.com	Naperville	IL	60563	630-983-1400	

Company	City	State	Zip	Phone	Fax
Solisco Inc 120 10e Rue	Scott	QC	G0S3G0	418-387-8908	
TF: 800-463-4188 ■ *Web:* www.solisco.com					
Solo Printing Inc 7860 NW 66th St	Miami	FL	33166	305-594-8699	599-5245
TF: 800-325-0118 ■ *Web:* www.soloprinting.com					
SOS Printing Inc 8135 Ronson Rd	San Diego	CA	92111	858-292-1800	
Southland Printing Company Inc 213 Airport Dr	Shreveport	LA	71107	318-221-8662	
TF: 800-241-8662 ■ *Web:* www.southlandprinting.com					
Southwest Offset Printing Company Inc 13650 Gramercy Pl	Gardena	CA	90249	310-323-0112	
Web: www.southwestoffset.com					
Sp Mount 1306 E 55th St	Cleveland	OH	44103	216-881-3316	
TF: 800-503-5022 ■ *Web:* www.spmount.com					
Spangler Graphics LLC 2930 S 44th St	Kansas City	KS	66106	913-722-4500	
Web: www.spanglergraphics.com					
Spartan Graphics Inc 200 Applewood Dr	Sparta	MI	49345	616-887-8243	
TF: 800-747-4477 ■ *Web:* spartangraphics.com					
Spectrum Litho 4300 Business Ctr Dr	Fremont	CA	94538	510-438-9192	
Web: www.spectrumlithograph.com					
Spectrum Printing Company LLC 4651 S Butterfield Dr	Tucson	AZ	85714	520-571-1114	
Web: www.spectrumprintingcompany.com					
Speedway Digital Printing Inc 475 4th St	San Francisco	CA	94107	415-543-5928	
Web: www.speedwayprinting.com					
Speedy Litho Inc 403 Catlin	Kelso	WA	98626	360-425-3610	
Web: speedylitho.com					
Sport Graphics Inc 3423 Park Davis Cir	Indianapolis	IN	46235	317-899-7000	
Web: www.sportg.com					
Springdot Inc 2611 Colerain Ave	Cincinnati	OH	45214	513-542-4000	
Web: www.springdot.com					
Sprint Copy Center 175 N Main St	Sebastopol	CA	95472	707-823-3900	
Web: sprintcopycenter.com					
Sprint Quality Printing Inc 3609 Silverside Rd	Wilmington	DE	19810	302-478-0720	
Web: www.sprintqp.com					
Sprint-Denver Inc 4999 Kingston St	Denver	CO	80239	303-371-0566	371-2341
Web: www.sprintdenver.com					
Square 1 Art LLC 5470 Oakbrook Pkwy Ste E	Norcross	GA	30093	678-906-2291	
TF: 888-332-3294 ■ *Web:* www.square1art.com					
St. Joseph Communications 50 MacIntosh Blvd	Concord	ON	L4K4P3	905-660-3111	
Web: www.stjoseph.com					
Stafford Printing Co 2707 Jefferson Davis Hwy	Stafford	VA	22554	540-659-4554	
TF: 800-774-6831 ■ *Web:* staffordprinting.com					
State Port Pilot 114 E Moore St	Southport	NC	28461	910-457-4568	
Web: stateportpilot.com					
Stella Color Inc 620 S Dakota St	Seattle	WA	98108	206-223-2303	
Web: www.stellacolor.com					
Stellar Printing Inc 3838 Ninth St	Long Island	NY	11101	718-361-1600	
Web: www.stellarprinting.com					
Steven Label Corp 11926 Burke St	Santa Fe Springs	CA	90670	562-698-9971	
Web: www.stevenlabel.com					
Stolze Printing 3435 Hollenberg Dr	Bridgeton	MO	63044	314-209-1997	
Web: www.stolze.com					
StorterChilds Printing Company Inc 1540 NE Waldo Rd	Gainesville	FL	32641	352-376-2658	
Web: www.storterchilds.com					
Strathmore Co 2000 Gary Ln	Geneva	IL	60134	630-232-9677	
Web: www.strath.com					
Strawbridge Studios Inc 3000 Hillsborough Rd	Durham	NC	27705	919-286-9512	
Web: www.strawbridge.net					
Streeter Printing Inc 9880 Via Pasar	San Diego	CA	92126	858-566-0866	
TF: 866-787-3383 ■ *Web:* www.streeterprinting.com					
Strine Printing Co Inc 30 Grumbacher Rd	York	PA	17406	717-767-6602	505-3227
Stuyvesant Press Inc 119 Coit St	Irvington	NJ	07111	973-399-3880	
Web: stuyvesantpress.com					
Success Printing & Mailing Inc 10 Pearl St	Norwalk	CT	06850	203-847-1112	
Web: www.successprint.com					
Suddekor LLC 240 Bowles Rd	Agawam	MA	01001	413-821-9000	
Web: www.suddekorllc.com					
Sun Graphics LLC 1818 Broadway	Parsons	KS	67357	620-421-6200	
Web: www.sun-graphics.com					
Sun Printing 1800 Grand Ave	Wausau	WI	54403	715-845-4911	
Web: www.sunprinting.com					
Sunbelt Printing & Graphics 1691 Sands Pl Ste E	Marietta	GA	30067	770-988-0812	
Web: www.sunbeltprinting.com					
Suncoast Forms & Systems Inc 1045 N Lime Ave	Sarasota	FL	34237	941-366-1123	
Web: www.suncoastforms.com					
Suncraft Technologies Inc 1301 Frontenac Rd	Naperville	IL	60563	630-369-7900	639-7070
Web: www.suncrafttechnologies.com					
Sunkist Graphics Inc 401 E Sunset Rd	Henderson	NV	89011	702-566-9008	
Web: www.sunkistgrfx.com					
Sunset Printing 4522 Rosemead Blvd	Pico Rivera	CA	90660	562-692-3950	
Web: sunsetprinting.wix.com/sunsetprinting					
Super Color Digital LLC 16761 Hale Ave	Irvine	CA	92606	949-622-0010	622-0050
TF: 800-979-4446 ■ *Web:* supercolor.com					
Suttle-Straus Inc 1000 Uniek Dr PO Box 370	Waunakee	WI	53597	608-849-1000	
Web: www.suttle-straus.com					
Swift Mailing Services Inc 600 Washington st Ste E	Bristol	PA	19007	215-638-4122	
Web: www.swiftmailing.com					
Swift Print Communication 1248 Research Blvd	Saint Louis	MO	63132	314-991-4300	
TF: 800-545-1141 ■ *Web:* www.swiftprint.com					
Symphony Printing Company Inc 19 21 Brook St	Belleville	NJ	07109	973-751-5100	
Web: www.symphonyprinting.com					
T K Direct 999 Commerce Crt	Buffalo Grove	IL	60089	312-296-7921	
Web: tkdirect.com					
Tandem Printing Inc 2970 Lexington Ave S	Saint Paul	MN	55121	651-289-2970	
Web: www.tandemprinting.com					
Tectonics Industries Inc 24680 Mound Rd	Warren	MI	48091	586-755-6522	
Web: tectonics.com					
Telepress Inc 19241 62nd Ave S	Kent	WA	98032	425-392-1660	
Web: telepress.com					
Tenenz Inc 9655 Penn S Ave	Minneapolis	MN	55431	800-888-5803	
TF: 800-888-5803 ■ *Web:* www.tenenz.com					
Tepel Brothers Printing Co 1725 John R Rd	Troy	MI	48083	248-743-2903	
Web: tepelbrothers.com					
Teton Machine Co 1805 NE Tenth Ave	Payette	ID	83661	208-642-9344	
Web: www.tetonmachine.com					
Teuteberg Inc 12200 W Wirth St	Wauwatosa	WI	53222	414-257-4110	
Web: www.teuteberg.com					
Tewell Warren Printing Co 4710 Lipan St	Denver	CO	80211	303-458-8505	
Web: www.tewellwarren.com					
Thrasher Printing Inc 814 Hanley Industrial Ct	Saint Louis	MO	63144	314-962-7979	
Web: www.thrasher-bcm.com					
Tidewater Direct LLC 300 Tidewater Dr	Centreville	MD	21617	410-758-1500	
Web: www.tidewaterdirect.com					
Tiger Press Administration 155 Industrial Dr	Northampton	MA	01060	413-585-1616	
Web: www.tigerpress.com					
Times Printing Company Inc 100 Industrial Dr	Random Lake	WI	53075	920-994-4396	994-2059*
**Fax:* Cust Svc ■ *TF:* 800-236-4396 ■ *Web:* www.timesprintingco.com					
Total Printing Systems 201 S Gregory St	Newton	IL	62448	800-465-5200	
TF: 800-465-5200 ■ *Web:* www.tps1.com					
Trabon Printing Company Inc 420 E Bannister Rd Ste	Kansas City	MO	64131	816-361-6279	
Web: www.trabongroup.com					
Transcontinental Inc 1 Pl Ville Marie Bureau 3315	Montreal	QC	H3B3N2	514-954-4000	954-4016
TSE: TCL.A ■ *Web:* tctranscontinental.com					
Transfer Express Inc 7650 Tyler Blvd	Mentor	OH	44060	440-918-1900	
TF: 800-622-2280 ■ *Web:* www.transferexpress.com					
Tranter Graphics Inc 8094 N State Rd 13	Syracuse	IN	46567	574-834-2626	
Web: www.trantergraphics.com					
Travel Tags Inc 5842 Carmen Ave	Inver Grove Heights	MN	55076	651-450-1201	
Web: www.traveltags.com					
Travers Printing Inc 32 Mission St	Gardner	MA	01440	978-632-0530	
TF: 800-696-0530 ■ *Web:* www.traversprinting.com					
Trend Offset Printing Services Inc 3791 Catalina St	Los Alamitos	CA	90720	562-598-2446	
Web: www.trendoffset.com					
Tri-State Financial Press LLC 109 N Fifth St	Saddle Brook	NJ	07663	201-226-9220	
Web: www.tsfpress.com					
TrialGraphix Inc 3300 Corporate Way	Hollywood	FL	33025	305-576-5400	
Web: www.trialgraphix.com					
Tricor Print Communications Inc 7931 N.E. Halsey St Ste 101	Portland	OR	97213	503-255-5595	
Web: www.tricorprint.com					
Tristar Web Graphics Inc 4010 Airline Dr	Houston	TX	77022	713-691-0005	
Web: www.tristarholdings.com					
Triune Color Corp 2605 N River Rd	Cinnaminson	NJ	08077	856-829-5600	
Web: www.triunecolor.com					
Trojan Press Inc 1635 Burlington St	Kansas City	MO	64116	816-221-6477	
Web: www.trojanpressinc.com					
Tucker Printers Inc 270 Middle Rd	Henrietta	NY	14467	585-359-3030	
Web: www.tuckerprinters.com					
Tucker-Castleberry Printing Inc 3500 McCall Pl	Atlanta	GA	30340	770-454-1580	
Web: www.tuckercastleberry.com					
Turner Plastic Innovations 1400 Production Dr	Burlington	KY	41005	859-525-9020	
Web: www.turnerplastic.com					
Tursso Companies Inc 223 Plato Blvd E	St. Paul	MN	55107	651-222-8445	
Web: www.tursso.com					
Tuttle Law Print Inc 414 Quality Ln	Rutland	VT	05701	800-776-7682	
TF: 800-776-7682 ■ *Web:* www.tuttleprinting.com					
Tvp Color Graphics Inc 230 Roma Jean Pkwy	Streamwood	IL	60107	630-837-3600	
Web: www.thinkvariable.com					
Two b Printing Inc 625 Ne 42nd St	Fort Lauderdale	FL	33334	954-566-4886	
Web: twobprinting.com					
Typecraft Press Inc 2403 Sidney St Ste 500	Pittsburgh	PA	15203	412-488-1600	
Web: www.typecraftpress.com					
U B S Printing Group Inc 2577 Research Dr	Corona	CA	92882	951-273-7900	
Web: www.ubsprint.com					
Ultra Flex Packaging Corp 975 Essex St	Brooklyn	NY	11208	718-272-9100	
Web: www.ultraflex.com					
Ultra-Tech Printing Co 5851 Crossroads Commerce	Grand Rapids	MI	49519	616-249-0500	
Web: www.utprinting.com					
Uni-Graphic Inc 110 Commerce Way	Woburn	MA	01801	781-231-7200	938-7727
Web: www.uni-graphic.com					
Unicom Graphics Ltd 4501 Manitoba Rd Se	Calgary	AB	T2G4B9	403-287-2020	
Web: www.unicomgraphics.com					
Unique Image Inc 19365 Bus Ctr Dr Ste 1	Northridge	CA	91324	818-727-7785	
Web: www.uniqueimageinc.com					
Unique Litho Inc 9 Inverness Dr E	Englewood	CO	80112	303-830-2999	
Web: www.uniquelitho.com					
United Reprographics LLC 1750 Fourth Ave S	Seattle	WA	98134	206-382-1177	
Web: www.unitedreprographics.com					
Universal Printing Co 1234 S Kings Hwy	Saint Louis	MO	63110	314-771-6900	771-7987
Web: www.universalprintingco.com					
USS Corp 780 Frelinghuysen Ave	Newark	NJ	07114	973-242-1110	
Web: usscorp.com					
Ussery Printing Company Inc 3402 Century Cir	Irving	TX	75062	972-438-8344	
Web: www.printussery.com					
Utley Brothers Inc 567 Robbins Dr	Troy	MI	48083	248-585-1700	
Web: www.utleybros.com					

Phone | Fax

Valassis Communications Inc
19975 Victor Pkwy ... Livonia MI 48152 734-591-3000 591-4994*
NYSE: VCI ■ **Fax:* Hum Res ■ *TF:* 800-437-0479 ■ *Web:* www.valassis.com

Valley Offset Printing Inc
160 S Sheridan Ave ... Valley Center KS 67147 316-755-0061
TF: 888-895-7913 ■ *Web:* www.valleyoffset.com

Valley Printing Company Inc
3919 Vanderbilt Rd ... Birmingham AL 35217 205-841-2746
Web: valleyprinting.net

Vectra Visual 3950 Business Pk Dr ... Columbus OH 43204 614-351-6868 351-4569
Web: vectravisual.com

Ventura Printing 1593 Palma Dr ... Ventura CA 93006 805-981-2600

Verified Label & Print Inc 7905 Hopi Pl ... Tampa FL 33634 813-290-7721
Web: www.verifiedlabel.com

Victorystore.Com Inc 5200 SW 30Th St ... Davenport IA 52802 866-241-2295
TF: 866-241-2295 ■ *Web:* www.victorystore.com

Villanti & Sons, Printers Inc 15 Catamount Dr ... Milton VT 05468 802-864-0723
Web: www.villanti.com

Vision Envelope Inc 2451 Executive St ... Charlotte NC 28208 704-392-9090
Web: www.visionenvelope.com

Vision Graphics Inc 5610 Boeing Dr ... Loveland CO 80538 970-679-9000
Web: www.visiongraphics-inc.com

Visions Inc 8801 Wyoming Ave N ... Brooklyn Park MN 55445 763-425-4251
Web: www.visionsfirst.com

Vista Color Corp 1401 NW 78th Ave ... Miami FL 33126 305-635-2000
Web: www.vistacolor.com

VistaPrint USA Inco 95 Hayden Ave ... Lexington MA 02421 781-652-6300
Web: www.vistaprint.com

Vox Printing Inc 4000 E Britton Rd ... Oklahoma City OK 73131 405-478-7500
Web: voxprinting.com

W&C Printing Company Inc 163 E Second St ... Winona MN 55987 507-452-2658
Web: www.wcprinting.com

Walker Printing Co 2501 E 5th St ... Montgomery AL 36107 334-832-4975
Web: www.walker360.com

Walter Snyder Printer Inc 691 River St ... Troy NY 12180 518-272-8881
TF: 888-272-9774 ■ *Web:* www.snyderprinter.com

Warren Printing & Mailing Inc
5000 Eagle Rock Blvd ... Los Angeles CA 90041 323-258-2621
TF: 888-468-6976 ■ *Web:* print-mail.com

Watermark Group Inc, The 4271 Gate Crst ... San Antonio TX 78217 210-599-0400
Web: www.thewatermarkgroup.com

Watkins Printing Co 1401 E 17th Ave ... Columbus OH 43211 614-297-8270
Web: watkinsprinting.com

Watson Label Products 10616 Trenton Ave ... Saint Louis MO 63132 314-493-9300 493-9390
TF: 800-678-6715 ■ *Web:* www.wlp.com

Watt Printing Co
4544 Hinckley Industrial Pkwy ... Cleveland OH 44109 216-398-2000
TF: 800-273-2170 ■ *Web:* www.wattprinters.com

Waveline Direct Inc 192 Hempt Rd ... Mechanicsburg PA 17050 717-795-8830
Web: www.wavelinedirect.com

We Print Today LLC 66 Summer St ... Kingston MA 02364 781-585-6021
Web: www.weprinttoday.com

Weatherall Printing Co 1349 Cliff Gookin Blvd ... Tupelo MS 38801 662-842-5284
TF: 800-273-6043 ■ *Web:* www.weatherallprinting.com

Web Offset Printing Company Inc
12198 44th St N ... Clearwater FL 33762 727-572-7488
Web: www.weboffsetprint.com

WebbMason Inc 10830 Gilroy Rd ... Hunt Valley MD 21031 410-785-1111
Web: www.webbmason.com

Weldon Williams & Lick Inc 711 N A St ... Fort Smith AR 72901 479-783-4113 783-7050
TF: 800-242-4995 ■ *Web:* www.wwlinc.com

Wells & Drew Companies 3414 Galilee Rd ... Jacksonville FL 32207 904-399-1510
Web: www.wellsdrew.com

Wells Printing Company Inc
6030 Perimeter Pkwy ... Montgomery AL 36116 334-281-3449
TF: 800-264-4958 ■ *Web:* www.wellsprinting.com

Wendling Printing Co 111 Beech St ... Newport KY 41071 859-261-8300
TF: 800-998-9553 ■ *Web:* www.wendlingprinting.net

Wentworth Printing Corp 101 N 12th St ... West Columbia SC 29169 803-796-9990
TF: 800-326-0784 ■ *Web:* www.wentworthprinting.com

West Metro Printing Co 33100 Industrial Rd ... Livonia MI 48150 734-522-0410
Web: www.westmetroprinting.com

West Penn Printing 103 Riverpark Dr ... New Castle PA 16101 724-856-3376
Web: westpennprinting.com

West Press Printing & Copying 1663 W Grant Rd ... Tucson AZ 85745 520-624-4939
TF: 888-637-0337 ■ *Web:* westpress.com

West-Camp Press Inc 39 Collegeview Rd ... Westerville OH 43081 614-882-2378
Web: www.westcamppress.com

Western Lithograph Co 4335 Directors Row ... Houston TX 77092 713-681-2100
Web: www.westernlithograph.com

Western Pad 391 Thor Pl ... Brea CA 92821 714-671-1900
Web: www.westernpad.com

Westland Enterprises Inc 3621 Stewart Rd ... Forestville MD 20747 301-736-0600
Web: www.westlandenterprises.com

Westland Printers Inc 14880 Sweitzer Ln ... Laurel MD 20707 301-384-7700 384-2616
Web: www.westlandprinters.com

Wetzel Brothers LLC 2401 E Edgerton ... Cudahy WI 53110 414-271-5444
Web: www.wetzelbrothers.com

Wildes-Spirit Design & Printing
4321 Charles Crossing Dr ... White Plains MD 20695 301-870-4141
Web: www.wildes-spirit.com

Wilen Direct 3333 SW 15th St ... Deerfield Beach FL 33442 954-246-5000
Web: wilendirect.com

William George Printing LLC
3469 Black and Decker Rd ... Hope Mills NC 28348 910-221-2700
Web: m.wgprinting.com

Williamson Printing Corp 6700 Denton Dr ... Dallas TX 75235 214-904-2100
Web: www.twpc.com

Wingate Packaging Inc 4347 Indeco Ct ... Cincinnati OH 45241 513-745-8600
Web: www.wingate-packaging.com

Winston Printing Company Inc
8095 N Point Blvd ... Winston-Salem NC 27106 336-759-0051
Web: www.winstonpackaging.com

Phone | Fax

Wisconsin Web Offset LLC
21045 Enterprise Ave ... Brookfield WI 53045 262-395-2000

Wizbang Solutions Inc 6747 E 50th Ave ... Commerce CO 80022 720-974-5623
Web: www.wizbangsolutions.com

Woelco Labeling Solutions Inc
107 Infield Ct ... Mooresville NC 28117 704-664-1027
Web: www.woelco.com

Wolf Printing 1200 Haines Rd ... York PA 17402 717-755-1560
Web: www.wolfprinting.com

Woolverton Printing Co
6714 Chancellor Dr ... Cedar Falls IA 50613 319-277-2616
Web: www.woolverton.com

World Internet Mktg Inc 8 S St ... Succasunna NJ 07876 973-252-0999
Web: www.eworldwire.com

Wright Printing Co 11616 I St ... Omaha NE 68137 402-334-0748

Xlibris Corp 1663 Liberty Dr Ste 200 ... Bloomington IN 47403 888-795-4274
TF: 888-795-4274 ■ *Web:* www.xlibris.com

Yellowdog Printing & Graphics LLC
490 S Santa Fe Dr Unit A ... Denver CO 80223 303-765-2000
Web: www.yellowdogprinting.com

Yoder & Armstrong Printing
627 E Baltimore Ave E ... Lansdowne PA 19050 610-622-6118
Web: yoderandarmstrong.com

Yurchak Printing Inc 920 Links Ave ... Landisville PA 17538 717-399-0209
Web: www.yurchak.com

Z Three - Printing Co 902 W Main St ... Teutopolis IL 62467 217-857-3153 857-3010
Web: www.threez.com

Zebra Graphics Inc 1611 Kentucky Ave ... Paducah KY 42003 270-443-4771
Web: www.zebragraphics.com

Zebra Print Solutions Inc
9401 Globe Ctr Dr Ste 130 ... Morrisville NC 27560 919-314-3700
Web: www.zebraprintsolutions.com

Zodiac Printing Corp 395 Oak Hill Rd ... Mountain Top PA 18707 570-474-9220
Web: www.zodiacink.com

Zomazz Inc 2 Harris Ct ... Monterey CA 93940 831-625-9877
Web: www.zomazz.com

Zoo Printing Inc 4730 Eastern Ave ... Bell CA 90201 310-253-7751
Web: www.zooprinting.com

Zookbinders Inc 151-K S Pfingsten Rd Ste ... Deerfield IL 60015 800-810-5745
TF: 800-810-5745 ■ *Web:* www.zookbinders.com

628 PRINTING & PHOTOCOPYING SUPPLIES

Phone | Fax

Abco Distribution Inc
6282 Proprietors Rd ... Worthington OH 43085 800-821-9435
TF: 800-821-9435 ■ *Web:* www.printingbyabco.com

Anderson & Vreeland Inc 8 Evans St ... Fairfield NJ 07004 973-227-2270
Web: andersonvreeland.com

Art Lithocraft Co 219 W 18th St ... Kansas City MO 64108 816-421-8335
Web: www.artlithocraft.com

Balance Innovations LLC 11011 Eicher Dr ... Lenexa KS 66219 913-599-1177
Web: balanceinnovations.com

Buckeye Business Products Inc
3830 Kelley Ave ... Cleveland OH 44114 800-837-4323 881-6105*
**Fax Area Code:* 216 ■ *TF:* 800-837-4323 ■ *Web:* www.buckeyebusiness.com

Chromaline Corp 4832 Grand Ave ... Duluth MN 55807 218-628-2217 628-3245
TF: 800-328-4261 ■ *Web:* www.chromaline.com

Color Imaging Inc
4350 Peachtree Industrial Blvd Ste 100 ... Norcross GA 30071 770-840-1090 783-9010*
**Fax Area Code:* 800 ■ *TF:* 800-783-1090 ■ *Web:* www.colorimaging.com

Convertech Inc 353 Richard Mine Rd ... Wharton NJ 07885 973-328-1850
Web: www.convertech.com

Drent Goebel North America Inc
2583 Chomedey Blvd ... Laval QC H7T2R2 450-687-7262
Web: www.rdpmarathon.com

DuraLine Imaging Inc 110 Commercial Blvd ... Flat Rock NC 28731 828-692-1301
TF: 800-982-3872 ■ *Web:* www.duralineimaging.com

Equipements De Transformation Imac (E.T.I.) Inc
1490-H Nobel St ... Boucherville QC J4B5H3 450-641-7900
Web: www.eticonverting.com

ExOne Co 127 Industry Blvd ... North Huntingdon PA 15642 724-863-9663
Web: www.exone.com

Glunz & Jensen K&F Inc 12633 Industrial Dr ... Granger IN 46530 574-272-9950
Web: www.glunz-jensen.com

Graphic Controls LLC 400 Exchange St ... Buffalo NY 14204 800-669-1535 347-2420
TF: 800-669-1535 ■ *Web:* www.graphiccontrols.com

Hurst Chemical Co 2360 Eastman Ave Ste 108 ... Oxnard CA 93030 800-723-2004
TF Cust Svc: 800-723-2004 ■ *Web:* www.hurstchemical.com

Image One Corp 13201 Capital Ave ... Oak Park MI 48237 248-414-9955 414-9951
TF: 800-799-5377 ■ *Web:* www.imageoneway.com

Ink Technology Corp 18320 Lanken Ave ... Cleveland OH 44119 216-486-6720 486-6003
TF: 800-633-2826 ■ *Web:* www.inktechnology.com

ITW Coding Products 111 W Pk Dr ... Kalkaska MI 49646 231-258-5521 258-6120
Web: www.codingproducts.com

Kase Equipment Corp 7400 Hub Pkwy ... Valley View OH 44125 216-642-9040
Web: www.kaseequip.com

Ko-Rec-Type Div Barouh Eaton Allen Corp
67 Kent Ave ... Brooklyn NY 11249 718-782-2601
Web: www.korectype.com

LexJet Corp 1680 Fruitville Rd 3rd Fl ... Sarasota FL 34236 941-330-1210 330-1220
TF: 800-453-9538 ■ *Web:* www.lexjet.com

Light Impressions 100 Carlson Rd ... Rochester NY 14610 800-975-6429
TF: 800-975-6429 ■ *Web:* www.lightimpressionsdirect.com

Micro Solutions Enterprises (MSE)
8201 Woodley Ave ... Van Nuys CA 91406 818-407-7500 407-7575
TF: 800-673-4968 ■ *Web:* www.mse-usa.com

NER Data Products Inc 307 S Delsea Dr ... Glassboro NJ 08028 888-637-3282 881-5524*
**Fax Area Code:* 856 ■ *TF:* 888-637-3282 ■ *Web:* www.nerdata.com

Pad Print Machinery of Vermont Inc
201 Tennis Way ... East Dorset VT 05253 802-362-0844
TF: 800-272-7764 ■ *Web:* www.epsvt.com

Phone | Fax

Perfecopy Co 103 W 61st St .... Westmont IL 60559 630-769-9901
Rayven Inc 431 Griggs St N .... Saint Paul MN 55104 651-642-1112 642-9497
TF Cust Svc: 800-878-3776 ■ *Web:* www.rayven.com
Ricoh Printing Systems America Inc
2390 Ward Ave Ste A .... Simi Valley CA 93065 805-578-4000 578-4001
Web: www.rpsa.ricoh.com
Rima Enterprises Inc
5340 Argosy Ave .... Huntington Beach CA 92649 714-893-4534
Web: www.rima-system.com
RVision Inc 2445 Fifth Ave Ste 450 .... San Diego CA 92101 619-233-1403
Web: www.rvisionusa.com
Spitz Inc 700 Brandywine Dr .... Chadds Ford PA 19317 610-459-5200
Web: www.spitzinc.com
Texas Lift-Off Correction Ribbon
1700 Surveyor Blvd Ste 110 .... Carrollton TX 75006 972-416-8100 416-9690
Thistle Roller Company Inc
209 Van Norman Rd .... Montebello CA 90640 562-948-3705
Web: thistleroller.com
Tomoegawa USA Inc 742 Glenn Ave .... Wheeling IL 60090 847-541-3001 459-7150
Web: www.tomoegawa.com
Western Printing Machinery Co
9229 Ivanhoe Ave .... Schiller Park IL 60176 847-678-1740
Web: www.wpm.com
WNC Supply LLC 37841 N 16th St .... Phoenix AZ 85086 623-594-4602 594-3769
TF: 800-538-5108 ■ *Web:* www.westnc.com
Xenetech Usa Inc 12139 Airline Hwy .... Baton Rouge LA 70817 225-752-0225
Web: www.xenetech.com

629 PRINTING & PUBLISHING EQUIPMENT & SYSTEMS

See Also Printers p. 2000

Phone | Fax

Apex Machine Co 3000 NE 12th Terr .... Fort Lauderdale FL 33334 954-566-1572 563-2844
Web: www.apexmachine.com
AWT World Trade Inc 4321 N Knox Ave .... Chicago IL 60641 773-777-7100 777-0909
Web: www.awt-gpi.com
Baldwin Technology Co Inc
2 Trap Falls Rd Ste 402 .... Shelton CT 06484 203-402-1000 402-5500
NYSE: BLD ■ *Web:* www.baldwintech.com
BMP America Inc 11625 Maple Ridge Rd .... Medina NY 14103 585-798-0950 798-4272
Web: www.bmpworldwide.com
Brackett Inc 75115 SE Forbes Ave Bldg 451 J .... Topeka KS 66619 785-862-2205 862-1127
TF: 800-255-3506 ■ *Web:* www.brackett-inc.com
Brandtjen & Kluge Inc
539 Blanding Woods Rd .... Saint Croix Falls WI 54024 715-483-3265 483-1640
TF: 800-826-7320 ■ *Web:* www.kluge.biz
Burgess Industries Inc (BII)
7500 Boone Ave N Ste 111 .... Brooklyn Park MN 55428 763-553-7800 553-9289
TF: 800-233-2589 ■ *Web:* www.burgessind.com
CODA Inc 30 Industrial Ave .... Mahwah NJ 07430 201-825-7400 825-8133
Web: www.codamount.com
Craftsmen Machinery Co
1257 Worcester Rd Unit 167 .... Framingham MA 01701 508-376-2001 376-2003
Web: www.craftsmenmachinery.com
Delphax Technologies Inc 6100 W 110th St .... Bloomington MN 55438 952-939-9000 939-1151*
OTC: DLPX ■ **Fax:* Cust Svc ■ *Web:* www.delphax.com
Goss International Americas Inc
121 Technology Dr .... Durham NH 03824 603-749-6600 750-6860
Web: www.gossinternational.com
Graphic Innovators Inc
855 Morse Ave .... Elk Grove Village IL 60007 847-718-1516 718-1517
Web: www.graphicinnovators.com
Gravograph-New Hermes Inc 2200 Northmont Pkwy .... Duluth GA 30096 770-623-0331 533-7637*
**Fax Area Code:* 800 ■ *TF:* 800-843-7637 ■ *Web:* www.gravograph.com
Heidelberg USA Inc 1000 Gutenberg Dr .... Kennesaw GA 30144 770-419-6500 419-6550
TF Cust Svc: 888-472-9655 ■ *Web:* www.heidelberg.com/us/en/index.jsp
LasscoWizer Inc 485 Hague St .... Rochester NY 14606 585-436-1934 464-8665
TF: 800-854-6595 ■ *Web:* www.lasscowizer.com
MAN Roland Inc 800 E Oak Hill Dr .... Westmont IL 60559 630-920-2000
Web: manrolandsheetfed.com
Mark Andy Inc
18081 Chesterfield Airport Rd .... Chesterfield MO 63005 636-532-4433 532-4701*
**Fax:* Cust Svc ■ *TF:* 800-700-6275 ■ *Web:* www.markandy.com
Pamarco Global Graphics 235 E 11th Ave .... Roselle NJ 07203 908-241-1200 241-4237
TF: 800-365-6510 ■ *Web:* www.pamarcoglobal.com
Presstek Inc 55 Executive Dr .... Hudson NH 03051 603-595-7000
NASDAQ: PRST ■ *TF:* 800-422-3616 ■ *Web:* www.presstek.com
Rosback Co 125 Hawthorne Ave .... Saint Joseph MI 49085 269-983-2582 983-2516
TF: 800-542-2420 ■ *Web:* www.rosbackcompany.com
Stevens Technology LLC 5700 E Belknap St .... Fort Worth TX 76117 817-831-3500 759-4080
Web: www.stevenstechnology.com
Stolle Machinery Co LLC 6949 S Potomac St .... Centennial CO 80112 303-708-9044 708-9045
Web: www.stollemachinery.com
Xerox Corp 45 Glover Ave PO Box 4505 .... Norwalk CT 06856 203-968-3000
NYSE: XRX ■ *TF:* 800-327-9753 ■ *Web:* www.xerox.com

630 PRISON INDUSTRIES

Prison industries are programs established by federal and state governments that provide work for inmates while they are incarcerated as well as on-the-job training to help them become employable on release. At the same time, prison industries provide quality goods and services at competitive prices.

Phone | Fax

Alabama Correctional Industries
1400 Lloyd St .... Montgomery AL 36107 334-261-3600 240-3162
TF: 800-224-7007 ■ *Web:* www.aci.alabama.gov
Arizona Correctional Industries
3701 W Cambridge Ave .... Phoenix AZ 85009 602-272-7600 255-3108
Web: aci.az.gov
Arkansas Correctional Industries (ACI)
6841 W. 13th St .... Pine Bluff AR 71602 870-730-0385 850-8440
TF: 877-635-7213 ■ *Web:* www.acicatalog.com

Phone | Fax

Badger State Industries (BSI)
3099 E Washington Ave PO Box 8990 .... Madison WI 53708 608-240-5200 240-3320
TF: 800-862-1086 ■ *Web:* www.buybsi.com
California Prison Industry Authority
560 E Natoma St .... Folsom CA 95630 916-358-2733 358-2660*
**Fax:* Cust Svc ■ *Web:* www.pia.ca.gov
Cornhusker State Industries
800 Pioneers Blvd .... Lincoln NE 68502 402-471-4597 471-1236
TF: 800-348-7537 ■ *Web:* www.nebraska.gov
Correctional Enterprises of Connecticut
24 Wolcott Hill Rd .... Wethersfield CT 06109 860-263-6839 263-6838
TF: 800-842-1146 ■ *Web:* www.ct.gov
Delaware Correctional Industries 245 McKee Rd .... Dover DE 19904 302-739-5601 739-1608
Web: doc.delaware.gov
Federal Prison Industries Inc
320 First St NW .... Washington DC 20534 800-827-3168
TF: 800-827-3168 ■ *Web:* www.unicor.gov
Georgia Correctional Industries
2984 Clifton Springs Rd .... Decatur GA 30034 404-244-5100 244-5141
TF: 800-282-7130 ■ *Web:* www.gci-ga.com
Idaho Correctional Industries
1301 N OrchaRd Rd Ste 110 .... Boise ID 83705 208-577-5555 577-5545
Web: www.ci.idaho.gov
Iowa Prison Industries (IPI)
1445 E Grand Ave .... Des Moines IA 50316 515-242-5770 242-5779
TF: 800-670-4537 ■ *Web:* www.iaprisonind.com
Kansas Correctional Industries PO Box 2 .... Lansing KS 66043 913-727-3249 727-2331
Web: kancorind.com
Kentucky Correctional Industries
1041 Leestown Rd .... Frankfort KY 40601 502-573-1040 573-1050
TF: 800-828-9524 ■ *Web:* www.kci.ky.gov
Louisiana Prison Enterprises
PO Box 94304 .... Baton Rouge LA 70804 225-342-6633 342-2022
Web: www.doc.louisiana.gov
Maryland Correctional Enterprises (MCE)
7275 Waterloo Rd .... Jessup MD 20794 410-540-5454 540-5570
Web: mce.md.gov
Massachusetts Correctional Industries
1 Industries Dr Bldg A PO Box 188 .... Norfolk MA 02056 508-850-1070 850-1091
TF: 800-222-2211 ■ *Web:* www.mass.gov
Michigan State Industries 5656 S Cedar St .... Lansing MI 48909 517-373-4277
Web: www.michigan.gov
Mississippi Prison Industries Corp
663 N State St .... Jackson MS 39202 601-969-5750 969-5757
Web: www.mpic.net
Missouri Vocational Enterprises
1717 Industrial Dr PO Box 1898 .... Jefferson City MO 65102 573-751-6663 751-9197
TF Sales: 800-392-8486 ■ *Web:* www.doc.mo.gov
New Hampshire Correctional Industries (NHCI)
105 Pleasant St PO Box 1806 .... Concord NH 03302 603-271-5600 271-5643
Web: www.nh.gov/nhdoc
New Jersey Bureau of State Use Industries
163 N Olden Ave PO Box 867 .... Trenton NJ 08625 800-321-6524 633-2495*
**Fax Area Code:* 609 ■ *TF:* 800-321-6524 ■ *Web:* www.state.nj.us/deptcor
New York Correctional Industries 550 Broadway .... Albany NY 12204 518-436-6321 436-6007
TF: 800-436-6321 ■ *Web:* www.corcraft.org
North Carolina Correction Enterprises
2020 Yonkers Rd .... Raleigh NC 27604 919-716-3600 716-3974
Web: www.doc.state.nc.us
Ohio Penal Industries (OPI) 1221 McKinley Ave .... Columbus OH 43222 614-752-0287 752-0303
TF: 800-237-3454 ■ *Web:* www.opi.state.oh.us
Oklahoma Correctional Industries
3402 N Martin Luther King Ave .... Oklahoma City OK 73111 405-425-7500
TF: 800-522-3565 ■ *Web:* www.ocisales.com
PEN Products 2010 E New York St .... Indianapolis IN 46201 317-955-6800 234-7635
TF: 800-736-2550 ■ *Web:* www.in.gov
Pennsylvania Correctional Industries
PO Box 47 .... Camp Hill PA 17001 717-425-7292 425-7291
TF General: 877-673-3724 ■ *Web:* www.cor.pa.gov/pci/pages/default.aspx
Prison Rehabilitative Industries & Diversified Enterprises Inc (PRIDE)
223 Morrison Rd Ste 200 .... Brandon FL 33511 813-324-8700
Web: www.prideenterprises.org
Rhode Island Correctional Industries
40 Howard Ave .... Cranston RI 02920 401-462-2611
Rough Rider Industries 3303 E Main Ave .... Bismarck ND 58506 701-328-6161 328-6164
TF: 800-732-0557 ■ *Web:* www.roughriderindustries.com
Silver State Industries 3955 W Russell Rd .... Las Vegas NV 89118 702-682-3147 486-9908
Web: www.ssi.nv.gov
South Carolina Prison Industries
4444 Broad River Rd .... Columbia SC 29210 803-896-8516 896-2173*
**Fax:* Cust Svc ■ *Web:* www.doc.sc.gov
Tennessee Rehabilitative Initiative in Correction (TRICOR)
240 Great Cir Rd Ste 310 .... Nashville TN 37228 615-741-5705 741-2747
TF: 800-958-7426 ■ *Web:* www.tricor.org
Texas Correctional Industries PO Box 4013 .... Huntsville TX 77342 936-437-6048 437-6040
Web: www.tci.tdcj.state.tx.us
Utah Correctional Industries
14072 S Pony Express Rd .... Draper UT 84020 801-576-7700 523-9753
Web: uci.utah.gov
Vermont Correctional Industries
103 S Main St .... Waterbury VT 05671 802-323-6214 241-1475
Web: vci.vermont.gov
Virginia Correctional Enterprises
8030 White Bark Terr .... Richmond VA 23237 804-743-4100
Web: www.govce.net
Washington Correctional Industries
801 88th Ave SE .... Tumwater WA 98501 360-725-9100 753-0219
Web: www.washingtonci.com
West Virginia Correctional Industries
617 Leon Sullivan Way .... Charleston WV 25301 304-558-6054 558-6056
TF: 800-525-5381 ■ *Web:* wvcorrectionalindustries.com

631 PROFESSIONAL EMPLOYER ORGANIZATIONS (PEOS)

Companies listed here contractually assume human resources responsibilities for client companies in exchange for a fee, thus allowing the client company to focus on its true company business. The PEO establishes and maintains an employer relationship with the workers assigned to its client companies, with the PEO and the client company each having specific rights and responsibilities toward the employees.

Phone *Fax*

A-1 Contract Staffing Inc 3829 Coconut Palm Dr. Tampa FL 33619 813-620-1661
Web: www.a1hr.com
AB Staffing Solutions LLC
2680 S Val Vista Dr Bldg 10 Ste 152 Gilbert AZ 85295 480-345-6668
Web: www.abstaffing.com
Abacus Corp 610 Gusryan St. Baltimore MD 21224 410-633-1900
Web: www.abacuscorporation.com
Abbacore LLC 7803 Cambridge Dr Prairie Village KS 66208 913-908-4654
Web: www.abbacore.com
Accion Labs US Inc 1121 Boyce Rd Ste 1400 Pittsburgh PA 15241 412-979-8111
Web: accionlabs.com
Accord Hum Res Inc 210 Pk Ave Ste 1200. Oklahoma City OK 73102 405-232-9888 232-9899
Adams Keegan Inc 6055 Primacy Pkwy Ste 300 Memphis TN 38119 901-683-5353 820-0472
TF: 800-621-1308 ■ *Web:* www.adamskeegan.com
ADP TotalSource Co 10200 Sunset Dr. Miami FL 33173 305-630-1000
TF: 800-447-3237 ■ *Web:* www.adp.com
Advanced Document Sciences Inc
29465 Elk View Dr Steamboat Springs CO 80487 970-875-0556
Web: www.adocs.com
Advice Media LLC PO Box 982064. Park City UT 84098 800-260-9497
TF: 800-260-9497 ■ *Web:* advicemedia.com
Agile Frameworks LLC 1826 Buerkle Rd Saint Paul MN 55110 651-487-3245
Web: www.agileframeworks.com
Alcott Group 71 Executive Blvd Farmingdale NY 11735 631-420-0100 420-1894
TF: 888-425-2688 ■ *Web:* www.alcottgroup.com
Alithya Group Inc 2875 Laurier Blvd Ste 1250 Quebec QC G1V2M2 418-650-2866
Web: www.alithya.com
Allevity HR & Payroll 870 Manzanita Ct Ste A. Chico CA 95926 530-345-2486 345-8486
TF: 800-447-8233 ■ *Web:* www.allevityhr.com
Allied Employer Group
4400 Buffalo Gap Rd Ste 4500 Abilene TX 79606 325-695-5822 692-9660
TF: 800-495-3836 ■ *Web:* www.coemployer.com
AlphaStaff Inc
800 Corporate Dr Ste 600. Fort Lauderdale FL 33334 954-267-1760 632-8090*
**Fax Area Code:* 866 ■ *TF:* 888-335-9545 ■ *Web:* www.alphastaff.com
Alta Consulting Services Inc
11000 NE 33rd Pl Ste 300 Bellevue WA 98004 425-576-1202
Web: www.altaconsulting.com
ALTRES Inc 967 Kapiolani Blvd Honolulu HI 96814 808-591-4940 591-4914
TF: 888-425-8737 ■ *Web:* www.altres.com
Assent Consulting Inc
2 Grand Central Twr 140 E 45th St. New York NY 10017 866-627-4473 610-3885*
**Fax Area Code:* 662 ■ *TF:* 866-627-4473 ■ *Web:* www.docsglobal.com
Axcet HR Solutions
Axet 8325 Lenexa Dr Ste 410. Lenexa KS 66214 913-383-2999 383-2949
TF: 800-801-7557 ■ *Web:* www.axcethr.com
B2 Digital Media LLC
3183 Airway Ave Ste F101 Costa Mesa CA 92627 949-945-3005
Web: www.b2digitalmedia.com
Barrett Business Services Inc
8100 NE Pkwy Dr Ste 200. Vancouver WA 98662 360-828-0700 828-0701
NASDAQ: BBSI ■ *TF:* 800-494-5669 ■ *Web:* www.barrettbusiness.com
Bco Inc 799 Middlesex Tpke. Billerica MA 01821 978-663-2525
Web: www.bco-inc.com
Beacon Hill Staffing Group LLC 152 Bowdoin St. Boston MA 02108 617-326-4000 227-1220
Web: www.beaconhillstaffing.com
Bedroc Inc 3351 Aspen Grove Dr Ste 350 Franklin TN 37067 615-815-1785
Web: www.bedroc.com
Bettinger The Company Inc
42 S 15th St Ste 1210. Philadelphia PA 19102 215-564-0700
Web: www.bettingerco.com
Beyond Ink LLC 82 Middle St Portland ME 04112 207-699-5775
Web: www.beyondink.com
BlueLine IT Group Inc 189 N Water St Rochester NY 14604 585-730-5977
Web: www.bluelineitgroup.com
BlueRange Technology Inc
9241 Globe Ctr Dr Ste 100. Morrisville NC 27560 905-829-5333
Web: www.bluerangetech.com
Brandmovers Inc 590 Means St Ste 250. Atlanta GA 30318 888-463-4933
TF: 888-463-4933 ■ *Web:* www.brandmovers.com
Burnett Cos Consolidated Inc
9800 Richmond Ave Ste 800 Houston TX 77042 713-977-4777 977-7533
Web: www.burnettspecialists.com
Cabedge Design 1105 17th Ave S. Nashville TN 37212 615-942-9937
Web: www.cabedge.com
Cardinal Path LLC 301 W Warner Rd Ste 136. Tempe AZ 85284 480-285-1622
Web: www.cardinalpath.com
Careers Express 234 Mall Blvd Ste 120 Kng Of Prussa PA 19406 610-768-1788
Web: careersexpress.com
Century II Staffing Inc
278 Franklin Rd Ste 350. Brentwood TN 37027 615-665-9060 665-1833
Web: www.centuryii.net
Challenge Enterprises of North Florida Inc
3530 Enterprise Way. Green Cove Springs FL 32043 904-284-9859
Web: www.ccar.org
Chipton-ross Inc 343 Main St. El Segundo CA 90245 310-414-7800 414-7808
TF: 800-927-9318 ■ *Web:* www.chiptonross.com
ClearEdge Partners Inc
8 Pleasant St Ste E-2 South Natick MA 01760 508-655-1022
Web: www.clearedgepartners.com
Co-Advantage Resources
3350 Buschwood Park Dr Ste 200 Tampa FL 33618 813-935-2000
TF: 800-868-1016 ■ *Web:* www.coadvantage.com
Cohen Brown Management Group
11835 Olympic Blvd Ste 920 Los Angeles CA 90064 310-966-1001
Web: www.cbmg.com
Compass Enterprise Solutions Inc
223 E State St. Geneva IL 60134 630-208-0200
Web: www.compass-solutions.com
Copper River Information Technology LLC
16600 Ctrfield Dr Ste 205. Eagle River AK 99577 703-234-9000
Web: www.copperriverit.com
CrowdSource Solutions Inc 33 Bronze Pointe Swansea IL 62226 855-276-9376
TF: 855-276-9376 ■ *Web:* www.crowdsource.com
Cubix Labs Inc
15308 Spencerville Ct Ste 201B. Burtonsville MD 20866 919-308-2385
Web: www.socialcubix.com
Cyber 360 Solutions Inc
1600 Providence Hwy Ste 15 Walpole MA 02081 781-438-4380
Web: www.cyber360solutions.com
Datacore Consulting LLC
5755 Granger Rd Ste 777 Independence OH 44131 216-398-8499
Web: www.datacoreonline.com
DBG Partners Inc 940 S Kimball Ave Ste 100 Southlake TX 76092 817-442-1060
Web: dbg.com
DecisionHR Inc
100 Carillon Pkwy Ste 350. St. Petersburg FL 33716 727-572-7331
Web: www.decisionhr.com
Dempton Groupe Conseil
1255, University St Ste 450 Montreal QC H3B3B6 514-657-3517
Web: www.dempton.com
Destiny Corp 2075 Silas Deane Hwy Rocky Hill CT 06067 860-721-1684
Web: www.destinycorp.com
Dismas Distribution Services LLC
6772 Kilowatt Cir Blacklick OH 43004 614-861-2525
Web: www.dismas.net
Diversified Hum Res Inc
3020 E Camelback Rd Ste 213 Phoenix AZ 85016 480-941-5588 553-4684*
**Fax Area Code:* 602 ■ *TF:* 888-870-5588 ■ *Web:* www.dhr.net
Doherty Employment Group 7625 Parklawn Ave. Edina MN 55435 952-832-8383 356-1953
TF Sales: 888-297-0495 ■ *Web:* www.dohertyemployment.com
Einstein HR Inc 3805 Crestwood Pkwy Ste 100 Duluth GA 30096 770-962-1700
Web: www.einsteinhr.com
Employee & Family Resources Inc (EFR)
505 Fifth Ave Ste 600 Des Moines IA 50309 515-288-9020
Web: www.efr.org
Employee Management Services 435 Elm St. Cincinnati OH 45202 513-651-3244 381-2764
TF: 888-651-1536 ■ *Web:* www.emshro.com
Employer's Hum Res Inc (EHRI)
75899 State Hwy 16 Wagoner OK 74467 918-485-9404 485-9317
Employers Choice Solutions Inc
22476 Sacramento Ave. Port Charlotte FL 33954 941-627-0777
Web: www.employerchoice.com
EMPO Corp 3100 W Lk St Ste 100 Minneapolis MN 55416 612-285-8707
Web: www.empocorp.com
Endeavour Software Technologies Inc
8140 N Mopac Expy Westpark 1 Ste 220 Austin TX 78759 512-464-1218
Web: www.techendeavour.com
eSoftware Professionals Inc
10450 SW Nimbus Ave Ste B Portland OR 97223 503-608-3601
Web: www.esopro.com
Find Your Dreams Inc
636 Plank Rd Ste 205 Clifton Park NY 12065 518-631-6227
Web: www.internetmarketingninjas.com
FrontPage Local 1660 Hotel Cir N Ste 600. San Diego CA 92108 800-521-7338
TF: 800-521-7338 ■ *Web:* www.frontpagelocal.com
G4S PLC 1395 University Blvd. Jupiter FL 33458 561-691-6669
Web: www.g4s.com
GetMeFriends 816 Camaron St. San Antonio TX 78212 210-722-0620
Web: www.getmefriends.com
GO2 Media Design Inc 40 Oakridge Pkwy. Peekskill NY 10566 914-734-1430
Web: www.go2mediadesign.com
HOV Services LLC 1305 Stephenson Hwy Ste. Royal Oak MI 48073 248-837-7100
Web: www.hovservices.com
HR Affiliates 1930 Bishop Ln # 111 Louisville KY 40218 502-485-9675
Web: www.hraffiliates.com
Human Capital
2055 Crooks Rd Lowr Level Rochester Hills MI 48309 888-736-9071
TF: 888-736-9071 ■ *Web:* www.human-capital.com
Human Resources Inc 2127 Espey Ct Ste 306. Crofton MD 21114 410-451-4202 451-4206
Web: www.hri-online.com
Iconma LLC 850 Stephenson Hwy Ste 612. Troy MI 48083 888-451-2519 489-8046*
**Fax Area Code:* 800 ■ *TF:* 888-451-2519 ■ *Web:* www.iconma.com
Identity Theft Resource Center
3625 Ruffin Rd Ste 204. San Diego CA 92123 858-693-7935
TF: 888-400-5530 ■ *Web:* www.idtheftcenter.org
Ignition Commerce Inc
710 Holcomb Bridge Rd Ste 100 Alpharetta GA 30075 770-640-6382
Web: www.ignitioncommerce.com
Ignition Ltd 161 Kimball Bridge Rd Ste 300 Alpharetta GA 30009 678-281-6402
Web: www.ignitionmsp.com
Inek Technologies LLC
9200 Indian Creek Pkwy Ste 187 Overland Park KS 66210 913-469-1066
Web: www.inekinfo.com
Innovate E-Commerce Inc 160 N Craig St Pittsburgh PA 15213 888-771-9606
TF: 888-771-9606 ■ *Web:* www.innovateec.com
Inspirage Inc 600 108th Ave NE Ste 540. Bellevue WA 98004 855-517-4250
TF: 855-517-4250 ■ *Web:* www.inspirage.com
Internet Solver Inc 11308 Aurora Ave Urbandale IA 50322 515-224-9229
Intrepidus Group Inc 119 Fifth Ave Ste 702 New York NY 10003 212-937-0458
Web: intrepidusgroup.com
Irontouch Managed Services Inc 540 Dado St. San Jose CA 95131 714-408-4700
Web: www.irontouchms.com
IT Staffing Inc 5 Bliss Court Ste 200. Woodcliff Lake NJ 07677 201-505-0493
Web: www.itstaffinc.com

	City	State	ZIP	Phone	Fax
Jackson Healthcare LLC 2655 Northwinds Pkwy *Web:* www.jacksonhealthcare.com	Alpharetta	GA	30009	770-643-5500	
JCS Consulting Group Inc 2775 Via De La Valle Ste 206 *Web:* jcsconsulting.com	San Diego	CA	92014	858-947-0101	
Jvt Advisors 35 New England Business Ctr Dr Ste 210 *Web:* www.jvtadvisors.com	Andover	MA	01810	978-683-4555	
Key2 Consulting LLC 1000 Peachtree Industrial Blvd Ste 6-289 *Web:* www.key2consulting.com	Suwanee	GA	30024	770-402-6938	
Konrad Group Inc 445 King St W 3rd Fl *Web:* www.konradgroup.com	Toronto	ON	M5V1K4	416-551-3684	
Laboratoires Bug-Tracker Inc 2030 Blvd Pie-IX Ste 307 *Web:* www.bug-tracker.com	Montreal	QC	H1V2C8	514-496-0093	
Legacy Engineering LLC 18662 Macarthur Blvd Ste 457 *Web:* www.legacyeng.com	Irvine	CA	92612	949-794-5860	794-5866
Lsg Solutions LLC 501 E 15th St Ste 200B *Web:* www.lsgsolutions.com	Edmond	OK	73013	405-285-2500	
Manpower Inc. 8170 W Sahara Ave Ste 207 *TF:* 888-333-1597 ■ *Web:* www.manpowerlv.com	Las Vegas	NV	89101	702-363-2626	363-0461
Marketleap Inc 359 Texas St *Web:* www.marketleap.com	San Francisco	CA	94107	415-642-7779	
Marvel Consultants Inc 28601 Chagrin Blvd Ste 210 *TF:* 800-338-1257 ■ *Web:* www.marvelconsultants.com	Cleveland	OH	44122	216-292-2855	292-7207
Mass Transmit Inc 333 Hudson St Ste 802 *Web:* masstransmit.com	New York	NY	10013	646-797-4349	
Miss Paige Ltd 8430 W Bryn Mawr Ste 625 *Web:* www.jobgiraffe.com	Chicago	IL	60631	773-693-0480	693-9071
Mitchell Martin Inc 307 W 38th St Ste 1305 **Fax Area Code:* 646 ■ *Web:* www.mitchellmartin.com	New York	NY	10018	212-943-1404	355-0229*
Modern Business Associates Inc 9455 Koger Blvd Ste 200 *Web:* www.mbahro.com	St. Petersburg	FL	33702	727-563-1500	
Moresource Inc 401 Vandiver Dr *Web:* www.moresource-inc.com	Columbia	MO	65202	573-443-1234	
Mountain Ltd 19 Yarmouth Dr Ste 301 *TF:* 800-322-8627 ■ *Web:* www.mountainltd.com	New Gloucester	ME	04260	207-688-6200	688-6212
Naviant Inc 201 Prairie Heights Dr *Web:* naviant.com	Verona	WI	53593	608-848-0924	
NETSHARE Inc 359 Bel Marin Keys Ste 24 *Web:* netshare.com	Novato	CA	94949	415-883-1700	
Nexio Group Inc, The 2050 de Bleury St Ste 500 *Web:* www.nexio.com	Montreal	QC	H3A2J5	514-798-3707	
Nomad Technology Group LLC 1315 Read St Unit C *Web:* nomadtechgroup.com	Evansville	IN	47710	812-618-4032	
NumbersOnly Inc 1520 State Hwy 130 N Ste 201 *Web:* www.numbersonly.com	North Brunswick	NJ	08902	732-940-0033	
Oasis Outsourcing 4511 Woodland Corporate Blvd *TF:* 866-709-9401 ■ *Web:* www.oasisadvantage.com	Tampa	FL	33614	813-864-8429	
Oasis Outsourcing Inc 2054 Vista Pkwy Ste 300 *TF General:* 888-627-4735 ■ *Web:* www.oasisadvantage.com	West Palm Beach	FL	33411	888-627-4735	274-4419
Omni Marketing Interactive 847 S Randall Rd Ste 312 *Web:* www.search-usability.com	Elgin	IL	60123	847-426-8978	
OmniTI Computer Consulting Inc 11830 W Market Pl Ste F *Web:* www.omniti.com	Fulton	MD	20759	240-646-0770	
OneSource Virtual HR Inc 5601 N MacArthur Blvd Ste 100 *Web:* www.onesourcevirtual.com	Irving	TX	75038	972-916-9847	
Optimum Outsourcing LLC 1300 Quail st #202 *Web:* www.optimumhr.net	Newport Beach	CA	92660	949-650-7800	
Optimum Staffing Inc 611 N Kingery Hwy Ste 105 *Web:* www.optimumlogistic.com	Bensenville	IL	60106	630-766-0694	
Optimus Information Inc 510-900 Howe St *Web:* www.optimusinfo.com	Vancouver	BC	V6Z2M4	604-736-4600	
OSF Global Services Inc 6655 Blvd Pierre Bertrand, 204-14 *TF:* 888-548-4344 ■ *Web:* www.osf-global.com	Quebec City	QC	G2K1M1	888-548-4344	
Outspoken Media Inc 4142 Mariner Blvd Ste 234 *Web:* outspokenmedia.com	Spring Hill	FL	34609	904-742-6477	
Paradime Solutions Inc 5800 Buford Hwy *Web:* www.paradimeinc.com	Norcross	GA	30071	770-441-6301	
Pay Plus Benefits Inc 1110 N Ctr Pkwy Ste B *TF:* 888-531-5781 ■ *Web:* www.payplusbenefits.com	Kennewick	WA	99336	509-735-1143	735-7668
Pencom Systems Inc 152 Remsen St *Web:* www.pencom.com	Brooklyn	NY	11201	718-923-1111	923-6065
People Lease Inc 689 Town Ctr Blvd Ste B *TF:* 800-723-3025 ■ *Web:* www.peoplelease.com	Ridgeland	MS	39157	601-987-3025	987-3029
Personnel Management Inc PO Box 6657 *TF:* 800-259-4126 ■ *Web:* www.pmiresource.com	Shreveport	LA	71136	318-869-4555	841-4350
PES Payroll Inc 4100 W Burbank Blvd *Web:* www.pespayroll.com	Burbank	CA	91505	818-729-0080	
Playlore Inc 69 Red Coat Rd *Web:* www.playlore.com	Westport	CT	06880	203-635-4306	
Primary Staffing Inc 4247 S Kedzie Ave *Web:* primary-staffing.net	Chicago	IL	60632	773-376-0486	
Professional Group Plans Inc (PGP) 225 Wireless Blvd Ste 200 *Web:* www.pgpbenefits.com	Hauppauge	NY	11788	631-951-9200	951-9623
Professional Staff Management Inc 6801 Lake Plaza Dr Ste D-405 *TF:* 800-967-5515 ■ *Web:* www.psmin.com	Indianapolis	IN	46220	317-816-7007	816-7005
Proficio Inc 16390 Bake Pkwy Ste 100 *Web:* www.proficio.com	Irvine	CA	92618	949-679-9188	
Progressive Employer Services 6407 Parkland Dr *TF:* 888-925-2990 ■ *Web:* www.progressiveemployer.com	Sarasota	FL	34243	941-925-2990	308-1789
Qualified Resources International LLC 78 Kenwood St *Web:* www.qristaffing.com	Cranston	RI	02907	401-946-1002	
Quinn Communications LC 1155 Main St Ste 109 *Web:* www.quinncom.net	Jupiter	FL	33458	561-622-7577	
RAM Enterprise Inc 1800 Boulder St *Web:* www.rcfdenver.org	Denver	CO	80211	303-433-7094	
Randstad Canada Group 810 Boul De Maisonneuve Quest *Web:* www.randstad.ca	Montreal	QC	H3A3E6	514-350-0033	
Rapidsoft Systems Inc 7 Diamond Ct *Web:* www.rapidsoftsystems.com	Princeton Junction	NJ	08550	609-439-4775	
Recon Management Services Inc 3649 S Beglis Pkwy *TF:* 888-301-4662 ■ *Web:* www.recon-group.com	Sulphur	LA	70665	337-583-4662	583-7565
Red Foundry Inc 1608 S Ashland Ave *TF:* 888-406-1099 ■ *Web:* www.redfoundry.com	Chicago	IL	60608	888-406-1099	
Redshift Business Networks Inc 1020 Railroad Ave Ste A *Web:* www.redshift-networks.com	Novato	CA	94945	415-462-6262	
REMPREX LLC 7501 S Quincy St Ste 100 *Web:* www.remprex.com	Willowbrook	IL	60527	630-910-0600	
Reserves Network, The 22021 Brookpark Rd *TF:* 866-876-2020 ■ *Web:* www.trnstaffing.com	Cleveland	OH	44126	440-779-6681	
Resource Management Inc 281 Main St Ste 5 *TF Cust Svc:* 800-508-0048 ■ *Web:* www.rmi-solutions.com	Fitchburg	MA	01420	800-508-0048	
RKL eSolutions LLC 1800 Fruitville Pk *Web:* www.rklesolutions.com	Lancaster	PA	17604	717-735-9109	
RMPersonnel Inc 4707 Montana Ave *TF:* 866-333-7176 ■ *Web:* www.rmpersonnel.com	El Paso	TX	79903	915-565-7674	565-7687
Rocket Whale Inc 3149 Mccully Dr NE *Web:* rocketwhale.com	Atlanta	GA	30345	404-219-1537	
ScaleMatrix Inc 5775 Kearny Villa Rd *Web:* www.scalematrix.com	San Diego	CA	92123	858-633-4300	
Slate Professional Resources Inc 800 W Main St Ste 204 *Web:* www.slateprofessional.com	Freehold	NJ	07728	732-303-6329	
SmartLink Internet Strategies Inc 8895 N Military Trl Ste B202 *Web:* thinksmartlink.com	Palm Beach Gardens	FL	33410	561-688-8155	
SourceGear LLC 115 N Neil St Ste 408 *Web:* www.sourcegear.com	Champaign	IL	61820	217-356-0105	
SPARK Experience Design LLC 7979 Old Georgetown Rd Ste 801 *Web:* sparkexperience.com	Bethesda	MD	20814	301-294-3340	
Spongelab Interactive Inc 662 King St W Ste 101 *Web:* www.spongelab.com	Toronto	ON	M5V1M7	416-703-9753	
SPR Consulting Sears Tower 233 S Wacker Dr Ste 3500 *Web:* spr.com	Chicago	IL	60606	312-756-1760	
Staff Management Inc 5919 Spring Creek Rd **Fax:* Hum Res ■ *Web:* www.staffmgmt.com	Rockford	IL	61114	815-282-3900	282-0515*
Staff One Inc 8111 LBJ Fwy **Fax Area Code:* 214 ■ *TF:* 800-771-7823 ■ *Web:* www.staffone.com	Dallas	TX	75251	800-771-7823	461-1141*
Strom Aviation Inc 109 S Elm St *TF:* 800-356-6440 ■ *Web:* www.stromaviation.com	Waconia	MN	55387	952-544-3611	
Summit Technical Services Inc 355 Centerville Rd *TF:* 800-643-7372 ■ *Web:* www.summit-technical.com	Warwick	RI	02886	401-736-8323	738-3341
Sycara Inc 6263 N Scottsdale Rd Ste 180 *TF:* 855-479-2272 ■ *Web:* www.sycaralocal.com	Scottsdale	AZ	85250	855-479-2272	
Synygy Pte. Ltd 2501 Seaport Dr *TF:* 877-883-5395 ■ *Web:* www.synygy.com	Chester	PA	19013	610-494-3300	
T & t Staff Management Inc 511 Executive Ctr Blvd *TF:* 800-598-1647 ■ *Web:* www.ttstaff.com	El Paso	TX	79902	915-771-0393	
Tech-Clarity Inc 2420 Martingale Rd Ste 100 *Web:* www.tech-clarity.com	Media	PA	19063	610-565-6302	
TekPartners 5810 Coral Ridge Dr Ste 250 *Web:* www.tekpartners.com	Coral Springs	FL	33076	954-656-8600	282-6070
TeleSearch Staffing Solutions 251 Re 206 *Web:* www.telesearch.com	Flanders	NJ	07836	973-927-7870	927-7880
Think Big Analytics Inc 520 San Antonio Rd Ste 210 *Web:* thinkbig.teradata.com	Mountain View	CA	94040	650-949-2350	
THINKstrategies Inc 22 Park Ave *Web:* www.thinkstrategies.com	Wellesley	MA	02481	781-431-2690	
Tiggee LLC 10809 Melanie Ct *Web:* www.tiggee.com	Oakton	VA	22124	703-880-3095	
Tilson HR Inc 1530 American Way Ste 200 *TF:* 800-276-3976 ■ *Web:* www.tilsonhr.com	Greenwood	IN	46143	317-885-3838	
Torry Harris Business Solutions Inc 536 Fayette St *Web:* www.thbs.com	Perth Amboy	NJ	08861	732-442-0049	
Training Assoc Corp, The 289 Tpke Rd *TF:* 800-241-8868 ■ *Web:* www.thetrainingassociates.com	Westborough	MA	01581	508-890-8500	890-8658
TriCore Solutions LLC 141 Longwater Dr Ste 100 *Web:* www.tricoresolutions.com	Norwell	MA	02061	617-774-5200	
TriNet Group Inc 1100 San Leandro Blvd Ste 300 *TF:* 888-874-6388 ■ *Web:* www.trinet.com	San Leandro	CA	94577	510-352-5000	352-6480

Phone Fax

VertitechIT Inc 4 Open Sq Way Ste 207 .... Holyoke MA 01040 413-268-1600
Web: vertitechit.com

Virsys12 LLC 5205 Maryland Way Ste 202 .... Brentwood TN 37027 615-800-6768
Web: virsys12.com

VJV IT 96 Linwood Plz. .... Fort Lee NJ 07024 800-614-7561
TF: 800-614-7561 ■ *Web:* www.vjvit.com

VS Management of NY Inc
3281 Veterans Memorial Hwy .... Ronkonkoma NY 11779 877-778-7648
TF: 877-778-7648 ■ *Web:* www.vsmgmt.com

Vuurr LLC 260 S Arizona Ave .... Chandler AZ 85225 480-525-8240
Web: www.vuurr.com

Willmott & Associates Inc
922 Waltham St Ste 103 .... Lexington MA 02421 781-863-5400
Web: www.willmott.com

Winterhawk Consulting LLC
1643 Williamsburg Sq .... Lakeland FL 33803 813-731-9665
Web: winterhawkconsulting.com

Yomari Information Services Inc
111 Third Ave S Ste 120 .... Minneapolis MN 55401 612-326-4852
Web: www.yomari.com

632 PUBLIC BROADCASTING ORGANIZATIONS

See Also Radio Networks p. 3013; Television Networks - Broadcast p. 3223

Phone Fax

Alabama Educational Television Commission
2112 11th Ave S Ste 400 .... Birmingham AL 35205 205-328-8756 251-2192
TF: 800-239-5233 ■ *Web:* www.aptv.org

Alabama Public Television (APT)
2112 11th Ave S Ste 400 .... Birmingham AL 35205 205-328-8756 251-2192
TF: 800-239-5233 ■ *Web:* www.aptv.org

Alaska Public Broadcasting Inc (APBI)
135 Cordova St. .... Anchorage AK 99501 907-277-6300
Web: www.akpb.org

American Public Television (APT)
55 Summer St 4th Fl. .... Boston MA 02110 617-338-4455 338-5369
Web: aptonline.org/aptweb.nsf/home?readform

Annenberg Media
1301 Pennsylvania Ave NW ste302 .... Washington DC 20004 800-532-7637 783-0333*
**Fax Area Code:* 202 ■ *TF:* 800-532-7637 ■ *Web:* www.learner.org

Arkansas Educational Television Network (AETN)
350 S Donaghey Ave .... Conway AR 72034 501-682-2386 682-4122
TF: 800-662-2386 ■ *Web:* www.aetn.org

Association of Independents in Radio (AIR)
42 Charles St 2nd Fl. .... Dorchester MA 02122 617-825-4400
Web: www.airmedia.org

Association of Public Television Stations (APTS)
2100 Crystal Dr Ste 700 .... Arlington VA 22202 202-654-4200 654-4236
Web: www.apts.org

Blue Ridge Public Television 1215 McNeil Dr .... Roanoke VA 24015 540-344-0991 344-2148
TF: 888-332-7788 ■ *Web:* www.blueridgepbs.org

California Public Radio
4100 Vachell Ln .... San Luis Obispo CA 93401 805-549-8855
TF: 800-549-8855 ■ *Web:* www.kcbx.org

Capitol Steps Productions Inc
210 N Washington St .... Alexandria VA 22314 703-683-8330
TF: 800-733-7837 ■ *Web:* www.capsteps.com

Commonwealth Club of California
595 Market St 2nd Fl .... San Francisco CA 94105 415-597-6700 597-6729
TF: 800-933-7548 ■ *Web:* www.commonwealthclub.org

Commonwealth Public Broadcasting
23 Sesame St .... Richmond VA 23235 804-320-1301
Web: www.ideastations.org

Connecticut Public Broadcasting Inc (CPBI)
1049 Asylum Ave .... Hartford CT 06105 860-278-5310
TF: 800-683-2112 ■ *Web:* www.cpbn.org

Corporation for Public Broadcasting (CPB)
401 Ninth St NW. .... Washington DC 20004 202-879-9600 879-9700
TF: 800-272-2190 ■ *Web:* www.cpb.org

East Tennessee Public Communications Corp
1611 E Magnolia Ave .... Knoxville TN 37917 865-595-0220 595-0300
TF: 844-686-2378 ■ *Web:* www.easttennesseepbs.org

Georgia Public Broadcasting (GPB)
260 14th St NW .... Atlanta GA 30318 800-222-6006
TF: 800-222-6006 ■ *Web:* www.gpb.org

GPB Education 260 14th St NW .... Atlanta GA 30318 404-685-2550 685-2556
TF: 888-501-8960 ■ *Web:* www.gpb.org

Hawaii Public Television 2350 Dole St .... Honolulu HI 96822 808-973-1000 973-1090
TF: 800-238-4847 ■ *Web:* www.pbshawaii.org

Idaho Public Television (IPTV) 1455 N Orchard St .... Boise ID 83706 208-373-7220 373-7245
TF: 800-543-6868 ■ *Web:* idahoptv.org

Independent Television Service (ITVS)
651 Brannan St Ste 410 .... San Francisco CA 94107 415-356-8383 356-8391
TF: 800-621-6196 ■ *Web:* www.itvs.org

Kentucky Educational Television (KET)
600 Cooper Dr .... Lexington KY 40502 859-258-7000 258-7399
TF: 800-432-0951 ■ *Web:* www.ket.org

KUAC FM/TV PO Box 755620 .... Fairbanks AK 99775 907-474-7491 474-5064
TF: 800-727-6543 ■ *Web:* kuac.org

Louisiana Public Broadcasting
7733 Perkins Rd .... Baton Rouge LA 70810 225-767-5660 767-4299
TF: 800-973-7246 ■ *Web:* lpb.org

Maine Public Broadcasting Network (MPBN)
65 Texas Ave .... Bangor ME 04401 207-941-1010 942-2857
TF: 800-884-1717 ■ *Web:* www.mpbn.net

Maryland Public Television (MPT)
11767 Owings Mills Blvd .... Owings Mills MD 21117 410-581-4201 581-4338
TF: 800-223-3678 ■ *Web:* www.mpt.org

Metropolitan Indianapolis Public Broadcasting Corp
1401 N Meridian St .... Indianapolis IN 46202 317-636-2020
Web: www.wfyi.org

Phone Fax

Michigan Public Media
535 W William St Ste 110 .... Ann Arbor MI 48103 734-764-9210
Web: www.michiganradio.org

Minnesota Public Radio (MPR) 480 Cedar St .... Saint Paul MN 55101 651-290-1212
TF: 800-228-7123 ■ *Web:* www.mpr.org

Mississippi Authority for Educational Television
3825 Ridgewood Rd .... Jackson MS 39211 601-432-6565 432-6311
TF: 800-850-4406 ■ *Web:* www.mpbonline.org

Montana Public Radio
32 Campus Dr University of Montana .... Missoula MT 59812 406-243-4931 243-3299
TF: 800-325-1565 ■ *Web:* www.mtpr.org

Montana Public Television
183 Visual Communications Bldg .... Bozeman MT 59717 866-832-0829 994-6545*
**Fax Area Code:* 406 ■ *TF:* 800-426-8243 ■ *Web:* www.montanapbs.org

National Captioning Institute (NCI)
3725 Concorde Pkwy Ste 100. .... Chantilly VA 20151 703-917-7600 917-9853
TF: 800-825-6758 ■ *Web:* www.ncicap.org

National Educational Telecommunications Assn (NETA)
939 S Stadium Rd. .... Columbia SC 29201 803-799-5517 771-4831
TF: 866-270-5141 ■ *Web:* www.netaonline.org

National Public Radio (NPR)
635 Massachusetts Ave NW .... Washington DC 20001 202-513-3232 513-3329
Web: www.npr.org

Nebraska Educational Telecommunications (NET)
1800 N 33rd St. .... Lincoln NE 68503 800-868-1868 472-1785*
**Fax Area Code:* 402 ■ *TF:* 800-868-1868 ■ *Web:* netdb.unl.edu

New Hampshire Public Television (NHPTV)
268 Mast Rd .... Durham NH 03824 603-868-1100 868-7552
TF: 800-639-8408 ■ *Web:* www.nhptv.org

NPR West 9909 Jefferson Blvd .... Culver City CA 90232 310-815-4200
Web: www.npr.org

Oregon Public Broadcasting Inc (OPB)
7140 SW Macadam Ave .... Portland OR 97219 503-244-9900
Web: www.opb.org

Prairie Public Broadcasting Inc 207 N Fifth St. .... Fargo ND 58102 701-241-6900 239-7650
TF: 800-359-6900 ■ *Web:* www.prairiepublic.org

Public Broadcasting Council of Central New York
506 Old Liverpool Rd PO Box 2400 .... Syracuse NY 13220 315-453-2424 451-8824
TF: 800-451-9269 ■ *Web:* www.wcny.org

Public Broadcasting Northwest Pennsylvania
8425 Peach St .... Erie PA 16509 814-864-3001 864-4077
TF: 800-727-8854 ■ *Web:* www.wqln.org

Public Broadcasting Service (PBS)
2100 Crystal Dr .... Arlington VA 22202 703-739-5000
TF: 866-864-0828 ■ *Web:* www.pbs.org

Radio Research Consortium Inc (RRC) PO Box 1309 ...... Olney MD 20830 301-774-6686 774-0976
Web: www.rrconline.org

Rhode Island PBS 50 Pk Ln .... Providence RI 02907 401-222-3636 222-3407
Web: www.ripbs.org

Rocky Mountain Public Broadcasting Network (RMPB)
1089 Bannock St .... Denver CO 80204 303-892-6666 620-5600
TF: 800-274-6666 ■ *Web:* www.rmpbs.org

Small Station Assn KRWG-TV PO Box 30001 .... Las Cruces NM 88003 575-646-2222 646-1974
TF: 877-308-2408 ■ *Web:* www.krwg.org

Smoky Hills Public Television (SHPTV)
604 Elm St .... Bunker Hill KS 67626 785-483-6990 483-4605
TF: 800-337-4788 ■ *Web:* www.shptv.org

South Carolina Educational Television Commission (ETV)
1101 George Rogers Blvd. .... Columbia SC 29201 803-737-3200
Web: www.scetv.org

South Dakota Public Broadcasting (SDPB)
555 N Dakota St PO Box 5000 .... Vermillion SD 57069 605-677-5861 677-5010
TF: 800-456-0766 ■ *Web:* www.sdpb.org

Station Resource Group (SRG)
6935 Laurel Ave Ste 202 .... Takoma Park MD 20912 301-270-2617 270-2618
Web: www.srg.org

Texas Public Radio (TPR)
8401 Datapoint Dr Ste 800 .... San Antonio TX 78229 210-614-8977 614-8983
TF: 800-622-8977 ■ *Web:* www.tpr.org

ThinkTV 110 S Jefferson St. .... Dayton OH 45402 937-220-1600 220-1642
TF: 800-247-1614 ■ *Web:* www.thinktv.org

TRAC Media Services
2030 E Speedway Blvd Ste 210 .... Tucson AZ 85719 520-299-1866 577-6077
TF: 888-299-1866 ■ *Web:* www.tracmedia.org

Twin Cities Public Television Inc
172 E Fourth St. .... Saint Paul MN 55101 651-222-1717 229-1282
TF: 866-229-1300 ■ *Web:* www.tpt.org

University of North Carolina Ctr for Public Television (UNC-TV)
10 TW Alexander Dr
PO Box 14900 .... Research Triangle Park NC 27709 919-549-7000 549-7201
TF: 800-906-5050 ■ *Web:* www.unctv.org

Vermont Public Television (VPT)
204 Ethan Allen Ave .... Colchester VT 05446 802-655-4800
TF: 800-639-7811 ■ *Web:* www.vpt.org

WAMC/Northeast Public Radio 318 Central Ave .... Albany NY 12206 518-465-5233 432-6974
TF: 800-323-9262 ■ *Web:* www.wamc.org

West Central Illinois Educational Telecommunications Corp
PO Box 6248 .... Springfield IL 62708 217-483-7887 483-1112
TF: 800-232-3605 ■ *Web:* www.networkknowledge.tv

WGBH Educational Foundation
1 Guest St Brighton Landing. .... Boston MA 02135 617-300-2000 300-1026
Web: www.wgbh.org

Wisconsin Educational Communications Board
3319 W Beltline Hwy .... Madison WI 53713 608-264-9600
TF: 800-422-9707 ■ *Web:* www.ecb.org

Wisconsin Public Radio (WPR) 821 University Ave ..... Madison WI 53706 800-747-7444 263-9763*
**Fax Area Code:* 608 ■ *TF:* 800-747-7444 ■ *Web:* www.wpr.org

Wisconsin Public Television (WPT)
821 University Ave .... Madison WI 53706 608-263-2121 263-9763
TF: 800-422-9707 ■ *Web:* www.wpt.org

Wyoming Public Television 2660 Peck Ave .... Riverton WY 82501 307-856-6944 856-3893
TF: 800-495-9788 ■ *Web:* wyomingpbs.org

633 PUBLIC INTEREST RESEARCH GROUPS (PIRGS) - STATE

See Also Consumer Interest Organizations p. 1761

Phone *Fax*

Alaska Public Interest Research Group (AkPIRG)
737 W Fifth Ave # 206 . . . . . Anchorage AK 99501 907-278-3661
Web: www.akpirg.org

California Public Interest Research Group (CAPIRG)
1107 Ninth St Ste 601 . . . . . Sacramento CA 95814 916-448-4516
Web: www.calpirg.org

Colorado Public Interest Research Group (COPIRG)
1543 Wazee St Ste 330. . . . . Denver CO 80202 303-573-7474
Web: www.copirg.org

Connecticut Public Interest Research Group (CONNPIRG)
2074 Park St. . . . . Hartford CT 06106 860-233-7554 233-7574
Web: www.connpirg.org

Florida Public Interest Research Group
926 E Pk Ave . . . . . Tallahassee FL 32301 850-224-3321 224-1310
Web: www.floridapirg.org

Georgia Public Interest Research Group (PIRG)
817 W Peachtree St NW Ste 204. . . . . Atlanta GA 30308 404-892-3405
Web: www.georgiapirg.org

Iowa Public Interest Research Group
3209 Ingersoll Ave . . . . . Des Moines IA 50312 515-282-4193
Web: www.iowapirg.org

Maryland Public Interest Research Group (MaryPIRG)
3121 St Paul St Ste 26 . . . . . Baltimore MD 21218 410-467-0439 366-2051
Web: www.marylandpirg.org

Massachusetts Public Interest Research Group (MASSPIRG)
44 Winter St 4th Fl . . . . . Boston MA 02108 617-292-4800 292-4800
Web: www.masspirg.org

New Hampshire Public Interest Research Group (NHPIRG)
30 S Main St Ste 301-A . . . . . Concord NH 03301 603-229-1343
Web: www.nhpirg.org

New Mexico Public Interest Research Group (NMPIRG)
PO Box 40173 . . . . . Albuquerque NM 87196 505-254-1244
Web: www.nmpirg.org

New York Public Interest Research Group (NYPIRG)
9 Murray St. . . . . New York NY 10007 212-349-6460 349-1366
TF: 800-342-3377 ■ *Web:* www.nypirg.org

North Carolina Public Interest Research Group (NCPIRG)
112 S Blount St . . . . . Raleigh NC 27601 919-833-2070
Web: www.ncpirg.org

Oregon State Public Interest Research Group (OSPIRG)
1536 SE 11th Ave. . . . . Portland OR 97214 503-231-4181
Web: www.ospirg.org

Pennsylvania Public Interest Research Group (PennPIRG)
1420 Walnut St Ste 650 . . . . . Philadelphia PA 19102 215-732-3747 732-4599
Web: www.pennpirg.org

Rhode Island Public Interest Research Group (RIPIRG)
9 S Angell St Second Fl-A . . . . . Providence RI 02906 401-608-1201
Web: www.ripirg.org

Texas Public Interest Research Group
815 Brazos Ste 600. . . . . Austin TX 78701 512-479-7287
Web: www.texpirg.org

US Public Interest Research Group (US PIRG)
218 D St SE . . . . . Washington DC 20003 202-546-9707 546-2461
Web: www.uspirg.org

Vermont Public Interest Research Group (VPIRG)
141 Main St Ste 6. . . . . Montpelier VT 05602 802-223-5221 223-6855
Web: www.vpirg.org

Washington State Public Interest Research Group
1402 Third Ave Ste 715 . . . . . Seattle WA 98101 206-568-2854
Web: www.washpirg.org

Wisconsin Public Interest Research Group (WISPIRG)
210 N Bassett St Ste 200 . . . . . Madison WI 53703 608-251-1918
Web: www.wispirg.org

634 PUBLIC POLICY RESEARCH CENTERS

Phone *Fax*

A Alfred Taubman Ctr for State & Local Government
Harvard Univ John F Kennedy School of Government
79 JFK St . . . . . Cambridge MA 02138 617-495-2199 496-1722
Web: www.hks.harvard.edu/centers/taubman

AARP Public Policy Institute 601 E St NW . . . . . Washington DC 20049 202-434-2277
TF: 888-687-2277 ■ *Web:* aarp.org/research/ppi

Acton Institute for the Study of Religion & Liberty
161 Ottawa Ave NW Ste 301. . . . . Grand Rapids MI 49503 616-454-3080 454-9454
TF: 800-345-2286 ■ *Web:* www.acton.org

Allegheny Institute for Public Policy
305 Mt Lebanon Blvd Ste 208 . . . . . Pittsburgh PA 15234 412-440-0079 440-0085
TF: 800-242-2184 ■ *Web:* www.alleghenyinstitute.org

American Assembly 475 Riverside Dr Ste 456. . . . . New York NY 10115 212-870-3500 870-3555
Web: www.americanassembly.org

American Enterprise Institute for Public Policy Research (AEI)
1150 17th St NW . . . . . Washington DC 20036 202-862-5800 862-7177
TF: 800-862-5801 ■ *Web:* www.aei.org

Ashbrook Ctr
401 College Ave Ashland University. . . . . Ashland OH 44805 419-289-5411
TF: 877-289-5411 ■ *Web:* www.ashbrook.org

Aspen Institute 1 DuPont Cir NW Ste 700 . . . . . Washington DC 20036 202-736-5823 467-0790
Web: www.aspeninstitute.org

Atlantic Council of the United States
1101 15th St NW 11th Fl . . . . . Washington DC 20005 202-463-7226 463-7241
TF: 800-311-9410 ■ *Web:* www.atlanticcouncil.org

Belfer Ctr for Science & International Affairs (BCSIA)
Harvard Univ John F Kennedy School of Government
79 JFK St . . . . . Cambridge MA 02138 617-495-1400 495-8963
Web: belfercenter.ksg.harvard.edu

Benton Foundation 1625 K St NW 11th Fl. . . . . Washington DC 20006 202-638-5770 638-5771
Web: www.benton.org

Brookings Institution
1775 Massachusetts Ave NW . . . . . Washington DC 20036 202-797-6000 797-6004
TF: 800-275-1447 ■ *Web:* www.brookings.edu

Capital Research Ctr 1513 16th St NW. . . . . Washington DC 20036 202-483-6900
TF: 800-459-3950 ■ *Web:* www.capitalresearch.org

Carnegie Council for Ethics in International Affairs (CCEIA)
Merrill House 170 E 64th St . . . . . New York NY 10065 212-838-4120 752-2432
Web: www.carnegiecouncil.org

Carnegie Endowment for International Peace
1779 Massachusetts Ave NW . . . . . Washington DC 20036 202-483-7600 483-1840
TF: 877-866-3070 ■ *Web:* www.carnegieendowment.org

Carter Ctr 1 Copenhill Ave 453 Freedom Pkwy . . . . . Atlanta GA 30307 404-420-5100 331-0283
TF: 800-550-3560 ■ *Web:* www.cartercenter.org

Cascade Policy Institute
4850 SW Scholls Ferry Rd Ste 103. . . . . Portland OR 97225 503-242-0900 242-3822
Web: www.cascadepolicy.org

Cato Institute 1000 Massachusetts Ave NW. . . . . Washington DC 20001 202-842-0200 842-3490
Web: www.cato.org

Center for American Progress
1333 H St NW 10th Fl. . . . . Washington DC 20005 202-682-1611 682-1867
Web: www.americanprogress.org

Center for Animals & Public Policy
Tufts Univ School of Veterinary Medicine
200 Westboro Rd . . . . . North Grafton MA 01536 508-839-7920 839-2953
TF: 888-748-8387 ■ *Web:* vet.tufts.edu

Center for Cognitive Liberty & Ethics
PO Box 73481 . . . . . Davis CA 95617 530-750-7912
TF: 888-950-6463 ■ *Web:* www.cognitiveliberty.org

Center for Equal Opportunity (CEO)
14 Pidgeon Hill Dr Ste 500. . . . . Sterling VA 20165 703-421-5443 421-6401
Web: www.ceousa.org

Center for Immigration Studies
1522 K St NW Ste 820 . . . . . Washington DC 20005 202-466-8185 466-8076
Web: www.cis.org

Center for International Development at Harvard University (CID)
Harvard Univ John F Kennedy School of Government
1 Eliot St Bldg 79 JFK St . . . . . Cambridge MA 02138 617-495-4112 496-8753
Web: www.hks.harvard.edu/centers/cid

Center for International Private Enterprise
1155 15th St NW Ste 700. . . . . Washington DC 20005 202-721-9200 721-9250
Web: www.cipe.org

Center for Law & Social Policy (CLASP)
1015 15th St NW Ste 400. . . . . Washington DC 20005 202-906-8000 842-2885
TF: 800-821-4367 ■ *Web:* www.clasp.org

Center for Mathematical Studies in Economics & Management Sciences
580 Leverone Hall 2001 Sheridan Rd. . . . . Evanston IL 60208 847-491-3527 491-2530
Web: www.kellogg.northwestern.edu/research/math

Center for Neighborhood Technology
2125 W N Ave. . . . . Chicago IL 60647 773-278-4800 278-3840
Web: www.cnt.org

Center for Policy Research
Syracuse University 426 Eggers Hall . . . . . Syracuse NY 13244 315-443-3114 443-1081
TF: 800-325-3535 ■ *Web:* www.maxwell.syr.edu

Center for Public Integrity
910 17th St NW 7th Fl . . . . . Washington DC 20006 202-466-1300 466-1101
Web: www.publicintegrity.org

Center for Public Leadership
Harvard Univ John F Kennedy School of Government
79 JFK St . . . . . Cambridge MA 02138 617-496-8866 496-3337
Web: www.centerforpublicleadership.org

Center for Responsive Politics
1101 14th St NW Ste 1030. . . . . Washington DC 20005 202-857-0044 857-7809
Web: www.opensecrets.org

Center for Security Policy 1920 L St NW. . . . . Washington DC 20036 202-835-9077 835-9066
Web: centerforsecuritypolicy.org

Center for Strategic & International Studies
1800 K St NW Ste 400 . . . . . Washington DC 20006 202-887-0200 775-3199
Web: www.csis.org

Center of the American Experiment (CAE)
8441 Wayzata Blvd Ste 350 . . . . . Golden Valley MN 55426 612-338-3605 338-3621
Web: www.americanexperiment.org

Center on Budget & Policy Priorities
820 First St NE Ste 510 . . . . . Washington DC 20002 202-408-1080 408-1056
Web: www.cbpp.org

Century Foundation, The
1 Whitehall St 15th Fl. . . . . New York NY 10004 212-535-4441
Web: www.tcf.org

Chicago Council on Global Affairs, The (CCGA)
332 S Michigan Ave Ste 1100 . . . . . Chicago IL 60604 312-726-3860 821-7555
Web: www.thechicagocouncil.org

Claremont Institute
937 W Foothill Blvd Ste E. . . . . Claremont CA 91711 909-621-6825 626-8724
Web: www.claremont.org

Committee for Economic Development (CED)
2000 L St NW Ste 700 . . . . . Washington DC 20036 202-296-5860 223-0776
TF: 800-676-7353 ■ *Web:* www.ced.org

Commonwealth Institute 186 Hampshire St. . . . . Cambridge MA 02139 617-547-4474 868-1267
Web: comw.org

Consortium for Policy Research in Education (CPRE)
University of Pennsylvania
3440 Market St Ste 560 . . . . . Philadelphia PA 19104 215-573-0700 573-7914
Web: www.cpre.org

Discovery Institute 208 Columbia St. . . . . Seattle WA 98104 206-292-0401 682-5320
Web: www.discovery.org

Earth Policy Institute
1350 Connecticut Ave NW Ste 403. . . . . Washington DC 20036 202-496-9290 496-9325
Web: www.earth-policy.org

EastWest Institute (EWI) 1 E 26th St 20th Fl . . . . . New York NY 10010 212-824-4100 824-4149
Web: www.eastwest.ngo

Economic Policy Institute
1333 H St NW Ste 300 E Twr . . . . . Washington DC 20005 202-775-8810 775-0819
Web: www.epi.org

Economic Strategy Institute
3050 K St NW Ste 220 . . . . . Washington DC 20007 202-965-9484 965-1104
Web: www.econstrat.org

Organization	City	State	ZIP	Phone	Fax
Employee Benefit Research Institute (EBRI) 1100 13th St NW Ste 878 *Web:* www.ebri.org	Washington	DC	20005	202-659-0670	775-6312
Employment Policies Institute 1090 Vermont Ave NW Ste 800 *Web:* www.epionline.org	Washington	DC	20005	202-463-7650	463-7107
Ethics & Public Policy Ctr 1730 M St NW *Web:* www.eppc.org	Washington	DC	20036	202-682-1200	408-0632
Faith & Reason Institute 1730 Rhode Island Ave NW Ste 212 *Web:* www.frinstitute.org	Washington	DC	20036	202-289-8775	393-7004
Food & Agricultural Policy Research Institute (FAPRI) Iowa State University 578 Heady Hall *Web:* www.fapri.iastate.edu	Ames	IA	50011	515-294-1183	294-6336
Foreign Policy Institute 1740 Massachusetts Ave NW Nitze Bldg *Web:* www.sais-jhu.edu	Washington	DC	20036	202-663-5600	663-5769
Foreign Policy Research Institute (FPRI) 1528 Walnut St Ste 610 *Web:* www.fpri.org	Philadelphia	PA	19102	215-732-3774	732-4401
Foundation for Economic Education (FEE) 30 S Broadway *TF:* 800-960-4333 ■ *Web:* www.fee.org	Irvington-on-Hudson	NY	10533	404-554-9980	
Free Congress Foundation 901 N Washington Ste 206 *Web:* www.freecongress.org	Alexandria	VA	22314	703-837-0030	
Goldwater Institute 500 E Coronado Rd *Web:* www.goldwaterinstitute.org	Phoenix	AZ	85004	602-462-5000	256-7045
Hauser Ctr for Nonprofit Organizations Harvard Univ John F Kennedy School of Government 79 JFK St *Web:* www.hks.harvard.edu/hauser	Cambridge	MA	02138	617-496-5675	495-0996
Heartland Institute 3939 N Wilke Rd Ste 903 *Web:* www.heartland.org	Arlington Heights	IL	60004	312-377-4000	377-5000
Heritage Foundation 214 Massachusetts Ave NE *TF:* 800-546-2843 ■ *Web:* www.heritage.org	Washington	DC	20002	202-546-4400	546-8328
Hoover Institution on War Revolution & Peace Stanford University 434 Galvez Mall *Web:* www.hoover.org	Stanford	CA	94305	650-723-1754	723-1687
Hudson Institute 1015 15th St NW Ste 600 *TF:* 888-554-1325 ■ *Web:* www.hudson.org	Washington	DC	20005	202-974-2400	974-2410
Independent Institute 100 Swan Way *TF:* 800-927-8733 ■ *Web:* www.independent.org	Oakland	CA	94621	510-632-1366	568-6040
Institute for Foreign Policy Analysis Inc 675 Massachusetts Ave 10th Fl *Web:* www.ifpa.org	Cambridge	MA	02139	617-492-2116	492-8242
Institute For Health Policy 3333 California St	San Francisco	CA	94118	415-476-4921	
Institute for Humane Studies 3434 Washington Blvd Ste 440 *TF:* 800-697-8799 ■ *Web:* www.theihs.org	Arlington	VA	22201	703-993-4880	993-4890
Institute for International Economics 1750 Massachusetts Ave NW *Web:* www.iie.com	Washington	DC	20036	202-328-9000	328-5432
Institute for Justice 901 N Glebe Rd Ste 900 *TF:* 888-322-6397 ■ *Web:* www.ij.org	Arlington	VA	22203	703-682-9320	682-9321
Institute for Philosophy & Public Policy Maryland School of Public Policy 3111 Van Munching Hall *Web:* www.msu.edu	College Park	MD	20742	301-405-4763	
Institute for Policy Studies (IPS) 1112 16th St NW Ste 600 *TF:* 877-564-6833 ■ *Web:* www.ips-dc.org	Washington	DC	20036	202-234-9382	
Institute for Research on the Economics of Taxation (IRET) 1710 Rhode Island Ave NW 11th Fl *Web:* www.iret.org	Washington	DC	20036	202-463-1400	463-6199
Institute for the North 1675 C St Ste 106 *Web:* www.institutenorth.org	Anchorage	AK	99501	907-786-6324	343-2466
Institute of Government & Public Affairs Univ of Illinois 1007 W Nevada St *TF:* 866-794-3340 ■ *Web:* igpa.uillinois.edu	Urbana	IL	61801	217-333-3340	244-4817
Institute of World Politics 1521 16th St NW *TF:* 888-566-9497 ■ *Web:* www.iwp.edu	Washington	DC	20036	202-462-2101	464-0335
Institute on Education & the Economy 525 W 120th St *Web:* www.tc.columbia.edu	New York	NY	10027	212-678-3091	678-3699
Inter-American Dialogue 1211 Connecticut Ave NW Ste 510 *Web:* www.thedialogue.org	Washington	DC	20036	202-822-9002	822-9553
International Ctr for Alcohol Policies (ICAP) 1519 New Hampshire Ave NW *Web:* www.icap.org	Washington	DC	20036	202-986-1159	986-2080
International Food Policy Research Institute (IFPRI) 2033 K St NW *Web:* www.ifpri.org	Washington	DC	20006	202-862-5600	467-4439
Joan Shorenstein Ctr on the Press Politics & Public Policy 79 John F Kennedy St *Web:* shorensteincenter.org	Cambridge	MA	02138	617-495-8269	495-8696
Joint Ctr for Housing Studies 1033 Massachusetts Ave *Web:* www.jchs.harvard.edu	Cambridge	MA	02138	617-495-7908	496-9957
Keystone Ctr 1628 St John Rd *Web:* www.keystone.org	Keystone	CO	80435	970-513-5800	262-0152
Levy Economics Institute of Bard College Blithewood Rd Bard College *Web:* www.levyinstitute.org	Annandale-on-Hudson	NY	12504	845-758-7700	758-1149
Malcolm Wiener Ctr for Social Policy John F Kennedy School of Government Harvard University 79 John F Kennedy St *TF:* 866-845-6596 ■ *Web:* www.hks.harvard.edu	Cambridge	MA	02138	617-496-4082	496-9053

Organization	City	State	ZIP	Phone	Fax
Manhattan Institute for Policy Research 52 Vanderbilt Ave 3rd Fl *Web:* www.manhattan-institute.org	New York	NY	10017	212-599-7000	599-3494
Manpower Demonstration Research Corp 16 E 34th St 19th Fl *TF:* 800-221-3165 ■ *Web:* www.mdrc.org	New York	NY	10016	212-532-3200	684-0832
Margaret Chase Smith Policy Ctr University of Maine York Complex Ste 4 *TF:* 877-486-2364 ■ *Web:* www.umaine.edu	Orono	ME	04469	207-581-1648	581-1266
Mathematica Inc PO Box 2393 *Web:* www.mathematica-mpr.com	Princeton	NJ	08543	609-799-3535	799-0005
Mershon Ctr 1501 Neil Ave *Web:* www.mershoncenter.osu.edu	Columbus	OH	43201	614-292-1681	292-2407
Milken Institute 1250 Fourth St *Web:* www.milkeninstitute.org	Santa Monica	CA	90401	310-570-4600	570-4601
National Academy on an Aging Society 1220 L St NW Ste 901 *Web:* www.agingsociety.org	Washington	DC	20005	202-408-3375	842-1150
National Ctr for Policy Analysis 12770 Coit Rd Ste 800 *Web:* www.ncpa.org	Dallas	TX	75251	972-386-6272	386-0924
National Ctr for Public Policy Research (NCPPR) 501 Capitol Ct NE Ste 200 *Web:* ncppr.org	Washington	DC	20002	202-543-4110	543-5975
National Ctr on Institutions & Alternatives 7222 Ambassador Rd **Fax Area Code:* 410 ■ *Web:* www.ncianet.org	Baltimore	MD	21244	443-780-1300	597-9656*
Nelson A Rockefeller Institute of Government 411 State St *Web:* www.rockinst.org	Albany	NY	12203	518-443-5522	443-5788
New America Foundation 1899 L St NW *Web:* www.newamerica.org	Washington	DC	20036	202-986-2700	986-3696
Northeast-Midwest Institute (NMI) 50 F St NW Ste 950 *Web:* www.nemw.org	Washington	DC	20001	202-544-5200	544-0043
Pacific Research Institute for Public Policy (PRI) 1 Embarcadero Ctr *Web:* www.pacificresearch.org	San Francisco	CA	94111	415-989-0833	989-2411
Panetta Institute for Public Policy, The California State University Monterey Bay 100 Campus Ctr Bldg 86E *Web:* www.panettainstitute.org	Seaside	CA	93955	831-582-4200	582-4082
Phoenix Ctr for Advanced Legal & Economic Public Policy Studies 5335 Wisconsin Ave NW Ste 440 *Web:* www.phoenix-center.org	Washington	DC	20015	202-274-0235	244-8257
Princeton Institute for International & Regional Studies (PIIRS) Princeton University Bendheim Hall *TF:* 888-486-3339 ■ *Web:* www.princeton.edu/piirs	Princeton	NJ	08544	609-258-4852	258-3988
Progress & Freedom Foundation (PFF) 1444 Eye St NW Ste 500 *Web:* www.pff.org	Washington	DC	20005	202-289-8928	289-6079
Progressive Policy Institute (PPI) 1101 14th St NW Ste 1250 *Web:* progressivepolicy.org	Washington	DC	20005	202-525-3926	525-3941
Public Agenda 6 E 39th St *TF:* 800-659-4044 ■ *Web:* www.publicagenda.org	New York	NY	10016	212-686-6610	889-3461
RAND Corp 1776 Main St *TF:* 877-584-8642 ■ *Web:* www.rand.org	Santa Monica	CA	90401	310-393-0411	393-4818
Reason Public Policy Institute 3415 S Sepulveda Blvd Ste 400 *TF:* 888-732-7668 ■ *Web:* www.reason.org	Los Angeles	CA	90034	310-391-2245	391-4395
Renewable Energy Policy Project (REPP) 1612 K St NW Ste 1200	Washington	DC	20006	202-293-2898	
Resources for the Future 1616 P St NW *Web:* www.rff.org	Washington	DC	20036	202-328-5000	939-3460
Robert J Dole Institute of Politics 2350 Petefish Dr *Web:* www.doleinstitute.org	Lawrence	KS	66045	785-864-4900	864-1414
Rockford Institute 928 N Main St *TF:* 800-383-0680 ■ *Web:* chroniclesmagazine.org	Rockford	IL	61103	815-964-5053	964-9403
Schneider Institute for Health Policy Brandeis University 415 S St *Web:* sihp.brandeis.edu	Waltham	MA	02454	781-736-3964	
Science & Environmental Policy Project 1600 S Eads St Ste 712-S *Web:* www.sepp.org	Arlington	VA	22202	212-664-4555	
Social Science Research Council (SSRC) 810 Seventh Ave *Web:* www.ssrc.org	New York	NY	10019	212-377-2700	377-2727
Tellus Institute 11 Arlington St *Web:* www.tellus.org	Boston	MA	02116	617-266-5400	266-8303
Urban Institute 2100 M St NW *TF:* 866-518-3874 ■ *Web:* www.urban.org	Washington	DC	20037	202-833-7200	
Weatherhead Ctr for International Affairs Harvard Univ 1737 Cambridge St *Web:* www.wcfia.harvard.edu	Cambridge	MA	02138	617-495-4420	495-8292
Weil Program on Collaborative Governance Ctr for Business & Government, The Harvard Univ John F Kennedy School of Government Weil Hall 79 JFK St *Web:* www.hks.harvard.edu/m-rcbg/wpcg	Cambridge	MA	02138	617-496-0587	496-6104
Winrock International 2101 Riverfront Dr *Web:* www.winrock.org	Little Rock	AR	72202	501-280-3000	280-3090
Woodrow Wilson International Ctr for Scholars 1 Woodrow Wilson Plz 1300 Pennsylvania Ave NW *Web:* wilsoncenter.org	Washington	DC	20004	202-691-4000	691-4001
World Policy Institute (WPI) 220 Fifth Ave 9th Fl *TF:* 800-207-8354 ■ *Web:* www.worldpolicy.org	New York	NY	10001	212-481-5005	481-5009
World Resources Institute (WRI) 10 G St NE Ste 800 *Web:* www.wri.org	Washington	DC	20002	202-729-7600	729-7610
Worldwatch Institute 1776 Massachusetts Ave NW *TF:* 877-539-9946 ■ *Web:* www.worldwatch.org	Washington	DC	20036	202-452-1999	296-7365

635 PUBLIC RECORDS SEARCH SERVICES

See Also Investigative Services *p. 2596*

Phone | Fax

Accufax PO Box 35563 Tulsa OK 74153 800-256-8898 936-3027*
**Fax Area Code:* 866 ■ *TF:* 800-256-8898 ■ *Web:* www.accufax-us.com

All-Search & Inspection Inc
1108 E S Union Ave Midvale UT 84047 801-984-8160 984-8170
TF: 800-227-3152 ■ *Web:* www.all-search.com

American Driving Records Inc
2860 Gold Tailings Ct PO Box 1970 Rancho Cordova CA 95670 916-456-3200 456-3332
TF: 800-766-6877 ■ *Web:* www.adr-inc.com

AmRent 250 E BRd St 21st Fl Columbus OH 43215 713-266-1870
TF: 800-324-4595 ■ *Web:* www.amrent.com

Applicant Insight Ltd
5396 School Rd PO Box 458 New Port Richey FL 34652 800-771-7703 890-6454
TF: 800-771-7703 ■ *Web:* applicantinsight.com

Apscreen Inc PO Box 80639 Rancho Santa Margarita CA 92688 949-646-4003 277-2733*
**Fax Area Code:* 888 ■ *TF:* 800-277-2733 ■ *Web:* www.apscreen.com

Background Bureau Inc
2019 Alexandria Pike Highland Heights KY 41076 859-781-3400 781-9540
TF: 800-854-3990 ■ *Web:* www.backgroundbureau.com

Background Information Services Inc
1800 30th St Ste 204 Boulder CO 80301 303-442-3960 442-1004
TF: 800-433-6010 ■ *Web:* www.bisi.com

Best Reports Inc PO Box 546 Richmond IL 60071 815-678-2703 839-7440
Web: www.bestreports.net

Capitol Lien Records & Research Inc
1010 N Dale St Saint Paul MN 55117 651-488-0100 488-0200
TF: 800-845-4077 ■ *Web:* www.capitollien.com

Capitol Services Inc 206 E 9th St Ste 1300 Austin TX 78701 800-345-4647 432-3622
TF: 800-345-4647 ■ *Web:* www.capitolservices.com

CARCO Group Inc 5000 Corporate Ct Holtsville NY 11742 631-862-9300 584-7094
TF: 800-645-4556 ■ *Web:* www.carcogroup.com

CCH Washington Service Bureau Inc
1015 15th St NW 10th Fl Washington DC 20005 202-312-6600
TF: 800-955-5219 ■ *Web:* www.wsb.com

CDI Credit Inc
6160 Peachtree Dunwoody Rd NE Ste B-210 Atlanta GA 30328 770-350-5070 394-2197
TF: 800-633-3961 ■ *Web:* www.cdicredit.com

Charles Jones LLC PO Box 8488 Trenton NJ 08650 800-792-8888 883-0677
TF: 800-792-8888 ■ *Web:* www.charlesjones.com

Colby Attorneys Service Company Inc
111 Washington Ave Ste 703 Albany NY 12210 800-832-1220
TF: 800-832-1220 ■ *Web:* www.colbyservice.com

CoreLogic SafeRent 7300 Westmore Rd Ste 3 Rockville MD 20850 866-873-3651 715-1212*
**Fax Area Code:* 240 ■ *TF:* 866-873-3651 ■ *Web:* www.corelogic.com

CT Lien Solutions 2727 Allen Pkwy Ste 1000 Houston TX 77019 800-833-5778 850-5194*
**Fax Area Code:* 877 ■ *TF:* 800-833-5778 ■ *Web:* ctliensolutions.com

D+H CollateralGuard RC (CSRS)
4126 Norland Ave Ste 200 Burnaby BC V5G3S8 604-637-4000 637-4001
TF: 866-873-9780 ■ *Web:* www.csrs.ca

Doc-U-Search Inc 63 Pleasant St PO Box 777 Concord NH 03301 800-332-3034 224-2794*
**Fax Area Code:* 603 ■ *TF:* 800-332-3034 ■ *Web:* www.docusearchinc.com

Driving Records Facilities PO Box 1086 Glen Burnie MD 21061 800-772-5510 760-5837*
**Fax Area Code:* 410 ■ *TF:* 800-772-5510 ■ *Web:* www.dr-rec-fac.com

Edge Information Management Inc
1682 W Hibiscus Blvd Melbourne FL 32901 321-722-3343 780-3299*
**Fax Area Code:* 800 ■ *TF:* 800-725-3343 ■ *Web:* www.edgeinformation.com

Employment Screening Services Inc
627 E Sprague St Ste 100 Spokane WA 99202 509-624-3851 321-2905*
**Fax Area Code:* 800 ■ *TF:* 800-473-7778 ■ *Web:* www.employscreen.com

Explore Information Services LLC
2900 Lone Oak Pkwy Ste 140 PO Box 21636 St. Paul MN 55121 800-531-9125 681-4476*
**Fax Area Code:* 651 ■ *TF:* 800-531-9125 ■ *Web:* www.exploredata.com

Fidelifacts 42 Broadway Ste 1548 New York NY 10004 212-425-1520 248-5619
TF: 800-678-0007 ■ *Web:* www.fidelifacts.com

Government Liaison Services Inc (GLS)
200 N Glebe Rd Ste 321 Arlington VA 22203 703-524-8200 525-8451
TF: 800-642-6564 ■ *Web:* www.trademarkinfo.com

HireRight Inc 5151 California Ave Irvine CA 92617 949-428-5800
TF: 800-400-2761 ■ *Web:* www.hireright.com

IMI Data Search Inc
275 E Hillcrest Dr Ste 102 Thousand Oaks CA 91360 805-495-1149 495-0310
TF: 800-860-7779 ■ *Web:* www.imidatasearch.com

Information Management Systems Inc
114 W Main St Ste 211 PO Box 2924 New Britain CT 06050 860-229-1119 225-5524
TF: 888-403-8347 ■ *Web:* www.imswebb.com

KnowX LLC 730 Peachtree St Atlanta GA 30308 404-541-0220 541-0260

Kress Employment Screening
320 Westcott St Ste 108 Houston TX 77007 713-880-3693 880-3694
TF: 888-636-3693 ■ *Web:* www.kressinc.com

Kroll Background America Inc
100 Centerview Dr Ste 300 Nashville TN 37214 615-320-9800
TF: 800-697-7189 ■ *Web:* www.kroll.com

Laborchex Co, The 2506 Lakeland Dr Ste 200 Jackson MS 39232 601-664-6760 844-2722*
**Fax Area Code:* 800 ■ *TF:* 800-880-0366 ■ *Web:* www.laborchex.com

Legal Data Resources Inc
2816 W Summerdale Ave Chicago IL 60625 773-561-2468
TF: 844-732-2437 ■ *Web:* www.ldrsearch.com

LegalEase Inc 211 E 43rd St Ste 2203 New York NY 10017 212-393-9070 580-4761*
**Fax Area Code:* 888 ■ *TF:* 800-393-1277 ■ *Web:* www.legaleaseinc.com

MLQ Attorney Services
2000 River Edge Pkwy Ste 885 Atlanta GA 30328 770-984-7007
TF: 800-446-8794 ■ *Web:* www.mlqattorneyservices.com

OPENonline 1650 Lk Shore Dr Ste 350 Columbus OH 43204 614-481-6999 481-6980
TF: 888-381-5656 ■ *Web:* www.openonline.com

Orange Tree Employment Screening
7275 Ohms Ln Minneapolis MN 55439 952-941-9040 941-9041
TF: 800-886-4777 ■ *Web:* www.orangetreescreening.com

Parasec Inc
2804 Gateway Oaks Dr Ste 200
PO Box 160568 Sacramento CA 95833 800-533-7272 603-5868
TF General: 800-533-7272 ■ *Web:* www.parasec.com

Penncorp Servicegroup Inc
600 N Second St Ste 401 Harrisburg PA 17101 717-234-2300 264-1137*
**Fax Area Code:* 800 ■ *TF:* 800-544-9050 ■ *Web:* www.penncorp.net/default/default.htm

Property Owners Exchange Inc
6630 Baltimore National Pk Ste 208 Catonsville MD 21228 410-719-0100
TF: 800-869-3200 ■ *Web:* www.poeknows.com

Questel Orbit 1725 Duke St Ste 625 Alexandria VA 22314 703-519-1820 519-1821
TF: 800-456-7248 ■ *Web:* www.questel.com

Quick Search 4155 Buena Vista Dallas TX 75204 214-358-2880
Web: quicksius.com

Record Search America Inc 1201 N Liberty St Boise ID 83704 208-375-1906

Rental Research Services Inc
7525 Mitchell Rd Ste 301 Eden Prairie MN 55344 952-935-5700 935-9212
TF: 800-328-0333 ■ *Web:* www.rentalresearch.com

Search Company International
1535 Grant St Ste 140 Denver CO 80203 303-863-1800 863-7767
TF: 800-727-2120 ■ *Web:* www.searchcompanyintl.com

Search Network Ltd
1503 42nd St Ste 210 West Des Moines IA 50266 515-223-1153
TF: 800-383-5050 ■ *Web:* www.searchnetworkltd.com

SearchTec Inc 314 N 12th St Ste 100 Philadelphia PA 19107 215-963-0888 851-8775
Web: www.searchtec.com

Securitech Inc 8230 E Broadway Blvd Tucson AZ 85710 520-721-0305
TF: 888-792-4473 ■ *Web:* www.hiresafe.com

TABB Inc PO Box 10 Chester NJ 07930 800-887-8222
TF: 800-887-8222 ■ *Web:* www.tabb.net

Thomson CompuMark 500 Victory Rd North Quincy MA 02171 617-479-1600 543-1983*
**Fax Area Code:* 800 ■ *TF:* 800-692-8833 ■ *Web:* trademarks.thomsonreuters.com

TML Information Services Inc
11655 Queens Blvd Forest Hills NY 11375 718-793-3737 544-2853

UCC Filing & Search Services Inc
1574 Village Sq Blvd Ste 100 Tallahassee FL 32309 850-681-6528 681-6528

Unisearch Inc 1780 Barnes Blvd SW Tumwater WA 98512 360-956-9500 531-1717*
**Fax Area Code:* 800 ■ *TF:* 800-722-0708 ■ *Web:* www.unisearch.com

USIS 7799 Leesburg Pk Ste 1100 Falls Church VA 22043 703-448-0178

Verified Credentials Inc
20890 Kenbridge Ct Lakeville MN 55044 952-985-7200 985-7218
TF: 800-473-4934 ■ *Web:* www.verifiedcredentials.com

Westlaw Court Express
1100 13th St NW Ste 300 Washington DC 20005 202-423-2163
TF: 877-362-7387 ■ *Web:* www.courtexpress.westlaw.com

636 PUBLIC RELATIONS FIRMS

See Also Advertising Agencies *p. 1695*

Phone | Fax

5W Public Relations LLC
1166 Ave of the Americas 4th Fl New York NY 10036 212-999-5585
Web: www.5wpr.com

A Larry Ross Communications Inc
4300 Marsh Ridge Rd Ste 114 Carrollton TX 75010 972-267-1111
Web: www.alarryross.com

A&A Merchandising Ltd 3250 Lakeshore Blvd W Toronto ON M8V1M1 416-503-3343
Web: www.aamerch.com

A&R Partners Inc 201 Baldwin Ave San Mateo CA 94401 650-762-2800
Web: www.arpartners.com

Abbi Agency Inc, The 275 Hill St Ste 250 Reno NV 89501 775-323-2977
Web: theabbiagency.com

Ackermann Public Relations & Marketing
1111 Northshore Dr Ste N-400 Knoxville TN 37919 865-584-0550 588-3009
TF General: 877-325-9453 ■ *Web:* www.ackermannpr.com

Admarc Southwest Ltd 10 Desta Dr Ste 170LL Midland TX 79705 432-687-1127
TF: 888-823-6272 ■ *Web:* admarc.com

Advocacy Solutions LLC
4 Richmond Sq Ste 300 Providence RI 02906 401-831-3700
Web: advocacysolutionsllc.com

Advocal 1000 Q St Sacramento CA 95811 916-446-6161
Web: www.advocal.com

Alcalde & Fay 2111 Wilson Blvd 8th Fl Arlington VA 22201 703-841-0626
Web: www.alcalde-fay.com

Allied Experiential 111 E 12 St 2nd Fl New York NY 10003 212-253-8777
Web: www.grandcentralmarketing.com

Amin Hallihan LLC 444 N Orleans St Fourth Fl Chicago IL 60654 312-466-1033
Web: www.amintalati.com

Andrea Obston Marketing Communications LLC
3 Regency Dr Bloomfield CT 06002 860-243-1447
Web: www.aomc.com

Andrew Edson & Associates Inc 89 Bounty Ln Jericho NY 11753 516-931-0873
Web: www.edsonpr.com

Anne Klein & Assoc Inc
1000 Atrium Way Ste 102 Mount Laurel NJ 08054 856-866-0411
Web: www.akleinpr.com

APCO Worldwide 700 12th St Washington DC 20005 202-778-1000 466-6002
Web: www.apcoworldwide.com

Apex Group
1201 1201 K St Ste 750 St Ste 750 Sacramento CA 95814 916-444-3116
Web: theapexgroup.net

Arment Dietrich Public Relations
PO Box 13013 Ste 4n Chicago IL 60613 312-878-6406
Web: www.armentdietrich.com

Articulon 2841 Plz Pl Ste 105 Raleigh NC 27612 919-232-5008
Web: www.articulon.com

Ascend Marketing LLC 3904 W Vickery Blvd Fort Worth TX 76107 817-886-0014
Web: ascend-marketing.com

Asher Agency Inc 535 W Wayne St Fort Wayne IN 46802 260-424-3373
Web: www.asheragency.com

Atomic Public Relations LLC
735 Market St 4th Fl San Francisco CA 94103 415-593-1400
Web: www.atomicpr.com

Phone Fax

AutoCom Associates
74 W Long Lk Rd Ste 103 .... Bloomfield Hills MI 48304 248-647-8621
Web: www.usautocom.com
Axia Public Relations 222 E Forsyth St .... Jacksonville FL 32202 904-416-1500
Web: www.axiapr.com
B & B Media Group 109 S Main St .... Corsicana TX 75110 903-872-0517
TF: 800-927-0517 ■ *Web:* www.tbbmedia.com
BackBay Communications Inc 20 Park Plz Ste 801 .... Boston MA 02116 617-556-9982
Web: www.backbaycommunications.com
Backbone Media LLC 69 Milk St Ste 306 .... Westborough MA 01581 508-366-2100
Web: backbonemedia.com
Baltz & Co 49 W 23rd St Fl 9 .... New York NY 10010 212-982-8300
Web: www.baltzco.com
Barnum Sales and Marketing
2720 Beechwood Dr Se .... Grand Rapids MI 49506 616-949-9408
Web: barnumsales.com
Barokas Public Relations
71 Columbia St Ste 325 .... Seattle WA 98104 206-264-8220
Web: www.barokas.com
barry r. epstein associates Inc
9273 Rutledge Ave .... Boca Raton FL 33434 561-852-0000
Web: www.publicrelations.nu
Bawmann Group Inc, The 1755 High St .... Denver CO 80218 303-320-7790
Web: www.morethanpr.com
Behan Communications Inc 86 Glen St .... New York NY 12801 518-792-3856
Web: www.behancommunications.com
Bender/Helper Impact (BHI)
11500 W Olympic Blvd Ste 655 .... Los Angeles CA 90064 310-473-4147
Web: www.bhimpact.com
Beyond Marketing 2001 Main St Ste 301 .... Wheeling WV 26003 304-232-4544
Web: www.beyondmk.com
Bianchi PR Inc 888 W Big Beaver Rd Ste 777 .... Troy MI 48084 248-269-1122
Web: www.bianchipr.com
Birch Tree Promotions 5 tyng st .... Newburyport MA 01950 978-270-3852
Web: www.birchtreepromotions.com
Birnbach Communications Inc
20 Devereux St Ste 3A .... Marblehead MA 01945 781-639-6701
Web: www.birnbachcom.com
Bite 345 Spear St Ste 750 .... San Francisco CA 94105 415-365-0222 365-0223
Web: www.biteglobal.com
Blattel Communications
250 Montgomery St Ste 1200 .... San Francisco CA 94104 415-397-4811
Web: www.blattel.com
Bleublancrouge Inc
606 rue Cathcart bureau 1007 .... Montreal QC H3B1K9 514-875-7007
Web: www.bleublancrouge.ca
Blick & Staff Communications Inc
130 S Bemiston Ste 501 .... St. Louis MO 63105 314-727-5700
Web: blickandstaff.com
Blue Plate Communications Inc 202 Bussey St .... Dedham MA 02026 781-453-0330
Web: www.blueplate.com
BluePoint Venture Marketing 17 Draper Rd .... Wayland MA 01778 978-509-8444
Web: www.bluepointmktg.com
Boardroom Communications Inc
Bank Of America Plaza 1776 N Pine Island Rd
Ste 320 .... Fort Lauderdale FL 33322 954-370-8999
TF: 877-773-4761 ■ *Web:* www.boardroompr.com
Boca Communications LLC 2159 Powell St .... San Francisco CA 94133 415-738-7718
Web: www.bocacommunications.com
Bohle Co, The 1625 Stanford St .... Santa Monica CA 90404 310-785-0515
Web: www.bohle.com
Bolt Public Relations 2911 State St Ste K .... Carlsbad CA 92008 760-730-7400
Web: www.boltpr.com
Bouvier Kelly Inc 212 S Elm St Ste 200 .... Greensboro NC 27401 336-275-7000
Web: www.bouvierkelly.com
Brandon Assoc 29 Commonwealth Ave Ste 901 .... Boston MA 02116 857-362-7360
Web: www.brandonassociatesllc.com
Brew Media Relations 250 Lafayette St Ste 3R .... New York NY 10012 212-677-4835
Web: www.brewpr.com
Bridge Global Strategies LLC
276 Fifth Ave Ste 205 .... New York NY 01001 212-583-1043
Web: www.bridgeny.com
Calhoun & Company Communications LLC
3275 Sacramento St .... San Francisco CA 94115 415-346-2929
Web: calhounwine.com
Calibre International LLC
6250 N Irwindale Ave .... Irwindale CA 91702 626-969-4660
Web: highcaliberline.com
Campbell Marketing & Communications
3200 Greenfield St Ste 280 .... Dearborn MI 48120 313-336-9000
Web: www.campbellmarketing.com
Carmichael Lynch Spong 110 N Fifth St .... Minneapolis MN 55403 612-334-6000 375-8501
Web: spongpr.com
Carol Fox & Associates 1412 W Belmont Ave .... Chicago IL 60657 773-327-3830
Web: www.carolfoxassociates.com
Carreno Group Inc 714 Parker St .... Houston TX 77007 713-426-4300
Web: www.carrenogroup.com
Carrot & Stick Inc 115 New St Ste A .... Decatur GA 30030 404-371-1891
Web: www.carrotandstick.com
Cary Francis Group Inc PO Box 321050 .... Franklin WI 53132 414-304-6400 421-4229
Casey Communications Inc
8301 Maryland Ave Ste 350 .... St. Louis MO 63105 314-721-2828
Web: www.caseycomm.com
Cassidy & Associates
700 13th St Nw Ste 400 .... Washington DC 20005 202-347-0773
Web: www.cassidy.com
Cerrell Assoc Inc 320 N Larchmont Blvd .... Los Angeles CA 90004 323-466-3445 466-8653
Web: www.cerrell.com
Chandler Chicco Agency 450 W 15th St 7th Fl .... New York NY 10011 212-229-8400 229-8496
Web: www.ccapr.com
Charles Ryan Assoc Inc
601 Morris St Ste 301 .... Charleston WV 25301 877-342-0161
TF: 877-342-0161 ■ *Web:* www.charlesryan.com

Phone Fax

CHEN PR Inc
Reservoir Pl 1601 Trapelo Rd Ste 360 .... Waltham MA 02451 781-466-8282
Web: www.chenpr.com
Clockwork Marketing Services Inc
10245 Centurion Pkwy N Ste 315 .... Jacksonville FL 32256 904-280-7960
Web: www.clockworkmarketing.com
Cohn & Wolfe 200 Fifth Ave .... New York NY 10010 212-798-9700 329-9900
Web: www.cohnwolfe.com
Colehour & Cohen 1011 Wern Ave Ste 702 .... Seattle WA 98104 206-262-0363
Web: www.cplusc.com
Colette Phillips Communications
1 Mckinley Sqr Fl 6 .... Boston MA 02109 617-357-5777
Web: cpcglobal.com
Compassionate Passages Inc
29869 White Hall Dr .... Farmington Hills MI 48331 248-592-9390
Web: compassionatepassages.org
Cone Inc 855 Boylston St .... Boston MA 02116 617-227-2111 227-2111
Web: www.conecomm.com
Connect PR 1 Market St 36th Fl .... San Francisco CA 94105 415-222-9691
TF: 800-455-8855 ■ *Web:* www.connectmarketing.com
Connect Public Relations 80 East 100 North .... Provo UT 84606 801-373-7888
Web: www.connectmarketing.com
Coyne Public Relations LLC
5 Wood Hollow Rd .... Parsippany NJ 07054 973-588-2000
Web: www.coynepr.com
Cramer-Krasselt 246 E Chicago St .... Milwaukee WI 53202 414-227-3500
Web: www.c-k.com
Crash Avenue LLC 640 S 4th St .... Louisville KY 40204 502-583-0333
Web: www.crash-avenue.com
Creatine Marketing 3840 Rosin Ct Ste 130 .... Sacramento CA 95834 916-302-4742
Web: creatinemarketing.com
Curt Pringle & Associates LLC
2400 E Katella Ave Ste 350 .... Anaheim CA 92806 714-939-9070
Web: curtpringle.com
D Exposito & Partners LLC
875 Sixth Ave 25th Fl .... New York NY 10001 646-747-8800
Web: www.newamericanagency.com
D.M. Reid Associates Ltd 50 Grove St Ste 227 .... Salem MA 01970 978-744-3818
Web: www.dmreid.com
Dakota Communications
2999 Overland Ave Ste 210 .... Los Angeles CA 90064 310-815-8444
Web: www.dakcomm.com
Dan Klores Communications Inc (DKC)
261 Fifth Ave .... New York NY 10016 212-685-4300 685-9024
Web: www.dkcnews.com
DAVIES 808 State St .... Santa Barbara CA 93101 805-963-5929
Web: www.daviespublicaffairs.com
Deardorff Associates 319 E Lea Blvd .... Wilmington DE 19802 302-764-7573
Web: www.deardorffassociates.com
Dehart & Company Public Relations LLC
1375 Lenoir Rhyne Blvd Se Ste 109 .... Hickory NC 28602 828-325-4966
Web: www.dehartandcompany.com
Denise Resnik And Associates Inc
717 E Maryland Ave Ste 110 .... Phoenix AZ 85014 602-956-8834
Web: www.resnikpr.com
Dennis Garberg & Associates Inc
14001 Marshall Dr .... Lenexa KS 66215 913-890-0900
Web: www.sunflowergroup.com
Dennis PR Group 41 Crossroads Ste 228 .... West Hartford CT 06117 860-523-7500
Web: www.dennispr.com
Deveney Communication Consulting LLC
2406 Chartres St .... New Orleans LA 70117 504-949-3999
Web: www.deveney.com
DeVries Public Relations 909 Third Ave .... New York NY 10022 212-546-8500
Web: www.devriesglobal.com
Digennaro Communications
18 W 21st St 6th Fl .... New York City NY 10010 212-966-9525
Web: www.digennaro-usa.com
Digiwaxx LLC 349 5th Ave 4th Fl .... New York NY 10016 212-665-8607
Web: www.digiwaxx.com
Dittoe Public Relations Inc
2815 E 62nd St Ste 300 .... Indianapolis IN 46220 317-202-2280
Web: www.dittoepr.com
Dix & Eaton Inc 200 Public Sq Ste 3900 .... Cleveland OH 44114 216-241-0405
Web: www.dix-eaton.com
Dixon Schwabl Advertising 1595 Moseley Rd .... Victor NY 14564 585-383-0380
Web: dixonschwabl.com
DJ Case & Assoc Inc 317 E Jefferson Blvd .... Mishawaka IN 46545 574-258-0100
Web: www.djcase.com
Doerr Associates 31 Church St .... Winchester MA 01890 781-729-9020
Web: mdoerr.com
Dovetail Public Relations
15951 Los Gatos Blvd Ste 16 .... Los Gatos CA 95032 408-395-3600
Web: www.dovetailpr.com
Downey Mcgrath Group Inc
1225 I St Nw Ste 600 .... Washington DC 20005 202-789-1110
Duffey Communications Inc
3379 Peachtree Rd NE Ste 300 .... Atlanta GA 30326 404-266-2600
Web: www.duffey.com
DVL Public Relations & Adv
700 12th Ave S Ste 400 .... Nashville TN 37203 615-244-1818
Web: www.dvl.com
DW Turner Inc 400 Gold Ave SW 12th Fl .... Albuquerque NM 87102 505-888-5877
Web: agenda-global.com
E. Boineau & Co 128 Beaufain St .... Charleston SC 29401 843-723-1462
Web: www.eboineauandco.com
Echo Media Group Inc 12711 Newport Ave Ste A .... Tustin CA 92780 714-573-0899
Web: www.echomediapr.com
Edelman Public Relations Worldwide
200 E Randolph Dr 63rd Fl .... Chicago IL 60601 312-240-3000 240-2900
Web: www.edelman.com
Edge Communications Inc
17328 Ventura Blvd Ste 324 .... Encino CA 91316 818-990-5001
Web: www.edgecommunicationsinc.com

Firm	City	State	ZIP	Phone	Fax
Eileen Koch & Co 230 S Hamilton Dr *Web:* www.eileenkoch.com	Beverly Hills	CA	90211	310-274-5586	
Eisbrenner Public Relations 2950 W Sq Lk Rd Ste 100 *Web:* www.eisbrenner.com	Troy	MI	48098	248-641-1446	
Elasticity LLC 1008 Locust Ave Ste 300 *Web:* goelastic.com	St. Louis	MO	63101	314-561-8253	
Entertainment Fusion Group Inc 8899 Beverly Blvd Ste 412 *Web:* www.efgpr.com	Los Angeles	CA	90048	310-432-0020	
Epoch 5 Public Relations 755 New York Ave *Web:* www.epoch5.com	Huntington	NY	11743	631-427-1713	
Equals Three Communications 7910 Woodmont Ave Ste 200	Bethesda	MD	20814	301-656-3100	652-5264
Erwin-Penland Inc 125 E Broad St *Web:* www.erwinpenland.com	Greenville	SC	29601	864-271-0500	
ES3 Inc 1625 Star Batt Dr	Rochester Hills	MI	48309	248-537-0110	
fama PR Inc Liberty Wharf 250 Northern Ave Ste 300 *Web:* www.famapr.com	Boston	MA	02210	617-986-5002	
Feinstein Kean Healthcare 245 First St Fl 10 *Web:* www.fkhealth.com	Cambridge	MA	02142	617-577-8110	
FIGHTER Interactive Inc 388 Beale St Ste 1014 *Web:* www.wearefighter.com	San Francisco	CA	94105	917-434-6102	
Fleishman-Hillard Inc 200 N Broadway *Web:* www.fleishmanhillard.com	Saint Louis	MO	63102	314-982-1700	
Focus Media Inc 10 Matthews St *Web:* www.focusmediausa.com	Goshen	NY	10924	845-294-3342	
Freeman Public Relations 16 Furler St *Web:* www.freemanpr.com	Totowa	NJ	07512	973-470-0400	
French West Vaughan 112 E Hargett St *Web:* fwv-us.com	Raleigh	NC	27601	919-832-6300	832-8322
Fresh Ideas Group Inc 2400 Spruce St Ste 100 *Web:* www.freshideasgroup.com	Boulder	CO	80302	303-449-2108	
Gally Public Affairs Inc 111 Cathedral St Ste 203 *Web:* www.gallypublicaffairs.com	Annapolis	MD	21401	410-990-0069	
Gard Communications 1140 SW 11th Ave Fl 3 *Web:* gardcommunications.com	Portland	OR	97205	503-221-0100	
Gelia, Wells & Mohr Inc 390 S Youngs Rd *Web:* www.gelia.com	Williamsville	NY	14221	716-629-3200	
Gibbs & Soell, Inc. 60 E 42nd St Fl 44 *Web:* www.gscommunications.com	New York	NY	10165	212-697-2600	697-2646
Giles Communications LLC 2975 Westchester Ave Ste 402 *Web:* giles.com	Purchase	NY	10577	914-644-3500	
Global Results Communications 9 Corporate Park Ste 250 *Web:* www.globalresultspr.com	Irvine	CA	92606	949-608-0276	
GMR Marketing LLC 5000 S Towne Dr *Web:* www.gmrmarketing.com	New Berlin	WI	53151	262-786-5600	
Gordon C James Public Relations Inc 4715 N 32nd St Ste 104 *Web:* www.gcjpr.com	Phoenix	AZ	85018	602-274-1988	
Gravina Smith & Matte Inc 4575 Via Royale Ste 214 *Web:* www.gravinasmith.com	Fort Myers	FL	33919	941-598-3001	
Green Bear Group 503 Seaport Ct Ste 105 *Web:* www.greenbeargroup.com	Redwood City	CA	94063	415-377-8431	
Griffin & Associates 119 Dartmouth Dr SE *Web:* www.griffinassoc.com	Albuquerque	NM	87106	505-764-4444	
Group Ist 494 8th Ave Fl 22 *Web:* www.groupist.com	New York	NY	10001	212-594-8787	
Gulf Coast Tmc 7670 Hwy 10 *TF:* 866-683-6636 ■ *Web:* www.gulfcoasttmc.com	Ethel	LA	70730	225-683-6636	
Hager Sharp Inc 1030 15th St NW Ste 600 E *Web:* www.hagersharp.com	Washington	DC	20005	202-842-3600	
Halliburton Investor Relations 14651 Dallas Pkwy Ste 800 *Web:* halliburtonir.com	Dallas	TX	75254	972-458-8000	
Harris, Deville & Associates Inc 521 Laurel St *Web:* hdaissues.com	Baton Rouge	LA	70801	225-344-0381	
Hawthorn Group LC 625 Slaters Ln # 100 *Web:* www.hawthorngroup.com	Alexandria	VA	22314	703-299-4499	299-4488
Hayzlett Companies Inc, The 2905 E Fireside Cir *Web:* hayzlett.com	Sioux Falls	SD	57103	650-697-6671	
Health Advocacy Strategies Llc 4126 E Madison St Ste 200 *Web:* www.hastrategies.com	Seattle	WA	98112	206-861-1000	
HG Marketing Group LLC 150 E State St *Web:* www.hgmarketing.com	Doylestown	PA	18901	215-340-3606	
Hicks Partners LLC 10 W Broad St Ste 900 *Web:* www.hickspartners.com	Columbus	OH	43215	614-221-2800	
Highwire Public Relations Inc 727 sansome st *Web:* www.highwirepr.com	San Francisco	CA	94111	415-963-4174	
Hill & Knowlton Inc 825 Third Ave *Web:* www.hillandknowlton.com	New York	NY	10022	212-885-0300	885-0570
HLB Communications Inc 875 N Michigan Ave	Chicago	IL	60611	312-649-0371	
HMA Public Relations 3610 N 44th St Ste 110 *Web:* hmapr.com	Phoenix	AZ	85018	602-957-8881	
Hubbell Group Inc, The 101 Derby St Ste 201 *Web:* www.hubbellgroup.com	Hingham	MA	02043	781-878-8882	
Hunter Public Relations 41 Madison Ave 5th Fl *TF:* 866-395-7710 ■ *Web:* www.hunterpr.com	New York	NY	10010	212-679-6600	679-6607
i.d.e.a. 444 W Beech St *Web:* www.theideabrand.com	San Diego	CA	92101	619-295-8232	
Impress Public Relations Inc 605 E Grant St Ste 106 *Web:* impresslabs.com	Phoenix	AZ	85004	602-443-0030	
Ink Inc 10561 Barkley St Ste 600 *Web:* www.inkincpr.com	Overland Park	KS	66212	816-753-6222	
InQuest Marketing Inc 9249 Ward Pkwy *Web:* www.inquestmarketing.com	Kansas City	MO	64114	816-994-0994	
Interprose Inc 2635 Steeplechase Dr *Web:* www.interprosepr.com	Reston	VA	20191	703-860-0577	
IPREX Inc 2861 Kingsland Ct *Web:* www.iprex.com	Atlanta	GA	30339	770-433-9084	
J P R Communications 5950 Canoga Ave Ste 430 *Web:* www.jprcom.com	Woodland Hills	CA	91367	818-884-8282	
J.C. Watts Companies 600 13th St Nw Ste 790 *Web:* www.wattsconsultinggroup.com	Washington	DC	20005	202-207-2854	
Jaffe Communications Inc 200 North Ave E *Web:* www.jaffecom.com	Westfield	NJ	07090	908-789-0700	
Jasculca/Terman & Assoc (JTPR) 730 N Franklin Ste 510 *Web:* www.jtpr.com	Chicago	IL	60654	312-337-7400	337-8189
Javelin Inc 1910 Locust St *Web:* javelinexperiential.com	Saint Louis	MO	63103	314-381-1450	
Jaymie Scotto & Associates LLC 295 Greenwich St Ste #551 *Web:* www.jaymiescotto.com	New York	NY	10007	201-839-0177	
Jones Agency, The 303 N Indian Canyon Dr *Web:* www.jonesagency.com	Palm Springs	CA	92262	760-325-1437	
Jones Huyett Partners Inc 3200 SW Huntoon St *Web:* jhpadv.com	Topeka	KS	66604	785-228-0900	
Kahn Media Inc 6900 Canby Ave Ste 102 *Web:* www.kahnmedia.com	Reseda	CA	91335	818-881-5246	
Katcher Vaughn & Bailey Public Relations Inc 401 Church St Ste 2100 *Web:* www.kvbpr.com	Nashville	TN	37219	615-248-8202	
KCSA Public Relations Worldwide 880 Third Ave # 6 *Web:* www.kcsa.com	New York	NY	10022	212-682-6300	697-0910
Keating & Co LLC 285 W Broadway Ste 460 *Web:* www.keatingco.com	New York	NY	10013	212-925-6900	
Keene Promotions Inc 450 Lexington St Ste 102 *Web:* www.keenepromotions.com	Auburndale	MA	02466	617-243-0101	
Kemper Lesnik Communications 500 Skokie Blvd 4th Fl *Web:* www.kemperlesnik.com	Northbrook	IL	60062	847-850-1818	559-0406
Ketchum 1285 Ave of the Americas *Web:* www.ketchum.com	New York	NY	10019	646-935-3900	935-4499
Kohnstamm Communications 400 Robert St N Ste 1450 *Web:* kohnstamm.com	Saint Paul	MN	55101	651-228-9141	
Kovak Likly Communications 23 Hubbard Rd *Web:* www.klcpr.com	Wilton	CT	06897	203-762-8833	
Krome Communications Inc 307 4th Ave *Web:* www.krome.com	Pittsburgh	PA	15222	412-471-0840	
Kurman Communications Inc 345 N Canal St Ste 1404 *Web:* kurman.com	Chicago	IL	60606	312-651-9000	
LaForce & Stevens 132 W 21st St *Web:* www.laforce-stevens.com	New York	NY	10011	212-242-9353	
Lanza Group LLC 1710 Defoor Ave NW Penthouse 2 *Web:* www.lanzagroup.com	Atlanta	GA	30318	404-350-0200	
Laura Davidson Public Relations Inc 72 Madison Ave Fl 11 Fl 8 *Web:* www.ldpr.com	New York	NY	10016	212-696-0660	
LeGrand Hart 1055 Auraria Pkwy Ste 200 *Web:* www.legrandhart.com	Denver	CO	80204	303-298-8470	
Lenzi Martin Communications 701 Hayes Ave	Oak Park	IL	60302	708-848-8404	
LEVICK LLC 1900 M St NW *Web:* levick.com	Washington	DC	20036	202-973-1300	
Linden Lab 945 Battery St *Web:* www.lindenlab.com	San Francisco	CA	94111	415-243-9000	
Lineo Group Ltd The 190 N Union St Ste 300 *Web:* www.lineogroup.com	Akron	OH	44304	330-475-1572	
Lois Paul & Partners (LPP) 1 Beacon St 2nd Fl *Web:* www.lpp.com	Boston	MA	02108	617-986-5700	
Love Communications 546 South 200 West *Web:* www.lovecomm.net	Salt Lake City	UT	84101	801-519-8880	
Lovio George Inc 681 W Forest Ave *Web:* www.loviogeorge.com	Detroit	MI	48201	313-832-2210	
Lukas Partners Inc 11915 P St Ste 100 *Web:* www.lukaspartners.com	Omaha	NE	68137	402-895-2552	
M Booth & Assoc Inc 300 Pk Ave S 12th Fl *Web:* www.mbooth.com	New York	NY	10010	212-481-7000	481-9440
Ma Cher (usa) Inc 1518 Abbot Kinney Blvd *Web:* www.macher.com	Venice	CA	90291	310-581-5222	
Maccabee Group Inc 211 N 1st St Ste 425 *Web:* www.maccabeegroup.com	Minneapolis	MN	55401	612-337-0087	
Makovsky + Co 16 E 34th St *Web:* www.makovsky.com	New York	NY	10016	212-508-9600	751-9710
Manning Selvage & Lee 375 Hudson St 14th Fl *Web:* northamerica.mslgroup.com	New York	NY	10014	646-500-7600	
Manzella Marketing Group 80 Sonwil Dr *Web:* manzellamarketing.com	Buffalo	NY	14225	716-681-6565	
Marcus Group Inc, The 150 Clove Rd Ste 11 *Web:* www.marcusgroup.com	Little Falls	NJ	07424	973-890-9590	
Martin Bontempo Matacera Bartlett Inc 212 W State St *Web:* www.mbigluckshaw.com	Trenton	NJ	08608	609-392-3100	

Firm	City	State	Zip	Phone	Fax
Marx Layne & Co 31420 NW Hwy. *Web:* www.marxlayne.com	Farmington Hills	MI	48334	248-855-6777	855-6719
Masto Public Relations Inc 1811 Western Ave *Web:* mastopr.com	Albany	NY	12203	518-786-6488	
Maximum Marketing Services Inc 833 W Jackson Blvd *Web:* www.maxmarketing.com	Chicago	IL	60607	312-226-4111	
McNally Temple Associates Inc 1817 Capitol Ave *Web:* www.mcnallytemple.com	Sacramento	CA	95811	916-447-8186	
McNeely Pigott & Fox 611 Commerce St Ste 2800 *TF:* 800-818-6953 ■ *Web:* www.mpf.com	Nashville	TN	37203	615-259-4000	259-4040
MCS Healthcare Public Relations 1420 US Hwy 206 Ste 100 *Web:* www.mcspr.com	Bedminster	NJ	07921	908-234-9900	470-4490
Mercury Public Affairs 137 Fifth Ave Ste 3 *Web:* www.mercuryllc.com	New York	NY	10010	212-681-1380	
Merkle Group Inc 7001 Columbia Gateway Dr *Web:* www.merkleinc.com	Columbia	MD	21046	443-542-4000	542-4758
Metis Communications Inc 294 Washington St *Web:* metiscomm.com	Boston	MA	02118	617-236-0500	
Mirrorball Group LLC 134 w 25th st *Web:* www.mirrorball.com	New York	NY	10001	212-604-9988	
Montesquieu Winery 8221 Arjons Dr. *TF:* 800-860-2378 ■ *Web:* www.montesquieu.com	San Diego	CA	92126	800-860-2378	
Morgan & Myers N 16 W 23233 Stone Ridge Dr Ste 200 *Web:* www.morganmyers.com	Weukesha	WI	53188	262-650-7260	
MSR Communications 832 Sansome St 2nd Fl *TF:* 866-247-6172 ■ *Web:* www.msrcommunications.com	San Francisco	CA	94111	415-989-9000	
Multi Marketing Corp 2033 N Fine Ave *Web:* multimarketingcorp.com	Fresno	CA	93727	559-454-9400	
MurphyEpson Inc 151 E Nationwide Blvd *Web:* murphyepson.com	Columbus	OH	43215	614-221-2885	
Neibart Group 20 Jay St Ste 820 *Web:* www.neibartgroup.com	Brooklyn	NY	11201	718-875-2300	
Nine Health Services Inc 1139 delaware st. *Web:* www.9healthfair.org	Denver	CO	80204	303-698-4455	
NM Marketing Communications Inc 706 Waukegan Rd. *Web:* www.nmmarketingbiz.com	Glenview	IL	60025	847-657-6011	
Nyhus Communications LLC 720 Third Ave Fl 12 *Web:* www.nyhus.com	Seattle	WA	98104	206-323-3733	
O'Malley Hansen Communications 180 N Wacker Dr Ste 400 *Web:* omalleyhansen.com	Chicago	IL	60606	312-377-0630	
O'reilly Public Relations 3403 10th St Ste 110 *Web:* www.oreillypr.com	Riverside	CA	92501	951-781-2240	
Ogden Ritnour 33 Sloan St *Web:* ogdenrit.com	Roswell	GA	30075	770-597-4703	
Ogilvy Public Relations Worldwide 636 11th Ave *Web:* www.ogilvypr.com	New York	NY	10036	212-880-5200	370-4636
Oliver Russell & Assoc Inc 217 S 11th St *Web:* www.oliverrussell.com	Boise	ID	83702	208-344-1734	344-1211
Otto Creative Marketing Inc 1611 Colley Ave *Web:* www.thinkotto.com	Norfolk	VA	23517	757-622-4050	
OutCast Agency, The 123 Townsend St 3rd Fl *Web:* www.outcastpr.com	San Francisco	CA	94107	415-392-8282	
Pacifico Inc 1190 Coleman Ave Ste 110 *Web:* www.pacifico.com	San Jose	CA	95110	408-327-8888	
Padilla Speer Beardsley Inc 1101 W River Pkwy Ste 400 *Web:* padillacrt.com	Minneapolis	MN	55415	612-455-1700	
Page One Public Relations Inc 2465 E Bayshore Rd Ste 348 *Web:* www.pageonepr.com	Palo Alto	CA	94303	650-565-9800	
Paul Werth Assoc Inc 10 N High St Ste300 *Web:* www.paulwerth.com	Columbus	OH	43215	614-224-8114	
Paul Wilmot Communications LLC 581 Sixth Ave *Web:* www.paulwilmot.com	New York	NY	10011	212-206-7447	
PepperCom Inc 470 Pk Ave S *Web:* www.peppercom.com	New York	NY	10016	212-931-6100	931-6159
Percepta LLC 290 Town Ctr Dr FairLn Plz N Ste 610 *Web:* www.percepta.com	Dearborn	MI	48126	313-390-0157	
Peritus Public Relations 2829 2nd Ave S Ste 335 *Web:* www.perituspr.com	Birmingham	AL	35233	205-267-6673	
Perry Communications Group Inc 925 L St Ste 1200 *Web:* perrycom.com	Sacramento	CA	95814	916-658-0144	
Picture Marketing Inc 1202 Grant Ave Ste D *Web:* www.picturemarketing.com	Novato	CA	94945	949-623-9889	
Porter Novelli International 75 Varick St 6th Fl *Web:* www.porternovelli.com	New York	NY	10013	212-601-8000	601-8101
Power PR 18103 Prairie Ave. *Web:* www.powerpr.com	Torrance	CA	90504	310-787-1940	
Pro Motion Inc 18405 Edison Ave. *Web:* www.promotion1.com	Chesterfield	MO	63005	636-449-3162	
Propheta Communications LLC 70 E 10th St Ste 6P *Web:* www.prophetacomm.com	New York	NY	10003	212-901-6914	
Prr (PRR) 1501 Fourth Ave Ste 550 *Web:* www.prrbiz.com	Seattle	WA	98101	206-623-0735	623-0731
Prx Inc 991 W Hedding St Ste 201 *Web:* www.prxdigital.com	San Jose	CA	95126	408-287-1700	

Firm	City	State	Zip	Phone	Fax
Public Conversations Project 46 Kondazian St *Web:* www.publicconversations.org	Watertown	MA	02472	617-923-1216	
Public Opinion Strategies LLC 214 N Fayette St *Web:* www.pos.org	Alexandria	VA	22314	703-836-7655	
Pyramid Communications Inc 1932 First Ave Ste 507 *Web:* pyramidcommunications.com	Seattle	WA	98101	206-374-7788	
Quest Corp of America Inc 3837 Northdale Blvd # 242 *Web:* qcausa.com	Tampa	FL	33624	813-926-2942	
R L f Communications Llc 301 N Elm St Ste 102 *Web:* rlfcommunications.com	Greensboro	NC	27401	336-553-1800	
R&J Public Relations LLC 1140 Route 22 E Ste 200 *Web:* www.randjsc.com	Bridgewater	NJ	08807	908-722-5757	
R&R Partners Inc 900 S Pavillion Ctr Dr *Web:* www.rrpartners.com	Las Vegas	NV	89144	702-228-0222	
Regan Communications Group Inc 106 Union Wharf *Web:* regancomm.com	Boston	MA	02109	617-488-2800	
Rendon Group Inc 1875 Conn Ave NW *Web:* www.rendon.com	Washington	DC	20009	202-745-4900	
Revive Public Relations LLC 915 Saint Vincent Ave. *Web:* www.thinkrevivehealth.com	Santa Barbara	CA	93101	805-617-2832	
RF|Binder Partners Inc 950 Third Ave 7th Fl. *Web:* www.rfbinder.com	New York	NY	10022	212-994-7600	
Richmond Public Relations 1411 Fourth Ave Ste 610 *Web:* www.richmondpr.com	Seattle	WA	98101	206-682-6979	
Richter7 280 South 400 West Ste 200 *Web:* www.richter7.com	Salt Lake City	UT	84101	801-521-2903	
Rinck Advertising 2 Great Falls Plz Unit 8 *Web:* www.rinckadvertising.com	Auburn	ME	04210	207-755-9470	
Riptide Communications Inc 2621 Palisade Ave Ste C *Web:* www.riptidecommunications.com	Bronx	NY	10463	212-260-5000	
RLM Public Relations Inc 989 Sixth Ave 3rd Fl *Web:* www.RLMpr.com	New York	NY	10018	212-741-5106	
RMR Assoc Inc 5870 Hubbard Dr *Web:* www.rmr.com	Rockville	MD	20852	301-230-0045	230-0046
Rob Bailey Communications 310 State Rt 17 *Web:* rbcpr.com	Upper Saddle River	NJ	07458	201-760-0200	
Ron Sachs Communications Inc 114 S Duval St *Web:* sachsmedia.com	Tallahassee	FL	32301	850-222-1996	
Rosen Group LLC, The 44 Wall St Ste 705 *Web:* rosengrouppr.com	New York	NY	10010	212-255-8455	
Rubin Communications Group Inc 4542 Bonney Rd Ste B *Web:* rubincommunications.com	Virginia Beach	VA	23462	757-456-5212	
Ruder Finn 301 E 57th St *Web:* www.ruderfinn.com	New York	NY	10022	212-593-6400	
Rulmeca Corp 6508 Windmill Way Ste B *Web:* www.rulmecacorp.com	Wilmington	NC	28405	910-794-9294	
Russo Partners LLC 729 Seventh Ave 17th Fl. *Web:* www.russopartnersllc.com	New York	NY	10019	212-845-4251	
S&S Public Relations Inc 150 N Upper Wacker Dr Ste 2010 *TF:* 800-287-2279 ■ *Web:* www.sspr.com	Chicago	IL	60606	800-287-2279	
Salter Mitchell Inc 117 S Gadsden St *Web:* www.saltermitchell.com	Tallahassee	FL	32301	850-681-3200	
SCG Governmental Affairs LLC 201 S Monroe St Ste 301 *Web:* www.scggov.com	Tallahassee	FL	32301	850-513-0004	
Schwartz Communications Inc 300 Fifth Ave *Web:* www.schwartzmsl.com	Waltham	MA	02451	781-684-0770	684-6500
Schwartz Ruth & Co 6 W 18th St Ste 6r *Web:* www.rcspr.com	New York	NY	10011	212-463-0684	
Scorr Marketing 2201 Central Ave Ste A *Web:* www.scorrmarketing.com	Kearney	NE	68847	308-237-5567	
Scott Public Relations 21201 Victory Blvd Ste 270 *Web:* scottpublicrelations.com	Canoga Park	CA	91303	818-610-0270	
Seigenthaler Public Relations Inc 115 29th Ave South *Web:* www.seig-pr.com	Nashville	TN	37212	615-244-1818	
Seyferth & Associates Inc 40 Monroe Ctr NW *TF:* 800-435-9539 ■ *Web:* www.seyferthpr.com	Grand Rapids	MI	49503	616-776-3511	
Shank Public Relations Counselors Inc 2611 Waterfront Pkwy E Dr Ste 310 *Web:* shankpr.com	Indianapolis	IN	46214	317-293-5590	
Shannon Systems LLC 173 Spark St *Web:* www.b2bgateway.net	Brockton	MA	02302	508-894-2150	
Shelton Group 12400 Coit Rd Ste 650 *Web:* www.sheltongroup.com	Dallas	TX	75251	972-239-5119	
SHIFT Communications LLC 275 Washington St Ste 410 *TF:* 800-494-8477 ■ *Web:* www.shiftcomm.com	Newton	MA	02458	617-779-1800	779-1899
Simon Public Relations Group Inc 200 S Broad St Ste 1160 *Web:* www.simonpr.com	Philadelphia	PA	19102	215-545-4715	
Sitrick & Co 1840 Century Pk E Ste 800 *TF:* 800-288-8809 ■ *Web:* www.sitrick.com	Los Angeles	CA	90067	310-788-2850	788-2855
Sloane & Co 7 Times Sq 17th Fl *Web:* www.sloanepr.com	New York	NY	10036	212-486-9500	486-9094

Phone | Fax

Smith Growth Partners
Mill Centre Penthouse 3000 Chestnut Ave Baltimore MD 21211 410-235-7004
Web: www.smithgrowthpartners.com

Southard Communications Inc
111 John St Ste 630 New York NY 10038 212-777-2220
Web: www.southardinc.com

Sparksight Inc 3520 Executive Ctr Dr Ste 150 Austin TX 78731 512-493-2070
Web: www.sparksight.com

Spitfire Strategies LLC 1800 M St NW Washington DC 20036 202-293-6200
Web: spitfirestrategies.com

Spread the News PR Inc 1236 Inverness Dr Lawrence KS 66049 785-842-8909
Web: www.spreadthenewspr.com

Stanton Public Relations & Marketing
880 Third Ave New York NY 10022 212-366-5300
Web: www.stantonprm.com

StartSampling Inc 195 E Elk Trail Carol Stream IL 60188 630-868-2000
Web: www.startsampling.com

Storefront Political Media
160 Pine St Ste 700 San Francisco CA 94111 415-834-0501
Web: www.storefrontpolitical.com

Strat@comm 1156 15th St NW Ste 800 Washington DC 20005 202-289-2001
Web: www.stratacomm.net

Sunshine Sachs & Associates
8409 santa monica blvd Los Angeles CA 90069 323-822-9300
Web: www.sunshinesachs.com

Taylor Global Inc 350 Fifth Ave New York NY 10118 212-714-1280 695-5685
Web: www.taylorstrategy.com

Tech Image Ltd 330 N Wabash Ave Ste 1900 Chicago IL 60611 847-279-0022
Web: www.techimage.com

Text 100 North America
100 Montgomery St San Francisco CA 94104 415-593-8400
Web: www.text100.com

Thomas Boyd Communications
117 N Church St Moorestown NJ 08057 856-642-6226
Web: thomasboyd.com

Thomas Collective Llc, The
37 W 28th St Fl 12 New York NY 10001 212-229-2294
Web: www.thethomascollective.com

Thomson Safaris 14 Mt Auburn St Watertown MA 02472 617-923-0426
TF: 800-235-0289 ■ *Web:* www.thomsonsafaris.com

Thorp & Co
150 Alhambra Cir Ste 900 Coral Gables Miami FL 33134 305-446-2700
Web: www.thorpco.com

Tierney Communications
200 S Broad St 10th Fl Philadelphia PA 19102 215-790-4100 790-4363
Web: www.hellotierney.com

Tonio Burgos & Associates Inc
115 Broadway Rm 1504 New York NY 10006 212-566-5600
Web: www.tonioburgos.com

TransMedia Group Inc
240 W Palmetto Park Rd Boca Raton FL 33432 561-750-9800
Web: www.transmediagroup.com

Tressel Communications 3122 Esperanza Dr Concord CA 94519 925-798-9421
Web: tresselpr.blogspot.com

TRIAD Strategies 240 N Third St 7th Fl Harrisburg PA 17101 717-238-2970
Web: www.triadstrategies.com

TSG Consulting Ii LLC 118 Capitol St Charleston WV 25301 304-345-1161
Web: tsgsolution.com

Tunheim Partners 8009 34th Ave S Minneapolis MN 55425 952-851-1600 851-1610
Web: www.tunheim.com

Turner Public Relations Inc
614 15th St 4th Fl Denver CO 80202 303-333-1402
Web: www.turnerpr.com

Van Aartrijk Group Inc, The
7411 Alban Sta Ct Ste B265 Springfield VA 22150 703-912-7974
Web: www.aartrijk.com

Vest Adv Mktg & PR 3007 Sprowl Rd Louisville KY 40299 502-267-5335
Web: www.vestadvertising.com

Viviani Associates Public Relations
160 Littleton Rd Ste 311 Parsippany NJ 07054 973-968-7929
Web: www.vivianipr.com

Voce Communications Inc
298 S Sunnyvale Ave Ste 101 Sunnyvale CA 94086 408-738-7840
Web: www.vocecommunications.com

Vox Public Relations Public Affairs
941 Oak St Eugene OR 97401 541-302-6620
Web: www.voxprpa.com

VPE Public Relations
1605 Hope St Ste 1202 Los Angeles CA 90012 626-403-3200
Web: vpe-pr.com

W2O Group 60 Francisco St San Francisco CA 94133 415-362-5018
Web: www.w2ogroup.com

Wagstaff Worldwide Inc
6725 W Sunset Blvd Ste 590 Los Angeles CA 90028 323-871-1151
Web: www.wagstaffworldwide.com

Walker Sands Communications LLC
121 N Jefferson St Chicago IL 60661 312-267-0066
Web: www.walkersands.com

Walt & Company Communications
2105 S Bascom Ave Ste 240 Campbell CA 95008 408-369-7200 369-7201
Web: www.walt.com

Warschawski 1501 Sulgrave Ave Ste 350 Baltimore MD 21209 410-367-2700
Web: www.warschawski.com

Weber Shandwick Worldwide 909 Third Ave New York NY 10022 212-445-8000
Web: www.webershandwick.com

Weidert Group Inc 901 S Lawe St Appleton WI 54915 920-731-2771
Web: www.weidert.com

Welcomm Inc 7975 Raytheon Rd Ste 340 San Diego CA 92111 858-279-1611
Web: www.welcomm.com

Widmeyer Communications
1129 20th St NW Ste 200 Washington DC 20036 202-667-0901 667-0902
Web: www.widmeyer.com

Winston Baker 4111 W Sunset Blvd Los Angeles CA 90029 310-922-1544
Web: www.winstonbaker.com

Phone | Fax

Wordsouth Public Relations Inc
53 Sam Ellis Dr Ste B Rainsville AL 35986 256-638-8856
Web: wordsouth.com

Zaiss & Co 11626 Nicholas St Omaha NE 68154 402-964-9293
Web: www.zaissco.com

Zapwater Communications Inc
118 N Peoria 4th Fl Chicago IL 60607 312-943-0333
Web: zapwater.com

Zeno Group 44 E 30th St Ste 11 New York NY 10016 212-299-8888
Web: www.zenogroup.com

Zeppos & Associates Inc
400 E Mason St Ste 200 Milwaukee WI 53202 414-276-6237
Web: www.zeppos.com

Zimmerman Agency, The
1821 Miccosukee Commons Tallahassee FL 32308 850-668-2222 656-4622
Web: www.zimmerman.com

Zone 5 25 Monroe St Ste 300 Albany NY 12210 518-242-7000
Web: www.zone5.com

PUBLICATIONS

See Magazines & Journals p. 2694; Newsletters p. 2825; Newspapers p. 2828

637 PUBLISHING COMPANIES

See Also Book Producers p. 1867; Literary Agents p. 2675; Magazines & Journals p. 2694; Newsletters p. 2825; Newspapers p. 2828

637-1 Atlas & Map Publishers

Phone | Fax

DeLorme 2 DeLorme Dr PO Box 298 Yarmouth ME 04096 207-846-7000 561-5105*
**Fax Area Code:* 800 ■ *TF Sales:* 800-452-5931 ■ *Web:* www.delorme.com

MARCOA Publishing Inc 9955 Black Mtn Rd San Diego CA 92126 858-695-9600 695-9641
TF: 800-854-2935 ■ *Web:* www.marcoa.com

Nystrom 4719 W 62nd St Indianapolis IN 46268 317-612-3901 329-3305

Rand McNally 9855 Woods Dr PO Box 7600 Skokie IL 60077 800-275-7263
TF: 800-275-7263 ■ *Web:* www.randmcnally.com

Simon & Schuster Interactive
1230 Ave of the Americas New York NY 10020 212-698-7000 632-8099
TF: 800-223-2336 ■ *Web:* www.simonandschuster.biz

637-2 Book Publishers

Phone | Fax

ABC-CLIO Inc 130 Cremona Dr Goleta CA 93117 805-968-1911 685-9685
TF: 800-368-6868 ■ *Web:* www.abc-clio.com

American Printing House for the Blind
1839 Frankfort Ave PO Box 6085 Louisville KY 40206 502-895-2405 899-2274
TF: 800-223-1839 ■ *Web:* www.aph.org

Antique Collectors Club 116 Pleasant St EastHampton MA 01027 413-529-0861
TF: 800-254-4100 ■ *Web:* businessfinder.masslive.com

Applewood Books Inc 1 River Rd Carlisle MA 01741 978-369-4172
TF General: 800-277-5312 ■ *Web:* www.applewoodbooks.com

Atlantic Publishing Co 315 E Washington St Starke FL 32091 800-814-1132 622-1875*
**Fax Area Code:* 352 ■ *TF:* 800-814-1132 ■ *Web:* www.atlantic-pub.com

Author House 1663 Liberty Dr Ste 200 Bloomington IN 47403 812-339-6000 339-6554
TF: 888-728-8467 ■ *Web:* www.authorhouse.com

Avalon Travel Publishing 1700 Fourth St Berkeley CA 94710 510-595-3664
Web: www.avalontravelbooks.com

Aviation Supplies & Academics Inc
7005 132nd Pl Se Newcastle WA 98059 425-235-1500
TF: 800-272-2359 ■ *Web:* asa2fly.com

Barron's Educational Series Inc
250 Wireless Blvd Hauppauge NY 11788 631-434-3311 434-3723
TF: 800-645-3476 ■ *Web:* www.barronseduc.com

Beacon Press Inc 24 Farnsworth St Boston MA 02210 617-742-2110 723-3097
Web: www.beacon.org

Behrman House Inc 11 Edison Pl Springfield NJ 07081 973-379-7200
Web: behrmanhouse.com

Bertelsmann SE & Co 1745 Broadway New York NY 10019 490-524-1800
Web: www.bertelsmann.com

Black Classic Press PO Box 13414 Baltimore MD 21203 410-242-6954
Web: www.blackclassicbooks.com

BOA Editions Ltd 250 N Goodman St Ste 306 Rochester NY 14607 585-546-3410 546-3913
Web: www.boaeditions.org

BRB Publications Inc PO Box 27869 Tempe AZ 85285 480-829-7475
TF: 800-929-3811 ■ *Web:* www.brbpub.com

Brillacademic Publishers Inc
2 liberty Sq 11th Fl Boston MA 02109 617-263-2323 263-2324
TF: 800-337-9255 ■ *Web:* www.brill.com

Browntrout Publishers Inc
201 Continental Blvd El Segundo CA 90245 310-607-9010 607-9011
TF: 800-777-7812 ■ *Web:* www.browntrout.com

Bureau of National Affairs Inc
1801 S Bell St Arlington VA 22202 703-341-3000
TF: 800-372-1033 ■ *Web:* www.bna.com

Candlewick Press Inc 99 Dover St Somerville MA 02144 617-661-3330 661-0565
Web: www.candlewick.com

Carroll Publishing Co
4701 Sangamore Rd Ste S-155 Bethesda MD 20816 301-263-9800 263-9801
TF: 800-336-4240 ■ *Web:* www.carrollpublishing.com

Catholic News Publishing Company Inc
210 N Ave New Rochelle NY 10801 914-632-1220
Web: catholicguides.com

Cengage Learning 10650 Tobben Dr Independence KY 41051 800-544-0550 647-4599*
**Fax Area Code:* 859 ■ *TF:* 800-544-0550 ■ *Web:* www.cengage.com

Cengage Learning PO Box 6904 Florence KY 41022 800-354-9706 487-8488
TF: 800-354-9706 ■ *Web:* www.cengage.com/highered

Phone Fax

Charles C Thomas Publisher
2600 S First St Springfield IL 62704 217-789-8980 789-9130
TF Sales: 800-258-8980 ■ *Web:* www.ccthomas.com

Chelsea Green Publishing Co
85 N Main St White River Junction VT 05001 802-295-6300
Web: chelseagreen.com

Children's Press 557 Broadway New York NY 10012 212-343-6100
Web: scholastic.co.in

Chronicle Books 680 Second St San Francisco CA 94107 415-537-4200 537-4460
TF: 800-722-6657 ■ *Web:* www.chroniclebooks.com

Clarion Books 215 Pk Ave S New York NY 10003 212-420-5800
Web: www.hmhco.com

Commemorative Brands Inc 7211 Cir S Rd Austin TX 78745 800-225-3687
TF: 800-225-3687 ■ *Web:* www.balfour.com

Corwin Press Inc 2455 Teller Rd Thousand Oaks CA 91320 805-499-9734 499-0871
TF Orders: 800-233-9936 ■ *Web:* www.corwin.com

CPP Inc 1055 Joaquin Rd Ste 200 Mountain View CA 94043 650-969-8901
TF: 800-624-1765 ■ *Web:* cpp.com

CRC Press LLC
6000 Broken Sound Pkwy NW Ste 300 Boca Raton FL 33487 561-994-0555 374-3401*
**Fax Area Code:* 800 ■ **Fax:* Cust Svc ■ *TF Cust Svc:* 800-272-7737 ■ *Web:* www.crcpress.com

Creative Communications For The Parish Inc
1564 Fencorp Dr Fenton MO 63026 636-305-9777 305-9333
TF: 800-325-9414 ■ *Web:* www.creativecommunications.com

Curriculum Assoc Inc 153 Rangeway Rd North Billerica MA 01862 800-225-0248 225-0248
TF: 800-225-0248 ■ *Web:* www.curriculumassociates.com

D & B 103 JFK Pkwy Short Hills NJ 07078 973-921-5500
NYSE: DNB ■ *TF:* 800-234-3867 ■ *Web:* www.dnb.com

Dalmation Press 113 Seaboard Ln Ste C-250 Franklin TN 37067 800-815-8696
TF: 800-815-8696 ■ *Web:* www.dalmatianpress.com

Dickinson Press Inc 5100 33rd St Se Grand Rapids MI 49512 616-957-5100
Web: dickinsonpress.com

Disney Consumer Products
500 S Buena Vista St Burbank CA 91521 818-560-1000 553-5402*
**Fax Area Code:* 215 ■ **Fax:* Cust Svc ■ *TF PR:* 855-553-4763 ■ *Web:* thewaltdisneycompany.com

Disney Publishing Worldwide Inc
44 S Broadway White Plains NY 10601 914-288-4100

Dolan Media Co 222 S Ninth St Ste 2300 Minneapolis MN 55402 612-317-9420 321-0563
Web: www.thedolancompany.com

Donning Company Publishers
184 Business Pk Dr Ste 206 Virginia Beach VA 23462 800-296-8572
TF: 800-296-8572 ■ *Web:* www.donning.com

Dorling Kindersley Publishing 375 Hudson St New York NY 10014 646-674-4047 674-4047
TF Cust Svc: 800-631-8571 ■ *Web:* www.dk.com/us

Educators Publishing Service Inc (EPS)
625 Mt Auburn St Third Fl PO Box 9031 Cambridge MA 02139 800-225-5750
TF: 800-225-5750 ■ *Web:* eps.schoolspecialty.com

EMC-Paradigm Publishing Co
875 Montreal Way Saint Paul MN 55102 651-290-2800 328-4564*
**Fax Area Code:* 800 ■ *TF:* 800-328-1452 ■ *Web:* newmountainlearning.com

Encyclopaedia Britannica Inc
331 N La Salle St Chicago IL 60654 312-347-7159 294-2104*
**Fax:* PR ■ *TF:* 800-323-1229 ■ *Web:* www.britannica.com

Ethan Ellenberg Literary Agency
548 Broadway New York NY 10012 212-431-4554
Web: ethanellenberg.com

FA Davis Co 1915 Arch St Philadelphia PA 19103 215-568-2270 568-5065
TF: 800-323-3555 ■ *Web:* www.fadavis.com

Feminist Press at the City University of New York
365 Fifth Ave Ste 5406 New York NY 10016 212-817-7915 817-1593
Web: www.feministpress.org

Financial Publishing Co PO Box 570 South Bend IN 46624 574-243-6040 243-6060
TF Cust Svc: 800-433-0090 ■ *Web:* www.financial-publishing.com

Forbes Inc 60 Fifth Ave New York NY 10011 212-620-2200
TF: 800-295-0893 ■ *Web:* www.forbes.com

Free Spirit Publishing Inc
217 Fifth Ave N Ste 200 Minneapolis MN 55401 612-338-2068
TF: 800-735-7323 ■ *Web:* freespirit.com

Gale Cengage Learning
27500 Drake Rd Farmington Hills MI 48331 248-699-4253 363-4253*
**Fax Area Code:* 877 ■ *TF Cust Svc:* 800-877-4253 ■ *Web:* www.gale.com

Glencoe/McGraw-Hill 8787 Orion Pl Columbus OH 43240 800-848-1567
TF: 800-848-1567 ■ *Web:* www.glencoe.com

Good Will Publishers Inc PO Box 269 Gastonia NC 28052 704-865-1256
TF: 800-219-4663 ■ *Web:* www.goodwillpublishers.com

Goodheart-Willcox Publisher
18604 W Creek Dr Tinley Park IL 60477 708-687-5000 409-3900*
**Fax Area Code:* 888 ■ *TF:* 800-323-0440 ■ *Web:* www.g-w.com

Government Research Service
1516 SW Boswell Ave Topeka KS 66604 785-232-7720 232-1615
TF: 800-346-6898 ■ *Web:* statelegislativesourcebook.com

Grade Finders Inc PO Box 944 Exton PA 19341 610-524-7070 269-7077
TF: 800-777-8074 ■ *Web:* www.gradefinders.com

Greenwood-Heinemann 361 Hanover St Portsmouth NH 03801 603-431-7894 431-7840
TF: 800-541-2086 ■ *Web:* www.heinemann.com

Grey House Publishing 4919 Rt 22 PO Box 56 Amenia NY 12501 518-789-8700 789-0556
TF: 800-562-2139 ■ *Web:* www.greyhouse.com

Grove/Atlantic Inc 841 Broadway 4th Fl New York NY 10003 781-314-0800 614-7886*
**Fax Area Code:* 212 ■ *Web:* www.groveatlantic.com

Hachette Book Group 237 Pk Ave New York NY 10017 800-759-0190 331-1664
TF: 800-759-0190 ■ *Web:* www.hachettebookgroup.com

Harlequin Enterprises Ltd
225 Duncan Mill Rd Don Mills ON M3B3K9 416-445-5860
TF: 888-343-9777 ■ *Web:* www.harlequin.com

Harlequin-Silhouette Books
233 Broadway Ste 1001 New York NY 10279 212-553-4200 227-8969
TF: 800-873-8635 ■ *Web:* www.harlequin.com

HarperCollins Publishers Inc 10 E 53rd St New York NY 10022 212-207-7000 207-6998
TF: 800-242-7737 ■ *Web:* www.harpercollins.com

Harris Connect LLC 1511 Rt 22 Ste C-25 Brewster NY 10509 800-516-4915
TF: 800-516-4915 ■ *Web:* www.harrisconnect.com

Harry N Abrams Inc 115 W 18th St 6th Fl New York NY 10011 212-206-7715 519-1210
Web: www.abramsbooks.com

Phone Fax

Health Communications Inc (HCI)
3201 SW 15th St Deerfield Beach FL 33442 954-360-0909 360-0034
TF Cust Svc: 800-441-5569 ■ *Web:* www.hcibooks.com

Holtzbrinck Publishers 175 Fifth Ave New York NY 10010 646-307-5151 420-9314*
**Fax Area Code:* 212 ■ *TF:* 800-221-7945 ■ *Web:* macmillan.com

Houghton Mifflin Company School Div
222 Berkeley St Boston MA 02116 617-351-3699
Web: www.eduplace.com

Houghton Mifflin Company Trade & Reference Div
222 Berkeley St Boston MA 02116 617-351-5000
Web: www.houghtonmifflinbooks.com

Human Kinetics 1607 N Market St Champaign IL 61820 217-351-5076 351-2674
TF: 800-747-4457 ■ *Web:* www.humankinetics.com

HW Wilson Co 10 Estes St Ipswich MA 01938 978-356-6500
TF: 800-653-2726 ■ *Web:* www.ebscohost.com

Inner Traditions International 1 Pk Row Rochester VT 05767 802-767-3174 767-3726
TF: 800-246-8648 ■ *Web:* www.innertraditions.com

Island Press 2000 M St NW Ste 650 Washington DC 20036 202-232-7933 234-1328
TF: 800-621-2736 ■ *Web:* www.islandpress.org

iUniverse 1663 Liberty Dr Bloomington IN 47403 812-330-2909 355-4085
TF: 800-288-4677 ■ *Web:* www.iuniverse.com

Jane's Information Group
110 N Royal St Ste 200 Alexandria VA 22314 703-683-3700
TF: 800-824-0768 ■ *Web:* www.janes.com

Jeppesen Sanderson Inc 55 Inverness Dr E Englewood CO 80112 303-799-9090 328-4153
TF: 800-621-5377 ■ *Web:* ww1.jeppesen.com

John Wiley & Sons Inc 111 River St Hoboken NJ 07030 201-748-6000 748-6088
NYSE: JW/A ■ *TF Sales:* 800-225-5945 ■ *Web:* www.wiley.com

Judaica Press Inc 123 Ditmas Ave Brooklyn NY 11218 718-972-6200
TF: 800-972-6201 ■ *Web:* www.judaicapress.com

Kendall/Hunt Publishing Co
4050 Westmark Dr PO Box 1840 Dubuque IA 52002 563-589-1000 772-9165*
**Fax Area Code:* 800 ■ **Fax:* Cust Svc ■ *TF Cust Svc:* 800-228-0810 ■ *Web:* www.kendallhunt.com

Kensington Publishing Corp 119 W 40th St New York NY 10018 212-407-1500 935-0699
TF: 800-221-2647 ■ *Web:* www.kensingtonbooks.com

Key Curriculum Press 1150 65th St Emeryville CA 94608 510-595-7000 541-2442*
**Fax Area Code:* 800 ■ *TF:* 800-338-3987 ■ *Web:* www.keycurriculum.com

Lawyers Diary & Manual
890 Mtn Ave Ste 300 New Providence NJ 07974 973-642-1440 642-4280*
**Fax:* Cust Svc ■ *TF:* 800-444-4041 ■ *Web:* www.lawdiary.com

Leadership Directories Inc
104 Fifth Ave 3rd Fl New York NY 10011 212-627-4140 645-0931
TF: 800-627-0311 ■ *Web:* www.leadershipdirectories.com

Lerner Publishing Group
1251 Washington Ave N Minneapolis MN 55401 800-328-4929 332-1132
TF: 800-328-4929 ■ *Web:* www.lernerbooks.com

LexisNexis Matthew Bender 744 Broad St Newark NJ 07102 973-820-2000
TF: 800-252-9257 ■ *Web:* www.lexisnexis.com

Lightning Source 1246 Heil Quaker Blvd La Vergne TN 37086 615-213-5815 213-4426
TF: 800-509-4156 ■ *Web:* www.lightningsource.com

Linden Publishing 2006 S Mary St Fresno CA 93721 559-233-6633 233-6933
TF Sales: 800-345-4447 ■ *Web:* www.woodworkerslibrary.com

Lippincott Williams & Wilkins
530 Walnut St Philadelphia PA 19106 215-521-8300 521-8902
Web: www.lww.com

Little Brown & Co 237 Pk Ave New York NY 10017 212-364-1100
TF Cust Svc: 800-759-0190 ■ *Web:* www.hachettebookgroup.com

Llewellyn Worldwide Inc 2143 Wooddale Dr Woodbury MN 55125 651-291-1970 291-1908
TF: 800-843-6666 ■ *Web:* www.llewellyn.com

Lonely Planet Publications 50 Linden St Oakland CA 94607 510-893-8555 893-8572
TF: 800-275-8555 ■ *Web:* www.lonelyplanet.com

LRP Publications 360 Hiatt Dr Palm Beach Gardens FL 33418 561-622-6520 622-2423
TF: 800-621-5463 ■ *Web:* www.lrp.com

Marquis Who's Who
300 Connell Dr Ste 2000 Berkeley Heights NJ 07922 908-673-1000 673-1189
TF: 800-473-7020 ■ *Web:* www.marquiswhoswho.com

McFarland & Company Inc
960 NC Hwy 88 W PO Box 611 Jefferson NC 28640 336-246-4460 246-5018
TF: 800-253-2187 ■ *Web:* www.mcfarlandbooks.com

McGraw-Hill Cos Inc
1221 Ave of the Americas New York NY 10020 212-512-2000
NYSE: MHFI ■ *Web:* www.mcgraw-hill.com

McGraw-Hill Higher Education Group
1333 Burr Ridge Pkwy Burr Ridge IL 60527 630-789-4000 755-5654*
**Fax Area Code:* 614 ■ *TF:* 800-634-3963 ■ *Web:* www.mheducation.com/highered/home-guest.html

McGraw-Hill Professional Publishing Group
2 Penn Plz 11th Fl New York NY 10121 877-833-5524
TF: 877-833-5524 ■ *Web:* www.mhprofessional.com

Mel Bay Publications Inc 1734 Gilsinn Ln Fenton MO 63026 636-257-3970 257-5062
TF: 800-863-5229 ■ *Web:* www.melbay.com

Meredith Corp 1716 Locust St Des Moines IA 50309 515-284-3000
NYSE: MDP ■ *Web:* www.meredith.com

Merriam-Webster Inc PO Box 281 Springfield MA 01102 413-734-3134 731-5979
Web: www.merriam-webster.com

Midwest Plan Service 122 Davidson Hall ISU Ames IA 50011 515-294-4337 294-9589
TF: 800-562-3618 ■ *Web:* www-mwps.sws.iastate.edu

Mike Murach & Assoc Inc 4340 N Knoll Fresno CA 93722 559-440-9071 440-0963
TF: 800-221-5528 ■ *Web:* www.murach.com

Moody's Corp
250 Greenwich St 7 World Trade Ctr New York NY 10007 212-553-0300
NYSE: MCO ■ *Web:* www.moodys.com

National Academy Press
500 Fifth St NW PO Box 285 Washington DC 20055 202-334-3313 334-2451*
**Fax:* Sales ■ *TF:* 800-624-6242 ■ *Web:* www.nap.edu

National Braille Press Inc 88 St Stephen St Boston MA 02115 617-266-6160 437-0456
TF: 888-965-8965 ■ *Web:* www.nbp.org

National Register Publishing Co
430 Mountain Ave Ste 400 New Providence NJ 07974 800-473-7020 673-1189*
**Fax Area Code:* 908 ■ *TF:* 800-473-7020 ■ *Web:* www.nationalregisterpub.com

National Underwriter Co 5081 Olympic Blvd Erlanger KY 41018 800-543-0874 692-2175*
**Fax Area Code:* 859 ■ *TF:* 800-543-0874 ■ *Web:* www.nationalunderwriter.com

Nerdy Books 135 Main St Flemington NJ 08822 908-788-4676
Web: www.nerdybooks.com

				Phone	Fax
New Generation Research Inc 225 Friend St Ste 801	Boston	MA	02114	617-573-9550	573-9554
TF: 800-468-3810 ■ *Web:* www.turnarounds.com					
New Readers Press 104 Marcellus St	Syracuse	NY	13204	315-422-9121	894-2100*
**Fax Area Code:* 866 ■ *TF:* 800-448-8878 ■ *Web:* www.newreaderspress.com					
Newkirk Products Inc 15 Corporate Cir	Albany	NY	12203	518-862-3200	862-3399
TF: 800-525-4237 ■ *Web:* www.newkirk.com					
Nielsen Business Media *Nielsen Co, The* 770 Broadway	New York	NY	10003	646-654-4500	
Web: www.nielsen.com					
Nightingale-Conant Corp 6245 W Howard St	Niles	IL	60714	800-557-1660	
TF Cust Svc: 800-557-1660 ■ *Web:* www.nightingale.com					
No Starch Press Inc 38 Ringold St	San Francisco	CA	94103	415-863-9900	863-9950
TF: 800-420-7240 ■ *Web:* www.nostarch.com					
Nolo.com 950 Parker St	Berkeley	CA	94710	800-728-3555	645-0895
TF: 800-728-3555 ■ *Web:* www.nolo.com					
Omnigraphics Inc PO Box 31-1640	Detroit	MI	48231	800-234-1340	875-1340
TF: 800-234-1340 ■ *Web:* www.omnigraphics.com					
Open Court Publishing Co 70 E Lake St Ste 800	Chicago	IL	60601	800-815-2280	701-1728*
**Fax Area Code:* 312 ■ *TF:* 800-815-2280 ■ *Web:* www.opencourtbooks.com					
Overlook Press 141 Wooster St	New York	NY	10012	212-673-2210	673-2296
TF: 800-527-9703 ■ *Web:* www.overlookpress.com					
Oxford University Press 198 Madison Ave	New York	NY	10016	212-726-6000	677-1303*
**Fax Area Code:* 919 ■ *TF Orders:* 800-445-9714					
Pathway Press 1080 Montgomery Ave NE	Cleveland	TN	37311	423-476-4512	
Web: www.pathwaypress.org					
Pearson Education Inc 1 Lake St	Upper Saddle River	NJ	07458	201-236-6716	
TF Cust Svc: 800-922-0579 ■ *Web:* www.pearsoned.com					
Pearson Education School Div 1900 E Lk Ave Ofc Ste B-110A	Glenview	IL	60025	800-348-4474	841-8939*
**Fax:* Cust Svc ■ *TF:* 800-348-4474 ■ *Web:* www.pearsonschool.com					
Pencor Services Inc 613 Third St	Palmerton	PA	18071	610-826-2552	
Web: www.pencor.com					
Penguin Group (USA) Inc 375 Hudson St	New York	NY	10014	212-366-2000	366-2933
TF Sales: 800-847-5515 ■ *Web:* penguin.com					
Penguin Random House 1745 Broadway	New York	NY	10019	212-782-9000	782-5157
TF: 800-733-3000 ■ *Web:* www.randomhouse.com					
Penguin Random House Inc *Bantam Dell Publishing Group* 1745 Broadway 10th Fl	New York	NY	10019	212-782-9000	
TF: 888-523-9292 ■ *Web:* www.penguinrandomhouse.com					
Perseus Books Group, The 210 American Dr	Jackson	TN	38301	731-426-6061	351-5073*
**Fax Area Code:* 800 ■ *TF:* 800-343-4499 ■ *Web:* perseusbooksgroup.com					
Peter Lang Publishing Inc 29 Broadway	New York	NY	10006	212-647-7706	647-7707
TF: 800-770-5264 ■ *Web:* www.peterlang.com					
Prentice-Hall Inc 1 Lake St	Upper Saddle River	NJ	07458	800-328-5999	
TF: 800-328-5999 ■ *Web:* www.pearsoned.com					
Price Books & Forms Inc 531 E Sierra Madre Ave	Glendora	CA	91741	800-423-8961	768-2162*
**Fax Area Code:* 626 ■ *TF:* 800-423-8961 ■ *Web:* www.autopricebooks.com					
PublicAffairs 250 W 57th St 15th Fl	New York	NY	10107	212-397-6666	340-8125
Web: www.publicaffairsbooks.com					
Publications International Ltd 7373 N Cicero Ave	Lincolnwood	IL	60712	847-676-3470	676-3671
TF General: 800-777-5582 ■ *Web:* pilbooks.com					
Quebecor Media Inc 612 Rue St Jacques	Montreal	QC	H3C4M8	514-380-1999	
Web: www.quebecor.com					
Rand McNally 9855 Woods Dr PO Box 7600	Skokie	IL	60077	800-275-7263	
TF: 800-275-7263 ■ *Web:* www.randmcnally.com					
Regnery Publishing Inc 300 New Jersey Ave NW	Washington	DC	20001	202-216-0600	216-0612
Web: www.regnery.com					
Rizzoli International Publications Inc 300 Pk Ave S 3rd Fl	New York	NY	10010	212-387-3400	387-3535
Web: www.rizzoliusa.com					
Rosen Publishing Group Inc, The 29 E 21st St	New York	NY	10010	800-237-9932	436-4643*
**Fax Area Code:* 888 ■ *TF:* 800-237-9932 ■ *Web:* www.rosenpublishing.com					
Rowman & Littlefield Publishers Inc 4501 Forbes Blvd Ste 200	Lanham	MD	20706	301-459-3366	429-5748
TF: 800-462-6420 ■ *Web:* rowman.com					
RR Bowker LLC 630 Central Ave	New Providence	NJ	07974	908-286-1090	219-0193*
**Fax:* Cust Svc ■ *TF:* 888-269-5372 ■ *Web:* www.bowker.com					
Sage Publications Inc 2455 Teller Rd	Thousand Oaks	CA	91320	805-499-9774	499-0871
TF: 800-818-7243 ■ *Web:* www.sagepub.com					
Sams Technical Publishing 9850 E 30th St	Indianapolis	IN	46229	800-428-7267	552-3910
TF Cust Svc: 800-428-7267 ■ *Web:* www.samswebsite.com					
Santillana USA Publishing Co 2023 NW 84th Ave	Doral	FL	33122	305-591-9522	248-9518*
**Fax Area Code:* 888 ■ *TF:* 800-245-8584 ■ *Web:* www.santillanausa.com					
School Annual Publishing Co 2568 Park Ctr Blvd	State College	PA	16801	800-436-6030	
TF: 800-436-6030 ■ *Web:* www.schoolannual.com					
Slack Inc 6900 Grove Rd	Thorofare	NJ	08086	856-848-1000	848-6091
TF: 800-257-8290 ■ *Web:* www.slackinc.com					
Sourcebooks Inc 1935 Brookdale Rd Ste 139	Naperville	IL	60563	630-961-3900	961-2168
TF: 800-432-7444 ■ *Web:* www.sourcebooks.com					
SRDS 1700 Higgins Rd	Des Plaines	IL	60018	800-851-7737	375-5001*
**Fax Area Code:* 847 ■ *TF:* 800-851-7737 ■ *Web:* login.srds.com					
Stackpole Books 5067 Ritter Rd	Mechanicsburg	PA	17055	717-796-0411	796-0412
Web: www.stackpolebooks.com					
Standard & Poor's Corp 55 Water St	New York	NY	10041	212-438-1000	
TF: 877-772-5436 ■ *Web:* www.standardandpoors.com					
Sterling Publishing Company Inc 387 Pk Ave S 5th Fl	New York	NY	10016	212-532-7160	213-2495
TF Cust Svc: 800-367-9692 ■ *Web:* www.sterlingpublishing.com					
Storey Publishing LLC 210 Mass Moca Way	North Adams	MA	01247	413-346-2100	346-2199*
**Fax:* Edit ■ *TF:* 800-827-7444 ■ *Web:* www.storey.com					
Sunset Publishing Corp 80 Willow Rd	Menlo Park	CA	94025	650-321-3600	
TF: 800-227-7346 ■ *Web:* www.sunset.com					
Taylor & Francis Group 6000 Broken Sound Pkwy NW Ste 300	Boca Raton	NY	33487	207-017-6000	
TF: 877-622-5543 ■ *Web:* www.taylorandfrancis.com					
Technology Marketing Corp 1 Technology Plz	Norwalk	CT	06854	203-852-6800	866-3326
TF Cust Svc: 800-243-6002 ■ *Web:* www.tmcnet.com					
Thomas Publishing Co 5 Penn Plaza	New York	NY	10001	212-695-0500	290-7362
TF: 800-733-1127 ■ *Web:* www.thomaspublishing.com					
Thorndike Press 10 Water St Ste 310	Waterville	ME	04901	800-223-1244	861-7501*
**Fax Area Code:* 207 ■ **Fax:* Sales ■ *TF:* 800-223-1244 ■ *Web:* www.gale.com/thorndike/thorndike/-/n-5p					
Torstar Corp 1 Yonge St	Toronto	ON	M5E1E6	416-869-4010	869-4183
TSE: TS.B ■ *Web:* www.torstar.com					
Townsend Press 439 Kelley Dr	West Berlin	NJ	08091	856-753-0554	225-8894*
**Fax Area Code:* 800 ■ *TF:* 800-772-6410 ■ *Web:* www.townsendpress.com					
Triumph Learning 136 Madison Ave	New York	NY	10016	800-221-9372	805-5723*
**Fax Area Code:* 866 ■ **Fax:* Cust Svc ■ *TF:* 800-221-9372 ■ *Web:* www.triumphlearning.com					
Tuttle Publishing 364 Innovation Dr	North Clarendon	VT	05759	802-773-8930	329-8885*
**Fax Area Code:* 800 ■ *TF Sales:* 800-526-2778 ■ *Web:* www.tuttlepublishing.com					
Unisystems Inc 155 E 55th St	New York	NY	10022	212-826-0850	759-9069
Web: www.modernpublishing.com					
University Press of America 4501 Forbes Blvd Ste 200	Lanham	MD	20706	301-459-3366	429-5746
TF: 800-462-6420 ■ *Web:* rowman.com					
Vantage Press Inc 419 Pk Ave S 18th Fl	New York	NY	10016	212-736-1767	
Verso Books 20 Jay St Ste 1010	Brooklyn	NY	11201	718-246-8160	246-8165
Web: www.versobooks.com					
Walch Education 40 Walch Dr	Portland	ME	04103	207-772-2846	772-3105
TF: 800-558-2846 ■ *Web:* www.walch.com					
Walsworth Publishing Co 306 N Kansas Ave	Marceline	MO	64658	660-376-3543	258-7798*
**Fax:* Hum Res ■ *TF:* 800-972-4968 ■ *Web:* www.walsworthyearbooks.com					
West Group 610 Opperman Dr	Eagan	MN	55123	651-687-7000	687-7551
TF Cust Svc: 800-328-4880 ■ *Web:* legalsolutions.thomsonreuters.com					
Wheatmark Inc 1760 E River Rd Ste 145	Tucson	AZ	85718	520-798-0888	798-3394
TF: 888-934-0888 ■ *Web:* www.wheatmark.com					
Wilderness Press c/o Keen Communications 2204 First Ave S Ste 102	Birmingham	AL	35233	800-443-7227	326-1012*
**Fax Area Code:* 205 ■ *TF:* 800-443-7227 ■ *Web:* www.wildernesspress.com					
Wiley Publishing Inc 111 River St	Hoboken	NJ	07030	201-748-6000	748-6088
TF: 800-225-5945 ■ *Web:* www.wiley.com/wileycda/section/index.html					
William H Sadlier Inc 9 Pine St	New York	NY	10005	800-221-5175	312-6080*
OTC: SADL ■ **Fax Area Code:* 212 ■ *TF:* 800-221-5175 ■ *Web:* www.sadlier.com					
William Morrow & Co 10 E 53rd St	New York	NY	10022	212-207-7000	
TF: 800-242-7737 ■ *Web:* www.harpercollins.com					
William S Hein & Company Inc 1285 Main St	Buffalo	NY	14209	716-882-2600	883-8100
TF: 800-828-7571 ■ *Web:* www.wshein.com					
Wilshire Book Co 9731 Variel Ave	Chatsworth	CA	91311	818-700-1522	700-1527
Web: www.mpowers.com					
Wimmer Cookbooks 4650 Shelby Air Dr	Memphis	TN	38118	901-362-8900	
Web: www.wimmerco.com					
Workman Publishing 225 Varick St	New York	NY	10014	212-254-5900	254-8098
TF: 800-722-7202 ■ *Web:* www.workman.com					
World Book Inc 233 N Michigan Ave Ste 2000	Chicago	IL	60601	312-729-5800	729-5600
TF: 800-967-5325 ■ *Web:* www.worldbook.com					
WW Norton & Company Inc 500 Fifth Ave 6th Fl	New York	NY	10110	212-354-5500	869-0856
TF: 800-233-4830 ■ *Web:* books.wwnorton.com					
Zaner-Bloser Inc 1201 Dublin Rd	Columbus	OH	43215	614-486-0221	487-2699
TF: 800-421-3018 ■ *Web:* www.zaner-bloser.com					
Zebra Books *Kensington Publishing Corp* 119 W 40th St	New York	NY	10018	212-407-1500	
TF: 800-221-2647 ■ *Web:* www.kensingtonbooks.com					

637-3 Book Publishers - Religious & Spiritual Books

				Phone	Fax
American Bible Society 1865 Broadway	New York	NY	10023	212-408-1200	408-1512
TF: 800-322-4253 ■ *Web:* www.americanbible.org					
Augsburg Fortress Publishers 510 Marquette Ave Ste 800	Minneapolis	MN	55402	612-330-3300	330-3455
TF: 800-426-0115 ■ *Web:* www.augsburgfortress.org					
Baker Book House Company Inc 6030 E Fulton St	Ada	MI	49301	616-676-9185	676-9573
TF Orders: 800-877-2665 ■ *Web:* www.bakerpublishinggroup.com					
Baker Book House Company Inc Revell Div 6030 E Fulton St	Ada	MI	49301	616-676-9185	676-9573
TF Orders: 800-877-2665 ■ *Web:* bakerpublishinggroup.com					
Bethany House Publishers 11400 Hampshire Ave S	Bloomington	MN	55438	616-676-9185	676-9573
TF: 800-328-6109 ■ *Web:* bakerpublishinggroup.com					
Brethren Press 1451 Dundee Ave	Elgin	IL	60120	800-441-3712	667-8188
TF: 800-441-3712 ■ *Web:* www.brethrenpress.com					
Broadman & Holman Publishers 127 Ninth Ave N MSN 114	Nashville	TN	37234	800-448-8032	251-3914*
**Fax Area Code:* 615 ■ *TF:* 800-448-8032 ■ *Web:* www.bhpublishinggroup.com					
Concordia Publishing House Inc 3558 S Jefferson Ave	Saint Louis	MO	63118	314-268-1000	268-1329
TF Cust Svc: 800-325-3040 ■ *Web:* www.cph.org					
Cook Communications Ministries 4050 Lee Vance View	Colorado Springs	CO	80918	719-536-0100	
TF: 800-708-5550 ■ *Web:* www.davidccook.com					
Deseret Book Co 57 W S Temple	Salt Lake City	UT	84111	801-534-1515	
TF: 800-453-4532 ■ *Web:* www.deseretbook.com					
DeVore & Sons Inc 9020 E 35th St N	Wichita	KS	67226	316-267-3211	
Web: www.devoreandsons.com					
Gospel Light Publications 1957 Eastman Ave	Ventura	CA	93003	805-644-9721	650-8173*
**Fax:* Mktg ■ *TF:* 800-446-7735 ■ *Web:* www.gospellight.com					
Hay House Inc PO Box 5100	Carlsbad	CA	92018	760-431-7695	650-5115*
**Fax Area Code:* 800 ■ *TF:* 800-654-5126 ■ *Web:* www.hayhouse.com					
Jewish Publication Society 2100 Arch St 2nd Fl	Philadelphia	PA	19103	215-832-0600	568-2017
TF: 800-234-3151 ■ *Web:* jps.org					
NavPress 3820 N 30th St	Colorado Springs	CO	80904	800-323-9400	
TF: 800-323-9400 ■ *Web:* www.navpress.com					
New Leaf Publishing Group PO Box 726	Green Forest	AR	72638	870-438-5288	
TF: 800-999-3777 ■ *Web:* www.nlpg.com					

					Phone	Fax
New World Library 14 Pamaron Way *TF:* 800-972-6657 ■ *Web:* www.newworldlibrary.com	Novato	CA	94949		415-884-2100	884-2199
Northwestern Publishing House 1250 N 113th St *TF Orders:* 800-662-6022 ■ *Web:* online.nph.net	Milwaukee	WI	53226		414-475-6600	475-7695
Oregon Catholic Press (OCP) 5536 NE Hassalo St *Fax Area Code: 800 ■ *TF:* 877-596-1653 ■ *Web:* www.ocp.org	Portland	OR	97213		503-281-1191	462-7329*
Our Sunday Visitor Inc 200 Noll Plaza *TF:* 800-348-2440 ■ *Web:* www.osv.com	Huntington	IN	46750		260-356-8400	356-8472
Pauline Books & Media 50 St Paul's Ave *TF Sales:* 800-876-4463 ■ *Web:* www.pauline.org	Boston	MA	02130		617-522-8911	524-8035
Review & Herald Publishing Assn 55 W Oak Ridge Dr *TF:* 800-456-3991 ■ *Web:* www.rhpa.org	Hagerstown	MD	21740		301-393-3000	393-3209
Standard Publishing Co 8805 Governors Hill Dr Ste 400 *Fax Area Code: 877 ■ *TF Orders:* 800-543-1353 ■ *Web:* www.standardpub.com	Cincinnati	OH	45249		513-931-4050	867-5751*
Standex International Corp Consumer Group 11 Keewaydin Dr *NYSE:* SXI ■ *TF:* 800-514-5275 ■ *Web:* www.standex.com	Salem	NH	03079		603-893-9701	893-7324
Thomas Nelson Inc 501 Nelson Pl PO Box 141000 *TF:* 800-251-4000 ■ *Web:* www.thomasnelson.com	Nashville	TN	37214		615-889-9000	889-5940
Tyndale House Publishers Inc 351 Executive Dr *TF:* 800-323-9400 ■ *Web:* www.tyndale.com	Carol Stream	IL	60188		800-323-9400	684-0247
United Methodist Publishing House 201 Eigth Ave S *TF:* 800-672-1789 ■ *Web:* umph.org	Nashville	TN	37203		615-749-6000	
Whitaker House/Anchor Distributors 1030 Hunt Vly Cir *TF General:* 800-444-4484 ■ *Web:* www.anchordistributors.com	New Kensington	PA	15068		724-334-7000	334-1200

637-4 Book Publishers - University Presses

				Phone	Fax
Catholic University of America Press 620 Michigan Ave NE 240 Leahy Hall *TF:* 800-537-5487 ■ *Web:* www.cua.edu	Washington	DC	20064	202-319-5052	319-4985
Columbia University Press 61 W 62nd St 3rd Fl *TF:* 800-944-8648 ■ *Web:* www.columbia.edu	New York	NY	10023	212-459-0600	459-3677
Cornell University Press 750 Cascadilla St PO Box 6525 *TF Sales:* 800-666-2211 ■ *Web:* www.cornellpress.cornell.edu	Ithaca	NY	14850	607-277-2338	277-6292
Duke University Press 905 W Main St Ste 18-B *Fax Area Code: 888 ■ *Fax: Cust Svc ■ *TF Cust Svc:* 888-651-0122 ■ *Web:* www.dukeupress.edu	Durham	NC	27701	919-687-3600	651-0124*
Gallaudet University Press 800 Florida Ave NE *TF:* 800-621-2736 ■ *Web:* gupress.gallaudet.edu	Washington	DC	20002	202-651-5488	651-5489
Harvard Business School Publishing 60 Harvard Way *Fax Area Code: 617 ■ *TF:* 800-795-5200 ■ *Web:* www.harvardbusiness.org	Boston	MA	02163	800-795-5200	783-7556*
Harvard University Press 79 Garden St *Fax Area Code: 800 ■ *TF:* 800-405-1619 ■ *Web:* www.hup.harvard.edu	Cambridge	MA	02138	617-495-2600	406-9145*
Indiana University Press 601 N Morton St *TF:* 800-842-6796 ■ *Web:* www.iupress.indiana.edu	Bloomington	IN	47404	812-855-8817	855-8507
Johns Hopkins University Press 2715 N Charles St *Fax: Orders ■ *TF Orders:* 800-537-5487 ■ *Web:* www.press.jhu.edu	Baltimore	MD	21218	410-516-6900	516-6998*
Michigan State University Press 1405 S Harrison Rd Ste 25 Manly Miles Bldg *Web:* msupress.org	East Lansing	MI	48823	517-355-9543	432-2611
MIT Press, The 1 Rogers St *Web:* www.mitpress.mit.edu	Cambridge	MA	02142	617-253-5646	253-1709
Naval Institute Press 291 Wood Rd *TF:* 800-233-8764 ■ *Web:* usni.org	Annapolis	MD	21402	410-268-6110	295-1049
Ohio State University Press 1070 Carmack Rd *Web:* www.ohiostatepress.org	Columbus	OH	43210	614-292-1462	292-2065
Ohio University Press 19 Cir Dr The Ridges *TF Sales:* 800-621-2736 ■ *Web:* www.ohioswallow.com	Athens	OH	45701	740-593-1154	593-4536
Oregon State University Press 1500 Jefferson St *TF Orders:* 800-426-3797 ■ *Web:* www.oregonstate.edu	Corvallis	OR	97331	541-737-3166	737-3170
Pennsylvania State University Press 820 N University Dr USB1 Ste C *TF:* 800-326-9180 ■ *Web:* www.psupress.org	University Park	PA	16802	814-865-1327	863-1408
Princeton University Press 41 William St *TF:* 800-777-4726 ■ *Web:* www.press.princeton.edu	Princeton	NJ	08540	609-258-4900	258-6305
Purdue University Press 504 W State St Stewart Ctr 370 *TF Orders:* 800-247-6553 ■ *Web:* www.thepress.purdue.edu	West Lafayette	IN	47907	765-494-2038	496-2442
Rutgers University Press 106 Somerset St 3rd Fl *TF:* 800-272-6817 ■ *Web:* rutgerspress.rutgers.edu	New Brunswick	NJ	08901	732-745-4935	445-7039
Stanford University Press 1450 Page Mill Rd *TF:* 800-621-2736 ■ *Web:* www.sup.org	Palo Alto	CA	94304	650-723-9434	725-3457
State University of New York Press (SUNY) 22 Corporate Woods Blvd 3rd Fl *TF:* 866-430-7869 ■ *Web:* www.sunypress.edu	Albany	NY	12211	518-472-5000	472-5038
Temple University Press 1852 N 10th St USB 305 *TF:* 800-621-2736 ■ *Web:* www.temple.edu/tempress	Philadelphia	PA	19122	215-926-2140	
Texas A & M University Press John H Lindsey Bldg 4354 TAMU *TF Orders:* 800-826-8911 ■ *Web:* www.tamu.edu	College Station	TX	77843	979-845-1436	847-8752
Texas Tech University Press 2903 Fourth St *TF:* 800-832-4042 ■ *Web:* ttupress.org	Lubbock	TX	79409	806-742-2982	742-2979
University of Alabama Press, The 200 Hackberry Ln Second Fl PO Box 870380 *TF Orders:* 800-621-2736 ■ *Web:* www.uapress.ua.edu	Tuscaloosa	AL	35487	205-348-5180	348-9201
University of Alaska Press 1760 Wwood Wy Ste 220 *TF:* 888-252-6657 ■ *Web:* www.uaf.edu	Fairbanks	AK	99709	907-474-5831	474-5502
University of Arizona Press, The 1510 E University Blvd PO Box 210055 *TF:* 800-426-3797 ■ *Web:* www.uapress.arizona.edu	Tucson	AZ	85721	520-621-1441	621-8899
University of Arkansas Press McIlroy House 105 McIlroy *TF:* 800-621-2736 ■ *Web:* www.uapress.com	Fayetteville	AR	72701	479-575-7258	575-6044
University of California Press 2120 Berkeley Way *Fax Area Code: 510 ■ *TF:* 800-343-4499 ■ *Web:* www.ucpress.edu	Berkeley	CA	94704	800-343-4499	643-7127*
University of Chicago Press 1427 E 60th St *TF Sales:* 800-621-2736 ■ *Web:* www.press.uchicago.edu	Chicago	IL	60637	773-702-7700	702-9756
University of Delaware Press 181 S College Ave Rm 200-A *Web:* www2.lib.udel.edu/udpress	Newark	DE	19717	302-831-1149	831-6549
University of Hawaii Press 2840 Kolowalu St *Fax Area Code: 800 ■ *TF:* 888-847-7377 ■ *Web:* www.uhpress.hawaii.edu	Honolulu	HI	96822	808-956-8255	650-7811*
University of Illinois Press 1325 S Oak St *TF:* 866-244-0626 ■ *Web:* www.press.uillinois.edu	Champaign	IL	61820	217-333-0950	244-8082
University of Iowa Press 119 W Pk Rd 100 Kuhl House *TF:* 800-621-2736 ■ *Web:* www.uiowapress.org	Iowa City	IA	52242	319-335-2000	335-2055
University of Massachusetts Press PO Box 429 *TF:* 800-562-0112 ■ *Web:* www.umass.edu/umpress	Amherst	MA	01004	413-545-2217	545-1226
University of Michigan Press 839 Greene St *TF:* 866-804-0002 ■ *Web:* www.press.umich.edu	Ann Arbor	MI	48104	734-764-4388	615-1540
University of Minnesota Press 111 Third Ave S Ste 290 *Web:* www.upress.umn.edu	Minneapolis	MN	55401	612-627-1970	627-1980
University of Missouri Press 2910 LeMone Blvd *TF:* 800-621-2736 ■ *Web:* press.umsystem.edu	Columbia	MO	65201	573-882-7641	884-4498
University of Nebraska Press 1111 Lincoln Mall *TF Orders:* 800-755-1105 ■ *Web:* www.nebraskapress.unl.edu	Lincoln	NE	68508	402-472-3581	
University of Nevada Press Morrill Hall MS 0166 *Web:* www.nvbooks.nevada.edu	Reno	NV	89557	775-784-6573	784-6200
University of North Carolina Press 116 S Boundary St *TF:* 800-848-6224 ■ *Web:* www.uncpress.unc.edu	Chapel Hill	NC	27514	919-966-3561	966-3829
University of North Texas Press 1155 Union Cir Ste 311336 *TF:* 800-826-8911 ■ *Web:* untpress.unt.edu	Denton	TX	76203	940-565-2142	565-4590
University of Pennsylvania Press 3902 Spruce St *TF Cust Svc:* 800-537-5487 ■ *Web:* www.upenn.edu/pennpress	Philadelphia	PA	19104	215-898-6261	898-0404
University of Pittsburgh Press 3400 Forbes Ave 5th Fl *TF Sales:* 800-621-2736 ■ *Web:* www.upress.pitt.edu	Pittsburgh	PA	15261	412-383-2456	383-2466
University of South Carolina Press 1600 Hampton St 5th Fl *TF Orders:* 800-768-2500 ■ *Web:* www.sc.edu/uscpress	Columbia	SC	29208	803-777-5243	777-0160
University of Tennessee Press 110 Conference Ctr 600 Henley St *Web:* utpress.org	Knoxville	TN	37996	865-974-3321	974-3724
University of Texas Press 2100 Comal St *TF Sales:* 800-252-3206 ■ *Web:* www.utexas.edu/utpress	Austin	TX	78722	512-471-7233	232-7178
University of Utah Press 295 South 1500 East Ste 5400 *TF:* 800-621-2736 ■ *Web:* www.uofupress.com	Salt Lake City	UT	84112	801-585-0082	581-3365
University of Virginia Press 210 Sprigg Ln PO Box 400318 *TF Orders:* 800-831-3406 ■ *Web:* www.upress.virginia.edu	Charlottesville	VA	22903	434-924-3469	982-2655
University of Washington Press 4333 Brooklyn Ave NE *TF:* 800-537-5487 ■ *Web:* www.washington.edu	Seattle	WA	98195	206-543-4050	543-3932
University of Wisconsin Press 1930 Monroe St 3rd Fl *Web:* www.wisc.edu	Madison	WI	53711	608-263-1110	263-1132
University Press of Colorado 5589 Arapahoe Ave Ste 206C *TF:* 800-621-2736 ■ *Web:* www.upcolorado.com	Boulder	CO	80303	720-406-8849	406-3443
University Press of Florida 15 NW 15th St *TF Sales:* 800-226-3822 ■ *Web:* www.upf.com	Gainesville	FL	32611	352-392-1351	392-7302
University Press of Kansas 2502 Westbrooke Cir *Web:* kuecprd.ku.edu/~upress/cgi-bin	Lawrence	KS	66045	785-864-4154	864-4586
University Press of Kentucky 663 S Limestone St *Fax: Mktg ■ *TF Sales:* 800-537-5487 ■ *Web:* www.kentuckypress.com	Lexington	KY	40508	859-257-8400	257-8481*
University Press of Mississippi 3825 Ridgewood Rd *TF:* 800-737-7788 ■ *Web:* www.upress.state.ms.us	Jackson	MS	39211	601-432-6205	432-6217
University Press of New England (UPNE) 1 Ct St Ste 250 *TF Orders:* 800-421-1561 ■ *Web:* www.upne.com	Lebanon	NH	03766	603-448-1533	448-9429
Vanderbilt University Press 2014 Broadway Ste 320 *TF:* 800-627-7377 ■ *Web:* vanderbilt.edu/university-press	Nashville	TN	37203	615-322-3585	343-8823
Wesleyan University Press 215 Long Ln *TF:* 800-421-1561 ■ *Web:* www.wesleyan.edu	Middletown	CT	06459	860-685-7711	685-7712
Yale University Press 302 Temple St *TF Sales:* 800-405-1619 ■ *Web:* www.yale.edu	New Haven	CT	06511	203-432-0960	
Yeshiva University Press 500 W 185th St *Web:* www.yu.edu	New York	NY	10033	212-960-5400	

637-5 Comic Book Publishers

				Phone	Fax
Archie Comic Publications Inc 325 Fayette Ave *Web:* www.archiecomics.com	Mamaroneck	NY	10543	914-381-5155	381-4015

				Phone	Fax
Dark Horse Comics Inc 10956 SE Main St *TF:* 800-862-0052 ■ *Web:* www.darkhorse.com	Milwaukie	OR	97222	503-652-8815	654-9440
DC Entertainment 1700 Broadway **Fax:* Mktg ■ *Web:* www.dccomics.com	New York	NY	10019	212-636-5400	636-5599*
Diamond Comic Distributors Inc 1966 Greenspring Dr Ste 300 *TF:* 800-452-6642 ■ *Web:* www.diamondcomics.com	Timonium	MD	21093	410-560-7100	560-7148
Fantagraphics Books 7563 Lk City Way NE *TF:* 800-657-1100 ■ *Web:* www.fantagraphics.com	Seattle	WA	98115	206-524-1967	524-2104
Viz Media 295 Bay St *Web:* www.viz.com	San Francisco	CA	94133	415-546-7073	546-7086

637-6 Directory Publishers

				Phone	Fax
ASD Data Services LLC PO Box 1184 *TF:* 877-742-7297 ■ *Web:* www.asd.com	Manchester	TN	37349	877-742-7297	
Bresser's Cross Index Directory Co 684 W Baltimore St *TF:* 800-995-0570 ■ *Web:* www.bressers.com	Detroit	MI	48202	313-874-0570	874-3510
BurrellesLuce 30 B Vreeland Rd PO Box 674 *TF:* 800-631-1160 ■ *Web:* www.burrellesluce.com	Florham Park	NJ	07932	973-992-6600	992-7675
Chain Store Guide 10117 Princess Palm Ave Ste 375 **Fax Area Code:* 813 ■ *TF:* 800-927-9292 ■ *Web:* www.chainstoreguide.com	Tampa	FL	33610	800-927-9292	627-6888*
Cincinnati Bell Directory (CBD) 312 Plum St Ste 600 *TF:* 800-877-0475 ■ *Web:* www.theberrycompany.com	Cincinnati	OH	45202	800-877-0475	
Cision US Inc 130 East Randolph St 7th Fl *Web:* www.cision.com	Chicago	IL	60601	312-922-2400	
Cole Information Services 3401 NW 39th St *TF:* 800-800-3271 ■ *Web:* www.coleinformation.com	Lincoln	NE	68524	402-555-5678	
Contractors Register Inc 800 E Main St PO Box 500 **Fax Area Code:* 914 ■ *TF:* 800-431-2584 ■ *Web:* www.thebluebook.com	Jefferson Valley	NY	10535	800-431-2584	243-0287*
DAG Media Inc 125-10 Queens Blvd Ste 14 *TF:* 800-261-2799 ■ *Web:* jewishyellow.com	Kew Gardens	NY	11415	718-263-8454	793-2522
Dataman Group Inc 22594 Lemon Tree Ln *Web:* datamangroup.com	Boca Raton	FL	33428	561-451-9302	
Diamond Mktg Solutions Group Inc 280 Madsen Dr *Web:* dmsolutions.com	Bloomingdale	IL	60108	630-523-5250	
Dickman Directories Inc 6145 Columbus Pk *TF:* 877-836-4154 ■ *Web:* dickmandirectories.com	Lewis Center	OH	43035	740-548-6130	548-2217
Downey Publishing Inc 2545 E Southlake Blvd *Web:* downeypublishing.com	Southlake	TX	76092	817-416-6661	
Genesis Publisher Services 3310 Eagle Pk Dr NE Ste 200 *TF:* 800-828-1022 ■ *Web:* www.genesispubservices.com	Grand Rapids	MI	49525	616-831-2800	831-0831
Haines & Company Inc 8050 Freedom Ave **Fax Area Code:* 330 ■ *TF:* 800-843-8452 ■ *Web:* www.haines.com	North Canton	OH	44720	800-843-8452	494-3862*
Hoover's Inc 5800 Airport Blvd *TF:* 800-486-8666 ■ *Web:* www.hoovers.com	Austin	TX	78752	512-374-4500	374-4501
InfoUSA Inc 1020 E First St *TF:* 800-321-0869 ■ *Web:* www.infousa.com	Papillion	NE	68046	800-321-0869	
LexisNexis Martindale-Hubbell 121 Chanlon Rd *TF:* 800-526-4902 ■ *Web:* www.martindale.com	New Providence	NJ	07974	800-526-4902	
Marc Publishing Co 600 Germantown Pk *TF:* 800-432-5478 ■ *Web:* www.marcpub.com	Lafayette Hill	PA	19444	610-834-8585	
Rasansky Law Firm 2525 McKinnon Ave Ste 625 *OTC:* ATTY ■ *TF:* 800-288-6763 ■ *Web:* www.1800attorney.com	Dallas	TX	75201	800-288-6763	
Stewart Directories Inc 50314 Kings Point Dr PO Box 326 **Fax Area Code:* 443 ■ *TF:* 800-311-0786 ■ *Web:* www.stewartdirectories.com	Frisco	NC	27936	800-311-0786	901-7570*
Valley Yellow Pages 1850 N Gateway Blvd *TF:* 800-350-8887 ■ *Web:* www.myyp.com	Fresno	CA	93727	559-251-8888	253-9729
Van Dam Inc 127 W 27 St *Web:* vandam.com	New York	NY	10011	212-929-0416	
World Chamber of Commerce Directory Inc 446 E 29th St *TF:* 888-883-3231 ■ *Web:* www.chamberdirectoryonline.com	Loveland	CO	80538	970-663-3231	
Yellow Book USA 398 RXR Plaza *TF:* 877-237-6120 ■ *Web:* www.yellowbook.com	Uniondale	NY	11556	917-861-5858	

637-7 Music Publishers

				Phone	Fax
Carl Fischer Inc 48 Wall St 28th Fl *TF:* 800-762-2328 ■ *Web:* www.carlfischer.com	New York	NY	10005	212-777-0900	477-6996
G Schirmer Inc 257 Pk Ave S 20th Fl *Web:* www.musicsalesclassical.com	New York	NY	10010	212-254-2100	254-2013
Hal Leonard Corp 960 E Mark St *TF:* 800-321-3408 ■ *Web:* www.halleonard.com	Winona	MN	55987	507-454-2920	454-8334
Lorenz Corp 501 E Third St *TF:* 800-444-1144 ■ *Web:* www.lorenz.com	Dayton	OH	45402	937-228-6118	223-2042
Malaco Music Group Inc 3023 W Northside Dr *TF Cust Svc:* 800-272-7936 ■ *Web:* www.malaco.com	Jackson	MS	39213	601-982-4522	982-4528
Mel Bay Publications Inc 1734 Gilsinn Ln *TF:* 800-863-5229 ■ *Web:* www.melbay.com	Fenton	MO	63026	636-257-3970	257-5062
Sony/ATV Music Publishing LLC 550 Madison Ave 5th Fl *Web:* www.sonyatv.com/cookiepolicy.php?re=lw==	New York	NY	10022	212-833-7730	
Theodore Presser Co 588 N Gulph Rd *TF:* 800-854-6764 ■ *Web:* www.presser.com	King of Prussia	PA	19406	610-592-1222	592-1229
Universal Music Publishing 2100 Colorado Ave *Web:* www.umusicpub.com	Santa Monica	CA	90404	310-235-4700	235-4900
Warner/Chappell Music Inc 10585 Santa Monica Blvd *Web:* www.warnerchappell.com	Los Angeles	CA	90025	310-441-8600	441-8780

637-8 Newspaper Publishers

				Phone	Fax
ABC Inc 77 W 66th St *Web:* www.abc.go.com	New York	NY	10023	212-456-7777	456-2795
Ada Evening News Corp PO Box 489 *Web:* theadanews.com	Ada	OK	74821	580-310-7500	332-8734
Afro-American Newspapers Co 2519 N Charles St **Fax Area Code:* 877 ■ *TF:* 800-237-6892 ■ *Web:* www.afro.com	Baltimore	MD	21218	410-554-8200	570-9297*
Alameda Times-Star 7677 Oakport St Ste 950 *TF:* 866-225-5277 ■ *Web:* alamedaca.gov	Oakland	CA	94604	510-208-6300	
Albany Herald Publishing Company Inc 126 N Washington St *TF:* 800-234-3725 ■ *Web:* www.albanyherald.com	Albany	GA	31702	229-888-9300	888-9357
Albert Lea Tribune, The 808 W Front St *TF:* 800-657-4996 ■ *Web:* www.albertleatribune.com	Albert Lea	MN	56007	507-373-1411	373-0333
Arizona Publishing Cos PO Box 1950 *TF:* 800-331-9303 ■ *Web:* www.azcentral.com	Phoenix	AZ	85001	602-444-8000	
Athens Messenger, The 9300 Johnson Rd *Web:* www.athensohiotoday.com	Athens	OH	45701	740-592-6612	592-4647
Athens Newspaper Inc PO Box 912 *Web:* athensga.com	Athens	GA	30603	706-549-6800	
Auburn Publishers Inc 25 Dill St *TF:* 800-878-5311 ■ *Web:* www.auburnpub.com	Auburn	NY	13021	315-253-5311	253-6031
Austin Daily Herald Inc 310 NE Second St *Web:* www.austindailyherald.com	Austin	MN	55912	507-433-8851	437-8644
Bliss Communications Inc PO Box 5001 *TF:* 800-422-7128 ■ *Web:* www.blissnet.net	Janesville	WI	53547	608-754-3311	
BMH Books 1104 Kings Hwy PO Box 544 *TF:* 800-348-2756 ■ *Web:* www.bmhbooks.com	Winona Lake	IN	46590	800-348-2756	
Boone Newspapers Inc 15222 Freeman's Bend Rd Northport PO Box 2370 *Web:* www.boonenewspapers.com	Tuscaloosa	AL	35403	205-330-4100	330-4140
Breese Publishing Co 8060 Old US Hwy 50 *Web:* www.breesepub.com	Breese	IL	62230	618-526-7211	526-2590
Breeze Newspaper 2510 Del Prado Blvd *Web:* www.breezenewspapers.com	Cape Coral	FL	33904	239-574-1110	
Brehm Communications Inc 16644 W Bernardo Dr # 300 *Web:* www.brehmcommunications.com	San Diego	CA	92127	858-451-6200	451-3814
Burlington Hawk Eye Co 800 S Main St PO Box 10 *TF:* 800-397-1708 ■ *Web:* www.thehawkeye.com	Burlington	IA	52601	319-754-8461	754-6824
Capital City Press Inc PO Box 588 *Web:* theadvocate.com	Baton Rouge	LA	70821	225-383-1111	
Capital Gazette Communications LLC 2000 Capital Dr *Web:* www.capitalgazette.com	Annapolis	MD	21401	410-268-5000	280-5953
Capital Newspapers 1901 Fish Hatchery Rd **Fax:* Cust Svc ■ *TF:* 888-798-4468 ■ *Web:* www.wiscnews.com	Madison	WI	53713	920-887-0321	887-8790*
Casa Grande Valley Newspaper Inc PO Box 15002 *TF:* 800-352-3796 ■ *Web:* www.trivalleycentral.com	Casa Grande	AZ	85130	520-836-7461	836-0343
Casiano Communications Inc 1700 Fernandez Juncos Ave *TF:* 844-723-2351	San Juan	PR	00909	787-728-3000	268-1001
Cheyenne Newspaper Inc 702 W Lincolnway *TF:* 800-561-6268 ■ *Web:* www.wyomingnews.com	Cheyenne	WY	82001	307-634-3361	633-3189
Chicago Tribune 3701 W Lake Ave **Fax Area Code:* 312 ■ *TF:* 800-874-2863	Glenview	IL	60026	847-486-9200	222-1172*
Christian Science Publishing Society 210 Massachusetts Ave P02-15 *TF:* 800-456-2220 ■ *Web:* www.csmonitor.com	Boston	MA	02115	617-450-2300	
Citizen Publishing Company Inc 260 Tenth St *Web:* www.windomnews.com	Windom	MN	56101	507-831-3455	831-3740
Columbia Star PO Box 5955 *Web:* www.thecolumbiastar.com	Columbia	SC	29250	803-771-0219	
Community Newspaper Co Inc 72 Cherry Hill Dr *TF:* 800-281-6498 ■ *Web:* www.wickedlocal.com	Beverly	MA	01915	978-739-1300	739-8501
Community Newspapers Inc 6605 SE Lake Rd *Web:* www.portlandtribune.com	Portland	OR	97222	503-684-0360	620-3433
Community Press Newspapers 394 Wards Corner Rd	Loveland	OH	45140	513-242-4300	242-2649
Consolidated Publishing Co PO Box 189 *TF:* 866-814-9253 ■ *Web:* www.annistonstar.com	Anniston	AL	36202	256-236-1551	241-1991
Coulter Press Inc 156 Church St	Clinton	MA	01510	978-368-0176	368-1151
Cox Media Group 6205 Peachtree Dunwoody Rd *Web:* www.coxmediagroup.com	Atlanta	GA	30328	678-645-0000	645-5002
Daily Globe, The 118 E McLeod Ave PO Box 548 *TF:* 800-236-2887 ■ *Web:* www.yourdailyglobe.com	Ironwood	MI	49938	906-932-2211	932-4211
Daily Journal Corp 915 E First St *NASDAQ:* DJCO ■ *Web:* www.dailyjournal.com	Los Angeles	CA	90012	213-229-5300	229-5481
Daily Progress 685 W Rio Rd *TF:* 866-469-4866 ■ *Web:* www.dailyprogress.com	Charlottesville	VA	22902	434-978-7200	978-7252
Daily Record Inc 6 Century Dr *Web:* www.dailyrecord.com	Parsippany	NJ	07054	973-428-6200	428-6666
Daily Record, The 11 E Saratoga St *Web:* www.thedailyrecord.com	Baltimore	MD	21202	443-524-8100	
Day Publishing Co 47 Eugene O'Neill Dr *TF:* 800-542-3354 ■ *Web:* www.theday.com	New London	CT	06320	860-442-2200	442-5599
Dayton Newspapers Inc 116 S Main St *Web:* www.daytondailynews.com	Dayton	OH	45409	937-225-2000	
Delphos Herald Inc 405 N Main St *TF:* 800-589-6950 ■ *Web:* www.delphosherald.com	Delphos	OH	45833	419-695-0015	692-7704
Denver Newspaper Agency 101 W Colfax Ave *TF:* 800-336-7678 ■ *Web:* www.denverpost.com	Denver	CO	80202	303-954-1010	954-1010

Company / Address	City	State	Zip	Phone	Fax
Derrick Publishing Co 1510 W First St *TF:* 800-352-1002 ■ *Web:* www.thederrick.com	Oil City	PA	16301	814-676-7444	677-8351
Desert Sun Publishing Co PO Box 2734 *TF Advertising:* 800-233-3741 ■ *Web:* desertsun.com	Palm Springs	CA	92263	760-322-8889	322-8889
Detroit Legal News Co 1409 Allen Rd Ste B *TF:* 800-875-5275 ■ *Web:* www.legalnews.com	Troy	MI	48083	248-577-6100	577-6111
Diocese of Steubenville Catholic Charities PO Box 969 *TF:* 800-339-7890 ■ *Web:* www.diosteub.org	Steubenville	OH	43952	740-282-3631	282-3327
Dispatch Printing Co 34 S Third St *TF:* 800-282-0263 ■ *Web:* www.dispatch.com	Columbus	OH	43215	614-461-5000	461-5565
Dow Jones & Company Inc 1211 Ave of the Americas *Web:* www.dowjones.com	New York	NY	10281	212-416-2000	416-2658
Eagle Publishing Co 75 S Church St *TF:* 800-245-0254 ■ *Web:* www.berkshireeagle.com	Pittsfield	MA	01201	413-447-7311	447-7311
East Hampton Star Inc, The 153 Main St PO Box 5002 *TF:* 844-324-0777 ■ *Web:* www.easthamptonstar.com	East Hampton	NY	11937	631-324-0002	324-7943
Eau Claire Press Co 701 S Farwell St *TF:* 800-236-8808 ■ *Web:* www.leadertelegram.com	Eau Claire	WI	54701	715-833-9200	833-9244
ECM Publishers Inc 4095 Coon Rapids Blvd *Web:* www.ecm-inc.com	Coon Rapids	MN	55433	763-712-2400	
Edward A Sherman Publishing Co 101 Malbone Rd *TF:* 800-320-2378 ■ *Web:* www.newportri.com	Newport	RI	02840	401-849-3300	849-3306
EW Scripps Co 312 Walnut St Ste 2800 *NYSE: SSP* ■ **Fax:* Hum Res ■ *TF:* 800-888-3000 ■ *Web:* www.scripps.com	Cincinnati	OH	45202	513-977-3000	977-3800*
Express-News Corp PO Box 2171 *TF:* 800-555-1551 ■ *Web:* www.mysanantonio.com	San Antonio	TX	78297	210-250-3000	
Feather Publishing Co Inc 287 Lawrence St *Web:* www.plumasnews.com	Quincy	CA	95971	530-283-0800	283-3952
Findlay Publishing Co 701 W Sandusky St *Web:* www.thecourier.com	Findlay	OH	45840	419-422-5151	422-2937
Finger Lakes Times 218 Genesse St PO Box 393 *TF:* 800-388-6652 ■ *Web:* www.fltimes.com	Geneva	NY	14456	315-789-3333	789-4077
Flashes Publishers Inc 595 Jenner Dr *Web:* www.flashespublishers.com	Allegan	MI	49010	269-673-2141	673-4761
Fort Wayne Newspapers Inc 600 W Main St *TF:* 800-444-3303 ■ *Web:* www.fortwayne.com	Fort Wayne	IN	46802	260-461-8444	
Forum Communications Co 101 Fifth St N *Web:* www.forumcomm.com	Fargo	ND	58102	701-235-7311	241-5406
Forward Publishing 125 Maiden Ln *Web:* www.forward.com	New York	NY	10038	212-889-8200	447-6406
Frankfort Publishing Co LLC 1216 Wilkinson Blvd PO Box 368 *Web:* www.state-journal.com	Frankfort	KY	40601	502-227-4556	227-2831
Freedom Communications Inc 17666 Fitch *TF:* 855-862-7238 ■ *Web:* www.freedom.com	Irvine	CA	92614	949-253-2300	474-7675
Galesburg Printing & Publishing Co 140 S Prairie St *TF:* 800-733-2767 ■ *Web:* www.galesburg.com	Galesburg	IL	61401	309-343-7181	343-2382
GateHouse Media Inc 350 Willowbrook Office Pk *NYSE: GHSE* ■ *Web:* www.gatehousemedia.com	Fairport	NY	14450	585-598-0030	248-2631
Gateway Newspapers 610 Beatty Rd *Web:* triblive.com	Monroeville	PA	15146	412-856-7400	856-7954
Gazette Newspapers Inc 9030 Comprint Ct *TF:* 888-670-7100 ■ *Web:* www.gazette.net	Gaithersburg	MD	20877	301-948-3120	
George J Foster Co Inc 150 Venture Dr *TF:* 800-462-2265 ■ *Web:* www.fosters.com	Dover	NH	03820	603-742-4455	749-7079
Gilmer Mirror Co 214 E Marshall St *Web:* www.gilmermirror.com	Gilmer	TX	75644	903-843-2503	843-5123
Glastonbury Citizen Inc PO Box 373 *TF:* 860-537-1772 ■ *Web:* www.glcitizen.com	Glastonbury	CT	06033	860-633-4691	657-3258
Glendale News Press 221 N Brand Ave *Web:* www.latimes.com/socal/glendale-news-press	Glendale	CA	91203	818-637-3200	241-1975
Goldsboro News-Argus 310 N Berkeley Blvd *Web:* www.newsargus.com	Goldsboro	NC	27534	919-778-2211	778-5408
Grant County Journal 29 A St SW	Ephrata	WA	98823	509-754-4636	
Gray Television Inc 4370 Peachtree Rd NE *NYSE: GTN* ■ *TF:* 888-835-2869 ■ *Web:* www.gray.tv	Atlanta	GA	30319	404-504-9828	
Greater Media Inc 35 Braintree Hill Pk Ste 300 *Web:* www.greater-media.com	Braintree	MA	02184	781-348-8600	
Guard Publishing Co PO Box 10188 *TF:* 800-377-7428 ■ *Web:* www.registerguard.com	Eugene	OR	97440	541-485-1234	
Hastings & Sons Publishing 38 Exchange St *TF:* 800-243-4636 ■ *Web:* www.itemlive.com	Lynn	MA	01901	781-593-7700	598-2891
Hearst Corp 300 W 57th St *Web:* www.hearst.com	New York	NY	10019	212-649-2275	
Hearst Newspapers 300 W 57th St *Web:* www.hearst.com/newspapers	New York	NY	10019	212-649-2000	
Herald Publishing Co PO Box 153 *TF:* 888-421-1866 ■ *Web:* www.jhvonline.com	Houston	TX	77001	713-630-0391	630-0404
Herald-Mail Co, The 100 Summit Ave PO Box 439 *TF:* 800-626-6397 ■ *Web:* www.heraldmailmedia.com	Hagerstown	MD	21741	301-733-5131	714-0245
Herald-Star 401 Herald Sq *TF:* 800-526-7987 ■ *Web:* heraldstaronline.com	Steubenville	OH	43952	740-283-4711	284-7355
Herald-Times Inc PO Box 909 *Web:* www.heraldtimesonline.com	Bloomington	IN	47402	812-332-4401	331-4285
Heritage Newspapers Inc 1 Heritage Pl Ste 100 *Web:* www.heritagenews.com	Southgate	MI	48195	734-246-0800	
Hersam Acorn Newspapers 16 Bailey Ave *TF:* 800-372-2790 ■ *Web:* hersamacorn.com	Ridgefield	CT	06877	203-438-6544	438-3395
Hi-Desert Publishing Co 56445 29 Palms Hwy *Web:* www.hidesertstar.com	Yucca Valley	CA	92284	760-365-3315	365-2650
High Plains Publishers Inc 1500 W Wyatt Earp Blvd *TF:* 800-452-7171 ■ *Web:* hpj.com	Dodge City	KS	67801	620-227-7171	227-7173
Home News Enterprises 333 Second St *TF:* 800-876-7811 ■ *Web:* homenewsenterprises.com	Columbus	IN	47201	800-876-7811	
Hubbard Publishing Co 127 E Chillicothe Ave PO Box 40 *TF:* 866-632-9992 ■ *Web:* www.examiner.org	Bellefontaine	OH	43311	937-592-3060	592-4463
Huse Publishing Co 525 Norfolk Ave PO Box 977 *TF:* 877-371-1020 ■ *Web:* www.norfolkdailynews.com	Norfolk	NE	68701	402-371-1020	371-5802
Hutchinson Leader Inc 36 Washington Ave W *Web:* www.crowrivermedia.com/hutchinsonleader	Hutchinson	MN	55350	320-587-5000	587-6104
Independent Publishing Co 1000 Williamston Rd *TF:* 800-859-6397 ■ *Web:* www.independentmail.com	Anderson	SC	29621	864-224-4321	260-1276
Indian Hill Journal 394 Wards Corner Ste 170	Loveland	OH	45140	513-248-8600	248-1938
Indiana Newspapers Inc 307 N Pennsylvania Pkwy *Web:* indystar.com	Indianapolis	IN	46206	317-444-4000	
Indiana Printing & Publishing Co 899 Water St PO Box 10 *TF:* 800-262-3077 ■ *Web:* www.indianagazette.com	Indiana	PA	15701	724-465-5555	465-8267
Isanti County News 234 S Main St *Web:* www.isanticountynews.com	Cambridge	MN	55008	763-689-1981	689-4372
Journal & Topics Newspapers 622 Graceland Ave *Web:* www.journal-topics.com	Des Plaines	IL	60016	847-299-5511	298-8549
Journal Graphics Inc 2840 NW 35th Ave *TF:* 888-609-6051 ■ *Web:* www.journalgraphics.com	Portland	OR	97210	503-790-9100	790-9043
Journal Publishing Co 1242 S Green St *TF:* 800-264-6397 ■ *Web:* djournal.com	Tupelo	MS	38804	662-842-2611	842-2233
Keene Publishing Corp PO Box 546 *TF:* 800-765-9994 ■ *Web:* www.sentinelsource.com	Keene	NH	03431	603-352-1234	352-0437
Knight Publishing Co 600 S Tryon St *TF:* 800-332-0686 ■ *Web:* www.charlotteobserver.com	Charlotte	NC	28202	704-358-5000	
Lake Charles American Press Inc PO Box 2893 *TF:* 800-737-2283 ■ *Web:* www.americanpress.com	Lake Charles	LA	70602	337-433-3000	494-4008
Lakeville Journal Co LLC 33 Bissell St PO Box 1688 *TF:* 800-553-2234 ■ *Web:* www.lakevillejournal.com	Lakeville	CT	06039	860-435-9873	435-4802
Lancaster Newspapers Inc 8 W King St PO Box 1328 *TF:* 800-809-4666 ■ *Web:* www.lancasteronline.com	Lancaster	PA	17603	717-291-8811	291-8728
Landmark Community Newspapers Inc 601 Taylorsville Rd *TF:* 800-939-9322 ■ *Web:* www.lcni.com	Shelbyville	KY	40065	502-633-4334	633-4447
Law Bulletin Publishing Co 415 N State St *Web:* www.lawbulletin.com	Chicago	IL	60654	312-644-7800	644-4255
Lawrence Daily Journal-World Co 609 New Hampshire St PO Box 888 *TF:* 800-578-8748 ■ *Web:* www2.ljworld.com	Lawrence	KS	66044	785-843-1000	843-4512
Leader Union, The 229 S Fifth St *Web:* www.leaderunion.com	Vandalia	IL	62471	618-283-3374	
Leaf Chronicle Co 200 Commerce St *Web:* www.theleafchronicle.com	Clarksville	TN	37040	931-552-1808	
Lee Enterprises Inc 201 N Harrison St Ste 600 *NYSE: LEE* ■ *Web:* www.lee.net	Davenport	IA	52801	563-383-2100	
Lee Publications Inc 6113 State Hwy 5 *Web:* www.leepub.com	Palatine Bridge	NY	13428	518-673-3237	673-3245
Livingston County Daily Press & Argus 323 E Grand River Ave *TF:* 888-999-1288 ■ *Web:* www.livingstondaily.com	Howell	MI	48843	517-548-2000	
Lowell Sun Publishing Co 491 Dutton St **Fax:* Edit ■ *TF Cust Svc:* 800-359-1300 ■ *Web:* www.lowellsun.com	Lowell	MA	01854	978-458-7100	970-4600*
Madison Newspapers Inc 1901 Fish Hatchery Rd *TF Sales:* 800-252-7723 ■ *Web:* host.madison.com	Madison	WI	53713	608-252-6200	252-6119
Magic Valley Newspapers 132 Fairfield St W *TF:* 800-658-3883 ■ *Web:* www.magicvalley.com	Twin Falls	ID	83301	208-733-0931	734-5538
Manhattan Media LLC 79 Madison Ave 16th Fl *Web:* www.manhattanmedia.com	New York	NY	10016	212-268-8600	268-0503
Marshall Independent 508 W Main St PO Box 411 *TF:* 877-276-6070 ■ *Web:* www.marshallindependent.com	Marshall	MN	56258	507-537-1551	537-1557
Maverick Media Inc 123 W 17th St *Web:* www.ncnewspress.com	Syracuse	NE	68446	402-269-2135	269-2392
McClatchy Newspapers 2100 Q St *TF:* 866-807-2200 ■ *Web:* www.mcclatchy.com	Sacramento	CA	95816	916-321-1000	321-1869
Media General Inc 333 E Franklin St *NYSE: MEG* ■ *Web:* www.media-general.com	Richmond	VA	23219	804-649-6000	
MediaNews Group Inc 101 W Colfax Ave *Web:* digitalfirstmedia.com	Denver	CO	80202	303-954-6360	954-6320
Memphis Publishing Co 495 Union Ave *TF Cust Svc:* 800-444-6397 ■ *Web:* local.commercialappeal.com	Memphis	TN	38103	901-529-2666	
Meridian Star Inc 814 22nd Ave *TF Cust Svc:* 800-232-2525 ■ *Web:* www.meridianstar.com	Meridian	MS	39301	601-693-1551	485-1275
MetroActive Publishing Inc 550 S First St *Web:* www.metroactive.com	San Jose	CA	95113	408-298-8000	298-0602
Mid-America Publishing Corp 9 Second St NW *TF:* 800-558-1244 ■ *Web:* www.hamptonchronicle.com	Hampton	IA	50441	641-456-2585	456-2587
Milford Daily News Co 197 Main St *TF:* 800-281-6498 ■ *Web:* www.milforddailynews.com	Milford	MA	01757	508-634-7522	634-7514
Mineral Daily News Tribune Inc 24 Armstrong St *Web:* www.newstribune.info	Keyser	WV	26726	304-788-3333	
Missouri Lawyers Media 319 N Fourth St *TF:* 800-635-5297 ■ *Web:* www.molawyersmedia.com	Saint Louis	MO	63102	314-421-1880	421-0436
Missourian Publishing Co 14 W Main St *TF:* 888-239-7701 ■ *Web:* www.emissourian.com	Washington	MO	63090	636-239-7701	239-0915
Moline Dispatch Publishing Co 1720 Fifth Ave *TF:* 800-660-2472 ■ *Web:* qconline.com	Moline	IL	61265	309-764-4344	797-0317
Morning Call Inc 101 N Sixth St **Fax:* Mktg ■ *TF:* 800-666-5492 ■ *Web:* www.mcall.com	Allentown	PA	18101	610-820-6500	820-6693*

Company	City	State	ZIP	Phone	Fax
Morris Communications Company LLC 725 Broad St *TF:* 800-622-6358 ■ *Web:* www.morris.com	Augusta	GA	30901	706-724-0851	828-3830
Morris Multimedia Inc 27 Abercorn St *Web:* www.morrismultimedia.com	Savannah	GA	31401	912-233-1281	232-4639
Mountain Home News 195 S Third E St PO Box 1330 *Web:* www.mountainhomenews.com	Mountain Home	ID	83647	208-587-3331	587-9205
Natchez Newspapers Inc 503 N Canal St *Web:* www.natchezdemocrat.com	Natchez	MS	39120	601-442-9101	442-7315
Native American Times PO Box 411 *TF:* 800-367-5390 ■ *Web:* www.nativetimes.com	Tahlequah	OK	74465	918-708-5838	431-0213
New Mexico Newspapers Inc PO Box 450 *Web:* www.daily-times.com	Farmington	NM	87499	505-325-4545	564-4630
New York News LP 450 W 33rd St 3rd Fl *Web:* www.nydailynews.com	New York	NY	10001	212-210-2100	643-7831
News Publishing Co 1126 Mills St PO Box 286 *Web:* www.npco.com	Black Earth	WI	53515	706-290-5330	
Newspapers of New England Inc PO Box 1177 *Web:* www.concordmonitor.com	Concord	NH	03302	603-224-5301	224-6949
Northwest Herald Inc PO Box 250 *TF:* 800-589-8910 ■ *Web:* www.nwherald.com	Crystal Lake	IL	60039	815-459-4040	459-5640
Northwest Publications 99 E State St *Fax: Edit ■ *Web:* www.rrstar.com	Rockford	IL	61104	815-987-1200	987-1365*
Oakland Press 48 W Huron St *TF:* 888-977-3677 ■ *Web:* www.theoaklandpress.com	Pontiac	MI	48342	248-332-8181	
Observer & Eccentric Newspapers 615 W Lafayette Second Level *TF:* 866-887-2737	Detroit	MI	48226	866-887-2737	
Observer Dispatch Inc 221 Oriskany Plz *Web:* www.uticaod.com	Utica	NY	13501	315-797-9150	
Observer Publishing Co 122 S Main St *TF:* 800-222-6397 ■ *Web:* www.observer-reporter.com	Washington	PA	15301	724-222-2200	225-2077
Ogden Newspapers Inc 1500 Main St *Web:* www.oweb.com	Wheeling	WV	26003	304-233-0100	233-2867
Ojai Valley News Inc 408 Bryant Cir # A *Web:* www.ojaivalleynews.com	Ojai	CA	93023	805-646-1476	646-4281
Oshkosh Northwestern Co 224 State St *TF:* 800-924-6168 ■ *Web:* www.thenorthwestern.com	Oshkosh	WI	54901	920-235-7700	
Our Sunday Visitor Inc 200 Noll Plaza *TF:* 800-348-2440 ■ *Web:* www.osv.com	Huntington	IN	46750	260-356-8400	356-8472
Owatonna Peoples Press 135 W Pearl St *Web:* www.southernminn.com	Owatonna	MN	55060	507-451-2840	444-2382
Pacific Palisades Post Co 839 Via de la Paz *Web:* palipost.com	Pacific Palisades	CA	90272	310-454-1321	454-1078
Pacific Publishing Co 636 Alaska St S PO Box 80156 *Web:* www.pacificpublishingcompany.com	Seattle	WA	98108	206-461-1300	
Paddock Publications Inc 155 E Algonquin Rd *Web:* www.dailyherald.com	Arlington Heights	IL	60005	847-427-4300	427-1301
Palm Beach Newspapers Inc PO Box 24700 *TF:* 800-432-7595 ■ *Web:* www.palmbeachpost.com	West Palm Beach	FL	33416	561-820-4100	
Papers Inc 206 S Main St *TF:* 800-733-4111 ■ *Web:* www.the-papers.com	Milford	IN	46542	574-658-4111	658-4701
Pennysaver 26522 La Alameda	Mission Viejo	CA	92691	949-614-2600	
PG Publishing Co 34 Blvd of the Allies *TF Cust Svc:* 800-228-6397 ■ *Web:* www.post-gazette.com	Pittsburgh	PA	15222	412-263-1100	263-1703
Philadelphia Tribune Co 520 S 16th St *Web:* www.phillytrib.com	Philadelphia	PA	19146	215-893-4050	735-3612
Phoenix Media Communications Group 126 Brookline Ave *TF:* 888-536-7464 ■ *Web:* www.thephoenix.com	Boston	MA	02215	617-536-5390	536-1463
Phoenix Newspapers Inc 200 E Van Buren St *Web:* azcentral.com	Phoenix	AZ	85004	602-444-8000	444-8044
Pioneer Newspapers Inc 221 First Ave W Ste 405 *Web:* pioneernewsgroup.com	Seattle	WA	98119	206-284-4424	
Pipestone Publishing Co PO Box 277 *TF:* 800-325-6440 ■ *Web:* www.pipestonestar.com	Pipestone	MN	56164	507-825-3333	825-2168
Ponca City Publishing Inc PO Box 191 *TF:* 866-765-3311 ■ *Web:* www.poncacitynews.com	Ponca City	OK	74602	580-765-3311	762-6397
Press-Enterprise Co PO Box 792 *TF:* 800-794-6397 ■ *Web:* www.pe.com	Riverside	CA	92502	951-684-1200	368-9023
Press-Enterprise Inc 3185 Lackawanna Ave *TF:* 888-484-6345 ■ *Web:* www.pressenterprise.net	Bloomsburg	PA	17815	570-784-2121	784-9226
Princeton Packet, The 300 Witherspoon St PO Box 350 *TF:* 888-747-1122 ■ *Web:* centraljersey.com	Princeton	NJ	08542	609-924-3244	921-2714
Progressive Communications Corp 18 E Vine St PO Box 791 *TF:* 800-772-5333 ■ *Web:* www.mountvernonnews.com	Mount Vernon	OH	43050	740-397-5333	397-1321
Progressive Publishing Co PO Box 291 *Web:* www.theprogressnews.com	Clearfield	PA	16830	814-765-5581	765-5165
Quebecor Media Inc 612 Rue St Jacques *Web:* www.quebecor.com	Montreal	QC	H3C4M8	514-380-1999	
Quincy Newspapers Inc 130 S Fifth St *TF:* 800-373-9444 ■ *Web:* www.whig.com	Quincy	IL	62301	217-223-5100	223-9757
Recorder Publishing Co 17 Morristown Rd	Bernardsville	NJ	07924	908-766-3900	766-6365
Reminder Press Inc 130 Old Town Rd PO Box 27 *TF:* 888-456-2211 ■ *Web:* courant.com/reminder-news	Vernon	CT	06066	860-875-3366	875-2089
Republican Co 1860 Main St *TF:* 800-828-5597 ■ *Web:* www.repub.com	Springfield	MA	01103	413-788-1000	788-1301
Republican-American Inc 389 Meadow St *TF:* 800-992-3232 ■ *Web:* www.rep-am.com	Waterbury	CT	06702	203-574-3636	596-9277
Richmond Times-Dispatch PO Box 85333 *TF:* 800-468-3382 ■ *Web:* www.richmond.com	Richmond	VA	23293	804-649-6000	819-1216
Rivertown Newspaper Group 2760 N Service Dr PO Box 15 *TF:* 800-535-1660 ■ *Web:* www.republican-eagle.com	Red Wing	MN	55066	651-388-8235	388-3404
Rock Valley Publishing LLC 11512 N Second St *Web:* www.rvpublishing.com	Machesney Park	IL	61115	815-877-4044	
Rome Sentinel Co 333 W Dominick St *Web:* www.romesentinel.com	Rome	NY	13440	315-337-4000	339-6281
Salisbury Post 131 W Innes St *TF:* 800-546-5664	Salisbury	NC	28144	704-633-8950	639-0003
San Angelo Standard Times Inc PO Box 5111 *TF:* 800-588-1884 ■ *Web:* www.gosanangelo.com	San Angelo	TX	76902	325-653-1221	659-8173
San Gabriel Valley Newspaper Group 1210 N Azusa Canyon Rd *Web:* www.sgvn.com	West Covina	CA	91790	626-962-8811	
Santa Barbara News-Press Publishing Co 715 Anacapa St *TF:* 800-654-3292 ■ *Web:* www.newspress.com	Santa Barbara	CA	93101	805-564-5200	966-6258
Scripps Howard Inc PO Box 5380 *TF:* 800-888-3000 ■ *Web:* www.scripps.com	Cincinnati	OH	45202	513-977-3000	
Singapore Press Holdings 529 14th St NW National Press Bldg Ste 916 *Web:* www.sph.com.sg	Washington	DC	20045	202-662-8726	662-8729
Sonoma Index-Tribune Inc 117 W Napa St *Web:* www.sonomanews.com	Sonoma	CA	95476	707-938-2111	938-1600
Sound Publishing Inc 11323 Commando Rd W Unit Main *Web:* www.soundpublishing.com	Everett	WA	98204	360-394-5800	394-5829
Southern Newspapers Inc (SNI) 5701 Woodway Dr *Web:* www.sninews.com	Houston	TX	77057	713-266-5481	266-1847
Star News 296 Third Ave *Web:* www.thestarnews.com	Chula Vista	CA	91910	619-427-3000	426-6346
Star-News Newspapers PO Box 840 *Web:* www.starnewsonline.com	Wilmington	NC	28402	910-343-2000	343-2210
Stonebridge Press Inc 25 Elm St *TF:* 800-536-5836 ■ *Web:* www.stonebridgepress.com	Southbridge	MA	01550	508-764-4325	764-8015
Suburban Life Publications 1101 W 31st St Ste 100 *TF:* 800-397-9397 ■ *Web:* www.mysuburbanlife.com	Downers Grove	IL	60515	630-368-1100	969-0228
Sun Newspapers 1801 Superior Ave *TF:* 800-362-8008 ■ *Web:* www.advance-ohio.com	Cleveland	OH	44114	216-999-3900	
Tacoma News Inc 1950 S State St *Web:* www.thenewstribune.com	Tacoma	WA	98405	253-597-8742	597-8274
TB Butler Publishing Co 410 W Erwin St *TF:* 800-333-9141 ■ *Web:* www.tylerpaper.com	Tyler	TX	75702	903-597-8111	595-0335
Tennessee Valley Printing Company Inc PO Box 2213 *TF:* 888-353-4612 ■ *Web:* www.decaturdaily.com	Decatur	AL	35609	256-353-4612	340-2392
This Week Community Newspapers 7801 N Central Dr PO Box 608 *TF:* 800-860-1267 ■ *Web:* www.thisweeknews.com	Lewis Center	OH	43035	740-888-6000	888-6006
Times & News Publishing Co 1570 Fairfield Rd PO Box 3669 *Web:* www.gettysburgtimes.com	Gettysburg	PA	17325	717-334-1131	334-4243
Times Herald Inc 410 Markley St PO Box 591 *TF:* 888-933-4233 ■ *Web:* www.timesherald.com	Norristown	PA	19404	610-272-2500	
Times News Publishing Co 707 S Main St *TF:* 800-488-0085 ■ *Web:* www.thetimesnews.com	Burlington	NC	27215	336-227-0131	228-1889
Times-Citizen Communications Inc 406 Stevens St PO Box 640 *TF:* 800-798-2691 ■ *Web:* www.timescitizen.com	Iowa Falls	IA	50126	641-648-2521	648-4765
Tribune Review Publishing Co 622 Cabin Hill Dr *TF:* 800-524-5700 ■ *Web:* pittsburghpennysaver.com	Greensburg	PA	15601	724-834-1151	838-5171
Truth Publishing Company Inc 421 S Second St *TF:* 800-585-5416 ■ *Web:* www.elkharttruth.com	Elkhart	IN	46516	574-294-1661	294-3895
Warrick Publishing Inc 204 W Locust St PO Box 266 *Web:* www.tristate-media.com	Boonville	IN	47601	812-897-2330	897-3703
Western Communications Inc 1777 SW Chandler Ave *Web:* www.bendbulletin.com	Bend	OR	97702	541-382-1811	383-0372
Western States Weeklies Inc PO Box 600600 *TF:* 800-628-9466 ■ *Web:* www.navydispatch.com	San Diego	CA	92160	619-280-2985	
Wick Communications Inc 333 W Wilcox Dr Ste 302 *Web:* www.wickcommunications.com	Sierra Vista	AZ	85635	520-458-0200	458-6166
William J Kline & Son Inc 1 Venner Rd *TF:* 800-453-6397	Amsterdam	NY	12010	518-843-1100	843-1338
Wooster Republican Printing Co 212 E Liberty St *TF:* 800-686-2958 ■ *Web:* www.the-daily-record.com	Wooster	OH	44691	330-264-1125	
Worcester Telegram & Gazette Inc 20 Franklin St PO Box 15012 *TF:* 800-678-6680 ■ *Web:* www.telegram.com	Worcester	MA	01615	508-793-9100	793-9313
World Publishing Co 315 S Boulder Ave *TF:* 800-444-6552 ■ *Web:* www.tulsaworld.com	Tulsa	OK	74102	918-583-2161	581-8353
Yankton Press & Dakotan 319 Walnut St PO Box 56 *TF:* 800-743-2968 ■ *Web:* www.yankton.net	Yankton	SD	57078	605-665-7811	665-1721
York Newspaper Co 1891 Loucks Rd *TF:* 800-559-3520 ■ *Web:* www.inyork.com	York	PA	17408	717-767-6397	772-8284
Your Houston News 523 N Sam Houston Pkwy E Ste 600 *Web:* www.yourhoustonnews.com	Houston	TX	77060	281-668-1100	

637-9 Periodicals Publishers

Company	City	State	ZIP	Phone	Fax
1105 Media Inc 9201 Oakdale Ave Ste 101 *Web:* www.1105media.com	Chatsworth	CA	91311	818-814-5200	734-1522
ABC Inc 77 W 66th St *Web:* www.abc.go.com	New York	NY	10023	212-456-7777	456-2795

Company / Address	City	State	ZIP	Phone	Fax
Access Intelligence LLC 4 Choke Cherry Rd 2nd Fl *TF:* 800-777-5006 ■ *Web:* www.accessintel.com	Rockville	MD	20850	301-354-2000	
ACTION On-Line Inc 4 S Central Ave Ste 1 *Web:* actionol.com	Saint Louis	MO	63105	314-726-4994	
Adler & Adler Publishers Inc 5530 Wisconsin Ave Ste 1460	Chevy Chase	MD	20815	301-654-4271	
Advantage Business Media 100 Enterprise Dr Ste 600 PO Box 912 **Fax:* Hum Res ■ *Web:* advantagemedia.com	Rockaway	NJ	07866	973-920-7000	920-7542*
Advertising Specialties Institute 4800 St Rd *TF:* 800-546-1350 ■ *Web:* www.asicentral.com	Trevose	PA	19053	215-942-8600	953-3045
Advisor Media Inc 4849 Viewridge Ave	San Diego	CA	92123	858-278-5600	
Adweek Directories 770 Broadway *Web:* www.adweek.com	New York	NY	10003	646-654-5000	
Affinity Group Inc 2575 Vista Del Mar *Web:* www.goodsamclub.com	Ventura	CA	93001	805-667-4100	
AHC Media LLC 3525 Piedmont Rd NE Bldg 6 Ste 400 **Fax:* Cust Svc ■ *TF Cust Svc:* 800-688-2421 ■ *Web:* www.ahcmedia.com	Atlanta	GA	30305	404-262-5476	262-5560*
Alexander Communications Group Inc 712 Main St Ste 187-B *TF:* 800-232-4317 ■ *Web:* www.alexcommgrp.com	Boonton	NJ	07005	973-265-2300	402-6056
American City Business Journals Inc 120 W Morehead St Ste 400 *Web:* www.bizjournals.com	Charlotte	NC	28202	704-973-1000	973-1001
American Lawyer Media Inc (ALM) 120 Broadway 5th Fl *TF:* 877-256-2472 ■ *Web:* www.alm.com	New York	NY	10271	212-457-9400	
American Media Inc 4 New York Plz *Web:* www.americanmediainc.com	New York	NY	10004	212-545-4800	
American Psychiatric Publishing Inc 1000 Wilson Blvd Ste 1825 *TF:* 800-368-5777 ■ *Web:* www.appi.org	Arlington	VA	22209	703-907-7322	907-1091
Amos Press Inc 911 S Vandemark Rd *TF:* 866-468-1622 ■ *Web:* www.amosmedia.com	Sidney	OH	45365	937-498-2111	498-0812
Annual Reviews 4139 El Camino Way *TF:* 800-523-8635 ■ *Web:* www.annualreviews.org	Palo Alto	CA	94303	650-493-4400	855-9815
APN Media LLC PO Box 20113 *TF:* 800-470-7599 ■ *Web:* www.ohranger.com	New York	NY	10023	212-581-3380	245-4226
Atlantic Information Services Inc 1100 17th St NW Ste 300 *TF:* 800-521-4323 ■ *Web:* www.aishealth.com	Washington	DC	20036	202-775-9008	331-9542
Augsburg Fortress Publishers 510 Marquette Ave Ste 800 *TF:* 800-426-0115 ■ *Web:* www.augsburgfortress.org	Minneapolis	MN	55402	612-330-3300	330-3455
AVN Media Network Inc 9400 Penfield Ave *Web:* www.avnmedianetwork.com	Chatsworth	CA	91311	818-718-5788	
Bauer Publishing Co LP 270 Sylvan Ave **Fax Area Code:* 201 ■ *Web:* www.bauerpublishing.com	Englewood Cliffs	NJ	07632	212-764-3344	569-5303*
BCC Research LLC 49 Walnut Pk Bldg 2 *TF:* 866-285-7215 ■ *Web:* www.bccresearch.com	Wellesley	MA	02481	781-489-7301	489-7308
Becker Communications 119 Merchant St Ste 300 *Web:* www.beckercommunications.com	Honolulu	HI	96813	808-533-4165	537-4990
Bertelsmann SE & Co 1745 Broadway *Web:* www.bertelsmann.com	New York	NY	10019	490-524-1800	
Bloomberg LP 731 Lexington Ave *Web:* www.bloomberg.com	New York	NY	10022	212-318-2000	893-5000
Boardroom Inc 281 Tresser Blvd 8th Fl **Fax Area Code:* 203 ■ *TF:* 800-274-5611 ■ *Web:* blinepubs.com	Stamford	CT	06901	800-274-5611	967-3086*
Bobit Business Media 3520 Challenger St **Fax:* Hum Res ■ *TF:* 888-239-2455 ■ *Web:* www.bobitbusinessmedia.com	Torrance	CA	90503	310-533-2400	533-2500*
Bureau of National Affairs Inc 1801 S Bell St *TF:* 800-372-1033 ■ *Web:* www.bna.com	Arlington	VA	22202	703-341-3000	
Business & Legal Reports Inc (BLR) 141 Mill Rock Rd E *TF:* 800-727-5257 ■ *Web:* www.blr.com	Old Saybrook	CT	06475	860-510-0100	510-7225
Business News Publishing Co 2401 W Big Beaver Rd Ste 700 *TF:* 800-837-7370 ■ *Web:* www.bnpmedia.com	Troy	MI	48084	248-362-3700	362-0317
Buyers Laboratory Inc 20 Railroad Ave *Web:* www.buyerslab.com	Hackensack	NJ	07601	201-488-0404	
Cabot Heritage Corp 176 N St PO Box 2049 *TF:* 800-326-8826 ■ *Web:* www.cabot.net	Salem	MA	01970	978-745-5532	745-1283
Cambridge Whos Who Publishing Inc 498 Rexcorp Plz 4th Fl *Web:* cambridgewhoswho.com	Uniondale	NY	11556	516-535-1515	
Card Player Media LLC 6940 O'Bannon Dr Ste 8 *Web:* www.cardplayer.com	Las Vegas	NV	89117	702-871-1720	
Challenge Publications Inc 9509 Vassar Ave Ste A *TF:* 800-562-9182 ■ *Web:* www.challengeweb.com	Chatsworth	CA	91311	818-700-6868	700-6282
Christianity Today International 465 Gundersen Dr *Web:* www.christianitytoday.com	Carol Stream	IL	60188	630-260-6200	260-0114
Coffey Communications Inc 1505 Business One Cir *Web:* coffeycomm.com	Walla Walla	WA	99362	509-525-0101	
CollegeBound Network 1200 S Ave Ste 202 *Web:* www.collegebound.net	Staten Island	NY	10314	718-761-4800	761-3300
Commodity Information Systems Inc 3030 NW Expy Ste 725 *TF:* 800-231-0477 ■ *Web:* www.cis-okc.com	Oklahoma City	OK	73112	405-604-8726	604-8726
Computer Economics Inc 2082 Business Ctr Dr Ste 240 *Web:* www.computereconomics.com	Irvine	CA	92612	949-831-8700	442-7688
Consumers Digest Inc 520 Lk Cook Rd Ste 500 *Web:* consumersdigest.com	Deerfield	IL	60015	847-607-3000	
Consumers Union of US Inc 101 Truman Ave *TF:* 800-927-4357 ■ *Web:* www.consumersunion.org	Yonkers	NY	10703	914-378-2000	
Cook Communications Ministries 4050 Lee Vance View *TF:* 800-708-5550 ■ *Web:* www.davidccook.com	Colorado Springs	CO	80918	719-536-0100	
Crain Communications Inc 1155 Gratiot Ave **Fax:* Hum Res ■ *TF:* 888-288-6954 ■ *Web:* www.crain.com	Detroit	MI	48207	313-446-6000	446-0361*
CRC Press LLC 6000 Broken Sound Pkwy NW Ste 300 **Fax Area Code:* 800 ■ **Fax:* Cust Svc ■ *TF Cust Svc:* 800-272-7737 ■ *Web:* www.crcpress.com	Boca Raton	FL	33487	561-994-0555	374-3401*
Cutter Information Corp 37 Broadway Ste 1 *TF:* 800-964-5118 ■ *Web:* www.cutter.com	Arlington	MA	02474	781-648-8700	648-8707
DataTrends Publications Inc PO Box 3221 **Fax Area Code:* 703 ■ *Web:* www.datatrendspublications.com	Leesburg	VA	20177	571-313-9916	771-9091*
Deal LLC, The 20 Broad St *TF Cust Svc:* 888-667-3325 ■ *Web:* www.thedeal.com	New York	NY	10005	212-313-9325	
Desert Homes Magazine 303 N Indian Canyon Dr PO Box 2724 *Web:* www.palmspringslife.com	Palm Springs	CA	92262	760-325-2333	
Desktop Engineering 1283 Main St PO Box 1039 *Web:* www.deskeng.com	Dublin	NH	03444	603-563-1631	563-8192
Disney Consumer Products 500 S Buena Vista St **Fax Area Code:* 215 ■ **Fax:* Cust Svc ■ *TF PR:* 855-553-4763 ■ *Web:* thewaltdisneycompany.com	Burbank	CA	91521	818-560-1000	553-5402*
Diversified Business Communications 121 Free St *Web:* divcom.com	Portland	ME	04101	207-842-5500	842-5503
Dupont Publishing Inc 3051 Tech Dr *Web:* dupontregistry.com	St Petersburg	FL	33716	727-573-9339	
E H Publishing Inc PO Box 989 *Web:* www.ehpub.com	Framingham	MA	01701	508-663-1500	663-1599
Earl G Graves Ltd 130 Fifth Ave 10th Fl *TF Cust Svc:* 800-727-7777 ■ *Web:* www.blackenterprise.com	New York	NY	10011	212-242-8000	
Economist Intelligence Unit 750 Third Ave 5th Fl *Web:* www.eiu.com	New York	NY	10017	212-554-0600	586-1181
Editorial Projects in Education 6935 Arlington Rd Ste 100 *Web:* www.edweek.org	Bethesda	MD	20814	301-280-3100	280-3200
EGW.com Inc 4075 Papazian Way *TF Cust Svc:* 800-546-4754	Fremont	CA	94538	510-668-0268	668-0280
Elliott Wave International (EWI) PO Box 1618 *TF Cust Svc:* 800-336-1618 ■ *Web:* www.elliottwave.com	Gainesville	GA	30503	770-536-0309	536-2514
Elsevier Science Ltd 360 Pk Ave S *TF:* 888-437-4636 ■ *Web:* www.elsevier.com	New York	NY	10010	212-989-5800	633-3990
Emerging Portfolio Fund Research Inc 80 Sherman St *Web:* www.epfr.com	Cambridge	MA	02140	617-864-4999	
Energy Intelligence Group 5 E 37th St 5th Fl *Web:* www.energyintel.com	New York	NY	10016	212-532-1112	532-4479
Entrepreneur Media Inc 18061 Fitch *TF:* 877-652-5295 ■ *Web:* www.entrepreneur.com	Irvine	CA	92614	949-261-2325	261-7729
Ernst Publishing Co LLC 1 Commerce Plaza 99 Washington Ave Ste 309 *TF:* 800-345-3822 ■ *Web:* marketing.ernstinfo.com	Albany	NY	12210	800-345-3822	252-0906
Essence Communications Inc 135 W 50th St 4th Fl **Fax Area Code:* 212 ■ *TF Sales:* 800-274-9398 ■ *Web:* www.essence.com	New York	NY	10020	800-274-9398	921-5173*
Euromoney Institutional Investor PLC 225 Pk Ave S *Web:* www.institutionalinvestor.com	New York	NY	10003	212-224-3300	
F+W, A Content + eCommerce Co 10151 Carver Rd Ste 200 *TF Sales:* 800-289-0963 ■ *Web:* www.fwcommunity.com	Cincinnati	OH	45236	513-531-2690	531-2690
Forbes Inc 60 Fifth Ave *TF:* 800-295-0893 ■ *Web:* www.forbes.com	New York	NY	10011	212-620-2200	
Forecast International 22 Commerce Rd *TF:* 800-451-4975 ■ *Web:* www.forecastinternational.com	Newtown	CT	06470	203-426-0800	426-1964
Forum Publishing Co 383 E Main St *TF:* 800-635-7654 ■ *Web:* www.forum123.com	Centerport	NY	11721	631-754-5000	
Gardner Publications Inc 6915 Valley Ave *TF:* 800-950-8020 ■ *Web:* www.gardnerweb.com	Cincinnati	OH	45244	513-527-8800	527-8801
Grace Communion International PO Box 5005 *TF:* 800-423-4444 ■ *Web:* www.gci.org	Glendora	CA	91740	626-650-2300	
Grand View Media Group Inc (GVMG) 200 Croft St Ste 1 *TF:* 888-431-2877 ■ *Web:* grandviewmedia.com	Birmingham	AL	35242	205-408-3700	408-3797
Grandstand Publishing LLC 990 Grove St Ste 400 *Web:* baseballdigest.com	Evanston	IL	60201	847-491-6440	491-0459
Greater Washington Publishing Inc 1800 Alexander Bell Dr Ste 120 *Web:* www.gwpi.net	Vienna	VA	20191	703-992-1100	893-8356
Gulf Publishing Company Inc 2 Greenway Plz Ste 1020 *Web:* www.gulfpub.com	Houston	TX	77046	713-529-4301	520-4433
Hanley-Wood LLC 1 Thomas Cir NW Ste 600 *TF:* 800-227-8839 ■ *Web:* www.hanleywood.com	Washington	DC	20005	202-452-0800	785-1974
Hart Publications Inc 1616 S Voss Rd Ste 1000 *TF:* 800-874-2544 ■ *Web:* www.hartenergy.com	Houston	TX	77057	713-260-6400	840-8585
Hatton Brown Publishers Inc PO Box 2268 *TF:* 800-669-5613 ■ *Web:* www.hattonbrown.net	Montgomery	AL	36102	334-834-1170	
Health Forum 155 North Wacker Drive Ste 400 *TF:* 800-621-6902 ■ *Web:* healthforum.com	Chicago	IL	60606	312-893-6800	
Healthy Directions LLC 7811 Montrose Rd *TF:* 866-599-9491 ■ *Web:* www.healthydirections.com	Potomac	MD	20854	866-599-9491	
Hearst Magazines Div 300 W 57th St *Web:* www.hearst.com	New York	NY	10019	212-649-2275	
Highlights for Children Inc 1800 Watermark Dr *TF Cust Svc:* 800-255-9517 ■ *Web:* www.highlights.com	Columbus	OH	43216	614-486-0631	324-1630
Hli Properties Inc 1003 Central Ave *TF:* 800-247-2000 ■ *Web:* www.hlipublishing.com	Fort Dodge	IA	50501	515-955-1600	

Company	City	State	Zip	Phone	Fax
Hobsons CollegeView 50 E Business Way Ste 300 *TF:* 800-927-8439 ■ *Web:* www.collegeview.com	Cincinnati	OH	45241	800-927-8439	891-8531
Homes & Land Magazine Affiliates LLC 1830 E Pk Ave *TF:* 800-277-7800 ■ *Web:* www.homesandland.com	Tallahassee	FL	32301	850-575-0189	574-2525
Honolulu Publishing Co Ltd 707 Richards St Ste PH3 *TF:* 800-272-5245 ■ *Web:* www.honolulupublishing.com	Honolulu	HI	96813	808-524-7400	531-2306
Horizon House Publications Inc (HHP) 685 Canton St *Web:* www.horizonhouse.com	Norwood	MA	02062	781-769-9750	762-9071
IEEE Computer Society Press 10662 Los Vaqueros Cir PO Box 3014 *TF:* 800-272-6657 ■ *Web:* computer.org/portal/web/cspress/home	Los Alamitos	CA	90720	714-821-8380	821-4010
Information Today Inc 143 Old Marlton Pike *TF:* 800-300-9868	Medford	NJ	08055	609-654-6266	654-4309
InfoWorld Media Group Inc 501 Second St 6 Fl *TF:* 800-227-8365 ■ *Web:* www.infoworld.com	San Francisco	CA	94107	415-243-0500	978-3120
Inside Washington Publishers 1919 S Eads St Ste 201 *TF:* 800-424-9068 ■ *Web:* www.iwpnews.com	Arlington	VA	22202	703-416-8500	416-8543
Institutional Investor Newsletters 225 Pk Ave S 8th Fl **Fax:* Cust Svc ■ *TF:* 800-437-9997 ■ *Web:* www.iinews.com	New York	NY	10003	212-224-3300	224-3491*
International Data Group Inc (IDG) 1 Exeter Plaza 15th Fl *TF Orders:* 800-343-4952 ■ *Web:* www.idg.com	Boston	MA	02116	617-534-1200	859-8642
Internet Business Network 303 Ross Dr *TF:* 866-497-6747	Mill Valley	CA	94941	415-377-2255	380-8245
Johnson Publishing Company Inc 200 S Michigan Ave *Web:* www.johnsonpublishing.com	Chicago	IL	60604	312-322-9200	
Journey Group Inc 418 Fourth St Ne *Web:* journeygroup.com	Charlottesville	VA	22902	434-961-2500	
JR O'Dwyer Co 271 Madison Ave 6th Fl *TF:* 866-395-7710 ■ *Web:* www.odwyerpr.com	New York	NY	10016	212-679-2471	683-2750
Latin Press Inc 2455 SW 27th Ave *Web:* www.latinpressinc.com	Miami	FL	33145	305-285-3133	
Laurin Publishing Co Inc 100 West St *TF:* 877-422-7300 ■ *Web:* www.photonics.com	Pittsfield	MA	01202	413-499-0514	442-3180
Lawrence Ragan Communications Inc 111 E Wacker Dr Ste 500 **Fax Area Code:* 312 ■ *TF:* 800-878-5331 ■ *Web:* www.ragan.com	Chicago	IL	60601	800-493-4867	960-4106*
Lebhar-Friedman Inc 425 Pk Ave	New York	NY	10022	212-756-5000	
LFP Inc 8484 Wilshire Blvd Ste 900 *Web:* hustler.com	Beverly Hills	CA	90211	323-651-5400	651-3525
Lionheart Publishing Inc 506 Roswell St *TF:* 888-303-5639 ■ *Web:* lionheartpub.com	Marietta	GA	30060	888-303-5639	
Lippincott Williams & Wilkins 530 Walnut St *Web:* www.lww.com	Philadelphia	PA	19106	215-521-8300	521-8902
Liturgical Publications Inc 2875 S James Dr *TF:* 800-876-4574 ■ *Web:* www.4lpi.com	New Berlin	WI	53151	262-785-1188	
LRP Publications 360 Hiatt Dr *TF:* 800-621-5463 ■ *Web:* www.lrp.com	Palm Beach Gardens	FL	33418	561-622-6520	622-2423
MAC Publishing LLC 501 Second St *Web:* www.macworld.com	San Francisco	CA	94107	415-243-0505	
Mary Ann Liebert Publishers Inc 140 Huguenot St 3rd Fl *TF:* 800-654-3237 ■ *Web:* www.liebertpub.com	New Rochelle	NY	10801	914-740-2100	740-2101
McGraw-Hill Cos Inc 1221 Ave of the Americas *NYSE: MHFI* ■ *Web:* www.mcgraw-hill.com	New York	NY	10020	212-512-2000	
McKnight's Long-Term Care News 1 Northfield Plz Ste 521 *TF:* 800-558-1703 ■ *Web:* www.mcknights.com	Northfield	IL	60093	847-784-8706	
Media Business Corp 1810 Platte St *Web:* mediabiz.com	Denver	CO	80202	303-271-9960	
Meister Media Worldwide 37733 Euclid Ave *TF Orders:* 800-572-7740 ■ *Web:* www.meistermedia.com	Willoughby	OH	44094	440-942-2000	942-0662
Mercedes Distribution Center Inc Brooklyn Navy Yard 63 Flushing Ave Ste 340 *Web:* www.mdist.com	Brooklyn	NY	11205	718-534-3000	
Meredith Corp 1716 Locust St *NYSE: MDP* ■ *Web:* www.meredith.com	Des Moines	IA	50309	515-284-3000	
Mergent Inc 477 Madison Ave Ste 410 *TF:* 800-937-1398 ■ *Web:* www.mergent.com	New York	NY	10022	212-413-7700	413-7670
Merion Publications Inc 2900 Horizon Dr *TF:* 800-355-1088 ■ *Web:* www.advanceweb.com	King of Prussia	PA	19406	610-278-1400	278-1425
Miles Media Group Inc 6751 Professional Pkwy W Ste 200 *TF:* 888-232-2499 ■ *Web:* www.see-florida.com	Sarasota	FL	34240	941-342-2300	
Moody's Corp 250 Greenwich St 7 World Trade Ctr *NYSE: MCO* ■ *Web:* www.moodys.com	New York	NY	10007	212-553-0300	
National Braille Press Inc 88 St Stephen St *TF:* 888-965-8965 ■ *Web:* www.nbp.org	Boston	MA	02115	617-266-6160	437-0456
National Catholic Reporter Publishing Co 115 E Armour Blvd *TF:* 800-333-7373 ■ *Web:* www.ncronline.org	Kansas City	MO	64111	816-531-0538	968-2292
Natural Mktg Institute Inc, The 272 Ruth Rd *Web:* www.nmisolutions.com	Harleysville	PA	19438	215-513-7300	
Nelson Publishing 2500 Tamiami Trl N *TF:* 800-226-6113 ■ *Web:* www.nelsonpub.com	Nokomis	FL	34275	941-966-9521	966-2590
News Corp 1211 Ave of the Americas *NASDAQ: NWSA* ■ *Web:* www.newscorp.com	New York	NY	10036	212-416-3400	
North American Publishing Co (NAPCO) 1500 Springarden St 12th Fl *TF:* 800-627-2689 ■ *Web:* www.napco.com	Philadelphia	PA	19130	215-238-5300	238-5457
Northstar Travel Media LLC 100 Lighting Way **Fax:* Hum Res ■ *Web:* www.northstartravelgroup.com	Secaucus	NJ	07094	201-902-2000	902-2045*
Our Sunday Visitor Inc 200 Noll Plaza *TF:* 800-348-2440 ■ *Web:* www.osv.com	Huntington	IN	46750	260-356-8400	356-8472
Pace Communications Inc 1301 Carolina St *Web:* www.paceco.com	Greensboro	NC	27401	336-378-6065	378-8273
Pacific Press 1350 N Kings Rd *TF Cust Svc:* 800-765-6955 ■ *Web:* www.pacificpress.com	Nampa	ID	83687	208-465-2500	465-2531
Paisano Publications LLC 28210 Dorothy Dr *TF:* 800-323-3484 ■ *Web:* www.paisanopub.com	Agoura Hills	CA	91301	818-889-8740	889-5214
Parade Publications Inc 711 Third Ave *Web:* parade.com	New York	NY	10017	212-450-7000	450-7287
Penton Media Inc 1300 E Ninth St *Web:* www.penton.com	Cleveland	OH	44114	216-696-7000	
Photosource International 1910 35th Rd *TF:* 800-786-6277 ■ *Web:* www.photosource.com	Osceola	WI	54020	715-248-3800	
Platts 2 Penn Plz 25th Fl *TF:* 800-752-8878 ■ *Web:* www.platts.com	New York	NY	10121	212-904-3070	
Pohly Co 867 Boylston St 5th Fl *TF:* 800-383-0888 ■ *Web:* www.pohlyco.com	Boston	MA	02116	617-451-1700	338-7767
Powersports Business Magazine 6420 Sycamore Ln N *Web:* www.powersportsbusiness.com	Maple Grove	MN	55369	763-383-4400	
Professional Sports Publications 519 Eigth Ave 25th Fl *Web:* www.pspsports.com	New York	NY	10018	212-697-1460	
Progressive Impressions 1 Hardman Dr *TF:* 800-644-0444 ■ *Web:* www.whateverittakes.com	Bloomington	IL	61701	309-664-0444	662-2055
Publications & Communications Inc 13552 Hwy 183 N Ste A *TF:* 800-678-9724 ■ *Web:* www.pcinews.com	Austin	TX	78750	512-250-9023	
Publications International Ltd 7373 N Cicero Ave *TF General:* 800-777-5582 ■ *Web:* pilbooks.com	Lincolnwood	IL	60712	847-676-3470	676-3671
Publishing Group of America Media 341 Cool Springs Blvd Ste 400	Franklin	TN	37067	615-468-6000	
Putman Media Inc 555 W Pierce Rd *TF:* 866-666-6033 ■ *Web:* www.putman.net	Itasca	IL	60143	630-467-1301	
Quebecor Media Inc 612 Rue St Jacques *Web:* www.quebecor.com	Montreal	QC	H3C4M8	514-380-1999	
Randall-Reilly Publishing Co 3200 Rice Mine Rd NE *TF Cust Svc:* 800-633-5953 ■ *Web:* randallreilly.com	Tuscaloosa	AL	35406	800-633-5953	
Renard Communications Inc 197 Mountain Ave	Springfield	NJ	07081	973-912-8550	
RentPath Inc 950 E Paces Ferry Rd NE Ste 2600 *TF:* 800-216-1423 ■ *Web:* rentpath.com	Norcross	GA	30092	678-421-3000	
RentPath, LLC 950 East Paces Ferry Rd NE Ste 2600 *TF:* 800-216-1423 ■ *Web:* rentpath.com	Atlanta	GA	30326	678-421-3000	
Review & Herald Publishing Assn 55 W Oak Ridge Dr *TF:* 800-456-3991 ■ *Web:* www.rhpa.org	Hagerstown	MD	21740	301-393-3000	393-3209
Sage Publications Inc 2455 Teller Rd *TF:* 800-818-7243 ■ *Web:* www.sagepub.com	Thousand Oaks	CA	91320	805-499-9774	499-0871
Saint Croix Press Inc 1185 S Knowles Ave *TF:* 800-826-6622 ■ *Web:* www.stcroixpress.com	New Richmond	WI	54017	715-246-5811	246-2486
Sandhills Publishing 120 W Harvest Dr *TF:* 800-331-1978 ■ *Web:* www.sandhills.com	Lincoln	NE	68521	402-479-2181	479-2195
Schaeffer's Investment Research Inc 5151 Pfeiffer Rd Ste 250 *TF:* 800-448-2080 ■ *Web:* www.schaeffersresearch.com	Cincinnati	OH	45242	513-589-3800	589-3810
Simba Information 60 Long Ridge Rd Ste 300 *TF:* 888-297-4622 ■ *Web:* simbainformation.com	Stamford	CT	06902	203-325-8193	325-8915
Simmons-Boardman Publishing Corp 55 Broad St 26th fl 12th Fl *TF:* 800-895-4389 ■ *Web:* www.simmonsboardman.com	New York	NY	10004	212-620-7200	633-1165
Singapore Press Holdings 529 14th St NW National Press Bldg Ste 916 *Web:* www.sph.com.sg	Washington	DC	20045	202-662-8726	662-8729
Sky Publishing Corp 90 Sherman St *TF:* 800-253-0245 ■ *Web:* skyandtelescope.com/a-brief-history-of-skytelescope	Cambridge	MA	02140	617-864-7360	864-6117
Slack Inc 6900 Grove Rd *TF:* 800-257-8290 ■ *Web:* www.slackinc.com	Thorofare	NJ	08086	856-848-1000	848-6091
Smithsonian Institution Business Ventures Div 600 Maryland Ave SW Ste 6000 *TF:* 800-521-5330 ■ *Web:* www.si.edu	Washington	DC	20024	202-633-6080	
Source Media Inc 1 State St Plz 27th Fl *TF:* 800-221-1809 ■ *Web:* www.sourcemedia.com	New York	NY	10004	212-803-8200	
Stamats Communications Inc 615 Fifth St SE *TF:* 800-553-8878 ■ *Web:* www.stamats.com	Cedar Rapids	IA	52401	319-364-6167	364-4278
Standard Publishing Co 8805 Governors Hill Dr Ste 400 **Fax Area Code:* 877 ■ *TF Orders:* 800-543-1353 ■ *Web:* www.standardpub.com	Cincinnati	OH	45249	513-931-4050	867-5751*
Strafford Publications Inc PO Box 13729 *TF:* 800-926-7926 ■ *Web:* www.straffordpub.com	Atlanta	GA	30324	404-881-1141	881-0074
Strang Communications 600 Rinehart Rd *Web:* www.charismamedia.com	Lake Mary	FL	32746	407-333-0600	333-7100
Sunset Publishing Corp 80 Willow Rd *TF:* 800-227-7346 ■ *Web:* www.sunset.com	Menlo Park	CA	94025	650-321-3600	
Sys-con Media Inc 577 Chestnut Ridge Rd **Fax:* Cust Svc ■ *Web:* www.sys-con.com	Woodcliff Lake	NJ	07677	201-802-3000	782-9600*
Taunton Press Inc 63 S Main St PO Box 5506 *Web:* www.taunton.com	Newtown	CT	06470	203-426-8171	426-3434
Tax Analysts 400 S Maple Ave *Web:* taxanalysts.com	Falls Church	VA	22046	703-533-4400	

Company	City	State	Zip	Phone	Fax
Tax Management Inc 1801 S Bell St *TF:* 800-372-1033 ■ *Web:* www.bna.com	Arlington	VA	22202	703-341-3000	
Testa Communications 25 Willowdale Ave *Web:* www.testa.com	Port Washington	NY	11050	516-767-2500	767-9335
Thompson Publishing Group Inc 805 15th St NW 3rd Fl *TF Cust Svc:* 800-677-3789 ■ *Web:* www.thompson.com	Washington	DC	20005	202-872-4000	296-1091
Time Inc 1271 Ave of the Americas *Web:* www.timeinc.com	New York	NY	10020	212-522-1212	
Transcontinental Inc 1100 Rene-Levesque Blvd W 24th Fl *TF:* 800-361-5479 ■ *Web:* tctranscontinental.com	Montreal	QC	H3B4X9	514-392-9000	
TransWorld Business 2052 Corte Del Nogal Ste 100 *TF General:* 800-788-7072 ■ *Web:* business.transworld.net	Carlsbad	CA	92011	760-722-7777	722-0653
United Methodist Publishing House 201 Eigth Ave S *TF:* 800-672-1789 ■ *Web:* umph.org	Nashville	TN	37203	615-749-6000	
University of Chicago Press Journals Div PO Box 37005 *TF:* 877-705-1878 ■ *Web:* www.press.uchicago.edu	Chicago	IL	60637	773-702-7700	753-0811
Vendome Group LLC 216 E 45th St 6th Fl **Fax Area Code:* 212 ■ *TF:* 800-519-3692 ■ *Web:* www.vendomegrp.com	New York	NY	10017	800-519-3692	228-1308*
Virgo Publishing Inc 3300 N Central Ave Ste 300 *Web:* www.vpico.com	Phoenix	AZ	85012	480-990-1101	990-0819
Viz Media 295 Bay St *Web:* www.viz.com	San Francisco	CA	94133	415-546-7073	546-7086
Warren Communications News Inc 2115 Ward Ct NW *TF:* 800-771-9202 ■ *Web:* www.warren-news.com	Washington	DC	20037	202-872-9200	318-8350
Weddings In Houston Lp 525 Arlington St *Web:* weddingsinhouston.com	Houston	TX	77007	713-464-4321	464-2880
West World Production Inc 420 N Camden Dr *Web:* www.wwpi.com	Beverly Hills	CA	90210	310-276-9500	
Wright's Media 2407 Timberloch Pl Ste B *TF:* 877-652-5295 ■ *Web:* wrightsmedia.com	The Woodlands	TX	77380	281-419-5725	
Yankee Publishing Inc PO Box 520 *TF:* 800-729-9265 ■ *Web:* yankeemagazine.com	Dublin	NH	03444	603-563-8111	563-8252
Ziff Davis Inc 28 E 28th St *Web:* www.ziffdavis.com	New York	NY	10016	212-503-3500	

637-10 Publishers (Misc)

Company	City	State	Zip	Phone	Fax
Allrecipescom Inc 413 Pine St Ste 500 *Web:* www.webconnoisseur.com	Seattle	WA	98101	206-292-3990	
AM Best Co Ambest Rd *TF:* 800-424-2378 ■ *Web:* www.ambest.com	Oldwick	NJ	08858	908-439-2200	439-3296
American Printing House for the Blind 1839 Frankfort Ave PO Box 6085 *TF:* 800-223-1839 ■ *Web:* www.aph.org	Louisville	KY	40206	502-895-2405	899-2274
Animax Interactive LLC 6627 Valjean Ave *Web:* www.animaxent.com	Van Nuys	CA	91406	818-787-4444	
Casino City Inc 95 Wells Ave Ste 125 *Web:* www.casinocitypress.com	Newton Center	MA	02459	617-332-2850	
Cathedral Press Inc 600 NE Sixth St *TF Cust Svc:* 800-874-8332 ■ *Web:* www.cathedralpress.com	Long Prairie	MN	56347	320-732-6143	732-3457
Chalk & Vermilion Fine Arts Inc 55 Old Post Rd Ste 2 *TF:* 800-877-2250 ■ *Web:* www.chalk-vermilion.com	Greenwich	CT	06830	203-869-9500	
Channing Bete Co 1 Community Pl **Fax Area Code:* 800 ■ **Fax:* Cust Svc ■ *TF:* 800-477-4776 ■ *Web:* www.channing-bete.com	South Deerfield	MA	01373	413-665-7611	499-6464*
Clement Communications Inc 3 Creek Pkwy *TF:* 800-253-6368 ■ *Web:* www.clement.com	Upper Chichester	PA	19061	610-459-4200	
Coastal Training Technologies Corp 500 Studio Dr *TF:* 866-333-6888 ■ *Web:* www.coastal.com	Virginia Beach	VA	23452	757-498-9014	498-3657
CSS Industries Inc 1845 Walnut St Ste 800 *NYSE: CSS* ■ *Web:* www.cssindustries.com	Philadelphia	PA	19103	215-569-9900	569-9979
Drivers License Guide Co 1492 Oddstad Dr *TF:* 800-227-8827 ■ *Web:* www.driverslicenseguide.com	Redwood City	CA	94063	650-369-4849	364-8740
EBSCO Publishing Inc 10 Estes St *TF:* 800-653-2726 ■ *Web:* www.ebscohost.com	Ipswich	MA	01938	978-356-6500	356-6500
Encyclopedia Britannica Inc 331 N Las Salle St *TF Cust Svc:* 800-323-1229 ■ *Web:* www.britannica.com	Chicago	IL	60654	312-347-7159	294-2104
Flyer.Com 201 Kelsey Ln *TF:* 800-995-4433 ■ *Web:* theflyer.com	Tampa	FL	33619	813-626-9430	
Force Mass Acceleration 20 W 22nd St Ste 601	New York	NY	10010	212-691-5000	
Forecast International 22 Commerce Rd *TF:* 800-451-4975 ■ *Web:* www.forecastinternational.com	Newtown	CT	06470	203-426-0800	426-1964
Genesis Press Inc 7112 Augusta Rd	Piedmont	SC	29673	864-552-2000	
Hadley House Co PO Box 219 **Fax Area Code:* 320 ■ *TF:* 800-423-5390 ■ *Web:* www.hadleyhouse.com	Cokato	MN	55321	800-423-5390	286-5815*
IDI Multimedia Inc 7250 Heritage Village Plz Ste 201 *Web:* www.idimultimedia.com	Gainesville	VA	20155	703-753-2141	
Imagination Publishing 600 W Fulton St Ste 600 *Web:* www.imaginepub.com	Chicago	IL	60661	312-887-1000	887-1003
InfoCommerce Group Inc 2 Bala Plaza Ste 300 *Web:* www.infocommercegroup.com	Bala Cynwyd	PA	19004	610-649-1200	471-0515
Innovative Integration Inc 2390-A Ward Ave *Web:* www.innovative-dsp.com	Simi Valley	CA	93065	805-578-4260	
Interactive Data Corp 32 Crosby Dr *TF:* 800-228-9715 ■ *Web:* www.interactivedata.com	Bedford	MA	01730	781-687-8500	687-8005
Kongregate Inc 660 Mission St Ste 400 *Web:* www.kongregate.com	San Francisco	CA	94105	415-618-0087	
Lifetouch Church Directories 1371 Portland Way N *TF:* 800-521-4611 ■ *Web:* www.lifetouch.com	Galion	OH	44833	419-468-4739	
Majesco Entertainment Co 160 Raritan Ctr Pkwy *NASDAQ: COOL* ■ *Web:* www.majescoent.com	Edison	NJ	08837	732-225-8910	225-8408
Mergent FIS Inc 580 Kingsley Pk Dr **Fax Area Code:* 704 ■ *TF:* 800-342-5647 ■ *Web:* www.mergent.com	Fort Mill	SC	29715	800-342-5647	559-6945*
Microcomputer Applications Inc 1025 W Seventh Ave *Web:* www.keylok.com	Denver	CO	80204	720-904-2252	
New York Graphic Society Ltd 129 Glover Ave *TF:* 800-221-1032 ■ *Web:* www.nygs.com	Norwalk	CT	06850	800-677-6947	
O'neil & Assoc Inc 495 Byers Rd *Web:* www.oneil.com	Miamisburg	OH	45342	937-865-0800	865-5858
OAG Worldwide 3025 Highland Pkwy Ste 200 *TF:* 800-342-5624 ■ *Web:* www.oag.com	Downers Grove	IL	60515	630-515-3230	515-3933
OmniPrint Inc 9700 Philadelphia Ct	Lanham	MD	20706	301-731-7000	
OneSource Information Services Inc 300 Baker Ave *TF:* 800-433-0287 ■ *Web:* avention.com	Concord	MA	01742	978-318-4300	318-4690
Post Asylum Inc 5642 Dyer St *Web:* www.postasylum.com	Dallas	TX	75206	214-363-0162	
PRS Group Inc, The Heritage Landing Dr Ste E Syracuse *Web:* www.prsgroup.com	New York	NY	13057	315-431-0511	
Reactrix Systems Inc PO Box 878 *Web:* www.reactrix.com	Ramsey	NJ	07446	240-342-6346	
San Dieguito Printers 1880 Diamond St *Web:* www.sd-print.com	San Marcos	CA	92078	760-744-0910	
Semantic Research Inc 4922 N Harbor Dr *Web:* www.semanticresearch.com	San Diego	CA	92106	619-222-4050	
ServerBeach Ltd 8500 Vicar Dr Ste 500 *Web:* www.peer1.com	San Antonio	TX	78218	210-798-4400	
Somerset Fine Arts PO Box 869 **Fax Area Code:* 713 ■ *TF Sales:* 800-444-2540 ■ *Web:* www.somersetfineart.com	Fulshear	TX	77441	800-444-2540	932-7861*
TechTarget 275 Grove St Ste 800 *TF:* 888-274-4111 ■ *Web:* www.techtarget.com	Newton	MA	02466	617-431-9200	431-9201
Thomson CenterWatch Inc 100 N Washington St Ste 301 *TF Cust Svc:* 800-765-9647 ■ *Web:* www.centerwatch.com	Boston	MA	02114	617-948-5100	948-5101
Washington Publishing Co 2107 Elliott Ave Ste 305 **Fax Area Code:* 775 ■ *Web:* www.wpc-edi.com	Seattle	WA	98121	425-562-2245	239-2061*
Wonderlic Inc 400 Lakeview Pkwy Ste 200 *TF:* 877-605-9496 ■ *Web:* www.wonderlic.com	Vernon Hills	IL	60061	847-680-4900	680-9492
Xperts Inc 4701 Cox Rd Ste 135 *Web:* www.xperts.com	Glen Allen	VA	23060	804-290-4272	
Zagat Survey LLC 76 9th Ave 4th Fl *Web:* www.zagat.com	New York	NY	10011	212-823-9335	

637-11 Technical Publishers

Company	City	State	Zip	Phone	Fax
Aircraft Technical Publishers 101 S Hill Dr **Fax:* Sales ■ *TF:* 800-227-4610 ■ *Web:* www.atp.com	Brisbane	CA	94005	415-330-9500	468-1596*
Applied Computer Research Inc (ACR) PO Box 41730 *Web:* www.itmarketintelligence.com	Phoenix	AZ	85080	602-885-5311	
Buyers Laboratory Inc 20 Railroad Ave *Web:* www.buyerslab.com	Hackensack	NJ	07601	201-488-0404	
Cambridge Information Group (CIG) 111 W 57th St *Web:* www.cambridgeinformationgroup.com	New York	NY	10019	212-897-6635	
Faulkner Information Services 7905 Browning Rd *TF:* 800-843-0460 ■ *Web:* www.faulkner.com	Pennsauken	NJ	08109	856-662-2070	662-0905
Health Forum 155 North Wacker Drive Ste 400 *TF:* 800-621-6902 ■ *Web:* healthforum.com	Chicago	IL	60606	312-893-6800	
Information Gatekeepers Inc (IGI) 1340 Soldiers Field Rd Ste 2 *TF:* 800-323-1088 ■ *Web:* www.igigroup.com	Brighton	MA	02135	617-782-5033	782-5735
JJ Keller & Assoc Inc 3003 Breezewood Ln PO Box 368 **Fax Area Code:* 800 ■ *TF:* 800-558-5011 ■ *Web:* www.jjkeller.com	Neenah	WI	54957	920-722-2848	727-7516*
Ken Cook Co 9929 W Silver Springs Dr *Web:* www.kencook.com	Milwaukee	WI	53225	414-466-6060	466-9275
Mitchell 1 14145 Danielson St **Fax:* Sales ■ *TF:* 888-724-6742 ■ *Web:* www.mitchell1.com	Poway	CA	92064	858-391-5000	746-8915*
Mitchell International Inc 6220 Greenwich Dr *TF:* 800-854-7030 ■ *Web:* www.mitchell.com	San Diego	CA	92122	858-368-7000	
O'Reilly & Assoc Inc 1005 Gravenstein Hwy N *TF:* 800-998-9938 ■ *Web:* www.oreilly.com	Sebastopol	CA	95472	707-829-0515	829-0104
TeleGeography Inc 1909 K St NW Ste 380 *Web:* www.telegeography.com	Washington	DC	20006	202-741-0020	741-0021
Thompson Publishing Group Inc 805 15th St NW 3rd Fl *TF Cust Svc:* 800-677-3789 ■ *Web:* www.thompson.com	Washington	DC	20005	202-872-4000	296-1091

638 PULP MILLS

See Also Paper Mills p. 2868; Paperboard Mills p. 2870

Company	City	State	Zip	Phone	Fax
A J Blosenski Inc 1600 Chestnut Tree Rd *Web:* www.ajblosenski.com	Honey Brook	PA	19344	610-942-2707	

Phone *Fax*

Alabama River Pulp Company Inc
Lena Landegger Hwy County Rd 39 .... Perdue Hill AL 36470 251-575-2000

Alberta-Pacific Forest Industries Inc
PO Box 8000 .... Boyle AB T0A0M0 780-525-8000 525-8028
TF: 800-661-5210 ■ *Web:* www.alpac.ca

Allied Paper Company LLC 5700 Plauche Ct .... Harahan LA 70123 504-733-5700
Web: www.alliedpapercompany.com

Arizona Pacific Pulp & Paper Inc
3209 S 36th St .... Phoenix AZ 85040 602-220-9200
Web: www.azpacificpaper.com

AV Nackawic Inc 103 Pinder Rd .... Nackawic NB E6G1W4 506-575-3314
Web: www.av-group.ca

Canadian Forest Products Ltd
5162 Northwood Pulp Mill Rd
PO Box 9000 .... Prince George BC V2L4W2 604-661-5241 962-3473*
**Fax Area Code:* 250 ■ **Fax:* Acctg ■ *Web:* www.canfor.com

Cheney Pulp & Paper Company Inc
1000 Anderson St .... Franklin OH 45005 937-746-9991
Web: www.cheneypulp.com

Cosmo Specialty Fibers Inc 1701 First St .... Cosmopolis WA 98537 360-500-4600
Web: www.cosmospecialtyfibers.com

Daishowa-Marubeni International Ltd
510 Burrard St Ste 700 .... Vancouver BC V6C3A8 604-684-4326
Web: www.dmi.ca

Donco Paper Supply Co
2100 Losantiville Ave .... Cincinnati OH 45237 513-731-0208 337-7891*
**Fax Area Code:* 312

Fox Converting Inc 1250 Cornell Rd .... Green Bay WI 54313 920-434-5272
Web: www.foxconverting.com

Gateway Products Recycling Inc
4223 E 49th St .... Cleveland OH 44125 216-341-8777
Web: www.gatewayrecycle.com

International Paper Co 6400 Poplar Ave .... Memphis TN 38197 901-419-9000
NYSE: IP ■ *TF Prod Info:* 800-223-1268 ■ *Web:* www.internationalpaper.com

KapStone Paper and Packaging Corp
300 Fibre Way PO Box 639 .... Longview WA 98632 360-425-1550
Web: www.kapstonepaper.com

Kimberly-Clark Corp 351 Phelps Dr .... Irving TX 75038 972-281-1200
NYSE: KMB ■ *TF:* 888-525-8388 ■ *Web:* www.kimberly-clark.com

Longhorn Recycling LP 5785 Fm 1346 .... San Antonio TX 78220 210-661-2341
Web: www.longhornrecycling.com

Mercer International
14900 Interurban Ave S Ste 282 .... Seattle WA 98168 604-684-1099
Web: www.mercerint.com

Nippon Paper Industries USA Co
1902 Marine Dr .... Port Angeles WA 98363 360-457-4474
Web: npiusa.com

Northern Pulp Nova Scotia Corp
260 Granton Abercrombie Branch Rd .... Abercrombie NS B2H5C6 902-752-8461
Web: www.northernpulp.ca

Omaha Paper Co 6936 L St .... Omaha NE 68117 402-331-3243
TF: 800-288-7026 ■ *Web:* www.omahapaper.com

Parsons & Whittemore Inc
4 International Dr .... Rye Brook NY 10573 914-937-9009 937-2259

Potlatch Corp 601 W First Ave Ste 1600 .... Spokane WA 99201 509-835-1500
NASDAQ: PCH ■ *Web:* www.potlatchcorp.com

Southern Cellulose Products Inc
105 W 45th St .... Chattanooga TN 37410 423-821-1561

639 PUMPS - MEASURING & DISPENSING

Phone *Fax*

AccuSport Inc 4310 Enterprise Dr Ste C .... Winston-Salem NC 27106 336-759-3300
Web: www.accusport.com

Alameda Applied Sciences Corp
3077 Teagarden St .... San Leandro CA 94577 510-483-4156
Web: www.aasc.net

American Sensor Technologies Inc
450 Clark Dr .... Mt Olive NJ 07828 973-448-1901
Web: www.astsensors.com

Apantec LLC 4500 N Cannon Ave .... Lansdale PA 19446 267-436-3991
Web: www.apantec.com

Apex Precision Technologies Inc
8824 Union Mills Dr .... Camby IN 46113 317-821-1000
Web: www.apexprecision.com

Assay Technology Inc 1382 Stealth St .... Livermore CA 94551 925-461-8880
TF: 800-833-1258 ■ *Web:* www.assaytech.com

ATC Inc 4037 Guion Ln .... Indianapolis IN 46268 317-328-8492
Web: www.atcinc.net

Belfort Instrument Co 727 S Wolfe St .... Baltimore MD 21231 410-342-2626
Web: www.belfortinstrument.com

Bennett Pump Co 1218 Pontaluna Rd .... Spring Lake MI 49456 231-798-1310 799-6202
TF: 800-235-7618 ■ *Web:* bennettpump.com

Brooks Utility Products Group
23847 Industrial Park Dr .... Farmington Hills MI 48335 248-477-0250
TF: 888-687-3008 ■ *Web:* www.brooksutility.com

Bubble Technology Industries Inc
31278 Hwy 17 .... Chalk River ON K0J1J0 613-589-2456
Web: www.bubbletech.ca

Chen Instrument Design Inc
4845 NW Camas Meadows Dr .... Camas WA 98607 360-833-8835
TF: 800-767-0119 ■ *Web:* www.cid-inc.com

ComSonics Electronic Mfg Services Inc
780 Keezletown Rd Ste 102 .... Weyers Cave VA 24486 540-434-7500
Web: www.cemsi.com

Controlled Access Inc 1515 W 130th St .... Hinckley OH 44233 330-273-6185
TF: 800-942-0829 ■ *Web:* www.controlledaccess.com

Daily Instruments Inc 5700 Hartsdale Dr .... Houston TX 77036 713-780-8600
Web: www.dailyinst.com

DICKEY-John Corp 5200 Dickey-John Rd .... Auburn IL 62615 217-438-3371
TF: 800-637-2952 ■ *Web:* www.dickey-john.com

Dyne Systems Company LLC
W209N17391 Industrial Dr .... Jackson WI 53037 262-677-9300
Web: www.dynesystems.com

Echometer Co 5001 Ditto Ln .... Wichita Falls TX 76302 940-767-4334
Web: www.echometer.com

Electro Static Technology
31 Winterbrook Rd .... Mechanic Falls ME 04256 207-998-5140
TF: 866-738-1857 ■ *Web:* www.est-static.com

Ferro Solutions Inc 5 Constitution Way .... Woburn MA 01801 781-935-7878
Web: www.ferrosi.com

Gagemaker LP 712 Southmore Ave .... Pasadena TX 77502 713-472-7360 472-7241
Web: gagemaker.com

Gasboy International Inc
7300 W Friendly Ave .... Greensboro NC 27420 336-547-5000 444-5569*
**Fax Area Code:* 800 ■ **Fax:* Cust Svc ■ *TF Sales:* 800-444-5579 ■ *Web:* www.gasboy.com

GEM Systems Inc 135 Spy Ct .... Markham ON L3R5H6 905-752-2202 752-2205
Web: www.gemsys.ca

Gerhart Systems & Controls Corp
754 Roble Rd Ste 140 .... Allentown PA 18109 610-264-2800
TF: 888-437-4278 ■ *Web:* gerhart.com

Gilbarco Inc 7300 W Friendly Ave .... Greensboro NC 27420 336-547-5000 547-5890*
**Fax:* Mktg ■ *Web:* www.gilbarco.com

Headwall Photonics Inc 601 River St .... Fitchburg MA 01420 978-353-4100
Web: www.headwallphotonics.com

Intelametrix 6246 Preston Ave .... Livermore CA 94551 925-606-7044
Web: www.intelametrix.com

Kamp Synergy 9434 N 107th St .... Milwaukee WI 53224 414-354-6700
Web: kampscada.com

Krohne Inc 7 Dearborn Rd .... Peabody MA 01960 978-535-6060
Web: www.krohne.com

Medicomp Inc 7845 Ellis Rd .... Melbourne FL 32904 321-794-3811
TF: 800-234-3278 ■ *Web:* www.medicompinc.com

Mehta Tech Inc 208 N 12th Ave .... Eldridge IA 52748 563-285-9151
Web: www.mehtatech.com

Motion Analysis Corp 3617 Wwind Blvd .... Santa Rosa CA 95403 707-579-6500
Web: www.motionanalysis.com

Nicol Scales 7239 Envoy Ct .... Dallas TX 75247 214-428-8181 428-8127
Web: www.nicolscales.com

O'Day Equipment Inc 1301 40th St NW .... Fargo ND 58102 701-282-9260 281-9770
TF: 800-654-6329 ■ *Web:* www.odayequipment.com

Pacific Precision Laboratories Inc
20447 Nordhoff St .... Chatsworth CA 91311 818-700-8977

Pajarito Scientific Security Corp
2532 Camino Entrada .... Santa Fe NM 87507 505-424-6660
Web: www.pajaritoscientific.com

Physical Acoustics Corp
195 Clarksville Rd .... Princeton Junction NJ 08550 609-716-4000
Web: www.physicalacoustics.com

Pressco Technology Inc 29200 Aurora Rd .... Cleveland OH 44139 440-498-2600
Web: www.pressco.com

Refraction Technology Inc 1600 10th St Ste A .... Plano TX 75074 214-440-1265
Web: www.reftek.com

Rexon Components Inc 24500 Highpoint Rd .... Beachwood OH 44122 216-292-7373
Web: www.rexon.com

Rice Lake Weighing Systems Inc
230 W Coleman St .... Rice Lake WI 54868 800-472-6703
TF: 800-472-6703 ■ *Web:* www.ricelakehockey.com

Spectec 9 Polaris Way .... Emigrant MT 59027 406-333-4967
Web: www.spectecsensors.com

Standard Imaging Inc 3120 Deming Way .... Middleton WI 53562 608-831-0025
TF: 800-261-4446 ■ *Web:* www.standardimaging.com

Thermtrol Corp 8914 Pleasantwood Ave NW .... North Canton OH 44720 330-497-4148
Web: www.thermtrol.com

THK America Inc 200 E Commerce Dr .... Schaumburg IL 60173 847-310-1111
Web: www.thk.com

Thwing-Albert Instrument Company Inc
14 W Collings Ave .... West Berlin NJ 08091 856-767-1000
Web: www.thwingalbert.com

Tuthill Transfer Systems 8500 S Madison .... Burr Ridge IL 60527 260-747-7529 747-3159
TF: 800-825-6937 ■ *Web:* www.tuthill.com

Vortek Instruments LLC
8475 W I25 Frontage Rd Ste 300 .... Longmont CO 80504 303-682-9999
Web: vortekinst.com

Xiris Automation Inc 1016 Sutton Dr Ste C5 .... Burlington ON L7L6B8 905-331-6660 331-6661
Web: www.xiris.com

640 PUMPS & MOTORS - FLUID POWER

Phone *Fax*

Applied Energy Company Inc (AEC)
1205 Venture Ct Ste 100 .... Carrollton TX 75006 214-355-4200 355-4201
TF: 800-580-1171 ■ *Web:* www.appliedenergyco.com

Bosch Rexroth Corp
5150 Prairie Stone Pkwy .... Hoffman Estates IL 60192 847-645-3600 645-6201
TF: 800-860-1055 ■ *Web:* www.boschrexroth.com/en/us

Bosch Rexroth Corp Piston Pump Div
8 Southchase Ct .... Fountain Inn SC 29644 864-967-2777 967-8900
TF: 877-266-7811 ■ *Web:* boschrexroth.com

Cross Manufacturing Inc
11011 King St Ste 210 .... Overland Park KS 66210 913-451-1233 451-1235
Web: www.crossmfg.com

Delta Power Co 4484 Boeing Dr .... Rockford IL 61109 815-397-6628 397-2526
Web: www.delta-power.com

Dynex Rivett Inc 770 Capitol Dr .... Pewaukee WI 53072 262-691-0300 691-0312
Web: www.dynexhydraulics.com

Fluid Metering Inc 5 Aerial Way Ste 500 .... Syosset NY 11791 516-922-6050 624-8261
TF: 800-223-3388 ■ *Web:* fluidmetering.com

Hydreco 1500 County Naple Blvd .... Charlotte NC 28273 704-295-7575 295-7574
Web: www.hydreco.com

Jetstream of Houston LLP 4930 Cranswick .... Houston TX 77041 713-462-7000 462-5387
TF: 800-231-8192 ■ *Web:* www.waterblast.com

Phone | Fax

Liquid Drive Corp 418 Hadley St. Holly MI 48442 248-634-5382
Web: www.liquiddrive.com

Milton Roy USA 201 Ivyland Rd. Ivyland PA 18974 215-441-0800 441-8620
Web: www.miltonroy.com

Mte Hydraulics 4701 Kishwaukee St. Rockford IL 61109 815-397-4701 399-5528
Web: www.mtehydraulics.com

Oilgear Co 2300 S 51st St PO Box 343924 Milwaukee WI 53219 414-327-1700 327-0532
Web: www.oilgear.com

Parker Hannifin Corp Hydraulic Pump/Motor Div
2745 Snapps Ferry Rd Greeneville TN 37745 423-639-8151 787-2418
Web: www.parker.com

Parker Hannifin Corp Nichols Portland Div
2400 Congress St. Portland ME 04102 207-774-6121 774-3601
Web: parker.com

Permco Inc 1500 Frost Rd Streetsboro OH 44241 330-626-2801 626-2805
TF: 800-628-2801 ■ *Web:* www.permco.com

Pnucor Inc 10525 Granite St PO Box 7209 Charlotte NC 28273 704-588-3333
Web: www.pnucor.com

Sauer-Danfoss 2800 E 13th St Ames IA 50010 515-239-6000 239-6318
NYSE: SHS ■ *Web:* powersolutions.danfoss.com

TexLoc Ltd 4700 Lone Star Blvd. Fort Worth TX 76106 817-625-5081
Web: www.texloc.com

TII Network Technologies Inc 141 Rodeo Dr. Edgewood NY 11717 631-789-5000 789-5063
NASDAQ: TIII ■ *TF:* 888-844-4720 ■ *Web:* tiitech.com

Viking Pump Inc 406 State St Cedar Falls IA 50613 319-266-1741 273-8157
Web: www.vikingpump.com

Voith Turbo Inc 25 Winship Rd. York PA 17406 717-767-3200 767-3210
Web: redirect.voith.com/index2.php?r=d939d1f104c0b

641 PUMPS & PUMPING EQUIPMENT (GENERAL USE)

See Also Industrial Machinery, Equipment, & Supplies p. 2559

Phone | Fax

Ace Pump and Supply 6013 Johnson St Hollywood FL 33024 954-981-7424
Web: acepumpandsupply.com

Ace Pump Corp PO Box 13187 Memphis TN 38113 901-948-8514 774-6147
Web: www.acepumps.com

Acme Dynamics Inc
3608 Sydney Rd PO Box 1780 Plant City FL 33566 813-752-3137 752-4580
TF: 800-622-9355 ■ *Web:* www.acmedynamics.com

Advanced Pressure Systems LP
701 S Persimmon St Ste 85 Tomball TX 77375 281-290-9950
Web: www.advancedpressuresystems.com

Aermotor Pumps Inc 293 Wright St. Delavan WI 53115 800-230-1816 230-1816
TF: 800-230-1816 ■ *Web:* www.aermotor.com

Air Systems International Inc
829 Juniper Crescent Chesapeake VA 23320 757-424-3967
TF: 800-866-8100 ■ *Web:* www.airsystems.com

American Machine & Tool Company Inc
400 Spring St Royersford PA 19468 610-948-3800 948-5300
TF: 888-268-7867 ■ *Web:* www.amtpump.com

Amico Corp 85 Fulton Way Richmond Hill ON L4B2N4 905-764-0800
TF: 877-462-6426 ■ *Web:* www.amico.com

Ampco Pumps Company Inc 2045 W Mill Rd. Glendale WI 53209 414-643-1852
TF: 800-737-8671 ■ *Web:* www.ampcopumps.com

Aqua-Dyne Inc 3620 W 11th St. Houston TX 77008 713-864-6929 864-0313
Web: www.aqua-dyne.com

AR Wilfley & Sons Inc
7350 E Progress Pl Ste 200 Englewood CO 80111 303-779-1777 779-1277
TF: 800-525-9930 ■ *Web:* www.wilfley.com

Armstrong International Inc
2081 SE Ocean Blvd 4th Fl. Stuart FL 34996 772-286-7175 286-1001
TF: 866-738-5125 ■ *Web:* www.armstronginternational.com

Armstrong Pumps Inc 93 E Ave North Tonawanda NY 14120 716-693-8813
Web: armstrongfluidtechnology.com

ASM Industries Inc Pacer Pumps Div
41 Industrial Cir Lancaster PA 17601 717-656-2161 656-0477
TF Cust Svc: 800-233-3861 ■ *Web:* www.pacerpumps.com

Banjo Corp 150 Banjo Dr Crawfordsville IN 47933 765-362-7367
Web: www.banjocorp.com

Barker Air & Hydraulics Inc
1308 Miller Rd Greenville SC 29607 864-288-3537
TF: 800-922-3324 ■ *Web:* www.barkerair.com

Barney's Pumps Inc 2965 Barney's Pumps Pl Lakeland FL 33812 863-665-8500 666-3858
Web: www.barneyspumps.com

Barrett Engineered Pumps Inc
1695 National Ave San Diego CA 92113 619-232-7867
Web: www.barrettpump.com

Bayou City Pump Inc 109 N Richey pasadena TX 77506 713-472-7722
Web: www.bayoucitypumpco.com

Beckett Corp 3250 Skyway Cir N Irving TX 75038 972-871-8000 871-8888
TF: 888-232-5388 ■ *Web:* www.beckettpumps.com

Berkeley Pumps 293 Wright St. Delavan WI 53115 262-728-5551 426-9446*
**Fax Area Code:* 800 ■ **Fax:* Cust Svc ■ *TF:* 866-582-2032 ■ *Web:* www.berkeleypumps.com

Blackmer 1809 Century Ave. Grand Rapids MI 49503 616-241-1611 241-3752
TF: 888-363-7886 ■ *Web:* www.psgdover.com

Buffalo Pumps Inc 874 Oliver St North Tonawanda NY 14120 716-693-1850 693-6303
Web: www.buffalopumps.com

Busch Vacuum Technics Inc
1740 Lionel Bertrand Boisbriand QC J7H1N7 450-435-6899
TF: 800-363-6360 ■ *Web:* busch.ca

Carver Pump Co 2415 Pk Ave. Muscatine IA 52761 563-263-3410 262-7688
Web: www.carverpump.com

Cascade Pump Co 10107 Norwalk Blvd Santa Fe Springs CA 90670 562-946-1414
Web: www.cascadepump.com

Cat Pumps 1681 94th Ln NE Minneapolis MN 55449 763-780-5440 780-2958
Web: www.catpumps.com

CDS-John Blue Co 290 Pinehurst Dr. Huntsville AL 35806 256-721-9090
TF: 800-253-2583 ■ *Web:* www.cds-johnblue.com

CIRCOR International Inc
30 Corporate Dr Ste 200 Burlington MA 01803 781-270-1200 270-1299
NYSE: CIR ■ *Web:* www.circor.com

Phone | Fax

CLYDE UNION Pumps 4600 W Dickman Rd. Battle Creek MI 49037 269-966-4600 962-5447
TF: 800-877-7867

Coffin Turbo Pump Inc 326 S Dean St. Englewood NJ 07631 201-568-2826 568-4716
TF: 800-568-9798 ■ *Web:* www.coffinturbopump.com

Colfax Corp 8730 Stony Pt Pkwy Ste 150 Richmond VA 23235 804-560-4070 560-4076
Web: www.colfaxcorp.com

Complete Pump Service 461 S Irmen Dr. Addison IL 60101 630-628-1600
Web: www.completepump.com

Corken Inc 3805 NW 36th St Oklahoma City OK 73112 405-946-5576 948-6664
TF: 800-631-4929 ■ *Web:* www.corken.com

Cornell Pump Co
16261 SE 130th Ave PO Box 6334 Clackamas OR 97015 503-653-0330 653-0338
Web: www.cornellpump.com

Crane Co 100 First Stamford Pl 4th Fl Stamford CT 06902 203-363-7300
NYSE: CR ■ *Web:* www.craneco.com

Crane Pumps & Systems 420 Third St Piqua OH 45356 937-778-8947 496-7629*
**Fax Area Code:* 780 ■ *Web:* www.cranepumps.com

CS & P Technologies LP 18119 Telge Rd Cypress TX 77429 713-467-0869 464-2089*
**Fax Area Code:* 832 ■ *TF:* 800-262-6103 ■ *Web:* www.csphouston.com

Custom Cylinders Inc 700 Industrial Dr Ste I Cary IL 60013 847-516-6467
Web: www.customcylinders.com

DADCO Inc 43850 Plymouth Oaks Blvd Plymouth MI 48170 734-207-1100
Web: www.dadco.net

Discflo Corp 10850 Hartley Rd. Santee CA 92071 619-596-3181
Web: www.discflo.com

Div 15 Sales Inc 12026 Roberts Rd. La Vista NE 68128 402-597-6353
Web: www.division-15.com

Ebara international corp 350 Salomon Cir. Sparks NV 89434 775-356-2796 356-2884
Web: www.ebaraintl.com

Environment One Corp 2773 Balltown Rd Niskayuna NY 12309 518-346-6161
Web: www.eone.com

Estabrook Corp 700 W Bagley Rd Berea OH 44017 440-234-8566
Web: www.estabrookcorp.com

Evans-Hydro 18128 S Santa Fe Ave. Rancho Dominguez CA 90221 310-608-5801
Web: evanshydro.com

F E Myers 1101 Myers Pkwy Ashland OH 44805 419-289-1144
TF: 855-274-8947 ■ *Web:* www.femyers.com

Flint & Walling Inc 95 N Oak St. Kendallville IN 46755 260-347-1600 347-6664
TF Sales: 800-345-9422 ■ *Web:* www.flintandwalling.com

Flowserve Corp 5215 N O'Connor Blvd Ste 2300 Irving TX 75039 972-443-6500 443-6800
NYSE: FLS ■ *TF:* 800-350-1082 ■ *Web:* www.flowserve.com

Fluid Equipment Development Company LLC
800 Ternes Dr. Monroe MI 48162 734-241-3935
Web: www.fedco-usa.com

Fluid Power Equipment Inc 6305 Cunningham Rd. Houston TX 77041 713-466-8088
Web: www.fluidpowerequipment.com

FMG Enterprises Inc 1125 Memorex Dr. Santa Clara CA 95050 408-982-0110
TF: 800-327-6177 ■ *Web:* www.fmgvacpump.com

Fortbrand Services Inc 50 Fairchild Ct Plainview NY 11803 516-576-3200
Web: www.fortbrand.com

Fristam Pumps USA LP 2410 Parview Rd. Middleton WI 53562 608-831-5001
Web: www.fristam.com

Gardner Denver Thomas - Products Div
1419 Illinois Ave. Sheboygan WI 53081 920-457-4891
Web: www.gd-thomas.com

GIW Industries Inc 5000 Wrightsboro Rd. Grovetown GA 30813 706-863-1011 860-5897
TF: 888-832-4449 ■ *Web:* www.ksb.com

Global Pump Company LLC 10162 E Coldwater Rd. Davison MI 48423 810-653-4828
Web: www.globalpump.com

Gorman-Rupp Co PO Box 1217 PO Box 1217 Mansfield OH 44901 419-755-1011
NYSE: GRC ■ *Web:* www.gormanrupp.com

Gorman-Rupp Industries 180 Hines Ave Bellville OH 44813 419-886-3001 886-2338
Web: www.gripumps.com

GPM Industries Inc 110 Gateway Dr. Macon GA 31210 478-471-7867
Web: www.gpmind.com

Graco Inc 88 11th Ave NE PO Box 1441 Minneapolis MN 55413 612-623-6000 623-6777*
NYSE: GGG ■ **Fax:* Hum Res ■ *TF Cust Svc:* 800-328-0211 ■ *Web:* www.graco.com

Graymills Corp 3705 N Lincoln Ave. Chicago IL 60613 773-477-4100 477-4133
TF: 877-465-7867 ■ *Web:* www.graymills.com

Great Plains Industries Inc 5252 E 36th St N. Wichita KS 67220 316-686-7361 686-6746
TF Sales: 800-835-0113 ■ *Web:* www.gpi.net

Grundfos Pumps Corp 17100 W 118th Terr Olathe KS 66061 913-227-3400 227-3500
Web: grundfos.com

Gusher Pumps 115 Industrial Dr Williamstown KY 41097 859-824-3100 824-7248
Web: www.gusher.com

Hale Products Inc 700 Spring Mill Ave Conshohocken PA 19428 610-825-6300 825-6440*
**Fax:* Cust Svc ■ *TF:* 800-220-4253 ■ *Web:* www.haleproducts.com

Hammelmann Corp 600 Progress Rd Dayton OH 45449 937-859-8777
TF: 800-783-4935 ■ *Web:* www.hammelmann.de

Harben Inc 2010 Ronald Regan Blvd Cumming GA 30041 770-889-9535 887-9411
TF: 800-327-5387 ■ *Web:* www.harben.com

Haskel International Inc 100 E Graham Pl Burbank CA 91502 818-843-4000 841-4291*
**Fax:* Sales ■ *TF:* 800-743-2720 ■ *Web:* www.haskel.com

Hayward Tyler Inc 480 Roosevelt Hwy Colchester VT 05446 802-655-4444 655-4682
Web: www.haywardtyler.com

Houston Grinding & Manufacturing Inc
3544 W 12th St. Houston TX 77008 713-869-3573

Hydromatic Pump Co 740 E Ninth St Ashland OH 44805 888-957-8677
TF: 888-957-8677 ■ *Web:* www.hydromatic.com

Hydromotion Inc 85 E Bridge St Spring City PA 19475 610-948-4150
Web: www.hydromotion.com

HydroPressure Cleaning Inc 413 Dawson Dr. Camarillo CA 93012 800-934-2399
TF: 800-934-2399 ■ *Web:* www.hydropressure.com

Hypro 375 Fifth Ave NW New Brighton MN 55112 651-766-6300 766-6600*
**Fax:* Sales ■ *TF Cust Svc:* 800-424-9776 ■ *Web:* www.hypropumps.com

IDEX Corp 1925 W Field Ct Ste 200 Lake Forest IL 60045 847-498-7070
NYSE: IEX ■ *Web:* www.idexcorp.com

Imo Pump 1710 Airport Rd. Monroe NC 28110 704-289-6511 289-9273*
**Fax:* Sales ■ *TF:* 888-478-6996 ■ *Web:* www.imo-pump.com

Ingersoll-Rand Co 800-E Beaty St Davidson NC 28036 704-655-4000
Web: www.ingersollrand.com

				Phone	Fax
Integrated Flow Solutions LLC 6461 Reynolds Rd. *TF:* 800-859-7867 ■ *Web:* www.ifsolutions.com	Tyler	TX	75708	903-595-6511	
ITT Corp 1133 Westchester Ave **Fax:* Mktg ■ *Web:* www.bellgossett.com	White Plains	NY	10604	914-641-2000	696-2950*
Iwaki America Inc 5 Boynton Rd *Web:* www.walchem.com	Holliston	MA	01746	508-429-1110	429-7433
Jit Cylinders 2201 Hwy 31 SW *Web:* www.jitindustries.com	Hartselle	AL	35640	256-751-2548	751-2189
Kappe Associates Inc 100 Wormans Mill Ct. *Web:* www.kappe-inc.com	Frederick	MD	21701	301-846-0200	
Kemlon Products & Development Co 1424 N Main St *Web:* www.kemlon.com	Pearland	TX	77581	281-997-3300	997-1300
Kerr Pump & Supply 12880 Cloverdale St *TF:* 800-482-8259 ■ *Web:* www.kerrpump.com	Oak Park	MI	48237	248-543-3880	543-3236
Kimray Inc 52 NW 42nd St. *Web:* www.kimray.com	Oklahoma City	OK	73118	405-525-6601	525-7520
Koshin America Corp 1218 Remington Rd. *TF:* 800-634-4092 ■ *Web:* koshinamerica.com	Schaumburg	IL	60173	847-310-0740	
Kraft Fluid Systems Inc 14300 Foltz Pkwy *TF:* 800-257-1155 ■ *Web:* www.kraftfluid.com	Strongsville	OH	44149	440-238-5545	238-5266
Lehigh Fluid Power Inc 1413 Rt 179 *TF:* 800-257-9515 ■ *Web:* www.lehighfluidpower.com	Lambertville	NJ	08530	800-257-9515	
LEWA Inc 132 Hopping Brook Rd *Web:* lewa-inc.com	Holliston	MA	01746	508-429-7403	
Liberty Pumps Inc 7000 Apple Tree Ave. *TF:* 800-543-2550 ■ *Web:* www.libertypumps.com	Bergen	NY	14416	585-494-1817	
Liquiflo Equipment Co 443 N Ave *Web:* www.liquiflo.com	Garwood	NJ	07027	908-518-0777	518-1847
Madden Manufacturing Inc PO Box 387 **Fax:* Sales ■ *TF:* 800-369-6233 ■ *Web:* www.maddenmfg.com	Elkhart	IN	46515	574-295-4292	295-7562*
Magnatex Pumps Inc 3575 W 12th St Ste 208 *Web:* www.magnatexpumps.com	Houston	TX	77008	719-329-0777	
McNally Industries LLC 340 W Benson Ave *TF:* 800-366-1410 ■ *Web:* www.northern-pump.com	Grantsburg	WI	54840	715-463-8300	463-5261
Met-Pro Corp Fybroc Div 700 Emlen Way *TF:* 800-392-7621 ■ *Web:* www.mp-gps.com	Telford	PA	18969	215-723-8155	723-2197
Met-Pro Corp Sethco Div 800 Emlen Way. *TF:* 800-645-0500 ■ *Web:* www.mp-gps.com	Telford	PA	18969	215-799-2577	799-0920
Micropump Inc 1402 NE 136th Ave. *TF Sales:* 800-222-9565 ■ *Web:* www.micropump.com	Vancouver	WA	98684	360-253-2008	253-8294
Moyno Inc 1895 W Jefferson St **Fax:* Mktg ■ *TF:* 877-486-6966 ■ *Web:* www.moyno.com	Springfield	OH	45506	937-327-3111	327-3177*
MP Pumps Inc 34800 Bennett Dr. *TF:* 800-563-8006 ■ *Web:* www.mppumps.com	Fraser	MI	48026	586-293-8240	293-8469
MWI Corp 33 N.W. 2nd St. *Web:* www.mwicorp.com	Deerfield Beach	FL	33441	954-426-1500	426-1582
Nagle Pumps Inc 1249 Ctr Ave **Fax:* Sales ■ *Web:* www.naglepumps.com	Chicago Heights	IL	60411	708-754-2940	754-2944*
National Pump Company LLC 7706 N 71st Ave *TF:* 800-966-5240 ■ *Web:* www.nationalpumpcompany.com	Glendale	AZ	85303	623-979-3560	
Neptune Chemical Pump Co PO Box 247 *TF:* 800-255-4017 ■ *Web:* www.psgdover.com	Lansdale	PA	19446	215-699-8700	699-0370
Neptune-Benson Inc 6 Jefferson Dr *TF:* 800-832-8002 ■ *Web:* www.neptunebenson.com	Coventry	RI	02816	401-821-2200	
NH Yates & Company Inc 117 Church Ln # C **Fax Area Code:* 888 ■ *TF:* 800-878-8181 ■ *Web:* www.nhyates.com	Cockeysville	MD	21030	800-878-8181	667-9201*
Nikkiso Pumps America Inc 3433 N Sam Houston Pkwy W Ste 400 *Web:* www.nikkisopumpsamerica.com	Houston	TX	77086	281-310-6747	
Odessa Pumps & Equipment Inc 3209 N County Rd W *Web:* www.odessapumps.com	Odessa	TX	79764	432-333-2817	333-2841
Oteco Inc PO Box 1849 *Web:* www.oteco.com	Houston	TX	77251	713-695-3693	695-3520
Packworld USA 539 S Main St *Web:* www.packworldusa.com	Nazareth	PA	18064	610-746-2765	
PACO Pumps Inc 902 Koomey Rd *TF:* 800-955-5847 ■ *Web:* www.paco-pumps.com	Brookshire	TX	77423	281-994-2700	
Paragon Products LLC 4475 Golden Foothill Pkwy *Web:* www.paragonproducts.net	El Dorado Hills	CA	95762	916-941-9717	
Patterson Pump Co 2129 Ayersville Rd *Web:* www.pattersonpumps.com	Toccoa	GA	30577	706-886-2101	886-0023
Peerless Pump Co 2005 ML King Jr St PO Box 7026 *TF:* 800-879-0182 ■ *Web:* www.peerlesspump.com	Indianapolis	IN	46207	317-925-9661	924-7388
Penn Air & Hydraulics Corp 1750 Industrial Hwy *TF:* 888-631-7638 ■ *Web:* www.pennair.com	York	PA	17402	717-840-8100	
Pentair Inc 5500 Wayzata Blvd Ste 800 *NYSE:* PNR ■ *Web:* www.pentair.com	Minneapolis	MN	55416	763-545-1730	656-5400
Pentair Water Pool & Spa 1620 Hawkins Ave *TF:* 800-831-7133 ■ *Web:* www.pentairpool.com	Sanford	NC	27330	800-831-7133	284-4151
Predator Systems Inc 600 PSI Dr *Web:* www.predatorsystemsinc.com	Boca Raton	FL	33431	561-394-9991	
Price Pump Co 21775 Eighth St E *Web:* www.pricepump.com	Sonoma	CA	95476	707-938-8441	
Procon Products 869 7 Oaks Blvd Ste 120 *Web:* www.proconpumps.com	Smyrna	TN	37167	615-355-8000	355-8001
Progressive Hydraulics Inc 350 N Midland Ave *Web:* www.phionline.com	Saddle Brook	NJ	07663	201-791-3400	
Pulsafeeder Inc 2883 Brighton-Henrietta Town Line Rd. *Web:* www.pulsa.com	Rochester	NY	14623	585-292-8000	424-5619
Ramrod Industries LLC 800 S Monroe St *Web:* www.ramrodindustries.com	Spencer	WI	54479	715-659-4996	
Randolph Austin Company Inc 2119 FM 1626 PO Box 988 *Web:* www.randolphaustin.com	Manchaca	TX	78652	512-282-1590	
RI Deppmann Co 20929 Bridge St. *Web:* www.deppmann.com	Southfield	MI	48033	248-354-3710	
Roper Pump Co 3475 Old Maysville Rd. *TF Sales:* 800-944-6769 ■ *Web:* www.roperpumps.com	Commerce	GA	30529	706-335-5551	335-5490
Roth Pump Co PO Box 4330 *TF:* 888-444-7684 ■ *Web:* www.rothpump.com	Rock Island	IL	61204	309-787-1791	787-5142
RS Corcoran Co 500 N Vine St *TF:* 800-637-1067 ■ *Web:* www.corcoranpumps.com	New Lenox	IL	60451	815-485-2156	485-2156
Scot Pump 6437 Pioneer Rd PO Box 286 *TF:* 888-835-0600 ■ *Web:* www.scotpump.com	Cedarburg	WI	53012	262-377-7000	377-7330
seepex Inc 511 Speedway Dr *Web:* www.seepex.com	Enon	OH	45323	937-864-7150	864-7157
Serfilco Ltd 2900 MacArthur Blvd *TF:* 800-323-5431 ■ *Web:* www.serfilco.com	Northbrook	IL	60062	847-559-1777	559-1141
Shanley Pump & Equipment Inc 2525 S Clearbrook Dr. *Web:* www.shanleypump.com	Arlington Heights	IL	60005	847-439-9200	
Shippensburg Pump Company Inc PO Box 279 *Web:* www.shipcopumps.com	Shippensburg	PA	17257	717-532-7321	
SHURflo Pump Mfg Company Inc 5900 Katella Ave. *TF:* 800-854-3218 ■ *Web:* www.shurflo.com	Cypress	CA	90630	562-795-5200	795-7554
SIHI Pumps Inc 303 Industrial Blvd *Web:* www.sihi-pumps.com	Grand Island	NY	14072	716-773-6450	773-2330
Simflo Pumps Inc 754 E Maley St PO Box 849 *TF:* 800-232-4142 ■ *Web:* www.simflo.com	Willcox	AZ	85644	520-384-2273	384-4042
Smith Pump Co Inc 301 M B Industrial *Web:* www.smithpump.com	Woodway	TX	76712	254-776-0377	776-0023
Standard Alloys & Mfg PO Box 969 *TF:* 800-231-8240 ■ *Web:* www.ksb.com/standard_alloys	Port Arthur	TX	77640	409-983-3201	983-7837
Stansteel Asphalt Plant Products 12700 Shelbyville Rd *Web:* www.stansteel.com	Louisville	KY	40243	502-245-1977	
Sulzer Pumps (US) Inc 2800 NW Front Ave *Web:* www.sulzer.com	Portland	OR	97210	503-205-3600	
Syncroflo Inc 6700 Best Friend Rd *Web:* www.syncroflo.com	Norcross	GA	30071	770-447-4443	
Systecon Inc 6121 Schumacher Pk Dr. *Web:* www.systecon.com	West Chester	OH	45069	513-777-7722	777-0259
TBK America Inc 3700 W Industries Rd *Web:* www.tbk-jp.com	Richmond	IN	47374	765-962-0147	
Textron Fluid & Power Inc 40 Westminster St *Web:* www.textron.com	Providence	RI	02903	401-421-2800	
Thompson Pump & Mfg Company Inc 4620 City Ctr Dr PO Box 291370 *TF:* 800-767-7310 ■ *Web:* www.thompsonpump.com	Port Orange	FL	32129	386-767-7310	761-0362
Thrush Company Inc Je Company Inc 340 W Eigth St *Web:* www.comteck.com	Peru	IN	46970	765-472-3351	
Townley Engineering & Manufacturing Company Inc 10551 SE 110th St Rd *Web:* www.townley.net	Candler	FL	32111	352-687-3001	
Tramco Pump Co 1500 W Adams St **Fax:* Sales ■ *Web:* www.tramcopump.com	Chicago	IL	60607	312-243-5800	243-0702*
TURBOCAM Inc 607 Calef Hwy *Web:* www.turbocam.com	Barrington	NH	03825	603-905-0200	
Tuthill Corp 8500 S Madison St. *TF:* 800-634-2695 ■ *Web:* www.tuthill.com	Burr Ridge	IL	60527	630-382-4900	382-4999
Tuthill Pump Group 12500 S Pulaski Rd *Web:* www.tuthillpump.com	Alsip	IL	60803	708-389-2500	388-0869
Ultimate Washer Inc 711 Commerce Way Ste 1 *TF:* 866-858-4982 ■ *Web:* www.ultimatewasher.com	Jupiter	FL	33458	561-741-7022	
V&P Hydraulic Products LLC 1700 Pittsburgh Dr. *Web:* www.vphyd.com	Delaware	OH	43015	740-203-3600	
Vanton Pump & Equipment Corp 201 Sweetland Ave *Web:* www.vanton.com	Hillside	NJ	07205	908-688-4216	686-9314
Vaughan Company Inc 364 Monte-Elma Rd *TF:* 888-249-2467 ■ *Web:* www.chopperpumps.com	Montesano	WA	98563	360-249-4042	249-6155
Viking Pump Inc 406 State St *Web:* www.vikingpump.com	Cedar Falls	IA	50613	319-266-1741	273-8157
Vogelsang USA 7966 State Rt 44 *TF:* 800-984-9400 ■ *Web:* vogelsangusa.com	Ravenna	OH	44266	330-296-3820	
Wanner Engineering Inc 1204 Chestnut Ave. *Web:* www.wannereng.com	Minneapolis	MN	55403	612-332-5681	
Warren Pumps LLC 82 Bridges Ave *Web:* www.warrenpumps.com	Warren	MA	01083	413-436-7711	
Warren Rupp Inc 800 N Main St. *Web:* www.warrenruppinc.com	Mansfield	OH	44902	419-524-8388	522-7867
Wastecorp Inc PO Box 70 *TF:* 888-829-2783 ■ *Web:* www.wastecorp.com	Grand Island	NY	14072	888-829-2783	
Waterous Co 125 Hardman Ave. *TF:* 800-488-1228 ■ *Web:* www.waterousco.com	South Saint Paul	MN	55075	651-450-5000	450-5090
Watson-Marlow Inc 37 Upton Technology Park *Web:* www.watson-marlow.com	Wilmington	MA	01887	978-658-6168	
Waukesha Cherry-Burrell Corp (WCB) 611 Sugar Creek Rd *TF:* 800-252-5200 ■ *Web:* www.spx.com	Delavan	WI	53115	262-728-1900	728-4904
Weil Pump Co W57 N14363 Doerr Wy PO Box 887 *Web:* www.weilpump.com	Cedarburg	WI	53012	262-377-1399	377-0515
Weir Floway Inc 2494 S Railroad Ave *Web:* weirminerals.com	Fresno	CA	93706	559-442-4000	
Weir Group, The 2701 S Stoughton Rd *Web:* weirminerals.com	Madison	WI	53716	608-221-2261	221-5807
Weir Minerals 225 N Cedar St. *Web:* www.weirminerals.com	Hazleton	PA	18201	570-455-7711	459-2586
Wilden Pump & Engineering Co 22069 Van Buren St *Web:* www.psgdover.com	Grand Terrace	CA	92313	909-422-1730	783-3440

Phone Fax

Yeomans Chicago Corp
3905 Enterprise Ct PO Box 6620 .... Aurora IL 60504 630-236-5500 236-5511
Web: www.yccpump.com

Zoeller Co 3649 Kane Run Rd. .... Louisville KY 40211 502-778-2731 774-3624
OTC: ZOLR ■ *TF:* 800-928-7867 ■ *Web:* www.zoeller.com

642 RACING & RACETRACKS

See Also Motor Speedways p. 2784

Phone Fax

Alameda County Fair Assn (ACFA)
4501 Pleasanton Ave .... Pleasanton CA 94566 925-426-7600 426-7599
TF: 800-874-9253 ■ *Web:* www.alamedacountyfair.com

Arlington Park
2200 W Euclid Ave PO Box 7 .... Arlington Heights IL 60006 847-385-7500 385-7251
Web: www.arlingtonpark.com

Atlantic City Racing Course (ACRC)
4501 Black Horse Pk .... Mays Landing NJ 08330 609-641-2190
Web: acracecourse.com

Balmoral Park 26435 S Dixie Hwy .... Crete IL 60417 708-672-1414 672-5932
Web: www.balmoralpark.com

Batavia Downs 8315 Pk Rd. .... Batavia NY 14020 585-343-3750
Web: www.westernotb.com

Bay Meadows Racing Association
2600 S Delaware St .... San Mateo CA 94403 650-573-4500
Web: baymeadows.com

Belmont Park 2150 Hempstead Tpke. .... Elmont NY 11003 516-488-6000
Web: www.nyra.com

Brainerd International Raceway
5523 Birchdale Rd .... Brainerd MN 56401 218-824-7223 824-7240
TF: 866-444-4455 ■ *Web:* www.brainerdraceway.com

Buffalo Raceway 5600 McKinley Pkwy .... Hamburg NY 14075 716-649-1280 649-0033
Web: www.buffaloraceway.com

Calder Casino & Race Course 21001 NW 27th Ave. .... Miami FL 33056 305-625-1311 620-2569
TF: 800-522-4700 ■ *Web:* www.caldercasino.com

Calgary Exhibition & Stampede Ltd
1410 Olympic Way S E .... Calgary AB T2G2W1 403-261-0101
TF: 888-883-3828 ■ *Web:* www.calgarystampede.com

Canterbury Park Holding Corp
1100 Canterbury Rd .... Shakopee MN 55379 952-445-7223 496-6400
NASDAQ: CPHC ■ *TF:* 800-340-6361 ■ *Web:* www.canterburypark.com

Cassia County Fairgrounds 1101 Elba Ave. .... Burley ID 83318 208-678-9150
Web: cassiacountyfair.com

Central Wyoming Fairgrounds
1700 Fairgrounds Rd .... Casper WY 82604 307-235-5775 266-4224
Web: www.centralwyomingfair.com

Charlotte Motor Speedway 5555 Concord Pkwy S .... Concord NC 28027 704-455-3200 455-2547
TF: 800-455-3267 ■ *Web:* www.charlottemotorspeedway.com

Churchill Downs Inc 700 Central Ave. .... Louisville KY 40208 502-636-4400
NASDAQ: CHDN ■ *TF:* 800-994-9909 ■ *Web:* www.churchilldowns.com

Colonial Downs 10515 Colonial Downs Pkwy. .... New Kent VA 23124 804-966-7223 966-1565*
**Fax:* PR ■ *TF:* 888-482-8722 ■ *Web:* www.colonialdowns.com

Columbus Races 822 15th St .... Columbus NE 68601 402-564-0133
Web: www.agpark.com

Dale Earnhardt Inc
1675 Dale Earnhardt Hwy 3 .... Mooresville NC 28115 704-662-8000
Web: www.daleearnhardtinc.com

Del Mar Thoroughbred Club
2260 Jimmy Durante Blvd .... Del Mar CA 92014 858-755-1141 755-1141
Web: www.dmtc.com

Delaware Racing Assn 777 Delaware Pk Blvd. .... Wilmington DE 19804 302-994-2521 994-3392
Web: www.delawarepark.com

Delta Downs Racetrack 2717 Delta Downs Dr .... Vinton LA 70668 800-589-7441
TF: 800-589-7441 ■ *Web:* www.deltadowns.com

Dover Downs Hotel & Casino 1131 N DuPont Hwy .... Dover DE 19901 302-674-4600
NYSE: DDE ■ *TF:* 800-711-5882 ■ *Web:* www.doverdowns.com

Dover International Speedway
1131 N DuPont Hwy PO Box 843 .... Dover DE 19901 302-883-6500 672-0100
TF: 800-441-7223 ■ *Web:* www.doverspeedway.com

Dover Motorsports Inc 1131 N Dupont Hwy .... Dover DE 19901 302-883-6500 672-0100
NYSE: DVD ■ *Web:* www.dovermotorsportsinc.com

DuQuoin State Fair 655 Executive Dr .... Du Quoin IL 62832 618-542-1515 542-1541
Web: www.agr.state.il.us/dq

Elko County Fairgrounds PO Box 2067 .... Elko NV 89803 775-738-3616 778-3468
Web: www.elkocountyfair.com

Ellis Park Race Course LLC 3300 US 41 .... Henderson KY 42420 812-425-1456
Web: www.ellisparkracing.com

Fair Grounds Race Course
1751 Gentilly Blvd .... New Orleans LA 70119 504-944-5515 948-1160
TF: 800-262-7983 ■ *Web:* www.fairgroundsracecourse.com

Fair Meadows at Tulsa 4609 E 21st St .... Tulsa OK 74114 918-743-7223
TF: 877-781-2660 ■ *Web:* exposquare.com

Fairmount Park 9301 Collinsville Rd .... Collinsville IL 62234 618-345-4300 436-1516*
**Fax Area Code:* 314 ■ *Web:* www.fairmountpark.com

Finger Lakes Gaming & Race Track
5857 Rt 96 .... Farmington NY 14425 585-924-3232 924-3967
TF: 877-846-7369 ■ *Web:* www.fingerlakesgaming.com

Finger Lakes Racing Assn 5857 Rt 96 .... Farmington NY 14425 585-924-3232 924-3967
Web: www.fingerlakesgaming.com

Flamboro Downs Ltd 967 Hwy 5 .... Hamilton ON L9H5E2 905-627-3561
Web: www.flamborodowns.com

Fonner Park 700 E Stolley Pk Rd. .... Grand Island NE 68801 308-382-4515 384-2753
Web: www.fonnerpark.com

Fort Erie Race Track
230 Catherine St PO Box 1130 .... Fort Erie ON L2A5N9 905-871-3200 994-3629
TF: 800-295-3770 ■ *Web:* www.forterieracing.com

Freehold Raceway 130 Pk Ave. .... Freehold NJ 07728 732-462-3800 462-2920
Web: www.freeholdraceway.com

Fresno District Fair 1121 S Chance Ave .... Fresno CA 93702 559-650-3247 650-3226
TF: 866-275-3772 ■ *Web:* www.fresnofair.com

Phone Fax

Gillespie County Fairgrounds
530 Fair Dr PO Box 526 .... Fredericksburg TX 78624 830-997-2359 997-4923
TF: 800-280-9531 ■ *Web:* gillespiefair.net

Global Gaming Solutions LLC 210 N Broadway .... Ada OK 74820 580-559-0886
Web: www.globalgamingsol.com

Golden Gate Fields 1100 Eastshore Hwy .... Berkeley CA 94710 510-559-7300 559-7467
Web: www.goldengatefields.com

Goshen Historic Track Inc 44 Pk Pl .... Goshen NY 10924 845-294-5333 294-3998
Web: www.goshenhistorictrack.com

Grand Prix of Long Beach 3000 Pacific Ave .... Long Beach CA 90806 562-981-2600
Web: www.gplb.com

Grand River Agricultural Society
7445 Wellington Rd Ste 21 .... Elora ON N0B1S0 519-846-5455
Web: www.grandriverraceway.com

Grays Harbor Raceway
32 Elma McCleary Rd PO Box 911 .... Elma WA 98541 360-482-4374 892-6582
TF: 800-667-7711 ■ *Web:* www.graysharborraceway.com

Harrington Raceway 15 W Rider Rd. .... Harrington DE 19952 302-398-7223
TF: 888-887-5687 ■ *Web:* casino.harringtonraceway.com

Hawthorne Race Course 3501 S Laramie Ave. .... Cicero IL 60804 708-780-3700 780-3677
Web: www.hawthorneracecourse.com

Hazel Park Raceway 1650 E 10 Mile Rd .... Hazel Park MI 48030 248-398-1000 398-5236
TF: 800-794-8001 ■ *Web:* www.hazelparkraceway.com

Hollywood Casino at Charles Town Races
750 Hollywood Dr. .... Charles Town WV 25414 304-725-7001
TF: 800-795-7001 ■ *Web:* www.hollywoodcasinocharlestown.com

Hollywood Casino at Penn National Race Course
777 Hollywood Blvd .... Grantville PA 17028 717-469-2211
Web: www.hollywoodpnrc.com

Hollywood Park Land Company LLC
1050 S Prairie Ave .... Inglewood CA 90301 310-419-1500
Web: www.hollywoodpark.com

Hoosier Park Racing & Casino
4500 Dan Patch Cir .... Anderson IN 46013 765-642-7223 608-2754
TF: 800-526-7223 ■ *Web:* www.hoosierpark.com

Humboldt County Fair 1250 Fifth St .... Ferndale CA 95536 707-786-9511 786-9450
Web: www.humboldtcountyfair.org

Illinois State Fairgrounds
801 E Sangamon Ave .... Springfield IL 62702 217-782-4231 524-6194
Web: www.agr.state.il.us

Indiana State Fairgrounds
1202 E 38th St .... Indianapolis IN 46205 317-927-7500 927-7695
Web: www.in.gov

Indianapolis Motor Speedway Corp
4790 W 16th St. .... Indianapolis IN 46222 317-492-8500
Web: indianapolismotorspeedway.com

Iowa Speedway LLC 3333 Rusty Wallace Dr. .... Newton IA 50208 641-791-8000
Web: www.iowaspeedway.com

Jefferson County Kennel Club Inc
3079 N Jefferson St .... Monticello FL 32344 850-997-2561
Web: www.jckcgreyhounds.com

Jerome County Fairgrounds 200 N Fir St. .... Jerome ID 83338 208-324-7209 324-7057
Web: www.jeromecountyfair.com

Joe Gibbs Racing Inc 13415 Reese Blvd W .... Huntersville NC 28078 704-944-5000
Web: www.joegibbsracing.com

Josephine County Fairgrounds
1451 Fairgrounds Rd PO Box 672 .... Grants Pass OR 97527 541-476-3215 476-1027
TF: 800-773-1162 ■ *Web:* www.co.josephine.or.us

Kentucky Downs LLC 5629 Nashville Rd .... Franklin KY 42135 270-586-7778
Web: www.kentuckydowns.com

Kyle Busch Motorsports Inc
351 Mazeppa Rd. .... Mooresville NC 28115 704-662-0000
Web: www.kylebuschmotorsports.com

Lake Erie Speedway 10700 Delmas Dr .... North East PA 16428 814-725-3303 725-3353
Web: www.lakeeriespeedway.com

Laurel Park Rt 198 & Racetrack Rd PO Box 130 .... Laurel MD 20724 301-725-0400 792-7775*
**Fax Area Code:* 410 ■ *TF:* 800-638-1859 ■ *Web:* www.laurelpark.com

Lone Star Park at Grand Prairie
1000 Lone Star Pkwy .... Grand Prairie TX 75050 972-263-7223
Web: www.lonestarpark.com

Los Alamitos Race Course
4961 Katella Ave. .... Los Alamitos CA 90720 714-820-2800
Web: www.losalamitos.com/laqhr

Los Angeles Turf Club Inc
285 W Huntington Dr .... Arcadia CA 91007 626-574-7223 446-1456

Maywood Park 8600 W N Ave. .... Melrose Park IL 60160 708-343-4800 343-2564
Web: www.maywoodpark.com

Meadowlands Racetrack 50 Rt 120 .... East Rutherford NJ 07073 201-843-2446
Web: www.meadowlandsracetrack.com

Meadows Racetrack 210 Racetrack Rd .... Washington PA 15301 724-225-9300
Web: www.meadowsgaming.com

Melbourne Greyhound Park 1100 N Wickham Rd .... Melbourne FL 32935 321-259-9800 259-3437
Web: www.mgpark.com

MetraPark 308 6th Ave N. .... Billings MT 59101 406-256-2400
TF: 800-366-8538 ■ *Web:* www.metrapark.com

Mile High Racing & Entertainment/Mile High
10750 E Iliff Ave .... Aurora CO 80014 303-751-5918
Web: www.mihiracing.com

Mohave County Fair Assn
2600 Fairgrounds Blvd .... Kingman AZ 86401 928-753-2636 753-8383
Web: www.mcfafairgrounds.org

Monmouth Park Racetrack 175 Oceanport Ave .... Oceanport NJ 07757 732-222-5100 571-5226
Web: www.monmouthpark.com

Montana State Fair 400 Third St NW. .... Great Falls MT 59404 406-727-8900 452-8955
Web: goexpopark.com

Mystique Casino 1855 Greyhound Pk Dr .... Dubuque IA 52001 563-582-3647
TF: 800-373-3647 ■ *Web:* www.mystiquedbq.com

Naples/Fort Myers Greyhound Track
10601 Bonita Beach Rd .... Bonita Springs FL 34135 239-992-2411
Web: www.naplesfortmyersdogs.com

New Mexico State Fair 300 San Pedro NE .... Albuquerque NM 87108 505-222-9700
Web: www.exponm.com

	City	State	Zip	Phone	Fax
New York Racing Assn (NYRA) 110-00 Rockaway Blvd PO Box 90 *Web:* www.nyra.com	Jamaica	NY	11420	718-641-4700	
Northfield Park Associates LLC 10705 Northfield Rd PO Box 374 *Web:* www.northfieldpark.com	Northfield	OH	44067	330-467-4101	
Northville Downs 301 S Ctr St *TF:* 888-349-7100 ■ *Web:* www.northvilledowns.com	Northville	MI	48167	248-349-1000	348-8955
Oaklawn Park 2705 Central Ave *TF General:* 800-625-5296 ■ *Web:* www.oaklawn.com	Hot Springs	AR	71901	501-623-4411	624-4950
Ocean Downs 10218 Racetrack Rd *Web:* www.oceandowns.com	Berlin	MD	21811	410-641-0600	
Ontario Lottery & Gaming Corp 70 Foster Dr Ste 800 *TF:* 800-563-5357 ■ *Web:* www.olg.ca	Sault Sainte Marie	ON	P6A6V2	705-946-6464	
Panther Racing LLC 5101 Decatur Blvd Ste P *Web:* www.pantherracing.com	Indianapolis	IN	46241	317-856-9500	
Penn National Gaming Inc 825 Berkshire Blvd Ste 200 *NASDAQ: PENN* ■ *TF:* 877-565-2112 ■ *Web:* www.hollywoodpnrc.com	Wyomissing	PA	19610	877-565-2112	
Pensacola Greyhound Track 951 Dog Track Rd *TF:* 800-345-3997 ■ *Web:* www.pensacolagreyhoundtrack.com	Pensacola	FL	32506	850-455-8595	
Petaluma Fairgrounds Speedway 100 Fairgrounds Dr *Web:* www.petaluma-speedway.com	Petaluma	CA	94952	707-763-7223	
Phoenix Greyhound Park 3801 E Washington St *Web:* www.phoenixgreyhoundpark.com	Phoenix	AZ	85034	602-273-7181	
Pinnacle Entertainment Inc 3980 Howard Hughes Pkwy *NYSE: PNK* ■ *TF:* 877-764-8750 ■ *Web:* www.pnkinc.com	Las Vegas	NV	89169	702-541-7777	
Pocatello Downs 10560 N Fairgrounds Rd *Web:* theracingjournal.com	Pocatello	ID	83202	208-238-1721	
Portland International Raceway 1940 N Victory Blvd *Web:* www.portlandraceway.com	Portland	OR	97217	503-823-7223	823-5896
Portland Meadows Horse Track 1001 N Schmeer Rd *Web:* www.portlandmeadows.com	Portland	OR	97217	503-285-9144	286-9763
Ravalli County Fair 100 Old Corvallis Rd *TF:* 800-225-6779 ■ *Web:* ravalli.us	Hamilton	MT	59840	406-363-3411	375-9152
Remington Park Race Track 1 Remington Pl *TF:* 866-456-9880 ■ *Web:* www.remingtonpark.com	Oklahoma City	OK	73111	405-424-1000	
Retama Park 1 Retama Pkwy *Web:* www.retamapark.com	Selma	TX	78154	210-651-7000	651-7097
Rockingham Park Rockingham Pk Blvd *Web:* www.rockinghampark.com	Salem	NH	03079	603-898-2311	898-7163
Sam Houston Race Park 7575 N Sam Houston Pkwy W *Web:* www.shrp.com	Houston	TX	77064	281-807-8700	807-8777
San Joaquin County Fairgrounds 1658 S Airport Way *Web:* sanjoaquinfairgrounds.com	Stockton	CA	95206	209-466-5041	466-5739
San Luis Rey Downs 5772 Camino Del Rey *Web:* www.slrd.com	Bonsall	CA	92003	760-414-3273	
Santa Anita Park 285 W Huntington Dr *Web:* www.santaanita.com	Arcadia	CA	91007	626-574-7223	
Santa Cruz County Fair & Rodeo 3142 Arizona 83 PO Box 85 *Web:* sonoitafairgrounds.com	Sonoita	AZ	85637	520-455-5553	455-5330
Sarasota Kennel Club Inc 5400 Bradenton Rd *Web:* www.sarasotakennelclub.com	Sarasota	FL	34234	941-355-7744	
Saratoga Gaming & Raceway 342 Jefferson St PO Box 356 *Web:* www.saratogacasino.com	Saratoga Springs	NY	12866	518-584-2110	
Saratoga Race Course 267 Union Ave *Web:* www.saratogaracetrack.com	Saratoga Springs	NY	12866	718-641-4700	
Scarborough Downs 90 Payne Rd *Web:* www.scarboroughdowns.com	Scarborough	ME	04070	207-883-4331	883-2020
Scioto Downs Inc 6000 S High St *TF:* 800-514-3849 ■ *Web:* www.sciotodowns.com	Columbus	OH	43207	614-295-4700	
Solano County Fair 900 Fairgrounds Dr *TF:* 800-700-2482 ■ *Web:* www.scfair.com	Vallejo	CA	94589	707-551-2000	642-7947
Sonoma County Fairgrounds 1350 Bennett Valley Rd *Web:* www.sonomacountyfair.com	Santa Rosa	CA	95404	707-545-4200	573-9342
Sports Creek Raceway 4290 Morrish Rd	Swartz Creek	MI	48473	810-635-3333	
Stewart-haas Racing LLC 6001 Haas Way *Web:* stewarthaasracing.com	Kannapolis	NC	28081	704-652-4227	
Sunland Park Racetrack & Casino 1200 Futurity Dr *TF:* 800-572-1142 ■ *Web:* www.sunland-park.com	Sunland Park	NM	88063	575-874-5200	
Tampa Bay Downs Inc 11225 Racetrack Rd *TF:* 800-200-4434 ■ *Web:* www.tampabaydowns.com	Tampa	FL	33626	813-855-4401	854-3539
Team Rahal Inc 4601 Lyman Dr *Web:* www.rahal.com	Hilliard	OH	43026	614-529-7000	
Technicon Engineering Services Inc 4539 N Brawley Ave Ste 108 *Web:* www.technicon.net	Fresno	CA	93722	559-276-9311	
Texas Motor Speedway Inc 3545 Lone Star Cir 6th Fl *Web:* www.texasmotorspeedway.com	Fort Worth	TX	76177	817-215-8510	
Thistledown Racing Club Inc 21501 Emery Rd *TF:* 800-522-4700 ■ *Web:* www.caesars.com	Cleveland	OH	44128	216-662-8600	662-5339
Tillamook County Fairgrounds 4603 E Third St PO Box 455 *Web:* www.tillamookfair.com	Tillamook	OR	97141	503-842-2272	842-3314
TrackMaster 2083 Old Middlefield Way Ste 206 *TF:* 800-334-3800 ■ *Web:* www.trackmaster.com	Mountain View	CA	94043	650-316-1020	
Turf Paradise Racetrack 1501 W Bell Rd *TF:* 800-639-8783 ■ *Web:* www.turfparadise.com	Phoenix	AZ	85023	602-942-1101	942-8659
Twin River Casino 100 Twin River Rd *TF:* 877-827-4837 ■ *Web:* www.twinriver.com	Lincoln	RI	02865	401-475-8505	
Walla Walla Racetrack 363 Orchard St *Web:* www.wallawallafairgrounds.com	Walla Walla	WA	99362	509-527-3247	527-3259
Western Montana Fair 1101 S Ave W *Web:* www.missoulafairgrounds.com	Missoula	MT	59801	406-721-3247	
Woodbine Entertainment Group Inc 555 Rexdale Blvd PO Box 156 *TF:* 888-675-7223 ■ *Web:* www.woodbineentertainment.com	Toronto	ON	M9W5L2	416-675-7223	
World Racing Group Inc 7575 D W Winds Blvd Ste D *Web:* www.worldracinggroup.com	Concord	NC	28027	704-795-7223	
XpressBet Inc 200 Racetrack Rd Bldg 26 *Web:* www.xpressbet.com	Washington	PA	15301	724-229-6918	
Yonkers Raceway 810 Yonkers Ave *Web:* empirecitycasino.com	Yonkers	NY	10704	914-968-4200	457-2537
Yuma County Fair 2520 E 32nd St *Web:* www.yumafair.com	Yuma	AZ	85365	928-726-4420	344-3480

643 RADIO COMPANIES

	City	State	Zip	Phone	Fax
Artistic Media Partners Inc 5520 E 75th St *Web:* www.artisticradio.com	Indianapolis	IN	46250	317-594-0600	594-9567
Backyard Broadcasting 4237 Salisbury Rd Ste 225 *Web:* www.bybradio.com	Jacksonville	FL	32216	904-674-0260	
Beasley Broadcast Group Inc 3033 Riviera Dr Ste 200 *NASDAQ: BBGI* ■ *Web:* www.bbgi.com	Naples	FL	34103	239-263-5000	263-8191
Bi-Coastal Media LLC 140 N Main St *Web:* www.bicoastalmedia.com	Lakeport	CA	95453	707-263-6113	263-0939
Bible Broadcasting Network Inc 11530 Carmel Commons Blvd PO Box 7300 *TF:* 800-888-7077 ■ *Web:* www.bbnradio.org	Charlotte	NC	28226	704-523-5555	522-1967
Birach Broadcasting Corp Tower 14 Ste 1190 *Web:* www.birach.com	Southfield	MI	48075	248-557-3500	557-2950
Bliss Communications Inc PO Box 5001 *TF:* 800-422-7128 ■ *Web:* www.blissnet.net	Janesville	WI	53547	608-754-3311	
Bonneville International Corp 55 N 300 W *Web:* www.bonneville.com	Salt Lake City	UT	84101	801-575-7500	575-5820
Bott Radio Network 10550 Barkley St Ste 100 *TF:* 800-875-1903 ■ *Web:* www.bottradionetwork.com	Overland Park	KS	66212	913-642-7770	642-1319
Brazos Valley Radio 1240 E Villa Maria Rd *Web:* www.brazosradio.com	Bryan	TX	77802	979-776-1240	
Bristol Broadcasting Company Inc 901 E Valley Dr PO Box 1389 *Web:* www.bristolbroadcasting.com	Bristol	VA	24203	276-669-8112	669-0541
Buckley Broadcasting Corp 166 W Putnam Ave	Greenwich	CT	06830	203-661-4307	622-7341
Canadian Broadcasting Corp (CBC) PO Box 3220 *Web:* www.cbc.radio-canada.ca	Ottawa	ON	K1Y1E4	514-597-6000	
Cherry Creek Radio 501 S Cherry St Ste 480 *Web:* www.cherrycreekradio.com	Denver	CO	80246	303-468-6500	468-6555
Crawford Broadcasting Co (CBC) 2821 S Parker Rd Ste 1205 *Web:* www.crawfordbroadcasting.com	Denver	CO	80014	303-433-5500	433-1555
Cromwell Group Inc 1824 Murfreesboro Rd 2nd Fl *Web:* www.cromwellradio.com	Nashville	TN	37217	615-361-7560	366-4313
Cumulus Media Inc 3280 Peachtree Rd Ste 2300 *NASDAQ: CMLS* ■ *Web:* www.cumulus.com	Atlanta	GA	30305	404-949-0700	949-0740
Curtis Media Group 3012 Highwoods Blvd Ste 200 *Web:* www.radio961.com	Raleigh	NC	27604	919-790-9392	882-1746
Delmarva Broadcasting Co PO Box 7492 *Web:* www.radiocenter.com	Wilmington	DE	19803	302-478-2700	
Eagle Communications Inc 2703 Hall St Ste 15 Ste 15 *TF:* 877-613-2453 ■ *Web:* www.eaglecom.net	Hays	KS	67601	785-625-5910	625-8030
Eagle Radio Inc 2703 Hall St Ste 15 *TF:* 877-613-2453 ■ *Web:* eaglecom.net	Hays	KS	67601	877-613-2453	
Educational Media Foundation 5700 W Oaks Blvd *TF General:* 800-525-5683 ■ *Web:* www.klove.com	Rocklin	CA	95765	916-251-1600	251-1650
Emmis Communications Corp 40 Monument Cir 1 Emmis Plz Ste 700 *NASDAQ: EMMS* ■ *Web:* www.emmis.com	Indianapolis	IN	46204	317-266-0100	631-3750
Entercom Communications Corp 401 City Ave Ste 809 *NYSE: ETM* ■ *TF:* 800-776-9437 ■ *Web:* www.entercom.com	Bala Cynwyd	PA	19004	610-660-5610	660-5620
Entravision Communications Corp 2425 Olympic Blvd Ste 6000 W *NYSE: EVC* ■ *Web:* www.entravision.com	Santa Monica	CA	90404	310-447-3870	447-3899
Family Radio 290 Hegenberger Rd *TF:* 800-543-1495 ■ *Web:* familyradio.org	Oakland	CA	94621	800-543-1495	
Far East Broadcasting Co Inc 15700 Imperial Hwy PO Box 1 *TF:* 800-523-3480 ■ *Web:* www.febc.org	La Mirada	CA	90638	800-523-3480	
Flinn Broadcasting 6080 Mt Moriah Rd Ext *Web:* www.flinn.com	Memphis	TN	38115	901-375-9324	375-0041
Forever Broadcasting 1 Forever Dr *Web:* www.forevermediainc.com	Hollidaysburg	PA	16648	814-941-9800	943-2754
Galaxy Communications LP 235 Walton St *Web:* www.galaxycommunications.com	Syracuse	NY	13202	315-472-9111	472-1888
Georgia-Carolina Radiocasting Cos LLC 233 Big A Rd *Web:* www.gacaradio.com	Toccoa	GA	30577	706-297-7264	297-7266
Greater Media Inc 35 Braintree Hill Pk Ste 300 *Web:* www.greater-media.com	Braintree	MA	02184	781-348-8600	

	City	State	Zip	Phone	Fax
Hall Communications Inc 404 W Lime St *Web:* www.hallradio.com	Lakeland	FL	33815	863-682-8184	
International Broadcasting Bureau 330 Independence Ave SW *Web:* www.bbg.gov	Washington	DC	20237	202-203-4000	203-4585
Keymarket Communications LLC 123 Blaine Rd	Brownsville	PA	15417	724-938-2000	938-7824
KVOC 218 N Wolcott St	Casper	WY	82601	307-265-1984	
Liberman Broadcasting Inc 1845 W Empire Ave *Web:* www.lbimedia.com	Burbank	CA	91504	818-729-5300	567-1062
Lotus Communications Corp 3301 Barham Blvd Ste 200 *Web:* www.lotuscorp.com	Los Angeles	CA	90068	323-512-2225	512-2224
Mahaffey Enterprises 3327 E Ridgeview St	Springfield	MO	65804	417-883-9180	
Main Line 25 Penncraft Ave # 4 *Web:* mix95.com	Chambersburg	PA	17201	717-263-0813	263-9649
Maritime Broadcasting System (MBS) 90 Lovett Lake Crt *Web:* www.mbsradio.com	Halifax	NS	B3S0H6	902-425-1225	423-2093
Mel Wheeler Inc 3934 Electric Rd Ste 107 *Web:* melwheelerinc.com	Roanoke	VA	24018	540-774-9200	
Mid-America Radio Group Inc 60 N Wayne St PO Box 1970	Martinsville	IN	46151	765-349-1485	
Midwest Communications Inc 904 Grand Ave **Fax:* Hum Res ■ *TF:* 877-945-4236 ■ *Web:* www.mwcradio.com	Wausau	WI	54403	715-842-1437	842-7061*
Midwest Family Broadcasting 2453 E Elm St *Web:* www.mwfmarketing.fm	Springfield	MO	65802	417-886-5677	886-2155
Multicultural Radio Broadcasting 27 William St 11th Fl *Web:* www.mrbi.net	New York	NY	10005	212-966-1059	
Newcap Radio (NCC) 745 Windmill Rd *Web:* www.ncc.ca	Dartmouth	NS	B3B1C2	902-468-7557	468-7558
Newfoundland Capital Corp Ltd 745 Windmill Rd *TSE: NCC.A* ■ *Web:* www.ncc.ca	Dartmouth	NS	B3B1C2	902-468-7557	468-7558
NextMedia Group Inc 6312 S Fiddlers Green Cir Ste 205E	Greenwood Village	CO	80111	303-694-9118	694-4940
Northeast Broadcasting Corp 288 S River Rd	Bedford	NH	03110	603-668-6400	668-6470
Northern Star Broadcasting LLC 3250 Racquet Club Dr *Web:* www.nsbroadcasting.com	Traverse City	MI	49684	231-922-4981	922-3633
NRG Media 2875 Mt Vernon Rd SE *Web:* www.nrgmedia.com	Cedar Rapids	IA	52403	319-862-0300	286-9383
Pamal Broadcasting Ltd 6 Johnson Rd *Web:* www.pamal.com	Latham	NY	12110	518-786-6600	
Quantum Communications Corp 1266 E Main St 6th Fl	Stamford	CT	06902	203-388-0048	388-0054
Radio Training Network Inc 5015 S Florida Ave	Lakeland	FL	33813	863-644-3464	
Renda Broadcasting Corp 900 Parish St 4th Fl *Web:* www.rendabroadcasting.com	Pittsburgh	PA	15220	412-875-1800	875-1801
Results Radio LLC 1355 N Dutton Ave Ste 225 **Fax Area Code:* 530	Santa Rosa	CA	95401	707-546-9185	244-9707*
Saga Communications Inc 73 Kercheval Ave *NYSE: SGA* ■ *TF:* 800-777-3674 ■ *Web:* sagacom.com	Grosse Pointe Farms	MI	48236	313-886-7070	886-7150
Shamrock Communications Inc 149 Penn Ave *TF:* 800-228-4637 ■ *Web:* www.thetimes-tribune.com	Scranton	PA	18503	570-348-9100	
Simmons Media Group Inc 216 W St George Blvd Ste 101 *Web:* www.simmonsmedia.com	St George	UT	84770	801-524-2600	
Spanish Broadcasting System Inc (SBS) 2601 S Bayshore Dr PH 2 *NASDAQ: SBSA* ■ *Web:* www.spanishbroadcasting.com	Coconut Grove	FL	33133	305-441-6901	446-5148
Tejas Broadcasting LLP 1300 Antelope St	Corpus Christi	TX	78401	361-883-1600	883-9303
Telesouth Communications Inc 6311 Ridgewood Rd *TF:* 888-808-8637 ■ *Web:* www.telesouth.com	Jackson	MS	39211	601-957-1700	956-5228
Three Eagles Communications Co 7600 CR 120 *Web:* www.threeeagles.com	Salida	CO	81201	402-466-1234	
Townsquare Media Inc 240 Greenwich Ave *Web:* www.townsquaremedia.com	Greenwich	CT	06830	203-861-0900	
Triad Broadcasting Company LLC 2511 Garden Rd Bldg A Ste 104	Monterey	CA	93940	831-655-6350	655-6355
Univision Communications Inc 605 Third Ave 12th Fl *Web:* corporate.univision.com	New York	NY	10158	212-455-5331	
VerStandig Broadcasting 10960 John Wayne Dr PO Box 788 *Web:* www.verstandig.com	Greencastle	PA	17225	717-597-9200	597-9210
Waitt Corp LLC 1125 S 103rd St Ste 425 *Web:* www.waittcompany.com	Omaha	NE	68124	402-697-8000	
Walt Disney Co 500 S Buena Vista St *NYSE: DIS* ■ **Fax:* Mail Rm ■ *Web:* thewaltdisneycompany.com	Burbank	CA	91521	818-560-1000	553-7210*
West Virginia Radio Corp 1251 Earl L Core Rd *Web:* wvaq.com	Morgantown	WV	26505	304-296-0029	
Zimmer Radio Group 3215 Lemone Industrial Blvd Ste 200 *TF:* 800-455-1099 ■ *Web:* www.zimmercommunications.com	Columbia	MO	65201	573-875-1099	875-2439

644 RADIO NETWORKS

	City	State	Zip	Phone	Fax
American Family Association PO Box 2440 *TF:* 800-326-4543 ■ *Web:* www.afa.net	Tupelo	MS	38803	662-844-5036	
Associated Press 1100 13th St NW Ste 700 *TF:* 800-824-5498 ■ *Web:* www.ap.org	Washington	DC	20005	202-641-9000	
BGC Partners Inc 499 Pk Ave *NASDAQ: BGCP* ■ *Web:* www.bgcpartners.com	New York	NY	10022	646-346-7000	346-6919
Black Radio Network 166 Madison Ave *TF:* 866-342-6892 ■ *Web:* www.blackradionetwork.com	New York	NY	10016	212-686-6850	686-7308
Bott Radio Network 10550 Barkley St Ste 100 *TF:* 800-875-1903 ■ *Web:* www.bottradionetwork.com	Overland Park	KS	66212	913-642-7770	642-1319
CBC Radio Canada 181 Queen St PO Box 3220 *Web:* www.cbc.ca	Ottawa	ON	K1P1K9	613-288-6000	
CBS Corp 51 W 52nd St *NYSE: CBS* ■ *Web:* www.cbscorporation.com	New York	NY	10019	212-975-4321	975-4516
CBS Radio Network 524 W 57th St *Web:* www.cbsnews.com	New York	NY	10019	212-975-3247	
CNN Radio Network 190 Marietta St Ste 1 *Web:* cnnradio.cnn.com	Atlanta	GA	30303	404-827-2750	
Crystal Media Networks 7201 Wisconsin Ave Ste 780 *Web:* www.crystalmedianetworks.com	Bethesda	MD	20814	240-223-0846	
Dial Global Inc Candler Tower 220 W 42nd St *Web:* www.westwoodone.com	New York	NY	10036	212-967-2888	
ESPN Radio Network 545 Middle St *Web:* www.espn.go.com/espnradio	Bristol	CT	06010	860-766-2000	766-2213
Family Life Communications Inc PO Box 35300 *TF:* 800-776-1070 ■ *Web:* www.myflr.org	Tucson	AZ	85740	800-776-1070	
Far East Broadcasting Co Inc 15700 Imperial Hwy PO Box 1 *TF:* 800-523-3480 ■ *Web:* www.febc.org	La Mirada	CA	90638	800-523-3480	
Hispanic Communications Network 50 F St NW 8th Floor *Web:* www.hcnmedia.com	Washington	DC	20001	202-637-8800	
Jones International Ltd 9697 E Mineral Ave *TF:* 800-525-7002 ■ *Web:* www.jones.com	Centennial	CO	80112	800-525-7002	
Learfield Communications Inc 505 Hobbs Rd *Web:* www.learfield.com	Jefferson City	MO	65109	573-893-7200	893-2321
Moody Global Ministries 820 N La Salle Blvd *Web:* moodyglobal.org	Chicago	IL	60610	312-329-4000	
Motor Racing Network (MRN) 555 MRN Dr *Web:* www.mrn.com/?homepage=true	Concord	NC	28027	704-262-6700	262-6811
Pacifica Radio Foundation 1925 ML King Jr Way *Web:* www.pacifica.org	Berkeley	CA	94704	510-849-2590	849-2617
Public Radio International (PRI) 401 Second Ave N Ste 500 *Web:* www.pri.org	Minneapolis	MN	55401	612-338-5000	330-9222
Radio America 1100 N Glebe Rd Ste 900 **Fax Area Code:* 571 ■ *TF:* 800-807-4703 ■ *Web:* www.radioamerica.com	Arlington	VA	22201	703-302-1000	480-4141*
Radio Free Asia 2025 M St NW Ste 300 *Web:* www.rfa.org	Washington	DC	20036	202-530-4900	530-7794
Radio Free Europe/Radio Liberty (RFE/RL) 1201 Connecticut Ave NW 4th Fl *Web:* www.rferl.org	Washington	DC	20036	202-457-6900	457-6992
Relevant Radio 1496 Bellevue St Ste 202 PO Box 10707 *TF:* 877-291-0123 ■ *Web:* www.relevantradio.com	Green Bay	WI	54311	877-291-0123	
Salem Radio Network 6400 N Beltline Rd Ste 210 *Web:* www.srnonline.com	Irving	TX	75063	972-831-1920	831-8626
SRN Broadcasting 307 E Washington	Lake Bluff	IL	60044	847-735-1995	
Tiger Financial News Network 601 Cleveland St Ste 618 *TF:* 877-518-9190 ■ *Web:* www.tfnn.com	Clearwater	FL	33755	727-467-9190	443-0869
Trident Communications 31 Timber Ln	Hilton Head Island	SC	29926	843-837-4978	
Triton Media Group 15303 Ventura Blvd Ste 1500 *Web:* www.tritondigital.com	Sherman Oaks	CA	91403	310-575-9700	
United Stations Radio Network 1065 Ave of the Americas 3rd Fl *TF:* 866-989-1975 ■ *Web:* www.unitedstations.com	New York	NY	10018	212-869-1111	869-1115
Voice of America Radio Network 330 Independence Ave SW *Web:* www.voanews.com	Washington	DC	20237	202-203-4959	
Yesterday USA Radio Networks, The 2001 Plymouth Rock Dr *TF:* 800-624-2272 ■ *Web:* www.yesterdayusa.com	Richardson	TX	75081	972-889-9872	889-2329

645 RADIO STATIONS

AAA	Adult Album Alternative	**NAC**	New Adult Contemporary
AC	Adult Contemporary	**Nost**	Nostalgia
Alt	Alternative	**NPR**	National Public Radio
CBC	Canadian Broadcasting Corp	**Oldies**	Oldies/80s
CHR	Contemporary Hit Radio	**Rel**	Religious
Clas	Classical	**Rock**	Rock
CR	Classic Rock	**Span**	Spanish
Ctry	Country	**Sports**	Sports
Ethnic	Multilingual	**Urban**	Urban
N/T	News/Talk	**Var**	Variety

See Also Internet Broadcasting p. 2593

	City	State	Zip	Phone	Fax
100.7 WLEV 2158 Ave C Ste 100 *Web:* www.wlevradio.com	Bethlehem	PA	18017	610-266-7600	
102.9 The Whale 869 Blue Hills Ave *Web:* www.1029thewhale.com	Bloomfield	CT	06002	860-243-1115	286-8257
107.9 The Bear 4270 Byrd Dr *Web:* 1079thebear.iheart.com	Loveland	CO	80538	970-461-2560	461-0118

Station / Address	City	State	Zip	Phone	Fax
92.5 FM WVNN 1717 Hwy 72 E	Athens	AL	35611	256-830-8300	232-6842
TF: 866-494-9866 ■ *Web:* www.wvnn.com					
97.1 THE WAVE 919 Ellegood St	Salisbury	MD	21801	410-219-3500	548-1543
Web: www.971thewave.com					
97.3 NOW Milwaukee 12100 W Howard Ave	Greenfield	WI	53228	414-545-8900	327-3200
Web: www.973now.com					
99.5 The River					
1203 Troy-Schenectady Rd Riverhill Ctr	Latham	NY	12110	518-452-4800	452-4855
TF: 800-995-9783 ■ *Web:* 995theriver.iheart.com					
99.5 WMAG 2-B PAI Pk	Greensboro	NC	27409	336-822-2000	
TF: 866-415-4158 ■ *Web:* 995wmag.iheart.com					
ALT 98.7 3400 W Olive Ave Ste 550	Burbank	CA	91505	818-559-2252	
Web: alt987fm.iheart.com					
ALT AZ 93.3 1167 W Javelina Ave	Mesa	AZ	85210	480-897-9300	
Web: altaz933.com					
AM 570 LA Sports 3400 W Olive Ave Ste 550	Burbank	CA	91505	818-559-2252	
TF: 866-987-2570 ■ *Web:* am570lasports.iheart.com					
Bell media 1640 Ouellette Ave	Windsor	ON	N8X1L1	519-258-8888	
Web: www.939theriverradio.com					
Big 920, The 12100 W Howard Ave	Greenfield	WI	53228	414-545-8900	
Web: www.thebig920.com					
BIG-FM 95.7 12100 W Howard Ave	Greenfield	WI	53228	414-545-8900	546-9654
Web: 957bigfm.iheart.com					
CBS Miami 194 NW 187th St	Miami	FL	33169	305-654-1700	
Web: miami.cbslocal.com/category/sports					
CBS Radio 1271 Ave of the Americas Fl 44	New York	NY	10020	248-855-5100	
Web: www.cbsradio.com					
CBV-FM 106.3 (CBC) PO Box 500 Stn A	Toronto	ON	M5W1E6	866-306-4636	
TF: 866-306-4636 ■ *Web:* www.cbc.radio-canada.ca					
CHML 875 Main St W	Hamilton	ON	L8S4R1	905-521-9900	540-2452
Web: 900chml.com					
CJXY-FM 107.9 (Rock) 875 Main St W Ste 900	Hamilton	ON	L8S4R1	905-521-9900	
Web: www.y108.ca					
CKLW-AM 800 (N/T) 1640 Ouellette Ave	Windsor	ON	N8X1L1	519-258-8888	258-0182
TF: 800-263-2559 ■ *Web:* www.am800cklw.com					
Entercom Boston 20 Guest St 3rd Fl	Boston	MA	02135	617-779-5800	
Web: www.entercom.com					
Family Stations Inc 290 Hegenberger Rd	Oakland	CA	94621	800-543-1495	
TF: 800-543-1495 ■ *Web:* familyradio.org					
Freedom 95 Radio 645 Industrial Dr	Franklin	IN	46131	317-736-4040	736-4781
TF: 800-278-9200 ■ *Web:* www.freedom95.us					
Fun 101.3 FM 1996 Auction Rd	Manheim	PA	17545	717-653-0800	653-0122
TF: 877-870-5678 ■ *Web:* www.fun1013.com					
Go 96.3 420 N Fifth St Ste 150	Minneapolis	MN	55401	612-659-4848	
Web: go963mn.com/connect					
Hot 103.1 1355 California St PO Box 968	Las Cruces	NM	88001	575-525-9298	525-9419
Web: www.hot103.fm					
K Light Radio 98 - 1016 Komo Mai Dr	Aiea	HI	96701	808-524-1040	487-1040
Web: www.klight.org					
KAAM-AM 770 (Nost) 3201 Royalty Row	Irving	TX	75062	972-445-1700	
Web: www.kaamradio.com					
KABX-FM 97.5 (Oldies) 1020 W Main St	Merced	CA	95340	209-723-2191	205-1013
TF: 800-350-3777 ■ *Web:* www.975kabx.com					
KACL-FM 98.7 (Oldies) 4303 Memorial Hwy	Mandan	ND	58554	701-663-9898	
Web: www.cool987fm.com					
KADI-FM 99.5 (Rel)					
5431 W Sunshine St	Brookline Station	MO	65619	417-831-0995	831-4026
Web: www.99hitfm.com					
KAJN-FM 102.9 (Rel)					
110 W Third St PO Box 1469	Crowley	LA	70527	337-783-1560	783-1674
Web: www.kajn.com					
KANU-FM 91.5 (NPR)					
1120 W 11th St Kansas Public Radio	Lawrence	KS	66044	785-864-4530	
TF: 888-577-5268 ■ *Web:* www.kansaspublicradio.org					
KBAQ-FM 89.5 (Clas) 2323 W 14th St	Tempe	AZ	85281	480-833-1122	774-8475
Web: www.kbaq.org					
KBBY-FM 95.1 (AC) 1376 Walter St	Ventura	CA	93003	805-642-8595	
TF: 888-288-9242 ■ *Web:* www.951kbby.com					
KBCO-FM 97.3 (AAA) 4695 S Monaco St	Denver	CO	80237	303-444-5600	
Web: kbco.iheart.com					
KBHE-FM 89.3 (NPR)					
555 N Dakota St PO Box 5000	Vermillion	SD	57069	605-677-5861	677-5010
TF: 800-456-0766 ■ *Web:* www.sdpb.org					
KBIA-FM 91.3 (NPR) 409 Jesse Hall	Columbia	MO	65211	573-882-3431	882-2636
TF: 800-292-9136 ■ *Web:* www.kbia.org					
KBRG-FM 100.3 (Span AC)					
750 Battery St Ste 200	San Francisco	CA	94111	888-808-1003	733-5766*
**Fax Area Code:* 415 ■ *TF:* 888-808-1003 ■ *Web:* www.univision.com/san-francisco/kbrg					
KBUE-FM 105.5 (Span) 1845 Empire Ave	Burbank	CA	91504	818-729-5300	
KBYZ-FM 96.5 (CR) 4303 Memorial Hwy	Mandan	ND	58554	701-663-9600	
TF: 888-663-9650 ■ *Web:* www.965thefox.com					
KCAQ-FM 104.7 (CHR)					
2284 S Victoria Ave Ste 2G	Ventura	CA	93003	805-289-1400	
TF: 877-440-1047 ■ *Web:* www.q1047.com					
KCBI-FM 90.9 (Rel) 411 Ryan Plz Dr	Arlington	TX	76011	817-792-3800	
Web: www.kcbi.org					
KCFR-FM 90.1 (NPR) 7409 S Alton Ct	Centennial	CO	80112	303-871-9191	733-3319
TF: 800-722-4449 ■ *Web:* www.cpr.org					
KCFX-FM 101.1 (CR) 5800 Foxridge Dr 6th Fl	Mission	KS	66202	913-514-3000	
Web: www.101thefox.net					
KCHZ-FM 95.7 (CHR) 5800 Foxridge Dr Fl 6	Mission	KS	66202	913-514-3000	
Web: www.957thevibe.com					
KCI 101 495 Benham St	Hamden	CT	06514	203-281-9600	281-2795
Web: kc101.iheart.com					
KCLR-FM 99.3 (Ctry)					
3215 Lemone Industrial Blvd Ste 200	Columbia	MO	65201	573-875-1099	
TF: 800-455-5257 ■ *Web:* www.clear99.com					
KCLU-FM 88.3 (NPR)					
60 W Olsen Rd Ste 4400	Thousand Oaks	CA	91360	805-493-3900	
Web: www.kclu.org					
KCMO-AM 710 (N/T) 5800 Foxridge Dr 6th Fl	Mission	KS	66202	913-514-3000	262-3946
Web: www.kcmotalkradio.com					
KCMO-FM 94.9 (Oldies) 5800 Foxridge Dr 6th Fl	Mission	KS	66202	913-514-3000	
Web: www.949kcmo.com					
KCMQ-FM 96.7 (CR)					
3215 Lemone Industrial Blvd Ste 200	Columbia	MO	65201	573-875-1099	
TF: 800-455-1967 ■ *Web:* www.kcmq.com					
KCRW-FM 89.9 (NPR) 1900 Pico Blvd	Santa Monica	CA	90405	310-450-5183	450-7172
TF: 877-527-9227 ■ *Web:* www.kcrw.com					
KCSD-FM 90.9 (NPR)					
555 N Dakota St PO Box 5000	Vermillion	SD	57069	605-677-5861	677-5010
TF: 800-456-0766 ■ *Web:* www.sdpb.org					
KCSM-FM 91.1 (Jazz) 1700 W Hillsdale Blvd	San Mateo	CA	94402	650-574-6586	
Web: www.kcsm.org					
KCSP-AM 610 (Sports) 7000 Squibb Rd	Mission	KS	66202	913-744-3600	
Web: 610sports.com					
KDB-FM 93.7 (Clas) 414 E Cota St	Santa Barbara	CA	93101	805-966-4131	966-4788
Web: www.kdb.com					
KDON-FM 102.5 (CHR) 903 N Main St	Salinas	CA	93906	831-755-8181	755-8193
TF: 888-558-5366 ■ *Web:* kdon.iheart.com					
Keymarket Communications					
56325 High Ridge Rd	Bellaire	OH	43906	740-676-5661	
Web: www.wyjkfm.com					
KEYY-AM 1450 (Rel) 307 S 1600 W	Provo	UT	84601	801-374-5210	
Web: www.keyradio.org					
KEZN-FM 103.1 (AC) 72-915 Parkview Dr	Palm Desert	CA	92260	760-340-9383	340-5756
KFAX-AM 1100 (Rel) 39138 Fremont Blvd	Fremont	CA	94538	510-713-1100	
Web: www.kfax.com					
KFI-AM 640 (N/T) 3400 W Olive Ave Ste 550	Burbank	CA	91505	818-559-2252	
Web: kfiam640.iheart.com					
KFRG-FM 95.1 (Ctry)					
900 E Washington St Ste 315	Colton	CA	92324	909-825-9525	825-0441
TF: 888-431-3764 ■ *Web:* kfrog.cbslocal.com					
KGNU-FM 88.5 (Var) 4700 Walnut St	Boulder	CO	80301	303-449-4885	
TF: 800-737-3030 ■ *Web:* www.kgnu.org					
KGOU-FM 106.3 (NPR) 860 Van Vleet Oval Rm 300	Norman	OK	73019	405-325-3388	325-7129
TF: 866-533-2470 ■ *Web:* www.kgou.org					
KGPR-FM 89.9 (NPR)					
2100 16th Ave S Rm G118	Great Falls	MT	59405	406-268-3739	268-3736
Web: www.kgpr.org					
KGRT-FM 103.9 (Ctry)					
1355 California St PO Box 968	Las Cruces	NM	88001	575-525-9298	525-9419
Web: www.kgrt.com					
KGY-FM 96.9 (Ctry) 1700 Marine Dr NE	Olympia	WA	98501	360-943-1240	
Web: www.kgyradio.com					
KHAY-FM 100.7 (Ctry) 1376 Walter St	Ventura	CA	93003	805-642-8595	
Web: www.khay.com					
KHOZ-FM 102.9 (Ctry) 1111 Radio Ave	Harrison	AR	72601	870-741-2301	
Web: www.1029thez.com					
KIIS-FM 102.7 (CHR) 3400 W Olive Ave Ste 550	Burbank	CA	91505	818-559-2252	729-2502
Web: kiisfm.iheart.com					
KIIX-AM 1410 (Sports) 4270 Byrd Dr	Loveland	CO	80538	970-461-2560	461-0118
Web: kiixcountry.iheart.com					
KIXI-AM 880 (Nost) 3650 131st Ave SE Ste 550	Bellevue	WA	98006	425-562-8964	653-1088
TF: 866-880-5494 ■ *Web:* www.kixi.com					
KJJY-FM 92.5 (Ctry) 4143 109th St	Urbandale	IA	50322	515-331-9200	
Web: 925nashicon.com					
KJLH-FM 102.3 (Urban) 161 N La Brea Ave	Inglewood	CA	90301	310-330-2200	
Web: www.kjlhradio.com					
KJZZ-FM 91.5 (NPR) 2323 W 14th St	Tempe	AZ	85281	480-834-5627	774-8475
Web: kjzz.org					
KKRQ-FM 100.7 (CR) 1 Stephen Atkins Dr	Iowa City	IA	52245	319-354-9500	354-9504
Web: kkrq.iheart.com					
KLBB-AM 1220 (Nost) 104 N Main St	Stillwater	MN	55082	651-439-5006	
Web: www.klbbradio.com					
KLTY-FM 94.9 (Rel) 6400 N Beltline Rd Ste 120	Irving	TX	75063	972-870-9949	
Web: www.klty.com					
KMBR-FM 95.5 (Rock) 750 Dewey Blvd Ste 1	Butte	MT	59701	406-494-4442	494-6020
Web: www.955kmbr.com					
KMBZ-AM 980 (N/T) 7000 Squibb Rd	Mission	KS	66202	913-744-3600	
Web: www.kmbz.com					
KMFC-FM 92.1 (Rel) 1249 E Hwy 22	Centralia	MO	65240	573-682-5525	
KNDR-FM 104.7 (Rel) 1400 NE Third St	Mandan	ND	58554	701-663-2345	663-2347
TF: 800-767-5095 ■ *Web:* www.kndr.fm					
KNOX-AM 1310 (N/T) 1185 Ninth St NE	Thompson	ND	58278	701-775-4611	772-0540
Web: www.knoxradio.com					
KNUS-AM 710 (N/T) 3131 S Vaughn Way Ste 601	Aurora	CO	80014	303-750-5687	696-8063
Web: www.710knus.com					
KNWI-FM 107.1 (Rel)					
3737 Woodland Ave Ste 300	West Des Moines	IA	50266	515-327-1071	
TF: 800-701-3123 ■ *Web:* life1071.com					
KOCP-FM 95.9 (CR) 2284 S Victoria Ave	Ventura	CA	93003	805-339-9590	
KOHL-FM 89.3 (CHR) 43600 Mission Blvd	Fremont	CA	94539	510-659-6221	659-6001
Web: www.kohlradio.com					
KOKZ-FM 105.7 (Oldies) 514 Jefferson St	Waterloo	IA	50701	319-234-2200	
Web: 1057kokz.com					
KOLA-FM 99.9 (Clas)					
1940 Orange Tree Ln Ste 200	Redlands	CA	92374	909-793-3554	
Web: www.kolafm.com					
KOPN-FM 89.5 (Var) 915 E Broadway	Columbia	MO	65201	573-874-1139	499-1662
TF: 800-895-5676 ■ *Web:* www.kopn.org					
KOST-FM 103.5 (AC) 3400 W Olive Ave Ste 550	Burbank	CA	91505	818-559-2252	260-9961
Web: kost1035.iheart.com					
KPCC-FM 89.3 (NPR) 1570 E Colorado Blvd	Pasadena	CA	91106	626-585-7000	585-7916
Web: www.scpr.org					
KPIG-FM 107.5 (AAA) 1110 Main St Ste 16	Watsonville	CA	95076	831-722-9000	
Web: www.kpig.com					
KPLU-FM 88.5 (NPR) 12180 Pk Ave S	Tacoma	WA	98447	253-535-7758	535-8332
TF: 800-677-5758 ■ *Web:* www.kplu.org					
KPVU-FM 91.3 (NPR)					
Prairie View A & M University MS 1415	Prairie View	TX	77446	936-261-3750	261-3769
TF: 877-241-1752 ■ *Web:* pvamu.edu/auxiliaryservices/kpvu					
KQFX-FM 104.3 (Span) 3639 Wolflin Ave	Amarillo	TX	79102	806-355-1043	

Station	City	State	Zip	Phone	Fax
KQKS-FM 107.5 (Urban) 4700 S Syracuse St Ste 1050 *Web:* www.ks1075.com	Denver	CO	80111	303-228-1075	
KQRC-FM 98.9 (Rock) 7000 Squibb Rd *Web:* www.989therock.com	Mission	KS	66202	913-744-3600	
KRKS-FM 94.7 (Rel) 3131 S Vaughn Way *Web:* www.947krks.com	Aurora	CO	80014	303-750-5687	696-8063
KRMD-FM 101.1 (Ctry) 270 Plz Loop *Web:* www.nashfm1011.com	Bossier City	LA	71111	318-549-8500	549-8505
KROX-AM 1260 (Var) 208 S Main St *TF:* 800-222-2537 ■ *Web:* www.kroxam.com	Crookston	MN	56716	218-281-1140	281-5036
KRWG-FM 90.7 (NPR) PO Box 3000 *Web:* krwg.org	Las Cruces	NM	88003	575-646-2222	646-1974
KSEA-FM 107.9 (Span) 608 E Boronda Rd Ste C *Web:* www.campesina.net	Salinas	CA	93906	831-754-1469	
KSKY-AM 660 (N/T) 6400 N Beltline Rd Ste 110 *Web:* www.660amtheanswer.com	Irving	TX	75063	972-870-9949	
KSME-FM 96.1 (CHR) 4270 Byrd Dr *TF:* 877-498-9600 ■ *Web:* kissfmcolorado.iheart.com	Loveland	CO	80538	970-461-2560	461-0118
KTMY-FM 107.1 (N/T) 3415 University Ave *Web:* www.mytalk1071.com	St. Paul	MN	55114	651-642-4107	647-2904
KTOM-FM 92.7 (Ctry) 903 N Main St *TF General:* 800-660-5866 ■ *Web:* ktom.iheart.com	Salinas	CA	93906	831-755-8181	755-8193
KTSD-FM 91.1 (NPR) 555 N Dakota St PO Box 5000 *TF:* 800-456-0766 ■ *Web:* www.sdpb.org	Vermillion	SD	57069	605-677-5861	677-5010
KTXY-FM 106.9 (AC) 3215 Lemone Industrial Blvd Ste 200 *TF:* 800-500-9107 ■ *Web:* www.y107.com	Columbia	MO	65201	573-875-1099	
KUAD-FM 99.1 (Ctry) 600 Main St **Fax Area Code:* 970 ■ *TF:* 800-500-2599 ■ *Web:* www.k99.com	Windsor	CO	80550	800-500-2599	686-7491*
KUAF 91.3 Public Radio 9 S School Ave *TF:* 800-522-5823 ■ *Web:* kuaf.com	Fayetteville	AR	72701	479-575-2556	575-8440
KUCR-FM 88.3 (Var) 691 W Linden St *Web:* www.kucr.org	Riverside	CA	92507	951-827-3737	827-3240
KUDL-FM 98.1 (AC) 7000 Squibb Rd *Web:* www.kmbz.com	Mission	KS	66202	913-744-3600	
KUNA-FM 96.7 (Span) 42-650 Melanie Pl *Web:* www.kesq.com	Palm Desert	CA	92211	760-773-0342	
KUPD-FM 97.9 (Rock) 1900 W Carmen St *Web:* www.98kupd.com	Tempe	AZ	85283	480-838-0400	
KUSP-FM 88.9 (NPR) 203 Eigth Ave *TF:* 800-655-5877 ■ *Web:* www.kusp.org	Santa Cruz	CA	95062	831-476-2800	476-2802
KUWC-FM 91.3 (NPR) 1000 E University Ave *Web:* www.uwyo.edu	Laramie	WY	82071	307-766-1121	
KUWJ-FM 90.3 (NPR) 1000 E University Ave *TF:* 800-729-5897 ■ *Web:* www.wyomingpublicmedia.org	Laramie	WY	82071	307-766-4240	766-6184
KUWS-FM 91.3 (NPR) 1805 Catlin Ave *TF:* 800-300-8530 ■ *Web:* www.kuws.fm	Superior	WI	54880	715-394-8530	394-8404
KVLC-FM 101.1 (Oldies) 101 Perkins Dr *TF:* 877-527-1011 ■ *Web:* www.101gold.com	Las Cruces	NM	88005	575-527-1111	
KWWR-FM 95.7 (Ctry) 1705 E Liberty St *Web:* info.kwwr.com	Mexico	MO	65265	573-581-5500	581-1801
KWYR-FM 93.7 (AC) PO Box 491 *TF:* 800-388-5997 ■ *Web:* www.kwyr.com	Winner	SD	57580	605-842-3333	842-3875
KXFG-FM 92.9 (Ctry) 900 E Washington Ste 315 *TF:* 888-431-3764 ■ *Web:* kfrog.cbslocal.com	Colton	CA	92324	909-825-9525	
KXXO-FM 96.1 (AC) 119 NE Washington St *Web:* www.mixx96.com	Olympia	WA	98501	360-943-9937	352-3643
KYCK-FM 97.1 (Ctry) 1185 Ninth St NE *Web:* www.97kyck.com	Thompson	ND	58278	701-775-4611	772-0540
KYGO-FM 98.5 (Ctry) 7800 E OrchaRd Rd Ste 400 *Web:* www.kygo.com	Greenwood Village	CO	80111	303-321-0950	
La Rockola 96.7FM 3101 W Fifth St *Web:* larockola967.estrellatv.com	Santa Ana	CA	92703	714-554-5000	554-9362
Magic 107.3 KMJK-FM 5800 Foxridge Dr Ste 600 *Web:* www.magic1073.com	Mission	KS	66202	816-576-7107	
Magic 590 6 Johnson Rd *Web:* albanymagic.com	Latham	NY	12047	518-786-6600	
Magic 98.9 351 Tilghman Rd *Web:* mymagic989.iheart.com	Salisbury	MD	21804	410-742-1923	742-2329
Majic 105.7 6200 Oak Tree Blvd 4th Fl *Web:* www.wmji.com	Independence	OH	44131	216-520-2600	
MEGA-FM 94.9 (Span CHR) 7601 Riviera Blvd *TF:* 877-599-2946 ■ *Web:* mega949.iheart.com	Miramar	FL	33023	954-862-2000	862-4015
NASH-FM 97.3 4143 109th St *Web:* www.nashfm973.com	Urbandale	IA	50322	515-331-9200	
NEW MOViN 92.5, The 3650 131st Ave SE Ste 550	Bellevue	WA	98006	425-653-9462	653-9464
Patriot AM 1150, The 3400 W Olive Ave Ste 550 *Web:* patriotla.iheart.com	Burbank	CA	91505	818-559-2252	
Queen B 51 Means Dr	Platteville	WI	53818	608-349-2000	349-2002
Radio Kansas 815 N Walnut St Ste 300 *TF:* 800-723-4657 ■ *Web:* www.radiokansas.org	Hutchinson	KS	67501	620-662-6646	
RadioU PO Box 1887 *TF:* 877-272-3468 ■ *Web:* www.radiou.com	Westerville	OH	43086	877-272-3468	
Real 92.3 FM 3400 W Olive Blvd Ste 550 *Web:* real923la.iheart.com	Burbank	CA	91505	818-559-2252	
Star 92.9 265 Hegeman Ave *TF:* 866-865-7827 ■ *Web:* www.star929.com	Colchester	VT	05446	802-655-0093	655-0478
Super Talk 1270 4303 Memorial Hwy *TF:* 844-255-7886 ■ *Web:* www.supertalk1270.com	Mandan	ND	58554	701-663-1270	
Trending Radio 93.3 N 72 W 12922 Good Hope Rd *Web:* www.b933fm.com	Menomonee Falls	WI	53051	414-778-1933	771-3036
Triad's 105.7 Man Up, The 2-B PAI Pk *TF:* 800-950-2482 ■ *Web:* 1057manup.iheart.com	Greensboro	NC	27409	336-822-2000	
WAAF-FM 107.3 (Rock) 20 Guest St 3rd Fl *Web:* www.waaf.com	Brighton	MA	02135	617-779-5800	
WAEB-AM 790 (N/T) 1541 Alta Dr Ste 400 *Web:* www.790waeb.com	Whitehall	PA	18052	610-434-1742	434-6288
WAEB-FM 104.1 (AC) 1541 Alta Dr 4th Fl *Web:* www.b104.com	Whitehall	PA	18052	610-434-1742	434-6288
WAFL-FM 97.7 (AC) 1666 Blairs Pond Rd *Web:* www.eagle977.com	Milford	DE	19963	302-422-7575	422-3069
WAJZ-FM 96.3 (Urban) 6 Johnson Rd *Web:* www.jamz963.com	Latham	NY	12110	518-786-6600	
WAKB-FM 100.9 (Urban) 6025 Broadcast Dr	North Augusta	SC	29841	803-279-2330	279-8149
WAKS-FM 96.5 (CHR) 6200 Oak Tree Blvd S 4th Fl *Web:* www.kisscleveland.com	Independence	OH	44131	216-520-2600	
WALK-FM 97.5 (AC) 234 Airport Plz Ste 5 *TF:* 877-263-7995 ■ *Web:* www.walk975.com	Farmingdale	NY	11735	631-475-5200	
WAPN-FM 91.5 (Rel) 1508 State Ave *Web:* www.wapn.net	Holly Hill	FL	32117	386-677-4272	
WAQY-FM 102.1 (CR) 45 Fisher Ave *Web:* www.rock102.com	East Longmeadow	MA	01028	413-525-4141	525-4334
WARO-FM 94.5 (CR) 2824 Palm Beach Blvd *Web:* 945thearrow.com	Fort Myers	FL	33916	239-479-5506	332-0767
WASH-FM 97.1 (AC) 1801 Rockville Pk Ste 601 *TF:* 866-927-4361 ■ *Web:* washfm.iheart.com	Rockville	MD	20852	240-747-2700	
WAVA-AM 780 (Rel) 1901 N Moore St Ste 200 **Fax Area Code:* 202 ■ *TF:* 888-976-6924 ■ *Web:* www.wava.com	Arlington	VA	22209	703-807-2266	342-3800*
WAVA-FM 105.1 (Rel) 1901 N Moore St Ste 200 *TF:* 888-293-9282 ■ *Web:* www.wava.com	Arlington	VA	22209	703-807-2266	
WAYJ-FM 88.7 (Rel) 1860 Boyscout Dr Ste 202	Fort Myers	FL	33907	239-936-1929	936-5433
WAYV-FM 95.1 (CHR) 8025 Black Horse Pike *TF:* 888-966-8146 ■ *Web:* www.951wayv.com	West Atlantic City	NJ	08232	609-484-8444	646-6331
WAYZ-FM 104.7 (Ctry) 10960 John Wayne Dr *TF:* 888-950-1047 ■ *Web:* www.wayz.com	Greencastle	PA	17225	717-597-9200	597-9210
WBAB-FM 102.3 (Rock) 555 Sunrise Hwy *Web:* www.wbab.com	West Babylon	NY	11704	631-587-1023	587-1282
WBACH 98 Main St	Ellsworth	ME	04605	207-667-9800	
WBAP-AM 820 (N/T) 3090 Olive St Ste 400 *Web:* www.wbap.com	Dallas	TX	75219	214-526-2400	
WBBN-FM 95.9 (Ctry) 4580 Hwy 15 N PO Box 6408 *Web:* www.b95country.com	Laurel	MS	39441	601-649-0095	649-8199
WBCI-FM 105.9 (Rel) 122 Main St *Web:* lifechangingradio.com	Topsham	ME	04086	207-725-9224	725-2686
WBEN-AM 930 (N/T) 500 Corporate Pkwy Ste 200 *TF:* 800-616-9236 ■ *Web:* www.wben.com	Amherst	NY	14226	716-843-0600	832-3080
WBGO-FM 88.3 (Jazz) 54 Pk Pl *Web:* www.wbgo.org	Newark	NJ	07102	973-624-8880	824-8888
WBIG-FM 100.3 (Oldies) 1801 Rockville Pk 6th fl *TF:* 800-493-1003 ■ *Web:* wbig.iheart.com	Rockville	MD	20852	240-747-2700	
WBLI-FM 106.1 (CHR) 555 Sunrise Hwy *Web:* www.wbli.com	West Babylon	NY	11704	631-669-9254	587-1282
WBON-FM 98.5 (Span) 3075 Veterans Memorial Hwy Ste 201 *Web:* www.lafiestali.com	Ronkonkoma	NY	11779	631-648-2500	648-2510
WBRB-FM 101.3 (Ctry) 1065 Radio Pk Dr *TF:* 877-232-7121 ■ *Web:* www.1013thebear.com	Mount Clare	WV	26408	304-623-6546	
WBTT-FM 105.5 (Urban) 13320 Metro Pkwy Ste 1 *Web:* 1055thebeat.iheart.com	Fort Myers	FL	33966	239-225-4300	225-4410
WBYT-FM 100(Ctry) 237 W Edison Rd *Web:* www.b100.com	Mishawaka	IN	46545	574-258-5483	258-0930
WBZN-FM 107.3 (CHR) 49 Acme Rd *Web:* z1073.com	Brewer	ME	04412	207-989-5631	
WBZO-FM 103.1 (Oldies) 234 Airport Plz Ste 5 *Web:* www.1031maxfm.com	Farmingdale	NY	11735	631-770-4200	
WCAR-AM 1090 (Rel) 32500 Pk Ln	Garden City	MI	48135	734-525-1111	
WCAT-FM 102.3 (Ctry) 728 N Hanover St *TF:* 888-513-5130 ■ *Web:* www.red1023.com	Carlisle	PA	17013	717-243-1200	
WCBK-FM 102.3 (Ctry) 1639 Burton Ln *Web:* www.wcbk.com	Martinsville	IN	46151	765-342-3394	342-5020
WCBM-AM 680 (N/T) 1726 Reisterstown Rd Ste 117 *Web:* www.wcbm.com	Pikesville	MD	21208	410-580-6800	580-6810
WCBN-FM 88.3 (Alt) University of Michigan 530 Student Activities Bldg *Web:* wcbn.org	Ann Arbor	MI	48109	734-763-3500	
WCKT-FM 107.1 (Ctry) 13320 Metro Pkwy Ste 1 **Fax:* Hum Res ■ *Web:* catcountry1071.iheart.com	Fort Myers	FL	33966	239-225-4300	225-4410*
WCLT-FM 100.3 (Ctry) PO Box 5150 *TF:* 800-837-9258 ■ *Web:* www.wclt.com	Newark	OH	43058	740-345-4004	
WCMR-AM 1270 (Rel) PO Box 307 *TF:* 800-522-9376 ■ *Web:* www.solidgospel1270.com	Elkhart	IN	46515	574-875-5166	875-6662
WCMS-FM 94.5 (Ctry) 103-D W Wood Hill Dr *Web:* www.wcms.com	Nags Head	NC	27959	252-480-4655	441-4827
WCNK-FM 98.7 (Ctry) 830 Crane Blvd *Web:* www.conchcountry.com	Sugarloaf Key	FL	33042	305-296-7511	
WCNY-FM 91.3 (NPR) 506 Old Liverpool Rd *TF:* 800-451-9269 ■ *Web:* www.wcny.org	Liverpool	NY	13088	315-453-2424	451-8824
WCPV-FM 101.3 (CR) 265 Hegeman Ave *TF:* 866-862-4267 ■ *Web:* www.1013espn.com	Colchester	VT	05446	802-655-0093	
WCQR-FM 88.3 (Rel) 2312 Oak St *TF:* 888-477-5676 ■ *Web:* www.wcqr.org	Gray	TN	37615	423-477-5676	477-7060
WCRZ-FM 107.9 (AC) 3338 E Bristol Rd *Web:* wcrz.com	Burton	MI	48529	810-743-1080	
WCSX-FM 94.7 (CR) 1 Radio Plz *Web:* www.wcsx.com	Ferndale	MI	48220	248-398-9470	
WCTL-FM 106.3 (Rel) 10912 Peach St *TF:* 800-568-8924 ■ *Web:* www.wctl.org	Waterford	PA	16441	814-796-6000	
WCTO-FM 96.1 (Ctry) 2158 Ave C Ste 100 *Web:* www.catcountry96.com	Bethlehem	PA	18017	610-266-7600	

Station / Address	City	State	Zip	Phone	Fax
WDAF-FM 106.5 (Ctry) 7000 Squibb Rd *Web:* www.1065thewolf.com	Mission	KS	66202	913-744-3600	
WDAI-FM 98.5 (Urban) 11640 Hwy 17 Bypass *Web:* www.985kissfm.net	Murrells Inlet	SC	29576	843-272-3000	
WDAS-FM 105.3 (Urban AC) 111 Presidential Blvd Ste 100 *TF:* 800-745-3000 ■ *Web:* wdasfm.iheart.com	Bala Cynwyd	PA	19004	610-784-3333	784-2098
WDEA-AM 1370 (Nost) 49 Acme Rd *Web:* wdea.am	Brewer	ME	04412	207-989-5631	
WDEV-AM 550 (N/T) 9 Stowe St PO Box 550 *Web:* www.wdevradio.com	Waterbury	VT	05676	802-244-7321	244-1771
WDEV-FM 96.1 (Clas) 9 Stowe St PO Box 550 *Web:* wdevradio.com	Waterbury	VT	05676	802-244-7321	244-1771
WDFN-AM 1130 (Sports) 27675 Halsted Rd *Web:* wdfn.iheart.com	Farmington Hills	MI	48331	248-324-5800	
WDIY-FM 88.1 (NPR) 301 Broadway *Web:* wdiy.org	Bethlehem	PA	18015	610-694-8100	954-9474
WDJA-AM 1420 (N/T) 2710 W Atlantic Ave *Web:* www.universo1420.com	Delray Beach	FL	33445	561-278-1420	
WDRM-FM 102.1 (Ctry) 26869 Peoples Rd *TF:* 866-302-0102 ■ *Web:* wdrm.iheart.com	Madison	AL	35756	256-309-2400	350-2653
WDSD-FM 94.7 (Ctry) 920 W Basin Rd Ste 400 *Web:* wdsd.iheart.com	New Castle	DE	19720	302-395-9800	
WEDR-FM 99.1 (Urban) 2741 N 29th Ave *TF:* 800-327-2323 ■ *Web:* www.wedr.com	Hollywood	FL	33020	305-444-4404	444-4404
WEEI-AM 850 (Sports) 20 Guest St 3rd Fl *TF:* 888-525-0850 ■ *Web:* www.weei.com	Brighton	MA	02135	617-779-3500	
WEKU-FM 88.9 (Clas) 521 Lancaster Ave 102 Perkins Bldg-EKU *TF:* 800-621-8890 ■ *Web:* www.weku.fm	Richmond	KY	40475	800-621-8890	
WEMU-FM 89.1 (NPR) PO Box 980350 *TF:* 888-299-8910 ■ *Web:* www.wemu.org	Ypsilanti	MI	48198	734-487-2229	487-1015
WERU-FM 89.9 (Var) 1186 Acadia Hwy *TF:* 800-643-6273 ■ *Web:* www.weru.org	East Orland	ME	04431	207-469-6600	469-8961
WETA-FM 90.9 (NPR) 2775 S Quincy St *Web:* www.weta.org/fm	Arlington	VA	22206	703-998-2600	
WEVO-FM 89.1 (N/T) 2 Pillsbury St 6th Fl *TF:* 800-639-4131 ■ *Web:* www.nhpr.org	Concord	NH	03301	603-228-8910	224-6052
WEZL-FM 103.5 (Ctry) 950 Houston Northcutt Blvd 2nd Fl *Web:* wezl.iheart.com	Mount Pleasant	SC	29464	843-884-2534	884-1218
WEZN-FM 99.9 (AC) 440 Wheelers Farm Rd Ste 302 *Web:* star999.com	Milford	CT	06461	203-783-8200	
WEZQ-FM 92.9 (AC) 49 Acme Rd PO Box 100 *Web:* 929theticket.com	Brewer	ME	04412	207-989-5631	
WFBY-FM 102.3 (CR) 1065 Radio Pk Dr *Web:* www.wfby.com	Mount Clare	WV	26408	304-623-6546	
WFCF-FM 88.5 (Var) Flagler College PO Box 1027 *TF:* 800-304-4208 ■ *Web:* www.flagler.edu	Saint Augustine	FL	32085	904-819-6449	826-0094
WFCR-FM 88.5 (NPR) University of Massachusetts 131 County Cir *Web:* nepr.net	Amherst	MA	01003	413-735-6600	732-7417
WFHB-FM 91.3 (Var) 108 W Fourth St *Web:* www.wfhb.org	Bloomington	IN	47404	812-323-1200	323-0320
WFHM-FM 95.5 (Rel) 4 Summit Pk Dr Ste 150 *Web:* www.955thefish.com	Cleveland	OH	44131	216-901-0921	
WFHN-FM 107.1 (CHR) 22 Sconticut Neck Rd *TF:* 877-854-9467 ■ *Web:* www.fun107.com	Fairhaven	MA	02719	508-999-6690	999-1420
WFIU-FM 103.7 Indiana University 1229 E Seventh St *TF:* 877-285-9348 ■ *Web:* indianapublicmedia.org	Bloomington	IN	47405	812-855-1357	855-5600
WFLY-FM 92.3 (CHR) 6 Johnson Rd *Web:* www.fly92.com	Latham	NY	12110	518-786-6600	
WFNT-AM 1470 (N/T) 3338 E Bristol Rd *Web:* wfnt.com	Burton	MI	48529	810-743-1080	742-5170
WFOY-AM 1240 (N/T) 567 Lewis Pt Rd Ext *Web:* www.1023newsradio.com	Saint Augustine	FL	32086	904-797-1955	
WFPG-FM 96.9 (AC) 950 Tilton Rd Ste 200 *TF:* 800-969-9374 ■ *Web:* www.literock969.com	Northfield	NJ	08225	609-645-9797	272-9224
WFRE-FM 99.9 (Ctry) 5966 Grove Hill Rd *Web:* www.wfre.com	Frederick	MD	21703	301-663-4181	682-8018
WFUV-FM 90.7 (Var) 441 E Fordham Rd Fordham University *TF:* 888-400-5520 ■ *Web:* www.wfuv.org	Bronx	NY	10458	718-817-4550	
WGAR-FM 99.5 (Ctry) 6200 Oak Tree Blvd S 4th Fl *TF:* 855-222-0995 ■ *Web:* www.wgar.com	Independence	OH	44131	216-520-2600	
WGBG-FM 98.5 (CR) 119 W Naylor Mill Rd *Web:* www.bigclassicrock.com	Salisbury	MD	21801	410-202-8102	
WGCU-FM 90.1 (NPR) 10501 FGCU Blvd S *Web:* www.wgcu.org	Fort Myers	FL	33965	239-590-2300	590-2310
WGEZ-AM 1490 (Oldies) 622 Public Ave *Web:* www.1490trueoldies.com	Beloit	WI	53511	608-365-8865	
WGGY-FM 101.3 (Ctry) 305 Hwy 315 *TF:* 800-570-1013 ■ *Web:* www.froggy101.com	Pittston	PA	18640	570-883-1111	
WGMD-FM 92.7 (N/T) PO Box 530 *TF:* 800-518-9292 ■ *Web:* www.wgmd.com	Rehoboth Beach	DE	19971	302-945-2050	945-3781
WGNA-FM 107.7 (Ctry) 1241 Kings Rd *Web:* www.wgna.com	Schenectady	NY	12303	518-881-1515	
WGNE-FM 99.9 (Ctry) 6440 Atlantic Blvd *TF:* 888-725-2345 ■ *Web:* www.999gatorcountry.com	Jacksonville	FL	32211	904-727-9696	721-9322
WGPA-AM 1100 (Var) 528 N New St	Bethlehem	PA	18018	610-866-8074	866-9381
WGR-AM 550 (Sports) 500 Corporate Pkwy Ste 200 *Web:* www.wgr550.com	Amherst	NY	14226	716-843-0600	832-3080
WGTS-FM 91.9 (Rel) 7600 Flower Ave *TF:* 800-700-1094 ■ *Web:* www.wgts.org	Takoma Park	MD	20912	301-891-4200	270-9191
WGTY-FM 107.7 (Ctry) 1560 Fairfield Rd PO Box 3179 *TF:* 800-366-9489 ■ *Web:* www.wgty.com	Gettysburg	PA	17325	717-334-3101	334-5822
WGY-AM 810 (N/T) 1203 Troy-Schenectady Rd *TF:* 800-825-5949 ■ *Web:* wgy.iheart.com	Latham	NY	12110	518-452-4800	452-4813
WHB-AM 810 (Sports) 6721 W 121st St *Web:* www.810whb.com	Overland Park	KS	66209	913-344-1500	
WHCC-FM 105.1 (Ctry) 304 State Rd 446 PO Box 7797 *Web:* www.whcc105.com	Bloomington	IN	47401	812-336-8000	336-7000
White River Broadcasting Station 3212 Washington St *Web:* www.wkkg.com	Columbus	IN	47203	812-372-4448	
WHLI-AM 1100 (Nost) 234 Airport Plz Ste 5 *Web:* www.whli.com	Farmingdale	NY	11735	631-770-4200	770-0101
WHQT-FM 105.1 (Urban) 2741 N 29th Ave *Fax Area Code: 954 ■ *Web:* www.hot105fm.com	Hollywood	FL	33020	305-444-4404	847-3223*
WHRB-FM 95.3 (Var) 389 Harvard St *Web:* www.whrb.org	Cambridge	MA	02138	617-495-4818	
WHVR-AM 1280 (Ctry) 275 Radio Rd *Web:* thepeak985.com	Hanover	PA	17331	717-637-3831	637-9006
WHYI-FM 100.7 (CHR) 7601 Riviera Blvd *Web:* y100.iheart.com	Miramar	FL	33023	954-862-2000	862-4013
WICO-AM 1320 (N/T) 919 Ellegood St PO Box 909 *Web:* www.wicoam.com	Salisbury	MD	21801	410-219-3500	
WILK-AM 980 (N/T) 305 Hwy 315 *Web:* www.wilknewsradio.com	Pittston	PA	18640	570-883-9800	
WIOQ-FM 102.1 (CHR) 111 Presidential Blvd Ste 100 *TF:* 800-521-1021 ■ *Web:* q102.iheart.com	Bala Cynwyd	PA	19004	610-784-3333	
WISN-AM 1130 (N/T) 12100 W Howard Ave *Web:* www.newstalk1130.com	Greenfield	WI	53228	414-545-8900	
WJDA-AM 1300 (N/T) 90 Everett Ave *Web:* www.wjda1300am.com	Chelsea	MA	02150	617-884-4500	
WJIB-AM 740 (AC) 443 Concord Ave *Web:* wjib.org	Cambridge	MA	02138	617-868-7400	
WJKK-FM 98.7 (AC) 265 Highpoint Dr *Web:* www.mix987.com	Ridgeland	MS	39157	601-956-0102	978-3980
WJMH-FM 102.1 (Urban) 7819 National Service Rd Ste 401 *Web:* www.102jamz.com	Greensboro	NC	27409	336-605-5200	
WJMI-FM 99.7 (Urban) 731 S Pear OrchaRd Rd Ste 27 *Web:* www.wjmi.com	Ridgeland	MS	39157	601-957-1300	
WJOY-AM 1230 (Nost) 70 Joy Dr *Web:* www.wjoy.com	South Burlington	VT	05403	802-658-1230	862-0786
WJPT-FM 106.3 (Nost) 20125 S Tamiami Trl *Web:* sunny1063.com	Estero	FL	33928	239-495-2100	
WJQK-FM 99.3 (Rel) 425 Centerstone Ct *TF:* 866-931-9936 ■ *Web:* www.jq99.com	Zeeland	MI	49464	616-931-9930	931-1280
WJRR-FM 101.1 (Alt) 2500 Maitland Ctr Pkwy Ste 401 *Web:* wjrr.iheart.com	Maitland	FL	32751	407-916-7800	916-7406
WJYY-FM 105.5 (CHR) *NH1 Media Center* 4 Church St NH1 Media Ctr *Web:* wjyy.nh1media.com	Concord	NH	03301	603-230-9000	228-2030
WKAR-AM 870 (NPR) Michigan State University 283 Communications Arts & Sciences Bldg *Web:* www.wkar.org	East Lansing	MI	48824	517-432-9527	
WKAR-FM 90.5 (NPR) Michigan State University 283 Comm Arts & Sciences Bldg *Web:* www.wkar.org	East Lansing	MI	48824	517-432-9527	
WKCQ-FM 98.1 (Ctry) 2000 Whittier St *TF:* 800-262-0098 ■ *Web:* www.98fmkcq.com	Saginaw	MI	48601	989-752-8161	752-8102
WKDD-FM 98.1 (AC) 7755 Freedom Ave *TF:* 888-533-4582 ■ *Web:* wkdd.iheart.com	North Canton	OH	44720	330-836-4700	836-5321
WKGM-AM 940 (Rel) 13379 Great Spring Rd *Web:* reverbnation.com	Smithfield	VA	23430	757-357-9546	
WKKV-FM 100.7 (Urban) 12100 W Howard Ave *Web:* www.v100.com	Greenfield	WI	53228	414-321-1007	546-9654
WKPT-AM 1400 (Nost) 222 Commerce St	Kingsport	TN	37660	423-246-9578	247-9836
WKQI-FM 95.5 (CHR) 27675 Halsted Rd *Web:* channel955.iheart.com	Farmington Hills	MI	48331	248-324-5800	
WKRR-FM 92.3 (CR) 192 E Lewis St *TF:* 800-762-5923 ■ *Web:* www.rock92.com	Greensboro	NC	27406	336-274-8042	274-5745
WKRZ-FM 98.5 (CHR) 305 Hwy 315 *Web:* www.985krz.com	Pittston	PA	18640	570-883-9850	
WKSE-FM 98.5 (CHR) 500 Corporate Pkwy Ste 200 *Web:* www.kiss985.com	Amherst	NY	14226	716-843-0600	
WKSU-FM 89.7 (NPR) 1613 E Summit St *TF:* 800-672-2132 ■ *Web:* www.wksu.org	Kent	OH	44242	330-672-3114	672-4107
WKTO-FM 88.9 (Rel) 900 Old Mission Rd *Web:* wkto.net	New Smyrna Beach	FL	32168	386-427-1095	
WKVV-FM 101.7 PO Box 2098 *TF:* 800-525-5683 ■ *Web:* www.klove.com	Omaha	NE	68103	800-525-5683	
WKZL-FM 107.5 (CHR) 192 E Lewis St *TF:* 800-682-1075 ■ *Web:* www.1075kzl.com	Greensboro	NC	27406	336-274-8042	274-5745
WKZW-FM 94.3 (AC) 4580 Hwy 15 N PO Box 6408 *Web:* www.kz94.com	Laurel	MS	39441	601-649-0095	649-8199
WLIF-FM 101.9 (AC) 1423 Clarkview Rd Ste 100 *Web:* todays1019.cbslocal.com	Baltimore	MD	21209	410-825-1000	
WLLL-AM 930 (Rel) PO Box 11375 *TF Cust Svc:* 888-224-9809	Lynchburg	VA	24506	434-385-9555	385-6073
WLUM-FM 102.1 (Rock) N 72 W 12922 Good Hope Rd *Web:* www.fm1021milwaukee.com	Menomonee Falls	WI	53051	414-771-1021	771-3036
WLXC-FM 98.5 (Urban) 1801 Charleston Hwy Ste J *Web:* www.kiss-1031.com	Cayce	SC	29033	803-796-7600	

				Phone	Fax
WLZX-FM 99.3 (Rock) 45 Fisher Ave	East Longmeadow	MA	01028	413-525-4141	525-4334
Web: www.lazer993.com					
WMBR-FM 88.1 (Var) 3 Ames St	Cambridge	MA	02142	617-253-4000	
Web: www.wmbr.org					
WMBS-AM 590 (Oldies) 44 S Mt Vernon Ave	Uniontown	PA	15401	724-438-3900	438-2406
Web: www.wmbs590.com					
WMGC-FM 105.1 (AC) 1 Radio Plz	Ferndale	MI	48220	248-414-5600	542-8800
Web: www.detroitsports1051.com					
WMGK-FM 102.9 (CR) 1 Bala Plz Ste 339	Bala Cynwyd	PA	19004	610-667-8500	
Web: www.wmgk.com					
WMGM-FM 103.7 (CR) 1601 New Rd	Linwood	NJ	08221	609-653-1400	601-0450
Web: www.1037wmgm.com					
WMID-AM 1340 (Nost) 8025 Black Horse Pk Ste 100	West Atlantic City	NJ	08232	609-484-8444	646-6331
Web: www.classicoldieswmid.com					
WMIL-FM 106.1 (Ctry) 12100 W Howard Ave	Greenfield	WI	53228	414-545-8900	327-3200
Web: www.fm106.com					
WMIT-FM 106.9 (Rel) 3 Porters Cove Rd	Asheville	NC	28805	828-285-8477	298-0117
TF: 800-330-9648 ■ *Web:* brb.org					
WMMJ-FM 102.3 (Urban AC) 8515 Georgia Ave 9th Fl	Silver Spring	MD	20910	301-306-1111	306-9540
Web: mymajicdc.hellobeautiful.com					
WMMR-FM 93.3 (Rock) 1 Bala Plz Ste 424	Bala Cynwyd	PA	19004	610-771-0933	771-9610
Web: www.wmmr.com					
WMPI-FM 105.3 (Ctry) 22 E McClain Ave	Scottsburg	IN	47170	812-752-3688	752-2345
TF: 800-441-1053 ■ *Web:* i1053country.com					
WMUM-FM 89.7 (NPR) 243 Carey Salem Rd	Cochran	GA	31014	478-301-5760	
TF: 800-222-4788 ■ *Web:* www.gpb.org/radio/stations/wmum					
WMXU-FM 106.1 (Urban) 200 Sixth St N Ste 205	Columbus	MS	39701	662-327-1183	
Web: www.mymix1061.com					
WMYX-FM 99.1 (AC) 11800 W Grange Ave	Hales Corners	WI	53130	414-529-1250	529-2122
Web: www.991themix.com					
WMZQ-FM 98.7 (Ctry) 1801 Rockville Pk 5th Fl	Rockville	MD	20852	240-747-2700	
TF: 800-505-0098 ■ *Web:* wmzq.iheart.com					
WNCS-FM 104.7 (AAA) 169 River St	Montpelier	VT	05602	802-223-2396	
Web: www.pointfm.com					
WNCW-FM 88.7 (AAA) PO Box 804	Spindale	NC	28160	828-287-8000	
TF: 800-245-8870 ■ *Web:* www.wncw.org					
WNIC-FM 100.3 (AC) 27675 Halsted Rd	Farmington Hills	MI	48331	248-324-5800	
Web: wnic.iheart.com					
WNIJ-FM 89.5 (NPR) 801 N First St	DeKalb	IL	60115	815-753-9000	
Web: www.northernpublicradio.org					
WNIU-FM 90.5 (Clas) 801 N First St	DeKalb	IL	60115	815-753-9000	
Web: www.northernpublicradio.org					
WNKU-FM 105.9 (Ctry) 301 Landrum Academic Ctr	Highland Heights	KY	41099	859-572-6500	
TF: 855-897-7897 ■ *Web:* www.wnku.org					
WNOG-AM 1270 (N/T) 2824 Palm Beach Blvd	Fort Myers	FL	33916	239-338-4326	
Web: www.tunein.com/radio/WNOG-1270-s21511					
WNOR-FM 98.7 (Rock) 870 Greenbrier Cir Ste 399	Chesapeake	VA	23320	757-366-9900	366-0022
Web: www.fm99.com					
WNSN-FM 101.5 (AC) 1301 E Douglas Rd	Mishawaka	IN	46545	574-233-3141	
TF: 855-757-1719 ■ *Web:* www.sunny1015.com					
WNST-AM 1570 (Sports) 1550 Hart Rd	Towson	MD	21286	410-821-9678	
Web: www.wnst.net					
WNUE-FM 98.1 (Span) 523 Douglas Ave	Altamonte Springs	FL	32714	407-774-2626	
Web: www.salsa981.com					
WNWV-FM 107.3 (NAC) 6133 Rockside Rd Ste 102	Independence	OH	44131	216-828-1073	
Web: 1073thewave.net					
WODE-FM 99.9 107 Paxinosa Rd W	Easton	PA	18040	610-258-6155	253-3384
TF: 800-733-2767 ■ *Web:* www.999thehawk.com					
WOGG-FM 94.9 (Ctry) 123 Blaine Rd	Brownsville	PA	15417	724-938-2000	
TF: 866-983-9898 ■ *Web:* www.froggyland.com					
WOGH-FM 103.5 (Ctry) 320 Market St	Steubenville	OH	43952	740-283-4747	
Web: www.froggyland.com					
WOGL-FM 98.1 (Oldies) 2 Bala Plz Ste 800	Bala Cynwyd	PA	19004	610-668-5900	668-5977
TF: 800-942-8998 ■ *Web:* wogl.cbslocal.com					
WOKO-FM 98.9 (Ctry) 70 Joy Dr	South Burlington	VT	05403	802-862-9890	862-0786
TF: 800-354-9890 ■ *Web:* www.woko.com					
WOKQ-FM 97.5 (Ctry) 292 Middle Rd PO Box 576	Dover	NH	03821	603-749-9750	
TF: 877-975-1037 ■ *Web:* www.wokq.com					
WOLC-FM 102.5 (Rel) 11890 Crisfield Ln PO Box 130	Princess Anne	MD	21853	410-543-9652	651-9652
WOMC-FM 104.3 (Oldies) 2201 Woodward Heights	Ferndale	MI	48220	248-327-2900	546-5446
Web: womc.cbslocal.com					
Woodward Communications Inc 801 Bluff St	Dubuque	IA	52001	800-553-4801	588-5739*
**Fax Area Code:* 563 ■ *TF:* 800-553-4801 ■ *Web:* www.wcinet.com					
WOSM-FM 103.1 (Rel) 4720 Radio Rd	Ocean Springs	MS	39564	228-432-1032	875-6461
WPCV-FM 97.5 (Ctry) 404 W Lime St	Lakeland	FL	33815	863-682-8184	683-2409
TF: 800-227-9797 ■ *Web:* www.wpcv.com					
WPGC-FM 95.5 (CHR) 4200 Parliament Pl Ste 300	Lanham	MD	20706	877-955-5267	383-9497*
**Fax Area Code:* 646 ■ *TF:* 877-955-5267 ■ *Web:* wpgc.cbslocal.com					
WPHI-FM 107.9 (Urban) 2 Bala Plaza Ste 700	Bala Cynwyd	PA	19004	610-538-1100	
Web: boomphilly.com					
WPHT-AM 1210 (N/T) 2 Bala Plz Ste 800	Bala Cynwyd	PA	19004	610-668-5800	668-5885
Web: tunein.com/radio/Talk-Radio-1210-WPHT-s21950					
WPLK-AM 800 (Nost) 1428 St Johns Ave	Palatka	FL	32177	386-325-5800	
Web: www.wplk.com					
WPLM-FM 99.1 (AC) 17 Columbus Rd	Plymouth	MA	02360	508-746-1390	830-1128
TF: 877-327-9991 ■ *Web:* www.easy991.com					
WPLR-FM 99.1 (Rock) 440 Wheelers Farm Rd Ste 302	Milford	CT	06461	203-783-8200	783-8399
Web: wplr.com					
WPOR-FM 101.9 (Ctry) 420 Western Ave	South Portland	ME	04106	207-774-4561	774-3788
Web: www.wpor.com					
WPRO-FM 92.3 (CHR) 1502 Wampanoag Trl	East Providence	RI	02915	401-433-4200	
TF: 800-638-0092 ■ *Web:* www.92profm.com					
WPST-FM 94.5 (AC) 619 Alexander Rd 3rd Fl	Princeton	NJ	08540	609-419-0300	419-0143
TF: 800-248-9778 ■ *Web:* www.wpst.com					
WPUR-FM 107.3 (Ctry) 950 Tilton Rd Ste 200	Northfield	NJ	08225	609-645-9797	
Web: www.catcountry1073.com					
WPWX-FM 92.3 (Urban) 6336 Calumet Ave	Hammond	IN	46324	773-734-4455	
Web: www.power92chicago.com					
WQBK-FM 103.9 (Rock) 1241 Kings Rd	Schenectady	NY	12303	518-881-1515	
Web: q103albany.com					
WQCB-FM 106.5 (Ctry) PO Box 100	Brewer	ME	04412	207-989-5631	
Web: q1065.fm					
WQFL-FM 100.9 (Rel) PO Box 2118	Omaha	NE	68103	888-937-2471	
TF: 888-937-2471 ■ *Web:* www.air1.com					
WQLZ-FM 92.7 (Rock) PO Box 460	Springfield	IL	62561	217-629-7077	629-7952
Web: www.wqlz.com					
WQTX-FM 92.1 (Oldies) 2495 Cedar St	Holt	MI	48842	517-699-0111	699-1880
WQUN-AM 1220 (Nost) 3085 Whitney Ave	Hamden	CT	06518	203-582-8984	582-5372
TF: 800-462-1944 ■ *Web:* www.qu.edu					
WRBR-FM 103.9 (Rock) 237 W Edison Rd	Mishawaka	IN	46545	574-258-5483	
Web: www.wrbr.com					
WRCH-FM 100.5 (AC) 10 Executive Dr	Farmington	CT	06032	860-677-6700	
TF: 800-530-1005 ■ *Web:* wrch.cbslocal.com					
WRDX-FM 92.9 (CR) 920 W Basin Rd Ste 400	New Castle	DE	19720	302-395-9800	
Web: www.iheart.com					
WRFQ-FM 104.5 (CR) 950 Houston Northcutt Blvd 2nd Fl	Mount Pleasant	SC	29464	843-884-2534	884-1218
Web: q1045.iheart.com					
WRKO-AM 680 (N/T) 20 Guest St 3rd Fl	Brighton	MA	02135	617-779-3400	
TF: 877-469-4322 ■ *Web:* www.wrko.com					
WROW-AM 6 Johnson Rd	Latham	NY	12110	518-786-6600	
Web: www.albanymagic.com					
WRVM-FM 102.7 (Rel) PO Box 212	Suring	WI	54174	920-842-2900	
TF: 888-225-9786 ■ *Web:* www.wrvmradio.org/pages/?p=3					
WRZK-FM 95.9 (Alt) 222 Commerce St	Kingsport	TN	37660	423-246-9578	247-9836
Web: www.wrzk.com					
WSAN-AM 1470 (Sports) 1541 Alta Dr Ste 400	Whitehall	PA	18052	610-434-1742	434-6288
Web: www.fox1470.com					
WSCI-FM 89.3 (NPR) 1101 George Rogers Blvd	Columbia	SC	29201	803-737-3200	
Web: www.scetv.org					
WSGL-FM 104.7 (AC) 10915 K-Nine Dr	Bonita Springs	FL	34135	239-495-8383	
Web: www.1047mixfm.com					
WSHU-FM 91.1 (NPR) 5151 Pk Ave	Fairfield	CT	06825	203-365-0425	
TF: 800-937-6045 ■ *Web:* www.wshu.org					
WSIC-AM 1400 (N/T) 1117 Radio Rd	Statesville	NC	28677	704-872-6345	873-6921
Web: www.wsicweb.com					
WSMK-FM 99.1 (Urban) 925 N Fifth St	Niles	MI	49120	269-683-4343	683-7759
Web: www.wsmkradio.com					
WSRS-FM 96.1 (AC) 96 Stereo Ln	Paxton	MA	01612	508-757-9696	757-1779
Web: 961srs.iheart.com					
WTAG-AM 580 (N/T) 96 Stereo Ln	Paxton	MA	01612	508-795-0580	757-1779
Web: wtag.iheart.com					
WTAK-FM 106.1 (CR) 26869 Peoples Rd	Madison	AL	35756	256-309-2410	350-2653
Web: wtak.iheart.com					
WTAM-AM 1100 (N/T) 6200 Oak Tree Blvd	Cleveland	OH	44131	216-520-2600	
Web: www.wtam.com					
WTFM-FM 98.5 (AC) 222 Commerce St	Kingsport	TN	37660	423-246-9578	247-9836
TF: 888-633-5452 ■ *Web:* www.wtfm.com					
WTIC-AM 1080 (N/T) 10 Executive Dr	Farmington	CT	06032	860-677-6700	284-9842
Web: connecticut.cbslocal.com					
WTIX-FM 94.3 (Oldies) 4539 N I-10 Service Rd 3rd Fl	Metairie	LA	70006	504-454-9000	
Web: www.wtixfm.com					
WTLN-AM 950 (Rel) 1188 Lakeview Dr	Altamonte Springs	FL	32714	407-682-9494	682-7005
Web: www.wtln.com					
WTMD-FM 89.7 (AAA) 8000 York Rd Towson University	Towson	MD	21252	410-704-8938	
WTPL-FM 107.7 (N/T) 501 S St 3rd Fl	Bow	NH	03304	603-545-0777	545-0781
Web: www.wtplfm.com					
WTRY-FM 98.3 (Oldies) 1203 Troy-Schenectady Rd	Latham	NY	12110	518-452-4884	452-4855
Web: 983try.iheart.com					
WTSR-FM 91.3 (Alt) College of New Jersey Kendall Hall PO Box 7718	Ewing	NJ	08628	609-771-3200	
Web: www.wtsr.org					
WTSS-FM 102.5 (AC) 500 Corporate Pkwy Ste 200	Amherst	NY	14226	716-843-0600	
Web: www.mystar1025.com					
WTSU-FM 89.9 (NPR) Troy University Wallace Hall	Troy	AL	36082	800-800-6616	670-3934*
**Fax Area Code:* 334 ■ *TF:* 800-800-6616 ■ *Web:* www.troypublicradio.org					
WTTH-FM 96.1 (Urban) 8025 Black Horse Pike Ste 100	West Atlantic City	NJ	08232	609-484-8444	646-6331
Web: www.961wtth.com					
WTTS-FM 92.3 (AAA) 400 One City Centre	Bloomington	IN	47404	812-332-3366	331-4570
TF: 800-923-9887 ■ *Web:* www.wttsfm.com					
WUMP-AM 730 (Sports) 3280 Peachtree Rd Ste 2300	Atlanta	GA	30305	256-830-8300	232-6842
TF: 866-485-9867 ■ *Web:* www.umpsports.com					
WUNC-FM 91.5 (NPR) 120 Friday Center Dr	Chapel Hill	NC	27517	919-445-9150	
TF: 800-962-9862 ■ *Web:* www.wunc.org					
WUSJ-FM 96.3 (Ctry) 265 Highpoint Dr	Ridgeland	MS	39157	601-956-0102	978-3980
Web: www.us963.com					
WVFJ-FM 93.3 (Rel) 1175 Senoia Rd	Tyrone	GA	30290	770-487-4500	
Web: georgia.thejoyfm.com					
WVPE-FM 88.1 (NPR) 2424 California Rd	Elkhart	IN	46514	574-674-9873	262-5700
TF: 888-399-9873 ■ *Web:* www.wvpe.org					
WVPS-FM 107.9 (NPR) 365 Troy Ave	Colchester	VT	05446	802-655-9451	655-2799
TF: 800-639-2192 ■ *Web:* www.vpr.net					
WWBN-FM 101.5 (Rock) 3338 E Bristol Rd	Burton	MI	48529	810-743-1080	742-5170
Web: banana1015.com					
WWDC-FM 101.1 (Rock) 1801 Rockville Pk 5th Fl	Rockville	MD	20852	240-747-2701	
TF: 866-913-2101 ■ *Web:* dc101.iheart.com					

Station / Address	City	State	Zip	Phone	Fax
WWDE-FM 101.3 (AC) 236 Clearfield Ave Ste 206 — *Web:* 2wd.com	Virginia Beach	VA	23462	757-497-2000	
WWGR-FM 101.9 (Ctry) 10915 K-Nine Dr — *TF:* 877-787-1019 ■ *Web:* www.gatorcountry1019.com	Bonita Springs	FL	34135	239-495-8383	495-0883
WWKA-FM 92.3 (Ctry) 4192 N John Young Pkwy — *TF:* 866-438-0220 ■ *Web:* www.k923orlando.com	Orlando	FL	32804	407-424-9236	299-4947
WWKX-FM 106.3 (Urban) 1502 Wampanoag Trail — *Web:* www.hot1063.com	East Providence	RI	02914	401-433-4200	
WWLI-FM 105.1 (AC) 1502 Wampanoag Trl — *Web:* www.literock105fm.com	East Providence	RI	02915	401-433-4200	
WWMJ-FM 95.7 (CR) 49 Acme Rd — *Web:* i95rocks.com	Brewer	ME	04412	207-989-5631	
WWRV-AM 1330 (Span Rel) 419 Broadway — *Web:* www.radiovision.net	Paterson	NJ	07501	973-881-8700	
WWTC-AM 1280 (N/T) 2110 Cliff Rd. — *Web:* www.am1280thepatriot.com	Eagan	MN	55122	651-405-8800	405-8222
WWUS-FM 104.1 (CR) 30336 Overseas Hwy — *Web:* www.us1radio.com	Big Pine Key	FL	33043	305-872-9100	872-1603
WWWS-AM 1400 (Urban) 500 Corporate Pkwy Ste 200 — *Web:* www.am1400solidgoldsoul.com	Amherst	NY	14226	716-843-0600	
WXBM-FM 102.7 (Ctry) 6565 N W St — *Web:* www.nashpensacola.com	Pensacola	FL	32505	850-310-9102	478-3971
WXCY-FM 103.7 (Ctry) 707 Revolution St — *TF:* 800-788-9929 ■ *Web:* www.wxcyfm.com	Havre de Grace	MD	21078	410-939-1100	939-1104
WXKB-FM 103.9 (CHR) 20125 S Tamiami Trl — *Web:* www.b1039.com	Estero	FL	33928	239-495-2100	
WXRL-AM 1300 (Ctry) PO Box 170 PO Box 170 — *Web:* www.wxrl.com	Lancaster	NY	14086	716-681-1313	
WXRR-FM 104.5 (Rock) 4580 Hwy 15 N — *Web:* www.rock104fm.com	Laurel	MS	39443	601-649-0095	
WXRV-FM 92.5 (AAA) 30 How St — *TF:* 800-352-9250 ■ *Web:* theriverboston.com	Haverhill	MA	01830	978-374-4733	373-8023
WXSS-FM 103.7 (CHR) 11800 W Grange Ave. — *Web:* www.1037kissfm.com	Hales Corners	WI	53130	414-529-1250	
WXTU-FM 92.5 (Ctry) 555 E City Ave Ste 330 — *Web:* 925xtu.cbslocal.com	Bala Cynwyd	PA	19004	610-667-9000	667-5978
WXXX-FM 95.5 (CHR) 118 Malletts Bay Ave. — *Web:* www.95triplex.com	Colchester	VT	05446	802-655-9550	655-1329
WYCB-AM 1340 (Rel) 8515 Georgia Ave 9th fl — *Web:* myspiritdc.hellobeautiful.com	Silver Spring	MD	20910	301-306-1111	306-9540
WYCR-FM 98.5 (AC) 275 Radio Rd. — *Web:* thepeak985.com	Hanover	PA	17331	717-637-3831	637-9006
WYJB-FM 95.5 (AC) 6 Johnson Rd. — *Web:* www.b95.com	Latham	NY	12110	518-786-6600	
WYNZ-FM 100.9 (Oldies) 420 Western Ave. — *Web:* rewind1009.com	South Portland	ME	04106	207-774-4561	774-3788
WZBA-FM 100.7 (CR) 11350 McCormick Rd Executive Plz 3 Ste 701	Hunt Valley	MD	21031	410-771-8484	771-1616
WZBC-FM 90.3 (Var) Boston College 107 McElroy Commons — *Web:* www.wzbc.org	Chestnut Hill	MA	02467	617-552-3511	
WZBT-FM 91.1 (Alt) 300 N Washington St Gettysburg College — *TF:* 800-431-0803 ■ *Web:* www.gettysburg.edu	Gettysburg	PA	17325	717-337-6300	
WZLX-FM 100.7 (CR) 83 Leo Birmingham Pkwy. — *Web:* wzlx.cbslocal.com	Brighton	MA	02135	617-746-5100	
WZMX-FM 93.7 (Urban) 10 Executive Dr — *Web:* hot937.cbslocal.com	Farmington	CT	06032	860-677-6700	
WZXL-FM 100.7 (Rock) 8025 Black Horse Pk Ste 100 — *Web:* www.wzxl.com	West Atlantic City	NJ	08232	609-484-8444	646-6331
WZZO-FM 95.1 (Rock) 1541 Alta Dr Ste 400 — *Web:* www.951zzo.com	Whitehall	PA	18052	610-434-1742	434-6288
XLTN-FM 104.5 (Span AC) 2403 Hoover Ave — *Web:* wp.1045radiolatina.com	National City	CA	91950	619-336-7800	420-1092
Your Network of Praise PO Box 2426 — *Web:* www.ynop.org	Havre	MT	59501	406-949-4308	

645-1 Abilene, TX

Station / Address	City	State	Zip	Phone	Fax
KACU-FM 89.7 (NPR) 1925 Campus Ct — *Web:* www.kacu.org	Abilene	TX	79699	325-674-2441	674-2417
KBCY-FM 99.7 (Ctry) 2525 S Danville Dr. — *Web:* www.kbcy.com	Abilene	TX	79605	325-793-9700	692-1576
KEAN-FM 105.1 (Ctry) 3911 S First St. — *TF:* 800-588-5326 ■ *Web:* www.keanradio.com	Abilene	TX	79605	325-676-5326	
KFGL-FM 100.7 (Oldies) 3911 S First St — *Web:* koolfmabilene.com	Abilene	TX	79605	325-676-5100	
KGNZ-FM 88.1 (Rel) 542 Butternut St. — *TF:* 800-588-8801 ■ *Web:* www.kgnz.com	Abilene	TX	79602	325-673-3045	672-7938
KKHR-FM 106.3 (Span) 402 Cypress St. — *Web:* www.radioabilene.com	Abilene	TX	79601	325-672-5442	
KULL-FM 92.5 (Oldies) 3911 S First St — *Web:* mix925abilene.com	Abilene	TX	79605	325-676-7711	

645-2 Akron, OH

Station / Address	City	State	Zip	Phone	Fax
Summit, The 65 Steiner Ave. — *TF:* 877-411-3662 ■ *Web:* thesummit.fm	Akron	OH	44301	330-761-3099	761-3103
WAKR-AM 1590 (N/T) 1795 W Market St	Akron	OH	44313	330-869-9800	
WNIR-FM 100.1 (N/T) PO Box 2170 — *Web:* www.wnir.com	Akron	OH	44309	330-673-2323	673-0301
WONE-FM 97.5 (Rock) 1795 W Market St — *TF:* 888-588-8436 ■ *Web:* www.wone.net	Akron	OH	44313	330-869-9800	869-9750
WQMX-FM 94.9 1795 W Market St — *Web:* www.wqmx.com	Akron	OH	44313	330-869-9800	
WZIP-FM 88.1 (Rock) 302 Buchtel Common — *Web:* www.wzip.fm	Akron	OH	44325	330-972-7105	

645-3 Albany, NY

Station / Address	City	State	Zip	Phone	Fax
WAMC-FM 90.3 (NPR) 318 Central Ave — *TF:* 800-323-9262 ■ *Web:* www.wamc.org	Albany	NY	12206	518-465-5233	432-6974

645-4 Albuquerque, NM

Station / Address	City	State	Zip	Phone	Fax
99.5 Magic FM 500 Fourth St NW 5th Fl — *Web:* www.995magicfm.com	Albuquerque	NM	87102	505-767-6700	767-9199
KANW-FM 89.1 (NPR) 2020 Coal Ave SE — *Web:* www.kanw.com	Albuquerque	NM	87106	505-242-7163	
KHFM 95.5 4125 Carlisle Blvd NE	Albuquerque	NM	87107	505-878-0980	878-0098
KHFM-FM 95.5 (Clas) 4125 Carlisle Blvd NE — *Web:* www.classicalkhfm.com	Albuquerque	NM	87107	505-878-0980	
KKSS-FM 97.3 (CHR) 8009 Marble Ave NE — *Web:* www.mykiss973.com	Albuquerque	NM	87110	505-254-7110	
KNML-AM 610 (Sports) 500 Fourth St NW 5th Fl — *TF:* 888-922-0610 ■ *Web:* www.610knml.com	Albuquerque	NM	87102	505-767-6700	767-6711
KUNM-FM 89.9 (NPR) 1University of New Mexico MSC 06 3520 — *TF:* 877-277-4806 ■ *Web:* www.kunm.org	Albuquerque	NM	87131	505-277-4806	277-6393

645-5 Amarillo, TX

Station / Address	City	State	Zip	Phone	Fax
KACV-FM 90 (Alt) PO Box 447 — *TF:* 800-766-0176 ■ *Web:* www.kacvfm.org	Amarillo	TX	79178	800-766-0176	
KATP-FM 101.9 (Ctry) 6214 W 34th St — *Web:* blakefm.com/help	Amarillo	TX	79109	806-355-9777	
KGNC-FM 97.9 (Ctry) 3505 Olsen Blvd Ste 117 — *Web:* www.kgncfm.com	Amarillo	TX	79109	806-355-9801	
KISS FM 96.9 6214 W 34th St — *Web:* kissfm969.com	Amarillo	TX	79109	806-355-9777	
KMXJ-FM 94.1 (AC) 6214 W 34th St — *Web:* www.mix941kmxj.com	Amarillo	TX	79109	806-355-9777	
KPRF-FM 98.7 (CHR) 6214 W 34th St — *TF:* 866-930-5225 ■ *Web:* 987jackfm.com	Amarillo	TX	79109	806-355-9777	
KZRK-FM 107.9 (Rock) 301 S Polk St Ste 100 — *Web:* www.amarillosrockstation.com	Amarillo	TX	79101	806-342-5200	

645-6 Anchorage, AK

Station / Address	City	State	Zip	Phone	Fax
KASH-FM 107.5 (Ctry) 800 E Dimond Blvd Ste 3-370 — *Web:* kashcountry1075.iheart.com	Anchorage	AK	99515	907-522-1515	743-5186
KATB-FM 89.3 (Rel) 6401 E Northern Lights Blvd. — *Web:* www.katb.org	Anchorage	AK	99504	907-333-5282	
KBBO-FM 92.1 (AC) 833 Gambell St. — *Web:* www.921bob.fm	Anchorage	AK	99501	907-344-4045	522-6053
KBRJ-FM 104.1 (Ctry) 301 Arctic Slope Ave Ste 200 — *Web:* www.kbrj.com	Anchorage	AK	99518	907-344-9622	
KEAG-FM 97.3 301 Arctic Slope Ave Ste 200 — *Web:* www.kool973.com	Anchorage	AK	99518	907-344-9622	
KENI-AM 650 (N/T) 800 E Dimond Blvd Ste 3-370 — *Web:* 650keni.iheart.com	Anchorage	AK	99515	907-522-1515	743-5186
KFAT-FM 92.9 (Urban) 833 Gambell — *Web:* 929kfat.com	Anchorage	AK	99501	907-344-4045	522-6053
KMXS-FM 103.1 (AC) 301 Arctic Slope Ave — *Web:* www.kmxs.com	Anchorage	AK	99518	907-344-9622	
KNBA-FM 90.3 (NPR) 3600 San Geronimo Dr Ste 480 — *TF:* 888-278-5622 ■ *Web:* www.knba.org	Anchorage	AK	99508	907-793-3500	793-3536
KSKA-FM 91.1 (NPR) 3877 University Dr — *Web:* www.alaskapublic.org	Anchorage	AK	99508	907-550-8400	
KWHL-FM 106.5 (Rock) 301 Arctic Slope Ave — *Web:* www.kwhl.com	Anchorage	AK	99518	907-344-9622	
Moose 96.3, The 833 Gambell St — *Web:* themoose963.com	Anchorage	AK	99501	907-344-4045	522-6053
New Northwest Broadcasters 833 Gambell St. — **Fax Area Code:* 206	Anchorage	AK	99501	907-344-4045	204-0214*

645-7 Ann Arbor, MI

Station / Address	City	State	Zip	Phone	Fax
WCBN-FM 88.3 (Alt) University of Michigan 530 Student Activities Bldg. — *Web:* wcbn.org	Ann Arbor	MI	48109	734-763-3500	

				Phone	Fax
WTKA-AM 1050 (N/T) 1100 Victors Way Ste 100 *Web:* www.wtka.com	Ann Arbor	MI	48108	734-302-8100	
WUOM-FM 91.7 (NPR) 535 W William St Ste 110 *TF:* 888-258-9866 ■ *Web:* www.michiganradio.org	Ann Arbor	MI	48103	734-764-9210	647-3488
WWWW-FM 102.9 (Ctry) 1100 Victors Way Ste 100 *Web:* www.w4country.com	Ann Arbor	MI	48108	734-302-8100	

645-8 Annapolis, MD

				Phone	Fax
WRNR-FM 103.1 112 Main St 3rd Fl *TF:* 877-762-1031 ■ *Web:* www.wrnr.com	Annapolis	MD	21401	410-626-0103	267-7634

645-9 Asheville, NC

				Phone	Fax
WCQS-FM 88.1 (NPR) 73 Broadway *TF:* 866-448-3881 ■ *Web:* www.wcqs.org	Asheville	NC	28801	828-210-4800	210-4801
WISE-AM 1310 (Sports) 1190 Patton Ave *Web:* espnasheville.com	Asheville	NC	28806	828-259-9695	253-5619
WKJV-AM 1380 70 Adams Hill Rd *TF:* 800-809-9558 ■ *Web:* www.wkjv.com	Asheville	NC	28806	828-252-1380	259-9427
WKSF-FM 99.9 (Ctry) 13 Summerlin Rd *TF:* 800-303-5477 ■ *Web:* 99kisscountry.iheart.com	Asheville	NC	28806	828-257-2700	255-7850
WSKY-AM 1230 (Rel) 40 Westgate Pkwy Ste 2 *Web:* www.wilkinsradio.com	Asheville	NC	28806	828-251-2000	
WTMT-FM 105.9 (Span) 1190 Patton Ave *Web:* 1059themountain.com	Asheville	NC	28806	828-259-9695	253-5619
WWNC-AM 570 (N/T) 13 Summerlin Rd *Web:* wwnc.iheart.com	Asheville	NC	28806	828-257-2700	255-7850

645-10 Atlanta, GA

				Phone	Fax
Cumulus Broadcasting Inc 3280 Peachtree Rd NW Ste 2300	Atlanta	GA	30305	478-746-6286	749-1393
Cumulus Media Inc 3280 Peachtree Rd NE Ste 2300 *Web:* www.cumulus.com	Atlanta	GA	30305	404-949-0700	949-0740
Life Radio Ministries Inc 100 S Hill St Ste 100 *Web:* www.wmvv.com	Griffin	GA	30223	770-229-2020	
Majic 107.5 101 Marietta St 12th Fl *Web:* majicatl.hellobeautiful.com	Atlanta	GA	30303	404-765-9750	688-7686
Majic ATL 107.5|97.5 101 Marietta St 12th Fl *Web:* majicatl.hellobeautiful.com	Atlanta	GA	30303	404-765-9750	688-7686
My Praise ATL 102.5 101 Marietta St 12th Fl *Web:* mypraiseatl.hellobeautiful.com	Atlanta	GA	30303	404-765-9750	688-7686
Rock 100.5 780 Johnson Ferry Rd NE 5th Fl *Web:* www.99x.com	Atlanta	GA	30342	404-741-7625	
WABE-FM 90.1 (NPR) 740 Bismark Rd NE *Web:* www.wabe.org	Atlanta	GA	30324	678-686-0321	
WACG-FM 90.7 (NPR) 2500 Walton Way *TF:* 800-222-4788 ■ *Web:* www.gpb.org	Atlanta	GA	30904	706-737-1661	
WALR-FM 104.1 (AC) 1601 W Peachtree St NE *Web:* www.kiss104fm.com	Atlanta	GA	30309	404-897-7500	897-6495
WAOK-AM 1380 (N/T) 1201 Peachtree St NE Ste 800 *Web:* atlanta.cbslocal.com	Atlanta	GA	30361	404-898-8900	898-8909
WCLK-FM 91.9 (Jazz) 111 James P Brawley Dr SW *TF:* 888-448-3925 ■ *Web:* www.wclk.com	Atlanta	GA	30314	404-880-8273	880-8869
WFSH-FM 104.7 (Rel) 2970 Peachtree Rd NW Ste 700 *Web:* www.thefishatlanta.com	Atlanta	GA	30305	404-995-7300	
WGST-AM 640 (N/T) 1819 Peachtree Rd NE Ste 700 *Web:* 640wgst.iheart.com	Atlanta	GA	30309	404-875-8080	367-1057
WHTA-FM 107.9 (Urban) 101 Marietta St 12th Fl *Web:* hotspotatl.com	Atlanta	GA	30303	404-765-9750	688-7686
Wilks Broadcast Group LLC 6470 E Johns Crossing Ste 450 *Web:* www.wilksbroadcastgroup.com	Duluth	GA	30097	678-240-8976	
WRAS *Georgia State University* 33 Gilmer St MSC 2A1220 *Web:* www2.gsu.edu	Atlanta	GA	30303	404-651-3504	
WRFG-FM 89.3 (Var) 1083 Austin Ave NE *Web:* www.wrfg.org	Atlanta	GA	30307	404-523-3471	
WSB-AM 750 (N/T) 1601 W Peachtree St NE *Web:* www.wsbradio.com	Atlanta	GA	30309	404-897-7500	897-7363
WSB-FM 98.5 (AC) 1601 W Peachtree St NE *Web:* www.b985.com	Atlanta	GA	30309	404-897-7500	897-7363
WSRV-FM 97.1 (AC) 1601 W Peachtree St *Web:* www.971theriver.com	Atlanta	GA	30309	404-897-7500	
WVEE-FM 103.3 (Urban) 1201 Peachtree St NE Ste 800 *Web:* v103.cbslocal.com	Atlanta	GA	30361	404-898-8900	898-8909
WZGC-FM 92.9 (CR) 1201 Peachtree St Ste 800 *Web:* atlanta.cbslocal.com/station/92-9-the-game	Atlanta	GA	30361	404-898-8900	

645-11 Augusta, GA

				Phone	Fax
WBBQ 104.3 2743 Perimeter Pkwy Bldg 100 Ste 300 *Web:* wbbq.iheart.com	Augusta	GA	30909	706-396-6000	396-6010
WGAC-AM 580 (N/T) 4051 Jimmie Dyess Pkwy *Web:* www.wgac.com	Augusta	GA	30909	706-396-7000	396-7100
WHHD-FM 98.3 (AC) 4051 Jimmie Dyess Pkwy *Web:* www.hd983.com	Augusta	GA	30909	706-396-7000	
WKXC-FM 99.5 (Ctry) 4051 Jimmie Dyess Pkwy *Web:* www.kicks99.com	Augusta	GA	30909	706-396-7000	

645-13 Augusta, ME

				Phone	Fax
WEBB-FM 98.5 (Ctry) 56 Western Ave Ste 13 *Web:* www.b985.fm	Augusta	ME	04330	207-623-4735	626-5948
WMME-FM 92.3 (CHR) 56 Western Ave Ste 13 *Web:* www.92moose.fm	Augusta	ME	04330	207-623-4735	626-5948

645-14 Austin, TX

				Phone	Fax
KAMX-FM 94.7 (AC) 4301 Westbank Dr Bldg B 3rd Fl *Web:* www.mix947.com	Austin	TX	78746	512-327-9595	
KAZI-FM 88.7 (Var) 8906 Wall St Ste 203 *Web:* www.kazifm.org	Austin	TX	78754	512-836-9544	836-9563
KGSR-FM 93.3 (Urban) 8309 N IH-35 *Web:* www.kgsr.com	Austin	TX	78753	512-832-4000	832-4071
KJCE-AM 1370 (N/T) 4301 Westbank Dr *Web:* www.talkradio1370am.com	Austin	TX	78746	512-327-9595	329-6252
KKMJ-FM 95.5 (AC) 4301 Westbank Dr Bldg B 3rd Fl *Web:* www.majic.com	Austin	TX	78746	512-327-9595	
KLBJ-AM 590 (N/T) 8309 N IH-35 *Web:* www.newsradioklbj.com	Austin	TX	78753	512-836-0590	
KLBJ-FM 93.7 (Rock) 8309 N IH-35 *Web:* www.klbjfm.com	Austin	TX	78753	512-832-4000	832-4081
KROX-FM 101.5 (Alt) 8309 N IH-35 *Web:* www.101x.com	Austin	TX	78753	512-832-4000	832-4071
KUT-FM 90.5 (NPR) University of Texas 1 University Stn PO Box A-0704 *Web:* www.kut.org	Austin	TX	78712	512-471-1631	471-3700
KVET-AM 1300 (Sports) 3601 S Congress Ave Bldg F *Web:* am1300thezone.iheart.com	Austin	TX	78704	512-684-7300	684-7441

645-15 Bakersfield, CA

				Phone	Fax
American General Media Corp 1400 Easton Dr Ste 144 *Web:* www.americangeneralmedia.com	Bakersfield	CA	93309	661-328-1410	
KBFP-FM 105.3 (Span) 1100 Mohawk St Ste 280 *Web:* www.iheart.com	Bakersfield	CA	93309	661-322-9929	
Kelly 95.3 FM 3651 Pegasus Dr Ste 107 *Web:* www.klly.com	Bakersfield	CA	93308	661-393-1900	
KGFM-FM 101.5 (AC) 1400 Easton Dr Ste 144-B *Web:* www.kgfm.com	Bakersfield	CA	93309	661-328-1410	328-0873
KIWI-FM 102.9 (Span) 5100 Commerce Dr *Web:* www.radiolobo.com	Bakersfield	CA	93309	661-327-9711	327-0797
KKBB-FM 99.3 (Oldies) 3651 Pegasus Dr Ste 107 *Web:* www.groove993.com	Bakersfield	CA	93308	661-393-1900	
KMYX-FM 92.5 (Span) 6313 Schirra Ct *Web:* www.campesina925.com	Bakersfield	CA	93313	661-837-0745	837-1612
KNZR-AM 1560 (N/T) 3651 Pegasus Dr Ste 107 *Web:* www.knzr.com	Bakersfield	CA	93308	661-393-1900	
KRAB-FM 106.1 (Rock) 1100 Mohawk St Ste 280 *Web:* krab.iheart.com	Bakersfield	CA	93309	661-322-9929	
KUZZ-FM 107.9 (Ctry) 3223 Sillect Ave *Web:* www.kuzzradio.com/home.shtml	Bakersfield	CA	93308	661-326-1011	328-7503

645-16 Baltimore, MD

				Phone	Fax
102.7Jack FM 711 W 40th St *TF:* 888-410-1027 ■ *Web:* 1027jackfm.iheart.com	Baltimore	MD	21211	410-366-7600	
WBAL-AM 1090 (N/T) 3800 Hooper Ave *Web:* www.wbal.com	Baltimore	MD	21211	410-467-3000	
WBJC-FM 91.5 (Clas) 6776 Reisterstown Rd Ste 202 *Web:* www.wbjc.com	Baltimore	MD	21215	410-580-5800	
WEAA-FM 88.9 (Jazz) 1700 E Cold Spring Ln *Web:* www.weaa.org	Baltimore	MD	21251	443-885-3564	885-8206
WERQ-FM 92.3 (Urban) 1705 Whitehead Rd *Web:* www.92q.com	Baltimore	MD	21207	410-481-9292	
WIYY-FM 97.9 (Rock) 3800 Hooper Ave *Web:* www.98online.com	Baltimore	MD	21211	410-889-0098	
WJZ-AM 1300 (N/T) 1423 Clarkview Rd Ste 100 *Web:* baltimore.cbslocal.com	Baltimore	MD	21209	410-481-1057	
WLIF-FM 101.9 (AC) 1423 Clarkview Rd Ste 100 *Web:* todays1019.cbslocal.com	Baltimore	MD	21209	410-825-1000	
WPOC-FM 93.1 (Country) 711 W 40th St Ste 350 *TF:* 866-962-5487 ■ *Web:* wpoc.iheart.com	Baltimore	MD	21211	410-366-7600	235-3899

Phone *Fax*

WRBS-FM 95.1 (Rel) 3500 Commerce Dr. . . . . Baltimore MD 21227 410-247-4100 247-4533
TF: 800-965-9324 ■ *Web:* www.951shinefm.com

WWMX-FM 106.5 (CHR)
1423 Clarkview Rd Ste 100. . . . . Baltimore MD 21209 410-825-1000 821-8256
Web: mix1065fm.cbslocal.com

WYPR-FM 88.1 (NPR) 2216 N Charles St. . . . . Baltimore MD 21218 410-235-1660 235-1161
TF: 866-789-8627 ■ *Web:* www.wypr.org

645-17 Bangor, ME

Phone *Fax*

WHCF-FM 88.5 (Rel) PO Box 5000. . . . . Bangor ME 04402 207-947-2751 947-0010
TF: 800-947-2577 ■ *Web:* www.whcffm.com

WHSN-FM 89.3 (Alt) 1 College Cir . . . . Bangor ME 04401 207-941-7116 947-3987
Web: www.whsn-fm.com

WMEH-FM 90.9 (NPR) 63 Texas Ave . . . . Bangor ME 04401 207-941-1010 761-0318
TF: 800-884-1717 ■ *Web:* www.mpbn.net

WVOM-FM 103.9 (N/T) 184 Target Industrial Cir . . . . Bangor ME 04401 207-947-9100
TF: 800-966-1039 ■ *Web:* www.wvomfm.com

645-18 Baton Rouge, LA

Phone *Fax*

WDGL-FM 98.1 (CR) 929-B Government St. . . . . Baton Rouge LA 70802 225-388-9898
Web: www.eagle981.com

WFMF-FM 102.5 (CHR)
5555 Hilton Ave Ste 500. . . . . Baton Rouge LA 70808 225-231-1860 231-1879
Web: wfmf.iheart.com

WJBO-AM 1150 (N/T)
5555 Hilton Ave Ste 500. . . . . Baton Rouge LA 70808 225-231-1860 231-1879
Web: wjbo.iheart.com

WRKF-FM 89.3 (NPR) 3050 Vly Creek Dr. . . . . Baton Rouge LA 70808 225-926-3050 926-3105
TF: 855-893-9753 ■ *Web:* www.wrkf.org

WYNK-FM 101.5 (Ctry)
5555 Hilton Ave Ste 500. . . . . Baton Rouge LA 70808 225-231-1860 231-1879
Web: wynkcountry.iheart.com

645-19 Billings, MT

Phone *Fax*

KBLG-AM 910 (N/T) 2075 Central Ave Ste 5 . . . . Billings MT 59102 406-652-5254

KCTR-FM 102.9 (Ctry) 27 N 27th St 23rd Fl. . . . . Billings MT 59101 406-248-7827 252-9577
Web: catcountry1029.com

KEWF-FM Radio Billings, LLC
222 N 32nd St 10th Fl . . . . Billings MT 59101 406-238-1000 238-1038
Web: www.985thewolf.com

KKBR-FM 97.1 (Oldies) 27 N 27th St 23rd Fl. . . . . Billings MT 59101 406-245-9700
Web: popcrush971.com

KMHK FM 28 N 27th St Crowne Plz 23rd Fl . . . . Billings MT 59101 406-294-1037
Web: kmhk.com

KRKX-FM 94.1 (CR) 2075 Central Ave . . . . Billings MT 59102 406-248-7777
Web: www.941ksky.com

KURL-AM 730 (Rel) 636 Haugen St. . . . . Billings MT 59101 406-245-3121 245-0822
Web: www.kurlradio.com

NewsTalk 95.5
27 N 27th St Crowne Plz 23rd Fl . . . . Billings MT 59101 406-248-7827
Web: newstalk955.com

Yellowstone Public Radio 1500 University Dr . . . . Billings MT 59101 406-657-2941 657-2977
TF: 800-441-2941 ■ *Web:* ypradio.org

645-20 Birmingham, AL

Phone *Fax*

105.5 WERC-FM 600 Beacon Pkwy W Ste 400 . . . . Birmingham AL 35209 205-439-9600 439-8390
Web: wercfm.iheart.com

WAPI-AM 1070 (N/T)
244 Goodwin Crest Dr Ste 300. Birmingham AL 35209 205-945-4646

WBHK-FM 98.7 (Urban)
2700 Corporate Dr Ste 115. . . . . Birmingham AL 35242 205-322-2987 290-1061
Web: 987kiss.com

WBHM-FM 90.3 (NPR) 650 11th St S. . . . . Birmingham AL 35233 205-934-2606 934-5075
TF: 800-444-9246 ■ *Web:* www.wbhm.org

WBPT-FM 106.9 (AC)
2700 Corporate Dr Ste 115. . . . . Birmingham AL 35242 205-916-1100 290-1061
Web: birminghamseagle.com

WDXB-FM 102.5 (Ctry)
600 Beacon Pkwy W Ste 400 . . . . Birmingham AL 35209 205-439-9600 439-8390
TF: 877-541-1966 ■ *Web:* 1025thebull.iheart.com

WJLD-AM 1400 (Var)
1449 Spaulding Ishkooda Rd . . . . Birmingham AL 35211 205-942-1776
Web: wjldradio.com

WJSR-FM 91.1 (CR)
Jefferson State Community College
2601 Carson Rd. . . . . Birmingham AL 35215 205-856-7702 815-8499
TF: 800-767-4984 ■ *Web:* www.angelfire.com/music2/wjsr

WZZK-FM 104.7 (Ctry)
2700 Corporate Dr Ste 115. . . . . Birmingham AL 35242 205-916-1100 290-1061
TF: 866-998-1047 ■ *Web:* wzzk.com

645-21 Bismarck, ND

Phone *Fax*

KKCT-FM 97.5 (CHR) 4303 Memorial Hwy. . . . . Mandan ND 58554 701-250-6602 250-6632
Web: www.hot975fm.com

KYYY-FM 92.9 (AC) 3500 E Rosser Ave . . . . Bismarck ND 58501 701-224-9393 222-1131
TF: 866-929-9393

645-22 Boise, ID

Phone *Fax*

KAWO-FM 104.3 (Ctry) 827 E Pk Blvd Ste 100 . . . . Boise ID 83712 208-344-6363
Web: www.wow1043.com

KBSX-FM 91.5 (NPR) 1910 University Dr. . . . . Boise ID 83725 208-426-3663 344-6631
Web: www.boisestatepublicradio.org

KBXL-FM 94.1 (Rel) 1440 S Weideman Ave. . . . . Boise ID 83709 208-377-3790 377-3792
TF: 877-207-2276 ■ *Web:* www.941thevoice.com

KIZN-FM 92.3 (Ctry) 1419 W Bannock St. . . . . Boise ID 83702 208-336-3670 336-3734
Web: www.kizn.com

KQXR-FM 100.3 (Rock) 5257 Fairview Ave . . . . Boise ID 83706 208-344-3511 947-6765
Web: www.xrock.com

KTIK-AM 1350 (Sports) 1419 W Bannock St . . . . Boise ID 83702 208-336-3670
TF: 866-296-1350 ■ *Web:* www.ktik.com

645-23 Boston, MA

Phone *Fax*

WBCN-FM 104.1 (Alt) 83 Leo Birmingham Pkwy. . . . . Boston MA 02135 617-931-1234 746-1402
Web: wzlx.cbslocal.com

WBMX-FM 104.1 83 Leo M Birmingham Pkwy. . . . . Boston MA 02135 617-931-1234
Web: mix1041.cbslocal.com

WBOS-FM 92.9 (AAA) 55 Morrissey Blvd. . . . . Boston MA 02125 617-822-9600
Web: www.myradio929.com

WBUR-FM 90.9 (NPR) 890 Commonwealth Ave . . . . Boston MA 02215 617-353-0909
TF: 800-909-9287 ■ *Web:* www.wbur.org

WBZ-AM 1030 (N/T) 1170 Soldiers Field Rd. . . . . Boston MA 02134 617-787-7000 787-7060
Web: boston.cbslocal.com

WGBH-FM 89.7 (NPR) 1 Guest St. . . . . Boston MA 02135 617-300-2000 300-1026
Web: www.wgbh.org

WKLB-FM 102.5 (Ctry) 55 Morrissey Blvd. . . . . Boston MA 02125 617-822-9600 822-6659*
**Fax:* News Rm ■ *TF:* 888-819-1025 ■ *Web:* country1025.com

WMJX-FM 106.7 (CHR) 55 Morrissey Blvd . . . . Boston MA 02125 617-822-9600
Web: www.magic1067.com

WODS-FM 103.3 (Oldies)
83 Leo Birmingham Pkwy. . . . . Brighton MA 02135 617-787-7500 787-7523
Web: 1033amppradio.cbslocal.com

WROR-FM 105.7 (Oldies) 55 Morrissey Blvd. . . . . Boston MA 02125 617-822-9600 822-6459
Web: www.wror.com

WUMB-FM 91.9 (Folk) 100 Morrissey Blvd . . . . Boston MA 02125 617-287-6900 287-6916
TF: 800-573-2100 ■ *Web:* www.wumb.org

645-24 Branson, MO

Phone *Fax*

HomeTown Daily News 202 Courtney St . . . . Branson MO 65616 417-334-6003
Web: www.hometowndailynews.com

KLFC-FM 88.1 (Rel) 205 W Atlantic St. . . . . Branson MO 65616 417-334-5532 335-2437
TF: 877-410-8592 ■ *Web:* www.klfcradio.com

645-25 Buffalo, NY

Phone *Fax*

WBFO-FM 88.7 (NPR) PO Box 1263. . . . . Buffalo NY 14240 716-845-7000 829-2277
Web: news.wbfo.org

WBLK-FM 93.7 (Urban) 14 Lafayette Sq Ste 1300 . . . . Buffalo NY 14203 716-852-9393
Web: www.wblk.com

WBNY-FM 91.3 (Alt) 1300 Elmwood Ave . . . . Buffalo NY 14222 716-878-5104 878-6600
Web: www.buffalostate.edu/wbny

WDCX-FM 99.5 (Rel) 625 Delaware Ave Ste 308 . . . . Buffalo NY 14202 716-883-3010 883-3606
TF: 800-684-2848 ■ *Web:* www.wdcxradio.com

WEDG-FM 103.3 (Alt) 50 James E Casey Dr. . . . . Buffalo NY 14206 716-881-4555 884-2931
Web: www.wedg.com

WGRF-FM 96.9 (CR) 50 James E Casey Dr. . . . . Buffalo NY 14206 716-881-4555
Web: www.97rock.com

WHTT-FM 104.1 (AC) 50 James E Casey Dr. . . . . Buffalo NY 14206 716-881-4555
Web: www.whtt.com

WNED-AM 970 (NPR) 140 Lower Terr . . . . Buffalo NY 14202 716-845-7000
Web: www.wned.org

WYRK-FM 106.5 (Ctry) 14 Lafayette Sq Ste 1200 . . . . Buffalo NY 14203 716-852-7444
Web: www.wyrk.com

645-26 Burlington, VT

Phone *Fax*

WIZN-FM 106.7 (Rock) 255 S Champlain St . . . . Burlington VT 05401 802-860-2440 860-1818
TF: 888-873-9496 ■ *Web:* www.wizn.com

645-27 Calgary, AB

Phone *Fax*

CBR-AM 1010 (N/T) 1724 Westmount Blvd NW . . . . Calgary AB T2N3G7 403-521-6000 521-6262*
**Fax:* News Rm ■ *Web:* cbc.ca/news/canada/calgary

CHQR-AM 770 (N/T) 200 Barclay Parade SW. . . . . Calgary AB T2P4R5 403-716-6500
Web: www.newstalk770.com

CJAY-FM 92.1 (CR) 1110 Ctr St NE Ste 300. . . . . Calgary AB T2E2R2 403-240-5800
Web: www.cjay92.com

CKMX-AM 1060 (Ctry) 1110 Ctr St NE Ste 300 . . . . Calgary AB T2E2R2 403-240-4100
Web: www.classiccountryam1060.com

645-28 Casper, WY

Station	City	State	Zip	Phone	Fax
KHOC-FM 102.5 (AC) 218 N Wolcott St *Web:* wyomingradio.com	Casper	WY	82601	617-822-9600	
KRVK-FM 107.9 (Rock) 150 N Nichols Ave *TF:* 800-442-2256 ■ *Web:* www.theriver1079.com	Casper	WY	82601	307-266-5252	
KTRS-FM 104.7 (CHR) 150 N Nichols Ave *TF:* 800-442-2256 ■ *Web:* www.kisscasper.com	Casper	WY	82601	307-266-5252	
KTWO-AM 1030 (Ctry) 150 N Nichols Ave *Web:* www.k2radio.com	Casper	WY	82601	307-266-5252	235-9143
KVOC-AM 1230 (Nost) 218 N Wolcott St	Casper	WY	82601	307-265-1984	
KWYY-FM 95.5 (Ctry) 150 N Nichols Ave *TF:* 800-339-4673 ■ *Web:* www.mycountry955.com	Casper	WY	82601	307-266-5252	

645-29 Cedar Rapids, IA

Station	City	State	Zip	Phone	Fax
96.5 FM KISS Country 600 Old Marion Rd NE *TF:* 800-258-0096 ■ *Web:* 965kisscountry.iheart.com	Cedar Rapids	IA	52402	319-395-0530	393-9600
KCCK-FM 88.3 (Jazz) 6301 Kirkwood Blvd SW *Web:* www.kcck.org	Cedar Rapids	IA	52404	319-398-5446	
KHAK-FM 98.1 (Ctry) 425 Second St SE 4th Fl *Web:* www.khak.com	Cedar Rapids	IA	52401	319-365-9431	
KMRY-AM 1450 (Nost) 1957 Blairs Ferry Rd NE *Web:* www.kmryradio.com	Cedar Rapids	IA	52402	319-393-1450	393-1407
KZIA-FM 102.9 (CHR) 1110 26th Ave SW *Web:* www.kzia.com	Cedar Rapids	IA	52404	319-363-2061	

645-30 Champaign, IL

Station	City	State	Zip	Phone	Fax
Rewind 92.5 2603 W Bradley Ave *Web:* www.rewind925.com	Champaign	IL	61821	217-352-4141	
WBGL-FM 91.7 (Rel) 4101 Fieldstone Rd PO Box 111 *TF Cust Svc:* 800-475-9245 ■ *Web:* www.wbgl.org	Champaign	IL	61822	217-359-8232	359-7374
WDWS-AM 1400 (N/T) 2301 S Neil St *TF:* 800-223-9397 ■ *Web:* news-gazette.com/wdws	Champaign	IL	61820	217-351-5300	351-5385
WEFT-FM 90.1 (Var) 113 N Market St *Web:* www.weft.org	Champaign	IL	61820	217-359-9338	
WIXY-FM 100.3 (Ctry) 2603 W Bradley Ave *Web:* www.wixy.com	Champaign	IL	61821	217-352-4141	352-1256
WLRW-FM 94.5 (CHR) 2603 W Bradley Ave *Web:* www.mix945.com	Champaign	IL	61821	217-352-4141	352-1256
WPCD-FM 88.7 (Rock) 2400 W Bradley Ave *Web:* wpcd.parkland.edu	Champaign	IL	61821	217-373-3790	
WPGU-FM 107.1 (Alt) 512 E Green St *Web:* www.wpgu.com	Champaign	IL	61820	217-337-8382	

645-31 Charleston, SC

Station	City	State	Zip	Phone	Fax
Apex Broadcasting Inc 2294 Clements Ferry Rd *Web:* www.apexbroadcasting.com	Charleston	SC	29492	843-972-1100	
WYBB-FM 98.1 (Alt) 59 Windermere Blvd *Web:* www.my98rock.com	Charleston	SC	29407	843-769-4799	

645-32 Charleston, WV

Station	City	State	Zip	Phone	Fax
WCHS-AM 58 (N/T) 1111 Virginia St E *Web:* www.58wchs.com	Charleston	WV	25301	304-342-8131	
WKWS-FM 96.1 (Ctry) 1111 Virginia St E *Web:* www.961thewolf.com	Charleston	WV	25301	304-342-8131	
WQBE-FM 97.5 (Ctry) 817 Suncrest Pl *TF:* 800-222-3697 ■ *Web:* www.wqbe.com	Charleston	WV	25303	304-344-9700	342-3118
WVAF-FM 1111 Virginia St E *Web:* www.v100.fm	Charleston	WV	25301	304-342-8131	

645-33 Charlotte, NC

Station	City	State	Zip	Phone	Fax
107.9 The Link 1 Julian Price Pl *TF:* 844-258-8477 ■ *Web:* www.1079thelink.com	Charlotte	NC	28208	704-570-1079	
Channel 96.1 801 Wood Ridge Ctr Dr *Web:* 1029thelake.iheart.com	Charlotte	NC	28217	704-714-9444	
WBAV-FM 101.9 (Urban AC) 1520 S Blvd Ste 300 *Web:* v1019.cbslocal.com	Charlotte	NC	28203	704-570-1019	227-8985
WBT-AM 1110 (N/T) 1 Julian Price Pl *Web:* www.wbt.com	Charlotte	NC	28208	704-570-1110	
WEND-FM 106.5 (Alt) 801 Wood Ridge Ctr Dr *TF:* 800-934-1065 ■ *Web:* 1065.iheart.com	Charlotte	NC	28217	704-714-9444	
WFAE-FM 90.7 (NPR) 8801 JM Keynes Dr Ste 91 *TF Cust Svc:* 800-876-9323 ■ *Web:* www.wfae.org	Charlotte	NC	28262	704-549-9323	547-8851
WFNZ-AM 610 (Sports) 1520 S Blvd Ste 300 *TF:* 866-570-9610 ■ *Web:* charlotte.cbslocal.com	Charlotte	NC	28203	704-319-9369	

645-34 Chattanooga, TN

Station	City	State	Zip	Phone	Fax
107.9 Nash Icon 821 Pineville Rd *Web:* www.1079nashicon.com	Chattanooga	TN	37405	423-756-6141	
WDEF-FM 92.3 (AC) 2615 S Broad St *Web:* www.sunny923.com	Chattanooga	TN	37408	423-321-6200	
WDOD-FM 96.5 (CHR) 2615 S Broad St *Web:* www.hits96.com	Chattanooga	TN	37408	423-321-6200	
WGOW-FM 102.3 (N/T) 821 Pineville Rd *Web:* www.wgow.com	Chattanooga	TN	37405	423-756-6141	
WSKZ-FM 106.5 (Rock) 821 Pineville Rd *Web:* www.wskz.com	Chattanooga	TN	37405	423-756-6141	266-3629
WUSY-FM 101 7413 Old Lee Hwy *Web:* us101country.iheart.com	Chattanooga	TN	37421	423-892-3333	899-7224
WUTC-FM 88.1 (NPR) 615 McCallie Ave 104 Cadek Hall Dept 1151 *TF:* 800-272-3900 ■ *Web:* www.wutc.org	Chattanooga	TN	37403	423-425-4756	425-2379

645-35 Cheyenne, WY

Station	City	State	Zip	Phone	Fax
KFBC-AM 1240 (N/T) 1806 Capitol Ave *Web:* www.kfbcradio.com	Cheyenne	WY	82001	307-634-4461	632-8586
KGAB-AM 650 (N/T) 1912 Capitol Ave Ste 300 *Web:* www.kgab.com	Cheyenne	WY	82001	307-632-4400	

645-36 Chicago, IL

Station	City	State	Zip	Phone	Fax
Chicago Public Radio 848 E Grand Ave *Web:* www.chicagopublicradio.org	Chicago	IL	60611	312-948-4600	
Chicago's wshe 100.3 130 E Randolph St Ste 2780 *Web:* wshechicago.com	Chicago	IL	60601	312-297-5100	297-5155
La Ley 107.9 150 N Michigan Ave Ste 1040 **Fax:* PR ■ *Web:* laley1079.lamusica.com	Chicago	IL	60601	312-920-9500	920-9515*
WBBM-AM 780 (N/T) 180 N Stetson Ste 1100 *Web:* chicago.cbslocal.com	Chicago	IL	60601	312-297-7800	297-7822
WBBM-FM 96.3 (CHR) 180 N Stetson Ste 963 *Web:* b96.cbslocal.com	Chicago	IL	60601	312-591-9696	297-7822
WBEZ-FM 91.5 (NPR) 848 E Grand Ave Navy Pier *Web:* www.wbez.org	Chicago	IL	60611	312-948-4600	
WDRV-FM 97.1 (CR) 875 N Michigan Ave Ste 1510 *Web:* www.wdrv.com	Chicago	IL	60611	312-274-9710	274-1304
WFMT-FM 98.7 (Clas) 5400 N St Louis Ave *Web:* www.wfmt.com	Chicago	IL	60625	773-279-2000	
WGCI-FM 107.5 (Urban) 233 N Michigan Ave Ste 2800 *Web:* wgci.iheart.com	Chicago	IL	60601	312-540-2000	
WGN Radio 720 (N/T) 435 N Michigan Ave *Web:* www.wgnradio.com	Chicago	IL	60611	312-222-4700	
WKSC-FM 103.5 (CHR) 233 N Michigan Ave Ste 2800 *Web:* 1035kissfm.iheart.com	Chicago	IL	60601	312-540-2000	
WLUP-FM 97.9 (CR) 222 Merchandise Mart Ste 230 *Web:* www.wlup.com	Chicago	IL	60654	312-245-1200	527-3620
WMBI-FM 90.1 (Rel) 820 N LaSalle Blvd *TF:* 877-376-2194 ■ *Web:* www.moodyradiochicago.fm	Chicago	IL	60610	312-329-4300	329-4468
WTMX-FM 101.9 (AC) 130 E Randolph St Ste 2700 1 Prudential Plz *Web:* www.wtmx.com	Chicago	IL	60601	312-946-1019	946-4747
WUSN-FM 99.5 (Ctry) 2 Prudential Plz Ste 1000 *Web:* us995.cbslocal.com	Chicago	IL	60601	312-649-0099	856-9586
WVAZ-FM 102.7 (Urban AC) 233 N Michigan Ave Ste 2800 *Web:* v103.iheart.com	Chicago	IL	60601	312-540-2000	938-4477
WVON-AM 1690 (N/T) 1000 E 87th St *Web:* www.wvon.com	Chicago	IL	60619	773-247-6200	

645-37 Cincinnati, OH

Station	City	State	Zip	Phone	Fax
WAKW-FM 93.3 (Rel) 6275 Collegevue Pl PO Box 24126 *TF:* 888-542-9393 ■ *Web:* www.mystar933.com	Cincinnati	OH	45224	513-542-9259	542-9333
WCKY-AM 1530 (N/T) 8044 Montgomery Rd Ste 650 *Web:* www.espn1530.com	Cincinnati	OH	45236	513-686-8300	
WCVX-AM 1050 (Rel) 635 W Seventh St Ste 400	Cincinnati	OH	45203	513-533-2500	
WGRR-FM 103.5 (Oldies) 4805 Montgomery Rd Ste 300 *Web:* www.wgrr.com	Cincinnati	OH	45212	513-241-9898	241-6689
WGUC-FM 90.9 (Clas) 1223 Central Pkwy *Web:* www.wguc.org	Cincinnati	OH	45214	513-241-8282	
WIZF-FM 101.1 (Urban) 705 Central Ave *TF:* 866-236-7588 ■ *Web:* wiznation.com	Cincinnati	OH	45202	513-679-6000	679-6014
WKFS-FM 107.1 (CHR) 8044 Montgomery Rd Ste 650 *Web:* www.kiss107.com	Cincinnati	OH	45236	513-686-8300	
WKRC-AM 550 (N/T) 8044 Montgomery Rd Ste 650 *Web:* www.55krc.com	Cincinnati	OH	45236	513-686-8300	

				Phone	Fax
WLW-AM 700 (N/T) 8044 Montgomery Rd Ste 650 *Web:* www.700wlw.com	Cincinnati	OH	45236	513-686-8300	
WNNF-FM 94.1 (AC) 4805 Montgomery Rd Ste 300 *Web:* nashfm941.com	Cincinnati	OH	45212	513-241-9898	241-6689
WRRM-FM 98.5 (AC) 4805 Montgomery Rd Ste 300 *Web:* www.warm98.com	Cincinnati	OH	45212	513-241-9898	241-6689
WUBE-FM 105.1 (Ctry) 2060 Reading Rd. *Web:* b105.com	Cincinnati	OH	45202	513-699-5105	699-5000
WVXU-FM 91.7 (NPR) 1223 Central Pkwy *Web:* www.wvxu.org	Cincinnati	OH	45214	513-352-9170	

645-38 Cleveland, OH

				Phone	Fax
Elyria-Lorain Broadcasting Co 538 Broad St 4th Fl. *Web:* www.elbc.net	Elyria	OH	44035	440-322-3761	
WCPN-FM 90.3 (NPR) 1375 Euclid Ave *Web:* wcpn.ideastream.org	Cleveland	OH	44115	216-916-6100	
WENZ-FM 107.9 (Urban) 2510 St Clair Ave NE *TF:* 800-440-1079 ■ *Web:* zhiphopcleveland.com	Cleveland	OH	44114	216-579-1111	771-4164
WERE-AM 1490 (N/T) 2510 St Clair Ave NE	Cleveland	OH	44114	216-579-1111	771-4164
WFHM-FM 95.5 (Rel) 4 Summit Pk Dr Ste 150 *Web:* www.955thefish.com	Cleveland	OH	44131	216-901-0921	
WJMO-AM 1300 (Rel) 2510 St Clair Ave NE *Web:* praisecleveland.hellobeautiful.com	Cleveland	OH	44114	216-579-1111	771-4164
WKNR-AM 850 (Sports) 1301 E Ninth St Ste 252 *Web:* espn.go.com/cleveland	Cleveland	OH	44114	216-583-9901	583-9550
WMMS-FM 100.7 (Rock) 6200 Oak Tree Blvd S 4th Fl. *Web:* www.wmms.com	Independence	OH	44131	216-986-8991	
WNCX-FM 98.5 (CR) 1041 Huron Rd *Web:* wncx.cbslocal.com	Cleveland	OH	44115	216-861-0100	696-0385
WZAK-FM 93.1 (Urban) 2510 St Clair Ave NE *Web:* wzakcleveland.hellobeautiful.com	Cleveland	OH	44114	216-579-1111	771-4164

645-39 Colorado Springs, CO

				Phone	Fax
KBIQ-FM 102.7 (Rel) 7150 Campus Dr Ste 150 *Web:* www.kbiqradio.com	Colorado Springs	CO	80920	719-531-5438	531-5588
KILO-FM 94.3 (Rock) 1805 E Cheyenne Rd *TF General:* 800-727-5456 ■ *Web:* kilo943.com	Colorado Springs	CO	80905	719-634-4896	634-5837
KKFM-FM 98.1 (CR) 6805 Corporate Dr Ste 130 *Web:* www.kkfm.com	Colorado Springs	CO	80919	719-593-2700	593-2727
KKMG-FM 98.9 (CHR) 6805 Corporate Dr Ste 130 *Web:* www.989magicfm.com	Colorado Springs	CO	80919	719-593-2700	593-2727
KRCC-FM 91.5 (NPR) 912 N Weber St *TF:* 800-748-2727 ■ *Web:* www.krcc.org	Colorado Springs	CO	80903	719-473-4801	473-7863
KVOR-AM 740 (N/T) 6805 Corporate Dr Ste 130 *TF:* 800-232-6459 ■ *Web:* www.kvor.com	Colorado Springs	CO	80919	719-540-0740	540-0740
MY 99.9 2864 S Cir Dr Ste 300 *Web:* my999radio.iheart.com	Colorado Springs	CO	80906	719-540-9200	579-0882
Y 96.9 2864 S Cir Dr Ste 300 *Web:* y969.iheart.com	Colorado Springs	CO	80906	719-540-9200	579-0882

645-40 Columbia, SC

				Phone	Fax
96.7 Steve FM 316 Greystone Blvd *Web:* 967stevefm.iheart.com	Columbia	SC	29210	803-343-1100	
WCOS-AM 1400 (Sports) 316 Greystone Blvd *Web:* foxsportsradio1400.iheart.com	Columbia	SC	29210	803-343-1100	748-9267
WCOS-FM 97.5 (Ctry) 316 Greystone Blvd *TF:* 800-570-9690 ■ *Web:* 975wcos.iheart.com	Columbia	SC	29210	803-343-1100	748-9267
WEPR-FM 90.1 (NPR) 1101 George Rogers Blvd *Web:* www.scetv.org	Columbia	SC	29201	803-737-3200	
WFMV-FM 95.3 (Rel) 2440 Milwood Ave *Web:* columbiainspiration.com	Columbia	SC	29205	803-939-9530	939-9469
WHMC-FM 90.1 (NPR) 1101 George Rogers Blvd *Web:* www.scetv.org	Columbia	SC	29201	803-737-3200	
WHXT-FM 103.9 (Urban) 1900 Pineview Rd *Web:* www.hot1039fm.com	Columbia	SC	29209	803-695-8600	
WLTR-FM 91.3 (NPR) 1101 George Rogers Blvd *Web:* www.scetv.org	Columbia	SC	29201	803-737-3200	
WMFX-FM 102.3 (CR) 1900 Pineview Rd *Web:* fox1023.com	Columbia	SC	29209	803-695-8600	
WNOK-FM 104.7 (CHR) 316 Greystone Blvd *Web:* wnok.iheart.com	Columbia	SC	29210	803-343-1100	
WVOC-AM 560 (N/T) 316 Greystone Blvd *Web:* wvoc.iheart.com	Columbia	SC	29210	803-343-1100	256-5255

645-41 Columbus, GA

				Phone	Fax
WCGQ-FM 107.3 (AC) 1820 Wynnton Rd *Web:* www.q1073.com	Columbus	GA	31906	706-327-1217	596-4600
WKCN-FM 99.3 (Ctry) 1820 Wynnton Rd *Web:* www.kissin993.com	Columbus	GA	31906	706-327-1217	596-4600
WRCG-AM 1420 (N/T) 1820 Wynnton Rd *TF:* 844-706-7625 ■ *Web:* www.1069rocks.com	Columbus	GA	31906	706-327-1217	596-4600

645-42 Columbus, OH

				Phone	Fax
WBNS-AM 1460 (Sports) 605 S Front St Ste 300 *Web:* www.971thefan.com	Columbus	OH	43215	614-460-3850	
WBNS-FM 97.1 (AC) 605 S Front St Ste 300 *TF:* 888-691-9710 ■ *Web:* www.971thefan.com	Columbus	OH	43215	614-460-3850	
WCBE-FM 90.5 (NPR) 540 Jack Gibbs Blvd *Web:* www.wcbe.org	Columbus	OH	43215	614-365-5555	365-5060
WCKX-FM 107.5 (Urban) 350 E First Ave Ste 100 *Web:* mycolumbuspower.com	Columbus	OH	43201	614-487-1444	487-5862
WCOL-FM 92.3 (Ctry) 2323 W Fifth Ave Ste 200 *TF:* 800-899-9265 ■ *Web:* wcol.iheart.com	Columbus	OH	43204	614-486-6101	487-2559
WLVQ-FM 96.3 (Rock) 4401 Carriage Hill Ln. *Web:* www.qfm96.com	Columbus	OH	43220	614-227-9696	
WMNI-AM 920 (Nost) 1458 Dublin Rd *Web:* www.wmni.com	Columbus	OH	43215	614-481-7800	
WNCI-FM 97.9 (CHR) 2323 W Fifth Ave Ste 200 *Web:* wnci.iheart.com	Columbus	OH	43204	614-486-6101	487-2559
WNND-FM 103.5 (NAC) 4401 Carriage Hill Ln *TF:* 877-984-8786 ■ *Web:* rewindcolumbus.com	Columbus	OH	43220	614-451-2191	451-1831
WOSU-AM 820 (NPR) 2400 Olentangy River Rd *Web:* www.wosu.org	Columbus	OH	43210	614-292-9678	292-7625
WRKZ-FM 99.7 (Rock) 1458 Dublin Rd *Web:* www.theblitz.com	Columbus	OH	43215	614-481-7800	
WSNY-FM 94.7 (AC) 4401 Carriage Hill Ln. *Web:* www.sunny95.com	Columbus	OH	43220	614-451-2191	451-1831
WTVN-AM 610 (N/T) 2323 W Fifth Ave Ste 200 *Web:* 610wtvn.iheart.com	Columbus	OH	43204	614-486-6101	487-2559

645-43 Corpus Christi, TX

				Phone	Fax
KEDT-FM 90.3 (NPR) 4455 S Padre Island Dr Ste 38 *TF:* 800-307-5338 ■ *Web:* www.kedt.org	Corpus Christi	TX	78411	361-855-2213	855-3877
KEYS-AM 1440 (N/T) 2117 Leopard St *Web:* www.1440keys.com	Corpus Christi	TX	78408	361-883-3516	882-9767
KFTX-FM 97.5 (Ctry) 1520 S Port Ave *Web:* www.kftx.com	Corpus Christi	TX	78405	361-883-5987	883-3648
KLUX-FM 89.5 (AC) 1200 Lantana St *Web:* www.goccn.org	Corpus Christi	TX	78407	361-289-6437	289-1420
KSAB-FM 99.9 (Span) 501 Tupper Ln *Web:* ksabfm.iheart.com	Corpus Christi	TX	78417	361-289-0111	289-5035
KZFM-FM 95.5 (CHR) 2117 Leopard St *Web:* www.hotz95.com	Corpus Christi	TX	78408	361-883-3516	

645-44 Dallas/Fort Worth, TX

				Phone	Fax
KBFB-FM 97.9 (Urban) 13331 Preston Rd Ste 1180 *TF:* 888-362-8683 ■ *Web:* thebeatdfw.com	Dallas	TX	75240	972-331-5400	331-5560
KDGE-FM 102.1 (Alt) 14001 N Dallas Pkwy Ste 300 *Web:* www.kdge.com	Dallas	TX	75240	214-866-8000	
KDMX-FM 102.9 (AC) 14001 N Dallas Pkwy Ste 300 *Web:* www.1029now.com	Dallas	TX	75240	214-866-8000	
KEGL-FM 97.1 (Rock) 14001 N Dallas Pkwy Ste 300 *Web:* www.kegl.com	Dallas	TX	75240	214-866-8000	
KERA-FM 90.1 (NPR) 3000 Harry Hines Blvd *TF:* 800-456-5372 ■ *Web:* www.kera.org	Dallas	TX	75201	214-871-1390	754-0635
KHKS-FM 106.1 (CHR) 14001 N Dallas Pkwy Ste 300 *Web:* www.1061kissfm.com	Dallas	TX	75240	214-866-8000	866-8008
Kidd Kraddick in The Morning 220 Las Colinas Blvd E Ste C- 210 *Web:* www.kiddlive.com	Irving	TX	75039	972-432-9094	
KJKK-FM 100.3 (Var) 4131 N Central Expy Ste 1000 *Web:* jackontheweb.cbslocal.com	Dallas	TX	75204	214-525-7000	
KKDA-FM 104 621 NW Sixth St *Web:* www.myk104.com	Grand Prairie	TX	75050	972-263-9911	
KLUV-FM 98.7 (Oldies) 4131 N Central Expy Ste 1000 *TF:* 855-987-5588 ■ *Web:* kluv.cbslocal.com	Dallas	TX	75204	214-525-7000	
KMVK-FM 107.5 (Urban) 4131 N Central Expy Ste 1000 *Web:* lagrande1075.cbslocal.com	Dallas	TX	75204	214-525-7000	
KRLD-AM 1080 (N/T) 4131 N Central Expy Ste 100 *TF:* 800-289-1080 ■ *Web:* dfw.cbslocal.com	Dallas	TX	75204	214-525-7000	
KVIL-FM 103.7 (AC) 4131 N Central Expy Ste 1000 *TF:* 877-787-1037 ■ *Web:* kvil.cbslocal.com	Dallas	TX	75204	214-525-7000	
KXT-FM 91.7 (Rel) 3000 Harry Hines Blvd *Web:* kxt.org	Dallas	TX	75201	214-871-1390	754-0635
KZPS-FM 92.5 (CR) 14001 N Dallas Pkwy Ste 300 *Web:* www.lonestar925.com	Dallas	TX	75240	214-866-8000	

Station	City	State	Zip	Phone	Fax
WRR-FM 101.1 (Clas) PO Box 159001 *Web:* www.wrr101.com	Dallas	TX	75315	214-670-8888	

645-45 Dayton, OH

Station	City	State	Zip	Phone	Fax
WDHT-FM 102.9 (Urban) 717 E David Rd *Web:* www.hot1029.com	Dayton	OH	45429	937-294-5858	
WDPR-FM 88.1 (Clas) 126 N Main St *Web:* discoverclassical.org	Dayton	OH	45402	937-496-3850	496-3852
WFCJ-FM 93.7 (Rel) PO Box 937 *Web:* www.wfcj.com	Dayton	OH	45449	937-424-1640	
WHIO-AM 1290 (N/T) 1414 Wilmington Ave *Web:* www.whio.com	Dayton	OH	45420	937-259-2111	259-2168
WHKO-FM 99.1 (Ctry) 1611 S Main St *Web:* www.k99online.com	Dayton	OH	45409	937-259-2111	259-2168
WING-AM 1410 (Sports) 717 E David Rd *Web:* www.wingam.com	Dayton	OH	45429	937-294-5858	
WONE-AM 980 (Sports) 101 Pine St *Web:* wone.iheart.com	Dayton	OH	45402	937-224-1137	224-5015
WROU-FM 92.1 (Urban AC) 717 E David Rd *Web:* www.921wrou.com	Dayton	OH	45429	937-294-5858	
WTUE-FM 104.7 (Rock) 101 Pine St *Web:* wtue.iheart.com	Dayton	OH	45402	937-224-1137	224-5015

645-46 Daytona Beach, FL

Station	City	State	Zip	Phone	Fax
WJLF 2925 Nw 39th Ave *Web:* www.thejoyfm.com	Gainesville	FL	32605	352-371-1457	
WVYB-FM 103.3 (CHR) 126 W International Speedway Blvd	Daytona Beach	FL	32114	386-255-9300	

645-47 Denver, CO

Station	City	State	Zip	Phone	Fax
KBPI-FM 106.7 (Rock) 4695 S Monaco St *Web:* kbpi.iheart.com	Denver	CO	80237	303-713-8000	713-8743
KOA-AM 850 (N/T) 4695 S Monaco Ave *Web:* koanewsradio.iheart.com	Denver	CO	80237	303-713-8000	713-8424
KOSI-FM 101(AC) 7800 E Orchard Rd Ste 400 *Web:* www.kosi101.com	Greenwood Village	CO	80237	303-967-2700	
KTCL-FM 93.3 (Alt) 4695 S Monaco St *Web:* area93.iheart.com	Denver	CO	80237	303-713-8000	713-8743
KUVO-FM 89.3 (Jazz) 2900 Welton St Ste 200 *TF:* 800-574-5886 ■ *Web:* www.kuvo.org	Denver	CO	80205	303-480-9272	291-0757
KWOF-FM 92.5 (Ctry) 720 S Colorado Blvd *Web:* www.925thewolf.com	Denver	CO	80246	303-832-5665	
KXKL-FM 105 (Oldies) 720 S Colorado Blvd Ste 1200 N *Web:* www.kool105.com	Denver	CO	80246	303-832-5665	
Mix 100 720 S Colorado Blvd Ste 1200N *Web:* www.mix100.com	Denver	CO	80246	303-832-5665	

645-48 Des Moines, IA

Station	City	State	Zip	Phone	Fax
107.5 Kiss Fm 2141 Grand Ave *Web:* 1075kissfm.iheart.com	Des Moines	IA	50312	515-245-8854	245-8902
Bus 100.3, The 2141 Grand Ave *Web:* thebusfm.iheart.com	Des Moines	IA	50312	515-245-8900	245-8902
KAZR-FM 103.3 (Rock) 1416 Locust St *Web:* www.lazer1033.com	Des Moines	IA	50309	515-280-1350	280-3011
KIOA-FM 93.3 (Oldies) 1416 Locust St *TF:* 877-984-8786 ■ *Web:* www.kioa.com	Des Moines	IA	50309	515-280-1350	280-3011
KSTZ-FM 102.5 (AC) 1416 Locust St *Web:* www.star1025.com	Des Moines	IA	50309	515-280-1350	280-3011
MORE 104 KMYR 1416 Locust St *Web:* more1041.com	Des Moines	IA	50309	515-280-1350	280-3011
WHO-AM 1040 (N/T) 2141 Grand Ave *Web:* whoradio.iheart.com	Des Moines	IA	50312	515-245-8900	245-8902

645-49 Detroit, MI

Station	City	State	Zip	Phone	Fax
WDET-FM 101.9 (NPR) 4600 Cass Ave Wayne State University *Web:* wdet.org	Detroit	MI	48201	313-577-4146	577-1300
WDRQ-FM 93.1 (Var) 3011 W Grand Blvd Fisher Bldg Ste 800 *Web:* nashfm931.com	Detroit	MI	48202	313-871-9300	
WDVD-FM 96.3 (AC) 3011 W Grand Blvd Fisher Bldg Ste 800 *Web:* www.963wdvd.com	Detroit	MI	48202	313-871-3030	
WGPR-FM 107.5 (Urban) 3146 E Jefferson Ave	Detroit	MI	48207	313-259-8862	259-6662
WJR-AM 760 (N/T) 3011 W Grand Blvd Ste 800 *Web:* www.wjr.com	Detroit	MI	48202	313-875-4440	
WMUZ-FM 103.5 (Rel) 12300 Radio Pl *Web:* www.wmuz.com	Detroit	MI	48228	313-272-3434	272-5045
WRIF-FM 101.1 (Rock) 1 Radio Plz Rd *Web:* www.wrif.com	Detroit	MI	48220	248-547-0101	542-8800

645-50 Dubuque, IA

Station	City	State	Zip	Phone	Fax
WDBQ-AM 1490 (N/T) 5490 Saratoga Rd *Web:* www.wdbqam.com	Dubuque	IA	52002	563-557-1040	
WDBQ-FM 107.5 (Oldies) 5490 Saratoga Rd *Web:* www.myq1075.com	Dubuque	IA	52002	563-557-1040	
WJOD-FM 103.3 (Ctry) 5490 Saratoga Rd *Web:* www.103wjod.com	Dubuque	IA	52002	563-557-1040	

645-51 Duluth, MN

Station	City	State	Zip	Phone	Fax
KBMX-FM 107.7 (AC) 14 E Central Entrance *Web:* www.mix108.com	Duluth	MN	55811	218-727-4500	
KDNW-FM 97.3 (Rel) 1101 E Central Entrance *Web:* life973.com	Duluth	MN	55811	218-722-6700	
KKCB-FM 105.1 (Ctry) 14 E Central Entrance *Web:* www.kkcb.com	Duluth	MN	55811	218-727-4500	
KLDJ-FM 101.7 (Oldies) 14 E Central Entrance *Web:* www.kool1017.com	Duluth	MN	55811	218-727-5665	
KTCO-FM 98.9 (Ctry) 715 E Central Entrance *Web:* katcountry989.com	Duluth	MN	55811	218-722-4321	722-5423
KUMD-FM 103.3 (Var) 1201 ordean Ct 130 Humanities Bldg Rm 130 *Web:* www.kumd.org	Duluth	MN	55812	218-726-7181	726-6571
WWJC-AM 850 (Rel) 1120 E McCuen St *Web:* www.wwjc.com	Duluth	MN	55808	218-626-2738	626-2585

645-52 Edmonton, AB

Station	City	State	Zip	Phone	Fax
CFBR-FM 100.3 (CR) 18520 Stony Plain Rd Ste 100 *Web:* www.thebearrocks.com	Edmonton	AB	T5S2E2	780-486-2800	
CHED-AM 630 (N/T) 5204 84th St *Web:* www.630ched.com	Edmonton	AB	T6E5N8	780-440-6300	
K-97 8882 170th St 2394 W Edmonton Mall *Web:* www.k97.fm	Edmonton	AB	T5T4M2	780-437-4996	

645-53 El Paso, TX

Station	City	State	Zip	Phone	Fax
KELP-AM 1590 (Rel) 6900 Commerce St *TF:* 800-658-6299 ■ *Web:* www.kelpradio.com	El Paso	TX	79915	915-779-0016	779-6641
KHEY-FM 96.3 (Ctry) 4045 N Mesa St *Web:* khey.iheart.com	El Paso	TX	79902	915-351-5400	351-3136
KINT-FM 93.9 (Span) 5426 N Mesa St *TF:* 866-560-5673 ■ *Web:* www.jose939.com	El Paso	TX	79912	915-581-1126	
KLAQ-FM 95.5 (Rock) 4180 N Mesa St *TF:* 844-305-6210 ■ *Web:* www.klaq.com	El Paso	TX	79902	915-880-4955	532-3334
KROD-AM 600 (N/T) 4180 N Mesa St *Web:* www.krod.com	El Paso	TX	79902	915-880-5763	
KSII-FM 93.1 (AC) 4180 N Mesa St. *Web:* kisselpaso.com	El Paso	TX	79902	915-544-9300	532-3334
KTEP-FM 88.5 (NPR) 500 W University Ave Cotton Memorial Bldg Rm 203 *Web:* www.ktep.org	El Paso	TX	79968	915-747-5152	
KTSM-AM 690 (N/T) 4045 N Mesa St *Web:* ktsmradio.iheart.com	El Paso	TX	79902	915-351-5400	351-3136
Univision Radio 2211 E Missouri Ave Ste S-300	El Paso	TX	79903	915-544-9797	544-1247

645-54 Erie, PA

Station	City	State	Zip	Phone	Fax
WFNN-AM 1330 (Sports) 1 Boston Store Pl *Web:* www.sportsradio1330.com	Erie	PA	16501	814-461-1000	
WJET-AM 1400 (N/T) 1 Boston Store Pl *Web:* www.jetradio1400.com	Erie	PA	16501	814-461-1000	
WQLN-FM 91.3 (NPR) 8425 Peach St *TF:* 800-727-8854 ■ *Web:* www.wqln.org	Erie	PA	16509	814-864-3001	864-4077
WRIE-AM 1260 (Sports) 471 Robison Rd *Web:* www.am1260thescore.com	Erie	PA	16509	814-868-5355	
WXKC-FM 99.9 (AC) 471 Robison Rd *Web:* www.classy100.com	Erie	PA	16509	814-868-5355	868-1876

645-55 Eugene, OR

Station	City	State	Zip	Phone	Fax
KDUK-FM 104.7 (CHR) 1500 Valley River Dr Ste 350 *Web:* www.kduk.com	Eugene	OR	97401	541-284-3600	484-5769
KKNU-FM 93.3 (Ctry) 925 Country Club Rd Ste 200 *Web:* kknu.fm	Eugene	OR	97401	541-484-9400	344-9424
KLCC-FM 89.7 (NPR) 4000 E 30th Ave *TF:* 800-922-3682 ■ *Web:* www.klcc.org	Eugene	OR	97401	541-463-6000	463-6046
KMGE-FM 94.5 (AC) 925 Country Club Rd Ste 200 *Web:* 945mixfm.com	Eugene	OR	97401	541-484-9400	344-9424
KODZ-FM 99.1 (CR) 1465 W Seventh Ave *Web:* www.kool991.com	Eugene	OR	97401	541-284-3600	

Station	City	State	Zip	Phone	Fax
KUGN-AM 590 (N/T) 1200 Executive Pkwy Ste 440 *Web:* www.kugn.com	Eugene	OR	97401	541-284-8500	485-0969
KZEL-FM 96.1 (CR) 1200 Executive Pkwy Ste 440 *Web:* www.96kzel.com	Eugene	OR	97401	541-284-8500	

645-56 Evansville, IN

Station	City	State	Zip	Phone	Fax
WABX-FM 107.5 (CR) 1162 Mt Auburn Rd *Web:* www.wabx.net	Evansville	IN	47720	812-424-8284	426-7928
WDKS-FM 106.1 (CHR) 117 SE Fifth St *TF:* 888-454-5477 ■ *Web:* 1061evansville.com	Evansville	IN	47708	812-425-4226	
WGBF-AM 1280 (N/T) 117 SE Fifth St *TF:* 877-437-5995 ■ *Web:* www.newstalk1280.com	Evansville	IN	47708	812-425-4226	
WGBF-FM 103.1 (Rock) 117 SE Fifth St *TF:* 888-900-9423 ■ *Web:* www.103gbfrocks.com	Evansville	IN	47708	812-425-4226	
WIKY-FM 104.1 (AC) 1162 Mt Auburn Rd *TF:* 800-866-5368 ■ *Web:* www.wiky.com	Evansville	IN	47720	812-424-8284	426-7928
WJLT-FM 105.3 (Oldies) 117 SE Fifth St *Web:* espnevansville.com	Evansville	IN	47708	812-421-1117	
WKDQ-FM 99.5 (Ctry) 117 SE Fifth St *Web:* www.wkdq.com	Evansville	IN	47708	812-425-4226	
WNIN-FM 88.3 (NPR) 405 Carpenter St *TF:* 855-888-9646 ■ *Web:* www.wnin.org	Evansville	IN	47708	812-423-2973	428-7548
WSTO-FM 96.1 (CHR) 1162 Mt Auburn Rd *TF:* 888-685-1961 ■ *Web:* hot96.com	Evansville	IN	47720	812-491-9468	426-7928

645-57 Fairbanks, AK

Station	City	State	Zip	Phone	Fax
KAKQ-FM 101.1 (AC) 546 Ninth Ave	Fairbanks	AK	99701	907-450-1000	457-2128
KCBF-AM 820 (Sports) 819 First Ave Ste A *Web:* www.820sports.com	Fairbanks	AK	99701	907-451-5910	451-5999
KFAR-AM 660 AM 819 First Ave Ste A *Web:* www.kfar660.com	Fairbanks	AK	99701	907-451-5910	451-5999
KFBX-AM 970 (N/T) 546 Ninth Ave *Web:* 970kfbx.iheart.com	Fairbanks	AK	99701	907-450-1000	450-1092
KIAK-FM 102.5 (Ctry) 546 Ninth Ave *Web:* kiak.iheart.com	Fairbanks	AK	99701	907-450-1000	457-2128
KSUA-FM 91.5 (Alt) 307 Capital Dr *Web:* www.ksuaradio.com	Fairbanks	AK	99709	907-474-7054	
KUAC-FM 89.9 (NPR) 312 Tanana Dr Ste 202 PO Box 755620 *TF:* 800-727-6543 ■ *Web:* www.kuac.org	Fairbanks	AK	99775	907-474-7491	474-5064

645-58 Fargo, ND

Station	City	State	Zip	Phone	Fax
Big 98.7 2720 Seventh Ave S *Web:* www.big987.com	Fargo	ND	58103	701-237-4500	235-9082
KDSU-FM 91.9 (NPR) 207 Fifth St N *TF:* 800-359-6900 ■ *Web:* www.prairiepublic.org	Fargo	ND	58102	701-241-6900	239-7651
KFGO-AM 790 (N/T) 1020 25th St S *Web:* www.kfgo.com	Fargo	ND	58103	701-237-5346	
KFJM-FM 90.7 (AAA) 207 N Fifth St *TF:* 800-366-6888 ■ *Web:* www.prairiepublic.org	Fargo	ND	58102	701-241-6900	239-7650
KFNW-FM 97.9 (Rel) 5702 52nd Ave S *Web:* www.life979.com	Fargo	ND	58104	701-282-5910	
KPFX-FM 107.9 (CR) 2720 Seventh Ave S *Web:* www.1079thefox.com	Fargo	ND	58103	701-237-4500	235-9082
KVOX-FM 99.9 (Ctry) 1020 S 25th St *Web:* www.froggyweb.com	Fargo	ND	58103	701-241-9936	
MIX-FM 101.9 (CR) 1020 25th St S *Web:* www.rock102online.com	Fargo	ND	58103	701-237-6257	235-4042
Q105.1 Rocks 2720 Seventh Ave S *Web:* www.q1051rocks.com	Fargo	ND	58103	701-237-4500	
WDAY-AM 970 (N/T) 301 Eigth St S *Web:* www.wday.com	Fargo	ND	58103	701-237-6500	
WDAY-FM 93.7 (CHR) 1020 25th St S *TF:* 877-478-5437 ■ *Web:* www.y94.com	Fargo	ND	58103	701-237-5346	237-0980

645-59 Flagstaff, AZ

Station	City	State	Zip	Phone	Fax
KAFF-AM 930 (Ctry) 1117 W Rt 66 *Web:* kaff.gcmaz.com	Flagstaff	AZ	86001	928-774-5231	779-2988
KAFF-FM 92.9 (Ctry) 1117 W Rt 66 *Web:* kaff.gcmaz.com	Flagstaff	AZ	86001	928-774-5231	779-2988
KMGN-FM 93.9 (CR) 1117 W Rt 66 *Web:* 939themountain.gcmaz.com	Flagstaff	AZ	86001	928-774-5231	779-2988
KNAU-FM 88.7 (NPR) PO Box 5764 PO Box 5764 *TF:* 800-523-5628 ■ *Web:* www.knau.org	Flagstaff	AZ	86011	928-523-5628	523-7647
KSED-FM 107.5 (Ctry) 2409 N Fourth St Ste 101 *Web:* www.koltcountry.com	Flagstaff	AZ	86004	928-779-1177	774-5179

645-60 Flint, MI

Station	City	State	Zip	Phone	Fax
FOX - WRSR The G-4511 Miller Rd *Web:* www.classicfox.com	Flint	MI	48507	810-720-9510	720-9513
WDZZ-FM 92.7 (Urban) 6317 Taylor Dr *Web:* www.wdzz.com	Flint	MI	48507	810-238-7300	
WWCK-FM 105.5 (CHR) 6317 Taylor Dr *Web:* www.wwck.com	Flint	MI	48507	810-238-7300	

645-61 Fort Smith, AR

Station	City	State	Zip	Phone	Fax
102.7 The Vibe 3101 Free Ferry Rd Ste E *Web:* www.1027thevibe.com	Fort Smith	AR	72903	479-452-0681	452-0873
B98-FM 97.9 311 Lexington Ave *TF:* 866-503-1398 ■ *Web:* kzbb.iheart.com	Fort Smith	AR	72901	479-782-8888	785-5946
KMAG-FM 99.1 (Ctry) 311 Lexington Ave *Web:* kmag991.iheart.com	Fort Smith	AR	72901	479-782-8888	785-5946
KOMS-FM 107.3 (Ctry) 3101 Free Ferry Rd Ste E *Web:* bigcountry1073.com	Fort Smith	AR	72903	479-452-0681	452-0873
KTCS-FM 99.9 (Ctry) 5304 Hwy 45 E *Web:* www.ktcs.com	Fort Smith	AR	72916	479-646-6151	
KWHN-AM 1320 (N/T) 311 Lexington Ave *Web:* kwhn.iheart.com	Fort Smith	AR	72901	479-782-8888	785-5946
KZKZ-FM 106.3 (Rel) 6420 S Zero St *Web:* www.kzkzfm.com	Fort Smith	AR	72903	479-646-6700	646-1373

645-63 Fort Wayne, IN

Station	City	State	Zip	Phone	Fax
89.1 WBOI 3204 Clairmont Ct *TF General:* 800-471-9264 ■ *Web:* wboi.org	Fort Wayne	IN	46808	260-452-1189	
98.9 the Bear WBYR 1005 Production Rd *Web:* www.989thebear.com	Fort Wayne	IN	46808	260-471-5100	471-5224
WBCL-FM 90.3 (Rel) 1025 W Rudisill Blvd *Web:* www.wbcl.org	Fort Wayne	IN	46807	260-745-0576	456-2913
WFWI 92.3 the Fort 1005 Production Rd *Web:* wowo.com	Fort Wayne	IN	46808	260-471-5100	
WJFX-FM 107.9 (CHR) 2000 Lower Huntington Rd *Web:* www.hot1079online.com	Fort Wayne	IN	46819	260-747-1511	
WLDE-FM 101.7 (Oldies) 347 W Berry St Ste 600 *TF:* 888-450-1017 ■ *Web:* fun1017.com	Fort Wayne	IN	46802	260-423-3676	422-5266
WMEE-FM 97.3 (AC) 2915 Maples Rd *Web:* www.wmee.com	Fort Wayne	IN	46816	260-447-5511	447-7546
WOWO-AM 1190 (N/T) 2915 Maples Rd *TF:* 800-333-1190 ■ *Web:* www.wowo.com	Fort Wayne	IN	46816	260-447-5511	447-7546

645-64 Fresno, CA

Station	City	State	Zip	Phone	Fax
103.7 The Beat 83 E Shaw Ave Ste 150 *Web:* thebeat1037.iheart.com	Fresno	CA	93710	559-230-4300	243-4301
KFRR-FM 104.1 (Rock) 1066 E Shaw Ave *Web:* newrock1041.fm	Fresno	CA	93710	559-230-0104	
KJWL-FM 99.3 (Nost) 1415 Fulton Ave *Web:* www.kjwl.com	Fresno	CA	93721	559-497-5118	497-9760
KMGV-FM 97.9 (Oldies) 1071 W Shaw Ave *Web:* www.mega979.com	Fresno	CA	93711	559-442-4850	490-4199
KMJ-AM 580 (N/T) 1071 W Shaw Ave *TF:* 800-776-5858 ■ *Web:* kmjnow.com	Fresno	CA	93711	559-490-5800	490-5878
KMJ-FM 105.9 1071 W Shaw Ave *TF:* 800-491-1899 ■ *Web:* www.kmjnow.com	Fresno	CA	93711	559-490-5800	490-5878
KPRX-FM 89.1 (NPR) 3437 W Shaw Ave Ste 101 *TF:* 800-275-0764 ■ *Web:* www.kvpr.org	Fresno	CA	93711	559-275-0764	
KSKS-FM 93.7 (Ctry) 1071 W Shaw Ave *TF:* 800-767-5477 ■ *Web:* www.ksks.com	Fresno	CA	93711	559-490-5800	
KVPR-FM 89.3 (NPR) 3437 W Shaw Ave Ste 101 *TF:* 800-275-0764 ■ *Web:* www.kvpr.org	Fresno	CA	93711	559-275-0764	
KWYE-FM 101.1 (CHR) 1071 W Shaw Ave *TF:* 800-345-9101 ■ *Web:* www.y101hits.com	Fresno	CA	93711	559-490-5800	
Softrock-FM 98.9 (AC) 83 E Shaw Ave Ste 150 *TF:* 800-423-5870 ■ *Web:* softrock989.iheart.com	Fresno	CA	93710	559-230-4300	243-4301

645-65 Grand Forks, ND

Station	City	State	Zip	Phone	Fax
Fox-FM 96.1 (CR), The 505 University Ave *Web:* 961thefox.iheart.com	Grand Forks	ND	58203	701-746-1417	746-1410
KJKJ-FM 107.5 (Rock) 505 University Ave *Web:* kjkj.iheart.com	Grand Forks	ND	58203	701-746-1417	746-1410
KZLT-FM 104.3 (AC) 1185 Ninth St NE *Web:* www.1043citiesfm.com	Thompson	ND	58278	701-775-4611	772-0540

645-66 Grand Rapids, MI

Station	City	State	Zip	Phone	Fax
WBCT-FM 93.7 (Ctry) 77 Monroe Ctr St NW Ste 1000 *TF:* 800-633-9393 ■ *Web:* b93.iheart.com	Grand Rapids	MI	49503	616-459-1919	732-3330
WCSG-FM 91.3 (Rel) 1159 E Beltline Ave NE *TF:* 800-968-4543 ■ *Web:* www.wcsg.org	Grand Rapids	MI	49525	616-942-1500	
WFGR-FM 98.7 (Oldies) 50 Monroe Ave NW Ste 500 *Web:* www.wfgr.com	Grand Rapids	MI	49503	616-451-4800	
WGRD-FM 97.9 (Rock) 50 Monroe Ave NW Ste 500 *TF:* 800-947-3979 ■ *Web:* www.wgrd.com	Grand Rapids	MI	49503	616-451-4800	451-9595
WGVU-FM 88.5 (NPR) 301 W Fulton St *TF:* 800-442-2771 ■ *Web:* www.wgvu.org	Grand Rapids	MI	49504	616-331-6666	

Station	City	State	Zip	Phone	Fax
Wlav 60 Monroe Ctr St NW 3rd Fl *Web:* wlav.com	Grand Rapids	MI	49503	616-774-8461	451-3299
WLHT-FM 95.7 (AC) 50 Monroe Ave NW Ste 500 *Web:* mychannel957.com	Grand Rapids	MI	49503	616-451-4800	
WOOD-AM 1300 (N/T) 77 Monroe Ctr St NW Ste 1000 *Web:* woodradio.iheart.com	Grand Rapids	MI	49503	616-459-1919	242-9373
WSNX-FM 104.5 (CHR) 77 Monroe Ctr St NW Ste 1000 *Web:* 1045snx.iheart.com	Grand Rapids	MI	49503	616-459-1919	242-9373

645-67 Green Bay, WI

Station	City	State	Zip	Phone	Fax
WDUZ-AM 1400 (Sports) 810 Victoria St *TF:* 855-724-1075 ■ *Web:* www.thefan1075.com	Green Bay	WI	54302	920-468-4100	468-0250
WIXX-FM 101.1 (CHR) 1420 Bellevue St *Web:* www.wixx.com	Green Bay	WI	54311	920-435-3771	321-2300
WNCY-FM 100.3 (Ctry) 1420 Bellevue St *TF:* 800-359-1003 ■ *Web:* www.wncy.com	Green Bay	WI	54311	920-435-3771	321-2300
WOGB-FM 103.1 (AC) 810 Victoria St *Web:* www.wogb.fm	Green Bay	WI	54302	920-468-4100	468-0250
WPNE-FM 89.3 (NPR) 2420 Nicolet Dr *TF:* 800-654-6228 ■ *Web:* www.wpr.org	Green Bay	WI	54311	920-465-2444	465-2576
WQLH-FM 98.5 (AC) 810 Victoria St *TF:* 855-782-7985 ■ *Web:* www.star98.net	Green Bay	WI	54302	920-468-4100	468-0250

645-68 Greenville, SC

Station	City	State	Zip	Phone	Fax
106.3 WORD 25 Garlington Rd *Web:* www.1063word.com	Greenville	SC	29615	864-271-9200	
92.5 WESC-FM 101 N Main St PO Box 100 *TF:* 800-248-0863 ■ *Web:* wescfm.iheart.com	Greenville	SC	29601	864-242-4660	271-3830
WFBC-FM 93.7 (CHR) 25 Garlington Rd *Web:* www.b937.com	Greenville	SC	29615	864-271-9200	242-1567
WJMZ-FM 107.3 (Urban) 220 N Main St Ste 402 *TF:* 800-767-1073 ■ *Web:* www.1073jamz.com	Greenville	SC	29601	864-235-1073	370-3403
WLFJ-FM 89.3 (Rel) 2420 Wade Hampton Blvd *TF:* 800-447-7234 ■ *Web:* www.hisradio.com	Greenville	SC	29615	864-292-6040	292-8428
WROQ-FM 101.1 (CR) 25 Garlington Rd *TF:* 888-257-0058 ■ *Web:* classicrock1011.com	Greenville	SC	29615	864-271-9200	242-1567
WTPT-FM 93.3 (Rock) 25 Garlington Rd *TF:* 800-774-0093 ■ *Web:* 933theplanetrocks.com	Greenville	SC	29615	864-271-9200	242-1567

645-69 Gulfport/Biloxi, MS

Station	City	State	Zip	Phone	Fax
107.1 The Monkey 9471 Three Rivers Rd Ste A *Web:* www.1071themonkey.net	Gulfport	MS	39503	228-388-1071	
WCPR-FM 97.9 (Rock) 9471 Three Rivers Rd Ste A *Web:* www.979cprrocks.com	Gulfport	MS	39503	228-388-2001	
WGCM-FM 102.3 (Oldies) 10250 Lorraine Rd *Web:* www.coast102.com	Gulfport	MS	39503	228-896-5500	
WJZD-FM 94.5 (Urban) 10211 Southpark Dr *Web:* www.wjzd.com	Gulfport	MS	39503	228-896-5307	896-5703
WQBB-FM 105.9 (CR) 9471 Three Rivers Rd Ste A *Web:* www.bob1059.com	Gulfport	MS	39503	228-388-2001	

645-70 Halifax, NS

Station	City	State	Zip	Phone	Fax
89.9 The Wave 90 Lovett Lake Ct *Web:* 899thewave.fm	Halifax	NS	B3S0H6	902-422-1651	
CFLT-FM 92.9 (Ctry) 6080 Young St 9th Fl *Web:* 929jackfm.ca	Halifax	NS	B3K5L2	902-493-7200	

645-71 Harrisburg, PA

Station	City	State	Zip	Phone	Fax
BOB 94.9 WRBT 600 Corporate Cir *TF:* 800-682-3047 ■ *Web:* bob949.iheart.com	Harrisburg	PA	17110	717-540-8800	540-9268
River 97.3 WRVV, The 600 Corporate Cir *Web:* theriver973.iheart.com	Harrisburg	PA	17110	717-540-8076	671-9973
WGRC FM Radio 101 Armory Blvd *Web:* www.wgrc.com	Lewisburg	PA	17837	570-523-1190	
WHP-AM 580 (N/T) 600 Corporate Cir *TF:* 888-251-7797 ■ *Web:* whp580.iheart.com	Harrisburg	PA	17110	717-540-8800	671-9973
WITF-FM 89.5 (NPR) 4801 Lindle Rd *TF:* 800-366-9483 ■ *Web:* www.witf.org	Harrisburg	PA	17111	717-704-3000	704-3659
WNNK-FM 104.1 (AC) 2300 Vartan Way *Web:* www.wink104.com	Harrisburg	PA	17110	717-238-1041	
WWKL-FM 92.1 (CHR) 2300 Vartan Way *Web:* www.hot935fm.com	Harrisburg	PA	17110	717-238-1041	

645-72 Hartford, CT

Station	City	State	Zip	Phone	Fax
ESPN Radio 1410 10 Columbus Blvd *Web:* newsradio1410.iheart.com	Hartford	CT	06106	860-723-6000	723-6195
Kiss 95.7 10 Columbus Blvd *Web:* kiss957.iheart.com	Hartford	CT	06106	860-723-6000	723-6195
Marlin Broadcasting 1039 Asylum Ave *Web:* www.beethoven.com	Hartford	CT	06105	860-525-1069	246-9084
Rock 106.9 WCCC, The 1039 Asylum Ave *Web:* www.wccc.com	Hartford	CT	06105	860-525-1069	
WHCN-FM 105.9 (CR) 10 Columbus Blvd *Web:* theriver1059.iheart.com	Hartford	CT	06106	860-723-6000	
WPKT-FM 90.5 (NPR) 1049 Asylum Ave *Web:* www.wnpr.org	Hartford	CT	06105	860-278-5310	
WRTC-FM 89.3 (Var) Trinity College 300 Summit St *Web:* www.wrtcfm.com	Hartford	CT	06106	860-297-2439	
WWYZ-FM 92.5 (Ctry) 10 Columbus Blvd *Web:* country925.iheart.com	Hartford	CT	06106	860-723-6000	

645-73 Honolulu, HI

Station	City	State	Zip	Phone	Fax
JAMZ-FM 93.9 (CHR) 650 Iwilei Rd Ste 400 *TF:* 800-745-3000 ■ *Web:* 939jamz.iheart.com	Honolulu	HI	96817	808-550-9200	550-9288
KAIM-FM 95.5 (Rel) 1160 N King St 2nd Fl *Web:* www.thefishhawaii.com	Honolulu	HI	96817	808-533-0065	524-2104
KCCN-FM 100.3 (CHR) 900 Ft St Ste 700 *Web:* kccnfm100.com	Honolulu	HI	96813	808-275-1000	
KDDB-FM 102.7 (CHR) 1000 Bishop St Ste 200 *Web:* www.1027dabomb.net	Honolulu	HI	96813	808-947-1500	
KDNN-FM 98.5 (Island) 650 Iwilei Rd Ste 400 *Web:* island985.iheart.com	Honolulu	HI	96817	808-550-9200	
KHVH-AM 830 (N/T) 650 Iwilei Rd Ste 400 **Fax:* Sales ■ *TF:* 888-565-8383 ■ *Web:* khvhradio.iheart.com	Honolulu	HI	96817	808-550-9200	550-9288*
KINE-FM 105.1 (AC) 900 Ft St Ste 700 *Web:* hawaiian105.com	Honolulu	HI	96813	808-275-1000	
KKOL-FM 107.9 (Oldies) 1160 N King St 2nd Fl *Web:* 1079koolgold.com	Honolulu	HI	96817	808-533-0065	524-2104
KRTR-FM 96.3 (AC) 900 Ft St Ste 700 *Web:* krater963.com	Honolulu	HI	96813	808-275-1000	
KSSK-FM 92.3 (AC) 650 Iwilei Rd Ste 400 *Web:* ksskradio.iheart.com	Honolulu	HI	96817	808-550-9200	
KUMU-FM 94.7 (AC) 1000 Bishop St Ste 200 *Web:* www.kumu.com	Honolulu	HI	96813	808-947-1500	
Star 101.9 650 Iwilei Rd Ste 400 **Fax:* Sales ■ *Web:* star1019.iheart.com	Honolulu	HI	96817	808-550-9200	550-9288*

645-74 Hot Springs, AR

Station	City	State	Zip	Phone	Fax
KHTO-FM 96.7 125 Corporate Terr *TF:* 888-507-9538 ■ *Web:* www.myhotsprings.com	Hot Springs	AR	71913	501-525-9700	
KLAZ-FM 105.9 (CHR) 208 Buena Vista Rd *TF:* 800-621-3362 ■ *Web:* www.klaz.com	Hot Springs	AR	71913	501-525-4600	525-4344
KLXQ-FM 101.9 (CR) 125 Corporate Terr *Web:* www.myhotsprings.com	Hot Springs	AR	71913	501-525-9700	
KQUS-FM 97.5 (Ctry) 125 Corporate Terr *Web:* www.myhotsprings.com	Hot Springs	AR	71913	501-525-9700	

645-75 Houston, TX

Station	City	State	Zip	Phone	Fax
KBXX-FM 97.9 (Urban) 24 Greenway Plaza Ste 900 *TF:* 888-407-4747 ■ *Web:* theboxhouston.com	Houston	TX	77046	713-623-2108	300-5751
KHMX-FM 96.5 (CHR) 24 Greenway Plz Ste 1900 *Web:* mix965houston.cbslocal.com	Houston	TX	77046	713-212-5965	
KKBQ-FM 92.9 (Ctry) 1990 Post Oak Blvd Ste 2300 *TF:* 877-745-6591 ■ *Web:* www.thenew93q.com	Houston	TX	77056	713-963-1200	
KKHT-FM 100.0 (Rel) 6161 Savoy Dr Ste 1200 *Web:* www.kkht.com	Houston	TX	77036	713-260-3600	
KKRW-FM 93.7 (CR) 2000 W Loop S Ste 300 *Web:* 937thebeathouston.com	Houston	TX	77027	713-212-8000	
KLAT-AM 1010 (Span N/T) 5100 SW Fwy *TF:* 800-646-6779 ■ *Web:* corporate.univision.com	Houston	TX	77056	713-407-1415	407-1400
KODA-FM 99.1 (AC) 2000 W Loop S Ste 300 *Web:* www.sunny99.com	Houston	TX	77027	713-212-8000	
KPRC-AM 950 (N/T) 2000 W Loop S Ste 300 *Web:* www.kprcradio.com	Houston	TX	77027	713-212-8000	
KRBE-FM 104.1 (CHR) 9801 Westheimer Rd Ste 700 *TF:* 888-955-2993 ■ *Web:* www.krbe.com	Houston	TX	77042	713-266-1000	954-2344
KSEV-AM 700 (N/T) 11451 Katy Fwy Ste 215 *Web:* www.ksevradio.com	Houston	TX	77079	281-588-4800	
KTBZ-FM 94.5 (Alt) 2000 W Loop S Ste 300 *Web:* www.thebuzz.com	Houston	TX	77027	713-212-8000	
KTHT-FM 1990 Post Oak Blvd Ste 2300 *TF:* 877-745-6591 ■ *Web:* www.countrylegends971.com	Houston	TX	77056	713-963-1200	622-5457
KTRH-AM 740 (N/T) 2000 W Loop S Ste 300 *Web:* www.ktrh.com	Houston	TX	77027	713-212-8000	
KUHF-FM 88.7 (Clas) 4343 Elgin St 3rd Fl *TF:* 877-252-0436 ■ *Web:* www.kuhf.org	Houston	TX	77204	713-743-0887	743-0868
Rovi Corporation 1990 Post Oak Blvd Ste 2300 *TF:* 877-745-6591 ■ *Web:* www.houstonseagle.com	Houston	TX	77056	713-963-1200	622-5457

645-76 Huntsville, AL

Station	City	State	Zip	Phone	Fax
Mix 96.9 8402 Memorial Pkwy SW *Web:* www.mix969huntsville.com	Huntsville	AL	35802	256-885-9797	885-9796

Station	City	State	Zip	Phone	Fax
WEUP-FM 103.1 (Urban) 2609 Jordan Ln NW *Web:* www.103weup.com	Huntsville	AL	35816	256-837-9387	837-9404
WJOU-FM 90.1 (Rel) 7000 Adventist Blvd *Web:* www.wjou.org	Huntsville	AL	35896	256-722-9990	837-7918
WLOR-AM 1550 (Oldies) 1555 the Boardwalk Ste 1 *Web:* sunny981.com	Huntsville	AL	35816	256-536-1568	536-4416
WLRH-FM 89.3 (NPR) University of Alabama-Huntsville John Wright Dr *TF:* 800-239-9574 ■ *Web:* www.wlrh.org	Huntsville	AL	35899	256-895-9574	

645-77 Indianapolis, IN

Station	City	State	Zip	Phone	Fax
93.9 The beat 6810 N Shadeland Ave *Web:* www.939thebeat.com	Indianapolis	IN	46220	317-842-9550	921-1996
Country 97.1 HANK FM 40 Monument Cir Ste 600 *Web:* www.hankfm.com	Indianapolis	IN	46204	317-266-9700	684-2021
HOT-FM 96.3 (CHR) 21 E St Joseph St *Web:* hot963.com	Indianapolis	IN	46204	317-266-9600	328-3870
Rockville Community School Corp Rockville Jr-Sr High School 506 N Beadle St *Web:* www.rockville.k12.in.us	Rockville	IN	47872	765-569-5686	
WFBQ-FM 94.7 (CR) 6161 Fall Creek Rd	Indianapolis	IN	46220	317-257-7565	254-9619
WFMS-FM 95.5 (Ctry) 6810 N Shadeland Ave *Web:* www.wfms.com	Indianapolis	IN	46220	317-842-9550	
WFYI-FM 90.1 1630 N Meridian St *Web:* www.wfyi.org	Indianapolis	IN	46202	317-636-2020	283-6645
WIBC-FM 93.1 (N/T) 40 Monument Cir Ste 400 *TF:* 800-571-9422 ■ *Web:* www.wibc.com	Indianapolis	IN	46204	317-266-9422	
WJJK-FM 104.5 (CR) 6810 N Shadeland Ave *Web:* www.1045wjjk.com	Indianapolis	IN	46220	317-842-9550	
WNDE-AM 1260 (Sports) 6161 Fall Creek Rd *Web:* foxsports975.iheart.com	Indianapolis	IN	46220	317-257-7565	254-9619
WNTR-FM 107.9 (AC) 9245 N Meridian St Ste 300 *Web:* www.indysmix.com	Indianapolis	IN	46260	317-816-4000	816-4035
WTLC-AM 1310 (Rel) 21 E St Joseph St *Web:* praiseindy.hellobeautiful.com	Indianapolis	IN	46204	317-266-9600	328-3870
WXNT-AM 1430 (N/T) 9245 N Meridian St Ste 300 *Web:* www.cbssports1430.com	Indianapolis	IN	46260	317-218-2264	
WYXB-FM 105.7 (AC) 40 Monument Cir Ste 600 *Web:* www.b1057.com	Indianapolis	IN	46204	317-681-1057	684-2021
WZPL-FM 99.5 (AC) 9245 N Meridian St Ste 300 *Web:* www.wzpl.com	Indianapolis	IN	46260	317-816-4000	

645-78 Jackson, MS

Station	City	State	Zip	Phone	Fax
WHLH-FM 95.5 (Rel) 1375 Beasley Rd *Web:* hallelujah955.iheart.com	Jackson	MS	39206	601-982-1062	362-1905
WJDX-AM 620 (Sports) 1375 Beasley Rd *Web:* wjdx.iheart.com	Jackson	MS	39206	601-982-1062	362-1905
WMAE-FM 89.5 (NPR) 3825 Ridgewood Rd *TF:* 800-850-4406 ■ *Web:* mpbonline.org	Jackson	MS	39211	601-432-6565	432-6746
WMAH-FM 90.3 (NPR) 3825 Ridgewood Rd *Web:* www.mpbonline.org	Jackson	MS	39211	601-432-6565	
Z-106.7 (WSTZ-FM) 1375 Beasley Rd *Web:* z106.iheart.com	Jackson	MS	39206	601-982-1062	362-1905

645-79 Jacksonville, FL

Station	City	State	Zip	Phone	Fax
107.3 Jack FM 11700 Central Pkwy *Web:* 1073jack.iheart.com	Jacksonville	FL	32224	904-636-0507	
93.3 The Beat 11700 Central Pkwy **Fax:* Sales ■ *Web:* wjbt.iheart.com	Jacksonville	FL	32224	904-636-0507	636-7971*
Jacksonville's Country WQIK 99.1 11700 Central Pkwy *Web:* 991wqik.iheart.com	Jacksonville	FL	32224	904-636-0507	
V101.5 11700 Central Pkwy *Web:* v1015.iheart.com	Jacksonville	FL	32224	904-636-0507	
WAPE-FM 95.1 (CHR) 8000 Belfort Pkwy Ste 100 *TF:* 800-475-9595 ■ *Web:* www.wape.com	Jacksonville	FL	32256	904-245-8500	245-8501
WCGL-AM 1360 (Rel) 3890 Dunn Ave Ste 804 *Web:* www.wcgl1360.com	Jacksonville	FL	32218	904-766-9955	765-9214
WEJZ-FM 96.1 (AC) 6440 Atlantic Blvd *Web:* www.wejz.com	Jacksonville	FL	32211	904-727-9696	721-9322
WFKS-FM 97.9 (CHR) 11700 Central Pkwy *Web:* 979kissfm.iheart.com	Jacksonville	FL	32224	904-636-0507	
WJCT-FM 89.9 100 Festival Pk Ave *Web:* www.wjct.org	Jacksonville	FL	32202	904-353-7770	
WJGL-FM 96.9 (CR) 8000 Belfort Pkwy *TF:* 800-438-1601 ■ *Web:* www.969theeagle.com	Jacksonville	FL	32256	904-245-8500	245-8501
WOKV-AM 690 (N/T) 8000 Belfort Pkwy Ste 100 *Web:* www.wokv.com	Jacksonville	FL	32256	904-245-8500	245-8501
WXXJ-FM 102.9 (AC) 8000 Belfort Pkwy *TF:* 800-460-6394 ■ *Web:* www.x1029.com	Jacksonville	FL	32256	904-245-8500	245-8501
WZNZ-AM 1460 (Rel) PO Box 51585 *Web:* www.qopradio.com	Jacksonville Beach	FL	32240	904-241-3311	

645-80 Jefferson City, MO

Station	City	State	Zip	Phone	Fax
KLIK-AM 1240 (N/T) 1002 Diamond Ridge Ctr Ste 400 *Web:* www.klik1240.com	Jefferson City	MO	65109	573-893-5100	

645-81 Johnson City, TN

Station	City	State	Zip	Phone	Fax
WETB-AM 790 (Rel) 231 Brandonwood Dr PO Box 4127	Johnson City	TN	37604	423-928-7131	928-8392
WETS-FM 89.5 (NPR) PO Box 70630 *TF:* 888-895-9387 ■ *Web:* etsu.edu/wets	Johnson City	TN	37614	423-439-6440	

645-82 Juneau, AK

Station	City	State	Zip	Phone	Fax
KTOO-FM 104.3 (NPR) 360 Egan Dr *Web:* www.ktoo.org	Juneau	AK	99801	907-586-1670	

645-83 Kansas City, KS & MO

Station	City	State	Zip	Phone	Fax
KCKC-FM 102.1 (AC) 508 Westport Rd Ste 202 *Web:* kc1021.com	Kansas City	MO	64111	816-753-4000	
KCUR-FM 89.3 (NPR) 4825 Troost Ave Ste 202 *TF:* 855-778-5437 ■ *Web:* www.kcur.org	Kansas City	MO	64110	816-235-1551	235-2864
KFKF-FM 94.1 (Ctry) 508 Westport Rd Ste 202 *Web:* www.kfkf.com	Kansas City	MO	64111	816-753-4000	
KKFI-FM 90.1 (Var) 3901 Main St Ste 203 *TF:* 888-931-0901 ■ *Web:* www.kkfi.org	Kansas City	MO	64111	816-931-3122	931-7078
KLJC-FM 88.5 (Rel) 15800 Calvary Rd *Web:* life885.com	Kansas City	MO	64147	816-331-8700	
KMXV-FM 93.3 (CHR) 508 Westport Rd Ste 202 *Web:* www.mix93.com	Kansas City	MO	64111	816-753-4000	
KPRS-FM 103.3 (Urban) 11131 Colorado Ave *TF:* 800-273-8255 ■ *Web:* www.kprs.com	Kansas City	MO	64137	816-763-2040	966-1055
KPRT-AM 1590 (Rel) 11131 Colorado Ave *Web:* www.kprt.com	Kansas City	MO	64137	816-763-2040	

645-84 Key West, FL

Station	City	State	Zip	Phone	Fax
WAIL-FM 99.5 (Rock) 830 Crane Blvd Ste 10 *Web:* www.sun103.com	Sugarloaf Key	FL	33042	305-296-7511	
WEOW-FM 92.7 (CHR) 5450 MacDonald Ave Ste 10 *Web:* www.weow927.com	Key West	FL	33040	305-296-7511	
WIIS-FM 107.1 Key West Radio 1075 Duval St Ste C17 *Web:* island1069.com	Key West	FL	33040	305-292-1071	
WKWF-AM 1600 (Sports) 830 Crane Blvd Ste 10 *Web:* www.sportsradio1600.com	Sugarloaf Key	FL	33042	305-294-2523	

645-85 Knoxville, TN

Station	City	State	Zip	Phone	Fax
NEWS TALK 98.7 4711 Old Kingston Pike **Fax:* News Rm ■ *TF:* 800-951-8255 ■ *Web:* www.newstalk987.com	Knoxville	TN	37919	865-588-6511	588-3725*
WCYQ-FM 93.1 (Oldies) 1533 Amherst Rd *Web:* www.q100country.com	Knoxville	TN	37909	865-824-1021	
WFIV-FM 105.3 (AAA) 517 Watt Rd *Web:* www.myi105.com	Knoxville	TN	37934	865-675-4105	
WIMZ-FM 103.5 (CR) 1100 Sharps Ridge Memorial Pk Dr *Web:* www.wimz.com	Knoxville	TN	37917	865-525-6000	
WITA-AM 1490 (Rel) 2914 Sanderson Rd *Web:* www.1490wita.com	Knoxville	TN	37921	865-588-2974	
WIVK-FM 107.7 (Ctry) 4711 Old Kingston Pike *TF:* 877-995-9961 ■ *Web:* www.wivk.com	Knoxville	TN	37919	865-588-6511	588-3725
WJBZ-FM 96.3 (Rel) 7101 Chapman Hwy *Web:* www.praise963.com	Knoxville	TN	37920	865-577-4885	
WJXB-FM 97.5 (AC) 1100 Sharps Ridge Rd *Web:* www.b975.com	Knoxville	TN	37917	865-525-6000	525-2000
WUOT-FM 91.9 (NPR) 209 Communications Bldg University of Tennessee *TF:* 888-266-9868 ■ *Web:* www.wuot.org	Knoxville	TN	37996	865-974-5375	974-3941
WWST-FM 102.1 (CHR) 1533 Amherst Rd *Web:* www.star1021fm.com	Knoxville	TN	37909	865-824-1021	

645-86 Lafayette, LA

Station	City	State	Zip	Phone	Fax
KJCB-AM 770 (Urban) 604 St John St	Lafayette	LA	70501	337-233-4262	235-9681

				Phone	Fax
KMDL-FM 97.3 (Ctry) 1749 Bertrand Dr. Web: 973thedawg.com	Lafayette	LA	70506	337-233-6000	
KPEL-AM 1420 (Sports) 1749 Bertrand Dr. Web: espn1420.com	Lafayette	LA	70506	337-233-6000	
KPEL-FM 105.1 (N/T) 1749 Bertrand Dr. Web: www.kpel965.com	Lafayette	LA	70506	337-233-6000	
KRKA-FM 107.9 (Urban) 1749 Bertrand Dr. Web: 1079ishot.com	Lafayette	LA	70506	337-233-6000	
KRRQ-FM 95.5 (Urban) 202 Galbert Rd. Web: www.krrq.com	Lafayette	LA	70506	337-232-1311	
KTDY-FM 99.9 (AC) 1749 Bertrand Dr. Web: 999ktdy.com	Lafayette	LA	70506	337-233-6000	
KXKC-FM 99.1 (Ctry) 202 Galbert Rd. Web: www.nashfm991.com	Lafayette	LA	70506	337-920-5952	

645-87 Lansing, MI

				Phone	Fax
WFMK-FM 99.1 (AC) 3420 Pine Tree Rd. Web: www.99wfmk.com	Lansing	MI	48911	517-394-7272	
WHZZ-FM 101.7 (AC) 600 W Cavanaugh Rd. Web: www.1017mikefm.com	Lansing	MI	48910	517-393-1320	393-0882
WIMI WJMS 222 S Lawrence St. Web: www.wimifm.com	Ironwood	MI	49938	906-932-2411	
WITL-FM 100.7 (Ctry) 3420 Pine Tree Rd. TF: 800-968-9485 ■ Web: www.witl.com	Lansing	MI	48911	517-394-7272	
WJIM-AM 1240 (N/T) 3420 Pine Tree Rd. Web: www.wjimam.com	Lansing	MI	48911	517-394-7272	
WJIM-FM 97.5 (CHR) 3420 Pine Tree Rd. Web: www.975now.com	Lansing	MI	48911	517-394-7272	
WLNZ-FM 89.7 (Var) 400 N Capitol Ave Ste 001. Web: www.lcc.edu	Lansing	MI	48933	517-483-1710	
WMMQ-FM 94.9 (CR) 3420 Pine Tree Rd. Web: www.wmmq.com	Lansing	MI	48911	517-394-7272	
WQHH-FM 96.5 (Urban) 600 W Cavanaugh. Web: www.power965fm.com	Lansing	MI	48910	517-393-1320	393-0882
WVFN-AM 730 (Sports) 3420 Pine Tree Rd. Web: thegame730am.com	Lansing	MI	48911	517-394-7272	

645-88 Las Vegas, NV

				Phone	Fax
Contact 93.1 The Party 2880 Meade Ave Ste 250. Web: 931theparty.iheart.com	Las Vegas	NV	89102	702-238-7300	732-4890
KCEP-FM 88.1 (Urban) 330 W Washington Ave. Web: kcep.power88lv.com	Las Vegas	NV	89106	702-648-0104	647-0803
KDWN-AM 720 (N/T) 1455 E Tropicana Ave Ste 800. TF: 888-695-2664 ■ Web: www.kdwn.com	Las Vegas	NV	89119	702-730-0300	736-8447
KENO-AM 1460 (Sports) 8755 W Flamingo Rd. Web: wearelv.com	Las Vegas	NV	89147	702-876-1460	
KKLZ-FM 96.3 2920 S Durango Dr Ste 800. Web: www.963kklz.com	Las Vegas	NV	89117	702-730-0300	736-8447
KKVV-AM 1060 (Rel) 3185 S Highland Dr Ste 13. Web: www.kkvv.com	Las Vegas	NV	89109	702-731-5588	
KMXB-FM 94.1 (AC) 7255 S Tenaya Way Ste 100. TF: 866-438-0220 ■ Web: mix941fm.cbslocal.com	Las Vegas	NV	89113	702-257-9400	257-2936
KNPR-FM 89.5 (NPR) 1289 S Torrey Pines Dr. TF: 888-258-9895 ■ Web: www.knpr.org	Las Vegas	NV	89146	702-258-9895	258-5646
KOMP-FM 92.3 (Rock) 8755 W Flamingo Rd. Web: www.komp.com	Las Vegas	NV	89147	702-876-3692	
KVEG-FM 97.5 (Urban) 3999 Las Vegas Blvd S Ste K. Web: www.kvegas.com	Las Vegas	NV	89119	702-736-6161	
KWNR-FM 95.5 (Ctry) 2880 Meade Ave Ste 250. Web: 955thebull.iheart.com	Las Vegas	NV	89102	702-238-7300	732-4890
KXNT-AM 840 (N/T) 7255 S Tenaya Way Ste 100. Web: lasvegas.cbslocal.com	Las Vegas	NV	89113	702-889-7300	
KXTE-FM 107.5 (Alt) 7255 S Tenaya Way Ste 100. Web: x1075lasvegas.cbslocal.com	Las Vegas	NV	89113	702-257-1075	889-7555
Sunny 106.5 - KSNE-FM 2880 Meade Ave Ste 250. Web: sunny1065.iheart.com	Las Vegas	NV	89102	702-238-7300	732-4890

645-89 Lexington/Frankfort, KY

				Phone	Fax
WBUL-FM 98.1 (Ctry) 2601 Nicholasville Rd. Web: wbul.iheart.com	Lexington	KY	40503	859-422-1000	
WFKY-FM 104.9 (Cty) 115 W Main St. Web: www.myfroggy1049.com	Frankfort	KY	40601	502-875-1130	
WGKS-FM 96.9 (AC) 401 W Main St Ste 301. Web: www.969kissfm.com	Lexington	KY	40507	859-233-1515	233-1517
WKYL-FM 102.1 (NAC) 102 Perkins Bldg 521 Lancaster Ave. TF: 800-621-8890 ■ Web: www.weku.fm	Richmond	KY	40475	800-621-8890	
WLAP-AM 630 (N/T) 2601 Nicholasville Rd. Web: wlap.iheart.com	Lexington	KY	40503	859-422-1000	422-1038
WUKY-FM 91.3 (NPR) 340 McVey Hall University of Kentucky. Web: wuky.org	Lexington	KY	40506	859-257-3221	

645-90 Lincoln, NE

				Phone	Fax
KBBK-FM 107.3 (AC) 4343 'O' St. Web: www.b1073.com	Lincoln	NE	68510	402-475-4567	
KFGE-FM 98.1 (Ctry) 4343 'O' St. Web: www.froggy981.com	Lincoln	NE	68510	402-475-4567	
KFRX-FM 106.3 (CHR) 3800 Cornhusker Hwy. TF: 800-523-9101 ■ Web: www.kfrxfm.com	Lincoln	NE	68504	402-466-1234	
KIBZ-FM 104.1 (Rock) 3800 Cornhusker Hwy. Web: www.kibz.com	Lincoln	NE	68504	402-466-1234	
Krvn Transmitter 73744 M Rd. Web: www.krvn.com	Holdrege	NE	68949	308-995-5541	
KTGL-FM 92.9 (CR) 3800 Cornhusker Hwy. Web: www.ktgl.com	Lincoln	NE	68504	402-466-1234	

645-91 Little Rock, AR

				Phone	Fax
KABF-FM 88.3 (Var) 2101 Main St # 200. *Fax Area Code: 504 ■ Web: www.kabf.org	Little Rock	AR	72206	501-372-6119	376-3952*
KABZ-FM 103.7 (N/T) 2400 Cottondale Ln. TF: 800-477-1037 ■ Web: www.1037thebuzz.com	Little Rock	AR	72202	501-661-1037	664-5871
KIPR-FM 92.3 (Urban) 700 Wellington Hills Rd. Web: www.power923.com	Little Rock	AR	72211	501-401-0200	
KKPT-FM 94.1 (CR) 2400 Cottondale Ln. TF: 800-844-0094 ■ Web: www.point941.com	Little Rock	AR	72202	501-664-9410	
KLAL-FM 107.7 (CHR) 700 Wellington Hills Rd. Web: www.alice1077.com	Little Rock	AR	72211	501-401-0200	
KOKY-FM 102.1 (Urban) 700 Wellington Hills Rd. Web: www.koky.com	Little Rock	AR	72211	501-401-0200	
KURB-FM 98.5 (AC) 700 Wellington Hills Rd. Web: www.b98.com	Little Rock	AR	72211	501-401-0200	

645-92 Los Angeles, CA

				Phone	Fax
KABC-AM 790 (N/T) 3321 S La Cienega Blvd PO Box 790. TF: 800-222-5222 ■ Web: www.kabc.com	Los Angeles	CA	90016	310-840-4900	
KFWB-AM 980 (N/T) 5777 W Century Blvd Ste 1110.	Los Angeles	CA	90045	408-440-0851	
KLOS-FM 95.5 (CR) 3321 S La Cienega Blvd. TF: 800-955-5567 ■ Web: www.955klos.com	Los Angeles	CA	90016	310-840-4828	
KNX-AM 1070 (N/T) 5670 Wilshire Blvd Ste 200. Web: losangeles.cbslocal.com	Los Angeles	CA	90036	323-957-4524	964-8398
KROQ-FM 106.7 (Alt) 5901 Venice Blvd. TF: 800-520-1067 ■ Web: kroq.cbslocal.com	Los Angeles	CA	90034	323-930-1067	
KRTH-FM 101.1 (Oldies) 5670 Wilshire Blvd Ste 200. TF: 800-232-5784 ■ Web: kearth101.cbslocal.com	Los Angeles	CA	90036	323-936-5784	933-6072
KSWD-FM 100.3 (Rock) 5900 Wilshire Blvd Ste 1900. TF: 888-696-1003 ■ Web: www.thesoundla.com	Los Angeles	CA	90036	323-634-1800	
KUSC-FM 91.5 (Clas) 1149 S Hill St Ste H100 PO Box 7913. TF: 877-587-2227 ■ Web: www.kusc.org	Los Angeles	CA	90015	213-225-7400	225-7410
Power 106 Radio 2600 W Olive Ave Ste 800. Web: www.power106.com	Burbank	CA	91505	818-953-4200	

645-93 Louisville, KY

				Phone	Fax
WAMZ-FM 97.5 (Ctry) 4000 Radio Dr. Web: wamz.iheart.com	Louisville	KY	40218	502-479-2222	479-2223
WFPK-FM 91.9 (AAA) 619 S Fourth St. Web: www.wfpk.org	Louisville	KY	40202	502-814-6500	
WFPL-FM 89.3 (NPR) 619 S Fourth St. Web: www.wfpl.org	Louisville	KY	40202	502-814-6500	
WGZB-FM 96.5 (Urban) 520 S Fourth Ave. Web: hiphopb965.com	Louisville	KY	40202	502-625-1220	
WHAS-AM 840 (N/T) 4000 One Radio Dr. TF: 800-444-8484 ■ Web: whas.iheart.com	Louisville	KY	40218	502-479-2222	479-2308
WLOU-AM 1350 (Rel) 2001 W Broadway. Web: www.wlouonline.com	Louisville	KY	40203	502-776-1240	
WQNU-FM 103.1 (Ctry) 612 S Fourth St. Web: www.qlouisville.com	Louisville	KY	40202	502-636-5023	
WVEZ-FM 106.9 (AC) 612 S 4th St. Web: www.1069play.com	Louisville	KY	40202	502-589-4800	589-1377
WXMA-FM 102.3 (AC) 520 S Fourth Ave. Web: www.themaxfm.com	Louisville	KY	40202	502-625-1220	

645-94 Lubbock, TX

				Phone	Fax
KFMX-FM 94.5 (Rock) 4413 82nd St Ste 300. Web: www.kfmx.com	Lubbock	TX	79424	806-798-7078	798-7052
KFYO-AM 790 (N/T) 4413 82nd St Ste 300. Web: www.kfyo.com	Lubbock	TX	79424	806-798-7078	

Station	City	State	Zip	Phone	Fax
KLLL-FM 96.3 (Ctry) 33 Briercroft Office Pk *Web:* www.klll.com	Lubbock	TX	79412	806-762-3000	
KONE-FM 101.1 (Rock) 33 Briercroft Office Pk *Web:* www.rock101.fm	Lubbock	TX	79412	806-762-3000	
KQBR-FM 99.5 (Ctry) 4413 82nd St Ste 300 *Web:* lonestar995fm.com	Lubbock	TX	79424	806-798-7078	798-7052
KZII-FM 102.5 (CHR) 4413 82nd St Ste 300 *Web:* 1025kiss.com	Lubbock	TX	79424	806-798-7078	798-7052

645-95 Macon, GA

Station	City	State	Zip	Phone	Fax
V 101.7 7080 Industrial Hwy *Web:* v1017.iheart.com	Macon	GA	31216	478-781-1063	781-6711
WDEN-FM 99.1 (Ctry) 544 Mulberry St 5th Fl *Web:* www.wden.com	Macon	GA	31201	478-746-6286	
WIBB-FM 97.9 (Urban) 7080 Industrial Hwy *TF:* 800-813-8418 ■ *Web:* wibb.iheart.com	Macon	GA	31216	478-781-1063	781-6711
WLZN-FM 92.3 (Urban) 544 Mulberry St 5th Fl *Web:* www.blazin923.com	Macon	GA	31201	478-330-6162	
WMAC-AM 940 (N/T) 544 Mulberry St 5th Fl *Web:* www.wmac-am.com	Macon	GA	31201	478-746-6286	
WMGB-FM 95.1 (CHR) 544 Mulberry St 5th Fl *Web:* www.allthehitsb951.com	Macon	GA	31201	478-646-9510	

645-96 Madison, WI

Station	City	State	Zip	Phone	Fax
Today's Q106 730 Rayovac Dr *Web:* www.q106.com	Madison	WI	53711	608-273-1000	
Triple M 105.5 fm 7601 Ganser Way *Web:* www.1055triplem.com	Madison	WI	53719	608-826-0077	
WERN-FM 88.7 (NPR) 821 University Ave **Fax Area Code:* 608 ■ *TF:* 800-747-7444 ■ *Web:* www.wpr.org	Madison	WI	53706	800-747-7444	263-9763*
WHA-AM 970 (NPR) 821 University Ave **Fax Area Code:* 608 ■ *TF:* 800-747-7444 ■ *Web:* www.wpr.org	Madison	WI	53706	800-747-7444	263-9763*
WHIT-AM 1550 (Nost) 730 Rayovac Dr *TF:* 800-422-7128 ■ *Web:* hankonline.net	Madison	WI	53711	608-273-1000	
WIBA-AM 1310 (N/T) 2651 S Fish Hatchery Rd *Web:* wiba.iheart.com	Madison	WI	53711	608-274-5450	274-5521
WIBA-FM 101.5 (CR) 2651 S Fish Hatchery Rd *Web:* wibafm.iheart.com	Madison	WI	53711	608-274-5450	274-5521
WJJO-FM 94.1 (Rock) 730 Rayovac Dr *Web:* www.wjjo.com	Madison	WI	53711	608-321-0941	
WMGN-FM 98.1 (AC) 730 Rayovac Dr *Web:* www.magic98.com	Madison	WI	53711	608-273-1000	441-0098
WTSO-AM 1070 (Sports) 2651 S Fish Hatchery Rd *Web:* thebig1070.iheart.com	Madison	WI	53711	608-274-5450	274-5521

645-97 Manchester, NH

Station	City	State	Zip	Phone	Fax
News Radio 610 70 Foundry St Ste 300 *Web:* nhnewsnetwork610.iheart.com	Manchester	NH	03102	603-625-6915	625-9255
WFEA-AM 1370 (Nost) 500 Commercial St *Web:* 1370wfea.com	Manchester	NH	03101	603-669-5777	669-4641
WMLL-FM 96.5 (CR) 500 Commercial St *TF:* 800-666-0957 ■ *Web:* 965themill.com	Manchester	NH	03101	603-669-5777	669-4641

645-98 Memphis, TN

Station	City	State	Zip	Phone	Fax
103.5 WRBO 5629 Murray Rd *Web:* www.1035wrbo.com	Memphis	TN	38119	901-682-1106	767-9531
600 WREC 2650 Thousand Oaks Blvd Ste 4100 *TF:* 800-474-9732 ■ *Web:* 600wrec.iheart.com	Memphis	TN	38118	901-259-1300	259-6456
98.9 The Vibe (WKIM-FM) 5629 Murray Rd *Web:* www.989thevibe.com	Memphis	TN	38119	901-682-1106	767-9531
K FM 97.1 2650 Thousand Oaks Blvd Ste 4100 *Web:* k97fm.iheart.com	Memphis	TN	38118	901-259-1300	259-6456
KWAM-AM 990 (N/T) 5495 Murray Rd *Web:* www.kwam990.com	Memphis	TN	38119	901-261-4200	261-4210
Rock 103 2650 Thousand Oaks Blvd Ste 4100 *Web:* rock103.iheart.com	Memphis	TN	38118	901-259-1300	259-6456
V101 2650 Thousand Oaks Blvd Ste 4100 *Web:* myv101.iheart.com	Memphis	TN	38118	901-259-1300	
WDIA-AM 1070 (Urban) 2650 Thousand Oaks Blvd Ste 4100 *TF:* 800-339-4673 ■ *Web:* mywdia.iheart.com	Memphis	TN	38118	901-259-1300	259-6456
WGKX-FM 105.9 (Ctry) 5629 Murray Rd *Web:* www.kix106.com	Memphis	TN	38119	901-682-1106	
WHAL-FM 95.7 (Rel) 2650 Thousand Oaks Blvd Ste 4100 *TF:* 888-302-6222 ■ *Web:* hallelujahfm.iheart.com	Memphis	TN	38118	901-259-1300	259-6456
WKNO-FM 91.1 (NPR) 900 Getwell Rd *TF:* 800-766-9566 ■ *Web:* www.wknofm.org	Memphis	TN	38111	901-325-6544	729-8176
WLOK-AM 1340 (Rel) 363 S Second St *Web:* www.wlok.com	Memphis	TN	38103	901-527-9565	528-0335
WRVR-FM 104.5 (AC) 1835 Moriah Woods Blvd Bldg 1 *Web:* www.1045theriver.com	Memphis	TN	38117	901-384-5900	767-6076
WXMX-FM 98.1 (Rock) 5629 Murray Rd *Web:* www.981themax.com	Memphis	TN	38119	901-535-9898	

645-99 Miami/Fort Lauderdale, FL

Station	City	State	Zip	Phone	Fax
El ZOL 106.7 FM 7007 NW 77th Ave *Web:* elzol.lamusica.com	Miami	FL	33166	305-444-9292	883-7701
POWER 96 194 NW 187th St *Web:* power96.cbslocal.com	Miami	FL	33169	305-654-1700	654-1715
WDNA-FM 88.9 (Jazz) 2921 Coral Way *Web:* www.wdna.org	Miami	FL	33145	305-662-8889	
WINZ-AM 940 (N/T) 7601 Riviera Blvd *Web:* 940winz.iheart.com	Miramar	FL	33023	954-862-2000	862-4013
WIOD-AM 610 (N/T) 7601 Riviera Blvd *Web:* wiod.iheart.com	Miramar	FL	33023	954-862-2000	
WKIS-FM 99.9 (Ctry) 194 NW 187th St *TF:* 866-978-0800 ■ *Web:* wkis.cbslocal.com	Miami	FL	33169	305-654-1700	654-1715
WLRN-FM 91.3 (NPR) 172 NE 15th St *Web:* www.wlrn.org	Miami	FL	33132	305-995-1717	995-2299
WLYF-FM 101.5 (AC) 20450 NW Second Ave **Fax Area Code:* 305 ■ *TF:* 877-790-1015 ■ *Web:* www.litemiami.com	Miami	FL	33169	877-790-1015	521-1414*
WMBM-AM 1490 (Rel) 13242 NW Seventh Ave *TF:* 800-721-9626 ■ *Web:* www.wmbm.com	North Miami	FL	33168	305-769-1100	769-9975
WMXJ-FM 102.7 (Oldies) 20450 NW Second Ave *TF:* 800-924-1027 ■ *Web:* www.thebeachmiami.com	Miami	FL	33169	305-521-5240	521-1414
WSUA-AM 1260 (Span) 2100 Coral Way Ste 201 *TF:* 877-453-5437 ■ *Web:* www.caracol1260.com	Miami	FL	33145	305-285-1260	
Zeta 92.3 7007 NW 77th Ave *Web:* zeta92.lamusica.com	Miami	FL	33166	305-444-9292	

645-100 Milwaukee, WI

Station	City	State	Zip	Phone	Fax
94.5 KTI Country 720 E Capitol Dr *Web:* www.wtmj.com/kticountry	Milwaukee	WI	53212	414-332-9611	967-5266
WAUK-AM 540 (Sports) 310 W Wisconsin Ave Ste 100 *TF:* 800-990-3776 ■ *Web:* espn.go.com/milwaukee	Milwaukee	WI	53203	414-273-3776	291-3776
WHAD-FM 90.7 (NPR) 310 W Wisconsin Ave Ste 750-E *TF:* 800-486-8655 ■ *Web:* www.wpr.org	Milwaukee	WI	53203	414-227-2040	227-2043
WHQG-FM 102.9 (Rock) 5407 W McKinley Ave *TF:* 877-777-1029 ■ *Web:* www.1029thehog.com	Milwaukee	WI	53208	414-978-9000	978-9001
WJMR-FM 98.3 (Urban) 5407 W McKinley Ave *Web:* jammin983.com	Milwaukee	WI	53208	414-978-9000	978-9001
WJYI-AM 1340 (Rel) 5407 W McKinley Ave *Web:* www.joy1340.com	Milwaukee	WI	53208	414-978-9000	978-9001
WKLH-FM 96.5 (CR) 5407 W McKinley Ave *Web:* www.wklh.com	Milwaukee	WI	53208	414-978-9000	
WTMJ-AM 620 (N/T) 720 E Capitol Dr *Web:* www.wtmj.com	Milwaukee	WI	53212	414-799-1620	967-5298
WUWM-FM 89.7 (NPR) 111 E Wisconsin Ave Ste 700 *Web:* www.wuwm.com	Milwaukee	WI	53202	414-227-3355	

645-101 Minneapolis/Saint Paul, MN

Station	City	State	Zip	Phone	Fax
KDWB-FM 101.3 (CHR) 1600 Utica Ave S Ste 400 *Web:* kdwb.iheart.com	Minneapolis	MN	55416	952-417-3000	417-3001
KFAN-AM 1130 (Sports) 1600 Utica Ave S Ste 400 *TF:* 800-320-5326 ■ *Web:* kfan.iheart.com	Minneapolis	MN	55416	952-417-3000	417-3001
KQRS-FM 92.5 (CR) 2000 SE Elm St *Web:* www.92kqrs.com	Minneapolis	MN	55414	612-617-4000	
KSTP-AM 1500 (N/T) 3415 University Ave *TF:* 877-615-1500 ■ *Web:* www.1500espn.com	Saint Paul	MN	55114	651-646-8255	
KSTP-FM 94.5 (AC) 3415 University Ave *Web:* www.ks95.com	Minneapolis	MN	55414	651-642-4141	647-2904
KXXR-FM 93.7 (Rock) 2000 SE Elm St *Web:* www.93x.com	Minneapolis	MN	55414	612-617-4000	676-8292
KZJK-FM 104.1 (Var) 625 Second Ave S *Web:* 1041jackfm.cbslocal.com	Minneapolis	MN	55402	612-370-0611	
WCCO-AM 830 (N/T) 625 Second Ave S Ste 200 *Web:* minnesota.cbslocal.com	Minneapolis	MN	55402	612-370-0611	
WLTE-FM 102.9 (AC) 625 Second Ave S Ste 200 *Web:* buzn1029.cbslocal.com	Minneapolis	MN	55402	612-370-0611	612-5653

645-102 Mobile, AL

Station	City	State	Zip	Phone	Fax
News Radio710 555 Broadcast Dr *Web:* newsradio710.iheart.com	Mobile	AL	36606	251-450-0100	479-3418
Rocket-FM 96.1 (CR), The 555 Broadcast Dr *Web:* 961therocket.iheart.com	Mobile	AL	36606	251-450-0100	479-3418
WABB-FM 97.5 (CHR) 1551 Springhill Ave	Mobile	AL	36604	251-432-5572	
WBHY-FM 88.5 (Rel) PO Box 1328 *TF:* 888-473-8488 ■ *Web:* www.goforth.org	Mobile	AL	36633	251-473-8488	
WGOK-AM 900 (Rel) 2800 Dauphin St Ste 104 *Web:* www.gospel900.com	Mobile	AL	36606	251-652-2064	652-2007
WNSP-FM 105.5 (Sports) 1100 Dauphin St Ste E *Web:* www.wnsp.com	Mobile	AL	36604	251-438-5460	438-5462

645-103 Monterey, CA

Station / Address	City	State	Zip	Phone	Fax
KCDU-FM 101.7 (AC) 60 Garden Ct Ste 300 *TF:* 800-365-8630 ■ *Web:* www.1017thebeach.com	Monterey	CA	93940	831-658-5200	658-5299
KHIP-FM 104.3 (CR) 60 Garden Ct Ste 300 *TF:* 877-762-5104 ■ *Web:* www.thehippo.com	Monterey	CA	93940	831-658-5200	658-5299

645-104 Montgomery, AL

Station / Address	City	State	Zip	Phone	Fax
WBAM-FM 98.9 (Ctry) 4101-A Wall St *Web:* bamacountry.com	Montgomery	AL	36106	334-244-0961	279-9563
WQKS 4101-A Wall St	Montgomery	AL	36106	334-244-0961	279-9563
WXFX-FM 95.1 (Rock) 1 Commerce St Ste 300 *Web:* www.wxfx.com	Montgomery	AL	36104	334-240-9274	240-9219

645-105 Morgantown, WV

Station / Address	City	State	Zip	Phone	Fax
WAJR-AM 1440 (N/T) 1251 Earl L Core Rd *Web:* www.wajr.com	Morgantown	WV	26505	304-296-0029	
WCLG-FM 100.1 (Rock) PO Box 885 *Web:* www.wclg.com	Morgantown	WV	26507	304-292-2222	292-2224
WKKW-FM 97.9 (Ctry) 1251 Earl L Core Rd *Web:* www.wkkwfm.com	Morgantown	WV	26505	304-296-0029	
WVAQ-FM 101.9 (CHR) 1251 Earl L Core Rd *Web:* www.wvaq.com	Morgantown	WV	26505	304-296-0029	
WWVU-FM 91.7 (Var) PO Box 6446 *Web:* u92.wvu.edu	Morgantown	WV	26506	304-293-3329	293-7363

645-106 Myrtle Beach, SC

Station / Address	City	State	Zip	Phone	Fax
WEZV-FM 105.9 (AC) 3926 Wesley St Ste 301 *Web:* www.wezv.com	Myrtle Beach	SC	29579	843-903-9962	
WKZQ-FM 96.1 (Rock) 1016 Ocala St *Web:* www.wkzq.net	Myrtle Beach	SC	29577	843-448-1041	626-5988
WMYB-FM 92.1 (AC) 1016 Ocala St *Web:* www.star921.net	Myrtle Beach	SC	29577	843-448-1041	
WRNN-FM 99.5 (N/T) 1016 Ocala St *Web:* www.wrnn.net	Myrtle Beach	SC	29577	843-448-1041	
WYAV-FM 104.1 (CR) 1016 Ocala St *Web:* wave104.net	Myrtle Beach	SC	29577	843-448-1041	626-5988

645-107 Naples, FL

Station / Address	City	State	Zip	Phone	Fax
WAVV-FM 101.1 (AC) 11800 Tamiami Trl E *TF:* 866-310-9288 ■ *Web:* www.wavv101.com	Naples	FL	34113	239-775-9288	793-7000
WAY Media Inc 1860 Boy Scout Dr Ste 202 *Web:* www.wayfm.com	Fort Myers	FL	33907	239-936-1929	

645-108 Nashville, TN

Station / Address	City	State	Zip	Phone	Fax
102.5 The Game 1824 Murfreesboro Rd *Web:* www.thegamenashville.com	Nashville	TN	37217	615-399-1029	361-9873
BIG 98, The 55 Music Sq W *Web:* thebig98.iheart.com	Nashville	TN	37203	615-664-2400	
River-FM 107.5 (CHR), The 55 Music Sq W *Web:* 1075theriver.iheart.com	Nashville	TN	37203	615-664-2400	664-2434
SuperTalk 99.7 WTN 10 Music Cir E *TF:* 800-618-7445 ■ *Web:* www.997wtn.com	Nashville	TN	37203	615-321-1067	
WBUZ-FM 102.9 (Alt) 1824 Murfreesboro Rd *Web:* www.1029thebuzz.com	Nashville	TN	37217	615-399-1029	361-9873
WCJK-FM 96.3 (Var) 504 Rosedale Ave *Web:* www.963jackfm.com	Nashville	TN	37211	615-259-4567	259-4594
WENO-AM 760 (Rel) 545 Mainstream Dr *Web:* www.760thegospel.com	Nashville	TN	37228	615-742-6506	
WJXA-FM 92.9 (AC) 504 Rosedale Ave *Web:* www.mix929.com	Nashville	TN	37211	615-737-0929	259-4594
WLAC-AM 1510 (N/T) 55 Music Sq W *TF:* 800-688-9522 ■ *Web:* wlac.iheart.com	Nashville	TN	37203	615-664-2400	744-4743
World Christian Broadcasting Corp 605 Bradley Ct *Web:* www.worldchristian.org	Franklin	TN	37067	615-371-8707	
WPLN-FM 90.3 (NPR) 630 Mainstream Dr *TF:* 877-760-2903 ■ *Web:* nashvillepublicradio.org	Nashville	TN	37228	615-760-2903	760-2904
WRLT-FM 100.1 (AAA) 1310 Clinton St Ste 200 *Web:* lightning100.com	Nashville	TN	37203	615-242-5600	296-9039
WSM-AM 650 (Ctry) 2644 McGavock Pk *Web:* wsmonline.com	Nashville	TN	37214	615-737-9650	
WSM-FM 95.5 (Ctry) 10 Music Cir E *Web:* 955nashicon.com	Nashville	TN	37203	615-321-1067	

645-109 New Haven, CT

Station / Address	City	State	Zip	Phone	Fax
Summit Handling Systems Inc 11 Defco Park Rd *Web:* www.summithandling.com	North Haven	CT	06473	203-239-5351	
WYBC-AM 1340 (Var) 142 Temple St Ste 203 *Web:* www.wybc.com	New Haven	CT	06510	203-776-4118	
WYBC-FM 94.3 (Urban) 440 Wheelers Farms Rd Ste 302 *Web:* www.943wybc.com	Milford	CT	06461	203-783-8200	783-8383

645-110 New Orleans, LA

Station / Address	City	State	Zip	Phone	Fax
KKND-FM 102.9 (Urban) 201 St Charles Ave Ste 201 *Web:* www.power1029.com	New Orleans	LA	70170	504-581-7002	566-4857
KMEZ-FM 106.7 (Oldies) 201 St Charles Ave Ste 201 *Web:* www.oldschool1067.com	New Orleans	LA	70170	504-581-7002	
NASH FM 92.3 201 St Charles Ave Ste 201 *Web:* www.nashfm923.com	New Orleans	LA	70170	504-581-7002	
WKBU-FM 95.7 (Rock) 400 Poydras St Ste 800 *Web:* www.bayou957.com	New Orleans	LA	70130	504-593-6376	
WLMG-FM 101.9 (AC) 400 Poydras St Ste 800 *Web:* www.magic1019.com	New Orleans	LA	70130	504-593-6376	
WNOE-FM 101.1 (Ctry) 929 Howard Ave *Web:* wnoe.iheart.com	New Orleans	LA	70113	504-679-7300	679-7345
WQUE-FM 93.3 (Urban) 929 Howard Ave *Web:* q93.iheart.com	New Orleans	LA	70113	504-679-7300	679-7345
WRNO-FM 99.5 (N/T) 929 Howard Ave *Web:* wrno.iheart.com	New Orleans	LA	70113	504-679-7300	679-7345
WSHO-AM 800 (Rel) 365 Canal St Ste 1175 *Web:* www.wsho.com	New Orleans	LA	70130	504-527-0800	527-0881
WWL-AM 870 (N/T) 400 Poydras St Ste 800 *Web:* www.wwl.com	New Orleans	LA	70130	504-593-6376	
WWL-FM 105.3 N/T) 400 Poydras St Ste 800 *Web:* www.wwl.com	New Orleans	LA	70130	504-593-6376	
WWNO-FM 89.9 (NPR) University of New Orleans Lake Frnt Campus *TF:* 800-286-7002 ■ *Web:* www.wwno.org	New Orleans	LA	70148	504-280-7000	280-6061
WWOZ-FM 90.7 (Var) 1008 N Peters St *Web:* www.wwoz.org	New Orleans	LA	70116	504-568-1239	558-9332
WYLD-AM 940 (Rel) 929 Howard Ave *TF:* 800-899-9265 ■ *Web:* am940.iheart.com	New Orleans	LA	70113	504-679-7300	679-7345
WYLD-FM 98.5 (Urban) 929 Howard Ave *Web:* wyldfm.iheart.com	New Orleans	LA	70113	504-679-7300	679-7345

645-111 New York, NY

Station / Address	City	State	Zip	Phone	Fax
Bear Used Office Furniture 256 E Jericho Tpke *Web:* www.computer-furniture.com	Mineola	NY	11501	516-741-7666	
NJTV 825 Eighth Avenue *TF:* 800-882-6622 ■ *Web:* www.njtvonline.org	New York	NY	10019	609-777-0031	
WABC-AM 770 (N/T) 2 Penn Plaza 17th Fl *Web:* www.wabcradio.com	New York	NY	10121	212-613-3800	613-3837
WAXQ-FM 104.3 (CR) 32 Ave of the Americas *TF:* 888-872-1043 ■ *Web:* www.q1043.com	New York	NY	10013	212-377-7900	
WBBR-AM 1130 (N/T) 731 Lexington Ave *Web:* www.bloomberg.com/radio	New York	NY	10022	212-318-2000	
WCBS-FM 101.1 (Oldies) 345 Hudson St 10th Fl *Web:* wcbsfm.cbslocal.com	New York	NY	10014	212-314-9200	
WFAN-AM 66 (Rel) 345 Hudson St *Web:* newyork.cbslocal.com	New York	NY	10014	212-314-9128	
WHTZ-FM 100.3 (CHR) 32 Ave of the Americas *TF:* 800-242-0100 ■ *Web:* www.z100.com	New York	NY	10013	212-377-7900	
WINS-AM 1010 (N/T) 345 Hudson St *Web:* newyork.cbslocal.com	New York	NY	10014	212-315-7036	
WKTU-FM 103.5 (CHR) 32 Ave of the Americas *Web:* www.ktu.com	New York	NY	10013	212-377-7900	
WLTW-FM 106.7 (AC) 32 Ave of the Americas 2nd Fl *TF:* 800-222-1067 ■ *Web:* www.1067litefm.com	New York	NY	10013	212-377-7900	
WNYC-AM 820 (NPR) 160 Varick St 7th Fl *Web:* www.wnyc.org	New York	NY	10013	646-829-4400	
WNYC-FM 93.9 (NPR) 160 Varick St 7th Fl *Web:* www.wnyc.org	New York	NY	10013	646-829-4400	
WOR-AM 710 (N/T) 32 Ave of the Americas 3rd Fl *Web:* www.wor710.com	New York	NY	10013	212-377-7900	
WPLJ-FM 95.5 (AC) 2 Penn Plaza 17th Fl *Web:* www.955plj.nyc	New York	NY	10121	212-613-8905	613-8956
WQHT-FM 97.1 (Urban) 395 Hudson St 7th Fl *TF:* 800-223-9797 ■ *Web:* www.hot97.com	New York	NY	10014	212-229-9797	929-8559
WQXR-FM 96.3 (Clas) 160 Varick St 8th Fl *Web:* www.wqxr.org	New York	NY	10013	646-829-4400	
WSJT-FM 94.1 (NAC) 1271 Avenue of Americas Ste 200 **Fax Area Code: 727* ■ *Web:* www.cbsradio.com	New York	NY	10020	212-649-9600	579-9250*
WWPR-FM 105.1 (Urban) 32 Ave of the Americas *TF:* 800-585-1051 ■ *Web:* www.power1051fm.com	New York	NY	10013	212-377-7900	

645-112 Norfolk/Virginia Beach, VA

Station / Address	City	State	Zip	Phone	Fax
92.1 The Beat 1003 Norfolk Sq *Web:* thebeatva.iheart.com	Norfolk	VA	23502	757-466-0009	
WGH 5589 Greenwich Rd Ste 200 *Web:* www.espnradio1310.com	Virginia Beach	VA	23462	757-671-1000	

Phone Fax

WGH-FM 97.3 (Ctry)
5589 Greenwich Rd Ste 200 .... Virginia Beach VA 23462 757-671-1000
Web: www.eagle97.com

WHRO-FM 90.3 (Clas) 5200 Hampton Blvd .... Norfolk VA 23508 757-889-9400 489-0007
Web: www.whro.org

WPTE-FM 94.9 (AC)
236 Clearfield Ave Ste 206 .... Virginia Beach VA 23462 757-497-2000
Web: www.pointradio.com

WVBW-FM 92.9 (Oldies)
5589 Greenwich Rd Ste 200 .... Virginia Beach VA 23462 757-671-1000
Web: www.929thewave.com

645-113 Ocean City, MD

Phone Fax

WOCM-FM 98.1 (AAA)
Irie Radio 117 W 49th St. .... Ocean City MD 21842 410-723-3683
Web: ocean98.com

645-114 Oklahoma City, OK

Phone Fax

KATT-FM 100.5 (Rock)
4045 NW 64th St Ste 600 .... Oklahoma City OK 73116 405-848-0100
Web: www.katt.com

KMGL-FM 104.1 (AC) 400 E Britton Rd. .... Oklahoma City OK 73114 405-478-5104
Web: www.magic104.com

KOMA-FM 92.5 (Oldies) 400 E Britton Rd .... Oklahoma City OK 73114 405-478-5104
Web: www.komaradio.com

KRXO-FM 107.7 (CR) 400 E Britton Rd. .... Oklahoma City OK 73114 405-478-5104
Web: www.krxo.com

KTOK-AM 1000 (N/T)
1900 Northwest Expy Ste 1000. .... Oklahoma City OK 73118 405-840-5271 858-5333
Web: ktok.iheart.com

KYIS-FM 98.9 (AC)
4045 NW 64th St Ste 600 .... Oklahoma City OK 73116 405-848-0100
Web: www.kyis.com

645-115 Omaha, NE

Phone Fax

KAT 103.7FM 5010 Underwood Ave .... Omaha NE 68132 402-561-2000 556-8937
Web: thekat.iheart.com

KFAB-AM 1110 (N/T) 5010 Underwood Ave .... Omaha NE 68132 402-561-2000 556-8937
Web: kfab.iheart.com

KIOS-FM 91.5 (NPR) 3230 Burt St .... Omaha NE 68131 402-557-2777 557-2559
Web: www.kios.org

KISS FM 96.1 5010 Underwood Ave .... Omaha NE 68132 402-558-9696
Web: 961kissonline.iheart.com

KQCH-FM 94.1 (CHR) 10714 Mockingbird Dr. .... Omaha NE 68127 402-938-9400
Web: www.channel941.com

KQKQ-FM 98.5 (CHR) 5011 Capitol Ave .... Omaha NE 68132 402-342-2000 827-5293
Web: pro.kqkq-fm.tritonflex.com

WBKL-FM 92.7 (Rel) PO Box 2098. .... Omaha NE 68103 800-525-5683
TF: 800-525-5683 ■ *Web:* www.klove.com

Z92 FM 10714 Mockingbird Dr. .... Omaha NE 68127 800-955-9230
TF: 800-955-9230 ■ *Web:* www.z92.com

645-116 Orlando, FL

Phone Fax

WCFB-FM 94.5 (AC) 4192 N John Young Pkwy .... Orlando FL 32804 407-294-2945 297-7595
Web: www.star945.com

WDBO-AM 580 (N/T) 4192 N John Young Pkwy .... Orlando FL 32804 321-281-2000
Web: www.news965.com

WJHM-FM 102 (Urban) 1800 Pembrook Dr Ste 400 ...... Orlando FL 32810 407-919-1000 816-9070
TF: 866-438-0220 ■ *Web:* 1019ampradio.cbslocal.com

WMMO-FM 98.9 (AC) 4192 N John Young Pkwy. .... Orlando FL 32804 321-281-2000 422-6538*
**Fax Area Code:* 407 ■ *Web:* www.wmmo.com

WOCL-FM 105.9 (Rock) 1800 Pembrook Dr Ste 400 ...... Orlando FL 32810 407-919-1000 919-1190
TF: 877-919-1059 ■ *Web:* 1059sunnyfm.cbslocal.com

WOMX-FM 105.1 (AC) 1800 Pembrook Dr Ste 400 .... Orlando FL 32810 407-919-1000 919-1190
TF: 877-919-1051 ■ *Web:* mix1051.cbslocal.com

WPYO-FM 95.3 (CHR) 4192 N John Young Pkwy. .... Orlando FL 32804 321-281-2000 291-6912*
**Fax Area Code:* 407 ■ *Web:* www.power953.com

WUCF-FM 89.9 (Jazz) PO Box 162199. .... Orlando FL 32816 407-823-0899
Web: www.wucf.ucf.edu

WWKA-FM 92.3 (Ctry) 4192 N John Young Pkwy .... Orlando FL 32804 407-424-9236 299-4947
TF: 866-438-0220 ■ *Web:* www.k923orlando.com

645-117 Ottawa, ON

Phone Fax

CBVE-FM 104.7 (CBC) PO Box 3220 Station C .... Ottawa ON K1Y1E4 866-306-4636
TF: 866-306-4636 ■ *Web:* www.cbc.radio-canada.ca

CFRA-AM 580 (N/T) 87 George St. .... Ottawa ON K1N9H7 613-789-2486
TF: 800-580-2372 ■ *Web:* www.cfra.com

CHEZ-FM 106.1 (CR) 2001 Thurston Dr .... Ottawa ON K1G6C9 613-736-2001
Web: www.chez106.com

CIWW-AM 1310 (Oldies) 2001 Thurston Dr. .... Ottawa ON K1G6C9 613-736-2001
Web: www.1310news.com

Ottawa-AM 1200 (Sports) 87 George St .... Ottawa ON K1N9H7 613-789-2486 738-5024
TF: 877-670-1200 ■ *Web:* www.tsn.ca/radio/ottawa-1200

645-118 Oxnard, CA

Phone Fax

KDAR-FM 98.3 (Rel) 500 E Esplanade Dr .... Oxnard CA 93036 805-485-8881
Web: www.kdar.com

KMLA-FM 103.7 (Span) 355 So 'A' St Ste 103. .... Oxnard CA 93030 805-385-5656 385-5690
Web: www.lam1037.com

KXLM-FM 102.9 (Span) 200 S Ste 400 .... Oxnard CA 93030 805-240-2070 240-5960
Web: www.radiolazer.com

645-119 Palm Springs, CA

Phone Fax

Desert Radio Group
1321 N Gene Autry Trl .... Palm Springs CA 92262 760-322-7890 322-5493

Jammin-FM 99.5 (Alt) 75153 Merle Dr Ste G .... Palm Desert CA 92211 760-568-4550
Web: www.jammin995fm.com

KCLB-FM 93.7 (Rock)
1321 N Gene Autry Trl .... Palm Springs CA 92262 760-322-7890
Web: 937kclb.com

KPLM-FM 106.1 (Ctry) 75153 Merle Dr Ste G .... Palm Desert CA 92211 760-568-4550
Web: www.thebig106.com

KPSI-AM 920 (N/T)
2100 Tahquitz Canyon Way .... Palm Springs CA 92262 760-325-2582
Web: www.newstalk920.com

KPSI-FM 100.5 (AC)
1321 N Gene Autry Trail .... Palm Springs CA 92262 760-323-1005
Web: www.mix1005.fm

645-120 Pensacola, FL

Phone Fax

WPCS-FM 89.5 (Rel) PO Box 18000. .... Pensacola FL 32523 850-479-6570
TF: 800-726-1191 ■ *Web:* www.rejoice.org

WPNN-AM 790 (N/T) 3801 N Pace Blvd .... Pensacola FL 32505 850-433-1141 433-1142
Web: talk790.com

WUWF-FM 88.1 (NPR) 11000 University Pkwy. .... Pensacola FL 32514 850-474-2787
TF: 800-239-9893 ■ *Web:* www.wuwf.org

645-121 Peoria, IL

Phone Fax

JMP Media LLC 331 Fulton St Ste 1200 .... Peoria IL 61602 309-637-3700
Web: www.jmpmedia.com

WCBU-FM 89.9 (NPR) 1501 W Bradley Ave .... Peoria IL 61625 309-677-3690
TF: 888-488-9228 ■ *Web:* peoriapublicradio.org

WCIC-FM 91.5 (Rel) 3902 W Baring Trace .... Peoria IL 61615 877-692-9242 692-9241*
**Fax Area Code:* 309 ■ *TF:* 877-692-9242 ■ *Web:* www.wcicfm.org

WFYR-FM 97.3 (Ctry) 120 Eaton St .... Peoria IL 61603 309-673-0973
Web: www.973nashfm.com

WGLO-FM 95.5 (CR) 120 Eaton St. .... Peoria IL 61603 309-676-9595 676-5000
Web: www.955glo.com

WXCL-FM 104.9 (Ctry) 331 Fulton St 12th Fl. .... Peoria IL 61602 309-637-3700
Web: www.1049thewolf.com

645-122 Philadelphia, PA

Phone Fax

KYW-NEWSRADIO 1060 (N/T)
400 Market St 10th Fl .... Philadelphia PA 19106 215-238-1060 238-4657
Web: philadelphia.cbslocal.com

WEMG-AM 1310 (Span)
1341 N Delaware Ave Ste 509. .... Philadelphia PA 19125 215-426-1900 426-1550

WHYY-FM 90.9 (NPR) 150 N Sixth St. .... Philadelphia PA 19106 215-351-1200 351-1211
Web: www.whyy.org

WRTI-FM 90.1 (NPR)
1509 Cecil B Moore Ave 3rd Fl. .... Philadelphia PA 19121 215-204-8405 204-7027
TF: 866-809-9784 ■ *Web:* www.wrti.org

WXPN-FM 88.5 (AAA) 3025 Walnut St .... Philadelphia PA 19104 215-898-6677 898-0707
Web: www.xpn.org

645-123 Phoenix, AZ

Phone Fax

KESZ-FM 99.9 (AC) 4686 E Van Buren St Ste 300. .... Phoenix AZ 85008 602-374-6000
Web: kez999.iheart.com

KNIX-FM 102.5 (Ctry)
4686 E Van Buren St Ste 300 .... Phoenix AZ 85008 602-374-6000 374-6035
Web: knixcountry.iheart.com

KOOL-FM 94.5 (Oldies) 840 N Central Ave. .... Phoenix AZ 85004 602-260-9494 440-6530
TF: 800-222-4357 ■ *Web:* kool.cbslocal.com

KSLX-FM 100.7 (CR)
4343 E Camelback Rd Ste 200 .... Phoenix AZ 85018 602-260-1007
Web: kslx.com

KTAR-FM 98.7 7740 N 16th St Ste 200. .... Phoenix AZ 85020 602-274-6200
Web: ktar.com

KZON-FM 101.5 (Urban) 840 N Central Ave. .... Phoenix AZ 85004 602-452-1000
Web: live1015phoenix.cbslocal.com

KZZP-FM 104.7 (CHR)
4686 E Van Buren St Ste 300 .... Phoenix AZ 85008 602-374-6000 374-6035
TF: 877-541-1966

La 105.9 4745 N Seventh St Ste 140 .... Phoenix AZ 85014 602-308-7900 308-7979
Web: www.univision.com/musica

645-124 Pierre, SD

Station	City	State	Zip	Phone	Fax
KCCR-AM 1240 106 W Capitol Ave *Web:* www.todayskccr.com	Pierre	SD	57501	605-224-1240	945-4270
KMLO-FM 100.7 (Ctry) 214 W Pleasant Dr *TF:* 800-658-5439 ■ *Web:* www.drgnews.com	Pierre	SD	57501	605-224-8686	224-8984
KPLO-FM 94.5 (Ctry) 214 W Pleasant Dr *TF General:* 800-658-5439 ■ *Web:* www.drgnews.com	Pierre	SD	57501	605-224-8686	224-8984

645-125 Pittsburgh, PA

Station	City	State	Zip	Phone	Fax
105.9 The X 200 Fleet St Fl 4 *Web:* 1059thex.iheart.com	Pittsburgh	PA	15220	412-937-1441	937-0323
KQV-AM 1410 (N/T) 650 Smithfield St Ste 620 Ctr City Towers *TF:* 888-272-7229 ■ *Web:* www.kqv.com	Pittsburgh	PA	15222	412-562-5900	562-5903
WDSY-FM 107.9 (Ctry) 651 Holiday Dr Foster Plz 2nd Fl *Web:* y108.cbslocal.com	Pittsburgh	PA	15220	412-920-9400	920-9449
WDUQ-FM 90.5 (NPR) 67 Bedford Sq *Web:* www.wesa.fm	Pittsburgh	PA	15203	412-381-9131	
WDVE-FM 102.5 (Rock) 200 Fleet St *Web:* dve.iheart.com	Pittsburgh	PA	15220	412-937-1441	937-0323
WKST-FM 96.1 (CHR) 200 Fleet St 4th Fl *Web:* 961kiss.iheart.com	Pittsburgh	PA	15220	412-937-1441	937-0323
WLTJ-FM 92.9 (AC) 650 Smithfield St Ste 2200 *Web:* www.q929fm.com	Pittsburgh	PA	15222	412-316-3342	316-3388
WQED-FM 89.3 (Clas) 4802 Fifth Ave *TF:* 800-876-1316 ■ *Web:* www.wqed.org	Pittsburgh	PA	15213	412-622-1436	622-7073
WSHH-FM 99.7 (AC) 900 Parish St 3rd Fl *Web:* www.wshh.com	Pittsburgh	PA	15220	412-875-9500	875-9474
WZPT-FM 100.7 (AC) 651 Holiday Dr Foster Plz 5 *Web:* starpittsburgh.cbslocal.com	Pittsburgh	PA	15220	412-920-9400	920-9449

645-126 Pocatello, ID

Station	City	State	Zip	Phone	Fax
KISU-FM 91.1 (NPR) Idaho State University 921 S Eigth Ave *Web:* www.isu.edu/kisufm	Pocatello	ID	83209	208-282-3691	282-4600
KZBQ-FM 93.7 (Ctry) PO Box 97 *Web:* www.kzbq.com	Pocatello	ID	83204	208-234-1290	234-9451
Pacific Empire Radio Corp 403 Capital St *Web:* pacempire.com	Lewiston	ID	83501	208-743-6564	

645-127 Portland, ME

Station	City	State	Zip	Phone	Fax
WRED-FM 95.9 (Urban) 779 Warren Ave *Web:* atlanticcoastradio.com	Portland	ME	04103	207-773-9695	761-4406
WTHT-FM 99.9 (Ctry) 477 Congress St 3rd Fl Annex *Web:* wtht.nh1media.com	Portland	ME	04101	207-797-0780	797-0368

645-128 Portland/Salem, OR

Station	City	State	Zip	Phone	Fax
106.7 The Eagle 13333 SW 68th Pkwy Ste 310 *Web:* 1067theeagle.iheart.com	Tigard	OR	97223	503-323-6400	323-6660
All Classical Portland 211 SE Caruthers St Ste 200 *TF:* 888-306-5277 ■ *Web:* www.allclassical.org	Portland	OR	97214	503-943-5828	802-9456
FM NEWS 101 KXL 1211 SW Fifth Ave Ste 6 *TF:* 877-733-1011 ■ *Web:* www.kxl.com	Portland	OR	97204	503-517-6000	
KBNP-AM 1410 (N/T) 278 SW Arthur St *TF:* 888-214-9237 ■ *Web:* www.kbnp.com	Portland	OR	97201	503-223-6769	
KBOO-FM 90.7 (Var) 20 SE Eigth Ave	Portland	OR	97214	503-231-8032	
KBZY-AM 1490 (AC) 2659 Commercial St SE Ste 204 *Web:* www.kbzy.com	Salem	OR	97302	503-362-1490	362-6545
KEX-AM 1190 (N/T) 13333 SW 68th Parkway Ste 310 *TF:* 888-457-4838 ■ *Web:* 1190kex.iheart.com	Tigard	OR	97223	503-323-6400	323-6660
KFIS-FM 104.1 (Rel) 6400 SE Lk Rd Ste 350 *Web:* www.thefishportland.com	Portland	OR	97222	503-786-0600	786-1551
KGON-FM 92.3 (CR) 0700 SW Bancroft St *TF:* 800-222-9236 ■ *Web:* www.kgon.com	Portland	OR	97239	503-223-1441	223-6909
KINK-FM 101.9 (AAA) 1211 SW Fifth Ave *Web:* www.kink.fm	Portland	OR	97204	503-517-6000	
KNRK-FM 94.7 (Alt) 0700 SW Bancroft St *TF:* 800-777-0947 ■ *Web:* www.947.fm	Portland	OR	97239	503-733-5470	
KOPB-FM 91.5 (NPR) 7140 SW Macadam Ave *Web:* www.opb.org	Portland	OR	97219	503-293-1905	
KPDQ-FM 93.9 (Rel) 6400 SE Lake Rd Ste 350 *TF:* 800-845-2162 ■ *Web:* www.kpdq.com	Portland	OR	97222	503-786-0600	786-1551
KWBY-AM 940 (Span) 1665 James St *Web:* lapantera940.com	Woodburn	OR	97071	503-981-9400	
KWJJ-FM 99.5 (Ctry) 0700 SW Bancroft St *TF:* 866-239-9653 ■ *Web:* www.thewolfonline.com	Portland	OR	97239	503-733-9653	223-6909
KXJM-FM 107.5 (AC) 13333 SW 68th Pkwy Ste 310 *Web:* jamn1075.iheart.com	Portland	OR	97223	503-248-1075	
KYKN-AM 1430 (N/T) PO Box 1430 *Web:* www.kykn.com	Salem	OR	97308	503-390-3014	390-3728
Rip city radio 620 13333 SW 68th Pkwy Ste 310 *Web:* ripcityradio.iheart.com	Tigard	OR	97223	503-323-6400	323-6664
WMBD-AM 1470 (N/T) 1211 SW 5th Ave Ste 750 *Web:* www.1470wmbd.com	Portland	OR	97204	309-637-3700	

645-129 Providence, RI

Station	City	State	Zip	Phone	Fax
94 HJY 75 Oxford St Ste 302 *Web:* 94hjy.iheart.com	Providence	RI	02905	401-781-9979	781-9329
WBRU-FM 95.5 (Alt) 88 Benevolent St *Web:* www.wbru.com	Providence	RI	02906	401-272-9550	272-9278
WHJJ-AM 920 (N/T) 75 Oxford St Ste 302 *Web:* 920whjj.iheart.com	Providence	RI	02905	401-781-9979	781-9329
WRNI-AM 1290 (NPR) 1 Union Stn *Web:* ripr.org	Providence	RI	02903	401-351-2800	351-0246

645-130 Quebec City, QC

Station	City	State	Zip	Phone	Fax
Nrj 98.9 900 Dyouville 1st Fl	Quebec	QC	G1R3P7	418-687-9900	687-3106

645-131 Raleigh/Durham, NC

Station	City	State	Zip	Phone	Fax
B93.9 new county 3100 Smoketree Ct 7th Fl *Web:* b939country.iheart.com	Raleigh	NC	27604	919-878-1500	
Foxy 104.3 Fm 8001-101 Creedmoor Rd *TF:* 800-321-5975 ■ *Web:* foxync.hellobeautiful.com	Raleigh	NC	27613	919-848-9736	848-4724
Foxy 107.1 8001-101 Creedmoor Rd *TF:* 800-467-3699 ■ *Web:* foxync.hellobeautiful.com	Raleigh	NC	27613	919-848-9736	848-4724
WKIX-FM 102.9 (Oldies) 4601 6 Forks Rd Ste 520 *Web:* www.kix1029.com	Raleigh	NC	27609	919-790-9392	510-6990
WKNC-FM 88.1 (Rock) 2810 Cates Ave *Web:* wknc.org	Raleigh	NC	27695	919-515-2401	
WNCU-FM 90.7 (NPR) PO Box 19875 *Web:* www.wncu.org	Durham	NC	27707	919-530-7445	530-5031
WNNL-FM 103.9 (Rel) 8001-101 Creedmoor Rd *TF:* 877-310-9665 ■ *Web:* thelightnc.hellobeautiful.com	Raleigh	NC	27613	919-848-9736	
WPTF-AM 680 (N/T) 3012 Highwoods Blvd Ste 201 *TF:* 800-662-7979 ■ *Web:* www.wptf.com	Raleigh	NC	27604	919-790-9392	790-8369
WQDR-FM 94.7 (Ctry) 3012 Highwoods Blvd Ste 201 *Web:* www.947qdr.com	Raleigh	NC	27604	919-876-6464	790-8893
WQOK-FM 97.5 (Urban) 8001-101 Creedmoor Rd *Web:* hiphopnc.com	Raleigh	NC	27613	919-863-4840	
WRAL-FM 101.5 (AC) 3100 Highwoods Blvd Ste 140 *TF:* 800-745-3000 ■ *Web:* www.wralfm.com	Raleigh	NC	27604	919-890-6101	890-6146
WRDU CLASSIC ROCK 100.7 3100 Smoketree Ct 7th Fl *Web:* wrdu.iheart.com	Raleigh	NC	27604	919-878-1500	876-8578
WRJD-AM 1410 (Rel) 707 Leon St	Durham	NC	27704	919-220-3226	
WSHA-FM 88.9 (Jazz) 118 E S St *TF:* 800-241-0421 ■ *Web:* www.shawu.edu	Raleigh	NC	27601	919-546-8430	546-8315
WXDU-FM 88.7 (Alt) PO Box 90689 *Web:* www.wxdu.org	Durham	NC	27708	919-684-2957	

645-132 Rapid City, SD

Station	City	State	Zip	Phone	Fax
KFXS-FM 100.3 (CR) 660 Flormann St Ste 100 *Web:* www.foxradio.com	Rapid City	SD	57701	605-394-4487	343-9012
KIMM-AM 1150 (Ctry) 11 Main St	Rapid City	SD	57701	605-342-1150	343-1096
KKMK-FM 93.9 (AC) 660 Flormann St Ste 100 *Web:* schurz.com/properties/radio/rushmore-media-company	Rapid City	SD	57709	605-343-6161	343-9012
KLMP-FM 88.3 1853 Fountain Plz Dr *Web:* www.klmp.com	Rapid City	SD	57702	605-342-6822	342-0854
KOUT-FM 98.7 (Ctry) 660 Flormann St Ste 100 *Web:* www.katradio.com	Rapid City	SD	57701	605-343-6161	343-9012
KRCS-FM 93.1 (CHR) 660 Flormann St Ste 100 *Web:* www.hot931.com	Rapid City	SD	57701	605-343-6161	343-9012

645-133 Reno/Carson City, NV

Station	City	State	Zip	Phone	Fax
KBUL-FM 98.1 (Ctry) 595 E Plumb Ln *Web:* www.nashfm981.com	Reno	NV	89502	775-789-6700	789-6767
KDOT-FM 104.5 (Rock) 2900 Sutro St *TF:* 800-227-1885 ■ *Web:* www.kdot.com	Reno	NV	89512	775-329-9261	323-1450
KLCA-FM 96.5 (Alt) 961 Matley Ln Ste 120 *TF:* 855-354-9111 ■ *Web:* www.alice965.com	Reno	NV	89502	775-829-1964	825-3183
KNIS-FM 91.3 (Rel) PO Box 21888 *TF:* 800-541-5647 ■ *Web:* www.pilgrimradio.com	Carson City	NV	89721	775-883-5647	
KODS-FM 103.7 (Oldies) 961 Matley Ln Ste 120 *TF:* 855-354-9111 ■ *Web:* www.river1037.com	Reno	NV	89502	775-829-1964	825-3183
KOZZ-FM 105.7 (CR) 2900 Sutro St *Web:* www.kozzradio.com	Reno	NV	89512	775-329-9261	323-1450
KRNO-FM 106.9 (AC) 961 Matley Ln Ste 120 *Web:* 1069morefm.com	Reno	NV	89502	775-829-1964	825-3183

Phone | Fax

KUUB-FM 94.5 (Ctry) 2900 Sutro St. .... Reno NV 89512 775-329-9261 323-1450
Web: www.espn945.com

645-134 Richmond, VA

Phone | Fax

106.5 The Beat 3245 Basie Rd .... Richmond VA 23228 804-474-0000 474-0096
Web: 1065thebeat.iheart.com

98.9 The Wolf 300 Arboretum Pl Ste 590 .... Richmond VA 23236 804-327-9902
Web: www.989wolf.com

99.3/105.7 KISS FM
2809 Emerywood Pkwy Ste 300 .... Richmond VA 23294 804-672-9299
Web: kissrichmond.hellobeautiful.com

Cox Radio Inc 812 Moorefield Pk Dr Ste 300 .... Richmond VA 23236 804-330-5700 862-3301

WBBT-FM 107.3 (Oldies)
300 Arboretum Pl Ste 590 .... Richmond VA 23236 804-327-9902 327-9911
Web: www.1073bbt.com

WCDX-FM 92.1 (Urban)
2809 Emerywood Pkwy Ste 300 .... Richmond VA 23294 804-672-9299
Web: ipowerrichmond.com

WRNL-AM 910 (Sports) 3245 Basie Rd .... Richmond VA 23228 804-474-0000 474-0096
Web: foxsportsrichmond.iheart.com

WRVA-AM 1140 (N/T) 3245 Basie Rd .... Richmond VA 23228 804-474-0000 474-0096
Web: 1140wrva.iheart.com

WRXL-FM 102.1 (Rock) 3245 Basie Rd .... Richmond VA 23228 804-474-0000 474-0096
Web: xl102richmond.iheart.com

WXGI-AM 950 (Sports) 701 German School Rd .... Richmond VA 23225 804-233-7666 233-7681
TF: 877-994-4950 ■ *Web:* www.espn950am.com

645-135 Riverside/San Bernardino, CA

Phone | Fax

KCAL-FM 96.7 (Rock)
1940 Orange Tree Ln Ste 200 .... Redlands CA 92374 909-793-3554
Web: www.kcalfm.com

KCXX-FM 103.9 (Alt)
242 E Airport Dr Ste 106 .... San Bernardino CA 92408 909-890-5904 890-9035
Web: www.x1039.com

KGGI-FM 99.1 (CHR) 2030 Iowa Ave Ste A .... Riverside CA 92507 951-684-1991 274-4949*
**Fax:* Sales ■ *TF:* 866-991-5444 ■ *Web:* 991kggi.iheart.com

KPRO-AM 1570 (Rel) 7351 Lincoln Ave .... Riverside CA 92504 951-688-1570 688-7009
Web: kpro1570.com

KSGN-FM 89.7 (Rel)
2048 Orange Tree Ln Ste 200 .... Redlands CA 92374 909-583-2150 583-2170
TF: 888-897-5746 ■ *Web:* www.ksgn.com

KUCR-FM 88.3 (Var) 691 W Linden St .... Riverside CA 92507 951-827-3737 827-3240
Web: www.kucr.org

KVCR-FM 91.9 (NPR)
701 S Mt Vernon Ave .... San Bernardino CA 92410 909-384-4444 885-2116
TF: 800-533-5827 ■ *Web:* www.kvcr.org

645-136 Roanoke, VA

Phone | Fax

Sunny 93.5 3807 Brandon Ave Ste 2350 .... Roanoke VA 24018 540-725-1220 725-1245
Web: sunny935.iheart.com

WFIR-AM 960 (N/T) 3934 Electric Rd SW .... Roanoke VA 24018 540-345-1511 342-2270
TF: 800-367-7623 ■ *Web:* wfir960.com

WSLQ-FM 99.1 (AC) 3934 Electric Rd SW .... Roanoke VA 24018 540-387-0234 342-2270
TF: 800-410-9936 ■ *Web:* www.q99fm.com

WVTF-FM 89.1 (NPR) 3520 Kingsbury Ln .... Roanoke VA 24014 540-989-8900 776-2727
TF: 800-856-8900 ■ *Web:* www.wvtf.org

WXLK-FM 92.3 (CHR) 3934 Electric Rd SW .... Roanoke VA 24018 540-774-9200
Web: www.k92radio.com

645-137 Rochester, MN

Phone | Fax

KFSI-FM 92.9 (Rel) 4016 28th St SE .... Rochester MN 55904 507-289-8585 529-4017
Web: www.kfsi.org

KRCH-FM 101.7 (CR)
1530 Greenview Dr SW Ste 200 .... Rochester MN 55902 507-288-3888 288-7815
Web: laser1017.iheart.com

KROC-AM 1340 (N/T) 122 SW Fourth St .... Rochester MN 55902 507-286-1010
Web: www.krocam.com/info/contact_us.php

KWEB-AM 1270 (Sports)
1530 Greenview Dr SW Ste 200 .... Rochester MN 55902 507-288-3888 288-7815
Web: fan1270.iheart.com

645-138 Rochester, NY

Phone | Fax

WBEE-FM 92.5 (Ctry) 70 Commercial St .... Rochester NY 14614 585-423-2900
Web: www.wbee.com

WBZA-FM 98.9 (CR) 70 Commercial St .... Rochester NY 14614 585-423-2900
Web: www.rochesterbuzz.com

WCMF-FM 96.5 (CR) 70 Commercial St .... Rochester NY 14614 585-423-2900
TF: 800-222-9196 ■ *Web:* www.wcmf.com

WDKX-FM 103.9 (Urban) 683 E Main St .... Rochester NY 14605 585-262-2050 262-2626
Web: www.wdkx.com

WHAM-AM 1180 (N/T) 100 Chestnut St .... Rochester NY 14604 585-454-4884 454-5081
Web: wham1180.iheart.com

WPXY-FM 97.9 (CHR) 70 Commercial St .... Rochester NY 14614 585-423-2900
Web: www.98pxy.com

WXXI-AM 1370 (NPR) PO Box 30021 .... Rochester NY 14603 585-325-7500 258-0339
Web: interactive.wxxi.org

Phone | Fax

WXXI-FM 91.5 (Clas) PO Box 30021 .... Rochester NY 14603 585-325-7500 258-0339
Web: interactive.wxxi.org

WZNE-FM 94.1 (Alt) 28 E Main St 8th Fl .... Rochester NY 14614 585-399-5700
Web: www.thezone941.com

645-139 Rockford, IL

Phone | Fax

WNTA-AM 1330 (N/T) 2830 Sandy Hollow Rd .... Rockford IL 61109 815-874-7861 874-2202
Web: www.lamovidaradiorockford.com

WROK-AM 1440 (N/T) 3901 Brendenwood Rd .... Rockford IL 61107 815-398-9765 484-2432
Web: www.1440wrok.com

645-140 Sacramento, CA

Phone | Fax

Capital Public Radio Inc 7055 Folsom Blvd .... Sacramento CA 95826 916-278-8900 278-8989
TF: 877-480-5900 ■ *Web:* www.capradio.org

KCTC-AM 1320 (Sports) 5345 Madison Ave .... Sacramento CA 95841 916-334-7777
Web: espn1320.net

KDND-FM 107.9 (CHR) 5345 Madison Ave .... Sacramento CA 95841 916-334-7777
Web: www.endonline.com

KFBK-AM 1530 (N/T)
1545 River Park Dr Ste 500 .... Sacramento CA 95815 916-929-5325
Web: kfbk.iheart.com

KHTK-AM 1140 (Sports) 5244 Madison Ave .... Sacramento CA 95841 916-338-9200 338-9208
TF: 800-920-1140 ■ *Web:* sacramento.cbslocal.com

KKDO-FM 94.7 (NAC) 5345 Madison Ave .... Sacramento CA 95841 916-334-7777
Web: www.radio947.net

KKFS-FM 103.9 (Rel)
1425 River Pk Dr Ste 520 .... Sacramento CA 95815 916-924-0710
Web: www.1039thefish.com

KRXQ-FM 98.5 (Rock) 5345 Madison Ave .... Sacramento CA 95841 916-334-7777
Web: www.krxq.net

KSEG-FM 96.9 (CR) 5345 Madison Ave .... Sacramento CA 95841 916-334-7777
Web: www.eagle969.com

KTKZ-AM 1380 (N/T)
1425 River Pk Dr Ste 520 .... Sacramento CA 95815 916-924-0710 924-1587
TF: 888-923-1380 ■ *Web:* www.am1380theanswer.com

KXPR-FM 88.9 (Clas) 7055 Folsom Blvd .... Sacramento CA 95826 916-278-8900 278-8989
TF: 877-480-5900 ■ *Web:* www.capradio.org

KYMX-FM 96.1 (AC) 280 Commerce Cir .... Sacramento CA 95815 916-923-6800
Web: kymx.cbslocal.com

KZZO-FM 100.5 (AC) 280 Commerce Cir .... Sacramento CA 95815 916-923-6800 927-6468
Web: now100fm.cbslocal.com

645-141 Saint Louis, MO

Phone | Fax

KEZK-FM 102.5 (AC) 3100 Market St .... Saint Louis MO 63103 314-531-0000
Web: kezk.cbslocal.com

KPNT-FM 105.7 (Alt) 401 S 18th St .... Saint Louis MO 63103 314-231-1057 621-3000
Web: 1057thepoint.com

KTRS-AM 550 (N/T) 638 Westport Plaza .... Saint Louis MO 63146 314-453-5500 453-9704
TF: 888-550-5877 ■ *Web:* www.ktrs.com

KWMU-FM 90.7 (NPR) 3651 Olive St .... Saint Louis MO 63108 314-516-5968
Web: www.kwmu.org

KYKY-FM Y98 (AC) 3100 Market St .... Saint Louis MO 63103 314-531-0000 531-9855
Web: y98.cbslocal.com

WEW-AM 770 (Var) 2740 Hampton Ave .... Saint Louis MO 63139 314-781-9397 781-8545
Web: www.wewradio.com

645-142 Salt Lake City, UT

Phone | Fax

KBEE-FM 98.7 (AC) 434 Bearcat Dr .... Salt Lake City UT 84115 801-485-6700
Web: www.b987.com

KBZN-FM 97.9 (NAC)
257 East 200 South Ste 400 .... Salt Lake City UT 84111 801-364-9836 364-8068
Web: www.kbzn.com

KEGA-FM 101.5 (Ctry)
50 West Broadway Ste 200 .... Salt Lake City UT 84101 801-524-2600
TF: 866-551-1015 ■ *Web:* www.1015theeagle.com

KJMY-FM 99.5 (Rock)
2801 S Decker Lk Dr .... Salt Lake City UT 84119 801-908-1300 908-1310
Web: my995fm.iheart.com

KLO-AM 1430 (N/T)
257 East 200 South Ste 400 .... Salt Lake City UT 84111 801-364-9836
TF: 866-627-1430 ■ *Web:* www.kloradio.com

KODJ-FM 94.1 (Oldies)
2801 S Decker Lk Dr .... Salt Lake City UT 84119 801-908-1300 908-1415
Web: 941kodj.iheart.com

KSL RADIO & TV 55 N 300 W .... Salt Lake City UT 84101 801-575-5555
Web: www.ksl.com

KSL-AM 1160 (N/T) 55 N 300 W .... Salt Lake City UT 84180 801-575-7600
Web: www.ksl.com

KSOP-AM 1370 (Ctry)
1285 West 2320 South .... Salt Lake City UT 84119 801-972-1043 974-0868
Web: www.cc1370.com

KSOP-FM 104.3 (Ctry)
1285 West 2320 South .... West Valley City UT 84119 801-972-1043
Web: www.ksopcountry.com

KUBL-FM 93.3 (Ctry) 434 Bearcat Dr .... Salt Lake City UT 84115 801-485-6700
Web: www.kbull93.com

KUER-FM 90.1 (NPR) 101 S Wasatch Dr .... Salt Lake City UT 84112 801-581-6625 581-6758
Web: www.kuer.org

Station	City	State	ZIP	Phone	Fax
KZHT-FM 97.1 (CHR) 2801 S Decker Lake Dr *TF:* 800-888-8499 ■ *Web:* 971zht.iheart.com	Salt Lake City	UT	84119	801-908-1300	908-1310
KZNS-AM 1280 (Sports) 301 W S Temple	Salt Lake City	UT	84101	801-670-1280	
U-FM 92.5 50 W Bdwy Ste 200 *Web:* u92slc.com	Salt Lake City	UT	84101	801-524-2600	643-1811

645-143 San Antonio, TX

Station	City	State	ZIP	Phone	Fax
930 AM The Answer 9601 McAllister Fwy Ste 1200 *TF:* 866-308-8867 ■ *Web:* 930amtheanswer.com	San Antonio	TX	78216	210-344-8481	
KCYY-FM 100.3 (Ctry) 8122 Datapoint Dr Ste 600 *Web:* www.y100fm.com	San Antonio	TX	78229	210-615-5400	615-5331
KISS-FM 99.5 (Rock) 8122 Datapoint Dr Ste 600 *TF:* 855-787-2227 ■ *Web:* www.kissrocks.com	San Antonio	TX	78229	210-615-5400	615-5331
KKYX-AM 680 (Ctry) 8122 Datapoint Dr Ste 600 *Web:* www.kkyx.com	San Antonio	TX	78229	210-615-5400	615-5330
KQXT-FM 101.9 (AC) 6222 NW IH-10 *Web:* q1019.iheart.com	San Antonio	TX	78201	210-736-9700	735-8811
KSLR-AM 630 (Rel) 9601 McAllister Fwy Ste 1200 *TF:* 800-247-4784 ■ *Web:* www.kslr.com	San Antonio	TX	78216	210-344-8481	340-1213
KSTX-FM 89.1 (NPR) 8401 Datapoint Dr Ste 800 *TF:* 800-622-8977 ■ *Web:* www.tpr.org	San Antonio	TX	78229	210-614-8977	614-8983
KTSA-AM 550 (N/T) 4050 Eisenhauer Rd *Web:* www.ktsa.com	San Antonio	TX	78218	210-654-5100	
KXXM-FM 96.1 (CHR) 6222 NW IH-10 *Web:* mix961.iheart.com	San Antonio	TX	78201	210-736-9700	735-8811
WOAI-AM 1200 (N/T) 6222 NW IH-10 *TF:* 800-707-5150 ■ *Web:* woai.iheart.com	San Antonio	TX	78201	210-736-9700	832-3149

645-144 San Diego, CA

Station	City	State	ZIP	Phone	Fax
iHeartMedia San Diego 9660 Granite Ridge Dr Ste 100 *Web:* star941fm.iheart.com	San Diego	CA	92123	858-292-2000	294-2916
KFMB-AM 760 (N/T) 7677 Engineer Rd *TF:* 800-760-5362 ■ *Web:* www.760kfmb.com	San Diego	CA	92111	858-292-7600	
KFMB-FM 100.7 (AC) 7677 Engineer Rd *Web:* www.sandiegojack.com	San Diego	CA	92111	858-571-8888	
KHTS-FM 93.3 (CHR) 9660 Granite Ridge Dr Ste 100 *Web:* channel933.iheart.com	San Diego	CA	92123	858-292-2000	294-2916
KLNV-FM 106.5 (Span) 600 W Broadway Ste 2150 *TF:* 800-879-4278 ■ *Web:* www.univision.com	San Diego	CA	92101	619-235-0600	
KOGO-AM 600 (N/T) 9660 Granite Ridge Dr Ste 100 *Web:* kogo.iheart.com	San Diego	CA	92123	858-292-2000	715-3675
KPBS-FM 89.5 (NPR) San Diego State University 5200 Campanile Dr *TF:* 888-399-5727 ■ *Web:* www.kpbs.org	San Diego	CA	92182	619-265-6438	594-3812
KSCF-FM 103.7 (N/T) 8033 Linda Vista Rd *TF:* 888-388-1037 ■ *Web:* energy1037.cbslocal.com	San Diego	CA	92111	858-571-7600	571-0326
KSDS-FM 88.3 (Jazz) 1313 Pk Blvd *Web:* www.jazz88.org	San Diego	CA	92101	619-388-3037	388-3928
KSON-FM 97.3 (Ctry) 1615 Murray Canyon Rd Ste 710 *Web:* www.kson.com	San Diego	CA	92108	619-291-9797	543-1353
KYXY-FM 96.5 (AC) 8033 Linda Vista Rd *TF:* 888-560-9650 ■ *Web:* kyxy.cbslocal.com	San Diego	CA	92111	858-571-7600	571-0326
XEMO-AM 860 (Span) 5030 Camino de la Siesta Ste 403 *Web:* www.uniradio.com	San Diego	CA	92108	619-497-0600	
XHRM-FM 92.5 (Oldies) 6160 Cornerstone Ct E Ste 150 *Web:* www.magic925.com	San Diego	CA	92121	858-888-7000	
XHTZ-FM 90.3 (Urban) 6160 Cornerstone Ct E Ste 150 *Web:* www.z90.com	San Diego	CA	92121	858-888-7000	
XTRA-FM 91.1 (Alt) 6160 Cornerstone Ct E Ste 150 *Web:* www.91x.com	San Diego	CA	92121	858-888-7000	

645-145 San Francisco, CA

Station	City	State	ZIP	Phone	Fax
98.5 KFOX 201 Third St Ste 1200 *TF:* 877-410-5369 ■ *Web:* www.kfox.com	San Francisco	CA	94103	877-410-5369	
Autonet Mobile Inc 3636 N Laughlin Rd Ste 150 *TF:* 800-977-2107 ■ *Web:* www.autonetmobile.com	Santa Rosa	CA	95403	415-223-0316	
CHFM-FM 95.9 (AC) 139 Townsend St *Web:* kiss959.com	San Francisco	CA	94107	403-246-9696	
KALW-FM 91.7 (NPR) 500 Mansell St *Web:* www.kalw.org	San Francisco	CA	94134	415-841-4121	841-4125
KCBS-AM 740 (N/T) 865 Battery St 3rd Fl *Web:* sanfrancisco.cbslocal.com	San Francisco	CA	94111	415-765-8758	765-4146
KFOG-FM 104.5 (CH) 750 Battery St 3rd Fl *Web:* www.kfog.com	San Francisco	CA	94111	415-995-6800	995-6829
KHTH-FM 101.7 (AC) 1410 Neotomas Ave Ste 200 *Web:* hot1017.com	Santa Rosa	CA	95405	707-543-0100	571-1097
KISQ-FM 98.1 (Urban AC) 340 Townsend St Ste 5101 *Web:* 981thebreeze.iheart.com	San Francisco	CA	94107	415-975-5555	
KITS-FM 105.3 (Alt) 865 Battery St *TF:* 800-696-1053 ■ *Web:* live105.cbslocal.com	San Francisco	CA	94111	800-696-1053	
KMVQ-FM 99.7 (AC) 865 Battery St **Fax Area Code: 415* ■ *TF:* 888-456-9970 ■ *Web:* 997now.cbslocal.com	San Francisco	CA	94111	888-456-9970	765-4152*
KOIT-FM 96.5 (AC) 201 Third St Ste 1200 *Web:* www.koit.com	San Francisco	CA	94103	415-777-0965	
KQED-FM 88.5 (NPR) 2601 Mariposa St *TF:* 800-723-3566 ■ *Web:* www.kqed.org	San Francisco	CA	94110	415-864-2000	
KRCB FM 5850 Labath Ave *Web:* www.krcb.org	Rohnert Park	CA	94928	707-584-2020	
KSAN-FM 107.7 (Alt) 750 Battery St 3rd Fl *TF:* 888-303-2663 ■ *Web:* www.1077thebone.com	San Francisco	CA	94105	415-995-6800	
Wild 94.9 340 Townsend St Ste 5101 *TF:* 888-333-9490 ■ *Web:* wild949.iheart.com	San Francisco	CA	94107	415-975-5555	538-1000

645-146 San Jose, CA

Station	City	State	ZIP	Phone	Fax
KBAY-FM 94.5 (AC) 190 Pk Ctr Plz Ste 200 *TF:* 800-948-5229 ■ *Web:* www.kbay.com	San Jose	CA	95113	408-287-5775	
KRTY-FM 95.3 (Ctry) 750 Story Rd *Web:* www.krty.com	San Jose	CA	95122	408-293-8030	
KXSC-FM 104.9 (Alt) PO Box 6375 *TF:* 888-966-5332 ■ *Web:* www.kdfc.com	Artesia	CA	90702	415-546-8710	

645-147 Santa Fe, NM

Station	City	State	ZIP	Phone	Fax
KBAC-FM 98.1 (AAA) 2502 Camino Entrada Ste C *TF:* 888-321-5123 ■ *Web:* www.santafe.com	Santa Fe	NM	87507	505-988-5222	
KSWV-AM 810 (Span) 102 Taos St *TF:* 800-873-3372 ■ *Web:* santafenewmexican.com	Santa Fe	NM	87505	505-983-3303	
KTRC-AM 1260 (N/T) 2502 Camino Entrada Ste C *TF:* 888-321-5123 ■ *Web:* www.santafe.com/ktrc	Santa Fe	NM	87507	505-471-1067	

645-148 Savannah, GA

Station	City	State	ZIP	Phone	Fax
97.3 Kiss Fm 245 Alfred St *TF:* 800-543-3548 ■ *Web:* 973kissfm.iheart.com	Savannah	GA	31408	912-964-7794	964-9414
WJCL-FM 96.5 (Ctry) 214 Television Cir *Web:* www.kix96.com	Savannah	GA	31406	912-961-9000	961-7070
WQBT-FM 94.1 (Urban) 245 Alfred St *Web:* 941thebeat.iheart.com	Savannah	GA	31408	912-964-7794	964-9414
WRHQ-FM 105.3 (Rock) 1102 E 52nd St *Web:* www.wrhq.com	Savannah	GA	31404	912-234-1053	354-6600
WSOK-AM 103.5 245 Alfred St *Web:* 1230wsok.iheart.com	Savannah	GA	31408	912-964-7794	964-9414
WSVH-FM 91.1 (NPR) 13040 Abercorn St Ste 8 **Fax Area Code: 404* ■ *TF:* 877-472-1227 ■ *Web:* gpb.org/savannah	Savannah	GA	31419	912-344-3565	362-4564*
WTKS-AM 1290 (N/T) 245 Alfred St *TF:* 877-263-7995 ■ *Web:* newsradio1290wtks.iheart.com	Savannah	GA	31408	912-964-7794	964-9414

645-149 Scranton, PA

Station	City	State	ZIP	Phone	Fax
Wejl 149 Penn Ave *Web:* nepasespnradio.com	Scranton	PA	18503	570-346-6555	346-6038
WEZX-FM 106.9 (Rock) 149 Penn Ave *TF:* 800-228-4637 ■ *Web:* www.rock107.com	Scranton	PA	18503	570-346-6555	346-6038
WVMW-FM 91.7 (Alt) 2300 Adams Ave *Web:* www.vmfm917.org	Scranton	PA	18509	570-348-6202	

645-150 Seattle/Tacoma, WA

Station	City	State	ZIP	Phone	Fax
106.1 Kiss Fm 645 Elliott Ave W Ste 400 *TF:* 888-343-1061 ■ *Web:* kissfmseattle.iheart.com	Seattle	WA	98119	206-494-2000	
KCMS-FM 105.3 (Rel) 19319 Fremont Ave N *Web:* www.spirit1053.com	Shoreline	WA	98133	206-546-7350	
KING-FM 98.1 (Clas) 10 Harrison St Ste 100 *Web:* www.king.org	Seattle	WA	98109	206-691-2981	691-2982
KIRO-FM 97.3 (N/T) 1820 Eastlake Ave E *Web:* www.mynorthwest.com	Seattle	WA	98102	206-726-7000	
KISW-FM 99.9 (Rock) 1100 Olive Way Ste 1650 *Web:* www.kisw.com	Seattle	WA	98101	206-285-7625	215-9355
KJAQ-FM 96.5 (Var) 1000 Dexter Ave N Ste 100 *TF:* 866-416-5225 ■ *Web:* jackseattle.cbslocal.com	Seattle	WA	98109	206-805-1100	805-0932
KJR-AM 950 (Sports) 351 Elliott Ave W Ste 300 *TF:* 800-829-0950 ■ *Web:* sportsradiokjr.iheart.com	Seattle	WA	98119	206-494-2000	286-2376
KNDD-FM 107.7 (Alt) 1100 Olive Way Ste 1650 *Web:* www.1077theend.com	Seattle	WA	98101	206-421-1077	
KOMO-AM 1000 (N/T) 140 Fourth Ave N Ste 340 *Web:* www.komonews.com	Seattle	WA	98109	206-404-4000	404-3646
KPLZ-FM 101.5 (AC) 140 Fourth Ave N Ste 340 *TF:* 888-821-1015 ■ *Web:* www.star1015.com	Seattle	WA	98109	206-404-4000	404-1015
KPTK-AM 1090 (N/T) 1000 Dexter Ave N Ste 100 *Web:* seattle.cbslocal.com	Seattle	WA	98109	206-805-1100	805-0922
KUOW-FM 94.9 (NPR) 4518 University Way NE Ste 310 *TF:* 800-289-5869 ■ *Web:* www.kuow.org	Seattle	WA	98105	206-543-2710	543-2720

Station	City	State	ZIP	Phone	Fax
KVI-AM 570 (N/T) 140 Fourth Ave N Ste 340 *TF:* 888-312-5757 ■ *Web:* www.kvi.com	Seattle	WA	98109	206-404-4000	404-3648
KZOK-FM 102.5 (CR) 1000 Dexter Ave N *TF:* 800-252-1025 ■ *Web:* kzok.cbslocal.com	Seattle	WA	98109	206-421-1025	

645-151 Shreveport, LA

Station	City	State	ZIP	Phone	Fax
KBTT-FM 103.7 (CHR) 208 N Thomas *Web:* kbtt.fm	Shreveport	LA	71137	318-222-3122	320-0102
KDAQ-FM 89.9 (NPR) 1 University Pl PO Box 5250 *TF:* 800-552-8502 ■ *Web:* www.redriverradio.org	Shreveport	LA	71115	318-798-0102	797-5265
KDKS-FM 102.1 (Urban) 208 N Thomas *Web:* www.kdks.fm	Shreveport	LA	71137	318-222-3122	320-0102
KLKL-FM 95.7 (Oldies) 208 N Thomas *Web:* www.klkl.fm	Shreveport	LA	71137	318-222-3122	
KRUF-FM 94.5 (CHR) 6341 W Port Ave *Web:* k945.com	Shreveport	LA	71129	318-688-1130	
KVKI-FM 96.5 (AC) 6341 W Port Ave *TF:* 800-487-1840 ■ *Web:* www.965kvki.com	Shreveport	LA	71129	318-688-1130	687-8574
KXKS-FM 93.7 (Ctry) 6341 W Port Ave *Web:* mykisscountry937.com	Shreveport	LA	71129	318-688-1130	

645-152 Sioux Falls, SD

Station	City	State	ZIP	Phone	Fax
KELO-AM 1320 (N/T) 500 S Phillips Ave *Web:* kelo.com	Sioux Falls	SD	57104	605-336-1320	336-0415
KELO-FM 92.5 (AC) 500 S Phillips Ave *Web:* www.kelofm.com	Sioux Falls	SD	57104	605-331-5350	336-0415
KIKN-FM 100.5 (Ctry) 5100 S Tennis Ln *Web:* www.kikn.com	Sioux Falls	SD	57108	605-361-0300	
KKLS-FM 104.7 (CHR) 5100 S Tennis Ln *Web:* www.hot1047.com	Sioux Falls	SD	57108	605-361-0300	
KMXC-FM 97.3 (AC) 5100 S Tennis Ln *Web:* www.mix97-3.com	Sioux Falls	SD	57108	605-361-0300	
KNWC-AM 96.5 (Rel) 6300 S Tallgrass Ave *TF:* 888-569-5692 ■ *Web:* life965.fm	Sioux Falls	SD	57108	605-339-1270	339-1271
KRRO-FM 103.7 (Rock) 500 S Phillips Ave *TF:* 800-283-4867 ■ *Web:* www.krro.com	Sioux Falls	SD	57104	605-331-5350	336-0415
KSOO-AM 1140 (N/T) 5100 S Tennis Ln *Web:* www.ksoo.com	Sioux Falls	SD	57108	605-361-0300	
KTWB-FM 101.9 (Ctry) 500 S Phillips Ave *TF:* 888-293-2832 ■ *Web:* www.ktwb.com	Sioux Falls	SD	57104	605-331-5350	336-0415
KXRB-AM 1000 (Ctry) 5100 S Tennis Ln *Web:* www.kxrb.com	Sioux Falls	SD	57108	605-361-0300	
KYBB-FM 102.7 (CR) 5100 S Tennis Ln *Web:* www.b1027.com	Sioux Falls	SD	57108	605-361-0300	

645-153 South Bend, IN

Station	City	State	ZIP	Phone	Fax
Federated Media 421 S Second St *Web:* www.federatedmedia.com	Elkhart	IN	46516	574-295-2500	
WNDV-FM 92.9 (CHR) 3371 Cleveland Rd Ste 300 *TF:* 800-242-0100 ■ *Web:* www.u93.com	South Bend	IN	46628	574-273-9300	273-9090

645-154 Spokane, WA

Station	City	State	ZIP	Phone	Fax
KBBD-FM 103.9 (AC) 1601 E 57th Ave *Web:* www.1039bobfm.com	Spokane	WA	99223	509-448-1000	448-7015
KDRK-FM 93.7 (Ctry) 1601 E 57th Ave *Web:* www.937thecat.com	Spokane	WA	99223	509-448-1000	448-7015
KGA-AM 1510 (N/T) 1601 E 57th Ave *Web:* www.1510kga.com	Spokane	WA	99223	509-448-1000	448-7015
KHTQ-FM 94 « (Rock) 500 W Boone Ave *Web:* www.rock945.com	Spokane	WA	99201	509-324-4200	
KISC-FM 98.1 (AC) 808 E Sprague Ave *Web:* kiss981.iheart.com	Spokane	WA	99202	509-242-2400	242-1160
KKZX-FM 98.9 (CR) 808 E Sprague Ave *Web:* 989kkzx.iheart.com	Spokane	WA	99202	509-242-2400	242-1160
KXLY-AM 920 (N/T) 500 W Boone Ave *Web:* www.kxly.com	Spokane	WA	99201	509-326-6760	
KZBD-FM 105.7 (Rock) 1601 E 57th Ave *Web:* www.now1057fm.com	Spokane	WA	99223	509-448-1000	
Spokane Public Radio 2319 N Monroe St *TF:* 800-328-5729 ■ *Web:* spokanepublicradio.org	Spokane	WA	99205	509-328-5729	328-5764

645-155 Springfield, IL

Station	City	State	ZIP	Phone	Fax
WDBR 103.7 3501 E Sangamon Ave *Web:* www.wdbr.com	Springfield	IL	62707	217-753-5400	753-7902
WFMB-AM 1450 (Sports) 3055 S Fourth St *Web:* www.sportsradio1450.com	Springfield	IL	62703	217-528-3033	528-5348
WFMB-FM 104.5 (Ctry) 3055 S Fourth St *Web:* www.wfmb.com	Springfield	IL	62703	217-528-3033	528-5348
WMAY-AM 970 (N/T) *Mid-West Family Broadcasting* 1510 N Third St *Web:* www.wmay.com	Riverton	IL	62561	217-629-7077	629-7952
WNNS-FM 98.7 (AC) PO Box 460 *Web:* www.wnns.com	Springfield	IL	62705	217-629-5483	629-7952
WQQL-FM 101.9 (Oldies) 3501 E Sangamon Ave *Web:* cool939.com	Springfield	IL	62707	217-753-5400	753-7902
WTAX-AM 1240 (N/T) 3501 E Sangamon Ave *Web:* www.wtax.com	Springfield	IL	62707	217-753-5400	753-7902
WUIS-FM 91.9 (NPR) University of Illinois at Springfield 1 University Plz WUIS-130 *TF:* 866-206-9847 ■ *Web:* www.wuis.org	Springfield	IL	62703	217-206-9847	
WXAJ-FM 99.7 (CHR) 3055 S Fourth St *Web:* www.997kissfm.com	Springfield	IL	62703	217-528-3033	528-5348
WYMG-FM 100.5 (CR) 3501 E Sangamon Ave *Web:* www.wymg.com	Springfield	IL	62707	217-753-5400	753-7902

645-156 Springfield, MA

Station	City	State	ZIP	Phone	Fax
MIX 93.1 1331 Main St 4th Fl *TF:* 888-293-9310 ■ *Web:* mix931.iheart.com	Springfield	MA	01103	413-781-1011	
WHYN-AM 560 (N/T) 1331 Main St 4th Fl *Web:* whyn.iheart.com	Springfield	MA	01103	413-781-1011	734-4434
WNNZ-AM 640 (NPR) 131 County Cir *Web:* nepr.net	Amherst	MA	01003	413-735-6600	
WSCB-FM 89.9 (Urban) 263 Alden St *TF:* 800-727-0504	Springfield	MA	01109	413-748-3000	748-3473
WTCC-FM 90.7 (Var) 1 Armory Sq *Web:* www.wtccfm.org	Springfield	MA	01105	413-736-2781	

645-157 Springfield, MO

Station	City	State	ZIP	Phone	Fax
105.9 KGBX 1856 S Glenstone Ave *TF:* 800-445-1059 ■ *Web:* kgbx.iheart.com	Springfield	MO	65804	417-890-5555	890-5050
KSMS-FM 90.5 (NPR) Missouri State University 901 S National Ave *TF:* 800-767-5768 ■ *Web:* www.ksmu.org	Springfield	MO	65804	417-836-5878	836-5889
KSMU-FM 91.1 (NPR) Missouri State University 901 S National Ave *TF:* 800-767-5768 ■ *Web:* www.ksmu.org	Springfield	MO	65897	417-836-5878	836-5889
KSPW-FM 96.5 (CHR) 2330 W Grand St *Web:* www.power965.com	Springfield	MO	65802	417-865-6614	865-9643
KSWF-FM 100.5 (Ctry) 1856 S Glenstone Ave *TF:* 844-289-7234 ■ *Web:* 1005thewolf.iheart.com	Springfield	MO	65804	417-890-5555	
KTOZ-FM 95.5 (AC) 1856 S Glenstone Ave *TF:* 800-757-9550 ■ *Web:* alice955.iheart.com	Springfield	MO	65804	417-890-5555	890-5050
KTTS-FM 94.7 (Ctry) 2330 W Grand St *TF:* 800-621-3362 ■ *Web:* www.ktts.com	Springfield	MO	65802	417-865-6614	865-9643
KTXR-FM 101.3 (AC) 3000 E Chestnut Expy *TF General:* 855-586-8852 ■ *Web:* 1013theoutlaw.com	Springfield	MO	65806	417-862-3751	869-7675
Meyer Communications Inc 3000 E Chestnut Expy *Web:* radiospringfield.com	Springfield	MO	65802	417-862-3751	

645-158 Stamford/Bridgeport, CT

Station	City	State	ZIP	Phone	Fax
WEBE-FM 108 (AC) 2 Lafayette Sq *TF:* 800-932-3108 ■ *Web:* www.webe108.com	Bridgeport	CT	06604	203-333-9108	384-0600
WICC-AM 600 (N/T) 2 Lafayette Sq *Web:* www.wicc600.com	Bridgeport	CT	06604	203-333-9108	384-0600
WPKN-FM 89.5 (Var) 244 University Ave *Web:* www.wpkn.org	Bridgeport	CT	06604	203-331-9756	

645-159 Stockton, CA

Station	City	State	ZIP	Phone	Fax
KWIN-FM 97.7 (CHR) 3127 Transworld Dr Ste 270 *TF:* 800-585-5946 ■ *Web:* www.kwin.com	Stockton	CA	95206	209-507-8500	
KYCC-FM 90.1 (Rel) 9019 W Ln *TF:* 800-654-5254 ■ *Web:* www.kycc.org	Stockton	CA	95210	209-477-3690	477-2762

645-160 Syracuse, NY

Station	City	State	ZIP	Phone	Fax
B104.7 Syracuse's Country Station 500 Plum St Ste 100 *Web:* b1047.iheart.com	Syracuse	NY	13204	315-472-9797	472-2323
Community Broadcasters LLC 199 Wealtha Ave *Web:* www.commbroadcasters.com	Watertown	NY	13601	315-782-1240	
TK99 235 Walton St *Web:* tk99.net	Syracuse	NY	13202	315-472-9111	472-1888
WAER-FM 88.3 (Jazz) 795 Ostram Ave *Web:* www.waer.org	Syracuse	NY	13210	315-443-4021	
WAQX-FM 95.7 1064 James St *Web:* www.95x.com	Syracuse	NY	13203	315-472-0200	472-1146
WKRL-FM 100.9 (Alt) 235 Walton St *Web:* syracuse.krock.com	Syracuse	NY	13202	315-472-9111	472-1888
WNTQ-FM 93.1 1064 James St *Web:* www.93q.com	Syracuse	NY	13203	315-472-0200	478-5625
WSYR-AM 570 (N/T) 500 Plum St Ste 400 *Web:* wsyr.iheart.com	Syracuse	NY	13204	315-472-9797	472-2323

	City	State	ZIP	Phone	Fax
WYYY iHeartMedia 500 Plum St Ste 400 Web: y94fm.iheart.com	Syracuse	NY	13204	315-472-9797	472-2323

645-161 Tallahassee, FL

	City	State	ZIP	Phone	Fax
WBZE-FM 98.9 (AC) 3411 W Tharpe St Web: www.mystar98.com	Tallahassee	FL	32303	850-201-3000	
WFSQ-FM 91.5 (Clas) 1600 Red Barber Plaza TF: 866-321-9378 ■ Web: www.wfsu.org	Tallahassee	FL	32310	850-487-3086	487-2611
WFSU-FM 88.9 (NPR) 1600 Red Barber Plaza TF: 800-322-9378 ■ Web: www.wfsu.org	Tallahassee	FL	32310	850-487-3086	487-2611
WGLF-FM 104.1 (CR) 3411 W Tharpe St Web: www.gulf104.com	Tallahassee	FL	32303	850-201-3000	
WHTF-FM 104.9 (CHR) 3000 Olson Rd Web: www.hot1049.com	Tallahassee	FL	32308	850-386-8004	422-1897
WTNT-FM 94.9 (Ctry) 325 John Knox Rd Bldg G Web: 949tnt.iheart.com	Tallahassee	FL	32303	850-422-3107	383-0747
X101.5 325 John Knox Rd Bldg G Web: x1015.iheart.com	Tallahassee	FL	32303	850-422-3107	383-0747

645-162 Tampa/Saint Petersburg, FL

	City	State	ZIP	Phone	Fax
Am860 The Answer 5211 W Laurel St Ste 101 Web: am860theanswer.com	Tampa	FL	33607	813-639-1903	639-1272
Cox Media Group Tampa 11300 Fourth St N Ste 300 TF: 888-723-9388 ■ Web: www.wduv.com	Saint Petersburg	FL	33716	727-579-2000	
Straight Way Radio LLC 407 N Howard Ave	Tampa	FL	33606	813-259-9867	
WDAE-AM 620 (Sports) 4002 W Gandy Blvd TF: 888-546-4620 ■ Web: 620wdae.iheart.com	Tampa	FL	33611	813-832-1000	832-1090
WHPT-FM 102.5 (CR) 11300 Fourth St N Ste 300 TF: 800-771-1025 ■ Web: www.theboneonline.com	Saint Petersburg	FL	33716	727-579-2000	579-2271
WQYK-AM 1010 (Ctry) 9721 Executive Ctr Dr N Ste 200 Web: wqyk.cbslocal.com	Saint Petersburg	FL	33702	727-579-1925	
WQYK-FM 99.5 (Ctry) 9721 Executive Ctr Dr N Ste 200 Web: wqyk.cbslocal.com	Saint Petersburg	FL	33702	727-579-1925	
WSUN-FM 97.1 (Alt) 11300 Fourth St N Ste 300 TF: 877-327-9797 ■ Web: www.97xonline.com	Saint Petersburg	FL	33716	727-579-2000	
WTBN-AM 570 (Rel) 5211 W Laurel St Ste 101 Web: www.letstalkfaith.com	Tampa	FL	33607	813-639-1903	639-1272
WUSF Public Broadcasting 4202 E Fowler Ave TVB100 Web: www.wusf.usf.edu	Tampa	FL	33620	813-974-8700	
WUSF-FM 89.7 (NPR) 4202 E Fowler Ave TVB 100 TF: 800-741-9090 ■ Web: wusf.usf.edu/radio	Tampa	FL	33620	813-974-8700	974-5016
WXGL-FM 107.3 (AC) 11300 Fourth St N Ste 300 TF: 800-242-1073 ■ Web: www.1073theeagle.com	Saint Petersburg	FL	33716	727-579-2000	578-0949

645-163 Toledo, OH

	City	State	ZIP	Phone	Fax
River-FM 101.5 (AC), The 125 S Superior St Web: 1015theriver.iheart.com	Toledo	OH	43604	419-244-8321	244-7631
WGTE-FM 91.3 (NPR) 1270 S Detroit Ave PO Box 30 Web: www.wgte.org	Toledo	OH	43614	419-380-4600	380-4710
WIOT-FM 104.7 (Rock) 125 S Superior St Web: wiot.iheart.com	Toledo	OH	43604	419-244-8321	244-7631
WRQN-FM 93.5 (Oldies) 3225 Arlington Ave TF: 866-240-1935 ■ Web: www.935wrqn.com	Toledo	OH	43614	419-725-5700	
WSPD-AM 1370 (N/T) 125 S Superior St TF: 800-745-3000 ■ Web: wspd.iheart.com	Toledo	OH	43604	419-244-8321	244-7631
WXKR-FM 94.5 (CR) 3225 Arlington Ave TF: 866-240-9945 ■ Web: www.wxkr.com	Toledo	OH	43614	419-725-5700	

645-164 Topeka, KS

	City	State	ZIP	Phone	Fax
KMAJ-AM 1440 (N/T) 825 S Kansas Ave Ste 100 TF: 877-297-1077 ■ Web: www.kmaj.com	Topeka	KS	66612	785-272-2122	272-6219
KMAJ-FM 107.7 (AC) 825 S Kansas Ave Ste 100 TF: 877-297-1077 ■ Web: www.kmaj.com	Topeka	KS	66612	785-272-2122	272-6219
KTPK-FM 106.9 (Ctry) 1210 SW Executive Dr Web: www.ktpk1069.com	Topeka	KS	66615	785-273-1069	
KWIC-FM 99.3 (Oldies) 825 S Kansas Ave Ste 100 Web: www.eagle993.com	Topeka	KS	66612	785-272-2122	272-6219
WIBW-AM 580 (N/T) 1210 SW Executive Dr Web: www.wibwnewsnow.com	Topeka	KS	66615	785-272-3456	228-7282
WIBW-FM 94.5 (Ctry) 1210 SW Executive Dr Web: www.94country.com	Topeka	KS	66615	785-272-3456	228-7282

645-165 Toronto, ON

	City	State	ZIP	Phone	Fax
CFNY-FM 102.1 (Alt) 25 Dock Side Dr Web: www.edge.ca	Toronto	ON	M5A0B5	416-870-3343	
CHIN-AM 1540 (Ethnic) 622 College St Web: www.chinradio.com	Toronto	ON	M6G1B6	416-531-9991	531-5274
CHIN-FM 100.7 (Ethnic) 622 College St Web: www.chinradio.com	Toronto	ON	M6G1B6	416-531-9991	531-5274

645-166 Trenton, NJ

	City	State	ZIP	Phone	Fax
Myat Inc 360 Franklin Tpke Web: www.myat.com	Mahwah	NJ	07430	201-684-0100	
WIMG-AM 1300 (Rel) PO Box 9078 Web: www.wimg1300.com	Trenton	NJ	08650	609-695-1300	278-1588
WKXW-FM 101.5 (N/T) 109 Walters Ave TF: 800-800-7822 ■ Web: www.nj1015.com	Trenton	NJ	08638	609-359-5300	359-5301

645-167 Tucson, AZ

	City	State	ZIP	Phone	Fax
HOT-FM 98.3 (Urban) 3202 N Oracle Rd Web: hot983.iheart.com	Tucson	AZ	85705	520-618-2100	
KFMA-FM Radio 3871 N Commerce Dr Web: www.kfma.com	Tucson	AZ	85705	520-407-4500	
KHYT-FM 107.5 (CR) 575 W Roger Rd Web: www.khit1075.com	Tucson	AZ	85705	520-887-1000	
KIIM-FM 99.5 (Ctry) 575 W Roger Rd Web: www.kiimfm.com	Tucson	AZ	85705	520-880-5446	887-6397
KLPX-FM 96.1 (Rock) 3871 N Commerce Dr Web: www.klpx.com	Tucson	AZ	85705	520-407-4500	
KMXZ-FM 94.9 7280 E Rosewood Web: www.mixfm.com	Tucson	AZ	85710	520-722-5486	
KNST-AM 3202 N Oracle Rd Web: knst.iheart.com	Tucson	AZ	85705	520-618-2100	
KRQQ-FM 93.7 (CHR) 3202 N Oracle Rd Web: krq.iheart.com	Tucson	AZ	85705	520-618-2100	
KUAT-FM 90.5 (Clas) PO Box 210067 Web: radio.azpm.org/classical	Tucson	AZ	85719	520-621-5828	

645-168 Tulsa, OK

	City	State	ZIP	Phone	Fax
92.1 The Beat 2625 S Memorial Dr Web: 921thebeat.iheart.com	Tulsa	OK	74129	918-388-5100	665-0555
92.9 BOB FM 4590 E 29th St Ste 711 Web: www.929bobfm.com	Tulsa	OK	74114	918-743-7814	
KFAQ-AM 1170 (N/T) 4590 E 29th St Web: www.1170kfaq.com	Tulsa	OK	74114	918-743-7814	
KHTT-FM 106.9 (CHR) 4590 E 29th St Web: www.khits.com	Tulsa	OK	74114	918-743-7814	
KJSR-FM 103.3 (CR) 7136 S Yale Ave Ste 500 Web: 1033theeagle.com	Tulsa	OK	74136	918-493-3434	493-2376
KMOD-FM 97.5 (Rock) 2625 S Memorial Dr Web: kmod.iheart.com	Tulsa	OK	74129	918-388-5100	665-0555
KRAV-FM 7136 S Yale Ave Ste 500 Web: www.mix96tulsa.com	Tulsa	OK	74136	918-491-9696	
KRMG-AM 740 (N/T) 7136 S Yale Ave Ste 500 TF: 855-297-9696 ■ Web: www.krmg.com	Tulsa	OK	74136	918-493-7400	493-2376
KVOO-FM 98.5 (Ctry) 4590 E 29th St Web: www.kvoo.com	Tulsa	OK	74114	918-743-7814	
KWEN-FM 95.5 (Ctry) 7136 S Yale Ave Ste 500 Web: www.k95tulsa.com	Tulsa	OK	74136	918-493-7400	
KXOJ-FM 100.9 (Rel) 2448 E 81st St Ste 5500 Web: www.kxoj.com	Tulsa	OK	74137	918-492-2660	
Public Radio 89.5 800 Tucker Dr TF: 888-594-5947 ■ Web: publicradiotulsa.org	Tulsa	OK	74104	918-631-2577	631-3695

645-169 Tupelo, MS

	City	State	ZIP	Phone	Fax
WSEL-FM 96.7 (Rel) Mississippi 6	Pontotoc	MS	38863	662-489-0297	
WWZD-FM 106.7 (Ctry) 5026 Cliff Gookin Blvd Web: wizard106.iheart.com	Tupelo	MS	38801	662-842-1067	844-2887

645-170 Tuscaloosa, AL

	City	State	ZIP	Phone	Fax
98 TXT 3900 11th Ave S Web: 98txt.iheart.com	Tuscaloosa	AL	35401	205-344-4589	366-9774
WHIL-FM 91.3 (NPR) 166 Reese Phifer Hall PO Box 870150 TF: 800-654-4262 ■ Web: apr.org	Tuscaloosa	AL	35487	205-348-6644	
WQZZ-FM 104.3 (Urban AC) 601 Greensboro Ave Ste 507	Tuscaloosa	AL	35401	205-345-4787	
WRTR-AM 105.9 (Sports) 3900 11th Ave S Web: talkradio1059.iheart.com	Tuscaloosa	AL	35401	205-344-4589	366-9774
WTBC-AM 1230 (N/T) 2110 McFarland Blvd E Ste C TF: 800-518-1977 ■ Web: www.wtbc1230.com	Tuscaloosa	AL	35404	205-758-5523	752-9696
WTSK-AM 790 (Rel) 142 Skyland Blvd Web: 790wtsk.com	Tuscaloosa	AL	35405	205-345-7200	349-1715
WTUG-FM 92.9 (Urban) 142 Skyland Blvd Web: www.wtug.com	Tuscaloosa	AL	35405	205-345-7200	
WUAL-FM 91.5 (NPR) 920 Paul W Bryant Dr Box 870370 TF: 800-654-4262 ■ Web: www.apr.org	Tuscaloosa	AL	35487	205-348-6644	

645-171 Vancouver, BC

	City	St	Zip	Phone	Fax
CHQM-FM 103.5 (AC) 969 Robson St Ste 500 *Web:* www.qmfm.com	Vancouver	BC	V6Z1X5	604-871-9000	871-2901

645-172 Washington, DC

	City	St	Zip	Phone	Fax
WAMU-FM 88.5 (NPR) 4000 Brandywine St NW American University Radio *Web:* www.wamu.org	Washington	DC	20016	202-885-1200	
WHUR-FM 96.3 (Urban AC) 529 Bryant St NW *TF:* 855-787-2227 ■ *Web:* accessatlanta.com	Washington	DC	20059	202-806-3500	
WMAL-AM 630 (N/T) 4400 Jenifer St NW *Web:* wmal.com	Washington	DC	20015	202-686-3100	
WRQX-FM 107.3 (AC) 4400 Jenifer St NW Ste 400 *Web:* www.mix1073.com	Washington	DC	20015	202-686-3100	686-3091
WTLP-FM 103.9 (N/T) 3400 Idaho Ave NW *Web:* www.wtop.com	Washington	DC	20016	202-895-5000	
WTOP-FM 103.5 (N/T) 3400 Idaho Ave NW *Web:* www.wtop.com	Washington	DC	20016	202-895-5000	

645-173 West Palm Beach, FL

	City	St	Zip	Phone	Fax
KOLL-FM 105.5 3071 Continental Dr *TF:* 888-415-1055 ■ *Web:* 1055online.iheart.com	West Palm Beach	FL	33407	561-616-6600	616-6677
Sunny 107.9 Radio *Palm Beach Broadcasting* 701 Northpoint Pkwy Ste 500 *TF:* 800-919-1079 ■ *Web:* www.sunny1079.com	West Palm Beach	FL	33407	561-616-4777	
WBZT-AM 1230 (N/T) 3071 Continental Dr *TF:* 800-889-0267 ■ *Web:* wbzt.iheart.com	West Palm Beach	FL	33407	800-889-0267	
WJNO-AM 1290 (N/T) 3071 Continental Dr *Web:* wjno.iheart.com	West Palm Beach	FL	33407	561-616-6600	616-6677
WKGR-FM 98.7 (CR) 3071 Continental Dr *Web:* gaterrocks.iheart.com	West Palm Beach	FL	33407	561-616-6600	616-6677
WLDI-FM 95.5 (CHR) 3071 Continental Dr *Web:* wild955.iheart.com	West Palm Beach	FL	33407	561-616-6600	
WMBX-FM 102.3 (Urban) 701 Northpoint Pkwy Ste 500 **Fax Area Code:* 561 ■ *TF:* 800-969-1023 ■ *Web:* www.x1023.com	West Palm Beach	FL	33407	800-969-1023	686-0157*
WXEL-FM 90.7 (NPR) 3401 S Congress Ave *TF:* 800-915-9935 ■ *Web:* www.wxel.org	West Palm Beach	FL	33426	561-737-8000	369-3067

645-174 Wheeling, WV

	City	St	Zip	Phone	Fax
Mix 97.3 1015 Main St *Web:* mix973wheeling.iheart.com	Wheeling	WV	26003	304-232-1170	234-0041
WEGW-FM 107.5 (Rock) 1015 Main St *Web:* www.iheart.com	Wheeling	WV	26003	304-232-1170	234-0041
WOVK-FM 98.7 (Ctry) 1015 Main St *Web:* wovk.iheart.com	Wheeling	WV	26003	304-232-1170	234-0041
WVKF Radio 1015 Main St *Web:* kisswheeling.iheart.com	Wheeling	WV	26003	304-232-1170	234-0036
WWVA-AM 1170 (N/T) 1015 Main St *Web:* newsradio1170.iheart.com	Wheeling	WV	26003	304-232-1170	234-0041

645-175 Wichita, KS

	City	St	Zip	Phone	Fax
KEYN-FM 103.7 (Oldies) 9111 E Douglas Ste 130 *Web:* www.keyn.com	Wichita	KS	67208	316-685-2121	
KFBZ-FM 105.3 (AC) 2120 N Woodlawn St Ste 352 *Web:* www.1053thebuzz.com	Wichita	KS	67208	316-685-2121	
KFDI-FM 101.3 (Ctry) 4200 N Old Lawrence Rd *Web:* www.kfdi.com	Wichita	KS	67219	316-838-9141	
KFH-AM 1240 (N/T) 9111 E Douglas Ste 130 *Web:* www.kfhradio.com	Wichita	KS	67207	316-685-2121	
KFTI-AM 1070 (Ctry) 4200 N Old Lawrence Rd *Web:* www.kfdi.com	Wichita	KS	67219	316-838-9141	
KICT-FM 95.1 (Rock) 4200 N Old Lawrence Rd *Web:* www.t95.com	Wichita	KS	67219	316-838-9141	
KMUW-FM 89.1 (NPR) 3317 E 17th St N *Web:* www.kmuw.org	Wichita	KS	67208	316-978-6789	978-3946
KNSS-AM 1330 (N/T) 2120 N Woodlawn St Ste 352 *Web:* www.knssradio.com	Wichita	KS	67208	316-685-2121	
KTHR 9323 E 37th St N **Fax Area Code:* 306	Wichita	KS	67226	316-436-1073	873-2372*
Power 93.9 2120 N Woodlawn St Ste 352 *Web:* www.power935.com	Wichita	KS	67208	316-685-2121	685-3408

645-176 Wilmington/Dover, DE

	City	St	Zip	Phone	Fax
Delmarva Broadcasting Company Inc 2727 Shipley Rd *Web:* www.delmarvabroadcasting.com	Wilmington	DE	19810	302-478-2700	
News Radio 1410 WDOV 1575 McKee Rd Ste 206 *Web:* wdov.iheart.com	Dover	DE	19904	302-395-9800	674-8621
Super 91.7 WMPH Mount Pleasant High School 5201 Washington St Ext *Web:* www.wmph.net	Wilmington	DE	19809	302-762-3671	
WDEL-AM 1150 (N/T) 2727 Shipley Rd *TF:* 800-544-1150 ■ *Web:* www.wdel.com	Wilmington	DE	19810	302-478-2700	478-0100
WJBR-FM 99.5 (AC) 812 Philadelphia Pk *Web:* www.wjbr.com	Wilmington	DE	19809	302-765-1160	
WSTW-FM 93.7 (CHR) 2727 Shipley Rd *TF:* 800-544-9370 ■ *Web:* www.wstw.com	Wilmington	DE	19810	302-478-2700	478-0100

645-177 Winnipeg, MB

	City	St	Zip	Phone	Fax
94.3 The Drive 177 Lombard Ave *Web:* www.943thedrive.ca	Winnipeg	MB	R3B0W5	204-944-1031	989-5291
CBW-AM 990 (CBC) 541 Portage Ave *Web:* cbc.ca/news/canada/manitoba	Winnipeg	MB	R3B2G1	204-788-3222	
CFQX-FM 104.1 (Ctry) 177 Lombard Ave 3rd Fl *Web:* www.qx104fm.com	Winnipeg	MB	R3B0W5	204-944-1031	989-5291
CITI-FM 92.1 (CR) 4-166 Osborne St *Web:* www.92citifm.ca	Winnipeg	MB	R3L1Y8	204-788-3400	
CJOB-AM 680 (N/T) 1440 Jack Blick Ave *Web:* www.cjob.com	Winnipeg	MB	R3G0L4	204-786-2471	783-4512

645-178 Winston-Salem, NC

	City	St	Zip	Phone	Fax
Centennial Broadcasting LLC 6201 Town Ctr Dr Ste 210 *Web:* www.centennialbroadcasting.com	Clemmons	NC	27012	336-766-2828	
WBFJ-FM 89.3 (Rel) 1249 Trade St *Web:* wbfj.fm	Winston-Salem	NC	27101	336-721-1560	
WFDD-FM 88.5 (NPR) 1834 Wake Forest Rd Ste 8850 *TF:* 800-262-8850 ■ *Web:* www.wfdd.org	Winston-Salem	NC	27109	336-758-8850	758-3083
WSJS-AM 600 (N/T) 875 W Fifth St *Web:* www.wsjs.com	Winston-Salem	NC	27101	336-777-3900	777-3915

645-179 Worcester, MA

	City	St	Zip	Phone	Fax
Signalfire Wireless Telemetry Inc 43 Broad St *Web:* www.signal-fire.com	Hudson	MA	01749	978-212-2868	
WCRN-AM 830 (N/T) 82 Franklin St *Web:* www.wcrnradio.com	Worcester	MA	01608	508-438-0965	
WCUW-FM 91.3 (Var) 910 Main St *Web:* www.wcuw.org	Worcester	MA	01610	508-753-1012	
WICN-FM 90.5 (NPR) 50 Portland St *TF:* 855-752-0700 ■ *Web:* www.wicn.org	Worcester	MA	01608	508-752-0700	752-7518
WORC-AM 1310 (Span) 122 Green St Ste 2L *Web:* www.megaworcester.com	Worcester	MA	01604	508-791-2111	
WVNE-AM 760 (Rel) 70 James St Ste 201 *Web:* lifechangingradio.com	Worcester	MA	01603	508-831-9863	831-7964
WWFX-FM 100.1 (CR) 250 Commercial St 5th Fl *Web:* www.pikefm.com	Worcester	MA	01608	508-752-1045	973-0824
WXLO-FM 104.5 (AC) 250 Commercial St *Web:* www.wxlo.com	Worcester	MA	01608	508-752-1045	793-0824

645-180 Youngstown, OH

	City	St	Zip	Phone	Fax
WBBW-AM 1240 (Sports) 4040 Simon Rd *Web:* www.wbbw.com	Youngstown	OH	44512	330-783-1000	
WYSU-FM 88.5 (Clas) Youngstown State University 1 University Plz *Web:* www.wysu.org	Youngstown	OH	44555	330-941-3363	941-1501

646 RADIO SYNDICATORS

	City	St	Zip	Phone	Fax
American Urban Radio Networks 960 Penn Ave 4th Fl *TF:* 800-456-4211 ■ *Web:* www.aurn.com	Pittsburgh	PA	15222	412-456-4000	456-4040
Associated Press 1100 13th St NW Ste 700 *TF:* 800-824-5498 ■ *Web:* www.ap.org	Washington	DC	20005	202-641-9000	
BGC Partners Inc 499 Pk Ave *NASDAQ: BGCP* ■ *Web:* www.bgcpartners.com	New York	NY	10022	646-346-7000	346-6919
Car Clinic Productions 5675 N Davis Hwy *TF:* 888-227-2546 ■ *Web:* www.carclinicnetwork.com	Pensacola	FL	32503	850-478-3139	477-0862
Crystal Media Networks 7201 Wisconsin Ave Ste 780 *Web:* www.crystalmedianetworks.com	Bethesda	MD	20814	240-223-0846	
Lichtenstein Creative Media Inc 1 Broadway 14th Fl *Web:* www.lcmedia.com	Cambridge	MA	02142	617-682-3700	
Media Syndication Services 236 Massachusetts Ave NE *Web:* buildbettermedia.com	Washington	DC	20002	202-544-4457	546-8435
MediaTracks Communications 2250 E Devon Ave Ste 151 *Web:* www.mediatracks.com	Des Plaines	IL	60018	847-299-9500	299-9501

Phone Fax

New Dimensions Radio Broadcasting Network
PO Box 7847 .... Santa Rosa CA 95407 707-468-5215
Web: www.newdimensions.org

North American Network Inc
5335 Wisconsin Ave NW .... Washington DC 20015 202-243-0592 243-0594
Web: www.radiospace.com

Radio America 1100 N Glebe Rd Ste 900 .... Arlington VA 22201 703-302-1000 480-4141*
**Fax Area Code:* 571 ■ *TF:* 800-807-4703 ■ *Web:* www.radioamerica.com

Radio Express Inc
1415 W Magnolia Blvd Ste 201 .... Burbank CA 91506 818-295-5800 295-5801
Web: www.radioexpress.com

Salem Radio Network 6400 N Beltline Rd Ste 210 .... Irving TX 75063 972-831-1920 831-8626
Web: www.srnonline.com

Strand Media Group
3955 Hwy 17 Bypass Ste D PO Box 1389 .... Murrells Inlet SC 29576 843-626-8911 626-6452
Web: www.strandmedia.com

Syndicated Solutions Inc PO Box 1078 .... Ridgefield CT 06877 203-431-0790 431-0792
Web: www.syndicatedsolutions.com

Syndication Networks Corp
8700 Waukegan Rd Ste 250 .... Morton Grove IL 60053 847-583-9000 583-9025
TF: 800-743-1988 ■ *Web:* syndication.net

Talk Radio Network (TRN) PO Box 3755 .... Central Point OR 97502 888-383-3733
TF: 888-383-3733 ■ *Web:* www.trncorporate.com

TM Century Inc 2002 Academy Ln Ste 110 .... Dallas TX 75234 972-406-6800 406-6890
Web: www.tmstudios.com

Transmedia 719 Battery St .... San Francisco CA 94111 415-956-3118 956-2595
TF: 800-229-7234 ■ *Web:* www.transmediasf.com

WCLV 1375 Euclid Ave Idea Ctr .... Cleveland OH 44115 216-916-6301 916-6365
TF: 877-399-3307 ■ *Web:* wclv.ideastream.org

WestStar Talk Radio Networks 2711 N 24th St .... Phoenix AZ 85008 602-381-8200 381-8221
Web: www.weststar.com

Whie Radio Station 1000 Memorial Dr .... Griffin GA 30223 770-227-9451
Web: wkeuradio.com

647 RADIO & TELEVISION BROADCASTING & COMMUNICATIONS EQUIPMENT

See Also Audio & Video Equipment p. 1816; Telecommunications Equipment & Systems p. 3217

Phone Fax

24eight LLC 711 Third Ave 11th Fl .... New York NY 10017 212-888-2248
Web: www.24eight.com

ACG Systems Inc 133 Defense Hwy Ste 206 .... Annapolis MD 21401 410-224-0224
Web: www.acgsys.com

Adrienne Electronics Corp
7225 Bermuda Rd Unit G .... Las Vegas NV 89119 702-896-1858
Web: www.adrielec.com

ADS-B Technologies LLC
900 Merrill Field Dr .... Anchorage AK 99501 907-258-2372
Web: www.ads-b.com

Advanced Media Technologies Inc
3150 SW 15th St .... Deerfield Beach FL 33442 954-427-5711
Web: www.amt.com

Advatech Pacific Inc
1711 W Greentree Dr Ste 112 .... Tempe AZ 85284 480-598-4005 598-6767
Web: www.advatechpacific.com

AeroSat Corp 62 Rt 101A Ste 2B .... Amherst NH 03031 603-879-0205
Web: www.aerosat.com

Aethercomm Inc 3205 Lionshead Ave .... Carlsbad CA 92010 760-208-6002
Web: www.aethercomm.com

AheadTek Inc 6410 Via Del Oro .... San Jose CA 95119 408-226-9991 226-9195
TF: 800-971-9191 ■ *Web:* www.aheadtek.com

Airbiquity Inc 1011 Western Ave Ste 600 .... Seattle WA 98104 206-219-2700 842-9259
TF: 888-334-7741 ■ *Web:* www.airbiquity.com

Alien Technology Corp
18220 Butterfield Blvd .... Morgan Hill CA 95037 408-782-3900 782-3910
TF: 866-734-3669 ■ *Web:* www.alientechnology.com

Aluma Tower Company Inc
1639 Old Dixie Hwy .... Vero Beach FL 32960 772-567-3423
Web: www.alumatower.com

Ambrado Inc
1301 W President George Bush Hwy Ste 150 .... Richardson TX 75080 972-696-6800
Web: www.ambrado.com

Andersen Manufacturing Inc
3125 N Yellowstone Hwy .... Idaho Falls ID 83401 208-523-6460
TF: 800-635-6106 ■ *Web:* andersenhitches.com

Antedo Inc 1475 Saratoga Ave Ste 190 .... San Jose CA 95129 408-253-1870
Web: www.antedo.com

Antenna Products Corp 101 SE 25th Ave .... Mineral Wells TX 76067 940-325-3301 325-0716
Web: www.antennaproducts.com

Antenna Technology Communications Inc
450 N McKemy Ave .... Chandler AZ 85226 480-844-8501
Web: www.atci.com

Antennas for Communications 2499 SW 60 Ave .... Ocala FL 34474 352-687-4121 687-1203
Web: www.afcsat.com

Apex Airtronics Inc 2465 Atlantic Ave .... Brooklyn NY 11207 718-485-8560 485-8564

AR Worldwide 160 Schoolhouse Rd .... Souderton PA 18964 215-723-8181 723-5688
Web: www.ar-worldwide.com

Arkansas Valley Communications
1201 E Eigth St .... Russellville AR 72801 479-968-1502
Web: www.avc-wireless.com

Arris 60 Decibel Rd .... State College PA 16801 814-238-2461 238-4065
TF: 800-233-2267 ■ *Web:* www.arris.com

Arris Group Inc 3871 Lakefield Dr .... Suwanee GA 30024 678-473-2000 473-8470
NASDAQ: ARRS ■ *TF:* 866-362-7747 ■ *Web:* www.arris.com

Artel Video Systems Corp 5B Lyberty Way .... Westford MA 01886 978-263-5775 263-9755
TF: 800-225-0228 ■ *Web:* www.artel.com

Ascom (US) Inc 598 Airport Blvd Ste 300 .... Morrisville NC 27560 919-234-2500
Web: www.ascom.us

Associated Industries
11347 Vanowen St .... North Hollywood CA 91605 818-760-1000 760-2142
Web: www.associated-ind.com

Phone Fax

Atrex Inc 175 Industrial Loop S .... Orange Park FL 32073 904-264-9086
TF: 800-874-4505 ■ *Web:* www.atrexinc.com

ATX Networks Corp 1-501 Clements Rd W .... Ajax ON L1S7H4 905-428-6068
TF: 800-565-7488 ■ *Web:* www.atxnetworks.com

Avi Systems Inc 9675 W 76th St Ste 200 .... Eden Prairie MN 55344 952-949-3700 949-6000
TF: 800-488-4954 ■ *Web:* www.avisystems.com

Avtech Corp 3400 Wallingford Ave N .... Seattle WA 98103 206-695-8000 695-8011
Web: www.avtcorp.com

Axcera Corp 103 Freedom Dr .... Lawrence PA 15055 724-873-8100 873-8105
TF: 800-215-2614 ■ *Web:* www.axcera.com

Ball Aerospace & Technologies Corp
1600 Commerce St .... Boulder CO 80301 303-939-4000 460-2315*
**Fax:* Mail Rm ■ *Web:* www.ball.com/aerospace

Barker & Williamson 603 Cidco Rd .... Cocoa FL 32926 321-639-1510 445-6031
Web: www.bwantennas.com

Beacon Wireless Solutions Inc
206 Laird Dr Ste 207 .... Toronto ON M4G3W5 416-696-7555
TF: 866-867-7770 ■ *Web:* www.beaconwireless.net

Blonder Tongue Laboratories Inc
1 Jake Brown Rd .... Old Bridge NJ 08857 732-679-4000 679-4353
NYSE: BDR ■ *TF:* 877-407-8033 ■ *Web:* www.blondertongue.com

BridgeWave Communications Inc
3350 Thomas Rd .... Santa Clara CA 95054 408-567-6900
Web: www.bridgewave.com

Broad Reach Engineering Co
1113 Washington Ave Ste 200 .... Golden CO 80401 303-216-9777
Web: www.broadreachengineering.com

Broadcast Electronics Inc 4100 N 24th St .... Quincy IL 62305 217-224-9600 224-9607
Web: www.bdcast.com

Broadcast International Group
10458 Nw 31st Ter .... Doral FL 33172 305-599-2112
Web: www.bigmiami.com

Cabot Coach Builders Inc 99 Newark St .... Haverhill MA 01832 978-374-4530
Web: www.royalelimo.com

CalAmp Corp 1401 N Rice Ave .... Oxnard CA 93030 805-987-9000 419-8498
NASDAQ: CAMP ■ *Web:* www.calamp.com

Canyon State Wireless 8 Corral Rd .... Sierra Vista AZ 85635 520-458-4772

Cattron Group International
58 W Shenango St .... Sharpsville PA 16150 724-962-3571 962-4310
Web: www.cattron.com

Celerity Systems Inc
8401 Greensboro Dr Ste 500 .... McLean VA 22102 703-848-1900 848-2139
Web: www.celerity.com

Channell 26040 Ynez Rd .... Temecula CA 92591 951-719-2600 296-2322
OTC: CHNL ■ *Web:* www.channell.com

Chaparral Communications Inc
950 S Bascom Ave Ste 3111 .... San Jose CA 95128 408-294-2900 294-6969
Web: www.chaparral.net

Coaxial Dynamics
6800 Lake Abrams Dr .... Middleburg Heights OH 44130 440-243-1100 243-1101
TF: 800-262-9425 ■ *Web:* www.coaxial.com

Cobalt Digital Inc 2506 Galen Dr .... Urbana IL 61802 217-344-1243
TF: 800-669-1691 ■ *Web:* www.cobaltdigital.com

Cobra Electronics Corp 6500 W Cortland St .... Chicago IL 60707 773-889-8870 889-8870
NASDAQ: COBR ■ *Web:* www.cobra.com

Cohu Inc 12367 Crosthwaite Cir .... Poway CA 92064 858-848-8100 848-8185
NASDAQ: COHU ■ *TF:* 800-685-5050 ■ *Web:* www.cohu.com

COMARK Communications 104 Feeding Hills Rd .... Southwick MA 01077 413-998-1100
TF: 800-288-8364 ■ *Web:* www.comarktv.com

Communications & Power Industries Inc Beverly Microwave Div (CPI-BMD)
150 Sohier Rd .... Beverly MA 01915 978-922-6000 922-2736
Web: cpii.com/division.cfm/8

Comtech PST Corp 105 Baylis Rd .... Melville NY 11747 631-777-8900
Web: www.comtechpst.com

Comtech Systems Inc 2900 Titan Row Ste 142 .... Orlando FL 32809 407-854-1950 851-6960
Web: www.comtechsystems.com

Comtech Telecommunications Corp
68 S Service Rd Ste 230 .... Melville NY 11747 631-962-7000 962-7001
NASDAQ: CMTL ■ *Web:* www.comtechtel.com

Concurrent 4375 River Green Pkwy Ste 100 .... Duluth GA 30096 678-258-4000 258-4300
NASDAQ: CCUR ■ *TF:* 877-978-7363 ■ *Web:* www.concurrent.com

Connecticut Radio Holding LLC
1208 Cromwell Ave Ste C .... Rocky Hill CT 06067 860-563-4867
Web: connradio.com

Conolog Corp 5 Columbia Rd .... Somerville NJ 08876 908-722-8081
OTC: CNLG ■ *TF:* 800-526-3984 ■ *Web:* iniven.com

Continental Electronics Corp
4212 S Buckner Blvd .... Dallas TX 75227 214-381-7161 381-4949
TF: 800-733-5011 ■ *Web:* www.contelec.com

Control Dynamics Corp 960 Louis Dr .... Warminster PA 18974 215-956-0700

Dage-MTI Inc 701 N Roeske Ave .... Michigan City IN 46360 219-872-5514 872-5559
Web: www.dagemti.com

Data Flow Systems Inc
605 N John Rodes Blvd .... Melbourne FL 32934 321-259-5009
Web: dataflowsys.com

Datron World Communications Inc
3030 Enterprise Ct .... Vista CA 92081 760-597-1500 597-1510
Web: www.dtwc.com

Dayton-Granger Inc 3299 SW Ninth Ave .... Fort Lauderdale FL 33315 954-463-3451 761-3172
Web: www.daytongranger.com

Destron Fearing 490 Villaume Ave .... South Saint Paul MN 55075 651-455-1621
TF: 800-328-0118 ■ *Web:* www.destronfearing.com

Diamond Antenna & Microwave Corp
59 Porter Rd .... Littleton MA 01460 978-486-0039 486-0079
Web: www.diamondantenna.com

Dielectric Communications Inc 22 Tower Rd .... Raymond ME 04071 207-655-8100
Web: www.dielectric.com

Digital Broadcast Inc 2731 NW 41 St Ste A .... Gainesville FL 32606 352-377-8344
Web: www.digitalbcast.com

Digital Video Group Inc
8529 Meadowbridge Rd Ste 100 .... Mechanicsville VA 23116 804-559-8850
Web: www.digitalvideogroup.com

Dnfcontrols 12843 Foothill Blvd Ste D .... Sylmar CA 91342 818-898-3380
Web: www.dnfcontrols.com

Company	City	State	ZIP	Phone	Fax
Eagle Comtronics Inc 7665 Henry Clay Blvd *TF:* 800-448-7474 ■ *Web:* www.eaglecomtronics.com	Liverpool	NY	13088	315-622-3402	622-3800
Earmark LLC 1125 Dixwell Ave *Web:* www.earmark.com	Hamden	CT	06514	203-777-2130	777-2886
Earthwave Technologies Inc 710 E 64th St *Web:* www.earthwavetech.com	Indianapolis	IN	46220	317-257-8740	
Eco-Site Inc 240 Leigh Farm Rd Ste 415 *Web:* eco-site.com	Durham	NC	27707	919-636-6810	
Edge Velocity Corp 68 Stiles Rd Ste G *Web:* www.edgevelocity.com	Salem	NH	03079	978-304-0142	
EFJohnson Technologies 1440 Corporate Dr *TF:* 800-328-3911 ■ *Web:* www.efjohnson.com	Irving	TX	75038	972-819-0700	819-0639
Empower Rf Systems Inc 316 W Florence Ave *Web:* www.empowerrf.com	Inglewood	CA	90301	310-412-8100	412-9232
Envivio Inc 400 Oyster Pt Blvd Ste 325 *Web:* www.envivio.com	South San Francisco	CA	94080	650-243-2700	
Etm Electromatic Inc 35451 Dumbarton Ct *Web:* www.etm-inc.com	Newark	CA	94560	510-797-1100	797-4358
Eventide Inc 1 Alsan Way *Web:* www.eventide.com	Little Ferry	NJ	07643	201-641-1200	
F H Video Inc 6137 Geary Blvd Fl 2 *Web:* www.fhvideo.com	San Francisco	CA	94121	415-221-6128	
Fidelity Technologies Corp 2501 Kutztown Rd *Web:* www.fidelitytech.com	Reading	PA	19605	610-929-3330	929-1969
First Signal LLC 1750 Enterprise Way Se Ste 107 *Web:* www.firstsignal.com	Marietta	GA	30067	770-988-8744	
Fleet Safety Equipment Inc 1100 Hemlock St *Web:* www.fleetsafety.com	North Little Rock	AR	72114	501-370-9500	
GAI-Tronics Corp 400 E Wyomissing Ave *TF:* 800-492-1212 ■ *Web:* www.gai-tronics.com	Mohnton	PA	19540	610-777-1374	775-6540
GCS Inc 7640 Omnitech Pl *Web:* www.globalcoms.com	Victor	NY	14564	585-742-9100	
General Dynamics SATCOM Technologies 3111 Fujita St *TF:* 888-874-7646 ■ *Web:* www.gdsatcom.com/prodelin.php	Torrance	CA	90505	828-464-4141	464-4147
General Dynamics SATCOM Technologies 1500 Prodelin Dr *TF:* 888-874-7646 ■ *Web:* www.gdsatcom.com	Newton	NC	28658	828-464-4141	464-5725
Globecomm Systems Inc 45 Oser Ave *NASDAQ: GCOM* ■ *TF:* 866-499-0223 ■ *Web:* www.globecommsystems.com	Hauppauge	NY	11788	631-231-9800	231-1557
GPSi LLC 25307 Dequindre Rd *Web:* www.guidepointsystems.com	Madison Heights	MI	48071	248-399-4731	
Guardian Mobility Corp 43 Auriga Dr *TF:* 888-817-8159 ■ *Web:* www.guardianmobility.com	Ottawa	ON	K2E7Y8	613-225-8885	
HAL Communications Corp 1201 W Kenyon Rd PO Box 365 *Web:* www.halcomm.com	Urbana	IL	61803	217-367-7373	367-1701
Harmonic Inc 4300 N First St *NASDAQ: HLIT* ■ *TF:* 800-322-2885 ■ *Web:* www.harmonicinc.com	San Jose	CA	95134	408-542-2500	542-2511
Harris Corp 1025 W NASA Blvd *NYSE: HRS* ■ *TF:* 800-442-7747 ■ *Web:* www.harris.com	Melbourne	FL	32919	321-727-9100	
Harris Corp Government Communication Systems Div 2400 Palm Bay Rd *Web:* www.govcomm.harris.com	Palm Bay	FL	32905	321-727-9100	
Harris Corp RF Communications Div 1680 University Ave *TF:* 866-264-8040 ■ *Web:* rf.harris.com	Rochester	NY	14610	585-244-5830	242-4755
Hitachi Kokusai Electric America Ltd 150 Crossways Pk Dr *TF:* 855-490-5124 ■ *Web:* www.hitachikokusai.us	Woodbury	NY	11797	516-921-7200	496-3718
Honeywell International Inc 101 Columbia Rd PO Box M6/LM *NYSE: HON* ■ *TF:* 877-841-2840 ■ *Web:* www.honeywell.com	Morristown	NJ	07962	480-353-3020	
iBiquity Digital Corp 65 Stanford Blvd Ste 202	Columbia	MD	21045	410-872-0186	
ICOM America Inc 2380 116th Ave NE *TF:* 800-872-4266 ■ *Web:* www.icomamerica.com	Bellevue	WA	98004	425-454-8155	454-1509
ID Systems Inc 123 Tice Blvd Ste 101 *NASDAQ: IDSY* ■ *TF:* 866-410-0152 ■ *Web:* www.id-systems.com	Woodcliff Lake	NJ	07677	201-996-9000	996-9144
Ikegami Electronics USA Inc 37 Brook Ave *TF:* 800-368-9171 ■ *Web:* www.ikegami.com	Maywood	NJ	07607	201-368-9171	569-1626
Imagine GPS Inc 6847 S Ea Ste 104 *TF:* 866-477-2489 ■ *Web:* www.gpscity.com	Las Vegas	NV	89119	702-990-5600	
Industrial Communications & Electronics Inc 40 Lone St *Web:* www.induscom.com	Marshfield	MA	02050	781-319-1100	
Information Station Specialists Inc 3368 88th Ave *Web:* www.theradiosource.com	Zeeland	MI	49464	616-772-2300	
Integral Systems Inc 6721 Columbia Gateway Dr	Columbia	MD	21046	443-539-5008	
IONX LLC 515 S Franklin St *Web:* www.ionxlive.com	West Chester	PA	19382	484-653-2600	
IPMobileNet LLC 1221 E Dyer Rd Ste 250 *Web:* www.ipmn.com	Santa Ana	CA	92705	714-434-6019	
Iteris Inc 1700 Carnegie Ave Ste 100 *NYSE: ITI* ■ *TF:* 888-254-5487 ■ *Web:* www.iteris.com	Santa Ana	CA	92705	949-270-9400	
Jampro Antennas Inc 6340 Sky Creek Dr *Web:* www.jampro.com	Sacramento	CA	95828	916-383-1177	383-1182
Jem Engineering LLC 8683 Cherry Ln *TF:* 877-317-1070 ■ *Web:* www.jemengineering.com	Laurel	MD	20707	301-317-1070	
Kairos Autonomi Inc 508 West 8360 South *Web:* www.kairosautonomi.com	Sandy	UT	84070	801-255-2950	
Kenwood USA Corp 2201 E Dominguez St *TF:* 800-536-9663 ■ *Web:* www.kenwoodusa.com	Long Beach	CA	90810	310-639-9000	
Kintronic Laboratories Inc 144 Pleasant Grove Rd *Web:* www.kintronic.com	Bluff City	TN	37618	423-878-3141	
Klein Electronics Inc 349 N Vinewood St *Web:* www.headsetusa.com	Escondido	CA	92029	760-781-3220	
Knight Sky LLC 7470-F New Technology Way *Web:* www.knight-sky.com	Frederick	MD	21703	240-252-1950	
Kongsberg Maritime Inc 5373 W Sam Houston Pkwy N Ste 200 *Web:* www.km.kongsberg.com	Houston	TX	77041	713-329-5580	329-5581
KVH Industries Inc 50 Enterprise Ctr *NASDAQ: KVHI* ■ *Web:* www.kvh.com	Middletown	RI	02842	401-847-3327	849-0045
Kyocera Communications Inc 9520 Towne Centre Dr *Web:* www.kyoceramobile.com	San Diego	CA	92121	858-882-1400	
L-3 Communications Corp 600 Third Ave 34-35 Fl *NYSE: LLL* ■ *TF:* 800-351-8483 ■ *Web:* www.l-3com.com	New York	NY	10016	212-697-1111	490-0731
L-3 Communications ESSCO 90 Nemco Way *TF:* 877-282-1168 ■ *Web:* www.l-3com.com	Ayer	MA	01432	978-568-5100	772-7581
L-3 Communications Telemetry East Div 1515 Grundy's Ln *TF:* 800-351-8483 ■ *Web:* www.l-3com.com	Bristol	PA	19007	267-545-7000	545-0100
L-3 Communications Telemetry West Div 9020 Balboa Ave *TF:* 800-351-8483 ■ *Web:* www.l-3com.com/tw	San Diego	CA	92123	858-694-7500	694-7538
Larcan Inc 228 Ambassador Dr	Mississauga	ON	L5T2J2	905-564-9222	564-9244
Lightspeed Aviation Inc 6135 Jean Rd *TF:* 800-332-2421 ■ *Web:* www.lightspeedaviation.com	Lake Oswego	OR	97035	503-968-3113	
Logitek Electronic Systems Inc 5622 Edgemoor Dr *TF:* 877-231-5870 ■ *Web:* www.logitekaudio.com	Houston	TX	77081	713-664-4470	
MCL Inc 501 S Woodcreek Rd *TF Support:* 800-743-4625 ■ *Web:* www.mcl.com	Bolingbrook	IL	60440	630-759-9500	759-5018
MDI Security Systems Inc 12500 Network Dr Ste 303 *TF:* 866-435-7634 ■ *Web:* www.mdisecure.com	San Antonio	TX	78249	210-477-5400	477-5401
Mesh Dynamics Inc 2953 Bunker Hill Ln Ste 400 *Web:* www.meshdynamics.com	Santa Clara	CA	95054	408-373-7700	
Metropolitan Communications 309 Commerce Dr Ste 100 *Web:* www.mcsradio.com	Exton	PA	19341	610-363-5858	
MFJ Enterprises Inc 300 Industrial Pk Rd *TF:* 800-647-1800 ■ *Web:* www.mfjenterprises.com	Starkville	MS	39759	662-323-5869	323-6551
Microphase Corp 587 Connecticut Ave *Web:* www.microphase.com	Norwalk	CT	06854	203-866-8000	866-6727
Microwave Networks Inc 4000 Greenbriar Ste 100A *Web:* www.microwavenetworks.com	Stafford	TX	77477	281-263-6500	263-6400
Midian Electronic Comm Systems 2302 E 22nd St *Web:* www.midians.com	Tucson	AZ	85713	520-884-7981	
Midland Instruments Ltd 20 Ed Connelly Dr Huronia Airport *Web:* www.midlandinstruments.com	Tiny	ON	L0L2J0	705-527-4447	527-5557
Millitech Inc 29 Industrial Dr E *Web:* www.millitech.com	NorthHampton	MA	01060	413-582-9620	
Minerva Networks Inc 2150 Gold St *TF:* 800-806-9594 ■ *Web:* www.minervanetworks.com	Santa Clara	CA	95002	408-567-9400	567-0747
MiTAC Digital Corp 471 El Camino Real *Web:* www.magellangps.com	Santa Clara	CA	95050	408-615-5100	
Mitsubishi International Corp 655 Third Ave *Web:* www.mitsubishicorp.com	New York	NY	10017	212-605-2000	
Modular Communications Systems 13309 Saticoy St *Web:* www.moducom.com	North Hollywood	CA	91605	818-764-1333	
Morcom International Inc 3656 Centerview Dr Unit 1 *Web:* www.morcom.com	Chantilly	VA	20151	703-263-9305	263-9308
Moseley Assoc Inc 82 Coromar Dr *Web:* www.moseleysb.com	Santa Barbara	CA	93117	805-968-9621	685-9638
MTSI Inc 541 Sterling Dr *Web:* www.mtsiinc.com	Richardson	TX	75081	972-669-0591	
Nanowave Technologies Inc 425 Horner Ave *Web:* www.nanowavetech.com	Etobicoke	ON	M8W4W3	416-252-5602	252-7077
Nautel Ltd 10089 Peggy'S Cove Rd *TF:* 877-662-8835 ■ *Web:* www.nautel.com	Hackett'S Cove	NS	B3Z3J4	902-823-3900	
Northway Communications Inc 105 E Oak St *Web:* www.northwaycom.com	Wausau	WI	54401	715-842-0841	
NSC Communications 6820 Power Line Dr *TF:* 800-543-1584 ■ *Web:* www.nsccom.com	Florence	KY	41042	859-727-6640	
Orbit/FR Inc 506 Prudential Rd *OTC: ORFR* ■ *Web:* www.orbitfr.com	Horsham	PA	19044	215-674-5100	674-5108
ParkerVision Inc 7915 Baymeadows Way *NASDAQ: PRKR* ■ *TF:* 800-532-8034 ■ *Web:* www.parkervision.com	Jacksonville	FL	32256	904-737-1367	731-0958
Pelco 3500 Pelco Way *TF:* 800-289-9100 ■ *Web:* www.pelco.com	Clovis	CA	93612	559-292-1981	348-1120
Pico Macom Inc 8880 Rehco Rd *TF:* 800-421-6511 ■ *Web:* www.picomacom.com	San Diego	CA	92121	858-546-5050	546-5051
PolarSat Inc 549 Meloche Ave *Web:* www.polarsat.com	Dorval	QC	H9P2W2	514-635-0040	635-0044
Powerwave Technologies Inc 1801 E St Andrew Pl *NASDAQ: PWAV*	Santa Ana	CA	92705	714-466-1000	466-5800
RA Miller Industries Inc 14500 168th Ave PO Box 858 *TF:* 888-845-9450 ■ *Web:* www.rami.com	Grand Haven	MI	49417	616-842-9450	842-2771
Radio Communication Service 510 S Pike E *Web:* www.radiocommsc.com	Sumter	SC	29150	803-773-9743	
Radio Frequency Systems 200 Pondview Dr *Web:* www.rfsworld.com	Meriden	CT	06450	203-630-3311	634-2273
Radio Holland USA Inc 8943 Gulf Fwy *Web:* imtech.com/en/imtechmarine-usa	Houston	TX	77017	713-378-2100	378-2101
Radio North 2682 Garfield Rd N Ste 22 *Web:* msatc.com	Traverse City	MI	49686	231-929-2934	
Rantec Microwave Systems Inc 24003 Ventura Blvd *Web:* www.rantecantennas.com	Calabasas	CA	91302	818-223-5000	223-5199

Phone Fax

RELM Wireless Corp 7100 Technology Dr....... West Melbourne FL 32904 321-984-1414 676-4403
NYSE: RWC ■ *TF Cust Svc:* 800-648-0947 ■ *Web:* www.relm.com

REVL Communications & Systems
650 W 58th Ave Ste J....... Anchorage AK 99518 907-563-8302
Web: www.revlinc.net

RF Products Inc 1500 Davis St....... Camden NJ 08103 856-365-5500 342-9757
Web: www.rfproducts.com

Ritron Wireless Solutions 505 W Carmel Dr....... Carmel IN 46032 317-846-1201
Web: www.ritron.com

RL Drake Co 9900 Springboro Pike....... Miamisburg OH 45342 937-746-4556 806-1510
TF: 800-777-8876 ■ *Web:* www.rldrake.com

Rockwell Collins Inc 400 Collins Rd NE....... Cedar Rapids IA 52498 319-295-1000 295-1542*
NYSE: COL ■ **Fax:* PR ■ *TF:* 888-721-3094 ■ *Web:* www.rockwellcollins.com

Ruckus Wireless Inc 350 W JAVA Dr....... Sunnyvale CA 94089 650-265-4200
Web: www.ruckuswireless.com

SAT Corp 931 Benecia Ave....... Sunnyvale CA 94085 408-530-1020
Web: www.sat.com

Satcom Scientific Inc 5644 Commerce Dr....... Orlando FL 32839 407-856-1050 855-7640
Web: www.satcomscientific.com

Satellite Systems Corp 101 Malibu Dr....... Virginia Beach VA 23452 757-463-3553 463-3891
Web: www.satsyscorp.com

SEA Com Corp 7030 220th St SW....... Mountlake Terrace WA 98043 425-771-2182 771-2650
Web: www.seacomcorp.com

SeaChange International Inc 50 Nagog Pk....... Acton MA 01720 978-897-0100 897-0132
NASDAQ: SEAC ■ *Web:* www.schange.com

SeaSpace Corp 12120 Kear Pl....... Poway CA 92064 858-746-1100
Web: www.seaspace.com

Secure Communication Systems Inc
1740 E Wilshire Ave....... Santa Ana CA 92705 714-547-1174 547-1343
Web: www.securecomm.com

SEKAI Electronics Inc 14600 Industry Cir....... La Mirada CA 90638 714-736-4180
Web: www.sekai-electronics.com

Sensor Systems Inc 8929 Fullbright Ave....... Chatsworth CA 91311 818-341-5366 341-9059
Web: www.sensorantennas.com

Setcom Corp 3019 Alvin DeVane Blvd Ste 560....... Austin TX 78741 650-965-8020
Web: www.setcomcorp.com

Shively Labs 188 Harrison Rd PO Box 389....... Bridgton ME 04009 207-647-3327 647-8273
TF: 888-744-8359 ■ *Web:* www.shively.com

Sierra Video Systems Inc
104 New Mohawk Rd....... Nevada City CA 95959 530-478-1000
Web: www.sierravideo.com

Silynx Communications Inc
9901 Belward Campus Dr Ste 150....... Rockville MD 20850 301-217-9223
Web: www.silynxcom.com

Simrex Corp 5490 Broadway St....... Lancaster NY 14086 480-926-6069
Web: www.simrex.com

Sirtrack Ltd 845 Pheasant Ln....... North Liberty IA 52317 905-836-6680
Web: www.sirtrack.co.nz

Skitter Inc 3720 Davinci Ct Ste 200....... Norcross GA 30092 678-894-8808
Web: www.skitter.tv

Skybox Imaging Inc
1061 Terra Bella Ave....... Mountain View CA 94043 650-316-6660

Sonetics Corp 7340 Sw Durham Rd....... Portland OR 97224 800-833-4558
TF: 800-833-4558 ■ *Web:* www.firecom.com

Space Micro Inc 10237 Flanders Ct....... San Diego CA 92121 858-332-0700
Web: www.spacemicro.com

Space Systems/Loral 3825 Fabian Way....... Palo Alto CA 94303 650-852-4000
TF: 800-332-6490 ■ *Web:* sslmda.com

Sunair Electronics LLC 3131 SW 42 St....... Fort Lauderdale FL 33312 954-400-5100
Web: www.sunairhf.com

Synergy Broadcast Systems 16115 Dooley Rd....... Addison TX 75001 800-601-6991
TF: 800-601-6991

Tachyon Networks Inc
9339 Carroll Park Dr Ste 150....... San Diego CA 92121 858-882-8100

Talk-a-Phone Co 7530 N Natchez Ave....... Niles IL 60714 773-539-1100 539-1241
Web: www.talkaphone.com

Talon Communications Inc
7795 Arjons Dr Ste 201....... San Diego CA 92126 858-653-0100
Web: www.taloncom.com

TCI International Inc 3541 Gateway Blvd....... Fremont CA 94538 510-687-6100 687-6101
TF: 877-247-3797 ■ *Web:* www.spx.com

Tecom Industries Inc
375 Conejo Ridge Ave....... Thousand Oaks CA 91361 805-267-0100 267-0181
TF: 866-840-8550 ■ *Web:* www.tecom-ind.com

Telemobile Inc 19840 Hamilton Ave....... Torrance CA 90502 310-538-5100 532-8526
Web: www.telemobile.com

Telepath Corp 49111 Milmont Dr....... Fremont CA 94538 510-656-5600
TF: 800-292-1700 ■ *Web:* www.telepathcorp.com

Telephonics Corp 815 Broad Hollow Rd....... Farmingdale NY 11735 631-755-7000 755-7200
Web: www.telephonics.com

Thales Communications Inc
22605 Gateway Ctr Dr....... Clarksburg MD 20871 240-864-7000 864-7920
TF: 800-258-4420 ■ *Web:* www.thalescomminc.com

TMC Design Corp 4325 Del Rey Blvd....... Las Cruces NM 88012 575-382-4600
Web: www.tmcdesign.us

TPL Communications
3825 Foothill Blvd Unit 206....... La Crescenta CA 91214 323-256-3000 254-3210
TF: 800-447-6937 ■ *Web:* www.tplcom.com

Trak Com Wireless Inc 101-3780 14th Ave....... Markham ON L3R9Y5 905-474-9935 474-9938
Web: www.trakcom.com

Tridon Communications 10017 Queen St....... Fort Mcmurray AB T9H4Y9 780-791-1002
Web: www.tridon.com

Troll Systems Corp 24950 Anza Dr....... Valencia CA 91355 661-702-8900
Web: www.trollsystems.com

TVU networks Corp 1225 Pear Ave Ste 100....... Mountain View CA 94043 650-969-6732
Web: www.tvunetworks.com

u-blox America Inc
1902 Campus Commons Dr Ste 310....... Reston VA 20191 703-483-3180
Web: www.u-blox.com

Phone Fax

UltiSat Inc
708 Quince Orchard Rd Ste 120....... Gaithersburg MD 20878 240-243-5100
Web: www.ultisat.com

Ultra Electronics Flightline Systems Inc
7625 Omni Tech Pl....... Victor NY 14564 585-924-4000 742-5397
TF: 888-959-9001 ■ *Web:* www.ultra-fei.com

Ultra Electronics-DNE Technologies Inc
50 Barnes Industrial Pk N....... Wallingford CT 06492 203-265-7151 265-9101
TF: 800-370-4485 ■ *Web:* www.dnetech.com

Unique Broadband Systems Ltd
400 Spinnaker Way Unit 1 10....... Vaughan ON L4K5Y9 905-669-8533
TF: 877-669-8533 ■ *Web:* www.uniquesys.com

Usglobalsat Inc 1308 John Reed Ct....... City Of Industry CA 91745 626-968-4145
Web: www.usglobalsat.com

Utah Scientific Inc
4750 Wiley Post Way Ste 150....... Salt Lake City UT 84116 801-575-8801
Web: www.utsci.com

VehSmart Inc 12180 Ridgecrest Rd Ste 412....... Victorville CA 92395 855-834-7627
TF: 855-834-7627 ■ *Web:* www.vehsmart.com

Verismo Networks Inc
5201 Great America Pkwy Ste 457....... Santa Clara CA 95054 408-598-3661
Web: www.verismonetworks.com

Vicon Industries Inc 89 Arkay Dr....... Hauppauge NY 11788 631-952-2288 951-2288
NYSE: VII ■ *TF Sales:* 800-645-9116 ■ *Web:* www.vicon-security.com

Wegener 11350 Technology Cir....... Johns Creek GA 30097 770-814-4000 623-0698
OTC: WGNR ■ *Web:* www.wegener.com

Wilcom Inc 73 Daniel Webster Hwy PO Box 508....... Belmont NH 03220 603-524-2622 524-3735
TF: 800-222-1898 ■ *Web:* www.wilcominc.com

Winegard Co 3000 Kirkwood St....... Burlington IA 52601 319-754-0600 754-0787
TF Cust Svc: 800-288-8094 ■ *Web:* www.winegard.com

Xcitex Inc 25 First St Ste 105....... Cambridge MA 02141 617-225-0080
TF: 800-780-7836 ■ *Web:* www.xcitex.com

Zephyrus Electronics Ltd 168 S 122nd E Ave....... Tulsa OK 74128 918-437-3333
Web: www.big-z.com

Zetron Inc 12034 134th Ct NE....... Redmond WA 98052 425-820-6363 820-7031
Web: www.zetron.com

648 RAIL TRANSPORT SERVICES

See Also Logistics Services (Transportation & Warehousing) p. 2681

Phone Fax

Aberdeen & Rockfish Railroad Co
101 E Main St....... Aberdeen NC 28315 910-944-2341 944-9738
TF: 800-849-8985 ■ *Web:* www.aberdeen-rockfish.com

Atlantic & Western Railway LP
136 S Steele St....... Sanford NC 27330 919-776-7521 774-4621

Bonneville Transloaders Inc (BTI)
642 S Federal Blvd....... Riverton WY 82501 307-856-7480 856-4623
Web: www.bonntran.com

Buffalo & Pittsburgh Railroad Inc (BPRR)
1200-C Scottsville Rd Ste 200....... Rochester NY 14624 585-463-3307 477-4947*
**Fax Area Code:* 800 ■ *TF:* 800-603-3385 ■ *Web:* www.gwrr.com

Burlington Northern & Santa Fe Railway (BNSF)
2650 Lou Menk Dr....... Fort Worth TX 76131 800-795-2673
TF: 800-795-2673 ■ *Web:* www.bnsf.com

Canadian National Railway Co
935 Rue de la Gauchetiere O....... Montreal QC H3B2M9 888-888-5909
TSE: CNR ■ *TF:* 888-668-4626 ■ *Web:* www.cn.ca

Canadian Pacific Railway Co
401 9 Ave SW Ste 500....... Calgary AB T2P4Z4 403-319-7000 704-3000*
**Fax Area Code:* 800 ■ **Fax:* Hum Res ■ *TF:* 888-333-6370 ■ *Web:* www.cpr.ca

Cedar Rapids & Iowa City Railway Co
2330 12th St SW....... Cedar Rapids IA 52404 319-786-3698
Web: www.crandic.com

CHEP USA 8517 S Pk Cir....... Orlando FL 32819 407-370-2437 355-6211
TF Cust Svc: 866-855-2437 ■ *Web:* www.chep.com

Chicago Southshore & South Bend Railroad
505 N Carroll Ave....... Michigan City IN 46360 219-874-9000 879-3754
TF: 800-356-2079 ■ *Web:* www.anacostia.com/railroads/css

Consolidated Rail Corp
1717 Arch St Ste 3210....... Philadelphia PA 19103 215-209-2000 209-4819
TF: 800-272-0911 ■ *Web:* www.conrail.com

CSX Transportation Inc 500 Water St....... Jacksonville FL 32202 904-359-3100
Web: www.csx.com

Dardanelle & Russellville Railroad Co
4416 S Arkansas Ave....... Russellville AR 72802 479-968-6455 968-2634
TF: 888-877-7267 ■ *Web:* up.com

El Dorado & Wesson Railway Co 900 SW Ave....... El Dorado AR 71730 870-863-7100 863-7130

Genesee & Wyoming Inc 66 Field Pt Rd....... Greenwich CT 06830 203-629-3722
NYSE: GWR ■ *Web:* www.gwrr.com

Georgetown Railroad Co
5300 S IH-35 PO Box 529....... Georgetown TX 78626 512-863-2538
TF: 888-456-6777

Illinois & Midland Railroad Inc
1500 N Grand Ave E....... Springfield IL 62702 217-788-8601 788-8630
Web: www.gwrr.com

Iowa Interstate Railroad
5900 Sixth St SW....... Cedar Rapids IA 52404 319-298-5400 298-5454
TF: 800-321-3884 ■ *Web:* www.iaisrr.com

Kansas City Southern Railway Co
427 W 12th St....... Kansas City MO 64105 816-983-1303
TF: 800-468-6527 ■ *Web:* www.kcsouthern.com

Lake State Railway Co 750 N Washington Ave....... Saginaw MI 48607 989-393-9800 757-2134
Web: www.lsrc.com

Louisiana & Delta Railroad Inc (LDRR)
402 W Washington St....... New Iberia LA 70560 337-364-9625
Web: www.gwrr.com

McCloud Railway Co 801 Industrial Way....... McCloud CA 96057 530-964-2141

Mississippi Export Railroad Co
4519 McInnis Ave....... Moss Point MS 39563 228-475-3322 475-3337
Web: mserailroad.com

				Phone	Fax
Modesto & Empire Traction Co 530 11th St *Web:* www.metrr.com	Modesto	CA	95354	209-524-4631	529-0336
Montana Rail Link Inc 101 International Way *TF:* 800-338-4750 ■ *Web:* www.montanarail.com	Missoula	MT	59808	406-523-1500	523-1493
New York Susquehanna & Western Railway Corp (NYSW) 1 Railroad Ave *TF General:* 800-366-6979 ■ *Web:* www.nysw.com	Cooperstown	NY	13326	607-547-2555	547-9834
Norfolk Southern Railway Co 3 Commercial Pl *TF:* 800-635-5768 ■ *Web:* www.nscorp.com	Norfolk	VA	23510	800-453-2530	
Paducah & Louisville Railway Inc 200 Clark St *Web:* www.palrr.com	Paducah	KY	42003	270-444-4300	
Pioneer Railcorp 1318 S Johanson Rd *OTC: PRRR* ■ *Web:* www.pioneer-railcorp.com	Peoria	IL	61607	309-697-1400	697-5387
Providence & Worcester Railroad Co 75 Hammond St *NASDAQ: PWX* ■ *TF:* 877-373-6374 ■ *Web:* www.pwrr.com	Worcester	MA	01610	508-755-4000	753-5548
Trans-Continental Systems Inc 10801 Evendale Dr *TF:* 800-525-8726 ■ *Web:* www.tcsohio.com	Cincinnati	OH	45241	513-769-4774	769-3215
Triple Crown Services 2720 Dupont Commerce Ct Ste 200 *TF:* 800-325-6510 ■ *Web:* www.triplecrownsvc.com	Fort Wayne	IN	46825	260-416-3600	416-3771
Union Pacific Railroad Co 1400 Douglas St **Fax Area Code:* 402 ■ *TF:* 888-870-8777 ■ *Web:* www.up.com	Omaha	NE	68179	888-870-8777	271-5572*
Union Railroad Co 1200 Penn Ave *Web:* www.tstarinc.com	Pittsburgh	PA	15222	412-433-7066	
Winston-Salem Southbound Railway Co 4550 Overdale Rd *TF:* 888-780-7245 ■ *Web:* www.ncrailways.org	Winston-Salem	NC	27107	336-788-9407	788-9085

649 RAIL TRAVEL

See Also Mass Transportation (Local & Suburban) p. 2731

				Phone	Fax
Buckingham Branch Railroad Co PO Box 336 *Web:* www.buckinghambranch.com	Dillwyn	VA	23936	434-983-3300	
Dakota Missouri Valley & Western Railroad Inc 3501 E Rosser Ave *Web:* www.dmvwrr.com	Bismarck	ND	58501	701-223-9282	
Dew Distribution Services Inc 2201 Touhy Ave *TF:* 800-837-3391 ■ *Web:* www.dewdist.com	Elk Grove Village	IL	60007	800-837-3391	
Grand Canyon Railway Inc 1201 W Rt 66 Ste 200 *Web:* www.thetrain.com	Flagstaff	AZ	86001	928-773-1976	
Idaho Northern & Pacific Railroad 119 N Commercial Ave *Web:* www.rgpc.com	Emmett	ID	83617	208-365-6353	
Indiana Rail Road Co, The 101 W Ohio St Ste 1600 *TF:* 888-596-2121 ■ *Web:* www.inrd.com	Indianapolis	IN	46204	317-262-5140	
Iowa Northern Railway Co 305 Second St SE Paramount Theatre Bldg Ste 400 *Web:* www.iowanorthern.com	Cedar Rapids	IA	52401	319-297-6000	
Louisville & Indiana Railroad Co 500 Willinger Ln *Web:* www.anacostia.com	Jeffersonville	IN	47130	812-288-0940	
National Railroad Passenger Corp 60 Massachusetts Ave NE *TF:* 800-872-7245 ■ *Web:* www.amtrak.com	Washington	DC	20002	202-906-3741	906-3285
Omega Rail Management 4721 Trousdale Dr Ste 206 *Web:* www.omegarail.com	Nashville	TN	37220	615-331-1900	
Pandrol Canada Ltd 6910 34th St *Web:* www.pandrolcanada.ca	Edmonton	AB	T6B2X2	780-413-4281	
Patriot Rail Company LLC 10060 Skinner Lk Dr *Web:* www.patriotrail.com	Jacksonville	FL	32246	904-423-2540	
Pinsly Railroad Company Inc 53 Southampton Rd *Web:* www.pinsly.com	Westfield	MA	01085	413-568-6426	
Shamokin Valley Railroad Co 356 Priestley Ave *Web:* www.nshr.com	Northumberland	PA	17857	570-473-7949	
Trinity Railway Express 1600 E Lancaster Ave *Web:* www.the-t.com	Fort Worth	TX	76102	817-215-8600	
Twin Cities & Western Railroad 2925 12th St E *TF:* 800-290-8297 ■ *Web:* www.tcwr.net	Glencoe	MN	55336	320-864-7200	
VIA Rail Canada Inc 3 Pl Ville-Marie PO Box 8116 *TF:* 800-681-2561 ■ *Web:* www.viarail.ca	Montreal	QC	H3C3N3	514-871-6000	871-6104

650 RAILROAD EQUIPMENT - MFR

See Also Transportation Equipment & Supplies - Whol p. 3262

				Phone	Fax
A Stucki Co 2600 Neville Rd *TF:* 888-266-6630 ■ *Web:* www.stucki.com	Pittsburgh	PA	15225	412-771-7300	771-7308
Adams & Westlake Ltd 940 N Michigan St *Web:* www.adlake.com	Elkhart	IN	46514	574-264-1141	264-1146
American Motive Power Inc 9431 Foster Wheeler Rd *Web:* www.americanmotivepower.com	Dansville	NY	14437	585-335-3131	
American Railcar Industries Inc 100 Clark St *NASDAQ: ARII* ■ *TF:* 800-489-9888 ■ *Web:* www.americanrailcar.com	Saint Charles	MO	63301	636-940-6000	940-6030
AMSTED Industries Inc 180 N Stetson St Ste 1800 *Web:* www.amsted.com	Chicago	IL	60601	312-645-1700	
Bombardier Transportation North America 1101 Parent St *Web:* www.bombardier.com	Saint-Bruno	QC	J3V6E6	450-441-2020	441-1515
CAD Railway Industries Ltd 155 boul. Montreal-Toronto (Hwy 2-20) *Web:* www.cadrail.ca	Lachine	QC	H8S1B4	514-634-3131	954-0431
CANAC Inc 6505 Trans-Canada Hwy Ste 405 *TF:* 800-588-4387 ■ *Web:* www.canac.com	St Laurent	QC	H4T1S3	514-734-4700	734-4850
Cando Contracting Ltd 740 Rosser Ave Fl 4 *TF:* 866-989-5310 ■ *Web:* www.candoltd.com	Brandon	MB	R7A0K9	204-725-2627	
Cardwell Westinghouse Co 8400 S Stewart Ave *Web:* www.wabtec.com	Chicago	IL	60620	773-483-7575	
Clark Filter Inc 3649 Hempland Rd *Web:* www.clarkfilter.com	Lancaster	PA	17601	717-285-5941	
Curran Group Inc 286 Memorial Ct *Web:* www.currangroup.com	Crystal Lake	IL	60014	815-455-5100	455-7894
Dayton-Phoenix Group Inc 1619 Kuntz Rd *TF:* 800-657-0707 ■ *Web:* www.dayton-phoenix.com	Dayton	OH	45404	937-496-3974	496-3969
Electro-Motive Diesel Inc 9301 W 55th St *TF:* 800-255-5355 ■ *Web:* www.emdiesels.com	La Grange	IL	60525	708-387-6000	387-6626
FreightCar America Inc 17 Johns St *NASDAQ: RAIL* ■ **Fax Area Code:* 814 ■ *TF:* 800-458-2235 ■ *Web:* www.freightcaramerica.com	Johnstown	PA	15901	800-458-2235	533-5010*
GE Aviation 1 Neumann Way *Web:* www.geaviation.com	Cincinnati	OH	45215	513-243-2000	
GE Transportation Rail 2901 E Lake Rd **Fax:* Hum Res ■ *TF Prod Info:* 800-285-6545 ■ *Web:* www.getransportation.com	Erie	PA	16531	814-875-2234	875-3591*
Graham-White Manufacturing Co 1242 Colorado St PO Box 1099 *Web:* www.grahamwhite.com	Salem	VA	24153	540-387-5600	387-5697
Gray Mfg Industries LLC 6258 Icehouse Rd *Web:* gmihornell.com	Hornell	NY	14843	607-281-1325	
Greenbrier Co 1 Centerpointe Dr Ste 200 *NYSE: GBX* ■ *TF:* 800-343-7188 ■ *Web:* www.gbrx.com	Lake Oswego	OR	97035	503-684-7000	684-7553
Harsco Rail (HTT) 2401 Edmund Rd PO Box 20 *Web:* www.harscorail.com	West Columbia	SC	29171	803-822-9160	822-8107
Holland Co 1000 Holland Dr *Web:* www.hollandco.com	Crete	IL	60417	708-672-2300	672-0119
Interstate Transport Inc 324 First Ave N *TF:* 866-281-1281 ■ *Web:* www.interstate-transport.com	St Petersburg	FL	33701	727-822-9999	
Kasgro Rail Corp 121 Rundle Rd *Web:* www.kasgro.com	New Castle	PA	16102	724-658-9061	
Kawasaki Rail Car Inc 29 Wells Ave Bldg 4 *Web:* www.kawasakirailcar.com	Yonkers	NY	10701	914-376-4700	
LB Foster Co 415 Holiday Dr *NASDAQ: FSTR* ■ *TF:* 800-255-4500 ■ *Web:* www.lbfoster.com	Pittsburgh	PA	15220	800-255-4500	
Loram Maintenance of Way 3900 Arrowhead Dr PO Box 188 *TF:* 800-328-1466 ■ *Web:* www.loram.com	Hamel	MN	55340	763-478-6014	478-6916
Miner Enterprises Inc 1200 E State St *TF:* 888-822-5334 ■ *Web:* www.minerent.com	Geneva	IL	60134	630-232-3000	232-3055
Motive Equipment Inc 8300 W Sleske Ct *Web:* www.motiveequipment.com	Milwaukee	WI	53223	414-446-3379	
National Railway Equipment Co (NREC) 14400 Robey St *TF:* 800-253-2905 ■ *Web:* www.nre.com	Dixmoor	IL	60426	708-388-6002	388-2487
New York Air Brake Co 748 Starbuck Ave **Fax:* Sales ■ *TF:* 888-836-6922 ■ *Web:* www.nyab.com	Watertown	NY	13601	315-786-5200	786-5675*
Nolan Co 1016 Ninth St SW *TF:* 800-297-1383 ■ *Web:* www.nolancompany.com	Canton	OH	44707	330-453-7922	453-7449
Pacific Coast Container Inc 432 Estudillo Ave *TF:* 800-458-4788 ■ *Web:* www.pcclogistics.com	San Leandro	CA	94577	510-346-6100	
Plasser American Corp 2001 Myers Rd PO Box 5464 *Web:* www.plasseramerican.com	Chesapeake	VA	23324	757-543-3526	494-7186
Portec Rail Products Inc 900 Old Freeport Rd *Web:* www.lbfoster-railtechnologies.com	Pittsburgh	PA	15238	412-782-6000	782-1037
Quantem Aviation Services Inc 175 Ammon Dr *Web:* qasllc.aero	Manchester	NH	03103	603-647-1717	
Racine Railroad Products Inc 1524 Frederick St PO Box 044577 *Web:* www.racinerailroad.com	Racine	WI	53404	262-637-9681	637-9069
Rail Car Service Co 584 Fairground Rd *TF:* 800-521-2151 ■ *Web:* www.parailcar.com	Mercer	PA	16137	724-662-3660	
Salco Products Inc 1385 101st St Ste A *Web:* www.salcoproducts.com	Lemont	IL	60439	630-783-2570	783-2590
Siemens Mobility 7464 French Rd *Web:* usa.siemens.com/infrastructure-cities/us/en	Sacramento	CA	95828	916-681-3000	
Southern Railway of British Columbia Ltd 2102 River Dr *Web:* www.sryraillink.com	New Westminster	BC	V3M6S3	604-521-1966	
Standard Car Truck Co 865 Busse Hwy *Web:* www.sctco.com	Park Ridge	IL	60068	847-692-6050	
Tealinc Ltd 1606 Rosebud Creek Rd *Web:* www.tealinc.com	Forsyth	MT	59327	406-347-5237	
Trackmobile Inc 1602 Executive Dr *Web:* www.trackmobile.com	LaGrange	GA	30240	706-884-6651	884-0390
Transco Railway Products Inc 820 Hopley Ave *TF:* 800-472-4592 ■ *Web:* www.transcorailway.com	Bucyrus	OH	44820	419-562-1031	562-3684
Transportation Research Corp 4305 Business Dr *Web:* www.varnaproducts.com	Cameron Park	CA	95682	530-676-7770	
Trinity Mining Service 109 48th St *TF:* 800-264-2583 ■ *Web:* www.trin-mine.com	Pittsburgh	PA	15201	412-682-4700	682-4725

Company	City	State	ZIP	Phone	Fax
Trinity Rail Group LLC 2525 N Stemmons Fwy *TF:* 800-631-4420 ■ *Web:* www.trinityrail.com	Dallas	TX	75207	214-631-4420	589-8623
Union Tank Car Co 175 W Jackson Blvd. *TF:* 866-535-7685 ■ *Web:* www.utlx.com	Chicago	IL	60604	312-431-3111	431-5125
Vapor Bus International 1010 Johnson Dr *TF:* 866-375-4126 ■ *Web:* www.vapordoors.com	Buffalo Grove	IL	60089	847-777-6400	520-2222
WABCO Freight Car Products Ltd 475 Seaman Dr. *Web:* www.wabtec.com	Stoney Creek	ON	L8E2R2	905-561-8700	561-8705
WABCO Locomotive Products 1001 Air Brake Ave *TF Cust Svc:* 877-922-2627 ■ *Web:* www.wabtec.com	Wilmerding	PA	15148	412-825-1000	825-1019
Wabtec Corp 1001 Air Brake Ave. *NYSE: WAB* ■ *TF Cust Svc:* 877-922-2627 ■ *Web:* www.wabtec.com	Wilmerding	PA	15148	412-825-1000	825-1019
Wabtec Corp WABCO Transit Div PO Box 11 *Web:* www.wabtec.com	Spartanburg	SC	29304	864-433-5900	433-0176
Watco Companies LLC 315 W Third St *TF:* 866-386-9321 ■ *Web:* www.watcocompanies.com	Pittsburg	KS	66762	620-231-2230	231-0812
Western Reman Industrial LLC 588 W Seventh St. *Web:* www.wriservices.com	Peru	IN	46970	765-472-2002	

651 RAILROAD SWITCHING & TERMINAL SERVICES

Company	City	State	ZIP	Phone	Fax
Belt Railway Co of Chicago 6900 S Central Ave *TF:* 877-772-5772 ■ *Web:* www.beltrailway.com	Bedford Park	IL	60638	708-496-4000	496-3037
Central California Traction Co 2201 W Washington St Ste 12 *Web:* www.cctrailroad.com	Stockton	CA	95203	209-466-6927	
East Erie Commercial Railroad 1030 Lawrence Pkwy	Erie	PA	16511	814-875-5437	
Indiana Harbor Belt Railroad Co 2721 161st St. *Web:* www.ihbrr.com	Hammond	IN	46323	219-989-4703	989-4707
Minnesota Commercial Railway 508 Cleveland Ave N *Web:* mnnr.net	Saint Paul	MN	55114	651-646-2010	646-8337
OmniTRAX Inc 252 Clayton St 4th Fl *Web:* www.omnitrax.com	Denver	CO	80206	303-398-4500	398-4540
Portland Terminal Railroad Co 3500 NW Yeon Ave.	Portland	OR	97210	503-241-9898	241-4494
Public Belt Railroad Commission 4822 Tchoupitulas St *TF Cust Svc:* 800-524-3421 ■ *Web:* nopb.com	New Orleans	LA	70115	504-896-7410	896-7452
Rail Link Inc 13901 Sutton Pk Dr S Ste 125 *TF:* 877-777-4778 ■ *Web:* gwrr.com	Jacksonville	FL	32224	904-223-1110	223-8710
Railserve Inc 1691 Phoenix Blvd Ste 110 *TF:* 800-345-7245 ■ *Web:* www.railserveinc.com	Atlanta	GA	30349	770-996-6838	996-6830
Rescar Inc 1101 31st St Ste 250 *TF:* 800-851-5196 ■ *Web:* www.rescar.com	Downers Grove	IL	60515	630-963-1114	963-6342
Roadrunner Transportation Systems Inc 4900 S Pennsylvania Ave *NYSE: RRTS* ■ *TF:* 800-831-4394 ■ *Web:* www.rrts.com	Cudahy	WI	53110	414-615-1500	615-1513
Terminal Railroad Assn of Saint Louis 415 S 18th St Ste 200 *Web:* www.terminalrailroad.com	Saint Louis	MO	63103	314-231-5196	
Vermont Railway Inc 1 Railway Ln *Web:* www.vermontrailway.com	Burlington	VT	05401	802-658-2550	
Wheeling & Lake Erie Railway Co 100 E First St *Web:* www.wlerwy.com	Brewster	OH	44613	330-767-3401	

652 REAL ESTATE AGENTS & BROKERS

Company	City	State	ZIP	Phone	Fax
33rd Co Inc 1800 Wooddale Dr Ste 100 *Web:* www.33rdcompany.com	Woodbury	MN	55125	651-777-5500	777-5501
4-D Properties 2870 N Swan Rd	Tucson	AZ	85712	520-325-9600	
A J Clarke Real Estate Corp 1035 River Rd	New Milford	NJ	07646	201-836-7464	
A to B Realty 1500 E Hamilton Ave Ste 105 *Web:* www.atobrealty.com	Campbell	CA	95008	408-626-4800	
Access Property Management 4 Walter E Foran Blvd Ste 311 *Web:* www.accesspm.com	Flemington	NJ	08822	908-806-2600	
Ackman-Ziff Real estate Group LLC 110 E 42nd St. *Web:* www.ackmanziff.com	New York	NY	10017	212-697-3333	
Advenir Real Estate 17501 Biscayne Blvd *Web:* advenir.net	Aventura	FL	33160	305-948-3535	
Advisor Group Inc, The 3000 Mcknight E Dr *Web:* www.theadvisorgroup.com	Pittsburgh	PA	15237	412-931-3900	
Alain Pinel Realtors Inc 12772 Saratoga-Sunnyvale Rd *Web:* www.apr.com	Saratoga	CA	95070	408-741-1111	
Aldrich-Thomas Group Inc 18 N Third St. *Web:* aldrich-thomas.com	Temple	TX	76501	254-773-4901	
Ale Solutions Inc 1 Illinois St Ste 300 *Web:* www.alesolutions.com	Saint Charles	IL	60174	630-513-6434	
All Power Brokers Real Estate Inc 847 N Hwy 49/88 Ste 1 *Web:* allpower.com	Jackson	CA	95642	209-223-0237	
Allen Morris Co 121 Alhambra Plz Ste 1600 *Web:* www.allenmorris.com	Coral Gables	FL	33134	305-443-1000	443-1462
Alterra Real Estate Advisors LLC 540 Officenter Pl Ste 260 *Web:* www.alterrare.com	Gahanna	OH	43230	614-365-9000	
America's Choice Home Loans LP 8584 Katy Fwy Ste 200 *Web:* www.achlonline.com	Houston	TX	77024	713-463-6779	
American Landmark Properties 8114 Lawndale Ave. *Web:* www.americanlandmark.com	Skokie	IL	60076	847-568-0808	
Amira Dba Rossum Realty Unlimited 3875 S Jones Blvd Ste 101	Las Vegas	NV	89103	702-368-1850	
Amtrust Realty Corp 250 Broadway Rm 3001 *Web:* www.amtrustre.com	New York	NY	10007	212-732-4776	
Anchor Realty Assoc Inc 1113 W Baker Rd Ste D *Web:* har.com	Baytown	TX	77521	281-427-4747	
Aquila Commercial LLC 1717 W Sixth St *Web:* www.aquilacommercial.com	Austin	TX	78703	512-684-3800	
Arcadia Assn of Realtors Inc 601 S First Ave *Web:* theaar.com	Arcadia	CA	91006	626-446-2115	
Aronov Realty 3500 Eastern Blvd *Web:* www.aronov.com	Montgomery	AL	36116	334-277-1000	272-0747
Arthur J Rogers & Co 1559 Elmhurst Rd *Web:* www.arthurjrogers.com	Elk Grove Village	IL	60007	847-297-2200	
Ascent Real Estate 2900 N Park Way *Web:* ascentrealestate.net	San Diego	CA	92104	619-814-3420	
Assist-2-Sell Inc 1610 Meadow Wood Ln. *TF:* 800-528-7816 ■ *Web:* www.assist2sell.com	Reno	NV	89502	775-688-6060	823-8823
Atlanta Intown Real Estate Services 181 10th St Ne *Web:* www.atlantaintown.com	Atlanta	GA	30309	404-881-1810	
Atlantic & Pacific Management 11075 Carmel Mtn Rd Ste 200 *Web:* www.apmanagement.net	San Diego	CA	92129	858-672-3100	
Atlantic Realty Partners Inc 3438 Peachtree Rd *Web:* www.goarp.com	Atlanta	GA	30326	404-591-2900	
Bailey Properties 106 Aptos Beach Dr *TF:* 800-347-6830 ■ *Web:* www.baileyproperties.com	Aptos	CA	95003	831-688-7009	
Baird & Warner Inc 120 S LaSalle St Ste 2000 *TF:* 888-661-1176 ■ *Web:* www.bairdwarner.com	Chicago	IL	60603	312-368-1855	368-1490
Bald Head Island Rentals LLC 21 Keelson Row *Web:* www.baldheadislandrentals.com	Bald Head Island	NC	28461	910-457-1702	
Barletta & Assoc Inc 1313 Campbell Rd Ste F *Web:* www.barlettainc.com	Houston	TX	77055	713-464-7700	464-3696
Barrington Management Company Inc 376 Massachusetts Ave *Web:* www.barrington-mgmt.com	Arlington	MA	02474	781-648-9600	
Barshop & Oles Company Inc 801 Congress Ave Ste 300 *Web:* www.barshopoles.com	Austin	TX	78701	512-477-1212	
Beach Realty & Construction 4826 N Croatan Hwy *TF:* 800-635-1559 ■ *Web:* www.beachrealtync.com	Kitty Hawk	NC	27949	252-261-3815	
Beatty Management Company Inc 6824 Elm St Ste 200 *Web:* www.beattycos.com	Mclean	VA	22101	703-821-0500	
Beco Management Inc 5410 Edson Ln Ste 200 *Web:* beconet.com	Rockville	MD	20852	301-816-1500	816-1501
Beer-wells Real Estate Services Inc 430 N Center St	Longview	TX	75601	903-753-2191	
Ben M Muller Realty Company Inc 1971 E Beltline Ave Ne Ste 240 *Web:* mullerrealty.com	Grand Rapids	MI	49525	616-456-7114	
Bently Holdings Corp 240 Stockton St. *Web:* www.kamalaspa.com	San Francisco	CA	94108	415-288-0202	
Bergman Real Estate 3259 SR- 28 *Web:* adkreal.com	North Creek	NY	12853	518-251-2122	
Berkeley Hills Real Estate Inc 1714 Solano Ave *Web:* www.berkhills.com	Berkeley	CA	94707	510-524-9888	
Birtcher Anderson Realty Management 31910 Del Obispo Ste 260 *Web:* birtcheranderson.com	San Juan Capistrano	CA	92675	949-545-0500	
Block Hawley Commercial Real Estate Services LLC 16253 Swingley Ridge Rd Ste 150 *Web:* blockhawley.com	Chesterfield	MO	63017	636-534-2900	
Blue Canoe Properties LLC 2120 16th Ave S	Birmingham	AL	35205	205-918-0921	
Bluestone & Hockley Real Estate Services 9320 SW Barbur Blvd Ste 300 *Web:* www.bluestonehockley.com	Portland	OR	97219	503-222-3800	
Bobeck Real Estate Company Inc 3333 W Hamilton Rd	Fort Wayne	IN	46814	260-432-1000	
Bosshardt Realty Services LLC 5542 NW 43rd St *TF:* 800-284-6110 ■ *Web:* www.bosshardtrealty.com	Gainesville	FL	32653	352-371-6100	
Boydell Development Co 743 Beaubien St	Detroit	MI	48226	313-964-0333	
Boys & Girls Club of Zionsville 1575 Mulberry st *Web:* www.bagcoz.org	Zionsville	IN	46077	317-873-6670	
Brack Capital Real Estate USA 885 Third Ave Ste no 2401 *Web:* www.brack-capital.com	New York	NY	10022	212-308-7200	
Bradford Allen 200 S Michigan Ave 18th Fl *Web:* www.bradfordallen.com	Chicago	IL	60604	312-994-5700	
Brady Sullivan Properties LLC 670 N Commercial St *Web:* www.bradysullivan.com	Manchester	NH	03101	603-622-6223	
Bray Real Estate 637 N Ave *TF:* 888-760-4251 ■ *Web:* www.brayandco.com	Grand Junction	CO	81501	970-242-8450	
Briarlane Rental Property Management Inc 85 Spy Ct Ste 100 *Web:* www.briarlane.ca	Markham	ON	L3R4Z4	905-944-9406	
Brookfield Residential Services Ltd 3190 Steeles Ave E Ste 200 *TF:* 800-949-0274 ■ *Web:* brookfieldcondominiums.com	Markham	ON	L3R1G9	416-510-8700	

				Phone	Fax

Brown Ken J Realtors 1618 S Western St .... Amarillo TX 79106 806-352-5617

Brownstone Real Estate Co 1840 Fishburn Rd .... Hershey PA 17033 717-533-6222
TF: 877-533-6222 ■ *Web:* www.brwnstone.com

Bulfinch Cos Inc
250 First Ave Ste 200 .... Needham Heights MA 02494 781-707-4000
Web: www.bulfinch.com

Bull Island Realty Inc 29 Holloway Rd .... Poquoson VA 23662 757-868-4663
Web: bullislandrealty.com

Burke & Assoc Professional Property Management
4974 N Fresno St Ste 106 .... Fresno CA 93726 559-225-6075

Burnac Corp 44 St Clair Ave W .... Toronto ON M4V3C9 416-964-3600
Web: www.burnac.com

Bwb Properties Inc 1384 North 450 East .... Orem UT 84097 801-222-3600

Cagan Management Group Inc
16554 Cagan Crossings Blvd Ste 4 .... Clermont FL 34714 352-242-2444
Web: www.cagan.com

Cambria Pines Realty Inc 746-A Main St .... Cambria CA 93428 805-927-8616
TF: 800-676-8616 ■ *Web:* cambriapinesrealty.com

Cambridge Realty Capital LLC
125 S Wacker Dr Ste 1800 .... Chicago IL 60606 312-357-1601
Web: www.cambridgecap.com

Camelot Homes
6607 N Scottsdale Rd Ste H100 .... Scottsdale AZ 85250 480-367-4300
Web: www.camelothomes.com

Cardinal Management Group 3704 Golf Trl Ln .... Fairfax VA 22033 703-591-1818
Web: cardinalmanagementgroup.com

Cardinal Pacific Escrow Inc
6615 E Pacific Coast Hwy Ste 240 .... Long Beach CA 90803 562-493-9393
Web: www.cardinalpacific.com

Carlson Real Estate Company Inc
301 Carlson Pkwy Ste 100 .... Minnetonka MN 55305 952-404-5000 404-5001
Web: carlsonrealestate.biz

Carolina Farms Real Estate 547 S Main St .... King NC 27021 336-983-5263
TF: 800-559-2113 ■ *Web:* www.carolinafarms.com

Carson Dunlop Home Inspections
407-120 Carlton St .... Toronto ON M5A4K2 416-964-9415
Web: www.carsondunlop.com

Castrop Wolfe Development Co
5775 Perimeter Dr Ste 290 .... Dublin OH 43017 614-793-2244
Web: www.cwbpm.com

Ceis Review Inc 8 Tannery Ln .... Camden ME 04843 207-230-2515
Web: ceisreview.com

Center for Real Estate Education & Research
210 S Poplar St .... New Washington IN 47162 812-333-2299

Central Management Inc (CMI)
820 Gessner Rd Ste 1525 .... Houston TX 77024 713-961-9777 961-5730
Web: www.cmirealestate.com

Century 21 A Property Shoppe 2033 N Main St .... Salinas CA 93906 831-663-2121

Century 21 Consolidated Real Estate
2820 Flamingo Rd .... Las Vegas NV 89121 702-732-7282

Century 21 Percy Fulton Ltd 2911 Kennedy Rd .... Toronto ON M1V1S8 416-298-8200
Web: www.century21toronto.com

CENTURY 21 Sweyer & Assoc
1630 Military Cutoff Rd .... Wilmington NC 28403 910-256-0021
Web: www.century21sweyer.com

Champions Real Estate Group LLC
6117 Richmond Ave Ste 120 .... Houston TX 77057 713-785-6666
Web: creg1.com

Chandler Properties 2799 California St .... San Francisco CA 94115 415-921-5733
Web: chandlerproperties.com

Chapin Hall Center For Children
1313 E 60th St .... Chicago IL 60637 773-753-5900
Web: www.chapinhall.org

Charles Dunn Co Inc 800 W Sixth St 6th Fl .... Los Angeles CA 90017 213-683-0500
Web: www.charlesdunn.com

Chris Smith Realty 306 Morris Ave .... Spring Lake NJ 07762 732-449-3777
Web: chrissmithrealty.com

Chromatin Inc 10 S Lasalle St Ste 2100 .... Chicago IL 60603 312-292-5400
Web: www.chromatininc.com

Cip Real Estate Property Services Inc
19762 Macarthur Blvd Ste 300 .... Irvine CA 92612 949-474-7030
Web: www.ciprealestate.com

Citi-Habitats Inc 250 Park Ave S 4th fl .... New York NY 10016 212-685-7777
Web: www.citihabitats.com

City Property Management Co
4645 E Cotton Gin Loop .... Phoenix AZ 85040 602-437-4777
Web: cityproperty.com

Cityfeetcom Inc 443 Park Ave S Ste 3A .... New York NY 10016 212-924-6450
Web: www.cityfeet.com

Claimsource One Services Group Inc
490 Sun Vly Dr Ste 103 .... Roswell GA 30076 404-252-1771

Clay Herman Realtor Inc
251 Park Rd Ste 710 .... Burlingame CA 94010 650-342-1141
Web: clayherman.com

Closing USA LLC 903 Elmgrove Rd .... Rochester NY 14624 585-454-1730
Web: www.closingusa.com

Cohen Financial LP 227 W Monroe St Ste 1000 .... Chicago IL 60606 312-346-5680 346-6669
Web: www.cohenfinancial.com

Cohen-Esrey Real Estate Services LLC
6800 W 64th St .... Overland Park KS 66202 913-671-3300 671-3301
Web: www.cohenesrey.com

Coldwell Banker Gundaker
2458 Old Dorsett Rd Ste 300 .... Maryland Heights MO 63043 314-298-5000
TF: 800-325-1978 ■ *Web:* www.coldwellbankerhomes.com/st-louis

Coldwell Banker Honig-Bell 950 Essington Rd .... Joliet IL 60435 815-744-1000
Web: www.cbhonig-bell.com

Coldwell Banker Howard Perry & Walston
1001 Wade Ave .... Raleigh NC 27605 919-782-5600
Web: www.hpw.com

Coldwell Banker Platinum Partners
6349 Abercorn St .... Savannah GA 31405 912-352-1222

Coldwell Banker Residential Brokerage
600 Grant St Ste 925 .... Denver CO 80203 303-409-1500 409-6336
TF All: 800-552-6787 ■ *Web:* www.coldwellbankerhomes.com/colorado

Coldwell Banker Residential Real Estate
5951 Cattleridge Ave .... Sarasota FL 34232 941-487-1400
TF: 888-937-6426 ■ *Web:* www.coldwellbankerhomes.com/florida

Coldwell Banker Schmidt Realtors
402 E Front St .... Traverse City MI 49686 231-922-2350
Web: www.cbgreatlakes.com

Coldwell Banker Select Professionals
1000 N Prince St .... Lancaster PA 17603 717-569-0608

Collett & Assoc LLC
1111 Metropolitan Ave Ste 700 .... Charlotte NC 28204 704-206-8300
Web: www.collettre.com/home

Collier Enterprises Management Inc
2550 Goodlette Rd N Ste 100 .... Naples FL 34103 239-261-4455
Web: www.collierenterprises.com

Colliers International
6606 W Broad St Ste 400 .... Richmond VA 23230 206-695-4200 782-1145*
**Fax Area Code:* 804 ■ *Web:* www.colliers.com

Colliers International 601 Union St Ste 4800 .... Seattle WA 98101 206-695-4200
Web: www.colliers.com

Colliers Parrish International Inc
1 Almaden Blvd Ste 300 .... San Jose CA 95113 408-282-4000
Web: www.colliersparrish.com

Colliers Pinkard
7172 Columbia Gateway Dr Ste 400 .... Columbia MD 21046 443-297-9000 543-0191
Web: www.colliers.com/markets/baltimore

Commercial Realty & Resources Corp
1415 Wyckoff Rd PO Box 1468 .... Wall NJ 07719 732-938-1111
Web: njresources.com

ConAm Management Corp
3990 Ruffin Rd Ste 100 .... San Diego CA 92123 858-614-7200
Web: www.conam.com

Conopco Realty & Development Inc
5448 Prairie Stone Pkwy Ste 250) .... Hoffman Estates IL 60192 847-645-5000 645-5050
Web: www.conopco.com

Constable Commercial Real Estate Services
2845 Moorpark Ave Ste 112 .... San Jose CA 95128 408-984-3700
Web: www.constablecommercial.com

Conterra Ultra Broadband LLC
2101 Rexford Rd Ste 200E .... Charlotte NC 28211 704-936-1800
TF: 800-634-1374 ■ *Web:* www.conterra.com

Corcoran Group Inc, The 660 Madison Ave .... New York NY 10021 212-355-3550
TF: 800-544-4055 ■ *Web:* www.corcoran.com

Core Partners LLC 320 Martin St Ste 140 .... Birmingham MI 48009 248-399-9999
Web: www.corepartners.net

Corus Realty Holdings Inc 6726 Curran St .... Mclean VA 22101 703-827-0075
Web: www.corushome.com

Costar Video Systems LLC
101 Wrangler Dr Ste 201 .... Coppell TX 75019 469-635-6800 446-8866
Web: www.costarvideo.com

Crosspoint Realty Services Inc
260 California St Fl 4 .... San Francisco CA 94111 415-288-6888
Web: crosspointrealty.com

Crye-Leike Inc 6525 N Quail Hollow Rd .... Memphis TN 38120 866-310-3102 758-5641*
**Fax Area Code:* 901 ■ *TF:* 866-310-3102 ■ *Web:* www.crye-leike.com

Cummings Properties LLC 200 W Cummings Pk .... Woburn MA 01801 781-935-8000
Web: www.meadowsestates.com

Cushman & Wakefield Inc
1290 Ave of the Americas .... New York NY 10019 212-841-7500 841-7867
Web: www.cushmanwakefield.com

Cutten Realty Inc 2120 Campton Rd Ste C .... Eureka CA 95503 707-445-8811
TF: 800-776-4458 ■ *Web:* cuttenrealty.com

Dana B Kenyon Co 5772 Timuquana Rd .... Jacksonville FL 32210 904-777-0833
Web: www.dbkenyon.com

Dana Group, The 6892 S Yosemite Ct .... Centennial CO 80112 303-694-7100
Web: www.danainvestments.com

Daniel Gale Sotheby's International Realty
187 Park Ave .... Huntington NY 11743 631-427-6600
Web: www.danielgale.com

Dart Appraisalcom 2600 W Big Beaver Rd Ste 540 .... Troy MI 48084 888-327-8123
TF: 888-327-8123 ■ *Web:* dartappraisal.com

Dartmouth Company Inc, The 351 Newbury St .... Boston MA 02115 617-262-6620
Web: www.dartco.com

Daum Commercial Real Estate Services
801 S Figueroa St Ste 600 .... Los Angeles CA 90017 213-626-9101
Web: www.daumcommercial.com

David Plunkett Realty LLC 8832 Riverside Dr .... Parker AZ 85344 928-667-1699
Web: davidplunkettrealty.com

Delois Smith All-Star Team Inc
4 Willow Bend Dr Ste 2A .... Hattiesburg MS 39402 601-545-3900
Web: deloissmith.com

Delphi Business Properties Inc
7100 Hayvenhurst Ave Ste 211 .... Van Nuys CA 91406 818-780-7878
Web: go2delphi.com

DelShah Capital LLC 114 E 13th St .... New York NY 10003 212-677-4506
Web: www.delshah.com

Development Planning & Financing Group Inc
27127 Calle Arroyo Ste 1910 .... San Juan Capistrano CA 92675 949-388-9269
Web: www.dpfg.com

DH Bader Management Services Inc
14435 Cherry Ln Ct Ste 210 .... Laurel MD 20707 301-953-1955
TF: 888-953-1955 ■ *Web:* dhbader.com

Diamond Realty Management Corp
790 Watervliet Shaker Rd Ste 2 .... Latham NY 12110 518-783-5000
Web: www.ambroselec.com

Discovery Green Conservancy 1500 Mckinney St .... Houston TX 77010 713-400-7336
Web: discoverygreen.com

DJM Capital Partners Inc
60 S Market St Ste 1120 .... San Jose CA 95113 408-271-0366
Web: www.djmcapital.com

Dominion First Realty Inc
2420 Maplewood Ave .... Richmond VA 23220 804-359-9200
Web: www.dominionfirst.com

Drake Commercial Lp
19310 Stone Oak Pkwy Ste 201 .... San Antonio TX 78258 210-402-6363
Web: drakecommercial.com

Phone Fax

Eakin Partners LLC
Roundabout Plz 1600 Division St Ste 600 .... Nashville TN 37203 615-250-1800
Web: www.eakinpartners.com

Eddy Group Ltd 660 St Anne St .... Bathurst NB E2A2N6 506-546-6631
Web: www.eddygroup.com

Edina Realty Inc 6800 France Ave S Ste 600 .... Edina MN 55435 952-928-5563
Web: www.edinarealty.com

Emerald Cos Inc 406 Ave D .... San Luis AZ 85349 337-264-9777
Web: emeraldcm.com/ecm

Emil Anderson Construction (EAC) Inc
907 Ethel St .... Kelowna BC V1Y2W1 250-762-9999 762-6171
Web: www.eac.bc.ca

Engel Realty Company Inc
951 Eighteenth St S Ste 200 .... Birmingham AL 35201 205-939-6800
Web: www.engelrealty.com

Enpria Inc 10260 SW Greenburg Rd Ste 850 .... Portland OR 97223 503-293-8444

Equine Canada 2685 Queensview Dr. .... Ottawa ON K2B8K2 613-248-3484
TF: 866-282-8395 ■ *Web:* www.equinecanada.ca

ERA Grizzard Real Estate 1300 W N Blvd .... Leesburg FL 34748 352-787-6966
Web: www.eragrizzard.com

ERA Naper Realty Inc 865 N Columbia St .... Naperville IL 60563 630-961-1776
Web: www.eranaper.com

ERA Wilder Realty 120A Columbia Ave PO Box 610 .... Chapin SC 29036 803-345-6713 772-9226
TF: 866-593-7653 ■ *Web:* www.era.com/era-wilder-realty-947c

Etkin Equities LLC
200 Franklin Ctr 29100 NW Hwy .... Southfield MI 48034 248-358-0800
Web: etkinllc.com

Fc Tucker Company Inc
9201 N Meridian St Ste 100 .... Indianapolis IN 46260 317-571-2200
Web: talktotucker.com

Fimc Commercial Realty 1619 S Tyler St .... Amarillo TX 79102 806-358-7151
TF: 800-658-2616 ■ *Web:* fimcrealty.com

Findwell 920 Dexter Ave N .... Seattle WA 98109 206-462-6200
Web: www.findwell.com

Firm Realty Inc 1930 Harrison St Ste 505 .... Hollywood FL 33020 954-926-2510
Web: www.firmrealty.com

Flans & Weiner Inc 16200 Ventura Blvd Ste 417 .... Encino CA 91436 818-501-4888
Web: flansweiner.com

Fortune Builders International
25082 Paseo Arboleda .... Lake Forest CA 92630 949-380-3080

FPI Management Inc 800 Iron Pt Rd .... Folsom CA 95630 916-357-5300 357-5310
Web: www.fpimgt.com

Fraser Forbes Co LLC 6862 Elm St Ste 620 .... Mclean VA 22101 703-790-9400
Web: www.fraserforbes.com

FREEMAN WEBB CO 3810 Bedford Ave Ste 300 .... Nashville TN 37215 615-271-2700
Web: www.freemanwebb.com

Frye Properties 300 W Freemason St .... Norfolk VA 23510 757-627-1980
Web: www.fryeproperties.com

Galman Group, The 261 Old York Rd Ofc .... Jenkintown PA 19046 215-886-2000

Garden State Mltple Lsting Services
1719 SR- 10 Ste 223 .... Parsippany NJ 07054 973-898-1900
Web: www.gsmls.com

Gart Cos Inc, The 299 Milwaukee St Ste 500 .... Denver CO 80206 303-333-1933
Web: www.gartcompanies.com

GEM Technology International Corp
2665 S Bayshore Dr Ste M103-5 .... Miami FL 33133 305-447-1344
Web: www.gemtechnology.com

Gerald A Teel Co 974 Campbell Rd Ste 204 .... Houston TX 77024 713-467-5858 467-0704
Web: www.gateel.com

Glacier Real Estate Finance Inc
2800 156th Ave Ste 210 .... Bellevue WA 98007 206-985-8200
Web: www.glacierres.com

Gorilla Capital Inc 1342 High St .... Eugene OR 97401 541-344-7867
Web: www.gorillacapital.com

Gove Group Real Estate LLC
70 Portsmouth Ave .... Stratham NH 03885 603-778-6400
TF: 866-778-6400 ■ *Web:* www.thegovegroup.com

Greater Fort Worth Assn of Realtors Inc
2650 Parkview Dr .... Fort Worth TX 76102 817-336-5165
Web: www.gfwar.org

Green Acres of America LLC
615 Lindsay St .... Chattanooga TN 37403 423-756-4082

Greg Malik Real Estate Group Inc
7450 Morro Rd .... Atascadero CA 93422 805-466-2540
Web: gregmalik.com

Gregg Distributors Ltd 16215-118 Ave .... Edmonton AB T5V1C7 780-447-3447
Web: www.greggdistributors.ca

Grubb Company Inc, The 1960 Mountain Blvd .... Oakland CA 94611 510-339-0400
Web: www.grubbco.com

Guarantee Real Estate Corp
5380 N Fresno Ave Ste 103 .... Fresno CA 93710 559-650-6088
Web: www.guarantee.com

GVD Commercial Properties Inc
1915 E Katella Ave Ste A .... Orange CA 92867 714-639-2131
Web: www.gvdcommercialproperties.com

H Pearce Real Estate Co 393 State St .... North Haven CT 06473 203-281-3400
TF: 800-373-3411 ■ *Web:* www.joelgalvin.com

Habitat Company LLC, The
350 W Hubbard St Ste 500 .... Chicago IL 60610 312-527-5400 527-7440
Web: www.habitat.com

Halstead Property LLC 770 Lexington Ave .... New York NY 10065 212-317-7800
Web: www.halstead.com

Hardin & Company Ltd 113 S 19th Ave Ste C .... Bozeman MT 59718 406-587-1211
Web: hardinre.com

Harold A Davison 1723 Claredon Ave NW .... Canton OH 44708 330-454-1244

Harry B Lucas Co
2828 E Trinity Mills Rd Ste 100 .... Carrollton TX 75006 972-991-4567
Web: www.harryblucascompany.com

Hart Corp 900 Jaymor Rd .... SouthHampton PA 18966 215-322-5100 322-5840
TF: 800-368-4278 ■ *Web:* www.hartcorp.com

Hart Realty Advisers Inc 1 Mill Pond Ln .... Simsbury CT 06070 860-651-4000
Web: www.hartadvisers.com

Phone Fax

Heartland Multiple Listing Service Inc
11150 Overbrook Rd Ste 125 .... Leawood KS 66211 913-661-1600
Web: matrix.heartlandmls.com

Heller Real Estate Group Inc, The
171 Saxony Rd Ste 205 .... Encinitas CA 92024 760-632-8408
Web: www.hellerthehomeseller.com

Help-U-Sell Real Estate
240 N Washington Blvd .... Sarasota FL 34236 941-951-7707
Web: www.helpusell.com

Henderson Properties Inc 919 Norland Rd .... Charlotte NC 28205 704-535-1122
Web: www.hendersonproperties.com

Herbert K Horita Realty Inc
98-150 Kaonohi St Ste B128 .... Aiea HI 96701 808-487-1561
Web: www.hicentral.com

Herbert Yentis & Company Inc
7300 City Line Ave .... Philadelphia PA 19151 215-878-7300
Web: yentis.com

Heritage Title Co
Frost Bank Tower Ste 1500 401 Congress Ave .... Austin TX 78701 512-505-5000
Web: reca.org

Herman & Kittle Properties Inc
500 E 96th St Ste 300 .... Indianapolis IN 46240 317-846-3111
Web: hermankittle.com

Hill & Company Real Estate Inc
1880 Lombard St .... San Francisco CA 94123 415-921-6000
Web: www.marinadistrictrealestate.com

Hilliker Corp 1401 S Brentwood Blvd Ste 650 .... St Louis MO 63144 314-781-0001
Web: www.hillikercorp.com

Hoban & Assoc Dba Coast Real Estate Services
2829 Rucker Ave .... Everett WA 98201 425-339-3638
TF: 800-339-3634 ■ *Web:* www.coastmgt.com

HomeGain.com Inc
6001 Shellmound St Ste 550 .... Emeryville CA 94608 510-655-0800 655-0848
TF: 888-542-0800 ■ *Web:* www.homegain.com

HomeServices of America Inc
333 S Seventh St 27th Fl .... Minneapolis MN 55402 888-485-0018 336-5572*
**Fax Area Code:* 612 ■ *TF:* 888-485-0018 ■ *Web:* www.homeservices.com

HomeSmart International LLC
8388 E Hartford Dr Ste 100 .... Scottsdale AZ 85255 602-230-7600
Web: homesmart.com

Horah Group, The
351 Manville Rd Ste 105 .... Pleasantville NY 10570 914-495-3200
Web: www.horah.com

Hospitality Real Estate Counselors
6400 S Fiddler'S Green Cir
Ste 1730 .... Greenwood Village CO 80111 303-267-0057
Web: www.hrec.com

Hotpadscom PO Box 53104 .... Washington DC 20009 202-232-1581
TF: 888-876-1992 ■ *Web:* hotpads.com

Housing Resources Group 1651 Bellevue Ave .... Seattle WA 98122 206-623-0506
Web: www.hrg.org

Howes & Jefferies Realtors 345 Fifth Ave S .... Clinton IA 52732 563-242-3265
Web: howesandjefferies.com

Hughes Commercial Properties Inc
935 S Main St Ste 202 .... Greenville NC 29603 864-233-0079
Web: www.hughescommercial.com

Hughes Marino Inc 1450 Front St .... San Diego CA 92101 619-238-2111
Web: www.hughesmarino.com

In-Rel Properties Inc
2328 10th Ave N Ste 401 .... Lake Worth FL 33461 561-533-0344
Web: in-rel.com

Industrial Realty Group LLC
11100 Santa Monica Blvd Ste 850 .... Los Angeles CA 90025 562-803-4761
Web: www.industrialrealtygroup.com

Inland Group Inc 2901 Butterfield Rd .... Oak Brook IL 60523 630-218-8000 218-4917
TF: 800-826-8228 ■ *Web:* www.inlandgroup.com

Inspirato with American Express
1625 Wazee St Ste 400 .... Denver CO 80202 303-586-7771
Web: www.inspirato.com

Institutional Real Estate Inc
2274 Camino Ramon .... San Ramon CA 94583 925-244-0500
Web: www.irei.com

Intereal Corp 520 Third St Ste 555 .... San Francisco CA 94107 415-778-3900

Iowa Realty Company Inc
3501 Westown Pkwy .... West Des Moines IA 50266 515-453-6222
TF: 800-247-2430 ■ *Web:* www.iowarealty.com

Irving A Miller Inc 2550 W Chester Pk .... Broomall PA 19008 610-356-1130

J & s Management 702 Marshall St Ste 420 .... Redwood City CA 94063 650-361-8350

J Rockcliff Realtors 15 Railroad Ave .... Danville CA 94526 925-855-4000
Web: www.rockcliff.com

Jack Conway 137 Washington St .... Norwell MA 02061 781-871-0080 878-2632
TF: 800-283-1030 ■ *Web:* www.jackconway.com

James R Mclauchlen Real Estate Inc
789 Hill St .... Southampton NY 11968 631-283-0448
Web: mclauchlen.com

Jameson Real Estate LLC 425 W N Ave .... Chicago IL 60610 312-751-0300

Janet Mcafee Real Estate 9889 Clayton Rd .... Saint Louis MO 63124 314-997-4800 997-0647
TF: 888-991-4800 ■ *Web:* www.janetmcafee.com

Javelina Partners 616 Texas St .... Fort Worth TX 76102 817-336-7109

JB Goodwin Real Estate Company Inc
3933 Steck Ave Ste 110 .... Austin TX 78759 512-502-7800
Web: www.jbgoodwin.com

Jersey Cape Realty Inc 739 Washington St .... Cape May NJ 08204 609-884-5800
TF: 800-643-0043 ■ *Web:* www.jerseycaperealty.com

JJ Clarke Enterprises Inc
2905 N Charles St .... Baltimore MD 21218 410-962-0241
Web: jjclarkeenterprises.com

JL Properties Inc 813 D St Ste 200 .... Anchorage AK 99501 907-279-8068
Web: www.jlproperties.com

John C R Kelly Realty
3535 Blvd Of The Allies .... Pittsburgh PA 15213 412-683-7300
Web: jcrkelly.com

John d Miller Real Estate Investments LLC
1370 W SR- 89A Ste 17 .... Sedona AZ 86336 928-254-0303
Web: johndmiller.com

				Phone	Fax

John Daugherty Realtors
520 Post Oak Blvd 6th Fl Houston TX 77027 713-626-3930 963-9588
TF: 800-231-2821 ■ *Web:* www.johndaugherty.com

John Stewart Company Inc
1388 Sutter St Fl 11 San Francisco CA 94109 415-345-4400 614-9175
Web: www.jsco.net

Jones Lang LaSalle IP Inc 200 E Randolph Dr Chicago IL 60601 312-782-5800
Web: www.jll.com

Joseph P Day Realty Corp 9 E 40th St New York NY 10016 212-889-7460
Web: www.jpday.com

Joyner Fine Properties (JFP)
2727 Enterprise Pkwy Richmond VA 23294 804-270-9440 967-2770
TF: 800-446-3858 ■ *Web:* www.joynerfineproperties.com

JR Realty 101 E Horizon Dr Henderson NV 89015 702-564-5142
TF: 800-541-6780 ■ *Web:* century21jrrealty.com

Kansas City Regional Assn of Realtors Inc, The
11150 Overbrook Rd Ste 100 Leawood KS 66211 913-498-1100
Web: www.kcrar.com

Keefe Real Estate 1155 E Geneva St Delavan WI 53115 262-728-8757
TF: 800-690-2292 ■ *Web:* www.keeferealestate.com

Keegan & Coppin Company Inc
1355 N Dutton Ave Santa Rosa CA 95401 707-528-1400
Web: www.keegancoppin.com

Keller Williams Realty Inc
807 Las Cimas Pkwy Ste 200 Austin TX 78746 512-327-3070 328-1433
Web: www.kw.com

Kelly Waters Inc 5 Clementine Pk Dorchester Center MA 02124 617-282-3620
Web: kellywaters.com

Kensington Realty Advisors Inc
100 N Riverside Plz Ste 2300 Chicago IL 60606 312-993-7800
Web: www.kra-net.com

Keystone Property Group Inc
1 Presidential Blvd Ste 300 Bala Cynwyd PA 19004 610-980-7000
TF: 866-980-1818 ■ *Web:* www.keystonepropertygroup.com

Kiemle & Hagood Co 601 W Main Ave Ste 400 Spokane WA 99201 509-838-6541 458-4014
Web: www.khco.com

Kindred Partners LLC 535 Mission St 22nd Fl San Mateo CA 94403 650-573-5500
Web: www.kindredpartners.com

Kislak Company Inc, The 1000 Rt 9 N Woodbridge NJ 07095 732-750-3000
Web: kislakrealty.com

Kline Scott Visco Commercial Real Estate Inc
117 W Patrick St Frederick MD 21701 301-694-8444
Web: klinescottvisco.com

KW Property Management LLC
8200 NW 33rd St Ste 300 Miami FL 33122 305-476-9188
Web: kwpmc.com

L a Tews Realty Inc 13011 Lazdins Cir Cypress TX 77429 281-807-3444
Web: www.latews.com

L b Property Management
4730 Woodman Ave Ste 200 Sherman Oaks CA 91423 888-400-7080
TF: 888-400-7080

L Peres & Assoc Inc 525 River Rd Edgewater NJ 07020 201-943-7717
Web: lperes.com

Land Home Financial Services Inc
1355 Willow Way Ste 250 Concord CA 94520 925-338-8200
Web: lhfs.com

Landmark Realty LLC 2205 Beckett St Bossier City LA 71111 318-747-0052
Web: www.landmarkrealty.org

Landshark Inc PO Box 1791 Boulder CO 80306 303-494-1229

LANE4 Property Group Inc 4705 Central St Kansas City MO 64112 816-960-1444
Web: www.lane4group.com

Lang Realty 2901 Clint Moore Rd Ste 9 Boca Raton FL 33496 561-998-0100
Web: www.langrealty.com

Latt Maxcy Corp 21299 Us Hwy 27 Lake Wales FL 33859 863-679-6700
Web: www.lattmaxcy.com

Latter & Blum Inc 430 Notre Dame St New Orleans LA 70130 504-525-1311 569-9336
Web: www.latterblum.com

Lawler-Wood LLC 1600 Riverview Tower Knoxville TN 37902 865-637-7777
Web: www.lawlerwood.com

LCB Assoc Inc 388 17th St Ste 200 Oakland CA 94612 510-763-7016
Web: www.lcbassociates.com

Lechner Realty Group Inc
13421 Manchester Rd Saint Louis MO 63131 314-909-8100 909-8105
Web: www.lechnerrealty.com

Lee & Assoc Commercial Real Estate Services Inc
13181 Crossroads Pkwy N Ste 300 City Of Industry CA 91746 562-699-7500
Web: www.lee-associates.com

Leisure World of Maryland
3701 Rossmoor Blvd Silver Spring MD 20906 301-598-1000
Web: www.lwmc.com

Lereta LLC 1123 Parkview Dr Covina CA 91724 626-339-5221
Web: www.lereta.com

Lewis Group 2766 Degen Dr Bonita CA 91902 619-470-9110
Web: www.mcmillinrealty.com

LG2 Environmental Solutions Inc
14785 Old St Augustine Rd Ste 4 Jacksonville FL 32258 904-288-8631
TF: 800-435-0072 ■ *Web:* www.lg2es.com

Lightstone Group, The 460 Pk Ave Ste 1300 New York NY 10022 212-616-9969
Web: www.lightstonegroup.com

Lincoln Equities Group LLC
1 Meadowlands Plz Ste 803 East Rutherford NJ 07073 201-460-3440
Web: www.lincolnequities.com

Lindy Property Management Co
207 Leedom St Jenkintown PA 19046 215-886-8030
Web: www.lindyproperty.com

Living Room Realtors Inc 1401 NE Alberta St Portland OR 97211 503-719-5588
Web: www.livingroomre.com

Loeb Properties Inc 825 Vly Brook Dr Memphis TN 38120 901-761-3333
Web: www.loebproperties.com

London Properties Ltd 6442 N Maroa Ave Fresno CA 93704 559-436-4000
Web: www.londonproperties.com

Long & Foster Realtors
14501 George Carter Way Chantilly VA 20151 703-653-8500
TF: 800-237-8800 ■ *Web:* www.longandfoster.com

Loopnet Inc 2100 E Rt 66 Glendora CA 91740 626-803-5000
Web: loopnet.com

Losvet Company LLC
260 S Beverly Dr Ste 301 Beverly Hills CA 90212 310-273-5364

Lucas Ltd 1200 Wilshire Blvd Ste 208 Los Angeles CA 90017 213-240-5990

Macdonald Realty 203 5188 Wminster Hwy Richmond BC V7C5S7 604-279-9822
TF: 877-278-3888 ■ *Web:* www.macrealty.com

MacPherson's Property Management Inc
18551 Aurora Ave N Ste 301 Shoreline WA 98133 206-542-6363 542-0783
TF: 800-962-6473 ■ *Web:* www.macphersons.com

Mad Inc Dba Century 21 Salvadori Realty
3500 N G St Merced CA 95340 209-383-6475
TF: 800-557-6033 ■ *Web:* c21salvadori.com

Major Properties Real Estate
1200 W Olympic Blvd Los Angeles CA 90015 213-747-4151 749-7972
Web: www.majorproperties.com

Mansermar Inc 2405 Satellite Blvd Ste 100 Duluth GA 30096 678-330-2000
Web: mansermar.com

Mar West Real Estate Inc
1049 Camino Del Mar Ste 12 Del Mar CA 92014 858-775-4917
Web: marwestcommercial.com

Marcus & Assoc Inc 1045 Mapunapuna St Honolulu HI 96819 808-839-7446
Web: www.marcusrealty.com

Massaro Properties LLC 120 Delta Dr Pittsburgh PA 15238 412-963-2800
Web: www.massaroproperties.com

Massey Knakal Realty Services Inc
275 Madison Ave 3rd Fl New York NY 10016 212-696-2500
Web: www.masseyknakal.com

Matrix Realty Group LLC 2066 Ridge Rd Homewood IL 60430 708-799-3600
Web: www.matrixrealtygroup.com

Mattson Resources Inc
7994 Swamp Flower Dr E Jacksonville FL 32244 904-772-6506

Max Hansen & Son Inc 200 Industrial Rd San Carlos CA 94070 650-595-5841

MCAP Service Corp 400-200 King St W Toronto ON M5H3T4 416-598-2665
TF: 800-387-4405 ■ *Web:* www.mcap.com

Mccaffery Interests Inc
875 N Michigan Ave Ste 1800 Chicago IL 60611 312-944-3777
Web: www.mccafferyinterests.com

Mccall & Almy Inc 1 Post Office Sq Ste 2800 Boston MA 02109 617-542-4141
Web: mccallalmy.com

McCann Realty Partners LLC
2520-B Gaskins Rd Richmond VA 23238 804-290-8870
Web: www.mrpapts.com

McEagle Properties LLC
1001 Boardwalk Springs Pl O'Fallon MO 63368 636-561-9300

Mcenearney Assoc Inc 109 S Pitt St Alexandria VA 22314 703-549-9292
TF: 877-624-9322 ■ *Web:* www.mcenearney.com

Mcwhirter Realty Partners LLC Formerly Mcwhirter Realty Corp
300 Galleria Pkwy Ste 300 Atlanta GA 30339 770-955-2000
Web: mcwrealty.com

MD Atkinson Company Inc
1401 19th St Ste 400 Bakersfield CA 93301 661-334-4800
Web: www.mdatkinson.com

MD Management Inc 5201 Johnson Dr Ste 100 Mission KS 66205 913-831-2996
Web: www.mdmgt.com

Me Cos Inc 635 Brooksedge Blvd Westerville OH 43081 614-818-4900 818-4901

Medve Group Inc 8390 Delmar Blvd Fl 1 Saint Louis MO 63124 314-569-0004
Web: www.medve.com

MEI Real Estate Services
5757 W Century Blvd Ste 605 Los Angeles CA 90045 310-258-0444
Web: www.meirealty.com

Menas Realty Co 4990 Mission Blvd San Diego CA 92109 619-276-5169
Web: www.menas.com

Merin Hunter Codman Inc
1601 Forum Pl Ste 200 West Palm Beach FL 33401 561-471-8000 471-9992
Web: www.mhcreal.com

Metcalfe Realty & Auction Company Inc
100 Castle Ridge Dr Edmonton KY 42129 270-432-7355
Web: metcalferealty.net

Mitsui Fudosan America Inc
1251 Ave of the Americas Ste 800 New York NY 10020 212-403-5600
Web: www.mfamerica.com

Morrison Ekre & Bart Management Services Inc
1215 E Missouri Ave Phoenix AZ 85014 602-279-5515
Web: mebapts.com

Morrow Realty Co Inc 809 22nd Ave Tuscaloosa AL 35401 205-759-5781
Web: www.morrowrealty.com

Mountain Thunder Lodge 50 Mountain Dr Breckenridge CO 80424 970-547-5650
Web: breckresorts.com

Mytina Inc Dba Real Estate Mortgage Exchange
842 Foothill Blvd La Canada Flintridge CA 91011 818-507-0077

Nai Hunneman 303 Congress St Boston MA 02210 617-457-3400
Web: www.naihunneman.com

National Church Residences Inc
2335 N Bank Dr Columbus OH 43220 800-388-2151 451-0351*
**Fax Area Code: 614* ■ *TF:* 800-388-2151 ■ *Web:* www.nationalchurchresidences.org

Nationwide Property & Appraisal Services LLC
10 Foster Ave Ste 3c Gibbsboro NJ 08026 856-258-6977
Web: onestopappraisals.com

Navarre Beach Realty 8305 Navarre Pkwy Navarre FL 32566 850-936-0700
Web: www.navarrebeachrealty.com

Nebo Agency Inc 197 East 100 North Ste 100 Payson UT 84651 801-465-2535

Net Lease Capital Advisors 1 Tara Blvd Nashua NH 03062 603-598-9500
Web: www.netleasecapital.com

New Bedford Management Corp
210 E 23rd St 5th Fl New York NY 10010 212-674-6123
Web: www.newbedfordmanagement.com

Newland Communities LLC
9820 Towne Centre Dr Ste 100 San Diego CA 92121 858-455-7503
Web: www.newlandcommunities.com

Newmark Grubb Knight Frank 1800 Larimer St Denver CO 80202 303-892-1111
Web: www.ngkf.com/home/about-our-firm/global-offices/us-offices/denver.aspx

Neyer Properties Inc 2135 Dana Ave Ste 200 Cincinnati OH 45207 513-563-7555
Web: www.neyer1.com

Phone | Fax

Nicholson Cos Inc, The 819 W Little Creek Rd Norfolk VA 23505 757-423-3281
Web: thenicholsoncompanies.com
Nicolson Porter & List
1300 W Higgins Rd Ste 104 Park Ridge IL 60068 847-698-7400
Web: nplchicago.com
North Orange County Escrow Corp
1370 Brea Blvd Ste 110 Fullerton CA 92835 714-526-5400 526-1744
Web: www.nocescrow.com/contact
North Pacific Management 1905 SE 10th Ave Portland OR 97214 503-425-1500
Web: www.northp.com
NP Dodge Real Estate 8701 W Dodge Rd Ste 300 Omaha NE 68114 402-397-4900
TF: 800-642-5008 ■ *Web:* www.npdodge.com
NRC Realty & Capital Advisors LLC
363 W Erie St Ste 300 E Chicago IL 60654 312-278-6800
Web: www.nrc.com
O'Neill Properties Group LP
2701 Renaissance Blvd 4th Fl King Of Prussia PA 19406 610-239-6100
Web: www.oneillproperties.com
Olive Real Estate Group
102 N Cascade Ave Ste 250 Colorado Springs CO 80903 719-598-3000 578-0089
Web: www.olivereg.com
Olmstead Properties Inc
575 Eighth Ave Rm 2400 New York NY 10018 212-564-6662
Web: olmsteadinc.com
Ontario Real Estate Assn 99 Duncan Mill Rd Don Mills ON M3B1Z2 416-445-9910
TF: 866-444-5557 ■ *Web:* www.orea.com
P J Morgan Real Estate Auctioneers
7801 Wakeley Plz Omaha NE 68114 402-397-7775
Web: www.pjmorgan.com
Pacific Coast Valuations
740 Corporate Ctr Dr Ste 200 Pomona CA 91768 909-623-4001
TF: 888-623-4001 ■ *Web:* www.pcvmurcor.com
Pacifica Hotel Co 1155 Coast Blvd Ste 1 La Jolla CA 92037 805-957-0095
Web: www.hcareers.com
Packard Cos, The 9555 Chesapeake Dr Ste 202 San Diego CA 92123 858-277-4305
Web: www.packard-1.com
Pan Pacific Ocean Hotel Inc
243 Kearny St San Francisco CA 94108 415-433-0177
Paragon Management Company LLC
4370 La Jolla Village Dr Ste 640 San Diego CA 92122 858-535-9000
Web: www.paragoncompany.com
Paramount Property Management Inc
473 Broadway Ste 500 Bayonne NJ 07002 201-858-8500
Web: www.paramountassets.com
Park Regency Real Estate
10146 Balboa Blvd Granada Hills CA 91344 818-363-6116
Web: parkregency.com
Partners Trust Real Estate Brokerage & Acquisitions
9378 Wilshire Blvd Ste 200 Beverly Hills CA 90212 310-500-3900
Web: www.thepartnerstrust.com
Patterson-Schwartz & Assoc Inc
7234 Lancaster Pike Ste 100A Hockessin DE 19707 302-234-5270
TF: 877-456-4663 ■ *Web:* www.pattersonschwartz.com
Peabody Properties Inc 536 Granite St Braintree MA 02184 781-794-1000
Web: www.ayerlofts.com
Pegasus Residential LLC
1750 Founders Pkwy Ste 180 Alpharetta GA 30009 678-347-2802
Web: www.pegasusresidential.com
Pembroke Commercial Realty Corp
4460 Corporation Ln Ste 300 Virginia Beach VA 23462 757-490-3141
Web: www.pembrokerealty.com
Pendleton Manor 414 Summit Dr Greenville SC 29609 864-271-7562
Web: pendletonmanor.com
Penn-Florida Cos
1515 N Federal Hwy Ste 306 Boca Raton FL 33432 561-750-1030
Web: www.pennflorida.com
Perennial Mgmt Ltd 40 Aberdeen Ave St John'S NL A1A5T3 709-754-2057
Web: perennialmanagement.ca
Phillips Property Management
6106 Macarthur Blvd Ste 102 Bethesda MD 20816 301-320-0422 229-0937
Web: www.phillipspm.com
Phoenix Realty & Trust Co PO Box 87420 Phoenix AZ 85080 602-494-0202
Pierce-Eislen Inc
9200 E Pima Ctr Pkwy Ste 150 Scottsdale AZ 85258 480-663-1149
Web: www.yardimatrix.com
PK Partners LLC
3610 River Crossing Pkwy Indianapolis IN 46240 317-817-8888
Web: pkpartners.com
Places Real Estate
400 Hibben St Ste 200 Mount Pleasant SC 29464 843-849-3636
Web: www.scplaces.com
Placitas Realty Inc 03 Homesteads Rd Ste A Placitas NM 87043 505-867-8000
PMCS-ICAP 829 W Genesee St Syracuse NY 13204 315-423-7962
TF: 800-245-7627 ■ *Web:* www.pmcs-icap.com
Preferred Properties of Venice Inc
325 W Venice Ave Venice FL 34285 941-485-9602
Web: www.veniceflproperties.com
Premier Real Estate Management LLC
19105 W Capitol Dr Ste 200 Brookfield NY 53045 262-790-4560
Web: www.premierremgmt.com
Premier Realty Group 2 N Sewalls Point Rd Stuart FL 34996 772-287-1777
TF: 800-915-8517 ■ *Web:* www.premierrealtygroup.com
Primera Partners LLC
111 Soledad St Ste 1250 San Antonio TX 78205 210-444-1400 444-1401
Web: primerapartners.com
Principal Properties Inc 3295 W 4 Ave Hialeah FL 33012 305-883-7555
Web: principalproperties.com
Pyramid Brokerage Co 5786 Widewaters Pkwy Syracuse NY 13214 315-445-1030
Web: www.pyramidbrokerage.com
Quad Cities Realty 1053 Ripon Ave Lewiston ID 83501 208-798-7798
TF: 877-798-7798 ■ *Web:* qcrhomes.com
Ramsey-Shilling Commercial Real Estate Services Inc
6711 Forest Lawn Dr Los Angeles CA 90068 323-851-6666
Web: www.ramsey-shilling.com

Phone | Fax

Ray Stone Inc 550 Howe Ave Ste 200 Sacramento CA 95825 916-649-7500
Web: www.raystoneinc.com
Raymond Group Inc, The
8333 Greenway Blvd Ste 200 Middleton WI 53562 608-833-4100
Web: www.raymondteam.com
RE/MAX International Inc 5075 S Syracuse St Denver CO 80237 303-770-5531 796-3599
TF Cust Svc: 800-525-7452 ■ *Web:* www.remax.com
RE/MAX of Western Canada Inc
1060 Manhattan Dr Ste 340 Kelowna BC V1Y9X9 250-860-3628
TF: 800-563-3622 ■ *Web:* www.remax.ca
RE/MAX Ontario-Atlantic 7101 Syntex Dr Mississauga ON L5N6H5 905-542-2400 542-3340
TF: 888-542-2499 ■ *Web:* www.remax.ca
RE/MAX Quebec Inc 1500 Cunard St Laval QC H7S2B7 450-668-7743 668-2115
TF: 800-361-9325 ■ *Web:* www.remax-quebec.com
Real Estate Institute of Bc
1750 - 355 Burrard St Vancouver BC V6C2G8 604-685-3702
TF: 800-667-2166 ■ *Web:* www.reibc.org
Real Estate One Inc 25800 NW Hwy Ste 100 Southfield MI 48075 248-304-6700 263-5966
TF: 800-521-0508 ■ *Web:* www.realestateone.com
Real Living First Service Realty
13155 SW 42nd St Ste 200 Miami FL 33175 305-551-9400 551-4965
TF: 800-899-8477 ■ *Web:* www.realliving.com
Real Living Inc 77 E Nationwide Blvd Columbus OH 43215 614-459-7400
Web: www.realliving.com
RealCapitalMarketscom LLC
5780 Fleet St Ste 130 Carlsbad CA 92008 760-602-5080
Web: www.rcm1.com
Realestateexpresscom
12977 N 40 Dr Ste 108 Saint Louis MO 63141 866-739-7277 205-1613*
**Fax Area Code:* 314 ■ *TF:* 866-739-7277 ■ *Web:* www.realestateexpress.com
Reality Interactive 386 Main St 6th Fl Middletown CT 06457 952-253-4700
Realogy Corp 175 Park Ave Madison NJ 07940 973-407-2000 407-7779
Web: www.realogy.com
Realty Executives International Inc
7600 N 16th St Ste 100 Phoenix AZ 85020 602-957-0747 224-5542
TF: 800-252-3366 ■ *Web:* www.realtyexecutives.com
Realty Plus Chicago Inc
453 E 111th St Apt 16 Chicago IL 60628 773-785-1400
Reata Real Estate Services LP
1100 NE Loop 410 Ste 400 San Antonio TX 78216 210-930-4111
Web: www.reatarealestate.com
Rebman Properties Inc
1014 W Fairbanks Ave Winter Park FL 32789 407-875-8001 875-8004
Web: www.rebmanproperties.com
Redstone Properties 1120 W SR- 89A Ste B2 Sedona AZ 86336 928-204-2500
Web: www.redstoneproperties.com
Redwood Adventure LLC
44075 Pipeline Plz Ste 225 Ashburn VA 20147 703-858-5676
Web: www.c21redwood.com
Reece & Nichols Realtors 11601 Granada Leawood KS 66211 913-945-3704 491-0930
Web: www.reecenichols.com
Regional Group of Cos Inc, The
1737 Woodward Dr 2nd Fl Ottawa ON K2C0P9 613-230-2100
Web: www.regionalgroup.com
Relocation Center Inc, The
1042 E Juneau Ave Milwaukee WI 53202 414-226-4200
TF: 800-783-5337
Remax Villa Realtors
7515 Bergenline Ave North Bergen NJ 07047 201-868-3100 868-9440
Web: www.remax-villa.com
RemoteReality Corp 100 Northfield Dr Ste 205 Windsor CT 06095 508-870-1500
Web: www.remotereality.com
Retail Planning Corp 35 Johnson Ferry Rd Marietta GA 30068 770-956-8383
Web: www.retailplanningcorp.com
Right at Home Properties PO Box 631154 Irving TX 75063 972-333-4164
Web: www.rightathomeproperties.com
RIS Media Inc 69 E Ave Norwalk CT 06851 203-855-1234
TF: 800-724-6000 ■ *Web:* www.rismedia.com
Ritchie Commercial 34 W Santa Clara St San Jose CA 95113 408-971-2700
Web: www.ritchiecommercial.com
Riverbay Corp 2049 Bartow Ave Bronx NY 10475 718-671-3050
Web: www.riverbaycorp.com
Rivercrest Realty Assoc
8816 Six Forks Rd Ste 201 Raleigh NC 27615 919-846-4046
Web: rivercrestrealty.com
RM Bradley 1 Financial Plz Hartford CT 06103 860-278-2040
Web: www.rmbradley.com
Roose & Ressler Lpa 243 E Liberty St Ste 230 Wooster OH 44691 330-263-5333
Web: theohiodisabilitylawyers.com
Rose Assoc Inc 200 Madison Ave New York NY 10016 212-210-6666
TF: 888-475-8860 ■ *Web:* www.rosenyc.com
Ross Realty Investments Inc
3325 S University Dr Ste 210 Davie FL 33328 954-452-5000 452-4700
TF: 800-370-4202 ■ *Web:* www.ross-realty.com
Rothman Goodman Managmnt Corp
27236 Grand Central Pkwy Floral Park NY 11005 718-224-2880
Rowell Auctions Inc 1303 Fourth St SW Moultrie GA 31768 229-985-8388
Web: rowellauctions.com
Rowley Properties Inc
1595 NW Gilman Blvd Ste 1 Issaquah WA 98027 425-392-6407
Web: www.rowleyproperties.com
Royal T Management 7419 N Cedar Ave Ste 102 Fresno CA 93720 559-447-9887
Web: royaltmanagement.com
Royco Inc
The World Bldg 8121 Georgia Ave
Ste 500 Silver Spring MD 20910 301-608-2212
Ruben Cos 600 Madison Ave New York NY 10022 212-293-9400
Web: www.rubenco.com
Russ Lyon Sotheby's International Realty
21040 N Pima Rd Scottsdale AZ 85255 480-502-3500
Web: www.russlyon.com
Russell & Jeffcoat Realtors Inc
1022 Calhoun St Columbia SC 29201 803-779-6000
Web: www.russellandjeffcoat.com

Company	City	State	Zip	Phone	Fax
Sachse Real Estate Company Inc 315 S Beverly Dr Ste 415 *Web:* www.sachsere.com	Beverly Hills	CA	90212	310-284-7100	
Salisbury Management Inc 120 Shrewsbury St *Web:* www.salisburymanagement.com	Boylston	MA	01505	508-869-0764	
Sam Hatfield Realty Inc 4470 Mansford Rd *TF:* 866-959-7474 ■ *Web:* samhatfield.com	Winchester	TN	37398	931-968-0500	
Sandor Development Co 5725 N Scottsdale Rd Ste C-195 *Web:* sandordev.com	Scottsdale	AZ	85250	480-949-9011	
Sandy River Co 509 Forest Ave PO Box 110 *Web:* sandyrivercompany.com	Portland	ME	04112	207-558-6053	
Select Group Real Estate Inc 409 Century Park Dr *Web:* selectgroupre.com	Yuba City	CA	95991	530-237-1800	
Selective First Realty 4110 Main St *Web:* selectivefirstrealty.com	Flushing	NY	11355	718-461-2510	
Semonin Realtors 4967 US Hwy 42 Ste 200 *TF:* 800-548-1650 ■ *Web:* www.semonin.com	Louisville	KY	40222	502-425-4760	
Sereno Group Real Estate 369 S San Antonio Rd *Web:* www.serenogroup.com	Los Altos	CA	94022	650-947-2900	
Shannon Oaks 2228 Hwy 167 S	Sheridan	AR	72150	870-942-3907	
Sheldon Gross Realty Inc 80 Main St *Web:* www.sheldongrossrealty.com	West Orange	NJ	07052	973-325-6200	
Shelter Canadian Properties Ltd 2600 Seven Evergreen Pl *Web:* www.scpl.com	Winnipeg	MB	R3L2T3	204-475-9090	
Shorewest Realtors Inc 17450 W N Ave *TF:* 800-434-7350 ■ *Web:* www.shorewest.com	Brookfield	WI	53008	262-827-4200	
Silicon Valley Assn of Realtors 19400 Stevens Creek Blvd Ste 100 *TF:* 877-699-6787 ■ *Web:* www.silvar.org	Cupertino	CA	95014	408-200-0100	200-0101
Situs Inc 4665 SW Fwy *Web:* www.situs.com	Houston	TX	77027	713-328-4403	355-5882
Skyline Properties South Inc 50 116th Ave SE Ste 120 *TF:* 800-753-6156 ■ *Web:* www.skylineproperties.com	Bellevue	WA	98004	425-455-2065	
Social Compact 113 S W St *Web:* www.socialcompact.org	Alexandria	VA	22314	202-547-2581	
Solari Enterprises Inc 1572 N Main St *Web:* www.solari-ent.com	Orange	CA	92867	714-282-2520	
Solid Earth Inc 113 Clinton Ave W *Web:* www.solidearth.com	Huntsville	AL	35801	256-536-0606	
Sotheby's International Realty 38 E 61st St *TF:* 866-899-4747 ■ *Web:* www.sothebysrealty.com	New York	NY	10065	212-606-7660	606-4199
Southwest Management Group Inc 622 W Maple St Ste H	Farmington	NM	87401	505-327-3611	
Southwest Property Management Corp 1044 Castello Dr Ste 206 *Web:* www.southwestpropertymanagement.com	Naples	FL	34103	239-261-3440	
St. Aubin Edwin & Co 4151 17 Mile Rd Ste A *Web:* www.michiganhousehunter.com	Sterling Heights	MI	48310	586-939-1400	
Stan Johnson Company Inc 6120 S Yale Ave Ste 813 *Web:* www.stanjohnsonco.com	Tulsa	OK	74136	918-494-2690	
Stan White Realty & Construction Inc 812 Ocean Trl *TF:* 800-753-6200 ■ *Web:* outerbanksrentals.com	Corolla	NC	27927	252-453-6131	
Steele Realty & Investment Company Inc 8900 Grant Line Rd *Web:* www.steelerealtyinc.com	Elk Grove	CA	95624	916-686-6500	686-8504
Stiles Realty Co 301 E Las Olas Blvd *Web:* www.stiles.com	Fort Lauderdale	FL	33301	954-627-9300	627-9305
Stout Management Co 10151 Park Run Dr *Web:* www.smc-lv.com	Las Vegas	NV	89145	702-227-0444	
StreamCo LLC 7130 Glen Forest Dr Ste 110 *Web:* streamco.com	Richmond	VA	23226	804-955-4397	
Strother Ventures II Inc 2929 Breezewood Ave Ste 200 *TF:* 855-753-6143 ■ *Web:* www.erastrother.com	Fayetteville	NC	28303	910-864-2327	
Studley Inc 399 Pk Ave 11th Fl *Web:* www.studley.com	New York	NY	10022	212-326-1000	326-1034
Stumbos & Company Real Estate 2251 Fair Oaks Blvd	Sacramento	CA	95825	916-646-4400	
Suburban Realty Inc 1055 Spring St *Web:* suburbanrealty.biz	Grafton	WI	53024	262-377-3060	
Sudberry Properties Inc 5465 Morehouse Dr Ste 260 *Web:* www.sudprop.com	San Diego	CA	92121	858-546-3000	
Sun Realty Inc 1500 S Croatan Hwy PO Box 1630 *Web:* www.sunrealtync.com	Kill Devil Hills	NC	27948	252-441-7033	
Surterre Properties Inc 1400 Newport Ctr Dr Ste 100 *Web:* www.surterreproperties.com	Newport Beach	CA	92660	949-717-7100	
Sutton Alliance LLC 515 Rockaway Ave *TF:* 866-435-6600 ■ *Web:* suttonalliance.com/progressive	Valley Stream	NY	11581	516-837-6100	
Tarbell Realtors 1403 N Tustin Ave Ste 380 *Web:* www.edwards.net	Santa Ana	CA	92705	714-972-0988	
Tarlton Properties Inc 1530 O'Brien Dr Ste C *Web:* www.tarlton.com	Menlo Park	CA	94025	650-330-3600	
Taylor Morrison Inc 4900 N Scottsdale Rd Ste 2000 *Web:* www.taylormorrison.com	Scottsdale	AZ	85251	480-840-8100	344-7001
TCN Worldwide 1755 N Collins Ste 207 *Web:* www.tcnworldwide.com	Richardson	TX	75075	972-769-8701	
Terrance F Wood Co 400 Mann St Ste 509	Crp Christi	TX	78401	361-888-8891	
Thalhimer Inc Morton G 11100 W Broad St *Web:* www.thalhimer.com	Glen Allen	VA	23060	804-648-5881	697-3479
Themlsonline Com Inc 11150 Commerce Dr N *TF:* 866-657-6654 ■ *Web:* www.themlsonline.com	Champlin	MN	55316	763-576-8286	
TheRedPincom Realty Inc 180 Bloor St W *Web:* www.theredpin.com	Toronto	ON	M5E1M2	416-800-0812	
THF Realty Inc 2127 Innerbelt Business Ctr Dr Ste 200 *Web:* www.thfrealty.com	St Louis	MO	63114	314-429-0900	
Tiempo Escrow Ii 18433 Amistad St *Web:* www.gotescrow.com	Fountain Valley	CA	92708	714-500-1500	
Tmmc 1404 Milbury St	Castle Rock	CO	80104	720-733-1369	
Tom J Keith & Assoc Inc 121 S Cool Spring St *Web:* www.keithvaluation.com	Fayetteville	NC	28301	910-323-3222	
Trammell Crow Co 2100 McKinney Ave Ste 800 *Web:* www.trammellcrow.com	Dallas	TX	75201	214-863-4101	863-4493
Travers Realty Corp 840 Newport Ctr Dr Ste 770 *Web:* www.traversrealty.com	Newport Beach	CA	92660	949-644-5900	
Tri Commercial Real Estate Services Inc 100 Pine St Ste 1000 *Web:* www.tricommercial.com	San Francisco	CA	94111	415-268-2200	268-2289
Tri Properties Inc 4309 Emperor Blvd Ste 110 *Web:* www.triprop.com	Durham	NC	27703	919-941-5745	
Tri-Land Kansas City Investors LLC 1 Wbrook Corporate Ctr Ste 520 *TF:* 800-441-7032 ■ *Web:* www.trilandproperties.com	Westchester	IL	60154	708-531-8210	
Trillium Residential LLC 230 W Fifth St *Web:* www.trilliumresidential.com	Tempe	AZ	85281	480-294-6300	
Trimark Properties LLC 321 SW 13th St *Web:* trimarkproperties.com	Gainesville	FL	32601	352-376-6223	
Trimont Real Estate Advisors Inc 3424 Peachtree Rd NE *Web:* www.trimontrea.com	Atlanta	GA	30326	404-420-5600	
Tvo North America 2500 Guerrero Dr	Carrollton	TX	75006	972-242-1517	
United Commercial Development Inc 7001 Preston Rd Ste 410 *Web:* www.ucdcorp.com	Dallas	TX	75205	214-224-4600	219-2080
United Country Real Estate Inc 2820 NW Barry Rd *TF:* 800-999-1020 ■ *Web:* www.unitedcountry.com	Kansas City	MO	64154	816-420-6200	
United Realty Group 8951 W Atlantic Blvd *Web:* urgfl.com	Coral Springs	FL	33071	954-670-5671	
Urdang Capital Management Inc 630 W Germantown Pk Ste 300 *Web:* centersquare.com	Plymouth Meeting	PA	19462	610-834-9500	
US Residential Group LLC 5001 Spring Valley Rd Ste 1000 E *Web:* www.usrgroup.com	Dallas	TX	75244	469-546-6400	
Vacation Palm Springs Real Estate Inc 1276 N Palm Canyon Dr Ste 211 *Web:* vacationpalmsprings.com	Palm Springs	CA	92262	760-778-7832	
Valuation Management Group LLC 1640 Powers Ferry Rd SE Bldg 15 Ste 100 *TF:* 866-799-7488 ■ *Web:* valuationmanagementgroup.com	Marietta	GA	30067	678-483-4420	
Victor International Corp 7640 Dixie Hwy Ste 100 *Web:* www.victorintl.com	Clarkston	MI	48346	248-364-2400	
Vintage Realty Co 330 Marshall St Ste 200 *Web:* www.vintagerealty.com	Shreveport	LA	71101	318-222-2244	
Virginia Cook Realtors LLC 5950 Sherry Ln Ste 110 *Web:* www.virginiacook.com	Dallas	TX	75225	214-696-8877	
Voit Real Estate Services Inc 101 Shipyard Way *Web:* www.voitco.com	Newport Beach	CA	92663	949-644-8648	
Walsh Property Management PO Box 2657 *TF:* 888-896-5510 ■ *Web:* www.walshpm.com	Castro Valley	CA	94546	510-888-8965	
Wangard Partners Inc 1200 N Mayfair Rd *Web:* www.wangard.com	Milwaukee	WI	53226	414-777-1200	
Waterfront Properties & Club Communities 825 Pkwy Ste 8 *Web:* www.waterfront-properties.com	Jupiter	FL	33477	561-746-7272	
Watson Realty Co 9101 Camino Media *Web:* www.watsonrealty.com	Bakersfield	CA	93311	661-327-5161	
Weichert Financial 6911 Laurel Bowie Rd Ste 100	Bowie	MD	20715	301-805-7788	
Weichert Realtors 1625 Rt 10 E *Web:* www.weichert.com	Morris Plains	NJ	07950	973-984-1400	984-4075
West Terrace Inc 1382 W Ninth St Ste 210 *Web:* yourerc.com	Cleveland	OH	44113	216-696-4466	
WestCorp Management Group LLC 6655 S Eastern Ave *Web:* www.westcorpmg.com	Las Vegas	NV	89119	702-307-2881	
Westcorp Properties Inc 200 College Plz 8215 - 112 St *Web:* www.westcorp.net	Edmonton	AB	T6G2C8	780-431-3300	
Western Development Corp 1228 31st St NW Ste 200 *Web:* www.westdev.com	Washington	DC	20007	202-338-5200	333-0223
Westsiderentalscom 1020 Wilshire Blvd *Web:* www.westsiderentals.com	Santa Monica	CA	90401	310-395-7368	
Wilkinson & Assoc Real Estate Inc 8604 Cliff Cameron Dr Ste 110 *Web:* www.wilkinsonandassociates.com	Charlotte	NC	28269	704-393-0048	
William C Smith & Company Inc 1100 New Jersey Ave SE *Web:* www.wcsmith.com	Washington	DC	20003	202-371-1220	371-9410
William Douglas Management Inc 4523 Park Rd Ste 201 A *Web:* www.wmdouglas.com	Charlotte	NC	28209	704-347-8900	
Williams & Williams Real Estate Auction 7120 S Lewis Ave Ste 200 *TF:* 800-801-8003 ■ *Web:* www.williamsauction.com	Tulsa	OK	74136	918-250-2012	
Wilson Meany Sullivan LLC 4 Embarcadero Ctr Ste 3330 *Web:* wilsonmeany.com	San Francisco	CA	94111	415-905-5300	

				Phone	Fax
Wilson Realty Exchange Inc 16910 15th Ave Ne *Web:* wilsonrealtyexchange.com	Shoreline	WA	98155	206-367-0200	
Wilwat Properties Inc 1958 Monroe Dr Ne *Web:* www.wilwatproperties.com	Atlanta	GA	30324	404-872-8666	
Windsor Co Ltd 101 W Liberty St *Web:* www.windsorhouseinc.com	Girard	OH	44420	330-545-1550	545-2444
Winter Management Corp 730 Fifth Ave 12th Fl *Web:* winter.com/history	New York	NY	10019	212-616-8900	616-8985
Wisconsin Management Co 2040 S Park St *Web:* wisconsinmanagement.com	Madison	WI	53713	608-258-2080	
Woodbury Corp 2733 E Parleys Way Ste 300 *Web:* www.woodburycorp.com	Salt Lake City	UT	84109	801-485-7770	485-0209
Woodfill & Pressler LLP 909 Fannin St 2 Houston Ctr Ste 1470	Houston	TX	77010	713-751-3080	
Youngwoo & Assoc LLC 435 Hudson St 4th Fl *Web:* www.iyoungwoo.com	New York	NY	10014	212-477-8008	
Zalco Realty Inc 8701 Georgia Ave Ste 300 *Web:* www.gjainc.com	Silver Spring	MD	20910	301-495-6600	
Zara Realty Holding Corp 166-07 Hillside Ave *Web:* www.zararealty.com	Jamaica	NY	11432	718-291-3331	
ZipRealty Inc 2000 Powell St Ste 300 *NASDAQ: ZIPR* ■ *TF:* 800-225-5947 ■ *Web:* www.ziprealty.com	Emeryville	CA	94608	510-735-2600	735-2850
ZRS Management LLC 2001 Summit Park Dr Ste 300 *Web:* zrsmanagement.com	Orlando	FL	32810	407-644-6300	

653 REAL ESTATE DEVELOPERS

See Also Construction - Building Contractors - Non-Residential p. 2060; Construction - Building Contractors - Residential p. 2073

				Phone	Fax
A & B Properties Inc 822 Bishop St *Web:* www.abprop.com	Honolulu	HI	96813	808-525-6676	525-8447
AG Spanos Cos 10100 Trinity Pkwy 5th Fl *Web:* www.agspanos.com	Stockton	CA	95219	209-478-7954	473-3703
Al Neyer Inc 302 W Third St Ste 800 *TF:* 877-271-6400 ■ *Web:* www.neyer.com	Cincinnati	OH	45202	513-271-6400	271-1350
Allen & O'Hara Inc PO Box 771889 *Web:* www.allenoharadev.com	Memphis	TN	38177	901-471-2080	471-2087
Alter Group 5500 W Howard St *Web:* www.altergroup.com	Skokie	IL	60077	847-676-4300	676-4302
Amerco Real Estate Co 2727 N Central Ave Ste 500 *Web:* www.amercorealestate.com	Phoenix	AZ	85004	602-263-6555	277-5824
American West Homes 250 Pilot Rd Ste 140 *Web:* www.americanwesthomes.com	Las Vegas	NV	89119	702-736-6434	617-0281
AMLI Residential Properties Trust 200 W Monroe St Ste 2200 *Web:* www.amli.com	Chicago	IL	60606	312-283-4700	283-4720
AMREP Corp 300 Alexander Pk Ste 204 *NYSE: AXR* ■ *Web:* www.amrepcorp.com	Princeton	NJ	08540	609-716-8200	716-8255
AMREP Southwest Inc 333 New Mexico 528 Ste 400 *Web:* www.amrepsw.com	Rio Rancho	NM	87124	505-892-9200	
Asset Plus Co 675 Bering Dr Ste 200 *Web:* www.assetpluscorp.com	Houston	TX	77057	713-782-5800	268-5111
AV Homes Inc 8601 N Scottsdale Rd Ste 225 *NASDAQ: AVHI* ■ *TF:* 800-284-6637 ■ *Web:* www.avhomesinc.com	Scottsdale	AR	85283	480-214-7400	
Barone Galasso & Assoc Inc 710 W Ivy *Web:* www.baronegalasso.com	San Diego	CA	92101	619-232-2100	
Beazer Homes 9202 N Meridian St Ste 300 *Web:* www.beazer.com	Indianapolis	IN	46260	317-574-1950	
Beazer Homes USA Inc 1000 Abernathy Rd Ste 1200 *NYSE: BZH* ■ *Web:* www.beazer.com	Atlanta	GA	30328	770-829-3700	481-0431
Bellmont Cabinet Co 13610 52nd St E Ste 300 *Web:* bellmontcabinets.com	Sumner	WA	98390	253-321-3011	
Belz Enterprises 100 Peabody Pl Ste 1400 *Web:* www.belz.com	Memphis	TN	38103	901-767-4780	
BPG Properties Ltd 1500 Market St 3200 Ctr Sq W *Web:* www.equuspartners.com	Philadelphia	PA	19102	215-496-0400	
Brooks Resources Corp 409 NW Franklin Ave *TF:* 877-475-9779 ■ *Web:* brooks-resources.com	Bend	OR	97701	541-382-1662	385-3285
Brothers Property Corp 2 Alhambra Plz Ste 1280 *Web:* www.brothersproperty.com	Coral Gables	FL	33134	305-285-1035	858-2733
Butler Real Estate 1540 Genessee St *Web:* www.butlermfg.com	Kansas City	MO	64102	816-968-3000	968-3720
Buzz Oates Construction LP 8615 Elder Creek Rd *Web:* www.buzzoates.com	Sacramento	CA	95828	916-379-3800	
Cadillac Fairview Ltd 20 Queen St W 5th Fl *Web:* www.cadillacfairview.com	Toronto	ON	M5H3R4	416-598-8200	598-8578
Cafaro Co 2445 Belmont Ave *Web:* www.cafarocompany.com	Youngstown	OH	44504	330-747-2661	743-2902
California Pacific Homes 38 Executive Pk Ste 200 *Web:* www.calpacifichomes.com	Irvine	CA	92614	949-833-6000	833-6133
Cannon Instrument Co 2139 High Tech Rd *Web:* www.cannoninstrument.com	State College	PA	16803	814-353-8000	
Cappelli Enterprises Inc 115 E Stevens Ave *Web:* www.cappelli-inc.com	Valhalla	NY	10595	914-769-6500	747-9268
Carlisle Corp 263 Wagner Pl *Web:* www.carlislecorp.com	Memphis	TN	38103	901-526-5000	
Casden Properties LLC 9090 Wilshire Blvd	Beverly Hills	CA	90211	310-274-5553	276-6486
Castle & Cooke Inc 10900 Wilshire Blvd Ste 1600 *Web:* www.castlecooke.net	Los Angeles	CA	90024	310-208-3636	
CenterCal Properties LLC 7455 SW Bridgeport Rd *Web:* www.centercal.com	Tigard	OR	97224	503-968-8940	
CFC Inc 320 W Eigth St Ste 200 *Web:* www.cfcproperties.com	Bloomington	IN	47402	812-332-0053	333-4680
Chelsea Investment Corp 5993 Avenida Encinas Ste 101 *Web:* www.chelseainvestco.com	Carlsbad	CA	92008	760-456-6000	456-6001
Christopherson Homes Inc 1315 Airport Blvd	Santa Rosa	CA	95403	707-524-8222	360-6208
Comstock Holding Companies Inc 1886 Metro Ctr Dr 4th Fl *NASDAQ: CHCI* ■ *Web:* comstockhomes.com	Reston	VA	20190	703-883-1700	760-1520
Connell Realty & Development Co 200 Connell Dr *Web:* www.connell-realestate.com	Berkeley Heights	NJ	07922	908-673-3700	673-3800
Conner Homes Co 846 108th Ave NE *Web:* www.connerhomes.com	Bellevue	WA	98004	425-455-9280	462-0426
Cooper Communities Inc 903 N 47th St *Web:* www.cooper-communities.com	Rogers	AR	72756	479-246-6500	
Corcoran Jennison Development Co 150 Mt Vernon St Bayside Ofc Ctr Ste 500 *Web:* www.corcoranjennison.com	Boston	MA	02125	617-822-7350	822-7352
Cornerstone Group 2100 Hollywood Blvd *TF:* 800-809-4099 ■ *Web:* www.theapartmentcorner.com	Hollywood	FL	33020	305-443-8288	
Coscan Homes LLC 5555 Ravenswood Rd	Fort Lauderdale	FL	33312	954-620-1000	
CountryTyme Inc 3451 Cincinnati-Zanesville Rd SW *TF:* 800-213-8365 ■ *Web:* www.countrytyme.com	Lancaster	OH	43130	740-475-6001	
Crescent Resources Inc 227 W Trade St Ste 1000 *Web:* crescentcommunities.com	Charlotte	NC	28202	980-321-6000	
Cullinan Properties Ltd 2020 W War Memorial Dr Ste 103 *Web:* www.cullinanproperties.com	Peoria	IL	61614	309-999-1700	
Darling Homes 2500 Legacy Dr Ste 100 **Fax Area Code: 972* ■ *Web:* www.darlinghomes.com	Frisco	TX	75034	469-252-2200	624-4106*
David Weekley Homes Inc 1111 N Post Oak Rd *TF:* 800-390-6774 ■ *Web:* www.davidweekleyhomes.com	Houston	TX	77055	713-963-0500	963-0322
De Anza Land & Leisure Corp 1615 Cordova St	Los Angeles	CA	90007	323-734-9951	734-2531
Deltona Corp 8014 SW 135th St Rd *TF:* 800-333-5866 ■ *Web:* www.deltona.com	Ocala	FL	34473	352-347-2322	307-8103
Desert Mountain Properties LP 37700 Desert Mountain Pkwy *Web:* www.desertmountain.com	Scottsdale	AZ	85262	480-488-2998	
Development Services of America 16100 N 71st St Ste 520 *Web:* www.developmentservicesofamerica.com/corpcenterseattle.html	Scottsdale	AZ	85254	480-927-4892	
Dixon Builders & Developers Inc 8050 Beckett Crt D Ste 213 *Web:* www.dixonbuilders.com	West Chester	OH	45069	513-887-6400	887-6643
Dominion Homes Inc 4900 Tuttle Crossing Blvd *Web:* www.dominionhomes.com	Dublin	OH	43016	614-356-5000	
Donohoe Cos Inc 2101 Wisconsin Ave NW *Web:* www.donohoe.com	Washington	DC	20007	202-333-0880	342-3924
Double Diamond Co 5495 Belt Line Rd Ste 200 *TF:* 800-324-7438 ■ *Web:* www.ddresorts.com	Dallas	TX	75254	214-706-9801	706-9878
DR Horton Inc 301 Commerce St Ste 500 *NYSE: DHI* ■ *TF:* 800-846-7866 ■ *Web:* www.drhorton.com	Fort Worth	TX	76102	817-390-8200	
Duffel Financial & Construction Co 1430 Willow Pass Rd Ste 220	Concord	CA	94520	925-603-8444	603-8440
EJM Development Co 9061 Santa Monica Blvd *Web:* www.ejmdevelopment.com	Los Angeles	CA	90069	310-278-1830	278-2965
Elliott Homes 340 Palladio Pkwy Ste 521	Folsom	CA	95630	916-984-1300	
Embrey Partners Ltd 1020 NE Loop 410 Ste 700 *Web:* www.embreydc.com	San Antonio	TX	78209	210-824-6044	824-7656
Emmer Group 2801 SW Archer Rd *Web:* www.emmergroup.com	Gainesville	FL	32608	352-376-2444	376-2260
Epcon Communities Inc 500 Stonehenge Pkwy *Web:* epconcommunities.com	Dublin	OH	43017	614-761-1010	
Ergon Properties Inc PO Box 1639 *Web:* www.ergonproperties.com	Jackson	MS	39215	601-933-3174	
Fieldstone Homes 12896 S Pony Express Rd Ste 400 *Web:* www.fieldstone-homes.com	Draper	UT	84020	801-233-8300	
First Hartford Corp 149 Colonial Rd *OTC: FHRT* ■ *Web:* www.firsthartford.com	Manchester	CT	06042	860-646-6555	646-8572
Flagship Properties Corp 1 Greenway Plz Ste 750 *Web:* flagshipco.com	Houston	TX	77046	713-623-6000	
Flournoy Development Co 900 Brookstone Ctr Pkwy *Web:* flournoycompanies.com	Columbus	GA	31904	706-324-4000	324-4150
Forest City Equity Services Inc 50 Public Sq Ste 1170	Cleveland	OH	44113	216-416-3500	
Forest City Ratner Cos (FCRC) 1 MetroTech Ctr N *Web:* www.forestcity.net	Brooklyn	NY	11201	718-923-8400	
Forsberg Real Estate Co 2422 Jolly Rd Ste 200 *Web:* www.lansingrealestate.com	Okemos	MI	48864	517-349-9330	349-7131
Friendswood Development Co 11506 Island Manor St **Fax Area Code: 281*	Pearland	TX	77584	713-436-6951	872-4207*
Gambone Bros Development Co 1030 W Germantown Pk PO Box 287 *Web:* www.gambone.com	Fairview Village	PA	19409	610-539-4700	539-2020

	Phone	Fax

Gatehouse Group Inc, The
120 Forbes Blvd Ste 180 .... Mansfield MA 02048 508-337-2500
Web: gatehousemgt.com

Gehan Homes 15725 N Dallas Pkwy Ste 300 .... Addison TX 75001 972-383-4300 383-4399
Web: www.gehanhomes.com

Gentry Homes Ltd 560 N Nimitz Hwy .... Honolulu HI 96809 808-599-5558 599-8347*
**Fax:* Sales ■ *Web:* www.gentryhawaii.com

Gilbane Inc 7 Jackson Walkway .... Providence RI 02903 401-456-5890 456-5996
TF: 800-445-2263 ■ *Web:* www.gilbaneco.com

Ginsburg Development Cos LLC (GDC)
100 Summit Lk Dr .... Valhalla NY 10595 914-747-3600 747-1608
Web: www.gdc-homes.com

GJ Grewe Inc 9109 Watson Rd .... Saint Louis MO 63126 314-962-6300
Web: www.gjgrewe.com

GL Homes of Florida Corp
1600 Sawgrass Corporate Pkwy Ste 400 .... Sunrise FL 33323 954-753-1730 753-4509
Web: www.glhomes.com

Gold Point Lodging & Realty Inc
100 S Main St .... Breckenridge CO 80424 970-453-1910
Web: www.grandtimber.com

Goldenberg Group Inc, The
630 Sentry Pkwy Ste 300 .... Blue Bell PA 19422 610-260-9600
Web: www.goldenberggroup.com

Goldrich & Kest Industries
5150 Overland Ave .... Culver City CA 90230 310-204-2050 204-1900
Web: www.gkind.com

Grand Homes Inc 5150 Keller Springs Rd .... Dallas TX 75001 214-750-6528 750-6849
Web: www.grandhomes.com

Greenwood Communities & Resorts Inc
104 Maxwell Ave .... Greenwood SC 29646 864-941-4044
Web: www.greenwoodcr.com

Haas & Haynie Corp
400 Oyster Pt Blvd Ste 123 .... South San Francisco CA 94080 650-588-5600
Web: www.hh1898.com

Hamilton Co, The 39 Brighton Ave .... Allston MA 02134 617-783-0039 783-0568
Web: www.thehamiltoncompany.com

Hamilton Partners Inc 300 Park Blvd Ste 500 .... Itasca IL 60143 630-250-9700
Web: www.hamiltonpartners.com

Hamlet Homes
308 East 4500 South Ste 200 .... Salt Lake City UT 84107 801-281-2223 281-2224
Web: www.hamlethomes.com

Harbour Homes LLC 400 N 34th St Ste 300 .... Seattle WA 98103 206-315-8130 315-8131
Web: www.harbourhomes.com

Harristown Development Corp 11 N 3rd St .... Harrisburg PA 17101 717-236-5061 236-8975
Web: strawberrysquare.com

Hartz Construction Co Inc
9026 Heritage Pkwy .... Woodridge IL 60517 630-228-3800 228-4910
Web: www.hartzhomes.com

Hearn Co, The 875 N Michigan Ave Ste 4100 .... Chicago IL 60611 312-408-3000 408-3010
Web: www.hearncompany.com

Hff Inc 301 Grant St Ste 600 .... Pittsburgh PA 15219 412-281-8714 281-2792
NYSE: HF ■ *Web:* www.hfflp.com

Highland Homes 5601 Democracy Dr Ste 300 .... Dallas TX 75024 972-789-3500
Web: www.highlandhomes.com

Hills Communities Inc 4901 Hunt Rd .... Cincinnati OH 45242 513-984-0300
Web: www.hillsinc.com

Hilton New Orleans Riverside
2 Poydras St .... New Orleans LA 70130 504-561-0500
Web: hiltonneworleansriverside.com

Hines Interest LP 2800 Post Oak Blvd .... Houston TX 77056 713-621-8000
TF: 888-782-7937 ■ *Web:* www.hines.com

Hoffman Homes for Youth PO Box 4777 .... Gettysburg PA 17325 717-359-7148 359-2600
Web: www.hoffmanhomes.com

Hofmann Co, The 1380 Galaxy Way .... Concord CA 94520 925-682-4830 682-4771
Web: www.hofmannhomes.com

Holiday Builders Inc
2293 W Eau Gallie Blvd .... Melbourne FL 32935 321-610-5172
TF: 866-431-2533 ■ *Web:* www.holidaybuilders.com

Hunt Midwest Enterprises Inc
8300 NE Underground Dr .... Kansas City MO 64161 816-455-2500
TF: 800-551-6877 ■ *Web:* www.huntmidwest.com

Hunt Midwest Residential Development
8300 NE Underground Dr .... Kansas City MO 64161 816-455-2500
TF: 800-551-6877 ■ *Web:* www.huntmidwest.com

IDI Group Cos 1700 N Moore St Ste 2020 .... Arlington VA 22209 703-558-7300 558-7377
Web: www.idigroup.com

Inland Real Estate Development Corp
2901 Butterfield Rd .... Oak Brook IL 60523 630-218-8000 990-5350
TF: 866-954-5692 ■ *Web:* www.inlandgroup.com

Instrument Development Corp Inc
820 Swan Dr .... Mukwonago WI 53149 262-363-7307
Web: www.idcwi.com

Intervest Construction Inc
2379 Beville Rd .... Daytona Beach FL 32119 844-349-6401
TF: 855-215-2974 ■ *Web:* www.icihomes.com

Irvine Co 550 Newport Ctr Dr .... Newport Beach CA 92660 949-720-2000 720-2218*
**Fax:* Hum Res ■ *Web:* www.irvinecompany.com

Iskalo Development Corp
Harbinger Sq 5166 Main St .... Williamsville NY 14221 716-633-2096
Web: www.iskalo.com

Ivory Homes 970 E Woodoak Ln .... Salt Lake City UT 84117 888-455-5561 747-7090*
**Fax Area Code:* 801 ■ *TF:* 888-455-5561 ■ *Web:* www.ivoryhomes.com

JA Billipp Co 6925 Portwest Dr Ste 130 .... Houston TX 77024 713-426-5000
TF: 800-216-9013 ■ *Web:* www.jabillipp.com

JAIR LYNCH Development Partners
1508 U St NW .... Washington DC 20009 202-462-1092
Web: www.jairlynch.com

JJ Gumberg Company Inc 1051 Brinton Rd .... Pittsburgh PA 15221 412-244-4000 244-9133
Web: www.jjgumberg.com

JMC Communities
2201 Fourth St N Ste 200 .... Saint Petersburg FL 33704 727-823-0022 821-2007
Web: www.jmccommunities.com

John Buck Co 225 W Washington St Ste 2300 .... Chicago IL 60606 312-993-9800 993-0857
Web: www.tjbc.com

John F Buchan Homes 2821 Northup Way Ste 100 .... Bellevue WA 98004 425-827-2266 827-0462
TF: 866-528-2426 ■ *Web:* www.buchan.com

John F Long Properties LLLP
5035 W Camelback Rd .... Phoenix AZ 85031 602-272-0421 846-7208*
**Fax Area Code:* 623 ■ *Web:* www.jflongproperties.com

John Wieland Homes & Neighborhoods
4125 Atlanta Rd SE .... Smyrna GA 30080 770-996-2400 907-3481
TF: 800-376-4663 ■ *Web:* www.jwhomes.com

Jupiter Realty Corp 401 Michigan Ave Ste 1300 .... Chicago IL 60611 312-642-6000 642-2316
Web: www.jupiterrealty.com

Kaiser Ventures LLC
3633 Inland Empire Blvd Ste 480 .... Ontario CA 91764 909-483-8500

KB Home 10990 Wilshire Blvd 7th Fl .... Los Angeles CA 90024 310-231-4000 231-4222
NYSE: KBH ■ *TF:* 800-304-0657 ■ *Web:* www.kbhome.com

Kettler 1751 Pinnacle Dr Ste 700 .... McLean VA 22102 703-641-9000 641-9630
Web: www.kettler.com

Keystone Builders Resource Group Inc
1207 Roseneath Rd .... Richmond VA 23230 804-354-8830 358-6976
Web: www.keybuild.com

Kravco Co 234 Mall Blvd .... King of Prussia PA 19406 610-854-2800
Web: www.kravco.com

Lancia Homes 9430 Lima Rd .... Fort Wayne IN 46818 260-489-4433
Web: www.lanciahomes.com

LCOR Inc 850 Cassatt Rd Ste 300 .... Berwyn PA 19312 610-251-9110 408-4420
Web: www.lcor.com

LeCesse Development Corp
650 S Northlake Blvd Ste 450 .... Altamonte Springs FL 32701 407-645-5575 645-0553
Web: www.lecesse.com

Legacy Property Group LLC
300 Marietta St NW Ste 304 .... Atlanta GA 30313 404-222-9100 222-9090
Web: www.legacyproperty.com

Legend Homes Corp 29256 SW Costa Cir E .... Wilsonville OR 97070 503-620-8080 598-8900
Web: www.legendhomes.com

Lord Baltimore Properties
6225 Smith Ave Ste B100 .... Baltimore MD 21209 410-415-7638 580-9250
Web: www.lordbaltimoreprop.com

Lozier Homes Corp 1203 114th Ave SE .... Bellevue WA 98004 425-454-8690 646-8695

Lu'ma Native Housing Society
2960 Nanaimo St .... Vancouver BC V5N5G3 604-876-0811
Web: lnhs.ca

M/I Homes Inc 3 Easton Oval .... Columbus OH 43219 614-418-8700 418-8080
NYSE: MHO ■ *TF:* 888-644-4111 ■ *Web:* www.mihomes.com

Magellan Development Group LLC
225 N Columbus Dr Ste 100 .... Chicago IL 60601 312-642-8869
Web: www.magellandevelopment.com

Maui Land & Pineapple Company Inc
120 Kane St PO Box 187 .... Kahului HI 96733 808-877-3351
Web: www.mauiland.com

McGuyer Homebuilders Inc (MHI)
7676 Woodway Ste 104 .... Houston TX 77063 713-952-6767 952-5637
Web: www.mcguyerhomebuilders.com

McKee Group 940 W Sproul Rd Ste 301 .... Springfield PA 19064 610-604-9800
Web: www.mckeebuilders.com

McStain Neighborhoods 7100 N Broadway Ste 5-H .... Denver CO 80221 303-494-5900
Web: www.mcstain.com

Meritage Homes Corp
17851 N 85th St Ste 300 .... Scottsdale AZ 85255 480-515-8100
NYSE: MTH ■ *Web:* www.meritagehomes.com

Metro Development Group
2502 N Rocky Point Dr Ste 1050 .... Tampa FL 33607 813-288-8078
Web: metrodevelopmentgroup.com

Mid-West Terminal Warehouse Company Inc
1700 Universal Ave .... Kansas City MO 64120 816-231-8811 231-0020
Web: www.mwtco.com

Miller & Smith Cos 8401 Greensboro Dr Ste 300 .... McLean VA 22102 703-821-2500
Web: www.millerandsmith.com

Mitchell Company Inc
41 W I-65 Service Rd N
Colonial Bank Ctr 3rd Fl .... Mobile AL 36608 251-380-2929 345-1264
Web: www.mitchellcompany.com

Mitsubishi Estate NY Inc
1221 Ave of the Americas 17th Fl .... New York NY 10020 212-698-2200 698-2211

Moceri Development Corp
3005 University Dr .... Auburn Hills MI 48326 248-340-9400 340-9401
Web: www.moceri.com

Morguard Investments Limited
55 City Centre Dr Ste 800 .... Mississauga ON L5B1M3 905-281-3800
Web: www.morguard.com

Morningside Equities Group Inc
223 W Erie St 3rd Fl .... Chicago IL 60654 312-280-7770
Web: www.morningsideusa.com

Narragansett Improvement Co
223 Allens Ave .... Providence RI 02903 401-331-7420 351-6444
Web: www.nicori.com

Newhall Land 25124 Springfield Ct Ste 300 .... Valencia CA 91355 661-255-4000 255-3960
Web: www.valencia.com

Newmark Knight Frank 125 Pk Ave .... New York NY 10017 212-372-2000 372-2426
Web: www.ngkf.com

Norwood Builders Inc 250 S NE Hwy Ste 300 .... Park Ridge IL 60068 847-655-7700 655-7701
Web: www.norwoodbuilders.com

NTS Development Co 10172 Linn Stn Rd .... Louisville KY 40223 502-426-4800 426-4994
Web: www.ntsdevelopment.com

NTS Realty Holdings LP 10172 Linn Stn Rd .... Louisville KY 40223 502-426-4800 426-4994
NYSE: NLP ■ *Web:* www.ntsdevelopment.com

Oil & Gas Asset Clearinghouse L P, The
500 N Sam Houston Pkwy W Ste 150 .... Houston TX 77067 281-873-4600
Web: www.ogclearinghouse.com

Olympia Group LLC
11411 Southern Highlands Pkwy Ste 300 .... Las Vegas NV 89141 702-220-6565
Web: www.olympiagroupcompanies.com

Orleans Homebuilders Inc 3333 St Rd Ste 101 .... Bensalem PA 19020 215-245-7500
Web: orleanshomes.com

Ovation Development Corp
6021 S Ft Apache Rd Ste 100 .... Las Vegas NV 89148 702-990-2390

				Phone	Fax
Pacific American Group LLC 104 Caledonia St *Web:* www.pacamgroup.com	Sausalito	CA	94965	415-331-3838	
Paparone Corp 702 N White Horse Pk. *Web:* www.paparonenewhomes.com	Stratford	NJ	08084	856-784-0550	
Paramount Group Inc 1633 Broadway Ste 1801 *Web:* www.paramount-group.com	New York	NY	10019	212-237-3100	
Parkit Enterprise Inc Suite 1088 - 999, W Hastings St *Web:* www.parkitenterprise.com	Vancouver	BC	V6C2W2	604-424-8700	
Peebles Corp, The 5937 Collins Ave *Web:* www.peeblescorp.com	Miami Beach	FL	33140	305-993-5050	
Picerne Real Estate Group 75 Lambert Lind Hwy *Web:* www.picerne.com	Warwick	RI	02886	401-732-3700	738-6452
Pineloch Management Inc 102 W Pineloch Ave Ste 10 *Web:* www.pineloch.com	Orlando	FL	32806	407-859-3550	650-0303
Pitcairn Properties Inc 165 Township Line Rd *Web:* www.pitcairnproperties.com	Jenkintown	PA	19046	215-690-3000	690-3100
Pizzuti Inc 629 N High St Ste 500 *Web:* www.pizzuti.com	Columbus	OH	43215	614-280-4000	280-5000
Porten Cos 333 NE Second St	Delray Beach	FL	33483	561-819-1109	
Post Properties Inc 4401 Northside Pkwy Ste 800 *NYSE: PPS* ■ *Web:* www.postproperties.com	Atlanta	GA	30327	404-846-5000	
Prairie Management & Development Inc 333 N Michigan Ave Ste 1700	Chicago	IL	60601	312-644-1055	
Prestige Properties & Development Company Inc 546 Fifth Ave	New York	NY	10036	212-944-0444	
Puget Western Inc 19515 N Creek Pkwy Ste 310 *Web:* pugetwestern.com	Bothell	WA	98011	425-487-6550	487-6565
Quadrant Corp 14725 SE 36 St *Web:* www.quadranthomes.com	Bellevue	WA	98006	425-455-2900	646-8300
Redd Brown & Williams 201 Bridge St PO Box 1720 *Web:* www.rbandw.com	Paintsville	KY	41240	606-789-8119	789-5414
Related Group of Florida 315 S Biscayne Blvd *Web:* www.relatedgroup.com	Miami	FL	33131	305-460-9900	460-9911
Related Midwest 350 W Hubbard St Ste 300 *Web:* www.relatedmidwest.com	Chicago	IL	60654	312-595-7400	
Republic Properties Corp 1280 MD Ave SW Ste 280 *Web:* www.republicpropertiescorp.com	Washington	DC	20024	202-552-5300	552-5320
Richman Group of Cos 340 Pemberwick Rd *Web:* www.therichmangroup.com	Greenwich	CT	06831	203-869-0900	869-1034
Richmond American Homes Inc 4350 S Monaco St *TF:* 888-402-4663 ■ *Web:* www.richmondamerican.com	Denver	CO	80237	303-773-1100	
Robson Communities 9532 E Riggs Rd **Fax Area Code:* 480 ■ *TF:* 800-732-9949 ■ *Web:* www.robson.com	Sun Lakes	AZ	85248	800-732-9949	895-0136*
S & A Custom Built Homes 2121 Old Gatesburg Rd Ste 200 *Web:* www.sahomebuilder.com	State College	PA	16803	814-231-4780	
Sabey Corp 12201 Tukwila International Blvd 4th Fl *Web:* www.sabey.com	Seattle	WA	98168	206-281-8700	282-9951
Schatten Properties Management Company Inc 1514 S St *TF:* 800-892-1315 ■ *Web:* www.schattenproperties.com	Nashville	TN	37212	615-329-3011	327-2343
Schostak Bros & Company Inc 17800 Laurel Pk Dr N Ste 200C *Web:* www.schostak.com	Livonia	MI	48152	248-262-1000	262-1814
Sea Pines Resort, The 32 Greenwood Dr *TF:* 866-561-8802 ■ *Web:* www.seapines.com	Hilton Head Island	SC	29928	843-785-3333	
Sea Trail Corp 75A Clubhouse Rd *TF:* 888-321-9048 ■ *Web:* www.seatrail.com	Sunset Beach	NC	28468	910-287-1100	
SEDA Construction Co 2120 Corporate Sq Blvd Ste 3 *Web:* www.sedaconstruction.com	Jacksonville	FL	32216	904-724-7800	727-9500
Shea Homes Inc 8800 N Gainey Ctr Dr Ste 370 *Web:* m.sheahomes.com	Scottsdale	AZ	85258	480-348-6000	
Shelter Group, The 218 N Charles St Ste 220 *Web:* www.thesheltergroup.com	Baltimore	MD	21201	410-962-0595	347-0587
Shodeen Inc 17 N First St *Web:* shodeen.com	Geneva	IL	60134	630-232-0300	
Silver Saddle Ranch & Club Inc 20751 Aristotle Dr *TF:* 888-430-8728 ■ *Web:* www.silversaddle.com	California City	CA	93505	760-373-8617	
Simpson Housing LLLP (SHLP) 8110 E Union Ave Ste 200 *Web:* www.simpsonhousing.com	Denver	CO	80237	303-283-4100	
Singh Homes Inc 7125 OrchaRd Lk Rd Ste 200 *Web:* www.singhweb.com	West Bloomfield	MI	48322	248-865-1600	865-1630
Skanska USA Inc 1616 Whitestone Expy. *Web:* www.skanska.com	Whitestone	NY	11356	718-767-2600	767-2663
SMS Settlement Services Inc 1004 W Taft Ave *Web:* www.smscorp.com	Orange	CA	92865	714-998-1111	
South Shore Harbor Development Ltd 2525 S Shore Blvd Ste 207	League City	TX	77573	281-334-7501	
Space Ctr Inc 2501 Rosegate *Web:* www.spacecenterinc.com	Saint Paul	MN	55113	651-604-4200	
Stanley Martin Cos 11111 Sunset Hills Rd Ste 200 *TF:* 800-446-4807 ■ *Web:* www.stanleymartin.com	Reston	VA	20190	703-964-5000	715-8076
Steiner & Assoc Inc 4016 Townsfair Way *Web:* www.steiner.com	Columbus	OH	43219	614-414-7300	414-7311
Stiles Corp 301 East Las Olas Blvd *Web:* www.stiles.com	Fort Lauderdale	FL	33301	954-627-9300	627-9288
Stratus Properties Inc 212 Lavaca St Ste 300 *NYSE: STRS* ■ *TF:* 800-690-0315 ■ *Web:* www.stratusproperties.com	Austin	TX	78701	512-478-5788	478-6340
Sueba USA Corp 1800 W Loop S Ste 1300 *Web:* www.suebausa.com	Houston	TX	77027	713-961-3588	961-1343
Susquehanna Real Estate 140 E Market St PO Box 2026 *Web:* www.susquehanna-realestate.com	York	PA	17401	717-848-5500	771-1430
TAK Construction 60 Walnut Ave Ste 400 *Web:* www.takgroupinc.com	Clark	NJ	07066	732-340-0700	
TELACU 5400 E Olympic Blvd 3rd Fl *Web:* www.telacu.com	Los Angeles	CA	90022	323-721-1655	724-3372
Timbercreek Asset Management Inc 25 Price St *Web:* www.timbercreek.com	Toronto	ON	M4W1Z1	416-306-9967	
Tm 1031 Exchange Inc 100 Wilshire Blvd Ste 1760 *Web:* www.tm1031exchange.com	Santa Monica	CA	90401	310-264-0497	
Toll Bros Inc 250 Gibraltar Rd *NYSE: TOL* ■ **Fax:* Mktg ■ *TF:* 855-897-8655 ■ *Web:* www.tollbrothers.com	Horsham	PA	19044	215-938-8000	938-8217*
Trammell Crow Co 2100 McKinney Ave Ste 800 *Web:* www.trammellcrow.com	Dallas	TX	75201	214-863-4101	863-4493
Trammell Crow Residential (TCR) 3889 Maple St. **Fax Area Code:* 614 ■ *Web:* tcr.com	Dallas	TX	75219	214-922-8400	861-7622*
TransCon Builders Inc 25250 Rockside Rd *TF:* 800-451-2608 ■ *Web:* www.transconbuilders.com	Cleveland	OH	44146	440-439-2100	439-6710
TW Lewis 850 W Elliot Rd Ste 101 *Web:* www.twlewis.com	Tempe	AZ	85284	480-820-0807	820-1455
Uniwell Corp 21172 Figueroa St	Carson	CA	90745	310-782-8888	
Victory Housing Inc 5430 Grosvenor Ln Ste 210 *Web:* www.victoryhousing.org	Bethesda	MD	20814	301-493-6000	493-9788
Village Builders 550 Greens Pkwy Ste 200 *Web:* www.lennar.com	Houston	TX	77067	281-873-4663	
Village Green Cos 30833 NW Hwy *TF:* 800-521-2220 ■ *Web:* www.villagegreen.com	Farmington Hills	MI	48334	248-851-9600	851-6161
Villages of Lake Sumter Inc 1000 Lk Sumter Landing *TF:* 800-245-1081 ■ *Web:* www.thevillages.com	The Villages	FL	32162	352-753-2270	
Vineland Construction Co 71 W Pk Ave *Web:* www.vinelandconstruction.com	Vineland	NJ	08360	856-794-4500	794-4721
Walt Disney Imagineering 500 S Vuenavista St **Fax Area Code:* 818 ■ *Web:* disneyworld.disney.go.com	Burbank	CA	91521	407-939-2273	544-7995*
Walters Group, The 2030 E Flamingo Rd *Web:* www.waltersgolf.com	Las Vegas	NV	89119	702-450-8001	
Walton Associated Company Inc 2001 Financial Way Ste 200	Glendora	CA	91741	626-963-8505	914-7016
Warren L & G Real Estate Inc 465 Van Wyck Lk Rd *Web:* www.warrenhomes.com	Fishkill	NY	12524	845-897-4126	
Waters Mcpherson Mcneill Pc 300 Lighting Way Seventh Fl PO Box 1560 *Web:* www.lawwmm.com	Secaucus	NJ	07096	201-863-4400	863-2866
Watson Land Co 22010 S Wilmington Ave *Web:* www.watsonlandcompany.com	Carson	CA	90745	310-952-6400	522-8788
Wave Crest Development Inc 530 Chestnut St *Web:* www.wavecrestdevelopment.com	Santa Cruz	CA	95060	831-423-2100	
WCI Communities Inc 24301 Walden Ctr Dr *TF:* 800-924-4005 ■ *Web:* www.wcicommunities.com	Bonita Springs	FL	34134	239-498-8200	
Western Golf Properties LLC 1 Spectrum Pointe Dr Ste 310 *Web:* www.cacm.org	Lake Forest	CA	92630	949-417-3251	
Weyerhaeuser Co 33663 Weyerhaeuser Way S *NYSE: WY* ■ *TF:* 800-525-5440 ■ *Web:* www.weyerhaeuser.com	Federal Way	WA	98003	253-924-2345	
Willard Cos Inc, The 75 Builders Pride Dr Ste 200 *Web:* www.thewillardcompanies.com	Hardy	VA	24101	540-721-5288	
Wispark LLC 301 W Wisconsin Ave Ste 400 *Web:* www.wispark.com	Milwaukee	WI	53203	414-274-4600	274-4640
Wooldridge Organization 395 Taylor Blvd Ste 120	Pleasant Hill	CA	94523	925-680-7979	
Zaremba Group 14600 Detroit Ave. *Web:* www.zarembagroup.com	Cleveland	OH	44107	216-221-6600	221-9742
Zicka Homes 7861 E Kemper Rd *Web:* www.zickahomes.com	Cincinnati	OH	45249	513-247-3500	247-3512

654 REAL ESTATE INVESTMENT TRUSTS (REITS)

				Phone	Fax
Acadia Realty Trust 1311 Mamaroneck Ave Ste 260 *NYSE: AKR* ■ *Web:* www.acadiarealty.com	White Plains	NY	10605	914-288-8100	
Alexandria Real Estate Equities Inc 385 E Colorado Blvd Ste 299 *NYSE: ARE* ■ *TF:* 800-776-9437 ■ *Web:* are.com	Pasadena	CA	91101	626-578-0777	
American Campus Communities Inc 12700 Hill Country Blvd Ste T-200 *NYSE: ACC* ■ *Web:* www.americancampus.com	Austin	TX	78738	512-732-1000	732-2450
AMLI Residential 200 W Monroe St Ste 2200 *Web:* www.amli.com	Chicago	IL	60606	312-283-4700	283-4720
Anworth Mortgage Asset Corp 1299 Ocean Ave 2nd Fl. *NYSE: ANH* ■ *Web:* www.anworth.com	Santa Monica	CA	90401	310-255-4493	434-0070
Apartment Investment & Management Co 4582 S Ulster St Pkwy Ste 1100 *NYSE: AIV* ■ *TF General:* 888-789-8600 ■ *Web:* www.aimco.com	Denver	CO	80237	303-691-4350	759-3226
Arbor Realty Trust Inc 333 Earle Ovington Blvd Ste 900 *NYSE: ABR* ■ *TF:* 800-272-6710 ■ *Web:* www.arborrealtytrust.com	Uniondale	NY	11553	800-272-6710	
Ashford Hospitality Trust Inc 14185 Dallas Pkwy Ste 1100 *NYSE: AHT* ■ *Web:* www.ahtreit.com	Dallas	TX	75254	972-490-9600	980-2705
AutoStar 114 Ave of the Americas Ste 39 *TF:* 800-288-6782	New York	NY	10036	212-930-9400	

	Phone	Fax
Benchmark Group 4053 Maple Rd Amherst NY 14226 *TF:* 800-876-0160 ■ *Web:* www.benchmarkgrp.com	716-833-4986	833-2954
BioMed Realty Trust Inc 17190 Bernardo Ctr Dr San Diego CA 92128 *NYSE: BMR* ■ *Web:* www.biomedrealty.com	858-485-9840	485-9843
BRT Realty Trust 60 Cutter Mill Rd Ste 303 Great Neck NY 11021 *NYSE: BRT* ■ *TF:* 800-450-5816 ■ *Web:* www.brtrealty.com	516-466-3100	
Camden Property Trust 11 Greenway Plz Ste 2400 Houston TX 77046 *NYSE: CPT* ■ **Fax:* Mktg ■ *TF:* 800-922-6336 ■ *Web:* www.camdenliving.com	713-354-2500	354-2700*
Canadian Real Estate Investment Trust (CREIT) 175 Bloor St E Ste 500 Toronto ON M4W3R8 *TSE: REF.UN* ■ *Web:* www.creit.ca	416-628-7771	628-7777
Capital Automotive Real Estate Services Inc 8270 Greensboro Dr Ste 950 McLean VA 22102 *Web:* www.capitalautomotive.com	703-288-3075	
CAPREIT 11200 Rockville Pk Ste 100 Rockville MD 20852 *Web:* www.capreit.com	301-231-8700	
Capstead Mortgage Corp 8401 N Central Expy Ste 800 Dallas TX 75225 *NYSE: CMO* ■ *TF:* 800-358-2323 ■ *Web:* www.capstead.com	214-874-2323	874-2398
Cedar Shopping Centers Inc 44 S Bayles Ave Ste 304 Port Washington NY 11050 *NYSE: CDR* ■ *Web:* www.cedarrealtytrust.com	516-767-6492	767-6497
Chesapeake Lodging Trust (CLT) 1997 Annapolis Exchange Pkwy Ste 410 Annapolis MD 21401 *NYSE: CHSP* ■ *TF:* 800-698-2820 ■ *Web:* www.chesapeakelodgingtrust.com	800-698-2820	
Choice Group 755 W Big Beaver Rd Troy MI 48084 *Web:* www.choiceproperties.com	248-362-4150	362-4154
Colonial Properties Trust 6584 Poplar Ave Memphis TN 38138 *NYSE: CLP* ■ **Fax Area Code:* 901 ■ *TF:* 866-620-1130 ■ *Web:* www.maac.com	866-620-1130	248-4188*
Commercial Properties Realty Trust 402 N Fourth St Baton Rouge LA 70802 *TF:* 800-648-9064 ■ *Web:* www.cprt.com	225-924-7206	924-1235
Corporate Office Properties Trust 6711 Columbia Gateway Dr Ste 300 Columbia MD 21046 *NYSE: OFC* ■ *Web:* www.copt.com	443-285-5400	285-7650
Cousins Properties Inc 191 Peachtree St NE Ste 500 Atlanta GA 30303 *NYSE: CUZ* ■ *Web:* www.cousinsproperties.com	404-407-1000	
DiamondRock Hospitality Co (DRHC) 3 Bethesda Metro Ctr Ste 1500 Bethesda MD 20814 *NYSE: DRH* ■ *TF:* 888-246-5941 ■ *Web:* www.drhc.com	240-744-1150	744-1199
Digital Realty Trust Inc 4 Embarcadero Ctr Ste 3200 San Francisco CA 94111 *NYSE: DLR* ■ *Web:* www.digitalrealty.com	415-738-6500	
Dividend Capital Trust 518 17th St Ste 1700 Denver CO 80202 *TF:* 866-324-7348 ■ *Web:* www.dividendcapital.com	303-228-2200	228-0128
Donahue Schriber Realty Group Inc 200 E Baker St Ste 100 Costa Mesa CA 92626 *Web:* www.donahueschriber.com	714-545-1400	545-4222
Duke Realty Corp 600 E 96th St Ste 100 Indianapolis IN 46240 *NYSE: DRE-M.CL* ■ *Web:* www.dukerealty.com	317-808-6000	808-6794
Dupont Fabros Technology Inc 1212 New York Ave NW Ste 900 Washington DC 20005 *NYSE: DFT* ■ *Web:* www.dft.com	202-728-0044	728-0220
Dynex Capital Inc 4991 Lk Brook Dr Ste 100 Glen Allen VA 23060 *NYSE: DX* ■ *Web:* www.dynexcapital.com	804-217-5800	
EastGroup Properties Inc 190 E Capitol St Ste 400 Jackson MS 39201 *NYSE: EGP* ■ *Web:* www.eastgroup.net	601-354-3555	352-1441
ECC Capital Corp 2600 E Coast Hwy Ste 250 Corona Del Mar CA 92625 *OTC: ECRO* ■ *Web:* www.ecccapital.com	949-954-7060	
Education Realty Trust Inc 530 Oak Ct Dr Ste 300 Memphis TN 38117 *NYSE: EDR* ■ *Web:* www.edrtrust.com	901-259-2500	
Equity Office Properties Trust 2 N Riverside Plz Ste 2100 Chicago IL 60606 *Web:* www.equityoffice.com	312-466-3300	
Essex Property Trust Inc 925 E Meadow Dr Palo Alto CA 94303 *NYSE: ESS* ■ *Web:* www.essexapartmenthomes.com	650-494-3700	494-8743
Federal Realty Investment Trust 1626 E Jefferson St Rockville MD 20852 *NYSE: FRT* ■ *TF:* 800-658-8980 ■ *Web:* www.federalrealty.com	301-998-8100	998-3700
FelCor Lodging Trust Inc 545 E John Carpenter Fwy Ste 1300 Irving TX 75062 *NYSE: FCH* ■ *Web:* www.felcor.com	972-444-4900	444-4949
First Industrial Realty Trust Inc 311 S Wacker Dr Ste 4000 Chicago IL 60606 *NYSE: FR* ■ *Web:* www.firstindustrial.com	312-344-4300	922-6320
First Potomac Realty Trust 7600 Wisconsin Ave 11th Fl Bethesda MD 20814 *NYSE: FPO* ■ *Web:* www.first-potomac.com	301-986-9200	986-5554
First Real Estate Investment 505 Main St Hackensack NJ 07602 *Web:* freitnj.com	201-488-6400	487-1798
Franklin Street Properties Corp 401 Edgewater Pl Ste 200 Wakefield MA 01880 *NYSE: FSP* ■ *TF:* 877-686-9496 ■ *Web:* www.franklinstreetproperties.com	781-557-1300	
Gables Residential Trust 3399 Peachtree Rd NE Ste 600 Atlanta GA 30326 *Web:* www.gables.com	561-997-9700	
GE Capital Solutions Franchise Finance 8377 E Hartford Dr Ste 200 Scottsdale AZ 85255 *TF:* 866-438-4333 ■ *Web:* www.gefranchisefinance.com	866-438-4333	
Ginkgo Residential LLC 301 S College St Ste 3850 Charlotte NC 28202 *Web:* ginkgores.com	704-944-0100	
Gramercy Capital Corp 420 Lexington Ave New York NY 10170 *NYSE: GKK* ■ *Web:* www.gptreit.com	212-297-1000	297-1090
Health Care Property Investors Inc 1920 Main St Ste 1200 Irvine CA 92614 *TF:* 800-690-6903 ■ *Web:* www.hcpi.com	949-407-0700	407-0800

	Phone	Fax
Healthcare Realty Trust Inc 3310 W End Ave Ste 700 Nashville TN 37203 *NYSE: HR* ■ *Web:* www.healthcarerealty.com	615-269-8175	269-8260
Highwoods Properties Inc 3100 Smoketree Ct Ste 600 Raleigh NC 27604 *NYSE: HIW* ■ *TF:* 866-449-6637 ■ *Web:* www.highwoods.com	919-872-4924	
HMG/Courtland Properties Inc 1870 S Bayshore Dr Coconut Grove FL 33133 *AMEX: HMG* ■ *Web:* hmgcourtland.com	305-854-6803	856-7342
Home Properties Inc 850 Clinton Sq Rochester NY 14604 *NYSE: HME* ■ *Web:* www.homeproperties.com	585-546-4900	
Horizon Group Properties Inc 5000 Hakes Dr Muskegon MI 49441 *Web:* www.horizongroup.com	231-798-9100	798-5100
Host Hotels & Resorts Inc 6903 Rockledge Dr Ste 1500 Bethesda MD 20817 *NYSE: HST* ■ *Web:* www.hosthotels.com	240-744-1000	
Impac Mortgage Holdings Inc 19500 Jamboree Rd Irvine CA 92612 *NYSE: IMH* ■ *TF:* 800-597-4101 ■ *Web:* www.impaccompanies.com	949-475-3600	
Inland Real Estate Corp 2901 Butterfield Rd Oak Brook IL 60523 *NYSE: IRC* ■ **Fax:* Investor Rel ■ *TF:* 888-331-4732 ■ *Web:* www.inlandgroup.com	630-218-8000	218-7357*
Innkeepers USA Trust 340 Royal Poinciana Way Ste 306 Palm Beach FL 33480 *Web:* www.innkeepersusa.com	561-835-1800	835-0457
InnSuites Hospitality Trust 1625 E Northern Ave Ste 105 Phoenix AZ 85020 *NYSE: IHT* ■ *TF:* 800-842-4242 ■ *Web:* www.innsuitestrust.com	602-944-1500	
Investors Real Estate Trust 1400 31st Ave Ste 60 Minot ND 58701 *NYSE: IRET*	701-837-4738	
iStar Financial Inc 1114 Ave of the Americas 39th Fl New York NY 10036 *NYSE: STAR* ■ *TF:* 888-603-5847 ■ *Web:* www.istarfinancial.com	212-930-9400	
Kilroy Realty Corp 12200 W Olympic Blvd Ste 200 Los Angeles CA 90064 *NYSE: KRC* ■ *Web:* www.kilroyrealty.com	310-481-8400	481-6501
Kimco Realty Corp 3333 New Hyde Pk Rd New Hyde Park NY 11042 *NYSE: KIM* ■ *TF:* 800-645-6292 ■ *Web:* www.kimcorealty.com	516-869-9000	
Kite Realty Group Trust 30 S Meridian St Ste 1100 Indianapolis IN 46204 *NYSE: KRG* ■ *TF:* 888-577-5600 ■ *Web:* www.kiterealty.com	317-577-5600	577-5605
KKR Asset Management LLC 555 California St Ste 5000 San Francisco CA 94104 *Web:* kkr.com	415-315-3620	391-3077
LaSalle Hotel Properties 3 Bethesda Metro Ctr Ste 1200 Bethesda MD 20814 *NYSE: LHO* ■ *Web:* www.lasallehotels.com	301-941-1500	941-1553
Lexington Corporate Properties Trust 1 Penn Plz Ste 4015 New York NY 10119 *TF:* 800-850-3948 ■ *Web:* www.lxp.com	212-692-7200	594-6600
Lexington Realty Trust Inc 1 Penn Plz Ste 4015 New York NY 10119 *Web:* www.lxp.com	212-692-7200	594-6600
Liberty Property Trust 500 Chesterfield Pkwy Malvern PA 19355 *NYSE: LPT* ■ *Web:* www.libertyproperty.com	610-648-1700	644-4129
LTC Properties Inc 2829 Townsgate Rd Ste 350 Westlake Village CA 91361 *NYSE: LTC* ■ *Web:* www.ltcreit.com	805-981-8655	981-8663
Macerich Co, The 401 Wilshire Blvd Ste 700 Santa Monica CA 90401 *NYSE: MAC* ■ *Web:* www.macerich.com	310-394-6000	395-2791
Mack-Cali Realty Corp 343 Thornall St Edison NJ 08837 *NYSE: CLI* ■ *TF:* 800-317-4445 ■ *Web:* www.mack-cali.com	732-590-1000	205-8237
Madison Park Financial Corp 155 Grand Ave Ste 1025 Oakland CA 94612 *Web:* www.mpfcorp.com	510-452-2944	452-2973
Medical Properties Trust Inc 1000 Urban Ctr Dr Ste 501 Birmingham AL 35242 *NYSE: MPW* ■ *Web:* www.medicalpropertiestrust.com	205-969-3755	
Meredith Enterprises Inc 3000 Sand Hill Rd Bldg 2 Ste 120 Menlo Park CA 94025 *Web:* www.meredithreit.com	650-233-7140	
MFA Mortgage Investments Inc 350 Pk Ave 20th Fl New York NY 10022 *Web:* www.mfafinancial.com	212-207-6400	207-6420
Monmouth Real Estate Investment Corp (MREIC) 3499 Rt 9 N Ste 3C Freehold NJ 07728 *NASDAQ: MNR* ■ *Web:* www.mreic.com	732-577-9996	
MPG Office Trust Inc 355 S Grand Ave Ste 3300 Los Angeles CA 90071 *Web:* brookfieldofficeproperties.com	213-626-3300	687-4758
National Health Investors Inc 222 Robert Rose Dr Murfreesboro TN 37129 *NYSE: NHI* ■ *Web:* nhireit.com	615-890-9100	
New York Mortgage Trust Inc (NYMT) 52 Vanderbilt Ave Ste 403 New York NY 10017 *NASDAQ: NYMT* ■ *TF:* 800-937-5449 ■ *Web:* www.nymtrust.com	212-792-0107	
Newcastle Investment Corp 1345 Ave of the Americas 46th Fl New York NY 10105 *NYSE: NCT* ■ *Web:* www.newcastleinv.com	212-798-6100	
NorthStar Realty Finance Corp 399 Pk Ave 18th Fl New York NY 10022 *NYSE: NRF* ■ *Web:* www.nrfc.com	212-547-2600	547-2700
Novastar Financial Inc 2114 Central Ste 600 Kansas City MO 64108 *TF:* 800-591-1137 ■ *Web:* www.novationcompanies.com	816-237-7000	
One Liberty Properties Inc 60 Cutter Mill Rd Ste 303 Great Neck NY 11021 *NYSE: OLP* ■ *TF:* 800-937-5449 ■ *Web:* 1liberty.com	516-466-3100	466-3132
Parkway Properties Inc 188 E Capitol St Ste 1000 Jackson MS 39201 *NYSE: PKY* ■ *TF:* 800-748-1667 ■ *Web:* www.pky.com	601-948-4091	949-4077
Pennsylvania Real Estate Investment Trust 200 S Broad St 3rd Fl Philadelphia PA 19102 *NYSE: PEI* ■ *TF:* 866-875-0700 ■ *Web:* www.preit.com	215-875-0700	546-7311

				Phone	Fax
PMC Commercial Trust 17950 Preston Rd Ste 600 .... / *NASDAQ: CMCT* ■ *TF:* 800-486-3223 ■ *Web:* cimgroup.com/pmc	Dallas	TX	75252	972-349-3200	349-3265
Post Properties Inc / 4401 Northside Pkwy Ste 800 .... / *NYSE: PPS* ■ *Web:* www.postproperties.com	Atlanta	GA	30327	404-846-5000	
ProLogis 4545 Airport Way .... / *NYSE: PLD* ■ *TF:* 800-566-2706 ■ *Web:* www.prologis.com	Denver	CO	80239	303-375-9292	567-5903
PS Business Parks Inc 701 Western Ave .... / *NYSE: PSB* ■ *TF Cust Svc:* 888-782-6110 ■ *Web:* www.psbusinessparks.com	Glendale	CA	91201	818-244-8080	242-0566
Public Storage Inc 701 Western Ave .... / *NYSE: PSA* ■ *TF Cust Svc:* 800-567-0759 ■ *Web:* www.publicstorage.com	Glendale	CA	91201	818-244-8080	
Ramco-Gershenson Properties Trust / 31500 NW Hwy Ste 300 .... / *NYSE: RPT* ■ *Web:* rgpt.com	Farmington Hills	MI	48334	248-350-9900	350-9925
Regency Centers 1 Independent Dr Ste 114 .... / *NYSE: REG* ■ *TF:* 800-950-6333 ■ *Web:* regencycenters.com	Jacksonville	FL	32202	904-598-7000	634-3428
Resource Capital Corp 712 Fifth Ave 12th Fl .... / *NYSE: RSO* ■ *Web:* www.resourcecapitalcorp.com	New York	NY	10019	212-506-3899	245-6372
RioCan Real Estate Investment Trust / 2300 Yonge St Ste 500 PO Box 2386 .... / *TSE: REI.UN.CA* ■ *TF:* 800-465-2733 ■ *Web:* www.riocan.com	Toronto	ON	M4P1E4	416-866-3033	866-3020
Simon Property Group Inc / 225 W Washington St .... / *NYSE: SPG* ■ *Web:* www.simon.com	Indianapolis	IN	46204	317-636-1600	
Simon Property Group, Inc. / 225 West Washington St .... / *Web:* www.premiumoutlets.com	Indianapolis	IN	46204	973-228-6111	
SL Green Realty Corp 420 Lexington Ave .... / *NYSE: SLG* ■ *Web:* www.slgreen.com	New York	NY	10170	212-594-2700	216-1790
Starwood Hotels & Resorts Worldwide Inc / 1111 Westchester Ave .... / *NYSE: HOT* ■ *TF Cust Svc:* 888-625-5144 ■ *Web:* www.starwoodhotels.com	White Plains	NY	10604	914-640-8100	640-8310
Strategic Hotels & Resorts / 200 W Madison St Ste 1700 .... / *NYSE: BEE* ■ *Web:* www.strategichotels.com	Chicago	IL	60606	312-658-5000	658-5799
Sun Communities Inc / 27777 Franklin Rd Ste 200 .... / *NYSE: SUI* ■ *Web:* www.suncommunities.com	Southfield	MI	48034	248-208-2500	208-2640
Tanger Factory Outlet Centers Inc / 3200 Northline Ave Ste 360 .... / *NYSE: SKT* ■ *TF:* 800-720-6728 ■ *Web:* www.tangeroutlet.com	Greensboro	NC	27408	336-292-3010	852-2096
Taubman Centers Inc / 200 E Long Lk Rd Ste 300 .... / *NYSE: TCO* ■ *TF:* 800-297-6003 ■ *Web:* www.taubman.com	Bloomfield Hills	MI	48303	248-258-6800	
Thayer Lodging Group / 1997 Annapolis Exchange # 550 .... / *Web:* www.thayerlodging.com	Annapolis	MD	21401	410-268-0515	
Transcontinental Realty Investors Inc / 1603 Lyndon B Johnson Fwy Ste 800 .... / *NYSE: TCI* ■ *TF:* 800-400-6407 ■ *Web:* www.transconrealty-invest.com	Dallas	TX	75234	469-522-4200	522-4299
United Mobile Homes Inc 3499 Rt 9 N Ste 3C .... / *NYSE: UMH* ■ *Web:* www.umh.com	Freehold	NJ	07728	732-577-9997	
Universal Health Realty Income Trust / 367 S Gulph Rd .... / *NYSE: UHT* ■ *Web:* www.uhrit.com	KingofPrussia	PA	19406	610-265-0688	
Urstadt Biddle Properties Inc / 321 Railroad Ave .... / *NYSE: UBA* ■ *Web:* www.ubproperties.com	Greenwich	CT	06830	203-863-8200	861-6755
Ventas Inc 353 N Clark St Ste 3300 .... / *NYSE: VTR* ■ *TF:* 877-483-6827 ■ *Web:* www.ventasreit.com	Chicago	IL	60654	877-483-6827	
Vornado Realty Trust 888 Seventh Ave .... / *NYSE: VNO* ■ *TF:* 800-294-1322 ■ *Web:* www.vno.com	New York	NY	10019	212-894-7000	902-9316
Washington Real Estate Investment Trust (WRIT) / 1775 I St NW .... / *NYSE: WRE* ■ *TF:* 800-565-9748 ■ *Web:* www.writ.com	Washington	DC	20006	301-984-9400	984-9610
Watson Land Co 22010 S Wilmington Ave .... / *Web:* www.watsonlandcompany.com	Carson	CA	90745	310-952-6400	522-8788
Weingarten Realty Investors / 2600 Citadel Plz Dr Ste 125 .... / *NYSE: WRI* ■ *TF:* 800-688-8865 ■ *Web:* www.weingarten.com	Houston	TX	77008	713-866-6000	866-6049
Westfield America Inc / 2049 Century Park E .... / *Web:* www.westfield.com	Century City	CA	90067	310-478-4456	
Winthrop Realty Trust 7 Bulfinch Pl Ste 500 .... / *NYSE: FUR* ■ *TF:* 800-622-6757 ■ *Web:* www.winthropreit.com	Boston	MA	02114	617-570-4614	570-4746
WP Carey & Company LLC / 50 Rockefeller Plz 2nd Fl .... / *NYSE: WPC* ■ *TF:* 800-972-2739 ■ *Web:* www.wpcarey.com	New York	NY	10020	212-492-1100	

655 REAL ESTATE MANAGERS & OPERATORS

See Also Hotels & Hotel Companies p. 2536; Retirement Communities p. 3136

				Phone	Fax
A&G Management Inc 7779 New York Ln .... / *Web:* aandgmanagement.com	Glen Burnie	MD	21061	410-766-8900	766-6557
Acadia Realty Trust / 1311 Mamaroneck Ave Ste 260 .... / *NYSE: AKR* ■ *Web:* www.acadiarealty.com	White Plains	NY	10605	914-288-8100	
Agellan Capital Partners Inc / 156 Front St W Ste 303 .... / *Web:* www.agellancapital.com	Toronto	ON	M5J2L6	416-593-6800	
Agree Realty Corp 70 E Long Lake Rd .... / *NYSE: ADC* ■ *Web:* www.agreerealty.com	Bloomfield Hills	MI	48304	248-737-4190	
Alexander Summer LLC 205 Robin Rd Ste 120 .... / *Web:* alexandersummer.com	Paramus	NJ	07652	201-712-1000	712-1274
Alexander's Inc 210 Rt 4 E .... / *NYSE: ALX* ■ *Web:* www.alx-inc.com	Paramus	NJ	07652	201-587-8541	708-6214
Alexandria Real Estate Equities Inc / 385 E Colorado Blvd Ste 299 .... / *NYSE: ARE* ■ *TF:* 800-776-9437 ■ *Web:* are.com	Pasadena	CA	91101	626-578-0777	
Allied Hotel Properties Inc / 515 W Pender St Ste 300 .... / *Web:* www.alliedhotels.com	Vancouver	BC	V6B6H5	604-669-5335	
American Assets Inc 11455 El Camino Real .... / *Web:* www.americanassetstrust.com	San Diego	CA	92130	858-350-2600	
American Golf Corp 2951 28th St .... / *TF:* 800-238-7267 ■ *Web:* www.americangolf.com	Santa Monica	CA	90405	310-664-4000	
American Motel Management / 2200 Northlake Pkwy Ste 277 .... / *TF:* 800-580-8258 ■ *Web:* www.americanmotelonline.com	Tucker	GA	30084	770-939-1801	939-1419
American Realty Investors Inc / 1800 Vly View Ln Ste 300 .... / *NYSE: ARL* ■ *TF:* 800-400-6407 ■ *Web:* www.americanrealtyinvest.com	Dallas	TX	75234	469-522-4200	522-4299
American Spectrum Realty Inc / 2401 Fountain View 7th Fl .... / *NYSE: AQQ* ■ *TF:* 888-315-2776 ■ *Web:* www.americanspectrum.com	Houston	TX	77057	713-706-6200	
Apartment Investment & Management Co / 4582 S Ulster St Pkwy Ste 1100 .... / *NYSE: AIV* ■ *TF General:* 888-789-8600 ■ *Web:* www.aimco.com	Denver	CO	80237	303-691-4350	759-3226
ARC Properties Inc 1401 Broad St .... / *Web:* www.arcproperties.com	Clifton	NJ	07013	973-249-1000	249-1001
Archstone-Smith Trust / 9200 E Panorama Cir Ste 400	Englewood	CO	80112	303-708-5959	708-5999
Arden Realty Inc / 11601 Wilshire Blvd 4th Fl .... / *Web:* www.ardenrealty.com	Los Angeles	CA	90025	310-966-2600	966-2699
Aronov Realty 3500 Eastern Blvd .... / *Web:* www.aronov.com	Montgomery	AL	36116	334-277-1000	272-0747
Belz Enterprises 100 Peabody Pl Ste 1400 .... / *Web:* www.belz.com	Memphis	TN	38103	901-767-4780	
Berkshire Property Advisors LLC / 1150 Sanctuary Pkwy Ste 150 .... / *Web:* www.berkshirecommunities.com	Alpharetta	MA	30009	617-646-2300	646-2375
Blue Ridge Real Estate Co PO Box 940 .... / *OTC: BLRGZ*	Blakeslee	PA	18610	570-443-8433	443-9544
Bob Harris Oil Co 905 S Main St	Cleburne	TX	76033	817-558-0615	
Boston Properties Inc 800 Boylston St .... / *NYSE: BXP* ■ *Web:* www.bostonproperties.com	Boston	MA	02199	617-236-3300	
Boyle Investment Co 5900 Poplar Ave Ste 100 .... / *Web:* www.boyle.com	Memphis	TN	38119	901-767-0100	766-4299
Bozzuto Group 7850 Walker Dr Ste 400 .... / *TF General:* 866-698-7513 ■ *Web:* www.bozzuto.com	Greenbelt	MD	20770	301-220-0100	220-3738
Bradford Cos 9400 N Central Expy Ste 500 .... / *Web:* www.bradford.com	Dallas	TX	75231	972-776-7000	776-7083
Brandywine Realty Trust / 555 E Lancaster Ave Ste 100 .... / *NYSE: BDN* ■ *TF:* 866-426-5400 ■ *Web:* www.brandywinerealty.com	Radnor	PA	19087	610-325-5600	325-5622
Brixmor Property Group / 420 Lexington Ave 7th Fl .... / *TF:* 800-468-7526 ■ *Web:* brixmor.com	New York	NY	10170	212-869-3000	
Broadstone Real Estate LLC 530 Clinton Sq .... / *Web:* www.broadstone.com	Rochester	NY	14604	585-287-6500	
Brookfield Office Properties Canada / 181 Bay St Ste 330 PO Box 770 .... / *NYSE: BPO* ■ *Web:* www.brookfieldofficepropertiescanada.com	Toronto	ON	M5J2T3	416-359-8555	359-8596
Brookfield Properties Corp (BOP) / 181 Bay St Ste 330 .... / *NYSE: BPO* ■ *TF:* 800-387-0825 ■ *Web:* www.brookfieldofficeproperties.com	Toronto	ON	M5J2T3	416-369-2300	369-2301
Brooklyn Navy Yard Development Corp / 63 Flushing Ave Bldg 292 3rd Fl .... / *Web:* brooklynnavyyard.org	Brooklyn	NY	11205	718-907-5900	643-9296
BVT Equity Holdings Inc / 400 Interstate N Pkwy Ste 700 .... / *Web:* www.bvt.com	Atlanta	GA	30339	770-618-3500	
Cadillac Fairview Ltd 20 Queen St W 5th Fl .... / *Web:* www.cadillacfairview.com	Toronto	ON	M5H3R4	416-598-8200	598-8578
Calista Corp 301 Calista Ct Ste A .... / *TF:* 800-277-5516 ■ *Web:* www.calistacorp.com	Anchorage	AK	99518	907-279-5516	272-5060
Camden Property Trust / 11 Greenway Plz Ste 2400 .... / *NYSE: CPT* ■ **Fax:* Mktg ■ *TF:* 800-922-6336 ■ *Web:* www.camdenliving.com	Houston	TX	77046	713-354-2500	354-2700*
CAPREIT 11200 Rockville Pk Ste 100 .... / *Web:* www.capreit.com	Rockville	MD	20852	301-231-8700	
Capstone Real Estate Investments LLC / 431 Office Park Dr .... / *Web:* www.capstonecompanies.com	Birmingham	AL	35223	205-414-6400	
Carneghi-blum & Partners Inc / 1602 The Alameda Ste 103 .... / *Web:* cbpappraisal.com	San Jose	CA	95126	408-535-0900	
Casto Realty 191 W Nationwide Blvd Ste 200 .... / *Web:* castolp.com	Columbus	OH	43215	614-228-5331	469-8376
CBH Homes 1977 E Overland Rd .... / *Web:* www.cbhhomes.com	Meridian	ID	83642	208-288-5560	
Cedar Shopping Centers Inc / 44 S Bayles Ave Ste 304 .... / *NYSE: CDR* ■ *Web:* www.cedarrealtytrust.com	Port Washington	NY	11050	516-767-6492	767-6497
Cencor Realty Services Inc / 3102 Maple Ave Ste 500 .... / *Web:* www.weitzmangroup.com	Dallas	TX	75201	214-954-0300	953-0860
CenterPoint Properties Trust 1808 Swift Dr .... / *Web:* centerpoint.com	Oak Brook	IL	60523	630-586-8000	586-8010
Charles E Lakin Enterprises / 8990 W Dodge Rd Ste 225	Omaha	NE	68114	402-393-5550	
Chrisken Property Management LLC / 345 N Canal St Ste 201 .... / *Web:* www.chrisken.com	Chicago	IL	60606	312-454-1626	454-1627
ClubCorp Inc 3030 Lyndon B Johnson Fwy Ste 600 .... / *TF:* 800-433-5079 ■ *Web:* www.clubcorp.com	Dallas	TX	75234	972-243-6191	
ClubLink Corp 15675 Dufferin St .... / *TF:* 800-661-1818 ■ *Web:* en.clublink.ca	King City	ON	L7B1K5	905-841-3730	841-1134
Codding Enterprises / 1400 Valley House Dr Ste 100 .... / *Web:* www.codding.com	Rohnert Park	CA	94928	707-795-3550	

	Phone	Fax

Colonial Properties Trust 6584 Poplar Ave ... Memphis TN 38138 866-620-1130 248-4188*
NYSE: CLP ■ **Fax Area Code:* 901 ■ *TF:* 866-620-1130 ■ *Web:* www.maac.com

Combined Properties Inc 300 Commercial St ... Malden MA 02148 781-321-7800 321-5144
Web: www.combinedproperties.com

Community Development Trust (CDT)
1350 Broadway Ste 700 ... New York NY 10018 212-271-5080 271-5079
Web: www.cdt.biz

Cornell & Assoc Inc 2633 E Lake Ave Ste 307 ... Seattle WA 98102 206-329-0085 329-4110
Web: www.cornellandassociates.com

Corporate Office Properties Trust
6711 Columbia Gateway Dr Ste 300 ... Columbia MD 21046 443-285-5400 285-7650
NYSE: OFC ■ *Web:* www.copt.com

Cousins Properties Inc
191 Peachtree St NE Ste 500 ... Atlanta GA 30303 404-407-1000
NYSE: CUZ ■ *Web:* www.cousinsproperties.com

Crescent Real Estate Equities Co
777 Main St Ste 2000 ... Fort Worth TX 76102 817-321-1566 321-2000
Web: www.crescent.com

Crombie REIT 115 King St ... Stellarton NS B0K1S0 902-755-8100 755-6477
Web: crombiereit.ca

Cushman & Wakefield Inc
1290 Ave of the Americas ... New York NY 10019 212-841-7500 841-7867
Web: www.cushmanwakefield.com

Daniel Corp 3660 Grandview Pkwy ... Birmingham AL 35243 205-443-4500
Web: www.danielcorp.com

Developers Diversified Realty Corp
3300 Enterprise Pkwy ... Beachwood OH 44122 216-755-5500 755-1500
NYSE: DDR ■ *TF:* 877-225-5337 ■ *Web:* ddr.com

Donahue Schriber Realty Group Inc
200 E Baker St Ste 100 ... Costa Mesa CA 92626 714-545-1400 545-4222
Web: www.donahueschriber.com

Douglas Allred Co
11452 El Camino Real Ste 200 ... San Diego CA 92130 858-793-0202 793-5363
Web: www.douglasallredco.com

Douglas Elliman Property Management
675 Third Ave 6th Fl ... New York NY 10017 212-370-9200
Web: www.ellimanpm.com

Draper & Kramer Inc 55 E Monroe St Ste 3900 ... Chicago IL 60603 312-346-8600 346-8600
Web: www.draperandkramer.com

Duke Realty Corp 600 E 96th St Ste 100 ... Indianapolis IN 46240 317-808-6000 808-6794
NYSE: DRE-M.CL ■ *Web:* www.dukerealty.com

EastGroup Properties Inc
190 E Capitol St Ste 400 ... Jackson MS 39201 601-354-3555 352-1441
NYSE: EGP ■ *Web:* www.eastgroup.net

Entertainment Properties Trust
909 Walnut Ste 200 ... Kansas City MO 64106 816-472-1700
NYSE: EPR ■ *Web:* www.eprkc.com

Equity Lifestyle Properties Inc
2 N Riverside Plz Ste 800 ... Chicago IL 60606 312-279-1400 279-1710
NYSE: ELS ■ *TF:* 800-274-7314 ■ *Web:* www.equitylifestyle.com

Equity Office Properties Trust
2 N Riverside Plz Ste 2100 ... Chicago IL 60606 312-466-3300
Web: www.equityoffice.com

Equity One Inc
1600 NE Miami Gardens Dr ... North Miami Beach FL 33179 305-947-1664 947-1734
NYSE: EQY ■ *Web:* www.equityone.com

Equity Residential 2 N Riverside Plz ... Chicago IL 60606 312-474-1300
NYSE: EQR ■ *Web:* www.equityapartments.com

Essex Property Trust Inc 925 E Meadow Dr ... Palo Alto CA 94303 650-494-3700 494-8743
NYSE: ESS ■ *Web:* www.essexapartmenthomes.com

Eugene Burger Management Corp
6600 Hunter Dr ... Rohnert Park CA 94928 707-584-5123 584-5124
TF: 800-788-0233 ■ *Web:* www.ebmc.com

Federal Realty Investment Trust
1626 E Jefferson St ... Rockville MD 20852 301-998-8100 998-3700
NYSE: FRT ■ *TF:* 800-658-8980 ■ *Web:* www.federalrealty.com

FelCor Lodging Trust Inc
545 E John Carpenter Fwy Ste 1300 ... Irving TX 75062 972-444-4900 444-4949
NYSE: FCH ■ *Web:* www.felcor.com

Festival Co 9841 Airport Blvd Ste 700 ... Los Angeles CA 90045 310-665-9600 665-9009
Web: www.festivalcos.com

First Industrial Realty Trust Inc
311 S Wacker Dr Ste 4000 ... Chicago IL 60606 312-344-4300 922-6320
NYSE: FR ■ *Web:* www.firstindustrial.com

First Real Estate Investment 505 Main St ... Hackensack NJ 07602 201-488-6400 487-1798
Web: freitnj.com

First Realty Management Corp
151 Tremont St PH 1 ... Boston MA 02111 617-423-7000
Web: www.frmboston.com

First Republic Corp of America
302 Fifth Ave Ste 6 Ste 6 ... New York NY 10001 212-279-6100 629-6848
NYSE: FRPC

FirstService Corp
1140 Bay St 1st Service Bldg Ste 4000 ... Toronto ON M5S2B4 416-960-9500 960-5333
TSE: FSV ■ *Web:* www.firstservice.com

Fisher Auction Company Inc
2112 E Atlantic Blvd Ste 210 ... Pompano Beach FL 33060 954-942-0917
Web: www.fisherauction.com

Flatley Co, The
35 Braintree Hill Office Pk ... Braintree MA 02184 781-848-2000 849-4430
Web: www.flatleyco.com

Forest City Residential Group
50 Public Sq Ste 1515 ... Cleveland OH 44113 216-416-3906
Web: www.forestcity.net

Freeport Ctr Assoc PO Box 160466 ... Clearfield UT 84016 801-825-9741 825-3587
Web: www.freeportcenter.com

G&L Realty Corp 439 N Bedford Dr ... Beverly Hills CA 90210 310-273-9930
Web: www.glrealty.com

Gene B Glick Company Inc
8425 Woodfield Crossing Blvd ... Indianapolis IN 46240 317-469-0400
Web: www.genebglick.com

General Growth Properties Inc
110 N Wacker Dr ... Chicago IL 60606 312-960-5000 960-5475
NYSE: GGP ■ *TF:* 888-395-8037 ■ *Web:* www.ggp.com

Ginkgo Residential LLC
301 S College St Ste 3850 ... Charlotte NC 28202 704-944-0100
Web: ginkgores.com

Goodale & Barbieri Co
818 W Riverside Ave Ste 300 ... Spokane WA 99201 509-459-6109 344-4939
Web: www.g-b.com

Grady Management Inc
8630 Fenton St Ste 625 ... Silver Spring MD 20910 301-587-3330
TF: 800-544-7239 ■ *Web:* www.gradymgt.com

Graham Cos 6843 Main St ... Miami Lakes FL 33014 305-821-1130 557-0313
Web: www.miamilakes.com

Great American Group Inc
21860 Burbank Blvd Ste 300 ... Woodland Hills CA 91367 818-884-3737 884-2976
OTC: GAMR ■ *TF:* 800-454-7328 ■ *Web:* www.greatamerican.com

Gundaker Property Management
2458 Old Dorsett Rd Ste 100 ... Maryland Heights MO 63043 314-298-5200 298-5096
TF: 800-325-1978 ■ *Web:* www.coldwellbankerhomes.com/st-louis

Gyrodyne Company of America Inc
1 Flowerfield Ste 24 ... Saint James NY 11780 631-584-5400 584-7075
NASDAQ: GYRO ■ *Web:* www.gyrodyne.com

H & R Retail Inc 2800 Quarry Lk Dr Ste 320 ... Baltimore MD 21209 410-308-0800 486-2733
Web: www.hrretail.com

Hall Financial Group 6801 Gaylord Pkwy Ste 100 ... Frisco TX 75034 972-377-1100 377-1170
Web: www.hallfinancial.com

Harrison & Lear Inc 2310 Tower Pl Ste 105 ... Hampton VA 23666 757-825-9100 838-2574
Web: www.harrison-lear.com

Hawaii Reserves Inc 55-510 Kamehameha Hwy ... Laie HI 96762 808-293-9201 293-6456
Web: www.hawaiireserves.com

Health Care Property Investors Inc
1920 Main St Ste 1200 ... Irvine CA 92614 949-407-0700 407-0800
TF: 800-690-6903 ■ *Web:* www.hcpi.com

Healthcare Realty Trust Inc
3310 W End Ave Ste 700 ... Nashville TN 37203 615-269-8175 269-8260
NYSE: HR ■ *Web:* www.healthcarerealty.com

Heitman LLC 191 N Wacker Dr Ste 2500 ... Chicago IL 60606 312-855-5700
Web: www.heitman.com

Hemstreet Development Co
16100 NW Cornell Rd Ste 100 ... Beaverton OR 97006 503-531-4000 531-4001
Web: www.hemstreet.com

Herb Redl Inc 80 Washington St Ste 100 ... Poughkeepsie NY 12601 845-471-3388 471-3851
Web: www.hredlproperties.com

Hersha Hospitality Trust
510 Walnut St 9th Fl ... Philadelphia PA 19106 215-238-1046 238-0157
NYSE: HT ■ *Web:* www.hersha.com

Hickel Investment Co 939 W Fifth Ave ... Anchorage AK 99501 907-343-2400
Web: hickelinvestment.com

Highwoods Properties Inc
3100 Smoketree Ct Ste 600 ... Raleigh NC 27604 919-872-4924
NYSE: HIW ■ *TF:* 866-449-6637 ■ *Web:* www.highwoods.com

Holiday Retirement Corp
5885 Meadows Rd Ste 500 ... Lake Oswego OR 97035 503-370-7070
TF: 800-322-0999 ■ *Web:* www.holidaytouch.com

Holladay Corp 3400 Idaho Ave NW Ste 500 ... Washington DC 20016 202-362-2400
Web: holladaycorp.com

Home Properties 11459 Cronhill Dr Ste P ... Owings Mills MD 21117 410-356-3320
NYSE: HME ■ *Web:* www.homeproperties.com

Home Properties Inc 850 Clinton Sq ... Rochester NY 14604 585-546-4900
NYSE: HME ■ *Web:* www.homeproperties.com

Horizon Group Properties Inc 5000 Hakes Dr ... Muskegon MI 49441 231-798-9100 798-5100
Web: www.horizongroup.com

Horning Bros
1350 Connecticut Ave NW Ste 800 ... Washington DC 20036 202-659-0700
Web: www.horningbrothers.com

Hospitality Properties Trust
255 Washington St ... Newton MA 02458 617-964-8389 969-5730
NYSE: HPT ■ *Web:* www.hptreit.com

Hunt Midwest Enterprises Inc
8300 NE Underground Dr ... Kansas City MO 64161 816-455-2500
TF: 800-551-6877 ■ *Web:* www.huntmidwest.com

Imperial Realty Company Inc
4747 W Peterson Ave ... Chicago IL 60646 773-736-4100 736-4541
Web: imperialrealtyco.com

Inland Group Inc 2901 Butterfield Rd ... Oak Brook IL 60523 630-218-8000 218-4917
TF: 800-826-8228 ■ *Web:* www.inlandgroup.com

Inland Real Estate Corp
2901 Butterfield Rd ... Oak Brook IL 60523 630-218-8000 218-7357*
NYSE: IRC ■ **Fax:* Investor Rel ■ *TF:* 888-331-4732 ■ *Web:* www.inlandgroup.com

Irvine Company Apartment Communities
110 Innovation Dr ... Irvine CA 92617 949-720-5600
Web: www.rental-living.com

Jim Wilson & Assoc Inc
2660 Eastchase Ln Ste 100 ... Montgomery AL 36117 334-260-2500 260-2533
Web: www.jwamalls.com

JJ Gumberg Company Inc 1051 Brinton Rd ... Pittsburgh PA 15221 412-244-4000 244-9133
Web: www.jjgumberg.com

JMG Realty Inc 5605 Glenridge Dr Ste 1010 ... Atlanta GA 30342 404-995-1111 995-1112
Web: www.jmgrealty.com

John F Long Properties LLLP
5035 W Camelback Rd ... Phoenix AZ 85031 602-272-0421 846-7208*
**Fax Area Code:* 623 ■ *Web:* www.jflongproperties.com

Jonas Equities 725 Church Ave ... Brooklyn NY 11218 718-871-6020
Web: www.jonasequities.com

Jones Lang LaSalle Inc 200 E Randolph Dr ... Chicago IL 60601 312-782-5800 782-4339
NYSE: JLL ■ *Web:* www.jll.com

Jones Lang LaSalle IP Inc 200 E Randolph Dr ... Chicago IL 60601 312-782-5800
Web: www.jll.com

JW Mays Inc 9 Bond St ... Brooklyn NY 11201 718-624-7400
NASDAQ: MAYS ■ *Web:* www.jwmays.com

Kilroy Realty Corp
12200 W Olympic Blvd Ste 200 ... Los Angeles CA 90064 310-481-8400 481-6501
NYSE: KRC ■ *Web:* www.kilroyrealty.com

Kimco Realty Corp 3333 New Hyde Pk Rd ... New Hyde Park NY 11042 516-869-9000
NYSE: KIM ■ *TF:* 800-645-6292 ■ *Web:* www.kimcorealty.com

	City	State	Zip	Phone	Fax
Kraus-Anderson Realty Co 4210 W Old Shakopee Rd; *Web:* www.krausanderson.com	Bloomington	MN	55437	952-881-8166	
Kravco Co 234 Mall Blvd; *Web:* www.kravco.com	King of Prussia	PA	19406	610-854-2800	
L & B Realty Advisors LLP 8750 N Central Expy Ste 800; *Web:* www.lbgroup.com	Dallas	TX	75231	214-989-0800	
Lexington Corporate Properties Trust 1 Penn Plz Ste 4015; *TF:* 800-850-3948 ■ *Web:* www.lxp.com	New York	NY	10119	212-692-7200	594-6600
Lexington Ctr Corp 430 W Vine St; *Web:* www.lexingtoncenter.com	Lexington	KY	40507	859-233-4567	253-2718
Liberty Property Trust 500 Chesterfield Pkwy; *NYSE: LPT* ■ *Web:* www.libertyproperty.com	Malvern	PA	19355	610-648-1700	644-4129
Lincoln Property Co 2000 McKinney Ave Ste 1000	Dallas	TX	75201	214-740-3300	740-3441
Lomax Cos, The 200 Highpoint Dr Ste 215; *Web:* www.thelomaxcos.com	Chalfont	PA	18914	215-822-1550	997-9582
Lone Oak Fund LLC 11611 San Vincente Blvd Ste 640; *Web:* www.loneoakfund.com	Los Angeles	CA	90049	310-826-2888	
Lowe Enterprises 11777 San Vicente Blvd Ste 900; *Web:* www.loweenterprises.com	Los Angeles	CA	90049	310-820-6661	207-1132
Macerich Co, The 401 Wilshire Blvd Ste 700; *NYSE: MAC* ■ *Web:* www.macerich.com	Santa Monica	CA	90401	310-394-6000	395-2791
Mack-Cali Realty Corp 343 Thornall St; *NYSE: CLI* ■ *TF:* 800-317-4445 ■ *Web:* www.mack-cali.com	Edison	NJ	08837	732-590-1000	205-8237
Macklowe Properties Inc 767 Fifth Ave; *Web:* www.macklowe.com	New York	NY	10153	212-265-5900	
Madison Marquette 909 Montgomery St Ste 200; *Web:* www.madisonmarquette.com	San Francisco	CA	94133	415-277-6800	
Madison Park Financial Corp 155 Grand Ave Ste 1025; *Web:* www.mpfcorp.com	Oakland	CA	94612	510-452-2944	452-2973
Madison Square Garden Corp 4 Pennsylvania Plz; *Web:* www.thegarden.com	New York	NY	10001	212-465-6000	
Maier Siebel Baber 80 E Sir Francis Drake Blvd 5th Fl; *Web:* www.msb-realestate.com	Larkspur	CA	94939	415-591-9900	
Majestic Realty Co 13191 Crossroads Pkwy N 6th Fl; *Web:* www.majesticrealty.com	City of Industry	CA	91746	562-692-9581	695-2329
Maxus Realty Trust Inc 104 Armour Rd PO Box 34729; *OTC: MRTI* ■ *Web:* www.mrti.com	North Kansas City	MO	64116	816-303-4500	221-1829
Mericle Commercial Real Estate Services 100 Baltimore Dr; *Web:* www.mericle.com	Wilkes-Barre	PA	18702	570-823-1100	823-0300
Merritt Properties LLC 2066 Lord Baltimore Dr; *Web:* www.merrittproperties.com	Baltimore	MD	21244	410-298-2600	298-9644
Mid-America Apartment Communities Inc (MAAC) 6584 Poplar Ave Ste 300; *NYSE: MAA* ■ *TF:* 866-620-1130 ■ *Web:* www.maac.com	Memphis	TN	38138	901-682-6600	682-6667
Mid-Atlantic PenFed Realty Berkshire Hathaway HomeServices (PCR) 3050 Chain Bridge Rd; *TF:* 866-225-5778 ■ *Web:* www.penfedrealty.com	Fairfax	VA	22030	703-691-7653	691-7662
Miller Valentine Group 4000 Miller Valentine Ct; *TF:* 877-684-7687 ■ *Web:* www.mvg.com	Dayton	OH	45439	937-293-0900	299-1564
Monmouth Real Estate Investment Corp (MREIC) 3499 Rt 9 N Ste 3C; *NASDAQ: MNR* ■ *Web:* www.mreic.com	Freehold	NJ	07728	732-577-9996	
MonteLago Village Resort 30 Strada di Villaggio; *Web:* www.montelagovillage.com	Henderson	NV	89011	702-564-4700	
Moody Rambin Interests 3003 W Alabama St; *Web:* www.moodyrambin.com	Houston	TX	77098	713-271-5900	773-5555
Mullan Enterprises Inc 2330 W Joppa Rd Ste 210; *Web:* www.mullancontr.com	Lutherville	MD	21093	410-494-9200	
National Realty & Development Corp 3 Manhattanville Rd; *Web:* www.nrdc.com	Purchase	NY	10577	914-694-4444	
NDC LLC 6312 S 27th St Ste 202; *Web:* www.ndcllc.com	Oak Creek	WI	53154	414-761-2040	761-3576
New England Development 1 Wells Ave; *Web:* www.nedevelopment.com	Newton	MA	02459	617-965-8700	243-7085
Newcastle Investment Corp 1345 Ave of the Americas 46th Fl; *NYSE: NCT* ■ *Web:* www.newcastleinv.com	New York	NY	10105	212-798-6100	
Norfolk Southern Corp 800 Princeton Ave; *TF:* 800-453-2530 ■ *Web:* www.nscorp.com	Bluefield	WV	24701	304-324-2400	
NorthMarq Capital Inc 3500 W American Blvd Ste 500; *Web:* www.northmarq.com	Bloomington	MN	55431	952-356-0100	
NTS Realty Holdings LP 10172 Linn Stn Rd; *NYSE: NLP* ■ *Web:* www.ntsdevelopment.com	Louisville	KY	40223	502-426-4800	426-4994
Omega Healthcare Investors Inc 200 International Cir Ste 3500; *NYSE: OHI* ■ *TF:* 877-511-2891 ■ *Web:* www.omegahealthcare.com	Hunt Valley	MD	21030	410-427-1700	
One Liberty Properties Inc 60 Cutter Mill Rd Ste 303; *NYSE: OLP* ■ *TF:* 800-937-5449 ■ *Web:* 1liberty.com	Great Neck	NY	11021	516-466-3100	466-3132
Oxford Development Co 301 Grant St; *Web:* www.oxford-pgh.com	Pittsburgh	PA	15219	412-261-1500	642-7543
Oxford Properties Group Inc 130 Adelaide St W Oxford Tower Ste 1100; *Web:* www.oxfordproperties.com	Toronto	ON	M5H3P5	416-865-8300	
Parkway Properties Inc 188 E Capitol St Ste 1000; *NYSE: PKY* ■ *TF:* 800-748-1667 ■ *Web:* www.pky.com	Jackson	MS	39201	601-948-4091	949-4077
Patriot Properties Inc 123 Pleasant St; *Web:* www.patriotproperties.com	Marblehead	MA	01945	781-586-9670	
Peek Properties 258 E Arapaho Rd 160	Richardson	TX	75081	972-783-6040	669-0586
Pennsylvania Real Estate Investment Trust 200 S Broad St 3rd Fl; *NYSE: PEI* ■ *TF:* 866-875-0700 ■ *Web:* www.preit.com	Philadelphia	PA	19102	215-875-0700	546-7311
Perini Management Services Inc 73 Mt Wayte Ave; *Web:* www.tutorperini.com	Framingham	MA	01701	508-628-2000	628-2357
Persis Corp 900 Ft St Mall Ste 1725; *Web:* www.persis.com	Honolulu	HI	96813	808-599-8000	526-4114
Peterson Cos, The 12500 Fair Lakes Cir Ste 400; *Web:* www.petersoncos.com	Fairfax	VA	22033	703-227-2000	631-6481
Picerne Real Estate Group 75 Lambert Lind Hwy; *Web:* www.picerne.com	Warwick	RI	02886	401-732-3700	738-6452
PM Realty Group 1000 Main St Ste 2400; **Fax:* Hum Res ■ *Web:* www.pmrg.com	Houston	TX	77002	713-209-5800	209-5702*
Portman Holdings LLC 303 Peachtree St NE Ste 575; *Web:* www.portmanholdings.com	Atlanta	GA	30303	404-614-5252	614-5400
PRC Group 40 Monmouth Pk Hwy; *Web:* www.prcgroup.com	West Long Branch	NJ	07764	732-222-2000	222-6410
Price Edwards & Co 210 Pk Ave Ste 1000; *Web:* www.priceedwards.com	Oklahoma City	OK	73102	405-843-7474	236-1849
Prime Group Realty Trust 330 N Wabash Ave Ste 2800; *Web:* www.rrpchicago.com	Chicago	IL	60611	312-917-1300	917-1310
Professional Community Management Inc 23726 Birtcher Dr; **Fax Area Code:* 949 ■ *TF:* 800-369-7260 ■ *Web:* www.associaonline.com	Lake Forest	CA	92630	800-369-7260	859-3729*
ProLogis 4545 Airport Way; *NYSE: PLD* ■ *TF:* 800-566-2706 ■ *Web:* www.prologis.com	Denver	CO	80239	303-375-9292	567-5903
PS Business Parks Inc 701 Western Ave; *NYSE: PSB* ■ *TF Cust Svc:* 888-782-6110 ■ *Web:* www.psbusinessparks.com	Glendale	CA	91201	818-244-8080	242-0566
Pyramid Cos 4 Clinton Sq; *Web:* www.pyramidmg.com	Syracuse	NY	13202	315-422-7000	472-4035
Ramco-Gershenson Properties Trust 31500 NW Hwy Ste 300; *NYSE: RPT* ■ *Web:* rgpt.com	Farmington Hills	MI	48334	248-350-9900	350-9925
RD Management LLC 810 Seventh Ave 10th Fl; *Web:* www.rdmanagement.com	New York	NY	10019	212-265-6600	459-9133
Real Foundation Inc 13737 Noel Rd Ste 900; *Web:* www.realfoundations.net	Dallas	TX	75240	214-292-7000	
Realty Income Corp 11995 El Camino Real; *NYSE: O* ■ *TF:* 877-924-6266 ■ *Web:* www.realtyincome.com	San Diego	CA	92130	858-284-5000	
Regency Centers 1 Independent Dr Ste 114; *NYSE: REG* ■ *TF:* 800-950-6333 ■ *Web:* regencycenters.com	Jacksonville	FL	32202	904-598-7000	634-3428
Richard E Jacobs Group Inc 25425 Ctr Ridge Rd; *Web:* www.rejacobsgroup.com	Cleveland	OH	44145	440-871-4800	808-6902
Rochdale Village Inc 169-65 137th Ave; *Web:* rochdalevillage.com	Jamaica	NY	11434	718-276-5700	
Rosen Assoc Management Corp 33 S Service Rd; *Web:* www.rosenmgmt.com	Jericho	NY	11753	516-333-2000	
Rossmar & Graham Community Assn Management Co 9362 E Raintree Dr; *Web:* fsresidential.com	Scottsdale	AZ	85260	480-551-4300	551-6000
Ruffin Cos 1522 S Florence St; *Web:* www.ruffinco.com	Wichita	KS	67209	316-942-7940	
RXR REALTY 625 Rex Plz; *Web:* www.rxrrealty.com	Uniondale	NY	11556	516-506-6000	506-6800
Sabey Corp 12201 Tukwila International Blvd 4th Fl; *Web:* www.sabey.com	Seattle	WA	98168	206-281-8700	282-9951
San Diego Family Housing LLC 3360 Murray Ridge Rd; *Web:* www.lincolnmilitary.com	San Diego	CA	92123	858-874-8100	
Sares-Regis Group 18802 Bardeen Ave; *Web:* www.sares-regis.com	Irvine	CA	92612	949-756-5959	756-5955
Saul Centers Inc 7501 Wisconsin Ave Ste 1500E; *NYSE: BFS* ■ *Web:* www.saulcenters.com	Bethesda	MD	20814	301-986-6200	986-6079
Saxe Real Estate Management Service 1999 Van Ness Ave; *Web:* www.saxerealestate.com	San Francisco	CA	94109	415-474-3171	447-8652
Schatten Properties Management Company Inc 1514 S St; *TF:* 800-892-1315 ■ *Web:* www.schattenproperties.com	Nashville	TN	37212	615-329-3011	327-2343
Sea Island Co PO Box 30351; *TF:* 800-732-4752 ■ *Web:* seaisland.com	Sea Island	GA	31561	912-638-3611	
Selig Enterprises Inc 1100 Spring St NW Ste 550; *Web:* www.seligenterprises.com	Atlanta	GA	30309	404-876-5511	875-2629
Seligman & Assoc 1 Town Sq Ste 1913; *Web:* www.seligmangroup.com	Southfield	MI	48076	248-862-8000	
Sen Plex Corp 938 Kohou St; *Web:* www.senplex.com	Honolulu	HI	96817	808-848-0111	
Senior Housing Properties Trust 255 Washington St; *NYSE: SNH* ■ *TF:* 866-511-5038 ■ *Web:* www.snhreit.com	Newton	MA	02458	617-796-8350	796-8349
Sentinel Real Estate Corp 1251 Ave of the Americas; *Web:* www.sentinelcorp.com	New York	NY	10020	212-408-5000	603-8253
Simon Property Group Inc 225 W Washington St; *NYSE: SPG* ■ *Web:* www.simon.com	Indianapolis	IN	46204	317-636-1600	
Simon Property Group, Inc. 225 West Washington St; *Web:* www.premiumoutlets.com	Indianapolis	IN	46204	973-228-6111	

Company / Address	City	State	Zip	Phone	Fax
SL Green Realty Corp 420 Lexington Ave. *NYSE: SLG* ■ *Web:* www.slgreen.com	New York	NY	10170	212-594-2700	216-1790
SonomaWest Holdings Inc 2064 Hwy 116 *Web:* sonomawestholdings.com	Sebastopol	CA	95472	707-824-2534	829-4630
SR Weiner & Assoc Inc 1330 Boylston St *Web:* www.wsdevelopment.com	Chestnut Hill	MA	02467	617-232-8900	734-4661
Stanmar Inc 321 Commonwealth Rd Ste 201 *Web:* www.stanmar-inc.com	Wayland	MA	01778	508-310-9922	
Stirling Properties 109 Northpark Blvd Ste 300 *TF:* 888-261-2022 ■ *Web:* www.stirlingprop.com	Covington	LA	70433	985-898-2022	898-2077
SUHRCO Management Inc 2010 156th Ave NE Ste 100 *Web:* suhrcorp.com	Bellevue	WA	98007	425-455-0900	462-1943
Sun Communities Inc 27777 Franklin Rd Ste 200 *NYSE: SUI* ■ *Web:* www.suncommunities.com	Southfield	MI	48034	248-208-2500	208-2640
Susquehanna Real Estate 140 E Market St PO Box 2026 *Web:* www.susquehanna-realestate.com	York	PA	17401	717-848-5500	771-1430
Tanger Factory Outlet Centers Inc 3200 Northline Ave Ste 360 *NYSE: SKT* ■ *TF:* 800-720-6728 ■ *Web:* www.tangeroutlet.com	Greensboro	NC	27408	336-292-3010	852-2096
Targa Real Estate Services Inc 720 S 348th St A2 *Web:* www.targarealestate.com	Federal Way	WA	98003	253-815-0393	815-0191
Taubman Centers Inc 200 E Long Lk Rd Ste 300 *NYSE: TCO* ■ *TF:* 800-297-6003 ■ *Web:* www.taubman.com	Bloomfield Hills	MI	48303	248-258-6800	
Thackeray Partners 5207 McKinney Ave Ste 200 *Web:* www.thackeraypartners.com	Dallas	TX	75205	214-360-7830	
Topa Management Co 1800 Ave of the Stars Ste 1400 *Web:* www.topamanagement.com	Los Angeles	CA	90067	310-203-9199	229-9788
Tower Properties Co 1000 Walnut St Ste 900 *Web:* www.towerproperties.com	Kansas City	MO	64106	816-421-8255	
Trammell Crow Co 2100 McKinney Ave Ste 800 *Web:* www.trammellcrow.com	Dallas	TX	75201	214-863-4101	863-4493
Transcontinental Realty Investors Inc 1603 Lyndon B Johnson Fwy Ste 800 *NYSE: TCI* ■ *TF:* 800-400-6407 ■ *Web:* www.transconrealty-invest.com	Dallas	TX	75234	469-522-4200	522-4299
Transwestern Commercial Services 1900 W Loop S Ste 1300 *Web:* www.transwestern.net	Houston	TX	77027	713-270-7700	270-6285
Tridel Corp 4800 Dufferin St Ste 200 *Web:* www.tridel.com	Toronto	ON	M3H5S9	416-661-9394	
TSI International Group 1 Robert Speck Pkwy *Web:* www.tsi-international.com	Mississauga	ON	L4Z4E8	905-602-7463	
Tucson Realty & Trust Co 333 N Wilmont Rd Ste 340 *Web:* www.tucsonrealty.com	Tucson	AZ	85711	520-577-7000	918-3031
Underwood Investments 11502 Juniper Ridge Dr *Web:* underwoodinvestments.com	Austin	TX	78759	512-336-1155	
United Capital Corp 9 Pk Pl *OTC: UCAP* ■ *Web:* www.unitedcapitalcorp.net	Great Neck	NY	11021	516-466-6464	829-4301
United Mobile Homes Inc 3499 Rt 9 N Ste 3C *NYSE: UMH* ■ *Web:* www.umh.com	Freehold	NJ	07728	732-577-9997	
Universal Health Realty Income Trust 367 S Gulph Rd *NYSE: UHT* ■ *Web:* www.uhrit.com	KingofPrussia	PA	19406	610-265-0688	
University City Housing (UCH) 3418 Sansom St *Web:* www.universitycityhousing.com	Philadelphia	PA	19104	215-222-2000	222-5449
Urban Retail Properties Co 111 E Wacker Dr Ste 2400 *Web:* www.urbanretail.com	Chicago	IL	60601	312-915-2000	
Urstadt Biddle Properties Inc 321 Railroad Ave *NYSE: UBA* ■ *Web:* www.ubproperties.com	Greenwich	CT	06830	203-863-8200	861-6755
USAA Real Estate Co 9830 Colonnade Blvd Ste 600 **Fax Area Code: 210* ■ *TF:* 800-531-8182 ■ *Web:* www.usrealco.com	San Antonio	TX	78230	800-531-8182	641-8425*
Vangard Investment Properties 118 N State College Blvd *Web:* www.vanguardproperty.com	Fullerton	CA	92831	714-446-0100	
Vann Realty Co 10330 Regency Pkwy Dr Ste 204 *Web:* www.vannrealtyco.com	Omaha	NE	68114	402-734-4800	
Ventas Inc 111 S Wacker Dr Ste 4800 *TF:* 877-483-6827 ■ *Web:* www.ventasreit.com	Chicago	IL	60606	312-660-3800	
Ventas Inc 353 N Clark St Ste 3300 *NYSE: VTR* ■ *TF:* 877-483-6827 ■ *Web:* www.ventasreit.com	Chicago	IL	60654	877-483-6827	
Vestar Development 2425 E Camelback Rd Ste 750 *Web:* www.vestar.com	Phoenix	AZ	85016	602-866-0900	955-2298
Viceroy Homes Ltd 414 Croft St E *Web:* www.viceroy.com	Port Hope	ON	L1A4H1	905-800-0712	
Village Green Cos 30833 NW Hwy *TF:* 800-521-2220 ■ *Web:* www.villagegreen.com	Farmington Hills	MI	48334	248-851-9600	851-6161
Vornado Realty Trust 888 Seventh Ave *NYSE: VNO* ■ *TF:* 800-294-1322 ■ *Web:* www.vno.com	New York	NY	10019	212-894-7000	902-9316
Wal-Mart Realty 2001 SE Tenth St *Web:* www.walmartrealty.com	Bentonville	AR	72716	479-273-4682	
Walton Street Capital LLC 900 N Michigan Ave Ste 1900 *Web:* www.waltonst.com	Chicago	IL	60611	312-915-2800	
Warren Properties Inc PO Box 469114 *TF:* 800-831-0804 ■ *Web:* www.warrenproperties.com	Escondido	CA	92046	800-831-0804	
Washington Real Estate Investment Trust (WRIT) 1775 I St NW *NYSE: WRE* ■ *TF:* 800-565-9748 ■ *Web:* www.writ.com	Washington	DC	20006	301-984-9400	984-9610
Weingarten Realty Investors 2600 Citadel Plz Dr Ste 125 *NYSE: WRI* ■ *TF:* 800-688-8865 ■ *Web:* www.weingarten.com	Houston	TX	77008	713-866-6000	866-6049
Westfield America Inc 2049 Century Park E *Web:* www.westfield.com	Century City	CA	90067	310-478-4456	
Westgate Management Co Inc 133 Franklin Corner Rd	Lawrence Township	NJ	08648	609-895-8890	895-0058
White Co 1600 S Brentwood Blvd Ste 770 *Web:* www.white-co.com	Saint Louis	MO	63144	314-961-4480	961-5903
Wings Event Center 3600 Van Rick Dr **Fax Area Code: 720* ■ *Web:* www.wingseventcenter.com/default.aspx	Kalamazoo	MI	49001	269-345-1125	258-3050*
Winthrop Realty Trust 7 Bulfinch Pl Ste 500 *NYSE: FUR* ■ *TF:* 800-622-6757 ■ *Web:* www.winthropreit.com	Boston	MA	02114	617-570-4614	570-4746
Woodmont Real Estate Services (WRES) 1050 Ralston Ave *Web:* www.wres.com	Belmont	CA	94002	650-592-3960	591-4577
WP Carey & Company LLC 50 Rockefeller Plz 2nd Fl *NYSE: WPC* ■ *TF:* 800-972-2739 ■ *Web:* www.wpcarey.com	New York	NY	10020	212-492-1100	
Wright Runstad & Co 1201 Third Ave Ste 2700 *Web:* www.wrightrunstad.com	Seattle	WA	98101	206-447-9000	223-8791
Zamias Services Inc 300 Market St *Web:* www.zamias.com	Johnstown	PA	15901	814-535-3563	536-5969

656 REALTOR ASSOCIATIONS - STATE

See Also Real Estate Professionals Associations p. 1799

Listed here are the state branches of the National Association of Realtors.

Company / Address	City	State	Zip	Phone	Fax
Alabama Assn of Realtors 522 Washington Ave PO Box 4070 *TF:* 800-446-3808 ■ *Web:* www.alabamarealtors.com	Montgomery	AL	36104	334-262-3808	263-9650
Alaska Assn of Realtors 4205 Minnesota Dr *TF:* 800-478-3763 ■ *Web:* www.alaskarealtors.com	Anchorage	AK	99503	907-563-7133	561-1779
Arizona Assn of Realtors 255 E Osborne Rd Ste 200 *TF:* 800-426-7274 ■ *Web:* www.aaronline.com	Phoenix	AZ	85012	602-248-7787	351-2474
Arkansas Realtors Assn 11224 Executive Ctr Dr *TF:* 888-333-2206 ■ *Web:* www.arkansasrealtors.com	Little Rock	AR	72211	501-225-2020	225-7131
Aspen Luxury Rentals 220 W Main St Ste 201 *Web:* www.luxuryhomerentalsaspen.com	Aspen	CO	81612	970-618-8290	
Axiom Xcell Inc 13230 Evening Creek Dr Ste 217 *Web:* www.axiomxcell.com	San Diego	CA	92128	858-683-6100	
Beach Properties of Hilton Head Inc 64 Arrow Rd PO Box 7408 *TF:* 800-671-5155 ■ *Web:* www.beach-property.com	Hilton Head Island	SC	29928	843-671-5155	
Buxton Co 2651 S Polaris Dr *Web:* www.buxtonco.com	Fort Worth	TX	76137	817-332-3681	
California Assn of Realtors 525 S Virgil Ave *Web:* www.car.org	Los Angeles	CA	90020	213-739-8200	480-7724
Carolina Designs Realty Inc 1197 Duck Rd *TF:* 800-368-3825 ■ *Web:* www.carolinadesigns.com	Kitty Hawk	NC	27949	252-261-3934	
Colorado Assn of Realtors 309 Inverness Way S *TF:* 800-944-6550 ■ *Web:* www.coloradorealtors.com	Englewood	CO	80112	303-790-7099	790-7299
Connecticut Assn of Realtors 111 Founders Plz Ste 1101 *TF:* 800-335-4862 ■ *Web:* www.ctrealtor.com	East Hartford	CT	06108	860-290-6601	290-6615
Countryside Asset Management Corp 7490 Clubhouse Rd Ste 201	Boulder	CO	80301	303-530-0700	
Delaware Assn of Realtors 134 E Water St *TF:* 800-305-4445 ■ *Web:* www.delawarerealtor.com	Dover	DE	19901	302-734-4444	734-1341
EMG Inc 222 Schilling Cir Ste 275 *Web:* www.emgcorp.com	Hunt Valley	MD	21031	410-785-6200	
Fine Hotels Corp Suite 402 One Washington St *Web:* finebergcompanies.com	Wellesley	MA	02481	781-431-1108	
Flaherty & Collins Properties Inc 8900 Keystone Crossing Ste 1200 *Web:* flco.com	Indianapolis	IN	46240	317-816-9300	
Florida Assn of Realtors 7025 Augusta National Dr *TF:* 800-669-4327 ■ *Web:* www.floridarealtors.org	Orlando	FL	32822	407-438-1400	438-1411
Georgia Assn of Realtors 3200 Presidential Dr *TF:* 866-280-0576 ■ *Web:* www.garealtor.com	Atlanta	GA	30340	770-451-1831	458-6992
Goodman Real Estate Inc 2801 Alaskan Way Ste 310 *Web:* www.goodmanre.com	Seattle	WA	98121	206-448-0259	
Grand Peaks Properties Inc 4582 S Ulster St Pkwy Ste 1200 *Web:* www.grandpeaks.com	Denver	CO	80237	720-889-9200	
Greater Capital Area Assn of Realtors 15201 Diamondback Dr Ste 100 *Web:* www.gcaar.com	Rockville	MD	20850	301-590-2000	
Growth Properties Investment Managers Inc 1329 Bristol Pike Ste 182 *Web:* www.gpim.net	Bensalem	PA	19020	215-546-5980	
Hawaii Assn of Realtors 1136 12th Ave Ste 220 *TF:* 866-693-6767 ■ *Web:* www.hawaiirealtors.com	Honolulu	HI	96816	808-733-7060	737-4977
Idaho Assn of Realtors 10116 W Overland Rd *TF:* 800-621-7553 ■ *Web:* www.idahorealtors.com	Boise	ID	83702	208-342-3585	336-7958
Illinois Assn of Realtors 522 S Fifth St *Web:* www.illinoisrealtor.org	Springfield	IL	62701	217-529-2600	529-3904
Indiana Assn of Realtors 7301 N Shadeland Ave Ste A *TF:* 800-284-0084 ■ *Web:* www.indianarealtors.com	Indianapolis	IN	46250	317-842-0890	842-1076

	City	State	Zip	Phone	Fax
Intracorp Projects Ltd 900-666 Burrard St Ste 204 *Web:* intracorp.ca	Vancouver	BC	V6C2X8	905-940-6555	
Iowa Assn of Realtors 1370 NW 114th St Ste 100 *TF:* 800-532-1515 ■ *Web:* www.iowarealtors.com	Clive	IA	50325	515-453-1064	453-1070
Jacobson Companies Inc, The 1334 S Fifth Ave *Web:* www.jacobsoncompanies.com	Yuma	AZ	85364	928-782-1801	
JEM Strapping Systems 116 Shaver St *TF:* 877-536-6584 ■ *Web:* www.jemline.com	Brantford	ON	N3T5M1	519-754-5432	
Kansas Assn of Realtors 3644 SW Burlingame Rd *TF:* 800-366-0069 ■ *Web:* www.kansasrealtor.com	Topeka	KS	66611	785-267-3610	267-1867
Kentucky Assn of Realtors 2801 Palumbo Dr Ste 202 *TF:* 800-264-2185 ■ *Web:* www.kar.com	Lexington	KY	40509	859-263-7377	263-7565
Maine Assn of Realtors 19 Community Dr *Web:* www.mainerealtors.com	Augusta	ME	04330	207-622-7501	623-3590
Mandelbaum Commercial Real Estate 2502 N Clark St Ste 204 *Web:* www.mandelbaumrealestate.com	Chicago	IL	60614	773-525-4700	
Maryland Assn of Realtors 2594 Riva Rd **Fax Area Code:* 301 ■ *TF:* 800-638-6425 ■ *Web:* www.mdrealtor.org	Annapolis	MD	21401	410-841-6080	261-8369*
Massachusetts Assn of Realtors 256 Second Ave *TF:* 800-725-6272 ■ *Web:* www.marealtor.com	Waltham	MA	02451	781-890-3700	890-4919
Mentor Group Inc, The 1775 E Palm Canyon Dr Ste 110-132	Palm Springs	CA	92264	760-325-6411	
MERIT Property Management Inc 1 Polaris Way Ste 100 *Web:* www.meritpm.com	Aliso Viejo	CA	92656	949-448-6000	
MetroList Services Inc 4640 Northgate Blvd Ste 100 *Web:* www.metrolistmls.com	Sacramento	CA	95834	916-922-7584	
Michael L. Shular 2682 S Mckenzie St *Web:* www.shularhospitality.com	Foley	AL	36535	251-943-9100	
Michigan Assn of Realtors 720 N Washington Ave *TF:* 800-454-7842 ■ *Web:* www.mirealtors.com	Lansing	MI	48906	517-372-8890	334-5568
Minnesota Assn of Realtors 5750 Lincoln Dr *TF:* 800-862-6097 ■ *Web:* www.mnrealtor.com	Minneapolis	MN	55436	952-935-8313	
Mississippi Assn of Realtors 4274 Lakeland Dr PO Box 321000 *TF:* 800-747-1103 ■ *Web:* www.msrealtors.org	Jackson	MS	39232	601-932-9325	932-0382
Missouri Assn of Realtors 2601 Bernadette Pl *TF:* 800-403-0101 ■ *Web:* www.missourirealtor.org	Columbia	MO	65203	573-445-8400	445-7865
MLS Property Information Network Inc 904 Hartford Tpke *Web:* www.mlspin.com	Shrewsbury	MA	01545	508-845-1011	
Montana Assn of Realtors 1 S Montana Ave Ste M1 *TF:* 800-477-1864 ■ *Web:* www.montanarealtors.org	Helena	MT	59601	406-443-4032	443-4220
Nebraska Realtors Assn 800 S 13th St Ste 200 *TF:* 800-777-5231 ■ *Web:* www.nebraskarealtors.com	Lincoln	NE	68508	402-323-6500	323-6501
Nevada Assn of Realtors 760 Margrave Dr Ste 200 *TF:* 800-748-5526 ■ *Web:* www.nvar.org	Reno	NV	89502	775-829-5911	829-5915
New Hampshire Assn of Realtors 115A Airport Rd *TF:* 800-335-4862 ■ *Web:* nhar.org	Concord	NH	03301	603-225-5549	228-0385
New Jersey Assn of Realtors 295 Pierson Ave *Web:* www.njrealtor.com	Edison	NJ	08837	732-494-5616	494-4723
New York State Assn of Realtors 130 Washington Ave *TF:* 800-462-7585 ■ *Web:* www.nysar.com	Albany	NY	12210	518-463-0300	462-5474
North Carolina Assn of Realtors Inc 4511 Weybridge Ln *TF:* 800-443-9956 ■ *Web:* www.ncrealtors.org	Greensboro	NC	27407	336-294-1415	299-7872
North Dakota Assn of Realtors 318 W Apollo Ave *TF:* 800-279-2361 ■ *Web:* www.ndrealtors.com	Bismarck	ND	58503	701-355-1010	258-7211
O'Keefe Drilling Co 2000 4 Mile Rd *Web:* www.okeefedrilling.com	Butte	MT	59701	406-494-3310	
Ohio Assn of Realtors 200 E Town St *Web:* www.ohiorealtors.org	Columbus	OH	43215	614-228-6675	228-2601
Oklahoma Assn of Realtors 9807 N Broadway *TF:* 800-375-9944 ■ *Web:* okrealtors.com	Oklahoma City	OK	73114	405-848-9944	848-9947
Oregon Assn of Realtors 2110 Mission St SE *TF:* 800-252-9115 ■ *Web:* oregonrealtors.org	Salem	OR	97308	503-362-3645	362-9615
Pennsylvania Assn of Realtors 500 N Twelfth St *TF:* 800-555-3390 ■ *Web:* www.parealtor.org	Lemoyne	PA	17043	717-561-1303	561-8796
Phoenix Housing Network 7050 S G St *Web:* ccswn.convio.net	Tacoma	WA	98408	253-471-5340	
Rainier Group Investment Advisory LLC 500 108th Ave N E Ste 2000 *TF:* 800-800-8974 ■ *Web:* rainiergroup.com	Bellevue	WA	98004	425-463-3000	
Real Estate Institute of Canada, The 5407 Eglinton Ave W Ste 208 *TF:* 800-542-7342 ■ *Web:* www.reic.ca	Toronto	ON	M9C5K6	416-695-9000	
Realtors Assn of New Mexico 2201 Bros Rd *TF:* 800-224-2282 ■ *Web:* www.nmrealtor.com	Santa Fe	NM	87505	505-982-2442	983-8809
Red Bell Real Estate LLC 1415 S Main St *Web:* www.redbellre.com	Salt Lake City	UT	84115	801-483-4300	
RedRock Consultants LLC 1450 Sutter St No. 527 *Web:* www.redrockconsultants.com	San Francisco	CA	94109	415-246-7625	
Rhode Island Assn of Realtors 100 Bignall St *TF:* 866-438-8345 ■ *Web:* www.riliving.com	Warwick	RI	02888	401-785-9898	941-5360
RPI Media Inc 265 Racine Dr Ste 201 *Web:* www.rpimedia.com	Wilmington	NC	28403	910-763-2100	
Ryness Company Inc, The 801 San Ramon Valley Blvd *Web:* www.ryness.com	Danville	CA	94526	925-820-3432	
Senior Resource Group 500 Stevens Ave Ste 100 *Web:* www.srgseniorliving.com	Solana Beach	CA	92075	858-792-9300	
Signature Homes Inc 4670 Willow Rd Ste 200 *TF:* 888-673-0200 ■ *Web:* www.sigprop.com	Pleasanton	CA	94588	925-463-1122	
SMI properties 5239 zMax Blvd *Web:* www.smiproperties.com	Harrisburg	NC	28075	704-455-9499	
South Carolina Assn of Realtors 3780 Fernandina Rd *TF:* 800-233-6381 ■ *Web:* www.screaltors.org	Columbia	SC	29210	803-772-5206	798-6650
South Dakota Assn of Realtors 204 N Euclid Ave *TF:* 800-227-5877 ■ *Web:* www.sdrealtor.org	Pierre	SD	57501	605-224-0554	224-8975
staySky Resort Management 7011 Grand National Dr Ste 104 *Web:* www.skyresortmanagement.com	Orlando	FL	32819	407-992-0430	
Surfside Realty Co Inc 213 S Ocean Blvd *Web:* www.surfsiderealty.com/	Surfside Beach	SC	29575	843-238-3435	
Tennessee Assn of Realtors (TAR) 901 19th Ave S *TF:* 877-321-1477 ■ *Web:* www.tarnet.com	Nashville	TN	37212	615-321-1477	321-4905
Texas Assn of Realtors 1115 San Jacinto Blvd Ste 200 *TF:* 800-873-9155 ■ *Web:* www.texasrealestate.com	Austin	TX	78701	512-480-8200	370-2390
Utah Assn of Realtors 230 W Towne Ridge Pkwy Ste 500 *TF:* 800-594-8933 ■ *Web:* www.utahrealtors.com	Sandy	UT	84070	801-676-5200	676-5225
Vermont Assn of Realtors 148 State St *Web:* www.vtrealtor.com	Montpelier	VT	05602	802-229-0513	
Virginia Assn of Realtors 10231 Telegraph Rd *TF:* 800-755-8271 ■ *Web:* www.varealtor.com	Glen Allen	VA	23059	804-264-5033	262-0497
Washington Assn of Realtors 504 14th Ave SE Ste 200 *TF General:* 800-562-6024 ■ *Web:* www.warealtor.org	Olympia	WA	98501	360-943-3100	
West Virginia Assn of Realtors 2110 Kanawha Blvd E *TF:* 800-445-7600 ■ *Web:* www.wvrealtors.com	Charleston	WV	25311	304-342-7600	343-5811
Wild Rose Entertainment LLC 5465 Mills Civic Pkwy Ste 400 *Web:* www.wildroseresorts.com	West Des Moines	IA	50266	515-327-1776	
Wisconsin Realtors Assn 4801 Forest Run Rd Ste 201 *TF:* 800-279-1972 ■ *Web:* www.wra.org	Madison	WI	53704	608-241-2047	241-2901
Wyoming Assn of Realtors 777 Overland Trail Ste 220 *TF:* 800-676-4085 ■ *Web:* www.wyorealtors.com	Casper	WY	82601	307-237-4085	237-7929

657 RECORDING COMPANIES

	City	State	Zip	Phone	Fax
ABKCO Music & Records Inc 85 Fifth Ave Ste 11 *Web:* www.abkco.com	New York	NY	10003	212-399-0300	
Alligator Records & Artist Management Inc PO Box 60234 *TF:* 800-344-5609 ■ *Web:* www.alligator.com	Chicago	IL	60660	773-973-7736	973-2088
American Gramaphone LLC 9130 Mormon Bridge Rd *TF:* 800-348-3434	Omaha	NE	68152	402-457-4341	457-4332
Balboa Records Inc 10900 Washington Blvd *Web:* www.balboarecords.com	Culver City	CA	90232	310-204-3792	204-0886
Cambria Music PO Box 374 *Web:* www.cambriamus.com	Lomita	CA	90717	310-831-1322	833-7442
Century Media 2323 W El Segundo Blvd *Web:* www.centurymedia.com	Hawthorne	CA	90250	323-418-1400	418-0118
Curb Records 48 Music Sq E *Web:* www.curb.com	Nashville	TN	37203	615-321-5080	
Domino Recording Co 55 Washington St Ste 454 *Web:* www.dominorecordco.com	Brooklyn	NY	11201	718-797-4229	
Dualtone Music Group 3 Mcferrin Ave *Web:* www.dualtone.com	Nashville	TN	37206	615-320-0620	320-0692
EMI Music Canada 1 Yonge St *Web:* www.emimusic.ca	Toronto	ON	M5E1W7	416-583-5000	
Geffen Records 2220 Colorado Ave *Web:* www.interscope.com	Santa Monica	CA	90404	310-865-1000	
Hollywood Records Inc 500 S Buena Vista St *Web:* www.hollywoodrecords.com	Burbank	CA	91521	818-560-5670	845-4313
Integrity Music 4050 Lee Vance View *TF:* 888-888-4726 ■ *Web:* www.integritymusic.com	Colorado Springs	CO	80918	719-536-0100	
Interscope Records 2220 Colorado Ave *Web:* www.interscope.com	Santa Monica	CA	90404	310-865-1000	865-1405
Jbi Studios 21434 Wyandotte St *Web:* www.jbistudios.com	Canoga Park	CA	91303	818-592-0056	
Mack Avenue Records Ii LLC 19900 Harper Ave *Web:* www.mackavenue.com	Harper Woods	MI	48225	313-640-8414	
Malaco Music Group Inc 3023 W Northside Dr *TF Cust Svc:* 800-272-7936 ■ *Web:* www.malaco.com	Jackson	MS	39213	601-982-4522	982-4528
Mcsd Studio 514 W 43rd St *Web:* mcsdstudio.com	Indianapolis	IN	46208	317-926-0773	
Mosaic Records 35 Melrose Pl *Web:* www.mosaicrecords.com	Stamford	CT	06902	203-327-7111	323-3526
Narada Productions Inc 4650 N Port Washington Rd	Milwaukee	WI	53212	414-961-8350	961-8351
Naxos of America Inc 1810 Columbia Ave *TF:* 877-629-6723 ■ *Web:* www.naxos.com	Franklin	TN	37064	615-771-9393	771-6747
Nightingale-Conant Corp 6245 W Howard St *TF Cust Svc:* 800-557-1660 ■ *Web:* www.nightingale.com	Niles	IL	60714	800-557-1660	
Nonesuch Records 3300 Warner Blvd *Web:* www.nonesuch.com	Burbank	CA	91505	212-275-2000	
Psychopathic Record 32575 Folsom Rd *Web:* www.psychopathicrecords.com	Farmington Hills	MI	48336	248-426-0800	

				Phone	Fax
Rainmaker Recording & Creative 1901 E Franklin St Ste 101 *Web:* www.rainmakerstudios.com	Richmond	VA	23223	804-771-9300	
RCA Records 550 Madison Ave *Web:* www.rcarecords.com	New York	NY	10022	212-930-4000	
Record Plant Inc 1032 N Sycamore Ave *Web:* www.recordplant.com	Hollywood	CA	90038	323-993-9300	466-8835
Rhino Records 3400 W Olive Ave **Fax Area Code:* 212 ■ *TF:* 800-827-4466 ■ *Web:* www.rhino.com	Burbank	CA	91505	800-546-3670	956-0529*
Righteous Babe Records 341 Delaware Ave PO Box 95 *TF:* 800-664-3769 ■ *Web:* www.righteousbabe.com	Buffalo	NY	14202	716-852-8020	852-2741
Silvercup Studios 3402 Starr Ave *Web:* www.silvercupstudios.com	Long Island	NY	11101	718-906-3000	
Skaggs Family Records PO Box 2478 *Web:* www.skaggsfamilyrecords.com	Hendersonville	TN	37077	615-264-8877	264-8899
Smithsonian Folkways Recordings 600 Maryland Ave SW Ste 200 *TF:* 800-410-9815 ■ *Web:* www.folkways.si.edu	Washington	DC	20024	202-633-6450	633-6477
Soar Corp (SOAR) 5200 Constitution Ave NE **Fax Area Code:* 215 ■ *TF:* 866-616-4450	Albuquerque	NM	87110	505-268-6110	464-0445*
Sony Music Entertainment 550 Madison Ave **Fax:* Sales ■ *Web:* www.sonymusic.com	New York	NY	10022	212-833-8000	833-5828*
Sony Music Nashville 1400 18th Ave S *Web:* www.sonymusicnashville.com	Nashville	TN	37212	615-301-4488	
SubPop Records 2013 Fourth Ave 3rd Fl *Web:* www.subpop.com	Seattle	WA	98121	206-441-8441	441-8245
Synchromesh Studios 1116 Ford Ave *Web:* www.synchromeshstudios.com	Birmingham	AL	35217	205-808-0808	
Telarc International Corp 23307 Commerce Pk Rd *Web:* concordmusicgroup.com/labels/telarc	Cleveland	OH	44122	216-464-2313	360-9663
Victory Records Inc 346 N Justine St 5th Fl *Web:* www.victoryrecords.com	Chicago	IL	60607	312-666-8661	666-8665
Walt Disney Studios 500 S Buena Vista St *Web:* www.disneyworld.disney.go.com	Burbank	CA	91521	407-939-5277	
Warner Bros Records 3300 Warner Blvd *Web:* www.warnerbrosrecords.com	Burbank	CA	91505	818-846-9090	
Warner Music Group 75 Rockefeller Plz 30th Fl *Web:* www.wmg.com	New York	NY	10019	212-275-2000	
Word Entertainment 25 Music Sq W *Web:* www.wordentertainment.com	Nashville	TN	37203	615-251-0600	726-7868
Worldly Voices LLC 2610 Westwood Dr *Web:* www.worldlyvoices.com	Nashville	TN	37204	615-321-8802	

658 RECORDING MEDIA - MAGNETIC & OPTICAL

See Also Photographic Equipment & Supplies p. 2939

				Phone	Fax
Allied Vaughn 7600 Parklawn Ste 300 *TF:* 800-323-0281 ■ *Web:* www.alliedvaughn.com	Minneapolis	MN	55435	952-832-3100	832-3179
Ampex Corp 500 Broadway **Fax:* Hum Res ■ *TF:* 800-835-5095 ■ *Web:* www.ampex.com	Redwood City	CA	94063	650-367-2011	367-4669*
Applied Data Resources Inc 1303 N Glenville Dr	Richardson	TX	75081	972-238-8111	
Athana Inc 1624 W 240 St *TF:* 800-421-1591 ■ *Web:* www.athana.com	Harbor City	CA	90710	310-539-7280	539-6596
Cine Magnetics Inc 100 Business Pk Dr *TF:* 800-431-1102 ■ *Web:* www.cminyla.com	Armonk	NY	10504	914-273-7500	273-7575
Cinram International Inc 2255 Markham Rd *Web:* cinramgroup.com	Scarborough	ON	M1B2W3	416-298-8190	
Conduant Corp 1501 S Sunset St Ste C *Web:* www.conduant.com	Longmont	CO	80501	303-485-2721	
Digital Excellence 300 York Ave *TF:* 800-608-8008 ■ *Web:* www.digx.com	Saint Paul	MN	55101	651-772-5100	771-5629
Duplication Factory Inc 4275 Norex Dr *Web:* www.duplicationfactory.com	Chaska	MN	55318	952-227-8106	
eScholar LLC 222 Bloomingdale Rd Ste 107 *Web:* www.escholar.com	White Plains	NY	10605	914-989-2900	
Farstone Technology Inc 1758-B N Shoreline Blvd **Fax Area Code:* 650 ■ *Web:* www.farstone.com	Mountain View	CA	94043	562-373-5370	969-4567*
Fujifilm Mfg USA Inc 211 Pucketts Ferry Rd *Web:* fujifilmusa.com/about	Greenwood	SC	29649	864-223-2888	
Imagine Express 2633 Minnehaha Ave *Web:* imagine-express.com	Minneapolis	MN	55406	612-728-1500	
Imation Corp 1 Imation Pl *NYSE: IMN* ■ *TF:* 888-466-3456 ■ *Web:* www.imation.com	Oakdale	MN	55128	651-704-4000	704-7100
LaserCard Corp 1875 N Shoreline Blvd *Web:* www.hidglobal.com	Mountain View	CA	94043	650-969-4428	969-3140
Maxell Corp of America 3 Garret Mountain Plaza 3rd Fl Ste 300 *Web:* www.maxell-usa.com	Woodland Park	NJ	07424	973-653-2400	653-2450
Mediostream Inc 4962 El Cmno Real 201 *Web:* www.mediostream.com	Los Altos	CA	94022	650-625-8900	625-9900
Peripheral Manufacturing Inc 4775 Paris St *TF:* 800-468-6888 ■ *Web:* www.periphman.com	Denver	CO	80239	303-371-8651	371-8643
Sony DADC US INC 1800 N Fruitridge Ave *Web:* www.sonydadc.com	Terre Haute	IN	47804	812-462-8100	
Stanton Magnetics Inc 772 S Military Trl *Web:* www.stantondj.com	Deerfield Beach	FL	33442	954-949-9600	
TDK Electronics Corp 525 RXR Plz *Web:* www.tdk.com	Uniondale	NY	11556	516-535-2600	
TDK USA Corp 525 RXR Plaza **Fax:* Sales ■ *Web:* www.tdk.com	Uniondale	NY	11556	516-535-2600	294-8318*
Verbatim Americas LLC 1200 W WT Harris Blvd *TF:* 800-538-8589 ■ *Web:* www.verbatim.com	Charlotte	NC	28262	704-547-6500	547-6609

				Phone	Fax
Viva Magnetics (Canada) Ltd 1663 Neilson Rd *Web:* www.vivacan.com	Scarborough	ON	M1X1T1	416-321-0622	

659 RECREATION FACILITY OPERATORS

See Also Bowling Centers p. 1875

				Phone	Fax
Clicks Billiards 3100 Monticello Ave Ste 350 *Web:* clicks.com	Dallas	TX	75205	214-521-7001	521-1449
Dave & Buster's Inc 2481 Manana Dr **Fax Area Code:* 302 ■ *TF:* 800-842-5369 ■ *Web:* www.daveandbusters.com	Dallas	TX	75220	214-357-9588	636-5454*

660 RECYCLABLE MATERIALS RECOVERY

Included here are companies that recycle post-consumer trash, tires, appliances, batteries, etc. as well as industrial recyclers of plastics, paper, wood, glass, solvents, and so on.

				Phone	Fax
A.J. Catagnus Inc 1299 W James St *Web:* www.ajcatagnus.com	Norristown	PA	19401	610-277-2727	
ACC Recycling Corp 1190 20th St N	Saint Petersburg	FL	33713	727-892-9216	822-4923
Active Recycling Company Inc 2000 W Slauson Ave *Web:* www.activelosangeles.com	Los Angeles	CA	90047	323-295-7774	
Advanced Environmental Recycling Technologies Inc 914 N Jefferson St *OTC: AERT* ■ *Web:* aert.com	Springdale	AR	72764	479-756-7400	
All American Recycling Corp 2 Hope St *Web:* allamericanrecyclingcorp.com	Jersey City	NJ	07307	201-656-3363	792-5693
Ambit Pacific Recycling Inc 16228 S Figueroa St *Web:* www.ambitpacific.com	Gardena	CA	90248	310-538-3798	327-7114
American Paper Recycling Corp 87 Central St *TF Cust Svc:* 800-762-6790 ■ *Web:* aprcorp.com	Mansfield	MA	02048	800-762-6790	
Apollo Wood Recovery Inc 14253 Whittram Ave *Web:* www.apollowood.com	Fontana	CA	92335	909-356-2735	
Appliance Recycling Centers of America Inc 7400 Excelsior Blvd *NASDAQ: ARCI* ■ *TF:* 800-452-8680 ■ *Web:* www.arcainc.com	Minneapolis	MN	55426	952-930-9000	930-1800
Arrow Value Recovery 9101 Burnet Rd Ste 203 *TF:* 800-393-7627 ■ *Web:* www.arrowvaluerecovery.com	Austin	TX	78758	800-393-7627	
Asbury Environmental Services 9119 Birch St *Web:* www.asburyenv.com	Spring Valley	CA	91977	619-463-1126	
Balcones Resources Inc 9301 Johnny Morris Rd *Web:* www.balconesresources.com	Austin	TX	78724	512-472-3355	
Bayshore Recycling Corp 75 Crows Mill Rd *Web:* bayshorerecycling.com	Keasbey	NJ	08832	732-738-6000	
Best Way of Indiana Inc 2577 Kentucky Ave *Web:* www.bestway-disposal.com	Indianapolis	IN	46221	317-484-3365	
Better Management Corp (BMC) 41738 Esterly Dr *TF:* 877-293-4300 ■ *Web:* www.bmcohio.com	Columbiana	OH	44408	330-482-7070	
Canusa Hershman Recycling Co 45 NE Industrial Rd *Web:* www.chrecycling.com	Branford	CT	06405	203-488-0887	483-9943
Chemtron Corp 35850 Schneider Ct *Web:* www.chemtron-corp.com	Avon	OH	44011	440-937-6348	
Clean Earth of North Jersey Inc 115 Jacobus Ave *TF:* 877-445-3478 ■ *Web:* cleanearthinc.com	South Kearny	NJ	07032	973-344-4004	344-8652
Continental Paper Grading Company Inc 1623 S Lumber St *Web:* www.cpgco.com	Chicago	IL	60616	312-226-2010	226-2025
Cycle-Tex Inc 702 S Thornton Ave # 101 *Web:* www.cycletex.com	Dalton	GA	30720	706-226-1116	
Dallas Waste Disposal & Recycling Inc 3303 Pluto St *Web:* www.dallasrecycling.net	Dallas	TX	75212	214-634-1831	
Eastern Sanitation Limited 17 Adam St *Web:* easternsanitation.com	Antigonish	NS	B2G2G1	902-863-1744	
Empire Recycling Corp North Genesee & Lee Sts *Web:* www.empirerecycling.com	Utica	NY	13503	315-724-7161	
Energy Answers Corp 79 N Pearl St *Web:* www.energyanswers.com	Albany	NY	12207	518-434-1227	436-6343
Federal International Inc 7935 Clayton Rd *Web:* www.federalinternational.com	Saint Louis	MO	63117	314-721-3377	721-2007
Friedman Recycling Co 3640 W Lincoln St *Web:* www.friedmanrecycling.com	Phoenix	AZ	85009	602-269-9324	
Fritz Enterprises Inc 1650 W Jefferson Ave *Web:* www.fritzinc.com	Trenton	MI	48183	734-362-3200	362-3250
Geep International 2501 N Great SW Pkwy *Web:* www.geepglobal.com	Grand Prairie	TX	75050	972-602-2900	
Giordano s Solid Waste Removal 110 N Mill Rd *TF:* 800-636-8625 ■ *Web:* www.giordanosrecycling.com	Vineland	NJ	08360	856-696-2068	
GreenMan Technologies Inc 7 Kimball Ln Bldg A *TF:* 866-994-7697 ■ *Web:* www.americanpowergroupinc.com	Lynnfield	MA	01940	781-224-2411	
Greentec International Inc 95 Struck Ct *TF:* 888-858-1515 ■ *Web:* www.greentec.com	Cambridge	ON	N1R8L2	519-624-3300	
Horry County Solid Waste Authority Inc 1886 Hwy 90 *Web:* www.solidwasteauthority.org	Conway	SC	29526	843-347-1651	
Hvf West LLC 6581 E Drexel Rd *Web:* www.hvfwest.com	Tucson	AZ	85706	520-750-9454	

	City	State	Zip	Phone	Fax
Jupiter Aluminum Corp 4825 Scott St *TF:* 800-392-7265 ■ *Web:* www.jupiteraluminum.com	Schiller Park	IL	60176	847-928-5930	928-0795
Marborg Industries 728 E Yanonali St *TF:* 800-798-1852 ■ *Web:* www.marborg.com	Santa Barbara	CA	93103	805-963-1852	962-0552
Marck Industries Inc 401 Main Ste E *Web:* www.marck.net	Cassville	MO	65625	417-847-5900	
MCF Systems Atlanta Inc 5353 Snapfinger Woods Dr *TF:* 800-828-3240 ■ *Web:* www.mcfsystems.com	Decatur	GA	30035	770-593-9434	
Mervis Industries Inc 3295 E Main St *TF:* 800-637-3016 ■ *Web:* www.mervis.com	Danville	IL	61834	217-442-5300	477-9245
Metal Management Mississippi Inc 304 W Bankhead St *Web:* www.simsmm.com	New Albany	MS	38652	662-534-3004	
Metro Recycling Co Inc 2424 Beekman St **Fax Area Code:* 519	Cincinnati	OH	45214	513-294-8711	836-1047*
Minergy Corp 1512 S Commercial St *Web:* www.minergy.com	Neenah	WI	54956	920-727-1919	727-1418
Newalta Corp 211 11 Ave SW *Web:* www.newalta.com	Calgary	AB	T2R0C6	403-806-7000	
North Shore Recycled Fibers Inc 53 Jefferson Ave *TF:* 800-225-2369	Salem	MA	01970	978-744-4330	744-8857
Pall Corp 2200 Northern Blvd *NYSE:* PLL ■ *TF:* 800-645-6532 ■ *Web:* www.pall.com	East Hills	NY	11548	516-484-5400	801-9754
Paper Tigers, The 2201 Waukegan Rd Ste 180 *TF:* 800-621-1774 ■ *Web:* www.papertigers.com	Bannockburn	IL	60015	847-919-6500	919-6501
Pioneer Paper Stock 155 Irving Ave N *TF:* 800-821-8512 ■ *Web:* www.pioneerintl.com	Minneapolis	MN	55405	612-374-2280	374-5982
Potential Industries Inc 922 E E St *Web:* potentialindustries.com	Wilmington	CA	90744	310-549-5901	513-1361
ReCommunity Recycling 809 W Hill St *Web:* www.recommunity.com	Charlotte	NC	28208	704-697-2000	375-2949
Recycle Ann Arbor Inc 2420 S Industrial Hwy *Web:* www.recycleannarbor.org	Ann Arbor	MI	48104	734-662-6288	
Recycling Center of Live Oak Inc, The 700 Houston Ave NW *Web:* www.biggreenball.org	Live Oak	FL	32064	386-364-5865	
Royal Waste Services Inc 18740 Hollis Ave *Web:* royalwaste.com	Hollis	NY	11423	718-468-8679	
Strategic Materials Inc 16365 Pk Ten Pl Ste 200 *Web:* www.strategicmaterials.com	Houston	TX	77084	281-647-2700	647-2710
Sun Valley Paper Stock Inc 11166 Pendleton St	Sun Valley	CA	91352	323-875-2613	
Texas Recycling Surplus Inc 2835 Congressman Ln *Web:* www.texasrecycling.com	Dallas	TX	75220	214-357-0262	
United Plastic Recycling Inc 3000 Selma Highway *Web:* unitedplasticrecycling.com	Montgomery	AL	36108	334-288-5002	
Utah Metal Works Inc (UMW) 805 Everett Ave *TF:* 877-221-0099 ■ *Web:* www.umw.com	Salt Lake City	UT	84116	801-503-9153	364-5676
Vexor Technology Inc 955 W Smith Rd *Web:* www.vexortechnology.com	Medina	OH	44256	330-721-9773	
Wise Recycling LLC 555 Wise Rd *Web:* www.wiserecycling.com	Clayton	NC	27520	919-553-9009	
WTE Corp 7 Alfred Cir *Web:* www.wte.com	Bedford	MA	01730	781-275-6400	275-8612

661 RECYCLED PLASTICS PRODUCTS

See Also Flooring - Resilient p. 2288

	City	State	Zip	Phone	Fax
Allen Ventures Inc 517 State Farm Rd *TF:* 877-423-9800 ■ *Web:* www.allenventures.com	Deerfield	WI	53531	608-423-9800	
Amazing Recycled Products Inc PO Box 312 *TF:* 800-241-2174 ■ *Web:* www.amazingrecycled.com	Denver	CO	80201	303-699-7693	699-2102
American Recycled Plastic Inc 773 N. Union Grove Rd *TF:* 866-417-5821 ■ *Web:* www.itsrecycled.com	Friendsville	TN	37737	865-738-3439	738-3731
Bedford Technology LLC 2424 Armour Rd PO Box 609 *TF:* 800-721-9037 ■ *Web:* plasticboards.com	Worthington	MN	56187	507-372-5558	372-5726
Everlast Plastic Lumber 800 Market St *Web:* plasticlumber.org	Auburn	PA	17922	570-754-7440	
GP Harmon Recycling LLC 2 Jericho Plz Ste 110 *Web:* www.eharmongp.com	Jericho	NY	11753	516-997-3400	997-3409
J-MacLumber Inc 4154 Faust St *Web:* www.maclumber.com	Bamberg	SC	29003	803-245-1700	245-1701
Koller Craft Plastic Products 1400 S Old Hwy PO Box 718 *Web:* www.koller-craft.com	Fenton	MO	63026	636-343-9220	343-1034
Parkland Plastics Inc 104 Yoder Dr PO Box 339 *TF:* 800-835-4110 ■ *Web:* www.parklandplastics.com	Middlebury	IN	46540	574-825-4336	
Plastic Lumberyard LLC 220 E Washington St *Web:* www.plasticlumberyard.com	Norristown	PA	19401	610-277-3900	277-3970
Plastic Recycling of Iowa Falls Inc 10252 Hwy 65 *TF:* 800-338-1438 ■ *Web:* www.plasticrecycling.us	Iowa Falls	IA	50126	641-648-5073	648-5074
Polymer Concentrates Inc 179 Woodlawn St *Web:* www.polymerconcentrates.com	Clinton	MA	01510	978-365-7335	368-0438
Renew Plastics PO Box 480 PO Box 480 *TF:* 800-666-5207 ■ *Web:* www.renewplastics.com	Luxemburg	WI	54217	920-845-2326	845-2335
Resco Plastics Inc 93783 Newport Ln *TF:* 800-266-5097 ■ *Web:* www.rescoplastics.com	Coos Bay	OR	97420	541-269-5485	
Witt Industries Inc 4600 Mason-Montgomery Rd **Fax Area Code:* 877 ■ *TF:* 800-543-7417 ■ *Web:* www.witt.com	Mason	OH	45040	800-543-7417	891-8200*

662 REFRACTORIES - CLAY

	City	State	Zip	Phone	Fax
BNZ Materials Inc 6901 S Pierce St Ste 260 *TF:* 800-999-0890 ■ *Web:* www.bnzmaterials.com	Littleton	CO	80128	303-978-1199	978-0308
HarbisonWalker International *ANH Refractories Co* 600 Grant St Ste 50 *Web:* thinkhwi.com	Pittsburgh	PA	15219	412-375-6800	562-6209
Magneco/Metrel Inc 223 W I- Rd *Web:* www.magneco-metrel.com	Addison	IL	60101	630-543-6660	543-1479
Minerals Technologies Inc 405 Lexington Ave *Web:* mineralstech.com	New York	NY	10174	212-878-1800	
Permatech Inc 911 E Elm St *Web:* www.permatech.net	Graham	NC	27253	336-578-0701	578-7758
RENO Refractories Inc 601 Reno Dr *TF:* 800-741-7366 ■ *Web:* www.renorefractories.com	Morris	AL	35116	205-647-0240	
RENO Refractories Inc Reftech Div 601 Reno Dr *TF General:* 800-741-7366 ■ *Web:* renorefractories.com	Morris	AL	35116	800-741-7366	
Resco Products Inc 2 Penn Ctr W Ste 430 *TF:* 888-283-5505 ■ *Web:* www.rescoproducts.com	Pittsburgh	PA	15276	412-494-4491	494-4571
Riverside Refractories Inc 201 Truss Ferry Rd *TF:* 800-924-0637 ■ *Web:* www.riversiderefractories.com	Pell City	AL	35128	205-338-3366	338-7456
Shenango Advanced Ceramics LLC 606 McCleary Ave *Web:* rescoproducts.com	New Castle	PA	16101	724-652-6668	
Utah Refractories Corp 2200 North 1200 West *Web:* utah-refractories-corp.com	Lehi	UT	84043	801-768-3591	768-2684
Whitacre Greer Fireproofing Inc 1400 S Mahoning Ave *TF Cust Svc:* 800-947-2837 ■ *Web:* www.wgpaver.com	Alliance	OH	44601	330-823-1610	823-5502

663 REFRACTORIES - NONCLAY

	City	State	Zip	Phone	Fax
Allied Mineral Products Inc 2700 Scioto Pkwy *Web:* www.alliedmineral.com	Columbus	OH	43221	614-876-0244	876-0981
C-E Minerals Inc 901 E Eigth Ave *Web:* www.ceminerals.com	King of Prussia	PA	19406	610-265-6880	337-8122
Fedmet Resources Corp PO Box 278 *TF:* 800-609-5711 ■ *Web:* www.fedmet.com	Montreal	QC	H3Z2T2	514-931-5711	931-8378
Magnesita Refractories Co 425 S Salem Church Rd **Fax:* Sales ■ *Web:* www.magnesita.com/?lang=en	York	PA	17403	717-792-3611	848-2294*
McDanel Advanced Ceramic Technologies LLC 510 Ninth Ave *Web:* www.ceramics.com/vesuvius	Beaver Falls	PA	15010	724-843-8300	359-1201
Minco Inc 510 Midway Cir *Web:* www.mincoitc.com	Midway	TN	37809	423-422-6051	422-4802
Minerals Technologies Inc 405 Lexington Ave *Web:* mineralstech.com	New York	NY	10174	212-878-1800	
New Castle Refractories Co Inc 915 Industrial St *TF:* 888-396-3566 ■ *Web:* www.refractoriesinstitute.org	New Castle	PA	16102	724-654-7711	654-6322
Permatech Inc 911 E Elm St *Web:* www.permatech.net	Graham	NC	27253	336-578-0701	578-7758
Plibrico Co 1010 N Hooker St *Web:* plibrico.com	Chicago	IL	60622	312-337-9000	337-9003
Ransom & Randolph Co 3535 Briarfield Blvd *TF:* 800-800-7496 ■ *Web:* www.ransom-randolph.com	Maumee	OH	43537	419-865-9497	865-9997
RENO Refractories Inc 601 Reno Dr *TF:* 800-741-7366 ■ *Web:* www.renorefractories.com	Morris	AL	35116	205-647-0240	
RENO Refractories Inc Reftech Div 601 Reno Dr *TF General:* 800-741-7366 ■ *Web:* renorefractories.com	Morris	AL	35116	800-741-7366	
TYK America Inc 301 BrickyaRd Rd *TF:* 800-569-9359 ■ *Web:* www.tykamerica.com	Clairton	PA	15025	412-384-4259	384-4242
Wahl Refractory Solutions LLC 767 OH-19 *TF:* 800-837-9245 ■ *Web:* www.wahlref.com	Fremont	OH	43420	419-334-2658	334-9445
Worldwide Refractories Inc 6th St	Tarentum	PA	15084	724-224-8800	224-3353

664 REFRIGERATION EQUIPMENT - MFR

See Also Air Conditioning & Heating Equipment - Commercial/Industrial p. 1720

	City	State	Zip	Phone	Fax
Adelt Mechanical Ltd 2640 Argentia Rd *Web:* www.adeltmechanical.com	Mississauga	ON	L5N6C5	905-812-7900	
Advance Energy Technologies Inc 1 Solar Dr *TF:* 800-724-0198 ■ *Web:* www.advanceet.com	Clifton Park	NY	12065	518-371-2140	371-0737
American Panel Corp 5800 SE 78th St *TF:* 800-327-3015 ■ *Web:* www.americanpanel.com	Ocala	FL	34472	352-245-7055	245-0726
Applied Process Cooling Corp 555 Price Ave **Fax Area Code:* 707 ■ *TF:* 877-231-6406 ■ *Web:* www.apcco.net	Redwood City	CA	94063	650-595-0665	433-1310*
Arctic Star Refrigeration Mfg Company Inc 3540 W Pioneer Pkwy *TF:* 800-229-6562 ■ *Web:* www.arcticstar.com	Arlington	TX	76013	817-274-1396	277-4828
Berg Co 2160 Industrial Dr *Web:* www.bergliquorcontrols.com	Monona	WI	53713	608-221-4281	221-1416
Bessam-Aire Inc 10145 Philipp Pkwy Unit B *TF:* 800-321-5992 ■ *Web:* www.bessamaire.com	Streetsboro	OH	44146	800-321-5992	
Beverage-Air Corp 3779 Champion Blvd *TF:* 800-845-9800 ■ *Web:* www.beverage-air.com	Winston-Salem	NC	27105	336-245-6400	245-6453
Burch Industries Inc 21381 Charles Craft Ln PO Box 1049 *Web:* www.burchindustries.com	Laurinburg	NC	28352	910-844-3688	844-3689

Phone | Fax

CIMCO Refrigeration 65 Villiers St ... Toronto ON M5A3S1 416-465-7581
TF: 800-267-1418 ■ *Web:* www.cimcorefrigeration.com

Coldmatic Products International LLC
8500 Keele St ... Concord ON L4K2A6 905-326-7600
Web: www.coldmatic.com

Compu-Aire Inc 8167 Byron Rd ... Whittier CA 90606 562-945-8971
Web: www.compu-aire.com

Contract Manufacturers Inc 729 N Fleishel Ave ... Tyler TX 75702 903-597-8297
Web: www.contractmanufacturersltd.com

CrownTonka Inc 15600 37th Ave N Ste 100 ... Plymouth MN 55446 763-541-1410 541-1563
TF: 800-523-7337 ■ *Web:* www.crowntonka.com

Custom Coolers LLC 5609 Azle Ave ... Fort Worth TX 76114 817-626-3737 626-1213
TF: 800-627-0488

Delfield Co 980 S Isabella Rd ... Mount Pleasant MI 48858 989-773-7981 773-3210
TF: 800-733-8821 ■ *Web:* www.delfield.com

Dole Refrigerating Co 1420 Higgs Rd ... Lewisburg TN 37091 931-359-6211 359-8664
TF: 800-251-8990 ■ *Web:* www.doleref.com

Eliason Corp 9229 Shaver Rd ... Portage MI 49024 269-327-7003 327-7006
TF Cust Svc: 800-828-3655 ■ *Web:* www.eliasoncorp.com

Federal Industries Div Standex Corp
215 Federal Ave ... Belleville WI 53508 800-356-4206 424-3234*
*Fax Area Code: 608 ■ *TF:* 800-356-4206 ■ *Web:* www.federalind.com

Follett Corp 801 Church Ln ... Easton PA 18040 610-252-7301 250-0169
TF Cust Svc: 800-523-9361 ■ *Web:* www.follettice.com

FRL Furniture 460 Grand Blvd ... Westbury NY 11590 516-333-4400 333-4759
TF: 800-529-4375 ■ *Web:* www.frlalternatives.com

Harris Environmental Systems Inc
11 Connector Rd ... Andover MA 01810 978-470-8600 475-7903
Web: www.harrisenv.com

Haws Corp 1455 Kleppe Ln ... Sparks NV 89431 775-359-4712 359-7424
TF: 888-640-4297 ■ *Web:* www.hawsco.com

Heatcraft Refrigeration Products
2175 W Pk Pl Blvd ... Stone Mountain GA 30087 770-465-5600 465-5990
TF: 800-321-1881 ■ *Web:* www.heatcraftrpd.com

Hill PHOENIX Inc 1003 Sigman Rd ... Conyers GA 30013 770-285-3264 285-3080
TF: 800-518-6630 ■ *Web:* www.hillphoenix.com

Honeywell Building Solutions Inc
1985 Douglas Dr N ... Golden Valley MN 55422 763-954-5421
Web: buildingsolutions.honeywell.com

Howe Corp 1650 N Elston Ave ... Chicago IL 60642 773-235-0200 235-1530
Web: www.howecorp.com

Hussmann Corp 12999 St Charles Rock Rd ... Bridgeton MO 63044 314-291-2000 298-4756
TF: 800-592-2060 ■ *Web:* www.hussmann.com

Ice Air LLC 80 Hartford Ave ... Mount Vernon NY 10553 914-668-4700
Web: www.ice-air.com

Ice-O-Matic 11100 E 45th Ave ... Denver CO 80239 303-371-3737 371-6296
TF: 800-423-3367 ■ *Web:* www.iceomatic.com

IMI Cornelius Inc 101 Broadway St W ... Osseo MN 55369 763-488-8200 488-4298
TF: 800-238-3600 ■ *Web:* www.cornelius.com

IntelliChoice Energy LLC 2355 W Utopia Rd ... Phoenix AZ 85027 623-879-4664
Web: www.iceghp.com

International Cold Storage Company Inc
215 E 13th St ... Andover KS 67002 316-733-1385 733-2434
TF: 800-835-0001 ■ *Web:* www.icsco.com

KDIndustries 1525 E Lake Rd ... Erie PA 16511 814-453-6761 455-6336
TF: 800-840-9577 ■ *Web:* www.kold-draft.com

Kloppenberg & Co 2627 W Oxford Ave ... Englewood CO 80110 303-761-1615 789-1741
TF: 800-346-3246 ■ *Web:* www.kloppenberg.com

Kolpak 2915 Tennessee Ave N ... Parsons TN 38363 731-847-5328 847-5387
TF: 800-826-7036 ■ *Web:* www.kolpak.com

Kysor Panel Systems 4201 N Beach St ... Fort Worth TX 76137 817-281-5121 281-5521
TF: 800-633-3426 ■ *Web:* www.kysorpanel.com

Lancer Corp 6655 Lancer Blvd ... San Antonio TX 78219 210-310-7000 310-7250
TF: 800-729-1500 ■ *Web:* www.lancercorp.com

Leer LP 206 Leer St ... New Lisbon WI 53950 608-562-7100 562-6022
TF Cust Svc: 800-766-5337 ■ *Web:* www.leerinc.com

Lytron Inc 55 Dragon Ct ... Woburn MA 01801 781-933-7300
Web: www.lytron.com

Manitowoc Ice 2110 S 26th St ... Manitowoc WI 54220 920-682-0161 683-7589*
*Fax: Sales ■ *TF:* 800-545-5720 ■ *Web:* www.manitowocice.com

McCann's Engineering & Manufacturing Co
4570 W Colorado Blvd ... Los Angeles CA 90039 818-637-7200 637-7222
TF: 800-423-2429 ■ *Web:* www.manitowocbeverage.com

Micro Matic USA Inc 10726 N Second St ... Machesney Park IL 61115 815-968-7557 968-0363*
*Fax: Sales ■ *TF:* 866-291-5756 ■ *Web:* www.micromatic.com

MicroMetl Corp
3035 N Shadeland Ave Ste 300 ... Indianapolis IN 46226 800-662-4822 524-5499*
*Fax Area Code: 317 ■ *TF:* 800-662-4822 ■ *Web:* www.micrometl.com

Morris & Assoc Inc 803 Morris Dr ... Garner NC 27529 919-582-9200 582-9100
Web: www.morris-associates.com

Nance International Inc 2915 Milam St ... Beaumont TX 77701 409-838-6127
TF: 877-626-2322 ■ *Web:* nanceinternational.com

Nor-Lake Inc 727 Second St PO Box 248 ... Hudson WI 54016 715-386-2323 386-6149
TF: 800-388-5253 ■ *Web:* www.norlake.com

Ontor Ltd 12 Leswyn Rd ... Toronto ON M6A1K3 416-781-5286
TF: 800-567-1631 ■ *Web:* www.ontor.com

Perlick Corp 8300 W Good Hope Rd ... Milwaukee WI 53223 414-353-7060 353-7069
TF: 800-558-5592 ■ *Web:* www.perlick.com

Refplus Inc 2777 Grande Allee ... Saint-Hubert QC J4T2R4 450-641-2665
Web: www.refplus.com

Scotsman Ice Systems
775 Corporate Woods Pkwy ... Vernon Hills IL 60061 847-215-4500 913-9844
TF Cust Svc: 800-726-8762 ■ *Web:* www.scotsman-ice.com

Semco Manufacturing Co 705 E Business 83 ... Pharr TX 78577 956-683-1411
Web: semcoice.com

Silver King Refrigeration Inc
1600 Xenium Ln N ... Minneapolis MN 55441 763-923-2441 553-1209
TF: 800-328-3329 ■ *Web:* www.silverking.com

Specific Systems Ltd 7655 E 41st St ... Tulsa OK 74145 918-663-9321
Web: specificsystems.com

Tigerflow Systems Inc 4034 Mint Way ... Dallas TX 75237 214-337-8780
Web: www.tigerflow.com

True Manufacturing Co 2001 E Terra Ln ... O'Fallon MO 63366 636-240-2400 272-2408
TF: 800-325-6152 ■ *Web:* www.truemfg.com

Turbo Refrigerating 1000 W Ormsby Ave ... Louisville KY 40210 502-635-3000 634-0479
TF: 800-853-8648 ■ *Web:* www.vogtice.com

Victory Refrigeration Inc
110 Woodcrest Rd ... Cherry Hill NJ 08003 856-428-4200 428-7299
TF: 800-523-5008 ■ *Web:* www.victoryrefrigeration.com

Vintage Air Inc 18865 Goll St ... San Antonio TX 78266 210-654-7171
TF: 800-862-6658 ■ *Web:* www.vintageair.com

Vogt Ice 1000 W Ormsby Ave Ste 19 ... Louisville KY 40210 502-635-3000 634-0479
TF: 800-853-8648 ■ *Web:* www.vogtice.com

WA Brown & Son Inc 209 Long Meadow Dr ... Salisbury NC 28147 704-636-5131
TF: 800-438-2316 ■ *Web:* www.wabrown.com

Weather-Rite LLC 616 N Fifth St ... Minneapolis MN 55401 612-338-1401
Web: www.weather-rite.com

Winvale Group LLC, The
1012 14th St NW 5th Fl ... Washington DC 20005 202-296-5505
Web: www.winvale.com

Xetex Inc 9405 Holly St NW ... Minneapolis MN 55433 612-724-3101
Web: www.xetexinc.com

665 REFRIGERATION EQUIPMENT - WHOL

See Also Plumbing, Heating, Air Conditioning Equipment & Supplies - Whol p. 2959

Phone | Fax

Abco Refrigeration Supply Corp
49-70 31st St ... Long Island NY 11101 718-937-9000 392-1296

Allied Supply Company Inc 1100 E Monument Ave ... Dayton OH 45402 937-224-9833 224-5648
TF: 800-589-5690 ■ *Web:* www.alliedsupply.com

Alpha Distributors Inc
4700 N Ronald St ... Harwood Heights IL 60706 708-867-5200
Web: www.alphadist.com

American Refrigeration Supplies
2632 E Chambers St ... Phoenix AZ 85040 602-243-2792 243-2893
Web: www.ars-net.com

Automatic Ice & Beverage Inc
1400 Tuscaloosa Ave SW ... Birmingham AL 35211 205-787-9640
Web: aibnow.com

Baker Distributing Co
14610 Breakers Dr Ste 100 ... Jacksonville FL 32258 800-217-4698
TF: 844-289-0033 ■ *Web:* www.bakerdist.com

Broich Enterprises Inc 6440 City W Pkwy ... Eden Prairie MN 55344 952-941-2270 941-3066
TF: 800-853-3508 ■ *Web:* www.arcticairco.com

Cannon Marketing Inc 4684 US Hwy 70 W ... Kinston NC 28504 252-527-3361
TF: 800-952-5913 ■ *Web:* www.1cmi.com

Cardinal Ice Equipment Inc
3311 Gilmore Industrial B ... Louisville KY 40213 502-966-4579
Web: iceguys.com

Dennis Supply Co PO Box 3376 ... Sioux City IA 51102 712-255-7637 255-4913
TF: 800-352-4618 ■ *Web:* www.dennissupply.com

Don Stevens Inc 980 Discovery Rd ... Eagan MN 55121 651-452-0872 452-4189
TF: 800-444-2299 ■ *Web:* www.donstevens.com

Downriver Refrigeration Supply Co
38170 N Executive Dr N ... Westland MI 48185 734-728-0795
Web: www.downriversupply.com

Ernest F Mariani Company Inc
573 West 2890 South ... Salt Lake City UT 84115 800-453-2927 531-9615*
*Fax Area Code: 801 ■ *TF:* 800-453-2927 ■ *Web:* efmco.com

Gustave A Larson Co PO Box 910 ... Pewaukee WI 53072 262-542-0200 542-1400
TF: 800-829-9609 ■ *Web:* www.galarson.com

Hart & Price Corp PO Box 36368 ... Dallas TX 75235 214-521-9129 350-4143
TF: 800-777-9129 ■ *Web:* www.hartprice.com

Insco Distributing Inc
12501 Network Blvd ... San Antonio TX 78249 210-690-8400 690-1524
TF: 855-282-4295 ■ *Web:* www.inscohvac.com

ISI Commercial Refrigeration LP 640 W 6th St ... Houston TX 77007 214-631-7980 631-6813
TF: 800-777-5070 ■ *Web:* www.isi-texas.com

Luce, Schwab & Kase Inc 9 Gloria Ln ... Fairfield NJ 07007 973-227-4840
TF: 800-458-7329 ■ *Web:* www.lskair.com

Minus Forty Technologies Corp
30 Armstrong Ave ... Georgetown ON L7G4R9 905-702-1441
TF: 800-800-5706 ■ *Web:* www.minusforty.com

Modern Ice Equipment & Supply Co
5709 Harrison Ave ... Cincinnati OH 45248 513-367-2101 367-5762
TF: 800-543-1581 ■ *Web:* www.modernice.com

Norm's Refrigeration & Ice Equipment Inc
1175 N Knollwood Cir ... Anaheim CA 92801 714-236-3600
TF: 800-933-4423 ■ *Web:* www.normsrefrigeration.com

Preston Refrigeration Company Inc
3200 Fiberglass Rd ... Kansas City KS 66115 913-621-1813 621-6962
Web: www.prestonrefrigeration.com

RE Lewis Refrigeration Inc
803 S Lincoln St PO Box 92 ... Creston IA 50801 641-782-8183 782-8156
TF Cust Svc: 800-264-0767 ■ *Web:* www.relewisinc.com

Redico Inc 1850 S Lee Ct ... Buford GA 30518 800-242-3920 614-1403*
*Fax Area Code: 770 ■ *TF:* 800-242-3920 ■ *Web:* www.redicoinc.com

Refricenter of Miami Inc 7101 NW 43rd St ... Miami FL 33166 305-477-8880 599-9323
Web: www.refricenter.net

Rogers Supply Company Inc PO Box 740 ... Champaign IL 61824 217-356-0166 356-1768
TF: 800-252-0406 ■ *Web:* www.rogerssupply.com

Schroeder America 5620 Business Park ... San Antonio TX 78218 210-662-8200
TF: 877-404-2488 ■ *Web:* schroederamerica.com

Sid Harvey Industries Inc 605 Locust St ... Garden City NY 11530 516-745-9200 222-9027
Web: www.sidharvey.com

Southern Refrigeration Corp
3140 Shenandoah Ave ... Roanoke VA 24017 540-342-3493 343-2163
TF: 800-763-4433 ■ *Web:* srcusa.com

Stafford-Smith Inc 3414 S Burdick St ... Kalamazoo MI 49001 269-343-1240 343-2509
TF: 800-968-2442 ■ *Web:* www.staffordsmith.com

Supermarket Systems Inc 6419 Bannington Rd ... Charlotte NC 28226 704-542-6000
TF: 800-553-1905 ■ *Web:* www.supermarketsystems.com

Phone *Fax*

SWH Supply Co 242 E Main St....................Louisville KY 40202 502-589-9287 585-3812
TF: 800-321-3598 ■ *Web:* www.swhsupply.com

Taylor Freezer Sales Company Inc
2032 Atlantic Ave....................Chesapeake VA 23324 800-768-6945 545-7908*
*Fax Area Code: 757 ■ *TF:* 800-768-6945 ■ *Web:* www.taylorfreezer.com

Thermo King of Houston LP 772 McCarty St..........Houston TX 77029 713-671-2700
Web: www.tkofhouston.net

Transport Refrigeration Inc 301 Lawrence Dr..........De Pere WI 54115 920-339-5700 339-5717
Web: thermokinggreenbay.com

United Refrigeration Inc
11401 Roosevelt Blvd....................Philadelphia PA 19154 215-698-9100 698-9493*
*Fax: Financial ■ *TF General:* 888-578-9100 ■ *Web:* www.uri.com

Vittitow Refrigeration 4103 Bishop Ln..........Louisville KY 40218 502-966-4444
Web: www.vittitow.com

Western Pacific Distributors Inc
1739 Sabre St....................Hayward CA 94545 510-732-0100 732-0155
Web: www.teamwpd.com

666 RELOCATION CONSULTING SERVICES

Phone *Fax*

Cartus Corp 40 Apple Ridge Rd....................Danbury CT 06810 203-205-3400 205-6575
Web: www.cartus.com

Coldwell Banker Gundaker
2458 Old Dorsett Rd Ste 300..........Maryland Heights MO 63043 314-298-5000
TF: 800-325-1978 ■ *Web:* www.coldwellbankerhomes.com/st-louis

Crye-Leike Inc 6525 N Quail Hollow Rd..........Memphis TN 38120 866-310-3102 758-5641*
*Fax Area Code: 901 ■ *TF:* 866-310-3102 ■ *Web:* www.crye-leike.com

RE/MAX LLC 5075 S Syracuse St....................Denver CO 80237 800-525-7452 796-3599*
*Fax Area Code: 303 ■ *TF:* 800-525-7452 ■ *Web:* www.remax.com

RELO Direct Inc 161 N Clark St Ste 1250..........Chicago IL 60601 312-384-5900
TF: 800-621-7356 ■ *Web:* www.relodirect.com

Relocation America 25800 NW Hwy Ste 210..........Southfield MI 48075 877-500-4466 263-0093*
*Fax Area Code: 248 ■ *TF:* 877-500-4466 ■ *Web:* relocationamericainternational.com

Runzheimer International Runzheimer Pk..........Rochester WI 53167 262-971-2200 971-2254
TF: 800-558-1702 ■ *Web:* www.runzheimer.com

SIRVA Inc 700 Oakmont Ln....................Terrace IL 60181 630-570-8900
TF: 888-444-4765 ■ *Web:* www.sirva.com

Windermere Relocation Inc
5424 Sand Point Way NE....................Seattle WA 98105 206-527-3801
TF: 866-740-9589 ■ *Web:* www.windermere.com

667 REMEDIATION SERVICES

See Also Environmental Organizations p. 1763; Consulting Services - Environmental p. 2097; Waste Management p. 3304

Remediation services include clean-up, restorative, and corrective work to repair or minimize environmental damage caused by lead, asbestos, mining, petroleum, chemicals, and other pollutants.

Phone *Fax*

911 Restoration Enterprises Inc
7721 Densmore Ave....................Van Nuys CA 91406 888-243-6653
TF: 888-243-6653 ■ *Web:* www.911restoration.com

AAA Environmental Inc 6679 Moore Rd..........Syracuse NY 13211 315-454-2000
Web: www.aaaenvironmentalinc.com

AAC Contracting Inc 175 Humboldt St..........Rochester NY 14610 585-527-8000
Web: www.aac-contracting.com

Abmech Inc 976 Forest Ave..........West Homestead PA 15120 412-462-7440
Web: www.abmechinc.com

Abscope Environmental Inc
7086 Commercial Dr....................Canastota NY 13032 315-697-8437
Web: www.abscope.com

Allstate Power Vac Inc 928 E Hazelwood Ave..........Rahway NJ 07065 732-815-0220 815-9892

Antea Group 5910 Rice Creek Pkwy Ste 100..........Saint Paul MN 55126 651-639-9449 639-9473
TF: 800-477-7411 ■ *Web:* www.anteagroup.com

BELFOR (Canada) Inc 3300 Bridgeway St..........Vancouver BC V5K1H9 604-432-1123
TF: 888-432-1123 ■ *Web:* www.belfor.com

Bristol Environmental Inc 1123 Beaver St..........Bristol PA 19007 215-788-6040
Web: www.beigroup.com

Brook Environmental & Engineering Corp
11419 Cronridge Dr Ste 10....................Owings Mills MD 21117 410-356-5073
Web: carrollcountytimes.com

Carylon Corp 2500 W Arthington St..........Chicago IL 60612 312-666-7700 666-5810
TF: 800-621-4342 ■ *Web:* www.carylon corp.com

Central Insulation Systems Inc
300 Murray Rd....................Cincinnati OH 45217 513-242-0600
TF: 800-544-7502 ■ *Web:* www.centralinsulation.com

Chemical Waste Management Inc
1001 Fannin St Ste 4000....................Houston TX 77002 713-512-6200
TF: 800-633-7871 ■ *Web:* www.wm.com

Clean Harbors Inc 42 Longwater Dr PO Box 9149..........Norwell MA 02061 781-792-5000
NYSE: CLH ■ *TF:* 800-282-0058 ■ *Web:* www.cleanharbors.com

Clean Street Inc 1937 W 169th St..........Gardena CA 90247 310-538-5888
Web: www.cleanstreet.com

Clean Venture/Cycle Chem Inc
201 S First St....................Elizabeth NJ 07206 908-355-5800 355-0562
TF: 800-347-7672 ■ *Web:* www.cyclechem.com

Contaminant Recovery Systems (CONREC)
9 Rocky Hill Rd....................Smithfield RI 02917 401-231-3770
Web: www.conrec.net

Crosby & Overton Inc 1610 W 17th St..........Long Beach CA 90813 562-432-5445 436-7540
TF: 800-827-6729 ■ *Web:* www.crosbyoverton.com

Custom Environmental Services Inc
8041 N I 70 Frontage Rd Unit 11....................Arvada CO 80002 303-423-9949
TF: 800-310-7445 ■ *Web:* www.customsvcs.com

Cyn Oil Corp 1771 Washington St..........Stoughton MA 02072 781-341-1777
Web: www.cynenv.com

Dec-Tam Corp 50 Concord St..........North Reading MA 01864 978-470-2860
Web: www.dectam.com

Denovo Constructors Inc 1302 W Randolph St..........Chicago IL 60607 312-733-9370
Web: www.denovogrp.com

Phone *Fax*

Ecology Control Industries Inc
255 Parr Blvd....................Richmond CA 94801 510-235-1393 235-3709
Web: www.ecologycontrol.com

EMR Inc 2110 Delaware St Ste B..........Lawrence KS 66046 785-842-9013
Web: www.emr-inc.com

Environmental Enterprises Inc (EEI)
10163 Cincinnati Dayton Rd....................Cincinnati OH 45241 513-772-2818
TF: 800-722-2818 ■ *Web:* www.eeienv.com

Envirovantage Inc 629 Calef Hwy Ste 200..........Epping NH 03042 603-679-9682
TF: 800-640-5323 ■ *Web:* www.envirovantage.com

Garner Environmental Services Inc
1717 W 13th St....................Deer Park TX 77536 281-930-1200
Web: www.garner-es.com

Greenleaf Environmental Group Inc
4943 Austin Park Ave....................Buford GA 30518 678-714-8420
Web: www.greenleafgroup.net

H & s Environmental Inc
160 E Main St Ste 2F....................Westborough MA 01581 508-366-7442
Web: www.hsenv.com

H Barber & Sons Inc 15 Raytkwich Rd..........Naugatuck CT 06770 203-729-9000
TF: 800-355-8318 ■ *Web:* hbarber.com

IEP Technologies LLC 400 Main St..........Ashland MA 01721 855-793-8407
TF: 855-793-8407 ■ *Web:* www.ieptechnologies.com

MCM Management Corp
35980 Woodward Ave Ste 210..........Bloomfield Hills MI 48304 248-932-9600 932-9638
Web: www.mcmmanagement.com

Metson Marine Inc 2060 Knoll Dr Ste 100..........Ventura CA 93003 805-658-2628
Web: www.metsonmarine.com

NACHER Corp, The 111 E Angus Dr..........Youngsville LA 70592 337-856-9144
Web: nacher.net

Paragon Environmental Construction Inc
5664 Mud Mill Rd....................Brewerton NY 13029 315-699-0840
Web: paragonec.net

Parc Specialty Contractors 1400 Vinci Ave..........Sacramento CA 95838 916-992-5405
Web: www.parcspecialty.com

Perma-Fix Environmental Services Inc
8302 Dunwoody Pl Ste 250....................Atlanta GA 30350 770-587-9898 587-9937
NASDAQ: PESI ■ *TF:* 800-365-6066 ■ *Web:* www.perma-fix.com

Perma-Fix Northwest Inc 2025 Battelle Blvd..........Richland WA 99354 509-375-5160 375-0613

PW Stephens Inc
15201 Pipeline Ln Unit B..........Huntington Beach CA 92649 714-892-2028 891-9807
TF: 800-750-7733 ■ *Web:* www.pwsei.com

R W Collins Co 7225 W 66th St..........Chicago IL 60638 708-458-6868
Web: www.rwcollins.com

Remediation Services Inc
2735 S 10th St PO Box 587..........Independence KS 67301 620-331-1200
Web: www.rsi-ks.com

S Brewer Enterprises
2151 Jamieson Ave Ste 1607....................Alexandria VA 22314 703-567-1284

Safety & Ecology Corp
2800 Solway Rd SEC Business Center..........Knoxville TN 37931 865-690-0501
Web: www.sec-tn.com

Safety-Kleen Corp
2600 N Central Expwy Ste 400..........Richardson TX 75080 800-323-5040 265-2990*
*Fax Area Code: 972 ■ *TF:* 800-669-5740 ■ *Web:* www.safety-kleen.com

SEACOR Holdings Inc
2200 Eller Dr PO Box 13038..........Fort Lauderdale FL 33316 954-523-2200 524-9185
NYSE: CKH ■ *TF:* 800-516-6203 ■ *Web:* www.seacorholdings.com

Sevenson Environmental Services Inc
2749 Lockport Rd....................Niagara Falls NY 14305 716-284-0431 284-7645
Web: www.sevenson.com

Sigma Environmental Services Inc
1300 W Canal St....................Milwaukee WI 53233 414-643-4200 643-4210
Web: www.thesigmagroup.com

Terra Contracting Services LLC
5787 Stadium Dr....................Kalamazoo MI 49009 269-375-9595
Web: www.terracontracting.net

US Ecology 300 E Mallard Dr Ste 300..........Boise ID 83706 208-331-8400 331-7900
NASDAQ: ECOL ■ *TF:* 800-590-5220 ■ *Web:* www.usecology.com/home.aspx

USA Environment LP 10234 Lucore St..........Houston TX 77017 713-425-6905
Web: www.usaenviro.com

Waste Control Specialists LLC
5430 LBJ Fwy Ste 1700....................Dallas TX 75240 972-715-9800 448-1419
Web: www.wcstexas.com

Winter Environmental
3350 Green Pointe Pkwy Ste 200..........Norcross GA 30092 404-588-3300 946-6494*
*Fax: Hum Res ■ *Web:* winterenv.wpengine.com

WRR Environmental Services 5200 Ryder Rd..........Eau Claire WI 54701 715-834-9624
TF: 800-727-8760 ■ *Web:* www.wrres.com

WRS Infrastructure & Environment Inc
221 Hobbs St Ste 108....................Tampa FL 33619 813-684-4400
Web: www.wrsie.com

Young's Environmental Cleanup Inc
G-5305 N Dort Hwy....................Flint MI 48505 810-789-7155
Web: www.youngsenvironmental.com

668 RESEARCH CENTERS & INSTITUTIONS

See Also Market Research Firms p. 2727; Public Policy Research Centers p. 2992; Testing Facilities p. 3237

Phone *Fax*

3D Biomatrix Inc
1600 Huron Pkwy Bldg 520 2nd Fl..........Ann Arbor MI 48109 734-272-4688
Web: 3dbiomatrix.com

Aaron Diamond AIDS Research Ctr
455 First Ave 7th Fl....................New York NY 10016 212-448-5000 725-1126
TF: 800-782-2737 ■ *Web:* www.adarc.org

Academy of Natural Sciences of Drexel University, The
1900 Benjamin Franklin Pkwy..........Philadelphia PA 19103 215-299-1000 299-1079
Web: www.ansp.org

ADA Technologies Inc
8100 Shaffer Pkwy Ste 130....................Littleton CO 80127 303-792-5615
TF: 800-232-0296 ■ *Web:* www.adatech.com

Name / Address	City	State	ZIP	Phone	Fax
Adaption Technologies Ventures Ltd 1009 Pruitt Rd *Web:* adpt-tech.com	Spring	TX	77380	281-465-3320	
Adherent Technologies Inc 11208 Cochiti SE *Web:* www.adherent-tech.com	Albuquerque	NM	87123	505-346-1688	
Adial Pharmaceuticals 414 E Water St *Web:* www.adialpharma.com	Charlottesville	VA	22902	434-422-9800	
Adlyfe Inc 9430 Key W Ave	Rockville	MD	20850	703-868-3050	
Advanced Cell Diagnostics Inc 3960 Point Eden Way *TF:* 877-576-3636 ■ *Web:* www.acdbio.com	Hayward	CA	94545	510-576-8800	
Advanced Focus 44 E 32nd St 4th Fl *Web:* www.advancedfocus.com	New York	NY	10016	212-217-2000	
Advanced Technology for Large Structural Systems Ctr (ATLSS) 117 ATLSS Dr *Web:* www.atlss.lehigh.edu	Bethlehem	PA	18015	610-758-3525	758-5902
Advantagene Inc 440 Lexington St *Web:* www.advantagene.com	Auburndale	MA	02466	617-916-5445	
Advion BioSciences Inc 19 Brown Rd *TF:* 877-523-8466 ■ *Web:* www.advion.com	Ithaca	NY	14850	607-266-0665	266-0749
Aegera Therapeutics Inc 810 ch Du Golf *Web:* www.aegera.com	Montreal	QC	H3E1A8	514-288-5532	288-9280
Aerodyne Research Inc 45 Manning Rd *Web:* www.aerodyne.com	Billerica	MA	01821	978-663-9500	663-4918
Aeronautical Systems Ctr (ASC) 5215 Thurlow St Bldg 70, Ste 4B *Web:* www.wpafb.af.mil/asc	Wright Patterson	OH	45433	937-522-3252	656-7088
Aeronix Inc 1775 W Hibiscus Blvd Ste 200 *Web:* www.aeronix.com	Melbourne	FL	32901	321-984-1671	
Aerospace Corp, The 2310 E El Segundo Blvd PO Box 92957 *Web:* www.aerospace.org	Los Angeles	CA	90009	310-336-5000	336-7055
Affinium Pharmaceuticals Ltd 200 Front St W Ste 3004 *Web:* pint.com	Toronto	ON	M5V3K2	416-645-6613	
Air Force Office of Scientific Research (AFOSR) 875 N Randolph St Ste 325 Rm 3112 *Web:* www.wpafb.af.mil	Arlington	VA	22203	703-696-7551	696-9556
Air Force Research Laboratory (AFRL) AFRL/PA 1864 Fourth St Bldg 15 Rm 225 **Fax Area Code:* 937 ■ *TF:* 800-222-0336 ■ *Web:* www.afsbirsttr.com	Wright-Patterson AFB	OH	45433	800-222-0336	255-2219*
Air Resources Laboratory 5830 University Research Ct Rm. 4204 *Web:* www.arl.noaa.gov	Silver Spring	MD	20740	301-713-0684	713-0119
Akebia Therapeutics Inc 245 St 1 Ste 1100 *Web:* www.akebia.com	Cambridge	MA	02142	617-871-2098	871-2099
Alaska Fisheries Science Ctr (AFSC) National Marine Fisheries Service 7600 Sand Pt Way NE Bldg 4 *Web:* www.afsc.noaa.gov	Seattle	WA	98115	206-526-4000	526-4004
Albany International Research Co 216 Airport Dr *TF:* 888-797-6735 ■ *Web:* www.albint.com	Rochester	NH	03867	603-330-5850	
Allied Business Intelligence Inc 249 S St *Web:* www.abiresearch.com	Oyster Bay	NY	11771	516-624-2500	
ALLPoints Research Inc 200 W First St Ste 100	Winston-Salem	NC	27101	336-896-2200	
American Institute for Cancer Research 1759 R St NW *TF:* 800-843-8114 ■ *Web:* www.aicr.org	Washington	DC	20009	202-328-7744	328-7226
American Institutes for Research 1000 Thomas Jefferson St NW *TF:* 877-334-3499 ■ *Web:* www.air.org	Washington	DC	20007	202-403-5000	403-5454
American Type Culture Collection (ATCC) 10801 University Blvd PO Box 1549 *TF Cust Svc:* 800-638-6597 ■ *Web:* www.atcc.org	Manassas	VA	20108	703-365-2700	365-2701
Ames Laboratory 111 TASF Iowa State University *Web:* www.ameslab.gov	Ames	IA	50011	515-294-9557	294-3226
Amunix Operating Inc 500 Ellis St *Web:* www.amunix.com	Mountain View	CA	94043	650-428-1800	
Anasys Instruments Corp 121 Gray Ave Ste 100 *Web:* www.anasysinstruments.com	Santa Barbara	CA	93101	805-730-3310	
Annapolis Micro Systems Inc 190 Admiral Cochrane Dr *Web:* www.annapmicro.com	Annapolis	MD	21401	410-841-2514	841-2518
Applied Physics Laboratory University of Washington 1013 NE 40th St PO Box 355640 *Web:* www.apl.washington.edu	Seattle	WA	98105	206-543-1300	543-6785
Applied Research Laboratory Pennsylvania State University N Atherton St PO Box 30 *Web:* www.arl.psu.edu	State College	PA	16804	814-865-6531	865-3105
Aptima Inc 12 Gill St Ste 1400 *Web:* www.aptima.com	Woburn	MA	01801	781-935-3966	935-4385
Aquarian Capital LLC 5345 Annabel Ln *Web:* www.aquariancapital.com	Plano	TX	75093	469-361-2177	
Arbor Research & Trading LLC 1000 Hart Rd Ste 260 *Web:* www.arborresearch.com	Barrington	IL	60010	847-304-1550	
Arca Biopharma Inc 11080 CirPoint Rd Ste 140 *NASDAQ: ABIO* ■ *Web:* www.arcabiopharma.com	Westminister	CO	80020	720-940-2100	208-9261
Arctic Research Consortium of the US (ARCUS) 3535 College Rd Ste 101 *Web:* www.arcus.org	Fairbanks	AK	99709	907-474-1600	474-1604
Argonne National Laboratory (ANL) 9700 S Cass Ave *TF:* 800-632-8990 ■ *Web:* www.anl.gov	Argonne	IL	60439	630-252-2000	
Atlantic Oceanographic & Meteorological Laboratory (AOML) 4301 Rickenbacker Cswy *Web:* www.aoml.noaa.gov	Miami	FL	33149	305-361-4300	361-4449
aTyr Pharma Inc 3545 General Atomics Ct Ste 250 *Web:* www.atyrpharma.com	San Diego	CA	92121	858-731-8389	
Autism Research Institute (ARI) 4182 Adams Ave *TF:* 866-366-3361 ■ *Web:* www.autism.com	San Diego	CA	92116	619-281-7165	563-6840
Avaxia Biologics Inc 128 Spring St Ste 620 *Web:* www.avaxiabiologics.com	Lexington	MA	02421	781-861-0062	
Avcom SMT Inc 213 E Broadway *Web:* www.avcomsmt.com	Westerville	OH	43081	614-882-8176	
Aveo Pharmaceuticals Inc 75 Sidney St *NASDAQ: AVEO* ■ *Web:* www.aveooncology.com	Cambridge	MA	02139	617-299-5000	995-4995
Axikin Pharmaceuticals Inc 6185 Cornerstone Ct Ste 106 *Web:* www.axikin.com	San Diego	CA	92121	858-458-1890	
Azaya Therapeutics Inc 12500 Network Blvd Ste 207 *Web:* www.azayatherapeutics.com	San Antonio	TX	78249	210-341-6600	
Baker Institute for Animal Health Cornell University College of Veterinary Medicine Hungerford Hill Rd	Ithaca	NY	14850	607-256-5600	256-5608
Barbara Ann Karmanos Cancer Institute 4100 John R St *TF:* 800-527-6266 ■ *Web:* www.karmanos.org	Detroit	MI	48201	800-527-6266	
Barrios Technology Inc 16441 Space Ctr Blvd Ste B-100 *Web:* www.barrios.com	Houston	TX	77058	281-280-1900	280-1901
Battelle Memorial Institute Inc 505 King Ave *TF:* 800-201-2011 ■ *Web:* www.battelle.org	Columbus	OH	43201	614-424-6424	424-5263
BC Systems Inc 200 Belle Mead Rd *Web:* www.bcpowersys.com	Setauket	NY	11733	631-751-9370	
Belle W Baruch Institute for Marine & Coastal Sciences University of S Carolina 609 EWS Bldg *Web:* artsandsciences.sc.edu	Columbia	SC	29208	803-777-5288	777-3935
Beltsville Human Nutrition Research Ctr USDA/ARS BARC-E Bldg 307-C Rm 117 10300 Baltimore Blvd *Web:* www.ars.usda.gov/main/site_main.htm?modecode=12-35-00-00	Beltsville	MD	20705	301-504-8157	504-9381
Bend Research Inc 64550 Research Rd *Web:* www.bendresearch.com	Bend	OR	97701	541-382-4100	382-2713
Berkeley Sensor & Actuator Ctr (BSAC) *University of California* 403 Cory Hall MC Ste 1774 *TF:* 800-549-1002 ■ *Web:* www-bsac.eecs.berkeley.edu	Berkeley	CA	94720	510-643-6690	643-6637
Beta Research Corp 6400 Jericho Tpke *Web:* www.betaresearch.com	Syosset	NY	11791	516-935-3800	
BioLegend Inc 11080 Roselle St *TF:* 877-246-5343 ■ *Web:* www.biolegend.com	San Diego	CA	92121	858-455-9588	
bioLytical Laboratories Inc 1108 - 13351 Commerce Pkwy *TF:* 866-674-6784 ■ *Web:* www.biolytical.com	Richmond	BC	V6V2X7	604-204-6784	
BioMarker Pharmaceuticals Inc 5941 Optical Ct *Web:* www.biomarkerinc.com	San Jose	CA	95138	408-257-2000	
Biomerix Corp 47757 Fremont Blvd *Web:* www.biomerix.com	Fremont	CA	94538	510-933-3450	
BioResource International Inc 4222 Emperor Blvd Ste 460 *Web:* www.briworldwide.com	Durham	NC	27703	919-993-3389	
BioVascular Inc 12230 El Camino Real Ste 100 *Web:* www.biovascularinc.com	San Diego	CA	92130	858-455-5000	
BN ImmunoTherapeutics Inc 595 Penobscot Dr *Web:* www.bavarian-nordic.com	Redwood city	CA	94063	650-681-4660	
Boyce Thompson Institute for Plant Research Inc Cornell University 533 Twr Rd *Web:* bti.cornell.edu	Ithaca	NY	14853	607-254-1234	254-1242
BPR Inc 4655 Wilfrid-Hamel Blvd *Web:* bpr.ca	Quebec	QC	G1P2J7	418-871-8151	871-9625
Brain Research Institute 695 Charles Young Dr S *Web:* www.bri.ucla.edu	Los Angeles	CA	90095	310-825-5061	206-5855
BrainCells Inc 3636 Nobel Dr Ste 215 *Web:* www.braincellsinc.com	San Diego	CA	92122	858-812-7700	
Brookhaven National Laboratory (BNL) PO Box 5000 *Web:* www.bnl.gov	Upton	NY	11973	631-344-8000	344-3000
Bureau of Economic Analysis (BEA) 1441 L St NW *Web:* www.bea.gov	Washington	DC	20005	202-606-9900	606-5311
C & C Market Research Inc 1115 S Waldron Rd Ste 207 *Web:* www.ccmarketresearch.com	Fort Smith	AR	72903	479-785-5637	
Caelum Research Corp 1700 Research Blvd Ste 250 *Web:* www.caelum.com	Rockville	MD	20850	301-424-8205	424-8183
California Pacific Medical Ctr Research Institute 475 Brannan St Ste 220 *TF:* 855-354-2778 ■ *Web:* www.cpmc.org/professionals/research	San Francisco	CA	94107	415-600-1600	600-1753
Cancer Research Ctr of Hawaii University of Hawaii 1236 Lauhala St *Web:* www.crch.org	Honolulu	HI	96813	808-586-3010	
CardioKinetix Inc 925 Hamilton Ave *Web:* www.cardiokinetix.com	Menlo Park	CA	94025	650-364-7016	
Carmell Therapeutics Corp 3636 Boulevard of the Allies *Web:* www.carmellrx.com	Pittsburgh	PA	15213	412-508-6519	
Carnegie Institution of Washington 1530 P St NW *Web:* www.carnegiescience.edu	Washington	DC	20005	202-387-6400	387-8092
Celator Pharmaceuticals Inc 303B College Rd E *Web:* celatorpharma.com	Princeton	NJ	08540	609-243-0123	

	City	State	Zip	Phone	Fax
Center for Advanced Biotechnology & Medicine *Rutgers The State University of New Jersey* 679 Hoes Ln *Web:* www3.cabm.rutgers.edu	Piscataway	NJ	08854	732-235-5310	235-5318
Center for Automation Research University of Maryland AV Williams Bldg 115 Rm 4413 *TF:* 800-868-0094 ■ *Web:* www.cfar.umd.edu	College Park	MD	20742	301-405-4526	314-9115
Center for Biofilm Engineering (CBE) Montana State University PO Box 173980 *Web:* www.biofilm.montana.edu	Bozeman	MT	59717	406-994-4770	994-6098
Center for Biophysical Sciences & Engineering (CBSE) University of Alabama CBSE 100 1720 2nd Ave S *Web:* www.uab.edu	Birmingham	AL	35294	205-934-5329	934-0480
Center for Crops Utilization Research Iowa State University 1041 Food Sciences Bldg *Web:* www.ccur.iastate.edu	Ames	IA	50011	515-294-0160	294-6261
Center for Education Rice University 320 IBC Bldg PO Box 1892 *Web:* www.centerforeducation.rice.edu	Houston	TX	77251	713-348-4827	348-4229
Center for Electromechanics University of Texas at Austin 10100 Burnet Rd Bldg 133 *Web:* www.utexas.edu/research/cem	Austin	TX	78758	512-471-4496	471-0781
Center for Engineering Logistics & Distribution University of Arkansas Dept of Industrial Engineering 4207 Bell Engineering Ctr *Web:* celdi.org	Fayetteville	AR	72701	479-575-2124	575-8431
Center for Global Change & Arctic System Research (CGC) *University of Alaska-Fairbanks* 505 N Chandalar Dr PO Box 757560 *Web:* www.cgc.uaf.edu	Fairbanks	AK	99775	907-474-5818	474-6722
Center for Global Change Science Massachusetts Institute of Technology 77 Massachusetts Ave *Web:* cgcs.mit.edu	Cambridge	MA	02139	617-253-4902	253-0354
Center for Grain & Animal Health Research 1515 College Ave **Fax Area Code:* 785 ■ *TF:* 800-627-0388 ■ *Web:* www.ars.usda.gov/main/site_main.htm?modecode=54300000	Manhattan	KS	66502	800-627-0388	776-2789*
Center for High Performance Software Research (HiPerSoft) Rice University 6100 Main St MS-41 *Web:* www.hipersoft.rice.edu	Houston	TX	77005	713-348-5186	348-3111
Center for Information Systems Research (CISR) Massachusetts Institute of Technology 5 Cambridge Ctr NE25 7th Fl *Web:* cisr.mit.edu	Cambridge	MA	02142	617-253-2348	253-4424
Center for Integrative Toxicology 1129 Farm Ln Rm 165 *Web:* iit.msu.edu	East Lansing	MI	48824	517-353-6469	355-4603
Center for International Trade in Forest Products (CINTRAFOR) University of Washington PO Box 352100 *Web:* www.cintrafor.org	Seattle	WA	98195	206-543-8684	685-0790
Center for Lesbian & Gay Studies (CLAGS) *University of New York* 365 Fifth Ave Rm 7115 *Web:* www.clags.org	New York	NY	10016	212-817-1955	817-1567
Center for Medical Agricultural & Veterinary Entomology (CMAVE) 1700 SW 23rd Dr *Web:* www.ars.usda.gov/saa/cmave	Gainesville	FL	32608	352-374-5901	374-5852
Center for Nanophysics & Advanced Materials University of Maryland *Web:* cnam.umd.edu	College Park	MD	20742	301-405-8285	405-3779
Center for Radiophysics & Space Research Cornell University 314 Space Sciences Bldg *Web:* www.astro.cornell.edu	Ithaca	NY	14853	607-255-1955	255-3433
Center for Research in Mathematics & Science Education San Diego State University 6475 Alvarado Rd Ste 206 *TF:* 800-573-8804 ■ *Web:* www.sci.sdsu.edu	San Diego	CA	92120	619-594-5090	594-1581
Center for Research on the Context of Teaching 520 Galvez Mall CERAS Bldg 4th Fl *Web:* cset.stanford.edu	Stanford	CA	94305	650-723-0572	
Center for Space Plasma & Aeronomic Research University of Alabama Huntsville *TF:* 800-824-2255 ■ *Web:* www.uah.edu	Huntsville	AL	35899	256-961-7403	961-7730
Center for Space Research University of Texas 3925 W Braker Ln Ste 200 *Web:* www.csr.utexas.edu	Austin	TX	78759	512-471-5573	471-3570
Center for Sustainable Environmental Technologies Iowa State University 1140 Biorenewables Research Laboratory *Web:* www.cset.iastate.edu	Ames	IA	50011	515-294-7936	294-3091
Center for the Study of Language & Information Stanford University Cordura Hall 210 Panama St *Web:* www-csli.stanford.edu	Stanford	CA	94305	650-725-3286	723-0758
Center for the Study of Teaching & Policy (CTP) University of Washington PO Box 353600 *Web:* www.depts.washington.edu	Seattle	WA	98195	206-221-4114	616-8158
Center on Education & Training for Employment Ohio State University 1900 Kenny Rd *TF:* 800-848-4815 ■ *Web:* cete.osu.edu	Columbus	OH	43210	614-292-6869	292-3742
Center on Human Development & Disability University of Washington 1701 NE Columbia Rd PO Box 357920 *TF:* 800-636-1089 ■ *Web:* www.depts.washington.edu/chdd	Seattle	WA	98195	206-543-2832	543-3561
Centers for Disease Control & Prevention (CDC) 1600 Clifton Rd NE *Web:* www.cdc.gov	Atlanta	GA	30333	404-639-7000	639-7111
National Center for Environmental Health 4770 Buford Hwy Bldg 101 *TF:* 800-232-4636 ■ *Web:* www.cdc.gov	Atlanta	GA	30341	404-639-3311	
National Institute for Occupational Safety & Health 200 Independence Ave SW *TF:* 800-356-4674 ■ *Web:* www.cdc.gov/niosh	Washington	DC	20201	404-639-3286	
Centrose LLC 918 Deming Way *Web:* www.centrosepharma.com	Madison	WI	53717	608-836-0207	
Charles River Laboratories Inc 251 Ballardvale St *NYSE: CRL* ■ **Fax Area Code:* 978 ■ *TF:* 800-772-3271 ■ *Web:* www.criver.com	Wilmington	MA	01887	781-222-6000	658-7132*
Charles Stark Draper Laboratory Inc 555 Technology Sq *Web:* www.draper.com	Cambridge	MA	02139	617-258-1000	258-1131
CHI Solutions Inc 801 W Ellsworth Rd Ste 202 *Web:* www.chisolutionsinc.com	Ann Arbor	MI	48108	734-662-6363	
Children's Nutrition Research Ctr USDA/ARS Baylor College of Medicine 1100 Bates St *Web:* www.bcm.edu/cnrc	Houston	TX	77030	713-798-6767	798-7046
Children's Research Institute Children's National Medical Ctr 111 Michigan Ave NW Research Fl 5 *TF:* 888-884-2327 ■ *Web:* www.childrensnational.org	Washington	DC	20010	888-884-2327	
Cibus Global 6455 Nancy Ridge Dr Ste 100 *Web:* www.cibus.com	San Diego	CA	92121	858-450-0008	
Clarassance Inc 9700 Great Seneca Hwy *Web:* www.clarassance.com	Rockville	MD	20850	301-452-2899	
Clark Martire & Bartolomeo 375 Sylvan Ave *Web:* www.cmbinc.com	Englewood Cliffs	NJ	07632	201-568-0011	
Cleveland Biolabs Inc 73 High St *NASDAQ: CBLI* ■ *Web:* www.cbiolabs.com	Buffalo	NY	14203	716-849-6810	
Climatronics Corp 140 Wilbur Pl *Web:* www.climatronics.com	Bohemia	NY	11716	631-567-7300	
CNA Corp 4825 Mark Ctr Dr *TF:* 800-344-0007 ■ *Web:* www.cna.org	Alexandria	VA	22311	703-824-2000	824-2949
Coastal & Marine Institute San Diego State University 4165 Spruance Rd *Web:* www.sci.sdsu.edu/cmi	San Diego	CA	92101	619-594-1308	
Cobalt Technologies Inc 500 Clyde Ave *Web:* cobalttech.com	Mountain View	CA	94043	650-230-0760	
Cogent Research LLC 125 Cambridge Park Dr *Web:* www.axiomresearch.com	Cambridge	MA	02140	617-441-9944	
Cold Spring Harbor Laboratory (CSHL) 1 Bungtown Rd *Web:* www.cshl.edu	Cold Spring Harbor	NY	11724	516-367-8800	367-8455
Colorado Ctr for Astrodynamics Research (CCAR) University of Colorado ECNT 320 UCB 431 *Web:* ccar.colorado.edu	Boulder	CO	80309	303-492-3105	492-2825
Columbia Environmental Research Ctr (CERC) 4200 New Haven Rd *TF:* 888-283-7626 ■ *Web:* www.cerc.usgs.gov	Columbia	MO	65201	573-875-5399	876-1896
Columbia Institute for Tele-Information (CITI) Columbia University 3022 Broadway Uris Hall Ste 1A *Web:* www8.gsb.columbia.edu/citi	New York	NY	10027	212-854-4222	854-1471
Comcor Environmental Ltd 320 Pinebush Rd Ste 12 *Web:* www.comcor.com	Cambridge	ON	N1T1Z6	519-621-6669	
Computer Emergency Response Team (CERT) 4500 Fifth Ave 4500 Fifth Ave *Web:* www.cert.org	Pittsburgh	PA	15213	412-268-7090	268-6989
Computer Science & Artificial Intelligence Laboratory (CSAIL) 32 Vassar St Bldg 32 *Web:* www.csail.mit.edu	Cambridge	MA	02139	617-253-5851	258-8682
Conservation & Production Research Laboratory (CPRL) USDA/ARS PO Box 10 *Web:* www.ars.usda.gov/main/site_main.htm?modecode=30-90-05-00	Bushland	TX	79012	806-356-5724	356-5750
Coriell Institute for Medical Research 403 Haddon Ave *TF:* 800-752-3805 ■ *Web:* www.coriell.org	Camden	NJ	08103	856-966-7377	
Cornell NanoScale Science & Technology Facility (CNF) Cornell University 250 Duffield Hall *Web:* www.cnf.cornell.edu	Ithaca	NY	14853	607-255-2329	255-8601
Courant Institute of Mathematical Sciences (CIMS) *New York University* 251 Mercer St *Web:* www.cims.nyu.edu	New York	NY	10012	212-998-1212	995-4121
Creare Inc 16 Great Hollow Rd *Web:* www.creare.com	Hanover	NH	03755	603-643-3800	643-4657
CRG Global Inc 3 Signal Ave Ste A *TF:* 800-831-1718 ■ *Web:* www.crgglobalinc.com	Ormond Beach	FL	32174	386-677-5644	
CureSearch for Children's Cancer 4600 East-West Hwy Ste 600 *TF:* 800-458-6223 ■ *Web:* www.curesearch.org	Bethesda	MD	20814	301-718-0047	
Curriculum Research & Development Group University of Hawaii 1776 University Ave *Web:* manoa.hawaii.edu	Honolulu	HI	96822	808-956-7961	956-9486
Dana-Farber Cancer Institute 44 Binney St **Fax:* PR ■ *TF:* 866-408-3324 ■ *Web:* www.dana-farber.org	Boston	MA	02115	617-632-3000	632-5520*
Data Sciences International 119 14th St NW Ste 100 *TF:* 800-262-9687 ■ *Web:* datasci.com/buxco	St. Paul	MN	55112	800-262-9687	
Data Storage Systems Ctr (DSSC) *Carnegie Mellon University ECE Dept* 5000 Forbes Ave *TF:* 800-864-8287 ■ *Web:* www.dssc.ece.cmu.edu	Pittsburgh	PA	15213	412-268-6600	268-3497
DEKA Research & Development Corp 340 Commercial St *Web:* www.dekaresearch.com	Manchester	NH	03101	603-669-5139	
Dell'Oro Group Inc 230 Redwood Shores Pkwy *Web:* www.delloro.com	Redwood City	CA	94065	650-622-9400	
Desert Research Institute 2215 Raggio Pkwy *Web:* www.dri.edu	Reno	NV	89512	775-673-7300	673-7397
Diabetes Research Institute 1450 NW Tenth Ave **Fax Area Code:* 305 ■ *TF:* 800-321-3437 ■ *Web:* www.diabetesresearch.org	Miami	FL	33136	954-964-4040	243-4404*

	City	State	Zip	Phone	Fax
Digital Monitoring Products Inc 2500 N Partnership Blvd *TF:* 800-641-4282 ■ *Web:* www.dmp.com	Springfield	MO	65803	417-831-9362	
Digitec Inc 2731 Van Dorn Rd *TF:* 888-761-3382	Milford	NE	68405	402-761-3382	
Discera Inc 1961 Concourse Dr *Web:* www.discera.com	San Jose	CA	95131	408-432-8600	
DisplayLink Corp 480 S California Ave Ste 305 *Web:* www.displaylink.com	Palo Alto	CA	94306	650-838-0481	
Diversified Laboratories Inc 4150 Lafayette Ctr Dr *Web:* www.diversifiedlaboratories.com	Chantilly	VA	20151	703-222-8700	222-0786
Dryden Flight Research Ctr PO Box 273 *Web:* www.nasa.gov/centers	Edwards	CA	93523	661-276-3311	276-3566
Dycor Technologies Ltd 1851 94 St *TF:* 800-663-9267 ■ *Web:* www.dycor.com	Edmonton	AB	T6N1E6	780-486-0091	486-3535
Earth Sciences & Resources Institute 901 Sumter St Ste 301 *Web:* www.esri.sc.edu	Columbia	SC	29208	803-777-4243	777-2972
Earth System Research Laboratory NOAA/ESRL 325 Broadway *Web:* www.esrl.noaa.gov	Boulder	CO	80305	303-497-6643	497-6951
Eastern Regional Research Ctr (ERRC) 600 E Mermaid Ln *Web:* www.ars.usda.gov/main/site_main.htm?modecode=19350000	Wyndmoor	PA	19038	215-233-6400	233-6559
Edison Biotechnology Institute Ohio University, Konneker Research Laboratories The Ridges *TF:* 800-444-2420 ■ *Web:* www.ohio.edu	Athens	OH	45701	740-593-4713	593-4795
Eikos Inc 2 Master Dr *TF:* 888-345-6712 ■ *Web:* www.eikos.com	Franklin	MA	02038	508-528-0300	
EmPower Research LLC 404 E 79th St Ste 16E *Web:* www.empowerresearch.com	New York	NY	10075	646-472-7908	
Enanta Pharmaceuticals Inc 500 Arsenal St *Web:* www.enanta.com	Watertown	MA	02472	617-607-0800	
Endacea Inc 2 Davis Dr *Web:* www.endacea.com	Research Triangle Park	NC	27709	919-406-1888	
Energy & Environmental Research Ctr (EERC) University of N Dakota, 15 N 23rd St S 9018 *Web:* www.eerc.und.nodak.edu	Grand Forks	ND	58202	701-777-5000	777-5181
Energy Institute Pennsylvania State University, Coal Utilization Laboratory Rm C211 *Web:* www.energy.psu.edu	University Park	PA	16802	814-865-3093	863-7432
Engineering Research Ctr for Net Shape Mfg 1971 Neil Ave Rm 339 *Web:* ercnsm.osu.edu	Columbus	OH	43210	614-292-9267	292-7219
Environmental Management Inc 5200 NE Hwy 33 *TF:* 800-510-8510 ■ *Web:* www.emiok.com	Guthrie	OK	73044	405-282-8510	
Environmental Science Assoc 225 Bush St Ste 1700 *Web:* www.esassoc.com	San Francisco	CA	94104	415-896-5900	896-0332
EPIEN Medical Inc 4225 White Bear Pkwy Ste 600 *TF:* 888-884-4675 ■ *Web:* www.epien.com	St Paul	MN	55110	651-653-3380	
Epiphany Biosciences Inc 1 California St Ste 2800 *Web:* www.epiphanybio.com	San Francisco	CA	94111	415-765-7193	
Epitomics Inc 863 Mitten Rd Ste 103 *TF:* 888-772-2226 ■ *Web:* www.epitomics.com	Burlingame	CA	94010	650-583-6688	
EPRI 3420 Hillview Ave *Web:* www.epri.com	Palo Alto	CA	94304	650-855-2000	
Eunice Kennedy Shriver Ctr 200 Trapelo Rd **Fax Area Code:* 781 ■ *Web:* www.umassmed.edu/shriver	Waltham	MA	02452	774-455-6562	642-0114*
Evans Data Corp 340 Soquel Ave *TF:* 800-831-3080 ■ *Web:* www.evansdata.com	Santa Cruz	CA	95062	831-425-8451	
Exponent Inc 149 Commonwealth Dr *NASDAQ: EXPO* ■ *TF:* 888-656-3976 ■ *Web:* www.exponent.com	Menlo Park	CA	94025	650-326-9400	326-8072
Expression Pathology Inc 9620 Medical Ctr Dr Ste100 *Web:* www.expressionpathology.com	Rockville	MD	20850	301-977-3654	
Federal Aviation Administration (FAA) 800 Independence Ave SW *TF:* 866-835-5322 ■ *Web:* www.faa.gov	Washington	DC	20591	866-835-5322	
Aviation Research Div 800 Independence Ave SW Rm 528A *TF:* 866-835-5322 ■ *Web:* www.faa.gov	Washington	DC	20591	202-267-9251	267-5320
Federal Judicial Ctr 1 Columbus Cir NE *Web:* www.fjc.gov	Washington	DC	20544	202-502-4000	
Fels Institute for Cancer Research & Molecular Biology Temple Univ School of Medicine, 3400 N Broad St *Web:* www.temple.edu	Philadelphia	PA	19140	215-707-6356	707-2783
Fermi National Accelerator Laboratory PO Box 500 *Web:* www.fnal.gov	Batavia	IL	60510	630-840-3000	840-4343
Florida Resources & Environmental Analysis Ctr *Florida State University* UCC 2200 FSU *Web:* www.freac.fsu.edu	Tallahassee	FL	32306	850-644-2007	644-7360
Florida Solar Energy Ctr 1679 Clearlake Rd *TF:* 877-777-4778 ■ *Web:* www.fsec.ucf.edu	Cocoa	FL	32922	321-638-1000	638-1010
Focus Forward LLC 950 W Valley Rd Ste 2700 *Web:* www.focusfwd.com	Wayne	PA	19087	215-367-4000	
Focus Pointe 100 E Penn Sq Ste 1200 *Web:* www.phonelab.com	Philadelphia	PA	19107	215-561-5500	
Focus Vision 7 River Park Pl E Ste 110 *Web:* www.decipherinc.com	Fresno	CA	93720	559-436-6940	
Food Research Institute University of Wisconsin Madison, 1550 Linden Dr *Web:* fri.wisc.edu	Madison	WI	53706	608-263-7777	263-1114
Fox Chase Cancer Ctr 333 Cottman Ave *TF:* 888-369-2427 ■ *Web:* www.foxchase.org	Philadelphia	PA	19111	215-728-6900	728-2682
Framingham Heart Study 73 Mt Wayte Ave Ste 2 *TF:* 800-854-7582 ■ *Web:* www.framinghamheartstudy.org	Framingham	MA	01702	508-935-3418	626-1262
Francis Bitter Magnet Laboratory Massachusetts Institute of Technology, 150 Albany St NW 14 *Web:* web.mit.edu/fbml	Cambridge	MA	02139	617-253-5478	253-5405
Fred Hutchinson Cancer Research Ctr 1100 Fairview Ave N PO Box 19024 *Web:* www.fredhutch.org/en.html	Seattle	WA	98104	206-667-5000	667-4051
Friends Research Institute Inc 1040 Pk Ave Ste 103 *TF:* 800-822-3677 ■ *Web:* www.friendsresearch.org	Baltimore	MD	21201	410-823-5116	823-5131
Social Research Ctr 1040 Pk Ave Ste 103 *TF:* 800-705-7757 ■ *Web:* www.friendsresearch.org	Baltimore	MD	21201	410-837-3977	752-4218
Functional Genetics Inc 708 Quince Orchard Rd	Gaithersburg	MD	20878	240-631-6790	
Galleon Pharmaceuticals Inc 213 Witmer Rd *Web:* www.galleonpharma.com	Horsham	PA	19044	267-803-1970	
Gas Technology Institute (GTI) 1700 S Mt Prospect Rd *Web:* www.gastechnology.org	Des Plaines	IL	60018	847-768-0500	768-0501
Gatorade Sports Science Institute 617 W Main St *TF:* 800-616-4774 ■ *Web:* www.gssiweb.org	Barrington	IL	60010	800-616-4774	
Gem Mobile Treatment Services Inc 2525 Cherry Ave Ste 105 *Web:* gem.evergreenes.com	Signal Hill	CA	90755	562-595-7075	
Gemmus Pharma Inc 409 Illinois St *Web:* www.gemmuspharma.com	San Francisco	CA	94158	415-978-2151	
Genemed Biotechnologies Inc 458 Carlton Ct S San Francisco *TF:* 877-436-3633 ■ *Web:* www.genemed.com	San Francisco	CA	94080	650-952-0110	
GenePharm Inc 1237 Midas Way *Web:* www.genepharminc.com	Sunnyvale	CA	94085	408-773-0106	
General Atomics 3550 General Atomics Ct PO Box 85608 *TF:* 800-669-6820 ■ *Web:* www.ga.com	San Diego	CA	92121	858-455-3000	455-3621
General Resonance LLC 1 Resonance Way	Havre De Grace	MD	21078	410-939-2343	
Genocea Biosciences Inc 100 Acorn Park Dr *Web:* www.genocea.com	Cambridge	MA	02140	617-876-8191	
Geophysical Fluid Dynamics Laboratory NOAA/OAR/GFDL 201 Forrestal Rd *Web:* www.gfdl.noaa.gov	Princeton	NJ	08540	609-452-6500	987-5063
Georgia Tech Fusion Research Ctr Boggs Bldg Rm 3-29 *Web:* www.frc.gatech.edu	Atlanta	GA	30332	404-894-3714	894-3733
Georgia Tech Research Institute (GTRI) *Georgia Institute of Technology* 250 14th St NW *Web:* www.gtri.gatech.edu	Atlanta	GA	30318	404-407-7400	894-9875
GFK Arbor LLC 1 W Third St *Web:* valientmarketresearch.com	Media	PA	19063	610-566-8700	
Giner Inc 89 Rumford Ave *Web:* www.ginerinc.com	Newton	MA	02466	781-529-0500	
Glen Research Corp 22825 Davis Dr *TF:* 800-327-4536 ■ *Web:* www.glenres.com	Sterling	VA	20164	703-437-6191	
Glenn Research Ctr 21000 Brookpark Rd *Web:* www.nasa.gov/centers/glenn/home	Cleveland	OH	44135	216-433-4000	433-8000
Goddard Institute for Space Studies 2880 Broadway *TF:* 888-661-1620 ■ *Web:* www.giss.nasa.gov	New York	NY	10025	212-678-5510	678-5552
Goddard Space Flight Ctr 8800 Greenbelt Rd **Fax:* PR ■ *Web:* www.nasa.gov/centers/goddard	Greenbelt	MD	20771	301-286-2000	286-1707*
Gongos Research Inc 2365 Pontiac Rd *Web:* www.gongos.com	Auburn Hills	MI	48326	248-239-2300	
Grand Forks Human Nutrition Research Ctr USDA/ARS 2420 Second Ave N PO Box 9034 *Web:* www.ars.usda.gov/Main/docs.htm?docid=3898	Grand Forks	ND	58202	701-795-8353	795-8395
Great Lakes Environmental Research Laboratory (GLERL) 4840 S State St *Web:* www.glerl.noaa.gov	Ann Arbor	MI	48108	734-741-2235	741-2055
Gustavson Assoc LLC 5757 Central Ave Ste D *Web:* www.gustavson.com	Boulder	CO	80301	303-443-2209	
H Lee Moffitt Cancer Ctr & Research Institute University of S Florida 12902 Magnolia Dr **Fax Area Code:* 813 ■ *TF:* 800-456-3434 ■ *Web:* www.moffitt.org	Tampa	FL	33612	888-663-3488	745-4064*
Hamner Institutes for Health Sciences, The 6 Davis Dr PO Box 12137 *Web:* www.thehamner.org	Research Triangle Park	NC	27709	919-558-1200	558-1400
Harry K Dupree Stuttgart National Aquaculture Research Ctr 2955 Hwy 130 E PO Box 1050 *Web:* www.ars.usda.gov/main/site_main.htm?modecode=62251000	Stuttgart	AR	72160	870-673-4483	673-7710
Harvard-Smithsonian Ctr for Astrophysics 60 Garden St *Web:* www.cfa.harvard.edu	Cambridge	MA	02138	617-495-7100	495-7468
Hatfield Marine Science Ctr 2030 SE Marine Science Dr *Web:* www.hmsc.oregonstate.edu	Newport	OR	97365	541-867-0100	867-0138
Hawaii Insitute of Geophysics & Planetology University of Hawaii, 1680 E-W Rd PO Box 602B *Web:* www.higp.hawaii.edu	Honolulu	HI	96822	808-956-8760	956-3188
Hazen Research Inc 4601 Indiana St *Web:* www.hazenresearch.com	Golden	CO	80403	303-279-4501	278-1528
HemoShear LLC 501 Locust Ave Ste 301 *Web:* www.hemoshear.com	Charlottesville	VA	22902	434-872-0196	872-0199
High Performance Computing Collaboratory PO Box 9627 *TF:* 800-521-4041 ■ *Web:* www.erc.msstate.edu	Mississippi State	MS	39762	662-325-8278	325-7692
Houston Advanced Research Ctr (HARC) 4800 Research Forest Dr *Web:* www.harcresearch.org	The Woodlands	TX	77381	281-364-6000	363-7914

	City	State	Zip	Phone	Fax
Howard Hughes Medical Institute 4000 Jones Bridge Rd *Web:* www.hhmi.org	Chevy Chase	MD	20815	301-215-8500	215-8863
Human Resources Research Organization (HumRRO) 66 Canal Ctr Plz Ste 400 *Web:* www.humrro.org	Alexandria	VA	22314	703-549-3611	549-9025
Hyperion Biotechnology Inc 13302 Langtry St *Web:* hyperionbiotechnology.com	San Antonio	TX	78248	210-493-7452	
Iconoculture Inc 244 First Ave N *Web:* iconoculture.cebglobal.com	Minneapolis	MN	55401	612-642-2222	
Idaho National Laboratory (INL) 2525 Fremont Ave *TF:* 866-495-7440 ■ *Web:* www.inl.gov	Idaho Falls	ID	83402	866-495-7440	
IFOS Inc 2363 Calle Del Mundo *Web:* www.ifos.com	Santa Clara	CA	95054	408-565-9000	
IIT Research Institute (IITRI) 10 W 35th St *Web:* www.iitri.org	Chicago	IL	60616	312-567-4000	
Immune Design Corp 1616 Eastlake Ave E Ste 310 *Web:* www.immunedesign.com	Seattle	WA	98102	206-682-0645	
Immunotope Inc The Pennsylvania Biotechnology Ctr 3805 Old Easton Rd *Web:* www.immunotope.com	Doylestown	PA	18902	215-253-4180	
in-sync Consumer Insight Corp 90 Eglinton Ave E Ste 403 *Web:* www.insyncstrategy.com	Toronto	ON	M4P2Y3	416-932-0921	
Indiana Molecular Biology Institute Indiana University 915 E 3rd St *Web:* imbi.bio.indiana.edu	Bloomington	IN	47405	812-855-4183	855-6082
Industrial Partnership for Research in Interfacial & Materials Engineering (IPRIME) University of Minnesota 151 Amundson Hall 421 Washington Ave SE *Web:* www.iprime.umn.edu	Minneapolis	MN	55455	612-626-9509	626-7246
Institute for Astronomy University of Hawaii 2680 Woodlawn Dr *TF:* 800-351-1330 ■ *Web:* www.ifa.hawaii.edu	Honolulu	HI	96822	808-956-8312	988-2790
Institute for Basic Research in Developmental Disabilities 1050 Forest Hill Rd *Web:* opwdd.ny.gov	Staten Island	NY	10314	718-494-0600	494-0833
Institute for Defense Analyses (IDA) 4850 Mark Ctr Dr *Web:* www.ida.org	Alexandria	VA	22311	703-845-2000	845-2588
Institute for Diabetes Obesity & Metabolism 700 Clinical Research Bldg 415 Curie Blvd *Web:* www.med.upenn.edu/physiol/faculty.html	Philadelphia	PA	19104	215-898-4365	898-5408
Institute for Molecular Virology (IMV) 413 RM Bock Laboratories 1525 Linden Dr *Web:* virology.wisc.edu	Madison	WI	53706	608-262-4540	262-4570
Institute for Physical Research & Technology (IPRT) *Iowa State University* 2156 Gilman Hall *Web:* www.iprt.iastate.edu	Ames	IA	50011	515-294-3045	294-2361
Institute for Research on Poverty University of Wisconsin Madison 1180 Observatory Dr 3412 William H Sewell Social Sciences Bldg *TF:* 866-301-1753 ■ *Web:* www.irp.wisc.edu	Madison	WI	53706	608-262-6358	265-3119
Institute for Scientific Analysis 390 Fourth St Ste D *Web:* www.scientificanalysis.org	San Francisco	CA	94107	415-777-2352	
Institute for Simulation & Training (IST) 3100 Technology Pkwy *Web:* www.ist.ucf.edu	Orlando	FL	32826	407-882-1300	658-5059
Institute for Social Behavioral & Economic Research University of California 2201 N Hall *Web:* www.isber.ucsb.edu	Santa Barbara	CA	93106	805-893-2548	893-7995
Institute for Social Research University of Michigan 426 Thompson St *Web:* home.isr.umich.edu	Ann Arbor	MI	48104	734-764-8354	936-9708
Institute for Systems Research University of Maryland 2173 AV Williams Bldg *TF:* 866-675-8967 ■ *Web:* www.isr.umd.edu	College Park	MD	20742	301-405-6615	314-9920
Institute for Telecommunications Sciences 325 Broadway *Web:* www.its.bldrdoc.gov	Boulder	CO	80305	303-497-5216	
Institute of Arctic & Alpine Research (INSTAAR) University of Colorado 1560 30th St PO Box 450 *Web:* instaar.colorado.edu	Boulder	CO	80309	303-492-6387	492-6388
Institute of Behavioral Science University of Colorado 1416 Broadway *Web:* www.colorado.edu/IBS	Boulder	CO	80302	303-492-8147	492-6924
Institute of Ecosystem Studies (IES) 2801 Sharon Tpke PO Box AB *Web:* www.caryinstitute.org	Millbrook	NY	12545	845-677-5343	677-5976
Institute of Education Sciences (IES) US Dept of Education 555 New Jersey Ave NW Rm 600 *Web:* www.ies.ed.gov	Washington	DC	20208	202-219-1385	219-1466
Institute of Gerontology University of Michigan 300 N Ingalls St *TF:* 877-865-2167 ■ *Web:* med.umich.edu	Ann Arbor	MI	48109	734-936-2107	936-2116
Institute of Human Origins (IHO) Arizona State Univ PO Box 874101 *Web:* iho.asu.edu	Tempe	AZ	85287	480-727-6580	727-6570
Institute of Materials Science University of Connecticut 97 N Eagleville Rd *TF:* 800-528-7411 ■ *Web:* www.ims.uconn.edu	Storrs	CT	06269	860-486-4623	486-4745
Intelligent Mechatronic Systems Inc 435 King St N *TF:* 866-818-6637 ■ *Web:* www.intellimec.com	Waterloo	ON	N2J2Z5	519-745-8887	
Intematix Corp 46410 Fremont Blvd *Web:* www.intematix.com	Fremont	CA	94538	510-933-3300	

	City	State	Zip	Phone	Fax
International Arctic Research Ctr (IARC) 930 Koyukuk Dr PO Box 757340 *Web:* www.iarc.uaf.edu	Fairbanks	AK	99775	907-474-6016	474-5662
International Ctr for Advanced Internet Research (iCAIR) 750 N Lk Shore Dr Ste 600 *Web:* www.icair.org	Chicago	IL	60611	312-503-0735	
International Institute of Tropical Forestry (IITF) Jardin Botanico Sur 1201 Calle Ceiba *Web:* www.fs.fed.us/global/iitf	San Juan	PR	00926	787-766-5335	766-6302
Ionian Technologies Inc 4940 Carroll Canyon Rd Ste 100 *Web:* www.ionian-tech.com	San Diego	CA	92121	858-642-0998	
Issues & Answers Network Inc 5151 Bonney Rd Ste 100 *Web:* www.issans.net	Virginia Beach	VA	23462	757-456-1100	
itherX Pharmaceuticals Inc 10790 Roselle St *Web:* www.itxpharma.com	San Diego	CA	92121	858-824-1100	
ITN Energy Systems Inc 8130 Shaffer Pkwy *Web:* www.itnes.com	Littleton	CO	80127	303-420-1141	
Jackson Laboratory, The 600 Main St *TF:* 800-422-6423 ■ *Web:* www.jax.org	Bar Harbor	ME	04609	207-288-6000	288-6076
James Cancer Hospital & Solove Research Institute, The 300 W Tenth Ave Ste 519 *Web:* cancer.osu.edu	Columbus	OH	43210	614-293-5066	293-3132
Jamie Whitten Delta States Research Ctr Experiment Stn Rd PO Box 225 *Web:* www.ars.usda.gov/main/site_main.htm?modecode=64-02-00-00	Stoneville	MS	38776	662-686-5265	686-5459
Jean Mayer USDA Human Nutrition Research Ctr on Aging 711 Washington St *Web:* hnrca.tufts.edu	Boston	MA	02111	617-556-3000	556-3344
Jet Propulsion Laboratory (JPL) 4800 Oak Grove Dr *Web:* www.jpl.nasa.gov	Pasadena	CA	91109	818-354-4321	
John A Volpe National Transportation Systems Ctr 55 Broadway *Web:* www.volpe.dot.gov	Cambridge	MA	02142	617-494-2000	
John F. Kennedy Space Ctr. *TF:* 866-737-5235 ■ *Web:* www.nasa.gov/centers/kennedy	Kennedy Space Center	FL	32899	321-867-5000	
Johns Hopkins University Applied Physics Laboratory 11100 Johns Hopkins Rd *Web:* www.jhuapl.edu	Laurel	MD	20723	240-228-5000	228-1093
Johnson Space Ctr 2101 NASA Pkwy *Web:* www.nasa.gov	Houston	TX	77058	281-483-0123	
Joint Institute for Laboratory Astrophysics (JILA) University of Colorado 440 UCB *Web:* jila.colorado.edu	Boulder	CO	80309	303-492-7789	492-5235
Joint Institute for Marine & Atmospheric Research University of Hawaii at Manoa 1000 Pope Rd MSB Bldg 312 *Web:* www.soest.hawaii.edu	Honolulu	HI	96822	808-956-8083	956-4104
Joint Institute for Marine Observations (JIMO) Scripps Institution of Oceanography -Univ of California 9500 Gilman Dr *Web:* www.jimo.ucsd.edu	La Jolla	CA	92093	858-534-4100	
Joseph Stokes Jr Research Institute Children's Hospital of Philadelphia 3615 Civic Ctr Blvd *Web:* stokes.chop.edu	Philadelphia	PA	19104	215-590-3800	590-3804
Joslin Diabetes Ctr 1 Joslin Pl *Web:* www.joslin.org	Boston	MA	02215	617-732-2400	732-2542
KemPharm Inc 2656Crosspark Rd Ste 100 *Web:* www.kempharm.com	Coralville	IA	52241	319-665-2575	665-2577
Kendle International Inc 441 Vine St 1200 Carew Twr *TF:* 800-733-1572 ■ *Web:* www.kendle.com	Cincinnati	OH	45202	513-381-5550	381-5870
Keweenaw Research Ctr Michigan Technological University 1400 Townsend Dr *Web:* www.mtukrc.org	Houghton	MI	49931	906-487-1885	487-2202
Knowledge Systems & Research Inc 120 Madison St 15th Fl *Web:* www.ksrinc.com	Syracuse	NY	13202	315-470-1350	
Kresge Hearing Research Institute (KHRI) 4605 Medical Science Unit *Web:* medicine.umich.edu/dept/kresge-hearing-research-institute	Ann Arbor	MI	48109	734-764-8110	764-0014
Laboratory for Laser Energetics 250 E River Rd *Web:* www.lle.rochester.edu	Rochester	NY	14623	585-275-5101	275-5960
Lamont-Doherty Earth Observatory 61 Rt 9w *Web:* www.ldeo.columbia.edu	Palisades	NY	10964	845-359-2900	359-2931
Langley Research Ctr 8 Lindbergh Wy *Web:* www.nasa.gov/centers/langley	Hampton	VA	23681	757-864-1000	
Lawrence Berkeley National Laboratory (LBNL) 1 Cyclotron Rd *Web:* www.lbl.gov	Berkeley	CA	94720	510-486-4000	486-7000
Advanced Light Source 1 Cyclotron Rd MS 6-2100 *Web:* www-als.lbl.gov	Berkeley	CA	94720	510-486-7745	486-4773
Lawrence Livermore National Laboratory (LLNL) 7000 E Ave PO Box 808 *Web:* www.llnl.gov	Livermore	CA	94550	925-422-1100	422-1370
LC Sciences LLC 2575 W Bellfort St Ste 270 *Web:* www.lcsciences.com	Houston	TX	77054	713-664-7087	
Learning Research & Development Ctr (LRDC) University of Pittsburgh 3939 O'Hara St *TF:* 800-397-0071 ■ *Web:* www.lrdc.pitt.edu	Pittsburgh	PA	15260	412-624-7020	624-9149
Learning Systems Institute 4600 University Ctr *Web:* www.lsi.fsu.edu	Tallahassee	FL	32306	850-644-2570	644-4952
Lerner Research Institute 9500 Euclid Ave *TF:* 800-223-2273 ■ *Web:* www.lerner.ccf.org	Cleveland	OH	44195	216-444-3900	444-3279
LifeSensors Inc 271 Great Vly Pkwy Ste 100 *Web:* www.lifesensors.com	Malvern	PA	19355	610-644-8845	

Phone | Fax

Lightwaves 2020 Inc 1323 Great Mall Dr. Milpitas CA 95035 408-503-8888
Web: www.lightwaves2020.com

LIMRA International Inc 300 Day Hill Rd Windsor CT 06095 860-688-3358 298-9555
TF: 800-235-4672 ■ *Web:* www.limra.com

Lincoln Laboratory
Massachusetts Institute of Technology
244 Wood St. Lexington MA 02420 781-981-5500 981-7086*
**Fax:* Hum Res ■ *TF:* 800-445-8667 ■ *Web:* www.ll.mit.edu

Lineagen Inc 2677 E Parleys Way Salt Lake City UT 84109 801-931-6200
TF: 888-888-6736 ■ *Web:* www.lineagen.com

Lodestar Research Corp
2400 Central Ave Ste P-5 Boulder CO 80301 303-449-9691 449-3865
Web: www.lodestar.com

Los Alamos National Laboratory (LANL)
PO Box 1663 Los Alamos NM 87545 505-667-7000
TF: 877-723-4101 ■ *Web:* www.lanl.gov

Los Angeles Biomedical Research Institute
1124 W Carson St Torrance CA 90502 877-452-2674 222-3640*
**Fax Area Code:* 310 ■ *TF:* 877-452-2674 ■ *Web:* www.labiomed.org

Lovelace Respiratory Research Institute (LRRI)
2425 Ridgecrest Dr SE Albuquerque NM 87108 505-348-9400 348-8541
TF: 800-700-1016 ■ *Web:* www.lrri.org

Lutonix Inc 9409 Science Ctr Dr New Hope MN 55428 763-445-2352
Web: www.lutonix.com

Mahoney Institute of Neurological Sciences
3535 Market St Mezzanine Philadelphia PA 19104 215-662-2560 349-8312
Web: www.med.upenn.edu

Mailman Research Ctr
McLean Hospital 115 Mill St Belmont MA 02478 617-855-2000
TF: 800-333-0338 ■ *Web:* mcleanhospital.org/research/mrc

Marine Biological Laboratory (MBL) 7 MBL St Woods Hole MA 02543 508-548-3705 540-6902
TF: 800-222-1222 ■ *Web:* www.mbl.edu

Marine Environmental Research Institute (MERI)
MERI Center for Marine Studies
55 Main St PO Box 1652 Blue Hill ME 04614 207-374-2135
Web: www.meriresearch.org

Marine Science Institute
University of California Santa Barbara CA 93106 805-893-4093 893-8062
Web: www.msi.ucsb.edu

Marinus Pharmaceuticals Inc
21 Business Park Dr Branford CT 06405 203-315-0566
Web: www.marinuspharma.com

Martec Group Inc, The 105 W Adams St Ste 2125 Chicago IL 60603 312-606-9690
TF: 888-811-5755 ■ *Web:* www.martecgroup.com

Massa Products Corp 280 Lincoln St Hingham MA 02043 781-749-4800
TF: 800-962-7543 ■ *Web:* www.massa.com

Massey Cancer Ctr
Virginia Commonwealth University
401 College St PO Box 980037 Richmond VA 23298 804-828-0450 828-8453
TF: 877-462-7739 ■ *Web:* www.massey.vcu.edu

MAX Technologies Inc
2051 Victoria Ave 3rd Fl Saint-Lambert QC J4S1H1 450-443-3332 443-1618
TF: 800-361-1629 ■ *Web:* www.maxt.com

MBI International 3815 Technology Blvd. Lansing MI 48910 517-337-3181 337-2122
Web: www.mbi.org

McArdle Laboratory for Cancer Research
University of Wisconsin Dept of Oncology
1400 University Ave Madison WI 53706 608-262-2177 262-2824
Web: mcardle.oncology.wisc.edu

McCrone Assoc Inc 850 Pasquinelli Dr Westmont IL 60559 630-887-7100 887-7417
Web: www.mccrone.com/materials-analysis

MCEER Red Jacket Quadrangle Buffalo NY 14260 716-645-3391 645-3733
Web: www.mceer.buffalo.edu

Mechanical Technology Inc
325 Washington Sq Ste 3 Albany NY 12205 518-533-2200 218-2500
NASDAQ: MKTY ■ *TF:* 800-937-5449 ■ *Web:* www.mechtech.com

Membrane Technology & Research Inc
1360 Willow Rd Ste 103 Menlo Park CA 94025 650-328-2228 328-6580
Web: www.mtrinc.com

Memorial Sloan-Kettering Cancer Ctr
1275 York Ave New York NY 10065 212-639-2000
TF: 800-525-2225 ■ *Web:* www.mskcc.org

Mersana Therapeutics Inc 840 Memorial Dr Cambridge MA 02139 617-498-0020
Web: www.mersana.com

Metabolon Inc
3410 Industrial Blvd Ste 103 West Sacramento CA 95691 916-371-7974
Web: www.lipomics.com

Metrics Inc 1240 Sugg Pkwy. Greenville NC 27834 252-752-3800 758-8522
Web: www.metricsinc.com

Miami Project to Cure Paralysis
1095 NW 14th Terr Lois Pope LIFE Ctr. Miami FL 33136 305-243-6001 243-6017
TF General: 800-782-6387 ■ *Web:* www.themiamiproject.org

Michigan Mfg Technology Ctr
47911 Halyard Dr Plymouth MI 48170 888-414-6682 451-4201*
**Fax Area Code:* 734 ■ *TF:* 888-414-6682 ■ *Web:* www.mmtc.org

Mid-Continent Research for Education & Learning (McREL)
4601 DTC Blvd Ste 500 Denver CO 80237 303-337-0990 337-3005
Web: www.mcrel.org

Midwest Research Institute (MRI)
425 Volker Blvd Kansas City MO 64110 816-753-7600 753-8420
Web: www.mriglobal.org

MIT Media Laboratory
Massachusetts Institute of Technology
77 Massachusetts Ave Bldg E15 Cambridge MA 02139 617-253-5960 258-6264
Web: www.media.mit.edu

MITRE Corp 202 Burlington Rd Bedford MA 01730 781-271-2000 271-2271
Web: www.mitre.org

Monell Chemical Senses Ctr
3500 Market St Philadelphia PA 19104 267-519-4700 519-4805
TF: 800-732-0999

Monteith Engineering Research Center
North Carolina State University
2410 Campus Shore Dr Centennial Campus Raleigh NC 27606 919-515-2030 515-5055
Web: www.ncsu.edu

Mote Marine Laboratory
1600 Ken Thompson Pkwy Sarasota FL 34236 941-388-4441 388-4312
Web: www.mote.org

MSU-DOE Plant Research Laboratory
612 Wilson Rd East Lansing MI 48824 517-353-2270 353-9168
TF: 800-875-5090 ■ *Web:* prl.natsci.msu.edu

NAHB Research Ctr
400 Prince Georges Blvd Upper Marlboro MD 20774 301-249-4000 430-6180
TF: 800-638-8556 ■ *Web:* www.homeinnovation.com

NanoBio Corp 2311 Green Rd Ste A. Ann Arbor MI 48105 734-302-4000
Web: www.nanobio.com

Nanotechnology Research Ctr
Georgia Institute of Technology
791 Atlantic Dr. Atlanta GA 30332 404-894-5100 894-5028
TF: 800-424-9300 ■ *Web:* ien.gatech.edu/nrc-transition-page

Nathan S Kline Institute for Psychiatric Research
140 Old Orangeburg Rd Orangeburg NY 10962 845-398-5500 398-5508
Web: www.rfmh.org/nki

National Astronomy & Ionosphere Ctr (NAIC)
Cornell University Space Sciences Bldg Ithaca NY 14853 607-255-3735 255-8803
Web: www.naic.edu

National Biodynamics Laboratory (NBDL)
University of New Orleans College of Engineering
2000 Lakeshore Dr. New Orleans LA 70148 888-514-4275 280-7413*
**Fax Area Code:* 504 ■ *TF:* 888-514-4275 ■ *Web:* www.uno.edu

National Bureau of Economic Research
1050 Massachusetts Ave Cambridge MA 02138 617-868-3900 868-2742
TF: 800-621-8476 ■ *Web:* www.nber.org

National Cancer Institute at Frederick
1050 Boyles St PO Box B Frederick MD 21702 301-846-1108 846-1494
Web: ncifrederick.cancer.gov

National Ctr for Agricultural Utilization Research
USDA/ARS 1815 N University St Peoria IL 61604 309-685-4011 681-6686
Web: www.ars.usda.gov/Main/docs.htm?docid=3153

National Ctr for Atmospheric Research (NCAR)
1850 Table Mesa Dr PO Box 3000 Boulder CO 80305 303-497-1000 497-8610*
**Fax:* PR ■ *Web:* www.ncar.ucar.edu

National Ctr for Computational Toxicology
US Environmental Protection Agency
109 TW Alexander Dr Research Triangle Park NC 27709 919-541-3850
Web: www.epa.gov

National Ctr for Ecological Analysis & Synthesis (NCEAS)
University of California Santa Barbara
735 State St Ste 300 Santa Barbara CA 93101 805-892-2500 892-2510
Web: www.nceas.ucsb.edu

National Ctr for Electron Microscopy (NCEM)
Lawrence Berkeley National Laboratory
MS 72-150 Berkeley CA 94720 510-486-4000 486-5888
Web: foundry.lbl.gov/facilities/ncem

National Ctr for Genetic Resources Preservation (NCGRP)
1111 S Mason St Fort Collins CO 80521 970-495-3200 221-1427
Web: www.ars.usda.gov/npa/ftcollins/ncgrp

National Ctr for Genome Resources
2935 Rodeo Pk Dr E Santa Fe NM 87505 505-995-4400 995-4432
TF: 800-450-4854 ■ *Web:* www.ncgr.org

National Ctr for Mfg Sciences (NCMS)
3025 Boardwalk Ann Arbor MI 48108 734-995-0300 995-1150
TF: 800-222-6267 ■ *Web:* www.ncms.org

National Ctr for Supercomputing Applications
University of Illinois Urbana-Champaign
1205 W Clark St Rm 1008 MC-257 Urbana IL 61801 217-244-0072 244-8195
Web: www.ncsa.illinois.edu

National Development & Research Institutes Inc
71 W 23rd St 8th Fl New York NY 10010 212-845-4400 438-0894*
**Fax Area Code:* 917 ■ *Web:* www.ndri.org

National Energy Research Scientific Computing Ctr (NERSC)
Lawrence Berkeley National Laboratory Berkeley CA 94720 510-486-5849 486-4300
TF: 800-666-3772 ■ *Web:* www.nersc.gov

National Energy Technology Laboratory (NETL)
3610 Collins Ferry Rd. Morgantown WV 26505 304-285-4764 285-4919
TF: 800-432-8330 ■ *Web:* www.netl.doe.gov

National Exposure Research Laboratory
US Environmental Protection Agency
TW Alexander Research Triangle Park NC 27709 202-564-6620 541-0605*
**Fax Area Code:* 919 ■ *Web:* www.epa.gov

National Hansen's Disease Program (NHDP)
1770 Physicians Pk Dr Baton Rouge LA 70816 800-221-9393
TF: 800-221-9393 ■ *Web:* hrsa.gov

National Health & Environmental Effects Research Laboratory
US Environmental Protection Agency
109 TW Alexander Dr Research Triangle Park NC 27709 202-564-6665 541-4324*
**Fax Area Code:* 919 ■ *Web:* www.epa.gov/nheerl

National High Magnetic Field Laboratory (NHMFL)
1800 E Paul Dirac Dr Tallahassee FL 32310 850-644-0311 644-8350

National Homeland Security Research Ctr
US Environmental Protection Agency
26 W Martin Luther King Dr Cincinnati OH 45268 513-569-7907 487-2555
TF: 888-372-7341 ■ *Web:* www.epa.gov

National Institute Child Health (CRMC)
6100 Executive Blvd Rockville MD 20852 301-435-6870

National Institute of Standards & Technology (NIST)
100 Bureau Dr Sp 1070 Gaithersburg MD 20899 301-975-6478 926-1630
TF: 800-877-8339 ■ *Web:* www.nist.gov
Boulder Laboratories 325 Broadway MS 104 Boulder CO 80305 301-975-6478 497-6235*
**Fax Area Code:* 303 ■ *Web:* www.boulder.nist.gov

National Institute on Disability & Rehabilitation Research (NIDRR)
400 Maryland Ave SW Washington DC 20202 202-245-6211 245-7323
Web: www.ed.gov/category/program/national-institute-disability-and-rehabilitation-research

National Institutes of Health (NIH)
9000 Rockville Pike Bethesda MD 20892 301-496-4000
Web: www.nih.gov
Clinical Ctr 10 Ctr Dr Bldg 10 Bethesda MD 20892 301-496-2563 402-2984
Web: www.cc.nih.gov

Phone | Fax

National Cancer Institute
Public Inquiries Office 6116 Executive Blvd
Rm 3036A .... Bethesda MD 20892 301-435-3848
TF: 800-422-6237 ■ *Web:* www.cancer.gov
National Eye Institute 2020 Vision Pl .... Bethesda MD 20892 301-496-5248 402-1065
Web: www.nei.nih.gov
National Human Genome Research Institute
31 Ctr Dr Bldg 31 Rm 4B09 .... Bethesda MD 20892 301-402-0911 402-2218
Web: www.genome.gov
National Institute of Arthritis & Musculoskeletal & Skin Diseases
31 Ctr Dr MSC 2350 Bldg 31 Rm 4C02 .... Bethesda MD 20892 301-496-8190 480-2814
Web: www.niams.nih.gov
National Institute of Dental & Craniofacial Research
31 Ctr Dr .... Bethesda MD 20892 301-496-3571 402-2185
Web: www.nidcr.nih.gov
National Institute of Environmental Health Sciences
PO Box 12233 .... Research Triangle Park NC 27709 919-541-3201 541-2260
Web: www.niehs.nih.gov
National Institute of General Medical Sciences
45 Ctr Dr MSC 6200 .... Bethesda MD 20892 301-496-7301
Web: www.nigms.nih.gov
National Institute of Mental Health
6001 Executive Blvd Rm 8184 MSC 9663 .... Bethesda MD 20892 301-443-4513 443-4279
TF: 866-615-6464 ■ *Web:* www.nimh.nih.gov
National Institute of Neurological Disorders & Stroke
PO Box 5801 .... Bethesda MD 20824 301-496-5751
TF: 800-352-9424 ■ *Web:* www.ninds.nih.gov
National Institute of Nursing Research
31 Ctr Dr Bldg 31 Rm 5B10 .... Bethesda MD 20892 301-496-8230 594-3405
Web: www.ninr.nih.gov
National Institute on Aging
31 Ctr Dr Bldg 31 Rm 5C27 MSC 2292 .... Bethesda MD 20892 301-496-1752 496-1072
Web: www.nia.nih.gov
National Institute on Alcohol Abuse & Alcoholism
5635 Fishers Ln MSC 9304 .... Bethesda MD 20892 301-443-3885 443-7043
Web: www.niaaa.nih.gov
National Institute on Deafness & Other Communication Disorders
31 Ctr Dr Bldg 31 Rm 3C35 .... Bethesda MD 20892 301-496-7243 402-0018
TF: 800-241-1044 ■ *Web:* www.nidcd.nih.gov

National Library of Medicine
Lister Hill National Center for Biomedical Communications
8600 Rockville Pike Bldg 38A 7th Fl .... Bethesda MD 20894 301-496-4441 480-3035
Web: www.lhncbc.nlm.nih.gov

National Optical Astronomy Observatories
950 N Cherry Ave .... Tucson AZ 85719 520-318-8163 318-8360
TF: 888-809-4012 ■ *Web:* www.noao.edu

National Radio Astronomy Observatory (NRAO)
520 Edgemont Rd .... Charlottesville VA 22903 434-296-0211 296-0278
Web: www.nrao.edu

National Renewable Energy Laboratory (NREL)
1617 Cole Blvd .... Golden CO 80401 303-275-3000 275-4053
Web: www.nrel.gov

National Research Ctr for Coal & Energy (NRCCE)
West Virginia University
385 Evansdale Dr PO Box 6064 .... Morgantown WV 26506 304-293-2867 293-3749
TF: 800-624-8301 ■ *Web:* www.nrcce.wvu.edu

National Research Ctr on English Learning & Achievement (CELA)
School of Education University of Albany B9
1400 Washington Ave .... Albany NY 12222 518-442-5026 442-5933
Web: www.albany.edu

National Risk Management Research Laboratory
US Environmental Protection Agency
26 Martin Luther King Dr .... Cincinnati OH 45268 513-569-7418 569-7680
Web: www.epa.gov/ordntrnt/ord/nrmrl

National Sedimentation Laboratory PO Box 1157 .... Oxford MS 38655 662-232-2924 281-5706
Web: www.ars.usda.gov/main/site_main.htm?modecode=64-08-05-00

National Severe Storms Laboratory (NSSL)
120 David L Boren Blvd .... Norman OK 73072 405-325-6907
Web: www.nssl.noaa.gov

National Soil Erosion Research Laboratory
USDA/ARS 275 S Russell St .... West Lafayette IN 47907 765-494-8689 494-5948
Web: www.ars.usda.gov/main/site_main.htm?modecode=36021500

National Technical Information Service (NTIS)
5285 Port Royal Rd .... Springfield VA 22161 703-605-6000 605-6900
TF Orders: 800-553-6847 ■ *Web:* www.ntis.gov

National Toxicology Program (NTP)
PO Box 12233 .... Research Triangle Park NC 27709 919-541-0530 541-3687
Web: ntp.niehs.nih.gov

National Undersea Research Ctr for Hawaii & the Western Pacific
University of Hawaii at Manoa
41-305 Kalanianaole Hwy .... Waimanalo HI 96795 808-956-6335 956-9772
TF: 888-800-0460

National Undersea Research Ctr for the Caribbean
Perry Institute for Marine Science Caribbean Marine Research Ctr
100 N US Hwy 1 Ste 202 .... Jupiter FL 33477 561-741-0192 741-0193
Web: www.perryinstitute.org

National Undersea Research Ctr for the Mid-Atlantic Bight
Institute of Marine & Coastal Sciences
Rutgers University 71 Dudley Rd .... New Brunswick NJ 08901 732-932-6555 932-8578
TF: 888-776-6537 ■ *Web:* www.marine.rutgers.edu

National Undersea Research Ctr for the North Atlantic & Great Lakes (NURC)
University of Connecticut at Avery Pt
1080 Shennecossett Rd .... Groton CT 06340 860-405-9121 445-2969
Web: nurtec.uconn.edu

National Undersea Research Ctr for the Southeastern US & Gulf of Mexico (NURC)
University of N Carolina at Wilmington
5600 Marvin K Moss Ln .... Wilmington NC 28409 910-962-2440 962-2444
Web: www.nurp.noaa.gov

National Wetlands Research Ctr
700 Cajundome Blvd .... Lafayette LA 70506 337-266-8500 266-8513
Web: www.usgs.gov/centers/wetland-and-aquatic-research-center-warc

National Wildlife Health Ctr
6006 Schroeder Rd .... Madison WI 53711 608-270-2400 270-2415
TF: 800-232-4636 ■ *Web:* www.nwhc.usgs.gov

National Wildlife Research Ctr
4101 LaPorte Ave .... Fort Collins CO 80521 970-266-6000 266-6032
Web: www.aphis.usda.gov

Nationwide Children's Hospital
700 Children's Dr .... Columbus OH 43205 614-722-2700 722-2716
Web: www.nationwidechildrens.org

Natural Hazards Ctr
University of Colorado 483 UCB .... Boulder CO 80309 303-492-6818 492-2151
Web: www.colorado.edu/hazards

Natural Resource Ecology Laboratory
Colorado State University
Campus Delivery 1499 .... Fort Collins CO 80523 970-491-1982 491-1965
Web: www.nrel.colostate.edu

Natural Resources Research Institute (NRRI)
University of Minnesota Duluth
5013 Miller Trunk Hwy .... Duluth MN 55811 218-720-4294 720-4219
TF: 800-234-0054 ■ *Web:* www.nrri.umn.edu

Naval Health Research Ctr (NHRC)
140 Sylvester Rd .... San Diego CA 92106 619-553-8400 553-9389
Web: www.med.navy.mil/sites/nhrc

Naval Institute for Dental & Biomedical Research (NDRI)
310-A B St Bldg 1-H .... Great Lakes IL 60088 847-688-1900
Web: www.dentalmercury.com

Naval Research Laboratory (NRL)
4555 Overlook Ave SW Code 1000 .... Washington DC 20375 202-767-3403 404-7419
Web: www.nrl.navy.mil

Naval Submarine Medical Research Laboratory (NSMRL)
PO Box 900 .... Groton CT 06349 703-681-9025 694-4809*
**Fax Area Code:* 860 ■ *Web:* www.med.navy.mil/sites/nsmrl/Pages/default.aspx

Naval Surface Warfare Ctr (NSWC)
1333 Isaac Hull Ave SE .... Washington Navy Yard DC 20376 202-781-4123
Web: www.navsea.navy.mil/nswc
Carderock Div 9500 MacArthur Blvd .... West Bethesda MD 20817 202-781-0000 227-3574*
**Fax Area Code:* 301 ■ *Web:* www.navsea.navy.mil/nswc/carderock
Dahlgren Div 6149 Welsh Rd Ste 203 .... Dahlgren VA 22448 877-845-5656
TF: 877-845-5656 ■ *Web:* www.navsea.navy.mil

Naval Undersea Warfare Ctr (NUWC)
1176 Howell St .... Newport RI 02841 401-832-7742 832-4396
Web: www.navsea.navy.mil/nuwc
Keyport Div 610 Dowell St .... Keyport WA 98345 360-396-2699 396-2387
Web: www.navsea.navy.mil/nuwc/keyport/default.aspx
Newport Div 1176 Howell St .... Newport RI 02841 401-832-7742 832-4661
Web: www.navsea.navy.mil/nuwc/default.aspx

Nebraska Ctr for Materials & Nanoscience
855 N 16th St N201 NANO .... Lincoln NE 68588 402-472-7886 472-2879
Web: www.unl.edu/ncmn

NEC Laboratories America Inc
4 Independence Way .... Princeton NJ 08540 609-520-1555
Web: www.nec-labs.com

Nereus Pharmaceuticals Inc
10480 Wateridge Cir .... San Diego CA 92121 858-587-4090
Web: www.nereuspharm.com

Neumedicines Inc 133 N Altadena Dr Ste 310 .... Pasadena CA 91107 626-844-3800
Web: www.neumedicines.com

Neurotech Pharmaceuticals Inc
900 Highland Corporate Dr .... Cumberland RI 02864 401-333-3880
Web: www.neurotechusa.com

Neurotez Inc 991 Hwy 22 Ste 200 A .... Bridgewater NJ 08807 908-998-1340
Web: neurotez.com

New England Primate Research Ctr (NEPRC)
1 Pine Hill Dr PO Box 9102 .... Southborough MA 01772 617-432-1000 786-3317*
**Fax Area Code:* 508 ■ *Web:* www.hms.harvard.edu

NGM Biopharmaceuticals Inc
630 Gateway Blvd .... South San Francisco CA 94080 650-243-5555
Web: www.ngmbio.com

NOAA's Undersea Research Program
Florida Keys Research Program
1315 EW Hwy .... Silver Spring MD 20910 301-734-1000 713-1967
Web: nurp.noaa.gov

Noblis 3150 Fairview Pk Dr S .... Falls Church VA 22042 703-610-2000
Web: www.noblis.org

Non-Intrusive Inspection Technology Inc
23031 Ladbrook Dr .... Dulles VA 20166 703-661-0283
Web: www.niitek.com

North American Science Assoc Inc
6750 Wales Rd .... Northwood OH 43619 419-666-9455 662-4386
TF: 866-666-9455 ■ *Web:* www.namsa.com

North Central Agricultural Research Laboratory (NGIRL)
USDA/ARS 2923 Medary Ave .... Brookings SD 57006 605-693-3241 693-5240
Web: www.ars.usda.gov/main/docs.htm?docid=2357

Northeast Fisheries Science Ctr
166 Water St .... Woods Hole MA 02543 508-495-2000 495-2258
Web: www.nefsc.noaa.gov

Northern Power Systems Inc 29 Pitman Rd .... Barre VT 05641 802-461-2955
TF: 877-906-6784 ■ *Web:* www.northernpower.com

Northern Prairie Wildlife Research Ctr
8711 37th St SE .... Jamestown ND 58401 701-253-5500 253-5553
Web: www.npwrc.usgs.gov

Northern Research Station
11 Campus Blvd Ste 200 .... Newtown Square PA 19073 610-557-4017 557-4095
Web: www.nrs.fs.fed.us

Northwest Fisheries Science Ctr
2725 Montlake Blvd E .... Seattle WA 98112 206-860-3200 860-3217
Web: www.nwfsc.noaa.gov

Notre Dame Radiation Laboratory
University of Notre Dame .... Notre Dame IN 46556 574-631-6163 631-8068
Web: www.rad.nd.edu

Oak Ridge National Laboratory (ORNL)
PO Box 2008 .... Oak Ridge TN 37831 865-576-2900 574-0595*
**Fax:* PR ■ *Web:* www.ornl.gov

Oceanic Institute 41-202 Kalanianaole Hwy .... Waimanalo HI 96795 808-259-7951 259-5971
Web: www.oceanicinstitute.org

Office of Naval Research (ONR)
875 N Randolph St Ste 1425 .... Arlington VA 22217 703-696-5031 696-5940
Web: onr.navy.mil

Phone | Fax

Office of Population Research
Princeton University Wallace Hall 2nd Fl .... Princeton NJ 08544 609-258-4870 258-1039
Web: www.opr.princeton.edu

Ohio State University Police, The
1680 Madison Ave .... Wooster OH 44691 330-287-0111 202-3579
TF: 800-358-4678 ■ *Web:* www.oardc.ohio-state.edu

Oklahoma Medical Research Foundation (OMRF)
825 NE 13th St .... Oklahoma City OK 73104 405-271-6673 271-7510
TF: 800-522-0211 ■ *Web:* www.omrf.org

Oracle Capital LLC 1985 E River Rd Ste 111 .... Tucson AZ 85718 520-319-9958
Web: www.oraclecapital.com

Orca Systems Inc 13025 Danielson St Ste 106 .... Poway CA 92064 858-679-9115
Web: www.orcasystems.com

Oregon National Primate Research Ctr (ONPRC)
3181 SW Sam Jackson Pk Rd .... Portland OR 97239 503-494-8311
Web: www.ohsu.edu

Pacific Disaster Ctr 1305 N Holopono St Ste 2 .... Kihei HI 96753 808-891-0525 891-0526
TF: 888-808-6688 ■ *Web:* www.pdc.org

Pacific Institute for Research & Evaluation
11720 Beltsville Dr Ste 900 .... Calverton MD 20705 301-755-2738 755-2799
Web: www.pire.org

Pacific International Ctr for High Technology Research (PICHTR)
1440 Kapiolani Blvd Ste 1225 .... Honolulu HI 96814 808-943-9581 943-9582
Web: www.pichtr.org

Pacific Island Ecosystems Research Ctr (PIERC)
12201 Sunrise Valley Dr Ste 615 .... Reston VA 20192 888-275-8747
TF: 888-275-8747 ■ *Web:* www.usgs.gov

Pacific Marine Environmental Laboratory (PMEL)
7600 Sand Pt Way NE .... Seattle WA 98115 206-526-6239 526-6815
Web: www.pmel.noaa.gov

Pacific Northwest National Laboratory (PNNL)
902 Battelle Blvd PO Box 999 .... Richland WA 99352 509-375-2121 375-2507*
**Fax:* Mail Rm ■ *TF:* 888-375-7665 ■ *Web:* www.pnl.gov

Pacific Northwest Research Station
333 SW First Ave .... Portland OR 97204 503-808-2100 808-2130
Web: www.fs.fed.us/pnw

Pacific Southwest Research Station
800 Buchanan St .... Albany CA 94710 510-559-6300 559-6440
Web: www.fs.fed.us/psw

Palo Alto Research Ctr Inc (PARC)
3333 Coyote Hill Rd .... Palo Alto CA 94304 650-812-4000 812-4970
Web: www.parc.com

PAREXEL International Corp 195 W St .... Waltham MA 02451 781-487-9900 487-0525
NASDAQ: PRXL ■ *TF:* 800-301-5033 ■ *Web:* www.parexel.com

Parker Mktg Research LLC 5405 Dupont Cir .... Milford OH 45150 513-248-8100
Web: parkerinsights.com

Parks Assoc Inc 15950 N Dallas Pkwy Ste 575 .... Dallas TX 75248 972-490-1113
TF: 800-727-5711 ■ *Web:* www.parksassociates.com

Patuxent Wildlife Research Ctr
12100 Beech Forest Rd .... Laurel MD 20708 301-497-5500 497-5505
Web: www.pwrc.usgs.gov

Peryam & Kroll Research Corp
6323 N Avondale Ave .... Chicago IL 60631 800-281-3155
TF: 800-747-5522

Pfenex Inc 10790 Roselle St .... San Diego CA 92121 858-352-4400
TF: 844-240-0005 ■ *Web:* www.pfenex.com

Phantom Laboratory Inc, The 2727 SR- 29 .... Greenwich NY 12834 518-692-1190 692-3329
TF: 800-525-1190 ■ *Web:* www.phantomlab.com

Pittsburgh Supercomputing Ctr
300 S Craig St .... Pittsburgh PA 15213 412-268-4960 268-5832
TF: 800-221-1641 ■ *Web:* www.psc.edu

Planet Biotechnology Inc 25571 Clawiter Rd .... Hayward CA 94545 510-887-1461
Web: www.planetbiotechnology.com

Plasma Science & Fusion Ctr
Massachusetts Institute of Technology
77 Massachusetts Ave NW16 .... Cambridge MA 02139 617-253-8100 253-0238
Web: www.psfc.mit.edu

Pleora Technologies Inc
340 Terry Fox Dr Ste 300 .... Kanata ON K2K3A2 613-270-0625 270-1425
TF: 888-687-6877 ■ *Web:* www.pleora.com

Plexxikon Inc 91 Bolivar Dr .... Berkeley CA 94710 510-647-4000
Web: plexxikon.com

Plum Island Animal Disease Ctr
1400 Independence Ave. SW .... Washington DC 20250 631-323-3200 323-2507
Web: www.ars.usda.gov/main/site_main.htm?modecode=19400000

Polisher Research Institute
Abramson Ctr for Jewish Life
1425 Horsham Rd .... North Wales PA 19454 215-371-1895 371-3015
Web: www.abramsoncenter.org/research/polisher-research-institute

Population Council
1 Dag Hammarskjold Plz 9th Fl .... New York NY 10017 212-339-0500 755-6052
Web: www.popcouncil.org

Population Research Ctr
University of Chicago 1155 E 60th St .... Chicago IL 60637 773-256-6315 256-6313
Web: popcenter.uchicago.edu

Population Research Institute
Pennsylvania State University
601 Oswald Tower .... University Park PA 16802 814-865-0486 863-8342
Web: www.pop.psu.edu

Positron Inc 5101 Buchan St Ste 220 .... Montreal QC H4P2R9 514-345-2200 345-2271
Web: www.positronpower.com

PPD Inc 929 N Front St .... Wilmington NC 28401 910-251-0081 762-5820
NASDAQ: PPDI ■ *Web:* www.ppdi.com

Precision Filters Inc 240 Cherry St .... Ithaca NY 14850 607-277-3550
Web: www.pfinc.com

Princeton Plasma Physics Laboratory (PPPL)
James Forrestal Campus Princeton University
PO Box 451 .... Princeton NJ 08543 609-243-2750 243-2751
TF: 800-772-2222 ■ *Web:* www.pppl.gov

Providence Health & Services (JWCI)
2200 Santa Monica Blvd .... Santa Monica CA 90404 310-582-7450 315-6148
TF: 800-262-6259 ■ *Web:* california.providence.org/saint-johns

Phone | Fax

Public Health Research Institute (PHRI)
International Ctr for Public Health
225 Warren St .... Newark NJ 07103 973-854-3100 854-3101
Web: www.phri.org

Quantiam Technologies Inc 1651 - 94 St NW .... Edmonton AB T6N1E6 780-462-0707 465-6603
TF: 877-461-0707 ■ *Web:* www.quantiam.com

Quintessence Biosciences Inc 505 S Rosa Rd .... Madison WI 53719 608-441-2950
Web: www.quintbio.com

Quintiles Transnational Corp
4820 Emperor Blvd .... Durham NC 27703 919-998-2000 998-2003
TF: 866-267-4479 ■ *Web:* www.quintiles.com

Radiant Research Inc
11500 Northlake Dr Ste 320 .... Cincinnati OH 45249 513-247-5500 247-5588
TF: 855-427-8839 ■ *Web:* www.radiantresearch.com

Regional Research Institute for Human Services (RRI)
Portland State University
1600 SW Fourth Ave Ste 900 .... Portland OR 97201 503-725-4040 725-2140
Web: www.rri.pdx.edu

Renaissance Computing Institute (RENCI)
100 Europa Dr Ste 540 .... Chapel Hill NC 27517 919-445-9640 445-9669
Web: www.renci.org

Research for Better Schools Inc
1500 Market St Centre Sq E .... Philadelphia PA 19102 215-568-6150 568-7260
Web: www.rbs.org

Research Foundation of City University of New York, The
230 W 41st St 7th Fl .... New York NY 10036 212-417-8300
Web: www.rfcuny.org

Research Institute on Addictions (RIA)
1021 Main St .... Buffalo NY 14203 716-887-2566 887-2252
Web: buffalo.edu/ria.html

Research Laboratory of Electronics
Massachusetts Institute of Technology
77 Massachusetts Ave Rm 36-413 .... Cambridge MA 02139 617-253-2519 253-1301
Web: www.rle.mit.edu

Research Triangle Institute
3040 Cornwallis Rd
PO Box 12194 .... Research Triangle Park NC 27709 919-541-6000 541-5985
TF: 800-334-8571 ■ *Web:* www.rti.org

Ricerca Biosciences LLC 7528 Auburn Rd .... Concord OH 44077 440-357-3300 354-6276
TF: 888-742-3722 ■ *Web:* www.ricerca.com

Rivel Research Group Inc 830 Post Rd E .... Westport CT 06880 203-226-0800
Web: www.rivel.com

Robotics Institute
Carnegie Mellon University
5000 Forbes Ave .... Pittsburgh PA 15213 412-268-3818 268-6436
TF: 800-767-8483 ■ *Web:* www.ri.cmu.edu

Rocky Mountain Research Station
US Forest Service 240 W Prospec .... Fort Collins CO 80526 970-498-1100 498-1010
Web: www.fs.fed.us/rm

Rodale Institute 611 Siegfriedale Rd .... Kutztown PA 19530 610-683-1400 683-8548
Web: www.rodaleinstitute.org

Rose F. Kennedy Ctr
Albert Einstein College of Medicine
1410 Pelham Pkwy S .... Bronx NY 10461 718-430-8500 918-7505
Web: www.einstein.yu.edu

Roswell Park Cancer Institute
Elm and Carlton St .... Buffalo NY 14263 716-845-2300
TF: 877-275-7724 ■ *Web:* www.roswellpark.org

Roubini Global Economics LLC
95 Morton St 6th Fl .... New York NY 10014 212-645-0010
Web: roubini.com

Roy J Carver Biotechnology Ctr 1206 W Gregory .... Urbana IL 61801 217-333-1695 244-0466
TF: 800-550-3033 ■ *Web:* www.biotech.illinois.edu

Russell Sage Foundation 112 E 64th St .... New York NY 10021 212-750-6000 371-4761
Web: www.russellsage.org

Rutgers Business School (RBS)
1 Washington Park 3rd Fl .... Newark NJ 07102 973-353-1821
Web: www.business.rutgers.edu/default.aspx?id=645

Sabrient Systems LLC
115 S La Cumbre Ln Ste 100 .... Santa Barbara CA 93105 805-730-7777
TF: 888-502-3605 ■ *Web:* www.sabrient.com

Safety Analysis & Forensic Engineering
5665 Hollister Ave .... Goleta CA 93117 805-964-0676 964-7669
TF: 800-426-7866 ■ *Web:* www.saferesearch.com

Salk Institute for Biological Studies
PO Box 85800 .... San Diego CA 92186 858-453-4100 552-8285
TF: 866-358-4354 ■ *Web:* www.salk.edu

San Diego Supercomputer Ctr (SDSC)
9500 Gilman Dr .... La Jolla CA 92093 858-534-5000 534-5056
Web: www.sdsc.edu

SanBio Inc 231 S Whisman Rd .... Mountain View CA 94041 650-625-8965
Web: www.san-bio.com

Sandelman & Assoc Inc
257 La Paloma Ste 1 .... San Clemente CA 92672 949-388-5600
TF: 888-897-7881 ■ *Web:* www.sandelman.com

Sandia National Laboratories - California (SNL)
7011 E Ave PO Box 969 .... Livermore CA 94551 925-294-3000
Web: www.sandia.gov

Sandia National Laboratories - New Mexico (SNL)
1515 Eubank SE PO Box 5800 .... Albuquerque NM 87123 505-845-0011
Web: www.sandia.gov

Sarnoff Corp 201 Washington Rd PO Box 5300 .... Princeton NJ 08543 609-734-2000
Web: sri.com/engage/products-solutions

Savannah River National Laboratory
Savannah River Site .... Aiken SC 29808 803-725-2854 725-1660
Web: srnl.doe.gov

SC&A Inc 1608 Spring Hill Rd Ste 400 .... Vienna VA 22182 703-893-6600 821-8236
Web: www.scainc.com

Schiefelbusch Institute for Life Span Studies
Univ of Kansas Robert Dole Human Development Ctr
1000 Sunnyside Ave Rm 1052 .... Lawrence KS 66045 785-864-4295 864-5323
Web: www.lsi.ku.edu/lsi

Science Applications International Corp
10260 Campus Pt Dr .... San Diego CA 92121 703-676-4300
Web: www.saic.com

Phone | Fax

Scripps Institution of Oceanography (SIO)
8622 Kennel Way .... La Jolla CA 92037 858-534-3624
Web: scripps.ucsd.edu

Scripps Research Institute
10550 N Torrey Pines Rd .... La Jolla CA 92037 858-784-1000 784-9004*
**Fax:* Hum Res ■ *Web:* www.scripps.edu

SEDL 4700 Mueller Blvd .... Austin TX 78723 512-476-6861 476-2286
TF: 800-476-6861 ■ *Web:* www.sedl.org

SEMATECH 2706 Montopolis Dr........ Austin TX 78741 512-356-3500
Web: www.sematech.org

Sensor Technology Systems Inc
2794 Indian Ripple Rd .... Beavercreek OH 45440 937-490-2509
Web: www.sts-eo.com

SERVE 5900 Summit Ave Ste 201 .... Browns Summit NC 27214 336-315-7400 315-7457
TF: 800-755-3277 ■ *Web:* www.serve.org

Shamrock Structures LLC 1440 Davey Rd .... Woodridge IL 60517 630-739-3215
Web: www.shamrockstructures.com

Sharp Laboratories Of America Inc
5750 NW Pacific Rim Blvd .... Camas WA 98607 360-817-8400 817-7544
Web: www.sharplabs.com

Shiley-Marcos Alzheimer's Disease Research Ctr
8950 Villa La Jolla Dr Ste C129........ La Jolla CA 92037 858-622-5800 622-1012
Web: www.adrc.ucsd.edu

Sidney Kimmel Comprehensive Cancer Ctr at Johns Hopkins
401 N Broadway The Harry & Jeanette Weinberg Bldg
Ste 1100........ Baltimore MD 21231 410-955-5222 955-6787
Web: www.hopkinsmedicine.org

SIS International Research Inc
11 E 22nd St 2nd Fl .... New York NY 10010 212-505-6805
Web: www.sisinternational.com

Siteman Cancer Ctr 4921 Parkview Pl .... Saint Louis MO 63110 314-362-5196
TF: 800-600-3606 ■ *Web:* www.siteman.wustl.edu

SIU's Advanced Coal and Energy Research Center
Southern Illinois University 504 W Grand........ Carbondale IL 62902 618-536-5521 453-7346
Web: acerc.siu.edu

Smith-Kettlewell Eye Research Institute
2318 Fillmore St........ San Francisco CA 94115 415-345-2000 345-8455
Web: www.ski.org

Smithsonian Environmental Research Ctr
647 Contees Wharf Rd PO Box 28 .... Edgewater MD 21037 443-482-2200 482-2380
Web: www.serc.si.edu

Smithsonian Tropical Research Institute (STRI)
9100 Panama City PL........ Washington DC 20521 703-487-3770 786-2557*
**Fax Area Code:* 202 ■ *Web:* www.stri.si.edu

SNBL USA Ltd 6605 Merrill Creek Pkwy........ Everett WA 98203 425-407-0121
Web: snbl.com

Social & Economic Sciences Research Ctr (SESRC)
Washington State University
Wilson Hall Rm 133 PO Box 644014........ Pullman WA 99164 509-335-1511 335-0116
TF: 800-932-5393 ■ *Web:* www.sesrc.wsu.edu

Socratic Technologies Inc
2505 Mariposa St........ San Francisco CA 94110 415-430-2200
TF: 800-576-2728 ■ *Web:* www.sotech.com

Software Engineering Institute (SEI)
4500 Fifth Ave .... Pittsburgh PA 15213 412-268-5800 268-6257*
**Fax:* Cust Svc ■ *TF:* 888-201-4479 ■ *Web:* www.sei.cmu.edu

Software Engineering Services Corp
1311 Ft Crook Rd S .... Bellevue NE 68005 402-292-8660 292-3271
TF: 800-244-1278 ■ *Web:* www.sessolutions.com

Somnus Therapeutics Inc
135 Us Hwy 202/206 Ste 9........ Bedminster NJ 07921 908-901-0300
Web: www.softekinfo.com

Southeast Fisheries Science Ctr
75 Virginia Beach Dr........ Miami FL 33149 305-361-4200 361-4219
Web: www.sefsc.noaa.gov

Southern California Earthquake Ctr
3651 Trousdale Pkwy Ste 169 .... Los Angeles CA 90089 213-740-5843 740-0011
Web: www.scec.org

Southern Regional Research Ctr (SRRC)
1100 Robert E Lee Blvd PO Box 19687........ New Orleans LA 70179 706-546-3527 286-4419*
**Fax Area Code:* 504 ■ *Web:* www.ars.usda.gov/main/site_main.htm?modecode=64350000

Southern Research Institute
2000 Ninth Ave S .... Birmingham AL 35205 205-581-2000 581-2726
TF: 800-967-6774 ■ *Web:* www.sri.org

Southern Research Station
USDA Forest Service 200 W.T. Weaver Blvd........ Asheville NC 28804 828-257-4300 257-4840
Web: www.srs.fs.usda.gov

Southwest National Primate Research Ctr (SNPRC)
Texas Biomedical Research Institute
PO Box 760549 .... San Antonio TX 78245 210-258-9400
Web: www.snprc.org

Southwest Research Institute (SwRI)
6220 Culebra Rd........ San Antonio TX 78238 210-684-5111 522-3496*
**Fax:* Hum Res ■ *Web:* swri.org

Space Dynamics Laboratory
1695 N Research Pkwy........ North Logan UT 84341 435-797-4600 797-4495
TF: 866-487-2365 ■ *Web:* www.sdl.usu.edu

Space Physics Research Laboratory
2455 Hayward St University of Michigan .... Ann Arbor MI 48109 734-936-7775 763-0437
Web: www.sprl.umich.edu

Space Science & Engineering Ctr
University of Wisconsin 1225 W Dayton St .... Madison WI 53706 608-262-0544 262-5974
TF: 866-391-1753 ■ *Web:* www.ssec.wisc.edu

Space Telescope Science Institute
3700 San Martin Dr .... Baltimore MD 21218 410-338-4700 338-4767
Web: www.stsci.edu

SPAWAR (SPAWAR) 53560 Hull St........ San Diego CA 92152 619-553-2717
Web: www.public.navy.mil/spawar/Pages/default.aspx

SPINS Inc 222 W hubbard St Ste 300........ Schaumburg IL 60654 847-908-1200
Web: www.spins.com

SRI International 333 Ravenswood Ave .... Menlo Park CA 94025 650-859-2000 326-5512
Web: www.sri.com

Stanford Cancer Ctr
875 Lake Blake Wilbur Dr........ Stanford CA 94305 650-498-6000 724-1433
TF: 800-422-6237 ■ *Web:* med.stanford.edu/cancer.html

Phone | Fax

Stanford Linear Accelerator Ctr (SLAC)
2575 Sand Hill Rd .... Menlo Park CA 94025 650-926-3300 926-4999
Web: www.slac.stanford.edu

Stanford Prevention Research Ctr (SPRC)
291 Campus Dr Li Ka Shing Bldg........ Stanford CA 94305 650-723-6254 725-6906
Web: prevention.stanford.edu

Stanford Synchrotron Radiation Lightsource (SSRL)
2575 Sand Hill Rd MS 69........ Menlo Park CA 94025 650-926-2079 926-3600
Web: www-ssrl.slac.stanford.edu

Stevenson Co, The
10002 Shelbyville Rd Ste 201........ Louisville KY 40223 502-271-5250
Web: www.stevensoncompany.com

Superclick Networks Inc
10222 Blvd Saint-Michel .... Montreal QC H1H5H1 514-847-0333

Supercomputing Institute for Digital Simulation & Advanced Computation
University of Minnesota
599 Walter Library 117 Pleasant St SE........ Minneapolis MN 55455 612-625-1818 624-8861
Web: www.msi.umn.edu

Survey Sampling International LLC
6 Research Dr........ Shelton CT 06484 203-567-7200
Web: www.surveysampling.com

Synchrotron Radiation Ctr (SRC)
3731 Schneider Dr .... Stoughton WI 53589 608-877-2000 877-2001
Web: www.src.wisc.edu

Synergy Co of Utah LLC, The
2279 S Resource Blvd .... Moab UT 84532 800-723-0277
TF: 800-723-0277 ■ *Web:* www.thesynergycompany.com

Syntron Bioresearch Inc 2774 Loker Ave W .... Carlsbad CA 92010 760-930-2200 930-2212
Web: www.syntron.net

Syracuse Research Corp (SRC)
7502 Round Pond Rd .... North Syracuse NY 13212 315-452-8000
TF: 800-724-0451 ■ *Web:* www.srcinc.com

Technology Service Corp
962 Wayne Ave Ste 800 .... Silver Spring MD 20910 301-565-2970 565-0673
TF: 800-324-7700 ■ *Web:* tsc.com

Tempra Technology Inc 6140 15th St E .... Bradenton FL 34203 941-739-8900
Web: www.tempratech.com

TERC 2067 Massachusetts Ave 2nd Fl........ Cambridge MA 02140 617-547-0430 349-3535
Web: www.terc.edu

Texas Ctr for Superconductivity
3201 Cullen Blvd Ste 202........ Houston TX 77204 713-743-8200 743-8201
Web: www.tcsuh.com

Therapeutics Inc 9025 Balboa Ave Ste 100 .... San Diego CA 92123 858-571-1800
Web: www.therapeuticsinc.com

Thomas Jefferson National Accelerator Facility
12000 Jefferson Ave........ Newport News VA 23606 757-269-7100 269-7363
Web: www.jlab.org

TMR Inc 450 Pkwy .... Broomall PA 19008 610-359-0696
Web: www.tmrinfo.com

Transportation Research Ctr Inc (TRC Inc)
10820 State Rt 347 PO Box B-67 .... East Liberty OH 43319 937-666-2011 666-5066
TF: 800-837-7872 ■ *Web:* www.trcpg.com

Transportation Technology Ctr Inc
55500 DOT Rd PO Box 11130 .... Pueblo CO 81001 719-584-0750 584-0711
Web: www.aar.com

Trex Enterprises Corp 10455 Pacific Ctr Ct........ San Diego CA 92121 858-646-5300 646-5301
TF: 800-626-5885 ■ *Web:* www.trexenterprises.com

TRICOR Systems Inc 1650 Todd Farm Dr........ Elgin IL 60123 847-742-5542
Web: www.tricor-systems.com

Tris Pharma Inc
2033 Rt 130 Brunswick Business Pk
Ste D........ Monmouth Junction NJ 08852 732-940-2800 940-2855
Web: www.trispharma.com

Turner-Fairbank Highway Research Ctr
6300 Georgetown Pike .... McLean VA 22101 800-424-9071 493-3170*
**Fax Area Code:* 202 ■ *TF:* 800-424-9071 ■ *Web:* www.fhwa.dot.gov

UAB Comprehensive Cancer Ctr
University of Alabama at Birmingham
1824 Sixth Ave S .... Birmingham AL 35294 205-934-4011
TF: 800-294-7780 ■ *Web:* www3.ccc.uab.edu

UNC Neuroscience Ctr
University of N Carolina
115 Mason Farm Rd CB 7250 .... Chapel Hill NC 27599 919-843-8536 966-1050
TF: 800-862-4938 ■ *Web:* www.med.unc.edu/neuroscience

University of Maryland Ctr for Environmental Science (UMCES)
2020 Horn Pt Rd........ Cambridge MD 21613 410-228-9250 228-3843
TF: 866-842-2520 ■ *Web:* www.umces.edu

University of Michigan Transportation Research Institute (UMTRI)
2901 Baxter Rd........ Ann Arbor MI 48109 734-764-6504 936-1081
Web: www.umtri.umich.edu

University of Texas Institute for Geophysics (UTIG)
JJ Pickle Research Campus Bldg 196
10100 Burnet Rd (RR2200)........ Austin TX 78758 512-471-6156 471-8844
Web: www.ig.utexas.edu

US Army Aeromedical Research Laboratory
MCMR-UAC Bldg 6901 .... Fort Rucker AL 36362 334-255-6920 255-6933
TF: 888-386-7635 ■ *Web:* www.usaarl.army.mil

US Army Armament Research Development & Engineering Ctr (ARDEC)
Technical & Industrial Liaison Officer........ Picatinny NJ 07806 973-724-9623 724-3044
Web: www.pica.army.mil

US Army Aviation & Missile Research Development & Engineering Ctr (AMRDEC)
5400 Bldg........ Redstone Arsenal AL 35898 256-313-5742 876-9142

US Army Corps of Engineers Institute for Water Resources
Hydrologic Engineering Ctr 609 Second St .... Davis CA 95616 530-756-1104 756-8250
Web: www.hec.usace.army.mil

US Army Engineer Research & Development Ctr (ERDC)
3909 Halls Ferry Rd .... Vicksburg MS 39180 601-634-3188 634-2388
TF: 800-522-6937 ■ *Web:* www.erdc.usace.army.mil

US Army Institute of Surgical Research (USAISR)
3698 Chambers Pass Ste B .... Fort Sam Houston TX 78234 210-539-3219 227-8502
Web: www.usaisr.amedd.army.mil

US Army Medical Research & Materiel Command (USAMRMC)
820 Chandler St .... Fort Detrick MD 21702 301-619-2471
Web: www.mrmc.smallbusopps.army.mil

Phone | Fax

US Army Medical Research Institute of Chemical Defense (USAMRICD)
3100 Ricketts Point Rd .... Aberdeen Proving Ground MD 21010 410-436-3276 436-1960
Web: usamricd.apgea.army.mil

US Army Medical Research Institute of Infectious Diseases (USAMRIID)
Attn: MCMR-UIZ-R 1425 Porter St .... Frederick MD 21702 301-619-2285
Web: www.usamriid.army.mil

US Army Research Laboratory (ARL)
Attn: AMSRD-ARL-O-PA 2800 Powder Mill Rd .... Adelphi MD 20783 301-394-2500 394-1174
Web: www.arl.army.mil

US Coast Guard Research & Development Ctr
1082 Shennecossett Rd .... Groton CT 06340 860-441-2600 441-2792
Web: www.uscg.mil/hq

US Dairy Forage Research Ctr (DFRC)
1925 Linden Dr W .... Madison WI 53706 608-890-0050
Web: ars.usda.gov

US Horticultural Research Laboratory
2001 S Rock Rd .... Fort Pierce FL 34945 772-462-5800 462-5986
Web: www.ars.usda.gov/Main/docs.htm?docid=7376

US Salinity Laboratory
USDA/ARS 450 W Big Springs Rd .... Riverside CA 92507 951-369-4815 369-4818
Web: www.ars.usda.gov/AboutUs/AboutUs.htm?modecode=53-10-20-00

US Vegetable Laboratory
USDA/ARS 2700 Savannah Hwy .... Charleston SC 29414 843-402-5300
Web: www.ars.usda.gov/main/docs.htm?docid=5953

USC Information Sciences Institute
4676 Admiralty Way Ste 1001 .... Marina del Rey CA 90292 310-822-1511 823-6714
Web: isi.edu

USGS Forest & Rangeland Ecosystem Science Ctr
777 NW Ninth St Ste 400 .... Corvallis OR 97330 541-750-1030 750-1069
Web: fresc.usgs.gov

USGS Leetown Science Ctr
11649 Leetown Rd .... Kearneysville WV 25430 304-724-4400 724-4410
Web: www.lsc.usgs.gov

USGS Northern Rocky Mountain Science Ctr (NRMSC)
2327 University Way Ste 2 .... Bozeman MT 59715 406-994-4293 994-6556
Web: www.usgs.gov/centers/norock/connect

USGS Southwest Biological Science Ctr
2255 N Gemini Dr MS-9394 .... Flagstaff AZ 86001 928-556-7094 556-7092
Web: sbsc.wr.usgs.gov

USGS Upper Midwest Environmental Sciences Ctr
2630 Fanta Reed Rd .... La Crosse WI 54603 608-783-6451 783-6066
Web: www.umesc.usgs.gov

USGS Western Fisheries Research Ctr
US Geological Survey 6505 NE 65th St .... Seattle WA 98115 206-526-6282 526-6654
Web: wfrc.usgs.gov

UT-Battelle LLC 1201 Oak Ridge Tpke Ste 100 .... Oak Ridge TN 37830 865-220-5101

Vanderbilt Kennedy Ctr for Research on Human Development
21st Ave S .... Nashville TN 37203 615-322-8240 322-8236
TF: 800-772-1213 ■ *Web:* vkc.mc.vanderbilt.edu

Venture Design Services Inc 1051 SE St .... Anaheim CA 92805 510-744-3720
Web: www.venture.com.sg

Virginia Institute of Marine Science (VIMS)
1208 Greate Rd PO Box 1346 .... Gloucester Point VA 23062 804-684-7000 684-7097
Web: www.vims.edu

Virobay Inc 1360 Willow Rd Ste 100 .... Menlo Park CA 94025 650-833-5700
Web: www.virobayinc.com

Visidyne Inc 111 S Bedford St Ste 103 .... Burlington MA 01803 781-273-2820 272-1068
Web: www.visidyne.com

Wadsworth Ctr
Biggs Laboratory New York Dept of Health
Empire State Plz PO Box 509 .... Albany NY 12201 518-474-2160
Web: www.wadsworth.org

Waisman Ctr
University of Wisconsin 1500 Highland Ave .... Madison WI 53705 608-263-5940 263-0529
TF: 888-428-8476 ■ *Web:* www.waisman.wisc.edu

Walter Reed Army Institute of Research (WRAIR)
MCMR-UWZ 503 Robert Grant Ave .... Silver Spring MD 20910 301-319-9471 319-9227
Web: wrair-www.army.mil

Washington National Primate Research Ctr (WNPRC)
1705 NE Pacific St PO Box 357330 .... Seattle WA 98195 206-543-0440 616-6771
Web: www.wanprc.org

WestEd 730 Harrison St 5th Fl .... San Francisco CA 94107 415-565-3000 565-3012
TF: 877-493-7833 ■ *Web:* www.wested.org

Western Environmental Technology Laboratories Inc
620 Applegate St .... Philomath OR 97370 541-929-5650
Web: www.wetlabs.com

Western Regional Research Ctr (WRRC)
800 Buchanan St .... Albany CA 94710 510-559-5600 559-5963
Web: www.ars.usda.gov/main/docs.htm?docid=5819

Western Research Institute 365 N Ninth St .... Laramie WY 82072 307-721-2011 721-2345
Web: westernresearch.org

Wisconsin Ctr for Education Research
University of Wisconsin Madison
1025 W Johnson St .... Madison WI 53706 608-263-4200 263-6448
Web: www.wcer.wisc.edu

Wisconsin National Primate Research Ctr
1220 Capitol Ct .... Madison WI 53715 608-263-3500 265-2067
TF: 800-833-7050 ■ *Web:* www.primate.wisc.edu

Wistar Institute 3601 Spruce St .... Philadelphia PA 19104 215-898-3700 898-3715
TF: 800-724-6633 ■ *Web:* wistar.org

WM Keck Ctr for Comparative & Functional Genomics
1201 W Gregory Dr .... Urbana IL 61801 217-244-3930 244-0466
Web: www.biotech.uiuc.edu

WM Keck Observatory 65-1120 Mamalahoa Hwy .... Kamuela HI 96743 808-885-7887 885-4464
Web: www.keckobservatory.org

Woods Hole Oceanographic Institution (WHOI)
266 Woods Hole Rd .... Woods Hole MA 02543 508-289-2282 457-2109*
**Fax:* Hum Res ■ *Web:* www.whoi.edu

Xenon Pharmaceuticals Inc 3650 Gilmore Way .... Burnaby BC V5G4W8 604-484-3300 484-3450
Web: www.xenon-pharma.com

Yale Child Study Ctr
Yale University 230 S Frontage Rd .... New Haven CT 06520 203-785-2540 785-7611
Web: www.medicine.yale.edu

Yerkes National Primate Research Ctr
Emory University 954 Gatewood Rd .... Atlanta GA 30322 404-727-7732 727-3108
Web: www.yerkes.emory.edu

669 RESORTS & RESORT COMPANIES

See Also Casinos p. 1894; Dude Ranches p. 2203; Hotels - Conference Center p. 2530; Hotels & Hotel Companies p. 2536; Spas - Hotel & Resort p. 3187

Alabama

Phone | Fax

Joe Wheeler Resort Lodge & Convention Ctr
4401 McLean Dr .... Rogersville AL 35652 256-247-5461 247-5471
TF: 800-544-5639 ■ *Web:* www.alapark.com/joewheeler

Perdido Beach Resort
27200 Perdido Beach Blvd .... Orange Beach AL 36561 251-981-9811 981-5670
TF: 800-634-8001 ■ *Web:* www.perdidobeachresort.com

StillWaters Resort 797 Moonbrook Dr .... Dadeville AL 36853 256-825-1353 825-1717
Web: www.stillwatersgolf.com

Alaska

Phone | Fax

Alyeska Prince Hotel & Resort
1000 Arlberg Ave PO Box 249 .... Girdwood AK 99587 907-754-1111 754-2200
TF: 800-880-3880 ■ *Web:* www.alyeskaresort.com

Pybus Point Lodge PO Box 33497 .... Juneau AK 99803 907-790-4866 790-4866
TF: 800-947-9287 ■ *Web:* pybuspoint.com

Alberta

Phone | Fax

Fairmont Banff Springs PO Box 960 .... Banff AB T1L1J4 403-762-2211 762-5755
TF: 800-441-1414 ■ *Web:* www.fairmont.com

Fairmont Chateau Lake Louise
111 Lk Louise Dr .... Lake Louise AB T0L1E0 403-522-3511 522-3834
TF: 800-441-1414 ■ *Web:* www.fairmont.com

Rimrock Resort Hotel, The
300 Mountain Ave PO Box 1110 .... Banff AB T1L1J2 403-762-3356 762-4132
TF: 888-746-7625 ■ *Web:* www.rimrockresort.com

Waterton Lakes Lodge Resort
101 Clematis Ave PO Box 4 .... Waterton Park AB T0K2M0 403-859-2150
TF: 888-985-6343 ■ *Web:* www.watertonlakeslodge.com

Arizona

Phone | Fax

Arizona Biltmore Resort & Spa
2400 E Missouri .... Phoenix AZ 85016 602-955-6600 381-7600
TF: 800-950-0086 ■ *Web:* www.arizonabiltmore.com

Arizona Golf Resort & Conference Ctr
425 S Power Rd .... Mesa AZ 85206 480-832-3202 981-0151
TF: 800-528-8282 ■ *Web:* www.arizonagolfresort.com

Arizona Grand Resort
8000 S Arizona Grand Pkwy .... Phoenix AZ 85044 602-438-9000 431-6535
TF: 866-267-1321 ■ *Web:* www.arizonagrandresort.com

Boulders Resort & Golden Door Spa
34631 N Tom Darlington Dr PO Box 2090 .... Carefree AZ 85377 480-488-9009
TF: 888-579-2631 ■ *Web:* www.theboulders.com

Camelback Inn JW Marriott Resort Golf Club & Spa
5402 E Lincoln Dr .... Scottsdale AZ 85253 480-948-1700
TF: 800-242-2635 ■ *Web:* www.marriott.com

Canyon Ranch Tucson 8600 E Rockcliff Rd .... Tucson AZ 85750 520-749-9000 749-1646
TF: 800-742-9000 ■ *Web:* www.canyonranchdestinations.com/tucson

Chaparral Suites Resort & Conference Ctr
5001 N Scottsdale Rd .... Scottsdale AZ 85250 480-949-1414 947-2675
TF: 866-534-1797 ■ *Web:* www.chaparralsuites.com

CopperWynd Resort & Club
13225 N Eagle Ridge Dr .... Fountain Hills AZ 85268 480-333-1900
TF: 877-707-7760 ■ *Web:* www.copperwynd.com

Doubletree Paradise Valley Resort
5401 N Scottsdale Rd .... Scottsdale AZ 85250 480-947-5400 443-9702
TF: 800-222-8733 ■ *Web:* www3.hilton.com

Enchantment Resort 525 Boynton Canyon Rd .... Sedona AZ 86336 800-826-4180 282-9249*
**Fax Area Code:* 928 ■ *TF:* 800-826-4180 ■ *Web:* www.enchantmentresort.com

Esplendor Resort at Rio Rico
1069 Camino Caralampi .... Rio Rico AZ 85648 520-281-1901
TF: 800-288-4746 ■ *Web:* www.esplendor-resort.com

Fairmont Scottsdale Princess
7575 E Princess Dr .... Scottsdale AZ 85255 480-585-4848 585-0086
TF: 800-257-7544 ■ *Web:* www.fairmont.com

FireSky Resort & Spa 4925 N Scottsdale Rd .... Scottsdale AZ 85251 480-945-7666 946-4056
TF: 800-528-7867 ■ *Web:* www.fireskyresort.com

Four Seasons Resort Scottsdale at Troon North
10600 E Crescent Moon Dr .... Scottsdale AZ 85262 480-515-5700 515-5599
TF: 800-332-3442 ■ *Web:* www.fourseasons.com

Francisco Grande Hotel & Golf Resort
26000 Gila Bend Hwy .... Casa Grande AZ 85222 520-836-6444 421-0544
TF General: 800-237-4238 ■ *Web:* www.franciscogrande.com

Gold Canyon Golf Resort
6100 S Kings Ranch Rd .... Gold Canyon AZ 85118 480-982-9090 830-5211
TF: 800-827-5281 ■ *Web:* www.gcgr.com

Hacienda del Sol Guest Ranch Resort
5501 N Hacienda Del Sol Rd .... Tucson AZ 85718 520-299-1501
TF: 800-728-6514 ■ *Web:* www.haciendadelsol.com

Harrah's Ak-Chin Casino Resort
15406 Maricopa Rd .... Maricopa AZ 85139 480-802-5000
TF General: 800-427-7247 ■ *Web:* www.totalrewards.com

Hilton Sedona Resort & Spa 90 Ridge Trl Dr .... Sedona AZ 86351 928-284-4040
TF General: 877-273-3762 ■ *Web:* www3.hilton.com/en/index.html

Phone Fax

JW Marriott Desert Ridge Resort & Spa
5350 E Marriott Dr . . . Phoenix AZ 85054 480-293-5000 293-3600
TF: 800-845-5279 ■ *Web:* www.marriott.com/hotels/travel/phxdr

Lake Powell Resorts & Marinas 100 Lakeshore Dr. . . . Page AZ 86040 888-896-3829 326-2670*
**Fax Area Code:* 580 ■ *TF:* 800-622-6317 ■ *Web:* www.travelok.com

Legacy Golf Resort 6808 S 32nd St. . . . Phoenix AZ 85042 602-305-5500 305-5501
TF: 888-828-3673 ■ *Web:* www.shellhospitality.com

Lodge at Ventana Canyon - A Wyndham Luxury Resort
6200 N Clubhouse Ln. . . . Tucson AZ 85750 520-577-1400
TF: 800-828-5701 ■ *Web:* www.thelodgeatventanacanyon.com

Loews Ventana Canyon Resort 7000 N Resort Dr . . . Tucson AZ 85750 520-299-2020 299-6832
TF: 800-234-5117 ■ *Web:* www.loewshotels.com

Los Abrigados Resort 160 Portal Ln . . . Sedona AZ 86336 928-282-1777 282-2614
TF: 877-374-2582 ■ *Web:* www.diamondresorts.com

Millennium Resort Scottsdale McCormick Ranch
7401 N Scottsdale Rd . . . Scottsdale AZ 85253 716-681-2400 991-5572*
**Fax Area Code:* 480 ■ *TF:* 800-243-1332 ■ *Web:* millenniumhotels.com

Omni Tucson National Golf Resort & Spa
2727 W Club Dr . . . Tucson AZ 85742 520-297-2271 297-7544
Web: www.tucsonnational.com

Orange Tree Golf & Conference Resort
10601 N 56th St . . . Scottsdale AZ 85254 480-948-6100 483-6074
TF: 866-729-7159 ■
Web: shellhospitality.com/en/orange-tree-golf-resort

Phoenician, The 6000 E Camelback Rd . . . Scottsdale AZ 85251 480-941-8200 947-4311
TF: 800-888-8234 ■ *Web:* www.thephoenician.com

Pointe Hilton at Squaw Peak Resort
7677 N 16th St . . . Phoenix AZ 85020 602-997-2626 875-1652*
**Fax Area Code:* 281 ■ *TF:* 800-685-0550 ■
Web: www3.hilton.com/en/hotels/arizona/pointe-hilton-tapatio-cliffs-resort-phxtcpr/index.html

Pointe Hilton Resort at Tapatio Cliffs
11111 N Seventh St . . . Phoenix AZ 85020 602-866-7500 875-1652*
**Fax Area Code:* 281 ■ *TF:* 800-947-9784 ■
Web: www3.hilton.com/en/hotels/arizona/pointe-hilton-tapatio-cliffs-resort-phxtcpr/index.html

Rancho de los Caballeros
1551 S Vulture Mine Rd . . . Wickenburg AZ 85390 928-684-5484
TF: 800-684-5030 ■ *Web:* www.ranchodeloscaballeros.com

Royal Palms Resort & Spa 5200 E Camelback Rd . . . Phoenix AZ 85018 602-840-3610 840-6927
TF: 800-672-6011 ■ *Web:* www.royalpalmshotel.com

Saguaro Lake Ranch 13020 Bush Hwy . . . Mesa AZ 85215 480-984-2194
Web: www.saguarolakeranch.com

Sanctuary on Camelback Mountain
5700 E McDonald Dr . . . Paradise Valley AZ 85253 480-948-2100
TF: 800-245-2051 ■ *Web:* www.sanctuaryoncamelback.com

Scottsdale Camelback Resort
6302 E Camelback Rd. . . . Scottsdale AZ 85251 480-947-3300
TF: 800-891-8585 ■ *Web:* www.scottsdalecamelback.com

Scottsdale Cottonwoods Resort & Suites
6160 N Scottsdale Rd . . . Scottsdale AZ 85253 480-991-1414 951-3350

Scottsdale Plaza Resort
7200 N Scottsdale Rd . . . Scottsdale AZ 85253 480-948-5000 998-5971
TF: 800-832-2025 ■ *Web:* www.scottsdaleplaza.com

Sheraton Wild Horse Pass Resort & Spa
5594 W Wild Horse Pass Blvd . . . Chandler AZ 85226 602-225-0100 225-0300
TF: 800-325-3535 ■ *Web:* www.wildhorsepassresort.com

Tanque Verde Guest Ranch
14301 E Speedway Blvd . . . Tucson AZ 85748 520-296-6275 721-9426
TF: 800-234-3833 ■ *Web:* www.tanqueverderanch.com

Westward Look Resort 245 E Ina Rd . . . Tucson AZ 85704 520-297-1151 297-9023
TF: 800-722-2500 ■ *Web:* www.westwardlook.com

Wigwam Golf Resort & Spa
300 E Wigwam Blvd . . . Litchfield Park AZ 85340 623-935-3811 935-3737
TF: 800-327-0396 ■ *Web:* wigwamarizona.com

Arkansas

Phone Fax

Arlington Resort Hotel & Spa
239 Central Ave . . . Hot Springs AR 71901 501-623-7771
TF: 800-643-1502 ■ *Web:* www.arlingtonhotel.com

Best Western Inn of the Ozarks
207 W Van Buren . . . Eureka Springs AR 72632 479-253-9768 253-9768
TF: 800-552-3785 ■ *Web:* www.bestwestern.com

Gaston's White River Resort 1777 River Rd. . . . Lakeview AR 72642 870-431-5202
Web: www.gastons.com

British Columbia

Phone Fax

Coast Hotels & Resorts Canada
1090 W Georgia St . . . Vancouver BC V6E3V7 604-682-7982 682-8942
Web: www.coasthotels.com

Delta Whistler Village Suites 4308 Main St . . . Whistler BC V0N1B4 604-905-3987
TF: 888-299-3987 ■ *Web:* www.deltahotels.com

Fairmont Chateau Whistler 4599 Chateau Blvd . . . Whistler BC V0N1B4 604-938-8000 938-2291
TF: 800-441-1414 ■ *Web:* www.fairmont.com

Four Seasons Resort Whistler
4591 Blackcomb Way . . . Whistler BC V0N1B4 604-935-3400 935-3455
Web: www.fourseasons.com/whistler

Harrison Hot Springs Resort & Spa
100 Esplanade Ave . . . Harrison Hot Springs BC V0M1K0 604-796-2244 796-3682
TF: 800-663-2266 ■ *Web:* www.harrisonresort.com

Hilton Whistler Resort & Spa
4050 Whistler Way . . . Whistler BC V0N1B4 604-932-1982 966-5093
TF: 800-515-4050 ■ *Web:* www.hiltonwhistler.com

Holiday Inn SunSpree Resort Whistler Village
4295 Blackcomb Way . . . Whistler BC V0N1B4 604-938-0878
Web: www.ihg.com

Holiday Trails Resorts (Western) Inc
53730 Bridal Falls Rd . . . Rosedale BC V0X1X1 604-794-7876 794-3756
TF: 800-663-2265 ■ *Web:* www.holidaytrailsresorts.com

Pan Pacific Whistler Mountainside
4320 Sundial Crescent . . . Whistler BC V0N1B4 604-905-2999 905-2995
TF: 888-905-9995 ■ *Web:* www.panpacific.com

Phone Fax

River Rock Casino Resort 8811 River Rd . . . Richmond BC V6X3P8 604-247-8900 207-2641
TF: 866-748-3718 ■ *Web:* www.riverrock.com

Tantalus Resort Lodge 4200 Whistler Way . . . Whistler BC V0N1B4 604-932-4146 932-2405
TF: 888-806-2299 ■ *Web:* www.tantaluslodge.com

Whistler Blackcomb Mountain Ski Resort
4545 Blackcomb Way . . . Whistler BC V0N1B4 604-932-3434 938-7527
TF: 800-766-0449 ■ *Web:* www.whistlerblackcomb.com

California

Phone Fax

Alisal Guest Ranch & Resort 1054 Alisal Rd . . . Solvang CA 93463 805-688-6411 688-2510
TF: 800-425-4725 ■ *Web:* www.alisal.com

Bacara Resort & Spa 8301 Hollister Ave . . . Santa Barbara CA 93117 805-968-0100 968-1800
TF: 855-968-0100 ■ *Web:* meritagecollection.com/bacararesort

Bahia Resort Hotel 998 W Mission Bay Dr . . . San Diego CA 92109 858-488-0551 488-7055
TF: 800-576-4229 ■ *Web:* www.bahiahotel.com

Barona Resort & Casino
1932 Wildcat Canyon Rd . . . Lakeside CA 92040 619-443-2300 443-2856
TF: 888-722-7662 ■ *Web:* www.barona.com

Bear Mountain Golf Course
43101 Gold Mine Dr PO Box 77 . . . Big Bear Lake CA 92315 909-866-5766
TF: 844-462-2327 ■ *Web:* www.bigbearmountainresorts.com

Calistoga Ranch 580 Lommel Rd . . . Calistoga CA 94515 707-254-2800 254-2825
TF: 800-942-4220 ■ *Web:* calistogaranch.aubergeresorts.com

Carmel Valley Ranch Resort 1 Old Ranch Rd. . . . Carmel CA 93923 831-625-9500 624-2858
TF: 866-405-5037 ■ *Web:* www.carmelvalleyranch.com

Casa Palmero 1518 Cypress Dr. . . . Pebble Beach CA 93953 831-622-6650 622-6655
TF: 800-654-9300 ■ *Web:* pebblebeach.com

Catalina Canyon Resort & Spa
888 Country Club Dr . . . Avalon CA 90704 310-510-0325 510-0900
Web: www.catalinacanyonresort.com

Chaminade 1 Chaminade Ln . . . Santa Cruz CA 95065 831-475-5600 476-4798
TF: 800-283-6569 ■ *Web:* www.chaminade.com

Claremont Resort & Spa 41 Tunnel Rd . . . Berkeley CA 94705 510-843-3000 848-6208
TF: 800-551-7266 ■ *Web:* www.fairmont.com/claremont-berkeley

Costanoa Coastal Lodge & Camp
2001 Rossi Rd . . . Pescadero CA 94060 650-879-1100 879-2275
TF: 877-262-7848 ■ *Web:* www.costanoa.com

Desert Hot Springs Spa Hotel
10805 Palm Dr . . . Desert Hot Springs CA 92240 760-329-6000
TF: 800-808-7727 ■ *Web:* www.dhsspa.com

Desert Springs Marriott Resort & Spa
74855 Country Club Dr . . . Palm Desert CA 92260 760-341-2211 341-1872
TF: 888-538-9459 ■ *Web:* www.marriott.com

Double Eagle Resort & Spa 5587 Hwy 158 . . . June Lake CA 93529 760-648-7004
Web: www.doubleeagle.com

Dr Wilkinson's Hot Springs Resort
1507 Lincoln Ave . . . Calistoga CA 94515 707-942-4102 942-4412
Web: www.drwilkinson.com

Elkhorn Golf Club 1050 Elkhorn Dr. . . . Stockton CA 95209 209-474-3900
Web: www.elkhorngc.com

Fairmont Sonoma Mission Inn & Spa, The
PO Box 1447 . . . Sonoma CA 95476 707-938-9000 938-4250
TF: 866-540-4499 ■ *Web:* www.fairmont.com/sonoma

Fess Parker's Doubletree Resort (FPDTR)
633 E Cabrillo Blvd. . . . Santa Barbara CA 93103 805-564-4333
TF: 800-879-2929 ■ *Web:* www.fessparkersantabarbarahotel.com

Flamingo Resort Hotel & Conference Ctr
2777 Fourth St . . . Santa Rosa CA 95405 707-545-8530 528-1404
TF: 800-848-8300 ■ *Web:* www.flamingoresort.com

Four Seasons Resort Santa Barbara
1260 Ch Dr. . . . Santa Barbara CA 93108 805-969-2261 565-8323
TF: 800-819-5053 ■ *Web:* www.fourseasons.com

Furnace Creek Inn & Ranch Resort
Hwy 190 . . . Death Valley CA 92328 760-786-2345 786-2514
TF: 800-236-7916 ■ *Web:* www.furnacecreekresort.com

Grand Pacific Palisades Resort & Hotel
5805 Armada Dr . . . Carlsbad CA 92008 760-827-3200 827-3210
TF: 800-725-4723 ■ *Web:* www.grandpacificpalisades.com

Greenhorn Creek Resort
711 McCauley Ranch Rd . . . Angels Camp CA 95222 209-729-8111 736-4728
TF: 888-736-5900 ■ *Web:* www.greenhorncreek.com

Handlery Hotel & Resort 950 Hotel Cir N . . . San Diego CA 92108 619-298-0511
TF: 800-676-6567 ■ *Web:* www.handlery.com

Harrah's Rincon Casino & Resort
777 Harrah's Rincon Way . . . Valley Center CA 92082 760-751-3100
TF: 800-522-4700 ■ *Web:* www.totalrewards.com

Hilton San Diego Resort
1775 E Mission Bay Dr. . . . San Diego CA 92109 619-276-4010 275-8944
TF: 800-445-8667 ■ *Web:* www.hilton.com

Hotel Del Coronado 1500 Orange Ave . . . Coronado CA 92118 619-435-6611 522-8262
TF: 800-468-3533 ■ *Web:* www.hoteldel.com

Indian Springs Resort & Spa
1712 Lincoln Ave . . . Calistoga CA 94515 707-942-4913 942-4919
TF: 800-877-3623 ■ *Web:* www.indianspringscalistoga.com

Indian Wells Resort Hotel
76-661 Hwy 111 . . . Indian Wells CA 92210 760-345-6466 772-5083
TF: 800-248-3220 ■ *Web:* www.indianwellsresort.com

Inn at Rancho Santa Fe
5951 Linea Del Cielo PO Box 869 . . . Rancho Santa Fe CA 92067 858-756-1131
TF: 800-843-4661 ■ *Web:* www.theinnatrsf.com

Inn at Spanish Bay, The 2700 17-Mile Dr. . . . Pebble Beach CA 93953 831-647-7500 622-3603
TF: 800-654-9300 ■ *Web:* www.pebblebeach.com

Knott's Berry Farm Resort
7675 Crescent Ave . . . Buena Park CA 90620 714-995-1111 220-5124
TF: 866-752-2444 ■ *Web:* www.knotts.com

L'Auberge Del Mar
1540 Camino del Mar PO Box 2880 . . . Del Mar CA 92014 858-259-1515 755-4940
TF: 800-245-9757 ■ *Web:* www.laubergedelmar.com

La Jolla Beach & Tennis Club
2000 Spindrift Dr . . . La Jolla CA 92037 858-454-7126 456-3805
TF: 888-828-0948 ■ *Web:* www.ljbtc.com

Phone | Fax

La Quinta Resort & Club
49-499 Eisenhower Dr ... La Quinta CA 92253 760-564-4111 564-7625
TF: 800-598-3828 ■ *Web:* www.laquintaresort.com

Laguna Cliffs Marriott Resort
25135 Pk Lantern ... Dana Point CA 92629 949-661-5000 661-5358
TF: 800-545-7483 ■ *Web:* www.lagunacliffs.com

Lake Arrowhead Resort & Spa
27984 Hwy 189 ... Lake Arrowhead CA 92352 909-336-1511 744-3088
TF: 800-800-6792 ■ *Web:* www.lakearrowheadresort.com

Lakeland Village Beach & Mountain Resort
3535 Lake Tahoe Blvd ... South Lake Tahoe CA 96150 530-544-1685
TF: 888-484-7094 ■ *Web:* lakeland--village.com

Le Parker Meridien Palm Springs
4200 E Palm Canyon Dr ... Palm Springs CA 92264 760-770-5000 324-2188
Web: www.starwoodhotels.com/lemeridien

Leisure Sports Inc
7077 Koll Ctr Pkwy Ste 110 ... Pleasanton CA 94566 925-600-1966 643-7950*
**Fax Area Code:* 949 ■ *TF:* 888-239-0930 ■ *Web:* clubsports.com

Lodge at Pebble Beach 1700 17-Mile Dr ... Pebble Beach CA 93953 831-624-3811 625-8598
TF: 800-654-9300 ■ *Web:* www.pebblebeach.com

Lodge at Sonoma - A Renaissance Resort & Spa
1325 Broadway ... Sonoma CA 95476 707-935-6600 935-6829
TF: 866-263-0758 ■ *Web:* www.marriott.com

Lodge at Torrey Pines Inn
11480 N Torrey Pines Rd ... La Jolla CA 92037 858-453-4420
Web: www.lodgeattorreypines.com

Loews Coronado Bay Resort
4000 Coronado Bay Rd ... Coronado CA 92118 619-424-4000 424-4400
TF: 800-815-6397 ■ *Web:* www.loewshotels.com/hotels/sandiego

Mammoth Mountain Resort
10001 Minaret Rd ... Mammoth Lakes CA 93546 760-934-2571 934-0615
TF: 800-626-6684 ■ *Web:* www.mammothmountain.com

Meadowood Napa Valley 900 Meadowood Ln ... Saint Helena CA 94574 707-963-3646 963-3532
TF: 800-458-8080 ■ *Web:* www.meadowood.com

Miramonte Resort & Spa
45000 Indian Wells Ln ... Indian Wells CA 92210 760-341-2200 568-0541
TF: 800-237-2926 ■ *Web:* www.miramonteresort.com

Montage Resort & Spa 30801 S Coast Hwy ... Laguna Beach CA 92651 949-715-6000
TF: 866-271-6953 ■ *Web:* montagehotels.com/lagunabeach

Morgan Run Resort & Club
5690 Cancha de Golf ... Rancho Santa Fe CA 92091 858-756-2471
TF Resv: 800-378-4653 ■ *Web:* www.clubcorp.com

Morongo Casino Resort & Spa
49500 Seminole Dr ... Cabazon CA 92230 951-849-3080
TF: 800-252-4499 ■ *Web:* www.morongocasinoresort.com

Mount Shasta Resort
1000 Siskiyou Lk Blvd ... Mount Shasta CA 96067 530-926-3030 926-0333
TF: 800-958-3363 ■ *Web:* www.mountshastaresort.com

Northstar-at-Tahoe PO Box 129 ... Truckee CA 96160 800-466-6784 562-3812*
**Fax Area Code:* 530 ■ *TF:* 800-466-6784 ■ *Web:* www.northstarcalifornia.com

Ojai Valley Inn & Spa 905 Country Club Rd ... Ojai CA 93023 805-640-2068 646-0904
TF: 800-422-6524 ■ *Web:* www.ojairesort.com

Pacific Palms Conference Resort
1 Industry Hills Pkwy ... City of Industry CA 91744 626-810-4455 964-9535
TF Cust Svc: 800-524-4557 ■ *Web:* www.pacificpalmsresort.com

Pala Casino Resort & Spa 35008 Pala-Temecula Rd ... Pala CA 92059 760-510-5100 510-5191
TF: 877-946-7252 ■ *Web:* www.palacasino.com

Pala Mesa Resort 2001 Old Hwy 395 ... Fallbrook CA 92028 760-728-5881 723-8292
TF: 800-722-4700 ■ *Web:* www.palamesa.com

Palm Mountain Resort & Spa
155 S BelaRdo Rd ... Palm Springs CA 92262 760-325-1301 323-8937
TF: 800-622-9451 ■ *Web:* www.palmmountainresort.com

Paradise Point Resort & Spa
1404 W Vacation Rd ... San Diego CA 92109 858-274-4630 581-5924
TF: 800-344-2626 ■ *Web:* www.paradisepoint.com

Pechanga Resort & Casino
45000 Pechanga Pkwy ... Temecula CA 92592 951-693-1819 695-7410
TF: 877-711-2946 ■ *Web:* www.pechanga.com

Quail Lodge Resort & Golf Club
8205 Valley Greens Dr ... Carmel CA 93923 831-624-2888
TF: 866-675-1101 ■ *Web:* www.quaillodge.com

Rancho Valencia Resort
5921 Valencia Cir PO Box 9126 ... Rancho Santa Fe CA 92067 858-756-1123 756-0165
TF: 800-548-3664 ■ *Web:* www.ranchovalencia.com

Renaissance Esmeralda Resort
44-400 Indian Wells Ln ... Indian Wells CA 92210 760-773-4444 346-9308
TF: 888-236-2427 ■ *Web:* www.marriott.com

Resort at Squaw Creek
400 Squaw Creek Rd PO Box 3333 ... Olympic Valley CA 96146 530-583-6300 581-6632
TF: 800-327-3353 ■ *Web:* www.squawcreek.com

Ritz-Carlton Half Moon Bay
1 Miramontes Pt Rd ... Half Moon Bay CA 94019 650-712-7000 712-7015
TF General: 800-241-3333 ■ *Web:* www.ritzcarlton.com

Ritz-Carlton Laguna Niguel, The
1 Ritz Carlton Dr ... Dana Point CA 92629 949-240-2000
TF: 800-542-8680 ■ *Web:* www.ritzcarlton.com/resorts/laguna_niguel

Saint Regis Monarch Beach Resort & Spa
1 Monarch Beach Resort ... Dana Point CA 92629 949-234-3200 234-3201
TF: 800-722-1543 ■ *Web:* www.stregismb.com

San Vicente Inn & Golf Course
24157 San Vicente Rd ... Ramona CA 92065 760-789-3788 788-6115
TF: 800-776-1289 ■ *Web:* www.sdcea.net

San Ysidro Ranch 900 San Ysidro Ln ... Santa Barbara CA 93108 805-565-1700 565-1995
Web: www.sanysidroranch.com

Sea Venture Resort 100 Ocean View Ave ... Pismo Beach CA 93449 805-773-4994 773-0924
TF: 800-443-7778 ■ *Web:* www.seaventure.com

Shadow Mountain Resort & Club
45-750 San Luis Rey ... Palm Desert CA 92260 760-346-6123
TF: 800-472-3713 ■ *Web:* www.shadowmountainresort.com

Silverado Resort & Spa 1600 Atlas Peak Rd ... Napa CA 94558 707-257-0200 257-2867
TF: 800-532-0500 ■ *Web:* www.silveradoresort.com

Snow Valley Mountain Resort
35100 State Hwy 18 PO Box 2337 ... Running Springs CA 92382 909-867-2751 867-7687
TF: 800-680-7669 ■ *Web:* www.snow-valley.com

Phone | Fax

Spa Resort, The 401 E Amado Rd ... Palm Springs CA 92262 800-854-1279
TF: 800-854-1279 ■ *Web:* www.sparesortcasino.com

Squaw Valley USA PO Box 2007 ... Olympic Valley CA 96146 800-403-0206 581-7106*
**Fax Area Code:* 530 ■ *TF:* 800-403-0206 ■ *Web:* squawalpine.com

Stonepine 150 E Carmel Vly Rd ... Carmel Valley CA 93924 831-659-2245 659-5160
Web: www.stonepineestate.com

Tahoe Seasons Resort
3901 Saddle Rd PO Box 16300 ... South Lake Tahoe CA 96150 530-541-6700 541-0653
Web: tahoeseasons.com

Temecula Creek Inn 44501 Rainbow Canyon Rd ... Temecula CA 92592 855-685-9299 676-8961*
**Fax Area Code:* 951 ■ *TF:* 877-517-1823 ■ *Web:* www.temeculacreekinn.com

Town & Country Resort Hotel
500 Hotel Cir N ... San Diego CA 92108 619-291-7131 291-3584
TF: 800-772-8527 ■ *Web:* www.destinationhotels.com/town-country

Two Bunch Palms Resort & Spa
67425 Two Bunch Palms Trl ... Desert Hot Springs CA 92240 760-329-8791 329-1874
TF: 800-472-4334 ■ *Web:* www.twobunchpalms.com

Ventana Inn 48123 Hwy 1 ... Big Sur CA 93920 831-667-2331 667-0573
TF: 800-628-6500 ■ *Web:* www.ventanainn.com

Welk Resort Branson 8860 Lawrence Welk Dr ... Escondido CA 92026 417-336-3575
TF: 800-505-9355 ■ *Web:* welkresorts.com

Welk Resort San Diego
8860 Lawrence Welk Dr ... Escondido CA 92026 760-749-3000 749-9537
TF Resv: 800-932-9355 ■ *Web:* welkresorts.com

Winner's Cir Resort 550 Via de la Valle ... Solana Beach CA 92075 858-755-6666 481-3706
TF: 800-874-8770 ■ *Web:* www.winnerscircleresort.com

Colorado

Phone | Fax

Aspen Meadows Resort 845 Meadows Rd ... Aspen CO 81611 970-925-4240 925-7790
TF: 800-452-4240 ■ *Web:* www.aspenmeadows.com

Aspen Skiing Co 117 ABC ... Aspen CO 81611 970-925-1220 925-2647
TF: 855-754-2863 ■ *Web:* www.aspensnowmass.com

Beaver Run Resort & Conference Ctr
620 Village Rd ... Breckenridge CO 80424 970-453-6000
TF: 800-525-2253 ■ *Web:* www.beaverrun.com

Broadmoor, The 1 Lake Ave ... Colorado Springs CO 80906 719-577-5775 577-5738
TF: 866-837-9520 ■ *Web:* www.broadmoor.com

C Lazy U Ranch
3640 Colorado Hwy 125 PO Box 379 ... Granby CO 80446 970-887-3344 887-3917
Web: www.clazyu.com

Copper Mountain Resort
209 Ten Mile Cir PO Box 3001 ... Copper Mountain CO 80443 970-968-2882 968-3155
TF: 888-219-2441 ■ *Web:* www.coppercolorado.com

Crested Butte Mountain Resort (CBMR)
12 Snowmass Rd PO Box 5700 ... Crested Butte CO 81225 877-547-5143 349-2250*
**Fax Area Code:* 970 ■ *TF:* 877-547-5143 ■ *Web:* www.skicb.com/cbmr

Destination Hotels & Resorts Inc
10333 E Dry Creek Rd Ste 450 ... Englewood CO 80112 303-799-3830 799-6011
TF: 855-893-1011 ■ *Web:* www.destinationhotels.com

Grand Lodge Crested Butte 6 Emmons Rd ... Crested Butte CO 81225 970-349-8000 349-4265
TF: 877-547-5143

Hot Springs Lodge & Pool
415 E Sixth St PO Box 308 ... Glenwood Springs CO 81602 970-945-6571 947-2950
TF: 800-537-7946 ■ *Web:* www.hotspringspool.com

Indian Hot Springs
302 Soda Creek Rd PO Box 1990 ... Idaho Springs CO 80452 303-989-6666
Web: www.indianhotsprings.com

Intrawest ULC 1621 18th St Ste 300 ... Denver CO 80202 303-749-8370
Web: www.intrawest.com

Inverness Hotel & Golf Club
200 Inverness Dr W ... Englewood CO 80112 303-799-5800 799-5874
TF: 800-346-4891 ■ *Web:* www.invernesshotel.com

Keystone Resort 21996 Hwy 6 PO Box 38 ... Keystone CO 80435 970-496-2316
TF: 877-625-1556 ■ *Web:* www.keystoneresort.com

Manor Vail Lodge 595 E Vail Vly Dr ... Vail CO 81657 970-476-5000
TF: 800-950-8245 ■ *Web:* www.manorvail.com

Mountain Lodge at Telluride
457 Mtn Village Blvd ... Telluride CO 81435 970-369-5000 369-4317
TF: 866-368-6867 ■ *Web:* www.mountainlodgetelluride.com

Omni Interlocken Resort
500 Interlocken Blvd ... Broomfield CO 80021 303-438-6600
TF: 800-843-6664 ■ *Web:* www.omnihotels.com

Park Hyatt Beaver Creek Resort & Spa
136 E Thomas Pl ... Avon CO 81620 970-949-1234 949-4164
TF Cust Svc: 800-233-1234 ■ *Web:* beavercreek.park.hyatt.com/en/hotel/home.html

Peaks Resort & Golden Door Spa
136 Country Club Dr ... Telluride CO 81435 800-789-2220
TF: 800-789-2220 ■ *Web:* www.thepeaksresort.com

Ritz-Carlton Bachelor Gulch 0130 Daybreak Ridge ... Avon CO 81620 970-748-6200 343-1070
TF: 800-241-3333 ■ *Web:* www.ritzcarlton.com

Saint Regis Resort Aspen 315 E Dean St ... Aspen CO 81611 970-920-3300
TF: 888-627-7198 ■ *Web:* www.stregisaspen.com

Snowmass Club PO Box G-2 ... Snowmass Village CO 81615 970-923-5600 923-6944
Web: www.snowmassclub.com

Sonnenalp Resort of Vail 20 Vail Rd ... Vail CO 81657 970-476-5656 476-1639
TF: 800-654-8312 ■ *Web:* www.sonnenalp.com

Steamboat Grand Resort Hotel & Conference Ctr
2300 Mt Werner Cir ... Steamboat Springs CO 80487 970-871-5500 871-5501
TF: 877-269-2628 ■ *Web:* www.steamboatgrand.com

Steamboat Ski & Resort Corp
2305 Mt Werner Cir ... Steamboat Springs CO 80487 970-879-6111 879-4757
TF: 877-237-2628 ■ *Web:* www.steamboat.com

Torian Plum Condo Resort
1855 Ski Time Sq Dr ... Steamboat Springs CO 80487 970-879-8811
TF: 800-228-2458 ■ *Web:* www.wyndhamvacationrentals.com

Vail Cascade Resort & Spa 1300 Westhaven Dr ... Vail CO 81657 970-476-7111 479-7020
TF: 800-420-2424 ■ *Web:* www.vailcascade.com

Vail Resorts Management Co
390 Interlocken Crescent Ste 1000 ... Broomfield CO 80021 303-404-1800 404-6415
NYSE: MTN ■ *TF:* 800-842-8062 ■ *Web:* www.vailresorts.com

				Phone	Fax
Village at Breckenridge Resort 535 S Pk Ave *Web:* www.breckenridgesports.com	Breckenridge	CO	80424	970-453-3000	
Wyndham Vacation Rentals 14 Sylvan Way **Fax Area Code:* 970 ■ *TF:* 800-467-3529 ■ *Web:* www.wyndhamvacationrentals.com	Vail	CO	81657	973-753-6300	476-7423*

Connecticut

				Phone	Fax
Heritage Hotel 522 Heritage Rd. *Web:* www.heritagesouthbury.com	Southbury	CT	06488	203-264-8200	264-5035
Interlaken Inn 74 Interlaken Rd Rt 12 *TF:* 800-222-2909 ■ *Web:* www.interlakeninn.com	Lakeville	CT	06039	860-435-9878	435-2980
Mohegan Sun Resort & Casino 1 Mohegan Sun Blvd *TF:* 888-226-7711 ■ *Web:* www.mohegansun.com	Uncasville	CT	06382	860-862-8150	
Saybrook Point Inn & Spa 2 Bridge St *TF:* 800-243-0212 ■ *Web:* www.saybrook.com	Old Saybrook	CT	06475	860-395-2000	
Water's Edge Resort & Spa 1525 Boston Post Rd PO Box 688 *TF:* 800-222-5901 ■ *Web:* www.watersedgeresortandspa.com	Westbrook	CT	06498	860-399-5901	399-8644

Florida

				Phone	Fax
Amelia Island Plantation 39 Beach Lagoon Rd. *TF:* 800-834-4900 ■ *Web:* www.villasofameliaisland.com	Amelia Island	FL	32034	904-261-6161	
Americano Beach Resort 1260 N Atlantic Ave *Web:* www.thesuitesatamericanobeach.com	Daytona Beach	FL	32118	386-255-7431	253-9513
Bahia Mar Beach Resort & Yachting Ctr 801 Seabreeze Blvd *TF:* 888-802-2442 ■ *Web:* doubletree3.hilton.com/en/hotels/florida/bahia-mar-fort-lauderdale-beach-a-doubletree-by-hilton-hotel-fllbmdt/index.html	Fort Lauderdale	FL	33316	954-764-2233	523-5424
Banyan Resort 323 Whitehead St *TF:* 866-371-9222 ■ *Web:* www.thebanyanresort.com	Key West	FL	33040	305-296-7786	294-1107
Bay Hill Golf Club & Lodge 9000 Bay Hill Blvd *TF:* 888-422-9445 ■ *Web:* www.bayhill.com	Orlando	FL	32819	407-876-2429	876-1035
Beachcomber Resort Hotel & Villas 1200 S Ocean Blvd *TF:* 800-231-2423 ■ *Web:* www.beachcomberresort.com	Pompano Beach	FL	33062	954-941-7830	942-7680
Biltmore Hotel & Conference Ctr of the Americas 1200 Anastasia Ave *TF Cust Svc:* 800-727-1926 ■ *Web:* www.biltmorehotel.com	Coral Gables	FL	33134	305-445-1926	
Bluewater Bay Resort 2000 Bluewater Blvd *TF:* 800-874-2128 ■ *Web:* www.bwbresort.com	Niceville	FL	32578	850-897-3613	897-2424
Boca Raton Resort & Club 501 E Camino Real *TF:* 888-543-1224 ■ *Web:* www.bocaresort.com	Boca Raton	FL	33432	561-447-3000	447-5073
Breakers, The 1 S County Rd *TF:* 888-273-2537 ■ *Web:* www.thebreakers.com	Palm Beach	FL	33480	561-655-6611	659-8403
Buena Vista Hospitality Group Inc 6750 Forum Dr Ste 316 *Web:* www.bvhg.com	Orlando	FL	32821	407-352-7161	352-2413
Buena Vista Palace Hotel & Spa 1900 N Buena Vista Dr *TF:* 866-397-6516 ■ *Web:* www.buenavistapalace.com	Lake Buena Vista	FL	32830	866-397-6516	
Casa Marina Resort & Beach Club 1500 Reynolds St *Web:* www.casamarinaresort.com	Key West	FL	33040	305-296-3535	296-4633
Casa Ybel Resort 2255 W Gulf Dr *TF:* 800-276-4753 ■ *Web:* www.casaybelresort.com	Sanibel Island	FL	33957	239-472-3145	
Choice Hotels International Inc 621 S Atlantic Ave *Web:* www.choicehotels.com/ascend	Ormond Beach	FL	32176	386-672-4550	
Club Med Sandpiper 4500 SE Pine Vly St *TF:* 888-932-2582 ■ *Web:* clubmed.co.in	Port Saint Lucie	FL	34952	772-398-5100	398-5103
Deauville Beach Resort 6701 Collins Ave *TF:* 800-327-6656 ■ *Web:* deauvillebeachresortmiami.com	Miami Beach	FL	33141	305-865-8511	861-2367
Disney's All-Star Movies Resort 1901 W Buena Vista Dr. *Web:* disneyworld.disney.go.com/resorts/all-star-movies-resort	Lake Buena Vista	FL	32830	407-939-7000	939-7111
Disney's All-Star Music Resort 1801 W Buena Vista Dr. *Web:* disneyworld.disney.go.com	Lake Buena Vista	FL	32830	407-939-6000	939-7222
Disney's All-Star Sports Resort 1701 W Buena Vista Dr. *Web:* www.disneyworld.disney.go.com	Lake Buena Vista	FL	32830	407-939-5000	939-7333
Disney's BoardWalk Resort 2101 N Epcot Resort Blvd. *Web:* disneyworld.disney.go.com	Lake Buena Vista	FL	32830	407-939-5100	939-5150
Disney's Caribbean Beach Resort 900 Cayman Way *Web:* disneyworld.disney.go.com/resorts/caribbean-beach-resort	Lake Buena Vista	FL	32830	407-934-3400	
Disney's Contemporary Resort 4600 N World Dr *Web:* disneyworld.disney.go.com/resorts/contemporary-resort	Lake Buena Vista	FL	32830	407-824-1000	824-3539
Disney's Coronado Springs Resort 1000 W Buena Vista Dr. *Web:* www.disneyworld.disney.go.com	Lake Buena Vista	FL	32830	407-939-1000	939-1001
Disney's Fort Wilderness Resort & Campground 4510 Ft Wilderness Trl *Web:* www.disneyworld.disney.go.com	Lake Buena Vista	FL	32830	407-824-2900	824-3508
Disney's Grand Floridian Resort & Spa 4401 Floridian Way *Web:* www.disneyworld.disney.go.com	Lake Buena Vista	FL	32830	407-824-3000	824-3186
Disney's Old Key West Resort 1510 N Cove Rd *Web:* disneyworld.disney.go.com/resorts/old-key-west-resort	Lake Buena Vista	FL	32830	407-827-7700	827-7710
Disney's Polynesian Resort 1600 Seven Seas Dr *Web:* disneyworld.disney.go.com/resorts/polynesian-resort	Lake Buena Vista	FL	32830	407-824-2000	824-3174
Disney's Pop Century Resort 1050 Century Dr *Web:* disneyworld.disney.go.com	Lake Buena Vista	FL	32830	407-938-4000	938-4040
Disney's Port Orleans Resort-French Quarter 2201 Orleans Dr *Web:* www.disneyworld.disney.go.com	Lake Buena Vista	FL	32830	407-934-5000	934-5353
Disney's Port Orleans Resort-Riverside 1251 Riverside Dr. *Web:* disneyworld.disney.go.com/resorts/port-orleans-resort-riverside	Lake Buena Vista	FL	32830	407-934-6000	934-5777
Disney's Wilderness Lodge 901 Timberline Dr. *Web:* disneyworld.disney.go.com/resorts/wilderness-lodge-resort	Lake Buena Vista	FL	32830	407-824-3200	824-3232
Disney's Yacht Club Resort 1700 EPCOT Resorts Blvd *Web:* www.disneyworld.disney.go.com	Lake Buena Vista	FL	32830	407-934-7000	934-3850
Don CeSar Beach Resort - A Loews Hotel 3400 Gulf Blvd **Fax:* Sales ■ *TF:* 888-430-4999 ■ *Web:* www.loewshotels.com	Saint Pete Beach	FL	33706	727-360-1881	360-1881*
Don Shula's Hotel & Golf Club 6842 Main St *Web:* www.donshulahotel.com	Miami Lakes	FL	33014	305-821-1150	820-8087
Doral Golf Resort & Spa 4400 NW 87th Ave *TF:* 800-713-6725 ■ *Web:* www.trumphotelcollection.com	Miami	FL	33178	305-592-2000	592-2000
DoubleTree Resort by Hilton Hotel Grand Key (DGKR) 3990 S Roosevelt Blvd *TF:* 888-844-0454 ■ *Web:* doubletree3.hilton.com	Key West	FL	33040	305-293-1818	296-6962
Eden Roc - A Renaissance Beach Resort & Spa 4525 Collins Ave *TF:* 855-433-3676 ■ *Web:* edenrocmiami.com	Miami Beach	FL	33140	305-531-0000	674-5555
Fisher Island Club & Resort 1 Fisher Island Dr *TF Resv:* 800-537-3708 ■ *Web:* www.fisherislandclub.com	Miami	FL	33109	305-535-6000	535-6003
Fontainebleau Miami Beach 4441 Collins Ave *TF:* 800-548-8886 ■ *Web:* fontainebleau.com	Miami Beach	FL	33140	305-538-2000	
Four Seasons Resort Palm Beach 2800 S Ocean Blvd *TF:* 800-432-2335 ■ *Web:* www.fourseasons.com/palmbeach	Palm Beach	FL	33480	561-582-2800	547-1374
Galleon Resort & Marina 617 Front St *TF:* 800-544-3030 ■ *Web:* www.galleonresort.com	Key West	FL	33040	305-296-7711	296-0821
Gaylord Palms Resort & Convention Ctr 6000 W Osceola Pkwy *Web:* www.marriott.com	Kissimmee	FL	34746	407-586-0000	
Grand Palms Hotel & Golf Resort 110 Grand Palms Dr *TF:* 800-327-9246 ■ *Web:* www.grandpalmsresort.com	Pembroke Pines	FL	33027	954-431-8800	435-5988
Grenelefe Golf & Tennis Resort 3271 Camelot Dr *Web:* www.thelefe.com	Haines City	FL	33844	863-422-7511	
Hammock Beach Resort 200 Ocean Crest Dr *TF:* 866-841-0287 ■ *Web:* www.hammockbeach.com	Palm Coast	FL	32137	386-246-5500	
Harborside Suites At Little Harbor 611 Destiny Dr **Fax Area Code:* 813 ■ *TF:* 800-327-2773 ■ *Web:* www.staylittleharbor.com	Ruskin	FL	33570	800-327-2773	922-6171*
Hard Rock Hotel at Universal Orlando Resort 5800 Universal Blvd *TF:* 888-430-4999 ■ *Web:* www.loewshotels.com	Orlando	FL	32819	407-503-2000	503-2010
Hawk's Cay Resort & Marina 61 Hawk's Cay Blvd *TF:* 888-395-5539 ■ *Web:* www.hawkscay.com	Duck Key	FL	33050	305-743-7000	743-5215
Hilton Longboat Key Beach Resort 4711 Gulf of Mexico Dr *Web:* www3.hilton.com/en/index.html	Longboat Key	FL	34228	941-383-2451	383-7979
Hilton Marco Island Beach Resort 560 S Collier Blvd *Web:* www3.hilton.com/en/index.html	Marco Island	FL	34145	239-394-5000	394-8410
Hilton Sandestin Beach Golf Resort & Spa 4000 Sandestin Blvd S *TF:* 800-559-1805 ■ *Web:* hiltonsandestinbeach.com	Destin	FL	32550	850-267-9500	267-3076
Holiday Inn Express & Suites Oceanfront 3301 S Atlantic Ave *TF:* 800-633-8464 ■ *Web:* www.ihg.com	Daytona Beach Shores	FL	32118	386-767-1711	
Holiday Inn Resort Lake Buena Vista 13351 SR 535 *TF Sales:* 866-808-8833 ■ *Web:* www.hiresortlbv.com	Orlando	FL	32821	407-239-4500	
Holiday Isle Beach Resort & Marina 84001 Overseas Hwy *TF:* 877-712-2842 ■ *Web:* www.holidayisle.com	Islamorada	FL	33036	305-664-2321	664-2703
Innisbrook Resort & Golf Club 36750 US Hwy 19 N *TF:* 800-492-6899 ■ *Web:* www.innisbrookgolfresort.com	Palm Harbor	FL	34684	727-942-2000	942-5576
Inverrary Resort 3501 Inverrary Blvd *Web:* inverrary.com	Fort Lauderdale	FL	33319	954-485-0500	
Janus Hotels & Resorts Inc 2300 Corporate Blvd NW Ste 232 *Web:* www.janushotels.com	Boca Raton	FL	33431	561-997-2325	997-5331
Jupiter Beach Resort 5 N A1A *TF:* 877-389-0571 ■ *Web:* www.jupiterbeachresort.com	Jupiter	FL	33477	561-746-2511	
JW Marriott Orlando Grande Lakes Resort 4040 Central Florida Pkwy *TF:* 800-576-5750 ■ *Web:* www.grandelakes.com	Orlando	FL	32837	407-206-2300	206-2301
Key Largo Grande Resort & Beach Club 97000 S Overseas Hwy *TF Resv:* 888-871-3437 ■ *Web:* www.keylargoresort.com	Key Largo	FL	33037	305-852-5553	
Key Largo Marriott Bay Resort 103800 Overseas Hwy *TF Resv:* 888-731-9056 ■ *Web:* www.marriottkeylargo.com	Key Largo	FL	33037	305-453-0000	
La Cita Country Club 777 Country Club Dr *Web:* www.lacitacc.com	Titusville	FL	32780	321-383-2582	267-4209
La Playa Beach & Golf Resort 9891 Gulf Shore Dr. *TF:* 800-237-6883 ■ *Web:* www.laplayaresort.com	Naples	FL	34108	239-597-3123	597-6278

Name / Address	City	State	Zip	Phone	Fax
Lago Mar Resort & Club 1700 S Ocean Ln — *TF:* 855-209-5677 ■ *Web:* www.lagomar.com	Fort Lauderdale	FL	33316	954-678-3915	
Little Palm Island Resort & Spa 28500 Overseas Hwy — *TF:* 800-343-8567 ■ *Web:* www.littlepalmisland.com	Little Torch Key	FL	33042	305-872-2524	
Lodge & Club at Ponte Vedra Beach 607 Ponte Vedra Blvd — **Fax Area Code: 904* ■ *TF:* 800-243-4304 ■ *Web:* www.pontevedra.com	Ponte Vedra Beach	FL	32082	888-839-9145	273-0210*
Longboat Key Club 220 Sands Point Rd — *TF:* 800-237-8821 ■ *Web:* www.longboatkeyclub.com	Longboat Key	FL	34228	941-383-8821	
Marco Beach Ocean Resort 480 S Collier Blvd — *TF:* 800-715-8517 ■ *Web:* www.marcoresort.com	Marco Island	FL	34145	239-393-1400	393-1401
Miami Beach Resort & Spa 4833 Collins Ave — *TF:* 866-765-9090 ■ *Web:* www.miamibeachresortandspa.com	Miami Beach	FL	33140	305-532-3600	534-7409
Mission Inn Resort & Club 10400 County Rd 48 — *TF:* 800-874-9053 ■ *Web:* www.missioninnresort.com	Howey in the Hills	FL	34737	352-324-3101	
Naples Bay Resort 1500 Fifth Ave S — *TF:* 866-605-1199 ■ *Web:* www.naplesbayresort.com	Naples	FL	34102	239-530-1199	
Naples Beach Hotel & Golf Club 851 Gulf Shore Blvd N — *TF:* 800-237-7600 ■ *Web:* www.naplesbeachhotel.com	Naples	FL	34102	239-261-2222	261-7380
Nickelodeon Family Suites by Holiday Inn 14500 Continental Gateway — *TF:* 877-642-5111 ■ *Web:* www.nickhotel.com	Orlando	FL	32821	407-387-5437	387-1488
Ocean Key Resort & Spa 0 Duval St — *TF:* 800-328-9815 ■ *Web:* www.oceankey.com	Key West	FL	33040	305-296-7701	
Ocean Manor Resort 4040 Galt Ocean Dr — *TF:* 800-955-0444 ■ *Web:* www.oceanmanor.com	Fort Lauderdale	FL	33308	954-566-7500	564-3075
Ocean Sands Resort & Spa 1350 N Ocean Blvd — *TF:* 800-721-7033 ■ *Web:* www.marriott.com/hotels/travel/fllpb-residence-inn-fort-lauderdale-pompano-beach-oceanfront	Pompano Beach	FL	33062	954-590-1000	590-1101
Omni Orlando Resort at Championsgate 1500 Masters Blvd — *TF:* 800-843-6664 ■ *Web:* www.omnihotels.com	Champions Gate	FL	33896	407-390-6664	
Orange Lake Country Club Inc (OLCC) 8505 W Irlo Bronson Memorial Hwy — *TF:* 800-877-6522 ■ *Web:* www.orangelake.com	Kissimmee	FL	34747	407-239-0000	239-5119
Palms, The 3025 Collins Ave — *TF:* 800-550-0505 ■ *Web:* www.thepalmshotel.com	Miami Beach	FL	33140	305-534-0505	534-0515
Park Shore Resort 600 Neapolitan Way — *TF:* 800-548-2077 ■ *Web:* www.sunstream.com/naples/park-shore	Naples	FL	34103	239-263-2222	263-0946
PGA National Resort & Spa 400 Ave of the Champions — *TF:* 800-633-9150 ■ *Web:* www.pgaresort.com	Palm Beach Gardens	FL	33418	561-627-2000	625-6204
Pier House Resort Caribbean Spa 1 Duval St — *TF:* 800-723-2791 ■ *Web:* www.pierhouse.com	Key West	FL	33040	305-296-4600	296-7569
Plantation Inn & Golf Resort 9301 W Ft Island Trl — *TF:* 800-632-6262 ■ *Web:* www.plantationoncrystalriver.com	Crystal River	FL	34429	352-795-4211	795-1156
Plaza Resort & Spa 600 N Atlantic Ave — *Web:* www.plazaresortandspa.com	Daytona Beach	FL	32118	386-255-4471	
Ponte Vedra Inn & Club 200 Ponte Vedra Blvd — *TF:* 800-234-7842 ■ *Web:* www.pontevedra.com	Ponte Vedra Beach	FL	32082	904-285-1111	285-1111
Portofino Bay Hotel at Universal Orlando - A Loews Hotel 5601 Universal Blvd — *TF:* 800-235-6397 ■ *Web:* www.loewshotels.com	Orlando	FL	32819	407-503-1000	503-1010
Quality Inn & Suites Naples Golf Resort 4100 Golden Gate Pkwy — *TF:* 800-277-0017 ■ *Web:* www.naplesgolfresort.com	Naples	FL	34116	239-455-1010	455-4038
Radisson Resort Parkway 2900 PkwyBlvd — *TF:* 800-333-3333 ■ *Web:* www.radisson.com	Kissimmee	FL	34747	407-396-7000	396-6792
Reach Resort 1435 Simonton St — *TF:* 888-318-4317 ■ *Web:* www.reachresort.com	Key West	FL	33040	305-296-5000	296-2830
Renaissance Orlando Resort at SeaWorld 6677 Sea Harbor Dr — *TF:* 800-327-6677 ■ *Web:* www.marriott.com/default.mi	Orlando	FL	32821	407-351-5555	351-9991
Renaissance Resort at World Golf Village 500 S Legacy Trl — *TF:* 888-740-7020 ■ *Web:* www.marriott.com/hotels/travel/jaxbr-world-golf-village-renaissance-st-augustine-resort	Saint Augustine	FL	32092	904-940-8000	940-8008
Renaissance Vinoy Resort & Golf Club 501 Fifth Ave NE — *TF:* 800-468-3571	Saint Petersburg	FL	33701	727-894-1000	
Resort at Singer Island 3800 N Ocean Dr — *TF:* 800-721-7033 ■ *Web:* marriott.com	Riviera Beach	FL	33404	561-340-1700	340-1705
Ritz-Carlton Amelia Island 4750 Amelia Island Pkwy — *TF:* 800-241-3333 ■ *Web:* www.ritzcarlton.com/resorts/amelia_island	Amelia Island	FL	32034	904-277-1100	261-9064
Ritz-Carlton Key Biscayne 455 Grand Bay Dr — *TF:* 800-241-3333 ■ *Web:* www.ritzcarlton.com/resorts/key_biscayne	Key Biscayne	FL	33149	305-365-4500	
Ritz-Carlton Naples 280 Vanderbilt Beach Rd — *Web:* www.ritzcarlton.com/resorts/naples	Naples	FL	34108	239-598-3300	
Ritz-Carlton Naples Golf Resort 2600 Tiburon Dr — *TF Resv:* 877-231-7916 ■ *Web:* www.ritzcarlton.com	Naples	FL	34109	239-593-2000	254-3300
Ritz-Carlton Orlando Grande Lakes 4012 Central Florida Pkwy — *TF:* 866-922-6882 ■ *Web:* www.ritzcarlton.com	Orlando	FL	32837	407-206-2400	
Ritz-Carlton Sarasota 1111 Ritz-Carlton Dr — *TF:* 800-241-3333 ■ *Web:* www.ritzcarlton.com	Sarasota	FL	34236	941-309-2000	
Rosen Hotels & Resorts Inc 9840 International Dr — *TF:* 800-204-7234 ■ *Web:* www.rosenhotels.com	Orlando	FL	32819	407-996-9840	996-0865
Royal Pacific Resort at Universal Orlando - A Loews Hotel 6300 Hollywood Way — *TF:* 800-235-6397 ■ *Web:* www.loewshotels.com	Orlando	FL	32819	407-503-3000	503-3010
Safety Harbor Resort & Spa 105 N Bayshore Dr — *TF:* 888-237-8772 ■ *Web:* www.safetyharborspa.com	Safety Harbor	FL	34695	727-726-1161	
Sandals Resorts International 4950 SW 72nd Ave — *TF:* 888-726-3257 ■ *Web:* www.sandals.com	Miami	FL	33155	305-284-1300	
Sandestin Golf & Beach Resort 9300 Emerald Coast Pkwy W — *TF:* 800-277-0800 ■ *Web:* www.sandestin.com	Sandestin	FL	32550	850-267-8000	
Sanibel Harbour Marriott Resort & Spa 17260 Harbour Pt Dr — *TF:* 800-767-7777 ■ *Web:* www.marriott.com	Fort Myers	FL	33908	239-466-4000	466-2266
Sawgrass Marriott Resort & Beach Club 1000 PGA Tour Blvd — *TF:* 800-228-9290 ■ *Web:* www.marriott.com	Ponte Vedra Beach	FL	32082	904-285-7777	285-0906
Sea Gardens Beach & Tennis Resort 615 N Ocean Blvd — *Web:* www.seagardens.com	Pompano Beach	FL	33062	954-943-6200	783-0047
Seminole Hard Rock Hotel & Casino Hollywood 1 Seminole Way — *TF:* 888-236-4848 ■ *Web:* www.theseminolecasinos.com	Hollywood	FL	33314	866-502-7529	
Sheraton Sand Key Resort 1160 Gulf Blvd — *TF:* 800-456-7263 ■ *Web:* www.sheratonsandkey.com	Clearwater Beach	FL	33767	727-595-1611	
South Seas Island Resort 5400 Plantation Rd — *TF:* 866-565-5089 ■ *Web:* www.southseas.com	Captiva	FL	33924	239-472-5111	472-7541
Standard, The 40 Island Ave — *Web:* standardhotels.com	Miami Beach	FL	33139	305-673-1717	
Sundial Beach & Golf Resort 1451 Middle Gulf Dr — *TF:* 866-717-2323 ■ *Web:* www.theinnsofsanibel.com	Sanibel	FL	33957	239-472-4151	
Sunset Beach Resort 3287 W Gulf Dr — *TF:* 866-565-5091 ■ *Web:* www.theinnsofsanibel.com	Sanibel Island	FL	33957	239-472-1700	
Sunset Key Guest Cottages at Westin Resort 245 Front St — *Web:* www.sunsetkeycottages.com	Key West	FL	33040	305-292-5300	292-5395
Trump International Sonesta Beach Resort 18001 Collins Ave — *TF:* 800-766-3782 ■ *Web:* www.sonesta.com	Sunny Isles Beach	FL	33160	305-692-5600	692-5601
Vanderbilt Beach Resort 9225 Gulf Shore Dr N — *TF:* 800-243-9076 ■ *Web:* www.vanderbiltbeachresort.com	Naples	FL	34108	239-597-3144	597-2199
Villas of Grand Cypress Golf Resort 1 N Jacaranda — *TF:* 800-835-7377 ■ *Web:* www.grandcypress.com	Orlando	FL	32836	407-239-4700	
Walt Disney World Dolphin 1500 Epcot Resorts Blvd — *TF:* 888-828-8850 ■ *Web:* www.swandolphin.com	Lake Buena Vista	FL	32830	407-934-4000	934-4884
Walt Disney World Resorts 4600 N World Dr — *Web:* disneyworld.disney.go.com	Lake Buena Vista	FL	32830	407-824-1000	827-2096
Walt Disney World Swan 1200 Epcot Resorts Blvd — *TF:* 888-828-8850 ■ *Web:* www.swandolphin.com	Lake Buena Vista	FL	32830	407-934-4000	934-4884
West Wind Inn 3345 W Gulf Dr — *TF:* 800-824-0476 ■ *Web:* www.westwindinn.com	Sanibel	FL	33957	239-472-1541	472-8134
Westin Diplomat Resort & Spa 501 Diplomat Pkwy — *Web:* www.diplomatgolf.com	Hallandale	FL	33009	954-883-4444	
Westin Key West Resort & Marina 245 Front St — *TF:* 866-837-4250 ■ *Web:* www.westinkeywestresort.com	Key West	FL	33040	305-294-4000	294-4086

Georgia

Name / Address	City	State	Zip	Phone	Fax
Barnsley Gardens 597 Barnsley Gardens Rd — *TF:* 877-773-2447 ■ *Web:* www.barnsleyresort.com	Adairsville	GA	30103	770-773-7480	773-1779
Brasstown Valley Resort 6321 US Hwy 76 — *TF:* 800-201-3205 ■ *Web:* www.brasstownvalley.com	Young Harris	GA	30582	706-379-9900	379-9999
Callaway Gardens 17800 Hwy 27 — *TF:* 800-225-5292 ■ *Web:* www.callawaygardens.com	Pine Mountain	GA	31822	706-663-2281	663-5122
Chateau Elan Resort & Conference Ctr 100 Rue Charlemagne — *TF:* 800-233-9463 ■ *Web:* www.chateauelan.com	Braselton	GA	30517	678-425-0900	425-6000
Forrest Hills Mountain Resort & Conference Ctr 135 Forrest Hills Rd — *TF:* 800-654-6313 ■ *Web:* forresthillsresort.com	Dahlonega	GA	30533	706-864-6456	
Jekyll Island Club Hotel 371 Riverview Dr — *TF:* 800-535-9547 ■ *Web:* www.jekyllclub.com	Jekyll Island	GA	31527	912-635-2600	635-2818
King & Prince Beach & Golf Resort 201 Arnold Rd — *TF:* 800-342-0212 ■ *Web:* www.kingandprince.com	Saint Simons Island	GA	31522	912-638-3631	638-7699
Lake Lanier Islands Resort 7000 Holiday Rd — *TF:* 800-840-5253 ■ *Web:* www.lanierislands.com	Buford	GA	30518	770-945-8787	271-7381
Reynolds Plantation 100 Linger Longer Rd — *TF:* 800-800-5250 ■ *Web:* www.reynoldslakeoconee.com	Greensboro	GA	30642	706-467-0600	
Ritz-Carlton Lodge Reynolds Plantation 1 Lk Oc1e Trl — *TF:* 877-231-7916 ■ *Web:* www.ritzcarlton.com	Greensboro	GA	30642	706-467-0600	
Sea Palms Golf & Tennis Resort 5445 Frederica Rd — *TF:* 800-841-6268 ■ *Web:* www.seapalms.com	Saint Simons Island	GA	31522	912-638-3351	634-8029
Sky Valley Golf Club 568 Sky Vly Way — *Web:* skyvalleycountryclub.com	Sky Valley	GA	30537	706-746-5302	
Villas by the Sea Resort 1175 N Beachview Dr — *TF:* 800-841-6262 ■ *Web:* www.villasbythesearesort.com	Jekyll Island	GA	31527	912-635-2521	635-2569

Hawaii

Name / Address	City	State	Zip	Phone	Fax
Fairmont Kea Lani 4100 Wailea Alanui Dr — *TF:* 800-659-4100 ■ *Web:* www.fairmont.com	Maui	HI	96753	808-875-4100	875-1200

Phone Fax

Fairmont Orchid Hawaii 1 N Kaniku Dr. . . . . Kohala Coast HI 96743 808-885-2000 885-5778
TF: 800-845-9905 ■ *Web:* www.fairmont.com/orchid

Four Seasons Resort Hualalai
100 Ka'upulehu Dr . . . . Kailua-Kona HI 96740 808-325-8000 325-8200
TF: 888-340-5662 ■ *Web:* www.fourseasons.com/hualalai

Four Seasons Resort Maui at Wailea
3900 Wailea Alanui Dr . . . . Wailea HI 96753 808-874-8000 874-2244
TF: 800-334-6284 ■ *Web:* www.fourseasons.com

Grand Hyatt Kauai Resort & Spa 1571 Poipu Rd. . . . . Koloa HI 96756 808-742-1234 742-1557
TF: 800-233-1234 ■ *Web:* kauai.grand.hyatt.com/en/hotel/home.html

Grand Wailea Resort & Spa
3850 Wailea Alanui Dr . . . . Wailea HI 96753 808-875-1234 879-4077
TF: 800-888-6100 ■ *Web:* www.grandwailea.com

Hanalei Bay Resort & Suites
5380 Honoiki Rd. . . . . Princeville HI 96722 808-826-6522
TF: 877-344-0688 ■ *Web:* www.hanaleibayresort.com

Hapuna Beach Prince Hotel 62-100 Kauna'oa Dr. . . . . . . Kamuela HI 96743 808-880-1111 880-3142
TF: 800-882-6060 ■ *Web:* www.princeresortshawaii.com

Hawaii Prince Hotel Waikiki, The
100 Holomoana St . . . . Honolulu HI 96815 888-977-4623 944-4491*
**Fax Area Code:* 808 ■ *TF:* 888-977-4623 ■ *Web:* www.princeresortshawaii.com

Hilton Hawaiian Village 2005 Kalia Rd. . . . . Honolulu HI 96815 808-949-4321 951-5458
TF: 800-445-8667 ■ *Web:* www.hilton.com

Hilton Waikoloa Village
425 Waikoloa Beach Dr . . . . Waikoloa HI 96738 808-886-1234 886-2900
TF: 866-931-1679 ■ *Web:* www.hiltonwaikoloavillage.com

Hyatt Regency Maui Resort & Spa
200 Nohea Kai Dr . . . . Lahaina HI 96761 808-661-1234 667-4497
TF: 800-633-7313 ■ *Web:* maui.regency.hyatt.com/en/hotel/home.html

Kapalua Villas, The 2000 Village Rd. . . . . Lahaina HI 96761 808-665-9170
TF: 800-545-0018 ■
Web: www.outrigger.com/hotels-resorts/hawaiian-islands/maui/the-kapalua-villas

Lodge at Koele 1 Keomoku Hwy . . . . Lanai City HI 96763 808-565-4000
Web: www.lodgeatkoele.com

Marriott Kaua'i Resort & Beach Club
3610 Rice St Kalapaki Beach . . . . Lihue HI 96766 808-245-5050 245-5049
TF: 800-220-2925 ■ *Web:* www.marriott.com

Mauna Kea Beach Hotel
62-100 Maunakea Beach Dr . . . . Island of Hawaii HI 96743 808-882-7222 882-5700
TF: 866-977-4589 ■ *Web:* www.princeresortshawaii.com

Mauna Lani Bay Hotel & Bungalows
68-1400 Mauna Lani Dr . . . . Kohala Coast HI 96743 808-885-6622 881-7000
TF: 800-367-2323 ■ *Web:* www.maunalani.com

Napili Kai Beach Club 5900 Honoapiilani Rd . . . . Lahaina HI 96761 808-669-6271 669-5740
TF: 800-367-5030 ■ *Web:* www.napilikai.com

Outrigger Enterprises Group 2375 Kuhio Ave . . . . Honolulu HI 96815 808-921-6941 369-9403*
**Fax Area Code:* 303 ■ *TF:* 800-462-6262 ■ *Web:* www.outrigger.com
Outrigger Hotels & Resorts 2375 Kuhio Ave . . . . Honolulu HI 96815 808-921-6941 926-4368*
**Fax:* Sales ■ *TF:* 800-688-7444 ■ *Web:* www.outrigger.com

Outrigger Kanaloa at Kona
78-261 Manukai St. . . . . Kailua-Kona HI 96740 808-322-9625
TF: 800-688-7444 ■ *Web:* www.outrigger.com

Outrigger Reef on the Beach 2169 Kalia Rd . . . . Honolulu HI 96815 808-923-3111 924-4957
TF: 800-688-7444 ■ *Web:* www.outrigger.com

Prince Resorts Hawaii 100 Holomoana St . . . . Honolulu HI 96815 808-956-1111 944-4491
TF: 888-977-4623 ■ *Web:* www.princeresortshawaii.com

Ritz-Carlton Kapalua 1 Ritz-Carlton Dr Kapalua . . . . Maui HI 96761 808-669-6200 669-1566
TF Resv: 800-262-8440 ■ *Web:* www.ritzcarlton.com/resorts/kapalua

Royal Hawaiian 2259 Kalakaua Ave . . . . Honolulu HI 96815 808-923-7311 931-7098
Web: royal-hawaiian.com

Royal Lahaina Resort 2780 Kekaa Dr . . . . Lahaina HI 96761 808-661-3611
TF: 800-222-5642 ■ *Web:* www.hawaiianhotels.com

Sheraton Kauai Resort 2440 Hoonani Rd. . . . . Koloa HI 96756 808-742-1661 742-4041
TF Resv: 800-325-3535 ■ *Web:* sheraton-kauai.com

Sheraton Maui Resort 2605 Kaanapali Pkwy. . . . . Lahaina HI 96761 808-661-0031 661-0458
TF: 866-716-8109 ■ *Web:* sheraton-maui.com

Sheraton Waikiki 2255 Kalakaua Ave. . . . . Honolulu HI 96815 808-922-4422
TF: 800-325-3535 ■ *Web:* sheraton-waikiki.com

Travaasa Hana 5031 Hana Hwy. . . . . Hana HI 96713 808-248-8211 248-7202
TF: 855-868-7282 ■ *Web:* travaasa.com

Turtle Bay Resort 57-091 Kamehameha Hwy. . . . . Kahuku HI 96731 808-293-6000 293-9147
TF: 866-475-2567 ■ *Web:* www.turtlebayresort.com

Wailea Beach Marriott Resort & Spa
3700 Wailea Alanui Dr . . . . Wailea HI 96753 808-879-1922 778-2049*
**Fax Area Code:* 817 ■ *TF:* 800-845-5279 ■ *Web:* www.marriott.com

Idaho

Phone Fax

Aston Hotel & Resorts Sunvalley
333 S Main St. . . . . Ketchum ID 83340 208-622-6400
TF: 877-997-6667 ■ *Web:* www.astonhotels.com

Coeur d'Alene Resort 115 S Second St. . . . . Coeur d'Alene ID 83814 208-765-4000 664-7276
TF: 800-688-5253 ■ *Web:* www.cdaresort.com

Red Lion Templin's Hotel on the River
414 E First Ave . . . . Post Falls ID 83854 208-773-1611 773-4192
TF: 800-733-5466 ■ *Web:* www.redlion.com

Sun Valley Resort 1 Sun Valley Rd. . . . . Sun Valley ID 83353 208-622-4111
TF: 800-786-8259 ■ *Web:* www.sunvalley.com

Illinois

Phone Fax

Eagle Ridge Inn & Resort 444 Eagle Ridge Dr . . . . Galena IL 61036 815-777-2444 777-4502
TF: 800-892-2269 ■ *Web:* www.eagleridge.com

Eaglewood Resort & Spa 1401 Nordic Rd. . . . . Itasca IL 60143 630-773-1400 773-1709
TF: 877-285-6150 ■ *Web:* www.eaglewoodresort.com

Pheasant Run Resort & Spa
4051 E Main St. . . . . Saint Charles IL 60174 630-584-6300
Web: www.pheasantrun.com

Indiana

Phone Fax

Belterra Casino Resort 777 Belterra Dr. . . . . Florence IN 47020 812-427-7777 427-7823
TF: 888-235-8377 ■ *Web:* www.belterracasino.com

Brickyard Crossing Golf Resort & Inn
4400 W 16th St. . . . . Indianapolis IN 46222 317-241-2500
Web: brickyardcrossing.com

Eagle Pointe Golf Resort 2250 E Pt Rd. . . . . Bloomington IN 47401 812-824-4040 824-6860
Web: www.eaglepointe.com

Fourwinds Resort & Marina
9301 Fairfax Rd . . . . Bloomington IN 47401 812-824-2628
TF: 800-824-2628 ■ *Web:* www.bestinboating.com

French Lick Resort 8670 W State Rd 56 . . . . French Lick IN 47432 812-936-9300 936-2100
TF: 888-936-9360 ■ *Web:* www.frenchlick.com

Potawatomi Inn
Pokagan State Pk 6 Ln 100A Lk James. . . . . Angola IN 46703 260-833-1077 833-4087
TF: 877-768-2928 ■ *Web:* www.in.gov/dnr/parklake/inns/potawatomi

Iowa

Phone Fax

Grand Harbor Resort & Waterpark 350 Bell St. . . . . Dubuque IA 52001 563-690-4000
TF: 866-690-4006 ■ *Web:* www.grandharborresort.com

Kansas

Phone Fax

Terradyne Resort Hotel & Country Club
1400 Terradyne Dr . . . . Andover KS 67002 316-733-2582
Web: www.terradyne-resort.com

Kentucky

Phone Fax

General Butler State Resort Park
1608 US Hwy 227. . . . . Carrollton KY 41008 502-732-4384 732-4270
TF: 866-462-8853 ■ *Web:* www.parks.ky.gov

Griffin Gate Marriott Resort
1800 Newtown Pk. . . . . Lexington KY 40511 859-231-5100 255-9944
TF: 800-228-9290 ■ *Web:* www.marriott.com

Lake Cumberland State Resort Park
5465 State Pk Rd . . . . Jamestown KY 42629 270-343-3111 343-5510
Web: www.state.ky.us

Maine

Phone Fax

Atlantic Oakes 119 Eden St . . . . Bar Harbor ME 04609 207-288-5801 288-8402
TF: 800-356-3585 ■ *Web:* www.barharbor.com

Bar Harbor Inn Oceanfront Resort
Newport Dr . . . . Bar Harbor ME 04609 207-288-3351
TF: 800-248-3351 ■ *Web:* www.barharborinn.com

Bethel Inn & Country Club
21 Broad St PO Box 49. . . . . Bethel ME 04217 207-824-2175 824-2233
TF: 800-654-0125 ■ *Web:* www.bethelinn.com

Black Point Inn Resort 510 Black Pt Rd . . . . Scarborough ME 04074 207-883-2500 883-9976
Web: www.blackpointinn.com

Cliff House Resort & Spa 591 Shore Rd. . . . . Cape Neddick ME 03902 207-361-1000 361-2122
Web: www.destinationhotels.com/cliff-house

Colony Hotel 140 Ocean Ave . . . . Kennebunkport ME 04046 207-967-3331
TF: 800-552-2363 ■ *Web:* www.thecolonyhotel.com

Inn by the Sea 40 Bowery Beach Rd . . . . Cape Elizabeth ME 04107 207-799-3134 799-4779
TF: 800-888-4287 ■ *Web:* www.innbythesea.com

Samoset Resort 220 Warrenton St . . . . Rockport ME 04856 207-594-2511 594-0722
TF: 800-341-1650 ■ *Web:* www.samosetresort.com

Sebasco Harbor Resort 29 Keynon Rd . . . . Phippsburg ME 04562 207-389-1161 389-2004
TF: 800-225-3819 ■ *Web:* www.sebasco.com

Spruce Point Inn
88 Grandview Ave PO Box 237. . . . . Boothbay Harbor ME 04538 207-633-4152
Web: www.sprucepointinn.com

Stage Neck Inn
8 Stage Neck Rd Rt 1A PO Box 70 . . . . York Harbor ME 03911 207-363-3850 363-2221
TF: 800-222-3238 ■ *Web:* www.stageneck.com

Sugarloaf/USA 5092 Access Rd. . . . . Carrabassett Valley ME 04947 207-237-2000 237-3768
TF: 800-843-5623 ■ *Web:* www.sugarloaf.com

Sunday River Ski Resort
15 S Ridge Rd PO Box 4500. . . . . Newry ME 04261 207-824-3500 824-5110
TF: 800-543-2754 ■ *Web:* sundayriver.com

Maryland

Phone Fax

Coconut Malorie Resort 200 59th St . . . . Ocean City MD 21842 410-723-6100
TF: 855-826-6361 ■
Web: vacationcondos.com/coconut-malorie-festiva-resort

Francis Scott Key Family Resort
12806 Ocean Gateway . . . . Ocean City MD 21842 410-213-0088 213-2854
TF: 800-213-0088 ■ *Web:* www.fskmotel.com

Harbourtowne Golf Resort & Conference Ctr
9784 Martingham Dr . . . . Saint Michaels MD 21663 410-745-9066
TF: 800-446-9066 ■ *Web:* www.harbourtowne.com

Ritz-Carlton Hotel Co LLC, The
4445 Willard Ave Ste 800. . . . . Chevy Chase MD 20815 301-547-4700 468-4069*
**Fax Area Code:* 801 ■ *TF:* 800-241-3333 ■ *Web:* www.ritzcarlton.com

Ritz-Carlton Huntington Hotel & Spa
4445 Willard Ave Ste 800. . . . . Chevy Chase MD 20815 301-547-4700 468-4069*
**Fax Area Code:* 801 ■ *TF:* 800-241-3333 ■ *Web:* www.ritzcarlton.com

Phone | Fax

Turf Valley Resort & Conference Ctr
2700 Turf Vly Rd ... Ellicott City MD 21042 410-465-1500
TF: 888-833-8873 ■ *Web:* www.turfvalley.com

Massachusetts

Phone | Fax

Bayside Resort Hotel
225 Massachusetts 28 ... West Yarmouth MA 02673 508-775-5669 775-8862
TF: 800-243-1114 ■ *Web:* www.baysideresort.com

Blue Water Resort 291 S Shore Dr ... South Yarmouth MA 02664 508-398-2288
TF: 800-367-9393 ■ *Web:* www.redjacketresorts.com/blue-water-resort.php

Canyon Ranch 165 Kemble St ... Lenox MA 01240 413-637-4100 637-0057
TF Resv: 800-742-9000 ■ *Web:* www.canyonranchdestinations.com

Cape Codder Resort & Spa
1225 Iyanough Rd Rt 132 Bearse's Way ... Hyannis MA 02601 508-771-3000
TF: 888-297-2200 ■ *Web:* www.capecodderresort.com

Captain Gosnold Village 230 Gosnold St ... Hyannis MA 02601 508-775-9111
Web: www.captaingosnold.com

Chatham Bars Inn 297 Shore Rd ... Chatham MA 02633 508-945-0096 945-6785
TF: 800-527-4884 ■ *Web:* www.chathambarsinn.com

Cranwell Resort Spa & Golf Club 55 Lee Rd ... Lenox MA 01240 413-637-1364 637-4364
TF: 800-272-6935 ■ *Web:* www.cranwell.com

New Seabury Resort 20 Red Brook Rd ... Mashpee MA 02649 508-539-8200 539-8634
TF: 877-687-3228 ■ *Web:* www.newseabury.com

Ocean Edge Resort & Golf Club 2907 Main St ... Brewster MA 02631 508-896-9000 896-9123
TF: 800-343-6074 ■ *Web:* www.oceanedge.com

Ocean Mist Resort 97 S Shore Dr ... South Yarmouth MA 02664 508-398-2633 398-2122
TF: 800-655-1972 ■ *Web:* www.oceanmistcapecod.com

Sea Crest Resort & Conference Ctr
350 Quaker Rd ... North Falmouth MA 02556 508-540-9400 548-0556
TF: 800-225-3110 ■ *Web:* www.seacrestbeachhotel.com

Michigan

Phone | Fax

Bay Valley Hotel & Resort
2470 Old Bridge Rd ... Bay City MI 48706 989-686-3500
TF: 888-241-4653 ■ *Web:* www.bayvalley.com

Boyne Highlands Resort
600 Highlands Dr ... Harbor Springs MI 49740 231-526-3000 526-3100
TF: 800-462-6963 ■ *Web:* www.boyne.com

Boyne Mountain Resort
11521 Huffman Lake Rd ... Boyne Falls MI 49713 231-549-6060 549-6094
TF: 800-462-6963 ■ *Web:* www.boyneresorts.com

Crystal Mountain Resort
12500 Crystal Mtn Dr ... Thompsonville MI 49683 231-378-2000 378-2998
TF: 800-968-7686 ■ *Web:* www.crystalmountain.com

Evergreen Resort 7880 Mackinaw Trail ... Cadillac MI 49601 800-634-7302 775-9621*
**Fax Area Code:* 231 ■ *TF:* 800-634-7302 ■ *Web:* www.evergreenresortmi.com

Garland Resort 4700 N Red Oak Rd ... Lewiston MI 49756 989-786-2211 786-1016
TF: 877-442-7526 ■ *Web:* www.garlandusa.com

Grand Traverse Resort & Spa
100 Grand Traverse Blvd PO Box 404 ... Acme MI 49610 231-534-6000
TF: 800-236-1577 ■ *Web:* www.grandtraverseresort.com

Homestead Resort, The 1 Wood Ridge Rd ... Glen Arbor MI 49636 231-334-5000 334-5246
Web: www.thehomesteadresort.com

Indianhead Mountain Resort
500 Indianhead Rd ... Wakefield MI 49968 800-346-3426 229-5920*
**Fax Area Code:* 906 ■ *TF:* 800-346-3426 ■ *Web:* www.indianheadmtn.com

Inn at Bay Harbor, The
3600 Village Harbor Dr ... Bay Harbor MI 49770 231-439-4000 439-4094
TF: 800-462-6963 ■ *Web:* www.innatbayharbor.com

Lakewood Shores Resort 7751 Cedar Lake Rd ... Oscoda MI 48750 989-739-2073
TF: 800-882-2493 ■ *Web:* www.lakewoodshores.com

Marsh Ridge Resort 4815 Old US Hwy 27 S ... Gaylord MI 49735 989-732-5552
Web: www.marshridge.com

Mission Point Resort 6633 Main St ... Mackinac Island MI 49757 800-833-7711
TF: 800-833-7711 ■ *Web:* www.missionpoint.com

Otsego Club 696 M-32 E Main St PO Box 556 ... Gaylord MI 49734 989-732-5181 732-0497
TF: 800-752-5510 ■ *Web:* www.otsegoclub.com

Shanty Creek Resort 5780 Shanty Creek Rd ... Bellaire MI 49615 231-533-8621
TF: 800-678-4111 ■ *Web:* www.shantycreek.com

Treetops Resort 3962 Wilkinson Rd ... Gaylord MI 49735 989-732-6711
TF: 866-348-5249 ■ *Web:* www.treetops.com

Minnesota

Phone | Fax

Arrowwood Resort & Conference Ctr
2100 Arrowwood Ln NW ... Alexandria MN 56308 320-762-1124 762-0133
TF Resv: 866-386-5263 ■ *Web:* www.arrowwoodresort.com

Breezy Point Resort 9252 Breezy Pt Dr ... Breezy Point MN 56472 218-562-7811 562-4510
TF: 800-432-3777 ■ *Web:* www.breezypointresort.com

Caribou Highlands Lodge
371 Ski Hill Rd PO Box 99 ... Lutsen MN 55612 218-663-7241
TF: 800-642-6036 ■ *Web:* www.caribouhighlands.com

Carlson
Radisson Hotels & Resorts
701 Carlson Pkwy ... Minnetonka MN 55305 763-212-5000
TF: 800-333-3333 ■ *Web:* www.carlson.com

Cascade Lodge 3719 W Hwy 61 ... Lutsen MN 55612 218-387-1112
TF: 800-322-9543 ■ *Web:* www.cascadelodgemn.com

Cragun's Conference & Golf Resort
11000 Cragun's Dr ... Brainerd MN 56401 800-272-4867 829-9188*
**Fax Area Code:* 218 ■ *TF:* 800-272-4867 ■ *Web:* www.craguns.com

Eagle's Nest Resort 6103 Lavaque Rd ... Duluth MN 55803 218-721-4147
Web: eaglesnestfishlake.com

Fair Hills Resort 24270 County Hwy 20 ... Detroit Lakes MN 56501 218-847-7638
TF Resv: 800-323-2849 ■ *Web:* www.fairhillsresort.com

Grand Casino Hinckley 777 Lady Luck Dr ... Hinckley MN 55037 800-472-6321
TF: 800-472-6321 ■ *Web:* www.grandcasinomn.com

Phone | Fax

Grand Casino Mille Lacs
777 Grand Ave PO Box 343 ... Onamia MN 56359 800-626-5825
TF: 800-626-5825 ■ *Web:* www.grandcasinomn.com

Grand Portage Lodge & Casino
PO Box 233 ... Grand Portage MN 55605 218-475-2401 475-2309
TF: 800-543-1384 ■ *Web:* www.grandportage.com

Grand View Lodge 23521 Nokomis Ave ... Nisswa MN 56468 218-963-2234
TF: 866-801-2951 ■ *Web:* www.grandviewlodge.com

Izatys Golf Resort 40005 85th Ave ... Onamia MN 56359 320-532-4574
Web: www.izatys.com

Lake Breeze Motel Resort 9000 Congdon Blvd ... Duluth MN 55804 218-525-6808 525-2986
TF: 800-738-5884 ■ *Web:* www.lakebreeze.com

Lutsen Resort 5700 W Hwy 61 PO Box 9 ... Lutsen MN 55612 218-663-7212 663-0145
TF: 800-258-8736 ■ *Web:* www.lutsenresort.com

Madden's on Gull Lake
11266 Pine Beach Peninsula ... Brainerd MN 56401 218-829-2811
TF: 800-642-5363 ■ *Web:* www.maddens.com

Ruttger's Bay Lake Lodge
25039 Tame Fish Lk Rd PO Box 400 ... Deerwood MN 56444 218-678-2885 678-2864
TF: 800-450-4545 ■ *Web:* www.ruttgers.com

Superior Shores Resort
1521 Superior Shores Dr ... Two Harbors MN 55616 218-834-5671
TF: 800-242-1988 ■ *Web:* www.superiorshores.com

Mississippi

Phone | Fax

Beau Rivage Resort & Casino 875 Beach Blvd ... Biloxi MS 39530 228-386-7111 386-7414
TF: 888-750-7111 ■ *Web:* www.beaurivage.com

Gulf Hills Hotel 13701 Paso Rd ... Ocean Springs MS 39564 228-875-4211 875-4213
TF: 866-875-4211 ■ *Web:* www.gulfhillshotel.com

IP Casino Resort & Spa 850 Bayview Ave ... Biloxi MS 39530 228-436-3000
TF Resv: 888-946-2847 ■ *Web:* www.ipbiloxi.com

Treasure Bay Casino & Hotel 1980 Beach Blvd ... Biloxi MS 39531 228-385-6000 385-6082
TF General: 800-747-2839 ■ *Web:* www.treasurebay.com

Missouri

Phone | Fax

Big Cedar Lodge 612 Devil's Pool Rd ... Ridgedale MO 65739 417-335-2777 335-2340
Web: www.bigcedar.com

Dogwood Hills Golf Resort
1252 State Hwy KK ... Osage Beach MO 65065 573-348-3153 348-0014
TF: 800-220-6571

Lilleys' Landing Resort 367 River Ln ... Branson MO 65616 417-334-6380 334-6311
TF: 866-545-5397 ■ *Web:* www.lilleyslanding.com

Lodge of Four Seasons
315 Four Seasons Dr PO Box 215 ... Lake Ozark MO 65049 573-365-3000
TF Resv: 888-265-5500 ■ *Web:* www.4seasonsresort.com

Peak Resorts 17409 Hidden Vly Dr ... Wildwood MO 63025 636-938-7474 549-0064
Web: www.peakresorts.com

Resort at Port Arrowhead, The
3080 Bagnell Dam Blvd PO Box 1930 ... Lake Ozark MO 65049 573-365-2334 365-6887
TF: 800-532-3575 ■ *Web:* theresortatportarrowhead.com

Tan-Tar-A Resort Golf Club & Spa
494 Tantara Dr PO Box 188TT ... Osage Beach MO 65065 573-348-3131 348-3206
TF Resv: 800-826-8272 ■ *Web:* www.tan-tar-a.com

Thousand Hills Golf Resort 245 S Wildwood Dr ... Branson MO 65616 417-336-5873 337-5740
TF: 877-262-0430 ■ *Web:* www.thousandhills.com

Montana

Phone | Fax

Big Sky Resort 1 L1 Mtn Trl PO Box 160001 ... Big Sky MT 59716 406-995-5000 995-5001
TF: 800-548-4486 ■ *Web:* www.bigskyresort.com

Fairmont Hot Springs Resort
1500 Fairmont Rd ... Fairmont MT 59711 406-797-3241 797-3337
TF: 800-332-3272 ■ *Web:* www.fairmontmontana.com

Glacier Park Inc PO Box 2025 ... Columbia Falls MT 59912 406-892-2525 892-1375
Web: www.glacierparkinc.com

Meadow Lake Resort 100 St Andrews Dr ... Columbia Falls MT 59912 406-892-8700 892-8731
TF: 800-321-4653 ■ *Web:* www.meadowlake.com

Rock Creek Resort 6380 US Hwy 212 ... Red Lodge MT 59068 406-446-1111
TF: 800-667-1119 ■ *Web:* www.rockcreekresort.com

Triple Creek Ranch 5551 W Fork Rd ... Darby MT 59829 406-821-4600 821-4666
TF: 800-654-2943 ■ *Web:* www.triplecreekranch.com

Nebraska

Phone | Fax

Radisson Palm Beach Shores Resort & Vacation Villas
11340 Blondo S Ste 100 ... Omaha NE 68164 800-615-7253
TF: 800-615-7253 ■ *Web:* www.radisson.com

Nevada

Phone | Fax

Alexis Park Resort 375 E Harmon Ave ... Las Vegas NV 89169 702-796-3300 796-4334
TF: 800-582-2228 ■ *Web:* www.alexispark.com

Aquarius Casino Resort 1900 S Casino Dr ... Laughlin NV 89029 702-298-5111
TF: 888-662-5825 ■ *Web:* www.aquariuscasinoresort.com

Atlantis Casino Resort 3800 S Virginia St ... Reno NV 89502 775-825-4700
TF: 800-723-6500 ■ *Web:* www.atlantiscasino.com

Bellagio Hotel & Casino
3600 Las Vegas Blvd S ... Las Vegas NV 89109 702-693-7111 693-8585
TF: 888-987-7111 ■ *Web:* www.bellagio.com

Casablanca Resort 950 W Mesquite Blvd ... Mesquite NV 89027 702-346-7529
TF: 800-459-7529 ■ *Web:* www.casablancaresort.com

Club Cal Neva Hotel Casino, The
38 E Second St PO Box 2071 ... Reno NV 89501 775-323-1046
TF: 877-777-7303 ■ *Web:* www.clubcalneva.com

Phone | Fax

Don Laughlin's Riverside Resort & Casino
1650 Casino Dr . . . Laughlin NV 89029 702-298-2535
TF: 800-227-3849 ■ *Web:* www.riversideresort.com

Golden Nugget Hotel 129 E Fremont St . . . Las Vegas NV 89101 702-385-7111 385-7111
TF: 800-634-3454 ■ *Web:* www.goldennugget.com

Golden Nugget Laughlin 2300 S Casino Dr . . . Laughlin NV 89029 702-298-7111 298-3023
TF: 800-950-7700 ■ *Web:* www.goldennugget.com

Grand Sierra Resort & Casino 2500 E Second St . . . Reno NV 89595 775-789-2000 789-2130
TF: 800-501-2651 ■ *Web:* www.grandsierraresort.com

Hard Rock Hotel & Casino 4455 Paradise Rd . . . Las Vegas NV 89169 702-693-5000 693-5331
TF: 800-693-7625 ■ *Web:* www.hardrockhotel.com

JW Marriott Resort Las Vegas
221 N Rampart Blvd . . . Las Vegas NV 89144 702-869-7777 869-7339
TF: 877-869-8777 ■ *Web:* www.marriott.com

Las Vegas Sands Corp 3355 Las Vegas Blvd S . . . Las Vegas NV 89109 702-414-1000 414-4884
NYSE: LVS ■ *Web:* www.sands.com

Mandalay Bay Resort & Casino
3950 Las Vegas Blvd S . . . Las Vegas NV 89119 702-632-7777 632-7234
TF: 877-632-7800 ■ *Web:* www.mandalaybay.com

MGM Grand Hotel & Casino
3799 Las Vegas Blvd S . . . Las Vegas NV 89109 702-891-1111 891-3036
TF: 877-880-0880 ■ *Web:* www.mgmgrand.com

Mirage, The 3400 Las Vegas Blvd S . . . Las Vegas NV 89109 702-791-7111 791-7414
TF: 800-627-6667 ■ *Web:* www.mirage.com

Monarch Casino & Resort Inc 3800 S Virginia St . . . Reno NV 89502 775-335-4600 332-9171
NASDAQ: MCRI ■ *Web:* www.monarchcasino.com

Monte Carlo Resort & Casino
3770 Las Vegas Blvd S . . . Las Vegas NV 89109 702-730-7777 730-7200
TF: 800-311-8999 ■ *Web:* www.montecarlo.com

Planet Hollywood Resort & Casino
3667 Las Vegas Blvd S . . . Las Vegas NV 89109 702-785-5555 785-5080
TF: 866-919-7472 ■ *Web:* www.caesars.com/planet-hollywood

Primm Valley Resort & Casino
31900 S Las Vegas Blvd . . . Primm NV 89019 800-926-4455
TF: 800-926-4455 ■ *Web:* www.primmvalleyresorts.com

Ridge Tahoe 400 Ridge Club Dr PO Box 5790 . . . Stateline NV 89449 775-588-3553 588-1551
TF: 800-334-1600 ■ *Web:* www.ridgetahoeresort.com

Treasure Island Hotel & Casino
3300 Las Vegas Blvd S . . . Las Vegas NV 89109 702-894-7111 894-7414
TF: 800-288-7206 ■ *Web:* www.treasureisland.com

Tropicana Resort & Casino
3801 Las Vegas Blvd S . . . Las Vegas NV 89109 702-739-2222
TF Resv: 800-462-8767 ■ *Web:* www.troplv.com

Venetian Resort Hotel & Casino
3355 Las Vegas Blvd S . . . Las Vegas NV 89109 702-414-1000 414-1100
TF: 866-659-9643 ■ *Web:* www.venetian.com

New Hampshire

Phone | Fax

Cranmore Mountain Resort
1 Skimobile Rd PO Box 1640 . . . North Conway NH 03860 603-356-5543 356-8526
TF: 800-786-6754 ■ *Web:* www.cranmore.com

Margate on Winnipesaukee, The 76 Lake St . . . Laconia NH 03246 603-524-5210
Web: www.themargate.com

Mount Washington Hotel & Resort Rt 302 . . . Bretton Woods NH 03575 603-278-1000
TF: 800-314-1752 ■ *Web:* www.brettonwoods.com

Waterville Valley Resort
1 Ski Area Rd PO Box 540 . . . Waterville Valley NH 03215 603-236-8311 236-4344
TF: 800-468-2553 ■ *Web:* www.waterville.com

White Mountain Hotel & Resort
2560 W Side Rd PO Box 1828 . . . North Conway NH 03860 603-356-7100 356-7100
TF: 800-533-6301 ■ *Web:* www.whitemountainhotel.com

New Jersey

Phone | Fax

Bally's Atlantic City 1900 Pacific Ave . . . Atlantic City NJ 08401 609-340-2000
TF: 800-772-7777 ■ *Web:* www.caesars.com/ballys-ac

Caesars Atlantic City Hotel Casino
2100 Pacific Ave . . . Atlantic City NJ 08401 609-348-4411
TF: 800-522-4700 ■ *Web:* www.totalrewards.com

Dolce International 28 W Grand Ave . . . Montvale NJ 07645 201-307-8700
Web: www.dolce.com

Montreal Inn Beach Dr & Madison Ave . . . Cape May NJ 08204 609-884-7011
TF: 800-525-7011 ■ *Web:* montrealbeachresort.com

Mountain Creek Resort 200 Rt 94 . . . Vernon NJ 07462 973-827-2000
Web: mountaincreek.com

Ocean Place Resort & Spa 1 Ocean Blvd . . . Long Branch NJ 07740 732-571-4000
Web: www.oceanplace.com

Resorts Casino Hotel 1133 Boardwalk . . . Atlantic City NJ 08401 800-334-6378
TF: 800-334-6378 ■ *Web:* www.resortsac.com

Tropicana Entertainment 2831 Boardwalk . . . Atlantic City NJ 08401 800-843-8767
OTC: TPCA ■ *TF:* 800-843-8767 ■ *Web:* www.tropicana.net

Trump Taj Mahal Casino Resort
1000 Boardwalk & Virginia Ave . . . Atlantic City NJ 08401 609-449-1000
TF: 800-426-2537 ■ *Web:* www.trumptaj.com

Wyndham Vacation Rentals 14 Sylvan Way . . . Parsippany NJ 07054 973-753-6300
TF: 800-467-3529 ■ *Web:* www.wyndhamvacationrentals.com

New Mexico

Phone | Fax

Angel Fire Resort PO Box 130 . . . Angel Fire NM 87710 575-377-6401
TF: 800-633-7463 ■ *Web:* www.angelfireresort.com

Inn of the Mountain Gods
287 Carrizo Canyon Rd . . . Mescalero NM 88340 800-545-9011
TF: 800-545-9011 ■ *Web:* www.innofthemountaingods.com

La Posada de Santa Fe Resort & Spa
330 E Palace Ave . . . Santa Fe NM 87501 505-986-0000 476-7425*
**Fax Area Code:* 970 ■ *TF:* 866-280-3810 ■ *Web:* rockresorts.com

Lifts West Condominium Resort Hotel
PO Box 330 . . . Red River NM 87558 505-754-2778 754-6617
TF: 800-221-1859 ■ *Web:* www.redrivernm.com/liftswest

New York

Phone | Fax

Bonnie Castle Resort 31 Holland St . . . Alexandria Bay NY 13607 315-482-4511
TF: 800-955-4511 ■ *Web:* www.bonniecastle.com

Canoe Island Lodge 3820 Lakeshore Dr . . . Diamond Point NY 12824 518-668-5592 668-2012
Web: www.canoeislandlodge.com

Doral Arrowwood Conference Resort
975 Anderson Hill Rd . . . Rye Brook NY 10573 844-214-5500 323-5500*
**Fax Area Code:* 914 ■ *TF:* 844-211-0512 ■ *Web:* www.arrowwood.com

Gurney's Montauk Resort & Seawater Spa
290 Old Montauk Hwy . . . Montauk NY 11954 631-668-2345
Web: www.gurneysmontauk.com

High Peaks Resort 2384 Saranac Ave . . . Lake Placid NY 12946 518-523-4411 523-1120
TF: 800-755-5598 ■ *Web:* highpeaksresort.com

Holiday Valley Resort
6557 Holiday Valley Rd PO Box 370 . . . Ellicottville NY 14731 716-699-2345 699-5204
TF: 800-323-0020 ■ *Web:* www.holidayvalley.com

Mohonk Mountain House 1000 Mtn Rest Rd . . . New Paltz NY 12561 845-255-1000
TF: 800-772-6646 ■ *Web:* www.mohonk.com

Montauk Yacht Club Resort & Marina
32 Star Island Rd . . . Montauk NY 11954 631-668-3100 668-6181
TF: 888-692-8668 ■ *Web:* www.montaukyachtclub.com

Otesaga, The 60 Lake St . . . Cooperstown NY 13326 607-547-9931 547-9675
TF: 800-348-6222 ■ *Web:* www.otesaga.com

Peek 'n Peak Resort 1405 Olde Rd . . . Clymer NY 14724 716-355-4141 355-4542
Web: www.pknpk.com

Point, The PO Box 1327 . . . Saranac Lake NY 12983 518-891-5674 891-1152
TF: 800-255-3530 ■ *Web:* thepointsaranac.com

Roaring Brook Ranch & Tennis Resort
Rte 9N S . . . Lake George NY 12845 518-668-5767
TF: 800-882-7665 ■ *Web:* www.roaringbrookranch.com

Rocking Horse Ranch Resort 600 Rt 44-55 . . . Highland NY 12528 845-691-2927
TF: 800-647-2624 ■ *Web:* www.rockinghorseranch.com

Sagamore, The 110 Sagamore Rd . . . Bolton Landing NY 12814 518-644-9400 743-6036
TF: 866-384-1944 ■ *Web:* www.thesagamore.com

Starwood Hotels & Resorts Worldwide Inc
1111 Westchester Ave . . . White Plains NY 10604 914-640-8100 640-8310
NYSE: HOT ■ *TF Cust Svc:* 888-625-5144 ■ *Web:* www.starwoodhotels.com
Saint Regis Hotels & Resorts
1111 Westchester Ave . . . White Plains NY 10604 914-640-8100 640-8310
TF: 888-625-4988 ■ *Web:* www.starwoodhotels.com

Villa Roma Resort & Conference Ctr
356 Villa Roma Rd . . . Callicoon NY 12723 845-887-4880 887-4824
TF: 800-533-6767 ■ *Web:* www.villaroma.com

Whiteface Club & Resort
373 Whiteface Inn Ln . . . Lake Placid NY 12946 518-523-2551 523-4278
Web: www.whitefaceclubresort.com

Woodcliff Hotel & Spa 199 Woodcliff Dr . . . Fairport NY 14450 585-381-4000 381-2673
TF: 800-365-3065 ■ *Web:* www.woodcliffhotelspa.com

North Carolina

Phone | Fax

Ballantyne Resort Hotel
10000 Ballantyne Commons Pkwy . . . Charlotte NC 28277 704-248-4000 248-4005
TF: 866-248-4824 ■ *Web:* www.theballantynehotel.com

Eseeola Lodge, The
175 Linville Ave PO Box 99 . . . Linville NC 28646 828-733-4311
TF: 800-742-6717 ■ *Web:* www.eseeola.com

Fontana Village Resort
300 Woods Rd PO Box 68 . . . Fontana Dam NC 28733 828-498-2211
TF: 800-849-2258 ■ *Web:* fontanavillage.com

Grove Park Inn Resort & Spa 290 Macon Ave . . . Asheville NC 28804 828-252-2711 253-7053
TF: 800-438-5800 ■ *Web:* www.omnihotels.com/hotels/asheville-grove-park

High Hampton Inn & Country Club
1525 Hwy 107 S . . . Cashiers NC 28717 828-743-2450 743-5991
TF: 800-334-2551 ■ *Web:* www.highhamptoninn.com

Holiday Inn SunSpree Resort Wrightsville Beach
1706 N Lumina Ave . . . Wrightsville Beach NC 28480 910-256-2231
TF: 888-211-9874 ■ *Web:* www.ihg.com

Hound Ears Lodge & Club 328 Shulls Mill Rd . . . Boone NC 28607 828-963-4321
Web: www.houndears.com

Maggie Valley Resort & Country Club
1819 Country Club Dr . . . Maggie Valley NC 28751 828-926-1616
TF: 800-438-3861 ■ *Web:* www.maggievalleyclub.com

Mid Pines Inn & Golf Club
1010 Midland Rd . . . Southern Pines NC 28387 910-692-2114 692-5349
TF: 800-747-7272 ■ *Web:* www.pineneedles-midpines.com

Pine Needles Lodge & Golf Club
PO Box 88 . . . Southern Pines NC 28388 910-692-7111 692-5349
TF: 800-747-7272 ■ *Web:* www.pineneedles-midpines.com

Pinehurst Resort & Country Club
80 Carolina Vista Dr . . . Pinehurst NC 28374 910-295-6811
TF: 800-487-4653 ■ *Web:* www.pinehurst.com

Pinnacle Inn Resort
301 Pinnacle Inn Rd . . . Beech Mountain NC 28604 828-387-2231
TF: 800-405-7888 ■ *Web:* www.pinnacleinn.com

Sanderling Resort & Spa 1461 Duck Rd . . . Duck NC 27949 252-261-4111 261-1638
TF: 800-701-4111 ■ *Web:* www.sanderling-resort.com

Waynesville Inn Golf & Country Club, The
176 Country Club Dr . . . Waynesville NC 28786 828-456-3551
TF: 800-627-6250 ■ *Web:* www.thewaynesvilleinn.com

Wolf Ridge Ski Resort 578 Vly View Cir . . . Mars Hill NC 28754 828-689-4111 689-9819
TF: 800-817-4111 ■ *Web:* www.skiwolfridgenc.com

North Dakota

Phone Fax

Prairie Knights Casino & Resort
7932 Hwy 24 ... Fort Yates ND 58538 701-854-7777 854-7786
TF: 800-425-8277 ■ *Web:* www.prairieknights.com

Nova Scotia

Phone Fax

Atlantica Hotel & Marina Oak Island
36 Treasure Dr PO Box 6 ... Western Shore NS B0J3M0 902-627-2600 627-2020
TF: 800-565-5075 ■ *Web:* www.atlanticaoakisland.com

Pines Resort, The 103 Shore Rd ... Digby NS B0V1A0 902-245-2511
TF: 800-667-4637 ■ *Web:* digbypines.ca

Ohio

Phone Fax

Atwood Lake Resort 2650 Lodge Rd ... Sherrodsville OH 44675 330-735-2211
Web: www.atwoodresort.com

Glenmoor Country Club 4191 Glenmoor Rd ... Canton OH 44718 330-966-3600 966-3611
Web: www.glenmoorcc.com

Hueston Woods Lodge & Conference Ctr
5201 Lodge Rd ... College Corner OH 45003 513-664-3500 523-1522
Web: huestonwoodslodge.com

Quail Hollow Resort
11080 Concord-Hambden Rd ... Painesville OH 44077 440-497-1100 350-3594
Web: www.quailhollowresort.com

Sawmill Creek Resort 400 Sawmill Creek Dr ... Huron OH 44839 419-433-3800 433-7610
TF: 800-729-6455 ■ *Web:* www.sawmillcreekresort.com

Oklahoma

Phone Fax

Fin & Feather Resort Inc 445889 Hwy 10-A ... Gore OK 74435 918-487-5148 487-5025
Web: finandfeather.publishpath.com

Lake Murray Resort Park 3323 Lodge Rd ... Ardmore OK 73401 580-223-6600 326-2670
TF: 800-622-6317 ■ *Web:* www.travelok.com

Quartz Mountain Resort & Conference Ctr
22469 Lodge Rd ... Lone Wolf OK 73655 580-563-2424 563-2422
TF: 877-999-5567 ■ *Web:* www.quartzmountainresort.com

Ontario

Phone Fax

Deerhurst Resort 1235 Deerhurst Dr ... Huntsville ON P1H2E8 705-789-6411 789-2431
TF Sales: 800-461-6522 ■ *Web:* www.deerhurstresort.com

Fallsview Casino Resort
6380 Fallsview Blvd ... Niagara Falls ON L2G7X5 888-325-5788 371-7952*
**Fax Area Code:* 905 ■ *TF:* 888-325-5788 ■ *Web:* www.fallsviewcasinoresort.com

Pinestone Resort 4252 County Rd Ste 21 ... Haliburton ON K0M1S0 705-457-1800 457-1783
TF: 800-461-0357 ■ *Web:* www.pinestone-resort.com

Oregon

Phone Fax

Black Butte Ranch
12930 Hawks BeaRd Rd PO Box 8000 ... Black Butte Ranch OR 97759 541-595-1252 595-2077
TF: 866-901-2961 ■ *Web:* www.blackbutteranch.com

Gearhart By the Sea 1157 N Marion Ave ... Gearhart OR 97138 503-738-8331 738-0881
TF: 800-547-0115 ■ *Web:* www.gearhartresort.com

Mount Bachelor Village Resort & Conference Ctr
19717 Mt Bachelor Dr ... Bend OR 97702 541-389-5900 388-7401
TF: 800-547-5204 ■ *Web:* www.mtbachelorvillage.com

Salishan Lodge & Golf Resort
PO Box 118 ... Gleneden Beach OR 97388 800-452-2300 764-3681*
**Fax Area Code:* 541 ■ *TF:* 800-452-2300 ■ *Web:* www.salishan.com

Seventh Mountain Resort 18575 SW Century Dr ... Bend OR 97702 541-382-8711
Web: www.seventhmountain.com

Sunriver Resort 17600 Ctr Dr PO Box 3609 ... Sunriver OR 97707 541-593-1000
TF: 800-547-3922 ■ *Web:* www.sunriver-resort.com

Timberline Lodge
27500 E Timberline Rd ... Government Camp OR 97028 503-272-3311
TF: 800-547-1406 ■ *Web:* www.timberlinelodge.com

Village Green Resort & Gardens
725 Row River Rd ... Cottage Grove OR 97424 541-942-2491 942-2386

Pennsylvania

Phone Fax

Allenberry Resort
1559 Boiling Springs Rd ... Boiling Springs PA 17007 717-258-3211 960-5280
TF: 800-430-5468 ■ *Web:* www.allenberry.com

Carroll Valley Golf Resort
78 Country Club Trail ... Carroll Valley PA 17320 717-642-8282 642-6534
TF: 855-784-0330 ■ *Web:* libertymountainresort.com

Cove Haven Pocono Palace
5222 Milford Rd ... East Stroudsburg PA 18302 800-432-9932 226-6982*
**Fax Area Code:* 570 ■ *TF:* 877-822-3333 ■ *Web:* www.covepoconoresorts.com

Felicita Resort 2201 Fishing Creek Vly Rd ... Harrisburg PA 17112 717-599-5301
Web: www.felicitaresort.com

Fernwood Resort 5785 Milford Rd ... East Stroudsburg PA 18302 888-337-6966 588-7112*
**Fax Area Code:* 570 ■ *TF:* 888-337-6966 ■ *Web:* fernwoodresortpoconos.com

Heritage Hills Golf Resort & Conference Ctr
2700 Mt Rose Ave ... York PA 17402 717-755-0123
TF: 877-782-9752 ■ *Web:* www.heritagehillsresort.com

Hershey Entertainment & Resorts Co
27 W Chocolate Ave ... Hershey PA 17033 800-437-7439
TF: 800-437-7439 ■ *Web:* www.hersheypa.com

Phone Fax

Hidden Valley Resort & Conference Ctr
1 Craighead Dr PO Box 4420 ... Hidden Valley PA 15502 814-443-8000 443-8254
TF: 800-452-2223 ■ *Web:* www.hiddenvalleyresort.com

Hotel Hershey, The 100 Hotel Rd ... Hershey PA 17033 717-533-2171 534-8887
Web: www.thehotelhershey.com

Lancaster Host Resort 2300 Lincoln Hwy E ... Lancaster PA 17602 717-299-5500
TF Resv: 800-233-0121 ■ *Web:* www.lancasterhost.com

Liberty Mountain Resort & Conference Ctr
78 Country Club Trl ... Carroll Valley PA 17320 717-642-8282
Web: www.libertymountainresort.com

Mountain Laurel Resort & Spa
Rt 940 PO Box 9 ... White Haven PA 18661 570-443-8411
TF: 888-243-9300 ■ *Web:* www.mountainlaurelresort.com

Nemacolin Woodlands Resort & Spa
1001 Lafayette Dr ... Farmington PA 15437 724-329-8555 329-6198
TF: 800-422-2736 ■ *Web:* www.nemacolin.com

Pocono Manor Golf Resort & Spa
1 Manor Dr Rt 314 ... Pocono Manor PA 18349 570-839-7111 839-3407
TF: 800-233-8150 ■ *Web:* www.poconomanor.com

Seven Springs Mountain Resort
777 Waterwheel Dr ... Champion PA 15622 814-352-7777
TF: 800-452-2223 ■ *Web:* www.7springs.com

Skytop Lodge 1 Skytop ... Skytop PA 18357 570-595-7401
TF: 800-345-7759 ■ *Web:* www.skytop.com

Split Rock Resort 100 Moseywood Rd ... Lake Harmony PA 18624 570-722-9111
TF: 800-255-7625 ■ *Web:* www.splitrockresort.com

Tamiment Resort & Conference Ctr
Bushkill Falls Rd ... Tamiment PA 18371 570-588-6652
TF: 800-233-8105 ■ *Web:* worldgolf.com

Willow Valley Resort & Conference Ctr
2400 Willow St Pike ... Lancaster PA 17602 717-464-0869 464-4784
Web: www.willowvalley.com

Woodlands Inn, The 1073 Hwy 315 ... Wilkes-Barre PA 18702 570-824-9831 824-8865
TF: 844-779-8472 ■ *Web:* www.choicehotels.com/ascend

Puerto Rico

Phone Fax

Caribe Hilton 1 San Geronimo St ... San Juan PR 00901 787-721-0303 725-8849
Web: www.caribehilton.com

El Conquistador Resort & Golden Door Spa
1000 El Conquistador Ave ... Fajardo PR 00738 787-863-1000 863-6500
TF Resv: 888-543-1282 ■ *Web:* www.elconresort.com

Las Casitas Village & Golden Door Spa
1000 El Conquistador Ave ... Fajardo PR 00738 787-863-1000
Web: www.lascasitasvillage.com

Ritz-Carlton San Juan, The
6961 Ave of the Governors Isla Verde ... Carolina PR 00979 787-253-1700 253-1777
TF: 800-241-3333 ■ *Web:* www.ritzcarlton.com/en/properties/sanjuan

Quebec

Phone Fax

Fairmont Le Chateau Montebello
392 Notre Dame St ... Montebello QC J0V1L0 819-423-6341 423-1133
TF: 800-441-1414 ■ *Web:* www.fairmont.com

Hotel Cheribourg 2603 Ch du Parc ... Orford QC J1X8C8 819-843-3308 843-2639
TF: 877-845-5344 ■ *Web:* www.hotelsvillegia.com

Hotel du Lac 121 Rue Cuttle ... Mont-Tremblant QC J8E1B9 819-425-2731 425-5617
TF: 800-567-8341 ■ *Web:* www.hoteldulac.ca/accueil

Manoir du Lac Delage 40 Ave du Lac ... Lac Delage QC G3C5C4 418-848-2551 848-1352
TF: 888-202-3242 ■ *Web:* www.lacdelage.com

Westin Resort Tremblant
100 Ch Kandahar ... Mont-Tremblant QC J8E1E2 819-681-8000
Web: www.westintremblant.com

Rhode Island

Phone Fax

Castle Hill Inn & Resort 590 Ocean Dr ... Newport RI 02840 401-849-3800 849-3838
TF: 888-466-1355 ■ *Web:* www.castlehillinn.com

Inn on Long Wharf 5 Washington St ... Newport RI 02840 401-847-7800
Web: extraholidays.com

South Carolina

Phone Fax

Barefoot Resort & Golf
4980 Barefoot Resort Bridge Rd ... North Myrtle Beach SC 29582 843-390-3200 390-3213
TF: 866-638-4818 ■ *Web:* www.barefootgolf.com

Bay Watch Resort & Conference Ctr
2701 S Ocean Blvd ... North Myrtle Beach SC 29582 843-272-4600
TF: 866-270-2172 ■ *Web:* oceanaresorts.com

Beach Colony Resort 5308 N Ocean Blvd ... Myrtle Beach SC 29577 843-449-4010 449-2810
TF General: 800-222-2141 ■ *Web:* www.beachcolony.com

Bluewater Resort 2001 S Ocean Blvd ... Myrtle Beach SC 29577 843-626-8345
TF: 800-845-6994 ■ *Web:* www.bluewaterresort.com

Breakers Resort 3002 N Ocean Blvd ... Myrtle Beach SC 29577 843-448-8082 626-5001
TF: 800-952-4507 ■ *Web:* www.breakers.com

Caravelle Resort Hotel & Villas
6900 N Ocean Blvd ... Myrtle Beach SC 29572 843-918-8000
TF: 800-507-9145 ■ *Web:* www.thecaravelle.com

Caribbean Resort & Villas
3000 N Ocean Blvd ... Myrtle Beach SC 29577 800-552-8509
TF: 800-552-8509 ■ *Web:* www.caribbeanresort.com

Compass Cove Ocean Resort
2311 S Ocean Blvd ... Myrtle Beach SC 29577 843-448-8373 448-5444
TF: 800-331-0934 ■ *Web:* www.compasscove.com

Coral Beach Resort & Suites
1105 S Ocean Blvd ... Myrtle Beach SC 29577 800-556-1754
TF: 800-843-2684 ■ *Web:* www.coralbeachmyrtlebeachresort.com

Phone | Fax

Disney's Hilton Head Island Resort
22 Harborside Ln .... Hilton Head Island SC 29928 843-341-4100 341-4130
Web: www.disneyvacationclub.disney.go.com

Hilton Charleston Harbor Resort & Marina
20 Patriots Pt Rd. .... Mount Pleasant SC 29464 843-856-0028 856-8333
Web: www.charlestonharborresort.com

Hilton Head Island Beach & Tennis Resort
40 Folly Field Rd .... Hilton Head Island SC 29928 843-842-4402
TF Resv: 800-475-2631 ■ *Web:* www.hhibeachandtennis.com

Hilton Myrtle Beach Resort
10000 Beach Club Dr .... Myrtle Beach SC 29572 843-449-5000 497-0168
TF: 800-445-8667 ■ *Web:* www.hilton.com

Holiday Inn Oceanfront at Surfside Beach
1601 N Ocean Blvd. .... Surfside Beach SC 29575 843-238-5601
Web: www.ihg.com

Kiawah Island Golf Resort
1 Sancturay Beach Dr .... Kiawah Island SC 29455 843-768-2121 768-2736*
**Fax:* Resv ■ *TF Resv:* 800-654-2924 ■ *Web:* www.kiawahresort.com/golf

Landmark Resort 1501 S Ocean Blvd .... Myrtle Beach SC 29577 843-448-9441
TF: 800-845-0658 ■ *Web:* www.landmarkresort.com

Litchfield Beach & Golf Resort
14276 Ocean Hwy. .... Pawleys Island SC 29585 843-237-3000 237-3282
TF: 888-766-4633 ■ *Web:* www.litchfieldbeach.com

Myrtle Beach Marriott Resort at Grande Dunes
8400 Costa Verde Dr .... Myrtle Beach SC 29572 843-449-8880 449-8669
Web: www.marriott.com

Myrtle Beach Resort Vacations
5905 S Kings Hwy PO Box 3936 .... Myrtle Beach SC 29578 843-238-1559 238-2424
TF: 888-627-3767 ■ *Web:* www.myrtle-beach-resort.com

Mystic Sea Resort 2105 S Ocean Blvd............ Myrtle Beach SC 29577 843-448-8446
TF: 800-443-7050 ■ *Web:* www.mysticsea.com

Ocean Reef Resort 7100 N Ocean Blvd .... Myrtle Beach SC 29572 843-449-4441 497-3041
TF: 888-322-6411 ■ *Web:* www.oceanreefmyrtlebeach.com

Palmetto Dunes Resort
4 Queen Folly Rd .... Hilton Head Island SC 29928 866-380-1778
TF: 866-380-1778 ■ *Web:* www.palmettodunes.com

Palms Resort 2500 N Ocean Blvd .... Myrtle Beach SC 29577 843-626-8334
TF: 800-300-1198 ■ *Web:* www.palmsresort.com

Patricia Grand Resort 2710 N Ocean Blvd .... Myrtle Beach SC 29577 843-448-8453
TF: 800-255-4763 ■ *Web:* www.oceanaresorts.com

Pawleys Plantation 70 Tanglewood Dr .... Pawleys Island SC 29585 843-237-6000
TF: 800-367-9959 ■ *Web:* www.pawleysplantation.com

Player's Club Resort
35 Deallyon Ave .... Hilton Head Island SC 29928 843-785-3355
TF: 800-497-7529 ■ *Web:* spinnakerresorts.com

Reef Resort 2101 S Ocean Blvd. .... Myrtle Beach SC 29577 843-448-1765
TF Cust Svc: 800-845-1212 ■ *Web:* www.reefmyrtlebeach.com

Resort at Seabrook Island
3772 Seabrook Island Rd .... Seabrook Island SC 29455 843-768-2500
Web: www.discoverseabrook.com

Sand Dunes Resort Hotel 201 74th Ave N. .... Myrtle Beach SC 29572 800-726-3783
TF: 800-726-3783 ■ *Web:* www.sandsresorts.com

Sea Mist Resort 1200 S Ocean Blvd. .... Myrtle Beach SC 29577 843-448-1551
TF: 800-793-6507 ■ *Web:* www.myrtlebeachseamist.com

Seacrest Oceanfront Resort on the South Beach
803 S Ocean Blvd. .... Myrtle Beach SC 29577 888-889-8113
TF: 888-889-8113 ■ *Web:* www.myrtlebeach-resorts.com

Shore Crest Vacation Villas
4709 S Ocean Blvd .... North Myrtle Beach SC 29582 843-361-3600
Web: www.bluegreenrentals.com

Wild Dunes Resort 5757 Palm Blvd .... Isle of Palms SC 29451 843-886-6000 886-2916
TF: 800-845-8880 ■ *Web:* www.wilddunes.com

Wyndham Vacation Resorts King Cotton Villas
1 King Cotton Rd .... Edisto Beach SC 29438 843-869-2561 869-2384
TF: 800-251-8736 ■ *Web:* www.clubwyndham.com/cw/home.page

South Dakota

Phone | Fax

Spearfish Canyon Resort
10619 Roughlock Falls Rd .... Lead SD 57754 605-584-3435 584-3990
TF: 877-975-6343 ■ *Web:* www.spfcanyon.com

Spring Creek Resort 28229 Spring Creek Pl .... Pierre SD 57501 605-224-8336
Web: www.springcreekventure.com

Tennessee

Phone | Fax

Brookside Resort 463 E Pkwy. .... Gatlinburg TN 37738 865-436-5611
TF: 800-251-9597 ■ *Web:* brooksideresort.com

Texas

Phone | Fax

Bahia Mar Resort & Conference Ctr
6300 Padre Blvd .... South Padre Island TX 78597 800-926-6926
TF: 800-926-6926 ■ *Web:* pirentals.com

Columbia Lakes Resort & Conference Ctr
188 Freeman Blvd. .... West Columbia TX 77486 979-345-5151
Web: www.columbialakesgolf.com

Four Seasons Resort & Club Dallas at Las Colinas
4150 N MacArthur Blvd .... Irving TX 75038 972-717-0700 717-2550
TF: 800-332-3442 ■ *Web:* www.fourseasons.com/dallas

Hilton Galveston Island Resort
5400 Seawall Blvd .... Galveston TX 77551 409-744-5000 740-2209
TF: 800-475-3386 ■ *Web:* www3.hilton.com/en/index.html

Houstonian Hotel Club & Spa
111 N Post Oak Ln .... Houston TX 77024 713-680-2626 680-2992
TF Resv: 800-231-2759 ■ *Web:* www.houstonian.com

Inn of the Hills River Resort
1001 Junction Hwy .... Kerrville TX 78028 830-895-5000 895-6020
TF: 800-292-5690 ■ *Web:* www.innofthehills.com

Phone | Fax

Omni Barton Creek Resort & Spa
8212 Barton Club Dr. .... Austin TX 78735 512-329-4000 329-4597
TF: 800-336-6158 ■ *Web:* www.omnihotels.com/hotels/austin-barton-creek

Quorum Hotels & Resorts
5429 Lyndon B Johnson Fwy #625 .... Dallas TX 75240 972-458-7265 991-5647
Web: www.quorumhotels.com

Rancho Viejo Resort & Country Club
1 Rancho Viejo Dr. .... Rancho Viejo TX 78575 956-350-4000 350-5696
TF: 800-531-7400

Rosewood Hotels & Resorts
500 Crescent Ct Ste 300. .... Dallas TX 75201 214-880-4200 880-4201
TF: 888-767-3966 ■ *Web:* www.rosewoodhotels.com

San Luis Resort Spa & Conference Ctr
5222 Seawall Blvd .... Galveston Island TX 77551 409-744-1500 744-8452
TF Cust Svc: 800-445-0090 ■ *Web:* www.sanluisresort.com

Silverleaf Resorts Inc
1221 Riverbend Dr Ste 120. .... Dallas TX 75247 214-631-1166 637-0585
TF: 800-613-0310 ■ *Web:* www.silverleafresorts.com

South Shore Harbour Resort & Conference Ctr
2500 S Shore Blvd .... League City TX 77573 281-334-1000 334-1157
TF Resv: 800-442-5005 ■ *Web:* www.sshr.com

Tanglewood Resort Hotel & Conference Ctr
290 Tanglewood Cir .... Pottsboro TX 75076 903-786-2968
TF: 800-833-6569 ■ *Web:* www.tanglewoodresort.com

Tapatio Springs Golf Resort & Conference Ctr
1 Resort Way .... Boerne TX 78006 855-627-2243
TF: 800-999-3299 ■ *Web:* www.tapatioresort.com

Utah

Phone | Fax

Alta Lodge PO Box 8040 .... Alta UT 84092 801-742-3500 742-3504
TF Cust Svc: 800-707-2582 ■ *Web:* www.altalodge.com

Deer Valley Resort Lodging PO Box 889 .... Park City UT 84060 435-645-6626 645-6538
TF: 800-558-3337 ■ *Web:* www.deervalley.com

Homestead Resort 700 N Homestead Dr .... Midway UT 84049 888-327-7220
TF: 888-327-7220 ■ *Web:* www.homesteadresort.com

Little America Hotels & Resorts
500 S Main St. .... Salt Lake City UT 84101 801-596-5700
TF: 800-281-7899 ■ *Web:* www.littleamerica.com

Park City Mountain Resort (PCMR)
1345 Lowell Ave PO Box 39 .... Park City UT 84060 435-649-8111 647-5374
TF: 800-222-7275 ■ *Web:* www.parkcitymountain.com

Rustler Lodge 10380 East Hwy 210 PO Box 8030............ Alta UT 84092 801-742-2200 742-3832
TF: 888-532-2582 ■ *Web:* www.rustlerlodge.com

Snowbasin Ski Resort 3925 E Snowbasin Rd .... Huntsville UT 84317 801-620-1100
TF: 888-437-5488 ■ *Web:* www.snowbasin.com

Snowbird Ski & Summer Resort
Hwy 210 PO Box 929000 .... Snowbird UT 84092 801-742-2222 947-8227
TF: 800-453-3000 ■ *Web:* www.snowbird.com

Solitude Ski Resort
12000 Big Cottonwood Canyon .... Solitude UT 84121 801-534-1400 517-7705
TF: 800-748-4754 ■ *Web:* www.skisolitude.com

Stein Eriksen Lodge 7700 Stein Way.................. Park City UT 84060 435-649-3700 649-5825
TF: 800-453-1302 ■ *Web:* www.steinlodge.com

Vermont

Phone | Fax

Basin Harbor Club 4800 Basin Harbor Rd. .... Vergennes VT 05491 802-475-2311 475-6545
TF: 800-622-4000 ■ *Web:* www.basinharbor.com

Equinox, The 3567 Main St .... Manchester Village VT 05254 802-362-4700 362-4861
TF: 800-362-4747 ■ *Web:* www.equinoxresort.com

Hawk Inn & Mountain Resort 75 Billings Rd .... Plymouth VT 05056 802-672-3811 672-5585
TF: 800-685-4295 ■ *Web:* www.hawkresort.com

Inn at Stratton Mountain
5 Village Lodge Rd .... Stratton Mountain VT 05155 802-297-2500
TF: 800-787-2886 ■ *Web:* www.stratton.com

Jay Peak Resort 830 Jay Peak Rd. .... Jay VT 05859 802-988-2611
TF: 800-451-4449 ■ *Web:* www.jaypeakresort.com

Killington Resort & Pico Mountain
4763 Killington Rd .... Killington VT 05751 802-422-6200 422-6113
TF: 800-621-6867 ■ *Web:* www.killington.com

Lake Morey Resort 1 Clubhouse Rd. .... Fairlee VT 05045 802-333-4311
TF: 800-423-1211 ■ *Web:* www.lakemoreyresort.com

Smugglers' Notch Resort
4323 Vermont Rt 108 S .... Jeffersonville VT 05464 802-644-8851 644-1230
TF: 800-451-8752 ■ *Web:* www.smuggs.com

Stowe Mountain Resort 5781 Mountain Rd .... Stowe VT 05672 802-253-3000
TF: 800-253-4754 ■ *Web:* www.stowe.com

Stoweflake Mountain Resort & Spa
1746 Mountain Rd PO Box 369 .... Stowe VT 05672 802-253-7355 253-6858
TF: 800-253-2232 ■ *Web:* www.stoweflake.com

Sugarbush Resort & Inn
1840 Sugarbush Access Rd .... Warren VT 05674 802-583-6300 583-6390
TF: 800-537-8427 ■ *Web:* www.sugarbush.com

Topnotch at Stowe Resort & Spa
4000 Mountain Rd .... Stowe VT 05672 800-451-8686 253-9263*
**Fax Area Code:* 802 ■ *TF:* 800-451-8686 ■ *Web:* www.topnotchresort.com

Trapp Family Lodge
700 Trapp Hill Rd PO Box 1428 .... Stowe VT 05672 802-253-8511
TF: 800-826-7000 ■ *Web:* www.trappfamily.com

Woodstock Inn & Resort 14 The Green. .... Woodstock VT 05091 802-457-1100 457-6699
TF: 800-448-7900 ■ *Web:* www.woodstockinn.com

Virginia

Phone | Fax

Alamar Resort Inn 311 16th St. .... Virginia Beach VA 23451 757-428-7582
TF: 800-346-5681 ■ *Web:* www.alamarresortinn.net

Boar's Head Inn 200 Ednam Dr. .... Charlottesville VA 22903 434-296-2181 972-6024
TF: 800-476-1988 ■ *Web:* www.boarsheadinn.com

Phone | Fax

Breakers Resort Inn 16th & Oceanfront .... Virginia Beach VA 23451 757-428-1821 422-9602
TF: 800-237-7532 ■ *Web:* www.breakersresort.com

Cavalier Hotel 4201 Atlantic Ave. .... Virginia Beach VA 23451 757-425-8555
Web: www.cavalierhotel.com

Crestline Hotels & Resorts
3950 University Dr Ste 301 .... Fairfax VA 22030 571-529-6100 529-6095
Web: www.crestlinehotels.com

Great Wolf Lodge Williamsburg
549 E Rochambeau Dr .... Williamsburg VA 23188 757-229-9700 229-9780
TF: 800-551-9653 ■ *Web:* www.greatwolf.com

Kingsmill Resort & Spa
1010 Kingsmill Rd .... Williamsburg VA 23185 757-253-1703 253-8246
TF: 800-832-5665 ■ *Web:* www.kingsmill.com

Lansdowne Resort 44050 Woodridge Pkwy .... Leesburg VA 20176 703-729-8400 729-4096
TF: 877-513-8400 ■ *Web:* www.lansdowneresort.com

Massanutten Resort 1822 Resort Dr .... McGaheysville VA 22840 540-289-9441 289-6981
Web: www.massresort.com

Shenvalee Golf Resort 9660 Fairway Dr .... New Market VA 22844 540-740-3181 740-8931
TF: 888-339-3181 ■ *Web:* www.shenvalee.com

Turtle Cay Resort 600 Atlantic Ave. .... Virginia Beach VA 23451 757-437-5565 437-9104
TF: 888-989-7788 ■ *Web:* www.vacationrentalsvabeach.com

Virginia Beach Resort Hotel & Conference Ctr
2800 Shore Dr .... Virginia Beach VA 23451 757-481-9000
TF: 800-468-2722 ■ *Web:* www.virginiabeachresort.com

Virginia Crossings Resort
1000 Virginia Ctr Pkwy .... Glen Allen VA 23059 804-727-1400
TF: 888-444-6553 ■ *Web:* www.wyndhamvirginiacrossings.com

Williamsburg Inn 136 E Francis St .... Williamsburg VA 23185 757-229-1000 220-7096
TF: 800-447-8679 ■ *Web:* www.colonialwilliamsburg.com

Washington

Phone | Fax

Alderbrook Resort & Spa 7101 E SR-106 .... Union WA 98592 360-898-2200 898-4610
TF: 800-622-9370 ■ *Web:* www.alderbrookresort.com

Campbell's Resort 104 W Woodin Ave PO Box 278 .... Chelan WA 98816 509-682-2561 682-2177
TF: 800-553-8225 ■ *Web:* www.campbellsresort.com

Coast Hotels & Resorts USA
2003 Western Ave Ste 500 .... Seattle WA 98121 206-826-2700 826-2701
Web: www.coasthotels.com

Desert Canyon Golf Resort
1030 Desert Canyon Blvd .... Orondo WA 98843 509-784-1111 784-2701
TF: 800-258-4173 ■ *Web:* www.desertcanyon.com

Freestone Inn at Wilson Ranch
31 Early Winters Dr. .... Mazama WA 98833 509-996-3906
TF: 800-639-3809 ■ *Web:* www.freestoneinn.com

Lake Quinault Lodge 345 S Shore Rd .... Quinault WA 98575 360-288-2900 288-2901
TF: 800-562-6672 ■ *Web:* www.olympicnationalparks.com

Little Creek Casino Resort 91 W State Rt 108 .... Shelton WA 98584 360-427-7711
TF: 800-667-7711 ■ *Web:* www.little-creek.com

Polynesian Resort, The
615 Ocean Shores Blvd NW .... Ocean Shores WA 98569 360-289-3361
TF: 800-562-4836 ■ *Web:* www.thepolynesian.com

Resort Semiahmoo 9565 Semiahmoo Pkwy .... Blaine WA 98230 360-318-2000 318-2087
TF: 855-917-3767 ■ *Web:* www.semiahmoo.com

Rosario Resort & Spa 1400 Rosario Rd .... Eastsound WA 98245 360-376-2222 376-2289
TF: 800-562-8820 ■ *Web:* www.rosarioresort.com

Salish Lodge & Spa 6501 Railroad Ave DE .... Snoqualmie WA 98065 425-888-2556 888-9634
TF: 800-272-5474 ■ *Web:* www.salishlodge.com

Sun Mountain Lodge
604 Patterson Lk Rd PO Box 1000 .... Winthrop WA 98862 509-996-2211 996-3133
TF: 800-572-0493 ■ *Web:* www.sunmountainlodge.com

West Virginia

Phone | Fax

Canaan Valley Resort & Conference Ctr
230 Main Lodge Rd .... Davis WV 26260 304-866-4121 866-2172
TF: 800-622-4121 ■ *Web:* www.canaanresort.com

Glade Springs Resort 255 Resort Dr .... Daniels WV 25832 866-562-8054
TF: 866-562-8054 ■ *Web:* www.gladesprings.com

Greenbrier, The 300 W Main St .... White Sulphur Springs WV 24986 304-536-1110 536-7854
TF: 800-453-4858 ■ *Web:* www.greenbrier.com

Lakeview Golf Resort & Spa 1 Lakeview Dr. .... Morgantown WV 26508 304-594-1111
TF: 800-624-8300 ■ *Web:* www.lakeviewresort.com

Oglebay Resort & Conference Ctr
465 Lodge Dr Oglebay Pk .... Wheeling WV 26003 304-243-4000
TF: 800-624-6988 ■ *Web:* www.oglebay-resort.com

Pipestem Resort State Park PO Box 150 .... Pipestem WV 25979 304-466-1800
TF: 800-225-5982 ■ *Web:* www.pipestemresort.com

Snowshoe Mountain Resort 10 Snowshoe Dr .... Snowshoe WV 26209 304-572-1000
TF: 877-441-4386 ■ *Web:* www.snowshoemtn.com

Stonewall Resort 940 Resort Dr .... Roanoke WV 26447 304-269-7400
TF: 888-278-8150 ■ *Web:* www.stonewallresort.com

Woods Resort & Conference Ctr
Mountain Lk Rd PO Box 5 .... Hedgesville WV 25427 800-248-2222 754-8146*
**Fax Area Code: 304* ■ *TF:* 800-248-2222 ■ *Web:* www.thewoods.com

Wisconsin

Phone | Fax

Abbey Resort & Fontana Spa 269 Fontana Blvd .... Fontana WI 53125 262-275-9000
TF: 800-709-1323 ■ *Web:* www.theabbeyresort.com

Alpine Resort 7715 Alpine Rd PO Box 200 .... Egg Harbor WI 54209 920-868-3000
Web: www.alpineresort.com

American Club, The 419 Highland Dr .... Kohler WI 53044 920-457-8000 457-0299
TF: 800-344-2838 ■ *Web:* www.americanclubresort.com

Chanticleer Inn 1458 E Dollar Lk Rd. .... Eagle River WI 54521 715-479-4486 479-0004
TF: 800-752-9193 ■ *Web:* www.chanticleerinn.com

Chula Vista Resort 2501 River Rd .... Wisconsin Dells WI 53965 608-254-8366 254-7653
TF: 800-388-4782 ■ *Web:* www.chulavistaresort.com

Phone | Fax

Devil's Head Resort & Convention Ctr
S 6330 Bluff Rd .... Merrimac WI 53561 608-493-2251 493-2176
TF: 800-472-6670 ■ *Web:* www.devilsheadresort.com

Fox Hills Resort & Convention Ctr
250 W Church St .... Mishicot WI 54228 920-755-2376
TF: 800-950-7615 ■ *Web:* www.foxhillsresort.com

Grand Geneva Resort & Spa
7036 Grand Geneva Way .... Lake Geneva WI 53147 262-248-8811 249-4763
TF: 800-558-3417 ■ *Web:* www.grandgeneva.com

Great Wolf Resorts Inc
525 Junction Rd Ste 6000 S .... Madison WI 53717 608-253-2222
NASDAQ: WOLF ■ *Web:* www.greatwolf.com

Heidel House Resort 643 Illinois Ave. .... Green Lake WI 54941 920-294-3344 294-6128
TF: 800-444-2812 ■ *Web:* www.heidelhouse.com

Holiday Acres Resort
4060 S Shore Dr PO Box 460 .... Rhinelander WI 54501 715-369-1500
TF: 800-261-1500 ■ *Web:* www.holidayacres.com

Lake Lawn Resort 2400 E Geneva St .... Delavan WI 53115 262-728-7950 728-2347
TF: 800-338-5253 ■ *Web:* www.lakelawnresort.com

Landmark Resort 7643 Hillside Rd .... Egg Harbor WI 54209 920-868-3205 868-2569
TF: 800-273-7877 ■ *Web:* www.thelandmarkresort.com

Maxwelton Braes Golf Resort
7670 Hwy 57 .... Baileys Harbor WI 54202 920-839-2321
Web: maxweltonbraes.com

Olympia Resort & Spa 1350 Royale Mile Rd .... Oconomowoc WI 53066 262-369-4999 369-4998
TF: 800-558-9573 ■ *Web:* www.olympiaresort.com

Osthoff Resort, The
101 Osthoff Ave PO Box 151 .... Elkhart Lake WI 53020 920-876-3366 876-3228
TF: 800-876-3399 ■ *Web:* www.osthoff.com

Tundra Lodge Resort & Waterpark
865 Lombardi Ave .... Green Bay WI 54304 920-405-8700 405-1997
TF: 877-886-3725 ■ *Web:* www.tundralodge.com

Wyoming

Phone | Fax

Amangani Resort 1535 NE Butte Rd .... Jackson WY 83001 307-734-7333 734-7332
TF: 877-734-7333 ■ *Web:* www.aman.com/resorts/amangani

Aramark Parks & Destinations
27655 Hwy 26 & 287 .... Moran WY 83013 307-543-2847 543-2391
TF: 866-278-4245 ■ *Web:* www.togwoteelodge.com

Four Seasons Resort Jackson Hole
7680 Granite Loop Rd PO Box 544 .... Teton Village WY 83025 307-732-5000 732-5001
TF: 800-914-5110 ■ *Web:* www.fourseasons.com/jacksonhole

Grand Targhee Resort 3300 E Ski Hill Rd .... Alta WY 83414 307-353-2300 353-8148
TF: 800-827-4433 ■ *Web:* www.grandtarghee.com

Grand Teton Lodge Co
5 Miles N Hwy 89 PO Box 250 .... Moran WY 83013 307-543-2811 543-3143*
**Fax:* Resv ■ *TF Resv:* 800-628-9988 ■ *Web:* www.gtlc.com

Jackson Hole Mountain Resort
3395 Cody Ln PO Box 290 .... Teton Village WY 83025 307-733-2292 739-2737
TF: 800-450-0477 ■ *Web:* www.jacksonhole.com

Jackson HoleResort Lodging
3200 W McCollister Dr PO Box 510 .... Teton Village WY 83025 307-733-3990
TF: 800-443-8613 ■ *Web:* www.jhrl.com

Jackson Lake Lodge PO Box 250 .... Moran WY 83013 307-543-2811 543-3143
TF: 800-628-9988 ■ *Web:* www.gtlc.com

Rusty Parrot Lodge & Spa PO Box 1657 .... Jackson WY 83001 307-733-2000 733-5566
TF: 800-458-2004 ■ *Web:* www.rustyparrot.com

Signal Mountain Lodge PO Box 50 .... Moran WY 83013 307-543-2831 543-2569
Web: www.signalmountainlodge.com

Snow King Resort
400 E Snow King Ave Jackson Hole .... Jackson WY 83001 307-733-5200 733-4086
TF: 800-522-5464 ■ *Web:* www.snowking.com

Teton Pines Resort & Country Club
3450 N Clubhouse Dr. .... Wilson WY 83014 307-733-1005 733-2860
Web: www.tetonpines.com

670 RESTAURANT COMPANIES

See Also Bakeries p. 1838; Food Service p. 2315; Franchises p. 2325; Ice Cream & Dairy Stores p. 2555

Phone | Fax

94th Aero Squadron Restaurants
16320 Raymer St .... Van Nuys CA 91406 818-994-7437
Web: www.94thvannuys.com/94thvannuys

Al Copeland Investments Inc
1001 Harimaw Ct S. .... Metairie LA 70001 504-830-1000 401-0401
TF: 800-401-0401 ■ *Web:* www.alcopeland.com

Aloha Restaurants Inc
204 Main St Ste 960 .... Newport Beach CA 92661 949-250-0331 673-5085
Web: aloharestaurants.com

Arby's Restaurant Group Inc
1155 Perimeter Ctr W .... Atlanta GA 30338 678-514-4100
Web: arbys.com

Arctic Cir Restaurants Inc PO Box 339 .... Midvale UT 84047 801-561-3620
Web: www.acburger.com

Ark Restaurants Corp 85 Fifth Ave 14th Fl .... New York NY 10003 212-206-8800 206-8814
NASDAQ: ARKR ■ *Web:* www.arkrestaurants.com

Aurelio's Pizza 18162 Harwood Ave .... Homewood IL 60430 708-798-8050 798-6692
Web: www.aureliospizza.com

Azteca Mexican Restaurants
15735 Ambaum Blvd SW .... Seattle WA 98166 206-243-7021
Web: www.aztecamex.com

BAB Inc 500 Lk Cook Rd Ste 475 .... Deerfield IL 60015 800-251-6101 405-8140*
OTC: BABB ■ **Fax Area Code: 847* ■ *TF:* 800-251-6101 ■ *Web:* www.babcorp.com

Back Yard Burgers Inc 500 Church St Ste 200 .... Nashville TN 37219 615-620-2300 620-2301
Web: www.backyardburgers.com

Baker's Burgers Inc
1875 Business Ctr Dr .... San Bernardino CA 92408 909-884-5233
Web: www.bakersdrivethru.com

Barbato's Italian Restaurants 3512 Buffalo Rd. .... Erie PA 16510 814-899-3423
Web: www.barbatos.com

Company	City	State	ZIP	Phone	Fax
Battleground Restaurant Group Inc 1337 Winstead Pl *Web:* www.brginc.com	Greensboro	NC	27408	336-272-9355	272-5568
Beef O'Bradys Inc 5660 W Cypress St Ste A *TF:* 800-728-8878 ■ *Web:* www.beefobradys.com	Tampa	FL	33607	813-226-2333	
Bennett's Bar-B-Que Inc 3538 Peoria St Ste 508 *Web:* www.bennettsbbq.com	Aurora	CO	80010	303-792-3088	
Bennigan's 5151 Beltline Rd Ste 300 *Web:* bennigans.com	Dallas	TX	75254	469-248-4419	
Bertucci's Restaurant Corp 155 Otis St *Web:* www.bertuccis.com	Northborough	MA	01532	508-351-2500	393-1231
BF Nashville 1101 Kermit Dr Ste 310	Nashville	TN	37217	615-399-9700	399-3373
Biaggi's Ristorante Italiano 1705 Clearwater Ave *Web:* www.biaggis.com	Bloomington	IL	61704	309-664-2148	664-2149
Bice Ristorante 7 E 54th St *Web:* www.bicenewyork.com	New York	NY	10022	212-688-1999	752-1329
Bickford's Family Restauarants Inc 37 Oak St Ext *TF:* 800-969-5653 ■ *Web:* www.bickfordsrestaurants.com	Brockton	MA	02301	800-969-5653	
Big Boy Restaurants International LLC 4199 Marcy St *Web:* www.bigboy.com	Warren	MI	48091	586-759-6000	
Big Buck Brewery & Steakhouse Inc 550 S Wisconsin Ave *Web:* www.bigbuck.com	Gaylord	MI	49735	989-732-5781	732-3990
Bill Miller Bar-B-Q Inc 2750 Bill Miller Ln PO Box 839925 **Fax:* Sales ■ *TF:* 800-339-3111 ■ *Web:* www.billmillerbbq.com	San Antonio	TX	78223	210-225-4461	302-1533*
Biscuitville Inc 1414 Yanceyville St *Web:* www.biscuitville.com	Greensboro	NC	27405	336-553-3700	
BJ's Restaurants Inc 7755 Ctr Ave Ste 300 *NASDAQ: BJRI* ■ *Web:* bjsrestaurants.com	Huntington Beach	CA	92647	714-500-2400	848-8287
Bob Evans Farms Inc 3776 S High St *NASDAQ: BOBE* ■ *TF:* 800-939-2338 ■ *Web:* www.bobevans.com	Columbus	OH	43207	800-939-2338	
Bobby Rubino's Place for Ribs 2501 N Federal Hwy *Web:* www.bobbyrubinos.com	Pompano Beach	FL	33064	954-781-7550	
Boddie-Noell Enterprises Inc (BNEINC) 1021 Noell Ln PO Box 1908 *Web:* www.bneinc.com	Rocky Mount	NC	27804	252-937-2000	937-6991
Bojangles' Restaurants Inc 9432 Southern Pine Blvd *TF:* 800-366-9921 ■ *Web:* www.bojangles.com	Charlotte	NC	28273	704-335-1804	
Bonefish Grill 2202 NW Shore Blvd *Web:* www.bonefishgrill.com	Tampa	FL	33607	813-282-1225	
Bongos Cuban Cafe 420 Jefferson Ave *Web:* www.bongoscubancafe.com	Miami Beach	FL	33139	305-695-7072	695-7160
Bono's Pit Bar-B-Q 10645 Phillips Hwy Ste 200 *Web:* www.bonosbarbq.com	Jacksonville	FL	32256	904-880-8310	880-8373
Boomerang Grille 9200 S Western *Web:* www.boomeranggrille.com	Oklahoma City	OK	73139	405-378-7049	
Boston Beanery Restaurants Inc 63 Don Knotts Blvd *Web:* www.bostonbeanery.com	Morgantown	WV	26508	304-594-0095	
Boston Market Corp 14103 Denver W Pkwy *TF General:* 866-977-9090 ■ *Web:* www.bostonmarket.com	Golden	CO	80401	303-278-9500	216-5339
Boston Pizza Restaurants LP 1501 LBJ Fwy Ste 450 *TF:* 866-277-8721 ■ *Web:* www.bostons.com	Dallas	TX	75234	972-484-9022	484-7630
BRAVO | BRIO Restaurant Group 777 Goodale Blvd Ste 100 *TF:* 888-452-7286 ■ *Web:* www.bbrg.com/index.html	Columbus	OH	43212	614-326-7944	326-7943
Briad Group, The 78 Okner Pkwy *Web:* www.briad.com	Livingston	NJ	07039	973-597-6433	597-6422
Brigantine Restaurants Inc 7889 Ostrow St *Web:* www.brigantine.com	San Diego	CA	92111	858-268-1030	268-5727
Brinker International Inc 6820 LBJ Fwy *NYSE: EAT* ■ *TF:* 800-983-4637 ■ *Web:* www.brinker.com	Dallas	TX	75240	972-980-9917	770-9593
Bristol Bar & Grille Inc 1321 BaRdstown Rd PO Box 4607 *Web:* bristolbarandgrille.com	Louisville	KY	40204	502-456-1702	
Brock & Company Inc 257 Great Vly Pkwy *TF:* 866-468-2783 ■ *Web:* www.brockco.com	Malvern	PA	19355	610-647-5656	647-0867
Bubba Gump Shrimp Co LLC 2501 Seawall Blvd *TF:* 800-552-6379 ■ *Web:* www.bubbagump.com	Galveston	TX	77550	409-766-4952	
Buca di Beppo 1204 Harmon Pl *Web:* www.bucadibeppo.com	Minneapolis	MN	55403	612-288-0138	341-0496
Buca Inc 1204 Harmon Pl *Web:* www.bucadibeppo.com	Minneapolis	MN	55403	612-288-0138	341-0496
Buck's Pizza Franchising Corp Inc PO Box 405 *TF:* 800-310-8848 ■ *Web:* www.buckspizza.com	Du Bois	PA	15801	800-310-8848	
Buddy's Bar-B-Q 5806 Kingston Pk *Web:* www.buddysbarbq.com	Knoxville	TN	37919	865-584-1924	588-7211
Buffalo Wild Wings Inc 5500 Wayzata Blvd Ste 1600 *NASDAQ: BWLD* ■ *Web:* www.buffalowildwings.com	Minneapolis	MN	55416	952-593-9943	593-9787
Buffalo's Franchise Concepts Inc 9606 Santa Monica Blvd Penthouse *Web:* www.buffaloscafe.com	Beverly Hills	CA	90210	310-402-0606	
Burger King Corp 5505 Blue Lagoon Dr *TF:* 866-394-2493 ■ *Web:* www.bk.com	Miami	FL	33126	305-378-3000	
Burgerville USA 109 W 17th St *TF:* 888-827-8369 ■ *Web:* www.burgerville.com	Vancouver	WA	98660	360-694-1521	694-9114
Cafe Express LLC 19443 Gulf Fwy *Web:* www.cafe-express.com	Webster	TX	77598	281-554-6999	554-5501
California Cafe Restaurants Old Town 50 University Ave Ste 260 *Web:* www.californiacafe.com	Los Gatos	CA	95030	408-354-8118	354-1400
California Pizza Kitchen Inc 18601 Airport Way Ste 135 *NASDAQ: CPKI* ■ *Web:* www.cpk.com	Santa Ana	CA	92707	949-252-6125	
Capital Restaurant Concepts Ltd (CRC) 1305 Wisconsin Ave NW *Web:* www.capitalrestaurants.com	Washington	DC	20007	202-339-6800	339-6801
Captain D's LLC 624 Grassmere Park Dr Ste 30 *TF:* 800-314-4819 ■ *Web:* www.captainds.com	Nashville	TN	37211	615-391-5461	
Carey Hilliard's Restaurants 11111 Abercom St *Web:* careyhilliards.com	Savannah	GA	31419	912-925-3225	
Carino's Italian 150 Cascade Mall Dr *Web:* www.carinos.com	Burlington	WA	98233	360-757-4535	
Carlson Restaurants 4201 Marsh Ln *TF:* 800-374-3297 ■ *Web:* www.carlson.com	Carrollton	TX	75007	972-662-5400	
Carrols Restaurant Group Inc 968 James St *NASDAQ: TAST* ■ *Web:* www.carrols.com	Syracuse	NY	13203	315-424-0513	
Carvers Steak & Chops 11940 Bernardo Plz Dr *Web:* www.carverssteak.com	San Diego	CA	92128	858-485-1262	
Cask 'n' Cleaver 8689 Ninth St *TF:* 800-995-4452 ■ *Web:* www.casknacleaver.com	Rancho Cucamonga	CA	91730	909-981-5771	981-9734
Catalina Restaurant Group Inc 2200 Faraday Ave Ste 250 *Web:* www.catalinarestaurantgroup.com	Carlsbad	CA	92008	760-804-5750	476-5141
CEC Entertainment Inc 3903 W Airport Frwy *NYSE: CEC* ■ *TF:* 888-778-7193 ■ *Web:* www.chuckecheese.com	Irving	TX	75062	972-258-8507	
Champps Entertainment Inc 19111 Dallas Pkwy Ste 370 *Web:* www.champps.com	Dallas	TX	75287	972-581-1171	
Charley's Grilled Subs 2500 Farmers Dr Ste 140 *TF:* 800-437-8325 ■ *Web:* www.charleys.com	Columbus	OH	43235	614-923-4700	923-4701
Chart House Restaurants 1510 W Loop S *Web:* www.chart-house.com	Houston	TX	77027	713-850-1010	
Checkers Drive-In Restaurants Inc 4300 W Cypress St Ste 600 *TF:* 800-800-8072 ■ *Web:* www.checkers.com	Tampa	FL	33607	813-283-7000	283-7208
Cheddar's Casual Cafe 700 I- 635 Service Rd *Web:* cheddars.com	Irving	TX	75063	972-409-0300	409-0302
Cheesecake Factory Inc 26901 Malibu Hills Rd *NASDAQ: CAKE* ■ *Web:* www.thecheesecakefactory.com	Calabasas Hills	CA	91301	818-871-3000	871-3001
Chefs International Inc 62 Broadway *Web:* www.lobster.com	Point Pleasant Beach	NJ	08742	732-295-0350	295-4514
Chelo's Inc 1725 Mendon Rd Ste 209 *Web:* www.chelos.com	Cumberland	RI	02864	401-312-6500	312-6501
Chesapeake Bay Seafood House Assoc LLC 1960 Gallows Rd Ste 200 *Web:* www.chesapeakerestaurants.com	Vienna	VA	22182	703-827-0320	893-1536
Chevys Inc 5660 Katella Ave Ste 100 *Web:* www.chevys.com	Cypress	CA	90630	858-205-1123	
Chick-fil-A Inc 5200 Buffington Rd *Web:* www.chick-fil-a.com	Atlanta	GA	30349	404-765-8000	
China Grill Management Inc (CGM) 60 W 53rd St *Web:* www.chinagrillmgt.com	New York	NY	10019	212-333-7788	
Chipotle Mexican Grill Inc 1401 Wynkoop St *NYSE: CMG* ■ *Web:* www.chipotle.com	Denver	CO	80202	303-595-4000	
Chuck's Steak House Inc 20 Segar St *Web:* www.chuckssteakhouse.com	Danbury	CT	06810	203-792-5555	
CiCi Enterprises LP 1080 W Bethel Rd	Coppell	TX	75019	972-745-4200	745-4203
City Barbeque Inc 6175 Emerald Pkwy *Web:* citybbq.com	Dublin	OH	43016	614-583-0999	
Clock Restaurants 902 Clint Moore Rd Ste 126	Boca Raton	FL	33487	561-994-3440	994-3655
Clyde's Restaurant Group 3236 M St NW *Web:* www.clydes.com	Washington	DC	20007	202-333-9180	625-7429
Corporate Chefs Inc 22 Parkridge Rd *Web:* www.corporatechefs.com	Haverhill	MA	01835	978-372-7400	
Cosi Inc 1751 Lk Cook Rd Ste 600 *NASDAQ: COSI* ■ *Web:* www.getcosi.com	Deerfield	IL	60015	847-597-8800	
Cousins Submarines Inc N83 W13400 Leon Rd *TF:* 800-238-9736 ■ *Web:* www.cousinssubs.com	Menomonee Falls	WI	53051	262-253-7700	253-7710
Cozymels Restaurant 2655 Grapevine Mills *Web:* www.cozymels.com	Grapevine	TX	76051	972-724-0277	
Cracker Barrel Old Country Store Inc PO Box 787 *NASDAQ: CBRL* ■ *TF:* 800-333-9566 ■ *Web:* www.crackerbarrel.com	Lebanon	TN	37088	615-444-5533	444-5533
Culver Franchising System Inc 1240 Water St *Web:* www.culvers.com	Prairie du Sac	WI	53578	608-643-7980	643-7982
D'Angelo Sandwich Shops 600 Providence Hwy *TF:* 800-727-2446 ■ *Web:* www.dangelos.com	Dedham	MA	02026	781-461-1200	461-1896
Darden Restaurants Inc (DRI) 1000 Darden Center Dr *NYSE: DRI* ■ *Web:* www.darden.com	Orlando	FL	32837	407-245-4000	
Davanni's Inc 1100 Xenium Ln N *Web:* www.davannis.com	Plymouth	MN	55441	952-927-2300	
DavCo Restaurants Inc 1657 Crofton Blvd *Web:* www.wendavco.com	Crofton	MD	21114	410-721-3770	793-0754
Debos Diners Inc 7625 Hamilton Pk Dr Ste 26 *Web:* debosdiners.com	Chattanooga	TN	37421	423-855-4650	
Del Taco Inc 25521 Commercentre Dr Ste 200 *TF Cust Svc:* 800-852-7204 ■ *Web:* www.deltaco.com	Lake Forest	CA	92630	949-462-9300	462-7444
Deli Management Inc 2400 Broadway *Web:* jasonsdeli.com	Beaumont	TX	77702	409-838-1976	
Deli Partners LLC 1608 Rogers Rd	Fort Worth	TX	76107	817-738-9355	
Denny's Corp 203 E Main St *NASDAQ: DENN* ■ *TF Cust Svc:* 800-733-6697 ■ *Web:* www.dennys.com	Spartanburg	SC	29319	864-597-8000	
Denny's Inc 203 E Main St **Fax:* Mktg ■ *Web:* www.dennys.com	Spartanburg	SC	29319	864-597-8000	597-7708*

Company	City	State	Zip	Phone	Fax
Dick's Last Resort 2211 N Lambar St *Web:* www.dickslastresort.com	Dallas	TX	75202	214-747-0001	
Dixie Restaurants Inc 1215 Rebsamen Pk Rd *Web:* www.dixiecafe.com	Little Rock	AR	72202	501-666-3494	666-8900
Dolly's Pizza Franchising Inc 1097 Union Lake Rd *Web:* www.dollyspizza.com	White Lake	MI	48386	248-360-6440	
Domino's Pizza Inc 30 Frank Lloyd Wright Dr *NYSE: DPZ* ■ *TF:* 800-253-8182 ■ *Web:* dominos.com	Ann Arbor	MI	48106	734-930-3030	
Don's Restaurants 8905 Lake Ave *Web:* www.strangcorp.com	Cleveland	OH	44102	216-961-6700	961-1966
Donatos Pizza 935 Taylor Stn Rd. **Fax Area Code:* 614 ■ *TF:* 800-366-2867 ■ *Web:* www.donatos.com	Columbus	OH	43230	800-366-2867	416-7701*
DRM Inc 5324 N 134th Ave. *Web:* www.drmarbys.com	Omaha	NE	68164	402-556-4098	573-0171
Dutchman Hospitality Group 4985 Walnut St PO Box 158 *Web:* www.dhgroup.com	Walnut Creek	OH	44687	330-893-2926	893-2637
Dynaco Inc 7050 N Fresno St Ste 210 *Web:* brg.co	Fresno	CA	93720	559-485-8520	256-5820
Eat'n Park Hospitality Group Inc 285 E Waterfront Dr PO Box 3000 *TF:* 800-947-4033 ■ *Web:* www.eatnpark.com	Homestead	PA	15120	412-461-2000	461-6000
Edo Japan International Inc 32 St SE Ste 4838 *TF:* 888-336-9888 ■ *Web:* www.edojapan.com	Calgary	AB	T2B2S6	403-215-8800	215-8801
Eegee's Inc 3360 E Ajo Way *Web:* www.eegees.com	Tucson	AZ	85713	520-294-3333	889-4340
Einstein Noah Restaurant Group Inc 555 Zang St Ste 300 *Web:* www.einsteinbros.com	Lakewood	CO	80228	303-568-8000	
El Centro Foods Inc 6930 1/2 Tujunga Ave	North Hollywood	CA	91605	818-766-4395	
El Fenix Corp 11075 Harry Hines Blvd. *TF:* 877-591-1918 ■ *Web:* www.elfenix.com	Dallas	TX	75229	972-241-2171	241-3031
El Pollo Loco 3535 Harbor Blvd Ste 100 *TF:* 877-375-4968 ■ *Web:* www.elpolloloco.com	Costa Mesa	CA	92626	714-599-5000	
El Torito Restaurants Inc 5660 Katella Ave Ste 100 *Web:* www.eltorito.com	Cypress	CA	90630	562-346-1200	
Elephant Bar Restaurant 10100 Stockdale Hwy *Web:* www.elephantbar.com	Bakersfield	CA	93311	661-663-3020	
Emeril's Homebase 829 St Charles Ave *Web:* www.emerils.com	New Orleans	LA	70130	504-524-4241	
Erik's Deli Cafe 365 Coral St *Web:* www.eriksdelicafe.com	Santa Cruz	CA	95060	831-458-1818	458-9797
Escape Enterprises Ltd 222 Neilston St *Web:* www.steakescape.com	Columbus	OH	43215	614-224-0300	224-6460
Famous Dave's of America Inc 12701 Whitewater Dr Ste 200 *NASDAQ: DAVE* ■ *TF:* 800-929-4040 ■ *Web:* www.famousdaves.com	Minnetonka	MN	55343	952-294-1300	
Fatburger North America Inc 9606 Santa Monica Blvd Penthouse Ste 200 *Web:* www.fatburger.com	Beverly Hills	CA	90210	310-319-1850	319-1863
Fatz Cafe 4324 Wade Hampton Blvd *Web:* www.fatz.com	Taylors	SC	29687	864-322-1331	322-1332
Fausto's Fried Chicken Inc 905 E Fourth St.	Dequincy	LA	70633	337-786-7264	
Faz Restaurants Inc 5121 HopyaRd Rd *Web:* www.fazrestaurants.com	Pleasanton	CA	94588	925-460-0444	469-1604
Figaro's Italian Pizza Inc 1500 Liberty St SE Ste 160 *TF:* 888-344-2767 ■ *Web:* www.figaros.com	Salem	OR	97302	503-371-9318	363-5364
Firehouse Restaurant Group Inc 3400 Kori Rd Ste 8 *Web:* www.firehousesubs.com	Jacksonville	FL	32257	904-886-8300	886-2111
Flamers Charbroiled Hamburgers 1515 International Pkwy Ste 2013 *TF:* 866-749-4889 ■ *Web:* www.flamersgrill.com	Heathrow	FL	32746	407-574-8363	
Flanigan's Enterprises Inc 5059 NE 18th Ave. *NYSE: BDL* ■ *Web:* www.flanigans.net	Fort Lauderdale	FL	33334	954-377-1961	
Fogo de Chao 14881 Quorum Dr Ste 750 *Web:* www.fogodechao.com	Dallas	TX	75254	972-960-9533	
Folks Southern Kitchen 1384 Buford Business Blvd Ste 500 *Web:* www.folkskitchen.com	Buford	GA	30518	770-904-6595	904-6805
Food Concepts International LP 2575 S Loop 289 *Web:* www.abuelos.com	Lubbock	TX	79423	806-785-8686	785-8866
Fosters Freeze LLC 630 Central Ave. *Web:* www.fostersfreeze.com	Alameda	CA	94501	510-521-1242	
Fox's Pizza Den Inc 4425 Willaim Penn Hwy *TF:* 800-899-3697 ■ *Web:* www.foxspizza.com	Murrysville	PA	15668	724-733-7888	
Friendly Ice Cream Corp 1855 Boston Rd. *TF:* 800-966-9970 ■ *Web:* www.friendlys.com	Wilbraham	MA	01095	413-731-4000	543-5844
Frisch's Restaurants Inc 2800 Gilbert Ave *NYSE: FRS* ■ *TF:* 800-873-3633 ■ *Web:* www.frischs.com	Cincinnati	OH	45206	513-961-2660	559-5160
Frullati Cafe & Bakery 9311 E Via de Ventura *TF:* 866-452-4252 ■ *Web:* www.frullati.com	Scottsdale	AZ	85258	480-362-4800	362-4812
Garden Fresh Restaurant Corp 15822 Bernardo Ctr Dr Ste A *TF:* 800-874-1600 ■ *Web:* www.souplantation.com	San Diego	CA	92127	858-675-1600	675-1616
Garduno's 10031 Coors Blvd NW. *Web:* www.gardunosrestaurants.com	Albuquerque	NM	87114	505-890-7000	
Gastronomy Inc 48 W Market St Ste 250 *Web:* marketstreetgrill.com	Salt Lake City	UT	84101	801-322-2020	363-5275
Gates Bar-B-Q 4621 Paseo Blvd *TF:* 800-662-7427 ■ *Web:* www.gatesbbq.com	Kansas City	MO	64110	816-923-0900	
Giorgio Restaurants 222 boul Saint Laurent *Web:* www.giorgio.ca	Montreal	QC	H2Y2Y3	514-845-4221	844-0071
Godfathers Pizza Inc 2808 N 108th St. *Web:* godfathers.com	Omaha	NE	68164	402-391-1452	
Gold Star Chili 650 Lunken Pk Dr *TF:* 800-643-0465 ■ *Web:* www.goldstarchili.com	Cincinnati	OH	45226	513-231-4541	624-4415
Golden Corral Corp 5151 Glenwood Ave *Web:* goldencorral.com	Raleigh	NC	27612	919-781-9310	881-4654
Golden Franchising Corp 1131 Rockingham Ste 250 *Web:* www.goldenchick.com	Richardson	TX	75080	972-831-0911	831-0401
Golden Griddle Corp, The 20 Woodlawn Rd E. *Web:* www.goldengriddleinc.com	Guelph	ON	N1H1G7	905-629-1460	
Good Eats Inc 12200 Stemmons Fwy Ste 100 *TF:* 800-275-1337 ■ *Web:* www.goodeatsgrill.com	Dallas	TX	75234	972-241-5500	
Good Times Restaurants Inc 141 Union Blvd Ste 400 *NASDAQ: GTIM* ■ *Web:* www.goodtimesburgers.com	Lakewood	CO	80228	303-384-1400	
Great Steak & Potato Co 9311 E Via de Ventura *TF:* 866-452-4252 ■ *Web:* www.thegreatsteak.com	Scottsdale	AZ	85258	480-362-4800	362-4812
Great Wraps! Inc 4 Executive Pk E Ste 315 *Web:* www.greatwraps.com	Atlanta	GA	30329	404-248-9900	248-0180
Griff's of America Inc 1202 Richardson Dr Ste 312 *Web:* griffshamburgers.com	Richardson	TX	75080	972-238-9561	
Grill Concepts Inc 6300 Canoga Ave Ste 600 *OTC: GLLC* ■ *Web:* www.dailygrill.com	Woodland Hills	CA	91367	818-251-7000	999-4745
Grinner's Food Systems Ltd 105 Walker *Web:* www.greco.ca	Truro	NS	B2N4B1	902-893-4141	
Grotto Pizza Inc 20376 Coastal Hwy *Web:* www.grottopizza.com	Rehoboth Beach	DE	19971	302-227-3567	227-4566
Hacienda Mexican Restaurants 1501 N Ironwood Dr *TF:* 800-541-3227 ■ *Web:* www.haciendafiesta.com	South Bend	IN	46635	800-541-3227	
Haddad Restaurant Group Inc 3100 Gillham Rd.	Kansas City	MO	64109	816-931-2261	931-9044
Hal Smith Restaurant Group Inc 3101 W Tecumseh Rd. *Web:* www.ehsrg.com	Norman	OK	73072	405-321-2600	
Happy Chef Systems Inc 51646 US Hwy 169	Mankato	MN	56001	507-388-2953	345-4585
Happy Joe's Inc 2705 Happy Joe Dr *Web:* www.happyjoes.com	Bettendorf	IA	52722	563-332-8811	332-5822
Hard Rock Cafe International Inc 6100 Old Pk Ln. *TF:* 888-519-6683 ■ *Web:* www.hardrock.com	Orlando	FL	32835	407-445-7625	445-7869
Hard Times Cafe 1404 King St *Web:* www.hardtimes.com	Alexandria	VA	22314	703-837-0050	837-0057
Harman Management Corp 199 First St Ste 212	Los Altos	CA	94022	650-941-5681	948-7532
Hero Systems Inc. 912 SW 3rd Ave *Web:* www.bigtownhero.com	Portland	OR	97204	503-228-4376	228-8778
High Plains Pizza Inc 7 W PkwyBlvd *Web:* highplainspizza.com	Liberal	KS	67901	620-624-5638	624-5411
Hillstone Restaurant Group 147 S Beverly Dr. *TF:* 800-230-9787 ■ *Web:* www.hillstone.com	Beverly Hills	CA	90212	310-385-7343	385-7119
Ho-Lee-Chow 2204 Danforth Ave. *Web:* www.holeechow.com	Toronto	ON	M4C1K3	416-996-3333	
Hof's Hut Restaurants Inc 2601 E Willow St *Web:* www.hofshut.com	Signal Hill	CA	90755	562-596-0200	430-0480
Holcomb Bridge at Grimes Bridge 690 Holcomb Bridge Rd *Web:* www.myfriendsplacedeli.com	Roswell	GA	30076	770-594-9117	
Holland Inc 109 W 17th St. *Web:* www.hollandinc.com	Vancouver	WA	98660	360-694-1521	694-9114
Homestyle Dining LLC 3701 W Plano Pkwy Ste 200 *Web:* www.ponderosasteakhouses.com	Plano	TX	75075	972-244-8900	588-5905
Hoss's Steak & Sea House 170 Patchway Rd *TF:* 800-992-4677	Duncansville	PA	16635	814-695-7600	695-3865
Hot Dog on a Stick 5942 Priestly Dr. *TF:* 877-639-2361 ■ *Web:* www.hotdogonastick.com	Carlsbad	CA	92008	760-930-0456	
Houlihan's Restaurants Inc 8700 State Line Rd Ste 100 *Web:* www.houlihans.com	Leawood	KS	66206	913-901-2500	901-2673
House of Blues Entertainment Inc 7060 Hollywood Blvd *Web:* www.houseofblues.com	Hollywood	CA	90028	323-769-4600	769-4787
Huddle House Inc 5901 Peachtree Dunwoody Ste B450 *Web:* www.huddlehouse.com	Atlanta	GA	30328	770-325-1300	
Humperdink's Texas LLC PO Box 542465	Dallas	TX	75354	214-358-4159	
Humpty's Restaurants International Inc 2505 Macleod Terr S *Web:* www.humptys.com	Calgary	AB	T2G5J4	403-269-4675	266-1973
Hungry Howie's Pizza & Subs Inc 30300 Stephenson Hwy Ste 200 *Web:* www.hungryhowies.com	Madison Heights	MI	48071	248-414-3300	414-3301
Hyde Park Restaurant Systems 26300 Chagrin Blvd Ste 1 *Web:* www.hydeparkrestaurants.com	Beachwood	OH	44122	216-464-0688	595-8267
Ignite Restaurant Group Inc 9900 Wpark Dr Ste 300 *Web:* igniterestaurants.com	Houston	TX	77063	713-366-7500	
IHOP Corp 450 N Brand Blvd *TF:* 866-444-5144 ■ *Web:* www.ihop.com	Glendale	CA	91203	818-240-6055	637-4730
Il Fornaio America Corp 770 Tamalpais Dr Ste 400 **Fax Area Code:* 408 ■ *TF:* 888-454-6246 ■ *Web:* www.ilfornaio.com	Corte Madera	CA	94925	415-945-0500	286-6632*
In-N-Out Burger Inc 4199 Campus Dr 9th Fl *TF Cust Svc:* 800-786-1000 ■ *Web:* www.in-n-out.com	Irvine	CA	92612	949-509-6200	509-6389

Phone | Fax

Interfoods of America Inc
9500 S Dadeland Blvd Ste 720 — Miami FL 33156 — 305-670-0746 670-0767

International Dairy Queen Corp
7505 Metro Blvd — Minneapolis MN 55439 — 952-830-0200 830-0270
TF: 866-793-7582 ■ *Web:* www.dairyqueen.com

International Restaurant Management Group Inc (IRMG)
4104 Aurora St — Coral Gables FL 33146 — 305-476-1611 476-9622
Web: www.irmgusa.com

Iron Hill Brewery 2502 W Sixth St — Wilmington DE 19805 — 302-472-2739
Web: www.ironhillbrewery.com

Isaac's Deli Inc 354 N Prince St Ste 220 — Lancaster PA 17603 — 717-394-0623 393-0955
Web: www.isaacsdeli.com

Islands Restaurants 5750 Fleet St Ste 120 — Carlsbad CA 92008 — 760-268-1800
Web: www.islandsrestaurants.com

J & S Cafeteria Inc 110 Westover Dr — High Point NC 27265 — 336-884-0404
Web: www.jandscafeteria.com

J A Sutherland Inc 228 MN St — Red Bluff CA 96080 — 530-529-1470 527-1959
Web: www.jasutherland.com

J Alexander's Corp 3401 W End Ave Ste 260 — Nashville TN 37203 — 615-269-1900 269-1999
NASDAQ: JAX ■ *TF:* 888-528-1991 ■ *Web:* www.jalexandersholdings.com

J Gilbert's Wood Fired Steaks
8700 State Line Rd Ste 100 — Leawood KS 66206 — 913-642-8070 901-2673
Web: www.jgilberts.com

Jack in the Box Inc 9330 Balboa Ave — San Diego CA 92123 — 858-571-2121
NASDAQ: JACK ■ *TF:* 800-955-5225 ■ *Web:* www.jackinthebox.com

Jack's Family Restaurants Inc
2831 19th St S — Homewood AL 35209 — 205-879-9321 945-8167
TF: 888-795-2707 ■ *Web:* www.eatatjacks.com

Jake's Pizza Enterprises Inc
1931 Rohlwing Rd Ste B — Rolling Meadows IL 60008 — 847-368-1990 368-1995

James Coney Island Inc 1750 Stebbins Dr — Houston TX 77043 — 713-932-1500 932-0061
Web: www.jamesconeyisland.com

Jan Cos 35 Sockanosset Cross Rd — Cranston RI 02920 — 401-946-4000 946-4392
TF: 888-693-6844 ■ *Web:* www.jancompanies.com

Jerry's Famous Deli Inc
12711 Ventura Blvd Ste 400 — Studio City CA 91604 — 818-766-8311 766-8315
Web: www.jerrysdeli.com

Jerry's Systems Inc
702 Russell Ave Ste 306 — Gaithersburg MD 20877 — 800-990-9176
TF: 800-990-9176 ■ *Web:* www.jerrysusa.com

Jet's America Inc 37501 Mound Rd — Sterling Heights MI 48310 — 586-268-5870 268-6762
Web: www.jetspizza.com

Jim's Restaurants 8520 Crownhill Blvd — San Antonio TX 78209 — 210-828-1493 822-8606
Web: www.jimsrestaurants.com

Jimmy John's Franchise Inc 2212 Fox Dr — Champaign IL 61820 — 217-356-9900 359-2956
TF: 800-546-6904 ■ *Web:* www.jimmyjohns.com

Jocks & Jills & Frankie's Sports Grill
4109 S Stream Blvd Ste 100-A — Charlotte NC 28217 — 770-209-0920
Web: www.jocks-frankies.com

Joey's Only Seafood Franchising Corp
514-42nd Ave SE — Calgary AB T2G1Y6 — 403-243-4584 243-8989
TF: 800-661-2123 ■ *Web:* www.joeys.ca

John Harvard's Brew House 33 Dunster St — Cambridge MA 02138 — 617-868-3585 868-4341
Web: www.johnharvards.com

JRN Inc 209 W Seventh St — Columbia TN 38401 — 931-381-3000
Web: kfc.com

K-Bob's USA Inc 141 E Palace Ave — Santa Fe NM 87501 — 505-982-3438
Web: k-bobs.com

K-Mac Enterprises Inc PO Box 6538 — Fort Smith AR 72906 — 479-646-2053 646-8748
TF: 800-947-9277 ■ *Web:* www.kmaccorp.com

Kahala Corp 9311 E Via de Ventura — Scottsdale AZ 85258 — 480-362-4800 362-4812
Web: www.blimpie.com

Keg Steakhouse 10100 Shellbridge Way — Richmond BC V6X2W7 — 604-276-0242 276-2681
Web: www.kegsteakhouse.com

Kellys Roast Beef Inc 605 Broadway Ste 300 — Saugus MA 01906 — 781-233-5700

KFC Corp 1441 Gardiner Ln — Louisville KY 40213 — 920-923-2321
TF: 800-225-5532 ■ *Web:* www.kfc.com

Kimpton Hotel & Restaurant Group LLC
222 Kearny St Ste 200 — San Francisco CA 94108 — 415-397-5572 296-8031
TF: 800-546-7866 ■ *Web:* www.kimptonhotels.com

King Taco Restaurants Inc 3421 E 14th St — Los Angeles CA 90023 — 323-266-3585 266-6565
Web: www.kingtaco.com

King's Seafood Co 3185 Airway Ave — Costa Mesa CA 92626 — 714-432-0400 432-0111
Web: www.kingsseafood.com

Kings Family Restaurants
1820 Lincoln Hwy — North Versailles PA 15137 — 412-823-0324
Web: www.kingsfamily.com

Kobe Japanese Steakhouse Inc
468 W Hwy 436 — Altamonte Springs FL 32714 — 407-862-6099
Web: www.kobesteakhouse.com

Kona Grill Inc 7150 E Camelback Rd Ste 220 — Scottsdale AZ 85251 — 480-922-8100 991-6811
NASDAQ: KONA ■ *TF:* 866-328-5662 ■ *Web:* www.konagrill.com

L & L Hawaiian Barbecue
931 University Ave Ste 202 — Honolulu HI 96826 — 808-951-9888
Web: www.hawaiianbarbecue.com

La Salsa Fresh Mexican Grill
320 Commerce Ste 100 — Irvine CA 92602 — 949-270-8900
TF: 866-452-7257 ■ *Web:* lasalsa.com

LaBelle Management Inc
405 S Mission Rd — Mount Pleasant MI 48858 — 989-772-2902 773-7521
Web: www.labellemgt.com

Lambert's Cafe Inc 2305 E Malone — Sikeston MO 63801 — 573-471-4261 471-7563
Web: www.throwedrolls.com

Lamppost Pizza Franchise Corp 3002 Dow Ave — Tustin CA 92780 — 714-731-6171
Web: www.lamppost-backstreet.com

Landry's Restaurants Inc 1510 W Loop S — Houston TX 77027 — 713-850-1010 632-4702*
**Fax Area Code:* 281 ■ *TF:* 800-552-6379 ■ *Web:* www.landrysinc.com

LaRosa's Inc 2334 Boudinot Ave — Cincinnati OH 45238 — 513-347-5660
Web: www.larosas.com

Lawry's Restaurants Inc
234 E Colorado Blvd Ste 500 — Pasadena CA 91101 — 626-440-5234
TF: 888-552-9797 ■ *Web:* www.lawrysonline.com

LEDO Pizza System Inc
2001 Tidewater Colony Dr — Annapolis MD 21401 — 410-721-6887 571-8395

Legal Sea Foods Inc 1 Seafood Way — Boston MA 02210 — 617-530-9000 530-9649
Web: www.legalseafoods.com

Lettuce Entertain You Enterprises Inc
5419 N Sheridan Rd — Chicago IL 60640 — 773-878-7340 878-8468
Web: www.leye.com

Levy Restaurants 980 N Michigan Ave — Chicago IL 60611 — 312-664-8200
Web: www.levyrestaurants.com

Libby Hill Seafood Restaurants Inc
4517 W Market St — Greensboro NC 27407 — 336-294-0505 292-6005
Web: www.libbyhill.com

Little Caesars Inc 2211 Woodward Ave — Detroit MI 48201 — 313-983-6409
TF: 800-722-3727 ■ *Web:* www.littlecaesars.com

Lone Star Steakhouse & Saloon Inc
5055 W Pk Blvd Ste 500 — Plano TX 75093 — 972-295-8600
Web: www.lonestarsteakhouse.com

Lone Star Texas Grill 472 Morden Rd Ste 101 — Oakville ON L6K3W4 — 905-845-5852
Web: www.lonestartexasgrill.com

Long John Silver's Restaurants Inc
9505 Williamsburg Plaza — Louisville KY 40222 — 502-815-6100
Web: www.ljsilvers.com

LongHorn Steakhouse 1000 Darden Ctr Dr — Orlando FL 32837 — 888-221-0642
TF: 888-221-0642 ■ *Web:* www.longhornsteakhouse.com

Luby's Inc 13111 NW Fwy Ste 600 — Houston TX 77040 — 713-329-6800
NYSE: LUB ■ *TF:* 800-886-4600 ■ *Web:* www.lubys.com

Lunan Corp 414 N Orleans St Ste 402 — Chicago IL 60654 — 312-645-9898 646-0654
Web: www.arbysrestaurants.com

Macayo Mexican Restaurants 12637 S 48th St — Phoenix AZ 85044 — 480-598-5101
Web: www.macayo.com

Maggiano's Little Italy
3000 Grapevine Mills pkwy — Grapevine TX 76051 — 214-360-0707
Web: www.maggianos.com

Magic Time Machine 8520 Crownhill Blvd — San Antonio TX 78209 — 210-828-1493
Web: www.magictimemachine.com

Malnati Organization Inc 3685 Woodhead Dr — Northbrook IL 60062 — 847-562-1814 562-1950
TF: 800-568-8646 ■ *Web:* www.loumalnatis.com

Mancha Development Co 2275 Sampson Ave Ste 201 — Corona CA 92879 — 951-271-4100 271-4110

Marie Callender Restaurant & Bakery
27101 Puerta Real Ste 260 — Mission Viejo CA 92691 — 800-776-7437
TF: 800-776-7437 ■ *Web:* mariecallenders.com

Maui Tacos International Inc
2001 Palmer Ave. Ste 105 — Larchmont NY 10538 — 866-388-3758
TF: 866-388-3758 ■ *Web:* www.mauitacos.com

Maui Wowi Inc
9311 E Via de Ventura Ste 300 — Scottsdale AZ 85258 — 303-781-7800
Web: www.mauiwowi.com

Maz Mezcal Inc 316 E 86th St — New York NY 10028 — 212-472-1599
Web: mazmezcal.com

McDonald's Corp 1 McDonald's Plz — Oak Brook IL 60523 — 630-623-3000
NYSE: MCD ■ *TF:* 800-244-6227 ■ *Web:* www.mcdonalds.com

McDonald's Restaurants of Canada Ltd
1 McDonald's Pl — Toronto ON M3C3L4 — 416-443-1000 446-3443
TF: 888-424-4622 ■ *Web:* www.mcdonalds.ca

Me-N-Ed's-Bullard/West
1731 W Bullard Ave Ste 101 — Fresno CA 93711 — 559-431-7331
Web: www.meneds.com

Melting Pot Restaurants Inc
8810 Twin Lakes Blvd — Tampa FL 33614 — 813-881-0055 889-9361
TF: 800-783-0867 ■ *Web:* www.meltingpot.com

Mercedes Restaurants Inc 2402 W Nebraska Ave — Peoria IL 61604 — 309-676-6443
Web: mercedesrestaurants.com

Meritage Hospitality Group Inc
3310 Eagle Park Dr Ste 205 — Grand Rapids MI 49525 — 616-776-2600
OTC: MHGU ■ *Web:* www.meritagehospitality.com

Mexican Restaurants Inc 1135 Edgebrook St — Houston TX 77034 — 713-943-7574 300-5859*
OTC: CASA ■ **Fax Area Code:* 832

Milio's Sandwiches 901 Deming Way Ste 202 — Madison WI 53717 — 608-662-3000 662-3001
Web: www.milios.com

Mirabile Investment Corp 1900 Whitten Rd — Memphis TN 38133 — 901-324-0450
Web: www.mic-memphis.com

Mitchco International Inc
4801 Sherburn Ln — Louisville KY 40207 — 502-896-9653 896-2989
Web: www.mitchcointernational.com

Mo's Restaurants 657 SW Bay Blvd — Newport OR 97365 — 541-265-7512 265-9323
Web: www.moschowder.com

Monical Pizza Corp 530 N Kinzie Ave — Bradley IL 60915 — 815-937-1890 937-9828
TF: 800-929-3227 ■ *Web:* monicals.com

Morgan's Foods Inc 4829 Galaxy Pkwy Ste S — Cleveland OH 44128 — 216-360-7500
Web: www.morgansfoods.com

Morton's The Steakhouse 400 Post St — San Francisco CA 94102 — 415-986-5830
Web: www.mortons.com

Mr Gatti's Inc 5912 Balcones Dr — Austin TX 78731 — 512-459-4796 454-4990
Web: www.mrgattis.com

Mr Goodcents Franchise Systems Inc
8997 Commerce Dr — DeSoto KS 66018 — 800-648-2368 583-3500*
**Fax Area Code:* 913 ■ *TF:* 800-648-2368 ■ *Web:* goodcentssubs.com

Mr Hero Restaurants
7010 Engle Rd Ste 100 — Middleburg Heights OH 44130 — 440-625-3080 625-3081
TF: 888-860-5082 ■ *Web:* www.mrhero.com

Mr Jim's Pizza Inc
Franchise Service Ctr
2521 Pepperwood St — Farmers Branch TX 75234 — 972-267-5467
TF: 800-583-5960 ■ *Web:* mrjims.pizza

Myriad Restaurant Group Inc 249 W Broadway — New York NY 10013 — 212-219-9500 219-2380
Web: www.myriadrestaurantgroup.com

Nancy's Pizza 7929 W 171st St — Tinley Park IL 60477 — 708-614-6100
Web: www.nancyspizza.com

Nathan's Famous Inc 1 Jericho Plz 2nd Fl — Jericho NY 11753 — 516-338-8500 338-7220
NASDAQ: NATH ■ *Web:* www.nathansfamous.com

National Coney Island Inc
27947 Groesback Hwy — Roseville MI 48066 — 586-771-7744 771-9578
Web: www.nationalconeyisland.com

Nations Foodservice Inc
11090 San Pablo Ave Ste 200 — El Cerrito CA 94530 — 510-237-1952
Web: nationsrestaurants.com

Phone | Fax

New York Fries 1220 Yonge St Ste 400 ... Toronto ON M4T1W1 416-963-5005
Web: www.newyorkfries.com

Newport Bay Restaurants
2865 NW Town Ctr Loop ... Portland OR 97006 503-645-2526
Web: www.newportbay.com

Nexdine LLC 905B S Main St Ste 203 ... Mansfield MA 02048 978-674-8464
Web: www.nexdine.com

Ninety-Nine Restaurant & Pubs 160 Olympia Ave ... Woburn MA 01801 781-933-8999
Web: www.99restaurants.com

Noble Roman's Pizza Inc
1 Virginia Ave Ste 300 ... Indianapolis IN 46204 317-634-3377
Web: www.nobleromans.com

Noodles & Co 520 Zang St ... Broomfield CO 80021 720-214-1900
Web: www.noodles.com

Norsan Group Inc 2445 Meadowbrook Pkwy ... Duluth GA 30096 678-242-1654 414-0617*
*Fax Area Code: 770 ■ *Web:* norsan.net

North Beach Pizza Inc 1462 Grant Ave ... San Francisco CA 94133 415-433-2444
Web: www.northbeachpizza.com

NPC International Inc 7300 W 129th St ... Overland Park KS 66213 913-327-5555 327-5850
TF: 866-299-1148 ■ *Web:* www.npcinternational.com

O'Charley's Inc 3038 Sidco Dr ... Nashville TN 37204 615-256-8500 782-5043
NASDAQ: CHUX ■ *Web:* ocharleys.com

Office Beer Bar & Grill
728 Thompson Ave Rt 22 W ... Bridgewater NJ 08805 732-469-0066
Web: www.office-beerbar.com

Old Chicago Restaurants
100 Superior Plaza Way Ste 100 ... Superior CO 80027 720-304-2048 664-4199*
*Fax Area Code: 303 ■ *Web:* www.oldchicago.com

Old Country Buffet Restaurants (OCB)
120 Chula Vista ... Hollywood Park TX 78232 509-484-5026
Web: www.oldcountrybuffet.com

Old Spaghetti Factory Inc (OSF)
0715 SW Bancroft St ... Portland OR 97239 503-225-0433 226-6214
Web: www.osf.com

Olga's Kitchen Inc 1940 Northwood Dr ... Troy MI 48084 248-362-0001 362-2013
Web: www.olgas.com

Olive Garden
1000 Darden Center Dr PO Box 695017 ... Orlando FL 32869 407-245-4336
Web: www.olivegarden.com

Orange Julius of America 7505 Metro Blvd ... Minneapolis MN 55439 952-830-0200
TF: 866-793-7582 ■ *Web:* www.dairyqueen.com

Original Pancake House Franchising Inc
8601 SW 24th Ave ... Portland OR 97219 503-246-9007
Web: www.originalpancakehouse.com

Outback Steakhouse Inc
2202 NW Shore Blvd 5th Fl ... Tampa FL 33607 813-282-1225 281-2114
Web: www.outback.com

PacPizza LLC 220 Porter Dr Ste 100 ... San Ramon CA 94583 925-838-8567 838-5801
Web: pacpizza.com

Palm Management Corp
1730 Rhode Island Ave NW Ste 900 ... Washington DC 20036 202-775-7256
TF: 800-388-7256 ■ *Web:* www.thepalm.com

Palm Restaurant
1730 Rhode Island Ave NW Ste 900 ... Washington DC 20036 202-775-7256
TF: 800-795-7256 ■ *Web:* www.thepalm.com

Palomino Restaurant Rotisseria Bar
1420 Fifth Ave ... Seattle WA 98101 206-623-1300
Web: www.palomino.com

Panchero's Mexican Grill
2475 Coral Ct Ste B ... Coralville IA 52241 319-545-6565
Web: www.pancheros.com

Panda Express 1717 Walnut Grove Ave ... Rosemead CA 91770 626-312-5401
TF: 800-877-8988 ■ *Web:* www.pandaexpress.com

Panda Restaurant Group Inc
1683 Walnut Grove Ave ... Rosemead CA 91770 626-799-9898 372-8288
TF: 800-877-8988 ■ *Web:* www.pandarg.com

Papa Gino's Inc 600 Providence Hwy ... Dedham MA 02026 781-461-1200 461-1896
TF: 800-727-2446 ■ *Web:* www.papaginos.com

Papa John's International Inc
2002 Papa John's Blvd ... Louisville KY 40299 502-261-7272
NASDAQ: PZZA ■ *TF:* 877-547-7272 ■ *Web:* www.papajohns.com

Papa Murphy's International Inc
8000 NE Pkwy Dr Ste 350 ... Vancouver WA 98662 360-260-7272 260-0500
Web: www.papamurphys.com

Pappas Restaurants Inc 13939 NW Fwy ... Houston TX 77040 713-869-0151 869-4932
TF: 877-277-2748 ■ *Web:* www.pappas.com

Pappas Seafood House 13939 NW Fwy ... Houston TX 77040 713-869-0151 869-4932
TF: 877-277-2748 ■ *Web:* www.pappas.com

Pappasito's Cantina 13070 Hwy 290 ... Houston TX 77040 713-462-0246
Web: www.pappasitos.com

Parco Ltd Co 998 Fremont Ave ... Dubuque IA 52003 563-557-1337

Pasta House Co 700 New Ballas Rd ... Saint Louis MO 63141 314-535-6644 531-2499
Web: www.pastahouse.com

Pasta Pomodoro Inc 851 Cherry Ave Ste 27 ... San Bruno CA 94066 415-241-5200 431-8940
Web: www.pastapomodoro.com

Pat O'Brien's International Inc
718 St Peter St ... New Orleans LA 70116 504-525-4823 582-6918
TF: 800-597-4823 ■ *Web:* www.patobriens.com

Patina Group 12700 Center Ct Dr S 9th Fl ... Cerritos CA 90703 866-972-8462
TF: 866-972-8462 ■ *Web:* www.patinagroup.com

Paul Revere's Pizza International Ltd
1570 42nd St NE ... Cedar Rapids IA 52402 319-395-9113
Web: www.paulreverespizza.com

Pei Wei 7676 E Pinnacle Peak Rd ... Scottsdale AZ 85255 480-888-3000
Web: www.peiwei.com

Penguin Point Franchise Systems Inc
2691 E US 30 ... Warsaw IN 46580 574-267-3107 267-3154
TF: 800-577-5755 ■ *Web:* www.penguinpoint.com

Pepe's Inc 1325 W 15th St ... Chicago IL 60608 312-733-2500
Web: www.pepes.com

Perkins Restaurant & Bakery
6075 Poplar Ave Ste 800 ... Memphis TN 38119 901-766-6400
TF: 800-877-7375 ■ *Web:* www.perkinsrestaurants.com

Peter Piper Inc 4745 N Seventh St Ste 350 ... Phoenix AZ 85014 480-609-6400
Web: www.peterpiperpizza.com

PF Chang's China Bistro Inc
7676 E Pinnacle Peak Rd ... Scottsdale AZ 85255 480-888-3000
NASDAQ: PFCB ■ *TF:* 866-732-4264 ■ *Web:* www.pfchangs.com

Piatti Restaurant Co 835 Fifth Ave ... San Rafael CA 94901 415-380-2525 380-2530
Web: www.piatti.com

Piccadilly Cafeterias Inc
3332 S Sherwood Forest Blvd ... Baton Rouge LA 70816 225-293-4853 445-4740*
*Fax Area Code: 318 ■ *Web:* www.piccadilly.com

Piccadilly Circus Pizza
1007 Okoboji Ave PO Box 188 ... Milford IA 51351 800-338-4340
TF: 800-338-4340 ■ *Web:* www.pcpizza.com

Pitt Grill Inc 928 Shady Ln ... Lake Charles LA 70601 337-479-1320 582-4297

Pizza Boli's 5721 Falls Rd 5725 Falls Rd ... Baltimore MD 21209 410-323-3278 323-7745
Web: www.pizzabolis.com

Pizza Factory Inc 49430 Rd 426 ... Oakhurst CA 93644 559-683-3377 683-6879
TF: 800-654-4840 ■ *Web:* www.pizzafactory.com

Pizza Inn Inc 3551 Plano Pkwy ... The Colony TX 75056 877-574-9924
NASDAQ: RAVE ■ *TF:* 877-574-9924 ■ *Web:* www.pizzainn.com

Pizza King Inc 221 Farabee Dr ... Lafayette IN 47905 765-447-2172
Web: theoriginalpizzaking.com

Pizza Plus Pizza Inc 299 Franklin Dr ... Blountville TN 37617 423-279-9335
Web: www.pizzaplusinc.com

Pizza Pro Inc 2107 N Second St PO Box 1285 ... Cabot AR 72023 501-605-1175 605-1204
TF: 800-777-7554 ■ *Web:* www.pizzapro.com

Pizza Ranch Inc 204 19th St SE ... Orange City IA 51041 800-321-3401
TF: 800-321-3401 ■ *Web:* www.pizzaranch.com

Planet Hollywood International Inc
4700 Millenia Blvd Ste 400 ... Orlando FL 32839 407-903-5500
Web: www.planethollywoodintl.com

Popeyes Louisiana Kitchen
5555 Glenridge Connector NE Ste 300 ... Atlanta GA 30342 404-459-4450
Web: www.popeyes.com

Potbelly Sandwich Works
222 Merchandise Mart Plz Ste 2300 ... Chicago IL 60654 312-951-0600
Web: www.potbelly.com

Pretzelmaker 1346 Oakbrook Dr Ste 170 ... Norcross GA 30093 877-639-2361
TF: 877-639-2361 ■ *Web:* pretzelmaker.com

Qdoba Restaurant Corp
4865 WaRd Rd Ste 500 ... Wheat Ridge CO 80033 720-898-2300 898-2396
Web: www.qdoba.com

Quality Dining Inc 4220 Edison Lakes Pkwy ... Mishawaka IN 46545 574-271-4600 271-4612
TF: 800-589-3820 ■ *Web:* www.qdi.com

Quiznos Corp 7595 Technology Way Ste 200 ... Denver CO 80237 720-359-3300
TF: 866-486-2783 ■ *Web:* www.quiznos.com

Rafferty's Inc
1750 Scottsville Rd Ste 2 ... Bowling Green KY 42104 270-842-0123
Web: www.raffertys.com

Rainforest Cafe 1510 W Loop S ... Houston TX 77027 713-850-1010
Web: www.rainforestcafe.com

Ram Restaurant & Brewery 10013 59th Ave SW ... Lakewood WA 98499 253-584-3191 588-9617

Ram's Horn Restaurant 26200 W 12 Mile Rd ... Southfield MI 48034 248-350-3430
Web: ramshornrestaurants.com

Red Hot & Blue Restaurants Inc
1600 Wilson Blvd ... Arlington VA 22209 703-276-7427
TF: 888-509-7100 ■ *Web:* www.redhotandblue.com

Red Robin Gourmet Burgers Inc
6312 S Fiddlers Green Cir
Ste 200-N ... Greenwood Village CO 80111 303-846-6000 846-6013
NASDAQ: RRGB ■ *Web:* www.redrobin.com

Republic Foods Inc
1101 Wootton Pkwy Ste 460 ... Rockville MD 20852 301-656-6687 656-3934
Web: www.republicfoods.com

Restaurant Assoc Inc 132 W 31st St Ste 601 ... New York NY 10001 212-613-5500
Web: www.restaurantassociates.com

Restaurant Developers Corp
7010 Engle Rd Ste 100 ... Cleveland OH 44130 440-625-3080
TF: 888-860-5082 ■ *Web:* www.mrhero.com

Restaurants Unlimited Inc
411 First Ave S Ste 200 ... Seattle WA 98104 206-634-0550
TF: 877-855-6106 ■ *Web:* www.r-u-i.com

Rib Crib Corp 4535 S Harvard Ave ... Tulsa OK 74135 918-712-7427
TF: 800-275-9677 ■ *Web:* www.ribcrib.com

Riscky's Barbecue 2314 Azle Ave ... Fort Worth TX 76164 817-624-8662 624-3777
Web: www.risckys.com

Roc Management & Assoc Inc
1601 Keokuk Ave ... Spirit Lake IA 51360 712-336-3933

Rockfish Seafood Grill
801 E Campbell Rd Ste 300 ... Richardson TX 75081 214-887-9400 821-0138

Rocky Rococo 105 E Wisconsin Ave ... Oconomowoc WI 53066 262-569-5580
TF: 800-888-7625 ■ *Web:* www.rockyrococo.com

Romano's Macaroni Grill 4535 Belt Line Rd ... Addison TX 75001 972-386-3831
Web: www.macaronigrill.com

Rosati's Pizza 28381 Davis Pkwy Ste 701 ... Warrenville IL 60555 630-393-2280 393-2281
Web: rosatispizza.com

Rosebud Restaurant 1419 W Diversey Pkwy ... Chicago IL 60614 773-325-9700
Web: www.rosebudrestaurants.com

Roy's Restaurants
321 West Katella Ave Ste 105 ... Anaheim CA 92802 949-261-2424
Web: www.roysrestaurant.com

RPM Pizza LLC 15384 Fifth St ... Gulfport MS 39503 228-832-4000 832-1092

Rubio's Restaurants Inc
1902 Wright Pl Ste 300 ... Carlsbad CA 92008 760-929-8226 929-8203
TF: 800-354-4199 ■ *Web:* www.rubios.com

Ruby Tuesday Inc 150 W Church Ave ... Maryville TN 37801 865-379-5700
NYSE: RT ■ *Web:* www.rubytuesday.com

Runza National Inc 5931 S 58th St ... Lincoln NE 68516 402-423-2394
Web: runza.com

Russ' Restaurants Inc 390 E Eigth St ... Holland MI 49423 616-396-6571 396-6755
TF: 800-521-1778 ■ *Web:* www.russrestaurants.com

Rusty's Pizza Parlors Inc
228 W Carrillo St Ste F ... Santa Barbara CA 93101 805-963-9127 962-5054
Web: www.rustyspizza.com

Phone Fax

Ruth's Hospitality Group Inc
1030 W Canton Ave Ste 100` Winter Park FL 32789 407-333-7440 833-9625
NASDAQ: RUTH ■ *TF Sales:* 800-544-0808 ■ *Web:* www.ruthschris.com

Sagebrush Steakhouse 129 Fast Ln Mooresville NC 28117 704-660-5939 799-6199
TF: 877-704-5939 ■ *Web:* www.sagebrushsteakhouse.com

Sandella's LLC 263 Farmington Ave Farmington CT 06030 203-544-9984 544-9981
Web: www.sandellas.com

Sasnak Management Corp 1877 N Rock Rd Wichita KS 67206 316-683-2611

Schwartz Bros Restaurants
325 118th Ave SE Ste 106 Bellevue WA 98005 425-455-3948 451-3573
Web: www.schwartzbros.com

Select Restaurants Inc
2000 Auburn Dr 1 Chagrin Highlands Cleveland OH 44122 216-464-6606
Web: www.selectrestaurants.com

Selrico Services Inc 717 W Ashby Pl San Antonio TX 78212 210-737-8220 737-7994
Web: selricoservices.com

SERVUS 4201 Mannheim Rd Ste A Jasper IN 47546 812-482-3212 482-4013
Web: www.greatservus.com

Shakey's USA 2200 W Valley Blvd Alhambra CA 91803 626-576-0616
Web: www.shakeys.com

Shari's Restaurant & Pies
9400 SW Gemini Dr Beaverton OR 97008 503-605-4299 605-4260
TF: 800-433-5334 ■ *Web:* www.sharis.com

Shoney's Restaurants Inc
1717 Elm Hill Pk Ste B1 Nashville TN 37210 615-231-2333
TF: 800-708-3558 ■ *Web:* www.shoneys.com

Shuhei Inc 23360 Chagrin Blvd Beachwood OH 44122 216-464-1720
Web: shuheirestaurant.com

Silver Diner Inc 12276 Rockville Pk Rockville MD 20852 301-770-0333 770-2832
TF: 866-561-0518 ■ *Web:* www.silverdiner.com

Sizzler Restaurants
25910 Acero Rd Ste 350 Mission Viejo CA 92691 855-895-9703
TF: 855-895-9703 ■ *Web:* www.sizzler.com

Sizzling Wok International Inc
2560 Shell Rd Richmond BC V6X0B8 604-207-8871

Skyline Chili Inc 4180 Thunderbird Ln Fairfield OH 45014 513-874-1188 874-3591
Web: www.skylinechili.com

Smith & Wollensky Restaurant Group Inc
318 N State St Chicago IL 60654 312-670-9900
Web: www.smithandwollensky.com

Smith Bros Restaurant Corp
16 N Marengo Ave Ste 609 Pasadena CA 91101 626-577-2400 577-8330
Web: www.smithbrothersrestaurants.com

Smitty's Canada Ltd 501 18th Ave SW Ste 600 Calgary AB T2S0C7 403-229-3838 229-3899
Web: www.smittys.ca

Snappy Tomato Pizza Co
6111 A Burgundy Hill Dr Burlington KY 41005 859-525-4680 525-4686
TF: 888-463-7627 ■ *Web:* www.snappytomato.com

Sobik's Subs 620 Crown Oak Ctr Dr Ste 104 Longwood FL 32750 407-671-2600 671-0260
Web: www.sobiks.com

Sonic Corp 300 Johnny Bench Dr Oklahoma City OK 73104 405-225-5000
NASDAQ: SONC ■ *TF:* 877-828-7868 ■ *Web:* sonicdrivein.com

Sonic Drive-in Restaurants
300 Johnny Bench Dr Oklahoma City OK 73104 405-225-5000
TF: 877-828-7868 ■ *Web:* www.sonicdrivein.com

Sonny Bryan's Smokehouse
12720 Hilcrest Rd Ste 910 Dallas TX 75230 214-350-1800 350-3738
Web: www.sonnybryans.com

Sonny's Franchise Co
2605 Maitland Ctr Pkwy Ste C Maitland FL 32751 407-660-8888
Web: www.sonnysbbq.com

Souplantation 15822 Bernardo Ctr Dr Ste A San Diego CA 92127 858-675-1600
Web: www.souplantation.com

Southern Multifoods Inc
101 E Cherokee St Jacksonville TX 75766 903-586-1524
Web: www.smi-tex.com

Spaghetti Warehouse Inc 1255 W I-20 Arlington TX 76017 817-557-0321 550-0908*
**Fax Area Code:* 972 ■ *Web:* www.meatballs.com

Spangles Inc 437 N Hillside St Wichita KS 67214 316-685-8817
Web: www.spanglesinc.com

Specialty Restaurants Corp
8191 E Kaiser Blvd Anaheim CA 92808 714-279-6100 998-7574
Web: www.specialtyrestaurants.com

Stanford's Restaurant & Bar 913 Lloyd Ctr Portland OR 97232 503-335-0811
Web: www.stanfords.com

Steak Escape 222 Neilston St Columbus OH 43215 614-224-0300 224-6460
Web: www.steakescape.com

Steak N Shake Co
3810 W Washington Holt Rd Indianapolis IN 46241 317-241-0483
TF: 877-785-6745 ■ *Web:* www.steaknshake.com

Strang Corp 8905 Lake Ave Cleveland OH 44102 216-961-6767 961-1966
Web: www.strangcorp.com

Strategic Restaurants Inc
3000 Executive Pkwy Ste 515 San Ramon CA 94583 925-328-3300 328-3333

Stuckey's Corp 8555 16th St Ste 850 Silver Spring MD 20910 301-585-8222
TF: 800-423-6171 ■ *Web:* www.stuckeys.com

Stuft Pizza Franchise Corp
50855 Washington St Ste 210 La Quinta CA 92253 760-777-1660 777-1948
Web: www.stuftpizza.com

Sub Station II Inc PO Box 2260 Sumter SC 29150 803-494-9709 775-2220
Web: www.substationii.com

Summerwood Corp 14 Balligomingo Rd Conshohocken PA 19428 610-520-1000
TF: 800-760-0950 ■ *Web:* www.summerwood.biz

Super Subby's Inc 8924 N Dixie Dr Dayton OH 45414 937-898-0996
Web: www.subbys.com

Sushi Doraku 1104 Lincoln Rd Miami Beach FL 33139 305-695-8383
Web: www.dorakusushi.com

Sweet Tomatoes 15822 Bernardo Ctr Dr Ste A San Diego CA 92127 858-675-1600
Web: www.souplantation.com

Tacala LLC 3750 Corporate Woods Dr Vestavia Hills AL 35242 205-443-9600 443-9700
Web: www.tacala.com

Taco Bell Corp 1 Glen Bell Way Irvine CA 92618 949-863-4000 863-2252
Web: www.tacobell.com

Phone Fax

Taco Cabana Inc 8918 Tesoro Dr Ste 200 San Antonio TX 78217 210-804-0990 804-1970
TF: 800-580-8668 ■ *Web:* www.tacocabana.com

Taco Mayo 10405 Greenbriar Pl Oklahoma City OK 73159 405-691-8226
Web: www.tacomayo.com/default.html

Taco Time International Inc
9311 E Via de Venutra Scottsdale AZ 85258 480-362-4800 362-4812
TF: 866-452-4252 ■ *Web:* www.tacotime.com

Tacoma Inc 328 E Church St Martinsville VA 24112 276-666-9417 666-9427
TF: 800-352-9417 ■ *Web:* www.gototaco.com

Tacos Mexico Inc 5120 E Olympic Blvd Los Angeles CA 90022 323-266-0482
Web: tacosmexico.com

Tavistock Restaurants LLC
6475 Christie Ave Ste 300 Emeryville CA 94608 510-594-4262
Web: tavistockrestaurants.com

Tavistock Restaurants LLC
4705 S Apopka Vineland Rd Ste 210 Orlando FL 32819 407-909-7101
TF: 800-424-2753 ■ *Web:* tavistockrestaurantcollection.com

Ted's Hot Dogs 95 Roger Chaffee Dr Amherst NY 14228 716-691-3731
Web: www.tedshotdogs.com

Tee Jaye's Country Place Restaurants
1363 Parsons Ave PO Box 6646 Columbus OH 43206 614-443-9773 443-0613
Web: www.barnyardbuster.com

Temple Square Hospitality Corp
15 E S Temple St 9th Fl Salt Lake City UT 84150 801-531-1000 539-3117
Web: www.templesquare.com

Texas Roadhouse Inc
6040 Dutchmans Ln Ste 400 Louisville KY 40205 502-426-9984
NASDAQ: TXRH ■ *TF:* 800-839-7623 ■ *Web:* www.texasroadhouse.com

Thompson Hospitality
1741 Business Center Dr Ste 200 Herndon VA 20170 703-964-5500 759-1538
Web: www.thompsonhospitality.com

Thundercloud Subs 1102 W Sixth St Austin TX 78703 512-479-8805 479-8806
Web: www.thundercloud.com

Tim Hortons Inc 874 Sinclair Rd Oakville ON L6K2Y1 905-845-6511 845-0265
NYSE: THI ■ *TF:* 888-601-1616 ■ *Web:* www.timhortons.com

Toarmina's Pizza 32785 Cherry Hill Rd Westland MI 48186 734-728-0060
Web: www.toarminas.com

TooJays Original Gourmet Deli
3654 Georgia Ave West Palm Beach FL 33405 561-659-9011 659-9703
Web: www.toojays.com

Trader Vic's Inc 9 Anchor Dr Emeryville CA 94608 510-653-3400
Web: www.tradervicsemeryville.com

Trail Dust Steak Houses Inc 2300 E Lamar Arlington TX 76006 817-640-6411
Web: www.traildust.com

Travaglini Enterprises 231 Chestnut St Meadville PA 16335 814-724-4880

Tri City Foods Inc 1400 Opus Pl Ste 900 Downers Grove IL 60515 630-598-3300
Web: www.3cityfoods.com

Tripps Restaurants 1605 Highwoods Blvd Greensboro NC 27410 336-272-9355 272-5568

TS Restaurants of California & Hawaii
2335 Kalakaua Ave Ste 116 Honolulu HI 96815 808-922-2268
Web: www.hulapie.com

Tubbys Grilled Submarines 31920 Groesbeck Hwy Fraser MI 48026 800-752-0644 293-5088*
**Fax Area Code:* 586 ■ *TF:* 800-752-0644 ■ *Web:* www.tubby.com

Tudor's Biscuit World PO Box 3603 Charleston WV 25336 304-343-4026
Web: www.tudorsbiscuitworld.com

Tumbleweed Inc 2301 River Rd Louisville KY 40206 502-893-0323 893-6676
TF: 866-719-3892 ■ *Web:* www.tumbleweedrestaurants.com

TWA Restaurant Group Inc
16012 Metcalf Ave Ste 1 Overland Park KS 66085 913-239-0266 239-9768

Uno Chicago Grill 100 Charles Pk Rd Boston MA 02132 617-323-9200
Web: www.unos.com

Uno Restaurant Corp 100 Charles Pk Rd Boston MA 02132 617-323-9200 323-6906
Web: www.unos.com

V & J Holding Cos Inc 6933 W Brown Deer Rd Milwaukee WI 53223 414-365-9003 365-9467
Web: www.vjfoods.com

Valentino's 2601 S 70th St Lincoln NE 68506 402-434-9350
TF: 888-289-8257 ■ *Web:* www.valentinos.com

Villa Enterprises Management Ltd Inc
25 Washington St Morristown NJ 07960 973-285-4800
Web: www.villapizza.com

Village Inn 400 W 48th Ave Denver CO 80216 303-296-2121
TF: 800-800-3644 ■ *Web:* www.villageinn.com

Viva Burrito Co 860 E 16th St Tucson AZ 85719 520-882-8713
Web: vivaburritoco.com

Vocelli Pizza 1005 S Bee St Pittsburgh PA 15220 412-919-2100 937-9204
Web: www.vocellipizza.com

Waffle House Inc 5986 Financial Dr Norcross GA 30071 770-729-5700 555-5555*
**Fax Area Code:* 555 ■ *Web:* www.wafflehouse.com

Wahoo's Fish Taco 2855 Pullman St Santa Ana CA 92705 949-222-0670 222-0750
Web: www.wahoos.com

Ward's Food Systems Inc
5133 Lincoln Rd Ext Hattiesburg MS 39402 601-268-9273
TF: 800-748-9273 ■ *Web:* wardsrestaurants.com

Weathervane Seafood Restaurant 306 US Rt 1 Kittery ME 03904 207-439-0330
TF: 800-914-1774 ■ *Web:* www.weathervaneseafoods.com

Wendy's International Inc 1 Dave Thomas Blvd Dublin OH 43017 614-764-3100 764-3330
Web: www.wendys.com

Whataburger Restaurants LP
300 Concord Plz PO Box 791990 San Antonio TX 78216 210-476-6000
Web: www.whataburger.com

Willie G's 1605 Post Oak Blvd Houston TX 77056 713-840-7190
Web: www.williegs.com

Winger's USA Inc 404 East 4500 South Ste A12 Murray UT 84107 801-261-3700
Web: www.wingers.info

Wingstop Restaurants Inc
1101 E Arapaho Rd Ste 150 Richardson TX 75081 972-686-6500
Web: www.wingstop.com

Wolfgang Puck Worldwide Inc
100 N Crescent Dr Ste 100 Beverly Hills CA 90210 310-432-1640 432-1640
Web: www.wolfgangpuck.com

World Wrapps 3023 80th Ave SE Ste 200 Mercer Island WA 98040 206-233-9727
Web: www.worldwrapps.com

Phone Fax

Yamashiro Inc 1999 N Sycamore Ave................Hollywood CA 90068 323-466-5125
Web: yamashirohollywood.com
Yard House Restaurant 620 Spectrum Center Dr..........Irvine CA 92618 949-753-9373
Web: www.yardhouse.com
Yaya's Flame Broiled Chicken 521 S Dort Hwy ....Flint MI 48503 810-235-6550 235-5210
Web: www.yayas.com
Yoshinoya Beef Bowl 991 Knox St .... Torrance CA 90502 310-527-6060 527-6050
TF: 800-576-8017 ■ *Web:* www.yoshinoyaamerica.com
Yum! Brands Inc 1441 Gardiner Ln...................Louisville KY 40213 502-874-8300
NYSE: YUM ■ *TF:* 800-225-5532 ■ *Web:* www.yum.com
Zero's Subs 3760 Virginia Beach Blvd............Virginia Beach VA 23452 757-463-9114
Web: zerossubs.com
Zyng Inc RPO Atwater PO Box 72108.................. Montreal QC H3J2Z6 514-288-8800 939-8808
TF: 888-328-9964 ■ *Web:* www.zyng.com

671 RESTAURANTS (INDIVIDUAL)

See Also Shopping/Dining/Entertainment Districts p. 1814; Restaurant Companies p. 3078
Individual restaurants are organized by city names within state and province groupings. (Canadian provinces are interfiled among the US states, in alphabetical order.)

Alabama

Phone Fax

Bottega 2240 Highland Ave S.....................Birmingham AL 35205 205-939-1000
Web: bottegarestaurant.com
Daniel George 2837 Culver Rd ....Birmingham AL 35223 205-871-3266 871-7266
Web: www.birminghammenus.com/danielgeorge
Dreamland BBQ 1427 14th Ave S ....Birmingham AL 35205 205-933-2133 933-9770
TF: 800-752-0544 ■ *Web:* www.dreamlandbbq.com
Fleming's Prime Steakhouse & Wine Bar
103 Summit Blvd ....Birmingham AL 35243 205-262-9463
Web: www.flemingssteakhouse.com
Highlands Bar & Grill 2011 11th Ave S..............Birmingham AL 35205 205-939-1400 939-1405
Web: www.highlandsbarandgrill.com
Hot & Hot Fish Club 2180 11th Ct S.................Birmingham AL 35205 205-933-5474
Web: www.birminghammenus.com
Jim-n-Nick's 1908 11th Ave S....................Birmingham AL 35205 205-320-1060
Web: jimnnicks.com
La Dolce Vita 1851 Montgomery Hwy...............Birmingham AL 35244 205-985-2909
Little Savannah 3811 Clairmont Ave...............Birmingham AL 35222 205-591-1119
Web: www.birminghammenus.com
Ming's Cuisine 514 Cahaba Pk Cir.................Birmingham AL 35242 205-991-3803
Web: mingsmenu.com
Niki's West 233 Finley Ave W ....Birmingham AL 35204 205-252-5751 252-8163
Web: nikiswest.com
Ocean 1218 20th St S............................Birmingham AL 35205 205-933-0999
Web: www.oceanbirmingham.com
PF Chang's China Bistro 233 Summit Blvd............Birmingham AL 35243 205-967-0040
Web: www.pfchangs.com
Ruth's Chris Steak House
2300 Woodcrest Pl....................Birmingham AL 35209 205-879-9995
Web: www.ruthschris.com
Sabor Latino Restaurant
112 Green Springs Hwy ....Birmingham AL 35209 205-942-9480 942-9428
Web: www.misaborlatino.webs.com
Shula's Steak House
1000 Riverchase Galleria ....Birmingham AL 35244 205-444-5750
Web: www.donshula.com
Sol Y Luna 2811 Seventh Ave S....................Birmingham AL 35233 205-322-1186 322-1708
Web: www.birminghammenus.com
Surin West 1918 11th Ave S.......................Birmingham AL 35205 205-324-1928
Web: www.surinwest.com
Taste of Thailand 3321 Lorna Rd...................Birmingham AL 35216 205-978-6863
Village Tavern 101 Summit Blvd.....................Birmingham AL 35243 205-970-1640 970-1641
Web: www.villagetavern.com
Sakana Grill 116 Second Ave SW ....Cullman AL 35055 403-290-1118 290-1120
Web: sakanagrill.ca
Cocina Superior 587 Brookwood Village............ Homewood AL 35209 205-259-1980 259-1987
Web: www.thecocinasuperior.com
Nabeel's Cafe 1706 Oxmoor Rd .... Homewood AL 35209 205-879-9292
Web: www.nabeels.com
J Alexanders 3320 Galleria Cir ....Hoover AL 35244 205-733-9995 733-8461
NASDAQ: JAX ■ *Web:* www.jalexandersholdings.com
Stix 3250 Galleria Cir.............................Hoover AL 35244 205-982-3070
Web: www.stixonline.com
Big Spring Cafe 2906 Governors Dr .... Huntsville AL 35805 256-539-9994
Cafe 302 2700 Winchester Rd NE.................... Huntsville AL 35811 256-852-3442
Dreamland Bar-B-Que Ribs
3855 University Dr .... Huntsville AL 35816 256-539-7427
Web: www.dreamlandbbq.com
Logan's Roadhouse 4249 Balmoral Dr SW............ Huntsville AL 35801 256-881-0584
Web: www.logansroadhouse.com
Rolo's Cafe 975 Airport Rd .... Huntsville AL 35802 256-883-7656
Scrugg's Barbeque 7529 Moores Mill Rd .... Huntsville AL 35811 256-859-6800
Web: www.scruggsbbq.com
Thai Garden Restaurant Inc
800 Wellman Ave NE ....Huntsville AL 35801 256-534-0122 564-7341
Web: www.ilovethaigarden.com/i_love_thai_garden/thai_garden_restaurant.html
Brick Pit 5456 Old Shell Rd.........................Mobile AL 36608 251-343-0001
Web: www.brickpit.com
Cafe 615 615 Dauphin St............................Mobile AL 36602 251-432-8434
Web: cafe615mobile.com
Downtowners 107 Dauphin St........................Mobile AL 36602 251-433-8868
Ruth's Chris Steak House 2058 Airport Blvd ....Mobile AL 36606 251-476-0516
Web: www.ruthschris.com
Saucy-Q Bar B Que 1111 Government St ....Mobile AL 36604 251-433-7427
Web: saucyqbbq.com
Dreamland Bar-B-Que Ribs
101 Tallapoosa St.................... Montgomery AL 36104 334-273-7427
Web: www.dreamlandbbq.com

Phone Fax

Island Delight Caribbean Restaurant
323 Airbase Blvd .... Montgomery AL 36108 334-264-0041
Ixtapa 6132 Atlanta Hwy .... Montgomery AL 36117 334-272-5232
King Buffet 2727 Bell Rd.......................... Montgomery AL 36117 334-273-8883
Lek's Taste of Thailand 5421 Atlanta Hwy .... Montgomery AL 36109 334-244-8994
Mings Garden Chinese Restaurant
1741 Eastern Bypass .... Montgomery AL 36117 334-277-8188
Web: www.mingsgardenmontgomery.com
Peyton's Place 5344 Atlanta Hwy.................. Montgomery AL 36109 334-396-3630
Web: peytonsplacelunch.tripod.com
Zoes Kitchen 7218 EastChase Pkwy .... Montgomery AL 36117 334-270-9115
Web: www.zoeskitchen.com
Baumhower's of Tuscaloosa
500 Harper Lee Dr .... Tuscaloosa AL 35404 205-556-5658 556-5639
Web: www.baumhowers.com
Bento 1306 University Blvd......................... Tuscaloosa AL 35401 205-758-7426
Buffalo Phil's 1149 University Blvd.................. Tuscaloosa AL 35401 205-758-3318
Web: buffalophils.com
Cypress Inn, The 501 Rice Mine Rd N .... Tuscaloosa AL 35406 205-345-6963 345-6997
Web: www.cypressinnrestaurant.com
DePalma's Italian Cafe
2300 University Blvd .... Tuscaloosa AL 35401 205-759-1879
Web: depalmasdowntown.com
Dreamland Bar-B-que 5535 15th Ave E............. Tuscaloosa AL 35405 205-758-8135
Web: www.dreamlandbbq.com
Evangeline's 1653 McFarland Blvd.................. Tuscaloosa AL 35406 205-752-0830
Web: www.evangelinesrestaurant.com
Kozy's Restaurant 3510 Loop Rd................... Tuscaloosa AL 35404 205-556-4112
Web: www.killionrestaurants.com
Los Tarascos 1759 Skyland Blvd.................... Tuscaloosa AL 35405 205-553-8896
Rama Jama's 1000 Paul Bryant Dr .... Tuscaloosa AL 35401 205-750-0901
Sol Azteca 1360 Montgomery Hwy Ste 128.........Vestavia Hills AL 35216 205-979-4902

Alaska

Phone Fax

Aladdin's Fine Mediterranean
4240 Old Seward Hwy ....Anchorage AK 99503 907-561-2373 563-5117
Web: www.aladdinsalaska.com
Bombay Deluxe 555 W Northern Lights Blvd...........Anchorage AK 99503 907-277-1200
Web: www.bombaydeluxe.com
Bradley House 11321 Old Seward Hwy...............Anchorage AK 99515 907-336-7177 336-7178
Web: alaskabradleyhouse.com
Club Paris 417 W Fifth Ave..........................Anchorage AK 99501 907-277-6332
Web: www.clubparisrestaurant.com
Crow's Nest
939 W Fifth Ave Hotel Captain Cook....................Anchorage AK 99501 907-343-2217
Don Jose's 2052 E Northern Lights Blvd ....Anchorage AK 99508 907-279-5111 279-2053
Web: www.alaskadonjoses.com
Glacier Brew House 737 W Fifth Ave..................Anchorage AK 99501 907-274-2739
Web: www.glacierbrewhouse.com
Gweenie's Old Alaska Restaurant
4333 SpenaRd Rd....................Anchorage AK 99517 907-243-2090
Web: gwenniesrestaurant.com
Jen's Restaurant 701 W 36th Ave ....Anchorage AK 99503 907-561-5367
Web: www.jensrestaurant.com
Kincaid Grill 6700 Jewel Lk Rd ....Anchorage AK 99502 907-243-0507 243-5110
Web: www.kincaidgrill.com
Kumagoro Restaurant 533 W Fourth Ave ....Anchorage AK 99501 907-272-9905
La Cabana 312 E Fourth Ave ....Anchorage AK 99501 907-272-0135
Web: alaskalacabana.com
Little Italy 2300 E 88th Ave........................Anchorage AK 99507 907-344-1515
Web: littleitalyalaska.com
Los Arcos 2000 E Dowling St........................Anchorage AK 99507 907-562-0477
Web: www.losarcosak.com
Marx Bros Cafe 627 W Third Ave ....Anchorage AK 99501 907-278-2133 258-6279
Web: www.marxcafe.com
Peking Wok 4000 W Dimond Blvd......................Anchorage AK 99502 907-248-1648
Web: pekingwokak.com
Sacks Cafe 328 G St ....Anchorage AK 99501 907-276-3546
Web: www.sackscafe.com
Sea Galley Restaurant 4101 Credit Union Dr ....Anchorage AK 99503 907-563-3520 563-6382
Web: seagalleyanchorage.com
Simon & Seafort's Saloon & Grill 420 L St...........Anchorage AK 99501 907-274-3502
Web: www.simonandseaforts.com
Southside Bistro 1320 Huffman Pk Dr ....Anchorage AK 99515 907-348-0088 348-0089
Web: www.southsidebistro.com
Villa Nova Restaurant
5121 Arctic Blvd Ste I....................Anchorage AK 99503 907-561-1660
Web: villanovaalaska.com
Alaska Salmon Bake In Alaskaland
2300 Airport Way....................Fairbanks AK 99701 907-452-7274
Web: www.akvisit.com/salmon.html
Cookie Jar 1006 Cadillac Ct.........................Fairbanks AK 99701 907-479-8319
Web: www.cookiejarfairbanks.com
Gambardella's Pasta Bella 706 Second Ave ....Fairbanks AK 99701 907-457-4992 456-3425
Web: www.gambardellas.com
Geraldo's 701 College Rd...........................Fairbanks AK 99701 907-452-2299 452-7634
Ivory Jack's 2581 Goldstream Rd ....Fairbanks AK 99709 907-455-6665 455-4254
Web: www.ivoryjacks.alaskansavvy.com
Lavelle's Bistro 575 First Ave.......................Fairbanks AK 99701 907-450-0555 450-0444
Web: www.lavellesbistro.com
Pump House, The 796 Chena Pump Rd ....Fairbanks AK 99709 907-479-8452 479-8432
Web: www.pumphouse.com
Soapy Smith's Pioneer Restaurant
543 Second Ave ....Fairbanks AK 99701 907-451-8380
Thai House 412 Fifth Ave............................Fairbanks AK 99701 907-452-6123
Web: thaihousefairbanks.com
Turtle Club 2098 Old Steese Hwy......................Fairbanks AK 99712 907-457-3883
Web: www.alaskanturtle.com
Vallata 2190 Goldstream Rd..........................Fairbanks AK 99709 907-455-6600
Zach's Catering 1717 University Ave S.................Fairbanks AK 99709 907-374-6531

Phone Fax

Seven Glaciers Restaurant 1000 Arlberg Ave ... Girdwood AK 99587 907-754-2111
Web: www.alyeska.com
Best Western Grandma's Feather Bed
9300 Glacier Hwy ... Juneau AK 99801 907-789-5005
TF: 888-781-5005 ■ *Web:* www.grandmasfeatherbed.com
El Sombrero 157 S Franklin St ... Juneau AK 99801 907-586-6770 586-6772
Web: elsombrerojuneau.com
Glacier Restaurant Lounge
1873 Shell Simmons Dr Ste 220 ... Juneau AK 99801 907-789-9538 789-3090
Gold Room 127 N Franklin St ... Juneau AK 99801 907-586-2660 586-8315
TF: 800-544-0970 ■ *Web:* www.westmarkhotels.com/juneau-food.php
Hangar On The Wharf 2 Marine Way Ste 106 ... Juneau AK 99801 907-586-5018 586-8173
Web: hangaronthewharf.com
Mi Casa 9200 Glacier Hwy ... Juneau AK 99801 907-789-3636 789-1969
Red Dog Saloon 278 S Franklin St ... Juneau AK 99801 907-463-3658
Web: www.reddogsaloon.com
Seong's Sushi Bar 740 W Ninth St ... Juneau AK 99801 907-586-4778
Web: seongssushibar.com

Alberta

Phone Fax

Abruzzo Ristorante 402 Eigth St SW ... Calgary AB T2P1Z9 403-237-5660
Web: abruzzoristorante.com
Aida's Mediterranean Bistro
2208 Fourth St SW ... Calgary AB T2S1W9 403-541-1189
Web: www.aidasbistro.ca
Antonio's Garlic Clove 2206 Fourth St SW ... Calgary AB T2S1W9 403-228-0866
Belvedere, The 107 Eigth Ave SW ... Calgary AB T2P1B4 403-265-9595
Web: www.thebelvedere.ca
Bonterra Trattoria 1016 Eigth St SW ... Calgary AB T2R1K2 403-262-8480
Web: www.bonterra.ca
Buddha's Veggie Restaurant
5802 MacLeod Trail SW ... Calgary AB T2H0J8 403-252-8830
Web: www.buddhasveggie.com
Buon Giorno Ristorante Italiano
823 17th Ave SW ... Calgary AB T2T0A1 403-244-5522
Web: buongiornoristoranteitaliano.ca
Caesar's Steak House 512 Fourth Ave SW ... Calgary AB T2P0J6 403-264-1222
Web: caesarssteakhouse.com
Carver's Steakhouse 2620 32nd Ave NE ... Calgary AB T1Y6B8 403-250-6327
Catch Oyster Bar/Seafood Restaurant
100 Eigth Ave SE ... Calgary AB T2G0K6 403-206-0000 206-0005
Web: hyatt.com
Chiante Cafe & Restaurant 2805 - 32 Ave NE ... Calgary AB T1Y6J1 403-291-2707 291-1615
Web: chianticafe.ca
Chianti Cafe 1438 17th Ave SW ... Calgary AB T2T0C8 403-229-1600
Web: www.chianticafe.ca
China Rose Restaurant 228 28th St SE ... Calgary AB T2A6J9 403-248-2711 248-6810
Web: www.chinarose.ca
Cilantro 338 17th Ave SW ... Calgary AB T2S0A8 403-229-1177 245-5239
Web: cilantrocalgary.com
Co Do Vietnamese Restaurant 1411 17th Ave SW ... Calgary AB T2T0C3 403-228-7798
Coup, The 924 17th Ave SW ... Calgary AB T2T0A2 403-541-1041
Web: www.thecoup.ca
Da Guido Ristorante 2001 Centre St N ... Calgary AB T2E2S9 403-276-1365
Web: www.daguido.ca
Ed's Restaurant 202 17th Ave SE ... Calgary AB T2G1H4 403-262-3500
Web: www.edsrestaurant.com
Fiore Cantina Italiana 638 17th Ave SW ... Calgary AB T2S0B4 403-244-6603
Web: www.fiore.ca
Hana Sushi 1807 Fourth St SW ... Calgary AB T2S1W2 403-229-1499
James Joyce Authentic Irish Pub
114 Eigth Ave SW ... Calgary AB T2P1B3 403-262-0708
Web: stthomasac.com
Joey Eau Claire
208 Barclay Parade SW
Ste 200 Eau Claire Market ... Calgary AB T2P4R4 403-263-6336
Web: joeyrestaurants.com/menu
KEG Steakhouse & Bar 7104 MacLeod Trl S ... Calgary AB T2H0L3 403-253-2534
Web: www.kegsteakhouse.com
La Chaumiere Restaurant Ltd
17th Ave SW Ste 139 ... Calgary AB T2S04A 403-228-5690 228-4448
Web: www.lachaumiere.ca
Limerick Traditional Public House
7304 MacLeod Trail SE ... Calgary AB T2H0L9 403-252-9190 252-9174
Web: calgarysbestpubs.com
Marathon Ethiopian Restaurant
130 Tenth St NW ... Calgary AB T2N1V3 403-283-6796
Web: marathonethiopian.com
Melrose Cafe & Bar 730 17th Ave SW ... Calgary AB T2S0B7 403-228-3566 228-5708
Web: www.melrosecalgary.com
Molly Malone's Irish Pub
1153 Kensington Crescent NW ... Calgary AB T2N3P7 403-296-3220
Web: www.mollymalonesyyc.com
Moti Mahal 1805 14 St SW ... Calgary AB T2T3T1 403-228-9990
Web: www.motimahal.ca
Q Haute Cuisine 100 LaCaille Pl SW ... Calgary AB T2P5E2 403-262-5554 237-6108
Web: www.qhautecuisine.com
Rajdoot 2424 Fourth St SW ... Calgary AB T2S2T4 403-245-0181 455-4017
Web: www.rajdoot.ca
Redwater Rustic Grille 9223 MacLeod Trl S ... Calgary AB T2J0P6 403-253-4266 253-9045
Web: www.redwatergrille.com
River Cafe 25 Prince's Island Pk ... Calgary AB T2P0R1 403-261-7670 261-8795
Web: www.river-cafe.com
Rouge 1240 Eigth Ave SE ... Calgary AB T2G0M7 403-531-2767 531-2768
Web: www.rougecalgary.com
Salt & Pepper 6515 Bowness Rd NW ... Calgary AB T3B0E8 403-247-4402
Web: www.saltnpepper.ca
Santorini Greek Taverna 1502 Centre St N ... Calgary AB T2E2R9 403-276-8363 276-8399
Web: www.santorinirestaurant.com
Silver Dragon Restaurant 106 Third Ave SE ... Calgary AB T2G0B6 319-366-6655

Phone Fax

Singapore Sam's 555 11th Ave SW Ste 101 ... Calgary AB T2R1P6 403-234-8088 266-6883
Web: www.singaporesams.com
Smuggler's Inn 6920 MacLeod Trl S ... Calgary AB T2H0L3 403-253-5355
Web: www.smugglers.ca
Thai Sa-On 351 Tenth Ave SW ... Calgary AB T2R0A5 403-264-3526 264-3526
Web: www.thai-sa-on.com
Villa Firenze 610 First Ave NE ... Calgary AB T2E0B6 403-264-4297
Web: villafirenze.ca
Vintage Chophouse & Tavern 320 11 Ave SW ... Calgary AB T2R0C5 403-262-7262
Web: www.vintagechophouse.com
Allegro Italian Kitchen 10011-109 St ... Edmonton AB T5J3S8 780-424-6644
Web: www.allegroitaliankitchen.ca
Ban Thai 15726 100th Ave ... Edmonton AB T5P0L1 780-444-9345
Web: www.banthai.com
Bul-Go-Gi House 8813 92 St NW ... Edmonton AB T6C3P9 780-466-2330
Web: www.edmontonkoreanfood.com
Cafe Mosaics 10844 82nd Ave ... Edmonton AB T6E2B3 780-433-9702
Web: cafemosaics.com
Characters 10257 105th St ... Edmonton AB T5J1E6 780-421-4100 425-1550
Web: www.characters.ca
Creperie, The 10220 103rd St NW ... Edmonton AB T5J4C9 780-420-6656
Web: www.thecreperie.com
Dan Shing 15912 Stony Plain Rd ... Edmonton AB T5P4A1 780-483-1143
Furusato 10012 82nd Ave ... Edmonton AB T6E1Y9 780-439-1335
Web: furusatojapaneserestaurant.com
Hardware Grill 9698 Jasper Ave ... Edmonton AB T5H3V5 780-423-0969
Web: www.hardwaregrill.com
Il Pasticcio Trattoria 11520 100th Ave ... Edmonton AB T5K1V4 780-488-9543
Web: www.ilpasticcio.ca
Julio's Barrio 10450 82nd Ave ... Edmonton AB T6E2A2 780-431-0774
Web: www.juliosbarrio.com
Khazana 10177 107th St ... Edmonton AB T5J1J5 780-702-0330 990-0342
Web: www.khazana.ab.ca
Louisiana Purchase Restaurant
10320 111th St NW ... Edmonton AB T5K1M9 780-420-6779
Web: www.louisianapurchase.ca
Normand's 11639 A Jasper Ave ... Edmonton AB T5K2S7 780-482-2600
TF: 866-308-4438 ■ *Web:* www.normands.com
Old Country Inn 9906 72nd Ave ... Edmonton AB T6E0Z3 780-433-3242
Web: oldcountryinnedmonton.com
Parkallen 7018 109th St ... Edmonton AB T6H3C1 587-520-6401
Web: www.parkallen.com
Pearl River Restaurant 4728 99th St NW ... Edmonton AB T6E5H5 780-435-2015 431-2758
Web: www.lusoft.ca/pearlriver
Red Ox Inn 9420 91st St ... Edmonton AB T6C1Z5 780-465-5727
Web: www.theredoxinn.com
Tasty Tom's Bistro 9965 82nd Ave NW ... Edmonton AB T6E1Z1 780-437-5761

Arizona

Phone Fax

Roy's 7151 W Ray Rd ... Chandler AZ 85226 480-705-7697
Web: www.roysrestaurant.com
Haus Murphy's 5739 W Glendale Ave ... Downtown Glendale AZ 85301 623-939-2480
Web: www.hausmurphys.com
August Moon Chinese Restaurant
1300 S Milton Rd ... Flagstaff AZ 86001 928-774-5280
Web: augustmoonflagstaff.com
Beaver Street Brewery 11 S Beaver St ... Flagstaff AZ 86001 928-779-0079
Web: www.beaverstreetbrewery.com
Black Barts Steakhouse Saloon
2760 E Butler Ave ... Flagstaff AZ 86004 928-779-3142
Web: www.blackbartssteakhouse.com
Brandy's 1500 E Cedar Ave Ste 40 ... Flagstaff AZ 86004 928-779-2187
Web: www.brandysrestaurant.com
Collins Irish Pub 2 N Laroux St ... Flagstaff AZ 86001 928-214-7363
Web: www.collinsirishpub.com
Cottage Place 126 W Cottage Ave ... Flagstaff AZ 86001 928-774-8431
Web: www.cottageplace.com
Dara Thai 14 S San Francisco St ... Flagstaff AZ 86001 928-774-0047
Web: darathaiflagstaff.com
Dehli Palace Cuisine of India
2700 S Woodlands Village Blvd ... Flagstaff AZ 86001 928-556-0019
El Capitan Fresh Mexican Grill
1800 S Milton Rd Ste 21 ... Flagstaff AZ 86001 928-774-1083
Web: www.elcapitanfmg.com
Granny's Closet 218 S Milton Rd ... Flagstaff AZ 86001 928-774-8331
Web: grannysclosetflagstaff.com
Josephine's 503 N Humphreys St ... Flagstaff AZ 86001 928-779-3400 226-0910
Web: www.josephinesrestaurant.com
La Fonda 1900 N Second St ... Flagstaff AZ 86004 928-779-0296
Web: lafondaflg.com
Little Thai Kitchen 1051 S Milton Rd ... Flagstaff AZ 86001 928-226-9422
Miz Zips Cafe 2924 E Rt 66 ... Flagstaff AZ 86004 928-526-0104
Mountain Oasis 11 E Aspen Ave ... Flagstaff AZ 86001 928-214-9270 214-0020
Sakura Restaurant 1175 W Rt 66 ... Flagstaff AZ 86001 928-773-8888
Web: www.radisson.com
Romeo's Euro Cafe 207 N Gilbert Rd Ste 105 ... Gilbert AZ 85234 480-962-4224
Web: www.eurocafe.com
Ajo Al's
Arrowhead 7458 W Bell Rd ... Glendale AZ 85308 623-334-9899
Web: www.ajoals.com
Babbo Italian Eatery 20211 N 67th Ave ... Glendale AZ 85308 623-566-9898 566-5561
Web: babboitalian.com
Bitz-Ee Mama's 7023 N 58th Ave ... Glendale AZ 85301 623-931-0562
Web: www.bitz-eemamas.com
Caramba 5421 W Glendale Ave ... Glendale AZ 85301 623-934-8888
Web: carambamex.com
Kiss the Cook Restaurant 72 Church St ... Glendale AZ 85301 802-863-4226
TF: 888-658-5477 ■ *Web:* www.kissthecook.net
La Perla Cafe 5912 W Glendale Ave ... Glendale AZ 85301 623-939-7561 939-0339

				Phone	Fax
Mimi's Cafe 7450 W Bell Rd *Web:* www.mimiscafe.com	Glendale	AZ	85308	623-979-4500	
Pedro's 4938 W Glendale Ave. *Web:* pedrosmexicanfood.com	Glendale	AZ	85301	623-937-0807	
Ah-So 1919 S Gilbert Rd *Web:* ahsomesa.com	Mesa	AZ	85204	480-497-1114	
Aloha Kitchen 2950 S Alma School Rd Ste 12	Mesa	AZ	85210	480-897-2451	
Baby Kay's Cajun Kitchen 2051 S Dobson Rd *Web:* www.babykayscajunkitchen.com	Mesa	AZ	85202	480-800-4811	
Bavarian Point Restaurant 4815 E Main St *Web:* www.bavarianpoint.net	Mesa	AZ	85205	480-830-0999	
Golden Gate 2640 W Baseline Rd	Mesa	AZ	85202	480-897-1335	
Hodori 1116 S Dobson Rd. *Web:* hodoriaz.com	Mesa	AZ	85202	480-668-7979	
On The Border mexican grill & cantina 1710 S Power Rd *Web:* www.ontheborder.com	Mesa	AZ	85206	602-247-7510	
Rosa's Mexican Grill 328 E University Dr *Web:* rosasgrill.com	Mesa	AZ	85201	480-964-5451	
SN Pacific Rim Asian Kitchen 1236 E Baseline Rd *Web:* www.asiaaz.com	Mesa	AZ	85204	480-892-0688	
El Chorro Lodge 5550 E Lincoln Dr. *Web:* www.elchorro.com	Paradise Valley	AZ	85253	480-948-5170	
Alexi's Grill 3550 N Central Ave Ste 120 *Web:* www.alexisgrillphx.com	Phoenix	AZ	85012	602-279-0982	
Alice Cooperstown 101 E Jackson St. *Web:* www.alicecooperstown.com	Phoenix	AZ	85004	602-253-7337	
Avanti's 2728 E Thomas Rd *Web:* www.avanti-az.com	Phoenix	AZ	85016	602-956-0900	
Barrio Cafe 2814 N 16th St *Web:* www.barriocafe.com	Phoenix	AZ	85006	602-636-0240	
Bill Johnson's Big Apple 3757 E Van Buren St. *Web:* www.billjohnsons.com	Phoenix	AZ	85008	602-275-2107	
Christopher's Crush 2502 E Camelback Rd *Web:* www.christophersaz.com	Phoenix	AZ	85016	602-522-2344	
Coup des Tartes 1725 E Osborn Rd *Web:* nicetartes.com	Phoenix	AZ	85016	602-212-1082	
Desert Jade 3215 E Indian School Rd *Web:* www.desertjade68.com	Phoenix	AZ	85018	602-954-0048	
Durant's Restaurant 2611 N Central Ave. *Web:* www.durantsaz.com	Phoenix	AZ	85004	602-264-5967	
Giuseppe's Italian Kitchen 2824 E Indian School Rd *Web:* giuseppeson28th.com	Phoenix	AZ	85016	602-381-1237	381-3669
Hard Rock Cafe 3 S Second St Ste 117 *Web:* www.hardrock.com	Phoenix	AZ	85004	602-261-7625	261-7635
India Palace 2941 W Bell Rd. *Web:* indiapalacephoenix.com	Phoenix	AZ	85053	602-942-4224	
La Pinata Mexican Food Restaurant 5521 N 7th Ave. *Web:* lapinatarestaurantaz.com	Phoenix	AZ	85013	602-279-1763	
Majerle's Sports Grill 24 N Second St. *Web:* www.majerles.com	Phoenix	AZ	85004	602-253-0118	
Melting Pot of Ahwatukee, The 3626 E Ray Rd *Web:* www.meltingpot.com	Phoenix	AZ	85044	480-704-9206	704-2973
Michelina's 3241 E Shea Blvd. *Web:* www.michelinasrestaurant.com	Phoenix	AZ	85028	602-996-8977	
Pizzeria Bianco 623 E Adams St. *Web:* www.pizzeriabianco.com	Phoenix	AZ	85004	602-258-8300	
Roy's 5350 E Marriott Dr. *Web:* www.roysrestaurant.com	Phoenix	AZ	85054	480-419-7697	
Ruth's Chris Steak House 2201 E Camelback Rd *Web:* www.ruthschris.com	Phoenix	AZ	85016	602-957-9600	
T Cook's 5200 E Camelback Rd *TF:* 800-672-6011 ■ royalpalmshotel.com/dining/tcooks-restaurant-phoenix	Phoenix	AZ	85018	602-808-0766	840-6927
Tarbell's 3213 E Camelback. *Web:* www.tarbells.com	Phoenix	AZ	85018	602-955-8100	
That's Italiano 3717 E Indian School Rd.	Phoenix	AZ	85018	602-778-9100	
Vincent Guerithault on Camelback 3930 E Camelback Rd. *Web:* www.vincentsoncamelback.com	Phoenix	AZ	85018	602-224-0225	956-5400
Arcadia Farms Cafe 7014 E First Ave *Web:* arcadiafarmscafe.com	Scottsdale	AZ	85251	480-941-5665	
Atlas Bistro 2515 N Scottsdale Rd Ste 18 *Web:* www.azeats.com	Scottsdale	AZ	85257	480-990-2433	
Blue Adobe Grille 10885 N Frank Lloyd Wright Blvd. *Web:* www.blueadobegrille.com	Scottsdale	AZ	85259	480-314-0550	
Cowboy Ciao Wine Bar & Grill 7133 E Stetson Dr. *Web:* www.cowboyciao.com	Scottsdale	AZ	85251	480-946-3111	
Don & Charlie's 7501 E Camelback Rd *Web:* www.donandcharlies.com	Scottsdale	AZ	85251	480-990-0900	
Fleming's Prime Steakhouse & Wine Bar 6333 N Scottsdale Rd. *Web:* www.flemingssteakhouse.com	Scottsdale	AZ	85250	480-596-8265	
George & Sons 11291 E Via Linda. *Web:* www.georgeandsonsasiancuisine.com	Scottsdale	AZ	85259	480-661-6336	
J & G's Steakhouse 6000 E Camelback Rd *Web:* www.spgrestaurantsandbars.com/united-states/arizona/scottsdale/jg-steakhouse	Scottsdale	AZ	85251	480-214-8000	214-8001
Jalapeno Inferno 23587 N Scottsdale. *Web:* www.jalapenoinferno.com	Scottsdale	AZ	85255	480-585-6442	
Kazimierz World Wine Bar 7137 E Stetson Dr. *Web:* www.kazbar.net	Scottsdale	AZ	85251	480-946-3004	
Kona Grill & Sushi Bar 7014 E Camelback Rd. *Web:* konagrill.com	Scottsdale	AZ	85251	480-429-1100	
Los Olivos Mexican Patio 7328 E Second St *Web:* losolivosrestaurants.com	Scottsdale	AZ	85251	480-946-2256	
Palm Court, The 7700 E McCormick Pkwy *Web:* www.destinationhotels.com/scottsdale-resort	Scottsdale	AZ	85258	480-991-9000	
Pane E Vino 8900 E Pinnacle Peak Rd *Web:* paneevinoaz.com	Scottsdale	AZ	85255	480-473-7900	
PF Chang's China Bistro 7135 E Camelback Rd. *Web:* pfchangs.com	Scottsdale	AZ	85251	480-949-2610	
PF Chang's China Bistro 7676 E. Pinnacle Peak Rd. *Web:* www.pfchangs.com	Scottsdale	AZ	85255	214-265-8669	
Rancho Pinot Grill 6208 N Scottsdale Rd. *Web:* www.ranchopinot.com	Scottsdale	AZ	85253	480-367-8030	443-0680
Remington's 7200 N Scottsdale Rd *Web:* scottsdaleplaza.com	Scottsdale	AZ	85253	480-951-5101	
Ruth's Chris Steak House 7001 N Scottsdale Rd Ste 290 *Web:* www.ruthschris.com	Scottsdale	AZ	85253	480-991-5988	991-6850
Salt Cellar 550 N Hayden Rd *Web:* www.saltcellarrestaurant.com	Scottsdale	AZ	85257	480-947-1963	941-0929
Sassi Ristorante 10455 E Pinnacle Peak Pkwy *Web:* www.sassi.biz	Scottsdale	AZ	85255	480-502-9095	
Sushi on Shea 7000 E Shea Blvd.	Scottsdale	AZ	85254	480-483-7799	
Taggia 4925 N Scottsdale Rd *Web:* www.taggiascottsdale.com	Scottsdale	AZ	85251	480-424-6095	
Veneto Trattoria 6137 N Scottsdale Rd *Web:* www.venetotrattoria.com	Scottsdale	AZ	85250	480-948-9928	
L'Auberge de Sedona 301 L'Auberge Ln *TF:* 855-905-5745 ■ *Web:* www.lauberge.com	Sedona	AZ	86336	928-282-1661	282-2885
Byblos Restaurant 3332 S Mill Ave *Web:* www.amdest.com	Tempe	AZ	85282	480-894-1945	
Caffe Boa 398 S Mill Ave. *Web:* www.cafeboa.com	Tempe	AZ	85281	480-968-9112	
Casey Moore's Oyster House 850 S Ash Ave *Web:* caseymoores.com	Tempe	AZ	85281	480-968-9935	
Cervantes 3318 S Mill Ave. *Web:* cervantesrestaurant.com	Tempe	AZ	85282	480-921-9113	
House of Tricks 114 E Seventh St. *Web:* www.houseoftricks.com	Tempe	AZ	85281	480-968-1114	968-0080
Pita Jungle 1250 E Apache Blvd *Web:* pitajungle.com	Tempe	AZ	85281	480-804-0234	
Urban Cafe 1212 E Apache Blvd. *Web:* www.theurbancafe.com	Tempe	AZ	85281	480-968-8888	
Wong's Place 1825 E Baseline Rd. *Web:* wongsplacetempe.com	Tempe	AZ	85283	480-838-8988	
Z'Tejas 20 W Sixth St *Web:* ztejas.com	Tempe	AZ	85281	480-377-1170	377-1167
Athens on Fourth Avenue 500 N Fourth Ave. *Web:* athenson4thave.com	Tucson	AZ	85705	520-624-6886	
Cafe Poca Cosa 110 E Pennington St. *Web:* cafepocacosatucson.com	Tucson	AZ	85701	520-622-6400	
Casa Molina 6225 E Speedway *Web:* www.casamolina.com	Tucson	AZ	85712	520-886-5468	
Char Thai 5039 Fifth St.	Tucson	AZ	85711	520-795-1715	
Delectables 533 N Fourth Ave. *Web:* www.delectables.com	Tucson	AZ	85705	520-884-9289	
El Charro Cafe 311 N Ct Ave *Web:* www.elcharrocafe.com	Tucson	AZ	85701	520-622-1922	
El Corral 2201 E River Rd. *Web:* elcorraltucson.com	Tucson	AZ	85718	520-299-6092	
Feast 3719 E Speedway *Web:* www.eatatfeast.com	Tucson	AZ	85712	520-326-9363	326-9245
Gandhi 150 W Ft Lowell Rd. *Web:* gandhicuisineofindia.com	Tucson	AZ	85705	520-292-1738	
Gold Room 245 E Ina Rd. *Web:* westwardlook.com	Tucson	AZ	85704	520-297-1151	
Grill at Hacienda del Sol 5501 N Hacienda del Sol Rd. *TF:* 800-728-6514 ■ *Web:* www.haciendadelsol.com	Tucson	AZ	85718	520-529-3500	
Jonathan's Tucson Cork 6320 E Tanque Verde Rd *Web:* www.jonathanscork.com	Tucson	AZ	85715	520-296-1631	
Kingfisher Bar & Grill 2564 E Grant Rd *Web:* www.kingfishertucson.com	Tucson	AZ	85716	520-323-7739	795-7810
Le Rendez-vous 3844 E Ft Lowell Rd *Web:* www.lerendez-vous.com	Tucson	AZ	85716	520-323-7373	
Mi Nidito Restaurant 1813 S Fourth Ave. *Web:* www.minidito.net	Tucson	AZ	85713	520-622-5081	
Michelangelo 420 W Magee Rd *Web:* www.michelangelotucson.com	Tucson	AZ	85704	520-297-5775	
Michelangelo Ristorante 420 W Magee Rd *Web:* www.michelangelotucson.com	Tucson	AZ	85704	520-297-5775	
Pastiche Modern Eatery 3025 N Campbell Ave *Web:* www.pasticheme.com	Tucson	AZ	85719	520-325-3333	
PF Chang's China Bistro 1805 E River Rd. *Web:* www.pfchangs.com	Tucson	AZ	85718	520-615-8788	
Sushi Ten 4500 E Speedway Blvd. *Web:* sushiten.webs.com	Tucson	AZ	85712	520-324-0010	
Thunder Canyon Brewery 7401 N La Cholla Blvd *Web:* thundercanyonbrewery.com	Tucson	AZ	85741	520-797-2652	
Wildflower 7037 N Oracle Rd. *Web:* www.foxrc.com/restaurants/wildflower-american-cuisine	Tucson	AZ	85704	520-219-4230	
Yoshimatsu 2660 N Campbell Ave. *Web:* www.yoshimatsuaz.com	Tucson	AZ	85719	520-320-1574	

Arkansas

				Phone	Fax
Catfish Cove 1615 Phoenix Ave.	Fort Smith	AR	72901	479-646-8835	646-8835
Taliano's Restaurant 201 N 14th St *Web:* talianos.net	Fort Smith	AR	72901	479-785-2292	785-2640
Back Porch Grill, The 4810 Central Ave *Web:* www.backporchgrill.com	Hot Springs	AR	71913	501-525-0885	
Cafe 1217 1217 Malvern Ave. *Web:* cafe1217.net	Hot Springs	AR	71901	501-318-1094	

Name / Address	City	State	Zip	Phone	Fax
Cajun Boilers 2806 Albert Pike Rd *Web:* cajunboilers.com	Hot Springs	AR	71913	501-767-5695	
Chuck's Southern Bar-B-Que 1118 Airport Rd	Hot Springs	AR	71913	501-760-3223	
Hamilton House Estate Bed & Breakfast 132 Van Lyell Terr *Web:* www.hamiltonhouseestate.com	Hot Springs	AR	71913	501-520-4040	520-4023
King's 3310 Central Ave	Hot Springs	AR	71913	501-318-1888	
McClard's Bar-B-Q 505 Albert Pike Rd *TF:* 866-622-5273 ■ *Web:* www.mcclards.com	Hot Springs	AR	71901	501-623-9665	
Mickey's CMB BBQ 1622 Pk Ave *Web:* www.mickeysbbq.net	Hot Springs National Park	AR	71901	501-624-1247	
1620 SAVOY 1620 Market St	Little Rock	AR	72211	501-221-1620	221-1921
Acadia 3000 Kavanaugh Blvd Ste 202 *Web:* www.acadiahillcrest.com	Little Rock	AR	72205	501-603-9630	
Anderson's Cajun Wharf 2400 Cantrell Rd *Web:* www.cajunswharf.com	Little Rock	AR	72202	501-375-5351	
Black Angus 10907 N Rodney Parham Rd *Web:* blackanguscafe.com	Little Rock	AR	72212	501-228-7800	
Brave New Restaurant (BNR) 2300 Cottondale Ln Ste 105 *Web:* www.bravenewrestaurant.com	Little Rock	AR	72202	501-663-2677	
Buffalo Grill 1611 Rebsamen Pk Rd *Web:* www.buffalogrilllr.com	Little Rock	AR	72211	501-296-9535	
Capers 14502 Cantrell Rd *Web:* www.capersrestaurant.com	Little Rock	AR	72223	501-868-7600	
Dave's Place 210 Ctr St *Web:* www.davesplacerestaurant.com	Little Rock	AR	72201	501-372-3283	
Doe's Eat Place 1023 W Marckham St *Web:* www.doeseatplace.net	Little Rock	AR	72201	501-376-1195	
El Chico 8409 I-30 *Web:* elchico.com	Little Rock	AR	72209	501-562-3762	
Fu Lin Chinese Restaurant 200 N Bowman Rd	Little Rock	AR	72211	501-225-8989	
Graffiti's Italian Restaurant 7811 Cantrell Rd *Web:* littlerockgraffitis.net	Little Rock	AR	72227	501-224-9079	
Loca Luna 3519 Old Cantrell Rd *Web:* www.localuna.com	Little Rock	AR	72202	501-663-4666	664-4176
Markham Street Grill & Pub 11321 W Markham St Ste 6 *Web:* markhamstreetpub.com	Little Rock	AR	72211	501-224-2010	
Shogun Japanese Steak House 2815 Cantrell Rd *Web:* www.shogunlr.com	Little Rock	AR	72202	501-666-7070	
Shorty Small's Great American Restaurant 11100 N Rodney Parham Rd *Web:* www.shortysmalls.com	Little Rock	AR	72212	501-224-3344	
Sonny Williams' Steak Room 500 President Clinton Ave *Web:* www.sonnywilliamssteakroom.com	Little Rock	AR	72201	501-324-2999	
Trio's 8201 Cantrell Rd *Web:* www.triosrestaurant.com	Little Rock	AR	72227	501-221-3330	221-1002

British Columbia

Name / Address	City	Prov	Postal Code	Phone	Fax
Afghan Horseman 1833 Anderson St *Web:* afghanhorsemen.com	Vancouver	BC	V6H4E5	604-873-5923	
Athene's 3618 W Broadway *Web:* athenesrestaurant.ca	Vancouver	BC	V6R2B7	604-731-4135	
Banana Leaf 820 W Broadway *Web:* www.bananaleaf-vancouver.com	Vancouver	BC	V5Z1J9	604-731-6333	
Bin 941 Tapas Parlour 941 Davie St *Web:* www.bin941.ca	Vancouver	BC	V6Z1B9	604-683-1246	683-1206
Bishop's 2183 W Fourth Ave *Web:* www.bishopsonline.com	Vancouver	BC	V6K1N7	604-738-2025	
Bistro Pastis 2153 Fourth Ave W *Web:* www.bistropastis.com	Vancouver	BC	V6K1N7	604-731-5020	
Blue Water Cafe 1095 Hamilton St *Web:* www.bluewatercafe.net	Vancouver	BC	V6B5T4	604-688-8078	688-8978
Bridges Restaurant 1696 Duranleau St *Web:* www.bridgesrestaurant.com	Vancouver	BC	V6H3S4	604-687-4400	
C Restaurant 2-1600 Howe St	Vancouver	BC	V6Z2L9	604-681-1164	605-8263
Cardero's 1583 Coal Harbour Quay *Web:* www.vancouverdine.com/carderos	Vancouver	BC	V6G3E7	604-669-7666	
Chambar 562 Beatty St *Web:* www.chambar.com	Vancouver	BC	V6B2L3	604-879-7119	879-7118
CinCin Ristorante 1154 Robson St *Web:* www.cincin.net	Vancouver	BC	V6E1B2	604-688-7338	688-7339
Cioppino's Mediterranean Grill & Enoteca 1133 Hamilton St *Web:* cioppinosyaletown.com	Vancouver	BC	V6B5P6	604-688-7466	
Coast 1054 Alberni St *Web:* www.glowbalgroup.com	Vancouver	BC	V6E1A3	604-685-5010	
Diva at the Met 645 Howe St *Web:* www.metropolitan.com/diva	Vancouver	BC	V6C2Y9	604-602-7788	
Five Sails Restaurant 999 Canada Pl Ste 410 *Web:* www.fivesails.ca	Vancouver	BC	V6C3E1	604-844-2855	682-6321
Glowbal Grill & Satay Bar 302 Water St *Web:* www.glowbalgroup.com	Vancouver	BC	V6B1B6	604-602-0835	
Go Fish! Ocean Emporium 1505 W First Ave	Vancouver	BC	V6J1E8	604-730-5040	
Gotham Steakhouse & Cocktail Bar 615 Seymour St *Web:* www.gothamsteakhouse.com	Vancouver	BC	V6B3K3	604-605-8282	605-8285
Las Margaritas Restaurante 1999 W Fourth Ave *Web:* www.lasmargaritas.com	Vancouver	BC	V6J1M7	604-734-7117	734-3528
Maurya Indian Cuisine 1643 W Broadway *Web:* www.mauryaindiancuisine.com	Vancouver	BC	V6J1W9	604-742-0622	
Mr Pickwick's 8620 Granville St	Vancouver	BC	V6P5A1	604-266-2340	
Original Tandoori Kitchen King 7215 Main St *Web:* originaltandoorikitchens.com	Vancouver	BC	V5X3J3	604-327-8900	
Ouisi Bistro 3014 Granville St *Web:* www.ouisibistro.com	Vancouver	BC	V6H3J8	604-732-7550	
Panos Greek Taverna 654 SE Marine Dr *Web:* panosgreekvancouver.ca	Vancouver	BC	V5X2T4	604-322-8824	
Pink Pearl Chinese Seafood 1132 E Hastings St *Web:* www.pinkpearl.com	Vancouver	BC	V6A1S2	604-253-4316	253-4316
Raincity Grill 1193 Denman St	Vancouver	BC	V6G2N1	604-685-7337	
Reef Caribbean Restaurants, The 4172 Main St *Web:* www.thereefrestaurant.com	Vancouver	BC	B8W1K9	604-874-5375	
Sawasdee Thai 4250 Main St *Web:* www.sawasdeethairestaurant.com	Vancouver	BC	V5V3P9	604-876-4030	
Sequoia Company of Restaurants 1583 Coal Harbour Quay *Web:* www.vancouverdine.com	Vancouver	BC	V6G3E7	604-687-5684	
Stepho's 1124 Davie St	Vancouver	BC	V6E1N1	604-683-2555	
Sun Sui Wah Seafood Restaurant 3888 Main St	Vancouver	BC	V5V3N9	604-872-8822	876-1638
Tojo's *Tojo's Restaurant* 1133 W Broadway *Web:* www.tojos.com	Vancouver	BC	V6H1G1	604-872-8050	872-8060
Yew Restaurant & Bar 791 W Georgia St 2nd Fl *Web:* www.fourseasons.com	Vancouver	BC	V6C2T4	604-692-4939	844-6749

California

Name / Address	City	State	Zip	Phone	Fax
Anaheim Marriott 700 W Convention Way *TF:* 800-845-5279 ■ *Web:* www.marriott.com	Anaheim	CA	92802	714-750-8000	750-9100
Anaheim White House 887 S Anaheim Blvd *Web:* www.anaheimwhitehouse.com	Anaheim	CA	92805	714-772-1381	772-7062
Catal Restaurant & Uva Bar 1510 Disneyland Dr *Web:* www.patinagroup.com	Anaheim	CA	92802	714-774-4442	
Catch, The 2100 E Katella Ave Ste 104 *Web:* www.catchanaheim.com	Anaheim	CA	92806	714-935-0101	
Cheesecake Factory 321 W Katella Ave *Web:* www.thecheesecakefactory.com	Anaheim	CA	92802	714-533-7500	
Hibachi Steak House 108 S Fairmont Blvd	Anaheim	CA	92808	714-998-4110	
JT Schmid's Restaurant & Brewery 2610 E Katella Ave *Web:* www.jtschmidsrestaurants.com	Anaheim	CA	92806	714-634-9200	634-9200
Merhaba 2801 W Ball Rd *Web:* merhabarestaurant.com	Anaheim	CA	92804	714-826-8859	
Naples 1550 S Disneyland Dr # 101 *Web:* www.patinagroup.com	Anaheim	CA	92802	714-776-6200	
Pepe's 2429 W Ball Rd *Web:* pepesmexicanfood.com	Anaheim	CA	92804	714-952-9410	
Polly's 173 Freedom Ave *Web:* www.pollypies.com	Anaheim	CA	92801	714-547-9681	
Rainforest Cafe 1515 S Disneyland Dr Downtown Disney *Web:* www.rainforestcafe.com	Anaheim	CA	92807	714-772-0413	
Ralph Brennan's Jazz Kitchen 1590 S Disneyland Dr Downtown Disney *Web:* www.rbjazzkitchen.com	Anaheim	CA	92802	714-776-5200	999-2123
Rosine's 721 S Weir Canyon Rd *Web:* www.rosines.com	Anaheim	CA	92808	714-283-5141	
Storytellers Cafe 1600 S Disneyland Dr *Web:* disneyland.disney.go.com	Anaheim	CA	92802	714-781-3463	
Tortilla Jo's 1510 Disneyland Dr Downtown Disney *Web:* www.patinagroup.com/tortillaJos	Anaheim	CA	92802	714-535-5000	
Benji's 4001 Rosedale Hwy	Bakersfield	CA	93308	661-328-0400	328-0423
Bill Lee's Bamboo Chopsticks 1203 18th St *Web:* www.billlees.com	Bakersfield	CA	93301	661-324-9441	324-7811
Bit of Germany 1901 Flower St	Bakersfield	CA	93305	661-325-8874	872-0854
Buck Owens' Crystal Palace Steakhouse 2800 Buck Owens Blvd *Web:* www.buckowens.com	Bakersfield	CA	93308	661-328-7560	
Cafe Med Restaurant 4809 Scottdale Hwy *Web:* www.cafemedrestaurant.com	Bakersfield	CA	93309	661-834-4433	
Chalet Basque 200 Oak St	Bakersfield	CA	93304	661-327-2915	
Chuy's Mesquite Broiler 2500 New Stine Rd *Web:* bajachuys.com	Bakersfield	CA	93309	661-833-3469	
Cope's Knotty Pine Cafe 1530 Norris Rd	Bakersfield	CA	93308	661-399-0120	
Imperial Chinese Restaurant 4525 Ming Ave *Web:* imperialchineseonline.com	Bakersfield	CA	93309	661-836-0288	
Izumo Sushi 4412 Ming Ave	Bakersfield	CA	93309	661-398-0608	
Jake's Tex-Mex Cafe 1710 Oak St *Web:* www.jakestexmex.com	Bakersfield	CA	93301	661-322-6380	322-3731
Mama Tosca's 9000 Ming Ave Ste K2-K3 *Web:* www.mamatoscas.com	Bakersfield	CA	93311	661-831-1242	
Mossman's Southwest 3610 Wible Rd *Web:* mossmanscatering.com	Bakersfield	CA	93309	661-832-5130	832-4783
Tahoe Joe's 9000 Ming Ave *Web:* www.tahoejoes.com	Bakersfield	CA	93311	661-664-7750	664-7732
Uricchio's Trattoria 1400 17th St *Web:* www.uricchios.com	Bakersfield	CA	93301	661-326-8870	326-8829
Wool Growers 620 E 19th St *Web:* woolgrowers.net	Bakersfield	CA	93305	661-327-9584	
Meritage at the Claremont 41 Tunnel Rd *Web:* www.fairmont.com/claremont-berkeley	Berkeley	CA	94705	510-549-8510	

Restaurant	City	State	ZIP	Phone	Fax
Belvedere, The 9882 S Santa Monica Blvd *Web:* peninsula.com	Beverly Hills	CA	90212	310-788-2306	788-2319
Crustacean 9646 Little Santa Monica Blvd *Web:* houseofan.com	Beverly Hills	CA	90210	310-205-8990	
Lawry's the Prime Rib 100 N La Cienega Blvd *TF:* 877-529-7984 ■ *Web:* www.lawrysonline.com	Beverly Hills	CA	90211	310-652-2827	657-5463
Mastro's Steakhouse 246 N Canon Dr *Web:* mastrosrestaurants.com	Beverly Hills	CA	90210	310-888-8782	
Matsuhisa Restaurant 129 N La Cienega Blvd *Web:* www.nobumatsuhisa.com	Beverly Hills	CA	90211	310-659-9639	659-0492
Ruth's Chris Steak House 224 S Beverly Dr. *Web:* www.ruthschris.com	Beverly Hills	CA	90212	310-859-8744	
Spago 176 N Canon Dr *Web:* www.wolfgangpuck.com	Beverly Hills	CA	90210	310-385-0880	385-0880
Tanzore 50 N La Cienega Blvd *Web:* tanzore.com	Beverly Hills	CA	90211	310-400-6800	
Anton & Michel PO Box 4917 *Web:* www.carmelsbest.com/antonmichel	Carmel	CA	93921	831-624-2406	
Casanova 5th Ave *Web:* www.casanovacarmel.com	Carmel	CA	93923	831-625-0501	625-9799
Flying Fish Grill Mission St *Web:* flyingfishgrill.com	Carmel	CA	93921	831-625-1962	
Grasing's 6th & Mission Sts. *Web:* www.grasings.com	Carmel	CA	93923	831-624-6562	624-7431
Pacific's Edge 120 Highland Dr *Web:* pacificsedge.com	Carmel	CA	93923	831-622-5445	
Rio Grill 101 the Crossroads *Web:* www.riogrill.com	Carmel	CA	93923	831-625-5436	
Robata Grill 3658 The Barnyard *Web:* robata-barnyard.com	Carmel	CA	93923	831-624-2643	
Bouchee Mission St and 7th Ave *Web:* www.andresbouchee.com	Carmel-By-The-Sea	CA	93923	831-626-7880	
Leon's at Desert Princess 28-555 Landau Blvd	Cathedral City	CA	92234	760-325-5002	
Aunt Emma's 700 E St *Web:* www.auntemmaspancakes.com	Chula Vista	CA	91910	619-427-2722	
Meakwan 230 Third Ave *Web:* www.meakwanthaicuisine.com	Chula Vista	CA	91910	619-426-5172	
Carmen & Family Bar-B-Q 41986 Fremont Blvd *Web:* carmenandfamilybbq.com	Fremont	CA	94538	510-657-5464	
China Chili 39116 State St	Fremont	CA	94538	510-791-1688	791-5181
Country Way 5325 Mowry Ave	Fremont	CA	94536	510-797-3188	
El Patio Restaurant 37311 Fremont Blvd. *Web:* elpatiooriginaldining.com	Fremont	CA	94536	510-796-1733	
Fremont Market Broiler 43406 Christy St. *Web:* www.marketbroiler.com	Fremont	CA	94538	510-791-8675	
Ho Chow Restaurant 47966 Warm Springs Blvd *Web:* www.hochow.com	Fremont	CA	94539	510-657-0683	
Massimo's 5200 Mowry Ave *Web:* www.massimos.com	Fremont	CA	94538	510-792-2000	792-7041
Norman's Family Restaurant 4949 Stevenson Blvd	Fremont	CA	94538	510-226-7777	
Papillon Restaurant 37296 Mission Blvd *Web:* www.papillonrestaurant.com	Fremont	CA	94536	510-793-6331	793-2789
Campagnia 1185 E Champlain Dr *Web:* www.campagnia.net	Fresno	CA	93720	559-433-3300	433-3066
Chopsticks 4783 E Olive Ave	Fresno	CA	93702	559-255-0489	
Livingstone's Restaurant & Pub 831 E Fern Ave. *Web:* towerdistrict.org	Fresno	CA	93728	559-485-5198	
Maxs Bistro 1784 W Bullard Ave *Web:* www.maxsbistro.com	Fresno	CA	93711	559-439-6900	439-7206
Ripe Tomato 5064 N Palm Ave *Web:* tripadvisor.com	Fresno	CA	93704	559-225-1850	
Sequoia Brewing Co 777 E Olive St *Web:* sequoiabrewing.com	Fresno	CA	93728	559-264-5521	
Thai House 1069 E Shaw Ave *Web:* 1jn.com	Fresno	CA	93710	559-221-7245	
Tokyo Garden 1711 Fulton St *Web:* tokyogardenfresno.com	Fresno	CA	93721	559-268-3596	
Yoshino Restaurant 6226 N Blackstone Ave	Fresno	CA	93710	559-431-2205	
Azteca 12911 Main St. *Web:* www.theazteca.com	Garden Grove	CA	92840	714-638-3790	
California Grill 11999 Harbor Blvd Hyatt Regency Orange County *TF:* 800-233-1234 ■ *Web:* orangecounty.regency.hyatt.com/en/hotel/home.html	Garden Grove	CA	92840	714-740-6047	740-0465
Carolina's 12045 Chapman Ave. *Web:* carolinasitalianrestaurant.com	Garden Grove	CA	92840	714-971-5551	
Casa De Soto 8562 Garden Grove Blvd *Web:* www.casadesoto.com	Garden Grove	CA	92844	714-530-4200	
Furiwa Seafood 13826 Brookhurst St *Web:* furiwa.com	Garden Grove	CA	92843	714-534-3996	
Joe's Crab Shack 12011 Harbor Blvd. *Web:* www.joescrabshack.com	Garden Grove	CA	92840	714-703-0505	
Pho 79 9941 W Hazard Ave *Web:* pho79.com	Garden Grove	CA	92844	714-531-2490	
Seafood Cove 8547 Westminster Blvd.	Garden Grove	CA	92844	714-895-7964	
Tokyo Love 12565 S Harbor Blvd.	Garden Grove	CA	92840	714-534-4751	
Barragan's 814 S Central Ave *Web:* barragansrestaurants.com	Glendale	CA	91204	818-243-1103	
Carousel Restaurant 304 N Brand Blvd *Web:* www.carouselrestaurant.com	Glendale	CA	91203	818-246-7775	246-6627
Damon's Steak House 317 N Brand Blvd. *Web:* www.damonsglendale.com	Glendale	CA	91203	818-507-1510	
Far Niente Ristorante 204 1/2 N Brand Blvd. *Web:* farnienteglendale.com	Glendale	CA	91203	818-242-3835	
Fresco Ristorante 514 S Brand Blvd *Web:* www.frescoristorante.com	Glendale	CA	91204	818-247-5541	247-1964
Gennaro's Ristorante 1109 N Brand Blvd *Web:* www.gennarosristorante.com	Glendale	CA	91202	818-243-6231	
La Cabanita 3447 N Verdugo Rd *Web:* cabanitarestaurant.com	Glendale	CA	91208	818-957-2711	
Max's of Manila 313 W Broadway *Web:* www.maxschicken.com	Glendale	CA	91204	818-637-7751	637-2325
Notte Luna 113 N Maryland Ave. *Web:* www.notteluna.com	Glendale	CA	91206	818-552-4100	552-3522
Panda Inn 111 E Wilson Ave *Web:* www.pandainn.com	Glendale	CA	91206	818-502-1234	
Scarantino's 1524 E Colorado St *Web:* www.scarantinos.com	Glendale	CA	91205	818-247-9777	
Tep Thai 209 W Wilson Ave *Web:* www.tepthai.com	Glendale	CA	91203	818-246-0380	
Two Guys From Italy 405 N Verdugo Rd *Web:* www.glendaletwoguysfromitaly.com	Glendale	CA	91206	818-240-0020	
Varouj's Kabobs 1110 S Glendale Ave	Glendale	CA	91205	818-243-9870	
Pine Mountain Lake Association 19228 Pine Mtn Dr *Web:* www.pinemountainlake.com	Groveland	CA	95321	209-962-8600	
Baci 18748 Beach Blvd *Web:* www.bacirestaurant.com	Huntington Beach	CA	92648	714-965-1194	
Beachfront 301 301 Main St. *Web:* www.beachfront301.com	Huntington Beach	CA	92648	714-374-3399	
Capone's Cucina 19688 Beach Blvd Ste 10 *Web:* www.caponescucina.com	Huntington Beach	CA	92646	714-593-2888	
Hyatt Regency Huntington Beach Resort & Spa 21500 Pacific Coast Hwy *TF:* 800-633-7313 ■ *Web:* huntingtonbeach.regency.hyatt.com/en/hotel/home.html	Huntington Beach	CA	92648	714-698-1234	845-4990
Longboard Restaurant & Pub 217 Main St *Web:* longboardpub.com	Huntington Beach	CA	92648	714-960-1896	
Lou's Brews & BBQ Grill 21501 Brookhurst St. *Web:* www.lousbbq.com	Huntington Beach	CA	92646	714-965-5200	
Mario's Mexican Food & Cantina 5 Points Plaza18603 Main St *Web:* mariosmexicanfoodcantina.com	Huntington Beach	CA	92648	714-842-5811	
Matsu Japanese Restaurant 18035 Beach Blvd. *Web:* matsusogood.com	Huntington Beach	CA	92648	714-848-4404	842-4049
Ruby's Diner 1 Main St *Web:* www.rubys.com	Huntington Beach	CA	92648	714-969-7829	
Sea Siam Restaurant 16103 Bolsa Chica St	Huntington Beach	CA	92649	714-846-8986	
Shades Restaurant 21100 Pacific Coast Hwy *Web:* www.waterfrontresort.com/dining/shades	Huntington Beach	CA	92648	714-845-8000	845-8424
Spark Woodfire Grill 300 Pacific Coast Hwy Ste 202	Huntington Beach	CA	92648	714-960-0996	960-7332
West Coast Club 21100 Pacific Coast Hwy Hilton Waterfront Beach Resort	Huntington Beach	CA	92648	714-845-8000	845-8425
Zubie's Dry Dock 9059 Adams Ave *Web:* zubiesdrydock.com	Huntington Beach	CA	92646	714-963-6362	
Baja Fresh 320 Commerce Ste 100 *TF:* 877-225-2373 ■ *Web:* www.bajafresh.com	Irvine	CA	92602	949-270-8900	270-8901
Marine Room, The 2000 Spindrift Dr *TF:* 866-644-2351 ■ *Web:* www.marineroom.com	La Jolla	CA	92037	858-459-7222	551-4673
Piatti 2182 Avenida de la Playa *Web:* piatti.com	La Jolla	CA	92037	858-454-1589	454-1799
Johnny Rockets 2 South Pointe Dr Ste 200	Lake Forest	CA	92630	703-415-3510	415-3510
Napoli Italian Restaurant 24960 Redlands Blvd *Web:* napoli-italian.com	Loma Linda	CA	92354	909-796-3770	478-7756
555 East 555 E Ocean Blvd. *Web:* www.555east.com	Long Beach	CA	90802	562-437-0626	
Alegria Cocina Latina Restaurant 115 Pine Ave *Web:* www.alegriacocinalatina.com	Long Beach	CA	90802	562-436-3388	
Attic, The 3441 E Broadway *Web:* theatticonbroadway.com	Long Beach	CA	90803	562-433-0153	
Bangkok Thai Cuisine 3426 E Fourth St *Web:* bangkokthaicuisinelbc.com	Long Beach	CA	90814	562-433-0093	
Belmont Brewing Co 25 39th Pl. *Web:* www.belmontbrewing.com	Long Beach	CA	90803	562-433-3891	434-0604
Cafe Piccolo 3222 E Broadway *Web:* www.cafepiccolo.com	Long Beach	CA	90803	562-438-1316	
Caffe La Strada 4716 E Second St *Web:* www.lastradalongbeach.com	Long Beach	CA	90803	562-433-8100	
Christy's On Broadway 3937 E Broadway *Web:* christysonbroadway.com	Long Beach	CA	90803	562-433-1171	
Crab Pot Restaurant & Bar, The 215 N Marina Dr. *Web:* www.crabpotlongbeach.com	Long Beach	CA	90803	562-430-0272	
George's Greek Cafe 5316 E Second St. *Web:* georgesgreekcafe.com	Long Beach	CA	90803	562-433-1755	
Green Field Churrascaria 5305 E Pacific Coast Hwy *Web:* greenfieldlongbeach.com	Long Beach	CA	90804	562-597-0906	
Joe's Crab Shack 6550 Marina Dr *Web:* joescrabshack.com	Long Beach	CA	90803	562-594-6551	
Johnny Rebs' Southern Roadhouse 4663 Long Beach Blvd *Web:* www.johnnyrebs.com	Long Beach	CA	90805	562-423-7327	
King's Fish House 100 W Broadway *Web:* www.kingsfishhouse.com	Long Beach	CA	90802	562-432-7463	435-6143
L'Opera 101 Pine Ave *Web:* www.lopera.com	Long Beach	CA	90802	562-491-0066	

	City	State	ZIP	Phone	Fax
La Traviata Restaurant 301 N Cedar Ave *Web:* www.latraviata301.com	Long Beach	CA	90802	562-432-8022	
Lucille's Smokehouse Bar-B-Que 7411 Carson St. *Web:* www.lucillesbbq.com	Long Beach	CA	90808	562-938-7427	
Nino's 3853 Atlantic Ave *Web:* ninoslongbeach.com	Long Beach	CA	90807	562-427-1003	
Parker's Lighthouse 435 Shoreline Village Dr. *Web:* www.parkerslighthouse.com	Long Beach	CA	90802	562-432-6500	436-3551
Phil Trani's 3490 Long Beach Blvd *Web:* philtrani.com	Long Beach	CA	90807	562-426-3668	
Reef Restaurant, The 880 S Harbor Scenic Dr *Web:* www.reefrestaurant.com	Long Beach	CA	90802	562-435-8013	
Roscoe's House of Chicken & Waffles 730 E Broadway *Web:* www.roscoeschickenandwaffles.com	Long Beach	CA	90802	562-437-8355	
Sir Winston's Restaurant & Lounge 1126 Queens Hwy. *TF:* 877-342-0738 ■ *Web:* www.queenmary.com	Long Beach	CA	90802	562-435-3511	
Sky Room 40 S Locust Ave *Web:* theskyroom.com	Long Beach	CA	90802	562-983-2703	
Utopia 445 E First St *Web:* www.utopiarestaurant.net	Long Beach	CA	90802	562-432-6888	
Yard House 401 Shoreline Village Dr *Web:* www.yardhouse.com	Long Beach	CA	90802	562-628-0455	
Shenandoah at the Arbor 10631 Los Alamitos Blvd *Web:* www.shenandoahatthearbor.com	Los Alamitos	CA	90720	562-431-1990	
Amalfi 143 N Brea Ave *Web:* www.amalfila.com	Los Angeles	CA	90036	323-938-2504	938-2252
Angeli Caffe 7274 Melrose Ave	Los Angeles	CA	90046	323-936-9086	938-9873
Angelini Osteria 7313 Beverly Blvd *Web:* www.angeliniosteria.com	Los Angeles	CA	90036	323-297-0070	297-0072
AOC Wine Bar & Restaurant 8700 W Third St *Web:* www.aocwinebar.com	Los Angeles	CA	90048	310-859-9859	
Bamboo Restaurant 10835 Venice Blvd *Web:* bamboorestaurant.net	Los Angeles	CA	90034	310-287-0668	
Ca'Brea 346 S La Brea Ave	Los Angeles	CA	90036	323-938-2863	938-8659
Cafe Pinot 700 W Fifth St *Web:* www.patinagroup.com	Los Angeles	CA	90071	213-239-6500	
Cafe Stella 3932 W Sunset Blvd *Web:* www.cafestella.com	Los Angeles	CA	90029	323-666-0265	666-0258
Carlitos Gardel 7963 Melrose Ave *Web:* www.carlitosgardel.com	Los Angeles	CA	90046	323-655-0891	
Cha Cha Cha 656 N Virgil Ave *Web:* www.theoriginalchachacha.com	Los Angeles	CA	90004	323-664-7723	664-7769
Chi Dynasty 1813 Hillhurst Ave *Web:* www.chidynasty.com	Los Angeles	CA	90027	323-667-3388	667-3393
Cicada 617 S Olive St *Web:* www.cicadarestaurant.com	Los Angeles	CA	90014	213-488-9488	488-9546
Engine Co No 28 644 S Figueroa St *Web:* www.engineco.com	Los Angeles	CA	90017	213-624-6996	
Farfalla Trattoria 1978 Hillhurst Ave *Web:* trattoriafarfalla.com	Los Angeles	CA	90027	323-661-7365	661-5956
Genghis Cohen 740 N Fairfax Ave *Web:* www.genghiscohen.com	Los Angeles	CA	90046	323-653-0640	
Gumbo Pot 6333 W Third St *Web:* www.thegumbopotla.com	Los Angeles	CA	90036	323-933-0358	
Hamasaku 11043 Santa Monica Blvd *Web:* www.hamasakula.com	Los Angeles	CA	90025	310-479-7636	
Harold & Belle's 2920 W Jefferson Blvd *Web:* haroldandbellesrestaurant.com	Los Angeles	CA	90018	323-735-9023	
Hilton Checkers Los Angeles 535 S Grand Ave *Web:* checkerslosangeles.hilton.com/diningcd.php	Los Angeles	CA	90071	213-624-0000	
Hu's Szechwan Restaurant 10450 National Blvd *Web:* www.husrestaurant.com	Los Angeles	CA	90034	310-837-0252	
IL Grano 11359 Santa Monica Blvd	Los Angeles	CA	90025	310-477-7775	477-7775
India's Oven 11645 Wilshire Blvd *Web:* www.laindiasoven.com	Los Angeles	CA	90025	310-207-5522	
India's Tandoori 5468 Wilshire Blvd *Web:* www.indiastandoori.net	Los Angeles	CA	90036	323-936-2050	936-0187
Ivy, The 113 N Robertson Blvd *Web:* theivyrestaurants.com	Los Angeles	CA	90048	310-274-8303	
JAR 8225 Beverly Blvd *Web:* www.thejar.com	Los Angeles	CA	90048	323-655-6566	
Jitlada 5233 1/2 W Sunset Blvd *Web:* jitladala.com	Los Angeles	CA	90027	323-667-9809	663-3104
Kendall's Brasserie & Bar 135 N Grand Ave *Web:* www.patinagroup.com/kendallsbrasserie	Los Angeles	CA	90012	213-972-7322	
Kitchen, The 4348 Fountain Ave *Web:* www.thekitchen.la	Los Angeles	CA	90029	323-664-3663	
La Barca 2414 S Vermont Ave	Los Angeles	CA	90007	323-735-6567	
Little Door 8164 W Third St *Web:* www.thelittledoor.com	Los Angeles	CA	90048	323-951-1210	
Locanda Veneta 8638 W Third St *Web:* www.locandaveneta.net	Los Angeles	CA	90048	310-274-1893	274-4217
Loteria! Grill 6333 W Third St *Web:* www.loteriagrill.com	Los Angeles	CA	90036	323-930-2211	
Lucques 8474 Melrose Ave *Web:* www.lucques.com	Los Angeles	CA	90069	323-655-6277	655-3925
Mario's Peruvian 5786 Melrose Ave	Los Angeles	CA	90038	323-466-4181	
Marouch 4905 Santa Monica Blvd *Web:* www.marouchrestaurant.com	Los Angeles	CA	90029	323-662-9325	664-4229
Moishe's 6333 W Third St *Web:* moishes-la.com	Los Angeles	CA	90036	323-936-4998	
Mori Sushi 11500 W Pico Blvd *Web:* www.morisushi.org	Los Angeles	CA	90064	310-479-3939	
Morton's the Steakhouse 435 S La Cienega Blvd *Web:* www.mortons.com	Los Angeles	CA	90048	310-246-1501	
Nick & Stef's Steakhouse 330 S Hope St *Web:* www.patinagroup.com	Los Angeles	CA	90071	213-680-0330	
Ocean Seafood 750 N Hill St *Web:* www.oceanseafoodchinatown.com	Los Angeles	CA	90012	213-687-3088	687-8549
Palms Thai 5900 Hollywood Blvd *Web:* palmsthai.com	Los Angeles	CA	90028	323-462-5073	
Papa Cristos 2771 W Pico Blvd *Web:* papacristos.com	Los Angeles	CA	90006	323-737-2970	737-3571
Patina 141 S Grand Ave *Web:* www.patinagroup.com	Los Angeles	CA	90012	213-972-3331	972-3531
Shabu Shabu House 127 Japanese Village Plz Mall	Los Angeles	CA	90012	213-680-3890	
Sunnin 1776 Westwood Blvd *Web:* www.sunnin.com	Los Angeles	CA	90024	310-475-3358	
Tam O'Shanter Inn 2980 Los Feliz Blvd *Web:* www.lawrysonline.com	Los Angeles	CA	90039	323-664-0228	664-4915
Taylor's Steak House 3361 W Eigth St *Web:* www.taylorssteakhouse.com	Los Angeles	CA	90005	213-382-8449	
Traxx Restaurant 800 N Alameda St *Web:* www.traxxrestaurant.com	Los Angeles	CA	90012	213-625-1999	
Tuk Tuk Thai 8875 W Pico Blvd *Web:* delivery.com	Los Angeles	CA	90035	310-860-1872	
Vermont 1714 N Vermont Ave *Web:* rockwell-la.com	Los Angeles	CA	90027	323-661-6163	
Versailles 10319 Venice Blvd *Web:* versaillescuban.com	Los Angeles	CA	90034	310-558-3168	558-1817
Water Grill 544 S Grand Ave *Web:* www.watergrill.com	Los Angeles	CA	90071	213-891-0900	629-1891
Nobu 3835 Crosscreek Rd *Web:* www.nobumatsuhisa.com	Malibu	CA	90265	310-317-9140	317-9136
Appetez 825 W Roseburg Ave	Modesto	CA	95350	209-577-5099	577-5598
Dewz 1505 J St	Modesto	CA	95354	209-549-1101	
El Rosal 3430 Tully Rd	Modesto	CA	95350	209-523-7871	
Fruit Yard, The 7948 Yosemite Blvd *Web:* www.thefruityard.com	Modesto	CA	95357	209-577-3093	577-0600
Fuzio Universal Pasta 1020 Tenth St Ste 100 *Web:* www.fuzio.com	Modesto	CA	95354	209-557-9711	557-9717
Galletto Ristorante 1101 J St *Web:* www.galletto.biz	Modesto	CA	95354	209-523-4500	
Marcella Restaurant 3507 Tully Rd *Web:* marcellasmexicanrestaurant.com	Modesto	CA	95356	209-577-3777	
MikiSushi 180 Leveland Ln	Modesto	CA	95350	209-524-3555	
Minnie's 107 McHenry Ave *Web:* minnies.58-s.com	Modesto	CA	95354	209-524-4621	524-6043
Noah's Hof Brau 1311 J St	Modesto	CA	95354	209-527-1090	527-8039
P Wexford's Pub 3313 McHenry Ave	Modesto	CA	95350	209-576-7939	576-7934
Papachino's 1212 J St *Web:* mypapachinos.com	Modesto	CA	95354	209-578-5225	
Strings Italian Cafe 2601 Oakdale Rd *Web:* stringscafe.com	Modesto	CA	95355	209-578-9777	
Tasty Thai 1401 Coffee Rd	Modesto	CA	95355	209-571-8424	571-8164
Torii Japanese Restaurant 2401 E Orangeburg Ave Ste 590	Modesto	CA	95355	209-529-8697	
Velvet Grill & Creamery 2204 McHenry Ave *Web:* www.velvetgrill.net	Modesto	CA	95350	209-544-9029	
Verona's Cucina Italiana 1700 McHenry Ave	Modesto	CA	95350	209-549-8876	
Abalonetti Seafood Trattoria 57 Fisherman's Wharf *Web:* www.restauranteur.com/abalonetti	Monterey	CA	93940	831-373-1851	373-2058
Bullwacker's 653 Cannery Row	Monterey	CA	93940	831-373-1353	373-0196
Cafe Fina 47 Fisherman's Wharf Ste 1 *TF:* 800-843-3462 ■ *Web:* www.cafefina.com	Monterey	CA	93940	831-372-5200	372-5209
Domenico's on the Wharf 50 Fisherman's Wharf # 1 *Web:* www.domenicosmonterey.com	Monterey	CA	93940	831-372-3655	372-2073
Epsilon Greek Restaurant 422 Tyler St *Web:* epsilonrestaurant.com	Monterey	CA	93940	831-655-8108	
Montrio 414 Calle Principal *Web:* www.montrio.com	Monterey	CA	93940	831-648-8880	
Old Fishermans Grotto 39 Fishermans Wharf *Web:* www.oldfishermansgrotto.com	Monterey	CA	93940	831-375-4604	375-0391
Rosine's 434 Alvarado St *Web:* www.rosinesmonterey.com	Monterey	CA	93940	831-375-1400	375-2636
Sardine Factory, The 701 Wave St *Web:* www.sardinefactory.com	Monterey	CA	93940	831-373-3775	
Tarpy's Roadhouse 2999 Monterey-Salinas Hwy *Web:* www.tarpys.com	Monterey	CA	93940	831-647-1444	
Whaling Station Prime Steaks & Seafood 763 Wave St *Web:* www.whalingstation.net	Monterey	CA	93940	831-373-3778	373-2460
Fleming's Prime Steakhouse & Wine Bar 1300 Dove St Ste 105 *Web:* www.flemingssteakhouse.com	Newport Beach	CA	92660	949-222-2223	222-0313
Banana Blossom Thai 4228 Pk Blvd *Web:* www.bananablossomthai.com	Oakland	CA	94602	510-336-0990	
Battambang 850 Broadway *Web:* themenupage.com	Oakland	CA	94607	510-839-8815	
Bay Wolf Restaurant 3853 Piedmont Ave *Web:* www.baywolf.com	Oakland	CA	94611	510-655-6004	
Dopo/Adesso 4293 Piedmont Ave *Web:* www.dopoadesso.com/dopo	Oakland	CA	94611	510-652-3676	
El Huarache Azteca 3842 International Blvd *Web:* elhuaracheazteca.net	Oakland	CA	94601	510-533-2395	
Everett & Jones Barbeque 126 Broadway *Web:* www.eandjbbq.com	Oakland	CA	94607	510-663-2350	663-8856
Holy Land 677 Rand Ave *Web:* holylandrestaurant.com	Oakland	CA	94610	510-272-0535	
Le Cheval Restaurant 1007 Clay St *Web:* www.lecheval.co	Oakland	CA	94607	510-763-8495	763-7610

				Phone	Fax
Legendary Palace 708 Franklin St	Oakland	CA	94607	510-663-9188	
Mama's Royal Cafe 4012 Broadway	Oakland	CA	94611	510-547-7600	
Web: mamasroyalcafeoakland.com					
Mezze					
Mezze Restaurant & Bar 3407 Lakeshore Ave	Oakland	CA	94610	510-663-2500	
Web: www.mezze.com					
Oliveto Cafe & Restaurant 5655 College Ave	Oakland	CA	94618	510-547-5356	
Web: www.oliveto.com					
Pho84 354 17th St	Oakland	CA	94612	510-832-1338	
Web: pho84.com					
Quinn's Lighthouse 1951 Embarcadero Cove	Oakland	CA	94606	510-536-2050	535-1285
Web: www.quinnslighthouse.com					
Jack London Square 2 Broadway	Oakland	CA	94607	510-444-3456	
Web: www.scottsjls.com					
Soi Four Bangkok Eatery 5421 College Ave	Oakland	CA	94618	510-655-0889	
Web: soifour.com					
Spettro 3355 Lakeshore Ave	Oakland	CA	94610	510-451-7738	
Web: themenupage.com					
Uzen Japanese Cuisine 5415 College Ave	Oakland	CA	94618	510-654-7753	
PlumpJack Cafe					
1920 Squaw Vly Rd PO Box 2407	Olympic Valley	CA	96146	530-583-1576	
Web: www.plumpjack.com					
Big Daddy O's Beach BBQ 2333 Roosevelt Blvd	Oxnard	CA	93035	805-984-0014	
BJ's Restaurant & Brewhouse 461 Esplanade Dr	Oxnard	CA	93030	805-485-1124	
Web: www.bjsrestaurants.com					
Cabo Seafood Grill & Cantina					
1041 S Oxnard Blvd	Oxnard	CA	93030	805-487-6933	487-6954
Web: www.caboseafoodgrill.com					
El Ranchero 131 W Second St	Oxnard	CA	93030	805-486-5665	
Kampai Japanese Restaurant 2367 N Oxnard Blvd	Oxnard	CA	93036	805-983-3333	
Korean Barbeque Swan 2061 N Oxnard Blvd	Oxnard	CA	93036	805-278-9611	
Pilar's Cafe 746 S 'A' St	Oxnard	CA	93030	805-487-1444	
Pirates Grub & Grog 450 S Victoria Ave	Oxnard	CA	93030	805-984-0046	
Web: www.piratesgrubngrog.net					
Plaza Grill 600 E Esplanade Dr	Oxnard	CA	93036	805-278-5070	
Favaloro's 545 Lighthouse Ave	Pacific Grove	CA	93950	831-373-8523	
Web: favalorosbignightbistro.com					
Passionfish 701 Lighthouse Ave	Pacific Grove	CA	93950	831-655-3311	
Web: www.passionfish.net					
Vito's Italian Restaurant					
1180 Forest Ave Ste A	Pacific Grove	CA	93950	831-375-3070	
Web: www.vitospacificgrove.com					
Pearl Dragon 15229 W Sunset Blvd	Pacific Palisades	CA	90272	310-459-9790	
Web: www.thepearldragon.com					
Al Dente Pasta 491 N Palm Canyon Dr	Palm Springs	CA	92262	760-325-1160	325-2199
Web: www.aldente-palmsprings.com					
Chop House 262 S Palm Canyon Dr	Palm Springs	CA	92262	760-320-4500	
Web: chophousepalmsprings.com					
El Mirasol Regional Cuisines of Mexico					
140 E Palm Canyon Dr	Palm Springs	CA	92264	760-323-0721	
Web: elmirasolrestaurants.com					
Europa Restaurant 1620 S Indian Trl	Palm Springs	CA	92264	760-327-2314	
TF: 800-245-2314 ■ *Web:* www.villaroyale.com					
Fisherman's Market & Grill					
235 S Indian Canyon Dr	Palm Springs	CA	92262	760-327-1766	
Web: www.fishermans.com					
Johanne's 196 S Indian Canyon Dr	Palm Springs	CA	92262	760-778-0017	
Web: www.johannesrestaurants.com					
John Henry's Cafe					
1785 E Tahquitz Canyon Way	Palm Springs	CA	92262	760-327-7667	
Web: johnhenryscafe.com					
Kaiser Grille 205 S Palm Canyon Dr	Palm Springs	CA	92262	760-323-1003	
Web: www.restaurantsofpalmsprings.com					
Las Casuelas Terraza					
222 S Palm Canyon Dr	Palm Springs	CA	92262	760-325-2794	327-4174
Web: lascasuelas.com					
Le Vallauris 385 W Tahquitz Canyon Way	Palm Springs	CA	92262	760-325-5059	
Web: www.palmsprings.com					
Melvyn's 200 W Ramon Rd	Palm Springs	CA	92264	760-325-2323	
Web: www.inglesideinn.com					
Norma's 4200 E Palm Canyon Dr	Palm Springs	CA	92264	760-770-5000	342-2188
Web: www.starwoodhotels.com/lemeridien					
Sammy G's 265 S Palm Canyon Dr	Palm Springs	CA	92262	760-320-8041	
Web: sammygsrestaurant.com					
Spencer's Restaurant 701 W Barista Rd	Palm Springs	CA	92262	760-327-3446	
Web: www.spencersrestaurant.com					
Thai Smile 651 N Palm Canyon Dr	Palm Springs	CA	92262	760-320-5503	320-5584
Web: thaismilepalmsprings.com					
Arroyo Chop House 536 S Arroyo Pkwy	Pasadena	CA	91105	626-577-7463	577-1089
Web: www.arroyochophouse.com					
Kabuki Japanese Restaurant					
3539 E Foothill Blvd Ste B	Pasadena	CA	91107	253-474-1650	
Parkway Grill 510 S Arroyo Pkwy	Pasadena	CA	91105	626-795-1001	796-6221
Web: www.theparkwaygrill.com					
Black Bear Diner 1880 Shasta St	Redding	CA	96001	602-843-1921	
Web: www.blackbeardiner.com					
Akina Teppan & Sushi 195 E Alessandro Blvd	Riverside	CA	92508	951-789-0443	
Chen Ling Palace 9856 Magnolia Ave	Riverside	CA	92503	951-351-8511	
Web: chenlingpalace.com					
City Cuisine 2586 Main St	Riverside	CA	92501	951-682-9566	682-8649
Duane's 3649 Mission Inn Ave	Riverside	CA	92501	951-784-0300	683-1342
TF: 800-843-7755 ■ *Web:* www.missioninn.com					
Kountry Folks 3653 La Sierra Ave	Riverside	CA	92505	951-354-0437	354-7728
Web: www.kountry.com					
Mario's Place 3646 Mission Inn Ave	Riverside	CA	92501	951-684-7755	
Web: www.mariosplace.com					
Sevilla Riverside 3252 Mission Inn Ave	Riverside	CA	92507	951-778-0611	
Web: www.cafesevilla.com					
33rd Street Bistro 3301 Folsom Blvd	Sacramento	CA	95816	916-455-2233	457-2189
Web: www.33rdstreetbistro.com					
Aioli Bodega Espanola 1800 L St	Sacramento	CA	95811	916-447-9440	
Web: aiolibodega.com					
Alamar Restaurant & Marina					
5999 Garden Hwy	Sacramento	CA	95837	916-922-0200	
Biba 2801 Capitol Ave	Sacramento	CA	95816	916-455-2422	455-0542
Web: www.biba-restaurant.com					
Caballo Blanco Restaurante					
5604 Franklin Blvd	Sacramento	CA	95824	916-428-6706	
Casablanca 3516 Fair Oaks Blvd	Sacramento	CA	95864	916-979-1160	
El Novillero 4216 Franklin Blvd	Sacramento	CA	95820	916-456-4287	456-4149
Web: www.elnov.com					
Enotria Cafe & Wine Bar					
1431 Del Paso Blvd	Sacramento	CA	95815	916-922-6792	
Web: enotria.com					
Ernesto's Mexican Food 1901 16th St	Sacramento	CA	95814	916-441-5850	
Web: www.ernestosmexicanfood.com					
Esquire Grill 1213 K St	Sacramento	CA	95814	916-448-8900	
Web: www.paragarys.com					
Firehouse, The 1112 Second St	Sacramento	CA	95814	916-442-4772	442-6617
Web: www.firehouseoldsac.com					
House of Chang 1589 W El Camino Ave	Sacramento	CA	95833	916-925-2138	
Il Fornaio 400 Capitol Mall	Sacramento	CA	95814	916-446-4100	
Web: www.ilfornaio.com					
JR's Texas Bar-B-Que 180 Otto Cir	Sacramento	CA	95822	916-424-3520	424-9915
Web: www.jrtexasbbq.com					
Kamon 2210 16th St	Sacramento	CA	95818	916-443-8888	
Web: jensaisushi.com					
Kaveri Madras Cuisine 1148 Fulton Ave	Sacramento	CA	95825	916-481-9970	
Web: kaverimadrascuisine.com					
Kitchen Restaurant, The 2225 Hurley Way	Sacramento	CA	95825	916-568-7171	
Web: thekitchenrestaurant.com					
Lemon Grass 601 Munroe St	Sacramento	CA	95825	916-486-4891	
Web: www.starginger.com					
Lucca Restaurant & Bar 1615 J St	Sacramento	CA	95814	916-669-5300	
Web: www.luccarestaurant.com					
MacQue's 8101 Elder Creek Rd	Sacramento	CA	95824	916-381-4119	
Web: www.macques.com					
Marrakech 1833 Fulton Ave	Sacramento	CA	95825	916-486-1944	
Web: www.marrakechrestaurant.com					
Nishiki Sushi 1501 16th St	Sacramento	CA	95814	916-446-3629	
Web: nishikisushi.com					
PF Chang's China Bistro 1530 J St Ste 100	Sacramento	CA	95814	916-288-0970	
Web: www.pfchangs.com					
Piatti Ristorante & Bar Sacramento					
571 Pavilions Ln	Sacramento	CA	95825	916-649-8885	649-8907
Web: www.piatti.com					
Rio City Cafe 1110 Front St	Sacramento	CA	95814	916-442-8226	
Web: www.riocitycafe.com					
Riverside Clubhouse 2633 Riverside Blvd	Sacramento	CA	95818	916-448-9988	
Web: www.riversideclubhouse.com					
Scott's Seafood Grill & Bar					
4800 Riverside Blvd	Sacramento	CA	95822	916-379-5959	489-2447
Web: www.scottsseafood.net					
Tapa the World 2115 J St	Sacramento	CA	95816	916-442-4353	
Web: www.tapatheworld.com					
Texas West Bar-B-Que 1600 Fulton Ave	Sacramento	CA	95825	916-483-7427	
Web: www.texaswestbbq.com					
Tower Cafe 1518 Broadway	Sacramento	CA	95818	916-441-0222	
Web: www.towercafe.com					
Waterboy, The 2000 Capitol Ave	Sacramento	CA	95811	916-498-9891	
Web: www.waterboyrestaurant.com					
Zinfandel Grille 2384 Fair Oaks Blvd	Sacramento	CA	95825	916-485-7100	
Web: zinfandelgrille.com					
Alfredo's Pizza & Pasta					
251 W Baseline St	San Bernardino	CA	92410	909-885-0218	
Web: alfredospizzaandpasta.com					
Lotus Garden 111 E Hospitality Ln	San Bernardino	CA	92408	909-381-6171	381-1757
Web: lotusgardensanbernardino.com					
Addison The Grand Del Mar					
5200 Grand Del Mar Way	San Diego	CA	92130	858-314-1900	
Web: www.addisondelmar.com					
Albie's Beef Inn 1201 Hotel Cir S	San Diego	CA	92108	619-291-1103	
Web: albiesbeefinn.com					
Andiamo 5950 Santo Rd	San Diego	CA	92124	858-277-3501	
Web: andiamo-ristorante.com					
Andre's 1235 Morena Blvd	San Diego	CA	92110	619-275-4114	276-4245
Web: www.andresrestaurantsd.com					
Anthony's Fish Grotto 1360 N Harbor Dr	San Diego	CA	92101	619-232-5103	425-8370
Web: www.anthonysfishgrotto.com					
Ashoka the Great 9474 Black Mountain Rd	San Diego	CA	92126	858-695-9749	695-9279
Web: ashokasd.com					
Bandar 845 Fourth Ave	San Diego	CA	92101	619-238-0101	
Web: www.bandarrestaurant.com					
Bernard'O Restaurant					
12457 Rancho BernaRdo Rd	San Diego	CA	92128	858-487-7171	487-7185
Web: bernardorestaurant.wordpress.com					
Berta's 3928 Twiggs St	San Diego	CA	92110	619-295-2343	
Web: www.bertasinoldtown.com					
Bertrand at Mister A's					
2550 Fifth Ave 12th Fl	San Diego	CA	92103	619-239-1377	239-1379
Web: www.asrestaurant.com					
Blue Point Coastal Cuisine 565 Fifth Ave	San Diego	CA	92101	619-233-6623	
Web: cohnrestaurants.com					
Buon Appetito 1609 India St	San Diego	CA	92101	619-238-9880	
Web: www.sandiegouniontribune.com					
Cafe Japengo 8960 University Ctr Ln	San Diego	CA	92122	858-450-3355	
Web: www.cafejapengo.com					
Cafe on Park 3831 Pk Blvd	San Diego	CA	92103	619-293-7275	
Web: cafeonpark.com					
Cafe Zucchero 1731 India St	San Diego	CA	92101	619-531-1731	
Web: www.cafezucchero.com					
Candelas 416 Third Ave	San Diego	CA	92101	619-702-4455	
Web: www.candelas-sd.com					
Celadon 3671 Fifth Ave	San Diego	CA	92103	619-297-8424	

Name / Address	City	State	ZIP	Phone	Fax
Cohn Restaurant Group 2225 Hancock St *Web:* www.cohnrestaurants.com	San Diego	CA	92110	619-236-1299	236-1300
Corvette Diner 2965 Historic Decatur Rd *Web:* cohnrestaurants.com	San Diego	CA	92103	619-542-1476	
De Medici 815 Fifth Ave *Web:* demedicisandiego.com	San Diego	CA	92101	619-702-7228	
Dobson's 956 Broadway Cir *Web:* www.dobsonsrestaurant.com	San Diego	CA	92101	619-231-6771	
Edgewater Grill 861 W Harbor Dr *Web:* www.edgewatergrill.com	San Diego	CA	92101	619-232-7581	
Emerald Chinese Seafood Restaurant 3709 Convoy St *Web:* www.emeraldrestaurant.com	San Diego	CA	92111	858-565-6888	
Field, The 544 Fifth Ave *Web:* www.thefield.com	San Diego	CA	92101	619-232-9840	232-9842
Fleming's Prime Steakhouse & Wine Bar 8970 University Ctr Ln *Web:* flemingssteakhouse.com	San Diego	CA	92122	858-535-0078	
French Market Grille 15717 Bernardo Heights Pkwy *Web:* frenchmarketgrille.com	San Diego	CA	92128	858-485-8055	673-5471
Georgia's Greek Cuisine 3550 Rosecrans St *Web:* www.georgiasgreekcuisine.com	San Diego	CA	92110	619-523-1007	523-2455
Greek Palace 8878 Clairmont Mesa Blvd *Web:* www.greekpalace.com	San Diego	CA	92123	858-573-0155	573-9645
Greystone the Steakhouse 658 Fifth Ave *Web:* www.greystonesteakhouse.com	San Diego	CA	92101	619-232-0225	233-3606
Hob-Nob Hill 2271 First Ave *Web:* hobnobhill.com	San Diego	CA	92101	619-239-8176	
Humphreys Restaurant 2241 Shelter Island Dr *Web:* humphreysrestaurant.com	San Diego	CA	92106	619-224-3577	224-9438
Ichiban 1449 University Ave *Web:* www.ichibansushisandiego.com	San Diego	CA	92103	619-299-7203	299-7514
Indigo Grill 1536 India St *Web:* www.cohnrestaurants.com	San Diego	CA	92101	619-234-6802	
Jack & Giulio's 2391 San Diego Ave *Web:* jackandgiulios.com	San Diego	CA	92110	619-294-2074	
Jasmine 4609 Convoy St *Web:* jasmineseafood.com	San Diego	CA	92111	858-268-0888	
JSix Restaurant 616 J St *Web:* www.jsixrestaurant.com	San Diego	CA	92101	619-531-8744	
La Gran Tapa 611 B St *Web:* www.lagrantapa.com	San Diego	CA	92101	619-234-8272	
Lou & Mickey's 224 Fifth Ave *Web:* www.louandmickeys.com	San Diego	CA	92101	619-237-4900	
Marriott International Inc 11966 El Camino Real **Fax Area Code:* 858 ■ *TF:* 888-236-2427 ■ *Web:* marriott.com/hotel-restaurants	San Diego	CA	92130	888-236-2427	369-6066*
Morton's the Steakhouse 285 J St *Web:* www.mortons.com	San Diego	CA	92101	619-696-3369	
Old Trieste 2335 Morena Blvd *Web:* places.singleplatform.com/old-trieste-restaurant/menu#	San Diego	CA	92110	619-276-1841	
Osteria Panevino 722 Fifth Ave *Web:* www.osteriapanevino.com	San Diego	CA	92101	619-595-7959	
Pampas Bar & Grill 8690 Aero Dr *Web:* www.pampasargentinegrill.com	San Diego	CA	92123	858-278-5971	
Panda Inn 506 Horton Plz *Web:* pandainn.com	San Diego	CA	92101	619-233-7800	
Park House Eatery 4574 Pk Blvd *Web:* www.parkhouseeatery.com	San Diego	CA	92116	619-295-7275	
PF Chang's China Bistro 7077 Friars Rd *Web:* www.pfchangs.com	San Diego	CA	92108	619-260-8484	
Phil's BBQ 3750 Sports Arena Blvd *Web:* www.philsbbq.net	San Diego	CA	92110	619-226-6333	
Princess Pub & Grille 1665 India St *Web:* www.princesspub.com	San Diego	CA	92101	619-702-3021	
Rama 327 Fourth Ave *Web:* www.ramarestaurant.com	San Diego	CA	92101	619-501-8424	
Rancho Bernardo Inn 17550 Bernardo Oaks Dr *Web:* www.ranchobernardoinn.com	San Diego	CA	92128	858-675-8500	675-8501
Rei do Gado 939 Fourth Ave *Web:* www.reidogado.net	San Diego	CA	92101	619-702-8464	
Roy's 8670 Genesee Ave *Web:* www.roysrestaurant.com	San Diego	CA	92122	858-455-1616	
Ruth's Chris Steakhouse 1355 N Harbor Dr *Web:* www.ruthschris.com	San Diego	CA	92101	619-233-1422	
Saigon on Fifth 3900 Fifth Ave *Web:* saigononfifth.menutoeat.com	San Diego	CA	92103	619-220-8828	
Star of India 1492 N Harbor Dr *Web:* lrstarofindia.com	San Diego	CA	92101	501-227-9900	
Star of the Sea 1360 N Harbor Dr *Web:* www.starofthesea.com	San Diego	CA	92101	619-232-7408	232-2128
Sushi Ota 4529 Mission Bay Dr *Web:* sushiota.com	San Diego	CA	92109	858-270-5670	
Taka Restaurant 555 Fifth Ave *Web:* www.takasushi.com	San Diego	CA	92101	619-338-0555	
Tapas Picasso 3923 Fourth Ave *Web:* tapas-picasso.com	San Diego	CA	92103	619-294-3061	
Taste of Thai 527 University Ave *Web:* tasteofthaisandiego.com	San Diego	CA	92103	619-291-7525	
Terra 7091 El Cajon Blvd *Web:* www.terrasd.com	San Diego	CA	92115	619-293-7088	293-7193
Tom Ham's Lighthouse 2150 Harbor Island Dr *Web:* www.tomhamslighthouse.com	San Diego	CA	92101	619-291-9110	
Westgate Hotel, The 1055 Second Ave *TF:* 800-522-1564 ■ *Web:* westgatehotel.com	San Diego	CA	92101	619-238-1818	557-3737
WineSellar & Brasserie 9550 Waples St Ste 115 *Web:* www.winesellar.com	San Diego	CA	92121	858-450-9557	
Absinthe Brasserie & Bar 398 Hayes St *Web:* www.absinthe.com	San Francisco	CA	94102	415-551-1590	255-2385
Acquerello 1722 Sacramento St *Web:* www.acquerello.com	San Francisco	CA	94109	415-567-5432	567-6432
Albona Ristorante Istriano 545 Francisco St *Web:* albonarestaurant.com	San Francisco	CA	94133	415-441-1040	
Alfred's Steakhouse 659 Merchant St *Web:* www.alfredssf.com	San Francisco	CA	94111	415-781-7058	397-1928
Anzu 222 Mason St Hotel Nikko *Web:* www.hotelnikkosf.com	San Francisco	CA	94102	415-394-1100	394-1102
asiaSF 201 Ninth St *Web:* www.asiasf.com	San Francisco	CA	94103	415-255-2742	
Atherton Hotel 685 Ellis St *Web:* www.athertonhotel.net	San Francisco	CA	94109	415-474-5720	
Aziza 5800 Geary Blvd *Web:* www.aziza-sf.com	San Francisco	CA	94121	415-752-2222	
Big Four Restaurant 1075 California St *Web:* big4restaurant.com	San Francisco	CA	94108	415-771-1140	
Bistro Aix 3340 Steiner St *Web:* www.bistroaix.com	San Francisco	CA	94123	415-202-0100	
Bix Restaurant 56 Gold St *Web:* www.bixrestaurant.com	San Francisco	CA	94133	415-433-6300	433-4574
Blue Mermaid Chowder House & Bar 471 Jefferson St *Web:* www.argonauthotel.com/fishermans-wharf-seafood-restaurants.aspx	San Francisco	CA	94109	415-771-2222	447-4014
Blue Plate, The 3218 Mission St *Web:* www.blueplatesf.com	San Francisco	CA	94110	415-282-6777	
Boulevard 1 Mission St *Web:* www.boulevardrestaurant.com	San Francisco	CA	94105	415-543-6084	495-2936
Campton Place Restaurant 340 Stockton St *Web:* www.camptonplacesf.com	San Francisco	CA	94108	415-955-5555	
Chaya Brasserie 132 The Embarcadero *Web:* www.thechaya.com	San Francisco	CA	94105	415-777-8688	
Chenery Park 683 Chenery St *Web:* www.chenerypark.com	San Francisco	CA	94131	415-337-8537	
Chez Papa Bistrot 1401 18th St	San Francisco	CA	94107	415-824-8205	
Chez Spencer 82 14th St *Web:* www.chezspencer.net	San Francisco	CA	94103	415-864-2191	
Crustacean 1475 Polk St 3rd Fl *Web:* houseofan.com	San Francisco	CA	94109	415-776-2722	
Delfina 3621 18th St *Web:* www.delfinasf.com	San Francisco	CA	94110	415-552-4055	
Ebisu 1283 Ninth Ave *Web:* www.ebisusushi.com	San Francisco	CA	94122	415-566-1770	
Farallon 450 Post St *Web:* www.farallonrestaurant.com	San Francisco	CA	94102	415-956-6969	834-1234
Fior D'Italia 2237 Mason St *Web:* www.fior.com	San Francisco	CA	94133	415-986-1886	
Firefly 4288 24th St *Web:* www.fireflyrestaurant.com	San Francisco	CA	94114	415-821-7652	821-1512
Foreign Cinema 2534 Mission St *Web:* www.foreigncinema.com	San Francisco	CA	94110	415-648-7600	
Frascati 1901 Hyde St *Web:* www.frascatisf.com	San Francisco	CA	94109	415-928-1406	
Fringale 570 Fourth St *Web:* www.fringalesf.com	San Francisco	CA	94107	415-543-0573	
Garcon Restaurant 1101 Valencia St *Web:* www.garconsf.com	San Francisco	CA	94110	415-401-8959	
Garibaldis 347 Presidio Ave *Web:* www.hurleyhafen.com	San Francisco	CA	94115	415-563-8841	
Greens Fort Mason Ctr Bldg A *Web:* www.greensrestaurant.com	San Francisco	CA	94123	415-771-6222	
Harris' Restaurant 2100 Van Ness Ave *Web:* www.harrisrestaurant.com	San Francisco	CA	94109	415-673-1888	673-8817
Hog Island Oyster Co 1 Ferry Bldg # 11A *Web:* hogislandoysters.com	San Francisco	CA	94111	415-391-7117	
House 1230 Grant Ave *Web:* www.thehse.com	San Francisco	CA	94133	415-986-8612	
House of Prime Rib 1906 Van Ness Ave *Web:* houseofprimerib.net	San Francisco	CA	94109	415-885-4605	
Hyde Street Seafood House 1509 Hyde St *Web:* hydestseafoodhouse.com	San Francisco	CA	94109	415-931-3474	
Indian Oven 233 Fillmore St *Web:* www.indianovensf.com	San Francisco	CA	94117	415-626-1628	
Isa 3324 Steiner St *Web:* www.isarestaurant.com	San Francisco	CA	94123	415-567-9588	
Jardiniere 300 Grove St *Web:* www.jardiniere.com	San Francisco	CA	94102	415-861-5555	861-5580
Kabuto Sushi 5121 Geary Blvd	San Francisco	CA	94118	415-752-5652	
Kokkari Estiatorio 200 Jackson St *Web:* www.kokkari.com	San Francisco	CA	94111	415-981-0983	982-0983
La Folie 2316 Polk St *Web:* www.lafolie.com	San Francisco	CA	94109	415-776-5577	776-3431
Little Nepal 925 Cortland Ave *Web:* www.littlenepalsf.com	San Francisco	CA	94110	415-643-3881	643-8088
Manora's Thai Cuisine 1600 Folsom St *Web:* www.manorathai.com	San Francisco	CA	94103	415-861-6224	
Masa's Restaurant 648 Bush St *Web:* www.masasrestaurant.com	San Francisco	CA	94108	415-989-7154	989-3141
Maykadeh 470 Green St *Web:* www.maykadehrestaurant.com	San Francisco	CA	94133	415-362-8286	
Millennium 580 Geary St *Web:* www.millenniumrestaurant.com	San Francisco	CA	94102	415-345-3900	
Morton's The Steakhouse 400 Post St *Web:* www.mortons.com	San Francisco	CA	94102	415-986-5830	
One Market 1 Market St *Web:* www.onemarket.com	San Francisco	CA	94105	415-777-5577	
Ozumo 161 Steuart St *Web:* www.ozumosanfrancisco.com	San Francisco	CA	94105	415-882-1333	
Pane e Vino 1715 Union St *Web:* www.paneevinotrattoria.com	San Francisco	CA	94123	415-346-2111	

				Phone	Fax
Piperade 1015 Battery St	San Francisco	CA	94111	415-391-2555	391-1159
Web: www.piperade.com					
Puccini & Pinetti 129 Ellis St	San Francisco	CA	94102	415-392-5500	
Web: pucciniandpinetti.com					
Quince 470 Pacific Ave	San Francisco	CA	94133	415-775-8500	775-8501
Web: www.quincerestaurant.com					
Restaurant Gary Danko 800 N Pt St	San Francisco	CA	94109	415-749-2060	
Web: www.garydanko.com					
Ristorante Bacco 737 Diamond St	San Francisco	CA	94114	415-282-4969	
Web: baccosf.com					
Roy's 575 Mission St	San Francisco	CA	94105	415-777-0277	
Web: www.roysrestaurant.com					
Ruth's Chris Steak House					
1601 Van Ness Ave	San Francisco	CA	94109	415-673-0557	
Web: www.ruthschris.com					
Scala's Bistro 432 Powell St	San Francisco	CA	94102	415-395-8555	
Web: www.scalasbistro.com					
Schroeder's Cafe 240 Front St	San Francisco	CA	94111	415-421-4778	
Web: www.schroederssf.com					
Seven Hills 1550 Hyde St	San Francisco	CA	94109	415-775-1550	
Web: sevenhillssf.com					
Silks 222 Sansome St	San Francisco	CA	94104	415-986-2020	
TF: 800-526-6566 ■ *Web:* www.mandarinoriental.com					
Slanted Door 1 Ferry Bldg Ste 3	San Francisco	CA	94111	415-861-8032	
Web: www.slanteddoor.com					
Sociale 3665 Sacramento St	San Francisco	CA	94118	415-921-3200	
Web: sfsociale.com					
South Park Cafe 108 S Pk St	San Francisco	CA	94107	415-495-7275	
Web: www.southparkcafe.com					
Town Hall 342 Howard St	San Francisco	CA	94105	415-908-3900	908-3700
Web: www.townhallsf.com					
Trattoria Contadina 1800 Mason St	San Francisco	CA	94133	415-982-5728	
Web: www.trattoriacontadina.com					
Tsunami Sushi & Sake Bar					
1306 Fulton St	San Francisco	CA	94117	415-567-7664	
Web: dajanigroup.net					
Venticello 1257 Taylor St	San Francisco	CA	94108	415-922-2545	
Web: www.venticello.com					
Yank Sing 49 Stevenson St	San Francisco	CA	94105	415-541-4949	
Web: www.yanksing.com					
Zuni Cafe & Grill 1658 Market St	San Francisco	CA	94102	415-552-2522	
Web: www.zunicafe.com					
71 Sainte Peter 71 N San Pedro St	San Jose	CA	95110	408-971-8523	938-3440
Web: www.71saintpeter.com					
Amber India 377 Santana Row Ste 1140	San Jose	CA	95128	408-248-5400	
Web: www.amber-india.com					
Aqui Cal-Mex Grill 1145 Lincoln Ave	San Jose	CA	95125	408-995-0381	
Web: aquicalmex.com					
Arcadia 100 W San Carlos St	San Jose	CA	95113	408-278-4555	
Web: michaelmina.net					
Bella Mia Restaurant & Bar 58 S First St	San Jose	CA	95113	408-280-1993	280-5624
Blowfish 355 Santana Row Ste 1010	San Jose	CA	95128	408-345-3848	
Web: www.blowfishsushi.com					
ChaatCafe.com 834 Blossom Hill Rd	San Jose	CA	95123	408-225-2233	
Web: www.chaatcafes.com					
Cheesecake Factory South San Jose					
925 Blossom Hill Rd	San Jose	CA	95123	408-225-6948	
Web: www.thecheesecakefactory.com					
Emile's 545 S Second St	San Jose	CA	95112	408-289-1960	998-1245
Web: www.emilesrestaurant.com					
Gecko Grill 855 N 13th St	San Jose	CA	95112	408-971-1826	
Grill on, The Alley, The 172 S Market St	San Jose	CA	95113	408-294-2244	294-2255
Web: www.thegrill.com					
Henry's Hi-life 301 W St John St	San Jose	CA	95110	408-295-5414	
Web: henryshilife.com					
House of Siam 151 S Second St	San Jose	CA	95113	408-295-3397	
Web: houseofsiamsanjose.com					
Korean Palace 2297A Stevens Creek Blvd	San Jose	CA	95128	408-947-8600	
Krung Thai 642 S Winchester Blvd	San Jose	CA	95128	408-260-8224	
Web: www.originalkrungthai.com					
La Foret 21747 Bertram Rd	San Jose	CA	95120	408-997-3458	
Web: www.laforetrestaurant.com					
La Pastaia 233 W Santa Clara St	San Jose	CA	95113	408-286-1000	
Web: www.destinationhotels.com/la-pastaia-restaurant					
Le Papillon 410 Saratoga Ave	San Jose	CA	95129	408-296-3730	247-7812
Web: www.lepapillon.com					
Left Bank 377 Santana Row	San Jose	CA	95128	408-984-3500	984-0300
Web: www.leftbank.com					
Menara 41 E Gish Rd	San Jose	CA	95112	408-453-1983	
Web: menara41.com					
Original Joe's 301 S First St	San Jose	CA	95113	408-292-7030	
Web: www.originaljoes.com					
Paolo's Restaurant					
333 W San Carlos St Ste 150	San Jose	CA	95110	408-294-2558	
Web: www.paolosrestaurant.com					
Picasso's 62 W Santa Clara St	San Jose	CA	95113	408-298-4400	
Web: www.picassostapas.com					
Rosy's Fish City 2882 Story Rd	San Jose	CA	95127	408-272-2088	
Straits Cafe 333 Santana Row Ste 1100	San Jose	CA	95128	408-246-6320	
Web: www.straitsrestaurants.com					
Sushi Factory Japanese Restaurant					
4632 Meridian Ave	San Jose	CA	95124	408-723-2598	
Web: www.sushifactorysj.com					
Teske's Germania 255 N First St	San Jose	CA	95113	408-292-0291	
Web: www.teskes-germania.com					
Tokyo Sushi 1716 Lundy Ave	San Jose	CA	95131	408-452-8868	452-8869
Tomisushi 4336 Moorpark Ave	San Jose	CA	95129	408-257-4722	
Web: www.tomisushi.us					
50 Forks 3601 W Sunflower Ave	Santa Ana	CA	92704	714-338-1325	
Web: www.artinstitutes.edu					
Antonello Ristorante 3800 S Plz Dr	Santa Ana	CA	92704	714-751-7153	751-8650
Web: www.antonello.com					
Colima 130 N Fairview St	Santa Ana	CA	92703	714-836-1254	543-6169
Web: www.colimarest.com					
Darya Restaurant 3800 S Plaza Dr	Santa Ana	CA	92704	714-557-6600	
Web: daryasouthcoastplaza.com					
El Gallo Giro 1442 S Bristol St	Santa Ana	CA	92704	714-549-2011	
Web: gallogiro.com					
Favori 3502 W First St	Santa Ana	CA	92703	714-531-6838	
Web: www.favorirestaurant.com					
Gypsy Den 125 N Broadway Ave	Santa Ana	CA	92701	714-835-8840	
Web: www.gypsyden.com					
Hacienda, The 1725 College Ave	Santa Ana	CA	92706	714-558-1304	
Web: tivoliterrace.com/wedding-packages					
Memphis 201 N Broadway	Santa Ana	CA	92701	714-564-1064	
Web: memphiscafe.com					
Olde Ship, The 1120 W 17th St	Santa Ana	CA	92706	714-550-6700	
Web: www.theoldeship.com					
Royal Khyber					
S Coast Plz Vlg 1621 W Sunflower Ave	Santa Ana	CA	92704	714-436-1010	
Web: www.royalkhyber.com					
Spoons California Grill 2601 Hotel Terr	Santa Ana	CA	92705	714-556-0700	
Web: www.spoonsoc.com					
Tangata 2002 N Main St	Santa Ana	CA	92706	714-550-0906	
Web: www.patinagroup.com					
Taqueria De Anda 1029 E Fourth St	Santa Ana	CA	92701	714-558-0856	
Web: taqueriadeanda.com					
Yellow Basket Restaurant 2860 S Main St	Santa Ana	CA	92707	714-545-8219	
Web: www.yellowbasket.com					
Border Grill					
Santa Monica 1445 Fourth St	Santa Monica	CA	90401	310-451-1655	394-2049
Web: www.bordergrill.com					
Chinois on Main 2709 Main St	Santa Monica	CA	90405	310-392-9025	396-5102
TF: 888-646-3387 ■ *Web:* www.wolfgangpuck.com					
Ivy at the Shore 1535 Ocean Ave	Santa Monica	CA	90401	310-393-3113	
Web: theivyrestaurant.com					
Josie 2424 Pico Blvd	Santa Monica	CA	90405	310-581-9888	581-4202
Melisse 1104 Wilshire Blvd	Santa Monica	CA	90401	310-395-0881	
Web: www.melisse.com					
Valentino Santa Monica 3115 Pico Blvd	Santa Monica	CA	90405	310-829-4313	315-2791
Web: valentinosantamonica.com					
Delius Restaurant 2951 Cherry Ave	Signal Hill	CA	90755	562-426-0694	426-0694
Web: www.deliusrestaurant.com					
Thai Nakorn 11951 Beach Blvd	Stanton	CA	90680	714-799-2031	
Web: thainakornrestaurant.com					
Angelina's 1563 E Fremont St	Stockton	CA	95205	209-948-6609	
Web: www.angelinas.com					
Bangkok Restaurant 3255 W Hammer Ln Ste 18	Stockton	CA	95209	209-476-8616	
Basil's 2324 Grand Canal Blvd	Stockton	CA	95207	209-478-6290	
Breadfruit Tree 8095 Rio Blanco Rd	Stockton	CA	95219	209-952-7361	
Web: www.breadfruittree.com					
Bud's Seafood Grill 314 Lincoln Ctr	Stockton	CA	95207	209-956-0270	
Web: www.budsseafood.com					
Chitiva's Salsa & Sports Bar & Grille					
445 W Weber Ave	Stockton	CA	95203	209-941-8605	
Web: www.chitiva.net					
Cocoro Bistro & Sushi Bar 2105 Pacific Ave	Stockton	CA	95204	209-941-6053	
Web: cocorobistro.com					
Dave Wong's 2828 W March Ln	Stockton	CA	95219	209-951-4152	
Web: davewongsrestaurant.com					
El Rancho Steak House 1457 E Mariposa Rd	Stockton	CA	95205	209-467-1529	467-1525
Garlic Bros 6629 Embarcadero Dr	Stockton	CA	95219	209-474-6585	
Web: garlicbrothersonline.com					
Hana Sushi 1101 E March Ln	Stockton	CA	95210	209-477-1667	
House of Shaw 227 Dorris Pl	Stockton	CA	95204	209-948-4300	
Mi Ranchito Cafe 425 S Ctr St	Stockton	CA	95203	209-946-9257	939-0227
Miguel's 7555 Pacific Ave	Stockton	CA	95207	209-951-1931	
Papapavlo's Bistro & Bar 501 N Lincoln Ctr	Stockton	CA	95207	209-477-6133	477-6132
Web: www.papapavlos.com					
Saigon 1904 Pacific Ave	Stockton	CA	95204	209-463-2274	
Sho Mi 419 Lincoln Ctr	Stockton	CA	95207	209-951-3525	
Web: shomirestaurant.com					
Stockton Joe's 236 Lincoln Ctr	Stockton	CA	95207	209-951-2980	
Web: modesto.backpage.com					
Yasso Yani Restaurant 326 E Main St	Stockton	CA	95202	209-464-3108	
Sushi Nozawa 11288 Ventura Blvd Ste C	Studio City	CA	91604	818-508-7017	
Web: sushinozawa.com					
Ca'del Sole 4100 Cahuenga Blvd	Toluka Lake	CA	91602	818-985-4669	
Web: www.cadelsole.com					
Rockenwagner					
3 Square Cafe + Bakery 1121 Abbot Kinney Blvd	Venice	CA	90291	310-399-6504	
Web: www.rockenwagner.com					
Chaya Brasserie 8741 Alden Dr	West Hollywood	CA	90048	310-859-8833	
Web: www.thechaya.com					
House of Blues 8430 W Sunset Blvd	West Hollywood	CA	90069	323-848-5100	
Web: www.houseofblues.com					
Vivoli Cafe & Trattoria of West Hollywood					
7994 Sunset Blvd	West Hollywood	CA	90046	323-656-5050	656-0419
Web: www.vivolicafe.com					
Wood Ranch Barbecue & Grill Inc					
2835 Townsgate Rd Ste 200	Westlake Village	CA	91361	805-719-9000	
Web: www.woodranch.com					
Eduardo's Border Grill 1830 Westwood Blvd	Westwood	CA	90025	310-475-2410	
Web: www.eduardosbordergrill.com					
Bistro Jeanty 6510 Washington St	Yountville	CA	94599	707-944-0103	944-0370
Web: www.bistrojeanty.com					

Colorado

				Phone	Fax
Cache Cache Bistro 205 S Mill St	Aspen	CO	81611	970-925-3835	
Web: www.cachecache.com					
Campo de Fiori 205 S Mill St	Aspen	CO	81611	970-920-7717	
Web: www.campodefiori.net					

				Phone	Fax
Hickory House Ribs *Aspen* 730 W Main St *Web:* www.hickoryhouseribs.com	Aspen	CO	81611	970-925-2313	
Matsuhisa 303 E Main St. *Web:* matsuhisaaspen.com	Aspen	CO	81611	970-544-6628	
Pinons 105 S Mill St. *Web:* www.pinons.net	Aspen	CO	81611	970-920-2021	
Syzygy 308 E Hawkins Ave *Web:* www.syzygyrestaurant.com	Aspen	CO	81611	970-925-3700	
Dozens 2180 S Havana St. *Web:* www.dozensrestaurant.com	Aurora	CO	80014	303-337-6627	
East Cafe Chinese Restaurant 15140 E Mississippi Ave	Aurora	CO	80012	303-369-6103	
El Alamo 1708 S Chambers Rd. *Web:* elalamogrande.comcastbiz.net	Aurora	CO	80017	720-535-5309	
Helga's German Restaurant 14197 E Exposition Ave *Web:* www.helgasdeli.com	Aurora	CO	80012	303-344-5488	
La Cueva 9742 E Colfax Ave. *Web:* www.lacueva.net	Aurora	CO	80010	303-367-1422	
Royal Hilltop 18581 E Hampden Ave. *Web:* www.royalhilltop.com	Aurora	CO	80013	303-690-7738	
Sam's No 3 2580 S Havana St *Web:* www.samsno3.com	Aurora	CO	80014	303-751-0347	
Senor Ric's 13200 E Mississippi Ave. *Web:* www.senorrics.net	Aurora	CO	80012	303-750-9000	
Summit Steakhouse, The 2700 S Havana St. *Web:* www.thesummitsteakhouse.com	Aurora	CO	80014	303-751-2112	
Bacaro 921 Pearl St	Boulder	CO	80302	303-444-4888	445-2422
Boulder ChopHouse & Tavern 921 Walnut St. *Web:* www.boulderchophouse.com	Boulder	CO	80302	303-443-1188	443-4876
Boulder Cork 3295 30th St *Web:* www.bouldercork.com	Boulder	CO	80301	303-443-9505	443-0193
Buff Restaurant 2600 Canyon Blvd *Web:* www.buffrestaurant.com	Boulder	CO	80302	303-442-9150	
Carelli's of Boulder 645 30th St *Web:* www.carellis.com	Boulder	CO	80303	303-938-9300	
Casa Alvarez 3161 Walnut St.	Boulder	CO	80301	303-546-0630	
Chautauqua Dining Hall 900 Baseline Rd *Web:* www.chautauqua.com	Boulder	CO	80302	303-440-3776	
Chez Thuy Restaurant 2655 28th St *Web:* www.chezthuy.com	Boulder	CO	80301	303-442-1700	
Falafel King Restaurant 5461 Wern Ave Unit B *Web:* falafelkingfoods.com	Boulder	CO	80301	303-449-9321	443-8965
Flagstaff House 1138 Flagstaff Rd *Web:* www.flagstaffhouse.com	Boulder	CO	80302	303-442-4640	442-8924
Greenbriar Inn, The 8735 N Foothills Hwy. *TF:* 800-253-1474 ■ *Web:* www.greenbriarinn.com	Boulder	CO	80302	303-440-7979	449-2054
Illegal Pete's 1447 Pearl St. *Web:* illegalpetes.com	Boulder	CO	80302	303-440-3955	
Japango 1136 Pearl St *Web:* www.boulderjapango.com	Boulder	CO	80302	303-938-0330	
Jax Fish House 928 Pearl St *Web:* jaxfishhouse.com/boulder	Boulder	CO	80302	303-444-1811	
L'Atelier 1739 Pearl St *Web:* www.latelierboulder.com	Boulder	CO	80302	303-442-7233	
Pasta Jays 1001 Pearl St *Web:* www.pastajays.com	Boulder	CO	80302	303-444-5800	
Ras Kassa's Ethiopian Restaurant 555 30th St *Web:* www.raskassas.com	Boulder	CO	80301	303-447-2919	
Spruce 2115 13th St	Boulder	CO	80302	303-442-4880	
Sushi Tora 2014 Tenth St *Web:* sushitoraboulder.com	Boulder	CO	80302	303-444-2280	
Sushi Zanmai 1221 Spruce St *Web:* www.sushizanmai.com	Boulder	CO	80302	303-440-0733	440-6676
Taj Restaurant 2630 Baseline Rd *Web:* tajcolorado.com	Boulder	CO	80305	303-494-5216	
Thyme on the Creek 1345 28th St *TF:* 866-866-8086 ■ *Web:* www.millenniumhotels.com	Boulder	CO	80302	303-998-3835	443-1480
Walnut Brewery 1123 Walnut St. *Web:* www.walnutbrewery.com	Boulder	CO	80302	303-447-1345	447-0067
Walnut Cafe 3073 Walnut St *Web:* www.walnutcafe.com	Boulder	CO	80301	303-447-2315	
Zolo Grill 2525 Arapahoe Ave *Web:* www.zologrill.com	Boulder	CO	80302	303-449-0444	
Amanda's Fonda 3625 W Colorado Ave	Colorado Springs	CO	80904	719-227-1975	578-0285
Bamboo Court 4935 Centennial Blvd. *Web:* bamboocourtcoloradosprings.com	Colorado Springs	CO	80919	719-599-7383	
Blue Star, The 1645 S Tejon St. *Web:* www.thebluestar.net	Colorado Springs	CO	80905	719-632-1086	
China Town 326 S Nevada Ave. *Web:* chinatown-restaurant.com	Colorado Springs	CO	80903	719-632-5151	
Edelweiss 34 E Ramona Ave *Web:* www.restauranteur.com	Colorado Springs	CO	80905	719-633-2220	
Flying W Ranch Inc 3330 Chuckwagon Rd. *TF:* 800-232-3599 ■ *Web:* www.flyingw.com	Colorado Springs	CO	80919	719-598-4000	598-4600
Fratelli 124 N Nevada Ave *Web:* www.fratelliristorante.com	Colorado Springs	CO	80903	719-575-9571	
IL Vicino 11 S Tejon St. *Web:* www.ilvicino.com	Colorado Springs	CO	80903	719-475-9224	
Jake & Telly's 2616 W Colorado Ave *Web:* www.jakeandtellys.com	Colorado Springs	CO	80904	719-633-0406	
Jun Japanese Restaurant 1760 Dublin Blvd	Colorado Springs	CO	80918	719-531-9368	
La Carreta 35 N Iowa Ave.	Colorado Springs	CO	80909	719-477-1157	
Luigi's 947 S Tejon St. *Web:* www.luigiscoloradosprings.com	Colorado Springs	CO	80903	719-632-7339	
MacKenzie's Chop House Restaurant 128 S Tejon St *Web:* www.mackenzieschophouse.com	Colorado Springs	CO	80903	719-635-3536	
Marigold Cafe 4605 Centennial Blvd. *Web:* marigoldcoloradosprings.com	Colorado Springs	CO	80919	719-599-4776	
Mason Jar, The 2925 W Colorado Ave *Web:* www.masonjarcolorado.com	Colorado Springs	CO	80904	719-632-4820	
Penrose Room 1 Lake Ave. *Web:* www.broadmoor.com	Colorado Springs	CO	80906	719-634-7711	
Pepper Tree, The 888 W Moreno Ave *Web:* www.peppertreecs.com	Colorado Springs	CO	80905	719-471-4888	471-0997
PF Chang's China Bistro 1725 Briargate Pkwy *Web:* www.pfchangs.com	Colorado Springs	CO	80920	719-593-8580	
Phantom Canyon Brewing Co 2 E Pikes Peak Ave *Web:* www.phantomcanyon.com	Colorado Springs	CO	80903	719-635-2800	635-9930
Uwes German Restaurant 31 Iowa Ave. *Web:* bestgermanrestaurant.com	Colorado Springs	CO	80909	719-475-1611	
1515 On Market 1515 Market St. *Web:* www.1515restaurant.com	Denver	CO	80202	303-571-0011	
Barolo Grill 3030 E Sixth Ave. *Web:* www.barologrilldenver.com	Denver	CO	80206	303-393-1040	333-9240
Bella Vista Mexican Restaurant 127 E 20th Ave	Denver	CO	80205	303-297-9020	297-8866
Bistro Vendome 1420 Larimer St *Web:* www.bistrovendome.com	Denver	CO	80202	303-825-3232	825-3240
Broker Restaurant, The 821 17th St. *Web:* www.thebrokerrestaurant.com	Denver	CO	80202	303-292-5065	292-2652
Cafe Brazil 4408 Lowell Blvd. *Web:* www.cafebrazildenver.com	Denver	CO	80211	303-480-1877	
Capital Grille 1450 Larimer St. *Web:* www.thecapitalgrille.com	Denver	CO	80202	303-539-2500	
Carmine's on Penn 92 S Pennsylvania. *Web:* www.carminescolorado.com	Denver	CO	80209	303-777-6443	777-4129
Celtic Tavern, The 1801 Blake St. *Web:* www.thecelticta vern.com	Denver	CO	80202	303-308-1795	308-1576
Corkhouse, The 4900 E Colfax Ave.	Denver	CO	80220	303-355-4488	
Damascus 2276 S Colorado Blvd.	Denver	CO	80222	303-757-3515	
El Taco de Mexico 714 Santa Fe Dr. *Web:* eltacodemexicodenver.com	Denver	CO	80204	303-623-3926	
Fado Irish Pub 1735 19th St Ste 150. *Web:* www.fadoirishpub.com	Denver	CO	80202	303-297-0066	
Hapa Sushi Grill & Sake Bar 2780 E Second Ave. *Web:* www.hapasushi.com	Denver	CO	80206	303-322-9554	355-3449
India's 8921 East Hampden Ave Ste F. *Web:* www.indiasrestaurant.com	Denver	CO	80231	303-755-4284	752-9814
Jax Fish House 1539 17th St. *Web:* jaxfishhouse.com/denver	Denver	CO	80202	303-292-5767	
Little India 330 E Sixth Ave *Web:* www.littleindiadenver.com	Denver	CO	80203	303-871-9777	
Luca d'Italia 711 Grant St *Web:* www.lucadenver.com	Denver	CO	80203	303-832-6600	
Maggiano's Little Italy 500 16th St *Web:* www.maggianos.com	Denver	CO	80202	303-260-7707	
Mizuna 225 E Seventh Ave *Web:* www.mizunadenver.com	Denver	CO	80203	303-832-4778	
New Saigon 630 S Federal Blvd *Web:* newsaigon.com	Denver	CO	80219	303-936-4954	
Panzano 909 17th St. *Web:* www.panzano-denver.com	Denver	CO	80202	303-296-3525	
Parisi 4401 Tennyson St. *Web:* www.parisidenver.com	Denver	CO	80212	303-561-0234	480-5514
PF Chang's China Bistro 1415 15th St *Web:* www.pfchangs.com	Denver	CO	80202	303-260-7222	
Potager 1109 Ogden St *Web:* www.potagerrestaurant.com	Denver	CO	80218	303-832-5788	
Solera 5410 E Colfax Ave *Web:* www.solerarestaurant.com	Denver	CO	80220	303-388-8429	
Sullivan's Steakhouse 1745 Wazee St. *Web:* sullivanssteakhouse.com	Denver	CO	80202	303-295-2664	
Sushi Den 1487 S Pearl St *Web:* www.sushiden.net	Denver	CO	80210	303-777-0826	
Tamayo 1400 Larimer St. *Web:* www.richardsandoval.com	Denver	CO	80202	720-946-1433	
Venice Ristorante & Wine Bar 1700 Wynkoop St. *Web:* www.veniceristorante.com	Denver	CO	80202	303-534-2222	
Wynkoop Brewing Co 1634 18th St *Web:* www.wynkoop.com	Denver	CO	80202	303-297-2700	297-2958
Zengo 1610 Little Raven St *Web:* www.richardsandoval.com	Denver	CO	80202	720-904-0965	
6512 Restaurant 6512 durango	Durango	CO	81301	970-247-9083	
Carver Brewing Co 1022 Main Ave. *Web:* www.carverbrewing.com	Durango	CO	81301	970-259-2545	
Christina's Grill & Bar 21382 Hwy 160 W.	Durango	CO	81303	970-382-3844	382-3865
Cyprus Cafe 725 E Second Ave *Web:* www.cypruscafe.com	Durango	CO	81301	970-385-6884	
East by Southwest 160 E College Dr *Web:* www.eastbysouthwest.com	Durango	CO	81301	970-247-5533	
Ken & Sue's 636 Main Ave *Web:* www.kenandsues.com	Durango	CO	81301	970-385-1810	
Lady Falconburgh's Barley Exchange 640 Main Ave	Durango	CO	81301	970-382-9664	382-9625
Mahogany Grille 699 Main Ave. *Web:* www.mahoganygrille.com	Durango	CO	81301	970-247-4433	259-2208
Red Snapper 144 E Ninth St. *Web:* www.durangoredsnapper.com	Durango	CO	81301	970-259-3417	
Bisetti's Italian Restaurant 120 S College Ave *Web:* www.bisettis.com	Fort Collins	CO	80524	970-493-0086	
Enzio's Italian Kitchen 126 W Mountain Ave *Web:* www.enzios.com	Fort Collins	CO	80524	970-484-8466	
Jay's Bistro 135 W Oak St *Web:* www.jaysbistro.net	Fort Collins	CO	80524	970-482-1876	482-1897

				Phone	Fax
Los Tarascos 622 S College Ave	Fort Collins	CO	80524	970-416-0265	416-8455
Web: lostarascos.com					
Moot House 2626 S College Ave	Fort Collins	CO	80525	970-226-2121	
Web: www.themoothouse.com					
Nimo's Sushi Bar & Japanese 921 E Harmony Rd Ste 104	Fort Collins	CO	80525	970-221-1040	
Web: www.nimossushi.com					
Rainbow Restaurant 212 W Laurel St	Fort Collins	CO	80521	970-221-2664	
Web: rainbowfortcollins.com					
South China 4613 S Mason St Unit D1	Fort Collins	CO	80525	970-225-6886	
Web: www.mingsouthchina.com					
Suehiro 4431 Corbett Dr	Fort Collins	CO	80525	970-672-8185	
Web: www.suehirojapaneserestaurant.com					
Young's Cafe 3307 S College Rd	Fort Collins	CO	80525	970-223-8000	
Web: www.youngscafe.com					
Sam Taylor's Barbeque 435 S Cherry St	Glendale	CO	80246	303-388-9300	388-2276
Web: samtaylorsbbq.com					
240 Union 240 Union Blvd	Lakewood	CO	80228	303-989-3562	989-3565
Web: www.240union.com					
Casa Bonita 6715 W Colfax Ave	Lakewood	CO	80214	303-232-5115	
Web: www.casabonitadenver.com					
Briarhurst Manor 404 Manitou Ave	Manitou Springs	CO	80829	719-685-1864	685-9638
TF: 877-685-1448 ■ *Web:* www.briarhurst.com					
Krabloonik 4250 Divide Rd PO Box 5517	Snowmass Village	CO	81615	970-923-3953	923-0246
Web: www.krabloonik.com					

Connecticut

				Phone	Fax
Bloodroot 85 Ferris St	Bridgeport	CT	06605	203-576-9168	
Web: www.bloodroot.com					
Captain's Cove Seaport 1 Bostwick Ave	Bridgeport	CT	06605	203-335-7104	335-6793
Web: www.captainscoveseaport.com					
Field Restaurant & Bar, The 3001 Fairfield Ave	Bridgeport	CT	06605	203-333-0043	
Web: www.fieldrestaurant.com					
Joseph's Steakhouse 360 Fairfield Ave	Bridgeport	CT	06604	203-337-9944	
Web: www.josephssteakhouse.com					
King & I 545 Broadbridge Rd	Bridgeport	CT	06610	203-374-2081	
Web: www.kingandict.com					
Ralph 'N Rich's 815 Main St	Bridgeport	CT	06604	203-366-3597	
Web: www.ralphnrichs.com					
Tony's Huntington Inn 437 Huntington Tpke	Bridgeport	CT	06610	203-374-5541	
Web: www.thpizza.com					
Vazzy's Brick Oven Restaurant 513 Broadbridge Rd	Bridgeport	CT	06610	203-371-8046	371-4293
Web: www.theoriginalvazzys.com					
Barcelona Restaurant & Wine Bar 4180 Black Rock Tpke	Fairfield	CT	06824	203-255-0800	
Web: www.barcelonawinebar.com					
Hana Tokyo Seafood & Steak House 1275 Post Rd	Fairfield	CT	06824	203-256-0800	
Web: www.hanatokyo.com					
Shiki Hana 222 Post Rd	Fairfield	CT	06824	203-259-5950	259-5428
Web: shikihanafairfield.com					
Asiana Cafe 130 E Putnam Ave	Greenwich	CT	06830	203-622-6833	861-2680
Web: www.asianacafe.com					
Barcelona Restaurant & Wine Bar 18 W Putnam Ave	Greenwich	CT	06830	203-983-6400	
Web: www.barcelonawinebar.com					
Elm Street Oyster House 11 W Elm St	Greenwich	CT	06830	203-629-5795	
Web: www.elmstreetoysterhouse.com					
L'Escale 500 Steamboat Rd	Greenwich	CT	06830	203-661-4600	
Web: www.lescalerestaurant.com					
Meli-Melo 362 Greenwich Ave	Greenwich	CT	06830	203-629-6153	
Web: melimelogreenwich.com					
Morello Bistro 253 Greenwich Ave	Greenwich	CT	06830	203-661-3443	661-3588
Web: www.morellobistro.com					
Penang Grill 55 Lewis St	Greenwich	CT	06830	203-861-1988	861-0003
Polpo 554 Old Post Rd	Greenwich	CT	06830	203-629-1999	
Web: www.polporestaurant.com					
Thomas Henkelmann Restaurant 420 Field Pt Rd	Greenwich	CT	06830	203-869-7500	869-7502
Web: www.homesteadinn.com					
Carbone's Ristorante 588 Franklin Ave	Hartford	CT	06114	860-296-9646	
Web: www.carbonesct.com					
City Steam Brewery Cafe 942 Main St	Hartford	CT	06103	860-525-1600	
Web: www.citysteambrewerycafe.com					
Coyote Flaco 635 New Britain Ave	Hartford	CT	06106	860-953-1299	
Web: www.mycoyoteflaco.com					
Ficara's 577 Franklin Ave	Hartford	CT	06114	860-296-3238	296-3238
Web: www.ficarasrestaurant.com					
First & Last Tavern 939 Maple Ave	Hartford	CT	06114	860-956-6000	
Web: www.firstandlasttavern.com					
Hot Tomato's 1 Union Pl	Hartford	CT	06103	860-249-5100	
Web: www.hottomatos.net					
Koji 17 Asylum St	Hartford	CT	06103	860-247-5654	677-5359
Max Downtown 185 Asylum St	Hartford	CT	06103	860-522-2530	246-5279
Web: www.maxrestaurantgroup.com					
New Park 1615 Pk St	Hartford	CT	06106	860-232-1565	
Oporto 2074 Park St	Hartford	CT	06106	860-233-3184	
Web: www.oportohartford.com					
Peppercorn's Grill 357 Main St	Hartford	CT	06106	860-547-1714	724-7612
Web: www.peppercornsgrill.com					
Trumbull Kitchen 150 Trumbull St	Hartford	CT	06103	860-493-7412	493-7416
Web: maxrestaurantgroup.com					
Vito's by the Park 26 Trumbull St	Hartford	CT	06103	860-244-2200	244-2210
Web: www.vitosct.com					
VIVO Seasonal Trattoria 200 Columbus Blvd	Hartford	CT	06103	860-760-2333	
Web: vivohartford.com					
Cavey's 45 E Ctr St	Manchester	CT	06040	860-643-2751	
Web: www.caveysrestaurant.com					
Adriana's 771 Grand Ave	New Haven	CT	06511	203-865-6474	
Web: adrianasnewhaven.com					
Akasaka 1450 Whalley Ave	New Haven	CT	06515	203-387-4898	397-3069
Archie Moore's Bar & Restaurant 188 1/2 Willow St	New Haven	CT	06511	203-773-9870	
Web: www.archiemoores.com					
Bangkok Garden 172 York St	New Haven	CT	06510	203-789-8684	
Web: www.bkkgardenct.com					
Bentara 76 Orange St	New Haven	CT	06510	203-562-2511	562-0892
Brazi's Italian Restaurant 201 Food Terminal Plz	New Haven	CT	06511	203-498-2488	
Web: brazis.com					
Carmen Anthony Steakhouse 660 State St	New Haven	CT	06511	203-773-1444	772-4853
Carmine's Tuscan Grill Ristorante 1500 Whalley Ave	New Haven	CT	06515	203-389-2805	
Web: www.carminestuscangrill.com					
Christopher Martin's 860 State St	New Haven	CT	06511	203-776-8835	777-8875
Web: www.christophermartins.com					
Claire's Corner Copia 1000 Chapel St	New Haven	CT	06510	203-562-3888	
Web: www.clairescornercopia.com					
Consiglio's 165 Wooster St	New Haven	CT	06511	203-865-4489	
Web: www.consiglios.com					
Fireside Restaurant 810 Woodward Ave	New Haven	CT	06512	203-466-1919	
Web: firesidebarandgrillct.com					
Mamoun's Falafel Restaurant 85 Howe St	New Haven	CT	06511	203-562-8444	
Web: www.mamouns.com					
Miya 68 Howe St	New Haven	CT	06511	203-777-9760	
Web: www.miyassushi.com					
Sage American Bar & Grill 100 S Water St	New Haven	CT	06519	203-787-3466	777-8274
Tre Scalini 100 Wooster St	New Haven	CT	06510	203-777-3373	787-5360
Web: www.trescalinirestaurant.com					
Union League Cafe 1032 Chapel St	New Haven	CT	06510	203-562-4299	562-6712
Web: unionleaguecafe.com					
Zaroka 148 York St	New Haven	CT	06511	203-776-8644	776-0051
Web: www.zaroka.com					
Zinc 964 Chapel St	New Haven	CT	06510	203-624-0507	
Web: www.zincfood.com					
Ruth's Chris Steak House 2513 Berlin Tpke	Newington	CT	06111	860-666-2202	
Web: www.ruthschris.com					
La Scogliera Restaurant 474 River Rd	Shelton	CT	06484	203-922-1179	922-1176
Web: www.lascoglierarestaurant.com					
Bobby Valentine's Sports Gallery Cafe 225 Main St	Stamford	CT	06901	203-348-0010	
Web: www.bobbyv.com					
Brasitas 954 E Main St	Stamford	CT	06902	203-323-3176	
Web: www.brasitas.com					
Columbus Park Trattoria 205 Main St	Stamford	CT	06901	203-967-9191	
Web: www.columbusparktrattoria.com					
Crab Shell 46 Southfield Ave	Stamford	CT	06902	203-967-7229	967-7233
Web: www.crabshell.com					
Eclisse Restaurant 700 Canal St	Stamford	CT	06902	203-325-3773	327-2308
Hugo's Restaurant 161 Stillwater Ave	Stamford	CT	06902	203-323-5577	
Kotobuki 457 Summer St	Stamford	CT	06901	203-359-4747	357-7522
Web: www.kotobukijapaneserestaurant.com					
Ole Mole 1030 High Ridge Rd	Stamford	CT	06905	203-461-9962	
Web: olemolestamford.com					
Tengda Asian Bistro 235 Bedford St	Stamford	CT	06901	203-625-5338	
Web: tengdaasian.com					
Arugula 953 Farmington Ave	West Hartford	CT	06107	860-561-4888	
Web: arugula-bistro.com					
Chengdu 179 Pk Rd	West Hartford	CT	06119	860-232-6455	232-3002
Web: chengduwesthartford.com					
Grant's 977 Farmington Ave	West Hartford	CT	06107	860-236-1930	
Web: billygrant.com					
Max's Oyster Bar 964 Farmington Ave	West Hartford	CT	06107	860-236-6299	233-6969
Web: www.maxrestaurantgroup.com					
Murasaki 23 LaSalle Rd	West Hartford	CT	06107	860-236-7622	
Web: murasakijapaneserestaurant.com					
Pond House Cafe 1555 Asylum Ave	West Hartford	CT	06117	860-231-8823	231-8731
Web: www.pondhousecafe.com					
Restaurant Bricco 78 LaSalle Rd	West Hartford	CT	06107	860-233-0220	
Web: www.billygrant.com					

Delaware

				Phone	Fax
Rusty Rudder Restaurant 113 Dickinson St	Dewey Beach	DE	19971	302-227-3888	
Web: rustyrudderdewey.com					
Starboard Restaurant 2009 Hwy 1	Dewey Beach	DE	19971	302-227-4600	
Web: www.thestarboard.com					
Two Seas Restaurant 1300 Delaware 1	Dewey Beach	DE	19971	302-227-2610	
Web: dinehere.us					
Roma Italian Restaurant 3 President Dr	Dover	DE	19901	302-678-1041	
Web: www.romadover.com					
US 13 Grill & Catering 1115 S Governors Ave	Dover	DE	19904	302-730-3551	
Where Pigs Fly 617 E Loockerman St	Dover	DE	19901	302-678-0586	
Web: wherepigsflyrestaurant.com					
Sambo's Tavern 283 Front St	Leipsic	DE	19901	302-674-9724	
Big Fish Grill 20298 Coastal Hwy	Rehoboth Beach	DE	19971	302-227-3474	
Web: www.bigfishgrill.com					
Blue Moon Restaurant 35 Baltimore Ave	Rehoboth Beach	DE	19971	302-227-6515	
Web: www.bluemoonrehoboth.com					
Dos Locos 208 Rehoboth Ave	Rehoboth Beach	DE	19971	302-227-3353	
Web: www.doslocos.com					
Jake's Seafood House Restaurant 29 Baltimore Ave	Rehoboth Beach	DE	19971	302-227-6237	
Web: www.jakesseafoodhouse.com					
Ristorante Zebra 32 Lake Ave	Rehoboth Beach	DE	19971	302-226-1160	
Web: ristorantezebra.us					

Phone Fax

Victoria's Restaurant
2 Olive Ave Boardwalk Plz Hotel . . . . . Rehoboth Beach DE 19971 302-227-0615
Web: boardwalkplaza.com

Blue Parrott Bar & Grille 1934 W Sixth St . . . . . Wilmington DE 19805 302-655-8990 655-9488
Web: www.blueparrotgrille.com

Bonhouse 4713 Kirkwood Hwy . . . . . Wilmington DE 19808 302-633-1218

Bull's Eye Saloon & Restaurant
3734 Kirkwood Hwy . . . . . Wilmington DE 19808 302-633-6557
Web: www.bullseyesaloon.com

Corner Bistro 3604 Silverside Rd . . . . . Wilmington DE 19810 302-477-1778
Web: www.mybistro.com

Eclipse Bistro 1020 N Union St. . . . . . Wilmington DE 19805 302-658-1588
Web: www.platinumdininggroup.com

Green Room at the Hotel duPont
11th & Market St . . . . . Wilmington DE 19801 302-594-3100 594-3108
TF: 800-441-9019 ■ *Web:* www.hoteldupont.com

Harry's Savoy Grill 2020 Naamans Rd . . . . . Wilmington DE 19810 302-475-3000 475-9990
Web: harryshospitalitygroup.com/harrys-savoy-grill

Harry's Seafood Grill 101 S Market St. . . . . . Wilmington DE 19801 302-777-1500 777-2406
Web: harryshospitalitygroup.com/harrys-seafood-grill

LaTolteca 2209 Concord Pk. . . . . . Wilmington DE 19803 302-778-4646
Web: authenticmex.com

Luigi Vitrone's Pastabilities
415 N Lincoln St. . . . . . Wilmington DE 19805 302-656-9822
Web: www.ljv-pastabilities.com

Melting Pot, The
1601 Concord Pike
Ste 43-47 Independence Mall. . . . . . Wilmington DE 19803 302-652-6358 652-8101
TF: 800-783-0867 ■ *Web:* www.meltingpot.com

Mexican Post 3100 Naamans Rd. . . . . . Wilmington DE 19810 302-478-3939 478-5599
Web: www.mexicanpost.com

Mikimoto's 1212 N Washington St . . . . . Wilmington DE 19801 302-656-8638 656-7423
Web: www.mikimotos.com

Moro 1307 N Scott St . . . . . Wilmington DE 19806 302-777-1800 777-2350
Web: www.mororestaurant.net

Mrs Robino's Restaurant 520 N Union St. . . . . . Wilmington DE 19801 302-652-9223
Web: www.mrsrobinos.com

Piccolina Toscana 1412 N DuPont St . . . . . Wilmington DE 19806 302-654-8001
Web: www.piccolinatoscana.com

Stanley's Tavern 2038 Foulk Rd. . . . . . Wilmington DE 19810 302-475-1887
Web: www.stanleystavern.com

Union City Grille 805 N Union St . . . . . Wilmington DE 19805 302-654-9780 654-0238

Valle Cucina Italiana 4752 Limestone Rd. . . . . . Wilmington DE 19808 302-998-9999
Web: www.vallecucina.com

Walter's Steak House & Saloon
802 N Union St. . . . . . Wilmington DE 19805 302-652-6780
Web: walters-steakhouse.com

District of Columbia

Phone Fax

15 Ria 1515 Rhode Island Ave NW . . . . . Washington DC 20005 202-742-0015 332-8436
Web: www.15ria.com

1789 Restaurant 1226 36th St NW. . . . . . Washington DC 20007 202-965-1789 337-1541
Web: www.1789restaurant.com

701 Restaurant 701 Pennsylvania Ave NW. . . . . . Washington DC 20004 202-393-0701
Web: www.701restaurant.com

Al Tiramisu 2014 P St NW. . . . . . Washington DC 20036 202-467-4466
Web: www.altiramisu.com

Ardeo 3311 Connecticut Ave NW . . . . . Washington DC 20008 202-244-6750
Web: www.ardeobardeo.com

Bistro Bis 15 E St NW. . . . . . Washington DC 20001 202-661-2700
Web: www.bistrobis.com

Bombay Club 815 Connecticut Ave NW. . . . . . Washington DC 20006 202-659-3727

Cactus Cantina 3300 Wisconsin Ave NW. . . . . . Washington DC 20016 202-686-7222
Web: www.cactuscantina.com

Cafe Atlantico 405 Eigth St NW . . . . . Washington DC 20004 202-393-0812 393-0555
Web: www.cafeatlantico.com

Cashion's Eat Place 1819 Columbia Rd NW. . . . . . Washington DC 20009 202-797-1819
Web: www.cashionseatplace.com

Ceiba 701 14th St NW. . . . . . Washington DC 20005 202-393-3983
Web: www.ceibarestaurant.com

Charlie Palmer Steak
101 Constitution Ave NW. . . . . . Washington DC 20001 202-547-8100
TF: 877-632-7800

City Lights of China
1731 Connecticut Ave NW . . . . . Washington DC 20009 202-265-6688 265-1369
Web: www.citylightsofchina.com

Coeur de Lion 926 Massachusetts Ave NW. . . . . . Washington DC 20001 202-414-0500 414-0513
Web: www.henleypark.com

Corduroy 1122 Ninth St NW . . . . . Washington DC 20001 202-589-0699
Web: corduroydc.com

Equinox 818 Connecticut Ave NW. . . . . . Washington DC 20006 202-331-8118 331-0809
Web: www.equinoxrestaurant.com

Filomena Ristorante 1063 Wisconsin Ave NW . . . . . Washington DC 20007 202-338-8800 338-8806

Hard Rock Cafe 999 E St NW . . . . . Washington DC 20004 202-737-7625
Web: www.hardrock.com

Heritage India 1337 Connecticut Ave NW. . . . . . Washington DC 20036 202-333-3120
Web: heritageindiausa.com

I Ricchi 1220 19th St NW. . . . . . Washington DC 20036 202-835-0459
Web: www.iricchi.net

Indique 3512 Connecticut Ave NW . . . . . Washington DC 20008 202-244-6600
Web: www.indique.com

Jaleo 480 Seventh St NW . . . . . Washington DC 20004 202-628-7949
Web: www.jaleo.com

Johnny's Half Shell 400 N Capitol St NW . . . . . Washington DC 20001 202-737-0400
Web: www.johnnyshalfshell.net

Jyoti 2433 18th St NW . . . . . Washington DC 20009 202-518-5892 518-5892
Web: jyotidc.com

Kaz Sushi Bistro 1915 I St NW. . . . . . Washington DC 20006 202-530-5500
Web: www.kazsushibistro.com

Phone Fax

Komi 1509 17th St NW . . . . . Washington DC 20036 202-332-9200 330-5909
Web: www.komirestaurant.com

Lebanese Taverna 2641 Connecticut Ave NW . . . . . Washington DC 20008 202-265-8681
Web: www.lebanesetaverna.com

Little Fountain Cafe 2339 18th St NW. . . . . . Washington DC 20009 202-462-8100
Web: www.littlefountaincafe.com

Loews Madison Hotel 1177 15th St NW . . . . . Washington DC 20005 202-862-1600
TF: 888-825-2436 ■ *Web:* loewshotels.com

Makoto 4822 MacArthur Blvd NW . . . . . Washington DC 20007 202-298-6866
Web: makotorestaurantdc.com

Marcel's 2401 Pennsylvania Ave NW. . . . . . Washington DC 20037 202-296-1166
Web: www.marcelsdc.com

Marrakesh 617 New York Ave NW. . . . . . Washington DC 20001 202-393-9393 737-3737

Montmarte 327 Seventh St SE. . . . . . Washington DC 20003 202-544-1244
Web: montmartredc.com

Morton's the Steakhouse
1050 Connecticut Ave NW . . . . . Washington DC 20036 202-955-5997 955-5889
Web: www.mortons.com

New Heights Restaurant 2317 Calvert St NW. . . . . . Washington DC 20008 202-234-4110
Web: www.newheightsrestaurant.com

Nora 2132 Florida Ave NW . . . . . Washington DC 20008 202-462-5143
Web: www.noras.com

Obelisk 2029 P St NW . . . . . Washington DC 20036 202-872-1180

Oceanaire Seafood Room 1201 F St NW . . . . . Washington DC 20004 202-347-2277
Web: www.theoceanaire.com

Old Ebbitt Grill 675 15th St NW . . . . . Washington DC 20005 202-347-4800
Web: www.ebbitt.com

Palena 3529 Connecticut Ave NW . . . . . Washington DC 20008 202-537-9250

Peacock Cafe 3251 Prospect St NW. . . . . . Washington DC 20007 202-625-2740 625-1402
Web: www.peacockcafe.com

Prime Rib, The 2020 K St NW. . . . . . Washington DC 20006 202-466-8811 466-2010
Web: www.theprimerib.com

Rice 1608 14th St NW. . . . . . Washington DC 20009 202-234-2400
Web: www.ricerestaurant.com

Sakana 2026 P St NW. . . . . . Washington DC 20036 202-887-0900

Sea Catch 1054 31st St NW. . . . . . Washington DC 20007 202-337-8855 337-7159
Web: www.seacatchrestaurant.com

Sushi Ko Glover Park
2309 Wisconsin Ave NW . . . . . Washington DC 20007 202-333-7594
Web: sushikorestaurants.com

Sushi Taro 1503 17th St NW . . . . . Washington DC 20036 202-462-8999
Web: www.sushitaro.com

Tabard Inn 1739 N St NW . . . . . Washington DC 20036 202-331-8528 785-6173
Web: www.tabardinn.com

Taberna Del Alabardero 1776 I St NW . . . . . Washington DC 20006 202-429-2200 775-3713
Web: www.alabardero.com

Tosca 1112 F St NW. . . . . . Washington DC 20004 202-367-1990 367-1999
Web: www.toscadc.com

Vidalia 1990 M St NW . . . . . Washington DC 20036 202-659-1990
Web: www.vidaliadc.com

Zaytinya 701 Ninth St NW . . . . . Washington DC 20001 202-638-0800 638-6969
Web: www.zaytinya.com

Florida

Phone Fax

Sandbar Seafood & Spirits 100 Spring Ave . . . . . Anna Maria FL 34216 941-778-0444 778-3997
Web: sandbar.groupersandwich.com

Chef Allen's 19088 NE 29th Ave . . . . . Aventura FL 33180 305-935-2900
Web: www.chefallens.com

Addison, The 2 E Camino Real . . . . . Boca Raton FL 33432 561-372-0568
Web: www.theaddison.com

Kathy's Gazebo Cafe 4199 N Federal Hwy. . . . . . Boca Raton FL 33431 561-395-6033
Web: www.kathysgazebo.com

Ke-e Grill 17940 N Military Trl. . . . . . Boca Raton FL 33496 561-995-5044
Web: wix.com

Le Vieux Paris 170 W Camino Real. . . . . . Boca Raton FL 33432 561-368-7910

Max's Grille 404 Plz Real. . . . . . Boca Raton FL 33432 561-368-0080
Web: www.maxsgrille.com

New York Prime 2350 Executive Ctr Dr NW . . . . . Boca Raton FL 33431 561-998-3881
Web: www.newyorkprime.com

Uncle Tai's 5250 Town Ctr Cir. . . . . . Boca Raton FL 33486 561-368-8806
Web: uncletais.com

Roy's 26831 S Bay Dr . . . . . Bonita Springs FL 34134 239-498-7697
Web: www.roysrestaurant.com

Caffe Vialetto 4019 Le Jeune Rd . . . . . Coral Gables FL 33134 305-446-5659 446-3532
Web: www.cafevialetto.com

Christy's 3101 Ponce de Leon Blvd . . . . . Coral Gables FL 33134 305-446-1400 446-3257
Web: www.christysrestaurant.com

Francesco 325 Alcazar Ave . . . . . Coral Gables FL 33134 305-446-1600
Web: www.francesco.com.pe

Maroosh 223 Valencia Ave. . . . . . Coral Gables FL 33134 305-476-9800 476-3999
Web: www.maroosh.com

Ortanique Restaurant 278 Miracle Mile . . . . . Coral Gables FL 33134 305-446-7710 446-9895
Web: ortaniquerestaurants.com

Pascal's on Ponce
2611 Ponce de Leon Blvd. . . . . . Coral Gables FL 33134 305-444-2024 444-9798
Web: www.pascalmiami.com

Ruth's Chris Steak House
2320 Salzedo St . . . . . Coral Gables FL 33134 305-461-8360
Web: www.ruthschris.com

Runyon's 9810 W Sample Rd . . . . . Coral Springs FL 33065 954-752-2333 752-2401
Web: www.runyonsofcoralsprings.com

Shorty's Bar-B-Q 5989 S University Dr. . . . . . Davie FL 33328 954-680-9900
Web: www.shortys.com

Angell & Phelps Chocolate Factory
154 S Beach St. . . . . . Daytona Beach FL 32114 386-252-6531
TF: 800-969-2634 ■ *Web:* angellandphelps.com

Anna's Trattoria 304 Seabreeze Blvd . . . . . Daytona Beach FL 32118 386-239-9624

Caribbean Jack's 721 Ballough Rd . . . . . Daytona Beach FL 32114 386-523-3000 252-7362
Web: www.caribbeanjacks.com

Name / Address	City	State	Zip	Phone	Fax
Cellar Restaurant, The 220 Magnolia Ave *Web:* www.thecellarrestaurant.com	Daytona Beach	FL	32114	386-258-0011	
Gene's Steak House 3674 W International Speedway Blvd	Daytona Beach	FL	32124	386-255-2059	
Ocean Deck 127 S Ocean Ave *Web:* www.oceandeck.com	Daytona Beach	FL	32118	386-253-5224	
Oyster Pub 555 Seabreeze Blvd *Web:* www.oysterpub.com	Daytona Beach	FL	32118	386-255-6348	
Pasha 919 W International Speedway Blvd *Web:* pashacafedaytona.com	Daytona Beach	FL	32114	386-257-7753	
Porto-Fino Restaurant 3124 S Atlantic Ave *Web:* portofinodaytona.com	Daytona Beach	FL	32118	386-767-9484	
Top of Daytona Restaurant 2625 S Atlantic Ave *Web:* topofdaytona.com	Daytona Beach	FL	32118	386-767-5791	
Baja Cafe Dos 1310 S Federal Hwy *Web:* www.bajacafedeerfield.com	Deerfield Beach	FL	33441	954-596-1305	
Tamarind Asian Grill & Sushi Bar 949 S Federal Hwy *Web:* www.tamarindgrill.com	Deerfield Beach	FL	33441	954-428-8009	
32 East 32 E Atlantic Ave *Web:* www.32east.com	Delray Beach	FL	33444	561-276-7868	
Fifth Avenue Grill 821 SE Fifth Ave Federal Hwy	Delray Beach	FL	33483	561-265-0122	
3030 Ocean 3030 Holiday Dr *Web:* www.3030ocean.com	Fort Lauderdale	FL	33316	954-765-3030	
Ambry 3016 E Commercial Blvd *Web:* ambryrestaurant.net	Fort Lauderdale	FL	33308	954-771-7342	
Bistro 17 1617 SE 17th St *Web:* marriott.com	Fort Lauderdale	FL	33316	954-626-1748	626-1717
Bistro Mezzaluna 1821 SE Tenth Ave *Web:* www.bistromezzaluna.com	Fort Lauderdale	FL	33316	954-522-9191	
Cafe Martorano 3343 E Oakland Pk Blvd *Web:* www.cafemartorano.com	Fort Lauderdale	FL	33308	954-561-2554	
Cafe Seville 2768 E Oakland Pk Blvd *Web:* www.cafeseville.com	Fort Lauderdale	FL	33306	954-565-1148	
Cafe Vico 1125 N Federal Hwy *Web:* www.cafevicorestaurant.com	Fort Lauderdale	FL	33304	954-565-9681	
Casa D'Angelo 1201 N Federal Hwy *Web:* casa-d-angelo.com	Fort Lauderdale	FL	33304	954-564-1234	
Casablanca Cafe 3049 Alhambra St *Web:* www.casablancacafeonline.com	Fort Lauderdale	FL	33304	954-764-3500	
Eduardo de San Angel 2822 E Commercial Blvd *Web:* www.eduardodesanangel.com	Fort Lauderdale	FL	33308	954-772-4731	772-0794
Greek Islands Taverna 3300 N Ocean Blvd *Web:* www.greekislandstaverna.com	Fort Lauderdale	FL	33308	954-565-5505	
Hi-Life Cafe 3000 N Federal Hwy	Fort Lauderdale	FL	33306	954-563-1395	
IL Mulino 1800 E Sunrise Blvd *Web:* www.ilmulinofl.com	Fort Lauderdale	FL	33304	954-524-1800	
Johnny V 625 E Las Olas Blvd *Web:* www.johnnyvlasolas.com	Fort Lauderdale	FL	33301	954-761-7920	761-3495
Las Vegas Cuban Cuisine 2807 E Oakland Pk Blvd *Web:* www.lasvegascubancuisine.com	Fort Lauderdale	FL	33934	954-564-1370	
Mango's 904 E Las Olas Blvd *Web:* www.mangosonlasolas.com	Fort Lauderdale	FL	33301	954-523-5001	
Nick's 3496 N Ocean Blvd *Web:* nicksitalianonline.com	Fort Lauderdale	FL	33308	954-563-6441	
PF Chang's China Bistro 2418 E Sunrise Blvd *Web:* www.pfchangs.com	Fort Lauderdale	FL	33304	954-565-5877	
Rainbow Palace 2787 E Oakland Pk Blvd *Web:* www.rainbowpalace.com	Fort Lauderdale	FL	33306	954-565-5652	
Sage 2378 N Federal Hwy *Web:* www.sagecafe.net	Fort Lauderdale	FL	33305	954-565-2299	
Sea Watch Restaurant 6002 N Ocean Blvd *Web:* www.seawatchontheocean.com	Fort Lauderdale	FL	33308	954-781-2200	
Sushi Rock Cafe 1515 E Las Olas Blvd	Fort Lauderdale	FL	33301	954-462-5541	
Thai on the Beach 901 N Ft Lauderdale Beach Blvd	Fort Lauderdale	FL	33304	954-565-0015	
Thai Spice 1514 E Commercial Blvd *Web:* www.thaispicefla.com	Fort Lauderdale	FL	33334	954-771-4535	
Timpano Italian Chophouse 450 E Las Olas Blvd *Web:* timpanochophouse.net	Fort Lauderdale	FL	33301	954-462-9119	
Tokyo Sushi 1499 SE 17th St *Web:* iluvtokyosushi.net	Fort Lauderdale	FL	33316	954-767-9922	
Tom Jenkins' Bar-B-Q 1236 S Federal Hwy *Web:* www.tomjenkins.net	Fort Lauderdale	FL	33316	954-522-5046	
Amelia's 235 S Main St Ste 107 *Web:* www.ameliasgainesville.com	Gainesville	FL	32601	352-373-1919	
David's Barbecue 5121 NW 39th Ave *Web:* davidsbbq.com	Gainesville	FL	32606	352-373-2002	
Emiliano's Cafe 7 SE First Ave *Web:* www.emilianoscafe.com	Gainesville	FL	32601	352-375-7381	
La Fiesta Mexican Restaurant 908 NW 69th Terrace	Gainesville	FL	32605	352-332-0878	332-0878
Leonardo's 706 706 W University Ave *Web:* www.leonardosgainesville.com	Gainesville	FL	32601	352-378-2001	
Mildred's Big City Food 3445 W University Ave *Web:* www.mildredsbigcityfood.com	Gainesville	FL	32607	352-371-1711	
Miya Sushi 3222 SW 35th Blvd *Web:* miyasushi.net	Gainesville	FL	32608	352-335-3030	
Northwest Grille 5115 NW 39th Ave	Gainesville	FL	32606	352-376-0500	
Sushi Matsuri 3418 SW Archer Rd	Gainesville	FL	32608	352-335-1875	
Tangelo's Grille 3121 Beach Blvd S *Web:* www.tangelosgrille.com	Gulfport	FL	33707	727-894-1695	
Molina's Ranch Restaurant 4090 E Eigth Ave *Web:* www.molinasranchrestaurant.com	Hialeah	FL	33013	305-693-4440	
Dave & Buster's 3000 Oakwood Blvd **Fax Area Code:* 214 ■ *TF:* 844-515-5157 ■ *Web:* www.daveandbusters.com	Hollywood	FL	33020	954-923-5505	904-2370*
Taverna Opa 800 N Ocean Dr *Web:* www.tavernaopa.com	Hollywood	FL	33019	954-922-2256	922-2258
Islamorada Fish Co 81532 Overseas Hwy PO Box 283 **Fax Area Code:* 305 ■ *TF:* 800-258-2559 ■ *Web:* www.ifcstonecrab.com	Islamorada	FL	33036	800-258-2559	664-5071*
BB's Restaurant & Bar 1019 Hendricks Ave *Web:* www.bbsrestaurant.com	Jacksonville	FL	32207	904-306-0100	306-0118
Biscotti's Restaurant 3556 St Johns Ave *Web:* www.biscottis.net	Jacksonville	FL	32205	904-387-2060	387-0051
Bistro Aix 1440 San Marco Blvd *Web:* www.bistrox.com	Jacksonville	FL	32207	904-398-1949	
Chart House 1501 River Pl Blvd *Web:* www.chart-house.com	Jacksonville	FL	32207	904-398-3353	
Dave & Buster's 7025 Salisbury Rd *Web:* www.daveandbusters.com	Jacksonville	FL	32256	904-296-1525	
Marker 32 14549 Beach Blvd *Web:* www.marker32.com	Jacksonville	FL	32250	904-223-1534	
Matthew's 2107 Hendricks Ave *Web:* www.matthewsrestaurant.com	Jacksonville	FL	32207	904-396-9922	396-5222
Pastiche 4260 Herschel St	Jacksonville	FL	32210	904-387-6213	
Ruth's Chris Steak House 1201 Riverplace Blvd *Web:* www.ruthschris.com	Jacksonville	FL	32207	904-396-6200	
Wine Cellar 1314 Prudential Dr *Web:* www.winecellarjax.com	Jacksonville	FL	32207	904-398-8989	
Dwight's Bistro 1527 Penman Rd *Web:* www.dwightsbistro.com	Jacksonville Beach	FL	32250	904-241-4496	
Eleven South 216 11th Ave S *Web:* www.elevensouth.com	Jacksonville Beach	FL	32250	904-241-1112	
Marlin Moon Grille 1183 Beach Blvd *Web:* www.marlinmoongrille.com	Jax Beach	FL	32250	904-372-4438	
A & B Lobster House 700 Front St *Web:* www.aandblobsterhouse.com	Key West	FL	33040	305-294-5880	294-6871
Ambrosia 1401 Simonton St *Web:* keywestambrosia.com	Key West	FL	33040	305-293-0304	
Bagatelle 115 Duval St *Web:* www.bagatellekeywest.com	Key West	FL	33040	305-296-6609	
Blue Heaven 729 Thomas St *Web:* www.blueheavenkw.homestead.com	Key West	FL	33040	305-296-8666	
BO's Fish Wagon 801 Caroline St *Web:* bosfishwagon.com	Key West	FL	33040	305-294-9272	
Cafe Marquesa 600 Fleming St *Web:* www.marquesa.com	Key West	FL	33040	305-292-1244	
Cafe Sole 1029 Southard St *Web:* cafesole.com	Key West	FL	33040	305-294-0230	
Camille's 1202 Simonton St *Web:* www.camilleskeywest.com	Key West	FL	33040	305-296-4811	
Duffy's Steak & Lobster House 1007 Simonton St *Web:* duffyskeywest.com	Key West	FL	33040	305-296-4900	
Grand Cafe Key West 314 Duval St *Web:* www.grandcafekeywest.com	Key West	FL	33040	305-292-4740	
Hard Rock Cafe Key West 313 Duval St *Web:* www.hardrock.com	Key West	FL	33040	305-293-0230	
Hog's Breath Saloon Key West 400 Front St Ste C *Web:* www.hogsbreath.com	Key West	FL	33040	305-296-4222	
Kelly's Caribbean Bar Grill & Brewery 301 Whitehead St *Web:* www.kellyskeywest.com	Key West	FL	33040	305-293-8484	296-0047
La Trattoria 524 Duval St *Web:* www.latrattoria.us	Key West	FL	33040	305-296-1075	
Louie's Backyard 700 Waddell Ave *Web:* www.louiesbackyard.com	Key West	FL	33040	305-294-1061	
Mangia Mangia 900 Southard St *Web:* www.mangia-mangia.com	Key West	FL	33040	305-294-2469	
Mangoes 700 Duval St *Web:* www.keywestmangoes.com	Key West	FL	33040	305-292-4606	
Margaritaville 500 Duval St *Web:* www.margaritavillekeywest.com	Key West	FL	33040	305-292-1435	
Michael's 532 Margaret St *Web:* www.michaelskeywest.com	Key West	FL	33040	305-295-1300	
Mo's 1116 White St	Key West	FL	33040	305-296-8955	
Pisces 1007 Simonton St *Web:* www.pisceskeywest.com	Key West	FL	33040	305-294-7100	
Square One 1075 Duval St *Web:* squareonekeywest.com	Key West	FL	33040	305-296-4300	
Turtle Kraals Restaurant & Bar 231 Margaret St *Web:* www.turtlekraals.com	Key West	FL	33040	305-294-2640	
Artist Point 901 Timberline Dr *Web:* disneyworld.disney.go.com	Lake Buena Vista	FL	32830	407-824-3200	
Bluezoo 1500 Epcot Resorts Blvd PO Box 22653 *Web:* www.swandolphin.com/bluezoo	Lake Buena Vista	FL	32830	407-934-1111	
Bongos Cuban Cafe 1498 E Buena Vista Dr *Web:* www.bongoscubancafe.com	Lake Buena Vista	FL	32830	407-828-0999	
California Grill Disney's Contemporary Resort 4600 N World Dr *Web:* disneyworld.disney.go.com	Lake Buena Vista	FL	32830	407-939-5277	

Name / Address	City	State	ZIP	Phone	Fax
Disney 4401 Grand Floridian Way Disney's Grand Floridian Resort *Web:* disneyworld.disney.go.com	Lake Buena Vista	FL	32830	407-934-7639	824-3186
House of Blues Orlando 1490 E Lk Buena Vista Dr *Web:* www.houseofblues.com	Lake Buena Vista	FL	32830	407-934-2583	
Blue Moon Fish Co 4405 W Tradewinds Ave *Web:* www.bluemoonfishco.com	Lauderdale-by-the-Sea	FL	33308	954-267-9888	267-9006
Rosey Baby 4587 N University Dr *Web:* www.roseybaby.com	Lauderhill	FL	33351	954-749-5627	
Cap's Place Island Restaurant 2765 NE 28th Ct *Web:* www.capsplace.com	Lighthouse Point	FL	33064	954-941-0418	
Le Bistro 4626 N Federal Hwy *Web:* www.lebistrorestaurant.com	Lighthouse Point	FL	33064	954-946-9240	
Chart House 201 Gulf of Mexico Dr *Web:* www.chart-house.com	Longboat Key	FL	34228	941-383-5593	
Euphemia Haye 5540 Gulf of Mexico Dr *Web:* www.euphemiahaye.com	Longboat Key	FL	34228	941-383-3633	
Harry's Continental Kitchens 525 St Judes Dr *Web:* www.harryskitchen.com	Longboat Key	FL	34228	941-383-0777	383-2029
Pattigeorge's 4120 Gulf of Mexico Dr. *Web:* www.pattigeorges.com	Longboat Key	FL	34228	941-383-5111	
Azul 500 Brickell Key Dr *Web:* www.mandarinoriental.com	Miami	FL	33131	305-913-8358	
Bali Cafe 109 NE Second Ave.	Miami	FL	33132	305-358-5751	
Bizcaya Grill 3300 SW 27th Ave *Web:* ritzcarlton.com	Miami	FL	33133	305-644-4675	
Bongos Cuban Cafe 601 Biscayne Blvd *Fax Area Code: 305 ■ *Web:* www.bongoscubancafe.com	Miami	FL	33132	786-777-2100	695-7160*
Bubba Gump Shrimp Co 401 Biscayne Blvd. *Web:* www.bubbagump.com	Miami	FL	33132	305-379-8866	
Cancun Grill 15406 NW 77th Ct. *Web:* cancungrillmiamilakes.com	Miami	FL	33016	305-826-8571	
Capital Grille 444 Brickell Ave. *Web:* www.thecapitalgrille.com	Miami	FL	33131	305-374-4500	
Captain's Tavern Restaurant Inc 9625 S Dixie Hwy *Web:* www.captainstavernmiami.com	Miami	FL	33156	305-666-5979	
Casa Juancho 2436 SW Eigth St *Web:* www.casajuancho.com	Miami	FL	33135	305-642-2452	642-2524
Garcia's 398 NW N River Dr *Web:* garciasmiami.com	Miami	FL	33128	305-375-0765	
Graziano's 9227 SW 40th St *Web:* grazianosgroup.com	Miami	FL	33165	305-225-0008	
La Loggia 68 W Flagler St. *Web:* laloggia.org	Miami	FL	33130	305-373-4800	
Lan Pan Asian Cafe 8332 S Dixie Hwy. *Web:* lanpanasian.com	Miami	FL	33143	305-661-8141	
Lombardi's 401 Biscayne Blvd *TF:* 888-286-3792 ■ *Web:* www.lombardifamilyconcepts.com	Miami	FL	33132	888-286-3792	
Melting Pot of Miami, The 11520 Sunset Dr *Web:* www.meltingpot.com	Miami	FL	33173	305-279-8816	598-8931
Morton's The Steakhouse 1200 Brickell Ave *Web:* www.mortons.com	Miami	FL	33131	305-400-9990	400-9989
Perricone's Marketplace & Cafe 15 SE Tenth St *Web:* www.perricones.com	Miami	FL	33131	305-374-9449	371-6647
Tony Chan's Water Club 1717 N Bayshore Dr. *Web:* www.tonychans.com	Miami	FL	33132	305-374-8888	
Tropical Chinese Restaurant 7991 SW 40th St *Web:* www.tropicalchinesemiami.com	Miami	FL	33155	305-262-7576	262-1552
Tutto Pasta 1751 SW Third Ave. *Web:* www.tuttopasta.com	Miami	FL	33129	305-857-0709	
Versailles 3555 SW Eigth St *Web:* versaillesrestaurant.com	Miami	FL	33135	305-444-0240	
A Fish Called Avalon 700 Ocean Dr *Web:* www.afishcalledavalon.com	Miami Beach	FL	33139	305-532-1727	
Cafe Prima Pasta 414 71st St *Web:* www.primapasta.com	Miami Beach	FL	33141	305-867-0106	
Escopazzo 1311 Washington Ave.	Miami Beach	FL	33139	305-674-9450	532-8770
Forge, The 432 41st St. *Web:* www.theforge.com	Miami Beach	FL	33140	305-538-8533	538-7733
Grillfish 1444 Collins Ave. *Web:* www.grillfish.com	Miami Beach	FL	33139	305-538-9908	
Hosteria Romana 429 Espanola Way *Web:* www.hosteriaromana.com	Miami Beach	FL	33139	305-532-4299	
Icebox Cafe 1855 Purdy Ave *Web:* www.iceboxcafe.com	Miami Beach	FL	33139	305-538-8448	
Joe's Stone Crab 11 Washington Ave. *TF:* 800-780-2722 ■ *Web:* www.joesstonecrab.com	Miami Beach	FL	33139	305-673-0365	
Macaluso's 1747 Alton Rd. *Web:* macalusosmiami.com	Miami Beach	FL	33139	305-604-1811	
Nemo 100 Collins Ave *Web:* www.mylesrestaurantgroup.com	Miami Beach	FL	33139	305-532-4550	
News Cafe 800 Ocean Dr *Web:* www.newscafe.com	Miami Beach	FL	33139	305-538-6397	538-7817
Nikki Beach 1 Ocean Dr S Beach	Miami Beach	FL	33139	305-538-1111	779-5895
Nobu 4525 Collins Ave *Web:* www.noburestaurants.com	Miami Beach	FL	33140	212-757-3000	
Pelican Cafe 826 Ocean Dr *Web:* www.pelicanhotel.com	Miami Beach	FL	33139	305-673-3373	
Prime 112 112 Ocean Dr *Web:* www.mylesrestaurantgroup.com	Miami Beach	FL	33139	305-532-8112	
Shula's Steak House 5225 Collins Ave *Web:* www.donshula.com	Miami Beach	FL	33140	305-341-6565	
Spris 731 Lincoln Rd *Web:* www.spris.cc	Miami Beach	FL	33139	305-673-2020	
SushiSamba 600 Lincoln Rd *Web:* www.sushisamba.com	Miami Beach	FL	33139	305-673-5337	
Tap Tap 819 Fifth St *Web:* www.taptaprestaurant.com	Miami Beach	FL	33139	305-672-2898	
Toni's Sushi Bar 1208 Washington Ave *Web:* www.tonisushi.com	Miami Beach	FL	33139	305-673-9368	
Yuca 501 Lincoln Rd *Web:* www.yuca.com	Miami Beach	FL	33139	305-532-9822	
Beverly Hills Cafe 7321 Miami Lakes Dr *Web:* www.thebeverlyhillscafe.com	Miami Lakes	FL	33014	305-558-8201	
El Novillo Restaurant 15450 New Barn Rd *Web:* www.elnovillorestaurant.com	Miami Lakes	FL	33014	305-819-2755	819-7570
Shula's Steak 2 15255 Bull Run Rd *Web:* www.donshula.com	Miami Lakes	FL	33014	305-820-8047	
Cheeseburger in Paradise 10562 US Hwy 98W *Web:* www.cheeseburgerinparadise.com	Miramar Beach	FL	32550	850-837-0197	837-0866
Bistro 821 821 Fifth Ave S *Web:* www.bistro821.com	Naples	FL	34102	239-261-5821	261-1972
Campiello 1177 Third St S *Web:* www.campiello.damico.com	Naples	FL	34102	239-435-1166	
Chop's City Grill 837 Fifth Ave S. *Web:* www.chopscitygrill.com	Naples	FL	34102	239-262-4677	
Dock at Crayton Cove 845 12th Ave S. *Web:* www.dockcraytoncove.com	Naples	FL	34102	239-263-9940	
Jasmine 7231 Radio Rd *Web:* jasminechinesefood.com	Naples	FL	34104	239-352-5528	
M Waterfront Grille 4300 Gulf Shore Blvd N *Web:* www.mwaterfrontgrille.com	Naples	FL	34103	239-263-4421	
McCormick & Schmick's 9114 Strada Place *Web:* www.mccormickandschmicks.com	Naples	FL	34108	407-226-6515	
Pazzo! 853 Fifth Ave S *Web:* gr8food.net	Naples	FL	34102	239-434-8494	
PF Chang's China Bistro 10840 Tamiami Trail N *Web:* www.pfchangs.com	Naples	FL	34109	239-596-2174	
Ristorante Ciao 835 Fourth Ave S. *Web:* www.ristoranteciao.com	Naples	FL	34102	239-263-3889	
Shula's Steak House 5111 Tamiami Trl N *Web:* www.donshula.com	Naples	FL	34103	239-430-4999	
Watermark Grille 11280 Tamiami Trl N *Web:* www.watermarkgrille.com	Naples	FL	34110	239-596-1400	
Yabba Island Grill 711 Fifth Ave S *Web:* www.yabbaislandgrill.com	Naples	FL	34102	239-262-5787	
Ruth's Chris Steak House 661 N Federal Hwy 1 *Web:* www.ruthschris.com	North Palm Beach	FL	33408	561-863-0660	
Ayothaya Thai Cuisine 7555 W Sand Lake *Web:* www.ayothayathaicuisineoforlando.com	Orlando	FL	32819	407-345-0040	
Bahama Breeze 8849 International Dr. *TF:* 877-500-9715 ■ *Web:* www.bahamabreeze.com	Orlando	FL	32819	407-248-2499	
Boheme, The 325 S Orange Ave *TF:* 866-663-0024 ■ *Web:* www.grandbohemianhotel.com/theboheme	Orlando	FL	32801	407-313-9000	313-9001
Cafe Tu Tu Tango 8625 International Dr. *Web:* www.cafetututango.com	Orlando	FL	32819	407-248-2222	352-3696
Capital Grille Offices, The 1000 Darden Ctr Dr *Web:* www.thecapitalgrille.com	Orlando	FL	32837	202-737-6200	
Cedar's 7732 W Sand Lk Rd *Web:* www.cedarsoforlando.com	Orlando	FL	32836	407-351-6000	
Charley's Steak House 8255 International Dr *Web:* www.talkofthetownrestaurants.com	Orlando	FL	32819	407-363-0228	
Chatham's Place Restaurant 7575 Doctor Philips Blvd *Web:* www.chathamsplace.com	Orlando	FL	32819	407-345-2992	345-0307
Cheesecake Factory 4200 Conroy Rd *Web:* www.thecheesecakefactory.com	Orlando	FL	32839	407-226-0333	
Christini's 7600 Dr Phillips Blvd *Web:* www.christinis.com	Orlando	FL	32819	407-345-8770	345-8700
Ciao Italia 6149 Westwood Blvd *Web:* www.ciaoitaliaonline.com	Orlando	FL	32821	407-354-0770	
Emeril's Orlando 6000 Universal Blvd Ste 702 *Web:* www.emerils.com	Orlando	FL	32819	407-224-2424	224-2525
Emeril's Tchoup Chop 6300 Hollywood Way *Web:* www.emerils.com	Orlando	FL	32819	407-503-2467	503-3344
Hard Rock Cafe 6050 Universal Blvd *Web:* www.hardrock.com	Orlando	FL	32819	407-351-7625	351-3983
Hemisphere 9300 Airport Blvd. *Web:* www.hyatt.com	Orlando	FL	32827	407-825-1234	
Hue Restaurant 629 E Central Blvd. *Web:* socothorntonpark.com	Orlando	FL	32801	407-849-1800	
Ichiban 19 S Orange Ave *Web:* www.shakaiorlando.com	Orlando	FL	32801	407-423-2688	
Julie's Waterfront 4201 S Orange Ave.	Orlando	FL	32806	407-240-2557	857-5850
K Restaurant & Wine Bar 1710 Edgewater Dr. *Web:* krestaurant.net	Orlando	FL	32804	407-872-2332	
Le Coq Au Vin 4800 S Orange Ave. *Web:* www.lecoqauvinrestaurant.com	Orlando	FL	32806	407-851-6980	
Linda's La Cantina 4721 E Colonial Dr *Web:* www.lindaslacantina.com	Orlando	FL	32803	407-894-4491	894-6415
Little Saigon 1106 E Colonial Dr *Web:* littlesaigonrestaurant.com	Orlando	FL	32803	407-423-8539	
Ming Court 9188 International Dr. *Web:* www.ming-court.com	Orlando	FL	32819	407-351-9988	
MoonFish 7525 W Sand Lk Rd *Web:* www.talkofthetownrestaurants.com	Orlando	FL	32819	407-363-7262	
Morton's The Steakhouse 7600 Doctor Phillips Blvd. *Web:* www.mortons.com	Orlando	FL	32819	407-248-3485	248-8559
Palm 5800 Universal Blvd Hard Rock Hotel *TF:* 866-333-7256 ■ *Web:* www.thepalm.com	Orlando	FL	32819	407-503-7256	503-2383
Roy's 7760 W Sand Lk Rd *Web:* www.roysrestaurant.com	Orlando	FL	32819	407-352-4844	
Ruth's Chris Steak House 7501 W Sand Lk Rd *Web:* www.ruthschris.com	Orlando	FL	32819	407-226-3900	

Name	City	State	ZIP	Phone	Fax
Seasons 52 7700 Sand Lk Rd *Web:* www.seasons52.com	Orlando	FL	32819	407-354-5212	
Sushi House of Orlando 8204 Crystal Clear Ln Ste 1300 *Web:* www.sushihouseint.com	Orlando	FL	32809	407-610-5921	
Thai House 2117 E Colonial Dr *Web:* www.thaihouseoforlando.net	Orlando	FL	32803	407-898-0820	898-1375
Vito's Chop House 8633 International Dr *Web:* www.talkofthetownrestaurants.com	Orlando	FL	32819	407-354-2467	
Cafe Boulud 301 Australian Ave *Web:* www.danielnyc.com	Palm Beach	FL	33480	561-655-6060	
Cafe Cellini 2505 S Ocean Blvd *Web:* cafecellini.com	Palm Beach	FL	33480	561-588-1871	
Cafe L'Europe 331 S County Rd *Web:* www.cafeleurope.com	Palm Beach	FL	33480	561-655-4020	
Chez Jean-Pierre Bistro 132 N County Rd *Web:* chezjean-pierre.com	Palm Beach	FL	33480	561-833-1171	
Echo 230A Sunrise Ave *TF:* 855-435-0061 ■ *Web:* www.echopalmbeach.com	Palm Beach	FL	33480	855-435-0061	
Trevini 150 Worth Ave *Web:* www.treviniristorante.com	Palm Beach	FL	33480	561-833-3883	
Cafe Chardonnay 4533 PGA Blvd *Web:* www.cafechardonnay.com	Palm Beach Gardens	FL	33418	561-627-2662	
Ironwood Grille 400 Ave of the Champions *Web:* www.pgaresort.com	Palm Beach Gardens	FL	33418	561-627-4852	
Capriccio 2424 N University Dr *Web:* www.capriccios.net	Pembroke Pines	FL	33024	954-432-7001	
Angus, The 1101 Scenic Hwy *Web:* www.anguspensacola.com	Pensacola	FL	32503	850-432-0539	
Fish House, The 600 S Barracks St *Web:* greatsouthernrestaurants.com	Pensacola	FL	32502	850-470-0003	470-0694
Horizen 3103 E Strong St *Web:* horizenpensacola.com	Pensacola	FL	32503	850-432-7899	
Jackson's Steakhouse 400 S Palafox St *Web:* greatsouthernrestaurants.com	Pensacola	FL	32502	850-469-9898	
Los Rancheros 7250 Plantation Rd *Web:* larumbamexicanrestaurant.com	Pensacola	FL	32504	850-476-1623	
McGuire's Irish Pub 600 E Gregory St *Web:* www.mcguiresirishpub.com	Pensacola	FL	32502	850-433-6789	
Melting Pot of Pensacola, The 418 Gregory St Ste 500 *TF:* 800-783-0867 ■ *Web:* www.meltingpot.com	Pensacola	FL	32501	850-438-4030	433-7664
Petrella's Italian Cafe 2174 W Nine Mile Rd *Web:* www.petrellasitaliancafe.com	Pensacola	FL	32534	850-471-9444	
Tokyo Japanese Steakhouse 312 E Nine Mile Rd *Web:* gotokyopensacola.com	Pensacola	FL	32514	850-479-9111	479-5881
Yamato Oriental Cuisine 131 N New Warrington Rd *Web:* www.yamatodining.com	Pensacola	FL	32506	850-453-3461	
India House 1711 N University Dr *Web:* www.indiahouserestaurant.com	Plantation	FL	33322	954-565-5701	
Cafe Maxx 2601 E Atlantic Blvd *Web:* www.cafemaxx.com	Pompano Beach	FL	33062	954-782-0606	782-0648
Palm-Aire Country Club in Pompano Beach 2600 N Palm Aire Dr *Web:* www.palmairegolf.com	Pompano Beach	FL	33069	954-975-6225	
JJ's Bistro de Paris 330 A1A N Ste 209 *Web:* www.jjbistro.com	Ponte Vedra	FL	32082	904-996-7557	
Booth's Bowery 3657 S Nova Rd *Web:* www.boothsbowery.com	Port Orange	FL	32129	386-761-9464	761-7518
Barnacle Bill's 14 Castillo Dr *Web:* www.barnaclebillsonline.com	Saint Augustine	FL	32084	904-824-3663	
Beachcomber Restaurant 2 A St	Saint Augustine	FL	32080	904-471-3744	
Cap's 4325 Myrtle St *Web:* www.capsonthewater.com	Saint Augustine	FL	32084	904-824-8794	
Cortesse's Bistro 1910 US 1	Saint Augustine	FL	32086	904-825-6775	
Creekside Dinery 160 Nix Boat Yard Rd *Web:* creeksidedinery.com	Saint Augustine	FL	32084	904-829-6113	
Kingfish Grill 252 Yacht Club Dr *Web:* www.kingfishgrill.com	Saint Augustine	FL	32084	904-824-2111	
Kings Head British Pub 6460 US Hwy 1 N *Web:* kingsheadbritishpub.com	Saint Augustine	FL	32095	904-823-9787	
Le Pavillon 45 San Marco Ave *Web:* www.lepav.com	Saint Augustine	FL	32084	904-824-6202	
Manatee Cafe 525 SR 16 Ste 106 Westgate Plz *Web:* www.manateecafe.com	Saint Augustine	FL	32084	904-826-0210	826-4080
Mikato Japanese Steak House 1092 S Ponce de Leon Blvd *Web:* mymikato.com	Saint Augustine	FL	32084	904-824-7064	
O'Steen's Restaurant 205 Anastasia Blvd *Web:* osteensrestaurant.com	Saint Augustine	FL	32080	904-829-6974	
Oasis Deck & Restaurant 4000 A1A *Web:* www.worldfamousoasis.com	Saint Augustine	FL	32080	904-471-3424	
Raintree, The 102 San Marco Ave *Web:* www.raintreerestaurant.com	Saint Augustine	FL	32084	904-824-7211	
Reef, The 4100 Coastal Hwy *Web:* www.thereefstaugustine.com	Saint Augustine	FL	32084	904-824-8008	
Salt Water Cowboy's 299 Dondanville Rd *Web:* www.saltwatercowboys.com	Saint Augustine	FL	32084	904-471-2332	
Santa Maria Restaurant 135 Avenida Menendez	Saint Augustine	FL	32084	904-829-6578	824-9214
South Beach Grill 45 Cubbedge Rd *Web:* www.southbeachgrill.net	Saint Augustine	FL	32080	904-471-8700	
Sunset Grill 421 A1A Beach Blvd *Web:* sunsetgrillea1a.com	Saint Augustine	FL	32080	904-471-5555	
9 Bangkok Restaurant 571 Central Ave *Web:* 9bangkok.info	Saint Petersburg	FL	33701	727-894-5990	826-6164
Athenian Garden 6940 22nd Ave N *Web:* www.atheniangardens.com	Saint Petersburg	FL	33710	727-345-7040	
Chattaway 358 22nd Ave S	Saint Petersburg	FL	33705	727-823-1594	
Marchand's Bar & Grill 501 Fifth Ave NE Renaissance Vinoy Resort *Web:* www.marriott.com	Saint Petersburg	FL	33701	727-824-8072	
Melting Pot ST Petersburg, The 2221 Fourth St N *Web:* www.meltingpot.com	Saint Petersburg	FL	33704	727-895-6358	894-7383
Red Mesa Restaurant 4912 Fourth St N *Web:* www.redmesarestaurant.com	Saint Petersburg	FL	33703	727-527-8728	
Siam Garden Thai Restaurant 3125 MLK St N *Web:* www.siamgardenthai1.com	Saint Petersburg	FL	33704	727-822-0613	
Ted Peter's Famous Smoked Fish 1350 Pasadena Ave S *Web:* tedpetersfish.com	Saint Petersburg	FL	33707	727-381-7931	
Tokyo Bay Japanese Restaurant & Sushi 5901 Sun Blvd *Web:* www.tokyobayrestaurant.com	Saint Petersburg	FL	33715	727-867-0770	
Cafe Amici 1371 Main St *Web:* www.cafeamicisrq.com	Sarasota	FL	34236	941-951-6896	
Cafe Baci 4001 S Tamiami Trl *Web:* www.cafebacisarasota.com	Sarasota	FL	34231	941-921-4848	923-8643
Captain Brian's Seafood Market & Restaurant 8421 N Tamiami Trl *Web:* www.captainbriansseafood.com	Sarasota	FL	34243	941-351-4492	
Chutney's Etc 1944 Hillview St *Web:* www.chutneysetc.com	Sarasota	FL	34239	941-954-4444	
Columbia 411 St Armands Cir *Web:* www.columbiarestaurant.com	Sarasota	FL	34236	941-388-3987	
Demetrio's 4410 S Tamiami Trail *Web:* www.demetriospizzeria.com	Sarasota	FL	34231	941-922-1585	
Mediterraneo 1970 Main St *Web:* mediterraneorest.com	Sarasota	FL	34236	941-365-4122	954-0106
Michael's on East 1212 E Ave S *Web:* bestfood.com	Sarasota	FL	34239	941-366-0007	953-3463
Morel Restaurant 3809 S Tuttle Ave *Web:* www.morelrestaurant.com	Sarasota	FL	34239	941-927-8716	
Old Salty Dog 1601 Ken Thompson Pkwy	Sarasota	FL	34236	941-388-4311	388-3902
Phillippi Creek Village Restaurant & Oyster Bar 5353 S Tamiami Trl *Web:* www.creekseafood.com	Sarasota	FL	34231	941-925-4444	
Saga Japanese Steak House 8383 S Tamiami Trl *Web:* sagasteakhouse.com	Sarasota	FL	34238	941-924-2800	
Selva Grill 1345 Main St *Web:* www.selvagrill.com	Sarasota	FL	34236	941-362-4427	362-2867
Ophelia's on the Bay 9105 Midnight Pass Rd *Web:* www.opheliasonthebay.net	Siesta Key	FL	34242	941-349-2212	
Songkran Thai Restaurant 2309 S Ridgewood Ave	South Daytona	FL	32119	386-760-0300	
Two Chefs 8287 S Dixie Hwy *Web:* twochefsrestaurant.com	South Miami	FL	33143	305-663-2100	
Rainforest Cafe 12801 W Sunrise Blvd *Web:* www.rainforestcafe.com	Sunrise	FL	33323	954-851-1015	
Andrew's 228 228 S Adams St *Web:* www.andrewsdowntown.com	Tallahassee	FL	32301	850-222-3444	222-2433
Bahn Thai Restaurant 1319 S Monroe St	Tallahassee	FL	32301	850-224-4765	
Barnacle Bill's 1830 N Monroe St *Web:* www.barnaclebills.com	Tallahassee	FL	32303	850-385-8734	385-6298
Bonefish Grill 3491 Thomasville Rd *Web:* www.bonefishgrill.com	Tallahassee	FL	32309	850-297-0460	
Cabo's Island Grill & Bar 1221 Apalachee Pkwy *Web:* www.cabosgrill.com	Tallahassee	FL	32301	850-878-7707	
Clusters & Hops 707 N Monroe St *Web:* www.winencheese.com	Tallahassee	FL	32303	850-222-2669	222-0469
Cypress, The 320 E Tennessee St *Web:* www.cypressrestaurant.com	Tallahassee	FL	32301	850-513-1100	
Georgio's 3425 Thomasville Rd *Web:* georgiostallahassee.com	Tallahassee	FL	32309	850-893-4161	
Kitcho 1415 Timberlane Rd Ste 121 *Web:* www.kitchorestaurant.com	Tallahassee	FL	32312	850-893-7686	
Longhorn Steakhouse 2400 N Monroe St *Web:* www.longhornsteakhouse.com	Tallahassee	FL	32303	850-385-4028	
Los Compadres 2102 W Pensacola St *Web:* bestmexicanfoodtallahassee.com	Tallahassee	FL	32304	850-576-8946	
Marie Livingston's Steakhouse & Saloon 2705 Apalachee Pkwy *Web:* marielivingstonsteakhouse.com	Tallahassee	FL	32301	850-562-2525	
Melting Pot, The 2727 N Monroe St *Web:* www.meltingpot.com	Tallahassee	FL	32303	850-386-7440	
Mom & Dad's 4175 Apalachee Pkwy *Web:* www.momanddadstally.com	Tallahassee	FL	32311	850-877-4518	
Samrat 2529 Apalachee Pkwy *Web:* samratindianrestaurantfl.com	Tallahassee	FL	32301	850-942-1993	942-8091
Z Bardhi 3596 Kinhega Dr *Web:* www.zbardhis.com	Tallahassee	FL	32312	850-894-9919	
Armani's Restaurant 2900 Bayport Dr *Web:* www.hyatt.com	Tampa	FL	33607	813-207-6800	
Bern's Steak House 1208 S Howard Ave *Web:* www.bernssteakhouse.com	Tampa	FL	33606	813-251-2421	
Byblos Cafe 2832 S MacDill Ave *Web:* www.bybloscafe.com	Tampa	FL	33629	813-805-7977	837-0951
Caffe Paridiso 4205 S MacDill Ave	Tampa	FL	33611	813-835-6622	835-9773

	City	State	ZIP	Phone	Fax
Capdevila at Lateresita 3248 W Columbus Dr *Web:* www.lateresitarestaurant.com	Tampa	FL	33607	813-879-9704	
Columbia Restaurant 2025 E 7th Ave *Web:* www.columbiarestaurant.com	Tampa	FL	33605	904-824-3341	
Columbia Restaurant 2025 E Seventh Ave. *Web:* www.columbiarestaurant.com	Tampa	FL	33605	813-248-3000	247-5881
Fleming's Prime Steakhouse & Wine Bar 4322 W Boy Scout Blvd *Web:* www.flemingssteakhouse.com	Tampa	FL	33607	813-874-9463	
Haven Restaurant 2208 W Morrison Ave *Web:* www.sideberns.com	Tampa	FL	33606	813-258-2233	
Jackson's Bistro 601 S Harbor Island Blvd *Web:* www.jacksonsbistro.com	Tampa	FL	33602	813-277-0112	277-0114
Jimbo's Pit BBQ 4103 W Kennedy Blvd *Web:* www.jimbosbarbq.com	Tampa	FL	33609	813-289-9724	289-1006
Kojak's House of Ribs 2808 W Gandy Blvd *Web:* kojaksbbq.net	Tampa	FL	33611	813-837-3774	
Mangroves Bar & Grille 208 S Howard Ave *Web:* www.mangroves-restaurants.com	Tampa	FL	33606	813-258-3302	
Melting Pot of Tampa, The 13164 N Dale Mabry Hwy *TF:* 800-783-0867 ■ *Web:* www.meltingpot.com	Tampa	FL	33618	813-962-6936	963-0125
Melting Pot, The 7886 Woodland Center Blvd *TF:* 800-783-0867 ■ *Web:* www.meltingpot.com	Tampa	FL	33614	865-971-5400	
Mise En Place 442 W Kennedy Blvd *Web:* miseonline.com	Tampa	FL	33606	813-254-5373	
Palm, The 205 Westshore Plz Dr *Web:* www.thepalm.com	Tampa	FL	33609	813-849-7256	
Roy's 4342 W Boy Scout Blvd *Web:* www.roysrestaurant.com	Tampa	FL	33607	813-873-7697	
Rusty Pelican 2425 N Rocky Pt Dr *Web:* www.therustypelican.com	Tampa	FL	33607	813-281-1943	
Sawatdee Thai Cuisine 10938 N 56th St *Web:* sawatdeethaioftampa.com	Tampa	FL	33617	813-985-2071	
Shula's Steak House 4860 W Kennedy Blvd *Web:* www.donshula.com	Tampa	FL	33609	813-286-4366	
Six Tables 4267 Henderson Blvd	Tampa	FL	33629	813-207-0527	
Taj Indian Cuisine 2734 E Fowler Ave *Web:* tajtampaindiancuisine.com	Tampa	FL	33612	813-971-8483	
Thai Terrace 2055 N Dale Mabry Hwy *Web:* thaiterrace.net	Tampa	FL	33607	813-877-8955	980-0444
Bimini Twist 8480 Okeechobee Blvd *Web:* mybiminitwist.com	West Palm Beach	FL	33411	561-784-2660	784-2660
Cabana 533 Clematis St *Web:* www.cabanarestaurant.com	West Palm Beach	FL	33401	561-833-4773	
City Cellar Wine Bar & Grill 700 S Rosemary Ave *Web:* bigtimerestaurants.com	West Palm Beach	FL	33401	561-366-0071	
La Sirena 6316 S Dixie Hwy *Web:* www.lasirenaonline.com	West Palm Beach	FL	33405	561-585-3128	
Maison Carlos 3010 S Dixie Hwy *Web:* www.maisoncarlos.com	West Palm Beach	FL	33405	561-659-6524	
Morton's the Steakhouse 777 S Flagler Dr *Web:* www.mortons.com	West Palm Beach	FL	33401	561-835-9664	835-4806
Okeechobee Steakhouse 2854 Okeechobee Blvd *Web:* www.okeesteakhouse.com	West Palm Beach	FL	33409	561-683-5151	
Raindancer Steak House 2300 Palm Beach Lakes Blvd *Web:* www.raindancersteakhouse.com	West Palm Beach	FL	33409	561-684-2810	
Rhythm Cafe 3800 S Dixie Hwy *Web:* www.rhythmcafe.cc	West Palm Beach	FL	33405	561-833-3406	
Stresa 2710 Okeechobee Blvd	West Palm Beach	FL	33409	561-615-0200	615-0200
Boondocks Restaurant 3948 S Peninsula Dr *Web:* boondocks-restaurant.com	Wilbur by the Sea	FL	32127	386-760-9001	
Old Florida Seafood House 1414 NE 26th St *Web:* www.oldflaseafood.com	Wilton Manors	FL	33305	954-566-1044	
Houston's 215 S Orlando Ave *Web:* www.hillstone.com	Winter Park	FL	32789	407-740-4005	
Ruth's Chris Steak House 1030 W. Canton Ave Ste 100 *Web:* www.ruthschris.com	Winter Park	FL	32789	314-783-9900	
Ruth's Chris Steak House 1030 W Canton Ave Ste 100 *Web:* www.ruthschris.com	Winter Park	FL	32789	407-622-2444	

Georgia

	City	State	ZIP	Phone	Fax
Di Paolo Cucina 8560 Holcomb Bridge Rd *Web:* www.dipaolorestaurant.com	Alpharetta	GA	30022	770-587-1051	
Village Tavern 11555 Rainwater Dr Haynes Rdg Rd *Web:* www.villagetavern.com	Alpharetta	GA	30009	770-777-6490	777-6492
10 Degrees South 4183 Roswell Rd NE *Web:* www.10degreessouth.com	Atlanta	GA	30342	404-705-8870	
Agave 242 Blvd SE *Web:* www.agaverestaurant.com	Atlanta	GA	30312	404-588-0006	
Anis Cafe & Bistro 2974 Grandview Ave *Web:* www.anisbistro.com	Atlanta	GA	30305	404-233-9889	
Annie's Thai Castle 3195 Roswell Rd NE *Web:* www.anniesthaifood.com	Atlanta	GA	30305	404-264-9546	
Antica Posta 519 E Paces Ferry Rd *Web:* www.anticaposta.com	Atlanta	GA	30305	404-262-7112	262-7335
Aria Restaurant 490 E Paces Ferry Rd NE *Web:* www.aria-atl.com	Atlanta	GA	30305	404-233-7673	
Atlanta Fish Market 265 Pharr Rd NE *Web:* www.buckheadrestaurants.com	Atlanta	GA	30305	404-240-1833	
Atlanta Grill 181 Peachtree St NE *Web:* www.ritzcarlton.com/en/Properties/Atlanta/Dining/AtlantaGrill/Default.htm	Atlanta	GA	30303	404-659-0400	
Atmosphere 1620 Piedmont Ave *Web:* www.atmospherebistro.com	Atlanta	GA	30324	678-702-1620	
Babette's Cafe 573 N Highland Ave *Web:* www.babettescafe.com	Atlanta	GA	30307	404-523-9121	
Bacchanalia 1198 Howell Mill Rd *Web:* starprovisions.com	Atlanta	GA	30318	404-365-0410	365-8020
Bangkok Thai 1492-A Piedmont Ave *Web:* www.bangkokatl.com	Atlanta	GA	30324	404-874-2514	
Baraonda 710 Peachtree St *Web:* www.baraondaatlanta.com	Atlanta	GA	30308	404-879-9962	
Basil's Restaurant & Tapas Bar 2985 Grandview Ave NE *Web:* www.basils.net	Atlanta	GA	30305	404-233-9755	
Beautiful Restaurant, The 2260 Cascade Rd SW *Web:* www.beautifulrestaurant-atlanta.com	Atlanta	GA	30311	404-752-5931	758-4767
Benihana 229 Peachtree St NE *Web:* www.benihana.com	Atlanta	GA	30303	404-522-9629	
Blue Ridge Grill 1261 W Paces Ferry Rd *Web:* www.blueridgegrill.com	Atlanta	GA	30327	404-233-5030	
BluePointe 3344 Peachtree Rd *Web:* www.buckheadrestaurants.com	Atlanta	GA	30326	404-237-9070	237-2387
Bone's Restaurant 3130 Piedmont Rd NE *Web:* www.bonesrestaurant.com	Atlanta	GA	30305	404-237-2663	233-5704
Buckhead Diner 3073 Piedmont Rd NE *Web:* www.buckheadrestaurants.com	Atlanta	GA	30305	404-262-3336	
Cafe Sunflower 2140 Peachtree Rd *Web:* www.cafesunflower.com	Atlanta	GA	30309	404-352-8859	
Cafe, The 3434 Peachtree Rd NE Ritz-Carlton Buckhead *TF:* 800-241-3333 ■ *Web:* www.ritzcarlton.com	Atlanta	GA	30326	404-237-2700	
Canoe 4199 Paces Ferry Rd NW *Web:* www.canoeatl.com	Atlanta	GA	30339	770-432-2663	
Capital Grille, The 255 E Paces Ferry Rd *Web:* www.thecapitalgrille.com	Atlanta	GA	30305	404-262-1162	
China Cooks 215 Northwood Dr	Atlanta	GA	30342	404-252-6611	
Chops/Lobster Bar 70 W Paces Ferry Rd NW *Web:* www.buckheadrestaurants.com	Atlanta	GA	30305	404-262-2675	240-6645
Eclipse di Luna 764 Miami Cir *Web:* www.eclipsediluna.com	Atlanta	GA	30324	404-846-0449	
Fat Matt's Rib Shack 1811 Piedmont Ave *Web:* www.fatmattsribshack.com	Atlanta	GA	30324	404-607-1622	
Figo Pasta/Osteria del Figo 1170 Collier Rd NW # B Ste B *Web:* www.figopasta.com	Atlanta	GA	30318	404-351-9667	
Floataway Cafe 1123 Zonolite Rd Ste 15 *Web:* www.starprovisions.com	Atlanta	GA	30306	404-892-1414	
Flying Biscuit Cafe 1655 McLendon Ave *Web:* www.flyingbiscuit.com	Atlanta	GA	30307	404-687-8888	
Fogo de Chao 3101 Piedmont Rd *Web:* www.fogodechao.com	Atlanta	GA	30305	404-266-9988	
Fritti 309 N Highland Ave *Web:* www.frittirestaurant.com	Atlanta	GA	30307	404-880-9559	
Georgia Grille 2290 Peachtree Rd	Atlanta	GA	30309	404-352-3517	
Grand China Restaurant 2975 Peachtree Rd NE *Web:* www.grandchinaatl.com	Atlanta	GA	30305	404-231-8690	231-5415
Hal's on Old Ivy 30 Old Ivy Rd *Web:* www.hals.net	Atlanta	GA	30342	404-261-0025	
Harry & Sons 820 N Highland Ave *Web:* surinofthailand.com	Atlanta	GA	30306	404-873-2009	
Haven 1441 Dresden Dr NE Ste 100 *Web:* www.havenrestaurant.com	Atlanta	GA	30319	404-969-0700	969-0701
Horseradish Grill 4320 Powers Ferry Rd *Web:* www.horseradishgrill.com	Atlanta	GA	30342	404-255-7277	847-0603
Hsu's Gourmet Chinese Restaurant 192 Peachtree Ctr Ave *Web:* www.hsus.com	Atlanta	GA	30303	404-659-2788	
Kyma 3085 Piedmont Rd *Web:* www.buckheadrestaurants.com	Atlanta	GA	30305	404-262-0702	841-9924
La Grotta 2637 Peachtree Rd *Web:* www.la-grotta.com	Atlanta	GA	30305	404-231-1368	
La Tavola Trattoria 992 Virginia Ave *Web:* www.latavolatrattoria.com	Atlanta	GA	30306	404-873-5430	
Le Mridien Atlanta Perimeterrestaurant 111 Perimeter Ctr W *Web:* www.lemeridienatlantaperimeter.com	Atlanta	GA	30346	770-396-6800	
Malaya 857 Collier Rd *Web:* malayaatlanta.com	Atlanta	GA	30318	404-609-9991	
Mali Restaurant 961 Amsterdam Ave NE *Web:* www.malirestaurant.com	Atlanta	GA	30306	404-874-1411	
McCormick & Schmick's 190 Marietta St NW *Web:* www.mccormickandschmicks.com	Atlanta	GA	30303	404-521-1236	521-1237
McKendrick's Steak House 4505 Ashford Dunwoody Rd *Web:* www.mckendricks.com	Atlanta	GA	30346	770-512-8888	
Morton's The Steakhouse 303 Peachtree Ctr Ave *Web:* www.mortons.com	Atlanta	GA	30308	404-577-4366	
Mu Lan 824 Juniper St NE *Web:* mulanatlanta.net	Atlanta	GA	30308	404-877-5797	
Nakato 1776 Cheshire Bridge Rd NE *Web:* www.nakatorestaurant.com	Atlanta	GA	30324	404-873-6582	874-7897
Nan Thai 1350 Spring St NW *Web:* www.nanfinedining.com	Atlanta	GA	30309	404-870-9933	870-9955
Nava 3060 Peachtree Rd	Atlanta	GA	30305	404-240-1984	
Nikolai's Roof 255 Courtland St NE *Web:* www.nikolaisroof.com	Atlanta	GA	30303	404-221-6362	
Nino's 1931 Chesire Bridge Rd *Web:* www.ninosatlanta.com	Atlanta	GA	30324	404-874-6505	
Nuevo Laredo 1495 Chattahoochee Ave *Web:* www.nuevolaredocantina.com	Atlanta	GA	30318	404-352-9009	
Pacific Rim Bistro 303 Peachtree Ctr Ave *Web:* www.pacificrimbistro.com	Atlanta	GA	30303	404-893-0018	

Name / Address	City	State	Zip	Phone	Fax
Palm Restaurant 3391 Peachtree Rd NE	Atlanta	GA	30326	404-814-1955	814-1985
Web: www.thepalm.com					
Park 75 75 14th St	Atlanta	GA	30309	404-253-3840	
Web: fourseasons.com					
Portofino 3199 Paces Ferry Pl	Atlanta	GA	30305	404-231-1136	
Web: www.portofinobistro.com					
Pricci 500 Pharr Rd	Atlanta	GA	30305	404-237-2941	
Web: www.buckheadrestaurants.com					
Rathbun's 112 Krog St Ste R	Atlanta	GA	30307	404-524-8280	524-8580
Web: www.kevinrathbun.com					
Ray's in the City 240 Peachtree St NW	Atlanta	GA	30303	404-524-9224	
Web: www.raysrestaurants.com					
Ritz-Carlton Dining Room 3434 Peachtree Rd	Atlanta	GA	30326	404-237-2700	
Web: ritzcarlton.com					
Ruth's Chris Steak House 267 Marietta St	Atlanta	GA	30313	404-223-6500	
Web: ruthschris.net					
Sotto Sotto Cucina Italiana 313 N Highland Ave	Atlanta	GA	30307	404-523-6678	
Web: www.sottosottorestaurant.com					
South City Kitchen 1144 Crescent Ave	Atlanta	GA	30309	404-873-7358	
Web: fifthgroup.com					
Surin of Thailand 810 N Highland Ave NE	Atlanta	GA	30306	404-892-7789	
Web: www.surinofthailand.com					
Tamarind Seed 1197 Peachtree St NW Ste 110	Atlanta	GA	30361	404-873-4888	873-4886
Web: www.tamarindseed.com					
Thai Chili 2169 Briarcliff Rd NE	Atlanta	GA	30329	404-315-6750	
Web: www.thaichilicuisine.com					
Tierra Restaurant 1425 Piedmont Ave NE	Atlanta	GA	30309	404-874-5951	
Web: tierrarestaurant.com					
Top Spice 3007 N Druid Hills Rd	Atlanta	GA	30329	404-728-0588	
Web: www.topspiceatlanta.com					
Veni-Vidi-Vici 41 Fourteenth St	Atlanta	GA	30309	404-875-8424	875-6533
Web: www.buckheadrestaurants.com					
Wisteria 471 N Highland Ave	Atlanta	GA	30307	404-525-3363	525-3313
Web: www.wisteria-atlanta.com					
Woodfire Grill 1782 Cheshire Bridge Rd	Atlanta	GA	30324	404-347-9055	347-9566
Web: www.woodfiregrill.com					
Yahoo Finance 3011 Paces Mill Rd SE	Atlanta	GA	30339	770-438-2282	438-0653
Web: finance.yahoo.com/news/website-three-simple-steps-simplewebtutorials-064900835.html					
Beamie's 865 Reynolds St	Augusta	GA	30901	706-724-6593	724-7466
California Dreaming 3241 Washington Rd	Augusta	GA	30907	706-860-6206	
Web: www.centraarchy.com					
Calvert's Restaurant 475 Highland Ave	Augusta	GA	30909	706-738-4514	
Web: www.calvertsrestaurant.com					
Formosa's 3830 Washington Rd	Augusta	GA	30907	706-855-8998	855-9742
French Market Grille 425 Highland Ave	Augusta	GA	30909	706-737-4865	
Web: www.thefrenchmarketgrille.com					
Luigi's 590 Broad St	Augusta	GA	30901	706-722-4056	
Web: www.luigisinc.com					
Rhinehart's Oyster Bar 3051 Washington Rd	Augusta	GA	30907	706-860-2337	
Web: rhineharts.com					
Sconyer's Bar-B-Que 2250 Sconyers Way	Augusta	GA	30906	706-790-5411	790-1505
Web: sconyersbar-b-que.com					
T's Restaurant 3416 Mike Pagett Hwy	Augusta	GA	30906	706-798-4145	793-8474
Web: www.tsrestaurant.com					
Villa Europa 3044 Deans Bridge Rd	Augusta	GA	30906	706-798-6211	798-0066
Web: www.villaeuropa.com					
Harmony Vegetarian Chinese Restaurant 4897 Buford Hwy Ste 109	Chamblee	GA	30341	770-457-7288	
Web: www.harmonyvegetarian.com					
Cafe Amici 2301 Airport Thwy Ste E2	Columbus	GA	31904	706-653-6361	653-6357
Country's Barbecue 2016 12th Ave	Columbus	GA	31901	706-327-7702	
TF General: 800-285-4267 ■ *Web:* www.countrysbarbecue.com					
Don Chuco's 5770 Milgen Rd	Columbus	GA	31907	706-561-3040	
Los Amigos Mexican Restaurant 5935 Veterans Pkwy	Columbus	GA	31909	706-322-1993	
Macon Road Barbecue 2703 Avalon Rd	Columbus	GA	31907	706-563-0542	
Mikata Japanese Steakhouse 5300 Sidney Simons Blvd	Columbus	GA	31904	706-327-5100	
Web: www.mikatasteakhouse.com					
Panda Garden 5600 Milgen Rd	Columbus	GA	31907	706-569-8487	569-8467
Shangri La Chinese Gourmet 4248 Buena Vista Rd	Columbus	GA	31907	706-568-7554	
Web: www.shangrilacolumbus.c					
Dawson's Kitchen 3360 Brookdale Ave	Macon	GA	31204	478-742-9852	
Web: www.dawsonskitchen.com					
Downtown Grill 562 Mulberry St Ln	Macon	GA	31201	478-742-5999	742-9708
Web: www.macondowntowngrill.com					
Marco 4581 Forsyth Rd	Macon	GA	31210	478-405-5660	
Web: www.marcomacon.com					
Natalia's 201 N Macon St	Macon	GA	31210	478-741-1380	
Web: natalias.net					
Saleem Fish Supreme 2198 Pio Nono Ave	Macon	GA	31206	478-788-8600	
Taj Indian Restaurant 5033 Brookhaven Rd Ste 300	Macon	GA	31206	478-785-8540	
Aqua Blue 1564 Holcomb Bridge Rd	Roswell	GA	30076	770-643-8886	643-8851
Web: www.aquablueatl.com					
5 Seasons Brewing Co 5600 Roswell Rd	Sandy Springs	GA	30342	404-255-5911	
Web: www.5seasonsbrewing.com					
17 Hundred 90 Restaurant 307 E President St	Savannah	GA	31401	912-236-7122	
Web: www.17hundred90.com					
45 Bistro 123 E Broughton St	Savannah	GA	31401	912-234-3111	
Web: www.marshallhouse.com					
Alligator Soul 114 Barnard St	Savannah	GA	31401	912-232-7899	
Web: alligatorsoul.com					
Belford's Savannah 315 W St Julian St	Savannah	GA	31401	912-233-2626	
Web: www.belfordssavannah.com					
Casbah 20 E Broughton St	Savannah	GA	31401	912-234-6168	
Web: www.casbahrestaurant.com					
Cotton Exchange Tavern 201 E River St	Savannah	GA	31401	912-232-7088	
Elizabeth on 37th 105 E 37th St	Savannah	GA	31401	912-236-5547	
Web: www.elizabethon37th.net					
Garibaldi Cafe 315 W Congress St	Savannah	GA	31401	912-232-7118	
Web: garibaldisavannah.com					
Huey's 115 E River St	Savannah	GA	31401	912-234-7385	
Web: hueysontheriver.net					
Lady & Sons, The 102 W Congress St	Savannah	GA	31401	912-233-2600	233-8283
Web: www.ladyandsons.com					
Olde Pink House 23 Abercorn St	Savannah	GA	31401	912-232-4286	
TF: 800-554-1187 ■ *Web:* plantersinnsavannah.com					
Pirates' House 20 E Broad St	Savannah	GA	31401	912-233-5757	
Web: www.thepirateshouse.com					
River House Seafood Restaurant 125 W River St	Savannah	GA	31401	912-234-1900	341-0277*
**Fax:* Orders ■ *Web:* www.savannahriverhouse.com					
Sapphire Grill 110 W Congress St	Savannah	GA	31401	912-443-9962	443-9964
Web: www.sapphiregrill.com					
Savannah ePASS 7000 LaRoche Ave	Savannah	GA	31406	912-352-8221	
Web: savannahepass.com					
Shell House Restaurant, The 8 Gateway Blvd	Savannah	GA	31419	912-927-3280	
Web: shellhouseseafoodsavannah.com					
Six Pence Pub 245 Bull St	Savannah	GA	31401	912-233-3151	
Web: www.sixpencepub.com					
Toucan Cafe 531 Stephenson Ave	Savannah	GA	31406	912-352-2233	352-2258
Web: www.toucancafe.com					
Uncle Bubba's Oyster House 104 Bryan Woods Rd	Savannah	GA	31410	912-897-6101	
Web: www.unclebubbas.com					
Wilkes Dining Room 107 W Jones St	Savannah	GA	31401	912-232-5997	
Web: mrswilkes.com					

Hawaii

Name / Address	City	State	Zip	Phone	Fax
Bravo 98-115 Kaonohi St	Aiea	HI	96701	808-487-5544	
Web: www.bravorestaurant.com					
3660 on the Rise 3660 Waialae Ave	Honolulu	HI	96816	808-737-1177	735-6105
Web: www.3660.com					
Alan Wong's 1857 S King St	Honolulu	HI	96826	808-949-2526	951-9520
Web: www.alanwongs.com					
Auntie Pasto's Restaurant 1099 S Beretania St	Honolulu	HI	96814	808-523-8855	523-8857
Web: www.auntiepastos.com					
Bali Steak & Seafood 2005 Kalia Rd	Honolulu	HI	96815	808-949-4321	
TF: 800-445-8667 ■ *Web:* www.hiltonhawaiianvillage.com/dining/bali-steak-and-seafood					
Chef Mavro 1969 S King St	Honolulu	HI	96826	808-944-4714	
Web: www.chefmavro.com					
Chuck's Steak House 2335 Kalakaua Ave	Honolulu	HI	96815	808-923-1228	
Web: www.chuckshawaii.com					
El Burrito 550 Piikoi St	Honolulu	HI	96814	808-596-8225	
Genki Sushi Hawaii 677 Ala Moana Blvd Ste 612	Honolulu	HI	96813	808-523-3315	523-3316
Web: www.genkisushiusa.com					
Gyotaku 1824 King St	Honolulu	HI	96826	808-949-4584	
Web: www.gyotakuhawaii.com					
Hard Rock Cafe International Inc 1837 Kapiolani Blvd	Honolulu	HI	96826	808-955-7383	
Web: www.hardrock.com					
Hee Hing 449 Kapahulu Ave	Honolulu	HI	96815	808-735-5544	732-6026
Web: www.heehinghawaii.com					
Hiroshi Eurasian Tapas 500 Ala Moana Blvd	Honolulu	HI	96813	808-533-4476	
Hoku's 5000 Kahala Ave	Honolulu	HI	96816	808-739-8888	739-8800
Web: www.kahalaresort.com					
Hy's Steak House 2440 Kuhio Ave	Honolulu	HI	96815	808-922-5555	926-5089
Web: hyswaikiki.com					
Keo's 2028 Kuhio Ave	Honolulu	HI	96815	808-951-9355	
Web: www.keosthaicuisine.com					
Kincaid's Fish Chop & Steak House 1050 Ala Moana Blvd	Honolulu	HI	96814	808-591-2005	
Web: www.kincaids.com					
Longhi's *Ala Moana Shopping Ctr* 1450 Ala Moana Blvd Ste 3001	Honolulu	HI	96814	808-947-9899	
Web: www.longhis.com					
Mariposa 1450 Ala Moana Blvd	Honolulu	HI	96814	808-951-3420	
Web: neimanmarcus.com					
Michel's 2895 Kalakaua Ave Colony Surf Hotel	Honolulu	HI	96815	808-923-6552	926-6063
Web: www.michelshawaii.com					
Morton's The Steakhouse 1450 Ala Moana Blvd	Honolulu	HI	96814	808-949-1300	947-9512
Web: www.mortons.com					
Ruth's Chris Steak House 500 Ala Moana Blvd Restaurant Row	Honolulu	HI	96813	808-599-3860	
Web: www.ruthschris.com					
Ryan's Grill at Ward Centre 1200 Ala Moana Blvd	Honolulu	HI	96814	808-591-9132	
Web: www.ryansgrill.com					
Sansei Seafood Restaurant & Sushi Bar *Waikiki Beach Marriot Resort & Spa* 2552 Kalakauna Ave	Honolulu	HI	96815	808-931-6286	
Web: www.sanseihawaii.com					
Shorebird Beach Broiler 2169 Kalia Rd Outrigger Reef Hotel	Honolulu	HI	96815	808-922-2887	
Web: www.shorebirdwaikiki.com					
Side Street Inn 1225 Hopaka St	Honolulu	HI	96814	808-591-0253	732-7333
Web: www.sidestreetinn.com					
Sorabol *Sorabol Korean Restaurant* 805 Keeaumoku St	Honolulu	HI	96814	808-947-3113	
Web: www.sorabolhawaii.com					
Stage Restaurant 1250 Kapiolani Blvd 2nd Fl	Honolulu	HI	96814	808-237-5429	
Web: www.stagerestauranthawaii.com					
Tanaka of Tokyo East 150 Kaiulani Ave 3rd Fl	Honolulu	HI	96815	808-922-4233	922-6948
Web: www.tanakaoftokyo.com					
Willows, The 901 Hausten St	Honolulu	HI	96826	808-952-9200	952-0050
Web: www.willowshawaii.com					

Name	City	State	Zip	Phone	Fax
Duke's Huntington Beach 130 Kai Malina Pkwy *Web:* www.hulapie.com	Lahaina	HI	96761	808-667-4800	
Assaggio 95-1249 Meheula Pkwy *Web:* assaggiohi.com	Mililani	HI	96789	808-623-5115	

Idaho

Name	City	State	Zip	Phone	Fax
Angell's Bar & Grill 999 W Main St *Web:* www.angellsbarandgrill.com	Boise	ID	83702	208-342-4900	
Barbacoa Grill 276 W Bobwhite Ct *Web:* www.barbacoa-boise.com	Boise	ID	83706	208-338-5000	
Bitter Creek Ale House 246 N Eigth St *Web:* bcrfl.com	Boise	ID	83702	208-429-6340	
Cottonwood Grille 913 W River St *Web:* www.cottonwoodgrille.com	Boise	ID	83702	208-333-9800	
Fujiyama 283 N Milwaukee St *Web:* www.fujiyamaboise.com	Boise	ID	83704	208-672-8227	672-8247
Joe's Crab Shack 2288 N Garden St *Web:* www.joescrabshack.com	Boise	ID	83706	208-336-9370	
Mai Thai 750 W Idaho St *Web:* www.maithaigroup.com	Boise	ID	83702	208-344-8424	344-2445
Reef 105 S Sixth St *Web:* www.reefboise.com	Boise	ID	83702	208-287-9200	
Shige Japanese Cuisine 100 N Eigth St Ste 215	Boise	ID	83702	208-338-8423	
Smoky Mountain Pizzeria Grill 408 E 41st St *Web:* www.smokymountainpizza.com	Boise	ID	83714	208-433-9596	433-9588
Bamboo Garden 1200 Yellowstone Ave *Web:* orderbamboogarden.com	Pocatello	ID	83201	208-238-2331	
Buddy's Italian Restaurant 626 E Lewis St	Pocatello	ID	83201	208-233-1172	
Mama Inez 390 Yellowstone Ave *Web:* mamainezid.com	Pocatello	ID	83201	208-234-7674	
Mandarin House 675 Yellowstone Ave Ste D *Web:* www.mandarinhouse.takeout1.com	Pocatello	ID	83201	208-233-6088	233-6089
Oliver's 130 S Fifth Ave *Web:* www.oliversdining.com	Pocatello	ID	83201	208-234-0672	

Illinois

Name	City	State	Zip	Phone	Fax
Bacaro 113 N Walnut St *Web:* www.bacarowinelounge.com	Champaign	IL	61820	217-398-6982	
Empire Chinese Restaurant 410 E Green St *Web:* cu-empire.com	Champaign	IL	61820	217-328-0832	
Fiesta Cafe 216 S First St *Web:* www.fiestacafe.com	Champaign	IL	61820	217-352-5902	
Li'l Porgy's Bar-B-Q 1917 W Springfield Ave *Web:* www.lilporgysbbq.com	Champaign	IL	61821	217-398-8575	
Radio Maria 119 N Walnut St *Web:* radiomariarestaurant.com	Champaign	IL	61820	217-398-7729	
Ryan's Family Steak House 1004 W Anthony Dr *Web:* www.ryans.com	Champaign	IL	61821	217-352-7403	
Taffie's 301 S Mattis Ave	Champaign	IL	61821	217-359-4201	
A Tavola 2148 W Chicago Ave *Web:* atavolachi.com	Chicago	IL	60622	773-276-7567	
Adobo Grill Chicago 1610 N Wells St *Web:* www.adobogrill.com	Chicago	IL	60610	312-266-7999	
Alinea 1723 N Halsted St *Web:* website.alinearestaurant.com	Chicago	IL	60614	312-867-0110	
Arun's 4156 N Kedzie Ave *Web:* www.arunsthai.com	Chicago	IL	60618	773-539-1909	539-2125
Atwood Cafe 1 W Washington St *Web:* atwoodrestaurant.com	Chicago	IL	60602	312-368-1900	
Avec Restaurant 615 W Randolph St *Web:* www.avecrestaurant.com	Chicago	IL	60661	312-377-2002	377-2008
Bacchanalia 2413 S Oakley Ave *Web:* www.bacchanaliainchicago.com	Chicago	IL	60608	773-254-6555	
BIN 36 161 N Jefferson St *Web:* www.bin36.com	Chicago	IL	60661	312-995-6560	
Blackbird 619 W Randolph St *Web:* www.blackbirdrestaurant.com	Chicago	IL	60661	312-715-0708	
Bongo Room 1470 N Milwaukee Ave *Web:* www.thebongoroom.com	Chicago	IL	60622	773-489-0690	
Buona Terra 2535 N California Ave *Web:* www.buona-terra.com	Chicago	IL	60647	773-289-3800	
Cafe Absinthe 1954 W N Ave *Web:* cafe-absinthe.com	Chicago	IL	60622	773-278-4488	
Capital Grille 633 N St Clair St *Web:* www.thecapitalgrille.com	Chicago	IL	60611	312-337-9400	
Chicago Chop House 60 W Ontario St *Web:* www.chicagochophouse.com	Chicago	IL	60654	312-787-7100	
Coco Pazzo 300 W Hubbard St *Web:* www.cocopazzochicago.com	Chicago	IL	60654	312-836-0900	
Everest 440 S LaSalle St 40th Fl *Web:* www.everestrestaurant.com	Chicago	IL	60605	312-663-8920	
F Gs Inc 815 W Van Buren St Ste 302 *Web:* fgs-inc.com	Chicago	IL	60607	312-421-3060	
Fat Willy's 2416 W Schubert Ave *Web:* www.fatwillys.com	Chicago	IL	60647	773-782-1800	
Francesca's on Taylor 1400 W Taylor St *Web:* www.francescarestaurants.com	Chicago	IL	60607	312-829-2828	829-2831
Frontera Grill 445 N Clark St *Web:* www.rickbayless.com	Chicago	IL	60654	312-661-1434	661-1830
Geja's Cafe 340 W Armitage Ave *Web:* www.gejascafe.com	Chicago	IL	60614	773-281-9101	
Gene & Georgetti 500 N Franklin St *Web:* www.geneandgeorgetti.com	Chicago	IL	60654	312-527-3718	527-2039
Gibsons Steakhouse 1028 N Rush St *Web:* www.gibsonssteakhouse.com	Chicago	IL	60611	312-266-8999	266-3327
Green Zebra 1460 W Chicago Ave *Web:* www.greenzebrachicago.com	Chicago	IL	60642	312-243-7100	226-3360
Indian Garden 247 E Ontario St 2nd Fl *Web:* www.indiangardenchicago.com	Chicago	IL	60611	312-280-4910	280-4934
Japonais Chicago 600 W Chicago Ave *Web:* japonaismorimoto.com	Chicago	IL	60610	312-822-9600	
Jin Ju 5203 N Clark St *Web:* jinjurestaurant.com	Chicago	IL	60640	773-334-6377	
Joe's Seafood Prime Steak & Stone Crab 60 E Grand Ave *Web:* www.leye.com	Chicago	IL	60611	312-379-5637	
Kiki's Bistro 900 N Franklin St *Web:* www.kikisbistro.com	Chicago	IL	60610	312-335-5454	
L20 Restaurant 2300 N Lincoln Pk W *Web:* www.l2orestaurant.com	Chicago	IL	60614	773-868-0002	
La Petite Folie 1504 E 55th St *Web:* www.lapetitefolie.com	Chicago	IL	60615	773-493-1394	
Lawry's the Prime Rib 100 E Ontario St *Web:* www.lawrysonline.com	Chicago	IL	60611	312-787-5000	
Le Colonial 937 N Rush St *Web:* www.lecolonialchicago.com	Chicago	IL	60611	312-255-0088	255-1108
Les Nomades 222 E Ontario St *Web:* www.lesnomades.net	Chicago	IL	60611	312-649-9010	649-0608
Merlo on Maple 16 W Maple St *Web:* www.merlochicago.com	Chicago	IL	60610	312-335-8200	335-8205
Mike Ditka's Restaurant 100 E Chestnut St *Web:* www.ditkasrestaurants.com	Chicago	IL	60611	312-587-8989	
Mirai Sushi 2020 W Div St *Web:* www.miraisushi.com	Chicago	IL	60622	773-862-8500	
MK Restaurant 868 N Franklin St *Web:* www.mkchicago.com	Chicago	IL	60610	312-482-9179	482-9171
Mon Ami Gabi 2300 N Lincoln Pk W *Web:* www.monamigabi.com	Chicago	IL	60614	773-348-8886	
Morton's the Steakhouse 1050 N State St *Web:* www.mortons.com	Chicago	IL	60610	312-266-4820	
Nacional 27 325 W Huron St *Web:* www.leye.com	Chicago	IL	60654	312-664-2727	
Naha 500 N Clark St *Web:* www.naha-chicago.com	Chicago	IL	60654	312-321-6242	
Nick's Fishmarket Grill & Bar 222 W Merchandise Mart Plaza #135 *Web:* www.nicks-fishmarket.com	Chicago	IL	60654	312-621-0200	
NoMI 800 N Michigan Ave *Web:* chicago.park.hyatt.com/en/hotel/home.html	Chicago	IL	60611	312-335-1234	239-4000
North Pond 2610 N Cannon Dr *Web:* www.northpondrestaurant.com	Chicago	IL	60614	773-477-5845	
Parthenon, The 314 S Halsted St *Web:* www.theparthenon.com	Chicago	IL	60661	312-726-2407	726-3203
Petterino's 150 N Dearborn St *Web:* www.petterinos.com	Chicago	IL	60601	312-422-0150	
Public Chicago 1301 N State Pkwy *Web:* www.publichotels.com	Chicago	IL	60610	312-787-3700	
Quartino 626 N State St *Web:* www.quartinochicago.com	Chicago	IL	60610	312-698-5000	
Rise Sushi & Sake Lounge 3401 N Southport Ave *Web:* www.risesushi.com	Chicago	IL	60657	773-525-3535	525-3522
Rockwell's Neighborhood Grill 4632 N Rockwell St *Web:* www.rockwellsgrill.com	Chicago	IL	60625	773-509-1871	
Roy's 720 N State St *Web:* www.roysrestaurant.com	Chicago	IL	60654	312-787-7599	
Sabatino's 4441 W Irving Pk Rd *Web:* www.sabatinoschicago.com	Chicago	IL	60641	773-283-8331	
Sai Cafe 2010 N Sheffield Ave *Web:* www.saicafe.com	Chicago	IL	60614	773-472-8080	472-0699
Salpicon 1252 N Wells St *Web:* www.salpicon.com	Chicago	IL	60610	312-988-7811	988-7715
Shanghai Terrace 108 E Superior St *Web:* chicago.peninsula.com	Chicago	IL	60611	312-573-6744	573-6697
Shaw's Crab House Chicago 21 E Hubbard St *Web:* www.shawscrabhouse.com	Chicago	IL	60611	312-527-2722	
South Water Kitchen 225 N Wabash Ave *Web:* www.southwaterkitchen.com	Chicago	IL	60601	312-236-9300	
Spiaggia 980 N Michigan Ave *Web:* www.spiaggiarestaurant.com	Chicago	IL	60611	312-280-2750	
Trattoria No 10 10 N Dearborn St *Web:* www.trattoriaten.com	Chicago	IL	60602	312-984-1718	
Tre Kronor 3258 W Foster Ave *Web:* trekronorrestaurant.com	Chicago	IL	60625	773-267-9888	
Tru 676 N St Clair St *Web:* www.trurestaurant.com	Chicago	IL	60611	312-202-0001	
University Club of Chicago 76 E Monroe St *Web:* www.ucco.com	Chicago	IL	60603	312-726-2840	726-0620
Vivere 71 W Monroe St *Web:* www.italianvillage-chicago.com	Chicago	IL	60603	312-332-4040	332-2656
Yoshi's Cafe 3257 N Halsted St *Web:* www.yoshiscafe.com	Chicago	IL	60657	773-248-6160	
Captain Merry Guesthouse & Fine Dining 399 Sinsinawa Ave *Web:* www.privatestay.com	East Dubuque	IL	61025	815-747-3644	
Abbington Distinctive Banquets 3s002 Il Route 53 *Web:* www.abbingtonbanquets.com	Glen Ellyn	IL	60137	630-942-8600	
Stonegate Conference & Banquet Centre, The 2401 W Higgins Rd *Web:* www.thestonegate.com	Hoffman Estates	IL	60169	847-884-7000	
Agatucci's 2607 N University St *Web:* agatuccis.com	Peoria	IL	61604	309-688-8200	
Fairview Farms 5911 Heuermann Rd *Web:* www.fairview-farm.com	Peoria	IL	61607	309-697-4111	
Fish House, The 4919 N University St *Web:* fishhousepeoria.com	Peoria	IL	61614	309-691-9358	

Name / Address	City	State	Zip	Phone	Fax
Flat Top Grill 5201 W War Memorial Dr *Web:* www.flattopgrill.com	Peoria	IL	61615	309-693-9966	
Jim's Downtown Steakhouse 110 SW Jefferson St *Web:* www.jimssteakhouse.net	Peoria	IL	61602	309-673-5300	673-9335
Sushigawa 2601 W Lake Ave	Peoria	IL	61615	309-679-9300	
Abreo 515 E State St *Web:* www.abreorockford.com	Rockford	IL	61104	815-968-9463	
Capri 313 E State St *Web:* caprirockford.com	Rockford	IL	61104	815-965-6341	
Cliffbreakers River Restaurant 700 W Riverside Blvd *Web:* www.cliffbreakers.com	Rockford	IL	61103	815-282-3033	282-6505
Garrett's Cafe 1631 N Bell School Rd *Web:* www.garrettsrestaurantbar.com	Rockford	IL	61107	815-484-9473	
Giovanni's Restaurant & Convention Ctr 610 N Bell School Rd *TF:* 877-926-8300 ■ *Web:* www.giodine.com	Rockford	IL	61107	815-398-6411	398-6416
Hoffman House 7550 E State St *Web:* www.hoffmanhouserockford.com	Rockford	IL	61108	815-397-5800	
Imperial Palace 3415 E State St *Web:* imperialpalacerockford.com	Rockford	IL	61108	815-227-1442	316-0721
JMK Nippon 2551 N Perryville Rd *Web:* jmkrockford.com	Rockford	IL	61107	815-877-0505	
Maria's Italian Restaurant 828 Cunningham St	Rockford	IL	61102	815-968-6781	
Octane Interlounge 124 N Main St *Web:* www.octane.net	Rockford	IL	61101	815-965-4012	
Olympic Tavern 2327 N Main St *Web:* www.theolympictavern.com	Rockford	IL	61103	815-962-8758	
Rathskeller, The 1132 Auburn St *Web:* derrathskeller.co	Rockford	IL	61103	815-963-2922	
Alexander's 620 N Bruns Ln *Web:* mercedesrestaurants.com	Springfield	IL	62702	217-793-0440	
Augie's Front Burner 109 S Fifth St *Web:* www.augiesfrontburner.com	Springfield	IL	62701	217-544-6979	
Chesapeake Seafood House 3045 Clear Lk Ave *Web:* www.chesapeakeseafoodhouse.com	Springfield	IL	62702	217-522-5220	
Fritz's Wagon Wheel Restaurant 2709 S MacArthur Blvd	Springfield	IL	62704	217-546-9888	726-5357
Indigo 3013 Lindbergh Blvd *Web:* www.indigocuisine.com	Springfield	IL	62704	217-726-3487	
Lime Street Cafe 951 S Durkin Dr	Springfield	IL	62704	217-793-1905	793-7860
Maldaner's 222 S Sixth St *Web:* www.maldaners.com	Springfield	IL	62701	217-522-4313	
Courier Cafe 411 N Race St *Web:* www.couriersilvercreek.com	Urbana	IL	61801	217-328-1811	
Kennedy's at Stone Creek 2560 Stone Creek Blvd	Urbana	IL	61802	217-384-8111	
Milo's Restaurant 2870 S Philo Rd *Web:* www.milosurbana.com	Urbana	IL	61802	217-344-8946	344-8922
Timpone's 710 S Goodwin Ave *Web:* www.timpones-urbana.com	Urbana	IL	61801	217-344-7619	

Indiana

Name / Address	City	State	Zip	Phone	Fax
Buffa Louie's 114 S Indiana Ave *Web:* www.buffalouies.com	Bloomington	IN	47408	812-333-3030	334-3945
Crazy Horse 214 W Kirkwood Ave *Web:* www.crazyhorseindiana.com	Bloomington	IN	47404	812-336-8877	
Dragon Chinese Restaurant 3261 W Third St	Bloomington	IN	47404	812-332-6610	
Esan Thai 221 E Kirkwood Ave *Web:* esanthairest.com	Bloomington	IN	47408	812-333-8424	
Fairfax Inn 8660 S Fairfax Rd *Web:* www.thefairfaxinn.com	Bloomington	IN	47401	812-824-8552	
Grazie Italian Eatery 106 W Sixth St *Web:* www.grazieitaliano.com	Bloomington	IN	47401	812-323-0303	
Irish Lion 212 W Kirkwood Ave *Web:* www.irishlion.com	Bloomington	IN	47404	812-336-9076	
Laughing Planet Cafe 322 E Kirkwood Ave *Web:* thelaughingplanetcafe.com	Bloomington	IN	47408	812-323-2233	323-1336
Le Petit Cafe 308 W Sixth St *Web:* lpc1977.com	Bloomington	IN	47404	812-334-9747	
Malibu Grill 106 N Walnut St *Web:* www.malibugrill.net	Bloomington	IN	47404	812-332-4334	333-2282
Michael's Uptown Cafe 102 E Kirkwood Ave *Web:* www.the-uptown.com	Bloomington	IN	47408	812-339-0900	
Mikado Japanese Restaurant 895 S College Mall Rd *Web:* www.btownmenus.com	Bloomington	IN	47401	812-333-1950	
Nick's English Hut 423 E Kirkwood Ave *Web:* www.nicksenglishhut.com	Bloomington	IN	47408	812-332-4040	
Scholars Inn Gourmet Cafe 717 N College Ave *TF:* 800-765-3466 ■ *Web:* www.scholarsinn.com	Bloomington	IN	47404	812-332-1892	
Trojan Horse 100 E Kirkwood Ave *Web:* www.thetrojanhorse.com	Bloomington	IN	47408	812-332-1101	
Upland Brewing Co 350 W 11th St *Web:* www.uplandbeer.com	Bloomington	IN	47404	812-336-2337	
Yogi's Grill & Bar 519 E Tenth St *Web:* www.yogis.com	Bloomington	IN	47408	812-323-9644	
Angelo's 305 Main St *Web:* angelosevansville.com	Evansville	IN	47708	812-428-6666	428-6699
Biaggi's 6401 E Lloyd Expy Ste 3 *Web:* www.biaggis.com	Evansville	IN	47715	812-421-0800	
Canton Inn Restaurant 947 N Pk Dr *Web:* www.cantoninnrestaurant.com	Evansville	IN	47710	812-428-6611	
Chopstick House 5412 E Indiana St *Web:* www.chopstickhouserestaurant.net	Evansville	IN	47715	812-473-5551	
Hacienda Mexican Restaurant 711 N First Ave *Web:* www.haciendafiesta.com	Evansville	IN	47710	812-423-6355	
Lorenzo's Bread Bistro 972 S Hebron Ave *Web:* lorenzosbistro.net	Evansville	IN	47714	812-475-9477	
Moe's Southwest Grill 6401 E Lloyd Expy *Web:* www.moes.com	Evansville	IN	47715	812-491-6637	
Raffi's 1100 N BurkehaRdt Rd	Evansville	IN	47715	812-479-9166	491-0318
Raffis Italian Cuisine 1100 N Burkhart Rd	Evansville	IN	47715	812-479-9166	491-0318
Western Rib-Eye & Ribs 1401 N Boeke Rd *Web:* www.westernribeye.com	Evansville	IN	47711	812-476-5405	
Wolf's Bar-B-Q Restaurant 6600 N First Ave *Web:* www.wolfsbarbq.com	Evansville	IN	47710	812-424-8891	424-8905
Baan Thai 3235 N Anthony Blvd *Web:* baanthaiin.com	Fort Wayne	IN	46805	260-471-2929	
Bandido's Inc 6060 E State Blvd *Web:* www.bandidos.com	Fort Wayne	IN	46815	260-493-0607	
Biaggi's 4010 W Jefferson Blvd *Web:* www.biaggis.com	Fort Wayne	IN	46804	260-459-6700	
Casa Ristoranti 7539 W Jefferson Blvd *Web:* www.casarestaurants.com	Fort Wayne	IN	46825	260-399-2455	745-5503
Club Soda 235 E Superior St *Web:* www.clubsodafortwayne.com	Fort Wayne	IN	46802	260-426-3442	426-4214
Cork'N Cleaver 221 E Washington Ctr Rd *Web:* corkncleaveronline.com	Fort Wayne	IN	46825	260-484-7772	
Don Hall's Old Gas House 305 E Superior St *Web:* www.donhalls.com	Fort Wayne	IN	46802	260-426-3411	
Double Dragon 117 W Wayne St	Fort Wayne	IN	46802	260-422-6426	
Eddie Merlot's 1502 Illinois Rd S *Web:* www.eddiemerlots.com	Fort Wayne	IN	46804	260-459-2222	459-8896
Flanagan's Restaurant & Pub 6525 Covington Rd *Web:* www.eatatflanagans.com	Fort Wayne	IN	46804	260-432-6666	432-6799
Logan's Roadhouse 6617 Lima Rd *Web:* www.logansroadhouse.com	Fort Wayne	IN	46818	260-487-9944	
Mi Pueblo IV 2419 W Jefferson Blvd *Fax Area Code: 408	Fort Wayne	IN	46802	260-432-6462	263-7780*
Rib Room 1235 E State Blvd *Web:* www.theribroom.com	Fort Wayne	IN	46805	260-483-9767	
Sakura 5828 W Jefferson Blvd	Fort Wayne	IN	46804	260-459-2022	
Taj Mahal 6410 W Jefferson Blvd *Web:* tajmahalindianrestaurant.net	Fort Wayne	IN	46804	260-432-8993	
Takaoka of Japan 305 E Superior St *Web:* donhalls.com	Fort Wayne	IN	46802	260-424-3183	
Amalfi 1351 W 86th St *Web:* www.amalfiristoranteitaliano.com	Indianapolis	IN	46260	317-253-4034	
Bonefish Grill 4501 E 82nd St *Web:* www.bonefishgrill.com	Indianapolis	IN	46250	317-863-3474	
Cheesecake Factory 8701 Keystone Xing Ste 4A *Web:* www.thecheesecakefactory.com	Indianapolis	IN	46240	317-566-0100	
Circle City Bar & Grille 350 W Maryland St *TF:* 877-640-7666 ■ *Web:* indymarriott.com	Indianapolis	IN	46225	317-405-6100	822-1002
Dunaway's 351 SE St *Web:* www.dunaways.com	Indianapolis	IN	46204	317-638-7663	
Fujiyama Japanese Steakhouse 5149 Victory Dr *Web:* www.fujiyama-indy.com	Indianapolis	IN	46203	317-787-7900	
Greek Islands Restaurant 906 S Meridian St *Web:* www.greekislandsrestaurant.com	Indianapolis	IN	46225	317-636-0700	
Hard Rock Cafe Indianapolis 49 S Meridian St *Web:* www.hardrock.com	Indianapolis	IN	46204	317-636-2550	
Hollyhock Hill 8110 N College Ave *Web:* www.hollyhockhill.com	Indianapolis	IN	46240	317-251-2294	
Iaria's Italian Restaurant 317 S College Ave *Web:* www.iariasrestaurant.com	Indianapolis	IN	46202	317-638-7706	
India Garden 830 Broad Ripple Ave *Web:* www.indiagardenindy.com	Indianapolis	IN	46220	317-253-6060	253-2832
India Palace 4213 Lafayette Rd *Web:* www.indiapalaceindy.com	Indianapolis	IN	46254	317-298-0773	
Iron Skillet Restaurant, The 2489 W 30th St *Web:* www.ironskillet.net	Indianapolis	IN	46222	317-923-6353	
Kona Jack's Fish Market & Sushi Bar 9419 N Meridian St *Web:* jacksarebetter.net	Indianapolis	IN	46260	317-843-1609	571-6987
Maggiano's Little Italy 3550 E 86th St *Web:* www.maggianos.com	Indianapolis	IN	46240	317-814-0700	
Mama Carolla's Old Italian Restaurant 1031 E 54th St *Web:* www.mamacarollas.com	Indianapolis	IN	46220	317-259-9412	
Marker, The 2544 Executive Dr *TF:* 877-999-3223 ■ *Web:* wyndham.com	Indianapolis	IN	46241	877-999-3223	
Melting Pot of Indianapolis, The 5650 E 86th St Ste A *TF:* 800-783-0867 ■ *Web:* www.meltingpot.com	Indianapolis	IN	46250	317-841-3601	841-1207
Mikado Japanese Restaurant 148 S Illinois St *Web:* indymikado.com	Indianapolis	IN	46225	317-972-4180	
Morton's the Steakhouse 41 E Washington St *Web:* www.mortons.com	Indianapolis	IN	46204	317-229-4700	
Oakley's Bistro 1464 W 86th St *Web:* www.oakleysbistro.com	Indianapolis	IN	46260	317-824-1231	824-0938
Oceanaire Seafood Room, The 30 S Meridian St Ste 100 *Web:* www.theoceanaire.com	Indianapolis	IN	46204	317-955-2277	

Phone Fax

Oh Yumm! Bistro 5615 N Illinois St .... Indianapolis IN 46208 317-251-5656
Web: www.ohyummbistro.com
Palomino 49 W Maryland St Ste 189 .... Indianapolis IN 46204 317-974-0400
Web: www.palomino.com
Plump's Last Shot 6416 Cornell Ave .... Indianapolis IN 46220 317-257-5867
Web: plumpslastshot.com
R Bistro 888 Massachusetts Ave. .... Indianapolis IN 46204 317-423-0312
Web: www.rbistro.com
Rathskeller Restaurant
401 E Michigan St .... Indianapolis IN 46204 317-636-0396 630-4652
Web: www.rathskeller.com
Rick's Cafe Boatyard 4050 Dandy Trl .... Indianapolis IN 46254 317-290-9300
Web: www.rickscafeboatyard.com
Saint Elmo Steak House
127 S Illinois St .... Indianapolis IN 46225 317-635-0636
Web: www.stelmos.com
Sakura 7201 N Keystone Ave .... Indianapolis IN 46240 317-259-4171 253-7846
Web: www.indysakura.com
Starwood Hotels & Resorts Worldwide Inc.
123 S Illinois St .... Indianapolis IN 46225 317-737-1600
Web: lemeridienindianapolis.com//go/restaurant.html
Yen Ching 9150 N Michigan Rd .... Indianapolis IN 46268 317-228-0868 228-0886
Web: www.yenchingwest.com
Bonefish Grill 620 W Edison Ave Ste 100 .... Mishawaka IN 46545 574-259-2663
Web: www.bonefishgrill.com
Hana Yori 3601 Grape Rd .... Mishawaka IN 46545 574-258-5817
Web: www.hanayori.com
Main Street Grille 112 N Main St .... Mishawaka IN 46544 574-254-4995
Web: www.mainstgrille.com
Carriage House 24460 Adams Rd .... South Bend IN 46628 574-272-9220
Web: www.carriagehousedining.com
Frankie's Barbecue 1621 W Washington St .... South Bend IN 46628 574-287-8993
Web: frankiesbbq.net
LaSalle Grill 115 W Colfax Ave .... South Bend IN 46601 574-288-1155
TF: 800-382-9323 ■ *Web:* www.lasallegrill.com
Matuba 2930 McKinley Ave .... South Bend IN 46615 574-251-0674 251-0675
Parisi's Italian Ristorante
1412 S Bend Ave .... South Bend IN 46617 574-232-4244
Web: www.parisisrestaurant.com
Rocco's 537 N St Louis Blvd .... South Bend IN 46617 574-233-2464
Web: roccosoriginalpizza.com
Simeri's Old Town Tap 1505 W Indiana Ave .... South Bend IN 46613 574-289-1361
Web: simerisoldtowntap.webs.com
Tippecanoe Place 620 W Washington St .... South Bend IN 46601 574-234-9077
Web: www.tippe.com
Volcano Restaurant 3700 Lincoln Way W .... South Bend IN 46628 574-287-5775
Web: volcanosb.com

Iowa

Phone Fax

Biaggi's Ristorante 320 Collins Rd NE .... Cedar Rapids IA 52402 319-393-6593
Web: biaggis.com
El Rancho 2747 16th Ave SW .... Cedar Rapids IA 52404 319-298-8844
Irish Democrat Pub 3207 First Ave SE .... Cedar Rapids IA 52402 319-364-9896
Web: www.irishdemocrat.net
Olive Tree Restaurant 2201 16th Ave SW .... Cedar Rapids IA 52404 319-364-0781
Texas Roadhouse 2605 Edgewood Rd SW .... Cedar Rapids IA 52404 319-396-3300 396-1500
Web: www.texasroadhouse.com
Third Base Sports Bar & Brewery
500 Blairs Ferry Rd NE .... Cedar Rapids IA 52402 319-378-9090
Web: www.3rdbasebrewery.com
Vito's 4100 River Ridge Dr NE .... Cedar Rapids IA 52402 319-393-8727 393-3981
Web: vitosonline.com
Zio Johno's Spaghetti House
2925 Williams Blvd SW .... Cedar Rapids IA 52404 319-396-1700
Web: www.ziojohnosonline.com
Cosi Cucina 1975 NW 86th St .... Clive IA 50325 515-278-8148
Web: www.cosicucina.com
Taste of Italy 8421 University Blvd .... Clive IA 50325 515-221-0743
Web: atasteofitalyia.com
Barattas 2320 S Union St .... Des Moines IA 50315 515-243-4516 243-5324
Web: barattas.com
China Chef Restaurant 5010 SW Ninth St .... Des Moines IA 50315 515-256-8005 256-1848
Chuck's Restaurant 3610 Sixth Ave .... Des Moines IA 50313 515-244-4104
Web: www.chucksdesmoines.com
Court Avenue Brewing Co 309 Ct Ave .... Des Moines IA 50309 515-282-2739 282-3789
Web: www.courtavebrew.com
Gino's Restaurant & Lounge 2809 Sixth Ave .... Des Moines IA 50313 515-282-4029
Iowa Beef Steakhouse 1201 E Euclid Ave .... Des Moines IA 50316 515-262-1138
Web: www.iowabeefsteakhouse.com
Latin King 2200 Hubbell Ave .... Des Moines IA 50317 515-266-4466
Web: www.tursislatinking.com
Raccoon River Brewing Co 200 Tenth St .... Des Moines IA 50309 515-362-5222 243-4317
Thai Flavors 1254 E 14th St .... Des Moines IA 50316 515-262-4658
Web: www.thaiflavorsiowa.com
Bridge Restaurant 31 Locust St .... Dubuque IA 52001 563-557-7280
Web: www.bridgerest.com
Champps Americana
3100 Dodge St Best Western Midway .... Dubuque IA 52003 563-690-2040
Web: www.champpsdubuque.com
Mario's Italian Restaurant 1298 Main St .... Dubuque IA 52001 563-556-9424
Web: mariosofdubuque.com
Pepper Sprout 378 Main St .... Dubuque IA 52001 563-556-2167
Web: www.peppersprout.com
Yen Ching 926 Main St .... Dubuque IA 52001 563-556-2574 556-2574
Web: yenchingdbq.com
Trostel's Greenbrier Restaurant
5810 Merle Hay Rd .... Johnston IA 50131 515-253-0124
Web: greenbriartrostels.com
Biaggi's 5990 University Ave .... West Des Moines IA 50266 515-221-9900
Web: www.biaggis.com
Rock Bottom Restaurant & Brewery
4508 University Ave .... West Des Moines IA 50266 515-267-8900 267-1400
Web: rockbottom.com
Waterfront Seafood Market
2900 University Ave .... West Des Moines IA 50266 515-223-5106
Web: www.waterfrontseafoodmarket.com

Kansas

Phone Fax

Arthur Bryant Barbecue
1702 Village W Pkwy .... Kansas City KS 66111 913-788-7500
Web: arthurbryantsbbq.com
Gates Bar-B-Que 1026 State Ave .... Kansas City KS 66102 913-621-1134
Web: www.gatesbbq.com
Los Amigos 2610 State Ave .... Kansas City KS 66102 913-281-4547
Rosedale Barbeque 600 SW Blvd .... Kansas City KS 66103 913-262-0343
Web: rosedalebarbeque.com
Vietnam Cafe 2200 W 39th St .... Kansas City KS 66103 913-262-8552
Web: thevietnamcafe.com
Fiorella's Jack Stack Barbecue
9520 Metcalf Ave .... Overland Park KS 66212 913-385-7427
Web: www.jackstackbbq.com
Garozzo's 9950 College Blvd .... Overland Park KS 66210 913-491-8300
Web: www.garozzos.com
Ruchi 11168 Antioch Rd .... Overland Park KS 66210 913-661-9088
Web: www.ruchicuisine.com
Blind Tiger Brewery & Restaurant
417 SW 37th St .... Topeka KS 66611 785-267-2739 267-7527
Web: www.blindtiger.com
Boss Hawg's 2833 SW 29th St .... Topeka KS 66614 785-273-7300
Web: www.bosshawgsbbq.com
Casa 3320 SW Topeka Blvd .... Topeka KS 66611 785-266-4503 266-4539
New City Cafe 4005 SW Gage Ctr Dr .... Topeka KS 66604 785-271-8646 271-8636
Paisano's 4043 SW Tenth St .... Topeka KS 66604 785-273-0100
Web: www.paisanoskansas.com
Pepe & Chela's 1001 SW Tyler St .... Topeka KS 66612 785-357-8332
Web: www.pepeandchelas.com
Bamboo Stix 2243 N Tyler Rd Ste 101 .... Wichita KS 67205 316-722-8886
Web: www.bamboostix.com
Cafe Bel Ami 229 E William St Ste 101 .... Wichita KS 67202 316-267-3433
Web: www.cafebelami.biz
Felipe's 2241 N Woodlawn .... Wichita KS 67220 316-652-0027
Web: www.felipeswichita.com
Great Wall 410 N Hillside Ave .... Wichita KS 67214 316-688-0881
Web: greatwallwichita.com
Harvest Kitchen & Bar 400 W Waterman .... Wichita KS 67202 316-613-6300 293-1200
Web: wichita.regency.hyatt.com/en/hotel/dining.html
IL Vicino 4817 E Douglas .... Wichita KS 67218 316-612-7085
Web: www.ilvicino.com
La Chinita 1451 N Broadway St .... Wichita KS 67214 316-267-1552 267-7097
Web: mexicancateringwichitaks.com
Larkspur Restaurant & Grill 904 E Douglas St .... Wichita KS 67202 316-262-5275 262-1292
Web: www.larkspuronline.com
NuWay Burgers 3441 E Harry .... Wichita KS 67218 316-684-6132
Web: www.nuwayburgers.com
PF Chang's China Bistro 1401 Waterfront Pkwy .... Wichita KS 67206 316-634-2211
Web: www.pfchangs.com
Sal's Japanese Steakhouse 6829 E Kellogg Dr .... Wichita KS 67207 316-682-8880
Sweet Basil 2424 N Woodlawn St .... Wichita KS 67220 316-651-0123
Web: 360wichita.com
Texas Roadhouse 6707 W Kellogg Dr .... Wichita KS 67209 316-943-8722 943-8730
Web: www.texasroadhouse.com

Kentucky

Phone Fax

Casa Fiesta 801 Louisville Rd .... Frankfort KY 40601 502-226-5010
Web: links2frankfort.com
China Buffet 1300 US Hwy 127 S .... Frankfort KY 40601 502-226-3400 226-3800
China Wok 111 E Wood Shopping Ctr .... Frankfort KY 40601 502-695-9388
Web: www.chinawokky.com
Jim's Seafood 950 Wilkinson Blvd .... Frankfort KY 40601 502-223-7448 227-7419
Web: jimseafood1.wix.com/jims-seafood
La Fiesta Grande 314 Versailles Rd .... Frankfort KY 40601 502-695-8378 695-8378
A La Lucie 159 N Limestone St .... Lexington KY 40507 859-252-5277 225-5027
Web: www.alalucie.com
Billy's Hickory Pit Bar B-Q 101 Cochran Rd .... Lexington KY 40502 859-269-9593 266-7865
Cheapside Bar & Grill 131 Cheapside St .... Lexington KY 40507 859-254-0046
Web: www.cheapsidebarandgrill.com
Dudley's 259 Westshort St .... Lexington KY 40507 859-252-1010 253-9383
Web: www.dudleysonshort.com
Durango's 2121 Richmond Rd .... Lexington KY 40502 859-268-0723
Gratz Park Inn 120 W Second St .... Lexington KY 40507 859-231-1777
TF: 800-752-4166 ■ *Web:* www.gratzparkinn.com
Hunan 115 Southland Dr .... Lexington KY 40503 859-278-3811
Web: hunanchineselexington.com
Malone's
Bluegrass Hospitality Group
3347 Tates Creek Rd .... Lexington KY 40502 859-335-6500
Web: www.bluegrasshospitality.com
Mansion at Griffin Gate 1800 Newtown Pk .... Lexington KY 40511 859-231-5100 288-6216
Web: www.mansionatgriffingate.com
Merrick Inn, The 1074 Merrick Dr .... Lexington KY 40502 859-269-5417
Web: themerrickinn.com
Natasha's Bistro & Bar 112 Esplanade .... Lexington KY 40507 859-259-2754
Web: www.beetnik.com
Portofino 249 E Main St .... Lexington KY 40507 859-253-9300 258-2488
Web: www.portofinolexington.com
211 Clover Lane 211 Clover Ln .... Louisville KY 40207 502-896-9570
Web: 211clover.com

Name	City	State	ZIP	Phone	Fax
610 Magnolia 610 Magnolia Ave. *Web:* www.610magnolia.com	Louisville	KY	40208	502-636-0783	
Against the Grain Brewery 401 E Main St Louisville Slugger Field. *Web:* www.atgbrewery.com	Louisville	KY	40202	502-515-0174	
August Moon 2269 Lexington Rd. *Web:* www.augustmoonbistro.com	Louisville	KY	40206	502-456-6569	
Bazo's Fresh Mexican Grill 4014 Dutchmans Ln *Web:* bazosgrill.com	Louisville	KY	40207	502-899-9600	
Buck's Restaurant 425 W Ormsby Ave *Web:* www.bucksrestaurantandbar.com	Louisville	KY	40203	502-637-5284	
De La Torre's 1606 BaRdstown Rd *Web:* www.delatorres.com	Louisville	KY	40205	502-456-4955	
El Mundo 2345 Frankfort Ave *Web:* www.502elmundo.com	Louisville	KY	40206	502-899-9930	
Equus 122 Sears Ave. *Web:* www.equusrestaurant.com	Louisville	KY	40207	502-897-9721	
Lilly's Bistro 1147 BaRdstown Rd *Web:* lillysbistro.com	Louisville	KY	40204	502-451-0447	
Lynn's Paradise Cafe 984 Barret Ave. *Web:* www.lynnsparadisecafe.com	Louisville	KY	40204	502-583-3447	583-0211
Pat's Steak House 2437 Brownsboro Rd *Web:* www.patssteakhouselouisville.com	Louisville	KY	40206	502-893-2062	893-2062
Porcini 2730 Frankfort Ave *Web:* www.porcinilouisville.com	Louisville	KY	40206	502-894-8686	
Ruth's Chris Steak House 6100 Dutchman's Ln 16th Fl. *Web:* www.ruthschris.com	Louisville	KY	40205	502-479-0026	
Shah's Mongolian Grill 9148 Taylorsville Rd. *Web:* www.shahsmongoliangrill.com	Louisville	KY	40299	502-493-0234	
Uptown Cafe 1624 BaRdstown Rd *Web:* www.uptownlouisville.com	Louisville	KY	40205	502-458-4212	
Vincenzo's 150 S Fifth St. *Web:* www.vincenzositalianrestaurant.com	Louisville	KY	40202	502-580-1350	580-1355
Yang Kee Noodle Club 7900 Shelbyville Rd *Web:* www.yangkeenoodle.com	Louisville	KY	40222	502-426-0800	426-9080

Louisiana

Name	City	State	ZIP	Phone	Fax
Albasha 5454 Bluebonnet Rd Ste G *Web:* www.albashabr.com	Baton Rouge	LA	70809	225-292-7988	
Boutin's 8322 Bluebonnet Blvd	Baton Rouge	LA	70810	225-819-9862	
Chimes Restaurant & Tap Room 3357 Highland Rd. *Web:* www.thechimes.com	Baton Rouge	LA	70802	225-383-1754	
Copelands of New Orleans 4957 Essen Ln. *Web:* www.copelandsofneworleans.com	Baton Rouge	LA	70809	225-769-1800	
Gino's 4542 Bennington Ave *Web:* www.ginosrestaurant.com	Baton Rouge	LA	70808	225-927-7156	
India's Restaurant 5230 Essen Ln	Baton Rouge	LA	70809	225-769-0600	
Juban's 3739 Perkins Rd *Web:* www.jubans.com	Baton Rouge	LA	70808	225-346-8422	387-2601
Mansur's 5720 Corporate Blvd Ste A *Web:* www.mansursontheboulevard.com	Baton Rouge	LA	70808	225-923-3366	
Melting Pot, The 5294 Corporate Blvd. *Web:* www.meltingpot.com	Baton Rouge	LA	70808	225-928-5677	928-5622
Mike Anderson's Seafood Restaurant 1031 W Lee Dr	Baton Rouge	LA	70809	225-766-7823	
Ninfa's Restaurant 4738 Constitution Ave. *Web:* tiojavis.com	Baton Rouge	LA	70808	225-924-0377	924-5620
Sullivan's Steakhouse 5252 Corporate Blvd. *Web:* sullivanssteakhouse.com	Baton Rouge	LA	70808	225-925-1161	
Thai Kitchen 4550 Concord Ave *Web:* www.thaikitchenla.com	Baton Rouge	LA	70808	225-346-1230	
L'Italiano 701 Barksdale Blvd. *Web:* litalianorestaurant.webs.com	Bossier City	LA	71111	318-747-7777	
Ralph & Kacoo's 1700 Old Minden Rd Ste 141 *Web:* ralphandkacoos.com	Bossier City	LA	71111	318-747-6660	747-9816
Antoni's Italian Cafe 1118 Coolidge Blvd Ste A.	Lafayette	LA	70503	337-232-8384	232-4311
Bailey's Seafood & Grill 5520-A Johnston St *Web:* www.baileyscss.com	Lafayette	LA	70503	337-988-6464	
Cafe Vermilionville 1304 W Pinhook Rd *Web:* www.cafev.com	Lafayette	LA	70503	337-237-0100	
Charley G's Seafood Grill 3809 Ambassador Caffery Pkwy *Web:* www.charleygs.com	Lafayette	LA	70503	337-981-0108	
Don's Seafood & Steakhouse 301 E Vermilion St	Lafayette	LA	70501	337-235-3551	235-6707
Prejean's Restaurant 3480 NE Evangeline Trwy *Web:* www.prejeans.com	Lafayette	LA	70507	337-896-3247	896-3278
Carreta's Grill 2320 Veterans Memorial Blvd *Web:* carretasgrillrestaurant.com	Metairie	LA	70002	504-837-6696	
Casa Garcia 8814 Veterans Memorial Blvd *Web:* casa-garcia.com	Metairie	LA	70003	504-464-0354	
Deanie's Seafood 1713 Lake Ave *Web:* www.deanies.com	Metairie	LA	70005	504-834-1225	
Drago's 3232 N Arnoult Rd *Web:* www.dragosrestaurant.com	Metairie	LA	70002	504-888-9254	
Fausto's Bistro 530 Veterans Memorial Blvd *Web:* www.faustosbistro.com	Metairie	LA	70005	504-833-7121	
Impastato's 3400 16th St *Web:* www.impastatos.com	Metairie	LA	70002	504-455-1545	
Peppermill Restaurant 3524 Severn Ave. *Web:* www.riccobonos.com	Metairie	LA	70002	504-455-2266	
Ruth's Chris Steak House 3633 Veterans Memorial Blvd. *Web:* www.ruthschris.com	Metairie	LA	70002	504-888-3600	
Siamese Thai Cuisine 6601 Veterans Memorial Blvd Ste 29-30 *Web:* www.siamesecuisine.com	Metairie	LA	70003	504-454-8752	
Sun Ray Grill 619 Pink St. *Web:* www.sunraygrill.com	Metairie	LA	70005	504-837-0055	
Vega Tapas Cafe 2051 Metairie Rd *Web:* www.vegatapascafe.com	Metairie	LA	70005	504-836-2007	
Vincent's 4411 Chastant St *Web:* www.vincentsitaliancuisine.com	Metairie	LA	70006	504-885-2984	
Acme Oyster House 724 Iberville St. *Web:* www.acmeoyster.com	New Orleans	LA	70130	225-906-2372	
Antoine's 713 St Louis St. *Web:* www.antoines.com	New Orleans	LA	70130	504-581-4422	
Arnaud's 813 Bienville St *TF:* 866-230-8895 ■ *Web:* www.arnaudsrestaurant.com	New Orleans	LA	70112	504-523-5433	
August 301 Tchoupitoulas St *Web:* www.rest-august.com	New Orleans	LA	70130	504-299-9777	
Bayona 430 Rue Dauphine *Web:* www.bayona.com	New Orleans	LA	70112	504-525-4455	522-0589
Bon Ton Cafe 401 Magazine St *Web:* www.thebontoncafe.com	New Orleans	LA	70130	504-524-3386	
Bourbon House Seafood & Oyster Bar 144 Bourbon St *Web:* www.bourbonhouse.com	New Orleans	LA	70130	504-522-0111	
Brigtsen's 723 Dante St *Web:* www.brigtsens.com	New Orleans	LA	70118	504-861-7610	
Broussard's Restaurant 819 Rue Conti. *Web:* www.broussards.com	New Orleans	LA	70112	504-581-3866	581-3873
Byblos 3218 Magazine St *Web:* www.byblosrestaurants.com	New Orleans	LA	70115	504-894-1233	894-1239
Cafe Degas 3127 Esplanade Ave *Web:* www.cafedegas.com	New Orleans	LA	70119	504-945-5635	943-5255
Cafe Giovanni 117 Rue Decatur St. *Web:* www.cafegiovanni.com	New Orleans	LA	70118	504-529-2154	
Ciro's Cote Sud 7918 Maple St *Web:* www.cotesudrestaurant.com	New Orleans	LA	70118	504-866-9551	
Clancy's 6100 Annunciation St. *Web:* clancysneworleans.com	New Orleans	LA	70118	504-895-1111	
Dick & Jenny's 4501 Tchoupitoulas St *Web:* www.dickandjennys.com	New Orleans	LA	70115	504-894-9880	
Elizabeth's 601 Gallier St. *Web:* elizabethsrestaurantnola.com	New Orleans	LA	70117	504-944-9272	
Emeril's 800 Tchoupitoulas St *Web:* www.emerils.com	New Orleans	LA	70130	504-528-9393	558-3925
Emeril's Delmonico 1300 St Charles Ave. *Web:* www.emerils.com	New Orleans	LA	70130	504-525-4937	595-2206
Galatoire's 209 Bourbon St *Web:* www.galatoires.com	New Orleans	LA	70130	504-525-2021	525-5900
GW Fins 808 Bienville St. *Web:* www.gwfins.com	New Orleans	LA	70112	504-581-3467	
Herbsaint Bar & Restaurant 701 St Charles Ave *Web:* herbsaint.com	New Orleans	LA	70130	504-524-4114	
Horinoya 920 Poydras St	New Orleans	LA	70112	504-561-8919	561-8919
Irene's Cuisine 539 St Phillip St.	New Orleans	LA	70116	504-529-8811	527-5273
Jacques-Imo's Cafe 8324 Oak St. *Web:* jacques-imos.com	New Orleans	LA	70118	504-861-0886	
K-Paul's Louisiana Kitchen 416 Chartres St. *Web:* www.kpauls.com	New Orleans	LA	70130	504-596-2530	
Kyoto 4920 Prytania St *Web:* kyotonola.com	New Orleans	LA	70115	504-891-3644	
La Crepe Nanou 1410 Robert St *Web:* www.lacrepenanou.com	New Orleans	LA	70115	504-899-2670	
Le Meritage at the Maison Dupuy 1001 Rue Toulouse. *Web:* www.maisondupuy.com	New Orleans	LA	70112	504-522-8800	
Liborio's 321 Magazine St *Web:* www.liboriocuban.com	New Orleans	LA	70130	504-581-9680	
Lilette 3637 Magazine St *Web:* www.liletterestaurant.com	New Orleans	LA	70115	504-895-1636	
Louisiana Bistro 337 Dauphine St *Web:* louisianabistro.net	New Orleans	LA	70112	504-525-3335	
Martinique Bistro 5908 Magazine St *Web:* www.martiniquebistro.com	New Orleans	LA	70115	504-891-8495	
Mat & Naddie's Restaurant 937 Leonidas St *Web:* www.matandnaddies.com	New Orleans	LA	70118	504-861-9600	
Mr B's Bistro 201 Royal St *Web:* www.mrbsbistro.com	New Orleans	LA	70130	504-523-2078	521-8304
Muriel's 801 Chartres St. *Web:* www.muriels.com	New Orleans	LA	70116	504-568-1885	568-9795
Ninja 8433 Oak St *Web:* ninjasushineworleans.com	New Orleans	LA	70118	504-866-1119	
NOLA 534 St Louis St. *Web:* www.emerils.com	New Orleans	LA	70130	504-522-6652	524-6178
Orleans Grapevine Wine Bar & Bistro 718 - 720 Orleans Ave *Web:* www.orleansgrapevine.com	New Orleans	LA	70116	504-523-1930	
Palace Cafe 605 Canal St *Web:* www.palacecafe.com	New Orleans	LA	70130	504-523-1661	
Pelican Club 312 Exchange Alley *Web:* www.pelicanclub.com	New Orleans	LA	70130	504-523-1504	522-2331
Port of Call 838 Esplanade Ave *Web:* portofcallnola.com	New Orleans	LA	70116	504-523-0120	
Red Fish Grill 115 Bourbon St. *Web:* www.redfishgrill.com	New Orleans	LA	70130	504-598-1200	
RioMar 800 S Peters St. *Web:* www.riomarseafood.com	New Orleans	LA	70130	504-525-3474	

	City	State	Zip	Phone	Fax
Sake Cafe 2830 Magazine St Web: sakecafeuptown.us	New Orleans	LA	70115	504-894-0033	
Sara's 724 Dublin St	New Orleans	LA	70118	504-861-0565	
Stella! 547 Saint Ann St Web: www.stanleyrestaurant.com/#private-events	New Orleans	LA	70116	504-587-0093	587-0092
Upperline 1413 Upperline St Web: www.upperline.com	New Orleans	LA	70115	504-891-9822	
Vincent's 7839 St Charles Ave Web: www.vincentsitaliancuisine.com	New Orleans	LA	70118	504-866-9313	
Bella Fresca Restaurant 6307 Line Ave Web: www.bellafresca.com	Shreveport	LA	71106	318-865-6307	
Chianti Restaurant 6535 Line Ave Web: chiantirestaurant.net	Shreveport	LA	71106	318-868-8866	
Copeland's of New Orleans 1665 E Industrial Loop Web: www.copelandsofneworleans.com	Shreveport	LA	71106	318-797-0143	
Ernest's Orleans Restaurant & Cocktail Lounge 1601 Spring St S Web: www.ernestsorleans.com	Shreveport	LA	71101	318-226-1325	425-0900
Mabry House 1540 Irving Pl	Shreveport	LA	71101	318-227-1121	227-1121
Ming Garden 1250 Shreveport Barksdale Hwy Web: chineserestaurantshreveport.com	Shreveport	LA	71105	318-861-2741	
Monjunis 1315 Louisiana Ave Web: www.monjunis.com	Shreveport	LA	71101	318-227-0847	
Superior Bar & Grill 6123 Line Ave Web: superiorgrill.com	Shreveport	LA	71106	318-869-3243	
Trejo's 9122 Mansfield Rd Web: trejosmexicanrestaurant.com	Shreveport	LA	71118	318-687-6192	
Village Grille 1313 Louisiana Ave	Shreveport	LA	71101	318-424-2874	

Maine

	City	State	Zip	Phone	Fax
Margaritas 390 Western Ave Web: www.margs.com	Augusta	ME	04330	207-622-7874	
Red Barn 455 Riverside Dr Web: theredbarnmaine.org	Augusta	ME	04330	207-623-9485	
Riverfront Barbeque & Grill 300 Water St Web: riverfrontbbq.com	Augusta	ME	04330	207-622-8899	
Bugaboo Creek Steak House 24 Bangor Mall Blvd Web: bugaboocreek.com	Bangor	ME	04401	207-945-5515	
China Light 571 Broadway Web: chinalightbangor.com	Bangor	ME	04401	207-947-6759	
Geaghan's Restaurant & Pub 570 Main St Web: www.geaghans.com	Bangor	ME	04401	207-945-3730	941-6758
Ichiban 226 Union St Web: bangorichiban.com	Bangor	ME	04401	207-262-9308	
Oriental Jade Bangor Mall Blvd Web: www.orientaljade.com	Bangor	ME	04401	207-947-6969	942-7170
Panda Garden 123 Franklin St Web: bangorpanda.com	Bangor	ME	04401	207-942-2704	
Thistle's 175 Exchange St Web: www.thistlesrestaurant.com	Bangor	ME	04401	207-945-5480	990-3836
Cafe Blue Fish 122 Cottage St Web: www.cafebluefishbarharbor.com	Bar Harbor	ME	04609	207-288-3696	
Geddy's Pub 19 Main St PO Box 955 Web: www.geddys.com	Bar Harbor	ME	04609	207-288-5077	288-9927
Havana 318 Main St Web: havanamaine.com	Bar Harbor	ME	04609	207-288-2822	
Mama DiMatteo's 34 Kennebec Pl Web: www.mamadimatteos.com	Bar Harbor	ME	04609	207-288-3666	
Michelle's 194 Main St Web: www.ivymanor.com	Bar Harbor	ME	04609	207-288-2138	
Poor Boy's Gourmet 300 Main St Web: www.poorboysgourmet.com	Bar Harbor	ME	04609	207-288-4148	
Rosalie's 46 Cottage St Web: rosaliespizza.com	Bar Harbor	ME	04609	207-288-5666	
Route 66 21 Cottage St Web: barharborroute66.com	Bar Harbor	ME	04609	207-288-3708	
Rupununi Bar & Grill 119 Main St Web: www.rupununi.com	Bar Harbor	ME	04609	207-288-2886	
West Street Cafe 76 W St Web: www.weststreetcafe.com	Bar Harbor	ME	04609	207-288-5242	
Ground Round 15 Main St Ste 210 Web: sparetimerec.com	Freeport	ME	04032	207-623-0022	
Bar Harbor Lobster Bakes 10 State Hwy 3 PO Box 177 Web: www.barharborlobsterbakes.com	Hulls Cove	ME	04644	207-288-4055	288-5767
Back Bay Grill 65 Portland St Web: www.backbaygrill.com	Portland	ME	04101	207-772-8833	
Benkay 2 India St Web: sushimanme.info	Portland	ME	04101	207-773-5555	
Blue Spoon 89 Congress St Web: bluespoonme.com	Portland	ME	04101	207-773-1116	
Cinque Terre 10 Dana St Web: www.vignolamaine.com	Portland	ME	04101	207-772-1330	
DiMillo's on the Water 25 Long Wharf Web: www.dimillos.com	Portland	ME	04101	207-772-2216	772-1081
Duckfat 43 Middle St Web: www.duckfat.com	Portland	ME	04101	207-774-8080	
Fore Street 288 Fore St Web: forestreet.biz	Portland	ME	04101	207-775-2717	
Gilbert's Chowder House 92 Commercial St Web: gilbertschowderhouse.com	Portland	ME	04101	207-871-5636	
Hugo's Restaurant 88 Middle St Web: www.hugos.net	Portland	ME	04101	207-774-8538	
Katahdin Restaurant 27 Forest Ave Web: www.katahdinrestaurant.com	Portland	ME	04101	207-774-1740	774-1740
Maria's 337 Cumberland Ave Web: mariasrestaurant.com	Portland	ME	04101	207-772-9232	
Pepperclub 78 Middle St Web: pepperclubrestaurant.com	Portland	ME	04101	207-772-0531	
Portland Lobster Co 180 Commercial St Web: www.portlandlobstercompany.com	Portland	ME	04112	207-775-2112	
Ri Ra Irish Pub & Restaurant 72 Commercial St Web: www.rira.com	Portland	ME	04101	207-761-4446	761-4447
Ribollita 41 Middle St Web: ribollitamaine.com	Portland	ME	04101	207-774-2972	
Sapporo Restaurant 230 Commercial St Web: www.sappororestaurant.com	Portland	ME	04101	207-772-1233	871-9275
Walter's Cafe 2 Portland Sq Web: www.waltersportland.com	Portland	ME	04101	207-871-9258	
Joe's Boathouse 1 Spring Pt Dr Web: www.joesboathouse.com	South Portland	ME	04106	207-741-2780	347-5718

Manitoba

	City	Prov	Postal Code	Phone	Fax
529 Wellington 529 Wellington Crescent Web: wowhospitality.ca	Winnipeg	MB	R3M0A1	204-487-8325	
Amici 326 Broadway Web: www.amiciwpg.com	Winnipeg	MB	R3C0S5	204-943-4997	943-0369
Bailey's 185 Lombard Ave Web: www.baileysprimedining.com	Winnipeg	MB	R3B0W4	204-944-1180	
Bella Vista 53 Maryland St	Winnipeg	MB	R3G1C3	204-775-4485	
Bombolini 326 Broadway Web: amiciwpg.com	Winnipeg	MB	R3C0S5	204-943-5066	943-0369
Cafe Carlo 243 Lilac St Web: www.cafecarlo.com	Winnipeg	MB	R3M2S2	204-477-5544	477-1652
East India Co 349 York Ave Web: www.eastindiaco.com	Winnipeg	MB	R3C3S9	204-947-3097	947-5019
Elephant & Castle/Delta Winnipeg Hotel 350 St Mary Ave Web: www.elephantcastle.com	Winnipeg	MB	R3C3J2	204-942-5555	
Fusion Grill 550 Academy Rd Web: fusiongrill.mb.ca	Winnipeg	MB	R3N0E3	204-489-6963	
Gasthaus Gutenberger 2583 Portage Ave Web: www.gasthausgutenberger.com	Winnipeg	MB	R3J0P5	204-888-3133	
Hy's Steakhouse & Cocktail Bar 1 Lombard Pl Main Fl Richardson Bldg Web: www.hyssteakhouse.com	Winnipeg	MB	R3B0X3	204-942-1000	
Ichiban 189 Carlton St Web: www.ichiban.ca	Winnipeg	MB	R3C3H7	204-925-7400	957-1697
King's Head Pub 120 King St Web: www.kingshead.ca	Winnipeg	MB	R3B1M3	204-957-7710	
Maxime 1131 St Mary's Rd *Fax Area Code: 207 ■ Web: maximesrestaurant.ca	Winnipeg	MB	R2M3T9	204-257-1521	257-1521*
Mei Ji Sushi 454 River Ave	Winnipeg	MB	R3L0C6	204-284-3996	
Mitchell Block, The 173 McDermot Ave Web: www.trevisirestaurant.com	Winnipeg	MB	R3B0S1	204-949-9032	
Mona Lisa 1697 Corydon Ave Web: www.monalisarestaurant.ca	Winnipeg	MB	R3N0J9	204-488-3684	489-1679
Pembina Village Restaurant 333 Pembina Hwy Web: www.pembinavillagerestaurant.com	Winnipeg	MB	R3L2E4	204-477-5439	
Resto Gare 630 Des Meurons St Web: www.restogare.com	Winnipeg	MB	R2H2P9	204-237-7072	
Sawatdee 555 Osborne St	Winnipeg	MB	R3L2B3	204-284-8424	
Toad in the Hole 112 Osborne St Web: toadinthehole.ca	Winnipeg	MB	R3L1Y5	204-284-7201	
Tropikis 878 Ellice Ave	Winnipeg	MB	R3G0C6	204-788-4733	
White Tower 3670 Roblin Blvd Web: weebly.com	Winnipeg	MB	R3R0E1	204-896-0406	

Maryland

	City	State	Zip	Phone	Fax
Cafe Normandie 185 Main St Web: www.cafenormandie.com	Annapolis	MD	21401	410-263-3382	
Cantler's Riverside Inn 458 Forest Beach Rd Web: www.cantlers.com	Annapolis	MD	21409	410-757-1311	757-6784
Castlebay Irish Pub 193-A Main St	Annapolis	MD	21401	410-626-0165	
Famous Dave's Barbeque 181 Jennifer Rd TF: 877-833-9335 ■ Web: www.famousdaves.com	Annapolis	MD	21401	410-224-2207	
Federal House Bar & Grille 22 Market Space Web: federalhouserestaurant.com	Annapolis	MD	21401	410-268-2576	280-0195
Galway Bay Irish Pub 63 Maryland Ave Web: www.galwaybayannapolis.com	Annapolis	MD	21401	410-263-8333	
Harry Browne's 66 State Cir Web: www.harrybrownes.com	Annapolis	MD	21401	410-263-4332	
Jalapenos 85 Forest Dr Web: jalapenosonline.com	Annapolis	MD	21401	410-266-7580	
Joss Cafe & Sushi Bar 195 Main St Web: josssushi.com	Annapolis	MD	21401	410-263-4688	
Lebanese Taverna 2478 Solomons Island Rd Annapolis Harbour Ctr Web: www.lebanesetaverna.com	Annapolis	MD	21401	410-897-1111	
Les Folies 2552 Riva Rd Web: www.lesfoliesbrasserie.com	Annapolis	MD	21401	410-573-0970	
Lewnes' Steakhouse 401 Fourth St Web: www.lewnessteakhouse.com	Annapolis	MD	21403	410-263-1617	
Main Ingredient 914 Bay Ridge Rd Web: www.themainingredient.com	Annapolis	MD	21403	410-626-0388	626-0204
Mangia 81 Main St Web: mangiasannapolis.com	Annapolis	MD	21401	410-268-1350	
Melting Pot of Annapolis, The 2348 Solomons Island Rd TF: 800-783-0867 ■ Web: www.meltingpot.com	Annapolis	MD	21401	410-266-8004	266-8431
O'Brien's Oyster Bar & Restaurant 113 Main St Web: www.obriensoysterbar.com	Annapolis	MD	21401	410-268-6288	267-7767

	City	State	Zip	Phone	Fax
O'Leary's Seafood Restaurant 310 Third St *Web:* www.olearysseafood.com	Annapolis	MD	21403	410-263-0884	
Osteria 177 177 Main St *Web:* www.osteria177.com	Annapolis	MD	21401	410-267-7700	
Paul's Homewood Cafe 919 W St *Web:* pauls.publishpath.com	Annapolis	MD	21401	410-267-7891	
Piccola Roma 200 Main St *Web:* piccolaromaannapolis.com	Annapolis	MD	21401	410-268-7898	
Red Hot & Blue Restaurants Inc 200 Old Mill Bottom Rd S *TF:* 888-509-7100 ■ *Web:* www.redhotandblue.com	Annapolis	MD	21401	410-626-7427	
Reynolds Tavern 7 Church Cir *Web:* www.reynoldstavern.org	Annapolis	MD	21401	410-295-9555	295-9559
Ruth's Chris Steak House 301 Severn Ave *Web:* www.ruthschris.com	Annapolis	MD	21403	410-990-0033	
Sam's on the Waterfront 2020 Chesapeake Harbour Dr E *Web:* www.samsonthewaterfront.com	Annapolis	MD	21403	410-263-3600	
Abacrombie Inn 58 W Biddle St	Baltimore	MD	21201	410-244-8413	
Akbar 823 N Charles St *Web:* www.akbar-restaurant.com	Baltimore	MD	21201	410-539-0944	
Aldo's 306 S High St *Web:* www.aldositaly.com	Baltimore	MD	21202	410-727-0700	
Ambassador Dining Room 3811 Canterbury Rd *Web:* www1.nyc.gov	Baltimore	MD	21218	410-366-1484	
Amicci's of Little Italy 231 S High St *Web:* www.amiccis.com	Baltimore	MD	21202	410-528-1096	
B - A Bolton Hill Bistro 1501 Bolton St *Web:* www.b-bistro.com	Baltimore	MD	21217	410-383-8600	
Ban Thai 340 N Charles St *Web:* www.banthai.us	Baltimore	MD	21201	410-727-7971	
Birches 641 S Montford Ave *Web:* www.birchesrestaurant.com	Baltimore	MD	21224	410-732-3000	
Black Olive 814 S Bond St *Web:* www.theblackolive.com	Baltimore	MD	21231	410-276-7141	276-7143
Brewers Art 1106 N Charles St *Web:* www.thebrewersart.com	Baltimore	MD	21201	410-547-6925	
Brightons Orangerie 550 Light St *Web:* sonesta.com	Baltimore	MD	21202	410-347-9750	659-5925
Carlyle, The 500 W University Pkwy *Web:* www.morgan-properties.com/thecarlyle	Baltimore	MD	21210	410-467-9890	
Charleston 1000 Lancaster St *Web:* www.charlestonrestaurant.com	Baltimore	MD	21202	410-332-7373	
Da Mimmo Italian Cuisine 217 S High St *Web:* www.damimmo.com	Baltimore	MD	21202	410-727-6876	727-1927
Dalesio's of Little Italy 829 Eastern Ave *Web:* www.dalesios.com	Baltimore	MD	21202	410-539-1965	
Dukem 1100 Maryland Ave *Web:* www.dukemrestaurant.com	Baltimore	MD	21201	410-385-0318	
Faidley's Seafood 203 N Paca St *Web:* www.faidleyscrabcakes.com	Baltimore	MD	21201	410-727-4898	
Gertrude's 10 Art Museum Dr *Web:* gertrudesbaltimore.com	Baltimore	MD	21218	410-889-3399	889-9689
Helmand, The 806 N Charles St *Web:* www.helmand.com	Baltimore	MD	21201	410-752-0311	
Henninger's Tavern 1812 Bank St *Web:* www.henningerstavern.com	Baltimore	MD	21231	410-342-2172	
Hull Street Blues 1222 Hull St *Web:* www.hullstreetblues.com	Baltimore	MD	21230	410-727-7476	576-2343
Ikaros 4901 Eastern Ave *Web:* www.ikarosrestaurant.com	Baltimore	MD	21224	410-633-3750	633-7881
Kali's Mezze 1606 Thames St *Web:* www.kalismezze.com	Baltimore	MD	21231	410-563-7600	
La Scala of Little Italy 1012 Eastern Ave *Web:* www.lascaladining.com	Baltimore	MD	21202	410-783-9209	783-5949
La Tavola 248 Albemarle St *Web:* www.la-tavola.com	Baltimore	MD	21202	410-685-1859	685-1891
Little Havana 1325 Key Hwy *Web:* www.littlehavanas.com	Baltimore	MD	21230	410-837-9903	
Louisiana Restaurant 1708 Aliceanna St *Web:* www.louisianasrestaurant.com	Baltimore	MD	21231	410-327-2610	
Mama's on the Half Shell 2901 O'Donnell St *Web:* www.mamasonthehalfshell.com	Baltimore	MD	21224	410-276-3160	
Matsuri Restaurant 1105 S Charles St *Web:* www.matsuri-restaurant.com	Baltimore	MD	21230	410-752-8561	
Morton's the Steakhouse 300 S Charles St *TF:* 800-552-6379 ■ *Web:* www.mortons.com	Baltimore	MD	21201	410-547-8255	547-8244
Nacho Mama's 2907 O'Donnell St *Web:* www.nachomamascanton.com	Baltimore	MD	21224	410-675-0898	
Peter's Inn 504 S Ann St *Web:* www.petersinn.com	Baltimore	MD	21231	410-675-7313	
Petit Louis Bistro 4800 Roland Ave *Web:* www.petitlouis.com	Baltimore	MD	21210	410-366-9393	
Red Maple 930 N Charles St *Web:* www.930redmaple.com	Baltimore	MD	21201	410-385-0520	
Rocco's Capriccio 846 Fawn St *Web:* roccosinlittleitaly.com	Baltimore	MD	21202	410-685-2710	
Ruth's Chris Steak House 600 Water St *Web:* www.ruthschris.com	Baltimore	MD	21202	410-783-0033	
Sabatino's 901 Fawn St *Web:* www.sabatinos.com	Baltimore	MD	21202	410-727-9414	837-6540
Samos 600 Oldham St *Web:* www.samosrestaurant.com	Baltimore	MD	21224	410-675-5292	
Sascha's 527 N Charles St *Web:* www.saschas.com	Baltimore	MD	21201	410-539-8880	
Sotto Sopra 405 N Charles St *Web:* sottosoprainc.com	Baltimore	MD	21201	410-625-0534	625-2642
Sushi-San Thai Jai Dee 2748 Lighthouse Pt *Web:* sushisanbaltimore.com	Baltimore	MD	21224	410-534-8888	534-8665
Suzie's Soba 1009 W 36th St	Baltimore	MD	21211	410-243-0051	
Tapas Teatro 1711 N Charles St *Web:* www.tapasteatro.com	Baltimore	MD	21201	410-332-0110	
Thai Arroy 1019 Light St *Web:* www.thaiarroy.com	Baltimore	MD	21230	410-385-8587	
Thai Landing 1207 N Charles St *Web:* www.thailandingmd.com	Baltimore	MD	21201	410-727-1234	
Tio Pepe 10 E Franklin St *Web:* tiopepebaltimore.com	Baltimore	MD	21202	410-539-4675	
Viccino 1317 N Charles St *Web:* www.viccino.com	Baltimore	MD	21201	410-347-0349	
La Fontaine Bleue Inc 7514 S Ritchie Hwy *TF:* 877-778-6863 ■ *Web:* www.lafontainebleu.com	Glen Burnie	MD	21061	410-760-4115	
Angler Restaurant 312 Talbot St *Web:* angleroc.net	Ocean City	MD	21842	410-289-7424	
BJ's On the Water 115 75th St *Web:* www.bjsonthewater.com	Ocean City	MD	21842	410-524-7575	524-7624
Bonfire, The 7009 Coastal Hwy *Web:* www.thebonfirerestaurant.com	Ocean City	MD	21842	410-524-7171	
Buxy's Salty Dog 2707 Philadelphia Ave *Web:* buxys.com	Ocean City	MD	21842	410-289-0973	289-0038
Coral Reef Restaurant 1701 Atlantic Ave *TF:* 866-627-8483 ■ *Web:* ocmdhotels.com	Ocean City	MD	21842	410-289-2612	289-3381
Fager's Island Restaurant 201 60th St *TF:* 855-432-4377 ■ *Web:* www.fagers.com	Ocean City	MD	21842	410-524-5500	723-2055
Harrison's Harbor Watch Restaurant 806 S Boardwalk *Web:* www.harborwatchrestaurant.com	Ocean City	MD	21842	410-289-5121	
JR's Place for Ribs 131st St & Coastal *Web:* www.jrsribs.com	Ocean City	MD	21842	410-250-3100	
Jules 11805 Coastal Hwy *Web:* ocjules.com	Ocean City	MD	21842	410-524-3396	
Macky's Bayside Bar & Grill 54th St on the Bay *Web:* www.mackys.com	Ocean City	MD	21842	410-723-5565	
Marina Deck 306 Dorchester St *Web:* www.marinadeckrestaurant.com	Ocean City	MD	21842	410-289-4411	
Nick's Original House of Ribs 14410 Coastal Highway *Web:* www.nickshouseofribs.com	Ocean City	MD	21842	410-250-1984	
Ocean City Maryland Hotels 6600 Coastal Hwy *TF:* 800-837-3588 ■ *Web:* www.ocmdhotels.com	Ocean City	MD	21842	410-524-5252	
Ocean Club Night Club 10100 Coastal Hwy *Web:* oceancity.com	Ocean City	MD	21842	410-703-1970	
Phillips Crab House 2004 N Philadelphia Ave *Web:* www.phillipsseafood.com	Ocean City	MD	21842	410-289-6821	
Tequila Mockingbird 130th St Montego Bay Shopping Ctr *Web:* www.octequila.com	Ocean City	MD	21842	410-250-4424	
Crab Alley 9703 Golf Course Rd *Web:* craballeyoc.com	West Ocean City	MD	21842	410-213-7800	213-1048

Massachusetts

	City	State	Zip	Phone	Fax
Outermost Inn 81 Lighthouse Rd *Web:* www.outermostinn.com	Aquinnah	MA	02535	508-645-3511	645-3514
29 Newbury 29 Newbury St *Web:* www.29newbury.com	Boston	MA	02116	617-536-0290	
75 Chestnut 75 Chestnut St *Web:* www.75chestnut.com	Boston	MA	02108	617-227-2175	227-3675
Abe & Louie's 793 Boylston St *Web:* www.abeandlouies.com	Boston	MA	02116	617-536-6300	
Addis Red Sea 544 Tremont St *Web:* www.addisredsea.com	Boston	MA	02116	617-426-8727	695-3677
Antico Forno 93 Salem St *Web:* www.anticofornoboston.com	Boston	MA	02113	617-723-6733	
Aquitaine 569 Tremont St *Web:* www.aquitaineboston.com	Boston	MA	02118	617-424-8577	
Assaggio 29 Prince St *Web:* www.assaggioboston.com	Boston	MA	02113	617-227-7380	742-3512
B & G Oysters 550 Tremont St *Web:* www.bandgoysters.com	Boston	MA	02116	617-423-0550	
Bin 26 Enoteca 26 Charles St *Web:* www.bin26.com	Boston	MA	02114	617-723-5939	
Blu 4 Avery St 4th Fl *Web:* www.blurestaurant.com	Boston	MA	02111	617-375-8550	
Bricco 241 Hanover St *Web:* www.bricco.com	Boston	MA	02113	617-248-6800	
Bristol, The 200 Boylston St *TF:* 800-819-5053 ■ *Web:* www.fourseasons.com	Boston	MA	02116	617-338-4400	423-0154
Brown Sugar Cafe 1033 Commonwealth Ave *Web:* www.brownsugarcafe.com	Boston	MA	02215	617-787-4242	
Butcher Shop, The 552 Tremont St *Web:* www.thebutchershopboston.com	Boston	MA	02118	617-423-4800	
Cantina Italiana 346 Hanover St *Web:* www.cantinaitaliana.com	Boston	MA	02113	617-723-4577	723-6357
Capital Grille 900 Boylston St *TF:* 866-518-9113 ■ *Web:* www.thecapitalgrille.com	Boston	MA	02115	866-518-9113	
Carmen 33 N Sq *Web:* www.carmenboston.com	Boston	MA	02113	617-742-6421	
Casa Romero 30 Gloucester St *Web:* www.casaromero.com	Boston	MA	02115	617-536-4341	
Davide 326 Commercial St *Web:* www.daviderestaurant.com	Boston	MA	02109	617-227-5745	
East Ocean City 27 Beach St *Web:* www.eastoceancity.com	Boston	MA	02111	617-542-2504	
Fleming's Prime Steakhouse & Wine Bar 217 Stuart St *Web:* www.flemingssteakhouse.com	Boston	MA	02116	617-292-0808	
Franklin Cafe 278 Shawmut Ave *Web:* www.franklincafe.com	Boston	MA	02118	617-350-0010	
Ginza 16 Hudson St	Boston	MA	02111	617-338-2261	426-3563

Name / Address	City	State	ZIP	Phone	Fax
Grill 23 & Bar 161 Berkeley St	Boston	MA	02116	617-542-2255	542-5114
Web: www.grill23.com					
Grotto 37 Bowdoin St	Boston	MA	02114	617-227-3434	
Web: www.grottorestaurant.com					
Hamersley's Bistro 553 Tremont St	Boston	MA	02116	617-423-2700	
India Quality 484 Commonwealth Ave	Boston	MA	02215	617-267-4499	267-4477
Web: www.indiaquality.com					
KO Prime 90 Tremont St	Boston	MA	02108	617-772-0202	772-5810
TF: 866-906-9090 ■ *Web:* www.ninezero.com					
L'Espalier 774-Bayleston St	Boston	MA	02199	617-262-3023	
Web: www.lespalier.com					
Lala Rokh 97 Mt Vernon St	Boston	MA	02108	617-720-5511	
Web: www.lalarokh.com					
Legal Sea Foods 26 Pk Plz	Boston	MA	02116	617-426-4444	
Web: www.legalseafoods.com					
Les Zygomates 129 S St	Boston	MA	02111	617-542-5108	482-8806
Web: winebar129.com					
Lucca 226 Hanover St	Boston	MA	02113	617-742-9200	
Web: www.luccaboston.com					
Mamma Maria's 3 N Sq	Boston	MA	02113	617-523-0077	
Web: www.mammamaria.com					
Meritage 70 Rowes Wharf	Boston	MA	02110	617-439-3995	
Web: www.meritagetherestaurant.com					
Metropolis Cafe 584 Tremont St	Boston	MA	02118	617-247-2931	
Web: www.metropolisboston.com					
Mistral 223 Columbus Ave	Boston	MA	02116	617-867-9300	351-2601
Web: www.mistralbistro.com					
Montien 63 Stuart St	Boston	MA	02116	617-338-5600	
Web: www.montien-boston.com					
No 9 PARK 9 Pk St	Boston	MA	02108	617-742-9991	
Web: www.no9park.com					
O Ya 9 E St Pl	Boston	MA	02111	617-654-9900	654-9909
Web: o-ya.restaurant					
Oak Room 138 St James Ave	Boston	MA	02116	617-585-7222	
Web: oaklongbarkitchen.com					
Oishii Boston 1166 Washington St	Boston	MA	02118	617-482-8868	482-8869
Web: www.oishiiboston.com					
Palm, The 200 Dartmouth St	Boston	MA	02116	617-867-9292	867-0789
TF: 866-333-7256 ■ *Web:* www.thepalm.com					
Peach Farm 4 Tyler St	Boston	MA	02111	617-482-1116	
Web: peachfarmboston.com					
Prezza 24 Fleet St	Boston	MA	02113	617-227-1577	
Web: www.prezza.com					
Ruby Room 155 Portland St	Boston	MA	02114	617-557-9950	557-0005
Web: www.onyxhotel.com/ruby-room/index.html					
Sakurabana 57 Broad St	Boston	MA	02109	617-542-4311	542-2320
Web: sakurabanaboston.com					
Smith & Wollensky 260 Franklin St Ste 240	Boston	MA	02110	215-545-1700	239-9219*
**Fax Area Code:* 857 ■ *Web:* www.smithandwollensky.com					
Sonsie 327 Newbury St	Boston	MA	02115	617-351-2500	
Web: www.sonsieboston.com					
Strega 379 Hanover St	Boston	MA	02113	617-523-8481	
Web: www.stregaristorante.com					
Tapeo 266 Newbury St	Boston	MA	02116	617-267-4799	
Web: www.tapeo.com					
Taranta 210 Hanover St	Boston	MA	02113	617-720-0052	507-0492
Web: www.tarantarist.com					
Teatro 177 Tremont St	Boston	MA	02111	617-778-6841	
Web: teatroboston.com					
Terramia Ristorante 98 Salem St	Boston	MA	02113	617-523-3112	
Web: www.terramiaristorante.com					
Tresca 233 Hanover St	Boston	MA	02113	617-742-8240	
Web: www.trescanorthend.com					
Troquet 140 Boylston St	Boston	MA	02116	617-695-9463	
Web: troquetboston.com					
Umbria 295 Franklin St	Boston	MA	02110	617-338-1000	
Web: www.umbriaprime.com					
Union Bar & Grille 1357 Washington St	Boston	MA	02118	617-338-5300	
Web: www.unionrestaurant.com					
Wagamama Quincy Market Bldg	Boston	MA	02109	617-742-9242	
Web: www.wagamama.us					
Ardeo 2671 Main St	Brewster	MA	02664	508-760-1500	
Web: www.dineardeo.com					
Bramble Inn 2019 Main St	Brewster	MA	02631	508-896-7644	
Web: www.brambleinn.com					
Chillingsworth 2449 Main St	Brewster	MA	02631	508-896-3640	
Web: www.chillingsworth.com					
Fireplace 1634 Beacon St	Brookline	MA	02446	617-975-1900	
Web: www.fireplacerest.com					
East Coast Grill & Raw Bar					
1271 Cambridge St	Cambridge	MA	02139	617-491-6568	868-4278
Web: www.eastcoastgrill.net					
Elephant Walk 2067 Massachusetts Ave	Cambridge	MA	02140	617-492-6900	
Web: www.elephantwalk.com					
Harvest 44 Brattle St	Cambridge	MA	02138	617-868-2255	
Web: www.harvestcambridge.com					
Helmand Restaurant 143 First St	Cambridge	MA	02142	617-492-4646	
Web: www.helmandrestaurantcambridge.com					
Oleana Restaurant 134 Hampshire St	Cambridge	MA	02139	617-661-0505	
Web: www.oleanarestaurant.com					
Red Pheasant 905 Rte 6A	Dennis	MA	02638	508-385-2133	
Web: www.redpheasantinn.com					
Nauset Beach Club 222 Main St	East Orleans	MA	02653	508-255-8547	
Web: www.nausetbeachclub.com					
Atria 137 Main St PO Box 561	Edgartown	MA	02539	508-627-5850	627-9389
Web: www.atriamv.com					
L'etoile 22 N Water St PO Box 2537	Edgartown	MA	02539	508-627-5187	
Web: www.letoile.net					
Water Street 131 N Water St	Edgartown	MA	02539	508-627-7000	
TF: 800-225-6005 ■ *Web:* www.harbor-view.com					
La Cucina Sul Mare 237 Main St	Falmouth	MA	02540	508-548-5600	
Web: www.lacucinasulmare.com					
Buca's Tuscan Roadhouse 4 Depot Rd	Harwich	MA	02645	508-432-6900	
Web: www.bucasroadhouse.com					
L'Alouette 787 Massachusetts 28	Harwich Port	MA	02646	508-430-0405	
Web: www.lalouettebistro.com					
Delaney House 500 Ehampton Rd	Holyoke	MA	01040	413-532-1800	
Web: logcabin-delaney.com					
Brazilian Grill 680 Main St	Hyannis	MA	02601	508-771-0109	
Web: www.braziliangrill-capecod.com					
Cooke's Seafood 1120 Iyannough Rd	Hyannis	MA	02601	508-775-0450	
Web: www.cookesseafood.com					
Fazio's Trattoria 294 Main St	Hyannis	MA	02601	508-775-9400	
Web: www.fazio.net					
Misaki Sushi 379 W Main St	Hyannis	MA	02601	508-771-3771	
Web: www.misakisushi.com					
Naked Oyster Bistro & Raw Bar 410 Main St	Hyannis	MA	02601	508-778-6500	
Web: www.nakedoyster.com					
Paddock, The 20 Scudder Ave	Hyannis	MA	02601	508-775-7677	771-9517
Sam Diego's 950 Iyanough Rd Rt 132	Hyannis	MA	02601	508-771-8816	771-0174
Web: www.samdiegos.com					
Tiki Port 714 Iyanough Rd	Hyannis	MA	02601	508-771-5220	771-2775
Web: www.tikiport.com					
Company of the Cauldron 5 India St	Nantucket	MA	02554	508-228-4016	
Web: www.companyofthecauldron.com					
Le Languedoc Bistro 24 Broad St	Nantucket	MA	02554	508-228-2552	228-4682
Web: languedocbistro.com					
Straight Wharf 6 Harbor Sq	Nantucket	MA	02554	508-228-4499	
Web: straightwharfrestaurant.com					
Topper's 120 Wauwinet Rd	Nantucket	MA	02584	508-228-8768	
Web: wauwinet.com					
Lumiere 1293 Washington St	Newton	MA	02465	617-244-9199	796-9178
Web: www.lumiererestaurant.com					
Abba 89 Old Colony Way	Orleans	MA	02653	508-255-8144	
Web: www.abbarestaurant.com					
Academy Ocean Grille 2 Academy Pl	Orleans	MA	02653	508-240-1585	
Web: www.academyoceangrille.com					
Captain Linnell House 137 Skaket Beach Rd	Orleans	MA	02653	508-255-3400	
Web: www.linnell.com					
Front Street 230 Commercial St	Provincetown	MA	02657	508-487-9715	
Web: www.frontstreetrestaurant.com					
Mews Restaurant & Cafe					
429 Commercial St	Provincetown	MA	02657	508-487-1500	487-3700
Web: mews.com					
Red Inn 15 Commercial St	Provincetown	MA	02657	508-487-7334	487-5115
TF: 866-473-3466 ■ *Web:* www.theredinn.com					
Ross' Grill					
237-241 Commercial St PO Box 304	Provincetown	MA	02660	508-487-8878	
Web: www.rossgrille.com					
Dali Restaurant 415 Washington St	Somerville	MA	02143	617-661-3254	661-2813
Web: www.dalirestaurant.com					
Riverway Lobster House					
1338 Massachusetts 28	South Yarmouth	MA	02664	508-398-2172	
Web: www.riverwaylobsterhouserestaurant.com					
A Touch of Garlic Restaurant					
427 White St	Springfield	MA	01108	413-736-7868	
Cafe Lebanon 1390 Main St	Springfield	MA	01103	413-737-7373	
Web: www.cafelebanon.com					
Casa De Nana 995 Boston Rd	Springfield	MA	01119	413-783-1549	
Web: www.casadenana.com					
Chef Wayne's Big Mamou 63 Liberty St	Springfield	MA	01103	413-732-1011	
Web: www.chefwaynes-bigmamou.com					
Lido's 555 Worthington St	Springfield	MA	01105	413-736-0887	
Web: www.lidosrestaurant.com					
Max's Tavern 1000 W Columbus Blvd	Springfield	MA	01105	413-746-6299	
Web: www.maxrestaurantgroup.com/tavern					
Pho Saigon 398 Dickinson St	Springfield	MA	01108	413-781-4488	
Web: phosaigonspringfield.com					
Salvatore's 1333 Boston Rd	Springfield	MA	01119	413-782-9968	796-7601
Web: www.salvatoresrestaurant.net					
Student Prince Cafe, The 8 Fort St	Springfield	MA	01103	413-734-7475	739-7303
Web: www.studentprince.com					
Theodore's Booze Blues & BBQ					
201 Worthington St	Springfield	MA	01103	413-736-6000	
Web: theodoresbbq.com					
Typical Sicilian 497 Belmont Ave	Springfield	MA	01108	413-739-7100	
Web: www.typicalsicilian.com					
Il Capriccio 888 Main St	Waltham	MA	02453	781-894-2234	
Web: www.bostonchefs.com					
Blue Ginger 583 Washington St	Wellesley	MA	02482	781-283-5790	
Web: www.ming.com					
Bistro 5 5 Playstead Rd	West Medford	MA	02155	781-395-7464	395-0130
Web: www.bistro5.com					
111 Chop House 111 Shrewsbury St	Worcester	MA	01604	508-799-4111	791-7224
Web: www.111chophouse.com					
Boynton Family Restaurant 117 Highland St	Worcester	MA	01609	508-756-8458	
Web: boyntonrestaurant.com					
Dalat Restaurant 425 Pk Ave	Worcester	MA	01610	508-753-6036	
Dino's 13 Lord St	Worcester	MA	01604	508-753-9978	
Web: www.dineatdinos.com					
El Basha 424 Belmont St	Worcester	MA	01604	508-797-0884	
Web: www.elbasharestaurant.com					
Flying Rhino Cafe 278 Shrewsbury St	Worcester	MA	01604	508-757-1450	754-8102
Web: flyingrhinocafe.com					
Leo's Ristorante 11 Leo Turo Wy	Worcester	MA	01604	508-753-9490	
Web: www.leosristorante.net					
Maxwell Silverman's Toolhouse Lincoln Sq	Worcester	MA	01608	508-755-1200	753-8217
Web: www.maxwellmaxine.com					
Nancy Chang 372 Chandler St	Worcester	MA	01602	508-752-8899	798-6688
Web: www.nancychang.com					
O'Connor's Restaurant & Bar					
1160 W Boylston St	Worcester	MA	01606	508-853-0789	853-2879
Web: www.oconnorsrestaurant.com					

	City	State	Zip	Phone	Fax
Sahara Restaurant 143 Highland St	Worcester	MA	01609	508-798-2181	
Web: eatsahara.com					
Sole Proprietor, The 118 Highland St	Worcester	MA	01609	508-798-3474	753-4889
Web: www.thesole.com					
Viva Bene 144 Commercial St	Worcester	MA	01608	508-799-9999	
Webster House Restaurant 1 Webster St	Worcester	MA	01603	508-757-7208	
Web: websterhouseweb.com					
Colonial House Inn 277 Main St Rt 6A	Yarmouth Port	MA	02675	508-362-4348	362-8034
TF: 800-999-3416 ■ *Web:* www.colonialhousecapecod.com/dine.html					
Inaho 157 Rt 6A	Yarmouth Port	MA	02675	508-362-5522	
Web: www.inahocapecod.com					

Michigan

	City	State	Zip	Phone	Fax
Amadeus 122 E Washington St	Ann Arbor	MI	48104	734-665-8767	
Web: www.amadeusrestaurant.com					
Arbor Brewing Co 114 E Washington St	Ann Arbor	MI	48104	734-213-1393	
Web: www.arborbrewing.com					
Argiero's 300 Detroit St	Ann Arbor	MI	48104	734-665-0444	
Web: argieros.net					
Blue Nile Ethiopian Restaurant - Ann Arbor, The 221 E Washington St	Ann Arbor	MI	48104	734-998-4746	
Web: www.bluenilemi.com					
Chia Shiang 2016 Packard St	Ann Arbor	MI	48104	734-741-0778	
Chop House Ann Arbor, The 322 S Main St	Ann Arbor	MI	48104	734-669-9977	
Web: thechophouseannarbor.com					
Cubs' Ac 1950 S Industrial Hwy	Ann Arbor	MI	48104	734-665-4474	
Web: www.coloniallanescubsac.com					
Earle, The 121 W Washington St	Ann Arbor	MI	48104	734-994-0211	
Web: www.theearle.com					
Gandy Dancer 401 Depot St	Ann Arbor	MI	48104	734-769-0592	769-0415
Web: www.muer.com					
Grizzly Peak Brewing Co 120 W Washington St	Ann Arbor	MI	48104	734-741-7325	
Web: www.grizzlypeak.net					
Knight's Steak House 2324 Dexter Ave	Ann Arbor	MI	48103	734-665-8644	
Web: www.knightsrestaurants.com					
Mediteranno Restaurant 2900 S State St	Ann Arbor	MI	48108	734-332-9700	
Web: mediterrano.com					
Metzger's German Restaurant 305 N Zeeb Rd	Ann Arbor	MI	48103	734-668-8987	
Web: www.metzgers.net					
Miki Japanese Restaurant 106 S First St	Ann Arbor	MI	48104	734-665-8226	
Pacific Rim 114 W Liberty St	Ann Arbor	MI	48104	734-662-9303	
Web: www.pacificrimbykana.com					
Paesano's 3411 Washtenaw Ave	Ann Arbor	MI	48104	734-971-0484	971-0419
Web: www.paesanosannarbor.com					
Prickly Pear Southwest Cafe 328 S Main St	Ann Arbor	MI	48104	734-930-0047	
Web: pricklypearcafe.com					
Raja Rani 400 S Div St	Ann Arbor	MI	48104	734-995-1545	995-5999
Sabor Latino 211 N Main St	Ann Arbor	MI	48104	734-214-7775	
Web: annarborsabor.com					
Shalimar 307 S Main St	Ann Arbor	MI	48104	734-663-1500	929-9129
Web: www.shalimarrestaurant.com					
Tuptim 4896 Washtenaw Ave	Ann Arbor	MI	48108	734-528-5588	528-2569
Web: www.tuptim.com					
Vinology 110 S Main St	Ann Arbor	MI	48104	734-222-9841	
Web: vinologya2.com					
West End Grill, The 120 W Liberty Ave	Ann Arbor	MI	48104	734-747-6260	
Web: westendgrillannarbor.com					
Zingerman's Roadhouse 2501 Jackson Rd	Ann Arbor	MI	48103	734-663-3663	
Web: www.zingermansroadhouse.com					
Andiamo 400 Renaissance Ctr Ste A403	Detroit	MI	48243	313-567-6700	567-6701
Web: www.andiamoitalia.com					
Armando's Mexican Restaurant 4242 W Vernor Hwy	Detroit	MI	48209	313-554-0666	
Web: www.mexicantown.com					
Atlas Global Bistro 3111 Woodward Ave	Detroit	MI	48201	313-831-2241	
Atwater Brewing Co 237 Joseph Campau Ave	Detroit	MI	48207	313-877-9205	
Web: atwaterbeer.com					
Cuisine 670 Lothrop Rd	Detroit	MI	48202	313-872-5110	
Web: www.cuisinerestaurant.com					
DaEdoardo Foxtown Grille 2203 Woodward Ave	Detroit	MI	48201	313-471-3500	471-3499
Web: daedoardo.net					
El Zocalo Mexican Restaurant 3400 Bagley St	Detroit	MI	48216	313-841-3700	
Web: elzocalodetroit.net					
Giovanni's Ristorante 330 S Oakwood Blvd	Detroit	MI	48217	313-841-0122	
Web: www.giovannisristorante.com					
Hard Rock Cafe 45 Monroe St	Detroit	MI	48226	313-964-7625	
TF: 888-519-6683 ■ *Web:* www.hardrock.com					
Hockeytown Cafe 2301 Woodward Ave	Detroit	MI	48201	313-471-3400	
Web: hockeytowncafe.com					
Iridescence 2901 Grand River Ave	Detroit	MI	48201	313-237-6732	
Web: www.motorcitycasino.com					
La Dolce Vita 17546 Woodward	Detroit	MI	48203	313-865-0331	
Web: ldvrestaurant.net					
Louisiana Creole Gumbo Restaurant 2051 Gratiot Ave	Detroit	MI	48207	313-567-1200	
Web: www.detroitgumbo.com					
Mario's 4222 Second Ave	Detroit	MI	48201	313-832-1616	832-1460
Web: www.mariosdetroit.com					
Opus One 565 E Larned St	Detroit	MI	48226	313-961-7766	
Web: www.opus-one.com					
Pegasus Taverna 558 Monroe St	Detroit	MI	48226	313-964-6800	964-0869
Web: pegasustavernas.com					
Roma Cafe 3401 Riopelle St	Detroit	MI	48207	313-831-5940	
Web: www.romacafe.com					
Small Plates 1521 Broadway St	Detroit	MI	48226	313-963-0702	963-0702
Web: www.smallplates.com					
Taqueria Mi Pueblo Mexican Restaurant 7278 Dix St	Detroit	MI	48209	313-841-3315	
Web: www.mipueblorestaurant.com					
Union Street 4145 Woodward Ave	Detroit	MI	48201	313-831-3965	831-2553
Web: www.unionstreetdetroit.com					
Vincente's Cuban Cuisine 1250 Library St	Detroit	MI	48226	313-962-8800	962-0898
Web: www.vicentesdetroit.com					
Whitney, The 4421 Woodward Ave	Detroit	MI	48201	313-832-5700	832-2159
Web: www.thewhitney.com					
Xochimilco Restaurant 3409 Bagley St	Detroit	MI	48216	313-843-0179	
Beggar's Banquet 218 Abbott Rd	East Lansing	MI	48823	517-351-4540	
Web: www.beggarsbanquet.com					
English Inn, The 677 S Michigan Rd	Eaton Rapids	MI	48827	517-663-2500	663-2643
TF: 800-858-0598 ■ *Web:* www.englishinn.com					
Blue Nile 545 W Nine-Mile Rd	Ferndale	MI	48220	248-547-6699	
Web: www.bluenilemi.com					
Badawest Restaurant 4018 Corruna Rd	Flint	MI	48532	810-232-2479	232-3326
Churchill's Food & Spirits 340 S Saginaw St	Flint	MI	48502	810-238-3800	
Web: churchillsflint.com					
Golden Moon 4527 Miller Rd	Flint	MI	48507	810-733-7030	
Web: goldenmoonflint.com					
Latina Restaurant & Pizzeria 1370 W Bristol Rd	Flint	MI	48507	810-767-8491	
Web: latinarestaurant.com					
Luigi's 2132 Davison Rd	Flint	MI	48506	810-234-9545	
Web: luigissince1955.com					
Redwood Steakhouse 5304 Gateway Ctr Dr	Flint	MI	48507	810-233-8000	233-8833
Web: theredwoodlodge.com					
Roma Pizzeria Flint G5227 N Saginaw St	Flint	MI	48505	810-787-1061	
Web: www.romaspizza.com					
Bavarian Inn 713 S Main St	Frankenmuth	MI	48734	989-652-9941	652-3481
Web: www.bavarianinn.com					
Beltline Bar 16 28th St SE	Grand Rapids	MI	49548	616-245-0494	245-3955
Web: beltlinebar.com					
Bistro Bella Vita 44 Grandville Ave SW	Grand Rapids	MI	49503	616-222-4600	222-4601
Web: www.bistrobellavita.com					
Bombay Cuisine 1420 Lake Dr	Grand Rapids	MI	49506	616-456-7055	
Brann's Steakhouse & Grille 401 Leonard St NW	Grand Rapids	MI	49504	616-454-9368	
Web: www.branns.com					
Charley's Crab Restaurant 63 Market St SW	Grand Rapids	MI	49503	616-459-2500	459-8142
Web: www.muer.com					
China Chef 4335 Lake Michigan Dr NW	Grand Rapids	MI	49534	616-791-4488	
Web: chinachef49534.com					
DoubleTree by Hilton Grand Rapids Airport Hotel 4747 28th St SE	Grand Rapids	MI	49512	616-957-0100	977-5632
Web: www.doubletreegrandrapids.com					
Maggie's Kitchen 636 Bridge St NW	Grand Rapids	MI	49504	616-458-8583	
Mikado 3971 28th St SE	Grand Rapids	MI	49512	616-285-7666	
Web: mikadogr.com					
Noto's Old World Italian 6600 28th St SE	Grand Rapids	MI	49546	616-493-6686	
Web: www.notosoldworld.com					
One Trick Pony 136 E Fulton St	Grand Rapids	MI	49503	616-235-7669	
Web: www.onetrick.biz					
San Chez 38 Fulton St W	Grand Rapids	MI	49503	616-774-8272	
Web: www.sanchezbistro.com					
Seoul Garden Restaurant 3321 28th St	Grand Rapids	MI	49512	616-956-1522	956-1801
Starbucks Corporation 187 Monroe Ave NW	Grand Rapids	MI	49503	616-774-2000	
Web: starbucks.com					
Tillman's 1245 Monroe Ave NW	Grand Rapids	MI	49505	616-451-9266	
Web: tillmansrestaurant.com					
Tre Cugini 122 Monroe Ctr NW	Grand Rapids	MI	49503	616-235-9339	235-9449
Web: trecugini.com					
XO Asian Cuisine 58 Monroe Ctr	Grand Rapids	MI	49503	616-235-6969	235-2801
Web: www.xoasiancuisine.com					
Z's Bar & Restaurant 168 Louis Campau	Grand Rapids	MI	49503	616-454-3141	
Web: www.zsbar.com					
Tokyo Grill & Sushi Restaurant 4478 Breton Rd SE	Kentwood	MI	49508	616-455-3433	
Web: tokyogrillsushi.com					
Christie's Bistro 925 S Creyts Rd	Lansing	MI	48917	517-323-4190	323-2180
Web: www.ihg.com					
Clara's 637 E Michigan Ave	Lansing	MI	48912	517-372-7120	
Web: www.claras.com					
Deluca's Restaurant 2006 W Willow St	Lansing	MI	48917	517-487-6087	
Web: www.delucaspizza.com					
Emil's 2012 E Michigan Ave	Lansing	MI	48912	517-482-4430	482-9390
House of Ing 4113 S Cedar St	Lansing	MI	48910	517-393-4848	393-6868
Web: www.houseofing.com					
Knight Cap, The 320 E Michigan Ave	Lansing	MI	48933	517-484-7676	
Web: www.theknightcap.com					
La Senorita 2706 Lk Lansing Rd	Lansing	MI	48912	517-485-0166	
Web: www.lasenorita.com					
Piazzano's Restaurant 1825 N Grand River Ave	Lansing	MI	48906	517-484-9922	
Web: www.piazzanos.com					
Apple Jade 300 N Clippert St	Lansing Charter Township	MI	48912	517-332-1111	
Gracie's Place 151 S Putnam St	Williamston	MI	48895	517-655-1100	
Web: www.graciesplacewilliamston.com					
Bangkok View 1233 28th St SW	Wyoming	MI	49509	616-531-8070	

Minnesota

	City	State	Zip	Phone	Fax
Lindey's Prime Steak House 3600 N Snelling Ave	Arden Hills	MN	55112	651-633-9813	
TF: 866-491-0538 ■ *Web:* www.theplaceforsteak.com					
Timber Lodge Steakhouse 7989 Southtown Ctr	Bloomington	MN	55431	218-722-2624	
Web: www.timberlodgesteakhouse.com					
Timber Lodge Steakhouse 7989 Southtown Dr	Bloomington	MN	55431	952-881-5509	
Web: www.timberlodgesteakhouse.com					

Name / Address	City	State	ZIP	Phone	Fax
Angie's Cantina 11 E Buchanan St *TF:* 800-706-7672 ■ *Web:* www.grandmasrestaurants.com/littleangies	Duluth	MN	55802	218-727-6117	
Bellisio's Italian Restaurant & Wine Bar 405 Lake Ave S *Web:* www.grandmasrestaurants.com	Duluth	MN	55802	218-727-4921	
Chinese Dragon 108 E Superior St	Duluth	MN	55802	218-723-4036	
Fitger's Brewery Complex 600 E Superior St *TF:* 888-348-4377 ■ *Web:* www.fitgers.com	Duluth	MN	55802	218-722-8826	722-8826
Grandma's Saloon & Grill 522 Lake Ave S *TF:* 800-706-7672 ■ *Web:* www.grandmasrestaurants.com/gmas_cp.htm	Duluth	MN	55802	218-727-4192	723-1986
Grandma's Sports Garden Bar & Grill 425 Lake Ave S *Web:* www.grandmasrestaurants.com/sportsgarden/family.htm	Duluth	MN	55802	218-722-4724	720-3804
India Palace 319 W Superior St	Duluth	MN	55802	218-727-8767	
Jade Fountain 305 N Central Ave *Web:* jadefountainduluth.com	Duluth	MN	55807	218-624-3517	
Lake Avenue Cafe 394 S Lake Ave Ste 107A *Web:* www.lakeavenuecafe.com	Duluth	MN	55802	218-722-2355	
New Scenic Cafe 5461 N Shore Dr *Web:* www.sceniccafe.com	Duluth	MN	55804	218-525-6274	
Old Chicago 327 Lake Ave S *Web:* www.oldchicago.com	Duluth	MN	55802	218-720-2966	
Porter's 200 W First St *Web:* hiduluth.com	Duluth	MN	55802	218-727-6746	722-0233
Sir Benedict's Tavern 805 E Superior St *Web:* www.sirbens.com	Duluth	MN	55802	218-728-1192	728-9878
Sneakers Sports Bar & Grill 207 W Superior St	Duluth	MN	55802	218-727-7494	
4 Bells Restaurant 1610 Harmon Pl *Web:* 4bells.com	Minneapolis	MN	55403	612-904-1163	
Alma 528 University Ave SE *Web:* www.restaurantalma.com	Minneapolis	MN	55414	612-379-4909	
Black Forest Inn 1 E 26th St *Web:* www.blackforestinnmpls.com	Minneapolis	MN	55404	612-872-0812	872-0423
Brit's Pub & Eating Establishment 1110 Nicollet Mall *Web:* www.britspub.com	Minneapolis	MN	55403	612-332-3908	332-8032
Broders Southside Pasta Bar 5000 Penn Ave S *Web:* www.broders.com	Minneapolis	MN	55419	612-925-9202	
Cafe Barbette 1600 W Lake St *Web:* www.barbette.com	Minneapolis	MN	55408	612-827-5710	
Cafe Lurcat 1624 Harmon Pl *Web:* www.cafelurcat.com	Minneapolis	MN	55403	612-486-5500	
Cafe Twenty-Eight 2724 W 43rd St	Minneapolis	MN	55410	612-926-2800	926-2804
Cave Vin 5555 Xerxes Ave S *Web:* cave-vin.net	Minneapolis	MN	55410	612-922-0100	
Christo's 2632 Nicollet Ave *Web:* www.christos.com	Minneapolis	MN	55408	612-871-2111	871-8129
Dakota Jazz Club & Restaurant 1010 Nicollet Ave *Web:* www.dakotacooks.com	Minneapolis	MN	55403	612-332-1010	
Erte Restaurant 323 13th Ave NE *Web:* www.ertedining.com	Minneapolis	MN	55413	612-623-4211	
Famous Dave's Bar-B-Que 3001 Hennepin Ave *Web:* www.famousdaves.com	Minneapolis	MN	55408	612-822-9900	
Fuji-Ya 600 W Lake St *Web:* www.fujiyasushi.com	Minneapolis	MN	55408	612-871-4055	
Gardens of Salonica 19 NE Fifth St *Web:* gardensofsalonica.com	Minneapolis	MN	55413	612-378-0611	
Local, The 931 Nicollet Mall *Web:* www.the-local.com	Minneapolis	MN	55402	612-904-1000	904-1005
Lucia's 1432 W 31st St *Web:* www.lucias.com	Minneapolis	MN	55408	612-825-1572	
Mandarin Kitchen 8766 Lyndale Ave S	Minneapolis	MN	55420	952-884-5356	
Manny's Steak House 825 Marquette Ave *Web:* www.mannyssteakhouse.com	Minneapolis	MN	55403	612-339-9900	341-2373
McCormick & Schmick's 800 Nicollet Mall *Web:* www.mccormickandschmicks.com	Minneapolis	MN	55402	612-338-3300	
Melting Pot, The 80 S Ninth St *Web:* www.meltingpot.com	Minneapolis	MN	55402	612-338-9900	312-2855
Mission American Kitchen 77 S Seventh St *Web:* www.missionamerican.com	Minneapolis	MN	55402	612-339-1000	339-8700
Modern Cafe 337 13th Ave NE	Minneapolis	MN	55413	612-378-9882	378-9882
Murray's 26 S Sixth St *Web:* www.murraysrestaurant.com	Minneapolis	MN	55402	612-339-0909	
Nami 251 N First Ave Ste 100	Minneapolis	MN	55401	612-333-1999	333-7449
Nicollet Island Inn 95 Merriam St *Web:* www.nicolletislandinn.com	Minneapolis	MN	55401	612-331-1800	331-6528
Oceanaire Seafood Room, The 50 S Sixth St *Web:* www.theoceanaire.com	Minneapolis	MN	55402	612-333-2277	
Prima 5325 Lyndale Ave S *Web:* primampls.com	Minneapolis	MN	55419	612-827-7376	827-7534
Quang 2719 Nicollet Ave *Web:* www.quangrestaurant.com	Minneapolis	MN	55408	612-870-4739	
Rainbow Chinese 2739 Nicollet Ave S *Web:* www.rainbowrestaurant.com	Minneapolis	MN	55408	612-870-7084	
Rock Bottom Brewery 800 LaSalle Plz *Web:* rockbottom.com	Minneapolis	MN	55402	612-332-2739	
Ruth's Chris Steak House 920 Second Ave S *Web:* www.ruthschris.com	Minneapolis	MN	55402	612-672-9000	
Salsa a la Salsa 1420 Nicollet Ave *Web:* www.salsaalasalsa.com	Minneapolis	MN	55403	612-813-1970	
Sapor Cafe & Bar 428 Washington Ave N *Web:* www.saporcafe.com	Minneapolis	MN	55401	612-375-1971	
Sawatdee 607 Washington Ave S *Web:* www.sawatdee.com	Minneapolis	MN	55415	612-338-6451	338-6498
Solera 900 Hennepin Ave	Minneapolis	MN	55403	612-338-0062	338-8871
Zelo 831 Nicollet Mall *Web:* zelomn.com	Minneapolis	MN	55402	612-333-7000	
Speak Easy 1001 30th Ave S *Web:* speakeasyrestaurant.com	Moorhead	MN	56560	218-233-1326	
Khan's Mongolian Barbecue 500 E 78th St *Web:* www.khansmongolianbarbecue.com	Richfield	MN	55423	612-861-7991	
Canadian Honker 1203 Second St SW *Web:* canadianhonker.com	Rochester	MN	55902	507-282-6572	
Fiesta Cafe Bar 1645 N Broadway *Web:* fiestacafeandbar.com	Rochester	MN	55906	507-288-1116	
India Garden 1107 N Broadway *Web:* indiagardenrestaurantmn.com	Rochester	MN	55906	507-288-6280	
Jenpachi Japanese Steak House 3160 Wellner NE *Web:* jenpachisteakhouse.com	Rochester	MN	55906	507-292-1688	
Kahler Grand Hotel, The 20 2nd Ave Sw Ste G13 *Web:* www.kahler.com	Rochester	MN	55902	507-280-6200	
Redwood Room 300 First Ave NW	Rochester	MN	55901	507-281-2978	
Roscoe's Root Beer & Ribs 603 Fourth St SE *Web:* roscoesbbq.com	Rochester	MN	55904	507-285-0501	
Sky Dragon Buffet 34 17th Ave NW	Rochester	MN	55901	507-281-1813	
Victoria's 7 First Ave NW *Web:* www.victoriasmn.com	Rochester	MN	55902	507-280-6232	280-6288
128 Cafe 128 Cleveland Ave N *Web:* the128cafe.com	Saint Paul	MN	55104	651-645-4128	
Beirut Restaurant 1385 Robert St S *Web:* www.beirutrestaurantanddeli.com	Saint Paul	MN	55118	651-457-4886	
Everest on Grand 1278 Grand Ave *Web:* www.everestongrand.com	Saint Paul	MN	55105	651-696-1666	
Forepaugh's 276 S Exchange St *Web:* www.forepaughs.com	Saint Paul	MN	55102	651-224-5606	
Fuji-Ya 465 N Wabasha St *Web:* www.fujiyasushi.com	Saint Paul	MN	55102	612-871-4055	
Green Mill Restaurant & Bar 1342 Grand Ave *Web:* www.greenmill.com	Saint Paul	MN	55105	651-203-3100	203-3101
Heartland 289 E Fifth St *Web:* www.heartlandrestaurant.com	Saint Paul	MN	55101	651-699-3536	
La Grolla 452 Selby Ave *Web:* lagrollastpaul.com	Saint Paul	MN	55102	651-221-1061	
Lexington, The 1096 Grand Ave *Web:* www.snapagency.com	Saint Paul	MN	55105	651-222-5878	
Luci Ancora 2060 Randolph Ave *Web:* luciancora.com	Saint Paul	MN	55105	651-698-6889	
Mai Village 394 University Ave *Web:* maivillage.net	Saint Paul	MN	55103	651-290-2585	
Mancini's Char House 531 Seventh St W *Web:* www.mancinis.com	Saint Paul	MN	55102	651-224-7345	
Moscow on the Hill 371 Selby Ave *Web:* www.moscowonthehill.com	Saint Paul	MN	55102	651-291-1236	
Muffuletta Cafe 2260 Como Ave *Web:* www.muffuletta.com	Saint Paul	MN	55108	651-644-9116	644-5329
Pad Thai Restaurant 1681 Grand Ave *Web:* padthaiongrand.com	Saint Paul	MN	55105	651-690-1393	
Pazzaluna 360 St Peter St *Web:* pazzaluna.com	Saint Paul	MN	55102	651-223-7000	227-1296
Peking Garden 1488 University Ave *Web:* www.pekinggardenmn.com	Saint Paul	MN	55104	651-644-0888	644-1738
Saji-Ya 695 Grand Ave *Web:* www.sajiya.com	Saint Paul	MN	55105	651-292-0444	
Sakura Japanese Restaurant 350 St Peter St *Web:* www.sakurastpaul.com	Saint Paul	MN	55102	651-224-0185	
St. Paul Grill, The 350 Market St *Web:* www.stpaulgrill.com	Saint Paul	MN	55102	651-224-7455	
Tavern on Grand 656 Grand Ave *Web:* www.tavernongrand.com	Saint Paul	MN	55105	651-228-9030	
Wild Onion 788 Grand Ave *Web:* www.wild-onion.net	Saint Paul	MN	55105	651-291-2525	

Mississippi

Name / Address	City	State	ZIP	Phone	Fax
Jazzeppi's 195 B Porter Ave	Biloxi	MS	39530	228-374-9660	374-9692
Mary Mahoney's 110 Rue Magnolia *Web:* www.marymahoneys.com	Biloxi	MS	39530	228-374-0163	
Mr Greek 1670 H Pass Rd	Biloxi	MS	39531	228-432-7888	432-8379
Eat With Us PO Box 1368 *TF:* 888-222-9550 ■ *Web:* eatwithusrestaurants.com	Columbus	MS	39703	662-327-6982	327-1672
Blow Fly Inn 1201 Washington Ave *Web:* blow-fly-inn.com	Gulfport	MS	39507	228-896-9812	
El Mexicano Inn 1215 30th Ave	Gulfport	MS	39501	228-863-3691	
Lil Ray's 500A Courthouse Rd *Web:* lilraysrestaurant.com	Gulfport	MS	39507	228-896-9601	
South China 548 Courthouse Rd	Gulfport	MS	39507	228-896-9832	
Bianchis Pizzeria 128 E Front St *Web:* www.bianchispizzeria.com	Hattiesburg	MS	39401	601-450-1263	
Donanelle's Bar & Grill 4321 U S Hwy 49 *Web:* www.donanelles.com	Hattiesburg	MS	39401	601-545-3860	
Front Porch Barbecue & Seafood 205 Thornhill Dr	Hattiesburg	MS	39401	601-264-3536	
La Fiesta Brava 6168 Hwy 49 N	Hattiesburg	MS	39401	601-584-9484	
Leatha's Bar-B-Que Inn 6374 US Hwy 98	Hattiesburg	MS	39402	601-271-6003	
Purple Parrot Cafe 3810 Hardy St *Web:* www.nsrg.com	Hattiesburg	MS	39402	601-264-0657	
Rayner's Seafood House 7343 Hwy 49	Hattiesburg	MS	39401	601-268-2639	
Sakura 6194 Hwy 49 *Web:* facebook.com	Hattiesburg	MS	39401	601-545-9393	
Walnut Cir Grill 115 Walnut St *Web:* www.walnutcirclegrill.com	Hattiesburg	MS	39401	601-544-2202	
Bonsai Japanese Steak House 1925 Lakeland Dr *Web:* facebook.com	Jackson	MS	39216	601-981-0606	

Name / Address	City	State	Zip	Phone	Fax
Bravo I-55 N Exit 100 *Web:* www.bravobuzz.com	Jackson	MS	39211	601-982-8111	362-2990
Elite Restaurant 141 E Capitol St	Jackson	MS	39201	601-352-5606	
Hal & Mal's 200 S Commerce St *Web:* www.halandmals.com	Jackson	MS	39204	601-948-0888	
Keifer's 710 Poplar Blvd.	Jackson	MS	39202	601-355-6825	355-0380
La Cazuela Mexican Grill 1401 E Ftification St *Web:* lacazuela.com	Jackson	MS	39202	601-353-3014	
Que Sera Sera 2801 N State St *Web:* queserams.com	Jackson	MS	39216	601-981-2520	981-2522
Sakura Bana 4800 I-55 N	Jackson	MS	39211	601-982-3035	982-3075
Thai House Restaurant 1405 Old Sq Rd	Jackson	MS	39211	601-982-9991	
Cancun Mexican Restaurant 201 N Gloster St *Web:* cancunmexicantupelo.com	Tupelo	MS	38804	662-842-9557	
China Capital 530 N Gloster St	Tupelo	MS	38804	662-841-0484	
Las Margaritas 123 S Industrial Rd.	Tupelo	MS	38801	662-844-7399	
Tellini's 504 S Gloster St *Web:* www.tellinis.com	Tupelo	MS	38801	662-620-9955	
Vanelli's 1302 N Gloster St *Web:* vanellis.com	Tupelo	MS	38802	662-844-4410	
Woody's 619 N Gloster St *Web:* woodyssteak.com	Tupelo	MS	38804	662-840-0460	

Missouri

Name / Address	City	State	Zip	Phone	Fax
Baldknobbers Restaurant 2845 W 76 Country Blvd *Web:* www.baldknobbers.com	Branson	MO	65616	417-334-7202	
Branson Cafe 120 W Main St *Web:* downtownbransoncafe.com	Branson	MO	65616	417-334-3021	
BT Bones 2280 Shepherd Hill Expy	Branson	MO	65616	417-335-2002	335-2109
Buckingham's Restaurant & Oasis 2820 W Hwy 76 *TF:* 800-725-2236 ■ *Web:* clarionhotelbranson.com	Branson	MO	65616	417-337-7777	
Casa Fuentes 1107 W Hwy 76 *Web:* www.casafuentes.com	Branson	MO	65616	417-339-3888	
Charlie's Steak-Ribs-Ale 3009 W State Hwy 76	Branson	MO	65616	417-334-6090	336-4038
Chateau Grille 415 N State Hwy 265 *TF:* 888-333-5253 ■ *Web:* www.chateauonthelake.com	Branson	MO	65616	417-334-1161	339-5566
Farmhouse Restaurant 119 W Main St *Web:* farmhouserestaurantbranson.com	Branson	MO	65616	417-334-9701	
Landry's Seafood House 2900 W Missouri Hwy 76 *Web:* www.landrysseafood.com	Branson	MO	65616	417-339-1010	
Plaza View 245 N Wildwood Dr *TF:* 800-850-6646 ■ *Web:* bransongrandplaza.com	Branson	MO	65616	417-335-2798	
Rocky's Italian Restaurant 120 N Sycamore St	Branson	MO	65616	417-335-4765	
Whipper Snapper's 2421 W Hwy 76 *Web:* www.bransonsbestrestaurant.com	Branson	MO	65616	417-334-3282	
Spiro's 1054 N Woods Mill Rd *Web:* www.spiros-restaurant.com	Chesterfield	MO	63017	314-878-4449	878-1090
Cardwell's 8100 Maryland Ave *Web:* www.cardwellsinclayton.com	Clayton	MO	63105	314-726-5055	
Addison's An American Grill 709 Cherry St *Web:* www.addisonsgrill.com	Columbia	MO	65201	573-256-1995	
Angelo's 4107 S Providence Rd *Web:* angelospizzaandsteak.com	Columbia	MO	65203	573-443-6100	
Bangkok Gardens 811 Cherry St *Web:* www.bangkokgardens.com	Columbia	MO	65201	573-874-3284	
CJ's in Tiger Country 704 E Broadway *Web:* www.cjsintigercountry.com	Columbia	MO	65201	573-442-7777	
Ernie's Cafe 1005 E Walnut St *Web:* erniescolumbia.com	Columbia	MO	65201	573-874-7804	
Flat Branch Pub & Brewing Co 115 S Fifth St *Web:* www.flatbranch.com	Columbia	MO	65201	573-499-0400	
Formosa Restaurant 913 E Broadway *Web:* www.formosatogo.com	Columbia	MO	65201	573-449-3339	
Italian Village Pizza 711 Vandiver Dr Ste B *Web:* theitalianvillagepizza.com	Columbia	MO	65202	573-442-8821	442-3571
Jack's Gourmet Restaurant 1903 Business Loop 70 E *Web:* www.jacksgourmetrestaurant.com	Columbia	MO	65201	573-449-3927	442-9881
Jimmy's Family Steak House 3101 S Providence Rd	Columbia	MO	65203	573-443-1796	
Murry's 3107 Green Meadows Way *Web:* murrysrestaurant.net	Columbia	MO	65203	573-442-4969	
Wine Cellar & Bistro 505 Cherry St *Web:* www.winecellarbistro.com	Columbia	MO	65201	573-442-7281	
54th Street Grill 18700 E 38th Terr *Web:* www.54thstreetgrill.com	Independence	MO	64057	816-795-7077	
El Maguey 3738 S Noland Rd	Independence	MO	64055	816-252-6868	
Englewood Cafe 10904 E Winner Rd	Independence	MO	64052	816-461-9588	
Gates Bar-B-Q 10440 E Us Hwy 40 *Web:* www.gatesbbq.com	Independence	MO	64055	816-353-5880	
Rheinland Restaurant 208 N Main St *Web:* www.rheinlandrestaurant.com	Independence	MO	64050	816-461-5383	
V's Italiano Ristorante 10819 E US Hwy 40 *Web:* www.vsrestaurant.com	Independence	MO	64055	816-353-1241	353-0004
Zio's Italian Kitchen 3901 S Bolger Dr *Web:* www.zios.com	Independence	MO	64055	816-350-1011	350-1211
Alexandro's 2125 Missouri Blvd *Web:* alexandrosandtgs.com	Jefferson City	MO	65109	573-634-7740	
Cajun Catfish House 6819 US Business 50 *Web:* www.cajuncatfishhouse.net	Jefferson City	MO	65109	573-893-4665	
Capitol Plaza Hotel 415 W McCarty St *TF:* 800-338-8088 ■ *Web:* capitolplazajeffersoncity.com	Jefferson City	MO	65101	573-635-1234	635-4565
Das Stein Haus 1436 Southridge Dr *Web:* www.dassteinhaus.com	Jefferson City	MO	65109	573-634-3869	
Hunan Restaurant 1416 Missouri Blvd. *Web:* hunan-restaurant.com	Jefferson City	MO	65109	573-634-5253	
Madison's Cafe 216 Madison St *Web:* www.madisonscafe.com	Jefferson City	MO	65101	573-634-2988	
Yen Ching Restaurant 2208 Missouri Blvd	Jefferson City	MO	65109	573-635-5225	
Arthur Bryant's Barbeque 1727 Brooklyn Ave *Web:* arthurbryantsbbq.com	Kansas City	MO	64127	816-231-1123	
Blue Bird Bistro 1700 Summit St *Web:* bluebirdbistro.com	Kansas City	MO	64108	816-221-7559	
Bluestem 900 Westport Rd *Web:* kansascitymenus.com/goodbye.html	Kansas City	MO	64111	816-561-1101	
Bo Ling's 4701 Jefferson St *Web:* www.bolings.com	Kansas City	MO	64112	816-753-1718	
Cafe Al Dente 412D Delaware *Web:* cafealdentekc.com	Kansas City	MO	64105	816-472-9444	
Californos 4124 Pennsylvania Ave *Web:* www.californos.com	Kansas City	MO	64111	816-531-7878	
Cascone's 3737 N Oak Trafficway *Web:* www.cascones.com	Kansas City	MO	64116	816-454-7977	
Cupini's Fresh Pasta & Panini 1809 Westport Rd *Web:* www.cupinis.com	Kansas City	MO	64111	816-753-7662	753-7564
EBT Restaurant 1310 Carondelet Dr *Web:* www.ebtrestaurant.com	Kansas City	MO	64114	816-942-8870	
Europa! 323 E 55th St *Web:* cafeeuropakc.com	Kansas City	MO	64113	816-523-1212	
Fiorella's Jack Stack Barbecue 13441 Holmes Rd *Web:* www.jackstackbbq.com	Kansas City	MO	64145	816-942-9141	
Garozzo's 526 Harrison St *Web:* www.garozzos.com	Kansas City	MO	64106	816-221-2455	
Grand Street Cafe 4740 Grand Ave *Web:* grandstreetkc.com	Kansas City	MO	64112	816-561-8000	
Grinders 417 E 18th St *Web:* grinderspizza.com	Kansas City	MO	64108	816-472-5454	
Houston's 4640 Wornall Rd *Web:* hillstone.com	Kansas City	MO	64112	816-561-8542	
Jasper's 1201 W 103rd St *Web:* www.jasperskc.com	Kansas City	MO	64114	816-941-6600	
Jess & Jim's Steakhouse 517 E 135th St *Web:* www.jessandjims.com	Kansas City	MO	64145	816-941-9499	
KatoSushi 6340 NW Barry Rd *Web:* www.katosushi.com	Kansas City	MO	64154	816-584-8883	
La Bodega 703 SW Blvd *Web:* labodegakc.com	Kansas City	MO	64108	816-472-8272	
Le Fou Frog 400 E Fifth St *Web:* www.lefoufrog.com	Kansas City	MO	64106	816-474-6060	
Lidia's Kansas City 101 W 22nd St *Web:* www.lidias-kc.com	Kansas City	MO	64108	816-221-3722	
Majestic Steakhouse 931 Broadway *Web:* www.majestickc.com	Kansas City	MO	64105	816-221-1888	
Malay Cafe 6003 NW Barry Rd	Kansas City	MO	64154	816-741-3616	
McCormick & Schmick's 448 W 47th St *Web:* www.mccormickandschmicks.com	Kansas City	MO	64112	816-531-6800	
New Peking 540 Westport Rd *Web:* newpekingkansas.com	Kansas City	MO	64111	816-531-6969	531-9188
Osteria Il Centro 5101 Main St *Web:* osteriailcentro.com	Kansas City	MO	64112	816-561-2369	
Peach Tree 6800 Eastwood TFWY *Web:* www.peachtreerestaurants.com	Kansas City	MO	64129	816-923-0099	
Pierpont's at Union Station 30 W Pershing Rd Union Station *Web:* www.herefordhouse.com	Kansas City	MO	64108	816-221-5111	
PotPie 904 Westport Rd *Web:* www.kcpotpie.com	Kansas City	MO	64111	816-561-2702	
Red Snapper 8430 Ward Pkwy *Web:* www.kcredsnapper.com	Kansas City	MO	64114	816-333-8899	
Smokin' Guns BBQ 1218 Swift Ave *Web:* www.smokingunsbbq.com	Kansas City	MO	64116	816-221-2535	221-2606
Streetcar Named Desire 2450 Grand Ave	Kansas City	MO	64108	816-472-5959	
Taj Mahal 7521 Wornall Rd *Web:* www.kctajmahal.com	Kansas City	MO	64114	816-361-1722	361-1654
Thai Place 4130 Pennsylvania Ave *Web:* www.kcthaiplace.com	Kansas City	MO	64111	816-753-8424	
Thomas Restaurant 1815 W 39th St *Web:* www.thomaskc.com	Kansas City	MO	64111	816-561-3663	
Blue Owl Restaurant, The 6116 Second St *Web:* www.theblueowl.com	Kimmswick	MO	63053	636-464-3128	
Chappell's Restaurant & Sports Museum 323 Armour Rd *Web:* chappellsrestaurant.com	North Kansas City	MO	64116	816-421-0002	
Al's Restaurant 1200 N First St *Web:* www.alsrestaurant.net	Saint Louis	MO	63102	314-421-6399	
Bandana's Bar-B-Q 11750 Gravois Rd *Web:* www.bandanasbbq.com	Saint Louis	MO	63127	314-849-1162	
Bar Italian Ristorante-Caffe 13 Maryland Plz *Web:* www.baritaliastl.com	Saint Louis	MO	63108	314-361-7010	
Broadway Oyster Bar 736 S Broadway *Web:* www.broadwayoysterbar.com	Saint Louis	MO	63102	314-621-8811	621-1995
Carmine's Steak House 20 S Fourth St *Web:* www.lombardosrestaurants.com	Saint Louis	MO	63102	314-241-1631	
Clark Street Grill 811 Spruce St *Web:* www.clarkstreetgrill.com	Saint Louis	MO	63102	314-552-5850	
Cunetto House of Pasta 5453 Magnolia Ave *Web:* www.cunetto.com	Saint Louis	MO	63139	314-781-1135	
Giovanni's 5201 Shaw Ave *Web:* www.giovannisonthehill.com	Saint Louis	MO	63110	314-772-5958	
Giuseppe's 4141 S Grand Blvd *Web:* www.giuseppesongrand.com	Saint Louis	MO	63118	314-832-3779	832-7598

Name	City	State	ZIP	Phone	Fax
House of India 8501 Delmar Blvd	Saint Louis	MO	63124	314-567-6850	
Web: www.hoistl.com					
I Love Mr Sushi 9443 Olive Blvd	Saint Louis	MO	63132	314-432-8898	
Web: mrsushistl.com					
Kemoll's 211 N Broadway	Saint Louis	MO	63102	314-421-0555	
Web: www.kemolls.com					
King & I 3157 S Grand Ave	Saint Louis	MO	63118	314-771-1777	
Web: kingandistl.squarespace.com					
Kreis' Restaurant 535 S Lindbergh Blvd	Saint Louis	MO	63131	314-993-0735	993-3020
Web: www.kreissteakhouse.com					
Lorenzo's Trattoria 1933 Edwards St	Saint Louis	MO	63110	314-773-2223	
Web: www.lorenzostrattoria.com					
LoRusso's Cucina 3121 Watson Rd	Saint Louis	MO	63139	314-647-6222	
Web: www.lorussos.com					
Mike Shannon's 620 Market St	Saint Louis	MO	63101	314-421-1540	
Web: www.shannonsteak.com					
Modesto 5257 Shaw Ave	Saint Louis	MO	63110	314-772-8272	
Web: www.saucecafe.com/modesto					
Nobu's 8643 Olive Blvd	Saint Louis	MO	63132	314-997-2303	
Web: www.nobusushistl.com					
Pho Grand 3195 S Grand Blvd	Saint Louis	MO	63118	314-664-7435	
Web: www.phogrand.com					
Sam's Steakhouse 10205 Gravois Rd	Saint Louis	MO	63123	314-849-3033	
Web: www.samssteakhouse.com					
Sidney Street Cafe 2000 Sidney St	Saint Louis	MO	63104	314-771-5777	771-7016
Web: www.sidneystreetcafestl.com					
Soulard's Restaurant 1731 S Seventh St	Saint Louis	MO	63104	314-241-7956	241-7956
Web: www.soulards.com					
SqWire's 1415 S 18th St	Saint Louis	MO	63104	314-865-3522	
Web: www.sqwires.com					
Tenderloin Room 232 N KingsHwy Blvd	Saint Louis	MO	63108	314-361-0900	
Web: www.tenderloinroom.com					
Trattoria Marcella 3600 Watson Rd	Saint Louis	MO	63109	314-352-7706	
Web: trattoriamarcella.com					
Tucker's Place					
Historic Soulard 2117 S 12th St	Saint Louis	MO	63104	314-772-5977	
Web: www.tuckersplacestl.com					
Vin de Set Rooftop Bar & Bistro					
2017 Chouteau Ave	Saint Louis	MO	63103	314-241-8989	
Web: www.1111-m.com					
Yemanja Brasil					
2900 Missouri Ave Pestalozzi St	Saint Louis	MO	63118	314-771-7457	771-0296
Web: www.yemanjabrasil.com					
Zia's 5256 Wilson Ave	Saint Louis	MO	63110	314-776-0020	
Web: www.zias.com					
Dominic's 5101 Wilson Ave	South Saint Louis	MO	63110	314-771-1632	
Web: www.dominicsrestaurant.com					
Bangkok City 1129 E Walnut St	Springfield	MO	65806	417-799-1221	
Web: wordpress.com					
Buckingham's BBQ 2002 S Campbell Ave	Springfield	MO	65807	417-886-9979	
Web: buckinghambbq.com					
China Star 1444 E Republic Rd	Springfield	MO	65804	417-887-9779	
Cielito Lindo Mexicano					
2953 S National Ave	Springfield	MO	65804	417-886-3320	
Gem of India 211 W Battlefield St	Springfield	MO	65807	417-881-9558	
Web: gemofindia.net					
Gilardi's 820 E Walnut St	Springfield	MO	65806	417-862-6400	
Web: www.gilardis.com					
Hemingway's Blue Water Cafe					
1935 S Campbell	Springfield	MO	65898	417-891-5100	887-5204
Web: restaurants.basspro.com					
Lucy's Chinese Food 3330 S Campbell	Springfield	MO	65807	417-882-5383	
Web: www.lucyschinesefood.com					
Metropolitan Grill 2931 E Battlefield	Springfield	MO	65804	417-889-4951	
Web: metropolitan-grill.com					
Nonna's Italian American Cafe 306 S Ave	Springfield	MO	65806	417-831-1222	
Web: nonnascafe.com					
Pappy's Place 943 N Main Ave	Springfield	MO	65802	417-866-8744	
Shanghai Inn 1937 N Glenstone Ave	Springfield	MO	65803	417-865-5111	
Springfield Brewing Co 305 S Market Ave	Springfield	MO	65806	417-832-8277	
Web: www.springfieldbrewingco.com					

Montana

Name	City	State	ZIP	Phone	Fax
Bistro Enzo 1502 Rehberg Ln	Billings	MT	59102	406-651-0999	
Web: bistroenzobillings.com					
Don Luis 15 N 26th St	Billings	MT	59101	406-256-3355	256-3359
Guadalajara Family Mexican 17 N 29th St	Billings	MT	59101	406-259-8930	259-8950
Jake's 2701 First Ave N	Billings	MT	59101	406-259-9375	
Web: jakesbillings.com					
Juliano's 2912 Seventh Ave N	Billings	MT	59101	406-248-6400	
Web: wordpress.com					
Montana Brewing Co 113 N 28th St	Billings	MT	59101	406-252-9200	
Web: www.montanabrewingcompany.com					
Rex, The 2401 Montana Ave	Billings	MT	59101	406-245-7477	
3-D International 1825 Smelter Ave	Black Eagle	MT	59414	406-453-6561	
Web: 3dinternationalrest.com					
Borrie's 1800 Smelter Ave	Black Eagle	MT	59414	406-761-0300	761-2021
Cattlemen's Cut Supper Club					
369 Vaughn Frontage Rd S	Great Falls	MT	59404	406-452-0702	
Web: cattlemenscut.com					
Dante's Creative Cuisine					
1325 Eigth Ave N	Great Falls	MT	59401	406-453-9599	453-9599
El Comedor 1120 25th St S	Great Falls	MT	59405	406-761-5500	761-5502
Maple Garden 5401 Ninth Ave S	Great Falls	MT	59405	406-727-0310	
Prime Cut Restaurant 3219 Tenth Ave S	Great Falls	MT	59405	406-727-2141	
Bert & Ernie's Saloon 361 N Last Chance Gulch	Helena	MT	59601	406-443-5680	
Web: www.bertanderniesofhelena.com					
Brewhouse Brew Pub & Grill 939 Getchell St	Helena	MT	59601	406-457-9390	457-9296
Web: atthebrewhouse.com					
Jade Garden Helena 3128 N Montana Ave	Helena	MT	59602	406-443-8899	443-8390
Web: jadegardenhelena.com					
Jorgenson's 1720 11th Ave	Helena	MT	59601	406-442-6380	
Web: www.jorgensons.com					
Mediterranean Grill 42 S Pk Ave	Helena	MT	59601	406-495-1212	
Web: www.mediterraneangrillhelena.com					
Miller's Crossing 52 S Pk Ave	Helena	MT	59601	406-442-3290	
Web: www.millerscrossing.biz					
Montana Club 24 W Sixth Ave	Helena	MT	59601	406-442-5980	
Web: www.mtclub.org					
On Broadway 106 Broadway	Helena	MT	59601	406-443-1929	
Web: onbroadwayinhelena.com					
Windbag Saloon & Grill 19 S Last Chance Gulch	Helena	MT	59601	406-443-9669	
Marysville House 153 Main St	Marysville	MT	59640	406-443-6677	
Jade Palace 1659 Rte 9	Wappingers Falls	MT	59102	406-656-8888	
Web: places.singleplatform.com					

Nebraska

Name	City	State	ZIP	Phone	Fax
Billy's 1301 H St	Lincoln	NE	68508	402-474-0084	
Web: www.billysrestaurant.com					
Doozy's 101 N 14th St Ste 3	Lincoln	NE	68508	402-438-1616	
Web: www.downtowndoozys.com					
El Toro 2600 S 48th St	Lincoln	NE	68506	402-488-3939	
Web: facebook.com					
Green Gateau 330 S Tenth St	Lincoln	NE	68508	402-477-0330	
Web: www.greengateau.com					
Imperial Palace 701 N 27th St	Lincoln	NE	68503	402-474-2688	
Web: imperialpalacene.net					
La Paz					
La PazMexican Restaurant 321 N Cotner Blvd	Lincoln	NE	68505	402-466-9111	
Web: www.getintolapaz.com					
Lazlo's Brewery & Grill 210 N Seventh St	Lincoln	NE	68508	402-434-5636	434-3291
Web: lazlosbreweryandgrill.com					
Mazatlan 211 N 70th St	Lincoln	NE	68505	402-464-7201	464-7527
Misty's Steakhouse & Brewery 200 N 11th St	Lincoln	NE	68508	402-476-7766	
Web: www.mistyslincoln.com					
Oven, The 201 N Eigth St	Lincoln	NE	68508	402-475-6118	
Web: www.theoven-lincoln.com					
Parthenon 56th & Hwy 2	Lincoln	NE	68516	402-423-2222	
Web: www.theparthenon.net					
Sher-E-Punjab 1601 Q St	Lincoln	NE	68508	402-477-3090	
Web: sherepunjablincoln.com					
Shogun 3700 S Ninth St	Lincoln	NE	68502	402-421-7100	
Tandoor 3530 Village Dr	Lincoln	NE	68516	402-423-2007	
Web: www.tandoorindiancuisinelincoln.com					
Tico's 317 S 17th St	Lincoln	NE	68508	402-475-1048	
Web: www.ticosoflincoln.com					
Ahmad's Persian 1006 Howard St	Omaha	NE	68102	402-341-9616	
Anthony's 7220 F St	Omaha	NE	68127	402-331-7575	
Web: www.anthonyssteakhouse.com					
Bangkok Cuisine 1905 Farnam St	Omaha	NE	68102	402-346-5874	
Biaggi's Ristorante Italiano					
13655 California St	Omaha	NE	68154	402-965-9800	
Web: biaggis.com					
Bohemian Cafe 1406 S 13th St	Omaha	NE	68108	402-342-9838	
Web: www.bohemiancafe.net					
Brother Sebastian's Steak House					
1350 S 119th St	Omaha	NE	68144	402-330-0300	330-4814
Web: www.brothersebastians.com					
Caniglia's Venice Inn 6920 Pacific St	Omaha	NE	68106	402-556-3111	
Web: canigliasveniceinn.com					
Cascio's Steak House 1620 S Tenth St	Omaha	NE	68108	402-345-8313	
Web: www.casciossteakhouse.com					
Charlie's on the Lake 4150 S 144th St	Omaha	NE	68137	402-894-9411	
Web: www.charliesonthelake.net					
Fleming's Prime Steakhouse & Wine Bar					
140 Regency Pkwy	Omaha	NE	68114	402-393-0811	
Web: www.flemingssteakhouse.com					
Gorat's Steakhouse 4917 Ctr St	Omaha	NE	68106	402-551-3733	
Web: www.goratsomaha.com					
Greek Islands 3821 Ctr St	Omaha	NE	68105	402-346-1528	345-7428
Web: greekislandsomaha.com					
HIRO 88 Restaurants 3655 N 129th St	Omaha	NE	68164	402-933-0091	
Web: www.hiro88.com					
Indian Oven 1010 Howard St	Omaha	NE	68102	402-342-4856	
Web: findmeglutenfree.com					
Jack & Mary's Restaurant 655 N 114th St	Omaha	NE	68154	402-496-2090	
Web: www.jackandmarysrestaurant.com					
Jaipur, The 10922 Elm St	Omaha	NE	68144	402-392-7331	
Web: jaipurindianfood.com					
Jazz A Louisiana Kitchen 1421 Farnam St	Omaha	NE	68102	402-342-3662	
Web: www.jazzkitchens.com					
Jim & Jennie's Greek Village 3026 N 90th St	Omaha	NE	68134	402-571-2857	
Web: jimandjennies.com					
Johnny's Cafe 4702 S 27th St	Omaha	NE	68107	402-731-4774	
Web: www.johnnyscafe.com					
Lo Sole Mio 3001 S 32nd Ave	Omaha	NE	68105	402-345-5656	
Web: www.losolemio.com					
McFoster's Natural Kind Cafe 302 S 38th St	Omaha	NE	68131	402-345-7477	
Web: mcfosters.com					
Mediterranean Bistro 1712 N 120th St	Omaha	NE	68154	402-493-3080	
Web: www.medbistro.com					
Taste of Thailand 15712 W Ctr Rd	Omaha	NE	68130	402-691-9991	
Web: www.totomaha.com					
Thai Spice 2933 N 108th St	Omaha	NE	68164	402-492-8808	
Web: www.thaispice.com					
Upstream Brewing Co 514 S 11th St	Omaha	NE	68102	402-344-0200	344-0451
Web: www.upstreambrewing.com					

Nevada

	City	State	Zip	Phone	Fax
Adele's 1112 N Carson St *Web:* www.adelesrestaurantandlounge.com	Carson City	NV	89701	775-882-3353	
China East 1810 Hwy 50 E	Carson City	NV	89701	775-885-6996	
Garibaldi's 307 N Carson St *Web:* garibaldisristoranteitaliano.com	Carson City	NV	89701	775-884-4574	
Glen Eagles 3700 N Carson St *Web:* www.gleneaglesrestaurant.com	Carson City	NV	89706	775-884-4414	
Grandma Hattie's 2811 S Carson St	Carson City	NV	89701	775-882-4900	
Heidi's 1020 N Carson St **Fax Area Code:* 775 ■ *Web:* heidislaketahoe.com	Carson City	NV	89701	530-544-8113	884-2091*
Ming's 2330 S Carson St *Web:* officialmobilesite.com	Carson City	NV	89701	775-887-8878	
Panda Kitchen 1986 Hwy 50 E *Web:* pandakitchencarsoncity.com	Carson City	NV	89701	775-882-8128	
Playa Azul 415 E William St	Carson City	NV	89701	775-883-2244	
Red's Old 395 Grill 1055 S Carson St *Web:* reds395.com	Carson City	NV	89701	775-887-0395	
Taqueria Uruaban 4601 Goni Rd	Carson City	NV	89706	775-883-7609	
Thurman's Ranch House 2943 Hwy 50 E	Carson City	NV	89701	775-883-1773	
Tito's 444 E William St	Carson City	NV	89701	775-885-0309	
Andre's 401 S Sixth St *Web:* andrelv.com	Las Vegas	NV	89101	702-385-5016	385-1742
Archi's Thai Kitchen 6360 W Flamingo Rd *Web:* archithai.com	Las Vegas	NV	89103	702-880-5550	
Aureole 3950 Las Vegas Blvd S *Web:* www.charliepalmer.com	Las Vegas	NV	89119	702-632-7401	
Bartolotta Ristorante diMare 3131 Las Vegas Blvd S *Web:* www.wynnlasvegas.com	Las Vegas	NV	89109	702-770-9966	
Border Grill Las Vegas 3950 Las Vegas Blvd S Mandalay Bay Resort & Casino *Web:* www.bordergrill.com	Las Vegas	NV	89119	702-632-7403	632-6945
Caesar's Palace 3570 Las Vegas Blvd S Caesar's Palace *TF:* 800-634-6001 ■ *Web:* www.caesars.com	Las Vegas	NV	89109	702-731-7110	
Caesars License Company LLC 3570 Las Vegas Blvd S *Web:* www.caesars.com	Las Vegas	NV	89109	702-731-7410	
Canaletto 3355 Las Vegas Blvd S *TF:* 866-659-9643 ■ *Web:* www.venetian.com	Las Vegas	NV	89109	702-414-1000	414-1100
Chicago Joe's 820 S Fourth St *Web:* www.chicagojoesrestaurant.com	Las Vegas	NV	89101	702-382-5637	
Craftsteak 3799 Las Vegas Blvd S *Web:* craftrestaurantsinc.com	Las Vegas	NV	89109	702-891-7318	
Del Frisco's Double Eagle Steak House 3925 Paradise Rd *Web:* www.delfriscos.com	Las Vegas	NV	89169	702-796-0063	
Delmonico Steakhouse 3355 Las Vegas Blvd S Venetian Resort Hotel & Casino *Web:* www.emerils.com	Las Vegas	NV	89109	702-414-3737	414-3838
Eiffel Tower Restaurant 3655 Las Vegas Blvd S *Web:* www.eiffeltowerrestaurant.com	Las Vegas	NV	89109	702-948-6937	942-0004
Emeril's New Orleans Fish House 3799 Las Vegas Blvd S MGM Grand Hotel *Web:* emerilsrestaurants.com/emerils-new-orleans-fish-house	Las Vegas	NV	89109	702-891-7374	891-7338
Ferraro's 4480 Paradise Rd *Web:* www.ferraroslasvegas.com	Las Vegas	NV	89169	702-364-5300	
Fiamma Trattoria 3799 Las Vegas Blvd S *Web:* mgmgrand.com	Las Vegas	NV	89109	702-891-7600	
Fleming's Prime Steakhouse & Wine Bar 8721 W Charleston Blvd *Web:* www.flemingssteakhouse.com	Las Vegas	NV	89117	702-838-4774	
Gandhi India's Cuisine 4080 Paradise Rd *Web:* www.gandhicuisine.com	Las Vegas	NV	89109	702-734-0094	734-3445
Grotto Ristorante 129 E Fremont St *TF:* 800-634-3454 ■ *Web:* www.goldennugget.com	Las Vegas	NV	89101	702-385-7111	
Hugo's Cellar 202 Fremont St *Web:* www.hugoscellar.com	Las Vegas	NV	89101	702-385-4011	
Le Cirque 3600 Las Vegas Blvd S *TF:* 888-987-6667 ■ *Web:* www.bellagio.com	Las Vegas	NV	89109	702-693-7111	693-8585
Lillie's Asian Cuisine 129 E Fremont St *TF:* 800-634-3454 ■ *Web:* www.goldennugget.com/dining/lillies.asp	Las Vegas	NV	89101	702-385-7111	
Lotus of Siam 953 E Sahara Ave *Web:* lotusofsiamlv.com	Las Vegas	NV	89104	702-735-3033	735-3033
McCormick & Schmick's 335 Hughes Ctr Dr *Web:* www.mccormickandschmicks.com	Las Vegas	NV	89169	702-836-9000	836-9500
Michael Mina 3600 Las Vegas Blvd S *Web:* michaelmina.net/restaurants/locations/mmlv.php	Las Vegas	NV	89109	702-693-7223	
Michael's 9777 Las Vegas Blvd S *TF:* 866-796-7111 ■ *Web:* www.southpointcasino.com	Las Vegas	NV	89183	702-796-7111	
N9ne Steakhouse 4321 W Flamingo Rd *Web:* www.palms.com	Las Vegas	NV	89103	702-933-9900	
Nob Hill 3799 Las Vegas Blvd S MGM Grand Hotel *TF Resv:* 800-929-1111 ■ *Web:* www.mgmgrand.com	Las Vegas	NV	89109	702-891-1111	891-3036
Olives 3600 Las Vegas Blvd S *Web:* cheftoddenglish.com	Las Vegas	NV	89109	702-693-8181	
Onda Ristorante 3400 Las Vegas Blvd S *Web:* www.mirage.com	Las Vegas	NV	89109	702-791-7111	
Osaka 4205 W Sahara Ave *Web:* lasvegas-sushi.com	Las Vegas	NV	89102	702-876-4988	
Osteria Del Circo 3600 Las Vegas Blvd S **Fax Area Code:* 702 ■ *TF:* 866-259-7111 ■ *Web:* www.bellagio.com/restaurants/circo.aspx	Las Vegas	NV	89109	888-987-6667	693-8585*
Pamplemousse 400 E Sahara Ave *Web:* www.pamplemousserestaurant.com	Las Vegas	NV	89104	702-733-2066	
PF Chang's China Bistro 3667 Las Vegas Blvd S *Web:* www.pfchangs.com	Las Vegas	NV	89109	702-836-0955	
Roy's 620 E Flamingo Rd *Web:* www.roysrestaurant.com	Las Vegas	NV	89119	702-691-2053	
Second Street Grill 200 E Fremont St *TF:* 800-634-6460 ■ *Web:* fremontcasino.com	Las Vegas	NV	89101	702-385-3232	
Smith & Wollensky 3767 Las Vegas Blvd S *Web:* www.smithandwollensky.com	Las Vegas	NV	89109	702-862-4100	
Spago 3500 Las Vegas Blvd S Ste G1 *TF:* 800-241-3333 ■ *Web:* www.wolfgangpuck.com	Las Vegas	NV	89109	702-369-6300	369-0361
Steak House 2880 Las Vegas Blvd S *Web:* circuscircus.com	Las Vegas	NV	89109	702-794-3767	
STRIPSTEAK 3950 Las Vegas Blvd S *Web:* www.mandalaybay.com	Las Vegas	NV	89119	702-632-7200	
Sushi Roku 3500 Las Vegas Blvd S *Web:* www.innovativedining.com	Las Vegas	NV	89109	702-733-7373	
SW Steakhouse 3131 Las Vegas Blvd S *TF:* 888-320-7123 ■ *Web:* wynnlasvegas.com	Las Vegas	NV	89109	702-770-7000	770-1570
Thai Spice 4433 W Flamingo Rd	Las Vegas	NV	89103	702-362-5308	
Trattoria Del Lupo 3950 Las Vegas Blvd S *TF:* 800-275-8273 ■ *Web:* www.wolfgangpuck.com/restaurants/fine-dining/3860	Las Vegas	NV	89119	702-740-5522	740-5533
Verandah 3960 Las Vegas Blvd S *Web:* www.fourseasons.com	Las Vegas	NV	89119	702-632-5000	632-5195
Willy & Jose's Mexican Cantina 5111 Boulder Hwy *TF:* 800-897-8696 ■ *Web:* samstownlv.com	Las Vegas	NV	89122	702-456-7777	
Wolfgang Puck's Bar & Grill 3799 Las Vegas Blvd S *Web:* www.wolfgangpuck.com	Las Vegas	NV	89109	702-891-3000	891-3263
Zeffirino Ristorante 3377 Las Vegas Blvd S *Web:* www.zeffirinolasvegas.com	Las Vegas	NV	89109	702-414-3500	
Atlantis Seafood Steakhouse 3800 S Virginia St Atlantis Casino Resort **Fax Area Code:* 775 ■ *TF:* 800-723-6500 ■ *Web:* www.atlantiscasino.com	Reno	NV	89502	800-723-6500	827-1518*
Bavarian World 595 Valley Rd *Web:* bavarianworldreno.com	Reno	NV	89512	775-323-7646	
Beaujolais Bistro 753 Riverside Dr *Web:* www.beaujolaisbistro.com	Reno	NV	89503	775-323-2227	
Black Bear Diner 2323 S Virginia St *Web:* www.blackbeardiner.com	Reno	NV	89502	775-827-5570	
Bricks 1695 S Virginia St *Web:* bricksrestaurant.com	Reno	NV	89502	775-786-2277	
Cafe de Thai 7499 Longly Ln *Web:* cafedethaireno.net	Reno	NV	89511	775-829-8424	
China East Restaurant 1086 S Virginia St	Reno	NV	89502	775-348-7020	348-1956
Flowing Tide Pub 10580 N McCarran Blvd *Web:* www.flowingtidepub.com	Reno	NV	89503	775-747-7707	
Golden Flower 205 W Fifth St *Web:* goldenflowerreno.com	Reno	NV	89503	775-323-1628	
Johnny's 4245 W Fourth St *Web:* johnnysristorante.com	Reno	NV	89523	775-747-4511	
La Strada 345 N Virginia St *Web:* eldoradoreno.com	Reno	NV	89501	775-348-9297	
Louis' Basque Corner 301 E Fourth St *Web:* louisbasquecorner.com	Reno	NV	89501	775-323-7203	
Paisan's 4826 Longley Ln *Web:* paisanscatering.com	Reno	NV	89502	775-826-9444	
Palais de Jade 960 W Moana Ln *Web:* www.palaisdejadereno.com	Reno	NV	89509	775-827-5233	
PF Chang's China Bistro 5180 S Kietzke Ln *Web:* www.pfchangs.com	Reno	NV	89511	775-825-9800	
Pho 777 Vietnamese Restaurant 102 E Second St	Reno	NV	89501	775-323-7777	
Pneumatic Diner 501 W First St	Reno	NV	89503	775-786-8888	
Romanza 2707 S Virginia St Peppermill Hotel Casino *TF:* 866-821-9996 ■ *Web:* www.peppermillreno.com	Reno	NV	89502	775-826-2121	
Sushi Club 294 E Moana Ln	Reno	NV	89502	775-828-7311	828-5426
Sushi Pier 1290 E Plumb Ln *Web:* mysushipier.com	Reno	NV	89502	775-825-6776	
Washoe Steakhouse 4201 W Fourth St *Web:* www.washoesteakhouse.com	Reno	NV	89523	775-786-1323	

New Hampshire

	City	State	Zip	Phone	Fax
Bedford Village Inn 2 Olde Bedford Way *TF:* 800-852-1166 ■ *Web:* www.bedfordvillageinn.com	Bedford	NH	03110	603-472-2001	
Angelina's Ristorante Italiano 11 Depot St *Web:* www.angelinasrestaurant.com	Concord	NH	03301	603-228-3313	
Barley House 132 N Main St *Web:* thebarleyhouse.com	Concord	NH	03301	603-228-6363	
Cheers 17 Depot St *Web:* www.cheersnh.com	Concord	NH	03301	603-228-0180	226-3459
Common Man, The 25 Water St *Web:* www.thecman.com	Concord	NH	03301	603-228-3463	
Corner View Restaurant 80 1/2 S St	Concord	NH	03301	603-229-4554	229-0932
Hermanos Cocina Mexicana 11 Hills Ave *Web:* www.hermanosmexican.com	Concord	NH	03301	603-224-5669	
Moritomo 32 Ft Eddy Rd *Web:* moritomonh.com	Concord	NH	03301	603-224-8363	
Red Blazer, The 72 Manchester St *Web:* www.theredblazer.com	Concord	NH	03301	603-224-4101	224-7118
Siam Orchid 12 N Main St *Web:* www.siamorchid.net	Concord	NH	03301	603-228-1529	
Szechuan Garden Restaurant 108 Fisherville Rd	Concord	NH	03303	603-226-2650	
Tea Garden Restaurant 184 N Main St *Web:* teagarden-nh.com	Concord	NH	03301	603-228-4420	
Belmont Hall & Restaurant 718 Grove St *Web:* www.belmontrestaurant.com	Manchester	NH	03103	603-625-8540	

Phone | Fax

Cactus Jacks Southwest Grill 782 S Willow St, Manchester NH 03103, 603-627-8600, 434-3200
Web: www.cactusjacksnh.com

Chateau Restaurant 201 Hanover St, Manchester NH 03104, 603-606-3026

Derryfield Restaurant, The 625 Mammoth Rd, Manchester NH 03104, 603-623-2880
Web: www.thederryfield.com

Don Quijote 362 Union St, Manchester NH 03103, 603-622-2246

Fratello's Ristorante Italiano 155 Dow St, Manchester NH 03101, 603-624-2022
Web: www.fratellos.com

Gaucho's Churrascaria 62 Lowell St, Manchester NH 03101, 603-669-9460
TF: 866-669-9460 ■ *Web:* www.gauchosbraziliansteakhouse.com

Lakorn Thai Restaurant 470 S Main St, Manchester NH 03102, 603-626-4545
Web: lakornthainh.com

Piccola Italia 815 Elm St, Manchester NH 03101, 603-606-5100
Web: www.piccolaitalianh.com

Shorty's 1050 Bicentennial Dr, Manchester NH 03104, 603-625-1730
Web: shortysmex.com

Szechuan House 245 Maple St, Manchester NH 03103, 603-669-8811
Web: szechuanhousenh.com

Thousand Crane 1000 Elm St, Manchester NH 03101, 603-634-0000
Web: thousandcranenh.com

Yard, The 1211 S Mammoth Rd, Manchester NH 03109, 603-623-3545, 625-8420
Web: www.theyardrestaurant.com

Castle In The Clouds Rt 171, Moultonborough NH 03254, 603-476-2352
Web: www.castleintheclouds.org

Lake Winnipesaukee Golf Club Llc 1 Lk Winnipesaukee Dr, New Durham NH 03855, 603-569-3055
Web: www.lwgcnh.com

Puritan Backroom Restaurant 245 Hooksett Rd, North Manchester NH 03104, 603-669-6890
Web: www.puritanbackroom.com

Margarita's 200 Griffin Rd Ste 1, Portsmouth NH 03801, 603-430-8905
Web: www.margs.com

New Jersey

Phone | Fax

Angelo's Fairmount Tavern 2300 Fairmount Ave, Atlantic City NJ 08401, 609-344-2439, 348-1043
Web: www.angelosfairmounttavern.com

Atlantic City Bar & Grill 1219 Pacific Ave, Atlantic City NJ 08401, 609-348-8080
Web: www.acbarandgrill.com

Bobby Flay Steak 1 Borgata Way, Atlantic City NJ 08401, 609-317-1000
Web: www.bobbyflaysteak.com

Cuba Libre 2801 Pacific Ave, Atlantic City NJ 08401, 609-348-6700
Web: www.cubalibrerestaurant.com

Dock's Oyster House 2405 Atlantic Ave, Atlantic City NJ 08401, 609-345-0092
Web: www.docksoysterhouse.com

Girasole Ristorante & Lounge 3108 Pacific Ave, Atlantic City NJ 08401, 609-345-5554
Web: www.girasoleac.com

Hard Rock Cafe Boardwalk at Virginia Ave, Atlantic City NJ 08401, 609-441-0007, 449-1836
Web: www.hardrock.com

Knife & Fork Inn, The 3600 Atlantic Ave, Atlantic City NJ 08401, 609-344-1133, 344-3533
Web: www.knifeandforkinn.com

Los Amigos 1926 Atlantic Ave, Atlantic City NJ 08401, 609-344-2293, 344-2373
Web: www.losamigosrest.com

Mexico 3810 Ventor Ave, Atlantic City NJ 08401, 609-344-0366
Web: mexicorestaurantbar.com

Mia Restaurant 2100 Pacific Ave, Atlantic City NJ 08401, 609-441-2345

Palm, The 2801 Pacific Ave, Atlantic City NJ 08401, 609-344-7256
Web: thepalm.com

PF Chang's China Bistro 2801 N Pacific Ave, Atlantic City NJ 08401, 609-348-4600
Web: www.pfchangs.com

Sea Blue 1 Borgata Way, Atlantic City NJ 08401, 609-317-1000, 317-1039
TF Cust Svc: 877-786-9900 ■ *Web:* www.theborgata.com

Sal Deforte's 1400 PkwyAve Serenity Plz, Ewing NJ 08628, 609-406-0123
Web: www.saldefortesristorante.com

Rams Head Inn 9 W White Horse Pike, Galloway NJ 08205, 609-652-1700
Web: ramsheadinn.com

Baja 104 14th St, Hoboken NJ 07030, 201-653-0610

Amelia's Bistro 187 Warren St, Jersey City NJ 07302, 201-332-2200
Web: ameliasbistro.com

Amiya 160 Green St, Harborside Financial Ctr Plz 5, Jersey City NJ 07311, 201-433-8000, 433-8866
Web: www.amiyarestaurant.com

Casa Dante 737 Newark Ave, Jersey City NJ 07306, 201-795-2750, 795-1225
Web: www.casadante.com

Confucius Asian Bistro 558 Washington Blvd, Jersey City NJ 07310, 201-386-8898, 386-8896
Web: confucius558.com

Iron Monkey 97 Greene St, Jersey City NJ 07302, 201-435-5756, 433-0762
Web: ironmonkey.com

Komegashi 103 Montgomery St, Jersey City NJ 07302, 201-433-4567
Web: www.komegashi.com

Laico's 67 Terhune Ave, Jersey City NJ 07305, 201-434-4115
Web: www.laicosjc.com

Liberty House 76 Audrey Zapp Dr, Jersey City NJ 07305, 201-395-0300
Web: www.libertyhouserestaurant.com

Light Horse Tavern 199 Washington St, Jersey City NJ 07302, 201-946-2028, 946-2029
Web: www.lighthorsetavern.com

Madame Claude Cafe 364 1/2 Fourth St, Jersey City NJ 07302, 201-876-8800
Web: www.madameclaudecafe.com

Marco & Pepe 289 Grove St, Jersey City NJ 07302, 201-860-9688
Web: www.marcoandpepe.com

Marker's Restaurant 153 Plaza II Harborside Financial Ctr, Jersey City NJ 07311, 201-433-6275, 433-0399
Web: www.markersrestaurant.com

Merchant, The 279 Grove St, Jersey City NJ 07302, 201-200-0202
Web: www.themerchantnj.com

Puccini's 1064 Westside Ave, Jersey City NJ 07306, 201-432-4111, 432-9026

Rita & Joe's 142 Broadway, Jersey City NJ 07306, 201-451-3606
Web: www.rita-joes.com

Acacia 2637 Lawrenceville Rd, Lawrenceville NJ 08648, 609-895-9885
Web: www.acacianj.com

Steve & Cookies By the Bay 9700 Amherst Ave, Margate NJ 08402, 609-823-1163
Web: www.steveandcookies.com

Adega Grill 130 Ferry St, Newark NJ 07105, 973-589-8830
Web: www.adegagrill.com

Campino Restaurant 70 Jabez St, Newark NJ 07105, 973-589-4004

Casa Vasca 141 Elm St, Newark NJ 07105, 973-465-1350
Web: casavascarestaurant.com

Don Pepe Restaurant & Catering 844 McCarter Hwy, Newark NJ 07102, 973-623-4662, 623-5402
Web: www.donpeperestaurant.com

Fernandes Steak House 158 Fleming Ave, Newark NJ 07105, 973-589-4344, 589-6312
Web: www.fernandessteakhouse.com

Fornos of Spain 47 Ferry St, Newark NJ 07105, 973-589-4767
Web: www.fornosrestaurant.com

Iberia Peninsula Restaurant 67 Ferry St, Newark NJ 07105, 973-344-5611, 344-2067
Web: www.iberiarestaurants.com

Maize
Maize Restaurant 50 Pk Pl, Newark NJ 07102, 973-733-2202
Web: www.maizerestaurant.com

Spain Restaurant 419 Market St, Newark NJ 07105, 973-344-0994, 344-2669
Web: www.spainrestaurant.com

Spanish Tavern 103 McWhorter St, Newark NJ 07105, 973-589-4959
Web: www.spanishtavern.com

Tony da Caneca 72 Elm Rd, Newark NJ 07105, 973-589-6882, 589-0036
Web: www.tonydacaneca.com

Albasha 1076 Main St, Paterson NJ 07503, 973-345-3700
Web: www.albashanj.com

Bonfire 999 Market St, Paterson NJ 07513, 973-278-2400
Web: www.bonfirerestaurant.com

Brownstone House 351 W Broadway, Paterson NJ 07522, 973-595-8582
Web: www.thebrownstone.com

D'Classico 58-60 Ellison St, Paterson NJ 07505, 973-569-4300

E & V Restaurant 320 Chamberlain Ave, Paterson NJ 07502, 973-942-4664
Web: www.evrestaurant.com

Hacienda Restaurant 102 McLean Blvd, Paterson NJ 07514, 973-345-1255
Web: haciendanj.com

Kikiriki 215 Market St, Paterson NJ 07505, 973-225-0336
Web: kikirikirestaurant.com

King Wok 712 Main St, Paterson NJ 07503, 973-881-8818

Patsy's 72 Seventh Ave, Paterson NJ 07524, 973-742-9596

Seven Bros Grill 846 Market St, Paterson NJ 07513, 973-684-2579

Tierras Colombians Restaurant 395 21st Ave, Paterson NJ 07513, 973-684-4066

Blue Point Grill 258 Nassau St, Princeton NJ 08542, 609-921-1211
Web: bluepointgrill.com

Cressi-Sub Usa Inc 3 Rosol Ln, Saddle Brook NJ 07663, 201-594-1450
Web: www.cressisubusa.com

Crab Trap 2 Broadway, Somers Point NJ 08244, 609-927-7377

Amici Milano Restaurant 600 Chesnut Ave, Trenton NJ 08611, 609-396-6300, 396-3926
Web: www.amicimilano.com

Blue Danube Elm & Adeline Sts, Trenton NJ 08611, 609-393-6133, 393-1596
Web: www.bluedanuberestaurant.net

Homestead Inn 800 Kuser Rd, Trenton NJ 08619, 609-890-9851

Yoshi Sono Japanese Restaurant 643 Eagle Rock Ave, West Orange NJ 07052, 973-325-2005, 325-2571

Birchwood Manor 111 N Jefferson Rd, Whippany NJ 07981, 973-887-1414
Web: birchwoodmanor.com

New Mexico

Phone | Fax

66 Diner 1405 Central Ave NE, Albuquerque NM 87106, 505-247-1421
Web: www.66diner.com

Antiquity 112 Romero St NW, Albuquerque NM 87104, 505-247-3545
Web: antiquityrestaurant.com

Artichoke Cafe 424 Central SE, Albuquerque NM 87102, 505-243-0200, 243-3365
Web: www.artichokecafe.com

Chama River Brewing Co 4939 Pan American Fwy, Albuquerque NM 87109, 505-342-1800
Web: www.chamariverbrewery.com

County Line 9600 Tramway Blvd NE, Albuquerque NM 87122, 505-856-7477
Web: www.countyline.com

El Pinto 10500 Fourth St NW, Albuquerque NM 87114, 505-898-1771, 890-0498
Web: www.elpinto.com

Forque Kitchen and Bar 330 Tijeras Ave NW, Hyatt Regency Albuquerque, Albuquerque NM 87102, 505-843-2700

Gold Street Caffe 218 Gold Ave SW, Albuquerque NM 87102, 505-765-1633
Web: goldstreetcaffe.com

High Finance Restaurant 40 Tramway Rd NE, Albuquerque NM 87122, 505-243-9742
Web: sandiapeakrestaurants.com

Monte Vista Fire Station 3201 Central Ave NE, Albuquerque NM 87106, 505-255-2424
Web: montevistafirestation.com

Mr Powdrell's Barbeque House 11301 Central Ave NE, Albuquerque NM 87123, 505-298-6766, 298-0025
Web: powdrellsbbq.webs.com

Pelican's Restaurant 9800 Montgomery Blvd NE, Albuquerque NM 87111, 505-298-7678
Web: pelicansabq.com

Ragin' Shrimp 3624 Central Ave SE, Albuquerque NM 87108, 505-254-1544
Web: www.raginshrimp.com

Ranchers Club of New Mexico 1901 University Blvd NE, Albuquerque NM 87102, 505-889-8071
Web: www.theranchersclubofnm.com

Phone Fax

Sadie's 6230 Fourth St NW....................... Albuquerque NM 87107 505-345-5339
Web: www.sadiessalsa.com

Samurai Grill & Sushi Bar
9500 Montgomery Blvd NE....................... Albuquerque NM 87111 505-275-6601 275-4146
Web: www.abqsamurai.com

Sandiago's Mexican Grill at the Tram
40 Tramway Rd NE....................... Albuquerque NM 87122 505-856-6692 856-6692
Web: www.sandiapeakrestaurants.com

Scalo Northern Italian Grill
3500 Central Ave SE....................... Albuquerque NM 87106 505-255-8781 265-7850
Web: www.scalonobhill.com

Seasons Rotisserie & Grill
2031 Mountain Rd NW....................... Albuquerque NM 87104 505-766-5100 766-5252
Web: www.seasonsabq.com

Yanni's Mediterranean Bar & Grill
3109 Central Ave NE....................... Albuquerque NM 87106 505-268-9250
Web: yannisandopabar.com

Zinc Wine Bar & Bistro
3009 Central Ave NE....................... Albuquerque NM 87106 505-254-9462
Web: zincabq.com

Chilito's 2405 S Valley Dr....................... Las Cruces NM 88005 575-526-4184
Web: chilitos.net

Farley's 3499 Foothills Rd....................... Las Cruces NM 88011 575-522-0466
Web: www.farleyspub.com

Los Compas Cafe 603 S Nevarez St....................... Las Cruces NM 88001 575-523-1778 527-5590

Mesilla Valley Kitchen 2001 E Lohman....................... Las Cruces NM 88001 575-523-9311
Web: www.mesillavalleykitchen.com

Mix Express 1001 E University Ave Ste D-3....................... Las Cruces NM 88001 575-532-2042 532-2046

Nellie's Cafe 1226 W Hadley Ave....................... Las Cruces NM 88005 575-524-9982

Roberto's 908 E Amador Ave....................... Las Cruces NM 88001 575-523-1851

Si Senor Restaurant 1551 E Amador Ave....................... Las Cruces NM 88001 575-527-0817
Web: www.sisenor.com

Spanish Kitchen 2960 N Main St....................... Las Cruces NM 88001 575-526-4275

Teriyaki Chicken House 805 El Paseo Rd....................... Las Cruces NM 88001 575-541-1696
Web: teriyakichickenhouse.com

Cattle Baron Restaurants Inc 901 S Main St....................... Roswell NM 88203 575-622-3311 623-8801
Web: www.cattlebaron.com

Andiamo 322 Garfield St....................... Santa Fe NM 87501 505-995-9595
Web: andiamosantafe.com

Annapurna Chai House 1620 St Michaels....................... Santa Fe NM 87505 505-988-9688
Web: www.chaishoppe.com

Bull Ring of Santa Fe, The
150 Washington Ave....................... Santa Fe NM 87501 505-983-3328
Web: santafebullring.com

Chow's Contemporary Chinese Food
720 St Michaels Dr....................... Santa Fe NM 87505 505-471-7120
Web: www.mychows.com

Coyote Cafe 132 W.Water St....................... Santa Fe NM 87501 505-983-1615
Web: www.coyotecafe.com

El Farol 808 Canyon Rd....................... Santa Fe NM 87501 505-983-9912
Web: www.elfarolsantafe.com

Fuego 330 E Palace Ave....................... Santa Fe NM 87501 505-986-0000
TF Sales: 855-811-0050 ■ *Web:* www.laposadadesantafe.com

Geronimo 724 Canyon Rd....................... Santa Fe NM 87501 505-982-1500
Web: www.geronimorestaurant.com

IL Vicino 321 W San Francisco St....................... Santa Fe NM 87501 505-986-8700

India Palace 227 Don Gaspar Ave....................... Santa Fe NM 87501 505-986-5859

Kohnami 313 S Guadalupe St....................... Santa Fe NM 87501 505-984-2002
Web: kohnamirestaurant.com

Maria's New Mexican Kitchen
555 W Cordova Rd....................... Santa Fe NM 87505 505-983-7929
Web: www.marias-santafe.com

Mariscos La Playa 537 W Cordova Rd....................... Santa Fe NM 87505 505-982-2790

Mu Du Noodles 1494 Cerrillos Rd....................... Santa Fe NM 87505 505-983-1411
Web: www.mudunoodles.com

Old House 309 W San Francisco St....................... Santa Fe NM 87501 505-988-4455 995-4543
TF: 800-955-4455 ■ *Web:* www.eldoradohotel.com

Rio Chama Steakhouse 414 Old Santa Fe Trl....................... Santa Fe NM 87501 505-955-0765
Web: www.riochamasteakhouse.com

Santacafe 231 Washington Ave....................... Santa Fe NM 87501 505-984-1788
Web: www.santacafe.com

Shed, The 113 1/2 E Palace Ave....................... Santa Fe NM 87501 505-982-9030
Web: www.sfshed.com

Tecolote Cafe 1203 Cerrillos Rd....................... Santa Fe NM 87505 505-988-1362
Web: tecolotecafe.com

Tomasita's Restaurant & Bar
500 S Guadalupe St....................... Santa Fe NM 87501 505-983-5721 983-0780
Web: www.tomasitas.com

Tortilla Flats 3139 Cerrillos Rd....................... Santa Fe NM 87507 505-471-8685
Web: tortillaflats.net

New York

Phone Fax

Cafe Capriccio 49 Grand St....................... Albany NY 12207 518-465-0439 465-6822
Web: www.cafecapriccio.com

Caffe Italia Ristorante 662 Central Ave....................... Albany NY 12206 518-459-8029 482-9433

CH Evans Brewing Company at the Albany Pump Station
19 Quackenbush Sq....................... Albany NY 12207 518-447-9000
Web: www.evansale.com

Desmond Albany Hotel, The
660 Albany-Shaker Rd....................... Albany NY 12211 518-869-8100
TF: 800-448-3500 ■ *Web:* www.desmondhotelsalbany.com

El Loco Mexican Cafe 465 Madison Ave....................... Albany NY 12210 518-436-1855
Web: ellocomexicancafe.com

El Mariachi 144 Washington Ave....................... Albany NY 12210 518-432-7580
Web: elmariachisrestaurant.com

Gandhi 1 Central Ave....................... Albany NY 12210 518-449-5577 449-8941
Web: www.albanygandhi.com

Ichiban 338 Central Ave....................... Albany NY 12206 518-432-0358
Web: ichibanjapanesechinese.com

Phone Fax

Jack's Oyster House 42 State St....................... Albany NY 12207 518-465-8854 434-2134
Web: www.jacksoysterhouse.com

My Linh 272 Delaware Ave....................... Albany NY 12209 518-465-8899 465-8898
Web: www.mylinhrestaurant.com

Provence 1475 Western Ave Stuyvesant Plz....................... Albany NY 12203 518-689-7777
Web: www.milano-restaurant.com/provence

Real Seafood Co 195 Wolf Rd....................... Albany NY 12205 518-458-2068
Web: www.reelseafoodco.com

Scotch & Sirloin 3999 Maple Rd....................... Amherst NY 14226 716-837-4900
Web: scotchnsirloinrestaurant.net

Taste of India 3192 SHERIDAN Dr....................... AMHERST NY 14226 716-837-0460
Web: www.tasteofindia.com

Erawan Thai Cuisine 42-31 Bell Blvd....................... Bayside NY 11361 718-428-2112
Web: www.erawanthaibayside.com

Roberto's 603 Crescent Ave....................... Bronx NY 10458 718-733-9503
Web: www.usmenuguide.com

Elia 8611 Third Ave....................... Brooklyn NY 11209 718-748-9891
Web: www.eliarestaurant.com/elia

Frankies 457 Court Street Spuntino
457 Ct St....................... Brooklyn NY 11231 718-403-0033 403-9260
Web: frankiesspuntino.com

Grocery, The 288 Smith St....................... Brooklyn NY 11231 718-596-3335
Web: www.thegroceryrestaurant.com

ICI Restaurant 246 DeKalb Ave....................... Brooklyn NY 11205 718-789-2778
Web: www.icirestaurant.com

Kai 20 Jay St Ste 530....................... Brooklyn NY 11201 718-250-4000 246-1325
TF: 888-832-7832 ■ *Web:* www.itoen.com

Peter Luger Steak House 178 Broadway....................... Brooklyn NY 11211 718-387-7400 387-3523
Web: www.peterluger.com

River Cafe 1 Water St....................... Brooklyn NY 11201 718-522-5200 875-0037
Web: www.rivercafe.com

Saul 200 Eastern Pkwy....................... Brooklyn NY 11238 718-935-9842
Web: www.saulrestaurant.com

Acropolis Family Restaurant 708 Elmwood Ave....................... Buffalo NY 14222 716-886-2977
Web: www.acropolisopa.com

Ambrosia 467 Elmwood Ave....................... Buffalo NY 14222 716-881-2196 881-2220

Bijou Grille, The 643 Main St....................... Buffalo NY 14203 716-847-1512 852-3041
Web: www.bijougrille.com

Bing's 1952 Kensington Ave....................... Buffalo NY 14215 716-839-5788
Web: www.bingsrestaurant.net

Blackthorn Restaurant & Pub 2134 Seneca St....................... Buffalo NY 14210 716-825-9327
Web: blackthornrestaurant.com

Duff's 3651 Sheridan Dr....................... Buffalo NY 14226 716-834-6234
Web: duffswings.com

Fat Bob's Smokehouse 41 Virginia Pl....................... Buffalo NY 14202 716-887-2971 332-1201
Web: www.fatbobs.com

Frank & Teressa's Anchor Bar & Restaurant
651 Delaware Ave....................... Buffalo NY 14202 716-883-1134
TF: 866-248-9623 ■ *Web:* www.anchorbar.com

Gigi's Restaurant 257 E Ferry St....................... Buffalo NY 14208 716-883-1438

Hutch's 1375 Delaware Ave....................... Buffalo NY 14209 716-885-0074
Web: www.hutchsrestaurant.com

Ilio DiPaolo's 3785 S Pk Ave....................... Buffalo NY 14219 716-825-3675 825-1054
Web: www.iliodipaolos.com

Left Bank 511 Rhode Island St....................... Buffalo NY 14213 716-882-3509
Web: www.leftbankrestaurant.com

Marco's 1085 Niagara St....................... Buffalo NY 14213 716-882-5539
Web: marcosbuffalo.com

Mother's 33 Virginia Pl....................... Buffalo NY 14202 716-882-2989

Oliver's 2095 Delaware Ave....................... Buffalo NY 14216 716-877-9662
Web: www.oliverscuisine.com

Pearl Street Grill & Brewery 76 Pearl St....................... Buffalo NY 14202 716-856-2337 849-0839
Web: pearlstreetgrill.com

Rue Franklin 341 Franklin St....................... Buffalo NY 14202 716-852-4416
Web: www.ruefranklin.com

Santasiero's 1329 Niagara St....................... Buffalo NY 14213 716-886-9197 884-9338

Salvatore's Italian Gardens 6461 Transit Rd....................... Depew NY 14043 716-683-7990
TF: 877-456-4097 ■ *Web:* www.salvatores.net

Tavern 104 Limestone Pl....................... Fayetteville NY 13066 315-637-8321

Bella Via 47-46 Vernon Blvd....................... Long Island NY 11101 718-361-7510

Alain Ducasse at the Essex House
60 W 55th St....................... New York NY 10019 646-943-7373 943-7330
Web: www.alain-ducasse.com

Annisa 13 Barrow St....................... New York NY 10014 212-741-6699
Web: www.annisarestaurant.com

Aquagrill Inc 210 Spring St....................... New York NY 10012 212-274-0505 274-0587
Web: www.aquagrill.com

Aquavit 65 E 55th St....................... New York NY 10022 212-307-7311
Web: www.aquavit.org

Aureole 135 W 42nd St....................... New York NY 10036 212-319-1660
TF: 800-889-7188 ■ *Web:* www.charliepalmer.com

Babbo 110 Waverly Pl....................... New York NY 10011 212-777-0303
Web: www.babbonyc.com

Balthazar 80 Spring St....................... New York NY 10012 212-965-1414
Web: www.balthazarny.com

Bar Americain 152 W 52nd St....................... New York NY 10019 212-265-9700
Web: www.baramericain.com

Barbuto 775 Washington St....................... New York NY 10014 212-924-9700 924-9300
Web: www.barbutonyc.com

BLT Prime 111 E 22nd St....................... New York NY 10010 212-995-8500
TF: 800-855-2880 ■ *Web:* www.e2hospitality.com/blt-prime-new-york

Blue Fin 1567 Broadway....................... New York NY 10036 212-918-1400
Web: bluefinnyc.com

Blue Hill 75 Washington Pl....................... New York NY 10011 212-539-1776 539-0959
Web: bluehillfarm.com

Blue Ribbon 97 Sullivan St....................... New York NY 10012 212-274-0404
Web: www.blueribbonrestaurants.com

Blue Water Grill 31 Union Sq W....................... New York NY 10003 212-675-9500
Web: bluewatergrillnyc.com

Bouley 163 Duane St....................... New York NY 10013 212-964-2525
Web: www.davidbouley.com

	City	State	ZIP	Phone	Fax
Cafe Boulud 20 E 76th St *Web:* www.danielnyc.com	New York	NY	10021	212-772-2600	
Cafe Centro 200 Pk Ave *Web:* patinagroup.com	New York	NY	10166	212-818-1222	
Casa Mono 52 Irving Pl *Web:* casamononyc.com	New York	NY	10003	212-253-2773	
Caviar Russe 538 Madison Ave 2nd Fl *Web:* www.caviarrusse.com	New York	NY	10022	212-980-5908	871-1842
Chanterelle 2 Harrison St	New York	NY	10013	212-966-6143	
Churrascaria Plataforma 316 W 49th St *Web:* plataformaonline.com	New York	NY	10019	212-245-0505	974-8250
Craft 43 E 19th St *Web:* www.craftrestaurantsinc.com	New York	NY	10003	212-780-0880	
Daniel 60 E 65th St *Web:* www.danielnyc.com	New York	NY	10065	212-288-0033	
Dawat 210 E 58th St *Web:* dawatny.com	New York	NY	10022	212-355-7555	
db Bistro Moderne 55 W 44th St *Web:* www.danielnyc.com	New York	NY	10036	212-391-2400	
Del Frisco's Restaurant Group, Inc. 1221 Ave of the Americas *Web:* www.delfriscos.com	New York	NY	10020	212-575-5129	
Del Posto 85 Tenth Ave *Web:* www.delposto.com	New York	NY	10011	212-497-8090	
Devi 8 E 18th St *Web:* www.devinyc.com	New York	NY	10003	212-691-1300	691-1695
Elle 300 W 57th St 24th Fl *Web:* elle.com	New York	NY	10019	212-903-5000	
Erminia 250 E 83rd St *Web:* erminiarestaurant.com	New York	NY	10028	212-879-4284	
Estiatorio Milos 125 W 55th St *Web:* www.milos.ca	New York	NY	10019	212-245-7400	
Felidia 243 E 58th St *Web:* www.felidia-nyc.com	New York	NY	10022	212-758-1479	
Four Seasons 99 E 52nd St *Web:* www.fourseasonsrestaurant.com	New York	NY	10022	212-754-9494	
Gordon Ramsay at the London 151 W 54th St *Web:* www.thelondonnyc.com	New York	NY	10019	212-468-8888	
Gotham Bar & Grill 12 E 12th St *Web:* www.gothambarandgrill.com	New York	NY	10003	212-620-4020	
Gramercy Tavern 42 E 20th St *Web:* www.gramercytavern.com	New York	NY	10003	212-477-0777	
Hangawi 12 E 32nd St *Web:* www.hangawirestaurant.com	New York	NY	10016	212-213-0077	689-0780
Harrison, The 355 Greenwich St	New York	NY	10013	212-274-9310	274-9376
IL Mulino 86 W Third St *Web:* www.ilmulino.com	New York	NY	10012	212-673-3783	
IL Palazzo 151 Mulberry St *Web:* littleitalynyc.com	New York	NY	10013	212-343-7000	
Jean Georges 1 Central Pk W *Web:* www.jean-georges.com	New York	NY	10023	212-299-3900	
Jewel Bako 239 E Fifth St *Web:* www.jewelbakosushi.com	New York	NY	10003	212-979-1012	
Joe Allen 326 W 46th St *Web:* www.joeallenrestaurant.com	New York	NY	10036	212-581-6464	
JoJo 160 E 64th St *Web:* jojorestaurantnyc.com	New York	NY	10021	212-223-5656	
Kuruma Zushi 7 E 47th St 2nd Fl *Web:* kurumazushi.com	New York	NY	10017	212-317-2802	317-2803
L'Absinthe Restaurant 227 E 67th St	New York	NY	10065	212-794-4950	794-1589
La Grenouille 3 E 52nd St *Web:* www.la-grenouille.com	New York	NY	10022	212-752-1495	
Le Perigord 405 E 52nd St *Web:* www.leperigord.com	New York	NY	10022	212-755-6244	
Lupa Osteria Romana 170 Thompson St *Web:* www.luparestaurant.com	New York	NY	10012	212-982-5089	
Maloney & Porcelli 37 E 50th St *Web:* www.maloneyandporcelli.com	New York	NY	10022	212-750-2233	
MAS (Farmhouse) 39 Downing St *Web:* masfarmhouse.com	New York	NY	10014	212-255-1790	255-0279
Masa 10 Columbus Cir Time Warner Ctr 4th Fl *Web:* www.masanyc.com	New York	NY	10019	212-823-9800	
Megu 62 Thomas St	New York	NY	10013	212-964-7777	
Mercer Kitchen 99 Prince St *Web:* www.jean-georges.com	New York	NY	10012	212-966-5454	
Michael Jordan's Steak House 23 Vanderbilt Ave *Web:* michaeljordansnyc.com	New York	NY	10017	212-655-2300	
Michael's New York 24 W 55th St *Web:* www.michaelsnewyork.com	New York	NY	10019	212-767-0555	
Naya Restaurant 1057 Second Ave *Web:* www.nayarestaurants.com	New York	NY	10022	212-319-7777	
NIOS Restaurant & Wine Bar 130 W 46th St *Web:* www.niosrestaurant.com	New York	NY	10036	212-485-2999	
Nobu 105 Hudson St *Web:* www.noburestaurants.com	New York	NY	10013	212-219-0500	
Oceana 120 W 49th St *Web:* www.oceanarestaurant.com	New York	NY	10020	212-759-5941	759-6076
Old Homestead Steakhouse 56 Ninth Ave *Web:* www.theoldhomesteadsteakhouse.com	New York	NY	10011	212-242-9040	727-1637
One if by Land Two if by Sea 17 Barrow St *Fax Area Code: 646 ■ *Web:* www.oneifbyland.com	New York	NY	10014	212-255-8649	304-2900*
Ouest 2315 Broadway	New York	NY	10024	212-580-1360	580-1360
Palm Restaurant 250 W 50th St *TF:* 866-333-7256 ■ *Web:* www.thepalm.com	New York	NY	10019	212-687-2953	
Pampano 209 E 49th St *Web:* www.richardsandoval.com	New York	NY	10017	212-751-4545	
Pearl Oyster Bar 18 Cornelia St *Web:* www.pearloysterbar.com	New York	NY	10014	212-691-8211	
Peasant 194 Elizabeth St *Web:* www.peasantnyc.com	New York	NY	10012	212-965-9511	965-8741
Periyali 35 W 20th St *Web:* www.periyali.com	New York	NY	10011	212-463-7890	
Picante Mexican Restaurant 3424 BRdway *Web:* www.picantesrestaurant.com	New York	NY	10031	337-896-1200	
Picholine 35 W 64th St *Web:* www.picholinenyc.com	New York	NY	10023	212-724-8585	
Po 31 Cornelia St *Web:* www.porestaurant.com	New York	NY	10014	212-645-2189	
Poke 343 E 85th St *Web:* www.pokesushinyc.com	New York	NY	10028	212-249-0569	
Post House, The 28 E 63rd St *Web:* www.theposthouse.com	New York	NY	10021	212-935-2888	
Prime Grill, The 25 W 56th St *Web:* www.theprimegrill.primehospitalityny.com	New York	NY	10019	212-692-9292	697-3652
Ramen-Ya 181 W Fourth St *Web:* www.ramen-ya.net	New York	NY	10014	212-989-5440	
Really Simple LLC 225 W 35th St Ste 1101 *Web:* www.reallysimple.com	New York	NY	10001	212-683-4696	
Remi 145 W 53rd St *Web:* remi-nyc.com	New York	NY	10019	212-581-4242	
Rothmann's Steakhouse & Grill 3 E 54th St *Web:* www.rothmanns54.com	New York	NY	10022	212-319-5500	
Scalini Fedeli 165 Duane St *Web:* www.scalinifedeli.com	New York	NY	10013	212-528-0400	
Sea Grill Restaurant 19 W 49th St *Web:* www.patinagroup.com	New York	NY	10020	212-332-7610	
Shun Lee Palace 155 E 55th St *Web:* www.shunleepalace.com	New York	NY	10022	212-371-8844	
Spain 245 E 47th St 36th Fl *Web:* www.spainun.org	New York	NY	10017	212-661-1050	949-7247
Sparks Steak House 210 E 46th St *Web:* www.sparkssteakhouse.com	New York	NY	10017	212-687-4855	557-7409
Spice Market 403 W 13th St *Web:* www.jean-georges.com	New York	NY	10014	212-675-2322	
Strip House 13 E 12th St *Web:* striphouse.com	New York	NY	10003	212-328-0000	
Sushi of Gari 402 E 78th St *Web:* sushiofgari.com	New York	NY	10075	212-517-5340	
Sushi Seki 1143 First Ave *Web:* sushiseki.com	New York	NY	10065	212-371-0238	
Sushi Yasuda 204 E 43rd St *Web:* www.sushiyasuda.com	New York	NY	10017	212-972-1001	972-1717
Sushi Zen 108 W 44th St *Web:* www.sushizen-ny.com	New York	NY	10036	212-302-0707	944-7710
Tamarind 43 E 22nd St # 42 *Web:* tamarindrestaurantsnyc.com	New York	NY	10010	212-674-7400	674-4449
Thalia 828 Eigth Ave *Web:* www.restaurantthalia.com	New York	NY	10019	212-399-4444	399-3268
Tocqueville 1 E 15th St *Web:* www.tocquevillerestaurant.com	New York	NY	10003	212-647-1515	
Tomoe Sushi 172 Thompson St *Web:* tomoesushi.com	New York	NY	10012	212-777-9346	
Trattoria dell'Arte 900 Seventh Ave *Web:* www.trattoriadellarte.com	New York	NY	10106	212-245-9800	
Triomphe 49 W 44th St *Web:* www.iroquoisny.com	New York	NY	10036	212-453-4233	
Union Square Cafe 21 E 16th St *Web:* unionsquarecafe.com	New York	NY	10003	212-243-4020	
Veritas 43 E 20th St *Web:* www.veritas-nyc.com	New York	NY	10003	212-353-3700	
Wallse 344 W 11th St *Web:* www.wallse.com	New York	NY	10014	212-352-2300	
Wolfgang's Steakhouse 4 Pk Ave *Web:* www.wolfgangssteakhouse.net	New York	NY	10016	212-889-3369	
Butcher Block 15 Booth Dr *Web:* www.butcherblockrestaurant.com	Plattsburgh	NY	12901	518-563-0920	
Agatina's 2967 Buffalo Rd *Web:* www.agatinas.com	Rochester	NY	14624	585-426-0510	
Aladdin's Natural Eatery 646 Monroe Ave *Web:* myaladdins.com/monroe.html	Rochester	NY	14607	585-442-5000	
Bacco's 263 Pk Ave *Web:* baccosristorante.com	Rochester	NY	14607	585-442-5090	
Bathtub Billy's 630 Ridge Rd W *Web:* www.bathtubbillys.com	Rochester	NY	14615	585-865-6510	
Benucci's 3349 Monroe Ave *Web:* www.benuccis.com	Rochester	NY	14618	585-264-1300	
Bernard's Grove 187 Long Pond Rd *Web:* www.bernardsgrove.com	Rochester	NY	14612	585-227-6405	
Brook House 920 Elmridge Ctr Dr	Rochester	NY	14626	585-723-9988	
California Rollin' 274 N Goodman St *Web:* californiarollin.com	Rochester	NY	14607	585-271-8990	
Edibles Restaurant & Bar 704 University Ave *Web:* www.ediblesrochester.com	Rochester	NY	14607	585-271-4910	
Elmwood Inn, The 1256 Mt Hope Ave *Web:* elmwoodinn.net	Rochester	NY	14620	585-271-5195	
Hogan's Hideaway 197 Pk Ave *Web:* www.hoganshideaway.com	Rochester	NY	14607	585-442-4293	
Lucano 1815 E Ave *Web:* www.ristorantelucano.com	Rochester	NY	14610	585-244-3460	
Mamasan 2800 Monroe Ave *Web:* www.mamasans.com	Rochester	NY	14618	585-461-3290	
Mario's Via Abruzzi 2740 Monroe Ave *Web:* www.mariosit.com	Rochester	NY	14618	585-271-1111	
Phillips European Restaurant 26 Corporate Woods *Web:* www.phillipseuropean.com	Rochester	NY	14623	585-272-9910	272-1778
Remington's Restaurant 425 Merchants Rd	Rochester	NY	14609	585-482-4434	
Salena's Mexican Restaurant 302 N Goodman St At the Vlg Gate *Web:* www.salenas.com	Rochester	NY	14607	585-256-5980	

Phone | Fax

Angelina's Ristorante 399 Ellis St. ... Staten Island NY 10307 718-227-2900 227-3329
Web: angelinasristorante.com
1060 at the Genesee Grande
1060 E Genesee St ... Syracuse NY 13210 315-476-9000
Web: 1060restaurant.com
Alto Cinco 526 Westcott St. ... Syracuse NY 13210 315-422-6399
Web: www.altocinco.net
Angotti's 725 Burnet Ave ... Syracuse NY 13203 315-472-8403
Blue Tusk 165 Walton St ... Syracuse NY 13202 315-472-1934
Web: www.bluetusk.com
Casa Di Copani 3414 Burnet Ave. ... Syracuse NY 13206 315-463-1031
Web: casadicopani.com
Delmonico's Italian Steakhouse Syracuse
2950 Erie Blvd E ... Syracuse NY 13224 315-445-1111 445-0257
Web: www.delmonicositaliansteakhouse.com
Joey's Restaurant 6594 Thompson Rd ... Syracuse NY 13206 315-432-0315
Web: joeysitalianrestaurant.com
King David's 129 Marshall St. ... Syracuse NY 13210 315-471-5000
Web: www.kingdavids.com
Lemon Grass 238 W Jefferson St ... Syracuse NY 13202 315-475-1111
Web: www.lemongrasscny.com
Luigi's 1524 Valley Dr. ... Syracuse NY 13207 315-492-9997
Mission, The 304 E Onondaga St ... Syracuse NY 13202 315-475-7344 475-7340
Web: themissionrestaurant.com
Phoebe's 900 E Genesee St ... Syracuse NY 13210 315-475-5154
Web: www.phoebessyracuse.com
Riley's 312 Pk St. ... Syracuse NY 13203 315-471-7111
Syracuse Suds Factory 320 S Clinton St. ... Syracuse NY 13202 315-471-2253
Web: s502965190.onlinehome.us
Thai Flavor 2863 Erie Blvd E ... Syracuse NY 13224 315-251-1366
Web: syracusethaiflavor.com
Tokyo-Seoul 3180 Erie Blvd E ... Syracuse NY 13214 315-449-2688
Web: tokyoseoulsyracuse.com
Jasmine 1330 Niagara Falls Blvd ... Tonawanda NY 14150 716-838-3011 332-0280
Web: www.jasthai.com
Scharf's Schiller Park Restaurant
2683 Clinton St ... West Seneca NY 14224 716-895-7249
Web: www.scharfsrest.com
Sripraphai 64-13 39th Ave ... Woodside NY 11377 718-899-9599
Web: sripraphairestaurant.com
Caridad & Louie's Restaurant 187 S Broadway ... Yonkers NY 10701 914-375-9777
La Lanterna 23 Grey Oaks Ave ... Yonkers NY 10710 914-476-3060 375-3008
Web: www.lalanterna.com
ranchogrande Highridge Plz ... Yonkers NY 10710 757-366-5128
Rory Dolan's 890 McLean Ave ... Yonkers NY 10704 914-776-2946 776-6538
Web: www.rorydolans.com
Tombolino Restaurant 356 Kimball Ave ... Yonkers NY 10704 914-237-1266 237-1254
Web: www.tombolinoristorante.com
Zuppa 59 Main St ... Yonkers NY 10701 914-376-6500 376-4900
Web: www.zupparestaurant.com

North Carolina

Phone | Fax

Charlotte Street Grill & Pub
157 Charlotte St ... Asheville NC 28801 828-252-2948
Web: charlottestreetpub.com
Doc Chey's Noodle House 37 Biltmore Ave. ... Asheville NC 28801 828-252-8220
Web: www.doccheys.com
Laughing Seed Cafe 40 Wall St ... Asheville NC 28801 828-252-3445
Web: laughingseed.jackofthewood.com
Market Place, The 20 Wall St ... Asheville NC 28801 828-252-4162 253-3120
Web: www.marketplace-restaurant.com
Moose Cafe 570 BrevaRd Rd ... Asheville NC 28806 828-255-0920 255-0042
Web: eatatthemoosecafe.com
Omni Grove Park Inn, The 290 Macon Ave ... Asheville NC 28804 828-252-2711 252-7053
Ristorante da Vincenzo 10 N Market St ... Asheville NC 28801 828-254-4698
Salsa 6 Patton Ave. ... Asheville NC 28801 828-252-9805 252-9805
Web: salsasnc.com
Savoy Restaurant & Martini Bar
641 Merrimon Ave ... Asheville NC 28804 828-253-1077
Web: www.savoyasheville.com
Tupelo Honey Cafe 12 College St. ... Asheville NC 28801 828-255-4863 255-4864
Web: www.tupelohoneycafe.com
Yoshida Japanese Steak House
4 Regent Pk Blvd ... Asheville NC 28806 828-252-5903 258-3514
Zambra! 85 W Walnut St. ... Asheville NC 28801 828-232-1060
Web: www.zambratapas.com
Ruth's Chris Steakhouse 2010 Renaissance Pk Pl ... Cary NC 27513 919-677-0033
Web: www.ruthschris.com
Aria Tuscan Grill 100 N Tryon St ... Charlotte NC 28202 704-376-8880
Web: www.sonomarestaurants.net
Baoding 4722 Sharon Rd Ste F ... Charlotte NC 28210 704-552-8899 552-8828
Web: baodingsouthpark.com
Barrington's 7822 Fairview Rd ... Charlotte NC 28226 704-364-5755
Web: www.barringtonsrestaurant.com
Big Ben British Pub & Restaurant
2000 S Blvd ... Charlotte NC 28203 704-817-9697
Web: www.bigbenpub.com
Bill Spoon's Barbecue 5524 S Blvd. ... Charlotte NC 28217 704-525-8865
Web: spoonsbarbecue.com
Blue Restaurant & Bar 206 N College St. ... Charlotte NC 28202 704-927-2583
Web: www.bluecharlotte.com
Bonterra Dining & Wine Room
1829 Cleveland Ave ... Charlotte NC 28203 704-333-9463
Web: www.bonterradining.com
Cajun Queen 1800 E Seventh St. ... Charlotte NC 28204 704-377-9017
Web: www.cajunqueen.net
Carpe Diem 1535 Elizabeth Ave ... Charlotte NC 28204 704-377-7976
Web: www.carpediemrestaurant.com
Ilios Noche 11508 Providence Rd ... Charlotte NC 28277 704-814-9882
Web: www.xeniahospitality.com

Phone | Fax

Mama Ricotta's 601 S Kings Dr ... Charlotte NC 28204 704-343-0148 377-7461
Web: www.mamaricottasrestaurant.com
McCormick & Schmick's 200 S Tryon St ... Charlotte NC 28202 704-377-0201 377-0208
TF: 800-552-6379 ■ *Web:* www.mccormickandschmicks.com
McNinch House 511 N Church St ... Charlotte NC 28202 704-332-6159 376-0212
Web: www.mcninchhouserestaurant.com
Melting Pot of Charlotte, The
901 S Kings Dr Ste 140B ... Charlotte NC 28204 704-334-4400 334-0535
TF: 800-783-0867 ■ *Web:* www.meltingpot.com
Mert's Heart & Soul 214 N College St ... Charlotte NC 28202 704-342-4222
Web: www.uptown2go.com
Mickey & Mooch The other Joint
8128 Providence Rd Ste 1200 ... Charlotte NC 28277 704-752-8080
Web: www.mickeyandmooch.com
Mimosa Grill 327 S Tryon St ... Charlotte NC 28202 704-343-0700
Web: www.harpersgroup.com
Miro Spanish Grille
12239 N Community House Rd ... Charlotte NC 28277 704-540-7374
Web: www.mirospanishgrille.com
Musashi 10110 Johnston Rd ... Charlotte NC 28210 704-543-5181
Web: www.musashi-nc.com
New South Kitchen & Bar
8140 Providence Rd Ste 300 ... Charlotte NC 28277 704-541-9990 541-1163
Web: www.newsouthkitchen.com
Nikko 1300 S Blvd ... Charlotte NC 28203 704-370-0100 370-0123
Web: www.nikkosushibar.net
Old Hickory House Restaurant
6538 N Tryon St ... Charlotte NC 28213 704-596-8014 596-0922
Portofino 3124 Eastway Dr ... Charlotte NC 28205 704-568-7933
Web: portofinos-us.com
Sullivan's Steakhouse 1928 S Blvd. ... Charlotte NC 28203 704-335-8228
Web: sullivanssteakhouse.com
Thai Orchid 4223 Providence Rd ... Charlotte NC 28211 704-364-1134
Web: thaiorchidrestaurantcharlotte.com
Toscana 6401 Morrison Blvd ... Charlotte NC 28211 704-367-1808
Web: conterestaurantgroup.com
Upstream
Harper's Restaurant Group
6902 Phillips Pl Ct. ... Charlotte NC 28210 704-556-7730 552-2793
Web: www.harpersgroup.com/upstream.asp
Villa Antonio 4707 S Blvd ... Charlotte NC 28217 704-523-1594 523-5697
Volare Ristorante Italiano
1523 Elizabeth Ave ... Charlotte NC 28204 704-370-0208
Web: www.volareristoranteitaliano.com
Zebra 4521 Sharon Rd. ... Charlotte NC 28211 704-442-9525
Web: www.zebrarestaurant.net
Bennett Pointe Grill & Bar
4625 Hillsborough Rd ... Durham NC 27705 919-382-9431
Web: www.bpgrill.com
Blue Corn Cafe 716 Ninth St ... Durham NC 27705 919-286-9600
Web: bluecorncafedurham.com
Bullock's Bar-B-Que 3330 Quebec Dr ... Durham NC 27705 919-383-3211 383-6202
Web: www.bullocksbbq.com
Cafe Parizade 2200 W Main St ... Durham NC 27705 919-286-9712
Web: www.parizadedurham.com
El Rodeo 3404 Westgate Dr ... Durham NC 27707 919-402-9190
Web: elrodeodurhamnc.com
Fairview Restaurant 3001 Cameron Blvd ... Durham NC 27705 919-493-6699
Web: washingtondukeinn.com
Fishmonger's 806 W Main St ... Durham NC 27701 919-682-0128
Hog Heaven Bar-B-Q 2419 Guess Rd ... Durham NC 27705 919-286-7447
Web: www.hogheavenbarbecue.com
Jamaica Jamaica 4857 NC Hwy 55 ... Durham NC 27713 919-544-1532
Kanki Japanese House of Steaks
3504 Mt Moriah Rd ... Durham NC 27707 919-401-6908 401-6843
Web: www.kanki.com
Kurama Seafood & Steakhouse
3644 Chapel Hill Blvd. ... Durham NC 27707 919-489-2669 489-4400
Web: www.kuramadurham.com
Nana's 2514 University Dr ... Durham NC 27707 919-493-8545 403-8487
Web: www.nanasdurham.com
Neo-Asia Restaurant 4015 University Dr. ... Durham NC 27707 919-489-2828 489-9898
Web: www.neo-china.com
Original Q Shack, The 2510 University Dr ... Durham NC 27707 919-402-4227
Web: theqshackoriginal.com
Satisfaction Restaurant 905 W Main St Ste 37 ... Durham NC 27701 919-682-7397
Web: www.satisfactionrestaurant.com
Shanghai Restaurant 3433 Hillsborough Rd ... Durham NC 27705 919-383-7581 383-7581
Web: www.shanghai.ypguides.net
Shiki Sushi 207 N Carolina 54 ... Durham NC 27713 919-484-4108
Web: shikitasu.com
Spice & Curry 2105 E Hwy 54 ... Durham NC 27713 919-544-7555
Torero's 800 W Main St ... Durham NC 27701 919-682-4197
Web: torerosmexicanrestaurants.com
Acropolis Restaurant 416 N Eugene St ... Greensboro NC 27401 336-273-3306 675-0913*
**Fax Area Code: 410*
Anton's 1628 Battleground Ave. ... Greensboro NC 27408 336-273-1386 273-1225
Asahi 4520 W Market St ... Greensboro NC 27407 336-855-8883
Bangkok Cafe 1203 S Holden Rd ... Greensboro NC 27407 336-855-9370
Boba House 332 S Tate St ... Greensboro NC 27403 336-379-7444
Web: www.bobahouse.com
Bonefish Grill 2100 Koury Blvd ... Greensboro NC 27407 336-851-8900
Web: www.bonefishgrill.com
Cafe Pasta 305 State St ... Greensboro NC 27408 336-272-1308
Web: www.cafepasta.com
Cooper's Ale House 5340 W Market St ... Greensboro NC 27409 336-294-0575
Web: www.coopersalehouse.com
Darryl's Wood Fired Grill 3300 High Pt Rd ... Greensboro NC 27407 336-294-1781 294-2242
Web: www.darrylswoodfiredgrill.com
George K's Catering & Banquet Hall
2108 Cedar Fork Dr ... Greensboro NC 27407 336-854-0008
Green Valley Grill 622 Green Vly Rd ... Greensboro NC 27408 336-854-2015 544-9000
Web: www.greenvalleygrill.com

	City	State	Zip	Phone	Fax
India Palace 413 Tate St	Greensboro	NC	27403	336-379-0744	
Leblon 106 S Holden Rd *Web:* leblonsteakhouse.com	Greensboro	NC	27407	336-294-2605	
Liberty Oak Restaurant & Bar 100 W Washington St Ste D *Web:* www.libertyoakrestaurant.com	Greensboro	NC	27401	336-273-7057	
Marisol 5834 High Pt Rd *Web:* www.themarisol.com	Greensboro	NC	27407	336-852-3303	
Monterrey 3724 Battleground Ave *Web:* monterrey29.com	Greensboro	NC	27410	336-282-5588	
Saigon 4205 High Pt Rd *Web:* www.saigonrestaurant.net	Greensboro	NC	27407	336-294-9286	
Sapporo Fantasy Japanese Steak 2939 C Battleground Ave	Greensboro	NC	27408	336-282-5345	282-5379
Southern Lights 2415 Lawndale Dr *Web:* southernlightsbistro.com	Greensboro	NC	27408	336-379-9414	
Stamey's Barbecue 2206 High Pt Rd *Web:* www.stameys.com	Greensboro	NC	27403	336-299-9888	
Taste of Thai 1500 Mill St *Web:* www.tasteofthaigreensboro.com	Greensboro	NC	27408	336-273-1318	
Undercurrent, The 327 Battleground Ave *Web:* www.undercurrentrestaurant.com	Greensboro	NC	27401	336-370-1266	
Village Tavern 1903 Westridge Rd *Web:* www.villagetavern.com	Greensboro	NC	27410	336-282-3063	
Villarosa Italian Restaurant & Grill 6010 Landmark Ctr Blvd *Web:* villarosa.us	Greensboro	NC	27407	336-294-8688	
Melting Pot of Greensboro, The 2045 S Hurstbourne Pkwy *Web:* www.meltingpot.com	Louisville	NC	27408	502-491-3125	
518 West 518 W Jones St	Raleigh	NC	27603	919-829-2518	
Angus Barn 9401 Glenwood Ave *TF:* 800-277-2270 ■ *Web:* www.angusbarn.com	Raleigh	NC	27617	919-781-2444	783-5568
Bella Monica 3121 EdwaRds Mill Rd Ste 103 *Web:* www.bellamonica.com	Raleigh	NC	27612	919-881-9778	
Bloomsbury Bistro 509 W Whitaker Mill Rd Ste 101 *Web:* www.bloomsburybistro.com	Raleigh	NC	27608	919-834-9011	834-9096
Caffe Luna 136 E Hargett St *Web:* www.cafeluna.com	Raleigh	NC	27601	919-832-6090	
Clyde Cooper's BBQ 109 E Davie St *Web:* clydecoopersbbq.com	Raleigh	NC	27601	919-832-7614	
Irregardless Cafe 901 W Morgan St *Web:* irregardless.com	Raleigh	NC	27603	919-833-8898	
Kanki Japanese House of Steaks 4500 Old Wake Forest Rd *Web:* www.kanki.com	Raleigh	NC	27609	919-782-9708	876-7699
Melting Pot of Raleigh, The 3100 Wake Forest Rd *Web:* www.meltingpot.com	Raleigh	NC	27609	919-878-0477	878-0815
Neo-Asia / Neo-China (Weekend Lunch Dim Sum) 6602 Glenwood Ave *Web:* www.neo-china.com	Raleigh	NC	27612	919-783-8383	783-8353
Nina's Ristorante 8801 Lead Mine Rd *Web:* ninasrestaurant.com	Raleigh	NC	27615	919-845-1122	
PF Chang's China Bistro 4325 Glenwood Ave *Web:* www.pfchangs.com	Raleigh	NC	27612	919-787-7754	
Rey's 1130 Buck Jones Rd *Web:* www.reysrestaurant.com	Raleigh	NC	27606	919-380-0122	
Saint-Jacques 6112 Falls of the Neuse Rd *Web:* saintjacquesfrenchcuisine.com	Raleigh	NC	27609	919-862-2770	862-2771
Second Empire 330 Hillsborough St *Web:* www.second-empire.com	Raleigh	NC	27603	919-829-3663	
ShabaShabu 3080 Wake Forest Rd *Web:* shabashabu.net	Raleigh	NC	27609	919-501-7755	501-7479
Sullivan's Steakhouse 410 Glenwood Ave Ste 100 *Web:* sullivanssteakhouse.com	Raleigh	NC	27603	919-833-2888	
Sushi Blues 301 Glenwood Ave *Web:* www.sushibluescafe.com	Raleigh	NC	27603	919-664-8061	664-8070
Waraji 5910 Duraleigh Rd *Web:* www.warajijapaneserestaurant.com	Raleigh	NC	27612	919-783-1883	
Zely & Ritz 301 Glenwood Ave *Web:* www.zelyandritz.com	Raleigh	NC	27603	919-828-0018	828-2937
Texas Steakhouse 711 Sutters Creek Blvd *Web:* www.texassteakhouse.com	Rocky Mount	NC	27804	252-443-3888	
1703 Restaurant 1703 Robin Hood Rd *Web:* www.localedge.com	Winston-Salem	NC	27104	336-725-5767	
A Noble Grille 380 Knollwood St *Web:* roosterskitchen.com/locations/a-noble-grille-winston-salem	Winston-Salem	NC	27103	336-777-8477	
Cha-Da Thai 420-J Jonestown Rd *Web:* chadathai-nc.com	Winston-Salem	NC	27104	336-659-8466	659-8458
Hill's Lexington Barbecue 4005 Patterson Ave *Web:* ncbbqsociety.com	Winston-Salem	NC	27105	336-767-2184	
ISE Sushi & Japanese Restaurant 121 Stark St *Web:* winstonsalemsushi.com	Winston-Salem	NC	27103	336-774-0433	
Midtown Cafe & Dessertery 151 S Stratford Rd *Web:* www.midtowncafews.com	Winston-Salem	NC	27104	336-724-9800	724-9830
MJM Reynolda Laundromat 2802 Reynolda Rd	Winston-Salem	NC	27106	336-724-4242	
Nawab Indian Cuisine 129 S Stratford Rd *Web:* www.nawabindiancuisine.com	Winston-Salem	NC	27104	336-725-3949	
Old Fourth Street Filling Station, The 871 W Fourth St *Web:* www.theoldfourthstreetfillingstation.com	Winston-Salem	NC	27101	336-724-7600	
Paul's Fine Italian Dining 3443-B Robinhood Rd *Web:* paulsfineitaliandining.com	Winston-Salem	NC	27106	336-768-2645	
Ryan's 719 Coliseum Dr *Web:* www.ryansrestaurant.com	Winston-Salem	NC	27106	336-724-6132	724-5761
Sampan Chinese Restaurant 985 Peters Creek Pkwy	Winston-Salem	NC	27103	336-777-8266	
Sweet Potatoes 529 N Trade St *Web:* www.sweetpotatoes-arestaurant.com	Winston-Salem	NC	27101	336-727-4844	
Szechuan Palace 3040 Healy Dr	Winston-Salem	NC	27103	336-768-7123	
Tokyo Japanese Steakhouse 1111 Salisbury Ridge Rd *Web:* www.tjsteakhouse.com	Winston-Salem	NC	27127	336-722-5009	
Vincenzo's 3449 Robinhood Rd *Web:* vincenzospizzawinstonsalemnc.com	Winston-Salem	NC	27106	336-765-3176	

North Dakota

	City	State	Zip	Phone	Fax
40 Steak & Seafood 1401 Interchange Ave	Bismarck	ND	58501	701-255-4040	258-7229
Bistro An American Cafe 1103 E Front Ave *Web:* www.bistro1100.com	Bismarck	ND	58504	701-224-8800	224-0398
China Garden 1929 N Washington St	Bismarck	ND	58501	701-224-0698	
Famous Dave's 401 E Bismarck Expy *Web:* www.famousdaves.com	Bismarck	ND	58504	701-530-9800	
Grand China 658 Kirkwood Mall *Web:* www.grandchinabismarck.com	Bismarck	ND	58504	701-222-1518	
Hong Kong Chinese Restaurant 1055 E Interstate Ave	Bismarck	ND	58503	701-223-2130	
Little Cottage Cafe 2513 E Main Ave	Bismarck	ND	58501	701-223-4949	
Peacock Alley 422 E Main St *Web:* www.peacock-alley.com	Bismarck	ND	58501	701-255-7917	
Space Aliens Grill & Bar 1304 E Century Ave *Web:* www.spacealiens.com	Bismarck	ND	58503	701-223-6220	
Walrus, The 1136 N 3rd St *Web:* www.thewalrus.com	Bismarck	ND	58501	701-250-0020	
Wood House Restaurant 1825 N 13th St	Bismarck	ND	58501	701-255-3654	
Alumni Center, The 1241 University Dr N *TF:* 800-279-8971 ■ *Web:* www.ndsualumni.com	Fargo	ND	58102	701-231-6800	
Bison Turf 1211 N University Dr *Web:* thebisonturfnd.com	Fargo	ND	58102	701-235-9118	
Cafe Aladdin 530 Sixth Ave N *Web:* cafealaddinfargo.com	Fargo	ND	58102	701-298-0880	
Granite City Food & Brewery Ltd (GCFB) 1636 42nd St SW *Web:* www.gcfb.com	Fargo	ND	58103	701-293-3000	
Juano's 402 Broadway	Fargo	ND	58102	701-232-3123	
Mexican Village 814 Main Ave *Web:* www.mexicanvillage.com	Fargo	ND	58103	701-293-0120	
Nine Dragons Restaurant 4525 17th Ave S *Web:* www.9dragonsrestaurant.com	Fargo	ND	58104	701-232-2411	
Seasons at Rose Creek 1500 Rose Creek Pkwy E	Fargo	ND	58104	701-235-5000	
Shang Hai 3051 25th St SW *Web:* fargoshanghai.com	Fargo	ND	58103	701-280-5818	
Timberlodge Steakhouse 1111 38th St SW *Web:* www.timberlodgesteakhouse.com	Fargo	ND	58103	952-881-5509	
China Garden 2550 32nd Ave S	Grand Forks	ND	58201	701-772-0660	
Eagle's Crest Grill 5301 S Columbia Rd *Web:* eaglescrestgrill.com	Grand Forks	ND	58201	701-787-3491	
Italian Moon 810 S Washington St *Web:* www.italianmoon.com	Grand Forks	ND	58201	701-772-7277	
Red Pepper 1011 University Ave *Web:* www.redpepper.com	Grand Forks	ND	58203	701-775-9671	
Sanders 1907 22 S Third St	Grand Forks	ND	58201	701-746-8970	

Nova Scotia

	City	Province	Postal Code	Phone	Fax
Chives Canadian Bistro 1537 Barrington St *Web:* www.chives.ca	Halifax	NS	B3J1Z4	902-420-9626	
Cousin's Restaurant 3545 Robie St *Web:* www.cousinsrestaurant.webs.com	Halifax	NS	B3K4S7	902-455-8931	
Da Maurizio *Fine Dining* 1496 Lower Water St *Web:* www.damaurizio.ca	Halifax	NS	B3J1R7	902-423-0859	
Dharma Sushi 1576 Argyle St	Halifax	NS	B3J2B3	902-425-7785	425-7250
Economy Shoe Shop Cafe & Bar 1663 Argyle St *Web:* www.economyshoeshop.ca	Halifax	NS	B3J2B5	902-423-8845	
Fid 1569 Dresden Row	Halifax	NS	B3J2K4	902-422-9162	422-0018
Five Fishermen Restaurant & Grill, The 1740 Argyle St *Web:* www.fivefishermen.com	Halifax	NS	B3J2B6	902-422-4421	
Great Wall 1649 Bedford Row *Web:* www.thegreatwall.ca	Halifax	NS	B3J3J4	902-422-6153	
Hamachi House 5190 Morris St *Web:* www.hamachirestaurants.com	Halifax	NS	B3J1B3	902-425-7711	444-4068
McKelvie's 1680 Lower Water St *Web:* www.mckelvies.com	Halifax	NS	B3J2Y3	902-421-6161	
Mexico Lindo 3635 Dutch Village Rd *Web:* www.mexicolindo.ca	Halifax	NS	B3N2S4	902-445-0996	
Murphy's Cable Wharf 1751 Lower Water St PO Box 2378 *Web:* www.mtcw.ca	Halifax	NS	B3J3E4	902-420-1015	423-7942
Wooden Monkey 1707 Grafton St *Web:* www.thewoodenmonkey.ca	Halifax	NS	B3J2C6	902-444-3844	
Your Father's Moustache 5686 Spring Garden Rd *Web:* www.yourfathersmoustache.ca	Halifax	NS	B3J1H5	902-423-6766	

Ohio

	City	State	Zip	Phone	Fax
Bill Hwang's Restaurant 879 Canton Rd *Web:* billhwangsrestaurant.com	Akron	OH	44312	330-784-7167	

Name	City	State	Zip	Phone	Fax
Bricco 1 W Exchange St	Akron	OH	44308	330-475-1600	
Web: www.briccoakron.com					
Dontino's La Vita Gardens 555 E Cuyahoga Falls Ave	Akron	OH	44310	330-928-9530	
Web: www.dontinos.com					
Duffy's Restaurant 231 Darrow Rd	Akron	OH	44305	330-784-5043	
Web: duffysrestaurantandgrill.com					
El Rincon 1485 S Arlington St	Akron	OH	44306	330-785-3724	785-2816
Gasoline Alley 870 N Cleveland Massillon Rd	Akron	OH	44333	330-666-2670	
Web: gasolinealleyinbath.com					
House of Hunan 12 E Exchange St Ste 1	Akron	OH	44308	330-253-1888	
Web: thehouseofhunan.com					
Hyde Park Grille 4073 Medina Rd	Akron	OH	44333	330-670-6303	670-6174
Web: www.hydeparkrestaurants.com					
Ido Bar & Grill 1537 S Main St	Akron	OH	44301	330-773-1724	
Web: www.idobar.com					
Ken Stewart's Grille 1970 W Market St	Akron	OH	44313	330-867-2555	
Web: kenstewarts.com					
Lanning's 826 N Cleveland-Massillon Rd	Akron	OH	44333	330-666-1159	
Web: www.lannings-restaurant.com					
Larry's Main Entrance 1964 W Market St	Akron	OH	44313	330-864-8162	
Luigi's 105 N Main St	Akron	OH	44308	330-253-2999	
Web: luigisrestaurant.com					
New Era Restaurant 10 Massillon Rd	Akron	OH	44312	330-784-0087	
Otani Japanese Seafood & Steakhouse 1684 Merriman Rd	Akron	OH	44313	330-836-1500	
Papa Joe's 1561 Akron Peninsula Rd	Akron	OH	44313	330-923-7999	923-8009
Web: papajoes.com					
Platinum Dragon 814 1/2 W Market St	Akron	OH	44303	330-434-8108	434-1908
Vaccaro's Trattoria 1000 Ghent Rd	Akron	OH	44333	330-666-6158	666-4558
Web: www.vactrat.com					
Antone's Italian Cafe 4837 Mahoning Ave	Austintown	OH	44515	330-793-0707	
Web: chadanthonys.com					
Asuka Japanese Cuisine 7381 Market St	Boardman	OH	44512	330-629-8088	
Web: asukajapanese.com					
Ambar 350 Ludlow Ave	Cincinnati	OH	45220	513-281-7000	281-7001
Web: www.ambarindia.com					
Amol India 354 Ludlow Ave	Cincinnati	OH	45220	513-961-3600	
Web: amolindiacincinnati.com					
Andy's Mediterranean Grille 906 Nassau St	Cincinnati	OH	45206	513-281-9791	
Web: www.andyskabob.com					
Bacall's Cafe 6118 Hamilton Ave	Cincinnati	OH	45224	513-541-8804	
Web: www.bacallscafe.com					
Ban Thai 792 Eastgate S Dr	Cincinnati	OH	45245	513-752-3200	
Barresi's 4111 Webster Ave	Cincinnati	OH	45236	513-793-2540	
Web: www.barresis.com					
BBQ Revue 4725 Madison Rd	Cincinnati	OH	45227	513-871-3500	
Big Art's BBQ 2796 Struble Rd	Cincinnati	OH	45251	513-825-4811	
Brown Dog Cafe 5893 Pfeiffer Rd	Cincinnati	OH	45242	513-794-1610	
Web: www.browndogcafe.com					
Celestial Restaurant 1071 Celestial St	Cincinnati	OH	45202	513-241-4455	241-4855
Web: www.thecelestial.com					
China Gourmet 3340 Erie Ave	Cincinnati	OH	45208	513-871-6612	
Web: thechinagourmet.com					
El Coyote 7404 State Rd	Cincinnati	OH	45230	513-232-5757	
Web: www.elcoyotecincy.com					
Hibachi Master 8160 Beechmont Ave	Cincinnati	OH	45255	513-474-9888	
Web: hibachimaster.com					
Jeff Ruby's Steakhouse 700 Walnut St	Cincinnati	OH	45202	513-321-8080	
Web: www.jeffruby.com					
Nectar Restaurant 1000 Delta Ave	Cincinnati	OH	45208	513-929-0525	
Web: www.tastenectar.com					
Nicholson's Tavern & Pub 625 Walnut St	Cincinnati	OH	45202	513-564-9111	
Web: www.tavernrestaurantgroup.com					
Nicola's 1420 Sycamore St	Cincinnati	OH	45202	513-721-6200	721-1777
Web: nicolasotr.com					
Palace, The 601 Vine St	Cincinnati	OH	45202	513-381-6006	651-0256
TF: 800-942-9000 ■ *Web:* www.palacecincinnati.com					
PF Chang's China Bistro 2633 Edmondson Rd	Cincinnati	OH	45209	513-531-4567	
Web: www.pfchangs.com					
Primavista 810 Matson Pl	Cincinnati	OH	45204	513-251-6467	251-4669
Web: www.pvista.com					
Restaurant at the Phoenix 812 Race St	Cincinnati	OH	45202	513-721-8901	
Web: www.thephx.com/restaurant					
Shanghai Mama's 216 E Sixth St	Cincinnati	OH	45202	513-241-7777	
Web: www.shanghaimamas.com					
TeakThai Cusine 1049-51 St Gregory St	Cincinnati	OH	45202	513-665-9800	
Web: www.teakthaicuisine.com					
Trio 7565 Kenwood Rd	Cincinnati	OH	45236	513-984-1905	
Web: www.triobistro.com					
Blue Point Grille 700 W St Clair Ave	Cleveland	OH	44113	216-875-7827	
Web: hrcleveland.com					
Bo Loong Restaurant 3922 St Clair Ave	Cleveland	OH	44114	216-391-3113	391-8407
China Jade 2190 Brookpark Rd	Cleveland	OH	44134	216-749-4720	
Web: www.chinajadecleveland.com					
Don's Lighthouse Grille 8905 Lake Ave	Cleveland	OH	44102	216-961-6700	
Web: www.donslighthouse.com					
Fahrenheit 2417 Professor Ave	Cleveland	OH	44113	216-781-8858	
Web: chefroccowhalen.com/fahrenheit-cleveland					
Fat Cats 2061 W Tenth St	Cleveland	OH	44113	216-579-0200	
Web: coolplacestoeat.com					
Fire 13220 Shaker Sq	Cleveland	OH	44120	216-921-3473	
Web: www.firefoodanddrink.com					
Flying Fig 2523 Market St	Cleveland	OH	44113	216-241-4243	
Web: www.theflyingfig.com					
Frank Sterles Slovenian Restaurant 1401 E 55th St	Cleveland	OH	44103	216-881-4181	
Web: www.sterlescountryhouse.com					
Gene's Place 3730 Rocky River Dr	Cleveland	OH	44111	216-252-1741	252-1742
Ginza Sushi House 1105 Carnegie Ave	Cleveland	OH	44115	216-589-8503	
Gusto 12022 Mayfield Rd	Cleveland	OH	44106	216-791-9900	
Web: www.gustolittleitaly.com					
Harp, The 4408 Detroit Ave	Cleveland	OH	44113	216-939-0200	939-0068
Web: www.the-harp.com					
Hyde Park Steakhouse 123 Prospect Ave W	Cleveland	OH	44115	216-344-2444	344-2726
Web: www.hydeparkrestaurants.com					
Johnny's Bar on Fulton 3164 Fulton Rd	Cleveland	OH	44109	216-281-0055	
Web: johnnyscleveland.com					
Johnny's Downtown 1406 W Sixth St	Cleveland	OH	44113	216-623-0055	
Web: www.johnnyscleveland.com					
Light Bistro 2801 Bridge Ave	Cleveland	OH	44113	216-771-7130	771-8130
Lolita 900 Literary Rd	Cleveland	OH	44113	216-771-5652	
Web: lolitarestaurant.com					
Mallorca 1390 W Ninth St	Cleveland	OH	44113	216-687-9494	
Web: www.clevelandmallorca.com					
Momocho Mod Mex 1835 Fulton Rd	Cleveland	OH	44113	216-694-2122	
Web: www.momocho.com					
Mortons the Steakhouse 1600 W Second St	Cleveland	OH	44113	216-621-6200	621-7745
Web: www.mortons.com					
Parallax 2179 W 11th St	Cleveland	OH	44113	216-583-9999	
Web: www.parallaxtremont.com					
Sans Souci 24 Public Sq	Cleveland	OH	44113	216-902-4095	
Web: www.sanssoucicleveland.com					
Siam Cafe 3951 St Clair Ave	Cleveland	OH	44114	216-361-2323	834-3181*
**Fax Area Code:* 615					
Sun Luck Garden 1901 S Taylor Rd	Cleveland	OH	44118	216-397-7676	
Sushi Rock 1276 W Sixth St	Cleveland	OH	44113	216-623-1212	
Tommy's Restaurant 1824 Coventry Rd	Cleveland	OH	44118	216-321-7757	
Web: www.tommyscoventry.com					
Villa Y Zapata 8505 Madison Ave	Cleveland	OH	44102	216-961-4369	
XO Prime Steaks 500 W St Claire Ave	Cleveland	OH	44113	216-861-1919	861-0374
Web: xoprimesteaks.com					
Cafe Tandoor 2096 S Taylor Rd	Cleveland Heights	OH	44118	216-371-8500	371-8560
Web: cafetandoorcleveland.com					
Mad Greek 2466 Fairmount Blvd	Cleveland Heights	OH	44106	216-421-3333	
Web: www.madgreekcleveland.com					
Aladdin's Eatery 2931 N High St	Columbus	OH	43202	614-262-2414	
Web: www.aladdinseatery.com					
Alana's Food & Wine 2333 N High St	Columbus	OH	43202	614-294-6783	
Web: www.alanas.com					
Anna's Greek Cuisine 7370 Sawmill Rd	Columbus	OH	43235	614-799-2207	
Web: annasgreekfood.com					
Barcelona 263 E Whittier St	Columbus	OH	43206	614-443-3699	444-0539
Web: www.barcelonacolumbus.com					
Barley's Smokehouse & Brewpub 1130 Dublin Rd	Columbus	OH	43215	614-485-0227	
Web: www.smokehousebrewing.com					
Basi Italia 811 Highland St	Columbus	OH	43215	614-294-7383	
Web: basi-italia.com					
Brio Tuscan Grille 3993 Easton Stn St	Columbus	OH	43219	614-416-4745	
Web: www.brioitalian.com					
Cafe Istanbul 3983 Worth Ave	Columbus	OH	43219	614-473-9144	
Web: www.cafeistanbul.com					
Cameron Mitchell Restaurants 515 Pk St	Columbus	OH	43215	614-291-3663	
Web: www.cameronmitchell.com					
Columbus Fish Market 1245 Olentangy River Rd	Columbus	OH	43212	614-291-3474	
Web: mitchellsfishmarket.com					
Due Amici 67 E Gay St	Columbus	OH	43215	614-224-9373	
Web: www.due-amici.com					
El Vaquero 2195 Riverside Dr	Columbus	OH	43221	614-486-4547	486-4050
Web: vaquerorestaurant.com					
G Michael's Bistro 595 S Third St	Columbus	OH	43215	614-464-0575	
Web: gmichaelsbistroandbar.com					
Haiku Poetic Food & Art 800 N High St	Columbus	OH	43215	614-294-8168	294-3868
Web: haikucolumbus.com					
Handke's Cuisine 520 S Front St	Columbus	OH	43215	614-621-2500	
Web: www.chefhandke.com					
Hunan House 2350 E Dublin Granville Rd	Columbus	OH	43229	614-895-3330	
Web: www.hunancolumbus.com					
Hyde Park Prime Steakhouse 569 N High St	Columbus	OH	43215	614-224-2204	
Web: hydeparkrestaurants.com					
Indian Oven 427 E Main St	Columbus	OH	43215	614-220-9390	
Web: www.indianoven.com					
Japanese Steak House 479 N High St	Columbus	OH	43215	614-228-3030	
Web: japanesesteakhousecolumbusoh.com					
Latitude 41 50 N Third St	Columbus	OH	43215	614-233-7541	
Web: www.latitude41restaurant.com					
Lemongrass 641 N High St	Columbus	OH	43215	614-224-1414	221-2535
Web: www.lemongrassfusion.com					
Lindey's 169 E Beck St	Columbus	OH	43206	614-228-4343	
Web: www.lindeys.com					
M at Miranova 2 Miranova PL Ste 100	Columbus	OH	43215	614-629-0000	221-5020
TF: 877-491-1267 ■ *Web:* www.matmiranova.com					
Martini Italian Bistro 445 N High St	Columbus	OH	43215	614-224-8259	224-8780
Web: www.martinimodernitalian.com					
Mitchell's Fish Market 1245 Olentangy River Rd	Columbus	OH	43212	614-291-3474	
Web: www.mitchellsfishmarket.com					
Mitchell's Ocean Club 4002 Easton Stn	Columbus	OH	43219	614-416-2582	416-2800
Web: www.ocean-prime.com/locations-menus/mitchells-ocean-club					
Mitchell's Steakhouse 45 N Third St	Columbus	OH	43215	614-621-2333	
Web: www.mitchellssteakhouse.com					
Refectory Resturant & Bistro 1092 Bethel Rd	Columbus	OH	43220	614-451-9774	
Web: www.therefectoryrestaurant.com					
Rigsby's Kitchen 698 N High St	Columbus	OH	43215	614-461-7888	
Web: www.rigsbyskitchen.com					
Rossi Bar & Kitchen 895 N High St	Columbus	OH	43215	614-299-2810	
Web: rossibarandkitchen.com					
Ruth's Chris Steak House 7550 High Cross Blvd	Columbus	OH	43235	614-885-2910	
Web: www.ruthschris.com					
Schmidt's Sausage Haus 240 E Kossuth St	Columbus	OH	43206	614-444-6808	445-3072
Web: www.schmidthaus.com					

Name / Address	City	State	ZIP	Phone	Fax
Shoku 1312 Grandview Ave	Columbus	OH	43212	614-485-9490	
Web: shokugrandview.com					
Smith & Wollensky 4145 the Strand W Easton Town Ctr	Columbus	OH	43219	614-416-2400	
Web: www.smithandwollensky.com					
Thai Taste 1178 Kenny Centre Mall	Columbus	OH	43220	614-451-7605	
Trattoria Roma 1447 Grandview Ave	Columbus	OH	43212	614-488-2104	
Web: www.trattoria-roma.com					
Windward Passage 4739 Reed Rd	Columbus	OH	43220	614-451-2497	
Akashi Sushi Bar 2020 Harshman Rd	Dayton	OH	45424	937-233-8005	
Web: akashidayton.com					
Amber Rose 1400 Valley St	Dayton	OH	45404	937-228-2511	
Web: www.theamberrose.com					
Barnsider 5202 N Main St	Dayton	OH	45415	937-277-1332	
Web: barnsider-restaurant.com					
Citilites 138 N Main St	Dayton	OH	45402	937-222-0623	222-1504
Web: victoriatheatre.com					
Dublin Pub 300 Wayne Ave	Dayton	OH	45410	937-224-7822	
Web: www.dubpub.com					
Elsa's 3618 Linden Ave	Dayton	OH	45410	937-252-9635	
Web: elsas.net					
Franco's Ristorante Italiano 824 E Fifth St	Dayton	OH	45402	937-222-0204	222-1380
Web: www.francos-italiano.com					
I-Zu Japanese Restaurant & Grocery 5252 N Dixie Dr	Dayton	OH	45414	937-277-9596	
Mamma DiSalvo's Italian Ristorante 1375 E Stroop Rd	Dayton	OH	45429	937-299-5831	299-1752
Web: www.mammadisalvo.com					
North China 6090 Far Hills Ave	Dayton	OH	45459	937-433-6837	
Web: northchinadayton.com					
Pine Club, The 1926 Brown St	Dayton	OH	45409	937-228-7463	228-5371
Web: www.thepineclub.com					
Thai9 11 Brown St	Dayton	OH	45402	937-222-3227	222-3235
Web: www.thai9restaurant.com					
La Petite France 3177 Glendale-Milford Rd	Evendale	OH	45241	513-733-8383	733-0038
Web: www.lapetitefrance.biz					
Max & Erma's 3750 W Market St	Fairlawn	OH	44333	330-666-1002	
Web: maxandermas.com					
Otani 1625 Golden Gate Plz	Mayfield Heights	OH	44124	440-442-7098	
Web: www.otanicleveland.com					
Dominic's 221 S Jefferson St	Medina	OH	44256	330-725-8424	
Web: www.dominicsitalianrestaurant.com					
Montgomery Inn 9440 Montgomery Rd	Montgomery	OH	45242	513-791-3482	992-8678*
**Fax Area Code:* 914 ■ *Web:* www.montgomeryinn.com					
356th Fighter Group 4919 Mt Pleasant Rd	North Canton	OH	44720	330-494-7418	494-5509
Phnom Penh 27080 Lorain Ave	North Olmsted	OH	44070	216-201-9141	
Web: ohiorestaurant.com					
Cousino's Steak House 1842 Woodville Rd	Oregon	OH	43616	419-693-0862	
Saffron Patch 20600 Chagrin Blvd Twr E Bldg	Shaker Heights	OH	44122	216-295-0400	295-1320
Web: www.thesaffronpatch.com					
Avenue Bistro Restaurant 6710 W Central Ave	Toledo	OH	43617	419-841-5944	842-1435
Web: centralavenuebistro.com					
Beirut 4082 Monroe St	Toledo	OH	43606	419-473-0885	
Web: beirutrestaurant.com					
Dolly & Joe's 1045 S Reynolds St	Toledo	OH	43615	419-385-2441	
Dorr Street Cafe 5243 Dorr St	Toledo	OH	43615	419-531-4446	
Web: dorrstreetcafe.com					
Eddie Lee's 4700 Nantucket Dr	Toledo	OH	43623	419-882-0616	
El Camino Real 2500 W Sylvania Ave	Toledo	OH	43613	419-472-0700	
Web: elcaminorealtoledo.com					
Fritz & Alfredo's 3025 N Summit St	Toledo	OH	43611	419-729-9775	
Web: toledostripletreat.com					
Georgio's Cafe International 426 N Superior St	Toledo	OH	43604	419-242-2424	
Web: www.georgiostoledo.com					
Mancy's 953 Phillips Ave	Toledo	OH	43612	419-476-4154	
Web: www.mancys.com					
Mango Tree 217 S Reynolds Rd	Toledo	OH	43615	419-536-2883	
Web: mangotreedining.com					
Manos Greek Restaurant & Bar 1701 Adams St	Toledo	OH	43604	419-244-4479	
Web: www.manosgreekrestaurant.com					
Real Seafood Co 22 Main St	Toledo	OH	43605	419-697-4400	
Web: mainstreetventuresinc.com					
Rockwell's 27 Broadway	Toledo	OH	43604	419-243-1302	243-9256
Web: www.mbaybrew.com/rockwells-steakhouse-lounge					
Rose Thai 5333 Monroe St	Toledo	OH	43623	419-841-8467	
Shorty's Bar-B-Cue 5111 Monroe St	Toledo	OH	43623	419-841-9505	
Web: www.mancys.com					
Tony Packo's 1902 Front St	Toledo	OH	43605	419-691-1953	
TF: 866-472-2567 ■ *Web:* www.tonypacko.com					
Ventura's 7742 W Bancroft St	Toledo	OH	43617	419-841-7523	
Web: toledostripletreat.com					
Zia's 20 Main St	Toledo	OH	43605	419-697-4559	
Web: mainstreetventuresinc.com					
China Dynasty 1689 W Ln Ave	Upper Arlington	OH	43221	614-486-7126	486-4131
Web: www.chinadynasty-cmh.com					
Kikyo 3706 Riverside Dr	Upper Arlington	OH	43221	614-457-5277	
Golden Dawn 1245 Logan Ave	Youngstown	OH	44505	330-746-0393	
Golden Hunan Restaurant 3111 Belmont Ave	Youngstown	OH	44505	330-759-7197	
Main Moon 1760 Belmont Ave	Youngstown	OH	44504	330-743-1638	
Nicolinni's 1912 S Raccoon Rd	Youngstown	OH	44515	330-799-9999	
Web: www.nicolinnis.com					
Station Square Restaurant 4250 Belmont Ave	Youngstown	OH	44505	330-759-8802	
Web: thestationsquare.com					
Upstairs Restaurant, The 4500 Mahoning Ave	Youngstown	OH	44515	330-793-5577	
Web: theupstairsrestaurant.com					
Youngstown Crab Co 3917 Belmont Ave	Youngstown	OH	44505	330-759-5480	
Web: www.youngstowncrabco.com					

Oklahoma

Name / Address	City	State	ZIP	Phone	Fax
Pelicans 291 N Air Depot Blvd	Midwest City	OK	73110	405-732-4392	
Web: pelicansok.com					
Ajanta 12215 N Pennsylvania Ave	Oklahoma City	OK	73120	405-752-5283	
Web: www.ajantaokc.com					
Alvarado's Mexican Restaurant 11641 S Western Ave	Oklahoma City	OK	73170	405-692-2007	
Web: www.alvaradosmexican.com					
Bricktown Brewery 1 N Oklahoma Ave	Oklahoma City	OK	73104	405-232-2739	
Web: www.bricktownbrewery.com					
Charleston's 5907 NW Expy St	Oklahoma City	OK	73132	405-721-0060	
Web: charlestons.ehsrg.com					
Coach House 6437 Avondale Dr	Oklahoma City	OK	73116	405-842-1000	843-9777
Deep Fork Grill 5418 N Western Ave	Oklahoma City	OK	73118	405-848-7678	840-0624
Web: www.deepforkgrill.com					
Dot Wo 3101 N Portland Ave	Oklahoma City	OK	73112	405-942-1376	
Web: www.dot-wo.com					
Earl's Rib Palace 6816 N Western Ave	Oklahoma City	OK	73116	405-843-9922	
Web: www.earlsribpalace.com					
Metro Wine Bar & Bistro 6418 N Western Ave	Oklahoma City	OK	73116	405-840-9463	
Web: www.metrowinebar.com					
Mickey Mantle's Steakhouse 7 Mickey Mantle Dr	Oklahoma City	OK	73104	405-272-0777	232-7111
Web: mickeymantlesteakhouse.com					
Musashi's Japanese Steakhouse 4315 N Western	Oklahoma City	OK	73118	405-602-5623	602-5574
Web: www.musashis.com					
Papa Dio's 10712 N May Ave	Oklahoma City	OK	73120	405-755-2255	
Web: papadiosokc.com					
Pearl's Oyster Bar 5641 N Classen Blvd	Oklahoma City	OK	73118	405-842-2102	840-0382
Web: pearlsokc.com					
PF Chang's China Bistro 13700 N Pennsylvania Ave	Oklahoma City	OK	73134	405-748-4003	
Web: www.pfchangs.com					
Redrock Canyon Grill 9221 Lk Hefner Pkwy	Oklahoma City	OK	73120	405-749-1995	
Web: redrockcanyongrill.com					
Royal Bavaria Brewery 3401 S Sooner Rd	Oklahoma City	OK	73165	405-799-7666	
Web: www.royal-bavaria.com					
Sushi Neko 4318 N Western	Oklahoma City	OK	73118	405-528-8862	521-9877
Web: www.sushineko.com					
Ted's Cafe Escondido 2836 NW 68th St	Oklahoma City	OK	73116	405-848-8337	
Web: tedscafe.com					
Tokyo Japanese Restaurant 7516 N Western Ave	Oklahoma City	OK	73116	405-848-6733	
Web: www.tokyookc.com					
Trapper's Fishcamp & Grill 4300 W Reno St	Oklahoma City	OK	73107	405-943-9111	
Web: pearlsokc.com/restaurants/trappers-fishcamp-grill					
Zio's Italian Kitchen 2035 S Meridian Ave	Oklahoma City	OK	73108	405-680-9999	685-7740
Web: www.zios.com					
Albert G's Bar-BQ 2748 S Harvard Ave	Tulsa	OK	74114	918-747-4799	
Web: www.albertgs.com					
Binh-Le 5903 E 31st St	Tulsa	OK	74135	918-835-7722	
Bodean Seafood Restaurant 3376 E 51st St	Tulsa	OK	74135	918-749-1407	
Web: www.bodean.net					
Brookside by Day 3313 S Peoria Ave	Tulsa	OK	74105	918-745-9989	
Web: brooksidebyday.com					
Chalkboard, The 1324 S Main St	Tulsa	OK	74119	918-582-1964	
Web: chalkboardtulsa.com					
Chimi's 1304 E 15th St	Tulsa	OK	74120	918-587-4411	
Web: chimismexican.com					
Doe's Eat Place 1350 E 15th St	Tulsa	OK	74120	918-585-3637	
Web: www.doestulsa.com					
French Hen 7143 S Yale Ave	Tulsa	OK	74136	918-492-2596	
Web: frenchhentulsa.net					
Fuji 8226 E 71st St	Tulsa	OK	74133	918-250-1821	
Web: www.fujisushibar.com					
In the Raw Sushi 3321 S Peoria	Tulsa	OK	74105	918-744-1300	
Web: www.intherawsushi.com					
India Palace Restaurant 6963 S Lewis Ave	Tulsa	OK	74136	918-492-8040	
Web: theindiapalacetulsa.com					
Joe's Crab Shack 7646 E 61st St	Tulsa	OK	74135	918-252-1010	
Web: joescrabshack.com					
Kilkenny's Irish Pub & Eatery 1413 E 15th St	Tulsa	OK	74120	918-582-8282	582-3931
Web: www.tulsairishpub.com					
Mahogany Prime Steak House 6823 S Yale Ave	Tulsa	OK	74136	918-494-4043	494-0209
Web: www.mahogany.ehsrg.com					
McGill's 1560 E 21st St	Tulsa	OK	74114	918-742-8080	
Web: dinemcgills.com					
New Hong Kong Restaurant 2623 E 11th St	Tulsa	OK	74104	918-585-5328	
PF Chang's China Bistro 1978 E 21st St	Tulsa	OK	74114	918-747-6555	
Web: www.pfchangs.com					
Polo Grill 2038 Utica Sq	Tulsa	OK	74114	918-744-4280	749-7082
Web: www.pologrill.com					
Ricardo's 5629 E 41st St	Tulsa	OK	74135	918-622-2668	
Web: ricardostulsa.com					
Spudder, The 6536 E 50th St	Tulsa	OK	74145	918-665-1416	
Web: www.thespudder.com					
Taste of China 11360 E 31st St	Tulsa	OK	74146	918-664-2252	
United States Beef Corp 4923 E 49th St	Tulsa	OK	74135	918-665-0740	
Web: www.usbeefcorp.com					
White Lion Pub 6927 S Canton Ave	Tulsa	OK	74136	918-491-6533	
Web: kelv.net					
Zio's 7111 S Mingo Rd	Tulsa	OK	74133	918-250-5999	252-1287
Web: zios.com					

Ontario

Phone Fax

Mandarin 8 Clipper Crt. Brampton ON L6W4T9 905-451-4100 456-3411
Web: www.mandarinrestaurant.com

Sodexo Canada Ltd
5420 N Service Rd Ste 501 Burlington ON L7L6C7 905-632-8592
Web: ca.sodexo.com

Grappa 690 The Queensway Etobicoke ON M8Y1K8 416-535-3337
Web: www.grapparestaurant.ca

Capone's 1701 Woodroffe Ave Nepean ON K2G1W2 613-226-6947
Web: www.capones.com

Beckta Dining & Wine 150 Elgin St. Ottawa ON K2P1L4 613-238-7063 231-7474
Web: www.beckta.com

Black Tomato 11 George St. Ottawa ON K1N8W5 613-789-8123
Web: www.theblacktomato.com

Blue Cactus Bar & Grill 2 ByWard Market Ottawa ON K1N7A1 613-241-7061
Web: www.bluecactusbarandgrill.com

Cafe Spiga 271 Dalhousie St Ottawa ON K1N7E5 613-241-4381
Web: www.cafespiga.com

Coriander 282 Kent St Ottawa ON K2P2A4 613-233-2828
Web: www.corianderthaiottawa.com

Fratelli 499 Terry Fox Dr Ottawa ON K2T1H7 613-592-0225
Web: www.fratelli.ca

Giovanni's 362 Preston St Ottawa ON K1S4M7 613-234-3156
Web: www.giovannis-restaurant.com

Golden Palace 2195 Carling Ave. Ottawa ON K2B7E8 613-820-8444
Web: goldenpalacerestaurant.ca

Green Door 198 Main St. Ottawa ON K1S1C6 613-234-9597
Web: www.greendoor.ca

Green Papaya 256 Preston St Ottawa ON K1R7R5 613-231-8424
Web: www.greenpapaya.ca

Heart & Crown 67 Clarence St. Ottawa ON K1N5P5 613-562-0674
Web: www.heartandcrown.ca

Indian Biriyani House 1589 Bank St Ottawa ON K1H7Z3 613-260-3893
Web: indianbiriyanihouse.ca

Island Jerk 1800 Bank St. Ottawa ON K1V0W3 613-737-5163

Juniper 245 Richmond Rd Ottawa ON K1Z6W7 613-728-0220 728-3993

Lemon Grass 331 Elgin St Ottawa ON K2P1M5 613-233-5000
Web: www.ottawalemongrass.com

Luxe Bistro 47 York St. Ottawa ON K1N5S7 613-241-8805
Web: www.luxebistro.com

Mamma Grazzi's Kitchen 25 George St. Ottawa ON K1N8W5 613-241-8656 241-5738
Web: www.mammagrazzis.com

Manx, The 370 Elgin St Ottawa ON K2P1N1 613-231-2070
Web: manxpub.com

Mekong 637 Somerset St W Ottawa ON K1R5K3 613-237-7717
Web: www.mekong.ca

Mezzanotte Cafe 50 Murray St Byward Market Ottawa ON K1N9M5 613-562-3978
Web: www.mezzanotte-bistro.com

Murray Street Kitchen 110 Murray St Ottawa ON K1N5M6 613-562-7244
Web: www.murraystreet.ca

New Mee Fung 350 Booth St. Ottawa ON K1R7K1 613-567-8228
Web: newmeefung.com

Nokham Thai 747 Richmond Rd Ottawa ON K2A3Z9 613-724-6135 724-6620
Web: nokhamthai.ca

Pancho Villa 361 Elgin St Ottawa ON K2P1M7 613-234-8872 234-7786

Pub Italia 434 1/2 Preston St. Ottawa ON K1S4N4 613-232-2326
Web: www.pubitalia.ca

Saigon 85 Clarence St. Ottawa ON K1N7B5 613-789-7934

Sante Restaurant 45 Rideau St 2nd Fl Ottawa ON K1N5W8 613-241-7113
TF: 877-241-8889 ■ *Web:* www.santerestaurant.com

Shanghai Restaurant 651 Somerset St W Ottawa ON K1R5K3 613-233-4001

Suisha Garden Japanese Restaurant
208 Slater St. Ottawa ON K1P5H8 613-236-9602
Web: japaninottawa.com

Sweet Basil 1585 Bank St Ottawa ON K1H7Z3 613-731-8424
Web: sweetbasilottawa.com

Tosca Ristorante 144 O'Connor St. Ottawa ON K2P2G7 613-565-3933
Web: www.tosca-ristorante.ca

Vineyards Wine Bar Bistro 54 York St Ottawa ON K1N5T1 613-241-4270 241-5538
Web: www.vineyards.ca

Vittoria Trattoria 35 William St Ottawa ON K1N6Z9 613-789-8959 730-5239
Web: www.vittoriatrattoria.com

Yangtze Dining Lounge 700 Somerset W Ottawa ON K1R6P6 613-236-0555
Web: www.yangtze.ca

Acqua Fine Foods 671 The Queensway Toronto ON M8Y1K8 416-368-7171 368-6171
Web: www.acqua.ca

Adega 33 Elm St Toronto ON M5G1H1 416-977-4338
Web: www.adegarestaurante.ca

Bangkok Garden 18 Elm St. Toronto ON M5G1G7 416-977-6748
Web: www.bangkokgarden.ca

Bar Mar 623 Mt Pleasant Rd Toronto ON M4S2M9 416-544-9035
Web: www.barmar.ca

Barberian's Steak House 7 Elm St Toronto ON M5G1H1 416-597-0335 597-1407
Web: www.barberians.com

Biagio 155 King St E Toronto ON M5C1G9 416-366-4040 366-4765
Web: www.biagioristorante.com

Bodega Restaurant 30 Baldwin St Toronto ON M5T1L3 416-977-1287 408-1941
Web: www.bodegarestaurant.com

Cafe 668 885 Dundas St W Toronto ON M6J1V9 416-703-0668
Web: www.cafe668.com

Chiado 864 College St Toronto ON M6H1A3 416-538-1910 588-8383
Web: www.chiadorestaurant.com

Coppi 3363 Yonge St. Toronto ON M4N2M6 416-484-4464
Web: www.coppi.ca

Courtyard Cafe 18 St Thomas St. Toronto ON M5S3E7 416-921-2921 921-9121
TF Cust Svc: 877-999-2767 ■ *Web:* www.windsorarmshotel.com

Dhaba 309 King St W Toronto ON M5V1J5 416-740-6622 740-4519
Web: www.dhaba.ca

Phone Fax

EDO Sushi 484 Eglinton Ave W Toronto ON M5N1A5 416-322-3033
Web: edorestaurants.com

Edo-ko 425 Spadina Rd. Toronto ON M5P2W3 416-482-8973
Web: edorestaurants.com

El Sol 1448 Danforth Ave. Toronto ON M4J1N4 416-405-8074
Web: elsol.ca

Far Niente 187 Bay St Toronto ON M5L1G5 416-214-9922
Web: www.farnienterestaurant.com

Fifth inc, The 221 Richmond St W Toronto ON M5V1W2 416-979-3000
Web: www.thefifth.com

Gandhi 554 Queen St W Toronto ON M5V2B7 416-504-8155

George 111 Queen St E Toronto ON M5C1S2 416-863-6006 368-6093
Web: www.georgeonqueen.com

Golden Thai 105 Church St Toronto ON M5C2G3 416-868-6668
Web: www.goldenthai.ca

Harbour Sixty Steakhouse 60 Harbour St Toronto ON M5J1B7 416-777-2111
Web: www.harboursixty.com

Hemispheres Restaurant & Bistro
108 Chestnut St Toronto ON M5G1R3 416-599-8000 977-9513
TF: 800-668-6600 ■ *Web:* www.metropolitan.com

Il Gatto Nero 720 College St Toronto ON M6G1C2 416-536-3132

Joso's 202 Davenport Rd Toronto ON M5R1J2 416-925-1903 925-6567
Web: josos.com

La Fenice 319 King St W Toronto ON M5V1J5 416-585-2377
Web: www.lafenice.ca

Lai Wah Heen 108 Chestnut St Toronto ON M5G1R3 416-977-9899
Web: laiwahheen.com

Le Papillon on Front 69 Front St E Toronto ON M5E1B5 416-367-0303
Web: papillononfront.com

Morton's of Chicago 4 Ave Rd Toronto ON M5R2E8 416-925-0648
Web: www.mortons.com

New Generation Sushi 493 Bloor St W Toronto ON M5S1Y2 416-963-8861
Web: newgenerationsushi.com

North 44 Degrees 2537 Yonge St Toronto ON M4P2H9 416-487-4897
Web: north44.mcewangroup.ca

Opus 37 Prince Arthur Ave. Toronto ON M5R1B2 416-921-3105
Web: www.opusrestaurant.com

ORO Restaurant 45 Elm St Toronto ON M5G1H1 416-597-0155
Web: www.ororestaurant.com

REDS Wine Tavern 77 Adelaide St W Toronto ON M5H1P9 416-862-7337
Web: www.redswinetavern.com

Ristorante SOTTO SOTTO 120 Ave Rd Toronto ON M5R2H4 416-962-0011
Web: www.sottosotto.ca

Rodney's Oyster House 469 King St W Toronto ON M5V1K4 416-363-8105 363-6638
Web: www.rodneysoysterhouse.com

Rol San 323 Spadina Ave Toronto ON M5T2E9 416-977-1128

Rosewater Supper Club 19 Toronto St Toronto ON M5C2R1 416-214-5888 214-2412
Web: www.libertygroup.com

Ruth's Chris Steak House
145 Richmond St W Hilton Toronto Hotel Toronto ON M5H2L2 416-955-1455
Web: www.ruthschris.com

Sassafraz 100 Cumberland St Toronto ON M5R1A6 416-964-2222 964-2402
Web: www.sassafraz.ca

Scaramouche Restaurant 1 Benvenuto Pl Toronto ON M4V2L1 416-961-8011
Web: www.scaramoucherestaurant.com

Signatures 220 Bloor St W Toronto ON M5S1T8 416-324-5885

Southern Accent 595 Markham St Toronto ON M6G2L7 416-536-3211 536-3548
Web: www.southernaccent.com

Spuntini 116 Ave Rd Toronto ON M5R2H4 416-962-1110 934-0179
Web: www.spuntini.ca

Trattoria Nervosa 75 Yorkville Ave. Toronto ON M5R1B8 416-961-4642
Web: www.eatnervosa.com

Young Thailand 936 King St W Toronto ON M5V1P5 416-366-8424
Web: www.youngthailand.com

Zucca Trattoria 2150 Yonge St. Toronto ON M4S2A7 416-488-5774
Web: www.zuccatrattoria.com

D'Arcy McGee's Irish Pub 199 Four Valley Dr Vaughan ON L4K0B8 613-230-4433
TF: 888-854-4402 ■ *Web:* darcymcgees.com

Oregon

Phone Fax

Skippers Seafood & Chowder House
2987 Santiam Hwy SE Albany OR 97322 541-926-8623
Web: www.skippersseafoodandchowder.com

Ambrosia Restaurant 174 E Broadway Eugene OR 97401 541-342-4141
Web: www.ambrosiarestaurant.com

Anatolia's 992 Willamette St Eugene OR 97401 541-343-9661
Web: poppisanatolia.com

Beppe & Gianni's Tratorria 1646 E 19th Ave Eugene OR 97403 541-683-6661
Web: beppeandgiannis.net

Cafe Soriah 384 W 13th Ave Eugene OR 97401 541-342-4410
Web: www.soriah.com

Chao Pra Ya Thai Cuisine 580 Adams St Eugene OR 97402 541-344-1706 344-1181

Chapala 136 Oakway ctr Eugene OR 97401 541-434-6113
Web: chapalamex.com

Fisherman's Market 830 W Seventh Ave Eugene OR 97402 541-484-2722
Web: eugenefishmarket.com

Jade Palace 906 W Seventh Ave Eugene OR 97402 541-344-9523
Web: jadepalaceeugene.com

Lotus Garden 810 Charnelton St Eugene OR 97401 541-344-1928
Web: lotusgardenveg.com

Maple Garden 1275 Alder St Eugene OR 97401 541-683-8128 683-1126
Web: www.eugenemaplegarden.com

Marche 296 E Fifth Ave. Eugene OR 97401 541-342-3612 342-3611
Web: www.marcherestaurant.com

McGrath's Fish House 1036 Vly River Way Eugene OR 97401 541-342-6404
Web: www.mcgrathsfishhouse.com

Morning Glory Cafe 450 Willamette St Eugene OR 97401 541-687-0709
Web: morninggloryeugene.com

Oregon Electric Station 27 E Fifth Ave Eugene OR 97401 541-485-4444 484-6149
Web: oesrestaurant.com

	City	State	Zip	Phone	Fax
Ring of Fire 1099 Chambers St *Web:* ringoffirerestaurant.wordpress.com	Eugene	OR	97402	541-343-8488	684-0732
Sixth Street Grill 55 W Sixth Ave *Web:* www.sixthstreetgrill.com	Eugene	OR	97401	541-485-2961	485-3080
Steelhead Brewery & Cafe 199 E Fifth Ave *Web:* www.steelheadbrewery.com	Eugene	OR	97401	541-686-2739	342-5338
Sushi Station 199 E Fifth Ave	Eugene	OR	97401	541-484-1334	
Vintage, The 837 Lincoln St *Web:* thevintageeugene.com	Eugene	OR	97401	541-349-9181	
3 Doors Down Cafe 1429 SE 37th St *Web:* www.3doorsdowncafe.com	Portland	OR	97214	503-236-6886	
Acadia 1303 NE Fremont St *Web:* www.acadiapdx.com	Portland	OR	97212	503-249-5001	
Amalfi's 4703 NE Fremont St *Web:* www.amalfisrestaurant.com	Portland	OR	97213	503-284-6747	
Andina 1314 NW Glisan *Web:* www.andinarestaurant.com	Portland	OR	97209	503-228-9535	
Baan Thai Restaurant 1924 SW BRdway *Web:* www.baanthai.ca	Portland	OR	97201	902-446-4301	
Basta's Trattoria 410 NW 21st Ave *Web:* www.bastastrattoria.com	Portland	OR	97209	503-274-1572	
Bluehour 250 NW 13th Ave *Web:* www.bluehouronline.com	Portland	OR	97209	503-226-3394	
Bombay Cricket Club Restaurant 1925 SE Hawthorne Blvd *Web:* www.bombaycricketclubrestaurant.com	Portland	OR	97214	503-231-0740	
Cafe Castagna 1752 SE Hawthorne Blvd. *Web:* www.castagnarestaurant.com	Portland	OR	97214	503-231-9959	
Cafe du Berry 6439 SW MacAdam Ave *Web:* cafeduberry.ypguides.net	Portland	OR	97239	503-244-5551	
Caffe Mingo 807 NW 21st Ave. *Web:* caffemingonw.com	Portland	OR	97209	503-226-4646	
Campbell's Bar-B-Q 8701 SE Powell Blvd *Web:* www.campbellsbbq.com	Portland	OR	97266	503-777-9795	
Canton Grill 2610 SE 82nd Ave *Web:* canton-grill.com	Portland	OR	97266	503-774-1135	
Castagna 1752 SE Hawthorne Blvd *Web:* www.castagnarestaurant.com	Portland	OR	97214	503-231-7373	
Cha! Cha! Cha! 1208 NW Glisan St. *Web:* chachachapdx.com	Portland	OR	97209	503-221-2111	
Chart House 5700 SW Terwilliger Blvd *Web:* www.chart-house.com	Portland	OR	97239	503-246-6963	
Clay's Smokehouse Grill 2932 SE Div St *Web:* clayssmokehouse.ypguides.net	Portland	OR	97202	503-235-4755	
El Gaucho 319 SW Broadway *Web:* www.elgaucho.com	Portland	OR	97205	503-227-8794	227-3412
Giorgio's 1131 NW Hoyt St. *Web:* www.giorgiospdx.com	Portland	OR	97209	503-221-1888	
Giuseppe's 17937 SE Stark St *Web:* giuseppespdx.com	Portland	OR	97233	503-669-8767	
Heathman Restaurant 1001 SW Broadway *Web:* www.heathmanrestaurantandbar.com	Portland	OR	97205	503-790-7752	
Higgins Restaurant & Bar 1239 SW Broadway *Web:* higginsportland.com	Portland	OR	97205	503-222-9070	
Iron Horse 6034 SE Milwaukie Ave. *Web:* www.portlandironhorse.com	Portland	OR	97202	503-232-1826	
Jake's Famous Crawfish 401 SW 12th Ave SW Stark *TF:* 800-552-6379 ■ *Web:* www.mccormickandschmicks.com	Portland	OR	97205	503-226-1419	220-1856
Jake's Grill 611 SW Tenth Ave *Web:* www.mccormickandschmicks.com	Portland	OR	97205	503-220-1850	226-8365
Kell's 112 SW Second Ave *Web:* www.kellsirish.com	Portland	OR	97204	503-227-4057	
Koji Osakaya 606 SW Broadway *Web:* www.koji.com	Portland	OR	97205	503-294-1169	294-1169
Lemongrass 1705 NE Couch St	Portland	OR	97232	503-231-5780	
London Grill 309 SW Broadway *Web:* www.coasthotels.com	Portland	OR	97205	503-228-2000	471-3924
McCormick & Schmick's Harborside 0309 SW Montgomery **Fax Area Code: 614* ■ *TF Resv:* 888-262-4386 ■ *Web:* www.mccormickandschmicks.com	Portland	OR	97201	503-220-1865	476-3663*
Mint Restaurant & Bar 816 N Russell St. *Web:* www.mintand820.com	Portland	OR	97227	503-284-5518	
Mio Sushi 2271 NW Johnson St. *Web:* www.miosushi.com	Portland	OR	97210	503-221-1469	827-4932
Morton's the Steakhouse 213 SW Clay St *Web:* www.mortons.com	Portland	OR	97201	503-248-2100	
Mother's Bistro & Bar 212 SW Stark St. *Web:* www.mothersbistro.com	Portland	OR	97204	503-464-1122	
Noble Rot 1111 E Burnside 4th Fl *Web:* www.noblerotpdx.com	Portland	OR	97214	503-233-1999	
Oba! 555 NW 12th Ave *Web:* www.obarestaurant.com	Portland	OR	97209	503-228-6161	228-2673
OM Seafood Restaurant 7632 SE Powell Blvd *Web:* omseafood.com	Portland	OR	97206	503-788-3128	
Paley's Place 1204 NW 21st Ave *Web:* www.paleysplace.net	Portland	OR	97209	503-243-2403	
Pambiche 2811 NE Glisan St *Web:* www.pambiche.com	Portland	OR	97232	503-233-0511	233-0495
Piazza Italia 1129 NW Johnson St *Web:* www.piazzaportland.com	Portland	OR	97209	503-478-0619	227-5199
Portland City Grill 111 SW Fifth Ave Unico US Bank Twr 30th Fl *Web:* www.portlandcitygrill.com	Portland	OR	97204	503-450-0030	
Red Star Tavern & Roast House 503 SW Alder St *Web:* www.redstartavern.com	Portland	OR	97204	503-222-0005	417-3334
Ringside SteakHouse, The 2165 W Burnside St. *Web:* www.ringsidesteakhouse.com	Portland	OR	97210	503-223-1513	223-6908
Saucebox 214 SW Broadway *Web:* www.saucebox.com	Portland	OR	97205	503-241-3393	
SinJu 1022 NW Johnson St. *Web:* www.sinjurestaurant.com	Portland	OR	97209	503-223-6535	
Slide Inn, The 2348 SE Ankeny *Web:* www.slideinnpdx.com	Portland	OR	97214	503-236-4997	
Southpark Seafood Grill & Wine Bar 901 SW Salmon St *Web:* southparkseafood.com	Portland	OR	97205	503-326-1300	
Stickers Asian Cafe 6808 SE Milwaukie Ave *Web:* www.stickersasiancafe.com	Portland	OR	97202	503-239-8739	
Sweet Basil 3135 NE Broadway *Web:* www.sweetbasilor.com	Portland	OR	97232	503-281-8337	
Thai Orchid 10075 SW Barbur Blvd *Web:* www.thaiorchidrestaurant.com	Portland	OR	97219	503-452-2544	
Veritable Quandary 1220 SW First Ave *Web:* veritablequandary.com	Portland	OR	97204	503-227-7342	
Adam's Rib 1210 State St. *Web:* adams-rib-smoke-house.com	Salem	OR	97301	503-362-2194	362-2196
Almost Home Restaurant & Steakhouse 3310 Market St NE	Salem	OR	97301	503-378-0100	
Casa Baez 1292 Lancaster Dr NE	Salem	OR	97301	503-371-3867	
Flight Deck Restaurant & Lounge 2680 Aerial Way *Web:* www.flightdeckrestaurant.com	Salem	OR	97302	503-581-5721	
India Palace 377 Ct St.	Salem	OR	97301	503-371-4808	
La Margarita Co 545 Ferry St SE *Web:* lamargaritasalem.com	Salem	OR	97301	503-362-8861	
Los Arcos Mexican Grill 4120 Commercial St SE	Salem	OR	97302	503-581-2740	
Los Baez 2920 Commercial St SE	Salem	OR	97302	503-363-3109	581-0701
Lucky Fortune 1401 Lancaster Dr NE *Web:* www.luckyfortunechinesesalem.com	Salem	OR	97301	503-399-9189	581-7810
Lum-Yuen 3190 Portland Rd NE *Web:* lumyuensalem.com	Salem	OR	97303	503-581-2912	
Macedonia 189 Liberty St NE *Web:* reedoperahouse.com	Salem	OR	97301	503-316-9997	316-9997
Marco Polo Global Restaurant 300 Liberty St SE	Salem	OR	97301	503-364-4833	364-4833

Pennsylvania

	City	State	Zip	Phone	Fax
Altland House 1 Ctr Sq Ste 100 *Web:* www.altlandhouse.com	Abbottstown	PA	17301	717-259-9535	
Aladdin 651 Union Blvd *Web:* aladdinlv.com	Allentown	PA	18109	610-437-4023	
Bay Leaf 935 W Hamilton St. *Web:* www.allentownbayleaf.com	Allentown	PA	18101	610-433-4211	
Ichiban 1914 Catasauqua Rd *Web:* ichibanpa.com	Allentown	PA	18109	610-266-7781	266-7783
Oasis Restaurant 2355 Schoenersville Rd	Allentown	PA	18109	610-264-1955	
Ritz Barbecue 302 17th St.	Allentown	PA	18104	610-432-0952	
Robata of Tokyo 39 S Ninth St *Web:* www.icloud.com	Allentown	PA	18102	610-821-6900	
Sunset Grille 6751 Ruppsville Rd *Web:* www.sunset-grille.com	Allentown	PA	18106	610-395-9622	
Youell's Oyster House 2249 Walnut St *Web:* youellsoysterhouse.com	Allentown	PA	18104	610-439-1203	
Cashtown Inn Restaurant 1325 Old Rt 30 PO Box 103 *TF:* 800-367-1797 ■ *Web:* cashtowninn.com	Cashtown	PA	17310	717-334-9722	334-4679
Bertrand's 18 N Pk Row *Web:* bertrandsbistro.com	Erie	PA	16501	814-871-6477	
Calamari's Squid Row 1317 State St *Web:* www.calamaris-squidrow.com	Erie	PA	16501	814-459-4276	
Colao's Ristorante 2826 Plum St. *Web:* colaos.com	Erie	PA	16508	814-866-9621	
Colony Pub & Grille 2670 W Eigth St. *Web:* colonypub.com	Erie	PA	16505	814-838-2162	
El Canelo 2709 W 12th St. *Web:* elcanelo.net	Erie	PA	16505	814-835-2290	
Hibachi Japanese Steak House 3000 W 12th St *Web:* www.hibachijapan.com	Erie	PA	16505	814-838-2495	
Hoss's Steak & Sea House 3302 W 26th St	Erie	PA	16506	814-838-6718	
Joe Roots Grill 2826 W Eigth St	Erie	PA	16505	814-836-7668	
Molly Brannigans 506 State St *Web:* www.mollybrannigans.com	Erie	PA	16501	814-453-7800	
Panos Restaurant 1504 W 38th St	Erie	PA	16508	814-866-0517	
Petra 3602 W Lake Rd. *TF:* 866-906-2931 ■ *Web:* www.petrarestaurant.com	Erie	PA	16505	814-838-7197	833-9543
Ricardo's 2112 E Lake Rd *Web:* ricardos-erie.com	Erie	PA	16511	814-455-4947	
Smokey Bones BBQ 2074 Interchange Rd. *Web:* www.smokeybones.com	Erie	PA	16565	814-868-3388	
Sullivan's Pub & Eatery 301 French St.	Erie	PA	16507	814-452-3446	
Syd's Place 2992 W Lake Rd	Erie	PA	16505	814-838-3089	
Avenue Restaurant, The 21 Steinwehr Ave.	Gettysburg	PA	17325	717-334-3235	334-5209
Blue & Gray Bar & Grill 2 Baltimore St	Gettysburg	PA	17325	717-334-1999	
Blue Parrot Bistro 35 Chambersburg St. *Web:* blueparrotbistro.com	Gettysburg	PA	17325	717-337-3739	
Dobbin House Inc 89 Steinwehr Ave *Web:* www.dobbinhouse.com/map.htm	Gettysburg	PA	17325	717-334-2100	334-6905
Dunlap's 90 Buford Ave *Web:* www.dunlapsrestaurant.com	Gettysburg	PA	17325	717-334-4816	334-2053
Ernie's Texas Lunch 58 Chambersburg St	Gettysburg	PA	17325	717-334-1970	
Farnsworth House Inn 401 Baltimore St *Web:* www.farnsworthhouseinn.com	Gettysburg	PA	17325	717-334-8838	
General Pickett's Buffet 571 Steinwehr Ave *Web:* generalpickettsbuffets.com	Gettysburg	PA	17325	717-334-7580	
Gettysburg Hotel 1 Lincoln Sq Best Western Gettysburg Hotel *TF:* 866-378-1797 ■ *Web:* www.hotelgettysburg.com	Gettysburg	PA	17325	717-337-2000	337-2075

	City	State	Zip	Phone	Fax
Herr Tavern & Public House 900 Chambersburg Rd	Gettysburg	PA	17325	717-334-4332	
TF: 800-362-9849 ■ *Web:* www.innatherrridge.com					
La Bella Italia 402 York St	Gettysburg	PA	17325	717-334-1978	
Web: labellaitalia.org					
Mamma Ventura 13 Chambersburg St	Gettysburg	PA	17325	717-334-5548	334-7231
Web: mammaventuras.com					
O'Rorke's Eatery & Spirits 44 Steinwehr Ave	Gettysburg	PA	17325	717-334-2333	
Web: ororkes.com					
Ping's Cafe 34 Baltimore St	Gettysburg	PA	17325	717-334-2234	
Web: www.pingscafe.com					
Aangan Classic Indian & Napalese Cuisine 3500 Walnut St	Harrisburg	PA	17109	717-909-7777	909-7979
Web: www.aanganonline.com					
Appalachian Brewing Co 50 N Cameron St	Harrisburg	PA	17101	717-221-1080	221-1083
Web: www.abcbrew.com					
Benihana 2517 Paxton St	Harrisburg	PA	17111	717-232-6731	
Web: www.benihana.com					
El Rodeo 4659 Jonestown Rd	Harrisburg	PA	17109	717-652-5340	
Web: elrodeopa.com					
Fuji Do Restaurant 1701 Paxton St	Harrisburg	PA	17104	717-232-1437	
Gabriella 3907 Jonestown Rd	Harrisburg	PA	17109	717-540-0040	
Web: gabriellaristorante.com					
Isaac's 421 Friendship Rd	Harrisburg	PA	17111	717-920-5757	920-3955
Web: www.isaacsdeli.com					
McGrath's Pub & Restaurant 202 Locust St	Harrisburg	PA	17101	717-232-9914	
Web: mcgrathspub.net					
Miyako 227 N Second St	Harrisburg	PA	17101	717-234-3250	
Molly Brannigans 31 N Second St	Harrisburg	PA	17101	717-260-9242	
Web: www.mollybrannigans.com					
Passage to India 520 Race St	Harrisburg	PA	17104	717-233-1202	
Web: www.passagetoindiaharrisburgpa.com					
Stocks on Second 211 N Second St	Harrisburg	PA	17101	717-233-6699	
Web: www.stocksonsecond.com					
Ted's Bar & Grill 6197 Allentown Blvd	Harrisburg	PA	17112	717-652-3832	
Web: tedsbarandgrill.com					
Vietnamese Garden 304 Reily St	Harrisburg	PA	17102	717-238-9310	
Wharf, The 6852 Derry St	Harrisburg	PA	17111	717-564-9920	
Web: www.thewharfbarandgrill.com					
Sullivan's Steakhouse 700 W DeKalb Pk	King of Prussia	PA	19406	610-878-9025	
Web: sullivanssteakhouse.com					
Carr's Restaurant 50 W Grant St	Lancaster	PA	17603	717-299-7090	
Web: www.carrsrestaurant.com					
El Serrano 2151 Columbia Ave	Lancaster	PA	17603	717-397-6191	
Web: www.elserrano.com					
Gibraltar 931 Harrisburg Ave	Lancaster	PA	17603	717-397-2790	
Web: www.kearesrestaurants.com					
La Fleur 2285 Lincoln Hwy E Continental Inn	Lancaster	PA	17602	717-299-0421	
Web: www.continentalinn.com/lafleur.asp					
Lancaster Brewing Co 302 N Plum St	Lancaster	PA	17602	717-391-6258	391-6015
Web: www.lancasterbrewing.com					
Loft Restaurant, The 201 W Orange St	Lancaster	PA	17603	717-299-0661	
Web: www.theloftlancaster.com					
Lombardo's 216 Harrisburg Ave	Lancaster	PA	17603	717-394-3749	
Web: www.lombardosrestaurant.com					
Pressroom Restaurant 26-28 W King St	Lancaster	PA	17603	717-399-5400	
Web: www.pressroomrestaurant.com					
Taj Mahal 2080 Bennet Ave	Lancaster	PA	17601	717-295-1434	295-7413
Web: www.tajlancaster.com					
Tony Wang's 2217 Lincoln Hwy E	Lancaster	PA	17602	717-399-1915	399-8475
Log Cabin 11 Lehoy Forest Dr	Leola	PA	17540	717-625-2142	
Web: www.logcabinrestaurant.com					
Brandstand Group Inc 686 Yorktown Rd	Lewisberry	PA	17339	717-932-4178	
Web: www.brandstandgroup.com					
Nana's Pasta House 1223 Springbrook Ave	Moosic	PA	18507	570-457-9612	
Web: www.nanaspastahouse.com					
New Amber Indian Restaurant 3505 Birney Ave	Moosic	PA	18507	570-344-7100	
Web: www.newamberindian.com					
Hickory Bridge Farm 96 Hickory Bridge Rd	Orrtanna	PA	17353	717-642-5261	
Web: www.hickorybridgefarm.com					
Alma de Cuba 1623 Walnut St	Philadelphia	PA	19103	215-988-1799	988-0807
Web: www.almadecubarestaurant.com					
Barclay Prime 237 S 18th St	Philadelphia	PA	19103	215-732-7560	732-7560
Web: www.barclayprime.com					
Bistro Romano 120 Lombard St	Philadelphia	PA	19147	215-925-8880	
Web: www.bistroromano.com					
Buddakan 325 Chestnut St	Philadelphia	PA	19106	215-574-9440	574-8994
Web: www.buddakan.com					
Capital Grille, The 1338 Chestnut St	Philadelphia	PA	19107	215-545-9588	
Web: www.thecapitalgrille.com					
Chloe 232 Arch St	Philadelphia	PA	19106	215-629-2337	
Web: www.chloebyob.com					
Continental, The 138 Market St	Philadelphia	PA	19106	215-923-6069	
Web: www.continentalmartinibar.com					
Cuba Libre Restaurant 10 S Second St	Philadelphia	PA	19106	215-627-0666	627-6193
Web: www.cubalibrerestaurant.com					
Cucina Forte 768 S Eigth St	Philadelphia	PA	19147	215-238-0778	
Web: cucinaforte.com					
Dahlak Restaurant inc 4708 Baltimore Ave	Philadelphia	PA	19143	215-726-6464	
Web: www.dahlakrestaurant.com					
El Vez 121 S 13th St	Philadelphia	PA	19107	215-928-9800	928-9889
Web: www.elvezrestaurant.com					
Fork 306 Market St	Philadelphia	PA	19106	215-625-9425	
Web: www.forkrestaurant.com					
Hikaru 607 S Second St	Philadelphia	PA	19147	215-627-7110	
Web: hikaruphilly.com					
Il Cantuccio 701 N Third St	Philadelphia	PA	19123	215-627-6573	627-6573
Karma 114 Chestnut St	Philadelphia	PA	19106	215-925-1444	
Web: karmaphiladelphia.com					
L'Angolo Ristorante 1415 Porter St	Philadelphia	PA	19145	215-389-4252	
Web: www.salentorestaurant.com					
La Famiglia 8 S Front St	Philadelphia	PA	19106	215-922-2803	
Web: www.lafamiglia.com					
Lacroix at the Rittenhouse 210 W Rittenhouse Sq	Philadelphia	PA	19103	215-790-2533	
Web: www.rittenhousehotel.com					
Macaroni's 9315 Old Bustleton Ave	Philadelphia	PA	19115	215-464-3040	
Web: macaronis.net					
Marrakesh 517 S Leithgow St	Philadelphia	PA	19147	215-925-5929	
Web: marrakesheastcoast.com					
Matyson 37 S 19th St	Philadelphia	PA	19103	215-564-2925	
Web: www.matyson.com					
McCormick & Schmick's 1 S Broad St	Philadelphia	PA	19107	215-568-6888	568-2066
Web: www.mccormickandschmicks.com					
Meritage Philadelphia 500 S 20th St	Philadelphia	PA	19103	215-985-1922	
Web: www.meritagephiladelphia.com					
Morimoto 723 Chestnut St	Philadelphia	PA	19106	215-413-9070	413-9075
Web: www.morimotorestaurant.com					
Morning Glory Diner 735 S Tenth St	Philadelphia	PA	19147	215-413-3999	
Web: www.themorninggglorydiner.com					
Morton's The Steakhouse 1411 Walnut St	Philadelphia	PA	19102	215-557-0724	557-9741
Web: www.mortons.com					
Osaka 8605 Germantown Pk	Philadelphia	PA	19118	215-242-5900	
Web: www.osakapa.com					
Palm Restaurant 200 S Broad St	Philadelphia	PA	19102	215-546-7256	546-3088
TF: 866-333-7256 ■ *Web:* www.thepalm.com					
Pod Restaurant 3636 Sansom St	Philadelphia	PA	19104	215-387-1803	
Web: www.podrestaurant.com					
Radicchio 402 Wood St	Philadelphia	PA	19106	215-627-6850	627-6801
Web: www.radicchio-cafe.com					
Rose Tattoo Cafe 1847 Callowhill St	Philadelphia	PA	19130	215-569-8939	
Web: www.rosetattoocafe.com					
Ruth's Chris Steakhouse 260 S Broad St	Philadelphia	PA	19102	215-790-1515	
Web: www.ruthschris.com					
Saloon 750 S Seventh St	Philadelphia	PA	19147	215-627-1811	
Web: www.saloonrestaurant.net					
Sansom Street Oyster House 1516 Sansom St	Philadelphia	PA	19102	215-567-7683	
Web: www.oysterhousephilly.com					
Scannicchio 2500 S Broad St	Philadelphia	PA	19145	215-468-3900	468-3900
Web: www.scannicchio.com					
Shiao Lan Kung 930 Race St	Philadelphia	PA	19107	215-928-0282	
Standard Tap 901 N 2nd St	Philadelphia	PA	19123	215-238-0630	
Web: news.standardtap.com.s86406.gridserver.com					
Susanna Foo 1720 Sansom St	Philadelphia	PA	19103	215-717-8968	688-8055*
**Fax Area Code:* 610 ■ *Web:* www.sugabyfoo.com					
Sweet Lucy's Smokehouse 7500 State Rd	Philadelphia	PA	19136	215-333-9663	331-3185
Web: www.sweetlucys.com					
Tai Lake Restaurant 134 N Tenth St	Philadelphia	PA	19107	215-922-0698	922-0347
Web: www.tailakeseafoodrest.com					
Tequilas 1602 Locust St	Philadelphia	PA	19103	215-546-0181	546-9953
Web: tequilasphilly.com					
Tre Scalini 1915 Passyunk Ave	Philadelphia	PA	19148	215-551-3870	
Web: trescaliniphiladelphia.com					
Umbria 7131 Germantown Ave	Philadelphia	PA	19119	215-242-6470	
Valanni Restaurant & Lounge 1229 Spruce St	Philadelphia	PA	19107	215-790-9494	
Web: www.valanni.com					
Vetri 1312 Spruce St	Philadelphia	PA	19107	215-732-3478	
Web: www.vetrifamily.com					
Vientiane Cafe 4728 Baltimore Ave	Philadelphia	PA	19143	215-726-1095	
Vietnam Palace Restaurant 222 N. 11th St	Philadelphia	PA	19107	215-592-9596	
Vietnam Restaurant 221 N 11th St	Philadelphia	PA	19107	215-592-1163	
Web: www.eatatvietnam.com					
White Dog Cafe 3420 Sansom St	Philadelphia	PA	19104	215-386-9224	
Web: www.whitedog.com					
Ali Baba 404 S Craig St	Pittsburgh	PA	15213	412-682-2829	
Web: www.alibabapittsburgh.com					
Amel's Restaurant 435 McNeilly Rd	Pittsburgh	PA	15226	412-563-3466	
Web: www.amelsrestaurantpgh.com					
Cafe du Jour 1107 E Carson St	Pittsburgh	PA	15203	412-488-9695	
Carlton Restaurant 500 Grant St 1 Mellon Bank Ctr	Pittsburgh	PA	15219	412-391-4152	281-1704
Web: www.thecarltonrestaurant.com					
Casbah 229 S Highland Ave	Pittsburgh	PA	15206	412-661-5656	
Web: casbahpgh.com					
Christos Mediterranean Grille 130 Sixth St	Pittsburgh	PA	15222	412-261-6442	
Web: christosmediterraneangrille.com					
Church Brew Works 3525 Liberty Ave	Pittsburgh	PA	15201	412-688-8200	
Web: www.churchbrew.com					
Eleven 1150 Smallman St	Pittsburgh	PA	15222	412-201-5656	201-5655
Web: www.bigburrito.com					
Grand Concourse 100 W Stn Sq Dr	Pittsburgh	PA	15219	412-261-1717	261-6041
Web: www.muer.com					
India Garden 328 Atwood St	Pittsburgh	PA	15213	412-682-3000	
Web: www.indiagarden.net					
Kaya 2000 Smallman St	Pittsburgh	PA	15222	412-261-6565	261-1526
Web: www.bigburrito.com					
Kiku 225 W Stn Sq Dr	Pittsburgh	PA	15219	412-765-3200	
Web: kikupittsburgh.net					
Lidia's Italy 1400 Smallman St	Pittsburgh	PA	15222	412-552-0150	
Web: www.lidias-pittsburgh.com					
Mallorca 2228 E Carson St	Pittsburgh	PA	15203	412-488-1818	488-1320
Web: mallorcarestaurantpgh.com					
Max's Allegheny Tavern 537 Suismon St	Pittsburgh	PA	15212	412-231-1899	
Web: www.maxsalleghenytavern.com					
Meat & Potatoes 649 Penn Ave	Pittsburgh	PA	15222	412-325-7007	
Web: meatandpotatoespgh.com					

Name	City	State	Zip	Phone	Fax
Morton's The Steakhouse 625 Liberty Ave *Web:* www.mortons.com	Pittsburgh	PA	15222	412-261-7141	261-7151
Mullaney's Harp & Fiddle 2329 Penn Ave *Web:* www.harpandfiddle.com	Pittsburgh	PA	15222	412-642-6622	
Nakama Japanese Steakhouse 1611 E Carson St *Web:* www.eatatnakama.com	Pittsburgh	PA	15203	412-381-6000	381-6643
Original Fish Market 1001 Liberty Ave *Web:* www.originalfishmarket.com	Pittsburgh	PA	15222	412-227-3657	
Penn Brewery, The 800 Vinial St *Web:* www.pennbrew.com	Pittsburgh	PA	15212	412-237-9400	
Pittsburgh Steak Co 1924 E Carson St *Web:* www.pghsteak.com	Pittsburgh	PA	15203	412-381-5505	488-6628
Pleasure Bar & Restaurant 4729 Liberty Ave *Web:* pleasurebarpittsburgh.com	Pittsburgh	PA	15224	412-682-9603	
Primanti Bros 46 18th St *Web:* primantibros.com	Pittsburgh	PA	15222	412-263-2142	
Ruth's Chris Steak House 6 PPG Pl *Web:* www.ruthschris.com	Pittsburgh	PA	15222	412-391-4800	
Sesame Inn 715 Washington Rd *Web:* sesameinn.com	Pittsburgh	PA	15228	412-341-2555	
Soba 5847 Ellsworth Ave *Web:* www.bigburrito.com	Pittsburgh	PA	15232	412-362-5656	
Spice Island Tea House 253 Atwood St *Web:* spiceislandteahouse.com	Pittsburgh	PA	15213	412-687-8821	
Sushi Kim 1241 Penn Ave	Pittsburgh	PA	15222	412-281-9956	281-9957
Tessaro's 4601 Liberty Ave *Web:* tessaros.com	Pittsburgh	PA	15224	412-682-6809	
Thai Place Restaurant 5528 Walnut St *Web:* www.thaiplacerestaurant.com	Pittsburgh	PA	15232	412-687-8586	
Tram's Kitchen 4050 Penn Ave	Pittsburgh	PA	15224	412-682-2688	
Umi 5849 Ellsworth Ave *Web:* bigburrito.com	Pittsburgh	PA	15232	412-362-6198	
Wilson's Bar-B-Q 700 N Taylor Ave	Pittsburgh	PA	15212	412-322-7427	
Cooper's Seafood House 701 N Washington Ave *Web:* www.coopers-seafood.com	Scranton	PA	18509	570-346-6883	
Foliage 122 N Main Ave	Scranton	PA	18504	570-347-1071	
Kelly's Pub & Eatery 1802 Cedar Ave *Web:* kpehotwings.com	Scranton	PA	18505	570-346-9758	
La Trattoria 522 Moosic St *Web:* thelatrattoria.com	Scranton	PA	18505	570-961-1504	
Osaka 244 Adams Ave *Web:* www.osakacuisine.com	Scranton	PA	18503	570-341-9600	
Russell's 1918 Ash St	Scranton	PA	18510	570-961-8949	
Stirna's 120 W Market St *Web:* stirnas.com	Scranton	PA	18508	570-343-5742	
Symposium 6021 Yonge St Unit 475	Toronto	PA	17603	416-449-3611	
Hunan Springs 4939 Hamilton Blvd *Web:* hunansprings.com	Wescosville	PA	18106	610-366-8338	366-7184

Quebec

Name	City	Prov	Postal Code	Phone	Fax
3 Amigos 1657 Ste Catherine W *Web:* www.3amigosrestaurant.com	Montreal	QC	H3H1L7	514-939-3329	
Ariel Restaurant 2072 Drummond St *Web:* www.arielrestaurant.com	Montreal	QC	H3G1W9	514-282-9790	
Beijing 92 Rue de la Gauchetiere O *Web:* www.restaurantbeijing.net	Montreal	QC	H2Z1C1	514-861-2003	
Bombay Mahal 1001 Rue Jean-Talon Ouest *Web:* www.restaurantbombaymahal.ca	Montreal	QC	H3N1T2	514-273-3331	
Buffet Maharaja 1481 Rene Levesque Blvd W *Web:* www.buffetmaharaja.com	Montreal	QC	H3G1T8	514-934-0655	
Carlos & Pepe's 1420 Peel St *Web:* carlospepes.com	Montreal	QC	H3A1S8	514-288-3090	
Chez la Mere Michel 1209 Rue Guy *Web:* www.chezlameremichel.ca	Montreal	QC	H3H2L3	514-934-0473	
Coco Rico 3907 St-Laurent Blvd	Montreal	QC	H2W1X9	514-849-5554	286-0967
Europea 1227 de la Montagne *Web:* www.europea.ca	Montreal	QC	H3G1Z2	514-397-9161	398-9718
Ferreira Cafe 1446 Peel St *Web:* www.ferreiracafe.com	Montreal	QC	H3A1S8	514-848-0988	
Frite Alors! 1562 Laurier St E *Web:* www.fritealors.com	Montreal	QC	H2J1H9	514-524-6336	
Globe Bar-Restaurant 3455 St Laurent Blvd	Montreal	QC	H2X2T6	514-284-3823	284-3531
Hwang-Kum 5908 Sherbrooke St W	Montreal	QC	H4A1X7	514-487-1712	
L'Entrecote St-Jean 2022 Peel St *Web:* www.lentrecotestjean.com	Montreal	QC	H3A2W5	514-281-6492	
L'Estaminet 1340 Fleury E *Web:* www.lestaminet.ca	Montreal	QC	H2C1R3	514-389-0596	
L'Express 3927 St Denis St *Web:* restaurantlexpress.com	Montreal	QC	H2W2M4	514-845-5333	843-7576
La Chronique 104 Ave Laurier Ouest *Web:* www.lachronique.qc.ca	Montreal	QC	H2T2N7	514-271-3095	
La Colombe 554 Duluth E *Web:* lacolomberestaurant.com	Montreal	QC	H2L1A9	514-849-8844	
La Mer 1840 Ren,L,vesque Est *Web:* lamer.ca	Montreal	QC	H2K4P1	514-522-3003	522-0467
Laloux 250 Pine Ave E *Web:* www.laloux.com	Montreal	QC	H2W1P3	514-287-9127	
Le Mas Des Oliviers Restaurant 1216 Rue Bishop *Web:* www.lemasdesoliviers.ca	Montreal	QC	H3G2E3	514-861-6733	
Le Nil Bleu 3706 St-Denis	Montreal	QC	H2X3L7	514-285-4628	
Les Chenets 2075 Rue Bishop	Montreal	QC	H3G2G2	514-844-1842	
Maestro SVP 3615 St Laurent Blvd *Web:* www.maestrosvp.com	Montreal	QC	H2X1V5	514-842-6447	
Milos 5357 du Parc Ave *Web:* www.milos.ca	Montreal	QC	H2V4G9	514-272-3522	
Moishes Steakhouse 3961 St Laurent Blvd *Web:* www.moishes.ca	Montreal	QC	H2W1Y4	514-845-3509	
Molivos 2310 Guy *Web:* molivos.ca	Montreal	QC	H3H2M2	514-846-8818	
Oishii Sushi 277 Bernard Ouest *Web:* www.oishii.ca	Montreal	QC	H2V1T5	514-271-8863	
Pho Bang New York 1001 St-Laurent Blvd	Montreal	QC	H2Z1J4	514-954-2032	
Pub St-Paul 124 St Paul St E *Web:* www.pubstpaul.com	Montreal	QC	H2Y1G6	514-874-0485	
Restaurant Gandhi 230 Rue St Paul Oeust *Web:* www.restaurantgandhi.com	Montreal	QC	H2Y1Z9	514-845-5866	
Restaurant Jano Grillades 3883 St-Laurent Blvd	Montreal	QC	H2W1X9	514-849-0646	849-3628
Restaurant Mysore 4216 St Laurent *Web:* restaurant-mysore.com	Montreal	QC	H2W1Z3	514-844-4733	
Ristorante DaVinci 1180 Bishop St *Web:* www.davinci.ca	Montreal	QC	H3G2E3	514-874-2001	
Rotisserie Italienne 1933 Sainte-Catherine St W *Web:* www.globeater.com	Montreal	QC	H3H1M4	514-935-4436	
Toque 900 Pl Jean-Paul Riopelle *Web:* www.restaurant-toque.com	Montreal	QC	H2Z2B2	514-499-2084	499-0292
Upstairs Jazz Bar & Grill 1254 MacKay St *Web:* www.upstairsjazz.com	Montreal	QC	H3G2H4	514-931-6808	
W Montreal Hotel 901 Victoria Sq *Web:* www.wmontrealhotel.com	Montreal	QC	H2Z1R1	514-395-3100	
YOY Sushi Bar 4526 St Denis St W	Montreal	QC	H2J2L3	514-844-9884	
LOEWS HOTELS 667 Madison Ave *Fax Area Code: 410 ■ *TF:* 800-235-6397 ■ *Web:* www.loewshotels.com	New York	NY	10065	615-340-2000	263-0084*
Chez Leveque 1030 Laurier Ave W *Web:* www.chezleveque.ca	Outremont	QC	H2V2K8	514-279-7355	
Apsara 71 Rue D'Auteuil *Web:* restaurantapsara.com	Quebec	QC	G1R4C3	418-694-0232	
Au Petit Coin Breton 1029 Rue Saint-Jean *Web:* aupetitcoinbreton.com	Quebec	QC	G1R1R6	418-694-0758	
Auberge du Tresor 20 Rue Sainte-Anne *TF:* 800-566-1876 ■ *Web:* www.aubergedutresor.com	Quebec	QC	G1R3X2	418-694-1876	694-0563
Aux Anciens Canadiens 34 rue Saint-Louis Casier postal 175 succursale Haute-Ville *Web:* www.auxancienscanadiens.qc.ca	Quebec	QC	G1R4P3	418-692-1627	692-5419
Charbon Steakhouse 450 Gare du Palais (old port) *Web:* charbonsteakhouse.com	Quebec	QC	G1K3X2	418-522-0133	
Ciccio Cafe 875 Claire-Fontaine	Quebec	QC	G1R3A8	418-525-6161	
Cochon Dingue Le 46 Champlain Blvd *Web:* www.cochondingue.com	Quebec	QC	G1R2A4	418-692-2013	
Cosmos Cafe 575 Grande Allee E *Web:* lecosmos.com	Quebec	QC	G1R2K4	418-640-0606	
Entrecote Saint Jean 1080 St Jean St *Web:* www.entrecotesaintjean.com	Quebec	QC	G1R1S4	418-694-0234	
L'Echaude 73 Rue Sault-au-Matelot St *Web:* www.echaude.com	Quebec	QC	G1K3Y9	418-692-1299	692-1133
La Cremailliere 73 rue Sainte-Anne	Quebec	QC	G1R3X4	418-692-2216	692-5202
La Grolla 815 Cote d'Abraham *Web:* www.restaurantlagrolla.com	Quebec	QC	G1R1A4	418-529-8107	
Laurie Raphael 117 Dalhousie St *TF:* 877-876-4555 ■ *Web:* www.laurieraphael.com	Quebec	QC	G1K9C8	418-692-4555	692-4175
Le Beffroi Steakhouse 775 Honore-Mercier Ave	Quebec	QC	G1R5M9	418-380-2638	
Le Saint-Amour 48 rue Sainte-Ursule *Web:* www.saint-amour.com	Quebec	QC	G1R4E2	418-694-0667	694-0967
Mistral Gagnant 160 St-Paul *Web:* mistralgagnant.ca	Quebec	QC	G1K3W1	418-692-4260	
Pub Saint-Alexandre 1087 St Jean St *Web:* www.pubstalexandre.com	Quebec	QC	G1R1S3	418-694-0015	694-0178
Pub St Patrick 1200 St-Jean St	Quebec	QC	G1R1S8	418-694-0618	694-2120
Restaurant Aviatic Club 450 de la Gare-du-Palais	Quebec	QC	G1K3X2	418-522-3555	522-6404
Restaurant Chez Rabelais 2 Rue Du Petit-Champlain	Quebec	QC	G1K4H5	418-522-3240	
Restaurant L'Initiale 54 St-Pierre St *Web:* restaurantinitiale.com	Quebec	QC	G1K4A1	418-694-1818	694-2387
D'Orsay Restaurant Pub 65 Rue de Buade *Web:* www.dorsayrestaurant.com	Vieux-Quebec	QC	G1R4A2	418-694-1582	694-1587
Le Continental 26 rue St-Louis *Web:* www.restaurantlecontinental.com	Vieux-Quebec	QC	G1R3Y9	418-694-9995	
Marie-Clarisse 12 du Petit-Champlain St	Vieux-Quebec	QC	G1K4H5	418-692-5085	
Le Lapin Saute 52 ru du Petit-Champlain *Web:* www.lapinsaute.com	Ville de Quebec	QC	G1K4H4	418-692-5325	

Rhode Island

Name	City	State	Zip	Phone	Fax
Basta 2195 Broad St *Web:* bastaonbroad.com	Cranston	RI	02905	401-461-2300	
22 Bowen's 22 Bowen's Wharf *Web:* www.22bowens.com	Newport	RI	02840	401-841-8884	841-8883
Black Pearl, The Bannister's Wharf *Web:* www.blackpearlnewport.com	Newport	RI	02840	401-846-5264	
Brick Alley Pub & Restaurant 140 Thames St *Web:* www.brickalley.com	Newport	RI	02840	401-849-6334	848-5640
Cafe Zelda 528 Lower Thames St *Web:* www.cafezelda.com	Newport	RI	02840	401-849-4002	
Christie's of Newport 14 Perry Mill Wharf *Web:* www.41north.com	Newport	RI	02840	401-847-5400	
Clarke Cooke House 1 Bannister's Wharf *Web:* www.bannistersnewport.com	Newport	RI	02840	401-846-4500	849-8750
Mamma Luisa 673 Thames St *Web:* www.mammaluisa.com	Newport	RI	02840	401-848-5257	
Mooring, The Sayer's Wharf *Web:* www.mooringrestaurant.com	Newport	RI	02840	401-846-2260	

				Phone	Fax
Red Parrot, The 348 Thames St *Web:* www.redparrotrestaurant.com	Newport	RI	02840	401-847-3800	
Restaurant Bouchard 505 Thames St *Web:* www.restaurantbouchard.com	Newport	RI	02840	401-846-0123	841-8565
Salvation Cafe 140 Broadway *Web:* www.salvationcafe.com	Newport	RI	02840	401-847-2620	
Sardella's Restaurant 30 Memorial Blvd W *Web:* www.sardellas.com	Newport	RI	02840	401-849-6312	
Scales & Shells Restaurant & Raw Bar 527 Thames St *Web:* www.scalesandshells.com	Newport	RI	02840	401-846-3474	
Spiced Pear 117 Memorial Blvd *TF:* 866-793-5664 ■ *Web:* thechanler.com	Newport	RI	02840	401-847-2244	
Thai Cuisine at Thames 517 Thames St *Web:* thaicuisinemenu.com	Newport	RI	02840	401-841-8822	845-8338
White Horse Tavern 26 Marlborough St *Web:* www.whitehorsenewport.com	Newport	RI	02840	401-849-3600	
Al Forno Restaurant 577 S Main St *Web:* alforno.com	Providence	RI	02903	401-273-9760	
Andreas 268 Thayer St *Web:* andreasri.com	Providence	RI	02906	401-331-7879	331-7300
Blue Grotto 210 Atwells Ave *Web:* www.bluegrottorestaurant.com	Providence	RI	02903	401-272-9030	
Camilles Restaurant 71 Bradford St *Web:* www.camillesonthehill.com	Providence	RI	02903	401-751-4812	
Capital Grille 1 Union Stn *Web:* www.thecapitalgrille.com	Providence	RI	02903	401-521-5600	
Capriccio 2 Pine St	Providence	RI	02903	401-421-1320	331-8732
Cassarino's Restaurant 177 Atwells Ave *Web:* www.cassarinosri.com	Providence	RI	02903	401-751-3333	
CAV Restaurant 14 Imperial Pl *Web:* www.cavrestaurant.com	Providence	RI	02903	401-751-9164	274-9107
Chez Pascal 960 Hope St *Web:* www.chez-pascal.com	Providence	RI	02906	401-421-4422	
Chilangos 447 Manton Ave	Providence	RI	02909	401-383-4877	
Classic Cafe 865 Westminster St *Web:* classiccaferi.com	Providence	RI	02903	401-273-0707	
Don Jose Tequila's 351 Atwells Ave *Web:* donjosetequilas.com	Providence	RI	02903	401-454-8951	
Haruki East 172 Wayland Ave *Web:* harukisushi.com	Providence	RI	02906	401-223-0332	
Hemenway's Seafood Grille 121 S Main St *TF:* 888-759-5557 ■ *Web:* www.hemenwaysrestaurant.com	Providence	RI	02903	401-351-8570	351-8594
Julian's 318 Broadway *Web:* www.juliansprovidence.com	Providence	RI	02909	401-861-1770	
Lot 401 44 Hospital St	Providence	RI	02903	401-490-3980	
Mandarin Garden 555 Chalkstone Ave	Providence	RI	02908	401-751-0144	
Mill's Tavern 101 N Main St *Web:* www.millstavernrestaurant.com	Providence	RI	02903	401-272-3331	
New Rivers Restaurant 7 Steeple St *Web:* www.newriversrestaurant.com	Providence	RI	02903	401-751-0350	
Nick's on Broadway 500 Broadway *Web:* nicksonbroadway.com	Providence	RI	02909	401-421-0286	
Not Just Snacks 833 Hope St *Web:* letseat.at	Providence	RI	02906	401-831-1150	
OPA Restaurant 230 Atwells Ave *Web:* opaprovidence.com	Providence	RI	02903	401-351-8282	
Pakarang 303 S Main St *Web:* www.pakarangrestaurant.com	Providence	RI	02903	401-453-3660	
Pane E Vino 365 Atwells Ave *Web:* www.panevino.net	Providence	RI	02903	401-223-2230	223-4322
Parkside Rotisserie & Bar 76 S Main St *Web:* www.parksideprovidence.com	Providence	RI	02903	401-331-0003	
Pot Au Feu 44 Custom House St *Web:* potaufeu.businesscatalyst.com	Providence	RI	02903	401-273-8953	273-8963
Providence Oyster Bar 283 Atwells Ave *Web:* www.providenceoysterbar.com	Providence	RI	02903	401-272-8866	
Sawaddee Thai Restaurant 93 Hope St *Web:* www.sawaddeerestaurant.com	Providence	RI	02906	401-831-1122	831-1121
Taste of India 230 Wickenden St *Web:* www.tasteofindiari.com	Providence	RI	02903	401-421-4355	751-1432
Ten Prime Steak & Sushi 55 Pine St *Web:* www.tenprimesteakandsushi.com	Providence	RI	02903	401-453-2333	
Tokyo Restaurant 388 Wickenden St	Providence	RI	02903	401-331-5330	
Waterman Grille, The 4 Richmond Sq *Web:* www.watermangrille.com	Providence	RI	02906	401-521-9229	521-9351
Wes' Rib House 38 Dike St *Web:* www.wesribhouse.com	Providence	RI	02909	401-421-9090	
XO Cafe 125 N Main St *Web:* www.xocafe.com	Providence	RI	02903	401-273-9090	

South Carolina

				Phone	Fax
Mi Tierra Mexican Restaurant 27 Mellichamp Dr Unit 101 *Web:* www.mitierrabluffton.com	Bluffton	SC	29910	843-757-7200	
39 Rue De Jean 39 John St *Web:* www.holycityhospitality.com	Charleston	SC	29403	843-722-8881	722-8835
82 Queen 82 Queen St *TF:* 800-849-0082 ■ *Web:* www.82queen.com	Charleston	SC	29401	843-723-7591	577-7463
Basil *Basil Thai Restaurant* 460 King St *Web:* www.eatatbasil.com	Charleston	SC	29403	843-724-3490	
Blossom Restaurant 171 E Bay St *Web:* magnolias-blossom-cypress.com	Charleston	SC	29401	843-722-9200	
Bubba Gump Shrimp Co 99 S Market St *Web:* www.bubbagump.com	Charleston	SC	29401	843-723-5665	
California Dreaming 1 Ashley Pointe Dr *Web:* www.centraarchy.com	Charleston	SC	29407	843-766-1644	
Carolina's 10 Exchange St *Web:* www.carolinasrestaurant.com	Charleston	SC	29401	843-724-3800	
Charleston Crab House 145 Wappoo Creek Dr *Web:* www.charlestoncrabhouse.com	Charleston	SC	29412	843-795-1963	762-4866
Charleston Grill 224 King St *Web:* www.charlestongrill.com	Charleston	SC	29401	843-577-4522	
Circa 1886 149 Wentworth St *Web:* www.circa1886.com	Charleston	SC	29401	843-853-7828	
Coast 39 John St *Web:* www.holycityhospitality.com	Charleston	SC	29403	843-722-8838	722-8835
Cru Cafe 18 Pinckney St *Web:* www.crucafe.com	Charleston	SC	29401	843-534-2434	
Cypress Lowcountry Grille 167 E Bay St *Web:* www.magnolias-blossom-cypress.com/cypresshome.asp?catid=20427	Charleston	SC	29401	843-727-0111	
FIG restaurant 232 Meeting St *Web:* www.eatatfig.com	Charleston	SC	29401	843-805-5900	
Fish 442 King St *Web:* www.fishrestaurantcharleston.com	Charleston	SC	29403	843-722-3474	937-0406
Fulton Five 5 Fulton St	Charleston	SC	29401	843-853-5555	853-6212
Grill 225 225 E Bay St *TF:* 877-440-2250 ■ *Web:* www.marketpavilion.com/grill225.cfm	Charleston	SC	29401	843-266-4222	723-4320
Hank's Seafood Restaurant 10 Hayne St *Web:* www.hanksseafoodrestaurant.com	Charleston	SC	29401	843-723-3474	
Harbor View Restaurant 301 Savannah Hwy *Web:* www.harborviewdining.com	Charleston	SC	29407	843-556-7100	
Hominy Grill 207 Rutledge Ave *Web:* www.hominygrill.com	Charleston	SC	29403	843-937-0930	
Il Cortile Del Re 193 King St *Web:* ilcortiledelre.com	Charleston	SC	29401	843-853-1888	
Jestine's Kitchen 251 Meeting St *Web:* jestineskitchen.com	Charleston	SC	29401	843-722-7224	
McCrady's 2 Unity Alley *Web:* www.mccradysrestaurant.com	Charleston	SC	29401	843-577-0025	
Middleton Place 4300 Ashley River Rd *TF:* 800-782-3608 ■ *Web:* www.middletonplace.org	Charleston	SC	29414	843-556-6020	766-4460
Peninsula Grill 112 N Market St *Web:* www.peninsulagrill.com	Charleston	SC	29401	843-723-0700	
Poogan's Porch 72 Queen St *Web:* www.poogansporch.com	Charleston	SC	29401	843-577-2337	
Slightly North of Broad 192 E Bay St *Web:* snobcharleston.com	Charleston	SC	29401	843-723-3424	724-3811
Sticky Fingers 235 Meeting St *Web:* www.stickyfingers.com	Charleston	SC	29401	843-853-7427	
Tristan 7671 Northwoods Blvd *Web:* tristanevents.com	Charleston	SC	29406	843-534-2155	
Trotters Restaurant 2008 Savannah Hwy *TF:* 800-334-6660 ■ *Web:* www.thetownandcountryinn.com	Charleston	SC	29401	843-571-1000	766-9444
Wasabi 61 State St	Charleston	SC	29401	843-577-5222	
Baan Sawan 2135 Devine St *Web:* baansawan.blogspot.com	Columbia	SC	29205	803-252-8992	
Blue Marlin 1200 Lincoln St *Web:* www.bluemarlincolumbia.com	Columbia	SC	29201	803-799-3838	
Delhi Palace 542 St Andrew Rd	Columbia	SC	29210	803-750-7760	750-7765
Eric's San Jose 6118 Garners Ferry Rd *Web:* ericssanjose.com	Columbia	SC	29209	803-783-6650	
Gervais & Vine 620-A Gervais St *Web:* www.gervine.com	Columbia	SC	29201	803-799-8463	
Hampton Street Vineyard 1201 Hampton St *Web:* www.hamptonstreetvineyard.com	Columbia	SC	29202	803-252-0850	931-0193
Melting Pot of Columbia, The 1410 Colonial Life Blvd *TF:* 800-783-0867 ■ *Web:* www.meltingpot.com	Columbia	SC	29210	803-731-8500	731-8569
Motor Supply Company Bistro 920 Gervais St *Web:* www.motorsupplycobistro.com	Columbia	SC	29201	803-256-6687	
Mr Friendly's New Southern Cafe 2001 Greene St *Web:* www.mrfriendlys.com	Columbia	SC	29205	803-254-7828	254-8219
Palmetto Pig 530 Devine St *Web:* palmettopig.com	Columbia	SC	29201	803-733-2556	
Saluda's 751 Saluda Ave *Web:* www.saludas.com	Columbia	SC	29205	803-799-9500	
Villa Tronco 1213 Blanding St *Web:* www.villatronco.com	Columbia	SC	29201	803-256-7677	256-4336
Yamato Steak House of Japan 360 Columbian Dr *Web:* www.yamatoinc.com	Columbia	SC	29212	803-407-0033	
Yesterday's Resturant & Tavern 2030 Devine St 5 Pts *Web:* www.yesterdayssc.com	Columbia	SC	29205	803-799-0196	
Zorba's 6169 St Andrews Rd	Columbia	SC	29212	803-772-4617	772-0342
Lemongrass Thai Cuisine 106 N Main St *Web:* www.lemongrassthai.net	Downtown Greenville	SC	29601	864-241-9988	
Addy's Dutch Cafe & Restaurant 17 E Coffee St *Web:* www.addysdutchcafe.com	Greenville	SC	29601	864-232-2339	
Augusta Grill 1818 Augusta Rd *Web:* www.augustagrill.com	Greenville	SC	29605	864-242-0316	
Blue Ridge Brewing Co 217 N Main St *Web:* www.blueridgebrewing.com	Greenville	SC	29601	864-232-4677	232-4680
Chicora Alley 608B S Main St *Web:* www.chicoraalley.com	Greenville	SC	29601	864-232-4100	
Chophouse '47 36 Beacon Dr *Web:* www.centraarchy.com/chophouse47.php	Greenville	SC	29615	864-286-8700	
Henry's Smokehouse 240 Wade Hampton Blvd *Web:* www.henryssmokehouse.com	Greenville	SC	29607	864-232-7774	232-7237
Irashiai Sushi Pub & Japanese Restaurant 115 Pelham Rd *Web:* www.irashiai.com	Greenville	SC	29615	864-271-0900	
Joy of Tokyo 15 Pelham Rd Ste A *Web:* joyoftokyo.tv	Greenville	SC	29615	864-232-2888	
Kanpai of Tokyo 533 Haywood Rd *Web:* www.kanpaioftokyo.com	Greenville	SC	29607	864-234-0334	
Larkin's on the River 318 S Main St *Web:* www.larkinsontheriver.com	Greenville	SC	29601	864-467-9777	

	City	State	Zip	Phone	Fax
Saskatoon 477 Haywood Rd *Web:* saskatoonrestaurant.com	Greenville	SC	29607	864-297-7244	
Soby's 207 S Main St *Web:* www.sobys.com	Greenville	SC	29601	864-232-7007	
Trattoria Giorgio 121 S Main St *Web:* trattoriagiorgio.net	Greenville	SC	29601	864-271-9166	
Alexander's Seafood Restaurant & Wine Bar 76 Queens Folly Rd *Web:* www.alexandersrestaurant.com	Hilton Head Island	SC	29928	843-785-4999	
Aunt Chilada's Easy Street Cafe 69 Pope Ave *Web:* auntchiladashhi.com	Hilton Head Island	SC	29928	843-785-7700	
Charlie's L'Etoile Verte 8 New Orleans Rd *Web:* www.charliesgreenstar.com	Hilton Head Island	SC	29928	843-785-9277	
CQ's Restaurant 140-A Lighthouse Rd Harbour Town *Web:* www.cqsrestaurant.com	Hilton Head Island	SC	29928	843-671-2779	
Crane's Tavern & Steakhouse 26 New Orleans Rd *Web:* cranestavern.com	Hilton Head Island	SC	29928	843-341-2333	
Crazy Crab 104 William Hilton Pkwy *Web:* www.thecrazycrab.com	Hilton Head Island	SC	29926	843-681-5021	
Fiesta Fresh Mexican Grill 51 New Orleans Rd Ste 4 *Web:* fiestafreshmexicangrill.com	Hilton Head Island	SC	29928	843-785-4788	
Hudson's Seafood House on the Docks 1 Hudsons Rd *Web:* www.hudsonsonthedocks.com	Hilton Head Island	SC	29926	843-681-2772	681-2774
Kingfisher Seafood & Steak House 18 Harborside Ln Shelter Cove Harbour *Web:* www.kingfisherseafood.com	Hilton Head Island	SC	29928	843-785-4442	
Mangiamo 2000 Main St *Web:* www.hhipizza.com	Hilton Head Island	SC	29926	843-682-2444	682-3355
Market Street Cafe 1 N Forest Beach Blvd *Web:* www.marketstreetcafe.com	Hilton Head Island	SC	29928	843-686-4976	
Marley's Island Grille 35 Office Pk Rd *Web:* marleyshhi.com	Hilton Head Island	SC	29928	843-686-5800	
Michael Anthony's Cucina Italiana 37 New Orleans Rd Ste L *Web:* www.michael-anthonys.com	Hilton Head Island	SC	29928	843-785-6272	
Old Fort Pub 65 Skull Creek Dr *Web:* oldfortpub.com	Hilton Head Island	SC	29926	843-681-2386	
Old Oyster Factory 101 Marshland Rd *Web:* www.oldoysterfactory.com	Hilton Head Island	SC	29926	843-681-6040	
Red Fish 8 Archer Rd *Web:* www.redfishofhiltonhead.com	Hilton Head Island	SC	29928	843-686-3388	
Sage Room 81 Pope Ave *Web:* www.thesageroom.com	Hilton Head Island	SC	29928	843-785-5352	
Salty Dog Cafe, The 232 S Sea Pines Dr *TF:* 877-725-8936 ■ *Web:* www.saltydog.com	Hilton Head Island	SC	29928	843-671-5199	
Santa Fe Cafe 807 William Hilton Pkwy *Web:* www.santafehhi.com	Hilton Head Island	SC	29928	843-785-3838	785-2496
Signe's Bakery & Cafe 93 Arrow Rd *TF:* 866-807-4463 ■ *Web:* www.signesbakery.com	Hilton Head Island	SC	29928	843-785-9118	785-6144
Smokehouse, The 34 Palmetto Bay Rd *Web:* www.smokehousehhi.com	Hilton Head Island	SC	29928	843-842-4227	
Steamer Seafood Co 1 N Forest Beach Dr Ste 28 Calligny Plz *Web:* www.steamerseafood.com	Hilton Head Island	SC	29928	843-785-2070	
Boathouse, The 101 Palm Blvd *Web:* www.boathouserestaurants.com	Isle of Palms	SC	29451	843-886-8000	
Bovine's 3979 Hwy 17 Business *Web:* www.bovinesrestaurant.com	Murrells Inlet	SC	29576	843-651-2888	
Bangkok House 318 N Kings Hwy	Myrtle Beach	SC	29577	843-626-5384	
Captain George's 1401 29th Ave *Web:* www.captaingeorges.com	Myrtle Beach	SC	29577	843-916-2278	
El Cerro Grande 108 S Kings Hwy	Myrtle Beach	SC	29577	843-946-9562	448-4431
Fiesta Del Burroloco 960 Jason Blvd *Web:* www.centraarchy.com	Myrtle Beach	SC	29577	843-626-1756	
Flamingo Grille 7050 N Kings Hwy *Web:* flamingogrill.com	Myrtle Beach	SC	29572	843-449-5388	
Giant Crab 9597 N Kings Hwy *Web:* www.giantcrab.com	Myrtle Beach	SC	29572	843-449-1097	
Melting Pot, The 5001 N Kings Hwy *Web:* www.meltingpot.com	Myrtle Beach	SC	29577	843-692-9003	692-9004
Miyabi 9732 N Kings Hwy *Web:* miyabimyrtlebeach.com	Myrtle Beach	SC	29572	843-449-9294	692-2274
Original Benjamin's, The 9593 N Kings Hwy *Web:* www.originalbenjamins.com	Myrtle Beach	SC	29572	843-449-0821	
Sea Captain's House 3002 N Ocean Blvd *Web:* www.seacaptains.com	Myrtle Beach	SC	29577	843-448-8082	
Senor Frogs 1304 Celebrity Cir Bldg R-8 *Web:* www.senorfrogs.com	Myrtle Beach	SC	29577	843-444-5506	
Sugami 4813 N Kings Hwy *Web:* sugamimyrtlebeach.com	Myrtle Beach	SC	29577	843-692-7709	
Thoroughbreds 9706 N Kings Hwy *Web:* www.thoroughbredsrestaurant.com	Myrtle Beach	SC	29572	843-497-2636	497-6474
Sea Blue 503 Hwy 17 N *Web:* www.seabluewinebar.com	North Myrtle Beach	SC	29582	843-249-8800	
Crabby Mike's Calabash Seafood 290 Hwy 17 N *Web:* www.crabbymikes.com	Surfside Beach	SC	29575	843-238-3524	238-3526

South Dakota

	City	State	Zip	Phone	Fax
Cattleman's Club Steakhouse & Lounge 29608 SD Hwy 34 *Web:* cattlemansclubsteakhouse.com	Pierre	SD	57501	605-224-9774	
Guadalajara 314 W Sioux Ave *Web:* restaurantdeguadlajara.com	Pierre	SD	57501	605-224-2771	
Jake's Good Time Place 620 S Cleveland *Web:* dexknows.com	Pierre	SD	57501	605-945-0485	
La Minestra 106 E Dakota Ave *Web:* www.laminestra.com	Pierre	SD	57501	605-224-8090	
Longbranch Restaurant & Lounge 351 S Pierre St	Pierre	SD	57501	605-224-6166	945-2240
Mad Mary's Steakhouse & Saloon 110 E Dakota Ave	Pierre	SD	57501	605-224-6469	
Outpost Lodge 28229 Cow Creek Rd *Web:* www.theoutpostlodge.com	Pierre	SD	57501	605-264-5450	
Botticelli Italian Restaurant 523 Main St *Web:* botticelliristorante.net	Rapid City	SD	57701	605-348-0089	
Colonial House 2501 Mt Rushmore Rd *Web:* www.colonialhousernb.com	Rapid City	SD	57701	605-342-4640	
Firehouse Brewing Co 610 Main St *Web:* firehousebrewing.com	Rapid City	SD	57701	605-348-1915	
Golden Phoenix 2421 W Main St	Rapid City	SD	57702	605-348-4195	
Hong Kong Buffet 927 E N St *Web:* cocopalaces.com	Rapid City	SD	57701	605-716-4664	
Hunan 1720 Mt Rushmore Rd *Web:* bhhunan.com	Rapid City	SD	57701	605-341-3888	
Minerva's 2111 N Lacrosse St *Web:* minervas.net	Rapid City	SD	57701	605-394-9505	
Mongolian Grill 1415 N Lacrosse St Ste 1 *Web:* mongoliangrill.com	Rapid City	SD	57701	519-645-6400	
Saigon 221 E N St *Web:* saigonrestaurantrc.com	Rapid City	SD	57701	605-348-8523	
Casa Del Rey 901 W Russell St *Web:* www.casadelrey.com	Sioux Falls	SD	57104	605-338-6078	
Cherry Creek Grill 3104 E 26th St *Web:* cherrycreek-grill.com	Sioux Falls	SD	57103	605-336-2333	
Dynasty 5326 W 26th St *Web:* www.dynastysf.com	Sioux Falls	SD	57106	605-361-7788	
Falls Landing 200 E Eigth St *Web:* falls-landing.com	Sioux Falls	SD	57103	605-336-2290	
Incas 3312 S Holly Ave *Web:* incasiouxfalls.com	Sioux Falls	SD	57105	605-367-1992	367-1993
Minerva's 301 S Phillips Ave *Web:* www.minervas.net	Sioux Falls	SD	57104	605-334-0386	334-9585
Sanaa's 401 E Eigth St *Web:* sanaacooks.com	Sioux Falls	SD	57103	605-275-2516	
Sushi Masa 423 S Phillips Ave	Sioux Falls	SD	57104	605-977-6968	

Tennessee

	City	State	Zip	Phone	Fax
Corky's 100 Franklin Rd *Web:* corkysbbq.com	Brentwood	TN	37027	615-373-1020	
212 Market Restaurant 212 Market St *Web:* www.212market.com	Chattanooga	TN	37402	423-265-1212	267-6757
Acropolis, The 2213 Hamilton Pl Blvd *Web:* www.acropolisgrill.com	Chattanooga	TN	37421	423-899-5341	
Amigo Mexican Restaurant 3805 Ringgold Rd *Web:* amigorestaurantonline.com	Chattanooga	TN	37412	423-624-4345	
Broad Street Grille at the Chattanoogan 1201 Broad St *Web:* www.chattanooganhotel.com	Chattanooga	TN	37402	423-424-3700	756-3404
China Moon 5600 Brainerd Rd *Web:* chinamoontn.com	Chattanooga	TN	37411	423-893-8088	855-5288
Chop House, The 2011 Gunbarrel Rd *Web:* www.thechophouse.com	Chattanooga	TN	37421	423-892-1222	
India Mahal 5970 Brainerd Rd	Chattanooga	TN	37421	423-510-9651	
Kanpai of Tokyo 2200 Hamilton Pl Blvd *Web:* www.kanpaioftokyo.com	Chattanooga	TN	37421	423-855-8204	
Mount Vernon Restaurant 3535 Broad St	Chattanooga	TN	37409	423-266-6591	
Na Go Ya 4921 Brainerd Rd *Web:* www.nagoyatn.com	Chattanooga	TN	37411	423-899-9252	
Porker's BBQ 1251 Market St	Chattanooga	TN	37402	423-267-2726	
Saint John's Restaurant 1278 Market St *Web:* www.stjohnsrestaurant.com	Chattanooga	TN	37402	423-266-4400	267-3004
Sekisui of Chattanooga 1120 Houston St *Web:* www.sekisuichattanooga.com	Chattanooga	TN	37402	423-267-4600	
Southern Star 1300 Broad St *Web:* www.southernstarrestaurant.com	Chattanooga	TN	37402	423-267-8899	
Sushi Nabe of Chattanooga 110 River St *Web:* www.sushinabechattanooga.com	Chattanooga	TN	37405	423-634-0171	
Terra Nostra 105 Frazier Ave *Web:* www.terranostratapas.com	Chattanooga	TN	37405	423-634-0238	
Jims Place Grille 3660 S Houston Levee *Web:* jimsplacegrille.com	Collierville	TN	38017	901-861-5000	
Alta Cucina 1200 N Roan St *Web:* www.altacucinajc.net	Johnson City	TN	37601	423-928-2092	
Bello Vita 2927 N Roan St	Johnson City	TN	37601	423-282-8600	
Cafe One 11 111 Broyles St Sunset Shopping Ctr Ste 1 *Web:* www.cafeone11jc.com	Johnson City	TN	37601	423-283-4633	
Cafe Pacific 1033 W Oakland Ave *Web:* www.cafepacificjtn.com	Johnson City	TN	37604	423-610-0117	
Dixie Barbecue Co 3301 N Roan St *Web:* dixiebarbeque.net	Johnson City	TN	37601	423-283-7447	

				Phone	Fax
Firehouse Restaurant 627 W Walnut St	Johnson City	TN	37604	423-929-7377	
Web: www.thefirehouse.com					
Harbor House Seafood 2510 N Roan St	Johnson City	TN	37601	423-282-5122	
Web: www.harborhousejc.com					
Horseshoe Restaurant & Lounge					
908 W Market St	Johnson City	TN	37604	423-928-8992	
Misaki Seafood & Steak House of Japan					
3104 Bristol Hwy	Johnson City	TN	37601	423-282-5451	
Moto Japanese Restaurant 2607 N Roan St	Johnson City	TN	37601	423-282-6686	282-0132
Peerless Steak House 2531 N Roan St	Johnson City	TN	37601	423-282-2351	283-0439
Web: www.peerlesseatout.com					
Red Pig Bar-B-Q 2201 Ferguson Rd	Johnson City	TN	37604	423-282-6585	282-6309
Bayou Bay Seafood House 7117 Chapman Hwy	Knoxville	TN	37920	865-573-7936	
Web: bayoubayseafoodhouseknoxville.com					
Bistro by the Tracks					
215 Brookview Centre Way Ste 109	Knoxville	TN	37919	865-558-9500	
Web: www.bistrobythetracks.com					
Buddy's Bar-B-Q 4401 Chapman Hwy	Knoxville	TN	37920	865-579-1747	579-3315
Web: buddysbarbq.com					
Calhoun's 10020 Kingston Pk	Knoxville	TN	37922	865-673-3444	
Web: calhouns.com					
Chesapeake's 600 Union Ave	Knoxville	TN	37902	865-673-3400	
Web: www.chesapeakes.com					
Chop House 9700 Kingston Pk	Knoxville	TN	37922	865-531-2467	693-4814
Web: thechophouse.com					
Downtown Grill & Brewery 424 S Gay St	Knoxville	TN	37902	865-633-8111	
Web: www.downtownbrewery.com					
King Tut's Grill 4132 Martin Mill Pk	Knoxville	TN	37920	865-573-6021	
Litton's Market & Restaurant & Bakery					
2803 Essary Dr	Knoxville	TN	37918	865-688-0429	
Web: www.littonsdirecttoyou.com/home.aspx					
Misaki Japanese Steak House					
8207 Kingston Pk	Knoxville	TN	37919	865-691-3121	691-3218
Nama Sushi Bar 506 S Gay St	Knoxville	TN	37902	865-633-8539	739-5819*
**Fax Area Code: 615 ■ Web:* www.namasushibar.com					
Naples Italian Restaurant 5500 Kingston Pk	Knoxville	TN	37919	865-584-5033	
Web: naplesitalianrestaurant.net					
Orangery, The 5412 Kingston Pk	Knoxville	TN	37919	865-588-2964	
Web: www.orangeryknoxville.com					
Pelanchos Mexican Grill					
1516 Downtown W Blvd	Knoxville	TN	37919	865-694-9060	
Web: www.pelanchos.com					
Savelli's 3055 Sutherland Ave	Knoxville	TN	37919	865-521-9085	
Web: savellisknoxville.com					
Sitar Indian Cuisine 6004 Kingston Pk	Knoxville	TN	37919	865-588-1828	
Web: sitarknoxville.com					
Tomato Head 12 Market Sq	Knoxville	TN	37902	865-637-4067	637-4019
Web: thetomatohead.com					
Wasabi Japanese Steak House 226 Lovell Rd	Knoxville	TN	37934	865-675-0201	
Web: www.wasabi-steakhouse.com					
Ye Olde Steak House 6838 Chapman Hwy	Knoxville	TN	37920	865-577-9328	
Web: www.yeoldesteakhouse.com					
Automatic Slim's 83 S Second St	Memphis	TN	38103	901-525-7948	
Web: www.automaticslimsmemphis.com					
Bar-B-Q Shop, The 1782 Madison Ave	Memphis	TN	38104	901-272-1277	
TF: 877-372-8237 ■ *Web:* dancingpigs.com					
BB King's Blues Club 143 Beale St	Memphis	TN	38103	901-524-5464	524-5454
Web: www.bbkings.com					
Benihana 912 Ridgelake Blvd	Memphis	TN	38120	901-767-8980	
Web: www.benihana.com					
Bhan Thai 1324 Peabody Ave	Memphis	TN	38104	901-272-1538	
Web: www.bhanthairestaurant.com					
Boscos Squared 827 S Main	Memphis	TN	38106	901-278-0087	
Web: www.boscosbeer.com					
Buckley's 5355 Poplar Ave	Memphis	TN	38119	901-683-4538	
Web: www.buckleysgrill.com					
Cafe 1912 243 S Cooper at Peabody	Memphis	TN	38104	901-722-2700	
Web: cafe1912.com					
Cafe Society 212 N Evergreen St	Memphis	TN	38112	901-722-2177	
Web: cafesocietymemphis.com					
Celtic Crossing Irish Pub & Restaurant					
903 S Cooper St	Memphis	TN	38104	901-274-5151	
Web: www.celticcrossingmemphis.com					
Central BBQ 2249 Central Ave	Memphis	TN	38104	901-272-9377	
Web: cbqmemphis.com					
Cupboard, The 1400 Union Ave	Memphis	TN	38104	901-276-8015	728-5518
Web: www.thecupboardrestaurant.com					
Erling Jensen Restaurant 1044 S Yates Rd	Memphis	TN	38119	901-763-3700	763-3800
Web: www.ejensen.com					
Folk's Folly Prime Steak House					
551 S Mendenhall Rd	Memphis	TN	38117	901-762-8200	
Web: www.folksfolly.com					
Frank Grisanti's 1022 S Shady Grove Rd	Memphis	TN	38120	901-761-9462	761-2245
Web: frankgrisanti.com					
Golden India 2097 Madison Ave	Memphis	TN	38104	901-728-5111	
Grill83 83 Madison Ave	Memphis	TN	38103	901-333-1224	
Web: www.eighty3memphis.com					
Grove Grill 4550 Poplar Ave	Memphis	TN	38117	901-818-9951	
Web: www.thegrovegrill.com					
Happy Mexican Restaurant & Cantina					
6080 Primacy Pkwy	Memphis	TN	38119	901-683-0000	
Web: www.happymexican.com					
Huey's 1927 Madison Ave	Memphis	TN	38104	901-726-4372	278-9073
Web: www.hueyburger.com					
India Palace 1720 Poplar Ave	Memphis	TN	38104	901-278-1199	
Jim Neely's Interstate Barbeque					
2265 S Third St	Memphis	TN	38109	901-775-2304	775-3149
Web: www.interstatebarbecue.com					
King's Palace Cafe 162 Beale St	Memphis	TN	38103	901-521-1851	
Melting Pot, The 2828 Wolfcreek Pkwy	Memphis	TN	38133	901-380-9500	
Web: www.meltingpot.com					

				Phone	Fax
Mollie's La Casita Restaurant					
2006 Madison Ave	Memphis	TN	38104	901-726-1873	
Web: www.mollyslacasita.com					
Owen Brennan's Restaurant 6150 Poplar Ave	Memphis	TN	38119	901-761-0990	761-9177
Web: www.brennansmemphis.com					
Saigon Le 51 N Cleveland St	Memphis	TN	38104	901-276-5326	
Sekisui 25 S Belvedere Blvd	Memphis	TN	38104	901-725-0005	
Web: www.sekisuiusa.com					
Sekisui Japanese Restaurant 4724 Poplar Ave	Memphis	TN	38117	901-767-7770	
Web: www.sekisuiusa.com					
Silky O'Sullivan's 183 Beale St	Memphis	TN	38103	901-522-9596	522-8462
Web: www.silkyosullivans.com					
Texas de Brazil 150 Peabody Pl Ste 103	Memphis	TN	38103	901-526-7600	526-7615
Web: www.texasdebrazil.com					
Valenti Mid-south Management LLC					
1775 Moriah Woods Blvd Ste 5	Memphis	TN	38117	901-684-1215	
Web: www.valentirestaurants.com					
Amerigo Nashville 1920 W End Ave	Nashville	TN	37203	615-320-1740	
Web: www.amerigo.net					
Anatolia 48 White Bridge Rd	Nashville	TN	37205	615-356-1556	356-1551
Web: www.anatolia-restaurant.com					
Antonios' of Nashville					
7097 Old HaRding Pike	Nashville	TN	37221	615-646-9166	
Web: antoniosofnashville.com					
Blackstone Restaurant & Brewery					
1918 W End Ave	Nashville	TN	37203	615-327-9969	327-4131
Web: blackstone-pub.com					
Bound'ry 911 20th Ave S	Nashville	TN	37212	615-321-3043	
Web: boundrynashville.com					
Chinatown 3900 Hillsboro Pk	Nashville	TN	37215	615-269-3275	
Web: nashvillechinatown.com					
Cock of the Walk 2624 Music Vly Dr	Nashville	TN	37214	615-889-1930	
Web: www.cockofthewalkrestaurant.com					
Copper Kettle Cafe 4004 Granny White Pk	Nashville	TN	37204	615-383-7242	383-7949
Web: copperkettlenashville.com					
Fleming's Prime Steakhouse & Wine Bar					
2525 W End Ave	Nashville	TN	37203	615-342-0131	
Web: www.flemingssteakhouse.com					
Goten Japanese Steak & Sushi Bar					
1719 W End Ave Ste 101W	Nashville	TN	37203	615-321-4537	321-3105
Hog Heaven 115 27th Ave N	Nashville	TN	37203	615-329-1234	
Web: www.hogheavenbbq.com					
Jack's Bar-B-Que 334 W Trinity Ln	Nashville	TN	37207	615-228-4600	228-4700
Web: www.jacksbarbque.com					
Jim 'N Nick's 7004 Charlotte Pk	Nashville	TN	37209	615-352-5777	
Web: jimnnicks.com					
Jimmy Kelly's 217 Louise Ave	Nashville	TN	37203	615-329-4349	
Web: www.jimmykellys.com					
Kalamata's 3764 Hillsboro Pike	Nashville	TN	37215	615-383-8700	
Web: www.eatatkalamatas.com					
Ken's 1108 Murfreesboro Pk	Nashville	TN	37217	615-321-2444	
Web: www.kensushi.com					
Kien Giang 5845 Charlotte Pk	Nashville	TN	37209	615-353-1250	
Kobe Steaks Nashville					
210 25th Ave N Ste 100	Nashville	TN	37203	615-327-9081	327-9083
Web: www.kobesteaks.net					
Korea House 6410 Charlotte Pk Ste 108	Nashville	TN	37209	615-352-2790	
Mad Platter, The 1239 Sixth Ave N	Nashville	TN	37208	615-242-2563	
Web: www.madplatternashville.com					
Margot Cafe & Bar 1017 Woodland St	Nashville	TN	37206	615-227-4668	
Web: margotcafe.com					
Melting Pot, The 166 Second Ave N	Nashville	TN	37201	615-742-4970	726-6328
Web: www.meltingpot.com					
Midtown Cafe 102 19th Ave S	Nashville	TN	37203	615-320-7176	
Web: www.midtowncafe.com					
Morton's The Steakhouse 618 Church St	Nashville	TN	37219	615-259-4558	726-2760
TF: 800-297-3276 ■ *Web:* www.mortons.com					
Palm, The 140 Fifth Ave S	Nashville	TN	37203	615-742-7256	742-9028
Web: www.thepalm.com					
Park Cafe 4403 Murphy Rd	Nashville	TN	37209	615-383-4409	383-4829
Web: parkcafenashville.com					
PF Chang's China Bistro 2525 W End Ave	Nashville	TN	37203	615-329-8901	
Web: www.pfchangs.com					
Rotier's 2413 Elliston Pl	Nashville	TN	37203	615-327-9892	
Web: rotiersrestaurant.com					
Ru San's 505 12th Ave S	Nashville	TN	37203	615-252-8787	
Web: rusansjapanese.com					
Ruth's Chris Steak House 2100 W End Ave	Nashville	TN	37203	615-320-0163	
Web: www.ruthschris.com					
Shalimar 3711 Hillsboro Pk	Nashville	TN	37215	615-269-8577	292-0330
Web: shalimarfinedining.com					
Siam Cafe 316 McCall St	Nashville	TN	37211	615-834-3181	
Sitar Indian Cuisine 116 21st Ave N	Nashville	TN	37203	615-321-8889	321-2688
Web: www.sitarnashville.com					
Sonobana Japanese Restaurant & Grocery					
40 White Bridge Rd	Nashville	TN	37205	615-356-6600	
Web: www.sonobananashville.com					
South Street Restaurant 907 20th Ave S	Nashville	TN	37212	615-320-5555	
Web: pansouth.net/southstreet					
Sperry's 5109 Harding Pike	Nashville	TN	37205	615-353-0809	353-0814
Web: www.sperrys.com					
Sunset Grill 2001 Belcourt Ave	Nashville	TN	37212	615-386-3663	
Web: www.sunsetgrill.com					
Tin Angel 3201 W End Ave	Nashville	TN	37203	615-298-3444	
Web: tinangel.net					
Valentino's 1907 W End Ave	Nashville	TN	37203	615-327-0148	
Web: www.valentinosnashville.com					
Yellow Porch, The 734 Thompson Ln	Nashville	TN	37204	615-386-0260	
Web: www.theyellowporch.com					

Texas

Phone — Fax

Abilene Seafood Tavern 1882 S Clack St . . . Abilene TX 79605 325-695-1770
Alfredo's Mexican Food 2849 S 14th St . . . Abilene TX 79605 325-698-0104
Catfish Corner 780 S Treadaway Blvd . . . Abilene TX 79602 325-672-3620
Cotton Patch Cafe 3302 S Clack St . . . Abilene TX 79606 325-691-0509
Web: www.cottonpatch.com
Cypress Street Station 158 Cypress St . . . Abilene TX 79601 325-676-3463 676-0715
Web: www.cypress-street.com
Eckos Restaurant 2410 Adam Ave . . . Abilene TX 79602 325-672-3792
Joe Allen's Pit Bar-B-Que 301 S 11th St . . . Abilene TX 79602 325-672-6082 672-3015*
Little Panda 1035 N Judge Ely Blvd . . . Abilene TX 79601 325-670-9393
Web: www.littlepandaonline.com
Lytle Land & Cattle Co 1150 E S 11th St . . . Abilene TX 79604 325-677-1925
Web: www.lytlelandandcattle.com
Towne Crier Steak House 818 US Hwy 80 E . . . Abilene TX 79601 325-673-4551
Web: www.townecriersteakhouse.com
Abuelo's Mexican Food Embassy
3501 W 45th Ave . . . Amarillo TX 79109 806-354-8294
Web: www.abuelos.com
Amarillo Club 600 S Tyler St . . . Amarillo TX 79101 806-373-4361
Web: amarilloclub.net
Big Texan Steak Ranch 7701 I-40 E . . . Amarillo TX 79118 806-372-6000
Web: www.bigtexan.com
BL Bistro 2203 S Austin St . . . Amarillo TX 79109 806-355-7838
Web: www.blbistro.com
Buns Over Texas 6045 SW 34th . . . Amarillo TX 79109 806-358-6808
Web: bunsovertexas.com
Coyote Bluff Cafe 2417 S Grand St . . . Amarillo TX 79103 806-373-4640
Web: coyotebluffcafe.com
Doug's Hickory Pit Bar B Que
3313 S Georgia St . . . Amarillo TX 79109 806-352-8471
Golden Light Cafe 2908 W Sixth Ave . . . Amarillo TX 79106 806-374-9237
Web: www.goldenlightcafe.com
Hoffbrau Steaks 7203-G IH- I-40 W . . . Amarillo TX 79106 806-358-6595
Web: www.hoffbrausteaks.com
Hummer's Sports Cafe 2600 Paramount Blvd . . . Amarillo TX 79109 806-353-0723 353-4249
Jorge's Taco Garcia Mexican Cafe
1100 S Ross St . . . Amarillo TX 79102 806-371-0411
Web: www.tacosgarcia.com
Kabuki Japanese Steakhouse 8130 I 40 W . . . Amarillo TX 79106 806-358-7799
Web: kabukiromanza.com
Macaroni Joe's 1619 S Kentucky St Ste 1500-D . . . Amarillo TX 79102 806-358-8990
Web: www.macaronijoes.com
My Thai 2029 Coulter Dr . . . Amarillo TX 79106 806-355-9541
Web: www.mythaiamarillo.com
Pacific Rim 2061 Paramount . . . Amarillo TX 79109 806-353-9179 358-7888
Web: www.pacificrimam.com
Ruby Tequila's 2001 S Georgia . . . Amarillo TX 79109 806-358-7829
Web: www.rubytequilas.com
Abuelo's Mexican Food Embassy
1041 IH- 20 W . . . Arlington TX 76017 817-468-2622
Web: www.abuelos.com
Arlington Steak House 1724 W Div St . . . Arlington TX 76012 817-275-7881 275-7881
Web: thearlingtonsteakhouse.com
Bigotes 1821 E Abram St . . . Arlington TX 76010 817-274-1350
Cacharel Restaurant & Grand Ballroom
2221 E Lamar Blvd . . . Arlington TX 76006 817-640-9981
Web: www.cacharel.net
La Isla 611 W Pk Row . . . Arlington TX 76010 817-460-1180
Mariano's Mexican Cuisine 2614 Majesty Dr . . . Arlington TX 76011 817-640-5118
Web: laharanch.com
Nagoya Japanese Restaurant
1155 W Arbrook Blvd . . . Arlington TX 76015 817-466-3688 466-3684
Web: www.txnagoya.com
Pappadeaux Seafood Kitchen
1304 E Copeland Rd . . . Arlington TX 76011 817-543-0545
Web: www.pappadeaux.com
Pappasito's Cantina
321 Rd to Six Flags St W . . . Arlington TX 76011 817-795-3535
Web: www.pappas.com
Piccolo Mondo 829 E Lamar Blvd . . . Arlington TX 76011 817-265-9174
Web: www.piccolomondo.com
Spring Creek Barbeque 2340 W I- 20 Ste 100 . . . Arlington TX 76017 817-467-0505
TF: 888-467-0505 ■ *Web:* www.springcreekbarbeque.com
Tandoor Indian Restaurant
1200 N Fielder Rd Ste 532 . . . Arlington TX 76012 817-261-6604
Web: www.tandoorrestaurant.net
Taste of Thai 2535 E Arkansas Ln . . . Arlington TX 76010 817-543-0110
Web: tasteofthaiarlington.com
Alborz Persian Cuisine
3300 W Anderson Ln Ste 300 . . . Austin TX 78757 512-420-2222
Web: www.alborzpersiancuisine.com
Asti Trattoria 408C E 43rd St . . . Austin TX 78751 512-451-1218
Web: www.astiaustin.com
Austin Land & Cattle Co 1205 N Lamar Blvd . . . Austin TX 78703 512-472-1813
Web: alcsteaks.com
Casa de Luz 1701 Toomey Rd . . . Austin TX 78704 512-476-2535
Web: www.casadeluz.org
Chez Nous 510 Neches St . . . Austin TX 78701 512-473-2413
Web: cheznousaustin.com
Chez Zee American Bistro 5406 Balcones Dr . . . Austin TX 78731 512-454-2666
Web: www.chez-zee.com
Clay Pit 1601 Guadalupe St . . . Austin TX 78701 512-322-5131
Web: www.claypit.com
Curra's Grill 614 E Oltorf St . . . Austin TX 78704 512-444-0012
Web: www.currasgrill.com
Cypress Grill 4404 W William Cannon Ste L . . . Austin TX 78749 512-358-7474
Web: www.cypressgrill.net

Phone — Fax

Din Ho's Chinese BBQ 8557 Research Blvd . . . Austin TX 78758 512-832-8788
Web: www.dinhochinesebbq.com
Dog & Duck Pub, The 2400 Webberville Rd . . . Austin TX 78702 512-479-0598
Web: www.dogandduckpub.com
Driskill Grill 604 Brazos St . . . Austin TX 78701 512-391-7162 391-7059
Web: www.driskillgrill.com
Eastside Cafe 2113 Manor Rd . . . Austin TX 78722 512-476-5858
Web: www.eastsidecafeaustin.com
El Sol Y La Luna 600 E Sixth St . . . Austin TX 78701 512-444-7770
Web: elsolylalunaaustin.com
Fado's Irish Pub 214 W Fourth St . . . Austin TX 78701 512-457-0172
Web: www.fadoirishpub.com
Fonda San Miguel 2330 W N Loop Blvd . . . Austin TX 78756 512-459-4121
Web: www.fondasanmiguel.com
Four Seasons Hotel Austin 98 San Jacinto Blvd . . . Austin TX 78701 512-478-4500 478-3117
Web: fourseasons.com
Green Pastures 811 W Live Oak St . . . Austin TX 78704 512-444-1888 444-3912
Habana 2728 S Congress Ave . . . Austin TX 78704 512-443-4252
Web: www.habanaaustin.com
Hudson's on the Bend 3509 Ranch Rd 620 N . . . Austin TX 78734 512-266-1369 266-1399
TF: 800-996-7655 ■ *Web:* www.hudsonsonthebend.com
Hula Hut 3825 Lk Austin Blvd . . . Austin TX 78703 512-476-4852
Web: www.hulahut.com
Hunan 1940 W William Cannon Dr . . . Austin TX 78745 512-443-8848
Web: www.hunanaustin.com
Hyde Park Bar & Grill 4206 Duval St . . . Austin TX 78751 512-458-3168
Web: www.hpbng.com
III Forks 111 Lavaca St . . . Austin TX 78701 512-474-1776
Web: www.3forks.com
Jeffrey's Restaurant 1204 W Lynn St . . . Austin TX 78703 512-477-5584 474-7279
Web: www.jeffreysofaustin.com
Kim Phung 7601 N Lamar Blvd Ste I . . . Austin TX 78752 512-451-2464
Web: kplamar.com
La Traviata 314 Congress Ave . . . Austin TX 78701 512-479-8131
Web: latraviata.net
Madam Mam's 2514 Guadalupe St . . . Austin TX 78705 512-472-8306
Web: madammam.com
Magnolia Cafe 2304 Lk Austin Blvd . . . Austin TX 78703 512-478-8645 494-1722
Web: www.magnoliacafeaustin.com
Mikado Ryotei 9033 Research Blvd . . . Austin TX 78758 512-833-8188
Web: www.mikadoryotei.com
Moonshine Patio Bar & Grill 303 Red River St . . . Austin TX 78701 512-236-9599
Web: www.moonshinegrill.com
Musashino Sushi Dokoro 3407 Greystone Dr . . . Austin TX 78731 512-795-8593
Web: www.musashinosushi.com
Oasis, The 6550 Comanche Trl . . . Austin TX 78732 512-266-2442
Web: www.oasis-austin.com
Rocco's Grill 12432 Bee Cave Rd Ste A106 . . . Austin TX 78738 512-263-8204
Web: www.roccosgrill.com
Ruth's Chris Steak House 107 W Sixth St . . . Austin TX 78701 512-477-7884
Web: ruthschris.com
Satay 3202 W Anderson Ln . . . Austin TX 78757 512-467-6731
Web: www.satayusa.com
Shoreline Grill 98 San Jacinto Blvd . . . Austin TX 78701 512-477-3300 477-6392
Web: www.shorelinegrill.com
Star of India 2900 W Anderson Ln Ste 12D . . . Austin TX 78757 512-452-8199
Web: www.starofindiaaustin.com
Sullivan's Steakhouse 300 Colorado St . . . Austin TX 78701 512-495-6504 495-6509
Web: sullivanssteakhouse.com
Sunflower 8557 Research Blvd . . . Austin TX 78758 512-339-7860
Sushi Japon 6801 N IH-35 . . . Austin TX 78752 512-323-6663 323-6789
Web: www.sushijaponaustin.com
Sushi Zushi 1611 W Fifth St . . . Austin TX 78703 512-474-7000
Web: www.sushizushi.com
Threadgill's 6416 N Lamar Blvd . . . Austin TX 78752 512-451-5440
Web: www.threadgills.com
Uchi 801 S Lamar Blvd . . . Austin TX 78704 512-916-4808
Web: www.uchiaustin.com
Umi Sushi Bar & Grill 5510 S IH-35 Ste 400 . . . Austin TX 78745 512-383-8681 383-8802
Web: umiaustin.com
Veggie Heaven 1914 Guadalupe St . . . Austin TX 78705 512-457-1013
Web: veggieheavenaustin.com
Vespaio 1610 S Congress Ave . . . Austin TX 78704 512-441-6100 441-7746
Web: austinvespaio.com
Wink Restaurant 1014 N Lamar Blvd Ste E . . . Austin TX 78703 512-482-8868 482-9477
Web: www.winkrestaurant.com
Z Tejas Grill 9400-A Arboreum Blvd . . . Austin TX 78759 512-346-3506 346-6328
Web: www.ztejas.com
Antonio's Mexican Village 840 Paredes Rd . . . Brownsville TX 78521 956-542-6504 542-1125
Blue Mermaid Cafe
119 Billy Mitchell Blvd . . . Brownsville TX 78521 956-544-2157
Camperos Grill & Bar 2500 N Expy 77/83 . . . Brownsville TX 78521 956-546-8172
Web: camperosgrillandbar.com
Cobbleheads Bar & Grill
3154 Central Blvd . . . Brownsville TX 78520 956-546-6224
Web: www.cobbleheads.com
Lotus Inn 905 N Expy . . . Brownsville TX 78520 956-542-5715
Web: lotuscafe.us
Oyster Bar I 157 E Levee St . . . Brownsville TX 78520 956-542-9786
Sylvia's Restaurant 1843 Southmost Rd . . . Brownsville TX 78521 956-542-9220
Vermillion, The 115 Paredes Line Rd . . . Brownsville TX 78521 956-542-9893
Web: www.thevermillion.com
Hunan Village Restaurant 1402 N Lp 336 W Ste A . . . Conroe TX 77304 936-539-6811
Web: www.hunanvillageconroe.com
Crawdaddy's 414 Starr St . . . Corpus Christi TX 78401 361-883-5432
El Rinconcitos 4025 Prescott St . . . Corpus Christi TX 78416 361-851-8020
Executive Surf Club 309 N Water St . . . Corpus Christi TX 78401 361-884-7873 882-2865
Web: www.watersmarketcc.com/executive-surf-club
Kiko's 5514 Everhart Rd . . . Corpus Christi TX 78411 361-991-1211
Web: kikosmexicanfood.com
Little Manila Lumpia House
2124 Waldron Rd . . . Corpus Christi TX 78418 361-937-5651

Name / Address	City	State	Zip	Phone	Fax
Mamma Mia's 128 N Mesquite St	Corpus Christi	TX	78401	361-883-3773	
Peoples 9738 Up River Rd *Web:* www.peoplesrestaurant.com	Corpus Christi	TX	78410	361-241-8087	
Pier 99 2822 N Shoreline Blvd *Web:* pier99restaurant.com	Corpus Christi	TX	78402	361-887-0764	
Republic of Texas Bar & Grill 900 N Shoreline Blvd *Web:* omnihotels.com	Corpus Christi	TX	78401	361-887-1600	886-3530
Snoopy's Pier 13313 S Padre Island Dr *Web:* snoopyspier.com	Corpus Christi	TX	78418	361-949-8815	
Thai Spice 523 N Water St *Web:* www.thaispice.com	Corpus Christi	TX	78401	361-883-8884	
Torch Restaurant 4425 S Alameda St	Corpus Christi	TX	78412	361-992-7491	
Vietnam Restaurant 701 N Water St *Web:* www.vietnam-restaurant.com	Corpus Christi	TX	78401	361-853-2682	
Water Street Market 309 N Water St *Web:* www.waterstmarketcc.com	Corpus Christi	TX	78401	361-882-8683	
Abacus *Kent Rathbun* 4511 McKinney Ave	Dallas	TX	75205	214-559-3111	559-3113
Al Biernat's 4217 Oak Lawn Ave *Web:* www.albiernats.com	Dallas	TX	75219	214-219-2201	219-2093
Amore 6931 Snider Plz *Web:* amoreitalian.net	Dallas	TX	75205	214-739-0502	
Anderson's BBQ House 5410 Harry Hines Blvd *Web:* www.mikeandersonsbbq.com	Dallas	TX	75235	214-630-0735	630-1686
Asian Mint 11617 N Central Expy Ste 135 *Web:* www.asianmint.com	Dallas	TX	75243	214-363-6655	
Avila's 4714 Maple Ave	Dallas	TX	75219	214-520-2700	
AW Shucks 3601 Greenville Ave *Web:* www.awshucksdallas.com	Dallas	TX	75206	214-821-9449	
Bob's Steak & Chop House 4300 Lemmon Ave *Web:* www.bobs-steakandchop.com	Dallas	TX	75219	214-528-9446	526-8159
Cafe Istanbul 5450 W Lovers Ln *Web:* www.cafe-istanbul.net	Dallas	TX	75209	214-902-0919	
Cafe Izmir 3711 Greenville Ave *Web:* www.cafeizmir.com	Dallas	TX	75206	214-826-7788	
Cafe Madrid 4501 Travis St *Web:* www.cafemadrid-dallas.com	Dallas	TX	75205	214-528-1731	
Cafe Pacific 24 Highland Pk Village *Web:* cafepacificdallas.com	Dallas	TX	75205	214-526-1170	
Capital Grille, The 500 Crescent Ct *Web:* www.thecapitalgrille.com	Dallas	TX	75201	214-303-0500	
Celebration Restaurant & Catering 4503 W Lovers Ln PO Box 7330 *Web:* www.celebrationrestaurant.com	Dallas	TX	75209	214-351-5681	904-1716
City Cafe 5757 W Lovers Ln *Web:* www.thecitycafedallas.com	Dallas	TX	75209	214-351-2233	
Cosmic Cafe 2912 Oak Lawn *Web:* www.cosmiccafedallas.com	Dallas	TX	75219	214-521-6157	521-9195
Deep Sushi 2624 Elm St *Web:* www.deepsushi.com	Dallas	TX	75226	214-651-1177	
Del Frisco's of dallas 5251 Spring Vly Rd *Web:* www.delfriscos.com	Dallas	TX	75254	972-490-9000	
Fadi's Mediterranean Grill 3001 Knox St *Web:* www.fadiscuisine.com	Dallas	TX	75205	214-528-1800	
Fearing's 2121 McKinney Ave *Web:* www.fearingsrestaurant.com	Dallas	TX	75201	214-922-4848	
French Room 1321 Commerce St *Web:* www.hoteladolphus.com	Dallas	TX	75202	214-742-8200	651-3575
Fuji Steakhouse & Sushi Bar 12817 Preston Rd *Web:* www.fujidallas.com	Dallas	TX	75230	972-661-5662	
Genghis Grill 18900 Dallas Pkwy Ste 150 *TF:* 888-436-4447 ■ *Web:* www.genghisgrill.com	Dallas	TX	75244	888-436-4447	
Grape, The 2808 Greenville Ave *Web:* www.thegraperestaurant.com	Dallas	TX	75206	214-828-1981	
Green Papaya 3211 Oak Lawn Ave Ste B *Web:* www.greenpapayadallas.com	Dallas	TX	75219	214-521-4811	
Hibiscus 2927 N Henderson *Web:* www.hibiscusdallas.com	Dallas	TX	75206	214-827-2927	
III Forks Steakhouse 17776 Dallas Pkwy *Web:* 3forks.com	Dallas	TX	75287	972-267-1776	267-1799
India Palace Restaurant 12817 Preston Rd Ste 105 *Web:* www.indiapalacedallas.com	Dallas	TX	75230	972-392-0190	
Jade Garden 4800 Bryan St	Dallas	TX	75204	214-821-0675	821-0675
Javier's Gourmet Mexicano 4912 Cole Ave *Web:* www.javiers.net	Dallas	TX	75205	214-521-4211	
Korea House 2598 Royal Ln *Web:* www.koreahousedallas.com	Dallas	TX	75229	972-243-0434	
La Duni Latin Cafe 4264 Oak Lawn Ave *Web:* www.laduni.com	Dallas	TX	75219	214-520-7300	520-7390
La Madeleine de Corps Inc 12201 Merit Dr Ste 900 *Web:* www.lamadeleine.com	Dallas	TX	75251	214-696-6962	692-8496
Lavendou 19009 Preston Rd Ste 200 *Web:* www.lavendou.com	Dallas	TX	75252	972-248-1911	248-1660
May Dragon 4848 Beltline Rd *Web:* www.maydragon.com	Dallas	TX	75254	972-392-9998	490-5023
Mercury Grill, The 11909 Preston Rd Ste 1418 *Web:* www.mcrowd.com	Dallas	TX	75240	972-960-7774	
MI PIACI 8411 Preston Rd Ste 132 *Web:* www.ilsole-dallas.com	Dallas	TX	75225	972-934-8424	
Morton's The Steakhouse 2222 McKinney Ave *Web:* www.mortons.com	Dallas	TX	75201	214-741-2277	748-6360
Nick & Sam's Grill 3008 Maple Ave *Web:* www.nick-sams.com	Dallas	TX	75201	214-871-7444	871-7663
Old Warsaw, The 2512 Maple Ave *Web:* www.oldwarsaw.com	Dallas	TX	75201	214-528-0032	
Palm The Restaurant 701 Ross Ave *Web:* www.thepalm.com	Dallas	TX	75202	214-698-0470	
Pappadeaux Seafood Kitchen 3520 Oak Lawn Ave *Web:* www.pappadeaux.com	Dallas	TX	75219	214-521-4700	
Primo's 3309 McKinney Ave *Web:* www.primosdallas.com	Dallas	TX	75204	214-220-0510	
Pyramid Grill 1717 N Akard St *Web:* www.pyramidrestaurant.com	Dallas	TX	75201	214-720-5249	
Reunion Tower 300 Reunion Blvd E *Web:* www.reuniontower.com	Dallas	TX	75207	214-651-1234	
Rosewood Hotels and Resorts LLC 2821 Turtle Creek Blvd *Web:* www.rosewoodhotels.com	Dallas	TX	75219	214-559-2100	528-4187
Royal Thai 5500 Greenville Ave *Web:* royalthaitexas.com	Dallas	TX	75206	214-691-3555	
Ruth's Chris Steak House 17840 Dallas Pkwy *Web:* www.ruthschris.com	Dallas	TX	75287	972-250-2244	
S & D Oyster Co 2701 McKinney Ave *Web:* sdoyster.com	Dallas	TX	75204	214-880-0111	
Saint Martin's Wine Bistro 3020 Greenville Ave *Web:* www.stmartinswinebistro.com	Dallas	TX	75206	214-826-0940	826-1229
Sammy's Barbeque 2126 Leonard St *Web:* sammystexasbbq.com	Dallas	TX	75201	214-880-9064	
Sevy's Grill 8201 Preston Rd Ste 100 *Web:* www.sevys.com	Dallas	TX	75225	214-265-7389	
Simply Fondue 2108 Greenville Ave **Fax Area Code:* 800 ■ *Web:* www.simplyfondue.com	Dallas	TX	75206	214-827-8878	378-9016*
Steel Restaurant & Lounge 3102 Oaklawn Ave *Web:* www.steeldallas.com	Dallas	TX	75219	214-219-9908	219-9929
Suze 4345 W NW Hwy *Web:* www.suzedallas.com	Dallas	TX	75220	214-350-6135	350-6178
Tei Tei Robata Bar 2906 N Henderson St *Web:* www.teiteirobata.com	Dallas	TX	75206	214-828-2400	
Teppo Yakitori & Sushi Bar 2014 Greenville Ave	Dallas	TX	75206	214-826-8989	
YO Ranch Steakhouse 702 Ross Ave *Web:* www.yoranchsteakhouse.com	Dallas	TX	75202	214-744-3287	
Ziziki's Restaurant & Bar 4514 Travis St Ste 122 *Web:* www.zizikis.com	Dallas	TX	75205	214-521-2233	
Salt Lick 18300 FM 1826 *Web:* www.saltlickbbq.com	Driftwood	TX	78619	512-858-4959	
Bella Napoli 6331 N Mesa St	El Paso	TX	79912	915-584-3321	584-3466
Cafe Central 109 N Oregon St *Web:* www.cafecentral.com	El Paso	TX	79901	915-545-2233	
Cappetto's 2711 N Stanton St *Web:* www.nuovocappetto.com	El Paso	TX	79902	915-532-0700	
Clock Family Restaurant 8409 Dyer St	El Paso	TX	79904	915-751-6367	
Dona Lupe Cafe 2919 Pershing Dr	El Paso	TX	79903	915-566-9833	
Edge of Texas Steakhouse 8690 Edge of Texas *Web:* theedgeoftexassteakhouse.com	El Paso	TX	79934	915-822-3343	
Forti's Mexican Elder 321 Chelsea St *Web:* fortisrestaurant.com	El Paso	TX	79905	915-772-0066	
Japanese Kitchen 4024 N Mesa St	El Paso	TX	79902	915-533-4267	542-1015
Julio's Cafe Corona 8050 Gateway Blvd E *Web:* julioscafecorona.com	El Paso	TX	79907	915-591-7676	592-1294
L & J Cafe 3622 E Missouri St *Web:* landjcafe.com	El Paso	TX	79903	915-566-8418	
Landry's Seafood House 6801 Gateway Blvd W *Web:* www.landrysseafood.com	El Paso	TX	79925	915-779-2900	
Mediterranean Cuisine 4111 N Mesa St	El Paso	TX	79902	915-542-1012	
Michelinos 3615 Rutherglen St	El Paso	TX	79925	915-592-1700	
Peking Garden 3306 Ft Blvd *Web:* pekinggarden2.com	El Paso	TX	79930	915-565-9090	565-9091
Pelican's Steak & Seafood 130 Shadow Mtn Rd *Web:* pelicanselpaso.com	El Paso	TX	79912	915-581-1392	
PF Chang's China Bistro 760 Sunland Pk Dr *Web:* www.pfchangs.com	El Paso	TX	79912	915-845-0166	
Pho Tre Bien 6946 Gateway E *Web:* www.photrebien.com	El Paso	TX	79915	915-598-0166	
Senor Fish 9530 Viscount Blvd Ste 1A	El Paso	TX	79925	915-598-3630	
State Line 1222 Sunland Pk Dr *Web:* www.countyline.com	El Paso	TX	79922	915-581-3371	
Trattoria Bella Sera 9449 Montana Ave *Web:* trattoriabellasera.com	El Paso	TX	79925	915-598-7948	
Cattleman's Steakhouse 3450 S Fabens Carlsbad Rd *Web:* www.cattlemanssteakhouse.com	Fabens	TX	79838	915-544-3200	
Blue Mesa Grill 1600 S University Dr *Web:* www.bluemesagrill.com	Fort Worth	TX	76107	817-332-6372	
Bonnell's 4259 Bryant Irvin Rd *Web:* bonnellstexas.com	Fort Worth	TX	76109	817-738-5489	
Byblos Byblos Lebanese Restaurant 1406 N Main St *Web:* www.byblostx.com	Fort Worth	TX	76106	817-625-9667	
Cafe Modern 3200 Darnell St *TF:* 866-824-5566 ■ *Web:* www.themodern.org	Fort Worth	TX	76107	817-738-9215	735-1161
Celaborelle Phoenician Buffet 2257 Hemphill St	Fort Worth	TX	76110	817-922-8118	
Del Frisco's Double Eagle Steak House 812 Main St *Web:* www.delfriscos.com	Fort Worth	TX	76102	817-877-3999	
Dixie House Cafe 6200 E Lancaster Ave *Web:* www.dixiehousecafe.com	Fort Worth	TX	76112	817-451-6180	
Edelweiss German Restaurant 3801 SW Blvd A *Web:* www.edelweissgermanrestaurant.com	Fort Worth	TX	76116	817-738-5934	
Fort Worth Chop House 301 Main St *Web:* www.fortworthchophouse.com	Fort Worth	TX	76102	817-336-4129	
H3 Ranch 105 E Exchange Ave Stockyards Hotel *Web:* www.h3ranch.com	Fort Worth	TX	76164	817-624-1246	624-2571
Joe T Garcia's 2201 N Commerce St *Web:* www.joets.com	Fort Worth	TX	76164	817-626-4356	
Keg, The 5760 SW Loop 820 *Web:* www.kegsteakhouse.com	Fort Worth	TX	76132	817-731-3534	

Restaurant	City	State	ZIP	Phone	Fax
La Familia Restaurant 841 Foch St.	Fort Worth	TX	76107	817-870-2002	
Lanny's Alta Cocina Mexicana 3405 W Seventh St *Web:* www.lannyskitchen.com	Fort Worth	TX	76107	817-850-9996	
Lonesome Dove Western Bistro 2406 N Main St *Web:* www.lonesomedovebistro.com	Fort Worth	TX	76164	817-740-8810	
Los Molcajetes 4320 Western Ctr Blvd *Web:* www.losmolcajetes.com	Fort Worth	TX	76137	817-306-9000	306-9033
Lucille's Stateside Bistro 4700 Camp Bowie Blvd *Web:* lucillesstatesidebistro.com	Fort Worth	TX	76107	817-738-4761	
Maharaja Restaurant 6308 Hulen Bend Blvd *Web:* maharajadfw.com	Fort Worth	TX	76132	817-263-7156	
MiCocina 509 Main St *Web:* micocinarestaurants.com	Fort Worth	TX	76102	817-877-3600	
Piranha 335 W Third St *Web:* www.piranhakillersushi.com	Fort Worth	TX	76102	817-348-0200	
Railhead Smokehouse 2900 Montgomery St *Web:* railheadsmokehouse.com	Fort Worth	TX	76107	817-738-9808	732-4059
Reata 310 Houston St *Web:* www.reata.net	Fort Worth	TX	76102	817-336-1009	
Saint Emilion 3617 W Seventh St *Web:* www.saint-emilionrestaurant.com	Fort Worth	TX	76107	817-737-2781	
Silver Fox Steakhouse 1651 S University Dr *Web:* www.silverfoxcafe.com	Fort Worth	TX	76107	817-332-9060	
Spiral Diner 1314 W Magnolia *Web:* www.spiraldiner.com	Fort Worth	TX	76104	817-332-8834	332-8834
Texas de Brazil 101 N Houston St *Web:* www.texasdebrazil.com	Fort Worth	TX	76102	817-882-9500	882-9503
Tres Jose's 4004 White Settlement Rd *Web:* tresjosestexmex.com	Fort Worth	TX	76107	817-763-0456	
West Side Cafe 7950 Camp Bowie W	Fort Worth	TX	76116	817-560-1996	
China Star 2425 W Walnut St *Web:* garlandchinastar.com	Garland	TX	75042	972-487-8311	
Crazy Catfish 1410 W Buckingham Rd	Garland	TX	75042	972-487-2100	
Ernesto's 1202 NW Hwy	Garland	TX	75041	972-681-8112	
Fish City Grill 445 Coneflower Dr *Web:* www.fishcitygrill.com	Garland	TX	75040	972-675-1600	
Golden Wok Buffet 1311 Plz Dr	Garland	TX	75041	972-686-8691	
Lucky China Buffet 1102 NW Hwy	Garland	TX	75041	972-270-3430	270-8839
Luna de Noche 7602 N Jupiter Rd *Web:* www.lunadenochetexmex.com	Garland	TX	75044	469-246-8271	
On the Border Cafe 1350 NW Hwy *Web:* ontheborder.com	Garland	TX	75041	972-865-7988	
Soulman's Barbeque 3410 Broadway Blvd *Web:* soulmans.com	Garland	TX	75043	972-271-6885	
Uncle Wing Chinese Restaurant 107 N First St	Garland	TX	75040	972-272-2775	
Yen China Cafe 1225 Belt Line Rd *Web:* garlandyenchinacafe.com	Garland	TX	75040	972-495-9779	
Grey Moss Inn 19010 Scenic Loop Rd *Web:* www.grey-moss-inn.com	Helotes	TX	78023	210-695-8301	695-3237
Arcodoro 5000 Westheimer Rd Ste 120 *Web:* www.arcodoro.com	Houston	TX	77056	713-621-6888	
Arcodoro & Pomodoro 5000 Westheimer Ste 120 *Web:* www.arcodoro.com	Houston	TX	77056	713-621-6888	
Armandos 2630 Westheimer Rd *Web:* www.armandosrestaurant.com	Houston	TX	77098	713-520-1738	
Ashiana Indian Restaurant 12610 Briar Forest Rd *Web:* ashianarestaurant.net	Houston	TX	77077	281-679-5555	493-0981
Babin's Seafood House 17485 Tomball Pkwy *Web:* www.babinsseafood.com	Houston	TX	77064	281-477-9300	
Backstreet Cafe 1103 S Shepherd Dr *Web:* www.backstreetcafe.net	Houston	TX	77019	713-521-2239	
Baker's Ribs 2223 S Voss Rd *Web:* www.bakersribs.com	Houston	TX	77057	713-977-8725	
Benjy's 2424 Dunstan Rd *Web:* www.benjys.com	Houston	TX	77005	713-522-7602	522-7655
Bocados Restaurant 1312 W Alabama St *Web:* www.bocadoshouston.com	Houston	TX	77006	713-523-5230	
Bonnie's Beef & Seafood Co 6867 Gulf Fwy *Web:* www.bonniesbeefandseafood.com	Houston	TX	77087	713-641-2397	
Brennan's of Houston 3300 Smith St *Web:* www.brennanshouston.com	Houston	TX	77006	713-522-9711	
Brenner's Steakhouse 10911 Katy Fwy *Web:* www.brennerssteakhouse.com	Houston	TX	77079	713-465-2901	
Cafe Rabelais 2442 Times Blvd *Web:* www.caferabelais.com	Houston	TX	77005	713-520-8841	
Carmelo's 14795 Memorial Dr *Web:* www.carmelosrestaurant.com	Houston	TX	77079	281-531-0696	
Charivari 2521 Bagby St *Web:* www.charivarirest.com	Houston	TX	77006	713-521-7231	
Churrasco's 2055 Westheimer Rd *Web:* www.cordua.com	Houston	TX	77098	713-527-8300	527-0847
Da Marco 1520 Westheimer Rd *Web:* www.damarcohouston.com	Houston	TX	77006	713-807-8857	
Damian's Cucina Italiana 3011 Smith St *Web:* www.damians.com	Houston	TX	77006	713-522-0439	522-4408
El Tiempo Cantina 3130 Richmond Ave *Web:* www.eltiempocantina.com	Houston	TX	77098	713-807-1600	
Empire Turkish Grill 12448 Memorial Dr *Web:* www.empireturkishgrill.com	Houston	TX	77024	713-827-7475	463-7719
Fadi's Mediterranean Cuisine 8383 Westheimer Rd *Web:* www.fadiscuisine.com	Houston	TX	77063	713-532-0666	
Fogo de Chao 8250 Westheimer Rd *Web:* www.fogodechao.com	Houston	TX	77063	713-978-6500	
Frenchie's 1041 NASA Pkwy *Web:* frenchiesvillacapri.com	Houston	TX	77058	281-486-7144	486-3952
Fung's Kitchen 7320 SW Fwy Ste 115 *Web:* eatatfungs.com	Houston	TX	77074	713-779-2288	271-2288
Goode Co Texas Barbecue 5109 Kirby Dr *Web:* www.goodecompany.com	Houston	TX	77098	713-522-2530	
Goode Company Seafood 2621 Westpark Dr *Web:* goodecompany.com	Houston	TX	77098	713-523-7154	
Hugo's 1600 Westheimer Rd *Web:* www.hugosrestaurant.net	Houston	TX	77006	713-524-7744	
Hunan Village 3311 S Shepherd Dr *Web:* houstonhunanvillage.com	Houston	TX	77098	713-528-4651	
Ibiza Food & Wine Bar 2450 Louisiana St *Web:* www.ibizafoodandwinebar.com	Houston	TX	77006	713-524-0004	
Indika 516 Westheimer Rd *Web:* www.indikausa.com	Houston	TX	77006	713-524-2170	984-1755
Jasmine Asian Cuisine 9938 Bellaire Blvd Ste D *Web:* jasmineasianrestaurant.com	Houston	TX	77036	713-272-8188	272-8187
Kam's 4500 Montrose Blvd *TF:* 800-510-3663 ■ *Web:* kamscuisine.com	Houston	TX	77006	713-529-5057	529-5486
Kiran's Restaurant & Bar 4100 Westheimer Rd *Web:* www.kiranshouston.com	Houston	TX	77027	713-960-8472	
Kubo's Sushi Bar & Grill 2414 University Blvd 200 *Web:* www.kubos-sushi.com	Houston	TX	77005	713-528-7878	528-9150
La Griglia 2002 W Gray St *Web:* www.lagrigliarestaurant.com	Houston	TX	77019	713-526-4700	526-9249
Lynn's Steakhouse 955 Dairy Ashford *Web:* www.lynnssteakhouse.com	Houston	TX	77079	281-870-0807	870-0888
Madras Pavilion 3910 Kirby Dr *Web:* madraspavilion.us	Houston	TX	77098	713-521-2617	
Maggiano's Little Italy Restaurant 2019 Post Oak Blvd *Web:* www.maggianos.com	Houston	TX	77056	713-961-2700	
Mark's American Cuisine 1658 Westheimer Rd *Web:* www.marks1658.com	Houston	TX	77006	713-523-3800	523-9292
Masraff's 1753 S Post Oak Ln *Web:* www.masraffs.com	Houston	TX	77056	713-355-1975	355-1965
Massa's 1160 Smith St *Web:* www.massas.com	Houston	TX	77002	713-650-0837	
Mockingbird Bistro 1985 Welch St *Web:* www.mockingbirdbistro.com	Houston	TX	77019	713-533-0200	533-0215
Morton's The Steakhouse 5000 Westheimer Rd *Web:* www.mortons.com	Houston	TX	77056	713-629-1946	629-4348
Nino's Vincent's Grappino di Nino 2817 W Dallas St *Web:* www.ninos-vincents.com	Houston	TX	77019	713-522-5120	
Noe Restaurant & Bar 4 Riverway *TF:* 800-809-6664	Houston	TX	77056	713-871-8181	871-0719
Oceanaire Seafood Room 5061 Westheimer Rd Ste 8050 *Web:* www.theoceanaire.com	Houston	TX	77056	832-487-8862	
Osaka Japanese Restaurant 515 Westheimer Rd	Houston	TX	77006	713-533-9098	
Palm Restaurant 6100 Westheimer Rd *TF:* 866-333-7256 ■ *Web:* www.thepalm.com	Houston	TX	77057	713-977-2544	977-3503
PF Chang's China Bistro 11685 Westheimer Rd *Web:* www.pfchangs.com	Houston	TX	77077	281-920-3553	
Piatto Ristorante 4925 W Alabama St *Web:* www.piattoristorante.com	Houston	TX	77056	713-871-9722	871-9190
Prego 2520 Amherst St *Web:* www.prego-houston.com	Houston	TX	77005	713-529-2420	
Rainbow Lodge 2011 Ella Blvd *TF:* 866-861-8666 ■ *Web:* www.rainbow-lodge.com	Houston	TX	77008	713-861-8666	
Reef 2600 Travis St *Web:* www.reefhouston.com	Houston	TX	77006	713-526-8282	
Rio Ranch 9999 Westheimer Rd *Web:* www.rioranch.com	Houston	TX	77042	713-952-5000	952-2263
Sabor! 5712 Bellaire Blvd	Houston	TX	77081	713-667-6001	
Saltgrass Steak House 520 Meyerland Plz Mall *Web:* www.saltgrass.com	Houston	TX	77096	713-665-2226	
Shiva 2514 Times Blvd *Web:* www.shivarestaurant.com	Houston	TX	77005	713-523-4753	523-4754
Spanish Flower 4701 N Main St *Web:* spanishflowersrestaurant.com	Houston	TX	77009	713-869-1706	869-1734
Spindletop 1200 Louisiana St *Web:* hyatt.com	Houston	TX	77002	713-375-4775	
Taste of Texas Restaurant 10505 Katy Fwy *Web:* www.tasteoftexas.com	Houston	TX	77024	713-932-6901	
Tony Mandola's Gulf Coast Kitchen 1212 Waugh Dr *Web:* www.tonymandolas.com	Houston	TX	77019	713-528-3474	528-4438
Tony's 3755 Richmond Ave *Web:* www.tonyshouston.com	Houston	TX	77046	713-622-6778	
Vieng Thai 6929 Long Pt St	Houston	TX	77055	713-688-9910	
Benihana 5400 Whitehall St *Web:* www.benihana.com	Irving	TX	75038	972-550-0060	
Bruno's 9462 N MacArthur Blvd *Web:* brunosristorante.com	Irving	TX	75063	972-556-2465	
Cool River Cafe 1045 Hidden Ridge *Web:* www.coolrivercafe.com	Irving	TX	75038	972-871-8881	871-8882
Danal's Mexican Restaurant 508 N O'Connor Rd *Web:* danals-restaurant.com	Irving	TX	75061	972-254-2666	
Empress of China 2648 N Belt Line Rd *Web:* www.eocrestaurant.com	Irving	TX	75062	972-252-7677	
Hanasho Japanese Restaurant 2938 N Belt Line Rd *Web:* www.hanashojapaneserestaurant.com	Irving	TX	75062	972-258-0250	
I Fratelli 7701 N MacArthur Blvd *Web:* www.ifratelli.net	Irving	TX	75063	972-501-9700	
Italian Cafe 387 Las Colinas Blvd E *Web:* italianitaliancafe.com	Irving	TX	75039	972-401-0000	401-9193
Jinbeh 301 E Las Colinas Blvd *Web:* www.jinbeh.com	Irving	TX	75039	972-869-4011	869-4311

Name / Address	City	State	ZIP	Phone	Fax
Keg Steakhouse & Bar 859 W John Carpenter Fwy *Web:* www.kegsteakhouse.com	Irving	TX	75039	972-556-9188	
Pasand Indian Cuisine 2600 N Belt Line Rd *Web:* www.pasandrestaurant.com	Irving	TX	75062	972-594-0693	594-8935
Pei Wei Asian Diner 7600 N MacArthur Blvd *Web:* peiwei.com	Irving	TX	75063	972-373-8000	
Piman Asian Bistro 4835 N O'Connor Rd *Web:* www.pimanasian.com	Irving	TX	75062	972-650-0001	
Rockfish Seafood Grill 7400 N MacArthur Blvd *Web:* www.rockfish.com	Irving	TX	75063	214-574-4111	
Sonny Bryan's Smoke House 4030 N MacArthur Blvd Ste 222 **Fax Area Code: 214* ■ *Web:* www.sonnybryans.com	Irving	TX	75038	972-650-9564	596-1081*
Texadelphia 7601 N MacArthur Blvd *Web:* www.texadelphia.com	Irving	TX	75063	972-432-0725	
Trevi's 221 Las Colinas Blvd *Web:* omnihotels.com	Irving	TX	75039	972-869-5550	556-0800
Via Real Restaurant 4020 N MacArthur Blvd *Web:* www.viareal.com	Irving	TX	75038	972-650-9001	541-0215
50 Yard Line Steakhouse 2549 Loop 289 S *Web:* 50-yardline.com	Lubbock	TX	79423	806-745-3991	
Bless Your Heart 3701 19th St	Lubbock	TX	79410	806-791-2211	791-5330
Cagle Steaks&BBQ 8732 Fourth St *Web:* www.caglesteaks.com	Lubbock	TX	79416	806-795-3879	
Choochai Thai Cuisine 2330 19th St	Lubbock	TX	79401	806-747-1767	
Fortune Cookie 7006 University Ave Ste 6 *Web:* lubbockfortunecookie.com	Lubbock	TX	79413	806-745-2205	
Gardski's 2009 Broadway *Web:* gardskisloft.com	Lubbock	TX	79401	806-744-2391	
India palace 3021 34th St	Lubbock	TX	79410	806-799-6772	
Jake's Sports Cafe 5025 50th St *Web:* www.jakes-sportscafe.com	Lubbock	TX	79414	806-687-5253	
Jazz Restaurant 3703C 19th St *Web:* www.jazzkitchen.com	Lubbock	TX	79410	806-799-2124	
Joe's Crab Shack 5802 W Loop S 289 *Web:* www.joescrabshack.com	Lubbock	TX	79424	806-797-8600	
Orlando's 2402 Ave Q *Web:* www.orlandos.com	Lubbock	TX	79411	806-747-5998	747-3501
Rudy's Country Store & Bar BQ 4930 S Loop 289 *Web:* www.rudysbbq.com	Lubbock	TX	79414	806-797-1777	
Texas Cafe & Bar 3604 50th St	Lubbock	TX	79413	806-792-8544	
Texas Land & Cattle Steak House 7202 Indiana Ave *Web:* www.txlc.com	Lubbock	TX	79423	806-791-0555	
Thai Thai 5018 50th St	Lubbock	TX	79414	806-791-0024	
Mesquite Championship Rodeo Inc 1818 Rodeo Dr *Web:* www.mesquiterodeo.com	Mesquite	TX	75149	972-285-8777	
Bavarian Grill 221 W Parker Rd *Web:* www.bavariangrill.com	Plano	TX	75023	972-881-0705	
Big Easy New Orleans Style Sandwiches 1915 N Central Expy Ste 200 *Web:* www.bigeasyplano.com	Plano	TX	75075	972-424-5261	
Blue Goose Cantina 4757 W Pk Blvd *Web:* www.bluegoosecantina.com	Plano	TX	75093	972-596-8882	
Bob's Steak & Chop House 5760 Legacy Dr Ste B1 *Web:* www.bobs-steakandchop.com	Plano	TX	75024	972-608-2627	
Chettinaad Palace 2205 N Central Expy *Web:* www.chettinaadpalace.com	Plano	TX	75075	469-229-9100	
Covino's 3265 Independence Pkwy *Web:* covinos.com	Plano	TX	75075	972-519-0345	
Fishmonger's Seafood 1901 N Central Expy *Web:* www.fishmongersplano.com	Plano	TX	75075	972-423-3699	
Greek Isles Grille & Taverna 3309 N Central Expy Ste 370 *Web:* greekislesgrille.com	Plano	TX	75023	972-423-7778	
Jade Palace 820 W Spring Creek Pkwy Ste 214 *Web:* www.jadepalacechinese.com	Plano	TX	75023	972-424-5578	
Japon Steak House & Sushi Bar 4021 Preston Rd *Web:* www.japonsteakhouseandsushi.com	Plano	TX	75093	972-781-2818	
Joe's Crab Shack 3320 Central Expressway *Web:* joescrabshack.com	Plano	TX	75023	972-423-2800	
Jorg's Cafe Vienna 1037 E 15th St *Web:* jorgscafevienna.com	Plano	TX	75074	972-509-5966	
Kosta's Cafe 4621 W Pk Blvd Ste 100 *Web:* www.kostascafe.com	Plano	TX	75093	972-596-8424	
Love & War In Texas 601 E Plano Pkwy *Web:* www.loveandwarintexas.com	Plano	TX	75074	972-422-6201	633-1225
Mango's Thai Cuisine 4701 W Pk Blvd Ste 104 *Web:* www.mangothaicuisine.com	Plano	TX	75093	972-599-0289	599-7013
Ojeda's 2001 Coit Rd Ste 102 *Web:* ojedasrestaurant.com	Plano	TX	75075	972-599-1300	
Osaka Sushi 5012 W Pk Blvd *Web:* osaka-plano.com	Plano	TX	75093	972-931-8898	
Paesano's 508 E 14th St *Web:* www.paesanosrestaurant.net	Plano	TX	75074	972-578-2727	
Patrizio's Restaurant 1900 Preston Rd *Web:* www.patriziorestaurant.com	Plano	TX	75093	972-964-2200	596-1743
Picasso's Italian Ristorante 4152 W Spring Creek Pkwy *Web:* www.picassosrestaurant.us	Plano	TX	75093	972-618-4143	
Posados Cafe 3421 N Central Expy *Web:* posados.com	Plano	TX	75023	972-509-4999	509-4949
Rockfish Seafood Grill 4701 W Pk Blvd Ste 105	Plano	TX	75093	972-599-2190	964-6898
Steve Fields Steak & Lobster Lounge 5013 W Pk Blvd *Web:* www.stevefields.com	Plano	TX	75093	972-596-7100	599-3950
Taste of the Islands 909 W Spring Creek Pkwy *Web:* tasteoftheislands.net	Plano	TX	75023	972-517-5900	
Vincent's 2432 Preston Rd	Plano	TX	75093	972-612-6208	
Piranha Killer Sushi 7100 Blvd 26 Ste 208 *Web:* www.piranhakillersushi.com	Richland Hills	TX	76180	682-626-5953	626-5954
Alamo Cafe 10060 W IH-10 *Web:* www.alamocafe.com	San Antonio	TX	78230	210-691-8827	
Anaqua Grill 555 S Alamo St **Fax Area Code: 817* ■ *TF:* 800-845-5279	San Antonio	TX	78205	210-229-1000	778-2049*
Biga on the Banks 203 S St Mary's St *Web:* www.biga.com	San Antonio	TX	78205	210-225-0722	
Boardwalk Bistro 4011 Broadway *Web:* www.boardwalkbistro.net	San Antonio	TX	78209	210-824-0100	824-0100
Bohanan's Prime Steaks & Seafood 219 E Houston St 2nd Fl *Web:* www.bohanans.com	San Antonio	TX	78205	210-472-2600	472-2276
Boudro's On the Riverwalk 421 E Commerce St *Web:* www.boudros.com	San Antonio	TX	78205	210-224-8484	225-2839
Cappy's 5011 Broadway St *Web:* www.cappysrestaurant.com	San Antonio	TX	78209	210-828-9669	
Chris Madrid's 1900 Blanco Rd *Web:* chrismadrids.com	San Antonio	TX	78212	210-735-3552	
Cove, The 606 W Cypress St *Web:* thecove.us	San Antonio	TX	78212	210-227-2683	
Crumpets 3920 Harry Wurzbach St *Web:* www.crumpetsa.com	San Antonio	TX	78209	210-821-5600	821-5624
Demo's 2501 N St Mary's St *Web:* www.demosgreekfood.com	San Antonio	TX	78212	210-732-7777	
El Mirador 722 S St Mary St *Web:* www.elmiradorsatx.com	San Antonio	TX	78205	210-225-9444	271-3236
Fig Tree 515 Villita St *Web:* www.figtreerestaurant.com	San Antonio	TX	78205	210-224-1976	271-9180
Formosa Garden 1011 NE Loop 410 *Web:* www.formosagarden.com	San Antonio	TX	78209	210-828-9988	826-2566
Golden Wok 8822 Wurzbach Rd *Web:* www.golden-wok.com	San Antonio	TX	78240	210-615-8282	
Hard Rock Cafe 111 W Crocket St *TF:* 888-519-6683 ■ *Web:* www.hardrock.com	San Antonio	TX	78205	210-224-7625	224-7693
India Oven 1031 Patricia *Web:* www.indiaoven.biz	San Antonio	TX	78213	210-366-1030	
India Palace Restaurant 8474 Fredericksburg Rd *Web:* www.indiapalacesa.com	San Antonio	TX	78229	210-692-5262	
Kirby's Steakhouse 123 N Loop 1604 E *Web:* www.kirbyssteakhouse.com	San Antonio	TX	78232	210-404-2221	404-2225
La Fogata 2427 Vance Jackson Rd *Web:* www.lafogata.com	San Antonio	TX	78213	210-340-1337	349-6467
Little Rhein Steakhouse 231 S Alamo St *Web:* www.littlerheinsteakhouse.com	San Antonio	TX	78205	210-225-2111	271-9180
Melting Pot of San Antonio, The 14855 Blanco Rd Ste 110 *TF:* 800-783-0867 ■ *Web:* www.meltingpot.com	San Antonio	TX	78216	210-479-6358	479-8106
Old San Francisco Steak House 10223 Sahara Dr *Web:* www.theoldsanfrancisco.com	San Antonio	TX	78216	210-342-2321	340-3135
Paesano's 555 E Basse Rd *Web:* www.prg-sa.com	San Antonio	TX	78209	210-828-5191	828-6329
Pappadeaux Seafood Kitchen 76 NE Loop 410 *Web:* www.pappadeaux.com	San Antonio	TX	78216	210-340-7143	
PF Chang's China Bistro 255 E Basse Rd *Web:* www.pfchangs.com	San Antonio	TX	78209	210-507-1000	
Piatti Ristorante & Bar San Antonio 255 E Basse Rd Ste 500 *Web:* www.piatti.com	San Antonio	TX	78209	210-832-0300	832-0303
Picante Grill 3810 Broadway *Web:* picantegrill.com	San Antonio	TX	78209	210-822-3797	
Rio Rio Cantina 421 E Commerce St *Web:* www.rioriorivenwalk.com	San Antonio	TX	78205	210-226-8462	226-8443
Ruth's Chris Steak House 7720 Jones-Maltsberger Rd *Web:* www.ruthschris.com	San Antonio	TX	78216	210-821-5051	
Silo 1133 Austin Hwy *Web:* www.siloelevatedcuisine.com	San Antonio	TX	78209	210-824-8686	
Texas Land & Cattle Steak House 9911 W IH- 10 *TF:* 855-685-1622 ■ *Web:* www.txlc.com	San Antonio	TX	78230	210-699-8744	699-8292
Zio's 12858 W IH-10 *Web:* www.zios.com	San Antonio	TX	78249	210-697-7222	697-7333
Tamolly's 5940 Summerhill Rd *Web:* www.tamollys.com	Texarkana	TX	75503	903-792-0732	

Utah

Name / Address	City	State	ZIP	Phone	Fax
Athenian 252 East 2500 South	Ogden	UT	84401	801-621-4911	395-2456
Bistro 258 258 25th St *Web:* bistro258.net	Ogden	UT	84404	801-394-1595	
Eastern Winds 3740 Washington Blvd *Web:* easternwindsrestaurant.com	Ogden	UT	84403	801-627-2739	627-2739
El Matador 2564 Ogden Ave *Web:* elmatadorogden.com	Ogden	UT	84401	801-393-3151	
Golden Dynasty 3433 Washington Blvd	Ogden	UT	84401	801-621-6789	
Javiers 703 Washington Blvd *Web:* javiersmexicanfood.com	Ogden	UT	84404	801-393-4747	
Jeremiah's 1307 West 1200 South *Web:* jeremiahsutah.com	Ogden	UT	84404	801-394-3273	627-6579
Prairie Schooner Restaurant 445 Pk Blvd *Web:* www.prairieschoonerrestaurant.com	Ogden	UT	84401	801-392-2712	
Rooster's 253 25th St *Web:* roostersbrewingco.com	Ogden	UT	84401	801-627-6171	
Ruby River Steak House 4286 Riverdale Rd *Web:* www.rubyriver.com	Ogden	UT	84405	801-622-2320	

	City	State	ZIP	Phone	Fax
Timber Mine 1701 Pk Blvd *Web:* www.timbermine.com	Ogden	UT	84401	801-393-2155	
Tona 210 25th St *Web:* www.tonarestaurant.com	Ogden	UT	84401	801-622-8662	
Union Grill 2501 Wall Ave *Web:* www.uniongrillogden.com	Ogden	UT	84401	801-621-2830	621-7946
Windy's Sukiyaki 3809 Riverdale Rd *Web:* www.windyssukiyaki.com	Ogden	UT	84405	801-621-4505	
Bombay House 463 N University Ave. *Web:* bombayhouse.com	Provo	UT	84601	801-373-6677	
Brick Oven 111 East 800 North *Web:* www.brickovenrestaurants.com	Provo	UT	84606	801-374-8800	
Demae Japanese Restaurant 82 W Ctr St *Web:* demae-japanese.com	Provo	UT	84601	801-374-0306	
Happy Sumo at the Riverwoods 4801 N University Ave *Web:* www.happysumosushi.com	Provo	UT	84604	801-225-9100	
Osaka Japanese Restaurant 46 W Ctr St.	Provo	UT	84601	801-373-1060	
OZZ - Event & Fun Ctr 490 N Freedom Blvd.	Provo	UT	84601	801-818-9000	
Ruby River Steakhouse 1454 S University Ave *Web:* www.rubyriver.com	Provo	UT	84601	801-371-0648	
Saigon Cafe 440 West 300 South *Web:* saigoncafeprovo.biz	Provo	UT	84601	801-812-1173	
Sam Hawk 660 N Freedom Blvd	Provo	UT	84601	801-377-7766	
Thai Ruby 744 East 820 North *Web:* thairubyfood.com	Provo	UT	84606	801-375-6840	
Tucanos Brazilian Grill 4801 N University Ave Unit 790 *Web:* www.tucanos.com	Provo	UT	84604	801-224-4774	
Aristo's 224 South 1300 East *Web:* aristosslc.com	Salt Lake City	UT	84102	801-581-0888	
Bambara Restaurant 202 S Main St *Web:* www.bambara-slc.com	Salt Lake City	UT	84101	801-363-5454	
Benihana of Tokyo 165 SW Temple *Web:* www.benihana.com	Salt Lake City	UT	84101	801-322-2421	
Blue Iguana 165 SW Temple *Web:* www.blueiguanarestaurant.net	Salt Lake City	UT	84101	801-533-8900	
Bombay House 2731 Parleys Way *Web:* www.bombayhouse.com	Salt Lake City	UT	84109	801-581-0222	
Cafe Madrid 5244 S Highland Dr. *Web:* www.cafemadrid.net	Salt Lake City	UT	84117	801-273-0837	
Cafe Rio 3025 East 3300 South *Web:* www.caferio.com	Salt Lake City	UT	84109	801-463-7250	
Cafe Trang 200 South 307 West *Web:* www.cafetrangrestaurant.com	Salt Lake City	UT	84101	801-539-1638	
Caffe Molise 55 West 100 South. *Web:* www.caffemolise.com	Salt Lake City	UT	84101	801-364-8833	
Christopher's Seafood & Steak House 134 W Pierpont Ave *Web:* www.christophersteakhouse.com	Salt Lake City	UT	84101	801-519-8515	
Citris Grill 2991 East 3300 South. *Web:* www.citrisgrill.com	Salt Lake City	UT	84109	801-466-1202	
Desert Edge Brewery 273 Trolley Sq. *Web:* www.desertedgebrewery.com	Salt Lake City	UT	84102	801-521-8917	
Em's 271 N Ctr St *Web:* www.emsrestaurant.com	Salt Lake City	UT	84103	801-596-0566	
Fleming's Prime Steakhouse & Wine Bar 20 South 400 West *Web:* www.flemingssteakhouse.com	Salt Lake City	UT	84101	801-355-3704	
Fresco Italian Cafe 1513 S 1500 E	Salt Lake City	UT	84105	801-486-1300	487-5379
Hong Kong Tea House 565 W 200 S *Web:* hongkongteahouse.yolasite.com	Salt Lake City	UT	84101	801-531-7010	531-7033
Koyo Restaurant 2275 East 33rd South *Web:* www.koyoslc.com	Salt Lake City	UT	84109	801-466-7111	
Lamb's Grill Cafe 169 S Main St *Web:* www.lambsgrill.com	Salt Lake City	UT	84111	801-364-7166	
Log Haven 6451 East Milcreek Canyon. *Web:* www.log-haven.com	Salt Lake City	UT	84109	801-272-8255	
Market Street Broiler 260 South 1300 East *Web:* marketstreetgrill.com	Salt Lake City	UT	84102	801-583-8808	
Market Street Oyster Bar 54 W Market St. *Web:* marketstreetgrill.com	Salt Lake City	UT	84101	801-531-6044	531-0730
Mazza 1515 S 1500 E *Web:* www.mazzacafe.com	Salt Lake City	UT	84105	801-484-9259	484-4277
New Yorker 60 W Market St. *Web:* newyorkerslc.com	Salt Lake City	UT	84101	801-363-0166	
Oasis Cafe 151 South 500 East *Web:* www.oasiscafeslc.com	Salt Lake City	UT	84102	801-322-0404	
Paris Bistro 1500 South 1500 East *Web:* www.theparis.net	Salt Lake City	UT	84105	801-486-5585	
PF Chang's China Bistro 174 W 300 S *Web:* www.pfchangs.com	Salt Lake City	UT	84101	801-539-0500	
Red Iguana 736 W N Temple St *Web:* www.rediguana.com	Salt Lake City	UT	84116	801-322-1489	
Red Rock Brewing Co 254 South 200 West *Web:* www.redrockbrewing.com	Salt Lake City	UT	84101	801-521-7446	
Rio Grande Cafe 270 S Rio Grande St.	Salt Lake City	UT	84101	801-364-3302	
Rodizio Grill 600 South 700 East *Web:* www.rodiziogrill.com	Salt Lake City	UT	84102	801-220-0500	
Rumbi Island Grill 358 South 700 East *Web:* rumbi.com	Salt Lake City	UT	84102	801-530-1000	
Sage's Cafe 234 W 900 S *Web:* www.sagescafe.com	Salt Lake City	UT	84101	801-322-3790	
Sampan 675 East 2100 South *Web:* www.esampan.com	Salt Lake City	UT	84106	801-467-3663	466-4120
Shogun 321 S Main St *Web:* shogunslc.com	Salt Lake City	UT	84111	801-364-7142	
Squatter's Pub Brewery 147 West Broadway *Web:* www.squatters.com	Salt Lake City	UT	84101	801-363-2739	
Thai Siam 1435 S State St *Web:* www.thaisiam.net	Salt Lake City	UT	84115	801-474-3322	
Tuscany 2832 East 6200 South *Web:* www.tuscanyslc.com	Salt Lake City	UT	84121	801-277-9919	
La Caille at Quail Run 9565 Wasatch Blvd *Web:* www.lacaille.com	Sandy	UT	84092	801-942-1751	944-8990

Vermont

	City	State	ZIP	Phone	Fax
Bove's of Vermont 68 Pearl St *Web:* www.boves.com	Burlington	VT	05403	802-864-6651	
Daily Planet 15 Ctr St *Web:* www.dailyplanet15.com	Burlington	VT	05401	802-862-9647	
Halvorson's Upstreet Cafe 16 Church St *Web:* halvorsonsupstreetcafe.com	Burlington	VT	05401	802-658-0278	
India House Restaurant 207 Colchester Ave.	Burlington	VT	05401	802-862-7800	
L'Amante 126 College St *Web:* www.lamante.com	Burlington	VT	05401	802-863-5200	
Leunig's Bistro 115 Church St *Web:* www.leunigsbistro.com	Burlington	VT	05401	802-863-3759	
New World Tortilla 696 Pine St *Web:* www.newworldtortilla.com	Burlington	VT	05401	802-865-1058	
Pauline's 1834 Shelburne Rd. *Web:* www.paulinescafe.com	Burlington	VT	05403	802-862-1081	
Ri Ra 123 Church St *Web:* www.rira.com	Burlington	VT	05401	802-860-9401	
Single Pebble 133 Bank St *Web:* www.asinglepebble.com	Burlington	VT	05401	802-865-5200	
Sweetwaters 120 Church St *Web:* www.sweetwatersvt.com	Burlington	VT	05401	802-864-9800	
Trattoria Delia 152 St Paul St. *Web:* www.trattoriadelia.com	Burlington	VT	05401	802-864-5253	
Chef's Table 118 Main St *Web:* neci.edu	Montpelier	VT	05602	802-229-9202	
China Star Chinese Restaurant 15 Main St.	Montpelier	VT	05602	802-223-0808	
House of Tang 114 River St. *Web:* houseoftang.com	Montpelier	VT	05602	802-223-6020	
J Morgan's Steakhouse 100 State St *Web:* www.capitolplaza.com	Montpelier	VT	05602	802-223-5222	
Julio's Restaurant 54 State St *Web:* www.julioscantina.com	Montpelier	VT	05602	802-229-9348	
Main Street Grill & Bar 118 Main St. *Web:* www.neci.edu	Montpelier	VT	05602	802-223-3188	
McGillicuddy's Irish Pub 14 Langdon St *Web:* mcgillicuddysvt.com	Montpelier	VT	05862	802-223-2721	
Sarducci's 3 Main St *Web:* www.sarduccis.com	Montpelier	VT	05602	802-223-0229	
Trader Duke's 1117 Williston Rd. *TF:* 800-445-8667 ■ *Web:* www.hilton.com	South Burlington	VT	05403	802-660-7523	660-7516
Peking Duck House 79 W Canal St *Web:* www.pekingduckhousevt.com	Winooski	VT	05404	802-655-7474	

Virginia

	City	State	ZIP	Phone	Fax
219 Restaurant 219 King St *Web:* www.219restaurant.com	Alexandria	VA	22314	703-549-1141	549-0035
A La Lucia 315 Madison St *Web:* www.alalucia.com	Alexandria	VA	22314	703-836-5123	548-9463
Afghan Restaurant 2700 Jefferson Davis Hwy *Web:* afghanrestaurantva.com	Alexandria	VA	22301	703-548-0022	
Akasaka Japanese Restaurant 514-C S Van Dorn St *Web:* akasakasushi.com	Alexandria	VA	22304	703-751-3133	
Atlantis Restaurant 3648 King St *Web:* alexandriaitalianfood.com	Alexandria	VA	22302	703-671-0250	
Bombay Curry Co 3110 Mt Vernon Ave The Calvert Bldg *Web:* www.bombaycurrycompany.com	Alexandria	VA	22305	703-836-6363	
Chart House Restaurant 1 Cameron St. *Web:* www.chart-house.com	Alexandria	VA	22314	703-684-5080	
Evening Star Cafe 2000 Mt Vernon Ave *Web:* www.eveningstarcafe.net	Alexandria	VA	22301	703-549-5051	
Finn & Porter 5000 Seminary Rd. *Web:* www.finnandporter.com	Alexandria	VA	22311	703-379-2346	845-7662
Fish Market 105 King St *Web:* www.fishmarketva.com	Alexandria	VA	22314	703-836-5676	684-9424
Geranio Ristorante 722 King St *Web:* www.geranio.net	Alexandria	VA	22314	703-548-0088	548-0091
Hee Been 6231 Little River Tpke. *Web:* www.heebeen.com	Alexandria	VA	22312	703-941-3737	
House of Dynasty 7550 Telegraph Rd. *Web:* www.houseofdynasty.com	Alexandria	VA	22315	703-922-5210	922-5211
IL Porto Ristorante 121 King St. *Web:* www.ilportoristorante.com	Alexandria	VA	22314	703-836-8833	
Indigo Landing Restaurant 1 Marina Dr. *Web:* indigolanding.com	Alexandria	VA	22314	703-548-0001	548-2296
La Bergerie 218 N Lee St. *Web:* www.labergerie.com	Alexandria	VA	22314	703-683-1007	519-6114
Landini Bros 115 King St. *Web:* www.landinibrothers.com	Alexandria	VA	22314	703-836-8404	549-3596
Le Refuge Restaurant 127 N Washington St. *Web:* www.lerefugealexandria.com	Alexandria	VA	22314	703-548-4661	
Morrison House 116 S Alfred St *TF:* 866-834-6628 ■ *Web:* www.morrisonhouse.com	Alexandria	VA	22314	703-838-8000	684-6283
Murphy's Grand Irish Pub 713 King St *Web:* www.murphyspub.com	Alexandria	VA	22314	703-548-1717	739-4583
Restaurant Eve 110 S Pitt St. *Web:* www.restauranteve.com	Alexandria	VA	22314	703-706-0450	706-0968

Name	City	State	Zip	Phone	Fax
Rocklands 25 S Quaker Ln *Web:* www.rocklands.com	Alexandria	VA	22314	703-778-8000	
RT's 3804 Mt Vernon Ave *Web:* www.rtsrestaurant.net	Alexandria	VA	22305	703-684-6010	548-0417
Satay Sarinah 512A S Van Dorn St *Web:* www.sataysarinah.com	Alexandria	VA	22304	703-370-4313	370-9672
Savio's 516 S Van Dorn St *Web:* www.saviosrestaurant.com	Alexandria	VA	22304	703-212-9651	
Shooter McGees 5239 Duke St *Web:* www.shootermcgees.com	Alexandria	VA	22304	703-751-9266	
Southside 815 815 S Washington St *Web:* www.southside815.com	Alexandria	VA	22314	703-836-6222	
Taqueria el Poblano 2400B Mt Vernon Ave *Web:* www.taqueriapoblano.com	Alexandria	VA	22301	703-548-8226	
Taverna Cretekou 818 King St *Web:* www.tavernacretekou.com	Alexandria	VA	22314	703-548-8688	683-2739
Tempo Restaurant 4231 Duke St *Web:* www.temporestaurant.com	Alexandria	VA	22304	703-370-7900	370-7902
Thai Lemon Grass Restaurant 506 S Van Dorn St	Alexandria	VA	22304	703-751-4627	
Union Street Public House 121 S Union St *Web:* www.unionstreetpublichouse.com	Alexandria	VA	22314	703-548-1785	
Vermilion 1120 King St *Web:* www.vermilionrestaurant.com	Alexandria	VA	22314	703-684-9669	
Warehouse Bar & Grill 214 King St *Web:* www.warehousebarandgrill.com	Alexandria	VA	22314	703-683-6868	683-6928
Wharf, The 119 King St *Web:* www.wharfrestaurant.com	Alexandria	VA	22314	703-836-2836	836-2830
Yamazato 6303 Little River Tpke *Web:* www.yamazato.net	Alexandria	VA	22312	703-914-8877	
Athena Pallas 556 22nd St S *Web:* www.athenapallas.com	Arlington	VA	22202	703-521-3870	521-3877
Bangkok 54 2919 Columbia Pk *Web:* www.bangkok54restaurant.com	Arlington	VA	22204	703-521-4070	
Bangkok Bistro 715 N Glebe Rd *Web:* www.bangkokbistrodc.com	Arlington	VA	22203	703-243-9669	
Cafe Asia 1550 Wilson Blvd *Web:* www.cafeasia.com	Arlington	VA	22209	703-741-0870	
Caribbean Grill 5183 Lee Hwy	Arlington	VA	22207	703-241-8947	
Carlyle 4000 Campbell Ave *Web:* www.greatamericanrestaurants.com	Arlington	VA	22206	703-931-0777	931-9420
Clarendon Grill 1101 N Highland St *Web:* www.cgrill.com	Arlington	VA	22201	703-524-7455	524-9598
Crystal Thai 4819 First St N *Web:* www.crystalthai.com	Arlington	VA	22203	703-522-1311	
El Paso Cafe 4235 N Pershing Dr *Web:* elpasocafeva.com	Arlington	VA	22203	703-243-9811	
El Pollo Rico 932 N Kennmore St *Web:* elpolloricorestaurant.com	Arlington	VA	22201	703-522-3220	
Freddie's Beach Bar & Restaurant 555 23rd St S *Web:* freddiesbeachbar.com	Arlington	VA	22202	703-685-0555	685-0877
Guajillo 1727 Wilson Blvd *Web:* guajillomexican.com	Arlington	VA	22201	703-807-0840	
Hunan Gate 4233 N Fairfax Dr *Web:* hunangate.com	Arlington	VA	22203	703-243-5678	
La Cote d'Or Cafe 6876 Lee Hwy *Web:* www.lacotedorcafe.com	Arlington	VA	22213	703-538-3033	573-0409
Laylalina Restaurant 5216 Wilson Blvd *Web:* layalinarestaurant.com	Arlington	VA	22205	703-525-1170	
Legal Sea Foods 2301 Jefferson Davis Hwy *Web:* www.legalseafoods.com	Arlington	VA	22202	703-415-1200	415-1464
McCormick & Schmick's 2010B Crystal Dr *Web:* www.mccormickandschmicks.com	Arlington	VA	22202	703-413-6400	413-7118
Melting Pot of Arlington, The 1110 N Glebe Rd *Web:* www.meltingpot.com	Arlington	VA	22201	703-243-4490	243-4547
Mexicali Blues 2933 Wilson Blvd *Web:* www.mexicali-blues.com	Arlington	VA	22201	703-812-9352	
Minh's 2500 Wilson Blvd *Web:* minhdcrestaurant.com	Arlington	VA	22201	703-525-2828	525-2829
Portabellos 2109 N Pollard St *Web:* portabellos.net	Arlington	VA	22207	703-528-1557	
Ray's the Steaks 2300 Wilson Blvd *Web:* raysthesteaks.com	Arlington	VA	22201	703-841-7297	
Rhodeside Grill 1836 Wilson Blvd *Web:* www.rhodesidegrill.com	Arlington	VA	22201	703-243-0145	
Ristorante Murali 1201 S Joyce St *Web:* www.muraliva.com	Arlington	VA	22202	703-415-0411	415-0410
Ruth's Chris Steak House 2231 Crystal Dr 11th Fl *Web:* www.ruthschris.com	Arlington	VA	22202	703-979-7275	
SoBe Seafood Co 3100 Clarendon Blvd	Arlington	VA	22201	703-527-1283	832-8840
Taqueria Poblano 2503 N Harrison St *Web:* www.taqueriapoblano.com	Arlington	VA	22207	703-237-8250	
THAI 4029 Campbell Ave *Web:* www.thaiinshirlington.com	Arlington	VA	22206	703-931-3203	
Thaiphoon 1301 S Joy St *Web:* www.thaiphoon.com	Arlington	VA	22202	703-413-8200	413-8868
Tutto Bene 501 N Randolph St	Arlington	VA	22203	703-522-1005	527-0863
Village Bistro, The 1723 Wilson Blvd *Web:* frenchitalianarlingtonva.com	Arlington	VA	22209	703-522-5222	
Court House Cafe 350 S Battlefield Blvd *Web:* gbcourthousecafe.com	Chesapeake	VA	23322	757-482-7077	
Daikichi Sushi Japanese Bistro 1400 N Battlefield Blvd *Web:* www.welovesushi.net	Chesapeake	VA	23320	757-549-0200	549-0200
El Loro 801 Volvo Pkwy Ste 114 *Web:* www.elloromexican.com	Chesapeake	VA	23320	757-436-3415	
Jade Garden Restaurant 1200 Battlefield Blvd N Ste 119 *Web:* gojadegarden.com	Chesapeake	VA	23320	757-436-1010	
Joe's Crab Shack 1568 Crossways Blvd *Web:* joescrabshack.com	Chesapeake	VA	23320	757-420-8330	
Kyoto Japanese Steak House & Sushi Bar 1412 Greenbrier Pkwy *Web:* kyotochesapeakeva.com	Chesapeake	VA	23320	757-420-0950	
Nagoya Sushi 109 Gainsborough Sq	Chesapeake	VA	23320	757-549-7977	549-3458
Pirate's Cove 109 Gainsborough Sq *Web:* piratescoveva.com	Chesapeake	VA	23320	757-549-7272	
Smokey Bones BBQ & Grill 1405 Greenbrier Pkwy *Web:* www.smokeybones.com	Chesapeake	VA	23320	757-361-6843	
Tida Thai Cuisine 1937 S Military Hwy *Web:* tidathai.com	Chesapeake	VA	23320	757-422-1027	
Awful Arthur's Seafood Co 6078 Mechanicsville Tpke *Web:* www.awfularthurs.com	Mechanicsville	VA	23111	804-559-4370	
Kabuto Inc 13158 Midlothian Tpke *Web:* kabutorichmond.com	Midlothian	VA	23113	804-379-7979	
Alfresco 11710 Jefferson Ave *Web:* www.alfrescoitalianrestaurant.com	Newport News	VA	23606	757-873-0644	
Chung Oak 15320 A & B Warwick Blvd	Newport News	VA	23608	757-874-3505	
Das Waldcafe 12529 Warwick Blvd	Newport News	VA	23606	757-930-1781	
Japan Samurai 12233 Jefferson Ave *Web:* japansamurainn.com	Newport News	VA	23602	757-249-4400	
Port Arthur 11137 Warwick Blvd *Web:* www.portarthurva.com	Newport News	VA	23601	757-599-6474	
RJ's Restaurant & Sports Pub 12743 Jefferson Ave	Newport News	VA	23602	757-874-4246	
Schlesinger's Chop House 1106 William Styron Sq S *Web:* www.schlesingerssteaks.com	Newport News	VA	23606	757-599-4700	
So Ya Japenese Restaurant 12715 Warwick Blvd Corner Shoppes Center	Newport News	VA	23606	757-930-0156	
456 Fish 456 Granby St *Web:* www.456fish.com	Norfolk	VA	23507	757-625-4444	
Banque, The 1849 E Little Creek Rd *Web:* thebanque.com	Norfolk	VA	23518	757-480-3600	
Bodega 442 Granby St *Web:* www.bodegaongranby.com	Norfolk	VA	23510	757-622-8527	
Empire Little Bar & Bistro, The 257 Granby St	Norfolk	VA	23510	757-626-3100	626-3124
Fellini's 3910 Colley Ave *Web:* fellinisva.com	Norfolk	VA	23508	757-625-3000	
Franco's 6200 N Military Hwy	Norfolk	VA	23518	757-853-0177	
Freemason Abbey 209 W Freemason St *Web:* www.freemasonabbey.com	Norfolk	VA	23510	757-622-3966	622-3592
Havana's 255 Granby St	Norfolk	VA	23510	757-627-5800	
Kotobuki 721 W 21st St *Web:* kotobukisushibar.com	Norfolk	VA	23517	757-628-1025	
Luna Maya 2010 Colley Ave and 21st St *Web:* www.lunamayarestaurant.com	Norfolk	VA	23517	757-622-6986	
Max & Erma's Restaurant 1500 N Military Hwy *Web:* www.maxandermas.com	Norfolk	VA	23502	757-625-7771	
Omar's Carriage House 313 W Bute St *Web:* omarscarriagehouse.com	Norfolk	VA	23510	757-622-4990	
Rajput Indian Cuisine 742 W 21st St *Web:* www.rajputonline.com	Norfolk	VA	23517	757-625-4634	
Regino's 3816 E Little Creek Rd *Web:* reginosrestaurantofnorfolk.com	Norfolk	VA	23518	757-588-4300	
Sai Gai Japanese Steakhouse 7521 Granby St	Norfolk	VA	23505	757-423-1000	
San Antonio Sams 1501 Colley Ave *Web:* www.sanantoniosams.com	Norfolk	VA	23517	757-623-0233	
Todd Jurich's Bistro 150 W Main St Ste 100 *Web:* www.toddjurichsbistro.com	Norfolk	VA	23510	757-622-3210	
Uptown Buffet 1050 N Military Hwy	Norfolk	VA	23502	757-893-9293	
Voila! 509 Botetourt St *Web:* voilainternationalcuisine.godaddysites.com	Norfolk	VA	23510	757-640-0343	
Acacia Mid-Town 2601 W Cary St *Web:* www.acaciarestaurant.com	Richmond	VA	23220	804-562-0138	
Amici 3343 W Cary St *Web:* www.amiciristorante.net	Richmond	VA	23221	804-353-4700	
Bella Italia 6407 Iron Bridge Rd *Web:* work-telephone-manners.com	Richmond	VA	23234	804-743-1116	
Capital Ale House 623 E Main St *Web:* www.capitalalehouse.com	Richmond	VA	23219	804-780-2537	
Cheesecake Factory 11800 W Broad St *Web:* www.thecheesecakefactory.com	Richmond	VA	23233	804-364-4300	
Helen's 2527 W Main St *Web:* helensrva.com	Richmond	VA	23220	804-358-4370	
India K'Raja 9051 W Broad St *Web:* www.indiakraja.com	Richmond	VA	23294	804-965-6345	
Lemaire 101 W Franklin St *Web:* www.lemairerestaurant.com	Richmond	VA	23220	804-649-4629	
Mamma 'Zu 501 S Pine St	Richmond	VA	23220	804-788-4205	
Mekong 6004 W Broad St *Web:* mekongisforbeerlovers.com	Richmond	VA	23230	804-288-8929	
Melting Pot of Richmond, The 9704 Gayton Rd *Web:* www.meltingpot.com	Richmond	VA	23233	804-741-3120	741-2781
Millie's 2603 E Main St *Web:* www.milliesdiner.com	Richmond	VA	23223	804-643-5512	648-4321
Old Original Bookbinder's 2306 E Cary St *Web:* bookbindersrichmond.com	Richmond	VA	23223	804-643-6900	
Palani Drive 401 Libbie Ave *Web:* www.palanidrive.com	Richmond	VA	23226	804-285-3200	
PF Chang's China Bistro 9212 Stony Pt *Web:* pfchangs.com	Richmond	VA	23235	804-253-0492	
Sam Miller's Restaurant 1210 E Cary St *Web:* www.sammillers.com	Richmond	VA	23219	804-644-5465	
Sine Irish Pub & Restaurant 1327 E Cary St *Web:* www.sineirishpub.com/cms_richmond	Richmond	VA	23218	804-649-7767	649-0661
Skilligalee 5416 Glenside Dr	Richmond	VA	23228	804-672-6200	755-1312

Name / Address	City	State	ZIP	Phone	Fax
Sticky Rice 2232 W Main St *Web:* www.ilovestickyrice.com	Richmond	VA	23220	804-358-7870	
Tobacco Company Restaurant 1201 E Cary St *Web:* www.thetobaccocompany.com	Richmond	VA	23219	804-782-9555	
Zeus Gallery Cafe 201 N Belmont Ave	Richmond	VA	23221	804-359-3219	
419 West 3865 Electric Rd *Web:* 419-west.com	Roanoke	VA	24018	540-776-0419	
Alexander's 105 S Jefferson St *Web:* alexandersva.com	Roanoke	VA	24011	540-982-6983	
Carlos Brazilian International Cuisine 4167 Electric Rd SW *Web:* carlosbrazilian.com	Roanoke	VA	24018	540-776-1117	
Coach & Four Restaurant 5206 Williamson Rd *Web:* www.coachandfour.com	Roanoke	VA	24012	540-362-4220	
El Toreo 3790 Peter's Creek Rd Ext SW *Web:* eltoreoroanoke.com	Roanoke	VA	24018	540-342-7060	
Frankie Rowland's Steakhouse 104 Jefferson St *Web:* frankierowlandssteakhouse.com	Roanoke	VA	24011	540-527-2333	
Kabuki Japanese Steak House 3503 Franklin Rd SW *Web:* kabukiva.com	Roanoke	VA	24014	540-981-0222	
Kobe Japanese Steak House 3214 Electric Rd. *Web:* www.kobesteakhouse.com	Roanoke	VA	24018	540-776-0008	
Metro! 14 Campbell Ave SE *Web:* www.metroroanoke.com	Roanoke	VA	24011	540-345-6645	
Nawab Indian Cuisine 118A Campbell Ave *Web:* www.nawabonline.com	Roanoke	VA	24011	540-345-5150	
Ragazzi's 3843 Electric Rd *Web:* www.ragazzis.com	Roanoke	VA	24018	540-989-9022	
Szechuan 5207 Bernard Dr *Web:* szechuan1.net	Roanoke	VA	24018	540-989-7947	
China Garden 1100 Wilson Blvd Twin Towers - Mall Level *Web:* chinagardenva.com	Rossyln	VA	22209	703-525-5317	525-5568
Woo Lae Oak 8240 Leesburg Pk *Web:* www.woolaeoak.com	Vienna	VA	22182	703-827-7300	827-7302
22nd St Raw Bar & Grill, The 202 22nd St *Web:* rawbarandgrille.com	Virginia Beach	VA	23451	757-491-2222	
Aberdeen Barn 5805 Northampton Blvd *Web:* www.aberdeenbarn.com	Virginia Beach	VA	23455	757-464-1580	
Aldo's Ristorante 1860 Laskin Rd *Web:* aldosvb.com	Virginia Beach	VA	23454	757-491-1111	
Boulevard Pizzeria & Italian Eatery 2935 Virginia Beach Blvd	Virginia Beach	VA	23452	757-463-1311	
Captain George's Seafood 1956 Laskin Rd. *Web:* www.captaingeorges.com	Virginia Beach	VA	23454	757-428-3494	
Ensenada 2824 Virginia Beach Blvd.	Virginia Beach	VA	23452	757-631-1090	
Hot Tuna Bar & Grill 2817 Shore Dr. *Web:* hottunavb.com	Virginia Beach	VA	23451	757-481-2888	
Il Giardino 910 Atlantic Ave *Web:* www.ilgiardino.com	Virginia Beach	VA	23451	757-422-6464	
Imperial Palace 4878 Princess Anne Rd. *Web:* elegantchinesedining.com	Virginia Beach	VA	23462	757-493-8838	
Kin's Wok 4001 Virginia Beach Blvd *Web:* kinswokvb.com	Virginia Beach	VA	23452	757-340-6898	
Lynnhaven Fish House 2350 Starfish Rd *Web:* www.lynnhavenfishhouse.net	Virginia Beach	VA	23451	757-481-0003	
Melting Pot of Virginia Beach, The 1564 Laskin Rd. *Web:* www.meltingpot.com	Virginia Beach	VA	23451	757-425-3463	
Mi Casita 3600 Bonney Rd. *Web:* micasitamexican.com	Virginia Beach	VA	23452	757-463-3819	
Mo Mo Sushi 1385 Fordham Dr.	Virginia Beach	VA	23464	757-366-3188	
Nara Sushi 1115 Independence Blvd Ste 104 *Web:* www.narasushi.com	Virginia Beach	VA	23455	757-456-5111	490-0109
North Beach Bar & Grill 3107 Atlantic Ave *TF:* 800-292-3297 ■ *Web:* hamptoninnvirginiabeachoceanfront.com	Virginia Beach	VA	23451	757-491-1800	
One Fish - Two Fish 2109 W Great Neck Rd *Web:* www.onefish-twofish.com	Virginia Beach	VA	23451	757-496-4350	
Otani 1532 Laskin Rd *Web:* otanigrill.com	Virginia Beach	VA	23451	757-425-0404	
PF Chang's China Bistro 4551 Virginia Beach Blvd *Web:* www.pfchangs.com	Virginia Beach	VA	23462	757-473-9028	
Plaza Azteca 4292 Holland Rd *Web:* plazaazteca.com	Virginia Beach	VA	23452	757-431-8135	
Reginella's 4000 Virginia Beach Blvd *Web:* reginellas.com	Virginia Beach	VA	23452	757-498-9770	
Steinhilbers Thalia 653 Thalia Rd *Web:* www.steinys.com	Virginia Beach	VA	23452	757-340-1156	
Tautog's 205 23rd St *Web:* www.tautogs.com	Virginia Beach	VA	23451	757-422-0081	
Waterman's Grill 415 Atlantic Ave *Web:* www.watermans.com	Virginia Beach	VA	23451	757-428-3644	
Zia Marie 4497 Lookout Rd	Virginia Beach	VA	23455	757-460-0715	
Aberdeen Barn 1601 Richmond Rd. *Web:* www.aberdeen-barn.com	Williamsburg	VA	23185	757-229-6661	
Blue Talon Bistro 420 Prince George St. *Web:* www.bluetalonbistro.com	Williamsburg	VA	23185	757-476-2583	
Captain George's Seafood Restaurant 5363 Richmond Rd. *Web:* www.captaingeorges.com	Williamsburg	VA	23188	757-565-2323	
Fat Canary 410 W Duke of Gloucester St. *Web:* fatcanarywilliamsburg.com	Williamsburg	VA	23185	757-229-3333	
Jefferson Restaurant 1453 Richmond Rd	Williamsburg	VA	23185	757-229-2296	
La Tolteca 3048 Richmond Rd.	Williamsburg	VA	23185	757-253-2939	
Le Yaca 1430 High St. *Web:* leyacawilliamsburg.com	Williamsburg	VA	23185	757-220-3616	
Nawab Indian Cuisine 204 Monticello Ave Monticello Shopping Ctr *Web:* www.nawabonline.com	Williamsburg	VA	23185	757-565-3200	
Old Chickahominy House 1211 Jamestown Rd *Web:* oldchickahominy.com	Williamsburg	VA	23185	757-229-4689	
Peking 120 Waller Mill Rd *Web:* peking-va.com	Williamsburg	VA	23185	757-229-2288	
Sal's 1242 Richmond Rd *Web:* www.salsbyvictor.com	Williamsburg	VA	23185	757-220-2641	
Seafare of Williamsburg 1632 Richmond Rd. *Web:* www.seafareofwilliamsburg.com/contact.php	Williamsburg	VA	23185	757-229-0099	
Second Street Restaurant & Tavern 140 Second St *Web:* www.secondst.com	Williamsburg	VA	23185	757-220-2286	
Trellis Restaurant 403 W Duke of Gloucester St *Web:* www.thetrellis.com	Williamsburg	VA	23185	757-229-8610	
Yorkshire Steak & Seafood Restaurant 700 York St. *Web:* www.theyorkshirerestaurant.com	Williamsburg	VA	23185	757-229-9790	

Washington

Name / Address	City	State	ZIP	Phone	Fax
Longhorn BBQ 635 C St SW *Web:* www.thelonghornbbq.com	Auburn	WA	98001	253-804-9600	804-5493
Budd Bay Cafe 525 Columbia St NW *Web:* www.buddbaycafe.com	Olympia	WA	98501	360-357-6963	
Casa Mia 716 Plum St *Web:* www.casamiarestaurants.com	Olympia	WA	98501	360-352-0440	
El Sarape 4043 Martin Way E *Web:* www.elsarape.net	Olympia	WA	98506	360-459-5525	
Emperor's Palace 400 Cooper Pt Rd SW *Web:* www.eprestaurant.com	Olympia	WA	98502	360-352-0777	
Fishbowl Brew Pub & Cafe 515 Jefferson St SE *Web:* www.fishbrewing.com/brewpub	Olympia	WA	98501	360-943-3650	943-6983
Gardner's Seafood & Pasta 111 Thurston Ave NW *Web:* gardnersrestaurant.com	Olympia	WA	98501	360-786-8466	
Koibito 1707 Harrison Ave NW *Web:* koibitosushi.com	Olympia	WA	98502	360-352-4751	
Lemon Grass Restaurant 212 Fourth Ave W	Olympia	WA	98501	360-705-1832	
Mekong 125 Columbia St NW	Olympia	WA	98501	360-352-9620	
Mercato 111 Market St NW *Web:* www.mercatoristorante.com	Olympia	WA	98501	360-528-3663	
Oyster House 320 Fourth Ave W *Web:* www.oysterhouse.com	Olympia	WA	98501	360-753-7000	
Ramblin Jack's 520 Fourth Ave E *Web:* www.ramblinjacks.com	Olympia	WA	98501	360-754-8909	
Saigon Rendez-vous 117 Fifth Ave SW *Web:* saigonrendezvous.com	Olympia	WA	98501	360-352-1989	
Trinacria Ristorante 113 Capitol Way N	Olympia	WA	98501	360-352-8892	
Urban Onion 116 Legion Way SE	Olympia	WA	98501	360-943-9242	
13 Coins 125 Boren Ave N *Web:* www.13coins.com	Seattle	WA	98109	206-682-2513	
Agua Verde Cafe 1303 NE Boat St *Web:* www.aguaverde.com	Seattle	WA	98105	206-545-8570	
Al Boccalino 1 Yesler Way *Web:* seattleslittleitaly.com	Seattle	WA	98104	206-622-7688	
Andaluca 407 Olive Way *Web:* www.andaluca.com	Seattle	WA	98101	206-382-6999	382-6997
Anthony's Pier 66 2201 Alaskan Way *Web:* www.anthonys.com	Seattle	WA	98121	206-448-6688	
Assaggio Ristorante 2010 Fourth Ave *Web:* www.assaggioseattle.com	Seattle	WA	98121	206-441-1399	
BluWater Bistro 102 Lakeside Ave *Web:* www.bluwaterbistro.com	Seattle	WA	98122	206-328-2233	
Brasserie Margaux 401 Lenora St *Web:* www.margauxseattle.com	Seattle	WA	98121	206-219-2224	
Brooklyn Seafood Steak & Oyster House 1212 Second Ave *Web:* thebrooklyn.com	Seattle	WA	98101	206-224-7000	
Cactus 4220 E Madison *Web:* www.cactusrestaurants.com	Seattle	WA	98112	206-324-4140	
Cafe Flora 2901 E Madison St *Web:* www.cafeflora.com	Seattle	WA	98112	206-325-9100	
Cafe Lago 2305 24th Ave E *Web:* www.cafelago.com	Seattle	WA	98112	206-329-8005	
Campagne 1600 Post Alley *Web:* cafecampagne.com	Seattle	WA	98101	206-728-2233	
Canlis Restaurant 2576 Aurora Ave N *Web:* www.canlis.com	Seattle	WA	98109	206-283-3313	283-1766
Chandler's Crabhouse 901 Fairview Ave N *Web:* www.schwartzbros.com/chandlers-crabhouse	Seattle	WA	98109	206-223-2722	223-9380
Chinook's at Salmon Bay 1900 W Nickerson St Ste 103 *Web:* anthonys.com	Seattle	WA	98119	206-283-4665	
Chiso Restaurant 3520 Fremont Ave N. *Web:* www.chisoseattle.com	Seattle	WA	98103	206-632-3430	
Cutters Bayhouse 2001 Western Ave *Web:* www.cuttersbayhouse.com	Seattle	WA	98121	206-448-4884	
Dahlia Lounge 2001 Fourth Ave *Web:* www.tomdouglas.com	Seattle	WA	98121	206-682-4142	
Daniel's Broiler 809 Fairview Pl N *Web:* www.schwartzbros.com	Seattle	WA	98109	425-990-6310	
El Gaucho 2505 First Ave *Web:* www.elgaucho.com	Seattle	WA	98121	206-728-1337	

Restaurant	City	State	Zip	Phone	Fax
El Gaucho-Aqua 2801 Alaskan Way Pier 70 *Web:* elgaucho.com	Seattle	WA	98121	206-956-9171	
Elliott's Oyster House 1201 Alaskan Way Pier 56 *Web:* www.elliottsoysterhouse.com	Seattle	WA	98101	206-623-4340	224-0154
Etta's Seafood 2020 Western Ave *Web:* www.tomdouglas.com	Seattle	WA	98121	206-443-6000	
Eva Restaurant 2227 N 56th St *Web:* evarestaurant.com	Seattle	WA	98103	206-633-3538	
Flying Fish 300 Westlake Ave N *Web:* www.flyingfishseattle.com	Seattle	WA	98109	206-728-8595	728-1551
Georgian, The 411 University St *TF:* 888-363-5022 ■ *Web:* fairmont.com	Seattle	WA	98101	206-621-7889	
Harvest Vine 2701 E Madison St *Web:* www.harvestvine.com	Seattle	WA	98112	206-320-9771	
Icon Grill 1933 Fifth Ave *Web:* www.icongrill.net	Seattle	WA	98101	206-441-6330	441-7037
Il Bistro 93-A Pike St *Web:* www.ilbistro.net	Seattle	WA	98101	206-682-3049	
Il Terrazzo Carmine 411 First Ave S *Web:* www.ilterrazzocarmine.com	Seattle	WA	98104	206-467-7797	
India Bistro 2301 NW Market St *Web:* www.seattleindiabistro.com	Seattle	WA	98107	206-783-5080	297-9069
Ivar's Acres of Clams 1001 Alaskan Way Pier 54 *Web:* www.ivars.com	Seattle	WA	98104	206-624-6852	624-4895
JaK's Grill 3701 NE 45th St *Web:* www.jaksgrill.com	Seattle	WA	98105	206-985-8545	
Kabul Afghan Cuisine 2301 N 45th St *Web:* www.kabulrestaurant.com	Seattle	WA	98103	206-545-9000	
Kingfish Cafe 602 19th Ave E *Web:* thekingfishcafe.com	Seattle	WA	98112	206-320-8757	
La Medusa 4857 Rainier Ave S *Web:* www.lamedusarestaurant.com	Seattle	WA	98118	206-723-2192	
La Rustica 4100 Beach Dr SW	Seattle	WA	98116	206-932-3020	
La Vita E Bella 2411 Second Ave *Web:* www.lavitaebella.us	Seattle	WA	98121	206-441-5322	
Le Gourmand 4100 4th Ave S *Web:* www.legourmandseattle.com	Seattle	WA	98134	206-588-9728	
Le Pichet 1933 First Ave *Web:* lepichetseattle.com	Seattle	WA	98101	206-256-1499	
Lola 2000 Fourth Ave *Web:* www.tomdouglas.com	Seattle	WA	98121	206-441-1430	
Maneki 304 Sixth Ave S *Web:* manekirestaurant.com	Seattle	WA	98104	206-622-2631	
Matt's in the Market 94 Pike St Ste 32 *Web:* www.mattsinthemarket.com	Seattle	WA	98101	206-467-7909	
McCormick's Fish House & Bar 722 Fourth Ave *Web:* www.mccormickandschmicks.com	Seattle	WA	98104	206-682-3900	667-0081
Metropolitan Grill 820 Second Ave *Web:* www.themetropolitangrill.com	Seattle	WA	98104	206-624-3287	389-0042
Morton's The Steakhouse 1511 Sixth Ave *Web:* www.mortons.com	Seattle	WA	98101	206-223-0550	223-0507
Nell's 6804 E Green Lk Way N *Web:* www.nellsrestaurant.com	Seattle	WA	98115	206-524-4044	
Pabla Indian Cuisine 1516 Second Ave *Web:* pablaindiacuisine.com	Seattle	WA	98101	206-623-2868	
Palace Kitchen 2030 Fifth Ave *Web:* www.tomdouglas.com	Seattle	WA	98121	206-448-2001	
Palisade 2601 W Marina Pl *Web:* www.palisaderestaurant.com	Seattle	WA	98199	206-285-1000	
Palomino 1420 Fifth Ave *Web:* www.palomino.com	Seattle	WA	98101	206-623-1300	
Paseo 4225 Fremont Ave N *Web:* www.paseorestaurants.com	Seattle	WA	98103	206-545-7440	
PF Chang's China Bistro 400 Pine St Ste 136 *Web:* www.pfchangs.com	Seattle	WA	98101	206-393-0070	
Phoenecia at Alki 2716 Alki Ave SW *Web:* www.phoeneciawestseattle.com	Seattle	WA	98116	206-935-6550	
Pink Door, The 1919 Post Alley *Web:* www.thepinkdoor.net	Seattle	WA	98101	206-443-3241	
Place Pigalle 81 Pike St *Web:* www.placepigalle-seattle.com	Seattle	WA	98101	206-624-1756	
Ponti Seafood Grill 3014 Third Ave N *Web:* www.pontiseafoodgrill.com	Seattle	WA	98109	206-284-3000	284-4768
Queen City Grill 2201 First Ave *Web:* www.queencitygrill.com	Seattle	WA	98121	206-443-0975	973-5345
Ray's Boathouse 6049 Seaview Ave NW *Web:* www.rays.com	Seattle	WA	98107	206-789-3770	781-1960
Restaurant Zoe 1318 E Union St *Web:* zoeseattle.com	Seattle	WA	98122	206-226-2010	
Rover's 2808 E Madison St *Web:* www.thechefinthehat.com	Seattle	WA	98112	206-328-6645	
Ruth's Chris Steak House 727 Pine St *Web:* www.ruthschris.com	Seattle	WA	98101	206-624-8524	
Salty's on Alki Beach 1936 Harbor Ave SW *Web:* www.saltys.com	Seattle	WA	98126	206-937-1600	937-1430
Serafina 2043 Eastlake Ave E *Web:* www.serafinaseattle.com	Seattle	WA	98102	206-323-0807	
Shiro's Sushi Restaurant 2401 Second Ave *Web:* www.shiros.com	Seattle	WA	98121	206-443-9844	
SkyCity Restaurant 400 Broad St *Web:* www.spaceneedle.com	Seattle	WA	98109	206-905-2100	
Sorrento Hotel 900 Madison St *TF:* 800-426-1265 ■ *Web:* www.hotelsorrento.com	Seattle	WA	98104	206-622-6400	
Sunfish 2800 Alki Ave SW	Seattle	WA	98116	206-938-4112	
Szmania's 3321 W McGraw St *Web:* www.szmanias.com	Seattle	WA	98199	206-284-7305	
Tango 1100 Pike St *Web:* tangorestaurant.com	Seattle	WA	98101	206-583-0382	
Ten Mercer 10 Mercer St *Web:* www.tenmercer.com	Seattle	WA	98109	206-691-3723	
Thai Heaven 352 Roy St *Web:* thaiheavenseattle.com	Seattle	WA	98109	206-285-1596	
Tilth Restaurant 1411 N 45th St *Web:* mariahinesrestaurants.com	Seattle	WA	98103	206-633-0801	633-0801
Tulio Ristorante 1100 Fifth Ave *Web:* www.tulio.com	Seattle	WA	98101	206-624-5500	
Volterra 5411 Ballard Ave NW *Web:* www.volterrarestaurant.com	Seattle	WA	98107	206-789-5100	
Wild Ginger Asian Restaurant 1401 Third Ave *Web:* www.wildginger.net	Seattle	WA	98101	206-623-4450	
Azar's 2501 N Monroe St *Web:* azarsrestaurant.com	Spokane	WA	99205	509-326-7171	
Cathay Inn 3714 N Div St *Web:* www.cathayinn.com	Spokane	WA	99207	509-326-2226	
China Dragon 27 E Queen Ave *Web:* chinadragonspokane.com	Spokane	WA	99207	509-483-5209	
Clinkerdagger 621 W Mallon Ave *Web:* www.clinkerdagger.com	Spokane	WA	99201	509-328-5965	
Downriver Grill 3315 W NW Blvd *Web:* www.downrivergrillspokane.com	Spokane	WA	99205	509-323-1600	
Elk Public House 1931 W Pacific Ave *Web:* wedonthaveone.com	Spokane	WA	99204	509-363-1973	
Linnie Thai Cuisine 1301 W Third Ave	Spokane	WA	99201	509-835-5800	
Luigi's 245 W Main St *Web:* www.luigis-spokane.com	Spokane	WA	99201	509-624-5226	
Luna 5620 S Perry St *Web:* www.lunaspokane.com	Spokane	WA	99223	509-448-2383	
Mamma Mia's 420 W Francis Ave *Web:* mammamiaspokane.com	Spokane	WA	99205	509-467-7786	
Ming Wah 1618 W Third Ave	Spokane	WA	99201	509-455-9474	
Mizuna 214 N Howard St *Web:* www.mizuna.com	Spokane	WA	99201	509-747-2004	
Mustard Seed 4750 N Div *Web:* www.mustardseedweb.com	Spokane	WA	99207	509-483-1500	
O'Doherty's Irish Grill 525 W Spokane Falls Blvd *Web:* odohertyspub.com	Spokane	WA	99201	509-747-0322	
Rancho Chico 2023 W NW Blvd *Web:* ranchochico.biz	Spokane	WA	99205	509-327-2723	
Shogun 821 E Third Ave *Web:* shogunspokane.com	Spokane	WA	99202	509-534-7777	
Spencer's 322 N Spokane Falls Ct *Web:* hhonors3.hilton.com/en/spencers-for-steaks-and-chops/index.html	Spokane	WA	99220	509-744-2372	744-2396
Taste of India 3110 N Div St	Spokane	WA	99207	509-327-7313	
Tomato Street North 6220 N Div *Web:* www.tomatostreet.com	Spokane	WA	99208	509-484-4500	
Twigs Bistro & Bar 808 W Main Ave *Web:* www.twigsbistro.com	Spokane	WA	99201	509-232-3376	755-0779
Anthony's at Point Defiance 5910 N Waterfront Dr *Web:* www.anthonys.com	Tacoma	WA	98407	253-752-9700	
Azteca 4801 Tacoma Mall Blvd *Web:* aztecamex.com	Tacoma	WA	98409	253-472-0246	
El Gaucho 2119 Pacific Ave *Web:* www.elgaucho.com	Tacoma	WA	98402	253-272-1510	
Europa Bistro 2515 N Proctor St *Web:* www.europabistro.net	Tacoma	WA	98406	253-761-5660	
Galanga 1129 Broadway *Web:* www.galangathai.com	Tacoma	WA	98402	253-272-3393	
Harmon Brewing Co 1938 Pacific Ave *Web:* harmonbrewingco.com	Tacoma	WA	98402	253-383-2739	
Indochine Asian Dining Lounge 1924 Pacific Ave *Web:* www.indochinedowntown.com	Tacoma	WA	98402	253-272-8200	
Johnny's Dock 1900 E D St *Web:* www.johnnysdock.com	Tacoma	WA	98421	253-627-3186	
Le-Le 1012 S Martin Luther King Jr Way *Web:* lelerestaurant.com	Tacoma	WA	98405	253-572-9491	
Lobster Shop South 4015 Ruston Way *Web:* wp.lobstershop.com	Tacoma	WA	98402	253-759-2165	752-9640
Marzano 516 Garfield St S *Web:* www.dinemarzano.com	Tacoma	WA	98444	253-537-4191	
Melting Pot, The 2121 Pacific Ave *Web:* www.meltingpot.com	Tacoma	WA	98402	253-535-3939	
Moctezuma's 4102 S 56th St *Web:* www.moctezumas.com	Tacoma	WA	98409	253-474-5593	
North China Garden 2303 Sixth Ave *Web:* northchinagardentacoma.com	Tacoma	WA	98403	253-572-5106	
Sakura Japanese Steakhouse 3630 S Cedar St	Tacoma	WA	98409	253-475-1300	
Southern Kitchen 1716 Sixth Ave *Web:* southernkitchen-tacoma.com	Tacoma	WA	98405	253-627-4282	
Stanley & Seafort's 115 E 34th St *Web:* www.stanleyandseaforts.com	Tacoma	WA	98404	253-473-7300	
Sushi Tama 3919 Sixth Ave	Tacoma	WA	98406	253-761-1014	
Tacos Guaymas 2630 S 38th St *Web:* www.tacosguaymas.com	Tacoma	WA	98409	253-471-2224	
Falls Terrace 106 Deschutes Way SW *Web:* www.fallsterrace.com	Tumwater	WA	98501	360-943-7830	
Beaches Restaurant & Bar 1919 SE Columbia River Dr *Web:* www.beachesrestaurantandbar.com	Vancouver	WA	98661	360-699-1592	699-0724
Cactus Ya Ya 15704 SE Mill Plain Blvd	Vancouver	WA	98684	360-944-9292	
Canton Chinese Buffet 1118 NE 78th St	Vancouver	WA	98665	360-576-8699	
Carol's Corner Cafe 7800 NE St Johns Blvd	Vancouver	WA	98665	360-573-6357	
Dragon King 1401 NE 78th St *Web:* dragonking78.com	Vancouver	WA	98665	360-574-6684	
Hudson's Bar & Grill 7805 NW Greenwood Dr *Web:* www.hudsonsbarandgrill.com	Vancouver	WA	98662	360-816-6100	
Jerusalem Restaurant & Cafe 106 E Evergreen Blvd *Web:* thejerusalemcafe.com	Vancouver	WA	98660	360-906-0306	

	City	State	ZIP	Phone	Fax
Joe's Crab Shack 101 SE Columbia Way *Web:* joescrabshack.com	Vancouver	WA	98661	360-693-9211	
Little Italy's Trattoria 901 Washington St. *Web:* www.littleitalystrattoria.com	Vancouver	WA	98660	360-737-2363	
McMenamins on the Columbia 1801 S Access Rd. *Web:* mcmenamins.com	Vancouver	WA	98661	360-699-1521	
Namaste Indian Cuisine 6300 NE 117th Ave. *Web:* www.namasteindiancuisine.com	Vancouver	WA	98662	360-891-5857	891-5906
Patrick's Hawaiian Cafe 316 SE 123rd Ave *Web:* www.hawaiiancafe.com	Vancouver	WA	98683	360-885-0881	
Thai Little Home 3214 E Fourth Plain Blvd. *Web:* thailittletogo.com	Vancouver	WA	98661	360-693-4061	
Thai Orchid 213 W 11th St. *Web:* www.thaiorchidvancouver.com	Vancouver	WA	98660	360-695-7786	
Tiger's Garden 312 W Eigth St *Web:* tigersgardenrestaurant.com	Vancouver	WA	98660	360-693-9585	
Who-Song & Larry's 111 SE Columbia Way *Web:* www.eltorito.com	Vancouver	WA	98661	360-695-1198	
Herbfarm, The 14590 NE 145th St *Web:* www.theherbfarm.com	Woodinville	WA	98072	425-485-5300	424-2925

West Virginia

	City	State	ZIP	Phone	Fax
Fifth Quarter 201 Clendenin St *Web:* fifthquarterofcharleston.com	Charleston	WV	25301	304-345-3933	
Laury's 350 MacCorkle Ave SE *Web:* www.laurysrestaurant.com	Charleston	WV	25314	304-343-0055	343-0078
Leonoro's Spaghetti House 1507 Washington St E *Web:* leonorosspaghettihouse.com	Charleston	WV	25311	304-343-1851	
Rio Grande 160 Ct St Ste 7	Charleston	WV	25301	304-344-8616	
Sitar of India 702 Lee St E. *Web:* sitarofindia.org	Charleston	WV	25311	304-346-3745	720-6260
Tidewater Grill 1060 Charleston Town Ctr *TF:* 888-456-3463 ■ *Web:* mainstreetventuresinc.com	Charleston	WV	25389	304-345-2620	345-5624
Whitewater Grille 200 Lee St E *TF:* 800-845-5279	Charleston	WV	25301	304-353-3636	353-3722
Cafe Bacchus 76 High St *Web:* cafebacchus.net	Morgantown	WV	26505	304-296-9234	
Casa D'Amici 485 High St *Web:* www.casadamici.com	Morgantown	WV	26507	304-292-4400	
Glasshouse Grille 709 Beechurst Ave. *Web:* www.theglasshousegrille.com	Morgantown	WV	26505	304-296-8460	
Great Chinese Buffet 5000 Greenbag Rd.	Morgantown	WV	26505	304-296-4050	
Hibachi Japanese Steak House 3091 University Ave *Web:* www.mangoeskeywest.com	Morgantown	WV	26505	304-598-7140	
Maxwell's 1 Wall St.	Morgantown	WV	26505	304-292-0982	
Oliverio's Ristorante on the Wharf 52 Clay St. *Web:* www.oliverios.sites.morgantowns.com	Morgantown	WV	26505	304-842-7388	296-2564
Peking House 1125 Van Voorhis Rd *Web:* pekinghousewv.com	Morgantown	WV	26505	304-598-3333	
Puglioni's 1137 Van Voorhis Rd *Web:* pugspasta.com	Morgantown	WV	26505	304-599-7521	
Voyagers Restaurant 110 Hartfield Rd. *Web:* www.alibabaexpress.com	Morgantown	WV	26505	304-777-4120	
Abbeys 145 Zane St	Wheeling	WV	26003	304-233-0729	
Coleman's Fish Market 2226 Centre Market.	Wheeling	WV	26003	304-232-8510	
Figaretti's 1035 Mt de Chantel Rd. *Web:* www.figarettis.net	Wheeling	WV	26003	304-243-5625	
Generations Restaurant & Pub 338 National Rd *Web:* www.generationswhg.com	Wheeling	WV	26003	304-232-7917	
Golden Chopsticks 329 N York St	Wheeling	WV	26003	304-232-2888	
Panda Chinese Kitchen 1133 Market St	Wheeling	WV	26003	304-232-7572	
River City Ale Works 1400 Main St *Web:* rivercitybanquets.com	Wheeling	WV	26003	304-233-4555	

Wisconsin

	City	State	ZIP	Phone	Fax
Crawdaddy's 1025 S Moorland Rd Ste 400 *TF:* 800-727-9477 ■ *Web:* foodspot.com/search/destination.aspx?fs=19985&st=1	Brookfield	WI	53005	414-778-2228	
Brett Favre's Steakhouse 1004 Brett Favre Pass *Web:* foodspot.com/clients	Green Bay	WI	54304	920-499-6874	
China Palace 213 N Washington St. *Web:* chinapalacegreenbay.com	Green Bay	WI	54301	920-433-0688	
Grazies Italian Grill 2851 S Oneida St *Web:* www.graziesitaliangrill.com	Green Bay	WI	54304	920-499-6365	
Hinterland Brewery & Restaurant 313 Dousman St. *Web:* www.hinterlandbeer.com	Green Bay	WI	54303	920-438-8050	
Kavarna 143 N Broadway *Web:* www.kavarna.com	Green Bay	WI	54303	920-430-3200	
Krolls West 1990 S Ridge Rd. *Web:* www.krollswest.com	Green Bay	WI	54304	920-497-1111	
Legends Brewhouse & Eatery 2840 Shawano Ave *Web:* legendseatery.com	Green Bay	WI	54313	920-662-1111	
Little Tokyo 121B N Broadway. *Web:* thegreenbaysushi.com	Green Bay	WI	54303	920-433-9323	433-9523
Los Banditos 1258 Main St *Web:* foodspot.com/clients/wi/greenbay/losbanditos/default.aspx?accid=13619	Green Bay	WI	54302	920-432-9462	
Luigi's Italian Bistro 2733 Mantiwoc Rd *Web:* luigisitalianbistro.com	Green Bay	WI	54311	920-468-4900	
Mackinaws Grill & Spirits 2925 Voyager Dr. *Web:* www.mackinaws.com	Green Bay	WI	54311	920-406-8000	
Mandarin Garden 2394 S Oneida St *Web:* mandaringardengreenbay.com	Green Bay	WI	54304	920-499-4459	429-2992
Rock Garden 1951 Bond St *Web:* comfortsuitesgb.com	Green Bay	WI	54303	920-497-4701	499-5242
Titletown Brewing Co 200 Dousman St. *Web:* www.titletownbrewing.com	Green Bay	WI	54303	920-437-2337	437-2739
Admiralty Room 666 Wisconsin Ave *TF:* 800-922-5512 ■ *Web:* isthmus.com	Madison	WI	53703	608-256-9071	
Babe's Grill & Bar 5614 Schroeder Rd *Web:* www.babesmadison.com	Madison	WI	53711	608-274-7300	274-3201
Bahn Thai Restaurant 944 Williamson St Ste 4.	Madison	WI	53703	608-256-0202	
Bandung Indonesian Restaurant 600 Williamson St *Web:* www.bandungrestaurant.com	Madison	WI	53703	608-255-6910	
Biaggi's 601 Junction Rd *Web:* www.biaggis.com	Madison	WI	53717	608-664-9288	
Blue Marlin 101 N Hamilton St	Madison	WI	53703	608-255-2255	
Blue Moon Bar & Grill 2535 University Ave. *Web:* www.bluemoonbar.com	Madison	WI	53705	608-233-0441	
Capitol Chophouse 9 E Wilson St. *Web:* chophouse411.com/chophouse_location_cch.asp	Madison	WI	53703	608-255-0165	
Eldorado Grill 744 Williamson St *Web:* eldoradogrillmadison.com	Madison	WI	53703	608-280-9378	
Eno Vino Wine Bar & Bistro 601 Junction Rd. *Web:* www.eno-vino.com	Madison	WI	53717	608-664-9565	
Essen Haus 514 E Wilson St *Web:* www.essen-haus.com	Madison	WI	53703	608-255-4674	258-8632
Famous Dave's Bar-B-Que 900 S Pk St *Web:* www.famousdaves.com	Madison	WI	53715	608-286-9400	
Husnu's 547 State St. *Web:* www.husnus.com	Madison	WI	53703	608-256-0900	
Imperial Garden 4214 E Washington Ave *Web:* imperialgardenmadison.com	Madison	WI	53704	608-249-0466	
Johnny Delmonico's 130 S Pinckney St. *Web:* www.foodfightinc.com	Madison	WI	53703	608-257-8325	
Jolly Bob's 1210 Williamson St. *Web:* jollybobs.com	Madison	WI	53703	608-251-3902	
L'Etoile 1 S Pinckney St *Web:* www.letoile-restaurant.com	Madison	WI	53703	608-251-0500	251-7577
La Hacienda 515 S Pk St.	Madison	WI	53715	608-255-8227	
Lao Laan-Xang 1146 Williamson St *Web:* www.laolaan-xang.com	Madison	WI	53703	608-280-0104	
Laredo's 694 S Whitney Way *Web:* laredosrestaurante.com	Madison	WI	53711	608-278-0585	
Lombardino's 2500 University Ave *Web:* www.lombardinos.com	Madison	WI	53705	608-238-1922	218-9810
Mariner's Inn, The 5339 Lighthouse Bay Dr *Web:* marinersmadison.com	Madison	WI	53704	608-246-3120	
Nau-Ti-Gal 5360 Westport Rd. *Web:* nautigal.com	Madison	WI	53704	608-246-3130	
Otto's Restaurant & Bar 6405 Mineral Pt Rd *Web:* www.ottosrestaurant.com	Madison	WI	53705	608-274-4044	274-1358
Pedro's Mexican Restaurante 3555 E Washington Ave *Web:* www.pedrosmexicanrestaurant.com	Madison	WI	53704	608-241-8110	241-8248
Porta Bella 425 N Frances St. *Web:* www.portabellarestaurant.biz	Madison	WI	53703	608-256-3186	256-1210
Sa Bai Thong 6802 ODANA Rd *Web:* www.sabaithong.com	Madison	WI	53719	608-238-3100	
Smoky's Club 3005 University Ave *Web:* www.smokysclub.com	Madison	WI	53705	608-233-2120	
State Street Brats 603 State St *Web:* www.statestreetbrats.com	Madison	WI	53703	608-255-5544	
Taj Indian Restaurant 1256 S Pk St *Web:* www.tajmadison.com	Madison	WI	53715	608-268-0772	
Tornado Club Steak House 116 S Hamilton St *Web:* tornadosteakhouse.com	Madison	WI	53703	608-256-3570	
Tutto Pasta 305 State St *Web:* www.foodspot.com	Madison	WI	53703	608-294-1000	
Wasabi Japanese Restaurant 449 State St *Web:* wasabi-madison.com	Madison	WI	53703	608-255-5020	
Captain Bill's Seafood Co 2701 Century Harbor Rd *Web:* www.capbills.com	Middleton	WI	53562	608-831-7327	
Alioto's 3041 N Mayfair Rd. *Web:* www.foodspot.com	Milwaukee	WI	53222	414-476-6900	476-6902
Apollo Cafe 1310 E Brady St *Web:* apollocafe.com	Milwaukee	WI	53202	414-272-2233	272-2344
Bacchus Restaurant 925 E Wells St *Web:* www.bacchusmke.com	Milwaukee	WI	53202	414-765-1166	
Beans & Barley 1901 E N Ave. *Web:* www.beansandbarley.com	Milwaukee	WI	53202	414-278-7878	
Botanas 816 S Fifth St *Web:* www.botanasrestaurant.com	Milwaukee	WI	53204	414-672-3755	
Caterina's Ristorante 9104 W Oklahoma Ave *Web:* www.caterinasristorante.com	Milwaukee	WI	53227	414-541-4200	
Cempazuchi 1205 E Brady St. *Web:* www.cempazuchi.com	Milwaukee	WI	53202	414-291-5233	
Coast 931 E Wisconsin Ave. *Web:* www.coastrestaurant.com	Milwaukee	WI	53202	414-727-5555	727-0777
Coquette Cafe 316 N Milwaukee St. *Web:* www.coquettecafe.com	Milwaukee	WI	53202	414-291-2655	
County Clare 1234 N Astor St *Web:* www.countyclare-inn.com	Milwaukee	WI	53202	414-272-5273	290-6300
Eddie Martini's 8612 W Watertown Plank Rd *Web:* www.foodspot.com	Milwaukee	WI	53226	414-771-6680	771-5034
Elsa's on the Park 833 N Jefferson St *Web:* www.elsas.com	Milwaukee	WI	53202	414-765-0615	
Emperor of China Restaurant 1010 E Brady St *Web:* www.emperorofchinarestaurant.com	Milwaukee	WI	53202	414-271-8889	
Filippo's 6915 W Lincoln Ave.	Milwaukee	WI	53219	414-321-4040	

	City	State	ZIP	Phone	Fax
Historic Turner Restaurant 1034 N Fourth St	Milwaukee	WI	53203	414-276-4844	276-0442
Web: www.foodspot.com					
Izumi's 2150 N Prospect Ave	Milwaukee	WI	53202	414-271-5258	
Web: www.izumis.com					
Jackson Grill 3736 W Mitchell St	Milwaukee	WI	53215	414-384-7384	
Web: www.jacksongrill.com					
Karl Ratzsch's Old World Restaurant 320 E Mason St	Milwaukee	WI	53202	414-276-2720	
Web: www.karlratzsch.com					
Kegels German Inn 5901 W National Ave	Milwaukee	WI	53214	414-257-9999	
Web: kegelsinn.com					
King & I, The 830 N Old World Third St	Milwaukee	WI	53203	414-276-4181	
Web: www.kingandirestaurant.com					
La Fuente 625 S Fifth St	Milwaukee	WI	53204	414-271-8595	
Mader's German Restaurant 1041 N Old World Third St	Milwaukee	WI	53203	414-271-3377	
Web: www.madersrestaurant.com					
Maharaja 1550 N Farwell Ave	Milwaukee	WI	53202	414-276-2250	
Milwaukee Chop House 633 N Fifth St	Milwaukee	WI	53203	414-226-2467	
Web: chophouse411.com/chophouse_location_mch.asp					
Mimma's Cafe 1307 E Brady St	Milwaukee	WI	53202	414-271-7337	
Web: www.mimmas.com					
Old Town 522 W Lincoln Ave	Milwaukee	WI	53207	414-672-0206	
Osteria del Mondo 1028 E Juneau Ave	Milwaukee	WI	53202	414-291-3770	291-0840
Web: www.getbianchini.com					
Packing House 900 E Layton Ave	Milwaukee	WI	53207	414-483-5054	483-3481
TF: 800-727-9477 ■ *Web:* www.foodspot.com/clients/wi/milwaukee					
Palms 221 N Broadway	Milwaukee	WI	53202	414-298-3000	
Safe House 779 N Front St	Milwaukee	WI	53202	414-271-2007	
Web: safe-house.com					
Sanford Restaurant 1547 N Jackson St	Milwaukee	WI	53202	414-276-9608	278-8509
Web: www.sanfordrestaurant.com					
Saraphino's 3074 E Layton Ave St Francis	Milwaukee	WI	53235	414-744-0303	
Saz's 5539 W State St	Milwaukee	WI	53208	414-453-2410	
Web: www.sazs.com					
Shahrazad 2847 N Oakland Ave	Milwaukee	WI	53211	414-964-5475	964-5471
Web: www.shahrazadrestaurant.com					
Singha Thai 2237 S 108th St	Milwaukee	WI	53227	414-541-1234	
Web: www.singhathaimilwaukee.com					
Speed Queen BBQ 1130 W Walnut St	Milwaukee	WI	53205	414-265-2900	
Web: www.foodspot.com					
Swig 217 N Broad Way St	Milwaukee	WI	53202	414-431-7944	
Web: www.swigmilwaukee.com					
Tandoor 1117 S 108th St	Milwaukee	WI	53214	414-777-1600	
Web: tandoorrestaurantmilwaukee.com					
Tess 2499 N Bartlett Ave	Milwaukee	WI	53211	414-964-8377	964-7790
Web: tess2499.com					
Third Ward Caffe 225 E St Paul Ave	Milwaukee	WI	53202	414-224-0895	
Web: foodspot.com/clients/wi/milwaukee/thirdwardcaffe					
Three Bros 2414 S St Clair St	Milwaukee	WI	53207	414-481-7530	595-8888*
**Fax Area Code:* 301					
Trocadero 1758 N Water St	Milwaukee	WI	53202	414-272-0205	
Web: www.trocaderomke.com					
Water Street Brewery 1101 N Water St	Milwaukee	WI	53202	414-272-1195	272-0406
Web: www.waterstreetbrewery.com					
Food Fight Restaurant 5111 Monona Dr	Monona	WI	53716	608-467-3130	
Web: www.foodfightinc.com					
Hammond Steakhouse 1402 N Fifth St	Superior	WI	54880	715-392-3269	
Web: hammondliquor.com					
Lan-Chi's Restaurant 1320 Belknap St	Superior	WI	54880	715-394-4496	395-2431
IL MITO Trattoria e Enoteca 6913 W N Ave	Wauwatosa	WI	53213	414-443-1414	
Web: www.ilmitotrattoriaeenoteca.com					

Wyoming

	City	State	ZIP	Phone	Fax
Dorn's Fireside 1745 Cy Ave	Casper	WY	82604	307-235-6831	
Web: dornsfireside.com					
Goose Egg Inn 10580 Goose Egg Rd	Casper	WY	82604	307-473-8838	
JS Chinese 116 W Second St	Casper	WY	82601	307-577-0618	
La Costa 1600 E Second St	Casper	WY	82601	307-235-6599	
Web: webs.com					
Mongolian Grill 4801 E Second St Ste 110	Casper	WY	82609	307-473-1033	
Poor Boys Steakhouse 739 N Ctr St	Casper	WY	82601	307-237-8325	
Web: poorboyssteakhouse.com					
Sanford's Grub & Pub 241 Ctr St	Casper	WY	82601	307-234-4555	
Web: thegrubandpub.com					
Silver Fox Restaurant & Lounge 3422 S Energy Ln	Casper	WY	82604	307-235-3000	
Web: www.silverfoxcasper.com					
Avanti 4620 Grandview Ave	Cheyenne	WY	82009	307-634-3432	
Web: avanticheyenne.com					
Casa de Trujillo 122 W Sixth St	Cheyenne	WY	82007	307-635-1227	
Good Friends 507 E Lincolnway	Cheyenne	WY	82001	307-778-7088	
Guadalajara 1745 Dell Range Blvd	Cheyenne	WY	82009	307-432-6803	
Korean House 3219 Snyder Ave	Cheyenne	WY	82001	307-638-7938	
Little Bear Inn 1700 Little Bear Rd	Cheyenne	WY	82009	307-634-3684	
Web: littlebearinn.com					
Renzios Greek Food 1400 Dell Range Blvd	Cheyenne	WY	82007	307-637-5411	
Web: renziosgreekfood.com					
T-Joe's Steakhouse & Saloon 12700 I-80 Service Rd	Cheyenne	WY	82009	307-634-8750	
Web: www.tjoessteakhouse.com					
Twin Dragons 1809 Carey Ave	Cheyenne	WY	82001	307-637-6622	
Bar-T-5 Covered Wagon Cook Out & Wild West Show 812 Cache Creek Dr	Jackson	WY	83001	307-733-5386	739-9183
TF: 800-772-5386 ■ *Web:* www.bart5.com					
Blue Lion Restaurant 160 N Millward St	Jackson	WY	83001	307-733-3912	
Web: www.bluelionrestaurant.com					
BonAppeThai 245 W Pearl St	Jackson	WY	83001	307-734-0245	
Web: bonappethai.com					
Bunnery Bakery & Restaurant, The 130 N Cache Dr	Jackson	WY	83001	307-733-5474	
Web: bunnery.com/restaurant2.php?					
Calico Restaurant & Bar Teton Village Rd	Jackson	WY	83014	307-733-2460	
Web: www.calicorestaurant.com					
Chinatown 850 W Broadway	Jackson	WY	83001	307-733-8856	
Gun Barrel Steak & Game House 862 W Broadway	Jackson	WY	83002	307-733-3287	733-6090
Web: www.gunbarrel.com					
Nikai Sushi 225 N Cache St PO Box 14250	Jackson	WY	83001	307-734-6490	734-6488
Web: www.nikaijh.com					
Ocean City 340 W Broadway	Jackson	WY	83001	307-734-9768	
Web: oceancitychinabistro.com					
Snake River Brewing Co 265 S Millward St	Jackson	WY	83001	307-739-2337	739-2296
Web: www.snakeriverbrewing.com					
Snake River Grill 84 E Broadway	Jackson	WY	83001	307-733-0557	
Web: www.snakerivergrill.com					
Sweetwater Restaurant 85 King St	Jackson	WY	83001	307-733-3553	
Web: sweetwaterjackson.com					
Thai Me Up 75 E Pearl St	Jackson	WY	83001	307-733-0005	
Web: www.thaijh.com					
Bubba's 100 Flat Creek Dr	Jackson Hole	WY	83001	307-733-2288	
Web: www.bubbasjh.com					
Mangy Moose PO Box 590	Teton Village	WY	83025	307-733-4913	
Web: mangymoose.com					

672 RETIREMENT COMMUNITIES

See Also Long-Term Care Facilities p. 2684

Listed here are senior communities where the majority of residents live independently but where nursing care and/or other personal care is available on-site. The listings in this category are organized alphabetically by state names.

	City	State	ZIP	Phone	Fax
Galleria Woods 3850 Galleria Woods Dr	Birmingham	AL	35244	205-206-6499	
Web: brookdale.com					
Westminster Village 500 Spanish Ft Blvd	Spanish Fort	AL	36527	251-626-2900	
Web: www.westminstervillageal.com					
Atria Campana del Rio 1550 E River Rd	Tucson	AZ	85718	520-299-1941	
Web: www.atriaseniorliving.com					
Atria Chandler Villas 101 S Yucca St	Chandler	AZ	85224	480-899-7650	
Web: www.atriaseniorliving.com					
Beatitudes Campus of Care 1610 W Glendale Ave	Phoenix	AZ	85021	602-995-2611	
Web: beatitudescampus.org					
Forum at Desert Harbor, The 13840 N Desert Harbor Dr	Peoria	AZ	85381	623-972-0995	796-8385*
**Fax Area Code:* 617 ■ *Web:* www.fivestarseniorliving.com/communities/az/peoria/the-forum-at-desert-harbor					
Forum at Tucson 2500 N Rosemont Blvd	Tucson	AZ	85712	520-325-4800	319-4076
Web: www.fivestarseniorliving.com/communities/az/tucson/the-forum-at-tucson					
Friendship Village of Tempe 2645 E Southern Ave	Tempe	AZ	85282	480-831-5000	
TF: 800-824-1112 ■ *Web:* www.friendshipvillageaz.com					
Glencroft 8611 N 67th Ave	Glendale	AZ	85302	623-939-9475	
Web: www.glencroft.com					
La Posada at Park Centre 350 E Morningside Rd	Green Valley	AZ	85614	520-648-8131	648-8397
Web: posadalife.org					
Terraces at Phoenix, The 7550 N 16th St	Phoenix	AZ	85020	602-906-4024	
TF: 800-836-4281 ■ *Web:* www.theterracesphoenix.com					
Butterfield Trail Village 1923 E Joyce Blvd	Fayetteville	AR	72703	479-442-7220	442-2019
Web: www.butterfieldtrailvillage.com					
H&H Total Care Services Inc 8382 156 St	Surrey	BC	V3S3R7	604-597-7931	
Web: www.hhtotalcare.com					
Atherton Baptist Homes 214 S Atlantic Blvd	Alhambra	CA	91801	626-863-1224	
TF: 800-340-4178 ■ *Web:* www.abh.org					
Atria Rancho Park 801 Cypress Way	San Dimas	CA	91773	626-275-4376	
Web: atriaranchopark.com					
Bixby Knolls Towers 3737 Atlantic Ave	Long Beach	CA	90807	562-426-6123	426-2571
Web: www.bixbyknollstowers.org					
Carmel Valley Manor 8545 Carmel Vly Rd	Carmel	CA	93923	831-624-1281	622-4543
TF: 800-544-5546 ■ *Web:* www.cvmanor.com					
Casa Dorinda 300 Hot Springs Rd	Santa Barbara	CA	93108	805-969-8011	969-8686
Web: casadorinda.org					
Castle Hill Retirement Village 3575 N Moorpark Rd	Thousand Oaks	CA	91360	805-492-2471	492-7431
Channing House 850 Webster St	Palo Alto	CA	94301	650-327-0950	
Web: www.channinghouse.org					
Covenant Village of Turlock 2125 N Olive Ave	Turlock	CA	95382	209-216-5610	565-3809*
**Fax Area Code:* 617 ■ *TF:* 800-485-7844 ■ *Web:* www.covenantvillageofturlock.org					
Eskaton Inc 5105 Manzanita Ave	Carmichael	CA	95608	916-334-0810	338-1248
Web: www.eskaton.org					
Eskaton Village 3939 Walnut Ave	Carmichael	CA	95608	916-974-2000	974-2022
TF: 800-300-3929 ■ *Web:* www.eskaton.org					
Freedom Village 23442 El Toro Rd	Lake Forest	CA	92630	949-472-4700	
TF: 800-584-8084 ■ *Web:* www.freedomvillage.org					
Grand Lake Gardens 401 Santa Clara Ave	Oakland	CA	94610	800-416-6091	
TF: 800-416-6091 ■ *Web:* www.grandlakegardens.com					
Hillcrest Convalescent Hospital Inc 3401 Cedar Ave	Long Beach	CA	90807	562-426-4461	
Web: www.hillcrestcare.com					
Hillcrest Homes 2705 Mtn View Dr	La Verne	CA	91750	909-392-4375	
Web: www.livingathillcrest.org					
Lake Park Retirement Residences 1850 Alice St	Oakland	CA	94612	510-835-5511	
TF: 866-384-3130 ■ *Web:* www.lakeparkretirement.org					
Los Gatos Meadows 110 Wood Rd	Los Gatos	CA	95030	408-354-0211	354-4193
Web: jtm-esc.org/lgm/index					

	City	State	ZIP	Phone	Fax
Morningside of Fullerton 800 Morningside Dr *TF:* 800-803-7597 ■ *Web:* www.morningsideoffullerton.com	Fullerton	CA	92835	714-256-8000	
Mount Miguel Covenant Village 325 Kempton St **Fax Area Code:* 617 ■ *Web:* www.mountmiguelcovenantvillage.org	Spring Valley	CA	91977	619-479-4790	565-3809*
O'Connor Woods 3400 Wagner Heights Rd *TF:* 800-957-3308 ■ *Web:* www.oconnorwoods.org	Stockton	CA	95209	209-956-3400	
Park Lane, The 200 Glenwood Cir *Web:* www.srgseniorliving.com/communities/monterey-ca-park-lane	Monterey	CA	93940	831-250-6159	
Peninsula Regent, The 1 Baldwin Ave *Web:* www.peninsularegent.com	San Mateo	CA	94401	650-579-5500	579-0446
People Creating Success Inc 2225 Sprerry Dr Ste 1500 *Web:* www.pcs-services.org	Ventura	CA	93003	805-644-9480	
Peppermint Ridge Inc 825 Magnolia Ave *Web:* peppermintridge.org	Corona	CA	92879	951-273-7320	
Piedmont Gardens 110 41st St *TF:* 800-496-8126 ■ *Web:* www.piedmontgardens.com	Oakland	CA	94611	510-596-2600	
Plymouth Village 900 Salem Dr *TF:* 800-391-4552 ■ *Web:* www.plymouthvillage.org	Redlands	CA	92373	909-793-9195	
Quaker Gardens 12151 Dale St **Fax:* Mktg ■ *Web:* rowntreegardens.org	Stanton	CA	90680	714-530-9100	530-0945*
Regents Point 19191 Harvard Ave **Fax Area Code:* 818 ■ *TF General:* 800-347-3735 ■ *Web:* www.thebegroup.org	Irvine	CA	92612	949-988-0849	247-3871*
Remington Club 16925 Hierba Dr *Web:* www.fivestarseniorliving.com/communities/ca/san-diego/the-remington-club	San Diego	CA	92128	858-673-6340	673-6318
Rosewood Retirement Community 1301 New Stine Rd *TF:* 800-984-4216 ■ *Web:* www.rosewoodretirement.org	Bakersfield	CA	93309	661-834-0620	
Samarkand, The 2550 Treasure Dr *Web:* thesamarkand.org	Santa Barbara	CA	93105	805-687-0701	687-3386
San Joaquin Gardens 5555 N Fresno St *Web:* theterracesatsanjoaquin.com	Fresno	CA	93710	559-435-1999	
Sequoias Portola Valley, The *Northern California Presbyterian Homes & Services* 501 Portola Rd *Web:* www.ncphs.org	Portola Valley	CA	94028	650-851-1501	851-5007
Sequoias San Francisco 1400 Geary Blvd *Web:* www.ncphs.org	San Francisco	CA	94109	415-922-9700	567-2576
Smith Ranch Homes 400 Deer Vly Rd Ste L *TF:* 800-772-6264 ■ *Web:* www.smithranchhomes.com	San Rafael	CA	94903	415-491-4918	491-0254
Solheim Lutheran Home (SLH) 2236 Merton Ave *TF:* 888-257-7518 ■ *Web:* www.solheimlutheran.org	Los Angeles	CA	90041	323-257-7518	255-3544
Spring Lake Village 5555 Montgomery Dr *TF:* 800-795-1267 ■ *Web:* jtm-esc.org	Santa Rosa	CA	95409	707-538-8400	
Tamalpais, The 501 Via Casitas *Web:* www.ncphs.org	Greenbrae	CA	94904	415-461-2300	461-0241
Terraces at Los Altos, The 2478 W El Camino Real *Web:* www.theterracesatlosaltos.com	Mountain View	CA	94040	650-917-9661	
Terraces of Los Gatos 800 Blossom Hill Rd *TF:* 800-673-1982 ■ *Web:* www.theterracesoflosgatos.com	Los Gatos	CA	95032	408-356-1006	
Valle Verde 900 Calle de los Amigos *TF:* 800-750-5089 ■ *Web:* www.valleverde.org	Santa Barbara	CA	93105	805-883-4000	
Villa Gardens 842 E Villa St *TF:* 800-958-4552 ■ *Web:* www.villagardens.org	Pasadena	CA	91101	626-463-5330	
Villa Marin 100 Thorndale Dr *TF:* 888-926-2030 ■ *Web:* www.villa-marin.com	San Rafael	CA	94903	415-492-2408	
Villa Valencia 24552 Paseo de Valencia *Web:* www.fivestarseniorliving.com/communities/ca/laguna-hills/villa-valencia	Laguna Hills	CA	92653	949-581-6111	837-1082
Village, The 2200 W Acacia Ave *TF:* 800-257-7888 ■ *Web:* thevillageriversidecounty.com	Hemet	CA	92545	951-658-3369	
Vista del Monte 3775 Modoc Rd *TF:* 800-736-1333 ■ *Web:* www.vistadelmonte.org	Santa Barbara	CA	93105	805-687-0793	
White Sands of La Jolla 516 Burchett St *TF:* 800-347-3735 ■ *Web:* www.thebegroup.org	Glendale	CA	92037	818-247-0420	247-3871
Heritage Club 2020 S Monroe St *TF:* 888-221-7317 ■ *Web:* brookdale.com/heritage-club-denver.aspx	Denver	CO	80210	303-758-3017	
Parkplace 111 Emerson St *Web:* brookdale.com/parkplace-.aspx	Denver	CO	80218	303-744-0400	
Villa Pueblo Towers 2501 E 104th Ave *Web:* centuraseniors.org	Thornton	CO	80233	303-255-4100	
Arbors of Hop Brook 403 W Ctr St *Web:* www.arborsct.com	Manchester	CT	06040	860-647-9343	
Covenant Village of Cromwell & Pilgrim Manor 52 Missionary Rd *Web:* www.covenantvillageofcromwell.org	Cromwell	CT	06416	860-635-2690	632-2407
Duncaster 40 Loeffler Rd *Web:* www.duncaster.org	Bloomfield	CT	06002	860-380-5006	242-8004
Elim Park Place 140 Cook Hill Rd *TF:* 800-994-1776 ■ *Web:* www.elimpark.org	Cheshire	CT	06410	203-272-3547	
Essex Meadows 30 Bokum Rd *TF:* 866-721-4838 ■ *Web:* www.essexmeadows.com	Essex	CT	06426	860-767-7201	
Evergreen Woods 88 Notch Hill Rd *TF General:* 866-413-6378 ■ *Web:* evergreenwoods.com	North Branford	CT	06471	203-488-8000	
Pomperaug Woods 80 Heritage Rd *TF:* 866-817-8935 ■ *Web:* www.pomperaugwoods.com	Southbury	CT	06488	203-262-6555	
Watermark at 3030 Park, The 3030 Pk Ave *Web:* www.watermarkcommunities.com/3030park	Bridgeport	CT	06604	203-502-7593	374-2871
Whitney Ctr 200 Leeder Hill Dr *TF:* 800-237-3847 ■ *Web:* www.whitneycenter.com	Hamden	CT	06517	203-848-2641	
Cokesbury Village 726 Loveville Rd *TF:* 800-530-2377 ■ *Web:* actsretirement.org	Hockessin	DE	19707	302-235-6000	
Methodist Country House 4830 Kennett Pk *TF:* 800-976-7610 ■ *Web:* www.actsretirement.org	Wilmington	DE	19807	302-654-5101	
Methodist Manor House 1001 Middleford Rd *TF:* 800-775-4593 ■ *Web:* www.actsretirement.org	Seaford	DE	19973	302-629-4593	
Stonegates 4031 Kennett Pk *Web:* www.stonegates.com	Greenville	DE	19807	302-658-6200	658-1510
Westminster Village 1175 Mckee Rd *Web:* www.presbyterianseniorliving.org	Dover	DE	19904	302-744-3600	
Ingleside Rock Creek 3050 Military Rd NW *Web:* www.ircdc.org	Washington	DC	20015	202-363-8310	
Knollwood 6200 Oregon Ave NW *TF:* 800-541-4255 ■ *Web:* www.armydistaff.org	Washington	DC	20015	202-541-0400	
Abbey Delray 2000 Lowson Blvd *TF:* 888-791-9363 ■ *Web:* lifespacecommunities.com/senior-living-delray-beach/ad	Delray Beach	FL	33445	561-454-2000	
Atria Meridian Assisted Living Community 3061 Donnelly Dr *Web:* www.atriaseniorliving.com	Lantana	FL	33462	561-902-1085	
Bay Village 8400 Vamo Rd *Web:* www.bayvillage.org	Sarasota	FL	34231	941-966-5611	966-4040
Covenant Village of Florida 9215 W Broward Blvd *Web:* www.covenantretirement.org	Plantation	FL	33324	954-472-2860	
East Ridge Retirement Village 19301 SW 87th Ave *Web:* www.eastridgeatcutlerbay.com	Miami	FL	33157	786-842-4596	
Edgewater Pointe Estates 23315 Blue Water Cir *TF General:* 888-339-2287 ■ *Web:* www.actsretirement.org	Boca Raton	FL	33433	561-391-6305	
Fleet Landing Retirement Community 1 Fleet Landing Blvd *TF General:* 877-591-6547 ■ *Web:* www.fleetlanding.com	Atlantic Beach	FL	32233	904-246-9900	246-9900
Florida Presbyterian Homes 16 Lk Hunter Dr *TF:* 866-294-3352 ■ *Web:* www.fphi.org	Lakeland	FL	33803	863-688-5521	
Gulf Coast Village 1333 Santa Barbara Blvd *Web:* www.gulfcoastvillage.com	Cape Coral	FL	33991	239-772-1333	
Harbour's Edge 401 E Linton Blvd *TF:* 888-417-9281 ■ *Web:* lifespacecommunities.com/senior-living-delray-beach/he	Delray Beach	FL	33483	561-272-7979	
Indian River Estates 2250 Indian Creek Blvd W *TF Mktg:* 800-544-0277 ■ *Web:* www.actsretirement.org	Vero Beach	FL	32966	772-562-7400	
John Knox Village 651 SW Sixth St **Fax Area Code:* 954 ■ *TF:* 800-998-5669 ■ *Web:* www.johnknoxvillage.com	Pompano Beach	FL	33060	800-998-5669	782-4044*
Lake Seminole Square 8333 Seminole Blvd *TF:* 866-785-9025 ■ *Web:* brookdale.com/lake-seminole-square.aspx	Seminole	FL	33772	727-228-7312	
Mayflower Retirement Community 1620 Mayflower Ct *TF:* 800-228-6518 ■ *Web:* www.themayflower.com	Winter Park	FL	32792	407-672-1620	671-6336
Mease Manor Retirement Living 700 Mease Plz *Web:* www.measemanor.com	Dunedin	FL	34698	727-738-3000	
Moorings Park 120 Moorings Pk Dr *TF:* 866-802-4302 ■ *Web:* www.mooringspark.org	Naples	FL	34105	239-643-9111	262-7040
Palace Renaissance & Royale 11355 SW 84th St *Web:* www.thepalace.org	Miami	FL	33173	305-270-7000	
Park Summit of Coral Springs 8500 Royal Palm Blvd *Web:* www.fivestarseniorliving.com/communities/fl/coral-springs/park-summit	Coral Springs	FL	33065	954-752-9500	755-9559
Plymouth Harbor 700 John Ringling Blvd *Web:* www.plymouthharbor.org	Sarasota	FL	34236	941-365-2600	
Saint Andrews Estates 6152 Verde Trail N *TF Mktg:* 866-897-3490 ■ *Web:* www.actsretirement.org	Boca Raton	FL	33433	561-487-4728	
Saint Mark Village 2655 Nebraska Ave *Web:* www.stmarkvillage.com	Palm Harbor	FL	34684	727-785-2580	
Sarasota-Manatee Jewish Housing Council Inc 1951 N Honore Ave *Web:* www.kobernickanchin.org	Sarasota	FL	34235	941-377-0781	
Shell Point Village 15101 Shell Pt Blvd *TF Mktg:* 800-780-1131 ■ *Web:* www.shellpoint.org	Fort Myers	FL	33908	239-466-1131	
Stratford Court 45 Katherine Blvd *TF:* 888-434-4648 ■ *Web:* www.sunriseseniorliving.com	Palm Harbor	FL	34684	727-787-1500	
Village on the Green 500 Village Pl *TF Mktg:* 888-541-3443 ■ *Web:* lifespacecommunities.com/senior-living-orlando	Longwood	FL	32779	407-682-0230	
Waterford, The 601 Universe Blvd *TF:* 888-335-1678 ■ *Web:* lifespacecommunities.com/senior-living-juno-beach	Juno Beach	FL	33408	561-627-3800	
Westminster Bradenton Manor 1700 21st Ave W *TF:* 877-382-9036 ■ *Web:* www.westminsterretirement.com	Bradenton	FL	34205	941-748-4161	
Westminster Oaks 4449 Meandering Way *TF:* 800-948-1881 ■ *Web:* www.westminsterretirement.com	Tallahassee	FL	32308	850-878-1136	
Westminster Towers 80 W Lucerne Cir *TF:* 877-382-9036 ■ *Web:* www.westminsterretirement.com	Orlando	FL	32801	407-841-1310	
Clairmont Place 2100 Clairmont Lake *Web:* clairmontplace.com	Decatur	GA	30033	404-633-8875	633-9417
Arcadia Retirement Residence 1434 Punahou St *Web:* arcadia.org/companies/arcadia	Honolulu	HI	96822	808-941-0941	949-4965
Admiral at the Lake 929 W Foster *Web:* admiral.kendal.org	Chicago	IL	60640	773-433-1800	
Birchwood Plaza 1426 W Birchwood *Web:* www.birchwoodplaza.com	Chicago	IL	60626	773-274-4405	
Church Creek 1250 W Central Rd *Web:* www.sunriseseniorliving.com	Arlington Heights	IL	60005	847-506-3200	
Clark-Lindsey Village 101 W Windsor Rd *TF:* 800-998-2581 ■ *Web:* www.clark-lindsey.com	Urbana	IL	61802	217-344-2144	
Covenant Retirement Communities Inc 5700 Old OrchaRd Rd *Web:* www.covenantretirement.org	Skokie	IL	60077	773-878-2294	
Friendship Manor 1209 21st Ave *TF:* 888-382-1222 ■ *Web:* www.friendshipmanor.org	Rock Island	IL	61201	309-786-9667	786-5611
Hallmark, The 2960 N Lk Shore Dr *Web:* brookdale.com	Chicago	IL	60657	773-880-2960	
Holmstad, The 700 W Fabyan Pkwy *Web:* www.covenantretirement.org	Batavia	IL	60510	630-879-4100	
Oak Crest DeKalb Area Retirement Ctr 2944 Greenwood Acres Dr *Web:* www.oakcrestdekalb.org	DeKalb	IL	60115	815-756-8461	
Providence Life Services 18601 N Creek Dr *TF:* 800-509-2800 ■ *Web:* www.providencelifeservices.com	Tinley Park	IL	60477	708-342-8100	342-8000

	City	State	Zip	Phone	Fax
Senior Lifestyle Corp 303 E Upper Wacker Dr Ste 2400 *Web:* www.seniorlifestyle.com	Chicago	IL	60601	312-673-4333	
Vi 71 S Wacker Dr *TF:* 800-421-1442 ■ *Web:* www.viliving.com	Chicago	IL	60606	312-803-8800	
Westminster Place 3200 Grant St *TF:* 888-285-3233 ■ *Web:* www.presbyterianhomes.org	Evanston	IL	60201	847-570-3422	
Westminster Village 2025 E Lincoln St *Web:* westminstervillageinc.com	Bloomington	IL	61701	309-663-6474	
Damar Services Inc 6067 Decatur Blvd *Web:* www.damar.org	Indianapolis	IN	46241	317-856-5201	
Four Seasons Retirement Ctr 1901 Taylor Rd *Web:* www.fourseasonsretirement.com	Columbus	IN	47203	812-372-8481	378-6184
Greencroft Retirement Communities Inc 1721 Greencroft Blvd *Web:* www.greencroft.org	Goshen	IN	46527	574-537-4000	
Greenwood Village South 295 Village Ln *Web:* www.greenwoodvillagesouth.com	Greenwood	IN	46143	317-881-2591	881-1299
Hoosier Village 5300 W 96th St *Web:* www.hoosiervillage.com	Indianapolis	IN	46268	317-873-3349	
Lutheran Life Villages 6701 S Anthony Blvd *Web:* www.lutheranlifevillages.org	Fort Wayne	IN	46816	260-447-1591	447-7369
Marquette 8140 Township Line Rd *Web:* www.marquetteseniorliving.org	Indianapolis	IN	46260	317-875-9700	
Meadowood Retirement Community 2455 Tamarack Trl *Web:* www.fivestarseniorliving.com/communities/in/bloomington/meadowood	Bloomington	IN	47408	812-336-7060	333-8917
Towne House, The 2209 St Joe Ctr Rd *Web:* www.townehouse.org	Fort Wayne	IN	46825	260-483-3116	969-8072
Wesley Manor 1555 N Main St *Web:* www.wesleymanor.org	Frankfort	IN	46041	765-659-1811	654-5596
Westminster Village 1120 E Davis Dr *Web:* www.westminstervillagein.com	Terre Haute	IN	47802	812-232-7533	
Friendship Village 600 Pk Ln *Web:* www.friendshipvillageiowa.com	Waterloo	IA	50702	319-291-8100	
Lifespace Communities Inc 100 E Grand Ave Ste 200 *Web:* www.lifespacecommunities.com	Des Moines	IA	50309	515-288-5805	
Meth-Wick Community 1224 13th St NW *Web:* www.methwick.org	Cedar Rapids	IA	52405	319-365-9171	
Western Home Communities 420 E 11th St *Web:* www.westernhomecommunities.org	Cedar Falls	IA	50613	319-277-2141	268-8338
Aldersgate Village 7220 SW Asbury Dr *Web:* www.aldersgatevillage.org	Topeka	KS	66614	785-478-9440	478-9104
Brewster Place 1205 SW 29th St *Web:* brewsterliving.org	Topeka	KS	66611	785-274-3350	
Delmar Gardens of Lenexa Inc 9701 Monrovia St *Web:* www.delmargardens.com	Lenexa	KS	66215	913-492-1130	
Kansas Christian Home 1035 SE Third St *Web:* kschristianhome.org	Newton	KS	67114	316-283-6600	283-6375
Larksfield Place 7373 E 29th St N *TF:* 866-232-8484 ■ *Web:* www.larksfieldplace.org	Wichita	KS	67226	316-858-3910	636-5790
Mennonite Friendship Communities 600 W Blanchard Rd *Web:* www.mennofriend.com	South Hutchinson	KS	67505	620-663-7175	
Prairie Mission Retirement Village 242 Carroll St *Web:* www.pmrv.com	Saint Paul	KS	66771	620-449-2400	
Wesley Towers 700 Monterey Pl *TF:* 888-663-9175 ■ *Web:* www.wesleytowers.com	Hutchinson	KS	67502	620-663-9175	
Forum at Brookside 200 Brookside Dr *Web:* www.fivestarseniorliving.com/communities/ky/louisville/the-forum-at-brookside	Louisville	KY	40243	502-245-3048	244-6327*
Treyton Oak Towers 211 W Oak St *Web:* www.treytonoaktowers.com	Louisville	KY	40203	502-589-3211	
Seniorsplus 8 Falcon Rd *TF:* 800-427-1241 ■ *Web:* www.seniorsplus.org	Lewiston	ME	04243	207-795-4010	795-4009
Asbury Methodist Village 201 Russell Ave *TF:* 800-327-2879 ■ *Web:* www.asburymethodistvillage.org	Gaithersburg	MD	20877	301-216-4100	
Bedford Court 3701 International Dr *Web:* www.sunriseseniorliving.com	Silver Spring	MD	20906	301-598-2900	
Broadmead 13801 York Rd *Web:* www.broadmead.org	Cockeysville	MD	21030	410-527-1900	
Carroll Lutheran Village 300 St Luke Cir *TF:* 877-848-0095 ■ *Web:* www.carrolllutheranvillage.org	Westminster	MD	21158	410-848-0090	848-8133
Charlestown Retirement Community (CCI) 715 Maiden Choice Ln *TF:* 800-917-8649 ■ *Web:* ericksonliving.com/catonsville/catonsville-senior-living.asp	Catonsville	MD	21228	410-242-2880	
Collington Episcopal Community 10450 Lottsford Rd **Fax Area Code:* 301 ■ *TF:* 888-257-9468 ■ *Web:* collington.kendal.org	Mitchellville	MD	20721	888-257-9468	925-7357*
Edenwald 800 Southerly Rd *Web:* www.edenwald.org	Baltimore	MD	21286	410-339-6000	583-8786
Fairhaven 7200 Third Ave *Web:* www.fairhavenccrc.org	Sykesville	MD	21784	410-795-8801	
Ginger Cove 4000 River Crescent Dr *TF:* 800-299-2683 ■ *Web:* www.gingercove.com	Annapolis	MD	21401	410-266-7300	
Glen Meadows 11630 Glen Arm Rd *TF:* 800-630-4689 ■ *Web:* www.presbyterianseniorliving.org/glen-meadows-retirement-community	Glen Arm	MD	21057	800-630-4689	
Heron Point of Chestertown 501 E Campus Ave *TF:* 800-327-9138 ■ *Web:* www.actsretirement.org	Chestertown	MD	21620	410-778-7300	810-2915
Homewood at Williamsport 16505 Virginia Ave *TF:* 877-849-9244 ■ *Web:* www.homewood.com	Williamsport	MD	21795	301-582-1750	582-1819
Roland Park Place 830 W 40th St *Web:* www.rolandparkplace.org	Baltimore	MD	21211	410-243-5700	243-4929
Brookhaven at Lexington 1010 Waltham St *Web:* www.aboutbrookhaven.org	Lexington	MA	02421	781-863-9660	
Carleton-Willard Village (CWV) 100 Old Billerica Rd *Web:* www.cwvillage.org	Bedford	MA	01730	781-275-8700	275-5787
Epoch Senior Living 51 Sawyer Rd Ste 500 *TF:* 877-376-2475 ■ *Web:* www.epochsl.com	Waltham	MA	02453	781-891-0777	891-0774
Fox Hill Village 10 Longwood Dr *Web:* foxhillvillage.com	Westwood	MA	02090	781-329-4433	461-2464
Loomis Communities 246 N Main St *TF:* 800-865-7655 ■ *Web:* www.loomiscommunities.org	South Hadley	MA	01075	413-532-5325	532-8676
Minuteman Senior Services 26 Crosby Dr *Web:* www.minutemansenior.org	Bedford	MA	01730	781-272-7177	
New Pond Village 180 Main St *Web:* www.norwoodma.brightviewseniorliving.com	Walpole	MA	02081	508-660-1555	668-8893
Willows, The 1 Lyman St *TF:* 800-464-8060 ■ *Web:* www.salmonhealth.com	Westborough	MA	01581	508-366-4730	898-3982
Friendship Village Kalamazoo 1400 N Drake Rd *TF:* 800-613-3984 ■ *Web:* www.friendshipvillagemi.com	Kalamazoo	MI	49006	269-381-0560	
Glacier Hills 1200 Earhart Rd *Web:* www.glacierhills.org	Ann Arbor	MI	48105	734-769-6410	769-3092
Marycrest Manor 15475 Middlebelt Rd *Web:* www.marycrestmanor.com	Livonia	MI	48154	734-427-9175	
Michigan Masonic Home 1200 Wright Ave *Web:* masonicpathways.com	Alma	MI	48801	989-463-3141	
Porter Hills 3600 E Fulton St *Web:* www.porterhills.org	Grand Rapids	MI	49546	616-949-4971	954-1795
Presbyterian Villages Of Michigan 25300 W Six Mile Rd *Web:* www.pvm.org	Redford	MI	48240	313-537-0000	
Vista Grande Villa 2251 Springport Rd *TF:* 800-889-8499 ■ *Web:* www.vistagrandevilla.com	Jackson	MI	49202	517-787-0222	787-6909
Covenant Village of Golden Valley 5800 St Croix Ave **Fax Area Code:* 617 ■ *TF:* 877-224-5051 ■ *Web:* www.covenantvillageofgoldenvalley.org	Minneapolis	MN	55422	763-546-6125	565-3809*
Friendship Village 8100 Highwood Dr *Web:* lifespacecommunities.com/senior-living-bloomington	Bloomington	MN	55438	952-831-7500	
Armed Forces Retirement Home - Gulfport 1800 Beach Dr **Fax Area Code:* 202 ■ *TF:* 800-422-9988 ■ *Web:* www.afrh.gov	Gulfport	MS	39507	800-422-9988	541-7519*
Methodist Senior Services 300 Airline Rd **Fax Area Code:* 601 ■ *Web:* www.mss.org	Columbus	MS	39702	662-327-6716	482-5567*
Beauvais Manor On The Park 3625 Magnolia Ave *Web:* www.beauvaismanor.com	Saint Louis	MO	63110	314-771-2990	
Bishop Spencer Place Redevelopment Corp 4301 Madison Ave *Web:* www.bishopspencerplace.org	Kansas City	MO	64111	816-931-4277	
Friendship Village of South County 12503 Village Cir Dr *Web:* www.friendshipvillagestl.com	Saint Louis	MO	63127	314-842-6840	525-7500
General Baptist Nursing Home US Hwy 62 W *Web:* generalbaptisthealthcare.com	Campbell	MO	63933	573-246-2155	
Kingswood Senior Living Community 10000 Wornall Rd **Fax:* Sales ■ *TF Sales:* 888-942-2715 ■ *Web:* kingswoodretirementliving.com	Kansas City	MO	64114	816-942-0994	942-2455*
Mother of Good Counsel Home 6825 Natural Bridge Rd *Web:* mogch.org	St. Louis	MO	63121	314-383-4765	
Parkside Meadows Retirement Community 2150 W Randolph St	Saint Charles	MO	63301	636-946-4966	940-0214
Village North Retirement Community 11160 Village N Dr *Web:* www.bethesdahealth.org/communities/10/village-north-retirement-community	Saint Louis	MO	63136	314-355-8010	
Eastmont Towers 6315 'O' St *Web:* www.eastmonttowers.com	Lincoln	NE	68510	402-486-2281	
Northfield Villa & Residency *Villa & Vista, The* 2550 21st St *Web:* www.northfieldretirement.net	Gering	NE	69341	308-436-3101	436-3493
Skyline Retirement Community 7300 Graceland Dr # 120B *Web:* skylinerc.com	Omaha	NE	68134	402-572-5750	
Havenwood-Heritage Heights Havenwood Campus 33 Christian Ave *TF:* 800-457-6833 ■ *Web:* www.hhhinfo.com	Concord	NH	03301	603-224-5363	
Kendal at Hanover 80 Lyme Rd *Web:* kah.kendal.org	Hanover	NH	03755	603-643-8900	643-7099
RiverMead Retirement Community 150 RiverMead Rd *TF:* 800-200-5433 ■ *Web:* rivermead.org	Peterborough	NH	03458	603-924-0062	
Cadbury Retirement Community 2150 Rt 38 *TF:* 800-422-3287 ■ *Web:* www.cadbury.org	Cherry Hill	NJ	08002	856-667-4550	667-3653
Crestwood Manor 50 Lacey Rd *TF General:* 877-467-1652 ■ *Web:* www.crestwoodmanoronline.org	Whiting	NJ	08759	732-849-4900	
Evergreens, The 309 Bridgeboro Rd *TF:* 877-673-8234 ■ *Web:* www.evergreens.org	Moorestown	NJ	08057	856-439-2000	
Franciscan Oaks 19 Pocono Rd *TF:* 800-237-3330 ■ *Web:* www.franciscanoaks.com	Denville	NJ	07834	973-586-6000	586-6030
Harrogate 400 Locust St *TF:* 888-551-5531 ■ *Web:* harrogatelifecare.org	Lakewood	NJ	08701	732-905-7070	905-4059
Medford Leas 1 Medford Leas Way *TF:* 800-331-4302 ■ *Web:* www.medfordleas.org	Medford	NJ	08055	609-654-3000	
New Jersey Firemen's Home 565 Lathrop Ave *Web:* www.njfh.org	Boonton	NJ	07005	973-334-0024	
La Vida Llena 10501 Lagrima de Oro NE *TF:* 800-922-1344 ■ *Web:* www.lavidallena.com	Albuquerque	NM	87111	505-293-4001	
Montebello on Academy, The 10500 Academy Rd NE *Web:* www.fivestarseniorliving.com/communities/nm/albuquerque/the-montebello-on-academy	Albuquerque	NM	87111	505-294-9944	294-1808
Andrus on Hudson 185 Old Broadway *Web:* andrusonhudson.org	Hastings On Hudson	NY	10706	914-478-3700	478-3541
Fountains at Millbrook, The 79 Flint Rd *Web:* www.watermarkcommunities.com	Millbrook	NY	12545	845-605-4457	
Freedom Village 5275 Rt 14 PO Box 24 *TF:* 800-842-8679 ■ *Web:* freedomvillageusa.com/1.4.html	Lakemont	NY	14857	607-243-8126	

	City	State	Zip	Phone	Fax
Kendal at Ithaca 2230 N Triphammer Rd TF: 800-253-6325 ■ Web: www.kai.kendal.org	Ithaca	NY	14850	607-266-5300	266-5353
People Inc 1219 N Forest Rd Web: www.people-inc.org	Williamsville	NY	14231	716-634-8132	
Arbor Acres 1240 Arbor Rd TF: 866-658-2724 ■ Web: www.arboracres.org	Winston-Salem	NC	27104	336-724-7921	
Bermuda Village 142 Bermuda Village Dr. TF Mktg: 800-843-5433 ■ Web: www.bermudavillage.net	Advance	NC	27006	800-843-5433	
Carol Woods Retirement Community 750 Weaver Dairy Rd TF: 800-518-9333 ■ Web: carolwoods.org	Chapel Hill	NC	27514	919-968-4511	
Carolina Meadows 100 Carolina Meadows TF: 800-458-6756 ■ Web: www.carolinameadows.org	Chapel Hill	NC	27517	919-942-4014	
Carolina Village 600 Carolina Village Rd Web: www.carolinavillage.com	Hendersonville	NC	28792	828-692-6275	
Covenant Village 1351 Robinwood Rd.	Gastonia	NC	28054	704-867-2319	861-8893
Deerfield Episcopal Retirement Community 1617 Hendersonville Rd TF: 800-284-1531 ■ Web: www.deerfieldwnc.org	Asheville	NC	28803	828-274-1531	274-0238
Forest at Duke 2701 Pickett Rd. TF: 800-474-0258 ■ Web: www.forestduke.org	Durham	NC	27705	919-490-8000	490-0887
Pines at Davidson 400 Avinger Ln TF: 877-574-8203 ■ Web: www.thepinesatdavidson.org	Davidson	NC	28036	704-896-1100	
Sharon Towers 5100 Sharon Rd Web: www.sharontowers.org	Charlotte	NC	28210	704-553-1670	
Springmoor Life Care Retirement Community 1500 Sawmill Rd Web: www.springmoor.org	Raleigh	NC	27615	919-848-7000	
Ability Center of Greater Toledo Inc 5605 Monroe St TF: 866-885-5733 ■ Web: www.abilitycenter.org	Sylvania	OH	43560	419-885-5733	
Breckenridge Village 36851 Ridge Rd Web: www.oprs.org	Willoughby	OH	44094	440-942-4342	
First Community Village 1800 Riverside Dr TF: 877-364-2570 ■ Web: www.nationalchurchresidences.org	Columbus	OH	43212	614-324-4455	
Friendship Village of columbus 5800 Forest Hills Blvd Web: www.fvcolumbus.org	Columbus	OH	43231	614-890-8282	890-2661
Hilltop Village 25900 Euclid Ave. Web: www.hilltopvillage.com	Euclid	OH	44132	216-261-8383	261-6816
Kendal at Oberlin 600 Kendal Dr *Fax Area Code: 440 ■ TF Mktg: 800-548-9469 ■ Web: www.kao.kendal.org	Oberlin	OH	44074	800-548-9469	775-9880*
Laurel Lake Retirement Community 200 Laurel Lk Dr. *Fax Area Code: 330 ■ TF: 866-650-2100 ■ Web: laurellake.org	Hudson	OH	44236	866-650-2100	655-1738*
Maple Knoll Communities Inc 11100 Springfield Pk TF: 800-272-3900 ■ Web: www.mapleknoll.org	Cincinnati	OH	45246	513-782-2400	
Methodist ElderCare Services 5155 N High St TF: 855-636-2225 ■ Web: www.wesleyridge.com/wesleyglen_home.aspx	Columbus	OH	43214	614-396-4990	436-6012
Otterbein Retirement Living Communities 580 N SR 741 TF: 888-513-9131 ■ Web: www.otterbein.org	Lebanon	OH	45036	513-933-5400	932-1054
Renaissance, The 26376 John Rd	Olmsted Township	OH	44138	440-235-7100	235-7115
Rockynol Retirement Community 1150 W Market St Web: www.oprs.org	Akron	OH	44313	330-867-2150	
Twin Towers 5343 Hamilton Ave Web: lec.org	Cincinnati	OH	45224	513-853-2000	853-2703
Westlake Village 28550 Westlake Village Dr TF: 855-308-2432	Westlake	OH	44145	855-308-2432	
Westminster-Thurber Community 717 Neil Ave Web: www.westminsterthurber.org	Columbus	OH	43215	614-228-8888	
Corn Heritage Village 106 W Adams St Apt 1 Web: cornheritage.org	Corn	OK	73024	580-343-2295	
Golden Oaks Village 5801 N Oakwood Rd TF: 800-259-0914 ■ Web: www.goldenoaks.com	Enid	OK	73703	580-249-2600	
Montereau Inc 6800 S Granite Ave Web: www.montereau.net	Tulsa	OK	74136	918-495-1500	
Spanish Cove 11 Palm Ave TF: 800-965-2683 ■ Web: www.spanishcove.com	Yukon	OK	73099	800-965-2683	
Kingsway Arms Retirement Residences Inc 208 Evans Ave Ste 115 Web: retirementliving.kingswayarms.com	Toronto	ON	M8Z1J7	647-288-2942	
Capital Manor 1955 Dallas Hwy NW Web: www.capitalmanor.com	Salem	OR	97304	503-967-3086	371-9021
Friendsview Retirement Community 1301 E Fulton St TF: 866-307-4371 ■ Web: friendsview.org	Newberg	OR	97132	503-538-3144	538-6371
Mennonite Village 5353 Columbus St SE TF: 866-453-4930 ■ Web: www.mennonitevillage.org	Albany	OR	97322	541-928-7232	917-1399
Rogue Valley Manor 1200 Mira Mar Ave TF: 800-848-7868 ■ Web: www.retirement.org/rvm	Medford	OR	97504	541-857-7214	857-7599
Willamette View 12705 SE River Rd TF: 800-446-0670 ■ Web: www.willametteview.org	Portland	OR	97222	503-654-6581	
Arbutus Park Retirement Community 207 Ottawa St Web: arbutusparkmanor.com	Johnstown	PA	15904	814-266-8621	
Beaumont at Bryn Mawr 601 N Ithan Ave Web: www.beaumontretirement.com	Bryn Mawr	PA	19010	610-526-7000	525-0293
Bethany Village 325 Wesley Dr Web: www.bethanyvillage.org	Mechanicsburg	PA	17055	717-766-0279	
Brittany Pointe Estates 1001 S Valley Forge Rd TF: 800-504-2287 ■ Web: www.actsretirement.org	Lansdale	PA	19446	215-855-4109	
Cornwall Manor 1 Boyd St TF: 800-222-2476 ■ Web: www.cornwallmanor.org	Cornwall	PA	17016	717-273-2647	
Cross Keys Village 2990 Carlisle Pk PO Box 128 TF Mktg: 888-624-8242 ■ Web: www.crosskeysvillage.org	New Oxford	PA	17350	717-624-5350	624-5252
Elm Terrace Gardens 660 N Broad St Web: www.elmterracegardens.org	Lansdale	PA	19446	215-361-5600	
Foulkeways at Gwynedd 1120 Meetinghouse Rd Web: www.foulkeways.org	Gwynedd	PA	19436	215-643-2200	646-2917
Foxdale Village 500 E Marylyn Ave TF: 800-253-4951 ■ Web: www.foxdalevillage.org	State College	PA	16801	814-272-2117	238-2920
Friendship Village of South Hills 1290 Boyce Rd Web: lifespacecommunities.com/senior-living-pittsburgh	Upper Saint Clair	PA	15241	724-941-3100	
Granite Farms Estates 1343 W Baltimore Pike TF: 888-499-2287 ■ Web: www.actsretirement.org	Media	PA	19063	610-358-3440	
Kendal at Longwood & Crosslands PO Box 100 TF: 800-216-1920 ■ Web: kcc.kendal.org	Kennett Square	PA	19348	610-388-1441	388-5503
Lebanon Valley Brethren Home 1200 Grubb Rd Web: www.lvbh.org	Palmyra	PA	17078	717-838-5406	
Lima Estates 411 N Middletown Rd. TF: 888-398-2287 ■ Web: www.actsretirement.org	Media	PA	19063	610-565-7020	
Lutheran Community at Telford 12 Lutheran Home Dr TF: 877-343-7518 ■ Web: www.lctelford.org	Telford	PA	18969	215-723-9819	723-3623
Meadowood 3205 Skippack Pike PO Box 670 Web: www.meadowood.net	Worcester	PA	19490	610-584-1000	584-3645
Menno Village 2075 Scotland Ave Web: www.mennohaven.org	Chambersburg	PA	17201	717-262-2373	
Moravian Hall Square 175 W N St. Web: www.moravian.com	Nazareth	PA	18064	610-746-1000	746-1023
Moravian Manor 300 W Lemon St Web: www.moravianmanor.org	Lititz	PA	17543	717-626-0214	
Moravian Village of Bethlehem 526 Wood St. Web: www.moravianvillage.com	Bethlehem	PA	18018	610-625-4885	
Normandy Farms Estates 1401 Morris Rd Web: www.normandyfarm.com	Blue Bell	PA	19422	215-616-8500	
Passavant Retirement Community 401 S Main St. TF: 888-498-7753 ■ Web: www.lutheranseniorlife.org	Zelienople	PA	16063	724-452-5400	
Pennswood Village 1382 Newtown-Langhorne Rd. TF: 888-454-1122 ■ Web: pennswood.org	Newtown	PA	18940	215-968-9110	
Peter Becker Community 800 Maple Ave Web: peterbeckercommunity.com	Harleysville	PA	19438	215-256-9501	
Philadelphia Protestant Home 6500 Tabor Rd Web: www.pphfamily.org	Philadelphia	PA	19111	215-697-8000	697-8137
Pine Run Community 777 Ferry Rd TF: 888-992-8992 ■ Web: www.pinerun.org	Doylestown	PA	18901	215-345-9000	
Quadrangle, The 3300 Darby Rd. Web: www.sunriseseniorliving.com	Haverford	PA	19041	610-642-3000	
Quarryville Presbyterian Retirement Community 625 Robert Fulton Hwy Web: www.quarryville.com	Quarryville	PA	17566	717-786-7321	
Riddle Village 1048 W Baltimore Pk Web: www.riddlevillage.com	Media	PA	19063	610-891-3700	891-3671
Rydal Park 1515 The Fairway Web: www.rydalpark.org	Rydal	PA	19046	215-885-6800	
Sherwood Oaks 100 Norman Dr TF: 800-642-2217 ■ Web: www.sherwood-oaks.com	Cranberry Township	PA	16066	724-776-8100	776-8468
Simpson House 2101 Belmont Ave Web: www.simpsonhouse.org	Philadelphia	PA	19131	215-878-3600	
Spring House Estates 728 Norristown Rd TF: 888-365-2287 ■ Web: www.actsretirement.org	Lower Gwynedd	PA	19002	215-628-8110	
Watermark at Logan Square 2 Franklin Town Blvd Web: www.watermarkcommunities.com/logansquare	Philadelphia	PA	19103	215-240-8915	
Waverly Heights 1400 Waverly Rd Web: www.waverlyheightsltd.org	Gladwyne	PA	19035	610-645-8600	645-8611
Westminster Village 803 N Wahneta St. TF: 888-563-8147 ■ Web: www.presbyterianseniorliving.org/westminster-village-in-allentown	Allentown	PA	18109	610-782-8300	782-8398
White Horse Village 535 Gradyville Rd Web: www.whitehorsevillage.org	Newtown Square	PA	19073	610-558-5000	558-5001
Willow Valley Lakes Manor 300 Willow Vly Lakes Dr. TF: 800-770-5445 ■ Web: www.willowvalleycommunities.org	Willow Street	PA	17584	717-464-0800	464-2560
CSSS d'Antoine-Labelle 515 boul Dr Albiny-Paquette Web: www.csssal.org	Mont-laurier	QC	J9L1K8	819-623-6127	
Bethea Baptist Retirement Community 157 Home Ave TF: 877-393-2867 ■ Web: bethearetirement.com	Darlington	SC	29532	843-393-2867	393-2458
Presbyterian Homes of SC 2817 Ashland Rd TF: 888-842-4855 ■ Web: preshomesc.org	Columbia	SC	29210	803-772-5885	772-5872
Westminster Towers 1330 India Hook Rd TF: 800-345-6026 ■ Web: www.westminstertowers.org	Rock Hill	SC	29732	803-328-5000	
White Oak Manor Inc 130 E Main St PO Box 3347 TF: 800-826-6762 ■ Web: www.whiteoakmanor.com	Spartanburg	SC	29304	864-582-7503	573-9107
Brookdale Senior Living Inc 111 Westwood Pl Ste 400 TF: 866-785-9025 ■ Web: brookdale.com	Brentwood	TN	37027	615-221-2250	221-2289
Army Residence Community 7400 Crestway TF: 800-725-0083 ■ Web: www.armyresidence.com	San Antonio	TX	78239	210-646-5316	646-5313
Bayou Manor 4141 S Braeswood Blvd Web: houstonretirement.org	Houston	TX	77025	713-666-2651	
Capital Senior Living Corp 14160 Dallas Pkwy Ste 300 NYSE: CSU ■ Web: www.capitalsenior.com	Dallas	TX	75254	972-770-5600	770-5666
Forum at Lincoln Heights 311 W Nottingham Pl Web: www.fivestarseniorliving.com/communities/tx/san-antonio/the-forum-at-lincoln-heights	San Antonio	TX	78209	210-824-2314	824-6556
Forum at Park Lane 7831 Pk Ln. Web: www.fivestarseniorliving.com/communities/tx/dallas/the-forum-at-park-lane	Dallas	TX	75225	214-369-9902	373-1836
Grace Presbyterian Village 550 E Ann Arbor Ave Web: www.gracepresvillage.org	Dallas	TX	75216	214-376-1701	376-4350

Phone Fax

John Knox Village of the Rio Grande Valley
1300 S Border Ave .... Weslaco TX 78596 956-968-4575
Web: johnknoxvillagergv.com

Manor Park Inc 2208 N Loop 250 W .... Midland TX 79707 432-689-9898 694-2551
TF: 800-523-9898 ■ *Web:* www.manorparkinc.org

Rolling Meadows 3006 McNiel Ave .... Wichita Falls TX 76309 940-691-7511
Web: www.rmeadows.com

Temple Meridian 4312 S 31st St .... Temple TX 76502 254-598-4019
TF: 855-444-7658 ■ *Web:* www.brookdale.com

Westminster Manor 4100 Jackson Ave .... Austin TX 78731 512-454-4643 371-7308
Web: westminsteraustintx.org

Brandermill Woods
14311 Brandermill Woods Trl. .... Midlothian VA 23112 804-744-1173 744-4894
Web: www.brandermillwoods.com

Colonnades, The 2600 Barracks Rd .... Charlottesville VA 22901 434-963-4198
Web: www.sunriseseniorliving.com

Covenant Woods 7090 Covenant Woods Dr .... Mechanicsville VA 23111 804-569-8000
Web: www.covenantwoods.com

Culpeper Baptist Retirement Community
12425 Village Loop .... Culpeper VA 22701 540-825-2411
TF: 800-894-2411 ■ *Web:* culpeperretirement.org

Fairfax, The 9140 Belvoir Woods Pkwy. .... Fort Belvoir VA 22060 703-799-1200
Web: sunriseseniorliving.com

Goodwin House 4800 Fillmore Ave .... Alexandria VA 22311 703-578-1000 824-1353
Web: www.goodwinhouse.org

Goodwin House Bailey's Crossroads
3440 S Jefferson St .... Falls Church VA 22041 703-820-1488
Web: www.goodwinhouse.org

Hermitage, The 1600 Westwood Ave .... Richmond VA 23227 804-474-1800
Web: www.hermitage-vumh.com

Jefferson, The 900 N Taylor St .... Arlington VA 22203 703-516-9455
Web: www.sunriseseniorliving.com

Lakewood Manor 1900 Lauderdale Dr .... Richmond VA 23238 804-740-2900 740-3774
TF: 866-521-9100 ■ *Web:* lakewoodwestend.org

Shenandoah Valley Westminster-Canterbury
300 Westminster-Canterbury Dr. .... Winchester VA 22603 540-665-5914
TF: 800-492-9463 ■ *Web:* www.svwc.org

Virginian, The 9229 Arlington Blvd. .... Fairfax VA 22031 703-385-0555
Web: www.thevirginian.org

Washington House 5100 Fillmore Ave .... Alexandria VA 22311 703-291-0188
Web: www.watermarkcommunities.com/washingtonhouse

Westminster-Canterbury of Lynchburg
501 VES Rd .... Lynchburg VA 24503 434-386-3500 386-3535
TF: 800-962-3520 ■ *Web:* www.wclynchburg.org

Westminster-Canterbury on Chesapeake Bay
3100 Shore Dr .... Virginia Beach VA 23451 757-496-1785
TF: 800-349-1722 ■ *Web:* www.wcbay.com

Westminster-Canterbury Richmond
1600 Westbrook Ave. .... Richmond VA 23227 804-264-6000 264-4579
TF: 800-445-9904 ■ *Web:* www.wcrichmond.org

Williamsburg Landing
5700 Williamsburg Landing Dr. .... Williamsburg VA 23185 757-565-6505
TF: 800-554-5517 ■ *Web:* www.williamsburglanding.com

Bayview Retirement Community 11 W Aloha St .... Seattle WA 98119 206-284-7330
Web: www.bayviewcommunity.org

Eastside Retirement Association
10901 17th Cir NE .... Redmond WA 98052 425-556-8100
Web: www.emeraldheights.com

Hearthstone at Green Lake, The
6720 E Green Lk Way N .... Seattle WA 98103 206-525-9666
Web: www.hearthstone.org

Judson Park 23600 Marine View Dr S .... Des Moines WA 98198 206-824-4000
TF: 800-401-4113 ■ *Web:* www.judsonpark.com

Panorama City 1751 Cir Ln SE .... Lacey WA 98503 360-456-0111 438-5901
TF: 800-999-9807 ■ *Web:* panorama.org

Park Shore 1630 43rd Ave E .... Seattle WA 98112 206-329-0770
Web: www.parkshore.org

Rockwood Retirement Community
2903 E 25th Ave .... Spokane WA 99223 509-536-6650 536-6662
TF: 800-727-6650 ■ *Web:* www.rockwoodretirement.org

Wesley Homes 815 S 216th St .... Des Moines WA 98198 206-824-5000 870-1209
TF: 866-937-5390 ■ *Web:* wesleyhomes.org

Fairhaven 435 W Starin Rd .... Whitewater WI 53190 262-473-2140 473-5468
TF: 877-624-2298 ■ *Web:* www.fairhaven.org

Milwaukee Catholic Home
2330 & 2462 N Prospect Ave .... Milwaukee WI 53211 414-224-9700 224-1666
Web: www.milwaukeecatholichome.org

Oakwood Village West 5565 Tancho Dr .... Madison WI 53705 608-230-4000
Web: www.oakwoodvillage.net

Saint John's On the Lake
1840 N Prospect Ave .... Milwaukee WI 53202 414-831-7300
Web: www.saintjohnsmilw.org

Village at Manor Park, The (VMP)
3023 S 84th St .... Milwaukee WI 53227 414-607-4100
Web: www.vmpcares.com

673 RETREATS - SPIRITUAL

The facilities listed here offer basic amenities and services such as bed linens, food preparation, maid service, etc. Although physical activity may play a role in the programs offered, the focus is on the spiritual.

Phone Fax

Ashram, The PO Box 8009 .... Calabasas CA 91372 818-222-6900
Web: www.theashram.com

Benedict Inn Retreat & Conference Ctr
1402 Southern Ave .... Beech Grove IN 46107 317-788-7581 782-3142
Web: benedictine.com

Bethany Retreat House
2202 Lituanica Ave .... East Chicago IN 46312 219-398-5047 398-9329
Web: www.bethanyretreathouse.org

Bishop's Ranch 5297 Westside Rd .... Healdsburg CA 95448 707-433-2440 433-3431
Web: www.bishopsranch.org

Bridge-Between Retreat Ctr, The
4471 Flaherty Ln. .... Denmark WI 54208 920-864-7230 864-7044
Web: www.bridge-between.com

Campion Renewal Ctr 319 Concord Rd .... Weston MA 02493 781-419-1337 894-5864
Web: www.campioncenter.org

Catholic Diocese of Buffalo
6892 Lake Shore Rd PO Box 816 .... Derby NY 14047 716-947-4708
Web: www.buffalodiocese.org

Chopra Ctr at La Costa Resort & Spa
2013 Costa del Mar Rd .... Carlsbad CA 92009 760-494-1600 494-1608
TF: 888-424-6772 ■ *Web:* www.chopra.com

Christ the King Retreat Ctr 621 First Ave S .... Buffalo MN 55313 763-682-1394 682-3453
Web: www.kingshouse.com

Conception Abbey PO Box 501 .... Conception MO 64433 660-944-3100 944-2811
Web: www.conceptionabbey.org

Elat Chayyim 116 Johnson Rd .... Falls Village CT 06031 800-398-2630 824-7228*
**Fax Area Code:* 860 ■ *TF:* 800-398-2630 ■ *Web:* hazon.org/isabella-freedman

Enders Island PO Box 399 .... Mystic CT 06355 860-536-0565 572-7655
Web: www.endersisland.com

Esalen Institute 55000 Hwy 1 .... Big Sur CA 93920 831-667-3000 667-2724
Web: www.esalen.org

Expanding Light 14618 Tyler Foote Rd .... Nevada City CA 95959 530-478-7518 478-7519
TF: 800-346-5350 ■ *Web:* www.expandinglight.org

Franciscan Spirituality Ctr 920 Market St .... La Crosse WI 54601 608-791-5295
Web: www.franciscanspiritualitycenter.org

Genesis Spiritual Life Ctr 53 Mill St. .... Westfield MA 01085 413-562-3627
Web: www.genesiscenter.us

Harbin Hot Springs
18424 Harbin Springs Rd PO Box 782 .... Middletown CA 95461 707-987-2477 987-0616
TF: 800-622-2477 ■ *Web:* www.harbin.org

Hollyhock PO Box 127 .... Mansons Landing BC V0P1K0 250-935-6576 935-6424
TF: 800-933-6339 ■ *Web:* www.hollyhock.ca

Holy Cross Monastery 1615 Rt 9W .... West Park NY 12493 845-384-6660 384-6031
Web: www.holycrossmonastery.com

Jesuit Ctr for Spiritual Growth
501 N Church Rd .... Wernersville PA 19565 610-670-3642
Web: jesuitcenter.org

Jesuit Retreat House 300 Manresa Way .... Los Altos CA 94022 650-917-4000
Web: www.jrclosaltos.org

Jesuit Spiritual Ctr 5361 S Milford Rd. .... Milford OH 45150 513-248-3500
Web: www.jesuitspiritualcenter.com

Kalani Oceanside Retreat
12-6860 Kapoho Kalapana Rd .... Pahoa HI 96778 808-965-7828 965-0527
TF: 800-800-6886 ■ *Web:* www.kalani.com

Kirkridge Retreat & Study Ctr 2495 Fox Gap Rd .... Bangor PA 18013 610-588-1793 588-8510
TF: 800-231-2222 ■ *Web:* www.kirkridge.org

Kordes Retreat Ctr 841 E 14th St .... Ferdinand IN 47532 812-367-2777
Web: www.thedome.org

Laurelville Mennonite Church Ctr
941 Laurelville Ln. .... Mount Pleasant PA 15666 724-423-2056 423-2096
TF: 800-839-1021 ■ *Web:* www.laurelville.org

Linwood Spiritual Ctr 50 Linwood Rd .... Rhinebeck NY 12572 845-876-4178 876-1920
Web: www.linwoodspiritualctr.org

Louhelen Baha'i School 3208 S State Rd .... Davison MI 48423 810-653-5033 653-7181
TF: 800-894-9716 ■ *Web:* louhelen.org

Loyola Retreat House 161 James St .... Morristown NJ 07960 973-539-0740 898-9839
Web: www.loyola.org

Manna House of Prayer 323 E Fifth St .... Concordia KS 66901 785-243-4428
Web: www.mannahouse.org

Marguerite Centre 700 Mackay St .... Pembroke ON K8A1G6 613-732-9925
Web: www.margueritecentre.com

Marie Joseph Spiritual Ctr 10 Evans Rd. .... Biddeford ME 04005 207-284-5671 286-1371
Web: www.mariejosephspiritual.org

Marycrest Assisted Living 2850 Columbine Rd .... Denver CO 80221 303-433-0282
Web: www.marycrest.org

Mercy Ctr 2300 Adeline Dr. .... Burlingame CA 94010 650-340-7474 340-1299
Web: www.mercy-center.org

Mercy Ctr at Madison 167 Neck Rd PO Box 191 .... Madison CT 06443 203-245-0401 245-8718
Web: www.mercybythesea.org

Mercy Ctr for Healing the Whole Person
520 W Buena Ventura .... Colorado Springs CO 80907 719-633-2302 633-1031
Web: www.mercycenter.com

Monastery of Saint Gertrude
465 Keuterville Rd .... Cottonwood ID 83522 208-962-3224 962-7212
Web: www.stgertrudes.org

Montserrat Jesuit Retreat House
600 N Shady Shores Dr PO Box 1390 .... Lake Dallas TX 75065 940-321-6020 321-6040
Web: www.montserratretreat.org

Mount Calvary Retreat House
PO Box 1296 .... Santa Barbara CA 93102 805-962-9855
Web: www.mount-calvary.org

Mount Carmel Ctr 4600 W Davis St .... Dallas TX 75211 214-331-6224
Web: www.mountcarmelcenter.org

Omega Institute for Holistic Studies
150 Lake Dr .... Rhinebeck NY 12572 845-266-4444 266-3769
TF: 800-944-1001 ■ *Web:* www.eomega.org

Our Lady of Fatima Retreat House
5353 E 56th St .... Indianapolis IN 46226 317-545-7681 545-0095
TF: 800-382-9836 ■ *Web:* www.archindy.org

Pecos Benedictine Monastery
Our Lady of Guadalupe Abbey PO Box 1080 .... Pecos NM 87552 505-757-6415
Web: www.pecosmonastery.org

Pendle Hill 338 Plush Mill Rd .... Wallingford PA 19086 610-566-4507 566-3679
TF: 800-742-3150 ■ *Web:* www.pendlehill.org

Priory Spirituality Ctr 500 College St NE .... Lacey WA 98516 360-438-2595 438-9236
Web: www.stplacid.org

Pumpkin Hollow Farm 1184 Rt 11 .... Craryville NY 12521 518-325-3583 325-5633
Web: www.pumpkinhollow.org

Quaker Hill Conference Ctr
10 Quaker Hill Dr .... Richmond IN 47374 765-962-5741
Web: www.qhcc.org/facilities.shtml

Redemptorist Retreat Ctr
1800 N Timber Trail Ln. .... Oconomowoc WI 53066 262-567-6900 567-0134
Web: redemptoristretreat.org

Name / Address	City	State	ZIP	Phone	Fax
Rowe Camp & Conference Ctr 22 Kings Hwy Rd PO Box 273 *Web:* www.rowecenter.org	Rowe	MA	01367	413-339-4954	339-5728
Saint Andrew's Abbey 31001 N Valyermo Rd *Web:* www.valyermo.com	Valyermo	CA	93563	661-944-2178	
Saint Anthony Retreat Ctr 300 E Fourth St *Web:* www.sarcenter.com	Marathon	WI	54448	715-443-2236	443-2235
Saint Francis Retreat Ctr 549 Mission VineyaRd Rd *Web:* www.stfrancisretreat.com	San Juan Bautista	CA	95045	831-623-4234	623-9046
Saint Meinrad Archabbey 200 Hill Dr *TF:* 800-682-0988 ■ *Web:* www.saintmeinrad.edu	Saint Meinrad	IN	47577	812-357-6585	357-6325
San Damiano Retreat Ctr 710 Highland Dr PO Box 767 *Web:* www.sandamiano.org	Danville	CA	94526	925-837-9141	837-0522
Satchidananda Ashram Yogaville (SAYVA) 108 Yogaville Way *TF Resv:* 800-858-9642 ■ *Web:* yogaville.org	Buckingham	VA	23921	434-969-3121	
Serra Retreat Ctr 3401 Serra Rd *Web:* www.serraretreat.com	Malibu	CA	90265	310-456-6631	456-9417
Shambhala Mountain Ctr 151 Shambhala Wy *TF:* 888-788-7221 ■ *Web:* www.shambhalamountain.org	Red Feather Lakes	CO	80545	970-881-2184	881-2909
Siena Ctr 5635 Erie St *Web:* racinedominicans.org	Racine	WI	53402	262-639-4100	
Song of the Morning Yoga Retreat Ctr 9607 Sturgeon Vly Rd *Web:* www.songofthemorning.org	Vanderbilt	MI	49795	989-983-4107	
Sophia Spirituality Ctr 751 S Eigth St *Web:* www.mountosb.org	Atchison	KS	66002	913-360-6173	
Spiritual Life Ctr 7100 E 45th St N *TF:* 800-348-2440 ■ *Web:* catholicdioceseofwichita.org	Wichita	KS	67226	316-744-0167	744-8072
Tabor Retreat Ctr 60 Anchor Ave *Web:* www.taborretreatcenter.org	Oceanside	NY	11572	516-536-3004	
Vivekananda Retreat Ridgely 101 Leggett Rd *Web:* www.ridgely.org	Stone Ridge	NY	12484	845-687-4574	687-4578
Wainwright House 260 Stuyvesant Ave *Web:* www.wainwright.org	Rye	NY	10580	914-967-6080	967-6114
Wisdom House Retreat & Conference Ctr 229 E Litchfield Rd *Web:* www.wisdomhouse.org	Litchfield	CT	06759	860-567-3163	567-3166
WomanWell 1784 La Crosse Ave	Saint Paul	MN	55119	651-739-7953	739-7475

674 ROLLING MILL MACHINERY

See Also Metalworking Machinery p. 2769

Name / Address	City	State	ZIP	Phone	Fax
Abbey International Ltd 11140 Ave Rd *Web:* www.abbeyintl.com	Perrysburg	OH	43552	419-874-4301	874-8200
Ampco-Pittsburgh Corp 600 Grant St Ste 4600 *NYSE:* AP ■ *Web:* www.ampcopittsburgh.com	Pittsburgh	PA	15219	412-456-4400	
Bonell Manufacturing Co 13521 S Halsted St *Web:* www.bonellmfg.com	Riverdale	IL	60827	708-849-1770	849-3434
Bradbury Company Inc 1200 E Cole *TF:* 800-397-6394 ■ *Web:* bradburygroup.com	Moundridge	KS	67107	620-345-6394	345-6381
Fairfield Machine Company Inc 1143 Lower Elkton Rd PO Box 27 *Web:* www.fairfieldmachine.com	Columbiana	OH	44408	330-482-3388	482-5052
Formtek Metal Forming Inc 4899 Commerce Pkwy *TF:* 800-631-0520 ■ *Web:* formtekgroup.com	Cleveland	OH	44128	216-292-4460	831-7948
Magnum Integrated Technologies Inc 200 First Gulf Blvd *TF:* 800-830-0642 ■ *Web:* www.mit-world.com	Brampton	ON	L6W4T5	905-595-1998	455-0422
T Sendzimir Inc 269 Brookside Rd *Web:* www.sendzimir.com	Waterbury	CT	06708	203-756-4617	
WHEMCO Inc 5 Hot Metal St **Fax Area Code:* 724 ■ *Web:* www.whemco.com	Pittsburgh	PA	15203	412-390-2700	539-0645*

675 ROYALTY TRUSTS

Name / Address	City	State	ZIP	Phone	Fax
ARC Resources Ltd 308 Fourth Ave SW Ste 1200 *TSE:* ARX ■ *TF:* 888-272-4900 ■ *Web:* www.arcresources.com	Calgary	AB	T2P0H7	403-503-8600	
Great Northern Iron Ore Properties 332 Minnesota St Rm W1290 *NYSE:* GNI ■ *TF:* 800-468-9716 ■ *Web:* www.gniop.com	Saint Paul	MN	55101	651-224-2385	224-2387
Harvest Energy Trust 700 2nd St SW Ste 2100 *TF:* 866-666-1178 ■ *Web:* www.harvestenergy.ca	Calgary	AB	T2P2W1	403-265-1178	
Hugoton Royalty Trust 2911 Turtle Creek Blvd, Ste 850 PO Box 962020 *NYSE:* HGT ■ *TF:* 855-588-7839	Dallas	TX	75219	214-209-2400	289-2431
Marine Petroleum Trust 2911 Turtle Creek Blvd Ste 850 *NASDAQ:* MARPS ■ *TF:* 800-758-4672 ■ *Web:* www.marps-marine.com	Dallas	TX	75219	800-758-4672	
North European Oil Royalty Trust 43 W Front St Ste 19A *NYSE:* NRT ■ *TF:* 800-368-5948 ■ *Web:* www.neort.com	Red Bank	NJ	07701	732-741-4008	741-3140
Pengrowth Energy Trust 222 Third Ave SW Ste 2100 *NYSE:* PGH ■ *TF:* 800-223-4122 ■ *Web:* www.pengrowth.com	Calgary	AB	T2P0B4	403-233-0224	265-6251
Penn West Energy Trust Penn W Plz 207 - 9th Ave SW Ste 200 *TF:* 866-693-2707 ■ *Web:* www.pennwest.com	Calgary	AB	T2P1K3	403-777-2500	777-2699
TAQA North Ltd 308-4th Ave *Web:* taqaglobal.com	Calgary	AB	T2P0H7	403-724-5000	724-5001
Texas Pacific Land Trust 1700 Pacific Ave Ste 2770 *NYSE:* TPL ■ *TF:* 877-231-7500 ■ *Web:* www.tpltrust.com	Dallas	TX	75201	214-969-5530	871-7139

676 RUBBER GOODS

Name / Address	City	State	ZIP	Phone	Fax
Aero Tec Labs Inc 45 Spear Rd Industrial Pk *TF:* 800-526-5330 ■ *Web:* www.atlinc.com	Ramsey	NJ	07446	201-825-1400	825-1962
Alliance Rubber Co 210 Carpenter Dam Rd **Fax Area Code:* 501 ■ *TF:* 800-626-5940 ■ *Web:* www.rubberband.com	Hot Springs	AR	71901	800-626-5940	262-3948*
Biltrite Corp 51 Sawyer Rd *TF:* 800-877-8775 ■ *Web:* www.biltrite.com	Waltham	MA	02454	781-647-1700	647-4205
BRP Manufacturing Co 637 N Jackson St *TF:* 800-858-0482 ■ *Web:* www.brpmfg.com	Lima	OH	45801	419-228-4441	222-5010
Dawson Mfg Co 1042 N Crystal Ave *Web:* www.dawsonmfg.com	Benton Harbor	MI	49022	269-925-0100	925-0997
Durable Products Inc PO Box 826 *TF:* 800-373-3502 ■ *Web:* www.durableproductsinc.com	Crossville	TN	38557	931-484-3502	456-7682
Dynatect Mfg 2300 S Calhoun Rd *Web:* www.dynatect.com	New Berlin	WI	53151	262-786-1500	786-3280
EAM World 5502 NW 37th Ave *Web:* www.theraft.com	Miami	FL	33142	305-871-4050	637-8632
Flexsys America LP 260 Springside Dr *TF:* 800-455-5622 ■ *Web:* www.eastman.com	Akron	OH	44333	330-666-4111	
Griswold Corp 1 River St PO Box 638 *TF:* 800-472-8788 ■ *Web:* www.griswoldcorp.com	Moosup	CT	06354	860-564-3321	564-9103
Hutchinson Aerospace & Industry Inc 82 S St **Fax:* Sales ■ *TF:* 800-227-7962 ■ *Web:* www.hutchinsonai.com	Hopkinton	MA	01748	508-417-7000	417-7224*
Interstate Foam & Supply Inc PO Box 338 *Web:* interstatefoamandsupply.com	Conover	NC	28613	828-459-9700	459-0300
Itran Precision Rubber 375 Metuchen Rd *Web:* www.itranrubber.com	South Plainfield	NJ	07080	908-754-8100	757-1820
Jet Rubber Company Inc 4457 Tallmadge Rd *Web:* www.jetrubber.com	Rootstown	OH	44272	330-325-1821	325-2876
Kent Elastomer Products Inc 1500 St Claire Ave *TF Cust Svc:* 800-331-4762 ■ *Web:* www.kentelastomer.com	Kent	OH	44240	330-673-1011	673-1351
Koneta Inc 1400 Lunar Dr *TF:* 800-331-0775 ■ *Web:* knrubber.com	Wapakoneta	OH	45895	419-739-4200	739-4247
Ludlow Composites Corp 2100 Commerce Dr **Fax Area Code:* 419 ■ *TF:* 800-628-5463 ■ *Web:* www.ludlow-comp.com	Fremont	OH	43420	800-628-5463	332-7776*
Mitchell Rubber Products Inc 10220 San Sevaine Way *TF:* 800-453-7526 ■ *Web:* www.mitchellrubber.com	Mira Loma	CA	91752	800-453-7526	
Mosites Rubber Company Inc PO Box 2115 *Web:* www.mositesrubber.com	Fort Worth	TX	76113	817-335-3451	870-1564
MSM Industries Inc 802 Swan Dr *TF:* 800-648-6648 ■ *Web:* www.msmind.com	Smyrna	TN	37167	615-355-4355	355-6874
Musson Rubber Company Inc 1320 E Archwood Ave *TF Cust Svc:* 800-321-2381 ■ *Web:* www.mussonrubber.com	Akron	OH	44306	330-773-7651	773-3254
National Rubber Technologies Corp 35 Cawthra Ave *TF:* 800-387-8501 ■ *Web:* www.knrubber.com	Toronto	ON	M6N5B3	416-657-1111	656-1231
Patch Rubber Co PO Box H *Web:* www.patchrubber.com	Roanoke Rapids	NC	27870	252-536-2574	
Pawling Corp 32 Nelson Hill Rd PO Box 200 **Fax Area Code:* 845 ■ *TF:* 800-431-3456 ■ *Web:* www.pawling.com	Wassaic	NY	12592	800-431-3456	373-9300*
Philpott Rubber Co 1010 Industrial Pkwy *Web:* www.philpottrubber.com	Brunswick	OH	44212	330-225-3344	225-1999
Plasticoid Co 249 W High St *Web:* www.plasticoid.com	Elkton	MD	21921	410-398-2800	398-2803
Proco Products Inc PO Box 590 *TF:* 800-344-3246 ■ *Web:* www.procoproducts.com	Stockton	CA	95201	209-943-6088	943-0242
R & K Industrial Products Co 1945 Seventh St *TF:* 800-842-7655 ■ *Web:* www.rkwheels.com	Richmond	CA	94801	510-234-7212	234-1923
Regupol America 33 Keystone Dr **Fax Area Code:* 717 ■ *TF:* 800-537-8737 ■ *Web:* www.regupol.com	Lebanon	PA	17042	800-537-8737	675-2199*
Rubber Industries Inc 200 Cavanaugh Dr *Web:* www.rubberindustries.com	Shakopee	MN	55379	952-445-1320	445-7934
Seismic Energy Products LP (SEP) 518 Progress Way	Athens	TX	75751	903-675-8571	677-4980
Shercon Inc 6262 Katella Ave *TF:* 888-227-5847 ■ *Web:* www.caplugs.com	Cypress	CA	90630	714-548-3999	
SMR Technologies Inc 93 Nettie Fenwick Rd *TF:* 800-767-6899 ■ *Web:* www.smrtech.com	Fenwick	WV	26202	304-846-6636	
Star-Glo Industries LLC 2 Carlton Ave *Web:* www.starglo.com	East Rutherford	NJ	07073	201-939-6162	939-4054
Swarco Industries Inc PO Box 89 *TF:* 800-216-8781 ■ *Web:* www.swarco.com	Columbia	TN	38402	931-388-5900	388-4039
Teknor Apex Co 505 Central Ave *TF:* 800-556-3864 ■ *Web:* www.teknorapex.com	Pawtucket	RI	02861	401-725-8000	725-8095
Vulcan Corp 30 Garfield Pl Ste 1040 *TF Sales:* 800-447-1146 ■ *Web:* www.vulcorp.com	Cincinnati	OH	45202	513-621-2850	

677 RUBBER GOODS - MECHANICAL

Mechanical rubber goods are rubber components used in machinery, such as o-rings, sprockets, sleeves, roller covers, etc.

Name / Address	City	State	ZIP	Phone	Fax
Acme Machell 2000 Airport Rd	Waukesha	WI	53187	262-521-2870	521-2894
AGC Inc 106 Evansville Ave *Web:* www.agcincorporated.com	Meriden	CT	06451	203-639-7125	235-6543
AirBoss of America Corp 16441 Yonge St *TSE:* BOS ■ *Web:* www.airbossofamerica.com	Newmarket	ON	L3X2G8	905-751-1188	751-1101
American National Rubber Co Main & High St **Fax:* Sales ■ *TF Cust Svc:* 800-624-3410 ■ *Web:* www.anr-co.com	Ceredo	WV	25507	304-453-1311	453-2347*
American Roller Co 1440 13th Ave *Web:* www.americanroller.com	Union Grove	WI	53182	262-878-8665	878-1932

Company	City	State	ZIP	Phone	Fax
Ames Corp 19 Ames Blvd *Web:* www.theamescorp.com	Hamburg	NJ	07419	973-827-9101	827-8893
Armada Rubber Mfg Co 24586 Armada Ridge Rd PO Box 579 *Web:* www.armadarubber.com	Armada	MI	48005	586-784-9135	784-5023
Ashtabula Rubber Co 2751 W Ave *Web:* www.ashtabularubber.com	Ashtabula	OH	44004	440-992-2195	992-7829
Atlantic India Rubber Co 1437 Kentucky Rt 1428 *TF:* 800-476-6638 ■ *Web:* www.atlanticindia.com	Hagerhill	KY	41222	606-789-9115	789-9098
BRC Rubber Group Inc PO Box 227 *Web:* www.brcrp.com	Churubusco	IN	46723	260-693-2171	693-6511
Buckhorn Rubber Products Inc 5151 Industrial Dr *Web:* www.buckhornrubber.com	Hannibal	MO	63401	573-221-8933	221-7144
Central Rubber & Plastics 17416 County Rd 34 *Web:* www.centralrubbercompany.com	Goshen	IN	46528	574-534-6411	
Colonial Diversified Polymer Products LLC 2055 Forrest St Ext PO Box 930 *Web:* www.colonialdpp.com	Dyersburg	TN	38025	731-287-3636	287-3691
Connor Corp 10633 Coldwater Rd Ste 200 *Web:* www.connorcorp.com	Fort Wayne	IN	46845	260-424-1601	
Da/Pro Rubber Inc 601 N Poplar Ave *Web:* www.daprorubber.com	Broken Arrow	OK	74012	918-258-9386	258-3286
Derby Cellular Products Inc 150 Roosevelt Dr	Derby	CT	06418	203-735-4661	
Fabreeka International Inc 1023 Tpke St *TF Cust Svc:* 800-322-7352 ■ *Web:* www.fabreeka.com	Stoughton	MA	02072	781-341-3655	341-3983
Finzer Roller Co 129 Rawls Rd *TF:* 888-486-1900 ■ *Web:* www.finzerroller.com	Des Plaines	IL	60018	847-390-6200	390-6201
Flexan Corp 6626 W Dakin St *Web:* www.flexan.com	Chicago	IL	60634	773-685-6446	685-6630
Flexible Products Co 2600 Auburn Ct *Web:* www.flexible-products.com	Auburn Hills	MI	48326	248-852-5500	852-8620
Grand River Rubber & Plastics Co 2029 Aetna Rd *Web:* www.grrp.com	Ashtabula	OH	44004	440-998-2900	
Griffith Rubber Mills 2625 NW Industrial St *TF:* 800-321-9677 ■ *Web:* griffithrubber.com	Portland	OR	97210	503-226-6971	226-6976
Hiawatha Rubber Co 1700 67th Ave N *Web:* www.hiawatharubber.com	Minneapolis	MN	55430	763-566-0900	566-9537
Holz Rubber Company Inc 1129 S Sacramento St *TF:* 800-285-1600 ■ *Web:* www.holzrubber.com	Lodi	CA	95240	209-368-7171	368-3246
IER Fujikura Inc 8271 Bavaria Rd *Web:* www.ierfujikura.com	Macedonia	OH	44056	330-425-7125	425-7596
Jamak Fabrication Inc 1401 N Bowie Dr *TF:* 800-543-4747 ■ *Web:* www.jamak.com	Weatherford	TX	76086	817-594-8771	594-8324
Jasper Rubber Products Inc 1010 First Ave *TF:* 800-457-7457 ■ *Web:* www.jasperrubber.com	Jasper	IN	47546	812-482-3242	482-0816
Johnson Bros Rubber Inc 42 W Buckeye St *Web:* www.johnsonbrosrubbercompany.com	West Salem	OH	44287	419-853-4122	
Jonal Laboratories Inc PO Box 743 *Web:* www.jonal.com	Meriden	CT	06450	203-634-4444	634-4448
Karman Rubber Co 2331 Copley Rd *Web:* www.karman.com	Akron	OH	44320	330-864-2161	864-2124
Kirkhill Manufacturing Co 12023 Woodruff Ave *Web:* www.rubbersales.com	Downey	CA	90241	562-803-1117	803-3117
Kirkhill-TA Co 300 E Cypress St *Web:* www.esterline.com	Brea	CA	92821	714-529-4901	529-6775
Lauren Mfg 2228 Reiser Ave SE *TF:* 800-683-0676 ■ *Web:* www.lauren.com	New Philadelphia	OH	44663	330-339-3373	339-1515
Lavelle Industries Inc 665 McHenry St *TF:* 800-528-3553 ■ *Web:* www.lavelle.com	Burlington	WI	53105	262-763-2434	763-5607
Longwood Elastomers Inc 706 Green Valley Rd Ste 212 *Web:* www.longwoodindustries.com	Greensboro	NC	27408	336-272-3710	272-3710
Lord Corp 111 Lord Dr *TF:* 877-275-5673 ■ *Web:* www.lord.com	Cary	NC	27511	919-468-5979	
Mantaline Corp 4754 E High St *Web:* www.mantaline.com	Mantua	OH	44255	330-274-2264	274-8850
MGI Coutier 603 W Seventh St *Web:* mgicoutier.com	Cadillac	MI	49601	231-775-6571	775-8731
Minor Rubber Company Inc 49 Ackerman St *TF:* 800-433-6886 ■ *Web:* www.minorrubber.com	Bloomfield	NJ	07003	973-338-6800	893-1399
MOCAP Inc 409 Parkway Dr *TF:* 800-633-6775 ■ *Web:* www.mocap.com	Park Hills	MO	63601	314-543-4000	543-4111
Molded Rubber & Plastic Corp 13161 W Glendale Ave *Web:* www.mrpcorp.com	Butler	WI	53007	262-781-7122	781-5353
Neff-Perkins Co 16080 Industrial Pkwy *Web:* www.neffp.com	Middlefield	OH	44062	440-632-1658	
OMNI Products Inc 3911 Dayton St *Web:* www.omnirail.com	Mchenry	IL	60050	815-344-3100	
Pamarco 171 E Marquardt Dr *TF Sales:* 800-323-7735 ■ *Web:* www.pamarcoglobal.com	Wheeling	IL	60090	847-459-6000	
Polymeric Technology Inc 1900 Marina Blvd	San Leandro	CA	94577	510-895-6001	
Polyneer Inc 259-D Samuel Barnet Blvd *Web:* www.polyneer.com	New Bedford	MA	02745	508-998-5225	
Precision Assoc Inc 3800 N Washington Ave *TF:* 800-394-6590 ■ *Web:* www.precisionassoc.com	Minneapolis	MN	55412	612-333-7464	342-2417
Precix Inc 744 Bellville Ave *TF:* 800-225-8505 ■ *Web:* www.precixinc.com	New Bedford	MA	02745	508-998-4000	998-4100
Prince Rubber & Plastics Company Inc 137 Arthur St *Web:* www.princerp.com	Buffalo	NY	14207	716-877-7400	877-0743
Quality Synthetic Rubber Inc 1700 Highland Rd *Web:* www.qsr-inc.com	Twinsburg	OH	44087	330-425-8472	425-7976
Reiss Manufacturing Inc 75 Mt Vernon Rd *Web:* www.reissbuilt.com	Englishtown	NJ	07726	732-446-6100	446-1394
RotaDyne Corp 8140 S Cass Ave *Web:* www.rotadyne.com	Darien	IL	60561	630-769-9700	769-9255
RPP Corp 12 Ballard Way *Web:* www.rppcorp.com	Lawrence	MA	01843	978-689-2800	
Sperry & Rice Mfg Company LLC 9146 US Hwy 52 *Web:* www.sperryrice.com	Brookville	IN	47012	765-647-4141	647-3302
Thermodyn Corp 3550 Silica Rd *TF:* 800-654-6518 ■ *Web:* www.thermodyn.com	Sylvania	OH	43560	419-841-7782	841-3139
Triangle Rubber Company Inc PO Box 95 *Web:* www.trianglerubberco.com	Goshen	IN	46527	574-533-3118	534-0416
Trostel Ltd 901 Maxwell St *Web:* www.trostel.com	Lake Geneva	WI	53147	262-248-4481	248-6406
Universal Polymer & Rubber Ltd 15730 Madison Rd *Web:* www.universalpolymer.com	Middlefield	OH	44062	440-632-1691	632-5761
Vail Rubber Works Inc 521 Langley Ave *Web:* www.vailrubber.com	Saint Joseph	MI	49085	269-983-1595	983-0155
Vernay Laboratories Inc 120 E S College St *Web:* www.vernay.com	Yellow Springs	OH	45387	937-767-7261	
Wabtec Rubber Products 269 Donohue Rd *Web:* www.wabtec.com	Greensburg	PA	15601	724-838-1317	832-5630
West American Rubber Co LLC 1337 Braden Ct *Web:* www.warco.com	Orange	CA	92868	714-532-3355	532-2238
YUSA Corp 151 Jamison Rd SW *Web:* yusa-oh.com	Washington Court House	OH	43160	740-335-0335	335-0330

678 SAFETY EQUIPMENT - MFR

See Also Medical Supplies - Mfr p. 2745; Personal Protective Equipment & Clothing p. 2926

Company	City	State	ZIP	Phone	Fax
ACR Electronics Inc 5757 Anglers Ave *TF:* 800-432-0227 ■ *Web:* www.acrartex.com	Fort Lauderdale	FL	33312	954-981-3333	983-5087
Adams Elevator Equipment Co 6310 W Howard St *TF:* 800-929-9247 ■ *Web:* www.adamselevator.com	Niles	IL	60714	847-581-2900	581-2949
Air Cruisers Co 1747 New Jersey 34 *Web:* zodiacaerospace.com/en/zodiac-aero-evacuation-systems-air-cruisers	Wall Township	NJ	07727	732-681-3527	681-9163
ALP Industries Inc 1229 W Lincoln Hwy *TF:* 800-220-2571 ■ *Web:* alpindustries.com	Coatesville	PA	19320	610-384-1300	384-7300
Amerex Corp 7595 Gadsden Hwy PO Box 81 *Web:* www.amerex-fire.com	Trussville	AL	35173	205-655-3271	655-3279
AmSafe Inc 1043 N 47th Ave *Web:* www.amsafe.com	Phoenix	AZ	85043	602-850-2850	850-2812
Ancra International LLC 4880 W Rosecrans Ave *TF:* 800-973-5092 ■ *Web:* www.ancra-llc.com	Hawthorne	CA	90250	310-973-5000	973-1138
Autoliv Inc 3350 Airport Rd *NYSE: ALV* ■ *Web:* www.autoliv.com	Ogden	UT	84405	801-625-8200	
Bradley Corp W 142 N 9101 Fountain Blvd *TF:* 800-272-3539 ■ *Web:* www.bradleycorp.com	Menomonee Falls	WI	53051	262-251-6000	251-5817
Buckeye Fire Equipment Co 110 Kings Rd PO Box 428 *Web:* www.buckeyef.com	Kings Mountain	NC	28086	704-739-7415	739-7418
Carsonite Composites LLC 19845 US Hwy 76 *TF:* 800-648-7916 ■ *Web:* www.carsonite.com	Newberry	SC	29108	803-321-1185	276-8940
CSE Corp 600 Seco Rd *TF:* 800-245-2224 ■ *Web:* www.csecorporation.com	Monroeville	PA	15146	412-856-9200	856-9203
Delta Scientific Corp 40355 Delta Ln *Web:* www.deltascientific.com	Palmdale	CA	93551	661-575-1100	575-1109
Encon Safety Products Co 6825 W Sam Houston Pkwy N PO Box 3826 *TF:* 800-283-6266 ■ *Web:* www.enconsafety.com	Houston	TX	77041	713-466-1449	466-1703
Energy Absorption Systems Inc 35 E Wacker Dr Ste 1100 *Web:* www.energyabsorption.com	Chicago	IL	60601	312-467-6750	467-1356
Gemtor Inc 1 Johnson Ave *TF:* 800-405-9048 ■ *Web:* www.gemtor.com	Matawan	NJ	07747	732-583-6200	290-9391
Hawkins Traffic Safety Supply 1255 E Shore Hwy **Fax Area Code:* 510 ■ *TF:* 800-772-3995 ■ *Web:* hawkinstraffic.com	Berkeley	CA	94710	800-236-0112	525-2861*
Key Safety Systems Inc 7000 Nineteen Mile Rd *OTC: BDTTZ* ■ *Web:* www.keysafetyinc.com	Sterling Heights	MI	48314	586-726-3800	726-4150
Mercedes Textiles Ltd 5838 Cypihot St *Web:* www.mercedestextiles.com	Ville Saint Laurent	QC	H4S1Y5	514-335-4337	335-9633
Monaco Enterprises Inc 14820 E Sprague Ave PO Box 14129 *Web:* www.monaco.com	Spokane	WA	99216	509-926-6277	924-4980
North American Fire Hose 910 E Noble Way *Web:* www.northamericanfirehose.com	Santa Maria	CA	93454	805-922-7076	922-0086
Ocenco Inc 10225 82nd Ave *Web:* www.ocenco.com	Pleasant Prairie	WI	53158	262-947-9000	947-9020
Peck & Hale LLC 180 Div Ave *Web:* www.peckhale.com	West Sayville	NY	11796	631-589-2510	589-2925
Peerless Chain Co 1416 E Sanborn St **Fax Area Code:* 800 ■ *TF:* 800-533-8056 ■ *Web:* www.peerlesschain.com	Winona	MN	55987	507-457-9100	356-1149*
Peerless Industrial Group PO Box 949 **Fax Area Code:* 503 ■ *TF:* 800-547-6806 ■ *Web:* www.peerlesschain.com	Clackamas	OR	97015	800-873-1916	656-4836*
Plastic Safety Systems Inc 2444 Baldwin Rd **Fax Area Code:* 216 ■ *TF:* 800-662-6338 ■ *Web:* pss-innovations.com	Cleveland	OH	44104	800-662-6338	231-2702*
Potter-Roemer 17451 Hurley St *TF:* 800-366-3473 ■ *Web:* www.potterroemer.com	City of Industry	CA	91744	626-855-4890	937-4777
Reflexite North America 315 S St *TF:* 800-654-7570 ■ *Web:* www.orafol.com	New Britain	CT	06051	860-223-9297	832-9267
Rite-Hite Corp 8900 N Arbon Dr *TF:* 800-456-0600 ■ *Web:* www.ritehite.com	Milwaukee	WI	53224	414-355-2600	355-9248
Rostra Precision Controls Inc 2519 Dana Dr *TF Cust Svc:* 800-782-3379 ■ *Web:* www.rostra.com	Laurinburg	NC	28352	910-276-4853	276-1354

Company / Address	City	State	ZIP	Phone	Fax
Safety Components International Inc 40 Emery St	Greenville	SC	29605	864-240-2692	
TF: 800-896-6926 ■ *Web:* www.safetycomponents.com					
Simulaids 16 Simulaids Dr PO Box 1289	Saugerties	NY	12477	845-679-2475	679-8996
Web: www.simulaids.com					
Takata Inc 2500 Takata Dr	Auburn Hills	MI	48326	248-373-8040	
Web: www.takata.com					
Tread Corp 176 Eastpark Dr	Roanoke	VA	24019	540-982-6881	344-7536
Web: www.treadcorp.com					

679 SAFETY EQUIPMENT - WHOL

Company / Address	City	State	ZIP	Phone	Fax
Allstar Fire Equipment Inc 12328 Lower Azusa Rd	Arcadia	CA	91006	626-652-0900	652-0920
TF: 800-425-5787 ■ *Web:* www.allstarfire.com					
Arbill PO Box 820542	Philadelphia	PA	19154	800-523-5367	426-5808
TF: 800-523-5367 ■ *Web:* www.arbill.com					
Brooks Equipment Company Inc 10926 David Taylor Dr Ste 300	Charlotte	NC	28269	800-826-3473	433-9265
TF: 800-826-3473 ■ *Web:* www.brooksequipment.com					
Broward Fire Equipment & Service Inc 101 SW Sixth St	Fort Lauderdale	FL	33301	954-467-6625	467-6640
TF: 800-866-3473 ■ *Web:* www.browardfire.com					
Calolympic Glove & Safety Company Inc 1720 Delilah St	Corona	CA	92879	951-340-2229	340-3337
TF: 800-421-6630 ■ *Web:* www.caloly-safety.com					
Choctaw-Kaul Distribution Co 3540 Vinewood Ave	Detroit	MI	48208	313-894-9494	894-7977
Web: www.choctawkaul.com					
Continental Safety Equipment 2935 Waters Rd Ste 140	Eagan	MN	55121	651-454-7233	454-3217
TF: 800-844-7003 ■ *Web:* www.csesafety.com					
Dunn Safety Products Inc 37 S Sangamon St	Chicago	IL	60607	312-666-5800	
Web: www.dunnsafety.com					
Empire Safety & Supply Inc 10624 Industrial Ave	Roseville	CA	95678	916-781-3003	882-9060*
**Fax Area Code:* 888 ■ *TF:* 800-995-1341 ■ *Web:* www.empiresafety.com					
Fire Fighters Equipment Co 3053 Rt 10 E	Denville	NJ	07834	973-366-4466	
Web: www.ffecnj.com					
Fire Protection Service Inc 8050 Harrisburg Blvd	Houston	TX	77012	713-924-9600	923-6272
Web: www.fps-usa.com					
International Fire Equipment Corp 500 Telser Rd	Lake Zurich	IL	60047	847-438-2343	438-1869
Web: www.intlfire.com					
La Grand Industrial Supply Co 2620 SW First Ave	Portland	OR	97201	503-224-5800	
Web: lagrandindustrial.net					
LaFrance Equipment Corp 516 Erie St	Elmira	NY	14904	607-733-5511	733-0482
TF: 800-873-8808 ■ *Web:* www.lafrance-equipment.com					
LN Curtis & Sons 1800 Peralta St	Oakland	CA	94607	510-839-5111	839-5325
TF: 800-443-3556 ■ *Web:* www.lncurtis.com					
Mid-Continent Safety 8225 E 35th St N	Wichita	KS	67226	316-522-0900	
TF General: 800-776-0956 ■ *Web:* www.midsafe.com/store/index.cfm					
Nardini Fire Equipment Company Inc 405 County Rd E W	Saint Paul	MN	55126	651-483-6631	483-6945
TF: 888-627-3464 ■ *Web:* www.nardinifire.com					
Orr Safety Corp 11601 Interchange Dr	Louisville	KY	40229	502-774-5791	776-8030
TF: 800-726-6789 ■ *Web:* www.orrsafety.com					
PK Safety Supply 1829 Clement Ave Ste 200	Alameda	CA	94501	510-337-8880	337-8890
TF: 800-829-9580 ■ *Web:* www.pksafety.com					
Reliable Fire Equipment Co 12845 S Cicero Ave	Alsip	IL	60803	708-597-4600	389-1150
Web: www.reliablefire.com					
Saf-T-Gard International Inc 205 Huehl Rd	Northbrook	IL	60062	847-291-1600	291-1610
TF: 800-548-4273 ■ *Web:* www.saftgard.com					
Safety Products Inc 3517 Craftsman Blvd	Lakeland	FL	33803	863-665-3601	330-0395*
**Fax Area Code:* 800 ■ *TF:* 800-248-6860 ■ *Web:* www.spisafety.com					
Safety Supply South Inc 100 Centrum Dr	Irmo	SC	29063	800-522-8344	
TF Cust Svc: 800-522-8344 ■ *Web:* www.safetysupplysouth.com					
Safeware Inc 3200 HubbaRd Rd	Landover	MD	20785	301-683-1234	683-1200
TF Cust Svc: 800-331-6707 ■ *Web:* www.safewareinc.com					
Sanderson Safety Supply Co 1101 SE Third Ave	Portland	OR	97214	503-238-5700	238-6443
Web: www.sandersonsafety.com					
Stauffer Glove & Safety PO Box 45	Red Hill	PA	18076	215-679-4446	679-5053
Web: my.stauffersafety.com					
Sun Devil Fire Equipment Inc 2929 W Clarendon Ave	Phoenix	AZ	85017	623-245-0636	495-9291*
**Fax Area Code:* 602 ■ *TF:* 800-536-3845 ■ *Web:* www.sundevilfire.com					
United Fire Equipment Co 335 N Fourth Ave	Tucson	AZ	85705	520-622-3639	882-3991
TF: 800-362-0150 ■ *Web:* unitedfire.net					
Wayest Safety Inc 3750 N I-44 Service Rd	Oklahoma City	OK	73112	405-942-7101	
TF: 800-256-1003 ■ *Web:* northernsafety.com/wayest					
Wenaas AGS Inc 12211 Parc Crest Dr Bldg Ste 100	Stafford	TX	77477	281-931-4300	931-4328
TF: 888-576-2668 ■ *Web:* www.wenaasusa.com					

680 SALT

See Also Spices, Seasonings, Herbs p. 2306

Companies listed here produce salt that may be used for a variety of purposes, including as a food ingredient or for deicing, water conditioning, or other chemical or industrial applications.

Company / Address	City	State	ZIP	Phone	Fax
Cargill Salt Inc PO Box 5621	Minneapolis	MN	55440	888-385-7258	
TF: 888-385-7258 ■ *Web:* www.cargill.com					
Compass Minerals International 9900 W 109th St Ste 100	Overland Park	KS	66210	913-344-9200	
NYSE: CMP ■ *TF Cust Svc:* 866-755-1743 ■ *Web:* www.compassminerals.com					
Morton Salt Inc 123 N Wacker Dr	Chicago	IL	60606	312-807-2000	807-2899*
**Fax:* Cust Svc ■ *TF:* 800-725-8847 ■ *Web:* www.mortonsalt.com					
North American Salt Co 9900 W 109th St Ste 100	Overland Park	KS	66210	913-344-9100	
Web: www.nasalt.com					
United Salt Corp 4800 San Felipe St	Houston	TX	77056	713-877-2600	877-2609
TF: 800-554-8658 ■ *Web:* www.unitedsalt.com					

681 SATELLITE COMMUNICATIONS SERVICES

See Also Cable & Other Pay Television Services p. 1887; Internet Service Providers (ISPs) p. 2596; Telecommunications Services p. 3219

Company / Address	City	State	ZIP	Phone	Fax
American International Radio Inc 3601 E Algonquin Rd Ste 800	Rolling Meadows	IL	60008	847-818-9999	
Web: www.airadio.com					
ARINC Inc 2551 Riva Rd	Annapolis	MD	21401	410-266-4000	573-3300
TF: 866-321-6060 ■ *Web:* www.arinc.com					
Broken Arrow Communications Inc 8316 Corona Loop NE	Albuquerque	NM	87113	505-877-2100	877-2101
Web: www.bacom-inc.com					
Bytemobile Inc 4988 Great America Pkwy	Santa Clara	CA	95054	408-327-7700	
Web: www.citrix.com					
Cableworks Communications Inc 3112 Main St Unit #3	Salisbury	NB	E4J2L6	506-372-9542	
Web: www.cableworkscommunications.com					
CapRock Communications Inc 4400 S Sam Houston Pkwy E	Houston	TX	77048	832-668-2300	668-2388
TF: 888-482-0289 ■ *Web:* www.harriscaprock.com					
Epoch Universal Inc 39 Musick	Irvine	CA	92618	949-268-3499	
Web: epochuniversal.com					
Fleet Management Solutions Inc 3426 Empresa Dr Ste 100	San Luis Obispo	CA	93401	805-787-0508	
Web: www.fmsgps.com					
Force10 Networks Inc 1415 N McDowell Blvd	Petaluma	CA	94954	707-665-4400	792-4938
TF: 866-600-5100 ■ *Web:* www.force10networks.com					
Globalstar LP 3200 Zanker Rd Bldg 260	San Jose	CA	95134	408-933-4000	933-4100
TF: 877-728-7466 ■ *Web:* www.globalstar.com					
Ground Control Systems Inc 3100 El Camino Real	Atascadero	CA	93422	805-783-4600	
Web: www.groundcontrol.com					
INSTALLS Inc 241 Main St 5th Fl	Buffalo	NY	14203	716-854-1994	
Web: www.installs.com					
Intelsat Ltd 3400 International Dr NW	Washington	DC	20008	703-559-6800	
Web: www.intelsat.com					
International Satellite Services Inc 1004 Collier Ctr Way Ste 205	Naples	FL	34110	239-598-2241	
Web: www.internationalsatelliteservices.com					
ISYS Technologies Inc 801 W Mineral Ave Ste 105	Littleton	CO	80120	303-290-8922	
Web: www.isystechnologies.com					
Lightriver Technologies Inc 2150 John Glenn Dre Ste 200	Concord	CA	94520	941-552-9410	299-9521*
**Fax Area Code:* 925 ■ *TF:* 888-544-4825 ■ *Web:* www.lightriver.com					
Linkus Enterprises Inc 5595 W San Madele Ave	Fresno	CA	93722	559-256-6600	
TF: 888-854-6587 ■ *Web:* linkuscorp.com					
MDU Communications International Inc 60 D Commerce Way	Totowa	NJ	07512	973-237-9499	237-9243
OTC: MDTV ■ *TF:* 866-286-9638 ■ *Web:* mymdu.com					
Microspace Communications Corp 3100 Highwoods Blvd Ste 120	Raleigh	NC	27604	919-850-4500	850-4518
Web: www.microspace.com					
Northstar Broadband LLC 3660 E Covington Ave Ste C	Post Falls	ID	83854	208-262-9394	
Web: www.northstarbroadband.net					
ORBCOMM 22970 Indian Creek Dr Ste 300	Sterling	VA	20166	703-433-6300	
TF Cust Svc: 800-607-0088 ■ *Web:* www.orbcomm.com					
Outerlink Corp 187 Ballardvale St Ste A260	Wilmington	MA	01887	978-284-6070	268-5444
TF: 877-688-3770 ■ *Web:* www.outerlink.com					
Quantum Dimension Inc 18672 Florida St Ste 302-D	Huntington Beach	CA	92648	714-893-6004	
Web: www.qdimension.com					
SES World Skies 4 Research Way	Princeton	NJ	08540	609-987-4000	987-4517*
**Fax:* Mktg ■ *Web:* www.ses.com					
Shaw Satellite Services Inc 2055 Flavelle Blvd	Mississauga	ON	L5K1Z8	905-403-2020	
Web: www.cancom.ca					
SpaceNet Inc 1750 Old Meadow Rd	McLean	VA	22102	703-848-1000	325-9202*
**Fax Area Code:* 800 ■ *TF:* 800-237-3513 ■ *Web:* www.spacenet.com					
SS8 Networks Inc 750 Tasman Dr	Milpitas	CA	95035	408-944-0250	428-3732
Web: www.ss8.com					
Star West Satellite Inc 580 Prong Horn Trl	Bozeman	MT	59718	406-522-8402	
TF: 888-814-8402 ■ *Web:* www.starwestsatellite.net					
Stratos Global Corp 6550 Rock Spring Dr Ste 650	Bethesda	MD	20817	301-214-8800	214-8801
TF: 800-563-2255 ■ *Web:* www.stratosglobal.com					
Telesat 1601 Telesat Ct	Ottawa	ON	K1B5P4	613-748-0123	748-8712
Web: www.telesat.com					
United Launch Alliance LLC Galileo Operations Ctr 9501 E Panorama Cir	Centennial	CO	80112	720-922-7100	
Web: www.ulalaunch.com					
ViaSat Inc 6155 El Camino Real	Carlsbad	CA	92009	760-476-2200	929-3941
NASDAQ: VSAT ■ *TF:* 855-463-9333 ■ *Web:* www.viasat.com					

682 SAW BLADES & HANDSAWS

See Also Tools - Hand & Edge p. 3253

Phone *Fax*

Blount Outdoor Products Group
4909 SE International Way ... Portland OR 97222 503-653-8881 653-4402
Web: blount.com

California Saw & Knife Works
721 Brannan St ... San Francisco CA 94103 415-861-0644 861-0406
TF: 888-729-6533 ■ *Web:* www.calsaw.com

Carlton Co 3901 SE Naef Rd ... Milwaukie OR 97267 503-659-8911
Web: carltonproducts.com

Contour Saws Inc 900 Graceland Ave ... Des Plaines IL 60016 800-259-6834
TF: 800-259-6834 ■ *Web:* contoursawsinc.com

Diamond Saw Works Inc 12290 Olean Rd ... Chaffee NY 14030 716-496-7417
TF: 800-828-1180 ■ *Web:* www.diamondsaw.com

Disston Precision Inc 6795 State Rd ... Philadelphia PA 19135 215-338-1200 338-7060
TF Cust Svc: 800-238-1007 ■ *Web:* www.disstonprecision.com

Great Neck Saw Manufacturing Inc
165 E Second St ... Mineola NY 11501 516-746-5352 746-5358
TF Cust Svc: 800-457-0600 ■ *Web:* www.greatnecksaw.com

ICS Blount Inc 4909 SE International Way ... Portland OR 97222 800-321-1240 653-4201*
**Fax Area Code:* 503 ■ *TF:* 800-321-1240 ■ *Web:* www.icsbestway.com

LS Starrett Co 121 Crescent St ... Athol MA 01331 978-249-3551 249-8495
NYSE: SCX ■ *TF:* 800-482-8710 ■ *Web:* www.starrett.com

Marvel Mfg Company Inc 3501 Marvel Dr ... Oshkosh WI 54902 920-236-7200 236-7209
TF: 800-472-9464 ■ *Web:* www.marvelsaws.com

MK Diamond Products Inc 1315 Storm Pkwy ... Torrance CA 90501 310-539-5221 539-5158
TF: 800-421-5830 ■ *Web:* www.mkdiamond.com

MK Morse Co 1101 11th St SE ... Canton OH 44707 330-453-8187 453-1111
TF: 800-733-3377 ■ *Web:* www.mkmorse.com

Simonds International 135 Intervale Rd ... Fitchburg MA 01420 800-343-1616 541-6224
TF: 800-343-1616 ■ *Web:* www.simondsint.com

683 SAWMILLS & PLANING MILLS

Phone *Fax*

Anderson-Tully Co 775 Ridgelake Blvd Ste 1050 ... Memphis TN 38120 901-576-1400
Web: www.andersontully.com

Anthony Forest Products Co
309 N Washington Ave ... El Dorado AR 71730 870-862-3414 863-4296
TF: 800-221-2326 ■ *Web:* www.anthonyforest.com

Anthony Timberlands Inc
111 S Plum St PO Box 137 ... Bearden AR 71720 870-687-3611 687-2283
Web: www.anthonytimberlands.com

Arbec Forest Products Inc
8770, Langelier Blvd Ste 216 ... Saint-leonard QC H1P3C6 514-327-3350
Web: www.arbec.ca

Balfour Lumber Company Inc 800 W Clay St ... Thomasville GA 31792 229-226-6086
Web: balfourlumber.com

Barrette-Chapais Ltee CP 248 Km 346 Rt 113 ... Chapais QC G0W1H0 418-745-2545
Web: www.barrette-chapais.qc.ca

Bayway Lumber & Home Center (inc)
400 Ashton Ave ... Linden NJ 07036 908-486-4480
Web: www.baywaylumber.com

Beadles Lumber Company Inc
900 Sixth St NE PO Box 3457 ... Moultrie GA 31776 229-985-6996
TF: 800-763-2400 ■ *Web:* www.beadleslumber.com

Beasley Forest Products Inc
712 Uvalda Hwy ... Hazlehurst GA 31539 912-375-5174
Web: www.beasleyforestproducts.com

Bennett Lumber Products Inc
3759 Hwy 6 PO Box 130 ... Princeton ID 83857 208-875-1121 875-0191
Web: blpi.com

Boisaco Inc 648, Chemin du Moulin ... Sacr?-coeur QC G0T1Y0 418-236-4633
Web: www.boisaco.com

Buse Timber & Sales Inc 3812 28th Pl NE ... Everett WA 98201 425-258-2577 259-6956
TF: 800-305-2577 ■ *Web:* www.busetimber.com

Buskirk Lumber Co 319 Oak St ... Freeport MI 49325 616-765-5103 765-3380
TF: 800-860-9663 ■ *Web:* www.buskirklumber.com

Canadian Forest Products Ltd
5162 Northwood Pulp Mill Rd
PO Box 9000 ... Prince George BC V2L4W2 604-661-5241 962-3473*
**Fax Area Code:* 250 ■ **Fax:* Acctg ■ *Web:* www.canfor.com

Carl Diebold Lumber Co 725 Nw Dunbar Ave ... Troutdale OR 97060 503-669-8226
Web: dieboldlumber.com

Carrier Lumber Ltd
4722 Continental Way ... Prince George BC V2N5S5 250-563-9271
Web: www.carrierlumber.bc.ca

Catawissa Wood & Components Inc
1015 W Valley Ave ... Elysburg PA 17824 570-644-1928 486-2800
Web: www.catlmbr.com

Cersosimo Lumber Co Inc 1103 Vernon St ... Brattleboro VT 05301 802-254-4508 477-6585*
**Fax Area Code:* 413 ■ *Web:* www.cersosimolumber.com

Charles City Forest Products
2200 Barnetts Rd ... Providence Forge VA 23140 804-966-2336
Web: ccforestproducts.com

Claude Howard Lumber Company Inc
600 Pk Ave ... Statesboro GA 30458 912-764-5407 764-6279
Web: sbcontract.com

Coastal Timbers Inc 1310 Jane St ... New Iberia LA 70563 337-369-3017 365-0003
Web: www.coastaltimbers.com

Collins Cos 1618 SW First Ave Ste 500 ... Portland OR 97201 800-329-1219 227-5349*
**Fax Area Code:* 503 ■ *TF:* 800-329-1219 ■ *Web:* www.collinsco.com

Collum's Lumber Products LLC
1723 Barnwell Hwy PO Box 535 ... Allendale SC 29810 803-584-3451
Web: www.collumlumber.com

Columbia Vista Corp PO Box 489 ... Vancouver WA 98666 360-892-0770 944-8229
Web: www.columbiavistacorp.com

Phone *Fax*

Conner Industries Inc
3800 Sandshell Dr Ste 235 ... Fort Worth TX 76137 817-847-0361
Web: www.connerindustries.com

Crone Lumber Company Inc 501 N Park Ave ... Martinsville IN 46151 765-342-2259
Web: www.cronelbr.com

Cronland Lumber Co PO Box 574 ... Lincolnton NC 28093 704-736-2691 735-8493
Web: www.cronlandlumber.com

Crownover Lumber Company Inc
501 Fairview Ave ... Mc Arthur OH 45651 740-596-5229
Web: www.crownoverlumber.com

Cumberland Lumber & Manufacturing Co
202 Red Rd ... McMinnville TN 37110 931-473-9542 473-6259

Cut - to - Size Technology Inc
345 S Fairbank St ... Addison IL 60101 630-543-8328
Web: www.cuttosizetech.com

Deltic Timber Corp PO Box 7200 ... El Dorado AR 71731 870-881-9400
NYSE: DEL ■ *Web:* www.deltic.com

DLH Nordisk Inc
2307 W Cone Boulvard Ste 200 ... Greensboro NC 27408 336-852-8341
Web: www.dlh.com/default.aspx

Domtar Corp 395 de Maisonneuve W ... Montreal QC H3A1L6 514-848-5555
NYSE: UFS ■ *TF:* 877-848-4466 ■ *Web:* www.domtar.com

DR Johnson Lumber Co 1991 Pruner Rd PO Box 66 ... Riddle OR 97469 541-874-2231 874-3337
Web: www.drjlumber.com

Dur-A-Flex Inc 95 Goodwin St ... East Hartford CT 06108 860-528-9838
Web: www.dur-a-flex.com

Dwight G Lewis Lumber Company Inc
1895 Pennsylvania 87 ... Hillsgrove PA 18619 570-924-3507

ECO Building Products Inc 909 W Vista Way ... Vista CA 92083 760-732-5826

Fitzgerald Lumber & Log Company Inc
403 E 29th St PO Box 188 ... Buena Vista VA 24416 540-261-3430
Web: www.fitzgeraldlumber.com

Fitzpatrick & Weller Inc
12 Mill St PO Box 490 ... Ellicottville NY 14731 716-699-2393 699-2893
Web: www.fitzweller.com

Forest Products Manufacturing Co 51 E 30th St ... Jasper IN 47547 812-482-5625 482-9148
Web: forestp.com

Frank Lumber Company Inc PO Box 79 ... Mill City OR 97360 503-897-2371
Web: franklumberco.com

Freeman Brothers Inc
2401 S Arkansas Ave ... Russellville AR 72802 479-968-4986 967-9989

Fulghum Industries 317 S Main St ... Wadley GA 30477 478-252-5223
TF: 800-841-5980 ■ *Web:* www.fulghum.com

Gram Lumber Co 985 NW Second St ... Kalama WA 98625 360-673-5231 673-5558
Web: rsgfp.com

Greenpak Development Inc 3001 Gateman Dr ... Parkersburg WV 26101 304-422-5461
Web: www.greenpak.com

Griffin Lumber Co 1284 Charity Hwy ... Woolwine VA 24185 276-930-2727
Web: www.griffithlumber.net

Groupe Savoie Inc 251, Rt 180 ... St-Quentin NB E8A2K9 506-235-2228 235-3200
Web: www.groupesavoie.com

Hampton Affiliates 9600 SW Barnes Rd Ste 200 ... Portland OR 97225 503-297-7691
TF: 888-310-1464 ■ *Web:* www.hamptonaffiliates.com

Hardwoods of Michigan Inc 430 Div St ... Clinton MI 49236 517-456-7431 456-4931
TF: 800-327-2812 ■ *Web:* www.hmilumber.com

Hartzell Hardwoods 1025 S Roosevelt Ave ... Piqua OH 45356 937-773-7054
Web: www.hartzellhardwoods.com

Hedstrom Lumber Company Inc
1504 Gunflint Trl ... Grand Marais MN 55604 218-387-2995 387-2204
Web: www.hedstromlumber.com

Hoge Lumber Co 701 S Main St ... New Knoxville OH 45871 419-753-2263 753-2963
Web: www.hoge.com

Hughes Hardwood International Inc
500 Hwy 13 S ... Collinwood TN 38450 931-724-6258 724-6259
Web: www.hugheshardwood.com

Hunt Forest Products
401 E Reynolds Dr PO Box 1263 ... Ruston LA 71273 318-255-2245 255-4048
TF: 800-390-8589 ■ *Web:* www.huntforpro.com

Impact Guns 2710 South 1900 West ... Ogden UT 84401 801-393-2474
TF: 888-505-3086 ■ *Web:* www.impactguns.com

Independence Lumber Inc 407 Lumber Ln ... Independence VA 24348 276-773-3744 773-3723
Web: www.indlbr.com

Indiana Dimension Inc 1621 W Market St ... Logansport IN 46947 888-875-4434
TF: 888-875-4434 ■ *Web:* indianadimension.com

Indiana Hardwood Specialists Inc
4341 N US Hwy 231 ... Spencer IN 47460 812-829-4866 829-4860
Web: indianahardwoodspec.com

Industrial Timber & Lumber Corp (ITL)
23925 Commerce Pk Rd ... Beachwood OH 44122 216-831-3140 831-4734
TF: 800-829-9663 ■ *Web:* www.itlcorp.com

Interfor Pacific Inc
2211 Rimland Dr Ste 220 ... Bellingham WA 98226 360-788-2299
Web: www.interfor.com

Jerry G Williams & Sons Inc
524 Brogden Rd PO Box 2430 ... Smithfield NC 27577 919-934-4115

JW Jones Lumber Company Inc
1443 Northside Rd ... Elizabeth City NC 27909 252-771-2497 771-8252
Web: mackeysferrysawmill.com

Kasco-Sharptech Corp 1569 Tower Grove Ave ... St. Louis MO 63110 314-771-1550
Web: www.kascosharptech.com

Kitchens Bros Manufacturing Co
4854 Reed Town Rd ... Utica MS 39175 601-885-6001 885-8501

Komo Machine Inc 1 Gusmer Dr ... Lakewood NJ 08701 732-719-6222
Web: www.komo.com

Kretz Lumber Company Inc W11143 County Hwy G ... Antigo WI 54409 715-623-5410
Web: www.kretzlumber.com

La Crete Sawmills Ltd Hwy 697 S PO Box 1090 ... La Crete AB T0H2H0 780-928-2292
Web: lacretesawmills.com

Langdale Forest Products Co
1202 Madison Hwy ... Valdosta GA 31603 229-333-2500 333-2533
Web: www.langdaleforest.com

Lewisohn Sales Company Inc
4001 Dell Ave ... North Bergen NJ 07047 201-864-0300
Web: www.lewisohn.com

				Phone	Fax
Lon Musolf Distributing Inc 985 E Berwood Ave. .... Vadnais Heights *Web:* www.lonmusolf.com		MN	55110	651-484-3020	
Louisiana-Pacific Corp 414 Union St Ste 2000 .... Nashville *NYSE: LPX* ■ *TF:* 888-820-0325 ■ *Web:* www.lpcorp.com		TN	37219	615-986-5600	986-5666
Maibec Inc 1984, 5e Rue .... Levis *TF:* 800-363-1930 ■ *Web:* www.maibec.com		QC	G6W5M6	418-659-3323	
Manke Lumber Company Inc 1717 Marine View Dr ...... Tacoma *TF:* 800-426-8488 ■ *Web:* www.mankelumber.com		WA	98422	253-572-6252	383-2489
Matson Lumber Company Inc 132 Main St .... Brookville *Web:* www.matsonlumber.com		PA	15825	814-849-5334	849-3811
MC Dixon Lumber Company Inc 605 W Washington St. .... Eufaula *Web:* www.dixonlumber.com		AL	36027	334-687-8204	687-8208
Menominee Tribal Enterprises PO Box 10 .... Neopit *Web:* www.mtewood.com		WI	54150	715-756-2311	799-4323
Merritt Bros Lumber Co Inc 5400 E Hwy 54 .... Athol *Web:* www.merrittbros.com		ID	83801	208-683-3321	683-3328
Mid South Lumber Inc 1115 C St. .... Meridian *Web:* www.mid-southlumber.com		MS	39301	601-483-4389	
Midwest Hardwood Corp 9540 83rd Ave N .... Maple Grove *Web:* www.midwesthardwood.com		MN	55369	763-425-8700	391-6740
Mill & Timber Products Ltd 12770- 116th Ave .... Surrey *Web:* www.millandtimber.com		BC	V3V7H9	604-580-2781	
Moose River Lumber Co Inc 25 Talpey Rd .... Moose River *Web:* pleasantriverlumber.com		ME	04945	207-668-4193	668-5381
Morgan Lumber Company Inc 628 Jeb Stuart Hwy ...... Red Oak *Web:* www.morganlumber.com		VA	23964	434-735-8151	
Nicholson Manufacturing Ltd 9896 Galaran Rd. .... Sidney *Web:* www.debarking.com		BC	V8L3S6	250-656-3131	
North American Forest Products Inc 27263 May St. .... Edwardsburg *Web:* www.nafpinc.com		MI	49112	269-663-8500	
Ochoco Lumber Co 200 SE Combs Flat Rd PO Box 668 .... Prineville		OR	97754	541-389-5000	382-6131
Ohio Valley Veneer Inc 165 No Name Rd .... Piketon		OH	45661	740-289-4979	
Oregon Canadian Forest Products Inc 31950 Comml St NW .... North Plains *Web:* www.ocfp.com		OR	97133	503-647-5011	647-0910
Pacific Fibre Products Inc 20 Fibre Way .... Longview *Web:* www.pacfibre.com		WA	98632	360-577-7112	
Parton Lumber Company Inc 251 Parton Rd. .... Rutherfordton *TF:* 800-624-1501 ■ *Web:* www.partonlumber.com		NC	28139	828-287-4257	
Pike Lumber Company Inc PO Box 247 .... Akron *TF:* 800-356-4554 ■ *Web:* www.pikelumber.com		IN	46910	574-893-4511	893-7400
Pleasant River Lumber Co 432 Milo Rd .... Dover-Foxcroft *Web:* www.pleasantriverlumber.com		ME	04426	207-564-8520	
Plummer Forest Products Inc 401 N Poltatch Rd. .... Post Falls *Web:* www.plummerforest.com		ID	83854	208-457-1060	
Potlatch Corp 601 W First Ave Ste 1600 .... Spokane *NASDAQ: PCH* ■ *Web:* www.potlatchcorp.com		WA	99201	509-835-1500	
Potlatch Corp Wood Products Div 805 Mill Rd PO Box 1388 .... Lewiston *Web:* www.potlatchcorp.com		ID	83501	509-835-1500	
Pyramid Mountain Lumber Inc 379 Boy Scout Rd PO Box 549 .... Seeley Lake *Web:* www.pyramidlumber.com		MT	59868	406-677-2201	677-2509
Riephoff Sawmill Inc 763 Rt 524 .... Allentown *Web:* www.riephoffsawmill.com		NJ	08501	609-259-7265	
Robbins Inc 4777 Eastern Ave .... Cincinnati *TF:* 800-543-1913 ■ *Web:* www.robbinsfloor.com		OH	45226	513-871-8988	871-7998
Robbins Lumber Co 53 Ghent Rd .... Searsmont *Web:* www.rlco.com		ME	04973	207-342-5221	342-5201
Rogers Lumber Company Inc 937 Hwy 7 N .... Camden *Web:* rogerspallet.com		AR	71701	870-574-0231	
Rosboro Lumber Co 2509 Main St .... Springfield *Web:* www.rosboro.com		OR	97477	541-746-8411	726-8919
Roseburg Forest Products Co PO Box 1088 .... Roseburg *TF:* 800-245-1115 ■ *Web:* www.roseburg.com		OR	97470	541-679-3311	
RSG Forest Products Inc 985 NW Second St .... Kalama *Web:* www.rsgfp.com		WA	98625	360-673-2825	673-5558
Rushmore Forest Products 23848 Hwy 385 PO Box 619 .... Hill City *TF:* 866-466-5254 ■ *Web:* neimanenterprises.com		SD	57745	605-574-2512	
Rutland Plywood Corp 1 Ripley Rd .... Rutland *Web:* www.rutply.com		VT	05701	802-747-4000	
Sandstorm Enterprises Inc 14 Summer St .... Malden *Web:* www.sandstorm.net		MA	02148	781-333-3200	
Scotch Gulf Lumber 1850 Conception St Rd .... Mobile *TF:* 800-496-3307 ■ *Web:* www.gulflumber.com		AL	36610	251-457-6872	452-7110
Scotch Lumber Co 119 W Main St PO Box 38 .... Fulton *TF:* 800-936-4424 ■ *Web:* scotchplywood.com		AL	36446	334-636-4424	
Scott Industries Inc 1573 Hwy 136 W PO Box 7 .... Henderson *TF:* 800-951-9276 ■ *Web:* www.scott-mfg.com		KY	42419	270-831-2037	831-2039
Seattle Snohomish Mill Co Inc 9525 Airport Way .... Snohomish		WA	98296	360-568-2171	
Seneca Sawmill Co 90201 Hwy 99 .... Eugene *Web:* www.senecasawmill.com		OR	97440	541-689-1011	
Sierra Forest Products 9000 Rd 234 .... Terra Bella *Web:* www.sierrafp.com		CA	93270	559-535-4893	
Sierra Pacific Industries 19794 Riverside Ave. .... Anderson *Web:* spi-ind.com		CA	96007	530-378-8000	378-8109
Simpson Timber Co 917 E 11th St .... Tacoma *Web:* www.simpson.com		WA	98421	253-779-6400	680-6855
Sims Bark Company Inc 1765 Spring Vly Rd .... Tuscumbia *Web:* www.simsbark.com		AL	35674	256-381-8323	
Smith Flooring Inc 1501 W Hwy 60 PO Box 99 .... Mountain View *Web:* www.smithflooring.com		MO	65548	417-934-2291	934-2295
South Coast Lumber Co 885 Railroad Ave PO Box 670 .... Brookings *Web:* www.socomi.com		OR	97415	541-469-2136	469-3487
Stella-Jones Inc 3100 de la Cote-Vertu Blvd Ste 300 .... St-laurent *Web:* www.stella-jones.com		QC	H4R2J8	514-934-8666	934-5327
Stimson Lumber Co 520 SW Yamhill St Ste 700 .... Portland *TF:* 800-445-9758 ■ *Web:* www.stimsonlumber.com		OR	97204	503-222-1676	222-2682
Sun Mountain Lumber 181 Greenhouse Rd .... Deer Lodge *Web:* www.sunmtnlumber.com		MT	59722	406-846-1600	
Swaner Hardwood Co Inc 5 W Magnolia Blvd PO Box 4200 .... Burbank *Web:* www.swanerhardwood.com		CA	91503	818-953-5350	846-3662
Teal-Jones Group, The 17897 Triggs Rd. .... Surrey *TF:* 888-995-8325 ■ *Web:* www.tealjones.com		BC	V4N4M8	604-587-8700	
Tembec Inc 800 Boul Rene Levesque O Bureau 1050 .... Montreal *TSE: TMB* ■ *TF:* 800-565-3021 ■ *Web:* www.tembec.com		QC	H3B1X9	514-871-0137	397-0896
Terminal Forest Products Ltd 12180 Mitchell Rd .... Richmond *Web:* www.terminalforest.com		BC	V6V1M8	604-717-1200	
TR Miller Mill Company Inc 215 Deer St PO Box 708 .... Brewton *TF:* 800-633-6740 ■ *Web:* www.trmillermill.com		AL	36427	251-867-4331	867-6882
Tucker Lumber Cos LLC 601 N Pearl St. .... Pageland *Web:* www.cmtuckerlumber.com		SC	29728	843-672-6135	672-5393
United Lumber & Remanufacturing LLC 980 Ford Rd .... Muscle Shoals *Web:* www.ufpi.com/united-lumber-reman		AL	35661	256-381-4151	
United Treating & Distribution LLC 338 D E Washington Ave .... Muscle Shoals *Web:* unitedtreating.com		AL	35661	256-248-0944	
Universal Forest Products Inc (UFPI) 2801 E Beltline Ave NE .... Grand Rapids *NASDAQ: UFPI* ■ *TF:* 800-598-9663 ■ *Web:* www.ufpi.com		MI	49525	616-364-6161	361-7534
USNR 1981 Schurman Way PO Box 310 .... Woodland *TF:* 800-289-8767 ■ *Web:* www.coemfg.com		WA	98674	360-225-8267	225-8017
West Coast Engineering Group Ltd 7984 River Rd .... Delta *Web:* www.wceng.com		BC	V4G1E3	604-946-1256	946-1203
West Fraser Timber Company Ltd (WFT) 501-858 Beatty St Ste 501 .... Vancouver *NYSE: WFT* ■ *Web:* www.westfraser.com		BC	V6B1C1	604-895-2700	681-6061
Westervelt Company Inc, The PO Box 48999 .... Tuscaloosa *Web:* www.westervelt.com		AL	35404	205-562-5000	562-5012
Weyerhaeuser Co 33663 Weyerhaeuser Way S .... Federal Way *NYSE: WY* ■ *TF:* 800-525-5440 ■ *Web:* www.weyerhaeuser.com		WA	98003	253-924-2345	

684 SCALES & BALANCES

See Also Laboratory Apparatus & Furniture p. 2625

				Phone	Fax
Advance Scale of MD LLC 2400 Egg Harbor Rd .... Lindenwold *TF:* 888-447-2253 ■ *Web:* advancescale.com		NJ	08021	856-627-0700	
Avery Weigh-Tronix Inc 1000 Armstrong Dr .... Fairmont **Fax:* Mktg ■ *TF:* 800-458-7062 ■ *Web:* www.averyweigh-tronix.com		MN	56031	507-238-4461	238-8258*
BRK Brands Inc 3901 Liberty St Rd .... Aurora *TF:* 800-323-9005 ■ *Web:* www.firstalert.com		IL	60504	630-851-7330	851-7452
Cardinal Detecto Scale Manufacturing Co 203 E Daugherty St. .... Webb City *TF:* 800-441-4237 ■ *Web:* www.cardet.com		MO	64870	417-673-4631	673-5001
Compuweigh Corp 50 Middle Quarter Rd .... Woodbury *Web:* www.compuweigh.com		CT	06798	203-262-9400	
Detecto Scale Co 203 E Daugherty St PO Box 151 .... Webb City *TF:* 800-641-2008 ■ *Web:* www.detecto.com		MO	64870	417-673-4631	673-4631
Emery Winslow Scale Co 73 Cogwheel Ln .... Seymour *TF:* 800-891-3952 ■ *Web:* www.emerywinslow.com		CT	06483	203-881-9333	881-9477
Fairbanks Scales Inc 821 Locust St .... Kansas City *TF:* 800-451-4107 ■ *Web:* www.fairbanks.com		MO	64106	816-471-0231	471-0241
Industrial Data Systems Inc 3822 E La Palma Ave .... Anaheim *TF:* 800-854-3311 ■ *Web:* www.industrialdata.com		CA	92807	714-921-9212	399-0286
Intercomp Co 3839 County Rd 116 .... Medina *TF:* 800-328-3336 ■ *Web:* www.intercompcompany.com		MN	55340	763-476-2531	476-2613
Jarden Consumer Solutions 2381 Executive Ctr Dr. .... Boca Raton *TF:* 800-777-5452 ■ *Web:* www.jardencs.com		FL	33431	561-912-4100	
Johnson Scale Company Inc 36 Stiles Ln .... Pine Brook **Fax Area Code:* 973 ■ *TF:* 800-572-2531 ■ *Web:* www.johnsonscale.net		NJ	07058	800-572-2531	882-8068*
LSI Robway Pty Ltd 9633 Zaka Rd .... Houston *Web:* www.loadsystems.com		TX	77064	281-664-1330	
Measurement Specialties Inc 1000 Lucas Way .... Hampton *NASDAQ: MEAS* ■ *TF:* 800-745-8008 ■ *Web:* www.meas-spec.com		VA	23666	757-766-1500	766-4297
Medela Inc 1101 Corporate Dr. .... Mchenry *Web:* www.medela.us		IL	60050	815-363-1166	
Merrick Industries Inc 10 Arthur Dr .... Lynn Haven **Fax:* Hum Res ■ *Web:* www.merrick-inc.com		FL	32444	850-265-3611	265-9768*
Mettler-Toledo International Inc 5 Barr Rd .... Ithaca **Fax Area Code:* 607 ■ *TF:* 800-836-0836 ■ *Web:* mt.com/hi-speed		NY	14850	800-836-0836	266-5478*
Ohaus Corp 19-A Chapin Rd PO Box 2033 .... Pine Brook *TF:* 800-672-7722 ■ *Web:* asiapacific.ohaus.com		NJ	07058	973-377-9000	944-7177
Premier Tech Industrial Equipment Group 1 Premier Ave .... Rivere-du-Loup *TF:* 866-571-7354 ■ *Web:* www.ptchronos.com		QC	G5R6C1	418-867-8884	862-6642
Schenck Trebel Corp 535 Acorn St .... Deer Park *TF:* 800-873-2357 ■ *Web:* www.schenck-usa.com		NY	11729	631-242-4010	242-5077
Scientech Inc 5649 Arapahoe Ave. .... Boulder *TF:* 800-525-0522 ■ *Web:* www.scientech-inc.com		CO	80303	303-444-1361	444-9229

				Phone	Fax
Setra Systems Inc 159 Swanson Rd *TF:* 800-257-3872 ■ *Web:* www.setra.com	Boxborough	MA	01719	978-263-1400	264-0292
Tanita Corp of America Inc 2625 S Clearbrook Dr *TF:* 800-826-4828 ■ *Web:* www.tanita.com	Arlington Heights	IL	60005	847-640-9241	640-9261
TCI Scales Inc PO Box 1648 *TF:* 800-522-2206 ■ *Web:* www.tciscales.com	Snohomish	WA	98291	425-353-4384	609-1021
Thayer Scale Corp 91 Schoosett St **Fax:* Cust Svc ■ *TF:* 855-784-2937 ■ *Web:* www.thayerscale.com	Pembroke	MA	02359	781-826-8101	826-0072*
Wisconsin Electrical Mfg Company Inc (WEM) 2501 S Moorland Rd PO Box 510767 *Web:* www.wemautomation.com	New Berlin	WI	53151	262-782-2340	782-2653
Yamato Corp 1775 S Murray Blvd *TF:* 800-538-1762 ■ *Web:* www.yamatocorp.com	Colorado Springs	CO	80916	719-591-1500	591-1045

685 SCHOOL BOARDS (PUBLIC)

				Phone	Fax
A.C. White Transfer & Storage Co Inc 1775 Founders Pkwy *Web:* www.atlantamovingcorp.com	Alpharetta	GA	30009	770-325-9100	325-9175
Abbeville County School District 60 400 Greenville St *Web:* www.acsd.k12.sc.us	Abbeville	SC	29620	864-366-5427	
Abbotsford Virtual School 33952 Pine St *Web:* avs.sd34.bc.ca	Abbotsford	BC	V2S2P3	604-859-9803	
Aberdeen School District 5 216 N G St *Web:* www.asd5.org	Aberdeen	WA	98520	360-538-2000	
Abrams Hebrew Academy 31 W College Ave *Web:* abramsonline.org	Yardley	PA	19067	215-493-1800	
Academy of Notre Dame De Namur 560 Sproul Rd *Web:* www.ndapa.org	Villanova	PA	19085	610-687-0650	
Acalanes Union High School Dist 1212 Pleasant Hill Rd *Web:* www.acalanes.k12.ca.us	Lafayette	CA	94549	925-280-3900	932-2336
Adair County Board of Education 1204 Greensburg St *Web:* adair.k12.ky.us	Columbia	KY	42728	270-384-2476	
Airport Community Schools 11270 Grafton Rd	Carleton	MI	48117	734-654-2414	654-3424
Akron Public Schools 70 N Broadway Ave *Web:* www.akronschools.com	Akron	OH	44308	330-761-1661	761-3225
Al Huda Islamic School 12227 Hawthorne Way *Web:* www.ichla.org	Hawthorne	CA	90250	310-973-0500	
Alamance-Burlington School District 1712 Vaughn Rd *TF:* 888-764-7001 ■ *Web:* www.abss.k12.nc.us	Burlington	NC	27217	336-570-6060	570-6218
Alameda Bible Church Home of Victory Christian School 220 El Pueblo Rd Nw *Web:* www.alamedabiblechurch.com	Albuquerque	NM	87114	505-898-2311	
Albany County School 1948 E Grand Ave *Web:* www.acsd1.org	Laramie	WY	82070	307-721-4400	
Albuquerque Public Schools (APS) 6400 Uptown Blvd NE **Fax:* Hum Res ■ *TF:* 866-563-9297 ■ *Web:* www.aps.edu	Albuquerque	NM	87110	505-880-3700	889-4883*
Alden Hebron High School 9604 Illinois St *Web:* www.alden-hebron.org	Hebron	IL	60034	815-648-2442	
Alexander Smith Academy Inc 10255 Richmond Ave Ste 100 *Web:* www.alexandersmith.com	Houston	TX	77042	713-266-0920	
Alisal Union Elementary School District 1205 E Market St *TF:* 800-782-7463 ■ *Web:* www.alisal.org	Salinas	CA	93905	831-753-5700	753-5709
Allegheny Valley School District 300 PEARL Ave *Web:* avsdweb.org	Cheswick	PA	15024	724-274-5300	274-8040
Allen Village School 706 W 42nd St *Web:* www.allenvillageschool.com	Kansas City	MO	64111	816-931-0177	
Allentown School District (ASD) 31 S Penn St *TF:* 877-262-1492 ■ *Web:* www.allentownsd.org	Allentown	PA	18105	484-765-4000	765-4140
Alpena Public Schools (Inc) 2373 Gordon Rd *Web:* www.alpenaschools.com	Alpena	MI	49707	989-358-5040	358-5041
Alta Loma School District 9390 Baseline Rd *Web:* www.alsd.k12.ca.us	Alta Loma	CA	91701	909-484-5151	484-5195
Amador County Unified School District 217 Rex Ave *Web:* www.amadorcoe.org	Jackson	CA	95642	209-223-1750	
Amarillo Independent School District (AISD) 7200 I- 40 W **Fax:* Hum Res ■ *Web:* amaisd.org	Amarillo	TX	79106	806-326-1000	354-4378*
American Quality Schools Corp 910 W. Van Buren St *Web:* www.aqs.org	Chicago	IL	60607	312-226-3355	
Ames Community School District 415 Stanton Ave *TF:* 800-262-3867 ■ *Web:* www.ames.k12.ia.us	Ames	IA	50014	515-268-6600	268-6633
Anaheim Elementary School District 1001 SE St *Web:* anaheimelementary.org	Anaheim	CA	92805	714-517-7500	
Anaheim Union High School District (AUHSB) 501 N Crescent Way **Fax:* Admin ■ *Web:* www.auhsd.us	Anaheim	CA	92801	714-999-3511	520-9752*
Anchor Bay School District 5201 County Line Rd Ste 100 *TF:* 800-285-4460 ■ *Web:* www.anchorbay.misd.net	Casco Township	MI	48064	586-725-2861	725-0290
Anchorage School District 3580 E Tudor Rd *Web:* www.asdk12.org	Anchorage	AK	99507	907-742-4000	742-4176
Anoka-Hennepin Independent School District 11 2727 N Ferry St *TF:* 800-729-6164 ■ *Web:* www.anoka.k12.mn.us	Anoka	MN	55303	763-506-1000	506-1003
Anthony Wayne Board of Education PO Box 2487 *Web:* www.anthonywayneschools.org	Whitehouse	OH	43571	419-877-5377	
Apollo-Ridge School District PO Box 219 *Web:* www.apolloridge.com	Spring Church	PA	15686	724-478-6000	
Apple Valley Unified School District (AVUSD) 12555 Navajo Rd *Web:* www.avusd.org	Apple Valley	CA	92308	760-247-8001	
Appling County Board of Education 249 Blackshear Hwy *TF:* 866-632-9992 ■ *Web:* www.appling.k12.ga.us	Baxley	GA	31513	912-367-8600	
Archway Programs Inc PO Box 668 *Web:* www.archwayprograms.org	Atco	NJ	08004	856-767-5757	
Arlington Central School District 144 Todd Hill Rd *TF:* 800-993-8982 ■ *Web:* www.arlingtonschools.org	LaGrangeville	NY	12540	845-486-4460	486-4457
Arlington School District 315 N French Ave *TF:* 888-535-0747 ■ *Web:* www.asd.wednet.edu	Arlington	WA	98223	360-618-6200	618-6221
Armbrae Academy 1400 Oxford St *Web:* www.armbrae.ns.ca	Halifax	NS	B3H3Y8	902-423-7920	
Armijo High School 824 Washington St *Web:* www.fsusd.org	Fairfield	CA	94533	707-422-7500	
Armstrong School District 410 Main St *TF:* 888-573-5733 ■ *Web:* www.asd.k12.pa.us	Ford City	PA	16226	724-763-5200	763-7295
Ashbury College 362 Mariposa Ave *Web:* www.ashbury.on.ca	Rockcliffe	ON	K1M0T3	613-749-5954	
Asheville Catholic School 12 Culvern St *Web:* www.ashevillecatholic.org	Asheville	NC	28804	828-252-7896	
Ashland Independent School District PO Box 3000 *TF:* 800-752-6200 ■ *Web:* www.ashland.kyschools.us	Ashland	KY	41105	606-327-2706	327-2705
Ashley Hall School 172 Rutledge Ave *Web:* ashleyhall.org	Charleston	SC	29403	843-722-4088	
Ashtabula Area City School District 2630 W 13th St *Web:* www.aacs.net	Ashtabula	OH	44004	440-992-1200	992-1209
Ashwaubenon School District 1055 Griffiths Ln *Web:* www.ashwaubenon.k12.wi.us	Green Bay	WI	54304	920-492-2900	492-2911
Athens City School District 25 S Plains Rd *Web:* www.athenscity.k12.oh.us	The Plains	OH	45780	740-797-4544	
Atkinson County School System 98 Roberts Ave E *TF:* 800-639-0850 ■ *Web:* www.atkinson.k12.ga.us	Pearson	GA	31642	912-422-7373	422-7369
Atlanta Public Schools 130 Trinity Ave SW *Web:* www.atlanta.k12.ga.us	Atlanta	GA	30303	404-802-3500	802-1803
Au Authum Ki Inc 4645 S Ash Ave Ste I1 *Web:* www.authumki.com	Tempe	AZ	85282	480-497-1997	377-1143
Auburn City School District PO Box 3270 *TF:* 866-632-9992 ■ *Web:* www.auburnschools.org	Auburn	AL	36831	334-887-2100	887-2107
Auburn Union School District 255 Epperle Ln *Web:* www.auburn.k12.ca.us	Auburn	CA	95603	530-885-7242	885-5170
Austin Elementary School 1900 Duncan St *Web:* www.pampaisd.net	Pampa	TX	79065	806-669-4760	
Austin Jewish Academy 7300 Hart Ln *Web:* www.austinjewishacademy.org	Austin	TX	78731	512-735-8350	
Ave Intervision LLC 1840 W State St *TF:* 800-448-9126 ■ *Web:* www.amvonet.com	Alliance	OH	44601	800-448-9126	
Avondale House 3611 Cummins St *Web:* www.avondalehouse.org	Houston	TX	77027	713-993-9544	
Avonworth School District 258 Josephs Ln *Web:* www.avonworth.k12.pa.us	Pittsburgh	PA	15237	412-369-8738	369-8746
Axis Construction Corp 125 Laser Ct *Web:* www.theaxisgroup.com	Hauppauge	NY	11788	631-243-5970	243-5973
Bakersfield City School District 1300 Baker St *Web:* www.bcsd.com	Bakersfield	CA	93305	661-631-4600	326-1485
Balboa City Schools 525 Hawthorn St *Web:* www.balboaschool.com	San Diego	CA	92101	619-298-2990	
Baltimore City Public Schools 200 E N Ave **Fax Area Code:* 410 ■ *Web:* www.baltimorecityschools.org	Baltimore	MD	21202	443-984-2000	545-0897*
Baltimore Polytechnic Institute 1400 W Cold Spring Ln *Web:* www.bpi.edu	Baltimore	MD	21209	410-396-7026	
Banks County Board of Education PO Box 248 *Web:* www.banks.k12.ga.us	Homer	GA	30547	706-677-2224	
Barbers Hill Isd (BHISD) 9600 Eagle Dr PO Box 1108 *Web:* www.bhisd.net	Mont Belvieu	TX	77580	281-576-2221	
Barnard & Sons Construction LLC 3054 Simpson Hwy 13 PO Box 517 *Web:* www.barnardandsons.com	Mendenhall	MS	39114	601-847-2420	847-0110
Barney Trucking Inc 235 State Rt 24 **Fax Area Code:* 435 ■ *TF:* 800-524-7930 ■ *Web:* www.barneytrucking.com	Salina	UT	84654	800-524-7930	529-7314*
Barstow School, The 11511 State Line Rd *Web:* www.barstowschool.org	Kansas City	MO	64114	816-942-3255	
Bartlett High School 701 W Schick Rd *Web:* www.u-46.org	Bartlett	IL	60103	630-372-4700	
Bastrop Isd 906 Farm St *Web:* www.bisdtx.org	Bastrop	TX	78602	512-772-7100	
Battle River Regional Div 5402 48a Ave *Web:* www.brsd.ab.ca	Camrose	AB	T4V0L3	780-672-6131	
Baugo Community School Indiana 29125 County Rd 22 W	Elkhart	IN	46517	574-293-8583	
Bay City Public Schools 910 N Walnut St *Web:* www.bcschools.net	Bay City	MI	48706	989-686-9700	686-7626
Bayview Glen Public School 42 Limcombe Dr *Web:* www.yrdsb.ca	Markham	ON	L3T2V5	905-889-2448	
Beam Construction Company Inc 601 E Main St *Web:* www.beamconstruction.com	Cherryville	NC	28021	704-435-3206	435-8412
Beantree Learning 43629 Greenway Corporate Dr *Web:* beantreelearning.com	Ashburn	VA	20147	571-223-3110	

Phone Fax

Bear Branch Elementary School
8909 Fm 1488 Rd . . . Magnolia TX 77354 281-356-4771
Web: www.magnoliaisd.org

Beaufort County Board of Education
321 Smaw Rd . . . Washington NC 27889 252-946-6593
Web: www.beaufort.k12.nc.us

Beaumont School 3301 N Park Blvd . . . Cleveland Heights OH 44118 216-321-2954
Web: www.beaumontschool.org

Beavercreek Board of Education 3040 Kemp Rd . . . Dayton OH 45431 937-426-1522 429-7517
Web: www.beavercreek.k12.oh.us

Bedford Public Schools 1623 W Sterns Rd . . . Temperance MI 48182 734-850-6000 850-6099
TF: 866-261-9184 ■ *Web:* www.bedford.k12.mi.us

Beemac Trucking 2747 Litionville Rd . . . Ambridge PA 15003 724-266-8781 266-5638
TF: 800-282-8781 ■ *Web:* beemactrucking.com

Belle Chasse Academy Inc 100 Fifth St . . . Belle Chasse LA 70037 504-433-5850
Web: www.bellechasseacademy.com

Bellefonte Area School District
318 N Allegheny St . . . Bellefonte PA 16823 814-355-4814
TF: 866-632-9992 ■ *Web:* www.basd.net

Belton School District 110 W Walnut St . . . Belton MO 64012 816-489-7000
Web: www.beltonschools.org

Bemidji Ind School District 31
3300 Gillett Dr NW . . . Bemidji MN 56601 218-333-3110
Web: www.bemidji.k12.mn.us

Berea City School District 390 Fair St . . . Berea OH 44017 216-898-8300 898-8551
Web: www.berea.k12.oh.us

Bernards Township Board of Education
101 Peachtree Rd . . . Basking Ridge NJ 07920 908-204-2600
Web: www.bernardsboe.com

Berrien Resa 711 Saint Joseph Ave . . . Berrien Springs MI 49103 269-471-7725
Web: www.berrienresa.org

Beth Ramacher Development Ctr
710 N Hughes Ave . . . Fresno CA 93728 559-497-3955
Web: www.fcoe.org

Bettendorf Community School District
3311 18th St . . . Bettendorf IA 52722 563-359-3681 359-3685
Web: www.bettendorf.k12.ia.us

Beverly Hills Unified School District
255 S Lasky Dr . . . Beverly Hills CA 90212 310-551-5100 277-6137
TF: 877-220-7229 ■ *Web:* www.bhusd.org

Bexley City School District
348 S Cassingham Rd . . . Columbus OH 43209 614-231-7611
TF: 800-282-1780 ■ *Web:* www.bexleyschools.org

Bialik Hebrew Day School 2760 Bathurst St . . . Toronto ON M6B3A1 416-783-3346
Web: bialik.ca

Big Spring Independent School District
708 E 11th Pl . . . Big Spring TX 79720 432-264-3600 264-3646
TF: 866-632-9992 ■ *Web:* www.bsisd.esc18.net

Biltmore Construction Company Inc
1055 Ponce De Leon Blvd . . . Belleair FL 33756 727-585-2084 585-2088
Web: www.biltmoreconstruction.com

Binghamton City School District (BCSD)
164 Hawley St PO Box 2126 . . . Binghamton NY 13902 607-762-8100
Web: binghamtonschools.org

Birmingham Board of Education (BCS)
2015 Pk Pl N . . . Birmingham AL 35203 205-231-4600
Web: www.bhamcityschools.org

Bishop George Ahr High School 1 Tingley Ln . . . Edison NJ 08820 732-549-1108
Web: www.bgahs.org

Bishop Kelly Foundation Inc 7009 W Franklin Rd . . . Boise ID 83709 208-375-6010
Web: www.bk.org

Bishop Loughlin Memorial High School
357 Clermont Ave . . . Brooklyn NY 11238 718-857-2700
Web: blmhs.org

Bishop Miege High School
5041 Reinhardt Dr . . . Roeland Park KS 66205 913-262-2700
Web: www.bishopmiege.com

Bishop O'Dowd High School 9500 Stearns Ave . . . OAKLAND CA 94605 510-577-9100
Web: www.bishopodowd.org

Bishop Whelan Elementary School
244 rue de la Presentation . . . Dorval QC H9S3L6 514-634-0550
Web: bishopwhelan.lbpsb.qc.ca

Black Horse Pike Regional School District
580 Erial Rd . . . Blackwood NJ 08012 856-227-4105 227-6835
Web: www.bhprsd.org

Blackburn Elementary School 10 E 25th St . . . Newton NC 28658 972-564-7008
Web: www.catawbaschools.net

Blackfoot School District 55
270 E Bridge St . . . Blackfoot ID 83221 208-785-8800 785-8809
Web: www.d55.k12.id.us

Blacksburg High 750 Imperial St . . . Christiansburg VA 24073 864-206-2378
Web: www.mcps.org

Blast Intermediate Unit 17
2400 Reach Rd . . . Williamsport PA 17701 570-323-8561
Web: www.iu17.org

Blount County Schools 204 Second Ave E . . . Oneonta AL 35121 205-625-4102
Web: www.blountboe.net

Blue Mountain School District Inc
PO Box 188 . . . Orwigsburg PA 17961 570-366-0515
Web: www.bmsd.org

Blythe Park Elementary School
735 Leesley Rd . . . Riverside IL 60546 708-447-2168
Web: www.district96.org

Boarder to Boarder Trucking Inc PO Box 328 . . . Edinburg TX 78541 956-316-4444 316-4445
TF: 800-678-8789 ■ *Web:* www.btbtrucking.com

Boces
Lower Hudson Regional Information Ctr 44 Executive Blvd
. . . Elmsford NY 10523 914-592-4203
Web: www.lhric.org

Bodwell High School
955 Harbourside Dr . . . North Vancouver BC V7P3S4 604-924-5056
Web: www.bodwell.edu

Boise City Independent School District
8169 W Victory Rd . . . Boise ID 83709 208-854-4000 854-4003
Web: www.sd01.k12.id.us

Phone Fax

Bookman Road Elementary School 1245 Bookman Rd . . . Elgin SC 29045 803-699-1724
Web: www.richland2.org

Borger High School 600 W First St . . . Borger TX 79007 806-273-1029
Web: www.borgerisd.net

Borough-Bogota Board-Education
1 Henry C Luthin Pl . . . Bogota NJ 07603 201-441-4800
Web: bogotaboe.com

Borton Lc 200 E First Ave . . . Hutchinson KS 67501 620-669-8211
Web: borton.biz

Boulder Country Day School
4820 Nautilus Court N . . . Boulder CO 80301 303-527-4931
Web: bouldercountryday.org

Bowling Green City Schools (BGCS)
137 Clough St . . . Bowling Green OH 43402 419-352-3576 352-1701
Web: www.bgcs.k12.oh.us

Bowling Green Independent School District
1211 Ctr St . . . Bowling Green KY 42101 270-746-2200
Web: b-g.k12.ky.us

Bozeman School District 7 PO Box 520 . . . Bozeman MT 59771 406-522-6000
Web: www.bsd7.org

Bradford Area School District Inc
PO Box 375 . . . Bradford PA 16701 814-362-3841
Web: www.bradfordareaschools.org

Brandon School Division 813 26th St . . . Brandon MB R7B2B6 204-729-3955
Web: www.bsd.ca

Breckinridge County School District
86 Airport Rd . . . Hardinsburg KY 40143 270-756-2186
TF: 800-325-1713 ■ *Web:* breckinridgecountyky.com

Brecksville Broadview Hts Csd
6638 Mill Rd . . . Brecksville OH 44141 440-740-4000 740-4004
Web: www.bbhcsd.org

Brentwood Christian School Association of Parents, Teachers & Friends
11908 N Lamar Blvd . . . Austin TX 78753 512-835-5983

Brentwood High School Pto 5304 Murray Ln . . . Brentwood TN 37027 615-472-4220
Web: www.ptobhs.org

Brentwood School 100 S Barrington Pl . . . Los Angeles CA 90049 310-476-9633 476-4087
Web: www.bwscampus.com

Bridges Public Charter School
1250 Taylor St Nw PO Box 60942 . . . Washington DC 20011 202-545-0515
Web: bridgespcs.org

Bristol-Warren Regional School District
151 State St . . . Bristol RI 02809 401-253-4000
Web: www.bw.k12.ri.us

Bronx Charter School for Excellence
1960 Benedict Ave . . . Bronx NY 10462 718-828-7301
Web: bronxexcellence.org

Brookhaven School District PO Box 540 . . . Brookhaven MS 39602 601-833-6661 833-4154
Web: www.brookhaven.k12.ms.us

Brookline College 2445 W Dunlap Ave Ste 100 . . . Phoenix AZ 85021 602-242-6265
TF: 800-793-2428 ■ *Web:* brooklinecollege.edu

Brooklyn Ascend Charter School
205 Rockaway Pkwy . . . Brooklyn NY 11212 718-240-9162
Web: www.ascendlearning.org

Brooks Elementary School 3225 Sangamon Dr . . . Dekalb IL 60115 815-754-9936
Web: www.dist428.org

Brookwood Middle School
1020 Hunters Ridge Dr . . . Genoa City WI 53128 262-279-1053
Web: www.genoacityschools.org

Broward County Public Schools
600 SE Third Ave . . . Fort Lauderdale FL 33301 754-321-0000 321-2701
Web: www.browardschools.com

Browne Academy 5917 Telegraph Rd . . . Alexandria VA 22310 703-960-3000
Web: www.browneacademy.org

Browning School Inc 52 E 62nd St . . . New York NY 10065 212-838-6280 355-5602
Web: www.browning.edu

Brownsville Area School Dist 5 Falcon Dr . . . Brownsville PA 15417 724-785-2021 785-4333
Web: www.basd.org

Brownsville Independent School District
1900 E Price Rd . . . Brownsville TX 78521 956-548-8000 548-8019
Web: www.bisd.us

Brunswick City School District 3643 Ctr Rd . . . Brunswick OH 44212 330-225-7731 273-0507
Web: www.bcsoh.org

Brunswick County Board of Education
35 Referendum Dr . . . Bolivia NC 28422 910-253-2900 253-2983
TF: 800-662-7030 ■ *Web:* www.bcswan.net

Bucher Elementary School 450 Candlewyck Rd . . . Lancaster PA 17601 717-569-4291
Web: www.mtwp.net

Buckingham Browne & Nichols School
46 Belmont St . . . Watertown MA 02472 617-547-6100
TF: 800-233-6329 ■ *Web:* www.bbns.org

Buckley School, The 3900 Stansbury Ave . . . Sherman Oaks CA 91423 818-783-1610
Web: www.buckley.org

Buffalo City School District 712 City Hall . . . Buffalo NY 14202 716-816-3500
Web: buffaloschools.org

Bullis Charter School 102 W Portola Ave . . . Los Altos CA 94022 650-947-4939
Web: www.bullischarterschool.com

Bulloch County Board of Education
150 Williams Rd Ste A . . . Statesboro GA 30458 912-212-8500 764-8436
Web: www.bulloch.k12.ga.us

Bullock Creek Public Schools
1420 S Badour Rd . . . Midland MI 48640 989-631-9022 631-2882
TF: 877-706-2508 ■ *Web:* www.bcreek.k12.mi.us

Burke County Public Schools
789 Burke Veterans Pkwy . . . Waynesboro GA 30830 706-554-5101 554-8051
Web: www.burke.k12.ga.us

Burnet Middle School 8401 Hathaway Dr . . . Austin TX 78757 512-414-3225
Web: www.austinisd.org

Bush School, The 3400 E Harrison St . . . Seattle WA 98112 206-322-7978
Web: bush.edu

Butler Area School District 110 Campus Ln . . . Butler PA 16001 724-287-8720
TF: 888-800-5583

Butler County Board of Education
215 Administrative Dr . . . Greenville AL 36037 334-382-2665
Web: www.butlerco.k12.al.us

Phone | Fax

Butts County Board of Education
181 N Mulberry St ... Jackson GA 30233 770-504-2300 504-2305
Web: www.butts.k12.ga.us
Cabarrus County School District
4401 Old Airport Rd ... Concord NC 28025 704-786-6191 786-6141
Web: cabarrus.k12.nc.us
Cabrillo Unified School District
498 Kelly Ave ... Half Moon Bay CA 94019 650-712-7100 726-0279
Web: www.cabrillo.k12.ca.us
Cache County School District
2063 N 1200 E ... North Logan UT 84341 435-752-3925 753-2168
TF: 888-837-6437 ■ *Web:* www.ccsdut.org
Caddo Mills Isd 100 Fox Ln ... Caddo Mills TX 75135 903-527-6056
Web: www.caddomillsisd.org
Caddo Parish School Board
1961 Midway Ave PO Box 32000 ... Shreveport LA 71130 318-603-6300 603-6559*
**Fax:* Hum Res ■ *Web:* caddo.k12.la.us
Cadillac Area Public Schools
421 S Mitchell St ... Cadillac MI 49601 231-876-5000
Web: vikingnet.org
Calhoun City of Schools Superintendents Offic
380 Barrett Rd ... Calhoun GA 30701 706-629-2900
Web: www.calhounschools.org
Calhoun County Board of Education
PO Box 2084 ... Anniston AL 36202 256-741-7400 237-5332
Web: www.calhoun.k12.al.us
Calhoun School Inc, The 160 W 74th St ... New York NY 10023 212-497-6500
Web: www.calhoun.org
Caliche Jr Sr. High School 301 Hagen St ... Sterling CO 80751 970-522-8200
Web: www.re1valleyschools.org
Calvary Church of Pacific
701 Palisades Dr ... Pacific Palisades CA 90272 310-454-6537
Web: www.calvarypalisades.org
Camden Central School District 51 Third St ... Camden NY 13316 315-245-2500
Web: www.camdenschools.org
Campbell Christian Schools
1075 E Campbell Ave ... Campbell CA 95008 408-370-4900
Web: www.campbellchristian.org
Campbell County Board of Education
101 Orchard Ln ... Alexandria KY 41001 859-635-2173 448-2428
TF: 800-942-3767 ■ *Web:* campbell.k12.ky.us
Campbell County Dept of Education
PO Box 843 ... Jacksboro TN 37757 423-562-8377 566-7562
Web: www.campbell.k12.tn.us
Campbell Union High School District
3235 Union Ave ... San Jose CA 95124 408-371-0960
Web: www.cuhsd.org
Campbell Union School District
155 N Third St ... Campbell CA 95008 408-364-4200
Web: www.campbellusd.org
Camphill Special School Inc
1784 Fairview Rd ... Glenmoore PA 19343 610-469-9236
Web: camphillspecialschool.org
Canandaigua City School District
143 N Pearl St ... Canandaigua NY 14424 585-396-3700
Web: www.canandaiguaschools.org
Canby School District 1130 S Ivy St ... Canby OR 97013 503-266-7861 266-0022
TF: 800-475-7785 ■ *Web:* www.canby.k12.or.us
Canton Public School District 403 Lincoln St ... Canton MS 39046 601-859-4110
Web: www.cantonschools.net
Capital High School 1500 Greenbrier St ... Charleston WV 25311 304-348-6500
Web: chs.kana.k12.wv.us
Cardinal Hayes High School 650 grand concourse ... Bronx NY 10451 718-292-6100
Cardinal O'hara High School 39 Ohara Rd ... Tonawanda NY 14150 716-695-2600
Web: www.cardinalohara.com
Carl Sandburg Jr High School
2600 Martin Ln ... Rolling Meadows IL 60008 847-963-7800
Web: www.ccsd15.net
Carlbrook School LLC, The
3046 Carlbrook Rd ... South Boston VA 24592 434-476-2406
Web: www.carlbrook.org
Carlinville Primary School
18456 Shipman Rd ... Carlinville IL 62626 217-854-9823
Web: www.carlinvilleschools.net
Carlthorp School 438 San Vicente Blvd ... Santa Monica CA 90402 310-451-1332
Web: carlthorp.org
Carlynton School District 435 Kings Hwy ... Carnegie PA 15106 412-429-8400
Web: www.carlynton.k12.pa.us
Carroll County Board of Ed
125 N Court St Ste 101 ... Westminster MD 21157 410-751-3000
Web: www.carrollk12.org
Cartersville School Board PO Box 3310 ... Cartersville GA 30120 770-382-3666
Web: www.cartersville.k12.ga.us
Cary Academy 1500 N Harrison Ave ... Cary NC 27513 919-677-3873
Web: www.caryacademy.org
Casa Di Mir Montessori School
90 E Latimer Ave ... Campbell CA 95008 408-370-3073
Web: www.casadimir.org
Case Raymond Elementary School
8565 Shasta Lily Dr ... Elk Grove CA 95624 916-681-8820
Web: egusd.net
Castilleja School Foundation
1310 Bryant St ... Palo Alto CA 94301 650-328-3160
Web: www.castilleja.org
Castle High School 3344 State Rt 261 ... Newburgh IN 47630 812-853-3331
Web: www.warrickschools.com
Catalina High School 3645 E Pima St ... Tucson AZ 85716 520-232-8400
Web: www.catalinahighschoolfoundation.org
Cataract Elementary School 6070 State Hwy 27 ... Sparta WI 54656 608-272-3111
Web: www.sparta.org
Cathedral High School 1253 Bishops Rd ... Los Angeles CA 90012 323-225-2438
Catholic High School 855 HEARTHSTONE DR ... Baton Rouge LA 70806 757-467-2881
Web: catholichigh.org

Centennial Independent School District No 12
4757 N Rd ... Circle Pines MN 55014 763-792-5000
Centennial School District
18135 SE Brooklyn ... Portland OR 97236 503-760-7990 762-3689
Web: csd28j.org
Centennial School District
433 Centennial Rd ... Warminster PA 18974 215-441-6000 441-5105
Web: www.centennialsd.org
Center Independent School Dist 404 Mosby St ... Center TX 75935 936-598-5642
Web: www.centerisd.org
Centinela Elementary School
1123 Marlborough Ave ... Inglewood CA 90302 310-680-5440
Web: inglewood.k12.ca.us
Central Montcalm Public School
1480 S Sheridan Rd ... Stanton MI 48888 989-831-5243
Web: www.central-montcalm.org
Central Union High School District
351 W Ross Ave ... El Centro CA 92243 760-336-4500 353-3606
Web: www.cuhsd.net
Centronia 1420 Columbia Rd Nw Fl 1 ... Washington DC 20009 202-332-4200
Web: www.centronia.org
Century Junior High School
10801 W 159th St ... Orland Park IL 60467 708-364-3500
Web: www.orland135.org
Champion Construction Corp
941 Forest Ave ... Staten Island NY 10310 718-818-8202 818-8238
Web: www.championcc.homestead.com
Chapa Elementary School 5670 N Doffing Rd ... Mission TX 78574 956-580-6150
Web: lajoyaisd.com
Chaparral Elementary School
451 Chaparral Dr ... Claremont CA 91711 909-398-0305
Chaparral High School 1600 N Cuyamaca St ... El Cajon CA 92020 619-956-4600
Web: chaparral.guhsd.net
Chariho Regional School District
455 Switch Rd ... Wood River Junction RI 02894 401-364-7575 415-6076
Web: www.chariho.k12.ri.us
Charleston County School District (CCSD)
75 Calhoun St ... Charleston SC 29401 843-937-6300 937-6300
TF: 800-255-7688 ■ *Web:* www.ccsdschools.com
Charleston School of Law LLC, The
81 Mary St ... Charleston SC 29403 843-329-1000
Web: www.charlestonlaw.edu
Charlevoix Public Schools
104 E St Marys Dr ... Charlevoix MI 49720 231-547-3200 547-0556
Web: www.rayder.net
Charlotte Latin Schools Inc
9502 Providence Rd ... Charlotte NC 28277 704-846-1100
Web: www.charlottelatin.org
Charlotte-Mecklenburg Schools
701 E ML King Jr Blvd ... Charlotte NC 28202 980-343-3000 343-5661
TF: 800-244-6224 ■ *Web:* www.cms.k12.nc.us
Chatham Central School District
50 Woodbridge Ave ... Chatham NY 12037 518-392-2400
Web: www.chathamcentralschools.com
Cherokee County Board of Education
221 W Main PO Box 769 ... Canton GA 30169 770-479-1871
Web: www.cherokee.k12.ga.us
Cherokee County School District 1
141 Twin Lk Rd PO Box 460 ... Gaffney SC 29342 864-206-2201
Web: www.cherokee1.k12.sc.us
Chester County School District 109 Hinton St ... Chester SC 29706 803-385-6122
Web: www.chester.k12.sc.us
Cheverus High School 267 Ocean Ave ... Portland ME 04103 207-774-6238
Web: www.cheverus.org
Chicago Board of Education 125 S Clark St ... Chicago IL 60603 773-553-1600 553-3543
Web: www.cps.edu/about_cps/pages/aboutcps.aspx
Chico Unified School District
1163 E Seventh St ... Chico CA 95928 530-891-3000 891-3220
Web: www.bcoe.org
Chignecto-central Regional 60 Lorne St ... Truro NS B2N3K3 902-897-8923
TF: 800-770-0008 ■ *Web:* www.ccrsb.ca
Childventures Early Learning Academy Inc
Burlington Campus 2180 Itabashi Way ... Burlington ON L7M5A5 905-637-8481
Web: www.childventures.ca
Chino Hills High School
16150 Pomona Rincon Rd ... Chino Hills CA 91709 909-606-7540
Web: chino.k12.ca.us
Chisum High School 3250 S Church St ... Paris TX 75462 903-737-2800
Web: www.chisumisd.org
Christ The King School Mothers Club Inc
4100 Colgate Ave ... Dallas TX 75225 214-365-1234
Web: www.cks.org
Christian County Public Schools
200 Glass Ave PO Box 609 ... Hopkinsville KY 42240 270-887-7000 887-1316
TF: 800-274-7374 ■ *Web:* www.christian.kyschools.us
Churchill County School District
545 E Richards St ... Fallon NV 89406 775-423-5184 423-2959
TF: 800-232-6382 ■ *Web:* www.churchill.k12.nv.us
Circleville City School District
388 Clark Dr ... Circleville OH 43113 740-474-4340 474-6600
TF: 800-418-6423 ■ *Web:* www.circlevillecityschools.org
Citrus County School District
1007 W Main St ... Inverness FL 34450 352-726-1931
Web: www.citrus.k12.fl.us
Clarendon Hall School 1140 S Dukes St ... Summerton SC 29148 803-485-3550
Clark County School District (CCSD)
5100 W Sahara Ave ... Las Vegas NV 89146 702-799-5000 799-5125
TF: 866-799-8997 ■ *Web:* www.ccsd.net
Cleveland Municipal School District (CMSD)
1380 E Sixth St ... Cleveland OH 44114 216-838-0000 361-2018*
**Fax:* Hum Res ■ *Web:* www.clevelandmetroschools.org
Clinton Public School District PO Box 300 ... Clinton MS 39060 601-924-7533
Web: www.clintonpublicschools.com
Clio Area School District 430 N Mill St ... Clio MI 48420 810-591-0500
Web: www.clioschools.org

Phone | Fax

Clovis Unified School District
1450 Herndon Ave ... Clovis CA 93611 559-327-9000 327-9109
TF: 800-498-9055 ■ *Web:* www.cusd.com

Clyde's Transfer Inc
8015 Industrial Pk Rd ... Mechanicsville VA 23116 804-746-1135 746-8898
TF: 800-342-8758 ■ *Web:* clydestransfer.com

Coachella Valley Unified School District
87-225 Church St ... Thermal CA 92274 760-399-5137

Cobleskill-Richmondville Central School District
155 Washington Ave ... Cobleskill NY 12043 518-234-4032
Web: www.crcs.k12.ny.us

Coil Construction Inc 209 E Broadway ... Columbia MO 65203 573-874-1444 443-3039
Web: www.coilconstruction.com

Coldwater Community Schools
401 Sauk River Dr ... Coldwater MI 49036 517-279-5910 279-7651
Web: www.coldwaterschools.org

Coleman Isd 2400 S Concho St ... Coleman TX 76834 325-625-4369
Web: www.coleman.netxv.net

Colfax Elementary School 24825 Ben Taylor Rd ... Colfax CA 95713 530-346-2202
Web: www.colfax.k12.ca.us

College Jean De Brebeuf
3200 Ch De La Cote-sainte-catherine ... Montreal QC H3T1C1 514-342-1320
Web: www.brebeuf.qc.ca

College Notre Dame, Quebec
3791 chemin Queen Mary ... Montreal QC H3V1A8 514-739-3371
Web: www.collegenotre-dame.qc.ca

College Regina Assumpta 1750 Rue Sauriol E ... Montreal QC H2C1X4 514-382-4121
Web: www.reginaassumpta.qc.ca

Collier County School Board 5775 Osceola Trl ... Naples FL 34109 239-377-0001 377-0336
Web: www.collierschools.com/site/default.aspx?pageid=1

Colorado Academy 3800 S Pierce St ... Denver CO 80235 303-986-1501
Web: www.coloradoacademy.org

Colorado Springs School District #11
1115 N El Paso St ... Colorado Springs CO 80903 719-520-2000 577-4546
TF: 800-273-8255 ■ *Web:* d11.org

Colts Neck High School 59 Five Points Rd ... Colts Neck NJ 07722 732-761-0190
Web: www.frhsd.com

Columbus City Schools 270 E State St ... Columbus OH 43215 614-365-5000 365-5652
Web: www.columbus.k12.oh.us

Columbus County Schools PO Box 729 ... Whiteville NC 28472 910-642-5168 640-1010
Web: www.columbus.k12.nc.us

Columbus Humanities Arts & Technology Academy
1333 Morse Rd ... Columbus OH 43229 614-261-1200
Web: columbushumanitiesata.org

Colusa County Office of Education 345 5th St ... Colusa CA 95932 530-458-0350

Community High School District 99
6301 Springside Ave ... Downers Grove IL 60516 630-795-7100
Web: csd99.org

Community Unit School District 200
130 W Pk Ave ... Wheaton IL 60189 630-682-2000 682-2227
Web: www.cusd200.org

Conestoga Valley School District
2110 Horseshoe Rd ... Lancaster PA 17601 717-397-2421 397-0442
TF: 800-732-0025 ■ *Web:* www.cvsd.k12.pa.us

Conneaut School District 219 W School Dr ... Linesville PA 16424 814-683-5900
Web: www.conneautsd.org

Conseil Des Ecoles Publique De L'est De L'ontario
2445 St Laurent Blvd ... Ottawa ON K1G6C3 613-742-8960
Web: www.cepeo.on.ca

Continental Development Corp
2041 Rosecrans Ave Ste 200 Ste 200 ... El Segundo CA 90245 310-640-1520 414-9279
Web: www.continentaldevelopment.com

Cooper High School 3639 Sayles Blvd ... Abilene TX 79605 325-691-1000
Web: abileneisd.org

Copperas Cove Independent School District
703 W Ave D ... Copperas Cove TX 76522 254-547-1227
TF: 866-632-9992 ■ *Web:* www.ccisd.com

Coquihalla Middle School 2975 Clapperton Ave ... Merritt BC V1K1A3 250-378-6104
Web: www.sd58.bc.ca

Cordova High School 1800 Berryhill Rd ... Cordova TN 38016 901-416-4540
Web: www.cadetsofcordova.org

Cornelia Connelly School of The Holy Child
2323 W Broadway ... Anaheim CA 92804 714-776-1717
Web: connellyschoolanaheim.org

Cornwall Lebanon School District
105 E Evergreen Rd ... Lebanon PA 17042 717-272-2031 274-2786
Web: www.clsd.k12.pa.us

Corona-Norco Unified School District
2820 Clark Ave ... Norco CA 92860 951-736-5000
Web: www.cnusd.k12.ca.us

Corunna Public School District
124 N Shiawassee St ... Corunna MI 48817 989-743-6338 743-4474
TF: 866-632-9992 ■ *Web:* www.corunna.k12.mi.us

Council Rock School District
30 N Chancellor St ... Newtown PA 18940 215-944-1000
Web: www.crsd.org

Counterpane Montessori Inc 839 Hwy 314 ... Fayetteville GA 30214 770-461-2304
Web: www.counterpane.org

Crane Country Day School
1795 San Leandro Ln ... Santa Barbara CA 93108 805-969-7732
Web: www.craneschool.org

Craven County School (CCS) 3600 Trent Rd ... New Bern NC 28562 252-514-6300 514-6351
Web: www.craven.k12.nc.us

Crawford Ausable School District
1135 N Old 27 ... Grayling MI 49738 989-344-3500
Web: www.casdk12.net

Crawford Central School District
11280 Mercer Pk ... Meadville PA 16335 814-724-3960
Web: www.craw.org

Crawford County School District
190 E Crusselle St PO Box 8 ... Roberta GA 31078 478-836-3131 836-3114
Web: www.crawfordcounty.schoolinsites.com

Creative Contractors Inc 620 Drew St ... Clearwater FL 33755 727-461-5522 447-4808
Web: www.creativecontractors.com

Phone | Fax

Crespi Carmelite High School Inc
5031 Alonzo Ave ... Encino CA 91316 818-345-1672
Web: www.crespi.org

Crete-Monee School District No 201-U
1500 S Sangamon St ... Crete IL 60417 708-367-8300
Web: www.cm201u.org

Crisp County Board of Education PO Box 729 ... Cordele GA 31015 229-276-3400 276-3406
Web: www.crispschools.org

Cristo Rey Jesuit High School 1852 W 22nd Pl ... Chicago IL 60608 773-890-6889
Web: www.cristorey.net

Crossroads School For Arts & Sciences
1714 21st St ... Santa Monica CA 90404 310-829-7391 828-5636
Web: www.xrds.org

Cuba Rushford Central School 5476 Rt 305 ... Cuba NY 14727 585-968-2650 968-2651
Web: www.crcs.wnyric.org

Cullman City School 301 First St Ne Ste 100 ... Cullman AL 35055 256-734-2233
Web: www.cullmancats.net

Cullman County Board of Education
PO Box 1590 ... Cullman AL 35056 256-734-2933
Web: www.ccboe.org

Culver City Unified School District (CCUSD)
4034 Irving Pl ... Culver City CA 90232 310-842-4220 842-4205
TF: 855-446-2673 ■ *Web:* www.ccusd.org

Cunningham-Limp Co
39300 W 12 Mile Rd Ste 200 ... Farmington Hills MI 48331 248-489-2300 489-2310
Web: www.cunninghamlimp.com

Curie Metropolitan High School
4959 S Archer Ave ... Chicago IL 60632 773-535-2100
Web: curiehs.org

Currituck County Board of Education
2958 Caratoke Hwy ... Currituck NC 27929 252-232-2223 232-3655
Web: www.currituck.k12.nc.us

Cushman School - Elementary School
592 Ne 60th St ... Miami FL 33137 305-757-1966
Web: www.cushmanschool.org

Cypress-Fairbanks Independent School District
PO Box 692003 ... Houston TX 77269 281-897-4000
Web: www.cfisd.net

D & T Trucking Inc
3686 140th St E PO Box 510 ... Rosemount MN 55068 651-480-7961
TF: 800-624-8130 ■ *Web:* bayandbay.com/index.php

Dallas Ctr - Grimes Community School District
1414 Walnut St Ste 200 ... Dallas Center IA 50063 515-992-3866
Web: dcgschools.com

Dallas Independent School District
3700 Ross Ave ... Dallas TX 75204 972-925-3700 925-4201
TF: 866-796-3682 ■ *Web:* www.dallasisd.org

Dallastown Area School District
700 New School Ln ... Dallastown PA 17313 717-244-4021
TF: 866-233-9796 ■ *Web:* www.dallastown.net

Dalton Public Schools
300 W Waugh St PO Box 1408 ... Dalton GA 30722 706-876-4000 226-4583
Web: www.daltonpublicschools.com

Dalton Schools Inc 108 E 89th St ... New York NY 10128 212-423-5200
Web: www.dalton.org

Dassel-Cokato Public Schools PO Box 1700 ... Cokato MN 55321 320-286-4100
Web: www.dc.k12.mn.us

Davie County Schools 220 Cherry St ... Mocksville NC 27028 336-751-5921 751-9013
Web: www.davie.k12.nc.us

Davis Elementary School 1050 Arlington Dr ... Costa Mesa CA 92626 714-424-7930
Web: davis.nmusd.us

Dawson County Board of Education, The
517 Allen St ... Dawsonville GA 30534 706-265-3246 265-1226
TF: 866-632-9992 ■ *Web:* www.dawsoncountyschools.org

Dayton City Schools 115 S Ludlow St ... Dayton OH 45402 937-542-3000 542-3188
Web: www.dps.k12.oh.us

De Soto Public School District 73
610 Vineland School Rd ... De Soto MO 63020 636-586-1000
Web: www.desoto.k12.mo.us

Decatur Isd Education Foundation Inc
501 E Collins St ... Decatur TX 76234 940-393-7100
Web: www.decaturisd.us

Decatur Public Schools 110 Cedar St ... Decatur MI 49045 269-423-6800
Web: raiderpride.org

Delano Union School District 1405 12th Ave ... Delano CA 93215 661-721-5000 725-2446
Web: www.duesd.org

Delaware City School District
248 N Washington St ... Delaware OH 43015 740-833-1100 833-1149
Web: www.dcs.k12.oh.us

Delaware Company Christian School
462 Malin Rd ... Newtown Square PA 19073 610-353-6522
Web: www.dccs.org

Delaware County Intermediate Unit
200 Yale Ave ... Morton PA 19070 610-938-9000 938-9887
TF: 800-441-3215 ■ *Web:* www.dciu.org

Dennis-Yarmouth Regional School District
296 Stn Ave ... South Yarmouth MA 02664 508-398-7600 398-7622
Web: www.dy-regional.k12.ma.us

Denver Public Schools 900 Grant St ... Denver CO 80203 720-423-3200 423-3413
TF: 866-726-0033 ■ *Web:* dpsk12.org

Des Moines Independent School District
901 Walnut St ... Des Moines IA 50309 515-242-7911 242-7579
TF: 800-452-1111 ■ *Web:* www.dmschools.org

Desert Sands Charter High School
44130 20th St W ... Lancaster CA 93534 877-360-5327
TF: 877-360-5327 ■ *Web:* www.dschs.org

Desoto Parish School District
201 Crosby St ... Mansfield LA 71052 318-872-2836 872-1324
TF: 888-741-0205 ■ *Web:* desotopsb.com

Destinta Theatres 215 Quassaick Ave ... New Windsor NY 12553 845-569-8181
Web: www.destinta.com

Detroit Community High School 12675 Burt Rd ... Detroit MI 48228 313-537-3570
Web: www.detcomschools.org

Detroit Public Schools 3031 W Grand Blvd ... Detroit MI 48202 313-873-7927 873-4564
TF: 800-656-4673 ■ *Web:* www.detroitk12.org

	City	State	Zip	Phone	Fax
Diamond Bar High School 21400 Pathfinder Rd *Web:* dbhs.wvusd.k12.ca.us	Diamond Bar	CA	91765	909-594-1405	
Dickenson County School District PO Box 1127 *TF:* 866-632-9992 ■ *Web:* www.dickenson.k12.va.us	Clintwood	VA	24228	276-926-4643	926-6374
Dillard Academy Charter School 504 W Elm St *Web:* www.dillardacademy.org	Goldsboro	NC	27530	919-581-0166	
Dinwiddie County Public School 14016 Boydton Plank Rd PO Box 7 *Web:* www.dinwiddie.k12.va.us	Dinwiddie	VA	23841	804-469-4190	469-4197
District of Columbia Public Schools (DCPS) 1200 First St NE *Web:* www.dcps.dc.gov	Washington	DC	20002	202-442-5885	442-5026
Division Scolaire Franco-Manitobaine No 49 1263 Dawson Rd *Web:* www.dsfm.mb.ca	Lorette	MB	R0A0Y0	204-878-9399	
Donegal School District 1051 Koser Rd *Web:* www.donegal.k12.pa.us	Mount Joy	PA	17552	717-653-1447	
Douglas County Board of Education 9030 Hwy 5 PO Box 1077 *Web:* www.douglas.k12.ga.us	Douglasville	GA	30134	770-651-2000	
Downey High School 11040 Brookshire Ave *Web:* www.dusd.net	Downey	CA	90241	562-869-7301	
Duarte Unified School District 1620 Huntington Dr *TF:* 888-225-7377 ■ *Web:* www.duarte.k12.ca.us	Duarte	CA	91010	626-599-5000	599-5069
Dublin Unified School District 7471 Larkdale Ave *Web:* www.dublin.k12.ca.us	Dublin	CA	94568	925-828-2551	829-6532
Dufour Petroleum LP 1374 US 11	Petal	MS	39465	601-583-9991	
Durham Academy Inc 3130 Pickett Rd *TF:* 888-904-9149 ■ *Web:* www.da.org	Durham	NC	27705	919-489-9118	
Duval County School System 1701 Prudential Dr *Web:* www.duvalschools.org	Jacksonville	FL	32207	904-390-2000	390-2586
Eagleville Elementary School S101w34511 County Rd Lo *Web:* www.masd.k12.wi.us/eves	LO Eagle	WI	53119	262-363-6258	
Earle Baum Center of The Blind 4539 Occidental Rd *Web:* www.earlebaum.org	Santa Rosa	CA	95401	707-523-3222	
Earlimart School District PO Box 11970 *Web:* www.earlimart.org	Earlimart	CA	93219	661-849-3386	
Early County School District 11927 Columbia St *Web:* www.early.k12.ga.us	Blakely	GA	39823	229-723-4337	
East Bernard Isd 723 College St *Web:* www.ebisd.org	East Bernard	TX	77435	979-335-7519	
East Cleveland Board of Education 14305 Shaw Ave *Web:* www.east-cleveland.k12.oh.us	Cleveland	OH	44112	216-268-6600	
East Maine School District 63 (EMSD) 10150 Dee Rd *TF:* 866-752-6850 ■ *Web:* www.emsd63.org	Des Plaines	IL	60016	847-299-1900	299-9963
East Penn School District 800 Pine St *Web:* www.eastpennsd.org	Emmaus	PA	18049	610-966-8300	
East Ramapo Central School District 105 S Madison Ave *Web:* www.ercsd.org	Spring Valley	NY	10977	845-577-6000	577-6038
East Side Union High School District 830 N Capitol Ave *Web:* www.esuhsd.org	San Jose	CA	95133	408-347-5000	347-5045
East Valley School District 361 12325 E Grace Ave *Web:* www.evsd.org	Spokane	WA	99216	509-924-1830	927-9500
Eastconn 376 Hartford Tpke *Web:* www.eastconn.org	Hampton	CT	06247	860-455-0707	
Eastern Nc School for The Deaf 1311 Us Hwy 301 N *Web:* encsd.net	Wilson	NC	27893	252-237-2450	
Easton Area School District Inc 1801 Bushkill Dr *Web:* www.eastonsd.org	Easton	PA	18040	610-250-2400	
Eastside Union School District 45006 30th St E *TF:* 877-263-7995 ■ *Web:* www.eastside.k12.ca.us	Lancaster	CA	93535	661-952-1200	952-1220
Ecampusalberta 1301 16 Ave Nw *TF:* 877-284-7248 ■ *Web:* www.ecampusalberta.ca	Calgary	AB	T2M0L4	403-284-8777	
Ecole De La Cle-des-champs 3858 Rue Principale *Web:* cle-des-champs.csvdc.qc.ca	Dunham	QC	J0E1M0	450-295-2722	
Edcouch-Elsa Independent School District PO Box 127 *Web:* www.eeisd.org	Edcouch	TX	78538	956-262-6000	262-6032
Edison School Elementary School 246 S Fair Ave *Web:* elmhurst205.org	Elmhurst	IL	60126	630-834-4272	
EdisonLearning Inc 900 S Gay St Ste 1000 *Web:* www.edisonlearning.com	Knoxville	TN	37902	865-329-3600	
Edwardsburg Public Schools 69410 Section St *Web:* www.edwardsburgpublicschools.org	Edwardsburg	MI	49112	269-663-1031	
Edwardsville Community School District 7 708 St Louis St *Web:* www.ecusd7.org	Edwardsville	IL	62025	618-656-1182	692-7423
El Campo Independent School District 700 W Norris St *Web:* www.ecisd.org	El Campo	TX	77437	979-543-6771	
El Centro Elementary School District 1256 Broadway St *Web:* www.ecesd.org	El Centro	CA	92243	760-352-5712	
El Monte City School District 3540 Lexington Ave *Web:* web.emcsd.org	El Monte	CA	91731	626-453-3700	
El Monte Union High School District 3537 Johnson Ave *Web:* www.emuhsd.k12.ca.us	El Monte	CA	91731	626-444-9005	448-8419
El Paso Independent School District 6531 Boeing Dr **Fax:* Hum Res ■ *Web:* episd.org	El Paso	TX	79925	915-779-3781	779-4280*
Elbert County Board of Education 50 Laurel Dr *Web:* www.elbert.k12.ga.us	Elberton	GA	30635	706-213-4000	
Elim Christian School 13020 S Central Ave *TF:* 877-935-4627 ■ *Web:* www.elimcs.org	Palos Heights	IL	60463	708-389-0555	
Elisabeth Morrow School, The 435 Lydecker St *Web:* elisabethmorrow.org	Englewood	NJ	07631	201-568-5566	
Ellington Elementary School 3001 Lindell Ave *Web:* www.qps.org	Quincy	IL	62301	217-222-5697	
Elmont Union Free School District 135 Elmont Rd *Web:* www.elmontschools.org	Elmont	NY	11003	516-326-5500	326-5574
Elmore County Public School System 100 H H Robison Dr PO Box 817 *Web:* www.elmoreco.com	Wetumpka	AL	36092	334-567-1200	
Elzinga & Volkers 86 E Sixth St *TF General:* 800-632-7734 ■ *Web:* www.elzinga-volkers.com	Holland	MI	49423	616-392-2383	392-3752
Emanuel County Board of Education PO Box 130 *Web:* www.emanuel.k12.ga.us	Swainsboro	GA	30401	478-237-6674	237-3404
Emek Hebrew Academy 15365 Magnolia Blvd *Web:* www.emek.org	Sherman Oaks	CA	91403	818-783-3663	
Encinitas Union School District Educational Facilities Corp 101 S Rancho Santa Fe Rd *Web:* www.eusd.k12.ca.us	Encinitas	CA	92024	760-944-4300	
Engineering Design Technologies (EDT) 1705 Entp Way SE Ste 200 *Web:* www.edtinc.net	Marietta	GA	30067	770-988-0400	988-0300
Ennis Independent School District 303 W Knox PO Box 1420 *Web:* www.ennis.k12.tx.us	Ennis	TX	75120	972-872-7000	875-8667
Ericson Elementary School 2309 Tulare St *Web:* fresnounified.org	Fresno	CA	93721	559-253-6450	
Erie 2-Chautauqua Cattaraugus Boces (ECCB) 8685 Erie Rd *TF:* 800-228-1184 ■ *Web:* www.e2ccb.org	Angola	NY	14006	716-549-4454	
Etiwanda School District (ESD) 6061 E Ave *TF:* 800-300-1506 ■ *Web:* www.etiwanda.k12.ca.us	Etiwanda	CA	91739	909-899-2451	899-1235
Eugene School District 4J 200 N Monroe St *Web:* www.4j.lane.edu	Eugene	OR	97402	541-687-3123	687-3691
Eureka Union School District 5455 Eureka Rd *Web:* www.eureka-usd.k12.ca.us	Granite Bay	CA	95746	916-791-4939	791-5527
Evanston/Skokie School District 65 1500 Mcdaniel Ave *Web:* www.district65.net	Evanston	IL	60201	847-859-8000	859-8707
Evergreen Public Schools 13501 NE 28th St PO Box 8910 *Web:* evergreenps.org	Vancouver	WA	98668	360-604-4000	892-5307
Evesham Township Board of Education 25 S Maple Ave *Web:* www.evesham.k12.nj.us	Marlton	NJ	08053	856-983-1800	
Exploris 401 Hillsborough St *Web:* www.exploris.org	Raleigh	NC	27603	919-715-3690	
Fairhill School & Diagnostic 16150 Preston Rd *Web:* fairhill.org	Dallas	TX	75248	972-233-1026	
Fairview Elementary School 300 Salem Dr *Web:* www.plymouth.k12.wi.us	Plymouth	WI	53073	920-892-2621	
Fannin County Board of Education 2290 E First St *TF:* 800-308-2145 ■ *Web:* www.fannin.k12.ga.us	Blue Ridge	GA	30513	706-632-3771	632-7583
Far Horizons Montessori 264 N Main St *Web:* www.farhorizonsmontessori.org	Orange	CA	92868	714-997-8333	
Farwest Freight Systems Inc 4504 E Vly Hwy E	Sumner	WA	98390	253-826-4565	
Fayette County Board of Education 210 Stonewall Ave *TF:* 800-550-5131 ■ *Web:* www.fcboe.org	Fayetteville	GA	30214	770-460-3535	460-8191
Fayette County Public Schools 701 E Main St **Fax:* Hum Res ■ *TF:* 877-597-2331 ■ *Web:* fcps.net	Lexington	KY	40502	859-381-4100	381-4271*
Ferndale School District 502 6041 Vista Dr PO Box 698 *Web:* ferndalesd.org	Ferndale	WA	98248	360-383-9200	383-9201
Ferry Transportation Inc 5 Thames Ave *Web:* www.ferrytrans.com	Laurel	MS	39440	601-425-5542	
First Bank Of Highland Park 1835 First St PO Box 546 *TF:* 877-651-7800 ■ *Web:* www.firstbankhp.com	Highland Park	IL	60035	847-432-7800	433-2156
First Farmers & Merchants National Bank 816 S Garden St PO Box 1148 *OTC:* FIME ■ *TF:* 800-882-8378 ■ *Web:* www.myfirstfarmers.com	Columbia	TN	38401	931-388-3145	380-8359
Flint Community Schools 923 E Kearsley St *Web:* www.flintschools.org	Flint	MI	48503	810-760-1000	
Floresville Independent School District 908 Tenth St *Web:* floresvilleathletics.us	Floresville	TX	78114	830-393-5300	
Floyd Blinsky Trucking Inc 210 Keys Rd *TF:* 800-537-9599 ■ *Web:* www.blinsky.com	Yakima	WA	98901	509-457-3484	457-0832
Floyd County Board of Education 600 Riverside Pkwy NE *Web:* www.floydboe.net	Rome	GA	30161	706-234-1031	236-1824
Foley High School 1 Pride Pl *Web:* www.foley.k12.mn.us	Foley	MN	36535	320-968-7246	

				Phone	Fax
Forest Hills Local School 7550 Forest Rd. *Web:* www.foresthills.edu	Cincinnati	OH	45255	513-231-3600	
Forest Lake Area School District 6100 210th St N *TF:* 866-632-9992 ■ *Web:* www.forestlake.k12.mn.us	Forest Lake	MN	55025	651-982-8100	982-8137
Forney Independent School District (Inc) 600 S Bois D ARC St *Web:* www.forneyisd.net	Forney	TX	75126	972-564-4055	
Forsyth County Board of Education 1120 Dahlonega Hwy *Web:* www.forsyth.k12.ga.us	Cumming	GA	30040	770-887-2461	781-6632
Fort Bragg Unified School District 312 S Lincoln St *TF:* 800-734-7793 ■ *Web:* www.fbusd.us	Fort Bragg	CA	95437	707-961-2850	
Fort Mill School District 4 120 E Elliott St *Web:* www.fortmillschools.org	Fort Mill	SC	29715	803-548-2527	547-4696
Fort Wayne Community Schools (FWCS) 1200 S Clinton St *Web:* www.fwcs.k12.in.us	Fort Wayne	IN	46802	260-467-2009	467-1186
Fort Worth Independent School District 100 N University Dr *Web:* fwisd.org	Fort Worth	TX	76107	817-871-2000	
Fox Chapel Area School District 611 Field Club Rd *Web:* www.fcasd.edu	Pittsburgh	PA	15238	412-967-2453	967-0697
Franklin Local School District PO Box 428 *TF:* 800-846-4976 ■ *Web:* www.franklinlocalschools.org	Duncan Falls	OH	43734	740-674-5203	
Franklin Special School District 507 New Hwy 96 W *Web:* www.fssd.org	Franklin	TN	37064	615-794-6624	790-4716
Franklin-Pierce Schools 315 129th St S *Web:* fpschools.org	Tacoma	WA	98444	253-298-3000	
Fredericksburg City Public Schools 817 Princess Anne St *TF:* 800-846-4464 ■ *Web:* www.cityschools.com	Fredericksburg	VA	22401	540-372-1130	372-1111
Free The Children 233 Carlton St *Web:* www.freethechildren.com	Toronto	ON	M5A2L2	416-925-5894	
Freedom Middle School 3016 Ridgeland Ave *Web:* www.bsd100.org	Berwyn	IL	60402	708-795-5800	
Fremont Public Schools 220 W Pine St *TF:* 800-822-9433 ■ *Web:* www.fremont.net	Fremont	MI	49412	231-924-2350	924-5264
Fremont Unified School District PO Box 5008 *TF:* 800-544-5248 ■ *Web:* www.fremont.k12.ca.us	Fremont	CA	94537	510-657-2350	770-9851
Fresno Unified School District 2309 Tulare St **Fax:* Hum Res ■ *Web:* www.fresno.k12.ca.us	Fresno	CA	93721	559-457-3000	457-3528*
Friends School of Wilmington Inc 350 Peiffer Ave *Web:* www.fsow.org	Wilmington	NC	28409	910-792-1811	
Friendship House PO Box 3778 *Web:* www.friendshiphousepa.org	Scranton	PA	18505	570-342-8305	344-1178
Frontier Central School District 5120 Orchard Ave	Hamburg	NY	14075	716-926-1710	
Fulton School District 58 2 Hornet Dr *TF:* 800-456-2634 ■ *Web:* www.fulton58.org	Fulton	MO	65251	573-590-8000	
Gainesville City Schools 508 Oak St *TF:* 800-533-0682 ■ *Web:* www.gcssk12.net	Gainesville	GA	30501	770-536-5275	287-2019
Galveston Independent School District (GISD) 3904 Ave PO Box 660 *TF:* 877-262-1492 ■ *Web:* www.gisd.org	Galveston	TX	77550	409-766-5100	762-8391
Garden Grove Unified School District 10331 Stanford Ave *Web:* www.ggusd.us	Garden Grove	CA	92840	714-663-6000	663-6100
Garfield Elementary School 1514 S Ninth Ave *Web:* www.maywood89.org	Maywood	IL	60153	708-450-2009	
Garland Independent School District (GISD) 501 S Jupiter PO Box 469026 *TF:* 800-252-5555 ■ *Web:* www.garlandisd.net	Garland	TX	75046	972-494-8201	485-4936
Gaston County School 943 Osceola St PO Box 1397 *Web:* www.gaston.k12.nc.us	Gastonia	NC	28054	704-866-6117	
Gateway Unified School Disrict 4411 Mtn Lakes Blvd *Web:* www.gateway-schools.org	Redding	CA	96003	530-245-7900	
Genesee Intermediate School District 2413 W Maple Ave *Web:* www.geneseeisd.org	Flint	MI	48507	810-591-4400	
Geneseo Community Unit School District 228 209 S College Ave *Web:* www.dist228.org	Geneseo	IL	61254	309-945-0450	945-0445
Geneva County Board of Education PO Box 250 *Web:* www.genevacountyschools.com	Geneva	AL	36340	334-684-5690	
Giddings Independent Schl Dst 2337 N Main St *Web:* giddingsisd.net	Giddings	TX	78942	979-542-2854	542-9264
Gilmer Junior High 111 Bruce St *Web:* www.gilmerisd.org	Gilmer	TX	75645	903-841-7600	
Gilroy Unified School District 7810 Arroyo Cir *Web:* www.gusd.k12.ca.us	Gilroy	CA	95020	408-847-2700	842-1158
Gladstone School District 115 17789 Webster Rd *TF:* 800-328-0272 ■ *Web:* www.gladstone.k12.or.us	Gladstone	OR	97027	503-655-2777	655-5201
Glen Ellyn School District 41 793 N Main St *Web:* www.d41.org	Glen Ellyn	IL	60137	630-790-6400	790-1867
Glen Grove Elementary School 3900 Glenview Rd *Web:* www.glenview34.org	Glenview	IL	60025	847-998-5030	
Glens Falls City School District 15 Quade St *Web:* www.gfsd.org	Glens Falls	NY	12801	518-792-1212	
Goleta Union School District 401 N Fairview Ave *Web:* www.goleta.k12.ca.us	Goleta	CA	93117	805-681-1200	
Goliad Independent School District PO Box 830 *Web:* www.goliadisd.org	Goliad	TX	77963	361-645-3259	
Gordon County Board of Education 205 Warrior Path PO Box 12001 *Web:* www.gcbe.org	Calhoun	GA	30703	706-629-7366	625-5671
Gordon Sevig Trucking Co (GSTC) 400 Hwy 151 E *Web:* www.gstcinc.com	Walford	IA	52351	319-846-5500	846-5541
Goshen County School District 1 626 W 25th Ave *Web:* www.goshen.k12.wy.us	Torrington	WY	82240	307-532-2171	532-7085
Grand Rapids Public Schools (GRPS) 1331 Franklin St SE PO Box 117 *Web:* www.grps.k12.mi.us	Grand Rapids	MI	49506	616-819-2000	819-2104
Grandview Heights City School District 1587 W Third Ave *Web:* www.ghcsd.org	Columbus	OH	43212	614-481-3600	
Granite Falls School District 307 N Alder Ave *TF:* 888-651-8931 ■ *Web:* www.gfalls.wednet.edu	Granite Falls	WA	98252	360-691-7717	691-4459
Grant Career Center 718 W Plane St *Web:* www.grantcareer.com	Bethel	OH	45106	513-734-6222	
Granville Central School District 58 Quaker St *Web:* www.granvillecsd.org	Granville	NY	12832	518-642-1051	642-4544
Grapeland Elementary School PO Box 249 *Web:* www.grapelandisd.net	Grapeland	TX	75844	936-687-2317	
Gratiot-Isabella Regional Education Service District 1131 E Ctr St PO Box 310 *Web:* giresd.net	Ithaca	MI	48847	989-875-5101	875-2858
Gray Transportation Inc 2459 GT Dr *TF:* 800-234-3930 ■ *Web:* www.graytran.com	Waterloo	IA	50703	319-234-3930	234-8841
Greenfield Union School District 1624 Fairview Rd *Web:* www.gfusd.k12.ca.us	Bakersfield	CA	93307	661-837-6000	832-2873
Greenwood School District 50 1855 Calhoun Rd PO Box 248 *TF:* 888-260-9430 ■ *Web:* www.gwd50.org	Greenwood	SC	29648	864-941-5400	941-5427
Grosse Ile Township Schools 23276 E River Rd *Web:* www.gischools.org	Grosse Ile	MI	48138	734-362-2555	
Guidance Charter School, The 1125 E Palmdale Blvd # B *Web:* www.thegcs.org	Palmdale	CA	93550	661-272-1701	
Guilford County Schools 617 W Market St *TF:* 866-286-7337 ■ *Web:* www.gcsnc.com	Greensboro	NC	27401	336-370-8100	370-8398
Gulf Coast Bank & Trust Co 200 St Charles Ave *TF:* 800-223-2060 ■ *Web:* www.gulfbank.com	New Orleans	LA	70130	504-561-6100	581-3583
Gulf County School District 150 Middle School Rd *Web:* www.gulf.k12.fl.us	Port Saint Joe	FL	32456	850-229-8256	229-6089
Guy Shavender Trucking Inc PO Box 206 *TF:* 800-682-2447 ■ *Web:* www.shavender.com	Pantego	NC	27860	252-943-3379	943-6434
Habersham County Board of Education 132 W Stanford Mill Rd PO Box 70 *Web:* www.habershamschools.com	Clarkesville	GA	30523	706-754-2118	754-1549
Hale County Board of Education 1115 Powers St *Web:* www.halek12.org	Greensboro	AL	36744	334-624-8836	
Halifax County Public Schools 1030 Mary Bethune St PO Box 1849 *TF:* 800-253-2687 ■ *Web:* www.halifax.k12.va.us	Halifax	VA	24558	434-476-2171	476-1858
Hall County Schools 711 Green St NW Ste 100 *TF:* 866-632-9992 ■ *Web:* www.hallco.org	Gainesville	GA	30501	770-534-1080	535-7404
Hamblen County Board of Education 210 E Morris Blvd *Web:* www.hcboe.net	Morristown	TN	37813	423-586-7700	586-7747
Hamburg Area School District (HASD) 701 Windsor St *Web:* www.hasdhawks.org	Hamburg	PA	19526	610-562-2241	562-2634
Hamilton City School District (HCSD) 533 Dayton St PO Box 627 *Web:* www.hamiltoncityschools.com	Hamilton	OH	45012	513-887-5000	887-5014
Hamilton County Dept of Education 3074 Hickory Vly Rd **Fax:* Hum Res ■ *Web:* www.hcde.org	Chattanooga	TN	37421	423-209-8400	209-8539*
Hamilton County Educational Service Ctr (HCESC) 11083 Hamilton Ave *TF:* 800-964-8211 ■ *Web:* www.hcesc.org	Cincinnati	OH	45231	513-674-4200	742-8339
Hanning Construction Inc 815 Swan St *Web:* www.hannigconstruction.com	Terre Haute	IN	47807	812-235-6218	235-1218
Hardee County School District PO Box 1678 *Web:* www.hardee.k12.fl.us	Wauchula	FL	33873	863-773-9058	
Harlandale Isd 102 Genevieve Dr *Web:* www.harlandale.net	San Antonio	TX	78214	210-989-4300	
Harlem Children's Zone Inc 35 E 125th St *Web:* www.hcz.org	New York	NY	10035	212-360-3255	289-0661
Harlingen High School 1201 Marshall St *Web:* hcisd.org	Harlingen	TX	78550	956-427-3600	
Harnett County Board of Education 1008 11th St PO Box 1029 *TF:* 800-942-3767 ■ *Web:* www.harnett.k12.nc.us	Lillington	NC	27546	910-893-8151	893-8839
Harrisburg School District Inc 1601 State St *Web:* www.hbgsd.k12.pa.us	Harrisburg	PA	17103	717-703-4000	
Hart County Board of Education PO Box 696 *Web:* www.hart.k12.ga.us	Hartwell	GA	30643	706-376-5141	376-7046
Hartford Public Schools 960 Main St **Fax:* Hum Res ■ *Web:* www.hartfordschools.org	Hartford	CT	06103	860-695-8000	722-8454*
Haslett Public School 5593 Franklin St *Web:* www.haslett.k12.mi.us	Haslett	MI	48840	517-339-8242	

Name / Address	City	State	Zip	Phone	Fax
Hatboro-Horsham School District 229 Meetinghouse Rd. *TF:* 866-771-3170 ■ *Web:* www.hatboro-horsham.org	Horsham	PA	19044	215-672-5660	420-5262
Hauppauge School District (HSP) 495 Hoffman Ln PO Box 6006 *Web:* www.hauppauge.k12.ny.us	Hauppauge	NY	11788	631-761-8208	
Hawaii Dept of Education Honolulu District Office 4967 Kilauea Ave *TF:* 800-437-8641 ■ *Web:* www.hawaiipublicschools.org	Honolulu	HI	96816	808-733-4950	733-4953
Hays Consolidated I S D 21003 I- 35 *Web:* www.hayscisd.net	Kyle	TX	78640	512-268-2141	268-2147
Hayward Unified School District (HUSD) 24411 Amador St PO Box 5000 *Web:* www.husd.k12.ca.us	Hayward	CA	94540	510-784-2600	784-2641
Hebrew Academy of The Five Towns & Rockaway Inc 389 Central Ave *Web:* www.haftr.org	Lawrence	NY	11559	516-569-3370	
Hemlock Public Schools District PO Box 260 *Web:* www.hemlock.k12.mi.us	Hemlock	MI	48626	989-642-5282	
Henderson Isd 200 N High St *Web:* www.hendersonisd.org	Henderson	TX	75652	903-657-8511	
Henry Carlson Co 1205 W Russell St *Web:* henrycarlson.com	Sioux Falls	SD	57104	605-336-2410	332-1314
Hereford Independent School District 601 N 25 Mile Ave *Web:* www.herefordisd.net	Hereford	TX	79045	806-363-7600	363-7699
Hertford County School District PO Box 158 *Web:* www.hertford.k12.nc.us	Winton	NC	27986	252-358-1761	
Highland Central School District 320 Pancake Hollow Rd *Web:* www.highland-k12.org	Highland	NY	12528	845-691-1000	
Highland Falls-Ft Montgomery School District PO Box 287 *Web:* www.hffmcsd.org	Highland Falls	NY	10928	845-446-9575	
Hillsboro City Schools 39 Willetsville Pk. *Web:* www.hillsboro.k12.oh.us	Hillsboro	OH	45133	937-393-3475	
Hillsboro Community Unit School District 3 1311 Vandalia Rd *Web:* www.hillsboroschools.net	Hillsboro	IL	62049	217-532-2942	532-3137
Hillsboro School District 3083 NE 49th Pl *Web:* www.hsd.k12.or.us	Hillsboro	OR	97124	503-844-1500	844-1540
Hillsborough County Public Schools 901 E Kennedy Blvd *TF:* 800-962-2873 ■ *Web:* www.sdhc.k12.fl.us	Tampa	FL	33602	813-272-4000	272-4073
Hillsborough Township Board of Education 379 S Branch Rd. *TF:* 800-272-1325 ■ *Web:* www.htps.us	Hillsborough	NJ	08844	908-431-6600	369-8286
Hilltop Elementary School 2615 W Lincoln Rd *Web:* www.d15.org	Mchenry	IL	60051	815-385-4421	
Hinds County School District 13192 Hwy 18 *Web:* www.hinds.k12.ms.us	Raymond	MS	39154	601-857-5222	857-8548
Hingham School District 220 Central St *Web:* www.hingham-ma.com	Hingham	MA	02043	781-741-1500	
Hoffmeier Inc 3210 N Lewis Ave *Web:* www.hoffmeier.com	Tulsa	OK	74110	918-428-5823	430-0820
Holiday Express Corp 721 S 28th St *TF:* 800-831-5078 ■ *Web:* www.holidayxpress.net	Estherville	IA	51334	712-362-5812	362-3019
Holland Patent Central School District 9601 Main St *Web:* www.hpschools.org	Holland Patent	NY	13354	315-865-7200	
Holland Public Schools 156 W 11th St *Web:* www.hollandpublicschools.org	Holland	MI	49423	616-494-2000	392-8225
Holmes District School Board (HDSB) 701 E Pennsylvania Ave *Web:* www.hdsb.org	Bonifay	FL	32425	850-547-9341	547-3568
Homer Central School District PO Box 500 *Web:* www.homercentral.org	Homer	NY	13077	607-749-7241	
Hopkins County Board-Education 320 S Seminary St *Web:* hopkins.k12.ky.us	Madisonville	KY	42431	270-825-6000	825-6072
Houston Independent School District 228 McCarty St. *TF:* 800-446-2821 ■ *Web:* www.houstonisd.org	Houston	TX	77029	713-556-6000	556-6006
Hueneme Elementary School Dist 205 N Ventura Rd *TF:* 866-431-2478 ■ *Web:* www.huensd.k12.ca.us	Port Hueneme	CA	93041	805-488-3588	488-1779
Humble Independent School District PO Box 2000 *Web:* www.humbleisd.net	Humble	TX	77347	281-641-1000	641-1050
Huntington Union Free School District 3 PO Box 1500 *Web:* www.hufsd.edu	Huntington	NY	11743	631-673-2185	
Huntsville Board of Education 200 White St. **Fax:* Hum Res ■ *TF:* 877-517-0020 ■ *Web:* www.huntsvillecityschools.org	Huntsville	AL	35801	256-428-6800	428-6838*
Hyde Park Central School District (Inc) PO Box 2033 *Web:* www.hpcsd.org	Hyde Park	NY	12538	845-229-4000	
Idaho Falls School District 91 Education Foundation Inc 690 John Adams Pkwy *TF:* 888-993-7120 ■ *Web:* www.d91.k12.id.us	Idaho Falls	ID	83401	208-525-7500	525-7596
Ilex Construction & Woodworking 3801 Northampton St NW Ste 3 *TF:* 866-551-4539 ■ *Web:* www.ilexconstruction.com	Washington	DC	20015	410-820-4393	820-4394
Iman Academy 10929 Almeda Genoa Rd. *Web:* www.imanacademy.org	Houston	TX	77034	713-910-3626	
Imperial High School 517 W Barioni Blvd *Web:* imperialhighschool.org	Imperial	CA	92251	760-355-3220	
Imperial Valley Rop 687 W State St. *Web:* www.ivrop.org	El Centro	CA	92243	760-482-2600	
Indianapolis Public Schools 120 E Walnut St *Web:* myips.org	Indianapolis	IN	46204	317-226-4000	
Ingleside High School 2807 Mustang Dr. *Web:* www.inglesideisd.org	Ingleside	TX	78362	361-776-2712	
J.M. Bozeman Enterprises Inc 166 Seltzer Ln. *TF General:* 800-472-1836 ■ *Web:* jmbozeman.com	Malvern	AR	72104	501-844-4060	
Jackson County Intermediate School District (JCISD) 6700 Browns Lk Rd *Web:* www.jcisd.org/site/default.aspx	Jackson	MI	49201	517-768-5200	
Jackson County School District 6 300 Ash St *TF:* 800-978-3040 ■ *Web:* www.district6.org	Central Point	OR	97502	541-494-6200	664-1637
Jackson County School District 9 PO Box 548 *Web:* www.eaglepnt.k12.or.us	Eagle Point	OR	97524	541-830-1200	
Jackson County School System 1660 Winder Hwy *TF:* 800-760-3727 ■ *Web:* www.jackson.k12.ga.us	Jefferson	GA	30549	706-367-5151	367-9457
Jackson Public Schools 662 S President St *Web:* www.jackson.k12.ms.us	Jackson	MS	39201	601-960-8700	960-8713
Jacksonville Independent School District PO Box 631 *TF:* 800-583-6908 ■ *Web:* www.jisd.org	Jacksonville	TX	75766	903-586-6511	586-3133
Jacksonville School District 117 516 Jordan St *Web:* jsd117.org	Jacksonville	IL	62650	217-243-9411	243-6844
Jaffrey-Rindge School District 81 Fitzgerald Dr Unit 2 *Web:* sau47.org	Jaffrey	NH	03452	603-532-8100	
James Jordan Middle School 7911 Winnetka Ave. *Web:* www.jamesjordanms.com	Winnetka	CA	91306	818-882-2496	
Jamesville-Dewitt Central School Dist (Inc) 6845 Edinger Dr PO Box 606 *Web:* www.jamesvilledewitt.org	Fayetteville	NY	13066	315-445-8340	445-8477
Jefferson Area Local School District 906 W Main St *Web:* www.west-jefferson.k12.oh.us	West Jefferson	OH	43162	614-879-7654	
Jefferson Davis Parish Parish Schools 203 E Plaquemine St PO Box 640 *Web:* www.webserver.jeffersondavis.org	Jennings	LA	70546	337-824-1834	
Jefferson Schools 2400 N Dixie Hwy *Web:* www.jeffersonschools.org	Monroe	MI	48162	734-289-5550	
Jenison Public Schools (JPS) 8375 20th Ave. *Web:* www.jpsonline.org	Jenison	MI	49428	616-457-1402	457-8090
Jennings County Schools 34 W Main St *TF:* 866-346-3724 ■ *Web:* www.jenningscounty-in.gov	North Vernon	IN	47265	812-346-4483	
Joan of Arc Academy 2221 Elmira Dr *Web:* joanofarcacademy.com	Ottawa	ON	K2C1H3	613-728-6364	
John Carroll School, The 703 Churchville Rd. *TF:* 800-422-0010 ■ *Web:* www.johncarroll.org	Bel Air	MD	21014	410-879-2480	
John Cooper School 1 John Cooper Dr *TF:* 800-295-1162 ■ *Web:* www.johncooper.org	The Woodlands	TX	77381	281-367-0900	
John Hersey High School 1900 E Thomas St *Web:* jhhs.d214.org	Arlington Heights	IL	60004	847-718-4800	
Johnston Community School District PO Box 10 *Web:* www.johnston.k12.ia.us	Johnston	IA	50131	515-278-0470	278-5884
Joliet Public School District 86 420 N Raynor Ave. *Web:* www.joliet86.org	Joliet	IL	60435	815-740-3196	
Jubilee Christian Center 105 Nortech Pkwy *Web:* jubilee.org	San Jose	CA	95134	408-262-0900	
Julian Charter School Inc 1704 Cape Horn *TF:* 866-853-0003 ■ *Web:* www.julianchaterschool.org	Julian	CA	92036	760-765-3847	
Junipero Serra High School 31422 Camino Capistrano *Web:* serra.capousd.ca.schoolloop.com	San Juan Capistrano	CA	92675	949-489-7216	
K12 Inc 2300 Corporate Pk Dr *NYSE:* LRN ■ *TF:* 866-512-2273 ■ *Web:* www.k12.com	Herndon	VA	20171	703-483-7000	483-7330
Kansas City Missouri School District 1211 McGee St. *Web:* www.kcpublicschools.org	Kansas City	MO	64106	816-418-7000	418-7766
Katherine Delmar Burke School 7070 California St. *Web:* www.kdbs.org	San Francisco	CA	94121	415-751-0177	
Kaweah High School 1107 Rocky Hill Dr. *Web:* www.kaweah.org	Exeter	CA	93221	559-592-4420	
KBT Inc 3885 W Michigan St **Fax Area Code:* 937 ■ *TF:* 800-860-9455	Sidney	OH	45365	800-860-9455	497-1870*
Kelseyville Unified School District 4410 Konocti Rd. *Web:* www.kusd.lake.k12.ca.us	Kelseyville	CA	95451	707-279-1511	
Kentwood Public Schools 5820 Eastern Ave SE. *Web:* www.kentwoodps.org	Grand Rapids	MI	49508	616-455-4400	455-4476
Keppel Union School District PO Box 186 *Web:* www.keppel.k12.ca.us	Pearblossom	CA	93553	661-944-2155	944-2933
Kern County High School District 5801 Sundale Ave. *Web:* www.khsd.k12.ca.us	Bakersfield	CA	93309	661-827-3100	827-3300
Kershaw County School District 2029 W DeKalb St *Web:* www.kcsdschools.net	Camden	SC	29020	803-432-8416	425-8918
Keystone School District 451 Huston Ave *Web:* www.keyknox.com	Knox	PA	16232	814-797-5921	
King City Union Elementary School District 800 Broadway St. *Web:* www.kcusd.org	King City	CA	93930	831-385-1144	
King's Academy Inc, The 8401 Belvedere Rd *Web:* www.tka.net	West Palm Beach	FL	33411	561-686-4244	
Kingsway College School 4600 Dundas St W. *Web:* www.kcs.on.ca	Etobicoke	ON	M9A1A5	416-234-5073	

				Phone	Fax
Kirkwood School District R-7 Inc 11289 Manchester Rd. *Web:* www.kirkwoodschools.org	Kirkwood	MO	63122	314-213-6100	984-0002
Klein Independent School District 7200 Spring Cypress Rd. *TF:* 888-703-0083 ■ *Web:* www.kleinisd.net	Spring	TX	77379	832-249-4000	
La Citadelle International Academy of Arts & Science 15 Mallow Rd *Web:* www.lacitadelleacademy.com	Toronto	ON	M3B1G2	416-385-9685	
La Mesa-Spring Valley School District 4750 Date Ave *Web:* www.lmsvsd.k12.ca.us	La Mesa	CA	91941	619-668-5700	
La Tercera Elementary School 1600 Albin Way *Web:* laterceraschool.org	Petaluma	CA	94954	707-765-4303	
Lab School of Washington, The 4759 Reservoir Rd Nw *Web:* www.labschool.org	Washington	DC	20007	202-965-6600	
Lafayette Parish School System 113 Chaplin Dr *Web:* www.lpssonline.com	Lafayette	LA	70508	337-521-7000	
Laingsburg Community School District 205 S Woodhull Rd *Web:* www.laingsburg.k12.mi.us	Laingsburg	MI	48848	517-651-2705	651-9075
Lake Superior Ind Sch Dist 381 1640 2 Hwy *TF:* 888-878-0136 ■ *Web:* www.isd381.k12.mn.us	Two Harbors	MN	55616	218-834-8201	834-8239
Lake Travis Independent School District 3322 Ranch Rd 620 S *Web:* www.laketravis.txed.net	Austin	TX	78738	512-533-6000	533-6001
Lake Washington School District 414 16250 NE 74th St PO Box 97039 *Web:* www.lwsd.org	Redmond	WA	98073	425-936-1200	936-1213
Lake Worth Independent School District (LWISD) 6805 Telephone Rd. *Web:* www.lwisd.org	Lake Worth	TX	76135	817-306-4200	237-2583
Lakeside Lutheran High School 231 Woodland Beach Rd *Web:* www.llhs.org	Lake Mills	WI	53551	920-648-2321	
Lamesa Independent School District PO Box 261 *TF:* 888-286-6700 ■ *Web:* www.lamesaisd.net	Lamesa	TX	79331	806-872-5461	872-6220
Lamphere Schools 31201 Dorchester Ave *Web:* www.lamphereschools.org	Madison Heights	MI	48071	248-589-1990	589-2618
Lancaster City School District 345 E Mulberry St. *TF:* 888-647-4729 ■ *Web:* www.lancaster.k12.oh.us	Lancaster	OH	43130	740-687-7300	
Lanier County Board of Education 247 S Hway 221 *Web:* www.lanier.k12.ga.us	Lakeland	GA	31635	229-482-3966	482-3020
Las Cruces Public Schools 505 S Main St Ste 249 **Fax:* Hum Res ■ *TF:* 888-222-1498 ■ *Web:* www.lcps.k12.nm.us	Las Cruces	NM	88001	575-527-5800	527-6658*
Laurel Highlands School District (LHSD) 304 Bailey Ave	Uniontown	PA	15401	724-437-2821	437-8929
Laurens County Board of Education 467 Firetower Rd *Web:* www.lcboe.net	Dublin	GA	31021	478-272-4767	277-2619
Lawrence Public Schools 110 McDonald Dr *TF:* 800-772-1213 ■ *Web:* www.usd497.org	Lawrence	KS	66044	785-832-5000	832-5016
Leadership Public Schools 344 Thomas L Berkley Way *Web:* www.leadps.org	Oakland	CA	94612	510-830-3780	225-2575
Lebanon City School District 700 Holbrook Ave. *Web:* www.lebanon.k12.oh.us	Lebanon	OH	45036	513-934-5770	
Leflore County School District 1901 Hwy 82 W *Web:* www.lefcsd.org	Greenwood	MS	38930	662-453-8566	
Lemont High School 800 Porter St. *Web:* lhs210.net	Lemont	IL	60439	630-257-5838	
Lenoir County Public School (LCPS) 2017 W Vernon Ave PO Box 729 *TF:* 888-684-8404 ■ *Web:* www.lenoir.k12.nc.us	Kinston	NC	28504	252-527-1109	527-6884
Leon County Schools (LCS) 2757 W Pensacola St	Tallahassee	FL	32303	850-487-7100	
Lewis S. Mills High School 24 Lyon Rd *TF:* 800-673-2411 ■ *Web:* www.region10ct.org	Burlington	CT	06013	860-673-0423	673-9128
Lexington City Board of Education 1010 Fair St *Web:* www.lexcs.org	Lexington	NC	27292	336-242-1527	
Lexington School District 4 607 E Fifth St. *Web:* www.lexington4.net	Swansea	SC	29160	803-568-1000	568-1020
Liberal High School 104 N Payne. *Web:* www.liberal.k12.mo.us	Liberal	MO	64762	417-843-2125	
Liberty Independent School District 1600 Grand Ave *Web:* www.libertyisd.net	Liberty	TX	77575	936-336-7215	
Liberty-Eylau Independent School District 2901 Leopard Dr. *Web:* www.leisd.net	Texarkana	TX	75501	903-832-1535	838-9444
Libertyville School District 70 1381 W Lake St *Web:* www.d70.k12.il.us	Libertyville	IL	60048	847-362-8393	
Light of Christ Rcssd 16 9301 19th Ave *Web:* www.loccsd.ca	North Battleford	SK	S9A3N5	306-445-6158	
Limestone County School District 300 S Jefferson St *Web:* www.lcsk12.org	Athens	AL	35611	256-232-5353	233-6461
Lincoln Public Schools PO Box 82889 **Fax:* Hum Res ■ *Web:* www.lps.org	Lincoln	NE	68510	402-436-1000	436-1620*
Lincoln Unified School District 2010 W Swain Rd. *Web:* www.lusd.net	Stockton	CA	95207	209-953-8700	
Lincoln-Way Central High School 1801 E Lincoln Hwy *Web:* www.lw210.org	New Lenox	IL	60451	815-462-2100	
Linden Kildare 205 Kildare Rd. *Web:* www.lkcisd.net	Linden	TX	75563	903-756-7071	
Little Cypress-Mauriceville Cisd Inc 6586 FM 1130 *Web:* www.lcmcisd.org	Orange	TX	77632	409-883-2232	
Little Friends Inc 140 N Wright St *Web:* littlefriendsinc.org	Naperville	IL	60540	630-355-6533	
Little Rock School District 810 W Markham St. **Fax:* Hum Res ■ *Web:* www.lrsd.org	Little Rock	AR	72201	501-447-1000	447-1162*
Locust Valley Central School District 22 Horse Hollow Rd *Web:* www.lvcsd.k12.ny.us	Locust Valley	NY	11560	516-277-5000	
Lompoc Unified School District 1301 N A St. *Web:* www.lusd.org	Lompoc	CA	93436	805-742-3300	735-8452
London City School District 380 Elm St. *Web:* www.london.k12.oh.us	London	OH	43140	740-852-5700	
Long County Board of Education PO Box 428. *Web:* www.longcountyps.com	Ludowici	GA	31316	912-545-2367	545-2380
Long Valley Charter School 436 Susan Dr 965 PO Box 7 *Web:* www.longvalleycs.org	Doyle	CA	96109	530-827-2395	
Longview School District 2715 Lilac St *TF:* 800-533-7881 ■ *Web:* www.longview.k12.wa.us	Longview	WA	98632	360-575-7000	575-7231
Los Alamitos Unified School District 10293 Bloomfield St. *Web:* www.losal.org	Los Alamitos	CA	90720	562-799-4700	799-4711
Los Altos School District 201 Covington Rd. *Web:* www.lasdschools.org	Los Altos	CA	94024	650-947-1150	947-0118
Los Angeles Unified School District (LAUSD) 333 S Beaudry Ave *TF:* 877-772-6273	Los Angeles	CA	90017	213-241-1000	
Los Banos California 645 Seventh St. *Web:* www.losbanos.org	Los Banos	CA	93635	209-827-7034	
Los Gatos Union Elementary School District 17010 Roberts Rd *Web:* www.lgusd.org	Los Gatos	CA	95032	408-335-2000	
Louis Riel School Division 900 St Mary's Rd *Web:* www.lrsd.net	Winnipeg	MB	R2M3R3	204-257-7827	
Louisville Municipal School District 112 S Columbus Ave PO Box 909 *Web:* www.louisville.k12.ms.us	Louisville	MS	39339	662-773-3411	773-4013
Loyola Academy 1100 Laramie *Web:* www.goramblers.org	Wilmette	IL	60091	847-256-1100	
Lubbock-Cooper Independent School District 16302 Loop 493 *Web:* www.lcisd.net	Lubbock	TX	79423	806-863-2282	
Luling Independent School District 212 E Bowie St *Web:* www.luling.txed.net	Luling	TX	78648	830-875-3191	
Lyons Elementary School District 103 4100 Joliet Ave *Web:* www.sd103.com	Lyons	IL	60534	708-783-4100	
Macomb Community Unit School District 185 323 W Washington St. *Web:* www.medfd.org	Macomb	IL	61455	309-833-4161	
Madera Unified School District 1902 HowaRd Rd *TF:* 800-322-6384 ■ *Web:* www.madera.k12.ca.us	Madera	CA	93637	559-675-4500	675-1186
Madison Local Board of Educuation 1379 Grace St. *Web:* www.madison-richland.k12.oh.us	Mansfield	OH	44905	419-589-2600	
Madison Metropolitan School District 545 W Dayton St. **Fax:* Hum Res ■ *Web:* www.madison.k12.wi.us	Madison	WI	53703	608-663-1879	204-0346*
Mahanoy Area School District 1 Golden Bear Dr *Web:* www.mabears.net	Mahanoy City	PA	17948	570-773-3443	
Maine Endwell Central School 712 Farm to Market Rd *Web:* www.me.stier.org	Endwell	NY	13760	607-754-1400	754-1650
Malvern Prep School 418 S Warren Ave *Web:* malvernprep.org	Malvern	PA	19355	484-595-1100	
Malverne Union Free School District 12 301 Wicks Ln *Web:* www.malverne.k12.ny.us	Malverne	NY	11565	516-887-6400	
Mandell School, The 795 Columbus Ave *Web:* www.mandellschool.org	New York	NY	10025	212-222-2925	
Manteno High School 443 N Maple St. *Web:* www.manteno5.org	Manteno	IL	60950	815-928-7100	
Manteo High School 829 Wingina St. *Web:* daretolearn.org	Manteo	NC	27954	252-473-5841	
Maple Valley School District 11090 Nashville Hwy *Web:* www.mvs.k12.mi.us	Vermontville	MI	49096	517-852-9699	
Marana Unified School District 6 11279 W Grier Rd Ste 127 *Web:* www.maranausd.org	Marana	AZ	85653	520-682-4757	616-4515
Mardel Inc 7727 SW 44th St *Web:* www.mardel.com	Oklahoma City	OK	73179	405-745-1300	745-1337
Marin Academy 1600 Mission Ave. *Web:* www.ma.org	San Rafael	CA	94901	415-453-4550	
Marine Military Academy Air Wing Inc 320 Iwo Jima Blvd *Web:* www.mma-tx.org	Harlingen	TX	78550	956-423-6006	
Marinette School District 2139 Pierce Ave *Web:* www.marinette.k12.wi.us	Marinette	WI	54143	715-735-1400	
Marion County Board of Education Inc 200 Gaston Ave *Web:* www.marionboe.com	Fairmont	WV	26554	304-367-2100	

Phone Fax

Marion Ctr Area School District
PO Box 156 Marion Center PA 15759 724-397-5551
Web: www.mcasd.net

Mark Young Construction Inc 7200 Miller Pl Frederick CO 80504 303-776-1449 776-1729
Web: www.markyoungconstruction.com

Marshall Independent School District (Inc)
1305 E Pinecrest Dr Marshall TX 75670 903-927-8701 935-0203
Web: www.marshallisd.com

Marshall Middle School 401 S Saratoga St Marshall MN 56258 507-537-6938
Web: swmn.org

Martin County West High School
16 W Fifth St Sherburn MN 56171 507-764-4661
Web: martin.k12.mn.us

Martinez Unified School District
921 Susana St Martinez CA 94553 925-335-5800 335-5960
Web: www.martinezusd.net

Massillon City School District
207 Oak Ave SE Massillon OH 44646 330-830-3900
Web: massillonschools.org

Masters Academy of Central Florida Inc, The
1500 Lukas Ln Oviedo FL 32765 407-971-2221

Mbc Computer Service Inc 11134 Downs Rd Pineville NC 28134 704-525-7590
Web: www.mbcservice.com

McCrory Construction Company LLC
1280 Assembly St PO Box 145 Columbia SC 29201 803-799-8100 254-9800
Web: www.mccroryconstruction.com

McIntosh County Board of Education
200 Pine St Darien GA 31305 912-437-6645
Web: www.mcintosh.k12.ga.us

Mclean School of Maryland Inc, The
8224 Lochinver Ln Potomac MD 20854 301-299-8277
Web: www.mcleanschool.org

McLeod Express LLC 5002 Cundiff Ct Decatur IL 62526 800-709-3936 875-7914*
**Fax Area Code:* 217 ■ *TF General:* 800-709-3936 ■ *Web:* www.mcleodexpress.com/default.asp

Mead School District 2323 E Farwell Rd Mead WA 99021 509-465-6000 465-6020
Web: www.mead354.org

Meadowridge School 12224 240 St Maple Ridge BC V4R1N1 604-467-4444
Web: www.meadowridge.bc.ca

Mechanicsburg Area School District (Inc)
100 E Elmwood Ave 2nd Fl Mechanicsburg PA 17055 717-691-4500
Web: www.mbgsd.org

Mecosta-Osceola Intermediate School District
15760 190th Ave Big Rapids MI 49307 231-796-3543
TF: 877-211-5253 ■ *Web:* www.moisd.org

Medford Township Board of Education
128 Rt 70 Ste 1 Medford NJ 08055 609-654-6416 654-7436
Web: www.medford.k12.nj.us

Melvindale-Northern Allen Park Public Schools
18530 Prospect St Melvindale MI 48122 313-389-3300 389-3312
Web: www.melnap.k12.mi.us

Memphis City Board of Education
2597 Avery Ave Memphis TN 38112 901-416-5300 416-5578
Web: www.mcsk12.net

Mentor Public Schools 6451 Center St Mentor OH 44060 440-255-4444
Web: www.mentorschools.net

Meramec Valley R-3 School District
126 N Payne St Pacific MO 63069 636-271-1400 271-1406
TF: 866-632-9992 ■ *Web:* www.mvr3.k12.mo.us

Merion Mercy Academy
511 Montgomery Ave Merion Station PA 19066 610-664-6655
Web: www.merion-mercy.com

Meriwether County Schools
2100 Gaston St PO Box 70 Greenville GA 30222 706-672-4297
Web: www.meriwether.k12.ga.us

Mesa Grande School Elementary School
9172 Third Ave Hesperia CA 92345 760-244-3709
Web: www.mesagrandeelementary.org

Metairie Park Country Day School Alumni Association Inc, The
300 Park Rd Metairie LA 70005 504-837-5204
Web: mpcds.com

Metropolitan Construction Services LLC (MCS)
2803 Butterfield Rd Ste 100 Oak Brook IL 60523 630-691-7200 691-7234
Web: www.metroconstructionllc.com

Metropolitan Nashville Public Schools (MNPS)
2601 Bransford Ave Nashville TN 37204 615-259-8531 214-8890
TF: 800-848-0298 ■ *Web:* www.mnps.org

Miami-Dade County Public Schools (M-DCPS)
1450 NE Second Ave Miami FL 33132 305-995-1000
Web: www.dadeschools.net

Michener Institute for Applied
222 Saint Patrick St Toronto ON M5T1V4 416-596-3101
TF: 800-387-9066 ■ *Web:* www.michener.ca

Mid-Central Educational Cooperative Office
612 Main Ave Platte SD 57369 605-337-2636
Web: midcentral-coop.org

Mid-East Career & Technology Centers
400 RichaRds Rd Zanesville OH 43701 740-454-0101 454-0731
Web: www.mid-east.k12.oh.us

Middlebury Community Schools
57853 Northridge Dr Middlebury IN 46540 574-825-9425 825-9426
TF: 866-632-9992 ■ *Web:* www.mcsin-k12.org

Middlesex County Educational Service Commission
1660 Stelton Rd Piscataway NJ 08854 732-777-9848
Web: www.mresc.k12.nj.us

Middlesex County Vocational & Technical High Schools
PO Box 1070 East Brunswick NJ 08816 732-257-3300
Web: www.mcvts.net

Middleton Cross Plains Area School District
7106 S Ave Middleton WI 53562 608-829-9000
Web: www.mcpasd.k12.wi.us

Middletown Area School District (Inc)
55 W Water St Middletown PA 17057 717-948-3300 948-3329
Web: www.raiderweb.org

Middletown City School 1515 Girard Ave Middletown OH 45044 513-423-0781 420-4579
Web: middletowncityschools.com

Midland High School 615 W Missouri Ave Midland TX 79701 989-923-5181
TF: 866-632-9992 ■ *Web:* www.midlandisd.net

Midwestern Intermediate Unit Iv
453 Maple St Grove City PA 16127 724-458-6700 458-5083
TF: 800-942-8035 ■ *Web:* www.miu4.org/site/default.aspx?pageid=1

Mifflin County School District
201 Eigth St Lewistown PA 17044 717-248-0148
Web: www.mcsdk12.org

Miken Builders Inc 32782 Cedar Dr Unit 1 Millville DE 19967 302-537-4444 537-4525
TF: 800-888-7501 ■ *Web:* www.mikenbuilders.com

Mildred High School 5475 S Us Hwy 287 Corsicana TX 75109 903-872-6505
Web: www.mildredisd.org

Milford Exempted Village School District
1039 St Rt 28 Milford OH 45150 513-831-9690 831-3208
Web: www.milfordschools.org

Milken Community High School
15800 Zeldins Way Los Angeles CA 90049 310-440-3500
Web: www.milkenschool.org

Millburn Township New Jersey Board Education
434 Millburn Ave Millburn NJ 07041 973-376-3600
Web: www.millburn.org

Miller Jordan Middle School
700 N Mccullough St San Benito TX 78586 956-361-6650
Web: mjms.sbcisd.net

Millet Learning Ctr 3660 Southfield Dr Saginaw MI 48601 989-777-2520
Web: www.sisd.cc

Milwaukee Public Schools 5225 W Vliet St Milwaukee WI 53208 414-475-8393 475-8722*
**Fax:* Hum Res ■ *Web:* mps.milwaukee.k12.wi.us/en/home.htm

Minisink Valley Central Sd PO Box 217 Slate Hill NY 10973 845-355-5100
Web: www.minisink.com

Minneapolis Public Schools
3345 Chicago Ave Minneapolis MN 55407 612-668-0000 668-0525
TF: 800-543-7709 ■ *Web:* www.mpls.k12.mn.us

Minnehaha Academy 3100 W River Pkwy Minneapolis MN 55406 612-729-8321
Web: www.minnehahaacademy.net

Minnetonka Public School Service Ctr
5621 County Rd 101 Minnetonka MN 55345 952-401-5000 401-5093
Web: www.minnetonka.k12.mn.us

Minnewaska Area High School
25122 State Hwy 28 Glenwood MN 56334 320-239-4820
Web: www.minnewaska.k12.mn.us

Minot Public School District 1
215 Second St SE Minot ND 58701 701-857-4400 857-4432
Web: minot.k12.nd.us

Minuteman Regional High School
758 Marrett Rd Lexington MA 02421 781-861-6500
Web: www.minuteman.org

Missouri School Boards Association
2100 I-70 Dr SW Columbia MO 65203 573-445-9920
TF: 800-221-6722 ■ *Web:* www.msbanet.org

Mitchell Elementary School 14429 Condon Ave Lawndale CA 90260 310-676-6140
Web: www.lawndale.k12.ca.us

Mobile County Public Schools
1 Magnum Pass PO Box 180069 Mobile AL 36618 251-221-4000 221-4545*
**Fax:* Hum Res ■ *TF:* 800-605-1033 ■ *Web:* www.mcpss.com

Modesto City Schools 426 Locust St Modesto CA 95351 209-576-4011 576-4846*
**Fax:* Hum Res ■ *TF:* 800-942-3767 ■ *Web:* monet.k12.ca.us

Mohawk Council of Akwesasne
Stn Main Po Box 579 Cornwall ON K6H5T3 613-575-2250
TF: 888-632-6273 ■ *Web:* www.akwesasne.ca

Monache High School 960 N Newcomb St Porterville CA 93257 559-782-7150
Web: mhs.portervilleschools.org

Monroe County Intermediate School District
1101 S Raisinville Rd Monroe MI 48161 734-242-5799
Web: www.monroeisd.us

Monrovia Unified School District
325 E Huntington Dr Monrovia CA 91016 626-471-2000
Web: www.monroviaschools.net

Monte Vista High School Keynoters
3131 Stone Vly Rd Danville CA 94526 925-552-5530
Web: www.mvkeynoters.org

Montebello Unified School District (MUSD)
123 S Montebello Blvd Montebello CA 90640 323-887-7900
Web: www.montebello.k12.ca.us

Montgomery Public Schools
307 S Decatur St PO Box 1991 Montgomery AL 36104 334-223-6700 269-3076
Web: www.mps.k12.al.us

Monticello Central School District
237 Forestburgh Rd Monticello NY 12701 845-794-7700
TF: 866-805-0990 ■ *Web:* www.monticelloschools.net

Montini Catholic High School 19w070 16th St Lombard IL 60148 630-627-6930
Web: montini.org

Montrose County School District Re-1j Inc
PO Box 10000 Montrose CO 81402 970-249-7726 249-7173
Web: www.mcsd.org

Mooresville Graded School District
305 N Main St Mooresville NC 28115 704-658-2530 663-3005
TF: 800-222-1222 ■ *Web:* www.mgsd.k12.nc.us

Morgan County Schools 1325 Pt Mallard Pkwy Decatur AL 35601 256-353-6442 309-2141
Web: www.morgank12.org

Moriah School of Engelwood
53 S Woodland St Englewood NJ 07631 201-567-0208
Web: www.moriahschool.org

Morris School District 31 Hazel St Morristown NJ 07960 973-292-2300
Web: www.morrisschooldistrict.org

Morris-Union Jointure Commission
340 Central Ave New Providence NJ 07974 908-464-7625
Web: www.mujc.org

Morton High School 500 Champion Dr Morton TX 79346 309-266-7182
Web: mortonisd.net

Mountain Empire Unified School District
3291 Buckman Springs Rd Pine Valley CA 91962 619-473-9022 473-9728
Web: www.meusd.k12.ca.us

Mountain Mission School 1760 Edgewater Dr Grundy VA 24614 276-935-2954
Web: mmskids.org

				Phone	Fax
Mountain View School District (MVSD) 3320 Gilman Rd *Web:* www.mtviewschools.com	El Monte	CA	91732	626-652-4000	652-4052
Mt Pleasant Central School District 825 Westlake Dr *Web:* www.mtplcsd.org	Thornwood	NY	10594	914-769-5500	769-3733
Mt Street Michael High School 4300 Murdock Ave *Web:* mtstmichael.org	Bronx	NY	10466	718-515-6400	
Mt. Lebanon School District 7 Horsman Dr *TF:* 800-222-3353 ■ *Web:* www.mtlsd.org	Pittsburgh	PA	15228	412-344-2000	344-2047
Mukwonago Area School District 385 County Rd NNE *Web:* www.masd.k12.wi.us	Mukwonago	WI	53149	262-363-6300	363-6272
Murray Co 1215 Fern Ridge Pkwy Ste 213 *TF:* 888-323-5560 ■ *Web:* www.murray-company.com	Saint Louis	MO	63141	314-576-2818	434-5780
N E Florida Educational Consortium 3841 Reid St *Web:* nefec.org	Palatka	FL	32177	386-329-3800	
Nashoba Regional School District Inc 50 Mechanic St *Web:* www.nrsd.net	Bolton	MA	01740	978-779-0539	
Nassau County School District 1201 Atlantic Ave *Web:* www.edline.net/pages/nassau_county_school_district	Fernandina Beach	FL	32034	904-491-9900	
National Children's Ctr Inc 6200 Second St NW *TF:* 866-632-9992 ■ *Web:* www.nccinc.org	Washington	DC	20011	202-722-2300	
National Outdoor Leadership School 284 Lincoln St *TF:* 800-710-6657 ■ *Web:* www.nols.edu	Lander	WY	82520	307-332-5300	332-1220
National School District 1500 N Ave *Web:* www.nsd.us	National City	CA	91950	619-336-7500	336-7521
Nationwide Magazine & Book Distributors Inc 3000 E Grauwyler Rd PO Box 170427 *TF General:* 800-777-9068 ■ *Web:* www.nationwidemagazine.com	Irving	TX	75017	972-438-7852	721-0613
Nebraska City Middle School 909 First Corso *Web:* www.nebcityps.org	Nebraska City	NE	68410	402-873-5591	
Netcong Elementary School 26 College Rd *Web:* www.netcongschool.org	Netcong	NJ	07857	973-347-0020	
Netivot Hatorah 18 Atkinson Ave *Web:* www.netivot.com	Thornhill	ON	L4J8C8	905-771-1234	
New Brighton Area School District 3225 43rd St *Web:* www.nbasd.org	New Brighton	PA	15066	724-843-1795	843-6144
New Haven Unified School District 34200 Alvarado Niles Rd *Web:* www.nhusd.k12.ca.us	Union City	CA	94587	510-471-1100	
New Lenox School District 122 (NLSD) 102 S Cedar Rd *Web:* www.nlsd122.org	New Lenox	IL	60451	815-485-2169	
New Trier Township High School District 203 7 Happ Rd *Web:* www.newtrier.k12.il.us	Northfield	IL	60093	847-446-7000	784-7500
New York City Dept of Education 65 Ct St *Web:* schools.nyc.gov	Brooklyn	NY	11201	718-935-4000	
Newberg School District 29 Jt 714 E Sixth St *Web:* www.newberg.k12.or.us	Newberg	OR	97132	503-554-5000	538-4374
Newton-Conover City Sch Dist 605 N Ashe Ave *Web:* www.newton-conover.org	Newton	NC	28658	828-464-3191	
Niagara Fresh Fruit Co 5796 Wilson Burt Rd *Web:* niagarafreshfruit.com	Burt	NY	14028	716-778-7631	778-8768
Niles Community School 111 Spruce St *TF:* 877-622-2321 ■ *Web:* nilesschools.schoolwires.net	Niles	MI	49120	269-683-0732	
Niskayuna Central School District (NCSD) 1239 Van Antwerp Rd *TF:* 866-893-6337 ■ *Web:* www.niskyschools.org	Schenectady	NY	12309	518-377-4666	377-4074
Noble & Greenough School 10 Campus Dr	Dedham	MA	02026	781-326-3700	
Nokomis Regional High School 266 Williams Rd *Web:* rsu19.org	Newport	ME	04953	207-368-4354	
Nordonia Hills School District 9370 Olde 8 Rd *Web:* www.nordoniaschools.org	Northfield	OH	44067	330-467-0580	
Norfolk Academy 1585 Wesleyan Dr *Web:* www.norfolkacademy.org	Norfolk	VA	23502	757-461-6236	
Norfolk Collegiate School 7336 Granby St *Web:* www.norfolkcollegiate.org	Norfolk	VA	23505	757-480-2885	
Norfolk Public Schools 800 E City Hall Ave *TF:* 800-846-4464 ■ *Web:* www.nps.k12.va.us	Norfolk	VA	23510	757-628-3843	628-3820
Norman Howard School 275 Pinnacle Rd *Web:* www.normanhoward.org	Rochester	NY	14623	585-334-8010	
Normandy School District 3855 Lcas Hunt Rd *Web:* www.normandy.k12.mo.us	Saint Louis	MO	63121	314-493-0400	493-0414
North Elementary School 1850 Hwy 351 *Web:* www.esc14.net	Abilene	TX	79601	254-559-6511	
North Hunterdon-Voorhees Regional High School District 1445 SR- 31 *Web:* www.nhvweb.net	Annandale	NJ	08801	908-735-2846	
North Love Christian School 5301 E Riverside Blvd *Web:* northlove.org	Rockford	IL	61114	815-877-6021	
North Mason School District Inc 71 E Campus Dr *Web:* www.nmsd.wednet.edu	Belfair	WA	98528	360-277-2300	
North Monterey County Unified School District 8142 Moss Landing Rd *Web:* www.nmcusd.org	Moss Landing	CA	95039	831-633-3343	
North Ridgeville City School District 5490 Mills Creek Ln *TF:* 877-644-6457 ■ *Web:* www.nrcs.k12.oh.us	North Ridgeville	OH	44039	440-327-4444	
North Rose-Wolcott Central School District 11631 Salter Colvin Rd *Web:* www.nrwcs.org	Wolcott	NY	14590	315-594-3141	594-2352

				Phone	Fax
North Sanpete School District Inc 390 East 700 South *Web:* www.nsh.nsanpete.k12.ut.us	Mount Pleasant	UT	84647	435-462-2452	462-3112
North Santiam School District 29 J 1155 N Third Ave *Web:* nsantiam.orvsd.org	Stayton	OR	97383	503-769-6924	769-3578
North Schuylkill School District 15 Academy Ln *Web:* www.northschuylkill.net	Ashland	PA	17921	570-874-0466	874-3334
North Shore School District 112 (NSSD) 1936 Green Bay Rd *Web:* www.nssd112.org	Highland Park	IL	60035	224-765-3000	
Northampton County School District 701 N Church St PO Box 158 *Web:* www.northampton.k12.nc.us	Jackson	NC	27845	252-534-1371	534-4631
Northeast Wyoming Board of Cooperative Educational Services Boces 410 N Miller Ave *Web:* www.newboces.com	Gillette	WY	82716	307-682-0231	
Northern Burlington County School District 160 Mansfield Rd E *Web:* www.nburlington.com	Columbus	NJ	08022	609-298-3900	
Northern Local School District 8700 Sheridan Dr *Web:* www.nlsd.k12.oh.us	Thornville	OH	43076	740-743-1303	743-3301
Northview Public School 4451 Hunsberger NE *TF:* 866-632-9992 ■ *Web:* www.nvps.net	Grand Rapids	MI	49525	616-363-4857	361-3494
Northwest Local School District (NWLSD) 3240 Banning Rd *Web:* www.nwlsd.org	Cincinnati	OH	45239	513-923-1000	923-3644
Northwest R-1 School District 2843 Community Ln *Web:* www.nwr1.k12.mo.us	High Ridge	MO	63049	636-677-3473	677-5480
Northwestern Lehigh Sch Dist 6493 Rt 309 *Web:* www.nwlehighsd.org	New Tripoli	PA	18066	610-298-8661	
Norwin School District 281 Mcmahon Dr *Web:* www.norwinsd.org	Irwin	PA	15642	724-861-3000	863-9467
Nye County School District Inc (NCSD) PO Box 113 *TF:* 800-796-6273 ■ *Web:* nyecounty.schoolinsites.com	Tonopah	NV	89049	775-482-6258	482-8573
O H Anderson Elementary School 666 Warner Ave S *Web:* www.mahtomedi.k12.mn.us	Saint Paul	MN	55115	651-407-2300	
Oak Creek-Franklin Joint School District 7630 S Tenth St	Oak Creek	WI	53154	414-768-5880	
Oak Meadows Elementary School 28600 Poinsettia St	Murrieta	CA	92563	951-246-4210	
Oakland Elementary School 2415 Brockton Ave *Web:* www.royaloakschools.com	Royal Oak	MI	48067	248-542-4406	
Oakland Schools Inc 2111 Pontiac Lk Rd *Web:* www.oakland.k12.mi.us	Waterford	MI	48328	248-209-2000	209-2206
Oakland Unified School District 1025 Second Ave *TF:* 888-604-4636 ■ *Web:* www.ousd.org	Oakland	CA	94606	510-879-8582	
Oceanside Union Free School District 11 145 Merle Ave *Web:* oceansideschools.org	Oceanside	NY	11572	516-678-1200	
Oconee County School District PO Box 146 *Web:* www.oconeeschools.org	Watkinsville	GA	30677	706-769-5130	769-3500
Ohio Council of Community Schools 3131 Executive Pkwy Ste 306 *Web:* ohioschools.org	Toledo	OH	43606	419-720-5200	
Ohio County Board of Education 315 E Union St *Web:* ohio.k12.ky.us	Hartford	KY	42347	270-298-3249	
Oklahoma City Public Schools 2500 NE 30th St *Web:* www.okcps.org	Oklahoma City	OK	73111	405-587-0000	
Olympia School District 1113 Legion Way SE *TF:* 855-846-8376 ■ *Web:* www.osd.wednet.edu	Olympia	WA	98501	360-596-6100	596-6111
Omaha Public Schools 3215 Cuming St *Web:* www.ops.org	Omaha	NE	68131	402-557-2222	
Oneida City School District Inc 565 Sayles St *Web:* www.oneidacsd.org	Oneida	NY	13421	315-363-2550	363-6728
Ontario Christian High School 931 W Philadelphia St	Ontario	CA	91762	909-984-1756	
Orange County Public Schools 445 W Amelia St *Fax: Hum Res ■ *TF:* 800-378-9264 ■ *Web:* www.ocps.net	Orlando	FL	32801	407-317-3200	317-3392*
Orangeburg Consolidated School District 5 578 Ellis Ave *Web:* www.ocsd5schools.org	Orangeburg	SC	29115	803-534-5454	533-7953
Oregon City School District 62 PO Box 2110 *Web:* ocsd62.org	Oregon City	OR	97045	503-785-8000	
Orleans Parish School Board 3520 General DeGaulle Dr *Web:* opsb.us	New Orleans	LA	70114	504-304-3520	
Oroville Union High School District 2211 Washington Ave *Web:* ouhsd.org	Oroville	CA	95966	530-538-2300	
Osprey Central School 408053 Grey Rd 4 *Web:* www.bwdsb.on.ca	Maxwell	ON	N0C1J0	519-922-2341	
Ossining Union Free School District 190 Croton Ave *TF:* 877-769-7447 ■ *Web:* www.ossiningufsd.org	Ossining	NY	10562	914-941-7700	941-7291
Oswego Community Unit School District 308 4175 SR- 71 *Web:* www.oswego308.org	Oswego	IL	60543	630-554-3447	554-2168
Our Lady Queen of Peace Catholic School 1600 Hwy 2004 *Web:* www.olqpschool.org	Richwood	TX	77531	979-265-3909	
Owatonna Senior High School 333 E School St *Web:* www.owatonna.k12.mn.us	Owatonna	MN	55060	507-444-8800	

				Phone	Fax
Owosso Public Schools 645 Alger St PO Box 340 *Web:* www.owosso.k12.mi.us	Owosso	MI	48867	989-723-8131	723-7777
Oxford Academy & Central School 50 S Washington Ave PO Box 192 *Web:* www.oxac.org	Oxford	NY	13830	607-843-2025	843-3241
Pacific Bldg Group 9752 Aspen Creek Ct Ste 150 *Web:* www.pacificbuildinggroup.com	San Diego	CA	92126	858-552-0600	552-0604
Pacific Ridge School 6269 El Fuerte St *Web:* www.pacificridge.org	Carlsbad	CA	92009	760-448-9820	
Paideia School Inc, The 1509 Ponce De Leon Ave NE *Web:* www.paideiaschool.org	Atlanta	GA	30307	404-377-3491	377-0032
Palisades Charter High School 15777 Bowdoin St *Web:* www.palihigh.org	Pacific Palisades	CA	90272	310-230-6623	
Palm Beach County School District, The 3300 Forest Hill Blvd **Fax:* Hum Res ■ *TF:* 866-930-8402 ■ *Web:* www.palmbeach.k12.fl.us	West Palm Beach	FL	33406	561-434-8000	434-8899*
Palmerton Area School District 680 Fourth St *TF:* 800-732-0999 ■ *Web:* www.palmerton.k12.pa.us	Palmerton	PA	18071	610-826-7101	826-4958
Palmyra Area School District 1125 Pk Dr *Web:* pasd.us	Palmyra	PA	17078	717-838-3144	
Paradise Valley Unified School District 15002 N 32nd St *Web:* www.pvschools.net	Phoenix	AZ	85032	602-449-2000	
Paramount 9338 Reseda Blvd Ste 102 *Web:* www.jennifer4homes.com	Northridge	CA	91324	626-458-0939	
Park County District No 6 919 Cody Ave *Web:* park6.org	Cody	WY	82414	307-587-4253	
Park Tudor School 7200 N College Ave *Web:* www.parktudor.org	Indianapolis	IN	46240	317-415-2700	
Parkland School District 1210 Springhouse Rd *Web:* www.parklandsd.org	Allentown	PA	18104	610-351-5503	351-5509
Parsons Elem. School 899 Hollywood St *Web:* nbtschools.org	North Brunswick	NJ	08902	732-289-3400	
Paul Risk Assoc Inc 11 W State St *Web:* www.paulrisk.com	Quarryville	PA	17566	717-786-7308	786-2848
Pawling Central School District 515 Rt 22 *Web:* www.pawlingschools.org	Pawling	NY	12564	845-855-4600	
Peace Wapiti Public School Division No 76 8611 108 St *Web:* www.pwsd76.ab.ca	Grande Prairie	AB	T8V4C5	780-532-8133	
Peach County School District Inc 523 Vineville St *TF:* 866-632-9992 ■ *Web:* www.peachschools.org	Fort Valley	GA	31030	478-825-5933	825-9970
Pearl City High School 100 S Summit St *Web:* www.pcwolves.net	Pearl City	IL	61062	815-443-2715	
Pembroke Hill School 400 W 51st St *Web:* www.pembrokehill.org	Kansas City	MO	64112	816-936-1200	
Peninsula High School 14105 Purdy Dr NW *Web:* www.phs.psd401.net	Gig Harbor	WA	98332	253-530-4400	
Penn Hills School District 260 Aster St *Web:* www.phsd.k12.pa.us	Pittsburgh	PA	15235	412-793-7000	793-6402
Penn. Manor Senior High School 100 E Cottage Ave *Web:* www.pennmanor.net	Millersville	PA	17551	717-872-9520	
Pennridge School District 1200 N Fifth St *Web:* pennridge.org	Perkasie	PA	18944	215-257-5011	
Penns Grove-Carneys Point Regional Board of Education 100 Iona Ave *TF:* 877-652-7624 ■ *Web:* pgcpschools.org	Penns Grove	NJ	08069	856-299-4250	299-5226
Perris Union High School District 155 E Fourth St *Web:* www.puhsd.org	Perris	CA	92570	951-943-6369	
Person Centered Services Inc 240 N Union St *Web:* www.pcs4dd.com	Stockton	CA	95205	209-466-2448	
Person County Public Schools 304 S Morgan St *TF:* 866-724-6650 ■ *Web:* www.person.k12.nc.us	Roxboro	NC	27573	336-599-2191	
Petaluma City Schools (PCS) 200 Douglas St *Web:* www.petalumacityschools.org	Petaluma	CA	94952	707-778-4813	
Phase North 6601 Xylon Ave N *Web:* www.district287.org	Minneapolis	MN	55428	763-533-3821	
Phillipsburg Board of Education 445 Marshall St *Web:* www.pburgsd.net	Phillipsburg	NJ	08865	908-454-3400	
Phoenix Elementary School District 1817 N Seventh St **Fax:* Hum Res ■ *Web:* phxschools.org	Phoenix	AZ	85006	602-257-3755	257-6077*
Phoenix Union High School District (PUHSD) 4502 N Central Ave *Web:* www.phxhs.k12.az.us	Phoenix	AZ	85012	602-764-1100	
Pickaway-Ross County Joint Vocational School District 895 Crouse Chapel Rd *Web:* pickawayross.com	Chillicothe	OH	45601	740-642-1200	
Pickens County School District (PCSD) 1348 Griffin Mill Rd *Web:* www.pickens.k12.sc.us	Easley	SC	29640	864-397-1000	855-8159
Pickerington Local School District 777 Long Rd *Web:* www.pickerington.k12.oh.us	Pickerington	OH	43147	614-833-2110	833-2143
Pima County School Superintendent 130 W Congress St 4th Fl **Fax:* Hum Res ■ *Web:* www.schools.pima.gov	Tucson	AZ	85701	520-740-8451	623-9308*
Pinckney Community Schools 2130 E MI 36 *Web:* www.pinckneyschools.org	Pinckney	MI	48169	810-225-3900	
Pine Grove Area School Dist 103 School St *Web:* www.pgasd.com	Pine Grove	PA	17963	570-345-2731	
Pine Road Elementary School 3737 Pine Rd *Web:* www.lmtsd.org	Huntingdon Valley	PA	19006	215-938-0290	

				Phone	Fax
Pinelands Regional School District PO Box 248 *Web:* www.prsdnj.org	Tuckerton	NJ	08087	609-296-3106	
Pinewood Preparatory School 1114 Orangeburg Rd *Web:* pinewoodprep.com	Summerville	SC	29483	843-873-1643	
Pittsburgh Public Schools (PPS) 341 S Bellefield Ave *Web:* www.pps.k12.pa.us	Pittsburgh	PA	15213	412-622-7920	
Pittsylvania County School Board 39 Bank St SE PO Box 232 *TF:* 888-440-6520 ■ *Web:* www.pcs.k12.va.us	Chatham	VA	24531	434-432-2761	432-9560
Placentia-Yorba Linda Unified School District (PYLUSD) 1301 E Orangethorpe Ave *Web:* www.pylusd.org	Placentia	CA	92870	714-996-2550	
Placer Union High School District PO Box 5048 *Web:* www.puhsd.k12.ca.us	Auburn	CA	95604	530-886-4400	886-4439
Plain Local School District 901 44th St NW *Web:* www.plainlocal.org	Canton	OH	44709	330-492-3500	493-5542
Plainfield Central School District 75 Canterbury Rd *Web:* www.plainfieldschools.org	Plainfield	CT	06374	860-564-6437	
Plainfield Community Consolidated School District 202 15732 S Howard St *Web:* www.psd202.org/pages/plainfieldsd202	Plainfield	IL	60544	815-577-4000	436-7824
Plainwell Community School District 600 School Dr *Web:* www.plainwellschools.org	Plainwell	MI	49080	269-685-5823	685-1108
Plaquemines Parish School Board 557 F Edward Hebert Blvd *TF:* 877-453-2721 ■ *Web:* www.ppsb.org	Belle Chasse	LA	70037	504-595-6400	392-4973
Pleasant Valley Sch District 600 Temple Ave *Web:* www.pvsd.k12.ca.us	Camarillo	CA	93010	805-482-2763	987-5511
Pleasantville Union Free School District 60 Romer Ave *Web:* www.pleasantvilleschools.com	Pleasantville	NY	10570	914-741-1400	741-1499
Pope John Paul Ii High School Office 1901 Jaguar Dr *Web:* pjp.org	Slidell	LA	70461	985-649-0914	
Portage Community School District 904 De Witt St *Web:* www.portage.k12.wi.us	Portage	WI	53901	608-742-4867	
Portland Public Schools 501 N Dixon St *TF:* 800-766-8206 ■ *Web:* www.pps.net	Portland	OR	97227	503-916-2000	916-3110
Portola School 300 Amador Ave *Web:* sbpsd.k12.ca.us	San Bruno	CA	94066	650-624-3175	
Positive Education Program Inc 3100 Euclid Ave *Web:* www.pepcleve.org	Cleveland	OH	44115	216-361-4400	361-8600
Poudre School District 2407 LaPorte Ave *Web:* psdschools.org	Fort Collins	CO	80521	970-482-7420	
Powhatan County School District 2320 Skaggs Rd *Web:* www.powhatan.k12.va.us	Powhatan	VA	23139	804-598-5700	
Prairie Lakes Area Education Agency 1235 Fifth Ave S *Web:* www.plaea.org	Fort Dodge	IA	50501	515-574-5500	
Prairie View Sr. High School 13731 Ks Hwy 152 *Web:* www.pv362.org	Lacygne	KS	66040	913-757-4447	
Preble-Shawnee School District 124 Bloomfield St	Camden	OH	45311	937-452-1283	
Prestwood Elementary School 343 E Macarthur St *Web:* prestwoodschool.org	Sonoma	CA	95476	707-935-6030	
Prince Edward County School District 35 Eagle Dr *Web:* www.pecps.k12.va.us	Farmville	VA	23901	434-315-2100	
Princeton Regional School District 25 Valley Rd Administration Bldg *TF:* 877-652-2873 ■ *Web:* www.prs.k12.nj.us	Princeton	NJ	08540	609-806-4200	
Prior Lake-Savage Area Public School District 719 4540 Tower St SE *TF:* 855-346-1650 ■ *Web:* www.priorlake-savage.k12.mn.us	Prior Lake	MN	55372	952-226-0000	226-0049
Proteus Inc 1830 N Dinuba Blvd *TF:* 888-776-9998 ■ *Web:* www.proteusinc.org	Visalia	CA	93291	559-733-5423	
Provision Ministry Group PO Box 19700 *TF:* 800-233-3880 ■ *Web:* www.provision.org	Irvine	CA	92623	800-233-3880	
Provo School District 280 West 940 North *Web:* www.provo.edu	Provo	UT	84604	801-374-4800	374-4808
Puget Sound Educational Service District 800 Oakesdale Ave SW *TF:* 800-664-4549 ■ *Web:* www.psesd.org	Renton	WA	98057	425-917-7600	
Pulaski County School District (PCPS) 202 N Washington Ave *Web:* www.pcva.us	Pulaski	VA	24301	540-994-2550	994-2552
Pullman School District 267 240 SE Dexter St *Web:* www.psd267.org	Pullman	WA	99163	509-332-3581	
Putnam Valley School District Inc 146 Peekskill Hollow Rd *TF:* 800-666-5327 ■ *Web:* www.pvcsd.org	Putnam Valley	NY	10579	845-528-8143	
Quaker Valley School District 203 Graham St *Web:* www.qvsd.org	Sewickley	PA	15143	412-749-3600	
Queensbury Union Free School 429 Aviation Rd *Web:* www.queensburyschool.org	Queensbury	NY	12804	518-824-5699	
Rabun County School District 963 Tiger Connector *TF:* 866-632-9992 ■ *Web:* www.rabun.k12.ga.us	Tiger	GA	30576	706-212-4350	782-6224
Radnor Township School Authority 135 S Wayne Ave *Web:* www.rtsd.org	Wayne	PA	19087	610-688-8100	

Name / Address	City	State	Zip	Phone	Fax
Ralston Middle School 8202 Lakeview St *Web:* ralstonschools.org	Omaha	NE	68127	402-331-4701	
Ramsey Board of Education 266 E Main St *Web:* www.ramsey.k12.nj.us	Ramsey	NJ	07446	201-785-2300	934-6623
RE Crawford Construction Inc 6771 Professional Pkwy W Ste 100 *Web:* www.recrawford.com	Sarasota	FL	34240	941-907-0010	
Red Clay Consolidated School District 1502 Spruce Ave	Wilmington	DE	19808	302-552-3700	
Red Lion Christian Academy 1390 Red Lion Rd *Web:* www.redlionca.org	Bear	DE	19701	302-834-2526	
Red River Valley School Division 233 Main St N *Web:* www.rrvsd.ca	Morris	MB	R0G1K0	204-746-2317	
Redmond School District 145 SE Salmon Ave *Web:* www.redmond.k12.or.us	Redmond	OR	97756	541-923-5437	923-5142
Redwood City School District (RCSD) 750 Bradford St *Web:* www.rcsd.k12.ca.us/site/default.aspx?pageid=1	Redwood City	CA	94063	650-423-2200	423-2294
Redwood Day School Parents & Guardians Association 3245 Sheffield Ave *Web:* www.rdschool.org	Oakland	CA	94602	510-534-0800	
Regis School 7330 Westview Dr *Web:* www.theregisschool.org	Houston	TX	77055	713-682-8383	
Retail Construction Services Inc (RCS) 11343 39th St N *Web:* www.retailconstruction.com	Lake Elmo	MN	55042	651-704-9000	704-9100
Reynolds School District 7 Inc 1204 NE 201st Ave *Web:* www.reynolds.k12.or.us	Fairview	OR	97024	503-661-7200	667-6932
Richland County School District One 1616 Richland St **Fax:* Hum Res ■ *Web:* www.richlandone.org	Columbia	SC	29201	803-231-7000	231-7417*
Richmond City Public Schools 301 N Ninth St *Web:* web.richmond.k12.va.us	Richmond	VA	23219	804-780-7700	780-4122
Richmond County School System 864 Broad St *Web:* www.rcboe.org/home.asp	Augusta	GA	30901	706-826-1000	
Ripon Elementary School 509 W Main St *Web:* riponusd.net	Ripon	CA	95366	209-599-4225	
River East Transcona School Division 589 Roch St *Web:* www.retsd.mb.ca	Winnipeg	MB	R2K2P7	204-667-7130	
River School 4880 Macarthur Blvd Nw *Web:* riverschool.net	Washington	DC	20007	202-337-3554	
River View Local School District 26496 SR- 60 *Web:* www.river-view.k12.oh.us	Warsaw	OH	43844	740-824-3521	
Riverdale Country School 5250 Fieldston Rd *Web:* www.riverdale.edu	Bronx	NY	10471	718-549-8810	519-2795
Riverside Unified School District (RUSD) 3380 14th St PO Box 2800 *Web:* www.rusdlink.org	Riverside	CA	92501	951-788-7135	
Riverton Elementary School 209 N Seventh St *Web:* www.rivertonschools.org	Riverton	IL	62561	217-629-6001	
Riverview Intermediate Unit Number 6 Administrative Offices 270 Mayfield Rd *Web:* www.riu6.org	Clarion	PA	16214	814-226-7103	
Robbinsdale Area Schools 4148 Winnetka Ave N *Web:* www.rdale.org	New Hope	MN	55427	763-504-8000	
Robert e Webber Institute for Worship Studies, The 151 Kingsley Ave *TF:* 800-282-2977 ■ *Web:* iws.edu	Orange Park	FL	32073	904-264-2172	
Robert Frost Middle School 2206 W 167th St	Markham	IL	60428	708-210-9929	
Robstown High School 609 W Hwy 44 *TF:* 800-446-3142 ■ *Web:* www.robstownisd.org	Robstown	TX	78380	361-387-5999	
Rochester City School District 131 W Broad St *Web:* www.rcsdk12.org	Rochester	NY	14614	585-262-8100	
Rocklin Academy, The 6532 Turnstone Way *Web:* www.rocklinacademy.com	Rocklin	CA	95765	916-632-6580	
Roman Catholic Diocese of Fresno 1550 N Fresno St *Web:* www.dioceseoffresno.org	Fresno	CA	93703	559-488-7400	
Rome City School District 508 E Second St *Web:* www.rcs.rome.ga.us	Rome	GA	30161	706-236-5050	802-4311
Romeo Community School District 316 N Main St *TF:* 888-427-6818 ■ *Web:* www.romeo.k12.mi.us	Romeo	MI	48065	586-752-0200	752-0228
Ronald C Wornick Jewish Day School 800 Foster City Blvd *Web:* www.wornickjds.org	Foster City	CA	94404	650-378-2600	
Ronald Reagan Middle School 620 Division St *Web:* dixonschools.org	Dixon	IL	61021	815-284-7725	
Roncalli High Sch. Sisters 2000 Mirro Dr *Web:* roncallijets.net	Manitowoc	WI	54220	920-682-8801	
Rose Tree Media School District 308 N Olive St *Web:* www.rtmsd.org	Media	PA	19063	610-627-6000	
Rosetta Stone Ltd 1919 N Lynn St 7th Fl *NYSE:* RST ■ **Fax Area Code:* 540 ■ *TF:* 800-788-0822 ■ *Web:* www.rosettastone.com	Arlington	VA	22209	800-788-0822	432-0953*
Roseville Joint Union High School District Fin Corp 1750 Cirby Way *Web:* www.rjuhsd.k12.ca.us	Roseville	CA	95661	916-786-2051	786-2681
Ross Valley School District 110 Shaw Dr *TF:* 800-322-6384 ■ *Web:* www.rossvalleyschools.org	San Anselmo	CA	94960	415-454-2162	
Round Rock ISD 1311 Round Rock Ave *Web:* www.roundrockisd.org	Round Rock	TX	78681	512-464-6000	
Rush-Henrietta Central School District 2034 Lehigh Stn Rd *Web:* www.rhnet.org	Henrietta	NY	14467	585-359-5000	359-5045
Rusk High School 203 E Seventh St *Web:* www.ruskisd.net	Rusk	TX	75785	903-683-5592	
Sachem Central School District At Holbrook 245 Union Ave *Web:* www.sachem.edu	Holbrook	NY	11741	631-471-1300	
Sacramento City Unified School District 5735 47th Ave *Web:* www.scusd.edu	Sacramento	CA	95824	916-643-7400	643-9440
Safford Unified School District 1 734 W 11th St *Web:* www.saffordusd.k12.az.us	Safford	AZ	85546	928-348-7000	
Saint Jude The Apostle School 7171 Glenridge Dr NE *Web:* saintjude.net	Atlanta	GA	30328	818-889-9483	
Saint Louis Public Schools 801 N 11th St **Fax:* Hum Res ■ *Web:* www.slps.org	Saint Louis	MO	63101	314-231-3720	345-2650*
Saint Patrick School 9040 Hutchins St *Web:* stpatrickwhitelake.org	White Lake	MI	48386	248-698-3240	
Salem-Keizer Public Schools 2450 Lancaster Dr NE **Fax:* Hum Res ■ *TF:* 877-293-1090 ■ *Web:* www.salkeiz.k12.or.us	Salem	OR	97305	503-399-3000	375-7802*
Salesian High School 2851 Salesian Ave	Richmond	CA	94804	510-234-4433	
Salin Bank 8455 Keystone Xing *TF:* 800-320-7536 ■ *Web:* www.salin.com	Indianapolis	IN	46240	317-452-8000	532-2263
Saline Area Schools 7265 Saline Ann Arbor Rd *Web:* www.salineschools.org	Saline	MI	48176	734-429-8000	
Salt Lake School District 440 East 100 South *Web:* slcschools.org	Salt Lake City	UT	84111	801-578-8599	578-8689
Sampson County Schools 437 Rowan Rd PO Box 439 *Web:* www.sampson.k12.nc.us	Clinton	NC	28329	910-592-1401	590-2445
San Antonio Independent School District (SAISD) 141 Lavaca St **Fax:* Hum Res ■ *TF:* 866-632-9992 ■ *Web:* www.saisd.net	San Antonio	TX	78210	210-554-2200	299-5600*
San Diego Jewish Academy 11860 Carmel Creek Rd *Web:* www.sdja.com	San Diego	CA	92130	858-704-3700	
San Diego Unified School District 4100 Normal St *Web:* www.sandiegounified.org	San Diego	CA	92103	619-725-8000	725-8001
San Francisco Unified School District 555 Franklin St *Web:* www.sfusd.edu	San Francisco	CA	94102	415-241-6000	
San Jacinto Valley Academy Inc 480 N San Jacinto Ave *Web:* www.sjva.net	San Jacinto	CA	92583	951-654-6113	
San Jose Unified School District 855 Lenzen Ave **Fax:* Hum Res ■ *TF:* 800-433-3243 ■ *Web:* www.sjusd.org	San Jose	CA	95126	408-535-6000	535-2377*
San Leandro Adult School 2255 Bancroft Ave *Web:* www.sanleandroadultschool.org	San Leandro	CA	94577	510-618-4420	
San Lorenzo Unified School District (SLZUSD) 15510 Usher St *Web:* www.slzusd.org	San Lorenzo	CA	94580	510-317-4600	
San Luis Obispo High School 1499 San Luis Dr *Web:* www.slcusd.org	San Luis Obispo	CA	93401	805-596-4040	
San Miguel Joint Un School Dst. 1601 L St *Web:* www.sanmiguelschools.org	San Miguel	CA	93451	805-467-3216	
San Ysidro School District 4350 Otay Mesa Rd *Web:* www.sysd.k12.ca.us	San Ysidro	CA	92173	619-428-4476	428-1505
Santa Barbara Unified School District 720 Santa Barbara St *Web:* www.sbunified.org	Santa Barbara	CA	93101	805-963-4338	
Santa Fe Independent School District PO Box 370 *Web:* www.sfisd.org	Santa Fe	TX	77510	409-925-3526	
Santa Fe Preparatory School 1101 Camino De Cruz Blanca *Web:* www.sfprep.org	Santa Fe	NM	87505	505-982-1829	
Santa Margarita Catholic High School 22062 antonio pkwy *Web:* www.eaglesfootball.com	Rancho Santa Margarita	CA	92688	949-766-6000	
Santa Maria-Bonita School Dist 708 S Miller St *Web:* www.smbsd.org	Santa Maria	CA	93454	805-928-1783	
Santee School District 9625 Cuyamaca St *Web:* www.santeesd.net	Santee	CA	92071	619-258-2300	
Saucon Valley School District 2097 Polk Vly Rd *TF:* 866-632-9992 ■ *Web:* svpanthers.org	Hellertown	PA	18055	610-838-7026	
Sauder School of Business 2389 Health Sciences Mall *Web:* www.sauder.ubc.ca	Vancouver	BC	V6T1Z2	604-822-8399	
Saugus High School 21900 Centurion Way *Web:* www.hartdistrict.org	Santa Clarita	CA	91350	661-297-3900	
Scarsdale Union Free School District 2 Brewster Rd *TF:* 888-837-6437 ■ *Web:* www.scarsdaleschools.k12.ny.us	Scarsdale	NY	10583	914-721-2410	
Schalmont Central School District 4 Sabre Dr *Web:* www.schalmont.org	Schenectady	NY	12306	518-355-9200	355-9203
School Board of Highlands County Florida PO Box 9300 *TF:* 877-357-7456 ■ *Web:* www.highlands.k12.fl.us	Sebring	FL	33871	863-471-5555	386-6179
School District of Cheltenham Township 2000 Ashbourne Rd *Web:* www.cheltenham.org	Elkins Park	PA	19027	215-886-9500	884-6929
School District of Hartford 675 E Rossman St *Web:* www.hartfordjt1.k12.wi.us	Hartford	WI	53027	262-673-3155	673-3548
School District of Philadelphia 440 N Broad St *Web:* www.phila.k12.pa.us	Philadelphia	PA	19130	215-400-4000	
School District of The Chathams 58 Meyersville Rd *TF:* 800-225-5425 ■ *Web:* www.chatham-nj.org	Chatham	NJ	07928	973-457-2500	

Name / Address	City	State	Zip	Phone	Fax
School Nurse Supply Co 1690 Wright Blvd *TF:* 800-485-2737 ■ *Web:* www.schoolnursesupplyinc.com	Schaumburg	IL	60193	800-485-2737	
Schools Wstrn Area Career & Techlgy Center; Main Ofc 688 Western Ave. *Web:* www.wactc.net	Canonsburg	PA	15317	724-746-2890	
Schuylkill Haven Area School Authority 120 Haven St *Web:* www.haven.k12.pa.us	Schuylkill Haven	PA	17972	570-385-6705	
Schuylkill Valley School District 929 Lakeshore Dr *Web:* www.schuylkillvalley.org	Leesport	PA	19533	610-926-1706	
Scotch Plains-Fanwood Board of Education 2280 Evergreen Ave *Web:* www.spfk12.org	Scotch Plains	NJ	07076	908-889-5331	889-9332
Scotts Valley Unified School District Inc 4444 Scotts Vly Dr Ste 5b. *Web:* www.svusd.santacruz.k12.ca.us	Scotts Valley	CA	95066	831-438-2312	
Scranton School District 425 N Washington Ave *Web:* www.scrsd.org	Scranton	PA	18503	570-348-3474	348-3563
Seaman Unified School District 345 901 NW Lyman Rd *Web:* www.seamanschools.org	Topeka	KS	66608	785-575-8600	575-8620
Seattle Public Schools PO Box 34165 *Web:* www.seattleschools.org	Seattle	WA	98124	206-252-0000	
Security Bancshares Co 735 11th St E PO Box 218 *Web:* www.security-banks.com	Glencoe	MN	55336	320-864-3171	864-5133
Seguin Independent School District 1221 E Kingsbury St. *TF:* 866-632-9992 ■ *Web:* www.seguin.k12.tx.us	Seguin	TX	78155	830-372-5771	379-0392
Seneca Falls School District 98 Clinton St *Web:* www.sfcs.k12.ny.us	Seneca Falls	NY	13148	315-568-5818	
Seton Home Study School 1350 Progress Dr *Web:* www.setonhome.org	Front Royal	VA	22630	540-636-9990	
Seven Arrows Elementary School Inc 15240 La Cruz Dr *Web:* www.sevenarrows.com	Pacific Palisades	CA	90272	310-230-0257	
Shamrock High School 100 S Illinois St	Shamrock	TX	79079	806-256-2241	
Shelton City School District 382 Long Hill Ave *Web:* www.sheltonpublicschools.org	Shelton	CT	06484	203-924-1023	
Shepherd Valley Waldorf School 6500 Dry Creek Pkwy *Web:* shepherdvalley.org	Niwot	CO	80503	303-652-0130	
Shikellamy School District 200 Island Blvd *Web:* www.shikbraves.org	Sunbury	PA	17801	570-286-3721	
Sidney Transportation Services 777 W Russell Rd PO Box 946 *TF:* 800-743-6391 ■ *Web:* www.sidneytransportationservices.com	Sidney	OH	45365	937-498-2323	
Silver Springs-Martin Luther School 512 W Township Line Rd *Web:* www.silver-springs.org	Plymouth Meeting	PA	19462	610-825-4440	
Sioux Falls School District 201 E 38th St **Fax:* Hum Res ■ *Web:* www.sf.k12.sd.us	Sioux Falls	SD	57105	605-367-7900	367-4637*
Siuslaw School District 97j 2111 Oak St *Web:* www.greatschools.org	Florence	OR	97439	541-997-2651	
Slaton Independent School District 140 E Panhandle St *Web:* www.slatonisd.net	Slaton	TX	79364	806-828-6591	
Sneed Elementary School 9855 Pagewood Ln *Web:* sneed.aliefisd.net	Houston	TX	77042	713-789-6979	
Snodgrass & Son's Construction Company Inc 2700 S George Washington Bldg *Web:* snodgrassconstruction.com	Wichita	KS	67210	316-687-3110	687-5853
Socrates Academy 3909 Weddington Rd *Web:* socratesacademy.us	Matthews	NC	28105	704-321-1711	
Solanco School District 121 S Hess St. *Web:* www.solanco.k12.pa.us	Quarryville	PA	17566	717-786-8401	786-8245
Solex Academy Inc 350 E Dundee Rd Ste 200 *TF:* 866-797-6539 ■ *Web:* www.solex.edu	Wheeling	IL	60090	847-229-9595	
Sonoma Valley Unified School District (SVUSD) 17850 Railroad Ave *Web:* www.svusdca.org	Sonoma	CA	95476	707-935-6000	
Sonoran Science Academy 5741 E Ironwood St. *Web:* www.sonoranschools.org	Tucson	AZ	85708	520-300-5699	
Souderton Area School District 760 Lower Rd *Web:* www.soudertonsd.org	Souderton	PA	18964	215-723-6061	723-8897
Soundview Preparatory School 370 Underhill Ave. *Web:* www.soundviewprep.org	Yorktown Heights	NY	10598	914-962-2780	
South Bay Union School District 601 Elm Ave *Web:* www.sbusd.org	Imperial Beach	CA	91932	619-628-1600	628-1608
South Haven Public Schools Inc 554 Green St. *Web:* www.shps.org	South Haven	MI	49090	269-637-0520	
South Kitsap School District 1962 Hoover Ave SE. *Web:* www.skitsap.wednet.edu	Port Orchard	WA	98366	360-874-7000	874-7068
South Orangetown School District (Inc), The 160 Van Wyck Rd *Web:* socsd.org	Blauvelt	NY	10913	845-680-1000	
South Plains Academy 4008 Ave R	Lubbock	TX	79412	806-744-0330	
South San Antonio Independent School District 5622 Ray Ellison Dr *Web:* www.southsanisd.net	San Antonio	TX	78242	210-977-7000	
South San Francisco Unified School District 398 B St *Web:* ssfusd.org	South San Francisco	CA	94080	650-877-8700	
South Summit School District 375 East 300 South *Web:* www.ssummit.k12.ut.us	Kamas	UT	84036	435-783-4301	
South Whidbey School Dist 206 PO Box 346 *Web:* www.sw.wednet.edu	Langley	WA	98260	360-221-6100	221-3835
Southern Lehigh School District 5775 Main St *TF:* 800-360-8989 ■ *Web:* www.slsd.org	Center Valley	PA	18034	610-282-3121	282-0193
Southern Regional High School District Board of Education 600 North Main St *TF:* 866-850-0511 ■ *Web:* www.srsd.net	Manahawkin	NJ	08050	609-597-9481	978-0298
Southern Tioga School District 241 Main St. *Web:* www.southerntioga.org	Blossburg	PA	16912	570-638-2183	
Southgate Community School District 14600 Dix Toledo Rd *TF:* 888-263-5897 ■ *Web:* www.southgateschools.com	Southgate	MI	48195	734-246-4600	283-6791
Southview Special Educatn Schl 12110 Clayton Rd. *Web:* www.ssdmo.org	St. Louis	MO	63131	314-989-8900	
Southwest Local School District 230 S Elm St. *Web:* www.southwestschools.org	Harrison	OH	45030	513-367-4139	
Southwestern Central School District 600 Hunt Rd *Web:* www.swcs.wnyric.org	Jamestown	NY	14701	716-664-1881	
Southwick Tolland Regional SD 86 Powder Mill Rd *Web:* www.stgrsd.org	Southwick	MA	01077	413-569-5391	
Spackenkill Union Free School Districts (Inc) 15 Croft Rd *Web:* www.spackenkillschools.org	Poughkeepsie	NY	12603	845-463-7800	
Sparta Area Schools 465 S Union St. *Web:* www.spartaschools.org	Sparta	MI	49345	616-887-8253	
Speech & Language Development 8699 Holder St *Web:* www.sldc.net	Buena Park	CA	90620	714-821-3620	
Splendora Independent School District 23419 FM 2090 Rd. *Web:* www.splendoraisd.org	Splendora	TX	77372	281-689-3128	689-7509
Spring-Ford Area School District 857 S Lewis Rd. *Web:* www.spring-ford.net	Royersford	PA	19468	610-705-6000	705-6245
Springfield Public School District #186 1900 W Monroe St *TF:* 877-632-7753 ■ *Web:* www.sps186.org	Springfield	IL	62704	217-525-3006	525-3005
Springfield Public Schools 1550 Main St. **Fax:* Hum Res ■ *Web:* www.springfieldpublicschools.com	Springfield	MA	01103	413-787-7100	787-7171*
Springfield Public Schools 1359 E St Louis St **Fax:* Mail Rm ■ *Web:* www.springfieldpublicschoolsmo.org	Springfield	MO	65802	417-523-0000	523-0196*
St. Anastasia School 8631 Stanmoor Dr. *Web:* www.st-anastasia.org	Los Angeles	CA	90045	310-645-8816	
St. Ann's Catholic School 365 N Cool Spring St *Web:* stbasilacademy.org	Fayetteville	NC	28301	910-483-3902	
St. Basil Academy High School 711 Fox Chase Rd *Web:* stbasilacademy.org	Jenkintown	PA	19046	215-885-3771	
St. Cecilia Catholic School 1310 Madison Ave. N. *Web:* www.saintceciliaschool.org	Bainbridge Island	WA	98110	714-544-1533	
St. Charles Inc 151 S 84th St *Web:* www.stcharlesinc.org	Milwaukee	WI	53214	414-476-3710	
St. Clair County Regional Educational Service Agency 499 Range Rd. *TF:* 800-294-9229 ■ *Web:* www.sccresa.org	Marysville	MI	48040	810-364-8990	
St. Edwards High School 13500 Detroit Ave. *Web:* www.sehs.net	Lakewood	OH	44107	216-221-3776	
St. Francis De Sales High School 2323 W Bancroft St. *Web:* www.sfstoledo.org	Toledo	OH	43607	419-531-1618	
St. Francis High School 1885 Miramonte Ave *Web:* www.sfhs.com	Mountain View	CA	94040	650-968-1213	
St. Francis Xavier High School 15 School St *Web:* www.sfxhs.com	Sumter	SC	29150	803-773-0210	
St. Henry District High School 3755 Scheben Dr *Web:* shdhs.org	Erlanger	KY	41018	859-525-0255	
St. Ignatius College Prep 2001 37th Ave *TF:* 888-225-5427 ■ *Web:* www.siprep.org	San Francisco	CA	94116	312-421-5900	
St. James Academy 3100 Monkton Rd *Web:* www.saintjamesacademy.org	Monkton	MD	21111	410-771-4816	
St. James Episcopal School 602 S Carancahua St *Web:* www.sjes.org	Corpus Christi	TX	78401	361-883-0835	
St. John Neumann Regional Catholic School 791 Tom Smith Rd Sw *Web:* www.sjnrcs.org	Lilburn	GA	30047	770-381-0557	
St. John The Apostle School 7421 Glenview Dr *Web:* stjs.org	Richland Hills	TX	76180	817-284-2228	
St. John Vianney High School 540 Line Rd *Web:* www.sjvhs.com	Holmdel	NJ	07733	732-739-0800	
St. Johns Unified District 450 S 13th St W *Web:* www.sjusd.net	Saint Johns	AZ	85936	928-337-2255	
St. Lukes Episcopal Day School 8833 Goodwood Blvd *Web:* www.stlukesbr.org	Baton Rouge	LA	70806	225-926-5343	
St. Margaret's School 1080 Lucas Ave *Web:* www.stmarg.ca	Victoria	BC	V8X3P7	250-479-7171	
St. Mary's Dominican High School Corp 7701 Walmsley Ave *Web:* www.stmarysdominican.org	New Orleans	LA	70125	504-865-9401	

Phone Fax

St. Mary's Home for Children
420 Fruit Hill Ave ... North Providence RI 02911 401-353-3900
Web: www.smhfc.org

St. Matthew Catholic School 11525 Elm Ln ... Charlotte NC 28277 704-544-2070
Web: www.charlottediocese.org

St. Olivier School 325 Beckwell Ave ... Radville SK S0C2G0 306-869-3221
Web: www.holyfamilyrcssd.ca

St. Paul Education Regional Division No 1
4901-47 St ... St Paul AB T0A3A3 780-645-3323
Web: www.stpauleducation.ab.ca

St. Paul High School
9635 Greenleaf Ave ... Santa Fe Springs CA 90670 562-698-6246
Web: stpaulhs.org

St. Sebastian's School 815 Broad Ave ... Belle Vernon PA 15012 724-929-5143
Web: www.stsebs.org

St. Stephen's Catholic School 16701 S St ... Omaha NE 68135 402-896-0754
Web: www.stephen.org

Steinhauer Elementary School
170 Frederick Ave ... Maple Shade NJ 08052 856-779-7323
Web: www.mapleshade.org

Stephen Mack Middle School
11810 Old River Rd ... Rockton IL 61072 815-624-2611
Web: rockton140.org

Stephenville Independent School District
2655 W Overhill Dr ... Stephenville TX 76401 254-968-4141
Web: www.sville.us

Stockton Unified School District
701 N Madison St ... Stockton CA 95202 209-933-7000 933-7031
Web: stocktonusd.net

Stoughton Area School District 320 N St ... Stoughton WI 53589 608-877-5000
Web: www.stoughton.k12.wi.us

Stow-Munroe Falls City School District
4350 Allen Rd ... Stow OH 44224 330-689-5445
Web: smfschools.org

Study (the) 3233 The Blvd ... Westmount QC H3Y1S4 514-935-9352
Web: www.thestudy.qc.ca

Sturgis Public Schools 107 W W St ... Sturgis MI 49091 269-659-1500
Web: www.sturgisps.org

Sugar Creek Board of Education
3757 Upper Bellbrook Rd ... Bellbrook OH 45305 937-848-6251
Web: www.sugarcreek.k12.oh.us

Summit Construction Company Inc
1107 Burdsal Pkwy PO Box 88126 ... Indianapolis IN 46208 317-634-6112 264-2529
Web: www.summitconst.com

Sumner School District 1202 Wood Ave ... Sumner WA 98390 253-891-6000 891-6098
TF: 866-548-3847 ■ *Web:* www.sumner.wednet.edu

Sunrise School Division 536 Park Ave ... Beausejour MB R0E0C0 204-268-4832
Web: www.sunrisesd.ca

Sunset Ridge School District 29
525 Sunset Ridge Rd ... Northfield IL 60093 847-881-9400 446-6388
Web: www.sunsetridge29.net

Surry County School
209 N Crutchfield St PO Box 364 ... Dobson NC 27017 336-386-8211 386-4279
Web: www.surry.k12.nc.us

Swan Valley School Dist 8380 Ohern Rd ... Saginaw MI 48609 989-921-3701
Web: swanvalleyschools.com

Sweet Home Central School District
1901 Sweet Home Rd ... Amherst NY 14228 716-250-1400
Web: sweethomeschools.org

Sweet Home School District 55
1920 Long St ... Sweet Home OR 97386 541-367-7126
Web: www.sweethome.k12.or.us

Sweetwater County School District 2
320 Monroe Ave ... Green River WY 82935 307-872-5500
Web: www.swcsd2.org

Syracuse City School District, The
725 Harrison St ... Syracuse NY 13210 315-435-4499
Web: www.syracusecityschools.com

Tahoe Truckee Unified School District (TTUSD)
11603 Donner Pass Rd ... Truckee CA 96161 530-582-2500 582-7606
Web: www.ttusd.org

Talbot County Public Schools PO Box 1029 ... Easton MD 21601 410-822-0330 820-4260
Web: www.tcps.k12.md.us

Tattnall County School
146 W Brazell St PO Box 157 ... Reidsville GA 30453 912-557-4726 557-3036
Web: www.tattnallschools.org

Taylor Independent School District
3101 N. Main St ... Taylor TX 76574 512-352-6361 365-3800
Web: www.taylorisd.org

Team Hardinger Transportation/Warehousing
1314 W 18th St ... Erie PA 16502 814-453-6587 453-4919
Web: www.team-h.com

Telfair County School District
212 W Huckabee St PO Box 240 ... McRae GA 31055 229-868-5661 868-5549
Web: www.telfairschools.org

Temecula Valley Unified School District School Facilities Corp
31350 Rancho Vista Rd ... Temecula CA 92592 951-676-2661 695-7121
Web: www.tvusd.k12.ca.us

Tempe Elementary Schools 3205 S Rural Rd ... Tempe AZ 85282 480-730-7100
Web: www.tempeschools.org

Templeton Unified School District
960 Old County Rd ... Templeton CA 93465 805-434-5800 434-5879
TF: 800-316-6142 ■ *Web:* tusd.ca.schoolloop.com

Tennyson High School 27035 Whitman St ... Hayward CA 94544 510-723-3190
Web: thslancers.com

Tforce Energy Services
6143 S Willow Ste 320 ... Greenwood Village CO 80111 877-234-1444 770-6461*
**Fax Area Code:* 303 ■ *TF:* 877-234-1444

TheAcademy.com
Contact Information 10223 McAllister
Ste 206 ... San Antonio TX 78216 210-530-2700

Thornapple Kellogg Schools
10051 Green Lk Rd ... Middleville MI 49333 269-795-3313 795-5492
Web: www.tkschools.org

Phone Fax

Thornton Fractional South High School
18500 Burnham Ave ... Lansing IL 60438 708-585-2000
Web: www.tfd215.org

Thunderbird School of Global Management
1 Global Pl ... Glendale AZ 85306 602-978-7000 978-9663
TF: 800-848-9084 ■ *Web:* www.thunderbird.edu

Thurman G Smith Elementary School
3600 Falcon Rd ... Springdale AR 72762 479-750-8846
Web: springdaleschools.org

Tipton County Schools 1580 Hwy 51 S ... Covington TN 38019 901-476-7148
Web: www.tipton-county.com

Tomball Independent School District
310 S Cherry St ... Tomball TX 77375 281-357-3100 357-3128
TF: 877-382-4357 ■ *Web:* www.tomballisd.net

Topeka Public Schools 624 SW 24th St ... Topeka KS 66611 785-295-3000 575-6162*
**Fax:* Hum Res ■ *Web:* www.topekapublicschools.net

Toppenish School District 202 306 Bolin Dr ... Toppenish WA 98948 509-865-4455 865-2067
TF: 888-730-1101 ■ *Web:* www.toppenish.wednet.edu

Torrance Unified School District
2335 Plz Del AMO ... Torrance CA 90501 310-972-6500
Web: www.tusd.org

Trenton Public School System
108 N Clinton Ave ... Trenton NJ 08609 609-656-4900 989-2682
Web: www.trenton.k12.nj.us

Tri-Valley Local School District PO Box 125 ... Dresden OH 43821 740-754-1442 754-6400
Web: www.tri-valley.k12.oh.us

Trinity Academy Inc 12345 E 21st St N ... Wichita KS 67206 316-634-0909
Web: www.trinityacademy.org

Trinity Area School District 231 Pk Ave ... Washington PA 15301 724-223-2000
Web: www.trinitypride.k12.pa.us

Trinity Elementary School
4410 Murfreesboro Rd ... Franklin TN 37067 615-472-4850
Web: www.wcs.edu

Triway Local School District 3205 Shreve Rd ... Wooster OH 44691 330-264-9491 262-3955
Web: www.triway.k12.oh.us

Tuckahoe Union Free School District
65 Siwanoy Blvd ... Eastchester NY 10709 914-337-6600
Web: tuckahoeschools.org

Tucson Unified School District No 1
1010 E Tenth St ... Tucson AZ 85719 520-225-6070 798-8767
Web: www.tusd1.org

Tulare Joint Union High School District
426 N Blackstone Ave ... Tulare CA 93274 559-688-2021 687-7317
TF: 800-942-3767 ■ *Web:* www.tulare.k12.ca.us

Tulsa Public Schools 3027 S New Haven Ave ... Tulsa OK 74114 918-746-6800 746-6144*
**Fax:* Hum Res ■ *TF:* 866-632-9992 ■ *Web:* tulsaschools.org

Tupelo Public School District 72 S Green St ... Tupelo MS 38804 662-841-8850 841-8887
Web: www.tupeloschools.com

Turner County Board of Education
423 N Cleveland St ... Ashburn GA 31714 229-567-3338 567-3285
Web: www.turner.k12.ga.us

Tuscarora Intermediate Unit 11
2527 US 522 S Hwy ... McVeytown PA 17051 717-899-7143
Web: www.tiu11.org

Twin Falls School District 411
201 Main Ave W ... Twin Falls ID 83301 208-733-6900 733-6987
TF: 800-726-0003 ■ *Web:* www.tfsd.k12.id.us

Twin Rivers Unified School District
3222 Winona Way ... North Highlands CA 95660 916-566-1628 566-3586
TF: 888-674-6854 ■ *Web:* www.twinriversusd.org

Unified School District 428
201 S Patton Rd ... Great Bend KS 67530 620-793-1500
Web: www.usd428.net

Unified School District of Antigo
120 S Dorr St ... Antigo WI 54409 715-627-4355 623-3279
TF: 800-795-3272 ■ *Web:* www.antigo.k12.wi.us

Union County Public Schools
510 S Mart St ... Morganfield KY 42437 270-389-1694 389-9806
Web: www.union.kyschools.us

Unity Elementary School
6846 Unity School Rd ... Brookport IL 62910 618-564-2582
Web: unity.massac.org

Unlimited Construction Services Inc
1696 Haleukana St ... Lihue HI 96766 808-241-1400 245-6611
Web: www.unlimitedhawaii.com

Upland Unified School District
390 N Euclid Ave ... Upland CA 91786 909-985-1864 949-7863
Web: www.upland.k12.ca.us

Upper Dauphin Area School District (UDASD)
5668 State Rt 209 ... Lykens PA 17048 717-362-8134 362-3050
TF: 866-632-9992 ■ *Web:* www.udasd.org

Upper Freehold Regional Board of Education (Inc)
27 High St ... Allentown NJ 08501 609-259-7292
Web: www.ufrsd.net

Upper Merion Area School District
435 Crossfield Rd ... King of Prussia PA 19406 610-205-6400 205-6433
Web: www.umasd.org

Upper Perkiomen School District
2229 E Buck Rd Ste 2 ... Pennsburg PA 18073 215-679-7961
Web: www.upsd.org

US Special Delivery Inc 821 E Blvd ... Kingsford MI 49802 906-774-1931 774-2032
TF: 800-821-6389 ■ *Web:* usspecial.com

Utica Community Schools (UCS)
11303 Greendale Dr ... Sterling Heights MI 48312 586-797-1000 797-1001
TF: 800-877-8339 ■ *Web:* www.uticak12.org

Uvalde Consolidated Independent School District
1000 North Getty St ... Uvalde TX 78801 830-278-6655
Web: www.ucisd.net

Vail Mountain School 3000 Booth Falls Rd ... Vail CO 81657 970-476-3850
Web: www.vms.edu/contact/contact-admissions

Val Verde Unified School District
975 Morgan St ... Perris CA 92571 951-940-6100
Web: www.valverde.edu

Name / Address	City	State	Zip	Phone	Fax
Valley Ctr-Pauma Unified School District 28751 Cole Grade Rd *Web:* www.vcpusd.net	Valley Center	CA	92082	760-749-0464	749-1208
Van Buren Public Schools (VBPS) 555 W Columbia Ave *Web:* www.vanburenschools.net	Belleville	MI	48111	734-697-9123	697-6385
Vancouver Talmud Torah Association 998 26th Ave W *Web:* www.talmudtorah.com	Vancouver	BC	V5Z2G1	604-736-7307	
Varnett School - East, The 804 Maxey Rd *Web:* www.varnett.org	Houston	TX	77013	713-637-6574	
Vernon Township Board of Education (Inc) PO Box 99 *Web:* www.vtsd.com	Vernon	NJ	07462	973-764-2900	
Vestal Central School District 201 Main St *Web:* vestal.stier.org	Vestal	NY	13850	607-757-2241	757-2227
Vestavia Hills Board of Education 1204 Montgomery Hwy *Web:* www.vestavia.k12.al.us	Birmingham	AL	35216	205-402-5100	
Victor Elementary School District (VESD) 15579 Eigth St	Victorville	CA	92395	760-245-1691	245-6245
Volmar Construction Inc 4400 Second Ave *Web:* www.volmar.com	Brooklyn	NY	11232	718-832-2444	499-4045
W. N. Morehouse Truck Line Inc 4010 Dahlman Ave *TF:* 800-228-9378 ■ *Web:* www.morehousetruckline.com	Omaha	NE	68107	402-733-2200	
Wahluke School District 73 411 E Saddle Mt Dr *Web:* www.wsd73.wednet.edu	Mattawa	WA	99349	509-932-4565	
Wake Christian Academy Inc 5500 Wake Academy Dr *Web:* www.wakechristianacademy.com	Raleigh	NC	27603	919-772-6264	
Wake County Public School System 3600 Wake Forest Rd *Web:* www.wcpss.net	Raleigh	NC	27609	919-850-1600	
Wakefield School District 60 Farm St *Web:* wakefieldpublicschools.org	Wakefield	MA	01880	781-246-6400	
Walbon & Company Inc 4230 Pine Bend Trial *Web:* www.walbon.com	Rosemount	MN	55068	651-437-2011	437-2087
Walker County Board of Education 1710 Alabama Ave PO Box 311 *TF:* 866-276-7735 ■ *Web:* www.walkercountyschools.com	Jasper	AL	35501	205-387-0555	221-5636
Wall Timber Products Inc 1825 Effingham Hwy *Web:* www.walltimber.com	Sylvania	GA	30467	912-863-5108	863-7478
Wallingford-Swarthmore School District 200 S Providence Rd *Web:* www.wssd.org	Wallingford	PA	19086	610-892-3470	
Wallkill Central School District (WCSD) 19 Main St PO Box 310 *Web:* www.wallkillcsd.k12.ny.us/education/district/district.php?sectionid=7785	Wallkill	NY	12589	845-895-7100	895-3630
Washington Company School District PO Box 716 *Web:* www.washington.k12.ga.us	Sandersville	GA	31082	478-552-3981	
Washington County Board of Education 802 Washington St *Web:* www.washingtonco.k12.nc.us	Plymouth	NC	27962	252-793-5171	793-5062
Washington International School 3100 Macomb St NW *Web:* www.wis.edu	Washington	DC	20008	202-243-1815	
Washington School District Inc 201 Allison Ave *TF:* 855-846-8376 ■ *Web:* www.washington.k12.pa.us	Washington	PA	15301	724-223-5085	223-5046
Washoe County School District 425 E Ninth St **Fax Area Code:* 814 ■ *Web:* www.washoeschools.net	Reno	NV	89512	775-348-0200	689-3962*
Watauga County Schools PO Box 1790 *Web:* www.watauga.k12.nc.us	Boone	NC	28607	828-264-7190	264-7196
Waterloo Community Unit School Dst 5 219 Pk St *Web:* www.wcusd5.net	Waterloo	IL	62298	618-939-3453	939-4578
Watertown-Mayer Public Schools 1001 Hwy 25 NW *Web:* www.wm.k12.mn.us	Watertown	MN	55388	952-955-0480	955-0251
Waxahachie Independent School District 411 N Gibson St *Web:* www.wisd.org	Waxahachie	TX	75165	972-923-4631	923-4759
Wayne Highlands School District 474 Grove St *Web:* www.waynehighlands.org	Honesdale	PA	18431	570-253-4661	253-9409
Weimar Junior High School 101 N W St	Weimar	TX	78962	979-725-9515	
Wellsboro Area School District 227 Nichols *Web:* www.wellsborosd.k12.pa.us	Wellsboro	PA	16901	570-724-4424	
West Clermont Local School District 4350 Aicholtz Rd Ste 220 *Web:* www.westcler.k12.oh.us	Cincinnati	OH	45245	513-943-5000	752-6158
West Fargo School District 6 207 Main Ave W *Web:* www.west-fargo.k12.nd.us	West Fargo	ND	58078	701-356-2000	356-2009
West Genesee Central School District 300 Sanderson Dr *Web:* www.westgenesee.org	Camillus	NY	13031	315-487-4562	487-2999
West Irondequoit Central School District 321 List Ave *Web:* www.westirondequoit.org	Rochester	NY	14617	585-342-5500	
West Millbrook Middle School Booster Club 8115 Strickland Rd *Web:* wmms.net	Raleigh	NC	27615	919-870-4050	
West Oaklane Charter School 7115 Stenton Ave *Web:* wolcs.org	Philadelphia	PA	19138	215-927-7995	
West Valley School District 208 8902 Zier Rd *Web:* www.wvsd208.org	Yakima	WA	98908	509-972-6000	
Western Placer Unified School District Finanacing Corp 600 Sixth St *Web:* www.wpusd.k12.ca.us	Lincoln	CA	95648	916-645-6350	
Western Suffolk Boces (suffolk 3) 507 Deer Park Rd *Web:* www.wsboces.org	Dix Hills	NY	11746	631-549-4900	
Westfield Board of Education Inc 302 Elm St *TF:* 800-355-2583 ■ *Web:* www.westfieldnjk12.org	Westfield	NJ	07090	908-789-4401	
Westminster School District 14121 Cedarwood St *TF:* 800-678-9133 ■ *Web:* www.wsdk8.us	Westminster	CA	92683	714-894-7311	899-2781
Wharton Independent School District 2100 N Fulton St *TF:* 800-818-3453 ■ *Web:* www.whartonisd.net	Wharton	TX	77488	979-532-3612	532-6228
Wheaton Academy 900 Prince Crossing Rd *Web:* wheatonacademy.org	West Chicago	IL	60185	630-562-7500	
Whitcomb School 25 Union St *Web:* mie.marlborough.schoolfusion.us	Marlborough	MA	01752	508-460-3547	
Whittier City School District 7211 Whittier Ave *Web:* www.whittiercity.k12.ca.us	Whittier	CA	90602	562-789-3000	907-9425
Wicomico County Board of Education PO Box 1538 *Web:* www.wcboe.org	Salisbury	MD	21802	410-677-4400	677-4444
William B Meyer Inc 255 Long Beach Blvd *TF:* 800-727-5985 ■ *Web:* www.williambmeyer.com	Stratford	CT	06615	203-375-5801	375-9820
Williams Valley School District 10400 US 209	Tower City	PA	17980	717-647-2181	
Williamsburg-James City County Educational Foundation Inc PO Box 8783 *Web:* wjccschools.org/web	Williamsburg	VA	23187	757-603-6400	
Williamsport Area School District 201 W Third St *TF:* 888-448-4642 ■ *Web:* www.wasd.org	Williamsport	PA	17701	570-327-5500	327-8122
Williamston Community Schools Inc 418 Highland St *Web:* www.gowcs.net	Williamston	MI	48895	517-655-4361	
Willoughby Eastlake City Schools 37047 Ridge Rd *Web:* www.weschools.org	Willoughby	OH	44094	440-946-5000	946-4671
Wills Point Independent School Distric 338 W N Commerce St *Web:* www.wpisd.com	Wills Point	TX	75169	903-873-3161	873-2462
Winchester-Thurston School 555 Morewood Ave *Web:* winchesterthurston.org	Pittsburgh	PA	15213	412-578-7500	578-7504
Windsor High School 6208 Us Hwy 61/67 *Web:* windsor.k12.mo.us	Imperial	MO	63052	636-464-4408	
Winnebago Community Unit District 323 304 E Mcnair Rd *Web:* www.winnebagoschools.org	Winnebago	IL	61088	815-335-2456	
Winston-Salem/Forsyth County Schools (WS/FCS) 1605 Miller St *Web:* www.wsfcs.k12.nc.us	Winston-Salem	NC	27103	336-727-2816	661-6572
Winton Woods City Schools 1215 W Kemper Rd *Web:* www.wintonwoods.org	Cincinnati	OH	45240	513-619-2300	619-2300
Woodland School District 50 1105 N Hunt Club Rd *Web:* www.dist50.net	Gurnee	IL	60031	847-596-5600	
Woodstock Community Unit School District 200 227 W Judd St *Web:* www.woodstockschools.org	Woodstock	IL	60098	815-338-8200	338-2005
Woodward Academy 1662 Rugby Ave *Web:* www.woodward.edu	College Park	GA	30337	404-765-4000	
Wooster City Board of Education 144 N Market St *Web:* www.woostercityschools.org	Wooster	OH	44691	330-264-0869	262-3407
Worcester Public Schools 20 Irving St *Web:* www.worcesterschools.org	Worcester	MA	01609	508-799-3115	799-3119
Wyoming Valley West School District 450 N Maple Ave *Web:* www.wvwspartans.org	Kingston	PA	18704	570-288-6551	288-1564
Wythe County Public Schools Foundation for Excellence Inc 1570 W Reservoir St *Web:* wytheexcellence.org	Wytheville	VA	24382	276-228-5411	
Xaverian Brothers High School Inc 800 clapboardtree st *Web:* www.xbhs.com	Westwood	MA	02090	781-326-6392	
Xavier High School Corporation of Middletown 181 Randolph Rd *Web:* xavierhighschool.org	Middletown	CT	06457	860-346-7735	
Yale Public Schools 315 E Chicago Ave *Web:* www.yale.k12.ok.us	Yale	OK	74085	918-387-2434	387-2503
Yancey County Schools Foundation Inc, The PO Box 190 *Web:* www.yanceync.net	Burnsville	NC	28714	828-682-6101	682-7110
Yeshivat Noam 70 W Century Rd *Web:* www.yeshivatnoam.org	Paramus	NJ	07652	201-261-1919	
York Catholic High School 601 E Springettsbury Ave *Web:* yorkcatholic.org	York	PA	17403	717-846-8871	
Zachary Community School Board 3755 Church St *Web:* zacharyschools.org	Zachary	LA	70791	225-658-4969	
Zanesville City School Board 160 N Fourth St *TF:* 866-280-7377 ■ *Web:* www.zanesville.k12.oh.us	Zanesville	OH	43701	740-454-9751	
Zumbrota-mazeppa Senior High School 705 Mill St *Web:* www.zmschools.us	Zumbrota	MN	55992	507-732-7395	

686 SCRAP METAL

See Also Recyclable Materials Recovery p. 3056

Company / Address	City	State	Zip	Phone	Fax
A Tenenbaum Company Inc 4500 W Bethany Rd — *Web:* www.trg.net	North Little Rock	AR	72117	501-945-0881	945-3865
Advantage Metals Recycling LLC 3005 Manchester Trfy — *TF:* 866-527-4733 ■ *Web:* www.advantagerecycling.com	Kansas City	MO	64129	816-861-2700	861-7670
Alco Iron & Metal Co 2140 Davis St — *Web:* www.alcometals.com	San Leandro	CA	94577	510-562-1107	562-1354
Allan Industries PO Box 999 — *Web:* allanrecyclers.com	Wilkes-Barre	PA	18703	570-826-0123	829-4099
Alter Trading Corp 700 Office Pkwy — *TF:* 888-337-2727 ■ *Web:* www.altertrading.com	Saint Louis	MO	63141	314-872-2400	872-2420
Amcep Metals 4484 E Tennessee St — *Web:* amcepmetals.com	Tucson	AZ	85714	520-748-1900	748-2752
AMG Resources Corp 2 Robinson Plaza # 350 — *TF:* 877-395-8338 ■ *Web:* www.amgresources.com	Pittsburgh	PA	15205	412-777-7300	331-0972
Azcon Corp 820 W Jackson Blvd Ste 425 — *Web:* azcon.net	Chicago	IL	60607	312-559-3100	559-1543
Baker Iron & Metal Company Inc 740 Rock Castle Ave — *Web:* www.bakeriron.com	Lexington	KY	40505	859-255-5676	252-3590
Borg Compressed Steel Corp 1032 N Lewis Ave — *Web:* yaffeco.net	Tulsa	OK	74110	918-587-2511	
Calbag Metals Co 2495 NW Nicolai St — *TF:* 800-398-3441 ■ *Web:* www.calbag.com	Portland	OR	97210	503-226-3441	228-0184
Cleveland Corp 42810 N Green Bay Rd — *TF:* 800-281-3464 ■ *Web:* www.clevelandcorp.com	Zion	IL	60099	847-872-7200	872-0827
Cohen Bros Inc 1723 Woodlawn Ave — *Web:* www.cohenusa.com	Middletown	OH	45044	513-422-3696	422-9018
Connell LP 1 International Pl 31st Fl — *Web:* www.connell-lp.com	Boston	MA	02110	617-391-5577	737-1617
Cycle Systems Inc 2580 Broadway SW	Roanoke	VA	24014	540-981-1211	
David J Joseph Co (DJJ) 300 Pike St — *Web:* www.djj.com	Cincinnati	OH	45202	513-419-6200	419-6222
Davis Industries Inc 9920 Richmond Hwy	Lorton	VA	22079	703-550-7402	
Dimco Steel Inc 3901 S Lamar St — *TF:* 877-428-8336 ■ *Web:* www.dimcosteel.com	Dallas	TX	75215	214-428-8336	428-1929
ELG Metals Inc 369 River Rd — *Web:* www.elg.de	McKeesport	PA	15132	412-672-9200	672-0824
FPT Pontiac Div 500 Collier Rd — *Web:* www.fptscrap.com	Pontiac	MI	48340	248-335-8141	
Franklin Iron & Metal Corp 1939 E First St — *Web:* franklinironandmetal.liveonatt.com	Dayton	OH	45403	937-253-8184	
Gachman Metals & Recycling Company Inc 2600 Shamrock Ave — *TF:* 800-749-0423 ■ *Web:* www.gachman.com	Fort Worth	TX	76107	817-334-0211	877-1528
Gershow Recycling Corp 71 Peconic Ave PO Box 526 — *Web:* www.gershow.com	Medford	NY	11763	631-289-6188	289-6368
Grossman Iron & Steel 5 N Market St — *TF:* 800-969-9423 ■ *Web:* www.grossmaniron.com	Saint Louis	MO	63102	314-231-9423	231-6983
Iron & Metals Inc 5555 Franklin St — *TF:* 800-776-7910 ■ *Web:* www.ironandmetals.com	Denver	CO	80216	303-292-5555	292-0513
Joe Krentzman & Son Inc 3175 Back Maitland Rd — *Web:* www.krentzman.net	Lewistown	PA	17044	717-543-4000	
Keywell LLC 7808 W College Dr — *Web:* www.keywell.com	Palos Heights	IL	60463	773-660-2060	
Langley Recycling 503 SE Branner St — *Web:* www.langleyrecycling.com	Topeka	KS	66607	785-234-2691	
Lionetti Assoc 450 S Front St — *TF:* 800-734-0910 ■ *Web:* www.lorcopetroleum.com	Elizabeth	NJ	07202	908-820-8800	820-8412
Louis Padnos Iron & Metal Co PO Box 1979 — *TF:* 800-442-3509 ■ *Web:* www.padnos.com	Holland	MI	49422	616-396-6521	396-7789
M Lipsitz & Co Inc 100 Elm St — *Web:* www.mlipsitzco.com	Waco	TX	76704	254-756-6661	752-0175
Mayer Pollock Steel Corp Industrial Hwy — *Web:* www.mayerpollock.com	Pottstown	PA	19464	610-323-5500	323-5506
Mervis Industries Inc 3295 E Main St — *TF:* 800-637-3016 ■ *Web:* www.mervis.com	Danville	IL	61834	217-442-5300	477-9245
Metal Exchange Corp 111 W Port Plaza Ste 350 — *Web:* www.metalexchangecorp.com	Saint Louis	MO	63146	314-434-3500	434-2196
Metalico Annaco Inc 943 Hazel St — *TF:* 800-966-1499 ■ *Web:* www.metalico.com	Akron	OH	44305	330-376-1400	376-9696
Metalsco Inc 1828 Craig Rd — *Web:* www.metalsco.com	Saint Louis	MO	63146	314-997-5200	997-5921
Metro Metals Northwest 5611 NE Columbia Blvd — *TF:* 800-610-5680 ■ *Web:* www.metrometalsnw.com	Portland	OR	97218	503-287-8861	287-5569
Mid State Trading Co 2525 Trenton Ave	Williamsport	PA	17701	570-326-9431	326-5028
Midland Iron & Steel Corp 3301 Fourth Ave — *Web:* midlanddavis.com	Moline	IL	61265	309-764-6723	764-6729
Miller Compressing Co 1640 W Bruce St	Milwaukee	WI	53204	414-671-5980	671-7191
Minkin Chandler Corp 15400 Oakwood Dr — *Web:* minkinchandler.weebly.com	Romulus	MI	48174	734-229-9200	
Northern Metal Recycling LLC 2800 Pacific St N — *Web:* www.northernmetalrecycling.com	Minneapolis	MN	55411	612-529-9221	
Omnisource Corp 2205 S Holt Rd — *Web:* www.omnisource.com	Indianapolis	IN	46241	317-381-5800	
OmniSource Corp 7575 W Jefferson Blvd — *TF:* 800-666-4789 ■ *Web:* www.omnisource.com	Fort Wayne	IN	46804	260-422-5541	423-8500
Pascap Company Inc 4250 Boston Rd — *Web:* pascapco.com	Bronx	NY	10475	718-325-7200	325-7595
Progress Rail Services 1600 Progress Dr PO Box 1037 — *TF:* 800-476-8769 ■ *Web:* www.progressrail.com	Albertville	AL	35950	256-505-6600	593-1249
PSC 5151 San Felipe Ste 1100 — **Fax Area Code:* 713 ■ *TF:* 800-726-1300 ■ *Web:* www.pscnow.com	Houston	TX	77056	800-726-1300	985-5318*
River Metals Recycling 2045 River Rd — *Web:* www.rmrecycling.com	Louisville	KY	40206	502-585-5331	587-8699
River Recycling Industries Inc 4195 Bradley Rd — *Web:* riverrecyclingind.com	Cleveland	OH	44109	216-459-2100	749-8107
Riverside Scrap Iron 2993 Sixth St — *Web:* www.riversidemetalrecycling.com	Riverside	CA	92507	951-686-2129	686-8933
Rocky Mountain Recycling (RMR) 6510 Brighton Blvd — *Web:* www.rmrscrap.com	Commerce	CO	80022	303-288-6868	288-0250
SA Recycling LLC 2411 N Glassell St — *TF:* 800-468-7272 ■ *Web:* www.sarecycling.com	Orange	CA	92865	714-632-2000	630-5836
Sadoff & Rudoy Industries LLP 240 W Arndt St — *TF General:* 877-972-3633 ■ *Web:* www.sadoff.com	Fond du Lac	WI	54936	920-921-2070	921-1283
SD Richman Sons Inc 2435 Wheatsheaf Ln — *Web:* www.sdrichmansons.com	Philadelphia	PA	19137	215-535-5100	288-1043
Simon Metals LLC 2202 E River St — *TF:* 800-562-8464 ■ *Web:* www.simonmetals.com	Tacoma	WA	98421	253-272-9364	
Sims Bros Inc 1011 S Prospect St PO Box 1170 — *TF:* 800-536-7465 ■ *Web:* www.simsbros.com	Marion	OH	43301	740-387-9041	
SLC Recycling Industries Inc 8701 E 8 Mile Rd — *Web:* fptscrap.com	Warren	MI	48089	586-759-6600	759-6518
Soave Enterprises LLC 3400 E Lafayette St — *Web:* www.soave.com	Detroit	MI	48207	313-567-7000	567-0966
Sugar Creek Scrap Inc 1201 W National Ave — *TF:* 800-466-7462 ■ *Web:* www.sugarcreekscrap.com	West Terre Haute	IN	47885	812-533-2147	
Tennessee Valley Recycling LLC 821 W College St — *Web:* tvrllc.com	Pulaski	TN	38478	931-363-3593	
Thalheimer Bros Inc 5550 Whitaker Ave — *Web:* www.thalheimerbrothers.com	Philadelphia	PA	19124	215-537-5200	533-3993
Thermo Fluids Inc 4301 W Jefferson St — *TF:* 800-350-7565 ■ *Web:* www.thermofluids.com	Phoenix	AZ	85043	602-272-2400	
Tri-State Iron & Metal Co 1725 E Ninth St — *TF:* 800-773-8409 ■ *Web:* www.tsimco.com	Texarkana	AR	71854	870-773-8409	
Tube City IMS Corp (TMS) 12 Monongahela Ave — *NYSE:* TMS ■ *TF:* 800-860-2442 ■ *Web:* www.tubecityims.com	Glassport	PA	15045	412-678-6141	675-8295
Tube City IMS Corp 1155 Business Ctr Dr Ste 200 — *TF General:* 800-860-2442 ■ *Web:* www.tubecityims.com	Horsham	PA	19044	215-956-5500	
Universal Steel Co, The 6600 Grant Ave — *Web:* univsteel.com	Cleveland	OH	44105	216-883-4972	
Upstate Shredding LLC 1 Recycle Dr Tioga Industrial Pk — *TF:* 800-245-3133 ■ *Web:* www.upstateshredding.com	Owego	NY	13827	607-687-7777	687-7746
Weiner Iron & Metal Corp PO Box 359	Pottsville	PA	17901	570-622-6543	622-3175
Western Scrap Processing Co 3315 Drennan Industrial Loop S — *Web:* www.westernscrap.com	Colorado Springs	CO	80910	719-390-7986	
Yaffe Cos Inc, The 1200 S G St — *TF:* 800-759-2333 ■ *Web:* yaffeco.net	Muskogee	OK	74403	918-687-7543	

687 SCREEN PRINTING

Company / Address	City	State	Zip	Phone	Fax
A Plus Designs Inc & Outfitters Plus Outlet Store 56988 635th St — *Web:* www.aplusdesignsinc.com	Atlantic	IA	50022	712-243-4379	
Ace Transfer Co 1017 Hometown St — *Web:* www.acetransco.com	Springfield	OH	45504	937-398-1103	
Action Screen Print Inc 30w260 Butterfield Rd Unit 203 — *Web:* actionscreen.com	Warrenville	IL	60555	630-393-1990	
Aim Screen Printing Supply LLC PO Box 9645 — *Web:* aimsupply.net	Naperville	IL	60567	630-357-4103	
Allied Advertising Agency Inc 3700 Blanco Rd — *Web:* www.alliedadvertising.com	San Antonio	TX	78212	210-732-7874	
Ares Sportswear Ltd 3704 Lacon Rd — *TF:* 800-439-8614 ■ *Web:* www.areswear.com	Hilliard	OH	43026	614-767-1950	
Art Brands LLC 225 Business Ctr Dr — *TF:* 877-755-4278 ■ *Web:* www.artbrands.com	Blacklick	OH	43004	614-755-4278	
Artco (US) Inc 1 Staery Pl — *Web:* www.artcoprinting.com	Rexburg	ID	83441	208-359-1000	
Atlantic Sportswear Inc 36 Waldron Way — *Web:* atlanticsportswearinc.com	Portland	ME	04103	207-797-5028	
Buffalo Specialties Inc 10706 Craighead Dr — *Web:* buffspec.com	Houston	TX	77025	713-271-6107	
Calaway Systems Inc 32 Lindburgh St — *Web:* www.calawaysystems.com	Courtland	AL	35618	256-637-2736	
Chimes Inc, The 4815 Seton Dr — *Web:* www.chimes.org	Baltimore	MD	21215	410-358-6400	
Designer Decal Inc 1120 E First Ave — *TF:* 800-622-6333 ■ *Web:* www.designerdecal.com	Spokane	WA	99202	509-535-0267	535-1476
Duck Co, The 5601 Gray St — *Web:* www.duckco.com	Arvada	CO	80020	303-423-5630	
E-Tec Marine Products Inc 7555 Garden Rd Bldg B — *Web:* www.etecmarine.com	West Palm Beach	FL	33404	561-848-8351	
Empire Screen Printing Inc N5206 Marco Rd PO Box 218 — *Web:* www.empirescreen.com	Onalaska	WI	54650	608-783-3301	783-3306

Company / Address	City	State	ZIP	Phone	Fax
Excel Screen Printing & Embroidery Inc 10507 Delta Pkwy. Web: www.excelscreenprinting.com	Schiller Park	IL	60176	847-801-5200	
Express Image Inc 2942 Rice St. Web: expressimage.com	Little Canada	MN	55113	651-482-8602	
F&E Sportswear Corp 1230 Newell Pkwy. TF: 800-523-7762 ■ Web: fandesportswear.us	Montgomery	AL	36110	334-244-6477	
Faux Pas Prints Inc 620 Papworth Ave. Web: www.fauxpasprints.com	Metairie	LA	70005	504-834-8342	
Fisher Printing Inc 8640 S Oketo Ave. Web: fisherprinting.com	Bridgeview	IL	60455	708-598-1500	
Flow-Eze Co 3209 Auburn St. TF: 800-435-4873 ■ Web: www.flow-eze.com	Rockford	IL	61101	815-965-1062	965-1329
Foresight Group Inc 619 E Hazel St. Web: www.foresightgr.com	Lansing	MI	48912	517-485-5700	
Garment Graphics LLC 220 W Ft Lowell Rd. Web: www.garmentgraphics.net	Tucson	AZ	85705	520-544-0529	
GFX International Inc 333 Barron Blvd. Web: www.gfxi.com	Grayslake	IL	60030	847-543-4600	
Gill Studios Inc 10800 Lackman Rd. Web: www.gill-line.com	Lenexa	KS	66219	913-888-4422	
Gillespie Graphics 27676 SW Pkwy Ave. TF: 800-547-6841 ■ Web: www.gillespie-graphics.com	Wilsonville	OR	97070	503-682-1122	
Graphic Trends Inc 7301 Adams St. Web: www.graphictrends.net	Paramount	CA	90723	562-531-2339	
Gwin's Commercial Printing & Engraving 957 Spring Hill Ave. Web: gwins.cc	Mobile	AL	36604	251-438-2226	
Haapanen Brothers Inc 1400 Saint Paul Ave. Web: hb-graphics.net	Gurnee	IL	60031	847-662-2233	
Hanson Sign & Screen Process Corp 82 Carter St. Web: www.hansonsign.com	Falconer	NY	14733	716-484-8564	
Image Sport Inc 1115 SE Westbrooke Dr. TF: 800-919-0520 ■ Web: www.imagesport.com	Waukee	IA	50263	515-987-7699	
Ink Enterprises 400 Casey Dr. Web: inkenterprises.com	Maumelle	AR	72113	501-851-6916	
Innerworkings Inc 600 W Chicago Ave Ste 850. NASDAQ: INWK ■ Web: www.inwk.com	Chicago	IL	60654	312-642-3700	
J.N. White Designs Digital Inc 129 N Ctr St PO Box 219. Web: www.jnwhitedesigns.com	Perry	NY	14530	585-237-5191	
Kapta Inc 2220 1re Av. Web: kapta.ca	Notre-dame-des-pins	QC	G0M1K0	418-774-5688	
Kay Automotive Graphics 57 Kay Industrial Dr. Web: www.kayautomotive.com	Lake Orion	MI	48359	248-377-4999	377-2097
Kerusso Activewear Inc 402 Hwy 62 Spur. TF: 800-424-0943 ■ Web: www.kerusso.com	Berryville	AR	72616	870-423-6242	
Killeen Dynamic Designs Inc 2100 E Stan Schlueter Loop Ste F. Web: www.dynamicdesignsinc.com	Killeen	TX	76542	254-628-8272	
Law Elder Law 2275 Church Rd. Web: lawelderlaw.com	Aurora	IL	60502	630-585-5200	
Litho Technical Services Inc 1600 W 92nd St. Web: lithotechusa.com	Bloomington	MN	55431	952-888-7945	
LSI Graphic Solutions Plus 9260 Pleasantwood Ave NW. Web: www.lsi-gsp.com	North Canton	OH	44720	330-494-9444	
M & M Designs Inc 1981 Quality Blvd. *Fax Area Code: 936 ■ TF: 800-627-0656 ■ Web: www.m-mdesigns.com	Huntsville	TX	77320	800-627-0656	295-9286*
Markley Enterprise Inc 800 Lillian St. Web: www.markleyent.com	Elkhart	IN	46516	574-295-4195	
Mastro Graphic Arts Inc 67 Deep Rock Rd. Web: www.mastrographics.com	Rochester	NY	14624	585-436-7570	
Mitographers Inc, The 4720 N Fourth Ave. TF: 800-221-6486 ■ Web: mito.com	Sioux Falls	SD	57104	605-336-1818	
Modagrafics Inc 5300 Newport Dr. Web: www.modagrafics.com	Rolling Meadows	IL	60008	847-392-3980	
Motson Graphics Inc 1717 Bethlehem Pk. TF: 800-972-1986 ■ Web: www.motson.com	Flourtown	PA	19031	215-233-0500	233-5014
New Life Industries Inc 140 Chappells Dairy Rd. Web: www.newlifeshopper.com	Somerset	KY	42503	606-679-3616	
NSO Press Inc 1921 E 68th Ave. Web: www.nsopress.com	Denver	CO	80229	303-227-1400	
Offset Impressions Inc 122 Mtn View Rd. Web: www.offsetimpress.com	Reading	PA	19607	610-378-1851	
Oscar Printing Co 57 Columbia Sq. Web: opportunitymart.com	San Francisco	CA	94103	415-626-8818	
Otis Graphics Inc 290 Grant Ave. Web: www.otisgraphics.com	Lyndhurst	NJ	07071	201-438-7120	
Petra Manufacturing Co 6600 W Armitage Ave. TF: 800-888-7387 ■ Web: www.petramanufacturing.com	Chicago	IL	60707	773-622-1475	
Pratt Corp 3035 N Shadeland Ave. Web: www.prattcorp.com	Indianapolis	IN	46226	317-924-3201	
Primary Color Inc 9239 Premier Row. TF: 800-581-9555 ■ Web: www.primarycolorinc.com	Dallas	TX	75247	214-630-8800	
Print Source Inc, The 404 S Tracy St. Web: www.ps-printsource.com	Wichita	KS	67209	316-945-7052	
Ram Graphics Inc 2408 S Pk Ave. TF: 800-531-4656 ■ Web: www.ramgraphics.com	Alexandria	IN	46001	800-531-4656	551-6846
Screen Graphics of Florida Inc 1801 N Andrews Ave. TF: 800-346-4420 ■ Web: www.screen-graphics.com	Pompano Beach	FL	33069	800-346-4420	
Screen Industry Art Inc 214 Industrial Park Dr. Web: businessdirectory.lebanondemocrat.com	Soddy Daisy	TN	37379	423-332-6190	
Screen Machine Inc 3855 Wabash Ave.	San Diego	CA	92104	619-281-3355	281-2033
Select Design Ltd 208 Flynn Ave Ste 1A. Web: www.selectdesign.com	Burlington	VT	05401	802-864-9075	
Selecto-Flash Inc 18 Central Ave. Web: www.selectoflash.com	West Orange	NJ	07052	973-677-3500	
Sensical Inc Decals 31115 Aurora Rd. Web: sensical.com	Solon	OH	44139	216-641-1141	
Serigraph Inc 3801 E Decorah Rd. Web: www.serigraph.com	West Bend	WI	53095	262-335-7200	335-7699
Service Graphics LLC 8350 Allison Ave. TF: 800-884-9876 ■ Web: www.mysgi.com	Indianapolis	IN	46268	317-471-8246	
Signcraft Screenprint Inc 100 A J Harle Dr. Web: www.signcraftinc.com	Galena	IL	61036	815-777-3030	
Silkworm Inc 102 S Sezmore Dr. TF: 800-826-0577 ■ Web: www.silkwormink.com	Murphysboro	IL	62966	618-687-4077	
Starline Printing Inc 7111 Pan American W Svc Ne. Web: www.starlineprinting.com	Albuquerque	NM	87109	505-345-8900	
Sun Line Products 1454 E Summitry Cir. Web: www.sunlineproducts.com	Katy	TX	77449	281-398-6655	
Technigraph Corp 850 W Third St. Web: www.technigraph.net	Winona	MN	55987	507-454-3830	454-6470
Technigraphics 3212 S Cravens Rd. Web: www.craftmarkid.com	Fort Worth	TX	76119	817-457-8412	
Thomas Graphics Inc 9501 N IH 35. Web: www.thomasgraphicsinc.com	Austin	TX	78753	512-719-3535	
Top Promotions Inc 8831 S Greenview Dr. Web: www.toppromotions.com	Middleton	WI	53562	608-836-9111	
Trau & Loevner Inc 838 Braddock Ave. Web: www.trau-loevner.com	Braddock	PA	15104	412-361-7700	361-8221
Triple Crown Products Inc 814 Ela Ave. Web: triplecrownproducts.com/index.aspx	Waterford	WI	53185	262-534-7878	
Trust-franklin Press Inc 41 Terminal Way. Web: www.trust-franklinpress.com	Pittsburgh	PA	15219	412-481-6442	
Vincent Printing Company Inc 1512 Sholar Ave. TF: 800-251-7262 ■ Web: www.vincentprinting.com	Chattanooga	TN	37406	800-251-7262	
Visual Impressions Inc 6600 W Calumet Rd. Web: www.visualimp.com	Milwaukee	WI	53223	414-354-9190	
Voss Signs LLC 112 Fairgrounds Dr. Web: www.vosssigns.com	Manlius	NY	13104	315-682-6418	
William Frick & Co 2600 Commerce Dr. Web: fricknet.com	Libertyville	IL	60048	847-918-3700	
Windy City Silkscreening 2715 S Archer Ave. Web: www.wcsshirts.com	Chicago	IL	60608	312-842-0030	

688 SCREENING - WOVEN WIRE

Company / Address	City	State	ZIP	Phone	Fax
ACS Industries Inc 1 New England Way. TF: 866-783-4838 ■ Web: www.acsindustries.com	Lincoln	RI	02865	401-769-4700	333-6088
Belleville Wire Cloth Inc 18 Rutgers Ave. TF: 800-631-0490 ■ Web: www.bwire.com	Cedar Grove	NJ	07009	973-239-0074	239-3985
Buffalo Wire Works Co 1165 Clinton St. TF: 800-828-7028 ■ Web: www.buffalowire.com	Buffalo	NY	14206	716-826-4666	826-8271
Cleveland Wire Cloth & Manufacturing Co 3573 E 78th St. TF: 800-321-3234 ■ Web: www.wirecloth.com	Cleveland	OH	44105	216-341-1832	341-1876
Edward J Darby & Son Inc 2200 N Eigth St PO Box 50049. TF: 800-875-6374 ■ Web: www.darbywiremesh.com	Philadelphia	PA	19133	215-236-2203	236-2203
Gerard Daniel Worldwide 34 Barnhart Dr. TF: 800-232-3332 ■ Web: www.gerarddaniel.com	Hanover	PA	17331	717-637-5901	633-7095
Halliburton Screen Co 3000 N Sam Houston Pkwy E. NYSE: HAL ■ Web: www.halliburton.com	Houston	TX	77032	281-871-4000	
Hanover Wire Cloth 500 E Middle St. Web: www.newyorkwireind.com	Hanover	PA	17331	717-637-3795	637-4766
Jelliff Corp 354 Pequot Ave. TF: 800-243-0052 ■ Web: www.jelliff.com	Southport	CT	06890	203-259-1615	255-7908
King Wire Partitions Inc 6044 N Figueroa St. Web: www.kingwireusa.com	Los Angeles	CA	90042	323-256-4848	
Metal Textiles 970 New Durham Rd. *Fax: Sales ■ Web: www.metexcorp.com	Edison	NJ	08818	732-287-0800	287-8546*
National Wire Fabric 701 Arkansas St.	Star City	AR	71667	870-628-4201	628-3700
TWP Inc 2831 Tenth St. TF: 800-227-1570 ■ Web: www.twpinc.com	Berkeley	CA	94710	510-548-4434	548-3073
United Capital Corp 9 Pk Pl. OTC: UCAP ■ Web: www.unitedcapitalcorp.net	Great Neck	NY	11021	516-466-6464	829-4301
Universal Wire Cloth Co 16 N Steel Rd. TF: 800-523-0575 ■ Web: www.universalwirecloth.com	Morrisville	PA	19067	215-736-8981	736-8994
Wayne Wire Cloth Products Inc 200 E Dresden St. Web: www.waynewire.com	Kalkaska	MI	49646	231-258-9187	258-5504
Western Wire Group 4025 NW Express Ave. Web: www.thewesterngroup.com	Portland	OR	97210	503-222-1644	
Wire Cloth Filter Manufacturing Co 611 St Charles Rd. Web: wireclothfilter.net	Maywood	IL	60153	708-410-1800	410-1807

689 SEATING - VEHICULAR

Company / Address	City	State	ZIP	Phone	Fax
Advanced Components Technologies Inc 91 - 16th St S	Northwood	IA	50459	641-324-2231	324-1231
American Metal Fab Inc 55515 Franklin Dr. Web: www.americanmetalfab.com	Three Rivers	MI	49093	269-279-5108	279-5356
Bridgewater Interiors LLC 4617 W Fort St. Web: bridgewater-interiors.com	Detroit	MI	48209	313-842-3300	842-3452
Custom Aircraft Interiors 3701 Industry Ave. Web: www.customaircraftinteriors.com	Lakewood	CA	90712	562-426-5098	490-0213

				Phone	Fax
Freedman Seating Co 4545 W Augusta Blvd *TF:* 800-443-4540 ■ *Web:* www.freedmanseating.com	Chicago	IL	60651	773-524-2440	252-7450
Gill Industries Inc 5271 Plainfield Ave NE *Web:* www.gill-industries.com	Grand Rapids	MI	49525	616-559-2700	559-8850
HO Bostrom Company Inc 818 Progress Ave *TF:* 800-332-5415 ■ *Web:* www.hobostrom.com	Waukesha	WI	53186	262-542-0222	542-3784
Johnson Controls Inc Automotive Systems Group 49200 Halyard Dr *Web:* www.johnsoncontrols.com	Plymouth	MI	48170	734-254-5000	
Kustom Fit/Hi-Tech Seating 8990 Atlantic Ave *Web:* www.kustomfit.com	South Gate	CA	90280	323-564-4481	
Milsco Mfg Co 9009 N 51st St *TF:* 800-255-0337 ■ *Web:* www.milsco.com	Milwaukee	WI	53223	414-354-0500	354-0508
Sears Manufacturing Co 1718 S Concord St PO Box 3667 *TF Cust Svc:* 800-553-3013 ■ *Web:* www.searsseating.com	Davenport	IA	52808	563-383-2800	383-2810
Seats Inc 1515 Industrial St *TF:* 800-443-0615 ■ *Web:* www.seatsinc.com	Reedsburg	WI	53959	608-524-8261	

690 SECURITIES BROKERS & DEALERS

See Also Commodity Contracts Brokers & Dealers p. 1996; Electronic Communications Networks (ECNs) p. 2226; Investment Advice & Management p. 2597; Mutual Funds p. 2818

				Phone	Fax
1&1 Internet Inc 701 Lee Rd Ste 300 **Fax Area Code:* 610 ■ *TF:* 877-461-2631 ■ *Web:* www.1and1.com	Chesterbrook	PA	19087	877-461-2631	560-1501*
195 Lumber Company Killeen Ltd 3032 S Ft Hood St *Web:* www.195lumberco.com	Killeen	TX	76542	254-634-2188	
1st Discount Brokerage Inc 8927 Hypoluxo Rd Ste A-5 *TF:* 888-642-2811 ■ *Web:* www.1db.com	Lake Worth	FL	33467	561-515-3200	515-3201
360 Trading Networks Inc 521 Fifth Ave 38th Fl *Web:* www.360t.com	New York	NY	10175	212-776-2900	
AB Watley Direct Inc 50 Broad St Ste 1614 **Fax Area Code:* 212 ■ *TF:* 877-993-4886	New York	NY	10004	646-753-9301	202-5204*
ABG Sundal Collier Inc 535 Madison Ave 17th Fl *Web:* www.abgsc.com	New York	NY	10022	212-605-3800	
Access Financial Resources Inc 3621 NW 63rd Ste A1 *Web:* afradvice.com	Oklahoma City	OK	73116	405-848-9826	
Access Securities Inc 30 Buxton Farm Rd *TF:* 800-331-6171 ■ *Web:* www.accesssecurities.com	Stamford	CT	06905	203-322-3377	
Acculease Construction Equipment Inc 63 Clifton St *Web:* www.acculease.com	Farmingdale	NY	11735	631-577-0101	
achoo! ALLERGY & AIR Products Inc 3411 Pierce Dr Ste 100 *Web:* www.achooallergy.com	Atlanta	GA	30341	770-455-9999	
Actinver Securities Inc 5075 Wheimer Rd Galleria Financial Tower Ste 650 *Web:* www.actinversecurities.com	Houston	TX	77056	713-885-9843	
Adventures Unlimited Press 1 Adventure Pl *Web:* www.adventuresunlimitedpress.com	Kempton	IL	60946	815-253-6390	
Akar Capital Management 8551 W Sunrise Blvd Ste 102A *Web:* akarcapital.com	Plantation	FL	33322	954-476-7011	
Alamo Capital Financial Services 201 N Civic Dr Ste 360 *Web:* www.alamocapital.com	Walnut Creek	CA	94596	925-472-5700	
Albert Fried & Company LLC 45 Broadway 24th Fl *Web:* www.albertfried.com	New York	NY	10006	212-542-8266	
Alchem Chemical Co 5360 Tulane Dr *Web:* www.alchemchemical.com	Atlanta	GA	30336	404-696-9202	
All-Phase Electric Supply Co 4216 Legacy Pkwy Ste D *Web:* all-phaselansing.com	Lansing	MI	48911	517-394-1461	
Allen & Co Inc 1401 South Florida Avenue *TF:* 800-950-2526	Lakeland	FL	33803	863-688-9000	688-4885
Allen & Company of Florida Inc 1401 S Florida Ave *Web:* alleninvestments.com	Lakeland	FL	33803	863-688-9000	
Allen C Ewing & Co 50 N Laura St Ste 3625 *Web:* www.allenewing.com	Jacksonville	FL	32202	904-354-5573	
Alliance Advisory & Securities Inc 3390 Auto Mall Dr *Web:* www.allianceadvisory.com	Westlake Village	CA	91362	805-371-8020	
Alpine Investors LP 3 Embarcadero Ctr Ste 2330 *Web:* www.alpine-investors.com	San Francisco	CA	94111	415-392-9100	
Alpine Securities Corp 39 Exchange Pl *Web:* www.alpine-securities.com	Salt Lake City	UT	84111	801-355-5588	
AmeriFile Inc 1940 W Oak Cir *Web:* www.amerifile.net	Marietta	GA	30062	770-420-1978	
Ameriprise Brokerage 70400 Ameriprise Financial Ctr *TF:* 800-535-2001 ■ *Web:* www.ameriprise.com	Minneapolis	MN	55474	800-535-2001	
Anachemia Canada Inc 255 Rue Norman *Web:* www.anachemia.com	Lachine	QC	H8R1A3	514-489-5711	
Andrew Garrett Inc 140 E 45th St 11th Fl *Web:* www.andrewgarrett.com	New York	NY	10017	212-682-8833	
Antaeus Capital Inc 1100 Glendon Ave PH Ste 9 *Web:* www.antaeuscap.com	Los Angeles	CA	90024	310-443-9000	443-9005
Ardour Capital Investments LLC 26 BRdway Ste 1107 *Web:* www.ardourcapital.com	New York City	NY	10004	212-375-2950	
Aronson + Johnson + Ortiz LP 230 S Broad St 20th Fl *Web:* www.ajopartners.com	Philadelphia	PA	19102	215-546-7500	
Arque Capital Ltd 7501 E McCormick Pkwy *Web:* www.arquecapital.com	Scottsdale	AZ	85258	602-971-9000	
Artspace.com Markets Inc 915 Broadway Ste 602 *Web:* www.artspace.com	New York	NY	10010	212-675-5804	
Atlantic Forest Products LLC 240 W Dickman St *Web:* www.atlanticforest.com	Baltimore	MD	21230	410-752-8092	
Atlas Advisors LLC 140 E 45th St 23rd Fl *Web:* www.atlasadvisors.com	New York	NY	10017	212-471-4100	
Auerbach Grayson & Company LLC 25 W 45th St *Web:* agco.com	New York	NY	10036	212-557-4444	
Ausdal Financial Partners 220 N Main St Ste 400 *Web:* www.ausdal.com	Davenport	IA	52801	563-326-2064	
Avalon Ventures 1134 Kline St *Web:* www.avalon-ventures.com	La Jolla	CA	92037	858-348-2180	
Avisen Securities Inc 3620 American River Dr Ste 145 *TF:* 800-230-7704 ■ *Web:* www.avisensecurities.com	Sacramento	CA	95864	916-480-2747	
AVM LP 777 Yamato Rd *Web:* www.avmlp.com	Boca Raton	FL	33431	561-544-4600	
B Riley & Company LLC 11100 Santa Monica Blvd Ste 800 *Web:* www.brileyco.com	Los Angeles	CA	90025	310-966-1444	
Baird Patrick & Company Inc 305 Plz Ten *TF:* 800-221-7747 ■ *Web:* www.bairdpatrick.com	Jersey City	NJ	07311	201-680-7300	680-7301
Banca IMI Securities Corp 1 William St *Web:* www.bancaimi.com	New York	NY	10004	212-326-1100	
Barclays Capital Inc 200 Pk Ave **Fax:* Hum Res ■ *TF:* 888-227-2275 ■ *Web:* www.investmentbank.barclays.com	New York	NY	10166	212-412-4000	412-7300*
BaxterBoo 7025 S Fulton St Ste 150 *TF:* 888-887-0063 ■ *Web:* www.baxterboo.com	Centennial	CO	80112	888-887-0063	
Bayview Capital Group LLC 214 Minnetonka Ave S *Web:* www.bayviewcap.com	Wayzata	MN	55391	952-345-2000	
BBS Securities Inc 4100 Yonge St Ste 507 *Web:* www.bbssecurities.com	Toronto	ON	M2P2B5	416-235-0200	
Bear Forest Products Inc 4685 Brookhollow Cir *Web:* www.bearfp.com	Riverside	CA	92509	951-727-1767	
Bell Supply Inc 7221 Rt 130 *TF:* 888-834-2371 ■ *Web:* www.bellsupplyinc.com	Pennsauken	NJ	08110	856-663-3900	665-2196
Bernard L Madoff Investment Securities Co 885 Third Ave 18th Fl *TF:* 800-334-1343 ■ *Web:* www.madofftrustee.com	New York	NY	10022	212-230-2424	
Berry-Shino Securities Inc 15100 N 78th Way Ste 100 *Web:* www.berry-shino.com	Scottsdale	AZ	85260	480-315-3660	
Berthel Fisher & Co 701 Tama St Bldg B PO Box 609 *TF:* 800-356-5234 ■ *Web:* www.berthel.com	Marion	IA	52302	319-447-5700	447-4250
BHK Securities LLC 2200 Lakeshore Dr Ste 250 *TF:* 888-529-2610 ■ *Web:* www.bhkllc.com	Birmingham	AL	35209	205-322-2025	
Bia Digital Partners Lp 15120 Enterprise Ct *Web:* www.biadigitalpartners.com	Chantilly	VA	20151	703-227-9600	
Big Ceramic Store LLC 543 Vista Blvd *Web:* www.bigceramicstore.com	Sparks	NV	89434	775-351-2888	
Black Canyon Capital LLC 2000 Ave of the Stars 11th Fl *Web:* www.blackcanyoncapital.com	Los Angeles	CA	90067	310-272-1800	
Blackstone Group 345 Pk Ave *Web:* www.blackstone.com	New York	NY	10154	212-583-5000	583-5749
Blowfish Direct LLC 11130 Holder St *TF:* 877-725-6934 ■ *Web:* www.blowfishoes.com	Cypress	CA	90630	877-725-6934	
Blue 9 Capital 145 Hudson St Ste 401 *Web:* www.blue9capital.com	New York	NY	10013	212-798-0400	
Blue Fire Capital LLC 311 S Wacker Dr Ste 2000 *Web:* www.bluefirecap.com	Chicago	IL	60606	312-242-0500	
Bluelinx Holdings Inc 4300 Wildwood Pkwy *Web:* www.bluelinxco.com	Atlanta	GA	30339	770-953-7000	
BluePointe Capital Management LLC 400 S El Camino Real Ste 760 *Web:* www.bluepointecapital.com	San Mateo	CA	94402	650-293-4545	
BNP Paribas 787 Seventh Ave *Web:* www.bnpparibas.com	New York	NY	10019	212-841-3000	841-2146
Bobcat of St. Louis 401 W Outer Rd *Web:* www.bobcatofstl.com	Valley Park	MO	63088	636-225-2900	
BOS Innovations Ltd 888 E Belvidere Rd Ste 218 *Web:* www.blacklight.com	Grayslake	IL	60030	847-665-1080	
Boston Partners 909 Third Ave 32nd Fl *Web:* www.robecoinvest.com	New York	NY	10022	212-908-9500	
Bourbon & Boots Inc 419 Main St *TF:* 877-791-8079 ■ *Web:* www.bourbonandboots.com	North Little Rock	AR	72114	855-623-3562	
Brant Securities Ltd Ste 300-220 Bay St Ste 300 *Web:* www.brantsec.com	Toronto	ON	M5J2W4	416-596-4545	
Bridgepoint Merchant Banking 816 P St Ste 200 *Web:* bridgepointmb.com	Lincoln	NE	68508	402-817-7900	
Brighton Securities Corp 1703 Monroe Ave *TF:* 800-388-1703 ■ *Web:* www.brightonsecurities.com	Rochester	NY	14618	585-473-3590	
Brill Securities Inc 152 W 57th St 16th Fl *TF:* 800-933-0800 ■ *Web:* www.brillsec.com	New York	NY	10019	212-957-5700	

Company	City	State	ZIP	Phone	Fax
Broadband Capital Management LLC 712 Fifth Ave 22nd Fl *Web:* www.broadbandcapital.com	New York	NY	10019	212-759-2020	
Bruml Capital Corp 1801 E Ninth St Ste 1620 *Web:* www.brumlcapital.com	Cleveland	OH	44114	216-771-6660	
BTIG LLC 600 Montgomery St 6th Fl *Web:* wwwca01.btig.com	San Francisco	CA	94111	415-248-2200	
Bull Wealth Management Group Inc 4100 Yonge St Ste 612 *TF:* 866-623-2053 ■ *Web:* www.bullwealth.com	Toronto	ON	M2P2B5	416-223-2053	
Burch & Company Inc 4151 N Mulberry Dr Ste 235 *Web:* www.burchco.com	Kansas City	MO	64116	816-842-4660	
Burgess Steel LLC 200 W Forest Ave *Web:* www.burgesssteel.com	Englewood	NJ	07631	201-871-3500	
Burgundy Asset Management Ltd Bay Wellington Tower Brookfield Pl 181 Bay St Ste 4510 *TF:* 888-480-1790 ■ *Web:* www.burgundyasset.com	Toronto	ON	M5J2T3	416-869-3222	
Burt Martin Arnold Securities Inc 608 Silver Spur Rd Ste 100 *Web:* www.bmasecurities.com	Rolling Hills Estates	CA	90274	310-544-3545	
Butler Capital Investments LLC 222 Court Sq Second Fl Ste 3 *Web:* www.butlercap.com	Charlottesville	VA	22902	434-295-5888	
BUYandHOLD.com Securities Corp *c/o Freedom Investments, Inc* 375 Raritan Ctr Pkwy Ste D *TF:* 800-646-8212 ■ *Web:* www.buyandhold.com	Edison	NJ	08837	800-646-8212	
Cabinets To Go LLC 6901 Crestwood Blvd *Web:* www.cabinetstogo.com	Birmingham	AL	35210	205-623-2209	
Cabrera Capital Markets LLC 10 S La Salle St Ste 1050 *Web:* www.cabreracapital.com	Chicago	IL	60603	312-236-8888	236-8936
Cal-Sierra Pipe LLC 3033 S 99 Hwy W Frontage Rd *Web:* www.calsierrapipe.com	Stockton	CA	95215	209-466-0988	
Caldwell Securities Ltd 150 King St W Ste 1710 *TF:* 800-387-0859 ■ *Web:* www.caldwellsecurities.com	Toronto	ON	M5H1J9	416-862-7755	
Calton & Assoc Inc 14497 N Dale Mabry Hwy *TF:* 800-942-0262 ■ *Web:* calton.com	Tampa	FL	33618	813-264-0440	962-8695
Camfour Inc 65 Wfield Industrial Park Rd	Westfield	MA	01085	413-564-2300	
Cantor Fitzgerald LP 499 Pk Ave *Web:* www.cantor.com	New York	NY	10022	212-938-5000	
Capital Lumber Company Inc 5110 N 40th St Ste 242 *Web:* www.capital-lumber.com	Phoenix	AZ	85018	602-381-0709	
Capitol Securities Management Inc 100 Concourse Blvd Glen Allen *Web:* www.capitolsecurities.com	Richmond	VA	23059	804-612-9700	
Capstone Investments Research Div 12760 High Bluff Dr Ste 120 *Web:* www.capstoneinvestments.com	San Diego	CA	92130	858-875-4500	
Carlyle Capital Markets Inc 14755 Preston Rd Ste510 *Web:* www.carlylecapitalmarkets.com	Dallas	TX	75254	972-404-8686	
Cedar Hill Associates LLC 120 S LaSalle St Ste 1750 *Web:* www.cedhill.com	Chicago	IL	60603	312-445-2900	
Centaurus Financial 2300 E Katella Ave Ste 200 *Web:* centaurusfinancial.com	Anaheim	CA	92806	714-456-1790	
Centurion Counsel Inc 1282 Pacific Oaks Pl *Web:* www.centurioncounsel.com	Escondido	CA	92029	760-471-8536	
Ceros Financial Services Inc 1445 Research Blvd Ste 530 *TF:* 866-842-3356 ■ *Web:* www.cerosfs.com	Rockville	MD	20850	866-842-3356	
Cetera Financial Group Inc 200 N Sepulveda Blvd Ste 1200 *TF:* 866-489-3100 ■ *Web:* www.cetera.com	El Segundo	CA	90245	866-489-3100	
Charles Schwab & Co Inc 211 Main St *TF Cust Svc:* 800-648-5300 ■ *Web:* www.schwab.com	San Francisco	CA	94105	415-667-1009	
Charter Brokerage LLC 383 Main Ave Ste 506 *Web:* charterbrokerage.net	Norwalk	CT	06851	203-840-7500	
Chase Plastic Services Inc 6467 Waldon Ctr Dr *TF:* 800-232-4273 ■ *Web:* www.chaseplastics.com	Clarkston	MI	48346	248-620-2120	
Chatsworth Securities LLC 95 East Putnam Ave *Web:* www.chatsworthgroup.com	Greenwich	CT	06830	203-629-2612	629-2375
Cheevers & Company Inc 440 S LaSalle St Ste 710 *TF:* 866-928-7643 ■ *Web:* www.cheeversco.com	Chicago	IL	60605	312-224-7922	
Chopper Trading LLC 141 W Jackson Blvd Ste 2201A *Web:* www.choppertrading.com	Chicago	IL	60604	312-628-3500	
Cinco Energy Land Services 9235 Katy Fwy Ste 400 *Web:* cincoland.com	Houston	TX	77024	713-463-6009	
City Securities Corp 30 S Meridian St Ste 600 *TF:* 800-800-2489 ■ *Web:* www.citysecurities.com	Indianapolis	IN	46204	317-634-4400	955-2509
CJS Securities Inc Westchester Financial Ctr 50 Main St Ste 325 *Web:* www.cjssecurities.com	White Plains	NY	10606	914-287-7600	
CL King & Associates Inc 9 Elk St *Web:* clking.com	Albany	NY	12207	518-431-3500	
Clark Food Service Equipment 2209 Old Philadelphia Pk *Web:* www.clarkfoodserviceequipment.biz	Lancaster	PA	17602	717-392-7363	
CLS Investments LLC 17605 Wright St *TF:* 888-455-4244 ■ *Web:* www.clsinvest.com	Omaha	NE	68130	402-493-3313	
CME Group Index Services LLC PO Box 300 *Web:* www.djindexes.com	Princeton	NJ	08543	609-520-7249	
CNBS Inc 7200 W 132nd St Ste 240 *TF:* 800-222-0978 ■ *Web:* www.cnbsnet.com	Overland Park	KS	66213	800-222-0978	
Cobblestone Capital Advisors LLC 140 Allens Creek Rd *TF:* 800-264-2769 ■ *Web:* cobblestonecap.com	Rochester	NY	14618	585-473-3333	
Colorado West Investments Inc 1731 E Niagara Rd *TF:* 888-249-9882 ■ *Web:* cowestinvest.com	Montrose	CO	81401	970-249-9882	
Columbia West Capital LLC 14624 N Scottsdale Rd Ste 124 *Web:* www.columbiawestcap.com	Scottsdale	AZ	85254	480-664-3949	
Community Banc Investments Inc 26 E Main St *Web:* www.cbibankstocks.com	New Concord	OH	43762	740-826-7601	
Compass Point Research & Trading LLC 1055 Thomas Jefferson St NW Ste 303 *Web:* www.compasspointllc.com	Washington	DC	20007	202-540-7300	
Conceptual Financial Planning Inc 3962 N Richmond St Ste B *TF:* 800-300-9500 ■ *Web:* www.viainsurance.com	Appleton	WI	54913	920-731-9500	
Concord International Investments Group LP 610 Fifth Ave 6th Fl *Web:* www.concordus.com	New York	NY	10022	212-759-2375	
Construction Book Express Inc 401 S Wright Rd *Web:* www.constructionbook.com	Janesville	WI	53546	608-743-8031	
Continental Stock Transfer & Trust Company Inc 17 Battery Pl *Web:* www.continentalstock.com	New York	NY	10004	212-509-4000	
Convergex Holdings LLC 1633 Broadway 48th Fl *TF:* 800-367-8998 ■ *Web:* www.convergex.com	New York	NY	10019	212-468-7713	
Corinthian Partners LLC 850 Third Ave Ste 16C *TF:* 800-899-8950 ■ *Web:* www.corinthianpartners.com	New York	NY	10022	212-287-1500	
CP Capital Securities Inc 1428 Brickell Ave Ste 600 *Web:* www.cpcapital.com	Miami	FL	33131	305-702-5500	
Credit Suisse 11 Madison Ave *TF:* 800-222-8977 ■ *Web:* www.credit-suisse.com	New York	NY	10010	212-325-2000	325-6665
Crest Industries Inc 231 Larkin Williams Industrial Ct *Web:* www.crestmidwest.com	Fenton	MO	63026	636-349-4800	
Cronin & Company Inc 800 Nicollet Mall Ste 2520 *Web:* www.cronincoinc.com	Minneapolis	MN	55402	612-339-8561	
Crowell Weedon & Co 1 Wilshire Blvd 26th Fl *TF:* 800-227-0319 ■ *Web:* www.davidsoncompanies.com/indv	Los Angeles	CA	90017	213-620-1850	244-9388
Currenex Inc 1230 Ave of the Americas 18th Fl *Web:* www.currenex.com	New York	NY	10020	212-340-1780	
Cutler Group LP 101 Montgomery St Ste 700 *Web:* www.cutlergrouplp.com	San Francisco	CA	94104	415-645-6745	
Cypress Asset Management Inc 4545 Post Oak Pl Dr Ste 205 *Web:* cypressasset.com	Houston	TX	77027	713-512-2100	
DA Davidson & Company Inc 8 Third St N *TF:* 800-332-5915 ■ *Web:* www.davidsoncompanies.com/indv	Great Falls	MT	59401	406-727-4200	791-7380
Daiwa Capital Markets America Inc Financial Sq 32 Old Slip *Web:* www.us.daiwacm.com	New York	NY	10005	212-612-7000	
DAK Group Ltd, The 195 Rt 17 S *Web:* www.dakgroup.com	Rochelle Park	NJ	07662	201-712-9555	
Davenport & Co LLC 901 E Cary St 1 James Center Ste 1100 *TF:* 800-846-6666 ■ *Web:* www.davenportllc.com	Richmond	VA	23219	804-780-2000	
Davidge Data Systems Corp 20 Exchange Pl 39th Fl *Web:* www.davidge.com	New York	NY	10005	212-269-0901	
Davidson Cos 8 Third St N PO Box 5015 *TF:* 800-332-5915 ■ *Web:* www.davidsoncompanies.com	Great Falls	MT	59401	406-727-4200	
Davidson's Inc 6100 Wilkinson Dr *Web:* www.galleryofguns.com	Prescott	AZ	86301	928-776-8055	
Decision Software Inc 116 John St *Web:* www.dsoftware.com	New York	NY	10038	212-385-1662	
DeMatteo Monness LLC 780 Third Ave 45th Fl *Web:* www.dmllc.com	New York	NY	10017	212-833-9900	
Demeter Advisory Group LLC 220 Halleck St Ste 220 *Web:* www.demetergroup.net	San Francisco	CA	94129	415-632-4400	
DH Capital LLC 810 Seventh Ave Ste 2005 *Web:* www.dhcapital.com	New York	NY	10019	212-774-3720	
DiscountMugs.com 12610 NW 115th Ave *TF:* 800-569-1980 ■ *Web:* www.discountmugs.com	Medley	FL	33178	800-569-1980	
DM Kelly & Co 3900 Ingersoll Ave Ste 300 *Web:* www.dmkc.com	Des Moines	IA	50312	515-221-1133	
Domestic Securities Inc 160 Summit Ave *TF:* 877-690-2274	Montvale	NJ	07645	201-505-9855	
Dot Com Holdings of Buffalo Inc 1460 Military Rd *TF:* 877-636-3673 ■ *Web:* www.dotcomholdingsofbuffalo.com	Buffalo	NY	14217	877-636-3673	
Dougherty & Company LLC 90 S Seventh St Ste 4300 *TF:* 800-328-4000 ■ *Web:* www.doughertymarkets.com	Minneapolis	MN	55402	612-376-4000	
Douglas P Bates 144 Genesee St	Auburn	NY	13021	315-253-2782	
Dowling & Yahnke Inc 12340 El Camino Real *Web:* dywealth.com	San Diego	CA	92130	858-509-9500	
Dresner Partners 20 N Clark St Ste 3550 *Web:* www.dresnerpartners.com	Chicago	IL	60602	312-726-3600	
Dreyfus Corp 200 Pk Ave *Web:* public.dreyfus.com	New York	NY	10166	212-495-1784	922-6880

Name / Address	City	State	Zip	Phone	Fax
DRW Trading Group 540 W Madison St Ste 2500 *Web:* www.drw.com	Chicago	IL	60661	312-542-1000	
Duncan-Williams Inc 6750 Poplar Ave Ste 300 *Web:* www.duncanwilliams.com	Memphis	TN	38138	901-260-6800	
Duquesne Capital Mgt LLC 40 W 57th St Fl 25	New York	NY	10019	212-397-8596	
E*Trade Financial Corp 1271 Ave of the Americas 14th Fl *NASDAQ:* ETFC ■ *TF:* 800-387-2331 ■ *Web:* about.etrade.com	New York	NY	10020	800-387-2331	
E1 Asset Management Inc 44 Wall St 9th Fl *Web:* e1am.com	New York	NY	10005	212-425-2670	
eBX LLC 65 Franklin St Ste 201 *TF:* 800-958-4813 ■ *Web:* www.levelats.com	Boston	MA	02110	617-350-1600	
ECMD Inc 2 Grandview St *TF:* 888-222-3961 ■ *Web:* www.ecmd.com	North Wilkesboro	NC	28659	336-667-5976	
EdgePoint Capital Advisors LLC 2000 Auburn Dr Ste 330 *Web:* www.edgepoint.com	Beachwood	OH	44122	216-831-2430	
Edward Jones 12555 Manchester Rd *Web:* www.edwardjones.com	Saint Louis	MO	63131	314-515-2000	515-3269
EFG Capital International Corp 701 Brickell Ave 9th Fl *Web:* www.efgcapital.com	Miami	FL	33131	305-482-8000	
EKRiley Investments LLC 1420 Fifth Ave Ste 3300 *Web:* www.ekriley.com	Seattle	WA	98101	206-832-1520	
Ellie Fashion Group Inc 1447 Second St 3rd Fl *TF:* 888-926-9615	Santa Monica	CA	90401	888-926-9615	
Ema Brokerage LLC 1300 Rt 73 Ste 306 *TF:* 855-267-5867 ■ *Web:* emabrokerage.com	Mount Laurel	NJ	08054	856-216-0211	
Emergent Financial Group Inc 3600 American Blvd W Ste 670 *Web:* www.emergentfinancial.com	Bloomington	MN	55431	952-829-1212	
Emerson Equity LLC 155 Bovet Rd Ste 725 *Web:* www.emersonequity.com	San Mateo	CA	94402	650-312-0200	
Endeavour Capital Inc 760 SW 9th Ave Ste 2300 *Web:* www.endeavourcapital.com	Portland	OR	97205	503-223-2721	
Energy Spectrum Advisors Inc 5956 Sherry Ln Ste 900 *Web:* www.energyspectrumadvisors.com	Dallas	TX	75225	214-987-6100	
Energynet.com Inc 7201 I-40 W Ste 319 *Web:* www.energynet.com	Amarillo	TX	79106	806-351-2953	354-2835
Envestnet Inc 35 E Wacker Dr Ste 2400 *Web:* www.envestnet.com	Chicago	IL	60601	312-827-2800	
Equinox Securities Inc 760 S Rochester Ave Ste E *Web:* www.equinoxsecurities.net	Ontario	CA	91761	909-218-8950	
Equitec Group LLC 111 W Jackson Blvd Fl 20 *Web:* www.eqtc.com	Chicago	IL	60604	312-692-5000	
Essex National Securities Inc 550 Gateway Dr *Web:* www.ensinet.com	Napa	CA	94558	707-258-5000	
Evans Investment Advisors LLC 6713 Perkins Rd	Baton Rouge	LA	70808	225-761-7870	
Everest Group Inc, The 9912 Carver Rd Ste 100 *Web:* www.everestrealestate.com	Cincinnati	OH	45242	513-769-2500	
Exane Inc 640 Fifth Ave 15th Fl *Web:* www.exane.com	New York	NY	10019	212-634-4990	
ExRx.net LLC 4236 Bell St *Web:* www.exrx.net	Kansas City	MO	64111	913-481-9335	
Fairbridge Capital Markets Inc 48 Carr 165 Ste 801 *Web:* www.fairbridgecap.com	Guaynabo	PR	00968	787-622-3473	
Fairmount Partners LP 100 Four Falls Corporate Ctr Ste 660 *Web:* fairmountpartners.com	West Conshohocken	PA	19428	610-260-6200	
Fastener Supply Co 13410 S Ridge Dr PO Box 7369 *TF:* 800-888-9519 ■ *Web:* www.fastenersupply.com	Charlotte	NC	28241	704-596-7634	598-0116
Fidus Partners LLC 227 W Trade St Ste 1910 *Web:* www.fiduspartners.com	Charlotte	NC	28202	704-334-2222	334-2202
Fieldpoint Private Bank & Trust 100 Field Pt Rd *TF:* 877-438-4338 ■ *Web:* www.fieldpointprivate.com	Greenwich	CT	06830	203-413-9300	
Fieldstone Partners 1800 Bering Dr Ste 430 *Web:* fieldstone.com	Houston	TX	77057	713-850-0080	
FIMAC Solutions LLC Denver Technological Ctr 5299 DTC Blvd Ste 950 *TF:* 877-789-5905 ■ *Web:* www.fimacsolutions.com	Greenwood Village	CO	80111	303-320-1900	
Financial America Securities Inc 1325 Carnegie Ave *Web:* www.fasinv.com	Cleveland	OH	44115	216-781-5060	
Financial Service Corp 2300 Windy Ridge Pkwy Ste 1100 *TF:* 800-547-2382 ■ *Web:* www.joinfsc.com	Atlanta	GA	30339	800-547-2382	
Financial West Investment Group Inc 4510 E Thousand Oaks Blvd *Web:* www.fwg.com	Westlake Village	CA	91362	805-497-9222	
Fincantieri Marine Systems North America Inc 800-C Principal Ct *TF:* 877-436-7643 ■ *Web:* www.fincantierimarinesystems.com	Chesapeake	VA	23320	757-548-6000	
First Dallas Securities 2905 Maple Ave *Web:* www.firstdallas.com	Dallas	TX	75201	214-954-1177	954-1281
First Heartland Capital Inc 1839 Lk St Louis Blvd	Lake Saint Louis	MO	63367	636-625-0900	
First London Securities Corp 2603 Fairmount St *Web:* www.firstlondon.com	Dallas	TX	75201	214-220-0699	
First Manhattan Co 399 Park Ave *Web:* www.firstmanhattan.com	New York	NY	10022	212-756-3300	
First New York Securities LLC 90 Pk Ave Fl 5 *Web:* www.firstny.com	New York	NY	10016	212-848-0600	
First Options of Chicago Inc 70 W Madison St Ste 2100 *Web:* www.pftctrading.com	Chicago	IL	60602	312-933-5884	
First Tryon Securities LLC 1355 Greenwood Cliff Ste 401 *Web:* www.firsttryon.com	Charlotte	NC	28204	704-372-6118	
FirstEnergy Capital Corp 311-6th Ave SW Ste 1100 *Web:* www.firstenergy.com	Calgary	AB	T2P3H2	403-262-0600	
Fisc Investment Services Corp 1849 Clairmont Rd *TF:* 800-241-3203 ■ *Web:* www.palmeragency.com	Decatur	GA	30033	404-321-1212	
Fisgard Capital Corp 3378 Douglas St *TF:* 866-382-9255 ■ *Web:* www.fisgard.com	Victoria	BC	V8Z3L3	250-382-9255	
Flagship Investment Group Inc 3939 W Ridge Rd Ste A-103 *Web:* raymondjames.com	Erie	PA	16506	814-835-1150	
Fogel International Inc 5110 N 32nd St Ste 206 *Web:* www.fogelinternational.com	Phoenix	AZ	85018	602-508-0728	
Force Capital Management LLC 767 Fifth Ave 12th Fl *Web:* www.bakercapital.com	New York	NY	10153	212-451-9150	
Fordham Financial Management Inc 14 Wall St *Web:* www.fordhamfinancial.com	New York	NY	10005	212-732-8500	
Forshaw Industries Inc 650 State St *Web:* www.forshaw.com	Charlotte	NC	28208	704-372-6790	
Franklin Templeton Investments 3344 Quality Dr *TF:* 800-632-2350 ■ *Web:* www.franklintempleton.com	Rancho Cordova	CA	95670	650-312-2000	
Freedom Investments Inc 375 Raritan Ctr Pkwy *TF:* 800-944-4033 ■ *Web:* www.freedominvestments.com	Edison	NJ	08837	800-944-4033	830-1855
Fremont Realty Capital 199 Fremont St Ste 2200 *Web:* www.fremontrealtycapital.com	San Francisco	CA	94105	415-284-8665	
Friedman Billings Ramsey Group Inc 1300 N 17th St Ste 1400 *TF:* 800-846-5050 ■ *Web:* www.fbr.com	Arlington	VA	22209	703-312-9500	
Frost Securities Inc 2727 N Harwood St Ste 1000 *Web:* www.frostbank.com/pages/business-investments-securities.aspx	Dallas	TX	75201	214-515-4435	515-4455
FSB Warner Financial 1001 Peoples Sq *TF:* 800-747-9999 ■ *Web:* fsbfs.com	Waterloo	IA	50702	319-235-6561	
Full Access Brokerage 1240 Charnelton St *TF:* 866-890-5743 ■ *Web:* fullaccess.org	Eugene	OR	97401	541-284-5070	
Galileo Global Advisors LLC 10 Rockefeller Plz Ste 1001 *Web:* galileoglobaladvisors.com	New York	NY	10020	212-332-6055	
Gar Wood Securities LLC 440 S LaSalle St Ste 2201 *Web:* www.garwoodsecurities.net	Chicago	IL	60605	312-566-0740	
Garban Capital Markets LLC 1100 Plaza Five *Web:* www.icap.com	Jersey City	NJ	07311	212-341-9900	
Gardner Rich & Co 401 S Financial Pl	Chicago	IL	60605	312-922-3333	922-2144
GBS Financial Corp 558 B St *Web:* www.gbsfinancial.com	Santa Rosa	CA	95401	707-568-2400	
GE Richards Graphic Supplies Company Inc 928 Links Ave *TF:* 800-233-0410 ■ *Web:* www.gerichards.com	Landisville	PA	17538	717-898-3151	
Geary Pacific Corp 1908 N Enterprise St *TF:* 800-444-3279 ■ *Web:* www.gearypacific.com	Orange	CA	92865	714-279-2950	
Geneos Wealth Management Inc 9055 E Mineral Cir Ste 200 *TF:* 888-812-5043 ■ *Web:* www.geneoswealth.com	Centennial	CO	80112	303-785-8470	
General Parts LLC 11311 Hampshire Ave S *Web:* generalparts.com	Bloomington	MN	55438	952-944-5800	
George K Baum & Co 4801 Main St Ste 500 Ste 500 *TF:* 800-821-7195 ■ *Web:* www.gkbaum.com	Kansas City	MO	64112	816-474-1100	283-5180
Georgeson Securities Corp 480 Washington Blvd 27th Fl *TF:* 800-428-0717 ■ *Web:* www.georgesonsecurities.com	Jersey City	NJ	07310	800-428-0717	
Gifts On Time LLC 80 Front St Ste 21 *Web:* www.giftsontime.com	Scituate	MA	02066	781-545-0799	
Gilford Securities Inc 777 Third Ave	New York	NY	10017	212-888-6400	826-9738
Gleacher & Co Inc 1290 Ave of the Americas *Web:* www.gleacher.com	New York	NY	10104	212-273-7100	
Glendale Securities Inc 15233 Ventura Blvd Ste 712 *Web:* www.glendalesecurities.com	Sherman Oaks	CA	91403	818-907-1505	
Glickenhaus & Co 546 Fifth Ave 7th Fl	New York	NY	10036	212-938-2100	983-8436
Global Arena Capital Corp 708 Third Ave 11th Fl *Web:* www.globalarenacapital.com	New York	NY	10017	212-508-4700	
Global Maxfin Investments Inc 100 Mural St Ste 201 *TF:* 866-666-5266 ■ *Web:* www.globalmaxfin.ca	Richmond Hill	ON	L4B1J3	416-741-1544	
Global Security Management Agency Inc 1781 Vineyard Dr *Web:* gsmasecurity.com	Antioch	CA	94509	925-262-4181	
Global Strategic Investments LLC 701 Brickell Ave Ste 1420 *Web:* www.gscorporation.com	Miami	FL	33131	305-373-3326	
GMP Securities LLC 331 Madison Ave *Web:* www.gmpsecuritiesllc.com	New York	NY	10017	212-692-5100	
GMS Group LLC, The 5 N Regent St Ste 513 *Web:* www.gmsgroup.com	Livingston	NJ	07039	973-535-5000	
Grace Financial Group LLC 83 Jobs Ln *Web:* www.gracefg.com	Southampton	NY	11968	631-287-4633	

Phone Fax

Great Pacific Fixed Income Securities Inc
151 Kalmus Dr Ste H-8 Costa Mesa CA 92626 714-619-3000 619-3018
TF: 800-284-4804 ■ *Web:* www.greatpac.com
GreenChem Industries LLC
222 Clematis St Ste 207 West Palm Beach FL 33401 561-659-2236
Web: www.greenchemindustries.com
Greenland (America) Inc
1905 Woodstock Rd Ste 2200 Roswell GA 30075 770-435-1100
Web: www.greenlandamerica.com
Greenspun Corp Inc, The
901 N Green Vly Pkwy Ste 210 Henderson NV 89074 702-259-4023
Gridley & Company LLC 10 E 53rd St 24th Fl New York NY 10022 212-400-9720
Web: www.gridleyco.com
Group One Trading LP 440 S La Salle Ste 3232 Chicago IL 60605 312-922-2620
Web: www.group1.com
Guzman & Co
One Guzman Plz 101 Aragon Ave Coral Gables Miami FL 33134 305-374-3600
Web: guzman.com
GVC Capital LLC
5350 S Roslyn St Ste 400 Greenwood Village CO 80111 303-694-0862 694-6287
Web: www.gvccap.com
GWN Securities Inc 11440 N Jog Rd Palm Beach Gardens FL 33418 561-472-2700
Web: www.gwnsecurities.com
Hampton Securities Ltd
141 Adelaide St W Ste 1800 Toronto ON M5H3L5 416-862-7800
TF: 877-225-0229 ■ *Web:* www.hamptonsecurities.com
Hanover Partners Inc
425 California St Ste 1700 San Francisco CA 94104 415-788-8680
Web: www.hanoverpartners.com
Hansen-Mueller Co 12231 Emmet St Ste 1 Omaha NE 68164 402-491-3385
Web: www.hansenmueller.com
Harch Capital Management LLC
7400 N Federal Hwy Ste A5 Boca Raton FL 33487 561-226-6199
Web: www.harchcapital.com
Harpeth Capital LLC 3100 W End Ave Ste 710 Nashville TN 37203 615-296-9840
Web: www.harpethcapital.com
Harris Financial Services Inc
940 Spokane Ave Whitefish MT 59937 406-862-4400
TF: 800-735-7895 ■ *Web:* harrisfsi.com
Hazlett Burt & Watson Inc 1300 Chapline St Wheeling WV 26003 304-233-3312
Web: www.hazlettburt.com
HC Wainwright & Co Inc 430 Park Ave 4th Fl New York NY 10022 212-356-0500
Web: www.hcwainwright.com
Heartland Investment Associates Inc
2202 Heritage Green Dr Hiawatha IA 52233 319-393-8913
Hencorp Inc 777 Brickell Ave Ste 1010 Miami FL 33131 305-373-9000
Web: www.hencorp.com
Henley & Company LLC 1290 RXR Plz Uniondale NY 11556 516-794-5520
Web: www.henleyandcompany.com
Henry H Armstrong Associates Inc
1 Gateway Ctr 420 Ft Duquesne Blvd
Ste 1825 Pittsburgh PA 15222 412-471-1551
Web: www.henryarmstrong.com
Hilco Industrial LLC
31555 W Fourteen Mile Rd Ste 207 Farmington Hills MI 48334 248-254-9999
Web: www.hilcoind.com
Hilco Merchant Resources LLC
5 Revere Dr Ste 206 Northbrook IL 60062 847-509-1100
Web: www.hilcomerchantresources.com
Hirzel Capital Management LLC
3963 Maple Ave Ste 170 Dallas TX 75129 214-999-0014
Web: www.hirzelcapital.com
Hogan-Knotts Financial Group, The
298 Broad St Red Bank NJ 07701 732-842-7400
TF: 800-801-3190 ■ *Web:* hkfg.biz
Horan Associates Inc 4990 E Galbraith Rd Cincinnati OH 45236 513-745-0707
Web: www.horanassoc.com
Houlihan Capital LLC
500 W Madison St Ste 2600 Chicago IL 60661 312-450-8600
Web: www.houlihan.com
Houston Asset Management Inc 1800 W Loop S Houston TX 77027 713-629-1534
Web: www.houstonassetmgmt.com
HoustonStreet Inc
1 New Hampshire Ave Ste 207 Portsmouth NH 03801 603-766-8716
Web: www.houstonstreet.com
Howe Barnes Hoefer & Arnett Inc
222 S Riverside Plz 7th Fl Chicago IL 60606 312-655-3000
Web: www.howebarnes.com
Huntleigh Securities Corp
7800 Forsyth Blvd 5th Fl Saint Louis MO 63105 314-236-2400 236-2401
TF: 800-727-5405 ■ *Web:* www.hntlgh.com
Hurlen Corp 9841 Bell Ranch Dr Santa Fe Springs CA 90670 562-941-5330
Web: kenigaero.com
Hutchinson Shockey Erley & Co
222 W Adams St Ste 1700 Chicago IL 60606 312-443-1550
Web: www.hsemuni.com
Icor Technology Inc 935 Ages Dr Ottawa ON K1G6L3 613-745-3600
TF: 877-483-7978 ■ *Web:* icortechnology.com
IDI Distributors Inc 8303 Audubon Rd Chanhassen MN 55317 952-279-6400
TF: 888-843-1318 ■ *Web:* idi-insulation.com
IEX Group Inc 4 World Trade Ctr 44th Fl New York NY 10007 646-568-2320
Web: iextrading.com
IKON Global Markets Inc
88 Pine St Wall St Plz 5th Fl New York NY 10005 212-482-8408
Web: www.ikongm.com
Illinois Fair Plan Association
130 East Randolph PO Box 81469 Chicago IL 60601 312-861-0385 861-0485
TF: 800-972-4480 ■ *Web:* www.illinoisfairplan.com
Impulse Technologies Ltd 920 Gana Crt Mississauga ON L5S1Z4 905-564-9266
TF: 800-667-5475 ■ *Web:* impulsetechnologies.com
Incapital LLC 200 S Wacker Dr Ste 3700 Chicago IL 60606 312-379-3700
Web: www.incapital.com
Incucomm Inc 5085 W Park Blvd Ste 100 Plano TX 75093 972-690-9494
Web: www.lone-star.com

Phone Fax

Index Funds Advisors Inc
19200 Von Karman Ave Ste 150 Irvine CA 92612 949-502-0050
TF: 888-643-3133 ■ *Web:* ifa.com
Industrial Source Inc 1574 W Sixth Ave Eugene OR 97402 541-344-1438
Web: www.industrialsource.com
Industrial Tube & Steel Corp 4658 Crystal Pkwy Kent OH 44240 330-474-5530
TF: 800-662-9567 ■ *Web:* www.industrialtube.com
Infinity Insurance Solutions LLC
10707 Barkley St Leawood KS 66211 913-338-3200
Web: www.infinityins.com
ING Financial Markets Llc
1325 Ave of the Americas New York NY 10019 646-424-6000 424-6060
Web: ing.com
Insight Capital Investments
4101 Gateway Dr Colleyville TX 76034 817-545-1959
Web: www.onealinvestments.com
Interwest Capital Corp
7724 Girard Ave Ste 300 La Jolla CA 92037 858-622-4900
Web: www.interwestcapital.com
Investec Ernst & Co 1 Battery Pk Plz 2nd Fl New York NY 10004 212-898-6200
Web: www.investec.com
Investment Professionals Inc
16414 San Pedro Ave Ste 150 San Antonio TX 78232 210-308-8800 308-8707
Web: www.invpro.com
Investors Security Company Inc
127 E Washington St Ste 101 Suffolk VA 23434 757-539-2396
Web: investorssecurity.com
Investrade Discount Securities
950 N Milwaukee Ave Ste 102 Glenview IL 60025 847-375-6080 367-8466*
**Fax Area Code:* 877 ■ **Fax:* Cust Svc ■ *TF Cust Svc:* 800-498-7120 ■ *Web:* www.investrade.com
Ironwood Capital Ltd 45 Nod Rd Avon CT 06001 860-409-2100
Web: www.ironwoodcap.com
Isaak Bond Investments Inc
3900 S Wadsworth Blvd Ste 590 Lakewood CO 80235 303-623-7500
TF: 800-279-4426 ■ *Web:* www.isaakbond.com
ITG Derivatives LLC 601 S LaSalle Ste 300 Chicago IL 60605 312-334-8000
Web: www.redskysecurities.com
ITG Inc 1 Liberty Plz 165 Broadway New York NY 10006 212-588-4000
TF: 800-215-4484 ■ *Web:* www.itginc.com
Janney Montgomery Scott LLC
1801 Market St Philadelphia PA 19103 215-665-6000
TF: 800-526-6397 ■ *Web:* www.janney.com
Javelin Capital Markets LLC
443 Park Ave S 10th Fl New York NY 10016 212-779-2300
Web: www.thejavelin.com
Jaypee International Inc
30 S Wacker Dr Ste 1700 Chicago IL 60606 312-655-7606
Web: www.jaypeeusa.com
JD Ford & Company LLC 650 S Cherry St Ste 1200 Denver CO 80246 303-333-3673
TF: 888-999-9495 ■ *Web:* www.jdford.com
Jefferies Group Inc 520 Madison Ave 10th Fl New York NY 10022 212-284-2300
NYSE: JEF ■ *Web:* www.jefferies.com
JJB Hilliard WL Lyons Inc
500 W Jefferson St Louisville KY 40202 502-588-8400 585-8901*
**Fax:* Hum Res ■ *TF:* 800-444-1854 ■ *Web:* www.hilliard.com
Jobast Holdings Inc 377 Oak St Ste 402 Garden City NY 11530 516-997-4490
Johnston Lemon & Company Inc
1101 Vermont Ave NW Ste 800 Washington DC 20005 202-842-5500 842-7185
JonesTrading Institutional Services LLC
32133 Lindero Canyon Rd Ste 208 Westlake Village CA 91361 818-991-5500
Web: www.jonestrading.com
Juniper Advisory LLC 191 N Wacker Dr Ste 900 Chicago IL 60606 312-506-3000
Web: www.juniperadvisory.com
Kane Reid Securities Group Inc
13024 Ballantyne Corporate Pl Ste 500 Charlotte NC 28277 877-495-5464
TF: 877-495-5464 ■ *Web:* www.tradeking.com
Katalyst Surgical LLC 754 Goddard Ave Chesterfield MO 63005 888-452-8259
TF: 888-452-8259 ■ *Web:* www.katalystsurgical.com
Kaufman Bros LP 800 Third Ave 30th Fl New York NY 10022 212-292-8100
Web: www.kbro.com
Keefe Bruyette & Woods Inc
787 Seventh Ave The Equitable Bldg 4th Fl New York NY 10019 212-887-7777
Web: www.kbw.com
Kelso & Company Inc 320 Pk Ave 24th Fl New York NY 10022 212-751-3939 223-2379
Web: www.kelso.com
Kidd & Company LLC 1455 E Putnam Ave Old Greenwich CT 06870 203-661-0070
Web: www.kiddcompany.com
Kingsdale Capital Markets Inc
55 University Ave Ste M002 Toronto ON M5J2H7 416-867-4550
Web: www.kingsdalecapital.com
KippsDeSanto & Co
8000 Towers Crescent Dr Ste 1200 Tysons Corner VA 22182 703-442-1400
Web: www.kippsdesanto.com
Knight Capital Group Inc
545 Washington Blvd Jersey City NJ 07310 201-222-9400 557-6853
NYSE: KCG ■ *TF:* 800-544-7508 ■ *Web:* www.kcg.com
Kohlberg Capital Corp 295 Madison Ave 6th Fl New York NY 10017 212-455-8300 983-7654
Web: www.kohlbergcapital.com
Kovack Securities Inc
6451 N Federal Hwy # 1201 Ste 1201 Fort Lauderdale FL 33308 954-782-4771 943-7331
TF: 800-711-4078 ■ *Web:* www.kovacksecurities.com
L B L Group 3631 S. Harbor Blvd Ste 200 Santa Ana CA 92704 657-232-0500
TF: 800-451-8037 ■ *Web:* www.lblgroup.com
Ladenburg Thalmann Financial Services Inc
4400 Biscayne Blvd 12th Fl Miami FL 33137 212-409-2000 572-4199*
NYSE: LTS ■ **Fax Area Code:* 305 ■ *TF:* 800-523-8425 ■ *Web:* www.ladenburg.com
Lake Shore Securities Lp
401 S La Salle St Ste 1000 Chicago IL 60605 312-663-1307
Web: www.lakeshoresecurities.com
Lasalle St Securities LLC
940 N Industrial Dr Elmhurst IL 60126 630-600-0500
Web: lasallest.com
Lasting Legacy Ltd 812 Busse Hwy Park Ridge IL 60068 847-685-8402
Web: raymondjames.com

Phone Fax

Laux & Co 672 W Liberty St Medina OH 44256 330-721-0100
Web: www.lauxco.com

Lazard 30 Rockefeller Plz New York NY 10112 212-632-6000
NYSE: LAZ ■ *TF:* 866-867-4070 ■ *Web:* www.lazard.com

Leader Capital Corp
919 N East 19th Ave Ste 200 Portland OR 97232 503-294-1010
Web: www.leadercapital.com

Leaders LLC 2 Portland Fish Pier Ste 214 Portland ME 04101 888-583-7770
TF: 888-583-7770 ■ *Web:* www.leaders-llc.com

Lebenthal Wealth Advisors 230 Park Ave Fl 32 New York NY 10169 212-425-6006 867-1787
TF: 877-425-6006 ■ *Web:* www.lebenthal.com

Legg Mason Inc (LMI) 100 International Dr Baltimore MD 21202 410-539-0000
NYSE: LM ■ *TF:* 800-822-5544 ■ *Web:* www.leggmason.com

Leigh Baldwin & Company LLC 1 Hopper St Ste 1 Utica NY 13501 315-734-1410
TF: 800-659-8044 ■ *Web:* www.leighbaldwin.com

Lenox Group LLC, The
3384 Peachtree Rd N E Ste 300 Atlanta GA 30326 404-419-1660
Web: www.lenoxgroupllc.com

Lepercq de Neuflize & Co
156 W 56th St Ste 1204 New York NY 10019 212-698-0700 262-0155
Web: www.lepercq.com

Lexington Investment Mortgage Company LLC
2365 Harrodsburg Rd Ste B375 Lexington KY 40504 859-224-7073
TF: 800-264-7073 ■ *Web:* www.lexinvest.com

Liberty Group LLC 3923 Grand Ave Oakland CA 94610 510-658-1880
Web: www.libertygroupllc.com

Liebherr-Canada Ltd 1015 Sutton Dr Burlington ON L7L5Z8 905-319-9222
Web: www.liebherr.com/en/deu/about-liebherr/liebherr-worldwide/canada/liebherr-in-canada.html

Lime Brokerage LLC 625 Broadway 12th Fl New York NY 10012 212-824-5000
Web: www.limebrokerage.com

Lincolnshire Management Inc
780 Third Ave 40th Fl New York NY 10017 212-319-3633 755-5457
Web: www.lincolnshiremgmt.com

Livingston Technologies
45 Horse Hill Rd Ste 105B Cedar Knolls NJ 07927 973-322-5671

Loop Capital Markets LLC
111 W Jackson Blvd Ste 1901 Chicago IL 60604 312-913-4900 913-4928
TF: 888-294-8898 ■ *Web:* www.loopcapital.com

Louisiana Chemical Equipment Company LLC
7911 Wrenwood Ste A Baton Rouge LA 70896 225-923-3602
Web: www.lcec.com

LPL Financial Services 75 State St 24th Fl Boston MA 02109 800-877-7210
TF: 800-877-7210

LTVtrade LLC 501 Madison Ave Ste 501 New York NY 10022 212-616-4600
Web: www.ltvtrade.com

Lyons Equipment Company Inc
5445 Nys Rt 353 Little Valley NY 14755 716-938-9175
Web: www.lyonstimbertalk.com

M Ramsey King Securities Inc
93 Tomlin Cir Burr Ridge IL 60527 630-789-0607
Web: mramseyking.com

Mackie Research Capital Corp
110 Nineth Ave SW 9th Fl Calgary AB T2P0T1 403-218-6375
TF: 888-292-0980 ■ *Web:* secure.mackieresearch.com/jenningscapital.php

Maguire Investments Inc
1862 S Broadway Ste 100 Santa Maria CA 93454 805-922-6901
Web: www.maguireinvest.com

Mailender Inc 9500 Glades Dr Hamilton OH 45011 513-942-5453
TF: 800-998-5453 ■ *Web:* www.mailender.com

Manhattan Beach Trading Inc
1926 E Maple Ave El Segundo CA 90245 310-647-4281
Web: www.mbtrading.com

Marco Polo Securities Inc
30 Vesey St 14th Fl New York NY 10007 212-220-2700
Web: mpsecurities.com

Marquette Partners LP 801 W Adams Ste 500 Chicago IL 60607 312-224-2400
Web: www.marquettepartners.com

Memorial Investments Corp
110 The American Rd Morris Plains NJ 07950 973-538-2808

Mercator Asset Management LP
5200 Town Ctr Cir Boca Ctr Ste 550 Boca Raton FL 33486 561-361-1079
Web: www.mercatorasset.com

Mercury Marine Ltd 8698 Escarpment Way Milton ON L9T0M1 905-636-1705

Mercy Home Care & Medical Supplies Inc
2001 McDonald Ave Brooklyn NY 11223 718-376-3131
Web: www.mercymedsupplies.com

Meridian Capital LLC
1809 Seventh Ave Ste 1330 Seattle WA 98101 206-623-4000 623-8221
Web: www.meridianllc.com

Meridian Equity Partners Inc
40 Wall St Ste 1704 New York NY 10005 212-500-6650
Web: meptraders.com

Merrion Group LLC 210 Elmer St Westfield NJ 07090 908-654-0033
Web: www.merriongroup.net

Mesa Products Inc 4445 S 74th E Ave Tulsa OK 74145 918-627-3188
Web: www.mesaproducts.com

Mesirow Financial Inc 350 N Clark St Chicago IL 60610 312-595-6000 595-4246*
**Fax:* Hum Res ■ *TF:* 888-681-0082 ■ *Web:* www.mesirowfinancial.com

Millennium Management LLC 666 Fifth Ave New York NY 10103 212-841-4100
Web: www.mlp.com

MISA Metal Processing of Tennessee Inc
104 Western Dr Portland TN 37148 615-325-5454
Web: www.misa.com

Mizuho Securities USA 1251 Sixth Ave New York NY 10020 212-282-3000
Web: www.mizuhosecurities.com

MKM Partners LLC
300 First Stamford Pl E 4th Fl Stamford CT 06902 203-861-9060
Web: www.mkmpartners.com

MLV & Co 1300 N17th St Ste 1400 Arlington NY 22209 212-542-5880
Web: www.mlvco.com

Moag & Company LLC 323 W Camden St Ste 400 Baltimore MD 21201 410-230-0105
Web: www.moagandcompany.com

Phone Fax

Money Concepts International Inc
11440 N Jog Rd Palm Beach Gardens FL 33418 561-472-2000
Web: www.moneyconcepts.com

Montgomery Investment Management Inc
6229 Executive Blvd Rockville MD 20852 301-897-9783
Web: www.miminvest.com

Morgan Stanley 1585 Broadway New York NY 10036 212-761-4000
NYSE: MS ■ *TF General:* 800-223-2440 ■ *Web:* www.morganstanley.com

Morgan Stanley Investment Management
1221 Ave of the Americas 5th Fl New York NY 10020 212-296-6600 452-0390*
**Fax Area Code:* 646 ■ *TF General:* 800-223-2440 ■ *Web:* www.morganstanley.com/im

MS Howells & Co 20555 N Pima Rd Ste 100 Scottsdale AZ 85255 480-563-2000
Web: www.mshowells.com

Municipal Capital Markets Group Inc
4851 Lyndon B Johnson Fwy Ste 200 Dallas TX 75244 972-386-0200
Web: www.municapital.com

Murfie Inc 7 N Pinckney St Ste 300 Madison WI 53703 608-515-8180
Web: www.murfie.com

Muzinich & Company Inc 450 Park Ave New York NY 10022 212-888-3413
Web: www.muzinich.com

NASDAQ OMX Commodities Clearing Co
311 S Wacker Dr Ste 1750 Chicago IL 60606 312-568-5900

National Alliance Capital Markets
515 Congress Ave Ste 2410 Austin TX 78701 512-609-1700
Web: www.natalliance.com

National Commerce Bank Services Inc
80 Monroe Ave Ste 250 Memphis TN 38103 800-264-2609
TF: 800-264-2609 ■ *Web:* www.ncbs.com

National Securities Corp
410 Park Ave 14th Fl New York NY 10022 212-417-8000
TF: 800-742-7730 ■ *Web:* www.nationalsecurities.com

Natixis Securities Americas LLC
1251 Ave of the Americas New York NY 10020 212-891-6100
Web: www.blr.natixis.com

Needham & Co Inc 445 Pk Ave 3rd Fl New York NY 10022 212-371-8300 751-1450
TF: 800-903-3268 ■ *Web:* www.needhamco.com

Neidiger Tucker Bruner Inc
9540 S Maroon Cir Ste 250 Englewood CO 80112 303-825-1825
Web: www.ntbinc.com

New Century Capital Partners Inc
1510 11th St Ste 1100 Santa Monica CA 90401 310-451-9073
Web: www.newcenturycap.com

New England Capital Partners Inc
1 Gateway Ctr Ste 405 Newton MA 02458 617-964-7300 964-7301
Web: www.necapitalpartners.com

Newbridge Securities Corp
1451 W Cypress Creek Rd Fort Lauderdale FL 33309 954-334-3450
TF: 877-447-9625 ■ *Web:* www.newbridgefinancial.com

Newport CH International LLC
1100 W Town & Country Rd Ste 1388 Orange CA 92868 714-572-8881
Web: www.newportch.com

Newport Group Securities Inc
300 International Pkwy Ste 270 Heathrow FL 32746 407-333-2905
Web: felc.com

NexBank Securities Inc 13455 Noel Rd Ste 2240 Dallas TX 75240 972-308-6700
Web: nexbank.com

NEXT Financial Holdings Inc
2500 Wilcrest Dr Ste 620 Houston TX 77042 713-789-7122
Web: www.nextfinancialholdings.com

Nollenberger Capital Partners Inc
101 California St Ste 3100 San Francisco CA 94111 415-402-6000
Web: www.nollenbergercapital.com

Nomura Securities International Inc
2 World Financial Ctr Bldg B New York NY 10281 212-667-9300
Web: www.nomura.com

Northeast Capital & Advisory Inc
7 Airport Pk Blvd Latham NY 12110 518-426-0100 786-0105
Web: www.northeastcapital.net

Northern Industrial Sales Ltd
3526 Opie Cres Prince George BC V2N2P9 250-562-4435
TF: 800-668-3317 ■ *Web:* www.northernindustrialsales.ca

Northern Trust Securities
50 S La Salle St 12th Fl Chicago IL 60603 312-630-6000
Web: www.northerntrust.com

Northstar Financial Services Group LLC
17605 Wright St Omaha NE 68130 402-895-1600
Web: nstar-financial.com

Northwest Bank & Trust Co
100 E Kimberly Rd Davenport IA 52806 563-388-2511
Web: www.northwestbank.com

Novasel & Schwarte Investments Inc
3170 Hwy 50 Ste 10 South Lake Tahoe CA 96150 530-577-5050

NSK Canada Inc 5585 Mcadam Rd Mississauga ON L4Z1N4 905-890-0740 890-0434
Web: nskamericas.com

Nunami Services LLC 410 17th St Ste 570 Denver CO 80202 303-914-2819
Web: www.stockborrow.net

Nuveen Investments Inc 333 W Wacker Dr Chicago IL 60606 312-917-7700
TF: 800-257-8787 ■ *Web:* www.nuveen.com

NYLIFE Securities Inc 51 Madison Ave Rm 251 New York NY 10010 800-695-4785
TF: 800-695-4785 ■ *Web:* www.newyorklife.com

Oberweis Securities Inc
3333 Warrenville Rd Ste 500 Lisle IL 60532 630-577-2300 245-0467
Web: www.oberweis.net

Octagon Capital Corp
181 University Ave Ste 400 Toronto ON M5H3M7 416-368-3322

Odeon Capital Group LLC
750 Lexington Ave 27th Fl New York NY 10022 212-257-6970
Web: www.odeoncap.com

Office Products Recycling Assoc Inc
100 W 18th Ave North Kansas City MO 64116 816-584-1000
Web: www.oprausa.com

Open E Cry LLC 9482 Wedgewood Blvd Ste 150 Powell OH 43065 614-792-2690

Orizon Investment Counsel LLC
16924 Frances St Ste 200 Omaha NE 68130 402-330-7008
Web: hsmcorizon.com

Phone Fax

Oscar Gruss & Son Inc 55 E 59th st 15th Fl. New York NY 10022 212-419-4000 317-5907
Web: www.oscargruss.com
Pacific Crest Securities Inc
111 SW Fifth Ave 42nd Fl. Portland OR 97204 503-248-0721
TF: 800-314-9837 ■ *Web:* www.pacific-crest.com
Packaging Material Direct Inc
30405 Solon Rd Ste 9. Solon OH 44139 440-914-0530
Web: www.packagingsuppliesbymail.com
Paint Applicator Corp of America
7 Harbor Park Dr. Port Washington NY 11050 516-284-3000
Web: www.pacoa.com
Palladium Equity Partners LLC
1270 Ave of the Americas. New York NY 10020 212-218-5150
Web: www.palladiumequity.com
Pangaea Partners Ltd 1210 N Wfield Rd. Madison WI 53717 608-347-0192
Web: www.pangaeapartners.com
PAR Capital Management Inc
1 International Pl Ste 2401 Boston MA 02110 617-526-8990
Web: www.parcapital.com
ParaCap Group LLC
6150 Parkland Blvd
Ste 250 Mayfield Heights Cleveland OH 44124 440-869-2100
Parchman Vaughan & Co LLC
Symphony Ctr Ste 120 1040 Park Ave Baltimore MD 21201 410-244-8971
Web: www.parchmanvaughan.com
Park Hill Group LLC 345 Park Ave 15th Fl New York NY 10154 212-583-5799
Web: www.parkhillgroup.com
Parnassus Investments
1 Market St Steuart Tower Ste 1600 San Francisco CA 94105 415-778-0200
Web: www.parnassus.com
Patriot Flooring Supply Inc 110 Commerce Way Woburn MA 01801 866-444-4433
TF: 866-444-4433 ■ *Web:* www.patriothardwoodfloors.com
Paulson Investment Company Inc
811 SW Naito Pkwy Ste 200. Portland OR 97204 503-243-6000
Web: www.paulsoninvestment.com
PDI Financial Group 601 N Lynndale Dr Appleton WI 54914 920-739-2303 739-2205
TF: 800-234-7341 ■ *Web:* www.pdifinancial.com
Pennsylvania Trust Co
5 Radnor Corp Ctr Ste 450 Radnor PA 19087 610-975-4300 975-4324
TF: 800-975-4316 ■ *Web:* penntrust.com
Penso Capital Markets LLC 68 Carman Ave. Cedarhurst NY 11516 516-791-3800
Web: penso.com
People's Securities Inc 850 Main St Bridgeport CT 06601 203-338-0800 338-3087*
**Fax:* Cust Svc ■ *TF:* 800-772-4400 ■ *Web:* psi.peoples.com
Perimeter Financial Corp
2 Queen St E Ste 1800 Toronto ON M5C3G7 416-703-7800
Web: www.pfin.ca
PERMAC Securities Inc
285 Grand Ave Bldg No 3. Englewood NJ 07631 646-820-8732
Web: www.victorsecurities.com
Phillips & Company Securities Inc
1300 Sw Fifth Ave Ste 2100 Portland OR 97201 503-224-0858
TF: 800-572-4765 ■ *Web:* www.phillipsandco.com
Pico Quantitative Trading LLC
120 Wall St 16th Fl. New York NY 10005 646-701-6120
Web: www.picotrading.com
Pikes Peak Financial Consultants
1544 Shane Cir. Colorado Springs CO 80907 719-266-8890
Piper Jaffray Cos
800 Nicollet Mall Ste 800. Minneapolis MN 55402 612-303-6000 303-1309*
NYSE: PJC ■ **Fax:* PR ■ *TF:* 800-333-6000 ■ *Web:* www.piperjaffray.com
Pita Communications LLC 40 Cold Spring Rd Rocky Hill CT 06067 860-293-0157
Web: www.pitacomm.com
Planesmart! Aviation LLC
Addison Airport 15841 Addison Rd Addison TX 75001 972-380-8004
TF: 888-228-4283 ■ *Web:* www.planesmart.com
Pointe Capital LLC 501 E Kennedy Blvd Ste 1400 Tampa FL 33602 813-202-7960
PolySource LLC 1003 Industrial Dr. Pleasant Hill MO 64080 816-540-5300
Web: www.polysource.net
Precision IBC Inc 8054 Mcgowin Dr Fairhope AL 36532 251-990-6789
TF: 800-544-7069 ■ *Web:* www.precisionibc.com
PRICE Futures Group Inc, The
141 W Jackson Blvd Ste 1340A Chicago IL 60604 312-264-4300
Web: www.pricegroup.com
Prime Capital Services Inc
11 Raymond Ave. Poughkeepsie NY 12603 845-485-3338
Web: www.primefs.com
Professional Sales & Service LC
3545 West 1500 South Salt Lake City UT 84104 801-977-3961
Web: pro-sales.com
Quality Oil Inc 55 N 400 E. Valparaiso IN 46383 219-462-2951
Questar Capital Corp
5701 Golden Hills Dr Minneapolis MN 55416 888-446-5872
TF: 888-446-5872 ■ *Web:* www.questarcapital.com
R Seelaus & Company Inc
25 Deforest Ave Ste 304 Summit NJ 07901 800-922-0584
TF: 800-922-0584 ■ *Web:* www.rseelaus.com
Radius Partners LLC 360 N Main St Ste 3104 Andover MA 01810 203-557-3845
Web: www.radiuspartnersllc.com
Raymond James Financial Inc
880 Carillon Pkwy Saint Petersburg FL 33716 727-567-1000 573-8622*
NYSE: RJF ■ **Fax:* Cust Svc ■ *TF:* 800-248-8863 ■ *Web:* www.raymondjames.com
RBC Capital Markets
155 Wellington St W 17th Fl. Toronto ON M5V3K7 416-842-3517
Web: www.rbcds.com
RBC Capital Markets 1 Liberty Plaza New York NY 10006 212-428-6200 428-6200*
**Fax:* Hum Res ■ *TF:* 800-387-1122 ■ *Web:* www.rbccm.com
RBC Dain Rauscher Inc
60 S Sixth St Dain Rauscher Plz. Minneapolis MN 55402 800-933-9946
TF: 800-933-9946 ■ *Web:* www.rbcwm-usa.com
RCI Capital Group Inc
1055 Dunsmuir St Ste 2184 Vancouver BC V7X1L3 604-689-0881
Web: www.rcicapitalgroup.com

Phone Fax

Reams Asset Management Company LLC
227 Washington St Columbus IN 47202 812-372-6606
Web: www.reamsasset.com
Redwood Capital Group LLC
885 Third Ave Ste 2500 New York NY 10022 212-508-7100
Web: www.redcapgroup.com
Regal Discount Securities Inc
950 Milwaukee Ave Ste 102 Glenview IL 60025 847-375-6024
Web: www.eregal.com
Renaissance Technologies Corp 800 Third Ave New York NY 10022 212-486-6780
Web: www.rentec.com
Residex LLC 248 Cox St. Roselle NJ 07203 908-272-4383
Web: www.residex.com
Reva Capital Markets LLC 45 Broadway 8th Fl. New York NY 10025 212-464-7363
Web: www.revacap.com
Rice Financial Products Co
55 Broad St 27th Fl. New York NY 10004 212-908-9200 908-9299
Web: www.ricefinancialproducts.com
RM Burritt Motors Inc 340 Rt 104 E Oswego NY 13126 315-343-8948
Web: www.burrittchevy.com
Robert W Baird & Company Inc PO Box 672 Milwaukee WI 53201 414-765-3500
TF: 800-792-2473 ■ *Web:* www.rwbaird.com
Roberts Mitani LLC 145 W 57th St 21st Fl. New York NY 10019 212-582-9800
Web: www.robertsmitani.com
Rockwell Automation Canada Inc
135 Dundas St Cambridge ON N1R5N9 519-623-1810 740-9871
Web: www.rockwellautomation.com/en_na/overview.page
Roehl & Yi Investment Advisors LLC
450 Country Club Rd Ste 160. Eugene OR 97401 541-683-2085
TF: 888-683-4343 ■ *Web:* roehl-yi.com
Roger a Soape Inc 450 Gears Rd Ste 780. Houston TX 77067 281-440-6347
Web: www.rasoape.com
Roosevelt & Cross Inc
1 Exchange Plz 55 Broadway 22nd Fl. New York NY 10006 212-344-2500
TF: 800-348-3426 ■ *Web:* www.roosevelt-cross.com
Ross Sinclaire & Associates LLC
700 Walnut St Ste 600 Cincinnati OH 45202 513-381-3939
Web: www.rsanet.com
Royal Alliance Assoc Inc
1 World Financial Ctr 14th Fl New York NY 10281 800-821-5100
TF: 800-821-5100 ■ *Web:* www.royalalliance.com
Royal Securities Co
4095 Chicago Dr SW Ste 120. Grandville MI 49418 616-538-2550 538-3360
TF: 800-421-3518 ■ *Web:* investwithjw.com
Rutberg & Company LLC
351 California St Ste 1100 San Francisco CA 94104 415-371-1186 371-1187
Web: www.rutbergco.com
SagePoint Financial Inc
2800 N Central Ave Ste 2100 Phoenix AZ 85004 800-552-3319
TF: 800-552-3319 ■ *Web:* www.sagepointfinancial.com
Salman Partners Inc
1095 W Pender St 17th Fl. Vancouver BC V6E2M6 604-685-2450
Web: www.salmanpartners.com
Samuel A Ramirez & Co Inc
61 Broadway Ste 2924 New York NY 10006 800-888-4086 248-0528*
**Fax Area Code:* 212 ■ *TF:* 800-888-4086 ■ *Web:* www.ramirezco.com
Sandler O'Neill + Partners LP
1251 Avenue of the Americas 6th Fl New York NY 10020 212-466-7800
TF: 800-635-6851 ■ *Web:* www.sandleroneill.com
Sands Brothers Asset Management
15 Valley Dr Greenwich CT 06831 203-661-7500
Web: www.sandsbros.com
Schroder Investment Management North America Inc (SIMNA)
875 Third Ave 22nd Fl New York NY 10022 800-730-2932 632-2954*
**Fax Area Code:* 212 ■ *TF:* 800-730-2932 ■ *Web:* www.schroders.com/us
Schroder US Holdings Inc 875 Third Ave New York NY 10022 212-641-3830
Web: www.schroders.com/en/us
Schwabe & Assoc Inc 8525 SW 92nd St Ste B6 Miami FL 33156 305-270-1990
Scotia Capital Markets 1 Liberty Plz New York NY 10006 212-225-5000 225-5090
TF: 877-294-3435 ■ *Web:* www.gbm.scotiabank.com
Scotttrade 8205 E Regal Ct Tulsa OK 74133 918-369-4333
Web: www.scottrade.com
Seasongood & Mayer LLC
414 Walnut St Ste 300 Cincinnati OH 45202 513-621-0580
Web: www.rbccm.com
Securities Center Inc, The 245 E St. Chula Vista CA 91910 619-426-3550
TF: 800-244-1718 ■ *Web:* www.securitiescenter.com
Securities Service Network Inc
9729 Cogdill Rd Ste 301 Knoxville TN 37932 866-843-4635
TF: 866-843-4635 ■ *Web:* www.ssnetwork.com
Seer Capital Management LP
1177 Ave of the Americas 34th Fl. New York NY 10036 212-850-9000
Web: seercap.com
Seidel & Shaw LLC 40 Exchange Pl New York NY 10005 212-269-9008
Sentinel Brokers Company Inc
20 Broadway Ste 1 Massapequa NY 11758 516-541-9100
SFE Investment Counsel Inc
801 S Figueroa St Ste 2100 Los Angeles CA 90017 213-612-0220
TF: 800-445-6320 ■ *Web:* www.sfeic.com
Shank Wealth Management LLC
2627 Chestnut Ridge Dr Ste 110 Kingwood TX 77339 281-359-3133
TF: 888-359-3133 ■ *Web:* shankwm.com
Shay Financial Services Inc
1000 Brickell Ave Ste 500. Miami FL 33131 305-379-6656
Web: www.shay.com
Shorcan Brokers Ltd 20 Adelaide St E Ste 1000 Toronto ON M5C2T6 416-360-2500
Web: www.shorcan.com
Shore Morgan Young
300 W Wilson Bridge Rd Worthington OH 43085 614-888-2117
TF: 800-288-2117 ■ *Web:* shoremorganyoung.com
Siebert Brandford Shank & Co LLC
100 Wall St 18th Fl. New York NY 10005 646-775-4850 576-9680
TF: 800-334-6800 ■ *Web:* www.sbsco.com
Sigma Financial Corp 300 Parkland Plz. Ann Arbor MI 48103 734-663-1611
Web: www.sigmafinancial.com

Company	City	State	Zip	Phone	Fax
SII Investments Inc 5555 W Grande Market Dr *Web:* www.siionline.com	Appleton	WI	54913	920-996-2600	
Silver Legacy Capital Corp 407 N Virginia St *TF:* 800-687-8733	Reno	NV	89501	800-687-8733	
Silverwood Partners LLC Silverwood Farm Pl 32 Pleasant St *Web:* www.silverwoodpartners.com	Sherborn	MA	01770	508-651-2194	
SMITH HAYES Financial Services Corp 1225 L St Ste 200 *Web:* www.smithhayes.com	Lincoln	NE	68508	402-476-3000	
South Street Securities LLC 825 Third Ave 35th Fl *Web:* www.southstreetsecurities.com	New York	NY	10022	212-824-0738	
Spartan Securities Group Ltd 15500 Roosevelt Blvd Ste 303 *Web:* www.spartansecurities.com	Clearwater	FL	33760	727-502-0508	
Spence Asset Management Inc 2455 E Missouri Ave Ste C *Web:* spenceassetmanagement.com	Las Cruces	NM	88001	575-556-8500	
Spencer Clarke LLC 40 Wall St Ste 1704 *Web:* www.spencerclarke.com	New York	NY	10005	212-446-6100	
SSI Investment Management Inc 9440 Santa Monica Blvd 8th Fl *Web:* www.ssi-invest.com	Beverly Hills	CA	90210	310-595-2000	
Standard Investment Chartered Inc 2801 Bristol St Ste 100 *Web:* www.standardinvestment.com	Costa Mesa	CA	92626	714-444-4300	
Starshak Winzenburg & Co 55 W Monroe St Ste 2530 *Web:* www.swandco.com	Chicago	IL	60603	312-444-9367	444-9519
Stephens Inc 111 Ctr St **Fax:* Mail Rm ■ *TF:* 800-643-9691 ■ *Web:* www.stephens.com	Little Rock	AR	72201	501-377-2000	377-2470*
Stern Brothers & Co 8000 Maryland Ave Ste 800 *Web:* www.sternbrothers.com	St. Louis	MO	63105	314-743-4005	
Sterne Agee & Leach Inc 800 Shades Creek Pkwy Ste 700 *TF:* 800-240-1438 ■ *Web:* www.sterneagee.com	Birmingham	AL	35209	205-949-3500	949-3607
Stifel Financial Corp 501 N Broadway *NYSE: SF* ■ *TF:* 800-679-5446 ■ *Web:* www.stifel.com	Saint Louis	MO	63102	800-679-5446	
Stifel Nicolaus & Co Inc 501 N Broadway *TF:* 800-679-5446 ■ *Web:* www.stifel.com	Saint Louis	MO	63102	314-342-2000	342-2151
Stock USA Investments Inc 1717 Rt 6 *Web:* www.speedtrader.com	Carmel	NY	10512	845-225-5132	
Stonegate Securities Inc 5950 Sherry Ln Ste 410 *Web:* www.stonegateinc.com	Dallas	TX	75225	214-987-4121	
Stonehenge Partners Inc 191 W Nationwide Blvd Ste 600 *TF:* 877-298-4409 ■ *Web:* www.stonehengepartners.com	Columbus	OH	43215	614-246-2500	
StormHarbour Securities LP 140 E 45th St Two Grand Central Tower 33rd Fl *Web:* www.stormharbour.com	New York	NY	10017	212-905-2500	
Success Trade Securities Inc 1900 L St N W Ste 525 *Web:* www.successtrade.com	Washington	DC	20036	202-466-6890	
Summer Street Capital Partners LLC 70 W Chippewa St Ste 500 *Web:* www.summerstreetcapital.com	Buffalo	NY	14202	716-566-2900	
Sunbelt Securities Inc 5065 Westheimer Ste 600 *Web:* www.sunbeltsecurities.com	Houston	TX	77056	713-965-9510	
SunTrust Robinson Humphrey Capital Markets 3333 Peachtree Rd NE *TF:* 800-634-7928 ■ *Web:* www.suntrustrh.com	Atlanta	GA	30326	404-926-5000	
SURFACExchange LLC 37 Brookside Dr *Web:* www.surfacexchange.com	Greenwich	CT	06830	203-987-6900	
Susquehanna International Group LLP 401 City Ave Ste 220 *Web:* www.sig.com	Bala Cynwyd	PA	19004	610-617-2600	
Sutter Securities Inc 220 Montgomery St Ste 1700 *Web:* www.suttersecurities.com	San Francisco	CA	94104	415-352-6300	
SWS Financial Services Inc 1201 Elm St Ste 3500 *Web:* www.burfordadvisors.com	Dallas	TX	75270	214-859-1800	
Symphony Asset Management Inc 555 California St *Web:* www.symphonyasset.com	San Francisco	CA	94104	415-676-4000	
Symphony Capital LLC 880 Third Ave 12th Fl *Web:* www.symphonycapital.com	New York	NY	10022	212-632-5400	632-5401
Synergy Advisors LLC 840 Apollo St Ste 213 *Web:* www.synergyadvisorsllc.com	El Segundo	CA	90245	310-414-3200	
Tano Capital LLC 1 Franklin Pkwy Bldg 970 2nd Fl *Web:* www.tanocapital.com	San Mateo	CA	94403	650-212-0330	
Tejas Inc 8226 Bee Caves Rd *Web:* www.tejassec.com	Austin	TX	78746	512-306-8222	306-1348
Thornhill Securities Inc 336 S Congress Ave Ste 200 *Web:* www.thornhillsecurities.com	Austin	TX	78704	512-472-7171	478-2616
TimeCapital Securities Corp 1 Roosevelt Ave *Web:* www.timecapital.com	Port Jefferson Station	NY	11776	631-331-1400	
Tocco Financial Services Inc 6236 E Pima Ste 190 *TF:* 877-881-1149 ■ *Web:* toccofinancial.com	Tucson	AZ	85712	520-881-1149	
Toll Cross Securities Inc Ste 200 1 Toronto St	Toronto	ON	M5C2V6	416-365-1960	
Topeka Capital Markets Inc 40 Wall St Ste 1702 *Web:* www.topekacapitalmarkets.com	New York	NY	10005	212-709-5701	
TradeHelm Inc 20 N Wacker Dr Ste 3550 *Web:* www.tradehelm.com	Chicago	IL	60606	918-561-6900	

Company	City	State	Zip	Phone	Fax
Tradelink Securities LLC 71 S Wacker Dr Ste 1900 *Web:* www.tradelinkllc.com	Chicago	IL	60606	312-264-2000	
Trader's Library LLC 6310 Stevens Forest Rd Ste 200 *Web:* www.traderslibrary.com	Columbia	MD	21046	410-964-0026	
TradeStation Group Inc 8050 SW Tenth St Ste 2000 *TF:* 800-871-3577 ■ *Web:* www.tradestation.com	Plantation	FL	33324	954-652-7000	652-7300
Trading Direct 160 Broadway E Bldg 7th Fl *TF:* 800-925-8566 ■ *Web:* www.tradingdirect.com	New York	NY	10038	212-766-0230	766-0914
TradingMarkets.com Inc 10 Exchange Pl Ste 1800 *Web:* www.tradingmarkets.com	Jersey City	NJ	07302	213-955-5858	
Tradition Asiel Securities Inc 75 Park Pl 4th Fl *Web:* www.tradition-na.com	New York	NY	10007	212-791-4500	
TranscriptionGear Inc 7280 Auburn Rd *Web:* www.transcriptiongear.com	Concord	OH	44077	440-392-9882	
Trefethen Advisors LLC 6710 E Camelback Rd Ste 100 *Web:* www.trefethenadvisors.com	Scottsdale	AZ	85251	480-922-9966	
Triton Capital Partners Ltd 566 W Lake St Ste 235 *Web:* www.tritoncap.com	Chicago	IL	60661	312-575-0190	
Trubee Collins & Company Inc 1350 One M & T Plz *Web:* www.trubeecollins.com	Buffalo	NY	14203	716-849-1401	
trueEX Group LLC 162 Fifth Ave *Web:* www.trueex.com	New York	NY	10010	646-786-8520	
Trumaker Inc 701 Sutter St Fl 5 *TF:* 855-623-3878 ■ *Web:* www.trumaker.com	San Francisco	CA	94109	855-623-3878	
TVC Capital LLC 11452 El Camino Real Ste 450 *Web:* www.tvccapital.com	San Diego	CA	92130	858-704-3261	
Twenty-First Securities Corp 780 Third Ave *Web:* www.twenty-first.com	New York	NY	10017	212-418-6000	
Two Sigma Investments LLC 100 Ave of the Americas 16th Fl *Web:* www.twosigma.com	New York	NY	10013	212-625-5700	
UBS Financial Services Inc 1285 Ave of the Americas *TF:* 800-221-3260 ■ *Web:* financialservicesinc.ubs.com	New York	NY	10019	212-713-2000	
UBS Warburg LLC 677 Washington Blvd *TF:* 800-221-3260 ■ *Web:* www.ubs.com	Stamford	CT	06901	203-719-3000	
Ulivi Wealth 369 S Glassell St *Web:* www.ulivi.com	Orange	CA	92866	714-771-6000	
Union Securities Ltd 700 W Georgia St Ste 900 *Web:* www.union-securities.com	Vancouver	BC	V7Y1H4	604-687-2201	
Vanguard Brokerage Services PO Box 1110 *TF:* 800-992-8327 ■ *Web:* investor.vanguard.com	Valley Forge	PA	19482	610-669-1000	669-6366
Veris Wealth Partners LLC 17 State St Ste 2450 *Web:* www.veriswp.com	New York	NY	10004	212-349-4172	
Veronis Suhler Stevenson (VSS) 55 E 52nd St 33rd Fl *Web:* www.vss.com	New York	NY	10055	212-935-4990	381-8168
vFinance Inc 1200 N Federal Hwy Ste 400 *Web:* www.vfinanceinvestments.com	Boca Raton	FL	33432	561-981-1000	
ViewTrade Securities Inc 525 Washington Blvd 24th Fl *Web:* www.viewtrade.com	Jersey City	NJ	07310	201-215-9850	
Vining Sparks IBG LP 775 Ridge Lk Blvd *Web:* www.viningsparks.com	Memphis	TN	38120	901-766-3000	
Virtual Brokers 4100 Yonge St Ste 415 *Web:* www.virtualbrokers.com	Toronto	ON	M2P2B5	416-288-8028	
Wachtel & Company Inc 1101 14th St NW Eigth Fl Ste 800 *Web:* www.wachtelco.com	Washington	DC	20005	202-898-1144	
Wallace Financial Group Inc 4390 Earney Rd *Web:* lpl.com	Woodstock	GA	30188	770-751-7411	
WallachBeth Capital LLC 100 Wall St Ste 6600 *Web:* www.wallachbeth.com	New York	NY	10005	646-237-8585	
Warbros Venture Partners PO Box 1033 *Web:* www.warbros.com	Westerly	RI	02891	401-596-8960	
Wayne Hummer Investments LLC 222 S Riverside Pz 28th Fl *TF:* 800-621-4477 ■ *Web:* www.wintrustwealth.com	Chicago	IL	60606	866-943-4732	
Wesbild Holdings Ltd 666 Burrard St Park Pl Ste 2650 *Web:* www.wesbild.com	Vancouver	BC	V6C2X8	604-694-8800	
Western International Securities Inc 70 S Lake Ave Ste 700 *TF:* 888-793-7717 ■ *Web:* www.wisdirect.com	Pasadena	CA	91101	888-793-7717	
WestPark Capital Inc 1900 Ave of the Stars Ste 310 *Web:* www.wpcapital.com	Los Angeles	CA	90067	310-843-9300	
William Blair & Company LLC 222 W Adams St *TF:* 800-621-0687 ■ *Web:* www.williamblair.com	Chicago	IL	60606	312-236-1600	236-1875
Wilson-Davis & Company Inc 236 South Main *Web:* www.wdco.com	Salt Lake City	UT	84101	801-532-1313	
Winetasting Network, The 578 Gateway Dr *TF:* 800-435-2225 ■ *Web:* www.winetasting.com	Napa	CA	94558	800-435-2225	
Wm Sword & Co Inc 90 Nassau St *Web:* swordrowe.com	Princeton	NJ	08542	609-924-6710	
Wolfe & Hurst Bond Brokers Inc 30 Montgomery St Ste 1040 *Web:* www.wolfehurstbbi.com	Jersey City	NJ	07302	201-938-0400	
Wolverton Securities Ltd 777 Dunsmuir St 17th Fl *TF:* 877-390-7771 ■ *Web:* www.wolverton.ca	Vancouver	BC	V7Y1J5	604-622-1000	

	City	State	ZIP	Phone	Fax
World Equity Group 1650 N Arlington Heights Rd Ste 100 *Web:* www.worldequitygroup.com	Arlington Heights	IL	60004	847-342-1700	
WR Hambrecht & Co 909 Montgomery St 3rd Fl *TF Cust Svc:* 855-753-6484 ■ *Web:* www.wrhambrecht.com	San Francisco	CA	94133	415-551-8600	
Wunderlich Securities Inc 6000 Poplar Ave Ste 150 *Web:* www.wunderlichsecurities.com	Memphis	TN	38119	901-251-1330	
Wyser-Pratte Management Company Inc 504 Guard Hill Rd *Web:* www.wyser-pratte.com	Bedford	NY	10506	914-234-4930	
Xpert Financial Inc 1825 S Grant St Ste 200 *Web:* www.xpertfinancial.com	San Mateo	CA	94402	650-212-1535	
Yellow Point Equity Partners LP 1285 W Pender St Ste 1000 *Web:* www.ypoint.ca	Vancouver	BC	V6E4B1	604-659-1898	
Ziegler Capital Markets Investment Services 200 S Wacker *Web:* ziegler.com	Chicago	IL	60606	414-978-6400	

691 SECURITIES & COMMODITIES EXCHANGES

	City	State	ZIP	Phone	Fax
Able Global Partners LLC 641 Lexington Ave 15th Fl *Web:* www.ableglobalps.com	New York	NY	10022	212-581-7011	
Accelon Capital 2470 El Camino Real Ste 210 *Web:* www.acceloncapital.com	Palo Alto	CA	94306	650-213-8353	
Advanced Equities Financial Corp 311 S Wacker Dr Ste 1650 *Web:* www.advancedequities.com	Chicago	IL	60606	312-377-5300	
Alinian Capital Group LLC 3343 W Commercial Blvd Ste 103 *Web:* www.alinian.com	Fort Lauderdale	FL	33309	954-495-2040	
Arcady Bay Partners LLC 40417 Aldie Springs Dr *Web:* www.arcadybay.com	Aldie	VA	20105	703-359-4773	
AtlasBanc Holdings Corp 301 S Missouri Ave *Web:* www.atlasbanc.com	Clearwater	FL	33756	727-446-6660	
Axial Inc 45 E 20th St 12th Fl *TF:* 800-860-4519 ■ *Web:* www.axial.net	New York	NY	10003	800-860-4519	
Bats Trading Inc 8050 Marshall Dr Ste 120 *Web:* www.batstrading.com	Lenexa	KS	66214	913-815-7000	
BizXchange Inc 3600 136th Pl SE Ste 270 *Web:* www.bizx.com	Bellevue	WA	98006	425-998-5055	
Border Gold Corp 15234 N Bluff Rd *TF:* 888-312-2288 ■ *Web:* www.bordergold.com	White Rock	BC	V4B3E6	604-535-3287	
Bulltick Capital Markets Holdings LLC 701 Brickell Ave Ste 2550 *Web:* www.bulltick.com	Miami	FL	33131	305-533-1541	
Cape Securities Inc 2005 Pennsylvania Ave *Web:* www.capesecurities.com	Mcdonough	GA	30253	678-583-1120	
Capital Growth Planning Inc 405 E Lexington Ave Ste 201 *Web:* www.capplan.com	El Cajon	CA	92020	619-440-7023	
Capital Guardian Holding LLC 1355 Greenwood Cliff Ste 250 *Web:* www.capitalguardianllc.com	Charlotte	NC	28204	704-705-1860	
CBOE Stock Exchange LLC 400 S LaSalle St *Web:* www.cboe.com/aboutcboe/legal/cbsx-regulatory.aspx	Chicago	IL	60605	312-786-7449	
Cedar Ventures LLC 2870 Peachtree Rd Ste 493 *Web:* cedarventures.com	Atlanta	GA	30305	404-239-8416	
Ceia USA Ltd 9155 Dutton Dr *Web:* www.ceia-usa.com	Twinsburg	OH	44087	330-405-3190	
Chapin Davis Investments 2 Village Sq Ste 200 *Web:* www.chapindavis.com	Baltimore	MD	21210	410-435-3200	
Chicago Board Options Exchange (CBOE) 400 S La Salle St *TF:* 800-678-4667 ■ *Web:* www.cboe.com	Chicago	IL	60605	312-786-5600	786-8818
Chicago Stock Exchange 440 S LaSalle St *Web:* chx.com	Chicago	IL	60605	312-663-2222	663-2721
CME Group Inc 20 S Wacker Dr *NASDAQ: CME* ■ *TF:* 866-716-7274 ■ *Web:* www.cmegroup.com	Chicago	IL	60606	312-930-1000	466-4410
Coker & Palmer Inc 1667 Lelia Dr *Web:* www.cokerpalmer.com	Jackson	MS	39216	601-354-0860	
Convergent Wealth Advisors LLC 12505 Park Potomac Ave Ste 400 *TF:* 888-444-6347 ■ *Web:* www.convergentwealth.com	Potomac	MD	20854	301-770-6300	
Culver Capital Group Inc 1600 Sunflower Ave Ste 120 *Web:* www.culvercapital.com	Costa Mesa	CA	92626	714-380-3000	
DN Partners LLC 180 N LaSalle St Ste 2630 *Web:* www.dnpartners.com	Chicago	IL	60601	312-332-7960	
England & Company LLC 888 17th St NW Ste 304 *Web:* www.englandco.com	Washington	DC	20006	202-386-6500	
Eris Exchange LLC 311 S Wacker Dr Ste 950 *Web:* www.erisfutures.com	Chicago	IL	60606	212-561-5472	
Farmington Capital Partners PO Box 1461 *Web:* www.farmingtoncapital.com	Hartford	CT	06144	860-284-1096	
FIRMA Foreign Exchange Corp 10205 101 St Edmonton City Ctr E Ste 400 *Web:* www.firmafx.com	Edmonton	AB	T5J4H5	780-426-4946	
FMA Advisory Inc 1631 N Front St *Web:* fma-advisory.com	Harrisburg	PA	17102	717-232-8850	
G2 Investment Group LLC 142 W 57th St 12th Fl *Web:* www.g2investmentgroup.com	New York	NY	10019	212-887-1150	
Geneva Trading USA LLC 190 S Lasalle St Ste 1800 *Web:* www.geneva-trading.com	Chicago	IL	60603	312-587-7000	
Granite Tower Capital 324 Traders Blvd E *Web:* www.granitetowercapital.com	Mississauga	ON	L4Z1W7	905-366-2551	
Ice Futures 1 N End Ave 13th Fl *Web:* www.theice.com	New York	NY	10282	212-748-4000	
Impetus Capital LLC 145 W 57th St 16 Fl *Web:* www.impetuscapital.com	New York	NY	10019	212-258-2782	
IPC Securities Corp 2680 Skymark Ave Ste 700 *TF:* 877-212-9799 ■ *Web:* www.ipcsecurities.com	Mississauga	ON	L4W5L6	905-212-9788	
JDB Capital Partners LLC 20645 N Pima Rd Ste 110 *Web:* www.jdbcapital.com	Scottsdale	AZ	85255	480-502-9200	
Jitney Trade Inc 360 St-Jacques St W Ste S-118 *Web:* www.jitneytrade.com	Montreal	QC	H2Y1P5	514-985-8080	
Kansas City Board of Trade 4800 Main St Ste 303 *Web:* www.cmegroup.com	Kansas City	MO	64112	816-753-7500	753-3944
KeyImpact Sales & Systems Inc 1701 Crossroads Dr *Web:* www.kisales.com	Odenton	MD	21113	410-381-1239	
Lazear Capital Partners Ltd 401 N Front St Ste 350 *Web:* www.lazearcapital.com	Columbus	OH	43215	614-221-1616	
Linch Capital LLC 3384 Peachtree Rd NW Ste 575 *Web:* www.linchcapital.com	Atlanta	GA	30326	404-334-7047	
Lucent Capital Inc 9454 Wilshire Blvd Ste 525 *Web:* www.lucentcapital.com	Beverly Hills	CA	90212	310-876-8454	
M3 Capital Partners 150 S Wacker Dr 31st Fl *Web:* www.mcp-llc.com	Chicago	IL	60606	312-499-8500	
MAM Global Financial Services 16161 Ventura Blvd *Web:* www.mamgfs.com	Encino	CA	91436	818-784-8752	
Manulife Securities Inc 500-1235 N Service Rd W *Web:* www.manulife.ca/wps/portal/site/manulifesecurities/home	Oakville	ON	L6M2W2	905-469-2100	
Market Street Consulting Group Inc 6965 El Camino Real Ste 105599 **Fax Area Code:* 888 ■ *Web:* www.marketstreetfs.com	Carlsbad	CA	92009	760-518-2310	621-5904*
MAS Capital Inc 2715 Coney Island Ave *TF:* 866-553-7493 ■ *Web:* www.mascapital.com	Brooklyn	NY	11235	866-553-7493	
MBF Clearing Corp 1 N End Ave World Financial Ctr Ste 1201 *Web:* www.mbfcc.com	New York	NY	10282	212-845-5000	
Milestone Partners LLC 6047 Tyvola Glen Cir *Web:* www.milestonex.com	Charlotte	NC	28217	704-414-6532	
Minneapolis Grain Exchange 400 S Fourth St 130 Grain Exchange Bldg *TF:* 800-827-4746 ■ *Web:* www.mgex.com	Minneapolis	MN	55415	612-321-7101	339-1155
Montreal Exchange 800 Victoria Sq Third Fl PO Box 61 *TF:* 800-361-5353 ■ *Web:* www.m-x.ca	Montreal	QC	H4Z1A9	514-871-2424	
MSB Fairway Capital Partners 1800 St James Pl Ste 450 *Web:* www.msbfairway.com	Houston	TX	77056	713-622-9961	
Nasdaq Stock Market Inc 165 Broadway *Web:* www.nasdaq.com	New York	NY	10006	212-401-8700	
National Stock Exchange (NSX) 101 Hudson St Ste 1200 *TF:* 800-843-3924 ■ *Web:* www.nsx.com	Jersey City	NJ	07302	201-499-3700	
Nations Financial Group Inc 4000 River Ridge Dr NE PO Box 908 *Web:* www.nationsfg.com	Cedar Rapids	IA	52406	319-393-9541	
NMS Capital Group LLC 433 N Camden Dr 4th Fl *TF:* 800-716-2080 ■ *Web:* nmscapital.com	Beverly Hills	CA	90210	800-716-2080	
NYSE Arce 115 Samsone St *TF:* 877-729-7291 ■ *Web:* www.nyse.com	San Francisco	CA	94104	877-729-7291	
NYSE Euronext 11 Wall St *NYSE: NYX* ■ *TF:* 866-873-7422 ■ *Web:* www.nyse.com	New York	NY	10005	212-656-3000	656-2126
Oliver Capital Partners Inc 102 3016 Fifth Ave NE *Web:* www.olcapa.com	Calgary	AB	T2A6K4	403-313-4645	
Partnership Capital Growth Advisors 1 Embarcadero Ctr PO Box 7 *Web:* www.pcg-investors.com	Los Gatos	CA	95031	415-705-8008	
Pavilion Financial Corp 1001 Corydon Ave Ste 300 *TF:* 866-954-5101 ■ *Web:* www.pavilioncorp.com	Winnipeg	MB	R3M0B6	204-954-5101	
Pelion Financial Group Inc 369 Lexington Ave Ste 311 *Web:* www.peliongroup.com	New York	NY	10017	917-639-5450	
ProFutures Inc 11719 Bee Cave Rd Ste 200 *Web:* www.profutures.com	Austin	TX	78738	512-263-3800	
RainMaker Securities LLC 500 N Michigan Ave Ste 600 *Web:* www.rainmakersecurities.com	Chicago	IL	60611	312-254-5048	
Raymond James (USA) Ltd 2200 - 925 W Georgia St *TF:* 877-570-7558 ■ *Web:* www.rjlu.com	Vancouver	BC	V6C3L2	877-570-7558	
Sprott Global Resource Investments Ltd 1910 Palomar Point Way Ste 200 *TF:* 800-477-7853 ■ *Web:* www.sprottglobal.com	Carlsbad	CA	92008	800-477-7853	
Stone Key Group LLC 411 W Putnam Ave Ste 110 *Web:* www.stonekey.com	Greenwich	CT	06830	203-930-3700	
TerraPass Inc 527 Howard St 4th Fl *Web:* www.terrapass.com	San Francisco	CA	94105	415-692-3411	

	Phone	Fax
Tigress Financial Partners LLC 500 Fifth Ave 15th Fl New York NY 10036 *Web:* www.tigressfp.com	212-430-8700	
Timucuan Asset Management Inc 200 W Forsyth St Ste 1600 Jacksonville FL 32202 *Web:* www.timucuan.com	904-356-1739	
Toronto Stock Exchange 130 King St W Toronto ON M5X1J2 *TF:* 888-873-8392 ■ *Web:* www.tmx.com	416-947-4670	947-4662
Trade Exchange of America 23200 Coolidge Hwy Oak Park MI 48237 *Web:* www.tradefirst.com	248-544-1350	
Unified Financial Services Inc 2353 Alexandria Dr Lexington KY 40504 *Web:* www.unified.com	859-422-0347	
VectorGlobal WMG Inc 801 Brickell Ave Ste 2500 (PH1) Miami FL 33131 *Web:* www.vectorglobalwmg.com	305-350-3350	
Wall Street Financial Group Inc 255 Woodcliff Dr Fairport NY 14450 *Web:* www.wsfg.com	585-267-8000	
Williams Financial Group Inc 2711 N Haskell Ave Cityplace Tower Ste 2900 Dallas TX 75204 *Web:* www.williams-financial.com	972-661-8700	
Wilmington Capital Securities LLC 600 Old Country Rd Ste 200 Garden City NY 11530 *Web:* wilmingtoncap.com	516-750-6200	
World Currency USA Inc 16 W Main St Marlton NJ 08053 *TF:* 888-593-7927 ■ *Web:* www.worldcurrencyusa.com	888-593-7927	

692 SECURITY PRODUCTS & SERVICES

See Also Audio & Video Equipment p. 1816; Fire Protection Systems p. 2285; Signals & Sirens - Electric p. 3185

	Phone	Fax
3M 639 N Rosemead Blvd Pasadena CA 91107 *Web:* www.cogentsystems.com	626-325-9600	
ADS Security LP 3001 Armory Dr Ste 100 Nashville TN 37204 *TF:* 800-448-8652 ■ *Web:* www.adsalarms.com	800-448-8652	
ADT Security Services Inc 14200 E Exposition Ave Aurora CO 80012 *TF:* 800-238-2455 ■ *Web:* www.adt.com	800-238-2455	
Advantor Systems Corp 12612 Challenger Pkwy Ste 300 Orlando FL 32809 **Fax:* Sales ■ *TF:* 800-238-2686 ■ *Web:* www.advantor.com	407-859-3350	857-1635*
AFA Protective Systems Inc 155 Michael Dr Syosset NY 11791 *OTC: AFAP* ■ *Web:* afap.com	516-496-2322	496-2848
Akal Security Inc 7 Infinity Loop Espanola NM 87532 *TF:* 888-325-2527 ■ *Web:* www.akalsecurity.com	505-692-6600	753-8689
Alken Inc 40 Hercules Dr Colchester VT 05446 *TF:* 800-357-4777 ■ *Web:* www.polhemus.com	802-655-3159	
Allied Fire & Security Inc 425 W Second Ave Spokane WA 99201 **Fax:* Acctg ■ *TF Acctg:* 888-333-2632 ■ *Web:* www.alliedfireandsecurity.com	509-321-8778	321-8767*
Alphacorp Inc 21351 Ridgetop Cir Dulles VA 20166 *Web:* www.alphacorpsecurity.com	801-977-8705	
AMAG Technology Inc 20701 Manhattan Pl Torrance CA 90501 *TF:* 800-889-9138 ■ *Web:* www.amag.com	310-518-2380	834-0685
American Locker Group Inc 815 S Main St Grapevine TX 76051 *OTC: ALGI* ■ *TF:* 800-828-9118 ■ *Web:* www.americanlocker.com	817-329-1600	421-8618
American Locker Security Systems Inc 608 Allen St Jamestown NY 14701 *TF Sales:* 800-828-9118 ■ *Web:* www.americanlocker.com	800-828-9118	
American Science & Engineering Inc 829 Middlesex Tpke Billerica MA 01821 *NASDAQ: ASEI* ■ *TF:* 800-225-1608 ■ *Web:* www.as-e.com	978-262-8700	
American Security Products Inc 11925 Pacific Ave Fontana CA 92337 *Web:* www.amsecusa.com	951-685-9680	685-9685
APi Systems Group Inc 10575 Vista Park Rd Dallas TX 75238 *TF General:* 877-828-1200 ■ *Web:* www.afpgusa.com/api-systems-group.php	214-291-1200	291-1340
Apollo Security Inc 2150 Boston Providence Hwy Walpole MA 02081 *Web:* apollointernational.com	508-660-1197	
Argyle Security Inc 12903 Delivery Dr San Antonio TX 78247 *Web:* isisecurity.com	210-495-5245	828-7300
Ascent Capital Group Inc 5251 DTC Pkwy Ste 1000 Greenwood Village CO 80111 *Web:* www.ascentcapitalgroupinc.com	303-628-5600	
Astrophysics Inc 21481 Ferrero Pkwy City Of Industry CA 91789 *Web:* www.astrophysicsinc.com	909-598-5488	
Authentix Inc 4355 Excel Pkwy Ste 100 Addison TX 75001 *TF:* 866-434-1402 ■ *Web:* www.authentix.com	469-737-4400	737-4409
B & G Security International 6631 Hwy 42 Rex GA 30273 *Web:* www.bgsecurity.com	770-507-6409	
Baltimore Alarm & Security 5314 Reistertown Rd Baltimore MD 21215 *Web:* www.baltoalarm.com	410-358-8600	
BI Inc 6400 Lookout Rd Boulder CO 80301 *TF:* 800-241-2911 ■ *Web:* www.bi.com	303-218-1000	218-1250
Black Hat Inc 1932 First Ave Ste 204 Seattle WA 98101 *TF:* 866-203-8081 ■ *Web:* www.blackhat.com	206-443-5489	
Bosch Security Systems 130 Perinton Pkwy Fairport NY 14450 *TF:* 800-289-0096 ■ *Web:* us.boschsecurity.com	585-223-4060	223-9180
Brivo Systems LLC 7700 Old Georgetown Rd Ste 300 Bethesda MD 20814 *TF Tech Supp:* 866-692-7486 ■ *Web:* www.brivo.com	301-664-5242	
BSM Wireless Inc 75 International Blvd Ste 100 Toronto ON M9W6L9 *TF:* 866-768-4771 ■ *Web:* www.bsmwireless.com	416-675-1201	
Carter Bros LLC 3015 RN Martin St East Point GA 30344 **Fax Area Code:* 404 ■ *TF:* 888-818-0152 ■ *Web:* carterbrothers.com	888-818-0152	767-2568*
Central Signaling 2033 Hamilton Rd Columbus GA 31904 *TF:* 800-554-1101 ■ *Web:* www.censignal.com	706-322-3756	
CFP Group Inc, The 1401 Chain Bridge Rd Ste 300 Mclean VA 22101 *Web:* www.thecfpgroup.com	703-752-0570	
Checkpoint Systems Inc 101 Wolf Dr Thorofare NJ 08086 *NYSE: CKP* ■ *TF:* 800-257-5540 ■ *Web:* www.checkpointsystems.com	856-848-1800	848-0937
CompuDyne Corp 2530 Riva Rd Ste 201 Annapolis MD 21401 *Web:* www.compudyne.com	410-224-4415	
Corby Industries Inc 1501 E Pennsylvania St Allentown PA 18109 *TF Sales:* 800-652-6729 ■ *Web:* www.corby.com	610-433-1412	435-1963
DEI Holdings Inc 1 Viper Way Vista CA 92081 *OTC: DEIX* ■ *TF:* 800-876-0800 ■ *Web:* deiholdings.com	760-598-6200	598-6400
Detector Electronics Corp 6901 W 110th St Minneapolis MN 55438 *Web:* det-tronics.com	952-941-5665	
Detex Corp 302 Detex Dr New Braunfels TX 78130 *TF:* 800-729-3839 ■ *Web:* www.detex.com	830-629-2900	620-6711
deView Electronics USA Inc 708 Vly Ridge Cir Ste 1 Lewisville TX 75057 *TF:* 877-433-8439 ■ *Web:* www.deviewelectronics.com	214-222-3332	
Diebold Inc 5995 Mayfair Rd North Canton OH 44720 *NYSE: DBD* ■ *TF:* 800-999-3600 ■ *Web:* www.diebold.com	330-490-4000	
Digital Security Controls (DSC) 3301 Langstaff Rd Concord ON L4K4L2 *TF:* 888-888-7838 ■ *Web:* www.dsc.com	905-760-3000	760-3004
Doyle Security Systems Inc 792 Calkins Rd Rochester NY 14623 *TF:* 866-463-6953 ■ *Web:* godoyle.com	585-244-3400	
eDist 97 McKee Dr Mahwah NJ 07430 **Fax Area Code:* 800 ■ *TF:* 800-800-6624 ■ *Web:* www.edist.com	201-512-1400	391-5078*
ELK Products Inc 3266 Us 70 W Connelly Springs NC 28612 *TF:* 800-797-9355 ■ *Web:* www.elkproducts.com	828-397-4200	
EZ Electric Inc 1250 Birchwood Dr Sunnyvale CA 94089 *Web:* www.ez-electric.com	408-734-4282	
Federal APD Inc (FAPD) 28100 Cabot Dr Ste 200 Novi MI 48377 *TF:* 877-992-7749 ■ *Web:* 3m.com	248-374-9600	
Felts Lock & Alarm Company Inc 4000 E Indiana St Evansville IN 47715 *Web:* www.feltsonline.com	812-473-4000	
Fiber SenSys LLC 2925 NW Aloclek Dr Ste 120 Hillsboro OR 97124 *TF:* 800-641-8150 ■ *Web:* www.fibersensys.com	503-692-4430	
FireKing Security Group 101 Security Pkwy New Albany IN 47150 *TF:* 800-457-2424 ■ *Web:* www.fireking.com	812-948-8400	
First Action Security Security Team Inc 18702 Crestwood Dr Hagerstown MD 21742 *TF Cust Svc:* 800-372-7447 ■ *Web:* www.firstactionteam.com	301-797-2124	
Fortress Technology Inc 51 Grand Marshall Dr Toronto ON M1B5N6 *TF:* 888-220-8737 ■ *Web:* www.fortresstechnology.com	416-754-2898	
Gateway Group One Inc 604-608 Market St Newark NJ 07105 *Web:* www.gatewaygroupone.com	973-465-8006	
GE Analytical Instruments Inc 6060 Spine Rd Boulder CO 80301 *TF:* 800-255-6964 ■ *Web:* www.geinstruments.com	303-444-2009	
Gentex Corp 600 N Centennial St Zeeland MI 49464 *NASDAQ: GNTX* ■ *Web:* www.gentex.com	616-772-1800	772-7348
George Risk Industries Inc 802 S Elm St Kimball NE 69145 *OTC: RSKIA* ■ *TF Sales:* 800-523-1227 ■ *Web:* www.grisk.com	308-235-4645	235-2609
Guardian Alarm 20800 Southfield Rd Southfield MI 48075 *TF:* 800-782-9688 ■ *Web:* www.guardianalarm.com	248-423-1000	423-3009
Hanchett Entry Systems Inc (HES) 22630 N 17th Ave Phoenix AZ 85027 *TF:* 800-626-7590 ■ *Web:* www.hesinnovations.com	623-582-4626	582-4641
HandyTrac Systems LLC 510 Staghorn Ct Alpharetta GA 30004 *TF:* 800-665-9994 ■ *Web:* www.handytrac.com	678-990-2305	
Hikvision USA Inc 908 Canada Ct City Of Industry CA 91748 *Web:* hikvision.com	909-895-0400	
Honeywell Automation & Control Solutions 11 W Spring St Freeport IL 61032 *Web:* www.honeywell.com	815-235-5500	
Honeywell Security Group 2 Corporate Ctr Dr Ste 100 Melville NY 11747 *TF:* 800-467-5875 ■ *Web:* www.security.honeywell.com	516-577-2000	
IDenticard Systems Inc 25 Race Ave FL 1 Lancaster PA 17603 *TF:* 800-233-0298 ■ *Web:* www.identicard.com	717-569-5797	569-2390
Infinova Corp 51 Stouts Ln Monmouth Junction NJ 08852 *Web:* www.infinova.com	732-355-9100	
Integrated Biometrics Inc 121 Broadcast Dr Spartanburg SC 29303 *TF:* 888-840-8034 ■ *Web:* www.integratedbiometrics.com	864-990-3711	
Interface Security Systems LLC 6340 International Pkwy Ste 100 Plano TX 75093 *TF:* 866-593-3480	972-996-2800	996-2801
ISS International Inc Aspen Corporate Park 1480 Us Hwy 9 N Ste 202 Woodbridge NJ 07095 *Web:* www.issccctv.com	732-855-1111	
Johnson Controls Fire & Security Solutions 5757 N Green Bay Ave PO Box 591 Milwaukee WI 53201 *Web:* www.johnsoncontrols.com/security	414-524-1200	
KWJ Engineering Inc 8430 Central Ave Ste C Newark CA 94560 *TF:* 800-472-6626 ■ *Web:* www.kwjengineering.com	510-794-4296	574-8341
Loomis Fargo & Co 2500 Citywest Blvd Ste 900 Houston TX 77042 *TF:* 866-383-5069 ■ *Web:* www.loomis.us	713-435-6700	
Lumenera Corp 7 Capella Ct Ottawa ON K2E8A7 *Web:* www.lumenera.com	613-736-4077	
Mace Security International Inc 240 Gibraltar Rd Ste 220 Horsham PA 19044 *OTC: MACE* ■ *Web:* corp.mace.com	267-317-4009	
Matrix Systems Inc 1041 Byers Rd Miamisburg OH 45342 *TF:* 800-562-8749 ■ *Web:* www.matrixsys.com	937-438-9033	438-0900
MDI Security Systems Inc 12500 Network Dr Ste 303 San Antonio TX 78249 *TF:* 866-435-7634 ■ *Web:* www.mdisecure.com	210-477-5400	477-5401
MMF Industries 1111 S Wheeling Rd Wheeling IL 60090 *TF:* 800-323-8181 ■ *Web:* www.mmfind.com	800-323-8181	

Company	City	State	ZIP	Phone	Fax
Monitronics International Inc 2350 Valley View Ln Ste 100 *TF Cust Svc:* 800-290-0709 ■ *Web:* www.monitronics.com	Dallas	TX	75234	972-243-7443	
MorphoTrust USA Inc 296 Concord Rd *TF:* 888-245-1114 ■ *Web:* www.morphotrust.com	Billerica	MA	01821	978-215-2400	
MSA Security 9 Murray St 2nd Fl *TF:* 800-286-2000 ■ *Web:* www.msasecurity.net	New York	NY	10007	212-509-1336	
NAPCO Security Systems Inc 333 Bayview Ave. *NASDAQ: NSSC* ■ *TF:* 800-645-9445 ■ *Web:* www.napcosecurity.com	Amityville	NY	11701	631-842-9400	842-9137
National Fingerprint Inc 6999 Dolan Rd. *TF:* 888-823-7873 ■ *Web:* www.nationalfingerprint.com	Glouster	OH	45732	740-767-3853	
New England Security Inc 10 Industrial Dr. *TF:* 800-556-7395 ■ *Web:* newenglandsecurityinc.com	Westerly	RI	02891	401-596-0660	
Norment Security Group Inc 2511 Midpark Dr *TF:* 800-466-3007 ■ *Web:* cornerstonedetention.com	Montgomery	AL	36109	334-281-8440	286-6421
Nortek Security & Control LLC 1950 Camino Vida Roble Ste 150 *TF Cust Svc:* 800-421-1587 ■ *Web:* www.nortekcontrol.com	Carlsbad	CA	92008	760-438-7000	931-1340
OpenEye Inc 23221 E Knox Ave. *Web:* www.openeye.net	Liberty Lake	WA	99019	509-232-5261	
Optex Inc 13661 Benson Ave Bldg C *TF:* 800-966-7839 ■ *Web:* www.optexamerica.com	Chino	CA	91710	909-993-5770	628-5560
OSI Systems Inc 12525 Chadron Ave *NASDAQ: OSIS* ■ *Web:* www.osi-systems.com	Hawthorne	CA	90250	310-978-0516	
Owlstone Nanotech Inc 761 Main Ave *Web:* www.owlstonenanotech.com	Norwalk	CT	06851	203-908-4848	
Paragon Systems Inc 13655 Dulles Technology Dr Ste 100 *Web:* www.parasys.com	Herndon	VA	20171	703-263-7176	
Parking Products Inc 2517 Wyandotte Rd *Web:* www.parkingproducts.com	Willow Grove	PA	19090	215-657-7500	
PCSC Corp 3541 Challenger St. *Web:* www.pcscsecurity.com	Torrance	CA	90503	310-303-3600	
Per Mar Security 1910 E Kimberly Rd *TF:* 800-473-7627 ■ *Web:* www.permarsecurity.com	Davenport	IA	52807	563-359-3200	359-6700
PerkinElmer Inc 940 Winter St *NYSE: PKI* ■ *Web:* www.perkinelmer.com	Waltham	MA	02451	203-925-4602	944-4904
protection One Alarm Monitoring 1035 N Third St Ste 101 *TF:* 800-438-4357 ■ *Web:* www.protection1.com	Lawrence	KS	66044	877-776-1911	
Public Safety Equipment Inc 10986 N Warson Rd *Web:* code3pse.com	St Louis	MO	63114	314-426-2700	
PV Labs Inc 1074 Cooke Blvd *Web:* www.pv-labs.com	Burlington	ON	L7T2Y8	905-667-7202	
Qualys Inc 1600 Bridge Pkwy *TF:* 866-801-6161 ■ *Web:* www.qualys.com	Redwood Shores	CA	94065	650-801-6100	801-6101
Radiance Technologies Inc 350 Wynn Dr *Web:* www.radiancetech.com	Huntsville	AL	35805	256-704-3400	704-3412
Revo America Inc 700 Freeport Pkwy Ste 100 *Web:* www.revoamerica.com	Coppell	TX	75019	469-464-2800	
Ronco Consulting Corp 6710 Oxon Hill Rd Ste 200 *Web:* www.roncoconsulting.com	Oxon Hill	MD	20745	240-493-3910	
RS2 Technologies LLC 400 Fisher St Ste G *Web:* www.rs2tech.com	Munster	IN	46321	219-836-9002	
Safeguards Technology LLC 75 Atlantic St. *Web:* www.safeguards.com	Hackensack	NJ	07601	201-488-1022	
Seco-Larm USA Inc 16842 Millikan Ave *TF:* 800-662-0800 ■ *Web:* www.seco-larm.com	Irvine	CA	92606	949-261-2999	261-7326
SecureUSA Inc 4250 Keith Bridge Rd Ste 160 *Web:* www.secureusa.net	Cumming	GA	30041	770-205-0789	
Securitas Security Services USA Inc 2 Campus Dr **Fax Area Code:* 323 ■ *TF:* 800-555-0906 ■ *Web:* www.securitas.com	Parsippany	NJ	07054	973-267-5300	832-0871*
Security Corp 22325 Roethel Dr *TF:* 877-374-5700 ■ *Web:* www.securitycorp.com	Novi	MI	48375	877-374-5700	
Security Defense Systems Corp 160 Pk Ave **Fax Area Code:* 973 ■ *TF:* 800-325-6339 ■ *Web:* www.securitydefense.com	Nutley	NJ	07110	800-325-6339	235-0132*
Security Signal Devices Inc 1740 N Lemon St. *TF:* 800-888-0444 ■ *Web:* www.ssdsystems.com	Anaheim	CA	92801	800-888-0444	
Sensormatic Electronics Corp 6600 Congress Ave *TF:* 800-327-1765 ■ *Web:* www.sensormatic.com	Boca Raton	FL	33487	561-912-6000	912-6097
Sentry Group 900 Linden Ave **Fax:* Cust Svc ■ *TF Cust Svc:* 800-828-1438 ■ *Web:* www.sentrysafe.com	Rochester	NY	14625	585-381-4900	381-2940*
Sentry Technology Corp 1881 Lakeland Ave. *OTC: SKVY* ■ **Fax Area Code:* 631 ■ *TF:* 800-645-4224 ■ *Web:* www.sentrytechnology.com	Ronkonkoma	NY	11779	800-645-4224	739-2124*
Sielox LLC 170 E Ninth Ave *TF:* 800-424-2126 ■ *Web:* www.sielox.com	Runnemede	NJ	08078	856-939-9300	
SIRCHIE Finger Print Laboratories Inc 100 Hunter Pl *TF:* 800-356-7311 ■ *Web:* www.sirchie.com	Youngsville	NC	27596	919-554-2244	554-2266
Sizemore Inc 2116 Walton Way *TF:* 800-445-1748 ■ *Web:* www.sizemoreinc.com	Augusta	GA	30904	706-736-1456	
Slomin's Inc 125 Lauman Ln *TF:* 800-252-7663 ■ *Web:* www.slomins.com	Hicksville	NY	11801	516-932-7000	
Sofradir EC Inc 373 Rt 46W *TF:* 800-759-9577 ■ *Web:* www.electrophysics.com	Fairfield	NJ	07004	973-882-0211	882-0997
Southern Folger Detention Equipment Co 4634 S Presa St *TF:* 888-745-0530 ■ *Web:* www.southernfolger.com	San Antonio	TX	78223	210-533-1231	533-2211
Teletrac Inc 7391 Lincoln Way *TF:* 800-500-6009 ■ *Web:* www.teletrac.com	Garden Grove	CA	92841	714-897-0877	379-6378
Texas Industrial Security 101 Summit Ave Ste 404 *Web:* www.txsecurity.com	Fort Worth	TX	76102	817-335-3046	335-3048
TrakLok Corp 11020 Solway School Rd Ste 105	Knoxville	TN	37931	865-927-4911	
Tyco Fire & Security 6600 Congress Ave *Web:* www.tyco.com	Boca Raton	FL	33487	561-912-6000	
Tyco International Ltd 9 Roszel Rd *NYSE: TYC* ■ *TF:* 800-685-4509 ■ *Web:* www.tyco.com	Princeton	NJ	08540	609-720-4200	720-4208
Unisec Inc 2555 Nicholson St **Fax Area Code:* 510 ■ *TF:* 800-982-4587 ■ *Web:* www.ultrabarrier.com	San Leandro	CA	94577	800-982-4587	352-6707*
Universal Security Instruments Inc 11407 Cronhill Dr. *TSE: UUU* ■ *TF:* 800-390-4321 ■ *Web:* www.universalsecurity.com	Owings Mills	MD	21117	410-363-3000	363-2218
VASCO Data Security International Inc 1901 S Meyers Rd Ste 210 *NASDAQ: VDSI* ■ *Web:* www.vasco.com	Oakbrook Terrace	IL	60181	630-932-8844	932-8852
Vector Security Inc 2000 Ericsson Dr *TF:* 800-832-8575 ■ *Web:* www.vectorsecurity.com	Warrendale	PA	15086	800-832-8575	
Verint Video Solutions 330 South Service Rd *TF:* 800-483-7468 ■ *Web:* www.verint.com	Melville	NY	11747	800-483-7468	
Winner International LLC 32 W State St *TF:* 800-258-2321 ■ *Web:* www.winner-intl.com	Sharon	PA	16146	724-981-1152	981-1034

693 SECURITY & PROTECTIVE SERVICES

See Also Investigative Services p. 2596

Company	City	State	ZIP	Phone	Fax
2GIG Technologies Inc 2961 West Maple Loop Dr Ste 300 *Web:* www.2gig.com	Lehi	UT	84043	801-221-9162	
5 Alarm Fire & Safety Equipment LLC 350 Austin Cir *TF:* 800-615-6789 ■ *Web:* www.5alarm.com	Delafield	WI	53018	262-646-5911	
A & R Security Service Inc 2552 W 135th St. *Web:* www.universalpro.com	Blue Island	IL	60406	708-389-3830	389-7734
A B S Advanced Business Solutions 600 S John Redditt Dr	Lufkin	TX	75904	936-639-4744	
A Bales Security Agency Inc 9700 Dr Martin Luther King Jr St N Ste 200 *Web:* www.balessecurity.com	Saint Petersburg	FL	33702	727-592-9101	
A Better Solution Inc 4303 Cedar Lk Cv *Web:* www.abs-consulting.com	Conley	GA	30288	770-252-1500	
AAA Alarm Systems Ltd 180 Nature Park Way *Web:* www.aaasecure.ca/aaa	Winnipeg	MB	R3P0X7	204-949-0078	
ABC Security Service Inc 1840 Embarcadero	Oakland	CA	94606	510-436-0666	
ABM Industries Inc 8020 W Doe Ste C *Web:* www.abm.com	Visalia	SC	93291	559-651-1612	
Accsense Inc 460 Ward Dr Ste E-2 *Web:* accsense.com	Santa Barbara	CA	93111	805-681-3500	
Accurate Controls 326 Blackburn St *Web:* www.accuratecontrols.com	Ripon	WI	54971	920-748-6603	
Accuvant Inc 1125 17th St Ste 1700 *TF:* 800-574-0896 ■ *Web:* www.accuvant.com	Denver	CO	80202	303-298-0600	298-0868
Action Security Inc 243 E Fifth Ave *TF:* 800-478-3785 ■ *Web:* actionsecurity.com	Anchorage	AK	99501	907-279-7050	
Admiral Security Services Inc 5550 W Touhy Ave Ste 101 *Web:* www.admiralsecuritychicago.com	Skokie	IL	60077	847-588-0888	
Advanced Alarm Systems Inc 101 Lindsey St *TF:* 800-442-5276 ■ *Web:* www.advancedalarmsystems.com	Fall River	MA	02720	508-675-1937	
Advent Security Corp 101 Roesch Ave *Web:* www.adventsecurity.com	Oreland	PA	19075	215-576-7111	
Aiphone Corp 1700 130th Ave NE *Web:* www.aiphone.com	Bellevue	WA	98005	425-455-0510	
AirScan Inc 3505 Murrell Rd *Web:* www.airscan.com	Rockledge	FL	32955	321-631-0005	
Aj Squared Security Inc 111 02 Jamaica Ave. *Web:* www.aj2security.com	Jamaica	NY	11418	718-849-2725	
Alarm Security Group LLC 12301 Kiln Court Ste A *Web:* www.asgsecurity.com	Beltsville	MD	20705	301-937-8880	
All American Private Security Inc 421 S Glendora Ave Ste 200 *Web:* www.allamericansecurity.com	West Covina	CA	91790	626-962-9620	
All Phase Security Inc 2959 Promenade St Ste 200 *Web:* www.allphasesecurity.com	West Sacramento	CA	95691	916-375-6640	
Allegiance Security Group LLC 2900 Arendell St Ste 18 *TF:* 866-747-2748 ■ *Web:* www.allegiancesecurityteam.com	Morehead City	NC	28557	252-247-1138	
Alliance Home Health Care Inc 5930 Hohman Ave Ste 102 *Web:* alliancehomehealthcare.net	Hammond	IN	46320	219-852-5101	
AlliedBarton Security Services 150 S Warner Rd *TF:* 866-703-7666 ■ *Web:* www.alliedbarton.com	King of Prussia	PA	19406	484-654-3800	
Alrod Enterprises Inc 119 N Sycamore St	Petersburg	VA	23803	804-732-3972	
Am-Gard Security Inc 600 Main St *TF:* 800-554-0412 ■ *Web:* www.am-gard.com	Pittsburgh	PA	15215	412-781-5800	
American Services Inc 1300 Rutherford Rd *TF:* 877-292-7450 ■ *Web:* www.american-services-inc.com	Greenville	SC	29609	864-292-7450	
Ameriguard Security Services Inc 5470 W Spruce Ave Ste 102 *Web:* ameriguard.publishpath.com	Fresno	CA	93722	559-271-5984	
Amherst Alarm Inc 435 Lawrence Bell Dr *Web:* www.amherstalarm.com	Amherst	NY	14221	716-632-4600	
Anderson Security Agency Ltd 2555 W Morningside Dr *Web:* www.andersonsecurity.com	Phoenix	AZ	85023	602-331-7000	
Andy Frain Services Inc 761 Shoreline Dr *TF:* 877-707-4771 ■ *Web:* www.andyfrain.com	Aurora	IL	60504	630-820-3820	
Apex3 Security 8750 W Bryn Mawr Ave *Web:* www.apex3security.com	Chicago	IL	60631	773-867-9204	
APG Security Inc 116 N Broadway *Web:* www.apgsecurity.com	South Amboy	NJ	08879	732-553-1537	

				Phone	Fax
Api Security Services & Investigations Inc 867 High St Ste D *Web:* apisecurity.us	Worthington	OH	43085	614-310-1980	
APL Access & Security Inc 115 S William Dillard Dr *TF:* 866-873-2288 ■ *Web:* www.aplsecurity.com	Gilbert	AZ	85233	480-497-9471	
Arkansas Automatic Sprinklers Inc 185 Arena Rd *Web:* www.arautosprinklers.com	Cabot	AR	72023	501-843-9392	
Armed Response Team, The 8200 Montgomery Blvd NE Ste 237 *Web:* www.armedresponseteam.com	Albuquerque	NM	87109	505-237-2278	
Arrow Security Patrols 60 Knickerbocker Ave *Web:* www.arrowsecurity.net	Bohemia	NY	11716	631-675-2430	
Asia Pacific Center for Security 2058 Maluhia Rd *Web:* www.apcss.org	Honolulu	HI	96815	808-971-8900	
ASP Inc 460 Brant St Ste 212 *Fax Area Code: 416 ■ *TF:* 877-552-5535 ■ *Web:* www.security-asp.com	Burlington	ON	L7R4B6	905-333-4242	481-1966*
Asset Protection Associates Inc 2305 Old Milton Pkwy *Web:* www.assetprotectionassociates.net	Alpharetta	GA	30005	678-566-0222	
ASSI Security Inc 1370 Reynolds Ave Ste 201 *Web:* www.assisecurity.com	Irvine	CA	92614	949-955-0244	
ASSIST Aviation Solutions LLC 117 Perimeter Rd *Web:* www.assist-us.com	Nashua	NH	03063	603-505-4668	
Atcc 757 Barbershop Rd	Edinburg	VA	22824	540-984-8443	
ATEK Access Technologies LLC 210 N.E. 10th Ave *Web:* atekcompanies.com	Brainerd	MN	56401	218-829-4719	
Avalon Fortress Security Corp 9697 N.W. E River Rd Number One Security Plz *Web:* www.avalonsecurity.com	Minneapolis	MN	55433	763-767-9111	
Avante Security Inc 1959 Leslie St *Web:* www.avantesecurity.com	Toronto	ON	M3B2M3	416-923-6984	
AWP Inc 826 Overholt Rd *TF:* 800-343-2650 ■ *Web:* www.awptrafficsafety.com	Kent	OH	44240	800-343-2650	
B b C Security & Communication Inc 401 Mclean Ave *Web:* bbcsecurity.com	Yonkers	NY	10705	914-969-4000	
Barnes Alarm Systems Inc 3201 Flagler Ave Ste 503 *Web:* www.barnesalarmsystems.net	Key West	FL	33040	305-294-6753	
BitRage NOVIS Corp 6816 Southpoint Pkwy Bldg 301 *Web:* www.bitrage.com	Jacksonville	FL	32216	904-674-0062	
Bms Integrated Services Inc 1277 Georgia St E *TF:* 866-676-0136 ■ *Web:* bmscom.com	Vancouver	BC	V6A2A9	604-676-0136	
Bonafide Security Solutions 3605 N 126th St *Web:* www.bonafidesafe.com	Brookfield	WI	53005	262-790-9400	
Bot Home Automation Inc 1523 26th St *Web:* www.ring.com	Santa Monica	CA	90404	310-929-7085	
Boyd & Assoc Inc 6319 Colfax Ave *Web:* www.boydsecurity.com	North Hollywood	CA	91606	818-752-1888	
Brink's Inc PO Box 619031 *TF:* 800-274-6575 ■ *Web:* www.brinks.com/en	Dallas	TX	75261	469-549-6000	
Brokers International Financial Services LLC 102 Se 13th St *TF:* 877-886-1939 ■ *Web:* www.brokersifs.com	Panora	IA	50216	641-755-4635	
Business Protection Specialists Inc 1296 E Victor Rd *Web:* www.securingpeople.com	Victor	NY	14564	585-394-5112	
By Taylor Made Irrigation 750 Barsby St	Vista	CA	92084	760-945-0118	
C & d Security Management Inc 306 Delaware Dr *Web:* www.canddsecurity.com	Colorado Springs	CO	80909	719-597-0750	
Cansec Systems Ltd 3105 Unity Dr Unit 9 *TF:* 877-545-7755 ■ *Web:* www.cansec.com	Mississauga	ON	L5L4L2	905-820-2404	
Cass 1810 Water Pl SE Ste 180 *Web:* www.cassecurity.com	Atlanta	GA	30339	770-916-0060	
Castlegarde Inc 4911 S W Shore Blvd *TF:* 866-751-3203 ■ *Web:* www.castlegarde.com	Tampa	FL	33611	813-872-4844	
Caveon LLC 6905 South 1300 East Ste 468 *Web:* www.caveon.com	Midvale	UT	84047	801-208-0103	
Cbm 2614 Hickory St *Web:* www.cbme.net	Santa Ana	CA	92707	714-424-9250	
CelAccess Systems Inc 13619 Inwood Rd Ste 360 *Web:* www.celaccess.com	Dallas	TX	75244	972-231-1999	
Central Defense Security 50 Vantage Way Ste 251 *Web:* www.centdef.com	Nashville	TN	37228	615-256-0300	
Checkview Corp 8180 upland cir *Web:* www.checkview.com	Chanhassen	MN	55317	952-227-5853	
Chubb Security Systems Inc 7700 Gulf Fwy *TF:* 800-513-3576 ■ *Web:* www.chubbedwards.com	Houston	TX	77017	800-513-3576	
Cincinnatus Consulting LLC 1721 Spruce St *Web:* www.cincinnatus-consulting.com	Philadelphia	PA	19103	267-872-0313	
CNB Technology USA Inc 2310 E Artesia Blvd *Web:* www.cnbusa.com	Long Beach	CA	90805	562-728-8500	
Code Blue Corp 92 E 64th St *Web:* www.codeblue.com	Holland	MI	49423	616-392-8296	
Command Security Corp 388 Westchester Ave Ste 1J/H *Web:* www.commandsecurity.com	Port Chester	NY	10573	914-937-2969	
Control Microsystems Inc 48 Steacie Dr *Web:* www2.schneider-electric.com	Kanata	ON	K2K2A9	613-591-1943	
Convergint Technologies LLC 1651 Wilkening Rd *Web:* www.convergint.com	Schaumburg	IL	60173	847-229-0222	
Cook Security Group Inc 5841 SE International Way *Web:* www.cooksecuritygroup.com	Milwaukie	OR	97222	503-786-5173	
Counterforce Inc 2740 Matheson Blvd E Unit 2A *TF:* 800-591-7374 ■ *Web:* www.counterforce.com	Mississauga	ON	L4W4X3	905-282-6200	
Counterstrike Corp 4956 Hayvenhurst Ave *Web:* www.counterstrike.com	Encino	CA	91316	818-906-7598	
Covenant Aviation Security LLC 400 Quadrangle Dr Ste A *Web:* www.covenantsecurity.com	Bolingbrook	IL	60440	630-631-6602	
Creative Security Company Inc 150 S Autumn St Ste B *Web:* www.creativesecurity.com	San Jose	CA	95110	408-295-2600	
Crimetek Security Services 3448 N Golden State Blvd *Web:* www.crimetek.com	Turlock	CA	95382	209-668-6208	
Criticom International Corp 715 W State Rd Ste 434 *TF:* 866-705-7705 ■ *Web:* www.criticominternational.com	Longwood	FL	32750	866-705-7705	
CTC International Group Inc 330 Clematis St Ste 220 *Web:* ctcintl.com	West Palm Beach	FL	33401	561-655-3111	
Custom Communications Inc 1661 Greenview Dr SW *Web:* www.custom-alarm.com	Rochester	MN	55902	507-288-5522	
Cypress Security LLC 478 Tehama St *TF:* 866-345-1277 ■ *Web:* www.cypress-security.com	San Francisco	CA	94103	866-345-1277	
DECO Inc 11140 Zealand Ave N *Web:* www.deco-inc.com	Champlin	MN	55316	763-576-9572	
Denco Security System LLC 4605 Clear Creek Pkwy	Northport	AL	35475	205-333-9931	
Destiny Networks Inc 15750 Vineyard Blvd Ste 120 *Web:* www.destinynetworks.com	Morgan Hill	CA	95037	408-779-0060	
Dial Security Inc 760 W Ventura Blvd *Web:* www.dialcomm.com	Camarillo	CA	93010	805-389-6700	
Diamond Group 13101 Preston Rd Ste 212 *Web:* www.thediamondgroup.ws	Dallas	TX	75240	972-788-1111	
DIGIOP Inc 3850 Priority Way S Dr Ste 200 *Web:* www.digiop.com	Indianapolis	IN	46240	317-489-0413	
Digistream Investigation 417 mace blvd *TF:* 800-747-4329 ■ *Web:* www.digistream.com	Davis	CA	95618	800-747-4329	
Digital Watchdog Inc 5436 W Crenshaw St *Web:* digital-watchdog.com	Tampa	FL	33634	813-888-9555	
Djg Investigative Services Inc 1370 Briar Creek Rd *Web:* djginvestigativeservices.com	Charlotte	NC	28205	704-536-8025	
Dk Security 5160 falcon view ave se *Web:* www.dksecurity.com	Grand rapids	MI	49512	616-656-0123	
DSA Detection LLC 120 Water St Ste 211 *Web:* www.dsadetection.com	North Andover	MA	01845	978-975-3200	
DSX Access Systems Inc 10731 Rockwall Rd *TF:* 888-419-8353 ■ *Web:* www.dsxinc.com	Dallas	TX	75238	214-553-6140	553-6147
Dynamic Security Inc 1102 Woodward Ave *Web:* www.dynamic.cc	Muscle Shoals	AL	35661	256-383-5798	
E P S 8845 Basil Western Rd *Web:* www.epsohio.com	Canal Winchester	OH	43110	614-834-9126	
East Coast Security Services Inc 68 Stiles Rd *TF:* 800-639-2086 ■ *Web:* www.ecss.com	Salem	NH	03079	603-898-6823	
Ebs Consultants Ltd Inc 1 freeland st *Web:* ebsconsultants.com	Monroe	NY	10950	845-774-8133	
ECSI International Inc 790 Bloomfield Ave Bldg C-1 *Web:* www.ecsiinternational.com	Clifton	NJ	07012	973-574-8555	
Edwards Company Inc 41 Woodford Ave *Web:* www.edwards-signals.com	Plainville	CT	06062	860-793-5301	
Electroworld Security Systems 867 E 26th St	Brooklyn	NY	11210	718-338-5831	
eLine Technology 1070 W 124th Ave Ste B-100 *Web:* www.elinetechnology.com	Westminster	CO	80234	303-938-1133	
Elite Investigations Ltd 538 W 29th St *Web:* www.eliteinvestigation.com	New York	NY	10001	212-629-3131	
EMERgency24 Inc 4179 W Irving Park Rd *Web:* www.emergency24.com	Chicago	IL	60641	773-777-0707	
eV Microelectronics Inc 373 Saxonburg Blvd *Web:* evproducts.com	Saxonburg	PA	16056	724-352-5288	
Excelsior Defense Inc 2232 Central Ave *TF:* 877-955-4636 ■ *Web:* www.excelsiordefense.com	Saint Petersburg	FL	33712	727-527-9600	
Execushield Inc 4104 24th St *Web:* www.execushield.com	San Francisco	CA	94114	415-508-0825	
Executive Technologies Corp 8731 Northpark Blvd Ste B *Web:* www.executivetechcorp.com	Charleston	SC	29406	843-824-5906	
FE Moran Security Solutions 201 W University Ave *Web:* www.femoranalarm.com	Champaign	IL	61820	217-403-6444	
Federal Protection Inc 2500 N Airport Commerce Ave *TF:* 800-299-5400	Springfield	MO	65803	800-299-5400	
Fidelco Guide Dog Foundation Inc 103 Vision Way *Web:* fidelco.org	Bloomfield	CT	06002	860-243-5200	
Finotex USA Corp 6942 NW 50th St *Web:* www.finotex.com	Miami	FL	33166	305-470-2400	
First Alarm Security & Patrol Inc 1111 Estates Dr *TF:* 800-684-1111 ■ *Web:* www.firstalarm.com	Aptos	CA	95003	831-476-1111	
FJC Security Services Inc 275 Jericho Tpke *TF:* 888-832-6352 ■ *Web:* www.fjcsecurity.com	Floral Park	NY	11001	516-328-6000	

Phone | Fax

Fluent Home Ltd 7319 104 St NW .... Edmonton AB T6E4B9 855-238-4826
TF: 855-238-4826 ■ *Web:* myfluenthome.com

Fluke Thermography
3550 Annapolis Ln N Ste 70 .... Plymouth MN 55447 763-383-8648
Web: en-us.fluke.com

Force One Security Solutions Inc
2175 Manana Dr .... Dallas TX 75220 214-550-1472
Web: www.forceone.com

G-S Company Inc, The 7920 Stansbury Rd .... Baltimore MD 21222 410-282-9549
Web: www.g-sco.com

Galaxy Integrated Technologies
100 Leo M Birmingham Pkwy .... Brighton MA 02135 617-202-6388
Web: www.galaxyintegrated.com

Garda World Security Corp 1390 Barre St .... Montreal QC H3C1N4 514-281-2811 281-2811
TSE: GW ■ *TF:* 800-859-1599 ■ *Web:* www.garda.com

General Security Services Corp
9110 Meadowview Rd .... Minneapolis MN 55425 952-858-5000
Web: www.gssc.net

Geutebruck Security Inc
750 Miller Dr Ste A-5 .... Leesburg VA 20175 703-378-4856
Web: geutebrueck.com

GHS Interactive Security Inc
2081 Arena Blvd Ste 260 .... Sacramento CA 95834 855-208-2447
TF: 855-208-2447 ■ *Web:* ghssecurity.com

Gillmore Security Systems Inc
26165 Broadway Ave .... Cleveland OH 44146 440-232-1000
TF: 800-899-8995 ■ *Web:* www.gillmoresecurity.com

Global Elite Group
825 E Gate Blvd Ste 301 .... Garden City NY 11530 516-414-0487
TF: 877-425-0999 ■ *Web:* www.globaleliteinc.com

Golden Glow Investigative & Protective Services
147 Belmont Blvd .... Elmont NY 11003 516-437-7486
Web: goldenglowsecurity.com

Grupo Golan Company Inc 18619 Long Lk Dr .... Boca Raton FL 33496 561-483-9972

Guard Systems Inc
1190 Monterey Pass Rd .... Monterey Park CA 91754 323-881-6711 261-7841
TF: 800-606-6711 ■ *Web:* www.guardsystemsinc.com

Guardian Alarm 20800 Southfield Rd .... Southfield MI 48075 248-423-1000 423-3009
TF: 800-782-9688 ■ *Web:* www.guardianalarm.com

Guardian Protection Services Inc
174 Thorn Hill Rd .... Warrendale PA 15086 855-779-2001 741-3541*
**Fax Area Code: 724* ■ *TF Cust Svc:* 877-314-7092 ■ *Web:* www.guardianprotection.com

guardNOW Inc 16209 Victory Blvd Ste 302 .... Van Nuys CA 91406 877-482-7366
TF: 877-482-7366 ■ *Web:* www.guardnow.com

Habitec Security Inc 2926 S Republic Blvd .... Toledo OH 43615 419-537-6768
TF: 888-422-4832 ■ *Web:* www.habitecsecurity.com

Hannon Security Services Inc
9036 Grand Ave S .... Minneapolis MN 55420 952-881-5865
TF: 800-328-3877 ■ *Web:* www.hannonsecurity.com

Hepaco Inc 2711 Burch Dr PO Box 26308 .... Charlotte NC 28269 704-598-9782 598-7823
TF: 800-888-7689 ■ *Web:* www.hepaco.com

Highcom Security Inc
2451 McMullen Booth Rd Ste 242 .... Clearwater FL 33759 727-592-9400
Web: highcomsecurity.com

Honor Guard Security Inc
1965 Bernice Rd Ste 1 NW .... Lansing IL 60438 708-418-3059
Web: www.hgsecurity.biz

Houston Harris Div Patrol Inc
6420 Richmond Ave .... Houston TX 77057 713-975-9922
TF: 877-975-9922 ■ *Web:* www.hhdpi.com

Huffmaster Crisis Management 1300 Combermere Dr .... Troy MI 48083 248-588-1600
Web: huffmaster.com

Hy-Safe Technology Inc 960 Commerce Dr .... Union Grove WI 53182 262-752-2400
Web: www.hysafe.com

IBI Armored Services Inc 37-06 61st St .... Woodside NY 11377 718-458-4000 458-5371
Web: www.ibiarmored.com

Imaging Locators Inc PO Box 3058 .... Pahrump NV 89048 775-751-6931
Web: www.imaginglocators.com

Information Network Assoc Inc
5235 N Front St .... Harrisburg PA 17110 717-599-5505
TF: 800-443-0824 ■ *Web:* www.ina-inc.com

InfraBasic LLC 440 Ninth Ave 11th Fl .... New York NY 10001 212-404-3099
Web: www.infrabasic.com

Innovative Industrial Solutions Inc
2830 Skyline Dr .... Russellville AR 72802 479-968-4266
TF: 888-684-8249 ■ *Web:* www.i-i-s.net

Inovonics Corp 397 S Taylor Ave .... Louisville CO 80027 303-939-9336
Web: www.inovonics.com

Intec Video Systems Inc
23301 Vista Grande Dr .... Laguna Hills CA 92653 949-859-3800
TF: 800-468-3254 ■ *Web:* www.intecvideo.com

Internal Intelligence Service Inc
9-25 Alling St Ist Fl .... Newark NJ 07102 973-242-5400
Web: www.internalintelligence.com

Ionit Technologies Inc 601 Academy Dr .... Northbrook IL 60062 847-205-9651
Web: www.ionitusa.com

IPC International Corp 2111 Waukegan Rd .... Bannockburn IL 60015 847-444-2000 444-2001

Ipss Inc 150 Isabella St .... Ottawa ON K1S1V7 613-232-2228 231-4888
TF: 866-532-2207 ■ *Web:* ipss.ca

isekurity Inc 24663 Mound Rd .... Warren MI 48091 877-838-5734
TF: 877-838-5734 ■ *Web:* www.isekurity.com

Isr 264 Main St .... Sugar Grove IL 60554 630-466-7800
Web: www.isr-usa.com

Itech Digital LLC 4287 W 96th St .... Indianapolis IN 46268 317-704-0440
TF: 866-733-6673 ■ *Web:* itechdigital.com

J & J Security Services Corp
2922 Howland Blvd Ste 2 .... Deltona FL 32725 386-789-5555
TF: 877-532-7233 ■ *Web:* www.jandjsecurity.com

JBM Patrol & Protection Corp
3110 Kingsley Way .... Madison WI 53713 608-222-5156
Web: jbmpatrol.com

JLS Security & Investigations Inc
2917 Carlisle Blvd NE .... Albuquerque NM 87110 505-400-3840
Web: www.hirejlssecurity.com

Phone | Fax

JMG Security Systems Inc
17150 Newhope St Ste 109 .... Fountain Valley CA 92708 714-545-8882
TF: 800-900-4564 ■ *Web:* www.jmgsecurity.com

Jupiter Group Inc, The Rt 590 .... Hamlin PA 18427 570-689-4722
Web: www.jupgroup.com

Kent Security Services Inc
14600 Biscayne Blvd .... North Miami Beach FL 33181 305-919-9400
TF: 800-273-5368 ■ *Web:* www.kentsecurity.com

Kimmons Security Services Inc
2000 S Dairy Ashford St Ste 430 .... Houston TX 77077 281-679-0070
Web: www.kimmonsinv.com

King Security Services Inc
1458 Howard St .... San Francisco CA 94103 415-556-5464
Web: www.kingsecurity.com

Knight Security Systems LLC
10105 Technology Blvd W Ste 100 .... Dallas TX 75220 214-350-1632
Web: www.knightsecurity.com

L3 Stratis 941 mercantile dr .... Hanover MD 21076 410-684-3019

Landmark Protection Inc
675 N First St Ste 800 .... San Jose CA 95112 408-293-6300
Web: www.landmarkprotection.com

Lantz Security Systems Inc
43440 Sahuayo St .... Lancaster CA 93535 661-949-3565
Web: www.lantzsecurity.com

Law Enforcement Assoc Corp (LEA)
120 Penmarc Dr Ste 125 .... Raleigh NC 27616 919-872-6210 872-6431
OTC: LAWEQ ■ *TF:* 800-354-9669 ■ *Web:* www.leacorp.com

Logitech WiLife 132 East 13065 South Ste 200 .... Draper UT 84020 801-316-4700
Web: online.wilife.com

Loomis Armored US Inc
2500 Citywest Blvd Ste 900 .... Houston TX 77042 713-435-6700
TF: 866-383-5069 ■ *Web:* www.loomis.us

LOREX Corp 3700 Koppers St Ste 504 .... Baltimore MD 21227 410-525-1905
Web: www.lorextechnology.com

Madison Security Group Inc 31 Kirk St .... Lowell MA 01852 978-459-5911
Web: www.madisonsg.com

Maloney Security Inc 1055 Laurel St .... San Carlos CA 94070 650-593-0163 593-1101
Web: www.maloneysecurityinc.com

Marlin Central Monitoring LLC
3600 Commerce Pl Ste 201 .... Kissimmee FL 34742 866-383-0333
TF: 866-383-0333 ■ *Web:* www.marlincentral.com

MaxBotix Inc 7594 S Long Lk Bay Rd .... Brainerd MN 56401 218-454-0766
Web: www.maxbotix.com

McRoberts Protective Agency Inc
87 Nassau St .... New York NY 10038 212-425-6500
TF: 800-866-7233 ■ *Web:* www.mcroberts1876.com

Merchants Building Maintenance LLC
606 Monterey Pass Rd .... Monterey Park CA 91754 800-560-6700
TF: 800-560-6700 ■ *Web:* www.mbmonline.com

Metrologic Instruments Inc 90 Coles Rd .... Blackwood NJ 08012 856-228-8100
Web: www.metrologic.com

Mijac Alarm
9339 Charles Smith Ave Ste 100 .... Rancho Cucamonga CA 91730 909-982-7612 481-0124
TF: 800-982-7612 ■ *Web:* www.mijacalarm.com

Mircom Technologies Ltd 25 Interchange Way .... Vaughan ON L4K5W3 905-660-4655 660-4113
TF: 888-660-4655 ■ *Web:* www.mircom.com

Monument Security Inc 5844 Price Ave .... Sacramento CA 95652 916-564-4234
TF: 877-506-1755 ■ *Web:* monumentsecurity.com

Murray Guard Inc 58 Murray Guard Dr .... Jackson TN 38305 731-668-3400 664-1343
TF: 800-238-3830 ■ *Web:* www.murrayguard.com

MVM Inc 44620 Guilford Dr .... Ashburn VA 20147 571-223-4500 223-4474
Web: www.mvminc.com

My Alarm Center LLC
3803 W Chester Pike Ste 100 .... Newtown Square PA 19073 866-484-4800
TF: 866-484-4800 ■ *Web:* www.myalarmcenter.com

Nabco Inc 1001 Corporate Dr Ste 205 .... Canonsburg PA 15317 724-746-9617
Web: www.nabcoinc.com

National Monitoring Center
26800 Aliso Viejo Pkwy Ste 250 .... Aliso Viejo CA 92656 800-662-1711
TF: 800-662-1711 ■ *Web:* www.nmccentral.com

Network Multi-Family Security Corp
4221 W John Carpenter Fwy .... Irving TX 75063 214-277-7000
TF: 800-541-3138 ■
Web: protection1.com/business/multifamily-security-systems

Nevis Networks Inc 295 Bernardo Ave .... Mountain View CA 94043 650-254-2500
Web: www.nevisnetworks.com

New York Merchants Protective Company Inc
75 W Merrick Rd .... Freeport NY 11520 516-561-5210
TF: 888-696-7911 ■ *Web:* www.nympc.com

Next Level Security Systems Inc
6353 Corte Del Abeto Ste 102 .... Carlsbad CA 92011 760-444-1410
Web: www.nlss.com

Norred & Associates Inc
600 S Central Ave Ste B-100 .... Atlanta GA 30354 404-761-5058
Web: www.norred.com

Northwest Protective Service Inc
801 S Fidalgo 2nd Fl .... Seattle WA 98108 206-448-4040 448-2461
Web: www.nwprotective.com

Northwestern Ohio Security Systems Inc
121 E High St .... Lima OH 45801 614-527-7037
TF: 800-833-6416 ■ *Web:* www.nwoss.com

Nuclear Security Services Corp
701 Willowbrook Centre Pkwy .... Willowbrook IL 60527 630-920-1488
Web: www.g4s.us

O'Gara Group Inc, The
9113 Le Saint Dr Ste 460 .... Fairfield OH 45014 513-338-0660
Web: www.ogaragroup.com

Okaloosa - Walton Security & Surveillancellc
593 Hubbard St .... Defuniak Springs FL 32435 850-892-4550
Web: okaloosa-waltonsecurityandsurveillance.com

Olympic Security Services Inc
631 Strander Blvd Ste A .... Seattle WA 98188 206-575-8531
Web: www.olympiksecurity.com

	City	State	Zip	Phone	Fax
Omega Security Service Inc 103 Yost Blvd Ste 100A *Web:* www.omega-security.com	Pittsburgh	PA	15221	412-349-0850	
OpSec Security Inc 1857 Colonial Village Ln *Web:* www.aotgroup.com	Lancaster	PA	17601	717-293-4110	
Optellios Inc 11 Penns Trl Ste 300 *Web:* www.optellios.com	Newtown	PA	18940	267-364-5298	
OSI Security Devices Inc 1580 Jayken Way *TF:* 800-711-6814 ■ *Web:* www.omnilock.com	Chula Vista	CA	91911	619-628-1000	
Pacific Security Integrations Inc 99-1285 Halawa Vly Rd *Web:* pacsecinc.com	Aiea	HI	96701	808-484-4000	
Pasek Corp 9 W Third St *TF:* 800-628-2822 ■ *Web:* www.pasek.com	South Boston	MA	02127	617-269-7110	
Pass Security LLC 340 Office Court Ste B *Web:* www.passsecurity.com	Fairview Heights	IL	62208	618-394-1144	
Patriot Security Inc 107 W 1st St *Web:* www.patriotsecurityinc.com	Humble	TX	77338	281-446-3736	
Patrol One 630 S Grand Ave Ste 101 *Web:* www.patrol-one.com	Santa Ana	CA	92705	714-541-0999	
Perey Turnstiles Inc 308 Bishop Ave *Web:* www.turnstile.com	Bridgeport	CT	06610	203-333-9400	
Perimeter Security Solutions Inc 1900 Fannin St *Web:* www.perimetersecuritysolutions.com	Vernon	TX	76384	940-552-2942	
Photo-scan of Los Angeles 743 Cochran St Ste C *Web:* www.pslasecurity.com	Simi Valley	CA	93065	805-581-4448	
Pierce County Security Inc 2002 99th St E *TF:* 800-773-4432 ■ *Web:* www.pcswa.com	Tacoma	WA	98445	253-535-4433	
Pivot Point Security 1245 Whitehorse Mercerville Rd *Web:* pivotpointsecurity.com	Trenton	NJ	08619	609-581-4600	
Point 2 Point Global Security Inc 14346 Jarrettsville Pike Ste 200 *Web:* www.p2pgsi.net	Phoenix	MD	21131	410-638-8788	
Pontis Research Inc 4195 E Thousand Oaks Blvd Ste 105 *Web:* www.pontisresearch.com	Westlake Village	CA	91362	805-777-7424	
Port Security International LLC 40 Calhoun St Ste 230 *Web:* www.securereports.com	Charleston	SC	29401	843-723-9255	
Post Alarm Systems Inc 47 E Saint Joseph St *Web:* www.postalarm.com	Arcadia	CA	91006	626-446-7159	
Premier Electronics Inc 465 Rockaway Ave	Valley Stream	NY	11581	516-837-3160	
Prestige Alarm & Specialty Products Inc 7640 Commerce Ln PO Box 9 *Web:* www.prestigealarm.com	Trussville	AL	35173	205-661-4822	
Prestige Security 5721 W Slauson Ave Ste 120 *TF:* 800-482-7303 ■ *Web:* www.prestigesecurity.com	Culver City	CA	90230	310-670-5999	
Pro Security Group 301B S Robinson Dr *TF:* 855-753-7766 ■ *Web:* prosecuritygroup.com	Robinson	TX	76706	254-753-7766	
Prodco International Inc 9408 Boul du Golf *TF:* 888-577-6326 ■ *Web:* www.prodcotech.com	Montreal	QC	H1J3A1	514-324-9796	
Protran Technology LLC 52 Paterson Ave *Web:* www.protrantechnology.com	Newton	NJ	07860	973-250-4176	
Pyro-Comm Systems Inc 15531 Container Ln *Web:* www.pyrocomm.com	Huntington Beach	CA	92649	714-902-8000	
R & d Professional Services LLC 3000 Keller Springs Rd Ste 200 *Web:* www.rndconsult.com	Carrollton	TX	75006	214-483-5342	
Rancho Santa Fe Protective Services Inc 1991 Vlg Pk Way Ste 100 *TF:* 800-303-8877 ■ *Web:* www.rsfsecurity.com	Encinitas	CA	92024	760-942-0688	
Ranger American Calle Marginal Lodi 605 Ave 65 Infanteria Villa Capri Rio Piedras *Web:* www.rangeramerican.com	San Juan	PR	00924	787-999-6060	
Rapid Focus Security LLC 253 Summer St Ste 303 *TF:* 855-793-1337 ■ *Web:* www.pwnieexpress.com	Boston	MA	02210	855-793-1337	
Rapid Response Monitoring Services Inc 400 W Division St *TF:* 800-558-7767 ■ *Web:* www.rrms.com	Syracuse	NY	13204	800-558-7767	
Razberi Technologies Inc 1628 Valwood Pkwy Ste 148 *Web:* www.razberi.net	Carrollton	TX	75006	469-828-3380	
Rebellion Photonics Inc 2327 Commerce St Ste 200 *Web:* rebellionphotonics.com	Houston	TX	77002	713-218-0101	
RECON Dynamics LLC 2300 Carillon Point *TF:* 877-480-3551 ■ *Web:* www.recondynamics.com	Kirkland	WA	98033	877-480-3551	
Redrock Security & Cabling Inc 6 Morgan Ste 150 *Web:* www.itredrock.com	Irvine	CA	92618	949-900-3460	
Redwire LLC 1136 Thomasville Rd *Web:* redwireus.com	Tallahassee	FL	32303	850-219-9473	
Regent Security Services Inc 2602 Commons Blvd *Web:* www.regentsecurity.com	Augusta	GA	30909	706-738-3113	
Reliance Protectron Security Services 4209-99 St Ste 102 *Web:* www.voxcom.com	Edmonton	AB	T6E5V7	780-462-1657	
RIEtech Global LLC 3700 Singer Blvd NE Ste A *Web:* www.rietechglobal.com	Albuquerque	NM	87109	505-299-6623	
RLE Technologies Inc 104 Racquette Dr *Web:* rletech.com	Fort Collins	CO	80524	970-484-6510	
Rochester Armored Car Company Inc 3937 Leavenworth St *Web:* www.rochesterarmoredcar.com	Omaha	NE	68105	402-558-9323	
Rodbat Security Services 8125 Somerset Blvd *TF:* 877-676-3228 ■ *Web:* www.rmiintl.com	Paramount	CA	90723	562-806-9098	
Safe Home Security Inc 55 Sebethe Dr *Web:* www.safehomesecurityinc.com	Cromwell	CT	06416	860-262-4000	
Safe Security PO Box 3888 Ste A *Web:* safesecurity.us	Silverdale	WA	98383	360-698-9800	
Safeguard Security & Communications Inc 8454 N 90th St *TF:* 800-426-6060 ■ *Web:* safeguardsecurity.com	Scottsdale	AZ	85258	480-609-6200	
Safety Service Systems Inc 4036 N Nashville Ave *Web:* www.safetyservicesystems.com	Chicago	IL	60634	773-282-4900	
Scarsdale Security Systems Inc 132 Montgomery Ave *Web:* scarsdalesecurity.com/index.html	Scarsdale	NY	10583	914-722-2200	
SDI Chicago 33 West Monroe Ste 400 *TF:* 888-968-7734 ■ *Web:* www.sdisolutions.com	Chicago	IL	60603	312-580-7500	580-7600
Secom International 9610 Bellanca Ave *Web:* www.secomintl.com	Los Angeles	CA	90045	310-641-1290	
Secure Mentem Inc 1910 Towne Centre Blvd Ste 250 *Web:* www.securementem.com	Annapolis	MD	21401	443-603-0200	
Securiguard Inc 6858 Old Dominion Dr Ste 307 *Web:* www.securiguardinc.com	Mclean	VA	22101	703-821-6777	
Security & Access Systems 3811 Rutledge Rd Ne *Web:* www.securityandaccess.com	Albuquerque	NM	87109	505-823-1561	
Security & Data Technologies Inc 101 Pheasant Run	Newtown	PA	18940	215-579-7000	579-7080
Security 101 LLC 2465 Mercer Ave Ste 101 *TF:* 888-909-4101 ■ *Web:* www.security101.com	West Palm Beach	FL	33401	888-909-4101	
Security America Inc 3412 Chesterfield Ave Ste *Web:* www.securityamerica.com	Charleston	WV	25304	304-925-4747	
Security Equipment Inc 13505 C St *Web:* www.sei-security.com	Omaha	NE	68144	402-333-3233	
Security Horizon Inc 5350 Tomah Dr Ste 3200 *Web:* www.securityhorizon.com	Colorado Springs	CO	80918	719-488-4500	
Security Information Systems Inc 6314 Kingspointe Pkwy Ste 3 *Web:* www.securitysoftware.com	Orlando	FL	32819	407-345-1550	
Security Instrument Corp of Delaware 309 W Newport Pk *Web:* www.securityinstrument.com	Wilmington	DE	19804	302-633-5621	
Security Management Systems Inc 225 Community Dr Ste 150 *Web:* www.securitymgt.com	Great Neck	NY	11021	516-450-3120	
Security Resource Group Inc 300-1914 Hamilton St *Web:* www.securityresourcegroup.com	Regina	SK	S4P3N6	306-522-0135	
SecurTek Monitoring Solutions Inc 70-1st Ave N *Web:* www.securtek.com/	Yorkton	SK	S3N1J6	306-786-4330	
Seico Security Systems 132 Court St *TF:* 800-272-0316 ■ *Web:* seicosecurity.com	Pekin	IL	61554	309-347-3200	
Select Engineered Systems 7991 W 26th Ave *TF:* 800-342-5737 ■ *Web:* www.selectses.com	Hialeah	FL	33016	305-823-5410	
Senstar Corp 119 John Cavanaugh Dr *Web:* senstar.com	Ottawa	ON	K0A1L0	613-839-5572	
Sentinel Offender Services LLC 201 Technology Dr *Web:* www.sentineladvantage.com	Irvine	CA	92618	949-453-1550	
Sentry 360 Security Inc 23807 West Andrew Rd Ste B *Web:* sentry360.com	Plainfield	IL	60585	630-355-3440	
Sentry Alarm Systems of America Inc 8 Thomas Owens Way *TF:* 800-424-7773 ■ *Web:* sentryalarm.com	Monterey	CA	93940	831-375-2727	
Sentry Security LLC 339 Egidi Dr *TF:* 888-272-7080 ■ *Web:* www.sentrysecurity.com	Wheeling	IL	60090	847-353-7200	
Sentry Watch Inc 1705 Holbrook St *TF:* 800-632-4961 ■ *Web:* www.sentrywatch.com	Greensboro	NC	27403	336-292-6468	
SFI Electronics Inc 400A Clanton Rd *Web:* www.sfi-electronics.com	Charlotte	NC	28217	704-522-0800	
SFRi LLC 242 California St *Web:* www.sfrillc.com	San Francisco	CA	94111	415-394-3900	
SIC Biometrics Inc 555 Larocque Rd *Web:* www.sic.ca	Valleyfield	QC	J6T4C8	450-424-2772	
Silver Shield Security Inc 2107 N First St Ste 100	San Jose	CA	95131	408-435-1111	
Simmons Investigative & Security Agency Inc 76 S Winter Park Dr *Web:* www.simmonssecurity.com	Casselberry	FL	32707	407-699-5308	
Smith Monitoring Inc 550 E 15th St *Web:* www.smithmonitoring.com	Plano	TX	75074	469-250-8866	
Smith Protective Services Inc 1801 Royal Ln Ste 250 *Web:* www.smithprotective.com	Dallas	TX	75229	214-631-4444	
SNUPI Technologies Inc 4512 University Way NE *Web:* www.wallyhome.com	Seattle	WA	98105	206-673-2707	
Sonavation Inc 3970 RCA Blvd Ste 7003 *Web:* sonavation.com	Palm Beach Gardens	FL	33410	561-209-1201	
St. James Security Services Inc 1604 Ave Ponce De Leon *Web:* www.stjamessecurity.com	San Juan	PR	00926	787-754-8448	
St. Moritz Security Services Inc 4600 Clairton Blvd *TF:* 800-218-9156 ■ *Web:* www.smssi.com	Pittsburgh	PA	15236	412-885-3144	
Staff Pro Inc 15272 Newsboy Cir *Web:* www.staffpro.com	Huntington Beach	CA	92649	714-230-7200	

				Phone	Fax
Stanley Correctional Services 14670 Cumberland Rd *Web:* stanleycorrectionalservices.com	Noblesville	IN	46060	317-776-3500	
Starr Security Services 601 W 51st St *Web:* starrsecurityservices.com	New York	NY	10019	212-767-1110	
Stealth Monitoring Inc 15182 Marsh Lane *TF:* 855-783-2584 ■ *Web:* www.stealthmonitoring.com	Dallas	TX	75001	214-341-0123	
Strongauth Inc 10846 Via San Marino *Web:* www.strongauth.com	Cupertino	CA	95014	408-331-2000	
Summit Security Services Inc 390 Rexcorp Plz W Tower - Lobby Level *TF:* 800-615-5888 ■ *Web:* www.summitsecurity.com	Uniondale	NY	11556	516-240-2400	
Superior Alarm Systems 9001 Canoga Ave *Web:* www.sassecurity.com	Canoga Park	CA	91304	818-700-7100	
Supreme Security Systems Inc 1565 Union Ave *Web:* www.supremesecurity.com	Union	NJ	07083	908-810-8822	
Tenable Protective Services Inc 2423 Payne Ave *Web:* www.anchor-security.com	Cleveland	OH	44114	216-361-0002	
Texas Dept of Public Safety 1001 E Coke Rd	Winnsboro	TX	75494	903-342-0982	
Titan Protection & Consulting Inc 9350 Metcalf Ave Ste 210 *Web:* www.tpcsecurity.com	Overland Park	KS	66212	913-441-0911	
Top Guard Inc 131 Kings Way Ste 100 *Web:* www.topguardinc.com	Hampton	VA	23669	757-722-3961	
Totevision 1319 Dexter Ave N Ste 20 *Web:* www.totevision.com	Seattle	WA	98109	206-623-6000	
Traffipax Inc 514 Progress Dr Ste D-E *Web:* www.traffipaxinc.com	Linthicum Heights	MD	21090	443-367-0007	
Trans-West Security Services Inc 4444 Grissom St *Web:* trans-west.net	Bakersfield	CA	93313	661-834-0711	
Triad Security Systems 971 Lehigh Ave *Web:* www.triadsecurity.com	Union	NJ	07083	908-964-5252	
Trident Security Service 4968 Dorchester Rd *Web:* www.tsecurityservices.com	Charleston	SC	29418	843-767-3855	
Triple s Alarm Company Inc 2820 Cantrell Rd *Web:* www.triplesalarm.com	Little Rock	AR	72202	501-664-4599	
Twin City Security Inc 519 Coon Rapids Blvd *Web:* www.twincitysecurity.com	Minneapolis	MN	55433	763-784-4160	
Tyco International Ltd 9 Roszel Rd *NYSE:* TYC ■ *TF:* 800-685-4509 ■ *Web:* www.tyco.com	Princeton	NJ	08540	609-720-4200	720-4208
UCIT Online Security 6441 Northam Dr *TF:* 866-756-7847 ■ *Web:* www.ucitonline.com	Mississauga	ON	L4V1J2	905-405-9898	
United Security Inc 4295 Arthur Kill Rd *Web:* www.usisecurity.com	Staten Island	NY	10309	718-967-6820	
Universal Protection Service 27134 Malibu Cove Colony Dr *Web:* universalpro.com	Malibu	CA	90265	310-589-5728	
Universal Services of America Inc 1551 N Tustin Ave Ste 650 *TF:* 866-877-1965 ■ *Web:* www.universalpro.com	Santa Ana	CA	92705	714-619-9700	619-9701
UPEK Inc 5900 Christie Ave *Web:* www.upek.com	Emeryville	CA	94608	510-420-2600	
US Protection Service LLC 5785 Emporium Sq *Web:* www.uspsvc.com	Columbus	OH	43231	614-794-4950	
US Security Assoc Inc 200 Mansell Ct 5th Fl *TF:* 800-730-9599 ■ *Web:* www.ussecurityassociates.com	Roswell	GA	30076	770-625-1500	625-1509
US Security Inc 4544 NW 10th St *TF:* 877-917-5566 ■ *Web:* www.ussecurity.com	Oklahoma City	OK	73127	405-947-3377	
Vanguard Products Group Inc 720 Brooker Creek Blvd Ste 223 *TF:* 877-477-4874 ■ *Web:* vanguardprotexglobal.com	Oldsmar	FL	34677	813-855-9639	
Verant Identification Systems Inc 2496 Ridge Rd W Ste 203 *TF:* 866-257-4351 ■ *Web:* www.verantid.com	Rochester	NY	14626	585-214-2451	
VeriTainer Corp The Beckstoffer House 1127 Pope St Ste 201 *Web:* www.veritainer.com	St. Helena	CA	94574	707-967-0944	
Vescom Corp 705 Main Rd N *TF:* 800-841-1769 ■ *Web:* www.vescomcorp.com	Hampden	ME	04444	207-945-5051	
VideoIQ Inc 900 Middlesex TurnPk Bldg 5 *Web:* www.videoiq.net	Billerica	MA	01821	781-222-3069	
Vinson Guard Service Inc 955 Howard Ave *TF:* 800-441-7899 ■ *Web:* www.vinsonguard.com	New Orleans	LA	70113	504-529-2260	
Voice Security Systems Inc 24591 Seth Cir *Web:* www.voice-security.com	Dana Point	CA	92629	949-493-4030	
Vss Security Services 1717 W Northern Ave Ste 200 *Web:* www.vss-security-services.com	Phoenix	AZ	85021	602-861-9900	
Weiser Security Services Inc 3939 Tulane Ave *Web:* www.weisersecurity.com	New Orleans	LA	70119	504-949-7558	
Whelan Security Co 1699 S Hanley Rd Ste 350 *TF:* 888-494-3526 ■ *Web:* www.whelansecurity.com	St Louis	MO	63144	314-644-3227	
Winfield Security Corp 35 W 35th St Fl 8 *Web:* www.winfieldsecurity.com	New York	NY	10001	212-947-3700	
Wyvern Consulting Ltd 10 N Main St *Web:* www.wyvernltd.com	Yardley	PA	19067	609-671-9300	
Xator Corp 543 Harbor Blvd Ste 501 *Web:* www.xatorcorp.com	Destin	FL	32541	850-460-2860	
Yale Assoc Inc 1150 Portion Rd *Web:* www.yaleassociates.com	Holtsville	NY	11742	631-320-3088	
Zinus Inc 30799 Wiegman Rd *Web:* zinus.com	Hayward	CA	94544	925-417-2100	
Zvetco Biometrics LLC 6820 Hanging Moss Rd *Web:* www.zvetcobiometrics.com	Orlando	FL	32807	407-681-0111	

694 SEED COMPANIES

See Also Farm Supplies p. 2281

Seed production and development companies (horticultural and agricultural).

				Phone	Fax
AgriGold Hybrids 5381 Akin Rd *TF:* 800-262-7333 ■ *Web:* www.agrigold.com	Saint Francisville	IL	62460	618-943-5776	
Albert Lea Seed House 1414 W Main St *TF:* 800-352-5247 ■ *Web:* www.alseed.com	Albert Lea	MN	56007	507-373-3161	373-7032
Ampac Seed Co 32727 Hwy 99 E *TF:* 800-547-3230 ■ *Web:* www.ampacseed.com	Tangent	OR	97389	541-928-1651	928-2430
Applewood Seed Co 5380 Vivian St *Web:* www.applewoodseed.com	Arvada	CO	80002	303-431-7333	467-7886
Barenbrug USA Inc 33477 Hwy 99 E PO Box 239 **Fax:* Sales ■ *Web:* www.barenbrug.com	Tangent	OR	97389	541-926-5801	926-9435*
Foremostco Inc 8457 NW 66th St **Fax Area Code:* 800 ■ *TF:* 800-421-8986 ■ *Web:* www.foremostco.com	Miami	FL	33166	305-592-8986	426-1362*
Gries Seed Farms Inc 2348 N Fifth St *TF:* 800-472-4797 ■ *Web:* seedtoday.com	Fremont	OH	43420	419-332-5571	
Harris Moran Seed Co PO Box 4938 **Fax Area Code:* 209 ■ *TF:* 800-808-7333 ■ *Web:* www.harrismoran.com	Modesto	CA	95352	800-320-4672	527-5312*
Johnny's Selected Seeds 955 Benton Ave *TF:* 877-564-6697 ■ *Web:* www.johnnyseeds.com	Winslow	ME	04901	207-861-3900	861-8363
JW Jung Seed Co 335 S High St *TF:* 800-297-3123 ■ *Web:* www.jungseed.com	Randolph	WI	53956	800-297-3123	692-5864
Keithly-Williams Seeds Inc 420 Palm Ave *TF:* 800-533-3465 ■ *Web:* www.keithlywilliams.com	Holtville	CA	92250	760-356-5533	356-2409
Latham Seed Co 131 180th St *TF:* 877-465-2842 ■ *Web:* www.lathamseeds.com	Alexander	IA	50420	641-692-3258	692-3250
Lebanon Seaboard Corp 1600 E Cumberland St *TF:* 800-233-0628 ■ *Web:* www.lebsea.com	Lebanon	PA	17042	717-273-1685	
Nunhems USA Inc 1200 Anderson Corner Rd **Fax:* Cust Svc ■ *TF Cust Svc:* 800-733-9505 ■ *Web:* www.nunhemsusa.com/www/NunhemsInternet.nsf/id/US_EN_Home	Parma	ID	83660	208-674-4000	674-4090*
Park Seed Co 1 Parkton Ave *TF Orders:* 800-845-3369 ■ *Web:* www.parkseed.com	Greenwood	SC	29647	800-845-3369	
Pennington Seed Inc 1280 AtlantaHwy *Web:* www.pennington.com/lawn-garden/grass-seed	Madison	GA	30650	706-342-1234	342-8071
Red River Commodities Inc 501 42nd St N *TF:* 800-437-5539 ■ *Web:* www.redriv.com	Fargo	ND	58102	701-282-2600	282-5325
Renee's Garden Seeds Inc 7389 W Zayante Rd *TF:* 888-880-7228 ■ *Web:* www.reneesgarden.com	Felton	CA	95018	831-335-7228	335-7227
Sakata Seed America Inc 18095 Serene Dr PO Box 880 *Web:* www.sakata.com	Morgan Hill	CA	95037	408-778-7758	778-7768
Sand Seed Service Inc 4765 Hwy 143 *TF:* 800-352-2228 ■ *Web:* www.sandsofiowa.com	Marcus	IA	51035	712-376-4135	376-4140
Schlessman Seed Co 11513 US Rt 250 *TF:* 888-534-7333 ■ *Web:* www.schlessman-seed.com	Milan	OH	44846	419-499-2572	499-2574
Seedway LLC 1734 Railroad Pl *TF:* 800-836-3710 ■ *Web:* www.seedway.com	Hall	NY	14463	585-526-6391	526-6832
Sharp Bros Seed Co 1005 S Sycamore *TF:* 800-462-8483 ■ *Web:* www.sharpseed.com	Healy	KS	67850	620-398-2231	398-2220
Stock Seed Farms 28008 Mill Rd *TF:* 800-759-1520 ■ *Web:* www.stockseed.com	Murdock	NE	68407	402-867-3771	867-2442
Stratton Seed Co 1530 Hwy 79 S *TF:* 800-264-4433 ■ *Web:* www.strattonseed.com	Stuttgart	AR	72160	870-673-4433	673-4290
W Atlee Burpee Co 300 Pk Ave *TF Cust Svc:* 800-333-5808 ■ *Web:* www.burpee.com	Warminster	PA	18974	215-674-4900	674-4170
Weeks Seed Company Inc 1050 Moye Blvd *TF:* 800-322-1234 ■ *Web:* www.weeksseeds.com	Greenville	NC	27834	252-757-1234	
Wetsel Inc 961 N Liberty St *TF Cust Svc:* 800-572-4018 ■ *Web:* bfgsupply.com	Harrisonburg	VA	22802	540-434-6753	

695 SEMICONDUCTOR MANUFACTURING SYSTEMS & EQUIPMENT

				Phone	Fax
Adcotron EMS Inc 12 Ch St Marine Industrial Pk *Web:* www.adcotron.com	Boston	MA	02210	617-598-3000	598-3001
Advanced Energy Industries Inc 1625 Sharp Pt Dr *NASDAQ:* AEIS ■ *TF:* 800-446-9167 ■ *Web:* www.advanced-energy.com	Fort Collins	CO	80525	970-221-4670	221-5583
Aehr Test Systems 400 Kato Terr *NASDAQ:* AEHR ■ *TF:* 800-962-4284 ■ *Web:* www.aehr.com	Fremont	CA	94539	510-623-9400	623-9450
Akrion Systems LLC 6330 Hedgewood Dr Ste 150 **Fax:* Sales ■ *Web:* www.akrionsystems.com	Allentown	PA	18106	610-391-9200	391-1982*
Amistar Automation Inc 1269 Linda Vista *Web:* www.amistarautomation.com	San Marcos	CA	92078	760-471-1700	471-9065
Amtech Systems Inc 131 S Clark Dr *NASDAQ:* ASYS ■ *Web:* www.amtechsystems.com	Tempe	AZ	85281	480-967-5146	968-3763
Applied Materials Inc 3050 Bowers Ave PO Box 58039 *NASDAQ:* AMAT ■ *TF:* 877-356-9175 ■ *Web:* www.appliedmaterials.com	Santa Clara	CA	95054	408-727-5555	
Applied Materials/Semitool 655 W Reserve Dr *TF:* 877-356-9175 ■ *Web:* www.appliedmaterials.com	Kalispell	MT	59901	406-752-2107	
ASM America Inc 3440 E University Dr *Web:* www.asm.com	Phoenix	AZ	85034	602-470-5700	437-1403
ASML US Inc 8555 S River Pkwy *Web:* www.asml.com	Tempe	AZ	85284	480-383-4422	
Axcelis Technologies Inc 108 Cherry Hill Dr *NASDAQ:* ACLS ■ *Web:* www.axcelis.com	Beverly	MA	01915	978-787-4000	787-4200
Brooks Automation Inc 15 Elizabeth Dr *NASDAQ:* BRKS ■ *TF:* 800-698-6149 ■ *Web:* www.brooks.com	Chelmsford	MA	01824	978-262-2400	262-2500
BTU International Inc 23 Esquire Rd *NASDAQ:* BTUI ■ *TF:* 800-998-0666 ■ *Web:* www.btu.com	North Billerica	MA	01862	978-667-4111	667-9068
Conceptronic Inc 1860 Smithtown Ave *Web:* www.conceptronic.com	Ronkonkoma	NY	11779	631-981-7081	981-7095

Phone Fax

Contact Systems Inc 50 Miry Brook Rd Danbury CT 06810 203-743-3837
Web: www.contactsystems.com

CVD Equipment Corp 1860 Smithtown Ave Ronkonkoma NY 11779 631-981-7081 981-7095
NASDAQ: CVV ■ *Web:* www.cvdequipment.com

Cymer Inc 17075 Thornmint Ct San Diego CA 92127 858-385-7300 385-7100
NASDAQ: CYMI ■ *Web:* www.cymer.com

Data I/O Corp 6464 185th Ave NE Ste 101 Redmond WA 98052 425-881-6444 881-6444
NASDAQ: DAIO ■ *TF:* 800-426-1045 ■ *Web:* dataio.com

Ebara Technologies Inc 51 Main Ave Sacramento CA 95838 916-920-5451 925-6654
TF: 800-535-5376 ■ *Web:* www.ebaratech.com

EG Systems LLC 6200 Village Pkwy Dublin CA 94568 408-528-3000 528-3562
Web: www.electroglas.com

EMCORE Corp 10420 Research Rd SE Albuquerque NM 87123 505-332-5000
NASDAQ: EMKR ■ *Web:* www.emcore.com

Engent Inc 3140 Northwoods Pkwy Ste 300A Norcross GA 30071 678-990-3320 990-3324
Web: www.engentaat.com

Entegris Inc 129 Concord Rd Bldg 2 Billerica MA 01821 978-436-6500 436-6735
NASDAQ: ENTG ■ *TF:* 877-695-7654 ■ *Web:* www.entegris.com

FormFactor Inc 7005 SouthFront Rd Livermore CA 94551 925-290-4000 290-4010
NASDAQ: FORM ■ *Web:* www.formfactor.com

Fortrend Corp 687 N Pastoria Ave Sunnyvale CA 94085 408-734-9311 734-4299
TF: 888-937-3637 ■ *Web:* www.fortrend.com

FSI International Inc 3455 Lyman Blvd Chaska MN 55318 952-448-5440 448-2825
NASDAQ: FSII ■ *Web:* www.tel.com

Gem City Engineering & Mfg Co, The 401 Leo St Dayton OH 45404 937-223-5544 226-1908
Web: www.gemcity.com

Gem Services USA Inc 2880 Lakeside Dr Santa Clara CA 95054 408-566-8866 566-8858
Web: www.gemservices.com

Global Communication Semiconductors Inc
23155 Kashiwa Ct Torrance CA 90505 310-530-7274 517-8200
Web: www.gcsincorp.com

I.B.I.S. Inc 30 Technology Pkwy S Ste 400 Norcross GA 30092 770-368-4000
TF: 866-714-8422 ■ *Web:* www.ibisinc.com

Imtec Acculine Inc 49036 Milmont Dr Fremont CA 94538 510-770-1800 770-1400
Web: www.imtecacculine.com

KDF Electronic & Vacuum Services Inc
10 Volvo Dr Rockleigh NJ 07647 201-784-5005 784-0202
Web: www.kdf.com

KLA-Tencor Corp 1 Technology Dr Milpitas CA 95035 408-875-3000 875-4144
NASDAQ: KLAC ■ *TF:* 800-600-2829 ■ *Web:* www.kla-tencor.com

Kokusai Semiconductor Equipment Corp
2460 N First St Ste 290 San Jose CA 95131 408-456-2750 456-2760
TF: 800-800-5321 ■ *Web:* www.ksec.com

Kulicke & Soffa Industries Inc (K&S)
1005 Virginia Dr Fort Washington PA 19034 215-784-6000 784-6001
NASDAQ: KLIC ■ *Web:* www.kns.com

Lam Research Corp 4650 Cushing Pkwy Fremont CA 94538 510-572-0200
NASDAQ: LRCX ■ *TF:* 800-526-7678 ■ *Web:* lamresearch.com

Lansdale Semiconductor Inc 5245 S 39th St Phoenix AZ 85040 602-438-0123 438-0138
Web: www.lansdale.com

Loranger International Corp 817 Fourth Ave Warren PA 16365 814-723-2250 723-5391
Web: www.loranger.com

Mattson Technology Inc 47131 Bayside Pkwy Fremont CA 94538 510-657-5900 492-5911
NASDAQ: MTSN ■ *TF:* 800-315-6607 ■ *Web:* www.mattson.com

MaxLinear Inc
2051 Palomar Airport Rd Ste 100 Carlsbad CA 92011 760-692-0711 444-8598
NYSE: MXL ■ *TF:* 888-505-4369 ■ *Web:* www.maxlinear.com

MCT Worldwide LLC 121 S Eigth St Ste 960 Minneapolis MN 55402 612-436-3240 436-3242
Web: www.mct.com

N J R Corp 125 Nicholson Ln San Jose CA 95134 408-321-0200 232-6060
TF: 800-800-5441 ■ *Web:* www.njr.com

Neutronix-Quintel (NXQ) 685 Jarvis Dr # A Morgan Hill CA 95037 408-776-5190 776-1039
Web: www.neutronixinc.com

Rudolph Technologies Inc
1 Rudolph Rd PO Box 1000 Flanders NJ 07836 973-691-1300
NASDAQ: RTEC ■ *TF:* 877-467-8365 ■ *Web:* www.rudolphtech.com

Semi-Kinetics Inc 20191 Windrow Dr Ste A Lake Forest CA 92630 949-830-7364 830-7385
Web: www.semi-kinetics.com

Sensitron Semiconductor 221 W Industry Ct Deer Park NY 11729 631-586-7600 586-6053
Web: www.sensitron.com

Shin-Etsu Microsi Inc 10028 S 51st St Phoenix AZ 85044 480-893-8898 893-8637
Web: www.microsi.com

Small Precision Tools Inc 1330 Clegg St Petaluma CA 94954 707-765-4545 778-2271
Web: www.smallprecisiontools.com

Spintrac Systems Inc 690 Aldo Ave Santa Clara CA 95054 408-980-1155 980-1267
Web: www.spintrac.com

Spire Corp 1 Patriots Pk Bedford MA 01730 978-649-6111 275-7470*
OTC: SPIR ■ **Fax Area Code:* 781 ■ *Web:* www.spiresolar.com

Tegal Corp 2201 S McDowell Blvd Petaluma CA 94954 707-763-5600
Web: www.collabrx.com

Tek-Vac Industries Inc 176 Express Dr S Brentwood NY 11717 631-436-5100 436-5154
Web: www.tekvac.com

Tokyo Electron America Inc 2400 Grove Blvd Austin TX 78741 512-424-1000 424-1001
TF: 800-828-6596 ■ *Web:* www.tel.com

Trio-Tech International 14731 Califa St Van Nuys CA 91411 818-787-7000 787-9130
NYSE: TRT ■ *Web:* www.triotech.com

Ultra Clean Holdings Inc 26462 Corporate Ave Hayward CA 94545 510-576-4400 576-4401
NASDAQ: UCTT ■ *Web:* www.uct.com

Ultratech Inc 3050 Zanker Rd San Jose CA 95134 408-321-8835 577-3378
NASDAQ: UTEK ■ *TF:* 800-222-1213 ■ *Web:* www.ultratech.com

United Memories Inc
4815 List Dr Ste 109 Colorado Springs CO 80919 719-594-4238
Web: www.unitedmemories.com

Universal Instruments Corp (UIC)
33 Broome Corporate Pk Conklin NY 13748 607-779-7522 779-4466
TF: 800-842-9732 ■ *Web:* uic.com

Varian Semiconductor Equipment Assoc Inc
35 Dory Rd Gloucester MA 01930 978-282-2000 283-6376
TF: 800-344-1111 ■ *Web:* www.vsea.com

Veeco Instruments Inc 1 Terminal Dr Plainview NY 11803 516-677-0200
NASDAQ: VECO ■ *TF:* 888-724-9511 ■ *Web:* www.veeco.com

696 SEMICONDUCTORS & RELATED DEVICES

See Also Electronic Components & Accessories - Mfr p. 2226; Printed Circuit Boards p. 2974

Phone Fax

8x8 Inc 810 W Maude Ave Sunnyvale CA 94085 408-727-1885 980-0432
NASDAQ: EGHT ■ *TF:* 888-898-8733 ■ *Web:* www.8x8.com

Actel Corp 2061 Stierlin Ct Mountain View CA 94043 650-318-4200 318-4600
TF: 800-262-1060 ■ *Web:* www.microsemi.com

Advanced Micro Devices Inc (AMD)
1 AMD Pl PO Box 3453 Sunnyvale CA 94088 408-749-4000
NYSE: AMD ■ *TF:* 800-538-8450 ■ *Web:* www.amd.com

Advanced Photonix Inc 2925 Boardwalk Ann Arbor MI 48104 734-864-5600 998-3474
NYSE: API ■ *Web:* www.advancedphotonix.com

Advantage Electronic Product Development
34 Garden Ctr Broomfield CO 80020 303-410-0292
TF: 866-841-5581 ■ *Web:* www.advantage-dev.com

Aeroflex Inc 35 S Service Rd PO Box 6022 Plainview NY 11803 516-694-6700 694-0658
TSE: ARX ■ *TF:* 800-843-1553 ■ *Web:* www.aeroflex.com

AKM Semiconductor Inc
1731 Technology Dr Ste 500 San Jose CA 95110 408-436-8580
Web: www.akm.com

Allegro Microsystems Inc 115 NE Cutoff Worcester MA 01606 508-853-5000 853-2431
Web: www.allegromicro.com

Alliance Semiconductor Corp
10755 Scripps Poway Pkwy Ste 302 San Diego CA 92131 415-984-8700
OTC: ALSC ■ *Web:* www.alsc.com

Altera Corp 101 Innovation Dr San Jose CA 95134 408-544-7000 544-6403*
NASDAQ: ALTR ■ **Fax:* Cust Svc ■ *TF Cust Svc:* 800-767-3753 ■ *Web:* www.altera.com

Amalfi Semiconductor Inc
475 Alberto Way Ste 200 Los Gatos CA 95032 408-399-5360

Ambarella Inc 2975 San Ysidro Way Santa Clara CA 95054 408-734-8888
Web: www.ambarella.com

American Arium 14811 Myford Rd Tustin CA 92780 714-731-1661 731-6344

Amkor Technology Inc 1900 S Price Rd Chandler AZ 85248 480-821-5000
NASDAQ: AMKR ■ *Web:* www.amkor.com

ANADIGICS Inc 141 Mt Bethel Rd Warren NJ 07059 908-668-5000 668-5068
NASDAQ: ANAD ■ *Web:* www.anadigics.com

Analog Devices Inc 3 Technology Way Norwood MA 02062 781-329-4700 461-3113
NASDAQ: ADI ■ *TF:* 800-262-5643 ■ *Web:* www.analog.com

Analogix Semiconductor Inc
3211 Scott Blvd Ste 103 Santa Clara CA 95054 408-988-8848
Web: www.analogix.com

Apogee Technology Inc 129 Morgan Dr Norwood MA 02062 781-551-9450 769-9107
OTC: ATCS ■ *Web:* www.apogeebio.com

Applied Micro Circuits Corp
215 Moffett Pk Dr Sunnyvale CA 94089 408-542-8600 542-8601
NASDAQ: AMCC ■ *Web:* www.apm.com

ARM Inc 141 Caspian Ct Sunnyvale CA 94089 408-734-5600 734-5050
Web: www.arm.com

Arsenal Capital Partners
100 Park Ave 31st Fl New York NY 10017 212-771-1717
Web: www.arsenalcapital.com

Ascent Solar Technologies Inc
12300 Grant St Thornton CO 80241 720-872-5000
Web: www.ascentsolar.com

Atmel Corp 2325 Orchard Pkwy San Jose CA 95131 408-441-0311 436-4200
NASDAQ: ATML ■ *Web:* www.atmel.com

AuthenTec Inc 100 Rialto Pl # 100 Melbourne FL 32901 321-308-1300 308-1430

Aware Inc 40 Middlesex Tpke Bedford MA 01730 781-276-4000 276-4001
NASDAQ: AWRE ■ *Web:* www.aware.com

Axsun Technologies Inc 1 Fortune Dr Billerica MA 01821 978-262-0049 262-0035
TF: 866-462-9786 ■ *Web:* www.axsun.com

AXT Inc 4281 Technology Dr Fremont CA 94538 510-438-4700 353-0668
NASDAQ: AXTI ■ *Web:* www.axt.com

B & B Electronics Manufacturing Co
PO Box 1040 Ottawa IL 61350 815-433-5100 433-5109
TF: 800-346-3119 ■ *Web:* www.bb-elec.com

BI Technologies Corp 4200 Bonita Pl Fullerton CA 92835 714-447-2300 447-2745
Web: www.bitechnologies.com

BKM Technology Partners LLC
3620 E Campbell Ave Ste A-2 Phoenix AZ 85018 480-922-4933
Web: www.bkmtechnologypartners.com

Broadcom Corp 1320 Ridder Park Dr Irvine CA 92617 408-433-8000 926-5203*
NASDAQ: BRCM ■ **Fax Area Code:* 949 ■ *TF:* 877-673-9442 ■ *Web:* www.broadcom.com

Busch Semiconductor Vacuum Group LLC
18430 Sutter Blvd Morgan Hill CA 95037 408-782-0800
Web: www.buschsvg.com

Calxeda Inc 7000 N Mopac Expy Ste 250 Austin TX 78731 512-961-3680

Cavium Inc 2315 Nfirst St San Jose CA 95131 408-943-7100
Web: investor.caviumnetworks.com

Celis Semiconductor Corp
5475 Mark Dabling Blvd Springs CO 80918 719-260-9133

CEVA Inc 1174 Castro St Ste 210 Mountain View CA 94040 650-417-7900
Web: www.ceva-dsp.com

Cirrus Logic Inc 2901 Via Fortuna Austin TX 78746 512-851-4000 851-4977
NASDAQ: CRUS ■ *TF:* 800-888-5016 ■ *Web:* www.cirrus.com

Clare Inc 78 Cherry Hill Dr Beverly MA 01915 978-524-6700 524-4700
TF: 800-272-5273 ■ *Web:* www.ixysic.com

Clearspeed Technology Inc 3031 Tisch Way San Jose CA 95128 408-557-2067
Web: www.clearspeed.com

Conexant Systems Inc 1901 Main St Ste 300 Irvine CA 92614 949-483-4600 370-8990*
**Fax Area Code:* 781 ■ *TF:* 888-855-4562 ■ *Web:* www.conexant.com

Cooper Crouse-Hinds MTL Inc
4300 Fortune Pl Ste A West Melbourne FL 32904 321-725-8000

Cree Inc 4600 Silicon Dr Durham NC 27703 919-313-5300
NASDAQ: CREE ■ *TF:* 800-533-2583 ■ *Web:* www.cree.com

Crossfield Technology LLC
3445 Executive Center Dr Ste 125 Austin TX 78731 512-795-0220
Web: www.crossfieldtech.com

Company	City	State	ZIP	Phone	Fax
Cypress Semiconductor Corp 198 Champion Ct *NASDAQ: CY* ■ **Fax:* Mktg ■ *TF:* 800-541-4736 ■ *Web:* www.cypress.com	San Jose	CA	95134	408-943-2600	943-4730*
Dakota Systems Inc 1057 Broadway Rd *Web:* www.dakotasystems.com	Dracut	MA	01826	978-275-0600	275-0606
Dallas Semiconductor Corp 4401 S Beltwood Pkwy **Fax:* Cust Svc ■ *Web:* www.maximintegrated.com	Dallas	TX	75244	972-371-3726	371-3715*
Deca Technologies Inc 7855 S River Pkwy Ste 111 *Web:* www.decatechnologies.com	Tempe	AZ	85284	480-345-9895	
Dialight Corp 1501 SR 34 *Web:* www.dialight.com	Farmingdale	NJ	07727	732-919-3119	751-5778
Diodes Inc 15660 N Dallas Pkwy Ste 850 *NASDAQ: DIOD* ■ **Fax Area Code:* 805 ■ *Web:* www.diodes.com	Dallas	TX	75248	972-385-2810	446-4850*
Dornerworks Ltd 3445 Lk Eastbrook Blvd SE *Web:* www.dornerworks.com	Grand Rapids	MI	49546	616-245-8369	
DSP Group Inc 2580 N First St Ste 460 *NASDAQ: DSPG* ■ *Web:* www.dspg.com	San Jose	CA	95131	408-986-4300	986-4323
E/g Electro-graph Inc 1491 Poinsettia Ave Ste 138 *Web:* plansee.com/en	Vista	CA	92081	760-438-9090	438-3923
EMCORE Corp 10420 Research Rd SE *NASDAQ: EMKR* ■ *Web:* www.emcore.com	Albuquerque	NM	87123	505-332-5000	
Enphase Energy Inc 1420 N Mcdowell Blvd *TF:* 877-797-4743 ■ *Web:* investor.enphase.com	Petaluma	CA	94954	707-763-4784	
Epson Electronics America Inc 150 River Oaks Pkwy *TF:* 800-228-3964 ■ *Web:* www.eea.epson.com	San Jose	CA	95134	408-922-0200	922-0238
Equator Technologies Inc 520 Pike St Ste 900	Seattle	WA	98101	206-267-4500	812-1285
ESS Technology Inc 48401 Fremont Blvd *Web:* www.esstech.com	Fremont	CA	94538	510-492-1088	492-1098
Exar Corp 48720 Kato Rd *NYSE: EXAR* ■ *TF:* 855-755-1330 ■ *Web:* www.exar.com	Fremont	CA	94538	510-668-7000	668-7011
Fairchild Imaging Inc 1801 McCarthy Blvd *TF:* 800-325-6975 ■ *Web:* www.fairchildimaging.com	Milpitas	CA	95035	408-433-2500	435-7352
Fairchild Semiconductor Corp 82 Running Hill Rd *NASDAQ: FCS* ■ *TF:* 800-341-0392 ■ *Web:* www.fairchildsemi.com	South Portland	ME	04106	207-775-8100	
GCT Semiconductor Inc 2121 Ringwood Ave *Web:* www.gctsemi.com	San Jose	CA	95131	408-434-6040	434-6050
Gel-Pak LLC 31398 Huntwood Ave *TF:* 888-621-4147 ■ *Web:* www.gelpak.com	Hayward	CA	94544	510-576-2220	576-2282
GHO Ventures LLC 92 Nassau St 2nd Fl *Web:* www.ghoventures.com	Princeton	NJ	08542	609-497-6333	
Global Equipment Services Corp 2372-East Qume Dr *Web:* www.geservs.com	San Jose	CA	95131	408-441-0682	
Global Solar Energy Inc 8500 S Rita Rd *TF:* 866-999-8422 ■ *Web:* www.globalsolar.com	Tucson	AZ	85747	520-546-6313	546-6318
Grinding & Dicing Services Inc 925 Berryessa Rd *Web:* www.wafergrind.com	San Jose	CA	95133	408-451-2000	
GSI Technology Inc 2360 Owen St *NASDAQ: GSIT* ■ *Web:* www.gsitechnology.com	Santa Clara	CA	95054	408-980-8388	980-8377
GT Advanced Technologies Inc 243 DANIEL WEBSTER Hwy *Web:* www.gtat.com	Merrimack	NH	03054	603-883-5200	
HEI Inc 1495 Steiger Lk Ln *TF:* 866-720-2397	Victoria	MN	55386	952-443-2500	443-2668
Hitachi Canada Ltd 5450 Explore Dr Ste 501 *TF:* 877-248-4237 ■ *Web:* www.hitachi.ca	Mississauga	ON	L4W5N1	905-629-9300	290-0141
Hitachi High Technologies America Inc 10 N Martingale Rd Ste 500 *Web:* www.hitachi-hightech.com/us	Schaumburg	IL	60173	847-273-4141	273-4407
Holt Integrated Circuits Inc 23351 Madero *Web:* www.holtic.com	Mission Viejo	CA	92691	949-859-8800	859-9643
Hynix Semiconductor America Inc 3101 N First St *Web:* www.hynix.com	San Jose	CA	95134	408-232-8000	232-8103
Hysitron Inc 9625 W 76th St *Web:* www.hysitron.com	Minneapolis	MN	55344	952-835-6366	
Hytel Group Inc 290 Industrial Dr *Web:* www.hytel.com	Hampshire	IL	60140	847-683-9800	683-7940
I-O Corp 14852 S Heritage Crest Way 1-A *Web:* www.iocorp.com	Bluffdale	UT	84065	801-973-6767	974-5683
i2a Technologies Inc 3399 W Warren Ave *Web:* www.ipac.com	Fremont	CA	94538	510-770-0322	
Ikanos Communications 47669 Fremont Blvd *NASDAQ: IKAN* ■ *Web:* www.ikanos.com	Fremont	CA	94538	510-979-0400	979-0500
Impinj Inc 400 Fairview Ave N Ste 1200	Seattle	WA	98109	206-517-5300	517-5262
Inabata America Corp 1270 Ave of the Americas Ste 602 *Web:* us.inabata.com	New York	NY	10020	212-586-7764	245-2876
Integrated Device Technology Inc 6024 Silver Creek Vly Rd *NASDAQ: IDTI* ■ *TF:* 800-345-7015 ■ *Web:* www.idt.com	San Jose	CA	95138	408-284-8200	284-2775
Integrated Silicon Solution Inc (ISSI) 1940 Zanker Rd *NASDAQ: ISSI* ■ *TF:* 800-379-4774 ■ *Web:* www.issi.com	San Jose	CA	95112	408-969-6600	969-7800
Intel Corp 2200 Mission College Blvd *NASDAQ: INTC* ■ *TF Cust Svc:* 800-628-8686 ■ *Web:* www.intel.in	Santa Clara	CA	95052	408-765-8080	
InterDigital Communications Corp 781 Third Ave *Web:* www.interdigital.com	King of Prussia	PA	19406	610-878-7800	878-7842
Intermolecular Inc 3011 N First St *TF:* 877-251-1860 ■ *Web:* www.intermolecular.com	San Jose	CA	95134	408-582-5700	
International Rectifier Corp 101 N Sepulveda Blvd *Web:* www.irf.com	El Segundo	CA	90245	310-322-3331	
Intersil Corp 1001 Murphy Ranch Rd *NASDAQ: ISIL* ■ *TF:* 888-468-3774 ■ *Web:* www.intersil.com	Milpitas	CA	95035	408-432-8888	434-5351
Invensense Inc 1197 Borregas Ave *NYSE: INVN* ■ *Web:* www.invensense.com	Sunnyvale	CA	94089	408-988-7339	988-8104
IQE Inc 119 Technology Dr *Web:* www.iqep.com	Bethlehem	PA	18015	610-861-6930	
Irvine Sensors Corp 3001 Redhill Ave B3-108vv *Web:* www.irvine-sensors.com	Costa Mesa	CA	92626	714-444-8700	
IXYS Corp 3540 Bassett St *NASDAQ: IXYS* ■ *Web:* www.ixys.com	Santa Clara	CA	95054	408-982-0700	748-9788
Jazz Semiconductor Inc 4321 Jamboree Rd *Web:* www.jazzsemi.com	Newport Beach	CA	92660	949-435-8000	435-8757
Johnstech International Corp 1210 New Brighton Blvd *Web:* www.johnstech.com	Minneapolis	MN	55413	612-378-2020	378-2030
Judson Technologies LLC 221 Commerce Dr *Web:* www.judsontechnologies.com	Montgomeryville	PA	18936	215-368-6900	362-6107
Kilopass Technology Inc 2895 Zanker Rd *Web:* www.kilopass.com	San Jose	CA	95134	408-980-8808	
Kleer Corp 19925 Stevens Creek Blvd Ste 111 *Web:* www.kleer.com	Cupertino	CA	95014	408-973-7255	
Kopin Corp 125 N Dr *NASDAQ: KOPN* ■ *Web:* www.kopin.com	Westborough	MA	01581	508-870-5959	822-1381
Kyocera Solar Inc 7812 E Acoma Dr Ste 2 *TF:* 800-544-6466 ■ *Web:* www.kyocerasolar.com	Scottsdale	AZ	85260	480-948-8003	483-6431
Laser Diode Inc 4 Olsen Ave *Web:* www.laserdiode.com	Edison	NJ	08820	732-549-9001	906-1559
Lattice Semiconductor Corp 5555 NE Moore Ct *NASDAQ: LSCC* ■ *TF:* 800-528-8423 ■ *Web:* www.latticesemi.com	Hillsboro	OR	97124	503-268-8000	268-8347
Lightel Technologies Inc 2210 Lind Ave SW Ste 100 *Web:* www.lighteltech.com	Renton	WA	98057	425-277-8000	
Lilliputian Systems Inc 36 Jonspin Rd	Wilmington	MA	01887	978-203-1700	
Linear Technology Corp 1630 McCarthy Blvd *NASDAQ: LLTC* ■ *TF:* 888-500-6973 ■ *Web:* www.linear.com	Milpitas	CA	95035	408-432-1900	434-0507
Lite Access Technologies Inc 6900 Graybar Rd Ste 1115-1215 *Web:* www.liteaccess.com	Richmond	BC	V6W0A5	604-247-4704	
Logic Devices Inc 1375 Geneva Dr *OTC: LOGC* ■ *TF:* 800-233-2518 ■ *Web:* www.logicdevices.com	Sunnyvale	CA	94089	408-542-5400	542-0080
LSI Computer Systems Inc 1235 Walt Whitman Rd *Web:* www.lsicsi.com	Melville	NY	11747	631-271-0400	271-0405
M Cubed Technologies Inc 921 Main St *Web:* www.mmmt.com	Monroe	CT	06468	203-452-2333	452-2335
M/A-COM Technology Solutions Inc 100 Chelmsford St *TF:* 800-366-2266 ■ *Web:* macom.com	Lowell	MA	01851	978-656-2500	
Macronix America Inc 680 N McCarthy Blvd *Web:* www.macronix.com	Milpitas	CA	95035	408-262-8887	262-8810
Magnum Semiconductor Inc 591 Yosemite Dr *Web:* www.magnumsemi.com	Milpitas	CA	95035	408-934-3700	
Marvell Technology Group Ltd 5488 Marvell Ln *NASDAQ: MRVL* ■ *Web:* www.marvell.com	Santa Clara	CA	95054	408-222-2500	988-8279
Maxim Integrated 6440 Oak Canyon Ste 100 *Web:* www.maximintegrated.com	Irvine	CA	92618	714-508-8800	
Maxim Integrated Products Inc 120 San Gabriel Dr *NASDAQ: MXIM* ■ *TF:* 888-629-4642 ■ *Web:* www.maximintegrated.com	Sunnyvale	CA	94086	408-737-7600	737-7194
Memsic Inc 1 Tech Dr Ste 325 *Web:* www.memsic.com	Andover	MA	01810	978-738-0900	
Micrel Inc 2180 Fortune Dr *NASDAQ: MCRL* ■ *TF:* 800-282-9855 ■ *Web:* www.micrel.com	San Jose	CA	95131	408-944-0800	474-1000
Microchip Technology Inc 2355 West Chandler Blvd *NASDAQ: MCHP* ■ **Fax Area Code:* 602 ■ *Web:* www.microchip.com	Chandler	AZ	85224	480-792-7200	687-4646*
Microchip Technology Inc 2355 W Chandler Blvd *NASDAQ: MCHP* ■ *TF:* 800-437-2767 ■ *Web:* www.microchip.com	Chandler	AZ	85224	480-792-7200	899-9210
MicroLink Devices Inc 6457 W Howard St *Web:* www.mldevices.com	Niles	IL	60714	847-588-3001	
Micropac Industries Inc 905 E Walnut St *OTC: MPAD* ■ *Web:* www.micropac.com	Garland	TX	75040	972-272-3571	487-6918
Microsemi Corp 2381 Morse Ave *NASDAQ: MSCC* ■ *TF:* 800-713-4113 ■ *Web:* www.microsemi.com	Irvine	CA	92614	949-221-7100	756-0308
Mindspeed Technologies Inc 4000 MacArthur Blvd *NASDAQ: MSPD* ■ *Web:* macom.com	Newport Beach	CA	92660	949-579-3000	
Mini-Circuits Laboratories Inc 13 Neptune Ave *TF:* 800-654-7949 ■ *Web:* www.minicircuits.com	Brooklyn	NY	11235	718-934-4500	332-4661
MIPS Technologies Inc 955 E Arques Ave *NASDAQ: MIPS* ■ **Fax Area Code:* 650 ■ *Web:* www.imgtec.com	Sunnyvale	CA	94085	408-530-5000	530-5150*
Monolithic Power Systems Inc (MPS) 6409 Guadalupe Mines Rd *NASDAQ: MPWR* ■ *Web:* www.monolithicpower.com	San Jose	CA	95120	408-826-0600	826-0601
Moschip Semiconductor Technology USA 3335 Kifer Rd *Web:* www.moschip.com	Santa Clara	CA	95051	408-737-7141	737-7708
MoSys Inc 3301 Olcott St *Web:* www.mosys.com	Santa Clara	CA	95054	408-418-7500	
N&K Technology Inc 80 Las Colinas Ln *Web:* www.nandk.com	San Jose	CA	95119	408-513-3800	
National Semiconductor Corp 2900 Semiconductor Dr *Web:* www.ti.com	Santa Clara	CA	95051	408-721-5000	739-9803
NeoPhotonics Corp 2911 Zanker Rd *Web:* www.neophotonics.com	San Jose	CA	95134	408-232-9200	
Netlist Inc 51 Discovery Ste 150 *Web:* www.netlist.com	Irvine	CA	92618	949-435-0025	

Company	City	State	Zip	Phone	Fax
Neurosky Inc 125 S Market St Ste 900 *Web:* www.neurosky.com	San Jose	CA	95113	408-600-0129	
Nikon Precision Inc 1399 Shoreway Rd *Web:* www.nikon.com	Belmont	CA	94002	650-508-4674	
NVE Corp 11409 Vly View Rd *NASDAQ: NVEC* ■ *TF:* 800-467-7141 ■ *Web:* www.nve.com	Eden Prairie	MN	55344	952-829-9217	996-1600
O2Micro International Ltd 3118 Patrick Henry Dr *NASDAQ: OIIM* ■ *Web:* www.o2micro.com	Santa Clara	CA	95054	408-987-5920	987-5929
Oclaro Inc 46429 Landing Pkwy *NASDAQ: OCLR* ■ *Web:* oclaro.com	Fremont	CA	94538	510-580-8828	
OEM Group Inc 2120 W Guadalupe Rd *Web:* www.oemgroupinc.com	Gilbert	AZ	85233	480-558-9200	
OmniVision Technologies Inc 4275 Burton Dr *NASDAQ: OVTI* ■ *Web:* www.ovt.com	Santa Clara	CA	95054	408-542-3000	542-3001
ON Semiconductor Corp 5005 E McDowell Rd *NASDAQ: ON* ■ *TF:* 800-282-9855 ■ *Web:* www.onsemi.com	Phoenix	AZ	85008	602-244-6600	
Optek Technology Inc 1645 Wallace Dr *TF:* 800-341-4747 ■ *Web:* www.optekinc.com	Carrollton	TX	75006	972-323-2200	323-2396
OSI Systems Inc 12525 Chadron Ave *NASDAQ: OSIS* ■ *Web:* www.osi-systems.com	Hawthorne	CA	90250	310-978-0516	
Peregrine Semiconductor Corp 9380 Carroll Pk Dr *Web:* www.psemi.com	San Diego	CA	92121	858-731-9400	731-9499
Pericom Semiconductor Corp 3545 N First St *NASDAQ: PSEM* ■ *TF:* 800-435-2336 ■ *Web:* www.pericom.com	San Jose	CA	95134	408-435-0800	435-1100
PerkinElmer Inc 940 Winter St *NYSE: PKI* ■ *Web:* www.perkinelmer.com	Waltham	MA	02451	203-925-4602	944-4904
Photronics Inc 15 Secor Rd *NASDAQ: PLAB* ■ *TF:* 800-292-9396 ■ *Web:* www.photronics.com	Brookfield	CT	06804	203-775-9000	
Pixelworks Inc 224 Airport Pkwy Ste 400 *NASDAQ: PXLW* ■ *Web:* www.pixelworks.com	San Jose	CA	95110	408-200-9200	200-9201
Plascore Inc 615 N Fairview St *TF:* 800-630-9257 ■ *Web:* www.plascore.com	Zeeland	MI	49464	616-772-1220	772-1289
Point Source Power Inc 132 Tharp Dr *Web:* www.pointsourcepower.com	Moraga	CA	94556	925-708-7845	
Power Integrations 5245 Hellyer Ave *NASDAQ: POWI* ■ *Web:* www.power.com	San Jose	CA	95138	408-414-9200	414-9201
Powerex Inc 173 Pavilion Ln *TF:* 800-451-1415 ■ *Web:* www.pwrx.com	Youngwood	PA	15697	724-925-7272	925-4393
Powerfilm Inc 2337 230th St *TF:* 888-354-7773 ■ *Web:* www.powerfilmsolar.com	Ames	IA	50014	515-292-7606	
QLogic Corp 26650 Aliso Viejo Pkwy *NASDAQ: QLGC* ■ *TF:* 800-662-4471 ■ *Web:* www.qlogic.com	Aliso Viejo	CA	92656	949-389-6000	389-6114
QuickLogic Corp 1277 Orleans Dr *NASDAQ: QUIK* ■ *Web:* www.quicklogic.com	Sunnyvale	CA	94089	408-990-4000	990-4040
Rambus Inc 1050 Enterprise Way Ste 700 *NASDAQ: RMBS* ■ *Web:* www.rambus.com	Sunnyvale	CA	94089	408-462-8000	462-8001
Ramtron International Corp 1850 Ramtron Dr *NASDAQ: RMTR* ■ *TF:* 800-541-4736 ■ *Web:* www.cypress.com	Colorado Springs	CO	80921	719-481-7000	481-9294
Rayotek Scientific Inc 11499 Sorrento Vly Rd *Web:* www.rayotek.com	San Diego	CA	92121	858-558-3671	
Raytek Inc 1201 Shaffer Rd *TF:* 800-227-8074 ■ *Web:* www.raytek.com	Santa Cruz	CA	95061	831-458-3900	425-4561
Raytheon RF Components (RRFC) 870 Winter St *Web:* www.raytheon.com	Waltham	MA	02451	781-522-3000	
RF Micro Devices Inc 7628 Thorndike Rd *NASDAQ: RFMD* ■ *TF:* 800-937-5449 ■ *Web:* www.rfmd.com	Greensboro	NC	27409	336-664-1233	931-7454
Samsung Semiconductors Inc 3655 N First St *TF General:* 800-726-7864 ■ *Web:* www.usa.samsungsemi.com	San Jose	CA	95134	408-544-4000	544-4980
Seiko Instruments USA Inc 21221 S Western Ave Ste 250 *TF Sales:* 800-688-0817 ■ *Web:* www.seikoinstruments.com	Torrance	CA	90501	310-517-7700	517-7709
Semiconductor Process Equipment Corp 27963 Franklin Pkwy *Web:* www.team-spec.com	Valencia	CA	91355	661-257-0934	
Semifab Inc 150 Great Oaks Blvd *Web:* www.semifab.com	San Jose	CA	95119	408-414-5928	
Semikron Inc 11 Executive Dr *Web:* semikron.com	Hudson	NH	03051	603-883-8102	
Semtech Corp 200 Flynn Rd *NASDAQ: SMTC* ■ *Web:* www.semtech.com	Camarillo	CA	93012	805-498-2111	498-3804
Senspex Inc 9798 Coors Blvd Nw Bldg B *Web:* www.senspex.com	Albuquerque	NM	87114	505-891-0034	
Sharp Microelectronics of the Americas 5700 NW Pacific Rim Blvd *Web:* www.sharpsma.com	Camas	WA	98607	360-834-2500	834-8903
Sheldahl Inc 1150 Sheldahl Rd *TF:* 800-927-3580 ■ *Web:* www.sheldahl.com	Northfield	MN	55057	507-663-8000	663-8545
Shin-Etsu Handotai America Inc PO Box 8965 *Web:* www.sehamerica.com	Vancouver	WA	98668	360-883-7053	883-7074
Showa Denko America 420 Lexington Ave Ste 2850 *Web:* www.showadenko.us	New York	NY	10170	212-370-0033	370-4566
Sigma Designs Inc 1778 Mcarthy Blvd *NASDAQ: SIGM* ■ *Web:* www.sigmadesigns.com	Milpitas	CA	95035	408-262-9003	
Silicon Laboratories Inc 400 W Cesar Chavez *NASDAQ: SLAB* ■ *TF:* 877-444-3032 ■ *Web:* www.silabs.com	Austin	TX	78701	512-416-8500	416-9669
Siliconix Inc 2201 Laurelwood Rd *Web:* www.vishay.com	Santa Clara	CA	95054	408-988-8000	567-8950
Siltronic Corp 7200 NW Front Ave **Fax Area Code:* 898 ■ **Fax:* Sales ■ *Web:* www.siltronic.com	Portland	OR	97210	503-243-2020	564-3219*
SkyFuel Inc 18300 W Hwy 72 *Web:* www.skyfuel.com	Arvada	CO	80007	303-330-0276	
Skyworks Solutions Inc 20 Sylvan Rd *NASDAQ: SWKS* ■ *Web:* www.skyworksinc.com	Woburn	MA	01801	781-376-3000	
Solar Solutions & Distribution LLC 2500 W Fifth Ave *TF:* 855-765-3478 ■ *Web:* www.soldist.com	Denver	CO	80204	303-948-6300	
Solatube International Inc 2210 Oak Ridge Way *TF:* 888-765-2882 ■ *Web:* www.solatube.com	Vista	CA	92081	760-477-1120	
Solid State Devices Inc 14701 Firestone Blvd *Web:* www.ssdi-power.com	La Mirada	CA	90638	562-404-4474	
Solitron Devices Inc 3301 Electronics Way *OTC: SODI* ■ **Fax:* Mktg ■ *Web:* www.solitrondevices.com	West Palm Beach	FL	33407	561-848-4311	863-5946*
Spectrolab Inc 12500 Gladstone Ave *TF:* 800-936-4888 ■ *Web:* www.spectrolab.com	Sylmar	CA	91342	818-365-4611	361-5102
SRS Labs Inc 2909 Daimler St *NASDAQ: SRSL* ■ *TF General:* 800-322-2885 ■ *Web:* dts.com	Santa Ana	CA	92705	949-442-1070	
STMicroelectronics NV 134 Vintage Park Blvd Ste 192 *TF:* 888-356-1766 ■ *Web:* www.st.com	Houston	TX	77070	844-786-4276	
Stretch Inc 1322 Orleans Dr *TF:* 800-468-6853 ■ *Web:* www.stretchinc.com	Sunnyvale	CA	94089	408-543-2700	747-5736
Sumitomo Electric Industries Ltd 2355 Zanker Rd *Web:* www.sei-device.com	San Jose	CA	95131	408-232-9500	428-9111
SunEdison Semiconductor Ltd 501 Pearl Dr *NASDAQ: SEMI* ■ **Fax:* Sales ■ *Web:* sunedisonsemi.com	Saint Peters	MO	63376	636-474-5000	474-5158*
SunPower Corp 77 Rio Robles *NASDAQ: SPWR* ■ *TF:* 800-786-7693	San Jose	CA	95134	408-240-5500	
Symetrix Corp 5055 Mark Dabling Blvd *Web:* www.symetrixcorp.com	Colorado Springs	CO	80918	719-594-6145	598-3437
Taiwan Semiconductor Mfg Company Ltd (TSMC) 2851 Junction Ave *NYSE: TSM* ■ *TF:* 877-248-4237 ■ *Web:* www.tsmc.com	San Jose	CA	95134	408-382-8000	382-8008
Teledyne DALSA Inc 888 East Arques Ave *Web:* www.teledynedalsa.com/imaging/markets/mv/ndt	Sunnyvale	CA	94085	408-736-6000	
Teledyne Electronics & Communications 1049 Camino Dos Rios *Web:* www.tet.com	Thousand Oaks	CA	91360	805-373-4545	
Tellurex Corp 1462 International Dr *TF:* 877-774-7468 ■ *Web:* www.tellurex.com	Traverse City	MI	49686	231-947-0110	
Tessera Technologies Inc 3099 Orchard Dr *NASDAQ: TSRA* ■ *Web:* www.tessera.com	San Jose	CA	95134	408-894-0700	894-0768
Texas Instruments Inc 12500 TI Blvd *NASDAQ: TXN* ■ *TF Cust Svc:* 800-336-5236 ■ *Web:* www.ti.com	Dallas	TX	75243	972-995-3773	927-6377
Tezzaron Semiconductor Corp 1415 Bond St Ste 111 *Web:* www.tachyonsemi.com	Naperville	IL	60563	630-505-0404	505-9292
Thorlabs Quantum Electronics Inc 10335 Guilford Rd *TF:* 877-226-8342 ■ *Web:* www.covega.com	Jessup	MD	20794	240-456-7100	456-7200
Time Domain Corp 4955 Corporate Dr Ste 101 Cummings Research Park *Web:* www.timedomain.com	Huntsville	AL	35805	256-922-9229	
Toppan Photomasks Inc 131 Old Settlers Blvd *Web:* www.photomask.com	Round Rock	TX	78664	512-310-6500	310-6544
Tosoh SMD Inc 3600 Gantz Rd *Web:* www.tosohsmd.com	Grove City	OH	43123	614-875-7912	875-0031
TranSwitch Corp 3 Enterprise Dr *Web:* www.websolutions.com	Shelton	CT	06484	203-929-8810	
Trident Microsystems Inc 1170 Kifer Rd	Sunnyvale	CA	94086	408-962-5000	
TriQuint Semiconductor Inc 2300 NE Brookwood Pkwy *NASDAQ: TQNT* ■ *TF:* 855-367-8768 ■ *Web:* www.triquint.com	Hillsboro	OR	97124	503-615-9000	615-8900
Tru-Si Technologies 657 N Pastoria Ave *Web:* www.trusi.com	Sunnyvale	CA	94085	408-720-3333	
Tvia Inc 4800 Great America Pkwy Ste 405 **Fax Area Code:* 972 ■ *Web:* www.tvia.com	Santa Clara	CA	95054	408-327-8033	612-2805*
United Microelectronics Corp 488 De Guigne Dr *NYSE: UMC* ■ *TF:* 800-990-1135 ■ *Web:* www.umc.com	Sunnyvale	CA	94085	408-523-7800	733-8090
Universal Display Corp 375 Phillips Blvd *NASDAQ: OLED* ■ *Web:* www.udcoled.com	Ewing	NJ	08618	609-671-0980	671-0995
Variosystems Inc 901 S Kimball Ave *Web:* www.variosystems.com	Southlake	TX	76092	817-416-7535	
Veritec Inc 2445 Winnetka Ave N *TF:* 866-546-1011 ■ *Web:* www.veritecinc.com	Golden Valley	MN	55427	763-253-2670	
VIA Technologies Inc 940 Mission Ct *TF:* 888-524-9382 ■ *Web:* www.viatech.com/en	Fremont	CA	94539	510-683-3300	687-4654
Vishay Intertechnology Inc 63 Lancaster Ave *NYSE: VSH* ■ *TF:* 800-567-6098 ■ *Web:* www.vishay.com	Malvern	PA	19355	610-644-1300	296-0657
Vishay Precision Group Inc 63 Lancaster Ave *NYSE: VPG* ■ **Fax Area Code:* 484 ■ *Web:* www.vishay.com	Malvern	PA	19355	610-644-1300	321-5301*
Vlsip Technologies Inc 750 Presidential Dr *Web:* www.vlsip.com	Richardson	TX	75081	972-437-5506	644-1286
Volterra Semiconductor Corp 47467 Fremont Blvd *NASDAQ: VLTR* ■ *Web:* www.maximintegrated.com	Fremont	CA	94538	510-743-1200	743-1600
Wabash Technologies 1375 Swan St PO Box 829 **Fax:* Sales ■ *TF:* 800-487-6865	Huntington	IN	46750	260-355-4100	355-4265*
Wafertech LLC 5509 NW Parker St *Web:* www.wafertech.com	Camas	WA	98607	360-817-3000	
Wallco Inc 53 E Jackson St # 55 *TF:* 800-392-5526 ■ *Web:* www.wallcoinc.com	Wilkes-Barre	PA	18701	570-823-6181	829-5952
West Coast Quartz Corp (WCQ) 1000 Corporate Way *Web:* www.westcoastquartz.com	Fremont	CA	94539	510-249-2160	651-4617
Winbond Electronics Corp America 2727 N First St *Web:* www.winbond.com	San Jose	CA	95134	408-943-6666	474-1600
Winslow Automation Inc 905 Montague Expy *Web:* www.winslowautomation.com	Milpitas	CA	95035	408-262-9004	956-0199
X-fab Texas Inc 2301 N University Ave *Web:* www.xfab.com	Lubbock	TX	79415	806-747-4400	747-3111

Phone Fax

Xilinx Inc 2100 Logic Dr. San Jose CA 95124 408-559-7778 559-7114
NASDAQ: XLNX ■ *TF:* 800-594-5469 ■ *Web:* www.xilinx.com

ZiLOG Inc 1590 Buckeye Dr. Milpitas CA 95035 408-513-1500 365-8535
Web: www.zilog.com

Zoran Corp 1390 Kifer Rd. Sunnyvale CA 94086 408-523-6500 523-6501
NASDAQ: ZRAN

697 SHEET METAL WORK

See Also Plumbing, Heating, Air Conditioning Contractors p. 2086; Roofing, Siding, Sheet Metal Contractors p. 2090

Phone Fax

A p Machine & Tool Inc 1301 Elm St Terre Haute IN 47807 812-232-4939
Web: apmachineandtool.com

A-1 Tool Corp 1425 Armitage Ave Melrose Park IL 60160 708-345-5000
Web: www.a1toolco.com

A2mg Inc 8601 E Us Hwy 40 Kansas City MO 64129 816-874-4500
Web: www.a2mg.com

Abalon Precision Mfg Corp 1040 Home St. Bronx NY 10459 718-589-5682 589-0300
TF: 800-888-2225

Abrams Airborne Manufacturing Inc
3735 N Romero Rd Tucson AZ 85705 520-887-1727 293-8807
Web: www.abrams.com

AC Horn & Co 1269 Majesty Dr Dallas TX 75247 214-630-3311
Web: www.achornmfg.com

Accede Mold & Tool Company Inc
1125 Lexington Ave Rochester NY 14606 585-254-6490
TF: 888-236-2427 ■ *Web:* www.accedemold.com

Accu-Fab Inc 801 Beacon Lk Dr Raleigh NC 27610 919-212-6400
Web: www.accufabnc.com

Accuduct Manufacturing Inc 316 Ellingson Rd. Algona WA 98001 253-939-7741
Web: www.accuduct.com

Ace Irrigation & Manufacturing Co
4740 E 39th St Kearney NE 68847 308-237-5173
Web: www.acenebraska.com

Acme Manufacturing Co 7601 State Rd Philadelphia PA 19136 215-268-1700 335-1905

Aero Trades Manufacturing Corp
65 Jericho Tpke Mineola NY 11501 516-746-3360 746-3417
Web: www.aerotrades.com

Aerospace Fabrications of Georgia Inc
305 Butler Industrial Dr Dallas GA 30132 770-505-8801
Web: www.afog.com

Ag Machining & Industries Inc
4607 S Windermere St Englewood CO 80110 303-783-0081
Web: www.agmachining.com

AHR Metals Inc 20 Division St Bessemer AL 35020 205-428-8888
Web: www.ahrmetals.com

Air Comfort Corp 2550 Braga Dr. Broadview IL 60155 708-345-1900 345-2730
TF: 800-466-3779 ■ *Web:* www.aircomfort.com

Air Conditioning Products Co 30350 Ecorse Rd Romulus MI 48174 734-326-0050 326-9632
Web: www.acpshutters.com

Air Vent Inc 4117 Pinnacle Pnt Dr Ste 400 Dallas TX 75211 800-247-8368 630-7413*
**Fax Area Code:* 214 ■ *TF:* 800-247-8368 ■ *Web:* www.airvent.com

Aircom Mfg Inc 6205 E 30th St. Indianapolis IN 46219 317-545-5383 542-7365
TF: 800-925-2426 ■ *Web:* www.aircommfg.com

Airecon Manufacturing Corp
5271 Brotherton Ct Cincinnati OH 45227 513-561-5522
Web: www.airecon.com

Airolite Company LLC PO Box 410 Schofield WI 54476 715-841-8757 841-8773
Web: www.airolite.com

Airtronics Metal Products Inc
1991 Senter Rd. San Jose CA 95112 408-977-7800 977-7810
Web: www.airtronics.com

All Metals Fabricating Inc 200 Allentown Pkwy Allen TX 75002 972-747-1234
Web: www.ametals.com

Allendale Machinery Systems Inc
16 Park Way Upper Saddle River NJ 07458 201-327-5215
Web: hfoallendale.com

Allied Tool & Die Company LLC
3807 S Seventh St Phoenix AZ 85040 602-276-2439
Web: www.alliedtool.com

Aluminum Line Products Co 24460 Sperry Cir. Westlake OH 44145 440-835-8880 835-8879
TF: 800-321-3154 ■ *Web:* www.aluminumline.com

American Aircraft Products Inc
15411 S Broadway Gardena CA 90248 310-532-7434
Web: www.americanaircraft.com

American Fabricators Inc 570 Metroplex Dr Nashville TN 37211 615-834-8700
Web: www.americanfabricators.com

American Warming & Ventilating Inc
7301 International Dr Holland OH 43528 419-865-5000 865-1375
Web: www.american-warming.com

Amtex Precision Fabrication 3920 Bahler Ave Manvel TX 77578 281-489-7042 489-1992
Web: www.amtexprecision.com

Amuneal Manufacturing Corp
4737 Darrah St Philadelphia PA 19124 215-535-3000
Web: www.amuneal.com

APX Enclosures Inc 200 Oregon St Mercersburg PA 17236 717-328-9399
Web: www.apx-enclosures.com

Arizona Precision Sheet Metal
2140 W Pinnacle Peak Rd. Phoenix AZ 85027 623-516-3700 516-3701
TF: 800-443-7039 ■ *Web:* www.apsm-jit.com

Arrow United Industries 450 Riverside Dr. Wyalusing PA 18853 570-746-1888 746-9286
Web: www.arrowunited.com

ASC Profiles Inc
2110 Enterprise Blvd West Sacramento CA 95691 916-372-0933 372-7606
TF Cust Svc: 800-360-2477 ■ *Web:* www.ascprofiles.com

Assembled Products 300 Hastings Dr Buffalo Grove IL 60089 847-215-1948
Web: www.aproducts.com

Associated Materials Inc
3773 State Rd Cuyahoga Falls OH 44223 330-929-1811 922-2296
TF: 800-257-4335 ■ *Web:* www.associatedmaterials.com

Phone Fax

Atlantic Air Enterprises Inc 856 Elston St Rahway NJ 07065 732-381-4000
Web: www.atlanticairent.com

Atlantic Ventilating & Equipment Co
25 Sebethe Dr Cromwell CT 06416 860-635-1300 632-7412

Atlas Mfg 2950 Weeks Ave SE Minneapolis MN 55414 612-331-2566 331-1295
Web: www.atlasmfg.com

ATS Systems Inc
30222 Esperanza Rancho Santa Margarita CA 92688 949-888-1744
TF: 800-321-1833 ■ *Web:* www.ats-s.com

Automated Quality Technologies Inc
563 Shoreview Park Rd. St Paul MN 55126 651-484-6544
TF: 800-250-9297 ■ *Web:* www.lionprecision.com

AW Mercer Inc 104 Industrial Dr PO Box 508 Boyertown PA 19512 610-367-8460 367-7491
Web: www.awmercer.com

Baldwin Metals Company Inc 1901 W Commerce St Dallas TX 75208 214-747-6722
Web: baldwinmetals.com

Ballew's Aluminum Products Inc 2 Shelter Dr Greer SC 29650 864-272-4453
TF: 800-231-6666 ■ *Web:* www.ballews.com

Bandy Inc 201 S International Rd Garland TX 75042 972-272-5455
Web: www.bandyco.com

Basmat Inc 1531 240th St Harbor City CA 90710 310-325-2063 325-9682
Web: www.mcstarlite.com

Bauer Manufacturing Inc 100 N Fm 3083 Rd. Conroe TX 77303 936-539-5030
Web: www.bauer-conroe.com

Berger Bldg Products Inc
805 Pennsylvania Blvd Feasterville PA 19053 215-355-1200 355-7738
TF Cust Svc: 800-523-8852 ■ *Web:* www.bergerbp.com

Bert R Huncilman & Son 115 Security Pkwy New Albany IN 47150 812-945-3544

Best Cutting Die Co 8080 Mccormick Blvd Skokie IL 60076 847-675-5522
Web: www.bestcuttingdie.com

BHW Sheet Metal Co 113 Johnson St Jonesboro GA 30236 770-471-9303 478-7923
Web: bhwsm.com

Blazing Technologies Inc 4631A Morgantown Rd Mohnton PA 19540 484-722-4800
Web: www.blazingtech.net

Branch Manufacturing Co 6420 Pine St. North Branch MN 55056 651-674-4441 674-4442
Web: www.branchmfg.com

Burgess Speciality Fabrication Inc
8222 Fawndale Ln Houston TX 77040 713-462-0293
Web: www.burgessfab.com

California Precision Products Inc
6790 Flanders Dr San Diego CA 92121 858-638-7300
Web: www.cal-precision.com

Captive-aire Systems Inc 4641 Paragon Pk Rd Raleigh NC 27616 919-882-2410 882-5204
TF: 800-334-9256 ■ *Web:* www.captiveaire.com

CEEMCO Inc 3330 E Kemper Rd. Cincinnati OH 45241 513-563-8822
Web: www.ceemco.com

Center Industries Corp 2505 S Custer Wichita KS 67217 316-942-8255
Web: www.centerindustries.com

Chantland-MHS 502 Seventh St N. Dakota City IA 50529 515-332-4045
Web: www.chantland.com

Chapco Inc 10 Denlar Dr Chester CT 06412 860-526-9535
Web: www.chapcoinc.com

Chapman Engineering Corp 2321 Cape Cod Way Santa Ana CA 92703 714-542-1942
Web: www.chapmanengineering.com

Chirch Global Mfg LLC 1150 Ridgeview Dr Mchenry IL 60050 815-385-5600
Web: www.chirchmfg.com

Christensen Industries 2990 S Main St Salt Lake City UT 84115 801-466-3334 466-1441
Web: www.christensenindustries.com

Ci Metal Fabrication 6205 St Louis St Meridian MS 39307 601-483-6281 693-6529
Web: www.cimetalfab.com

CID Performance Tooling Inc 6 Willey Rd Saco ME 04072 207-286-3319
TF: 800-964-2331 ■ *Web:* www.cidtools.com

Cincinnati Ventilating Company Inc
7410 Industrial Rd Florence KY 41042 859-371-1320
Web: www.cvc-fab.com

Clark Specialty Co Inc 323 West Morris St. Bath NY 14810 607-776-3193 776-3190
Web: www.clarkspecialty.com

Cody Company Inc 4200 N I-45 Ennis TX 75119 972-875-5884 875-0308
Web: www.codycompany.com

Coltwell Industries Inc 55 Winans Ave Cranford NJ 07016 908-276-7600
Web: www.coltwell.com

Computer Components Corp
2751 S Hampton Rd Philadelphia PA 19154 215-676-7600 464-7876
Web: compcomp.com

Connell LP 1 International Pl 31st Fl Boston MA 02110 617-391-5577 737-1617
Web: www.connell-lp.com

Contech Construction Products Inc
9025 Centre Pt Dr Ste 400 West Chester OH 45069 513-645-7000 645-7993
TF: 800-338-1122 ■ *Web:* www.conteches.com

Continuous Metal Technology 439 W Main St Ridgway PA 15853 814-772-9274
Web: www.powdered-metal.com

Corchran Inc 1340 State St S. Waseca MN 56093 507-835-3910 835-1382
Web: www.corchran.com

Cortec Precision Sheet Metal Inc
2231 Will Wool Dr San Jose CA 95112 408-278-8540
Web: www.cortecprecision.com

Craftech Metal Forming Inc
24100 Water Ave Ste B Perris CA 92570 951-940-6444
Web: www.craftechmetal.com

Craftsman Custom Metals LLC
3838 N River Rd Schiller Park IL 60176 847-655-0040
Web: www.ccm.com

Crown Products Company Inc
6390 Phillips Hwy Jacksonville FL 32216 904-737-7144 737-3533
TF: 800-683-7144 ■ *Web:* www.crownproductsco.com

Custom Metalcraft Inc
2332 E Division PO Box 10587 Springfield MO 65808 417-862-0707
Web: www.custom-metalcraft.com

CWR Mfg Corp 7000 Fly Rd. Syracuse NY 13057 315-437-1032 437-1493
Web: www.cwronline.com

Dalsin Industries Inc 9111 Grand Ave S Bloomington MN 55420 952-881-2260
Web: www.dalsinind.com

Company	City	State	ZIP	Phone	Fax
Danco Metal Products Inc 760 Moore Rd *Web:* www.dancometal.com	Avon Lake	OH	44012	440-871-2300	
Daria Metal Fabricators 1507 W Park Ave *Web:* www.dariametalfabricators.com	Perkasie	PA	18944	215-453-2110	
Data Transformation Corp 1 Penn Plz Ste 4515 *Web:* www.dtcss.com	New York	NY	10119	212-563-7565	
Data-Matique 2110 Sherwin St *TF:* 866-706-0981 ■ *Web:* www.data-matique.com	Garland	TX	75041	972-272-3446	
Datagenic Tool & Die Inc 4280 Motor Ave	Culver City	CA	90232	310-253-9918	
Datamation Systems Inc 125 Louis St *Web:* www.pc-security.com	South Hackensack	NJ	07606	201-329-7200	
Dauntless Molds 806 N Grand Ave *Web:* www.dauntlessmolds.com	Covina	CA	91724	626-966-4494	
Daviess County Metal Sales Inc 9929 E US Hwy 50 *TF:* 800-279-4299 ■ *Web:* www.dcmetal.com	Cannelburg	IN	47519	812-486-4299	
Davis Tool & Die Company Inc 888 Bolger Ct *Web:* www.davistool.com	Fenton	MO	63026	636-343-0828	
Dawson Metal Company Inc 825 Allen St *Web:* www.dawsonmetal.com	Jamestown	NY	14701	716-664-3815	664-3485
Defabco Inc 3765 E Livingston Ave *Web:* www.defabco.com	Columbus	OH	43227	614-231-2700	
Detronic Industries Inc 35800 Beattie Dr *Web:* www.detronic.com	Sterling Heights	MI	48312	586-977-5660	939-5340
Domaille Engineering LLC 7100 Dresser Dr Ne *Web:* www.domailleengineering.com	Rochester	MN	55906	507-281-0275	
Du-Mont Co 7800 N Pioneer Ct	Peoria	IL	61615	309-692-7240	693-2937
Duggan Manufacturing LLC 50150 Ryan Rd Ste 15 *Web:* www.dugganmfg.com	Shelby Township	MI	48317	586-254-7400	
Dura-Bilt Products Inc PO Box 188 *Web:* www.durabilt.com	Wellsburg	NY	14894	570-596-2000	
Durand Forms Inc 6200 Equitable Rd **Fax Area Code:* 989 ■ *TF:* 800-545-6342 ■ *Web:* www.durandforms.com	Kansas City	MO	64120	800-545-6342	288-2128*
Duratrack Inc 950 Morse Ave *Web:* www.duratrack.com	Elk Grove Village	IL	60007	847-806-0202	
Duwest Tool & Die Inc 8400 Madison Ave *Web:* duwesttool.com	Cleveland	OH	44102	216-631-1060	
Dynamic Tool Company Inc 1421 Vanderbilt Dr *Web:* dynamicdesignfabrication.com	El Paso	TX	79935	915-598-2330	
Eagle Cornice Co Inc 89 Pettaconsett Ave *Web:* www.eaglecornice.com	Cranston	RI	02920	401-781-5978	781-6570
EDAK Inc 630 Distribution Dr *Web:* www.edak.com	Melbourne	FL	32904	321-674-6804	
Edco & Arrowhead Products Inc 8700 Excelsior Blvd *TF:* 800-333-2580 ■ *Web:* www.edcoproducts.com	Hopkins	MN	55343	952-945-2680	938-4950
EDM Zap Parts Inc 1108 Front St Ste 2 *TF:* 800-759-2839 ■ *Web:* www.edmzap.com	Lisle	IL	60532	630-852-1699	
El Dorado Molds Inc 2691 Mercantile Dr *Web:* www.eldoradomolds.com	Rancho Cordova	CA	95742	916-635-4558	
Electro-Space Fabricators Inc 300 W High St *Web:* www.esfinc.com	Topton	PA	19562	610-682-7181	
Electromet Corp 879 Commonwealth Ave *Web:* www.electromet.com	Hagerstown	MD	21740	301-797-5900	
Elimetal Inc 1515 Boul Pitfield *Web:* elimetal.com	St Laurent	QC	H4S1G3	514-956-7400	956-8110
Elixir Industries Inc 24800 Chrisanta Dr Ste 210 *TF:* 800-421-1942 ■ *Web:* www.elixirind.com	Mission Viejo	CA	92691	949-860-5000	860-5011
Endicott Precision Inc 1328 Campville Rd *Web:* www.endicottprecision.com	Endicott	NY	13760	607-754-7076	
Engravers Metal Fabricators 124 Imperial St *Web:* www.emfinc.net	Merritt Island	FL	32952	321-453-3670	
Enprotech Corp 4259 E 49th St *Web:* www.enprotech.com	Cleveland	OH	44125	216-206-0081	
Enprotech Mechanical Services Inc 2200 Olds Ave *Web:* www.enpromech.com	Lansing	MI	48915	517-372-0950	
Epic Metals Corp 11 Talbot Ave *TF:* 877-696-3742 ■ *Web:* www.epicmetals.com	Rankin	PA	15104	412-351-3913	351-3913
Evansville Sheet Metal Works Inc 1901 W Maryland St *Web:* www.esmw.com	Evansville	IN	47712	812-423-7871	
EVS Metal Inc 1 Kenner Ct *Web:* www.evsmetal.com	Riverdale	NJ	07457	973-839-4432	
Exact Inc 5285 Ramona Blvd	Jacksonville	FL	32205	904-783-6640	
Experi-Metal Inc 6385 Wall St *Web:* www.experi-metal.com	Sterling Heights	MI	48312	586-977-7800	977-6981
Eze Lap Diamond Products 3572 Arrowhead Dr *TF:* 800-843-4815 ■ *Web:* www.eze-lap.com	Carson City	NV	89706	775-888-9500	
Fabrication Concepts Corp 1800 E St Andrew Pl *Web:* www.fabcon.com	Santa Ana	CA	92705	714-881-2000	881-2001
Fabrico Inc 10 Old Webster Rd	Oxford	MA	01540	508-987-5900	
Falstrom Co 147 Falstrom Ct *Web:* www.falstromcompany.com	Passaic	NJ	07055	973-777-0013	777-6396
Flat Rock Metal Inc (FRM) 26601 W Huron River Dr PO Box 1090 *Web:* www.frm.com	Flat Rock	MI	48134	734-782-4454	782-5640
Flexbar Machine Corp 250 Gibbs Rd *TF:* 800-879-7575 ■ *Web:* www.flexbar.com	Islandia	NY	11749	631-582-8440	
Floturn Inc 4236 Thunderbird Ln *Web:* www.floturn.com	Fairfield	OH	45014	513-860-8040	860-8044
Frank M Booth Inc 222 Third St *Web:* www.frankbooth.com	Marysville	CA	95901	530-742-7134	742-8109
Fred Christen & Sons Co 714 George St *Web:* toledochamber.com	Toledo	OH	43608	419-243-4161	243-1292
Frost Roofing Inc 2 Broadway St *Web:* www.frost-roofing.com	Wapakoneta	OH	45895	419-739-2701	
FS Tool Corp 71 Hobbs Gate *TF:* 800-387-9723 ■ *Web:* www.fstoolcorp.com	Markham	ON	L3R9T9	905-475-1999	
G&G Steel Inc PO Box 179 *Web:* www.ggsteel.com	Russellville	AL	35653	256-332-6652	332-0143
Gasbarre Products Inc 590 Division St *Web:* www.gasbarre.com	Dubois	PA	15801	814-371-3015	
Gauthier Industries Inc 3105 22nd St NW *Web:* www.gauthind.com	Rochester	MN	55901	507-289-0731	
Gentek Bldg Products Inc 11 Craigwood Rd *TF:* 800-548-4542 ■ *Web:* www.gentekinc.com	Avenel	NJ	07001	732-381-0900	
Gerome Mfg Co Inc 80 Laurel View Dr *Web:* www.geromemfg.com	Smithfield	PA	15478	724-438-8544	437-5608
Gerref Industries 206 N York St *Web:* www.gerref.com	Belding	MI	48809	616-794-3110	
Gilbert Mechanical Contractors Inc 4451 W 76th St *Web:* www.gilbertmech.com	Edina	MN	55435	952-835-3810	835-4765
Girtz Industries Inc 5262 N E Shafer Dr *Web:* www.girtz.com	Monticello	IN	47960	574-278-7510	
Global Power Equipment Group Inc 400 E Las Colinas Blvd Ste 400 *NASDAQ: GLPW* ■ *Web:* www.globalpower.com	Irving	TX	75039	214-574-2700	853-4744
Goldberg Bros Inc 8000 E 40th Ave *Web:* www.goldbergbrothers.com	Denver	CO	80207	303-321-1099	388-0749
Gomez & Associates Company LLC 3216 Industry Dr Ste C *Web:* www.cryogenics.net	North Charleston	SC	29418	843-552-4552	
Gordons Specialties Inc 720 W Wintergreen Rd *Web:* www.gsihighway.com	Hutchins	TX	75141	972-225-1660	
Grayd-A Metal Fabricators 13233 Florence Ave *Web:* www.grayd-a.com	Santa Fe Springs	CA	90670	562-944-8951	944-2326
Greene Metal Products Inc 24500 Capital Blvd	Clinton Township	MI	48036	586-465-6800	465-0136
Group Manufacturing Services Inc 1928 Hartog Dr *Web:* www.groupmanufacturing.com	San Jose	CA	95131	408-436-1040	
H & H Industrial Corp 7612 Rt 130 *TF:* 800-982-0341 ■ *Web:* www.hhindustrial.com	Pennsauken	NJ	08110	856-663-4444	663-4446
H & S Manufacturing Co 2913 Singleton St *Web:* www.hsmfg.com	Rowlett	TX	75088	972-475-4747	
Hagerty Steel & Aluminum Co 601 N Main *Web:* www.hagertysteel.com	East Peoria	IL	61611	309-699-7251	
Hamilton Form Company Ltd 7009 Midway Rd *Web:* www.hamiltonform.com	Fort Worth	TX	76118	817-590-2111	595-1110
Handy Industries LLC 600 W Second Ave PO Box 223 *Web:* www.handyindustries.com	Sully	IA	50251	641-752-5446	
Harrington Mold 1906 S Quaker Ridge Pl *Web:* www.harringtonmold.com	Ontario	CA	91761	909-923-2627	
HASCO America Inc 270 Rutledge Rd Unit B *Web:* www.hasco.com	Fletcher	NC	28732	828-650-2600	
Hawkeye Industries Inc 1126 N Eason Blvd *Web:* hawkeye.ws	Tupelo	MS	38804	662-842-3333	
Herold Precision Metals LLC 1370 Hammond Rd White Bear Township *Web:* www.heroldprecision.com	Saint Paul	MN	55110	651-490-5550	
Herr Industrial Inc 610 E Oregon Rd *Web:* www.herrindustrial.com	Lititz	PA	17543	717-569-6619	
Hi-Tech Fabrication Inc Leesville Industrial Park 8900 Midway W Rd *TF:* 800-359-7249 ■ *Web:* www.htfi.com	Raleigh	NC	27617	919-781-2552	
HiMEC Mechanical 1400 Seventh St NW *Web:* www.himec.com	Rochester	MN	55901	507-281-4000	281-5206
HM White Inc 12855 Burt Rd *Web:* paintfinishingsystems.com	Detroit	MI	48223	313-531-8477	
HS Die & Engineering Inc 0-215 Lk Michigan Dr NW *Web:* www.hsdie.com	Grand Rapids	MI	49534	616-453-5451	
Humanetics II Ltd 1700 Columbian Club Dr *Web:* www.humanetics.com	Carrollton	TX	75006	972-416-1304	
Hutchinson Manufacturing Inc 720 Hwy 7 W PO Box 487 *TF:* 800-795-1276 ■ *Web:* www.hutchmfg.com	Hutchinson	MN	55350	320-587-4653	
Hydraulic Technology Inc 3833 Cincinnati Ave *Web:* www.hydraulictechnology.com	Rocklin	CA	95765	916-645-3317	
IMCO Inc 858 N Lenola Rd	Moorestown	NJ	08057	856-235-7254	
IMM Inc 758 Isenhauer Rd *Web:* www.imm.net	Grayling	MI	49738	989-344-7662	
In-place Machining Company Inc 3811 N Holton St *TF:* 800-833-3575 ■ *Web:* inplace.com	Milwaukee	WI	53212	414-562-2000	
Industrial Air Inc 428 Edwardia Dr PO Box 8769 *Web:* www.industrialairinc.com	Greensboro	NC	27409	336-292-1030	855-7763
Industrial Louvers Inc 511 Seventh St S *TF:* 800-328-3421 ■ *Web:* www.industriallouvers.com	Delano	MN	55328	763-972-2981	972-2911
Industrial Revolution Inc 9225 151st Ave NE *TF:* 888-297-6062 ■ *Web:* www.industrialrev.com	Redmond	WA	98052	425-883-6600	
Irving Tool & Mfg Company Inc 2249 Wall St *Web:* irvingtool.com	Garland	TX	75041	972-926-4000	926-4099
J & E Metal Fabricators 1 Coan Pl *Web:* www.metalfab.com	Metuchen	NJ	08840	732-548-9650	
J & K Contracting 8903 Pioneer Rd	Neenah	WI	54956	920-836-9539	
Jaquith Industries Inc 600 E Brighton Ave *Web:* www.jaquith.com	Syracuse	NY	13210	315-478-5700	478-5707
Jensen Bridge & Supply Co 400 Stoney Creek Dr *Web:* www.jensenbridge.com	Sandusky	MI	48471	810-648-3000	648-3549

				Phone	Fax
John W McDougall Company Inc (JWMCD) 3731 Amy Lynn Dr *Web:* www.jwmcd.com	Nashville	TN	37218	615-321-3900	329-9069
Jones Metal Products Inc 3201 Third Ave *TF:* 800-967-1750 ■ *Web:* jonesmetalinc.com	Mankato	MN	56001	507-625-4436	625-2994
Jor-Mac Company Inc 155 E Main St *Web:* www.jor-mac.com	Lomira	WI	53048	920-269-8500	
Juniper Industries Inc 72-15 Metropolitan Ave PO Box 148 *Web:* www.juniperind.com	Middle Village	NY	11379	718-326-2546	326-3786
K y Diamond Ltd 2645 Rue Diab *Web:* kydiamond.ca	St Laurent	QC	H4S1E7	514-333-5606	339-5493
Kees Inc 400 Industrial Dr *Web:* www.kees.com	Elkhart Lake	WI	53020	920-876-3391	
Kingsbury Corp 15 Business Center Dr *Web:* www.optimation.us	Swanzey	NH	03446	603-352-5212	
Kirk Williams Company Inc 2734 Home Rd *Web:* www.kirkwilliamsco.com	Grove City	OH	43123	614-875-9023	
Klauer Manufacturing Co 1185 Roosevelt Ext PO Box 59 *Web:* www.klauer.com	Dubuque	IA	52004	563-582-7201	582-2022
Krueger Sheet Metal Co 731 N Superior St *Web:* kruegersheetmetal.com	Spokane	WA	99202	509-489-0221	489-6539
KSM Industries Inc N 115 W 19025 Edison Dr *Web:* www.ksmindustries.com	Germantown	WI	53022	262-251-9510	251-4865
Kuest Corp PO Box 33007 *Web:* www.kuestcorp.com	San Antonio	TX	78265	210-655-1220	655-1220
Laciny Bros Inc 6622 Vernon Ave *Web:* www.lacinybros.com	Saint Louis	MO	63130	314-862-8330	
Landmark Manufacturing Corp 28100 Quick Ave *Web:* www.landmarkfab.com	Gallatin	MO	64640	660-663-2185	663-2417
LB Foster Co 415 Holiday Dr *NASDAQ: FSTR* ■ *TF:* 800-255-4500 ■ *Web:* www.lbfoster.com	Pittsburgh	PA	15220	800-255-4500	
Leader Industries Inc 2509 Cruzen St *Web:* www.leaderindustries.com	Nashville	TN	37211	615-256-3500	
Lewis Corp 15136 W Hunziker Rd *Web:* www.lcorp.com	Pocatello	ID	83202	208-238-1202	
Lifetime Nut Covers Inc 720 320th St *Web:* lifetimenutcovers.com	Britt	IA	50423	641-565-3566	
Limco Airepair Inc 5304 S Lawton Ave *Web:* www.limcoairepair.com	Tulsa	OK	74107	918-445-4300	445-2210
Link-Burns Mfg Company Inc 253 American Way *TF:* 800-457-4358 ■ *Web:* linkburns.com	Voorhees	NJ	08043	856-429-6844	
Lippincott Marine 3420 Main St *TF:* 877-437-4193 ■ *Web:* www.lippincottmarine.com	Grasonville	MD	33701	410-827-9300	
Livers Bronze Co 4621 E 75th Terr *Web:* www.liversbronze.com	Kansas City	MO	64132	816-300-2828	300-0864
Lyco Manufacturing Inc 115 Commercial Dr *Web:* www.lycomfg.com	Columbus	WI	53925	920-623-4152	
Lynx Enterprises 724 E Grant Line Rd Ste B *Web:* lynxenterprises.com	Tracy	CA	95304	209-833-3400	
M K Specialty Metal Fabricators 725 W Wintergreen Rd *TF:* 866-814-4617 ■ *Web:* www.mkspecialty.com	Hutchins	TX	75141	972-225-6562	
M&M Manufacturing Co 4001 Mark IV Pkwy *TF:* 866-706-3999 ■ *Web:* www.mmmfg.com	Fort Worth	TX	76106	817-336-2311	
M2 Global Inc 5714 Epsilon *Web:* www.m2global.com	San Antonio	TX	78249	210-561-4800	561-4852
Mac Cal Company Inc 1737 Junction Ave *Web:* www.maccal.com	San Jose	CA	95112	408-441-1435	
Maddox Metal Works Inc 4116 Bronze Way *Web:* www.maddoxmetalworks.com	Dallas	TX	75237	214-333-2311	337-8169
Magic Metals Inc 3401 Bay St *Web:* www.magicmetals.com	Union Gap	WA	98903	509-453-1690	
Magnus-hitech Industries Inc 1605 Lake St *Web:* www.magnushitech.com	Melbourne	FL	32901	321-724-9731	
Majestic Industries Inc 15378 Hallmark Ct *Web:* www.majesticind.net	Macomb	MI	48042	586-786-9100	
Majestic Metals Inc 7770 Washington St *Web:* majesticmetals.com	Denver	CO	80229	303-288-6855	
Malmberg Engineering Inc 550 Commerce Way *Web:* malmbergengineering.com	Livermore	CA	94551	925-606-6500	
Mantz Automation Inc 1630 Innovation Way *Web:* www.mantzautomation.com	Hartford	WI	53027	262-673-7560	
Mapes Panels LLC 2929 Cornhusker Hwy PO Box 80069 *TF:* 800-228-2391 ■ *Web:* mapes.com	Lincoln	NE	68504	800-228-2391	737-6756
Matcor Metal Fabrication Inc 1021 W Birchwood St *Web:* www.matcor-matsu.com	Morton	IL	61550	309-266-7176	263-1866
Mayco Industries LLC 18 W Oxmoor Rd *TF:* 800-749-6061 ■ *Web:* www.maycoindustries.com	Birmingham	AL	35209	205-942-4242	945-8704
Mayville Products Corp 403 Degner Ave *TF:* 800-558-7297 ■ *Web:* optimastantron.com/en/optima-stantron	Mayville	WI	53050	920-387-3000	387-7196
McCorvey Sheet Metal Works LP 8610 Wallisville Rd *TF:* 800-580-7545 ■ *Web:* www.mccorvey.com	Houston	TX	77029	713-672-7545	672-0509
McFarlane Inc 3473 N Washington St *Web:* mcfarlane-e3.com	Grand Forks	ND	58203	701-772-9511	
McGill Airflow Corp 900 Pinder Ave **Fax Area Code:* 614 ■ *Web:* www.mcgillairflow.com	Grinnell	IA	50112	641-236-1580	829-1291*
McHone Metal Fabricators Inc 10300 County Rd 304 *Web:* www.kwikbilt.com	Terrell	TX	75160	972-524-7775	
Mech-Tronics Corp 1635 N 25th Ave *Web:* www.mech-tronics.com	Melrose Park	IL	60160	708-344-9823	344-0067
Melanson Company Inc, The 353 W St *Web:* www.melanson.com	Keene	NH	03431	603-352-4232	
Menches Tool & Die Inc 30995 San Benito St *TF:* 877-592-2328 ■ *Web:* www.menches.com	Hayward	CA	94544	510-476-1160	
Mercury Aircraft Inc 17 Wheeler Ave *Web:* www.mercurycorp.com	Hammondsport	NY	14840	607-569-4200	569-4306
Metal Standard Corp 286 Hedcor St *Web:* www.metalstd.com	Holland	MI	49423	616-396-4890	
Metal Trades Inc PO Box 129 *Web:* www.metaltrades.com	Hollywood	SC	29449	843-889-6441	
Metal-Fab Inc 3025 May St *TF:* 800-835-2830 ■ *Web:* www.mtlfab.com	Wichita	KS	67213	316-943-2351	943-2717
Metalcraft Technologies Inc 526 N Aviation Way *Web:* www.metalcraft.net	Cedar City	UT	84720	435-586-3871	586-0289
Metaltech Inc 206 Prospect Ave	Saint Louis	MO	63122	314-965-4550	965-4234
Metalworks Inc 902 E Fourth St *Web:* metalworks1.com	Ludington	MI	49431	231-845-5136	845-1043
Metcam Inc 305 Tidwell Cir *TF:* 888-394-9633 ■ *Web:* www.metcam.com	Alpharetta	GA	30004	770-475-9633	442-3425
Mid-Continent Engineering Inc 405 35th Ave NE *Web:* www.mid-continent.com	Minneapolis	MN	55418	612-781-0260	782-1320
Middle Atlantic Products Inc 300 Fairfield Rd *Web:* www.middleatlantic.com	Fairfield	NJ	07004	973-839-1011	
Milbank Mfg Company Inc 4801 Deramus Ave *Web:* www.milbankworks.com	Kansas City	MO	64120	816-483-5314	483-6357
Miller-Leaman 800 Orange Ave *TF:* 800-881-0320 ■ *Web:* www.millerleaman.com	Daytona Beach	FL	32114	386-248-0500	
Missouri Metals LLC 9970 Page Boulvard *Web:* www.missourimetals.com	St. Louis	MO	63132	314-222-7100	
Mitchell Metal Products Inc 19250 Hwy 12 E PO Box 789 *TF:* 800-258-6137 ■ *Web:* www.mitchellmetal.net	Kosciusko	MS	39090	662-289-7110	289-7112
Models & Tools 51400 Bellestri Ct *Web:* www.modelsandtools.com	Shelby Township	MI	48315	586-580-6900	
Modern Tool Inc 1200 Northdale Blvd *Web:* www.moderntoolinc.com	Coon Rapids	MN	55448	763-754-7337	
Morse Industries Inc 25811 74th Ave S *TF:* 800-325-7513 ■ *Web:* www.morseindustries.com	Kent	WA	98032	800-325-7513	
Multi-metal & Manufacturing Company Inc 1500 E Interstate 30 *Web:* www.multi-metal.com	Rockwall	TX	75087	972-771-1376	
Murray Sheet Metal Co Inc 3112 Seventh St *TF:* 800-464-8801 ■ *Web:* www.murraysheetmetal.com	Parkersburg	WV	26104	304-422-5431	428-4623
Myrmidon Corp 10555 W Little York Rd *Web:* myrmcorp.com	Houston	TX	77041	713-880-0044	880-4720
N-fab Inc 14925 Stuebner Airline Rd Ste 207 *Web:* www.n-fab.com	Houston	TX	77069	281-880-6322	
Napco Ply Gem Inc 5020 Weston Pkwy Ste 400 *TF:* 800-786-2726 ■ *Web:* www.plygem.com/wps/portal/home/brands/napco	Cary	MO	27153	888-975-9436	842-3991
National Fabtronix Inc 28800 Hesperian Blvd *Web:* www.natfab.com	Hayward	CA	94545	510-785-3135	785-1253
National Metal Fabricators 2395 Greenleaf Ave *TF:* 800-323-8849 ■ *Web:* www.nmfrings.com	Elk Grove Village	IL	60007	847-439-5321	439-4774
New Age Metal Fabricating Company Inc 26 Daniel Rd *Web:* www.namf.com	Fairfield	NJ	07004	973-227-9107	
Newjac Inc 415 S Grant St *TF:* 800-827-3259 ■ *Web:* www.newjac.com	Lebanon	IN	46052	765-483-2190	
Noll Manufacturing Co 1320 Performance Dr	Stockton	CA	95206	209-234-1600	234-5925
Northern Manufacturing Company Inc 132 N Railroad St *Web:* www.northernmfg.com	Oak Harbor	OH	43449	419-898-2821	
Northwest Precision Fabricators Inc 1765 Red Soils Ct Ste 100 *Web:* www.nwprecision.com	Oregon City	OR	97045	503-557-1951	
Nsa Industries LLC 210 Pierce Rd PO Box 54 *Web:* www.nsaindustries.com	St. Johnsbury	VT	05819	802-748-5007	748-0067
Nu-Way Industries Inc 555 Howard Ave *TF:* 888-488-5631 ■ *Web:* www.nuwayindustries.com	Des Plaines	IL	60018	847-298-7710	635-8650
OMAX Corp 21409 72nd Ave S *TF:* 800-838-0343 ■ *Web:* www.omax.com	Kent	WA	98032	253-872-2300	
Panavise Products Inc 7540 Colbert Dr *TF:* 800-759-7535 ■ *Web:* www.panavise.com	Reno	NV	89511	775-850-2900	
Paramount Precision Products Inc 15255 W Eleven Mile Rd	Oak Park	MI	48237	248-543-2100	
Passaic Metal Products Co 5 Central Ave *Web:* www.pampco.com	Clifton	NJ	07015	973-546-9000	
Pegasus Manufacturing Inc 422 Timber Ridge Rd *Web:* www.pegasusmfg.com	Middletown	CT	06457	860-635-8811	
Petersen Aluminum Corp 1005 Tonne Rd **Fax Area Code:* 800 ■ *TF:* 800-323-1960 ■ *Web:* www.pac-clad.com	Elk Grove Village	IL	60007	847-228-7150	722-7150*
PKM Steel Service Inc 228 E Ave A *Web:* www.pkmsteel.com	Salina	KS	67401	785-827-3638	
Platt & Labonia Co 70 Stoddard Ave *TF:* 800-505-9099 ■ *Web:* www.plattlabonia.com	North Haven	CT	06473	203-239-5681	234-7978
Poly Tech Diamond Co 4 E St PO Box 6 *Web:* www.polytechdiamond.com	North Attleboro	MA	02760	508-695-3561	
Precise Industries Inc 610 Neptune Ave *Web:* www.preciseind.com	Brea	CA	92821	714-482-2333	
Precision Kidd Steel Company Inc 1 Quality Way *Web:* www.precisionkidd.com	Aliquippa	PA	15001	724-378-7670	
Precorp Inc 2024 N Chappel Dr *Web:* www.precorp.net	Spanish Fork	UT	84660	801-798-5425	
Pro Fabrication Inc 201 First St *Web:* www.pro-fabrication.com	Madison Lake	MN	56063	507-243-3441	
Protocase Inc 46 Wabana Court Harbourside Industrial Park *Web:* www.protocase.com	Sydney	NS	B1P0B9	902-567-3335	
PTMW Inc 5040 NW US Hwy 24 *Web:* www.ptmw.com	Topeka	KS	66618	785-232-7792	

Company	City	State	ZIP	Phone	Fax
Puritan Manufacturing Inc 1302 Grace St *Web:* www.purmfg.com	Omaha	NE	68110	402-341-3753	
QPM Aerospace Inc 14341 Fryelands Blvd *Web:* www.qpm2000.com	Monroe	WA	98272	360-794-9925	
Qual-fab Inc 34250 Mills Rd *Web:* www.qual-fab.net	Avon	OH	44011	440-327-5000	
Quality Industries Inc 130 Jones Blvd. *Web:* www.qualityindustries.com	La Vergne	TN	37086	615-793-3000	
Quality Metal Fabricators Inc 2610 E Fifth Ave. *Web:* www.qmf.com	Tampa	FL	33605	813-831-7320	
Quality Metal Products Inc Orange Rd PO Box 273 *TF:* 888-251-2805 ■ *Web:* www.qualmet.com	Dallas	PA	18612	570-333-4248	333-4967
Quality Tool Inc 1220 Energy Park Dr. *Web:* www.qualitytool.com	Saint Paul	MN	55108	651-646-7433	
Rain Trade Corp 19 Skokie Vly Rd *Web:* www.guttersupply.com	Lake Bluff	IL	60044	847-283-0006	
Recovered Energy Inc 11455 N Rio Vista Rd. *Web:* www.recoveredenergy.com	Pocatello	ID	83202	208-637-0645	
RF Knox Company Inc 4865 Martin Ct SE *Web:* www.rfknox.com	Smyrna	GA	30082	770-434-7401	433-1783
RG Smith Co 1249 Dueber Ave SW *Web:* www.rgscontractors.com	Canton	OH	44706	330-456-3415	456-9638
Roll Forming Corp (RFC) 1070 Brooks Industrial Rd *Web:* www.rfcorp.com	Shelbyville	KY	40065	502-633-4435	
Rollex Corp 800 Chasa Ave *TF Cust Svc:* 800-251-3300 ■ *Web:* www.rollex.com	Elk Grove Village	IL	60007	847-437-3000	437-7561
RuMar Manufacturing Corp 925 S St. *Web:* www.rumar.com	Mayville	WI	53050	920-387-2104	387-2367
Ruskin Manufacturing Co 3900 Doctor Greaves Rd *Web:* www.ruskin.com	Grandview	MO	64030	816-761-7476	765-8955
S & S X-Ray Products Inc 10625 Telge Rd *TF:* 800-231-1747 ■ *Web:* www.ss-technology.com	Houston	TX	77095	281-815-1300	
Saferack Manufactoring 219 Safety Ave *Web:* www.saferack.com	Andrews	SC	29510	843-264-8096	
Saint Regis Culvert Inc 202 Morrell St *TF:* 800-527-4604 ■ *Web:* www.stregisculvert.com	Charlotte	MI	48813	517-543-3430	543-2313
Schadegg Mechanical Inc 225 Bridgepoint Dr S *Web:* www.schadegg-mech.com	St. Paul	MN	55075	651-292-9933	
Serra Corp 3590 Snell Ave *Web:* www.serracorp.com	San Jose	CA	95133	510-651-7333	657-5860
Seyer Industries Inc 66 Patmos Ct *Web:* www.seyerind.com	St. Peters	MO	63376	636-928-1190	
Sheet Metal Engineers Inc 383 Tower Rd	Augusta	GA	30907	706-863-6575	
Ship & Shore Environmental Inc 2474 N Palm Dr *Web:* www.shipandshore.com	Signal Hill	CA	90755	562-997-0233	
Simpson Dura-Vent Inc 877 Cotting Ct *TF:* 800-835-4429 ■ *Web:* www.duravent.com	Vacaville	CA	95688	707-446-1786	446-4740
SMT Inc 7300 ACC Blvd *TF:* 888-214-4804 ■ *Web:* www.smtcoinc.com	Raleigh	NC	27617	919-782-4804	781-1498
Soldream Inc 203 Hartford Tpke *Web:* www.soldream.com	Tolland	CT	06084	860-871-6883	
Southbridge Sheet Metal Works Inc 441 Main St *Web:* ssmwusa.com	Sturbridge	MA	01566	508-347-7800	347-9118
Southwark Metal Mfg Company Inc 2800 Red Lion Rd *TF:* 800-523-1052 ■ *Web:* southwarkmetal.com	Philadelphia	PA	19114	215-735-3401	735-0411
Spartan Carbide 34110 Riviera *Web:* www.spartancarbide.com	Fraser	MI	48026	586-285-9786	
Special Products & Manufacturing Inc 2625 Discovery Blvd. *Web:* www.spmfg.com	Rockwall	TX	75032	972-771-8851	771-8563
Specialty Fabrications Inc 2674 Westhills Ct *Web:* www.specfabinc.com	Simi Valley	CA	93065	805-579-9730	
Spencer Fabrications Inc 29511 County Rd 561 *TF:* 866-277-3623 ■ *Web:* www.spenfab.com	Tavares	FL	32778	352-343-0014	
Spray Enclosure Technologies Inc 1427 N Linden Ave *Web:* www.spraytech.com	Rialto	CA	92376	909-419-7011	
STANDARD Iron & Wire Works Inc 524 Pine St *Web:* www.std-iron.com	Monticello	MN	55362	763-295-8700	
Standard Metal Products 1541 W 132nd St *Web:* www.sheet-metal.com	Gardena	CA	90249	310-532-9861	
Standley Batch Systems Inc 505 Aquamsi St *Web:* www.standleybatch.com	Cape Girardeau	MO	63702	573-334-2831	
Star Precision LLC 7300 Miller Dr *Web:* www.starprecision.com	Longmont	CO	80504	303-926-0559	
Streimer Sheet Metal Works Inc 740 N Knott St *TF:* 888-288-3828 ■ *Web:* www.streimer.com	Portland	OR	97227	503-288-9393	288-3327
Structures Unlimited Inc 166 River Rd *TF:* 800-225-3895 ■ *Web:* www.structuresunlimitedinc.com	Bow	NH	03304	603-645-6539	625-0798
Superior Air Handling Corp 200 East 700 South *Web:* www.sahco.com	Clearfield	UT	84015	801-776-1997	
Sureway Tool & Engineering 2959 Hart Ct *Web:* www.surewaytool.com	Franklin Park	IL	60131	847-451-1784	
Swift Atlanta 3605 Swiftwater Park Dr. *Web:* www.swiftatlanta.com	Suwanee	GA	30024	770-945-1084	
T & C Industries Inc PO Box 629 *TF:* 800-426-6447 ■ *Web:* www.royal-basket.com	Darien	WI	53114	262-882-1227	
Tarus Products Inc 38100 Commerce Dr *Web:* www.tarus.com	Sterling Heights	MI	48312	586-977-1400	
Taylor Dynamometer Inc 3602 W Wheelhouse Rd *Web:* www.taylordyno.com	Milwaukee	WI	53208	414-755-0040	
Technifab Products Inc 10339 N Industrial Park Dr *Web:* www.technifab.com	Brazil	IN	47834	812-442-0520	
Tella Tool & Mfg 1015 N Ridge Ave *Web:* www.tellatool.com	Lombard	IL	60148	630-495-0545	495-3056
Tenere Inc 700 Kelly Ave *Web:* www.tenere.com	Dresser	WI	54009	715-247-4242	
TF System The Vertical ICF Inc 3030c Holmgren Way *TF:* 800-360-4634 ■ *Web:* tfsystem.com	Green Bay	WI	54304	920-983-9960	
TH Martin Inc 8500 Brookpark Rd *Web:* www.thmartin.net	Cleveland	OH	44129	216-741-2020	
Thybar Corp 913 S Kay Ave *TF:* 800-666-2872 ■ *Web:* www.thybar.com	Addison	IL	60101	630-543-5300	543-5309
Titan Air Inc 13901 16th St *Web:* www.titan-air.com	Osseo	WI	54758	715-597-2050	
Tobar Industries 912 Olinder Ct *Web:* www.tobar-ind.com	San Jose	CA	95122	408-494-3530	
Top Tool Co 3100 84th Ln Ne *Web:* www.toptool.com	Blaine	MN	55449	763-786-0030	
Trend Technologies LLC 4626 Eucalypus Ave. *Web:* www.trendtechnologies.com	Chino	CA	91710	909-597-7861	597-2284
Tru-Fab Technology Inc 34820 Lakeland Blvd *Web:* www.trufab.com	Eastlake	OH	44095	440-954-9760	
Unist 4134 36th St SE *TF:* 800-253-5462 ■ *Web:* www.unist.com	Grand Rapids	MI	49512	616-949-0853	
United McGill Corp 1 Mission Pk. *Web:* www.unitedmcgill.com	Groveport	OH	43125	614-829-1200	829-1291
United Tool & Stamping Company of North Carolina Inc 2817 Enterprise Ave *TF:* 800-883-6087 ■ *Web:* www.uts-nc.com	Fayetteville	NC	28306	910-323-8588	
Unruh Fire Inc 100 Industrial Dr *Web:* www.unruhfire.com	Sedgwick	KS	67135	316-772-5400	
USAch Technologies Inc 1524 Davis Rd. *Web:* www.usach.com	Elgin	IL	60123	847-888-0148	
V M Systems 3125 Hill Ave *Web:* www.vmsystemsinc.com	Toledo	OH	43607	419-535-1044	
Valley Joist 3019 Gault Ave N *TF:* 800-263-0324 ■ *Web:* www.valleyjoist.com	Fort Payne	AL	35967	256-845-2330	845-2597
Valley Tool & Die Inc 10020 York Theta Dr. *Web:* www.valcocleve.com	North Royalton	OH	44133	440-237-0160	
Vander Bend Manufacturing LLC 2701 Orchard Pkwy *Web:* www.vander-bend.com	San Jose	CA	95134	408-240-3500	
Vaughn Mfg Company Inc 757 Douglas Ave. *Web:* www.vaughnmfg.com	Nashville	TN	37207	615-262-5775	
Vector Industries Inc 1520 - 80th St SW Bldg B *Web:* www.vectorindustries.com	Everett	WA	98203	425-347-6696	
Vent Products Company Inc 1901 S Kilbourn Ave.	Chicago	IL	60623	773-521-1900	521-5613
Vent-A-Hood Ltd 1000 N Greenville Ave *Web:* www.ventahood.com	Richardson	TX	75081	972-235-5201	231-0663
Versatile Fabrication 2708 Ninth St *Web:* versatile-fabrication.com	Muskegon	MI	49444	231-739-7115	
Virtual Solutions LLC 21644 N Ninth Ave Ste 201 *Web:* www.vsols.com	Phoenix	AZ	85027	623-580-0775	
Voisard Mfg Inc 60 Scott St *Web:* www.voisard.com	Shiloh	OH	44878	419-896-3191	896-2127
Votaw Precision Technologies Inc 13153 Lakeland Rd *Web:* www.votaw.com	Santa Fe Springs	CA	90670	562-944-0661	
Western Bay Sheet Metal Inc 2311 Marconi Ct. *Web:* www.westernbay.net	San Diego	CA	92154	619-233-1753	
Western Industries Inc Watertown Metal Products Div 1141 S Tenth St *Web:* www.westernind.com	Watertown	WI	53094	920-261-0660	261-3832
Wiley Metal Fabricating Inc 4589 N Wabash Rd. *Web:* www.wileymetal.com	Marion	IN	46952	765-671-7865	
Wilson Manufacturing Co 4725 Green Park Rd *TF:* 800-634-5248 ■ *Web:* www.wilsonmfg.com	Saint Louis	MO	63123	314-416-8900	
Wilson Tool International Inc 12912 Farnham Ave *TF:* 800-328-9646 ■ *Web:* www.wilsontool.com	White Bear Lake	MN	55110	651-286-6001	
Wisco Products Inc 109 Commercial St *TF:* 800-367-6570 ■ *Web:* www.wiscoproducts.com	Dayton	OH	45402	937-228-2101	228-2407
Wolfe Engineering Inc 3040 N First St *Web:* www.e-wolfe.com	San Jose	CA	95134	408-232-2600	
Woodings Industrial Corp 218 Clay Ave. *Web:* www.woodingsindustrial.com	Mars	PA	16046	724-625-3131	
Wyoming Machine Inc 30680 Forest Blvd. *Web:* www.wyomingmachine.com	Stacy	MN	55079	651-462-4156	
York Metal Fabricators Inc 27 Ne 26th St *TF:* 800-255-4703 ■ *Web:* www.yorkmetal.com	Oklahoma City	OK	73105	405-528-7495	

698 SHIP BUILDING & REPAIRING

Company	City	State	ZIP	Phone	Fax
Al Larson Boat Shop Inc 1046 S Seaside Ave *Web:* larsonboat.com	San Pedro	CA	90731	310-514-4100	831-4912
Allied Marine & Industrial Inc 118 W St. *Web:* www.allmind.com	Port Colborne	ON	L3K4C9	905-834-8275	
Allied Shipyard Inc 310 Ledet Ln	Larose	LA	70373	985-693-3323	693-3687

Company	City	State	Zip	Phone	Fax
Allison Marine Contractors Inc 9828 Hwy 182 E *Web:* www.allisonmarine.net	Amelia	LA	70340	985-631-2000	
Austal USA LLC 100 Addsco Rd. *Web:* www.austal.com	Mobile	AL	36602	251-434-8000	
Bath Iron Works Corp 700 Washington St *Web:* gdbiw.com	Bath	ME	04530	207-443-3311	442-1567
Bay Diesel Corp 3736 Cook Blvd *Web:* www.baydiesel.com	Chesapeake	VA	23323	757-485-0075	
Bay Ship & Yacht Co 2900 Main St Ste 2100 *Web:* www.bay-ship.com	Alameda	CA	94501	510-337-9122	337-0154
Bay Shipbuilding Co 605 N Third Ave *Web:* bayshipbuildingcompany.com	Sturgeon Bay	WI	54235	920-743-5524	
Boland Marine & Mfg Company Inc 1000 Tchoupitoulas St *Web:* www.bolandmarine.com	New Orleans	LA	70130	504-581-5800	581-5814
Bollinger Algiers Inc 434 Powder St *Web:* www.bollingershipyards.com	New Orleans	LA	70114	504-362-7960	361-1679
Bollinger Gretna 4640 Peters Rd *Web:* bollingershipyards.com	Harvey	LA	70058	504-367-8080	
Bollinger Shipyards Inc 8365 Louisiana 308 *Web:* www.bollingershipyards.com	Lockport	LA	70374	985-532-2554	532-7225
C & G Boat Works Inc 401 Cochran Bridge Causeway Hwy 98 *Web:* www.cgboatworks.com	Mobile	AL	36603	251-694-1300	
Colonna's Shipyard Inc 400 E Indian River Rd *TF:* 800-265-6627 ■ *Web:* www.colonnaship.com	Norfolk	VA	23523	757-545-2414	543-2480
Conrad Industries Inc 1501 Front St *Web:* www.conradindustries.com	Morgan City	LA	70380	985-384-3060	385-4090
Continental Maritime of San Diego Inc 1995 Bay Front St *TF:* 877-631-0020 ■ *Web:* www.continentalmaritime.com	San Diego	CA	92113	619-234-8851	696-7358
Dakota Creek Industries Inc 820 Fourth St PO Box 218 *Web:* www.dakotacreek.com	Anacortes	WA	98221	360-293-9575	293-6432
Davis Boat Works Inc 99 Jefferson Ave *Web:* www.davisboat.com	Newport News	VA	23607	757-247-0101	
Derecktor Shipyards Inc 311 E Boston Post Rd *Web:* www.derecktor.com	Mamaroneck	NY	10543	914-698-5020	
Detyens Shipyards Inc 1670 Drydock Ave Bldg 236 Ste 200 *Web:* www.detyens.com	North Charleston	SC	29405	843-308-8000	308-8059
Earl Industries LLC 2 Harper Ave *TF:* 800-433-8442 ■ *Web:* www.nasscoearl.com	Portsmouth	VA	23707	757-215-2500	215-2504
Elevating Boats LLC 201 Dean Ct *TF:* 800-843-2895 ■ *Web:* www.ebi-inc.com	Houma	LA	70363	985-868-9655	868-9656
Elliott Bay Design Group LLC 5305 Shilshole Ave NW Ste 100 *Web:* www.ebdg.com	Seattle	WA	98107	206-782-3082	
Essex Boat Works Inc Ferry St PO Box 37 *Web:* essexboatworks.com	Essex	CT	06426	860-767-8276	767-1729
Fraser Shipyards Inc 1 Clough Ave *Web:* www.frasershipyards.com	Superior	WI	54880	715-394-7787	394-2807
General Dynamics Electric Boat Corp (GDEB) 75 Eastern Pt Rd **Fax:* Hum Res ■ *Web:* gdeb.com	Groton	CT	06340	860-433-3000	433-1400*
General Dynamics NASSCO 2798 E Harbor Dr *Web:* www.nassco.com	San Diego	CA	92113	619-544-3400	544-3541
General Ship Repair Corp, The 1449 Key Hwy *Web:* www.generalshiprepair.com	Baltimore	MD	21230	410-752-7620	
Gladding-Hearn Shipbuilding 1 Riverside Ave PO Box 300 *Web:* www.gladding-hearn.com	Somerset	MA	02726	508-676-8596	672-1873
Goltens New York Corp 160 Van Brunt St *Web:* www.goltens.com	Brooklyn	NY	11231	718-855-7200	802-1147
Greenbrier Co 1 Centerpointe Dr Ste 200 *NYSE:* GBX ■ *TF:* 800-343-7188 ■ *Web:* www.gbrx.com	Lake Oswego	OR	97035	503-684-7000	684-7553
Gulf Copper & Mfg Corp 7200 Hwy 87 *Web:* www.gulfcopper.com	Port Arthur	TX	77642	409-989-0300	985-6349
Gulf Craft LLC 320 Boro Ln *Web:* www.gulfcraft.com	Franklin	LA	70538	337-828-2580	828-2586
Hodgdon Yachts Inc 14 School St *Web:* www.hodgdonyachts.com	East Boothbay	ME	04544	207-633-4194	
Horizon Shipbuilding Inc 13980 Shell Belt Rd *Web:* www.horizonshipbuilding.com	Bayou La Batre	AL	36509	251-824-1660	
Huntington Ingalls Industries 4101 Washington Ave *NYSE:* HII ■ *Web:* www.huntingtoningalls.com	Newport News	VA	23607	757-380-2000	
Huntington Ingalls Shipbuilding Inc 1000 Access Rd *Web:* ingalls.huntingtoningalls.com	Pascagoula	MS	39567	228-935-1122	
Indmar Products Company Inc 5400 Old Millington Rd *Web:* www.indmar.com	Millington	TN	38053	901-353-9930	
International Submarine Engineering Ltd 1734 Broadway St *Web:* www.ise.bc.ca	Port Coquitlam	BC	V3C2M8	604-942-5223	942-7577
Irving Shipbuilding Inc 3099 Barrington St *Web:* www.irvingshipbuilding.com	Halifax	NS	B3K5M7	902-423-9271	
J. M. Martinac Shipbuilding Corp 401 E 15th St *Web:* www.martinacship.com	Tacoma	WA	98421	253-572-4005	
Jupiter Marine International Holdings 1103 12th AveEast *Web:* www.jupitermarine.com	Palmetto	FL	34221	941-729-5000	
Kvichak Marine Industries 469 NW Bowdoin Pl *Web:* www.kvichak.com	Seattle	WA	98107	206-545-8485	545-3504
Lake Union Drydock Co 1515 Fairview Ave E *Web:* ludd.com	Seattle	WA	98102	206-323-6400	
Leevac Shipyards Inc 111 Bunge St *TF:* 800-244-3262 ■ *Web:* leevac.com	Jennings	LA	70546	337-824-2210	824-2970
Lyon Shipyard Inc PO Box 2180 *Web:* www.lyonshipyard.com	Norfolk	VA	23501	757-622-4661	
Malibu Boats LLC 5075 Kimberly Way *Web:* www.maliboats.com	Loudon	TN	37774	209-383-7469	
Malin International Ship Repair & Drydock Inc 320 77th St Pier 41 *Web:* www.malinshiprepair.com	Galveston	TX	77554	409-740-3314	
MARCO Global 4259 22nd Ave W *TF:* 866-966-2726 ■ *Web:* www.marcoglobal.com	Seattle	WA	98199	206-285-3200	282-8520
Marine Hydraulics International Inc (MHI) 543 E Indian River Rd *Web:* www.mhi-shiprepair.com	Norfolk	VA	23523	757-545-6400	545-8169
Marine Systems Inc 116 Capital Blvd *Web:* www.kirbycorp.com	Houma	LA	70360	985-223-7100	
Marinette Marine Corp 1600 Ely St **Fax:* Cust Svc ■ *Web:* marinettemarine.com	Marinette	WI	54143	715-735-9341	735-3516*
Marisco Ltd 91-607 Malakole Rd *Web:* www.marisco.net	Kapolei	HI	96707	808-682-1333	
Metro Machine Corp PO Box 1860 PO Box 1860 **Fax:* Hum Res ■ *Web:* www.memach.com	Norfolk	VA	23501	757-543-6801	494-0430*
Mitsubishi Heavy Industries America Inc 630 Fifth Ave Ste 2650 *Web:* www.mitsubishitoday.com	New York	NY	10111	212-969-9000	262-2113
Mship Co 401 W A St Ste 2125 *Web:* www.mshipco.com	San Diego	CA	92101	619-232-8937	
Newport Shipyard 1 Washington St *Web:* www.newportshipyard.com	Newport	RI	02840	401-846-6000	846-6001
Nichols Bros Boat Builders Inc 5400 Cameron Rd *Web:* www.nicholsboats.com	Freeland	WA	98249	360-331-5500	331-7484
North River Boats Inc 1750 Green Siding Rd *Web:* www.northriverboats.com	Roseburg	OR	97471	541-673-2438	
Northrop Grumman Newport News 13560 Jefferson Ave **Fax:* Hum Res ■ *TF:* 888-493-7386 ■ *Web:* www.newport-news.org	Newport News	VA	23603	757-886-7777	886-7920*
Ocean Shipholdings Inc 16211 Pk Ten Pl *Web:* www.oceanshipholdings.com	Houston	TX	77084	281-579-3700	579-0671
Orange Shipbuilding Co Inc 710 Market St *Web:* www.conradindustries.com	Orange	TX	77631	409-883-6666	
Pacific Fisherman Inc 5351 24th Ave NW *TF:* 877-644-6148 ■ *Web:* pacificfishermen.com	Seattle	WA	98107	206-784-2562	784-1986
Pacific Shipyards International LLC 41 Sand Island Access Rd PO Box 31328 *Web:* www.pacificshipyards.com	Honolulu	HI	96819	808-848-6211	848-6279
Pacord Inc 240 W 30th St *Web:* l-3mps.com	National City	CA	91950	619-336-2200	
Pocock Racing Shells 615 80Th St Sw *TF:* 888-762-6251 ■ *Web:* www.pocock.com	Everett	WA	98203	425-438-9048	
Robishaw Engineering Inc 10106 Mathewson Ln *TF:* 800-877-1706 ■ *Web:* www.flexifloat.com	Houston	TX	77043	713-468-1706	468-5822
SeaArk Boats 728 W Patton PO Box 803 *Web:* seaarkboats.com	Monticello	AR	71655	870-367-9755	
Southwest Shipyard L P 18310 Market St *Web:* www.swslp.com	Channelview	TX	77530	281-860-3200	860-3215
Stabbert Mantime Management 2629 Nw 54th St Ste 201 *Web:* www.stabbertmaritime.com	Seattle	WA	98107	206-547-6161	
Swiftships Inc 1105 Levee Rd *Web:* www.swiftships.com	Morgan City	LA	70380	985-384-1700	380-2559
Tecnico Corp 831 Industrial Ave *TF General:* 800-786-2207 ■ *Web:* www.tecnicocorp.com	Chesapeake	VA	23324	757-545-4013	
Trinity Marine Products Inc 2525 N Stemmons Fwy *TF:* 877-876-5463 ■ *Web:* www.trin.net	Dallas	TX	75207	214-589-8446	
United States Marine Inc 10011 Lorraine Rd *Web:* www.usmi.com	Gulfport	MS	39503	228-679-1005	
Victoria Shipyards Company Ltd 825 Admirals Rd *Web:* www.seaspan.com/victoria-shipyards	Victoria	BC	V9A2P1	250-380-1602	
VT Halter Marine Inc 900 Bayou Casotte Pkwy *Web:* www.vthaltermarine.com	Pascagoula	MS	39581	228-696-6888	696-6899

699 SHUTTERS - WINDOW (ALL TYPES)

Company	City	State	Zip	Phone	Fax
Atlantic Premium Shutters 29797 Beck Rd *TF:* 866-288-2726 ■ *Web:* thetapcogroup.com/brands/atlantic	Wixom	MI	48393	248-668-6408	
Champion Window Mfg Inc 12121 Champion Way *TF:* 877-424-2674 ■ *Web:* www.championwindow.com	Cincinnati	OH	45241	513-346-4600	346-4614
Commonwealth Laminating & Coating Inc 345 Beaver Creek Dr *TF General:* 888-321-5111 ■ *Web:* www.suntekfilms.com	Martinsville	VA	24112	276-632-4991	632-0173
Perfect Shutters Inc 12213 Rte 173 *TF:* 800-548-3336 ■ *Web:* www.shuttersinc.com	Hebron	IL	60034	815-648-2401	648-4510
Roll Shutter Systems Inc 21633 N 14th Ave *TF:* 800-551-7655 ■ *Web:* www.rollshuttersystemsusa.com	Phoenix	AZ	85027	623-869-7057	
Roll-A-Way Inc 1661 Glenlake Ave **Fax Area Code:* 630 ■ *TF:* 866-749-5424 ■ *Web:* www.roll-a-way.com	Itasca	IL	60143	866-749-5424	980-6364*
Rolling Shield Inc 2500 NW 74th Ave **Fax Area Code:* 305 ■ *TF:* 800-474-9404 ■ *Web:* www.rollingshield.com	Miami	FL	33122	800-474-9404	436-5523*
Shutter Mill Inc 8517 S Perkins Rd *TF:* 800-416-6455 ■ *Web:* www.kirtz.com	Stillwater	OK	74074	405-377-6455	377-1010
Sunburst Shutters 6480 W Flamingo Rd Ste D *TF:* 877-786-2877 ■ *Web:* www.sunburstshutters.com	Las Vegas	NV	89103	702-367-1600	367-8525
Tapco Group 29797 Beck Rd *TF:* 800-521-7567 ■ *Web:* www.tapcogroup.com	Wixom	MI	48393	248-668-6400	668-6466

700 SIGNALS & SIRENS - ELECTRIC

Company	City	State	Zip	Phone	Fax
ADDCO LLC 240 Arlington Ave E *TF:* 800-616-4408 ■ *Web:* www.addco.com	Saint Paul	MN	55117	651-488-8600	558-3600
ECCO 833 W Diamond St **Fax Area Code:* 800 ■ *TF:* 800-635-5900 ■ *Web:* www.eccolink.com	Boise	ID	83705	208-395-8000	688-3226*
Econolite Control Products Inc 3360 E La Palma Av *TF:* 800-225-6480 ■ *Web:* www.econolite.com	Anaheim	CA	92806	714-630-3700	630-6349
Federal Signal Corp Emergency Products Div 2645 Federal Signal Dr. *TF:* 800-264-3578 ■ *Web:* www.fedsig.com	University Park	IL	60466	708-534-3400	
Harrington Signal Co 2519 Fourth Ave. *Web:* www.harringtonsignal.com	Moline	IL	61265	309-762-0731	762-8215
Rothenbuhler Engineering 524 Rhodes Rd PO Box 708 *Web:* www.rothenbuhlereng.com	Sedro Woolley	WA	98284	360-856-0836	856-2183
Safetran Traffic Systems Inc 1485 Garden of the Gods Rd. *Web:* www.safetran-traffic.com	Colorado Springs	CO	80907	719-599-5600	599-3853
Western Cullen Hayes Inc 2700 W 36th Pl *Web:* wch.com	Chicago	IL	60632	773-254-9600	254-1110
Whelen Engineering Company Inc 51 Winthrop Rd & Rt 145 *Web:* www.whelen.com	Chester	CT	06412	860-526-9504	526-4078
WL Jenkins Co 1445 Whipple Ave SW *Web:* www.wljenkinsco.com	Canton	OH	44710	330-477-3407	477-8404

701 SIGNS

See Also Displays - Exhibit & Trade Show p. 2196; Displays - Point-of-Purchase p. 2197; Signals & Sirens - Electric p. 3185

Company	City	State	Zip	Phone	Fax
Ace Sign Systems Inc 3621 W Royerton Rd *Web:* www.acesign.com	Muncie	IN	47304	765-288-1000	
Ad Art Co 3260 E 26th St *TF:* 800-266-7522 ■ *Web:* www.adartco.com	Los Angeles	CA	90058	323-981-8941	980-0515
Ad Display Sign Systems Inc 27255 Katy Fwy *Web:* addisplaysigns.com	Katy	TX	77494	281-392-2828	392-7446
Adamsahern Sign Solutions Inc 30 Arbor St Ste 3 *Web:* www.adamsahern.com	Hartford	CT	06106	860-523-8835	
Advance Corp Braille-Tac Div 8200 97th St S *TF:* 800-328-9451 ■ *Web:* www.advancecorp.com	Cottage Grove	MN	55016	651-771-9297	771-2121
Advantage Sign Supply Inc 3939 N Greenbrooke SE *Web:* advantagesgs.com	Grand Rapids	MI	49512	616-554-3300	
Allen Industries Inc 6434 Burnt Poplar Rd *TF:* 800-967-2553 ■ *Web:* www.allenindustries.com	Greensboro	NC	27409	336-668-2791	668-7875
Always a Good Sign 407 Bloomfield Dr Ste 3 *Web:* alwaysagoodsign.com	West Berlin	NJ	08091	856-753-7800	
American Porcelain Enamel Co 203 W Church St	Crandall	TX	75114	972-427-6654	
Anza Inc 312 Ninth Ave SE Ste B *Web:* www.anza.com	Watertown	SD	57201	605-886-3889	
APCO Graphics Inc 388 Grant St SE *TF:* 877-988-2726 ■ *Web:* www.apcosigns.com	Atlanta	GA	30312	404-688-9000	
Apex Digital Imaging Inc 16057 Tampa Palms Blvd W *TF:* 866-973-3034 ■ *Web:* www.apexdigitalimaging.com	Tampa	FL	33647	813-973-3034	
Art Guild Inc 300 Wolf Dr *Web:* www.artguildinc.com	West Deptford	NJ	08086	856-853-7500	
Artcraft Signs Co 1717 S Acoma St *Web:* www.artcraftsign.com	Denver	CO	80223	303-777-7771	778-7175
ASC Signal Corp 1120 Jupiter Rd Ste 102 *Web:* www.cpii.com/division.cfm/13	Plano	TX	75074	214-291-7654	
ASL Services 3700 Commerce Blvd Ste 216 *TF:* 888-744-6275 ■ *Web:* www.aslservices.com	Kissimmee	FL	34741	407-518-7900	
Atlantic Sign Media Inc 151 McArthur Ln. *Web:* atlanticsignmedia.com	Burlington	NC	27217	336-584-1375	584-3848
Banana Banner Signs 3148 Duke St. *Web:* bananabanner.com	Alexandria	VA	22314	703-522-6262	
Beyond Digital Imaging 36 Apple Creek Blvd *TF:* 888-689-1888 ■ *Web:* www.bdimaging.com	Markham	ON	L3R4Y4	905-415-1888	415-1583
Brady Corp 6555 W Good Hope Rd. *NYSE:* BRC ■ **Fax Area Code:* 800 ■ **Fax:* Cust Svc ■ *TF Cust Svc:* 800-541-1686 ■ *Web:* www.bradycorp.com	Milwaukee	WI	53223	414-358-6600	292-2289*
Budget 1 Hour Signs Inc 2535 E Indian School Rd *Web:* budgetsignsaz.com	Phoenix	AZ	85016	602-955-4686	
Caasco Signs 2719 Texas Ave **Fax Area Code:* 281 ■ *Web:* creativesigntc.com	Texas City	TX	77590	409-945-4929	332-1503*
California Neon Products Inc 4530 Mission Gorge Pl. *TF:* 800-822-6366 ■ *Web:* www.cnpsigns.com	San Diego	CA	92120	619-283-2191	283-9503
Carousel Signs & Designs Inc 2312 Commerce Ctr Dr Ste B *Web:* www.carouselsigns.com	Rockville	VA	23146	804-620-3200	
Century Graphics & Metals Inc 550 S N Lake Blvd Ste 1000 **Fax Area Code:* 407 ■ *TF:* 800-327-5664 ■ *Web:* www.centurygraphics.com	Altamonte Springs	FL	32701	800-327-5664	262-8291*
Club Colors Inc 420 E State Pkwy. *Web:* www.clubcolors.com	Schaumburg	IL	60173	847-490-3636	
Coast 2 Coast Sign Surveys Inc 7704 Basswood Dr *Web:* www.c2csurveys.com	Chattanooga	TN	37416	423-296-9000	

Company	City	State	Zip	Phone	Fax
Colorado Time Systems 1551 E 11th St. *TF:* 800-279-0111 ■ *Web:* www.colotime.com	Loveland	CO	80537	970-667-1000	667-5876
Couch & Philippi Inc 10680 Fern Ave PO Box A. *TF Orders:* 800-854-3360 ■ *Web:* www.couchandphilippi.com	Stanton	CA	90680	714-527-2261	827-2077
Cummings Signs Inc 15 Century Blvd Ste 200 *TF:* 800-489-7446 ■ *Web:* cummingsbrandnew.com	Nashville	TN	37214	800-489-7446	
Di Highway Sign & Structure Corp 40 Greenman Ave *Web:* www.dihighway.com	New York Mills	NY	13417	315-736-8312	
DiAZiT Company Inc 941 US 1 Hwy *TF Cust Svc:* 800-334-6641 ■ *Web:* www.diazit.com	Youngsville	NC	27596	919-556-5188	556-3757
Douglas Corp 9650 Valley View Rd *Web:* www.douglascorp.com	Eden Prairie	MN	55344	952-941-2944	942-3125
Doyle Signs Inc 232 W IH- Rd *Web:* www.doylesigns.com	Addison	IL	60101	630-543-9490	543-9493
Dualite Sales & Service Inc 1 Dualite Ln *TF:* 800-543-7271 ■ *Web:* www.dualite.com	Williamsburg	OH	45176	513-724-7100	724-7100
Dynasign Corp 44040 Fremont Blvd. *Web:* www.dynasign.net	Fremont	CA	94538	510-405-5988	
Eastern Metal/USA-SIGN 1430 Sullivan St. *TF Sales:* 800-872-7446 ■ *Web:* www.usa-sign.com	Elmira	NY	14901	607-734-2295	734-8783
Everbrite Inc 4949 S 110th St PO Box 20020 *TF:* 800-558-3888 ■ *Web:* www.everbrite.com	Greenfield	WI	53220	414-529-3500	529-7191
Fairmont Sign Company Inc 3750 E Outer Dr *Web:* www.fairmontsign.com	Detroit	MI	48234	313-368-4000	
FASTSIGNS International Inc 2542 Highlander Way *TF:* 800-327-8744 ■ *Web:* www.fastsigns.com	Carrollton	TX	75006	972-447-0777	248-8201
Federal Heath Sign Co 4602 N Ave *Web:* www.federalheath.com	Oceanside	CA	92056	760-941-0715	941-0719
FLOORgraphics Inc 200 American Metro Blvd	Hamilton Township	NJ	08619	609-528-9200	
Formetco Inc 2963 Pleasant Hill Rd *TF:* 800-367-6382 ■ *Web:* www.formetco.com	Duluth	GA	30096	770-476-7000	
Forms & Surfaces Inc 30 Pine St *Web:* www.forms-surfaces.com	Pittsburgh	PA	15223	412-781-9003	
GableSigns Inc 7440 Ft Smallwood Rd *TF:* 800-854-0568 ■ *Web:* www.gablesigns.com	Baltimore	MD	21226	410-255-6400	437-5336
Gemini Inc 103 Mensing Way *TF:* 800-538-8377 ■ *Web:* www.geminisignproducts.com	Cannon Falls	MN	55009	507-263-3957	263-4887
George Patton Assoc Inc 55 Broadcommon Rd. *TF:* 800-572-2194 ■ *Web:* www.displays2go.com	Bristol	RI	02809	401-247-0333	
Gopher Sign Co 1310 Randolph Ave *TF:* 800-383-3156 ■ *Web:* www.gophersign.com	Saint Paul	MN	55105	651-698-5095	699-3727
Gordon Sign 2930 W Ninth Ave. *Web:* www.gordonsign.com	Denver	CO	80204	303-629-6121	629-1024
Grandwell Industries Inc 6109 S NC HWY 55 *TF Cust Svc:* 800-338-6554 ■ *Web:* www.grandwell.com	Fuquay Varina	NC	27526	919-557-1221	552-9830
Graphic Specialties Inc 3110 Washington Ave N. *TF:* 800-486-4605 ■ *Web:* www.signsbygsi.com	Minneapolis	MN	55411	612-522-5287	
Gulf Coast Signs of Sarasota Inc 1713 Northgate Blvd. *Web:* www.gulfcoastsigns.com	Sarasota	FL	34234	941-355-8841	
Hackley Architectural Signage Inc 1999 Alpine Way *Web:* www.hackley.net	Hayward	CA	94545	510-940-2608	
Hall Signs Inc 4495 W Vernal Pk **Fax Area Code:* 812 ■ *TF:* 800-284-7446 ■ *Web:* www.hallsigns.com	Bloomington	IN	47404	800-284-7446	332-9816*
Hallmark Nameplate Inc 1717 E Lincoln Ave *TF:* 800-874-9063 ■ *Web:* www.hallmarknameplate.com	Mount Dora	FL	32757	352-383-8142	
Hawkins Traffic Safety Supply 1255 E Shore Hwy **Fax Area Code:* 510 ■ *TF:* 800-772-3995 ■ *Web:* hawkinstraffic.com	Berkeley	CA	94710	800-236-0112	525-2861*
Highland Containers 100 Ragsdale Rd *Web:* www.stronghaven.com	Jamestown	NC	27282	336-887-5400	
Hy-Ko Products Co 60 Meadow Ln *TF:* 800-292-0550 ■ *Web:* www.hy-ko.com	Northfield	OH	44067	330-467-7446	467-7442
Icon Identity Solutions 1418 Elmhurst Rd. **Fax Area Code:* 847 ■ *TF:* 888-724-0380 ■ *Web:* www.iconid.com	Elk Grove Village	IL	60007	888-724-0380	364-1517*
Image National Inc 16265 Star Rd *Web:* www.imagenational.com	Nampa	ID	83687	208-345-4020	336-9886
Insignia Systems Inc 8799 Brooklyn Blvd *NASDAQ:* ISIG ■ *TF:* 800-874-4648 ■ *Web:* www.insigniasystems.com	Minneapolis	MN	55445	763-392-6200	392-6222
International Display Systems Inc 5008 Veterans Memorial Hwy. *Web:* www.idsmenus.com	Holbrook	NY	11741	631-218-1802	
International Patterns Inc 50 Inez Dr.	Bay Shore	NY	11706	631-952-2000	
Interstate Highway Sign Corp 7415 Lindsey Rd. *Web:* www.interstatesigns.com	Little Rock	AR	72206	501-490-4242	490-1090
Kessler Sign Co 5804 Poe Ave. *TF:* 800-686-1870 ■ *Web:* www.kesslersignco.com	Dayton	OH	45414	937-898-0633	
Kieffer & Company Inc 3322 Washington Ave **Fax Area Code:* 920 ■ *TF:* 800-458-4394 ■ *Web:* www.kieffersigns.com	Sheboygan	WI	53081	800-458-4394	451-3360*
King Signs & Graphics 3858 Jackson River Rd.	Monterey	VA	24465	540-468-2932	
LaFrance Corp 1 LaFrance Way PO Box 5002 *Web:* www.lafrancecorp.com	Concordville	PA	19331	610-361-4300	361-4301
Lake Shore Industries Inc (LSI) 1817 Poplar St PO BOX 3427 **Fax Area Code:* 814 ■ *TF:* 800-458-0463 ■ *Web:* www.lsisigns.com	Erie	PA	16508	800-458-0463	453-4293*
Lauretano Sign Group 1 Tremco Dr *Web:* www.lauretano.com	Terryville	CT	06786	860-582-0233	583-0949
LNI Custom Manufacturing Inc 12536 Chadron Ave *TF:* 800-338-3387 ■ *Web:* www.lnisigns.com	Hawthorne	CA	90250	310-978-2000	
LSI Industries Inc 10000 Alliance Rd. *NASDAQ:* LYTS ■ *Web:* www.lsi-industries.com	Cincinnati	OH	45242	513-793-3200	984-1335
Lynn Sign 8 Gleason St	Andover	MA	01810	978-470-1194	

Company / Address	City	State	Zip	Phone	Fax
M-R Sign Company Inc 1706 First Ave N TF: 800-231-5564 ■ Web: www.mrsigncompany.com	Fergus Falls	MN	56537	218-736-5681	736-4070
Magnetsigns Adv Inc 4225 38th St TF: 800-219-8977 ■ Web: www.magnetsigns.com	Camrose	AB	T4V3Z3	780-672-8720	672-8716
MC Sign Company Inc 8959 Tyler Blvd TF: 800-627-4460 ■ Web: www.mcsign.com	Mentor	OH	44060	440-953-2280	
McLoone 75 Sumner St TF: 800-624-6641 ■ Web: www.mcloone.com	La Crosse	WI	54603	608-784-1260	782-3711
National Sign Corp 1255 Westlake Ave N Web: www.nationalsigncorp.com	Seattle	WA	98109	206-282-0700	285-3091
National Stock Sign Co 1040 El Dorado Ave TF: 800-462-7726 ■ Web: nationalstocksign.com	Santa Cruz	CA	95062	831-476-2020	476-1734
NW Sign Industries Inc 360 Crider Ave Web: www.nwsignindustries.com	Moorestown	NJ	08057	856-802-1677	
O'Ryan Group Inc 4010 Pilot Ste 108 TF: 800-253-0750 ■ Web: www.oryangroup.com	Memphis	TN	38118	901-794-4610	794-3206
Pannier Graphics 345 Oak Rd TF: 800-544-8428 ■ Web: www.panniergraphics.com	Gibsonia	PA	15044	724-265-4900	
Pattison Sign Group 555 Ellesmere Rd *Fax Area Code: 855 ■ TF: 800-268-6536 ■ Web: www.pattisonsign.com	Scarborough	ON	M1R4E8	416-759-1111	759-9560*
Philadelphia Sign Co 707 W Spring Garden St Web: www.philadelphiasign.com	Palmyra	NJ	08065	856-829-1460	829-8549
Poblocki Sign Company LLC 922 S 70th St TF: 800-776-7064 ■ Web: www.poblocki.com	West Allis	WI	53214	414-453-4010	453-3070
Precision Solar Controls Inc 2985 Market St TF: 800-686-7414 ■ Web: www.precisionsolarcontrols.com	Garland	TX	75041	972-278-0553	
Prismaflex Inc 1645 Queens Way E Web: www.prismaflex.com	Mississauga	ON	L4X3A3	905-279-9793	279-1330
Progressive Promotions Inc 145 Cedar Ln Web: progressivepromotions.com	Englewood	NJ	07631	201-945-0500	
Protection Services Inc 635 Lucknow Rd TF: 866-489-1234 ■ Web: www.protectionservices.com	Harrisburg	PA	17110	717-236-9307	236-1281
Quality Manufacturing Inc 969 Labore Industrial Ct TF: 800-243-5473 ■ Web: www.qualitymanufacturing.com	Saint Paul	MN	55110	651-483-5473	483-1101
Quiel Bros Sign Co 272 S 'I' St Web: www.quielsigns.com	San Bernardino	CA	92410	909-885-4476	888-2239
Recognition Specialties Inc 1710 Harbeck Rd Web: nicebadge.com	Grants Pass	OR	97527	541-476-3166	
SA-SO Co 525 N Great SW Pkwy Web: www.sa-so.com	Arlington	TX	76011	972-641-4911	660-3684
Safeway Sign Co 9875 Yucca Rd TF: 800-637-7233 ■ Web: www.safewaysign.com	Adelanto	CA	92301	760-246-7070	246-5512
Scioto Sign Company Inc 6047 US Rt 68 N TF: 800-572-4686 ■ Web: www.sciotosigns.com	Kenton	OH	43326	419-673-1261	675-3298
SFC Graphics 110 E Woodruff Ave TF: 800-537-1130 ■ Web: www.sfcgraphics.com	Toledo	OH	43604	419-255-1283	
Sign Builders Inc 4800 Jefferson Ave PO Box 28380 *Fax Area Code: 205 ■ TF: 800-222-7330 ■ Web: www.signbuilders.com	Birmingham	AL	35228	800-222-7330	923-2124*
Sign Designs Inc 204 Campus Way TF: 800-421-7446 ■ Web: www.signdesigns.com	Modesto	CA	95352	209-524-4484	521-0272
Sign Resource Inc 6135 District Blvd Web: www.signresource.net	Maywood	CA	90270	323-771-2098	
Sign-A-Rama 2121 Vista Pkwy TF All: 800-776-8105 ■ Web: www.signarama.com	West Palm Beach	FL	33411	561-640-5570	640-5580
Signs by Tomorrow USA Inc 8681 Robert Fulton Dr TF: 800-765-7446 ■ Web: www.signsbytomorrow.com	Columbia	MD	21046	410-312-3600	312-3520
Signs Now 5368 Dixie Hwy Ste 1 TF: 800-356-3373 ■ Web: www.signsnow.com	Waterford	MI	48329	248-596-8600	596-8601
Signtech Electrical Adv Inc 4444 Federal Blvd *Fax Area Code: 866 ■ TF: 877-885-1135 ■ Web: www.signtech.com	San Diego	CA	92102	619-527-6100	275-6115*
Signtex Imaging LP 1225 Alma St Ste C Web: www.signtex.com	Tomball	TX	77375	281-351-2776	
Signtronix 1445 W Sepulveda Blvd *Fax Area Code: 310 ■ *Fax: Sales ■ TF: 800-729-4853 ■ Web: www.signtronix.com	Torrance	CA	90501	800-729-4853	539-3554*
Spectrum Corp 10048 Easthaven Blvd TF: 800-392-5050 ■ Web: www.specorp.com	Houston	TX	77075	713-944-6200	944-1290
Spotlight Promotions Inc 2000 Van Ness Ave Ste 101 Web: www.spotlightsf.com	San Francisco	CA	94109	415-202-7100	
Stouse Inc 300 New Century Pkwy Web: www.stouse.com	New Century	KS	66031	913-764-5757	
STOUT 6425 W Florissant Ave Web: www.stoutsign.com	Saint Louis	MO	63136	314-385-4600	
Tool Sport & Sign Co 1060 S Lapeer Rd Web: toolsportandsign.com	Oxford	MI	48371	248-969-5850	
Tube Art Group (TAG) 11715 SE Fifth St TF: 800-562-2854 ■ Web: www.tubeart.com	Bellevue	WA	98005	206-223-1122	223-1123
Turnroth Sign Company Inc 1207 E Rock Falls Rd	Rock Falls	IL	61071	815-625-1155	625-1158
U s Nameplate Company Inc Hwy 30 W TF: 800-553-8871 ■ Web: www.usnameplate.com	Mount Vernon	IA	52314	319-895-8804	
Vomar Products Inc 7800 Deering Ave Web: www.vomarproducts.com	Canoga Park	CA	91304	818-610-5115	610-5123
Vomela Co, The 274 E Fillmore Ave TF: 800-645-1012 ■ Web: www.vomela.com	Saint Paul	MN	55107	651-228-2200	228-2295
Walter Haas & Sons Inc 123 W 23rd St TF: 800-552-3845 ■ Web: www.haasprint.com	Hialeah	FL	33010	305-883-2257	883-0598
Werner Tool & Mfg Co Inc 12301 E McNichols Rd Web: www.trivision.com	Detroit	MI	48205	313-526-6020	
White Way Sign 451 Kingston Ct Web: www.whiteway.com	Mount Prospect	IL	60056	847-391-0200	
World Wide Concessions Inc 1950 Old Cuthbert Rd Ste M TF: 888-377-7666 ■ Web: www.wwconcessions.com	Cherry Hill	NJ	08034	856-933-9900	
Worldwide Sign Systems 446 N Cecil St TF: 800-874-3334 ■ Web: www.wwsign.com	Bonduel	WI	54107	800-874-3334	
Young Electric Sign Co 2401 Foothill Dr TF: 866-779-8357 ■ Web: www.yesco.com	Salt Lake City	UT	84109	801-464-4600	483-0998
Zumar Industries Inc 9719 Santa Fe Springs Rd TF: 800-654-7446 ■ Web: www.zumar.com	Santa Fe Springs	CA	90670	562-941-4633	941-4643

702 SILVERWARE

See Also Cutlery p. 2177; Metal Stampings p. 2758

Company / Address	City	State	Zip	Phone	Fax
Empire Silver Company Inc 6520 New Utrecht Ave	Brooklyn	NY	11219	718-232-3389	232-0680
Great American Products Inc 1661 S Seguin Ave Web: www.gap1.com	New Braunfels	TX	78130	830-620-4400	620-8430
Metallics Inc W7274 County Hwy Z PO Box 99 Web: www.metallics.net	Onalaska	WI	54650	608-781-5200	781-2254
Old Newbury Crafters 36 Main St Ste 2 TF: 800-343-1388	Amesbury	MA	01913	800-343-1388	
Olde Country Reproductions Inc 722 W Market St TF Cust Svc: 800-358-3997 ■ Web: www.pewtarex.com	York	PA	17405	717-848-1859	845-7129
Pfaltzgraff Co PO Box 21769 *Fax: Cust Svc ■ TF: 800-999-2811 ■ Web: www.pfaltzgraff.com	York	PA	17402	800-999-2811	717-2481*
Salisbury Inc 29085 Airpark Dr TF: 855-255-5309 ■ Web: salisburyinc.net	Easton	MD	21601	410-770-4901	
Towle Silversmiths PO Box 21379 TF: 800-264-0758 ■ Web: www.lifetimesterling.com	York	PA	17402	800-264-0758	
Tropar Manufacturing Inc 5 Vreeland Rd Web: www.airflyte.com	Florham Park	NJ	07932	973-822-2400	
Utica Cutlery Co 820 Noyes St PO Box 10527 Web: www.uticacutlery.com	Utica	NY	13503	315-733-4663	733-6602
Woodbury Pewterers Inc 860 Main St S TF: 800-648-2014 ■ Web: www.woodburypewter.com	Woodbury	CT	06798	800-648-2014	

703 SIMULATION & TRAINING SYSTEMS

Company / Address	City	State	Zip	Phone	Fax
Bemco Inc 2255 Union Pl Web: www.bemcoinc.com	Simi Valley	CA	93065	805-583-4970	583-5033
CACI MTL Systems Inc 2685 Hibiscus Way Web: www.caci.com	Beavercreek	OH	45431	937-426-3111	
CAE Inc 8585 Cote de Liesse NYSE: CAE ■ TF: 866-999-6223 ■ Web: www.cae.com	Saint Laurent	QC	H4T1G6	514-341-6780	341-7699
Cubic Corp 9333 Balboa Ave PO Box 85587 NYSE: CUB ■ TF: 800-937-5449 ■ Web: www.cubic.com	San Diego	CA	92186	858-277-6780	505-1523
Cubic Defense Systems 9333 Balboa Ave TF: 800-937-5449 ■ Web: www.cubic.com	San Diego	CA	92123	858-277-6780	505-1524
Doron Precision Systems Inc 150 Corporate Dr PO Box 400 Web: www.doronprecision.com	Binghamton	NY	13904	607-772-1610	772-6760
DRS C3 Systems LLC 400 Professional Dr TF: 800-694-5005 ■ Web: www.drs.com	Gaithersburg	MD	20879	301-921-8100	921-8010
Energy Concepts Inc 404 Washington Blvd TF: 800-621-1247 ■ Web: www.eci-info.com	Mundelein	IL	60060	847-837-8191	
Environmental Tectonics Corp 125 James Way OTC: ETCC ■ Web: www.etcusa.com	SouthHampton	PA	18966	215-355-9100	357-4000
Evans & Sutherland Computer Corp 770 Komas Dr OTC: ESCC ■ TF Sales: 800-327-5707 ■ Web: www.es.com	Salt Lake City	UT	84108	801-588-1000	
Faac Inc 1229 Oak Valley Dr TF: 877-322-2387 ■ Web: www.faac.com	Ann Arbor	MI	48108	734-761-5836	761-5368
Frasca International Inc 906 E Airport Rd Web: www.frasca.com	Urbana	IL	61802	217-344-9200	344-9207
Malwin Electronics Corp 52 E 22nd St Web: www.malwin.com	Paterson	NJ	07514	973-881-1500	
Meggitt Training Systems Inc 296 Brogdon Rd TF: 800-813-9046 ■ Web: www.meggitttrainingsystems.com	Suwanee	GA	30024	678-288-1090	288-1515
Nida Corp 300 S John Rodes Blvd TF: 800-327-6432 ■ Web: www.nida.com	Melbourne	FL	32904	321-727-2265	727-2655
Ternion Corp 2223 Drake Ave Web: www.ternion.com	Huntsville	AL	35805	256-881-9933	881-9957

704 SMART CARDS

Company / Address	City	State	Zip	Phone	Fax
CardLogix 16 Hughes Ste 100 TF: 866-392-8326 ■ Web: www.cardlogix.com	Irvine	CA	92618	949-380-1312	380-1428
Clever Devices Ltd 300 Crossways Pk Dr TF: 800-872-6129 ■ Web: www.cleverdevices.com	Woodbury	NY	11797	516-433-6100	
Credit Card Systems Inc 180 Shepard Ave TF: 800-747-1269 ■ Web: www.ccsplastech.com	Wheeling	IL	60090	847-459-8320	
DataCard Corp 11111 Bren Rd W TF: 800-328-8623 ■ Web: www.datacard.com	Minnetonka	MN	55343	952-933-1223	933-7971
MDI Security Systems Inc 12500 Network Dr Ste 303 TF: 866-435-7634 ■ Web: www.mdisecure.com	San Antonio	TX	78249	210-477-5400	477-5401
Perfect Plastic Printing Corp 311 Kautz Rd Web: www.perfectplastic.com	Saint Charles	IL	60174	630-584-1600	584-0648
Smart Card Integrators Inc (SCI) 2424 N Ontario St Web: www.sci-s.com	Burbank	CA	91504	818-847-1022	847-1454

705 SNOWMOBILES

See Also Sporting Goods p. 3193

Name / Address	City	State	Zip	Phone	Fax
Arctic Cat Inc 601 Brooks Ave S *NASDAQ: ACAT* ■ *Web:* www.arcticcat.com	Thief River Falls	MN	56701	218-681-8558	
Polaris Industries Inc 2100 Hwy 55 *NYSE: PII* ■ *Web:* www.polaris.com	Medina	MN	55340	763-542-0500	542-0599
Yamaha Motor Corp USA 6555 Katella Ave *TF Cust Svc:* 800-656-7695 ■ *Web:* www.yamaha-motor.com	Cypress	CA	90630	800-656-7695	

SOFTWARE

See Computer Software p. 2026

706 SPAS - HEALTH & FITNESS

See Also Health & Fitness Centers p. 2456; Spas - Hotel & Resort p. 3187; Weight Loss Centers & Services p. 3311

Facilities listed here provide multi-day programs designed to increase health and well-being. Types of programs offered include (but are not limited to) relaxation, smoking cessation, weight loss, and physical fitness.

Name / Address	City	State	Zip	Phone	Fax
Amerispa 90 Rue de Stanstead St Ste 101 *TF:* 866-263-7477 ■ *Web:* www.amerispa.ca	Bromont	QC	J2L1K6	450-534-2717	
Balancing Pool 2350, 330 - 5th Ave SW *Web:* www.balancingpool.ca	Calgary	AB	T2P0L4	403-539-5350	
Birdwing Spa 21398 575th Ave *Web:* www.birdwingspa.com	Litchfield	MN	55355	320-693-6064	693-7026
Black Hills Health & Education Ctr PO Box 19 *TF Cust Svc:* 866-757-0160 ■ *Web:* bhhec.org	Hermosa	SD	57744	605-255-4101	255-4687
Body/Mind Restoration Retreats 56 Lieb Rd *Web:* www.bodymindretreats.com	Spencer	NY	14883	607-277-7779	
Bremerton Swimming Pool 50 Magnuson Way *Web:* www.ci.bremerton.wa.us	Bremerton	WA	98310	360-473-5376	
Briar Ridge Country Club Inc 123 Country Club Dr *Web:* www.briarridgecc.com	Schererville	IN	46375	219-322-1605	
Cal-a-Vie Spa 29402 Spa Havens Way *TF:* 866-772-4283 ■ *Web:* www.cal-a-vie.com	Vista	CA	92084	760-945-2055	630-0074
Calistoga Spa Hot Springs 1006 Washington St *TF:* 866-822-5772 ■ *Web:* www.calistogaspa.com	Calistoga	CA	94515	707-942-6269	942-4214
City of Fairhope: Adult & Tourist Recreation Center 352 Morphy Ave *Web:* www.cofairhope.com	Fairhope	AL	36532	251-928-7081	
City of Wetaskiwin Recreation 4705-50 Ave *Web:* www.wetaskiwin.ca	Wetaskiwin	AB	T9A2E9	780-361-4444	
Clark Oil Company Inc 720 Station St *Web:* www.clark-oil.com	Waynesboro	MS	39367	601-735-4847	
Classic Golf Management Inc 103 Weatherstone Dr Ste 710 *Web:* www.cgmgolf.com	Woodstock	GA	30188	770-928-1600	
Cooper Wellness Program 12230 Preston Rd *TF:* 800-444-5192 ■ *Web:* cooperaerobics.com	Dallas	TX	75230	972-386-4777	
Core Fitness LLC 8000 NE Pkwy Dr Ste 220 *Web:* stairmaster.com	Vancouver	WA	98662	360-326-4090	
Coyotes Ice LLC 9375 E Bell Rd *Web:* www.coyotesice.com	Scottsdale	AZ	85260	480-585-6354	
Deerfield Spa 650 Resica Falls Rd *TF:* 800-852-4494 ■ *Web:* www.deerfieldspa.com	East Stroudsburg	PA	18302	570-223-0160	
Downtown Swimming Pool 324 Gold St *Web:* www.downtowngrand.com	Kingman	AZ	86401	928-753-8155	
Dr Wilkinson's Hot Springs Resort 1507 Lincoln Ave *Web:* www.drwilkinson.com	Calistoga	CA	94515	707-942-4102	942-4412
Duke Diet & Fitness Ctr (DFC) 501 Douglas St *TF:* 800-235-3853 ■ *Web:* dukemedicine.org/treatments/treatments/weight-loss-and-wellness	Durham	NC	27705	800-235-3853	
Golden Door 777 Deer Springs Rd *TF:* 866-420-6414 ■ *Web:* www.goldendoor.com	San Marcos	CA	92069	760-744-5777	471-2393
Grand Wailea Resort & Spa 3850 Wailea Alanui Dr *TF:* 800-888-6100 ■ *Web:* www.grandwailea.com	Wailea	HI	96753	808-875-1234	879-4077
Green Mountain at Fox Run 262 Fox Ln PO Box 358 *TF:* 800-448-8106 ■ *Web:* www.fitwoman.com	Ludlow	VT	05149	802-228-8885	228-8887
Green Valley Spa & Resort 1871 W Canyon View Dr *TF:* 800-237-1068 ■ *Web:* www.greenvalleyspa.com	Saint George	UT	84770	800-237-1068	
Hamilton Bulldogs Hockey Club 101 York Blvd *Web:* www.hamiltonbulldogs.com/	Hamilton	ON	L8R3L4	905-529-8500	
Heartland Spa 1237 E 1600 N Rd *TF:* 800-545-4853 ■ *Web:* www.heartlandspa.com	Gilman	IL	60938	800-545-4853	
Hills Health Ranch 4871 Caribou Hwy 97 PO Box 26	108 Mile Ranch	BC	V0K2Z0	250-791-5225	
Hilton Head Health Institute 14 Valencia Rd *TF:* 800-292-2440 ■ *Web:* www.hhhealth.com	Hilton Head Island	SC	29928	843-785-3919	
Himalayan Institute Ctr for Health & Healing 952 Bethany Tpke *Web:* www.himalayaninstitute.org	Honesdale	PA	18431	570-253-5551	
Hippocrates Health Institute Life-Change Ctr 1443 Palmdale Ct *TF:* 800-842-2125 ■ *Web:* www.hippocratesinst.org	West Palm Beach	FL	33411	561-471-8876	471-9464
Kohala Spa 69-425 Waikoloa Beach Dr *Web:* www.kohalaspa.com	Waikoloa	HI	96738	808-886-2828	886-2953
Kripalu Ctr for Yoga & Health 57 Interlaken Rd *TF:* 800-741-7353 ■ *Web:* www.kripalu.org	Stockbridge	MA	01262	413-448-3400	448-3384
Landings Yacht Golf and Tennis Club Inc, The 4420 Flagship Dr *Web:* www.landingsygtc.com	Fort Myers	FL	33919	239-482-3211	
Lodge & Spa at Cordillera 2205 Cordillera Way *TF:* 800-877-3529 ■ *Web:* www.cordilleralodge.com	Edwards	CO	81632	970-926-2200	926-2486
Miraval AZ Resort & Spa 5000 E Via Estancia Miraval **Fax Area Code:* 520 ■ *TF:* 800-232-3969 ■ *Web:* www.miravalresorts.com	Tucson	AZ	85739	800-232-3969	825-5163*
Nautilus Plus Inc 3550, 1Šre Rue *Web:* www.nautilusplus.com	St-hubert	QC	J3Y8Y5	514-666-5814	
Northern Pines on Crescent Lake Bed & Breakfast Plus 31 Big Pine Rd *Web:* people.maine.com	Raymond	ME	04071	207-655-7624	
Oaks at Ojai 122 E Ojai Ave *TF:* 800-753-6257 ■ *Web:* www.oaksspa.com	Ojai	CA	93023	805-646-5573	
Ocean Waters Spa 600 N Atlantic Ave *TF:* 844-284-2685 ■ *Web:* plazaresortandspa.com	Daytona Beach	FL	32118	386-267-1660	
Ojo Caliente Mineral Springs Resort 50 Los Banos Dr PO Box 68 *TF:* 800-222-9162 ■ *Web:* www.ojospa.com	Ojo Caliente	NM	87549	505-583-2233	583-2045
One on One Athc Clb - Brarwood 2875 Boardwalk St *Web:* 1on1club.com	Ann Arbor	MI	48104	734-761-4440	
Optimum Health Institute 6970 Central Ave *TF:* 800-993-4325 ■ *Web:* www.optimumhealth.org	Lemon Grove	CA	91945	619-464-3346	
Oregon Recreation Dept 5330 Seaman Rd *Web:* state.or.us	Oregon	OH	43616	419-698-7146	
Owen Sound Minor Hockey Group P.O. Box 13 *Web:* owensoundminorhockey.com	Owen Sound	ON	N4K5P1	519-372-2717	
Preventure Inc 2006 Nooseneck Hill Rd *Web:* www.preventure.com	Coventry	RI	02816	401-385-9312	
Pritikin Longevity Ctr & Spa 8755 NW 36th St **Fax:* Resv ■ *TF:* 800-327-4914 ■ *Web:* www.pritikin.com	Doral	FL	33178	305-935-7131	935-7371*
Raj, The 1734 Jasmine Ave *TF:* 800-248-9050 ■ *Web:* www.theraj.com	Fairfield	IA	52556	641-472-9580	472-2496
Sagestone Spa & Salon *Red Mountain Resort* 1275 East Red Mtn Cir *TF:* 877-246-4453 ■ *Web:* www.redmountainresort.com	Ivins	UT	84738	435-673-4905	
Spa at Coeur d'Alene 115 S Second St *TF:* 800-684-0514 ■ *Web:* cdaresort.com/discover/spa	Coeur d'Alene	ID	83814	208-765-4000	
Spa at Peninsula Beverly Hills 9882 S Santa Monica Blvd *TF:* 800-462-7899 ■ *Web:* www.peninsula.com/beverly_hills/en	Beverly Hills	CA	90212	310-551-2888	788-2319
Spa at The Setai 2001 Collins Ave **Fax Area Code:* 305 ■ *TF:* 888-625-7500 ■ *Web:* www.thesetaihotel.com	Miami Beach	FL	33139	888-625-7500	520-6600*
Spa Radiance 3011 Fillmore St *Web:* www.sparadiance.com	San Francisco	CA	94123	415-346-6281	
Structure House 3017 Pickett Rd *TF:* 800-553-0052 ■ *Web:* www.structurehouse.com/?nocookies=true	Durham	NC	27705	919-493-4205	490-0191
Tennessee Fitness Spa 299 Natural Bridge Pk Rd *TF:* 800-235-8365 ■ *Web:* www.tennesseefitnessspa.com	Waynesboro	TN	38485	931-722-5589	722-9113
Tracie Martyn Salon 59 Fifth Ave Ste 1 *TF:* 866-862-7896 ■ *Web:* www.traciemartyn.com	New York	NY	10003	212-206-9333	206-8399
Two Bunch Palms Resort & Spa 67425 Two Bunch Palms Trl *TF:* 800-472-4334 ■ *Web:* www.twobunchpalms.com	Desert Hot Springs	CA	92240	760-329-8791	329-1874
Uchee Pines Lifestyle Ctr 30 Uchee Pines Rd PO Box 75 *TF:* 877-824-3374 ■ *Web:* ucheepines.org	Seale	AL	36875	334-855-4764	855-9014
Vail Cascade Resort & Spa 1300 Westhaven Dr *TF:* 800-420-2424 ■ *Web:* www.vailcascade.com	Vail	CO	81657	970-476-7111	479-7020
Vail Racquet Club Inc 4695 Racquet Club Dr *Web:* vailracquetclub.com	Vail	CO	81657	970-476-4840	
Wiesbaden Hot Springs 625 5th St PO Box 349 *Web:* www.wiesbadenhotsprings.com	Ouray	CO	81427	970-325-4347	325-4358

707 SPAS - HOTEL & RESORT

See Also Spas - Health & Fitness p. 3187

Name / Address	City	State	Zip	Phone	Fax
100 Fountain Spa at the Pillar & Post Inn 48 John St PO Box 48 *TF:* 888-669-5566 ■ *Web:* www.vintage-hotels.com	Niagara-on-the-Lake	ON	L0S1J0	905-468-2123	468-3551
74 State LLC 74 State St *Web:* www.74state.com	Albany	NY	12207	518-434-7410	
Abbey Resort & Fontana Spa 269 Fontana Blvd *TF:* 800-709-1323 ■ *Web:* www.theabbeyresort.com	Fontana	WI	53125	262-275-9000	
Abhasa Waikiki Spa at the Royal Hawaiian Hotel 2259 Kalakaua Ave *Web:* www.abhasa.com	Honolulu	HI	96815	808-922-8200	
Accent Inns Ltd 3233 Maple St *Web:* www.accentinns.com	Victoria	BC	V8X4Y9	250-475-7500	
AdVantis Hospitality Alliance LLC 615 N Highland Ste 2A *TF:* 866-218-4782 ■ *Web:* www.vistarez.com	Murfreesboro	TN	37130	615-904-6133	
Alamo City Riverwalk Plaza Hotel 100 Villita St *Web:* www.riverwalkplaza.com	San Antonio	TX	78205	210-225-1234	
Aliante Gaming LLC 7300 Aliante Pkwy *Web:* www.aliantegaming.com	North Las Vegas	NV	89084	702-692-7777	
Allegria Spa at the Park Hyatt Beaver Creek 100 E Thomas Pl *Web:* www.allegriaspa.com	Avon	CO	81620	970-748-7500	748-7501
Aloft Broomfield Denver 8300 Arista Pl *TF:* 866-716-8143 ■ *Web:* www.aloftbroomfielddenver.com	Broomfield	CO	80021	303-635-2000	

Phone | Fax

Aloft Chicago O'hare 9700 Balmoral Ave ... Rosemont IL 60018 847-671-4444
TF: 866-716-8143 ■ *Web:* www.aloftchicagoohare.com

Alpine Lodge 434 Indian Creek Cir ... Branson MO 65616 417-338-2514
TF: 888-563-4388 ■ *Web:* www.alpinelodgeresort.com

AM Resorts LLC 7 Campus Blvd ... Newtown Square PA 19073 610-359-6500
Web: www.amresorts.com

Amadeus Spa at the Marriott Napa Valley
3425 Solano Ave ... Napa CA 94558 707-254-3330
Web: marriott.com/hotels/travel/sfonp-napa-valley-marriott-hotel-and-spa

Amoray Dive Resort Inc 104250 Overseas Hwy ... Key Largo FL 33037 305-451-3595
TF: 800-426-6729 ■ *Web:* www.amoray.com

Anara Spa at the Hyatt Regency Kauai
1571 Poipu Rd ... Koloa HI 96756 808-742-1234
Web: www.anaraspa.com

Ancient Cedars Spa at the Wickaninnish Inn
500 Osprey Ln PO Box 250 ... Tofino BC V0R2Z0 250-725-3113 725-3110
TF: 800-333-4604 ■ *Web:* www.wickinn.com

Andre Balazs Properties 23 E Fourth St Fl 5 ... New York NY 10002 212-226-5656
Web: www.andrebalazsproperties.com

Antoine du Chez 2700 E Second Ave ... Denver CO 80206 303-320-6012 996-1061
Web: www.antoineduchez.com

Aquae Sulis Spa at the JW Marriott Resort Las Vegas
221 N Rampart Blvd ... Las Vegas NV 89144 702-869-7807
TF: 877-869-8777 ■ *Web:* www.marriott.com

Aquaterra Spa at the Surf & Sand Resort
1555 S Coast Hwy ... Laguna Beach CA 92651 949-376-2772
TF: 877-741-5908 ■ *Web:* www.surfandsandresort.com

Aria Spa & Club at the Vail Cascade Resort
1300 Westhaven Dr ... Vail CO 81657 970-479-5942 476-7405
TF: 888-824-5772 ■ *Web:* vailcascade.com/colorado-mountain-spa.php

Arizona Biltmore Resort & Spa
2400 E Missouri ... Phoenix AZ 85016 602-955-6600 381-7600
TF: 800-950-0086 ■ *Web:* www.arizonabiltmore.com

Arlington Residence Court Hotel
1200 N Courthouse Rd ... Arlington VA 22201 703-524-4000
Web: www.arlingtoncourthotel.com

Au Naturel Wellness & Medical Spa at the Brookstreet Hotel
525 Legget Dr ... Ottawa ON K2K2W2 613-271-1800
TF: 888-826-2220 ■ *Web:* www.brookstreethotel.com

Auberge De La Fontaine b & b Inn
1301 Rue Rachel E ... Montreal QC H2J2K1 514-597-0166
TF: 800-597-0597 ■ *Web:* www.aubergedelafontaine.com

Baccarat New York LLC 20 W 53rd St ... New York NY 10019 212-790-8800
TF: 866-957-5139 ■ *Web:* www.baccarathotels.com

Bartell Hotels 4875 N Harbor Dr ... San Diego CA 92106 619-224-1556
Web: www.bartellhotels.com

Bathhouse at Calistoga Ranch 580 Lommel Rd ... Calistoga CA 94515 707-254-2820 254-2825
Web: calistogaranch.aubergeresorts.com

Battery Wharf Hotel & Spa, The
3 Battery Wharf ... Boston MA 02109 617-994-9000
TF: 877-794-6218 ■ *Web:* www.batterywharfhotelboston.com

Beekman Arms-delamater Inn Inc
6387 Mill St ... Rhinebeck NY 12572 845-876-7077
Web: www.beekmandelamaterinn.com

Belamar Hotel, The
3501 Sepulveda Blvd ... Manhattan Beach CA 90266 310-750-0300
Web: www.thebelamar.com

Best Western Tuscan Inn 425 N Point St ... San Francisco CA 94133 415-561-1100
TF: 800-648-4626 ■ *Web:* www.tuscanhotel.com

Bittersweet Ski Resort Snowline 600 River Rd ... Otsego MI 49078 269-694-2032
Web: www.skibittersweet.com

Blue Haven Resort 1851 Lk Shore Dr ... Branson MO 65616 417-334-3917
Web: www.branson.com

Bluestar Resort & Golf LLC
8800 N Gainey Ctr Dr Ste 350 ... Scottsdale AZ 85258 480-348-6519
Web: www.bluestargolf.com

Boutique Spa at the Ritz-Carlton Georgetown
3100 S St NW ... Washington DC 20007 202-912-4175
TF: 800-241-3333 ■ *Web:* www.ritzcarlton.com

Boxer Hotel, The 107 Merrimac St ... Boston MA 02114 617-624-0202
Web: www.theboxerboston.com

Brampton (City of) 2 Wellington St W ... Brampton ON L6Y4R2 905-874-2600
Web: www.brampton.ca

Canyon Ranch SpaClub at the Venetian
3355 Las Vegas Blvd S Ste 1159 ... Las Vegas NV 89109 702-414-3606 414-3801
TF: 877-220-2688 ■ *Web:* www.canyonranchdestinations.com

Cape Codder Resort & Spa
1225 Iyanough Rd Rt 132 Bearse's Way ... Hyannis MA 02601 508-771-3000
TF: 888-297-2200 ■ *Web:* www.capecodderresort.com

Capella Hotels & Resorts
3384 Peachtree Rd Ste 375 ... Atlanta GA 30326 404-649-7030
Web: www.capellahotels.com

Carefree Resort & Conference Ctr
37220 Mule Train Rd ... Carefree AZ 85377 888-692-4343
TF: 888-692-4343 ■ *Web:* www.carefree-resort.com

Carneros Inn, The 4048 Sonoma Hwy ... Napa CA 94559 707-299-4900 299-4950
TF: 888-400-9000 ■ *Web:* www.thecarnerosinn.com

Casa Marina Hotel & Restaurant
691 First St N ... Jacksonville Beach FL 32250 904-270-0025
Web: www.casamarinahotel.com

Centre for Well-Being at the Phoenician
6000 E Camelback Rd ... Scottsdale AZ 85251 800-843-2392
TF: 800-843-2392 ■ *Web:* www.thephoenician.com

Century City Fitness Club & Spa
10220 Constellation Blvd ... Century City CA 90067 310-286-2900
Web: www.equinox.com

CEPA Le Baluchon Inc
3550 chemin des Trembles ... Saint-Paulin QC J0K3G0 819-268-2555
TF: 800-789-5968 ■ *Web:* www.baluchon.com

Chateau Resort & Conference Center, The
300 Camelback Rd ... Tannersville PA 18372 570-629-5900
TF: 800-245-5900 ■ *Web:* chateauresort.com

Chateau Rouge 1505 S Broadway Ave ... Red Lodge MT 59068 406-446-1601
TF: 800-926-1601 ■ *Web:* www.chateaurouge.com

Cheeca Lodge & Spa
81801 Overseas Hwy Mile Marker 82 ... Islamorada FL 33036 305-664-4651
TF: 800-327-2888 ■ *Web:* www.cheeca.com

Cliff Spa at Snowbird Hwy 210 PO Box 929000 ... Snowbird UT 84092 801-933-2225
TF: 800-453-3000 ■ *Web:* www.snowbird.com

Columbia Room Inc 1108 E Marina Way ... Hood River OR 97031 541-386-2200
TF: 800-828-7873 ■ *Web:* www.hoodriverinn.com

Condado Vanderbilt Hotel Towers
1055 Ashford Ave ... San Juan PR 00907 787-721-5500
Web: www.condadovanderbilt.com

Coral Kay Resort 2300 Caravelle Cir ... Kissimmee FL 34746 407-787-0718
TF: 866-357-3682 ■ *Web:* www.staycoralcay.com

Cranwell Resort Spa & Golf Club 55 Lee Rd ... Lenox MA 01240 413-637-1364 637-4364
TF: 800-272-6935 ■ *Web:* www.cranwell.com

Crowne plaza Hotels & Resorts
2270 Hotel Cir N ... San Diego CA 92108 619-297-1101
Web: www.ihg.com

Cupertino Inn 10889 N De Anza Blvd ... Cupertino CA 95014 408-996-7700
Web: m.cupertinoinn.com

Deer Lodge Hotels Ltd 106 Circle Dr ... Saskatoon SK S7L4L6 306-242-8881
TF: 800-578-7878 ■ *Web:* www.travelodge.ca

Delta Montreal Hotel
475 President Kennedy Ave ... Montreal QC H3A1J7 514-286-1986

Disney's Grand Floridian Spa
4401 Floridian Wy ... Lake Buena Vista FL 32830 407-824-2332 824-3186*
**Fax:* Cust Svc ■ *TF:* 800-169-0730 ■ *Web:* disneyworld.disney.go.com

Dmi 235 W Jefferson Ave ... Naperville IL 60540 630-428-1000
Web: www.dmihotels.com

Econo Lodge 2934 Polynesian Isle Blvd ... Kissimmee FL 34746 407-787-4100
Web: www.choicehotels.com/econo-lodge

Edward Thomas Companies, The
9950 Santa Monica Blvd ... Beverly Hills CA 90212 310-859-9366
Web: www.edwardthomasco.com

El Caribe Resort 2125 S Atlantic Ave ... Daytona Beach FL 32118 386-252-1558
TF: 800-445-9889 ■ *Web:* elcaribe.com

Elite Island Resorts Inc
1065 SW 30th Ave ... Deerfield Beach FL 33442 954-481-8787
Web: www.eliteislandresorts.com

Elizabeth Arden Red Door Spa at Mystic Marriott Hotel & Spa
625 N Rd ... Groton CT 06340 860-446-2500 446-2696
TF: 866-449-7390 ■ *Web:* www.marriott.com

Elizabeth Arden Red Door Spa at the Seaview Marriott Resort & Spa
400 E Fairway Ln ... Galloway NJ 08205 609-404-4100
Web: www.reddoorspas.com

Embassy San Diego - Downtown #66378
601 Pacific Hwy ... San Diego CA 92101 619-233-9922
Web: embassysuites3.hilton.com/en/hotels/california/embassy-suites-by-hilton-san-diego-bay-downtown-sandnes/index.html

Embassy Suites Tysons Corner Hotel
8517 Leesburg Pk ... Vienna VA 22182 703-883-0707
Web: embassysuites3.hilton.com/en/index.html

Emerson Resort & Spa 5340 Rt 28 ... Mount Tremper NY 12457 845-688-2828
TF: 877-688-2828 ■ *Web:* www.emersonresort.com

EZ8 Motels Inc 2484 Hotel Cir Pl ... San Diego CA 92108 619-291-4824
TF: 855-413-1222 ■ *Web:* www.ez8motels.com

Felicita Resort 2201 Fishing Creek Vly Rd ... Harrisburg PA 17112 717-599-5301
Web: www.felicitaresort.com

Festival Inn, The 1144 Ontario St ... Stratford ON N5A6Z3 519-273-1150
TF: 800-463-3581 ■ *Web:* www.festivalinnstratford.com

Ford Hotel Supply Company Inc
2204 N Broadway ... Saint Louis MO 63102 314-231-8400
TF: 800-472-3673 ■ *Web:* www.fordstl.com

Four Seasons Spa at the Four Seasons Hotel Las Vegas
3960 Las Vegas Blvd S ... Las Vegas NV 89119 702-632-5302
TF: 800-332-3442 ■ *Web:* www.fourseasons.com/lasvegas

Four Seasons Spa at the Four Seasons Hotel Los Angeles at Beverly Hills
300 S Doheny Dr ... Los Angeles CA 90048 310-786-2229
TF: 800-819-5053 ■ *Web:* www.fourseasons.com/losangeles

Four Seasons Spa at the Four Seasons Resort Jackson Hole
7680 Granite Loop Rd PO Box 544 ... Teton Village WY 83025 307-732-5120
TF: 800-819-5053 ■ *Web:* www.fourseasons.com/jacksonhole

Four Seasons Spa at the Four Seasons Resort Maui
3900 Wailea Alanui Dr ... Wailea HI 96753 808-874-2925
TF: 800-334-6284 ■ *Web:* www.fourseasons.com/maui

Four Seasons Spa at the Four Seasons Resort Santa Barbara
1260 Ch Dr ... Santa Barbara CA 93108 805-565-8250
TF General: 800-819-5053 ■ *Web:* www.fourseasons.com/santabarbara

Fox Harb'r Resort & Spa 1337 Fox Harbour Rd ... Wallace NS B0K1Y0 902-257-1801 257-1852
TF: 866-257-1801 ■ *Web:* www.foxharbr.com

Galvestonian Condominium Association
1401 E Beach Dr ... Galveston TX 77550 409-765-6161
TF: 888-526-6161 ■ *Web:* www.galvestonian.com

Garden Spa at MacArthur Place
29 E MacArthur St ... Sonoma CA 95476 707-933-3193 933-9833
TF: 800-722-1866 ■ *Web:* www.macarthurplace.com

Gaylord Texan Resort & Convention Center
1501 Gaylord Trl ... Grapevine TX 76051 817-778-2000
Web: www.marriott.com/hotels/travel/dalgt-gaylord-texan-resort-and-convention-center

General Hotels Corp
2501 S High School Rd ... Indianapolis IN 46241 317-243-1000
Web: genhotels.com

Glacial Waters Spa at Grand View Lodge
23521 Nokomis Ave ... Nisswa MN 56468 218-963-2234
TF: 866-801-2951 ■ *Web:* www.grandviewlodge.com

Global Sports Consultants LLC
196 Route 202 N ... Far Hills NJ 07931 908-766-1001
Web: www.jetsetsports.com

Gold Key Resorts Phr Career Center
313 Laskin Rd Ste 103 ... Virginia Beach VA 23451 757-213-4344
Web: goldkeyphr.com

				Phone	Fax
Grand Hotel & Conference Center Peoria 4400 N Brandywine Dr *Web:* travelodgepeoria.com	Peoria	IL	61614	309-686-8000	
Grand Hotel Marriott Resort Golf Club & Spa 1 Grand Blvd PO Box 639 *TF:* 800-544-9933 ■ *Web:* www.marriott.com	Point Clear	AL	36564	251-928-9201	928-1149
Grand Lodge of The Order of The Sons of Hermann in the State of Texas 515 S Saint Marys St *Web:* www.texashermannsons.org	San Antonio	TX	78205	210-892-0254	
Greek Peak Ski Resort 2000 State Rt 392 *Web:* greekpeakmtnresort.com	Cortland	NY	13045	607-835-6111	
Green Valley Ranch Resort Casino & Spa 2300 Paseo Verde Pkwy *TF Resv:* 866-782-9487 ■ *Web:* greenvalleyranch.sclv.com	Henderson	NV	89052	702-617-7777	
Greenbrier, The 300 W Main St *TF:* 800-453-4858 ■ *Web:* www.greenbrier.com	White Sulphur Springs	WV	24986	304-536-1110	536-7854
Groupe Germain Inc 1200 des-Soeurs-du-Bon-Pasteur Ste 500 *Web:* www.groupegermain.com	Quebec	QC	G1S0B1	418-687-1123	
Groupe Riotel Hospitality Inc 250 Ave du Phare Est *TF:* 877-566-2651 ■ *Web:* www.riotel.com	Matane	QC	G4W3N4	418-566-2651	
Grouse Mountain Resorts Ltd 6400 Nancy Greene Way *Web:* www.grousemountain.com	North Vancouver	BC	V7R4K9	604-984-0661	
Grove Park Inn Resort & Spa 290 Macon Ave *TF:* 800-438-5800 ■ *Web:* www.omnihotels.com/hotels/asheville-grove-park	Asheville	NC	28804	828-252-2711	253-7053
Guildford Ventures Ltd 15269 104th Ave *Web:* www.sheratonguildford.com	Surrey	BC	V3R1N5	604-582-9288	
Hard Rock Hotel Palm Springs 150 S Indian Canyon Dr *Web:* www.hrhpalmsprings.com	Palm Springs	CA	92262	760-325-9676	
Hibiscus Spa at the Myrtle Beach Marriott Resort at Grande Dunes 8400 Costa Verde Dr *Web:* www.csspagroup.com	Myrtle Beach	SC	29572	843-692-3730	
Hilton Akron Fairlawn 3180 W Market St *Web:* www.akronhilton.com	Fairlawn	OH	44333	330-867-5024	
Hilton Mystic Hotel 20 Coogan Blvd *Web:* www.hiltonmystic.com	Mystic	CT	06355	860-572-0731	
Hilton Pasadena Hotel 168 S Los Robles Ave *Web:* www.daytonahilton.com	Pasadena	CA	91101	626-577-1000	
Hilton Short Hills 41 JFK Pkwy *TF:* 800-445-8667 ■ *Web:* www3.hilton.com/en/hotels/new-jersey/hilton-short-hills-ewrshhh/index.html	Short Hills	NJ	07078	973-379-0100	379-6870
Hilton Suites Toronto/Markham Conference Centre & Spa 8500 Warden Ave *TF:* 800-445-8667 ■ *Web:* www3.hilton.com	Markham	ON	L6G1A5	905-470-8500	477-8611
Hilton Tampa Airport Westshore, The 2225 N Lois Ave *Web:* www3.hilton.com	Tampa	FL	33607	813-877-6688	
Holly Shores Best Holiday 491 Route 9 *TF:* 877-494-6559 ■ *Web:* www.hollyshores.com	Cape May	NJ	08204	609-886-1234	
Home2 Suites by Hilton 4035 Sycamore Dairy Rd *Web:* home2suites3.hilton.com/en/index.html	Fayetteville	NC	28303	910-223-1170	
Homestead Resort 700 N Homestead Dr *TF:* 888-327-7220 ■ *Web:* www.homesteadresort.com	Midway	UT	84049	888-327-7220	
Horizon Hotels Ltd 99 Corvett Way Ste 302 *Web:* www.horizonhotels.com	Eatontown	NJ	07724	732-935-9553	
Hotel 373 Fifth Avenue 373 Fifth Ave *Web:* www.373uhotels.com	New York	NY	10016	212-213-3388	
Hotel Elegante Event & Conference Center 2886 South Cir Dr *Web:* www.hotelelegante.com	Colorado Springs	CO	80906	719-576-5900	
Hotel Mortagne 1228 Rue Nobel *TF:* 877-655-9966 ■ *Web:* www.hotelmortagne.com	Boucherville	QC	J4B5H1	450-655-9966	
Hotel Nelligan 106 Rue Saint-paul Ouest *Web:* hotelnelligan.com	Montreal	QC	H2Y1Z3	514-788-2040	
Hotel Sorella 800 sorella ct *Web:* www.hotelsorella-citycentre.com	Houston	TX	77024	713-973-1600	
Hotel Valencia Riverwalk 150 E Houston St *TF:* 855-596-3387 ■ *Web:* www.hotelvalencia-riverwalk.com	San Antonio	TX	78205	210-227-9700	
Hotels at Home Inc 208 Passaic Ave *Web:* www.hotelsathome.com	Fairfield	NJ	07004	973-882-8437	
Hualalai Resort Corp At Historic Ka'upulehu Post Office Box 1119 *Web:* www.hualalairesort.com	Kailua-kona	HI	96745	808-325-8455	
Hualalai Sports Club & Spa at the Four Seasons Resort Hualalai 100 Kaupulehu Dr *Web:* www.fourseasons.com/hualalai	Kaupulehu-Kona	HI	96740	808-325-8440	
Hutton Hotel, The 1808 W End Ave *Web:* www.huttonhotel.com	Nashville	TN	37203	615-340-9333	
Hyatt Boston Harbor 101 Harborside Dr *Web:* bostonharbor.regency.hyatt.com/en/hotel/home.html	Boston	MA	02128	617-568-1234	
Hyatt Deerfield 1750 Lk Cook Rd *Web:* deerfield.regency.hyatt.com/en/hotel/home.html?icamp=hyattdeerfieldredirect	Deerfield	IL	60015	847-945-3400	
Hyatt Regency Scottsdale Resort at Gainey Ranch 7500 E Doubletree Ranch Rd *TF:* 800-233-1234 ■ *Web:* scottsdale.regency.hyatt.com/en/hotel/home.html	Scottsdale	AZ	85258	480-483-5558	483-5544
Hyatt Rosemont 6350 N River Rd *Web:* rosemont.hyatt.com	Rosemont	IL	60018	847-518-1234	
Il Fornello Management Ltd 112 Isabella St *Web:* www.ilfornello.com	Toronto	ON	M4Y1P1	416-920-9410	
Imc Resort Services LLC 2 Corpus Christie Pl Ste C104 *Web:* www.imcresortservices.com	Hilton Head Island	SC	29928	843-785-4775	
Indian Springs Resort & Spa 1712 Lincoln Ave *TF:* 800-877-3623 ■ *Web:* www.indianspringscalistoga.com	Calistoga	CA	94515	707-942-4913	942-4919

				Phone	Fax
Jefferson Hotel Washington Dc, The 1200 16th St Nw *TF:* 877-313-9749 ■ *Web:* www.jeffersondc.com	Washington	DC	20036	202-448-2300	
Jiminy Peak Mountain Resort LLC 37 Corey Rd *Web:* www.jiminypeak.com	Hancock	MA	01237	413-738-5500	
Jurlique Spa 4925 N Scottsdale Rd *TF:* 800-528-7867 ■ *Web:* www.fireskyresort.com	Scottsdale	AZ	85251	480-424-6072	
JW Starr Pass Resort & Spa 3800 W Starr Pass Blvd **Fax Area Code:* 817 ■ *TF:* 800-845-5279 ■ *Web:* www.marriott.com	Tucson	AZ	85745	520-792-3500	778-2049*
Kea Lani Spa at the Fairmont Kea Lani Maui 4100 Wailea Alanui Dr *TF:* 800-659-4100 ■ *Web:* www.fairmont.com	Maui	HI	96753	808-875-2229	875-1200
Kelco Management & Development Inc 1020 Oriental Gardens Rd *Web:* www.kelcohotels.com	Jacksonville	FL	32207	904-858-9919	
Kohler Waters Spa 444 Highlands Dr *TF:* 866-928-3777 ■ *Web:* www.americanclubresort.com	Kohler	WI	53044	920-457-7777	
L.A. Hotel Downtown, The 333 S Figueroa St *Web:* www.thelahotel.com	Los Angeles	CA	90071	213-617-1133	
Labovitz Enterprises 227 W First St 880 Missabe Bldg Ste 950 *Web:* www.labovitzenterprises.com	Duluth	MN	55802	218-727-7765	
Lafayette Park Hotel 3287 Mt Diablo Blvd *TF:* 855-382-8632 ■ *Web:* www.lafayetteparkhotel.com	Lafayette	CA	94549	925-283-3700	284-1621
Lake Austin Spa Resort 1705 S Quinlan Pk Rd *TF:* 800-847-5637 ■ *Web:* www.lakeaustin.com	Austin	TX	78732	512-372-7380	266-1572
Lake Natoma Ltd 702 Gold Lk Dr *Web:* www.lakenatomainn.com	Folsom	CA	95630	916-932-2769	
Larry Blumberg & Associates Inc 2733 Ross Clark Cir *Web:* lbaproperties.com	Dothan	AL	36301	334-793-6855	
Lexington New York City, The 511 Lexington Ave 48th St *Web:* www.lexingtonhotelnyc.com	New York	NY	10017	212-755-4400	
Lido Beach Resort 700 Ben Franklin Dr *Web:* www.lidobeachresort.com	Sarasota	FL	34236	941-388-2161	
Living Spa at El Monte Sagrado 317 Kit Carson Rd *TF:* 855-846-8267 ■ *Web:* www.elmontesagrado.com	Taos	NM	87571	575-758-3502	737-2985
Lodgco Management LLC 5225 E Pickard Rd *Web:* lodgco.net	Mount Pleasant	MI	48858	989-773-2400	
Lodging Dynamics Hospitality Group LLC 5314 North River Run Dr Ste 310 *Web:* www.lodgingdynamics.com	Provo	UT	84604	801-919-3440	
Los Willows Inn & Spa 530 Stewart Canyon Rd *Web:* www.loswillows.com	Fallbrook	CA	92028	760-731-9400	
Luxe City Center Hotel 1020 S Figueroa St *Web:* www.luxecitycenter.com	Los Angeles	CA	90015	213-748-1291	
Magnuson Hotels PO Box 1434 *Web:* www.magnusonhotels.com	Spokane	WA	99210	509-747-8713	
Manga Hotels Inc 3279 Caroga Dr *Web:* www.mangahotels.com	Mississauga	ON	L4V1A3	905-672-4821	
Marcus Whitman Hotel & Conference Center LLC 6 W Rose St *Web:* www.marcuswhitmanhotel.com	Walla Walla	WA	99362	509-525-2200	
Marina del Rey Hotel 13534 Bali Way *Web:* www.marinadelreyhotel.com	Marina Del Rey	CA	90292	310-301-1000	
Massage Ctr at Mohonk Mountain House 1000 Mtn Rest Rd *TF:* 800-772-6646 ■ *Web:* www.mohonk.com	New Paltz	NY	12561	845-255-1000	
MHG of Pensacola, Florida LLC 481 Creighton Rd *Web:* www.mckibbon.com	Pensacola	FL	32504	850-484-7022	
Mii Amo at Enchantment Resort 525 Boynton Canyon Rd *TF:* 888-749-2137 ■ *Web:* www.miiamo.com	Sedona	AZ	86336	928-203-8500	282-9249
MileNorth Chicago Hotel 166 E Superior St *Web:* www.milenorthhotel.com	Chicago	IL	60611	312-787-6000	
Milestone Hospitality Management LLC 717 Light St *Web:* www.milestonehotels.com	Baltimore	MD	21230	561-981-8828	
Mirbeau Inn & Spa 851 W Genesee St *TF:* 877-647-2328 ■ *Web:* www.mirbeau.com	Skaneateles	NY	13152	315-685-5006	
Mirror Lake Inn Resort & Spa 77 Mirror Lk Dr *Web:* www.mirrorlakeinn.com	Lake Placid	NY	12946	518-523-2544	523-2871
MODERN Honolulu, The 1775 Ala Moana Blvd *Web:* www.themodernhonolulu.com	Honolulu	HI	96815	808-943-5800	
Mokara Hotel & Spa 212 W Crockett St *TF:* 866-605-1212 ■ *Web:* www.omnihotels.com/hotels/san-antonio-mokara	San Antonio	TX	78205	210-396-5800	226-0389
Montecito Inn Inc 1295 Coast Village Rd *TF:* 800-843-2017 ■ *Web:* www.montecitoinn.com	Santa Barbara	CA	93108	805-969-7854	
Moonstone Hotel Properties Inc 2905 Burton Dr *Web:* www.moonstonehotels.com	Cambria	CA	93428	805-927-4200	
Morrissey Hospitality Companies Inc 345 St Peter St Ste 2000 *Web:* www.morrisseyhospitality.com	Saint Paul	MN	55102	651-221-0815	
Motif Seattle 1415 Fifth Ave *Web:* www.motifseattle.com	Seattle	WA	98101	206-971-8000	
Mountain Laurel Spa at Stonewall Resort 940 Resort Dr *TF:* 888-278-8150 ■ *Web:* www.stonewallresort.com	Roanoke	WV	26447	304-269-8881	
Music Road Hotel LLC 303 Henderson Chapel Rd *Web:* www.musicroadhotel.com	Pigeon Forge	TN	37863	865-429-7700	

Phone | Fax

Na Ho'ola Spa at Hyatt Regency Waikiki Resort
2424 Kalakaua Ave Honolulu HI 96815 808-923-1234 926-3415
TF: 800-233-1234 ■ *Web:* waikiki.regency.hyatt.com/en/hotel/home.html

New Suncadia LLC 3600 Suncadia Trl Cle Elum WA 98922 509-649-6400
Web: www.suncadiaresort.com

Northern Rockies Lodge
Mile 462 Alaska Hwy Muncho Lake BC V0C1Z0 250-776-3481
Web: www.northernrockieslodge.com

Oak Hotels Inc 2424 State Route 52 Hopewell Junction NY 12533 845-223-3603
Web: www.oakhotels.com

Ocean Drive Clevelander Inc
1020 Ocean Dr Miami Beach FL 33139 305-534-2700
Web: www.clevelander.com

Ocean House Hotel Partners LLC
1 Bluff Ave Watch Hill RI 02891 401-584-7000
Web: www.oceanhouseri.com

Ohio House Motel 600 N La Salle Dr Chicago IL 60654 312-943-6000
TF: 866-601-6446 ■ *Web:* www.ohiohousemotel.com

Omni Interlocken Resort
500 Interlocken Blvd Broomfield CO 80021 303-438-6600
TF: 800-843-6664 ■ *Web:* www.omnihotels.com

Omni Rancho Las Palmas Resort & Spa
41000 Bob Hope Dr Rancho Mirage CA 92270 760-568-2727 568-5845
TF: 866-423-1195 ■
Web: www.omnihotels.com/hotels/palm-springs-rancho-las-palmas/spa

Osprey Valley Resorts 18821 Main St Alton ON L7K1R1 519-927-9034
TF: 800-833-1561 ■ *Web:* www.ospreyvalleygolf.com

P Saa 5142 State St PO Box 27 White Haven PA 18661 570-443-0963
Web: skipa.com

Pacific Hospitality Group LLC 2532 Dupont Dr Irvine CA 92612 949-861-4700
Web: www.pacifichospitality.com

Pala Casino Resort & Spa 35008 Pala-Temecula Rd Pala CA 92059 760-510-5100 510-5191
TF: 877-946-7252 ■ *Web:* www.palacasino.com

Palm Garden Hotel 495 N Ventu Park Rd Thousand Oaks CA 91320 805-716-4200
Web: www.palmgardenhotel.com

Peaks Resort & Golden Door Spa
136 Country Club Dr Telluride CO 81435 800-789-2220
TF: 800-789-2220 ■ *Web:* www.thepeaksresort.com

Pineapple Hospitality Co
155 108th Ave NE Ste 350 Bellevue WA 98004 425-455-5825
Web: www.staypineapple.com

Portofino Spa at Portofino Island Resort
10 Portofino Dr Pensacola FL 32561 850-916-5000
TF: 866-849-0223 ■ *Web:* www.portofinoisland.com

Post Ranch Inn Hwy 1 PO Box 219 Big Sur CA 93920 831-667-2200
Web: www.postranchinn.com

Promise Hotels Inc 2201 N 77th E Ave Tulsa OK 74115 918-858-2779
Web: www.promisehotels.com

Rainbow Courts Motel & Apartments
915 E Cameron Ave Rockdale TX 76567 512-446-2361
Web: www.rainbowcourts.com

Raindance Spa at the Lodge at Sonoma Renaissance Resort
1325 Broadway Sonoma CA 95476 707-935-6600
TF: 866-263-0758 ■ *Web:* www.marriott.com

Raleigh, The 1775 Collins Ave Miami Beach FL 33139 305-534-6300
Web: www.raleighhotel.com

Ramada Hotel & Suites Lethbridge
2375 Mayor Magrath Dr S Hwy 4 and Mayor Magrath Dr
Lethbridge AB T1K7M1 403-380-5050
Web: www.wyndhamhotels.com/ramada/lethbridge-alberta/ramada-lethbridge-ab/overview

Ramada Mall of America
2300 E American Blvd Bloomington MN 55425 952-548-3609
Web: www.ramadamoa.com

Renoir Hotel 45 McAllister St San Francisco CA 94102 415-626-5200
Web: www.renoirhotel.com

Residence Inn Mystic 40 Whitehall Ave Mystic CT 06355 860-536-5150
TF: 888-268-7222 ■ *Web:* www.lakesregion.org

Resort at Squaw Creek
400 Squaw Creek Rd PO Box 3333 Olympic Valley CA 96146 530-583-6300 581-6632
TF: 800-327-3353 ■ *Web:* www.squawcreek.com

Revere Hotel Boston Common 200 Stuart St Boston MA 02116 617-482-1800
TF: 855-673-8373 ■ *Web:* www.reverehotel.com

Revive Spa at the JW Marriott Desert Ridge Resort Phoenix
5350 E Marriott Dr Phoenix AZ 85054 480-293-3700
TF: 800-845-5279 ■ *Web:* www.marriott.com

Ritz-Carlton Hotel Company, The
4445 Willard Ave Ste 800 Chevy Chase MD 20815 301-547-4700 467-7188*
**Fax Area Code:* 706 ■ *TF:* 800-876-7280 ■ *Web:* www.ritzcarlton.com

Ritz-Carlton Hotel Company, The
1111 Ritz-Carlton Dr Sarasota FL 34236 866-922-6882 468-4069*
**Fax Area Code:* 801 ■ *TF:* 800-241-3333 ■ *Web:* www.ritzcarlton.com

Ritz-Carlton Tysons Corner, The
1700 Tysons Blvd McLean VA 22102 703-506-4300 506-2694
TF: 800-241-3333 ■ *Web:* www.ritzcarlton.com

Safety Harbor Resort & Spa
105 N Bayshore Dr Safety Harbor FL 34695 727-726-1161
TF: 888-237-8772 ■ *Web:* www.safetyharborspa.com

Saint Regis Aspen 315 E Dean St Aspen CO 81611 970-920-3300
TF General: 888-627-7198 ■ *Web:* www.stregisaspen.com

Sanctuary Beach Resort Monterey Bay
3295 Dunes Rd Marina CA 93933 831-883-9478
TF: 855-693-6583 ■ *Web:* www.thesanctuarybeachresort.com

Sea Spa at Loews Coronado Bay Resort
4000 Loews Coronado Bay Rd Coronado CA 92118 619-424-4000 424-4000
TF: 800-815-6397 ■ *Web:* www.loewshotels.com

Seasons Restaurant at Highland Lake Inn
86 Lilly Pad Ln Flat Rock NC 28731 828-696-9094
TF: 800-635-5101 ■ *Web:* hlinn.com

Secret Garden Spa at the Prince of Wales Hotel
6 Picton St Niagara-on-the-Lake ON L0S1J0 905-468-3246 468-5521
TF: 888-669-5566 ■ *Web:* www.vintage-hotels.com

Senator Inn & Spa of Augusta 284 Western Ave Augusta ME 04330 207-622-8800 622-8803
TF: 877-772-2224 ■ *Web:* www.senatorinn.com

ShaNah Spa at the Bishop's Lodge
1297 Bishop Santa Fe NM 87506 505-983-6377
Web: www.bishopslodge.com

Shell Island Ocean Front Suites
2700 N Lumina Ave Wrightsville Beach NC 28480 910-256-8696
TF: 800-689-6765 ■ *Web:* www.shellisland.com

Sheraton Agoura Hills Hotel
30100 Agoura Rd Agoura Hills CA 91301 818-707-1220
TF: 866-716-8134 ■ *Web:* www.sheratonagourahills.com

Sheraton Denver Tech Center Hotel
7007 S Clinton St Greenwood Village CO 80112 303-799-6200
Web: www.sheratondenvertech.com

Sheraton Fishermans Wharf (San Francisco, CA)
2500 Mason St San Francisco CA 94133 415-362-5500
TF: 866-716-8134 ■ *Web:* www.sheratonatthewharf.com

Sheraton Gunter Hotel 205 E Houston St San Antonio TX 78205 210-227-3241
TF: 866-716-8134 ■ *Web:* www.sheratongunter.com

Sheraton North Houston Hotel At George Bush Intercontinental
15700 JFK Blvd Houston TX 77032 281-442-5100
Web: www.sheratonnorthhouston.com

Sheraton Phoenix Downtown Hotel
340 N Third St Phoenix AZ 85004 602-262-2500
TF: 866-716-8134 ■ *Web:* www.sheratonphoenixdowntown.com

Sheraton Raleigh Hotel 421 S Salisbury St Raleigh NC 27601 919-834-9900
TF: 866-716-8134 ■ *Web:* www.sheratonraleigh.com

Sheraton Safari Hotel & Suites
12205 S Apopka Vineland Rd Orlando FL 32836 407-239-0444
TF: 800-325-3535 ■ *Web:* www.sheratonlakebuenavistaresort.com

Sheraton Washington North Hotel
4095 Powder Mill Rd Beltsville MD 20705 301-937-4422
TF: 866-716-8134 ■ *Web:* www.sheratoncollegeparknorth.com

Shui Spa at Crowne Pointe Historic Inn
82 Bradford St Provincetown MA 02657 508-487-6767 487-5554
TF: 877-276-9631 ■ *Web:* www.crownepointe.com

Sixty Hotels 54 Thompson St New York NY 10012 877-431-0400
TF: 877-431-0400 ■ *Web:* sixtyhotels.com

SLS Hotel South Beach 1701 Collins Ave Miami Beach FL 33139 305-674-1701
Web: slshotels.com

Sofitel Philadelphia Hotel
120 S 17th St Philadelphia PA 19103 215-569-8300
Web: www.sofitel.com

Soho House Beach House LLC
4385 collins ave Miami Beach FL 33140 786-507-7900
Web: www.sohobeachhouse.com

Solage Calistoga 755 Silverado Trl Calistoga CA 94515 707-266-7531
Web: www.solagecalistoga.com

Sole East LLC 90 Second House Rd Montauk NY 11954 631-668-2105
Web: www.soleeast.com

Spa & Fitness Club at the Four Seasons Hotel Washington
2800 Pennsylvania Ave NW Washington DC 20007 202-944-2022
TF: 800-819-5053 ■ *Web:* www.fourseasons.com/washington

Spa at Big Cedar Lodge 612 Devil's Pool Rd Ridgedale MO 65739 417-339-5201 779-5363
TF: 800-225-6343 ■ *Web:* www.bigcedar.com

Spa at Eagle Crest Resort
1522 Cline Falls Hwy Redmond OR 97756 541-923-9647
TF: 800-682-4786 ■ *Web:* www.eagle-crest.com

Spa at Kingsmill Resort
1010 Kingsmill Rd Williamsburg VA 23185 757-253-8230
TF: 800-965-4772 ■ *Web:* www.kingsmill.com

Spa at Le Merigot JW Marriott Beach Hotel Santa Monica
1740 Ocean Ave Santa Monica CA 90401 310-395-9700 395-9200
TF: 888-236-2427 ■ *Web:* www.marriott.com

Spa at Pebble Beach 1518 Cypress Dr Pebble Beach CA 93953 831-649-7615
TF: 800-654-9300 ■ *Web:* www.pebblebeach.com

Spa at Pinehurst Resort
80 Carolina Vista Dr PO Box 4000 Pinehurst NC 28374 910-235-8320
TF: 800-487-4653 ■ *Web:* www.pinehurst.com

Spa at the Beverly Wilshire, The
9500 Wilshire Blvd Beverly Hills CA 90212 310-385-7023
TF: 800-545-4000 ■ *Web:* www.fourseasons.com

Spa at the Bodega Bay Lodge
103 Coast Hwy 1 Bodega Bay CA 94923 707-875-3525
TF: 888-875-2250 ■ *Web:* www.bodegabaylodge.com

Spa at the Breakers 1 S County Rd Palm Beach FL 33480 561-653-6656
TF: 888-273-2537 ■ *Web:* www.thebreakers.com

Spa at the Broadmoor 1 Lake Ave Colorado Springs CO 80906 719-634-7711
TF: 800-634-7711 ■ *Web:* www.broadmoor.com

Spa at the Buena Vista Palace Resort in the Walt Disney World Resort
1900 Buena Vista Dr Lake Buena Vista FL 32830 407-827-3200
TF: 866-397-6516 ■
Web: www.buenavistapalace.com/services_and_activities/spa.cfm

Spa at the Camelback Inn JW Marriott Resort Golf Club & Spa
5402 E Lincoln Dr Scottsdale AZ 85253 480-596-7040 596-7000
TF: 800-922-2635 ■
Web: www.marriott.com/spas/phxcb-jw-marriott-scottsdale-camelback-inn-resort-and-spa/the-spa-at-camelback-inn-/5014642/home-page.mi

Spa at the Chattanoogan 1201 S Broad St Chattanooga TN 37402 423-756-3400 756-3404
TF: 800-619-0018 ■ *Web:* www.chattanooganhotel.com

Spa at the Diplomat Country Club
501 Diplomat Pkwy Hallandale FL 33009 954-883-4900
Web: www.diplomatresort.com

Spa at the Equinox Resort
3567 Main St Manchester Village VT 05254 800-362-4747 362-4861*
**Fax Area Code:* 802 ■ *TF:* 800-362-4747 ■ *Web:* www.equinoxresort.com

Spa at the Fairmont Inn Sonoma Mission Inn
100 Boyes Blvd Sonoma CA 95476 707-938-9000
TF: 877-289-7354 ■ *Web:* www.fairmont.com

Spa at the Hotel Hershey 100 Hotel Rd Hershey PA 17033 717-520-5888
TF: 877-772-9988 ■ *Web:* www.chocolatespa.com

Spa at the JW Marriott Desert Springs Resort Palm Desert
74855 Country Club Dr Palm Desert CA 92260 760-341-2211 778-2049*
**Fax Area Code:* 817 ■ *TF:* 800-845-5279 ■ *Web:* www.marriott.com

Name / Address	City	State	Zip	Phone	Fax
Spa at the Marriott Harbor Beach Resort 3030 Holiday Dr *Web:* www.marriott.com	Fort Lauderdale	FL	33316	954-765-3032	
Spa at the Norwich Inn 607 W Thames St *TF:* 800-275-4772 ■ *Web:* www.thespaatnorwichinn.com	Norwich	CT	06360	860-886-2401	
Spa at the Orlando World Ctr Marriott Resort & Convention Ctr 8701 World Ctr Dr *Web:* www.marriott.com	Orlando	FL	32821	407-238-8705	238-8777
Spa at the PGA National Resort 450 Ave of the Champions *TF:* 800-633-9150 ■ *Web:* www.pgaresort.com	Palm Beach Gardens	FL	33418	561-627-3111	
Spa at the Ponte Vedra Inn & Club 302 Ponte Vedra Blvd *Web:* www.pvspa.com	Ponte Vedra Beach	FL	32082	904-273-7700	273-7706
Spa at the Ritz-Carlton Amelia Island 4750 Amelia Island Pkwy *TF:* 800-241-3333 ■ *Web:* www.ritzcarlton.com	Amelia Island	FL	32034	904-277-1087	
Spa at the Ritz-Carlton Bachelor Gulch 0130 Daybreak Ridge *TF:* 800-241-3333 ■ *Web:* www.ritzcarlton.com	Avon	CO	81620	970-748-6200	343-1126
Spa at the Ritz-Carlton Half Moon Bay 1 Miramontes Pt Rd *TF:* 800-241-3333 ■ *Web:* www.ritzcarlton.com	Half Moon Bay	CA	94019	650-712-7040	
Spa at the Ritz-Carlton New Orleans 921 Canal St *TF:* 800-241-3333 ■ *Web:* www.ritzcarlton.com	New Orleans	LA	70112	504-670-2929	670-2930
Spa at the Saddlebrook Resort 5700 Saddlebrook Way *TF:* 800-729-8383	Wesley Chapel	FL	33543	813-907-4419	
Spa at the Sagamore 110 Sagamore Rd *TF:* 866-384-1944 ■ *Web:* www.thesagamore.com	Bolton Landing	NY	12814	518-743-6081	
Spa at the Sanderling Resort 1461 Duck Rd *TF:* 855-412-7866 ■ *Web:* www.sanderling-resort.com	Duck	NC	27949	252-261-7744	261-1352
Spa at the Vail Marriott Mountain Resort 715 W Lionshead Cir *TF:* 800-648-0720 ■ *Web:* www.marriott.com	Vail	CO	81657	970-479-5004	
Spa at the Villagio Inn 6481 Washington St *TF:* 800-351-1133 ■ *Web:* www.villagio.com	Yountville	CA	94599	707-948-5050	
Spa at White Oaks Conference Resort 253 Taylor Rd *TF:* 800-263-5766 ■ *Web:* www.whiteoaksresort.com	Niagara-on-the-Lake	ON	L0S1J0	905-641-2599	
Spa Esmeralda at the Renaissance Esmeralda Resort 44400 Indian Wells Ln **Fax Area Code:* 817 ■ *TF:* 800-845-5279 ■ *Web:* www.marriott.com	Indian Wells	CA	92210	760-836-1265	778-2049*
Spa Gaucin at the Saint Regis Monarch Beach 1 Monarch Beach Resort *TF:* 800-722-1543	Dana Point	CA	92629	949-234-3367	234-3365
Spa Grande at the Grand Wailea Resort Maui 3850 Wailea Alanui Dr *TF:* 800-772-1933 ■ *Web:* www.grandwailea.com/spa	Wailea	HI	96753	808-875-1234	
Spa La Quinta at La Quinta Resort 49499 Eisenhower Dr *TF:* 877-527-7721 ■ *Web:* www.laquintaresort.com	La Quinta	CA	92253	760-777-4800	
Spa Moana at the Hyatt Regency Maui Resort & Spa 200 Nohea Kai Dr *TF:* 800-233-1234 ■ *Web:* maui.regency.hyatt.com/en/hotel/home.html	Lahaina	HI	96761	808-667-4725	667-4503
Spa Shiki at the Lodge of Four Seasons 315 Horseshoe Bend Pkwy *TF:* 800-843-5253 ■ *Web:* spashiki.com	Lake Ozark	MO	65049	573-365-8108	365-8101
Spa Suites at Kahala Hotel & Resort 5000 Kahala Ave *TF:* 800-367-2525 ■ *Web:* www.kahalaresort.com	Honolulu	HI	96816	808-739-8938	
Spa Terre at LaPlaya Beach & Golf Resort 9891 Gulf Shore Dr *TF:* 800-237-6883 ■ *Web:* www.laplayaresort.com	Naples	FL	34108	239-597-3123	597-6278
Spa Terre at Paradise Point Resort 1404 Vacation Rd *TF:* 800-344-2626 ■ *Web:* www.paradisepoint.com	San Diego	CA	92109	858-581-5998	
Spa Terre at the Hotel Viking 1 Bellevue Ave *TF:* 800-556-7126 ■ *Web:* www.hotelviking.com	Newport	RI	02840	401-847-3300	
Spa Terre at the Inn & Spa at Loretto 211 Old Santa Fe Trl *TF:* 800-727-5531 ■ *Web:* www.destinationhotels.com/inn-at-loretto	Santa Fe	NM	87501	505-984-7997	
Spa Toccare at Borgata Hotel Casino 1 Borgata Way *TF:* 877-448-5833 ■ *Web:* www.theborgata.com	Atlantic City	NJ	08401	609-317-7555	317-1039
Spa Torrey Pines at the Lodge at Torrey Pines 11480 N Torrey Pines Rd *Web:* www.spatorreypines.com	La Jolla	CA	92037	858-777-6690	
SpaHalekulani at the Halekulani Hotel 2199 Kalia Rd *TF:* 800-367-2343 ■ *Web:* www.halekulani.com	Honolulu	HI	96815	808-931-5322	
Spire Hospitality LLC 111 S Pfingsten Rd Ste 425 *Web:* www.spirehotels.com	Deerfield	IL	60015	847-498-6650	
Sportsmen's Lodge Hotel 12825 Ventura Blvd *Web:* www.sportsmenslodge.com	Studio City	CA	91604	818-769-4700	
Springmaid Beach Resort 3200 S Ocean Blvd *TF:* 866-764-8501 ■ *Web:* springmaidbeach.com	Myrtle Beach	SC	29577	866-764-8501	
Staybridge Suites Hotel 6095 Emerald Pkwy *Web:* www.ihg.com/staybridge/hotels/us/en/reservation	Dublin	OH	43016	614-734-9882	
Stillwater Spa at the Hyatt Regency Newport 1 Goat Island *TF:* 800-233-1234 ■ *Web:* newport.regency.hyatt.com/en/hotel/home.html	Newport	RI	02840	401-851-3225	851-3201
Studio 6 PO Box 809092 *TF:* 855-249-0891 ■ *Web:* www.staystudio6.com	Dallas	TX	75380	614-601-4060	
Sundestin Beach Resort 1040 Hwy 98 E *Web:* sundestinresort.com	Destin	FL	32541	850-586-1775	
Sunstone Hotel Properties Inc 903 Calle Amanecer Ste 100 *Web:* www.sunstonehotels.com	San Clemente	CA	92673	949-369-4000	
Sunway Hotel Group Inc 8500 College Blvd *Web:* www.sunwayhotel.com	Overland Park	KS	66210	913-345-2111	
Taboo Resort Golf & Spa 1209 Muskoka Beach Rd *TF:* 800-461-0236	Gravenhurst	ON	P1P1R1	705-687-2233	687-7474
Tampa Marriott Waterside Hotel & Marina 700 S Florida Ave *TF:* 888-268-1616 ■ *Web:* www.marriott.com	Tampa	FL	33602	813-204-6300	204-6342
Ten Thousand Waves Japanese Health Spa 3451 Hyde Pk Rd *Web:* www.tenthousandwaves.com	Santa Fe	NM	87501	505-982-9304	
TMI Hospitality Inc 4850 32nd Ave South *TF:* 800-210-8223 ■ *Web:* www.tharaldson.com	Fargo	ND	58104	701-235-1060	
Toll House Hotel 140 S Santa Cruz Ave *Web:* www.tollhousehotel.com	Los Gatos	CA	95030	408-395-7070	
Treasure Island Resort & Casino 5734 Sturgeon Lk Rd *Web:* www.ticasino.com	Welch	MN	55089	651-385-2786	
Trump Soho New York 246 Spring St *TF:* 855-878-6700 ■ *Web:* www.trumphotelcollection.com/soho	New York	NY	10013	212-842-5500	
Tulalip Resort Casino 10200 Quil Ceda Blvd *TF:* 888-272-1111 ■ *Web:* www.tulalipresortcasino.com	Tulalip	WA	98271	888-272-1111	
Turtle Cove Spa at Mountain Harbor Resort 181 Club House Dr *Web:* www.turtlecovespa.com	Mount Ida	AR	71957	870-867-1220	
Urgo Hotels LP 6710A Rockledge Dr Ste 420 *Web:* www.urgohotels.com	Bethesda	MD	20817	301-657-2130	
Vail Mountain Lodge & Spa, The 352 E Meadow Dr *TF:* 888-794-0410 ■ *Web:* www.vailmountainlodge.com	Vail	CO	81657	970-476-0700	
Verandah Club, The 2201 Stemmons Fwy *Web:* www.verandahclub.com	Dallas	TX	75207	214-761-7878	
W Fort Lauderdale Hotel & Residences 401 N Ft Lauderdale Beach Blvd *Web:* www.wfortlauderdalehotel.com	Fort Lauderdale	FL	33304	954-414-8200	
Well Spa at Miramonte Resort 45000 Indian Wells Ln *TF:* 800-237-2926 ■ *Web:* www.miramonteresort.com	Indian Wells	CA	92210	760-837-1652	
Westglow Resort & Spa 224 Westglow Cir *TF:* 800-562-0807 ■ *Web:* www.westglowresortandspa.com	Blowing Rock	NC	28605	828-295-4463	
Westin Harbour Castle 1 Harbour Sq *Web:* www.westinharbourcastletoronto.com	Toronto	ON	M5J1A6	416-869-1600	
Westin Kierland Resort & Spa 6902 E Greenway Pkwy *TF:* 800-354-5892 ■ *Web:* www.kierlandresort.com	Scottsdale	AZ	85254	480-624-1000	624-1001
Westin Maui Resort & Spa, The 2365 Kaanapali Pkwy *TF:* 866-716-8112 ■ *Web:* www.westinmaui.com	Lahaina	HI	96761	808-667-2525	661-5764
Westin Mission Hills Resort 71333 Dinah Shore Dr *TF:* 866-716-8108 ■ *Web:* www.westinmissionhills.com	Rancho Mirage	CA	92270	760-328-5955	
Westin Resort & Spa 4090 Whistler Way *TF:* 888-627-8979 ■ *Web:* www.westinwhistler.com	Whistler	BC	V0N1B4	604-905-5000	
Willow Stream Spa at Fairmont Scottsdale Princess 7575 E Princess Dr *TF:* 800-908-9540 ■ *Web:* www.fairmont.com	Scottsdale	AZ	85255	480-585-2732	585-0086
Willow Stream Spa at the Fairmont Banff Springs 405 Spray Ave *TF:* 800-404-1772 ■ *Web:* www.fairmont.com	Banff	AB	T1L1J4	403-762-1772	
Willow Stream Spa at the Fairmont Empress 633 Humboldt St *TF:* 866-854-7444 ■ *Web:* www.fairmont.com	Victoria	BC	V8W1A6	250-995-4650	
Wingate by Wyndham Calgary Hotel 400 Midpark Way SE *TF:* 800-228-1000 ■ *Web:* www.wingatebywyndhamcalgary.com	Calgary	AB	T2X3S4	403-514-0099	
Wintergreen Resort Rt 664 PO Box 706 *TF:* 855-699-1858 ■ *Web:* www.wintergreenresort.com	Wintergreen	VA	22958	855-699-1858	

708 SPEAKERS BUREAUS

Name / Address	City	State	Zip	Phone	Fax
3 Arts Entertainment Inc 9460 Wilshire Blvd *Web:* 3arts.com	Beverly Hills	CA	90212	310-888-3200	
Abrams Artists Agency 750 N San Vicente Blvd E tower 11th Fl *Web:* www.abramsartists.com	Los Angeles	CA	90069	310-859-0625	
Add Rob Litho LLC 11 W Passaic St *Web:* www.addroblitho.com	Rochelle Park	NJ	07662	201-556-0700	
AEI Speakers Bureau 214 Lincoln St Ste 113 *TF:* 800-447-7325 ■ *Web:* aeispeakers.com	Allston	MA	02134	617-782-3111	782-3444
Agency For the Performing Arts Inc 405 S Beverly Dr *Web:* www.apa-agency.com	Beverly Hills	CA	90212	310-888-4200	
Ambassador Speakers Bureau PO Box 50358 *Web:* www.ambassadorspeakers.com	Nashville	TN	37205	615-370-4700	661-4344
Anderson Daymon Worldwide LLC 1301 Fourth Ave NW Ste 100 *Web:* www.adww.com	Issaquah	WA	98027	425-313-1505	
Atlantic Speakers Bureau 980 Rt 730 *Web:* www.atlanticspeakersbureau.com	Scotch Ridge	NB	E3L5L2	506-465-0990	
Atlas Performing Arts Center 1333 H St Ne *Web:* atlasarts.org	Washington	DC	20002	202-399-7993	
Barber & Assoc 1308 Sumac Dr *Web:* www.barberandassociates.com	Knoxville	TN	37919	865-388-5296	
Bronx Defenders, The 860 Courtlandt Ave *Web:* www.bronxdefenders.org	Bronx	NY	10451	718-838-7878	

				Phone	Fax
Brooks International Speakers Bureau 763 Santa Fe Dr *Web:* www.brooksinternational.com	Denver	CO	80204	303-825-8700	
Capitol City Speakers Bureau 1620 S Fifth St *TF:* 800-397-3183 ■ *Web:* www.capcityspeakers.com	Springfield	IL	62703	217-544-8552	544-1496
Debt Marketplace Inc, The 10440 Pioneer Blvd Ste 2 *Web:* debtmarketplace.com	Santa Fe Springs	CA	90670	562-903-7220	
Eclipse Advertising Inc 2255 N Ontario St Ste 230 *Web:* www.eclipseadvertising.com	Burbank	CA	91504	818-238-9388	
Elk Valley Rancheria 2332 Howland Hill Rd *TF:* 866-464-4680 ■ *Web:* www.elk-valley.com	Crescent City	CA	95531	707-464-4680	
Everingham & Kerr Inc 1300 Route 73 Ste 103 *Web:* www.everkerr.com	Mount Laurel	NJ	08054	856-546-6655	
Executive Speakers Bureau 8567 Cordes Cir *TF:* 800-754-9404 ■ *Web:* www.executivespeakers.com	Germantown	TN	38139	901-754-9404	756-4237
Florexpo LLC 1960 Kellogg Ave *TF:* 800-830-3567 ■ *Web:* www.florexpo.com	Carlsbad	CA	92008	800-830-3567	
Glyphic Technologies Inc 1001 Ave Of The Amrcas *Web:* www.glytec.com	New York	NY	10018	212-625-9170	
Greater Talent Network Inc 437 Fifth Ave *TF:* 800-326-4211 ■ *Web:* www.greatertalent.com	New York	NY	10016	212-645-4200	627-1471
H2f Comedy Productions 102 E Magnolia Blvd *Web:* www.flapperscomedy.com	Burbank	CA	91502	818-845-9721	
Harry Walker Agency Inc (HWA) 355 Lexington Ave 21st Fl *Web:* www.harrywalker.com	New York	NY	10017	646-227-4900	
Infinedi LLC 1437 S Boulder Ave Ste 1030 *Web:* www.infinedi.net	Tulsa	OK	74145	918-249-4450	
International Speakers Bureau Inc 2128 Boll St *Web:* business-bankruptcies.com	Dallas	TX	75204	214-744-3885	
J Reynolds & Company Inc 369 Sansom Blvd	Saginaw	TX	76179	817-369-3775	
Janas Consulting 201 S Lk Ave Ste 302 *Web:* www.janascorp.com	Pasadena	CA	91101	626-432-7000	
Joanne Rile Artists Management Inc 93 York Rd Ste 222 *Web:* www.rilearts.com	Jenkintown	PA	19046	215-885-6400	
Justifacts Credential Verification Inc 5250 Logan Ferry Rd *TF:* 800-356-6885 ■ *Web:* www.justifacts.com	Murrysville	PA	15668	412-798-4790	
Keppler Speakers Bureau 3030 Clarendon Blvd 7th Fl *Web:* www.kepplerspeakers.com	Arlington	VA	22201	703-516-4000	516-4819
Key Speakers Bureau Inc 3500 E Coast Hwy Ste 6 *TF:* 800-675-1175 ■ *Web:* www.keyspeakers.com	Corona del Mar	CA	92625	949-675-7856	675-1478
Laser Rite Technologies Inc 1744 Independence Blvd *Web:* www.laserrite.com	Sarasota	FL	34234	941-955-2737	
Leading Authorities Inc 1990 M St Ste 800 *TF:* 800-773-2537 ■ *Web:* www.leadingauthorities.com	Washington	DC	20036	202-783-0300	783-0301
Lytmos Group Inc 400 SW Longview Blvd Ste 290 *Web:* www.lytmos.com	Lees Summit	MO	64081	816-347-9449	
MediVista Media LLC 1100 Spring St Ste 750 *Web:* www.everwell.com	Atlanta	GA	30309	404-817-7767	
National Speakers Bureau 1177 W Bdwy Ste 300 *TF:* 800-661-4110 ■ *Web:* www.nsb.com	Vancouver	BC	V6H1G3	604-734-3663	734-8906
National Speakers Bureau Inc 14047 W Petronalla Dr Ste 102 *TF:* 800-323-9442 ■ *Web:* www.nationalspeakers.com	Libertyville	IL	60048	847-295-1122	367-5499
Powerzone Volleyball Inc 3 Luger Rd *Web:* www.powerzonevb.com	Denville	NJ	07834	973-983-8208	
Publicitas North America 330 Seventh Ave Fl 5 *Web:* www.publicitas.com	New York	NY	10001	212-330-0720	
Santa Barbara Speakers Bureau LLC (SBSB) PO Box 30768 *Web:* www.sbsb.net	Santa Barbara	CA	93130	805-682-7474	
Semple Brown Design PC 1160 Santa Fe Dr *Web:* www.sbdesign-pc.com	Denver	CO	80204	303-571-4137	
Six Degrees LLC 8040 E Gelding Dr *Web:* www.six-degrees.com	Scottsdale	AZ	85260	480-627-9850	
Solix Inc 30 Lanidex Plz W PO Box 685 *TF:* 800-200-0818 ■ *Web:* www.solixinc.com	Parsippany	NJ	07054	973-581-6700	
Speak Inc Speakers Bureau 10680 Treena St Ste 230 *TF:* 800-677-3324 ■ *Web:* www.speakinc.com	San Diego	CA	92131	858-228-3771	228-3989
Speakers Guild Inc 35 Discovery Hill Rd *Web:* businessfinder.masslive.com	East Sandwich	MA	02537	508-888-6702	
Speakers Unlimited PO Box 27225 *TF:* 888-333-6676 ■ *Web:* www.speakersunlimited.com	Columbus	OH	43227	614-864-3703	864-3876
Speakers.com 1125 W St Ste 200 *Web:* www.speakers.com	Annapolis	MD	21401	410-897-1970	
Steven Barclay Agency 12 Western Ave *TF:* 888-965-7323 ■ *Web:* www.barclayagency.com	Petaluma	CA	94952	707-773-0654	778-1868
Venture Opportunities Inc 13140 Coit Rd Ste 211 *Web:* www.bizdealmaker.com	Dallas	TX	75240	972-783-1662	
Walters International Speakers Bureau 18825 Hicrest Rd	Glendora	CA	91741	626-335-8069	
Washington Speakers Bureau 1663 Prince St *Web:* www.washingtonspeakers.com	Alexandria	VA	22314	703-684-0555	684-9378
WME | IMG SPEAKERS 304 Pk Ave S *Web:* www.imgspeakers.com	New York	NY	10010	212-774-6735	
World Class Speakers & Entertainers 5200 Kanan Rd Ste 210 *Web:* www.wcspeakers.com	Agoura Hills	CA	91301	818-991-5400	

709 SPEED CHANGERS, INDUSTRIAL HIGH SPEED DRIVES, GEARS

See Also Aircraft Parts & Auxiliary Equipment p. 1726; Automotive Parts & Supplies - Mfr p. 1830; Controls & Relays - Electrical p. 2146; Machine Shops p. 2688; Motors (Electric) & Generators p. 2787; Power Transmission Equipment - Mechanical p. 2967

				Phone	Fax
Amarillo Gear Co 2401 W Sundown Ln *Web:* www.amarillogear.com	Amarillo	TX	79118	806-622-1273	622-3258
Auburn Gear Inc 400 E Auburn Dr *Web:* www.auburngear.com	Auburn	IN	46706	260-925-3200	925-4725
Avion Technologies Inc 1203 Lorimar Dr *Web:* www.avion-tech.com	Mississauga	ON	L5S1M9	905-670-1570	670-1568
Bison Gear & Engineering Corp 3850 Ohio Ave *TF:* 800-282-4766 ■ *Web:* www.bisongear.com	Saint Charles	IL	60174	630-377-4327	377-6777
BMT Aerospace USA Inc 18559 Malyn Blvd *Web:* www.bmtaerospace.com	Fraser	MI	48026	586-285-7700	
Bonfiglioli USA 3541 Hargrave Ct *Web:* www.bonfiglioliusa.com	Hebron	KY	41048	859-334-3333	
Charles Bond Co 11 Green St PO Box 105 *Web:* www.bondgear.com	Christiana	PA	17509	610-593-5171	
Chicago Gear-DO James Corp 2823 W Fulton St *Web:* www.oc-gear.com	Chicago	IL	60612	773-638-0508	638-7161
Cleveland Gear Co 3249 E 80th St *TF:* 800-423-3169 ■ *Web:* www.clevelandgear.com	Cleveland	OH	44104	216-641-9000	641-2731
Columbia Gear Corp 530 County Rd 50 *TF:* 800-323-9838 ■ *Web:* www.columbiagear.com	Avon	MN	56310	320-356-7301	356-2131
Cone Drive Operations Inc - A Textron Co 240 E 12th St **Fax Area Code:* 888 ■ *TF Sales:* 888-994-2663 ■ *Web:* www.conedrive.com	Traverse City	MI	49685	231-946-8410	907-2663*
Cotta Transmission Company LLC 1301 Prince Hall Dr *Web:* www.cotta.com	Beloit	WI	53511	608-368-5600	368-5605
Curtis Machine Company Inc 2500 E Trl St *TF:* 800-835-9166 ■ *Web:* www.curtismachine.com	Dodge City	KS	67801	620-227-7164	
Dalton Gear Co 212 Colfax Ave N *TF:* 800-328-7485 ■ *Web:* www.daltongear.com	Minneapolis	MN	55405	612-374-2150	374-2467
Designatronics Inc 2101 Jericho Tpke *TF Orders:* 800-345-1144 ■ *Web:* www.sdp-si.com	New Hyde Park	NY	11040	516-328-3300	326-8827
Electro Sales Inc 100 Fellsway W	Somerville	MA	02145	617-666-0500	628-2800
Emerson Industrial Automation 8000 W Florissant Ave PO Box 4100 *TF:* 888-213-0970 ■ *Web:* www.emerson.com	St Louis	MO	63136	952-995-8000	
Fairchild Industrial Products Co 3920 Westpoint Blvd **Fax:* Sales ■ *TF:* 800-334-8422 ■ *Web:* www.fairchildproducts.com	Winston-Salem	NC	27103	336-659-3400	659-9323*
Fairfield Mfg Company Inc 2309 Concord Rd *Web:* www.oerlikon.com	Lafayette	IN	47909	765-772-4000	772-4001
Gear Motions Inc 1750 Milton Ave *Web:* www.gearmotions.com	Syracuse	NY	13209	315-488-0100	488-0196
Geartronics Industries Inc 100 Chelmsford Rd *Web:* www.geartronics.com	North Billerica	MA	01862	978-663-6566	667-3130
Hankscraft Inc 300 Wengel Dr *Web:* www.hankscraft.com	Reedsburg	WI	53959	608-524-4341	524-4342
HECO Inc 2350 Del Monte St *Web:* www.hecogear.com	West Sacramento	CA	95691	916-372-5411	
Horsburgh & Scott Co 5114 Hamilton Ave *Web:* www.horsburgh-scott.com	Cleveland	OH	44114	216-431-3900	432-5850
Hub City Inc 2914 Industrial Ave *TF:* 800-482-2489 ■ *Web:* www.hubcityinc.com	Aberdeen	SD	57401	605-225-0360	225-0567
Imperial Electric Co 1503 Exeter Rd *Web:* www.imperialelectric.com	Akron	OH	44306	330-734-3600	734-3601
Industrial Motion Control LLC 1444 S Wolf Rd *Web:* www.camcoindex.com	Wheeling	IL	60090	847-459-5200	459-3064
Koellmann Gear Corp 8 Industrial Park *Web:* www.koellmann.com	Waldwick	NJ	07463	201-447-0200	
Kurz Electric Solutions Inc 1325 McMahon Dr *TF:* 800-776-3629 ■ *Web:* www.kurz.com	Neenah	WI	54956	920-886-8200	886-8201
L & H Industrial 913 L J Ct *Web:* www.lnh.net	Gillette	WY	82718	307-682-7238	686-1646
Leedy Manufacturing Co 210 Hall St SW *Web:* www.leedymfg.com	Grand Rapids	MI	49507	616-245-0517	245-3888
Leeson Electric Corp 2100 Washington St *Web:* www.leeson.com	Grafton	WI	53024	262-377-8810	
Lenze 630 Douglas St *TF:* 800-217-9100 ■ *Web:* www.lenze.com/en-us/home	Uxbridge	MA	01569	508-278-9100	
Martin Sprocket & Gear Inc 3100 Sprocket Dr PO Box 91588 *Web:* www.martinsprocket.com	Arlington	TX	76015	817-258-3000	258-3333
Milwaukee Gear Co 5150 N Port Washington Rd *Web:* www.milwaukeegear.com	Milwaukee	WI	53217	414-962-3532	962-2774
Nixon Gear Inc 1750 Milton Ave *Web:* gearmotions.com/about-gear-motions/nixon-gear-oliver-gear	Syracuse	NY	13209	315-488-0100	488-0196
Nuttall Gear LLC 2221 Niagra Falls Blvd *TF:* 800-724-6710 ■ *Web:* www.nuttallgear.com	Niagara Falls	NY	14304	716-298-4100	298-4101
Oliver Gear Inc 1120 Niagara St *Web:* www.gearmotions.com	Buffalo	NY	14213	716-885-1080	885-1145
Overton Chicago Gear Inc 530 Westgate Dr *Web:* www.ocgear.com	Addison	IL	60101	630-543-9570	543-7440
Peerless-Winsmith Inc 172 Eaton St *Web:* www.winsmith.com	Springville	NY	14141	716-592-9310	592-9362

Phone Fax

Perfection Gear Inc 9 N Bear Creek Rd .... Asheville NC 28806 828-253-0000 253-2649
Web: www.perfectiongear.com

Piller Inc 45 Turner Rd .... Middletown NY 10941 800-597-6937 692-0295*
**Fax Area Code:* 845 ■ *TF:* 800-597-6937 ■ *Web:* www.piller.com

Precision Technology USA Inc
225 Glade View Dr .... Roanoke VA 24012 540-857-9871
Web: www.pt-usa.net

Regal-Beloit Corp 200 State St........................ Beloit WI 53511 608-364-8800 364-8818
NYSE: RBC ■ *TF:* 800-672-6495 ■ *Web:* www.regalbeloit.com

Regal-Beloit Corp Durst Div PO Box 298................ Beloit WI 53512 608-365-2563 365-2182
TF: 800-356-0775 ■ *Web:* www.durstdrives.com

Richmond Gear PO Box 238 .... Liberty SC 29657 864-843-9231 843-1276
TF Sales: 800-934-2727 ■ *Web:* www.richmondgear.com

Rush Gears Inc 550 Virginia Dr .... Fort Washington PA 19034 800-523-2576 635-6273
TF: 800-523-2576 ■ *Web:* www.rushgears.com

Schafer Gear Works Inc 4701 Nimtz Pkwy .... South Bend IN 46628 574-234-4116 234-4115
Web: schaferindustries.com/schafer-gear-works/about-schafer-gear-works

SEW-Eurodrive Inc 1295 Old Spartanburg Hwy .... Lyman SC 29365 864-439-7537 439-0566
Web: www.seweurodrive.com

Standard Machine Ltd 868-60th St E............... Saskatoon SK S7K8G8 306-931-3343
TF: 800-329-4327 ■ *Web:* www.standardmachine.ca

Sterling Electric Inc 7997 Allison Ave............ Indianapolis IN 46268 317-872-0471 872-0907
TF Cust Svc: 800-654-6220 ■ *Web:* www.sterlingelectric.com

Sumitomo Machinery Corp of America
4200 Holland Blvd .... Chesapeake VA 23323 757-485-3355 485-7490
TF: 800-762-9256 ■ *Web:* www.sumitomodrive.com

Superior Gearbox Co 803 W Hwy 32.................. Stockton MO 65785 417-276-5191 276-3492
TF: 800-346-5745 ■ *Web:* www.superiorgearbox.com

TECO-Westinghouse Motor Co 5100 N IH-35...... Round Rock TX 78681 512-255-4141 244-5512
TF: 800-451-8798 ■ *Web:* www.tecowestinghouse.com

Textron Fluid & Power Inc
40 Westminster St .... Providence RI 02903 401-421-2800
Web: www.textron.com

710 SPORTING GOODS

See Also All-Terrain Vehicles p. 1733; Bicycles & Bicycle Parts & Accessories p. 1859; Boats - Recreational p. 1864; Cord & Twine p. 2161; Exercise & Fitness Equipment p. 2276; Firearms & Ammunition (Non-Military) p. 2285; Gym & Playground Equipment p. 2448; Handbags, Totes, Backpacks p. 2449; Motor Vehicles - Commercial & Special Purpose p. 2785; Personal Protective Equipment & Clothing p. 2926; Snowmobiles p. 3187; Swimming Pools p. 3213; Tarps, Tents, Covers p. 3215

Phone Fax

40-Up Tackle Co 16 Union Ave PO Box 442 .... Westfield MA 01086 413-562-0385
Web: www.40uptackleco.com

Abel Automatics Inc 165 Aviador St................ Camarillo CA 93010 805-484-8789 482-0701
TF: 866-511-7444 ■ *Web:* www.abelreels.com

Acushnet Co 333 Bridge St .... Fairhaven MA 02719 508-979-2000 979-3927*
**Fax:* Hum Res ■ *TF:* 800-225-8500 ■ *Web:* www.acushnetcompany.com

AcuSport Corp 1 Hunter Pl..................... Bellefontaine OH 43311 937-593-7010 592-5625*
**Fax:* Sales ■ *TF:* 800-543-3150 ■ *Web:* www.acusport.com

Adams Golf 2801 E Plano Pkwy .... Plano TX 75074 972-673-9000 398-8818

Adams USA Inc 610 S Jefferson Ave................ Cookeville TN 38501 800-426-9784 526-8357*
**Fax Area Code:* 931 ■ *TF:* 800-426-9784 ■ *Web:* www.adamsusa.com

Air Chair Inc
2175 N Kiowa Blvd Ste 101 .... Lake Havasu City AZ 86403 928-505-2226 505-2229
Web: www.airchair.com

Aldila Inc 14145 Danielson St Ste B .... Poway CA 92064 858-513-1801 513-1870
OTC: ALDA ■ *TF:* 800-854-2786 ■ *Web:* www.aldila.com

Alpine Archery 3101 N S Hwy PO Box 319 .... Lewiston ID 83501 208-746-4717
Web: www.alpinearchery.com

American Classic Sales
1142 South 2475 West........................ Salt Lake City UT 84104 801-977-3935

American Sports 74 Albe Dr Ste 1.................... Newark DE 19702 302-369-9480 250-4024
TF: 866-207-3179 ■ *Web:* www.americansports.com

AMF Bowling Worldwide Inc
7313 Bell Creek Rd...................... Mechanicsville VA 23111 800-342-5263
TF: 800-342-5263 ■ *Web:* www.amf.com

Aqua-Leisure Industries Inc PO Box 239............... Avon MA 02322 866-807-3998
TF: 866-807-3998 ■ *Web:* www.aqualeisure.com

Aqualung America Inc 2340 Cousteau Ct .... Vista CA 92083 760-597-5000 597-4900
TF: 800-446-2671 ■ *Web:* www.aqualung.com

Arrow Surfboards 1115 Thompson Ave Ste 7 .... Santa Cruz CA 95062 831-462-2791
Web: www.arrowsurfshop.com

Atomic USA 2030 Lincoln Ave .... Ogden UT 84401 800-258-5020 334-4503*
**Fax Area Code:* 801 ■ *TF:* 800-258-5020 ■ *Web:* www.atomic.com

Bankshot Sports Organization
330-U N Stonestreet Ave Ste 504................. Rockville MD 20852 301-309-0260 309-0263
TF: 800-933-0140 ■ *Web:* www.bankshot.com

BAUER 100 Domain Dr.............................. Exeter NH 03833 603-430-2111 430-3010
Web: www.bauer.com

Bauer Premium Fly Reels 585 Clover Ln Ste 1 .... Ashland OR 97520 541-488-8246 488-8244
TF: 888-484-4165 ■ *Web:* www.bauerflyreel.com

Bell Sports Corp 6225 N St Hwy 161 Ste 300 .... Irving TX 75038 469-417-6600 492-1639
TF: 866-525-2357 ■ *Web:* www.bellhelmets.com/en_eu

Big Rock Sports LLC 173 Hankison Dr............... Newport NC 28570 252-808-3500 726-8352
TF: 800-334-2661 ■ *Web:* www.bigrocksports.com

Biscayne Rod Manufacturing Inc
425 E Ninth St .... Hialeah FL 33010 305-884-0808
TF: 866-969-0808 ■ *Web:* www.biscaynerod.com

Bison Inc 603 L St................................. Lincoln NE 68508 402-474-3353 638-0698*
**Fax Area Code:* 800 ■ *TF:* 800-247-7668 ■ *Web:* www.bisoninc.com

Bombardier Recreational Products (BRP)
565 de la Montagne .... Valcourt QC J0E2L0 450-532-2211 532-5133
Web: www.brp.com

Bravo Sports Corp
12801 Carmenita Rd...................... Santa Fe Springs CA 90670 562-484-5100 484-5183
TF Cust Svc: 800-234-9737 ■ *Web:* www.bravosportscorp.com

Phone Fax

Bridgestone Golf Inc
15320 Industrial Pk Blvd NE........................ Covington GA 30014 770-787-7400
TF: 800-358-6319 ■ *Web:* www.bridgestonegolf.com

Brine Inc 32125 Hollingsworth Ave..................... Warren MI 48092 800-968-7845 446-1162*
**Fax Area Code:* 586 ■ **Fax:* Cust Svc ■ *TF:* 800-968-7845 ■ *Web:* www.brine.com

Brunswick Corp 1 N Field Ct.................... Lake Forest IL 60045 847-735-4700 735-4765
NYSE: BC ■ *Web:* www.brunswick.com

Bullet Weights Inc 182 S Apollo Dr .... Alda NE 68810 308-382-7436 382-2906
Web: www.bulletweights.com

Callaway Golf Co 2180 Rutherford Rd.................. Carlsbad CA 92008 760-931-1771 931-8013
NYSE: ELY ■ *TF:* 800-588-9836 ■ *Web:* www.callawaygolf.com

Carstens Industries Inc 733 W Main St.............. Melrose MN 56352 320-256-3919 256-4052
Web: www.carstensindustries.com

Cascade Designs Inc 4000 First Ave S................. Seattle WA 98134 206-505-9500 505-9525
TF Cust Svc: 800-531-9531 ■ *Web:* www.cascadedesigns.com

Catalyst 109 N Orlando Ave .... Cocoa Beach FL 32931 321-783-1530 799-1643

Century Sports Inc
1995 Rutgers University Blvd .... Lakewood NJ 08701 732-905-4422 901-7766
TF Sales: 800-526-7548 ■ *Web:* www.centurysportsinc.com

Century Tool & Mfg 90 McMillen Rd .... Antioch IL 60002 800-635-3831 395-3305*
**Fax Area Code:* 847 ■ *TF:* 800-635-3831 ■ *Web:* www.centurycamping.com

Champion Shuffleboard Ltd
7216 Burns St.................................. Richland Hills TX 76118 817-284-3499 595-1506
TF: 800-826-7856 ■ *Web:* www.championshuffleboard.com

Cleveland Golf Co 5601 Skylab Rd............ Huntington Beach CA 92647 800-999-6263 889-5890*
**Fax Area Code:* 714 ■ *TF Cust Svc:* 800-999-6263 ■ *Web:* www.clevelandgolf.com

Cobra Mfg Co Inc 7909 E 148th St S.................. Bixby OK 74008 918-366-7484
TF: 800-352-6272 ■ *Web:* www.cobraarchery.com

Coleman Co 1100 Stearns Dr........................ Sauk Rapids MN 56379 320-252-1642 453-8585*
**Fax Area Code:* 415 ■ *TF:* 800-835-3278 ■ *Web:* www.coleman.com

Coleman Company Inc 3600 N Hydraulic............... Wichita KS 67219 800-835-3278
TF Cust Svc: 800-835-3278 ■ *Web:* www.coleman.com

Columbia Industries Inc PO Box 746 .... Hopkinsville KY 42240 270-881-1200
TF: 800-531-5920 ■ *Web:* www.columbia300.com

Confluence Watersports Co
575 Mauldin Rd Ste 200.......................... Greenville SC 29607 800-595-2925
TF: 800-595-2925 ■ *Web:* confluenceoutdoor.com

Connelly Skis Inc 20621 52nd Ave W .... Lynnwood WA 98036 425-775-5416 778-9590
Web: www.connellyskis.com

Cortland Line Company Inc 3736 Kellogg Rd .... Cortland NY 13045 607-756-2851 753-8835
Web: www.cortlandline.com

Coverstar LLC 1795 West 200 North .... Lindon UT 84042 801-373-4777 373-5095
TF: 800-617-7283 ■ *Web:* www.coverstar.com

Creative Playthings Ltd 33 Loring Dr .... Framingham MA 01702 508-620-0900 872-3120
Web: www.creativeplaythings.com

Current Designs PO Box 247.......................... Winona MN 55987 507-454-5430 454-5448
Web: www.cdkayak.com

Daisy Outdoor Products 400 W Stribling Dr............ Rogers AR 72756 479-636-1200 636-1601
TF: 800-643-3458 ■ *Web:* www.daisy.com

Daiwa Corp 11137 Warland Dr .... Cypress CA 90630 562-802-9589
TF: 800-736-4653 ■ *Web:* www.daiwa.com

Douglas Industries Co 3441 S 11th Ave................ Eldridge IA 52748 563-285-4162 285-4163
TF: 800-553-8907 ■ *Web:* www.douglas-sports.com

Dover Saddlery Inc 525 Great Rd PO Box 1100.......... Littleton MA 01460 978-952-8062
NASDAQ: DOVR ■ *TF:* 800-406-8204 ■ *Web:* www.doversaddlery.com

Dynastar 1413 Crt Dr .... Park City UT 84098 435-252-3300
Web: www.dynastar.com

Eagle One Golf Products Inc
1340 N Jefferson St .... Anaheim CA 92807 714-983-0050
TF: 800-448-4409 ■ *Web:* www.eagleonegolf.com

Eastaboga Tackle Mfg Co Inc 261 Mudd St .... Eastaboga AL 36260 256-831-9682 835-2524
Web: www.eastabogatackle.com

Easton Tru-Flite LLC 2709 S Freeman Rd............ Monticello IN 47960 574-583-5131
Web: eastonarchery.com

Easy Rider Canoe & Kayak Co PO Box 88108 .... Seattle WA 98138 425-228-3633 277-8778
Web: www.easyriderkayaks.com

Ebonite International Inc PO Box 746 .... Hopkinsville KY 42241 270-881-1200 881-1201
TF: 800-326-6483 ■ *Web:* www.ebonite.com

Eddyline Kayaks 11977 Westar Ln .... Burlington WA 98233 360-757-2300 757-2302
Web: www.eddyline.com

Eppinger Manufacturing Co 6340 Schaefer Rd......... Dearborn MI 48126 313-582-3205
TF: 888-771-8277 ■ *Web:* www.eppinger.net

Escalade Inc 817 Maxwell Ave........................ Evansville IN 47711 812-467-1200
NASDAQ: ESCA ■ *TF Cust Svc:* 800-426-1421 ■ *Web:* www.escaladesports.com

Facility Merchandising Inc
5959 Topanga Canyon Blvd Ste 125............ Woodland Hills CA 91367 818-703-6690
Web: www.facilitymerchandising.com

Folbot Inc 4209 Pace St .... Charleston SC 29405 843-744-3483 744-7783
TF: 800-533-5099 ■ *Web:* www.folbot.com

Franklin Sports Inc
17 Campanelli Pkwy PO Box 508................... Stoughton MA 02072 781-344-1111 341-0333
TF: 800-225-8649 ■ *Web:* www.franklinsports.com

G & H Decoys Inc PO Box 1208 .... Henryetta OK 74437 918-652-3314
TF Orders: 800-443-3269 ■ *Web:* www.ghdecoys.com

Game Country Inc 2403 Commerce Ln .... Albany GA 31707 229-883-4706 883-4766
Web: www.gamecountry.biz

Gamma Sports 200 Waterfront Dr.................... Pittsburgh PA 15222 412-323-0335 323-0317
TF: 800-333-0337 ■ *Web:* www.gammasports.com

Gared Sports Inc 707 N Second St Ste 202........... Saint Louis MO 63102 314-421-0044 421-6014
TF: 800-325-2682 ■ *Web:* www.garedsports.com

Gexco 3460 Vine St .... Norco CA 92860 951-735-4951
Web: gexcoenterprises.com

Gill Athletics Inc 2808 Gemini Ct .... Champaign IL 61822 217-367-8438 367-8440
TF Cust Svc: 800-637-3090 ■ *Web:* www.gillathletics.com

Goal Sporting Goods Inc
37 Industrial Pk Rd PO Box 236........................ Essex CT 06426 800-334-4625 767-9121*
**Fax Area Code:* 860 ■ *TF:* 800-334-4625 ■ *Web:* www.goalsports.com

Goals & Poles 7575 Jefferson Hwy................ Baton Rouge LA 70806 225-923-0622
TF: 800-275-0317 ■ *Web:* www.goalsandpoles.com

Goalsetter Systems Inc 1041 Cordova Ave........... Lynnville IA 50153 800-362-4625 594-3343*
**Fax Area Code:* 641 ■ *TF:* 800-362-4625 ■ *Web:* www.goalsetter.com

				Phone	Fax
Golf Instruments Co 3210 Production Ave Unit A Web: www.golfinstruments.com	Oceanside	CA	92058	760-722-1129	967-7268
Golfsmith International Inc 11000 N IH-35 TF Sales: 800-396-0099 ■ Web: www.golfsmith.com	Austin	TX	78753	512-821-4050	837-1245
GolfWorks, The 4820 Jacksontown Rd PO Box 3008 TF: 800-848-8358 ■ Web: www.golfworks.com	Newark	OH	43055	740-328-4193	323-0311
Green Grass Golf Corp 282 Newbridge Rd Web: www.greengrassgolf.com	Hicksville	NY	11801	516-935-6722	935-7064
Grundmann's Athletic Co 3018 Galleria Dr Web: www.grundmanns.com	Metairie	LA	70001	504-833-6602	833-6899
Harlick & Company Inc 893 American St Web: www.harlick.com	San Carlos	CA	94070	650-593-2093	593-9704
HEAD USA Inc 1 Selleck St TF: 800-874-3235 ■ Web: www.head.com	Norwalk	CT	06855	800-874-3235	
Hillerich & Bradsby Company Inc 800 W Main St TF: 800-282-2287 ■ Web: www.slugger.com	Louisville	KY	40202	502-585-5226	585-1179
Hireko Trading Company Inc 16185 Stephens St *Fax Area Code: 888 ■ TF: 800-367-8912 ■ Web: www.hirekogolf.com	City of Industry	CA	91745	800-367-8912	367-8912*
Hobie Cat Co 4925 Oceanside Blvd TF: 800-462-4349 ■ Web: www.hobiecat.com	Oceanside	CA	92056	760-758-9100	758-1841
Hoyt 543 N Neil Armstrong Rd Web: hoyt.com	Salt Lake City	UT	84116	801-363-2990	537-1470
Hunter Company Inc 3300 W 71st Ave TF: 800-676-4868 ■ Web: www.huntercompany.com	Westminster	CO	80030	303-427-4626	
Hunter's Specialties Inc 6000 Huntington Ct NE Web: www.hunterspec.com	Cedar Rapids	IA	52402	319-395-0321	395-0326
International Billiards Inc 2311 Washington Ave Web: www.intlbilliards.com	Houston	TX	77007	713-869-3237	
Intex Recreation Corp 1665 Hughes Way PO Box 1440 TF Cust Svc: 800-234-6839 ■ Web: www.intexcorp.com	Long Beach	CA	90801	800-234-6839	
J & B Importers Inc 11925 SW 128th St Web: jbi.bike/web	Miami	FL	33186	305-238-1866	235-8056
Jayhawk Bowling Supply Inc 355 N Iowa St PO Box 685 TF: 800-255-6436 ■ Web: www.jayhawkbowling.com	Lawrence	KS	66044	785-842-3237	842-9667
Jerry's Sport Ctr Inc 100 Capital Rd TF: 800-234-2612 ■ Web: www.jerryssportscenter.com	Jenkins Township	PA	18640	800-234-2612	388-8452
Johnson Outdoors Inc 555 Main St NASDAQ: JOUT ■ TF: 800-468-9716 ■ Web: www.johnsonoutdoors.com	Racine	WI	53403	262-631-6600	631-6601
Jugs Sports 11885 SW Herman Rd *Fax Area Code: 503 ■ TF: 800-547-6843 ■ Web: www.jugssports.com	Tualatin	OR	97062	800-547-6843	691-1100*
K2 Sports 4201 Sixth Ave S TF: 800-426-1617 ■ Web: www.k2sports.com	Seattle	WA	98108	206-805-4800	
Kawasaki Motors Corp USA PO Box 25252 TF: 866-802-9381 ■ Web: www.kawasaki.com	Santa Ana	CA	92799	949-770-0400	460-5600
Kent Sporting Goods Company Inc 433 Pk Ave S Web: www.kentwatersports.com	New London	OH	44851	419-929-7021	929-1769
KL Industries Inc 1790 Sun Dolphin Dr TF: 800-733-2727 ■ Web: www.klindustries.com	Muskegon	MI	49444	231-733-2725	739-4502
Kolpin Powersports 9955 59th Ave N *Fax: Cust Svc ■ TF: 877-956-5746 ■ Web: www.kolpin.com/powersports	Plymouth	MN	55442	920-928-3118	928-3687*
Kwik Goal Ltd 140 Pacific Dr *Fax Area Code: 800 ■ TF: 800-531-4252 ■ Web: www.kwikgoal.com	Quakertown	PA	18951	215-536-2200	778-8869*
Lakes Mall LLC, The 5600 Harvey St Web: www.thelakesmall.com	Muskegon	MI	49444	231-798-7104	
Lamartek Inc 175 NW Washington St TF Orders: 800-495-1046 ■ Web: www.diverite.com	Lake City	FL	32055	386-752-1087	755-0613
Lamiglas Inc 1400 Atlantic Ave Web: www.lamiglas.com	Woodland	WA	98674	360-225-9436	225-5050
Laughing Loon 344 GaRdiner Rd Web: www.laughingloon.com	Jefferson	ME	04348	207-549-3531	
Lifetime Products Inc Freeport Ctr Bldg D-11 PO Box 160010 TF: 800-242-3865 ■ Web: www.lifetime.com	Clearfield	UT	84016	801-776-1532	
Linden Surfboards 1027 S Cleveland St Web: www.lindensurfboards.com	Oceanside	CA	92054	760-722-8956	722-8972
Lobster Sports Inc 7340 Fulton Ave TF: 800-210-5992 ■ Web: www.lobstersports.com	North Hollywood	CA	91605	818-764-6000	764-6061
Local Motion Inc 870 Kawaiahao St Web: www.localmotionhawaii.com	Honolulu	HI	96813	808-523-7873	521-6413
Louisville Golf Club Co 2320 Watterson Trail TF: 800-456-1631 ■ Web: www.louisvillegolf.com	Louisville	KY	40299	502-491-5490	491-6189
MacNeill Engineering Company Inc 140 Locke Dr PO Box 735 TF: 800-652-4267 ■ Web: www.champspikes.com	Marlborough	MA	01752	508-481-8830	303-4923
Manns Bait Co 1111 State Docks Rd *Fax Area Code: 334 ■ TF: 800-841-8435 ■ Web: www.mannsbait.com	Eufaula	AL	36027	800-841-8435	687-4352*
Maravia Corp of Idaho 602 E 45th St TF: 800-223-7238 ■ Web: www.maravia.com	Boise	ID	83714	208-322-4949	322-5016
Marble Arms (MA) 420 Industrial Pk Dr Web: www.marblearms.com	Gladstone	MI	49837	906-428-3710	428-3711
Mares America Corp 1 Selleck St TF: 800-874-3236 ■ Web: www.mares.com	Norwalk	CT	06855	203-855-0631	866-9573
Martin Archery Inc 3134 Heritage Rd Web: www.martinarchery.com	Walla Walla	WA	99362	509-529-2554	529-2186
Master Industries Inc 14420 Myford Rd Web: www.masterindustries.com	Irvine	CA	92606	714-918-4650	
Master Pitching Machine 4200 NE Birmingham Rd Web: www.masterpitch.com	Kansas City	MO	64117	816-452-0228	452-7581
Mitsven Surfboards 1157 Cushman Ave Web: mitsvensurfboards.com	San Diego	CA	92110	619-299-7873	
Mizuno USA 4925 Avalon Ridge Pkwy TF: 800-966-1211 ■ Web: www.mizunousa.com	Norcross	GA	30071	770-441-5553	448-3234
Moultrie Feeders 150 Industrial Rd TF: 800-653-3334 ■ Web: www.moultriefeeders.com	Alabaster	AL	35007	205-664-6700	664-6706
Murrey International Inc 14150 S Figueroa St TF: 800-421-1022 ■ Web: murreybowling.com	Los Angeles	CA	90061	310-532-6091	217-0504
National Billiard Manufacturing Co 3315 Eugenia Ave TF: 800-543-0880 ■ Web: www.nationalbilliard.com	Covington	KY	41015	859-431-4129	431-4179
Nicklaus Design 11780 US Hwy 1 Ste 500 Web: www.nicklaus.com	North Palm Beach	FL	33408	561-227-0300	227-0548
North Face, The 14450 Doolittle Dr TF: 855-500-8639 ■ Web: www.thenorthface.com	San Leandro	CA	94577	877-992-0111	
NuStep Inc 5111 Venture Dr Ste 1 Web: www.nustep.com	Ann Arbor	MI	48108	734-769-3939	
O'Brien International 14615 NE 91st St TF: 800-662-7436 ■ Web: www.obrien.com	Redmond	WA	98052	425-202-2100	
O'Neill Wetsuits USA 1071 41st Ave PO Box 6300 *Fax Area Code: 831 ■ TF: 800-538-0764 ■ Web: www.oneill.com	Santa Cruz	CA	95063	800-538-0764	475-0544*
Ocean Kayak 125 Gilman Falls Ave Bldg B *Fax Area Code: 207 ■ TF: 800-852-9257 ■ Web: www.oceankayak.com	Old Town	ME	04468	800-852-9257	827-3647*
Ocean Management Systems Inc 2021 Goshen Turnpike Web: www.omsdive.com	Wallkill	NY	12589	619-236-1203	
Oceanic USA 2002 Davis St TF: 800-435-3483 ■ Web: www.oceanicworldwide.com	San Leandro	CA	94577	510-562-0500	569-5404
Old Town Canoe Co 125 Gilman Falls Ave Bldg B TF: 800-343-1555 ■ Web: www.oldtowncanoe.com	Old Town	ME	04468	207-827-5513	827-3647
Orvis International Travel 178 Conservation Way TF: 800-547-4322 ■ Web: www.orvis.com	Sunderland	VT	05250	802-362-8790	362-8795
Parker Compound Bows Inc PO Box 105 Web: www.parkerbows.com	Mint Spring	VA	24463	540-337-5426	
Penn Fishing Tackle Manufacturing Co 3028 W Hunting Pk Ave Web: pennfishing.com	Philadelphia	PA	19132	215-229-9415	
Penn Inc 306 S 45th Ave *Fax Area Code: 888 ■ *Fax: Cust Svc ■ TF: 800-289-7366 ■ Web: www.pennracquet.com	Phoenix	AZ	85043	800-289-7366	329-7366*
Pentair Ltd 1351 Rt 55 TF: 888-711-7487 ■ Web: www.pentaircommercial.com/products/index.php	Lagrangeville	NY	12540	845-463-7200	463-7291
PIC Skate 22 Village Dr TF: 800-882-3448 ■ Web: www.picskate.com	Riverside	RI	02915	401-490-9334	438-5419
Ping Inc 2201 W Desert Cove Ave PO Box 82000 TF: 800-474-6434 ■ Web: www.ping.com	Phoenix	AZ	85071	800-474-6434	
Poolmaster Inc 770 Del Paso Rd TF: 800-854-1492 ■ Web: www.poolmaster.com	Sacramento	CA	95834	916-567-9800	567-9880
Powell Skate One Corp 30 S La Patera Ln TF: 800-288-7528 ■ Web: www.skateone.com	Santa Barbara	CA	93117	805-964-1330	964-0511
Precision Shooting Equipment Inc 2727 N Fairview Ave TF: 800-477-7789 ■ Web: www.pse-archery.com	Tucson	AZ	85705	520-884-9065	884-1479
Prince Global Sports LLC 1 Advantage Ct TF All: 800-283-6647 ■ Web: www.princetennis.com	Bordentown	NJ	08505	609-291-5800	291-5900
Reebok-CCM Hockey Inc 3400 Raymond Lasnir Web: www.thehockeycompany.com	Montreal	QC	H4R3L3	514-461-8000	
Resilite Sports Products PO Box 764 TF: 800-843-6287 ■ Web: www.resilite.com	Sunbury	PA	17801	570-473-3529	473-8988
Riedell Shoes Inc 122 Cannon River Ave TF: 800-698-6893 ■ Web: www.riedellskates.com	Red Wing	MN	55066	651-388-8251	385-5500
RL Winston Rod Co 500 S Main St PO Box 411 Web: www.web.winstonrods.com	Twin Bridges	MT	59754	406-684-5674	684-5533
Roller Derby Skate Corp PO Box 930 Web: www.rollerderby.com	Litchfield	IL	62056	217-324-3961	324-2213
Rome Specialty Company Inc Rosco Div 501 W Embargo St TF: 800-794-8357 ■ Web: www.roscoinc.com	Rome	NY	13440	315-337-8200	339-2523
Ross Reels 11 Ponderosa Ct Web: www.rossreels.com	Montrose	CO	81401	970-249-0606	
RSR Group Inc 4405 Metric Dr TF: 800-541-4867 ■ Web: www.rsrgroup.com	Winter Park	FL	32792	407-677-1000	677-4489
Sampo Inc 119 Remsen Rd Web: www.sampoinc.com	Barneveld	NY	13304	315-896-2606	896-6575
Saunders Archery Co 1874 14th Ave PO Box 1707 TF Cust Svc: 800-228-1408 ■ Web: www.sausa.com	Columbus	NE	68601	402-564-7176	564-3260
Scott Fly Rod Co 2355 Air Pk Way *Fax Area Code: 970 ■ TF: 800-728-7208 ■ Web: www.scottflyrod.com	Montrose	CO	81401	800-728-7208	249-4172*
Scott USA Inc PO Box 2030 TF: 800-292-5874 ■ Web: www.scott-sports.com	Sun Valley	ID	83353	208-622-1000	622-1005
Sea Eagle Boats Inc 19 N Columbia St Ste 1 TF: 800-748-8066 ■ Web: www.seaeagle.com	Port Jefferson	NY	11777	631-791-1799	473-7398
Seeker Rod Co 1340 W Cowles St Web: seekerrods.com	Long Beach	CA	90813	562-491-0076	
Shakespeare Fishing Tackle Co 7 Science Ct TF Cust Svc: 800-466-5643 ■ Web: www.shakespeare-fishing.com	Columbia	SC	29203	803-754-7000	
Sheldons' Inc 626 Ctr St Web: www.mepps.com	Antigo	WI	54409	715-623-2382	623-3001
Shimano American Corp 1 Holland Dr Web: www.shimano.com	Irvine	CA	92618	949-951-5003	768-0920
Simms Fishing Products Corp 101 Evergreen Dr TF: 800-217-4667 ■ Web: www.simmsfishing.com	Bozeman	MT	59715	406-585-3557	585-3562
Spalding PO Box 90015 *Fax Area Code: 877 ■ TF: 855-253-4533 ■ Web: www.spalding.com	Bowling Green	KY	42103	855-253-4533	729-4800*
Sport Supply Group Inc 1901 Diplomat Dr Web: www.sportsupplygroup.com	Dallas	TX	75234	972-484-9484	
Sportco Sporting Goods Inc 2580 E Sunset Rd Web: sportcolasvegas.com	Las Vegas	NV	89120	702-739-9750	739-9021

				Phone	Fax
Sportline Inc 555 Taxter Rd Ste 210 *Web:* www.sportline.com	Elmsford	NY	10523	914-964-5200	
Standard Golf Co 6620 Nordic Dr *Web:* www.standardgolfcompany.com	Cedar Falls	IA	50613	319-266-2638	266-9627
Stewart Surfboards 2102 S El Camino Real *Web:* www.stewartsurfboards.com	San Clemente	CA	92672	949-492-1085	492-2344
Storm Products Inc 165 South 800 West *TF:* 800-369-4402 ■ *Web:* www.stormbowling.com	Brigham City	UT	84302	435-723-0403	734-0338
Summit Treestands LLC 715 Summit Dr *Web:* www.summitstands.com	Decatur	AL	35601	256-353-0634	353-9818
Talon 1552 Down River Dr PO Box 907 *Web:* www.talon-graphite.com	Woodland	WA	98674	360-225-8247	225-7737
TaylorMade - Adidas Golf 5545 Fermi Ct *TF Cust Svc:* 800-555-1212 ■ *Web:* www.taylormadegolf.com	Carlsbad	CA	92008	760-918-6000	918-6014
Tecnica USA 19 Technology Dr *Web:* tecnicausa.com	West Lebanon	NH	03784	603-298-8032	298-5790
Toobs Inc 347 Quintana Rd *TF:* 800-795-8662 ■ *Web:* www.toobs.com	Morro Bay	CA	93442	800-795-8662	
True Temper Sports 8275 Tournament Dr Ste 200 *TF:* 800-355-8783 ■ *Web:* www.truetemper.com	Memphis	TN	38125	901-746-2000	746-2160
Underwater Kinetics (UK) 13400 Danielson St *TF:* 800-852-7483 ■ *Web:* www.uwkinetics.com	Poway	CA	92064	858-513-9100	513-3602
Victoria Skimboards 2955 Laguna Canyon Rd Ste 1 *Web:* ocean.victoriaskimboards.com	Laguna Beach	CA	92651	949-494-0059	494-5485
Weed USA Inc 5780 Harrow Glen Ct *TF:* 800-933-3758 ■ *Web:* www.weedusa.com	Galena	OH	43021	740-548-3881	548-3882
West Coast Trends 17811 Jamestown Ln *TF:* 800-736-4568 ■ *Web:* www.clubglove.com	Huntington Beach	CA	92647	714-843-9288	843-9020
Wiley Waterski and Wakeboard Pro Shop 1417 S Trenton *TF:* 800-962-0785 ■ *Web:* www.wileyski.com	Seattle	WA	98108	206-762-1300	762-7339
Wilson Sporting Goods Co 8750 W Bryn Mawr Ave *TF:* 800-874-5930 ■ *Web:* www.wilson.com	Chicago	IL	60631	773-714-6400	714-4565
Wittek Golf Supply Co Inc 3865 N Commercial Ave *TF:* 800-869-1800 ■ *Web:* www.wittekgolf.com	Northbrook	IL	60062	847-943-2399	412-9591
Worldwide Golf Shops Inc 1421 Village Wy *TF:* 888-216-5252 ■ *Web:* www.worldwidegolfshops.com	Santa Ana	CA	92705	714-543-8284	
Worth Co, The 214 Sherman Ave PO Box 88 *TF:* 800-944-1899 ■ *Web:* www.worthco.com	Stevens Point	WI	54481	715-344-6081	344-3021
Wright & McGill Co 4245 E 46th Ave **Fax Area Code:* 303 ■ *Web:* www.wright-mcgill.com	Denver	CO	80216	720-941-8700	321-4750*
Yakima Bait Company Inc PO Box 310 *TF:* 800-527-2711 ■ *Web:* www.yakimabait.com	Granger	WA	98932	509-854-1311	854-2263
Yamaha Motor Corp USA 6555 Katella Ave *TF Cust Svc:* 800-656-7695 ■ *Web:* www.yamaha-motor.com	Cypress	CA	90630	800-656-7695	
Yonex Corp 20140 S Western Ave *TF:* 800-449-6639 ■ *Web:* www.yonex.com	Torrance	CA	90501	310-793-3800	

711 SPORTING GOODS STORES

				Phone	Fax
2nd Swing Inc 13031 Ridgedale Dr *Web:* www.2ndswing.com	Minnetonka	MN	55305	952-546-1906	
2nd Wind Exercise Equipment Inc 7585 Equitable Dr *Web:* www.2ndwindexercise.com	Eden Prairie	MN	55344	952-544-5249	544-5053
3balls.com 319 Manley St Ste 1 *TF:* 888-289-0300 ■ *Web:* www.3balls.com	West Bridgewater	MA	02379	888-289-0300	
5 Star Equine Products Inc 4589 Hwy 71 S *Web:* www.5starequineproducts.com	Hatfield	AR	71945	870-389-6328	
A T R Sales Inc 41 Talbot Rd *Web:* www.atrsales.com	Northborough	MA	01532	508-393-8529	
Academy Sports & Outdoors 1800 N Mason Rd *TF:* 888-922-2336 ■ *Web:* www.academy.com	Katy	TX	77449	281-646-5200	
Action Water Sports 4155 32nd Ave *Web:* www.actionwater.com	Hudsonville	MI	49426	616-896-3100	
Advanced Cable Ties Inc 245 Suffolk Ln *Web:* www.advancedcableties.com	Gardner	MA	01440	978-630-3900	
Adventure 16 Inc 4620 Alvarado Canyon Rd **Fax:* Hum Res ■ *Web:* www.adventure16.com	San Diego	CA	92120	619-283-2362	283-7956*
Aero Tech Designs Cycling Apparel 1132 Fourth Ave *TF:* 800-783-8326 ■ *Web:* www.aerotechdesigns.com	Coraopolis	PA	15108	412-262-3255	
AFP International LLC 1730 Berkeley St *Web:* www.afproducts.com	Santa Monica	CA	90404	310-559-9949	
Alabama Outdoors Inc 3054 Independence Dr *TF:* 800-870-0011 ■ *Web:* www.alabamaoutdoors.com	Birmingham	AL	35209	205-870-1919	870-5505
Alaska Mining & Diving Supply Inc 3222 Commercial Dr *Web:* akmining.com	Anchorage	AK	99501	907-277-1741	
Allstar Fasteners Inc 1550 Arthur Ave *Web:* www.allstarfasteners.com	Elk Grove Village	IL	60007	847-640-7827	
Alpina Sports Corp 93 Etna Rd *Web:* www.alpinasports.com	Lebanon	NH	03766	603-448-3101	448-1586
Alpine Accessories Ski, Snowboard, Paddle Board Shop 9219 S State Rt 31 *Web:* www.alpineaccessories.com	Lake In The Hills	IL	60156	847-854-4754	
Ambush Boarding Co 2555 Cobb Pl Ln Nw *Web:* www.ambushboardco.com	Kennesaw	GA	30144	770-420-9111	
American Outfitters Ltd 3700 Sunset Ave *TF:* 800-397-6081 ■ *Web:* www.americanoutfitters.com	Waukegan	IL	60087	847-623-3959	
Ammo Alley LLC 11562 County Rd 395 *Web:* www.wholesalehunter.com	Hartsburg	MO	65039	573-634-6196	
Anaconda Sports Inc 85 Katrine Ln *Web:* www.anacondasports.com	Lake Katrine	NY	12449	845-336-4024	
Andy & Bax Sporting Goods & Gi Surplus 324 Se Grand Ave *Web:* www.andyandbax.com	Portland	OR	97214	503-234-7538	
Apple Saddlery 1875 Innes Rd *TF:* 800-867-8225 ■ *Web:* www.applesaddlery.com	Ottawa	ON	K1B4C6	613-744-4040	
Arco Ideas & Design Inc 212 N Tennessee St *Web:* www.arcoideas.com	Cartersville	GA	30120	770-386-2799	
ASLU LLC 12087 Landon Dr *Web:* www.activerideshop.com	Mira Loma	CA	91752	951-934-4200	
Aspen Ski & Board Co 1170 E Powell Rd *TF:* 877-861-0777 ■ *Web:* aspenskiandboard.com	Lewis Center	OH	43035	614-848-6600	
Associated Electrics Inc 26021 Commercentre Dr *Web:* www.teamassociated.com	Lake Forest	CA	92630	949-544-7500	
Athletic Supply Co 16101 NE 87th St *TF:* 800-732-9259 ■ *Web:* www.kimmelathletic.com	Redmond	WA	98052	425-882-1456	497-4727
Athletic Training Equipment Company Inc 655 Spice Island Dr *Web:* www.atecsports.com	Sparks	NV	89431	775-352-2800	
Atlantic Firearms LLC 10337 Bunting Rd *Web:* www.atlanticfirearms.com	Bishopville	MD	21813	410-352-5183	
Atomic Aquatics Inc 16742 Burke Ln *Web:* atomicaquatics.com	Huntington Beach	CA	92647	714-375-1433	
Austad's Golf 2801 E 10th St *TF Cust Svc:* 800-444-1234 ■ *Web:* www.austads.com	Sioux Falls	SD	57103	605-331-4653	
Backcountry Gear LLC 1855 W Second Ave *TF:* 800-953-5499 ■ *Web:* www.backcountrygear.com	Eugene	OR	97402	541-485-4007	
Backwoods 3300 N IH35 Ste 149 *Web:* www.backwoods.com	Austin	TX	78705	512-583-1700	370-3636
Backwoods Guns & Wildlife Taxidermy Inc 3322 Us Rt 60 *Web:* backwoodsgunstore.com	Huntington	WV	25705	304-521-6888	
Backyard Adventures Inc 14201 Interstate 27 *Web:* www.crownofminnesota.com	Amarillo	TX	79119	806-622-1220	
Barnes Bullets Inc 38 N Frontage Rd *Web:* www.barnesbullets.com	Mona	UT	84645	435-856-1000	
Barts Water Sports 7581 E 800 N *TF:* 800-348-5016 ■ *Web:* www.bartswatersports.com	North Webster	IN	46555	574-834-7666	
Baseball Express Inc 5750 NW Pkwy Ste 100 *TF:* 800-937-4824 ■ *Web:* www.baseballexpress.com	San Antonio	TX	78249	210-348-7000	525-9339
Basilius Inc 4338 S Ave *Web:* www.basilius.com	Toledo	OH	43615	419-536-5810	
Bass Pro Shops Outdoor World 1935 S Campbell Ave *Web:* www.basspro.com	Springfield	MO	65807	417-887-7334	885-0072
Beads Galore International Inc 3320 S Priest Dr Ste 3 *TF:* 800-424-9577 ■ *Web:* www.beadsgalore.com	Tempe	AZ	85282	480-921-3949	
Bell Lifestyle Products Inc 3164 Pepper Mill Ct *TF:* 800-333-7995 ■ *Web:* www.belllifestyleproducts.com	Mississauga	ON	L5L4X4	800-333-7995	
Bent Gate Mountaineering 1313 Washington Ave *TF:* 877-236-8428 ■ *Web:* www.bentgate.com	Golden	CO	80401	303-271-9382	
Berg's Ski & Snowboard Shop 367 W 13th Ave *TF:* 800-800-1953 ■ *Web:* www.bergsskishop.com	Eugene	OR	97401	541-683-1300	
Berts Bikes & Sports 4050 Southwestern Blvd *Web:* www.bertsbikes.com	Orchard Park	NY	14127	716-646-0028	
Beval Saddlery Ltd 50 Pine St *Web:* www.beval.com	New Canaan	CT	06840	203-966-7828	
Bicycle Garage of Indy Inc 4340 E 82nd St *TF:* 800-238-7389 ■ *Web:* bgifitness.com	Indianapolis	IN	46250	317-842-4140	
Bicycle Warehouse 4670 Santa Fe St *Web:* www.bicyclewarehouse.com	San Diego	CA	92109	858-273-7300	
Big 5 Sporting Goods Corp 2525 E El Segundo Blvd *NASDAQ: BGFV* ■ *TF:* 800-898-2994 ■ *Web:* big5sportinggoods.com	El Segundo	CA	90245	310-536-0611	
Bike Gallery Portland Inc 5329 NE Sandy Blvd *Web:* bikegallery.com	Portland	OR	97213	503-281-9800	
Bike Line Corp 700 Lawrence Dr *Web:* www.bikeline.com	West Chester	PA	19380	610-429-4370	
Bike USA Inc 2811 Brodhead Rd *Web:* www.bikeusainc.com	Bethlehem	PA	18020	610-868-7652	
Bilenky Cycle Works Inc 5319 N Second St *Web:* www.bilenky.com	Philadelphia	PA	19120	215-329-4744	
Birdie Golf Balls Golf Equipment 208 Margate Ct *TF:* 800-333-7271 ■ *Web:* www.birdiegolfballstore.com	Margate	FL	33063	954-973-2741	
Bit of Britain Inc 141 Union School Rd *Web:* www.bitofbritain.com	Oxford	PA	19363	610-998-0400	
Black Bart International Llc 155 Blue Heron Blvd E Ste R2 *Web:* www.blackbartlures.com	West Palm Beach	FL	33404	561-842-4550	
Black Box Inc 2777 Loker Ave W Unit A *Web:* www.blackboxdist.com	Carlsbad	CA	92010	760-804-3300	
Black Hills Shooters Supply Inc 2875 Creek Dr *Web:* www.bhshooters.com	Rapid City	SD	57703	605-348-4477	
Blade-Tech Industries Inc 5530 184th St East *TF:* 877-331-5793 ■ *Web:* www.blade-tech.com	Puyallup	WA	98375	253-655-8059	
Blue Quill Angler Inc 1532 Bergen Pkwy *Web:* www.bluequillangler.com	Evergreen	CO	80439	303-674-4700	
Blue Ribbon Products Fishng Tackl Dlr 1701 W Academy St *Web:* www.bettstackle.net	Fuquay Varina	NC	27526	919-552-2226	
Blue Sky Cycling Inc 2530 Randolph St *TF:* 800-585-4137 ■ *Web:* www.blueskycycling.com	Huntington Park	CA	90255	323-585-3934	

Phone | Fax

Blue Sky Sports Center of Euless LLC
7801 Main St — The Colony TX 75056 469-384-3400
Web: www.blueskysportscenter.com

Bob Reeves Brass Mouthpieces
25574 Rye Canyon Rd Ste D — Valencia CA 91355 661-775-8820
TF: 800-837-0980 ■ *Web:* www.bobreeves.com

Bob Ward & Sons Inc 3015 Paxson St — Missoula MT 59801 406-728-3220 728-5230
TF: 800-800-5083 ■ *Web:* www.bobwards.com

Body Bar Inc 1942 Broadway St Ste 314 — Boulder CO 80302 303-938-6865
Web: www.bodybars.com

Boyne Country Sports 1200 Bay View Rd — Petoskey MI 49770 231-439-4906
TF: 800-462-6963 ■ *Web:* www.boyne.com

Brainsport The Running Store
704 Broadway Ave — Saskatoon SK S7N1B4 306-244-0955
Web: www.brainsport.ca

Brighton Feed & Saddlery 370 N Main St — Brighton CO 80601 303-659-0721
Web: www.brightonsaddlery.com

Brooklyn Gallery of Coins & Stamps Inc
8725 4th Ave — Brooklyn NY 11209 718-745-5701 745-2775
Web: brooklyngallery.com

Buchbinder Tunick & Company LLP
1 Penn Plz Ste 5335 — New York NY 10119 212-695-5003
Web: www.buchbinder.com

Burghardt Sporting Goods
14660 W Capitol Dr — Brookfield WI 53005 262-790-1170
TF: 866-790-6606 ■ *Web:* www.burghardtsportinggoods.com

Busy Body Home Fitness 9990 Empire St — San Diego CA 92126 800-466-3348 258-5744*
**Fax Area Code:* 949 ■ *TF:* 800-466-3348 ■ *Web:* www.busybody.com

C W I Inc 650 Three Springs Raod — Bowling Green KY 42104 888-626-7576
TF: 888-626-7576 ■ *Web:* www.campingworld.com

C Walters Intercoastal Corp Inc
20081 Ellipse — Foothill Ranch CA 92610 949-448-9940
Web: www.destinationwater.com

Cabela's Inc 1 Cabela Dr — Sidney NE 69160 308-254-5505
NYSE: CAB ■ *TF:* 800-237-8888 ■ *Web:* www.cabelas.com

Cabela's Outdoor Adventures Inc
610 Glover Rd Ste A — Sidney NE 69162 800-346-8747
TF: 800-346-8747 ■ *Web:* www.cabelasoutdooradventures.com

Cambria Bicycle Outfitter
1645 Commerce Way — Paso Robles CA 93446 707-579-5400
Web: www.cambriabike.com

Campmor Inc 400 Corporate Dr PO Box 680 — Mahwah NJ 07430 201-335-9064
Web: campmor.com

Cannon Sports Inc 11614 Pendleton Steet — Sun Valley CA 91352 818-683-1000
Web: www.cannonsports.com

CAP Barbell Inc 10820 Westpark — Houston TX 77042 713-977-3090
Web: www.capbarbell.com

Capt Harrys Fishing Supply Company Inc
8501 Nw Seventh Ave — Miami FL 33150 305-374-4661
TF: 800-327-4088 ■ *Web:* www.captharry.com

Carbite Golf Inc 5816 Dryden Pl — Carlsbad CA 92008 760-929-1410
Web: www.carbitegolf.com

Carl's Golfland Inc
1976 S Telegraph Rd — Bloomfield Hills MI 48302 248-335-8095
TF: 877-412-2757 ■ *Web:* www.carlsgolfland.com

Cascade Bicycle Club
7400 Sand Point Way Ne Ste 101s — Seattle WA 98115 206-522-3222
Web: www.cascade.org

Centaur Products Inc 6855 Antrim Ave — Burnaby BC V5J4M5 604-430-3088
Web: www.centaurproducts.com

Century Martial Art Supply Inc
1000 Century Blvd — Oklahoma City OK 73110 405-732-2226
TF Sales: 800-626-2787 ■ *Web:* www.centurymartialarts.com

Century Tool & Gage Co 200 S Alloy Dr — Fenton MI 48430 810-629-0784
Web: www.centurytool.com

Champions for Life Sports Center
453 Grant Ave Rd — Auburn NY 13021 315-252-9305
Web: championsforlife.org

Champs Sports 311 Manatee Ave W — Bradenton FL 34205 941-748-0577 741-7582*
**Fax:* Mktg ■ *TF:* 800-991-6813

Channel Islands Surfboards Inc
36 Anacapa St — Santa Barbara CA 93101 805-966-7213
Web: www.almerrick.com

Chicagoland Bicycle Federation
9 W Hubbard St Ste 402 — Chicago IL 60654 312-427-3325
Web: www.activetrans.org

Chick's 18011 S Dupont Hwy — Harrington DE 19952 302-398-4630
TF: 800-444-2441 ■ *Web:* chicksaddlery.com

Christy Sports LLC 875 Parfet St — Lakewood CO 80215 303-237-6321
Web: www.christysports.com

CIC Photonics Inc 9000 Washington St — Albuquerque NM 87113 505-343-9500
Web: www.cicp.com

City Bikes 8401 Connecticut Ave Ste 111 — Chevy Chase MD 20815 301-652-1777
Web: www.citybikes.com

Clear Water Outdoor LLC 744 W Main St — Lake Geneva WI 53147 262-348-2420
Web: www.clearwateroutdoor.com

CMC Rescue Inc 41 Aero Camino — Goleta CA 93117 805-562-9120
Web: www.cmcrescue.com

CMMG Inc 620 County Rd 118 — Fayette MO 65248 660-248-2293
Web: www.cmmginc.com

Coghlan's Ltd 121 Irene St — Winnipeg MB R3T4C7 204-284-9550
TF: 877-264-4526 ■ *Web:* www.coghlans.com

Cole Sport Inc 1615 Park Ave — Park City UT 84060 435-649-4800
TF: 800-345-2938 ■ *Web:* www.colesport.com

Colonial Country Club Inc
3735 Country Club Cir — Fort Worth TX 76109 817-927-4200
Web: www.colonialfw.com

Colorado Ski Country USA Inc
1444 Wazee S Ste 320 — Denver CO 80202 303-837-0793
Web: www.coloradoski.com

Concept Molds Inc 12273 N Us 131 — Schoolcraft MI 49087 269-679-2100 679-2157
Web: www.conceptmolds.com

Condor Outdoor Products 5268 Rivergrade Rd — Irwindale CA 91706 800-552-2554
TF: 800-552-2554 ■ *Web:* www.condoroutdoor.com

Coontail Corner 5466 Park St — Boulder Junction WI 54512 715-385-2582
TF: 888-874-0885 ■ *Web:* coontailsports.com

Cosfibel Inc 60 E 42nd St Ste 2301 — New York NY 10165 212-867-4133
Web: www.cosfibelgroup.com

Cox Sales Co 2035 Cook Dr — Salem VA 24153 540-345-2636
Web: www.glue4you.com

Crown Enterprises Inc 145 Hutton Ranch Rd — Kalispell MT 59901 406-755-6484 758-7425
Web: www.sportsmanskihaus.com

Cycle-safe Inc
5211 Cascade Rd Se Ste 210 — Grand Rapids MI 49546 616-954-9977
TF: 888-950-6531 ■ *Web:* cyclesafe.com

Cyclone Bicycle Supply 135 SE Main St 101 — Portland OR 97214 503-226-0696
Web: cyclonebicycle.com

CZ-USA Inc 3327 N Seventh St — Kansas City KS 66117 913-321-1811
Web: cz-usa.com

D & R Sports Ctr Inc 8178 W Main St — Kalamazoo MI 49009 269-372-2277 372-9072
TF: 800-992-1520 ■ *Web:* www.dandrsports.com

D&S Pump & Supply Co 3784 Danbury Rd — Brewster NY 10509 845-279-3784
Web: www.dspumpco.com

Daddies Board Shop LLC 7126 NE Sandy Blvd — Portland OR 97218 503-281-5123
Web: www.daddiesboardshop.com

Dallas Athletic Club
4111 Dallas Athletic Club Dr — Dallas TX 75228 972-279-6517
Web: www.dallasathleticclub.org

Dan Bailey Fly Shop 209 W Park St — Livingston MT 59047 406-222-1673
Web: www.dan-bailey.com

Dan's Competition Inc 1 Competition Way — Mount Vernon IN 47620 812-838-2691
Web: www.danscomp.com

Darien Sport Shop Inc, The 1127 Post Rd — Darien CT 06820 203-655-2575
Web: dariensport.com

Dart World Inc 140 Linwood St — Lynn MA 01905 781-581-6035
TF: 800-225-2558 ■ *Web:* www.dartworld.com

Dave'S Pawn Shop 1576 N Main St — Crossville TN 38555 931-484-8947
Web: davespawnshop.com

Del-Ton Inc 330 Aviation Pkwy — Elizabethtown NC 28337 910-645-2172
Web: www.del-ton.com

Delta Mold Inc 9415 Stockport Pl — Charlotte NC 28273 704-588-6600
Web: www.deltamold.com

Dharma Trading Co 1604 Fourth St — San Rafael CA 94901 415-456-1211
TF: 800-542-5227 ■ *Web:* dharmatrading.com

DHM Adhesives Inc 509 S Wall St Ste A — Calhoun GA 30701 706-629-7960
Web: www.dhmadhesives.com

Diamond Supply Co 451 N Fairfax Ave — Los Angeles CA 90036 323-966-5970
Web: www.diamondsupplyco.com

Diamond Tour 203 E Lincoln Hwy — Dekalb IL 60115 815-787-2649
Web: www.diamondtour.com

Dick's Sporting Goods Inc 345 Ct St — Coraopolis PA 15108 724-273-3400
Web: www.dickssportinggoods.com

Direct Sports Inc 1720 Curve Rd — Pearisburg VA 24134 800-456-0072
TF: 800-456-0072 ■ *Web:* directsports.com

Dive N' Surf Inc 504 N Broadway — Redondo Beach CA 90277 310-372-8423
Web: www.divensurf.com

Divers Supply Inc 2396 Belle Chasse Hwy — Gretna LA 70056 504-392-2800
Web: divers-supply.com

Dixie Gun Works Inc
1412 W Reelfoot Ave PO Box 130 — Union City TN 38281 731-885-0700 885-0440
TF Orders: 800-238-6785 ■ *Web:* dixiegunworks.com

Dollamur LP 1734 E El Paso St — Fort Worth TX 76102 817-534-3344
Web: www.dollamur.com

Dolphin Swim School Inc
1530 El Camino Ave — Sacramento CA 95815 916-929-8188
TF: 800-436-5744 ■ *Web:* www.dolphinscuba.com

Doms Outdoor Outfitters 1870 First St — Livermore CA 94550 925-447-9629
Web: www.domsoutdoor.com

Double J Saddlery Inc 2243 US Hwy 77A S — Yoakum TX 77995 361-293-6364
Web: www.doublejsaddlery.com

Dowdle Sports Inc 4415 Donelson Dr — Eads TN 38028 901-466-7706
Web: www.dowdlesports.com

Downtown Athletic Store Inc
1180 Seminole Trail Ste 210 — Charlottesville VA 22901 434-975-3696 975-2845
TF: 800-348-2649 ■ *Web:* www.downtownathletic.com

Duke's Source for Sports 3876 Bloor St W — Etobicoke ON M9B1L3 416-233-2011
Web: www.sourceforsports.com

Duluth Pack 365 Canal Park Dr — Duluth MN 55802 218-722-1707
TF: 800-777-4439 ■ *Web:* www.duluthpack.com

Dynamic Tool & Design Inc
W133 N5180 Campbell Dr — Menomonee Falls WI 53051 262-783-6340
Web: www.dyntool.com

Eagle Grips Inc 460 Randy Rd — Carol Stream IL 60188 630-260-0400
TF: 800-323-6144 ■ *Web:* eaglegrips.com

Eagle Quest Golf Centers Inc
1001 United Blvd — Coquitlam BC V3K4S8 604-523-6400
Web: www.eaglequestgolf.com

Earth Sports LLC
746 W Algonquin Rd — Arlington Heights IL 60005 847-439-1400
Web: www.erehwon.com

Earth Treks Rockville Climbing Center Llc
7125 Columbia Gateway Dr Ste C — Columbia MD 21046 410-872-0060
Web: www.earthtreksclimbing.com

Eastern Mountain Sports 1 Vose Farm Rd — Peterborough NH 03458 603-924-7231
TF: 888-463-6367 ■ *Web:* www.ems.com

Eastern Skateboard Supply Inc
6612 Amsterdam Way — Wilmington NC 28405 910-791-8240
Web: www.easternskatesupply.com

Easy Picker Golf Products Inc
415 Leonard Blvd N — Lehigh Acres FL 33971 239-368-6600
Web: www.easypicker.com

Efinger Sporting Goods Company Inc
513 W Union Ave — Bound Brook NJ 08805 732-356-0604 356-0604
Web: www.efingersports.com

Phone Fax

Electra Bicycle Company LLC
3270 Corporate View Ste A. . . . . Vista CA 92081 760-607-2453
Web: www.electrabike.com

Entest Inc 2015 Midway Rd Ste 114. . . . . Carrollton TX 75006 972-980-9876 960-7044
Web: www.entest.net

Equinox Ltd 1307 Park Ave. . . . . Williamsport PA 17701 570-322-5900
Web: www.equinoxltd.com

Evaporated Coatings Inc
2365 Maryland Rd . . . . . Willow Grove PA 19090 215-659-3080
Web: www.evaporatedcoatings.com

Excel Sports Boulder 2045 32nd St . . . . . Boulder CO 80301 303-444-6737
Web: www.excelsports.com

Exerplay Inc 12001 State Hwy 14 N. . . . . Cedar Crest NM 87008 505-281-0151
Web: www.exerplay.com

Eyeline Golf 2990 W 29th St Unit 7 . . . . . Greeley CO 80631 970-353-0393
Web: www.eyelinegolf.com

Fairway Golf Inc 5040 Convoy St . . . . . San Diego CA 92111 858-268-1702
Web: www.fairwaygolfusa.com

Fanzz 2657 South 1030 West. . . . . Salt Lake City UT 84119 801-325-2700
TF: 888-326-9946 ■ *Web:* www.fanzz.com

Farwest Sports Inc 4602 20th St E. . . . . Fife WA 98424 253-922-2581
Web: sportco.com

Fibar Group LLC, The
80 Business Park Dr Suit 300. . . . . Armonk NY 10504 914-273-8770
TF: 800-342-2721 ■ *Web:* www.fibar.com

Fin-feather-fur Outfitters 652 Us Hwy 250 E. . . . . Ashland OH 44805 419-281-2557
Web: www.finfeatherfur.com

Finlandia Sauna Products Inc
14010 Sw 72nd Ave Ste B . . . . . Portland OR 97224 503-684-8289
TF: 800-354-3342 ■ *Web:* www.finlandiasauna.com

First to The Finish Inc 1325 N Broad St. . . . . Carlinville IL 62626 800-747-9013
TF: 800-747-9013 ■ *Web:* www.firsttothefinish.com

Fisher Athletic Equipment Inc
2060 Cauble Rd . . . . . Salisbury NC 28144 704-636-5713
Web: www.fisherathletic.com

Fishtech 5802 W Dempster St . . . . . Morton Grove IL 60053 847-966-5900
Web: www.fishtechmg.com

Fitness Club Warehouse Inc
2210 S Sepulveda Blvd. . . . . Los Angeles CA 90064 310-235-2040
TF: 800-348-4537 ■ *Web:* www.fitnessblowout.com

Fitness Marketing Systems LLC
427 N Theard St 239. . . . . Covington LA 70433 504-723-9649
Web: www.netprofitexplosion.com

Fitness Zone 3439 Colonnade Pkwy Se 800 . . . . . Birmingham AL 35243 800-875-9145
TF: 800-875-9145 ■ *Web:* www.fitnesszone.com

Flite Hockey Inc 3400 Ridgeway Dr Unit 2 . . . . . Mississauga ON L5L0A2 905-828-6030
Web: www.flitehockey.com

Florida Custom Mold Inc 1806 Gunn Hwy. . . . . Odessa FL 33556 813-343-5080
Web: www.fla-mold.com

Flow Sports Inc 1021 Calle Recodo. . . . . San Clemente CA 92673 949-361-5260
Web: www.flow.com

Fly Fishing Shop E 67296 Hwy 26 . . . . . Welches OR 97067 503-622-4607
Web: www.flyfishusa.com

Foreman Tool & Mold Corp
3850 Swenson Ave. . . . . Saint Charles IL 60174 630-377-6389
Web: www.foremantool.com

Forzani Group Ltd 824 41st Ave NE. . . . . Calgary AB T2E3R3 403-717-1400
Web: www.fglsports.com

Fourteen Company Ltd
18271 W McDurmott St Ste F. . . . . Irvine CA 92614 949-852-8811
Web: www.fourteengolf.com

Fox Creek Leather Inc
2029 Elk Creek Pkwy . . . . . Independence VA 24348 276-773-3131
TF: 800-766-4165 ■ *Web:* www.foxcreekleather.com

Fram Trak Industries Inc 205 Hallock Ave. . . . . Middlesex NJ 08846 732-424-8400
Web: www.framtrak.com

Frank's Great Outdoors 1212 N. Huron Rd . . . . . Linwood MI 48634 989-697-5341
Web: www.franksgreatoutdoors.com

Free Flite Inc 2949 Canton Rd Ste 1000 . . . . . Marietta GA 30066 770-422-5237
Web: www.freeflite.com

Freebord Manufacturing Inc
455 Irwin St Unit 104 . . . . . San Francisco CA 94107 415-285-2673
Web: www.freebord.com

Freeline Sports Inc 10 Hughes Ste A-107. . . . . Irvine CA 92618 949-770-3478
Web: freelinedistribution.com

French Creek Outfitters Inc
270 Schuylkill Rd . . . . . Phoenixville PA 19460 610-933-7200
Web: www.frenchcreekoutfitters.com

Gander Mountain Co 180 Fifth St E Ste 1300. . . . . Saint Paul MN 55101 651-325-4300
Web: gandermountain.com

Garber C s & Sons Inc 7928 Boyertown Pk. . . . . Boyertown PA 19512 610-689-9500
Web: www.csgarber.com

Gazelle Sports 3930 28th St Se . . . . . Grand Rapids MI 49512 616-940-9888
Web: www.gazellesports.com

Gem Manufacturing Company Inc
78 Brookside Rd. . . . . Waterbury CT 06708 203-574-1466
Web: www.gemmfg.com

Genesis Bicycles 126 Bushkill St . . . . . Easton PA 18042 610-253-1140
Web: genesisbicycles.com

Gerry Cosby & Company Inc
11 Pennsylvania Plz . . . . . New York NY 10001 212-563-6464 967-0876
TF: 877-563-6464 ■ *Web:* www.cosbysports.com

Getboards.com 40905 Big Bear Blvd . . . . . Big Bear Lake CA 92315 909-878-3155
Web: www.getboards.com

Ggi Worldwide Inc 552 Forest Crest Lk . . . . . St. Louis MO 63367 636-561-4900
Web: ggiww.com

Girl Skateboard Company Inc, The
22500 S Vermont Ave. . . . . Torrance CA 90502 310-783-1900
Web: www.girlskateboards.com

Gita Sporting Goods Ltd
12500 Steele Creek Rd . . . . . Charlotte NC 28273 704-588-7555
Web: www.gitabike.com

Phone Fax

Gold Tip LLC 368 S Gold Tip Dr . . . . . Orem UT 84058 801-229-1666
Web: www.goldtip.com

Golf & Ski Warehouse Inc
290 Plainfield Rd . . . . . West Lebanon NH 03784 603-298-8282
Web: www.golfskiwarehouse.com

Golf Etc of America Inc 2201 Commercial Ln . . . . . Granbury TX 76048 817-579-5263
TF: 800-806-8633 ■ *Web:* www.golfetc.com

Golf Shack Inc 1631 N Bell School Rd. . . . . Rockford IL 61107 815-397-3709
TF: 888-446-5390 ■ *Web:* www.golfshack.com

Golf Shoe Centers of America
9899 N Kings Hwy . . . . . Myrtle Beach SC 29572 843-497-0507
Web: www.golfshoesonly.com

Golfballs.com Inc 126 Arnould Blvd . . . . . Lafayette LA 70506 337-210-4653
Web: www.golfballs.com

Golfer's Warehouse Inc 75 Brainard Rd. . . . . Hartford CT 06114 860-522-6829
Web: www.golferswarehouse.com

Golfsmith International Inc 11000 N IH-35 . . . . . Austin TX 78753 512-821-4050 837-1245
TF Sales: 800-396-0099 ■ *Web:* www.golfsmith.com

Good Sports Outdoor Outfitters
12730 W Interstate 10 Ste 300 . . . . . San Antonio TX 78230 210-694-0881
Web: www.goodsports.com

Graf & Sons Whlse. Dept Inc 4050 S Clark St. . . . . Mexico MO 65265 573-581-2266
TF: 800-531-2666 ■ *Web:* www.grafs.com

Great Skate Hockey Supl Co 3395 Sheridan Dr . . . . . Buffalo NY 14226 716-838-5100
TF: 800-828-7496 ■ *Web:* www.greatskate.com

Green Top Sporting Goods Corp PO Box 1015 . . . . . Glen Allen VA 23060 804-550-2188 550-2693
Web: www.greentophuntfish.com

Gregg's Greenlake Cycle 7007 Woodlawn Ave NE . . . . . Seattle WA 98115 206-523-1822
Web: www.greggscycles.com

Guildcraft Inc 100 Fire Tower Dr. . . . . Tonawanda NY 14150 800-345-5563
TF: 800-345-5563 ■ *Web:* www.guildcraftinc.com

Gulf States Distributors Inc
6000 E Shirley Ln. . . . . Montgomery AL 36117 334-271-2010
Web: www.gulfstatesdist.com

Gunsite Academy Inc 2900 W Gunsite Rd . . . . . Paulden AZ 86334 928-636-4565
Web: www.gunsite.com

Gym Source 40 E 52nd St . . . . . New York NY 10022 212-688-4222 750-2886
TF: 800-496-3499 ■ *Web:* www.gymsource.com

H & s Sports Plus 8015 Summerfield Rd . . . . . Lambertville MI 48144 734-847-3881
Web: hssportsplus.com

H E Anderson Company Inc 2100 Anderson Dr . . . . . Muskogee OK 74403 918-687-4426
Web: www.heanderson.com

Haddrell's Point Tackle & Supply
47 Windermere Blvd. . . . . Charleston SC 29407 843-573-3474
Web: www.haddrellspoint.com

Half Hitch Tackle Company Inc
2206 Thomas Dr. . . . . Panama City FL 32408 850-234-2621
TF: 888-668-9810 ■ *Web:* www.halfhitch.com

Half Moon Outfitters 15 E Broughton St . . . . . Savannah GA 31401 912-201-9393
Web: www.recarts.com

Hansen Surfboards 1105 S Coast Hwy 101. . . . . Encinitas CA 92024 760-753-6595
TF: 800-480-4754 ■ *Web:* www.hansensurf.com

Harbinger Sports Inc 35 Executive Ct . . . . . Napa CA 94558 707-257-5838
Web: www.harbingersports.com

Hawaiian Island Creations Inc 348 Hahani St . . . . . Kailua HI 96734 808-266-6730
Web: www.hicsurf.com

Heerema Co 200 Sixth Ave. . . . . Hawthorne NJ 07506 973-423-0505
TF: 800-346-4729 ■ *Web:* www.heeremacompany.com

Hibbett Sporting Goods Inc
451 Industrial Ln . . . . . Birmingham AL 35211 205-942-4292 912-7290
Web: www.hibbett.com

His Tackle Box Inc
40 Chestnut Ave . . . . . South San Francisco CA 94080 650-588-1200
Web: www.histackleboxshop.com

Hoigaards Inc 5425 Excelsior Blvd . . . . . Minneapolis MN 55416 952-929-1351 929-2669
TF: 800-266-8157 ■ *Web:* www.hoigaards.com

Holabird Sports LLC 9220 Pulaski Hwy. . . . . Middle River MD 21220 410-687-6400
TF: 866-860-1416 ■ *Web:* www.holabirdsports.com

Holiday Diver Inc 180 Gulf Stream Way. . . . . Dania Beach FL 33004 954-925-7630
TF: 800-348-3872 ■ *Web:* www.diversdirect.com

Hometown Sportswear Inc
3692 Us Rt 60 E . . . . . Barboursville WV 25504 304-736-4021
TF: 888-770-7223 ■ *Web:* hometownsportswear.com

Hopkins Sporting Goods Inc
5485 NW Beaver Dr . . . . . Johnston IA 50131 515-270-0132
TF: 800-362-2937 ■ *Web:* www.hopkinssportinggoods.com

Horse of Course Tack Shop
506 W Will Rogers Blvd . . . . . Claremore OK 74017 918-341-6293
Web: thehorseofcourse.com

Hot Melt Technologies Inc
1723 W Hamlin Rd . . . . . Rochester Hills MI 48309 248-853-2011
Web: www.hotmelt-tech.com

Hunter Banks Company Inc 29 Montford Ave . . . . . Asheville NC 28801 828-252-3005
Web: hunterbanks.com

Hunter'S Friend LLC 340 Low Gap Frk . . . . . Oil Springs KY 41238 606-297-1011
Web: huntersfriend.com

Ice Box Sports Center
21902 Telegraph Rd . . . . . Brownstown Twp MI 48183 734-676-5500
Web: www.norianproperties.com

In The Swim Inc 320 Industrial Dr . . . . . West Chicago IL 60185 630-876-0040 766-5329*
**Fax Area Code:* 800 ■ *TF:* 800-288-7946 ■ *Web:* www.intheswim.com

Industrial Ride Shop
3111 W Chandler Blvd Ste 2198. . . . . Chandler AZ 85226 480-812-8881
Web: www.industrialrideshop.com

Ironmind Enterprises Inc
11992 Charles Dr . . . . . Grass Valley CA 95945 530-272-3579
Web: www.ironmind.com

Island Surf
1450 Miracle Strip Pkwy SE. . . . . Fort Walton Beach FL 32548 800-272-2065
TF: 800-272-2065 ■ *Web:* www.islandsurf.com

Isometric Tool & Design Inc
330 Wisconsin Dr. . . . . New Richmond WI 54017 715-246-7005
Web: www.isotool.com

Company / Address	City	State	Zip	Phone	Fax
J & G Sales Inc 440 Miller Vly Rd *Web:* jgsales.com	Prescott	AZ	86301	928-445-9650	
J. & M. Golf Inc 319 Industrial Dr *Web:* jandmgolf.com	Griffith	IN	46319	219-922-1787	
Jan's Mountain Outfitters 1600 Pk Ave PO Box 280 *TF:* 800-745-1020 ■ *Web:* www.jans.com	Park City	UT	84060	435-649-4949	649-7511
Jax Outdoor Gear 1200 N College Ave *Web:* jaxmercantile.com	Fort Collins	CO	80524	970-221-0544	
Jay's Sporting Goods Inc 8800 S Clare Ave *Web:* www.jayssportinggoods.com	Clare	MI	48617	989-386-3475	386-3496
Joes Sporting Goods - Ski Shop Inc 33 County Rd B E *Web:* www.joessportinggoods.com	Saint Paul	MN	55117	651-209-7800	
Jumping Brook Country Club 210 Jumping Brook Rd *Web:* www.jumpingbrookcc.com	Neptune	NJ	07753	732-922-3653	
Karla Colletto Swimwear Inc 319d Mill St Ne *Web:* www.karlacolletto.com	Vienna	VA	22180	703-281-3262	
Keep Me in Stitches 14833 N Dale Mabry Hwy *Web:* www.kmisinc.com	Tampa	FL	33618	813-908-3889	
Killer Dana Surf Shop 24621 Del Prado *Web:* www.killerdana.com	Dana Point	CA	92629	949-489-8380	
Kinnucan's 1199 S Donahue Dr Ste F *Web:* www.kinnucans.com	Auburn	AL	36832	334-887-6100	
Kirkham's Outdoor Products 3125 S State St *TF:* 800-453-7756 ■ *Web:* www.kirkhams.com	Salt Lake City	UT	84115	801-486-4161	
Kittery Trading Post 301 US 1 **Fax Area Code:* 207 ■ *TF:* 888-587-6246 ■ *Web:* www.kitterytradingpost.com	Kittery	ME	03904	603-334-1157	439-8001*
Kitty Hawk Kites Inc 306 W Lk Dr Unit K *Web:* www.kittyhawk.com	Kill Devil Hills	NC	27948	252-441-4127	
Kona Sports Center 103 E Rio Grande Ave *Web:* www.konasurfco.com	Wildwood	NJ	08260	609-522-7899	
Korney Board Aids Sporting 312 Harrison Ave *TF:* 800-842-7772 ■ *Web:* www.kbacoach.com	Roxton	TX	75477	903-346-3269	
Kreinik Manufacturing Company Inc 1708 Gihon Rd *TF:* 800-537-2166 ■ *Web:* www.kreinik.com	Parkersburg	WV	26101	304-422-8900	
Kwik Industries Inc 4725 Nall Rd *Web:* kwikind.com	Dallas	TX	75244	972-458-9761	458-0948
Lacrosse Unlimited Inc 59 Gilpin Ave *Web:* www.lacrosseunlimited.com	Hauppauge	NY	11788	631-582-2500	
Lancaster Archery Supply Inc 2195a Old Phila Pk *Web:* www.lancasterarchery.com	Lancaster	PA	17602	717-394-7229	
Laux Sporting Goods Inc 25 Pineview Dr *Web:* www.lauxsportinggoods.com	Amherst	NY	14228	716-691-3367	691-4393
Lee's Cyclery 202 W Laurel St *Web:* www.leescyclery.com	Fort Collins	CO	80521	970-482-6006	
Leisure Fitness Inc 231 Executive Dr Ste 15 *Web:* www.leisurefitness.com	Newark	DE	19702	302-224-5000	
Leisure Pro 42 W 18th St *TF:* 800-637-6880 ■ *Web:* www.leisurepro.com	New York	NY	10011	212-645-1234	
Lombardi Sports Inc 1600 Jackson St *Web:* www.lombardisports.com	San Francisco	CA	94109	415-771-0600	
Lone Mountain Sports Mountain Vlg *Web:* www.lonemountainsports.net	Big Sky	MT	59716	406-995-4471	
Look Cycle Usa 6300 San Ignacio Ave Ste G *TF:* 866-430-5665 ■ *Web:* www.lookcycle.com	San Jose	CA	95119	408-363-1406	
Love to Swim & Tumble School 15502 Huebner Rd Ste 111 *Web:* www.love-to-swim.com	San Antonio	TX	78248	210-492-2606	
Lumberjack Building Centers 3470 Pointe Tremble Rd *Web:* www.lumber-jack.com	Algonac	MI	48001	810-794-4921	
Macks Prairie Wings 2335 Hwy 63 N *Web:* www.mackspw.com	Stuttgart	AR	72160	870-673-6960	
Mad Dogg Athletics Inc 2111 Narcissus Ct *Web:* www.spinning.com	Venice	CA	90291	310-823-7008	
Magasin Latulippe 637 Rue Saint-vallier O *Web:* latulippe.com	Quebec	QC	G1N1C6	418-529-0024	
Magnum Research Inc 7110 University Ave NE *Web:* www.magnumresearch.com	Minneapolis	MN	55432	763-574-1868	
Mancom Manufacturing Inc 1335 Osprey Dr	Ancaster	ON	L9G4V5	905-304-6141	
Marin Mountain Bikes Inc 265 Bel Marin Keys Blvd *Web:* www.marinbikes.com	Novato	CA	94949	415-382-6000	
Markwort Sporting Goods Co 1101 Research Blvd *Web:* markwort.com	St. Louis	MO	63132	314-652-8935	
Marman Industries Inc 1701 Earhart *Web:* marman.com	La Verne	CA	91750	909-392-2136	
Martin Kilpatrick Table Tennis 4482 Technology Dr NW *Web:* www.butterflyonline.com	Wilson	NC	27896	252-291-4770	
Mass Movement Inc 65 Green St Ste 1 *Web:* www.massmovement.com	Foxboro	MA	02035	508-543-2073	
Mathews Inc 919 River Rd *Web:* www.mathewsinc.com	Sparta	WI	54656	608-269-2728	
MC Sports 3070 Shaffer Ave SE *TF:* 800-626-1762 ■ *Web:* www.mcsports.com	Grand Rapids	MI	49512	616-942-2600	942-2786
McCormick's Enterprises Inc 216 W Campus Dr Ste 101 *Web:* www.mccormicksnet.com	Arlington Heights	IL	60004	847-398-8680	
Medallion Athletic Products Inc 150 River Park Rd *TF:* 888-600-3412 ■ *Web:* www.medallionathletics.com	Mooresville	NC	28117	704-660-3000	
Mel Cotton's Sales & Rentals Inc 1266 W San Carlos St *Web:* www.melcottons.com	San Jose	CA	95126	408-287-5994	298-3536
Midwest Gun & Supply Inc 16 E Peoria *Web:* midwestgunandsupply.com	Paola	KS	66071	913-557-4867	
Midwest Mountaineering Inc 309 Cedar Ave S *Web:* www.midwestmtn.com	Minneapolis	MN	55454	612-339-3433	
Midwest Sports Supply Inc 11613 Reading Rd *TF:* 800-334-4580 ■ *Web:* www.midwestsports.com	Cincinnati	OH	45241	513-956-4900	
Mikasa Sports Usa Inc 1821 Kettering *Web:* www.mikasasports.com	Irvine	CA	92614	949-863-1588	
Mike's Archery Center Inc 413 Franklin Ave Ne *Web:* www.mikesarcherycenter.com	Saint Cloud	MN	56304	320-251-2242	
Minco Tool & Mold Co 5690 Webster St *Web:* www.mincogroup.com	Dayton	OH	45414	937-890-7905	
Mission Bicycles Inc 766 Valencia St *Web:* missionbicycle.com	San Francisco	CA	94110	415-683-6166	
Mitchell Golf Equipment Co 954 Senate Dr *Web:* www.mitchellgolf.com	Dayton	OH	45459	937-436-1314	
Modell's Sporting Goods 498 Seventh Ave 20th Fl *TF:* 888-645-8667 ■ *Web:* www.modells.com	New York	NY	10018	800-275-6633	
MOL (America) Inc 700 E Butterfield Rd Ste 150 *Web:* www.molpower.com	Lombard	IL	60148	630-812-3700	
Mold Craft Inc 200 Stillwater Rd PO Box 458 *Web:* www.mold-craft.com	Willernie	MN	55090	651-426-3216	
Moldex 823 Bessemer St *Web:* www.moldexcorp.com	Meadville	PA	16335	814-337-3190	
Mollusk Surf Shop LLC 4500 Irving St *Web:* mollusksurfshop.com	San Francisco	CA	94122	415-564-6300	
Monogram Center 437 Amboy Ave *Web:* www.njtees.com	Perth Amboy	NJ	08861	732-442-1800	
Motion Fitness LLC 1400 W Northwest Hwy *Web:* www.motionfitness.com	Palatine	IL	60067	847-963-8969	
Motrec Inc 200 rue Des PME St *Web:* www.motrec.com	Sherbrooke	QC	J1C0R2	819-846-2010	
Mountain Equipment Co-operative 149 W Fourth Ave *Web:* www.mec.ca	Vancouver	BC	V5Y4A6	604-707-3300	
Mountain Tools Inc 225 Crossroads Blvd *Web:* www.mtntools.com	Carmel	CA	93923	831-620-0911	
Mud Hole Custom Tackle Inc 400 Kane Ct *TF:* 866-790-7637 ■ *Web:* www.mudhole.com	Oviedo	FL	32765	407-447-7637	
Mueller Recreational Products Inc 4825 S 16th St *Web:* www.muellers.com	Lincoln	NE	68512	402-423-8888	
Mystic Valley Wheel Works Inc 480 Trapelo Rd *Web:* www.wheelworks.com	Belmont	MA	02478	617-489-3577	
Nagel Gun & Sports Shop 6201 San Pedro Ave *Web:* nagelsguns.net	San Antonio	TX	78216	210-342-5420	
National Sports Center Foundation, The 1700 105th Ave Ne *Web:* www.nscsports.org	Minneapolis	MN	55449	763-785-5600	
Nerel Corp Dba Wheat Ridge Cyclery 7085 W 38th Ave	Wheat Ridge	CO	80033	303-424-3221	
New York Golf Center 131 W 35th St *Web:* www.nygolfcenter.com	New York	NY	10001	212-564-2255	
Nicros Inc 845 Phalen Blvd *TF:* 800-699-1975 ■ *Web:* www.nicros.com	Saint Paul	MN	55106	651-778-1975	
Nill Bros Sports 2814 S 44th St *TF:* 800-748-7221 ■ *Web:* www.nillbros.com	Kansas City	KS	66106	913-384-4242	384-0107
NLC Products Inc 3801 Woodland Heights Rd Ste 100 *Web:* www.huntsmart.com	Little Rock	AR	72212	501-227-9050	
No Fault Sports Products 2101 Briarglen Dr *TF:* 800-462-7766 ■ *Web:* nofaultsports.com	Houston	TX	77027	713-683-7101	
Nordica USA Corp 5 Commerce Ave *Web:* www.nordica.com	West Lebanon	NH	03784	603-298-6900	
North Carolina Railroad Co 2809 Highwoods Blvd Ste 100 *Web:* www.ncrr.com	Raleigh	NC	27604	919-954-7601	
North Shore Country Club 1340 Glenview Rd *Web:* www.north-shorecc.org	Glenview	IL	60025	847-729-1200	
Northern Wholesale Supply Inc 6800 Otter Lk Rd *TF:* 800-333-7777 ■ *Web:* www.northernwholesale.com	Lino Lakes	MN	55038	651-429-1515	
Northland Fishing Tackle LLC 1001 Naylor Dr Se *TF:* 800-786-3474 ■ *Web:* www.northlandtackle.com	Bemidji	MN	56601	218-751-6723	
Northwest Outlet 1814 Belknap St *TF:* 800-569-8142 ■ *Web:* www.northwestoutlet.com	Superior	WI	54880	715-392-9838	
Notubes 202 Daniel Zenker Dr *Web:* www.notubes.com	Big Flats	NY	14814	607-562-2877	
Nova Fitness Equipment 4511 S 119th Cir *TF:* 800-949-6682 ■ *Web:* www.novafitnessequipment.com	Omaha	NE	68137	402-343-0552	
NRC Sports Inc 603 Pleasant St *TF:* 800-243-5033 ■ *Web:* www.nrcsports.com	Paxton	MA	01612	800-243-5033	
Okuma Fishing Tackle Corp 2310 E Locust Ct *Web:* www.okumafishing.com	Ontario	CA	91761	909-923-2828	
Old Harbor Outfit 480 Barnum Ave *Web:* www.oldharboroutfitters.com	Bridgeport	CT	06608	203-540-5150	

Name / Address	City	State	ZIP	Phone	Fax
Olympia Sports 5 Bradley Dr *Web:* www.olympiasports.net	Westbrook	ME	04092	207-854-2794	854-4168
Omega Sports Inc 130 S Walnut Cir *Web:* www.omegasports.net	Greensboro	NC	27409	336-854-0797	
Onion River Sports Inc 20 Langdon St *Web:* www.onionriver.com	Montpelier	VT	05602	802-229-9409	
Otis Technology 6987 Laura St PO Box 582 *Web:* www.otistec.com	Lyons Falls	NY	13368	315-348-4300	
Out-fit 25 W Easy St Ste 304 *TF:* 800-376-3339 ■ *Web:* www.out-fit.net	Simi Valley	CA	93065	805-584-1500	
Outcast Sporting Gear 2021 E Wilson Ln *Web:* aireindustrial.net	Meridian	ID	83642	208-955-0476	
Outdoor Sports Center 80 Danbury Rd *Web:* www.outdoorsports.com	Wilton	CT	06897	203-762-8797	
Outdoor Ventures 10579 S Main St *TF:* 866-710-2846 ■ *Web:* www.outdoorventureshayward.com	Hayward	WI	54843	715-634-4447	
Palco Marketing Inc 8555 Revere Ln N *Web:* www.palcosports.com	Maple Grove	MN	55369	763-559-5539	
Palos Sports Inc 11711 S Austin Ave *TF:* 800-233-5484 ■ *Web:* www.palossports.com	Alsip	IL	60803	708-396-2555	
Pape's Archery Inc 250 Terry Blvd *Web:* www.papesinc.com	Louisville	KY	40229	502-955-8118	
Paragon Sporting Goods Corp 867 Broadway 18th St *TF:* 800-961-3030 ■ *Web:* www.paragonsports.com	New York	NY	10003	212-255-8889	929-1831
Pedigree Ski Shop Inc 355 Mamaroneck Ave *Web:* www.pedigreeskishop.com	White Plains	NY	10605	914-948-2995	948-1599
Peloton Cycles Inc 1310 E Eisenhower Blvd *Web:* peloton-cycles.com	Loveland	CO	80537	970-669-5595	
Perani's Hockey World 1600 Cochran Rd *Web:* hockeyworld.com	Pittsburgh	PA	15220	412-343-5857	
Perform Better Inc 11 Amflex Dr *Web:* www.everythingtrackandfield.com	Cranston	RI	02921	401-942-9363	
Performance Inc 1 Performance Way **Fax Area Code:* 919 ■ *TF Cust Svc:* 800-727-2453 ■ *Web:* www.performancebike.com	Chapel Hill	NC	27514	800-727-2453	942-5431*
Peter Glenn Ski & Sports 2901 W Oakland Pk Blvd *TF:* 800-818-0946 ■ *Web:* www.peterglenn.com	Fort Lauderdale	FL	33311	954-484-3606	
PETZL America Inc Freeport Ctr Bldg M-7 *Web:* www.petzl.com	Clearfield	UT	84016	801-926-1310	
Planet Bike 2402 Vondron Rd *TF:* 866-256-8510 ■ *Web:* www.planetbike.com	Madison	WI	53718	608-256-8510	
Playnation of Wnc 542 Hendersonville Rd *Web:* playnationofwnc.com	Asheville	NC	28803	828-776-2731	
Playspace Designs Inc 6321 S Heughs Canyon Dr *Web:* www.playspacedesign.com	Salt Lake City	UT	84121	801-274-0212	
Playwell Group, The 4743 Iberia Ave Ste C *TF:* 800-726-1816 ■ *Web:* www.playwellgroup.com	Dallas	TX	75207	800-726-1816	
Playworks Inc 340 Blalock Rd *Web:* www.playworksinc.com	Boiling Springs	SC	29316	780-453-6903	
Power Gripps Usa Inc 41 Pomola Ave *Web:* www.versagripps.com	Sorrento	ME	04677	207-422-2051	
Price Point Mail Order Ltd 1490 W Walnut Pkwy *TF:* 800-774-2376 ■ *Web:* www.pricepoint.com	Rancho Dominguez	CA	90220	800-774-2376	
Pro Hockey Life Sporting Goods Inc 4440 Autoroute 440 *Web:* www.prohockeylife.com	Laval	QC	H7T2P7	450-681-8440	
Pro Performance Sports LLC 2081 Faraday Ave *TF:* 877-225-7275 ■ *Web:* www.sklz.com	Carlsbad	CA	92008	877-225-7275	
Pro Sports Memorabilia Inc 725 Landwehr Rd *TF:* 888-950-5399 ■ *Web:* www.prosportsmemorabilia.com	Northbrook	IL	60062	888-950-5399	
Proactive Sports Inc 1200 SE Second Ave *TF:* 800-369-8642 ■ *Web:* proactivesports.com	Canby	OR	97013	503-263-8583	
Proline Distributors Inc 1191 S Rogers Cir *Web:* www.prolinedist.com	Boca Raton	FL	33487	561-241-7000	
Protek Cargo 1568 Airport Blvd *TF:* 800-439-1426 ■ *Web:* www.protekcargo.com	Napa	CA	94558	707-254-9627	
Pummills Sporting Goods Inc 2400 W 16th St *Web:* www.pummillsports.com	Sedalia	MO	65301	660-826-0150	
Quarq Technology Inc 3100 First Ave *Web:* www.quarq.com	Spearfish	SD	57783	605-642-2226	
R K Sport Inc 26900 Jefferson Ave *Web:* www.stretchformingcorp.com	Murrieta	CA	92562	951-894-7883	
Randall Scott Cycle Company LLC 2897 Mapleton Ave Ste 100 *Web:* www.rscycle.com	Boulder	CO	80301	720-214-0714	
RD Rogers Co, The 515 N Garfield Cir *Web:* www.pushpedalpull.com	Sioux Falls	SD	57104	605-334-7740	
Recreation Unlimited Inc 15150 Herriman Blvd Ste B *Web:* recreationunltd.com	Noblesville	IN	46060	317-773-3545	
Recreational Equipment Inc (REI) 6750 S 228th St *TF Orders:* 800-426-4840 ■ *Web:* www.rei.com	Kent	WA	98032	253-395-3780	891-2523
Redden Marine Supply Inc 1411 Roeder Ave *TF:* 800-426-9284 ■ *Web:* www.reddenmarine.com	Bellingham	WA	98225	360-733-0250	
Reeds Family Outdoor Outfitters 522 Minnesota Ave NW *TF:* 800-346-0019 ■ *Web:* www.reedssports.com	Walker	MN	56484	800-346-0019	
Reliable Racing Supply Inc 643 Glen St *TF:* 800-223-4448 ■ *Web:* www.reliableracing.com	Queensbury	NY	12804	518-793-5677	
Retail Concepts Inc 10560 Bissonnet St Ste 100 *Web:* www.retailconcepts.cc	Stafford	TX	77099	281-340-5000	
Rhino Gun Safes 607 Garber St *Web:* www.rhinosafe.com	Caldwell	ID	83605	208-454-5545	
Rich n Ton Calls Inc 2315 Hwy 63 N *Web:* www.rntcalls.com	Stuttgart	AR	72160	870-673-4274	
Richardson Bike Mart Inc 1451 W Campbell Rd *Web:* bikemart.com	Richardson	TX	75080	972-644-1466	
Ride Inc 8160 304th Ave SE *Web:* www.rideinc.com	Preston	WA	98050	425-222-6015	
Risse Racing Technology Inc 1240 Redwood Blvd *Web:* www.risseracing.com	Redding	CA	96003	530-246-8700	
RJR Fashion Fabrics 2203 Dominguez Way *TF:* 800-422-5426 ■ *Web:* www.rjrfabrics.com	Torrance	CA	90501	310-222-8782	
Robart Manufacturing Co 625 N 12th St *Web:* www.robart.com	Saint Charles	IL	60174	630-584-7616	
Rock Creek Outfitters 1530 Riverside Dr *Web:* www.rockcreek.com	Chattanooga	TN	37406	423-266-8200	
Rome Snowboards Corp 1 Derby Ln Ste 4 *Web:* www.romesnowboards.com	Waterbury	VT	05676	802-244-1758	
Ron Jon Surf Shop 3850 S Banana River Blvd *TF:* 888-757-8737 ■ *Web:* www.ronjonsurfshop.com	Cocoa Beach	FL	32931	321-799-8888	799-8805
Royal Oaks Country Club Club House 7915 Greenville Ave *Web:* roccdallas.com	Dallas	TX	75231	214-691-6091	
Royer Corp 805 East St *TF:* 800-457-8997 ■ *Web:* www.royercorp.com	Madison	IN	47250	812-265-3133	
Rubenstein & Ziff Inc 1055 American Blvd E *Web:* www.quiltworksonline.com	Minneapolis	MN	55420	952-854-1460	
Ruby Hill Golf Shop 3400 W Ruby Hill Dr *Web:* rubyhill.com	Pleasanton	CA	94566	925-417-5850	
Rudolph Brothers 6550 Oley Speaks Way *TF:* 800-600-9508 ■ *Web:* www.rudolphbros.com	Canal Winchester	OH	43110	614-833-0707	
Runner's Edge Inc, The 3195 N Federal Hwy *TF:* 888-361-1950 ■ *Web:* runnersedgeboca.com	Boca Raton	FL	33431	561-361-1950	
Runners Forum of Carmel Inc 620 Station Dr *Web:* www.runnersforum.com	Carmel	IN	46032	317-844-1558	
Rusted Moon Outfitters Inc 6410 Cornell Ave *Web:* www.rustedmoonoutfitters.com	Indianapolis	IN	46220	317-253-4453	
San Juan Golf & Country Club Golf Shop 806 Golf Course Rd *Web:* www.sjgolfclub.com	Friday Harbor	WA	98250	360-378-2254	
Scottsdale Gun Club 14860 N Northsight Blvd *Web:* www.scottsdalegunclub.com	Scottsdale	AZ	85260	480-348-1111	
Scouts Canada 1345 Baseline Rd *Web:* www.scouts.ca	Ottawa	ON	K2C0A7	613-225-2770	
Scuba Com Inc 1752 Langley Ave *TF:* 800-347-2822 ■ *Web:* www.scuba.com	Irvine	CA	92614	949-221-9300	
Seattle Golf Club Pro Shop LLC 210 Nw 145th St *Web:* www.seattlegolfclub.com	Shoreline	WA	98177	206-363-8811	
SeeMore Putter Co, The 277 Mallory Sta Ste 119 *Web:* www.seemore.com	Franklin	TN	37067	615-435-8015	
Shatz Norman C Company Inc 3570 St Rd *Web:* www.shatzusa.com	Bensalem	PA	19020	215-245-5511	
Shuert Industries Inc 6600 Dobry Rd *Web:* www.shuert.com	Sterling Heights	MI	48314	586-254-4590	
Sierra Bullets LLC 1400 W Henry St *Web:* www.sierrabullets.com	Sedalia	MO	65301	660-827-6300	
SKI Pro 1924 W Eigth St *Web:* www.skipro.com	Mesa	AZ	85201	480-962-6910	
Ski Stop 197 S Service Rd *Web:* www.sunandski.com	Plainview	NY	11803	516-249-7980	
Skiershop PO Box 1542 *Web:* www.skiershop.com	Stowe	VT	05672	802-253-9400	
Slocum Adhesives Corp 2500 Carroll Ave *Web:* www.slocumadhesives.com	Lynchburg	VA	24501	434-847-5671	
Soccer 4 All 1306 Fm 1092 Rd Ste 101 *Web:* www.soccer4all.com	Missouri City	TX	77459	281-499-6665	
Sonoma Outfitters 2412 Magowan Dr *TF:* 800-290-1920 ■ *Web:* www.sonomaoutfitters.com	Santa Rosa	CA	95405	707-528-1920	
South Hills Country Club Golf Shop 2655 S Citrus St *Web:* www.southhillscountryclub.org	West Covina	CA	91791	626-339-1231	
Spokes Etc Inc 1545 N Quaker Ln *Web:* www.spokesetc.com	Alexandria	VA	22302	703-820-2200	
Sporting Goods Intelligence Inc 442 Featherbed Ln *Web:* www.sginews.com	Glen Mills	PA	19342	610-459-4040	
Sports Authority Inc, The 1050 W Hampden Ave *Web:* sportsauthority.com	Englewood	CO	80110	303-200-5050	
Sports Excellence Corporation Inc 151 Alston Bureau 100 *Web:* sportsexcellence.com	Pointe-Claire	QC	H9R5V9	418-687-0133	
Sports Imports Inc 4000 Parkway Ln *Web:* www.sportsimports.com	Hilliard	OH	43026	614-771-0246	
Sports One Inc 9640 SW Sunshine Court Ste 400 *Web:* www.etzelagency.com	Portland	OR	97005	503-721-7477	
Sports Promotion Network PO Box 200548 **Fax Area Code:* 866 ■ *TF:* 800-460-9989 ■ *Web:* www.gotospn.com	Arlington	TX	76006	800-460-9989	300-5333*
Sports Warehouse Inc 181 Suburban Rd *Web:* www.tennis-warehouse.com	San Luis Obispo	CA	93401	805-781-6464	

Name / Address	City	State	Zip	Phone	Fax
Sportsman's Warehouse 7035 High Tech Dr *Web:* www.sportsmanswarehouse.com	Midvale	UT	84047	801-566-6681	
Spot-Hogg Archery Products 125 Smith St *TF:* 888-302-7768 ■ *Web:* spot-hogg.com	Harrisburg	OR	97446	541-995-3702	
Spyder Ii 65 Pier Ave *Web:* www.spydersurf.com	Hermosa Beach	CA	90254	310-374-2494	
St. Bernard Sports 5570 W Lovers Ln Ste 388 *Web:* www.saintbernard.com	Dallas	TX	75209	214-357-9700	357-0107
Starline Inc 1300 W Henry St *TF:* 800-280-6660 ■ *Web:* starlinebrass.com	Sedalia	MO	65301	660-827-6640	
STI International Inc 114 Halmar Cove *Web:* stiguns.com	Georgetown	TX	78628	512-819-0656	
Stic-adhesive Products Company Inc 3950 Medford St *Web:* www.sticadhesive.com	Los Angeles	CA	90063	323-268-2956	
Stoneybrook West Golf Club LLC 15501 Towne Commons Blvd *Web:* www.stoneybrookgolf.com	Winter Garden	FL	34787	407-877-8533	
Stretch Boards 983 Tower Pl *Web:* www.stretchboards.com	Santa Cruz	CA	95062	831-479-7309	
Summit Canyon Mountaineering 732 Grand Ave *Web:* summitcanyon.com	Glenwood Springs	CO	81601	970-945-6994	
Summit Hut 5045 E Speedway Blvd *TF:* 800-499-8696 ■ *Web:* www.summithut.com	Tucson	AZ	85712	520-325-1554	795-7350
Sun & Ski Sports 10560 Bissonnet St Ste 100 *TF:* 866-786-3869 ■ *Web:* www.sunandski.com	Houston	TX	77099	281-340-5000	
Sun & Snow Sports Inc 3780 Jackson Rd Ste J *Web:* www.sunandsnow.com	Ann Arbor	MI	48103	734-663-9515	
Sundance Beach 59 S La Patera Ln *TF:* 877-968-0036 ■ *Web:* www.sundancebeach.com	Goleta	CA	93117	877-968-0036	
Super Runners Shop Inc 355 New York Ave *Web:* www.superrunnersshop.com	Huntington	NY	11743	631-549-3006	
Surf Associates Inc 1701 N Federal Hwy *Web:* www.bcsurf.com	Fort Lauderdale	FL	33305	954-563-1366	
Surf Technicians LLC 2685 Mattison Ln *Web:* www.surftech.com	Santa Cruz	CA	95062	831-479-4944	
Switlik Parachute Company Inc 1325 E State St *Web:* www.switlik.com	Trenton	NJ	08609	609-587-3300	
Syndrome Distribution Inc 1410 Vantage Ct *Web:* www.syndromedist.com	Vista	CA	92081	760-560-0440	
Tabata U.S.A. Inc 2380 Mira Mar Ave *Web:* www.tusa.com	Long Beach	CA	90815	562-498-3708	
Tack Room Too Inc 201 Lee St Sw *TF:* 800-258-2581 ■ *Web:* www.tackroomtoo.com	Tumwater	WA	98501	360-357-4268	
Tactics Boardshop 375 W 4th Ave Ste 202 *Web:* www.boardtactics.com	Eugene	OR	97401	541-349-0087	
Tahoe Mountain Sports 11200 Donner Pass Rd Ste 5e *TF:* 866-891-9177 ■ *Web:* www.tahoemountainsports.com	Truckee	CA	96161	866-891-9177	
Tam O'shanter Country Club 5051 Orchard Lk Rd *Web:* www.blendedlearningworkshop.com	West Bloomfield	MI	48323	248-855-1900	
Team Estrogen Inc 21350 NW Mauzey Rd *Web:* www.teamestrogen.com	Hillsboro	OR	97124	503-924-2030	
Tennis Express 11022 Westheimer Rd *Web:* www.tennisexpress.com	Houston	TX	77042	713-781-4848	781-1237
Tennis Pro Shop 19101 Peninsula Club Dr *Web:* www.thepeninsulaclub.com	Cornelius	NC	28031	704-896-7676	
Texford Battery Co 2002 Milby St *TF:* 866-301-0125 ■ *Web:* www.texford.com	Houston	TX	77003	713-222-0125	
Tie Fast Vest Tools 847 W Fifth St *Web:* tie-fast.com	Chico	CA	95928	530-345-4261	
Toledo Physical Education Supply Inc 5101 Advantage Dr *TF:* 800-225-7749 ■ *Web:* www.tpesonline.com	Toledo	OH	43612	419-726-8122	
Toledo Ticket Co 3963 Catawba St *Web:* www.toledoticket.com	Toledo	OH	43612	419-476-5424	
Total Hockey Inc 5833 Suemandy Rd *Web:* www.totalhockey.net	Saint Peters	MO	63376	636-397-6370	
Traditions Performance Firearms 1375 Boston Post Rd *Web:* www.traditionsfirearms.com	Old Saybrook	CT	06475	860-388-4656	
Treads Bicycle Outfitters 16701 E Iliff Ave *Web:* www.treads.com	Aurora	CO	80013	303-750-1671	
Trek Bicycle Superstore 4240 Kearny Mesa Rd Ste 108 *Web:* www.trekbicyclesuperstore.com	San Diego	CA	92111	858-974-8735	
Trek Bicycles of American Fork 356 North 750 West Ste D11 *Web:* trekaf.com	American Fork	UT	84003	801-763-1222	
Trek Bikes of Ventura 4060 E Main St *Web:* www.trekbikesofventura.com	Ventura	CA	93003	805-644-8735	
Tri-State Pumps Inc 1162 Chastain Rd *TF:* 800-868-4631 ■ *Web:* www.tsppumps.com	Liberty	SC	29657	864-843-8100	
Triathlete Sports 186 Exchange St *TF:* 800-635-0528 ■ *Web:* www.triathletesports.com	Bangor	ME	04401	207-990-2013	
Trijicon Inc 49385 Shafer Ave PO Box 930059 *Web:* www.trijicon.com	Wixom	MI	48393	248-960-7700	
TriSports.com 4495 S Coach Dr *TF:* 888-293-3934 ■ *Web:* www.trisports.com	Tucson	AZ	85714	888-293-3934	
Tum Yeto Inc 2001 Commercial St *Web:* www.tumyeto.com	San Diego	CA	92113	619-232-7523	
Turbo 2 n 1 Grip 46460 Continental Dr *TF:* 800-530-9878 ■ *Web:* www.turbogrips.com	Chesterfield	MI	48047	586-598-3948	
Turner's Outdoorsman 11738 Sanmarino St Ste A *Web:* www.turners.com	Rancho Cucamonga	CA	91730	909-923-3009	
U.S. Kids Golf LLC 3040 Northwoods Pkwy *TF:* 888-387-5437 ■ *Web:* www.uskidsgolf.com	Norcross	GA	30071	770-441-3077	
Ultimate Paint Ball 7075 Stormy Ln *Web:* www.ultimatepaintball.com	Bonne Terre	MO	63628	573-358-1300	
Val Surf Inc 4810 Whitsett Ave *TF:* 888-825-7873 ■ *Web:* www.valsurf.com	Valley Village	CA	91607	818-769-6977	
Vance Outdoors Inc 3723 Cleveland Ave *Web:* www.vanceoutdoors.com	Columbus	OH	43224	614-471-7000	
Viking Ski Shop Inc 3422 W Fullerton Ave *Web:* vikingskishop.com	Chicago	IL	60647	773-276-1222	
Volquartsen Custom Ltd 24276 240th St PO Box 397 *Web:* volquartsen.com	Carroll	IA	51401	712-792-4238	
Vyatek Sports Inc 1711 W University Dr Ste 155 *Web:* www.vyatek.com	Tempe	AZ	85281	480-998-2046	
Wapsi Fly Co 27 County Rd 458 *Web:* www.wapsifly.com	Mountain Home	AR	72653	870-425-9500	
Warehouse Skateboards Inc 1638 Military Cutoff Rd Ste 101 *Web:* www.warehouseskateboards.com	Wilmington	NC	28403	910-509-9599	
Warrior Custom Golf Inc 15 Mason Ste A *TF:* 800-600-5113 ■ *Web:* www.warriorcustomgolf.com	Irvine	CA	92618	949-699-2499	
Waterline Technologies Inc 620 N Santiago St *Web:* waterlinetechnologies.com	Santa Ana	CA	92701	714-564-9100	
Wave Loch Inc 210 Westbourne St *Web:* www.waveloch.com	La Jolla	CA	92037	858-454-1777	
Western Power Sports Inc 601 E Gowen Rd *TF:* 800-999-3388 ■ *Web:* www.wps-inc.com	Boise	ID	83716	208-376-8400	375-8901
Wheel & Sprocket 6940 N Santa Monica Blvd *Web:* www.wheelandsprocket.com	Fox Point	WI	53217	414-247-8100	
Wheel & Sprocket Inc 5722 S 108th St *TF:* 866-995-9918 ■ *Web:* wheelandsprocket.com	Hales Corners	WI	53130	414-529-6600	
Wilmette Bicycle & Sport Shop 605 Green Bay Rd *Web:* wwww.wilmettesportshop.com	Wilmette	IL	60091	847-251-1404	
Worldwide Golf Co 560 E 2100 S *Web:* www.worldwidegolfshops.com	Salt Lake City	UT	84106	801-487-8233	466-5713
WrestlingGearCom Ltd 655 W Grand Ave Ste 140 *Web:* www.wrestlinggear.com	Elmhurst	IL	60126	630-832-0500	
Xs Sight Systems Inc 2401 Ludelle St *TF:* 888-744-4880 ■ *Web:* www.xssights.com	Fort Worth	TX	76105	817-536-0136	
Zimmer Enterprises Inc 911 Senate Dr *Web:* www.pbj-sport.com	Dayton	OH	45459	937-428-1057	

712 SPORTS COMMISSIONS & REGULATORY AGENCIES - STATE

Name / Address	City	State	Zip	Phone	Fax
Arizona Racing Dept 1110 W Washington St Ste 260 *Web:* racing.az.gov	Phoenix	AZ	85007	602-364-1700	364-1703
Arkansas Racing Commission 1509 W Seventh St Rm 505 *Web:* www.dfa.arkansas.gov	Little Rock	AR	72201	501-682-1467	682-5273
California Athletic Commission 1430 Howe Ave *Web:* www.dca.ca.gov	Sacramento	CA	95825	916-263-2195	263-2197
California Horse Racing Board 1010 Hurley Way Rm 300 *Web:* www.chrb.ca.gov	Sacramento	CA	95825	916-263-6000	263-6042
Delaware Harness Racing Commission 2320 S Dupont Hwy *Web:* dda.delaware.gov	Dover	DE	19901	302-698-4599	697-6287
Delaware Thoroughbred Racing Commission 2320 S DuPont Hwy *Web:* dda.delaware.gov	Dover	DE	19901	302-698-4599	
Energy and Environment Cabinet 500 Mero St Ste 5 *Web:* www.eec.ky.gov	Frankfort	KY	40601	502-564-3350	564-3969
Idaho Racing Commission 700 S Stratford Dr *Web:* isp.idaho.gov	Meridian	ID	83642	208-884-7080	884-7098
Illinois Racing Board 100 W Randolph St Ste 5-700 **Fax Area Code:* 866 ■ *Web:* www2.illinois.gov	Chicago	IL	60601	312-814-2600	323-0273*
Indiana Horse Racing Commission 150 W Market St Ste 530 *Web:* www.in.gov	Indianapolis	IN	46204	317-233-3119	233-4470
Kentucky Horse Racing Authority 4063 Iron Works Pkwy Bldg B *Web:* khrc.ky.gov	Lexington	KY	40511	859-246-2040	246-2039
Louisiana Racing Commission 320 N Carrollton Ave Ste 2-B *Web:* horseracing.louisiana.gov	New Orleans	LA	70119	504-483-4000	483-4898
Maryland Racing Commission 500 N Calvert St Rm 201 *Web:* www.dllr.state.md.us	Baltimore	MD	21202	410-230-6320	
Maryland State Athletic Commission 500 N Calvert St Rm 304 *Web:* www.dllr.state.md.us/license/occprof/athlet.html	Baltimore	MD	21202	410-230-6223	333-6314
Massachusetts State Boxing Commission 1 Ashburton Pl Rm 1301 *Web:* www.mass.gov/mbc	Boston	MA	02108	617-727-3200	727-5732
Massachusetts State Racing Commission 1 Ashurton Pl 11th Fl *Web:* www.mass.gov	Boston	MA	02108	617-727-2581	
Michigan Racing Commissioners Office 525 W Allegan St PO Box 30773 *Web:* www.michigan.gov	Lansing	MI	48909	517-335-1420	241-3018

	City	State	Zip	Phone	Fax
Nebraska State Racing Commission 5903 Walker Ave. *Web:* nebraskaracingcommission.com	Lincoln	NE	68507	402-471-4155	
Nevada State Athletic Commission 555 E Washington Ave Ste 3300 *Web:* www.boxing.nv.gov	Las Vegas	NV	89101	702-486-2575	486-2577
New Jersey Racing Commission 140 E Front St *Web:* www.njpublicsafety.org	Trenton	NJ	08625	609-292-0613	599-1785
New Jersey State Athletic Control Board 25 Market St 1st Fl W Wing *Web:* www.state.nj.us/lps/sacb	Trenton	NJ	08625	609-292-0317	292-3756
New Mexico Racing Commission 4900 Alameda NE *Web:* www.nmrc.state.nm.us	Albuquerque	NM	87113	505-222-0700	222-0713
New York Athletic Commission 123 William St 20th Fl *TF:* 866-269-3769 ■ *Web:* www.dos.ny.gov	New York	NY	10038	212-417-5700	417-4987
North Dakota Racing Commission 500 N Ninth St *Web:* www.ndracingcommission.com	Bismarck	ND	58501	701-328-4290	
Ohio Racing Commission 77 S High St 18th Fl *Web:* www.racing.ohio.gov	Columbus	OH	43215	614-466-2757	466-1900
Pennsylvania State Athletic Commission 2601 N Third St *Web:* www.dos.pa.gov/pages/default.aspx	Harrisburg	PA	17110	717-787-5720	783-0824
South Dakota Gaming Commission 221 W Capitol Ave Ste 101 *Web:* sd.gov	Pierre	SD	57501	605-773-6050	773-6053
Texas Racing Commission 8505 Cross Pk Dr Ste 110 *Web:* txrc.state.tx.us	Austin	TX	78754	512-833-6699	833-6907
Utah Sports Commission 201 S Main St Ste 2002 *Web:* www.utahsportscommission.com	Salt Lake City	UT	84111	801-328-2372	328-2389
Washington Horse Racing Commission 6326 Martin Way Ste 209 *Web:* www.whrc.wa.gov	Olympia	WA	98516	360-459-6462	459-6461
West Virginia Racing Commission 900 Pennsylvania Ave Ste 533 *Web:* www.racing.wv.gov	Charleston	WV	25302	304-558-2150	558-6319

SPORTS FACILITIES

See Motor Speedways p. 2784; Racing & Racetracks p. 3011; Stadiums & Arenas p. 3204

713 SPORTS TEAMS - BASEBALL

See Also Sports Organizations p. 1778

	City	State	Zip	Phone	Fax
Major League Baseball (Office of the Commissioner) 245 Pk Ave 31st Fl **Fax:* PR ■ *TF Cust Svc:* 866-800-1275 ■ *Web:* mlb.mlb.com	New York	NY	10167	212-931-7800	949-5654*
Arizona Diamondbacks 401 E Jefferson St *Web:* arizona.diamondbacks.mlb.com	Phoenix	AZ	85004	602-462-6500	462-6600
Atlanta Braves PO Box 4064 *TF:* 800-326-4000 ■ *Web:* atlanta.braves.mlb.com	Atlanta	GA	30302	404-522-7630	614-1329
Baltimore Orioles Oriole Park 333 W Camden St *Web:* orioles.com	Baltimore	MD	21201	410-685-9800	
Boston Red Sox Fenway Pk 4 Yawkey Way *Web:* boston.redsox.mlb.com	Boston	MA	02215	617-226-6000	236-6797
Brooklyn Cyclones 1904 Surf Ave MCU Park *Web:* www.brooklyncyclones.com	Brooklyn	NY	11224	718-449-8497	
Camden Riversharks 401 N Delware Ave	Camden	NJ	08102	856-963-2600	
Chicago Cubs 1060 W Addison St Ste 1 **Fax:* PR ■ *Web:* chicago.cubs.mlb.com	Chicago	IL	60613	773-404-2827	404-4129*
Chicago White Sox US Cellular Field 333 W 35th St *Web:* chicago.whitesox.mlb.com	Chicago	IL	60616	312-674-1000	
Cincinnati Reds 100 Joe Nuxhall Way *TF:* 877-647-7337 ■ *Web:* cincinnati.reds.mlb.com	Cincinnati	OH	45202	513-381-7337	765-7342
Cleveland Indians 2401 Ontario St **Fax:* Cust Svc ■ *Web:* cleveland.indians.mlb.com	Cleveland	OH	44115	216-420-4487	420-4799*
Colorado Rockies Coors Field 2001 Blake St **Fax:* PR ■ *Web:* colorado.rockies.mlb.com	Denver	CO	80205	303-292-0200	312-2115*
Delaware 87ers 24 Vardry St Ste 201 *Web:* www.nbadleague.com	Greenville	SC	29601	864-248-1100	
Detroit Tigers Comerica Pk 2100 Woodward Ave **Fax:* PR ■ *TF:* 866-800-1275 ■ *Web:* detroit.tigers.mlb.com	Detroit	MI	48201	313-962-4000	471-2138*
Houston Astros Minute Maid Pk 501 Crawford St *TF:* 800-771-2303 ■ *Web:* houston.astros.mlb.com	Houston	TX	77002	713-259-8000	799-9562
Kansas City Royals Kauffman Stadium 1 Royal Way *TF Sales:* 800-676-9257 ■ *Web:* kansascity.royals.mlb.com	Kansas City	MO	64129	816-921-8000	921-5775
Lancaster Barnstormers & Keystone Baseball 650 N Prince St *Web:* www.lancasterbarnstormers.com	Lancaster	PA	17603	717-509-1340	
Los Angeles Angels of Anaheim Angel Stadium 2000 Gene Autry Way **Fax:* PR ■ *Web:* losangeles.angels.mlb.com	Anaheim	CA	92806	714-940-2000	940-2205*
Los Angeles Dodgers Dodger Stadium 1000 Elysian Pk Ave **Fax:* PR ■ *Web:* losangeles.dodgers.mlb.com	Los Angeles	CA	90012	323-224-1500	224-1269*
Miami Marlins Marlins Park 501 Marlins Way *Web:* marlins.com	Miami	FL	33125	305-480-1300	
Milwaukee Brewers Miller Pk 1 Brewers Way *TF:* 877-722-6458 ■ *Web:* milwaukee.brewers.mlb.com	Milwaukee	WI	53214	414-902-4452	902-4588
Minnesota Twins Metrodome 34 Kirby Puckett Pl *TF:* 800-338-9467 ■ *Web:* minnesota.twins.mlb.com	Minneapolis	MN	55415	612-375-1366	
New Britain Rock Cats 230 John Karbonic Way S Main St New Britain Stadium *Web:* www.milb.com/index.jsp	New Britain	CT	06051	860-224-8383	
New York Mets Shea Stadium 123-01 Roosevelt Ave *TF:* 888-652-7467 ■ *Web:* newyork.mets.mlb.com	Flushing	NY	11368	718-507-6387	507-6395
New York Yankees Yankee Stadium 161st St & River Ave *Web:* newyork.yankees.mlb.com	Bronx	NY	10451	718-293-4300	293-8431
Norfolk Tides Baseball 150 Park Ave Harbor Park *Web:* www.milb.com/index.jsp	Norfolk	VA	23510	757-622-2222	
Oakland Athletics 7000 Coliseum Way *Web:* oakland.athletics.mlb.com	Oakland	CA	94621	510-638-4900	568-3770
Philadelphia Phillies Citizens Bank Pk 1 Citizens Bank Pk Way *Web:* philadelphia.phillies.mlb.com	Philadelphia	PA	19148	215-463-1000	
Pittsburgh Pirates 115 Federal St PO Box 7000 *TF:* 800-289-2827 ■ *Web:* pittsburgh.pirates.mlb.com	Pittsburgh	PA	15212	412-321-2827	
Reading Phillies Baseball Club 1900 Centre Ave *Web:* tickets.readingphillies.com	Reading	PA	19612	610-375-8469	
San Diego Padres Petco Pk 100 Park Blvd *Web:* sandiego.padres.mlb.com	San Diego	CA	92101	619-795-5000	795-5035
San Francisco Giants AT & T Pk 24 Willie Mays Plaza 24 Willie Mays Plz *Web:* sanfrancisco.giants.mlb.com	San Francisco	CA	94107	415-972-2000	
Seattle Mariners Safeco Field 1250 First Ave S *TF:* 800-255-7932 ■ *Web:* seattle.mariners.mlb.com	Seattle	WA	98134	206-346-4000	346-4050
Spokane Indians Baseball Club 602 N Havana St *Web:* spokane.indians.milb.com	Spokane	WA	99202	509-535-2922	
St. Louis Cardinals Busch Stadium 700 Clark St *Web:* cardinals.com	St. Louis	MO	63102	314-345-9600	
St. Paul Saints Baseball Club Inc 1771 Energy Park Dr *Web:* www.saintsbaseball.com	Saint Paul	MN	55108	651-644-6659	
Tampa Bay Rays Tropicana Field 1 Tropicana Dr St *Web:* raysbaseball.com	Petersburg	FL	33705	727-825-3137	
Texas Rangers Rangers Ballpark in Arlington 1000 Ballpark Way *TF:* 866-800-1275 ■ *Web:* texas.rangers.mlb.com	Arlington	TX	76011	817-273-5222	273-5190
Toledo Mud Hens Baseball Club Inc 406 Washington St *Web:* www.milb.com/index.jsp?sid=t512	Toledo	OH	43604	419-725-4367	
Toronto Blue Jays 1 Blue Jays Way Ste 3200 **Fax:* PR ■ *TF:* 888-654-6529 ■ *Web:* toronto.bluejays.mlb.com	Toronto	ON	M5V1J1	416-341-1000	341-1250*
Washington Nationals Nationals Park 1500 S Capitol St *Web:* nationals.com	SE. Washington	DC	20003	202-675-6287	
Winston-Salem Dash 926 Brookstown Ave *Web:* www.milb.com	Winston-salem	NC	27101	336-714-2287	

714 SPORTS TEAMS - BASKETBALL

See Also Sports Organizations p. 1778

714-1 National Basketball Association (NBA)

	City	State	Zip	Phone	Fax
National Basketball Association (NBA) 645 Fifth Ave *Web:* www.nba.com	New York	NY	10022	212-407-8000	832-3861
Atlanta Hawks Centennial Tower 101 Marietta St NW Ste 1900 *Web:* www.nba.com/hawks	Atlanta	GA	30303	404-827-3800	827-3880
Boston Celtics 226 Cswy St 4th Fl *Web:* www.nba.com	Boston	MA	02114	617-854-8000	367-4286
Charlotte Bobcats 333 E Trade St *Web:* www.nba.com/bobcats	Charlotte	NC	28202	704-688-8600	
Chicago Bulls 1901 W Madison St *Web:* www.nba.com	Chicago	IL	60612	312-455-4000	
Cleveland Cavaliers Quicken Loans Arena 1 Ctr Ct **Fax:* PR ■ *TF:* 800-332-2287 ■ *Web:* www.nba.com	Cleveland	OH	44115	216-420-2000	420-2298*
Dallas Mavericks 2909 Taylor St *Web:* www.nba.com	Dallas	TX	75226	214-747-6287	658-7121
Denver Nuggets 1000 Chopper Cir *Web:* www.nba.com	Denver	CO	80204	303-405-1100	405-1315
Detroit Pistons Palace at Auburn Hills 5 Championship Dr *Web:* www.nba.com	Auburn Hills	MI	48326	248-377-0100	377-4262
Golden State Warriors 1011 Broadway **Fax Area Code:* 404 ■ *TF:* 866-648-4668 ■ *Web:* www.nba.com	Oakland	CA	94607	510-986-2200	827-3880*
Houston Rockets 1510 Polk St **Fax:* Hum Res ■ *TF:* 866-648-4668 ■ *Web:* www.nba.com/rockets	Houston	TX	77002	713-758-7200	758-7396*
Indiana Pacers Conseco Fieldhouse 125 S Pennsylvania St *Web:* www.nba.com/pacers	Indianapolis	IN	46204	317-917-2500	917-2599

	City	State	Zip	Phone	Fax
Los Angeles Clippers Staples Ctr 1111 S Figueroa St Ste 1100 *TF:* 855-895-0872 ■ *Web:* www.nba.com/clippers	Los Angeles	CA	90015	213-742-7100	742-7550
Los Angeles Lakers 555 N Nash St *TF:* 866-648-4668 ■ *Web:* www.nba.com/lakers	El Segundo	CA	90245	310-426-6000	426-6105
Memphis Grizzlies FedExForum 191 Beale St *Web:* www.nba.com/grizzlies	Memphis	TN	38103	901-205-1234	205-1235
Miami Heat American Airlines Arena 601 Biscayne Blvd *Web:* www.nba.com	Miami	FL	33132	786-777-1000	777-1615
Milwaukee Bucks Bradley Ctr 1001 N Fourth St *Web:* www.nba.com	Milwaukee	WI	53203	414-227-0500	227-0543
Minnesota Timberwolves Target Ctr 600 First Ave N *TF:* 855-895-0872 ■ *Web:* www.nba.com	Minneapolis	MN	55403	612-673-1600	673-1699
New Jersey Nets Nets Champion Ctr 390 Murray Hill Pkwy *TF:* 800-346-6387 ■ *Web:* www.nba.com	East Rutherford	NJ	07073	201-935-8888	
New Orleans Pelicans 1450 Poydras St *Web:* www.nba.com	New Orleans	LA	70113	504-593-4700	
New York Knicks Madison Sq Garden 2 Pennsylvania Plz 14th Fl **Fax:* PR ■ *Web:* www.nba.com/knicks	New York	NY	10121	212-465-6471	465-6498*
Orlando Magic 8701 Maitland Summit Blvd *Web:* www.nba.com	Orlando	FL	32810	407-916-2400	916-2953
Philadelphia 76ers 3601 S Broad St *Web:* www.nba.com	Philadelphia	PA	19148	215-339-7600	339-7615
Phoenix Suns US Airways Ctr 201 E Jefferson St *TF:* 866-648-4668 ■ *Web:* www.nba.com/suns	Phoenix	AZ	85004	602-379-7900	379-7990
Sacramento Kings ARCO Arena 1 Sports Pkwy *TF:* 866-746-7622 ■ *Web:* www.nba.com/kings	Sacramento	CA	95834	916-928-0000	928-0727
San Antonio Spurs 1 AT & T Ctr *Web:* www.nba.com/spurs	San Antonio	TX	78219	210-444-5000	444-5003
Seattle SuperSonics 1201 Third Ave Ste 1000 *TF:* 800-743-7021 ■ *Web:* www.nba.com	Seattle	WA	98101	206-281-5800	281-5839
Trail Blazers Inc 1 N Center Ct St Ste 200 *Web:* www.trailblazers.org	Portland	OR	97227	503-234-9291	
Utah Jazz 301 W S Temple St Energy Solutions Arena **Fax:* PR ■ *Web:* www.nba.com	Salt Lake City	UT	84101	801-325-2500	325-2578*
Washington Wizards Verizon Ctr 601 F St NW *Web:* www.nba.com	Washington	DC	20004	202-661-5000	

714-2 Women's National Basketball Association (WNBA)

	City	State	Zip	Phone	Fax
Women's National Basketball Assn (WNBA) 645 Fifth Ave *Web:* www.wnba.com	New York	NY	10022	212-688-9622	
Chicago Sky 20 W Kinzie St Ste 1000 *TF:* 877-329-9622 ■ *Web:* www.wnba.com	Chicago	IL	60610	312-828-9550	
Detroit Shock 5 Championship Dr Palace at Auburn Hills	Auburn Hills	MI	48326	248-377-0100	377-0584
Houston Comets 1730 Jefferson St **Fax:* Hum Res ■ *Web:* www.wnba.com	Houston	TX	77003	713-739-7442	739-7709*
Indiana Fever Conseco Fieldhouse 125 S Pennsylvania St *TF:* 877-275-9007 ■ *Web:* www.wnba.com/fever	Indianapolis	IN	46204	317-917-2500	917-2899
Los Angeles Sparks 865 S Figueroa St Ste 104 *TF:* 888-694-3278 ■ *Web:* www.wnba.com	Los Angeles	CA	90017	213-929-1300	929-1325
Minnesota Lynx 600 First Ave N Target Ctr *Web:* www.wnba.com/lynx	Minneapolis	MN	55403	612-673-1600	673-8407
Mohegan Sun 1 Mohegan Sun Blvd *TF:* 877-962-2849 ■ *Web:* www.wnba.com	Uncasville	CT	06382	860-862-4000	862-4010
New York Liberty Madison Sq Garden 2 Pennsylvania Plz *Web:* www.wnba.com/liberty	New York	NY	10121	212-564-9622	465-6250
Phoenix Mercury US Airways Ctr 201 E Jefferson St *Web:* www.wnba.com/mercury	Phoenix	AZ	85004	602-514-8333	514-8303
San Antonio Silver Stars 1 AT & T Ctr *Web:* wnba.com/stars	San Antonio	TX	78219	210-444-5090	444-5003
Washington Mystics 627 N Glebe Rd Ste 850 *TF:* 877-962-2849 ■ *Web:* www.wnba.com	Arlington	VA	22203	202-266-2200	266-2220

715 SPORTS TEAMS - FOOTBALL

See Also Sports Organizations p. 1778

715-1 Arena Football League (AFL)

	City	State	Zip	Phone	Fax
Arena Football League (AFL) 640 N LaSalle St Ste 557 *Web:* www.arenafootball.com	Chicago	IL	60654	312-465-2200	496-3055
Arizona Rattlers 201 East Jefferson St Ste 120 *Web:* www.azrattlers.com	Phoenix	AZ	85004	602-514-8383	
New York Islanders 1255 Hempstead Tpke *TF:* 800-843-5678 ■ *Web:* islanders.nhl.com	Uniondale	NY	11553	516-501-6700	501-6762

715-2 Canadian Football League (CFL)

	City	Prov	Postal Code	Phone	Fax
Canadian Football League 50 Wellington St E 3rd Fl *TF:* 855-264-4242 ■ *Web:* www.cfl.ca	Toronto	ON	M5E1C8	416-322-9650	322-9651
BC Lions 10605 135th St *Web:* www.bclions.com	Surrey	BC	V3T4C8	604-930-5466	583-7882
Calgary Stampeders 1817 Crowchild Trail NW McMahon Stadium *Web:* www.stampeders.com	Calgary	AB	T2M4R6	403-289-0205	
Montreal Alouettes 1260 boul Robert-Bourassa Ste 100 *Web:* www.montrealalouettes.com	Montreal	QC	H3B3B9	514-871-2266	871-2277
Saskatchewan Roughriders 1910 Piffles Taylor Way PO Box 1966 *TF:* 888-474-3377 ■ *Web:* www.riderville.com	Regina	SK	S4P3E1	306-569-2323	566-4280
Toronto Argonauts 1 Blue Jays Way Ste 3300 *Web:* www.argonauts.ca	Toronto	ON	M5V1J3	416-341-2700	
Winnipeg Blue Bombers Investors Group Field315 Chancellor Matheson Rd *Web:* www.bluebombers.com	Winnipeg	MB	R3T1Z2	204-784-2583	783-5222

715-3 National Football League (NFL)

	City	State	Zip	Phone	Fax
Arizona Cardinals 8701 S Hardy Dr *TF:* 800-999-1402 ■ *Web:* www.azcardinals.com	Tempe	AZ	85284	602-379-0101	379-1819
Atlanta Falcons 4400 Falcon Pkwy *Web:* www.atlantafalcons.com	Flowery Branch	GA	30542	770-965-3115	965-3185
Baltimore Ravens 1101 Russell St *Web:* www.baltimoreravens.com	Baltimore	MD	21230	410-261-7283	
Buffalo Bills Ralph Wilson Stadium 1 Bills Dr *TF:* 877-228-4257 ■ *Web:* www.buffalobills.com	Orchard Park	NY	14127	716-648-1800	
Carolina Panthers Bank of America Stadium 800 S Mint St *TF:* 888-297-8673 ■ *Web:* www.panthers.com	Charlotte	NC	28202	704-358-7000	358-7618
Chicago Bears 1000 Football Dr *Web:* www.chicagobears.com	Lake Forest	IL	60045	847-295-6600	295-8986
Cincinnati Bengals 1 Paul Brown Stadium *TF:* 866-621-8383 ■ *Web:* www.bengals.com	Cincinnati	OH	45202	513-621-3550	621-3570
Cleveland Browns 76 Lou Groza Blvd *Web:* www.clevelandbrowns.com	Berea	OH	44017	440-891-5000	891-5009
Dallas Cowboys 1 Cowboys Pkwy *Web:* www.dallascowboys.com	Irving	TX	75063	972-556-9900	556-9304
Denver Broncos 13655 Broncos Pkwy *Web:* www.denverbroncos.com	Englewood	CO	80112	303-649-9000	
Detroit Lions 222 Republic Dr *TF:* 800-745-3000 ■ *Web:* www.detroitlions.com	Allen Park	MI	48101	313-216-4000	216-4056
Green Bay Packers 1265 Lombardi Ave PO Box 10628 *Web:* www.packers.com	Green Bay	WI	54304	920-569-7500	569-7301
Houston Texans 2 NRG Park *Web:* www.houstontexans.com	Houston	TX	77054	832-667-2002	
Indianapolis Colts 7001 W 56th St *TF:* 800-805-2658 ■ *Web:* www.colts.com	Indianapolis	IN	46254	317-297-2658	297-8971
Kansas City Chiefs Arrowhead Stadium 1 Arrowhead Dr *TF:* 800-332-6048 ■ *Web:* www.chiefs.com	Kansas City	MO	64129	816-920-9300	920-4315
Miami Dolphins 7500 SW 30th St *Web:* www.miamidolphins.com	Davie	FL	33314	305-943-8000	
Minnesota Vikings 9520 Viking Dr *TF:* 877-722-6458 ■ *Web:* www.vikings.com	Eden Prairie	MN	55344	952-828-6500	828-6540
New Orleans Saints 5800 Airline Dr *Web:* www.neworleanssaints.com	Metairie	LA	70003	504-733-0255	731-1782
New York Giants 1925 Giants Dr *Web:* www.giants.com	East Rutherford	NJ	07073	201-935-8111	
Oakland Raiders 1220 Harbor Bay Pkwy *TF:* 800-724-3377 ■ *Web:* www.raiders.com	Alameda	CA	94502	510-864-5000	864-5134
Philadelphia Eagles NovaCare Complex 1 NovaCare Way *Web:* www.philadelphiaeagles.com	Philadelphia	PA	19145	215-463-2500	339-5464
Pittsburgh Steelers 3400 S Water St *Web:* www.steelers.com	Pittsburgh	PA	15203	412-432-7800	432-7878
San Diego Chargers 4020 Murphy Canyon Rd *TF:* 877-242-7437 ■ *Web:* www.chargers.com	San Diego	CA	92123	858-874-4500	292-2760
San Francisco 49ers 4949 Centennial Blvd *Web:* www.49ers.com	Santa Clara	CA	95054	408-562-4949	727-4937
Seattle Seahawks 12 Seahawks Way *TF:* 888-635-4295 ■ *Web:* www.seahawks.com	Renton	WA	98056	888-635-4295	
Tampa Bay Buccaneers 1 Buccaneer Pl *Web:* www.buccaneers.com	Tampa	FL	33607	813-870-2700	
Tennessee Titans 460 Great Cir Rd *TF:* 800-334-4628 ■ *Web:* www.titansonline.com	Nashville	TN	37228	615-565-4000	565-4006
Washington Redskins 21300 Redskin Pk Dr *Web:* www.redskins.com	Ashburn	VA	20147	703-726-7000	726-7086

716 SPORTS TEAMS - HOCKEY

See Also Sports Organizations p. 1778

	City	State	Zip	Phone	Fax
National Hockey League (NHL) 1185 Ave of the Americas *Web:* www.nhl.com	New York	NY	10036	212-789-2000	789-2020

				Phone	Fax
Anaheim Ducks 2695 E Katella Ave *Fax Area Code: 714 ■ TF: 877-945-3946 ■ Web: ducks.nhl.com	Anaheim	CA	92806	877-945-3946	940-2953*
Boston Bruins 100 Legends Way Web: bruins.nhl.com	Boston	MA	02114	617-624-1900	523-7184
Buffalo Sabres HSBC Arena 1 Seymour H Knox III Plz TF: 888-467-2273 ■ Web: sabres.nhl.com	Buffalo	NY	14203	716-855-4100	855-4115
Calgary Flames Pengrowth Saddledome 555 Saddledome Rise SE *Fax: PR ■ Web: flames.nhl.com	Calgary	AB	T2G2W1	403-777-2177	777-2195*
Carolina Hurricanes RBC Ctr 1400 EdwaRds Mill Rd TF: 800-521-7521 ■ Web: hurricanes.nhl.com	Raleigh	NC	27607	919-467-7825	462-7030
Chicago Blackhawks 1901 W Madison St *Fax: PR ■ Web: blackhawks.nhl.com	Chicago	IL	60612	312-455-7000	455-7041*
Colorado Avalanche Pepsi Ctr 1000 Chopper Cir Web: avalanche.nhl.com	Denver	CO	80204	303-405-1100	
Columbus Blue Jackets Nationwide Arena 200 W Nationwide Blvd Ste Level Web: bluejackets.nhl.com	Columbus	OH	43215	614-246-4625	246-4007
Dallas Stars 2601 Ave of the Stars Web: stars.nhl.com	Frisco	TX	75034	214-387-5500	387-5599
Detroit Red Wings Joe Louis Arena 600 Civic Ctr Dr *Fax: PR ■ Web: redwings.nhl.com	Detroit	MI	48226	313-396-7444	567-0296*
Edmonton Oilers 11230 110th St TF: 866-414-4625 ■ Web: oilers.nhl.com	Edmonton	AB	T5G3H7	780-414-4000	409-5890
Florida Panthers BankAtlantic Ctr 1 Panther Pkwy *Fax: Sales ■ Web: panthers.nhl.com	Sunrise	FL	33323	954-835-7000	835-7200*
Los Angeles Kings Staples Ctr 1111 S Figueroa St TF: 888-546-4752 ■ Web: kings.nhl.com	Los Angeles	CA	90015	213-742-7100	
Minnesota Wild 317 Washington St TF: 866-242-5006 ■ Web: wild.nhl.com	Saint Paul	MN	55102	651-602-6000	222-1055
Montreal Canadiens Bell Centre 1260 de la Gauchetiere St W *Fax: PR ■ TF: 800-363-8162 ■ Web: canadiens.nhl.com	Montreal	QC	H3B5E8	514-989-2841	925-2144*
Nashville Predators 501 Broadway Web: predators.nhl.com	Nashville	TN	37203	615-770-2355	770-2341
New York Islanders 1535 Old Country Rd TF: 800-843-5678 ■ Web: islanders.nhl.com	Plainview	NY	11803	516-501-6700	501-6729
New York Rangers 2 Pennsylvania Plz Web: rangers.nhl.com	New York	NY	10121	212-465-6553	465-6494
Ontario Minor Hockey Association Inc 3-25 Brodie Dr Web: www.omha.net	Richmond Hill	ON	L4B3K7	905-780-6642	
Ottawa Senators 1000 Palladium Dr Scotia Bank Pl TF: 800-444-7367 ■ Web: senators.nhl.com	Kanata	ON	K2V1A5	613-599-0100	
Philadelphia Flyers Wachovia Ctr 3601 S Broad St Web: flyers.nhl.com	Philadelphia	PA	19148	215-465-4500	389-9476
Phoenix Coyotes 6751 N Sunset Blvd Ste 200 TF: 877-448-4483 ■ Web: coyotes.nhl.com	Glendale	AZ	85305	623-772-3200	772-3201
Pittsburgh Penguins 1001 Fifth Avenue TF: 800-642-7367 ■ Web: penguins.nhl.com	Pittsburgh	PA	15219	412-642-1300	642-1859
Reading Royals Hockey Club 645 Penn St 3rd Fl Web: www.royalshockey.com	Reading	PA	19601	610-898-7825	
San Jose Sharks HP Pavilion at San Jose 525 W Santa Clara St TF: 800-755-5050 ■ Web: sharks.nhl.com	San Jose	CA	95113	408-287-7070	999-5797
Tampa Bay Lightning St Pete Times Forum 401 Channelside Dr TF: 800-745-3000 ■ Web: lightning.nhl.com	Tampa	FL	33602	813-301-6500	301-1482
Toronto Maple Leafs Air Canada Ctr 40 Bay St Ste 400 Web: mapleleafs.nhl.com	Toronto	ON	M5J2X2	416-815-5700	359-9205
Vancouver Canucks 800 Griffiths Way TF: 877-788-3937 ■ Web: canucks.nhl.com	Vancouver	BC	V6B6G1	604-899-7400	899-7401
Washington Capitals 627 N Glebe Rd Ste 850 Web: capitals.nhl.com	Arlington	VA	22203	202-266-2200	

717 SPORTS TEAMS - SOCCER

See Also Sports Organizations p. 1778

				Phone	Fax
Major League Soccer (MLS) 420 Fifth Ave 7th Fl Web: www.mlssoccer.com	New York	NY	10018	212-450-1200	
Big League Dreams USA LLC 16333 Fairfield Ranch Rd Web: www.bigleaguedreams.com	Chino Hills	CA	91709	909-287-6900	
Bobcats Basketball LLC 333 E Trade St Web: www.timewarnercablearena.com	Charlotte	NC	28202	704-688-9000	
Chicago Fire 7000 S Harlem Ave TF: 888-657-3473 ■ Web: www.chicago-fire.com	Bridgeview	IL	60455	708-594-7200	496-6050
Colorado Rapids 6000 Victory Way Web: www.coloradorapids.com	Commerce	CO	80022	303-727-3500	727-3536
Colorado Storm Soccer Assoc 7002 S Revere Pkwy Ste 60 Web: www.shippertmedical.com	Centennial	CO	80112	303-799-0151	
Columbus Crew SC MAPFRE Stadium 1 Black & Gold Blvd Web: nationals.com	Columbus	OH	43211	614-447-2739	447-4109
DC United 2400 E Capitol St SE Web: www.dcunited.com	Washington	DC	20003	202-587-5000	587-5400
FC Dallas 9200 World Cup Way Ste 202 Web: www.fcdallas.com/stadium	Frisco	TX	75034	214-705-6700	705-6799
Global Sports & Entertainment Inc 300 N Continental Blvd Ste 140 Web: www.globalsports-ent.com	El Segundo	CA	90245	310-414-2690	
Houston Dynamo 1001 Avenida de las Americas Ste 200 Web: www.houstondynamo.com	Houston	TX	77010	713-276-7500	276-7580
Los Angeles Galaxy Home Depot Ctr 18400 Avalon Blvd Ste 200 TF: 877-342-5299 ■ Web: www.lagalaxy.com	Carson	CA	90746	310-630-2200	630-2250
Manchester Monarchs 555 Elm St Web: www.manchestermonarchs.com	Manchester	NH	03101	603-626-7825	
Milwaukee Wave LLC 510 W Kilbourn Ave TF: 800-745-3000 ■ Web: www.milwaukeewave.com	Milwaukee	WI	53203	414-224-9283	224-9290
Montreal Impact Stade Saputo 4750 Sherbrooke East St Web: nationals.com	Montreal	QC	H1V3S8	514-328-3668	328-1287
Monumental Sports & Entertainment LLC 601 F St NW Web: www.monumentalsports.com	Washington	DC	20004	202-628-3200	
MVP Sports Spot 3701 32nd St SE Web: www.soccerspot.net	Grand Rapids	MI	49512	616-464-1000	
Natick Junior Redmen 15 W St Web: www.natickma.gov/184/police-department	Natick	MA	01760	508-653-9900	
New England Revolution Gillette Stadium 1 Patriot Pl TF: 877-438-7387 ■ Web: www.revolutionsoccer.net	Foxboro	MA	02035	877-438-7387	
New York City FC 600 Third Ave 30th Fl Web: raysbaseball.com	New York	NY	10016	212-738-5900	738-5901
New York Red Bulls 600 Cape May St TF: 877-727-6223 ■ Web: www.newyorkredbulls.com	Harrison	NJ	07029	877-727-6223	
Richmond Kickers Soccer Club Inc 2001 Maywill St Ste 203 Web: www.richmondkickers.com	Richmond	VA	23230	804-644-5425	
Suwanee Sports Academy 3640 Burnette Rd Web: ssasports.com	Suwanee	GA	30024	770-614-6686	
Swix Sport USA Inc 600 Research Dr Web: www.swixsport.com	Wilmington	MA	01887	978-657-4820	

718 SPRINGS - HEAVY-GAUGE

				Phone	Fax
Automatic Spring Products Corp 803 Taylor Ave Web: www.automaticspring.com	Grand Haven	MI	49417	616-842-7800	842-4380
Barnes Group Inc 123 Main St NYSE: B ■ Web: barnesgroupinc.com	Bristol	CT	06011	860-583-7070	
General Wire Spring Co 1101 Thompson Ave TF: 800-245-6200 ■ Web: www.generalwirespring.com	McKees Rocks	PA	15136	412-771-6300	771-6317
Pa-Ted Spring Company Inc 137 Vincent P Kelly Rd Web: patedspring.com	Bristol	CT	06010	860-582-6368	583-1044
Perfection Spring & Stamping Corp 1449 E Algonquin Rd Web: www.pss-corp.com	Mount Prospect	IL	60056	847-437-3900	437-1322
Rockford Spring Co 3801 S Central Ave Web: www.rockfordspring.com	Rockford	IL	61102	815-968-3000	968-3100
Service Spring Corp 4370 Moline Martin Rd TF: 800-752-8522 ■ Web: www.sscorp.com	Millbury	OH	43447	419-838-6081	838-6071
Southern Spring & Stamping Inc 401 Sub Stn Rd TF: 800-450-5882 ■ Web: www.southernspring.com	Venice	FL	34285	941-488-2276	485-9156
Stanley Spring & Stamping Corp 5050 W Foster Ave Web: www.stanleyspring.com	Chicago	IL	60630	773-777-2600	

719 SPRINGS - LIGHT-GAUGE

				Phone	Fax
American Coil Spring Co 1041 E Keating Ave Web: americancoil.com	Muskegon	MI	49442	231-726-4021	
Atlantic Spring PO Box 650 TF: 877-231-6474 ■ Web: www.mw-ind.com	Flemington	NJ	08822	908-788-5800	788-0511
Century Spring Corp 222 E 16th St TF: 800-237-5225 ■ Web: www.centuryspring.com	Los Angeles	CA	90015	213-749-1466	749-3802
Connecticut Spring & Stamping Corp 48 Spring Ln *Fax: Cust Svc ■ Web: ctspring.com	Farmington	CT	06034	860-677-1341	677-7199*
Dudek & Bock Spring Mfg Co 5100 W Roosevelt Rd Web: www.dudek-bock.com	Chicago	IL	60644	773-379-4100	379-4108
Economy Spring & Stamping Co 29 DePaolo Dr TF: 800-237-5225 ■ Web: www.mw-ind.com	Southington	CT	06489	860-621-7358	621-7882
Exacto Spring Corp 1201 Hickory St Web: www.exacto.com	Grafton	WI	53024	262-377-3970	377-3854
Fennell Spring LLC 295 Hemlock St Web: www.fennellspring.com	Horseheads	NY	14845	607-739-3541	739-7601
General Wire Spring Co 1101 Thompson Ave TF: 800-245-6200 ■ Web: www.generalwirespring.com	McKees Rocks	PA	15136	412-771-6300	771-6317
Hickory Springs Mfg Co 235 Second Ave NW TF: 800-438-5341 ■ Web: www.hsmsolutions.com	Hickory	NC	28601	800-438-5341	
John Evans' Sons Inc 1 Spring Ave PO Box 885 Web: www.springcompany.com	Lansdale	PA	19446	215-368-7700	368-9019
Lee Spring Company Inc 140 58th St Unit 3C TF: 800-110-2500 ■ Web: www.leespring.com	Brooklyn	NY	11220	718-236-2222	236-3919

				Phone	Fax
Leggett & Platt Inc Number 1 Leggett Rd PO Box 757 *NYSE:* LEG ■ *TF:* 800-888-4569 ■ *Web:* www.leggett.com	Carthage	MO	64836	417-358-8131	358-6996
Maryland Precision Spring Co 8900 Kelso Dr *Web:* www.mw-ind.com	Baltimore	MD	21221	410-391-7400	687-9223
Mastercoil Spring 4010 Albany *Web:* www.mastercoil.com	McHenry	IL	60050	815-344-0051	344-0071
Michigan Spring & Stamping LLC 2700 Wickham Dr *Web:* www.msands.com	Muskegon	MI	49441	231-755-1691	755-3449
Micromatic Spring & Stamping Company Inc 45 N Church St *Web:* www.micromaticspring.com	Addison	IL	60101	847-671-6600	671-3452
Mid-West Spring & Stamping Co 1404 Joliet Rd Unit C *TF:* 800-619-0909 ■ *Web:* www.mwspring.com	Romeoville	IL	60446	630-739-3800	
Monticello Spring Corp 3137 Freeman Rd PO Box 705 *Web:* www.monticellospring.com	Monticello	IN	47960	574-583-8090	583-9299
Newcomb Spring Corp 235 Spring St *TF:* 888-579-3051 ■ *Web:* www.newcombspring.com	Southington	CT	06489	860-621-0111	621-7048
Pa-Ted Spring Company Inc 137 Vincent P Kelly Rd *Web:* patedspring.com	Bristol	CT	06010	860-582-6368	583-1044
Perfection Spring & Stamping Corp 1449 E Algonquin Rd *Web:* www.pss-corp.com	Mount Prospect	IL	60056	847-437-3900	437-1322
Peterson Spring 21200 Telegraph Rd *Web:* www.pspring.com	Southfield	MI	48033	248-799-5400	357-3176
Plymouth Spring Company Inc 281 Lake Ave *Web:* www.plymouthspring.com	Bristol	CT	06010	860-584-0594	584-0943
Precision Coil Spring Co 10107 Rose Ave *Web:* www.pcspring.com	El Monte	CA	91731	626-444-0561	444-3712
QS/Togo Inc 355 Jay St *Web:* www.qsti.com	Coldwater	MI	49036	517-278-2391	279-4680
R & L Spring Co 1097 Geneva Pkwy *Web:* www.rlspring.com	Lake Geneva	WI	53147	262-249-7854	249-7866
Rockford Spring Co 3801 S Central Ave *Web:* www.rockfordspring.com	Rockford	IL	61102	815-968-3000	968-3100
Rowley Spring & Stamping Corp 210 Redstone Hill Rd *Web:* www.rowleyspring.com	Bristol	CT	06010	860-582-8175	
Southern Spring & Stamping Inc 401 Sub Stn Rd *TF:* 800-450-5882 ■ *Web:* www.southernspring.com	Venice	FL	34285	941-488-2276	485-9156
Spring Dynamics Inc 7378 Research Dr *TF:* 888-274-8432 ■ *Web:* www.springdynamics.com	Almont	MI	48003	810-798-2622	798-2902
Spring Engineers Inc 9740 Tanner Rd *TF:* 800-899-9488 ■ *Web:* springhouston.com	Houston	TX	77041	713-690-9488	690-1199
Stanley Spring & Stamping Corp 5050 W Foster Ave *Web:* www.stanleyspring.com	Chicago	IL	60630	773-777-2600	
Twist Inc 47 S Limestone St *Web:* www.twistinc.com	Jamestown	OH	45335	937-675-9581	675-6781
Walker Corp 1555 Vintage Ave *Web:* www.walkercorp.com	Ontario	CA	91761	909-390-4300	
Winamac Coil Spring Inc 512 N Smith St *Web:* www.winamaccoilspring.com	Kewanna	IN	46939	574-653-2186	653-2645
Wire Products Company Inc 14601 Industrial Pkwy *Web:* www.universalfabassembly.com/index.html	Cleveland	OH	44135	216-267-0777	267-7972
Yost Superior Co PO Box 1487 *Web:* www.yostsuperior.com	Springfield	OH	45501	937-323-7591	323-5180

720 STADIUMS & ARENAS

See Also Convention Centers p. 2148; Performing Arts Facilities p. 2912

				Phone	Fax
500 Festival Inc 500 Festival Bldg 21 Virginia Ave Ste 500 *Web:* www.500festival.com	Indianapolis	IN	46204	317-927-3378	
Air Canada Centre 40 Bay St *Web:* www.theaircanadacentre.com	Toronto	ON	M5J2X2	416-815-5500	
Alamodome 100 Montana St *TF:* 800-884-3663 ■ *Web:* www.alamodome.com	San Antonio	TX	78203	210-207-3663	207-3646
Albert Lea City Arena 701 Lk Chapeau Dr *Web:* cityofalbertlea.org	Albert Lea	MN	56007	507-377-4374	
Alerus Ctr 1200 42nd St S *Web:* www.aleruscenter.com	Grand Forks	ND	58201	701-792-1200	746-6511
Allen County War Memorial Coliseum 4000 Parnell Ave *TF:* 800-745-3000 ■ *Web:* www.memorialcoliseum.com	Fort Wayne	IN	46805	260-482-9502	484-1637
Allstate Arena 6920 Mannheim Rd *Web:* rosemont.com/allstate	Rosemont	IL	60018	847-635-6601	635-6606
Aloha Stadium 99-500 Salt Lk Blvd *Web:* www.alohastadium.hawaii.gov	Honolulu	HI	96818	808-483-2500	483-2823
American Airlines Arena 601 Biscayne Blvd *Web:* www.aaarena.com	Miami	FL	33132	786-777-1000	
American Airlines Ctr 2500 Victory Ave *TF:* 800-745-3000 ■ *Web:* www.americanairlinescenter.com	Dallas	TX	75219	214-222-3687	
Angel Stadium 2000 Gene Autry Way *TF:* 866-800-1275 ■ *Web:* losangeles.angels.mlb.com	Anaheim	CA	92806	714-940-2000	940-2244
Arrowhead Stadium 1 Arrowhead Dr **Fax:* PR ■ *Web:* www.chiefs.com/arrowhead	Kansas City	MO	64129	816-920-9300	923-4719*
Arts Midwest 2908 Hennepin Ave Ste 200 *Web:* www.artsmidwest.org	Minneapolis	MN	55408	612-341-0755	
AT & T Park 24 Willie Mays Plaza	San Francisco	CA	94107	415-972-1800	
AT&T Ctr 1 AT&T Ctr Pkwy *TF Resv:* 800-745-3000 ■ *Web:* www.attcenter.com	San Antonio	TX	78219	210-444-5000	444-5100
Bank of America Stadium 800 S Mint St *Web:* www.panthers.com	Charlotte	NC	28202	704-358-7000	
Bankers Life Fieldhouse 125 S Pennsylvania St *Web:* www.bankerslifefieldhouse.com	Indianapolis	IN	46204	317-917-2500	
Bay Area Renaissance Festival at Mosi 11315 N 46th St *Web:* bayarearenfest.com	Tampa	FL	33617	813-983-0111	
Big Night Entertainment Group 33 Union St 2nd Fl *Web:* www.bneg.com	Boston	MA	02108	617-338-4343	
Big Sandy Superstore Arena 1 Civic Ctr Plz *Web:* www.bigsandyarena.com	Huntington	WV	25701	304-696-5990	
Billy Bob's Texas 2520 Rodeo Plz *Web:* billybobstexas.com	Fort Worth	TX	76164	817-624-7117	
BMO Harris Bradley Center 1001 N Fourth St *Web:* www.bmoharrisbradleycenter.com	Milwaukee	WI	53203	414-227-0400	
Bon Secours Wellness Arena 650 N Academy St *Web:* bonsecoursarena.com	Greenville	SC	29601	864-241-3800	250-4939
Bridgestone Arena 501 Broadway *Web:* www.bridgestonearena.com	Nashville	TN	37203	615-770-2000	
British Columbia Place Stadium 777 Pacific Blvd *Web:* www.bcplace.com	Vancouver	BC	V6B4Y8	604-669-2300	661-3412
Broome County Veterans Memorial Arena 1 Stuart St *Web:* broomearenaforum.com	Binghamton	NY	13901	607-778-1528	
Busch Stadium 700 Clark St *Web:* stlouis.cardinals.mlb.com	Saint Louis	MO	63102	314-345-9600	345-9523
Camp Randall Stadium 1440 Monroe St *Web:* www.uwbadgers.com	Madison	WI	53711	608-262-1866	
Canal Park Stadium 300 S Main St *TF:* 888-223-6000 ■ *Web:* www.milb.com	Akron	OH	44308	330-253-5151	
Chase Field 401 E Jefferson St *Web:* azchasefield.com	Phoenix	AZ	85004	602-462-6500	
Cincinnati Gardens 2250 Seymour Ave *Web:* www.cincygardens.com	Cincinnati	OH	45212	513-631-7793	351-5898
Clark County Event Center at The Fairgrounds 17402 Ne Delfel Rd *Web:* www.clarkcofair.com	Ridgefield	WA	98642	360-397-6180	
Columbus Civic Ctr 400 Fourth St *TF:* 800-745-3000 ■ *Web:* www.columbusciviccenter.org	Columbus	GA	31901	706-653-4482	
Coors Field 2001 Blake St *Web:* colorado.rockies.mlb.com	Denver	CO	80205	303-292-0200	312-2115
Cowtown Coliseum 121 E Exchange Ave *TF:* 888-269-8696 ■ *Web:* stockyardsrodeo.com	Fort Worth	TX	76164	817-625-1025	
David S Palmer Arena 100 W Main St *Web:* www.palmerarena.com	Danville	IL	61832	217-431-2424	431-6444
DCU Ctr 50 Foster St *Web:* www.dcucenter.com	Worcester	MA	01608	508-755-6800	929-0111
Denver Coliseum 4600 Humboldt St *Web:* www.denvercoliseum.com	Denver	CO	80216	720-865-2475	
Dodger Stadium 1000 Elysian Pk Ave *Web:* losangeles.dodgers.mlb.com/index.jsp?c_id=la	Los Angeles	CA	90012	323-224-1500	224-1269
Dort Event Ctr 3501 Lapeer Rd	Flint	MI	48503	810-744-0580	744-2906
Dunkin' Donuts Ctr 1 LaSalle Sq *Web:* www.dunkindonutscenter.com	Providence	RI	02903	401-331-0700	
Ed Smith Stadium 2700 12th St *Web:* baltimore.orioles.mlb.com	Sarasota	FL	34237	941-954-4101	365-1587
Endeavor Hall 6008 Center St *Web:* cityofclayton.org	Clayton	CA	94517	925-673-7300	
Eyebeam Atelier 540 W 21st St *Web:* www.eyebeam.org	New York	NY	10011	212-937-6580	
Family Arena 2002 Arena Pkwy *Web:* www.familyarena.com	Saint Charles	MO	63303	636-896-4242	896-4205
FARGODOME 1800 N University Dr *TF:* 855-694-6367 ■ *Web:* www.fargodome.com	Fargo	ND	58102	701-241-9100	237-0987
FedEx Field 1600 FedEx Way *Web:* www.redskins.com	Landover	MD	20785	301-276-6000	276-6001
FedEx Forum 191 Beale St *TF:* 866-648-4668 ■ *Web:* www.nba.com/grizzlies	Memphis	TN	38103	901-205-1234	205-1235
Fenway Park 4 Yawkey Way *TF:* 877-733-7699 ■ *Web:* boston.redsox.mlb.com	Boston	MA	02215	617-226-6000	226-6682
Fiesta San Antonio Commission Inc, The 2611 Broadway St *TF:* 877-723-4378 ■ *Web:* www.fiesta-sa.org	San Antonio	TX	78215	210-227-5191	
First Niagara Ctr 1 Seymour Knox III Plz *TF:* 888-223-6000 ■ *Web:* www.firstniagaracenter.com	Buffalo	NY	14203	716-855-4100	855-4122
Florida Repertory Theatre Inc 2267 Bay St *TF:* 877-787-8053 ■ *Web:* www.floridarep.org	Fort Myers	FL	33901	239-332-4665	
Ford Field 2000 Brush St Ste 200 *Web:* www.detroitlions.com	Detroit	MI	48226	313-262-2000	262-2808
Frank Erwin Ctr 1701 Red River PO Box 2929 *Web:* www.uterwincenter.com	Austin	TX	78701	512-471-7744	471-9652
Freeman Coliseum 3201 E Houston St *Web:* www.freemancoliseum.com	San Antonio	TX	78219	210-226-1177	226-5081
Georgia Dome 1 Georgia Dome Dr NW *TF:* 888-333-4406 ■ *Web:* www.gadome.com	Atlanta	GA	30313	404-223-9200	223-8011
Gila River Arena 9400 W Maryland Ave *Web:* gilariverarena.com	Glendale	AZ	85305	623-772-3800	772-3201
Gillette Stadium 1 Patriots Pl *Web:* www.gillettestadium.com	Foxboro	MA	02035	508-543-8200	
Globe Life Park In Arlington 1000 Ballpark Way *Web:* Www.texas.rangers.mlb.com	Arlington	TX	76011	817-273-5222	
Golden Spike Event Ctr 1000 North 1200 West *Web:* www.goldenspikeeventcenter.com	Ogden	UT	84404	801-399-8798	
Greater Austin Performing Arts Center Inc 701 W Riverside Dr *Web:* thelongcenter.org	Austin	TX	78704	512-457-5100	

Name / Address	City	State	Zip	Phone	Fax
Greensboro Coliseum Complex 1921 W Lee St *Web:* www.greensborocoliseum.com	Greensboro	NC	27403	336-373-7400	373-2170
Hampton Coliseum 1000 Coliseum Dr PO Box 7309 *Web:* www.hamptoncoliseum.org	Hampton	VA	23666	757-838-5650	838-2595
Harvey Wheeler Community Ctr 1276 Main St *Web:* www.concordnet.org	Concord	MA	01742	978-318-3020	
Hawthorne Direct Inc 300 N 16th St *Web:* www.hawthornedirect.com	Fairfield	IA	52556	641-472-3800	
Heinz Field 100 Art Rooney Ave *Web:* www.steelers.com	Pittsburgh	PA	15212	412-697-7181	697-7701
Hersheypark Arena & Stadium 550 W Hersheypark Dr *Web:* www.hersheyentertainment.com/giant-center	Hershey	PA	17033	717-534-3911	534-8996
Hippodrome State Theatre 25 SE Second Pl *Web:* thehipp.org	Gainesville	FL	32601	352-373-5968	
Honda Ctr 2695 E Katella Ave *TF:* 877-945-3946 ■ *Web:* www.hondacenter.com	Anaheim	CA	92806	714-704-2400	704-2443
Houston Arts Alliance 3201 Allen Pkwy Ste 250 *Web:* www.houstonartsalliance.com	Houston	TX	77019	713-527-9330	
Hubert H Humphrey Metrodome 900 S Fifth St *Web:* msfa.com	Minneapolis	MN	55415	612-332-0386	332-8334
i Wireless Ctr 1201 River Dr *TF:* 800-745-3000 ■ *Web:* www.iwirelesscenter.com	Moline	IL	61265	309-764-2001	764-2192
Independence Stadium 3301 Pershing Blvd *Web:* campingworldindependencebowl.com	Shreveport	LA	71109	318-673-7789	
Iowa State Fair (state House) Po Box 57130 *Web:* www.iowastatefair.org	Des Moines	IA	50317	515-262-3111	
Jacksonville Municipal Stadium 1 EverBank Field Dr **Fax:* Mktg ■ *Web:* www.jaguars.com	Jacksonville	FL	32202	904-633-6000	633-6055*
Jacksonville Veterans Memorial Arena 300 A Philip Randolph Blvd *Web:* www.jaxevents.com	Jacksonville	FL	32202	904-630-3900	854-0601
James J. Eagan Civic Center 1 James J Eagan Dr *Web:* www.florissantmo.com	Florissant	MO	63033	314-921-4466	
Jcd Sports Group Inc 1300 Park of Commerce Ste 272 *Web:* www.jcdsportsgroup.com	Delray Beach	FL	33445	561-265-0255	
JHE Production Group Inc 6427 Saddle Creek Ct *Web:* www.gojhe.com	Harrisburg	NC	28075	704-455-8888	
Kansas Coliseum 1279 E 85th St N *Web:* www.kansascoliseum.com	Park City	KS	67147	316-440-0888	
Kauffman Stadium 1 Royal Way **Fax Area Code:* 816 ■ *TF:* 800-676-9257 ■ *Web:* kansascity.royals.mlb.com	Kansas City	MO	64129	512-434-1542	921-5775*
Kemper Arena & American Royal Centers 1701 American Royal Ct *TF:* 800-767-7700 ■ *Web:* www.visitkc.com	Kansas City	MO	64102	816-221-5242	
Kentucky Fair & Expo Ctr 937 Phillips Ln *Web:* www.kyfairexpo.org	Louisville	KY	40209	502-367-5000	367-5139
Key Arena 305 Harrison St *Web:* www.seattlecenter.com	Seattle	WA	98109	206-684-7202	
LA STAGE Alliance 4200 Chevy Chase Dr *Web:* www.lastagealliance.com	Los Angeles	CA	90039	213-614-0556	
Ladd-Peebles Stadium 1621 Virginia St *Web:* www.laddpeeblesstadium.com	Mobile	AL	36604	251-208-2500	208-2514
Lambeau Field Atrium 1265 Lombardi Ave *Web:* www.packers.com	Green Bay	WI	54304	920-569-7500	569-7301
Laredo Energy Arena 6700 Arena Blvd *Web:* www.learena.com	Laredo	TX	78041	956-791-9192	523-7777
LC Walker Arena & Conference Ctr 955 Fourth St *Web:* www.lcwalkerarena.com	Muskegon	MI	49440	231-724-5225	
Long Beach Arena 300 E Ocean Blvd *Web:* longbeachcc.com	Long Beach	CA	90802	562-436-3636	436-9491
Los Angeles Memorial Coliseum & Sports Arena 3939 S Figueroa St *Web:* www.lacoliseum.com	Los Angeles	CA	90037	213-747-7111	
LP Field 1 Titans Way *Web:* www.titansonline.com	Nashville	TN	37213	615-565-4300	
Lubbock Municipal Auditorium/Coliseum 1625 13th St *TF:* 800-735-2989 ■ *Web:* www.mylubbock.us/departmental-websites/departments/civic-center/home	Lubbock	TX	79415	806-775-2242	775-3240
Lucas Oil Stadium 500 S Capitol Ave *Web:* www.icclos.com	Indianapolis	IN	46225	317-262-8600	
M&T Bank Stadium 1101 Russell St *Web:* www.baltimoreravens.com	Baltimore	MD	21230	410-261-7283	
Macon Centreplex Coliseum 200 Coliseum Dr *TF:* 877-532-6144 ■ *Web:* www.maconcentreplex.org	Macon	GA	31217	478-751-9152	751-9154
Martin Luther King Jr Arena 301 W Oglethorpe Ave *Web:* www.savannahga.gov	Savannah	GA	31401	912-651-6550	651-6552
Meeting House, The 5885 Robert Oliver Pl *Web:* www.themeetinghouse.org	Columbia	MD	21045	410-730-4090	
Mellon Arena 1001 Fifth Ave *Web:* www.consolenergycenter.com	Pittsburgh	PA	15219	412-642-1800	
Mercedes-Benz Superdome 1500 Girod St PO Box 52439	New Orleans	LA	70112	504-587-3663	587-3848
MetraPark Arena 308 Sixth Ave N *TF:* 800-366-8538 ■ *Web:* www.metrapark.com	Billings	MT	59101	406-256-2400	
Michigan Stadium 1201 S Main St University of Michigan *TF:* 866-296-6849 ■ *Web:* www.mgoblue.com	Ann Arbor	MI	48104	734-647-2583	764-3221
Minute Maid Park 501 Crawford St *TF:* 877-927-8767 ■ *Web:* houston.astros.mlb.com	Houston	TX	77002	713-259-8000	259-8981
Mississippi Veterans Memorial Stadium 2531 N State St *Web:* www.ms-veteransstadium.com	Jackson	MS	39216	601-354-6021	354-6019
Mullins Ctr 200 Commonwealth Ave University of Massachusetts *Web:* www.mullinscenter.com	Amherst	MA	01003	413-545-3001	
Municipal Auditorium Arena 1321 Baltimore Ave *TF:* 800-767-7700 ■ *Web:* visitkc.com/convention-center/index.aspx	Kansas City	MO	64105	816-691-3800	
Musicians On Call Inc 39 W 32nd St Ste 1103 *Web:* www.musiciansoncall.org	New York	NY	10001	212-741-2709	
Nassau Veterans Memorial Coliseum 1255 Hempstead Tpke *TF:* 800-745-3000 ■ *Web:* www.nassaucoliseum.com	Uniondale	NY	11553	516-794-9300	794-9389
Nationwide Arena 200 W Nationwide Blvd *Web:* www.nationwidearena.com	Columbus	OH	43215	614-246-2000	246-4300
Norfolk Scope Arena 201 E Brambleton Ave *TF:* 800-745-3000 ■ *Web:* www.sevenvenues.com	Norfolk	VA	23510	757-664-6464	664-6990
North Charleston Coliseum & Convention Ctr 5001 Coliseum Dr *Web:* www.northcharlestoncoliseumpac.com	North Charleston	SC	29418	843-529-5050	529-5010
Northwest Washington Fair Association 1775 Front St *Web:* www.nwwafair.com	Lynden	WA	98264	360-354-4111	
Oakland Arena & McAfee Coliseum 7000 Coliseum Way *Web:* www.coliseum.com	Oakland	CA	94621	510-569-2121	
Ohio Stadium 411 Woody Hayes Dr *Web:* www.ohiostatebuckeyes.com	Columbus	OH	43210	614-292-7572	292-0506
Olympic Ctr Arena 2634 Main St *TF:* 800-462-6236 ■ *Web:* www.orda.org	Lake Placid	NY	12946	518-523-1655	523-9275
Oriole Park at Camden Yards 333 Camden St *TF:* 888-848-2473 ■ *Web:* baltimore.orioles.mlb.com	Baltimore	MD	21201	410-547-6100	
Palace of Auburn Hills 6 Championship Dr *Web:* www.palacenet.com	Auburn Hills	MI	48326	248-377-0100	
Paul Brown Stadium 1 Paul Brown Stadium *TF:* 866-621-8383 ■ *Web:* www.bengals.com/stadium/index.html	Cincinnati	OH	45202	513-621-3550	621-3570
Petco Park 100 Pk Blvd *TF:* 866-800-1275 ■ *Web:* sandiego.padres.mlb.com	San Diego	CA	92101	619-795-5000	
Philips Arena 1 Philips Dr *Web:* www.philipsarena.com	Atlanta	GA	30303	404-878-3000	
PNC Arena 1400 EdwaRds Mill Rd *TF:* 800-745-3000 ■ *Web:* www.thepncarena.com	Raleigh	NC	27607	919-861-2300	861-2310
PNC Park 115 Federal St *TF:* 866-800-1275 ■ *Web:* www.pittsburgh.pirates.mlb.com/pit/ballpark	Pittsburgh	PA	15212	412-321-2827	
Power Balance Pavilion 1 Sports Pkwy *Web:* www.sleeptrainarena.com	Sacramento	CA	95834	916-928-0000	
Pratt Fine Arts Center 1902 S Main St *Web:* www.pratt.org	Seattle	WA	98144	206-328-2200	
Qualcomm Stadium 9449 Friars Rd *TF:* 800-400-7115 ■ *Web:* www.sandiego.gov/qualcomm	San Diego	CA	92108	619-641-3100	283-0460
Quicken Loans Arena 1 Ctr Ct *TF:* 888-894-9424 ■ *Web:* www.theqarena.com	Cleveland	OH	44115	216-420-2000	
Qwest Arena 233 S Capitol Blvd *Web:* www.centurylinkarenaboise.com	Boise	ID	83702	208-424-2200	424-2222
Rabobank Arena Theater & Convention Ctr 1001 Truxtun Ave *Web:* rabobankarena.com	Bakersfield	CA	93301	661-852-7300	861-9904
Ralph Wilson Stadium 1 Bills Dr *TF:* 877-228-4257 ■ *Web:* www.buffalobills.com	Orchard Park	NY	14127	716-648-1800	
Ravinia Festival Association 418 Sheridan Rd *Web:* www.ravinia.org	Highland Park	IL	60035	847-266-5000	
Raymond James Stadium 4201 N Dale Mabry Hwy *Web:* www.tampasportsauthority.com	Tampa	FL	33607	813-350-6500	673-4308
Reno Rodeo Association 1350 N Wells Ave *Web:* www.ci.reno.nv.us	Reno	NV	89512	775-329-3877	
Richmond Coliseum 601 E Leigh St *TF:* 800-228-9290 ■ *Web:* www.richmondcoliseum.net	Richmond	VA	23219	804-780-4970	780-4606
Robert F Kennedy Stadium 2400 E Capitol St SE *Web:* eventsdc.com/venues/rfkstadium/contactinfo.aspx	Washington	DC	20003	202-608-1100	
Rockford MetroCentre 300 Elm St *TF:* 800-745-3000 ■ *Web:* thebmoharrisbankcenter.com	Rockford	IL	61101	815-968-5600	968-5451
Roger Dean Stadium 4751 Main St *Web:* www.rogerdeanstadium.com	Jupiter	FL	33458	561-775-1818	691-6886
Rogers Arena 800 Griffiths Way *Web:* rogersarena.com	Vancouver	BC	V6B6G1	604-899-7400	
Rogers Centre 1 Blue Jays Way Ste 3000 *Web:* www.rogerscentre.com	Toronto	ON	M5V1J1	416-341-3000	
Rose Bowl 1001 Rose Bowl Dr *Web:* www.rosebowlstadium.com	Pasadena	CA	91103	626-577-3100	405-0992
Royal Farms Arena 201 W Baltimore St *Web:* www.royalfarmsarena.com	Baltimore	MD	21201	410-347-2020	
Rupp Arena 430 W Vine St *Web:* www.rupparena.com	Lexington	KY	40507	859-233-4567	253-2718
Safeco Field 1250 First Ave S *Web:* seattle.mariners.mlb.com	Seattle	WA	98134	206-346-4000	346-4050
San Jose Municipal Stadium 588 E Alma Ave *Web:* www.milb.com	San Jose	CA	95112	408-297-1435	297-1453
Scottrade Ctr 1401 Clark Ave *Web:* www.scottradecenter.com	Saint Louis	MO	63103	314-622-5400	622-5410
Scottsdale Stadium 7408 E Osborn Rd *TF:* 877-229-5042 ■ *Web:* www.scottsdaleaz.gov/stadium	Scottsdale	AZ	85251	480-312-2856	312-7729
Seattle Ctr 305 Harrison St *Web:* www.seattlecenter.com	Seattle	WA	98109	206-684-7200	
Seattle Theatre Group 911 Pine St *TF:* 877-784-4849 ■ *Web:* www.stgpresents.org	Seattle	WA	98101	206-467-5510	
Selland Arena 700 M St *Web:* www.fresnoconventioncenter.com	Fresno	CA	93721	559-445-8100	445-8110
Show Me Ctr 1333 N Sprigg St *Web:* www.showmecenter.biz	Cape Girardeau	MO	63701	573-651-2297	651-5054

	City	State	ZIP	Phone	Fax
Sioux Falls Arena 1201 NW Ave	Sioux Falls	SD	57104	605-367-7288	338-1463
TF: 800-338-3177 ■ *Web:* www.sfarena.com					
Sky Sox Stadium 4385 Tutt Blvd Security Service Field	Colorado Springs	CO	80922	719-597-1449	597-2491
TF: 866-698-4253 ■ *Web:* www.milb.com					
Soccer City LLC 5770 Springdale Rd	Cincinnati	OH	45247	513-741-8480	
Web: indoorsoccercity.com					
Soldier Field 1410 S Museum Campus Dr	Chicago	IL	60605	312-235-7000	235-7030
Web: www.soldierfield.net					
Sovereign Bank Arena 81 Hamilton Ave	Trenton	NJ	08611	609-656-3200	656-3201
Web: www.sunnationalbankcenter.com					
Sports Authority Field at Mile High 1701 Bryant St	Denver	CO	80204	720-258-3000	258-3050
Web: www.sportsauthorityfieldatmilehigh.com					
Staples Ctr 1111 S Figueroa St	Los Angeles	CA	90015	213-742-7100	
Web: www.staplescenter.com					
State Fair & Exposition 1001 Beulah Ave	Pueblo	CO	81004	719-404-2018	
TF: 800-876-4567 ■ *Web:* www.coloradostatefair.com					
Studio Theatre 1501 14th St NW	Washington	DC	20005	202-232-7267	
Web: www.studiotheatre.org					
Sullivan Arena 1600 Gambell St	Anchorage	AK	99501	907-279-0618	274-0676
Sun Devil Stadium 500 E Veterans Way Arizona State University	Tempe	AZ	85281	480-965-3482	965-1261
TF: 888-786-3857 ■ *Web:* www.thesundevils.com/viewarticle.dbml?atclid=208254937					
Sun Life Stadium 347 Don Shula Dr	Miami Gardens	FL	33056	305-943-8000	
Web: www.newmiamistadium.com					
Taco Bell Arena 1910 University Dr	Boise	ID	83725	208-426-1900	426-1998
Web: www.tacobellarena.com					
Tacoma Dome Arena & Exhibition Hall 2727 E 'D' St	Tacoma	WA	98421	253-272-3663	593-7620*
**Fax:* Mktg ■ *Web:* www.tacomadome.org					
Target Ctr Arena 600 First Ave N	Minneapolis	MN	55403	612-673-1300	673-1387
Web: www.targetcenter.com					
Thomas & Mack Ctr/Sam Boyd Stadium 4505 S Maryland Pkwy PO Box 450003	Las Vegas	NV	89154	702-895-3761	
Web: thomasandmack.com					
Times Union Ctr 51 S Pearl St	Albany	NY	12207	518-487-2000	487-2020
TF: 866-308-3394 ■ *Web:* www.timesunioncenter-albany.com					
Toyota Ctr 1510 Polk St	Houston	TX	77002	713-758-7200	758-7315
TF: 866-446-8849 ■ *Web:* www.houstontoyotacenter.com					
Tropicana Field 1 Tropicana Dr	Saint Petersburg	FL	33705	727-825-3137	825-3204
TF: 888-326-7297					
United Ctr 1901 W Madison St	Chicago	IL	60612	312-455-4500	
Web: www.unitedcenter.com					
University of Phoenix Stadium 1 Cardinals Dr	Glendale	AZ	85305	623-433-7100	
Web: www.azcardinalsstadium.com					
US Cellular Ctr 370 First Ave E	Cedar Rapids	IA	52401	319-398-5211	
TF: 800-745-3000 ■ *Web:* www.uscellularcenter.com					
US Cellular Field 333 W 35th St	Chicago	IL	60616	312-674-1000	674-5104*
**Fax:* Hum Res ■ *Web:* chicago.whitesox.mlb.com/cws/ballpark/index.jsp					
US Olympic Training Ctr 1750 E Boulder St	Colorado Springs	CO	80909	719-866-4618	325-8995
TF: 800-775-8762 ■ *Web:* www.teamusa.org					
US Olympic Training Ctr 196 Old Military Rd	Lake Placid	NY	12946	518-523-2600	
Web: teamusa.org/about-the-usoc					
Valley View Casino Ctr 3500 Sports Arena Blvd	San Diego	CA	92110	619-224-4171	224-3010
TF: 800-745-3000 ■ *Web:* www.valleyviewcasinocenter.com					
Van Andel Arena 130 Fulton St W	Grand Rapids	MI	49503	616-742-6600	742-6197
Web: www.vanandelarena.com					
Verizon Arena 1 Verizon Arena Way	North Little Rock	AR	72114	501-340-5660	
TF: 800-745-3000 ■ *Web:* www.verizonarena.com					
Verizon Ctr 601 F St NW	Washington	DC	20004	202-628-3200	
Web: verizoncenter.monumentalsportsnetwork.com					
Verizon Wireless Arena 555 Elm St	Manchester	NH	03101	603-644-5000	644-1575
Web: www.verizonwirelessarena.com					
Webster Bank Arena 600 Main St	Bridgeport	CT	06604	203-345-2300	335-1719
TF: 800-745-3000 ■ *Web:* www.websterbankarena.com					
Will Rogers Memorial Ctr 3401 W Lancaster Ave	Fort Worth	TX	76107	817-392-7469	392-8170
Web: fortworthtexas.gov					
Winnipeg Centennial Folk Festival Inc, The 211 Bannatyne Ave Ste 203	Winnipeg	MB	R3B3P2	204-231-0096	
TF: 866-301-3823 ■ *Web:* www.winnipegfolkfestival.ca					
Winnipeg Goldeyes Baseball Club Inc 1 Portage Ave E	Winnipeg	MB	R3B3N3	204-982-2273	
Web: www.goldeyes.com					
Winston-Salem Entertainment-Sports Complex 2825 University Pkwy	Winston-Salem	NC	27105	336-758-2410	727-2922
Web: www.ljvm.com					
Wrigley Field 1060 W Addison St	Chicago	IL	60613	773-404-2827	404-4129
TF: 866-800-1275 ■ *Web:* chicago.cubs.mlb.com					
Yankee Stadium 161st St & River Ave	Bronx	NY	10451	718-293-4300	293-8431
Web: newyork.yankees.mlb.com					
Zed Ink Inc 228 Main St Ste 17	Venice	CA	90291	310-460-2424	
Web: zedink.com					

721 STAFFING SERVICES

See Also Employment Offices - Government p. 2243; Employment Services - On-line p. 2244; Executive Recruiting Firms p. 2275; Modeling Agencies p. 2777; Professional Employer Organizations (PEOs) p. 2989; Talent Agencies p. 3214

	City	State	ZIP	Phone	Fax
ABM Industries Inc 8020 W Doe Ste C	Visalia	SC	93291	559-651-1612	
Web: www.abm.com					
Accounting Principals 10151 Deerwood Park Blvd Ste 400	Jacksonville	FL	32256	800-981-3849	
TF: 800-981-3849 ■ *Web:* www.accountingprincipals.com					
Ace Personnel (AP) 5909 Woodson Rd	Mission	KS	66202	913-384-1100	
Web: www.acepersonnel.com					
Acentron Technologies Inc 12028 Olympic Club Dr	Charlotte	NC	28277	704-335-0030	675-1061*
**Fax Area Code:* 864					
Adecco Inc 175 Broad Hollow Rd	Melville	NY	11747	631-844-7650	844-7614*
**Fax:* Mktg ■ *TF General:* 800-978-3729 ■ *Web:* www.adeccousa.com					
Advantage Resourcing 220 Norwood Pk S	Norwood	MA	02062	781-251-8000	676-7172*
**Fax Area Code:* 325 ■ *TF:* 800-343-4314 ■ *Web:* www.advantageresourcing.com					
Aerotek Inc 7301 Pkwy Dr	Hanover	MD	21076	410-694-5100	
TF: 800-237-6835 ■ *Web:* www.aerotek.com					
Allegis Group Inc 7301 Pkwy Dr	Hanover	MD	21076	410-579-3000	540-7556
TF: 800-927-8090 ■ *Web:* www.allegisgroup.com					
Allied Health Group LLC 145 Technology Pkwy NW	Norcross	GA	30092	800-741-4674	
TF: 800-355-6150 ■ *Web:* www.alliedhealth.com					
ALTRES Inc 967 Kapiolani Blvd	Honolulu	HI	96814	808-591-4940	591-4914
TF: 888-425-8737 ■ *Web:* www.altres.com					
American Healthcare Services LLC 1000 John R Ste 250	Troy	MI	48083	248-588-9700	774-0780*
**Fax Area Code:* 540 ■ *TF:* 866-227-9998					
AMN Healthcare Services Inc 12400 High Bluff Dr Ste 100	San Diego	CA	92130	866-871-8519	282-1211*
NYSE: AHS ■ **Fax Area Code:* 800 ■ *TF:* 866-871-8519 ■ *Web:* www.amnhealthcare.com					
APEX Systems Inc 4400 Cox Rd Ste 100	Glen Allen	VA	23060	804-254-2600	254-7290
TF: 800-452-7391 ■ *Web:* www.apexsystemsinc.com					
AppleOne Employment Services Inc 327 W Broadway	Glendale	CA	91204	310-750-3400	265-5514*
**Fax Area Code:* 818 ■ *TF:* 800-872-2677 ■ *Web:* www.appleone.com					
Aquent LLC 711 Boylston St	Boston	MA	02116	617-535-5000	429-6244*
**Fax Area Code:* 208 ■ *TF:* 855-767-6333 ■ *Web:* www.aquent.com					
ARC Industries Inc 2879 Johnstown Rd	Columbus	OH	43219	800-734-7007	342-5680*
**Fax Area Code:* 614 ■ *TF:* 800-734-7007 ■ *Web:* www.arcind.com					
Area Temps Inc 1228 Euclid Ave	Cleveland	OH	44115	440-646-1333	
TF: 866-995-5627 ■ *Web:* www.areatemps.com					
Artech Information Systems LLC 240 Cedar Knolls Rd Ste 100	Cedar Knolls	NJ	07927	973-998-2500	998-2599
TF: 800-950-9496 ■ *Web:* www.artechinfo.com					
Attorney Resource 3300 Oak Lawn Ave Ste 510	Dallas	TX	75219	214-922-8050	871-3041
Web: www.attorneyresource.com					
BarkerGilmore LLC 1387 Fairport Rd Ste 845	Fairport	NY	14450	585-598-6555	
Web: www.barkergilmore.com					
Bartech Group 17199 N Laurel Pk Dr Ste 224	Livonia	MI	48152	734-953-5050	
TF: 800-828-4410 ■ *Web:* www.bartechgroup.com					
Bay Area Anesthesia Inc PO Box 1547	Ukiah	CA	95482	707-462-9420	
TF: 800-327-8427 ■ *Web:* www.fastgas.com					
Bergaila & Assoc Inc 1155 Dairy Ashford Rd Ste 600	Houston	TX	77079	281-496-0803	496-4705
Web: www.bergaila.com					
Bolton Group 2860 Carradale Dr	Roseville	CA	95661	916-783-4486	
Web: www.boltongrp.com					
Bowdoin Group Inc, The 40 William St	Wellesley	MA	02481	781-239-9933	
Web: www.bowdoingroup.com					
Brentwood Group Ltd, The 4949 SW Meadows Rd Ste 140	Lake Oswego	OR	97035	503-697-8136	
Web: www.brentwoodgroup.com					
Brooke Chase Associates Inc 1543 Second St Ste 201	Sarasota	FL	34236	877-374-0039	
TF: 877-374-0039 ■ *Web:* www.brookechase.com					
C & A Industries Inc 13609 California St	Omaha	NE	68154	402-891-0009	891-9461
TF: 800-574-9829 ■ *Web:* www.ca-industries.com					
Calian Technology Ltd 340 Legget Dr Ste 101	Ottawa	ON	K2K1Y6	613-599-8600	599-8650
TSE: CTY ■ *TF:* 877-225-4264 ■ *Web:* www.calian.com					
CareerStaff Unlimited Inc 6363 N State Hwy 161 Ste 525	Irving	TX	75038	888-993-4599	
TF: 888-993-4599 ■ *Web:* www.therapistsunlimited.com					
CDI Corp 1717 Arch St 35th Fl	Philadelphia	PA	19103	215-569-2200	
NYSE: CDI ■ *Web:* www.cdicorp.com					
Cejka Search Inc 4 Cityplace Dr Ste 300	Saint Louis	MO	63141	314-726-1603	726-0026
TF: 800-678-7858 ■ *Web:* www.cejkasearch.com					
Command Ctr Inc 3609 S Wadsworth Blvd Ste 250	Lakewood	ID	80235	866-464-5844	
OTC: CCNI ■ *TF:* 866-464-5844 ■ *Web:* www.commandonline.com					
CompHealth Inc 6440 S Millrock Dr Ste 175 Ste 175	Salt Lake City	UT	84121	801-930-3000	
TF: 800-453-3030 ■ *Web:* www.chghealthcare.com					
Compunnel Software Group Inc 103 Morgan Ln Ste 102	Plainsboro	NJ	08536	800-696-8128	
TF: 800-696-8128 ■ *Web:* www.compunnel.com					
Computer Consulting Assoc International (CCAII) 200 Pequot Ave	Southport	CT	06890	203-255-8966	
Web: www.ccaii.com					
Computer Enterprises Inc (CEI) 1000 Omega Dr Ste 1150	Pittsburgh	PA	15205	412-341-3541	341-0519
Web: www.ceiamerica.com					
Consultnet LLC 10813 S River Front Pkwy Ste 150	South Jordan	UT	84095	801-208-3700	208-3643
TF: 888-215-9675 ■ *Web:* consultnet.com					
Continuum Legal 1651 Old Meadow Rd Ste 600	McLean	VA	22102	703-734-7474	734-8839
Web: www.continuumlegal.com					
CORESTAFF Services 1775 St James Pl	Houston	TX	77056	713-438-1400	
Web: www.corestaff.com					
Cox Elearning Consultants Llc 3848 Macgregor Cmn	Livermore	CA	94551	925-373-6558	
Web: www.coxec.com					
CPC Logistics Inc 14528 S Outer 40 Rd Ste 210	Chesterfield	MO	63017	314-542-2266	542-0666
TF: 800-274-3746 ■ *Web:* www.callcpc.com					

Phone Fax

Cross Country Healthcare Inc
6551 Pk of Commerce Blvd .... Boca Raton FL 33487 561-998-2232 998-8533
NASDAQ: CCRN ■ *TF:* 800-347-2264 ■ *Web:* www.crosscountryhealthcare.com

CyberStaff America Ltd 253 W 35th St .... New York NY 10001 212-244-2300

Davis Cos 325 Donald J Lynch Blvd .... Marlborough MA 01752 763-231-0700 481-8519*
**Fax Area Code:* 508 ■ *TF:* 800-482-9494 ■ *Web:* www.daviscos.com

Debbie's Staffing Services Inc
4431 Cherry St Ste 50 .... Winston-Salem NC 27105 336-744-2393 776-1661
Web: www.debbiesstaffing.com

Design Group Staffing Inc 10012 Jasper Ave .... Edmonton AB T5J1R2 780-428-1505 428-7095
Web: dg.ca

DLH Holdings Corp
1776 Peachtree St NW Ste 300S .... Atlanta GA 30309 770-554-3545
NASDAQ: DLHC ■ *Web:* www.dlhcorp.com

Dressler Associates 624 University Ave .... Palo Alto CA 94301 650-323-0456
Web: www.dresslerassociates.com

Duran Human Capital Partners Inc
300 Orchard City Dr Ste 142 .... Campbell CA 95008 408-540-0070 540-0073
TF: 800-287-9682 ■ *Web:* www.duranhcp.com

Durham Cos Inc 6300 Transit Rd .... Depew NY 14043 716-684-3333 681-7408
TF: 800-633-7724 ■ *Web:* www.durhamstaffing.com

Durham Exchange Club Industries Inc
1717 E Lawson St .... Durham NC 27703 919-596-1341 596-6380
Web: www.deci.org

Eagle Professional Resources Inc
67 Yonge St Ste 200 .... Toronto ON M5E1J8 613-234-1810 861-8401*
**Fax Area Code:* 416 ■ *TF:* 800-281-2339 ■ *Web:* www.eagleonline.com

Elinvar Corp 1804 Hillsborough St .... Raleigh NC 27605 919-878-4454
Web: www.elinvar.com

Energy Services Group International Inc (ESG)
3601 La Grange Pkwy .... Toano VA 23168 757-741-4040 741-4045
Web: www.esgi.net

Ensearch Management Consultants
905 E Cotati Ave .... Cotati CA 94931 888-667-5627 795-6200*
**Fax Area Code:* 707 ■ *TF:* 888-667-5627 ■ *Web:* www.ensearch.com

Entegee Inc 70 BlanchaRd Rd Ste 102 .... Burlington MA 01803 781-221-5800 221-4544
TF: 800-368-3433 ■ *Web:* www.entegee.com

Execupharm Inc 500 N Gulph Rd Ste 120 .... King Of Prussia PA 19406 610-272-8771 272-8056
Web: www.execupharm.com

Express Employment Professionals
8516 NW Expy .... Oklahoma City OK 73162 405-840-5000
TF: 800-222-4057 ■ *Web:* www.expresspros.com

G&A Partners 4801 Woodway Dr Ste 210W .... Houston TX 77056 713-784-1181 784-2705
TF: 800-253-8562 ■ *Web:* www.gnapartners.com

General Employment Enterprises Inc
1 Tower Ln Ste 2200 .... Oakbrook Terrace IL 60181 630-954-0400 954-0447
NYSE: JOB ■ *Web:* www.generalemployment.com

Gibson Arnold & Assoc
5433 Westheimer Rd Ste 1016 .... Houston TX 77056 713-572-3000 572-4664
TF: 800-879-2007 ■ *Web:* www.gibsonarnold.com

Godshall & Godshall Personnel Po Box 1984 .... Greenville SC 29602 864-242-3491
Web: www.sccareersearch.com

Hawkins Assoc Inc 909 NE Loop 410 Ste 104 .... San Antonio TX 78209 210-349-9911 349-3393
Web: www.hawkinspersonnel.com

Headway Corporate Resources Inc
421 Fayetteville St Ste 1020 .... Raleigh NC 27601 919-376-4929
Web: www.headwaycorp.com

Helbling & Associates Inc
9000 Brooktree Rd Ste 150 .... Wexford PA 15090 724-935-7500
Web: www.helblingsearch.com

Hire Image LLC 6 Alcazar Ave .... Johnston RI 02919 401-490-2202
TF: 888-433-0090 ■ *Web:* www.hireimage.com

Integrity Staffing Solutions Inc
700 Prides Crossing Ste 300 .... Newark DE 19713 302-661-8776 661-8779
TF: 888-458-8367 ■ *Web:* www.integritystaffing.com

Interim HealthCare Inc
1601 Sawgrass Corporate Pkwy .... Sunrise FL 33323 954-858-6000 858-2720
TF: 800-338-7786 ■ *Web:* www.interimhealthcare.com

IPC Technologies Inc
7200 Glen Forest Dr Ste 100 .... Richmond VA 23226 804-622-7288
TF: 877-947-2835 ■ *Web:* www.ipctech.com

J2t Recruiting Consultants Inc
4101 S Quebec St .... Denver CO 80237 303-741-6122
Web: j2t-recruiting.com

Janou Pakter Inc 5 W 19th St .... New York NY 10011 212-989-1288
Web: www.janoupakter.com

Jean Simpson Personnel Services Inc
1318 Shreveport Barksdale .... Shreveport LA 71105 318-869-3494
Web: www.jeansimpson.com

Joule Inc 1245 US Rt 1 S .... Edison NJ 08837 732-548-5444 494-6346
TF: 800-341-0341 ■ *Web:* www.jouleinc.com

Judge Group Inc
300 Conshohocken State Rd Ste 300 .... West Conshohocken PA 19428 610-667-7700 667-1058
TF: 888-228-7162 ■ *Web:* www.judge.com

Justin Bradley 1725 I St Nw Ste 300 .... Washington DC 20006 202-457-8400
Web: www.justinbradley.com

Kelly Law Registry Inc 999 W Big Beaver Rd .... Troy MI 48084 248-362-4444
Web: www.kellyservices.us

Kelly Services Inc 999 W Big Beaver Rd .... Troy MI 48084 248-362-4444
NASDAQ: KELYA ■ *Web:* www.kellyservices.com

Kforce Inc 1001 E Palm Ave .... Tampa FL 33605 813-552-5000 552-1482
NASDAQ: KFRC ■ *TF:* 877-453-6723 ■ *Web:* www.kforce.com

Kimco Staffing Services Inc 17872 Cowan Ave .... Irvine CA 92614 949-752-6996 752-7298
TF: 800-649-5627 ■ *Web:* kimco.com

Labor Finders International Inc
11426 N Jog Rd .... Palm Beach Gardens FL 33418 561-627-6507 627-6556
TF: 800-864-7749 ■ *Web:* www.laborfinders.com

Lakeshore Staffing Inc 1 N Franklin St .... Chicago IL 60606 312-251-7575
Web: www.livinglakeshore.com

LJ Gonzer Assoc Inc 14 Commerce Dr Ste 305 .... Cranford NJ 07016 908-709-9494 709-9077
TF: 866-692-4538 ■ *Web:* www.gonzer.com

Lucas Assoc Inc 3384 Peachtree Rd Ste 900 .... Atlanta GA 30326 800-466-4489
TF: 800-515-0819 ■ *Web:* www.lucasgroup.com

Phone Fax

Lumen Legal 1025 N Campbell Rd .... Royal Oak MI 48067 248-597-0400 597-0410
TF: 877-933-1330 ■ *Web:* www.lumenlegal.com

Magnum Staffing Services Inc
2900 Smith St Ste 250 .... Houston TX 77006 713-658-0068 523-3621
Web: www.magnumstaffing.com

Major Legal Services
1301 E Ninth St Ste 1414 .... Cleveland OH 44114 216-579-9782
Web: majorlegalservices.com

ManpowerGroup 100 Manpower Pl .... Milwaukee WI 53212 414-961-1000
NYSE: MAN ■ *Web:* www.manpower.us

Marketstar Corp 2475 Washington Blvd .... Ogden UT 84401 801-393-1155 393-4115
Web: www.marketstar.com

Medical Staffing Assoc Inc
6731 Whittier Ave 3rd Fl .... McLean VA 22101 800-235-5105 893-7358*
**Fax Area Code:* 703 ■ *TF:* 800-235-5105 ■ *Web:* www.medstaffer.com

Medical Staffing Network Holdings Inc
901 Yamato Rd Ste 110 .... Boca Raton FL 33431 800-676-8326
TF: 800-676-8326 ■ *Web:* www.msnhealth.com

Medvantx Inc 5626 Oberlin Dr Ste 110 .... San Diego CA 92121 858-625-2990 625-2999
TF: 866-744-0621 ■ *Web:* www.medvantx.com

Minute Men Staffing Services
3740 Carnegie Ave .... Cleveland OH 44115 216-426-9675 426-2246
TF: 877-873-8856 ■ *Web:* www.minutemeninc.com

Motion Recruitment Partners
131 Clarendon St 3rd Fl .... Boston MA 02116 617-585-6500 536-9154
Web: www.motionrecruitment.com

National Engineering Service Corp
72 Mirona Rd .... Portsmouth NH 03801 603-431-9740 637-2562*
**Fax Area Code:* 800 ■ *TF:* 800-562-3463 ■ *Web:* www.nesc.com

Nextgen Information Services Inc
906 Olive St Ste 1100 .... Saint Louis MO 63101 314-588-1212 588-1211
Web: www.nextgen-is.com

North Highland Co, The
3333 Piedmont Rd NE Ste 1000 .... Atlanta GA 30305 404-233-1015 233-4930
Web: www.northhighland.com

Nursefinders Inc 12400 High Bluff Dr .... San Diego CA 92130 877-214-4105
TF: 800-445-0459 ■ *Web:* www.nursefinders.com

On Assignment Inc 26745 Malibu Hills Rd .... Calabasas CA 91301 818-878-7900
NYSE: ASGN ■ *Web:* www.onassignment.com

Orion International Consulting Group Inc
912 Capital of Texas Hwy S Ste 220 .... Austin TX 78746 512-327-7111 327-4286
TF: 800-336-7466 ■ *Web:* www.orioninternational.com

Oxford Global Resources Inc
100 Cummings Ctr Ste 206L .... Beverly MA 01915 978-236-1182 236-1077
TF: 800-426-9196 ■ *Web:* www.oxfordcorp.com

Peak Technical Services Inc
583 Epsilon Dr .... Pittsburgh PA 15238 412-696-1080 696-1083
TF: 888-888-7325 ■ *Web:* www.peaktechnical.com

Pinnacle Staffing Inc
127 Tanner Rd PO Box 17589 .... Greenville SC 29606 864-297-4212 987-7351
Web: pinnaclestaffing.com

Plus Group Inc, The (TPG)
7425 Janes Ave Ste 201 .... Woodridge IL 60517 630-515-0500 515-0510
Web: www.theplusgroup.com

Premier Staffing Services of New York Inc
1 N Broadway Ste 801 .... White Plains NY 10601 914-428-2233 428-5547
Web: www.thepremiergroup.com

Prime Staffing Inc 3806 N Cicero Ave .... Chicago IL 60641 773-685-9399 685-9565

Principal Technical Services Inc
9960 Research Dr Ste 200 .... Irvine CA 92618 888-787-3711 268-4040*
**Fax Area Code:* 949 ■ *TF:* 888-787-3711 ■ *Web:* www.ptsstaffing.com

Pro Staff Personnel Services
2999 W County Rd 42 Ste 220 .... Burnsville MN 55306 952-892-3240
Web: www.prostaff.com

Professional Placement Inc
4040 E Camelback Ste 235 .... Phoenix AZ 85018 602-955-0870 955-0604
Web: www.proplacement.com

Professional Staffing Group 155 Federal St .... Boston MA 02110 617-250-1000
Web: www.psgstaffing.com

Profiles International Inc 5205 Lk Shore Dr .... Waco TX 76710 254-751-1644 776-5405
TF: 866-751-1644 ■ *Web:* www.profilesinternational.com

PRWT Services Inc 1835 Market St 8th Fl .... Philadelphia PA 19103 215-569-8810 569-9893
Web: www.prwt.com

Raymond International
410 High St PO Box 591 .... Santa Cruz CA 95061 831-429-1234
Web: www.globalrecruiter.com

RCM Technologies Inc
2500 McClellan Ave Ste 350 .... Pennsauken NJ 08109 856-356-4500 356-4600
NASDAQ: RCMT ■ *TF:* 800-322-2885 ■ *Web:* www.rcmt.com

Remedy Temp Inc 3820 State St .... Santa Barbara CA 93105 805-882-2200 898-7111
TF: 800-688-6162 ■ *Web:* www.remedystaff.com

Resources Global Professionals
17101 Armstrong Ave .... Irvine CA 92614 714-430-6400 433-6100
NASDAQ: RECN ■ *TF:* 800-900-1131 ■ *Web:* www.rgp.com

Right at Home Inc 6464 Crt St Ste 150 .... Omaha NE 68106 402-697-7537 697-0289
TF: 877-697-7537 ■ *Web:* www.rightathome.net

Robert Half International Inc
2884 Sand Hill Rd Ste 200 .... Menlo Park CA 94025 650-234-6000
NYSE: RHI ■ *Web:* www.roberthalf.com

Robert Half International Inc Accountemps Div
2884 Sand Hill Rd Ste 200 .... Menlo Park CA 94025 855-396-4598
TF: 855-396-4598 ■ *Web:* www.roberthalf.com

Robert Half International Inc OfficeTeam Div
2884 Sand Hill Rd Ste 200 .... Menlo Park CA 94025 650-234-6000 234-6998*
**Fax:* Mktg ■ *Web:* www.roberthalf.com

Roth Staffing Cos LP 333 City Blvd W Ste 100 .... Orange CA 92868 714-939-8600 939-8688
Web: www.rothstaffing.com

Sacramento Employment & Training Agency
925 Del Paso Blvd .... Sacramento CA 95815 916-263-3800
Web: www.seta.net

Salem Group, The
2 TransAm Plz Dr Ste 170 .... Oakbrook Terrace IL 60181 630-932-7000 932-7010
TF: 877-768-7141 ■ *Web:* www.saleminc.com

Company	City	State	ZIP	Phone	Fax
SEEK Careers/Staffing Inc 1160 Opportunity Dr *Web:* www.seekcareers.com	Grafton	WI	53024	262-377-8888	375-6677
Select Staffing 3820 State St *TF:* 800-688-6162 ■ *Web:* www.selectstaffing.com	Santa Barbara	CA	93105	805-882-2200	898-7111
Shimento 1350 Hayes St *TF:* 877-211-8708 ■ *Web:* www.shimento.com	Benicia	CA	94510	877-211-8708	
Show Pros Entertainment Services Inc PO Box 12599 *Web:* www.showprostaff.com	Charlotte	NC	28220	704-525-3784	525-3785
Sigma Systems Inc 201 Boston Post Rd Ste 201 *Web:* www.sigmainc.com	Marlborough	MA	01752	508-925-3200	
Silicon Valley Staffing 2336 Harrison St *TF:* 877-660-6000 ■ *Web:* www.svsjobs.com	Oakland	CA	94612	510-923-9898	923-9313
Softworld Inc 281 Winter St Ste 301 *TF:* 877-899-1166 ■ *Web:* www.softworldinc.com	Waltham	MA	02451	781-466-8882	466-8885
SOS Staffing Services Inc 2650 S Decker Lk Blvd Ste 500 *Web:* elwoodstaffing.com/redirect.html	Salt Lake City	UT	84119	801-484-4400	
Sourcing Interests Group (SIG) 221 N Hogan St #389 *Web:* www.sig.org	Jacksonville	FL	32202	904-310-9560	
Southwest Medical Assoc Inc 638 E Market St PO Box 2168 **Fax Area Code:* 361 ■ *TF:* 800-929-4854 ■ *Web:* www.swmed.com	Rockport	TX	78382	800-929-4854	729-8854*
Special Counsel Inc 10201 Centurion Pkwy N Ste 400 *TF:* 800-737-3436 ■ *Web:* www.specialcounsel.com	Jacksonville	FL	32256	904-737-3436	360-2307
Sterling Computer Corp 600 Stevens Port Dr Ste 200 *TF:* 877-242-4074 ■ *Web:* www.sterlingcomputers.com	Dakota Dunes	SD	57049	605-242-4000	242-4001
Stivers Staffing Services Inc 200 W Monroe St Ste 1300 *Web:* www.stivers.com	Chicago	IL	60606	312-558-3550	
Superior Technical Resources Inc 250 International Dr *TF:* 800-568-8310 ■ *Web:* superiorgroup.com	Williamsville	NY	14221	716-929-1400	633-2026
Surgical Staff Inc 120 St Matthews Ave *TF:* 800-339-9599 ■ *Web:* surgicalstaffinc.net	San Mateo	CA	94401	650-558-3999	558-3949
Sysazzle Inc 15815 S. 46th St Ste 116, *TF:* 800-862-9545 ■ *Web:* sysazzle.com	Phoenix	AZ	85048	800-862-9545	
TAJ Technologies Inc 1168 Northland Dr *TF:* 877-825-2801 ■ *Web:* www.tajtech.com	Mendota Heights	MN	55120	651-688-2801	688-8321
Target Solutions Inc 530 Causeway Dr *Web:* www.targetsol.com	Wrightsville Beach	NC	28480	910-509-1800	
Team Health Inc 265 Brookview Ctr Way Ste 400 *TF:* 800-342-2898 ■ *Web:* www.teamhealth.com	Knoxville	TN	37919	865-693-1000	539-8030
TEKsystems Inc 7437 Race Rd *TF:* 888-519-0776 ■ *Web:* www.teksystems.com	Hanover	MD	21076	410-540-7700	540-7556
Temporary Solutions Inc 10550 Linden Lk Plz Ste 200 *TF:* 888-222-0457 ■ *Web:* www.eeihr.com	Manassas	VA	20109	703-361-2220	368-3594
Thinkpath Inc 9080 Springboro Pk Ste 300 *Web:* www.thinkpath.com	Miamisburg	OH	45342	937-291-8374	
Thompson Technologies Inc 114 Townpark Dr Ste 100 *TF:* 888-794-7947 ■ *Web:* www.thompsontalent.com	Kennesaw	GA	30144	770-794-8380	794-8381
Transforce Inc 5520 Cherokee Ave Ste 200 *TF:* 800-308-6989 ■ *Web:* www.transforce.com	Alexandria	VA	22150	703-838-5580	838-5585
True Blue Inc PO Box 2910 *NYSE: TBI* ■ **Fax Area Code:* 877 ■ *TF:* 800-610-8920 ■ *Web:* www.trueblue.com	Tacoma	WA	98401	253-383-9101	733-0399*
TSR Inc 400 Oser Ave Ste 150 *NASDAQ: TSRI* ■ *Web:* www.tsrconsulting.com	Hauppauge	NY	11788	631-231-0333	435-1428
UltraStaff 1818 Memorial Dr Ste 200 *TF:* 800-522-7707 ■ *Web:* www.ultrastaff.com	Houston	TX	77007	713-522-7100	522-0744
US Legal Support Inc 363 N Sam Houston Pkwy E Ste 900 *TF:* 800-567-8757 ■ *Web:* www.uslegalsupport.com	Houston	TX	77060	713-653-7100	653-7171
Vaco 5410 Maryland Way Ste 460 *Web:* www.vaco.com	Brentwood	TN	37027	615-324-8226	324-8245
VMC Consulting Corp 11611 Willows Rd NE *TF:* 877-393-8622 ■ *Web:* www.vmc.com	Redmond	WA	98052	425-558-7700	
Volt Services Group 1065 Ave of the Americas 20th Fl *NYSE: VISI* ■ *Web:* volt.com	New York	NY	10018	212-704-2400	
White Glove Placement Inc 85 Bartlett St *TF:* 866-387-8100 ■ *Web:* whiteglovecare.com	Brooklyn	NY	11206	718-387-8181	387-8359
Winston Resources Inc 122 E 42nd St Ste 320 *Web:* www.winstonresources.com	New York	NY	10168	212-557-5000	682-1056
Wolff r L & Associates 2138 Richmond Ave *Web:* rlwolff.com	Houston	TX	77098	713-523-2655	
Workstream Inc 2200 Lucien Way Ste 201	Maitland	FL	32751	407-475-5500	475-5517
York Solutions LLC 1 Westbrook Corporate Ctr Ste 910 *TF:* 877-700-9675 ■ *Web:* www.yorksolutions.net	Westchester	IL	60154	708-531-8362	

722 STAGE EQUIPMENT & SERVICES

Company	City	State	ZIP	Phone	Fax
Angstrom Lighting 12224 Montague St *Web:* www.angstromlighting.com	Pacoima	CA	91331	323-960-0113	
Apollo Design Technology Inc 4130 Fourier Dr *TF:* 800-288-4626 ■ *Web:* www.internetapollo.com	Fort Wayne	IN	46818	260-497-9191	497-9192
ARTEC Consultants Inc 114 W 26th St Ste 11 *Web:* www.artecconsultants.com	New York	NY	10001	212-242-0120	645-8635
BlueScreen LLC 137 N Larchmont Ste 508 *Web:* www.bluescreen.com	Los Angeles	CA	90004	323-467-7572	
Chapman/Leonard Studio Equipment Inc 12950 Raymer St *TF:* 888-883-6559 ■ *Web:* www.chapman-leonard.com	North Hollywood	CA	91605	818-764-6726	764-6730
Creative Stage Lighting Company Inc 149 Rt 28 N PO Box 567 *Web:* www.creativestagelighting.com	North Creek	NY	12853	518-251-3302	251-2908
Dreamworld Backdrops 6450 Lusk Blvd Ste E-106 *TF:* 800-737-9869 ■ *Web:* www.dreamworldbackdrops.com	San Diego	CA	92121	800-737-9869	
Fisher Dachs Assoc 22 W 19th St 6th Fl *Web:* www.fda-online.com	New York	NY	10011	212-691-3020	633-1644
Grosh Scenic Rentals 4114 Sunset Blvd **Fax Area Code:* 323 ■ *TF:* 877-363-7998 ■ *Web:* www.grosh.com	Los Angeles	CA	90029	877-363-7998	664-7526*
High End Systems Inc 2105 Gracy Farms Ln *TF:* 800-890-8989 ■ *Web:* www.highend.com	Austin	TX	78758	512-836-2242	837-5290
Holzmueller Productions Corp 1000 25th St *Web:* www.holzmueller.com	San Francisco	CA	94107	415-826-8383	826-2608
Janson Industries 1200 Garfield Ave SW *TF:* 800-548-8982 ■ *Web:* www.jansonindustries.com	Canton	OH	44706	330-455-7029	455-5919
Lycian Stage Lighting 1144 Kings Hwy PO Box D *Web:* www.lycian.com	Sugar Loaf	NY	10981	845-469-2285	469-5355
Musson Theatrical Inc 890 Walsh Ave *TF:* 800-843-2837 ■ *Web:* www.musson.com	Santa Clara	CA	95050	408-986-0210	986-9552
Production Resource Group LLC 539 Temple Hill Rd *Web:* www.prg.com	New Windsor	NY	12553	845-567-5700	567-5800
Rosco Laboratories Inc 52 Harbor View Ave *TF:* 800-767-2669 ■ *Web:* www.rosco.com	Stamford	CT	06902	203-708-8900	708-8919
Schuler & Shook 750 N Orleans St Ste 400 *Web:* www.schulershook.com	Chicago	IL	60654	312-944-8230	
Screen Works 2201 W Fulton St *TF Cust Svc:* 800-294-8111 ■ *Web:* www.thescreenworks.com	Chicago	IL	60612	312-243-8265	243-8290
Secoa Inc 8650 109th Ave N *TF:* 800-328-5519 ■ *Web:* www.secoa.com	Champlin	MN	55316	763-506-8800	506-8844
Syracuse Scenery & Stage Lighting Company Inc 101 Monarch Dr *TF:* 800-453-7775 ■ *Web:* www.syracusescenery.com	Liverpool	NY	13088	315-453-8096	453-7897
Triangle Scenery Drapery & Lighting Co 1215 Bates Ave *Web:* www.tridrape.com	Los Angeles	CA	90029	323-662-8129	662-8120

723 STEEL - MFR

Company	City	State	ZIP	Phone	Fax
A Finkl & Sons Co 2011 N Southport Ave *TF:* 800-343-2562 ■ *Web:* www.finkl.com	Chicago	IL	60614	773-975-2510	348-5347
Action Sales & Metal Company Inc 1625 E Pacific Coast Hwy *Web:* actionsalesmetal.com	Wilmington	CA	90744	310-549-5666	
Air-Cure Inc 8501 Evergreen Blvd *Web:* www.aircure.com	Minneapolis	MN	55433	763-717-0707	
AK Steel Corp 9227 Centre Pt Dr *NYSE: AKS* ■ **Fax Area Code:* 312 ■ *TF:* 800-331-5050 ■ *Web:* www.aksteel.com	West Chester	OH	45069	513-425-5000	601-4332*
Aleris International Inc 25825 Science Pk Dr Ste 400 *TF:* 866-266-2586 ■ *Web:* www.aleris.com	Beachwood	OH	44122	216-910-3400	910-3650
Allegheny Technologies Inc 1000 Six PPG Pl *NYSE: ATI* ■ *TF Sales:* 800-258-3586 ■ *Web:* www.atimetals.com	Pittsburgh	PA	15222	412-394-2800	
American Tank & Fabricating Co (AT&F) 12314 Elmwood Ave *TF:* 800-544-5316 ■ *Web:* www.atfco.com	Cleveland	OH	44111	216-252-1500	251-4963
ATI Allegheny Ludlum Corp 100 River Rd *TF Sales:* 800-258-3586 ■ *Web:* www.atimetals.com	Brackenridge	PA	15014	724-224-1000	
Block Steel Corp 6101 Oakton St *Web:* www.blocksteel.com	Skokie	IL	60077	847-966-3000	966-5906
Borgeson Universal Company Inc 91 Technology Park Dr *Web:* borgeson.com	Torrington	CT	06790	860-482-8283	
Bushwick Metals LLC 560 N Washington Ave *TF:* 888-399-4070 ■ *Web:* www.bushwickmetals.com	Bridgeport	CT	06604	888-399-4070	
Cadillac Casting Inc 1500 Fourth Ave *Web:* cadillaccasting.com	Cadillac	MI	49601	231-779-9600	
Calstrip Steel Corp 7140 Bandini Blvd *Web:* calstripsteel.com	Los Angeles	CA	90040	323-726-1345	722-8269
Canam Group Inc 11535 First Ave Bureau 500 *TSE: CAM* ■ *TF:* 877-499-6049 ■ *Web:* groupecanam.com/en	Saint-Georges	QC	G5Y7H5	418-228-8031	
Carpenter Specialty Alloys Operations 101 W Bern St *TF:* 800-654-6543 ■ *Web:* www.cartech.com/contact.aspx?id=3858	Reading	PA	19601	610-208-2000	208-3716
Carpenter Technology Corp PO Box 14662 *NYSE: CRS* ■ *TF:* 800-654-6543 ■ *Web:* www.cartech.com	Reading	PA	19612	610-208-2000	208-3716
Cascade Steel Rolling Mills Inc (CSRM) 3200 N Hwy 99 W PO Box 687 *TF:* 800-283-2776 ■ *Web:* www.cascadesteel.com	McMinnville	OR	97128	503-472-4181	434-5739
Central Illinois Steel Co 3141 WEST 36TH PLACE	Chicago	IL	62626	217-854-3251	854-4771
Charleston Steel & Metal Co 3038 Hwy 52 *Web:* www.charlestonsteelandmetal.com	Mt. Holly	SC	29461	843-722-7278	
Charter Mfg Company Inc 1212 W Glen Oaks Ln *Web:* www.chartermfg.com	Mequon	WI	53092	262-243-4700	
Chicago Heights Steel Acquisition Corp 211 E Main St *Web:* chs.com	Chicago Heights	IL	60411	708-756-5648	756-5628
Claret Medical Inc 1745 Copperhill Pkwy Ste 1 *Web:* www.claretmedical.com	Santa Rosa	CA	95403	707-528-9300	
Colibri Technologies Inc 293 Lesmill Rd *Web:* colibritech.com	North York	ON	M3B2V1	416-483-0100	

Phone | Fax

Commercial Metals Co (CMC)
6565 N MacArthur Blvd Ste 800 Irving TX 75039 214-689-4300 689-4300
NYSE: CMC ■ *Web:* www.cmc.com

Corey Steel Co 2800 S 61st Ct Cicero IL 60804 708-735-8000 735-8100
TF: 800-323-2750 ■ *Web:* www.coreysteel.com

Creform Corp PO Box 830 Greer SC 29652 864-989-1700 877-3863
TF: 800-839-8823 ■ *Web:* www.creform.com

Crucible Materials Corp 575 State Fair Blvd Syracuse NY 13209 315-487-4111 470-9358*
**Fax:* Sales ■ *TF:* 800-365-1180 ■ *Web:* www.crucible.com

D-M-E Co 70 E Hillis St Youngwood PA 15697 724-925-7291 925-2424
TF: 800-626-6653 ■ *Web:* dme.net

Delphinus Medical Technologies LLC
46701 Commerce Ctr Dr Plymouth MI 48170 734-233-3088
Web: www.delphinusmt.com

Dunkirk Specialty Steel Corp 830 Brigham Rd Dunkirk NY 14048 716-366-1000 366-0478
Web: www.dunkirkspecialtysteel.com

E&h Steel Corp 3635 Alabama 134 Midland City AL 36350 334-983-6405 983-6173
Web: www.ehsteel.com

Electralloy Corp 175 Main St Oil City PA 16301 814-678-4100 678-4100
TF: 800-458-7273 ■ *Web:* www.electralloy.com

Ellwood Engineered Castings Co
7158 Hubbard Masury Rd Hubbard OH 44425 330-534-8668
Web: ellwoodengineeredcastings.com

F & D Head Co 3040 E Peden Rd Fort Worth TX 76179 817-236-8773 236-1061
Web: www.fwfdhead.com

Feroleto Steel Company Inc
300 Scofield Ave Bridgeport CT 06605 203-366-3263 366-8058
TF: 800-243-2839 ■ *Web:* www.feroletosteel.com

Gerdau Ameristeel 2300 Oklahoma 97 Sand Springs OK 74063 918-245-1335 245-9343

Gerdau AmeriSteel Corp
4221 W Boy Scout Blvd Ste 600 Tampa FL 33607 813-286-8383
TF Sales: 800-876-7833 ■ *Web:* www.gerdau.com

Gibraltar Industries Inc 3556 Lakeshore Rd Buffalo NY 14219 716-826-6500 826-1589*
NASDAQ: ROCK ■ **Fax:* Sales ■ *TF:* 800-247-8368 ■ *Web:* www.gibraltar1.com

GO Carlson Inc
350 Marshallton Thorndale Rd Downingtown PA 19335 610-384-2800 383-3429
TF: 800-338-5622 ■ *Web:* www.electralloy.com

Greer Steel Co 624 Blvd Dover OH 44622 330-343-8811 343-1700
TF Sales: 800-388-2868 ■ *Web:* www.greersteel.com

Guided Delivery Systems Inc
2355 Calle de Luna Santa Clara CA 95054 408-727-1105
Web: www.gdsmed.com

Gulf Coast Machine & Supply Company Inc
6817 Industrial Rd Beaumont TX 77705 409-842-1311 842-4621
TF: 800-231-3032 ■ *Web:* www.gulfco.com

Harris Steel Co 1223 S 55th Ct Cicero IL 60804 708-656-5500 656-0151
Web: www.harrissteelco.com

Heidtman Steel Products Inc 2401 Front St Toledo OH 43605 419-691-4646 698-1150
Web: www.heidtman.com

Huron Valley Steel Corp
1650 W Jefferson Ste 100 Trenton MI 48183 734-479-3500 479-3413
Web: www.hvsc.net

Image Diagnostics Inc 310 Authority Dr Fitchburg MA 01420 978-829-0009
Web: www.imagediagnostics.com

Intsel Steel Distributors LP
11310 W Little York Houston TX 77041 713-937-9500 937-1091
TF: 800-762-3316 ■ *Web:* www.intselsteel.com

Jersey Shore Steel Co
70 Maryland Ave PO Box 5055 Jersey Shore PA 17740 570-753-3000 753-3782
TF: 800-833-0277 ■ *Web:* www.jssteel.com

JFE Steel Corp 350 Pk Ave 27th Fl New York NY 10022 212-310-9320 308-9292
Web: www.jfe-steel.co.jp

Kardium Inc 12851 Rowan Pl Ste 100 Richmond BC V6V2K5 604-248-8891
Web: www.kardium.com

Kentucky Electric Steel LLC
2704 S Big Run Rd W Ashland KY 41102 606-929-1200 929-1219
TF: 800-333-3012 ■ *Web:* www.kentuckyelectricsteel.com

KMA Manufacturing LLC 685 State St Vanport PA 15009 724-371-3059
Web: www.kma-usa.com

Kobe Steel USA Inc 535 Madison Ave 5th Fl New York NY 10022 212-751-9400 355-5564
Web: www.kobelco.co.jp

LBIW Inc 2020 W 14th St Long Beach CA 90813 562-432-5451

LOKRING Technology LLC 38376 Apollo Pkwy Willoughby OH 44094 440-942-0880
TF: 800-876-2323 ■ *Web:* www.lokring.com

Lynchburg Steel & Specialty Co
275 Francis Ave Monroe VA 24574 434-929-0951 929-2613
Web: lynchburgsteel.com

Metalex Corp
1530 Artaius Pkwy PO Box 399 Libertyville IL 60048 847-362-8300 362-7939
TF: 800-323-0792 ■ *Web:* www.metlx.com

Mevion Medical Systems Inc
300 Foster Sreet Littleton MA 01460 978-540-1500
Web: www.stillriversystems.com

Mill Steel Co 5116 36th St SE Grand Rapids MI 49512 800-247-6455 977-9411*
**Fax Area Code:* 616 ■ *TF:* 800-247-6455 ■ *Web:* www.millsteel.com

Millerbernd Manufacturing Co 622 6th St S Winsted MN 55395 320-485-2111 485-4420
Web: www.millerberndmfg.com

Mobisante Inc 8201 164th Ave NE Ste 200 Redmond WA 98052 425-605-0600
Web: www.mobisante.com

Moore Erection LP 19921 Fm 2252 San Antonio TX 78266 210-648-7461 648-1340
TF: 800-656-6673 ■ *Web:* melpsteel.com

Niagara Corp 667 Madison Ave New York NY 10021 212-317-1000 317-1001
TF: 877-289-2277 ■ *Web:* www.niagaralasalle.com

Nisshin USA LLC
1701 Golf Rd
Continental Tower 3 Ste 1004 Rolling Meadows IL 60008 847-290-5100 290-0826
Web: www.nisshin-steel.co.jp

Nucor Corp 1915 Rexford Rd Charlotte NC 28211 704-366-7000 362-4208
NYSE: NUE ■ *TF:* 800-294-1322 ■ *Web:* www.nucor.com

Nucor Corp Cold Finish Div
2800 N Governor Williams Hwy Darlington SC 29540 704-366-7000 395-8759*
**Fax Area Code:* 843 ■ **Fax:* Sales ■ *TF:* 800-333-0590 ■ *Web:* www.nucor.com

Phone | Fax

Nucor Corp Steel Div 1455 Hagan Ave Huger SC 29450 843-336-6000
Web: www.nucorsteel.com

Nucor-Yamato Steel Co
5929 E State Hwy 18 Blytheville AR 72315 870-762-5500 762-1130
TF: 800-289-6977 ■ *Web:* www.nucoryamato.com

Reference Metals Company Inc
1000 Old Pond Rd Bridgeville PA 15017 412-221-7008
Web: cbmm.com.br

Regional Fabricators Inc 1905 Diver Dr New Iberia LA 70560 337-367-3488
Web: www.regionalfab.com

ROHN Products LLC 1 Fairholm Ave Peoria IL 61603 309-566-3000
Web: www.rohnnet.com

Sandmeyer Steel Co 1 Sandmeyer Ln Philadelphia PA 19116 215-464-7100 677-1430
TF: 800-523-3663 ■ *Web:* www.sandmeyersteel.com

Schnitzer Steel Industries Inc
6241 SE 111th Ave Portland OR 97266 503-224-9900
NASDAQ: SCHN ■ *Web:* www.schnitzersteel.com

Scion Steel Inc 21555 Mullin Ave Warren MI 48089 586-755-4000 757-5210
TF: 800-288-2127 ■ *Web:* www.scionsteel.com

Shasta Inc 300 Steel St Aliquippa PA 15001 724-378-8280
Web: shastainc.com

Standard Steel LLC 500 N Walnut St Burnham PA 17009 717-248-4911 248-8050
Web: www.standardsteel.com

Steel Dynamics Inc
7575 W Jefferson Blvd Ste 200 Fort Wayne IN 46804 260-969-3500 969-3590
NASDAQ: STLD ■ *TF:* 866-740-8700 ■ *Web:* www.steeldynamics.com

Steel of West Virginia Inc
17th St & Second Ave Huntington WV 25703 304-696-8200 529-1479
TF: 800-624-3492 ■ *Web:* www.swvainc.com

Tempel Steel Co 5500 N Wolcott Ave Chicago IL 60640 773-250-8000 250-8910*
**Fax:* Cust Svc ■ *Web:* www.tempel.com

Tenaris 530-8th Ave SW Ste 400 Calgary AB T2P3S8 403-767-0100 767-0299
Web: www.tenaris.com

Thompson Steel Co 120 Royall St Canton MA 02021 781-828-8800
Web: www.thompsonsteelco.com

Tube Products Corp 14420 Ewing Ave S Burnsville MN 55306 952-894-2817

TWB Co 1600 Nadeau Rd Monroe MI 48162 734-289-6400 289-6555
Web: www.twbcompany.com

Ulbrich Stainless Steels & Special Metals Inc (USSM)
57 Dodge Ave North Haven CT 06473 203-239-4481 239-7479*
**Fax:* Sales ■ *TF:* 800-243-1676 ■ *Web:* www.ulbrich.com

Union Electric Steel Corp 726 Bell Ave Carnegie PA 15106 412-429-7655 276-1711
Web: www.uniones.com

United Performance Metals 3475 Symmes Rd Hamilton OH 45015 513-860-6500 874-6857
TF: 888-282-3292 ■ *Web:* www.upmet.com

US Steel Corp 600 Grant St Pittsburgh PA 15219 412-433-6791
NYSE: X ■ *Web:* www.ussteel.com

USS-POSCO Industries 900 Loveridge Rd Pittsburg CA 94565 925-439-6000 439-6722
TF: 800-877-7672 ■ *Web:* www.ussposco.com

Western Steel Inc Attn Fred Campbell
3360 Davey Allison Blvd Hueytown AL 35023 205-744-2230
Web: westernsteelinc.com

Worthington Specialty Processing
4905 S Meridian Rd Jackson MI 49201 517-789-0200
Web: worthingtonindustries.com

Worthington Steel Co
200 W Old Wilson Bridge Rd Columbus OH 43085 614-438-3210
TF: 800-944-3733 ■ *Web:* worthingtonindustries.com

724 STONE (CUT) & STONE PRODUCTS

Phone | Fax

Adam Ross Cut Stone Co 1003 Broadway Albany NY 12204 518-463-6674 463-0710
Web: www.adamrosscutstone.com

Akdo Intertrade Inc 1435 State St Bridgeport CT 06605 203-336-5199
TF: 800-811-2536 ■ *Web:* www.akdo.com

American Slate Co 1900 Olympic Blvd Walnut Creek CA 94596 925-977-4880
Web: www.americanslate.com

Austin Countertops 11108 Bluff Bend Dr Austin TX 78753 512-835-5100 339-1796
Web: www.austincountertops.com

AZ Countertops Inc 1445 S Hudson Ave Ontario CA 91762 909-983-5386 983-5495
TF: 800-266-3524 ■ *Web:* azcountertopsinc.com

Benson Stone Co 1100 11th St Rockford IL 61104 815-227-2000 227-2001
Web: www.bensonstone.com

Biesanz Stone Co Inc 4600 Goodview Rd Winona MN 55987 507-454-4336 454-8140
Web: www.biesanzstone.com

Briar Hill Stone Co, The
12470 State Rt 520 PO Box 457 Glenmont OH 44628 330-377-5100
Web: www.briarhillstone.com

Bristol Memorial Works Inc 797 King St Bristol CT 06010 860-583-1654
TF: 888-987-7821

Bybee Stone Company Inc
6293 N Matthews Dr Ellettsville IN 47429 812-876-2215
TF: 800-457-4530 ■ *Web:* www.bybeestone.com

C & H Stone Company Inc
4000 S Rockport Rd Bloomington IN 47403 812-336-2560 331-7292
Web: chstoneinc.com

Cold Spring Granite Inc
17482 Granite W Rd Cold Spring MN 56320 320-685-3621 685-8490
TF: 800-328-5040 ■ *Web:* www.coldspringusa.com

Coldspring 17482 Granite W Rd Cold Spring MN 56320 800-328-5040 473-4881
TF: 800-328-5040 ■ *Web:* www.coldspringusa.com

Columbus Marble Works Corp 2415 Hwy 45 N Columbus MS 39705 662-328-1477
TF Cust Svc: 800-647-1055 ■ *Web:* www.columbusmarbleworks.net

Continental Cast Stone Manufacturing Inc
22001 W 83rd St Shawnee KS 66227 800-989-7866 422-7272*
**Fax Area Code:* 913 ■ *TF:* 800-989-7866 ■ *Web:* www.continentalcaststone.com

Dakota Granite Co 48391 150th St PO Box 1351 Milbank SD 57252 605-432-5580 432-6155
TF: 800-843-3333 ■ *Web:* dakotagranite.com

Dakota Marble Inc 902 W 19th St Yankton SD 57078 605-665-7241 665-7241
TF: 800-697-7241 ■ *Web:* www.dakotamarble.com

Phone Fax

Daprato Rigali Inc 6030 N NW Hwy Chicago IL 60631 773-763-5511
Web: www.dapratorigali.com
Dutch Quality Stone Inc 18012 Dover Rd Mount Eaton OH 44659 330-359-7866
Web: www.dutchqualitystone.com
Environmental Materials LLC
6300 E Stapleton Dr S Denver CO 80216 303-309-3040
Web: www.estoneworks.com
Finger Lakes Stone Company Inc 33 Quarry Rd Ithaca NY 14850 607-273-4646 273-4692
Web: www.fingerlakesstone.net
Glenrock International Inc 985 E Linden Ave Linden NJ 07036 908-862-3433 862-0430
TF: 800-453-6762 ■ *Web:* glenrock.com
Hilltop Slate
3 County Rt 21 PO Box 201 Middle Granville NY 12849 518-642-2270 642-1220
Web: www.hilltopslate.com
Intercontinental Marble Corp 8228 NW 56th St Miami FL 33166 305-591-2207
Web: www.intercontinentalmarble.com
Keystone Retaining Wall Systems Inc
4444 W 78th St Minneapolis MN 55435 952-897-1040
TF: 800-642-3887 ■ *Web:* www.keystonewalls.com
Kollmann Monumental Works Inc
1915 W Div St Saint Cloud MN 56301 320-251-8010
Web: www.kollmann.com
Kotecki Rock of Ages Memorials
3636 Pearl Rd Cleveland OH 44109 216-749-2880
Web: www.koteckifamilymemorials.com
Little Falls Granite Works 10802 Hwy 10 Little Falls MN 56345 800-862-2417
TF: 800-862-2417 ■ *Web:* lfgranite.com
Mankato-Kasota Stone Inc 818 N Willow St Mankato MN 56001 507-625-2746
Web: www.mankato-kasota-stone.com
Maryland Materials Inc 233 Stevenson Rd North East MD 21901 410-287-8177
Web: www.marylandmaterials.com
Monumental Sales Inc
537 22nd Ave N PO Box 667 Saint Cloud MN 56302 320-251-6585 251-6547
TF: 800-442-1660 ■ *Web:* www.sunburstmemorials.com
North Carolina Granite Corp
151 Granite Quarry Trl PO Box 151 Mount Airy NC 27030 336-786-5141 719-2623
TF: 800-227-6242 ■ *Web:* www.ncgranite.com
Northfield Block Co 1 Hunt Ct Mundelein IL 60060 847-949-3600 816-9072
TF: 800-358-3003 ■ *Web:* northfieldblock.com
Polycor Inc 139 St-Pierre St Quebec QC G1K8B9 418-692-4695
Web: www.polycor.com
RJ Marshall Co 26776 W 12-Mile Rd Southfield MI 48034 248-353-4100 338-7900*
**Fax Area Code:* 800 ■ *TF Cust Svc:* 888-514-8600 ■ *Web:* www.rjmarshall.com
Rock of Ages Corp 560 Graniteville Rd Graniteville VT 05654 802-476-3119
TF: 800-421-0166 ■ *Web:* www.rockofages.com
Solidia Technologies Inc 11 Colonial Dr Piscataway NJ 08854 908-315-5901
Web: www.solidiatech.com
Starrett Tru-Stone Technologies Div
1101 Prosper Dr PO Box 430 Waite Park MN 56387 320-251-7171 259-5073
TF: 800-959-0517 ■ *Web:* www.starrett.com
StonePeak Ceramics Inc 314 W Superior Ste 201 Chicago IL 60610 312-506-2800
Web: www.stonepeakceramics.com
Tri-State Cut Stone & Brick Co
10333 Van's Dr Frankfort IL 60423 815-469-7550 464-5096
Web: www.stone-brick.com
Vermont Structural Slate Company Inc
3 Prospect St PO Box 98 Fair Haven VT 05743 802-265-4933 265-3865
TF: 800-343-1900 ■ *Web:* www.vermontstructuralslate.com
Vetter Stone Co (VSC) 23894 Third Ave Mankato MN 56001 507-345-4568 345-4777
TF: 800-878-2850 ■ *Web:* www.vetterstone.com
WE Neal Slate Co 2840 Hwy 25 Watertown MN 55388 952-955-3340 955-3341
Web: www.nealslate.com
Winona Monument Company Inc 174 W Third St Winona MN 55987 507-452-4672
WS Hampshire Inc 365 Keyes Ave Hampshire IL 60140 847-683-4400 683-4407
TF: 800-541-0251 ■ *Web:* www.wshampshire.com

725 STUDENT ASSISTANCE PROGRAMS

Phone Fax

Alabama Commission on Higher Education
100 N Union St PO Box 302000 Montgomery AL 36104 334-242-1998 242-0268
Web: ache.alabama.gov
Alabama Prepaid Affordable College Tuition (PACT) Program
100 N Union St Ste 660 Montgomery AL 36130 334-242-7514
TF: 800-252-7228 ■ *Web:* www.treasury.state.al.us
Alaska Commission on Postsecondary Education
PO Box 110510 Juneau AK 99811 907-465-2962 465-5316
TF: 800-441-2962 ■ *Web:* acpe.alaska.gov
Arkansas Financial Aid Office
114 Silas Hunt Hall Fayetteville AR 72701 479-575-3806 575-7790
TF: 800-547-8839 ■ *Web:* finaid.uark.edu
California Student Aid Commission
PO Box 419027 Rancho Cordova CA 95741 916-526-8999 526-8002
TF: 888-224-7268 ■ *Web:* www.csac.ca.gov
Colorado CollegeInvest 1560 Broadway Ste 1700 Denver CO 80202 303-376-8800 296-4811
TF: 800-448-2424 ■ *Web:* collegeinvest.org
Council for Opportunity in Education
1025 Vermont Ave NW Ste 900 Washington DC 20005 202-347-7430 347-0786
Web: www.coenet.us
DC Tuition Assistance Grant Program
810 First St NE Washington DC 20001 202-727-2824 727-2834
TF: 877-485-6751 ■ *Web:* www.osse.dc.gov
Dollars for Scholars
Scholarship America 1 Scholarship Way Saint Peter MN 56082 507-931-1682 931-9168
TF: 800-248-8080 ■ *Web:* www.scholarshipamerica.org
EdVest PO Box 55244 Boston MA 02205 888-338-3789 266-2647*
**Fax Area Code:* 608 ■ *TF:* 888-338-3789 ■ *Web:* www.edvest.com
FastWeb Inc 444 N Michigan Ave Ste 600 Chicago IL 60611 444-536-1212 467-0638*
**Fax Area Code:* 312 ■ *TF:* 800-829-1040 ■ *Web:* www.fastweb.com
FinAid Page LLC PO Box 2056 Cranberry Township PA 16066 724-538-4500 538-4502
TF: 800-433-3243 ■ *Web:* www.finaid.org

Phone Fax

Florida Prepaid College Board
PO Box 6567 Tallahassee FL 32314 800-552-4723 309-1766*
**Fax Area Code:* 850 ■ **Fax:* Cust Svc ■ *TF:* 800-552-4723 ■ *Web:* www.myfloridaprepaid.com
Florida Student Financial Assistance Office
1940 N Monroe St Ste 70 Tallahassee FL 32303 850-410-5200 488-3612
TF: 888-827-2004 ■ *Web:* www.floridastudentfinancialaid.org
Georgia Student Finance Commission
2082 E Exchange Pl Ste 200 Tucker GA 30084 770-724-9000 724-9089
TF: 800-505-4732 ■ *Web:* www.gsfc.org
Harry S Truman Scholarship Foundation
712 Jackson Pl NW Washington DC 20006 202-395-4831 395-6995
Web: www.truman.gov
Hawaii Postsecondary Education Commission
2444 Dole St Bachman Hall Rm 209 Honolulu HI 96822 808-956-8213 956-5156
TF: 877-531-2333 ■ *Web:* hawaii.edu
Idaho Scholarship Office
650 W State St Rm 307 PO Box 83720 Boise ID 83720 208-334-2270 334-2632
Web: www.boardofed.idaho.gov
Illinois Student Assistance Commission
1755 Lake Cook Rd Deerfield IL 60015 847-948-8500 831-8549*
**Fax:* Cust Svc ■ *TF:* 800-899-4722 ■ *Web:* collegeillinois.org
Indiana Students Assistance Commission
150 W Market St Ste 500 Indianapolis IN 46204 317-232-2350 232-3260
TF: 888-528-4719 ■ *Web:* www.in.gov
Iowa College Student Aid Commission
603 E 12th St Fl 5th Des Moines IA 50319 515-725-3400 725-3401
TF: 800-383-4222 ■ *Web:* www.iowacollegeaid.gov
Kansas Board of Regents, The
1000 SW Jackson St Ste 520 Topeka KS 66612 785-296-3421 296-0983
Web: www.kansasregents.org
Kentucky Higher Education Assistance Authority (KHEAA)
100 Airport Rd Frankfort KY 40602 800-928-8926
TF: 800-928-8926 ■ *Web:* www.kheaa.com
Louisiana Office of Student Financial Assistance (LOSFA)
602 N Fifth St PO Box 91202 Baton Rouge LA 70802 225-219-1012 208-1496
TF: 800-259-5626 ■ *Web:* www.osfa.la.gov
Maine Finance Authority of Maine (FAME)
5 Community Dr PO Box 949 Augusta ME 04332 207-623-3263 623-0095
TF: 800-228-3734 ■ *Web:* www.famemaine.com
Maryland Student Financial Assistance Office
839 Bestgate Rd Ste 400 Annapolis MD 21401 410-260-4565 260-3200
TF: 800-974-0203 ■ *Web:* www.mhec.state.md.us
Michigan Education Trust (MET) PO Box 30198 Lansing MI 48909 517-335-4767 373-6967
TF General: 800-638-4543 ■ *Web:* www.setwithmet.com
Michigan Student Financial Services Bureau
Austin Bldg 430 W Allegan Lansing MI 48922 888-447-2687 335-6792*
**Fax Area Code:* 517 ■ *TF General:* 800-642-5626 ■ *Web:* www.michigan.gov/mistudentaid
Minnesota Office of Higher Education
1450 Energy Pk Dr Ste 350 Saint Paul MN 55108 651-642-0567 642-0675
TF: 800-657-3866 ■ *Web:* www.ohe.state.mn.us
Mississippi Student Financial Aid Office
3825 Ridgewood Rd Jackson MS 39211 601-432-6997 432-6527
TF: 800-327-2980 ■ *Web:* www.ihl.state.ms.us/financialaid
Montana Higher Education Board of Regents
2500 Broadway St PO Box 203201 Helena MT 59620 406-444-6570 444-1469
TF: 877-501-1722 ■ *Web:* www.mus.edu
Morris K Udall Foundation 130 S Scott Ave Tucson AZ 85701 520-901-8500 670-5530
Web: www.udall.gov
National Merit Scholarship Corp
1560 Sherman Ave Ste 200 Evanston IL 60201 847-866-5100 866-5113
Web: www.nationalmerit.org
Nebraska Coordinating Commission for Postsecondary Educatio
140 N Eigth St Ste 300 PO Box 95005 Lincoln NE 68509 402-471-2847 471-2886
Web: www.ccpe.state.ne.us
New Hampshire Postsecondary Education Commission
64 South St Ste 300 Concord NH 03301 603-271-2555 271-2696
TF: 800-735-2964 ■ *Web:* www.nh.gov
New Jersey Higher Education Student Assistance Authority
4 Quakerbridge Plaza PO Box 540 Trenton NJ 08625 609-584-4480 588-7389
TF: 800-792-8670 ■ *Web:* www.hesaa.org
New York Higher Education Services Corp
99 Washington Ave Albany NY 12255 518-473-1574 473-3749
TF: 888-697-4372 ■ *Web:* www.hesc.ny.gov
North Carolina State Education Assistance Authority (NCSEAA)
PO Box 14103 Research Triangle Park NC 27709 919-549-8614 549-8481
TF: 800-700-1775 ■ *Web:* www.ncseaa.edu
North Dakota Student Financial Assistance Program
600 E Blvd Ave 10th Fl Dept 215 Bismarck ND 58505 701-328-2960 328-2961
Web: www.ndus.nodak.edu
Ohio Tuition Trust Authority
580 S High St Ste 208 Columbus OH 43215 614-752-9400
TF Cust Svc: 800-233-6734 ■ *Web:* www.collegeadvantage.com
Oklahoma State Regents for Higher Education
655 Research Pkwy Ste 200 Oklahoma City OK 73104 405-225-9100 225-9235
Web: www.okhighered.org
Oregon Student Assistance Commission
1500 Valley River Dr Ste 100 Eugene OR 97401 541-687-7400
Web: oregonstudentaid.gov
Pennsylvania Higher Education Assistance Agency
1200 N Seventh St Harrisburg PA 17102 800-233-0557 720-3901*
**Fax Area Code:* 717 ■ *TF:* 800-233-0557 ■ *Web:* www.pheaa.org
Scholarship America
1 Scholarship Way PO Box 297 Saint Peter MN 56082 507-931-1682 931-9168
TF: 800-537-4180 ■ *Web:* www.scholarshipamerica.org
South Carolina Higher Education Tuition Grants Commission
115 Atrium Wy Ste 102 Columbia SC 29203 803-896-1120 896-1126
TF: 877-382-4357 ■ *Web:* www.sctuitiongrants.com
Tennessee Student Assistance Corp
404 James Robertson Pkwy Ste 1510 Nashville TN 37243 615-741-1346 741-6101
Web: www.state.tn.us/tsac
Tennessee Treasurer
Tennessee State Capitol
1st Fl 600 Charlotte Ave Nashville TN 37243 615-741-2956
Web: www.treasury.state.tn.us

Phone | Fax

Texas Higher Education Coordinating Board
1200 E Anderson Ln ... Austin TX 78752 512-427-6101 427-6169
Web: www.thecb.state.tx.us

Thurgood Marshall Scholarship Fund
901 F St NW Ste 300 ... Washington DC 20004 212-573-8888 573-8497
TF: 866-632-9992 ■ *Web:* tmcf.org

Utah Higher Education Assistance Authority
PO Box 145112 ... Salt Lake City UT 84114 801-321-7294 366-8431
TF: 877-336-7378 ■ *Web:* www.uheaa.org

Vermont Student Assistance Corp (VSAC)
PO Box 2000 ... Winooski VT 05404 802-655-9602 654-3765
TF: 800-642-3177 ■ *Web:* www.vsac.org

Virginia College Savings Plan
9001 Arboretum Pkwy ... Richmond VA 23236 804-786-0719
TF: 888-567-0540 ■ *Web:* www.virginia529.com

Virginia State Council of Higher Education
101 N 14th St 9th Fl ... Richmond VA 23219 804-225-2600 225-2604
Web: www.schev.edu

Washington Higher Education Coordinating Board
917 Lakeridge Way PO Box 43430 ... Olympia WA 98504 360-753-7800 753-7808
Web: www.wsac.wa.gov

West Virginia Higher Education Policy Commission
1018 Kanawha Blvd E Ste 700 ... Charleston WV 25301 304-558-2101
TF: 888-825-5707 ■ *Web:* wvhepc.com

Wisconsin Higher Educational Aids Board (HEAB)
131 W Wilson S PO Box 7885 ... Madison WI 53707 608-267-2206 267-2808
Web: www.heab.state.wi.us

Wyoming Community College Commission
2300 Capitol Ave Fl 5 Ste B ... Cheyenne WY 82002 307-777-7763 777-6567
Web: communitycolleges.wy.edu

726 SUBSTANCE ABUSE TREATMENT CENTERS

See Also Self-Help Organizations p. 1777; General Hospitals - Canada p. 2494; General Hospitals - US p. 2496; Psychiatric Hospitals p. 2523

Phone | Fax

AdCare Hospital of Worcester
107 Lincoln St ... Worcester MA 01605 508-799-9000 753-3733
TF: 800-252-6465 ■ *Web:* www.adcare.com

Aletheia House 201 Finley Ave W ... Birmingham AL 35204 205-324-6502
Web: specialkindofcaring.org

Anchor Hospital 5454 Yorktowne Dr ... Atlanta GA 30349 770-991-6044
TF: 866-667-8797 ■ *Web:* www.anchorhospital.com

Anthony Louis Ctr 115 Forestview Ln ... Plymouth MN 55441 763-542-9212 542-9248
Web: www.anthonylouiscenter.com

Apex Behavioral Health Western Wayne PLLC
1547 S Wayne Rd ... Westland MI 48186 734-729-3133
Web: www.apexwesternwayne.com

Applewood Centers Inc 2525 E 22nd St ... Cleveland OH 44115 216-696-5800
Web: www.applewoodcenters.org

APT Foundation 1 Long Wharf Dr Ste 321 ... New Haven CT 06511 203-781-4600
TF: 855-378-4373 ■ *Web:* aptfoundation.org

Area Mental Health Center 531 Campusview ... Garden City KS 67846 620-276-7689
Web: compassbh.org

AREBA Casriel Inc (ACI) 500 W 57th St ... New York NY 10019 212-293-3000 293-3020
TF: 800-724-4444 ■ *Web:* www.acirehab.org

Arizona Foundation for the Handicapped
3146 E Windsor Ave ... Phoenix AZ 85008 602-956-0400
Web: www.azafh.com

Arms Acres 75 Seminary Hill Rd ... Carmel NY 10512 845-225-3400
TF: 800-989-2676 ■ *Web:* www.armsacres.com

Baltimore Behavioral Health (BBH)
1101 W Pratt St ... Baltimore MD 21223 410-962-7180 962-7194
TF: 800-789-2647 ■ *Web:* baltimorecity.md.networkofcare.org

Blue Hills Hospital 500 Vine St ... Hartford CT 06112 860-293-6400 293-6470
Web: www.ct.gov

Bradford Health Services
2101 Magnolia Ave S Ste 518 ... Birmingham AL 35205 205-251-7753 251-7760
TF: 800-217-2849 ■ *Web:* www.bradfordhealth.com

CenterPointe Inc 2633 P St ... Lincoln NE 68503 402-475-8717
Web: www.centerpointe.org

Central Street Health Ctr 26 Central St ... Somerville MA 02143 617-591-6033 591-6452
TF: 800-909-2677 ■ *Web:* www.challiance.org

Child Guidance Resource Centers
2000 Old W Chester Pk ... Havertown PA 19083 484-454-8700
Web: www.cgrc.org

Circle Family Care 3919 N Albany Ave ... Chicago IL 60618 773-478-4747
Web: www.cfhcn.org

Clear Brook Lodge 890 Bethel Hill Rd ... Shickshinny PA 18655 570-864-8615

Clear Brook Manor 1100 E Northampton St ... Laurel Run PA 18706 800-582-6241
TF: 800-582-6241 ■ *Web:* clearbrookinc.com

Coleman Professional Services 24 7 Emergency C
3920 Lovers Ln ... Ravenna OH 44266 330-296-3555
TF: 800-673-1347 ■ *Web:* www.colemanservices.org

Columbia Community Mental Health
58646 McNulty Way ... Saint Helens OR 97051 503-397-5211
Web: www.ccmh1.com

COMHAR Inc 100 W Lehigh Ave ... Philadelphia PA 19133 215-203-3000
Web: comhar.org

Community Partnership of The Ozarks Inc
330 N Jefferson Ave Ste A ... Springfield MO 65806 417-888-2020
Web: www.commpartnership.org

Conifer Park 79 Glenridge Rd ... Schenectady NY 12302 518-399-6446 952-8228
TF: 800-989-6446 ■ *Web:* www.coniferpark.com

Cornerstone Medical Arts Ctr Hospital
159-05 Union Tpke ... Fresh Meadows NY 11366 718-906-6700
TF: 800-233-9999 ■ *Web:* www.cornerstoneny.com

Daymark Recovery Services Inc Stanly Center
1000 N First St Ste 1 ... Albemarle NC 28001 704-983-2117
TF: 866-275-9552 ■ *Web:* www.daymarkrecovery.org

Phone | Fax

Dayton Rehabilitation Institute
1 Elizabeth Pl ... Dayton OH 45417 937-424-8200
TF: 800-765-4772 ■ *Web:* reliantdayton.com

Detroit Central City Community Mental Health Inc
10 Peterboro St ... Detroit MI 48201 313-831-3160
Web: www.dcccmh.org

Eagleville Hospital 100 Eagleville Rd ... Eagleville PA 19408 610-539-6000 539-6249
TF General: 800-255-2019 ■ *Web:* www.eagleville.org

El Rincon Community Clinic 3809 W Grand Ave ... Chicago IL 60651 773-276-0200
Web: elrinconclinic.org

Fairbanks Hospital 8102 Clearvista Pkwy ... Indianapolis IN 46256 317-849-8222 849-8222
TF: 800-225-4673 ■ *Web:* fairbankscd.org

Family Behavioral Resources Inc
400 Oakbrook Dr Oakbrook Commons Ste 2300
PO Box 879 ... Greensburg PA 15601 724-850-8118
Web: www.familybehavioralresources.com

Family Guidance Center of Warren County Inc
492 Route 57 W ... Washington NJ 07882 908-689-1000
Web: www.fgcwc.org

Fellowship Hall Inc 5140 Dunstan Rd ... Greensboro NC 27405 336-621-3381
TF: 800-659-3381 ■ *Web:* www.fellowshiphall.com

Florida Ctr for Addictions & Dual Disorders
100 W College Dr ... Avon Park FL 33825 863-452-3858 452-3863
Web: tchsonline.org

Fountain House Inc 425 W 47th St ... New York NY 10036 212-582-0340
Web: www.fountainhouse.org

Friary of Lakeview Ctr, The
4400 Hickory Shores Blvd ... Gulf Breeze FL 32563 850-932-9375 934-1281
TF: 800-332-2271 ■ *Web:* www.thefriary.org

Gateway Foundation Inc 1080 E Pk St ... Carbondale IL 62901 877-505-4673
TF: 877-505-4673 ■ *Web:* www.recovergateway.org

Gaudenzia 106 W Main St ... Norristown PA 19401 610-239-9600 239-9195
Web: www.gaudenzia.org

Glenbeigh Health Source 2863 SR 45 ... Rock Creek OH 44084 440-563-3400 563-9619
TF: 800-234-1001 ■ *Web:* www.glenbeigh.com

Grand Lake Mental Health Center Inc
114 W Delaware ... Nowata OK 74048 918-273-1841
Web: www.glmhc.net

Greenleaf Ctr 2209 Pineview Dr ... Valdosta GA 31602 229-671-6700 242-1252
TF: 800-247-2747 ■ *Web:* www.greenleafhospital.com

Griffin Memorial Hospital 900 E Main St ... Norman OK 73071 405-321-4880
TF General: 800-955-3468 ■ *Web:* ok.gov

Gulf Coast Mental Health Center
1600 Broad Ave ... Gulfport MS 39501 228-863-1132
Web: www.gcmhc.com

Hamm Memorial Psychiatric Clnc
408 Saint Peter St Ste 429 ... Saint Paul MN 55102 651-224-0614
Web: www.hammclinic.org

Hampton Behavioral Health Center
650 Rancocas Rd ... Westampton NJ 08060 800-603-6767
TF: 800-603-6767 ■ *Web:* hamptonhospital.com

Harmony Foundation Inc
1600 Fish Hatchery Rd ... Estes Park CO 80517 970-586-4491
TF: 866-686-7867 ■ *Web:* www.harmonyfoundationinc.com

Hathaway-Sycamores Child & Family Services
210 S DeLacey Ave Ste 110 ... Pasadena CA 91105 626-395-7100
Web: www.hathaway-sycamores.org

Hazelden Chicago 867 N Dearborn St ... Chicago IL 60610 312-943-3534
TF: 800-257-7810 ■ *Web:* www.hazelden.org

Hazelden Ctr for Youth & Families (HCYF)
11505 36th Ave N ... Plymouth MN 55441 763-509-3800 559-0149
TF: 800-257-7810 ■ *Web:* www.hazelden.org

Hazelden Foundation
15251 Pleasant Vly Rd ... Center City MN 55012 651-213-4200
TF: 800-257-7810 ■ *Web:* www.hazelden.org

Hazelden New York 322 Eigth Ave 12th Fl ... New York NY 10001 212-420-9520 420-9664
TF: 800-257-7800 ■ *Web:* www.hazelden.org

Hazelden Springbrook 1901 Esther St ... Newberg OR 97132 503-554-4300 537-7007
TF: 866-866-4662 ■ *Web:* www.hazelden.org

HealthSource Saginaw 3340 Hospital Rd ... Saginaw MI 48603 989-790-7700
TF: 800-662-6848 ■ *Web:* www.healthsourcesaginaw.org

Highland Ridge Hospital 7309 South 180 West ... Midvale UT 84047 801-569-2153
TF: 800-821-4357 ■ *Web:* www.highlandridgehospital.com

Impact Drug & Alcohol Treatment Ctr
1680 N Fair Oaks Ave PO Box 93607 ... Pasadena CA 91103 626-798-0884 798-6970
TF: 866-734-4200 ■ *Web:* www.impacthouse.com

Indian Creek Foundation 420 Cowpath Rd ... Souderton PA 18964 267-203-1500
Web: www.indcreek.org

Judson Center Inc 4410 W 13 Mile Rd ... Royal Oak MI 48073 248-549-4339
Web: www.judsoncenter.org

Julian F Keith Alcohol & Drug Abuse Treatment Ctr
201 Tabernacle Rd ... Black Mountain NC 28711 828-257-6200 257-6300

Keystone Ctr 2001 Providence Ave ... Chester PA 19013 610-876-9000 876-5441
TF: 800-558-9600 ■ *Web:* www.keystonecenter.net

La Hacienda Treatment Ctr 145 La Hacienda Way ... Hunt TX 78024 830-238-4222 238-3120
TF: 800-749-6160 ■ *Web:* www.lahacienda.com

Lifetime Recovery 10290 Southton Rd ... San Antonio TX 78223 210-633-0201
Web: www.lifetimerecoverytx.org

Livengrin Foundation 4833 Hulmeville Rd ... Bensalem PA 19020 215-638-5200
TF: 800-245-4746 ■ *Web:* www.livengrin.org

Malvern Institute 940 W King Rd ... Malvern PA 19355 610-647-0330
TF: 888-643-3869 ■ *Web:* www.malverninstitute.com

Miami Valley Family Care Center
922 W Riverview Ave ... Dayton OH 45402 937-223-7217
Web: www.cssmv.org

Mid-south Health Systems
102 Sw Larkspur Dr ... Walnut Ridge AR 72476 870-886-7924
Web: www.mshs.org

Missouri Home Therapy
11636 W Florissant Ave ... Saint Louis MO 63033 314-246-0137
Web: www.missourihometherapy.com

				Phone	Fax
Mohave Mental Health Clinic Inc 3505 Western Ave. *TF:* 888-757-8111 ■ *Web:* www.mmhc-inc.org	Kingman	AZ	86409	928-757-8111	
Momentum For Mental Health 438 N White Rd *Web:* www.momentumformentalhealth.org	San Jose	CA	95127	408-254-6828	
Monadnock Family Services 64 Main St Ste 201 *Web:* www.mfs.org	Keene	NH	03431	603-357-4400	
Mount Regis Ctr 405 Kimball Ave *TF:* 877-217-3447 ■ *Web:* www.mtregis.com	Salem	VA	24153	877-217-3447	
Mountain Manor Treatment Ctr 9701 Keysville Rd. *TF:* 800-537-3422 ■ *Web:* www.mountainmanor.org	Emmitsburg	MD	21727	301-447-2361	
New Directions Inc 30800 Chagrin Blvd *TF:* 800-750-6709 ■ *Web:* www.newdirect.org	Cleveland	OH	44124	216-591-0324	591-1243
Nicasa 31979 N Fish Lk Rd *Web:* www.nicasa.org	Round Lake	IL	60073	847-546-6450	
Nordoff-Robbins Music Therapy Clinic 26 Washington Pl *Web:* steinhardt.nyu.edu	New York	NY	10003	212-998-5151	
North Oklahoma County Mental Health Center 4436 NW 50th St *Web:* www.northcare.com	Oklahoma City	OK	73112	405-858-2700	
Northeast Guidance Center 2900 Conner Bldg A *Web:* www.neguidance.org	Detroit	MI	48215	313-308-1400	
Nulton Diagnostic & Treatment Center PC 214 College Park *Web:* www.nulton.com	Johnstown	PA	15904	814-262-0025	
Oaklawn Psychiatric Center Inc 330 Lakeview Dr *Web:* www.oaklawn.org	Goshen	IN	46527	574-533-1234	
Oesterlen-services for Youth Inc 1918 Mechanicsburg Rd. *Web:* oesterlen.org	Springfield	OH	45503	937-399-6101	
Omni Behavioral Health 2904 14th St Apt 3 *Web:* www.omnibehavioralhealth.com	Columbus	NE	68601	402-562-7933	
OnTrack Inc 221 W Main St *Web:* www.ontrackrecovery.org	Medford	OR	97501	541-772-1777	
Oriana House Inc 885 E Buchtel Ave PO Box 1501 *Web:* www.orianahouse.org	Akron	OH	44305	330-535-8116	
Osceola Mental Health Inc 206 Park Pl Blvd *Web:* www.ppbh.org	Kissimmee	FL	34741	407-846-0023	
Ozark Guidance Center Inc 2400 S 48th St *Web:* www.ozarkguidance.org	Springdale	AR	72762	479-750-2020	
Palmetto Lowcountry Behavioral Health LLC 2777 Speissegger Dr *Web:* palmettobehavioralhealth.com	North Charleston	SC	29405	843-747-5830	
Park Center Inc 909 E State Blvd *Web:* www.parkcenter.org	Fort Wayne	IN	46805	260-481-2700	
Peak Wellness Center 1263 N 15th St *Web:* www.peakwellnesscenter.org	Laramie	WY	82072	307-745-8915	
Perception Programs Inc 54 N St *Web:* perceptionprograms.org	Willimantic	CT	06226	860-450-7122	
Phoenix House Foundation Inc (PHF) 164 W 74th St 4th Fl *TF:* 888-671-9392 ■ *Web:* www.phoenixhouse.org	New York	NY	10023	888-671-9392	
Postgraduate Center for Mental Health Residence 516 W 50th St *Web:* www.pgcmh.org	New York	NY	10019	212-246-0898	
Prestera Center for Mental Health Services Inc 3375 Us Route 60 *Web:* www.prestera.org	Huntington	WV	25705	304-525-7851	
Progress Unlimited Inc 11431 Cronhill Dr Ste C *Web:* www.progressunlimited.org	Owings Mills	MD	21117	410-363-8550	
Prototypes 1000 N Alameda St Ste 390 *Web:* www.prototypes.org	Los Angeles	CA	90012	213-542-3838	
Providence Behavioral Health Hospital 1233 Main St *Web:* www.mercycares.com	Holyoke	MA	01040	413-536-5111	
Reconnect Mental Health Services 2150 Islington Ave *Web:* www.reconnect.on.ca	Etobicoke	ON	M9P3V4	416-248-2050	
Ridgeview Institute Inc 3995 S Cobb Dr *Web:* www.ridgeviewinstitute.com	Smyrna	GA	30080	770-434-4567	
Rimrock Foundation 1231 N 29th St *TF:* 800-227-3953 ■ *Web:* www.rimrock.org	Billings	MT	59101	406-248-3175	248-3821
Riverside General Hospital (RGH) *Houston Recovery Ctr* 4514 Lyons Ave *Web:* riversidegeneralhospital.org	Houston	TX	77020	713-331-2501	
Rivervalley Behavioral Health Hospital 1100 Walnut St PO Box 1637 *TF:* 800-755-8477 ■ *Web:* www.rvbh.com	Owensboro	KY	42302	270-689-6800	
Riverwood Center 1485 M 139 *Web:* riverwoodcenter.org	Benton Harbor	MI	49022	269-925-0585	
Rutland Mental Health Services Inc 78 S Main St *Web:* www.rmhsccn.org	Rutland	VT	05701	802-775-2381	
Safety Council of The Ozarks 1111 S Glenstone Ave Ste 1-103 *Web:* nscozarks.org	Springfield	MO	65804	417-869-2121	
Samaritan Village 138-02 Queens Blvd *TF:* 800-532-4357 ■ *Web:* samaritanvillage.org	Briarwood	NY	11435	718-206-2000	206-2399
Schick Shadel Hospital 12101 Ambaum Blvd SW **Fax Area Code: 206* ■ *TF:* 800-500-6395 ■ *Web:* schickshadel.com	Seattle	WA	98146	800-500-6395	431-9142*
Senior World 6501 N Sheridan Rd *Web:* ipmr.org	Peoria	IL	61614	309-495-4530	
Serenity Lane 616 E 16th Ave *TF:* 800-543-9905 ■ *Web:* www.serenitylane.org	Eugene	OR	97401	541-687-1110	687-9041
Sierra Tucson Inc 39580 S Lago Del Oro Pkwy *TF:* 800-842-4487 ■ *Web:* www.sierratucson.com/?nocookies=true	Tucson	AZ	85739	520-624-4000	818-5869
Spectrum Programs Inc 11031 NE Sixth Ave.	Miami	FL	33161	305-757-0602	757-2387
Spencer Recovery Centers Inc 1316 S Coast Hwy *TF:* 800-334-0394 ■ *Web:* www.spencerrecovery.com	Laguna Beach	CA	92651	800-334-0394	
Talbott Recovery Campus 5448 Yorktowne Dr *TF:* 800-445-4232 ■ *Web:* www.talbottcampus.com	Atlanta	GA	30349	770-994-0185	994-2024
Turning Point Hospital 3015 Veterans Pkwy PO Box 1177 *TF:* 800-342-1075 ■ *Web:* www.turningpointcare.com	Moultrie	GA	31776	229-985-4815	
Turning Point of Tampa 6227 Sheldon Rd *TF:* 800-397-3006 ■ *Web:* www.tpoftampa.com	Tampa	FL	33615	813-882-3003	885-6974
Twin Town Treatment Ctr 1706 University Ave *Web:* meridianprograms.com	Saint Paul	MN	55104	651-645-3661	
Upper Bay Counseling & Support Services Inc 200 Booth St *Web:* www.upperbay.org	Elkton	MD	21921	410-996-5104	
Valley Forge Medical Ctr & Hospital 1033 W Germantown Pk *TF:* 888-539-8500 ■ *Web:* www.vfmc.net	Norristown	PA	19403	610-539-8500	539-0910
Villa of Hope 3300 Dewey Ave *Web:* www.villaofhope.org	Rochester	NY	14616	585-865-1550	865-5219
Village South Inc 3050 Biscayne Blvd 9th Fl *TF:* 800-443-3784 ■ *Web:* www.villagesouth.com	Miami	FL	33137	305-573-3784	576-1348
Wake County Alcoholism Treatment Ctr 3000 Falstaff Rd *Web:* www.wakegov.com	Raleigh	NC	27610	919-250-1500	
Walter B Jones Alcohol & Drug Abuse Treatment Ctr 2577 W Fifth St *TF:* 800-422-1884 ■ *Web:* ncdhhs.gov	Greenville	NC	27834	252-830-3426	
Warwick Manor Behavioral Health 3680 Warwick Rd *Web:* www.warwickmanor.org	East New Market	MD	21631	410-943-8108	
Westbridge Inc 1361 Elm St Ste 207 *Web:* www.westbridge.org	Manchester	NH	03101	603-634-4446	
Willingway Hospital 311 Jones Mill Rd *TF:* 800-242-9455 ■ *Web:* www.willingway.com	Statesboro	GA	30458	912-764-6236	764-7063
Wilmington Treatment Ctr 2520 Troy Dr **Fax Area Code: 910* ■ *TF:* 877-762-3750 ■ *Web:* www.wilmingtontreatment.com?nocookies=true	Wilmington	NC	28401	877-762-3750	762-7923*
Youth Home Inc 20400 Colonel Glenn Rd *TF:* 800-728-6452 ■ *Web:* www.youthhome.org	Little Rock	AR	72210	501-821-5500	

727 SURVEYING, MAPPING, RELATED SERVICES

See Also Engineering & Design p. 2252

				Phone	Fax
AD Potts & Assoc Inc 11524 Jefferson Ave	Newport News	VA	23601	757-595-4610	
Adams & Clark Inc 1720 W Fourth Ave *Web:* adamsandclark.com	Spokane	WA	99204	509-747-4600	
Aerotech Mapping Inc 2580 Montessouri St *Web:* www.atmlv.com	Las Vegas	NV	89117	702-228-6277	
Allen & Major Associates Inc 100 Commerce Way *Web:* www.allenmajor.com	Woburn	MA	01888	781-935-6889	
Atzl Scatassa & Zigler Land Surveyors & Engineers PC 234 N Main St	New City	NY	10956	845-634-4694	
Austin Exploration Inc 10333 Westoffice Dr *Web:* austinex.com	Houston	TX	77042	713-780-7141	780-3118
B H Suhr & Company Inc 840 Custer *Web:* bhsuhr.com	Evanston	IL	60202	847-864-6315	
Bock & Clark Corp 3550 W Market St Ste 200 *Web:* www.bockandclark.com	Akron	OH	44333	330-665-4821	
Bowman Consulting Group 14020 Thunderbolt Pl # 300 *Web:* www.bowmanconsulting.com	Chantilly	VA	20151	703-464-1000	481-8410
Brill J Michael & Associates 5053 Ritter Rd Ste 200 *Web:* www.jmichaelbrill.com	Mechanicsburg	PA	17055	717-691-0200	
Campbell & Associates Inc 1923 Bailey Rd Ste A *Web:* www.campbellsurvey.com	Cuyahoga Falls	OH	44221	330-945-4117	
Chastain Homer L & Associates LLP 5 N Country Club Rd *Web:* hlcllp.com	Decatur	IL	62521	217-422-8544	
Coast Surveying Inc 15031 Pkwy Loop Ste B *Web:* coastsurvey.com	Tustin	CA	92780	714-918-6266	
Cochrane Technologies Inc PO Box 81276 *TF:* 800-346-3745 ■ *Web:* www.cochranetech.com	Lafayette	LA	70598	337-837-3334	837-7134
Cooper Aerial Survey Co 1692 W Grant Rd *Web:* cooperaerial.com	Tucson	AZ	85745	520-884-7580	
Core Design Inc 14711 NE 29th Pl Ste 101 *Web:* www.coredesigninc.com	Bellevue	WA	98007	425-885-7877	
D W Smith Associates LLC 1450 State Rte 34 Ste 101 *Web:* www.dwsmith.com	Wall Township	NJ	07753	732-363-5850	
Day & Zimmermann Group Inc 1818 Market St *TF:* 877-319-0270 ■ *Web:* www.dayzim.com	Philadelphia	PA	19130	215-299-8000	
Doyle & Wachtstetter Inc 131 Commerce St *Web:* www.dw-surveyor.com	Clute	TX	77531	979-265-3622	
Fronterra Integrated Geosciences LLC 3403 Marquart *Web:* www.fronterrageo.com	Houston	TX	77027	713-634-0777	
Fugro Chance Inc 6100 Hillcroft St *Web:* www.fugrochance.com	Houston	TX	77081	713-346-3700	
Fugro Pelagos Inc 3574 Ruffin Rd *Web:* www.fugro-pelagos.com	San Diego	CA	92123	858-292-8922	292-5308
Gabriel E Senor PC 90 N Central Ave	Hartsdale	NY	10530	914-422-0070	
Geodetic Designs 2300 N Grand River Ave *Web:* geodeticdesigns.com	Lansing	MI	48906	517-908-0008	

Company	City	State	Zip	Phone	Fax
Geokinetics Management Inc 1500 Citywest Blvd Ste 800 *Web:* www.geokinetics.com	Houston	TX	77042	713-850-7600	
Geophysics GPR International Inc 100 - 2545 Delorimier Stree *TF:* 800-672-4774 ■ *Web:* www.geophysicsgpr.com	Longueuil	QC	J4K3P7	450-679-2400	
GeoStrata Resources Inc 9727 Horton Rd SW *Web:* www.geostrata.ca	Calgary	AB	T2V2X5	403-319-0922	
Geotech Ltd 245 Industrial Pkwy N *Web:* www.geotech.ca	Aurora	ON	L4G4C4	905-841-5004	
Ghiotto & Assoc Inc 2426 Phillips Hwy *Web:* www.ghiotto.com	Jacksonville	FL	32207	904-886-0071	
Greene & Bradford Inc 3501 Constitution Dr *Web:* greeneandbradford.com	Springfield	IL	62711	217-793-8844	
Ground Penetrating Radar Systems Inc 7540 New West Rd *Web:* www.gp-radar.com	Toledo	OH	43617	419-843-9804	
GX Technology Corp 2105 CityWest Blvd Ste 900 *Web:* www.iongeo.com	Houston	TX	77042	713-789-7250	
Gymo, Architecture, Engineering & Land Surveying PC 220 Sterling St *Web:* www.gymopc.com	Watertown	NY	13601	315-788-3900	
H2 Engineering Surveying LLC 8880 N Hess St *TF:* 877-700-9909 ■ *Web:* h2survey.com	Hayden	ID	83835	208-772-6600	
HadenStanziale PA 2200 W Main St Ste 560 *Web:* www.hadenstanziale.com	Durham	NC	27705	919-286-7440	
Hagedorn Inc 1924 Broadway St Ste B	Vancouver	WA	98663	360-696-4428	
Hanover Design Services PA 1123 Floral Pkwy	Wilmington	NC	28403	910-343-8002	
Hillwig-Goodrow Inc 31407 Outer Hwy 10 *Web:* hillwig-goodrow.com	Redlands	CA	92373	909-794-2673	
HRG Pllc 416 W Third St *Web:* hrgpllc.com	Owensboro	KY	42301	270-683-7558	
Huitt-Zollars Inc 1717 McKinney Ave Ste 1400 *TF:* 866-667-6572 ■ *Web:* www.huitt-zollars.com	Dallas	TX	75202	214-871-3311	871-0757
Ingersoll Watson & Mcmachen Inc 1133 E Milham Rd *Web:* iwmeng.com	Portage	MI	49002	269-344-6165	
Inland Aerial Surveys Inc 7117 Arlington Ave Ste A *Web:* inlandaerial.com	Riverside	CA	92503	951-687-4252	
Intermap Technologies Inc 8310 S Vly Hwy Ste 400 *Web:* www.intermap.com	Englewood	CO	80112	303-708-0955	
Joseph A. Schudt & Associates Inc 19350 S Harlem Ave *Web:* www.jaseng.com	Frankfort	IL	60423	708-720-1000	
JSD Professional Services Inc 161 Horizon Dr Ste 101 *Web:* www.jsdinc.com	Verona	WI	53593	608-848-5060	
KCI Technologies Inc 936 Ridgebrook Rd *TF:* 800-572-7496 ■ *Web:* kci.com	Sparks	MD	21152	410-316-7800	316-7817
Keystone Aerial Surveys Inc 9800 Ashton Rd *Web:* www.keystoneaerialsurveys.com	Philadelphia	PA	19114	215-677-3119	
Lamp, Rynearson & Associates Inc 14710 W Dodge Rd Ste 100 *Web:* www.lra-inc.com	Omaha	NE	68154	402-496-2498	
Landiscor 7310 N 16th St Ste 275 *TF:* 866-221-8578 ■ *Web:* www.landiscor.com	Phoenix	AZ	85020	602-248-8989	
Landpoint Surveys Inc 611 El Dorado Rd *Web:* www.landpoint.net	Magnolia	AR	71753	870-234-6384	
Lewis Yockey & Brown Inc 505 N Main St *Web:* www.lybinc.com	Bloomington	IL	61701	309-829-2552	
Loureiro Engineering Associates 100 Northwest Dr *Web:* www.loureiro.com	Plainville	CT	06062	860-747-6181	
MacDonald Dettwiler & Assoc Ltd 13800 Commerce Pkwy *TSE:* MDA ■ *Web:* www.mdacorporation.com	Richmond	BC	V6V2J3	604-278-3411	231-2768
Mackie Consultants LLC 9575 W Higgins Rd Ste 500 *Web:* www.mackieconsult.com	Rosemont	IL	60018	847-696-1400	
Northeast Civil Solutions Inc 381 Payne Rd *Web:* www.northeastcivilsolutions.com	Scarborough	ME	04074	207-883-1000	883-1001
NuTech Energy Alliance Ltd 7702 FM 1960 E Ste 300 *Web:* www.nutechenergy.com	Houston	TX	77346	281-812-4030	
Poepping Stone Bach & Assoc Inc Engr 100 S 54th St PO Box 709 *Web:* psba.com	Quincy	IL	62305	217-223-4605	
Print-O-Stat Inc 1011 W Market St *TF:* 800-711-8014 ■ *Web:* www.printostat.com	York	PA	17404	717-854-7821	846-4084
Quantapoint Inc 275 Curry Hollow Rd *Web:* www.quantapoint.com	Pittsburgh	PA	15236	412-653-0100	653-2940
Quantec Geoscience Ltd 146 Sparks Ave *Web:* www.quantecgeoscience.com	Toronto	ON	M2H2S4	416-306-1941	
R e Warner & Associates Inc 25777 Detroit Rd Ste 200 *Web:* www.rewarner.com	Westlake	OH	44145	440-835-9400	
R&M Consultants Inc 9101 Vanguard Dr *Web:* www.rmconsult.com	Anchorage	AK	99507	907-522-1707	
Ramsey Land Surveying LLC 8718 SW Pkwy	Austin	TX	78735	512-301-9398	
Raudenbush Engineering Inc 29 S Union St *Web:* raudeng.com	Middletown	PA	17057	717-944-0883	
Rice Assoc Inc 10625 Gaskins Way *Web:* ricesurveys.com	Manassas	VA	20109	703-968-3200	
Rouse-sirine Associates Ltd 333 Office Sq Ln *TF:* 800-276-2023 ■ *Web:* www.rouse-sirine.com	Virginia Beach	VA	23462	757-490-2300	
Sidwell Co Inc 675 Sidwell Ct *TF:* 877-743-9355 ■ *Web:* www.sidwellco.com	Saint Charles	IL	60174	630-549-1000	549-1111
Surdex Corp 520 Spirit of St Louis Blvd *Web:* www.surdex.com	Chesterfield	MO	63005	636-368-4400	
Surveying Services Inc 41 Heritage Sq	Jackson	TN	38305	731-664-0807	
T3 Global Strategies Inc 10 Emerson Ln Ste 808	Bridgeville	PA	15017	412-221-2003	
Teletrac Inc 7391 Lincoln Way *TF:* 800-500-6009 ■ *Web:* www.teletrac.com	Garden Grove	CA	92841	714-897-0877	379-6378
Terra Remote Sensing Inc 1962 Mills Rd *Web:* www.terraremote.com	Sidney	BC	V8L5Y3	250-656-0931	
Tim Miller Assoc Inc 10 N St *Web:* timmillerassociates.com	Cold Spring	NY	10516	845-265-4400	
Wade-Trim Group Inc 500 Griswold Ave Ste 2500 *TF:* 800-482-2864 ■ *Web:* www.wadetrim.com	Detroit	MI	48226	313-961-3650	961-0898

728 SWIMMING POOLS

Company	City	State	Zip	Phone	Fax
Anthony & Sylvan Pools Corp 3739 Easton Rd Rt 611 *TF:* 800-366-7958 ■ *Web:* www.anthonysylvan.com	Doylestown	PA	18901	215-489-5600	
Delair Group LLC 8600 River Rd *TF:* 800-235-0185 ■ *Web:* jerith.com/delgard	Delair	NJ	08110	215-676-4068	
Fox Pool Corp 3490 BoaRd Rd *TF:* 800-723-1011 ■ *Web:* www.foxpool.com	York	PA	17406	717-764-8581	
Gary Pools Inc 438 Sandau Rd *Web:* www.garypools.com	San Antonio	TX	78216	210-341-5153	341-5154
Hoffinger Industries Inc 315 Sebastian St	West Helena	AR	72390	870-572-3466	572-9711
Hornerxpress Inc 5755 Powerline Rd *TF:* 800-432-6966 ■ *Web:* www.hornerxpress.com	Fort Lauderdale	FL	33309	954-772-6966	772-6970
Imperial Pools Inc 33 Wade Rd *TF:* 800-444-9977 ■ *Web:* www.imperialpoolsb2b.com	Latham	NY	12110	518-786-1200	786-0954
Mission Pools of Escondido 755 W Grand Ave *Web:* www.missionpools.com	Escondido	CA	92025	760-743-2605	
Morgan Bldg Systems Inc 2800 McCree Rd *TF:* 800-935-0321 ■ *Web:* www.morganusa.com	Garland	TX	75041	972-864-7300	
Radiant Pools Div Trojan Leisure Products LLC 440 N Pearl St *TF:* 866-697-5870 ■ *Web:* www.radiantpools.com	Albany	NY	12207	518-434-4161	432-6554
Viking Pools Inc 121 Crawford Rd PO Box 96 *TF:* 800-854-7665 ■ *Web:* www.vikingpools.net	Williams	CA	95987	530-473-5319	473-5393
Vogue Pool Products 7050 St Patrick St *TF:* 800-363-3232 ■ *Web:* www.piscinesvogue.com	LaSalle	QC	H8N1V2	514-363-3232	363-1772

729 SWITCHGEAR & SWITCHBOARD APPARATUS

See Also Transformers - Power, Distribution, Specialty p. 3259; Wiring Devices - Current-Carrying p. 3313

Company	City	State	Zip	Phone	Fax
Acorn Technology 23103 Miles Rd *Web:* www.acorntechnology.com	Cleveland	OH	44128	216-663-1244	
Actelis Networks Inc 6150 Stevenson Blvd *Web:* www.actelis.com	Fremont	CA	94538	510-545-1045	
Atkinson Industries Inc 1801 E 27th St Terr *Web:* www.azz.com	Pittsburg	KS	66762	620-231-6900	231-7154
AudioCodes Inc 27 World'S Fair Dr *Web:* audiocodes.com	Somerset	NJ	08873	732-469-0880	
AZZ Inc 3100 W Seventh St Ste 500 *Web:* www.azz.com	Fort Worth	TX	76107	817-810-0095	336-5354
Bel Fuse Inc 206 Van Vorst St *NASDAQ:* BELFA ■ *TF:* 800-235-3873 ■ *Web:* www.belfuse.com	Jersey City	NJ	07302	201-432-0463	432-9542
Cleaveland Price Inc 14000 Rt 993 *Web:* www.cleavelandprice.com	Trafford	PA	15085	724-864-4177	
Cole Instrument Corp 2650 S Croddy Way **Fax:* Sales ■ *Web:* www.cole-switches.com	Santa Ana	CA	92704	714-556-3100	241-9061*
Components Corp of America 5950 Berkshire Ln # 1550 *Web:* www.components-corp-amer.com	Dallas	TX	75225	214-969-0166	969-5905
Comus International Inc 454 Allwood Rd *Web:* www.comus-intl.com	Clifton	NJ	07012	973-777-6900	
Custom Control Solutions Inc 8500 Fowler Ave *Web:* www.ccsinc-florida.com	Pensacola	FL	32534	850-473-8704	
CW Industries 130 James Way *Web:* www.cwind.com	SouthHampton	PA	18966	215-355-7080	355-1088
Delta Systems Inc 1734 Frost Rd *Web:* phoenixtechnologyit.com	Streetsboro	OH	44241	330-626-2811	
Electroswitch Corp 180 King Ave *Web:* www.electroswitch.com	Weymouth	MA	02188	781-335-5200	335-4253
FIC Corp 12216 Parklawn Dr *Web:* www.ficcorp.com	Rockville	MD	20852	301-881-8124	
Grayhill Inc 561 W Hillgrove Ave *Web:* www.grayhill.com	La Grange	IL	60525	708-354-1040	354-2820
Guardian Electric Mfg Company Inc 1425 Lake Ave *TF:* 800-762-0369 ■ *Web:* www.guardian-electric.com	Woodstock	IL	60098	815-334-3600	337-0377
HVB AE Power Systems Inc 7250 Mcginnis Ferry Rd *TF:* 866-362-0798 ■ *Web:* hvbi.hitachi.us	Suwanee	GA	30024	770-495-1755	
Indak Manufacturing Corp 1915 Techny Rd *Web:* www.indak.com	Northbrook	IL	60062	847-272-0343	
Indicon Corp 6125 Center Dr Ste 110	Sterling Heights	MI	48312	586-274-0505	
Inertia Engineering 6665 Hardaway Rd *Web:* www.inertiaworks.com	Stockton	CA	95215	209-931-1670	
Instruments Inc 7263 Engineer Rd Ste G *Web:* www.instrumentsinc.com	San Diego	CA	92111	858-571-1111	571-0188

	City	State	Zip	Phone	Fax
ITW Switches 195 E Algonquin Rd TF: 800-544-3354 ■ Web: www.itwswitches.com	Des Plaines	IL	60016	847-876-9400	876-9440
JMS North America Corp 22320 Foothill Blvd Ste 350 Web: www.jmsna.net	Hayward	CA	94541	510-888-9090	
Kasa Industrial Controls Inc 418 E Ave B TF: 800-755-5272 ■ Web: www.kasacontrols.com	Salina	KS	67401	785-825-7181	825-1663
Keystone Electrical Manufacturing Co 2511 Bell Ave Web: www.keystoneemc.com	Des Moines	IA	50321	515-283-2567	283-0418
Kraus & Naimer 760 New Brunswick Rd Web: www.krausnaimer.com	Somerset	NJ	08873	732-560-1240	560-8823
LayerZero Power Systems Inc 1500 Danner Dr Web: www.layerzero.com	Aurora	OH	44202	440-399-9000	
Littelfuse Inc 8755 W Higgins Rd Ste 500 NASDAQ: LFUS ■ TF Sales: 800-227-0029 ■ Web: www.littelfuse.com	Chicago	IL	60631	773-628-1000	
Logic Technologies Inc 117 Bellamy Pl Web: logictechnologies.com	Stockbridge	GA	30281	770-389-4964	
Lumitex Inc 8443 Dow Cir TF: 800-969-5483 ■ Web: www.lumitex.com	Strongsville	OH	44136	440-243-8401	243-8402
Mac Products Inc 60 Pennsylvania Ave PO Box 469 Web: www.macproducts.net	Kearny	NJ	07032	973-344-0700	344-5368
Marathon Special Products 13300 Van Camp Rd PO Box 468 Web: www.marathonsp.com	Bowling Green	OH	43402	419-352-8441	352-0875
MCC Control Systems LP 859 Cotting Ct Ste G Web: www.mcccontrolsystems.com	Vacaville	CA	95688	707-449-0341	
Mechanical Products Co 1112 N Garfield St Web: www.mechprod.com	Lombard	IL	60148	630-953-4100	
Mersen Inc 374 Merrimac St Web: www.mersen.com	Newburyport	MA	01950	978-462-6662	462-7934
Mitsubishi Electric Power Products Inc Thorn Hill Industrial Park 530 Keystone Dr Web: www.meppi.com	Warrendale	PA	15086	724-772-2555	
Multitech Industries Inc 350 Village Dr Web: www.multitechind.com	Carol Stream	IL	60188	630-784-9200	784-9225
Norberg-ies 4237 S 74th E Ave TF: 800-739-9145 ■ Web: www.nema7.com	Tulsa	OK	74145	918-665-6888	
Otto Engineering Inc 2 E Main St TF: 888-234-6886 ■ Web: www.ottoexcellence.com	Carpentersville	IL	60110	847-428-7171	428-1956
Pacs Industries Inc 61 Steamboat Rd Web: www.pacsswitchgearllc.com	Great Neck	NY	11024	516-465-7100	829-9557
Powell Industries Inc 8550 Mosely Dr NASDAQ: POWL ■ TF: 800-480-7273 ■ Web: www.powellind.com	Houston	TX	77075	713-944-6900	947-4453
Power Distribution Inc 4200 Oakleys Ct TF: 800-225-4838 ■ Web: smithspower.com/brands/pdi	Richmond	VA	23223	804-737-9880	
Powercon Corp PO Box 477 TF: 800-638-5055 ■ Web: www.powerconcorp.com	Severn	MD	21144	410-551-6500	551-8451
Professional Power Products Inc 448 W Madison St Web: www.professionalpowerproducts.com	Darien	WI	53114	262-882-9000	882-9010
PSI Control Solutions Inc 5808 Long Creek Park Dr Web: psicontrolsolutions.com	Charlotte	NC	28269	704-596-5617	
Reliance Controls Corp 2001 Young Ct TF: 800-634-6155 ■ Web: www.reliancecontrols.com	Racine	WI	53404	262-634-6155	634-6436
Revere Control Systems Inc 2240 Rocky Ridge Rd TF: 800-536-2525 ■ Web: www.reverecontrol.com	Birmingham	AL	35216	205-824-0004	824-0439
Romac Supply Company Inc 7400 Bandini Blvd Web: www.romacsupply.com	Commerce	CA	90040	323-721-5810	
Russelectric Inc 99 Industrial Pk Rd TF: 800-225-5250 ■ Web: www.russelectric.com	Hingham	MA	02043	781-749-6000	
S & C Electric Co 6601 N Ridge Blvd TF: 800-621-5546 ■ Web: www.sandc.com	Chicago	IL	60626	773-338-1000	338-3657
Satin American Corp 40 Oliver Terr *Fax Area Code: 203 ■ TF: 877-356-5050 ■ Web: www.satinamerican.com	Shelton	CT	06484	877-356-5050	929-9684*
Sigma-Netics Inc 2 N Corporate Dr Web: www.sigmanetics.com	Riverdale	NJ	07457	973-227-6372	
Southwest Electric Co PO Box 82639 Web: www.swelectric.com	Oklahoma City	OK	73148	405-869-1100	
SPD Electrical Systems 13500 Roosevelt Blvd Web: l-3com.com	Philadelphia	PA	19116	215-677-4900	
Tapeswitch Corp 100 Schmitt Blvd TF: 800-234-8273 ■ Web: www.tapeswitch.com	Farmingdale	NY	11735	631-630-0442	630-0454
Taqua LLC 740 E Campbell Rd Ste 200 Web: www.taqua.com	Richardson	TX	75081	972-692-1800	437-2762
TopWorx Inc 3300 Fern Vly Rd Web: www2.emersonprocess.com	Louisville	KY	40213	502-969-8000	969-5911
Turner Electric LLC 131 Enterprise Dr Web: www.turnerswitch.com	Edwardsville	IL	62025	618-797-5000	
Uniforce Technologies Inc 1805 E Fifth St	North Little Rock	AR	72114	501-945-3283	

730 TABLE & KITCHEN SUPPLIES - CHINA & EARTHENWARE

See Also

	City	State	Zip	Phone	Fax
Bradshaw International Inc 9409 Buffalo Ave Web: www.bradshawintl.com	Rancho Cucamonga	CA	91730	909-476-3884	476-3616
Hall China Co 672 Fiesta Dr PO Box 989 *Fax Area Code: 800 ■ Web: www.hlcdinnerware.com/hall_china	Newell	WV	26050	330-385-2900	837-4950*
Heritage Mint Ltd PO Box 13750 TF: 888-860-6245 ■ Web: www.heritagemint.com	Scottsdale	AZ	85267	480-860-1300	
Homer Laughlin China Co 672 Fiesta Dr TF: 800-452-4462 ■ Web: hlcdinnerware.com	Newell	WV	26050	304-387-1300	387-0593
Lenox Corp PO Box 2006 TF: 800-223-4311 ■ Web: www.lenox.com	Bristol	PA	19007	800-223-4311	
Lipper International Inc 235 Washington St TF: 800-243-3129 ■ Web: www.lipperinternational.com	Wallingford	CT	06492	203-269-8588	284-8637
Luna Garcia 201 San Juan Ave TF: 800-905-9975 ■ Web: www.lunagarcia.com	Venice	CA	90291	310-396-8026	
Original Hartstone Pottery, The 1719 Dearborn St Web: www.hartstonepottery.com	Zanesville	OH	43701	740-452-9000	452-5369
Pfaltzgraff Co PO Box 21769 *Fax: Cust Svc ■ TF: 800-999-2811 ■ Web: www.pfaltzgraff.com	York	PA	17402	800-999-2811	717-2481*
True West 8549 PR 2414 PO Box 441 Web: www.truewesthome.com	Royse City	TX	75189	972-636-7922	635-2059
Waterford Wedgwood USA Inc 1330 Campus Pkwy Web: wedgwood.com	Wall	NJ	07753	732-938-5800	

731 TALENT AGENCIES

See Also Literary Agents p. 2675; Modeling Agencies p. 2777

	City	State	Zip	Phone	Fax
Buddy Lee Attractions Inc 38 Music Sq E Ste 300 Web: www.buddyleeattractions.com	Nashville	TN	37203	615-244-4336	726-0429
CAA Sports 2000 Ave of the Stars Web: sports.caa.com	Los Angeles	CA	90067	424-288-2000	288-2900
CESD Talent Agency Inc 10635 Santa Monica Blvd Ste 130 Web: www.cesdtalent.com	Los Angeles	CA	90025	310-475-2111	
CM Artists New York 127 W 96th St Ste 13 B Web: www.cmartists.com	New York	NY	10025	212-864-1005	864-1066
Columbia Artists Management LLC 1790 Broadway Web: www.cami.com	New York	NY	10019	212-841-9500	841-9744
Creative Artists Agency Inc (CAA) 2000 Ave of the Stars Web: www.caa.com	Los Angeles	CA	90067	424-288-2000	288-2900
Don Buchwald & Assoc 6500 Wilshire Blvd Ste 2200 Web: www.buchwald.com	Los Angeles	CA	90048	323-655-7400	655-7470
Endeavor Agency 9601 Wilshire Blvd 3rd Fl Web: www.wmeentertainment.com	Beverly Hills	CA	90210	310-859-4000	285-9010
Gersh Agency 9465 Wilshire Blvd Web: www.gershcomedy.com	Beverly Hills	CA	90212	310-274-6611	
Gersh Agency, The (TGA) 41 Madison Ave 33rd Fl Web: www.gershcomedy.com	New York	NY	10010	212-997-1818	
Gorfaine/Schwartz Agency 4111 W Alameda Ave Ste 509 Web: www.gsamusic.com	Burbank	CA	91505	818-260-8500	260-8522
Great North Artists Management 350 Dupont St Web: tamac.ca	Toronto	ON	M5R1V9	416-925-2051	925-3904
Hartig Hilepo Agency Ltd 54 W 21st St Ste 610 Web: hartighilepo.com	New York	NY	10010	212-929-1772	929-1266
HS International 9871 Irvine Ctr Dr Web: www.hsi.net	Irvine	CA	92618	949-753-9153	753-9253
IMG Artists 7 W 54th St Web: www.imgartists.com	New York	NY	10019	212-994-3500	994-3550
IMG Inc 1360 E Ninth St Web: img.com	Cleveland	OH	44114	216-522-1200	522-1145
Innovative Artists 1505 Tenth St Web: www.innovativeartists.com	Santa Monica	CA	90401	310-656-0400	656-0456
Kraft-Engel Management 15233 Ventura Blvd Ste 200 Web: www.kraft-engel.com	Sherman Oaks	CA	91403	818-380-1918	380-2609
Media Talent Group 9200 Sunset Blvd Ste 550	West Hollywood	CA	90069	310-275-7900	275-7910
Monterey International 200 W Superior St Ste 202 Web: www.montereyinternational.net	Chicago	IL	60654	312-640-7500	640-7515
Monterey Peninsula Artists/Paradigm 404 W Franklin St Web: www.paradigmagency.com	Monterey	CA	93940	831-375-4889	
Nettwerk 1650 W Second Ave Web: www.nettwerk.com	Vancouver	BC	V6J4R3	604-654-2929	654-1993
One Entertainment 12 W 57th St Ste 1	New York	NY	10019	212-974-3900	
Original Artists 9465 Wilshire Blvd Ste 870	Beverly Hills	CA	90212	310-275-6765	
Paradigm Talent & Literary Agency 360 N Crescent Dr N Bldg Web: paradigmagency.com	Beverly Hills	CA	90210	310-288-8000	288-2000
Parseghian Planco LLC 322 Eigth Ave Ste 601	New York	NY	10001	212-777-7786	
Peter Strain & Assoc 5455 Wilshire Blvd Ste 1812 Web: natacharoi.com	Los Angeles	CA	90036	323-525-3391	
Randsman Artist Management 250 W 57th St Ste 2401 Web: www.randsman.com	New York	NY	10107	212-290-2281	
Rogers & Cowan Pacific Design Ctr 8687 Melrose Ave 7th Fl Web: www.rogersandcowan.com	Los Angeles	CA	90069	310-854-8100	
Rosebud Agency PO Box 170429 Web: www.rosebudus.com	San Francisco	CA	94117	415-386-3456	386-0599
Sfx Live Nation 5335 Wisconsin Ave NW	Washington	DC	20015	202-686-2000	
Shapiro/West & Assoc 141 El Camino Dr Ste 205	Beverly Hills	CA	90212	310-278-8896	278-7238
Stone Manners Agency 9911 W Pico Blvd Ste 1400	Los Angeles	CA	90035	323-655-1313	389-1577
TalentWorks 3500 W Olive Ave Ste 1400 Web: www.talentworks.us	Burbank	CA	91505	818-972-4300	955-6411

Phone | Fax

United Talent Agency Inc (UTA)
9336 Civic Ctr Dr . . . . . Beverly Hills CA 90210 310-273-6700 247-1111
Web: www.unitedtalent.com

William Morris Agency
1325 Ave of the Americas . . . . . New York NY 10019 212-586-5100 246-3583
Web: www.wma.com

William Morris Agency 1600 Div St Ste 300 . . . . . Nashville TN 37203 615-963-3000 963-3090
Web: www.wma.com

William Morris Agency
1500 S Douglas Rd Ste 230 . . . . . Coral Gables FL 33134 305-938-2000 938-2002
Web: www.wma.com

TAPE - ADHESIVE

See Medical Supplies - Mfr p. 2745

732 TAPE - CELLOPHANE, GUMMED, MASKING, PRESSURE SENSITIVE

See Also Medical Supplies - Mfr p. 2745

Phone | Fax

3M Canada Co 300 Tartan Dr . . . . . London ON N5V4M9 888-364-3577 479-4453*
**Fax Area Code:* 800 ■ *TF:* 888-364-3577 ■ *Web:* 3m.com/intl/ca

Adchem Corp 1852 County Rd 58 . . . . . Riverhead NY 11901 631-727-6000 727-6010
Web: www.adchem.com

Adhesive Applications Inc 41 O'Neill St . . . . . EastHampton MA 01027 413-527-7120 527-7249
Web: www.stik-2.com

American Biltrite Inc 57 River St . . . . . Wellesley Hills MA 02481 781-237-6655 237-6880
OTC: ABLT ■ *Web:* www.ambilt.com

American Biltrite Inc Tape Products Div (ABI)
105 Whittendale Dr . . . . . Moorestown NJ 08057 856-778-0700 224-6325*
**Fax Area Code:* 888 ■ *TF:* 888-224-6325 ■ *Web:* www.abitape.com

Avery Dennison Corp 207 Goode Ave . . . . . Glendale CA 91203 626-304-2000
NYSE: AVY ■ *TF Cust Svc:* 888-567-4387 ■ *Web:* www.averydennison.com

Avery Dennison Specialty Tapes Div
250 Chester St Bldg 5 . . . . . Painesville OH 44077 626-304-2000 358-3341*
**Fax Area Code:* 440 ■ *TF:* 866-462-8379 ■ *Web:* www.averydennison.com

Bemis Company Inc
1 Neenah Ctr Fourth Fl PO Box 669 . . . . . Neenah WI 54957 920-727-4100
NYSE: BMS ■ *Web:* www.bemis.com

Brady Coated Products 6555 W Good Hope Rd . . . . . Milwaukee WI 53223 414-358-6600 541-1686*
**Fax Area Code:* 800 ■ *TF:* 800-662-1191 ■
Web: www.bradyid.com/en-us/standards-and-compliance/custom-coating-services/overview

Brite-Line LLC 10660 E 51st Ave . . . . . Denver CO 80239 888-201-6448 208-0758
TF: 888-201-6448 ■ *Web:* www.brite-line.com

Decker Tape Products Inc 6 Stewart Pl . . . . . Fairfield NJ 07004 973-227-5350 808-9418
TF: 800-227-5252 ■ *Web:* www.deckertape.com

DeWAL Industries Inc 15 Ray Trainor Dr . . . . . Narragansett RI 02882 401-789-9736 783-6780
TF: 800-366-8356 ■ *Web:* www.dewal.com

Eternabond 75 E Div St . . . . . Mundelein IL 60060 847-837-9400 837-9449
TF: 888-336-2663 ■ *Web:* www.eternabond.com

FiberMark Inc 161 Wellington Rd . . . . . Brattleboro VT 05301 802-257-0365
Web: www.fibermark.com

Gaska-Tape Inc 1810 W Lusher Ave . . . . . Elkhart IN 46517 574-294-5431 293-4504
TF: 800-423-1571 ■ *Web:* www.gaska.com

Harris Industries Inc
5181 Argosy Ave . . . . . Huntington Beach CA 92649 714-898-8048 898-7108
TF: 800-222-6866 ■ *Web:* www.harrisind.com

Hawkeye International Ltd
5760 VT Rt 100 . . . . . North Hyde Park VT 05665 802-635-7500 635-7900
Web: www.hawkeyeintl.com/home.htm

Holland Mfg Co Inc 15 Main St PO Box 404 . . . . . Succasunna NJ 07876 973-584-8141 584-6845
TF: 800-345-0492 ■ *Web:* www.hollandmfg.com

JHL Industries 10012 Nevada Ave . . . . . Chatsworth CA 91311 818-882-2233 882-4350
TF: 800-255-6636 ■ *Web:* www.jhlindustries.com

Kruse Adhesive Tape Inc
1610 E McFadden Ave . . . . . Santa Ana CA 92705 714-640-2130 640-2134
TF: 800-992-7702 ■ *Web:* www.krusetape.com

M & C Specialties Co 90 James Way . . . . . SouthHampton PA 18966 215-322-1600 322-1620
TF Cust Svc: 800-441-6996 ■ *Web:* www.mcspecialties.com

Neptco Inc 30 Hamlet St . . . . . Pawtucket RI 02861 401-722-5500 722-6378
TF: 800-354-5445 ■ *Web:* www.neptco.com

Plymouth Rubber Company Inc
275 Tpke St Ste 310 . . . . . Canton MA 02021 781-828-0220 828-6041
Web: www.plymouthrubber.com

Presto Tape Inc 1626 Bridgewater Rd . . . . . Bensalem PA 19020 215-245-8555 245-8554
TF: 800-331-1373 ■ *Web:* www.prestotape.com

Pro Tapes & Specialties PO Box 53026 . . . . . Newark NJ 07101 732-346-0900 729-7440
TF: 800-345-0234 ■ *Web:* www.protapes.com

Shurtape Technologies LLC
1712 Eigth St Dr SE . . . . . Hickory NC 28602 828-322-2700 335-7651*
**Fax Area Code:* 800 ■ *TF:* 888-442-8273 ■ *Web:* www.shurtape.com

TapeSouth Inc 10302 Deerwood Pk Ste 125 . . . . . Jacksonville FL 32256 904-642-1800 642-7006
Web: www.tapesouth.com

Tesa Tape Inc 5825 Carnegie Blvd . . . . . Charlotte NC 28209 704-554-0707 852-8831*
**Fax Area Code:* 800 ■ **Fax:* Cust Svc ■ *TF:* 800-426-2181 ■ *Web:* www.tesatape.com

Thomas Tape Co 1713 Sheridan Ave . . . . . Springfield OH 45505 937-325-6414 325-2850
Web: www.thomastape.com

Tommy Tape 378 Four Rod Rd . . . . . Berlin CT 06037 860-378-0111 378-0113
TF: 888-866-8273 ■ *Web:* www.tommytape.com

Venture Tape Corp 30 Commerce Rd . . . . . Rockland MA 02370 781-331-5900
Web: venturetape.com

VIBAC Canada Inc 12250 Industrial Blvd . . . . . Montreal QC H1B5M5 514-640-0250 640-1577
TF: 800-557-0192 ■ *Web:* www.vibacgroup.com

WTP Inc PO Box 937 . . . . . Coloma MI 49038 269-468-3399
TF: 800-521-0731 ■ *Web:* www.wtp-inc.com

733 TARPS, TENTS, COVERS

See Also Bags - Textile p. 1837; Sporting Goods p. 3193

Phone | Fax

Aero Industries Inc 4243 W Bradbury Ave . . . . . Indianapolis IN 46241 317-244-2433 244-1311
TF Sales: 800-535-9545 ■ *Web:* www.aeroindustries.com

American Pavilion 1706 Warrington Ave . . . . . Danville IL 61832 217-443-0800 443-9619
TF: 800-424-9699 ■ *Web:* www.americanpavilion.com

Anchor Industries Inc 1100 Burch Dr . . . . . Evansville IN 47725 812-867-2421 867-1429
TF: 800-544-4445 ■ *Web:* www.anchorinc.com

Canvas Products Co 274 S Waterman St . . . . . Detroit MI 48209 313-496-1000
TF: 877-293-1669 ■ *Web:* www.canvaspc.com

Canvas Specialty PO BOX 22268 . . . . . Los Angeles CA 90040 323-722-1156
Web: www.can-spec.com

Carefree of Colorado 2145 W Sixth Ave . . . . . Broomfield CO 80020 303-469-3324
Web: www.carefreeofcolorado.com

Clamshell Structures Inc 1101 Maulhardt Ave . . . . . Oxnard CA 93030 805-988-1340 988-2266
TF: 800-360-8853 ■ *Web:* www.clamshell.com

Commonwealth Canvas Inc 5 Perkins Way . . . . . Newburyport MA 01950 978-499-3900 499-3933
TF: 877-922-6827 ■ *Web:* www.commonwealthcanvas.com

CR Daniels Inc 3451 Ellicott Ctr Dr . . . . . Ellicott City MD 21043 410-461-2100 461-2987
TF: 800-933-2638 ■ *Web:* www.crdaniels.com

DC Humphrys Inc 5744 Woodland Ave . . . . . Philadelphia PA 19143 215-724-8181 724-8706
TF Sales: 800-645-2059 ■
Web: www.sbcontract.com/contractor/1661625/d-c-humphrys-co-inc-in-philadelphia-pa.htm

Diamond Brand Canvas Products
145 Cane Creek Industrial Pk Rd Ste 1 . . . . . Fletcher NC 28732 828-684-9848
TF Sales: 800-459-6262 ■ *Web:* www.diamondbrand.com

Eide Industries Inc 16215 Piuma Ave . . . . . Cerritos CA 90703 562-402-8335 924-2233
TF: 800-422-6827 ■ *Web:* www.eideindustries.com

Estex Mfg Co Inc 402 E Broad St PO Box 368 . . . . . Fairburn GA 30213 800-749-1224 964-7534*
**Fax Area Code:* 770 ■ *TF:* 800-749-1224 ■ *Web:* www.estexmfg.com

Fisher Canvas Products Inc 415 St Mary St . . . . . Burlington NJ 08016 800-892-6688 239-2728*
**Fax Area Code:* 609 ■ *TF:* 800-892-6688 ■ *Web:* www.fishercanvas.com

Harry Miller Co Inc 850 Albany St . . . . . Boston MA 02119 617-427-2300 442-1152
Web: www.harrymiller.com

John Johnson Co 274 S Waterman St . . . . . Detroit MI 48209 313-496-0600 496-0252
TF: 800-991-1394 ■ *Web:* www.johnjohnsonco.com

Johnson Outdoors Inc 555 Main St . . . . . Racine WI 53403 262-631-6600 631-6601
NASDAQ: JOUT ■ *TF:* 800-468-9716 ■ *Web:* www.johnsonoutdoors.com

Loop-Loc Ltd 390 Motor Pkwy . . . . . Hauppauge NY 11788 631-582-2626 582-2636
TF: 800-562-5667 ■ *Web:* www.looploc.com

Mauritzon Inc 3939 W Belden Ave . . . . . Chicago IL 60647 773-235-6000
Web: www.mauritzononline.com

Midwest Canvas Corp 4635 W Lake St . . . . . Chicago IL 60644 773-287-4400 854-2017
Web: www.midwestcanvas.com

North Sails Group LLC 125 Old Gate Ln . . . . . Milford CT 06460 203-877-7621 874-6059
Web: www.northsails.com/us

Rainier Industries Ltd 18375 Olympic Ave S . . . . . Tukwila WA 98188 425-251-1800 251-5065
TF: 800-869-7162 ■ *Web:* www.rainier.com

Robertson Manufacturing Inc
112 Woodland Ave . . . . . West Grove PA 19390 610-869-9600 869-6365
TF: 800-260-5423

Shur-Co Inc 2309 Shur-Lok St PO Box 713 . . . . . Yankton SD 57078 605-665-6000 665-0501
TF: 800-474-8756 ■ *Web:* www.shurco.com

Steele Canvas Basket Corp
201 William St PO Box 6267 IMCN . . . . . Chelsea MA 02150 617-889-0202 889-0524
TF: 800-541-8929 ■ *Web:* steelecanvas.com

Trimaco LLC
2300 Gateway Centre Blvd Ste 200 . . . . . Morrisville NC 27560 919-674-3460 674-3461
TF: 800-325-7356 ■ *Web:* www.trimaco.com

Troy Sunshade Co 607 Riffle Ave . . . . . Greenville OH 45331 937-548-2466
TF: 800-833-8769 ■ *Web:* bagsbytroy.com

Universal Fabric Structures Inc
2200 Kumry Rd . . . . . Telford PA 18969 215-529-9921 529-9936
TF: 800-634-8368 ■ *Web:* www.ufsinc.com

Webb Manufacturing Co 1241 Carpenter St . . . . . Philadelphia PA 19147 215-336-5570 336-4422
Web: www.webbmfg.com

734 TAX PREPARATION SERVICES

Phone | Fax

1-2-3 Payroll & HR Services Inc PO Box 96 . . . . . Holtsville NY 11742 631-654-1811
Web: www.1-2-3payroll.com

Abdo Eick & Meyers LLP 5201 Eden Ave . . . . . Edina MN 55436 952-835-9090
Web: www.aemcpas.com

AccessPoint LLC
28800 Orchard Lake Rd . . . . . Farmington Hills MI 48334 866-513-3861
TF: 866-513-3861 ■ *Web:* www.accesspointhr.com

Accume Partners LLC 341 New Albany Rd . . . . . Moorestown NJ 08057 856-914-9500
Web: www.accumepartners.com

Active Professionals Inc
9647b Folsom Blvd . . . . . Sacramento CA 95827 888-838-5086
TF: 888-838-5086 ■ *Web:* activeprofessionalconferences.com

Acumen Fiscal Agent LLC
4542 E Inverness Ave Ste 210 . . . . . Mesa AZ 85206 480-497-0343
Web: www.acumenfiscalagent.com

Adamy Valuation Advisors
50 Louis St NW Ste 405 . . . . . Grand Rapids MI 49503 616-284-3700
Web: www.adamyvaluation.com

Advantage One Tax Consulting Inc
20610 Quarterpath Trace Cir . . . . . Sterling VA 20165 703-584-5533
Web: www.aotax.com

AFJ Consulting Group
5455 Wilshire Blvd Ste 2020 . . . . . Los Angeles CA 90036 323-782-9391
Web: www.afjconsulting.com

Alliance Benefit Group Financial Services Corp
201 E Clark St PO Box 1206 . . . . . Albert Lea MN 56007 507-377-2919
Web: www.abgfs.com

Company	City	State	Zip	Phone	Fax
AmCheck Inc 5030 E Sunrise Dr *Web:* www.amcheck.com	Phoenix	AZ	85044	480-763-5900	
APA Services 4150 International Plz Tower I Ste 510 *TF:* 877-425-5023 ■ *Web:* www.apaservices.net	Fort Worth	TX	76109	877-425-5023	
Arthur Consulting Group Inc 31355 Oak Crest Dr Ste 200 *Web:* www.arthurconsulting.com	Westlake Village	CA	91361	818-735-4800	
Audit Technology Group 1850 W Winchester Rd *Web:* www.atgaudits.com	Libertyville	IL	60048	847-281-8703	
Audits & Systems Inc C/O 464 Central Rd	Northfield	IL	60093	847-446-5244	
Avitus Group PO Box 81590 *TF:* 800-454-2446 ■ *Web:* www.avitusgroup.com	Billings	MT	59108	800-454-2446	
Barry W James & Associates LLP 721 E Texas Ave *Web:* www.bwjames.com	Baytown	TX	77520	281-420-1040	
Bayerkohler & Graff Ltd 11132 Zealand Ave N *TF:* 866-315-2771 ■ *Web:* bayergraff.com	Champlin	MN	55316	763-427-2542	
BCRS Assoc LLC 77 Water St *Web:* bcrsllc.com	New York	NY	10005	212-440-0800	
BDB Payroll Inc 768 Bedford Ave *TF:* 800-729-7687 ■ *Web:* www.bdbpayroll.com	Brooklyn	NY	11205	718-522-2000	
Bederson LLP 405 Northfield Ave *Web:* www.bederson.com	West Orange	NJ	07052	973-736-3333	
Benefit Administrative Services International Corp 9246 Portage Industrial Dr *Web:* www.basiconline.com	Portage	MI	49024	269-327-1922	
BGBC Partners LLP 300 N Meridian St Ste 1100 *Web:* bgbc.us	Indianapolis	IN	46204	317-633-4700	
Bradley & Associates 201 S Capitol Ave Ste 910 *Web:* www.bradleycpa.com	Indianapolis	IN	46225	317-237-5500	
Building Block Computer 3209 Terminal Dr Ste 100 *Web:* www.bbcusa.com	Saint Paul	MN	55121	651-687-9435	
Cannon & Co 5605 Murray Ave *Web:* www.cannoncpa.com	Memphis	TN	38119	901-761-1710	
Canyon Tax & Bookkeeping Service 22342 Avenida Empresa Ste 280 *Web:* canyontax.com	Rancho Santa Margarita	CA	92688	949-888-2829	
CAPS LLC 10600 Virginia Ave *Web:* www.capspayroll.com	Culver City	CA	90232	310-280-0755	
Carlisle Tax Credit Advisors LLC 33 Union St 2nd Fl *Web:* www.carlisletaxcredits.com	Boston	MA	02108	617-500-8620	
CASA Payroll Service LLC 3120 Fire Rd *Web:* www.casapayroll.com	Egg Harbor Township	NJ	08234	609-383-0677	383-0907
CeFO Inc 88 Inverness Cir E Ste L107 *Web:* www.cefo.net	Englewood	CO	80112	720-506-4105	
Central Tax Inc 534 Notre-Dame St *Web:* www.centraletaxes.com	Repentigny	QC	J6A2T8	450-585-8293	
CF & Company LLP 8750 N Central Expy Ste 300 *Web:* www.cfllp.com	Dallas	TX	75231	972-387-4300	
Christopher Smith Leonard Bristow Stanell & Wells PA Suntrust Bank Bldg 1001 Third Ave W Ste 700 *Web:* www.cslcpa.com	Bradenton	FL	34205	941-748-1040	
City of Bay Village Ohio 350 Dover Ctr Rd *Web:* www.cityofbayvillage.com	Bay Village	OH	44140	440-899-3412	
Clairmount Group Plc 18424 Mack Ave *Web:* clairmount.com	Grosse Pointe Farms	MI	48236	313-642-1102	
COBRA Solutions Inc 4500 S Lakeshore Dr *Web:* www.cobra-solutions.com	Tempe	AZ	85282	480-831-6078	
Cohen & Co 1350 Euclid Ave Ste 800 *Web:* www.cohencpa.com	Cleveland	OH	44115	216-579-1040	
Collabrus Inc 111 Sutter St Ste 900 *Web:* www.collabrus.com	San Francisco	CA	94104	415-288-1826	
Connolly Consulting Associates Inc 50 Danbury Rd *Web:* www.cotiviti.com/healthcare	Wilton	CT	06897	203-529-2000	
Cordano Severson & Assoc Ltd 2321 Plainfield Rd *Web:* csatax.com	Crest Hill	IL	60403	815-744-1900	
Corporate Payroll Services Inc 1000 Miller Ct W *Web:* www.corpay.com	Norcross	GA	30071	770-446-7289	
Cort Software Inc 855 S W Yates Dr Ste 201 *Web:* www.nuviewinc.com	Bend	OR	97702	541-617-5100	
Crowe Horwath International 488 Madison Ave Ste 202 *Web:* www.crowehorwath.net	New York	NY	10022	212-808-2000	
Cytak Inc 444 de Haro Ste 210 *Web:* www.cytak.com	San Francisco	CA	94107	415-738-1650	
Daddy Don'S Tax Service 8235 Santa Monica Blvd Ste 210 *Web:* daddydon.com	West Hollywood	CA	90046	323-656-7532	
Davidson & Company LLP 1200 - 609 Granville St Pacific Centre *Web:* www.davidson-co.com	Vancouver	BC	V7Y1G6	604-687-0947	
Dawson & Associates 3250 Mary St *Web:* www.flacpa.com	Coconut Grove	FL	33133	305-443-1500	
Defense Finance & Accounting Service 8899 E 56th St *TF:* 888-332-7411 ■ *Web:* www.dfas.mil	Indianapolis	IN	46249	888-332-7411	
Diverse Staffing Inc 1800 E Lambert Rd Ste 100 *Web:* www.dss-staffing.com	Brea	CA	92821	714-482-0499	

Company	City	State	Zip	Phone	Fax
DuCharme McMillen & Assoc Inc 6610 Mutual Dr *Web:* www.dmainc.com	Fort Wayne	IN	46825	260-484-8631	482-8152
Eastridge Workforce Solutions 2375 Northside Dr Ste 360 *TF:* 877-862-2632 ■ *Web:* www.eastridge.com	San Diego	CA	92108	619-296-8735	
EBS Associates Inc 7150 SW Hampton St Ste 200 *Web:* www.teachmequickbooks.com	Tigard	OR	97223	503-885-0776	
Employer Flexible 7850 N Sam Houston Parkway W Ste 100 *TF:* 866-501-4942 ■ *Web:* www.employerflexible.com	Houston	TX	77064	866-501-4942	
Employer Solutions Group Inc 4844 North 300 West Ste 100 *Web:* www.esghr.com	Provo	UT	84604	801-223-7007	
EP Canada Film Services Inc 130 Bloor St W Ste 500 *Web:* epcanada.com	Toronto	ON	M5S1N5	416-923-9255	
Etonien LLC 222 N Sepulveda Blvd Ste 1507 *Web:* www.etonien.com	El Segundo	CA	90245	310-321-5800	
Exactax Inc 2301 W Lincoln Ave Ste 100 *TF:* 844-327-6740 ■ *Web:* www.exactax.com	Anaheim	CA	92801	714-284-4802	
Exerve Inc 2909 Langford Rd Ste 400B *TF:* 800-364-0637 ■ *Web:* www.exerve.com	Norcross	GA	30071	770-447-1566	
Farm Business Consultants Inc 150 3015 Fifth Ave Ne *TF:* 800-265-1002 ■ *Web:* www.fbc.ca	Calgary	AB	T2A6T8	403-735-6105	
Farm Financial Strategies 2029 400th St *Web:* farmestate.com	Osage	IA	50461	641-732-3636	
Feldman Financial Advisors Inc 1001 Connecticut Ave NW Ste 840 *Web:* www.feldmanfinancial.com	Washington	DC	20036	202-467-6862	
Fesnak & Associates LLP 1777 Sentry Pkwy W Ste 300 *TF:* 800-274-3978 ■ *Web:* rsmus.com/who-we-are/welcome-fesnak-llp.html	Blue Bell	PA	19422	267-419-2200	
Fgmk LLC 2801 Lakeside Dr 3rd Fl *Web:* www.fgmk.net	Bannockburn	IL	60015	847-374-0400	
Fiducial 1370 Ave of the Americas 31st Fl *TF:* 866-343-8242 ■ *Web:* www.fiducial.com	New York	NY	10019	212-207-4700	308-2613
Fiducial 10100 Old Columbia Rd *TF:* 800-323-9000 ■ *Web:* www.fiducial.com	Columbia	MD	21046	410-290-8296	910-5903
Financial Intelligence LLC 1451 Grant Rd Ste 200 *Web:* www.financial-intelligence.com	Mountain View	CA	94040	650-264-2252	
First Choice Software LLC PO Box 1657 *Web:* www.fcs-software.com	West Chester	PA	19380	610-436-6825	
Fortune Industries Inc 6402 Corporate Dr *Web:* www.ffi.net	Indianapolis	IN	46278	317-532-1374	
G&J Seiberlich & Company LLP 3264 Villa Ln *Web:* www.gjscollp.com	Napa	CA	94558	707-224-7948	
Global Tax Network US LLC 750 Boone Ave N Ste 102 *Web:* www.gtn.com	Minneapolis	MN	55427	763-746-4556	
Goff Backa Alfera & Company LLC 3325 Saw Mill Run Blvd *Web:* www.gbaco.com	Pittsburgh	PA	15227	412-885-5045	
H & R Block Tax Services Inc 4400 Main St *TF:* 800-472-5625 ■ *Web:* www.hrblock.com	Kansas City	MO	64111	800-472-5625	
Harding & Carbone Inc 3903 Bellaire Blvd *Web:* www.hctax.com	Houston	TX	77025	713-664-1215	
Harrison Accountancy Corp 2850 Mesa Verde Dr E Ste 101	Costa Mesa	CA	92626	714-966-0644	
HK Payroll Services 2345 JFK Rd *Web:* www.hkpayroll.com	Dubuque	IA	52004	563-556-0123	
Industry Consulting Group Inc 2777 N Stemmons Fwy Ste 940 *Web:* www.icgtax.com	Dallas	TX	75207	972-991-0391	
Infiniti HR LLC 3905 National Dr Ste 400 *Web:* www.infinitihr.com	Burtonsville	MD	20866	301-841-6380	
Innovative Employee Solutions Inc 9665 Granite Ridge Dr Ste 420 *Web:* www.innovativeemployeesolutions.com	San Diego	CA	92123	858-715-5100	
Inova Payroll Inc 176 Thompson Ln Ste 204 *TF:* 888-244-6106 ■ *Web:* www.inovapayroll.com	Nashville	TN	37211	615-921-0600	
Jackson Hewitt Inc 3 Sylvan Way Ste 301 *OTC:* JHTXQ ■ *TF:* 800-234-1040 ■ *Web:* www.jacksonhewitt.com	Parsippany	NJ	07054	800-234-1040	
JD Clark & Co 2225 Washington Blvd Ste 300 *Web:* www.jdclark.com	Ogden	UT	84401	801-737-4000	
JG Tax Group 1430 S Federal Hwy *TF:* 866-477-5291 ■ *Web:* www.jgtaxgroup.com	Deerfield Beach	FL	33441	866-477-5291	
Johnson & Sheldon PC 500 S Taylor Plz II Ste 200 *Web:* www.amacpas.com	Amarillo	TX	79105	806-371-7661	
Kafafian Group Inc, The 2001 Rt 46 Ste 310 *Web:* www.kafafiangroup.com	Parsippany	NJ	07054	973-299-0300	299-1002
Karuna Advisors LLP 1550 El Camino Real Ste 250 *Web:* www.karunaadvisors.com	Menlo Park	CA	94025	650-328-2758	
Katz Cassidy An Accountancy Corp 11400 W Olympic Blvd Ste 1050 *Web:* www.katzcassidy.com	Los Angeles	CA	90064	310-477-6300	
KMJ Corbin & Company LLP 555 Anton Blvd Ste 1000 *Web:* www.corbincocpa.com	Costa Mesa	CA	92626	714-380-6565	
Knight James E & Associates Pc 14825 Saint Marys Ln *TF:* 800-772-1213 ■ *Web:* www.ktjcpas.com	Houston	TX	77079	281-493-5080	
Liberty Tax Service Inc 1716 Corporate Landing Pkwy *TF Cust Svc:* 800-790-3863 ■ *Web:* www.libertytax.com	Virginia Beach	VA	23454	757-493-8855	493-0169

Phone Fax

LINK Staffing Services Inc
1800 Bering Dr Ste 800 ... Houston TX 77057 713-784-4400
Web: www.linkstaffing.com
Lippa Assoc Inc 3633 Camino Del Rio S 207 ... San Diego CA 92108 619-283-2581
Maahs & Vanlahr PC 3911 Old Lee Hwy Ste 43E ... Fairfax VA 22030 703-691-8632
Web: maahsandvanlahrcpa.com
MaloneBailey LLP 9801 Westheimer Rd Ste 1100 ... Houston TX 77042 713-343-4286
Web: www.malonebailey.com
Martini Iosue & Akpovi CPAs
16830 Ventura Blvd Ste 415 ... Encino CA 91436 818-789-1179
Web: www.miacpas.com
Maxwell Locke & Ritter LLP
401 Congress Ave Ste 1100 ... Austin TX 78701 512-370-3200
Web: www.mlrpc.com
Meadows Urquhart Acree & Cook LLP
1802 Bayberry Court Ste 102 ... Richmond VA 23226 804-249-5786
Web: www.muacllp.com
Medical Practice Partners
29 Naek Rd ... Vernon Rockville CT 06066 860-872-2289
Web: www.healthwisema.com
Mengel Metzger Barr & Company LLP
100 Chestnut St Ste 1200 ... Rochester NY 14604 585-423-1860
Web: www.mengelmetzgerbarr.com
Michael West & Assoc 5356 Clayton Rd Ste 216 ... Concord CA 94521 925-676-7437
Web: westfinancial.net
Mid-Atlantic Diamond Ventures
1801 Liacouras Walk 503 Alter Hall ... Philadelphia PA 19122 215-204-3082
Web: www.fox.temple.edu
Moody Famiglietti & Andronico LLP
1 Highwood Dr ... Tewksbury MA 01876 978-557-5300
Web: mfa-cpa.com
Morgan Jacoby Thurn Boyle & Assoc PA
700 20th St ... Vero Beach FL 32960 772-562-4158
Web: www.mjtbcpa.com
Morrissey Family Businesses Inc
5919 Spring Creek Rd ... Rockford IL 61114 815-282-4600
Web: www.morrisseyfamily.com
MTS Consulting LLC 7444 Long Ave ... Skokie IL 60077 847-675-6666
Web: www.mtsconsulting.com
Multistate Tax Commission
444 N Capitol St Nw Ste 425 ... Washington DC 20001 202-624-8699
Web: www.mtc.gov
National Tax Search LLC
130 S Jefferson St Ste 300 ... Chicago IL 60661 312-233-6440
Web: www.nationaltaxsearch.com
Nextaff LLC 11225 College Blvd Ste 250 ... Overland Park KS 66210 913-562-5620
Web: www.nextaff.com
Ogden Cos Inc 606 Green Meadow N ... Colleyville TX 76034 817-656-8570
Opportune LLP 711 Louisiana St Ste 3100 ... Houston TX 77002 713-490-5050
Web: www.opportune.com
Payce Inc 1220B E Joppa Rd Ste 324 ... Towson MD 21286 443-279-9000
Web: www.paycepayroll.com
Paycom 7501 W Memorial Rd ... Oklahoma City OK 73142 800-580-4505
TF: 800-580-4505 ■ *Web:* www.paycomonline.com
Payworks Inc 1565 Willson Pl ... Winnipeg MB R3T4H1 866-788-3500 779-0538*
**Fax Area Code:* 204 ■ *TF:* 866-788-3500 ■ *Web:* www.payworks.ca
Perry-Smith & Company LLP
400 Capital Mall Ste 1200 ... Sacramento CA 95814 916-441-1000
Web: www.perry-smith.com
Phyphar Inc 29 Walter Hammond Pl ... Waldwick NJ 07463 201-444-4648
Web: www.phyphar.com
Premier Tax & Financial Services
121 W 27th St Ste 1003A ... New York NY 10001 212-807-8201
Web: premiertaxandfinancial.com
Premium Transportation Staffing Inc
190 Highland Dr ... Medina OH 44256 330-722-7974
Web: www.premiumtransportation.com
PrO Unlimited Inc 301 Yamato Rd Ste3199 ... Boca Raton FL 33431 800-291-1099
TF: 800-291-1099 ■ *Web:* www.prounlimited.com
Pursuit of Excellence Inc
10440 N Central Expy Ste 1250 ... Dallas TX 75231 214-452-7881
Web: poehr.com
Quantum Management Services Ltd
2000 McGill College Ave Ste 1800 ... Montreal QC H3A3H3 514-842-5555 849-8846
TF: 800-978-2688 ■ *Web:* www.quantum.ca
Questco LLC 100 Commercial Cir Bldg B ... Conroe TX 77304 936-756-1980
Web: questco.net
Quigley Tax Service SC
5822 W Fond Du Lac Ave ... Milwaukee WI 53218 414-461-1800
Web: quigleytaxserv.com
Relevante Inc 1235 Westlakes Dr Ste 280 ... Berwyn PA 19312 484-403-4100
Web: www.relevante.com
Resourcing Edge Inc 1309 Ridge Rd Ste 200 ... Rockwall TX 75087 214-771-4411
Web: www.resourcingedge.com
Revenew International LLC
9 Greenway PlZ Ste 1950 ... Houston TX 77046 281-276-4500
Web: www.revenew.net
Richter LLP 1981 McGill College 11th Fl ... Montreal QC H3A0G6 514-934-3400
Web: www.richter.ca
Rockoff Harlan & Rasof Ltd 3818 Oakton St ... Skokie IL 60076 847-675-7777
Web: www.rhrcpa.com
Rose Financial Services LLC
2 Research Pl Ste 300 ... Rockville MD 20850 301-527-1130
Web: www.rosefinancial.com
Rubino & McGeehin Consulting Group Inc
6903 Rockledge Dr Ste 1200 ... Bethesda MD 20817 301-564-3636
Web: www.rubino.com
Rylander Clay & Opitz LLP
3200 Riverfront Dr Ste 200 ... Fort Worth TX 76107 817-332-2301 338-4608
Web: www.rylander-cpa.com
Safstrom & Company PS
1411 Fourth Ave Ste 1120 ... Seattle WA 98101 206-622-6456
Web: safstrom.com

Phone Fax

SALT Group, The 1845 Sidney Baker St ... Kerrville TX 78028 830-257-1290
TF: 888-257-1266 ■ *Web:* thesaltgroup.com
Sam S Sloven CPA Inc 3025 S Parker Rd Ste 733 ... Aurora CO 80014 303-750-0050
Schechter Dokken Kanter CPA'S
100 Washington Ave S Ste 1600 ... Minneapolis MN 55401 612-332-5500
Web: www.sdkcpa.com
Shwiff Levy & Polo LLP
433 California St Ste 1000 ... San Francisco CA 94104 415-291-8600
Web: www.slpconsults.com
Sidney Tax Service Inc 115 Second St Ne ... Sidney MT 59270 406-433-3131
Silver Creek Financial ServicesInc
175 Hwy 82 ... Lostine OR 97857 541-569-2272
TF: 866-569-0020 ■ *Web:* silvercreekteam.com
Silver Freedman Taff & Tiernan LLP
3299 K St NW Ste 100 ... Washington DC 20007 202-295-4500
Web: www.sftlaw.com
Silver Lerner Schwartz Fertel
8707 Skokie Blvd Ste 400 ... Skokie IL 60077 847-676-2000
Web: www.slsf.com
Skoda Minotti 6685 Beta Dr ... Cleveland OH 44143 440-449-6800
Web: www.skodaminotti.com
StaffingSolutions Inc 1390 S Eufaula Ave ... Eufaula AL 36027 334-687-7460
Web: www.staffingsolutions.com
Sterlings Bookkeeping & Tax Services
5418 Saint Charles Ave ... Dallas TX 75223 214-330-4682
Web: www.sterlingstax.com
Strategic Compliance Solutions LLC
18 Mallard Point Rd ... Essex CT 06426 860-767-3006
Web: www.strategiccompliancesolutions.com
Swan Employer Services Inc
1306 East 74th Ave Ste 200 ... Anchorage AK 99518 907-344-7926
Web: www.swanhr.com
Sweeney Conrad PS 2606 116th Ave NE 200 ... Bellevue WA 98004 425-629-1990
Web: sweeneyconrad.com
Talagy Inc 245 Riverside Ave Ste 250 ... Jacksonville FL 32202 904-224-1400 224-1410
Tax Savvy 401 S Birmingham St ... Wylie TX 75098 972-442-5226
Web: www.taxsavvy.biz
Tax Smart Accounting Services
19616 E Benwood St ... Covina CA 91724 626-974-5152
Web: www.taxsmartaccounting.com
TGG Accounting 10188 Telesis Ct Ste 130 ... San Diego CA 92121 760-697-1033
Web: www.tgg-accounting.com
Thurman Campbell Group PLC
324 Franklin St ... Clarksville TN 37040 931-552-7474
Web: www.tccpas.com
Traphagen Financial Group
234 Kinderkamack Rd ... Oradell NJ 07649 201-262-1040
Web: www.tfgllc.com
TravisWolff Independent Advisors & Accountants
15950 N Dallas Pkwy Ste 600 ... Dallas TX 75248 972-661-1843
Web: www.traviswolff.com
Utilisave LLC 129 W 27th St 11th Fl ... New York NY 10001 718-382-4500
Web: www.utilisave.com
Valuation Advisory Group Inc, The
445 Pharr Rd NE ... Atlanta GA 30305 404-841-0992
Web: www.valuationadvisory.com
Verified Audit Circulation Inc
900 Larkspur Landing Cir ... Larkspur CA 94939 415-461-6006
TF: 800-775-3332 ■ *Web:* www.verifiedaudit.com
Vic's Accounting 897 Henderson Hwy ... Winnipeg MB R2K2L8 204-668-3441
Web: allyear.ca
Victory Education Partners Inc
12 W 21st St Fl 8 ... New York NY 10010 212-265-1742
Web: victoryep.com
Walthall Drake & Wallace LLP
6300 Rockside Rd ... Cleveland OH 44131 216-573-2330
Web: www.walthall.com
Wayne Long & Co
1502 Mill Rock Way Ste 200 ... Bakersfield CA 93311 661-664-0909
Web: welcpa.com
Windes & McClaughry Accountancy Corp
Landmark Sq 111 W Ocean Blvd 22nd Fl ... Long Beach CA 90802 562-435-1191
Web: www.windes.com
WISS & Company LLP 354 Eisenhower Pkwy ... Livingston NJ 07039 973-994-9400
Web: www.wiss.com
Wm Stukey & Associates LLC
1705 W Northwest Hwy Ste 220 ... Grapevine TX 76051 817-481-3265
Web: www.midcitiescpa.com
Wolfe & Co 99 High St ... Boston MA 02110 617-439-9700
Web: www.wolfandco.com
Xpitax LLC 10 Forbes Rd W ... Braintree MA 02184 781-303-0136
Web: www.xpitax.com
Zimmermans Acctg & Tax Service Inc
804 Carpenter Ave ... Iron Mountain MI 49801 906-774-4529

735 TELECOMMUNICATIONS EQUIPMENT & SYSTEMS

See Also Modems p. 1999; Radio & Television Broadcasting & Communications Equipment p. 3037

Phone Fax

ABB Flexible Automation Inc 12040 Regency Pkwy ... Cary NC 27518 919-856-2360 807-5022
Web: www.abb.com
ADTRAN Inc 901 Explorer Blvd ... Huntsville AL 35806 256-963-8000 963-8004
NASDAQ: ADTN ■ *TF:* 800-923-8726 ■ *Web:* www.adtran.com
AirNet Communications Corp
3950 Dow Rd Ste C ... Melbourne FL 32934 321-984-1990
Web: www.aircom.com
Airspan Networks Inc 777 Yamato Rd Ste 105 ... Boca Raton FL 33431 561-893-8670 893-8671
OTC: AIRO ■ *Web:* www.airspan.com
AltiGen Communications Inc
410 E Plumeria Dr ... San Jose CA 95134 408-597-9000 597-9020
OTC: ATGN ■ *TF:* 888-258-4436 ■ *Web:* www.altigen.com

	City	State	Zip	Phone	Fax
Amtelco 4800 Curtin Dr TF: 800-356-9148 ■ Web: www.amtelco.com	McFarland	WI	53558	608-838-4194	838-8367
AOC Technologies Inc 6690 Amador Plz Rd Ste 110 Web: www.aoctech.com	Dublin	CA	94568	925-875-0808	
Argon ST Inc 12701 Fair Lakes Cir Ste 800 Web: www.argonst.com	Fairfax	VA	22033	703-322-0881	322-0885
AT & T Inc 175 E Houston St PO Box 2933 NYSE: AT&T ■ TF: 800-351-7221 ■ Web: www.att.com	San Antonio	TX	78299	210-821-4105	
Atris Inc 1151 S Trooper Rd Ste E TF: 800-724-3384 ■ Web: www.atris.biz	Norristown	PA	19403	800-724-3384	
Audiovox Corp 180 Marcus Blvd NASDAQ: VOXX ■ TF: 800-645-4994 ■ Web: www.voxxintl.com	Hauppauge	NY	11788	631-231-7750	
Aurora Networks Inc 5400 Betsy Ross Dr TF: 888-287-6726 ■ Web: www.aurora.com	Santa Clara	CA	95054	408-235-7000	
Axesstel Inc 6815 Flanders Dr Ste 210 OTC: AXST ■ Web: www.axesstel.com	San Diego	CA	92121	858-625-2100	625-2110
Bo-Sherrel Company Inc 3340 Tree Swallow Pl	Fremont	CA	94555	510-792-0354	797-2038
Call One Inc 400 Imperial Blvd PO Box 9002 TF: 800-749-3160 ■ Web: www.calloneonline.com	Cape Canaveral	FL	32920	321-783-2400	799-9222
Ceragon Networks Inc 10 Forest Ave NASDAQ: CRNT ■ Web: www.ceragon.com	Paramus	NJ	07652	201-845-6955	845-5665
Charles Industries Ltd 5600 Apollo Dr TF: 800-458-4747 ■ Web: www.charlesindustries.com	Rolling Meadows	IL	60008	847-806-6300	806-6231
CiDRA Corp 50 Barnes Pk N TF: 877-243-7277 ■ Web: www.cidra.com	Wallingford	CT	06492	203-265-0035	294-4211
CIENA Corp 1201 Winterson Rd NASDAQ: CIEN ■ TF: 800-921-1144 ■ Web: www.ciena.com	Linthicum	MD	21090	410-694-5700	694-5750
ClearOne Communications Inc 5225 Wiley Post Way TF: 800-945-7730 ■ Web: www.clearone.com	Salt Lake City	UT	84116	801-975-7200	977-0087
CoAdna Photonics Inc 733 Palomar Ave Web: www.coadna.com	Sunnyvale	CA	94085	408-736-1100	
COM DEV International Ltd 155 Sheldon Dr TSE: CDV ■ Web: www.comdev.ca	Cambridge	ON	N1R7H6	519-622-2300	622-1691
Comarco Inc 25541 Commerce Ctr Dr OTC: CMRO ■ Web: www.comarco.com	Lake Forest	CA	92630	949-599-7400	
Comarco Wireless Technologies Inc 25541 Commerce Ctr Dr	Lake Forest	CA	92630	949-599-7400	599-1415
Communication Technologies Inc 14151 Newbrook Dr Ste 400 TF: 888-266-8358 ■ Web: www.comtechnologies.com	Chantilly	VA	20151	703-961-9080	961-1330
Communications Systems Inc 10900 Red Cir Dr NASDAQ: JCS ■ Web: www.commsystems.com	Minnetonka	MN	55343	952-996-1674	
Communications Test Design Inc 1339 Enterprise Dr TF: 800-223-3910 ■ Web: www.ctdi.com	West Chester	PA	19380	610-436-5203	
Compunetix Inc 2420 Mosside Blvd TF: 800-879-4266 ■ Web: www.compunetix.com	Monroeville	PA	15146	412-373-8110	373-2720
Consolidated Communications Holdings Inc 121 S 17th St NASDAQ: CNSL ■ Web: consolidated.com	Mattoon	IL	61938	217-235-3311	235-3311
Cyber Digital Inc 400 Oser Ave Ste 1650 OTC: CYBD ■ Web: www.cyberdigitalinc.com	Hauppauge	NY	11788	631-231-1200	231-1446
Digital Voice Corp 1201 S Beltline Rd Ste 150 TF Cust Svc: 800-777-8329 ■ Web: www.digitalvoicecorp.com	Coppell	TX	75019	469-635-6500	635-6500
DynaMetric Inc 717 S Myrtle Ave TF: 800-525-6925 ■ Web: www.dynametric.com	Monrovia	CA	91016	626-358-2559	359-5701
Dynamic Concepts Inc (DCI) 1730 17th St NE Web: www.dcihq.com	Washington	DC	20002	202-944-8787	526-7233
Ecessa Corp 13755 1st Ave N Ste 100 TF: 800-669-6242 ■ Web: www.ecessa.com	Plymouth	MN	55441	763-694-9949	551-0664
ECI Telecom Ltd 5100 NW 33rd Ave Ste 150 Web: www.ecitele.com	Fort Lauderdale	FL	33309	954-772-3070	351-4404
Electro Standards Laboratories Inc 36 Western Industrial Dr TF: 877-943-1164 ■ Web: www.electrostandards.com	Cranston	RI	02921	401-943-1164	
Electronic Tele-Communications Inc 1915 MacArthur Rd OTC: ETCIA ■ TF: 888-746-4382 ■ Web: www.etcia.com	Waukesha	WI	53188	262-542-5600	542-1524
Ericsson Inc 6300 Legacy Dr Web: www.ericsson.com	Plano	TX	75024	972-583-0000	
Ever Win International Corp 17579 Railroad St Web: www.everwin.com	City Of Industry	CA	91748	626-810-8218	
FleetBoss Global Positioning Solutions Inc 241 O'Brien Rd TF: 877-265-9559 ■ Web: www.fleetboss.com	Fern Park	FL	32730	407-265-9559	265-0365
Fujitsu America Inc 1250 E Arques Ave TF: 800-538-8460 ■ Web: www.fujitsu.com	Sunnyvale	CA	94085	408-746-6200	746-6260
GAI-Tronics Corp 400 E Wyomissing Ave TF: 800-492-1212 ■ Web: www.gai-tronics.com	Mohnton	PA	19540	610-777-1374	775-6540
General DataComm Inc 6 Rubber Ave Web: www.gdc.com	Naugatuck	CT	06770	203-729-0271	723-2883
Genesys Telecommunications Laboratories Inc 2001 Junipero Serra Blvd TF: 888-436-3797 ■ Web: genesys.com	Daly City	CA	94014	650-466-1100	466-1260
GN US Inc 77 NE Blvd TF: 800-327-2230 ■ Web: www.jabra.com	Nashua	NH	03062	603-598-1100	598-1122
Harris Corp 1025 W NASA Blvd NYSE: HRS ■ TF: 800-442-7747 ■ Web: www.harris.com	Melbourne	FL	32919	321-727-9100	
Honeywell International Inc 101 Columbia Rd PO Box M6/LM NYSE: HON ■ TF: 877-841-2840 ■ Web: www.honeywell.com	Morristown	NJ	07962	480-353-3020	
Hughes Network Systems LLC 11717 Exploration Ln TF: 800-461-9330 ■ Web: www.hughes.com	Germantown	MD	20876	301-428-5500	428-1868
I Wireless 4135 NW Urbandale Dr TF Cust Svc: 888-550-4497 ■ Web: www.iwireless.com	Urbandale	IA	50322	515-258-7000	
iDirect Technologies Inc 13865 Sunrise Valley Dr Ste 100 TF: 888-362-5475 ■ Web: www.idirect.net	Herndon	VA	20171	703-648-8118	648-8014
Infinera Corp 140 Caspian Ct NASDAQ: INFN ■ TF: 877-742-3427 ■ Web: www.infinera.com	Sunnyvale	CA	94089	408-572-5200	572-5454
InnoMedia Inc 1901 McCarthy Blvd Web: www.innomedia.com	Milpitas	CA	95035	408-432-5400	941-8152
ISCO International LLC 1450 Arthur Ave Ste A TF: 888-948-4726 ■ Web: www.iscointl.com	Elk Grove Village	IL	60007	224-222-1666	222-1691
ITUS Corp 12100 Wilshire Blvd Ste 1275 OTC: COPY ■ Web: ctipatents.com	Los Angeles	CA	90025	631-549-5900	
JTech Communications Inc 6413 Congress Ave Ste 150 *Fax Area Code: 561 ■ TF: 800-321-6221 ■ Web: www.jtech.com	Boca Raton	FL	33487	800-321-6221	995-2260*
Kaiam Corp 39655 Eureka Dr Web: www.kaiamcorp.com	Newark	CA	94560	510-344-2231	
L-3 Communications Corp 600 Third Ave 34-35 Fl NYSE: LLL ■ TF: 800-351-8483 ■ Web: www.l-3com.com	New York	NY	10016	212-697-1111	490-0731
Lantronix Inc 167 Technology Dr NASDAQ: LTRX ■ TF Orders: 800-526-8766 ■ Web: www.lantronix.com	Irvine	CA	92618	949-453-3990	450-7249
LCC International Inc 7900 Westpark Dr Ste A300 Web: www.lcc.com	McLean	VA	22102	703-873-2000	873-2100
Mercury Systems Inc 267 Lowell Rd Ste 101 NASDAQ: MRCY ■ Web: rf.mrcy.com	Hudson	NH	03051	603-546-4100	
Metro-Tel Corp 290 NE 68 St TF: 888-998-8300	Miami	FL	33138	402-498-2964	
Microlog Corp 401 Professional Dr Ste 125 Web: www.mlog.com	Gaithersburg	MD	20879	301-540-5500	
Microphase Corp 587 Connecticut Ave Web: www.microphase.com	Norwalk	CT	06854	203-866-8000	866-6727
Microsemi-RFIS 1000 Avenida Acaso Web: www.microsemi.com	Camarillo	CA	93012	805-388-1345	484-2191
Mitel Networks Corp 350 Legget Dr PO Box 13089 TF: 800-722-1301 ■ Web: www.mitel.com	Kanata	ON	K2K2W7	613-592-2122	
Molex Premise Networks 2222 Wellington Ct TF: 866-733-6659 ■ Web: www.molexpn.com	Lisle	IL	60532	630-969-4550	969-1352
Motorola Inc IDEN Group 8000 W Sunrise Blvd TF: 800-102-2344 ■ Web: motorola-mobility-en-in.custhelp.com	Plantation	FL	33322	800-102-2344	
Movius Interactive 11360 Lakefield Dr Web: www.moviuscorp.com	Duluth	GA	30097	770-283-1000	
NDS Americas 3500 Highland Ave TF: 866-398-8749 ■ Web: www.cisco.com	Costa Mesa	CA	92626	714-434-2100	
NEC America Inc 6555 N State Hwy 161 TF Cust Svc: 866-632-3226 ■ Web: www.necam.com	Irving	TX	75039	214-262-2000	
Network Equipment Technologies Inc 6900 Paseo Padre Pkwy NASDAQ: NWK	Fremont	CA	94555	510-713-7300	574-4000
NextIO Inc 8303 N MoPac Expy	Austin	TX	78759	512-439-5350	439-5391
NICE Systems Inc 301 Rt 17 N 10th Fl TF: 800-994-4498 ■ Web: www.nice.com	Rutherford	NJ	07070	201-964-2600	964-2610
Nokia Inc 200 S Mathilda Ave NYSE: NOK ■ Web: www.nokia.com	Sunnyvale	CA	94086	408-737-0900	
Norsat International Inc 110-4020 Viking Way TSE: NII ■ TF: 800-644-4562 ■ Web: www.norsat.com	Richmond	BC	V6V2N2	604-821-2800	821-2801
Numerex Corp 1600 Parkwood Cir 5th Fl NASDAQ: NMRX ■ TF: 800-665-5686 ■ Web: www.numerex.com	Atlanta	GA	30339	770-693-5950	693-5951
Oplink Communications Inc 46335 Landing Pkwy NASDAQ: OPLK ■ Web: www.oplink.com	Fremont	CA	94538	510-933-7200	933-7300
Optelian Inc 1700 Enterprise Way SE Ste 101 Web: www.optelian.com	Marietta	GA	30067	770-690-9575	
Optoplex Corp 3374-3390 Gateway Blvd Web: www.optoplex.com	Fremont	CA	94538	510-490-9930	
Orion Systems Inc 602 Masons Mill Business Pk Web: www.orionsystemsinc.net	Huntingdon Valley	PA	19006	215-659-1207	659-4234
OSRAM Sylvania Inc 100 Endicott St Web: www.sylvania.com	Danvers	MA	01923	978-777-1900	750-2152
PBE Group, The 1459 Wittens Mill Rd Web: pbegrp.com	Tazewell	VA	24630	276-988-5505	988-6820
Pics Telecom International Corp 1920 Lyell Ave TF: 800-521-7427 ■ Web: www.picstelecom.com	Rochester	NY	14606	585-295-2000	295-2020
Plantronics Inc 345 Encinal St NYSE: PLT ■ TF: 800-544-4660 ■ Web: www.plantronics.com	Santa Cruz	CA	95060	831-426-5858	426-6098
Polycom Inc 4750 Willow Rd TF: 800-765-9266 ■ Web: www.polycom.com	Pleasanton	CA	94588	800-765-9266	
Protel Inc 4150 Kidron Rd TF: 800-925-8882 ■ Web: www.protelinc.com	Lakeland	FL	33811	863-644-5558	646-5855
Proxim Wireless Corp 1561 Buckeye Dr OTC: PRXM ■ TF: 800-229-1630 ■ Web: www.proxim.com	Milpitas	CA	95035	408-383-7600	383-7680
Pulse Communications Inc 2900 Towerview Rd *Fax: Cust Svc ■ TF Cust Svc: 800-381-1997 ■ Web: www.pulse.com	Herndon	VA	20171	703-471-2900	471-2951*
Qualcomm Inc 5775 Morehouse Dr NASDAQ: QCOM ■ Web: www.qualcomm.com	San Diego	CA	92121	858-587-1121	658-2100
Quintron Systems Inc 2105 S Blosser Rd Web: www.quintron.com	Santa Maria	CA	93458	805-928-4343	928-9914
RAD Data Communications Ltd 900 Corporate Dr TF: 800-444-7234 ■ Web: www.rad.com	Mahwah	NJ	07430	201-529-1100	529-1157
Redcom Laboratories Inc 1 Redcom Ctr Web: www.redcom.com	Victor	NY	14564	585-924-7550	924-6572
RFL Electronics Inc 353 Powerville Rd Web: www.rflelect.com	Boonton	NJ	07005	973-334-3100	334-3863
SAJE Technology LLC 765 Dixon Ct Web: www.saje-tech.com	Hoffman Estates	IL	60192	847-756-7603	496-4515

Phone Fax

Samsung Telecommunications America LLP
1301 E Lookout Dr .... Richardson TX 75082 972-761-7000 761-7001
TF: 800-726-7864 ■ *Web:* www.samsung.com

Sanyo Fisher Co 21605 Plummer St .... Chatsworth CA 91311 818-998-7322 717-2759

Siemens Canada Ltd 1550 Appleby Line .... Burlington ON L7L6X7 905-319-3600
Web: www.siemens.com

SmarTrunk Systems Inc 867 Bowsprit Rd .... Chula Vista CA 91914 619-426-3781 426-3788
Web: www.smartrunk.com

Sonetronics Inc PO Box L .... West Belmar NJ 07719 732-681-5016 681-5216
Web: www.sonetronics.com

Star Dynamics Corp 100 Outwater Ln .... Garfield NJ 07026 973-340-3883 340-1530
Web: www.stardynamic.com

STM Wireless Inc 2 Faraday .... Irvine CA 92618 949-273-6800
Web: emcsatcom.com

Superior Essex Communications LP
6120 Powers Ferry Rd Ste 150 .... Atlanta GA 30339 770-657-6000 657-6652
TF: 800-551-8948 ■ *Web:* www.superioressex.com

Suttle 1001 E Hwy 212 .... Hector MN 55342 320-848-6711 848-6218
TF: 800-852-8662 ■ *Web:* www.suttlesolutions.com

Symetrics Industries Inc 1615 W NASA Blvd .... Melbourne FL 32901 321-254-1500 259-4122
Web: www.symetrics.com

Symmetricom Inc 2300 Orchard Pkwy .... San Jose CA 95131 408-433-0910 428-7998
NASDAQ: SYMM ■ *TF:* 888-367-7966 ■ *Web:* microsemi.com/index.php

System Engineering International Inc (SEI)
5115 Pegasus Ct Ste Q .... Frederick MD 21704 301-694-9601 694-9608
TF: 800-765-4734 ■ *Web:* www.seipower.com

TAG Solutions LLC 12 Elmwood Rd .... Albany NY 12204 518-292-6500 292-6510
TF: 800-724-0023 ■ *Web:* www.tagsolutions.com

Taylored Systems Inc
14701 Cumberland Rd Ste 100 .... Noblesville IN 46060 317-776-4000 776-4004
Web: www.taylored.com

Technical Communications Corp 100 Domino Dr .... Concord MA 01742 978-287-5100 371-1280
NASDAQ: TCCO ■ *TF:* 800-952-4082 ■ *Web:* www.tccsecure.com

Tekelec 5200 Paramount Pkwy .... Morrisville NC 27560 919-460-5500 460-0877
NASDAQ: TKLC ■ *TF:* 800-633-0738 ■
Web: oracle.com/us/corporate/acquisitions/tekelec/index.html

Tel Electronics Inc
313 S 740 E St Ste 1 .... American Fork UT 84003 801-756-9606 756-9135
TF: 800-748-5022 ■ *Web:* www.tel-electronics.com

Telco Systems Inc 15 Berkshire Rd .... Mansfield MA 02048 781-255-2120 255-2122
TF: 800-227-0937 ■ *Web:* www.telco.com

Telect Inc 23321 E Knox Ave .... Liberty Lake WA 99019 509-926-6000 926-8915
TF Cust Svc: 800-551-4567 ■ *Web:* www.telect.com

Telemobile Inc 19840 Hamilton Ave .... Torrance CA 90502 310-538-5100 532-8526
Web: www.telemobile.com

Tellabs Inc 1415 W Diehl Rd .... Naperville IL 60563 630-798-8800 798-2000
NASDAQ: TLAB ■ *Web:* www.tellabs.com

Teo Technologies Inc 11609 49th Pl W .... Mukilteo WA 98275 425-349-1000 349-1010
TF: 800-524-0024 ■ *Web:* www.teotech.com

Tollgrade Communications Inc
3120 Unionville Rd Ste 400 .... Cranberry Township PA 16066 412-820-1400 820-1530
TF Cust Svc: 800-878-3399 ■ *Web:* www.tollgrade.com

Toshiba America Inc
1251 Ave of the Americas Ste 4100 .... New York NY 10020 212-596-0600 593-3875
TF: 800-457-7777 ■ *Web:* www.toshiba.com

Tricomm Services Corp
1247 N Church St Ste 8 .... Moorestown NJ 08057 856-914-9001 914-9065
TF: 800-872-2401 ■ *Web:* www.tricommcorp.com

TSI Global Cos 700 Fountain Lakes Blvd .... Saint Charles MO 63301 636-949-8889 925-2111
TF: 800-875-5605 ■ *Web:* www.tsi-global.com

Uniden America Corp 4700 Amon Carter Blvd .... Fort Worth TX 76155 817-858-3300 858-3300*
**Fax:* Hum Res ■ *TF Cust Svc:* 800-297-1023 ■ *Web:* www.uniden.com

UTStarcom Inc 1732 North First St Ste 220 .... San Jose CA 95112 408-453-4557 996-7273*
NASDAQ: UTSI ■ **Fax Area Code:* 510 ■ *TF:* 877-547-6340 ■ *Web:* www.utstar.com

Valcom Inc 5614 Hollins Rd .... Roanoke VA 24019 540-563-2000 362-9800
TF: 800-825-2661 ■ *Web:* www.valcom.com

Vbrick Systems Inc 12 Beaumont Rd .... Wallingford CT 06492 203-265-0044 265-6750
TF: 866-827-4251 ■ *Web:* www.vbrick.com

VCON Inc 578 Main St .... Hackensack NJ 07601 201-883-1220
Web: www.clearone.com

Vela Research LP 5540 Rio Vista Dr .... Clearwater FL 33760 727-507-5300 507-5312
Web: www.vela.com

Veramark Technologies Inc
1565 Jefferson Rd .... Rochester NY 14623 585-381-6000 383-6800

VTech Communications Inc
9590 SW Gemini Dr Ste 120 .... Beaverton OR 97008 503-596-1200 644-9887
TF: 800-595-9511 ■ *Web:* www.vtech.com

Westell Technologies Inc 750 N Commons Dr .... Aurora IL 60504 630-898-2500 375-4931*
NASDAQ: WSTL ■ **Fax:* Sales ■ *TF:* 800-323-6883 ■ *Web:* www.westell.com

Wireless Telecom Group Inc 25 Eastmans Rd .... Parsippany NJ 07054 973-386-9696 386-9191
NYSE: WTT ■ *Web:* www.wirelesstelecomgroup.com

XETA Technologies Inc 1814 W Tacoma St .... Broken Arrow OK 74012 918-664-8200 664-6876

Zhone Technologies Inc 7001 Oakport St .... Oakland CA 94621 510-777-7000 777-7001
NASDAQ: ZHNE ■ *TF:* 877-946-6320 ■ *Web:* www.zhone.com

736 TELECOMMUNICATIONS SERVICES

Phone Fax

4L Communications Inc 1555 Regent Ave W .... Winnipeg MB R2C4J2 204-336-0606
Web: www.4lcommunications.com

Access America 673 Emory Vly Rd .... Oak Ridge TN 37830 865-482-2140 482-2306
TF: 800-860-2140 ■ *Web:* www.accessam.com

Access Point Inc 1100 Crescent Green .... Cary NC 27518 919-851-4838
TF: 877-419-4274 ■ *Web:* www.accesspointinc.com

Accessory Export LLC 4105 Indus Way .... Riverside CA 92503 951-687-1140
Web: www.empirecase.com

Acotel Interactive Inc 80 Pine St 29th Fl .... New York NY 10005 212-400-1212
Web: www.flycell.com

ACT Conferencing
1526 Cole Blvd Bldg 3 Ste 300 .... Lakewood CO 80401 303-233-3500 238-0096
TF: 800-433-2900

Advanced Telecom Services Inc
1150 1st Ave Ste 105 .... King of Prussia PA 19406 610-688-6000
Web: www.atsmobile.com

AirIQ Inc 1845 Sandstone Manor Ste 10 .... Pickering ON L1W3W9 905-831-6444
TF: 888-606-6444 ■ *Web:* airiq.com

Airvoice Wireless LLC
2425 Franklin Rd .... Bloomfield Hills MI 48302 888-944-2355
TF: 888-944-2355 ■ *Web:* www.airvoicewireless.com

Alaska Communications Systems Group Inc
600 Telephone Ave .... Anchorage AK 99503 907-563-8000 297-3100
NASDAQ: ALSK ■ *TF:* 800-808-8083 ■ *Web:* www.alaskacommunications.com

Allstream Corp 200 Wellington St W .... Toronto ON M5V3G2 416-345-2000
TF Cust Svc: 888-288-2273 ■ *Web:* www.allstream.com

AmeriCom Inc PO Box 2146 .... Sandy UT 84091 801-571-2446 257-6643*
**Fax Area Code:* 775 ■ *TF:* 800-820-6296 ■ *Web:* www.americom.com

Aperto Networks Inc 598 Gibraltar Dr .... Milpitas CA 95035 408-719-9977 719-9970
Web: www.apertonet.com

AT & T Inc 175 E Houston St PO Box 2933 .... San Antonio TX 78299 210-821-4105
NYSE: AT&T ■ *TF:* 800-351-7221 ■ *Web:* www.att.com

Auragan LLC PO Box 1501 .... New Canaan CT 06840 866-644-2872
TF: 866-644-2872 ■ *Web:* www.advection.net

Bell Aliant Regional Communications
1505 Barrington St Maritime Ctr .... Halifax NS B3J3K5 800-267-1110
TSE: BA ■ *TF:* 800-555-1212 ■ *Web:* www.bellaliant.ca

Bell Canada 1050 Beaver Hall Hill .... Montreal QC H2Z1S4 800-667-0123
TF: 800-667-0123 ■ *Web:* www.bell.ca

Birch Communications Inc
2300 Main St 6th Fl .... Kansas City MO 64108 816-300-3000
TF: 866-424-5100 ■ *Web:* www.birch.com

Bledsoe Telephone Co-op Corp (BTC)
338 Cumberland Ave PO Box 609 .... Pikeville TN 37367 423-447-2121 447-2498
TF: 888-382-1222 ■ *Web:* www.bledsoe.net

Bluegrass Cellular Inc 2902 Ring Rd .... Elizabethtown KY 42701 270-769-0339
TF: 800-928-2355 ■ *Web:* www.bluegrasscellular.com

Blumerich Communications Service
6403 W Pierson Rd .... Flushing MI 48433 810-659-5000
Web: www.blumerich.com

Brazoria Telephone Co 314 W Texas St .... Brazoria TX 77422 979-798-2121
Web: www.btel.com

Broadview Networks Holdings Inc
800 Westchester Ave Ste N-501 .... Rye Brook NY 10573 914-922-7000 922-7001
TF: 800-260-8766 ■ *Web:* www.broadviewnet.com

Bruce Telecom 3145 Hwy 21 PO Box 80 .... Tiverton ON N0G2T0 519-368-2000
Web: www.brucetelecom.com

Cap Rock Telephone Co-op Inc PO Box 300 .... Spur TX 79370 806-271-3336
Web: www.caprock-spur.com

Cavalier Telephone LLC 2134 W Laburnum Ave .... Richmond VA 23227 800-442-2410 422-4200*
**Fax Area Code:* 804 ■ *TF:* 800-683-3944

Cellhire USA LLC 3520 W Miller Rd Ste 100 .... Garland TX 75041 214-355-5200
TF: 877-244-7242 ■ *Web:* www.cellhire.com

Cellular Communications Inc
825 25th St S Ste 109 .... Fargo ND 58103 701-241-4394
Web: www.cellcominc.com

Century Interactive LLC
1505 Federal St Ste 200 .... Dallas TX 75201 817-713-2329
TF: 877-921-7992 ■ *Web:* callbox.com/?ci

Cesium Telecom Inc 5798 Ferrier .... Montreal QC H4P1M7 514-798-8686
TF: 877-798-8686 ■ *Web:* www.cesiumonline.com

Cincinnati Bell Inc 221 E Fourth St .... Cincinnati OH 45202 513-397-9900
NYSE: CBB ■ *TF:* 800-387-3638 ■ *Web:* www.cincinnatibell.com

Circa Enterprises Inc 206-5 Richard Way SW .... Calgary AB T3E7M8 403-258-2011
Web: www.circaent.com

Citizens Telephone Co-op PO Box 137 .... Floyd VA 24091 540-745-2111 745-3791
TF: 800-941-0426 ■ *Web:* www.citizens.coop

Co-op Communciations Inc
412 Washington Ave .... Belleville NJ 07079 800-833-2700
TF: 800-833-2700 ■ *Web:* www.cooperativenet.com

Commenco Inc 4901 Bristol Ave .... Kansas City MO 64129 816-753-2166
TF: 800-292-9725 ■ *Web:* www.commenco.com

Commonwealth Telephone Co
1 Newbury St Ste 103 .... Peabody MA 01960 978-536-9500
TF: 800-439-7170 ■ *Web:* www.commonwealthtel.com

Communication Services Inc 2151 E Broadway Rd .... Tempe AZ 85282 480-905-8689 905-8818
Web: www.com-serv.com

Comporium Communications 332 E Main St .... Rock Hill SC 29730 888-403-2667 326-5708*
**Fax Area Code:* 803 ■ *TF:* 866-922-5922 ■ *Web:* www.comporium.com

Computer Consulting Operations Specialists Inc
600 Corporate Pointe .... Culver City CA 90230 310-568-5000 417-7991
Web: www.ccops.com

Conference Plus Inc 1051 E Woodfield Rd .... Schaumburg IL 60173 847-619-6100
Web: conferenceplus.com

Convergent Media Systems Corp
190 Bluegrass Vly Pkwy 1 Convergent Ctr .... Alpharetta GA 30005 770-369-9000 369-9100
Web: www.convergent.com

Corporate Telephone Services 184 W Second St .... Boston MA 02127 617-625-1200
TF: 800-274-1211 ■ *Web:* corptelserv.com

Criticom Inc 4211 Forbes Blvd .... Lanham MD 20706 301-306-0600
TF: 800-449-3384 ■ *Web:* www.ultra-3eti.com

D2 Technologie 2119 Boul Marcel-laurin .... Saint-laurent QC H4R1K4 514-904-5888
Web: d2technologie.com

Dakota Central Telecommunications Co-op
630 Fifth St N .... Carrington ND 58421 701-652-3184 674-8121
TF: 800-771-0974 ■ *Web:* www.daktel.com

Deltacom Inc 7037 Old Madison Pike .... Huntsville AL 35806 800-239-3000
TF: 800-239-3000 ■ *Web:* www.deltacom.com

deltathree Inc 75 Broad St .... New York NY 10004 212-500-4850 500-4888
PINK: DDDC ■ *TF:* 888-335-8230 ■ *Web:* deltathree.com

Develcon Inc 401 Magnetic Dr Units 15-17 .... Toronto ON M3J3H9 416-385-1390
Web: www.develcon.com

Digerati Technologies Inc
3463 Magic Dr Ste 355 .... San Antonio TX 78229 210-614-7240
OTC: DTGI ■ *Web:* www.digerati-inc.com

Company	City	State	ZIP	Phone	Fax
Eastex Telephone Co-op Inc PO Box 150 *TF:* 800-232-7839 ■ *Web:* www.eastex.com	Henderson	TX	75653	903-854-1000	
EATELCORP Inc 913 S Burnside Ave *TF:* 800-621-4211 ■ *Web:* eatel.com	Gonzales	LA	70737	225-621-4300	
Electronique Mercier Ltee 162 Rue Fraser *Web:* www.emercier.com	Riviere-du-loup	QC	G5R1C8	418-862-7269	
Empire Telephone Corp 34 Main St PO Box 349 *TF:* 800-338-3300 ■ *Web:* www.empiretelephone.com	Prattsburgh	NY	14873	607-522-3712	
Etex Telephone Co-op Inc 1013 Hwy 155 N *Web:* www.etex.net	Gilmer	TX	75644	903-797-2711	
Excel Telecommunications 433 Las Colinas Blvd Ste 400 *TF:* 877-668-0808 ■ *Web:* www.excel.com	Irving	TX	75039	972-910-1900	
FairPoint Communications Inc 521 E Morehead St Ste 250 *NASDAQ: FRP* ■ *TF:* 866-740-2764 ■ *Web:* www.fairpoint.com	Charlotte	NC	28202	704-344-8150	
Farmers Telecommunications Co-op (FTC) 144 McCurdy Ave N PO Box 217 *TF:* 866-638-2144 ■ *Web:* www.farmerstel.com	Rainsville	AL	35986	256-638-2144	638-4830
Farmers Telephone Co-op Inc 1101 E Main St *TF:* 888-218-5050 ■ *Web:* www.ftc-i.net	Kingstree	SC	29556	843-382-2333	382-2333
Faxaway 417 Second Ave W *TF:* 800-906-4329 ■ *Web:* www.faxaway.com	Seattle	WA	98119	206-301-7000	301-7500
FaxBack Inc 7007 SW Cardinal Ln Ste 105 *TF:* 800-329-2225 ■ *Web:* www.faxback.com	Portland	OR	97224	503-597-5350	597-5399
FiberTower Corp 185 Berry St Ste 4800 *OTC: FTWRQ* ■ *Web:* www.fibertower.com	San Francisco	CA	94107	415-659-3500	
Fido Solutions Inc 800 De La Gauchetiere St W Ste 4000 *Web:* www.fido.ca	Montreal	QC	H5A1K3	514-933-3436	
Filer Mutual Telephone Co PO Box 89 *Web:* www.filertel.com	Filer	ID	83328	208-326-4331	326-3190
Frontier Communications Corp 3 High Ridge Pk *NASDAQ: FTR* ■ *TF:* 800-877-4390 ■ *Web:* www.frontier.com	Stamford	CT	06905	203-614-5600	614-4602
Fusion Telecommunications International Inc 420 Lexington Ave Ste 1718 *OTC: FSNN* ■ *TF:* 888-301-1721 ■ *Web:* fusionconnect.com	New York	NY	10170	212-201-2400	972-7884
General Communication Inc 2550 Denali St Ste 1000 *NASDAQ: GNCMA* ■ *TF:* 800-770-7886 ■ *Web:* www.gci.com	Anchorage	AK	99503	907-265-5600	868-5676
GetWireless LLC 10901 Red Cir Dr *Web:* www.getwirelessllc.com	Minnetonka	MN	55343	952-890-6669	
Global Domains International Inc 701 Palomar Airport Rd Ste 300 *Web:* www.worldsite.ws	Carlsbad	CA	92009	760-602-3000	602-3099
Golden West Telecommunications 415 Crown St PO Box 411 *TF:* 866-279-2161 ■ *Web:* www.goldenwest.com	Wall	SD	57790	605-279-2161	279-2727
GPShopper LLC 584 Broadway Ste 904 *Web:* www.gpshopper.com	New York	NY	10012	212-488-2222	
Granite Telecommunications LLC 100 Newport Ave Ext *TF:* 866-847-1500 ■ *Web:* www.granitenet.com	Quincy	MA	02171	617-933-5500	328-0312
Graphnet Inc 40 Fultron St 28th Fl *TF:* 800-327-1800 ■ *Web:* www.graphnet.com	New York	NY	10038	212-994-1100	994-1199
GTT Communications Inc 7900 Tysons One Pl Ste 1450 *NYSE: GTT* ■ *Web:* www.gtt.net	McLean	VA	22102	703-442-5500	
GTX Corp 117 W Ninth St Ste 1214 *TF:* 877-489-3019 ■ *Web:* www.gtxcorp.com	Los Angeles	CA	90015	213-489-3019	
Guadalupe Valley Telephone Co-op (GVTC) 36101 FM 3159 *TF:* 800-367-4882 ■ *Web:* www.gvtc.com	New Braunfels	TX	78132	830-885-4411	885-2400
Guidance Solutions Inc 4134 Del Rey Ave *Web:* www.guidance.com	Marina del Rey	CA	90292	310-754-4000	754-4010
Hargray Communications 856 William Hilton Pkwy PO Box 5986 *TF:* 800-726-1266 ■ *Web:* www.hargray.com	Hilton Head Island	SC	29938	843-341-1501	
Harrisonville Telephone Co 213 S Main St PO Box 149 *TF:* 888-482-8353 ■ *Web:* htc.net	Waterloo	IL	62298	618-939-6112	939-4826
Hayneville Telephone Company Inc PO Box 175 *Web:* www.htcnet.net	Hayneville	AL	36040	334-548-2101	548-2051
Hop-on Inc PO Box 940 Ste 222 *Web:* hop-on.com	Temecula	CA	92593	949-756-9008	
Horry Telephone Co-op Inc (HTC) 3480 Hwy 701 N PO Box 1820 *TF:* 800-824-6779 ■ *Web:* www.htcinc.net	Conway	SC	29528	843-365-2151	365-0855
iBasis Inc 20 Second Ave *Web:* www.ibasis.com	Burlington	MA	01803	781-505-7500	505-7300
Idc Communications 1385 Niakwa Rd E *Web:* www.idccommunications.com	Winnipeg	MB	R2J3T3	204-255-8389	
IDT Corp 520 Broad St *NYSE: IDT* ■ *Web:* www.idt.net	Newark	NJ	07102	973-438-1000	
Ingenicomm Inc 14120 Parke Long Court Ste 210 *Web:* www.ingenicomm.net	Chantilly	VA	20151	703-665-4333	
Integra Telecom Inc 1201 NE Lloyd Blvd Ste 500 *TF General:* 866-468-3472 ■ *Web:* www.integratelecom.com	Portland	OR	97232	503-453-8000	453-8221
Inter-Community Telephone Co (ICTC) PO Box 8 *TF:* 800-350-9137 ■ *Web:* www.ictc.com	Nome	ND	58062	701-924-8815	924-8808
InterCall 8420 W Bryn Mawr Ste 1100 *TF:* 800-374-2441 ■ *Web:* www.intercall.com	Chicago	IL	60631	773-399-1600	399-1588
Interop Technologies LLC 13500 Powers Ct *Web:* www.interoptechnologies.com	Fort Myers	FL	33912	239-425-3000	
Intrado Inc 1601 Dry Creek Dr *TF:* 877-262-3775 ■ *Web:* www.intrado.com	Longmont	CO	80503	720-494-5800	494-6600
Iridium Satellite LLC 6701 Democracy Blvd *Web:* www.iridium.com	Bethesda	MD	20817	301-571-6200	571-6250
IVCi LLC 601 Old Willets Path *TF:* 800-224-7083 ■ *Web:* www.ivci.com	Hauppauge	NY	11788	631-273-5800	273-7277
J2 Global Communications Inc 6922 Hollywood Blvd 8th Fl *TF Sales:* 888-718-2000 ■ *Web:* www.j2global.com	Los Angeles	CA	90028	323-860-9200	
Japan Telecom America Inc 100 Wall St Ste 1803 *Web:* www.jt-america.com	New York	NY	10005	212-422-4650	
Kaplan Telephone Company Inc (KTC) 220 N Cushing Ave *TF:* 866-643-7171 ■ *Web:* www.ktconline.net	Kaplan	LA	70548	337-643-7171	643-6000
KDDI America Inc 825 Third Ave Ste 3 *Web:* kddia.com	New York	NY	10022	212-295-1200	295-1080
Kennebec Telephone Company Inc 220 S Main St *TF:* 888-868-3390 ■ *Web:* www.kennebectelephone.com	Kennebec	SD	57544	605-869-2220	869-2221
Kentec Communications Inc 710 W Main St *Web:* kci.net	Sterling	CO	80751	970-522-8107	
Lambeau Telecom 1807 N Ctr St *TF Cust Svc:* 800-444-4014 ■ *Web:* bcntele.com	Beaver Dam	WI	53916	920-887-3148	
Liberty Global Inc 12300 Liberty Blvd *NASDAQ: LBTYA* ■ *Web:* www.libertyglobal.com	Englewood	CO	80112	303-220-6600	220-6601
LICT Corp 401 Theodore Fremd Ave *TF:* 800-690-6903 ■ *Web:* www.lictcorp.com	Rye	NY	10580	914-921-8821	921-6410
Lightower Fiber Networks 80 Central St *TF:* 888-583-4237 ■ *Web:* www.lightower.com	Boxborough	MA	01719	978-264-6000	
Linkedin Corp 2029 Stierlin Ct *Web:* www.linkedin.com	Mountain View	CA	94043	650-687-3600	
Matanuska Telephone Assn Inc 1740 S Chugach St *TF:* 800-478-3211 ■ *Web:* www.mta-telco.com	Palmer	AK	99645	907-745-3211	
Mckay Brothers LLC 2355 broadway *Web:* www.mckay-brothers.com	Oakland	CA	94612	312-948-9188	
Mercury Wireless LLC 2825 se california ave *TF:* 800-354-4915 ■ *Web:* www.mercurywireless.com	Topeka	KS	66605	800-354-4915	
Microserve 276 Fifth Ave Ste 1011 *Web:* www.mserve.com	New York	NY	10001	212-683-2811	
Midcontinent Communications PO Box 5010 *TF:* 800-888-1300 ■ *Web:* www.midco.com	Sioux Falls	SD	57117	605-274-9810	
Modern Wireless Inc 1163 N Patt St *Web:* www.modernwirelessusa.com	Anaheim	CA	92801	714-535-6399	
Molalla Communications Co 211 Robbins St PO Box 360 *TF:* 800-332-2344 ■ *Web:* www.molalla.com	Molalla	OR	97038	503-829-1100	829-7781
Motricity Inc 601 - 108th Ave NE, Ste 800 *Web:* www.motricity.com	Bellevue	WA	98004	425-957-6200	
Multiband Corp 9449 Science Ctr Dr *NASDAQ: MBND* ■ *Web:* www.multibandusa.com	New Hope	MN	55428	763-504-3000	504-3060
National Field Service Corp (NFS) 162 Orange Ave *Web:* nfsco.com	Suffern	NY	10901	845-368-1600	368-1989
NativeX LLC 1900 Medical Arts Ave S *Web:* nativex.com	Sartell	MN	56377	320-257-7500	
Neocell Wireless 1500 Royal York Rd *Web:* www.neocell.ca	Etobicoke	ON	M9P3B6	416-241-6626	
Net Access Corp 2300 15th St Ste 300 *TF:* 800-638-6336 ■ *Web:* www.cologix.com	Denver	CO	80202	973-590-5000	590-5080
Net Talk.Com Inc 1080 NW 163rd Dr *Web:* www.nettalk.com	Miami	FL	33169	305-621-1200	
Net2Phone Inc 520 Broad St *TF:* 800-386-6438 ■ *Web:* www.net2phone.com	Newark	NJ	07102	973-438-3111	412-2829
Netwolves Corp 4710 Eisenhower Blvd Ste E-8 *Web:* www.netwolves.com	Tampa	FL	33634	813-579-3200	882-0209
Network Communications International Corp (NCIC) PO Box 551 *TF:* 800-382-2887 ■ *Web:* www.ncic.com	Longview	TX	75601	903-757-4455	247-2057
Network Services LLC 2065 Kensington Ave *Web:* www.ns-wny.com	Amherst	NY	14226	716-839-5309	839-5301
New Global Telecom Inc 143 Union Blvd Ste 400	Lakewood	CO	80228	303-278-0700	278-0728
New Ulm Telecom Inc 27 N Minnesota St *OTC: NULM* ■ *TF:* 888-873-6853 ■ *Web:* www.newulmtel.net	New Ulm	MN	56073	507-354-4111	354-1982
Nexius Inc 825 Market St Ste 250 *Web:* www.nexius.com	Allen	TX	75013	703-650-7777	
NII Holdings Inc 1875 Explorer St Ste 1000 *NASDAQ: NIHD* ■ *Web:* www.nii.com	Reston	VA	20190	703-390-5100	
North Central Telephone Co-op Corp PO Box 70 *TF:* 800-795-3272 ■ *Web:* www.nctc.com	Lafayette	TN	37083	615-666-2151	
North State Communications 111 N Main St *Web:* www.northstate.net	High Point	NC	27261	336-886-3600	887-7418
NTELOS Holdings Corp 1154 Shenandoah Village Dr *NASDAQ: NTLS* ■ *TF:* 877-468-3567 ■ *Web:* www.ntelos.com	Waynesboro	VA	22980	540-946-3500	
NTT DoCoMo USA Inc 757 Third Ave 16th Fl *TF:* 888-362-6661 ■ *Web:* www.docomo-usa.com	New York	NY	10017	888-362-6661	
O1 Communications Inc 4359 town ctr blvd Ste 217 **Fax Area Code:* 916 ■ *TF:* 888-444-1111 ■ *Web:* www.o1.com	El Dorado hills	CA	95762	888-444-1111	933-6958*
Oakes Motor Sports 1210 S Seventh St *Web:* www.oakesmotorsports.com	Oakes	ND	58474	469-215-4591	
Omnitracs LLC 10290 Campus Point Dr *TF:* 888-627-2716 ■ *Web:* www.omnitracs.com	San Diego	CA	92121	800-647-3325	
Oncologix Tech Inc 206 Crown St SW	Grand Rapids	MI	49548	616-977-9933	
Otelco Inc 505 Third Ave E *NASDAQ: OTT* ■ *TF:* 866-471-7888 ■ *Web:* www.otelco.net	Oneonta	AL	35121	205-625-3574	
OTZ Telephone Co-op Inc PO Box 324 *TF:* 800-478-3111 ■ *Web:* otz.net	Kotzebue	AK	99752	907-442-3114	

				Phone	Fax
Ovation Wireless Management Inc 19315 W Catawba Ave Ste 220	Cornelius	NC	28031	704-714-2111	
Web: www.ovationwm.com					
Over-The-Air Wireless Inc 844 NW 49th St	Seattle	WA	98107	206-357-5020	
Web: www.otawireless.com					
P & R Communications Service Inc 700 E First St	Dayton	OH	45402	937-512-8100	
Web: www.pandrcommunications.com					
Panhandle Telecommunication Systems Inc (PTSI) 2222 NW Hwy	Guymon	OK	73942	580-338-2556	
TF: 800-562-2556 ■ Web: www.ptci.net					
Penasco Valley Telecommunications (PVT) 4011 W Main St	Artesia	NM	88210	800-505-4844	746-4142*
*Fax Area Code: 575 ■ TF: 800-505-4844 ■ Web: www.pvt.com					
Pioneer Long Distance Inc PO Box 539	Kingfisher	OK	73750	888-782-2667	
TF: 888-782-2667 ■ Web: www.pldi.net					
Pioneer Telephone Assn Inc PO Box 707	Ulysses	KS	67880	620-356-3211	356-3242
TF: 800-308-7536 ■ Web: www.pioncomm.net					
Pioneer Telephone Co-op Inc 108 E Roberts Ave PO Box 539	Kingfisher	OK	73750	405-375-0411	699-3053*
*Fax: Mktg ■ Web: www.ptci.com					
Pratt Communications 2913 Tech Ctr	Santa Ana	CA	92705	714-540-6840	
TF General: 800-980-2323 ■ Web: www.prattcommunications.com					
Preston Mobility Inc 13071 Vanier Pl Ste 128	Richmond	BC	V6V2J1	604-629-8526	
Web: www.prestonmobility.com					
Primus Telecommunications (PTGi) 7901 Jones Ranch Dr Ste 900	McLean	VA	22102	703-902-2800	902-2814
NYSE: PTGI ■ TF: 866-385-3360 ■ Web: www.ptgi.com					
PRTC Inc (PRTC) 292 Robertson Blvd Walterboro	Walterboro	SC	29488	864-682-3131	
Web: www.prtcnet.com					
PWR LLC 6402 Deere Rd	Syracuse	NY	13206	315-701-0210	701-0217
TF: 800-342-0878 ■ Web: www.pwrllc.com					
Qualicom Systems Inc 2100 Electronics Ln	Fort Myers	FL	33912	239-481-8700	
Web: www.lightningradio.net					
Questar InfoComm Inc 180 East 100 South PO Box 45433	Salt Lake City	UT	84145	801-324-5856	
TF: 800-729-6790 ■ Web: www.questarpipeline.com					
QuickPlay Media Inc 190 Liberty St 2nd Fl	Toronto	ON	M6K3L5	416-916-7529	
Web: www.quickplay.com					
Redknee Solutions Inc 2560 Matheson Blvd E Ste 500	Mississauga	ON	L4W4Y9	905-625-2622	
Web: www.redknee.com					
Reiko Wireless 1218 flushing ave	Brooklyn	NY	11237	212-213-1102	
TF: 888-797-3456 ■ Web: www.reikowireless.com					
Reserve Telephone Company Inc PO Box T	Reserve	LA	70084	985-536-1111	536-4815
TF: 888-611-6111 ■ Web: www.rtconline.com					
RFIP Inc 100 W Wilshire Blvd Ste C4	Oklahoma City	OK	73116	405-286-0928	
Web: rfip.com					
Rnk Inc 333 Elm St Ste 310	Dedham	MA	02026	781-613-6000	297-2091
TF: 877-323-2486					
Rogers Communications Inc 333 Bloor St E 10th Fl	Toronto	ON	M4W1G9	416-935-7777	935-3599
TSE: RCI.B ■ Web: www.rogers.com					
Rogers Wireless Communications Inc 333 Bloor St. E, 4th Fl	Toronto	ON	M4W1G9	888-764-3771	
TF: 800-575-9090 ■ Web: www.rogers.com					
Rural Telephone Service Company Inc PO Box 158	Lenora	KS	67645	785-567-4281	567-4401
TF: 877-625-7872 ■ Web: www.nex-tech.com					
Russell Cellular Inc 5624 S Hwy FF	Battlefield	MO	65619	417-886-7542	
Web: www.russellcellular.com					
S & P Communications 6712 Randolph Blvd	San Antonio	TX	78233	210-656-5073	
Web: www.spcomm.com					
Sage Telecom Inc 3300 E Renner Rd Ste 350 Bldg 2	Richardson	TX	75082	214-495-4700	
Web: www.sagetelecom.net					
Sandhill TelephoneCo-op Inc PO Box 519	Jefferson	SC	29718	843-658-3434	658-7700
Web: www.shtc.net					
Securus Technologies Inc 14651 Dallas Pkwy	Dallas	TX	75254	972-277-0300	277-0301
TF: 800-844-6591 ■ Web: www.securustech.net					
Shawnee Telephone Co PO Box 69	Equality	IL	62934	618-276-4211	
TF: 800-461-3956 ■ Web: myshawnee.net					
Shenandoah Telecommunications Co 500 Shentel Way	Edinburg	VA	22824	540-984-5224	984-3438
NASDAQ: SHEN ■ TF: 800-743-6835 ■ Web: www.shentel.com					
SignalPoint Communications Corp 433 Hackensack Ave Continental Plz 6th Fl	Hackensack	NJ	07601	201-968-9797	968-1886
TF: 877-928-3292 ■ Web: www.signalpointcommunications.com					
Sirius Canada Inc 135 Liberty St	Toronto	ON	M6K1A7	888-539-7474	
TF: 888-539-7474 ■ Web: www.siriusxm.ca					
Skyline Telephone Membership Corp PO Box 759	West Jefferson	NC	28694	336-877-3111	
TF: 877-475-9546 ■ Web: www.skyline.org					
SkyTel Corp PO Box 2469	Jackson	MS	39225	800-759-8737	
TF Cust Svc: 800-759-8737 ■ Web: www.skytel.com					
Smart City Networks 5795 W Badura Ave Ste 110	Las Vegas	NV	89118	702-943-6000	943-6001
TF: 888-446-6911 ■ Web: www.smartcity.com					
Smithville Communications Inc 1600 W Temperance St	Ellettsville	IN	47429	812-876-2211	339-3313
Web: www.smithville.com					
SnapOne Inc 3490 Route 1 Bldg 16	Princeton	NJ	08540	609-720-1900	
Solarus 440 E Grand Ave	Wisconsin Rapids	WI	54494	715-421-8111	421-6081
TF: 800-421-9282 ■ Web: www.solarus.net					
SoundBite Communications Inc 22 Crosby Dr	Bedford	MA	01730	650-466-1100	466-1260
NASDAQ: SDBT ■ TF: 888-436-3797 ■ Web: genesys.com/soundbite					
Southern Communications Services Inc 5555 Glenridge Connector Ste 500	Atlanta	GA	30342	800-818-5462	443-1533*
*Fax Area Code: 678 ■ TF: 800-818-5462 ■ Web: www.southernlinc.com					
Spotwave Wireless Inc 500 Van Buren St Box 550	Kemptville	ON	K0G1J0	613-591-1662	
TF: 866-704-9750 ■ Web: www.spotwave.com					

				Phone	Fax
Startec Global Communications Corp 11300 Rockville Pike Ste 900	Rockville	MD	20852	301-610-4300	329-2882*
*Fax Area Code: 877 ■ TF: 800-827-3374 ■ Web: www.startec.com					
Statmon Technologies Corp 385, 736 N Western Ave Ste	Lake Forest	IL	60045	847-604-5366	
Web: www.statmon.com					
T-Mobile USA Inc 12920 SE 38th St	Bellevue	WA	98006	425-383-4000	
TF: 800-318-9270 ■ Web: www.t-mobile.com					
Tango Networks Inc 3801 Parkwood Blvd	Frisco	TX	75034	469-229-6000	
Web: www.tango-networks.com					
TDS Telecommunications Corp 525 Junction Rd	Madison	WI	53717	608-664-4000	830-5569
TF: 866-571-6662 ■ Web: www.tdstelecom.com					
TelAlaska Inc 201 E 56th St	Anchorage	AK	99518	907-563-2003	565-5539
TF: 888-570-1792 ■ Web: www.telalaska.com					
Telecom Management Inc 39 Darling Ave	South Portland	ME	04106	207-774-9500	
Web: www.pioneertelephone.com					
Telefonica USA Inc 1111 Brickell Ave 10th Fl	Miami	FL	33131	305-925-5300	373-1685
Web: www.us.telefonica.com					
Telephone Service Co 2 Willipie St	Wapakoneta	OH	45895	419-739-2200	739-2299
TF: 800-743-5707 ■ Web: www.telserco.com					
Telephone Systems International Inc (TSI) 4400 Marsh Landing Blvd Ste 3	Ponte Vedra Beach	FL	32082	904-686-1470	
Web: www.tsiglobe.com					
Teligent Inc 105 Lincoln Ave	Buena	NJ	08310	800-656-0793	
TF: 800-656-0793 ■ Web: www.teligent.com					
Thumb Cellular Ltd. Partnership 82 S Main St	Pigeon	MI	48755	989-453-4333	
TF: 800-443-5057 ■ Web: www.thumbcellular.com					
Total Telcom Inc 540 1632 Dickson Ave	Kelowna	BC	V1Y7T2	250-860-3762	
TF: 877-860-3762 ■ Web: www.totaltelcom.com					
Tower Ventures LLC 4091 Viscount Ave	Memphis	TN	38118	901-794-9494	
Web: www.towerventures.com					
TracFone Wireless Inc 9700 NW 112th Ave	Miami	FL	33178	305-640-2000	
TF: 800-876-5753 ■ Web: www.tracfone.com					
Trans National Communications International Inc (TNCI) 2 Charlesgate W	Boston	MA	02215	617-369-1000	
TF: 800-800-8400 ■ Web: www.tncii.com					
Twin Lakes Telephone Co-op 200 Telephone Ln	Gainesboro	TN	38562	931-268-2151	
TF Cust Svc: 800-644-8582 ■ Web: www.twlakes.net					
United Utilities Inc 5450 A St	Anchorage	AK	99509	907-561-1674	273-5322
TF: 800-478-2020 ■ Web: www.unicom-alaska.com					
Unitel Inc PO Box 165	Unity	ME	04988	207-948-3900	
TF: 888-760-1048 ■ Web: www.unitelme.com					
Universal Service Administrative Co (USAC) 2000 L St NW Ste 200	Washington	DC	20036	202-776-0200	776-0080
TF: 888-641-8722 ■ Web: www.usac.org					
Universal Service Administrative Company Schools & Libraries Div 2000 L St NW Ste 200	Washington	DC	20036	888-203-8100	276-8736
TF: 888-203-8100 ■ Web: www.usac.org					
Upper Peninsula Telephone Co PO Box 86	Carney	MI	49812	906-639-2111	
TF: 800-950-8506 ■ Web: www2.michbbs.com					
US Cellular Corp (USCC) 8410 W Bryn Mawr Ave Ste 700	Chicago	IL	60631	773-399-8900	
NYSE: USM ■ TF: 888-944-9400 ■ Web: www.uscellular.com					
USA Datanet Corp 109 S Warren St Ste 602	Syracuse	NY	13202	800-566-8655	
TF: 800-566-8655					
USA Mobility Inc 6677 Richmond Hwy	Alexandria	VA	22306	703-660-6677	660-6994
TF: 800-231-2556 ■ Web: www.usamobility.com					
Valley Telephone Co-op Inc 752 E Maley St	Willcox	AZ	85643	520-384-2231	384-2831
TF: 800-421-5711 ■ Web: www.vtc.net					
VeriSign Inc 350 Ellis St	Mountain View	CA	94043	650-426-3100	961-7300
NASDAQ: VRSN ■ TF Sales: 866-893-6565 ■ Web: www.verisign.com					
Verizon Business 1 Verizon Way	Basking Ridge	NJ	07920	908-559-2000	
TF Cust Svc: 877-297-7816 ■ Web: www.verizonenterprise.com					
Verizon Communications Inc 140 W St	New York	NY	10007	212-395-1000	
NYSE: VZ ■ Web: www.verizon.com					
Verizon Wireless 180 Washington Valley Rd	Bedminster	NJ	07921	908-306-7000	306-6927*
*Fax: Hum Res ■ TF: 800-922-0204 ■ Web: www.verizonwireless.com					
Virgin Mobile USA Inc 10 Independence Blvd	Warren	NJ	07059	908-607-4000	607-4822
TF: 888-322-1122 ■ Web: www.virginmobileusa.com					
Voicecom 5900 Windward Pkwy Ste 500	Alpharetta	GA	30005	888-468-3554	
TF: 888-468-3554 ■ Web: intelliverse.com					
Vonage Holdings Corp 23 Main St	Holmdel	NJ	07733	732-528-2600	834-0189
NYSE: VG ■ TF: 877-862-2562 ■ Web: www.vonage.com					
Vox Mobile LLC 6200 Oak Tree Blvd Ste 450	Independence	OH	44131	216-525-0191	
Web: voxmobile.com					
Wabash Telephone Co-op Inc PO Box 299	Louisville	IL	62858	618-665-3311	665-4188
TF: 800-228-9824 ■ Web: www.wabashtelephone.coop					
Warwick Valley Telephone Co 47 Main St PO Box 592	Warwick	NY	10990	845-986-8080	986-6699
NASDAQ: WWVY ■ TF Cust Svc: 800-952-7642 ■ Web: www.wvtc.com					
Wavedivision Holdings LLC 401 Kirkland Prk Pl Ste 500	Kirkland	WA	98033	425-576-8200	576-8221
TF: 866-928-3123 ■ Web: www.wavebroadband.com					
Webtech Wireless Inc 4299 Canada Way Ste 215	Burnaby	BC	V5G1H3	604-434-7337	
Web: www.webtechwireless.com					
West Central Wireless 3389 Knickerbocker Rd	San Angelo	TX	76904	325-223-6680	
Web: www.wcc.net					
West River Co-op Telephone Co (WRCTC) 801 Coleman Ave PO Box 39	Bison	SD	57620	605-244-5213	
TF: 888-464-9513 ■ Web: www.sdplains.com					
West River Telecommunications Co-op PO Box 467	Hazen	ND	58545	701-748-2211	748-6800
TF: 800-748-7220 ■ Web: www.westriv.com					
West Texas Rural TelephoneCo-op Inc PO Box 1737	Hereford	TX	79045	806-364-3331	276-5219
TF: 888-440-4331 ■ Web: www.wtrt.net					
Windstream Corp 4001 Rodney Parham Rd	Little Rock	AR	72212	501-748-7000	
Web: www.windstream.com					
Wireless Mike's 301 S 21st St	Mattoon	IL	61938	217-235-9300	
Web: wirelessmikes.com					

Phone Fax

WQN Inc 14911 Quorum Dr Ste 140 .... Dallas TX 75254 866-661-6176
OTC: WQNI ■ *TF:* 866-661-6176 ■ *Web:* www.wqn.com

XO Communications Inc 13865 Sunrise Vly Dr .... Herndon VA 20171 703-547-2000 547-2881
TF: 866-349-0134 ■ *Web:* www.xo.com

Yak Communications Corp 48 Yonge St Ste 1200 .... Toronto ON M5E1G6 877-925-4925 216-9923*
**Fax Area Code:* 866 ■ *TF:* 877-925-4925 ■ *Web:* www.yak.ca

York Telecom Corp 81 Corbett Way .... Eatontown NJ 07724 732-413-6000 413-6060
TF: 866-836-8463 ■ *Web:* www.yorktel.com

737 TELEMARKETING & OTHER TELE-SERVICES

Both inbound and outbound telephone marketing as well as other tele-services are included here.

Phone Fax

Aegis Communications Group Inc
8201 Ridgepoint Dr .... Irving TX 75063 972-830-1800 830-1801
Web: www.aegisglobal.com

Alta Resources 120 N Commercial St .... Neenah WI 54956 877-464-2582 727-9954*
**Fax Area Code:* 920 ■ *TF:* 877-464-2582 ■ *Web:* www.altaresources.com

America's Call Center Inc
7901 Baymeadows Way Ste 14 .... Jacksonville FL 32256 904-224-2000
TF: 800-598-2580 ■ *Web:* www.webcallusa.com

American Home Base 428 Childers St .... Pensacola FL 32534 850-857-0860 484-8661
TF General: 800-549-0595 ■ *Web:* www.amhomebase.com

Ameridial Inc 4535 Strausser St NW .... North Canton OH 44720 800-445-7128 497-5500*
**Fax Area Code:* 330 ■ *TF:* 800-445-7128 ■ *Web:* www.ameridial.com

Aria Communications Corp
717 W Saint Germain St .... St. Cloud MN 56301 800-955-9924
TF: 800-955-9924 ■ *Web:* www.ariacallsandcards.com

Ask Telemarketing Inc 5815 Carmichael Rd .... Montgomery AL 36117 334-387-2758
Web: www.asktelemarketing.com

Blue Valley Tele-Communications Inc
1559 Pony Express Hwy .... Home KS 66438 785-799-3311
Web: www.bluevalley.net

Bluestem Brands Inc
6509 Flying Cloud Dr .... Eden Prairie MN 55344 952-656-3700 656-4112
Web: bluestembrands.silkroad.com

Calling Solutions By Phone Power Inc
2200 McCullough Ave .... San Antonio TX 78212 210-801-9630
TF Cust Svc: 800-683-5500 ■ *Web:* www.callingsolutions.com

Concept Services Ltd 230 Quadral Dr. Ste A .... Wadsworth OH 44281 330-336-2571
Web: www.conceptservicesltd.com

Connection, The 11351 Rupp Dr .... Burnsville MN 55337 952-948-5488
TF Sales: 800-883-5777 ■ *Web:* www.theconnectioncc.com

Convergys Corp 201 E Fourth St .... Cincinnati OH 45202 513-723-7000
NYSE: CVG ■ *TF:* 888-284-9900 ■ *Web:* www.convergys.com

Dale Corp 28091 Dequindre .... Madison Heights MI 48071 248-542-2400 542-6007
Web: www.dalecorporation.com

DialAmerica Marketing Inc 960 MacArthur Blvd .... Mahwah NJ 07495 201-327-0200 327-4066
Web: www.dialamerica.com

EBSCO TeleServices
4150 Belden Village Ave NW Ste 401 .... Canton OH 44718 330-492-5105

Evolve IP LLC 989 Old Eagle School Rd Ste 815 .... Wayne PA 19087 610-964-8000
Web: www.evolveip.net

Gage 10000 Hwy 55 .... Minneapolis MN 55441 763-595-3800 595-3871
Web: www.gage.com

Harte-Hanks Response Management
2800 Wells Branch Pkwy .... Austin TX 78728 512-434-1100
TF: 800-456-9748 ■ *Web:* hartehanks.com

Hartington Telemarketing Inc
318 318 S Robinson Ave Ave .... Hartington NE 68739 402-254-2255
Web: www.hartel.net

Holden Marketing Support Services
5000 Lima St .... Denver CO 80239 720-374-3700

InfoCision Management Corp 325 Springside Dr .... Akron OH 44333 330-668-1400 668-1401
TF: 800-210-6269 ■ *Web:* www.infocision.com

Inktel Direct Corp 13975 NW 58th Ct .... Miami Lakes FL 33014 305-523-1100
Web: www.inktel.com

InService America Inc 129 Vista Centre Dr .... Forest VA 24551 434-316-7400
Web: www.inserviceamerica.com

Insight Tele - Services Inc
17117 W 9 Mile Rd Ste 800 .... Southfield MI 48075 248-552-8866
Web: www.insightteleservices.com

Integretel Inc 5883 Rue Ferrari .... San Jose CA 95138 408-362-4000
TF: 888-302-2750

Intelemark LLC 4545 E Shea Blvd Ste 280 .... Phoenix AZ 85028 602-943-7111
Web: www.intelemark.com

iSky 1700 Pennsylvania Ave NW Ste 560 .... Washington DC 20006 855-475-4759
TF: 855-475-4759 ■ *Web:* www.isky.com

Julie Inc 3275 Executive Dr .... Joliet IL 60431 815-741-5000
TF: 800-892-0123 ■ *Web:* www.illinois1call.com

Kipany Productions Ltd 32 E 39th St .... New York NY 10016 212-883-8300
Web: www.kipany.com

Kowal & Associates Inc 5 Cambridge Ctr .... Cambridge MA 02142 617-577-0700
Web: www.kowalassociates.com

Lester Inc 19 Business Pk Dr .... Branford CT 06405 203-488-5265 483-0408
TF: 800-999-5265 ■ *Web:* www.lesterusa.com

Lexicon Marketing Corp
6380 Wilshire Blvd .... Los Angeles CA 90048 323-782-7400
Web: www.lexiconmarketing.com

LiveBridge Inc 7303 SE Lk Rd .... Portland OR 97267 503-652-6000
Web: www.livebridge.com

Mars Stout Inc 4500 Majestic Dr .... Missoula MT 59808 406-721-6280
TF: 800-451-6277 ■ *Web:* www.marsstout.com

Meyer Assoc Inc 14 Seventh Ave N .... Saint Cloud MN 56303 320-259-4000 259-4044
TF: 800-676-9233

Miratel Solutions Inc 2501 Steeles Ave W .... North York ON M3J2P1 416-650-7850
TF: 866-647-2835 ■ *Web:* www.miratelinc.com

My Receptionist 800 Wisconsin St Ste 410 .... Eau Claire WI 54703 800-686-0162
TF: 800-686-0162 ■ *Web:* www.myreceptionist.com

Phone Fax

Nordia Inc 5200 Blvd de l'Ormiere .... Quebec QC G1P4B2 418-864-7359
Web: www.nordia.ca

ProCom Inc 28838 US Hwy 69 PO Box 27 .... Lamoni IA 50140 641-784-8841
TF: 800-433-9893 ■ *Web:* www.procom-inc.com

Psi Contact Center
3160 Haggerty Rd Ste D .... West Bloomfield MI 48323 248-624-2400
Web: www.psicontactcenter.com

Quez Media Marketing 1138 Prospect Ave E .... Cleveland OH 44115 216-910-0202
Web: www.quezmedia.com

Research First Consulting Inc
8 Mockingbird Lane .... Gulfport MS 39507 205-995-8866
Web: www.researchfirst.com

Results Telemarketing Inc
499 E Sheridan St Ste 400 .... Dania Beach FL 33004 954-921-2400 923-8070
Web: www.resultstel.com

Sage Advantage
9414 E San Salvador Dr Ste 250 .... Scottsdale AZ 85258 480-941-0094
Web: www.sageadvantage.com

Sisk Kathy Enterprises 1874 Polson Ave .... Clovis CA 93611 559-323-1472
Web: kathysiskenterprises.com

SITEL Corp 2 American Ctr Ste 900 .... Nashville TN 37203 615-301-7100
TF: 866-957-4835 ■ *Web:* www.sitel.com

Synergy Solutions Inc
2340 E Beardsley Rd Ste 110 .... Phoenix AZ 85024 602-296-1600
Web: www.synergysolutionsinc.com

Telax Voice Solutions 365 Evans Ave Ste 302 .... Toronto ON M8Z1K2 416-207-0630
TF: 888-808-3529 ■ *Web:* www.telax.com

Tele Business USA 1945 Techny Rd Ste 3 .... Northbrook IL 60062 877-315-8353 480-6055*
**Fax Area Code:* 847 ■ *TF:* 877-315-8353 ■ *Web:* www.tbiz.com

TeleDevelopment Services Inc
4816 Brecksville Rd Ste 2 .... Richfield OH 44286 330-659-4441
Web: www.teledevelopment.com

Teleperformance USA
1991 South 4650 West .... Salt Lake City UT 84104 801-257-5800
Web: www.teleperformance.com

Telerx 723 Dresher Rd .... Horsham PA 19044 267-942-3300 347-6010*
**Fax Area Code:* 215 ■ *TF:* 800-283-5379 ■ *Web:* www.telerx.com

TeleServices Direct
5305 Lakeview Pkwy S Dr .... Indianapolis IN 46268 317-216-2240
Web: www.teleservicesdirect.com

TeleTech Holdings Inc 9197 S Peoria St .... Englewood CO 80112 303-397-8100
NASDAQ: TTEC ■ *TF General:* 800-835-3832 ■ *Web:* www.teletech.com

Telexpertise Inc
7790 E Arapahoe Rd Ste 240 .... Centennial CO 80112 720-200-0590
TF: 877-767-6762 ■ *Web:* www.telexpertise.com

Thomas L Cardella & Associates Inc
4515 20th Ave SW .... Cedar Rapids IA 52404 319-730-4028
Web: www.tlcassociates.com

Thumbs-Up Telemarketing Inc
11861 Westline Industrial Dr Ste 600 .... Saint Louis MO 63146 314-821-8111
Web: thumbsupinc.com

Torcom 25 Kessel Ct .... Madison WI 53711 608-276-0709
Web: torco.com

TRG Holdings LLC 1700 Pennsylvania Ave NW .... Washington DC 20006 202-289-9898
Web: www.ibexglobal.com

Turn-Key Solutions Inc
4920 W Thunderbird Ave Ste C-120 .... Glendale AZ 85306 602-863-0269
Web: www.tksnation.com

Urban Data Solutions Inc
589 Eighth Ave 15th Fl .... New York NY 10018 212-931-6330
Web: www.u-data.com

USA 800 Inc 9808 E 66th Terr .... Kansas City MO 64133 816-358-1303 358-8845
TF: 800-821-7539 ■ *Web:* www.usa800.com

USAN Inc 3080 Northwoods Cir .... Norcross GA 30071 770-670-2278
Web: www.usan.com

VibrantAds LLC 2115 W Crescent Ave Ste 220 .... Anaheim CA 92801 714-400-9898
Web: www.vibrantads.com

VOX Data 1155 Metcalfe St 18th Fl .... Montreal QC H3B2V6 514-871-1920
TF: 800-861-9599 ■ *Web:* www.voxdata.com

West Corp 11808 Miracle Hills Dr .... Omaha NE 68154 800-232-0900
TF Sales: 800-232-0900 ■ *Web:* www.west.com

Working Solutions 1820 Preston Pk Blvd Ste 2000 .... Plano TX 75093 972-964-4800 964-4802
TF: 866-857-4800 ■ *Web:* www.workingsolutions.com

Young America Corp 10 S 5th St 7th Fl .... Minneapolis MN 55402 800-533-4529
TF: 800-533-4529 ■ *Web:* www.yaengage.com

Your Selling Team 100 Spectrum Ctr Dr Ste 700 .... Irvine CA 92618 888-387-8002
TF: 888-387-8002 ■ *Web:* www.yoursellingteam.com

TELEVISION - CABLE

See Cable & Other Pay Television Services p. 1887; Television Networks - Cable p. 3223

738 TELEVISION COMPANIES

Phone Fax

A. Smith & Company Productions Inc
9911 W Pico Blvd Ste 128 .... Los Angeles CA 90035 310-432-4800
Web: www.asmithco.com

Acme Communications Inc
2101 E Fourth St Ste 202 .... Santa Ana CA 92705 714-245-9499 245-9494
PINK: ACME ■ *Web:* www.acmecommunications.com

Allbritton Communications Co
1000 Wilson Blvd Ste 2700 .... Arlington VA 22209 703-647-8700
Web: allbritton.com

Ask Associates Inc 1201 Wakarusa Ste C-1 .... Lawrence KS 66049 785-841-8194
TF: 800-315-4333 ■ *Web:* www.askusa.com

California Oregon Broadcasting Inc
125 S Fir St .... Medford OR 97501 541-779-5555 779-5564
Web: www.kobi5.com

Phone Fax

Capitol Broadcasting Co Inc
2619 Western Blvd Raleigh NC 27606 919-890-6000 890-6095
TF: 800-234-4857 ■ *Web:* capitolbroadcasting.com

CBS Television Stations Group 51 W 52nd St New York NY 10019 212-975-4321 975-3154
Web: www.cbs.com

Christian Television Network Inc (CTN)
6922 142nd Ave N Largo FL 33771 727-535-5622 531-2497
TF: 800-716-7729 ■ *Web:* www.ctnonline.com

Communications Corp of America
700 St John St Ste 300 Lafayette LA 70501 337-237-1142

Community Educational Television
10902 S Wilcrest Dr Houston TX 77099 281-561-5828 561-9793
Web: myedutv.org

CW Network LLC, The 3300 Olive Ave Burbank CA 91505 818-977-2500
Web: www.cwtv.com

Diversified Business Communications
121 Free St Portland ME 04101 207-842-5500 842-5503
Web: divcom.com

Elevation Ltd 1027 33rd St Nw Ste 260 Washington DC 20007 202-380-3230
Web: www.elevation-us.com

Emmis Communications Corp
40 Monument Cir 1 Emmis Plz Ste 700 Indianapolis IN 46204 317-266-0100 631-3750
NASDAQ: EMMS ■ *Web:* www.emmis.com

Entravision Communications Corp
2425 Olympic Blvd Ste 6000 W Santa Monica CA 90404 310-447-3870 447-3899
NYSE: EVC ■ *Web:* www.entravision.com

EW Scripps Co 312 Walnut St Ste 2800 Cincinnati OH 45202 513-977-3000 977-3800*
NYSE: SSP ■ **Fax:* Hum Res ■ *TF:* 800-888-3000 ■ *Web:* www.scripps.com

Fisher Communications Inc
140 Fourth Ave N Ste 500 Seattle WA 98109 206-404-7000 404-6037
NASDAQ: FSCI ■ *Web:* www.sbgi.net

Flinn Broadcasting 6080 Mt Moriah Rd Ext Memphis TN 38115 901-375-9324 375-0041
Web: www.flinn.com

Fort Group Inc
100 Challenger Rd 8th Fl Ridgefield Park NJ 07660 201-445-0202
Web: www.fortgroupinc.com

Forum Communications Co 101 Fifth St N Fargo ND 58102 701-235-7311 241-5406
Web: www.forumcomm.com

Fox Television Stations Inc
1999 S Bundy Dr Los Angeles CA 90025 310-584-2000 584-2012
Web: www.foxla.com

Freedom Communications Inc 17666 Fitch Irvine CA 92614 949-253-2300 474-7675
TF: 855-862-7238 ■ *Web:* www.freedom.com

Gannett Company Inc 7950 Jones Branch Dr McLean VA 22107 703-854-6000
NYSE: GCI ■ *Web:* www.gannett.com

Granite Broadcasting Corp
767 Third Ave 34th Fl New York NY 10017 212-826-2530 826-2858
Web: www.granitetv.com

Gray Television Inc 4370 Peachtree Rd NE Atlanta GA 30319 404-504-9828
NYSE: GTN ■ *TF:* 888-835-2869 ■ *Web:* www.gray.tv

Kota 518 St Joseph St Rapid City SD 57701 605-342-2000 342-7305

LeSea Broadcasting Corp
61300 S Ironwood Rd South Bend IN 46614 574-291-8200 291-9043
TF: 800-365-3732 ■ *Web:* www.lesea.com

Lieberman Productions 455 Ninth St San Francisco CA 94103 415-955-0855
Web: www.lieberman.com

Media General Broadcast Group
333 E Franklin St Richmond VA 23219 804-649-6000
TF: 800-937-5449 ■ *Web:* www.mediageneral.com

Meredith Corp 1716 Locust St Des Moines IA 50309 515-284-3000
NYSE: MDP ■ *Web:* www.meredith.com

Metrovision Production Group LLC
508 W 24th St New York NY 10011 212-989-1515
Web: www.metrovision-nyc.com

Morgan Murphy Broadcasting Group
7025 Raymond Rd Madison WI 53719 608-271-4321 271-6111
Web: www.channel3000.com

Morris Multimedia Inc 27 Abercorn St Savannah GA 31401 912-233-1281 232-4639
Web: www.morrismultimedia.com

Omnivision Entertainment Inc
The Film Ctr 630 Ninth Ave Ste 810 New York NY 10036 212-582-2199
Web: www.mydamnchannel.com

On Event Services LLC 6550 McDonough Dr Norcross GA 30093 770-457-0966
TF: 800-967-2419 ■ *Web:* www.oneventservices.com

Pappas Telecasting Cos 823 W Center Ave Visalia CA 93291 559-733-7800 733-7878

Quincy Newspapers Inc 130 S Fifth St Quincy IL 62301 217-223-5100 223-9757
TF: 800-373-9444 ■ *Web:* www.whig.com

Raycom Media Inc
201 Monroe St RSA Tower 20th Fl Montgomery AL 36104 334-206-1400 206-1555
Web: www.raycommedia.com

Red River Broadcasting Co LLC 2001 London Rd Duluth MN 55812 218-728-1622
Web: www.fox21online.com

Roadtrip Productions Ltd
1626 Placentia Ave Costa Mesa CA 92627 949-764-9121
Web: roadtripnation.com

Saga Communications Inc
73 Kercheval Ave Grosse Pointe Farms MI 48236 313-886-7070 886-7150
NYSE: SGA ■ *TF:* 800-777-3674 ■ *Web:* sagacom.com

Sarkes Tarzian Inc
205 N College Ave Ste 800 Bloomington IN 47404 812-332-7251 331-4575

Sinclair Broadcast Group Inc
10706 Beaver Dam Rd Hunt Valley MD 21030 410-568-1500 568-1533
NASDAQ: SBGI ■ *Web:* www.sbgi.net

Smart MultiMedia Inc 1113 Vine St Ste 239 Houston TX 77002 713-574-6690
Web: www.smartgeometrics.com

Tribune Co 435 N Michigan Ave Chicago IL 60611 312-222-9100
Web: www.tribune.com

Univision Television Group Inc
5999 Ctr Dr Los Angeles CA 90045 310-846-2800
TF: 800-594-5387 ■ *Web:* www.univision.com

Verite Inc 608 West 9320 South Sandy UT 84070 801-553-1101
Web: www.verite.com

Visual Data Media Services Inc
610 N Hollywood Way Burbank CA 91505 818-558-3363
Web: www.visualdatamedia.com

Weigel Broadcasting 26 N Halstead St Chicago IL 60661 312-705-2600 705-2656
Web: www.metv.com

Wicks Group of Cos LLC 405 Pk Ave Ste 702 New York NY 10022 212-838-2100 223-2109
Web: www.wicksgroup.com

WMFE 11510 E Colonial Dr Orlando FL 32817 407-273-2300
Web: www.wmfe.org

WYOMedia Inc 1856 Skyview Dr Casper WY 82601 307-577-5923 577-5928

Xanadoo Co 225 City Ave Ste 100 Bala Cynwyd PA 19004 610-934-7000 341-1835

ZGS Communications 2000 N 14th St Ste 400 Arlington VA 22201 703-528-5656 526-0879
Web: www.zgsgroup.com

739 TELEVISION NETWORKS - BROADCAST

Phone Fax

ABC Inc 77 W 66th St New York NY 10023 212-456-7777 456-2795
Web: www.abc.go.com

CBS Broadcasting Inc 51 W 52nd St New York NY 10019 212-975-4321
Web: www.cbs.com

CBS Corp 51 W 52nd St New York NY 10019 212-975-4321 975-4516
NYSE: CBS ■ *Web:* www.cbscorporation.com

Fox Broadcasting Co 10201 W Pico Blvd Los Angeles CA 90035 310-369-1350
Web: www.fox.com

Nstreams Technologies Inc 1914 Junction Ave San Jose CA 95131 408-734-8889 734-8886

Public Broadcasting Service (PBS)
2100 Crystal Dr Arlington VA 22202 703-739-5000
TF: 866-864-0828 ■ *Web:* www.pbs.org

Raycom Sports Inc 1900 W Morehead St Charlotte NC 28208 704-378-4400
Web: raycomsports.com

Univision Communications Inc
1999 Ave of the Stars Ste 3050 Los Angeles CA 90067 310-348-3672
Web: www.univision.com

740 TELEVISION NETWORKS - CABLE

Phone Fax

A&E Television Networks LLC 235 E 45th St New York NY 10017 212-210-1400 210-1308
Web: www.aenetworks.com

Accent Health 60 E 42nd St Ste 1543 New York NY 10165 800-235-4930 349-7299*
**Fax Area Code:* 813 ■ *TF:* 800-235-4930 ■ *Web:* www.accenthealth.com

AMC Networks Inc 11 Penn Plaza 2nd Fl New York NY 10001 212-324-8500
NASDAQ: AMCX ■ *Web:* www.amcnetworks.com

Artv 1400 Rene-Levesque Blvd E Bureau A-53-1 Montreal QC H2L2M2 514-597-3636
Web: www.artv.ca

Asian Television Network (ATN) 330 Cochrane Dr Markham ON L3R8E4 905-948-8199 948-8108
Web: www.asiantelevision.com

Auto Ch 332 W Broadway Ste 1604 Louisville KY 40202 502-992-0200 992-0201
Web: www.theautochannel.com

BBC America 1120 Ave of the Americas 5th Fl New York NY 10036 212-705-9300
Web: www.bbcamerica.com

Bell Media Inc
Bell Media Inc 299 Queen St W Toronto ON M5V2Z5 416-924-6664
Web: www.bellmedia.ca

BET Networks & BET Interactive LLC
1235 W St NE Washington DC 20018 202-608-2000
Web: www.bet.com

Book Television 299 Queen St W Toronto AB M5V2Z5 416-384-8000 591-5117
Web: www.booktelevision.com

Business News Network (BNN) 299 Queen St W Toronto ON M5V2Z5 416-384-6600
TF: 855-326-6266 ■ *Web:* www.bnn.ca

C-SPAN Extra 400 N Capitol St NW Ste 650 Washington DC 20001 202-737-3220
Web: www.c-span.org

C-SPAN3 400 N Capitol St NW Ste 650 Washington DC 20001 202-737-3220
Web: www.c-span.org

Cable Public Affairs Ch (CPAC) PO Box 81099 Ottawa ON K1P1B1 877-287-2722 567-2749*
**Fax Area Code:* 613 ■ *TF:* 877-287-2722 ■ *Web:* www.cpac.ca

Cable Satellite Public Affairs Network (C-SPAN)
400 N Capitol St NW Ste 650 Washington DC 20001 202-737-3220
Web: www.c-span.org

Cartoon Network Inc, The 1015 Techwood Drive Atlanta GA 30318 404-878-0694
Web: www.cartoonnetwork.com

Christian Broadcasting Network (CBN)
977 Centerville Tpke Virginia Beach VA 23463 757-226-7000 226-2017
TF: 800-759-0700 ■ *Web:* www.cbn.com

Cinemax 1100 Ave of the Americas New York NY 10036 212-512-1000
Web: www.cinemax.com

Classic Arts Showcase PO Box 828 Burbank CA 91503 323-878-0283 878-0329
Web: www.classicartsshowcase.org

CNBC Inc 900 Sylvan Ave Englewood Cliffs NJ 07632 201-735-2622
Web: www.cnbc.com

Comedy Central 1775 Broadway New York NY 10019 212-767-8600 767-8592
Web: cc.com

Country Music Television (CMT)
330 Commerce St Nashville TN 37201 615-335-8400 335-8614
Web: www.cmt.com

CRN Digital Talk Radio 10487 Sunland Blvd Sunland CA 91040 818-352-7152 352-3229
TF: 866-554-7387 ■ *Web:* www.crntalk.com

Cross TV 370 W Camino Gardens Blvd Ste 300 Boca Raton FL 33432 561-367-7454
TF: 877-276-7788 ■ *Web:* www.crosstv.com

Crown Media Holdings Inc
12700 Ventura Blvd Ste 200 Studio City CA 91604 818-755-2400
NASDAQ: CRWN ■ *TF:* 800-479-7328 ■ *Web:* www.hallmarkchannel.com

CTV Edmonton 18520 Stony Plain Rd NW Edmonton AB T5S1A8 780-483-3311

Daystar Television Network
3901 Hwy 121 PO Box 610546 Bedford TX 76021 817-571-1229 571-7458
TF: 800-329-0029 ■ *Web:* daystar.com

Deep Dish TV 339 Lafayette St 3rd Fl New York NY 10012 212-473-8933
Web: www.deepdishtv.org

Phone Fax

Discovery Comm Latin America
6505 Blue Lagoon Dr Ste 190 ... Miami FL 33126 786-273-4700
Web: corporate.discovery.com

Discovery Communications Inc
1 Discovery Pl ... Silver Spring MD 20910 240-662-2000
NASDAQ: DISCA ■ *TF:* 877-324-5850 ■ *Web:* corporate.discovery.com

Discovery Life Cannel 1 Discovery Pl ... Silver Spring MD 20910 240-662-2000
Web: www.discoverylife.com

Documentary Ch 1207 16th Ave S ... Nashville TN 37212 615-322-9333
Web: www.pivot.tv

E! Entertainment Television
5750 Wilshire Blvd ... Los Angeles CA 90036 323-954-2400 954-2621*
**Fax Area Code:* 213 ■ *Web:* www.eonline.com

ESPN 545 Middle St ... Bristol CT 06010 877-710-3776
TF: 877-710-3776 ■ *Web:* www.espn.go.com

ESPN Classic Canada 299 Queen St W ... Toronto ON M5V2Z5 416-384-3139
Web: www.tsn.ca

ESPN Classic Inc ESPN Plaza ... Bristol CT 06010 877-710-3776
TF: 877-710-3776 ■ *Web:* espn.go.com

ESPN Deportes 2 Alhambra Plz 9th Fl ... Coral Gables FL 33134 305-567-3797
TF: 800-337-6783 ■ *Web:* espndeportes.espn.go.com

Eternal Word Television Network (EWTN)
5817 Old Leeds Rd ... Irondale AL 35210 205-271-2900
Web: www.ewtn.com

EVINE Live Inc 6740 Shady Oak Rd ... Eden Prairie MN 55344 800-676-5523
TF: 800-676-5523 ■ *Web:* www.evine.com

FOX News Ch 1211 Ave of the Americas ... New York NY 10036 212-301-3000 301-8274*
**Fax:* News Rm ■ *Web:* www.foxnews.com

FOX Sports Net 10201 W Pico Blvd ... Los Angeles CA 90035 310-369-7069
Web: www.foxsports.com

Free Speech TV (FSTV) PO Box 44099 ... Denver CO 80201 303-542-4813
Web: www.freespeech.org

God's Learning Ch (GLC) PO Box 61000 ... Midland TX 79711 432-563-0420 563-1736
TF: 800-707-0420 ■ *Web:* www.glc.us.com

Hallmark Ch 12700 Ventura Blvd Ste 200 ... Studio City CA 91604 818-755-2400
TF: 888-390-7474 ■ *Web:* www.hallmarkchannel.com

Hispanic Information & Telecommunications Network Inc
63 Flushing Ave Unit 281 ... Brooklyn NY 11205 212-966-5660 966-5725
Web: www.hitn.org

History Ch
A&E Television Networks LLC
235 E 45th St 2nd Fl ... New York NY 10017 212-210-1400
TF: 888-371-5848 ■ *Web:* www.history.com

Idea Channel 2002 Filmore Ave Ste 1 ... Erie PA 16506 814-833-7107 833-7415
Web: theideachannel.tv

iN DEMAND 345 Hudson St 17th Fl ... New York NY 10014 646-638-8200 486-0855
Web: www.indemand.com

Ion Media Networks
601 Clearwater Pk Rd ... West Palm Beach FL 33401 561-659-4122 597-5903*
**Fax Area Code:* 646 ■ **Fax:* PR ■ *TF:* 800-987-9936 ■ *Web:* www.ionmedianetworks.com

Les Chaines Tele Astral
1800 Ave McGill College Bureau 1600 ... Montreal QC H3A3J6 514-938-3320 939-3151
Web: www.bellmedia.ca

Liberty Ch 1971 University Blvd ... Lynchburg VA 24506 434-582-2000
TF: 800-332-1883 ■ *Web:* www.liberty.edu

MSG Network 2 Pennsylvania Plz ... New York NY 10121 212-465-6741 465-6024
Web: www.msgnetworks.com/index.html

MTV Networks 1515 Broadway ... New York NY 10036 212-846-6000 422-6630*
**Fax Area Code:* 201 ■ *Web:* www.mtv.com

MTV Networks On Campus Inc (MTVU)
1540 Broadway 33rd Fl ... New York NY 10036 877-800-4483
TF: 877-800-4483 ■ *Web:* www.mtvu.com

NASA TV 300 E St SW ... Washington DC 20546 202-358-0000 358-4338
TF: 877-546-1574 ■ *Web:* www.nasa.gov

New England Cable News (NECN) 160 Wells Ave ... Newton MA 02459 617-630-5000 630-5055
Web: www.necn.com

New England Sports Network (NESN)
480 Arsenal St Bldg 1 ... Watertown MA 02472 617-536-9233 536-7814
Web: www.nesn.com

NFL Network 345 Park Avenue ... New York NY 10154 212-450-2000 681-7599
TF: 800-724-3377 ■ *Web:* www.nfl.com/nflnetwork

Nickelodeon 1515 Broadway 38th Fl ... New York NY 10036 212-258-7500 258-7705
Web: www.nick.com

Oasis TV Inc 2029 Century Pk E Ste 400 ... Los Angeles CA 90067 310-553-4300
Web: www.otvlive.tv

Outdoor Ch 43445 Business Pk Dr Ste 103 ... Temecula CA 92590 951-699-6991
NASDAQ: OUTD ■ *TF:* 800-770-5750 ■ *Web:* www.outdoorchannel.com

Ovation The Arts Network
2850 Ocean Pk Blvd Ste 225 ... Santa Monica CA 90405 310-430-7575
Web: www.ovationtv.com

Pet Network 105 Gordon Baker Rd 8th Fl ... Toronto ON M2H3P8 416-756-2404 756-5526
Web: www.thepetnetwork.tv

QVC Inc 1200 Wilson Dr ... West Chester PA 19380 484-701-1000
TF: 800-367-9444 ■ *Web:* www.qvc.com

Resort Sports Network
Outside Television 33 Riverside Ave 4th Fl ... Westport CT 06880 203-221-9240
TF: 888-795-9488 ■ *Web:* www.outsidetelevision.com

SCOLA 21557 270th St ... McClelland IA 51548 712-566-2202 566-2502
Web: www.scola.org

Score, The 500 King St W 4th Fl ... Toronto ON M5V1L9 416-479-8812 361-2045
Web: thescore.com

Scripps Networks LLC 9721 Sherrill Blvd ... Knoxville TN 37932 865-694-2700
Web: www.diynetwork.com

Shopping Ch, The
Credit Card Dept 59 Ambassador Dr ... Mississauga ON L5T2P9 888-202-0888
TF: 888-202-0888 ■ *Web:* www.theshoppingchannel.com

Showtime Networks Inc 1633 Broadway 15th Fl ... New York NY 10019 212-708-1600 708-1217
Web: www.sho.com

SoapNet LLC 500 S Buena Vista St ... Burbank CA 91521 818-560-1000

Starz Encore Group LLC 8900 Liberty Cir ... Englewood CO 80112 720-852-7700
Web: www.starz.com

Starz LLC 8900 Liberty Cir ... Englewood CO 80112 720-852-7700
Web: www.starz.com

Phone Fax

Stornoway Communications
105 Gordon Baker Rd 8th Fl ... Toronto ON M2H3P8 416-756-2404
Web: www.stornoway.com

Sundance Ch 1633 Broadway ... New York NY 10019 212-708-1500
Web: sundance.tv

TBS Superstation Inc 1050 Techwood Dr NW ... Atlanta GA 30318 404-827-1700
Web: www.tbs.com

TCT Ministries Inc 11717 N Rt 37 PO Box 1010 ... Marion IL 62959 618-997-4700 993-9778
TF: 800-232-9855 ■ *Web:* www.tct.tv

Telelatino Network Inc (TLN) 5125 Steeles Ave W ... Toronto ON M9L1R5 416-744-8200 744-0966
TF: 800-551-8401 ■ *Web:* www.tlntv.com

Teletoon Canada Inc
181 Bay St Ste 100 Brookfield Pl ... Toronto ON M5J2T3 416-956-2060
Web: www.teletoon.com

Tennis Ch 2850 Ocean Pk Blvd Ste 150 ... Santa Monica CA 90405 310-314-9400 314-9433
Web: www.tennischannel.com

TFC USA 150 Shoreline Dr ... Redwood City CA 94065 650-508-6000
TF: 800-345-2465 ■ *Web:* www.tfc-usa.com

Total Living Network (TLN) 2880 Vision Ct ... Aurora IL 60506 630-801-3838 801-3839
Web: www.tln.com

Travel Ch LLC 5425 Wisconsin Ave Ste 500 ... Chevy Chase MD 20815 301-244-7500
Web: www.travelchannel.com

Trinity Broadcasting Network (TBN) PO Box A ... Santa Ana CA 92711 714-832-2950
TF: 888-731-1000 ■ *Web:* www.tbn.org

Turner Broadcasting System Inc (TBS) 1 CNN Ctr ... Atlanta GA 30303 404-827-1700
Web: www.turner.com

Turner Classic Movies (TCM) 1050 Techwood Dr NW ... Atlanta GA 30318 404-827-1700
Web: www.tcm.turner.com

TV Asahi America Inc 875 Third Ave 3rd Fl ... New York NY 10022 212-644-6300 644-0003
Web: www.tv-asahi.net

TV One 1010 Wayne Ave 10th Fl ... Silver Spring MD 20910 301-755-0400 429-3202
Web: tvone.tv

USA Network 30 Rockefeller Plaza 21st Fl ... New York NY 10112 212-664-4444 664-6365
Web: www.usanetwork.com

VH1 Classic 1515 Broadway 21st Fl ... New York NY 10036 212-275-6661
Web: www.vh1.com

Video Hits One (VH1) 1515 Broadway 20th Fl ... New York NY 10036 800-745-1892 422-6630*
**Fax Area Code:* 201 ■ **Fax:* Hum Res ■ *TF:* 800-745-1892 ■ *Web:* www.vh1.com

W Network 25 Dockside Dr ... Toronto ON M5A0B5 416-479-6784
Web: www.wnetwork.com

Weather Ch Inc, The
300 I N Pkwy Po Box 724554 ... Atlanta GA 30339 770-226-0000 226-2632
TF: 866-843-0392 ■ *Web:* www.weather.com

Weather Network, The 2655 Bristol Cir ... Oakville ON L6H7W1 905-829-1159 829-5800
Web: www.theweathernetwork.com

WGN America 2501 W Bradley Pl ... Chicago IL 60618 773-528-2311
Web: www.wgnamerica.com

Worship Network PO Box 428 ... Safety Harbor FL 34695 800-728-8723
TF: 800-728-8723 ■ *Web:* www.worship.net

741 TELEVISION STATIONS

ABC	American Broadcasting Co	**PBS**	Public Broadcasting Service
CBC	Canadian Broadcasting Corp	**QS**	Television Quatre Saisons
CBS	Columbia Broadcasting System	**SRC**	Societe Radio-Canada
CTV	Canadian Television Network	**TBN**	Trinity Broadcasting Network
Fox	Fox Broadcasting Co	**Tele**	Telemundo Communications Group
GTN	Global Television Network	**TVA**	Groupe TVA
Ind	Independent	**Uni**	Univision Television Network
NBC	National Broadcasting Co	**UPN**	United Paramount Network
PAX	Paxson Communications Corp	**WB**	Warner Bros Television

See Also Internet Broadcasting p. 2593

Phone Fax

CBET-TV Ch 9 (CBC) 825 Riverside Dr W ... Windsor ON N9A5K9 519-255-3411
Web: cbc.ca/news/canada/windsor

CFCM-TV Ch 4 (TVA) 1000 Myrand Ave ... Sainte-Foy QC G1V2W3 514-526-9251 688-0413*
**Fax Area Code:* 418 ■ *Web:* tva.canoe.ca

Channel 45 WHFT TV 3324 Pembroke Rd ... Hollywood FL 33021 954-962-1700
Web: tbn.org

CKVR-TV Ch 3 (Ind) 299 Queen St W ... Toronto ON M5V2Z5 416-384-5000
TF: 866-690-6179 ■ *Web:* www.ctv.ca

EW Scripps Co, The 1866 E Chisholm ... Nampa ID 83687 208-336-0500 381-6682
Web: www.kivitv.com

Iowa Public Television 6450 Corporate Dr ... Johnston IA 50131 515-242-3100 725-9836
TF: 800-532-1290 ■ *Web:* www.iptv.org

KAAL-TV Ch 6 (ABC) 1701 Tenth Pl NE ... Austin MN 55912 507-437-6666 433-9560
Web: www.kaaltv.com

KABC-TV Ch 7 (ABC) 500 Cir Seven Dr ... Glendale CA 91201 818-863-7777 863-7080

KAFT-TV Ch 13 (PBS) 350 S Donaghey Ave ... Conway AR 72034 501-682-2386 682-4122
TF: 800-662-2386 ■ *Web:* www.aetn.org

KAIL-TV Ch 7 1590 Alluvial Ave ... Clovis CA 93611 559-299-9753 299-1523
Web: www.kail.tv

KARE-TV Ch 11 (NBC) 8811 State Hwy 55 ... Golden Valley MN 55427 763-546-1111
TF: 888-966-4532 ■ *Web:* www.kare11.com

KAZT-TV Ch 7 (Ind) 3211 Tower Rd ... Prescott AZ 86305 928-778-6770
Web: aztv.com

KBHE-TV Ch 9 (PBS)
555 N Dakota St PO Box 5000 ... Vermillion SD 57069 800-333-0789 677-5010*
**Fax Area Code:* 605 ■ *TF:* 800-333-0789 ■ *Web:* www.sdpb.org

KBYU-TV Ch 11 (PBS)
2000 Ironton Blvd Brigham Young University ... Provo UT 84606 801-422-8450 422-8478
TF: 800-298-5298 ■ *Web:* www.kbyutv.org

KCAL-TV Ch 9 (Ind) 4200 Radford Ave ... Studio City CA 91604 818-655-2000
Web: losangeles.cbslocal.com

KCBA-TV Ch 35 (Fox) 1550 Moffett St ... Salinas CA 93905 831-422-3500 422-9365
Web: www.kionrightnow.com

KCBS-TV Ch 2 (CBS) 4200 Radford Ave ... Studio City CA 91604 818-655-2000
Web: losangeles.cbslocal.com

				Phone	Fax
KCTV-TV Ch 5 (CBS) 4500 Shawnee Mission Pkwy *Web:* www.kctv5.com	Fairway	KS	66205	913-677-5555	677-7243
KCWC-TV Ch 4 (PBS) 2660 Peck Ave *TF:* 800-495-9788 ■ *Web:* wyomingpbs.org	Riverton	WY	82501	307-856-6944	856-3893
KCWY-TV Ch 13 (NBC) 141 Progress Cir *Web:* kcwy13.com	Mills	WY	82644	307-577-0013	577-5251
KDTX-TV Ch 58 (TBN) 2823 W Irving Blvd *Web:* www.tbn.org	Irving	TX	75061	972-313-1333	
KESQ-TV Ch 3 (ABC) 42650 Melanie Pl *TF:* 888-776-8538 ■ *Web:* www.kesq.com	Palm Desert	CA	92211	760-318-8528	343-7480
KETG-TV Ch 9 (PBS) 350 S Donaghey Ave *TF:* 800-662-2386 ■ *Web:* www.aetn.org	Conway	AR	72034	501-682-2386	682-4122
KETS-TV Ch 2 (PBS) 350 S Donaghey Ave *TF:* 800-662-2386 ■ *Web:* www.aetn.org	Conway	AR	72034	501-682-2386	682-4122
KFBB-TV 3200 Old Havre Hwy *TF:* 877-509-9785 ■ *Web:* www.kfbb.com	Black Eagle	MT	59414	406-453-4377	
KFPX-TV Ch 39 (I) 4570 114th St	Urbandale	IA	50322	515-331-3939	331-1312
KGBT-TV Ch 4 (CBS) 9201 W Expy 83 *Web:* www.valleycentral.com	Harlingen	TX	78552	956-366-4444	366-4494
KICU-TV Ch 36 (Ind) 2102 Commerce Dr *Web:* www.ktvu.com	San Jose	CA	95131	408-953-3636	
KIMT-TV Ch 3 (CBS) 112 N Pennsylvania Ave *TF:* 800-323-4883 ■ *Web:* www.kimt.com	Mason City	IA	50401	641-423-2540	423-9309
KION-TV Ch 46 (CBS) 1550 Moffett St *Web:* www.kionrightnow.com	Salinas	CA	93905	831-422-3500	422-9365
KIVI-TV Ch 6 (ABC) 1866 E Chisholm Dr *Web:* www.kivitv.com	Nampa	ID	83687	208-336-0500	381-6682
KMAX-TV Ch 31 (CBS) 2713 Kovr Dr *TF:* 800-374-8813 ■ *Web:* sacramento.cbslocal.com	West Sacramento	CA	95605	916-374-1313	374-1304
KMBH-TV Ch 60 (PBS) 1701 Tennessee St	Harlingen	TX	78550	956-421-4111	
KMIR-TV Ch 6 (NBC) 72920 Parkview Dr *Web:* kmir.com	Palm Desert	CA	92260	760-568-3636	
KMIZ-TV Ch 17 (ABC) 501 Business Loop 70 E *TF:* 800-345-4109 ■ *Web:* www.abc17news.com	Columbia	MO	65201	573-449-0917	875-7078
KMOS-TV Ch 6 (PBS) University of Central Missouri *Fax Area Code: 660 ■ *TF:* 800-753-3436 ■ *Web:* www.kmos.org	Warrensburg	MO	64093	800-753-3436	543-8863*
KMSP-TV Ch 9 (Fox) 11358 Viking Dr *Web:* www.fox9.com	Eden Prairie	MN	55344	952-944-9999	942-0455
KNTV-TV Ch 11 (NBC) 2450 N First St *Web:* www.nbcbayarea.com	San Jose	CA	95131	408-432-6221	
KNWA-TV Ch 51 (NBC) 609 W Dickson St 3rd Flr *Web:* www.nwahomepage.com	Fayetteville	AR	72701	479-571-5100	
KOAA-TV Ch 5/30 (NBC) 2200 Seventh Ave *Web:* www.koaa.com	Pueblo	CO	81003	719-544-5781	295-6677
KOMU-TV Ch 8 (NBC) 5550 Hwy 63 S *TF:* 800-286-3932 ■ *Web:* www.komu.com	Columbia	MO	65201	573-884-6397	
KPDX-TV Ch 49 (MNT) 14975 NW Greenbrier Pkwy *TF:* 866-906-1249 ■ *Web:* www.kptv.com	Beaverton	OR	97006	503-906-1249	548-6920
KPLC-TV Ch 7 (NBC) 320 Div St *Web:* www.kplctv.com	Lake Charles	LA	70601	337-439-9071	437-7600
KPLO-TV Ch 6 (CBS) 501 S Phillips Ave *TF:* 800-888-5356 ■ *Web:* www.keloland.com	Sioux Falls	SD	57104	605-336-1100	
KPTV-TV Ch 12 (Fox) 14975 NW Greenbrier Pkwy *TF:* 866-906-1249 ■ *Web:* www.kptv.com	Beaverton	OR	97006	503-906-1249	548-6920
KPXD-TV Ch 68 (I) 600 Six Flags Dr Ste 652	Arlington	TX	76011	817-633-6843	633-3176
KPXE-TV Ch 50 (I) 4220 Shawnee Mission Pkwy Ste 110 B *Web:* www.ionmedianetworks.com	Fairway	KS	66205	913-722-0798	722-1217
KQED Inc 50 W San Fernando St Ste 110 *Web:* www.kqed.org	San Jose	CA	95131	415-864-2000	
KRCG-TV Ch 13 (CBS) 10188 Old Hwy 54 N *Web:* krcgtv.com	New Bloomfield	MO	65063	573-896-5144	896-5193
KRGV-TV Ch 5 (ABC) 900 E Expy PO Box 5 *Web:* www.krgv.com	Weslaco	TX	78596	956-968-5555	973-5016
KSBW-TV Ch 8 (NBC) 238 John St *Web:* www.ksbw.com	Salinas	CA	93901	831-758-8888	424-3750
KSMO-TV Ch 62 (MNT) 4500 Shawnee Mission Pkwy *Web:* www.kctv5.com	Fairway	KS	66205	913-677-5555	
KSMQ-TV Ch 15 (PBS) 2000 Eigth Ave NW *TF:* 800-658-2539 ■ Web: www.ksmq.org	Austin	MN	55912	507-433-0678	
KSTW-TV Ch 11 (CW) 1000 Dexter Ave N Ste 205 *TF:* 866-313-5789 ■ *Web:* cwseattle.cbslocal.com	Seattle	WA	98109	206-441-1111	861-8915
KTBN-TV Ch 40 (TBN) 2442 Michelle Dr *TF:* 888-731-1000 ■ Web: www.tbn.org	Tustin	CA	92780	714-832-2950	
KTNL-TV Ch 13 (CBS/I) 520 Lake St *Web:* www.cbssoutheastak.com	Sitka	AK	99835	907-747-5749	
KTSC-TV Ch 8 (PBS) 2200 Bonforte Blvd *Web:* www.rmpbs.org	Pueblo	CO	81001	719-543-8800	549-2208
KTSD-TV Ch 10 (PBS) 555 N Dakota St PO Box 5000 *Fax Area Code: 605 ■ *TF:* 800-333-0789 ■ *Web:* www.sdpb.org	Vermillion	SD	57069	800-333-0789	677-5010*
KTSF-TV Ch 26 (Ind) 100 Valley Dr *TF:* 800-772-1213 ■ *Web:* www.ktsf.com	Brisbane	CA	94005	415-468-2626	467-7559
KTVU-TV Ch 2 (Fox) 2 Jack London Sq *Web:* www.ktvu.com	Oakland	CA	94607	510-834-1212	272-9957
KUSD-TV Ch 2 (PBS) 555 N Dakota St PO Box 5000 *Fax Area Code: 605 ■ *TF:* 800-333-0789 ■ *Web:* www.sdpb.org	Vermillion	SD	57069	800-333-0789	677-5010*
KUSM-TV Ch 9 (PBS) Visual Communications Bldg Rm 183 *TF:* 800-426-8243 ■ *Web:* www.montanapbs.org	Bozeman	MT	59717	406-994-3437	994-6545
KVEA-TV Ch 52 (Tele) 3000 W Alameda Ave *Web:* www.telemundo52.com	Burbank	CA	91523	202-237-2280	
KVVU-TV Ch 5 (Fox) 25 TV 5 Dr *Web:* www.fox5vegas.com	Henderson	NV	89014	702-435-5555	451-4220
KWKB-TV Ch 20 (CW) 1547 Baker Ave *Web:* kwkb.com	West Branch	IA	52358	319-643-5952	
KWPX-TV Ch 33 (I) 8112-C 304th Ave SE PO Box 426 *TF:* 888-467-2988 ■ *Web:* www.ionmedianetworks.com	Preston	WA	98050	425-222-6010	222-6032
KWWL-TV Ch 7 (NBC) 500 E Fourth St *TF:* 800-947-7746 ■ *Web:* www.kwwl.com	Waterloo	IA	50703	319-291-1200	291-1255
KWYB-TV Ch 18 (ABC) 3825 Harrison Ave *Web:* www.abcfoxmontana.com	Butte	MT	59701	406-782-7185	723-9269
KXLF-TV Ch 4 (CBS) 1003 S Montana St *Web:* www.kxlf.com	Butte	MT	59701	406-496-8400	782-8906
Liberman Broadcasting, INC 1845 Empire Ave *Web:* www.lbimedia.com	Burbank	CA	91504	818-729-5300	
South Carolina ETV Commission 1041 George Rogers Blvd *Web:* www.scetv.org	Columbia	SC	29201	843-524-0808	
UNC-TV Ch 4 (PBS) 10 TW Alexander Dr PO Box 14900 *TF:* 800-906-5050 ■ *Web:* www.unctv.org	Research Triangle Park	NC	27709	919-549-7000	549-7201
WADL-TV Ch 38 (Fox) 35000 Adell Dr *Web:* www.wadldetroit.com	Clinton Township	MI	48035	586-790-3838	
WAND-TV Ch 17 (ABC) 904 S Side Dr *Web:* www.wandtv.com	Decatur	IL	62521	217-424-2500	424-2583
WAOE-TV Ch 59 (MNT) 2907 Springfield Rd *Web:* www.my59.tv	East Peoria	IL	61611	309-674-5900	674-5959
WAVY-TV Ch 10 (NBC) 300 Wavy St *Web:* www.wavy.com	Portsmouth	VA	23704	757-393-1010	
WBBZ-TV Ch 67 (Ind) 4545 Transit Rd Ste 750 *Web:* www.wbbz.tv	Williamsville	NY	14221	716-630-9229	630-9233
WBIN TV 11 A St *Web:* www.wbintv.com	Derry	NH	03038	603-845-1000	
WBND-TV Ch 57 (Ind) 53550 Generations Dr *Web:* www.abc57.com	South Bend	IN	46635	574-344-5500	344-5094
WBNX-TV Ch 55 (CW) 2690 State Rd *TF:* 800-282-0515 ■ *Web:* www.wbnx.com	Cuyahoga Falls	OH	44223	330-922-5500	929-2410
WBOC-TV Ch 16 (CBS) 1729 N Salisbury Blvd *Web:* www.wboc.com	Salisbury	MD	21801	410-749-1111	742-5190
WBRE-TV Ch 28 (NBC) 62 S Franklin St *TF:* 800-367-9222 ■ *Web:* www.pahomepage.com	Wilkes-Barre	PA	18701	570-823-2828	829-0440
WCAU-TV Ch 10 (NBC) 10 Monument Rd *TF:* 800-847-9228 ■ *Web:* www.nbcphiladelphia.com	Bala Cynwyd	PA	19004	610-668-5510	
WCAX-TV Ch 3 (CBS) 30 Joy Dr *Web:* www.wcax.com	South Burlington	VT	05403	802-658-6300	652-6399
WCBB-TV Ch 10 (PBS) 1450 Lisbon St *TF:* 800-884-1717 ■ *Web:* www.mpbn.net	Lewiston	ME	04240	207-783-9101	783-5193
WCBD-TV Ch 2 (NBC) 210 W Coleman Blvd *Web:* www.counton2.com	Mount Pleasant	SC	29464	843-884-2222	881-3410
WCBI-TV Ch 4 (CBS) 201 Fifth St S *Web:* www.wcbi.com	Columbus	MS	39701	662-327-4444	328-5222
WCIA-TV Ch 3 (CBS) PO Box 20 *TF:* 800-676-3382 ■ *Web:* www.illinoishomepage.net	Champaign	IL	61824	217-356-8333	402-9750
WCLF-TV Ch 22 (Ind) PO Box 6922 *Web:* www.ctnonline.com	Clearwater	FL	33758	727-535-5622	531-2497
WCTX-TV Ch 59 (MNT) 8 Elm St	New Haven	CT	06510	203-782-5900	
WCVB-TV Ch 5 (ABC) 5 TV Pl *Web:* www.wcvb.com	Needham	MA	02494	781-449-0400	433-4510
WCYB-TV Ch 5 (NBC) 101 Lee St *Web:* www.wcyb.com	Bristol	VA	24201	276-645-1555	
WDAM-TV Ch 7 (NBC) PO Box 16269 *TF:* 800-844-9326 ■ *Web:* www.wdam.com	Hattiesburg	MS	39404	601-544-4730	584-9302
WDSC-TV 1200 W International Speedway Blvd *TF:* 866-273-5825 ■ *Web:* www.daytonastate.edu/wdsc	Daytona Beach	FL	32114	386-506-4415	506-4427
WEAO-TV Ch 49 (PBS) 1750 Campus Ctr Dr *TF:* 800-544-4549 ■ *Web:* westernreservepublicmedia.org	Kent	OH	44240	330-677-4549	678-0688
WEAR-TV Ch 3 (ABC) 4990 Mobile Hwy *Fax Area Code: 410 ■ *TF:* 800-772-1213 ■ *Web:* www.weartv.com	Pensacola	FL	32506	850-456-3333	568-1691*
WECT-TV Ch 6 (NBC) 322 Shipyard Blvd *Web:* www.wect.com	Wilmington	NC	28412	910-791-8070	791-9535
WEEK-TV Ch 25 (NBC) 2907 Springfield Rd *Web:* www.cinewsnow.com	East Peoria	IL	61611	309-698-2525	698-9335
WEHT-TV Ch 25 (ABC) 800 Marywood Dr *TF:* 800-879-8542 ■ *Web:* www.tristatehomepage.com	Henderson	KY	42420	270-826-9566	
WELF-TV Ch 23 (TBN) 384 S Campus Rd *Web:* www.tbn.org	Lookout Mountain	GA	30750	706-820-1663	
WENH-TV Ch 11 (PBS) 268 Mast Rd *TF:* 800-639-8408 ■ *Web:* www.nhptv.org	Durham	NH	03824	603-868-1100	868-7552
WESH-TV Ch 2 (NBC) 1021 N Wymore Rd *Web:* www.wesh.com	Winter Park	FL	32789	407-645-2222	539-7948
WETA-TV Ch 26 (PBS) 2775 S Quincy St *Web:* www.weta.org	Arlington	VA	22206	703-998-2600	
WEYI-TV Ch 25 (NBC) 2225 W WillaRd Rd *Web:* nbc25news.com	Clio	MI	48420	810-687-1000	687-4925
WFFF-TV Ch 44 (Fox) 298 Mountain View Dr *TF:* 888-344-7233 ■ *Web:* www.mychamplainvalley.com	Colchester	VT	05446	802-660-9333	660-8673
WFMY-TV Ch 2 (CBS) 1615 Phillips Ave *TF:* 800-593-3692 ■ *Web:* wfmynews2.com	Greensboro	NC	27405	336-379-9369	273-9433
WFMZ-TV Ch 69 (Ind) 300 E Rock Rd *Web:* www.wfmz.com	Allentown	PA	18103	610-478-6500	791-9994
WFSB-TV Ch 3 (CBS) 333 Capital Blvd *Web:* www.wfsb.com	Rocky Hill	CT	06067	860-728-3333	728-0263
WFXT-TV Ch 25 (Fox) 25 Fox Dr *TF:* 877-369-2563 ■ *Web:* www.myfoxboston.com	Dedham	MA	02026	781-467-2525	
WGAL-TV Ch 8 (NBC) 1300 Columbia Ave *Web:* www.wgal.com	Lancaster	PA	17604	717-393-5851	295-7457
WGBH-TV Ch 2 (PBS) 1 Guest St *TF:* 800-492-1111 ■ *Web:* www.wgbh.org	Brighton	MA	02135	617-300-2000	300-1026
WGGS-TV Ch 16 (Ind) 3409 Rutherford Rd Ext *TF General:* 800-849-3683 ■ *Web:* www.wggs16.com	Taylors	SC	29687	864-244-1616	292-8481

Station	City	State	Zip	Phone	Fax
WGHP-TV Ch 8 (Fox) 2005 Francis St *TF:* 800-808-6397 ■ *Web:* myfox8.com	High Point	NC	27263	336-841-8888	
WGPX-TV Ch 16 (I) 1114 N Ohenry Blvd	Greensboro	NC	27405	336-272-9227	272-9298
WHKY-TV Ch 14 (Ind) PO Box 1059 *Web:* www.whky.com	Hickory	NC	28603	828-322-1290	322-8256
WHLT-TV Ch 22 (CBS) 5912 Hwy 49 Cloverleaf Mall Ste A *Web:* www.whlt.com	Hattiesburg	MS	39401	601-545-2077	545-3589
WHMB-TV Ch 40 (Ind) 10511 Greenfield Ave *Web:* whmb.lesea.com	Noblesville	IN	46060	317-773-5050	776-4051
WHOI-TV Ch 19 (ABC) 2907 Springfield Rd *Web:* www.cinewsnow.com	East Peoria	IL	61611	309-698-2525	
WICD-TV Ch 15 (ABC) 2680 E Cook St *Web:* www.newschannel20.com	Springfield	IL	62703	217-753-5620	
WILL-TV Ch 12 (PBS) 300 N Goodwin Ave *Web:* www.will.illinois.edu	Urbana	IL	61801	217-333-7300	333-7151
WITV-TV Ch 7 (PBS) 1101 Geroge Rogers Blvd *TF:* 800-277-3245 ■ *Web:* www.scetv.org	Columbia	SC	29201	803-737-3200	737-3476
WJAR-TV Ch 10 (NBC) 23 Kenney Dr *Web:* www.turnto10.com	Cranston	RI	02920	401-455-9100	455-9140
WJBK-TV Ch 2 (Fox) PO Box 2000 *Web:* www.fox2detroit.com	Southfield	MI	48037	248-557-2000	
WJLA-TV Ch 7 (ABC) 1100 Wilson Blvd *Web:* www.wjla.com	Arlington	VA	22209	703-236-9552	236-2331
WJYS-TV Ch 62 (Ind) 18600 Oak Pk Ave *Web:* www.wjys.tv	Tinley Park	IL	60477	708-633-0001	
WKAR-TV Ch 23 (PBS) MSU *Web:* wkar.org/tv	East Lansing	MI	48824	517-884-4700	
WKBD-TV Ch 50 (CW) 26905 W 11-Mile Rd *Web:* cwdetroit.cbslocal.com	Southfield	MI	48034	248-355-7000	355-7000
WKMJ-TV Ch 68 (PBS) 600 Cooper Dr *TF:* 800-432-0951 ■ *Web:* www.ket.org	Lexington	KY	40502	859-258-7000	258-7399
WKNO-TV Ch 10 (PBS) 7151 Cherry Farms Rd *TF:* 877-717-7822 ■ *Web:* www.wkno.org	Cordova	TN	38016	901-729-8765	729-8176
WKPC-TV Ch 15 (PBS) 600 Cooper Dr *TF:* 800-432-0951 ■ *Web:* www.ket.org	Lexington	KY	40502	859-258-7000	258-7399
WKPT-TV Ch 19 (ABC) 222 Commerce St *TF:* 855-646-1390 ■ *Web:* www.abc19.tv	Kingsport	TN	37660	423-246-9578	
WLAE-TV Ch 32 (PBS) 3330 N Cswy Blvd Ste 345 *Web:* www.wlae.com	Metairie	LA	70002	504-866-7411	840-9838
WLGA-TV Ch 66 (CW) 1501 13th Ave *Web:* www.wlgatv.com	Columbus	GA	31901	706-257-6703	
WLIW-TV Ch 21 (PBS) 825 Eighth Ave *Web:* www.wliw.org	New York	NY	10019	212-560-8021	
WLNY-TV Ch 55 (Ind) 270 S Service Rd Ste 55 *Web:* newyork.cbslocal.com	Melville	NY	11747	631-777-8855	
WLOX-TV Ch 13 (ABC) 208 Debuys Rd *Web:* www.wlox.com	Biloxi	MS	39531	228-896-1313	
WMDT-TV Ch 47 (ABC) 202 Downtown Plz *Web:* www.wmdt.com	Salisbury	MD	21801	410-742-4747	742-5767
WMGM NBC40.Net 1601 New Rd	Linwood	NJ	08221	609-927-4440	927-7014
WMHT-TV Ch 17 (PBS) 4 Global View *Web:* www.wmht.org	Troy	NY	12180	518-880-3400	880-3409
WMTW-TV Ch 8 (ABC) 99 Danville Corner Rd *TF:* 800-248-6397 ■ *Web:* www.wmtw.com	Auburn	ME	04210	207-782-1800	783-7371
WMUR-TV Ch 9 (ABC) 100 S Commercial St *Web:* www.wmur.com	Manchester	NH	03101	603-669-9999	641-9005
WMYD-TV Ch 20 (MNT) 2777 Franklin Rd Ste 1220 *TF:* 800-825-0770 ■ *Web:* wxyz.com/tv20detroit	Southfield	MI	48034	248-355-2020	
WNEM-TV Ch 5 (CBS) 107 N Franklin St *TF:* 800-522-9636 ■ *Web:* www.wnem.com	Saginaw	MI	48607	989-755-8191	
WNEP-TV Ch 16 (ABC) 16 Montage Mtn Rd *Fax: News Rm ■ *TF:* 800-982-4374 ■ *Web:* www.wnep.com	Moosic	PA	18507	570-346-7474	341-1344*
WNET PO Box 5776 *TF:* 800-882-6622 ■ *Web:* www.njtvonline.org	Englewood	NJ	07631	609-777-0031	
WNJU-TV Ch 47 (Tele) 2200 Fletcher Ave 6th Fl *TF:* 877-478-3536 ■ *Web:* www.telemundo47.com	Fort Lee	NJ	07024	877-478-3536	
WNOL-TV Ch 38 (CW) 1 Galeria Blvd Ste 850 *Web:* wgno.com	Metairie	LA	70001	504-525-3838	
WOFL-TV Ch 35 (Fox) 35 Skyline Dr *Web:* www.fox35orlando.com	Lake Mary	FL	32746	407-644-3535	741-5189
WOI-TV Ch 5 (ABC) 3903 Westown Pkwy *Fax: Sales ■ *TF:* 800-858-5555 ■ *Web:* weareiowa.com/home	West Des Moines	IA	50266	515-457-9645	457-1034*
WOUC-TV Ch 44 (PBS) 35 S College St *TF:* 800-456-2044 ■ *Web:* www.woub.org	Athens	OH	45701	740-593-1771	593-0240
WOWK-TV Ch 13 (CBS) 555 Fifth Ave *TF:* 800-333-7636 ■ *Web:* www.tristateupdate.com	Huntington	WV	25701	304-525-1313	523-0545
WPBF-TV Ch 25 (ABC) 3970 RCA Blvd Ste 7007 *Web:* www.wpbf.com	Palm Beach Gardens	FL	33410	561-694-2525	624-1089
WPLG-TV Ch 10 (ABC) 3401 W Hallandale Beach Blvd *Fax Area Code: 305 ■ *Fax: News Rm ■ *Web:* www.local10.com	Pembroke Park	FL	33023	954-364-2500	375-2480*
WPMT-TV Ch 43 (Fox) 2005 S Queen St *TF:* 866-976-8747 ■ *Web:* www.fox43.com	York	PA	17403	717-843-0043	814-5530
WPNE-TV Ch 38 (PBS) 821 University Ave *Web:* www.wpt.org	Madison	WI	53706	608-263-2121	
Wpri TV 25 Catamore Blvd	East Providence	RI	02914	401-438-7200	228-1774
WPTZ-TV Ch 5 (NBC) 5 Television Dr *Web:* www.wptz.com	Plattsburgh	NY	12901	518-561-5555	
WPXD-TV Ch 31 (I) 3975 Varsity Dr *TF:* 888-467-2988 ■ *Web:* www.ionmedianetworks.com	Ann Arbor	MI	48108	734-973-7900	973-7906
WPXL-TV Ch 49 (I) 3900 Veterans Blvd Ste 202	Metairie	LA	70002	504-887-9795	887-1518
WPXT-TV Ch 12 (CW) 4 Ledgeview Dr *Web:* ourmaine.com	Westbrook	ME	04092	207-774-0051	774-6849
WPXW-TV Ch 66 (I) 6199 Old Arrington Ln	Fairfax Station	VA	22039	703-503-7966	503-1225
WQCW-TV Ch 30 (CW) 800 Gallia St	Portsmouth	OH	45662	740-353-3391	
WRBW-TV Ch 65 (MNT) 35 Skyline Dr *Web:* www.fox35orlando.com/my65	Lake Mary	FL	32746	407-644-3535	741-5189
WRGB-TV Ch 6 (CBS) 1400 Balltown Rd *Web:* www.cbs6albany.com	Schenectady	NY	12309	518-346-6666	
WSAZ-TV Ch 3 (NBC) PO Box 2115 *Web:* www.wsaz.com	Huntington	WV	25721	304-697-4780	690-3066
WSBT-TV Ch 22 (CBS) 1301 E Douglas Rd *TF:* 877-634-7181 ■ *Web:* www.wsbt.com	Mishawaka	IN	46545	574-232-6397	289-0622
WSCV-TV Ch 51 (NBC) 15000 SW 27th St *Web:* www.telemundo51.com	Miramar	FL	33027	954-622-7710	
WSET-TV Ch 13 (ABC) 2320 Langhorne Rd *TF:* 800-639-7847 ■ *Web:* www.wset.com	Lynchburg	VA	24501	434-528-1313	847-0458
WSKY-TV Ch 4 (Ind) 218 Salters Creek Rd *Web:* www.sky4tv.com	Hampton	VA	23661	757-382-0004	382-0365
WSRE-TV Ch 23 (PBS) 1000 College Blvd *Web:* www.wsre.org	Pensacola	FL	32504	850-484-1200	484-1255
WSYR-TV Ch 9 (ABC) 5904 Bridge St *Web:* www.localsyr.com	East Syracuse	NY	13057	315-446-9999	251-1567
WTAT-TV Ch 24 (Fox) 4301 Arco Ln *Web:* www.foxcharleston.com	North Charleston	SC	29418	843-744-2424	554-9649
WTGL-TV Ch 45 (Ind) 31 Skyline Dr *Web:* www.tv45.org	Lake Mary	FL	32746	407-215-6745	215-6789
WTIU-TV Ch 30 (PBS) 1229 E Seventh St *TF:* 800-662-3311 ■ *Web:* www.wtiu.indiana.edu	Bloomington	IN	47405	812-855-5900	855-0729
WTJP-TV Ch 60 (TBN) 313 Rosedale Ave *Web:* www.tbn.org	Gadsden	AL	35901	256-546-8860	
WTLH-TV Ch 49 (Fox) 950 Commerce Blvd *Web:* fox49.tv	Midway	FL	32343	850-576-4990	576-0200
WTLJ-TV Ch 54 (Ind) 10290 48th Ave	Allendale	MI	49401	616-895-4154	
WTNH-TV Ch 8 (ABC) 8 Elm St *Fax: Mktg ■ *Web:* www.wtnh.com	New Haven	CT	06510	203-784-8888	789-2010*
WTVA-TV Ch 9 (NBC) 1359 Beech Springs Rd *Web:* www.wtva.com	Saltillo	MS	38866	662-842-7620	
WTVJ-TV Ch 6 (NBC) 15000 SW 27th St *Web:* www.nbcmiami.com	Miramar	FL	33027	954-622-6000	
WTXL-TV Ch 27 (ABC) 1620 Commerce Blvd *Web:* www.wtxl.com	Midway	FL	32343	850-893-3127	
WUGA-TV Ch 32 (PBS) 120 Hooper St *Web:* www.uga.edu	Athens	GA	30602	706-542-3000	
WUNI-TV Ch 27 (Uni) 33 Fourth Ave *Web:* noticias.entravision.com/nueva-inglaterra	Needham	MA	02494	781-433-2727	433-2750
WUNL-TV Ch 26 (PBS) 10 TW Alexander Dr PO Box 14900 *Web:* www.unctv.org	Research Triangle Park	NC	27709	919-549-7000	
WVIT-TV Ch 30 (NBC) 1422 New Britain Ave *TF:* 800-523-9848 ■ *Web:* www.nbcconnecticut.com	West Hartford	CT	06110	860-521-3030	
WVNY-TV Ch 22 (ABC) 298 Mountain View Dr *Web:* www.mychamplainvalley.com	Colchester	VT	05446	802-660-9333	660-8673
WWJ-TV Ch 62 (CBS) 26905 W 11-Mile Rd *Web:* detroit.cbslocal.com	Southfield	MI	48034	248-355-7000	
WWMT-TV Ch 3 (CBS) 590 W Maple St *Fax Area Code: 269 ■ *TF:* 800-875-3333 ■ *Web:* www.wwmt.com	Kalamazoo	MI	49008	800-875-3333	388-8322*
WWOR-TV Ch 9 (MNT) 9 Broadcast Plaza *Web:* www.my9nj.com	Secaucus	NJ	07096	201-330-2148	
WXXV-TV Ch 25 (Fox) 14351 Hwy 49 N *Web:* www.wxxv25.com	Gulfport	MS	39503	228-832-2525	832-4442
WXYZ-TV Ch 7 (ABC) 20777 W 10-Mile Rd *TF:* 800-825-0770 ■ *Web:* www.wxyz.com	Southfield	MI	48037	248-827-7777	827-9444
WYES-TV Ch 12 (PBS) 111 Veterans Blvd Ste 250 *Web:* www.wyes.org	Metairie	LA	70005	504-486-5511	840-9954
WYOU-TV Ch 22 (CBS) 62 S Franklin St *TF:* 855-241-5144 ■ *Web:* www.pahomepage.com	Wilkes-Barre	PA	18701	570-961-2222	829-0440
WYPX-TV Ch 55 (I) 1 Charles Blvd *Web:* www.ionmedianetworks.com	Guilderland	NY	12084	518-464-0143	464-0633
WYZZ-TV Ch 43 (Fox) 2714 E Lincoln St *Web:* www.centralillinoisproud.com	Bloomington	IL	61701	309-661-4343	

741-1 Abilene, TX

Station	City	State	Zip	Phone	Fax
KRBC-TV Ch 9 (NBC) 4510 S 14th St *Web:* www.bigcountryhomepage.com	Abilene	TX	79605	325-692-4242	692-8265
KTAB-TV Ch 32 (CBS) 4510 S 14th St *Web:* www.bigcountryhomepage.com	Abilene	TX	79605	325-695-2777	695-9922
KTXS-TV Ch 12 (ABC) 4420 N Clack St *Fax: News Rm ■ *Web:* www.ktxs.com	Abilene	TX	79601	325-677-2281	672-5307*

741-2 Albany, NY

Station	City	State	Zip	Phone	Fax
WNYT-TV Ch 13 (NBC) 715 N Pearl St *TF:* 800-999-9698 ■ *Web:* www.wnyt.com	Albany	NY	12204	518-436-4791	434-0659
WTEN-TV Ch 10 (ABC) 341 Northern Blvd *Fax: News Rm ■ *Web:* www.news10.com	Albany	NY	12204	518-436-4822	426-4792*

741-3 Albuquerque/Santa Fe, NM

Station	City	State	Zip	Phone	Fax
KASY-TV Ch 50 (MNT) 8341 Washington St NE	Albuquerque	NM	87113	505-247-1743	
KNAT-TV Ch 23 (TBN) 1510 Coors Blvd NW *Web:* www.tbn.org	Albuquerque	NM	87121	505-836-6585	
KNME-TV Ch 5 (PBS) 1130 University Blvd NE University of New Mexico *TF:* 800-328-5663 ■ *Web:* www.newmexicopbs.org	Albuquerque	NM	87102	505-277-2121	

Station	City	State	Zip	Phone	Fax
KOAT-TV Ch 7 (ABC) 3801 Carlisle Blvd NE *TF:* 877-871-0165 ■ *Web:* www.koat.com	Albuquerque	NM	87107	505-884-7777	
KOB-TV Ch 4 (NBC) 4 Broadcast Plz SW *Web:* www.kob.com	Albuquerque	NM	87104	505-243-4411	764-2522
KRQE-TV Ch 13 (CBS) 13 Broadcast Plz SW *TF:* 800-283-4227 ■ *Web:* www.krqe.com	Albuquerque	NM	87104	505-243-2285	

741-4 Amarillo, TX

Station	City	State	Zip	Phone	Fax
KACV-TV Ch 2 (PBS) PO Box 447 *Web:* www.kacvtv.org	Amarillo	TX	79178	806-371-5222	371-5258
KAMR-TV Ch 4 (NBC) 1015 S Fillmore St *Web:* myhighplains.com	Amarillo	TX	79101	806-383-3321	220-0941
KCIT-TV Ch 14 (Fox) 1015 S Fillmore St *Web:* www.myhighplains.com	Amarillo	TX	79101	806-383-3321	322-0123
KFDA-TV Ch 10 (CBS) 7900 Broadway *Web:* www.newschannel10.com	Amarillo	TX	79105	806-383-1010	

741-5 Anchorage, AK

Station	City	State	Zip	Phone	Fax
KAKM-TV Ch 7 (PBS) 3877 University Dr *Web:* www.alaskapublic.org	Anchorage	AK	99508	907-550-8400	550-8401
KTBY-TV Ch 4 (Fox) 2700 E Tudor Rd *TF:* 877-304-1313 ■ *Web:* www.youralaskalink.com	Anchorage	AK	99507	907-561-1313	561-1377
KTUU-TV Ch 2 (NBC) 701 E Tudor Rd Ste 220 *Web:* www.ktuu.com	Anchorage	AK	99503	907-762-9202	563-3318
KTVA-TV Ch 11 (CBS) 1001 Northway Dr St 202 *Web:* www.ktva.com	Anchorage	AK	99508	907-274-1111	334-9427
KYUR-TV Ch 13 (ABC) 2700 E Tudor Rd *TF:* 877-304-1313 ■ *Web:* www.youralaskalink.com	Anchorage	AK	99507	907-561-1313	561-8934

741-6 Asheville, NC/Greenville, SC/Spartanburg, SC

Station	City	State	Zip	Phone	Fax
WLOS-TV Ch 13 (ABC) 110 Technology Dr **Fax Area Code:* 410 ■ *TF:* 800-419-6356 ■ *Web:* www.wlos.com	Asheville	NC	28803	828-684-1340	568-1691*
WMYA-TV Ch 40 (MNT) 33 Villa Rd *Web:* www.my40.tv	Greenville	SC	29615	828-684-1340	
WRET-TV Ch 49 (PBS) PO Box 4069 *Web:* www.scetv.org	Spartanburg	SC	29305	864-503-9371	
WSPA-TV Ch 7 (CBS) 250 International Dr *TF:* 866-946-6349 ■ *Web:* www.wspa.com	Spartanburg	SC	29303	864-576-7777	
WYFF-TV Ch 4 (NBC) 505 Rutherford St *TF:* 800-453-9933 ■ *Web:* www.wyff4.com	Greenville	SC	29609	864-242-4404	240-5305

741-7 Atlanta, GA

Station	City	State	Zip	Phone	Fax
WAGA-TV Ch 5 (Fox) 1551 Briarcliff Rd NE **Fax:* News Rm ■ *Web:* www.fox5atlanta.com	Atlanta	GA	30306	404-898-0100	898-0169*
WATL-TV Ch 36 (MNT) 1 Monroe Pl *Web:* 11alive.com	Atlanta	GA	30324	404-892-1611	885-7639
WGCL-TV Ch 46 (CBS) 425 14th St NW *Web:* cbs46.com	Atlanta	GA	30318	404-327-3194	327-3004
WPBA-TV Ch 30 (PBS) 740 Bismark Rd NE *Web:* www.pba.org	Atlanta	GA	30324	678-686-0321	686-0356
WSB-TV Ch 2 (ABC) 1601 W Peachtree St NE *Web:* www.wsbtv.com	Atlanta	GA	30309	404-897-7000	897-7370
WUPA-TV Ch 69 (CW) 2700 NE Expy Bldg A *Web:* cwatlanta.cbslocal.com	Atlanta	GA	30345	404-325-6929	633-4567
WXIA-TV Ch 11 (NBC) 1 Monroe Pl **Fax:* News Rm ■ *Web:* www.11alive.com	Atlanta	GA	30324	404-892-1611	881-0675*

741-8 Augusta, GA

Station	City	State	Zip	Phone	Fax
WAGT-TV Ch 26 (NBC) 1336 Augusta W Pkwy *Web:* www.nbc26.tv	Augusta	GA	30909	706-826-0026	
WFXG-TV Ch 54 (Fox) 3933 Washington Rd *Web:* www.wfxg.com	Augusta	GA	30907	706-650-5400	650-8411
WRDW-TV Ch 12 (CBS) PO Box 1212 *TF:* 866-591-2502 ■ *Web:* www.wrdw.com	Augusta	GA	30903	803-278-1212	279-8316

741-9 Austin, TX

Station	City	State	Zip	Phone	Fax
FOX 7 Austin 119 E Tenth St *Web:* www.fox7austin.com	Austin	TX	78701	512-476-7777	495-7060
KEYE-TV Ch 42 (CBS) 10700 Metric Blvd *TF:* 800-621-3362 ■ *Web:* www.keyetv.com	Austin	TX	78758	512-835-0042	490-2111
KLRU-TV Ch 18 (PBS) 2504-B Whitis Ave *Web:* www.klru.org	Austin	TX	78712	512-471-4811	475-9090
KNVA-TV Ch 54 (CW) 908 W ML King Jr Blvd *Web:* www.thecwaustin.com	Austin	TX	78701	512-478-5400	476-1520
KVUE-TV Ch 24 (ABC) 3201 Steck Ave **Fax:* News Rm ■ *Web:* www.kvue.com	Austin	TX	78757	512-459-6521	533-2233*
KXAN News 908 W Martin Luther King Jr Bl *Web:* www.kxan.com	Austin	TX	78701	512-476-3636	

741-10 Bakersfield, CA

Station	City	State	Zip	Phone	Fax
KERO-TV Ch 23 (ABC) 321 21st St **Fax:* News Rm ■ *Web:* www.turnto23.com	Bakersfield	CA	93301	661-637-2323	323-5538*
KGET-TV Ch 17 (NBC) 2120 L St *Web:* www.kerngoldenempire.com	Bakersfield	CA	93301	661-283-1700	
KUVI-TV Ch 45 (MNT) 5801 Truxtun Ave	Bakersfield	CA	93309	661-324-0045	

741-11 Baltimore, MD

Station	City	State	Zip	Phone	Fax
WBAL-TV Ch 11 (NBC) 3800 Hooper Ave *TF:* 800-622-4121 ■ *Web:* www.wbaltv.com	Baltimore	MD	21211	410-467-3000	
WBFF-TV Ch 45 (Fox) 2000 W 41st St *Web:* www.foxbaltimore.com	Baltimore	MD	21211	410-467-4545	467-5090
WJZ-TV Ch 13 (CBS) 3725 Malden Ave *Web:* baltimore.cbslocal.com	Baltimore	MD	21211	410-466-0013	578-7502

741-12 Bangor, ME

Station	City	State	Zip	Phone	Fax
WABI-TV Ch 5 (CBS) 35 Hildreth St *Web:* wabi.tv	Bangor	ME	04401	207-947-8321	941-9378
WLBZ-TV Ch 2 (NBC) 329 Mt Hope Ave *TF:* 800-244-6306 ■ *Web:* www.wlbz2.com	Bangor	ME	04401	207-942-4821	
WMEB-TV Ch 12 (PBS) 63 Texas Ave *TF:* 800-884-1717 ■ *Web:* www.mpbn.net	Bangor	ME	04401	207-941-1010	942-2857
WVII-TV Ch 7 (ABC) 371 Target Industrial Cir *TF General:* 888-820-8458 ■ *Web:* www.foxbangor.com	Bangor	ME	04401	207-945-6457	

741-13 Baton Rouge, LA

Station	City	State	Zip	Phone	Fax
BRProud 10000 Perkins Rd *Web:* www.brproud.com	Baton Rouge	LA	70810	225-766-3233	768-9293
KLPB-TV Ch 24 (PBS) 7733 Perkins Rd *TF:* 800-272-8161 ■ *Web:* www.lpb.org	Baton Rouge	LA	70810	225-767-5660	
KLTS-TV Ch 24 (PBS) 7733 Perkins Rd *Web:* www.lpb.org	Baton Rouge	LA	70810	225-767-5660	767-4299
NBC 33 TV 10000 Perkins Rd *Web:* www.brproud.com	Baton Rouge	LA	70810	225-766-3233	768-9293
WAFB-TV Ch 9 (CBS) 844 Government St *TF:* 888-677-2900 ■ *Web:* www.wafb.com	Baton Rouge	LA	70802	225-215-4700	
WBRZ-TV Ch 2 (ABC) 1650 Highland Rd *Web:* theadvocate.com	Baton Rouge	LA	70802	225-387-2222	
WLPB-TV Ch 27 (PBS) 7733 Perkins Rd *TF:* 800-272-8161 ■ *Web:* www.lpb.org	Baton Rouge	LA	70810	225-767-5660	

741-14 Billings, MT

Station	City	State	Zip	Phone	Fax
KSVI-TV Ch 6 (ABC) 445 S 24th St W *Web:* www.yourbigsky.com	Billings	MT	59102	406-652-4743	652-6963
KTVQ-TV Ch 2 (CBS) 3203 Third Ave N *TF:* 800-908-4490 ■ *Web:* www.ktvq.com	Billings	MT	59101	406-252-5611	252-9938
KULR-TV Ch 8 (NBC) 2045 Overland Ave *Web:* www.kulr8.com	Billings	MT	59102	406-656-8000	652-8207

741-15 Birmingham, AL

Station	City	State	Zip	Phone	Fax
WABM-TV Ch 68 (MNT) 800 Concourse Pkwy Ste 200 *Web:* www.wabm68.com	Birmingham	AL	35244	205-403-3340	
WBIQ-TV Ch 10 (PBS) 2112 11th Ave S Ste 400 *TF:* 800-239-5233 ■ *Web:* www.aptv.org	Birmingham	AL	35205	205-328-8756	251-2192
WBRC-TV Ch 6 (Fox) 1720 Vly View Dr *Web:* www.wbrc.com	Birmingham	AL	35209	205-322-6666	583-4356
WCFT-TV Ch 33 (ABC) 800 Concourse Pkwy Ste 200 *TF:* 800-784-8669 ■ *Web:* www.abc3340.com	Birmingham	AL	35244	205-403-3340	
WEIQ-TV Ch 42 (PBS) 2112 11th Ave S Ste 400 *TF:* 800-239-5233 ■ *Web:* www.aptv.org	Birmingham	AL	35205	205-328-8756	251-2192
WHIQ-TV Ch 24 (PBS) 2112 11th Ave S Ste 400 *TF:* 800-239-5233 ■ *Web:* www.aptv.org	Birmingham	AL	35205	205-328-8756	251-2192
WTTO-TV Ch 21 (CW) 651 Beacon Pkwy W Ste 105 *Web:* www.wtto21.com/birmingham_al	Birmingham	AL	35209	205-943-2168	290-2114
WVTM-TV Ch 13 (NBC) 1732 Valley View Dr *TF:* 844-248-7698 ■ *Web:* www.wvtm13.com	Birmingham	AL	35209	205-933-1313	558-7389

741-16 Bismarck, ND

Station	City	State	Zip	Phone	Fax
KBMY-TV Ch 17 (ABC) 1811 N 15th St *Web:* wday.com	Bismarck	ND	58501	701-223-1700	

Phone | Fax

KFYR-TV Ch 5 (NBC) 200 N Fourth St .... Bismarck ND 58501 701-255-5757 255-8220
Web: www.kfyrtv.com

KNDX-TV Ch 26 (Fox) 3130 E Broadway Ave .... Bismarck ND 58501 701-355-0026

KXMB-TV Ch 12 (CBS) 1811 N 15th St .... Bismarck ND 58501 701-223-9197
Web: www.kxnet.com

741-17 Boise, ID

Phone | Fax

KTVB-TV Ch 7 (NBC) 5407 Fairview .... Boise ID 83706 208-375-7277 223-4650*
**Fax Area Code:* 313 ■ *TF:* 800-537-8939 ■ *Web:* www.ktvb.com

741-18 Boston, MA

Phone | Fax

WHDH-TV Ch 7 (NBC) 7 Bulfinch Pl .... Boston MA 02114 617-725-0777
Web: whdh.com

741-19 Brownsville, TX

Phone | Fax

KVEO-TV Ch 23 (NBC) 394 N Expy .... Brownsville TX 78521 956-544-2323 544-4636
Web: www.rgvproud.com

741-20 Buffalo, NY

Phone | Fax

WGRZ-TV Ch 2 (NBC) 259 Delaware Ave .... Buffalo NY 14202 716-849-2200 849-7602
Web: www.wgrz.com

WIVB-TV Ch 4 (CBS) 2077 Elmwood Ave .... Buffalo NY 14207 716-874-4410 874-8173*
**Fax:* News Rm ■ *TF:* 800-794-3687 ■ *Web:* www.wivb.com

WKBW-TV Ch 7 (ABC) 7 Broadcast Plaza .... Buffalo NY 14202 716-845-6100 840-7820*
**Fax:* News Rm ■ *TF:* 888-373-7888 ■ *Web:* www.wkbw.com

WNED-TV Ch 17 (PBS) Horizons Plz PO Box 1263 .... Buffalo NY 14240 716-845-7000 845-7036
Web: www.wned.org

WNYO-TV Ch 49 (MNT) 699 Hertel Ave Ste 100 .... Buffalo NY 14207 716-447-3200 875-4919
Web: www.mytvbuffalo.com

WUTV-TV Ch 29 (Fox) 699 Hertel Ave Ste 100 .... Buffalo NY 14207 716-447-3200 875-4919
Web: www.wutv29.com

741-21 Calgary, AB

Phone | Fax

CBC 1724 Westmount Blvd NW .... Calgary AB T2N3G7 403-521-6000 521-6079
Web: www.cbc.ca

CFCN-TV Ch 3 (CTV) 80 Patina Rise SW .... Calgary AB T3H2W4 403-240-5600 240-5689
Web: calgary.ctvnews.ca

741-22 Casper, WY

Phone | Fax

KGWC-TV Ch 14 (CBS) 1856 Skyview Dr .... Casper WY 82601 307-234-1111 234-4005

KTWO-TV Ch 2 (ABC) 1896 Skyview Dr .... Casper WY 82601 307-237-3711 234-9866
Web: www.k2tv.com

Wyo Media Inc 1856 Skyview Dr .... Casper WY 82601 307-577-5923 577-5928

741-23 Cedar Rapids, IA

Phone | Fax

KCRG-TV Ch 9 (ABC) 501 Second Ave SE .... Cedar Rapids IA 52401 319-398-8393
TF: 800-332-5443 ■ *Web:* www.kcrg.com

KFXA-TV Ch 28 (Fox)
600 Old Marion Rd NE .... Cedar Rapids IA 52402 800-462-8782 395-7028*
**Fax Area Code:* 319 ■ *TF:* 800-222-5426 ■ *Web:* cbs2iowa.com

KGAN-TV Ch 2 (CBS) 600 Old Marion Rd NE .... Cedar Rapids IA 52402 319-395-9060 395-0987
TF: 800-642-6140 ■ *Web:* www.cbs2iowa.com

KPXR-TV Ch 48 (I)
1957 Blairs Ferry Rd NE .... Cedar Rapids IA 52402 319-378-1260
Web: www.iontelevision.com

741-24 Charleston, SC

Phone | Fax

WCIV-TV Ch 4 (ABC) PO Box 22165 .... Charleston SC 29413 843-881-4444 849-2519*
**Fax:* News Rm ■ *Web:* www.abcnews4.com

WCSC-TV Ch 5 (CBS) 2126 Charlie Hall Blvd .... Charleston SC 29414 843-577-6397
Web: www.live5news.com

741-25 Charleston, WV

Phone | Fax

WCHS-TV Ch 8 (ABC) 1301 Piedmont Rd .... Charleston WV 25301 304-346-5358 346-4765
TF: 888-696-9247 ■ *Web:* www.wchstv.com

WVAH-TV Ch 11 (Fox) 1301 Piedmont Rd .... Charleston WV 25301 304-346-5358 346-4765
Web: www.wvah.com

741-26 Charlotte, NC

Phone | Fax

WAXN-TV Ch 64 (ABC) 1901 N Tryon St .... Charlotte NC 28206 704-335-4786
TF: 855-336-0360 ■ *Web:* www.wsoctv.com

WBTV-TV Ch 3 (CBS) 1 Julian Price Pl .... Charlotte NC 28208 704-374-3500
Web: www.wbtv.com

WCCB-TV Ch 18 (Fox) 1 Television Pl .... Charlotte NC 28205 704-372-1800
Web: wccbcharlotte.com

WCNC-TV Ch 36 (NBC) 1001 Wood Ridge Ctr Dr .... Charlotte NC 28217 704-329-3636
Web: www.wcnc.com

WMYT-TV Ch 12 (MNT) 3501 Performance Rd .... Charlotte NC 28214 704-398-0046 393-8407
Web: www.fox46charlotte.com/about/wmyt

WSOC-TV Ch 9 (ABC) 1901 N Tryon St .... Charlotte NC 28206 704-338-9999 335-4736
TF: 855-336-0360 ■ *Web:* www.wsoctv.com

WTVI-TV Ch 42 (PBS) 3242 Commonwealth Ave .... Charlotte NC 28205 704-372-2442 335-1358
Web: www.wtvi.org

741-27 Chattanooga, TN

Phone | Fax

WDEF-TV Ch 12 (CBS) 3300 Broad St .... Chattanooga TN 37408 423-785-1200 785-1271
Web: www.wdef.com

WRCB-TV Ch 3 (NBC) 900 Whitehall Rd .... Chattanooga TN 37405 423-267-5412
Web: www.wrcbtv.com

WTCI-TV Ch 45 (PBS) 7540 Bonnie Shire Dr .... Chattanooga TN 37416 423-702-7800 702-7823
Web: www.wtcitv.org

WTVC-TV Ch 9 (ABC) 4279 Benton Dr .... Chattanooga TN 37406 423-756-5500 757-7400
Web: www.newschannel9.com

741-28 Cheyenne, WY

Phone | Fax

KGWN-TV Ch 5 (CBS) 2923 E Lincolnway .... Cheyenne WY 82001 307-634-7755
Web: www.kgwn.tv

741-29 Chicago, IL

Phone | Fax

WCIU-TV Ch 26 (Ind) 26 N Halsted St .... Chicago IL 60661 312-705-2600
Web: www.wciu.com

WCPX-TV Ch 38 (I) 333 S Desplaines St Ste 101 .... Chicago IL 60661 312-376-8520 575-8735
Web: www.ionmedianetworks.com

WFLD-TV Ch 32 (Fox) 205 N Michigan Ave .... Chicago IL 60601 312-565-5532 819-1332
Web: www.fox32chicago.com

WGN-TV Ch 9 (CW) 2501 W Bradley Pl .... Chicago IL 60618 773-528-2311
Web: www.wgntv.com

WMAQ-TV Ch 5 (NBC) 454 N Columbus Dr NBC Twr .... Chicago IL 60611 312-836-5555 527-5925
Web: www.nbcchicago.com

WPWR-TV Ch 50 (Fox) 205 N Michigan Ave .... Chicago IL 60601 312-565-5532 819-1332
Web: www.fox32chicago.com/my50chicago

WTTW-TV Ch 11 (PBS) 5400 N St Louis Ave .... Chicago IL 60625 773-583-5000 583-3046
Web: www.wttw.com

WYCC-TV Ch 20 (PBS) 6258 S Union Ave .... Chicago IL 60621 773-224-3300 783-2906
Web: www.wycc.org

741-30 Cincinnati, OH

Phone | Fax

WCET-TV Ch 48 (PBS) 1223 Central Pkwy .... Cincinnati OH 45214 513-381-4033 381-7520
Web: www.cetconnect.org

WCPO-TV Ch 9 (ABC) 1720 Gilbert Ave .... Cincinnati OH 45202 513-721-9900 721-7717
Web: www.wcpo.com

WKRC-TV Ch 12 (CBS) 1906 Highland Ave .... Cincinnati OH 45219 513-763-5500 421-3820
TF: 877-889-5610 ■ *Web:* www.local12.com

WLWT-TV Ch 5 (NBC) 1700 Young St .... Cincinnati OH 45202 513-412-5000
Web: www.wlwt.com

WSTR-TV Ch 64 (MNT) 5177 Fishwick Dr .... Cincinnati OH 45216 513-641-4400 242-2633
Web: www.star64.tv

WXIX-TV Ch 19 (Fox)
635 W Seventh St 19 Broadcast Plz .... Cincinnati OH 45203 513-421-1919 421-3022
Web: fox19.com

741-31 Cleveland/Akron, OH

Phone | Fax

Ideastream 1375 Euclid Ave .... Cleveland OH 44115 216-916-6100
Web: wviz.ideastream.org

WDLI-TV Ch 17 (TBN) PO Box A .... Santa Ana CA 92711 714-832-2950
TF: 888-731-1000 ■ *Web:* www.tbn.org

WEWS-TV Ch 5 (ABC) 3001 Euclid Ave .... Cleveland OH 44115 216-431-5555 431-3666
Web: www.newsnet5.com

WJW-TV Ch 8 (Fox) 5800 S Marginal Rd .... Cleveland OH 44103 216-431-8888 391-9559
Web: fox8.com

WKYC-TV Ch 3 (NBC) 1333 Lakeside Ave E .... Cleveland OH 44114 216-344-3333 344-3314
TF: 877-790-7370 ■ *Web:* www.wkyc.com

741-32 Colorado Springs, CO

Phone | Fax

KKTV-TV Ch 11 (CBS)
3100 N Nevada Ave .... Colorado Springs CO 80907 719-634-2844 634-3741
Web: www.kktv.com

Station	City	State	ZIP	Phone	Fax
KXRM-TV Ch 21 (Fox) 560 Wooten Rd *Web:* www.fox21news.com	Colorado Springs	CO	80915	719-596-2100	591-4180

741-33 Columbia, SC

Station	City	State	ZIP	Phone	Fax
ABC Columbia 5807 Shakespeare Rd *Web:* abccolumbia.com	Columbia	SC	29223	803-754-7525	
WACH-TV Ch 57 (Fox) 1400 Pickens St Ste 6 *Web:* www.wach.com	Columbia	SC	29201	803-252-5757	212-7270
WHMC-TV Ch 23 (PBS) 1101 George Rogers Blvd *Web:* www.scetv.org	Columbia	SC	29201	803-737-3200	
WIS-TV Ch 10 (NBC) 1111 Bull St *Web:* www.wistv.com	Columbia	SC	29201	803-799-1010	758-1155
WLTX-TV Ch 19 (CBS) 6027 Garner's Ferry Rd *Web:* www.wltx.com	Columbia	SC	29209	803-776-3600	695-3714
WRLK-TV Ch 35 (PBS) 1101 George Rogers Blvd *TF:* 800-922-5437 ■ *Web:* www.scetv.org	Columbia	SC	29201	803-737-3200	

741-34 Columbus, GA

Station	City	State	ZIP	Phone	Fax
WLTZ-TV Ch 38 (NBC) 6140 Buena Vista Rd *Web:* www.wltz.com	Columbus	GA	31907	706-561-3838	563-8467
WRBL-TV Ch 3 (CBS) 1350 13th Ave *Web:* www.wrbl.com	Columbus	GA	31901	706-323-3333	323-0841
WTVM-TV Ch 9 (ABC) 1909 Wynnton Rd *Web:* www.wtvm.com	Columbus	GA	31906	706-494-5400	322-7527

741-35 Columbus, OH

Station	City	State	ZIP	Phone	Fax
WBNS-TV Ch 10 (CBS) 770 Twin Rivers Dr **Fax:* News Rm ■ *Web:* www.10tv.com	Columbus	OH	43215	614-460-3700	460-2891*
WCMH-TV Ch 4 (NBC) 3165 Olentangy River Rd *Web:* www.nbc4i.com	Columbus	OH	43202	614-263-4444	263-0166
WOSU-TV Ch 34 (PBS) 2400 Olentangy River Rd *Web:* wosu.org/2012/television	Columbus	OH	43210	614-292-9678	292-7625
WSYX-TV Ch 6 (ABC) 1261 Dublin Rd **Fax:* News Rm ■ *Web:* www.abc6onyourside.com	Columbus	OH	43215	614-481-6666	481-6624*
WTTE-TV Ch 28 (Fox) 1261 Dublin Rd *Web:* www.myfox28columbus.com	Columbus	OH	43215	614-481-6666	481-6624

741-36 Corpus Christi, TX

Station	City	State	ZIP	Phone	Fax
KEDT-TV Ch 16 (PBS) 4455 S Padre Island Dr Ste 38 *TF:* 800-307-5338 ■ *Web:* www.kedt.org	Corpus Christi	TX	78411	361-855-2213	855-3877
KIII-TV Ch 3 (ABC) 5002 S Padre Island Dr *TF:* 800-882-9539 ■ *Web:* www.kiiitv.com	Corpus Christi	TX	78411	361-986-8300	
KRIS-TV Ch 6 (NBC) 301 Artesian St *Web:* www.kristv.com	Corpus Christi	TX	78401	361-886-6100	
KZTV-TV Ch 10 (CBS) 301 Artesian St **Fax:* News Rm ■ *Web:* www.kztv10.com	Corpus Christi	TX	78401	361-883-7070	884-8111*

741-37 Dallas/Fort Worth, TX

Station	City	State	ZIP	Phone	Fax
KDFW FOX 4 400 N Griffin St *Web:* www.fox4news.com	Dallas	TX	75202	214-720-4444	720-3263
KERA-TV Ch 13 (PBS) 3000 Harry Hines Blvd *Web:* www.kera.org	Dallas	TX	75201	214-871-1390	
KTVT-TV Ch 11 (CBS) 5233 Bridge St *Web:* dfw.cbslocal.com	Fort Worth	TX	76103	817-451-1111	496-7739
KXAS-TV Ch 5 (NBC) 3900 Barnett St *Web:* www.nbcdfw.com	Fort Worth	TX	76103	817-429-5555	654-6325
KXTX-TV Ch 39 (Tele) 4805 Amon Carter Blvd *TF:* 877-266-8365 ■ *Web:* www.telemundodallas.com	Fort Worth	TX	76155	877-266-8365	
WFAA-TV Ch 8 (ABC) 606 Young St Communications Ctr *Web:* www.wfaa.com	Dallas	TX	75202	214-748-9631	

741-38 Dayton, OH

Station	City	State	ZIP	Phone	Fax
WDTN-TV Ch 2 (NBC) 4595 S Dixie Ave *Web:* www.wdtn.com	Dayton	OH	45439	937-293-2101	296-7147
WHIO-TV Ch 7 (CBS) 1414 Wilmington Ave *Web:* whio.com/	Dayton	OH	45420	937-259-2111	259-2005
WPTD-TV Ch 16 (PBS) 110 S Jefferson St *TF:* 800-247-1614 ■ *Web:* www.thinktv.org	Dayton	OH	45402	937-220-1600	220-1642

741-39 Denver, CO

Station	City	State	ZIP	Phone	Fax
KCEC-TV Ch 50 (Uni) 777 Grant St 5th Fl *Web:* www.entravision.com	Denver	CO	80203	303-832-0050	832-3410
KCNC-TV Ch 4 (CBS) 1044 Lincoln St *Web:* denver.cbslocal.com	Denver	CO	80203	303-861-4444	830-6380
KDVR-TV Ch 31 (Fox) 100 E Speer Blvd *TF:* 888-397-3742 ■ *Web:* kdvr.com	Denver	CO	80203	303-595-3131	
KMGH-TV Ch 7 (ABC) 123 E Speer Blvd *Web:* www.thedenverchannel.com	Denver	CO	80203	303-832-7777	832-0119
KRMA-TV Ch 6 (PBS) 1089 Bannock St *TF:* 800-274-6666 ■ *Web:* www.rmpbs.org	Denver	CO	80204	303-892-6666	620-5600
KUSA-TV Ch 9 (NBC) 500 Speer Blvd *Web:* www.9news.com	Denver	CO	80203	303-871-9999	698-4700
KWGN-TV Ch 2 (CW) 100 E Speer Blvd *Web:* kwgn.com	Denver	CO	80203	303-595-3131	

741-40 Des Moines, IA

Station	City	State	ZIP	Phone	Fax
KCCI-TV Ch 8 (CBS) 888 Ninth St *Web:* www.kcci.com	Des Moines	IA	50309	515-247-8888	244-0202
KDSM-TV Ch 17 (Fox) 4023 Fleur Dr *Web:* www.kdsm17.com	Des Moines	IA	50321	515-287-1717	287-0064
WHO-TV Ch 13 (NBC) 1801 Grand Ave **Fax:* News Rm ■ *TF:* 800-777-8398 ■ *Web:* www.whotv.com	Des Moines	IA	50309	515-242-3500	242-3796*

741-41 Detroit, MI

Station	City	State	ZIP	Phone	Fax
WDIV-TV Ch 4 (NBC) 550 W Lafayette Blvd *Web:* www.clickondetroit.com	Detroit	MI	48226	313-222-0500	

741-42 Duluth, MN

Station	City	State	ZIP	Phone	Fax
KDLH-TV Ch 3 (CBS) 246 S Lake Ave *Web:* www.northlandsnewscenter.com	Duluth	MN	55802	218-720-9600	720-9660
KQDS-TV Ch 21 (Fox) 2001 London Rd *Web:* www.fox21online.com	Duluth	MN	55812	218-728-1622	728-1557
WDIO-TV Ch 10 (ABC) 10 Observation Rd *TF:* 800-477-1013 ■ *Web:* www.wdio.com	Duluth	MN	55811	218-727-6864	727-4415
WDSE-TV Ch 8 (PBS) 632 Niagara Ct *TF:* 888-563-9373 ■ *Web:* www.wdse.org	Duluth	MN	55811	218-788-2831	

741-43 Edmonton, AB

Station	City	State	ZIP	Phone	Fax
CFRN-TV Ch 3 (CTV) 18520 Stony Plain Rd *Web:* edmonton.ctvnews.ca	Edmonton	AB	T5S1A8	780-483-3311	489-5883

741-44 El Paso, TX

Station	City	State	ZIP	Phone	Fax
ElPaso Proud 801 N Oregon St *Web:* www.elpasoproud.com	El Paso	TX	79902	915-532-5421	496-4590
KCOS-TV Ch 13 (PBS) 9050 Viscount Blvd Ste A-440 *Web:* www.kcostv.org	El Paso	TX	79925	915-590-1313	594-5394
KFOX-TV Ch 14 (Fox) 6004 N Mesa St *Web:* www.kfoxtv.com	El Paso	TX	79912	915-833-8585	833-8717
KTDO-TV Ch 48 (Tele) 10033 Carnegie Ave	El Paso	TX	79925	915-591-9595	591-9896
KVIA-TV Ch 7 (ABC) 4140 Rio Bravo St **Fax:* News Rm ■ *TF:* 800-433-7300 ■ *Web:* www.kvia.com	El Paso	TX	79902	915-496-7777	532-0505*

741-45 Erie, PA

Station	City	State	ZIP	Phone	Fax
WFXP-TV Ch 66 (Fox) 8455 Peach St *Web:* www.yourerie.com	Erie	PA	16509	814-864-2400	
WICU-TV Ch 12 (NBC) 3514 State St *TF:* 800-454-8812 ■ *Web:* www.erietvnews.com	Erie	PA	16508	814-454-5201	454-3753
WJET-TV Ch 24 (ABC) 8455 Peach St *Web:* yourerie.com	Erie	PA	16509	814-864-2400	868-3041
WQLN-TV Ch 54 (PBS) 8425 Peach St *TF:* 800-727-8854 ■ *Web:* www.wqln.org	Erie	PA	16509	814-864-3001	864-4077
WSEE-TV Ch 35 (CBS) 3514 State St *TF:* 888-697-2217 ■ *Web:* www.erietvnews.com	Erie	PA	16508	814-454-5201	

741-46 Eugene, OR

Station	City	State	ZIP	Phone	Fax
KEZI-TV Ch 9 (ABC) PO Box 7009 *Web:* www.kezi.com	Eugene	OR	97408	541-485-5611	686-8004
KVAL-TV Ch 13 (CBS) 4575 Blanton Rd PO Box 1313 *Web:* www.kval.com	Eugene	OR	97405	541-342-4961	342-2635

741-47 Evansville, IN

Station	City	State	ZIP	Phone	Fax
WEVV-TV Ch 44 (CBS) 44 Main St *Web:* www.wevv.com	Evansville	IN	47708	812-464-4444	465-4559
WFIE-TV Ch 14 (NBC) 1115 Mt Auburn Rd *TF:* 800-832-0014 ■ *Web:* www.14news.com	Evansville	IN	47720	812-426-1414	425-2482
WNIN-TV Ch 9 (PBS) 405 Carpenter St *TF:* 855-888-9646 ■ *Web:* www.wnin.org	Evansville	IN	47708	812-423-2973	428-7548

741-48 Fairbanks, AK

Station	City	State	ZIP	Phone	Fax
KATN-TV Ch 2 (ABC) 516 2nd Ave Ste 400 *Web:* www.youralaskalink.com	Fairbanks	AK	99701	907-452-2125	
KTVF-TV Ch 11 (NBC) 3650 Braddock St. *TF:* 855-255-5975 ■ *Web:* www.webcenter11.com	Fairbanks	AK	99701	907-458-1800	458-1820
KUAC-TV Ch 9 (PBS) University of Alaska PO Box 755620 *TF:* 800-727-6543 ■ *Web:* kuac.org	Fairbanks	AK	99775	907-474-7491	474-5064

741-49 Fargo/Grand Forks, ND

Station	City	State	ZIP	Phone	Fax
KBME-TV Ch 3 (PBS) 207 N Fifth St *TF:* 800-359-6900 ■ *Web:* www.prairiepublic.org	Fargo	ND	58102	701-241-6900	239-7650
KFME-TV Ch 13 (PBS) 207 N Fifth St *TF:* 800-359-6900 ■ *Web:* www.prairiepublic.org	Fargo	ND	58102	701-241-6900	239-7650
KGFE-TV Ch 2 (PBS) 207 N Fifth St *TF:* 800-359-6900 ■ *Web:* www.prairiepublic.org	Fargo	ND	58102	701-241-6900	239-7650
KVLY-TV Ch 11 (NBC) 1350 21st Ave S *TF:* 800-450-5844 ■ *Web:* www.valleynewslive.com	Fargo	ND	58103	701-237-5211	232-0493
KXJB-TV Ch 4 (CBS) 1350 21st Ave S *TF:* 877-571-0774 ■ *Web:* www.valleynewslive.com	Fargo	ND	58103	701-237-5211	232-0493
WDAY-TV Ch 6 (ABC) 301 S Eigth St *Web:* www.inforum.com	Fargo	ND	58103	701-237-6500	
WDAZ-TV Ch 8 (ABC) 2220 S Washington St *TF:* 877-382-4357 ■ *Web:* www.wdaz.com	Grand Forks	ND	58201	701-775-2511	241-5217

741-50 Flint, MI

Station	City	State	ZIP	Phone	Fax
WJRT-TV Ch 12 (ABC) 2302 Lapeer Rd **Fax:* News Rm ■ *Web:* www.abclocal.go.com	Flint	MI	48503	810-233-3130	257-2812*
WSMH-TV Ch 66 (Fox) 3463 W Pierson Rd *Web:* www.wsmh.com	Flint	MI	48504	810-785-8866	

741-51 Fort Smith, AR

Station	City	State	ZIP	Phone	Fax
KFSM-TV Ch 5 (CBS) 318 N 13th St *Web:* 5newsonline.com	Fort Smith	AR	72902	479-783-3131	783-3295
KHBS-TV Ch 40 (ABC) 2415 N Albert Pike *TF General:* 855-253-7122 ■ *Web:* www.4029tv.com	Fort Smith	AR	72904	479-783-4040	785-5375

741-52 Fort Wayne, IN

Station	City	State	ZIP	Phone	Fax
WANE-TV Ch 15 (CBS) 2915 W State Blvd *Web:* www.wane.com	Fort Wayne	IN	46808	260-424-1515	
WFWA-TV Ch 39 (PBS) 2501 E Coliseum Blvd *TF:* 888-484-8839 ■ *Web:* www.wfwa.org	Fort Wayne	IN	46805	260-484-8839	
WPTA-TV Ch 21 (ABC) 3401 Butler Rd *Web:* www.21alive.com	Fort Wayne	IN	46808	260-483-0584	483-2568

741-53 Fresno, CA

Station	City	State	ZIP	Phone	Fax
KFSN-TV Ch 30 (ABC) 1777 G St *Web:* abc30.com	Fresno	CA	93706	559-442-1170	
KFTV-TV Ch 21 (Uni) 601 W Univision Plaza **Fax Area Code:* 604 ■ *TF:* 866-783-2645 ■ *Web:* www.univision.com/fresno/kftv	Fresno	CA	93650	559-222-2121	251-7898*
KGPE CBS47 5035 E McKinley Ave *Web:* www.yourcentralvalley.com	Fresno	CA	93727	559-222-2411	
KMPH-TV Ch 26 (Fox) 5111 E McKinley Ave *TF:* 800-101-2045 ■ *Web:* kmph-kfre.com	Fresno	CA	93727	559-453-8850	255-9626
KNXT-TV Ch 49 (Ind) 1550 N Fresno St *Web:* www.knxt.tv	Fresno	CA	93703	559-488-7440	488-7444
KSEE-TV Ch 24 (NBC) 5035 E McKinley Ave *Web:* www.yourcentralvalley.com	Fresno	CA	93727	559-222-2411	
Valley PBS 1544 Van Ness Ave *Web:* www.kvpt.org	Fresno	CA	93721	559-266-1800	650-1880

741-54 Grand Rapids, MI

Station	City	State	ZIP	Phone	Fax
WGVU-TV Ch 35 (PBS) 301 W Fulton St *TF:* 800-442-2771 ■ *Web:* www.wgvu.org	Grand Rapids	MI	49504	616-331-6666	
WOOD-TV Ch 8 (NBC) 120 College Ave SE *Web:* www.woodtv.com	Grand Rapids	MI	49503	616-456-8888	
WOTV-TV Ch 4 (ABC) 120 College Ave *Web:* www.wotv4women.com	Grand Rapids	MI	49503	616-456-8888	456-9169
WXMI-TV Ch 17 (Fox) 3117 Plz Dr NE *Web:* www.fox17online.com	Grand Rapids	MI	49525	616-364-8722	364-8506
WZPX-TV Ch 43 (I) 2610 Horizon Dr SE Ste E *TF:* 800-987-9936 ■ *Web:* www.ionmedianetworks.com	Grand Rapids	MI	49546	616-222-4343	493-2677
WZZM-TV Ch 13 (ABC) 645 3-Mile Rd NW *Web:* www.wzzm13.com	Grand Rapids	MI	49544	616-785-1313	785-1301

741-55 Great Falls, MT

Station	City	State	ZIP	Phone	Fax
KRTV-TV Ch 3 (CBS) PO Box 2989 *Web:* www.krtv.com	Great Falls	MT	59403	406-791-5400	

741-56 Green Bay, WI

Station	City	State	ZIP	Phone	Fax
NBC 26 1391 N Rd *Web:* www.nbc26.com	Green Bay	WI	54313	920-494-2626	490-2500
WBAY-TV Ch 2 (ABC) 115 S Jefferson St *TF:* 800-261-9229 ■ *Web:* www.wbay.com	Green Bay	WI	54301	920-432-3331	432-1190
WCWF-TV Ch 14 (CW) 787 Lombardi Ave *Web:* www.cw14online.com	Green Bay	WI	54304	920-494-8711	494-8782
WFRV-TV Ch 5 (CBS) 1181 E Mason St *Web:* www.wearegreenbay.com	Green Bay	WI	54301	920-437-5411	437-4576
WLUK-TV Ch 11 (Fox) 787 Lombardi Ave *TF:* 800-242-8067 ■ *Web:* www.fox11online.com	Green Bay	WI	54304	920-494-8711	

741-57 Harrisburg, PA

Station	City	State	ZIP	Phone	Fax
WHP-TV Ch 21 (CBS) 3300 N Sixth St *Web:* www.local21news.com	Harrisburg	PA	17110	717-238-2100	
WHTM-TV Ch 27 (ABC) 3235 Hoffman St *Web:* www.abc27.com	Harrisburg	PA	17110	717-236-2727	236-1263

741-58 Hartford, CT

Station	City	State	ZIP	Phone	Fax
WTIC-TV Ch 61 (Fox) 285 Broad St *Web:* fox61.com	Hartford	CT	06115	860-527-6161	293-0178

741-59 Helena, MT

Station	City	State	ZIP	Phone	Fax
KTVH 100 W Lyndale Ave Ste A *Web:* www.ktvh.com	Helena	MT	59601	406-457-1212	442-5106

741-60 Honolulu, HI

Station	City	State	ZIP	Phone	Fax
KBFD-TV Ch 32 (Ind) 1188 Bishop St Ste PH 1 *Web:* www.kbfd.com	Honolulu	HI	96813	808-521-8066	521-5233
KHET-TV Ch 11 (PBS) 2350 Dole St *Web:* www.pbshawaii.org	Honolulu	HI	96822	808-973-1000	973-1090
KHNL-TV Ch 8 (NBC) 420 Waiakamilo Rd Ste 205 *Web:* www.hawaiinewsnow.com	Honolulu	HI	96817	808-847-3246	845-3616
KHON-TV Ch 2 (Fox) 88 Piikoi St *TF:* 877-926-8300 ■ *Web:* www.khon2.com	Honolulu	HI	96814	808-591-4278	593-2418
KIKU-TV Ch 20 (Ind) 737 Bishop St Mauka Twr Ste 1430 *Web:* www.kikutv.com	Honolulu	HI	96813	808-847-2021	841-3326
KITV-TV Ch 4 (ABC) 801 S King St *Web:* www.kitv.com	Honolulu	HI	96813	808-535-0240	536-8993
KPXO-TV Ch 66 (I) 875 Waimanu St Ste 630 *TF:* 800-987-9936 ■ *Web:* ionmedia.tv	Honolulu	HI	96813	808-591-1275	
KWHE-TV Ch 14 (Ind) 1188 Bishop St Ste 502 *TF:* 800-218-1414 ■ *Web:* kwhe.lesea.com	Honolulu	HI	96813	808-538-1414	526-0326

741-61 Houston, TX

Station	City	State	ZIP	Phone	Fax
KETH-TV Ch 14 (TBN) 10902 S Wilcrest Dr *Web:* myedutv.org	Houston	TX	77099	281-561-5828	561-9793
KHOU-TV Ch 11 (CBS) 1945 Allen Pkwy *Web:* www.khou.com	Houston	TX	77019	713-526-1111	
KPRC-TV Ch 2 (NBC) 8181 SW Fwy *Web:* www.click2houston.com	Houston	TX	77074	713-222-2222	771-4930
KPXB-TV Ch 49 (I) 256 N Sam Houston Pkwy E Ste 49	Houston	TX	77060	281-820-4900	
KRIV-TV Ch 26 (Fox) 4261 SW Fwy **Fax:* News Rm ■ *Web:* www.fox26houston.com	Houston	TX	77027	713-479-2600	479-2859*
KTBU-TV Ch 55 (Ind) 7007 NW 77th Ave *NASDAQ: SBSA* ■ **Fax Area Code:* 866 ■ *Web:* www.spanishbroadcasting.com	Miami	FL	33166	305-441-6901	269-1521*
KTMD-TV Ch 47 (Tele) 1235 N Loop W Ste 125 *Web:* www.telemundohouston.com	Houston	TX	77008	713-974-4848	
KTRK-TV Ch 13 (ABC) 3310 Bissonnet St *Web:* abc13.com	Houston	TX	77005	713-666-0713	
KUHT-TV Ch 8 (PBS) 4343 Elgin St *Web:* houstonpublicmedia.org	Houston	TX	77204	713-748-8888	
KXLN-TV Ch 45 (Uni) 5100 SW Fwy *Web:* www.univision.com/houston/kxln	Houston	TX	77056	713-662-4545	965-2604

741-62 Huntsville, AL

Station	City	State	ZIP	Phone	Fax
WAAY-TV Ch 31 (ABC) 1000 Monte Sano Blvd SE **Fax:* News Rm ■ *TF:* 888-407-4747 ■ *Web:* www.waaytv.com	Huntsville	AL	35801	256-533-3131	728-7118*

				Phone	Fax
WAFF-TV Ch 48 (NBC) 1414 Memorial PkwyNW *Web:* www.waff.com	Huntsville	AL	35801	256-533-4848	534-4101
WHDF-TV Ch 15 (CW) 200 Andrew Jackson Way *Web:* www.lbgtv.com	Huntsville	AL	35801	256-536-1550	
WHNT-TV Ch 19 (CBS) PO Box 19 *TF:* 800-533-8819 ■ *Web:* www.whnt.com	Huntsville	AL	35804	256-533-1919	536-9468
WZDX-TV CH 54 (Fox) 1309 N Memorial Pkwy *Web:* www.rocketcitynow.com	Huntsville	AL	35801	256-533-5454	203-8320

741-63 Indianapolis, IN

				Phone	Fax
WFYI-TV Ch 20 (PBS) 1630 N Meridian St *Web:* www.wfyi.org	Indianapolis	IN	46202	317-636-2020	283-6645
WISH-TV Ch 8 (CBS) 1950 N Meridian St *Web:* www.wishtv.com	Indianapolis	IN	46202	317-923-8888	931-2242
WRTV-TV Ch 6 (ABC) 1330 N Meridian St **Fax:* News Rm ■ *TF:* 877-667-4265 ■ *Web:* www.theindychannel.com	Indianapolis	IN	46202	317-635-9788	269-1445*
WTHR-TV Ch 13 (NBC) 1000 N Meridian St *Web:* www.wthr.com	Indianapolis	IN	46204	317-636-1313	636-3717
WTTV-TV Ch 4 (CW) 6910 Network Pl *Web:* fox59.com	Indianapolis	IN	46278	317-632-5900	
WXIN-TV Ch 59 (Fox) 6910 Network Pl *Web:* www.fox59.com	Indianapolis	IN	46278	317-632-5900	

741-64 Jackson, MS

				Phone	Fax
WAPT-TV Ch 16 (ABC) 7616 Ch 16 Way *Web:* www.wapt.com	Jackson	MS	39209	601-922-1607	
WJTV-TV Ch 12 (CBS) 1820 TV Rd *Web:* www.wjtv.com	Jackson	MS	39204	601-372-6311	
WLBT-TV Ch 3 (NBC) 715 S Jefferson St *Web:* www.msnewsnow.com	Jackson	MS	39201	601-948-3333	355-7830

741-65 Jacksonville, FL

				Phone	Fax
WCWJ-TV Ch 17 (CW) 9117 Hogan Rd *Web:* www.yourjax.com	Jacksonville	FL	32216	904-641-1700	642-7201
WJCT-TV Ch 7 (PBS) 100 Festival Pk Ave *Web:* www.wjct.org	Jacksonville	FL	32202	904-353-7770	
WJXT-TV Ch 4 (Ind) 4 Broadcast Pl **Fax:* News Rm ■ *Web:* www.news4jax.com	Jacksonville	FL	32207	904-399-4000	393-9822*
WJXX-TV Ch 25 (ABC) 1070 E Adams St *Web:* www.firstcoastnews.com	Jacksonville	FL	32202	904-354-1212	
WTLV-TV Ch 12 (NBC) 1070 E Adams St *Web:* www.firstcoastnews.com	Jacksonville	FL	32202	904-354-1212	

741-66 Jefferson City, MO

				Phone	Fax
KNLJ-TV Ch 25 (Ind) 311 W Dunklin *Web:* www.knlj.tv	Jefferson City	MO	65101	573-896-5105	

741-67 Johnson City, TN

				Phone	Fax
WJHL-TV Ch 11 (CBS) 338 E Main St **Fax Area Code:* 804 ■ *TF:* 800-861-5255 ■ *Web:* www.wjhl.com	Johnson City	TN	37601	423-926-2151	887-7062*

741-68 Juneau, AK

				Phone	Fax
KATH-TV Ch 5 (NBC) 1107 W Eigth St *Web:* www.kath.tv	Juneau	AK	99801	907-586-8384	586-8394
KJUD-TV Ch 8 (ABC) 2700 E Tudor Rd *TF:* 877-304-1313 ■ *Web:* www.youralaskalink.com	Anchorage	AK	99507	907-561-1313	561-1377
KTOO-TV Ch 3 (PBS) 360 Egan Dr *Web:* www.ktoo.org	Juneau	AK	99801	907-586-1670	

741-69 Kansas City, KS & MO

				Phone	Fax
KCPT-TV Ch 19 (PBS) 125 E 31st St *Web:* www.kcpt.org	Kansas City	MO	64108	816-756-3580	
KCWE-TV Ch 29 (CW) 6455 Winchester Ave *Web:* www.kmbc.com/kcwe/index.html	Kansas City	MO	64133	816-221-2900	
KMBC-TV Ch 9 (ABC) 6455 Winchester Ave *Web:* www.kmbc.com	Kansas City	MO	64133	816-221-9999	
KMCI-TV Ch 38 (Ind) 4720 Oak St *Web:* www.kshb.com	Kansas City	MO	64112	816-753-4141	
KSHB-TV Ch 41 (NBC) 4720 Oak St *TF:* 800-222-1222 ■ *Web:* www.kshb.com	Kansas City	MO	64112	816-753-4141	
WDAF-TV Ch 4 (Fox) 3030 Summit *Web:* www.fox4kc.com	Kansas City	MO	64108	816-753-4567	

741-70 Knoxville, TN

				Phone	Fax
Rev Rocket, LLC 9000 Executive Pk Dr Bldg D Ste 300 *Web:* foxville43.revrocket.us	Knoxville	TN	37923	865-693-4343	691-6904
WATE-TV Ch 6 (ABC) 1306 Broadway *Web:* www.wate.com	Knoxville	TN	37917	865-637-6666	525-4091
WBIR-TV Ch 10 (NBC) 1513 Hutchinson Ave *Web:* www.wbir.com	Knoxville	TN	37917	865-637-1010	637-6380
WBXX-TV Ch 20 (CW) 10427 Cogdill Rd Ste 100 *Web:* www.lbgtv.com	Knoxville	TN	37932	865-777-9220	777-9221
WKOP-TV Ch 17 (PBS) 1611 E Magnolia Ave *Web:* www.etptv.org	Knoxville	TN	37917	865-595-0220	
WVLT-TV Ch 8 (CBS) 6450 Papermill Dr *Web:* www.local8now.com	Knoxville	TN	37919	865-450-8888	450-8869

741-71 Lafayette, LA

				Phone	Fax
KATC-TV Ch 3 (ABC) 1103 Eraste Landry Rd *Web:* www.katc.com	Lafayette	LA	70506	337-235-3333	
KLFY-TV Ch 10 (CBS) 1808 Eraste Landry Rd PO Box 90665 *Web:* www.klfy.com	Lafayette	LA	70509	337-981-4823	

741-72 Lansing, MI

				Phone	Fax
WILX-TV Ch 10 (NBC) 500 American Rd *TF:* 888-345-4124 ■ *Web:* www.wilx.com	Lansing	MI	48911	517-393-0110	393-8555
WLAJ-TV Ch 3 (ABC) 5815 S Pennsylvania Ave *Web:* www.wlns.com	Lansing	MI	48911	517-394-5300	
WLNS-TV Ch 6 (CBS) 2820 E Saginaw St *Web:* www.wlns.com	Lansing	MI	48912	517-372-8282	374-7610
WSYM-TV Ch 47 (Fox) 600 W St Joseph St Ste 47 *Web:* www.fox47news.com	Lansing	MI	48933	517-484-7747	484-3144

741-73 Las Vegas, NV

				Phone	Fax
KINC-TV Ch 15 (Uni) 500 Pilot Rd Ste D *Web:* www.entravision.com	Las Vegas	NV	89119	702-434-0015	434-0527
KLVX-TV Ch 10 (PBS) 3050 E Flamingo *Web:* www.vegaspbs.org	Las Vegas	NV	89121	702-799-1010	
KTNV-TV Ch 13 (ABC) 3355 S Valley View Blvd *Web:* www.ktnv.com	Las Vegas	NV	89102	702-876-1313	876-2237
Sinclair Broadcast Group, Inc 10706 Beaver Dam Rd *Web:* www.sbgi.net	Cockeysville	MD	21030	410-568-1500	

741-74 Lexington, KY

				Phone	Fax
WDKY-TV Ch 56 (Fox) 836 Euclid Ave Ste 201 *TF:* 888-404-5656 ■ *Web:* www.foxlexington.com	Lexington	KY	40502	859-269-5656	293-1578
WKYT-TV Ch 27 (CBS) 2851 Winchester Rd **Fax:* News Rm ■ *Web:* www.wkyt.com	Lexington	KY	40509	859-299-0411	293-1578*
WTVQ-TV Ch 36 (ABC) 6940 Man O War Blvd *Web:* www.wtvq.com	Lexington	KY	40509	859-294-3636	

741-75 Lincoln, NE

				Phone	Fax
KLKN-TV Ch 8 (ABC) 3240 S Tenth St *Web:* www.klkntv.com	Lincoln	NE	68502	402-434-8000	436-2236
KOLN-TV Ch 10 (CBS) 840 N 40th *TF:* 800-475-1011 ■ *Web:* www.1011now.com	Lincoln	NE	68503	402-467-4321	467-9210
NET Radio 1800 N 33rd St *TF:* 800-868-1868 ■ *Web:* www.netnebraska.org	Lincoln	NE	68503	800-868-1868	

741-76 Little Rock, AR

				Phone	Fax
KATV-TV Ch 7 (ABC) 401 S Main St *Web:* www.katv.com	Little Rock	AR	72201	501-324-7777	
KTHV-TV Ch 11 (CBS) 720 S Izard St *TF:* 800-621-3362 ■ *Web:* www.thv11.com	Little Rock	AR	72201	501-376-1111	376-1645

741-77 Los Angeles, CA

				Phone	Fax
KCET-TV Ch 28 (PBS) 4401 Sunset Blvd *Web:* www.kcet.org	Los Angeles	CA	90027	323-666-6500	
KJLA-TV Ch 57 (Ind) 2323 Corinth Ave *TF:* 800-588-5788 ■ *Web:* www.kjla.com	Los Angeles	CA	90064	310-943-5288	943-5299
KLCS-TV Ch 58 (PBS) 1061 W Temple St *Web:* www.klcs.org	Los Angeles	CA	90012	213-241-4000	481-1019
KSCI-TV Ch 18 (Ind) 1990 S Bundy Dr Ste 850 *Web:* www.la18.tv	Los Angeles	CA	90025	310-478-1818	479-8118
KTLA-TV Ch 5 (CW) 5800 W Sunset Blvd *Web:* ktla.com	Los Angeles	CA	90028	323-460-5500	460-5333
KTTV FOX 11 1999 S Bundy Dr *Web:* www.foxla.com	Los Angeles	CA	90025	310-584-2000	
KTTV-TV Ch 11 (Fox) 1999 S Bundy Dr *Web:* www.foxla.com	Los Angeles	CA	90025	310-584-2000	584-2024

741-78 Louisville, KY

Station	City	State	ZIP	Phone	Fax
WAVE-TV Ch 3 (NBC) 725 S Floyd St PO Box 32970 *TF:* 800-223-2579 ■ *Web:* www.wave3.com	Louisville	KY	40203	502-585-2201	561-4115
WDRB-TV Ch 41 (Fox) 624 W Muhammad Ali Blvd *Web:* www.wdrb.com	Louisville	KY	40203	502-584-6441	589-5559
WHAS-TV Ch 11 (ABC) 520 W Chestnut *Web:* www.whas11.com	Louisville	KY	40202	502-582-7711	582-7279
WLKY-TV Ch 32 (CBS) 1918 Mellwood Ave. *Web:* www.wlky.com	Louisville	KY	40206	502-893-3671	896-0725

741-79 Lubbock, TX

Station	City	State	ZIP	Phone	Fax
KAMC-TV Ch 28 (ABC) 7403 S University Ave *Web:* everythinglubbock.com	Lubbock	TX	79423	806-745-2345	748-2250
KCBD-TV Ch 11 (NBC) 5600 Ave A *Web:* www.kcbd.com	Lubbock	TX	79404	806-744-1414	749-1111
KLBK-TV Ch 13 (CBS) 7403 S University Ave *Web:* everythinglubbock.com	Lubbock	TX	79423	806-745-2345	748-2250
KTTZ-TV Ch 5 (PBS) 17th & Indiana Ave PO Box 42161 *Web:* www.kttz.org	Lubbock	TX	79409	806-742-2209	742-1274

741-80 Macon, GA

Station	City	State	ZIP	Phone	Fax
WGNM-TV Ch 64 (Ind) 178 Steven Dr *Web:* www.wgnm.com	Macon	GA	31210	478-474-8400	474-4777
WMAZ-TV Ch 13 (CBS) 1314 Gray Hwy. *Web:* www.13wmaz.com	Macon	GA	31211	478-752-1313	752-1331
WMGT-TV Ch 41 (NBC) 301 Poplar St. *Web:* 41nbc.com	Macon	GA	31201	478-745-4141	742-2626

741-81 Madison, WI

Station	City	State	ZIP	Phone	Fax
NBC15 615 Forward Dr. *Web:* nbc15.com	Madison	WI	53711	608-274-1515	271-5194
WHA-TV Ch 21 (PBS) 821 University Ave *Web:* www.wpt.org	Madison	WI	53706	608-263-2121	
WISC-TV Ch 3000 (CBS) 7025 Raymond Rd *Web:* www.channel3000.com	Madison	WI	53719	608-271-4321	271-0800
WKOW-TV Ch 27 (ABC) 5727 Tokay Blvd *Web:* www.wkow.com	Madison	WI	53719	608-274-1234	274-9514
WMSN-TV Ch 47 (Fox) 7847 Big Sky Dr *Web:* www.fox47.com	Madison	WI	53719	608-833-0047	

741-82 Memphis, TN

Station	City	State	ZIP	Phone	Fax
WHBQ-TV Ch 13 (Fox) 485 S Highland St *Web:* www.fox13memphis.com	Memphis	TN	38111	901-320-1313	320-1366
WMC-TV Ch 5 (NBC) 1960 Union Ave *Web:* wmcactionnews5.com	Memphis	TN	38104	901-726-0555	278-7633
WPTY-TV Ch 24 (ABC) 2701 Union Ave Ext *Web:* www.localmemphis.com	Memphis	TN	38112	901-323-2430	
WREG-TV Ch 3 (CBS) 803 Ch Three Dr *Web:* www.wreg.com	Memphis	TN	38103	901-543-2333	543-2167

741-83 Miami/Fort Lauderdale, FL

Station	City	State	ZIP	Phone	Fax
WBFS-TV Ch 33 (MNT) 8900 NW 18th Terr. *Web:* miami.cbslocal.com	Miami	FL	33172	305-591-4444	477-3040
WFOR-TV Ch 4 (CBS) 8900 NW 18th Terr *Web:* miami.cbslocal.com	Miami	FL	33172	305-591-4444	477-3040
WLRN-TV Ch 17 (PBS) 172 NE 15th St *Web:* www.wlrn.org	Miami	FL	33132	305-995-1717	995-2299
WPBT-TV Ch 2 (PBS) 14901 NE 20th Ave **Fax:* News Rm ■ *TF:* 800-222-9728 ■ *Web:* www.wpbt2.org	Miami	FL	33181	305-949-8321	944-4211*
WSFL-TV Ch 39 (CW) 200 E Las Olas Blvd 11th Fl *Web:* www.southflorida.com	Fort Lauderdale	FL	33301	954-627-7349	355-2000
WSVN-TV Ch 7 (Fox) 1401 79th St Cswy. *Web:* www.wsvn.com	Miami	FL	33141	305-751-6692	

741-84 Milwaukee, WI

Station	City	State	ZIP	Phone	Fax
WCGV-TV Ch 24 (MNT) 4041 N 35th St *Web:* www.my24milwaukee.com	Milwaukee	WI	53216	414-815-4100	
WDJT-TV Ch 58 (CBS) 809 S 60th St. *Web:* www.cbs58.com	Milwaukee	WI	53214	414-777-5800	777-5802
WISN-TV Ch 12 (ABC) 759 N 19th St. *Web:* www.wisn.com	Milwaukee	WI	53233	414-342-8812	342-7505
WITI-TV Ch 6 (Fox) 9001 N Green Bay Rd **Fax:* News Rm ■ *Web:* www.fox6now.com	Milwaukee	WI	53209	414-355-6666	586-2141*
WMVS-TV Ch 10 1036 N Eigth St. *Web:* www.mptv.org	Milwaukee	WI	53233	414-271-1036	297-8549
WPXE-TV Ch 55 (I) 6161 N Flint Rd Ste F	Milwaukee	WI	53209	414-247-0117	247-1302
WTMJ-TV Ch 4 (NBC) 720 E Capitol Dr. *Web:* www.tmj4.com	Milwaukee	WI	53212	414-332-9611	967-5378
WVCY-TV Ch 30 (Ind) 3434 W Kilbourn Ave *TF:* 800-729-9829 ■ *Web:* www.vcyamerica.org	Milwaukee	WI	53208	414-935-3000	935-3015
WVTV-TV Ch 18 (CW) 4041 N 35th St. *Web:* super18tv.com	Milwaukee	WI	53216	414-815-4100	203-2300

741-85 Minneapolis/Saint Paul, MN

Station	City	State	ZIP	Phone	Fax
KSTP-TV Ch 5 (ABC) 3415 University Ave W *Web:* www.kstp.com	Saint Paul	MN	55114	651-646-5555	642-4409
KTCA-TV Ch 2 (PBS) 172 E Fourth St *Web:* www.tpt.org	Saint Paul	MN	55101	651-222-1717	
KTCI-TV Ch 17 (PBS) 172 E Fourth St *Web:* www.tpt.org	Saint Paul	MN	55101	651-222-1717	
WCCO-TV Ch 4 (CBS) 90 S 11th St *Web:* minnesota.cbslocal.com	Minneapolis	MN	55403	612-339-4444	330-2767
WUCW-TV Ch 23 (CW) 1640 Como Ave *Web:* thecw23.com	Saint Paul	MN	55108	651-646-2300	646-1220

741-86 Mobile, AL

Station	City	State	ZIP	Phone	Fax
WALA-TV Ch 10 (Fox) 1501 Satchel Paige Dr *Web:* www.fox10tv.com	Mobile	AL	36606	251-434-1010	
WKRG-TV Ch 5 (CBS) 555 Broadcast Dr *Web:* www.wkrg.com	Mobile	AL	36606	251-479-5555	473-8130
WMPV-TV Ch 21 (TBN) 1668 W I-65 Service Rd S *Web:* www.tbn.org	Mobile	AL	36693	251-661-2101	
WPMI-TV Ch 15 (NBC) 661 Azalea Rd *Web:* www.local15tv.com	Mobile	AL	36609	251-602-1500	602-1550

741-87 Montgomery, AL

Station	City	State	ZIP	Phone	Fax
WAIQ-TV Ch 26 (PBS) 1255 Madison Ave **Fax Area Code:* 334 ■ *TF:* 800-239-5239 ■ *Web:* www.aptv.org	Montgomery	AL	36107	205-328-8756	264-7045*
WAKA-TV Ch 8 (CBS) 3020 Eastern Blvd. *TF:* 800-467-0401 ■ *Web:* www.waka.com	Montgomery	AL	36116	334-271-8888	244-7859
WCOV-TV Ch 20 (Fox) 1 W Cov Ave *Web:* www.wcov.com	Montgomery	AL	36111	334-288-7020	288-5414
WNCF-TV Ch 32 (ABC) 3251 Harrison Rd *TF:* 800-467-0424 ■ *Web:* www.alabamanews.net	Montgomery	AL	36109	334-270-2834	272-6444
WSFA-TV Ch 12 (NBC) 12 E Delano Ave **Fax:* News Rm ■ *Web:* www.wsfa.com	Montgomery	AL	36105	334-288-1212	613-8303*

741-88 Montreal, QC

Station	City	State	ZIP	Phone	Fax
CFCF-TV Ch 12 (CTV) 1205 Papineau Ave. *Web:* montreal.ctvnews.ca	Montreal	QC	H2K4R2	514-273-6311	273-1973

741-89 Myrtle Beach, SC

Station	City	State	ZIP	Phone	Fax
WBTW-TV Ch 13 (CBS) 101 McDonald Ct. *Web:* www.wbtw.com	Myrtle Beach	SC	29588	843-293-1301	
WFXB-TV Ch 43 (Fox) 3364 Huger St. *Web:* www.wfxb.com	Myrtle Beach	SC	29577	843-828-4300	828-4343

741-90 Naples/Fort Myers, FL

Station	City	State	ZIP	Phone	Fax
WBBH-TV Ch 20 (NBC) 3719 Central Ave *Web:* www.nbc-2.com	Fort Myers	FL	33901	239-939-2020	936-7771
WFTX-TV Ch 4 (Fox) 621 SW Pine Island Rd. *Web:* www.fox4now.com	Cape Coral	FL	33991	239-574-3636	574-2025
WGCU-TV Ch 30 (PBS) 10501 FGCU Blvd. *Web:* www.wgcu.org	Fort Myers	FL	33965	239-590-2300	590-2310
WINK-TV Ch 11 (CBS) 2824 Palm Beach Blvd *Web:* www.winknews.com	Fort Myers	FL	33916	239-334-1111	
WZVN-TV Ch 26 (ABC) 3719 Central Ave. *TF:* 888-232-8635 ■ *Web:* www.abc-7.com	Fort Myers	FL	33901	239-939-2020	936-7771

741-91 Nashville, TN

Station	City	State	ZIP	Phone	Fax
WKRN-TV Ch 2 (ABC) 441 Murfreesboro Rd *TF:* 800-222-5555 ■ *Web:* www.wkrn.com	Nashville	TN	37210	615-369-7222	369-7329
WNPT-TV Ch 8 (PBS) 161 Rains Ave *Web:* www.wnpt.org	Nashville	TN	37203	615-259-9325	248-6120
WSMV-TV Ch 4 (NBC) 5700 Knob Rd *Web:* www.wsmv.com	Nashville	TN	37209	615-353-4444	
WUXP-TV Ch 30 (MNT) 631 Mainstream Dr *Web:* www.mytv30web.com	Nashville	TN	37228	615-259-5617	
WZTV-TV Ch 17 (Fox) 631 Mainstream Dr. *Web:* www.fox17.com	Nashville	TN	37228	615-259-5617	259-5684

741-92 New Orleans, LA

				Phone	Fax
WDSU-TV Ch 6 (NBC) 846 Howard Ave *TF:* 888-925-4127 ■ *Web:* www.wdsu.com	New Orleans	LA	70113	504-679-0600	679-0752
WHNO-TV Ch 20 (Ind) 839 St Charles Ave. *Web:* whno.lesea.com	New Orleans	LA	70130	504-681-0120	681-0180
WUPL-TV Ch 54 (MNT) 1024 N Rampart St. *Web:* www.wupltv.com	New Orleans	LA	70116	504-529-4444	
WVUE-TV Ch 8 (Fox) 1025 S Jefferson Davis Pkwy *Web:* www.fox8live.com	New Orleans	LA	70125	504-486-6161	483-1543
WWL-TV Ch 4 (CBS) 1024 N Rampart St *Web:* www.wwltv.com	New Orleans	LA	70116	504-529-4444	

741-93 New York, NY

				Phone	Fax
PIX 11 220 E 42nd St *Web:* pix11.com	New York	NY	10017	212-949-1100	
WABC-TV Ch 7 (ABC) 7 Lincoln Sq *Web:* www.abclocal.go.com	New York	NY	10023	917-260-7000	
WCBS-TV Ch 2 (CBS) 51 W 52th St *Web:* newyork.cbslocal.com	New York	NY	10019	212-975-4321	975-9387
WNBC-TV Ch 4 (NBC) 30 Rockefeller Plz *Web:* www.nbcnewyork.com	New York	NY	10112	212-664-4444	
WNET-TV Ch 13 (PBS) 450 W 33rd St *Web:* www.thirteen.org	New York	NY	10001	212-560-1313	560-1314
WNYW-TV Ch 5 (Fox) 205 E 67th St *Web:* www.fox5ny.com	New York	NY	10065	212-452-5500	249-1182
WPXN-TV Ch 31 (I) 810 Seventh Ave 30th Fl *TF:* 800-987-9936 ■ *Web:* www.ionmedianetworks.com	New York	NY	10019	212-603-8419	664-5918
WTBY-TV Ch 54 (TBN) 111 E 15th St *Web:* www.tbn.org	New York	NY	10003	714-731-1000	

741-94 Norfolk/Virginia Beach, VA

				Phone	Fax
WHRO-TV Ch 15 (PBS) 5200 Hampton Blvd *Web:* www.whro.org	Norfolk	VA	23508	757-889-9400	489-0007
WTKR-TV Ch 3 (CBS) 720 Boush St. *TF:* 866-347-2423 ■ *Web:* www.wtkr.com	Norfolk	VA	23510	757-446-1000	622-1807
WTVZ-TV Ch 33 (MNT) 900 Granby St. *Web:* www.mytvz.com	Norfolk	VA	23510	757-622-3333	623-1541
WVEC-TV Ch 13 (ABC) 613 Woodis Ave *Web:* www.13newsnow.com	Norfolk	VA	23510	757-625-1313	628-5855

741-95 Oklahoma City, OK

				Phone	Fax
KETA-TV Ch 13 (PBS) PO Box 14190 *TF:* 800-879-6382 ■ *Web:* www.oeta.tv	Oklahoma City	OK	73113	405-848-8501	
KFOR-TV Ch 4 (NBC) 444 E Britton Rd. *Web:* www.kfor.com	Oklahoma City	OK	73114	405-424-4444	
KOCB-TV Ch 34 (CW) 1228 E Wilshire Blvd *Web:* www.cwokc.com	Oklahoma City	OK	73111	405-843-2525	478-4343
KOCO-TV Ch 5 (ABC) 1300 E Britton Rd. *Web:* www.koco.com	Oklahoma City	OK	73131	405-478-3000	
KOKH-TV Ch 25 (Fox) 1228 E Wilshire Blvd *Web:* www.okcfox.com	Oklahoma City	OK	73111	405-843-2525	478-4343
KOPX-TV Ch 62 (I) 13424 Railway Dr. *Web:* ionmedia.tv	Oklahoma City	OK	73114	405-478-9562	
KWTV-TV Ch 9 (CBS) 7401 N Kelley Ave. *TF:* 888-550-5988 ■ *Web:* www.news9.com	Oklahoma City	OK	73111	405-843-6641	841-9989

741-96 Omaha, NE

				Phone	Fax
KETV-TV Ch 7 (ABC) 2665 Douglas St. *TF:* 800-279-5388 ■ *Web:* www.ketv.com	Omaha	NE	68131	402-345-7777	522-7740
KMTV Action 3 News 10714 Mockingbird Dr **Fax Area Code:* 414 ■ *TF:* 800-800-6619 ■ *Web:* www.kmtv.com	Omaha	NE	68127	402-592-3333	967-5378*
KPTM 42.2 FM 4625 Farnam St. *Web:* www.fox42kptm.com	Omaha	NE	68132	402-554-4282	
KXVO-TV Ch 15 (CW) 4625 Farnam St. *Web:* www.kxvo.com	Omaha	NE	68132	402-554-1500	554-4290
WOWT-TV Ch 6 (NBC) 3501 Farnam St *TF:* 866-434-8587 ■ *Web:* www.wowt.com	Omaha	NE	68131	402-346-6666	233-7887

741-97 Orlando, FL

				Phone	Fax
ION Media Networks Inc 7091 Grand National Dr Ste 100 *Web:* www.ionmedia.tv	Orlando	FL	32819	407-370-5600	363-1759
WFTV-TV Ch 9 (ABC) 490 E S St *Web:* www.wftv.com	Orlando	FL	32801	407-841-9000	
WKMG-TV Ch 6 (CBS) 4466 N John Young Pkwy *TF:* 800-435-7352 ■ *Web:* www.clickorlando.com	Orlando	FL	32804	407-521-1200	521-1204

741-98 Ottawa, ON

				Phone	Fax
CJOH-TV Ch 13 (CTV) 87 George St *Web:* ottawa.ctvnews.ca	Ottawa	ON	K1N9H7	613-224-1313	

741-99 Peoria, IL

				Phone	Fax
WMBD-TV Ch 31 (CBS) 3131 N University St *Web:* www.centralillinoisproud.com	Peoria	IL	61604	309-688-3131	686-8650
WTVP-TV Ch 47 (PBS) 101 State St *TF:* 800-837-4747 ■ *Web:* www.wtvp.org	Peoria	IL	61602	309-677-4747	677-4730

741-100 Philadelphia, PA

				Phone	Fax
KYW-TV Ch 3 (CBS) 1555 Hamilton St. *Web:* philadelphia.cbslocal.com	Philadelphia	PA	19130	215-977-5333	238-4545
WHYY-TV Ch 12 (PBS) 150 N Sixth St *Web:* www.whyy.org	Philadelphia	PA	19106	215-351-1200	351-3352
WPHL-TV Ch 17 (MNT) 5001 Wynnefield Ave *Web:* phl17.com	Philadelphia	PA	19131	215-878-1700	
WPPX-TV Ch 61 (I) 3901 B Main St Ste 301	Philadelphia	PA	19127	215-482-4770	482-4777
WPSG-TV Ch 57 (CW) 1555 Hamilton St.	Philadelphia	PA	19130	215-977-5700	977-5658
WPVI-TV Ch 6 (ABC) 4100 City Line Ave. *Web:* www.abclocal.go.com	Philadelphia	PA	19131	215-878-9700	581-4530
WTXF-TV Ch 29 (Fox) 330 Market St. **Fax:* News Rm ■ *Web:* www.fox29.com	Philadelphia	PA	19106	215-925-2929	982-5494*

741-101 Phoenix, AZ

				Phone	Fax
ION Media Networks 2777 E Camelback Rd Ste 220 *TF:* 888-796-6988 ■ *Web:* www.ionmedianetworks.com/business/stations?station=56	Phoenix	AZ	85016	602-340-1466	
KASW-TV Ch 61 (CW) 5555 N Seventh Ave.	Phoenix	AZ	85013	480-661-6161	207-3327
KNXV-TV Ch 15 (ABC) 515 N 44th St *TF:* 800-222-4357 ■ *Web:* www.abc15.com	Phoenix	AZ	85008	602-273-1500	
KPAZ-TV Ch 21 (TBN) 3551 E McDowell Rd *Web:* www.tbn.org	Phoenix	AZ	85008	602-273-1477	
KSAZ-TV Ch 10 (Fox) 511 W Adams St *TF:* 888-369-4762 ■ *Web:* fox10phoenix.com	Phoenix	AZ	85003	602-257-1234	
KTVK-TV Ch 3 (Ind) 5555 N Seventh Ave. *Web:* www.azfamily.com	Phoenix	AZ	85013	602-207-3333	207-3477

741-102 Pittsburgh, PA

				Phone	Fax
WPGH-TV Ch 53 (Fox) 750 Ivory Ave *Web:* www.wpgh53.com/pittsburgh_pa	Pittsburgh	PA	15214	412-931-5300	
WPMY-TV Ch 22 (MNT) 750 Ivory Ave *Web:* 22thepoint.com	Pittsburgh	PA	15214	412-931-5300	931-4284
WPXI-TV Ch 11 (NBC) 4145 Evergreen Rd. *Web:* www.wpxi.com	Pittsburgh	PA	15214	412-237-1100	
WQED-TV Ch 13 (PBS) 4802 Fifth Ave. *TF:* 800-876-1316 ■ *Web:* www.wqed.org	Pittsburgh	PA	15213	412-622-1370	622-6413
WTAE-TV Ch 4 (ABC) 400 Ardmore Blvd **Fax:* News Rm ■ *Web:* www.wtae.com	Pittsburgh	PA	15221	412-242-4300	244-4628*

741-103 Pocatello, ID

				Phone	Fax
KIFI-TV Ch 8 (ABC) 1915 N Yellowstone Hwy *Web:* www.localnews8.com	Idaho Falls	ID	83401	208-525-8888	522-1930
KISU-TV Ch 10 (PBS) 921 S Eighth Ave S-8111 *TF:* 800-543-6868 ■ *Web:* www.idahoptv.org	Pocatello	ID	83209	208-282-2857	
KPVI-TV Ch 6 (NBC) 902 E Sherman St *Web:* www.kpvi.com	Pocatello	ID	83201	208-232-6666	233-6678

741-104 Portland, ME

				Phone	Fax
WCSH-TV Ch 6 (NBC) 1 Congress Sq *TF:* 800-464-1213 ■ *Web:* www.wcsh6.com	Portland	ME	04101	207-828-6666	828-6620
WGME-TV Ch 13 (CBS) 81 Northport Dr *Web:* www.wgme.com	Portland	ME	04103	207-797-1313	

741-105 Portland, OR

				Phone	Fax
KATU-TV Ch 2 (ABC) 2153 NE Sandy Blvd *Web:* www.katu.com	Portland	OR	97232	503-231-4222	
KGW-TV Ch 8 (NBC) 1501 SW Jefferson St *TF:* 800-669-9777 ■ *Web:* www.kgw.com	Portland	OR	97201	503-226-5000	
KOIN-TV Ch 6 (CBS) 222 SW Columbia St. *Web:* www.koin.com	Portland	OR	97201	503-464-0600	

741-106 Providence, RI

				Phone	Fax
WLNE-TV Ch 6 (ABC) 10 Orms St Web: www.abc6.com	Providence	RI	02904	401-453-8000	331-4431
WSBE-TV Ch 36 (PBS) 50 Pk Ln Web: www.ripbs.org	Providence	RI	02907	401-222-3636	222-3407

741-107 Raleigh/Durham, NC

				Phone	Fax
WNCN-TV Ch 17 (NBC) 1205 Front St Web: www.wncn.com	Raleigh	NC	27609	919-836-1717	
WRAL-TV Ch 5 (CBS) 2619 Western Blvd TF: 800-245-9725 ■ Web: www.wral.com	Raleigh	NC	27606	919-821-8555	821-8541
WRAZ-TV Ch 50 (Fox) 512 S Mangum St TF: 877-369-5050 ■ Web: www.fox50.com	Durham	NC	27701	919-595-5050	
WTVD-TV Ch 11 (ABC) 411 Liberty St Web: www.abclocal.go.com	Durham	NC	27701	919-683-1111	

741-108 Rapid City, SD

				Phone	Fax
KEVN-TV Ch 7 (Fox) 2001 Skyline Dr PO Box 677 *Fax Area Code: 202 ■ Web: www.blackhillsfox.com	Rapid City	SD	57709	605-394-7777	747-7791*
KNBN-TV Ch 27 (NBC) 2424 S Plz Dr Web: www.newscenter1.tv	Rapid City	SD	57702	605-355-0024	355-9274
KOTA-TV Ch 3 (ABC) 518 St Joseph St TF: 866-558-4554 ■ Web: www.kotatv.com	Rapid City	SD	57701	605-342-2000	342-7305

741-109 Reno/Carson City, NV

				Phone	Fax
KNPB-TV Ch 5 (PBS) 1670 N Virginia St Web: www.knpb.org	Reno	NV	89503	775-784-4555	784-1438
KOLO-TV Ch 8 (ABC) 4850 Ampere Dr *Fax: News Rm ■ Web: www.kolotv.com	Reno	NV	89502	775-858-8888	858-8855*
KRXI-TV Ch 11 (Fox) 4920 Brookside Ct Web: www.foxreno.com	Reno	NV	89502	775-856-1100	856-2116
KTVN-TV Ch 2 (CBS) 4925 Energy Way Web: www.ktvn.com	Reno	NV	89502	775-858-2222	861-4298

741-110 Richmond, VA

				Phone	Fax
WCVE-TV Ch 23 (PBS) 23 Sesame St TF: 800-476-8440 ■ Web: ideastations.org	Richmond	VA	23235	804-320-1301	
WRIC-TV Ch 8 (ABC) 301 Arboretum Pl Web: www.wric.com	Richmond	VA	23236	804-330-8888	330-8881
WRLH-TV Ch 35 (Fox) 1925 Westmoreland St Web: www.foxrichmond.com	Richmond	VA	23230	804-358-3535	358-1495
WTVR-TV Ch 6 (CBS) 3301 W Broad St *Fax: Sales ■ Web: www.wtvr.com	Richmond	VA	23230	804-254-3600	342-3418*
WUPV-TV Ch 65 (CW) 5710 Midlothian Tpke Web: www.cwrichmond.tv	Richmond	VA	23225	804-230-1212	
WWBT-TV Ch 12 (NBC) 5710 Midlothian Tpke Web: www.nbc12.com	Richmond	VA	23225	804-230-1212	

741-111 Roanoke, VA

				Phone	Fax
WFXR-TV Ch 27 (Fox) 5305 Valleypark Dr Ste 1 Web: www.virginiafirst.com	Roanoke	VA	24019	540-344-2127	345-1912
WSLS-TV Ch 10 (NBC) PO Box 10 TF: 855-447-7647 ■ Web: www.wsls.com	Roanoke	VA	24022	540-981-9110	343-2059

741-112 Rochester, MN

				Phone	Fax
KTTC-TV Ch 10 (NBC) 6301 Bandel Rd NW TF: 800-288-1656 ■ Web: www.kttc.com	Rochester	MN	55901	507-288-4444	288-6324
KXLT-TV Ch 47 (Fox) 6301 Bandel Rd NW TF: 800-452-4368 ■ Web: www.myfox47.com	Rochester	MN	55901	507-252-4747	252-5050

741-113 Rochester, NY

				Phone	Fax
WHAM-TV Ch 13 (ABC) 4225 W Henrietta Rd Web: www.13wham.com	Rochester	NY	14623	585-334-8700	334-8719
WHEC-TV Ch 10 (NBC) 191 E Ave Web: www.whec.com	Rochester	NY	14604	585-546-5670	546-5688
WROC-TV Ch 8 (CBS) 201 Humboldt St *Fax: News Rm ■ Web: www.rochesterfirst.com	Rochester	NY	14610	585-288-8400	288-1505*
WUHF-TV Ch 31 (Fox) 201 Humbolt St Web: www.rochesterfirst.com	Rochester	NY	14610	585-232-3700	288-1505
WXXI-TV Ch 21 (PBS) PO Box 30021 Web: interactive.wxxi.org	Rochester	NY	14603	585-325-7500	258-0335

741-114 Rockford, IL

				Phone	Fax
WIFR-TV Ch 23 (CBS) 2523 N Meridian Rd Web: www.wifr.com	Rockford	IL	61101	815-987-5300	965-0981
WREX-TV Ch 13 (NBC) 10322 Auburn Rd *Fax: News Rm ■ Web: www.wrex.com	Rockford	IL	61103	815-335-2213	335-2055*
WTVO-TV Ch 17 (ABC) 1917 N Meridian Rd Web: www.mystateline.com	Rockford	IL	61101	815-963-5413	

741-115 Sacramento, CA

				Phone	Fax
KCRA-TV Ch 3 (NBC) 3 Television Cir Web: www.kcra.com	Sacramento	CA	95814	916-446-3333	
KQCA-TV Ch 58 (MNT) 3 Television Cir Web: www.kcra.com	Sacramento	CA	95814	916-446-3333	
KTXL-TV Ch 40 (Fox) 4655 Fruitridge Rd Web: www.fox40.com	Sacramento	CA	95820	916-454-4422	739-0559
KVIE-TV Ch 6 (PBS) 2030 W El Camino Ave TF: 800-347-5843 ■ Web: www.kvie.org	Sacramento	CA	95833	916-929-5843	929-7215

741-116 Saint Louis, MO

				Phone	Fax
KDNL-TV Ch 30 (ABC) 1215 Cole St Web: www.abcstlouis.com	Saint Louis	MO	63106	314-436-3030	
KETC-TV Ch 9 (PBS) 3655 Olive St TF: 855-482-5382 ■ Web: ninenet.org	Saint Louis	MO	63108	314-512-9000	512-9005
KMOV-TV Ch 4 (CBS) 1 Memorial Dr Web: www.kmov.com	Saint Louis	MO	63102	314-621-4444	621-4775
KSDK-TV Ch 5 (NBC) 1000 Market St Web: www.ksdk.com	Saint Louis	MO	63101	314-421-5055	

741-117 Salt Lake City, UT

				Phone	Fax
Good 4 Utah 2175 W 1700 S Web: www.4utah.com	Salt Lake City	UT	84104	801-975-4444	924-8099
KJZZ-TV Ch 14 (Ind) 301 West South Temple Web: www.kjzz.com	Salt Lake City	UT	84101	801-537-1414	
KPNZ-TV Ch 24 (Ind) 1845 Empire Ave Web: www.lbimedia.com	Burbank	CA	91504	818-729-5300	
KSL-TV Ch 5 (NBC) PO Box 1160 TF: 800-862-9098 ■ Web: www.ksl.com	Salt Lake City	UT	84110	801-575-5555	575-5560
KSTU-TV Ch 13 (Fox) 5020 Amelia Earhart Dr Web: fox13now.com	Salt Lake City	UT	84116	801-536-1313	
KUED-TV Ch 7 (PBS) 101 Wasatch Dr Rm 215 TF: 800-477-5833 ■ Web: www.kued.org	Salt Lake City	UT	84112	801-581-7777	585-5096
KUPX-TV Ch 16 (I) 466C Lawndale Dr TF: 888-467-2988 ■ Web: www.ionmedia.tv	Salt Lake City	UT	84115	801-474-0016	463-9667
KUTV-TV Ch 2 (CBS) 299 S Main St Ste 150 *Fax: News Rm ■ TF: 866-438-0220 ■ Web: www.kutv.com	Salt Lake City	UT	84111	801-839-1234	839-1235*

741-118 San Antonio, TX

				Phone	Fax
KABB-TV Ch 29 (Fox) 4335 NW Loop 410 TF: 888-538-8541 ■ Web: www.foxsanantonio.com	San Antonio	TX	78229	210-366-1129	377-4758
KENS-TV Ch 5 (CBS) 5400 Fredericksburg Rd Web: www.kens5.com	San Antonio	TX	78229	210-366-5000	
KLRN-TV Ch 9 (PBS) 501 Broadway St TF: 800-627-8193 ■ Web: www.klrn.org	San Antonio	TX	78215	210-270-9000	270-9078
KMYS-TV Ch 35 (MNT) 4335 NW Loop 410 *Fax: News Rm ■ Web: www.kmys.tv	San Antonio	TX	78229	210-366-1129	377-4758*
KSAT-TV Ch 12 (ABC) 1408 N St Mary's St Web: www.ksat.com	San Antonio	TX	78215	210-351-1200	
KVDA-TV Ch 60 (Tele) 6234 San Pedro Ave	San Antonio	TX	78216	210-340-8860	

741-119 San Diego, CA

				Phone	Fax
KFMB-TV Ch 8 (CBS) 7677 Engineer Rd Web: www.cbs8.com	San Diego	CA	92111	858-571-8888	560-0627
KGTV-TV Ch 10 (ABC) 4600 Airway Web: www.10news.com	San Diego	CA	92102	619-237-1010	527-0369
KNSD-TV Ch 39 (NBC) 225 Broadway Web: www.nbcsandiego.com	San Diego	CA	92101	619-231-3939	
KPBS-TV Ch 15 (PBS) 5200 Campanile Dr TF: 888-399-5727 ■ Web: www.kpbs.org	San Diego	CA	92182	619-594-1515	594-3812
KSWB-TV Ch 5 (Fox) 7191 Engineer Rd *Fax: News Rm ■ Web: www.fox5sandiego.com	San Diego	CA	92111	858-492-9269	268-0401*
KUSI-TV Ch 51 (Ind) 4575 Viewridge Ave Web: www.kusi.com	San Diego	CA	92123	858-571-5151	
XETV-TV Ch 6 (CW) 8253 Ronson Rd TF: 866-700-6397 ■ Web: www.cw6sandiego.com	San Diego	CA	92111	858-279-6666	279-0061

741-120 San Francisco, CA

Station	City	State	ZIP	Phone	Fax
KBHK-TV Ch 44 (CW) 855 Battery St	San Francisco	CA	94111	415-765-8144	
Web: cwsanfrancisco.cbslocal.com					
KGO-TV Ch 7 (ABC) 900 Front St	San Francisco	CA	94111	415-954-7777	
Web: www.abclocal.go.com					
KQED-TV Ch 9 (PBS) 2601 Mariposa St	San Francisco	CA	94110	415-864-2000	553-2254
TF: 866-573-3123 ■ *Web:* www.kqed.org					

741-121 San Juan, PR

Station	City	State	ZIP	Phone	Fax
WKAQ-TV Ch 2 (Tele) PO Box 366222	San Juan	PR	00936	787-758-2222	
Web: www.telemundopr.com					

741-122 Savannah, GA

Station	City	State	ZIP	Phone	Fax
WJCL-TV Ch 22 (ABC) 1375 Chatham Pkwy 3rd Fl	Savannah	GA	31405	912-925-0022	921-2235
Web: www.wjcl.com					
WSAV-TV Ch 3 (NBC) 1430 E Victory Dr	Savannah	GA	31404	912-651-0300	
Web: www.wsav.com					

741-123 Seattle/Tacoma, WA

Station	City	State	ZIP	Phone	Fax
KBTC-TV Ch 28 (PBS) 2320 S 19th St	Tacoma	WA	98405	253-680-7700	680-7725
TF: 888-596-5282 ■ *Web:* www.kbtc.org					
KCPQ-TV Ch 13 (Fox) 1813 Westlake Ave N	Seattle	WA	98109	206-674-1313	
Web: q13fox.com					
KCTS-TV Ch 9 (PBS) 401 Mercer St	Seattle	WA	98109	206-728-6463	443-6691
TF: 800-443-9991 ■ *Web:* kcts9.org					
KING 5 Television 333 Dexter Ave N	Seattle	WA	98109	206-448-5555	448-4525
TF: 877-564-2261 ■ *Web:* www.king5.com					
KIRO-TV Ch 7 (CBS) 2807 Third Ave	Seattle	WA	98121	206-728-7777	
Web: www.kiro7.com					
KOMO-TV Ch 4 (ABC) 140 Fourth Ave N	Seattle	WA	98109	206-404-4000	404-4422
Web: www.komonews.com					
KONG-TV Ch 16 (Ind) 333 Dexter Ave N	Seattle	WA	98109	206-448-5555	448-4525
Web: www.king5.com					

741-124 Shreveport, LA

Station	City	State	ZIP	Phone	Fax
KSLA-TV Ch 12 (CBS) 1812 Fairfield Ave	Shreveport	LA	71101	318-222-1212	677-6703
TF: 800-444-5752 ■ *Web:* www.ksla.com					
KTAL-TV Ch 6 (NBC) 3150 N Market St	Shreveport	LA	71107	318-629-6000	334-0288*
**Fax Area Code:* 903 ■ *TF:* 800-259-4929 ■ *Web:* www.arklatexhomepage.com					
KTBS-TV Ch 3 (ABC) 312 E Kings Hwy	Shreveport	LA	71104	318-861-5800	219-4601
TF: 866-543-3296 ■ *Web:* www.ktbs.com					

741-125 Sioux Falls, SD

Station	City	State	ZIP	Phone	Fax
KDLT-TV Ch 46 (NBC) 3600 S Westport Ave	Sioux Falls	SD	57106	605-361-5555	361-3982
TF: 800-727-5358 ■ *Web:* kdlt.com					
KELO-TV Ch 11 (CBS) 501 S Phillips Ave	Sioux Falls	SD	57104	605-336-1100	
TF: 800-888-5356 ■ *Web:* www.keloland.com					
KSFY-TV Ch 13 (ABC) 300 N Dakota Ave Ste 100	Sioux Falls	SD	57104	605-336-1300	336-2067
Web: www.ksfy.com					
KTTW-TV Ch 7 (Fox) 2817 W 11th St	Sioux Falls	SD	57104	605-338-0017	338-7173
Web: www.kttw.com					

741-126 South Bend, IN

Station	City	State	ZIP	Phone	Fax
WNDU-TV Ch 16 (NBC) PO Box 1616	South Bend	IN	46634	574-284-3000	284-3009
Web: www.wndu.com					
WNIT Public Television 300 W Jefferson Blvd PO Box 7034	South Bend	IN	46601	574-675-9648	289-3441
TF: 877-411-3662 ■ *Web:* www.wnit.org					
WSJV-TV Ch 28 (Fox) PO Box 28	South Bend	IN	46624	574-679-9758	294-1267
TF: 800-435-3803 ■ *Web:* www.fox28.com					

741-127 Spokane, WA

Station	City	State	ZIP	Phone	Fax
KAYU-TV Ch 28 (Fox) 4600 S Regal St	Spokane	WA	99223	509-448-2828	
Web: www.myfoxspokane.com					
KHQ-TV Ch 6 (NBC) 1201 W Sprague Ave	Spokane	WA	99201	509-448-6000	448-4644
Web: www.khq.com					
KREM-TV Ch 2 (CBS) 4103 S Regal St	Spokane	WA	99223	509-448-2000	425-1307*
**Fax Area Code:* 870 ■ *TF:* 888-404-3922 ■ *Web:* www.krem.com					
KSKN-TV Ch 22 (CW) 4103 S Regal St	Spokane	WA	99223	509-448-2000	425-1307*
**Fax Area Code:* 870 ■ *TF:* 888-404-3922 ■ *Web:* www.krem.com					
KSPS Public TV 3911 S Regal St	Spokane	WA	99223	509-443-7800	
TF: 800-735-2377 ■ *Web:* www.ksps.org					
KXLY-TV Ch 4 (ABC) 500 W Boone Ave	Spokane	WA	99201	509-324-4000	
Web: www.kxly.com					

741-128 Springfield, IL

Station	City	State	ZIP	Phone	Fax
WICS-TV Ch 20 (ABC) 2680 E Cook St	Springfield	IL	62703	217-753-5620	753-5681*
**Fax:* News Rm ■ *Web:* newschannel20.com					
WRSP-TV Ch 55 (Fox) 3003 Old Rochester Rd	Springfield	IL	62703	217-523-8855	
Web: foxillinois.com					

741-129 Springfield, MA

Station	City	State	ZIP	Phone	Fax
WESTERN MASS NEWS 1300 Liberty St	Springfield	MA	01104	413-733-4040	471-7338*
**Fax Area Code:* 816 ■ *TF:* 877-872-2756 ■ *Web:* www.westernmassnews.com					
WGBY-TV Ch 57 (PBS) 44 Hampden St	Springfield	MA	01103	413-781-2801	731-5093
Web: www.wgby.org					
WWLP-TV Ch 22 (NBC) PO Box 2210	Springfield	MA	01102	413-377-2200	377-2261
Web: www.wwlp.com					

741-130 Springfield, MO

Station	City	State	ZIP	Phone	Fax
KOLR-TV Ch 10 (CBS) 2650 E Div St	Springfield	MO	65803	417-862-1010	831-4209
Web: ozarksfirst.com					
KOZK-TV Ch 21 (PBS) 901 S National Ave	Springfield	MO	65897	417-836-3500	836-3569
TF: 866-684-5695 ■ *Web:* www.optv.org					
KSPR-TV Ch 33 (ABC) 1359 St Louis St	Springfield	MO	65802	417-831-1333	
TF: 877-248-6922 ■ *Web:* www.kspr.com					
KYTV-TV Ch 3 (NBC) PO Box 3500	Springfield	MO	65808	417-268-3000	268-3364
TF: 888-476-6988 ■ *Web:* www.ky3.com					

741-131 Syracuse, NY

Station	City	State	ZIP	Phone	Fax
WCNY-TV Ch 24 (PBS) 506 Old Liverpool Rd PO Box 2400	Syracuse	NY	13220	315-453-2424	451-8824
TF: 800-638-5163 ■ *Web:* www.wcny.org					
WNYS-TV Ch 43 (MNT) 1000 James St	Syracuse	NY	13203	315-472-6800	471-8889
Web: foxsyracuse.com					
WSYT-TV Ch 68 (Fox) 1000 James St	Syracuse	NY	13203	315-472-6800	471-8889
Web: www.foxsyracuse.com					

741-132 Tallahassee, FL

Station	City	State	ZIP	Phone	Fax
WCTV-TV Ch 6 (CBS) 1801 Halstead Blvd	Tallahassee	FL	32309	850-893-6666	
TF: 888-297-9461 ■ *Web:* www.wctv.tv					
WFSU-TV Ch 11 (PBS) 1600 Red Barber Plz	Tallahassee	FL	32310	850-487-3170	487-3093
TF: 800-322-9378 ■ *Web:* www.wfsu.org					
WTWC-TV Ch 40 (NBC) 8440 Deerlake Rd S	Tallahassee	FL	32312	850-893-4140	
Web: www.wtwc40.com					

741-133 Tampa/Saint Petersburg, FL

Station	City	State	ZIP	Phone	Fax
WEDU-TV Ch 3 (PBS) 1300 N Blvd	Tampa	FL	33607	813-254-9338	253-0826
Web: www.wedu.org					
WFLA-TV Ch 8 (NBC) PO Box 1410	Tampa	FL	33601	813-228-8888	225-2770
TF: 800-338-0808 ■ *Web:* www.wfla.com					
WFTS-TV Ch 28 (ABC) 4045 N Himes Ave	Tampa	FL	33607	813-354-2828	
TF: 877-833-2828 ■ *Web:* www.abcactionnews.com					
WMOR-TV Ch 32 (Ind) 7201 E Hillsborough Ave	Tampa	FL	33610	813-626-3232	626-1961
Web: www.mor-tv.com					
WTOG-TV Ch 44 (CW) 365 105th Terr NE	Saint Petersburg	FL	33716	727-576-4444	
Web: cwtampa.cbslocal.com					
WTSP-TV Ch 10 (CBS) 11450 Gandy Blvd N	Saint Petersburg	FL	33702	727-577-1010	576-6924
TF: 877-248-6922 ■ *Web:* www.wtsp.com					
WTTA-TV Ch 38 (MNT) 7622 Bald Cypress Pl	Tampa	FL	33614	813-228-8888	225-2770
Web: wfla.com/category/great-38					
WTVT-TV Ch 13 (Fox) 3213 W Kennedy Blvd	Tampa	FL	33609	813-876-1313	871-3135
Web: www.fox13news.com					
WUSF-TV Ch 16 (PBS) 4202 E Fowler Ave	Tampa	FL	33620	813-974-4000	974-4806
TF: 800-654-3703 ■ *Web:* www.wusftv.usf.edu					

741-134 Toledo, OH

Station	City	State	ZIP	Phone	Fax
WGTE-TV Ch 30 (PBS) PO Box 30	Toledo	OH	43614	419-380-4600	380-4710
Web: www.wgte.org					
WLMB-TV Ch 40 (Ind) 825 Capital Commons Dr	Toledo	OH	43615	419-720-9562	720-9563
TF: 800-218-5740 ■ *Web:* www.wlmb.com					
WNWO-TV Ch 24 (NBC) 300 S Byrne Rd	Toledo	OH	43615	419-535-0024	535-8936
Web: nbc24.com					
WTOL-TV Ch 11 (CBS) 730 N Summit St	Toledo	OH	43604	419-248-1111	244-7104
Web: www.wtol.com					
WTVG-TV Ch 13 (ABC) 4247 Dorr St	Toledo	OH	43607	419-531-1313	534-3898
Web: www.13abc.com					

741-135 Topeka, KS

Station	City	State	Zip	Phone	Fax
KSNT-TV Ch 27 (NBC) 6835 NW Hwy 24 *TF:* 800-222-8477 ■ *Web:* ksnt.com	Topeka	KS	66618	785-582-4000	
KTWU-TV Ch 11 (PBS) 1700 College *TF:* 800-866-5898 ■ *Web:* www.ktwu.org	Topeka	KS	66621	785-670-1111	670-1112
WIBW-TV Ch 13 (CBS) 631 SW Commerce Pl. *Web:* www.wibw.com	Topeka	KS	66615	785-272-6397	272-1363

741-136 Toronto, ON

Station	City	State	Zip	Phone	Fax
CICA-TV Ch 19 (Ind) 2180 Yonge St Stn Q PO Box 200 *TF:* 800-613-0513 ■ *Web:* tvo.org	Toronto	ON	M4T2T1	416-484-2600	484-4234
CITY-TV Ch 57 (Ind) 33 Dundas St E. *TF:* 888-336-9978 ■ *Web:* www.citytv.com/toronto	Toronto	ON	M5B1B8	416-764-3003	

741-137 Tucson, AZ

Station	City	State	Zip	Phone	Fax
KGUN-TV Ch 9 (ABC) 7280 E Rosewood St *Web:* www.kgun9.com	Tucson	AZ	85710	520-722-5486	733-7050
KOLD-TV Ch 13 (CBS) 7831 N Business Pk Dr *Web:* www.tucsonnewsnow.com	Tucson	AZ	85743	520-744-1313	744-5235
KUAT-TV Ch 6 (PBS) University of Arizona Modern Languages Bldg 1423 E University Blvd *Web:* stations.fcc.gov/station-profile/kuat-tv	Tucson	AZ	85721	520-621-5828	621-9664
KVOA-TV Ch 4 (NBC) 209 W Elm PO Box 5188 *Web:* www.kvoa.com	Tucson	AZ	85703	520-792-2270	620-1309

741-138 Tulsa, OK

Station	City	State	Zip	Phone	Fax
KJRH-TV Ch 2 (NBC) 3701 S Peoria Ave *Web:* www.kjrh.com	Tulsa	OK	74105	918-743-2222	748-1436
KOKI-TV Ch 23 (Fox) 2625 S Memorial Dr *Web:* www.fox23.com	Tulsa	OK	74129	918-491-0023	
KOTV-TV Ch 6 (CBS) PO Box 6 *TF:* 888-434-8248 ■ *Web:* www.newson6.com	Tulsa	OK	74101	918-732-6000	732-6185
KTUL-TV Ch 8 (ABC) PO Box 8 *Web:* www.ktul.com	Tulsa	OK	74101	918-445-8888	445-9316
KWHB-TV Ch 47 (Ind) 8835 S Memorial Dr. *Web:* kwhb.lesea.com	Tulsa	OK	74133	918-254-4701	254-5614

741-139 Washington, DC

Station	City	State	Zip	Phone	Fax
WDCW-TV 2121 Wisconsin Ave NW Ste 350 *Web:* dcw50.com	Washington	DC	20007	202-965-5050	
WHUT-TV Ch 32 (PBS) 2222 Fourth St NW *Web:* www.whut.org	Washington	DC	20059	202-806-3200	806-3300
WRC-TV Ch 4 (NBC) 4001 Nebraska Ave NW *Web:* www.nbcwashington.com	Washington	DC	20016	202-885-4000	
WTTG FOX 5 & myfoxdc 5151 Wisconsin Ave NW *Web:* www.fox5dc.com	Washington	DC	20016	202-244-5151	895-3340
WTTG-TV Ch 5 (Fox) 5151 Wisconsin Ave NW *TF:* 866-756-3587 ■ *Web:* www.fox5dc.com	Washington	DC	20016	202-244-5151	
WUSA-TV Ch 9 (CBS) 4100 Wisconsin Ave NW. *Web:* www.wusa9.com	Washington	DC	20016	202-895-5999	

741-140 West Palm Beach, FL

Station	City	State	Zip	Phone	Fax
WFGC-TV Ch 61 (Ind) 1900 S Congress Ave Ste A *Web:* www.wfgctelevision.com	West Palm Beach	FL	33406	561-642-3361	967-5961
WFLX-TV Ch 29 (Fox) 4119 W Blue Heron Blvd *TF:* 844-555-1329 ■ *Web:* www.wflx.com	West Palm Beach	FL	33404	561-845-2929	863-1238
WPTV-TV Ch 5 (NBC) 1100 Banyan Blvd. **Fax:* News Rm ■ *Web:* www.wptv.com	West Palm Beach	FL	33401	561-655-5455	653-5719*
WTVX-TV Ch 34 (CW) 1700 Palm Beach Lakes Blvd *Web:* cw34.com	West Palm Beach	FL	33401	561-681-3434	
WXEL-TV Ch 42 (PBS) PO Box 6607 *TF:* 800-915-9935 ■ *Web:* www.wxel.org	West Palm Beach	FL	33405	561-737-8000	369-3067

741-141 Wheeling, WV

Station	City	State	Zip	Phone	Fax
WTRF-TV Ch 7 (CBS) 96 16th St **Fax:* News Rm ■ *Web:* www.yourohiovalley.com	Wheeling	WV	26003	304-232-7777	233-5822*

741-142 Wichita, KS

Station	City	State	Zip	Phone	Fax
KAKE-TV Ch 10 (ABC) 1500 NW St *Web:* www.kake.com	Wichita	KS	67203	316-943-4221	943-5374
KPTS-TV Ch 8 (PBS) 320 W 21 St *TF:* 800-794-8498 ■ *Web:* www.kpts.org	Wichita	KS	67203	316-838-3090	838-8586
KSAS-TV Ch 24 (Fox) 316 NW St. *Web:* www.foxkansas.com	Wichita	KS	67203	316-942-2424	942-8927
KSCW-TV Ch 33 (CW) 2815 E 37th St N *Web:* kwch.com/kscw-crew/-/22425548/-/cxwku6/-/index.html	Wichita	KS	67219	316-838-1212	
KSNW-TV 833 N Main St *TF:* 800-432-3924 ■ *Web:* www.ksn.com	Wichita	KS	67203	316-265-3333	292-1195
KWCH-TV Ch 12 (CBS) 2815 E 37th St N *TF:* 888-512-6397 ■ *Web:* www.kwch.com	Wichita	KS	67219	316-838-1212	

741-143 Winnipeg, MB

Station	City	State	Zip	Phone	Fax
CTV-TV Ch 5 (CTV) 345 Graham Ave Ste 400 **Fax:* News Rm ■ *TF:* 800-461-1542 ■ *Web:* winnipeg.ctvnews.ca	Winnipeg	MB	R3C5S6	204-788-3300	788-3399*

741-144 Winston-Salem, NC

Station	City	State	Zip	Phone	Fax
WMYV-TV Ch 48 (MNT) 3500 Myer Lee Dr. *Web:* www.my48.tv	Winston-Salem	NC	27101	336-722-4545	723-8217
WXII-TV Ch 12 (NBC) 700 Coliseum Dr. *Web:* www.wxii12.com	Winston-Salem	NC	27106	336-721-9944	721-0856
WXLV-TV Ch 45 (ABC) 3500 Myer Lee Dr. *Web:* www.abc45.com	Winston-Salem	NC	27101	336-722-4545	723-8217

741-145 Youngstown, OH

Station	City	State	Zip	Phone	Fax
WFMJ-TV Ch 21 (NBC) 101 W Boardman St. *TF:* 800-488-9365 ■ *Web:* www.wfmj.com	Youngstown	OH	44503	330-744-8611	742-2472
WKBN-TV Ch 27 (CBS) 3930 Sunset Blvd *Web:* www.wkbn.com/default.aspx	Youngstown	OH	44512	330-782-1144	782-3504
WKBN/WYFX 3930 Sunset Blvd *Web:* www.wkbn.com	Youngstown	OH	44512	330-782-1144	782-3504
WYFX-TV Ch 62 (Fox) 3930 Sunset Blvd. *Web:* www.wkbn.com	Youngstown	OH	44512	330-782-1144	782-3504

742 TELEVISION SYNDICATORS

Television syndicators are companies that produce programming in-house and market and distribute the programs to networks on a national or regional basis.

Company	City	State	Zip	Phone	Fax
A Taste of New York Inc 10 Roberta Ln *Web:* www.tasteofny.com	Syosset	NY	11791	516-677-0239	
ABC NewsOne 47 W 66th St *Web:* abcnews.extremereach.com/pg/ntaxnji=/abcnewsone	New York	NY	10023	212-456-4110	
American Public Television (APT) 55 Summer St 4th Fl. *Web:* aptonline.org/aptweb.nsf/home?readform	Boston	MA	02110	617-338-4455	338-5369
Associated Press 1100 13th St NW Ste 700. *TF:* 800-824-5498 ■ *Web:* www.ap.org	Washington	DC	20005	202-641-9000	
Babe Winkelman Productions PO Box 407. *TF:* 800-333-0471 ■ *Web:* www.winkelman.com	Brainerd	MN	56401	800-333-0471	
bieMEDIA LLC 511 Broadway *Web:* biemedia.com	Denver	CO	80203	303-825-2275	
CBS Newspath 524 W 57th St. *Web:* www.cbsnewspath.com	New York	NY	10019	212-975-6121	
CBS Television Distribution 2450 Colorado Ave Ste 500E *Web:* www.cbstvd.com	Santa Monica	CA	90404	310-264-3300	264-3301
Disney ABC Domestic Television 500 S Buena Vista St *Web:* www.disneyabc.tv	Burbank	CA	91521	818-560-9300	560-5296
Five Star Productions 42 N Swinton Ave *Web:* www.swoolleyentertainment.com	Delray Beach	FL	33444	561-279-7827	
Guthy-Renker Television Network 3340 Ocean Pk Blvd *TF:* 888-651-6607 ■ *Web:* www.guthy-renker.com	Santa Monica	CA	90405	310-581-6250	581-3232
Hearst Entertainment & Syndication Group 300 W 57th St. *Web:* hearst.com/entertainment	New York	NY	10019	212-969-7553	
Independent Television Service (ITVS) 651 Brannan St Ste 410 *TF:* 800-621-6196 ■ *Web:* www.itvs.org	San Francisco	CA	94107	415-356-8383	356-8391
Information Television Network 6650 Pk of Commerce Blvd *Web:* www.itvisus.com	Boca Raton	FL	33487	561-997-7771	997-5208
Initiative Corp 5700 Wilshire Blvd Ste 400 *Web:* initiative.com	Los Angeles	CA	90036	323-370-8000	
Ivanhoe Broadcast News 2745 W Fairbanks Ave *Web:* www.ivanhoe.com	Winter Park	FL	32789	407-740-0789	740-5320
K Rcr Tv News Channel 7 Tv 755 Auditorium Dr *TF:* 800-222-5727 ■ *Web:* www.krcrtv.com	Redding	CA	96001	530-243-7777	
National Educational Telecommunications Assn (NETA) 939 S Stadium Rd. *TF:* 866-270-5141 ■ *Web:* www.netaonline.org	Columbia	SC	29201	803-799-5517	771-4831
RCTV International 4380 NW 128th St *Web:* www.rctvintl.com	Opa Locka	FL	33054	305-688-7475	

Phone Fax

Thomson Reuters 3 Times Sq....................New York NY 10036 646-223-4000
Web: www.thomsonreuters.com

WPT Enterprises Inc (WPTE)
5700 Wilshire Blvd Ste 350....................Los Angeles CA 90036 949-225-2600
Web: www.worldpokertour.com

743 TESTING FACILITIES

Phone Fax

2b Technologies Inc 2100 Central Ave Ste 105..........Boulder CO 80301 303-273-0559
Web: www.twobtech.com

4P Therapeutics LLC 9005 Westside Pkwy..........Alpharetta GA 30009 678-325-4975
Web: www.4ptherapeutics.com

A & E Testing 1514 Rochester St....................Lima NY 14485 585-624-4500
Web: www.shawndra.com

A&L Great Lakes Laboratories Inc
3505 Conestoga Dr....................Fort Wayne IN 46808 260-483-4759
Web: www.algreatlakes.com

Absolute Standards Inc 44 Rossotto Dr..........Hamden CT 06514 203-281-2917
Web: www.absolutestandards.com

Accusource Inc 1240 E Ontario Ave Ste 102-140..........Corona CA 92881 951-734-8882
TF: 888-649-6272 ■ *Web:* www.accusource-online.com

Accutest Laboratories 2235 Rt 130 Bldg B..........Dayton NJ 08810 732-329-0200 329-3499
Web: www.accutest.com

Achaogen Inc
7000 Shoreline Ct Ste 371..........South San Francisco CA 94080 650-266-1120
Web: www.achaogen.com

Acme Analytical Laboratories Ltd
1020 Cordova St E....................Vancouver BC V6A4A3 604-253-3158
TF: 800-990-2263 ■ *Web:* www.acmelab.com

Actimis Pharmaceuticals Inc
10835 Rd To The Cure Ste 200....................San Diego CA 92121 858-458-1890
Web: www.actimis.com

Activation Laboratories Ltd
1336 Sandhill Dr....................Ancaster ON L9G4V5 905-648-9611
TF: 888-228-5227 ■ *Web:* www.actlabs.com

Acutus Medical Inc 2210 Faraday Ave Ste 100..........Carlsbad CA 92008 442-232-6080
Web: www.acutusmedical.com

Adamson Analytical Laboratories Inc
200 Crouse Dr....................Corona CA 92879 951-549-9657 549-9659
Web: www.adamsonlab.com

ADPEN Laboratories Inc
11757 Central Pkwy....................Jacksonville FL 32224 904-645-9169
Web: www.adpen.com

AEDC Public Affairs
100 Kindell Dr Ste B-213....................Arnold AFB TN 37389 931-454-5655 454-6720*
**Fax:* Hum Res ■ *Web:* www.arnold.af.mil

Aegis Sciences Corp 515 Great Cir Rd..........Nashville TN 37228 615-255-2400
Web: www.aegislabs.com

Aerotech Laboratories Inc 1501 W Knudsen Dr..........Phoenix AZ 85027 623-780-4800
Web: www.emlab.com

Affinimark Technologies Inc
300 George St Ste 561....................New Haven CT 06511 201-676-3676
Web: www.affinimark.com

AgaMatrix Inc 7C Raymond Ave....................Salem NH 03079 603-328-6000
Web: www.agamatrix.com

Aircraft X-Ray Labs Inc
5216 Pacific Blvd....................Huntington Park CA 90255 323-587-4141 588-6410
Web: www.aircraftxray.com

Akron Rubber Development Laboratory Inc
2887 Gilchrist Rd....................Akron OH 44305 330-794-6600
TF: 866-778-2735 ■ *Web:* www.ardl.com

Akros Pharma Inc 302 Carnegie Ctr Ste 300..........Princeton NJ 08540 609-919-9570
Web: www.akrospharma.com

Alere Toxicology Services Inc 1111 Newton St..........Gretna LA 70053 504-361-8989
Web: www.aleretoxicology.com

ALine Inc 2206 E Gladwick St..........Rancho Dominguez CA 90220 877-707-8575
TF: 877-707-8575 ■ *Web:* www.alineinc.com

All Metals Processing of Orange County Inc
8401 Standustrial St....................Stanton CA 90680 714-828-8238 828-4552
Web: www.allmetalsprocessing.com

All-Tronics Medical Systems Inc
3289 E 55th St....................Cleveland OH 44127 216-429-3000
Web: www.all-tronics.net

Allegro Diagnostics Inc
6 Clock Tower Pl Ste 225....................Maynard MA 01754 978-938-4866
Web: investor.veracyte.com

Allegro Ophthalmics LLC
31473 Rancho Viejo Rd Ste 204..........San Juan Capistrano CA 92675 949-940-8130
Web: www.allegroeye.com

Alliance Source Testing LLC
214 Central Cir SW....................Decatur AL 35603 256-351-0121
Web: www.stacktest.com

Altran Solutions USA 2525 Rt 130 S..........Cranbury NJ 08512 609-409-9790 409-8622
TF: 855-425-8726 ■ *Web:* www.altran-na.com

Alturas Analytics Inc 1324 Alturas Dr..........Moscow ID 83843 208-883-3400
TF: 877-344-1279 ■ *Web:* www.alturasanalytics.com

Alverix Inc 2590 N First St Ste 100..........San Jose CA 95131 408-432-8372
Web: www.alverix.com

ALZA Corp 700 Eubanks Dr....................Vacaville CA 95688 707-453-6400
Web: jnj.com

American Standards Testing Bureau Inc
PO Box 583....................New York NY 10274 212-943-3160 825-2250

Amplicon Express Inc 2345 Ne Hopkins Ct..........Pullman WA 99163 509-332-8080
TF: 877-332-8080 ■ *Web:* ampliconexpress.com

Ana-Lab Corp PO Box 9000....................Kilgore TX 75663 903-984-0551 984-5914
Web: www.ana-lab.com

AnaBios Corporation Inc
San Diego Science Ctr 3030 Bunker Hill St
Ste 312....................San Diego CA 92109 858-427-4808
Web: www.anabios.com

Phone Fax

Anabolic Laboratories Inc ÿ17802 Gillette Ave..........Irvine CA 92614 949-863-0340
Web: www.anaboliclabs.com

Analysts Inc 22750 Hawthorne Blvd Ste 220..........Torrance CA 90505 800-336-3637 320-0970*
**Fax Area Code:* 310 ■ *TF:* 800-336-3637 ■ *Web:* www.analystsinc.com

Analytica Group-environmental Laboratories
4307 Arctic Blvd....................Anchorage AK 99503 907-258-2155

Analytics Corp 10329 Stony Run Ln..........Ashland VA 23005 804-365-3000
TF: 800-888-8061 ■ *Web:* analyticscorp.com

Anatek Labs Inc 1282 Alturas Dr..........Moscow ID 83843 208-883-2839
Web: www.anateklabs.com

Anatom-e Information Systems Ltd
7505 Fannin St Ste 422....................Houston TX 77054 469-231-4568
Web: www.anatom-e.com

Andro Diagnostics Inc 12521 Gulf Fwy..........Houston TX 77034 409-762-0678
Web: www.androdx.com

Animal & Plant Health Inspection Service (APHIS)
National Veterinary Services Laboratories
2300 Dayton Ave....................Ames IA 50010 515-663-7200
Web: www.aphis.usda.gov

Anrad Corp 4950 Levy St....................St Laurent QC H4R2P1 514-856-6920
Web: www.anrad.com

Apotex Fermentation Inc 50 Scurfield Blvd..........Winnipeg MB R3Y1G4 204-989-6830
Web: www.apoferm.com

Aqua Test Inc
28620 Maple Valley Black Diamond Rd SE..........Maple Valley WA 98038 425-432-9360
Web: aquatestinc.com

Arcadia Biosciences Inc 202 Cousteau Pl Ste 200..........Davis CA 95618 530-756-7077
Web: www.arcadiabio.com

Astro Pak Corp 270 E Baker St Ste 100..........Costa Mesa CA 92626 866-492-7876 434-1376*
**Fax Area Code:* 714 ■ *TF:* 888-278-7672 ■ *Web:* www.astropak.com

Atlantic Pharmaceuticals Inc
1 Glenlake Pkwy Ste 700....................Atlanta GA 30328 678-638-6170
Web: www.atlanticpharma.com

Atlas Testing Laboratories Inc
9820 Sixth St....................Rancho Cucamonga CA 91730 909-373-4130
Web: www.atlastesting.com

AXON Connected LLC
2322 Blue Stone Hills Dr Ste 20..........Harrisonburg VA 22801 540-558-8596
Web: www.axonconnected.com

Balazs Analytical Laboratory
46409 Landing Pkwy....................Fremont CA 94538 510-624-4000
Web: www.balazs.com

Ballantine Laboratories Inc
312 Old Allerton Rd....................Annandale NJ 08801 908-713-7742 713-7743
Web: www.ballantinelabs.com

Benaroya Research Institute 1201 Ninth Ave..........Seattle WA 98101 206-342-6500
Web: www.benaroyaresearch.org

Benchmark International 2710 W Fifth Ave..........Eugene OR 97402 541-484-9212 344-2735
Web: www.benchmark-intl.com

BERTL Inc 20 Just Rd Ste 130....................Fairfield NJ 07004 973-882-0200
Web: www.bertl.com

Beta Analytic Inc 4985 SW 74th Ct..........Miami FL 33155 305-667-5167
Web: www.betaanalytic.com

Bio-Research Products Inc
323 W Cherry St....................North Liberty IA 52317 319-626-6707
TF: 800-326-3511 ■ *Web:* www.bio-researchprod.com

BioFlorida
525 Okeechobee Blvd Ste 1500..........West Palm Beach FL 33401 561-653-3839
Web: www.biofIorida.com

Bion Enterprises Ltd 455 State St Ste 100..........Des Plaines IL 60016 847-544-5044
Web: www.bionenterprises.com

BIOPAC Systems Inc 42 Aero Camino..........Goleta CA 93117 805-685-0066
TF: 877-524-6722 ■ *Web:* www.biopac.com

BIOQUELL Inc 702 Electronic Dr Ste 200..........Horsham PA 19044 215-682-0225
Web: www.bioquell.com

Biosan Laboratories Inc 1950 Tobsal Ct..........Warren MI 48091 586-755-8970
TF: 800-253-6800 ■ *Web:* www.biosan.com

BioStratum Inc 4825 Creekstone Dr Ste 200..........Durham NC 27703 919-572-6515
Web: www.biostratum.com

Biotech Clinical Laboratories Inc
25775 Meadowbrook....................Novi MI 48375 248-912-1700
Web: biotechclinical.com

Biothera Inc 3388 Mike Collins Dr..........Eagan MN 55121 651-675-0300
Web: www.biotherapharma.com

bioTheranostics Inc
9640 Towne Centre Dr Ste 200..........San Diego CA 92121 858-587-5870
TF: 877-886-6739 ■ *Web:* www.biotheranostics.com

BioWa Inc 9420 Athena Cir....................La Jolla CA 92037 858-952-7200
Web: kyowa-kirin.com/biowa

Boca Biolistics LLC
4851 W Hillsboro Blvd Ste A7..........Coconut Creek FL 33073 954-573-1200
Web: bocabio.com

Bosch Automotive Proving Grounds
32104 State Rd 2....................New Carlisle IN 46552 574-654-4000
Web: www.bosch.us

Brain Tunnelgenix Technologies Corp
375 Mather St....................Hamden CT 06514 203-870-9611
Web: www.braintunnelgenix.com

Brook Environmental & Engineering Corp
11419 Cronridge Dr Ste 10..........Owings Mills MD 21117 410-356-5073
Web: carrollcountytimes.com

Brooks Rand Labs LLC 18804 N Crk Pkwy Ste 100..........Bothell WA 98011 206-632-6206
Web: brooksapplied.com

Brunswick Laboratories LLC
200 Turnpike Rd....................Southborough MA 01772 508-281-6660
Web: www.brunswicklabs.com

Caldwell Manufacturing Inc 2605 Manitou Rd..........Rochester NY 14624 585-352-3790
Web: www.caldwellmfgco.com

Camin Cargo Control Inc 230 Marion Ave..........Linden NJ 07036 908-862-1899 523-0616*
**Fax:* Hum Res ■ *TF:* 800-756-8798 ■ *Web:* www.camincargo.com

Cancer Care Ontario 620 University Ave..........Toronto ON M5G2L7 416-971-9800
Web: www.cancercare.on.ca

Phone Fax

CanWest DHI 660 Speedvale Ave W .... Guelph ON N1K1E5 519-824-2320
TF: 800-549-4373 ■ *Web:* www.canwestdhi.com

CardioNexus Corp 710 N Post Oak Rd Ste 103 .... Houston TX 77024 281-769-4201
Web: www.cardionexus.com

Cardiovascular Research Foundation
111 E 59th St .... New York NY 10022 646-434-4500
Web: www.crf.org

Carlson Testing Inc 8430 SW Hunziker .... Tigard OR 97223 503-684-3460
Web: www.carlsontesting.com

Carrot Medical LLC
22122 20th Ave SE Ste H-166 .... Bothell WA 98021 425-318-8089
TF: 866-492-3533 ■ *Web:* carrotmedical.com

Catalyst Biosciences Inc
260 Littlefield Ave .... South San Francisco CA 94080 650-871-0761
Web: www.catalystbiosciences.com

CD Diagnostics Inc 650 Naamans Rd Ste 100 .... Claymont DE 19703 302-367-7770
Web: cddiagnostics.com

Chardon Laboratories Inc
7300 Tussing Rd .... Reynoldsburg OH 43068 614-860-1000
Web: chardonlabs.com

Chemir Analytical Services Inc
2672 Metro Blvd .... Maryland Heights MO 63043 314-291-6620
Web: www.chemir.com

Cherney Microbiological Services Ltd
1110 S Huron Rd .... Green Bay WI 54311 920-406-8300
Web: cherneymicro.com

Christian Alliance for Humanitarian Aid Inc
4401 Rice Dyer Rd .... Pearland TX 77581 281-412-2285
Web: christian-alliance.org

Claro Scientific LLC
10100 Dr Martin Luther King St N .... St. Petersburg FL 33716 727-568-1213
Web: clarosci.com

CME Associates 439 N Pearl St .... Albany NY 12204 518-432-5820
Web: www.cmeassociates.com

Coherex Medical Inc
3598 West 1820 South .... Salt Lake City UT 84104 801-433-9900
Web: www.coherex.com

Columbia Analytical Services Inc
1317 S 13th Ave .... Kelso WA 98626 360-577-7222 425-9096
Web: www.caslab.com

Compact Membrane Systems Inc 335 Water St .... Newport DE 19804 302-999-7996
Web: www.compactmembrane.com

Con-Test Analytical Laboratory
39 Spruce St 2 .... East Longmeadow MA 01028 413-525-2332
Web: www.contestlabs.com

Consano Medical Inc 101 Mississippi St .... San Francisco CA 94107 415-779-6682
Web: www.consanomed.com

Construction Testing & Engineering Inc
1441 Montiel Rd Ste 115 .... Escondido CA 92026 760-746-4955 839-2895*
**Fax Area Code: 209* ■ *Web:* www.cte-inc.net

Copernicus Group Inc, The
1 Triangle Dr Ste 100 .... Durham NC 27713 919-465-4310
Web: www.cgirb.com

Cosmed Group Inc 28 Narragansett Ave .... Jamestown RI 02835 401-423-2003
Web: www.cosmedgroup.com

Craft Technologies Inc
4344 Frank Price Church Rd .... Wilson NC 27893 252-206-7071
Web: www.crafttechnologies.com

Criterion Laboratories Inc
3370 Progress Dr Ste J .... Bensalem PA 19020 215-244-1300
Web: www.criterionlabs.com

Cryogenic Experts Inc 531 Sandy Cir .... Oxnard CA 93036 805-981-4500
Web: www.cexi.com

CSP Assoc Inc
55 Cambridge Pkwy Riverfront 2 .... Cambridge MA 02142 617-225-2828
Web: www.cspassociates.com

CTLGroup 5400 Old OrchaRd Rd .... Skokie IL 60077 847-965-7500 965-6541
TF: 800-522-2285 ■ *Web:* www.ctlgroup.com

Curtis & Tompkins Ltd 2323 Fifth St .... Berkeley CA 94710 510-486-0900
Web: curtisandtompkins.com

Cyl-tec Inc 971 W Industrial Dr .... Aurora IL 60506 630-844-8800
TF: 888-429-5832 ■ *Web:* cyl-tec.com

D L s Electronic Systems Inc
1250 Peterson Dr .... Wheeling IL 60090 847-537-6400
Web: www.dlsemc.com

D-Tech Optoelectronics Inc USA
18007 Cortney Ct .... City Of Industry CA 91748 626-956-1100
Web: www.dtechopto.com

Dairyland Laboratories Inc 217 E Main St .... Arcadia WI 54612 608-323-2123
Web: www.dairylandlabs.net

Dako Colorado Inc 4850 Innovation Dr .... Fort Collins CO 80525 970-226-2200
Web: www.dakocytomation.com

DALSA Corp 605 McMurray Rd .... Waterloo ON N2V2E9 519-886-6000
Web: www.dalsa.com.

Daniel B Stephens & Assoc Inc
6020 Academy Ne Ste 100 .... Albuquerque NM 87109 505-822-9400
Web: www.dbstephens.com

Davinci Biosciences LLC 1239 victoria st .... Costa mesa CA 92627 949-515-2828
Web: www.dvbiologics.com

Dayton T Brown Inc 1175 Church St .... Bohemia NY 11716 631-589-6300 589-0046
TF: 800-232-6300 ■ *Web:* www.dtb.com

DDL Inc 10200 Vly View Rd Ste 101 .... Eden Prairie MN 55344 952-941-9226
Web: www.testedandproven.com

DHL Analytical 2300 Double Creek Dr .... Round Rock TX 78664 512-388-8222
Web: www.dhlanalytical.com

Diw Group Inc Dba Specialized Engineering
4845 International Blvd .... Frederick MD 21703 301-607-4180

Dominion Diagnostics LLC
211 Circuit Dr .... North Kingstown RI 02852 401-667-0800
Web: dominiondiagnostics.com

DRG International Inc 841 Mountain Ave .... Springfield NJ 07081 973-564-7555
Web: www.drg-international.com

Phone Fax

Dugway Proving Ground 5124 Kister Ave .... Dugway UT 84022 435-831-2178
Web: www.dugway.army.mil

DyAnsys Inc 577 Airport Blvd Ste 610 .... Burlingame CA 94010 321-276-1070
Web: www.dyansys.com

Dyna Flex Ltd PO Box 99 .... Saint Ann MO 63074 314-426-4020
Web: www.dynaflex.com

E Pi Bio Analytical 9095 W Harristown Blvd .... Niantic IL 62551 217-963-2143
TF: 866-963-2143 ■ *Web:* www.eplbas.com

Eastern Analytical Inc 25 chenell dr .... Concord NH 03301 603-228-0525
Web: easternanalytical.com

Eccs Nationwide Mobile Laboratories
2525 Advance Rd .... Madison WI 53718 608-221-8700
Web: www.eccsmobilelab.com

Edward S Babcock & Sons Inc
6100 Quail Vly Ct .... Riverside CA 92507 951-653-3351
Web: www.babcocklabs.com

Elektro Assemblies Inc 522 NW Sixth Ave .... Rochester MN 55901 507-288-9308
Web: elektroassemblies.com

Element Materials Technology
5405 E Schaaf Rd .... Cleveland OH 44131 216-524-1450 524-1459
Web: www.element.com

Ellis & Associates Inc
7064 Davis Creek Rd .... Jacksonville FL 32256 904-880-0960
TF: 800-273-0960 ■ *Web:* www.ellisassoc.com

Embryotech Laboratories Inc 140 Hale St .... Haverhill MA 01830 978-373-7300
TF: 800-673-7500 ■ *Web:* www.embryotech.com

Empirical Testing Corp
4628 Northpark Dr .... Colorado Springs CO 80918 719-264-9937
Web: empiricaltech.com

ENCO Laboratories Inc 10775 Central Port Dr .... Orlando FL 32824 407-826-5314
Web: encolabs.com

Endotronix Inc
1005 Internationale Pkwy Ste 104 .... Woodridge IL 60517 877-363-6879
TF: 877-363-6879 ■ *Web:* www.endotronix.com

Energy Laboratories Inc
2393 Old Salt Creek Rd .... Casper WY 82601 307-995-3200
Web: solarenergy.com

eNeura Therapeutics LLC
715 North Pastoria Ave .... Sunnyvale CA 94085 408-245-6400
Web: www.eneura.com

Engineering Dynamics Inc
3925 S Kalamath St .... Englewood CO 80110 303-761-4367
Web: www.engdynamics.com

Enthalpy Analytical Inc 800-1 Capitola Dr .... Durham NC 27713 919-850-4392
Web: www.enthalpy.com

EnviroLogix Inc
500 Riverside Industrial Pkwy .... Portland ME 04103 207-797-0300
TF: 866-408-4597 ■ *Web:* www.envirologix.com

Environ Laboratories LLC
9725 Girard Ave S .... Minneapolis MN 55431 952-888-7795
Web: environlab.com

Environmental Enterprises Inc (EEI)
10163 Cincinnati Dayton Rd .... Cincinnati OH 45241 513-772-2818
TF: 800-722-2818 ■ *Web:* www.eeienv.com

Ettl Engineers & Consultants Inc
1717 E Erwin St .... Tyler TX 75702 903-595-4421
Web: www.ettlinc.com

Eurofins Product Safety Labs Inc
2394 Hwy 130 Ste E .... Dayton NJ 08810 732-438-5100
Web: www.productsafetylabs.com

Evans Analytical Group 810 Kifer Rd .... Sunnyvale CA 94086 408-530-3500 530-3501
Web: www.eag.com

Evena Medical Inc
339 S San Antonio Rd Ste 1C .... Los Altos CA 94022 650-209-0398
Web: www.evenamed.com

Everist Genomics Inc 709 W Ellsworth Rd .... Ann Arbor MI 48108 855-383-7478
TF: 855-383-7478 ■ *Web:* www.everisthealth.com

Evogen Inc 10513 W 84th Ter .... Lenexa KS 66214 913-948-5640
Web: www.evogen.com

Excalibre Engineering 9201 Irvine Blvd .... Irvine CA 92618 949-454-6603
TF: 877-922-5427 ■ *Web:* www.excaliburengineering.com

EyeMarker Systems Inc
886 Chestnut Ridge Rd 6th Fl .... Morgantown WV 26506 304-598-1101
Web: www.eyemarkersystems.com

Falcon Genomics Inc
2661 Clearview Rd Ste 1 .... Allison Park PA 15101 412-486-1108
Web: www.falcongenomics.com

Fenway Community Health Center Inc
1340 Boylston St .... Boston MA 02215 617-859-1256
Web: www.fenwayhealth.org

Forensic Fluids Laboratories Inc
225 Parsons St .... Kalamazoo MI 49007 269-492-7700
TF: 866-492-2517 ■ *Web:* www.forensicfluids.com

Forensic It 57 E Southcrest Cir .... Edwardsville IL 62025 314-677-3950
TF: 877-483-3284 ■ *Web:* www.forensicit.us

Freedom Meditech Inc
5090 Shoreham Pl Ste 109 .... San Diego CA 92122 858-638-1433
Web: www.freedom-meditech.com

Froehling & Robertson Inc 3015 Dumbarton Rd .... Richmond VA 23228 804-264-2701 264-1202
Web: www.fandr.com

Frontage Laboratories LLC 700 Pennsylvania Dr .... Exton PA 19341 610-232-0100
Web: www.frontagelab.com

Frontier Geosciences Inc
414 Pontius Ave N Ste B .... Seattle WA 98109 206-622-6960
Web: www.frontiergs.com

Fruit Growers Laboratory Inc
853 Corporation St .... Santa Paula CA 93060 805-392-2000
Web: www.fglinc.com

Future Path Medical Holding Company LLC
7757 Auburn Rd Ste 21 .... Concord OH 44077 440-354-4044
Web: www.future-path.net

G & R Labs 2996 scott blvd .... Santa Clara CA 95054 408-986-0377
Web: www.grlabs.com

Name / Address	City	State	ZIP	Phone	Fax
Galbraith Laboratories Inc 2323 Sycamore Dr *Web:* www.galbraith.com	Knoxville	TN	37921	865-546-1335	
Galson Laboratories Inc 6601 Kirkville Rd *Web:* www.galsonlabs.com	East Syracuse	NY	13057	315-432-5227	
Gamma Medica Inc 12 Manor Pkwy Unit 3 *Web:* www.gammamedica.com	Salem	NH	03079	603-952-4441	
GE Healthcare Bio-Sciences Corp 800 Centennial Ave *Web:* www.gelifesciences.com	Piscataway	NJ	08855	732-457-8000	
GenePOC Inc 360 Rue Franquet Porte 3 Technology Park *Web:* www.genepoc-diagnostics.com	Quebec	QC	G1P4N3	418-650-3535	
General Genetics Corp MSC3ARP, Box 30001 3655 Research Dr *Web:* www.ggcdna.com	Las Cruces	NM	88003	575-646-7850	
Geneva Laboratories Inc 1001 Proctor Dr *Web:* www.genevalabs.com	Elkhorn	WI	53121	262-723-5669	
Genmab Inc 902 Carnegie Ctr Ste 301 *Web:* www.genmab.com	Princeton	NJ	08540	609-430-2481	
Genome Diagnostics Inc 80 S Lk Ave Ste 680 *Web:* genomedx.com	Pasadena	CA	91101	626-529-0516	
Glidewell Laboratories Inc 4141 MacArthur Blvd *TF:* 800-854-7256 ■ *Web:* www.glidewelldental.com	Newport Beach	CA	92660	800-854-7256	
Global ID Group 504 N Fourth St *Web:* www.global-id-group.com	Fairfield	IA	52556	641-472-9979	
Global X-Ray & Testing Corp PO Box 1536 *Web:* www.globalxray.com	Morgan City	LA	70381	985-631-2426	
Glytec LLC 770 Pelham Rd Ste 210 *Web:* www.glytecsystems.com	Greenville	SC	29615	864-370-3297	
Groupe PARIMA Inc 4450 Cousens Rue *Web:* groupeparima.com	Montreal	QC	H4S1X6	514-338-3780	
GVI Medical Devices Corp 1470 Enterprise Pkwy *Web:* www.gvimd.com	Twinsburg	OH	44087	330-963-4083	
H&H X-Ray Services Inc 104 Enterprise St *Web:* www.hhxray.com	West Monroe	LA	71292	318-949-4349	
H.P. White Laboratory Inc 3114 Scarboro Rd *Web:* www.hpwhite.com	Street	MD	21154	410-838-6550	
H2m Labs Inc 575 Broadhollow Rd *Web:* www.h2mlabs.com	Melville	NY	11747	631-694-3040	
Hawk Mountain Lab Inc 201 W Clay Ave *Web:* hawkmtnlabs.com	Hazle Township	PA	18202	570-455-6011	
Health-Chem Diagnostics LLC 3341 SW 15th St *Web:* www.healthchemdiagnostics.com	Pompano Beach	FL	33069	954-979-3845	
Healthsense Inc 1191 Northland Dr Ste 100 *Web:* www.healthsense.com	Mendota Heights	MN	55120	952-400-7300	
Helixis Inc 5421 Avenida Encinas Ste B *Web:* support.illumina.com	Carlsbad	CA	92008	760-688-0104	
Heron Systems Inc 20945 Great Mills Rd Ste 201 *Web:* www.heronsystems.com	Lexington Park	MD	20653	301-866-0330	
HNP Pharmaceuticals 381 Van Ness Ave Ste 1507 *Web:* www.hnppharmaceuticals.com	Torrance	CA	90501	310-783-7450	
Hoffman Engineering Corp PO Box 4430 *Web:* www.hoffmanengineering.com	Stamford	CT	06907	203-425-8900	425-8910
HORIBA ABX Diagnostics Inc 34 Bunsen Dr *Web:* eurofex.horiba.com	Irvine	CA	92618	949-453-0500	
Huffman Laboratories Inc 4630 Indiana St *TF:* 877-886-6225 ■ *Web:* www.huffmanlabs.com	Golden	CO	80403	303-278-4455	
Huron Technologies International Inc 550 Parkside Dr Unit B6 *Web:* www.hurondigitalpathology.com	Waterloo	ON	N2L5V4	519-886-9013	
Hydro-Photon Inc 262 Ellsworth Rd *Web:* www.steripen.com	Blue Hill	ME	04614	207-374-5800	
Hydro-stat Inc 1111 Sw First Way *Web:* www.hydrostat.com	Deerfield Beach	FL	33441	954-428-7677	
Hydrox Laboratories Inc 825 Tollgate Rd *Web:* www.hydroxlabs.com	Elgin	IL	60123	847-468-9400	
HyGreen Inc 3630 SW 47th Ave Ste 100 *TF:* 877-574-9473 ■ *Web:* hygreen.com	Gainesville	FL	32608	877-574-9473	
iHealth Lab Inc 719 N Shoreline Blvd *TF:* 855-816-7705 ■ *Web:* www.ihealthlabs.com	Mountain View	CA	94043	855-816-7705	
Ikonisys Inc 5 Science Park *TF:* 866-456-6832 ■ *Web:* www.ikonisys.com	New Haven	CT	06511	203-776-0791	
Immuno Concepts NA Ltd 9825 Goethe Rd Ste 350 *TF:* 800-251-5115 ■ *Web:* www.immunoconcepts.com	Sacramento	CA	95827	916-363-2649	
Impulse Devices Inc 12731A Loma Rica Dr *Web:* www.burstenergies.com	Grass Valley	CA	95945	530-913-9753	
Indyne Inc 11800 Sunrise Vly Dr Ste 250 *Web:* www.indyneinc.com	Reston	VA	20191	703-903-6900	903-4997
InformationWEEK Labs 600 Community Dr *Web:* www.informationweek.com	Manhasset	NY	11030	516-562-5000	562-5036
InforMedix Holdings Inc Georgetowne Park 5880 Hubbard Dr *Web:* www.informedix.com	Rockville	MD	20852	301-984-1566	
Inovatia Laboratories LLC 120 E Davis St *TF:* 800-280-1912 ■ *Web:* inovatia.com	Fayette	MO	65248	660-248-1911	
Insero Health Inc 1951 NW 7th Ave 3rd Fl Rm 13140 *Web:* insero.co	Miami	FL	33136	786-300-4600	
Insight Service 20338 Progress Dr *Web:* www.testoil.com	Strongsville	OH	44149	216-251-2510	
Integrated BioTherapeutics Inc 21 Firstfield Rd Ste 100 *Web:* www.integratedbiotherapeutics.com	Gaithersburg	MD	20878	240-454-8934	
InterCorr International Inc 14503 Bammel N Houston Ste 300 *Web:* www.intercorr.com	Houston	TX	77014	281-444-2282	
International Down & Feather Testing Laboratory 1455 S 1100 E *Web:* www.idfl.com	Salt Lake City	UT	84105	801-467-7611	467-7711
Intertek Automotive Research 5404 Bandera Rd *Web:* intertek.com/petroleum	San Antonio	TX	78238	210-684-2310	684-6074
Introtek International LP 150 Executive Dr *Web:* www.introtek.com	Edgewood	NY	11717	631-242-5425	
Iris Diagnostics Inc 9172 Eton Ave	Chatsworth	CA	91311	818-527-7000	
iScreen Vision Inc 110 Timber Creek Dr Ste 2 *Web:* www.iscreenvision.com	Cordova	TN	38018	901-201-6132	
Isotech Laboratories Inc 1308 Parkland Ct *Web:* www.isotechlabs.com	Champaign	IL	61821	217-398-3490	
ITEL Laboratories Inc 6745 Philips Industrial Blvd *Web:* www.itelinc.com	Jacksonville	FL	32256	904-363-0196	
IVDiagnostics Inc 9800 Connecticut Dr *Web:* www.ivdiagnostics.com	Crown Point	IN	46307	219-840-0007	
JANX Integrity Group Inc 8500 E Michigan Ave *Web:* www.janx.net	Parma	MI	49269	517-531-8210	
JDP Therapeutics Inc 823 Jays Dr *Web:* www.jdptherapeutics.com	Lansdale	PA	19446	215-661-8557	
JM Test Systems Inc 7323 Tom Dr *TF:* 800-353-3411 ■ *Web:* www.jmtest.com	Baton Rouge	LA	70806	225-925-2029	
Kanomax Usa 250 W 57th St Ste 816 *Web:* kanomax-usa.com	New York	NY	10107	212-489-3755	
Kar Laboratories Inc 4425 Manchester Rd *Web:* karlabs.com	Kalamazoo	MI	49001	269-381-9666	
Kett Engineering Corp 15500 Erwin St Ste 1029 *TF:* 877-372-6799 ■ *Web:* www.ketteng.com	Van Nuys	CA	91411	818-908-5388	908-5323
Keweenaw Research Ctr Michigan Technological University 1400 Townsend Dr *Web:* www.mtukrc.org	Houghton	MI	49931	906-487-1885	487-2202
Kineticorp 3955 E Exposition Ave *Web:* www.kineticorp.com	Denver	CO	80209	303-733-1888	
Koehler Instrument Company Inc 1595 Sycamore Ave *Web:* www.koehlerinstrument.com	Bohemia	NY	11716	631-589-3800	
L&g Engineering Laboratory LLC 2100 W Expressway 83 *TF:* 888-565-9813 ■ *Web:* www.lgengineers.com	Mercedes	TX	78570	956-565-9813	
Labstat International ULC 262 Manitou Dr *Web:* www.labstat.com	Kitchener	ON	N2C1L3	519-748-5409	
Laclede Inc 2103 E University Dr *Web:* www.laclede.com	Rancho Dominguez	CA	90220	310-605-4280	
Lambda Technologies 3929 Virginia Ave *Web:* www.lambdatechs.com	Cincinnati	OH	45227	513-561-0883	
Lancaster Laboratories Inc 2425 New Holland Pk PO Box 12425 *Web:* www.lancasterlabs.com	Lancaster	PA	17605	717-656-2300	656-2681
Lark Technologies Inc 9441 W Sam Houston Pkwy S Ste 103 *Web:* www.lark.com	Houston	TX	77099	713-779-3663	
LaserGen Inc 8052 El Rio St *Web:* www.lasergen.com	Houston	TX	77054	713-747-3380	
Laucks Testing Laboratories Inc 940 S Harney St *Web:* pacelabs.com	Seattle	WA	98108	206-767-5060	767-5063
Lavipharm Laboratories Inc 69 Princeton - Hightstown Rd *Web:* www.lavipharm.com	East Windsor	NJ	08529	609-371-6500	
Ledoux & Company Inc 359 Alfred Ave *Web:* www.ledoux.com	Teaneck	NJ	07666	201-837-7160	837-1235
Leica Microsystems Inc 1700 Leider Ln *Web:* www.leica-microsystems.com/contact/service	Buffalo Grove	IL	60089	847-405-0123	
Life Medical Technologies Inc 3 Forest View Dr Hopewell Jct *Web:* www.lifemt.com	East Fishkill	NY	12533	845-896-1230	
Lumed Science Inc 375 S Logan St *Web:* www.lumedscience.com	Denver	CO	80209	303-775-3762	
MagiQ Technologies Inc 11 Ward St *Web:* www.magiqtech.com	Somerville	MA	02143	617-661-8300	
Magna Chek Inc 32701 Edward Ave *TF:* 800-582-8947 ■ *Web:* www.magnachek.com	Madison Heights	MI	48071	248-597-0089	597-0440
Magnetic Inspection Laboratory Inc 1401 Greenleaf Ave *Web:* www.milinc.com	Elk Grove Village	IL	60007	847-437-4488	437-4538
Matech Advanced Materials Inc 31304 Via Colinas Ste 102 *Web:* www.matech.us	Westlake Village	CA	91362	818-991-8500	
Materials Engineer & Testing 125 Valley Ct *Web:* www.meandt.com	Oak Ridge	TN	37830	865-482-7762	
Maxwell Sensors Inc 10020 Pioneer Blvd Ste 103 *Web:* www.maxwellsensors.com	Santa Fe Springs	CA	90670	562-801-2088	
Mayer Laboratories Inc 1950 Addison St Ste 101 *Web:* www.mayerlabs.com	Berkeley	CA	94704	510-229-5300	
Mccloy Engineering LLC 3701 Port Union Rd *Web:* www.accutektesting.com	Fairfield	OH	45014	513-984-4112	
MEC Dynamics Corp 90 Rose Orchard Way *Web:* www.mecdynamics.com	San Jose	CA	95134	408-428-9427	
Medelis Inc 5870 FLwring Sage Ct Ste 200 *Web:* www.medelis.com	Reno	NV	89511	775-851-9460	
Medpace Medical Device Inc 3787 95th Ave NE Ste 100 *Web:* www.medpace.com	Minneapolis	MN	55014	612-234-8500	

Phone Fax

Metcut Research Inc 3980 Rosslyn Dr . . . . Cincinnati OH 45209 513-271-5100 271-9511
TF: 877-847-1985 ■ Web: www.metcut.com

Michelson Laboratories Inc 6280 Chalet Dr . . . . .Commerce CA 90040 562-928-0553
Web: michelsonlab.com

Micro Precision Calibration Inc
22835 Industrial Pl. . . . . Grass Valley CA 95949 530-268-1860
Web: www.microprecision.com

Micro-Clean Inc 177 N Commerce Way . . . . .Bethlehem PA 18017 610-867-5302
TF: 800-523-9852 ■ Web: www.microcln.com

Microbac Laboratories Inc
101 Bellevue Rd Ste 301. . . . . Pittsburgh PA 15229 412-459-1060
Web: microbac.com

Microbial Insights Inc
2340 Stock Creek Blvd. . . . . Rockford TN 37853 865-573-8188
Web: www.microbe.com

MicroFluidic Systems 1252 Quarry Ln Ste B. . . . . .Pleasanton CA 94566 510-354-0400

Micronics Inc 8463 154th Ave NE Bldg G . . . . .Redmond WA 98052 425-895-9197
Web: micronics.net

Midwest Institute For Clinical Research Inc
8803 N Meridian St . . . . .Indianapolis IN 46260 317-705-7050
Web: micr.com

Midwest Laboratories Inc 13611 B St . . . . .Omaha NE 68144 402-334-7770
Web: www.midwestlabs.com

Miltenyi Biotec Inc 2303 Lindbergh St. . . . . Auburn CA 95602 530-888-8871
Web: www.miltenyibiotec.com

mImage Inc, The 1194 West 4800 South . . . . Salt Lake City UT 84127 801-207-8281
Web: www.thermimage.com

Mineral Labs Inc 309 Pkwy Dr . . . . Salyersville KY 41465 606-349-6145
Web: minerallabs.com

Mira Vista Diagnostics LLC
4444 Decatur Blvd Ste 300. . . . . .Indianapolis IN 46241 317-856-2681
Web: www.miravistalabs.com

Modern Industries Inc 613 W 11th St . . . . Erie PA 16501 814-455-8061 453-4382
Web: modernind.com

Molecular Sciences Institute
2168 Shattuck Ave . . . . .Berkeley CA 94704 510-647-0690
Web: www.molsci.org

Morgan Schaffer Systems Inc
8300, rue Saint-Patrick Bureau 150 LaSalle . . . . Montreal QC H8N2H1 514-739-1967
Web: www.morganschaffer.com

Morphotek Inc 210 Welsh Pool Rd . . . . .Exton PA 19341 610-423-6100
Web: www.morphotek.com

Morse Laboratories LLC 1525 Fulton Ave . . . . .Sacramento CA 95825 916-481-3141
Web: morselabs.com

Mountain Research LLC 825 25th St. . . . . Altoona PA 16601 814-949-2034
TF: 800-837-4674 ■ Web: www.mountainresearch.com

MSE Technology Applications Inc
200 Technology Way . . . . Butte MT 59701 406-494-7100 494-7230
Web: www.mse-ta.com

Nanolab Technologies Inc 1708 McCarthy Blvd. . . . . . . .Milpitas CA 95035 408-433-3320
Web: www.nanolabtechnologies.com

Nanotechnology Research & Education Ctr
University of S Florida College of Engineering
4202 E Fowler Ave ENB 118. . . . . .Tampa FL 33620 813-974-3780 974-3610
Web: www.nrec.usf.edu

National Air & Radiation Environmental Laboratory (NAREL)
US Environmental Protection Agency
540 S Morris Ave . . . . Montgomery AL 36115 334-270-3400 270-3454
Web: www.epa.gov

National Technical Systems Inc
24007 Ventura Blvd Ste 200. . . . . Calabasas CA 91302 818-591-0776 591-0899
NASDAQ: NTSC ■ TF: 800-879-9225 ■ Web: www.nts.com

National X-Ray Corp 2310 S Dock Str Ste 110. . . . . Palmetto Fl 34221? 941-870-3069

NDS Surgical Imaging LLC 5750 Hellyer Ave . . . . San Jose CA 95138 408-776-0085
Web: www.ndssi.com

Neotropix Inc 351 Phoenixville Pk. . . . . .Malvern PA 19355 610-296-8660
Web: www.neotropix.com

Neuisys LLC 1500 Pinecroft Rd Ste 212 . . . . Greensboro NC 27407 877-299-9052
TF: 877-299-9052 ■ Web: www.neuisys.com

Neuro Diagnostic Devices Inc
3701 Market St 3rd Fl. . . . . Philadelphia PA 19104 215-966-6207
Web: www.neurodiagnosticdevices.com

Neuronetrix Inc 1044 E Chestnut St . . . . .Louisville KY 40204 502-561-9040
Web: www.neuronetrix.com

NeuroVigil Inc 7606 Fay Ave . . . . La Jolla CA 92037 858-454-5134
Web: www.neurovigil.com

Newport Partners LLC
3760 Tanglewood Ln . . . . .Davidsonville MD 21035 301-889-0017
TF: 866-302-0017 ■ Web: newportpartnersllc.com

Next Breath LLC 1450 S Rolling Rd . . . . .Baltimore MD 21227 410-455-5904
Web: www.nextbreath.net

Nikkiso Cryo Inc 4661 Eaker St. . . . . North Las Vegas NV 89081 702-643-4900
Web: nikkisocryo.com

Norchem Drug Testing Laboratory
1760 E Route 66 . . . . .Flagstaff AZ 86004 928-526-1011
TF: 844-284-1843 ■ Web: www.norchemlab.com

Northwest Aerospace Technologies Inc
2210 Hewitt Ave Ste 300. . . . . .Everett WA 98201 425-257-2044

Northwest Labs of Seattle 241 S Holden St. . . . . Seattle WA 98108 206-763-6252 763-3949
Web: www.nwlabs1896.com

Norwich Clinical Research Associates Ltd
74 E Main St. . . . . .Norwich NY 13815 607-334-5850
Web: www.ncra.com

Norwich Pharma Services 6826 State Hwy 12. . . . . .Norwich NY 13815 607-335-3000
Web: www.norwichpharma.com

Nova Biologicals Inc 1775 N Loop 336 Ste 4 . . . . Conroe TX 77301 936-756-5333
Web: www.novatx.com

NOVX Systems Inc 9133 Leslie St Ste 110. . . . . Richmond Hill ON L4B4N1 905-474-5051
TF: 877-879-6689 ■ Web: www.novxsystems.com

Nsl Analytical 4450 Cranwood Pkwy . . . . Cleveland OH 44128 216-447-1550
TF: 877-560-3943 ■ Web: www.nslanalytical.com

NU Laboratories Inc 312 Old Allerton Rd. . . . . Annandale NJ 08801 908-713-9300 713-9001
Web: www.nulabs.com

Phone Fax

NutriCorp International 4025 Rhodes Dr. . . . . .Windsor ON N8W5B5 888-446-8874
TF: 888-446-8874 ■ Web: www.nutricorp.com

NuView Life Sciences Inc
1389 Center Dr Ste 250 . . . . Park City UT 84098 888-902-7779
TF: 888-902-7779 ■ Web: www.nuviewinfo.com

Octapharma Plasma Inc 10644 Westlake Dr. . . . . Charlotte NC 28273 704-654-4600
Web: octapharmaplasma.com

Ok Kosher Certification 391 Troy Ave . . . . Brooklyn NY 11213 718-756-7500
Web: www.ok.org

On-Q-ity Inc 610 Lincoln St N Bldg 3rd Fl. . . . . Waltham MA 02451 781-895-8100
Web: www.On-Q-ity.com

Oncoscope Inc 324 Blackwell St Ste 1120 . . . . Durham NC 27701 919-251-8030
Web: www.oncoscope.com

Ornim Inc 23462 Thornewood Dr . . . . Santa Clarita CA 91321 661-310-0240
Web: www.ornim.com

Pacific States Marine Fisheries Commissi
205 SE Spokane St Ste 100 . . . . .Portland OR 97202 503-650-5400
Web: www.psmfc.org

Parabase Genomics Inc
100 Morrissey Blvd University of Massachusetts Venture Development Ctr Wheatley Hall
3rd Fl . . . . .Boston MA 02125 857-288-0838
Web: www.parabasegenomics.com

Passport Systems Inc
70 Treble Cove Rd 1st Fl . . . . .Billerica MA 01862 978-263-9900
Web: www.passportsystems.com

PCAS-Nanosyn LLC 3331 - B Industrial Dr . . . . Santa Rosa CA 95403 707-526-4526
Web: nanosyn.com

Perritt Laboratories Inc
145 S Main St PO Box 147. . . . . Hightstown NJ 08520 609-443-4848
Web: www.childsafepackaginggroup.com

Pharmout Laboratories Inc 1151 Sonora Ct. . . . . Sunnyvale CA 94086 408-481-3090
Web: www.pharmoutlabs.net

Phenova Inc 6390 Joyce Dr Ste 100 . . . . .Golden CO 80403 303-940-0033
Web: www.phenova.com

Phoenix Environmental Laboratories Inc
587 Middle Tpke E . . . . Manchester CT 06040 860-645-3513
Web: www.phoenixlabs.com

Pikes Peak Test Labs Inc
4750 Edison Ave. . . . . Colorado Springs CO 80915 719-596-0802
Web: www.pptli.com

Pipette Calibration Services Inc
81 Deborah Rd . . . . Newton MA 02459 617-964-0039
Web: www.pipettecal.com

PMRS Inc 202 Precision Rd. . . . . Horsham PA 19044 267-960-3300
Web: www.pmrsinc.com

PPD Development Inc 929 N Front St. . . . . Wilmington NC 28401 910-251-0081 762-5820
Web: www.ppdi.com

Premier Integrity Solutions Inc
7 Jamestown St . . . . .Russell Springs KY 42642 270-866-3144
Web: www.premierintegrity.com

PreventionGenetics LLC 3700 Downwind Dr. . . . . Marshfield WI 54449 715-387-0484
Web: www.preventiongenetics.com

Prezacor Inc 170 Cold Soil Rd . . . . .Princeton NJ 08540 609-896-1122
Web: prezacor.com

Pria Diagnostics LLC 3475 Edison Way Ste F. . . . . Menlo Park CA 94025 650-298-9777
Web: www.priadiagnostics.com

Product Evaluation Systems Inc
637 Donohoe Rd. . . . . Latrobe PA 15650 724-834-8848
Web: www.productevaluationsystems.com

Provista Diagnostics Inc
17301 N Perimeter Dr. . . . . Scottsdale AZ 85255 855-552-7439
TF: 855-552-7439 ■ Web: www.provistadx.com

PTS Laboratories 8100 Secura Way. . . . . .Santa Fe Springs CA 90670 562-907-3607
Web: www.ptslabs.com

QC Laboratories Inc 10810 Northwest Fwy. . . . . .Houston TX 77092 713-472-8378
Web: www.qclabs.com

Quadrants Scientific Inc
10840 Thornmint Rd Ste 110 . . . . San Diego CA 92127 858-618-4708
Web: www.quadscience.com

Qualtech Laboratories Inc 104 Green Grove Rd . . . . Ocean NJ 07712 732-918-0207
Web: www.qualtechlabsinc.com

Quanta Laboratories 3199 De La Cruz Blvd . . . . Santa Clara CA 95054 408-988-0770
Web: www.quantalabs.com

Quantex Laboratories 22 Distribution Blvd . . . . .Edison NJ 08817 732-248-3335
Web: www.quantexlabs.com

Quantum Laboratories Inc 28221 Beck Rd Ste A-11. . . . . .Wixom MI 48393 248-348-8378
Web: www.quantumlaboratories.com

Radiometrics Midwest Corp 12 E Devonwood. . . . . . Romeoville IL 60446 815-293-0772 293-0820
Web: www.radiomet.com

Red Rock Research Ctr
5701 W Charleston Blvd Ste 100 . . . . Las Vegas NV 89146 702-602-6839
Web: www.redrockmedical.com

Redwood Toxicology Laboratory Inc
3650 W Wind Blvd . . . . Santa Rosa CA 95403 707-577-7959
Web: www.redwoodtoxicology.com

Resuscitation International LLC
17797 N Perimeter Dr Ste 105 . . . . Scottsdale AZ 85255 480-240-9495
Web: resusintl.com

Retlif Inc Testing Laboratories
795 Marconi Ave . . . . .Ronkonkoma NY 11779 631-737-1500 737-1497
Web: www.retlif.com

RMC Research Corp 1000 Market St Bldg 2 . . . . Portsmouth NH 03801 603-422-8888
Web: www.rmcresearchcorporation.com

Rndt Inc Nondestructive Testing & Research Services
228 Maple Ave . . . . .Johnstown PA 15901 814-535-5448
Web: www.rndt.net

Robin Hood Foundation 826 Broadway 9th Fl . . . . .New York NY 10003 212-227-6601
Web: www.robinhood.org

Rothe Development Inc 4614 Sinclair Rd . . . . .San Antonio TX 78222 210-648-3131
Web: www.rothe.com

Sanford Consortium For Regenerative Medicine
2880 torrey pines scenic dr . . . . La jolla CA 92037 858-246-1071
Web: www.sanfordconsortium.org

Phone Fax

Schneider Laboratories Inc 2512 W Cary St Richmond VA 23220 804-353-6778
TF: 800-785-5227 ■ *Web:* slabinc.com
Scion Medical Technologies LLC 90 Oak St Newton MA 02464 888-582-6211
TF: 888-582-6211 ■ *Web:* www.scionmedtech.com
SDK Laboratories 1000 Corey Rd Hutchinson KS 67501 620-665-5661
Web: www.sdklabs.com
Selerity Technologies Inc
1950 South 900 West Ste S3 Salt Lake City UT 84104 801-978-2295
Web: www.selerity.com
Sensiotec Inc
Georgia Tech Venture Ctr 75 5th St NW
Ste 348 Atlanta GA 30308 404-526-6236
Web: www.sensiotec.com
Sentinel Integrity Solutions Inc
6606 Miller Rd 2 Houston TX 77049 281-457-2225
Web: sentinelintegrity.com
SGS Canada Inc 6490 Vipond Dr Mississauga ON L5T1W8 905-364-3757 364-0344
TF General: 877-747-7658 ■ *Web:* www.sgs.ca
SGS US Testing Company Inc
291 Fairfield Ave Fairfield NJ 07004 973-575-5252 575-7175
Web: www.sgsgroup.us.com
SHINE Medical Technologies Inc
2555 Industrial Dr Ste 140 Monona WI 53713 608-210-1060
Web: shinemed.com
Shuster Laboratories Inc 85 John Rd Canton MA 02021 781-821-2200
Web: www.shusterlabs.com
Siamab Therapeutics Inc 1396 Poinsettia Ave Vista CA 92081 858-623-0276
Web: www.siamab.com
Sigma Test Labs 1480 W 178th St Gardena CA 90248 310-324-9427 532-6216
Web: www.sigmatestlabs.com
Simco Electronics 1178 Bordeaux Dr Sunnyvale CA 94089 408-734-9750 734-9754
TF: 866-299-6029 ■ *Web:* www.simco.com
Sky Cylinder Testing 2220 Lexington Rd Evansville IN 47720 812-423-1759
Web: www.skycylinder.com
Smithers Group Inc, The 425 W Market St Akron OH 44303 330-762-7441
Web: smithers.com
Sonivate Medical Inc
8305 SW Creekside Pl Ste C Beaverton OR 97008 503-616-4357
Web: sonivate.com
Sonoscan Inc 2149 Pratt Blvd Elk Grove Village IL 60007 847-437-6400 437-1550
Web: www.sonoscan.com
Southern Petroleum Lab Inc
8850 Interchange Dr Houston TX 77054 713-660-0901 219-3309*
**Fax Area Code:* 225 ■ *TF:* 877-775-5227 ■ *Web:* www.spl-inc.com
SOV Therapeutics Inc 101 Guymon Ct Morrisville NC 27560 919-601-2208
Web: www.sovtherapeutics.com
Spectrasonics Inc 440 Woodcrest Rd Ste 310 Wayne PA 19087 610-964-0713
Web: www.spectrasonics.com
Spectrum Analytical Inc 830 Silver St Agawam MA 01001 413-789-9018 789-4076
TF: 800-789-9115 ■ *Web:* www.spectrum-analytical.com
Speedie & Assoc Inc 3331 E Wood St Phoenix AZ 85040 602-997-6391 943-5508
TF: 800-628-6221 ■ *Web:* www.speedie.net
SRS Medical Systems Inc
76 Treble Cove Rd Bldg 3 North Billerica MA 01862 978-663-2800
Web: www.srsmedical.com
St. Louis Testing Laboratories
2810 Clark Ave Saint Louis MO 63103 314-531-8080 531-8085
Web: www.labinc.com
Standard Laboratories Inc
147 11th Ave Ste 100 South Charleston WV 25303 304-744-6800
Web: standardlabs.com
Stimwave Technologies Inc
901 E Las Olas Blvd Ste 201 Fort Lauderdale FL 33301 786-565-3342
TF: 800-965-5134 ■ *Web:* stimwave.com
Summers Laboratories Inc
103 Gp Clement Dr Collegeville PA 19426 610-454-1471
Web: www.sumlab.com
Sun Ten Laboratories Inc 9250 Jeronimo Rd Irvine CA 92618 949-587-0509
Web: www.sunten.com
Syagen Technology Inc 1411 Warner Ave Tustin CA 92780 714-258-4400
TF: 877-258-8250 ■ *Web:* www.syagen.com
Synergy Environmental Lab Inc
1990 Prospect Ct Appleton WI 54914 920-830-2455
Web: synergy-lab.net
TecMed Inc 1603 Capitol Ave Ste 209 Cheyenne WY 82001 307-509-9653
Web: tecmed.com
Tension Member Technology
5721 Research Dr Huntington Beach CA 92649 714-898-5641
Web: www.tmtlabs.com
Terra Tek Inc 5599 San Felipe 17th Fl Houston TX 77056 713-375-3535
Web: www.slb.com
Test Devices Inc 571 Main St Hudson MA 01749 978-562-6017
Web: www.testdevices.com
Test Inc 2323 4th St Peru IL 61354 815-224-1650
Web: testinc.com/
TestAmerica Laboratories Inc
4625 E Cotton Ctr Blvd Ste 189 Phoenix AZ 85040 602-437-3340 454-9303
TF: 866-785-5227 ■ *Web:* www.testamericainc.com
Testcountry 6310 Nancy Ridge Dr Ste 103 San Diego CA 92121 858-784-6904
TF: 866-237-7976 ■ *Web:* www.testcountry.com
TGR Industrial Services
8777 Tallyho Rd Bldg 1 Houston TX 77061 281-487-8800
Web: www.tulsagammaray.com
Therapeutic Monitoring Services LLC
134 LaSalle St Ste 4 New Orleans LA 70112 504-208-9696
Web: www.tmsbioscience.com
Thornton Laboratories Testing & Inspection Services
1145 E Cass St Tampa FL 33602 813-223-9702 223-9332
Web: www.thorntonlab.com
Thought Technology Ltd 2180 Belgrave Ave Montreal QC H4A2L8 514-489-8251
TF: 800-361-3651 ■ *Web:* www.thoughttechnology.com

Phone Fax

Tourney Consulting Group LLC
3401 Midlink Dr Kalamazoo MI 49048 269-384-9980
Web: tourneyconsulting.com
Toxikon Corp 15 Wiggins Ave Bedford MA 01730 781-275-3330 271-1138
TF: 800-458-4141 ■ *Web:* www.toxikon.com
Transportation Research Ctr Inc (TRC Inc)
10820 State Rt 347 PO Box B-67 East Liberty OH 43319 937-666-2011 666-5066
TF: 800-837-7872 ■ *Web:* www.trcpg.com
Transportation Technology Ctr Inc
55500 DOT Rd PO Box 11130 Pueblo CO 81001 719-584-0750 584-0711
Web: www.aar.com
TransTech Pharma Inc
4170 Mendenhall Oaks Pkwy High Point NC 27265 336-841-0300
Web: vtvtherapeutics.com
TriLink BioTechnologies Inc
9955 Mesa Rim Rd San Diego CA 92121 858-546-0004
TF: 800-863-6801 ■ *Web:* www.trilinkbiotech.com
Triumf 4004 Wesbrook Mall Vancouver BC V6T2A3 604-222-1047
Web: www.triumf.ca
Truesdail Laboratories Inc 14201 Franklin Ave Tustin CA 92780 714-730-6239 730-6462
Web: www.truesdail.com
Tulsa Welding School Inc 2545 E 11th St Tulsa OK 74104 918-587-6789
Web: www.weldingschool.com
Twin City Testing 662 Cromwell Ave Saint Paul MN 55114 651-645-3601 659-7348
Web: www.element.com
Twining Laboratories of Southern California Inc
3310 Airport Way Long Beach CA 90806 562-426-3355 426-6424
Web: twininginc.com
Tyzx Inc 3715 Haven Ave Ste 110 Menlo Park CA 94025 650-282-4500
UL CCS 47173 Benicia St Fremont CA 94538 510-771-1000
Web: www.northamerica-ul.com
UL LLC 1559 King St Enfield CT 06082 860-749-8371 749-8234
TF: 800-903-5660 ■ *Web:* www.ul.com
UL LLC (UL) 2600 NW Lk Rd Camas WA 98607 877-854-3577 817-6278*
**Fax Area Code:* 360 ■ *TF:* 877-854-3577 ■ *Web:* www.ul.com
US Army Yuma Proving Ground 301 C St Bldg 300 Yuma AZ 85365 928-328-2163 328-6249
V t e C Laboratories Inc 212 Manida St Bronx NY 10474 718-542-8248
Web: www.vteclabs.com
Valley Lea Laboratories
4609 Grape Rd Ste D-4 Mishawaka IN 46545 574-272-8484 272-8485
Verichem Laboratories Inc
90 Narragansett Ave Providence RI 02907 401-461-0180
TF: 800-552-5859 ■ *Web:* www.verichemlabs.com
Verium Diagnostics Inc
4480 Lk Forest Dr Ste 412 Cincinnati OH 45242 513-429-4340
Web: www.veriumdiagnostics.com
VeroScience LLC 1334 Main Rd Tiverton RI 02878 401-816-0525
Web: www.veroscience.com
VHG Labs Inc 276 Abby Rd Manchester NH 03103 603-622-7660
Web: www.vhglabs.com
Vibranalysis Inc 220 Plz Western Auto Trujillo Alto PR 00976 787-283-7500
Web: www.vibranalysispr.com
Vibrant Corp 8330A Washington Pl NE Albuquerque NM 87113 505-314-1488
Web: www.vibrantndt.com
ViOptix Inc 47224 Mission Falls Ct Fremont CA 94539 510-226-5860
Web: www.vioptix.com
Vista Analytical Laboratory Inc
1104 Windfield Way El Dorado Hills CA 95762 916-673-1520 673-0106
Web: vista-analytical.com
VJ Technologies Inc 89 Carlough Rd Bohemia NY 11716 631-589-8800
TF: 800-858-9729 ■ *Web:* www.vjt.com
Vocal Laboratories Inc
10925 Valley View Rd Ste 202 Eden Prairie MN 55344 952-941-6580
Web: www.vocalabs.com
Wadsworth Ctr
Biggs Laboratory New York Dept of Health
Empire State Plz PO Box 509 Albany NY 12201 518-474-2160
Web: www.wadsworth.org
Wallops Flight Facility
Office of Public Affairs Wallops Island VA 23337 757-824-1579 824-1971
Web: www.nasa.gov
Water Spigot Inc, The 5806 E Hwy 22 Panama City FL 32404 850-871-1900
Web: thewaterspigot.com
WaveTec Vision Systems Inc
66 Argonaut Ste 170 Aliso Viejo CA 92656 949-273-5970
Weecycle Environmental Consulting Inc
5375 Western Ave Ste B Boulder CO 80301 303-413-0452
TF: 800-875-7033 ■ *Web:* www.www.weecycle-env.com
Westmoreland Mechanical Testing & Research Inc
PO Box 388 Youngstown PA 15696 724-537-3131 537-3151
Web: www.wmtr.com
WIL Research Laboratories Inc 1407 George Rd Ashland OH 44805 419-289-8700 289-3650
Web: www.wilresearch.com
WinMed Inc Dundee Park Bldg 17 Door 6 Andover MA 01810 978-590-4246
Web: www.winmed-inc.com
Wirebenders, The 2075 Lincoln Ave Ste A San Jose CA 95125 408-265-5576
Web: www.thewirebenders.com
X-Ray Industries Inc 1961 Thunderbird Troy MI 48084 248-362-2242
Web: www.xritesting.com
XBiotech USA Inc
8201 E Riverside Dr Bldg 4 Ste 100 Austin TX 78744 512-386-2900
Web: www.xbiotech.com
Zyomyx Inc 6519 Dumbarton Cir Fremont CA 94555 510-265-8000

744 TEXTILE MACHINERY

Phone Fax

AB Carter Inc 4801 York Hwy Gastonia NC 28052 704-865-1201
Web: www.abcarter.com

Company	City	State	ZIP	Phone	Fax
Advanced Innovative Technologies LLC 530 Wilbanks Dr. *Web:* www.aitequipment.com	Ball Ground	GA	30107	770-479-1900	479-4179
Andritz Kusters Inc 201 Zima Pk Dr *Web:* www.andritz.com	Spartanburg	SC	29301	864-587-4848	
Belmont Textile Machinery Co 1212 W Catawba St PO Box 568 *Web:* www.btmc.com	Mount Holly	NC	28120	704-827-5836	827-8551
Bowman Hollis Manufacturing Inc 2925 Old Steele Creek Rd *TF:* 888-269-2358 ■ *Web:* www.bowmanhollis.com	Charlotte	NC	28208	704-374-1500	333-5520
Custom Industries Inc 215 Aloe Rd *Web:* www.customindustries.com	Greensboro	NC	27409	336-299-2885	
Eastman Machine Co 779 Washington St *TF:* 800-872-5571 ■ *Web:* www.eastmancuts.com	Buffalo	NY	14203	716-856-2200	856-1140
Entec Composite Machines Inc 300 West 2975 South *Web:* www.entec.com	Salt Lake City	UT	84115	801-486-8721	484-4363
Gaston County Dyeing Machine Co PO Box 308 *Web:* www.gaston-county.com	Stanley	NC	28164	704-822-5000	822-0753
Gerber Technology Inc 24 Industrial Pk Rd W *TF:* 800-826-3243 ■ *Web:* www.gerbertechnology.com	Tolland	CT	06084	860-871-8082	
GTP Inc 1801 Rutherford Rd *Web:* www.globaltextilepartner.com	Greenville	SC	29609	864-288-5475	
Handy Kenlin Group, The 29 E Hintz Rd *Web:* www.handykenlin.com	Wheeling	IL	60090	847-459-0900	459-0902
HH Arnold Co Inc 529 Liberty St *TF:* 866-868-9603 ■ *Web:* www.hharnold.com	Rockland	MA	02370	781-878-0346	878-7944
Hix Corp 1201 E 27th Terr *TF:* 800-835-0606 ■ *Web:* www.hixcorp.com	Pittsburg	KS	66762	620-231-8568	231-1598
Ioline Corp 14140 NE 200th St *TF:* 800-598-0029 ■ *Web:* www.ioline.com	Woodinville	WA	98072	425-398-8282	398-8383
Lawson-Hemphill Inc 1658 G A R Hwy Ste 6 *Web:* www.lawsonhemphill.com	Swansea	MA	02777	508-679-5364	679-5396
Lummus Corp 225 Bourne Blvd PO Box 929 *TF:* 800-458-6687 ■ *Web:* www.lummus.com	Savannah	GA	31408	912-447-9000	447-9250
Mayer Industries Inc PO Box 1466 *Web:* mayerind.com	Orangeburg	SC	29116	803-536-3500	536-2545
MB Industries Inc 9205 Rosman Hwy *Web:* www.m-bindustries.com	Rosman	NC	28772	828-862-4201	862-4297
McCoy-Ellison Inc 1101 Curtis St PO Box 967 *Web:* www.mccoymachinery.com	Monroe	NC	28111	704-289-5413	283-0480
Morrison Berkshire Inc 865 S Church St *Web:* www.morrisonberkshire.com	North Adams	MA	01247	413-663-6501	
Petty Machine Company Inc 2403 Forbes Rd	Gastonia	NC	28056	704-864-3254	861-1937
Rando Machine Corp 1071 Rt 31 PO Box 614 *Web:* www.randomachine.com	Macedon	NY	14502	315-986-2761	986-7943
Standex International Corp Mullen Testers Div 939 Chicopee St *Web:* www.mullentesters.com	Chicopee	MA	01013	413-536-1311	536-1367
Stork Prints America Inc 3201 Rotary Dr *Web:* www.spgprints.com	Charlotte	NC	28269	704-598-7171	
Thermopatch Corp 2204 Erie Blvd E *TF:* 800-252-6555 ■ *Web:* www.thermopatch.biz/us/en	Syracuse	NY	13224	315-446-8110	445-8046
Tompkins Bros Company Inc 623 Oneida St *Web:* www.tompkinsusa.com	Syracuse	NY	13202	315-422-8763	422-8762
TrimMaster 4860 N Fifth St Hwy *TF:* 800-356-4237 ■ *Web:* www.trimmaster.com	Temple	PA	19560	610-921-0203	929-8833
Tubular Textile Machinery 113 Woodside Dr PO Box 2097 *Web:* www.navisglobal.com	Lexington	NC	27292	336-956-6444	956-1795
Tuftco Corp 2318 S Holtzclaw Ave *TF:* 800-288-3826 ■ *Web:* www.tuftco.com	Chattanooga	TN	37408	423-698-8601	698-0842
Tuftco Finishing Systems Inc 100 W Industrial Blvd *TF:* 800-288-3826 ■ *Web:* www.tuftco.com	Dalton	GA	30720	706-277-1110	277-4334
Wardwell Braiding Machine Co 1211 High St *Web:* www.wardwell.com	Central Falls	RI	02863	401-724-8800	723-2690
West Point Industries 2021 Stateline Rd PO Box 589 *Web:* www.westpoint.com	West Point	GA	31833	706-643-2101	643-2100

745 TEXTILE MILLS

745-1 Broadwoven Fabric Mills

Company	City	State	ZIP	Phone	Fax
Alice Mfg Company Inc 208 E First Ave *Web:* www.alicemfgco.com	Easley	SC	29640	864-859-6323	859-6328
American Cotton Growers Textile Div (ACG) PO Box 2827 *TF:* 800-333-8011 ■ *Web:* pcca.com/services/denim	Lubbock	TX	79408	806-763-8011	762-7400
American Fiber & Finishing Inc PO Box 2488 *Web:* www.affinc.com	Albemarle	NC	28001	704-983-6102	983-1850
American Silk Mills Corp 75 Stark St *Web:* www.americansilk.com	Plains	PA	18705	570-822-7147	829-7044
Central Textiles Inc 237 Mill Ave *Web:* ctextiles.com	Central	SC	29630	864-639-2491	639-4513
Circa 1801 1 Jacquard Dr	Connelly Springs	NC	28612	828-397-7003	
Cone Denim LLC 804 Green Valley Rd Ste 300	Greensboro	NC	27408	336-379-6220	379-6287
Copland Fabrics Inc 1714 Carolina Mill Rd *Web:* www.coplandfabrics.com	Burlington	NC	27217	336-226-0272	226-6452
Covington Industries Inc 470 Seventh Ave Ste 900 *Web:* covingtonfabric.com	New York	NY	10018	212-689-2200	
Culp Inc 1823 Eastchester Dr *NYSE:* CFI ■ *Web:* www.culpinc.com	High Point	NC	27265	336-889-5161	
DeRoyal Textiles 141 E York St *TF:* 800-845-1062 ■ *Web:* www.deroyal.com	Camden	SC	29020	803-432-2403	424-5112
Faribault Woolen MillCo 1500 NW Second Ave *Web:* faribaultmill.com	Faribault	MN	55021	507-412-5510	
Fortune Fabrics Inc *Wyoming Weavers* 315 Simpson St *Web:* www.wyomingweavers.com	Swoyersville	PA	18704	570-288-3667	283-2124
Garnet Hill Inc 231 Main St **Fax Area Code:* 888 ■ *TF:* 800-870-3513 ■ *Web:* www.garnethill.com	Franconia	NH	03580	603-823-5545	842-9696*
Glen Raven Inc 232 Glen Raven Rd *Web:* www.glenraven.com	Glen Raven	NC	27217	336-227-6211	226-8133
Greenwood Mills Inc 300 Morgan Ave *Web:* www.greenwoodmills.com	Greenwood	SC	29646	864-227-2121	
Hamrick Mills Inc 515 W Buford St PO Box 48 *TF:* 800-600-4305 ■ *Web:* www.hamrickmills.com	Gaffney	SC	29341	864-489-4731	
Henry Glass & Co 49 W 37th St **Fax Area Code:* 212 ■ *TF:* 800-294-9495 ■ *Web:* www.henryglassfabrics.com	New York	NY	10018	917-229-1080	532-3525*
Inman Mills 300 Pk Rd PO Box 207 *Web:* www.inmanmills.com	Inman	SC	29349	864-472-2121	472-0261
JB Martin Co 645 Fifth Ave Ste 400 *TF:* 800-223-0525 ■ *Web:* www.jbmartin.com	New York	NY	10022	212-421-2020	421-1460
Juniata Fabrics Inc 1301 Broadway	Altoona	PA	16601	814-944-9381	944-1938
Keystone Weaving Mills Inc 1349 Cumberland St	Lebanon	PA	17042	717-272-4665	272-4840
KM Fabrics Inc 2 Waco St *TF:* 800-873-7326	Greenville	SC	29611	864-295-2550	295-3356
Kuraray America Inc 2625 Bay Area Blvd Ste 600 *TF:* 800-423-9762 ■ *Web:* www.kuraray.us.com	Houston	TX	77058	281-909-5800	
Lantal Textiles Inc 1300 Langenthal Dr PO Box 965 *TF:* 800-334-3309 ■ *Web:* www.lantal.com	Rural Hall	NC	27045	336-969-9551	
Milliken & Co 920 Milliken Rd **Fax:* Hum Res ■ *Web:* www.milliken.com	Spartanburg	SC	29303	864-503-2020	503-2100*
Mount Vernon Mills Inc 503 S Main St PO Box 100 *Web:* www.mvmills.com	Mauldin	SC	29662	864-688-7100	688-7215
Polymer Group Inc 9335 Harris Corners Pkwy *Web:* www.polymergroupinc.com	Charlotte	NC	28269	704-697-5100	697-5116
Precision Fabrics Group Inc 301 N Elm St Ste 600 *TF:* 800-284-8001 ■ *Web:* www.precisionfabrics.com	Greensboro	NC	27401	336-510-8000	510-8004
Raxon Fabrics 261 Fifth Ave *Web:* www.raxon.com	New York	NY	10016	212-532-6816	481-9361
Scalamandre Silks Inc 350 Wireless Blvd *TF:* 800-932-4361 ■ *Web:* scalamandre.com	Hauppauge	NY	11788	631-467-8800	467-9448
Stonecutter Mills Corp 230 Spindale St *OTC:* STCMA ■ *Web:* www.stonecuttermills.com	Spindale	NC	28160	828-286-2341	287-7280
Trelleborg Coated Systems US Inc 790 Reeves St **Fax Area Code:* 864 ■ *TF:* 800-344-0714 ■ *Web:* www.trelleborg.com	Spartanburg	SC	29301	800-344-0714	595-2273*
Tweave LLC 138 Barrows St PO Box AV *Web:* www.gehring-tricot.com	Norton	MA	02766	508-285-6701	285-2904
Valdese Weavers LLC 1000 Perkins Rd SE *Web:* www.valdeseweavers.com	Valdese	NC	28690	828-874-2181	874-3920
Vectorply Corp 3500 Lakewood Dr *TF:* 800-577-4521 ■ *Web:* www.vectorply.com	Phenix City	AL	36867	334-291-7704	291-7743
Warm Co 5529 186th Pl SW *TF:* 800-234-9276 ■ *Web:* www.warmcompany.com	Lynnwood	WA	98037	425-248-2424	248-2422
WestPoint Home Inc 28 E 28th St Ste 2 *Web:* martex.com	New York	NY	10016	212-930-2000	

745-2 Coated Fabric

Company	City	State	ZIP	Phone	Fax
Adell Plastics Inc 4530 Annapolis Rd *TF:* 800-638-5218 ■ *Web:* www.adellplas.com	Baltimore	MD	21227	410-789-7780	789-2804
Alpha Assoc Inc 145 Lehigh Ave *TF:* 800-631-5399 ■ *Web:* www.alphainc.com	Lakewood	NJ	08701	732-634-5700	634-1430
Beckmann Converting Inc 14 Pk Dr *Web:* www.beckmannconverting.com	Amsterdam	NY	12010	518-842-0073	842-0282
Bondcote Corp PO Box 729 *TF:* 800-368-2160 ■ *Web:* www.bondcote.com	Pulaski	VA	24301	540-980-2640	980-5636
Bradford Industries Inc 1857 Middlesex St *Web:* www.bradfordind.com	Lowell	MA	01851	978-459-4100	459-2597
Brookwood Laminating 275 Putnam Rd *Web:* www.brookwoodcos.com	Wauregan	CT	06387	860-774-5001	774-5002
Cellusuede Products Inc 500 N Madison St *Web:* www.cellusuede.com	Rockford	IL	61107	815-964-8619	964-7949
Cooley Group 50 Esten Ave *TF Cust Svc:* 800-992-0072 ■ *Web:* www.cooleygroup.com	Pawtucket	RI	02860	401-724-9000	
Dazian Inc 18 Central Blvd **Fax Area Code:* 201 ■ *TF:* 877-232-9426 ■ *Web:* www.dazian.com	South Hackensack	NJ	07606	877-232-9426	549-1055*
Deccofelt Corp 555 S Vermont Ave *TF Cust Svc:* 800-543-3226 ■ *Web:* www.deccofelt.com	Glendora	CA	91741	626-963-8511	963-4981
Der-Tex Corp 1 Lehner Rd **Fax Area Code:* 207 ■ *TF:* 800-669-0364 ■ *Web:* www.dertexcorp.com	Saco	ME	04072	800-669-0364	669-9026*
Duracote Corp 350 N Diamond St *TF:* 800-321-2252 ■ *Web:* www.duracote.com	Ravenna	OH	44266	330-296-3487	296-5102
Emtex Inc 42 Cherry Hill Dr # B *Web:* www.emtexinc.com	Danvers	MA	01923	978-907-4500	
Flexfirm Products Inc 2300 N Chico Ave *Web:* www.flexfirmproducts.com	South El Monte	CA	91733	626-448-7627	579-5116
Haartz Corp 87 HaywaRd Rd *Web:* www.haartz.com	Acton	MA	01720	978-264-2600	264-2601
Herculite Products Inc 105 E Sinking Springs Ln **Fax:* Acctg ■ *TF Cust Svc:* 800-772-0036 ■ *Web:* www.herculite.com	Emigsville	PA	17318	717-764-1192	764-5211*
ICG/Holliston 905 Holliston Mills Rd **Fax Area Code:* 800 ■ *TF:* 800-251-0451 ■ *Web:* www.holliston.com	Church Hill	TN	37642	423-357-6141	325-0351*

	City	State	Zip	Phone	Fax
Middlesex Research Mfg Company Inc 27 Apsley St	Hudson	MA	01749	978-562-3697	562-7446
TF: 800-424-5188 ■ *Web:* www.middlesexresearch.com					
OMNOVA Solutions Inc 175 Ghent Rd	Fairlawn	OH	44333	330-869-4200	
NYSE: OMN ■ *Web:* www.omnova.com					
Polyguard Products Inc PO Box 755	Ennis	TX	75120	972-875-8421	875-9425
TF: 800-541-4994 ■ *Web:* www.polyguardproducts.com					
Reflexite Corp 120 Darling Dr	Avon	CT	06001	860-676-7100	676-7199
TF: 800-654-7570 ■ *Web:* www.orafol.com					
Seaman Corp 1000 Venture Blvd	Wooster	OH	44691	330-262-1111	263-6950
TF: 800-927-8578 ■ *Web:* www.seamancorp.com					
Swift Textile Metalizing LLC 23 Britton Dr	Bloomfield	CT	06002	860-243-1122	243-0848
Web: www.swift-textile.com					
Taconic 136 Coonbrook Rd PO Box 69	Petersburg	NY	12138	518-658-3202	658-3204
TF: 800-833-1805 ■ *Web:* www.4taconic.com					
Twitchell Corp 4031 Ross Clark Cir	Dothan	AL	36303	334-792-0002	
TF General: 800-633-7550 ■ *Web:* www.twitchellcorp.com					
Uniroyal Engineered Products LLC 1800 Second St Ste 970	Sarasota	FL	34236	941-906-8580	
Web: www.naugahyde.com					
WL Gore & Assoc Inc 551 Papermill Rd	Newark	DE	19711	302-738-4880	738-7710
Web: www.gore.com					

745-3 Industrial Fabrics

	City	State	Zip	Phone	Fax
Albany International Corp 1373 Broadway PO Box 1907	Albany	NY	12204	518-445-2200	
NYSE: AIN ■ *TF:* 888-797-6735 ■ *Web:* www.albint.com					
Amatex Corp 1032 Stambridge St	Norristown	PA	19404	610-277-6100	277-6106
TF: 800-441-9680 ■ *Web:* www.amatex.com					
AMETEK Inc Chemical Products Div 455 Corporate Blvd	Newark	DE	19702	302-456-4400	456-4444
TF Orders: 800-441-7777 ■ *Web:* www.ametekfpp.com					
AstenJohnson 4399 Corporate Rd	Charleston	SC	29405	843-747-7800	202-6278
TF: 800-529-7990 ■ *Web:* www.astenjohnson.com					
Belton Industries Inc 1205 Hanby Rd PO Box 127	Belton	SC	29627	864-338-5711	338-5594
TF: 800-845-8753 ■ *Web:* www.beltonindustries.com					
BGF Industries Inc 3802 Robert Porcher Way	Greensboro	NC	27410	800-476-4845	545-0233*
**Fax Area Code:* 336 ■ *TF:* 800-476-4845 ■ *Web:* www.bgf.com					
Carthage Mills 4243 Hunt Rd	Cincinnati	OH	45242	513-794-1600	794-3434
TF Sales: 800-543-4430 ■ *Web:* www.carthagemills.com					
Clear Edge Technical Fabrics 7160 Northland Cir N	Minneapolis	MN	55428	763-535-3220	535-6040
TF: 800-328-3036 ■ *Web:* www.clear-edge.com/products/technical-fabrics					
Fablok Mills Inc 140 Spring St	Murray Hill	NJ	07974	908-464-1950	464-6520
Web: www.fablokmills.com					
FH Bonn Co 4300 Gateway Blvd	Springfield	OH	45502	937-323-7024	323-0388
TF: 800-323-0143 ■ *Web:* www.fhbonn.com					
Firestone Fibers & Textiles Co 100 Firestone Ln PO Box 1369	Kings Mountain	NC	28086	704-734-2132	734-2104
TF: 800-441-1336 ■ *Web:* www.firestonefibers.com					
HFI LLC 2421 McGaw Rd	Obetz	OH	43207	614-491-0700	491-1899
Web: hfi-inc.com					
Mutual Industries Inc 707 W Grange St	Philadelphia	PA	19120	215-927-6000	927-3388
TF: 800-523-0888 ■ *Web:* www.mutualindustries.com					
Newtex Industries Inc 8050 Victor Mendon Rd	Victor	NY	14564	585-924-9135	924-4645
TF: 800-836-1001 ■ *Web:* www.newtex.com					
Sefar Printing Solutions Inc 111 Calumet St	Depew	NY	14043	716-683-4050	685-9469
TF: 800-995-0531 ■ *Web:* www.sefar.com					
Stern & Stern Industries Inc 188 Thacher St PO Box 556	Hornell	NY	14843	212-972-4040	
Web: www.sternandstern.com					
TenCate Geosynthetics North America 365 S Holland Dr	Pendergrass	GA	30567	706-693-2226	693-4400
TF: 888-795-0808 ■ *Web:* www.tencate.com					
TenCate Protective Fabrics USA 6501 Mall Blvd	Union City	GA	30291	800-241-8630	
TF: 800-241-8630 ■ *Web:* www.tencate.com					
Tex-Tech Industries Inc 1 City Ctr 11th Fl	Portland	ME	04101	207-933-4404	
Web: www.textechindustries.com					
Ultrafabrics LLC 303 S Broadway	Tarrytown	NY	10591	914-460-1730	631-3572
TF: 877-309-6648 ■ *Web:* www.ultrafabricsllc.com					
Weavexx 51 Flex Way	Youngsville	NC	27596	919-556-7235	556-2432
Web: www.xerium.com					
Wendell Fabrics Corp 108 E Church St PO Box 128	Blacksburg	SC	29702	864-839-6341	839-2911
Web: www.wendellfabrics.com					

745-4 Knitting Mills

	City	State	Zip	Phone	Fax
Alamac American Knits LLC 1885 Alamac Rd	Lumberton	NC	28358	910-739-2811	618-2292
Web: www.alamacusa.com					
Apex Mills Corp 168 Doughty Blvd	Inwood	NY	11096	516-239-4400	239-4951
TF: 800-989-2739 ■ *Web:* www.apexmills.com					
Asheboro Elastics Corp 150 N Pk St	Asheboro	NC	27203	336-629-2626	629-3782
Web: www.aecnarrowfabrics.com					
Cellunet Mfg Co 1006 Jacksonville Rd	Burlington Township	NJ	08016	609-386-1147	
Clover Knits Inc 1075 Jackson Heights	Clover	SC	29710	803-222-3021	222-4105
Contempora Fabrics Inc 351 Contempora Dr	Lumberton	NC	28358	910-738-7131	738-9575
Web: www.contemporafabrics.com					
Darlington Fabrics Corp 36 Beach St	Westerly	RI	02891	401-315-6279	
Web: www.darlingtonfabrics.com					
Draper Knitting Co 28 Draper Ln	Canton	MA	02021	781-828-0029	828-3034
TF: 800-808-7707 ■ *Web:* www.draperknitting.com					
Elastic Fabrics of America 3112 Pleasant Garden Rd	Greensboro	NC	27406	336-275-9401	378-2631
Web: www.elasticfabrics.com					
Fab Industries Corp 98 Cutter Mill Rd Ste 412-N	Great Neck	NY	11021	516-498-3200	498-3200
Web: fab-industries.com					
Gehring Textiles Inc 1225 Franklin Ave Ste 300	Garden City	NY	11530	516-747-4555	747-8885
Web: www.gehring-tricot.com					
Hornwood Inc 766 Hailey's Ferry Rd	Lilesville	NC	28091	704-848-4121	848-4555
Web: www.hornwoodinc.com					
Klauber Bros Inc 980 Ave of the Americas 2nd Fl	New York	NY	10018	212-686-2531	481-7194
Web: www.klauberlace.com					
Lace For Less Inc 1500 Main Ave Ste 3	Clifton	NJ	07011	973-478-2955	478-8746
TF: 800-533-5223 ■ *Web:* www.parislace.com					
Minnesota Knitting Mills 1450 Mendota Heights Rd	Saint Paul	MN	55120	651-452-2240	
Web: www.mnknit.com					
MoCaro Industries Inc 2201 Mocaro Dr	Statesville	NC	28677	704-878-6645	873-6139
Web: www.mocaro.com					
Monterey Mills Inc 1725 E Delavan Dr	Janesville	WI	53546	608-754-2866	754-3750
TF: 800-255-9665 ■ *Web:* www.montereymills.com					
Russ-Knits Inc 520 E Main St	Candor	NC	27229	910-974-4114	974-4023
Web: www.russknits.com					
Westchester Lace & Textiles Inc 3901 Liberty Ave	North Bergen	NJ	07047	201-864-2150	864-2116
Web: www.westchesterlace.com					

745-5 Narrow Fabric Mills

	City	State	Zip	Phone	Fax
Advance Fiber Technologies Corp 344 Lodi St	Hackensack	NJ	07601	201-488-2700	489-5656
American Cord & Webbing Co 88 Century Dr	Woonsocket	RI	02895	401-762-5500	762-5514
Web: www.acw1.com					
Avery Dennison 950 German St	Lenoir	NC	28645	800-444-4947	
TF: 800-444-4947 ■ *Web:* www.rbis.averydennison.com					
Bally Ribbon Mills 23 N Seventh St	Bally	PA	19503	610-845-2211	845-8013
Web: www.ballyribbon.com					
Carolina Narrow Fabric Co 1100 N Patterson Ave	Winston-Salem	NC	27101	336-631-3000	631-3060
Web: www.carolinanarrowfabric.com					
Conrad-Jarvis Corp 217 Conant St	Pawtucket	RI	02860	401-722-8700	726-8860*
**Fax:* Orders ■ *Web:* conrad-jarvis.com					
ELC Industries LLC 1439 Dave Lyle Blvd Ste 16-C	Rock Hill	SC	29730	803-980-7600	980-7676
Web: ricebraid.com					
Fulflex Inc 32 Justin Holden Dr	Brattleboro	VT	05301	802-257-5256	257-5602*
**Fax:* Cust Svc ■ *TF:* 800-283-2500 ■ *Web:* www.fulflex.com					
Hickory Brands Inc (HBI) 429 27th St NW	Hickory	NC	28601	800-438-5777	422-3279
TF: 800-438-5777 ■ *Web:* www.hickorybrands.com					
Hope Global Engineered Textile Solutions 50 Martin St	Cumberland	RI	02864	401-333-8990	334-6442
TF General: 800-854-7139 ■ *Web:* www.hopeglobal.com					
JRM Industries Inc 1 Mattimore St	Passaic	NJ	07055	973-779-9340	779-8017
TF: 800-533-2697 ■ *Web:* www.jrm.com					
Julius Koch USA Inc 387 Church St	New Bedford	MA	02745	508-995-9565	995-8434
TF Sales: 800-522-3652 ■ *Web:* www.jkusa.com					
Murdock Webbing Co 27 Foundry St	Central Falls	RI	02863	401-724-3000	
TF: 800-375-2052 ■ *Web:* www.murdockwebbing.com					
Name Maker Inc 4450 Commerce Cir PO Box 43821	Atlanta	GA	30336	404-691-2237	691-7711
TF: 800-241-2890 ■ *Web:* www.namemaker.com					
Narricot Industries LP 928 Jaymore Rd Ste C150	SouthHampton	PA	18966	215-322-3900	
Web: www.narricot.com					
Narrow Fabric Industries Corp 701 Reading Ave	Reading	PA	19611	610-376-2891	
TF: 877-523-6373 ■ *Web:* readingeagle.com					
NFA Corp 850 Boylston St Ste 428	Chestnut Hill	MA	02467	617-232-6060	
Rhode Island Textile Co 211 Columbus Ave	Pawtucket	RI	02862	401-722-3700	726-2840
TF: 800-556-6488 ■ *Web:* www.ritextile.com					
Ross Matthews Mills Inc 657 Quarry St	Fall River	MA	02723	508-677-0601	
TF: 800-753-7677					
Sequins International Inc 60-01 31st Ave	Woodside	NY	11377	718-204-0002	204-0999
Web: www.sequinsdirect.com					
Shelby Elastics Inc 639 N Post Rd PO Box 2405	Shelby	NC	28150	704-487-4301	481-9348
TF: 800-562-4507 ■ *Web:* www.shelbyelastics.com					
South Carolina Elastic Co 201 S Carolina Elastic Rd	Landrum	SC	29356	864-457-3388	
TF: 800-845-6700 ■ *Web:* www.ritextile.com					
Southern Weaving Co 1005 W Bramlett Rd	Greenville	SC	29611	864-233-1635	240-9302
TF: 800-849-8962 ■ *Web:* www.southernweaving.com					
State Narrow Fabrics Inc 2902 Borden Ave	Long Island	NY	11101	718-392-8787	392-9421
Web: www.statenarrow.com					
Sturges Mfg Company Inc 2030 Sunset Ave PO Box 59	Utica	NY	13502	315-732-6159	732-2314
Web: www.sturgesstraps.com					
Tape Craft Corp 200 Tape Craft Dr	Oxford	AL	36203	800-521-1783	236-6718*
**Fax Area Code:* 256 ■ *TF Cust Svc:* 800-521-1783 ■ *Web:* www.tapecraft.com					
Trimtex Company Inc 400 Pk Ave	Williamsport	PA	17701	570-326-9135	326-4250
Wayne Mills Co Inc 130 W Berkley St	Philadelphia	PA	19144	215-842-2134	438-8599
TF: 800-220-8053 ■ *Web:* www.waynemills.com					

745-6 Nonwoven Fabrics

	City	State	Zip	Phone	Fax
Acme Felt Works Co 6500 Stanford Ave	Los Angeles	CA	90001	323-752-3778	752-7164
Aetna Felt Corp 2401 W Emaus Ave	Allentown	PA	18103	610-791-0900	791-5791
TF: 800-526-4451 ■ *Web:* www.aetnafelt.com					

Company / Address	City	State	ZIP	Phone	Fax
Airtex Consumer Products a Div of Federal Foam Technologies 150 Industrial Pk Blvd; **Fax Area Code:* 320 ■ *TF:* 800-851-8887 ■ *Web:* www.airtex.com	Cokato	MN	55321	800-851-8887	286-2428*
American Felt & Filter Co 361 Walsh Ave; *Web:* www.affco.com	New Windsor	NY	12553	845-561-3560	563-4422
Cerex Advanced Fabrics Inc 610 Chemstrand Rd; *TF:* 800-572-3739 ■ *Web:* www.cerex.com	Cantonment	FL	32533	850-968-0100	937-3342
Clark-Cutler-McDermott Co (CCMcD) 5 Fisher St	Franklin	MA	02038	508-528-1200	528-1406
Fiber Bond Corp 110 Menke Rd; *Web:* www.fiberbond.net	Michigan City	IN	46360	219-879-4541	874-7502
Fisher Textiles Inc 139 Business Pk Dr; *TF:* 800-554-8886 ■ *Web:* www.fishertextiles.com	Indian Trail	NC	28079	704-821-8870	821-8880
Foss Mfg Co LLC 11 Merrill Industrial Dr; *TF:* 800-343-3277 ■ *Web:* www.fossmfg.com	Hampton	NH	03842	603-929-6000	929-6010
Hobbs Bonded Fibers Inc 200 Commerce Dr; *TF:* 800-433-3357 ■ *Web:* www.hobbsbondedfibers.com	Waco	TX	76710	254-741-0040	772-7238
National Nonwovens PO Box 150; *TF:* 800-333-3469 ■ *Web:* www.nationalnonwovens.com	EastHampton	MA	01027	413-527-3445	527-9570
Orr Felt Co 750 S Main St; *Web:* www.orrfelt.com	Piqua	OH	45356	937-773-0551	778-9670
Sellars 6565 N 60th St; *TF:* 800-237-8454 ■ *Web:* sellarscompany.com	Milwaukee	WI	53223	414-353-5650	353-5707
Texollini Inc 2575 E El Presidio St; *Web:* www.texollini.com	Long Beach	CA	90810	310-537-3400	537-3500
Tietex International 3010 N Blackstock Rd; *TF:* 800-843-8390 ■ *Web:* www.tietex.com	Spartanburg	SC	29301	864-574-0500	574-9490
Trenton Mills LLC 400 Factory St PO Box 107; *Web:* www.trentonmills.com	Trenton	TN	38382	731-855-1323	855-9000

745-7 Textile Dyeing & Finishing

Company / Address	City	State	ZIP	Phone	Fax
Advanced Textile Composites 700 E Parker St; *Web:* www.advtextile.com	Scranton	PA	18509	570-207-7000	207-7070
Albert Screen Print Inc 3704 Summit Rd; *Web:* www.albertinc.com	Norton	OH	44203	330-753-7559	753-1612
Aurora Textile Finishing Co 911 N Lake St PO Box 70; *TF:* 800-864-0303 ■ *Web:* www.auroratextile.com	Aurora	IL	60507	630-892-7651	
Bradford Printing & Finishing LLC 460 Bradford Rd	Bradford	RI	02808	401-377-2231	377-2234
Buckeye Fabric Finishing Co 1260 E Main St; *Web:* www.buckeyefabric.com	Coshocton	OH	43812	740-622-3251	
Carlisle Finishing 3863 Carlisle Chester Hwy; *Web:* www.itg-global.com/companies/carlisle_finishing.html	Carlisle	SC	29031	864-466-4100	427-4501
Como Textile Prints Inc 193 E Railway Ave	Paterson	NJ	07503	973-279-2950	881-8450
Coral Dyeing & Finishing Corp 555 E 31st St	Paterson	NJ	07513	973-278-0272	278-9490
Cosmo 12 Kent Way Ste 201 PO Box 737; *Web:* www.cosmofabric.net	Byfield	MA	01922	978-462-7311	465-6223
Cranston Print Works Co 1381 Cranston St; *TF:* 800-876-2756 ■ *Web:* www.cpw.com	Cranston	RI	02920	401-943-4800	275-9333
Deep River Dyeing & Finishing Company Inc 225 Poplar St PO Box 217; *Web:* deepriverdyeing.com	Randleman	NC	27317	336-498-4181	498-7252
Duro Textiles LLC 110 Chace St; *Web:* www.duroindustries.com	Fall River	MA	02724	508-675-0101	677-6791
GJ Littlewood & Son Inc 4045 Main St; *Web:* www.littlewooddyers.com	Philadelphia	PA	19127	215-483-3970	483-6129
Hanes Dye & Finish Inc 600 NW Blvd; *Web:* www.hanescompanies.com	Winston-Salem	NC	27101	336-725-1391	777-3895
Harodite Industries Inc 66 S St; *Web:* www.harodite.com	Taunton	MA	02780	508-824-6961	880-0696
Holt Sublimation Printing & Products 2208 Air Pk Dr	Burlington	NC	27215	336-222-3600	229-7580
Huffman Finishing Co 4919 Hickory Blvd	Granite Falls	NC	28630	828-396-1741	
Kenyon Industries Inc 36 Sherman Ave; *Web:* www.brookwoodcos.com	Kenyon	RI	02836	401-364-3400	364-6130
Microfibres Inc 1 Moshassuck St; *Web:* www.microfibres.com	Pawtucket	RI	02904	401-725-4883	722-8520
Parthenon Prints Inc PO Box 2505; *Web:* www.parthenonprints.com	Panama City	FL	32402	850-769-8321	769-5374
Royal Carolina Corp 7305 Old Friendly Rd; *Web:* www.royalcarolina.com	Greensboro	NC	27410	336-292-8845	294-2396
Westex Inc 122 W 22nd St; *TF:* 866-493-7839 ■ *Web:* www.westex.com	Oak Brook	IL	60523	773-523-7000	523-0965
William J Dixon Company Inc 756 Springdale Dr; *Web:* www.wjdixon.com	Exton	PA	19341	610-524-1131	
Wolfe Dye & Bleach Works Inc 25 Ridge Rd; *Web:* www.wolfedyeandbleachworks.com	Shoemakersville	PA	19555	610-562-7639	
Yates Bleachery Co 503 Flintstone Rd; *Web:* www.yatesbleachery.info	Flintstone	GA	30725	706-820-1531	820-9459

745-8 Textile Fiber Processing Mills

Company / Address	City	State	ZIP	Phone	Fax
Buffalo Industries Inc 99 S Spokane St; *TF:* 800-683-0052 ■ *Web:* www.buffaloindustries.com	Seattle	WA	98134	206-682-9900	682-9907
Claremont Flock LLC 107 Scott Dr; *Web:* www.claremontflock.com	Leominster	MA	01453	978-534-6191	534-7352
Fabritech Inc 5740 Salmen St; *TF:* 888-733-5009 ■ *Web:* www.fabritechonline.com	New Orleans	LA	70123	504-733-5009	
Fiber Conversion Inc 15 E Elm St; *Web:* fiberconversion.net	Broadalbin	NY	12025	518-883-3431	
JE Herndon Company Inc 1020 J E Herndon Access Rd; *TF:* 800-277-0500 ■ *Web:* jeherndon.com	Kings Mountain	NC	28086	704-739-4711	734-0621
Leigh Fibers Inc 1101 Syphrit Rd; *Web:* www.leighfibers.com	Wellford	SC	29385	864-439-4111	439-4116
Norman W Paschall Co Inc 1 Paschall Rd; *Web:* www.paschall.com	Peachtree City	GA	30269	770-487-7945	487-0840
Oklahoma Waste & Wiping Rag Company Inc 2013 SE 18th St	Oklahoma City	OK	73129	405-670-3100	670-3993
Royal Processing Co 5710 Old Concord Rd; *Web:* steinfibers.com	Charlotte	NC	28213	704-599-2804	599-2805
RSM Co 811 Pressley Rd PO Box 31605; *Web:* www.rsmcompany.com	Charlotte	NC	28231	704-525-6851	525-8368
Spectro Coating Corp 101 Scott Dr; *Web:* www.spectrocoating.com	Leominster	MA	01453	978-534-1800	534-4155

745-9 Yarn & Thread Mills

Company / Address	City	State	ZIP	Phone	Fax
Carolina Mills Inc 618 Newton Rd; *Web:* www.carolinamills.com	Maiden	NC	28650	828-428-9911	
Chargeurs Wool USA 178 Wool Rd	Jamestown	SC	29453	843-257-2212	257-4579
Charles Craft Inc 21381 Charles Craft Ln; *TF:* 800-275-4117 ■ *Web:* www.commonthread.us	Laurinburg	NC	28352	910-844-3521	844-3045
Chesterfield Yarn Mills Inc 201 N Maple St; *Web:* www.chesterfieldwraps.com	Pageland	SC	29728	843-672-7211	672-7210
Clover Yarns Inc 1030 Tanyard Branch Trl	Clover	VA	24534	434-454-7151	454-6725
Coats North America 3430 Toringdon Way Ste 301; *TF:* 800-631-0965 ■ *Web:* www.coats.com	Charlotte	NC	28277	704-329-5800	329-5279
Crescent Woolen Mills Co 1016 School St; *Web:* crescentwoolenmills.com	Two Rivers	WI	54241	920-793-3331	793-3818
Dillon Yarn Inc 1019 Titan Rd; *Web:* dillonyarn.com	Dillon	SC	29536	843-774-7353	
DMC Corp 10 Basin Dr Ste 130; *Web:* www.dmc-usa.com	Kearny	NJ	07032	973-589-0606	589-8931
Eddington Thread Manufacturing Co PO Box 446; *TF:* 800-220-8901 ■ *Web:* www.edthread.com	Bensalem	PA	19020	215-639-8900	639-8900
Glen Raven Inc 232 Glen Raven Rd; *Web:* www.glenraven.com	Glen Raven	NC	27217	336-227-6211	226-8133
Hickory Yarns Inc 1025 Tenth St NE; *Web:* www.hickoryyarns.com	Hickory	NC	28601	828-322-1550	322-1627
Interstock Premium Cabinets LLC 6300 Bristol Pike; *TF:* 800-896-9842 ■ *Web:* www.interstockcabinets.com	Levittown	PA	19057	267-288-1200	288-1206
Kent Wool 671 Runnymede Rd; *Web:* www.kentwool.com	Pickens	SC	29671	864-878-6367	878-2723
Liberty Throwing Company Inc 214 Pringle St; *Web:* www.libertythrowing.com	Kingston	PA	18704	570-287-1114	283-3531
Lion Brand Yarn Co 135 Kero Rd; *TF:* 800-795-5466 ■ *Web:* www.lionbrand.com	Carlstadt	NJ	07072	212-243-8995	
Meridian Specialty Yarns Inc 312 Colombo St SW; *Web:* www.msyg.com	Valdese	NC	28690	828-874-2151	874-3780
Parkdale Mills Inc 531 Cotton Blossom Cir; *TF:* 800-331-1843 ■ *Web:* www.parkdalemills.com	Gastonia	NC	28054	704-874-5000	874-5175
Pharr Yarns LLC 100 Main St PO Box 1939; *Web:* www.pharryarns.com	McAdenville	NC	28101	704-824-3551	824-0072
Regal Mfg Co Inc 990 Third Ave SE	Hickory	NC	28602	828-328-5381	
RL Stowe Mills Inc 100 N Main St	Belmont	NC	28012	704-825-5314	825-6608
Sapona Mfg Company Inc 2478 Cedar Falls Rd; *Web:* www.saponamfg.com	Cedar Falls	NC	27230	336-625-2727	626-0876
Supreme Corp 325 Spence Rd; *TF:* 888-604-6975 ■ *Web:* supremecorporation.com	Conover	NC	28613	828-322-6975	322-7881
Swift Spinning Inc 16 Corporate Ridge Pkwy; *TF:* 800-849-1252 ■ *Web:* www.swiftspinning.com	Columbus	GA	31907	706-323-6303	
Tuscarora Yarns Inc 8760 E Franklin St; *TF:* 800-849-6527 ■ *Web:* www.tuscarorayarns.com	Mount Pleasant	NC	28124	704-436-6527	436-9461
Ultrafab Inc 1050 Hook Rd; *Web:* www.ultrafab.com	Farmington	NY	14425	585-924-2186	924-7680
Unifi Inc 7201 W Friendly Ave; *NYSE:* UFI ■ *Web:* www.unifi.com	Greensboro	NC	27410	336-294-4410	316-5422
Universal Fibers Inc PO Box 8930; *Web:* www.universalfibers.com	Bristol	VA	24203	276-669-1161	669-3304

746 TEXTILE PRODUCTS - HOUSEHOLD

Company / Address	City	State	ZIP	Phone	Fax
1888 Mills LLC 1520 Kensington Rd Ste 115; **Fax Area Code:* 630 ■ *TF:* 800-346-3660 ■ *Web:* www.1888mills.com	Oak Brook	IL	60523	800-346-3660	586-9303*
American Textile Co 10 N Linden St; *TF Cust Svc:* 800-289-2826 ■ *Web:* www.americantextile.com	Duquesne	PA	15110	412-948-1020	948-1002
Arden Cos 30400 Telegraph Rd Ste 200; *TF:* 800-876-7336 ■ *Web:* www.ardencompanies.com	Bingham Farms	MI	48025	248-415-8500	415-8520
Ascot Enterprises Inc 503 S Main St; *Web:* www.ascotent.com	Nappanee	IN	46550	574-773-7751	773-2894
Bardwil Industries Inc 1071 Ave of the Americas 4th Fl; *Web:* bardwilhome.com	New York	NY	10018	212-944-1870	869-3599
Biddeford Blankets 300 Terr Dr; **Fax Area Code:* 847 ■ *TF:* 800-789-6441 ■ *Web:* biddefordblankets.com	Mundelein	IL	60060	800-789-6441	566-6431*
Biederlack of America 11501 Bedford Rd NE	Cumberland	MD	21502	301-759-3633	759-3837
Brentwood Originals Inc 20639 S Fordyce Ave; *Web:* www.brentwoodoriginals.com	Carson	CA	90810	310-637-6804	639-9710

Phone *Fax*

Carole Fabrics Inc PO Box 1436.......... Augusta GA 30903 706-863-4742
TF: 800-241-0920 ■ *Web:* carolefabrics.com

CHF Industries Inc 1 Pk Ave 9th Fl .... New York NY 10016 212-951-7800
TF Cust Svc: 800-243-7090 ■ *Web:* www.chfindustries.com

Cotton Goods Manufacturing Co
259 N California Ave.......... Chicago IL 60612 773-265-0088 265-0096
Web: www.cottongoodsmfg.com

Creative Bath Products 250 Creative Dr .... Central Islip NY 11722 631-582-8000 582-2020
Web: www.creativebath.com

Crown Crafts Inc 916 S Burnside .... Gonzales LA 70737 225-647-9100 647-8331
NASDAQ: CRWS ■ *TF:* 800-433-9560 ■ *Web:* www.crowncrafts.com

Custom Drapery Blinds & Shutters
3402 E T C Jester.......... Houston TX 77018 713-225-9211 227-0808
TF: 800-929-9211 ■ *Web:* www.cdbas.com

Echota Fabrics Inc 1394 US 41 N .... Calhoun GA 30701 706-629-9750 629-5229
TF: 800-763-9750 ■ *Web:* www.echotafabrics.com

Franco Mfg Company Inc 555 Prospect St .... Metuchen NJ 08840 732-494-0500 494-8270
Web: franco-mfg.com

Haleyville Drapery Manufacturing Co
1050 Hill Ave .... Haleyville AL 35565 205-486-9257

Hollander Home Fashions Corp
6501 Congress Avenue Ste 300 .... Boca Raton FL 33487 561-997-6900 997-8738
TF: 800-233-7666 ■ *Web:* www.hollander.com

Kaslen Textiles 6099 Triangle Dr .... Commerce CA 90040 323-588-7700 838-0346
TF: 800-777-5789 ■ *Web:* www.kaslentextiles.com

Kay Dee Designs Inc 177 Skunk Hill Rd .... Hope Valley RI 02832 800-537-3433 539-2210*
**Fax Area Code:* 401 ■ *TF:* 800-537-3433 ■ *Web:* www.kaydeedesigns.com

Kellwood Co 600 Kellwood Pkwy.......... Chesterfield MO 63017 314-576-3100 576-3434
Web: www.kellwood.com

Lafayette Venetian Blind Inc
3000 Klondike Rd. PO Box 2838 .... West Lafayette IN 47996 800-342-5523 423-2402*
**Fax Area Code:* 765 ■ *TF:* 800-342-5523 ■ *Web:* www.lafvb.com

Louis Hornick & Co Inc 117 E 38th St .... New York NY 10016 212-679-2448 779-7098
Web: www.louishornick.com

Louisville Bedding Co 10400 Bunsen Way.......... Louisville KY 40299 502-491-3370 495-5346
Web: www.loubed.com

Manual Woodworkers & Weavers Inc
3737 HowaRd Gap Rd.......... Hendersonville NC 28792 828-692-7333 696-2961
TF: 800-542-3139 ■ *Web:* www.manualww.com

Marietta Drapery & Window Coverings Company Inc
22 Trammel St PO Box 569 .... Marietta GA 30064 770-428-3335 423-3398*
**Fax:* Mktg ■ *TF Mktg:* 800-762-4774 ■ *Web:* www.mariettadrapery.com

Miller Industries Inc 7 Canal St.......... Lisbon Falls ME 04252 207-353-4371 353-5900

Newport Layton Home Fashions Inc
8515 N Columbia Blvd.......... Portland OR 97203 503-283-4864 283-4895
Web: www.newportlayton.com

Pacific Coast Feather Co 1964 Fourth Ave S .... Seattle WA 98134 206-624-1057
TF: 888-297-1778 ■ *Web:* www.pacificcoast.com

Paramount Industrial Cos Inc
1112 Kingwood Ave .... Norfolk VA 23502 757-855-3321 855-2029
Web: www.paramountsleep.com

Pendleton Woolen Mills Inc 220 NW Broadway.......... Portland OR 97209 503-226-4801 535-5502
TF: 800-760-4844 ■ *Web:* www.pendleton-usa.com

Perfect Fit Industries Inc 230 Fifth Ave .... New York NY 10010 212-679-6656

Phoenix Down Corp 85 US 46.......... Totowa NJ 07512 973-812-8100 812-9077
Web: www.phoenixdown.com

Riegel Consumer Products 51 Riegel Rd.......... Johnston SC 29832 803-275-2541 275-2219
TF: 800-845-3251 ■ *Web:* www.riegellinen.com

S Lichtenberg & Co Inc 295 Fifth Ave Rm 918 .... New York NY 10016 212-689-4510
Web: www.lichtenberg.com

Samson Manufacturing Co 231 E 13th St.......... Waynesboro GA 30830 706-554-2129

Saturday Knight Ltd 2100 Section Rd.......... Cincinnati OH 45237 513-641-1400 242-2805
Web: skltd.com

Surefit Inc 6575 Snowdrift Rd Ste 101 .... Allentown PA 18106 888-796-0500 336-8995*
**Fax Area Code:* 610 ■ *TF:* 888-796-0500 ■ *Web:* www.surefit.net

Tuway American Group Inc, The
2820 W Maple Rd Ste 101 .... Troy MI 48084 248-649-8790 649-3666
Web: www.tuwaymops.com

United Feather & Down Inc 414 E Golf Rd .... Des Plaines IL 60016 847-296-6610 296-6616
TF: 888-297-1778 ■ *Web:* www.ufandd.com

Wesco Fabrics Inc 4001 Forest St .... Denver CO 80216 303-388-4101 388-3908
TF: 800-950-9372 ■ *Web:* www.wescofabrics.com

747 THEATERS - BROADWAY

See Also Performing Arts Facilities p. 2912; Theater Companies p. 2924; Theaters - Resident p. 3246

Phone *Fax*

Al Hirschfeld Theatre 302 W 45th St .... New York NY 10036 212-239-6262
TF: 800-432-7780 ■ *Web:* www.telecharge.com

Ambassador Theaters 219 W 49th St .... New York NY 10019 212-239-6200
Web: ambassadortheater.com

American Airlines Theatre 227 W 42nd St.......... New York NY 10036 212-719-1300 869-8817
Web: www.roundabouttheatre.org

August Wilson 245 W 52nd St.......... New York NY 10019 212-239-6200 520-3420*
**Fax Area Code:* 415 ■ *Web:* www.telecharge.com

Biltmore Theatre 261 W 47th St.......... New York NY 10036 212-399-3000
Web: www.manhattantheatreclub.com

Boca Del Lupo 1422 William St .... Vancouver BC V5L2P7 604-684-2622
Web: bocadellupo.com

Booth Theatre 222 W 45th St.......... New York NY 10036 212-239-6200 520-3420*
**Fax Area Code:* 415 ■ *TF:* 800-432-7780 ■ *Web:* www.telecharge.com

Broadhurst Theatre 235 W 44th St.......... New York NY 10036 212-239-6200 520-3420*
**Fax Area Code:* 415 ■ *TF:* 800-447-7400 ■ *Web:* telecharge.com/go.aspx?md=102&pid=7793

Circle in the Square Theatre 1633 Broadway.......... New York NY 10019 212-239-6200 520-3420*
**Fax Area Code:* 415 ■ *Web:* www.telecharge.com

Helen Hayes Theatre 240 W 44th St.......... New York NY 10036 212-239-6200 520-3420*
**Fax Area Code:* 415 ■ *TF:* 800-447-7400 ■ *Web:* telecharge.com/go.aspx?md=102&pid=8417

Imperial Theatre 249 W 45th St .... New York NY 10036 212-239-6200 520-3420*
**Fax Area Code:* 415 ■ *TF:* 800-447-7400 ■ *Web:* www.telecharge.com

Phone *Fax*

Jacobs Theatre 242 W 45th St .... New York NY 10036 212-239-6200 520-3420*
**Fax Area Code:* 415 ■ *TF:* 800-447-7400 ■ *Web:* www.telecharge.com

Longacre Theatre 220 W 48th St .... New York NY 10036 212-239-6200 520-3420*
**Fax Area Code:* 415 ■ *TF:* 800-447-7400 ■ *Web:* www.telecharge.com

Lyceum Theatre 149 W 45th St.......... New York NY 10036 212-239-6200
TF: 800-432-7780 ■ *Web:* www.telecharge.com

Majestic Theatre 245 W 44th St.......... New York NY 10036 212-239-6200 520-3420*
**Fax Area Code:* 415 ■ *TF:* 800-447-7400 ■ *Web:* www.telecharge.com

Minskoff Theatre 200 W 45th St.......... New York NY 10036 212-869-0550
TF: 800-714-8452 ■ *Web:* minskofftheatre.com

Ottawa Fringe Festival 100-2 Daly Ave .... Ottawa ON K1N6E2 613-232-6162
Web: ottawafringe.com

Palace Theatre 1564 Broadway.......... New York NY 10036 212-730-8200
Web: palacetheatreonbroadway.com

Richard Rodgers Theatre 226 W 46th St.......... New York NY 10036 212-221-1211
TF: 866-755-3075 ■ *Web:* richardrodgerstheatre.com

Roundabout Theatre Co 231 W 39th St Ste 1200.......... New York NY 10018 212-719-9393 869-8817
Web: www.roundabouttheatre.org

Shubert Theatre 225 W 44th St.......... New York NY 10036 212-239-6200 520-3420*
**Fax Area Code:* 415 ■ *Web:* www.telecharge.com

Studio 54 Theatre 254 W 54th St .... New York NY 10019 212-719-1300
Web: www.roundabouttheatre.org

Tix Bay Area 1119 Market St 2nd Fl .... San Francisco CA 94103 415-430-1140
Web: www.theatrebayarea.org

Wing It Productions Inc
5510 University Way Ne.......... Seattle WA 98105 206-352-8291
Web: www.wingitproductions.org

748 THEATERS - MOTION PICTURE

Phone *Fax*

AMC Star Theatres 25333 W 12-Mile Rd .... Southfield MI 48034 248-368-1802
TF: 888-262-4386 ■ *Web:* www.amctheatres.com

AMC Theatres 920 Main St .... Kansas City MO 64105 816-221-4000
TF: 877-341-6397 ■ *Web:* www.amctheatres.com

Artisan Cinema & Sound LLC
9171 E Bell Rd Ste 100.......... Scottsdale AZ 85260 480-538-1071
Web: www.iintegrations.net

Brenden Theatres 531 Davis St .... Vacaville CA 95688 707-469-0190
Web: www.brendentheatres.com

Carmike Cinemas Inc 1301 First Ave.......... Columbus GA 31901 706-576-3400
NASDAQ: CKEC ■ *Web:* www.carmike.com

Celebration! Cinema
2121 Celebration Ave.......... Grand Rapids MI 49525 616-530-7469
Web: www.celebrationcinema.com

Chakeres Theatres Inc 200 N Murray St.......... Springfield OH 45503 937-323-6447
Web: www.chakerestheatres.com

Cinemark USA Inc 3900 Dallas Pkwy Ste 500.......... Plano TX 75093 972-665-1000 665-1004
TF: 800-246-3627 ■ *Web:* www.cinemark.com

Cineplex Entertainment LP 1303 Yonge St.......... Toronto ON M4T2Y9 416-323-6600 323-7228
TF: 800-333-0061 ■ *Web:* www.cineplex.com

Classic Cinemas 603 Rogers St.......... Downers Grove IL 60515 630-968-1600 968-1626
Web: www.classiccinemas.com

Clearview Cinema Group Inc
97 Main St Ste A.......... Florham Park NJ 07932 908-918-2000
Web: www.bowtiecinemas.com

Cobb Theatres LLC
2000-B Southbridge Pkwy Ste 100.......... Birmingham AL 35209 205-802-7766
Web: www.cobbtheatres.com

Coming Attractions Theatres
1644 Ashland St Unit 5.......... Ashland OR 97520 541-488-1021
Web: www.catheatres.com

Community Theater 100 S St.......... Morristown NJ 07960 973-455-1607
TF: 888-278-7769 ■ *Web:* www.mayoarts.org

Crest Theater 1013 K St.......... Sacramento CA 95814 916-442-5189
Web: www.thecrest.com

De Anza Land & Leisure Corp
1615 Cordova St.......... Los Angeles CA 90007 323-734-9951 734-2531

Decurion Corp, The 120 N Robertson Blvd.......... Los Angeles CA 90048 310-659-9432
Web: www.decurion.com

Dickinson Theaters Inc 6801 W 107th St .... Overland Park KS 66211 913-432-2334
Web: www.dtmovies.com

Eastern Federal Corp 901 E Blvd .... Charlotte NC 28203 704-377-3495
Web: easternfederal.com

Fairfield Theater 70 Sanford St.......... Fairfield CT 06824 203-319-1404
Web: fairfieldtheatre.org

Harkins Theatres 7511 E Mcdonald Dr.......... Scottsdale AZ 85250 480-627-7777
Web: www.harkinstheatres.com

Hollywood Blvd a Cinema Bar & Eatery
1001 75th St Ste 153 .... Woodridge IL 60517 630-427-1880
Web: www.atriptothemovies.com

Hollywood Theater Holdings Inc
919 SW Taylor St Ste 800.......... Portland OR 97205 503-221-7090 796-0229
Web: www.regmovies.com

IMAX Corp 2525 Speakman Dr .... Mississauga ON L5K1B1 905-403-6500 403-6450
NYSE: IMAX ■ *Web:* www.imax.com

Kerasotes ShowPlace Theatres LLC
224 N Des Plaines Ave.......... Chicago IL 60661 312-756-3360
Web: showplaceicon.com

Landmark Theaters 2222 S Barrington Ave .... Los Angeles CA 90064 310-473-6701
TF Cust Svc: 888-724-6362 ■ *Web:* www.landmarktheatres.com

Magnolia Pictures LLC 49 W 27th St 7th Fl.......... New York NY 10001 212-924-6701
Web: www.magpictures.com

Malco Theatres Inc 5851 Ridgeway Ctr Pkwy.......... Memphis TN 38120 901-761-3480 681-2044
Web: www.malco.com

Marcus Corp 100 E Wisconsin Ave.......... Milwaukee WI 53202 414-905-1000
NYSE: MCS ■ *Web:* www.marcuscorp.com

Marcus Theatres Corp
100 E Wisconsin Ave Ste 2000.......... Milwaukee WI 53202 414-905-1000 920-2250
TF Cust Svc: 800-274-0099 ■ *Web:* marcustheatres.com

	City	State	Zip	Phone	Fax
Metropolitan Theaters Corp 8727 W Third St *Web:* www.metrotheatres.com	Los Angeles	CA	90048	310-858-2800	858-2860
National Amusements Inc 846 University Ave *Web:* www.showcasecinemas.com	Norwood	MA	02062	781-461-1600	326-1306
New Federal Theatre 292 Henry St *Web:* www.newfederaltheatre.org	New York	NY	10002	212-353-1176	
Open Air Cinema LLC 1402 West 400 South *Web:* www.openaircinema.us	Orem	UT	84058	801-796-6800	
Pacific Theatres Corp 120 N Robertson Blvd *Web:* www.pacifictheatres.com	Los Angeles	CA	90048	310-657-8420	
Reading International Inc 6100 Center Dr Ste 900 *NASDAQ: RDI* ■ *Web:* www.readingrdi.com	Los Angeles	CA	90045	213-235-2240	235-2229
Regal Entertainment Group 7132 Regal Ln *NYSE: RGC* ■ *TF Cust Svc:* 877-835-5734 ■ *Web:* www.regmovies.com	Knoxville	TN	37918	865-922-1123	922-3188
Regency Theatres Inc 1440 Eastman Ave *Web:* www.regencymovies.com	Ventura	CA	93003	805-658-6544	
Southern Theatres LLC 305 Baronne St Ste 900 *Web:* www.thegrandtheatre.com	New Orleans	LA	70112	504-297-1133	
United Entertainment Corp 3601 18th St S Ste 104 *Web:* www.uecmovies.com	Saint Cloud	MN	56301	320-203-1003	
Virginia Air & Space Center 600 Settlers Landing Rd *Web:* www.vasc.org	Hampton	VA	23669	757-727-0900	
Vittum Theater 1012 N Noble St *Web:* www.vittumtheater.org	Chicago	IL	60642	773-342-4141	
Wometco Enterprises Inc 3195 Ponce De Leon Blvd *Web:* miamiseaprison.com	Coral Gables	FL	33134	305-529-1400	529-1466

749 THEATERS - RESIDENT

See Also Performing Arts Facilities p. 2912; Theater Companies p. 2924; Theaters - Broadway p. 3245

All of the theaters listed here are members of the League of Resident Theatres (LORT). In order to become a member of LORT, each theater must be incorporated as a non-profit, IRS-approved organization; must rehearse each self-produced production for a minimum of three weeks; must have a playing season of 12 weeks or more; and must operate under a LORT-Equity contract.

	City	State	Zip	Phone	Fax
5th Avenue Theatre Association 1308 Fifth Ave *Web:* www.5thavenue.org	Seattle	WA	98101	206-625-1900	
A Contemporary Theatre (ACT) 700 Union St Kreielsheimer Pl *TF:* 888-584-4849 ■ *Web:* www.acttheatre.org	Seattle	WA	98101	206-292-7660	292-7670
Actors Theatre of Louisville 316 W Main St *TF:* 800-428-5849 ■ *Web:* www.actorstheatre.org	Louisville	KY	40202	502-584-1205	561-3300
Alabama Shakespeare Festival 1 Festival Dr *TF:* 800-841-4273 ■ *Web:* www.asf.net	Montgomery	AL	36117	334-271-5300	271-5348
Alley Theatre 615 Texas Ave *Web:* www.alleytheatre.org	Houston	TX	77002	713-220-5700	222-6542
Alliance Theatre Co 1280 Peachtree St NE Woodruff Arts Ctr *Web:* www.alliancetheatre.org	Atlanta	GA	30309	404-733-4650	733-4625
American Repertory Theatre (ART) 64 Brattle St *Web:* www.americanrepertorytheater.org	Cambridge	MA	02138	617-495-2668	495-1705
Arden Theatre Co 40 N Second St *Web:* www.ardentheatre.org	Philadelphia	PA	19106	215-922-8900	922-7011
Arena Stage 1101 Sixth St SW *Web:* www.arenastage.org	Washington	DC	20024	202-554-9066	488-4056
Arkansas Repertory Theatre 601 Main St PO Box 110 *TF:* 866-684-3737 ■ *Web:* www.therep.org	Little Rock	AR	72201	501-378-0445	378-0012
Asolo Repertory Theatre 5555 N Tamiami Tr *TF:* 800-361-8388 ■ *Web:* www.asolorep.org	Sarasota	FL	34243	941-351-9010	351-5796
Barter Theatre 127 W Main St *Web:* www.bartertheatre.com	Abingdon	VA	24210	276-628-3991	619-3335
Bb Riverboats Inc 101 Riverboat Row *TF:* 800-261-8586 ■ *Web:* www.bbriverboats.com	Newport	KY	41071	859-261-8500	
Berkeley Repertory Theatre 2025 Addison St *TF:* 888-427-8849 ■ *Web:* www.berkeleyrep.org	Berkeley	CA	94704	510-647-2949	647-2975
Berkshire Theatre Festival 83 E Main St *Web:* www.berkshiretheatregroup.org	Stockbridge	MA	01262	413-298-5576	298-3368
Capital Repertory Theatre 432 State St *Web:* www.capitalrep.org	Schenectady	NY	12305	518-462-4531	881-1823
Center Stage 700 N Calvert St *Web:* www.centerstage.org	Baltimore	MD	21202	410-986-4000	539-3912
City Theatre Co 1300 Bingham St *Web:* www.citytheatrecompany.org	Pittsburgh	PA	15203	412-431-4400	431-5535
Clarence Brown Theatre *University of Tennessee* 206 McClung Tower *Web:* www.clarencebrowntheatre.com	Knoxville	TN	37996	865-974-5161	974-4867
Comedy Works Inc 1226 15th St *Web:* www.comedyworks.com	Denver	CO	80202	303-595-3637	
Court Theatre 5535 S Ellis Ave *Web:* www.courttheatre.org	Chicago	IL	60637	773-702-7005	834-1897
Dallas Theater Ctr 3636 Turtle Creek Blvd *Web:* www.dallastheatercenter.org	Dallas	TX	75219	214-526-8210	521-7666
Delaware Theatre Co 200 Water St *Web:* www.delawaretheatre.org	Wilmington	DE	19801	302-594-1104	594-1107
Fringe Theatre Adventures Society 10330 84 Ave Nw *Web:* www.fringetheatre.ca	Edmonton	AB	T6E2G9	780-448-9000	
Geffen Playhouse 10886 Le Conte Ave *Web:* www.geffenplayhouse.org	Los Angeles	CA	90024	310-208-5454	208-8383
Genesee Theatre 221 N Genesee St *Web:* www.geneseetheatre.com	Waukegan	IL	60085	847-782-2366	
George Street Playhouse 9 Livingston Ave *Web:* www.georgestreetplayhouse.org	New Brunswick	NJ	08901	732-246-7717	247-9151
Geva Theatre Ctr 75 Woodbury Blvd *Web:* www.gevatheatre.org	Rochester	NY	14607	585-232-1366	232-4031
Goodman Theatre 170 N Dearborn St *Web:* www.goodmantheatre.org	Chicago	IL	60601	312-443-3811	443-3821
Goodspeed Musicals PO Box A *Web:* www.goodspeed.org	East Haddam	CT	06423	860-873-8664	873-2329
Great Lakes Theater Festival 1501 Euclid Ave Ste 300 *Web:* www.greatlakestheater.org	Cleveland	OH	44115	216-241-5490	241-6315
Guthrie Theater 818 S Second St *TF Resv:* 877-447-8243 ■ *Web:* www.guthrietheater.org	Minneapolis	MN	55415	612-377-2224	225-6004
Hartford Stage Co 50 Church St *Web:* www.hartfordstage.org	Hartford	CT	06103	860-527-5151	247-8243
Huntington Theatre Co 264 Huntington Ave Boston University Theatre *Web:* www.huntingtontheatre.org	Boston	MA	02115	617-266-7900	353-8300
Kansas City Repertory Theatre 4949 Cherry St *Web:* www.kcrep.org	Kansas City	MO	64110	816-235-2700	235-5508
La Jolla Playhouse PO Box 12039 *Web:* www.lajollaplayhouse.org	La Jolla	CA	92039	858-550-1070	550-1075
Laguna Playhouse, The 606 Laguna Canyon Rd PO Box 1747 *Web:* www.lagunaplayhouse.com	Laguna Beach	CA	92651	949-497-2787	497-6948
Lincoln Ctr Theater 150 W 65th St **Fax Area Code:* 212 ■ *TF:* 800-432-7250 ■ *Web:* www.lct.org	New York	NY	10023	800-432-7250	873-0761*
Maltz Jupiter Theatre 1001 E Indiantown Rd *TF:* 800-445-1666 ■ *Web:* www.jupitertheatre.org	Jupiter	FL	33477	561-743-2666	743-0107
Manhattan Theatre Club Inc 311 W 43rd St 8th Fl *Web:* www.manhattantheatreclub.com	New York	NY	10036	212-399-3000	
Massey Theatre 735 Eighth Ave *Web:* vcn.bc.ca	New Westminster	BC	V3M2R2	604-517-5900	
McCarter Theatre 91 University Pl *Web:* www.mccarter.org	Princeton	NJ	08540	609-258-6500	497-0369
Merrimack Repertory Theatre 132 Warren St *Web:* www.mrt.org	Lowell	MA	01852	978-654-7550	654-7575
Milwaukee Repertory Theater 108 E Wells St *Web:* www.milwaukeerep.com	Milwaukee	WI	53202	414-224-1761	224-9097
New Repertory Theatre 200 Dexter Ave *Web:* www.newrep.org	Watertown	MA	02472	617-923-7060	
Northlight Theatre 9501 Skokie Blvd *Web:* www.northlight.org	Skokie	IL	60077	847-673-6300	679-1879
Old Globe Theatre 1363 Old Globe Way *Web:* www.oldglobe.org	San Diego	CA	92101	619-231-1941	231-5879
One Yellow Rabbit Performance Theatre 225 8 Ave Se *Web:* oyr.org	Calgary	AB	T2G0K8	403-264-3224	
Opera Atelier 157 King St E *Web:* www.operaatelier.com	Toronto	ON	M5C1G9	416-703-3767	
Oregon Shakespeare Festival 15 S Pioneer St *TF:* 800-219-8161 ■ *Web:* www.orshakes.org	Ashland	OR	97520	541-482-2111	
Pasadena Playhouse, The 39 S El Molino Ave *TF:* 800-733-2767 ■ *Web:* www.pasadenaplayhouse.org	Pasadena	CA	91101	626-356-7529	204-7399
People's Light & Theatre Co 39 Conestoga Rd *TF:* 800-732-0999 ■ *Web:* www.peopleslight.org	Malvern	PA	19355	610-647-1900	640-9521
Philadelphia Theatre Co 230 S Broad St 10th Fl *Web:* www.philadelphiatheatrecompany.org	Philadelphia	PA	19107	215-985-1400	985-5800
Pittsburgh Public Theater 621 Penn Ave *TF:* 800-732-0999 ■ *Web:* www.ppt.org	Pittsburgh	PA	15222	412-316-8200	316-8219
PlayMakers Repertory Co 150 Country Club Rd *Web:* www.playmakersrep.org	Chapel Hill	NC	27599	919-962-7529	
Portland Ctr Stage (PCS) 128 NW Eleventh Ave *Web:* www.pcs.org	Portland	OR	97209	503-445-3700	445-3701
Portland Stage Co PO Box 1458 *Web:* www.portlandstage.org	Portland	ME	04104	207-774-1043	774-0576
Prince Music Theater 1412 Chestnut St *Web:* www.princetheater.org	Philadelphia	PA	19102	267-239-2941	
Repertory Theatre of Saint Louis 130 Edgar Rd PO Box 191730 *Web:* www.repstl.org	Saint Louis	MO	63119	314-968-7340	968-9638
River Center-performing Arts Po Box 2425 *Web:* rivercenter.org	Columbus	GA	31902	706-256-3607	
Roundabout Theatre Co 231 W 39th St Ste 1200 *Web:* www.roundabouttheatre.org	New York	NY	10018	212-719-9393	869-8817
San Jose Repertory Theatre 101 Paseo de San Antonio	San Jose	CA	95113	408-367-7255	367-7236
Seattle Repertory Theatre (SRT) 155 Mercer St PO Box 900923 *TF:* 877-900-9285 ■ *Web:* www.seattlerep.org	Seattle	WA	98109	206-443-2210	443-2379
Shakespeare & Company Inc 70 Kemble St *Web:* www.shakespeare.org	Lenox	MA	01240	413-637-1199	
Shakespeare Theatre 516 Eigth St SE *TF:* 877-487-8849 ■ *Web:* www.shakespearetheatre.org	Washington	DC	20003	202-547-3230	547-0226
South Coast Repertory 655 Town Ctr Dr *Web:* www.scr.org	Costa Mesa	CA	92626	714-708-5500	708-5576
Spotlight on Kids 20 S Main St Ste 22 *Web:* www.janesvillepac.org	Janesville	WI	53545	608-758-1451	
Stagestruck 121 W Chestnut St *Web:* stagestruck.org	Goldsboro	NC	27530	919-736-4530	
Syracuse Stage 820 E Genesee St *Web:* www.syracusestage.org	Syracuse	NY	13210	315-443-4008	443-9846

Phone Fax

TADA 15 W 28th St 3rd Fl. New York NY 10001 212-252-1619
Web: www.tadatheater.com

Theatre For A New Audience
154 Christopher St Ste 3D New York NY 10014 212-229-2819 229-2911
TF: 866-811-4111 ■ *Web:* www.tfana.org

TheatreWorks 350 Twin Dolphin Dr Redwood City CA 94065 650-463-1950 463-1963
Web: www.theatreworks.org

Trinity Repertory Co 201 Washington St Providence RI 02903 401-521-1100 751-5577
Web: www.trinityrep.com

Victory Gardens Theater 2257 N Lincoln Ave Chicago IL 60614 773-549-5788
Web: victorygardens.org

Wilma Theater 265 S Broad St Philadelphia PA 19107 215-893-9456 893-0895
TF: 800-732-0999 ■ *Web:* www.wilmatheater.org

Winnipeg Fringe Festival 174 Market Ave Winnipeg MB R3B0P8 204-956-1340
Web: www.winnipegfringe.com

Yale Repertory Theatre
1120 Chapel St PO Box 1257 New Haven CT 06505 203-432-1234 432-6423
TF: 800-973-2837 ■ *Web:* www.yalerep.org

750 TICKET BROKERS

Phone Fax

All American Ticket Service
2616 Philadelphia Pike Ste E Claymont DE 19703 800-669-0571 798-6552*
**Fax Area Code:* 302 ■ *TF:* 800-669-0571 ■ *Web:* www.allamericantickets.com

Americana Tickets NY 1535 Broadway New York NY 10036 212-581-6660 262-9627
TF: 800-833-3121 ■ *Web:* www.americanaticketsny.com

Barter Depot 1107 W Veterans Hwy Jackson NJ 08527 732-833-2273
Web: barterdepot.com

Broadway.com 729 Seventh Ave New York NY 10019 212-541-8457 541-4892
TF: 800-762-3929 ■ *Web:* broadway.com

Casual Apparel Inc 139 S Main St Sparta TN 38583 931-836-3004

Front Row USA Entertainment
900 N Federal Hwy Ste 200 Hallandale FL 33009 305-940-8499
TF: 800-277-8499 ■ *Web:* www.frontrowusa.com

Great Seats Inc
7338 Baltimore Ave Ste 108A College Park MD 20740 301-985-6250 985-6254
TF: 800-664-5056 ■ *Web:* www.greatseats.com

REZ-1 Inc 100 William St Ste 100 Wellesley MA 02481 617-928-5000
Web: www.rez1.com

Select-A-Ticket Inc 25 Rt 23 S Riverdale NJ 07457 973-839-6100 839-0870
TF: 800-735-3288 ■ *Web:* www.selectaticket.com

Theatre Development Fund
1501 Broadway 21st Fl New York NY 10036 212-221-0885 768-1563
TF: 888-424-4685 ■ *Web:* www.tdf.org

Ticket Heaven Inc 440 Knoll St Ste 144 Wheaton IL 60187 630-260-0626 260-4831

Ticket Source Inc
5516 E Mockingbird Ln Ste 100 Dallas TX 75206 214-821-9011 821-9060
TF: 800-557-6872 ■ *Web:* www.ticketsource.com

Tickets.com Inc 555 Anton Blvd 11th Fl Costa Mesa CA 92626 714-327-5400 327-5410
TF: 800-352-0212 ■ *Web:* www.tickets.com

TicketWeb Inc PO Box 77250 San Francisco CA 94103 866-777-8932
TF Cust Svc: 866-777-8932 ■ *Web:* www.ticketweb.com

Western States Ticket Service
143 W McDowell Rd Phoenix AZ 85003 602-254-3300
TF: 800-326-0331 ■ *Web:* www.wstickets.com

Wincup GP LLC 358 Chinook Cir Lake Mary FL 32746 407-619-4157
Web: www.wincupgp.com

751 TILE - CERAMIC (WALL & FLOOR)

Phone Fax

American Marazzi Tile Inc 359 Clay Rd Sunnyvale TX 75182 972-232-3801 226-5629
TF: 800-289-8453 ■ *Web:* marazziusa.com

Ann Sacks Tile & Stone Inc 8120 NE 33rd Dr Portland OR 97211 503-281-7751 287-8807
TF: 800-278-8453 ■ *Web:* www.annsacks.com

Armstrong World Industries Inc
2500 Columbia Ave Lancaster PA 17603 717-397-0611 396-6133*
NYSE: AWI ■ **Fax:* Hum Res ■ *TF Cust Svc:* 800-233-3823 ■ *Web:* www.armstrong.com

B & W Tile Mfg Company Inc
14600 S Western Ave Gardena CA 90249 310-538-9579 538-2190
Web: www.bwtile.com

Crossville Porcelain Stone/USA
PO Box 1168 Crossville TN 38557 931-484-2110 484-2110
TF: 800-221-9093 ■ *Web:* www.crossvilleinc.com

Curran Group Inc 286 Memorial Ct Crystal Lake IL 60014 815-455-5100 455-7894
Web: www.currangroup.com

Dal-Tile International Inc 7834 Hawn Fwy Dallas TX 75217 214-398-1411 309-4553
TF: 800-933-8453 ■ *Web:* www.daltile.com

Deutsche Steinzeug America Inc (DSA)
367 Curie Dr Alpharetta GA 30005 770-442-5500 442-5502
Web: www.deutsche-steinzeug.de

Ege Seramik America Inc
5600 Oakbrook Pkwy Ste 280 Norcross GA 30093 678-291-0888 291-0832
Web: www.egeseramik-usa.com

Endicott Tile LLC 57120 707 Rd Endicott NE 68350 402-729-3315 729-5804
Web: www.endicott.com

Epro Tile Inc 10890 E CR 6 Bloomville OH 44818 866-818-3776 343-8453
TF: 866-818-3776 ■ *Web:* www.eprotile.com

Florida Tile Industries Inc
998 Governors Ln Ste 300 Lexington KY 40513 859-219-5200
TF Cust Svc: 800-352-8453 ■ *Web:* www.floridatile.com

Florim USA Inc 300 International Blvd Clarksville TN 37040 931-645-5100 647-5974
Web: www.florimusa.com

Interceramic USA 2333 S Jupiter Rd Garland TX 75041 214-503-5500 503-5555
Web: www.interceramicusa.com

Interstyle Ceramics & Glass Ltd
3625 Brighton Ave Burnaby BC V5A3H5 604-421-7229 421-7544
TF: 800-667-1566 ■ *Web:* interstyleglass.com

Ironrock Capital Inc 1201 Millerton St SE Canton OH 44707 330-484-4887
Web: www.ironrock.com

Phone Fax

Jefferson Ceramic Tile Company Inc
405 S Main St Jefferson WI 53549 920-674-5725

ME Tile 447 Atlas Dr Nashville TN 37211 888-348-8453
TF: 888-348-8453 ■ *Web:* www.metile.com

Meredith Collection 1201 Millerton St SE Canton OH 44707 330-484-1656 484-9380
TF: 888-325-3945 ■ *Web:* www.meredithtile.com

Metropolitan Ceramics 1201 Millerton St SE Canton OH 44707 800-325-3945
TF: 800-325-3945 ■ *Web:* www.metroceramics.com

Nudo Products Inc 1500 Taylor Ave Springfield IL 62703 217-528-5636 528-8722
TF: 800-826-4132 ■ *Web:* www.nudo.com

Summitville Tiles Inc 15364 Ohio 644 Summitville OH 43962 330-223-1511 223-1414
Web: www.summitville.com

Wood Pro Inc 421 Washington St PO Box 363 Auburn MA 01501 508-832-3291 832-9847
TF: 800-786-5577 ■ *Web:* www.woodproinc.com

752 TIMBER TRACTS

Phone Fax

American Lumber Distributors & Brokers Inc
2405 Republic Blvd Birmingham AL 35201 205-791-0155
Web: www.americanlumber1.com

Authentic Pine Floors Inc 4042 Hwy 42 Locust Grove GA 30248 800-283-6038
TF: 800-283-6038 ■ *Web:* www.authenticpinefloors.com

Boething Treeland Farms Inc
23475 Long Valley Rd Woodland Hills CA 91367 818-883-1222 712-6979
Web: boethingtreeland.com

Boise Cascade LLC 1111 W Jefferson St Ste 300 Boise ID 83702 208-384-6161 384-7189
Web: www.bc.com

Bulbman 3101 Orange Grove Ave North Highlands CA 95660 916-920-3234
Web: www.bulbman.com

Cherry Lake Tree Farm 7836 Cherry Lk Rd Groveland FL 34736 352-429-2171
Web: www.cherrylake.com

Crescent Resources Inc
227 W Trade St Ste 1000 Charlotte NC 28202 980-321-6000
Web: crescentcommunities.com

Deltic Timber Corp PO Box 7200 El Dorado AR 71731 870-881-9400
NYSE: DEL ■ *Web:* www.deltic.com

Dutchman Tree Farms 9689 W Walker Rd Manton MI 49663 231-839-7901
Web: www.dutchmantreefarms.com

Federal Wage & Labor Institute
7001 W 43rd St Houston TX 77092 713-690-5676
TF: 800-767-9243 ■ *Web:* www.fwlli.com

Gillies & Prittie Inc
151 Pleasant Hill Rd Scarborough ME 04074 207-883-7815
Web: www.gilliesandprittie.com

Haida Corp PO Box 89 Hydaburg AK 99922 907-285-3721
TF: 800-478-3721 ■ *Web:* haidacorporation.com

Holiday Tree Farms Inc 800 NW Cornell Ave Corvallis OR 97330 541-753-3236 757-8028
TF: 800-289-3684 ■ *Web:* www.holidaytreefarm.com

Industrial Timber & Lumber Corp (ITL)
23925 Commerce Pk Rd Beachwood OH 44122 216-831-3140 831-4734
TF: 800-829-9663 ■ *Web:* www.itlcorp.com

JM Huber Corp 499 Thornall St 8th Fl Edison NJ 08837 732-549-8600 549-2239*
**Fax:* Hum Res ■ *TF:* 877-418-0038 ■ *Web:* www.huber.com

Keim Lumber Company Inc
4465 State Rt 557 PO Box 40 Charm OH 44617 330-893-2251
Web: www.keimlumber.com

Kohltech International Ltd 583 MacElmon Rd Debert NS B0M1G0 902-662-3100
TF: 800-565-4396 ■ *Web:* www.kohltech.com

Koopman Lumber Company Inc
665 Church St Whitinsville MA 01588 508-234-4545
Web: www.koopmanlumber.com

Lester Group, The
101 E Commonwealth Blvd Martinsville VA 24115 276-632-2195 632-2117
Web: www.lestergroup.com

McShan Lumber Company Inc PO Box 27 McShan AL 35471 205-375-6277 375-2773
TF: 800-882-3712 ■ *Web:* www.mcshanlumber.com

Mendocino Redwood Company LLC
850 Kunzler Ranch Rd Ukiah CA 95482 707-463-5110
Web: www.hrcllc.com

Moonworks 1137 Park E Dr Woonsocket RI 02895 800-975-6666
TF: 800-975-6666 ■ *Web:* www.moonworkshome.com

Moulures M Warnet Mouldings Inc
100 Rue Marius-Warnet Blainville QC J7C5P9 450-437-1209 437-3679
Web: www.mwarnet.com

Olympic Resource Management
19950 Seventh Ave NE Ste 200 Poulsbo WA 98370 360-697-6626 697-1156
NASDAQ: POPE ■ *Web:* www.orminc.com

Pike Lumber Company Inc PO Box 247 Akron IN 46910 574-893-4511 893-7400
TF: 800-356-4554 ■ *Web:* www.pikelumber.com

Pioneer Millworks 1180 Commercial Dr Farmington NY 14425 585-924-9970
TF: 800-951-9663 ■ *Web:* www.pioneermillworks.com

Ring's End Inc 181 W Ave Darien CT 06820 203-655-2525
Web: www.ringsend.com

Rossi Building Materials Inc
835 Stewart St Fort Bragg CA 95437 707-964-4086
Web: www.rossi-ace.com

Roy O Martin 2189 Memorial Dr PO Box 1110 Alexandria LA 71301 318-448-0405 473-2624
Web: www.royomartin.com

Shell Lumber & Hardware Co 2733 SW 27th Ave Miami FL 33133 305-856-6401
Web: www.shelllumber.com

Sierra Pacific Industries
19794 Riverside Ave Anderson CA 96007 530-378-8000 378-8109
Web: spi-ind.com

Starker Forests Inc 7240 SW Philomath Blvd Corvallis OR 97333 541-929-2477 929-2178
Web: www.starkerforests.com

Westervelt Company Inc, The PO Box 48999 Tuscaloosa AL 35404 205-562-5000 562-5012
Web: www.westervelt.com

Weyerhaeuser Co 33663 Weyerhaeuser Way S Federal Way WA 98003 253-924-2345
NYSE: WY ■ *TF:* 800-525-5440 ■ *Web:* www.weyerhaeuser.com

Yule Tree Farms LLC 8804 S Heinz Rd Canby OR 97013 503-651-2114 651-2665
TF: 888-970-8733

753 TIMESHARE COMPANIES

See Also Hotels & Hotel Companies p. 2536

				Phone	Fax
Bluegreen Corp 4960 Conference Way N Ste 100 ... *NYSE:* BXG ■ *TF:* 800-456-2582 ■ *Web:* bluegreenvacations.com	Boca Raton	FL	33431	561-912-8000	912-8100
Central Florida Investments Inc 5601 Windhover Dr ... *Web:* www.westgateresorts.com	Orlando	FL	32819	407-351-3351	352-8935
Diamond Resorts International 3745 Las Vegas Blvd S ... *Web:* www.diamondresorts.com	Las Vegas	NV	89109	702-261-1000	
Disney Vacation Club 1390 Celebration Blvd ... *TF:* 800-500-3990 ■ *Web:* www.disneyvacationclub.disney.go.com	Celebration	FL	34747	407-566-3100	
Festiva Resorts 1 Vance Gap Rd ... **Fax:* Financial ■ *TF Resv:* 866-933-7848 ■ *Web:* festiva.com	Asheville	NC	28805	828-254-3378	254-2285*
Four Seasons Hotels & Resorts 1165 Leslie St ... *TF:* 800-332-3442 ■ *Web:* www.fourseasons.com	Toronto	ON	M3C2K8	416-449-1750	441-4374
Hilton Grand Vacations Company LLC 6355 Metro W Blvd Ste 180 ... *TF:* 800-230-7068 ■ *Web:* www.hiltongrandvacations.com	Orlando	FL	32835	407-722-3100	521-3112
Hyatt Vacation Ownership Inc 140 Fountain Pkwy N Ste 570 ... *TF:* 800-926-4447 ■ *Web:* www.hyatt.com	Saint Petersburg	FL	33716	727-803-9400	803-9401
Interval International Inc 6262 Sunset Dr PO Box 431920 ... *TF:* 800-828-8200 ■ *Web:* www.intervalworld.com	Miami	FL	33143	305-666-1861	667-2072
Marriott Vacation Club International 6649 Westwood Blvd Ste 500 ... *TF:* 800-307-7312 ■ *Web:* www.marriottvacationclub.com	Orlando	FL	32821	407-206-6000	
One Napili Way 5355 Lower Honoapiilani Hwy ... *Web:* www.onenapiliway.com	Lahaina	HI	96761	808-669-2007	
Resort Condominiums International (RCI) 9998 N Michigan Rd ... *TF:* 800-338-7777 ■ *Web:* www.rci.com	Carmel	IN	46032	317-805-8000	
Royal Aloha Vacation Club 1505 Dillingham Blvd Ste 212 ... *TF:* 800-367-5212 ■ *Web:* www.ravc.com	Honolulu	HI	96817	808-847-8050	841-5467
Shell Vacations Club 40 Skokie Blvd Ste 350 ... *Web:* www.shellvacationsclub.com	Northbrook	IL	60062	847-564-4600	
Silverleaf Resorts Inc 1221 Riverbend Dr Ste 120 ... *TF:* 800-613-0310 ■ *Web:* www.silverleafresorts.com	Dallas	TX	75247	214-631-1166	637-0585
Sunchaser Vacation Villas 5129 Riverview Gate Rd ... *TF Resv:* 877-451-1250 ■ *Web:* www.sunchaservillas.ca	Fairmont Hot Springs	BC	V0B1L1	250-345-4545	345-6166
Tempus Resorts International 7380 Sand Lake Rd Ste 600 ... *TF:* 877-747-4747 ■ *Web:* www.tempusresorts.com	Orlando	FL	32819	407-226-1000	
Vacation Internationale 1417 116th Ave NE ... *TF:* 800-444-6633 ■ *Web:* www.vacationinternationale.com	Bellevue	WA	98004	425-454-8429	456-0536
WorldMark the Club 9805 Willows Rd NE ... *TF:* 800-722-3487 ■ *Web:* www.worldmarktheclub.com	Redmond	WA	98052	425-498-1950	

754 TIRES - MFR

				Phone	Fax
Albert Tire LLC 39 Phoenix Dr ... *Web:* www.alberttire.com	West Deptford	NJ	08086	856-663-0574	
Bridgestone Americas Holding Inc 535 Marriott Dr ... *TF Cust Svc:* 877-201-2373 ■ *Web:* www.bridgestoneamericas.com/en/index	Nashville	TN	37214	615-937-1000	937-3621
Callaghan Tire 1511 38th Ave E ... *Web:* www.callaghantire.com	Bradenton	FL	34208	941-746-6188	
Coker Tire Co 1317 Chestnut St ... *Web:* www.cokertire.com	Chattanooga	TN	37402	423-265-6368	
Continental Tire North America Inc 1800 Continental Blvd ... **Fax:* Mktg ■ *TF:* 877-235-0102 ■ *Web:* www.conti-online.com	Charlotte	NC	28273	704-583-3900	583-8947*
Cooper Tire & Rubber Co 701 Lima Ave ... *NYSE:* CTB ■ *TF:* 800-854-6288 ■ *Web:* www.coopertire.com	Findlay	OH	45840	419-423-1321	424-4108
Dunlop Tires 3045 Sheridan Dr ... *TF:* 800-845-8378 ■ *Web:* www.dunloptires.com/en-US	Amherst	NY	14226	800-522-7458	
Goodyear Tire & Rubber Co 200 Innovation Way ... *NASDAQ:* GT ■ **Fax:* Cust Svc ■ *TF Cust Svc:* 800-321-2136 ■ *Web:* www.goodyear.com	Akron	OH	44316	330-796-2121	796-2222*
Hankook Tire America Corp 1450 Valley Rd ... *TF:* 800-426-8252 ■ *Web:* www.hankooktire.com/us	Wayne	NJ	07470	973-633-9000	633-0028
Hercules Tire & Rubber Co 16380 E US Rt 224 - 200 ... *TF:* 800-677-9535 ■ *Web:* www.herculestire.com	Findlay	OH	45840	419-425-6400	425-6404
Hercules Tire Sales Inc 10130 E 51st St ... *Web:* www.herculestiresales.com	Tulsa	OK	74146	918-627-7353	
K&M Tire Inc 965 Spencerville Rd PO Box 279 ... *TF:* 877-879-5407 ■ *Web:* www.kmtire.com	Delphos	OH	45833	419-695-1061	
Kal Tire Ltd 1540 Kalamalka Lk Rd PO Box 1240 ... *Web:* www.kaltire.com	Vernon	BC	V1T6N6	250-542-2366	
La Cie Canada Tire Inc 21500 Transcanadienne ... *TF:* 888-267-5097 ■ *Web:* www.cdatire.com	Baie-D'Urfe	QC	H9X4B7	514-457-0155	457-1158
Lyna Manufacturing Inc 1125 15th St W ... *TF:* 800-993-4007 ■ *Web:* tirelyna.com	North Vancouver	BC	V7P1M7	604-990-0988	
Martin Wheel Company Inc 342 W Ave ... *TF:* 800-462-7846 ■ *Web:* www.martinwheelco.com	Tallmadge	OH	44278	330-633-3278	633-3303
Michelin North America Inc 1 PkwyS PO Box 19001 ... **Fax:* Cust Svc ■ *TF Cust Svc:* 800-847-3435 ■ *Web:* www.michelin.com	Greenville	SC	29602	864-458-5000	458-6359*
Mickey Thompson Tires 4600 Prosper Dr ... *TF:* 800-222-9092 ■ *Web:* www.mickeythompsontires.com	Stow	OH	44224	330-928-9092	928-0503
Millennium Industrial Tires LLC 433 Lane Dr ... *Web:* www.millenniumtire.com	Florence	AL	35630	256-764-2900	
Mitchell Industrial Tire Co 2915 Eigth Ave PO Box 71839 ... **Fax:* Sales ■ *TF:* 800-251-7226 ■ *Web:* www.mitco.com	Chattanooga	TN	37407	423-698-4442	697-7143*
OTR Wheel Engineering Inc 6 Riverside Industrial Park NE ... *Web:* www.otrwheel.com	Rome	GA	30161	706-235-9781	
Pete's Road Service Inc 2230 E Orangethorpe Ave ... *Web:* www.petesrs.com	Fullerton	CA	92831	714-446-1207	
Purcell Tire & Rubber Co 301 N Hall St ... **Fax:* Hum Res ■ *Web:* www.purcelltire.com	Potosi	MO	63664	573-438-2131	438-2151*
Robbins LLC 3415 Thompson St ... **Fax Area Code:* 800 ■ *TF:* 800-633-3312 ■ *Web:* www.robbinsllc.com	Muscle Shoals	AL	35661	256-383-5441	821-7918*
SolidBoss Worldwide Inc 200 Veterans Blvd ... *TF:* 888-258-7252 ■ *Web:* www.solidboss.com	South Haven	MI	49090	269-637-6356	637-6356
Specialty Tires of America Inc 1600 Washington St ... *TF:* 800-622-7327 ■ *Web:* www.stausaonline.com	Indiana	PA	15701	724-349-9010	349-8192
Superior Tire & Rubber Corp 1818 Pennsylvania Ave W PO Box 308 ... *TF Cust Svc:* 800-289-1456 ■ *Web:* www.superiortire.com	Warren	PA	16365	814-723-2370	726-0740
Tech International 200 E Coshocton St ... *TF:* 800-336-8324 ■ *Web:* www.techtirerepairs.com	Johnstown	OH	43031	740-967-9015	967-1039
Titan Tire Co 2345 E Market St ... *TF:* 800-872-2327 ■ *Web:* www.titan-intl.com	Des Moines	IA	50317	515-265-9200	265-9301
Toyo Tire USA Corp 6261 Katella Ave Ste 2B ... *TF:* 800-678-3250 ■ *Web:* toyotires.com	Cypress	CA	90630	800-678-3250	
Turbo Wholesale Tires Inc 5793 Martin Rd ... *Web:* turbotiresonline.com	Irwindale	CA	91706	626-856-1400	
Valley Tire Company Inc 1002 Arentzen Blvd ... *Web:* www.valleytireco.com	Charleroi	PA	15022	724-417-9564	
Yokohama Tire Corp 601 S Acacia Ave ... *TF:* 800-423-4544 ■ *Web:* www.yokohamatire.com	Fullerton	CA	92831	714-870-3800	

755 TIRES & TUBES - WHOL

				Phone	Fax
4 Wheel Parts 8227-100 Ave ... *Web:* www.4wheelparts.com	Fort St. John	BC	V1J1W7	250-787-2566	
A & E Tire Inc 3855 E 52nd Ave ... *Web:* www.aetire.com	Denver	CO	80216	303-308-6900	
Allied Oil & Supply Inc 2209 S 24th St ... *TF:* 800-333-3717 ■ *Web:* www.alliedoil.com	Omaha	NE	68108	402-344-4343	344-4360
American Tire Depot 1123 W Commonwealth Ave ... **Fax Area Code:* 562 ■ *TF:* 855-333-2823 ■ *Web:* www.americantiredepot.com	Fullerton	CA	92833	714-525-2306	677-3956*
Aperia Technologies Inc 1616 Rollins Rd ... *Web:* www.aperiatech.com	Burlingame	CA	94010	415-494-9624	
Ball Tire & Gas Inc 620 S Ripley Blvd ... *Web:* balltire.net	Alpena	MI	49707	989-354-4186	356-2080
Bauer Built Inc PO Box 248 ... *TF:* 800-268-5114 ■ *Web:* www.bauerbuilt.com	Durand	WI	54736	715-672-4295	
Ben Tire Distributors Ltd 203 E Madison St PO Box 158 ... **Fax Area Code:* 217 ■ *TF:* 800-252-8961 ■ *Web:* www.bentire.com	Toledo	IL	62468	800-252-8961	849-3019*
Best-One Tire & Service LLC 101 N Polk St ... *Web:* www.bestonetire.com	Monroe	IN	46772	260-692-6171	
BFGoodrich Tires Inc 1 Pkwy S ... *TF:* 877-788-8899 ■ *Web:* www.bfgoodrichtires.com	Greenville	SC	29602	877-788-8899	
Bridgestone Canada Inc 5770 Hurontario St Ste 400 ... *Web:* www.bridgestone.com	Mississauga	ON	L5R3G5	905-890-1990	890-1991
Brookside Equipment 7707 Mosley Rd ... *Web:* www.brooksideusa.com	Houston	TX	77017	713-943-7100	943-9102
Clark Tire & Auto Supply Co Inc 220 S Ctr St ... *Web:* www.clarktire.com	Hickory	NC	28602	828-322-2303	324-2906
Community Imports Inc 8340 W 159th St ... *Web:* www.communityhonda.com	Orland Park	IL	60462	708-364-2600	
CRM Co 15800 S Avalon Blvd ... *Web:* www.crmrubber.com	Rancho Dominguez	CA	90220	310-538-2222	
Cross-Midwest Tire Co 401 S 42nd St ... *Web:* www.crossmidwest.com	Kansas City	KS	66106	913-321-3003	
Dapper Tire Company Inc 4025 Lockridge St ... *TF:* 800-266-7172 ■ *Web:* www.dappertire.com	San Diego	CA	92102	619-266-1397	266-2384
De Ronde Tire Supply Inc 95 Rapin Pl ... *TF:* 800-227-4647 ■ *Web:* www.etrucktire.com	Buffalo	NY	14211	716-897-6690	893-5716
Dealer Tire LLC 3711 Chester Ave ... *Web:* www.dealertire.com	Cleveland	OH	44114	216-432-0088	
East Bay Tire Co 2200 Huntington Dr Unit C ... *TF:* 800-831-8473 ■ *Web:* eastbaytire.com	Fairfield	CA	94533	707-437-4700	437-4800
Eddie's Tire Service Inc 3077 Valley Rd ... *Web:* www.eddiestireservice.com	Berkeley Springs	WV	25411	304-258-1368	258-1777
Eurotire Inc 200 S Biscayne Blvd 55th Fl ... *Web:* www.eurotire.net	Miami	FL	33131	305-900-2850	
Free Service Tire Co Inc PO Box 6187 ... *TF:* 855-646-1423 ■ *Web:* www.freeservicetire.com	Johnson City	TN	37602	423-979-2250	979-2262
Friend Tire Co 11 Industrial Dr ... **Fax Area Code:* 417 ■ *TF:* 800-950-8473 ■ *Web:* www.friendtire.com	Monett	MO	65708	800-950-8473	235-3062*
Goodyear Canada Inc 450 Kipling ... *Web:* www.goodyear.ca	Toronto	ON	M8Z5E1	416-201-4300	
Grismer Tire Co PO Box 337 ... *Web:* www.grismertire.com	Dayton	OH	45401	937-643-2526	
K&W Tire Company Inc 735 N Prince St ... *Web:* www.kwtire.com	Lancaster	PA	17603	717-397-3596	
Kauffman Tire Inc 2832 Anvil Block Rd ... *Web:* www.kauffmantire.com	Ellenwood	GA	30294	404-762-4944	

Company	City	State	ZIP	Phone	Fax
Ken Jones Tire Inc 73 Chandler St *TF:* 800-225-9513 ■ *Web:* www.kenjones.com	Worcester	MA	01609	508-755-5255	755-4397
Kenda USA 7095 Americana Pkwy *TF:* 866-536-3287 ■ *Web:* www.kendatire.com	Reynoldsburg	OH	43068	614-866-9803	866-9805
Kumho Tire USA Inc 10299 Sixth St *TF:* 800-445-8646 ■ *Web:* www.kumhotireusa.com	Rancho Cucamonga	CA	91730	909-428-3999	
Lakin General Corp 2044 N Dominick St *Web:* www.lakincorp.com	Chicago	IL	60614	773-871-6675	
Lakin Tire West Inc 15305 Spring Ave *TF:* 800-488-2752 ■ *Web:* www.lakintire.com	Santa Fe Springs	CA	90670	562-802-2752	802-7584
Michelin North America (Canada) Inc 3020 Jacques-Bureau Ave *Web:* www.michelin.ca	Laval	QC	H7P6G2	450-978-4700	
Michelin North America Inc 1 PkwyS PO Box 19001 **Fax:* Cust Svc ■ *TF Cust Svc:* 800-847-3435 ■ *Web:* www.michelin.com	Greenville	SC	29602	864-458-5000	458-6359*
Net Driven 280 Eureka St *Web:* gatewaytire.net	Batesville	MS	38606	662-563-1143	
OK Tire Stores Inc 19082 21st Ave *Web:* www.oktire.com	Surrey	BC	V3S3M3	604-542-7999	542-7990
Parrish Tire Company Inc 5130 Indiana Ave *TF:* 800-849-8473 ■ *Web:* www.parrishtire.com	Winston-Salem	NC	27106	336-767-0202	744-2716
Pete's Tire Barns Inc 275 E Main St *Web:* www.petestire.com	Orange	MA	01364	978-544-8811	
Petro Amigos Supply Inc 777 N Eldridge Pkwy Ste 400 *Web:* www.petro-amigos.com	Houston	TX	77079	281-497-0858	
Piedmont Truck Tires Inc PO Box 18228 *TF:* 800-274-8473 ■ *Web:* www.piedmonttrucktires.com	Greensboro	NC	27419	336-668-0091	
Pomps Tire Service Inc 1123 Cedar St *TF:* 800-236-8911 ■ *Web:* www.pompstire.com	Green Bay	WI	54301	920-435-8301	435-1546
Reliable Tire Co 805 N Blackhorse Pk **Fax Area Code:* 856 ■ *TF All:* 800-342-3426 ■ *Web:* www.reliabletire.com	Blackwood	NJ	08012	800-342-3426	232-6583*
Snyder Tire 401 Cadiz Rd *TF:* 800-967-8473 ■ *Web:* www.snydertire.com	Steubenville	OH	43953	740-264-5543	
Solideal USA Inc 306 Forsyth Hall Dr	Charlotte	NC	28273	704-374-9700	
Southeastern Wholesale Tire Co 4721 Trademark Dr *TF General:* 800-849-9215 ■ *Web:* www.southeasterntireonline.com	Raleigh	NC	27610	919-832-3900	861-4357
Southern Tire Mart LLC 529 Industrial Park *Web:* www.stmtires.com	Columbia	MS	39429	601-424-3200	
Steepleton Tire Co 777 S Lauderdale St *Web:* steepletontire.com	Memphis	TN	38126	901-774-6440	774-6445
T BC Corp 4770 Hickory Hill Rd *TF:* 866-822-4968 ■ *Web:* www.tbcbrands.com	Memphis	TN	38141	866-822-4968	
Ted Wiens Tire & Auto Centers 1701 Las Vegas Blvd S *Web:* www.tedwiens.com	Las Vegas	NV	89104	702-732-2382	
Terry's Tire Town Inc 2360 W Main St PO Box 2405 *TF:* 800-235-2921	Alliance	OH	44601	800-235-2921	
Tire Centers LLC 310 Inglesby Pkwy *TF:* 800-603-2430 ■ *Web:* www.tirecenters.com	Duncan	SC	29334	864-329-2700	329-2900
Tire Rack 7101 Vorden Pkwy *TF:* 888-541-1777 ■ *Web:* www.tirerack.com	South Bend	IN	46628	574-287-2345	236-7707
Tire Warehouse Inc 7500 NW 35 Terr *TF:* 877-235-0102 ■ *Web:* www.tiregroup.com	Miami	FL	33122	305-696-0096	696-5926
Tire Wholesalers Co Inc 1783 E 14-Mile Rd *Web:* twitire.com	Troy	MI	48083	248-589-9910	589-9919
Tire's Warehouse Inc 240 Teller St *TF:* 800-655-8851 ■ *Web:* tireswarehouse.net	Corona	CA	92879	951-808-0111	808-9062
Tire-Rama Inc 1429 Grand Ave *TF:* 800-828-1642 ■ *Web:* www.tirerama.com	Billings	MT	59102	406-245-4006	
TO Haas Tire Co Inc 2400 'O' St *TF:* 866-393-5204 ■ *Web:* www.tohaastire.com	Lincoln	NE	68510	402-474-1525	474-0336
Tyres International Inc 4637 Allen Rd *Web:* www.tyres1.com	Stow	OH	44224	330-374-1000	
WD Tire Warehouse Inc 3805 E Livingston Ave *Web:* www.wdtire.com	Columbus	OH	43227	614-461-8944	461-0136
Wheels Etc 17521 Mesa St **Fax Area Code:* 760 ■ *TF:* 800-758-4737 ■ *Web:* www.wheels-etc.com	Hesperia	CA	92345	909-350-8200	949-1000*

756 TOBACCO & TOBACCO PRODUCTS

Company	City	State	ZIP	Phone	Fax
Abel Reel, The 165 Aviador St *TF:* 866-511-7444 ■ *Web:* www.abelreels.com	Camarillo	CA	93010	805-484-8789	482-0701
Albert H Notini & Sons Inc 225 Aiken St *TF:* 800-366-8464 ■ *Web:* www.ahnotini.com	Lowell	MA	01854	978-459-7151	458-7692
Alliance One International Inc 8001 Aerial Ctr Pkwy PO Box 2009 *NYSE: AOI* ■ *TF:* 800-937-5449 ■ *Web:* www.aointl.com	Morrisville	NC	27560	919-379-4300	379-4346
AMCON Distributing Co 7405 Irvington Rd *NYSE: DIT* ■ *TF:* 888-201-5997 ■ *Web:* www.amcon.com	Omaha	NE	68122	402-331-3727	331-4834
Burklund Distributors Inc 2500 N Main St Ste 3 *TF:* 800-322-2876 ■ *Web:* www.burklund.com	East Peoria	IL	61611	309-694-1900	694-6788
Caldwell Wholesale Company Inc 9630 Saint Vincent Ave *Web:* caldwell-wholesale.com	Shreveport	LA	71106	318-869-3101	
Carolina Group 2405 Westwood Ave Ste 101 **Fax Area Code:* 336	Richmond	VA	23230	804-349-4796	335-7414*
Cigar.com Inc 1911 Spillman Dr **Fax Area Code:* 877 ■ *TF:* 800-357-9800 ■ *Web:* www.cigar.com	Bethlehem	PA	18015	800-357-9800	464-2872*
Commonwealth Altadis Inc 5900 N Andrews Ave Ste 1000 *Web:* www.altadisusa.com	Fort Lauderdale	FL	33309	954-772-9000	938-7811
Domestic Tobacco Co 830 N Prince St	Lancaster	PA	17603	717-393-0613	397-2381
Eby-Brown Co 280 W Shuman Blvd Ste 280 *TF:* 800-553-8249 ■ *Web:* www.eby-brown.com	Naperville	IL	60563	630-778-2800	778-2830
Finck Cigar Co 414 Vera Cruz St *TF Orders:* 800-221-0638 ■ *Web:* www.finckcigarcompany.com	San Antonio	TX	78207	210-226-4191	226-2825
Flue-Cured Tobacco Co-op 1304 Annapolis Dr *Web:* www.ustobaccofarmer.com	Raleigh	NC	27608	919-821-4560	821-4564
Hail & Cotton Inc 2500 S Main St *Web:* www.hailcotton.com	Springfield	TN	37172	615-384-9576	
Holts Cigar Co 1522 Walnut St *TF:* 800-523-1641 ■ *Web:* www.holts.com	Philadelphia	PA	19102	215-732-8500	732-4988
J Polep Distribution Services Inc 705 Meadow St *TF:* 800-447-6537 ■ *Web:* www.jpolep.com	Chicopee	MA	01013	413-592-4141	592-5870
JC Newman Cigar Co 2701 16th St *TF Orders:* 800-477-1884 ■ *Web:* www.cigarfamily.com	Tampa	FL	33605	813-248-2124	247-2135
Keilson-Dayton Co 107 Commerce Pk Dr *TF:* 800-759-3174 ■ *Web:* keilsondayton.com	Dayton	OH	45404	937-236-1070	236-2124
Klafter's Inc 216 N Beaver St *TF:* 800-922-1233 ■ *Web:* www.klafters.com	New Castle	PA	16101	800-922-1233	
Macon Cigar & Tobacco Company Inc 575 12th St *Web:* www.mctweb.com	Macon	GA	31201	478-743-2236	744-0903
Mathew Zechman Company Inc 152 Resar Ct	Elyria	OH	44035	440-366-2442	
Modern Distributors Inc 817 W Columbia St *TF:* 800-880-5543 ■ *Web:* teammodern.com	Somerset	KY	42501	606-679-1178	
National Tobacco Company LP 5201 Interchange Way *TF Cust Svc:* 800-579-0975 ■ *Web:* zigzag.com	Louisville	KY	40229	502-778-4421	
Oliva Tobacco Co 3104 N Armenia Ave *Web:* olivatobacco.com	Tampa	FL	33607	813-248-4921	
Philip Morris USA 2325 Bells Rd *TF:* 800-343-0975 ■ *Web:* www.altria.com/our-companies/philipmorrisusa/pages/default.aspx	Richmond	VA	23234	804-274-2000	
Queen City Wholesale Inc 1001 E 8th PO Box 1083 *Web:* queencitywholesale.com	Sioux Falls	SD	57103	605-336-3215	
Reynolds American Inc 401 N Main St PO Box 2990 *NYSE: LO* ■ *TF:* 877-390-5533 ■ *Web:* www.reynoldsamerican.com	Winston-Salem	NC	27101	336-741-2000	
Reynolds American Inc PO Box 2990 *NYSE: RAI* ■ *Web:* www.reynoldsamerican.com	Winston-Salem	NC	27102	336-741-7693	
RJ Reynolds Tobacco Co 401 N Main St *Web:* www.rjrt.com	Winston-Salem	NC	27102	336-741-5000	741-2998
Star Scientific Inc 4470 Cox Rd Ste 110 *NASDAQ: RCPI* ■ *Web:* rockcreekpharmaceuticals.com	Glen Allen	VA	23060	804-527-1970	
Swisher International Inc 459 E 16th St *Web:* www.swisher.com	Jacksonville	FL	32206	904-353-4311	
Tobacco Superstores Inc 3550 Commerce Rd *Web:* tobaccosuper.com	Forrest City	AR	72335	870-633-0099	
Universal Leaf Tobacco Co Inc 1501 N Hamilton St PO Box 25099 **Fax:* Hum Res ■ *Web:* www.universalcorp.com	Richmond	VA	23260	804-359-9311	254-3584*

757 TOOL & DIE SHOPS

Company	City	State	ZIP	Phone	Fax
A & M Tool & Die Company Inc 64 Mill St *Web:* www.am-tool.com	Southbridge	MA	01550	508-764-3241	
A Finkl & Sons Co 2011 N Southport Ave *TF:* 800-343-2562 ■ *Web:* www.finkl.com	Chicago	IL	60614	773-975-2510	348-5347
ABA-PGT Inc 10 Gear Dr PO Box 8270 *Web:* www.abapgt.com	Manchester	CT	06040	860-649-4591	643-7619
Able Wire Edm Inc 440 W Atlas St *Web:* www.ableedm.com	Brea	CA	92821	714-255-1967	
Abrasive-Form Inc 454 Scott Dr *Web:* www.abrasive-form.com	Bloomingdale	IL	60108	630-893-7800	893-6313
Advance Industrial Machine LLP W6335 Design Dr *Web:* www.aim-msm.com	Greenville	WI	54942	920-757-6786	
Aegis Sales & Engineering Inc 5411 Industrial Rd *Web:* www.aegisparts.com	Fort Wayne	IN	46825	260-483-4160	
Aeromet Industries Inc 739 S Arbogast St *Web:* www.aerometindustries.com	Griffith	IN	46319	219-924-7442	
Aerostar Aerospace Manufacturing Inc 2688 E Rose Garden Ln *Web:* www.aerostaraerospace.com	Phoenix	AZ	85050	602-861-1145	
Afa Systems Inc 8 Tilbury Ct *Web:* www.afasystemsinc.com	Brampton	ON	L6T3T4	905-873-2532	
Ahaus Tool & Engineering Inc PO Box 280 *Web:* www.ahaus.com	Richmond	IN	47375	765-962-3571	962-3426
Akron Special Machinery Inc 2740 Cory Ave *Web:* www.polinggroup.com	Akron	OH	44314	330-753-1077	
Alco Industries Inc 820 Adams Ave Ste 130 *Web:* www.alcoind.com	Norristown	PA	19403	610-666-0930	666-0752
Alcona Tool & Machine Inc PO Box 340 *Web:* www.alconatool.com	Lincoln	MI	48742	989-736-8151	736-6717
Alden Tool Company Inc 199 New Pk Dr *Web:* www.aldentool.com	Berlin	CT	06037	860-828-3556	828-8872
Alliance Carolina Tool & Mold Corp 125 Glenn Bridge Rd *Web:* www.alliance-carolina.com	Arden	NC	28704	828-684-7831	
Alliance Precision Plastics 1220 Lee Rd *Web:* www.allianceppc.com	Rochester	NY	14606	585-426-5310	426-5081
Allied Pacific 2951 E La Palma Ave *Web:* www.allied-pacific.com	Anaheim	CA	92806	714-630-8145	
Allways Precision Inc 14001 Van Dyke Rd *Web:* allwaysprecision.com	Plainfield	IL	60544	815-577-1600	
Alpha Precision Machining Inc 19652 70th Ave South *Web:* www.alphapre.com	Kent	WA	98032	253-395-7381	
Alt's Tool & Machine Inc 10926 Woodside Ave N *Web:* www.altstool.com	Santee	CA	92071	619-562-6653	

Company	City	State	ZIP	Phone	Fax
Altest Corp 898 Faulstich Ct *Web:* www.altestcorp.com	San Jose	CA	95112	408-436-9900	
American Tool & Mold Inc 1700 Sunshine Dr *Web:* www.a-t-m.com	Clearwater	FL	33765	727-447-7377	447-0125
Ams Production Machining Inc 800 Andico Rd *Web:* www.amsmachining.com	Plainfield	IN	46168	317-838-9273	
Anchor Tool & Die Co 12200 Brookpark Rd *TF:* 888-341-8910 ■ *Web:* www.anchor-mfg.com	Cleveland	OH	44130	216-362-1850	265-7833
Apex Tool Works Inc 3200 Tollview Dr *Web:* www.apextool.com	Rolling Meadows	IL	60008	847-394-5810	394-2739
Arlington Machine & Tool Co 90 New Dutch Ln *Web:* www.arlingtonmachine.com	Fairfield	NJ	07004	973-276-1377	
Armin Industries 1500 N La Fox St *Web:* www.armin-ind.com	South Elgin	IL	60177	847-742-1864	742-0253
Armstrong Mold Corp 6910 Manlius Ctr Rd *Web:* www.armstrongmold.com	East Syracuse	NY	13057	315-437-1517	437-9198
Arobotech Systems Inc 1524 E Avis Dr *Web:* www.arobotech.com	Madison Heights	MI	48071	248-588-9080	
Astro Tool & Machine Company Inc 810 Martin St *Web:* www.astrotoolco.com	Rahway	NJ	07065	732-382-2450	382-6394
Ateliers Lesage Inc (les) 1330 Rue Soucy *Web:* ateliersleage.com	Saint-hubert	QC	J4T1A3	450-445-5088	
Atlas Machining & Welding Inc 777 Smith Ln *Web:* www.atlasmw.com	Northampton	PA	18067	610-262-1374	
Atlas Tool Inc 29880 Groesbeck Hwy *Web:* www.atlastool.com	Roseville	MI	48066	586-778-3570	778-3931
Atscott Manufacturing Company Inc 1150 Holstein Dr NE *Web:* www.atscott.com	Pine City	MN	55063	320-629-2501	
Attodyne Inc 1 Westside Dr Unit 6 *Web:* www.attodynelasers.com	Toronto	ON	M9C1B2	416-840-9096	
Austro Mold Inc 3 Rutter St	Rochester	NY	14606	585-458-1410	458-0963
Autodie LLC 44 Coldbrook St NW *Web:* www.autodie.com	Grand Rapids	MI	49503	616-454-9361	356-1429
Aztalan Engineering Inc 100 S Industrial Dr *Web:* www.aztalan.com	Lake Mills	WI	53551	920-648-3411	
Baum Machine Inc N253 Stoney Brook Rd *Web:* www.baummachine.com	Appleton	WI	54915	920-738-6613	
Bent River Machine Inc 951 Rio Torcido *Web:* www.bent-river.com	Clarkdale	AZ	86324	928-634-7568	
Bilco Tool Corp 30076 Dequindre Rd *Web:* www.bilcotool.com	Warren	MI	48092	586-574-9300	574-9340
Birdsall Tool & Gage Co 24735 Crestview Ct *Web:* www.birdsalltool.com	Farmington Hills	MI	48335	248-474-5150	
Bowden Manufacturing Corp 4590 Beidler Rd *TF:* 800-876-8970 ■ *Web:* bowdenmfg.com	Willoughby	OH	44094	440-946-1770	
Brinkman Tool & Die Inc 325 Kiser St *Web:* www.brinkmantool.com	Dayton	OH	45404	937-222-1161	222-2079
Buckeye Machine Fabricators Inc 610 E Lima St *Web:* www.buckeyemachine.com	Forest	OH	45843	419-273-2521	
Busch Precision Inc 8200 N Faulkner Rd *Web:* www.buschprecision.com	Milwaukee	WI	53224	414-362-7300	
Byran Company Inc, The 779 Avery Blvd N *Web:* thebryancompany.com	Ridgeland	MS	39157	601-956-1533	
C & H Machine Inc 943 S Andreasen Dr *Web:* www.c-hmachine.com	Escondido	CA	92029	760-746-6459	
C&A Tool Engineering Inc 4100 N US 33 PO Box 94 *Web:* www.catool.com	Churubusco	IN	46723	260-693-2167	693-3633
C.B.S. Boring & Machine Company Inc 33750 Riviera Dr *Web:* www.cbsboring.com	Fraser	MI	48026	586-294-7540	
CA Spalding Co 1011 Cedar Ave *Web:* www.caspalding.com	Croydon	PA	19021	267-550-9000	
Caco-Pacific Corp 813 N Cummings Rd *Web:* www.cacopacific.com	Covina	CA	91724	626-331-3361	966-4219
Calmax Technology Inc 526 Laurelwood Rd *Web:* www.calmaxtechnology.com	Santa Clara	CA	95054	408-748-8660	
Canadian Tool & Die Ltd 1331 Chevrier Blvd *TF:* 800-204-4150 ■ *Web:* www.canadiantool.com	Winnipeg	MB	R3T1Y4	204-453-6833	
Carlson Tool & Manufacturing Corp W57 N14386 Doerr Way PO Box 85 *TF:* 800-532-2252 ■ *Web:* www.carlsontool.com	Cedarburg	WI	53012	262-377-2020	377-1751
Carr Lane Mfg 4200 Carr Ln Ct *Web:* www.carrlane.com	Saint Louis	MO	63119	314-647-6200	647-5736
Cbw Automation 3939 automation way *TF:* 800-229-9500 ■ *Web:* www.cbwautomation.com	Fort collins	CO	80525	970-229-9500	
Chicago Cutting Die Co 3555 Woodhead Dr *Web:* www.chicagocuttingdie.com	Northbrook	IL	60062	847-509-5800	509-0355
Chicago Mold Engineering Co 615 Stetson Ave *Web:* www.chicagomold.com	Saint Charles	IL	60174	630-584-1311	584-8695
Church Metal Spinning Co 5050 N 124th St *TF:* 877-461-6460 ■ *Web:* www.churchmetal.com	Milwaukee	WI	53225	414-461-6460	
Claret Canada Inc 1400 Rue Joliot-curie *Web:* claretnet.com	Boucherville	QC	J4B7L9	450-449-5774	
Classic Turning Inc 3000 E S St *Web:* www.classicturning.com	Jackson	MI	49201	517-764-1335	
Cleveland Punch & Die Co 666 Pratt St PO Box 769 *TF:* 888-451-4342 ■ *Web:* www.clevelandpunch.com	Ravenna	OH	44266	888-451-4342	451-6877
Clifty Engineering & Tool Company Inc 2949 Clifty Dr *Web:* www.cliftyengineering.com	Madison	IN	47250	812-273-3272	273-3272
CMMC Machine Inc 2081 Hayter St *Web:* www.cmmcmachine.com	North Charleston	SC	29405	843-554-0993	
CNC Machine Products Inc 1709 W 20th St *Web:* www.cncmp.com	Joplin	MO	64804	417-782-2627	
Coast Composites Inc 1395 S Lyon St *Web:* www.coastcomposites.com	Santa Ana	CA	92705	949-455-0665	455-0061
Coastal Casting Service Inc 2903 Gano St *Web:* coastalcasting.com	Houston	TX	77009	713-223-4439	
Cockburn Enterprises Inc PO Box 2369	Muscle Shoals	AL	35662	256-381-3620	381-9146
Cole Tool & Die Co 241 Ashland Rd *TF:* 800-837-2653 ■ *Web:* www.coletool.com	Mansfield	OH	44905	419-522-1272	522-5506
Colonial Machine Co 1041 Mogadore Rd *Web:* www.colonial-machine.com	Kent	OH	44240	330-673-5859	673-5859
Comet Die & Engraving Co 909 Larch Ave *Web:* www.cometdie.com	Elmhurst	IL	60126	630-833-5600	833-2644
Composidie Inc 1295 Rt 380 *Web:* www.composidie.com	Apollo	PA	15613	724-727-3466	727-3788
Custom Mold Engineering Inc 9780 S Franklin Dr *TF:* 800-448-2005 ■ *Web:* www.custommold.com	Franklin	WI	53132	414-421-5444	
D & D Manufacturing Inc 500 Territorial Dr *Fax Area Code: 630 ■ *TF:* 888-300-6869 ■ *Web:* www.ddmfg.com	Bolingbrook	IL	60440	888-300-6869	759-0043*
D-M-E Co 29111 Stephenson Hwy *TF:* 800-626-6653 ■ *Web:* www.dme.net	Madison Heights	MI	48071	248-398-6000	544-5705
Danly IEM 6779 Engle Rd Ste A-F *Fax Area Code: 440 ■ *TF:* 800-652-6462 ■ *Web:* www.danly.com	Cleveland	OH	44130	800-652-6462	239-7605*
Dayton Progress Corp 500 Progress Rd *Web:* www.daytonprogress.com	Dayton	OH	45449	937-859-5111	859-5353
Decatur Mold Tool & Engineering Inc 3330 N State Rd 7 PO Box 387 *Web:* www.decaturmold.com	North Vernon	IN	47265	812-346-5188	346-7357
Del-Tech Manufacturing Inc 9703 Penn Rd *TF:* 800-736-7733 ■ *Web:* www.deltech.ca	Prince George	BC	V2N5T6	250-564-3585	
Delaware Machinery & Tool 700 S Mulberry St *Web:* www.delawaredynamics.com	Muncie	IN	47302	765-284-3335	289-7185
Deluxe Stitcher Company Inc 3747 acorn ln *TF:* 800-634-0810 ■ *Web:* deluxestitcher.com	Franklin Park	IL	60131	800-634-0810	
Delva Tool & Machine Corp 1603 Industrial Hwy *Web:* www.delvatool.com	Cinnaminson	NJ	08077	856-786-8700	786-8708
Demmer Corp 1600 N Larch St Ste 1 *Web:* www.demmercorp.com	Lansing	MI	48906	517-321-3600	321-7449
Detroit Tool & Engineering Co 1107 Springfield Rd *Web:* www.detroittool.com	Lebanon	MO	65536	417-720-8108	
Diamond Die & Mold Co 35401 Groesbeck Hwy *Web:* www.diamond-die.com	Clinton Township	MI	48035	586-791-0700	791-5419
Diamond Tool & Die Inc 508 29th Ave *TF:* 800-227-1084 ■ *Web:* www.dtdjobshop.com	Oakland	CA	94601	510-534-7050	534-0454
Die Services International 45000 Van Born Rd *Web:* www.dieservicesinternational.com	Belleville	MI	48111	734-699-3400	699-4081
Diemasters Manufacturing Inc 2100 Touhy Ave *Web:* www.thediemasters.com	Elk Grove Village	IL	60007	847-640-9900	640-9900
Dominion Technologies Inc 15736 Sturgeon St *Web:* www.dominiontec.com	Roseville	MI	48066	586-773-3303	773-2730
Domino Machine Inc 4040 98 St NW *Web:* www.dominomachine.com	Edmonton	AB	T6L3E3	780-462-1354	
Du Hadaway Tool & Die Shop Inc 801 Dawson Dr *Web:* duhadawaytool.com	Newark	DE	19713	302-366-0113	
Durre Brothers Welding & Machine Shop Inc 405 S Chestnut *Web:* www.durrebros.com	Minonk	IL	61760	309-432-2512	
Eagle Rock Technologies Inc 1 Eagle Rock Dr *Web:* www.eaglerockonline.com	Bath	PA	18014	610-759-5200	
EF Precision Design Inc 2301 Computer Rd *TF:* 800-536-3900 ■ *Web:* www.efgroup.com	Willow Grove	PA	19090	215-784-0861	
Ehrhardt Tool & Machine Co 25 Central Industrial Dr *TF:* 877-386-7856 ■ *Web:* www.ehrhardttool.com	Granite City	IL	62040	314-436-6900	436-6905
Electro-Magnetic Products Inc 355 Crider Ave *Web:* www.empmags.com	Moorestown	NJ	08057	856-235-3011	722-0566
Elizabeth Carbide Die Company Inc 601 Linden St *Web:* www.eliz.com	McKeesport	PA	15132	412-751-3000	754-0755
Estee Mold & Die Inc 1467 Stanley Ave *Web:* www.esteemold.com	Dayton	OH	45404	937-224-7853	228-0257
Esterline & Sons Mfg 6508 Old Clifton Rd *Web:* esterlineandsons.com	Springfield	OH	45502	937-265-5278	
Euclid Industries Inc 1655 Tech Dr *Web:* www.euclidindustries.com	Bay City	MI	48706	989-686-8920	
Ewart-Ohlson Machine Company Inc, The 1435 Main St PO Box 359 *Web:* www.ewart-ohlson.com	Cuyahoga Falls	OH	44222	330-928-2171	
Excel Machinery Ltd 12100 I-40 E *Web:* www.excelmach.com	Amarillo	TX	79120	806-335-1553	
Excel Tool Inc 2020 First Ave *Web:* www.exceleti.com	Seymour	IN	47274	812-522-6880	522-6524
Falmouth Scientific Inc 1400 Route 28A *Web:* www.falmouth.com	Cataumet	MA	02534	508-564-7640	
Ferriot Inc 1000 Arlington Cir *Web:* ferriot.com	Akron	OH	44306	330-786-3000	786-3001
First Tool Corp 612 Linden Ave *Web:* www.firsttoolcorp.com	Dayton	OH	45403	937-254-6197	254-0625
Fischer Tool & Die Corp 7155 Industrial Dr *Web:* www.fischertool.com	Temperance	MI	48182	734-847-4788	847-5027

Company	City	State	ZIP	Phone	Fax
Fisher Products LLC 1320 W 22nd Pl *Web:* www.fisherproductsllc.com	Tulsa	OK	74107	918-582-2204	
Formex Metal Industries Inc N2b-221 Riverbend Dr *Web:* www.formexmetal.com	Kitchener	ON	N2B2E8	519-745-2260	
Fort Wayne Wire Die Inc 2424 American Way *Web:* www.fwwd.com	Fort Wayne	IN	46809	260-747-1681	747-4269
Frizzelle & Parsons Die Sinking Co 6602 John Deere Rd *Web:* www.frizzelle-parsons.com	Moline	IL	61265	309-796-1030	
Futuramic Tool & Engineering Co 24680 Gibson Dr *Web:* www.futuramic.com	Warren	MI	48089	586-758-2200	758-0641
Future Products Tool Corp 885 Rochester Rd S *Web:* www.future-products.com	Troy	MI	48083	248-588-1060	588-7303
General Carbide Corp 1151 Garden St *TF:* 800-245-2465 ■ *Web:* www.generalcarbide.com	Greensburg	PA	15601	724-836-3000	836-6274
General Tool Co 101 Landy Ln *TF:* 800-314-9817 ■ *Web:* www.gentool.com	Cincinnati	OH	45215	513-733-5500	733-5604
Global Concepts Enterprise Inc 785 Waverly Ct *Web:* www.globalconcepts.com	Holland	MI	49423	616-355-7657	355-7662
GlobalDie 1130 Minot Ave PO Box 1120 *TF:* 800-910-3747 ■ *Web:* www.globaldie.com	Auburn	ME	04211	207-514-7252	514-7202
Greenville Tool & Die Co 1215 S Lafayette St *Web:* www.gtd.com	Greenville	MI	48838	616-754-5693	754-5500
Gremada Industries Inc 825 28th St SW Unit E *Web:* www.gremada.com	Fargo	ND	58103	701-356-0814	
Grinding Products Company Inc 11084 E 9 Mile Rd *Web:* grindingproducts.net	Warren	MI	48089	586-757-2118	
Guill Tool & Engineering Company Inc 10 Pike St *Web:* guill.com	West Warwick	RI	02893	401-828-7600	823-5310
Hahn Manufacturing Co 5332 Hamilton Ave *Web:* www.hahnmfg.com	Cleveland	OH	44114	216-391-9300	
Hampton Machine Shop Inc 900 39th St *Web:* www.hampmach.com	Newport News	VA	23607	757-380-8500	
Harig Manufacturing Corp 5757 W Howard St *Web:* www.harigmfg.com	Niles	IL	60714	847-647-9500	647-8351
Hercules Machine Tool & Die Co 13920 E Ten-Mile Rd *Web:* www.hmtd.com	Warren	MI	48089	586-778-4120	778-0070
Holdren Brothers Inc 301 Runkle *Web:* www.holdrenbrothers.com	West Liberty	OH	43357	937-465-7050	
Houston Dynamic Service Inc 8150 Lawndale *Web:* www.houstondynamic.com	Houston	TX	77012	713-928-6200	
Howmet TMP Corp 3960 S Marginal Rd *Web:* www.alcoa.com/howmet	Cleveland	OH	44114	216-361-5229	391-4842
Hudson Tool & Die Co *Hudson Technologies* 1327 N US 1 **Fax:* Sales ■ *Web:* www.hudson-technologies.com	Ormond Beach	FL	32174	386-672-2000	676-6212*
Hydro Carbide 4439 State Rte 982 *TF:* 800-245-2476 ■ *Web:* www.hydrocarbide.com	Latrobe	PA	15650	724-539-9701	539-8140
Hygrade Precision Technologies Inc 329 Cooke St *TF:* 800-457-1666 ■ *Web:* www.hygrade.com	Plainville	CT	06062	860-747-5773	747-3179
Incoe Corp 1740 E Maple Rd *Web:* www.incoe.com	Troy	MI	48083	248-616-0220	616-0225
Indian Creek Fabricators 1350 Commerce Pk Dr *TF:* 877-769-5880 ■ *Web:* www.indiancreekfab.com	Tipp City	OH	45371	937-667-5818	667-4093
Ivanhoe Tool & Die Company Inc 590 Thompson Rd *Web:* www.ivanhoetool.com	Thompson	CT	06277	860-923-9541	923-2497
Ivarson Inc 3100 W Green Tree Rd *Web:* ivarsoninc.com	Milwaukee	WI	53209	414-351-0700	
J & J Machine Inc 12655 Industrial Blvd *Web:* www.jandjmachine.com	Elk River	MN	55330	763-421-0114	
J & M Machine Products Inc 1821 Manor Dr *Web:* www.jmmachine.com	Muskegon	MI	49441	231-755-1622	
Jaco Engineering 879 S E St *Web:* www.jacoengineering.com	Anaheim	CA	92805	714-991-1680	
Jade Corp 3063 Philmont Ave *Web:* www.jadecorp.com	Huntingdon Valley	PA	19006	215-947-3333	947-6838
Jasco Tools Inc 1390 Mt Read Blvd *Web:* www.jascotools.com	Rochester	NY	14606	585-254-7000	254-2655
Jennings International Corp 3 Blue Heron Dr *Web:* www.jenningsinternational.com	Collegeville	PA	19426	610-831-1600	
Jo-Ad Industries Inc 31465 Stephenson Hwy *Web:* www.jo-ad.com	Madison Heights	MI	48071	248-588-4810	588-3448
Jones Metal Products Co 200 N Ctr St *TF:* 888-868-6535 ■ *Web:* www.jmpforming.com	West Lafayette	OH	43845	740-545-6381	545-9690
Kalow Technologies Inc 238 Innovation Dr *Web:* www.kalowtech.com	North Clarendon	VT	05759	802-775-4633	
Kalt Manufacturing Co, The 36700 Sugar Ridge Rd *Web:* www.kaltmfg.com	North Ridgeville	OH	44039	440-327-2102	
Kell-Strom Tool Co 214 Church St *Web:* www.kell-strom.com	Wethersfield	CT	06109	860-529-6851	257-9694
Kenmode Tool & Engineering Co 820 W Algonquin Rd *Web:* kenmode.com	Algonquin	IL	60102	847-658-5041	658-9150
Kennedy Tool & Die Inc 325 W Main St *Web:* www.ktdmold.com	Birdsboro	PA	19508	610-582-8735	
Lane Punch Corp 281 Ln Pkwy **Fax Area Code:* 800 ■ *Web:* www.lanepunch.com	Salisbury	NC	28146	704-633-3900	227-6725*
Lansing Tool & Engineering Inc 1313 S Waverly Rd *Web:* www.lansingtool.com	Lansing	MI	48917	517-372-2550	
Leader Engineering Fabrication Inc 695 Independence Dr *Web:* www.leaderengineeringfabrication.com	Napoleon	OH	43545	419-592-0008	
Leech Tool & Die Works Inc 13144 Dickson Rd *Web:* www.leechind.com	Meadville	PA	16335	814-336-2141	337-0354
Lenhardt Tool & Die Co 3100 E Broadway *Web:* www.lenhardttool.com	Alton	IL	62002	618-462-1075	462-6306
Lou-Rich Machine Tool Inc 505 W Front St *TF:* 800-893-3235 ■ *Web:* www.lou-rich.com	Albert Lea	MN	56007	507-377-8910	373-7110
Mack Engineering Corp 3215 E 26th St *Web:* www.mackengineering.com	Minneapolis	MN	55406	612-721-2471	
Macro Engineering & Technology Inc 199 Traders Blvd E *Web:* www.macroeng.com	Mississauga	ON	L4Z2E5	905-507-9000	
Mahuta Tool Corp N118W19137 Bunsen Dr *TF:* 888-686-4940 ■ *Web:* www.mahutatool.com	Germantown	WI	53022	262-502-4100	
Manda Machine Co 2683 Myrtle Springs Ave *Web:* www.mandamachine.com	Dallas	TX	75220	214-352-5946	
Master Machine & Tool Company Inc 5857 Jefferson Ave *Web:* www.master-machine.com	Newport News	VA	23605	757-245-6653	
Master Precision Machining Inc 2199 Ronald St *Web:* master-precision.com	Santa Clara	CA	95050	408-727-0185	
Mate Precision Tooling Inc 1295 Lund Blvd *TF:* 800-328-4492 ■ *Web:* www.matept.com	Anoka	MN	55303	763-421-0230	421-0285
May Tool & Mold Company Inc 2922 Wheeling Ave *Web:* www.mayinc.com	Kansas City	MO	64129	816-923-6262	923-6277
McAfee Tool & Die Inc 1717 Boettler Rd *Web:* www.mcafeetool.com	Uniontown	OH	44685	330-896-9555	896-9549
Meta Manufacturing Corp 8901 Blue Ash Rd *Web:* metamfg.com	Cincinnati	OH	45242	513-793-6382	
Metal Technologies of Murfreesboro Inc 314 W Broad St *Web:* www.metaltechnc.com	Murfreesboro	NC	27855	252-398-4041	
Metro Mold & Design Inc 20600 County Rd 81 *Web:* www.metromold.com	Rogers	MN	55374	763-428-8310	
Microcast Technologies Corp (MTC) 1611 W Elizabeth Ave *Web:* www.mtcnj.com	Linden	NJ	07036	908-523-9503	523-0910
Mid-State Machine Products Inc 83 Verti Dr *TF:* 800-341-4672 ■ *Web:* hnprecision.com	Winslow	ME	04901	207-873-6136	
Midwest Tool & Engineering Co 112 Webster St *Web:* www.themidwesttool.com	Dayton	OH	45402	937-224-0756	224-0757
Milwaukee Bearing & Machining Inc W134N5235 Campbell Dr *Web:* www.milwaukeebearing.com	Menomonee Falls	WI	53051	262-783-1100	
Moeller Mfg Company Inc Punch & Die Div 43938 Plymouth Oaks Blvd *TF:* 800-521-7613 ■ *Web:* www.moellerpunch.com	Plymouth	MI	48170	734-416-0000	416-2200
Mold Base Industries Inc 7501 Derry St **Fax Area Code:* 717 ■ *TF:* 800-241-6656 ■ *Web:* www.moldbase.com	Harrisburg	PA	17111	800-241-6656	564-2250*
Mold Masters International Inc 7500 Clover Ave *Web:* www.moldmastersintl.com	Mentor	OH	44060	440-953-0220	953-1016
Mold-A-Matic Corp 147 River St *TF:* 866-886-2626 ■ *Web:* www.mamco-molding.com	Oneonta	NY	13820	607-433-2121	432-7861
Motor-Services Hugo Stamp Inc 3190 SW Fourth Ave *Web:* www.mshs.com	Fort Lauderdale	FL	33315	954-763-3660	
MS Willett Inc 220 Cockeysville Rd *Web:* www.mswillett.com	Cockeysville	MD	21030	410-771-0460	771-6972
Multifeeder Technology Inc 4821 White Bear Pkwy *Web:* www.multifeeder.com	Saint Paul	MN	55110	651-407-3100	
National Tool & Mfg Company Inc 100 N 12th St	Kenilworth	NJ	07033	908-276-1600	
Nexxa Industries Ltd 1-4380 76 Ave Se *Web:* www.nexxaindustries.com	Calgary	AB	T2C2J2	403-720-1996	
NGInstruments Inc 4643 N State Rd 15 *Web:* www.nginstruments.com	Warsaw	IN	46582	574-268-2112	
Nitek Laser Inc 305 Rt du Port *Web:* www.niteklaser.com	Nicolet	QC	J3T1R7	819-293-4887	
Nolte Precise Manufacturing Inc 6850 Colerain Ave *Web:* www.nolteprecise.com	Cincinnati	OH	45239	513-923-3100	
Nor-Arc Steel Fabricators 331567 Hwy 11 *Web:* www.norarc.com	Earlton	ON	P0J1E0	705-563-2656	
Northland Machine Inc 35234 US Hwy 2 *Web:* www.northlandmachine.com	Grand Rapids	MN	55744	218-328-6479	
Northwestern Tools Inc 3130 Valleywood Dr *TF:* 800-236-3956 ■ *Web:* www.northwesterntools.com	Dayton	OH	45429	937-298-9994	298-3715
Nypromold Inc 144 Pleasant St *Web:* www.nypromold.com	Clinton	MA	01510	978-365-4547	365-4548
O Keller Tool Engineering Co 12701 Inkster Rd	Livonia	MI	48150	734-425-4504	
Oakdale Precision Inc 7022 Sixth St N *Web:* www.oakdaleprecision.com	Oakdale	MN	55128	651-730-7700	
Oberg Industries Inc 2301 Silverville Rd PO Box 368 *TF:* 866-487-2365 ■ *Web:* www.oberg.com	Freeport	PA	16229	724-295-2121	295-2588
Odc Tooling & Molds 119 Roger St *Web:* www.odctooling.com	Waterloo	ON	N2J3Z6	519-576-8950	
Ohlinger Industries Inc 1211 W Melinda Ln *Web:* www.ohlingerind.com	Phoenix	AZ	85027	602-285-0911	
OKL Can Line Inc 11235 Sebring Dr *Web:* www.oklcan.com	Cincinnati	OH	45240	513-825-1655	
Ontario Die Co of America 1755 Busha Hwy *Web:* www.ontariodie.com	Marysville	MI	48040	810-987-5060	987-3688
Ort Tool & Die Corp 6555 S Dixie Hwy **Fax Area Code:* 734 ■ *Web:* www.orttool.com	Erie	MI	48133	419-242-9553	848-4308*

Company	City	State	ZIP	Phone	Fax
Owens Precision Inc 5966 Morgan Mill Rd *Web:* www.owensprecision.com	Carson City	NV	89701	775-883-4690	
Panoramic Corp 4321 Goshen Rd *TF:* 800-654-2027 ■ *Web:* www.pancorp.com	Fort Wayne	IN	46818	800-654-2027	
Paragon Die & Engineering Co 5225 33rd St SE *Web:* www.paragondie.com	Grand Rapids	MI	49512	616-949-2220	949-2536
Paslin Co 25303 Ryan Rd *Web:* www.paslin.com	Warren	MI	48091	586-758-0200	758-6602
PCS Co 34488 Doreka Dr. *TF:* 800-521-0546 ■ *Web:* www.pcs-company.com	Fraser	MI	48026	586-294-7780	294-7799
Peddinghaus Corp 300 N Washington Ave *TF:* 800-786-2448 ■ *Web:* www.peddinghaus.com	Bradley	IL	60915	815-937-3800	937-4003
Penn Manufacturing Industries Inc 506 Stump Rd *Web:* www.pennmfg.com	Mongtomeryville	PA	18936	215-362-1217	
Penn State Tool & Die Corp 260 Westec Dr *Web:* www.pennstatetool.com	Mount Pleasant	PA	15666	724-613-5500	
Penn United Technology Inc 799 N Pike Rd *TF:* 866-572-7537 ■ *Web:* www.pennunited.com	Cabot	PA	16023	724-352-1507	352-4970
Pennsylvania Tool & Gages Inc PO Box 534 *TF:* 877-827-8285 ■ *Web:* www.patool.com	Meadville	PA	16335	814-336-3136	333-9131
Permac Industries Inc 14401 Ewing Ave S *Web:* www.permacindustries.com	Burnsville	MN	55306	952-894-7231	
PHB Inc 7900 W Ridge Rd *Web:* www.phbcorp.com	Fairview	PA	16415	814-474-5511	474-3091
Phillips Precision Inc 7 Paul Kohner Pl *Web:* www.phillipsprecision.com	Elmwood Park	NJ	07407	201-797-8820	
Phinney Tool & Die Co 11023 West Center St Ext *Web:* www.phinneytool.com	Medina	NY	14103	585-798-3000	798-5612
PhotoMachining Inc 4 Industrial Dr Unit number 4 *Web:* www.photomachining.com	Pelham	NH	03076	603-882-9944	
Piedmont Precision Machine Company Inc 150 Airside Dr *Web:* www.ppmmach.com	Danville	VA	24540	434-793-0677	
Pioneer Manufacturing Inc 740 Beechcroft Rd *Web:* www.pioneerleveler.com	Spring Hill	TN	37174	931-486-2296	
Plasidyne Engineering & Manufacturing Inc 3230 E 59th St *Web:* www.plasidyne.com	Long Beach	CA	90805	562-531-0510	531-1377
Porter Precision Products Inc 2734 Banning Rd *TF:* 800-543-7041 ■ *Web:* www.porterpunch.com	Cincinnati	OH	45239	513-923-3777	923-1111
Power Brake Dies Inc 263 W 154th St *Web:* www.powerbrakedies.com	South Holland	IL	60473	708-339-5951	339-7737
Precision Component Industries 5325 Southway St SW *Web:* www.precision-component.com	Canton	OH	44706	330-477-6287	477-1052
Precision Fasteners Tooling Inc 11530 Western Ave *Web:* www.precisionfastenertooling.com	Stanton	CA	90680	714-898-8558	891-4988
Precision Tool Die & Machine Co Inc 6901 Preston Hwy *TF:* 877-511-9695 ■ *Web:* www.nth-works.com	Louisville	KY	40219	877-511-9695	
Prikos & Becker Tool Co 8109 N Lawndale Ave *Web:* prikosandbecker.com	Skokie	IL	60076	847-675-3910	675-3913
Producto Machine Co 800 Union Ave *TF Cust Svc:* 800-722-2606	Bridgeport	CT	06607	203-367-8675	367-0418
Progress Pump & Machine Services Inc 918 Kennedy Ave *Web:* www.progresspump.com	Schererville	IN	46375	219-322-3700	
Prospect Mold Inc 1100 Main St *Web:* www.prospectmold.com	Cuyahoga Falls	OH	44221	330-929-3311	920-1338
Proto-1 Manufacturing LLC 10 Tower Rd *Web:* www.proto1mfg.com	Winneconne	WI	54986	920-582-4491	
Quality Metalcraft Inc 33355 Glendale St *Web:* www.qualitymetalcraft.com	Livonia	MI	48150	734-261-6700	261-5180
Rand Machine Products Inc PO Box 72 *Web:* www.randmachine.com	Falconer	NY	14733	716-708-4583	665-3374
Raymath Company Inc 2323 W State Rt 55 *Web:* raymath.com	Troy	OH	45373	937-335-1860	
Reber Machine & Tool Company Inc 1112 S Liberty *Web:* rebermachine.com	Muncie	IN	47302	765-288-0297	
Reddog Industries Inc 2012 E 33rd St *Web:* www.reddog-erie.com	Erie	PA	16510	814-898-4321	899-5671
Reed City Tool & Die Inc 603 E Church St *Web:* www.reedcitytool.com	Reed City	MI	49677	231-832-7500	
Reliance Tool & Manufacturing Co 900 N State St Ste 101 *Web:* www.reliancetool.com	Elgin	IL	60123	847-695-1234	695-0931
Reuther Mold & Mfg Co 1225 Munroe Falls Ave *Web:* www.reuthermold.com	Cuyahoga Falls	OH	44221	330-923-5266	923-9930
Reynolds Manufacturing Co 501 38th St *Web:* www.reynoldsmfg.com	Rock Island	IL	61201	309-788-7443	
Richardson Manufacturing Co 2209 Old Jacksonville Rd *Web:* www.rmc-bigcnc.com	Springfield	IL	62704	217-546-2249	546-9433
Rocheleau Tool & Die Company Inc 117 Industrial Rd *Web:* www.rocheleautool.com	Fitchburg	MA	01420	978-345-1723	345-5972
Rome Tool & Die Company Inc 113 Hemlock St *TF:* 800-241-3369 ■ *Web:* stemco.com	Rome	GA	30161	706-234-6743	234-1242
RotoMetrics Group 800 Howerton Ln *TF:* 800-325-3851 ■ *Web:* www.rotometrics.com	Eureka	MO	63025	636-587-3600	587-3701
Ryan Manufacturing Inc 6606 Machmueller St *Web:* ryanmfg.com	Schofield	WI	54476	715-359-2565	
SB Whistler & Sons Inc PO Box 270 *TF:* 800-828-1010 ■ *Web:* www.sbwhistler.com	Medina	NY	14103	585-318-4630	798-5612
Schaffer Specialty Welding Inc 109 Industrial Ave *Web:* www.schafferwelding.com	Milltown	WI	54858	715-825-2424	
Schoitz Engineering Inc 4901 Sergeant Rd Hwy 63 S *Web:* www.schoitz.com	Waterloo	IA	50704	319-234-6615	234-0368
Schroeder & Bogardus Die Company Inc 1130 Red Gum St *Web:* www.schroederinc.com	Anaheim	CA	92806	714-630-2270	630-1739
Scribner Associates Inc 150 E Connecticut Ave *Web:* www.scribner.com	Southern Pines	NC	28387	910-695-8884	
Sea-Lect Plastic Corp 3420 Smith Ave *Web:* sealectplastics.com	Everett	WA	98201	425-339-0288	
Serapid Inc 34100 Mound Rd *TF:* 800-663-4514 ■ *Web:* www.serapid.com	Sterling Heights	MI	48310	586-274-0774	
Sidney Tool & Die Inc 1950 Campbell Rd *Web:* www.sidneytool.com	Sidney	OH	45365	937-492-6121	498-9601
Sirois Tool Company Inc 169 White Oak Dr *Web:* www.siroistool.com	Berlin	CT	06037	860-828-5327	
SMI Manufacturing Inc 13312 E Hardy Toll Rd *Web:* www.ameriforgegroup.com	Houston	TX	77039	281-449-0345	
Specialized Products Ltd 200 Summer St *Web:* www.specializedproductsltd.com	Clintonville	WI	54929	715-823-3727	
Specialty Design & Mfg Co PO Box 4039 *TF:* 800-720-0867 ■ *Web:* www.specialtydesign.com	Reading	PA	19606	610-779-1357	370-0269
SPX Corp OTC Div 655 Eisenhower Dr. *TF:* 800-533-6127 ■ *Web:* www.otctools.com	Owatonna	MN	55060	507-455-7000	
Stanfordville Machine & Manufacturing Inc 29 Victory Ln *Web:* www.stanfordville.com	Poughkeepsie	NY	12603	845-868-2266	
Stanley Machining & Tool Corp 425 Maple Ave *Web:* www.stanleymachining.com	Carpentersville	IL	60110	847-426-4560	
Stephens Machine Inc 1600 E Dodge St *Web:* www.stephensmachine.com	Kokomo	IN	46902	765-459-4017	
Sterling Process Engineering & Services Inc 333 McCormick Blvd *TF:* 800-783-7875 ■ *Web:* www.sterlingpe.com	Columbus	OH	43213	614-868-5151	
Sulzer Machine & Manufacturing Inc 2475 Spring Brook Rd *Web:* www.sulzermachine.com	Mosinee	WI	54455	715-443-2569	
SUNBELT Machine Works Corp 13411 Redfish Ln *Web:* sunbeltmachine.com	Stafford	TX	77477	281-499-0051	
Superior Die Set Corp 900 W Drexel Ave **Fax Area Code:* 800 ■ *TF:* 800-558-6040 ■ *Web:* www.supdie.com	Oak Creek	WI	53154	414-764-4900	657-0855*
Superior Die Tool & Machine Co 2301 Fairwood Ave *TF:* 800-292-2181 ■ *Web:* www.superior-dietool.com	Columbus	OH	43207	614-444-2181	444-8712
Superior Jig Inc 1540 N Orangethorpe Way *Web:* www.sji.net	Anaheim	CA	92801	714-525-4777	525-8798
Swan Engineering & Machine Co 2611 State St *Web:* swanengr.com	Bettendorf	IA	52722	563-355-2671	355-5380
Swihart Industries Inc 5111 Webster St *Web:* www.swihartindustries.com	Dayton	OH	45414	937-277-4796	
Swissline Precision Mfg. Inc 23-A Ashton Pkwy *Web:* www.swisslineprecision.com	Cumberland	RI	02864	401-333-8888	
Sylhan LLC 210 Rodeo Dr *Web:* www.sylhan.com	Edgewood	NY	11717	631-243-6600	
Techfab Gauthier Inc 470, ave Laurendeau *Web:* techfab.com	Montreal East	QC	H1B5M2	514-640-8451	
Texas Shapes Inc 6470 Rupley Cir Ste 1	Houston	TX	77087	713-641-1000	
TOG Manufacturing Company Inc 1454 S State St *Web:* www.togmanufacturing.com	North Adams	MA	01247	413-664-6711	
Tom Smith Industries 500 Smith Dr	Clayton	OH	45315	937-832-1555	832-1577
Toolcraft Products Inc 1265 Mc Cook Ave *Web:* www.toolcraftproducts.com	Dayton	OH	45404	937-223-8271	223-1408
Tools & Production Co 4924 N Encinita Ave *Web:* www.toolsandproduction.com	Temple City	CA	91780	626-286-0213	286-3398
Triangle Tool Corp 8609 W Port Ave *Web:* ttool.net	Milwaukee	WI	53224	414-357-7117	357-7610
Tru-Cut Inc 1145 Allied Dr *Web:* www.trucut.com	Sebring	OH	44672	330-938-9806	938-9342
Uniloy Milacron Inc 5550 S Occidental Rd Ste B *Web:* www.milacron.com/our-brands/uniloy	Tecumseh	MI	49286	517-424-8756	423-5671
Unipunch Products Inc 311 Fifth St NW *TF:* 800-828-7061 ■ *Web:* www.unipunch.com	Clear Lake	WI	54005	800-828-7061	453-3994
United Standard Industries Inc 2062 Lehigh Ave *Web:* www.unitedstandard.com	Glenview	IL	60026	847-724-0350	
Usinatech Inc 1099 Chemin Ely *Web:* usinatech.com	Melbourne	QC	J0B2B0	819-826-3774	
V&L Tool Inc 2021 MacArthur Rd *Web:* www.vltool.com	Waukesha	WI	53188	262-547-1226	
VRC Inc 696 W Bagley Rd *Web:* www.vrcmfg.com	Berea	OH	44017	440-243-6666	
W Machine Works Inc 13814 Del Sur St *Web:* www.wmwcnc.com	San Fernando	CA	91340	818-890-8049	
Walker Tool & Die Inc 2411 Walker Ave NW *TF:* 877-925-5378 ■ *Web:* www.walkertool.com	Grand Rapids	MI	49544	616-453-5471	453-3765
Waterflood Service & Sales Ltd 1314 Third St Box 1490 *Web:* www.waterflood.com	Estevan	SK	S4A2L7	306-634-7212	
Weldangrind Ltd 10323 174 St NW *TF:* 866-226-2414 ■ *Web:* www.weldangrind.ca	Edmonton	AB	T5S1H1	780-484-3030	

Phone Fax

Wesco Machine Products Inc
S84W18569 Enterprise Dr .... Muskego WI 53150 262-679-4799
Web: wescomachine.com

Westland Corp 1735 S Maize Rd........ Wichita KS 67209 316-721-1144 721-1495
TF: 800-247-1144 ■ *Web:* reiloyusa.com

Windsor Beach Technologies Inc
7321 Klier Dr .... Fairview PA 16415 814-474-4900
Web: www.windsorbeach.com

Wirtz Mfg Company Inc
1105 24th St PO Box 5006........ Port Huron MI 48061 810-987-7600 987-8135
Web: www.wirtzusa.com

Wyatt Precision Machine Inc
3301 E 59th St .... Long Beach CA 90805 562-634-0524
Web: www.wyattprecisionmachine.com

X-L Engineering Corp 6150 W Mulford St .... Niles IL 60714 847-965-3030
Web: www.xleng.com

Yarema Die & Engineering Co Inc
300 Minnesota Rd .... Troy MI 48083 248-585-2830 616-1422
TF: 800-937-9311 ■ *Web:* www.yarema.com

758 TOOLS - HAND & EDGE

See Also Lawn & Garden Equipment p. 2645; Metalworking Devices & Accessories p. 2768; Saw Blades & Handsaws p. 3144

Phone Fax

Adjustable Clamp Co 404 N Armour St .... Chicago IL 60642 312-666-0640 666-2723
Web: www.adjustableclamp.com

Allway Tools Inc 1255 Seabury Ave .... Bronx NY 10462 718-792-3636 823-9640
TF: 800-422-5592 ■ *Web:* www.allwaytools.com

Ames Taping Tools Inc
3350 Breckinridge Blvd Ste 100........ Duluth GA 30096 800-303-1827 243-2658*
**Fax Area Code: 770* ■ *TF:* 800-408-2801 ■ *Web:* www.amestools.com

Ames True Temper Inc 465 Railroad Ave........ Camp Hill PA 17011 800-393-1846
TF: 800-393-1846 ■ *Web:* www.ames.com

Arrow Fastener Co Inc 271 Mayhill St........ Saddle Brook NJ 07663 201-843-6900 843-3911
TF: 800-776-2228 ■ *Web:* www.arrowfastener.com

BARCO Industries Inc 1020 MacArthur Rd........ Reading PA 19605 800-234-8665 374-6320*
**Fax Area Code: 610* ■ *TF Cust Svc:* 800-234-8665 ■ *Web:* www.barcotools.com

Bondhus Corp 1400 E Broadway St PO Box 660........ Monticello MN 55362 763-295-2162 295-4440
TF Cust Svc: 800-328-8310 ■ *Web:* www.bondhus.com

Cal-Van Tools 4300 Waterleaf Ct........ Greensboro NC 27410 800-537-1077 299-4003*
**Fax Area Code: 336* ■ *TF:* 800-537-1077 ■ *Web:* www.cal-vantools.com

Channellock Inc 1306 S Main St .... Meadville PA 16335 800-724-3018 962-2583
TF Cust Svc: 800-724-3018 ■ *Web:* www.channellock.com

Charles GG Schmidt & Company Inc
301 W Grand Ave .... Montvale NJ 07645 201-391-5300 391-3565
TF: 800-724-6438 ■ *Web:* www.cggschmidt.com

Consolidated Devices Inc (CDI)
19220 San Jose Ave........ City of Industry CA 91748 626-965-0668 810-2759
TF: 800-525-6319 ■ *Web:* www.cditorque.com

Cooper Industries 600 Travis St Ste 5400 .... Houston TX 77002 713-209-8400 209-8995
NYSE: ETN ■ *TF:* 866-853-4293 ■ *Web:* www.cooperindustries.com

Cornwell Quality Tools 667 Seville Rd .... Wadsworth OH 44281 330-336-3506 336-3337
TF: 800-321-8356 ■ *Web:* www.cornwelltools.com

CS Osborne & Company Inc 125 Jersey St........ Harrison NJ 07029 973-483-3232 484-3621
Web: www.csosborne.com

CTA Manufacturing Corp 263 Veterans Blvd........ Carlstadt NJ 07072 201-896-1000 896-1378
Web: www.ctatools.com

Danaher Corp
2200 Pennsylvania Ave NW Ste 800........ Washington DC 20037 202-828-0850 828-0860
NYSE: DHR ■ *TF:* 800-833-9200 ■ *Web:* www.danaher.com

Daniels Manufacturing Corp 526 Thorpe Rd........ Orlando FL 32859 407-855-6161 855-6884
Web: www.dmctools.com

Dasco Pro Inc 340 Blackhawk Pk Ave .... Rockford IL 61104 815-962-3727
TF: 800-327-2690 ■ *Web:* dascopro.com

Duo-Fast Corp 2400 Galvin Dr........ Elgin IL 60123 847-783-5500 783-5500
TF Cust Svc: 888-386-3278 ■ *Web:* www.itwindfast.com

Empire Level Manufacturing Corp
929 Empire Dr PO Box 800........ Mukwonago WI 53149 800-558-0722 368-2127*
**Fax Area Code: 262* ■ *TF:* 800-558-0722 ■ *Web:* www.empirelevel.com

Enderes Tool Co 1103 Hershey St........ Albert Lea MN 56007 800-874-7776 891-1202*
**Fax Area Code: 952* ■ *TF:* 800-874-7776 ■ *Web:* www.enderes.com

Estwing Manufacturing Co 2647 Eigth St .... Rockford IL 61109 815-397-9558 397-8665
Web: www.estwing.com

Everhard Products Inc 1016 Ninth St SW........ Canton OH 44707 330-453-7786
TF: 800-225-0984 ■ *Web:* www.everhard.com

Fiskars Brands Inc 2537 Daniels St........ Madison WI 53718 866-348-5661
TF: 866-348-5661 ■ *Web:* www2.fiskars.com

Fletcher-Terry Company Inc 65 Spring Ln........ Farmington CT 06032 860-677-7331 676-8858
TF Cust Svc: 800-843-3826 ■ *Web:* www.fletcherviscom.com

General Machine Products Company Inc
3111 Old Lincoln Hwy .... Trevose PA 19053 215-357-5500 357-6216
TF Tech Supp: 800-345-6009 ■ *Web:* www.gmptools.com

General Tools Mfg Company LLC 80 White St........ New York NY 10013 212-431-6100 431-6499
TF: 800-697-8665 ■ *Web:* www.generaltools.com

Grobet File Company of America Inc
750 Washington Ave........ Carlstadt NJ 07072 201-939-6700 939-5067
TF: 800-847-4188 ■ *Web:* www.grobetusa.com

Hastings Fiber Glass Products Inc
770 Cook Rd PO Box 218........ Hastings MI 49058 269-945-9541 945-4623
Web: www.hfgp.com

Hexacon Electric Co 161 W Clay Ave .... Roselle Park NJ 07204 908-245-6200 245-6176
Web: www.hexaconelectric.com

Huther Bros Inc 1290 University Ave .... Rochester NY 14607 585-473-9462

Hyde Tools Co 54 Eastford Rd........ Southbridge MA 01550 508-764-4344 765-5250
TF: 800-872-4933 ■ *Web:* www.hydetools.com

Johnson Level & Tool Mfg Company Inc
6333 W Donges Bay Rd .... Mequon WI 53092 262-242-1161 242-0189
Web: www.johnsonlevel.com

Jonard Industries Corp 134 Marbledale Rd........ Tuckahoe NY 10707 914-793-0700 793-4527
Web: www.jonard.com

Phone Fax

Ken-Tool Co 768 E N St........ Akron OH 44305 330-535-7177 872-4929*
**Fax Area Code: 800* ■ *Web:* www.kentool.com

Klein Tools Inc 450 Bond St........ Lincolnshire IL 60069 800-553-4676
TF Cust Svc: 800-553-4676 ■ *Web:* www.kleintools.com

Leatherman Tool Group Inc
12106 NE Ainsworth Cir........ Portland OR 97220 503-253-7826 253-7830
TF: 800-847-8665 ■ *Web:* www.leatherman.com

Lisle Corp 813 E Main St........ Clarinda IA 51632 712-542-5101 542-6591
Web: www.lislecorp.com

LS Starrett Co 121 Crescent St .... Athol MA 01331 978-249-3551 249-8495
NYSE: SCX ■ *TF:* 800-482-8710 ■ *Web:* www.starrett.com

Mac Tools Inc 505 N Cleveland Ave........ Westerville OH 43082 614-755-7000
TF: 800-622-8665 ■ *Web:* www.mactools.com

Malco Products Inc
14080 State Hwy 55 NW PO Box 400........ Annandale MN 55302 320-274-8246 274-2269
TF: 800-328-3530 ■ *Web:* www.malcoproducts.com

Marshalltown Co 104 S Eigth Ave .... Marshalltown IA 50158 641-753-5999 753-6341
TF: 800-888-0127 ■ *Web:* www.marshalltown.com

Matco Tools 4403 Allen Rd........ Stow OH 44224 330-926-5332 926-5320
TF: 866-289-8665 ■ *Web:* www.matcotools.com

Mayhew Steel Products Inc
199 Industrial Blvd........ Turners Falls MA 01376 413-863-4860 863-8464
TF: 800-872-0037 ■ *Web:* www.mayhew.com

MIBRO Group 111 Sinnott Rd........ Toronto ON M1L4S6 416-285-9000
TF: 866-941-9006 ■ *Web:* www.mibro.com

Newell Rubbermaid Inc Irwin Tools Div
8935 Northpointe Executive Dr........ Huntersville NC 28078 704-987-4555
TF: 800-866-5740 ■ *Web:* www.irwin.com

QEP Co Inc 1001 Broken Sound Pkwy NW Ste A .... Boca Raton FL 33487 561-994-5550 241-2830
OTC: QEPC ■ *TF Sales:* 800-777-8665 ■ *Web:* www.qep.com

Red Devil Inc 1437 S Boulder........ Tulsa OK 74119 800-423-3845 585-8120*
**Fax Area Code: 918* ■ *TF:* 800-423-3845 ■ *Web:* www.reddevil.com

Reed Manufacturing Co 1425 W Eigth St........ Erie PA 16502 814-452-3691 455-1697
TF: 800-456-1697 ■ *Web:* www.reedmfgco.com

Relton Corp 317 Rolyn Dr PO Box 60019 .... Arcadia CA 91066 323-681-2551 446-9671*
**Fax Area Code: 626* ■ *TF Cust Svc:* 800-423-1505 ■ *Web:* www.relton.com

Ridge Tool Co 400 Clark St........ Elyria OH 44035 440-323-5581 323-5204
Web: www.ridgid.com

Ripley Co 46 Nooks Hill Rd .... Cromwell CT 06416 860-635-2200 635-3631
TF: 800-528-8665 ■ *Web:* www.ripley-tools.com

Seymour Mfg Co Inc PO Box 248........ Seymour IN 47274 812-522-2900 522-6109
TF: 800-815-7253 ■ *Web:* www.seymourmfg.com

Snap-on Inc 2801 80th St .... Kenosha WI 53143 262-656-5200 656-5577
NYSE: SNA ■ *TF:* 877-762-7664 ■ *Web:* www.snapon.com

Stabila Inc 332 Industrial Dr PO Box 402 .... South Elgin IL 60177 800-869-7460 488-0051*
**Fax Area Code: 847* ■ *TF:* 800-869-7460 ■ *Web:* www.stabila.com

Stanley Tools Inc 480 Myrtle St........ New Britain CT 06053 800-262-2161
TF Cust Svc: 800-262-2161 ■ *Web:* www.stanleytools.com

Stride Tool Inc Imperial Div
30333 Emerald Vly Pkwy .... Glenwillow OH 44139 440-247-4600 527-6383*
**Fax Area Code: 800* ■ *TF:* 888-467-8665 ■ *Web:* imperial-tools.com

Superior Tool Co 100 Hayes Dr Unit C........ Cleveland OH 44131 216-398-8600 398-8691
TF Cust Svc: 800-533-3244 ■ *Web:* www.superiortool.com

Tamco Inc 1466 Delberts Dr........ Monongahela PA 15063 724-258-6622 258-6692
TF: 800-826-2672 ■ *Web:* www.tamcotools.com

Triumph Twist Drill Co Inc 1 SW 7th St........ Chisholm MN 55719 218-263-3891 263-3887
TF: 800-942-1501 ■ *Web:* triumphtwistdrill.com

Ullman Devices Corp 664 Danbury Rd........ Ridgefield CT 06877 203-438-6577 431-9064
TF: 800-784-7796 ■ *Web:* www.users.ntplx.net/~ullman

Vaughan & Bushnell Manufacturing Co
11414 Maple Ave........ Hebron IL 60034 815-648-2446 648-4300
TF: 800-435-6000 ■ *Web:* vaughanmfg.com

Wall Lenk Corp 1950 Dr Martin Luther King Jr........ Kinston NC 28501 252-527-4186
Web: www.wlenk.com

Walter Meier Mfg Inc 427 New Sanford Rd........ La Vergne TN 37086 615-793-8900
Web: www.wiltontools.com

Warner Manufacturing Co
13435 Industrial Pk Blvd .... Plymouth MN 55441 763-559-4740
TF: 800-444-0606 ■ *Web:* www.warnertool.com

Wheeler-Rex Inc
3744 Jefferson Rd PO Box 688........ Ashtabula OH 44005 440-998-2788 992-2925
TF: 800-321-7950 ■ *Web:* www.wheelerrex.com

Zephyr Mfg Company Inc 201 Hindry Av........ Inglewood CA 90301 310-410-4907
TF: 800-624-3944 ■ *Web:* zephyrtoolgroup.com

TOOLS - MACHINE

See Machine Tools - Metal Cutting Types p. 2692; Machine Tools - Metal Forming Types p. 2693

759 TOOLS - POWER

See Also Lawn & Garden Equipment p. 2645; Metalworking Devices & Accessories p. 2768

Phone Fax

Alpine Power Systems Inc 24355 Capitol........ Redford MI 48239 313-531-6600 531-2950
TF: 877-769-3762 ■ *Web:* www.alpinepowersystems.com

American Pneumatic Tool Inc
9949 Tabor Pl........ Santa Fe Springs CA 90670 562-204-1555 204-1773
TF: 800-532-7402 ■ *Web:* www.apt-tools.com

Atlas Copco Tools & Assembly Systems
2998 Dutton Rd .... Auburn Hills MI 48326 248-373-3000 373-3001
TF: 800-859-3746 ■ *Web:* atlascopco.com/us/tools/us

Blackstone Industries Inc 16 Stoney Hill Rd........ Bethel CT 06801 203-792-8622 796-7861
TF: 800-272-2885 ■ *Web:* www.blackstoneind.com

Chicago Pneumatic Tool Co 1800 Overview Dr........ Rock Hill SC 29730 803-817-7000 228-9096*
**Fax Area Code: 800* ■ **Fax:* Hum Res ■ *TF:* 800-624-4735 ■ *Web:* www.cp.com

Cooper Industries 600 Travis St Ste 5400 .... Houston TX 77002 713-209-8400 209-8995
NYSE: ETN ■ *TF:* 866-853-4293 ■ *Web:* www.cooperindustries.com

Dremel Inc 4915 21st St........ Racine WI 53406 262-554-1390 554-7654
TF: 800-437-3635 ■ *Web:* www.dremel.com

				Phone	Fax
Dynabrade Inc 8989 Sheridan Dr	Clarence	NY	14031	716-631-0100	631-2073
TF Cust Svc: 800-828-7333 ■ *Web:* www.dynabrade.com					
Enerpac PO Box 3241	Milwaukee	WI	53201	262-293-1600	781-1049*
**Fax:* Cust Svc ■ *TF Cust Svc:* 800-433-2766 ■ *Web:* www.enerpac.com					
Florida Pneumatic Manufacturing Corp					
851 Jupiter Pk Ln	Jupiter	FL	33458	561-744-9500	575-9134
TF: 800-327-9403 ■ *Web:* www.florida-pneumatic.com					
Greenlee Textron Inc 4455 Boeing Dr	Rockford	IL	61109	800-435-0786	451-2632
TF: 800-435-0786 ■ *Web:* www.greenlee.com					
Hilti Inc 5400 S 122nd E Ave	Tulsa	OK	74146	918-252-6000	879-7000*
**Fax Area Code:* 800 ■ *TF Cust Svc:* 800-879-8000 ■ *Web:* www.us.hilti.com					
Hougen Manufacturing Inc 3001 Hougen Dr	Swartz Creek	MI	48473	810-635-7111	635-8277
TF Orders: 800-426-7818 ■ *Web:* www.hougen.com					
Makita USA Inc 14930 Northam St	La Mirada	CA	90638	714-522-8088	522-8133
TF: 800-462-5482 ■ *Web:* www.makitausa.com					
Master Appliance Corp 2420 18th St	Racine	WI	53403	262-633-7791	633-9745
TF: 800-558-9413 ■ *Web:* www.masterappliance.com					
Milwaukee Electric Tool Corp					
13135 W Lisbon Rd	Brookfield	WI	53005	262-781-3600	638-9582*
**Fax Area Code:* 800 ■ **Fax:* Orders ■ *TF:* 800-729-3878 ■ *Web:* www.milwaukeetool.com					
P & F Industries Inc 445 Broadhollow Rd	Melville	NY	11747	631-694-9800	694-9804
NASDAQ: PFIN ■ *TF:* 800-327-9403 ■ *Web:* www.pfina.com					
Paslode 888 Forest Edge Dr	Vernon Hills	IL	60061	847-634-1900	634-6602
TF Cust Svc: 800-682-3428 ■ *Web:* www.paslode.com					
Pioneer Tool & Forge Inc 101 Sixth St	New Kensington	PA	15068	724-337-4700	337-4707
TF: 800-359-6408 ■ *Web:* www.breakersteel.com					
Pneutek 17 Friars Dr	Hudson	NH	03051	603-883-1660	882-9165
TF: 800-431-8665 ■ *Web:* www.pneutek.com					
Powernail Co 1300 Rose Rd	Lake Zurich	IL	60047	847-634-3000	634-4943
TF: 800-323-1653 ■ *Web:* www.powernail.com					
Ridge Tool Co 400 Clark St	Elyria	OH	44035	440-323-5581	323-5204
Web: www.ridgid.com					
Robert Bosch Tool Corp					
1800 W Central Rd	Mount Prospect	IL	60056	224-232-2000	232-3169
TF: 877-267-2499 ■ *Web:* www.boschtools.com					
Ryobi Technologies Inc					
1428 Pearman Dairy Rd	Anderson	SC	29625	800-525-2579	261-9435*
**Fax Area Code:* 864 ■ *TF:* 800-525-2579 ■ *Web:* www.ryobitools.com					
SENCO Products Inc 4270 Ivy Pt Blvd	Cincinnati	OH	45245	800-543-4596	388-3100*
**Fax Area Code:* 513 ■ *TF Tech Supp:* 800-543-4596 ■ *Web:* www.sencobrands.com					
Shopsmith Inc 6530 Poe Ave	Dayton	OH	45414	937-898-6070	722-3965*
OTC: SSMH ■ **Fax Area Code:* 800 ■ *TF Cust Svc:* 800-543-7586 ■ *Web:* www.shopsmith.com					
Sioux Tools Inc 250 Snap-on Dr	Murphy	NC	28906	828-835-9765	835-9685
TF Orders: 800-722-7290 ■ *Web:* www.siouxtools.com					
Speedgrip Chuck Inc 2000 E Industrial Pkwy	Elkhart	IN	46516	574-294-1506	294-2465
Web: www.speedgrip.com					
Stanley Assembly Technologies Div					
5335 Avion Pk Dr	Cleveland	OH	44143	440-461-5500	461-2710
TF: 877-787-7830 ■ *Web:* www.stanleyengineeredfastening.com					
Stihl Inc 536 Viking Dr	Virginia Beach	VA	23452	757-486-9100	340-0377*
**Fax Area Code:* 303 ■ *TF Cust Svc:* 800-467-8445 ■ *Web:* www.stihlusa.com					
Suhner Manufacturing Inc 43 Anderson Rd	Rome	GA	30161	706-235-8046	235-8045
Web: www.suhner.com					
Thomas C Wilson Inc 21-11 44th Ave	Long Island	NY	11101	718-729-3360	361-2872
TF: 800-230-2636 ■ *Web:* www.tcwilson.com					

760 TOUR OPERATORS

See Also Bus Services - Charter p. 1880; Travel Agencies p. 3264

				Phone	Fax
Academy Bus LLC 111 Paterson Ave	Hoboken	NJ	07030	201-420-7000	420-8087
TF: 800-442-7272 ■ *Web:* www.academybus.com					
Acadia National Park Tours 53 Main St	Bar Harbor	ME	04609	207-288-0300	
Web: www.nationalparktours.com					
Adventure Alaska Tours Inc PO Box 64	Hope	AK	99605	907-782-3730	782-3725
TF: 800-365-7057 ■ *Web:* www.adventurealaskatours.com					
Adventure Connection PO Box 475	Coloma	CA	95613	530-626-7385	626-9268
TF: 800-556-6060 ■ *Web:* www.raftcalifornia.com					
Adventure Ctr Inc 1311 63rd St Ste 200	Emeryville	CA	94608	510-654-1879	654-4200
Adventure Life South America					
1655 S Third St W Ste 1	Missoula	MT	59801	406-541-2677	541-2676
TF: 800-344-6118 ■ *Web:* www.adventure-life.com					
Adventures Out West 1680 S 21st St	Colorado Springs	CO	80904	800-755-0935	
TF: 800-755-0935 ■ *Web:* www.advoutwest.com					
Africa Adventure Co, The					
5353 N Federal Hwy Ste 300	Fort Lauderdale	FL	33308	954-491-8877	491-9060
TF: 800-882-9453 ■ *Web:* www.africa-adventure.com					
African Travel Inc 330 N Brand Blvd Ste 950	Glendale	CA	91203	818-507-7893	507-5802
TF: 800-421-8907 ■ *Web:* www.africantravelinc.com					
Agape Tours & Charter					
3306 Cumberland Ave	Wichita Falls	TX	76301	940-767-4935	
Web: agapetourstx.com					
Agentours Inc 126 W Portal Ave	San Francisco	CA	94127	415-661-5200	
Web: agentours.com					
AHI International Corp					
8550 W Bryn Mawr Ave Ste 600	Chicago	IL	60631	800-323-7373	318-5000*
**Fax Area Code:* 847 ■ *TF:* 800-323-7373 ■ *Web:* www.ahitravel.com					
Alaska Heritage Tours Inc 509 W Fourth Ave	Anchorage	AK	99501	907-777-2805	
Web: www.alaskaheritagetours.com					
All Aboard Travel PO Box 90074	Chattanooga	TN	37412	423-499-9977	
TF: 800-499-9877 ■ *Web:* www.allaboardchatt.com					
Alpha Omega Tours & Charters					
419 N Jefferson St PO Box 97	Medical Lake	WA	99022	509-299-5595	299-5545
Web: www.alphaomegatoursandcharters.com					
Alpine Adventure Trails Tours Inc					
7495 Lower Thomaston Rd	Macon	GA	31220	888-478-4004	477-4117*
**Fax Area Code:* 478 ■ *TF:* 888-478-4004 ■ *Web:* www.swisshiking.com					
AmaWaterways 26010 Mureau Rd	Calabasas	CA	91302	800-626-0126	
TF: 800-626-0126					
Ambassadors Group Inc 110 S Ferrall St	Spokane	WA	99202	509-534-6200	
NASDAQ: EPAX					
American Trails West (ATW) 92 Middle Neck Rd	Great Neck	NY	11021	516-487-2800	487-2855
TF: 800-645-6260 ■ *Web:* www.atwteentours.com					
AmericanTours International LLC (ATI)					
6053 W Century Blvd	Los Angeles	CA	90045	310-641-9953	216-5807
Web: www.americantours.com					
Anderson Coach & Travel 1 Anderson Plz	Greenville	PA	16125	724-588-8310	588-0257
TF: 800-345-3435 ■ *Web:* www.goanderson.com					
ATS Tours 300 Continental Blvd Ste 350	El Segundo	CA	90245	888-410-5770	643-0032*
**Fax Area Code:* 310 ■ *TF:* 888-410-5770 ■ *Web:* travel2-us.com					
Backroads 801 Cedar St	Berkeley	CA	94710	510-527-1555	527-1444
TF: 800-462-2848 ■ *Web:* www.backroads.com					
Badger Coaches Inc 5501 Femrite Dr	Madison	WI	53718	608-255-1511	
TF: 800-442-8259 ■ *Web:* www.badgerbus.com					
Banff Adventures Unlimited					
211 Bear St Bison Courtyard	Banff	AB	T1L1A8	403-762-4554	
TF: 800-644-8888 ■ *Web:* www.banffadventures.com					
Beamers Hells Canyon Tours & Excursions					
PO Box 1243	Lewiston	ID	83501	509-758-4800	758-3643
TF: 800-522-6966 ■ *Web:* www.hellscanyontours.com					
Bestway Tours & Safaris 8678 Greenall Ave	Burnaby	BC	V5J3M6	604-264-7378	264-7774
TF: 800-663-0844 ■ *Web:* www.bestway.com					
Big Five Tours & Expeditions 1551 SE Palm Ct	Stuart	FL	34994	772-287-7995	287-5990
TF: 800-244-3483 ■ *Web:* www.bigfive.com					
Blue Grass Tours Inc 817 Enterprise Dr	Lexington	KY	40510	859-233-2152	
Web: www.bluegrasstours.com					
Bonaventure Tours 8 Boudreau Ln	Haute-Aboujagane	NB	E4P5N1	506-532-3674	532-6487
TF: 800-561-1213 ■ *Web:* www.aboutbonaventuretours.com					
Borderland Tours 2875 W Hilltop Rd	Portal	AZ	85632	520-558-2351	
Web: www.borderland-tours.com					
Boston Duck Tours Ltd 4 Copley Pl Ste 310	Boston	MA	02116	617-450-0065	
TF: 800-226-7442 ■ *Web:* www.bostonducktours.com					
Breakaway Tours 3300 Bloor St Ste 1800	Toronto	ON	M8X2X2	416-915-9880	915-9881
TF: 800-465-4257 ■ *Web:* www.breakawaytours.com					
Brendan Vacations 21625 Prairie St	Chatsworth	CA	91311	800-687-1002	
TF: 800-687-1002 ■ *Web:* www.brendanvacations.com					
Brewster Rocky Mountain Adventures PO Box 370	Banff	AB	T1L1A5	403-762-5454	673-2100
Web: www.brewsteradventures.com					
Brewster Travel Canada					
100 Gopher St PO Box 1140	Banff	AB	T1L1J3	403-762-6700	762-6750
TF: 866-606-6700 ■ *Web:* www.brewster.ca					
Burke International Tours Inc PO Box 890	Newton	NC	28658	828-465-3900	
TF: 800-476-3900 ■ *Web:* www.burkechristiantours.com					
California Parlor Car Tours					
500 Sutter St Ste 401	San Francisco	CA	94102	415-474-7500	673-1539
TF: 800-227-4250 ■ *Web:* www.calpartours.com					
Centennial Travelers 311 S College Ave	Fort Collins	CO	80524	970-484-4988	
TF: 800-223-0675 ■ *Web:* www.centennialtravel.com					
Chicago Supernatural Tours PO Box 557544	Chicago	IL	60655	708-499-0300	
Web: www.ghosttour.com					
Churchill Nature Tours PO Box 429	Erickson	MB	R0J0P0	204-636-2968	636-2557
TF: 877-636-2968 ■ *Web:* www.churchillnaturetours.com					
Classic Student Tours 75 Rhoads Ctr Dr	Dayton	OH	45458	937-439-0032	439-0041
TF: 800-860-0246 ■ *Web:* classicstudenttours.com					
Club Europa 802 W Oregon St	Urbana	IL	61801	217-344-5863	344-4072
TF: 800-331-1882 ■ *Web:* www.clubeuropatravel.com					
Coach Tours Ltd 475 Federal Rd	Brookfield	CT	06804	203-740-1118	
TF: 800-822-6224 ■ *Web:* www.coachtour.com					
Complete Travel Services 3841 Nostrand Ave	Brooklyn	NY	11235	718-934-9400	891-8681
Contemporary Tours					
1400 Old Country Rd Ste 100	Westbury	NY	11590	516-484-5032	
TF: 800-627-8873 ■ *Web:* www.contemporarytours.com					
Contiki Holidays 801 E Katella Ave 3rd Fl	Anaheim	CA	92805	714-935-0808	
TF: 800-944-5708 ■ *Web:* www.contiki.com					
Convexx 6865 S Ea Ste 101	Las Vegas	NV	89119	702-450-7662	
Web: www.convexx.com					
Cook Inlet Region Inc 2525 C St Ste 500	Anchorage	AK	99503	907-274-8638	
Web: www.ciri.com					
Cultural Experiences Abroad (CEA)					
2999 N 44th St Ste 200	Phoenix	AZ	85018	480-557-7900	557-7926
TF: 800-266-4441 ■ *Web:* www.ceastudyabroad.com					
D & m Tours Inc 117 E Seventh St	Paterson	NJ	07524	520-512-7843	
Dash Tours 1024 Winnipeg St	Regina	SK	S4R8P8	306-352-2222	757-4126
TF: 800-265-0000 ■ *Web:* dashtours.com					
Delta Tour & Travel Services Inc					
3360 Flair Dr Ste 102	El Monte	CA	91731	626-300-0033	
Web: deltatours.com					
Dipert Travel & Transportation Ltd					
PO Box 580	Arlington	TX	76004	800-433-5335	543-3728*
**Fax Area Code:* 817 ■ *TF:* 800-433-5335 ■ *Web:* www.dandipert.com					
Earthwatch Institute 114 Western Ave	Boston	MA	02134	978-461-0081	461-2332
TF: 800-776-0188 ■ *Web:* www.earthwatch.org					
Eco Park Resort at Mt. St. Helens Inc					
14000 Spirit Lk Hwy	Toutle	WA	98649	360-274-7007	
Web: www.ecoparkresort.com/tours.htm					
Educational Tours 1123 Sterling Rd	Inverness	FL	34450	800-343-9003	
TF: 800-343-9003 ■ *Web:* www.edtours-us.com					
Educational Travel Consultants (ETC)					
PO Box 1580	Hendersonville	NC	28793	828-693-0412	692-1591
TF: 800-247-7969 ■ *Web:* www.educationaltravelconsultants.com					
Educational Travel Tours Inc PO Box 9028	Trenton	NJ	08650	609-587-1550	587-1550
Web: www.educationaltraveltours.com					
EF Tours 2 Education Cir	Cambridge	MA	02141	877-205-9909	
TF: 800-872-8439 ■ *Web:* www.eftours.com					
Esplanade Tours 160 Commonwealth Ave Ste U-1A	Boston	MA	02116	617-266-7465	262-9829
TF: 800-628-4893 ■ *Web:* esplanadetravel.com					
Explorica Inc 145 Tremont St	Boston	MA	02111	888-310-7120	310-7088
TF: 888-310-7120 ■ *Web:* www.explorica.com					
Fantastic Tours & Travel 6143 Jericho Tpke	Commack	NY	11725	631-462-6262	462-2311
TF: 800-552-6262 ■ *Web:* www.fantastictours.com					
Festive Holidays Inc					
5501 New Jersey Ave	Wildwood Crest	NJ	08260	609-522-6316	729-8606
TF: 800-257-8920 ■ *Web:* www.festiveholidays.com					

Name / Address	City	State	Zip	Phone	Fax
Flathead Lake Lodge & Ranch 150 Flathead Lodge Rd. *Web:* flatheadlakelodge.com	Bigfork	MT	59911	406-837-4391	
Friendly Excursions Inc PO Box 69. *TF:* 800-775-5018 ■ *Web:* www.friendlyexcursions.net	Sunland	CA	91041	818-353-7726	353-3903
Frontiers International Travel PO Box 959. *TF:* 800-245-1950 ■ *Web:* www.frontierstravel.com	Wexford	PA	15090	724-935-1577	935-5388
Gadabout Vacations 1801 E Tahquitz Canyon Way Ste 100. *TF:* 800-952-5068 ■ *Web:* www.gadaboutvacations.com	Palm Springs	CA	92262	760-325-5556	325-5127
General Tours 53 Summer St. **Fax Area Code:* 603 ■ *TF:* 800-221-2216 ■ *Web:* alexanderroberts.com	Keene	NH	03431	800-221-2216	357-4548*
Gerber Tours Inc 100 Crossways Park Dr W Ste 400. *TF:* 800-645-9145 ■ *Web:* www.gerbertours.com	Woodbury	NY	11797	516-826-5000	
Global Educational Tours 7216 Madison Ave Ste U	Indianapolis	IN	46227	317-787-2787	787-2765
Globus 5301 S Federal Cir. *TF:* 866-755-8581 ■ *Web:* www.globusjourneys.com	Littleton	CO	80123	866-755-8581	
Go Next 8000 W 78th St Ste 345. *TF:* 800-842-9023 ■ *Web:* www.gonext.com	Minneapolis	MN	55439	952-918-8950	918-8975
Go West Adventures Inc PO Box 882319. *Web:* www.gowestadventures.com	Los Angeles	CA	90009	310-216-2522	216-2638
Go...With Jo! Tours & Travel Inc 910 Dixieland Rd. *TF:* 800-999-1446 ■ *Web:* www.gowithjo.com	Harlingen	TX	78552	956-423-1446	
Good Time Tours 455 Corday St. *TF:* 800-446-0886 ■ *Web:* www.goodtimetours.com	Pensacola	FL	32503	850-476-0046	476-7637
Good Times Travel Inc 17132 Magnolia St. *TF:* 888-488-2287 ■ *Web:* www.goodtimestravel.com	Fountain Valley	CA	92708	714-848-1255	848-2855
Grand European Tours 6000 Meadows Rd Ste 520. *TF:* 877-622-9109 ■ *Web:* www.getours.com	Lake Oswego	OR	97035	503-718-2262	718-5198
Gray Line Worldwide 1835 Gaylord St. *TF:* 800-472-9546 ■ *Web:* www.grayline.com	Denver	CO	80206	303-394-6920	394-6950
Green Tortoise Adventure Travel & Hostels 494 Broadway. *TF:* 800-867-8647 ■ *Web:* www.greentortoise.com	San Francisco	CA	94133	415-834-1000	956-4900
Greene Coach Charters & Tours Inc 126 Bohannon Ave	Greeneville	TN	37745	423-638-8271	638-5541
Group Voyagers Inc 5301 S Federal Cir. *Web:* www.globusandcosmos.com	Littleton	CO	80123	303-703-7000	
Gutsy Women Travel LLC 801 E Katella Ave. *TF:* 866-464-8879 ■ *Web:* www.gutsywomentravel.com	Anaheim	CA	92806	866-464-8879	
Hagey Coach & Tours Nrt 210 Schoolhouse Rd. *TF:* 800-544-2439 ■ *Web:* hagey.com	Souderton	PA	18964	215-723-4381	
Hampton Golf Inc 10401 Deerwood Park Blvd Ste No. 2130. *Web:* www.hamptongolfclubs.com	Jacksonville	FL	32256	904-564-9129	
Harbor Cruises LLC 1 Long Wharf. *Web:* www.bostonharborcruises.com	Boston	MA	02110	617-227-4321	
Hesselgrave International PO Box 30768. *TF:* 800-457-5522 ■ *Web:* www.hesselgravetours.com	Bellingham	WA	98228	360-734-3570	734-3588
Historic Tours of America Inc 201 Front St Ste 224. *TF General:* 800-844-7601 ■ *Web:* www.historictours.com	Key West	FL	33040	305-296-3609	292-8902
Hole in One International 6195 Ridgeview Ct Ste A. *TF:* 800-827-2249 ■ *Web:* www.holeinoneinternational.com	Reno	NV	89519	775-828-4653	
Holiday River Expeditions 544 East 3900 South. *TF:* 800-624-6323 ■ *Web:* www.bikeraft.com	Salt Lake City	UT	84107	801-266-2087	266-1448
Holiday Tours Inc 10367 Randleman Rd. *Web:* www.holidaytoursinc.com	Randleman	NC	27317	336-498-9000	498-2204
Isram World of Travel Inc 90 John St Ste 602. **Fax Area Code:* 212 ■ *TF:* 800-223-7460 ■ *Web:* www.isram.com	New York	NY	10038	800-223-7460	370-1477*
Jade Travel Group 139 Keefer St Ste 202. *Web:* www2.jadetours.com	Vancouver	BC	V6A1X3	604-689-5885	
JALPAK International Hawaii Inc 2270 Kalakaua Ave Ste 1600	Honolulu	HI	96815	808-926-4500	923-4635
Jasmine's China Adventure Tours 6044 Laguna Villa Way	Elk Grove	CA	95758	916-683-1790	
Julian Tours 1721 Crestwood Dr. *TF:* 800-541-7936 ■ *Web:* www.juliantours.com	Alexandria	VA	22302	703-379-2300	379-5030
Katmai Coastal Bear Tours PO Box 1503. *TF:* 800-532-8338 ■ *Web:* www.katmaibears.com	Homer	AK	99603	907-235-8337	
Ker & Downey Inc 6703 Hwy Blvd. *TF:* 800-423-4236 ■ *Web:* www.kerdowney.com	Katy	TX	77494	281-371-2500	371-2514
Kincaid Coach Lines Inc 9207 Woodend Rd. *TF:* 800-998-1901 ■ *Web:* www.kincaidcoach.com	Kansas City	KS	66111	913-441-6200	441-0068
Knight Inlet Grizzly Bear Adventure Tours 8841 Driftwood Rd. *Web:* www.grizzlytours.com	Black Creek	BC	V9J1A8	250-337-1953	337-1914
Lakefront Lines Inc 13315 Brookpark Rd. *Web:* www.lakefrontlines.com	Brook Park	OH	44142	216-267-8810	
Landmark Tours 1304 University Ave NE Ste 201. *TF:* 888-231-8735 ■ *Web:* landmark-tours.com	Minneapolis	MN	55413	651-490-5408	
Lemhi Ventures Inc 315 East Lk St Ste 304. *Web:* www.lemhiventures.com	Wayzata	MN	55391	952-908-9680	
Lindblad Expeditions 96 Morton St 9th Fl. *TF:* 800-397-3348 ■ *Web:* www.expeditions.com	New York	NY	10014	212-765-7740	265-3770
Macy's Travel 700 Nicollet Mall. *TF:* 800-316-6166 ■ *Web:* www.travel.carlsonwagonlit.com	Minneapolis	MN	55402	800-316-6166	
Maupintour Inc 2690 Weston Rd Ste 200. *TF:* 800-255-4266 ■ *Web:* www.maupintour.com	Weston	FL	33331	954-653-3820	888-9082
Mayflower Tours Inc 1225 Warren Ave PO Box 490. *TF:* 800-323-7604 ■ *Web:* www.mayflowertours.com	Downers Grove	IL	60515	630-435-8500	960-3575
Micato Safaris 15 W 26th St 11th Fl. *TF:* 800-642-2861 ■ *Web:* www.micato.com	New York	NY	10010	212-545-7111	545-8297
Mid-American Coaches Inc 4530 Hwy 47. *TF:* 866-944-8687 ■ *Web:* www.mid-americancoaches.com	Washington	MO	63090	866-944-8687	
Midnight Sun Adventure Travel 1027 Pandora Ave. *TF:* 800-255-5057 ■ *Web:* www.midnightsuntravel.com	Victoria	BC	V8V3P6	250-480-9409	483-7422
MLT Inc 700 Central Ave. *Web:* www.mltvacations.com	Atlanta	GA	30354	404-559-2270	
Monograms 5301 S Federal Cir. *TF:* 866-270-9841 ■ *Web:* monograms.com	Littleton	CO	80123	866-270-9841	
Montana River Outfitters 923 Tenth Ave N. *TF:* 800-800-8218 ■ *Web:* www.montanariveroutfitters.com	Great Falls	MT	59401	406-761-1677	
Moose Travel Network 192 Spadina Ave Unit 408. *TF:* 888-244-6673 ■ *Web:* www.moosenetwork.com	Toronto	ON	M5T2C2	604-297-0255	297-0228
Mountain Travel Sobek 1266 66th St Ste 4. *TF:* 888-831-7526 ■ *Web:* www.mtsobek.com	Emeryville	CA	94608	510-594-6000	594-6001
Musiker Discovery Programs Inc 1326 Old Northern Blvd. *Web:* www.summerdiscovery.com	Roslyn	NY	11576	516-621-3939	625-3438
National Events Inc 9672 South 700 East Ste 200. *Web:* www.nationaleventservices.com	Sandy	UT	84070	801-495-9118	
Natural Habitat Adventures PO Box 3065. *TF:* 800-543-8917 ■ *Web:* www.nathab.com	Boulder	CO	80307	303-449-3711	449-3712
Networld Inc 300 Lanidex Plz Ste 1. *TF:* 800-992-3411 ■ *Web:* www.networldinc.com	Parsippany	NJ	07054	973-884-7474	
Off the Beaten Path 7 E Beall St. *TF:* 800-445-2995 ■ *Web:* www.offthebeatenpath.com	Bozeman	MT	59715	406-586-1311	587-4147
Olivia Cruises & Resorts 434 Brannan St. *TF:* 800-631-6277 ■ *Web:* www.olivia.com	San Francisco	CA	94107	415-962-5700	962-5710
On Tour 201 Cortsen Rd	Pleasant Hill	CA	94523	925-930-9135	
Onondaga Coach Corp PO Box 277. *TF:* 800-451-1570 ■ *Web:* www.onondagacoach.com	Auburn	NY	13021	315-255-2216	255-0925
Orange Belt Stages PO Box 949. *TF:* 800-266-7433 ■ *Web:* www.orangebelt.com	Visalia	CA	93279	559-733-4408	733-0538
Overseas Adventure Travel 347 Congress St. *TF:* 800-221-0814 ■ *Web:* www.oattravel.com	Boston	MA	02210	800-221-0814	
Panorama Balloon Tours 2683 Via De La Valle 625G. *TF:* 800-455-3592 ■ *Web:* www.gohotair.com	Del Mar	CA	92014	800-455-3592	
Perillo Tours 577 Chestnut Ridge Rd. *TF:* 800-431-1515 ■ *Web:* www.perillotours.com	Woodcliff Lake	NJ	07677	201-307-1234	307-1808
Pilgrim Tours & Travel Inc 3071 Main St PO Box 268. *TF:* 800-322-0788 ■ *Web:* www.pilgrimtours.com	Morgantown	PA	19543	610-286-0788	286-6262
Pink Jeep Tours Las Vegas Inc 3629 W Hacienda Ave. *TF:* 800-873-3662 ■ *Web:* www.pinkjeeptours.com	Las Vegas	NV	89118	702-895-6777	
Pioneer Golf Inc 609 Castle Ridge Rd. Ste 335. *TF:* 800-262-5725 ■ *Web:* www.pioneergolf.com	Austin	TX	78746	512-327-2680	327-8120
Pitmar Tours 7549 140th St Ste 9. *TF:* 877-596-9670 ■ *Web:* www.pitmartours.com	Surrey	BC	V3W5J9	604-596-9670	596-3444
Polynesian Adventure Tours Inc 2880 Kilihau St. **Fax:* Resv ■ *TF:* 800-622-3011 ■ *Web:* www.polyadhawaiitours.com	Honolulu	HI	96819	808-833-3000	833-3473*
Premier Alaska Tours Inc 1900 Premier Ct. *TF:* 888-486-8725 ■ *Web:* www.premieralaskatours.com	Anchorage	AK	99502	907-279-0001	
Premier Tours 21 S 12th St 9th Fl. *TF:* 800-545-1910 ■ *Web:* www.premiertours.com	Philadelphia	PA	19107	800-545-1910	
Presley Tours Inc 16 Presley Pk Dr PO Box 58. *TF:* 800-621-6100 ■ *Web:* www.presleytours.com	Makanda	IL	62958	618-549-0704	
REI Adventures PO Box 1938. *TF:* 800-622-2236 ■ *Web:* www.rei.com/adventures	Sumner	WA	98390	253-437-1100	395-8160
Richmond Tours 1828 Hylan Blvd. *TF:* 800-766-3868	Staten Island	NY	10305	718-979-3111	979-7143
Rivers Oceans & Mountains Adventures Inc (ROAM) 2485 Hwy 3A. *TF:* 888-639-1114 ■ *Web:* www.iroamtheworld.com	Nelson	BC	V1L6K7	888-639-1114	
Roberts Hawaii Inc 680 Iwilei Rd Ste 700. *TF:* 800-831-5541 ■ *Web:* www.robertshawaii.com	Honolulu	HI	96817	808-523-7750	522-7872
Royal Coach Tours 630 Stockton Ave. *TF:* 800-927-6925 ■ *Web:* www.royal-coach.com	San Jose	CA	95126	408-279-4801	286-1410
Royal Tours Inc PO Box 372 PO Box 372. *Web:* www.gowithgaynelle.com	Smithfield	VA	23431	757-569-7616	
RSVP Vacations 2535 25th Ave S. **Fax Area Code:* 612 ■ *TF:* 800-328-7787	Minneapolis	MN	55406	310-432-2300	729-2809*
Scenic Airlines Inc 3900 Paradise Rd Ste 223. *TF:* 866-235-9422 ■ *Web:* www.scenic.com	Las Vegas	NV	89169	702-638-3300	639-3275
Short Hills Tours 46 Chatham Rd Ste 1. *TF:* 800-348-6871 ■ *Web:* www.shorthillstours.com	Short Hills	NJ	07078	973-467-2113	467-3353
Silver Fox Tours & Motorcoaches 3 Silver Fox Dr. *TF:* 800-342-5998 ■ *Web:* www.silverfoxcoach.com	Millbury	MA	01527	508-865-6000	865-4660
Silverado Stages Inc 241 Prado Rd. *TF:* 888-383-8109 ■ *Web:* www.silveradostages.com	San Luis Obispo	CA	93401	805-545-8400	545-8404
Sixthman LTD 1040 Blvd SE Ste J. *Web:* www.sixthman.net	Atlanta	GA	30312	770-738-6013	
South of the Border Tours 7937 E Coronado Rd	Tucson	AZ	85750	520-760-4000	760-3999
Sports Leisure Vacations 9812 Old Winery Pl. *TF:* 800-951-5556 ■ *Web:* www.sportsleisure.com	Sacramento	CA	95827	916-361-2051	
Sports Travel Inc 60 Main St PO Box 50. *TF:* 800-662-4424 ■ *Web:* www.sportstravelandtours.com	Hatfield	MA	01038	413-247-7678	247-5700
Storm Chasing Adventure Tours 1627 W Main St Ste 105. *Web:* www.stormchasing.com	Bozeman	MT	59715	970-367-5395	
Straight A Tours & Travel 6881 Kingspointe Pkwy Ste 18. *TF:* 800-237-5440 ■ *Web:* straightatours.com	Orlando	FL	32819	407-896-1242	896-1151
Student Tours Inc 60 W Ave. *TF:* 800-331-7093 ■ *Web:* www.studenttoursinc.com	Vineyard Haven	MA	02568	508-693-5078	693-8627
Student Travel Services Inc 1413 Madison Pk Dr. **Fax Area Code:* 410 ■ *TF:* 800-648-4849 ■ *Web:* www.ststravel.com	Glen Burnie	MD	21061	800-648-4849	787-9580*

				Phone	Fax
Summit Performance Group LLC 100 Leverne St ... Web: www.summitpg.com	Mammoth Lakes	CA	93546	760-924-7813	
Sunny Land Tours Inc 21 Old Kings Rd N Ste B-212 ... TF: 800-783-7839 ■ Web: www.sunnylandtours.com	Palm Coast	FL	32137	386-449-0059	449-0060
Super Holiday Tours 116 Gatlin Ave ... *Fax Area Code: 407 ■ TF: 800-327-2116 ■ Web: www.superholiday.com	Orlando	FL	32806	800-327-2116	851-0071*
Tag-A-Long Expeditions 452 N Main St ... TF: 800-453-3292 ■ Web: www.tagalong.com	Moab	UT	84532	435-259-8946	259-8990
Talbot Tours Inc 1952 Camden Ave ... Web: www.talbottours.com	San Jose	CA	95124	408-879-0101	
Tauck World Discovery 10 Norden Pl ... *Fax: Hum Res ■ TF: 800-468-2825 ■ Web: www.tauck.com	Norwalk	CT	06855	203-899-6500	899-6612*
Team America Inc 33 W 46th St Frnt 3 ... Web: www.teamamericany.com	New York	NY	10036	212-221-5938	
Tempest Tours Inc 711 E Lamar Blvd ... Web: www.tempesttours.com	Arlington	TX	76011	817-274-9313	
Timberwolf Tours Ltd 51404 RR 264 Ste 34 ... *Fax Area Code: 866 ■ TF: 888-467-9697 ■ Web: www.timberwolftours.com	Spruce Grove	AB	T7Y1E4	780-470-4966	339-3960*
Toto Tours Ltd 1326 W Albion Ave ... TF: 800-565-1241 ■ Web: www.tototours.com	Chicago	IL	60626	773-274-8686	274-8695
Tour East Holidays (Canada) Inc 15 Kern Rd ... Web: www.toureast.com	North York	ON	M3B1S9	416-929-8017	
TOUR GCX Partners Inc 450 Park Ave ... Web: www.tourgcx.com	New York	NY	10016	212-685-2200	
Touram Limited Partnership 1440 St Catherine St W Ste 800 ... Web: vacations.aircanada.com	Montreal	QC	H3G1R8	514-876-0700	
Travcoa 100 N Sepulveda Blvd Ste 1700 ... TF: 800-992-2003 ■ Web: www.travcoa.com	El Segundo	CA	90245	310-649-7104	649-7106
Tri-State Travel 4349 Industrial Pk Dr ... TF: 800-779-4869 ■ Web: www.tristatetravel.com	Galena	IL	61036	815-777-0820	777-8128
Uncharted Outposts Inc 9 Village Ln ... Web: www.unchartedoutposts.com	Santa Fe	NM	87505	505-795-7710	
Upstate Tours & Travel 207 Geyser Rd ... TF: 800-237-5252 ■ Web: www.upstatetours.com	Saratoga Springs	NY	12866	518-584-5252	584-1092
USA Student Travel 5080 Robert J Mathews Pkwy ... TF: 800-448-4444 ■ Web: www.usastudenttravel.com	El Dorado Hills	CA	95762	916-939-6805	939-6806
V I P Meetings & Conventions 1515 Palisades Dr Ste I ... Web: vipmeetings.com	Pacific Palisades	CA	90272	310-459-4691	
VBT Bicycling & Walking Vacations 614 Monkton Rd ... TF: 800-245-3868 ■ Web: www.vbt.com	Bristol	VT	05443	802-453-4811	
VentureOut 575 Pierce St Ste 604 ... TF: 888-431-6789 ■ Web: www.venture-out.com	San Francisco	CA	94117	415-626-5678	626-5679
VIP Tour & Charter Bus Co 129-137 Fox St ... TF General: 800-231-2222 ■ Web: www.vipchartercoaches.com	Portland	ME	04101	207-772-4457	772-7020
Vip Tours of California Inc 9830 Bellanca Ave ... Web: www.viptoursofcalifornia.com	Los Angeles	CA	90045	310-641-8114	
Visit America Inc 330 Seventh Ave 20th Fl ... Web: www.visitamerica.com	New York	NY	10001	212-683-8082	
Wade Tours Inc 797 Burdeck St ... TF: 800-955-9233 ■ Web: www.wadetours.com	Schenectady	NY	12306	518-355-4500	355-4942
Walking Adventures International 14612 NE Fourth Plain Rd Ste A ... *Fax Area Code: 360 ■ TF: 800-779-0353 ■ Web: www.walkingadventures.com	Vancouver	WA	98682	800-779-0353	260-1131*
West Coast Connection 1725 Main St Ste 215 ... TF: 800-767-0227 ■ Web: www.westcoastconnection.com	Weston	FL	33326	954-888-9780	888-9781
White Mountain Adventures 131 Eagle Crescent PO Box 4259 ... TF: 800-408-0005 ■ Web: www.whitemountainadventures.com	Banff	AB	T1L1A6	403-760-4403	
White Star Tours 26 E Lancaster Ave ... TF: 800-437-2323 ■ Web: www.whitestartours.com	Reading	PA	19607	610-775-5000	775-7155
Wilderness Travel 1102 Ninth St ... TF: 800-368-2794 ■ Web: www.wildernesstravel.com	Berkeley	CA	94710	510-558-2488	558-2489
Wildland Adventures Inc 3516 Ne 155th St ... TF: 800-345-4453 ■ Web: wildland.com	Lake Forest Park	WA	98155	206-365-0686	
Wings Tours Inc 11350 McCormick Rd Ste 703 ... TF: 800-869-4647	Hunt Valley	MD	21031	410-771-0925	771-0928
WorldPass Travel Group LLC 5080 Robert J Matthews Pkwy ... Web: www.goworldpass.com	El Dorado Hills	CA	95762	916-939-6805	939-6806
WorldStrides 218 W Water St Ste 400 ... *Fax Area Code: 434 ■ TF General: 800-999-7676 ■ Web: worldstrides.com/discoveries	Charlottesville	VA	22902	800-999-7676	982-8690*

761 TOY STORES

				Phone	Fax
A2Z Science & Nature Store 57 King St ... Web: a2zscience.com	NorthHampton	MA	01060	413-586-1611	584-7253
Alabama Card Systems Inc 500 Gene Reed Dr Ste 102 ... TF: 800-985-7507 ■ Web: alabamacard.com	Birmingham	AL	35215	205-833-1116	833-1160
Artists Club, The 13118 Ne Fourth St ... Web: www.knitpicks.com	Vancouver	WA	98684	360-260-8900	
Aruze Gaming America Inc 745 Grier Dr ... Web: www.aruzegaming.com	Las Vegas	NV	89119	702-361-3166	
Bennett Mineral Co PO Box 28 ... Web: www.bennettmineral.com	Walkerton	VA	23177	804-769-0546	
Build-A-Bear Workshop Inc 1954 Innerbelt Business Ctr Dr ... NYSE: BBW ■ TF: 888-560-2327 ■ Web: www.buildabear.com	Saint Louis	MO	63114	314-423-8000	423-8188
Creative Kid Stuff 3939 E 46th St ... TF: 800-353-0710 ■ Web: www.creativekidstuff.com	Minneapolis	MN	55406	612-929-2431	876-3981
CRT Custom Products Inc 7532 Hickory Hills Ct ... TF: 800-453-2533 ■ Web: www.crtcustomproducts.com	Whites Creek	TN	37189	615-876-5490	
Daron Worldwide Trading Inc 24 Stewart Pl Unit 4 ... TF: 800-776-2324 ■ Web: www.daronwwt.com	Fairfield	NJ	07004	973-882-0035	
Digital Engineering Systems Corp 2450 Scott Blvd Ste 300 ... TF: 888-788-1898 ■ Web: www.digi-eng.com	Santa Clara	CA	95050	408-970-8551	
Discount School Supplies 2 Lower Ragsdale Rd Ste 125 ... TF: 800-919-5238 ■ Web: www.discountschoolsupply.com	Monterey	CA	93940	800-919-5238	919-5235
Fat Brain Toys LLC 1405 N 205th St Ste 120 ... Web: www.fatbraintoys.com	Elkhorn	NE	68022	402-779-3181	
Fibre Craft Materials Corp 6400 W Howard St ... Web: www.fibrecraft.com	Niles	IL	60714	847-929-5600	
Funagain Games of Ashland 1660 Ashland St ... Web: funagain.com	Ashland St	OR	97520	541-482-1939	
Galt Toys 900 N Michigan Ave ... Web: www.galtbaby.com	Chicago	IL	60611	312-440-9550	
Game Informer 724 N First St Fl 3 ... Web: www.gameinformer.com	Minneapolis	MN	55401	612-486-6100	
Glitterex Corp 7 Commerce Dr ... Web: glitterex.com	Cranford	NJ	07016	908-272-9121	
Globalstor Data Corp 9960 Congoga Ave Unit D9 ... Web: www.globalstor.com	Chatsworth	CA	91311	818-701-7771	
Great Lakes Dart Manufacturing Inc S84 W19093 Enterprise Dr ... TF: 800-225-7593 ■ Web: www.gldproducts.com	Muskego	WI	53150	262-679-8730	
Happy Hen Toys Ltd 7246 W Foster Ave ... Web: www.happyhentoys.com	Chicago	IL	60656	847-831-3630	
Hobbytown USA 1233 Libra Dr ... Web: www.hobbytown.com	Lincoln	NE	68512	402-434-5050	
Horizon Dart Supply 2415 S 50th St ... Web: www.horizondarts.com	Kansas City	KS	66106	913-236-9111	
Hosung NY Inc 300 Kingsland Ave ... Web: www.hosungny.com	Brooklyn	NY	11222	718-389-8233	
Jeson Enterprises Inc 504 NE Fifth Ave ... Web: www.craftwarehouse.com	Camas	WA	98607	360-834-7728	
Learning Express Inc 29 Buena Vista St ... TF: 888-725-8697 ■ Web: www.learningexpress.com	Devens	MA	01434	978-889-1000	889-1010
M B Klein Inc 243-A Cockeysville Rd Ste A ... Web: www.modeltrainstuff.com	Cockeysville	MD	21030	410-229-9995	
Magic Beans LLC 312 Harvard St ... Web: www.mbeans.com	Brookline	MA	02446	617-264-2326	
Make It Better LLC 1150 Wilmette Ave Ste J ... Web: www.makeitbetter.net	Wilmette	IL	60091	847-256-4642	
Mary Maxim Ltd 75 Scott Ave ... TF: 888-442-2266 ■ Web: www.marymaxim.ca	Paris	ON	N3L3G5	888-442-2266	
MGA Entertainment Inc 16300 Roscoe Blvd Ste 150 ... TF: 800-222-4685 ■ Web: www.mgae.com	Van Nuys	CA	91406	818-894-2525	894-8094
Mobile Id Solutions Inc 1574 N Batavia St Ste 1 ... Web: www.mobileidsolutions.com	Orange	CA	92867	714-922-1134	
Mountain Boy Sledworks Inc 1070 Greene St ... Web: www.mountainboysleds.com	Silverton	CO	81433	970-387-5077	
NetWire Inc 165 Nantasket Beach Ave ... Web: www.netwire.com	Hull	MA	02045	781-925-1700	
Next Level Games Inc 208 Robson St 4th Fl ... Web: www.nextlevelgames.com	Vancouver	BC	V6B6A1	604-484-6111	
Northstar Ceramic Trading LLC 14500 East Beltwood Pkwy ... Web: www.northstarceramics.com	Dallas	TX	75244	972-392-3800	392-3808
Outset Media Corp 106-4226 Commerce Cir ... Web: www.outsetmedia.com	Victoria	BC	V8Z6N6	250-592-7374	592-7522
Perfect Game Softball LLC 850 Twixt Town Rd NE ... Web: perfectgame.org	Cedar Rapids	IA	52402	319-298-2923	
Plaster Fun Time 400 Highland Ave Ste 9 ... Web: www.plasterfuntime.com	Salem	MA	01970	978-745-7788	
Pollard Games Inc 504 34th Ave ... Web: www.amgam.com	Council Bluffs	IA	51501	712-366-9553	
Pun's Toy Shop 839 1/2 Lancaster Ave ... Web: punstoys.com	Bryn Mawr	PA	19010	610-525-9789	527-5514
Reel Games Inc 1501 NE 13th Ave ... Web: www.reelgamesinc.com	Fort Lauderdale	FL	33304	954-563-8253	
Thinkfun Inc 1321 Cameron St ... Web: www.thinkfun.com	Alexandria	VA	22314	703-549-4999	
Thinkway Toys Inc 8885 Woodbine Ave ... Web: www.thinkwaytoys.com	Markham	ON	L3R5G1	905-470-8883	
Toys 'R' Us (Canada) Ltd 2777 Langstaff Rd ... Web: www.toysrus.ca	Concord	ON	L4K4M5	905-660-2000	
Trainworld Associates LLC 751 Mcdonald Ave ... TF: 800-541-7010 ■ Web: www.trainworld.com	Brooklyn	NY	11218	718-436-7072	
Village Toy Shop 2100 Patriot Blvd ... Web: www.kohlchildrensmuseum.org	Glenview	IL	60026	847-832-6908	
WB Games Inc 12131 113th Ave NE Ste 300 ... Web: www.wbgames.com	Kirkland	WA	98034	425-216-3200	
Workshop Inc, The 339 Broadway ... Web: www.northeastcareer.org	Menands	NY	12204	518-465-5201	

762 TOYS, GAMES, HOBBIES

See Also Baby Products p. 1836; Bicycles & Bicycle Parts & Accessories p. 1859; Games & Entertainment Software p. 2030

				Phone	Fax
Airmate Co Inc 16280 County Rd D ... TF: 800-544-3614 ■ Web: www.airmatecompany.com	Bryan	OH	43506	419-636-3184	636-4210

Phone Fax

American Girl Inc 8400 Fairway Pl ... Middleton WI 53562 608-836-4848 836-1999
TF Orders: 800-845-0005 ■ *Web:* www.americangirl.com

American Plastic Toys Inc 799 Ladd Rd ... Walled Lake MI 48390 248-624-4881 624-4918
TF: 800-521-7080 ■ *Web:* www.americanplastictoys.com

Atlas Model Railroad Company Inc
378 Florence Ave ... Hillside NJ 07205 908-687-0880 687-8857
TF Orders: 800-872-2521 ■ *Web:* www.atlasrr.com

Bachmann Industries Inc 1400 E Erie Ave ... Philadelphia PA 19124 215-533-1600 744-4699
TF Cust Svc: 800-356-3910 ■ *Web:* www.bachmanntrains.com

Ball Bounce & Sport Inc/Hedstrom Plastics
1 Hedstrom Dr ... Ashland OH 44805 419-289-9310 281-3371
TF: 800-765-9665 ■ *Web:* www.hedstrom.com

Bravo Sports Corp
12801 Carmenita Rd ... Santa Fe Springs CA 90670 562-484-5100 484-5183
TF Cust Svc: 800-234-9737 ■ *Web:* www.bravosportscorp.com

Buffalo Games Inc 220 James E Casey Dr ... Buffalo NY 14206 855-895-4290
TF: 855-895-4290 ■ *Web:* www.buffalogames.com

Cardinal Industries Inc 21-01 51st Ave ... Long Island NY 11101 718-784-3000 482-7877
TF: 800-622-8339 ■ *Web:* www.cardinalgames.com

Cepia LLC 121 Hunter Ave ... Saint Louis MO 63124 314-725-4900 725-4919
TF: 800-225-9319 ■ *Web:* www.cepiallc.com

Commonwealth Toy & Novelty Co
45 W 25th St 7th Fl ... New York NY 10010 212-242-4070 645-4279
Web: commonwealthtoy.com

Creativity for Kids 9450 Allen Dr ... Cleveland OH 44125 216-643-4660 643-4663
TF: 800-311-8684 ■ *Web:* www.fabercastell.com

Dentt Inc 10450 S State St ... Sandy UT 84070 801-561-3821
Web: hammondtoy.com

Douglas Cuddle Toys Company Inc
69 Krif Rd PO Box D ... Keene NH 03431 603-352-3414 352-1248
TF: 800-992-9002 ■ *Web:* www.douglascuddletoy.com

Electronic Arts Inc (EA)
209 Redwood Shores Pkwy ... Redwood City CA 94065 650-628-1500
NASDAQ: EA ■ *Web:* www.ea.com

Estes-Cox Corp 1295 H St ... Penrose CO 81240 719-372-6565 372-3419
TF: 800-525-7561 ■ *Web:* www.estesrockets.com

Fisher-Price Inc 636 Girard Ave ... East Aurora NY 14052 716-687-3000 687-3476
TF: 800-432-5437 ■ *Web:* www.fisher-price.com

Five Below Inc 1818 Market St Ste 2000 ... Philadelphia PA 19103 215-546-7909 546-8099
TF: 866-935-8852 ■ *Web:* www.fivebelow.com

Gayla Industries Inc PO Box 920800 ... Houston TX 77292 800-231-7508 682-1357*
**Fax Area Code: 713* ■ *TF:* 800-231-7508 ■ *Web:* www.gaylainc.com

Goffa International Corp 930 Flushing Ave ... Brooklyn NY 11206 718-361-8883 361-0506
Web: www.goffausa.com

Great Planes Model Distributors
PO Box 9021 ... Champaign IL 61826 217-398-3630 398-1104
TF: 800-637-7660 ■ *Web:* www.gpmd.com

Guidecraft USA 55508 Hwy 19 W ... Winthrop MN 55396 507-647-5030 647-3254
TF: 800-524-3555 ■ *Web:* www.guidecraft.com

Gund Inc 1 Runyons Ln ... Edison NJ 08817 732-248-1500 248-1968
TF Cust Svc: 800-448-4863 ■ *Web:* www.gund.com

Hasbro Inc 1027 Newport Ave ... Pawtucket RI 02861 401-431-8697 431-8082*
NASDAQ: HAS ■ **Fax:* Cust Svc ■ *TF:* 800-242-7276 ■ *Web:* www.hasbro.com

Imperial Toy LLC 16641 Roscoe Pl ... North Hills CA 91343 818-536-6500 536-6501
Web: www.imperialtoy.com

International Playthings Inc
75D Lackawanna Ave ... Parsippany NJ 07054 973-316-2500 316-5883
TF: 800-631-1272 ■ *Web:* www.intplay.com

JAKKS Pacific Inc 21749 Baker Pkwy ... Walnut CA 91789 909-594-7771
NASDAQ: JAKK ■ *TF:* 877-875-2557 ■ *Web:* www.jakks.com

LeapFrog Enterprises Inc
6401 Hollis St Ste 100 ... Emeryville CA 94608 510-420-5000
NYSE: LF ■ *TF:* 800-701-5327 ■ *Web:* leapfrog.com

Learning Resources 380 N Fairway Dr ... Vernon Hills IL 60061 847-573-8400 573-8425
TF: 800-222-3909 ■ *Web:* www.learningresources.com

LEGO Systems Inc 555 Taylor Rd ... Enfield CT 06082 860-763-6731
TF: 877-518-5346 ■ *Web:* www.lego.com

Lionel .com LLC 26750 23 Mile Rd ... Chesterfield MI 48051 586-949-4100
TF: 800-454-6635 ■ *Web:* www.lionel.com

Little Tikes Co, The 2180 Barlow Rd ... Hudson OH 44236 800-321-0183
TF Cust Svc: 800-321-0183 ■ *Web:* www.littletikes.com

Losi 4710 E Guasti Rd ... Ontario CA 91761 909-390-9595 390-5356
TF: 888-899-5674 ■ *Web:* www.losi.com

Mag-Nif Inc 8820 E Ave ... Mentor OH 44060 800-869-5463 974-0449*
**Fax Area Code: 440* ■ *TF:* 800-869-5463 ■ *Web:* www.magnif.com

Maple City Rubber Co 55 Newton St PO Box 587 ... Norwalk OH 44857 419-668-8261 668-1275
TF: 800-841-9434 ■ *Web:* www.maplecityrubber.com

Mattel Inc 333 Continental Blvd ... El Segundo CA 90245 310-252-2000
NASDAQ: MAT ■ *TF:* 800-524-8697 ■ *Web:* www.mattel.com

Midwest Products Company Inc 400 S Indiana St ... Hobart IN 46342 219-942-1134 947-2347*
**Fax:* Sales ■ *TF Orders:* 800-348-3497 ■ *Web:* www.midwestproducts.com

Model Rectifier Corp 80 Newfield Ave ... Edison NJ 08837 732-225-2100 225-0091
Web: www.modelrec.com

Nintendo of America Inc 4820 150th Ave NE ... Redmond WA 98052 425-882-2040 882-3585
TF Cust Svc: 800-255-3700 ■ *Web:* www.nintendo.com

Ohio Art Co 1 Toy St ... Bryan OH 43506 419-636-3141
OTC: OART ■ *TF:* 800-800-3141 ■ *Web:* www.world-of-toys.com

Original Appalachian Artworks Inc
1721 Hwy 75 S PO Box 714 ... Cleveland GA 30528 706-865-2171
Web: www.cabbagepatchkids.com

Paul K Guillow Inc
40 New Salem St PO Box 229 ... Wakefield MA 01880 781-245-5255 245-4738
Web: www.guillow.com

Pepperball Technologies Inc
6540 Lusk Blvd Ste C137 ... San Diego CA 92121 858-638-0236
TF: 877-887-3773 ■ *Web:* www.pepperball.com

Pioneer National Latex Co 5000 E 29th St N ... Wichita KS 67220 316-685-2266 329-3864*
**Fax Area Code: 800* ■ *TF:* 800-386-4438 ■ *Web:* www.pioneernational.com

Plaid Enterprises Inc 3225 Westech Dr ... Norcross GA 30092 678-291-8100 291-8368*
**Fax:* Mktg ■ *TF:* 800-842-4197 ■ *Web:* www.plaidonline.com

Playmobil USA Inc 26 Commerce Dr ... Cranbury NJ 08512 609-409-1263 395-3015
Web: www.playmobil.com

Phone Fax

Pressman Toy Corp 121 New England Ave ... Piscataway NJ 08854 732-562-1590 562-8407
TF Cust Svc: 800-800-0298 ■ *Web:* www.pressmantoy.com

Radio Flyer Inc 6515 W Grand Ave ... Chicago IL 60707 773-637-7100 637-8874
TF: 800-621-7613 ■ *Web:* www.radioflyer.com

SEGA of America Inc
350 Rhode Island St Ste 400 ... San Francisco CA 94103 415-701-6000 701-6001
Web: www.sega.com

SIG Mfg Company Inc 401 S Front St ... Montezuma IA 50171 641-623-5154 623-3922
TF Sales: 800-247-5008 ■ *Web:* www.sigmfg.com

Sony Computer Entertainment America Inc
919 E Hillsdale Blvd ... Foster City CA 94404 650-655-8000 655-8001
Web: playstation.com/en-us/home

Spin Master Ltd 450 Front St W ... Toronto ON M5V1B6 416-364-6002 364-5097
TF: 800-622-8339 ■ *Web:* www.spinmaster.com

Steiff North America 24 Albion Rd Ste 220 ... Lincoln RI 02865 401-312-0080
TF: 888-978-3433 ■ *Web:* www.steiffusa.com

Swibco Inc 4810 Venture Rd ... Lisle IL 60532 630-968-8900 367-7943*
**Fax Area Code: 800* ■ *TF:* 877-794-2261 ■ *Web:* www.swibco.com

Tara Toy Corp 40 Adams Ave ... Hauppauge NY 11788 631-273-8697 273-8583
Web: www.taratoy.com

Testor Corp 440 Blackhawk Pk Ave ... Rockford IL 61104 815-962-6654 962-7401
TF: 800-837-8677 ■ *Web:* www.testors.com

TOMY International Inc
1111 W 22nd St Ste 320 ... Oak Brook IL 60523 800-704-8697 573-7575*
**Fax Area Code: 630* ■ *TF:* 800-704-8697 ■ *Web:* tomy.com

Tonner Doll Co 301 Wall St PO Box 4410 ... Kingston NY 12402 845-339-9537 339-1259
TF: 800-794-2107 ■ *Web:* www.tonnerdoll.com

Troxel Co Hwy 57 ... Moscow TN 38057 901-877-6875 877-6942
Web: www.troxel.com

Uncle Milton Industries Inc
29209 Canwood St Ste 120 ... Agoura CA 91301 818-707-0800 707-0878
TF General: 800-869-7555 ■ *Web:* www.unclemilton.com

Universal Mfg Co Inc 5030 Mackey S ... Overland Park KS 66203 913-815-6230 815-6240
TF: 800-524-5860 ■ *Web:* www.umcprint.com

University Games Corp 2030 Harrison St ... San Francisco CA 94110 415-503-1600 503-0085
TF: 800-347-4818 ■ *Web:* www.ugames.com

Upper Deck Co LLC 5909 Sea Otter Pl ... Carlsbad CA 92010 800-873-7332 929-3512*
**Fax Area Code: 760* ■ *TF Cust Svc:* 800-873-7332 ■ *Web:* www.upperdeck.com

Vermont Teddy Bear Company Inc
6655 Shelburne Rd ... Shelburne VT 05482 802-985-3001 985-1304
TF: 800-988-8277 ■ *Web:* vermontteddybear.com

VTech Electronics North America LLC
1155 W Dundee St Ste 130 ... Arlington Heights IL 60004 847-400-3600 400-3601
TF: 800-521-2010 ■ *Web:* www.vtechkids.com

Wham-O Inc 6301 Owensmouth Ave Ste 700 ... Woodland Hills CA 91367 888-942-6650
TF: 888-942-6650 ■ *Web:* www.wham-o.com

Wiffle Ball Inc 275 Bridgeport Ave PO Box 193 ... Shelton CT 06484 203-924-4643 924-9433
Web: www.wiffle.com

William K Walthers Inc 5601 W Florist Ave ... Milwaukee WI 53218 414-527-0770 527-4423
TF: 800-877-7171 ■ *Web:* www.walthers.com

Wizards of the Coast Inc
1600 Lind Ave SW Ste 400 ... Renton WA 98057 425-226-6500 204-5818
TF: 800-324-6496 ■ *Web:* company.wizards.com

TRAILERS - TRUCK

See Truck Trailers p. 3270

763 TRAILERS (TOWING) & TRAILER HITCHES

Phone Fax

Blessey Marine Services Inc
1515 River Oaks Rd E ... Harahan LA 70123 504-734-1156 734-1195
Web: www.blessey.com

Bright Co-op Inc 803 W Seale St ... Nacogdoches TX 75964 936-564-8378 564-3281
TF: 800-562-0730 ■ *Web:* www.brightcoop.com

Cequent Towing Products 47774 Anchor Ct W ... Plymouth MI 48170 800-521-0510 656-3009*
**Fax Area Code: 734* ■ *TF:* 800-521-0510 ■ *Web:* www.draw-tite.com

Cequent Trailer Products 1050 Indianhead Dr ... Mosinee WI 54455 715-693-1700 693-1799
TF: 800-604-9466 ■ *Web:* www.fultonperformance.com

CM Trailers Inc 200 County Rd PO Box 680 ... Madill OK 73446 580-795-5536 575-5218*
**Fax Area Code: 903* ■ *TF:* 888-268-7577 ■ *Web:* www.cmtrailers.com

Com-Fab Inc 4657 Price HilliaRds Rd ... Plain City OH 43064 740-857-1107 857-1757
TF: 866-522-1794 ■ *Web:* www.comfab-inc.com

Dethmers Manufacturing Co (DEMCO) 4010 320th St ... Boyden IA 51234 712-725-2311 725-2380
TF: 800-543-3626 ■ *Web:* www.demco-products.com

EZ Loader Boat Trailers Inc
717 N Hamilton St ... Spokane WA 99202 509-489-0181 489-5729
TF: 800-398-5623 ■ *Web:* www.ezloader.com

Gardner Cryogenics 2136 City Line Rd ... Bethlehem PA 18017 610-264-4523
Web: www.gardnercryo.com

Gooseneck Trailer Mfg Co
4400 E Hwy 21 PO Box 832 ... Bryan TX 77808 979-778-0034 778-0615
TF Cust Svc: 800-688-5490 ■ *Web:* www.gooseneck.net

Hawkeye Leisure Trailers Ltd 1419 11th St N ... Humboldt IA 50548 515-332-1802 332-1833
Web: www.yachtclubtrailers.com

Karavan Trailers Inc
100 Karavan Dr PO Box 27 ... Fox Lake WI 53933 920-928-6200 928-6201
Web: www.karavantrailers.com

Load Rite Trailers Inc
265 Lincoln Hwy ... Fairless Hills PA 19030 215-949-0500 949-1385
TF: 800-562-3783 ■ *Web:* www.loadrite.com

Mac-Lander Inc 509 E Maple ... Milton IA 52570 641-656-4271 656-4225
Web: www.mac-lander.com

Midwest Industries Inc 122 E State Hwy 175 ... Ida Grove IA 51445 712-364-3365 364-3361
TF: 800-859-3028 ■ *Web:* www.shorelandr.com

Rigid Hitch Inc 3301 W Burnsville Pkwy ... Burnsville MN 55337 952-895-5001 895-9150
TF Cust Svc: 800-624-7630 ■ *Web:* www.rigidhitch.com

Sundowner Trailers Inc 9805 S State Hwy 48 ... Coleman OK 73432 580-937-4255
TF: 800-654-3879 ■ *Web:* www.sundownertrailer.com

Take 3 Trailers Inc 1808 Hwy 105 ... Brenham TX 77833 979-337-9568
TF: 800-428-2533 ■ *Web:* www.take3trailers.com

Phone | Fax

TriMas Corp
39400 Woodward Ave Ste 130 ... Bloomfield Hills MI 48304 248-631-5450 631-5455
Web: www.trimascorp.com

Unique Functional Products Corp
135 Sunshine Ln ... San Marcos CA 92069 760-744-1610 744-4709
TF: 800-854-1905 ■ *Web:* www.ufpnet.com

764 TRAINING & CERTIFICATION PROGRAMS - COMPUTER & INTERNET

Phone | Fax

AAIM Employers' Association LLC
1600 S Brentwood Ste 400 ... St. Louis MO 63144 314-968-3600
Web: www.aaimea.org

Agencia International Inc
110 W 40th St Ste 603 ... New York NY 10018 212-391-1306
Web: www.agencianyc.com

Altima Technologies Inc 2300 Cabot Dr Ste 535 ... Lisle IL 60532 630-281-6464
Web: www.altimatech.com

Animation Mentor 1400 65th St Ste 250 ... Emeryville CA 94608 877-326-4628
TF: 877-326-4628 ■ *Web:* www.animationmentor.com

ASPE Inc 114 Edinburgh S Dr Ste 200 ... Cary NC 27511 877-800-5221
TF: 877-800-5221 ■ *Web:* aspetraining.com

Bilingual Education Institute
6060 Richmond Ave Ste 180 ... Houston TX 77057 713-789-4555
Web: www.bei.edu

Career Step LLC 4692 North 300 West Ste 150 ... Provo UT 84604 801-489-9393
Web: www.careerstep.com

Computer Workshop Inc, The
5131 Post Rd Ste 102 ... Dublin OH 43017 614-798-9505
TF: 800-639-3535 ■ *Web:* www.tcworkshop.com

Computers 4 Kids 19 E Broadway St ... Oviedo FL 32765 434-817-1121
Web: www.computers4kids.us

Compuworks Ltd 600 W Cummings Park Ste 6950 ... Woburn MA 01801 413-499-0607
Web: www.bill-dixon.com

Coyne College Inc 330 N Green St ... Chicago IL 60607 773-577-8100
TF: 800-707-1922 ■ *Web:* www.coynecollege.edu

ECO Canada 308 - 11th Ave SE Ste 200 ... Calgary AB T2G0Y2 403-233-0748
Web: www.eco.ca

Gainshare Inc 3110 N Central Ave Ste 160 ... Phoenix AZ 85012 602-266-8500
Web: www.interfacett.com

Global Knowledge Training LLC
9000 Regency Pkwy Ste 500 ... Cary NC 27518 919-461-8600 461-8646
TF: 800-268-7737 ■ *Web:* www.globalknowledge.com

Hands on Technology Transfer Inc
1 Village Sq Ste 8 ... Chelmsford MA 01824 978-250-4299
Web: traininghott.com

Hatsize Learning Corp 555 11 Ave SW Ste 200 ... Calgary AB T2R1P6 403-538-3295
Web: hatsize.com

Health & Safety Institute Inc 1450 Westec Dr ... Eugene OR 97402 800-447-3177
TF: 800-447-3177 ■ *Web:* www.hsi.com

It4ce Inc 1200 Aerowood Dr ... Mississauga ON L4W2S7 905-206-9947
TF: 877-470-0008 ■ *Web:* it4ce.com

Learning Tree International Inc
1831 Michael Faraday Dr ... Reston VA 20190 703-709-9119
OTC: LTRE ■ *TF Cust Svc:* 800-843-8733 ■ *Web:* www.learningtree.com

Metex Inc 789 Don Mills Rd Ste 218 ... North York ON M3C1T5 416-203-8388
TF: 866-817-8137 ■ *Web:* www.metex.com

Milwaukee Rescue Mission 830 n 19th st ... Milwaukee WI 53233 414-344-2211
Web: www.milmission.org

Minact Inc 5220 Keele St ... Jackson MS 39206 601-362-1631 362-5771
Web: www.minact.com

MindLeaders.com Inc 5500 Glendon Ct Ste 200 ... Dublin OH 43016 614-781-7300 781-6510
TF: 800-223-3732

Moore Group, The 112 Brooke Ave ... Norfolk VA 23510 757-627-1015
Web: www.themooregroup.com

My Service Depot 8774 Cotter St ... Lewis Center OH 43035 888-518-0818
TF: 888-518-0818 ■ *Web:* www.myservicedepot.com

Natural Healing College 446 E Vine St ... Stockton CA 95202 209-390-8076
Web: naturalhealingcollege.com

Nevada Area Vocational School
900 W Ashland St ... Nevada MO 64772 417-448-2090
Web: www.nevada.k12.mo.us

New Horizons Computer Learning Centers Inc
1900 S State College Blvd Ste 450 ... Anaheim CA 92806 714-940-8000
TF: 888-236-3625 ■ *Web:* www.newhorizons.com

New Horizons Worldwide Inc
1900 S State College Blvd Ste 450 ... Anaheim CA 92806 888-236-3625
TF: 888-236-3625 ■ *Web:* www.newhorizons.com

Next Level Purchasing
1315 Coraopolis Heights Rd Ste 2002 ... Moon Township PA 15108 412-294-1990
Web: www.nextlevelpurchasing.com

On-Track Computer Training Corp
885 W Georgia St 4th Fl ... Vancouver BC V6B3E8 604-683-0020
Web: www.on-track.com

Online Marketing Institute
2088 Union St Ste 3 ... San Francisco CA 94123 415-450-9524
Web: www.onlinemarketinginstitute.org

Optimum Talent Inc 25 York St Ste 1802 ... Toronto ON M5J2V5 416-364-2605
TF: 877-364-2605 ■ *Web:* www.optimumtalent.com

PAR Springer-Miller Systems Inc
782 Mountain Rd ... Stowe VT 05672 802-253-7377
Web: www.springermiller.com

Parker University 2540 Walnut Hill Ln ... Dallas TX 75229 972-438-6932
TF: 800-637-8337 ■ *Web:* www.parkerproproducts.com

PowerScore Inc 57 Hasell St ... Charleston SC 29401 800-545-1750
TF: 800-545-1750 ■ *Web:* www.powerscore.com

Preferred Solutions Inc
17199 N Laurel Pk Ste 260 ... Livonia MI 48152 248-679-0130
Web: www.prefsol.com

Productivity Point International Inc
2950 Gateway Ctr Blvd ... Morrisville NC 27560 919-379-5611

Prospero Learning Solutions Inc
1075 Bay St Ste 500 ... Toronto ON M5S2B1 416-360-0606
Web: www.prosperolearning.com

Reading-muhlenberg Area Vocational-technical Schoo
2615 Warren Rd ... Reading PA 19604 610-921-7300
Web: www.rmctc.org

Region 4 Education Service Center
7145 W Tidwell Rd ... Houston TX 77092 713-462-7708
Web: www.esc4.net

Rockford Career College 1130 s alpine rd ... Rockford IL 61108 815-965-8616

Software Answers Inc
6770 W Snowville Rd Ste 200 ... Brecksville OH 44141 440-526-0095
Web: software-answers.com

Total Seminars LLC 12929 Gulf Fwy Ste 105 ... Houston TX 77034 281-922-4166
Web: totalsem.com

Training Objectives Corp 8940 Sw 67th Pl ... Portland OR 97223 503-245-3387
Web: trainingobjectives.com

Trivac Ltd 3050 Regent Blvd Ste 310 ... Irving TX 75063 469-484-5400
Web: www.trivac.com

UAW Labor Employment & Training Corp
3965 S Vermont Ave ... Los Angeles CA 90037 323-730-7900
Web: www.letc.com

Unicom Technologies Inc 1011 Hwy 6 S ... Houston TX 77077 281-496-3606
Web: www.unicom-tech.com

Workgroup Connections Inc
1000 St Louis Union Station Grand Central Bldg
Ste 205 ... St. Louis MO 63103 314-436-2233
Web: www.wgcinc.com

765 TRAINING PROGRAMS - CORPORATE

Phone | Fax

AchieveGlobal Inc
8875 Hidden River Pkwy Ste 400 ... Tampa FL 33637 800-566-0630 631-5796*
**Fax Area Code:* 813 ■ *TF:* 800-566-0630 ■ *Web:* www.mhiglobal.com/achieveglobal

ActionCOACH 5781 S Ft Apache Rd ... Las Vegas NV 89148 702-795-3188 795-3183
TF: 888-483-2828 ■ *Web:* www.actioncoach.com

Acumen Learning LLC 226 N Orem Blvd ... Orem UT 84057 801-224-5444
Web: acumenlearning.com

Allen Interactions Inc
1120 Centre Pointe Dr Ste 800 ... Mendota Heights MN 55120 651-203-3700
Web: www.alleninteractions.com

Baker Communications Inc 10101 SW Fwy #630 ... Houston TX 77074 713-627-7700 587-2051
TF: 877-253-8506 ■ *Web:* www.bakercommunications.com

Briljent LLC 7615 W Jefferson Blvd ... Fort Wayne IN 46804 260-434-0990
Web: www.briljent.com

Center for Creative Leadership
1 Leadership Pl PO Box 26300 ... Greensboro NC 27438 336-545-2810 282-3284
Web: www.ccl.org

Christy Capital Management Inc 2939 Mcmanus Rd ... Macon GA 31220 478-314-2160
TF: 866-331-7749 ■ *Web:* www.christycapital.com

ClickSafety.com Inc
2185 N California Blvd Ste 425 ... Walnut Creek CA 94596 800-971-1080
TF: 800-971-1080 ■ *Web:* www.clicksafety.com

Creative Training Techniques International Inc
14530 Martin Dr ... Eden Prairie MN 55344 952-829-1954 829-0260
TF: 800-383-9210 ■ *Web:* www.bobpikegroup.com

Crestcom International Ltd
6900 E Belleview Ave ... Greenwood Village CO 80111 303-267-8200
Web: www.crestcomleadership.com

Dale Carnegie & Assoc Inc 290 Motor Pkwy ... Hauppauge NY 11788 800-231-5800
TF: 800-231-5800 ■ *Web:* www.dalecarnegie.com

Don Hutson Organization
516 Tennessee St Ste 219 ... Memphis TN 38103 901-767-0000
TF: 800-647-9166 ■ *Web:* www.donhutson.com

Elite Business Services PO Box 9630 ... Rancho Santa Fe CA 92067 800-204-3548 756-4781*
**Fax Area Code:* 858 ■ *TF:* 800-204-3548 ■ *Web:* www.eliteworldwide.com

Executive Enterprises Institute
12 Skyline Dr ... Hawthorne NY 10532 914-517-1122
TF: 877-334-4273 ■ *Web:* sp.smartpros.com/pages/index.aspx

Forum Corp 265 Franklin St 4th Fl ... Boston MA 02110 617-523-7300 371-3300
Web: www.forum.com

Franklin Covey Co 2200 West PkwyBlvd ... Salt Lake City UT 84119 801-817-1776
NYSE: FC ■ *TF:* 800-827-1776 ■ *Web:* www.franklincovey.com

Fred Pryor Seminars 9757 Metcalf Ave ... Overland Park KS 66212 800-780-8476 967-8842*
**Fax Area Code:* 913 ■ *TF:* 800-780-8476 ■ *Web:* www.pryor.com

Frontline Group of Texas LLC
15021 Katy Fwy Ste 575 ... Houston TX 77094 281-453-6000
TF: 800-285-5512 ■ *Web:* www.frontline-group.com

Greenlining Institute, The
1918 University Ave Ste 2 ... Berkeley CA 94704 510-926-4000
Web: greenlining.org

HealthStream Inc 209 Tenth Ave S Ste 450 ... Nashville TN 37203 615-301-3100 301-3200
NASDAQ: HSTM ■ *TF:* 800-933-9293 ■ *Web:* www.healthstream.com

Hinda Incentives Inc 2440 W 34th St ... Chicago IL 60608 773-890-5900 890-4606
TF: 866-487-2365 ■ *Web:* www.hinda.com

Insight Information 214 King St W Ste 300 ... Toronto ON M5H3S6 416-777-2020 777-1292*
**Fax Area Code:* 866 ■ *TF:* 888-777-1707 ■ *Web:* www.insightinfo.com

Inspirica Ltd 850 Seventh Ave Ste 403 ... New York NY 10019 212-245-3888
Web: www.inspirica.com

Invitechange LLC 110 Third Ave N Ste 102 ... Edmonds WA 98020 425-778-3505
TF: 877-228-2622 ■ *Web:* www.invitechange.com

ITC Learning Corp 1616 Anderson Rd Ste 109 ... McLean VA 22102 800-638-3757 852-7174*
**Fax Area Code:* 703 ■ *TF:* 800-638-3757 ■ *Web:* www.itclearning.com

Leadership Management Inc 4567 Lk Shore Dr ... Waco TX 76710 254-776-2060 772-9588
TF: 800-568-1241 ■ *Web:* www.lmi-world.com

Levinson Institute Inc 28 Main St Ste 100 ... Jaffrey NH 03452 603-532-4700 532-4750
TF: 800-290-5735 ■ *Web:* levinsonandco.com

Mandel Communications Inc
820 Bay Ave Ste 113 ... Capitola CA 95010 831-475-8202
Web: www.mandel.com

Phone Fax

National Businesswomen's Leadership Assn
PO Box 419107 .... Kansas City MO 64141 913-432-7755 432-0824
TF: 800-258-7246 ■ *Web:* www.nationalseminarstraining.com

National Seminars Training
6900 Squibb Rd .... Shawnee Mission KS 66202 913-432-7755 432-0824
TF: 800-258-7246 ■ *Web:* www.nationalseminarstraining.com

Netlan Technology Center Inc
39 W 37th St Fl 11 .... New York NY 10018 212-730-5900
Web: www.netlan.com

Nexient Learning Canada Inc
1809 Barrington St Ste 900 .... Halifax NS B3J3K8 902-429-4357
Web: www.globalknowledge.com/ca-en/?utm_source=direct&utm_medium=redirect&utm_campaign=gkca

NTL Institute 1901 S Bell St Ste 300 .... Arlington VA 22202 703-548-1500
Web: www.ntl.org

Pacific Institute 1709 Harbor Ave SW .... Seattle WA 98126 206-628-4800 587-6007
TF: 800-426-3660 ■ *Web:* www.thepacificinstituteretail.com

Patch Plus Consulting Inc 3 Raleigh Cir Ste B .... Medford NJ 08055 609-792-6204
Web: www.patchplusconsulting.com

Pm Resource Group LLC 219 Scott St Ste 165 .... Beaufort SC 29902 404-247-6968
Web: www.pmresourcegroup.com

Priority Management Systems Inc
11160 Silversmith Pl .... Richmond BC V7A5E4 604-214-7772
TF: 800-437-1032 ■ *Web:* www.prioritymanagement.com

Productivity Inc 375 Bridgeport Ave 3rd Fl .... Shelton CT 06484 203-225-0451 225-0771
TF: 800-966-5423 ■ *Web:* www.productivityinc.com

Results-Based Leadership Group
3507 N University Ave Ste 175 .... Provo UT 84604 801-373-4238
Web: www.rbl.net

Rockhurst University Continuing Education Ctr Inc
PO Box 419107 .... Kansas City MO 64141 913-432-7755 432-0824
TF: 800-258-7246 ■ *Web:* www.nationalseminarstraining.com

Safety Sam Inc 2626 S Roosevelt St Ste 2 .... Tempe AZ 85282 866-478-6980
TF: 866-478-6980 ■ *Web:* www.safetyservicescompany.com

Sandler Sales Institute 10411 Stevenson Rd .... Stevenson MD 21153 410-653-1993 358-7858
Web: www.sandler.com

Situation Management Systems Inc
98 Spit Brook Rd Ste 201 .... Nashua NH 03062 603-897-1200
Web: situationmanagementsystems.com

Skillpoint Alliance 201 E 2nd St Ste B .... Austin TX 78701 512-323-6773
Web: www.skillpointalliance.org

SkillSoft PLC 107 NE Blvd .... Nashua NH 03062 603-324-3000
TF: 877-545-5763 ■ *Web:* www.skillsoft.com

SmartPros Ltd 12 Skyline Dr .... Hawthorne NY 10532 914-345-2620 345-2603
NASDAQ: SPRO ■ *Web:* sp.smartpros.com

Speakeasy Inc
3438 Peachtree Rd Ste 1000 Phipps Twr .... Atlanta GA 30326 404-541-4800 541-4848
Web: www.speakeasyinc.com

Team Business LLC 1410 Belt St .... Baltimore MD 21230 410-837-1414
Web: www.teambusiness.com

Telemedia Inc
750 W Lk Cook Rd Rd Ste 250 .... Buffalo Grove IL 60089 847-808-4000
Web: www.tpctraining.com

Teleos Leadership Inst LLC
7837 Old York Rd .... Elkins Park PA 19027 267-620-9999
Web: teleosleaders.com

Toastmasters International
23182 Arroyo Vista .... Rancho Santa Margarita CA 92688 949-858-8255 858-1207
Web: www.toastmasters.org

US Learning Inc 516 Tennessee St Ste 219 .... Memphis TN 38103 901-767-0000
TF: 800-647-9166 ■ *Web:* www.uslearning.com

Veriforce LLC 19221 I-45 S Ste 200 .... Shenandoah TX 77385 800-426-1604
TF: 800-426-1604 ■ *Web:* www.veriforce.com

Visual Awareness Technologies & Consulting Inc
3611 W Swann Ave .... Tampa FL 33609 813-207-5055
Web: www.vatcinc.com

Voice Pro Inc 2055 Lee Rd Ste 101 .... Cleveland OH 44118 216-932-8040
TF: 800-261-0104 ■ *Web:* www.voiceproinc.com

Wilson Learning Corp 8000 W 78th St Ste 200 .... Edina MN 55439 952-944-2880 828-8835
TF: 800-328-7937 ■ *Web:* www.wilsonlearning.com

Xcelerate Media Inc 61 W Bridge St .... Dublin OH 43017 614-336-9722
Web: www.xceleratemedia.com

Zenger Folkman Co 1550 N Technology Way Bldg D .... Orem UT 84097 801-705-9375
Web: zengerfolkman.com

766 TRAINING PROGRAMS (MISC)

See Also Children's Learning Centers p. 1937; Training & Certification Programs - Computer & Internet p. 3258; Training Programs - Corporate p. 3258

Phone Fax

Academy for Guided Imagery Inc
10780 Santa Monica Blvd Ste 290 .... Los Angeles CA 90025 800-726-2070 727-2070
TF: 800-726-2070 ■ *Web:* www.acadgi.com

American College of Orgonomy 4419 Rt 27 .... Princeton NJ 08545 732-821-1144 821-0174
Web: www.orgonomy.org

Audio-Digest Foundation
1577 E Chevy Chase Dr .... Glendale CA 91206 818-240-7500 240-7379
TF: 800-423-2308 ■ *Web:* www.audio-digest.org

Canter & Assoc LLC 12975 Coral Tree Pl .... Los Angeles CA 90066 310-578-4700 301-7512
TF Cust Svc: 800-669-9011 ■ *Web:* www.canter.net

Ed Necco & Assoc 178 Private Dr .... South Point OH 45680 513-771-9600 894-1132*
**Fax Area Code:* 740 ■ *TF:* 866-996-3226 ■ *Web:* www.necco.org

Executive Protection Institute
16 Penn Plz Ste 1570 .... New York NY 10001 212-268-4555 563-4783
TF: 800-947-5827 ■ *Web:* www.personalprotection.com

Global University 1211 S Glenstone Ave .... Springfield MO 65804 417-862-9533 865-7167
TF: 800-443-1083 ■ *Web:* www.globaluniversity.edu

Megatech Corp 525 Woburn St .... Tewksbury MA 01876 978-937-9600
Web: www.megatechcorp.com

Mission Essential Personnel LLC
4343 Easton Commons Ste 100 .... Columbus OH 43219 614-416-2345
TF: 888-542-3447 ■ *Web:* www.missionessential.com

Outward Bound 910 Jackson St .... Golden CO 80401 207-510-7533 510-7535
TF: 866-467-7651 ■ *Web:* www.outwardbound.org

Penland School of Crafts
67 Doras Trl PO Box 37 .... Penland NC 28765 828-765-2359 765-7389
Web: www.penland.org

Smith & Wesson Academy 299 Page Blvd .... Springfield MA 01104 413-846-6461 736-0776
Web: www.smith-wesson.com

Yamaha Music Education System
6600 Orangethorpe Ave .... Buena Park CA 90620 714-522-9011
Web: usa.yamaha.com

767 TRANSFORMERS - POWER, DISTRIBUTION, SPECIALTY

Phone Fax

3 Sixty Manufacturing
6288 San Ignacio Ave Ste E .... San Jose CA 95119 408-365-0360

Active Power Inc 2128 W Breaker Ln .... Austin TX 78758 512-836-6464 836-4511
NASDAQ: ACPW ■ *TF:* 800-625-1731 ■ *Web:* www.activepower.com

Adcomm Inc 89 Leuning St Ste 9 .... South Hackensack NJ 07606 201-342-6349
Web: adcomminc.com

Advanced Conversion Technology Inc
2001 Fulling Mill Rd .... Middletown PA 17057 717-939-2300
Web: www.actpower.com

AFP Transformers Inc 206 Talmedge Rd .... Edison NJ 08817 732-248-0305 248-0542
TF: 800-843-1215 ■ *Web:* www.afp-transformers.com

Airex Corp 15 Lilac Ln .... Somersworth NH 03878 603-841-2040
Web: www.airex.com

Algonquin Power 2845 Bristol Cir .... Oakville ON L6H7H7 905-465-4500
Web: www.algonquinpower.com

ATCO Power Ltd 919-11 Ave SW Ste 400 .... Calgary AB T2R1P3 403-209-6900
Web: www.atcopower.com

Bodine Co PO Box 460 .... Collierville TN 38027 901-853-7211 853-5009
TF: 800-223-5728 ■ *Web:* www.bodine.com

Cam Tran Company Ltd 203 Purdy Rd .... Colborne ON K0K1S0 905-355-3224
Web: www.camtran.com

Central Moloney Inc 2400 W Sixth Ave .... Pine Bluff AR 71601 870-534-5332 536-4002
Web: www.centralmoloneyinc.com

CG Power Systems USA Inc 1 Pauwels Dr .... Washington MO 63090 636-239-9300
Web: cgglobal.com

Controlled Power Co 1955 Stephenson Hwy .... Troy MI 48083 248-528-3700 528-0411
TF: 800-521-4792 ■ *Web:* www.controlledpwr.com

Cooper Power Systems Inc 2300 Badger Dr .... Waukesha WI 53187 262-896-2400 896-2313
Web: www.cooperindustries.com

Core Power Services Inc 37428 Centralmont Pl .... Fremont CA 94536 510-796-6682
Web: www.cpspower.com

Datatronic Distribution Inc 28151 Hwy 74 .... Romoland CA 92585 951-928-7700
Web: www.datatronics.com

DC Group Inc 1977 W River Rd N .... Minneapolis MN 55411 800-838-7927 529-9518*
**Fax Area Code:* 612 ■ *TF:* 800-838-7927 ■ *Web:* www.dc-group.com

Delta Star Inc 270 Industrial Rd .... San Carlos CA 94070 800-892-8673
TF: 800-892-8673 ■ *Web:* www.deltastar.com

Delta Transformers Inc
1311-A rue Ampere .... Boucherville QC J4B5Z5 450-449-9774
Web: www.delta.xfo.com

Dynapower Corp 85 Meadowland Dr .... South Burlington VT 05403 802-860-7200
Web: www.dynapower.com

Electric Research & Mfg Co-op Inc
PO Box 1228 .... Dyersburg TN 38025 731-285-9121
TF: 800-238-5587 ■ *Web:* www.ermco-eci.com

Energy Transformation Systems Inc
43353 Osgood Rd .... Fremont CA 94539 510-656-2012
TF: 800-752-8208 ■ *Web:* www.etslan.com

Ensign Corp 201 Ensign Rd .... Bellevue IA 52031 563-872-3900 872-4575
TF: 888-797-8658 ■ *Web:* www.ensigncorp.com

Federal Pacific PO Box 8200 .... Bristol VA 24203 276-669-4084 669-1869
Web: www.federalpacific.com

Grand Transformers Inc 1500 Marion Ave .... Grand Haven MI 49417 616-842-5430
Web: www.gtipower.com

Hitran Corp 362 SR- 31 .... Flemington NJ 08822 908-782-5525 782-9733
Web: www.hitrancorp.com

Howard Industries Inc 3225 Pendorff Rd .... Laurel MS 39440 601-425-3151 649-8090
Web: www.howard-ind.com

Hunterdon Transformer Co 75 Industrial Dr .... Alpha NJ 08865 908-454-2400 454-6266
Web: www.hunterdontransformer.com

Ideal Power Inc 4120 Freidrich Ln Ste 100 .... Austin TX 78744 512-264-1542
Web: www.idealpower.com

Jefferson Electric Inc 9650 S Franklin Dr .... Franklin WI 53132 414-209-1620
Web: www.jeffersonelectric.com

Johnson Electric Coil Co 821 Watson St .... Antigo WI 54409 715-627-4367 623-2812
TF: 800-826-9741 ■ *Web:* www.johnsoncoil.com

Lamination Specialties Corp
235 N Artesian Ave .... Chicago IL 60612 312-243-2181 243-2873
Web: www.laminationspecialties.com

Legend Power Systems Inc 1480 Frances St .... Vancouver BC V5L1Y9 604-420-1500 420-1533
TF: 866-772-8797 ■ *Web:* legendpower.com

Maruson Technology Corp
18557 Gale Ave .... City Of Industry CA 91748 626-912-8388 912-8680
TF: 888-627-8766 ■ *Web:* marusonusa.com

Megatran Electric Ltd
860 Lucien Beaudin .... St. Jean-sur-richelieu QC J2X5V5 450-346-6622
Web: www.megatran.qc.ca

Mesta Electronics Inc
11020 Parker Dr .... North Huntingdon PA 15642 412-754-3000 754-3016
TF: 800-535-6798 ■ *Web:* www.mesta.com

MGM Transformer Co 5701 Smithway St .... Commerce CA 90040 323-726-0888 726-8224
TF: 800-423-4366 ■ *Web:* www.mgmtransformer.com

Micrometals Inc 5615 E La Palma Ave .... Anaheim CA 92807 714-970-9400
Web: www.micrometals.com

Mirus International Inc 31 Sun Pac Blvd .... Brampton ON L6S5P6 905-494-1120
TF: 888-866-4787 ■ *Web:* www.mirusinternational.com

Moloney Electric Inc 35 Leading Rd .... Toronto ON M9V4B7 416-534-9226
Web: www.moloney-electric.com

				Phone	Fax
Morlan & Associates Inc 6625 McVey Blvd. *Web:* www.flex-core.com	Columbus	OH	43235	614-889-6152	
MTE Corp PO Box 9013 *TF:* 800-455-4683 ■ *Web:* www.mtecorp.com	Menomonee Falls	WI	53051	262-253-8200	253-8222
Myers Power Products Inc 2950 E Philadelphia St *Web:* www.myerspowerproducts.com	Ontario	CA	91761	909-923-1800	
Neeltran Inc 71 Pickett District Rd. *Web:* www.neeltran.com	New Milford	CT	06776	860-350-5964	350-5024
Niagara Transformer Corp 1747 Dale Rd *TF:* 800-817-5652 ■ *Web:* www.niagaratransformer.com	Buffalo	NY	14225	716-896-6500	896-8871
Norlake Mfg Co 39301 Taylor Pkwy *Web:* www.norlakemfg.com	Elyria	OH	44035	440-353-3200	353-3232
North American Substation Services LLC 190 N Westmonte Dr *Web:* www.northamericansubstationservices.com	Altamonte Springs	FL	32714	407-788-3717	
Nova Power Solutions 23020 Eaglewood Ct Ste 100 *TF:* 800-999-6682 ■ *Web:* www.novapower.com	Sterling	VA	20166	800-999-6682	
Olsun Electrics Corp 10901 Commercial St. **Fax Area Code:* 815 ■ *TF:* 800-336-5786 ■ *Web:* www.olsun.com	Richmond	IL	60071	800-336-5786	678-4909*
Pauwels Canada Inc 101 Rockman St *Web:* www.cgglobal.com	Winnipeg	MB	R3T0L7	204-452-7446	
Philips Advance Light Elctro 10275 W Higgins Rd **Fax Area Code:* 888 ■ *TF:* 800-322-2086 ■ *Web:* www.usa.lighting.philips.com	Rosemont	IL	60018	847-390-5000	423-1882*
Power Partners Inc 200 Newton Bridge Rd *Web:* abb.com	Athens	GA	30607	706-548-3121	
Powersmiths International Corp 10 Devon Rd *TF:* 800-747-9627 ■ *Web:* www.powersmiths.com	Brampton	ON	L6T5B5	905-791-1493	
Powertronix Inc 1120 Chess Dr *Web:* www.powertronix.com	Foster City	CA	94404	650-345-6800	
PWR LLC 6402 Deere Rd *TF:* 800-342-0878 ■ *Web:* www.pwrllc.com	Syracuse	NY	13206	315-701-0210	701-0217
Quality Transformer & Electronics 963 Ames Ave. *Web:* www.qte.com	Milpitas	CA	95035	408-263-8444	263-8448
Raf Technologies Inc 200 Lexington Ave *TF:* 888-876-6424	Deland	FL	32724	386-736-1698	736-7338
Rantec Power Systems Inc 1173 Los Olivos Ave. *Web:* www.rantec.com	Los Osos	CA	93402	805-596-6000	
RE Uptegraff Manufacturing Co 120 Uptegraff Dr PO Box 182 *Web:* www.uptegraff.com	Scottdale	PA	15683	724-887-7700	887-4748
Saunders Electronics 192 Gannett Dr *Web:* saunderselectronics.com	South Portland	ME	04106	207-228-1888	
Shallbetter Inc 3110 Progress Dr *Web:* www.shallbetter.com	Oshkosh	WI	54901	920-232-8888	
Shape LLC 2105 Corporate Dr *TF:* 800-367-5811 ■ *Web:* www.shapellc.com	Addison	IL	60101	630-620-8394	620-0784
Southern States LLC 30 Georgia Ave *Web:* www.southernstatesllc.com	Hampton	GA	30228	770-946-4562	
Sparta Capital Ltd 303-6707 Elbow Drive SW *Web:* www.spartacapital.com	Calgary	AB	T2V0E5	306-491-6323	
T & R Electric Supply Company Inc 308 SW Third St *TF:* 800-843-7994 ■ *Web:* www.t-r.com	Colman	SD	57017	605-534-3555	534-3861
T. A. Pelsue Co 2500 S Tejon St *Web:* www.pelsue.com	Englewood	CO	80110	303-936-7432	
Toronto Hydro Corp 14 Carlton St *Web:* www.torontohydro.com	Toronto	ON	M5B1K5	416-542-3000	
Unique Lighting Systems Inc 1240 Simpson Way **Fax Area Code:* 760 ■ *TF:* 800-955-4831 ■ *Web:* www.uniquelighting.com	Escondido	CA	92029	800-955-4831	740-0977*
VanTran Industries Inc 7711 Imperial Dr *TF:* 800-433-3346 ■ *Web:* www.vantran.com	Waco	TX	76712	254-772-9740	772-0016
Victor Products USA 322 Commerce Pk Dr *Web:* www.victorproductsusa.com	Cranberry Township	PA	16066	724-776-4900	776-3855
Virginia Transformer Corp 220 Glade View Dr *TF:* 800-882-3944 ■ *Web:* www.vatransformer.com	Roanoke	VA	24012	540-345-9892	342-7694
Warner Power LLC 40 Depot St *Web:* www.warnerpower.com	Warner	NH	03278	603-456-3111	456-3754
Waukesha Electric Systems Inc 400 S Prairie Ave *TF:* 800-835-2732 ■ *Web:* www.spxtransformersolutions.com	Waukesha	WI	53186	262-547-0121	
WEG Electric Corp 6655 Sugarloaf Pkwy *Web:* www.weg.net	Duluth	GA	30097	678-249-2000	
Winkle Electric Company Inc., The 1900 Hubbard Rd *Web:* www.winkle.com	Youngstown	OH	44501	330-744-5303	

768 TRANSLATION SERVICES

See Also Language Schools p. 2626

				Phone	Fax
A William Roberts Jr & Assoc Inc 234 Seven Farms Dr Ste 210 *Web:* scheduledepo.com	Charleston	SC	29492	843-722-8414	
A2z Global LLC 6981 N Park Dr *Web:* a2zglobal.com	Pennsauken	NJ	08109	856-910-0300	
ABLE Innovations LLC 1100 Lakeway Dr Ste 200 *Web:* www.ableinnovations.com	Bellingham	WA	98229	360-714-1390	
Agnew Multilingual 741 Lakefield Rd Ste C *Web:* www.agnew.com	Westlake Village	CA	91361	805-494-3999	
Arch Language Network Inc 1885 University Ave W Ste 75 *Web:* www.archlanguage.com	Saint Paul	MN	55104	651-789-7897	
Argo Translation Inc 2420 Ravine Way Ste 200 *TF:* 888-961-9291 ■ *Web:* www.argotrans.com	Glenview	IL	60025	847-901-4075	
Asist Translation Services 4891 Sawmill Rd Ste 200 *Web:* www.asisttranslations.com	Columbus	OH	43235	614-451-6744	
Back to Basics Learning Dynamics Inc 6 Stone Hill Rd *Web:* backtobasicslearning.com	Wilmington	DE	19803	302-594-0754	
Birnbaum Interpreting Services 8730 Georgia Ave Ste 210 *TF:* 800-471-6441 ■ *Web:* www.bisworld.com	Silver Spring	MD	20910	301-587-8885	
Boston Language Institute Inc 648 Beacon St Kenmore Sq *TF:* 877-998-3500 ■ *Web:* www.bostonlanguage.com	Boston	MA	02215	617-262-3500	262-3595
Bridge-world Language Center Inc, The 110 Second St S Ste 213 *TF:* 800-835-6870 ■ *Web:* www.bridgelanguage.com	Waite Park	MN	56387	320-259-9239	
CanTalk (Canada) Inc 70 Arthur St Ste 250 *Web:* www.cantalk.com	Winnipeg	MB	R3B1G7	204-982-1245	
Certified Languages International LLC 4724 SW Macadam Ave *Web:* www.certifiedlanguages.com	Portland	OR	97239	503-525-9601	
Cosmopolitan Translation Bureau Inc 53 W Jackson Blvd Ste 1260 *Web:* www.cosmopolitantranslation.net	Chicago	IL	60604	312-726-2610	
Cyracom International Inc 5780 N Swan Rd *Web:* cyracom.com	Tucson	AZ	85718	520-745-9447	
Deaf Hearing Communication Centre Inc 630 Fairview Rd Ste 100 *Web:* www.dhcc.org	Swarthmore	PA	19081	610-604-0450	
Deaf-Talk Inc 14 E Main St *Web:* dtinterpreting.com	Carnegie	PA	15106	412-563-3177	
Dialog One Llc 2380 Wycliff St Ste 200 *Web:* www.dialog-one.com	Saint Paul	MN	55114	651-379-8600	
Excelsys 3230 N Braeswood Blvd *Web:* excelsys.org	Houston	TX	77025	713-662-0172	
Fluent Language Solutions Inc 8801 JM Keynes Dr Ste 400 *Web:* www.fluentls.com	Charlotte	NC	28262	704-532-7446	
Ganser German Translations 602 Fairway Rd	Belton	MO	64012	816-561-3777	
Geo Group 6 Odana Ct Ste 205 *Web:* www.thegeogroup.com	Madison	WI	53719	608-230-1000	
Glyph Language Services Inc 126 Nw Canal St Ste 110 *Web:* glyphservices.com	Seattle	WA	98107	206-315-0994	
Imani Lee Translations Services; Ili International Services; Ili Business s 11297 Senda Luna Llena Bldg B *Web:* www.imanilee.com	San Diego	CA	92130	858-523-9733	
Independent Living Resource Center Inc, The 423 W Victoria St *Web:* www.ilrc-trico.org	Santa Barbara	CA	93101	805-963-1350	
Interpreters Unlimited Inc 11199 Sorrento Vly Rd Ste 203 *TF:* 800-726-9891 ■ *Web:* www.interpretersunlimited.com	San Diego	CA	92121	800-726-9891	
Iverson Language Associates Inc 1661 N Farwell Ave. *Web:* iversonlang.com	Milwaukee	WI	53202	414-271-1144	
JLS Language Corp 135 Willow Rd. *Web:* www.jls.com	Menlo Park	CA	94025	650-321-9832	
Kane Transport Inc 40925 403rd Ave *TF:* 800-892-8557 ■ *Web:* www.kanetransport.com	Sauk Centre	MN	56378	320-352-2762	352-6141
Language Line Services 1 Lower Ragsdale Dr Bldg 2 *TF:* 800-752-6096 ■ *Web:* www.languageline.com	Monterey	CA	93940	800-752-6096	
Language Services Associates Inc 455 Business Ctr Dr - Ste 100 *TF:* 800-305-9673 ■ *Web:* www.lsaweb.com	Horsham	PA	19044	800-305-9673	
Language World Services Inc 7220 Fair Oaks Blvd Ste D *Web:* www.languageworldservices.com	Carmichael	CA	95608	916-333-5247	
Legal Interpreting Services Inc 26 Court St Ste 1005 *Web:* www.lis-translations.com	Brooklyn	NY	11242	718-237-8919	
Lingualinx Language Solutions Inc 433 River St *Web:* lingualinx.com	Troy	NY	12180	518-388-9000	
Linguistics Systems Inc 201 Broadway **Fax Area Code:* 617 ■ *TF:* 877-654-5006 ■ *Web:* www.linguist.com	Cambridge	MA	02139	877-654-5006	864-5186*
Lionbridge Technologies Inc 1050 Winter St Ste 2300 *NASDAQ: LIOX* ■ *Web:* lionbridge.com	Waltham	MA	02451	781-434-6000	434-6034
Master Translating Services Inc 10651 N Kendall Dr Ste 220 *Web:* www.mastertranslating.com	Miami	FL	33176	305-279-2484	
Masterword Services, International Inc 303 Stafford St *TF:* 866-716-4999 ■ *Web:* www.masterword.com	Houston	TX	77079	281-589-0810	
McElroy Translation Co 910 W Ave *Web:* www.mcelroytranslation.com	Austin	TX	78701	512-472-6753	
Merritt Interpreting Services 3626 N Hall St Ste 504 *TF:* 866-761-2585 ■ *Web:* www.mis-interpreting.com	Dallas	TX	75219	214-969-5585	
Mill Neck Manor School for The Deaf 40 Frost Mill Rd *Web:* millneck.org	Mill Neck	NY	11765	516-922-3818	
MotionPoint Corp Lyons Technology Ctr 4661 Johnson Rd Ste 14 *Web:* www.motionpoint.com	Coconut Creek	FL	33073	954-421-0890	
One Planet Corp 850 Ridge Ave *Web:* www.one-planet.net	Pittsburgh	PA	15212	412-323-1050	
Opies Transport Inc 21 Hwy FF PO Box 89 *Web:* www.opiestransport.com	Eldon	MO	65026	573-392-6525	
Pals International 900 Wilshire Dr Ste 105 *Web:* www.palsintl.com	Troy	MI	48084	248-362-2060	

Phone | Fax

Professional Translating Services Inc
Douglas Rd — Coral Gables FL 33134 305-371-7887
Web: www.protranslating.com

Russtech Inc 1338 Vickers Rd — Tallahassee FL 32303 850-562-9811
Web: www.russtechinc.com

Schreiber Translations Inc
51 Monroe St Ste 101 — Rockville MD 20850 301-424-7737
Web: www.schreibernet.com

SimulTrans LLC 455 N Whisman Rd Ste 400 — Mountain View CA 94043 650-605-1300
Web: www.simultrans.com

Spanish-American Translating
330 Eagle Ave — West Hempstead NY 11552 516-481-3339
TF: 800-870-5790 ■ *Web:* arleneboas.com

Syntes Language Group 7465 E Peakview Ave — Centennial CO 80111 303-779-1288
Web: www.syntes.com

Traducta Inc 35 Bella-vista St — Saint-basile-le-grand QC J3N1L1 450-461-2252
Web: www.traducta.com

Translations International Inc
2821 15th Ave S — St. Cloud MN 56301 320-217-2775
Web: www.tiinc.com

TransPerfect Translations Inc
3 Pk Ave 39th Fl — New York NY 10016 212-689-5555 689-1059
Web: www.transperfect.com

Verbatim Solutions LLC
5200 South Highland Dr Ste 201 — Salt Lake City UT 84117 801-273-5700
Web: www.verbatimsolutions.com

Versacom Inc 1501 Ave McGill College 6th Fl — Montreal QC H3A3M8 514-397-1950
Web: www.versacom.ca

Vocalink Language Services
405 W First St Unit A — Dayton OH 45402 937-223-1415
TF: 877-492-7754 ■ *Web:* www.vocalink.net

769 TRANSPLANT CENTERS - BLOOD STEM CELL

Phone | Fax

Arthur G James Cancer Hospital & Richard J Solove Research Institute
Bone Marrow Transplant Program
300 W Tenth Ave Ste 519 — Columbus OH 43210 800-293-5066 293-4044*
**Fax Area Code:* 614 ■ *TF:* 800-293-5066 ■ *Web:* cancer.osu.edu

Blood & Marrow Transplant Group of Georgia (BMTGA)
5670 Peachtree Dunwoody Rd Ste 1000 — Atlanta GA 30342 404-255-1930 255-1939
Web: www.bmtga.com

Blood Donor Ctr at Presbyterian/St Luke's Medical Ctr
1719 E 19th Ave — Denver CO 80218 303-839-6000
TF: 800-231-2222 ■ *Web:* www.pslmc.com

Children's Hospital Bone Marrow Transplant Program
LSU Health Science Ctr
200 Henry Clay Ave — New Orleans LA 70118 504-896-9740 896-9758
Web: www.chnola.org

Children's Hospital of New York-Presbyterian
Pediatric Blood & Marrow Transplantation Program
3959 Broadway — New York NY 10032 212-305-5593 305-8428
TF: 866-463-2778 ■ *Web:* nyp.org/kids

Children's Hospital of Orange County Blood & Donor Services
505 S Main St — Orange CA 92868 714-509-8339
TF: 800-228-5234 ■ *Web:* www.choc.org

Children's Hospital of Philadelphia Stem Cell Transplant Program
3401 Civic Ctr Blvd — Philadelphia PA 19104 800-879-2467 590-4744*
**Fax Area Code:* 215 ■ *TF:* 800-879-2467 ■ *Web:* www.chop.edu

City of Hope National Medical Ctr Hematology & Hematopoietic Cell Transplantation Div
1500 E Duarte Rd — Duarte CA 91010 626-256-4673 301-8888
TF: 800-826-4673 ■ *Web:* cityofhope.org

Cleveland Clinic Bone Marrow Transplantation Program
9500 Euclid Ave — Cleveland OH 44195 216-444-0261 445-7444
TF: 800-223-2273 ■ *Web:* my.clevelandclinic.org

Dana-Farber Cancer Institute Stem Cell/Bone Marrow Transplant Program
450 Brookline Ave Dana 2 — Boston MA 02115 617-632-3591 632-4139
TF: 866-408-3324 ■ *Web:* www.dana-farber.org

Duke Clinical Research & Treatment Ctr
Bone Marrow & Stem Cell Transplant Program
2400 Pratt St — Durham NC 27710 919-668-1002 668-1091
Web: dukemedicine.org

Fairfax PET Imaging Ctr
8503 Arlington Blvd Ste 120 Lowr Level — Fairfax VA 22031 703-698-4441
TF: 800-358-8831 ■ *Web:* www.inova.org

Froedtert Hospital Bone Marrow Transplant Program
9200 W Wisconsin Ave — Milwaukee WI 53226 414-805-3666
TF: 800-272-3666 ■ *Web:* www.froedtert.com

H Lee Moffitt Cancer Ctr & Research Institute Blood & Marrow Transplantation Program
12902 Magnolia Dr — Tampa FL 33612 888-663-3488
TF: 888-663-3488 ■ *Web:* www.moffitt.org

Hahnemann University Hospital
230 N Broad St — Philadelphia PA 19102 215-762-7000
Web: www.hahnemannhospital.com
Bone Marrow Transplant Program
230 N Broad St MS 451 — Philadelphia PA 19102 215-762-7000
Web: www.hahnemannhospital.com

Helen DeVos Children's Hospital Pediatric Hematology/Oncology Program
100 Michigan NE — Grand Rapids MI 49503 616-391-9000 391-9430
TF: 866-989-7999 ■ *Web:* www.helendevoschildrens.org

Indiana University Cancer Ctr Bone Marrow & Stem Cell Transplant Team
550 N University Blvd — Indianapolis IN 46202 317-948-6997
TF: 888-600-4822 ■ *Web:* cancer.iu.edu

James Graham Brown Cancer Ctr
529 S Jackson St — Louisville KY 40202 502-562-4369
TF: 866-530-5516 ■ *Web:* www.kentuckyonehealth.org/browncancercenter

Karmanos Cancer Institute Bone Marrow/Stem Cell Transplant Program
4100 John R — Detroit MI 48201 800-527-6266
TF: 800-527-6266 ■ *Web:* www.karmanos.org

Lombardi Comprehensive Cancer Ctr at Georgetown University Bone Marrow Transplantation Program
3800 Reservoir Rd NW — Washington DC 20057 202-444-0275
Web: lombardi.georgetown.edu

Phone | Fax

Blood & Marrow Transplant Program
86 Jonathan Lucas St — Charleston SC 29425 843-792-9300
Web: www.muschealth.org/index.html

Mount Sinai Hospital Bone Marrow Transplant Program
19 E 98th St — New York NY 10029 212-241-6021
TF: 866-682-9380 ■ *Web:* www.mountsinai.org

North Shore-Long Island Jewish Health System
Bone Marrow & Blood Cell Transplant Program
300 Community Dr — Manhasset NY 11030 516-562-8973 734-8836
TF: 888-321-3627 ■ *Web:* www.northwell.edu

Northwestern Memorial Hospital
251 E Huron St — Chicago IL 60611 312-926-2000
Web: www.nmh.org

Oregon Health & Science University
Bone Marrow Transplant Program (OHSU)
3181 SW Sam Jackson Pk Rd — Portland OR 97239 503-494-1617 494-7086
TF: 800-222-1222 ■ *Web:* www.ohsu.edu

OU Medical Ctr
Bone Marrow Transplant Program
1 S Bryant 7th Fl — Oklahoma City OK 73104 405-271-8042
Web: www.oumedicine.com

Penn State Milton S Hershey Medical Ctr Bone Marrow Transplantation Program
500 University Dr — Hershey PA 17033 717-531-1657 531-1656
TF: 800-243-1455 ■ *Web:* www.pennstatehershey.org

Roswell Park Cancer Institute Blood & Marrow Transplantation Program
Elm & Carlton Sts — Buffalo NY 14263 716-845-3516
TF: 800-685-6825 ■ *Web:* www.roswellpark.org

Saint Jude Children's Research Hospital Stem Cell Transplantation Div
262 Danny Thomas Pl — Memphis TN 38105 901-595-3300
TF: 800-822-6344 ■ *Web:* www.stjude.org

Scripps Green Hospital Blood & Marrow Transplant Ctr
10666 N Torrey Pines Rd — La Jolla CA 92037 858-554-8597
Web: scripps.org

Seattle Cancer Care Alliance
825 Eastlake Ave E PO Box 19023 — Seattle WA 98109 206-288-1024 288-1025
TF: 800-804-8824 ■ *Web:* www.seattlecca.org

St. Francis Healthcare System of Hawaii
2226 Liliha St Ste 227 — Honolulu HI 96817 808-547-8030
Web: www.stfrancishawaii.org

Stanford University School of Medicine Blood & Marrow Transplant Program
300 Pasteur Dr Rm H-3249 MC 5623 — Stanford CA 94305 650-723-0822 725-8950
TF: 888-275-5724 ■ *Web:* bmt.stanford.edu

Strong Memorial Hospital
Stem Cell Transplantation Ctr
601 Elmwood Ave — Rochester NY 14642 585-275-1941 275-5590
Web: www.urmc.rochester.edu

Texas Children's Hospital Stem Cell & Bone Marrow Transplant Program
6701 Fannin St 14th Fl — Houston TX 77030 832-824-5800
Web: texaschildrens.org

Texas Transplant Institute
7700 Floyd Curl Dr — San Antonio TX 78229 210-575-3817 575-4113
TF: 800-298-7824 ■
Web: sahealth.com/locations/texas-transplant-institute

Thomas Jefferson University Hospital Blood & Marrow Transplant Unit
125 S Ninth St 2nd Fl — Philadelphia PA 19107 215-955-6000 955-0412
Web: www.jefferson.edu

Tufts-New England Medical Ctr
Bone Marrow Transplant Program
800 Washington St PO Box 15265 — Boston MA 02111 617-636-5000
Web: www.tuftsmedicalcenter.org

UMass Memorial Medical Ctr
Bone Marrow Transplant Program
55 Lake Ave N — Worcester MA 01655 508-334-1000 334-7983
Web: umassmemorialhealthcare.org/umass-memorial-medical-center

University Medical Ctr Blood & Marrow Transplantation Program
1400 Morreene Rd PO Box 24-5176 — Durham NC 27705 520-694-0111 694-5009
TF: 800-524-5928 ■ *Web:* www.uahealth.com

University Medical Ctr Bone Marrow & Blood Stem Cell Transplant Program (UMC)
602 Indiana Ave — Lubbock TX 79415 806-775-8200
Web: www.umchealthsystem.com

University of California San Diego Medical Ctr Blood & Marrow Transplantation Program
3855 Health Sciences Dr — La Jolla CA 92093 858-657-7000
Web: www.cancer.ucsd.edu

University of Kansas Medical Ctr
Bone Marrow/Hematopoietic Stem Cell Transplant Program
3901 Rainbow Blvd — Kansas City KS 66160 913-588-5000
Web: kumc.edu

University of Maryland Greenebaum Cancer Ctr
22 S Greene St Ste N9E17 — Baltimore MD 21201 410-328-7904
TF: 800-888-8823 ■ *Web:* www.umm.edu/cancer/canc_stem.html

University of Miami Hospital & Clinics (UMHC)
Sylvester Comprehensive Cancer Ctr
1475 NW 12th Ave — Miami FL 33136 305-243-1000
TF: 800-545-2292 ■ *Web:* www.sylvester.org

University of Michigan Cancer Ctr Adult Blood and Marrow Transplantation Clinic
1540 E Hospital Dr 9th Fl — Ann Arbor MI 48109 734-232-8838
Web: www.cancer.med.umich.edu

University of Mississippi Medical Ctr Bone Marrow Transplant Program (UMMC)
2500 N State St — Jackson MS 39216 601-354-6655 984-6289
Web: www.umc.edu

University of Nebraska Medical Ctr Bone Marrow & Stem Cell Transplantation Program (Adults)
987400 Nebraska Medical Ctr — Omaha NE 68198 402-559-2000
TF: 800-922-0000 ■ *Web:* www.nebraskamed.com

University of Pittsburgh Medical Ctr (UPMC)
Horizon 110 N Main St — Greenville PA 16125 724-588-2100
TF: 888-447-1122 ■ *Web:* www.upmc.com
Stem Cell Transplantation Program
5150 Centre Ave — Pittsburgh PA 15232 412-235-1052
Web: www.upmccancercenter.com

University of Texas Southwestern Medical Ctr Dallas
Hematopoietic Cell Transplant Program
2201 Inwood Rd 2nd Fl — Dallas TX 75390 214-645-4673
TF: 866-645-6455 ■ *Web:* www.utsouthwestern.edu
Blood & Marrow Transplant Program
50 N Medical Dr — Salt Lake City UT 84132 801-581-2121 585-5825
TF General: 800-824-2073 ■ *Web:* www.healthcare.utah.edu/hospital

Phone | Fax

VA Puget Sound Health Care System - Seattle Div
1660 S Columbian Way .... Seattle WA 98108 206-762-1010
TF: 800-329-8387 ■ *Web:* www.va.gov

Vanderbilt University Medical Ctr Stem Cell Transplant Program
1301 22nd Ave S Ste B902 .... Nashville TN 37232 615-591-9890
Web: www.vanderbilthealth.com

VCU Massey Cancer Center
Bone Marrow Transplant Program
401 College St PO Box 980037 .... Richmond VA 23298 804-828-4360
Web: www.massey.vcu.edu

Westchester Medical Ctr Advanced Imaging
Bone Marrow & Hematopoietic Stem Cell Transplant program
19 Bradhurst Ave Ste 2100 .... Hawthorne NY 10532 914-493-1448 493-2428
Web: www.westchestermedicalcenter.com

Winship Cancer Institute of Emory University
1365 Clifton Rd NE .... Atlanta GA 30322 404-778-1900 843-5615*
**Fax Area Code:* 678 ■ *TF:* 888-946-7447 ■ *Web:* www.winshipcancer.emory.edu

Yale-New Haven Hospital Blood Stem Cell Transplant Unit
20 York St .... New Haven CT 06510 203-688-4242
Web: www.ynhh.org

770 TRANSPORTATION EQUIPMENT & SUPPLIES - WHOL

Phone | Fax

A & K Railroad Materials Inc
1505 S Redwood Rd .... Salt Lake City UT 84104 801-974-5484 972-2041*
**Fax:* Sales ■ *TF Sales:* 800-453-8812 ■ *Web:* www.akrailroad.com

A D I Services 210 Commerce Cir .... Kearneysville WV 25430 304-870-4384
Web: www.adiservices.com

AAR Aircraft Turbine Ctr
1100 N Wood Dale Rd 1 AAR Pl .... Wood Dale IL 60191 630-227-2000 227-2329
TF General: 800-422-2213 ■ *Web:* www.aarcorp.com

AAR Corp 1100 N Wood Dale Rd 1 AAR Pl .... Wood Dale IL 60191 630-227-2000 227-2019
NYSE: AIR ■ *TF:* 800-422-2213 ■ *Web:* www.aarcorp.com

AAR Defense Systems & Logistics
1100 N Wood Dale Rd 1 AAR Pl .... Wood Dale IL 60191 630-227-2000
TF: 877-227-9200 ■
Web: aarcorp.com/parts/inventory-management-programs/defense-programs

AAR Distribution
1100 N Wood Dale Rd 1 AAR Pl .... Wood Dale IL 60191 630-227-2000
TF: 800-422-2213 ■ *Web:* www.aarcorp.com

Aero Hardware & Parts Company Inc
130 Business Pk Dr .... Armonk NY 10504 914-273-8550 273-8612
Web: www.aerohardwareparts.com

Aero Products Component Services Inc
551 N 40th St .... Show Low AZ 85901 928-537-1000
Web: www.aeroproducts.com

Aero Recip (Canada) Ltd 540 Marjorie St .... Winnipeg MB R3H0S9 204-788-4765 786-2775
Web: www.aerorecip.com

Aerodirect Inc 860 Chaddick Dr Bldg A .... Wheeling IL 60090 847-325-4971
Web: www.aerodirect.com

Aeronautical Systems Inc
43671 Trade Ctr Pl Ste 100 .... Sterling VA 20166 703-996-8090
Web: www.aeronautical.com

AeroSolutions Group Inc
10681 Frank Marshall Ln .... Manassas VA 20110 703-257-7008
Web: www.aerosolutions.com

AerSale Inc 121 Alhambra Plz Ste 1700 .... Coral Gables FL 33134 305-764-3200
Web: www.aersale.com

Africair Inc 13551 SW 132nd Ave # 1 .... Miami FL 33186 305-255-6973
Web: www.africair.com

Agility 480 Production Ave .... Madison AL 35758 256-772-7743
Web: www.agility.com/en/pages/default.aspx

Aim Mro Holdings Inc
8500 Glendale Milford Rd .... Camp Dennison OH 45111 513-831-2938 831-3859
Web: www.aimmro.com

AIRCO Group 1853 S Eisenhower Ct .... Wichita KS 67209 316-945-0445 945-8014
Web: www.airco-ict.com

Airline Spares America Inc (ASA)
1022 E Newport Ctr Dr .... Deerfield Beach FL 33442 954-429-8600 429-8388
Web: www.asaspares.com

Airparts Company Inc 2310 NW 55th Ct .... Fort Lauderdale FL 33309 954-739-3575 739-9514
TF: 800-392-4999 ■ *Web:* www.airpartsco.com

Alamo Aircraft Ltd
2538 SW 36th St PO Box 37343 .... San Antonio TX 78237 210-434-5577 434-1030
Web: alamoaircraft.com

All-system Aerospace Int'l Inc 75 Beacon Dr .... Holbrook NY 11741 631-582-9200 582-9353
Web: allsystem.com

Allied International Corp 7 Hill St .... Bedford Hills NY 10507 914-241-6900 241-6985
Web: www.alliedinter.com

ALSTOM Signaling Inc 1025 John St .... West Henrietta NY 14586 585-783-2000
Web: www.alstomsignalingsolutions.com

American Equipment Co (AMECO)
4775 Technology Way Ste 208 .... Boca Raton FL 33431 561-997-2080 997-2110
Web: www.ameco.net

American General Supplies Inc
7840 Airpark Rd .... Gaithersburg MD 20879 301-590-9200 590-3069
Web: www.agsusa.com

Amex International Inc
1615 L St Nw Ste 340 .... Washington DC 20036 202-429-0222
Web: www.amexdc.com

Amsted Rail Company Inc
311 S Wacker Dr Ste 5300 .... Chicago IL 60606 312-922-4501
Web: www.amstedrail.com

Andantex USA Inc 1705 Valley Rd .... Wanamassa NJ 07712 732-493-2812
Web: www.andantex.com

Argo International Corp 160 Chubb Ave .... Lyndhurst NJ 07071 201-561-7010
TF: 877-274-6468 ■ *Web:* www.argointl.com

Arrow Trading Inc
5290 NW 20th Terr Hngr 57-101 .... Fort Lauderdale FL 33309 954-771-9366
Web: www.arrowtrading.com

ASC Industries Inc 1227 Corporate Dr W .... Arlington TX 76006 817-640-1300 649-2685
Web: www.ascintl.com

Atlantic Track & Turnout Co
270 N Broad St .... Bloomfield NJ 07003 973-748-5885 748-4520
TF: 800-631-1274 ■ *Web:* www.atlantictrack.com

Aviall Inc
2750 Regent Blvd Dallas Fort Worth Airport .... Dallas TX 75261 972-586-1985 586-1361
Web: www.aviall.com

Aviojet Corp 76 Brookside Dr .... Upper Saddle River NJ 07458 201-825-3111 825-6950
Web: www.aviojet.com

BBB Tank Services Inc 9225 Leopard St .... Corpus Christi TX 78409 361-241-1001
Web: www.bbbtankservices.com

Bearing Belt & Chain Inc 729 E Buckeye .... Phoenix AZ 85034 602-252-6541
Web: bbcarizona.com

Beier Radio Inc 1150 N Causeway Blvd .... Mandeville LA 70471 504-341-0123
Web: www.beierradio.com

Bell Fork Lift Inc 34660 Centaur Dr .... Clinton Township MI 48035 586-415-5200
Web: www.bellforklift.com

Birmingham Rail & Locomotive Company Inc
PO Box 530157 .... Birmingham AL 35253 205-424-7245 424-7436
TF: 800-241-2260 ■ *Web:* www.bhamrail.com

Burke Handling Systems 431 Hwy 49 S .... Jackson MS 39218 601-939-6600
Web: www.burkehandling.com

Burkle North America Inc 11105 Knott Ave .... Cypress CA 90630 714-379-5090
Web: burkleamerica.com

Cardinal Carryor Inc 1055 Grade Ln .... Louisville KY 40213 502-363-6641
Web: www.cardinalcarryor.com

Cargo Equipment Corp 640 Church Rd .... Elgin IL 60123 847-741-7272
TF: 888-557-8727 ■ *Web:* www.cargoequipmentcorp.com

Centurion Investments Inc
18377 Edison Ave .... Chesterfield MO 63005 636-532-2674
Web: www.avmats.com

Chand LLC 157 Hwy 654 .... Mathews LA 70375 985-532-2512 532-3262
Web: www.chand.com

Christensen Shipyards Ltd
4400 Se Columbia Way .... Vancouver WA 98661 360-695-3238
Web: www.christensenyachts.com

Core Inc 6590 W Rogers Cir .... Boca Raton FL 33487 561-241-4580
Web: www.core-aerospace.com

Corland Co 327 s Isis Ave .... Inglewood CA 90301 310-670-3720
Web: www.coreland.com

Corporate Jet Support Inc 1 Graphic Pl .... Moonachie NJ 07074 201-807-0784
Web: www.corpjetsupport.com

Cosgrove Aircraft Service Inc 70 Oser Ave .... Hauppauge NY 11788 631-231-6111
Web: www.cosgroveaircraft.com

Cromer Material Handling Inc 4701 Oakport St .... Oakland CA 94601 510-534-6566
Web: www.cromer.com

Crown Xpress Transport
9931 Via De La Amistad .... San Diego CA 92154 619-671-9611
Web: www.crownxt.com

DAC International Inc 6702 McNeil Dr .... Austin TX 78729 512-331-5323 331-4516
TF: 800-527-2531 ■ *Web:* www.dacint.com

Davanac Inc 1936 St. Regis .... Dorval QC H9P1H6 514-421-0177 421-0188
Web: www.davanac.com

Defender Industries Inc 42 Great Neck Rd .... Waterford CT 06385 860-701-3400 701-3424
TF: 800-628-8225 ■ *Web:* www.defender.com

Derco Aerospace Inc 8000 W Tower Ave .... Milwaukee WI 53223 414-355-3066
Web: www.dercoaerospace.com

Dodson Aviation Inc 2110 Montana Rd .... Ottawa KS 66067 785-242-4000
Web: www.dodson.com

Donovan Marine Inc 6316 Humphreys St .... Harahan LA 70123 504-488-5731
TF: 800-347-4464 ■ *Web:* www.donovanmarine.com

Dreyfus-Cortney & Lowery Bros Rigging
4400 N Galvez St .... New Orleans LA 70117 504-944-3366 947-8557
TF: 800-228-7660 ■ *Web:* www.dcl-usa.com

Dutch Valley Supply Company Inc (DVS)
970 Progress Ctr Ave .... Lawrenceville GA 30043 770-513-0612 513-0716
Web: www.dutchvalley.com

E-Z-GO Division of Textron Inc
1451 Marvin Griffin Rd .... Augusta GA 30906 706-798-4311 771-4609
TF: 800-241-5855 ■ *Web:* ezgo.com

East Air Corp 337 Second St .... Hackensack NJ 07601 201-487-6060 487-5938
Web: www.eastair.com

Edmo Distributors Inc
12830 E Mirabeau Pkwy .... Spokane Valley WA 99216 509-535-8280 535-8266
TF: 800-235-3300 ■ *Web:* www.edmo.com

Ellett Industries Ltd
1575 Kingsway Ave .... Port Coquitlam BC V3C4E5 604-941-8211
Web: www.ellett.ca

ERS Industries Inc 1005 Indian Church Rd .... West Seneca NY 14224 716-675-2040 675-0300
TF: 800-993-6446 ■ *Web:* www.ersindustries.com

Expert Industries Inc 848 E 43rd St .... Brooklyn NY 11210 718-434-6060
Web: www.rubiconhx.com

Farrell e d Company Inc 1225 E Second St .... Jamestown NY 14701 716-488-1759
Web: www.edfarrell.com

Fatair Inc 17033 Evergreen Pl .... City of Industry CA 91745 626-839-7513 839-7523

Fieldtech Avionics & Instruments Inc
4151 N Main St .... Fort Worth TX 76106 817-625-2719
Web: www.ftav.com

First Aviation Services Inc
15 Riverside Ave .... Westport CT 06880 203-291-3300 291-3330
Web: www.firstaviation.com

Fisheries Supply Co 1900 N Northlake Way .... Seattle WA 98103 206-632-4462 634-4600
TF: 800-426-6930 ■ *Web:* www.fisheriessupply.com

FleetPro Ocean Inc
4770 Biscayne Blvd Penthouse A .... Miami FL 33137 305-573-6355
Web: www.fleetpro-psm.com

Flight Director Inc 100 Michael Angelo Way .... Austin TX 78728 512-834-2000 833-6097
Web: flightdirector.com

Fokker Services Inc
5169 Southridge Pkwy Ste 100 .... Atlanta GA 30349 770-991-4373
Web: www.twincitytesting.com

Formsprag Clutch Inc 23601 Hoover Rd .... Warren MI 48089 586-758-5000
Web: www.formsprag.com

Phone Fax

Freundlich Supply Co Inc
2200 Arthur Kill Rd ... Staten Island NY 10309 718-356-1500 356-3661
TF: 800-221-0260 ■ *Web:* www.fresupco.com

Furuno USA Inc 4400 NW Pacific Rim Blvd ... Camas WA 98607 360-834-9300
Web: www.furuno.com

General Aviation Services LLC
1155 E Ensell Rd ... Lake Zurich IL 60047 847-726-5000 726-7668
Web: www.genav.com

Georgetown Rail Equipment Co
111 Cooperative Way Ste 100 ... Georgetown TX 78626 512-869-1542
Web: www.georgetownrail.com

Global Parts Support Inc 2799 SW 32nd Ave ... Hollywood FL 33023 954-989-5988
Web: www.globalpartssupport.com

Gulf Marine & Industrial Supplies Inc
5501 Jefferson Hwy ... New Orleans LA 70123 504-525-6252 525-4761
Web: www.gulfmarine.net

Handling Systems Inc 2659 E Magnolia St ... Phoenix AZ 85034 602-275-2228
Web: www.handlingsystems.com

Heli-Mart Inc 3184 Airway Ave Unit E ... Costa Mesa CA 92626 714-755-2999 755-2995
TF: 800-826-6899 ■ *Web:* www.helimart.com

Helicopter Support Inc (HSI) 124 Quarry Rd ... Trumbull CT 06611 203-416-4000 416-4291
TF: 800-795-6051

Heubel Material Handling Inc
6311 NE Equitable Rd ... Kansas City MO 64120 800-283-4177
TF: 800-283-4177 ■ *Web:* www.heubelshaw.com

Holloway Houston Inc 5833 Armour Dr ... Houston TX 77020 713-674-5631
Web: www.hhilifting.com

Hy-Tek Material Handling Inc
2222 Rickenbacker Pkwy W ... Columbus OH 43217 614-497-2500
Web: www.hy-tek.net

IHI Inc 150 E 52nd St Fl 24 ... New York NY 10022 212-599-8100 599-8111
Web: www.ihiincus.com

Industry-Railway Suppliers Inc
811 Golf Ln ... Bensenville IL 60106 630-766-5708 766-0017
TF: 800-728-0029 ■ *Web:* www.industryrailway.com

Integrated Procurement Technologies Inc
320 Storke Rd Ste 100 ... Goleta CA 93117 805-682-0842
Web: www.iptsb.com

Intermountain Air LLC 301 N 2370 W ... Salt Lake City UT 84116 801-322-1645
TF: 800-433-9617 ■ *Web:* keystoneaviation.com

Jerry's Marine Service
100 SW 16th St ... Fort Lauderdale FL 33315 800-432-2231 525-0361*
**Fax Area Code:* 954 ■ **Fax:* Sales ■ *TF:* 800-432-2231 ■ *Web:* jms.qwik-order.com

Jet International Company LLC
1811 Elmdale Ave ... Glenview IL 60026 847-657-8666 657-9197
Web: www.jetinternational.com

JJ MacKay Canada Ltd 1342 Abercrombie Rd ... New Glasgow NS B2H5C6 902-752-5124
TF: 888-462-2529 ■ *Web:* www.mackaymeters.com

JMA Railroad Supply Co
927 N Shields Ave ... Carol Stream IL 60188 812-522-7200 522-1150
Web: www.jmarail.com

Kalmar RT Center LLC 103 Guadalupe Dr ... Cibolo TX 78108 210-599-6541
Web: www.kalmarrt.com

Kampi Components Co Inc 88 Canal Rd ... Fairless Hills PA 19030 215-736-2000 736-9000
Web: www.kampi.com

KAPCO/VALTEC 3120 Enterprise St ... Brea CA 92821 714-223-5400 996-3490
Web: www.kapcousa.com

Kellogg Marine Supply Inc 5 Enterprise Dr ... Old Lyme CT 06371 860-434-6002 628-1304*
**Fax Area Code:* 800 ■ *TF:* 800-243-9303 ■ *Web:* www.kelloggmarine.com

Kelsan Technologies Corp
1140 W 15th St ... North Vancouver BC V7P1M9 604-984-6100
Web: www.kelsan.com

KP McNamara Company Inc 3972 Hamilton Ave ... Cleveland OH 44114 216-361-8955
Web: www.kpmcnamara.com

Lagrange Products Inc 607 S Wayne St ... Fremont IN 46737 260-495-3025
Web: www.lagrangeproducts.com

Lat-Lon LLC 2300 S Jason St ... Denver CO 80223 303-937-7406
Web: www.lat-lon.com

Lewis Marine Supply Co Inc
220 SW 32nd St ... Fort Lauderdale FL 33315 954-523-4371
Web: www.lewismarine.com

Madison Components LLC
1 Merrill Industrial Dr Ste 19 ... Hampton NH 03842 603-758-1780
Web: www.madisoncomponentsllc.com

Magno International Lp 11014 Nw 33rd St Ste 100 ... Doral FL 33172 305-392-4726
Web: www.magnointl.com

Marine Depot 14271 Corporate Dr ... Garden Grove CA 92843 800-566-3474
TF: 800-566-3474 ■ *Web:* www.marinedepot.com

Mark C Pope Associates 2215 Birmingham Dr ... Albany GA 31705 229-435-2473
Web: www.markcpope.com

Markey Machinery Company Inc
7266 Eigth Ave S ... Seattle WA 98108 206-622-4697
TF: 800-637-3430 ■ *Web:* www.markeymachinery.com

Material Handling Products Corp
6601 Joy Rd ... East Syracuse NY 13057 315-437-2891
TF: 866-980-4788 ■ *Web:* www.mhpcorp.com

Mecanex USA Inc 119 White Oak Dr ... Berlin CT 06037 860-828-6531
Web: www.mecanexusa.com

Mediterranean Shipping Company (USA) Inc
420 Fifth Ave 37th St 8th Fl ... New York NY 10018 212-764-4800
Web: www.msc.com/usa

Meridian Aerospace Group Ltd
3796 Vest Mill Rd ... Winston-Salem NC 27106 336-765-5560
Web: airunion.us

Mitchell Aircraft 1160 Alexander Ct ... Cary IL 60013 847-516-3773
Web: www.mitchellair.com

MJLF & Associates 300 First Stamford Place ... Stamford CT 06902 203-326-2800
Web: www.mjlf.com

Modern Track Machinery 1415 Davis Rd ... Elgin IL 60123 847-697-7510
Web: www.geismar-mtm.com

Muncie Power Products Inc 201 E Jackson St ... Muncie IN 47305 765-284-7721
Web: www.munciepower.com

Norlift of Oregon Inc
7373 Se Milwaukie Expy ... Portland OR 97222 503-659-5438
TF: 888-716-2478 ■ *Web:* www.norliftor.com

NTE Aviation Ltd
1800 Waters Ridge Dr Ste 400 ... Lewisville TX 75057 972-353-3933 353-3923
Web: www.nteaviation.com

O'halloran International Inc
3311 Adventureland Dr ... Altoona IA 50009 515-967-3300 967-0206
TF: 800-800-6503 ■ *Web:* www.ohallorans.com

Omni Jet Trading Ctr 9415 Jet Ln Ste 3 ... Easton MD 21601 410-820-7300 820-5082
Web: www.omnijet.com

Orkal Industries LLC 333 Westbury Ave ... Carle Place NY 11514 516-333-2121
Web: www.orkal.com

Ottosen Propeller & Accessories Inc
105 S 28th St ... Phoenix AZ 85034 602-275-8514
Web: www.hartzellprop.com

Pacific Meridian Group 222 Juana Ave ... San Leandro CA 94577 510-618-1600
Web: pacificfarms.com

Parker-Hannifin Corp 1160 Ctr Rd ... Avon OH 44011 440-937-6211 937-5409
TF: 800-272-5464 ■ *Web:* parker.com

PartsBase Inc 905 Clint Moore Rd ... Boca Raton FL 33487 561-953-0700 953-0793
TF Cust Svc: 888-322-6896 ■ *Web:* www.partsbase.com

Paxton Co 1111 Ingleside Rd ... Norfolk VA 23502 757-853-6781 853-7709
TF: 800-234-7290 ■ *Web:* www.paxtonco.com

Polywest Ltd 110-3240 Idylwyld Dr N ... Saskatoon SK S7L5Y7 306-956-7788
Web: www.polywest.ca

Rail Exchange Inc 1150 State St ... Chicago Heights IL 60411 708-757-3317
Web: railexchangeinc.com

Railhead Corp 12549 S Laramie Ave ... Alsip IL 60803 708-844-5500
TF: 800-235-1782 ■ *Web:* www.railheadcorp.com

Rails Co 101 Newark Way ... Maplewood NJ 07040 973-763-4320 763-2585
TF: 800-217-2457 ■ *Web:* www.railsco.com

Railtech Ltd 325 Lee Ave ... Montreal QC H9X3S3 514-457-4760 457-7111
TF: 877-759-3653 ■ *Web:* www.railtech.ca

Relli Technology Inc 1200 S Rogers Cir ... Boca Raton FL 33487 561-886-0200 886-0201
Web: www.relli.com

Ringfeder Power Transmission USA Corp
165 Carver Ave ... Westwood NJ 07675 201-666-3320
Web: www.ringfeder.com

RS Braswell Company Inc 485 S Cannon Blvd ... Kannapolis NC 28082 704-933-2269
Web: www.rsbraswell.com

S-Line Cargo Control & Safety Products
11414 Mathis ... Dallas TX 75234 800-687-9900
TF: 800-687-9900 ■ *Web:* www.s-line.com

Sabine Universal Products Inc
945 Houston Ave ... Port Arthur TX 77640 409-985-2448
Web: supus.com

Satair USA Inc 3993 Trade Port Blvd Ste 100 ... Atlanta GA 30354 404-675-6333 675-6311
Web: www.satair.com

SEA BOX Inc 1 SEA BOX Dr ... Cinnaminson NJ 08077 856-303-1101
Web: www.seabox.com

Sea-Dog Corp 3402 Smith Ave ... Everett WA 98201 425-259-0194
Web: www.sea-dog.com

Shea Concrete Products Inc 87 Haverhill Rd ... Amesbury MA 01913 978-388-1509
Web: www.sheaconcrete.com

Simtech Inc 66A Floydville Rd ... East Granby CT 06026 860-653-2408
Web: www.simtech-inc.com

SkyTech Inc
701 Wilson Pt Rd Ste 3 PO Box 4942 ... Baltimore MD 21220 410-574-4144
TF: 800-394-1334 ■ *Web:* www.skytechinc.com

Sooner Lift Inc 3401 S Purdue St ... Oklahoma City OK 73179 405-682-1400
TF: 800-593-2830 ■ *Web:* www.soonerlift.com

Spencer Industries Inc 19308 68th Ave S ... Kent WA 98032 253-796-1100 796-1101*
**Fax:* Sales ■ *TF:* 800-367-5646 ■ *Web:* web.applied.com

Standard Equipment Company Inc
75 Beauregard St ... Mobile AL 36602 251-432-1705
TF: 800-239-3442 ■ *Web:* www.standardequipmentco.com

Steiner Shipyard Inc
8640 Hemley St PO Box 742 ... Bayou La Batre AL 36509 251-824-4143 824-4178
Web: www.steinershipyard.com

Sunbelt Industrial Trucks
1617 Terre Colony Ct ... Dallas TX 75212 214-819-4150
Web: www.sunbelt-industrial.com

Superior Tank Company Inc
9500 Lucas Ranch Rd ... Rancho Cucamonga CA 91730 909-912-0580
Web: superiortank.com

Talgo Inc 505 Fifth Ave S Ste 170 ... Seattle WA 98104 206-254-7051
Web: www.talgo.com/index.php/es/home.php

Tank Connection LLC 3609 N 16th St ... Parsons KS 67357 620-423-3010
Web: www.tankconnection.com

Tanks-A-Lot Ltd 1810 Yellowhead Trail N.E. ... Edmonton AB T6S1B4 780-472-8265 478-5699
TF: 800-661-5667 ■ *Web:* www.tanks-a-lot.com

TBS Shipping Services Inc
612 E Grassy Sprain Rd ... Yonkers NY 10710 914-961-1000
Web: www.tbsship.com

Tex-air Parts Inc 3724 N Commerce St ... Fort Worth TX 76106 817-624-9882
Web: www.texair.com

Tom's Aircraft Maintenance Inc
2641 E Spring St ... Long Beach CA 90806 562-426-5331
Web: www.tomsaircraft.com

Tornado Alley Turbo 300 Airport Rd ... Ada OK 74820 580-332-3510
TF: 877-359-8284 ■ *Web:* www.taturbo.com

TPS Aviation Inc 1515 Crocker Ave ... Hayward CA 94544 510-475-1010 475-8817
Web: tpsaviation.com

Tranergy Inc 726 Foster Ave ... Bensenville IL 60106 630-238-9338
Web: tranergy.com

Transmarine Navigation Corp
301 E Ocean Blvd Ste 590 ... Long Beach CA 90802 562-951-8260
Web: www.transmarine.com

Tri-Lift Inc 180 Main St Annex ... New Haven CT 06512 203-467-1686
Web: www.triliftinc.com

Trupar America Inc 160 Wilson Rd ... Bentleyville PA 15314 724-239-2220
Web: www.trupar.com

Phone *Fax*

Turbo Resources International Inc
5780 W Oakland St. . . . Chandler AZ 85226 480-961-3600 961-1775
Web: www.turboresources.com

Unical Aviation Inc 680 S LemonAve. . . . City of Industry CA 91789 909-348-1700
Web: www.unical.com

Unirex Inc 9310 E 37th St N. . . . Wichita KS 67226 316-636-1228 636-5482
Web: www.unirexinc.com

United Aerospace Corp 9800 Premier Pkwy . . . Miramar FL 33025 954-364-0085 364-0089
Web: unitedaerospace.com

Unity Railway Supply Company Inc
805 Golf Ln. . . . Bensenville IL 60106 630-595-4560
Web: www.unityrailway.com

Valley Power Systems Inc
425 S Hacienda Blvd . . . City of Industry CA 91745 626-333-1243 369-7096
TF: 800-924-4265 ■ *Web:* www.valleypowersystems.com

Van Bortel Aircraft Inc 4912 S Collins. . . . Arlington TX 76018 817-468-7788 468-7886
TF: 800-759-4295 ■ *Web:* www.vanbortel.com

Washington Chain & Supply Inc
2901 Utah Ave S PO Box 3645. . . . Seattle WA 98124 206-623-8500 621-9834
TF: 800-851-3429 ■ *Web:* www.wachain.com

West Marine Inc 500 Westridge Dr. . . . Watsonville CA 95076 831-728-2700
NASDAQ: WMAR ■ *TF:* 800-262-8464 ■ *Web:* www.westmarine.com

Western Branch Diesel Inc
3504 Shipwright St. . . . Portsmouth VA 23703 757-673-7000 673-7190
Web: www.westernbranchdiesel.com

Yingling Aircraft Inc 2010 Airport Rd . . . Wichita KS 67209 316-943-3246 943-2484
TF: 800-835-0083 ■ *Web:* www.yinglingaviation.com

ZAP 501 Fourth St . . . Santa Rosa CA 95401 707-525-8658 525-8692
OTC: ZAAP ■ *TF Orders:* 800-251-4555 ■ *Web:* www.zapworld.com

771 TRAVEL AGENCIES

See Also Tour Operators p. 3254; Travel Agency Networks p. 3265

Phone *Fax*

ABC Global Services 6400 Shafer Ct Ste 310. . . . Rosemont IL 60018 800-722-5179
TF: 800-722-5179 ■ *Web:* www.abccst.com

Adelman Travel Group
6980 N Port Washington Rd. . . . Milwaukee WI 53217 414-352-7600 352-3900
TF Cust Svc: 800-248-5562 ■ *Web:* www.adelmantravel.com

ADTRAV Travel Management 4555 S Lake Pkwy. . . . Birmingham AL 35244 205-444-4800
TF: 800-476-2952 ■ *Web:* www.adtrav.com

AESU Travel Inc 3922 Hickory Ave . . . Baltimore MD 21211 410-366-5494 366-6999
TF: 800-638-7640 ■ *Web:* www.aesu.com

Alamo Travel Group Inc 8930 Wurzbach Rd . . . San Antonio TX 78240 210-593-0084 614-2448
TF: 800-692-5266 ■ *Web:* www.alamotravel.com

Alaska Tour & Travel
9170 Jewel Lk Rd Ste 202 PO Box 221011. . . . Anchorage AK 99502 907-245-0200 245-0400
TF: 800-208-0200 ■ *Web:* www.alaskatravel.com

Alaska Travel Adventures Inc
9085 Glacier Hwy Ste 301 . . . Juneau AK 99801 907-789-0052 789-1749
TF: 800-323-5757 ■ *Web:* www.alaskarv.com

All Aboard Cruise Ctr PO Box 540685. . . . Grand Prairie TX 75054 972-262-4638

All Aboard Cruises Inc 11114 SW 127th Ct. . . . Miami FL 33186 305-385-8657 419-4873*
**Fax Area Code:* 786 ■ *TF:* 800-883-8657 ■ *Web:* www.allaboardcruises.com

All Cruise Travel 1723 Hamilton Ave . . . San Jose CA 95125 408-295-1200 295-2254
TF: 800-227-8473 ■ *Web:* www.allcruise.com

All-Inclusive Vacations Inc 1595 Iris St . . . Lakewood CO 80215 303-980-6483
TF: 866-980-6483 ■ *Web:* www.all-inclusivevacations.com

American Express Travel Service Co
200 Vesey St American Express Tower C . . . New York NY 10285 212-640-5574 640-0404
Web: travel.americanexpress.com

Apple Vacations Inc 101 NW Pt Blvd . . . Elk Grove Village IL 60007 800-517-2000 640-1950*
**Fax Area Code:* 847 ■ *TF:* 800-517-2000 ■ *Web:* www.applevacations.com

Avanti Destinations Inc 1629 SW Salmon St . . . Portland OR 97205 503-295-1100 422-9505*
**Fax Area Code:* 800 ■ *TF:* 800-422-5053 ■ *Web:* www.avantidestinations.com

Balboa Travel Management Inc
5414 Oberlin Dr Ste 300. . . . San Diego CA 92121 858-678-3300 678-3399
TF: 800-359-8773 ■ *Web:* www.balboa.com

Best Travel Inc 8600 W Bryn Mawr Ave . . . Chicago IL 60631 773-380-0150 380-7028
TF: 800-927-7357 ■ *Web:* www.besttravel.com

Bon Voyage Travel 1640 E River Rd Ste 115 . . . Tucson AZ 85718 520-797-1110 797-2408
TF: 800-439-7963 ■ *Web:* bvtravel.com

Brownell World Travel
216 Summit Blvd Ste 220. . . . Birmingham AL 35243 205-802-6222
TF: 800-999-3960 ■ *Web:* www.brownelltravel.com

Burkhalter Travel Agency 6501 Mineral Pt Rd. . . . Madison WI 53705 608-833-5200
TF: 800-556-9286 ■ *Web:* www.burkhaltertravel.com

Carefree Vacations Inc
11885 Carmel Mt Rd Ste 906 . . . San Diego CA 92128 858-450-4060
TF: 800-266-3476 ■ *Web:* www.carefreevacations.com

Cass Tours 2621 Green River Rd Ste 105-222. . . . Corona CA 92882 951-371-3511
TF: 800-593-6510 ■ *Web:* www.casstours.com

Casto Travel Inc 2560 N First St Ste 150 . . . San Jose CA 95131 408-984-7000 984-7007
TF: 800-832-3445 ■ *Web:* www.casto.com

City Escape Holidays
13470 Washington Blvd Ste 101 . . . Marina del Rey CA 90292 800-222-0022 827-5575*
**Fax Area Code:* 310 ■ *TF:* 800-222-0022 ■ *Web:* www.cityescapeholidays.com

Classic Custom Vacations 5893 Rue Ferrari . . . San Jose CA 95138 800-635-1333
TF: 800-635-1333 ■ *Web:* www.classicvacations.com

Clipper Navigation Inc
2701 Alaskan Way Pier 69 . . . Seattle WA 98121 206-443-2560 443-2583
TF: 800-888-2535 ■ *Web:* www.clippervacations.com

Conlin Travel Inc 3270 Washtenaw Ave . . . Ann Arbor MI 48104 734-677-0900 677-0901
TF: 800-426-6546 ■ *Web:* www.conlintravel.com

Corporate Travel Management Group
450 E 22nd St. . . . Lombard IL 60148 630-691-8000
TF: 866-545-6789 ■ *Web:* www.corptrav.com

Covington International Travel
4401 Dominion Blvd. . . . Glen Allen VA 23060 804-747-7077 273-0009
TF: 800-922-9238 ■ *Web:* www.covingtontravel.com

Phone *Fax*

Crown Travel & Cruises 240 Newton Rd Ste 106 . . . Raleigh NC 27615 919-870-1986 870-1666
TF: 800-869-7447 ■ *Web:* www.crowncruise.com

Cruise Brokers 2803 W Busch Blvd Ste 100. . . . Tampa FL 33618 813-288-9597 932-9650
TF: 800-409-1919 ■ *Web:* www.cruisebrokers.com

Cruise Concepts 1329 Eniswood Pkwy. . . . Palm Harbor FL 34683 727-784-7245
TF: 800-752-7963 ■ *Web:* www.cruiseconcepts.com

Cruise Connection LLC 7932 N Oak Ste 210. . . . Kansas City MO 64118 816-420-8688 420-8667
TF: 800-572-0004 ■ *Web:* www.cruiseconnectionllc.com

Cruise Connections Inc
3411 Healy Dr Ste D. . . . Winston-Salem NC 27103 800-248-7447 701-1156*
**Fax Area Code:* 215 ■ *TF:* 800-248-7447 ■ *Web:* cruisedriveflystay.com

Cruise People Inc
10191 W Sample Rd Ste 215 . . . Coral Springs FL 33065 954-753-0069 340-1968
TF: 800-642-2469 ■ *Web:* www.cruisepeople.com

Cruise People Ltd
1252 Lawrence Ave E Ste 210. . . . Don Mills ON M3A1C3 416-444-2410
TF: 800-268-6523 ■ *Web:* www.thecruisepeople.ca

Cruise Shop, The 700 Pasquinelli Dr Ste C . . . Westmont IL 60559 630-325-7447 321-1669
TF: 800-622-6456 ■ *Web:* vikingtvl.com

Cruise Specialists Inc
221 First Ave W Ste 210. . . . Seattle WA 98119 206-285-5600
Web: cruisespecialists.com

Cruise Vacation Ctr 2042 Central Pk Ave . . . Yonkers NY 10710 800-803-7245 337-8672*
**Fax Area Code:* 914 ■ *TF:* 800-803-7245 ■ *Web:* www.cruisevacationcenter.com

Cruise Web Inc 3901 Calverton Blvd Ste 350 . . . Calverton MD 20705 240-487-0155
TF: 800-377-9383 ■ *Web:* www.cruiseweb.com

CruiseOne Inc
1201 W Cypress Creek Rd Ste 100. . . . Fort Lauderdale FL 33309 800-278-4731
TF: 800-278-4731 ■ *Web:* www.cruiseone.com

Cruises Cruises 6604 Antoine Dr . . . Houston TX 77091 713-681-9866 957-2076
TF: 800-245-9806 ■ *Web:* www.cruisescruises.net

Cruises Inc
1201 W Cypress Creek Rd Ste 100. . . . Fort Lauderdale FL 33309 888-282-1249
TF Cust Svc: 888-282-1249 ■ *Web:* www.cruisesinc.com

Direct Travel 95 New Jersey 17. . . . Paramus NJ 07652 201-847-9000
TF: 800-831-1366 ■ *Web:* www.dt.com

E Tour & Travel 3626 Quadrangle Blvd Ste 400 . . . Orlando FL 32817 407-515-2400 658-1768
TF Sales: 800-339-5120 ■ *Web:* www.etourandtravel.com

Elegant Voyages 1802 Keesling Ct. . . . San Jose CA 95125 408-239-0300 239-0304
TF: 800-555-3534 ■ *Web:* www.elegantvoyages.com

Euro Lloyd Travel Inc
1640 Hempstead Tpke . . . East Meadow NY 11554 516-228-4970 228-8258
TF: 800-334-2724 ■ *Web:* www.lcc-eurolloyd.com

Friendly Cruises
3081 S Sycamore Village Dr. . . . Superstition Mountain AZ 85118 480-358-1496
TF: 888-842-1786 ■ *Web:* www.friendlycruises.com

Gant Travel Management
400 W Seventh St Ste 233 . . . Bloomington IN 47404 800-742-4198
TF Cust Svc: 800-742-4198 ■ *Web:* www.ganttravel.com

Gil Tours Travel Inc
1511 Walnut St 2nd Fl . . . Philadelphia PA 19102 215-568-6655 568-0696
TF: 800-223-3855 ■ *Web:* www.giltravel.com

Giselle's Travel Inc
1300 Ethan Way Ste 100. . . . Sacramento CA 95825 916-922-5500 679-3090
TF: 800-782-5545 ■ *Web:* www.globaltrav.com

Global Travel 900 W Jefferson St . . . Boise ID 83702 208-387-1000
TF: 800-584-8888 ■ *Web:* www.globaltrav.com

GOGO WorldWide Vacations 69 Spring St . . . Ramsey NJ 07446 800-254-3477 934-3764*
**Fax Area Code:* 201 ■ *TF:* 800-254-3477 ■ *Web:* www.gogowwv.com

Golden Sports Tours 301 W Parker Rd Ste 206 . . . Plano TX 75023 800-966-8258 578-0786*
**Fax Area Code:* 972 ■ *TF:* 800-966-8258 ■ *Web:* www.goldensports.com

Gwin's Travel Planners Inc
212 N Kirkwood Rd. . . . Saint Louis MO 63122 314-822-1957
TF: 800-433-9211 ■ *Web:* www.gwins.com

HRG North America 16 E 34th St 3rd Fl . . . New York NY 10016 212-404-8800
Web: www.hrgworldwide.com

Islands in the Sun Cruises & Tours Inc
121 Bayview . . . Grasonville MD 21638 410-827-3812 782-2371*
**Fax Area Code:* 443 ■ *TF:* 800-278-7786 ■ *Web:* www.crus-sun.com

Japan Travel Bureau USA Inc 156 W 56th St. . . . New York NY 10019 212-698-4900 586-9686
TF: 800-235-3523 ■ *Web:* www.jtbusa.com

JourneyCorp 350 Madison Ave 15th Fl . . . New York NY 10017 212-753-5511
Web: www.journeycorp.com

Kintetsu International 1290 Ave Ste 900 . . . New York NY 10104 212-259-9600 259-9625
Web: www.kintetsu.com

Lawyers' Travel Service 71 Fifth Ave . . . New York NY 10003 800-431-1112
TF General: 800-431-1112 ■ *Web:* www.lawyerstravel.com

Liberty Travel Inc 69 Spring St . . . Ramsey NJ 07446 201-934-3500
TF: 888-271-1584 ■ *Web:* www.libertytravel.com

Lorraine Travel Bureau Inc
377 Alhambra Cir . . . Coral Gables FL 33134 305-446-4433
TF: 800-666-8911 ■ *Web:* www.lorrainetravel.com

Mark Travel Corp 8907 N Port Washington Rd. . . . Milwaukee WI 53217 414-228-7472 351-1207
Web: www.marktravel.com

Marvel Aero International Inc
21 Rancho Cir. . . . Lake Forest CA 92630 949-829-8031

Maupin Travel Inc 2501 Blue Ridge Rd . . . Raleigh NC 27607 919-821-2146 829-0232
TF: 800-786-2738 ■ *Web:* www.maupintravel.com

MC & A Inc 615 Piikoi St Ste 1000 . . . Honolulu HI 96814 808-589-5500 589-5501
TF General: 877-589-5589 ■ *Web:* www.mcahawaii.com

Merit Travel Group Inc 111 Peter St Ste 200. . . . Toronto ON M5V2H1 416-364-3775
TF: 800-268-5940 ■ *Web:* www.merit.ca

Miller Travel Services Inc 4380 W 12th St. . . . Erie PA 16505 814-833-8888
TF: 800-989-8747 ■ *Web:* www.millertravel.com

Montrose Travel 2355 Honolulu Ave . . . Montrose CA 91020 800-766-4687
TF: 800-766-4687 ■ *Web:* www.montrosetravel.com

More Hawaii for Less Inc
11 Ash Tree Ln Ste 290 . . . Irvine CA 92660 949-724-5050
TF: 800-967-6687 ■ *Web:* www.hawaii4less.com

National Discount Cruise Co
1401 N Cedar Crest Blvd Ste 110. . . . Allentown PA 18104 610-439-4883
TF: 800-788-8108 ■ *Web:* www.nationaldiscountcruise.com

Northstar Cruises 80 Bloomfield Ave Ste 102 . . . Caldwell NJ 07006 800-249-9360
TF: 800-249-9360 ■ *Web:* www.northstarcruises.com

	City	State	Zip	Phone	Fax
Ocean One Cruise Outlet 3264 Marilynn St *TF:* 888-353-1922	Lancaster	CA	93536	661-949-2873	949-3311
Omega World Travel Inc 3102 Omega Office Pk Dr *TF:* 800-756-6342 ■ *Web:* omegatravel.com	Fairfax	VA	22031	703-359-0200	359-8880
Orvis International Travel 178 Conservation Way *TF:* 800-547-4322 ■ *Web:* www.orvis.com	Sunderland	VT	05250	802-362-8790	362-8795
Outdoor Connection Inc 424 Neosho *Web:* www.outdoor-connection.com	Burlington	KS	66839	620-364-5500	364-5563
Paradise Island Vacations 1000 S Pine Island Rd Ste 800 *TF Resv:* 888-877-7525 ■ *Web:* www.atlantis.com	Plantation	FL	33324	954-809-2000	
Pleasant Holidays LLC 2404 Townsgate Rd *TF:* 800-742-9244 ■ *Web:* www.pleasantholidays.com	Westlake Village	CA	91361	818-991-3390	
Premier Golf 4355 River Green Pkwy *TF:* 866-260-4409 ■ *Web:* www.premiergolf.com	Duluth	GA	30096	770-291-4202	291-5157
Prestige Travel & Cruises Inc 6175 Spring Mountain Rd *TF:* 800-758-5693 ■ *Web:* www.prestigecruises.com	Las Vegas	NV	89146	702-251-5552	
Professional Travel Inc 25000 Great Northern Corporate Ctr Ste 170 *TF:* 800-247-0060 ■ *Web:* www.protrav.com	Cleveland	OH	44070	440-734-8800	734-4528
Protravel International Inc 515 Madison Ave 10th Fl *TF:* 800-227-1059 ■ *Web:* www.protravelinc.com	New York	NY	10022	212-755-4550	593-4907
Regal Travel 615 Piikoi St Ste 104 *TF:* 800-799-0865 ■ *Web:* www.regaltravel.com	Honolulu	HI	96814	808-566-7620	
Rich Worldwide Travel Inc 500 Mamaroneck Ave *TF:* 800-431-1130	Harrison	NY	10528	914-835-7600	835-1666
Rocky Mountain Escape PO Box 5029 *Web:* www.ecolodge.com	Hinton	AB	T7V1X3	780-865-0124	
Roeder Travel Ltd 9805 York Rd *TF:* 800-379-9887 ■ *Web:* www.roedertravel.com	Cockeysville	MD	21030	410-667-6090	
Seaside Golf Vacations 218 Main St *TF:* 877-732-6999 ■ *Web:* www.seasidegolf.com	North Myrtle Beach	SC	29582	877-732-6999	
SGH Golf Inc 6805 Mt Vernon Ave *TF:* 800-284-8884 ■ *Web:* www.sghgolf.com	Cincinnati	OH	45227	513-984-0414	984-9648
Sita World Travel Inc 16250 Ventura Blvd *TF:* 800-421-5643 ■ *Web:* www.sitatours.com	Encino	CA	91436	818-990-9530	
Sports Empire PO Box 6169 *TF:* 800-255-5258 ■ *Web:* www.sports-empire.com	Lakewood	CA	90714	562-920-2350	920-1828
Star Travel Services Inc 1025 Acuff Rd *TF:* 800-542-1687 ■ *Web:* www.startravelservices.com	Bloomington	IN	47404	812-336-6811	331-6670
Sterling Cruises & Travel 8700 W Flagler St *TF:* 800-435-7967 ■ *Web:* www.cruisewin.com	Miami	FL	33174	305-592-2522	592-7442
Stevens Travel Management Inc 119 W 40th St 14th Fl *TF:* 800-275-7400 ■ *Web:* www.stevenstravel.com	New York	NY	10018	212-696-4300	679-5072
Studentcity.com Inc 8 Essex Ctr Dr **Fax Area Code:* 978 ■ *TF:* 888-777-4642 ■ *Web:* www.studentcity.com	Peabody	MA	01960	888-777-4642	573-2069*
Sun Islands Hawaii Inc 438 Hobron Ln Ste 222 *Web:* www.sunislandshawaii.com	Honolulu	HI	96815	808-926-3888	922-6951
SunQuest Vacations 77-6435 Kuakini Hwy *TF:* 800-367-5168 ■ *Web:* www.sunquest-hawaii.com	Kailua-Kona	HI	96740	808-329-6438	
Sunsational Cruises 2470 E Glen Canyon Rd **Fax Area Code:* 520 ■ *TF:* 800-239-6252 ■ *Web:* www.sunsationalcruises.com	Green Valley	AZ	85614	480-491-6248	445-6812*
Tenenbaum's Vacation Stores Inc 300 Market St *TF:* 800-545-7099 ■ *Web:* www.tenenbaums.com	Kingston	PA	18704	570-288-8747	
TNT Vacations 2 Charlesgate W *Web:* www.funjet.com	Boston	MA	02215	617-262-9200	
Tower Travel Management 53 Ogden Ave **Fax Area Code:* 630 ■ *TF:* 800-542-9700 ■ *Web:* www.towertravel.com	Clarendon Hills	IL	60514	800-542-9700	954-3040*
Tramex Travel Inc 4505 Spicewood Springs Rd Ste 200 *TF:* 800-527-3039 ■ *Web:* www.tramex.com	Austin	TX	78759	512-343-2201	343-0022
Transat AT Inc 300 Leo-Pariseau St Ste 600 *TSE:* TRZ.B ■ *TF:* 800-387-0825 ■ *Web:* www.transat.com	Montreal	QC	H2X4C2	514-987-1616	987-8035
Travel & Transport Inc 2120 S 72nd St *TF:* 800-228-2545 ■ *Web:* www.travelandtransport.com	Omaha	NE	68124	402-399-4500	
Travel Destinations Management Group Inc 110 Painters Mill Rd *TF:* 800-635-7307 ■ *Web:* www.traveldest.com	Owings Mills	MD	21117	410-363-3111	363-1816
Travel Holdings Inc 220 E Central Pkwy Ste 4000 *Web:* www.travelholdings.com	Altamonte Springs	FL	32701	407-667-8700	
Travel Impressions Ltd 465 Smith St *TF:* 800-284-0044 ■ *Web:* www.travimp.com	Farmingdale	NY	11735	631-845-8000	845-8095
Travel Inc 4355 River Green Pkwy *TF:* 888-439-1831 ■ *Web:* www.travelinc.com	Duluth	GA	30096	770-291-4100	
Travel Team Inc 2495 Main St *TF:* 800-245-8326 ■ *Web:* profile.thetravelteam.com	Buffalo	NY	14214	716-862-7600	862-7650
Travelennium Inc 556 Colonial Rd *TF:* 800-844-4924 ■ *Web:* www.travelennium.com	Memphis	TN	38117	901-767-0761	766-0126
Traveline Travel Agencies Inc 4074 Erie St *TF:* 888-700-8747 ■ *Web:* www.traveline.com	Willoughby	OH	44094	440-602-8020	946-3613
Travelmore 212 W Colfax Ave *Web:* www.travelleaders.com	South Bend	IN	46601	574-232-3061	
Travelong Inc 135 W 50th St Ste 500 *TF:* 800-537-6043	New York	NY	10020	212-736-2166	763-0496
TravelStore Inc 11601 Wilshire Blvd *TF:* 800-850-3224 ■ *Web:* www.travelstore.com	Los Angeles	CA	90025	310-575-5540	575-5541
Tzell Travel Group 119 W 40th St 14th Fl *Web:* www.tzell.com	New York	NY	10018	212-944-2121	944-7100
Ultramar Travel Management International 14 E 47th St 5th Fl **Fax Area Code:* 212 ■ *TF:* 888-856-2929 ■ *Web:* www.ultramartravel.com	New York	NY	10017	888-856-2929	856-0129*
Valerie Wilson Travel Inc 475 Pk Ave S *TF:* 800-776-1116 ■ *Web:* www.valeriewilsontravel.com	New York	NY	10016	212-532-3400	779-7073
Virtuoso 505 Main St Ste 5 **Fax Area Code:* 212 ■ *TF:* 800-401-4274 ■ *Web:* www.virtuoso.com	Fort Worth	TX	76102	817-870-0300	588-8240*
World Travel Bureau Inc 618 N Main St *TF:* 800-899-3370 ■ *Web:* www.wtbtvl.com	Santa Ana	CA	92701	714-835-8111	835-8124
World Travel Holdings (WTH) 100 Fordham Rd Bldg C Bldg C *TF:* 877-958-7447 ■ *Web:* www.worldtravelholdings.com	Wilmington	MA	01887	617-424-7990	424-1943
World Travel Inc 1724 W Schuylkill Rd *TF:* 877-265-1881 ■ *Web:* www.worldtravelinc.com	Douglassville	PA	19518	610-327-9000	
Worldwide Holidays Inc 7800 Red Rd Ste 112 *TF:* 800-327-9854 ■ *Web:* www.galapagoscruises.net	South Miami	FL	33143	305-665-0841	661-1457
Worldwide Travel & Cruise Assoc Inc 150 S University Dr Ste E *TF:* 800-881-8484 ■ *Web:* www.cruiseco.com	Plantation	FL	33324	954-452-8800	446-9008
Wright Travel Inc 2505 21st Ave S 5th Fl *TF:* 800-577-0888 ■ *Web:* www.wrighttravel.net	Nashville	TN	37212	615-783-1111	783-1100

772 TRAVEL AGENCY NETWORKS

See Also Travel Agencies p. 3264

A travel agency network is a consortium of travel agencies in which a host agency provides technology, marketing, distribution, customer support, and other services to the network member agencies in exchange for a percentage of the member agencies' profits.

	City	State	Zip	Phone	Fax
Abbey Travel Ltd 522 N Washington St *Web:* www.wehrlitravel.com	Naperville	IL	60563	630-420-0400	
Affordabletours.com 11150 Cash Rd *Web:* www.affordabletours.com	Stafford	TX	77477	281-269-2600	269-2690
Air Apparent Inc 5432 W 104th St *Web:* www.air-apparent.com	Los Angeles	CA	90045	310-649-0064	
Airtreks Inc 7 Spring St *Web:* www.airtreks.com	San Francisco	CA	94104	415-977-7100	
Alice Travel Luxury Cruises & Tour 277 Fairfield Rd Ste 218 *TF:* 800-229-2542 ■ *Web:* www.alicetravel.com	Fairfield	NJ	07004	800-229-2542	
All Direct Travel Services Inc 19000 Macarthur Blvd Ste 625 *TF:* 800-862-1516 ■ *Web:* www.alldirecttravel.com	Irvine	CA	92612	949-474-8100	
Allied T Pro Inc 500 Seventh Ave *Web:* alliedtpro.azurewebsites.net	New York	NY	10036	212-596-1000	313-9800
Altour International Inc 1270 Ave of the Americas 15th Fl Ste 2911 *Web:* www.altour.com	New York	NY	10020	212-897-5000	
American Express Company Inc World Financial Ctr 200 Vesey St *NYSE:* AXP ■ *TF:* 800-528-4800 ■ *Web:* www.americanexpress.com	New York	NY	10285	212-640-2000	640-0404
Arizona Sports & Tourism Authority 1 Cardinals Dr *Web:* www.az-sta.com	Glendale	AZ	85305	623-433-7500	
ARTA Travel 5700 W Plano Pkwy Ste 1400 *Web:* www.artatravel.com	Plano	TX	75093	972-422-4000	422-2331
Baskow & Associates 2948 E Russell Rd *Web:* www.baskow.com	Las Vegas	NV	89120	702-733-7818	
BCD Travel USA LLC 6 Concourse Parkway **Fax Area Code:* 404 ■ *Web:* www.bcdtravel.us	Atlanta	GA	30328	678-441-5200	815-6555*
Berkeleys Northside Travel Inc 1824 Euclid Ave *TF:* 800-575-3411 ■ *Web:* www.berkeley4travel.com	Berkeley	CA	94709	510-843-1000	
Caldwell Travel Inc 5341 Virginia Way *Web:* www.travelcaldwell.com	Brentwood	TN	37027	615-327-2720	
Carlson Wagonlit Travel Inc 701 Carlson Pkwy **Fax Area Code:* 763 ■ *TF:* 800-213-7295 ■ *Web:* www.carlsonwagonlit.com	Minnetonka	MN	55305	800-213-7295	212-2409*
Cascadia Motivation Inc 4646 Riverside Dr Ste 14 *Web:* www.cascadiamotivation.com	Red Deer	AB	T4N6Y5	403-340-8687	342-5644
Chamber Discoveries Inc 1300 E Shaw Ave Ste 127 *Web:* www.chamberdiscoveries.com	Fresno	CA	93710	559-244-6600	
Chartered Business Valuators 277 Wellington St W Ste 710 *TF:* 866-770-7315 ■ *Web:* www.cicbv.ca	Toronto	ON	M5V3H2	416-977-1117	
Classic Travel Inc 4767 Okemos Rd *TF:* 800-643-3449 ■ *Web:* www.classictravelusa.com	Okemos	MI	48864	517-349-6200	
ClosingCorp Inc 6165 Greenwich Dr Ste 300 *Web:* www.closing.com	San Diego	CA	92122	858-551-1500	
Club Cruise 1509 Grass Vly Hwy *Web:* clubcruise.com	Auburn	CA	95603	530-889-2582	
Colpitts World Travel 875 Providence Hwy *Web:* www.colpittswt.com	Dedham	MA	02026	781-326-7800	
Corniche Group Inc, The 8721 W Sunset Blvd Ste 200	West Hollywood	CA	90069	310-854-6000	
Corporate Incentive Travel Inc 685 S Washington St *Web:* www.corporateincentivetravel.net	Alexandria	VA	22314	703-683-0123	
Corporate Travel Service 23420 Ford Rd Ste 1 *Web:* ctscentral.net	Dearborn Heights	MI	48127	313-565-8888	
CP Franchising LLC 3300 University Dr *TF:* 800-683-0206 ■ *Web:* www.cruiseplanners.com	Coral Springs	FL	33065	954-344-8060	755-5898
Cruise & Travel Store 5435 Scotts Vly Dr	Scotts Valley	CA	95066	831-438-8844	
Cruise Brothers, The 950 Wellington Ave *TF:* 800-827-7779 ■ *Web:* www.cruisebrothers.com	Cranston	RI	02910	800-827-7779	
Cruise Deals.com 11111 Carmel Commons Blvd Ste 210 *TF:* 800-668-6414 ■ *Web:* www.cruisedeals.com	Charlotte	NC	28226	704-542-6414	
Cruisecheapcom 220 Congress Park Dr Ste 140 *TF:* 800-543-1915 ■ *Web:* www.cruisecheap.com	Delray Beach	FL	33445	561-243-2100	

Name / Address	City	State	ZIP	Phone	Fax
CruiseOne Inc 1201 W Cypress Creek Rd Ste 100 *TF:* 800-278-4731 ■ *Web:* www.cruiseone.com	Fort Lauderdale	FL	33309	800-278-4731	
Cultural Tourism DC 1250 H St Nw Ste 1000 *Web:* www.culturaltourismdc.org	Washington	DC	20005	202-661-7581	
D&F Travel Inc 338 Central Ave Ste 320 *TF:* 800-832-3516 ■ *Web:* www.dfbuses.com	Dunkirk	NY	14048	800-832-3516	
Destinations Unlimited Inc 5020 Council St Ne *Web:* www.duagency.com	Cedar Rapids	IA	52402	319-393-1359	
Discovery World Travel Inc 1045 Pennsylvania Ave *Web:* www.tldiscovery.com	Sheboygan	WI	53081	920-459-2963	
Do All Travel Company Inc 4620 18th Ave *Web:* www.doalltravel.com	Brooklyn	NY	11204	718-972-6000	
Dude Girl LLC 11854 Kitzbuhel Rd *Web:* www.dudegirl.com	Truckee	CA	96161	530-550-3247	
Ecuatours Travel Agency Inc 154 Giralda Ave *Web:* www.ecuatours.com	Coral Gables	FL	33134	305-446-3999	
Elkhorn Bus Service Inc 511 S Lincoln St *Web:* www.jonestravel.com	Elkhorn	WI	53121	262-723-4309	
Empire Travel Services 2080 Wern Ave *Web:* www.empiretravel.com	Guilderland	NY	12084	518-869-0738	
Ensemble Travel 256 W 38th St 11th Fl *TF:* 800-576-2378 ■ *Web:* www.ensembletravel.com	New York	NY	10018	212-545-7460	
Executive Travel Consultants Ltd 345 118th Ave Se Ste 130 *Web:* www.etctravel.com	Bellevue	WA	98005	425-453-8200	
Executive Travel Inc 1212 O St *Web:* www.executivetravel.com	Lincoln	NE	68508	402-435-8888	
Expedition Trips.com 6553 California Ave Sw *TF:* 877-412-8527 ■ *Web:* www.expeditiontrips.com	Seattle	WA	98136	206-547-0700	
Flathead Travel Service 500 Main St *Web:* www.flatheadtravel.com	Kalispell	MT	59901	406-752-8700	
Forest Travel Agency 2440 Ne Miami Gardens Dr Ste 107 *Web:* www.fnbromney.com	Miami	FL	33180	305-932-5560	
Fredericton Tourism 11 Carleton St *Web:* www.fredericton.ca	Fredericton	NB	E3B4Y7	506-460-2041	
Fredson Travel Inc 11077 Biscayne Blvd Ste 401	Miami	FL	33161	305-577-8422	
Frosch International Travel Inc 1 Greenway Plz Ste 800 *TF:* 800-866-1623 ■ *Web:* www.froschtravel.com	Houston	TX	77046	800-866-1623	
Future Media Concepts Inc 299 Broadway Ste 1510 *Web:* www.fmctraining.com	New York	NY	10007	212-233-3500	
Gateway Travel Service Inc 28470 W 13 Mile Rd Ste 200 *TF:* 800-423-4898 ■ *Web:* www.gatewaytrvl.com	Farmington Hills	MI	48334	248-432-8600	
Georgia Hardy Tours 20 Eglinton Ave East *TF:* 800-813-4509 ■ *Web:* www.ghardytours.com	Toronto	ON	M4R1K8	416-483-7533	
Global Enterprises Inc 7951 Shoal Creek Ste 200	Austin	TX	78757	512-451-8280	
Global Travel International 2600 Lk Lucien Dr Ste 201 *TF:* 800-715-4440 ■ *Web:* www.globaltravel.com	Maitland	FL	32751	407-660-7800	875-0711
Globe Vacation Inc 13527 Roosevelt Ave Ste 2 *Web:* wkka.com	Flushing	NY	11354	718-539-3385	
Goway Travel Ltd 3284 Yonge St Ste 300 *TF:* 800-665-4432 ■ *Web:* www.goway.com	Toronto	ON	M4N3M7	416-322-1034	
Great GetAways Inc 313 Cambridge St *Web:* www.ggatravel.com	Boston	MA	02114	617-720-6100	
Great Southern Travel 3424 S National *Web:* www.greatsoutherntravel.com	Springfield	MO	65807	417-888-4488	
GTI Corporate Travel 111 Township Line Rd *TF:* 800-223-3863 ■ *Web:* gtitravel.com	Jenkintown	PA	19046	215-379-6800	
Gulliver's Travel Service Inc 2800 S Hulen Ste 110 *Web:* www.gullivers.com	Fort Worth	TX	76109	817-924-7766	
Handa Travel Services Ltd 2269 Riverside Dr Billings Bridge Plz	Ottawa	ON	K1H8K2	613-731-1111	
Happy Time Tours & Travel 1475 Walsh St W *TF:* 800-473-5955 ■ *Web:* www.httours.com	Thunder Bay	ON	P7E4X6	807-473-5955	
Hari World Travel Inc 3400 Peachtree Rd Ne Ste 815 *Web:* www.ymdesign.com	Atlanta	GA	30326	404-233-5005	
Hispano Unidos Multiservice Inc 6051 Arlington Blvd *Web:* www.tm.org	Falls Church	VA	22044	703-534-9800	
HMJ Inc 212 W Colfax Ave *TF:* 800-347-7986 ■ *Web:* www.travelmore.com	South Bend	IN	46601	574-232-3061	
Holiday Travel of America 6405 El Camino Real *Web:* www.htoa.com	Carlsbad	CA	92009	760-431-8600	
Hume Travel Corp 401 WGeorgia St Ste 1680 *TF:* 800-663-9787 ■ *Web:* www.hume-travel.com	Vancouver	BC	V6B5A1	604-682-7581	
Hunter Travel Managers 4683 Chabot Dr Ste 385 *TF:* 800-876-8785 ■ *Web:* www.hunterworldtravel.com	Pleasanton	CA	94588	925-463-0560	
Inn at Wall Street Ltd, The 9 S William St *Web:* www.thewallstreetinn.com	New York	NY	10004	212-747-1500	
Interval Servicing International Co 3363 W Commercial Blvd Ste 202 *Web:* www.intervalservicing.com	Ft Lauderdale	FL	33309	954-485-5400	484-6343
Kahala Travel 3838 Camino Del Rio N Ste 300 *TF:* 800-852-8338 ■ *Web:* www.kahalatravel.com	San Diego	CA	92108	619-282-8300	
Luxe Travel Management Inc 16450 Bake Pkwy Ste 100 *Web:* www.luxetm.com	Irvine	CA	92618	949-336-1000	
Luxury Link LLC 5200 W Century Blvd Ste 410 *TF:* 888-297-3299 ■ *Web:* www.luxurylink.com	Los Angeles	CA	90045	310-215-8060	
Mansour Travel Company Inc 345 N Maple Dr Ste 210 *Web:* www.mansourtravel.com	Beverly Hills	CA	90210	310-276-2768	
Market Square Travel LLC 13756 83rd Way N *Web:* www.tvlleaders.com	Maple Grove	MN	55369	763-231-8870	
MAST Vacation Partners Inc 635 Butterfield Rd Ste 150 *TF:* 855-824-9288 ■ *Web:* www.mvptravel.com	Oakbrook Terrace	IL	60181	630-889-9817	889-9832
Meridican Incentive Consultants 16 Esna Park Dr Ste 103 *Web:* www.meridican.com	Markham	ON	L3R5X1	905-477-7700	
Metro Travel & Tours 9298 Central Ave Ne Ste 222 *Web:* metrotravel.biz	Minneapolis	MN	55434	763-784-0560	
Morris Murdock LLC 515 South 700 East Ste 1B *Web:* www.morrismurdock.com	Salt Lake City	UT	84102	801-483-6441	
Music Celebrations International 1440 S Priest Dr Ste 102 *TF:* 800-395-2036 ■ *Web:* www.musiccelebrations.com	Tempe	AZ	85281	480-894-3330	
National Travel Systems LP 4314 S Loop 289 Ste 300 *Web:* www.nationaltravelsystems.com	Lubbock	TX	79413	806-794-3336	
New Wave Travel 1075 Bay St *TF:* 800-463-1512 ■ *Web:* www.newwavetravel.net	Toronto	ON	M5S2B1	416-928-3113	
Newser LLC 222 N Columbus Dr Unit D *Web:* www.newser.com	Chicago	IL	60601	312-284-2300	
Nexion 6225 N State Hwy 161 Ste 450 *TF:* 800-949-6410 ■ *Web:* www.nexion.com	Irving	TX	75038	408-280-6410	271-2039
Ohio Travel Association 130 E Chestnut St Ste 301 *TF:* 800-896-4682 ■ *Web:* www.ohiotravel.org	Columbus	OH	43215	614-572-1931	
Ohio Travel Bag Manufacturing Co 6481 Davis Industrial Pkwy *Web:* www.ohiotravelbag.com	Solon	OH	44139	440-498-1955	
Pan American Travel Services 320 East 900 South *TF:* 800-364-4359 ■ *Web:* www.panam-tours.com	Salt Lake City	UT	84111	801-364-4300	
Panda Travel 1017 Kapahulu Ave Fl 2 *TF:* 800-303-6702 ■ *Web:* www.pandaonline.com	Honolulu	HI	96816	808-734-1961	
Paratransit Services Inc 4810 Auto Ctr Way Ste Z *Web:* www.paratransit.net	Bremerton	WA	98312	360-377-7176	
Peak Travel Group Inc 1723 Hamilton Ave *Web:* www.rainbowtraveler.com	San Jose	CA	95125	408-286-2633	
Premiere Travel Services Inc 7900 Westpark Dr Ste A60 *TF:* 800-458-8670 ■ *Web:* www.premieretravel.com	Mclean	VA	22102	703-893-2288	
RADIUS 7700 Wisconsin Ave Ste 400 *TF:* 800-989-3059 ■ *Web:* www.radiustravel.com	Bethesda	MD	20814	301-718-9500	
Raptim Humanitarian Travel 6420 Inducon Dr W Ste A *TF:* 800-272-7846 ■ *Web:* www.raptim.org	Sanborn	NY	14132	716-754-9232	754-2881
Raritan Center Travel II 110 Fieldcrest Ave *Web:* www.sairealestate.com	Edison	NJ	08837	732-417-1600	
Red Label Vacations Inc 5450 Explorer Dr Ste 100 *TF:* 866-573-3824 ■ *Web:* www.redtag.ca	Mississauga	ON	L4W5N1	905-283-6020	
Results Travel 701 Carlson Pkwy *TF:* 800-456-4000 ■ *Web:* www.carlson.com	Minnetonka	MN	55305	763-212-5000	
Rick Steves' Europe Through The Back Door 130 Fourth Ave N *Web:* www.ricksteves.com	Edmonds	WA	98020	425-771-8303	
Ritz Tours & Travel Inc 233 El Camino Real *Web:* www.ritztours.com	Millbrae	CA	94030	650-259-9983	
Riverside Travel Group Inc 709 NE 102nd Av *Web:* www.riversidetravel.com	Portland	OR	97220	503-255-2950	
Royal Travel & Tours Inc 122 N First St *Web:* www.royal-travel.com	Dekalb	IL	60115	815-758-8172	
S Di Travel & Incentives 152 W Huron St Ste 200 *Web:* www.sditravel.com	Chicago	IL	60654	312-587-8200	
S&L Travel Partners Inc 210 Aspen Airport Business Ctr Ste AA *Web:* www.ski.com	Aspen	CO	81611	970-925-9500	
Sabre Travel Network 3150 Sabre Dr *Web:* www.sabretravelnetwork.com/home	Southlake	TX	76092	682-605-1000	
Signal Travel & Tours Inc 219 E Main St *TF:* 800-811-1522 ■ *Web:* www.signaltravel.com	Niles	MI	49120	269-684-2880	
Simlab.net 579 Pompton Ave *Web:* www.simlab.net	Cedar Grove	NJ	07009	973-571-0055	
Strong Travel Services Inc 8214 Westche Ste 670 *TF:* 800-747-5670 ■ *Web:* www.strongtravel.com	Dallas	TX	75225	214-361-0027	
Sunwing Travel Group Inc 27 Fasken Dr *Web:* www.sunwing.ca	Toronto	ON	M9W1K6	416-620-4955	
Tangerine Travel Ltd 16017 Juanita Woodinville Way Ne Ste 201 *TF:* 800-678-8202 ■ *Web:* www.tangerinetravel.com	Bothell	WA	98011	425-822-2333	
Texas Travel Industry Association 3345 Bee Cave Rd Ste 102A *Web:* www.ttia.org	Austin,	TX	78746	512-328-8842	
There & Back Again Travel 35 E Broad St *Web:* www.thereandbackagain.com	Savannah	GA	31401	912-920-8222	
Thor Travel Services Inc 12202 Airport Way Ste 150 *TF:* 800-825-1071 ■ *Web:* www.thortravelservices.com	Broomfield	CO	80021	303-439-4100	
Top of the World Travel 5105 - 48 St *Web:* www.topoftheworldtravel.com	Yellowknife	NT	X1A1N5	867-766-6000	
Tour Edge Golf Manufacturing Inc 1301 Pierson Dr *Web:* www.touredge.com	Batavia	IL	60510	630-584-4777	
Tourbillon International LLC 11 W 25th St 8th Fl	New York	NY	10010	212-627-7732	

				Phone	Fax
Tourism Richmond Inc South Tower 5811 Cooney Rd Ste 205	Richmond	BC	V6X3M1	604-821-5474	
TF: 877-247-0777 ■ *Web:* www.tourismrichmond.com					
Trading Places International Inc 23807 Aliso Creek Rd Ste 100	Laguna Niguel	CA	92677	949-448-5150	
Web: www.tradingplaces.com					
Travel & Cruise 4331 Wyoming Blvd Ne	Albuquerque	NM	87111	505-299-7766	
Web: www.rgtravel.com					
Travel Berkley Springs 127 Fairfax St	Berkeley Springs	WV	25411	304-258-9147	
TF: 800-447-8797 ■ *Web:* www.berkeleysprings.com					
Travel Management Partners Inc 7208 Falls of Neuse Rd Ste 220	Raleigh	NC	27615	919-782-3810	
Web: www.tmptravel.com					
Travel One Inc 8009 34th Ave S 15th Fl	Minneapolis	MN	55425	952-854-2551	
TF: 800-247-1311 ■ *Web:* www.traveloneinc.com					
Travel Oriented Inc 15490 S Western Ave	Gardena	CA	90249	310-329-2800	
Web: traveloriented.com					
Travel Society Inc 650 S Cherry St Ste 200	Denver	CO	80246	303-321-0900	
Web: www.travelsociety.com					
Travel Turf Inc 7540 Windsor Dr Ste 202	Allentown	PA	18195	610-391-9094	
Web: www.wcv.com					
Travel Wizard LLC 4380 Redwood Hwy Ste 6	San Rafael	CA	94903	415-446-5252	
Web: www.travelwizard.com					
Travel-On Ltd 9000 Virginia Manor Rd Ste 201	Beltsville	MD	20705	240-387-4000	
Web: www.tvlon.com					
Travelex International Inc 2061 N Barrington Rd	Hoffman Estates	IL	60169	847-882-0400	882-1212
TF: 800-882-0499 ■ *Web:* travelexinternational.com					
Travelmart Inc, The 28011 Clemens Rd	Westlake	OH	44145	440-835-8220	
Web: ww.thetravelmart.com					
Travelsavers Inc 71 Audrey Ave	Oyster Bay	NY	11771	516-624-0500	624-6024
Web: www.travelsavers.com					
TRAVELVIDEOSTORE.com Inc 5420 Boran Dr	Tampa	FL	33610	813-630-9778	
Web: www.travelvideostore.com					
UNIGLOBE Travel USA LLC 18662 MacArthur Blvd Ste 100	Irvine	CA	92612	949-623-9000	
TF: 877-438-4338 ■ *Web:* www.uniglobetravelusa.com					
Vacation.com Inc 1650 King St Ste 450	Alexandria	VA	22314	800-843-0733	548-6815*
**Fax Area Code:* 703 ■ *TF:* 800-843-0733 ■ *Web:* www.vacation.com					
Vacations To Go Inc 5851 San Felipe St Ste 500	Houston	TX	77057	713-974-2121	
Web: www.vacationstogo.com					
Van Zile Travel Services 3540 Winton Pl	Rochester	NY	14623	585-244-1100	
Web: www.vanzile.com					
Venuequest LLC 695 Arboreal Ct	Alpharetta	GA	30022	678-909-4089	
Web: www.venuequest.com					
Virtuoso 505 Main St Ste 5	Fort Worth	TX	76102	817-870-0300	588-8240*
**Fax Area Code:* 212 ■ *TF:* 800-401-4274 ■ *Web:* www.virtuoso.com					
Wcities.com Inc 512 Second St 2nd Fl	San Francisco	CA	94107	415-495-8090	
Web: www.wcities.com					
West University Travel 3622 University Blvd	Houston	TX	77005	713-665-4767	
Web: westuniversitytravel.com					
Western Assn of Travel Agencies (WESTA) 5933 NE Win Sivers Dr Ste 202	Portland	OR	97220	503-251-8170	
Westwood Partners LLC 51 W 52nd St 12th Fl	New York	NY	10019	212-672-3350	757-4640
Web: www.westwood-partners.com					
Whaley Childrens Center 1201 N Grand Traverse St	Flint	MI	48503	810-234-3603	
Web: www.whaleychildren.org					
Wilcox Travel Sandals 1 W Pack Sq Ste 1700	Asheville	NC	28801	828-210-8197	
Web: www.wilcoxtravel.com					
World Travel Service Inc 10201 Parkside Dr	Knoxville	TN	37922	865-777-1600	
Web: www.worldtrav.com					
World Travel Services LLC 7645 E 63rd St Ste 101	Tulsa	OK	74133	918-743-8856	
Web: www.worldtraveltoday.com					
World Ventures Tours & Travel Inc 6601 Kingston Pike Sequoyah Pl	Knoxville	TN	37919	865-588-7426	
Web: www.wvtt.com					
WorldClass Travel Network 7831 Southtown Ctr Ste A	Bloomington	MN	55431	952-835-8636	835-2340
TF: 800-234-3576 ■ *Web:* www.worldclassnetwork.net					
WorldTEK Event & Travel Management 1 Audubon Ste 400	New Haven	CT	06511	203-772-0470	865-2034
TF: 800-233-5989 ■ *Web:* www.worldtek.com					
Worldview Travel Management Co 101 W Fourth St Ste 400	Santa Ana	CA	92701	714-540-7400	
Web: www.worldviewtravel.com					
Wyndham Jade LLC 202 E Main Ave	Rockford	IA	50468	641-756-3385	
Web: www.wynjade.com					
Your Travel Agent Corporate 321 N Pine St	Spartanburg	SC	29302	864-583-3054	
Web: www.ytavacations.com					

TRAVEL INFORMATION - CITY

See Convention & Visitors Bureaus p. 2152

773 TRAVEL SERVICES - ONLINE

See Also Hotel Reservations Services p. 2529

				Phone	Fax
BedandBreakfast.com 700 Brazos St Ste B-700	Austin	TX	78701	512-322-2700	320-0883
TF Sales: 800-462-2632 ■ *Web:* www.bedandbreakfast.com					
Cruises.com 100 Fordham Rd Bldg C	Wilmington	MA	01887	800-288-6006	
TF: 800-288-6006 ■ *Web:* www.cruises.com					
Hidden America PO Box 4262	River Edge	NJ	07661	201-487-1190	
Web: journeysinto.com					
Hospitality Enterprises 4220 Howard Ave	New Orleans	LA	70125	504-529-4567	
Web: www.bigeasy.com					
Hotwire.com 655 Montgomery St Ste 600	San Francisco	CA	94111	415-343-8400	343-8401
TF Cust Svc: 866-468-9473 ■ *Web:* www.hotwire.com					
Kayak.com 7 Market St Ste 300	Stamford	CT	06902	203-899-3100	899-3125
Web: www.kayak.co.in					
LastMinuteTravel.com Inc 220 E Central Pkwy Ste 4000	Altamonte Springs	FL	32701	407-667-8700	667-8850
TF: 800-442-0568 ■ *Web:* www.lastminutetravel.com					
Lonely Planet Online 150 Linden St	Oakland	CA	94607	510-250-6400	893-8572
TF: 800-275-8555 ■ *Web:* www.lonelyplanet.com					
National Recreation Reservation Service (NRRS) PO Box 140	Ballston Spa	NY	12020	518-885-3639	
TF: 877-444-6777 ■ *Web:* www.recreation.gov					
Priceline.com LLC 800 Connecticut Ave	Norwalk	CT	06854	800-774-2354	
NASDAQ: PCLN ■ *TF:* 800-774-2354 ■ *Web:* www.priceline.com					
ReserveAmerica Holdings Inc 2480 Meadowvale Blvd Ste 120	Mississauga	ON	L5N8M6	877-444-6777	286-0371*
**Fax Area Code:* 905 ■ *TF:* 877-444-6777 ■ *Web:* www.reserveamerica.com					
Travelzoo Inc 590 Madison Ave 37th Fl	New York	NY	10022	212-484-4900	521-4230
NASDAQ: TZOO ■ *Web:* www.travelzoo.com					
TripAdvisor LLC 464 Hillside Ave Ste 304	Needham	MA	02494	781-444-1113	444-1146
Web: www.tripadvisor.com					
Vacation.com Inc 1650 King St Ste 450	Alexandria	VA	22314	800-843-0733	548-6815*
**Fax Area Code:* 703 ■ *TF:* 800-843-0733 ■ *Web:* www.vacation.com					
Yahoo! Travel 701 First Ave	Sunnyvale	CA	94089	408-349-5080	349-7821
Web: www.yahoo.com/style/tagged/travel					

774 TRAVEL & TOURISM INFORMATION - CANADIAN

				Phone	Fax
Canadian Tourism Commission 1055 Dunsmuir St PO Box 49230	Vancouver	BC	V7X1L2	604-638-8300	
Web: en.destinationcanada.com					
Consumer Benefit Services Inc 1620 Bond St	Naperville	IL	60563	630-420-6200	
Web: www.consumerbenefit.com					
Lion World Travel 33 Kern Rd	Toronto	ON	M3B1S9	416-920-5466	
Web: www.lionworldtravel.com					
Mason Horvath Inc 1250 Homer St Ste 502	Vancouver	BC	V6B1C6	604-899-9401	
Web: www.masonhorvath.com					
Nova Scotia Dept of Tourism & Culture 1800 Argyle St PO Box 456	Halifax	NS	B3J2R5	902-425-5781	424-2668
TF: 800-565-0000 ■ *Web:* www.novascotia.com					
NWT Tourism PO Box 610	Yellowknife	NT	X1A2N5	867-873-7200	873-4059
TF: 800-661-0788 ■ *Web:* www.spectacularnwt.com					
Ontario Tourism Marketing Partnership Corp 10 Dundas St E Ste 900	Toronto	ON	M7A2A1	905-282-1721	
TF: 800-668-2746 ■ *Web:* www.ontariotravel.net					
Prince Edward Island Tourism PO Box 2000	Charlottetown	PE	C1A7N8	902-368-4000	368-4438
TF: 800-463-4734 ■ *Web:* www.gov.pe.ca					
Tourism New Brunswick PO Box 6000	Fredericton	NB	E3B5H1	800-561-0123	
TF: 800-561-0123 ■ *Web:* www.tourismnewbrunswick.ca					
Tourism Saskatchewan 1621 Albert St	Regina	SK	S4P2S5	306-787-9600	787-6293
TF: 877-237-2273 ■ *Web:* tourismsaskatchewan.com					
Tourism Winnipeg 259 Portage Ave Ste 300	Winnipeg	MB	R3B2A9	204-943-1970	
Web: www.tourismwinnipeg.com					
Tourism Yukon PO Box 2703	Whitehorse	YT	Y1A2C6	800-661-0494	
TF: 800-661-0494 ■ *Web:* www.travelyukon.com					
Travel Manitoba 155 Carlton St 7th Fl	Winnipeg	MB	R3C3H8	204-927-7800	927-7828
TF: 800-665-0040 ■ *Web:* www.travelmanitoba.com					
TravelNow com Inc 4124 S Mccann Ct Ste 418	Springfield	MO	65804	417-864-3600	
Web: www.travelnow.com					
Yyz Travel American Express 7851 Dufferin St	Thornhill	ON	L4J3M4	905-660-7000	
Web: www.yyztravel.com					

775 TRAVEL & TOURISM INFORMATION - FOREIGN TRAVEL

See Also Embassies & Consulates - Foreign, in the US p. 2238

				Phone	Fax
A P F Travel Inc 1721 Garvey Ave Fl 2	Alhambra	CA	91803	626-282-9988	
Web: www.apftravel.com					
Action Travel Center Inc 5900 Harper Rd	Solon	OH	44139	440-248-4949	
Web: www.actiontvl.com					
Air Land & Sea Travel Wedding Crdn 126 North Orlando Ave	Cocoa Beach	FL	32931	321-783-4900	
Web: www.als-travel.com					
All World Travel Inc 314 Gilmer St	Sulphur Springs	TX	75482	903-885-0896	
TF: 866-298-6067 ■ *Web:* www.allworldtravel.com					
Anguilla Tourist Marketing Office 246 Central Ave	White Plains	NY	10606	914-287-2400	
TF: 800-553-4939 ■ *Web:* ivisitanguilla.com					
Antigua & Barbuda Dept of Tourism & Trade 305 E 47th St 6th Fl	New York	NY	10017	212-541-4117	541-4789
TF: 888-268-4227 ■ *Web:* www.antigua-barbuda.org					
Aruba Tourism Authority 1750 Powder Springs St Ste 190	Marietta	GA	30064	404-892-7822	
TF: 800-862-7822 ■ *Web:* www.aruba.com					
Atlas Travel International Inc 1 Maple St Ste 3	Milford	MA	01757	508-478-8626	
Web: www.atlastravel.com					
Austrian Tourist Office PO Box 1142	New York	NY	10108	212-944-6880	730-4568
Web: www.austria.info/us					
Bahamas Tourism Office 1200 S Pine Island Rd Ste 750	Plantation	FL	33324	954-236-9292	236-9282
TF: 800-327-7678 ■ *Web:* www.bahamas.com					
Baker Travel Inc 23832 Rockfield Blvd	Lake Forest	CA	92630	949-458-1818	
Web: www.bakertravel.com					

Listing	City	State	Zip	Phone	Fax
Belgian Tourist Office 220 E 42nd St Ste 3402 *Web:* www.visitbelgium.com	New York	NY	10017	212-758-8130	355-7675
Bermuda Dept of Tourism 675 Third Ave 20th Fl *TF:* 800-223-6106 ■ *Web:* www.gotobermuda.com	New York	NY	10017	212-818-9800	983-5289
Bike Friday Travel Systems 3364 W 11th Ave *TF:* 800-777-0258 ■ *Web:* bikefriday.com	Eugene	OR	97402	541-687-0487	
Blue Ribbon Travel-american 3601 W 76th St Ste 190 *TF:* 800-626-5309 ■ *Web:* www.blueribbontravel.com	Minneapolis	MN	55435	952-835-2724	
Bonaire Government Tourist Office 80 Broad St Ste 3202 32nd Fl *TF:* 877-267-2572 ■ *Web:* www.infobonaire.com	New York	NY	10004	212-956-5912	956-5913
Byrne's Northpoint Travel 1213 Sheridan Rd *Web:* byrnestravel.com	Winthrop Harbor	IL	60096	847-872-9223	
Caa Niagara 155 Main St E *TF:* 800-263-7272 ■ *Web:* www.caaniagara.ca	Grimsby	ON	L3M1P2	905-945-5555	
Canyon Creek Travel Inc 333 W Campbell Rd Ste 440 *TF:* 800-952-1998 ■ *Web:* www.canyoncreektravel.com	Richardson	TX	75080	972-238-1998	
Caribbean Tourism Organization 80 Broad St 32nd Fl *Web:* www.onecaribbean.org	New York	NY	10004	212-635-9530	635-9511
Cayman Islands Dept of Tourism 350 Fifth Ave *TF:* 800-235-5888 ■ *Web:* www.caymanislands.ky	New York	NY	10118	212-889-9009	889-9125
Cayman Islands Dept of Tourism 8300 NW 53rd St Ste 103 *Web:* www.caymanislands.ky	Miami	FL	33166	305-599-9033	599-3766
Centro De Servicios & Viajes Inc 525 "H" st *Web:* centrodeservicios.org	Union City	CA	94587	510-675-5620	
China National Tourist Office 370 Lexington Ave Ste 912 *Web:* www.cnto.org	New York	NY	10017	212-760-8218	760-8809
China Travel Service Chicago Inc 2145b S China Pl *TF:* 800-793-8856 ■ *Web:* www.nexusholidays.com	Chicago	IL	60616	312-328-0688	
Croatian National Tourist Office 350 Fifth Ave Ste 4003 *TF:* 800-829-4416 ■ *Web:* www.croatia.hr	New York	NY	10118	212-279-8672	279-8683
Cyprus Tourism Organization 13 E 40th St *Web:* www.visitcyprus.com	New York	NY	10016	212-683-5280	683-5282
Dominican Republic Tourist Board 136 E 57th St Ste 805 *Web:* www.dominicanrepublic.com	New York	NY	10022	212-588-1012	
Duncan Hill Travel Ltd 2700 Beverly St *TF:* 888-748-0391 ■ *Web:* www.duncanhilltravel.ca	Duncan	BC	V9L5C7	250-748-0391	
Egyptian Tourist Authority 45 Rockefeller Plaza Ste 2305 *Web:* www.egypt.travel	New York	NY	10011	212-332-2570	
Europ Assistance USA Services Inc 4330 East-West Hwy Ste 1000 *Web:* www.europassistance-usa.com	Bethesda	MD	20814	240-330-1000	
Fiji Visitors Bureau 5777 W Century Blvd Ste 220 *TF:* 800-932-3454 ■ *Web:* www.fiji.travel	Los Angeles	CA	90045	310-568-1616	670-2318
French Government Tourist Office 9454 Wilshire Blvd Ste 210 *Web:* us.france.fr/	Beverly Hills	CA	90212	310-271-6665	276-2835
German National Tourist Office 122 E 42nd St Ste 2000 *Web:* www.germany.travel/en	New York	NY	10168	212-661-7176	
Go Travel 205 Parnell St *Web:* gotravel.com	Merritt Island	FL	32953	321-453-1702	
Go West Tours Inc 790 Eddy St at Van Ness *Web:* www.gowesttours.com	San Francisco	CA	94109	415-837-0154	
Golden Anchor Travel 1909 Southwood St *TF:* 800-299-1125 ■ *Web:* www.goldenanchortravel.com	Sarasota	FL	34231	941-922-4070	
Greek National Tourism Organization 305 E 47th St *Web:* www.visitgreece.gr	New York	NY	10017	212-421-5777	
Guided Tours of Trois-Rivieres 1457 Rue Notre Dame *TF:* 800-313-1123 ■ *Web:* www.tourismetroisrivieres.com	Trois-Rivieres	QC	G9A4X4	819-375-1122	375-0022
Hong Kong Tourism Board 5670 Wilshire Blvd Ste 1230 **Fax Area Code:* 310 ■ *TF:* 800-282-4582 ■ *Web:* www.discoverhongkong.com	Los Angeles	CA	90036	323-938-4582	208-1869*
Hong Kong Tourism Board 370 Lexington Ave 2nd Fl *Web:* www.discoverhongkong.com	New York	NY	10017	212-421-3382	421-8428
India Tourist Office 3550 Wilshire Blvd Ste 204 *TF General:* 800-425-1414 ■ *Web:* www.incredibleindia.org	Los Angeles	CA	90010	213-380-8855	380-6111
India Tourist Office 1270 Ave of the Americas Ste 303 *Web:* www.incredibleindia.org	New York	NY	10020	212-586-4901	582-3274
Irish Tourist Board 345 Pk Ave 17th Fl *Web:* www.tourismireland.com	New York	NY	10154	212-418-0800	371-9052
Israel Government Tourist Office 800 Second Ave 16th Fl **Fax Area Code:* 323 ■ *TF:* 877-248-8687 ■ *Web:* www.goisrael.com	New York	NY	10017	212-499-5660	658-6543*
Italian Government Tourist Board 500 N Michigan Ave Ste 1046 *Web:* www.italiantourism.com	Chicago	IL	60611	312-644-0996	644-3019
Italian Government Tourist Board 10850 Wilshire Blvd Ste 575 *Web:* www.italiantourism.com	Los Angeles	CA	90024	310-820-1898	470-7788
Italian Government Tourist Board 45 Rockefeller Plz # 1965 *Web:* www.italia.it	New York	NY	10111	212-245-5618	
Jamaica Tourist Board 5201 Blue Lagoon Dr Ste 670 *TF:* 800-526-2422 ■ *Web:* www.visitjamaica.com	Miami	FL	33126	305-665-0557	
Japan National Tourist Organization 515 S Figueroa St Ste 1470 *Web:* us.jnto.go.jp	Los Angeles	CA	90071	213-623-1952	623-6301
Japan National Tourist Organization 11 W 42nd St *Web:* us.jnto.go.jp	New York	NY	10110	212-757-5640	307-6754
Jordan Tourism Board (JTB) 1307 Dolley Madison Blvd Ste 2A *TF:* 877-733-5673 ■ *Web:* www.visitjordan.com	McLean	VA	22101	703-243-7404	243-7406
Kenya Tourism Board 6033 West Century Blvd Ste 900 **Fax Area Code:* 952 ■ *TF:* 800-223-6486 ■ *Web:* www.magicalkenya.com	Los Angeles	CA	90045	310-649-7718	914-6946*
Korea National Tourism Organization 2 Executive Dr Ste 750 *TF:* 800-868-7567 ■ *Web:* english.visitkorea.or.kr	Fort Lee	NJ	07024	201-585-0909	585-9041
Maritime Travel Inc 202-2000 Barrington St Cogswell Tower *Web:* www.maritimetravel.ca	Halifax	NS	B3J3K1	902-420-1554	
Martinique Promotion Bureau 825 Third Ave 16th Fl *Web:* www.martinique.org	New York	NY	10022	212-838-6887	
Mexico Tourism Board (CSTM) 225 N Michigan Ave Ste 1800 *TF General:* 800-446-3942 ■ *Web:* www.visitmexico.com	Chicago	IL	60601	800-446-3942	
Mexico Tourism Board 4507 San Jacinto St *TF:* 800-446-3942 ■ *Web:* www.visitmexico.com	Houston	TX	77004	713-772-2581	
Mexico Tourism Board 1399 SW St 1st Ave *TF:* 800-446-3942 ■ *Web:* www.visitmexico.com	Miami	FL	33130	786-621-2909	
Mexico Tourism Board 152 Madison Ave Ste 1800 *TF:* 800-446-3942 ■ *Web:* www.visitmexico.com	New York	NY	10016	212-308-2110	
Ministry of Tourism of Dominican Republic 848 Brickell Ave *TF:* 888-358-9594 ■ *Web:* godominicanrepublic.com	Miami	FL	33131	305-358-2899	
Monaco Government Tourist Office 565 Fifth Ave 23rd Fl *TF:* 800-753-9696 ■ *Web:* www.visitmonaco.com	New York	NY	10017	212-286-3330	
Morley Companies Inc 1 Morley Plz *Web:* www.morleycompanies.com/home	Saginaw	MI	48603	989-791-2550	
Netherlands Board of Tourism & Conventions 215 Park Ave S *Web:* www.holland.com	New York	NY	10003	212-370-7360	370-9507
New Zealand Tourism Board 501 Santa Monica Blvd Ste 300 *Web:* www.newzealand.com/travel	Santa Monica	CA	90401	310-395-7480	395-5453
Nova Tours & Travel Inc 504 Vine St *TF:* 800-543-6682 ■ *Web:* www.novatours.com	Liverpool	NY	13088	315-451-0260	
Philippine Dept of Tourism 556 Fifth Ave 1st Fl Mezzanine *Web:* www.tourism.gov.ph	New York	NY	10036	212-575-7915	302-6759
Plaza Travel 16530 Ventura Blvd Ste 106 *TF:* 800-347-4447 ■ *Web:* www.plazatravel.com	Encino	CA	91436	818-990-4053	
Polish National Tourist Office 5 Marina View Plz Ste 303b *Web:* www.poland.travel	Hoboken	NJ	07030	201-420-9910	584-9153
Puerto Rico Tourism Co Paseo La Princesa *TF:* 800-866-7827 ■ *Web:* topuertorico.org	Old San Juan	PR	00902	787-721-2400	722-1093
Rail Europe Inc 44 S Broadway 11th Fl *TF:* 800-361-7245 ■ *Web:* www.raileurope.com	White Plains	NY	10601	914-682-2999	
Romanian National Tourist Office 355 Lexington Ave 19th Fl *Web:* www.romaniatourism.com	New York	NY	10017	212-545-8484	
Roseborough Travel Agency Inc 140 E Indiana Ave *Web:* roseboroughtravel.com	Deland	FL	32724	386-734-7245	
Russian National Tourist Office 224 W 30th St Ste 701 *TF:* 877-221-7120 ■ *Web:* www.russia-travel.com	New York	NY	10001	646-473-2233	473-2205
Saint Lucia Tourist Board 800 Second Ave Ste 910 *TF:* 800-456-3984 ■ *Web:* www.stlucia.org/?src=orgredirection	New York	NY	10017	212-867-2950	867-2795
Saint Vincent & the Grenadines Tourist Information Office 801 Second Ave 21st Fl *TF:* 800-729-1726	New York	NY	10017	212-687-4981	
SaveOnResorts.com 6727 Flanders Dr Ste 220 *Web:* www.saveonresorts.com	San Diego	CA	92121	858-625-0630	
Scandinavian Tourist Boards 655 Third Ave *Web:* www.goscandinavia.com	New York	NY	10017	212-885-9700	
Skyland Escapes.ca 445 Sixth Ave W *Web:* www.escapes.ca	Vancouver	BC	V5Y1L3	604-685-6885	
Swedish Travel & Tourism Council Grand Central Stn PO Box 4649 *Web:* www.visitsweden.com	New York	NY	10163	212-885-9700	885-9710
Switzerland Tourism 608 Fifth Ave Ste 202 *TF:* 800-794-7795 ■ *Web:* www.myswitzerland.com	New York	NY	10020	212-757-5944	262-6116
Tahiti Tourism 300 Continental Blvd Ste 160 *Web:* www.tahiti-tourisme.com	El Segundo	CA	90245	310-414-8484	414-8490
Taiwan Visitors Assn 1 E 42nd St Ste 9 *Web:* www.taiwan.net.tw	New York	NY	10017	212-867-1632	867-1635
Taiwan Visitors Assn 555 Montgomery St Ste 505 *Web:* www.taiwan.net.tw	San Francisco	CA	94111	415-989-8677	989-7242
Tourism Australia 6100 Ctr Dr Ste 1150 *Web:* www.australia.com	Los Angeles	CA	90045	310-695-3200	695-3201
Tourism Authority of Thailand 611 N Larchmont Blvd 1st Fl *Web:* www.tourismthailand.org	Los Angeles	CA	90004	323-461-9814	461-9834
Tourism Authority of Thailand 61 Broadway Ste 2810 *Web:* www.tourismthailand.org	New York	NY	10006	212-432-0433	269-2588

Name / Address	City	State	Zip	Phone	Fax
Tourism Malaysia (MTPB) 120 E 56th St 15th Fl *Web:* www.malaysia.travel/en/us	New York	NY	10022	212-754-1113	754-1116
Tourism Malaysia 818 W Seventh St Ste 970 *TF:* 800-336-6842 ■ *Web:* www.tourism.gov.my	Los Angeles	CA	90017	213-689-9702	689-1530
Tourism Medicine Hat 8 Gehring Rd Se *Web:* www.tourismmedicinehat.com	Medicine Hat	AB	T1B4W1	403-527-6422	
Tourism Saskatoon 202 Fourth Ave N *TF:* 800-567-2444 ■ *Web:* www.tourismsaskatoon.com	Saskatoon	SK	S7K0K1	306-242-1206	
Tourist Office of Spain 845 N Michigan Ave Ste 915-E *Web:* www.spain.info	Chicago	IL	60611	312-642-1992	642-9817
Tourist Office of Spain 8383 Wilshire Blvd Ste 960 *Web:* www.spain.info	Beverly Hills	CA	90211	323-658-7188	658-1061
Travel Network Corp, The 1920 Ave Rd *TF:* 888-666-8747 ■ *Web:* www.thetravelnetwork.com	Toronto	ON	M5M4A1	416-789-3271	
Turks & Caicos Islands Tourism Office 225 W 35th St Ste 1200 *TF:* 800-241-0824 ■ *Web:* www.turksandcaicostourism.com	New York	NY	10001	646-375-8830	375-8835
VEGAS.com LLC 2370 Corporate Cir 3rd Fl *Web:* www.vegas.com	Henderson	NV	89074	702-992-7990	
Vip Cruises & Travel 22 Cleveland Ter *Web:* www.myvipcruises.com	West Orange	NJ	07052	985-626-9104	
Visit Florida 2540 W Executive Ctr Cir Ste 200 *Web:* www.visitflorida.org	Tallahassee	FL	32301	850-488-5607	
Voyages Groupe Ideal Inc 5415 Pare St Ste 1 *TF:* 800-342-9554 ■ *Web:* www.groupeideal.ca	Montreal	QC	H4P1P7	514-342-9554	
Voyages Michel Barrette 100 Rue Saint-joseph *Web:* voyagesmichelbarrette.com	Alma	QC	G8B7A6	418-668-3078	
Welcome Aboard Travel Ltd 107 S State St *Web:* welcomeaboard.net	Dover	DE	19901	302-678-9480	
Williamsburg Travel Management Companies 570 W Crossville Rd Ste 102 *Web:* willtrav.com	Roswell	GA	30075	770-650-5515	

776 TREE SERVICES

See Also Landscape Design & Related Services p. 2626

Name / Address	City	State	Zip	Phone	Fax
ABC Professional Tree Services Inc 201 Flint Ridge Rd *Web:* www.abctree.com	Webster	TX	77598	281-280-1100	
Acres Enterprises Inc 610 W Liberty St *Web:* www.acresgroup.com	Wauconda	IL	60084	847-526-4554	
Adco Services Inc 1532 W Olympic Blvd *Web:* www.adcoservices.com	Montebello	CA	90640	323-725-2581	
Akehurst Landscaping Service Inc 712 Philadelphia Rd *Web:* www.akehurst.com	Joppa	MD	21085	410-538-4018	
Alaska Snow Removal 2134 E 88th Ave *Web:* www.akplow.com	Anchorage	AK	99507	907-349-5000	
Arbor Masters Tree & Landscape Inc 8250 Cole Pkwy *Web:* www.arbormasters.com	Shawnee	KS	66227	913-441-8888	
Arbor Tree Surgery Inc 802 Paso Robles St *TF:* 800-247-8733 ■ *Web:* www.arbortree.com	Paso Robles	CA	93446	805-239-1239	
Arborwell Inc 2337 American Ave *Web:* www.arborwell.com	Hayward	CA	94545	510-881-4260	
Asplundh Tree Expert Co 708 Blair Mill Rd *TF:* 800-248-8733 ■ *Web:* www.asplundh.com	Willow Grove	PA	19090	215-784-4200	784-4493
Atlas Environmental Services Inc 9032 Olive Dr *Web:* www.atlastree.com	Spring Valley	CA	91977	619-463-1707	
BCI Inc 848 Marshall Phelps Rd *Web:* www.thebutlerco.com	Windsor	CT	06095	860-688-8024	
Blue Ridge Landscape & Design Inc 172-12 Imboden Dr *Web:* www.blueridgelandscape.com	Winchester	VA	22603	540-869-0000	
Breezy Hill Nursery Inc 7530 288th Ave *Web:* www.breezyhillnursery.com	Salem	WI	53168	262-537-2111	
CableTest Systems Inc 400 Alden Rd *Web:* www.cabletest.com	Markham	ON	L3R4C1	905-475-2607	
Care of Trees Inc 2371 Foster Ave *TF:* 888-661-8268 ■ *Web:* www.thecareoftrees.com	Wheeling	IL	60090	888-661-8268	
CoCal Landscape Services Inc 12570 E 39th Ave *Web:* www.cocal.com	Denver	CO	80239	303-399-7877	
Cti Property Services 5916 Triangle Dr *Web:* www.ctipropertyservices.com	Raleigh	NC	27617	919-787-3789	
Davey Tree Expert Co 1500 N Mantua St **Fax:* Hum Res ■ *TF:* 800-445-8733 ■ *Web:* www.davey.com	Kent	OH	44240	330-673-9511	673-7089*
David J. Frank Landscape Contracting Inc N120 W21350 Freistadt Rd *Web:* www.davidjfrank.com	Germantown	WI	53022	262-255-4888	
Dejana Industries Inc 30 Sagamore Hill Dr *Web:* www.dejanaindustries.com	Port Washington	NY	11050	516-944-3100	
Del Conte's Landscaping Inc 41900 Boscell Rd *Web:* www.visionrecycling.com	Fremont	CA	94538	510-353-6030	
Down To Earth Landscaping Inc 705 Wright-Debow Rd *Web:* www.downtoearthlandscaping.com	Jackson	NJ	08527	732-833-7702	
Embark Tree & Landscape Services 2700 Palo Pinto *Web:* lmchouston.com	Houston	TX	77080	713-462-3261	
FA Bartlett Tree Expert Co 1290 E Main St *TF:* 877-227-8538 ■ *Web:* www.bartlett.com	Stamford	CT	06902	203-323-1131	353-0808
Floralawn Inc 135 Contractors Way *Web:* www.floralawn.com	Lakeland	FL	33801	863-668-0494	
Gachina Landscape Management Inc 1130 O'Brien Dr *Web:* www.gachina.com	Menlo Park	CA	94025	650-853-0400	
Gardeners' Guild Inc 2780 Goodrick Ave *Web:* www.gardenersguild.com	Richmond	CA	94801	510-439-3700	
Grover Landscape Services Inc 6224 Stoddard Rd *Web:* www.groverlandscapeservices.com	Modesto	CA	95356	209-545-4401	
Hou-scape Inc 17725 Telge Rd *Web:* www.hou-scape.com	Cypress	TX	77429	281-579-6741	
Kimball Property Maintenance 12717 South 125 East *Web:* kimballpm.com	Draper	UT	84020	801-571-3351	
Lawn Dawg Inc 39 Simon St., Unit 14 *TF:* 888-993-3294 ■ *Web:* www.lawndawg.com	Nashua	NH	03060	888-993-3294	
Lewis Tree Service Inc 300 Lucius Gordon Dr *TF:* 800-333-1593 ■ *Web:* www.lewistree.com	West Henrietta	NY	14586	585-436-3208	235-5864
MainScapes Inc 20400 New Hampshire Ave *Web:* www.mainscapes.com	Brinklow	MD	20861	301-260-0190	
Maldonado Nursery & Landscaping Inc 16348 Nacogdoches Rd *Web:* mnlsa.com	San Antonio	TX	78247	210-599-1219	
Metco Landscape Inc 2200 Rifle St *Web:* www.metcolandscape.com	Aurora	CO	80011	303-421-3100	
Nature's Trees Inc 550 Bedford Rd *Web:* www.savatree.com	Bedford Hills	NY	10507	914-241-4999	
Nelson Tree Service Inc 3300 Office Pk Dr Ste 205 *TF:* 800-522-4311 ■ *Web:* www.nelsontree.com	Dayton	OH	45439	937-294-1313	294-8673
Odyssey Landscaping Company Inc 800 W Eight Mile Rd *Web:* odysseylandscape.com	Stockton	CA	95209	209-952-9752	
Paramount Landscape & Maintenance Inc 402 W Orion St *Web:* www.paramountlandscape.com	Tempe	AZ	85283	480-668-6109	
Pattillo Grounds Management 289 N Price Rd	Sugar Hill	GA	30518	678-288-1010	
Peabody Landscape Construction Inc 2253 Dublin Rd *Web:* www.peabodylandscape.com	Columbus	OH	43228	614-488-2877	
Rainbow Treecare Inc 11571 K-Tel Dr *Web:* www.rainbowtreecare.com	Minnetonka	MN	55343	952-922-3810	
Realty Landscaping Corp 2585 Second St Pk *Web:* www.realtylandscaping.com	Newtown	PA	18940	215-598-7334	
Shade Tree Service Company Inc 520 S Hwy Dr *Web:* www.stsco.net	Fenton	MO	63026	636-343-1212	343-5660
Sunworld Landscape & Construction LLC 451 E Sunset Rd *Web:* www.sunworldllc.com	Henderson	NV	89011	702-598-1711	
Ted Hosmer Interprises Inc 1249 Lehigh Station Rd *Web:* www.tedhosmer.com	Henrietta	NY	14467	585-334-3620	
Terry Hughes Tree Service Inc 15802 Fairview Rd *Web:* www.hughestree.com	Gretna	NE	68028	402-558-8198	
Three C's Landscaping Inc 32124 Utica Rd *Web:* www.threecslandscaping.com	Fraser	MI	48026	586-415-4850	
Treepeople Inc 12601 Mulholland Dr *Web:* www.treepeople.org	Beverly Hills	CA	90210	818-753-4600	
Trees Inc 650 N Sam Houston Pkwy E Ste 205 *TF:* 866-865-9617 ■ *Web:* www.treesinc.com	Houston	TX	77060	281-447-1327	260-0728
Twin Oaks Landscaping Inc 997 Harvey Rd *Web:* www.twinoakslandscaping.com	Oswego	IL	60543	630-554-3399	
United Lawnscape Inc 62170 Van Dyke Rd *Web:* www.unitedlawnscape.com	Washington	MI	48094	586-752-5000	
Van Zelst Inc 39400 N Hwy 41 *Web:* www.vanzelst.com	Wadsworth	IL	60083	847-623-3580	
Waverly Landscape Associates Inc 1010 Pleasant St *Web:* www.waverlylandscape.com	Belmont	MA	02478	617-484-3360	
West Coast Turf 42-540 Melanie Pl *Web:* www.westcoastturf.com	Palm Desert	CA	92211	760-340-7300	
West Tree Service Inc 6300 Forbing Rd *Web:* www.westtree.com	Little Rock	AR	72209	501-568-5111	
Wolf Tree Experts Inc 3310 Greenway Dr *Web:* www.wolftreeinc.com	Knoxville	TN	37918	865-687-3400	

777 TROPHIES, PLAQUES, AWARDS

Name / Address	City	State	Zip	Phone	Fax
Architectural Bronze Aluminum Corp 655 Deerfield Rd Ste 100 **Fax Area Code:* 847 ■ *TF:* 800-339-6581 ■ *Web:* www.architecturalbronze.com	Deerfield	IL	60015	800-339-6581	266-7301*
Au Sable Woodworking Co PO Box 108 *TF:* 800-248-9261 ■ *Web:* www.ausablewood.com	Frederic	MI	49733	989-348-7086	
Award Products Inc 4830 N Front St *Web:* directory.hawaiitribune-herald.com	Philadelphia	PA	19120	215-457-9414	
Bruce Fox Inc 1909 McDonald Ln *Web:* www.brucefox.com	New Albany	IN	47150	812-945-3511	945-0275
Champion Awards Inc 3649 Winplace Rd *Web:* www.gochampion.net	Memphis	TN	38118	901-365-4830	
Classic Medallics Inc 520 S Fulton Ave *TF:* 800-221-1348 ■ *Web:* www.classic-medallics.com	Mount Vernon	NY	10550	914-530-6259	530-6258
Crown Trophy 529 N State Rd *Web:* www.crowntrophy.com	Briarcliff Manor	NY	10510	914-941-0020	941-3039
F & H Ribbon Co Inc 3010 S Pipeline Rd *TF:* 800-877-5775 ■ *Web:* www.fhribbon.com	Euless	TX	76040	800-877-5775	344-3010
Jostens Inc 3601 Minnesota Ave Ste 400 **Fax:* Hum Res ■ *TF:* 800-235-4774 ■ *Web:* www.jostens.com	Minneapolis	MN	55435	952-830-3300	830-3293*
Metallic Arts Inc 914 N Lake Rd *TF:* 800-541-3200 ■ *Web:* www.metallicarts.com	Spokane	WA	99212	509-489-7173	483-1759

	Phone	Fax

Plastic Dress-Up Co 11077 Rush St. South El Monte CA 91733 626-442-7711 442-1814
Web: www.pdu.com

Regalia Manufacturing Co 2018 Fourth Ave Rock Island IL 61201 309-788-7471 788-0788
TF: 800-798-7471 ■ *Web:* www.regaliamfg.com

RS Owens & Co 5535 N Lynch Ave Chicago IL 60630 773-282-6000
Web: www.rsowens.com

Trophyland USA Inc 7001 W 20th Ave Hialeah FL 33014 800-327-5820 823-4836*
**Fax Area Code:* 305 ■ *TF:* 800-327-5820 ■ *Web:* www.trophyland.com

US Bronze Sign Co 811 Second Ave New Hyde Park NY 11040 516-352-5155 352-1761
TF: 800-872-5155 ■ *Web:* www.usbronze.com

Wilson Trophy Co 1724 Frienza Ave Sacramento CA 95815 916-927-9733 927-9955
TF: 800-635-5005 ■ *Web:* www.wilsontrophy.com

TRUCK BODIES

See Motor Vehicles - Commercial & Special Purpose p. 2785

778 TRUCK RENTAL & LEASING

	Phone	Fax

Barco Rent a Truck
717 South 5600 West Salt Lake City UT 84104 801-532-7777
TF: 800-453-4761 ■ *Web:* www.barcorentatruck.com

Brody Transportation Co Inc
621 S Bentalou St. Baltimore MD 21223 410-947-7000 947-5858

Calmont Leasing Ltd
14610 Yellowhead Trail NW Edmonton AB T5L3C5 855-474-2568
TF: 855-474-2568 ■ *Web:* www.calmont.ca

Carco National Lease Inc 2905 N 32nd St Fort Smith AR 72904 479-441-3200
TF: 800-643-2596 ■ *Web:* carcotrans.com

DeCarolis Truck Rental Inc 333 Colfax St Rochester NY 14606 585-254-1169 458-4072
TF: 800-666-1169 ■ *Web:* www.decarolis.com

Idealease Inc 430 N Rand Rd North Barrington IL 60010 847-304-6000 304-0076
TF: 800-435-3273 ■ *Web:* www.idealease.com

Interstate NationaLease 2700 Palmyra Rd. Albany GA 31707 229-883-7250
Web: inlleasing.com

Kris Way Truck Leasing Inc
43 Hemco Rd Ste 1 South Portland ME 04106 207-799-8593 799-8657
Web: www.kris-way.com

Lily Transportation Corp 145 Rosemary St. Needham MA 02494 781-449-8811 449-7128
Web: www.lily.com

Mendon Truck Leasing & Rental
8215 Foster Ave Brooklyn NY 11236 718-209-9886
Web: www.mendonleasing.com

MHC Kenworth 1524 N Corrington Ave. Kansas City MO 64120 816-483-7035 483-4391
TF: 888-259-4826 ■ *Web:* mhc.com

National Truck Leasing System
450 S Summit Ave Oakbrook IL 60181 630-953-8878 953-0040
TF: 800-729-6857 ■ *Web:* nationalease.com

PACCAR Leasing Corp 777 106th Ave NE Bellevue WA 98004 425-468-7877 468-8211
TF: 800-759-2979 ■ *Web:* www.paclease.com

Rush Enterprises Inc
555 IH 35 S Ste 500 New Braunfels TX 78130 830-626-5200 626-5310
NASDAQ: RUSHA ■ *TF:* 800-973-7874 ■ *Web:* www.rushenterprises.com

Ryder System Inc 11690 NW 105th St Miami FL 33178 305-500-3726
NYSE: R ■ *TF:* 800-297-9337 ■ *Web:* www.ryder.com

Star Leasing Co 4080 Business Pk Dr. Columbus OH 43204 614-278-9999 340-3137
TF: 888-771-1004 ■ *Web:* www.starleasing.com

Star Truck Rentals Inc
3940 Eastern Ave SE Grand Rapids MI 49508 616-243-7033 243-7498
TF: 800-748-0468 ■ *Web:* startruckrentals.com

Superstition Trailers LLC 535 N 51st Ave. Phoenix AZ 85043 602-415-0222
Web: www.stlaz.com

U-Haul International Inc 2727 N Central Ave Phoenix AZ 85004 800-528-0361 263-6772*
**Fax Area Code:* 602 ■ *TF:* 800-528-0361 ■ *Web:* www.uhaul.com

779 TRUCK TRAILERS

See Also Motor Vehicles - Commercial & Special Purpose p. 2785

	Phone	Fax

4-Star Trailers Inc 10000 NW Tenth St Oklahoma City OK 73127 405-324-7827 324-8423
TF: 800-848-3095 ■ *Web:* www.4startrailers.com

Alta-Fab Structures Ltd 504-13 Ave Nisku AB T9E7P6 780-955-7733
TF: 800-252-7990 ■ *Web:* www.altafab.com

American Carrier Equipment Trailer Sales LLC
2285 E Date Ave Fresno CA 93706 559-442-1500 442-3618
TF: 800-344-2174 ■ *Web:* www.americancarrierequipment.com

Arkansas Trailer Manufacturing Co
3200 S Elm St. Little Rock AR 72204 501-666-5417 666-1787
TF: 800-666-5417 ■ *Web:* arkansastrailer.com

Austin-Westran LLC 602 E Blackhawk Dr. Byron IL 61010 815-234-2811 234-3009
Web: www.austinwestran.com

Barrett Trailers Inc 1831 Hardcastle Blvd Purcell OK 73080 405-527-5050 527-3206
Web: www.barrett-trailers.com

Beall Corp 9200 N Ramsey Blvd. Portland OR 97203 855-219-5686 289-3528*
**Fax Area Code:* 503 ■ *TF:* 855-219-5686 ■ *Web:* www.bealltrailers.com

Brenner Tank LLC 450 Arlington Ave Fond du Lac WI 54935 920-922-5020 922-3303
Web: www.brennertank.com

Bri-Mar Mfg LLC 1080 S Main St Chambersburg PA 17201 717-263-6116 263-6479
TF: 800-732-5845 ■ *Web:* www.bri-mar.com

Circle J Trailers 312 W Simplot Blvd Caldwell ID 83605 208-459-0842 459-0106
TF: 800-247-2535 ■ *Web:* www.circlejtrailers.com

Clement Industries Inc PO Box 914 Minden LA 71058 318-377-2776 377-2776
TF Cust Svc: 800-562-5948 ■ *Web:* www.clementind.com

CM Trailers Inc 200 County Rd PO Box 680 Madill OK 73446 580-795-5536 575-5218*
**Fax Area Code:* 903 ■ *TF:* 888-268-7577 ■ *Web:* www.cmtrailers.com

Cottrell Inc 2125 Candler Rd. Gainesville GA 30507 770-532-7251 535-2831
TF Sales: 800-827-0132 ■ *Web:* www.cottrelltrailers.com

Dakota Mfg Company Inc 1909 S Rowley St. Mitchell SD 57301 605-996-5571 996-5572
TF: 800-232-5682 ■ *Web:* traileze.com

	Phone	Fax

Dexter Chassis Group 501 Miller Dr White Pigeon MI 49099 269-483-7681
Web: dexterchassisgroup.com

Doonan Trailer Corp 36 NE Hwy 156 Great Bend KS 67530 620-792-6222 792-3308
Web: www.doonan.com

East Mfg Corp 1871 State Rt 44 PO Box 277 Randolph OH 44265 330-325-9921 325-7851
TF: 888-405-3278 ■ *Web:* www.eastmfg.com

Featherlite Trailers Hwy 63 & 9 PO Box 320 Cresco IA 52136 563-547-6000 547-6100
TF: 800-800-1230 ■ *Web:* www.fthr.com

Fontaine Trailer Co
430 Letson Rd PO Box 619 Haleyville AL 35565 205-486-5251
TF: 800-821-6535 ■ *Web:* www.fontainetrailer.com

Great Dane Trailers Inc 602 E Lathrop Ave. Savannah GA 31415 912-644-2100
Web: greatdanetrailers.com

Hesse Inc 6700 St John Ave. Kansas City MO 64123 816-483-7808 241-9010
TF: 800-821-5562 ■ *Web:* www.grouphesse.com

Holden Industries Inc
5624 S State Hwy 43 South West City MO 64863 417-762-3218
Web: www.holdentrailers.com

Hudson Bros Trailer Manufacturing Inc
1508 Hwy 218 W Indian Trail NC 28079 704-753-4723
Web: www.hudsontrailers.com

K-Dee Supply Inc 621 E Lake St Lake Mills WI 53551 920-648-8202 648-2903
TF: 800-268-3681

Kentucky Trailer 7201 Logistics Dr Louisville KY 40258 502-637-2551 636-3675
TF: 888-598-7245 ■ *Web:* www.kytrailer.com

Kentucky Trailer Technologies
1240 N Pontiac Trial Walled Lake MI 48390 248-960-9700 960-7775
TF: 866-638-6080 ■ *Web:* www.kytrailer.com

LBT Inc 11502 "I" St Omaha NE 68137 402-333-4900 333-0685
TF: 888-528-7278 ■ *Web:* www.lbt-inc.com

Ledwell & Son Enterprises 3300 Waco St Texarkana TX 75501 903-838-6531 831-2719*
**Fax:* Sales ■ *TF:* 888-533-9355 ■ *Web:* www.ledwell.com

Liberty Industries Inc 130 E Cemetery Rd. Fillmore IN 46128 765-246-4031
Web: www.liberty-industries.com

Loadcraft Industries Inc 3811 N Bridge St. Brady TX 76825 325-597-2911
Web: www.loadcraft.com

Mac Trailer Mfg Inc 14599 Commerce St NE Alliance OH 44601 330-823-9900 823-0232
TF: 800-795-8454 ■ *Web:* www.mactrailer.com

Magic Tilt Trailers Inc
2161 Lions Club Rd Clearwater FL 33764 727-535-5561 539-8472
Web: www.boattrailers.com

Maurer Mfg 1300 38th Ave W PO Box 160 Spencer IA 51301 712-262-2992 262-1022
TF: 888-274-6010 ■ *Web:* www.maurermfg.com

MCT Industries Inc 7451 Pan American Fwy Albuquerque NM 87109 505-345-8651 345-2597
TF: 800-876-8651 ■ *Web:* www.mct-ind.com

Merritt Equipment Co 9339 Hwy 85 Henderson CO 80640 303-289-2286 288-6127
TF: 800-634-3036 ■ *Web:* www.merrittequipment.com

Mickey Truck Bodies Inc
1305 Trinity Ave PO Box 2044 High Point NC 27261 336-882-6806 889-6712
TF: 800-334-9061 ■ *Web:* www.mickeybody.com

Midwest Systems 5911 Hall St. Saint Louis MO 63147 314-389-6280 389-9443
TF: 800-383-6281 ■ *Web:* www.mwsystems.com

Nu Van Technology Inc 2155 Hwy 1187 Mansfield TX 76063 817-477-1734

Performance Co, The 1263 US Hwy 59 N Cleveland TX 77328 281-593-8888
Web: www.performancetruck.com

Pitts Enterprises Inc 5734 Hwy 431 Pittsview AL 36871 334-855-4754
Web: www.pittstrailers.com

Polar Service Centers
7600 E Sam Houston Pkwy N Houston TX 77049 281-459-6400
TF: 800-955-8558 ■ *Web:* www.polartank.com

Polar Tank Trailer Inc
12810 County Rd 17 Holdingford MN 56340 320-746-2255 746-2937
TF: 800-826-6589 ■ *Web:* www.polartank.com

Redneck Trailer Supplies 2100 NW By-Pass Springfield MO 65803 417-864-5210 864-7764
TF: 877-973-3632 ■ *Web:* www.redneck-trailer.com

Rogers Bros Corp 100 Orchard St. Albion PA 16401 814-756-4121 756-4830
TF: 800-441-9880 ■ *Web:* www.rogerstrailers.com

Royal Camp Services Ltd 7111 - 67 St. Edmonton AB T6B3L7 780-463-8000
TF: 877-884-2267 ■ *Web:* www.royalcamp.com

Schutt Industries Inc
185 Industrial Ave. Clintonville WI 54929 715-823-8025
Web: www.schuttindustries.com

Schwend Inc 28945 Johnston Rd Dade City FL 33523 352-588-2220 588-2221
TF: 800-243-7757 ■ *Web:* www.schwendinc.com

Stoughton Trailers LLC 416 S Academy St Stoughton WI 53589 608-873-2500 873-2575
Web: www.stoughtontrailers.com

Summit Trailer Sales Inc 1 Summit Plz Summit Station PA 17979 570-754-3511 754-7025
TF: 800-437-3729 ■ *Web:* www.summittrailer.com

Superior Fabrication Inc 801 S Eastern Ave. Elk City OK 73644 580-243-5693
Web: www.superiorfab.com

Timpte Inc 1827 Industrial Dr David City NE 68632 402-367-3056 367-4340
TF: 888-256-4884 ■ *Web:* www.timpte.com

Towmaster Inc 61381 US Hwy 12 Litchfield MN 55355 320-693-7900 693-7921
TF: 800-462-4517 ■ *Web:* towmaster.com

Trail King Industries Inc
147 Industrial Pk Rd Brookville PA 15825 814-849-2342 849-5063
TF: 800-545-1549 ■ *Web:* www.trailking.com

Trailiner Corp PO Box 5270 Springfield MO 65801 417-866-7258 866-1168
TF: 800-833-8209 ■ *Web:* www.trailiner.com

Trailstar Mfg Corp
20700 Harrisburg-Westville Rd PO Box 2086 Alliance OH 44601 330-821-9900 821-6941
Web: trailstarintl.com

Travis Body & Trailer Inc 13955 FM529 Houston TX 77041 713-466-5888 466-3238
TF: 800-535-4372 ■ *Web:* www.travistrailers.com

Trinity Trailer Manufacturing Inc
8200 S Eisenman Rd Boise ID 83716 208-336-3666 336-3741
TF: 800-235-6577 ■ *Web:* www.trinitytrailer.com

Truck Equipment Service Co 800 Oak St. Lincoln NE 68521 402-476-3225 476-3726
TF: 800-869-0363 ■ *Web:* www.cornhusker800.com

Utility Tool & Trailer Co
151 E 16th St PO Box 360 Clintonville WI 54929 715-823-3167 823-5274
Web: www.uttwi.com

Phone | Fax

Utility Trailer Mfg Co
17295 E Railroad St, City of Industry CA 91748 — 626-965-1541 965-2790
TF: 800-874-6807 ■ *Web:* www.utilitytrailer.com

Vanco USA Trailer Mfg
1170 Florence Rd PO Box 98, Florence NJ 08518 — 609-499-4141 499-8865
Web: www.vancotrailers.com

Vantage Trailers Inc 29335 Hwy Blvd, Katy TX 77494 — 281-391-2664
TF: 800-826-8245 ■ *Web:* www.vantagetrailer.com

VE Enterprises Inc PO Box 369, Springer OK 73458 — 580-653-2171 653-2773
Web: www.veenterprises.com

Wabash National Corp
1000 Sagamore PkwyS PO Box 6129, Lafayette IN 47903 — 765-771-5300 771-5474
NYSE: WNC ■ *TF Sales:* 866-877-5062 ■ *Web:* www.wabashnational.com

Wells Cargo Inc 1503 W McNaughton St, Elkhart IN 46514 — 574-264-9661 264-5938
TF: 800-348-7553 ■ *Web:* www.wellscargo.com

Western Trailer Co 251 W Gowen Rd, Boise ID 83716 — 208-344-2539 344-1521
TF: 888-344-2539 ■ *Web:* www.westerntrailer.com

Wilson Trailer Co 4400 S Lewis Blvd, Sioux City IA 51106 — 712-252-6500 252-6510
TF: 800-798-2002 ■ *Web:* www.wilsontrailer.com

Witzco Trailers Inc 6101 McIntosh Rd, Sarasota FL 34238 — 941-922-5301 924-2402
TF: 800-462-4123 ■ *Web:* www.witzco.com

780 TRUCKING COMPANIES

See Also Logistics Services (Transportation & Warehousing) p. 2681; Moving Companies p. 2789

Phone | Fax

A & A Express Inc PO Box 707, Brandon SD 57005 — 605-582-2402 582-7300
TF: 800-658-3549 ■ *Web:* www.aaexpressinc.com

AAA Cooper Transportation 1751 Kinsey Rd, Dothan AL 36303 — 334-793-2284 794-3353
TF: 800-633-7571 ■ *Web:* www.aaacooper.com

Aaa Moving & Storage Inc
747 E Ship Creek Ave, Anchorage AK 99501 — 888-927-3330 276-1986*
**Fax Area Code:* 907 ■ *TF:* 866-641-4446 ■ *Web:* www.alliedalaska.com

ABF Freight Systems Inc
3801 Old Greenwood Rd, Fort Smith AR 72903 — 479-785-8913 785-8800*
**Fax:* Cust Svc ■ *TF:* 800-610-5544 ■ *Web:* www.abfs.com

Ace Doran Hauling & Rigging Co Inc
1601 Blue Rock St, Cincinnati OH 45223 — 513-681-7900 681-7908
TF: 800-829-0929 ■ *Web:* www.acedoran.com

Ace Relocation Systems Inc
5608 Eastgate Dr, San Diego CA 92121 — 858-677-5500 677-5587
TF: 800-453-0964 ■ *Web:* www.acerelocation.com

Acme Truck Line Inc 1180 Destrehan Ave, Harvey LA 70058 — 504-368-2510 368-2510
TF: 800-825-6246 ■ *Web:* www.acmetruck.com

Action Carrier Inc
1720 S Southeastern Ave Ste 220, Sioux Falls SD 57103 — 605-335-5500

Admiral-Merchants Motor Freight Inc
215 S 11th St, Minneapolis MN 55403 — 612-332-4819 332-4765

Alabama Motor Express Inc
10720 E US Hwy 84 E, Ashford AL 36312 — 800-633-7590 899-2311*
**Fax Area Code:* 334 ■ *TF:* 800-633-7590 ■ *Web:* www.amxtrucking.com

Alan Ritchey Inc
740 S I-35 E Frontage Rd, Valley View TX 76272 — 940-726-3276 726-5335
TF: 800-877-0273 ■ *Web:* www.alanritchey.com

All American Moving Group LLC PO Box 271277, Memphis TN 38167 — 901-353-3900 353-4113
TF: 800-467-2900 ■ *Web:* www.allamericanmoving.com

Allegheny Design Management Inc
1154 Parks Industrial Dr, Vandergrift PA 15690 — 724-845-7336 845-9889
TF: 800-927-2611 ■ *Web:* www.alleghenydesignmgmt.com

Allied Automotive Group
2302 ParkLake Dr Bldg 15 Ste 600, Atlanta GA 30345 — 800-476-2058
TF: 800-476-2058

Ameril-Co Carriers Inc 1702 E Overland, Scottsbluff NE 69361 — 308-635-3157 635-1447
TF: 800-445-5400 ■ *Web:* www.americo-carriers.com

Amstan Logistics 101 Knightsbridge Dr, Hamilton OH 45011 — 513-863-4627
TF: 800-322-5546 ■ *Web:* www.amstan.com

Anderson Trucking Service Inc
725 Opportunity St PO Box 1377, Saint Cloud MN 56301 — 320-255-7400 255-7494
TF: 800-328-2316 ■ *Web:* www.atsinc.com

Anson County School District 320 Camden Rd, Wadesboro NC 28170 — 704-694-4417 694-7479
Web: www.ansonschools.org

Apgar Brothers Trucking Co 200 Apgar Dr, Somerset NJ 08873 — 732-356-3900

Ards Trucking Company Inc
4190 Alligator Rd, Timmonsville SC 29161 — 843-393-5101
TF: 877-273-7297 ■ *Web:* www.ardtrucking.com

ARG Trucking Corp 369 Bostwick Rd, Phelps NY 14532 — 315-789-8871 789-8879*
**Fax:* Hum Res ■ *TF:* 800-334-1314 ■ *Web:* www.wadhams.com

Arkansas Best Corp (ABC)
3801 Old Greenwood Rd PO Box 10048, Fort Smith AR 72903 — 479-785-6000 785-8927
NASDAQ: ARCB ■ *Web:* arcb.com

Arlo G. Lott Trucking Inc 257 S 100 E, Jerome ID 83338 — 208-324-5053 324-8668
TF: 800-443-5688 ■ *Web:* arloglotttrucking.com

Armellini Express Lines Inc
3446 SW Armellini Ave, Palm City FL 34990 — 772-287-0575 221-3284*
**Fax:* Cust Svc ■ *TF:* 800-327-7887 ■ *Web:* www.armellini.com

Arnold Transportation Services Inc
9523 Florida Mining Blvd, Jacksonville FL 32257 — 972-986-3154
TF: 800-846-4321 ■ *Web:* www.arnoldtrans.com

Associated Petroleum Carriers Inc
PO Box 2808, Spartanburg SC 29304 — 864-573-9301
TF Cust Svc: 800-573-9301 ■ *Web:* www.apccorporate.com

Atkinson Freight Lines Co 2950 State Rd, Bensalem PA 19020 — 215-639-2678

Averitt Express Inc 1415 Neal St, Cookeville TN 38501 — 800-283-7488
TF: 800-283-7488 ■ *Web:* www.averittexpress.com

B-D-R Transport Inc 7994 US Rt 5, Westminster VT 05158 — 802-463-0606
TF: 800-421-0126 ■ *Web:* www.bdrtransport.com

Baggett Transportation Co 2 S 32nd St, Birmingham AL 35233 — 888-224-4388 320-2329*
**Fax Area Code:* 205 ■ *TF:* 800-633-8982 ■ *Web:* www.baggetttransport.com

Bailey's Express Inc 61 Industrial Pk Rd, Middletown CT 06457 — 860-632-0388 632-9089
TF: 800-523-3758 ■ *Web:* www.baileysxpress.com

Barlow 1305 Grand Dd SE, Faucett MO 64448 — 816-238-3373
TF: 800-688-1202 ■ *Web:* www.barlowtruckline.com

Phone | Fax

Bastian Trucking Inc 440 South Main, Aurora UT 84620 — 435-529-7453
TF: 800-452-5126 ■ *Web:* www.bastiantrucking.com

Baylor Trucking Inc 9269 E State Rd 48, Milan IN 47031 — 812-623-2020
TF: 800-322-9567 ■ *Web:* www.baylortrucking.com

Bayshore Transportation System Inc
901 Dawson Dr, Newark DE 19713 — 302-366-0220
TF: 800-523-3319 ■ *Web:* www.bayshoreallied.com

Beam Mack Sales & Service Inc
2674 W Henrietta Rd, Rochester NY 14623 — 585-424-4860 272-8851
TF: 877-650-8789 ■ *Web:* www.beammack.com

Beaver Express Service LLC
4310 Oklahoma Ave PO Box 1147, Woodward OK 73802 — 580-256-6460 256-6239
TF: 800-593-2328 ■ *Web:* www.beaverexpress.com

Bee Trucking Inc 9540 Ball St, San Antonio TX 78217 — 210-646-7211 646-6218

Beelman Truck Co 1 Racehorse Dr, East Saint Louis IL 62205 — 618-646-5300
TF Sales: 800-541-5918 ■ *Web:* www.beelman.com

Beeville Independent School District
201 N St Marys St, Beeville TX 78102 — 361-358-7111 358-7837
Web: www.beevilleisd.net

Benton Express Inc
1045 S River Industrial Blvd SE, Atlanta GA 30315 — 404-267-2200 267-2201
TF: 888-423-6866

Besl Transfer Co 5700 Este Ave, Cincinnati OH 45232 — 513-242-3456 242-4013
TF: 800-456-2375 ■ *Web:* www.besl.com

Bestway Enterprises Inc 3877 Luker Rd, Cortland NY 13045 — 607-753-8261 753-9948
Web: www.bestwaylumber.com

Big G Express Inc PO Box 1650, Shelbyville TN 37162 — 800-684-9140
TF: 800-955-9140 ■ *Web:* www.biggexpress.com

Bilkays Express Co 2400 Bedle Place, Linden NJ 07036 — 908-289-2400 289-6364
TF: 800-526-4006 ■ *Web:* Www.bilkays.com

Bob's Transport & Storage Company Inc
7980 Tar Bay Dr, Jessup MD 20794 — 410-799-0832 799-0951
Web: www.bobstransport.com

Boyd Bros Transportation Inc 3275 Alabama 30, Clayton AL 36016 — 334-775-1400 775-1433
TF: 800-700-2693 ■ *Web:* www.boydbros.com

Britt Trucking & Construction Co
1900 Seminole Rd, Lamesa TX 79331 — 806-872-3353

Brooke County Schools 1201 Pleasant Ave, Wellsburg WV 26070 — 304-737-3481 737-3480
Web: www.edline.net/pages/brookecountyschools

Brph Cos Inc
5700 N Harbor City Blvd Ste 400, Melbourne FL 32940 — 321-254-7666 259-4703
Web: www.brph.com

Bryan Systems 14020 US 20A Hwy, Montpelier OH 43543 — 800-745-2796 485-6653*
**Fax Area Code:* 419 ■ *TF:* 800-745-2796 ■ *Web:* www.bryansystems.com

Buchanan Hauling & Rigging
4625 Industrial Rd, Fort Wayne IN 46825 — 260-471-1877 471-8878
TF: 888-544-4285 ■ *Web:* www.buchananhauling.com

Buddy Moore Trucking Inc PO Box 10047, Birmingham AL 35202 — 205-949-2260
TF: 866-704-1598 ■ *Web:* www.buddymooretrucking.com

Bulk Transit Corp 7177 Industrial Pkwy, Plain City OH 43064 — 614-873-4632 873-3393
TF: 800-345-2855 ■ *Web:* www.bulktransit.com

Bulkmatic Transport Co 2001 N Cline Ave, Griffith IN 46319 — 800-535-8505 972-7655*
**Fax Area Code:* 219 ■ *TF:* 800-535-8505 ■ *Web:* www.bulkmatic.com

Bulkmatic Transport Co 205 Butler Cir SW, Vernon AL 35592 — 205-695-7132 695-9500

Burnet Consolidated Independent School District
208 E Brier Ln, Burnet TX 78611 — 512-756-2124 756-7498
Web: www.burnet.txed.net

Burns Motor Freight Inc 500 Seneca Trl N, Marlinton WV 24954 — 304-799-6106 799-4257
TF: 800-598-5674 ■ *Web:* www.burnsmotorfreight.com

Butler Transport Inc 347 N James St, Kansas City KS 66118 — 913-321-0047 342-5725
TF: 800-345-8158 ■ *Web:* www.butlertransport.com

Cal-ark Inc PO Box 990, Mabelvale AR 72103 — 501-455-3399
TF: 888-422-5275 ■ *Web:* www.calark.com

Calex Express Inc 58 Pittston Ave, Pittston PA 18640 — 570-603-0180 603-0940
TF: 800-292-2539 ■ *Web:* www.calexlogistics.com

California Cartage Company Inc
2931 Redondo Ave, Long Beach CA 90806 — 888-537-1432 427-6855*
**Fax Area Code:* 562 ■ *TF:* 888-537-1432 ■ *Web:* www.calcartage.com

Cardinal Transport Inc 7180 E Reed Rd, Coal City IL 60416 — 815-634-4443 634-8267
TF: 800-435-9302 ■ *Web:* www.cardinaltransport.com

Cargo Transporters Inc
3390 N Oxford St PO Box 850, Claremont NC 28610 — 828-459-3282 459-3292
Web: www.cargotransporters.com

Carroll Fulmer Logistics Corp
8340 American Way, Groveland FL 34736 — 352-429-5000 429-0350*
**Fax:* Mktg ■ *Web:* www.cfulmer.com

Cassens Transport Co 145 N Kansas St, Edwardsville IL 62025 — 618-656-3006 692-7316
Web: www.cassens.com/transport

Cedar Rapids Truck Ctr Inc
9201 Sixth St SW, Cedar Rapids IA 52404 — 319-848-6230 848-4302
TF: 866-602-1597 ■ *Web:* www.cedarrapidstruckcenter.com

Celadon Trucking Services Inc
9503 E 33rd St, Indianapolis IN 46235 — 317-972-7000 890-9428
TF: 800-235-2366 ■ *Web:* www.celadontrucking.com

Centra Financial Holdings Inc
101 Venture Dra, Morgantown WV 26508 — 304-598-2000
Web: www.bankwithunited.com

Central Freight Lines Inc PO Box 2638, Waco TX 76702 — 800-782-5036 741-5370*
**Fax Area Code:* 254 ■ *TF:* 800-782-5036 ■ *Web:* www.centralfreight.com

Central Petroleum Transport Inc (CPT)
6115 Mitchell St, Sioux City IA 51111 — 712-258-6357 258-8592
TF: 800-798-6357 ■ *Web:* www.cptrans.com

Central Refrigerated Service Inc
5175 W 2100 S, West Valley City UT 84120 — 801-924-7000 924-7142
TF: 800-777-0069

Chadderton Trucking Inc 40 Stewart Way, Sharon PA 16146 — 724-981-5050 981-1615
TF: 800-327-6868 ■ *Web:* www.chaddertontrucking.com

Charles G Lawson Trucking 7815 Mobile Hwy, Hope Hull AL 36043 — 334-284-3220 281-4672

Chester Bross Construction Co 6739 CR 423, Palmyra MO 63461 — 573-221-5958 221-1892
Web: www.cbrossgroup.com

Christenson Transportation Inc
2001 W Old Rt 66, Strafford MO 65757 — 417-866-5993 447-0864
TF: 800-980-2493 ■ *Web:* www.christensontrans.com

Company	City	State	ZIP	Phone	Fax
Clipper Americas Inc 2500 City W Blvd Ste 500 *Web:* www.clipper-group.com	Houston	TX	77042	713-953-2200	953-2201
Coastal Transport Co Inc 1603 Ackerman Rd *TF:* 800-523-8612 ■ *Web:* coastaltransport.com	San Antonio	TX	78219	210-661-4287	
Coleman American Moving Services Inc PO Box 960 *TF:* 877-693-7060 ■ *Web:* www.colemanallied.com	Midland City	AL	36350	866-929-1482	
Colonial Freight Systems Inc 10924 McBride Ln *TF:* 800-826-1402 ■ *Web:* www.cfsi.com	Knoxville	TN	37932	865-966-9711	966-3649
Colonial Truck Co 1833 Commerce Rd *TF:* 800-234-8782 ■ *Web:* www.colonialtruck.com	Richmond	VA	23224	804-232-3492	
Combined Transport Inc 5656 Crater Lake Ave *TF:* 800-547-2870 ■ *Web:* www.combinedtransport.com	Central Point	OR	97502	541-734-7418	826-2001
Comcar Industries Inc 502 E Bridgers Ave *TF Cust Svc:* 800-524-1101 ■ *Web:* www.comcar.com	Auburndale	FL	33823	863-967-1101	965-1023
Commercial Storage & Distribution Co 432 Richmond Rd	Texarkana	TX	75503	903-794-2202	
Con-Way Freight 2211 Old Earhart Rd *TF:* 800-755-2728	Ann Arbor	MI	48105	734-994-6600	
Container Port Group 1340 Depot St Ste 103 *Web:* www.containerport.com	Cleveland	OH	44116	440-333-1330	333-1520
Cooke Trucking Co Inc 1759 S Andy Griffith Pkwy *TF:* 800-888-9502 ■ *Web:* www.cooketrucking.com	Mount Airy	NC	27030	336-786-5181	789-7132
Corvallis School District 509 J 1555 SW 35th St PO Box 3509J *Web:* www.csd509j.net	Corvallis	OR	97333	541-757-5811	
Covenant Transport Inc 400 Birmingham Hwy *NASDAQ: CVTI* ■ *TF:* 800-334-9686 ■ *Web:* www.covenanttransport.com	Chattanooga	TN	37419	423-821-1212	821-5442
Cox Transportation Services Inc 10448 Dow Gil Rd *TF:* 800-288-8118 ■ *Web:* www.truckingforamerica.com	Ashland	VA	23005	804-798-1477	798-1299
CR England & Sons Inc 4701 West 2100 South *TF:* 800-453-8826 ■ *Web:* www.crengland.com	Salt Lake City	UT	84120	801-972-2712	
Craig Transportation Co 26699 Eckel Rd *TF:* 800-521-9119 ■ *Web:* www.craigtransportation.com	Perrysburg	OH	43551	419-872-3333	874-9372
Cresco Lines Inc 15220 S Halsted St *TF:* 800-323-4476 ■ *Web:* www.crescolines.com	Harvey	IL	60426	708-339-1186	339-1186
Crete Carrier Corp 400 NW 56th St PO Box 81228 **Fax:* Mktg ■ *TF Cust Svc:* 800-998-4095 ■ *Web:* www.cretecarrier.com	Lincoln	NE	68528	402-475-9521	479-2073*
Crook County School District 1 108 N Fourth St PO Box 830 *Web:* www.crook1.com	Sundance	WY	82729	307-283-2299	283-1810
Crossett Inc 201 S Carver St *TF General:* 800-876-2778 ■ *Web:* www.crossettinc.com	Warren	PA	16365	800-876-2778	
CRST International Inc 3930 16th Ave SW PO Box 68 **Fax Area Code:* 319 ■ **Fax:* Sales ■ *TF:* 800-736-2778 ■ *Web:* www.crst.com	Cedar Rapids	IA	52406	800-736-2778	390-2649*
Crysteel Truck Equipment Inc 55248 Ember Rd *TF General:* 800-722-0588 ■ *Web:* www.crysteeltruckequipment.com	Lake Crystal	MN	56055	507-726-6041	
CTI Inc 11105 Norrth Casa Grande Hwy *TF:* 800-362-4952 ■ *Web:* www.cti-az.com	Rillito	AZ	85654	520-624-2348	682-3509
CTL Distribution Inc 4201 Bonnie Mine Rd *TF:* 800-237-9088 ■ *Web:* www.ctltrans.com	Mulberry	FL	33860	863-428-2373	428-1731
Curtiss Arlin Trucking Inc 582 SW First St Ste 1	Montevideo	MN	56265	320-269-5581	269-9417
D M Bowman Inc 10226 Governor Ln Blvd Ste 4009 *TF:* 800-326-3274 ■ *Web:* www.dmbowman.com	Williamsport	MD	21795	301-582-2784	223-5968
D&D Sexton Inc PO Box 156 *TF:* 800-743-0265 ■ *Web:* www.ddsextoninc.com	Carthage	MO	64836	417-358-8727	358-5669
D. P. Curtis Trucking Inc 1450 South Hwy 118 **Fax Area Code:* 435 ■ *TF:* 800-257-9151 ■ *Web:* www.dpcurtis.com	Richfield	UT	84701	800-257-9151	896-6553*
Daggett Truck Line Inc 32717 County Rd 10 *TF:* 800-262-9393 ■ *Web:* daggetttruck.com	Frazee	MN	56544	218-334-3711	334-2566
Dahlsten Truck Line Inc 101 W Edgar PO Box 95 *TF:* 800-228-4313 ■ *Web:* www.dahlsten.com	Clay Center	NE	68933	402-762-3511	762-3592
Daily Express Inc 1072 Harrisburg Pk *TF:* 800-735-3136 ■ *Web:* www.dailyexp.com	Carlisle	PA	17013	717-243-5757	240-2103
Dakota Line Inc PO Box 476 *TF:* 800-532-5682 ■ *Web:* www.dakotalines.com	Vermillion	SD	57069	605-624-5228	624-5338
Dana Transport Inc 210 Essex Ave E *TF:* 800-733-3262 ■ *Web:* www.danacompanies.com	Avenel	NJ	07001	732-750-9100	636-7441
Davis Express Inc PO Box 1276 *TF:* 800-874-4270 ■ *Web:* www.davis-express.com	Starke	FL	32091	800-874-4270	
Daylight Transport 1501 Hughes Way Ste 200 *TF:* 800-468-9999 ■ *Web:* dylt.com	Long Beach	CA	90810	800-468-9999	
Deboer Transportation Inc PO Box 145 *Web:* www.deboertrans.com	Blenker	WI	54415	715-652-2911	
Decker Truck Line Inc 4000 Fifth Ave S *TF:* 800-247-2537 ■ *Web:* www.deckertruckline.com	Fort Dodge	IA	50501	515-576-4141	
Dejana Truck & Utility Equipment Company Inc 490 Pulaski Rd *TF:* 877-335-2621 ■ *Web:* www.dejana.com	Kings Park	NY	11754	631-544-9000	544-0942
Devine Intermodal 3870 Ch Dr *Web:* www.devineintermodal.com	West Sacramento	CA	95691	916-371-4430	371-0355
Diamond Transportation System Inc 5021 21st St *Web:* diamondtrans.net	Racine	WI	53406	262-554-5400	
Dick Lavy Trucking Inc 8848 State Rt 121 *TF:* 800-345-5289 ■ *Web:* www.dicklavytrucking.com	Bradford	OH	45308	937-448-2104	448-2312
Dilmar Oil Company Inc 1951 W Darlington St PO Box 5629 *TF:* 800-922-5823 ■ *Web:* www.dilmar.com	Florence	SC	29501	800-922-5823	
Dino's Trucking Inc 9615 Continental Indus Dr *TF:* 800-771-7805 ■ *Web:* www.dinoslogistics.com	Saint Louis	MO	63123	314-631-3001	638-3562
Dircks Moving Services Inc 4340 W Mohave St *TF:* 800-523-5038 ■ *Web:* www.dircks.com	Phoenix	AZ	85043	602-267-9401	267-8188
Don Hummer Trucking Corp 1486 Hwy 6 NW PO Box 310 *TF:* 866-248-6637 ■ *Web:* www.donhummertrucking.com	Oxford	IA	52322	319-828-2000	828-2105
Dts Cos Inc 1640 Monad Rd *TF:* 800-755-5855 ■ *Web:* www.dtsb.com	Billings	MT	59101	406-245-4695	245-5404
Dun Transportation & Stringing Inc 304 Reynolds Ln *Web:* www.duntrans.com	Sherman	TX	75092	903-891-9660	891-9660
Duncan & Son Lines Inc 23860 W US Hwy 85 *TF:* 800-528-4283 ■ *Web:* www.duncanandson.com	Buckeye	AZ	85326	623-386-4511	386-3656
Duncan Machinery Movers Inc 2004 Duncan Machinery Dr *Web:* www.dmmlex.com	Lexington	KY	40504	859-233-7333	233-7365
Eagle Express Lines Inc 925 W 175th St *Web:* www.eagleexpresslines.com	Homewood	IL	60473	708-333-8400	333-4747
Eagle Transport Corp 300 S Wesleyan Blvd Ste 202 *TF:* 800-776-9937 ■ *Web:* www.eagletransportcorp.com	Rocky Mount	NC	27804	252-937-2464	937-2198
Earl L Henderson Trucking Inc 206 W Main St *TF:* 800-447-8084 ■ *Web:* www.hendersontrucking.com	Salem	IL	62881	618-548-4667	548-6204
Epes Carriers Inc 3400 Edgefield Ct *TF:* 800-869-3737 ■ *Web:* www.epestransport.com	Greensboro	NC	27409	336-668-3358	668-7008
Equity Transportation Company Inc 3685 Dykstra Dr NW *Web:* equityinc.com	Grand Rapids	MI	49544	616-466-5647	
Erickson Transport Corp 2255 N Packer Rd	Springfield	MO	65803	417-862-6741	
Essex County Public Schools 109 Cross St PO Box 756 *Web:* www.essex.k12.va.us	Tappahannock	VA	22560	804-443-4366	443-4498
Estes Express Lines Inc 3901 W Broad St PO Box 25612 **Fax:* Sales ■ *Web:* www.estes-express.com	Richmond	VA	23230	804-353-1900	353-8001*
Evans Dedicated Systems Inc PO Box 9 *TF:* 800-427-6387 ■ *Web:* www.evansdedicated.com	Maywood	CA	90270	323-725-2928	726-0796
EW Wylie Corp 1520 Second Ave NW *TF Cust Svc:* 800-437-4132 ■ *Web:* www.wylietrucking.com	West Fargo	ND	58078	701-282-5550	281-0415
Falcon Express Inc 2250 E Church St *TF:* 800-544-6566 ■ *Web:* www.falconexp.com	Philadelphia	PA	19124	215-992-3140	992-3150
Fauquier County Public Schools 320 Hospital Dr Ste 40 *Web:* www.schoolcenter.fcps1.org	Warrenton	VA	20186	540-422-7017	
FedEx Freight East 942 S Shady Grove Rd *Web:* www.fedex.com	Memphis	TN	38120	901-818-7500	
Fenix Constructors Inc 215 Drew St SW *Web:* www.fenixci.com	Ardmore	OK	73401	580-223-4313	223-4315
FFE Transportation Inc 1145 Empire Central Pl *TF:* 800-569-9200 ■ *Web:* www.ffeinc.com	Dallas	TX	75247	214-630-8090	819-5625
First Class Services Inc 9355 US Hwy 60 E *TF General:* 800-467-8684 ■ *Web:* www.firstclassservices.com	Lewisport	KY	42351	270-295-3746	
Firstexpress Inc 1135 Freightliner Dr **Fax Area Code:* 615 ■ *TF:* 800-848-9203 ■ *Web:* firstexpress.com	Nashville	TN	37210	800-848-9203	244-1448*
Five Star Trucking Inc 4380 Glenbrook Rd *TF:* 800-321-3658 ■ *Web:* www.fivestartrucking.com	Willoughby	OH	44094	440-953-9300	
Fort Edward Express Company Inc 1402 Rt 9 *TF:* 800-342-1233 ■ *Web:* bulktransporter.com	Fort Edward	NY	12828	518-792-6571	
Forward Air Corp 430 Airport Rd PO Box 1058 *NASDAQ: FWRD* ■ *TF:* 800-726-6654 ■ *Web:* www.forwardair.com	Greeneville	TN	37744	423-636-7100	636-7221
Frank C. Alegre Trucking Inc PO Box 1508 *TF:* 800-769-2440 ■ *Web:* www.alegretrucking.com	Lodi	CA	95241	209-334-2112	367-0572
Fry-Wagner Moving & Storage Co 3700 Rider Trl S *TF:* 800-899-4035 ■ *Web:* www.fry-wagner.com	Earth City	MO	63045	314-291-4100	
Gabler Trucking Inc 5195 Technology Ave *Web:* www.hcgabler.com	Chambersburg	PA	17201	717-261-1492	709-0017
Godfrey Trucking Inc 6173 West 2100 South *TF:* 800-444-7669 ■ *Web:* www.godfreytrucking.com	West Valley City	UT	84128	801-972-0660	972-0709
Gordon Trucking Inc 151 Stewart Rd SW *TF:* 800-426-8486 ■ *Web:* www.gordontrucking.com	Pacific	WA	98047	253-863-7777	863-5328
Grammer Industries Inc 6320 E State St *TF:* 800-333-7410 ■ *Web:* www.grammerindustries.com	Columbus	IN	47201	812-579-5655	579-5643
Greatwide Logistics Services LLC 12404 Pk Central Dr Ste 300S *Web:* www.greatwide.com	Dallas	TX	75251	972-228-7300	
Green Transfer & Storage Co 10099 N Portland Rd *Web:* greentransfer.com	Portland	OR	97203	503-286-0673	
Groendyke Transport Inc 2510 Rock Island Blvd *TF:* 800-843-2103 ■ *Web:* www.groendyke.com	Enid	OK	73701	580-234-4663	234-1216
Gully Transportation Inc 3820 Wismann Ln *Web:* www.gullyicx.com	Quincy	IL	62305	217-224-0770	224-9885
Guy M Turner Inc 4514 S Holden Rd PO Box 7776 *TF:* 800-432-4859 ■ *Web:* www.guymturner.com	Greensboro	NC	27406	336-294-4660	294-6668
H & M International Transportation Inc 485B Rt 1 S *TF:* 800-446-4685 ■ *Web:* www.hmit.net	Iselin	NJ	08830	732-510-4640	510-4697
H & W Trucking Company Inc 1772 N Andy Griffith Pkwy PO Box 1545 *TF:* 800-334-9181 ■ *Web:* www.hwtrucking.com	Mount Airy	NC	27030	336-789-2188	789-7973
H O Wolding Inc PO Box 217 *TF:* 800-950-0054 ■ *Web:* www.howolding.com	Amherst	WI	54406	715-824-5513	824-5018
Hallamore Motor Transportation Inc 795 Plymouth St **Fax Area Code:* 920 ■ *Web:* www.hallamore.com	Holbrook	MA	02343	781-767-2000	683-6277*
Harbor Express Inc 501 Quay Ave *Web:* harbor-express.com	Wilmington	CA	90744	310-513-6478	835-3794

Company	City	State	Zip	Phone	Fax
Harrisonburg City Public Schools (HCPS) 317 S Main St *Web:* www.harrisonburg.k12.va.us	Harrisonburg	VA	22801	540-434-9916	434-5196
Hazen Transport Inc 27050 Wick Rd **Fax Area Code:* 734 ■ *TF:* 800-251-2120 ■ *Web:* www.hazentransport.com	Taylor	MI	48180	313-292-2120	946-4452*
Heartland Express Inc 901 N Kansas Ave *NASDAQ: HTLD* ■ **Fax Area Code:* 319 ■ *TF:* 800-654-1175 ■ *Web:* www.heartlandexpress.com	North Liberty	IA	52317	800-654-1175	626-3311*
High Country Transportation Inc PO Box 700 *TF:* 800-635-7687 ■ *Web:* www.highcountrytrans.com	Cortez	CO	81321	800-635-7687	
Highway Transport Logistics Inc (HTL) 6420 Baum Dr *Web:* www.hytt.com	Knoxville	TN	37919	865-584-8631	
Hirschbach Motor Lines Inc 18355 US Hwy 20 **Fax Area Code:* 800 ■ *TF:* 800-554-2969 ■ *Web:* www.hirschbach.com	East Dubuque	IL	61025	402-494-5000	772-2500*
Holman Transportation Services Inc 1010 Holman Ct *TF:* 800-375-2416 ■ *Web:* holmantransport.com	Caldwell	ID	83605	208-454-0779	454-2226
Hot-Line Freight System Inc PO Box 205 *TF:* 800-468-4686 ■ *Web:* www.hotlinefreight.com	West Salem	WI	54669	608-486-1600	486-1601
Houff Transfer Inc 46 Houff Rd *TF:* 800-476-4683 ■ *Web:* www.houff.com	Weyers Cave	VA	24486	540-234-9233	234-9011
Howard F Baer Inc 1301 Foster Ave *TF:* 800-447-7430 ■ *Web:* hbitransport.com	Nashville	TN	37210	615-255-7351	726-1529
Howard Sheppard Inc PO Box 797 *TF:* 800-846-1726 ■ *Web:* www.howardsheppard.com	Sandersville	GA	31082	478-552-5127	552-6973
Howell's Motor Freight Inc PO Box 12308 *TF:* 800-444-0585 ■ *Web:* www.howellsmotor.com	Roanoke	VA	24024	540-966-3200	966-3202
Hribar Trucking Inc 1521 Waukesha Rd *Web:* hribarlogistics.com	Caledonia	WI	53108	262-835-4401	
HVH Transportation Inc 181 E 56th Ave Ste 200 *TF:* 800-525-4844 ■ *Web:* www.hvhtransportation.com	Denver	CO	80216	303-292-3656	292-9713
Indian River Transport Co 2580 Executive Rd *TF:* 800-877-2430 ■ *Web:* www.indianrivertransport.com	Winter Haven	FL	33884	863-324-2430	326-9702
Interstate Distributor Co 11707 21st Ave S **Fax Area Code:* 253 ■ *TF:* 800-426-8560 ■ *Web:* www.intd.com	Tacoma	WA	98444	800-426-8560	538-4430*
Irvin Dick Inc 475 Wilson Ave	Shelby	MT	59474	406-434-5862	
J & J Motor Service Inc 2338 S Indiana Ave *Web:* jjexhibitors.com	Chicago	IL	60616	312-225-3323	225-9873
J A T of Fort Wayne Inc 5031 Industrial Rd *Web:* www.jatoffortwayne.com	Fort Wayne	IN	46825	260-482-8447	482-9990
J P Noonan Transportation Inc 415 W St *TF:* 800-922-8026 ■ *Web:* www.jpnoonan.com	West Bridgewater	MA	02379	508-583-2880	587-0317
J R C Transportation Inc 47 Maple Ave PO Box 366 *Web:* www.jrctransportation.com	Thomaston	CT	06787	860-283-0207	
J-Mar Enterprises Inc PO Box 4143 *TF:* 800-446-8283 ■ *Web:* www.j-mar-enterprises.com	Bismarck	ND	58502	701-222-4518	255-7587
Jack B Kelley Inc 801 S Fillmore St Ste 505 *TF:* 800-225-5525 ■ *Web:* www.jackbkelley.com	Amarillo	TX	79101	806-353-3553	356-9327
Jack Cooper Transport Co Inc 1100 Walnut St Ste 2400 *Web:* www.jackcooper.com	Kansas City	MO	64106	816-983-4000	983-5000
Jack Gray Transport Inc 4600 E 15th Ave	Gary	IN	46403	219-938-7020	938-0127
Jaro Transportation Services Inc 975 Post Rd *TF:* 800-451-3447 ■ *Web:* www.jarotrans.com	Warren	OH	44483	330-393-5659	393-5906
Jerry Lipps Inc 3888 Nash Rd *TF:* 800-325-3331 ■ *Web:* www.jerrylippsinc.com	Cape Girardeau	MO	63702	573-335-8204	335-4483
Jet Star Inc 10825 Andrade Dr *TF:* 800-969-4222 ■ *Web:* www.jetstarinc.com	Zionsville	IN	46077	317-873-4222	873-4361
JH Walker Trucking Company Inc 152 N Hollywood Rd *TF:* 800-535-5992 ■ *Web:* www.jhwalkertrucking.com	Houma	LA	70364	985-868-8330	873-5210
Jim Palmer Trucking Inc 9730 Derby Dr *TF:* 888-698-3422 ■ *Web:* www.jimpalmertrucking.com	Missoula	MT	59801	406-721-5151	829-6271
JNJ Express Inc 3935 Old Getwell Rd PO Box 30983 *TF:* 888-383-7157 ■ *Web:* www.jnjexpress.com	Memphis	TN	38130	901-362-3444	362-2331
Johnson Carlier Inc 738 S 52nd St **Fax Area Code:* 480 ■ *Web:* www.johnsoncarlier.com	Tempe	AZ	85281	602-275-2222	921-9255*
Jones Motor Company Inc 900 W Bridge St PO Box 137 *TF:* 800-825-6637 ■ *Web:* www.jonesmotor.com	Spring City	PA	19475	610-948-7900	948-5660
KAG West 4076 Seaport Blvd *TF:* 800-547-1587 ■ *Web:* www.thekag.com	West Sacramento	CA	95691	916-371-8241	372-1760
Kahului Trucking & Storage Inc 140 Hobron Ave *Web:* kahuluitrucking.com	Kahului	HI	96732	808-877-5001	877-0572
Kaplan Trucking Co 6600 Bessemer Ave *Web:* www.kaplantrucking.com	Cleveland	OH	44127	216-341-3322	341-3348
Kauai Commercial Company Inc 1811 Leleiona St	Lihue	HI	96766	808-245-1985	245-2079
Keim T S Inc 1249 N Ninth St PO Box 226 *TF:* 800-255-2450 ■ *Web:* keimts.com	Sabetha	KS	66534	800-255-2450	
Keith Titus Corp PO Box 920 *TF:* 800-233-2126 ■ *Web:* www.pagetrucking.com	Weedsport	NY	13166	315-834-6681	834-9687
Kenan Advantage Group Inc (KAG) 4366 Mt Pleasant St NW *TF:* 800-969-5419 ■ *Web:* www.thekag.com	North Canton	OH	44720	330-491-0474	409-2786
Kenan Transport Co 100 Europa Ctr Ste 320 *TF:* 866-821-3444 ■ *Web:* thekag.com	Chapel Hill	NC	27517	919-967-8221	929-5295
Kenworth Sales Co 2125 Constitution Blvd *TF General:* 800-222-7831 ■ *Web:* www.kenworthsalesco.com	West Valley City	UT	84119	801-487-4161	467-3820
Key Energy 2210 W Broadway *Web:* www.keyenergy.com	Sweetwater	TX	79556	325-236-6611	
Kildeer Countryside Community Consolidated School District 96 1050 Ivy Hall Ln *Web:* www.kcsd96.org	Buffalo Grove	IL	60089	847-459-4260	459-2344
KLLM Inc 135 Riverview Dr *TF:* 800-925-5556 ■ *Web:* www.kllm.com	Richland	MS	39218	800-925-1000	
Knight Transportation Inc 5601 W Buckeye Rd *NYSE: KNX* ■ *TF:* 800-489-2000 ■ *Web:* www.knighttrans.com	Phoenix	AZ	85043	602-269-2000	269-8409
Kruepke Trucking Inc 2881 Hwy P *TF Cust Svc:* 800-798-5000 ■ *Web:* kruepketrucking.com	Jackson	WI	53037	262-677-3155	677-3206
Kuntzman Trucking Inc 13515 Oyster Rd *TF:* 800-362-9779 ■ *Web:* www.kmantrucking.com	Alliance	OH	44601	330-821-9160	821-9163
La Rosa Del Monte Express Inc 1133-35 Tiffany St *TF:* 800-452-7672 ■ *Web:* www.larosadelmonte.com	Bronx	NY	10459	718-991-3300	893-1948
Landair Corp 1110 Myers St *TF:* 888-526-3247 ■ *Web:* www.landair.com	Greeneville	TN	37743	888-526-3247	
Landmark Construction Group Inc 300 NW 61st St Ste 100 *Web:* landmarkokc.com	Oklahoma City	OK	73118	405-843-8041	
Landmark International Trucks Inc 4550 Rutledge Pk *TF:* 800-968-9999 ■ *Web:* www.landmarktrucks.com	Knoxville	TN	37914	865-637-4881	
Landstar Express America Inc 13410 Sutton Pk Dr S **Fax:* Hum Res ■ *TF:* 800-872-9400 ■ *Web:* www.Landstar.com	Jacksonville	FL	32224	904-398-9400	398-9400*
Landstar Inway Inc 13410 Sutton Pk Dr S *TF:* 800-435-7352 ■ *Web:* landstar.com	Jacksonville	FL	61102	800-872-9400	
Lanter Delivery Systems Inc 1 Caine Dr *Web:* www.lanterdeliverysystems.com	Madison	IL	62060	618-452-5300	452-5931
Lawrence Companies (LTS) 872 Lee Hwy PO Box 7667 *TF:* 800-336-9626 ■ *Web:* www.lawrencecompanies.com	Roanoke	VA	24019	540-966-4000	966-4555
LCT Transportation Services 26444 County Rd 33 *Web:* citysearch.com/guide/orlando-fl-metro	Okahumpka	FL	34762	352-326-8900	
Liberty Moving & Storage Inc 350 Moreland Rd *Web:* www.libertymoving.com	Commack	NY	11725	631-234-3000	234-3639
Lightning Transportation Inc 16820 Blake Rd *TF:* 800-233-0624 ■ *Web:* www.lightningtrans.com	Hagerstown	MD	21740	301-582-5700	582-5898
Linden Bulk Transportation Company Inc 4200 Tremley Pt Rd *Web:* www.lindenbulk.com	Linden	NJ	07036	908-862-3883	
Linden Warehouse & Distribution Co Inc 1300 Lower Rd *TF:* 800-333-2855 ■ *Web:* www.lindencompanies.com	Linden	NJ	07036	908-862-1400	862-7539
Liquid Transport Corp 8470 Allison Pt Blvd Ste 400 *TF:* 800-942-3175 ■ *Web:* www.liquidtransport.com	Indianapolis	IN	46250	317-841-4200	841-8259
Lisa Motor Lines 1145 Empire Central Pl PO Box 655888 *TF:* 800-569-9200 ■ *Web:* www.ffeinc.com	Dallas	TX	75247	214-630-8090	
LL Smith Trucking Inc 711 Rail Rd	Riverton	WY	82501	307-856-2491	
Lockwood Bros Inc 220 Salters Creek Rd *Web:* www.lockwoodbrothers.com	Hampton	VA	23661	757-722-1946	
Lynden Transport Inc 3027 Rampart Dr **Fax Area Code:* 907 ■ *TF:* 800-327-9390 ■ *Web:* www.lynden.com	Anchorage	AK	99501	800-327-9390	257-5155*
Mail Contractors of America 3809 Roundtop Dr N	Little Rock	AR	72117	501-280-0500	280-0111
Market Transport Ltd 110 N Marine Dr *TF:* 800-547-0781 ■ *Web:* markettransport.com	Portland	OR	97217	503-283-2405	289-3567
Marten Transport Ltd 129 Marten St *NASDAQ: MRTN* ■ *TF:* 800-395-3000 ■ *Web:* www.marten.com	Mondovi	WI	54755	715-926-4216	926-5609
Martin Enterprises Inc 4315 Meyer Rd *Web:* truckdriver.com	Fort Wayne	IN	46806	260-447-5591	447-4026
Martin Trucking Inc 1015 W City Limits St	Hugoton	KS	67951	620-544-4920	544-4990
Mason City School District 211 NE St *Web:* www.masonohioschools.com	Mason	OH	45040	513-398-0474	
Matheson Trucking Inc 9785 Goethe Rd **Fax Area Code:* 919 ■ *TF:* 800-455-7678 ■ *Web:* www.mathesoninc.com	Sacramento	CA	95827	916-685-2330	685-8875*
Maverick USA Inc 13301 Valentine Rd *TF:* 800-289-6600 ■ *Web:* www.maverickusa.com	North Little Rock	AR	72117	501-955-1255	955-4670
Mawson & Mawson Inc 1800 Old Lincoln Hwy PO Box 248 *TF:* 800-262-9766 ■ *Web:* www.mawsonandmawson.com	Langhorne	PA	19047	215-750-1100	750-0396
May Trucking Co 4185 Brooklake Rd PO Box 9039 **Fax Area Code:* 503 ■ *TF:* 800-547-9169 ■ *Web:* www.maytrucking.com	Salem	OR	97305	800-547-9169	390-8836*
Mayfield Transfer Company Inc 3200 W Lake St *TF:* 800-222-2959 ■ *Web:* www.mfld.net	Melrose Park	IL	60160	708-681-4440	681-4483
McC Construction Corp 5990 Greenwood Plaza Blvd Ste 205	Greenwood	CO	80111	303-741-0404	741-0505
McKenzie Tank Lines Inc 1966 Commonwealth Ln *TF:* 800-828-6495 ■ *Web:* www.mckenzietank.com	Tallahassee	FL	32303	850-576-1221	574-2351
MCT Transportation LLC 1600 E Benson Rd *TF Cust Svc:* 800-843-9904 ■ *Web:* mcttrans.com	Sioux Falls	SD	57104	605-339-8400	339-8407
Melloul-Blamey Construction Ltd 55 Commerce Ctr *Web:* www.melloul.com	Greenville	SC	29615	864-627-0302	627-0804
Melton Truck Lines Inc 808 N 161 E Ave *Web:* www.meltontruck.com	Tulsa	OK	74116	918-234-8000	270-9401
Mercer County State Bancorp Inc 3279 S Main St *Web:* www.mcsbank.com	Sandy Lake	PA	16145	724-376-7015	
Mercer Transportation Co 1128 W Main St PO Box 35610 *TF:* 800-626-5375 ■ *Web:* www.mercer-trans.com	Louisville	KY	40232	502-584-2301	
Mergenthaler Transfer & Storage 1414 N Montana Ave *TF General:* 800-826-5463 ■ *Web:* www.mergenthaler.net	Helena	MT	59601	406-442-9470	442-4340
Mid Seven Transportation Co 2323 Delaware Ave *Web:* www.mid7.com	Des Moines	IA	50317	515-266-5181	266-1457
Middlesboro Independent School District 220 N 20th St PO Box 959 *Web:* mboro.k12.ky.us	Middlesboro	KY	40965	606-242-8800	242-8805
Midwest Motor Express Inc 5015 E Main Ave *TF:* 800-741-4097 ■ *Web:* www.mmeinc.com	Bismarck	ND	58502	701-223-1880	224-1405

Phone Fax

Milan Express Company Inc 1091 Kefauver Dr. Milan TN 38358 731-686-7428
TF: 800-231-7303 ■ *Web:* www.milanexpress.com

Miller Transporters Inc 5500 Hwy 80 W. Jackson MS 39209 601-922-8331 923-2535
TF Cust Svc: 800-645-5378 ■ *Web:* www.millert.com

Milton Transportation Inc
5505 State Rt 405 PO Box 355 Milton PA 17847 570-742-8774
Web: www.miltontrans.com

Minuteman Trucks Inc 2181 Providence Hwy. Walpole MA 02081 508-668-3112
TF: 800-231-8458 ■ *Web:* www.minutemantrucks.com

Morris School District 54 54 White Oak Dr. Morris IL 60450 815-942-0056 942-0240
Web: www.morris54.org

Morristown Drivers Service Inc
PO Box 2158 Morristown TN 37816 423-581-6048 581-9696
Web: www.mdstrucking.com

Murrows Transfer Inc PO Box 4095 High Point NC 27263 336-475-6101 475-1240
TF Cust Svc: 800-669-2928 ■ *Web:* www.murrows.com

National Carriers Inc 1501 E Eigth St Liberal KS 67901 620-624-1621
TF: 800-835-9180 ■ *Web:* www.nationalcarriers.com

National Highway Express Co
971 Old Henderson St PO Box 20262 Columbus OH 43220 614-459-4900
TF: 800-837-5700

Nationwide Truck Brokers Inc (NTB)
4203 Roger B Chaffee Memorial Blvd SE
Ste 2 Grand Rapids MI 49548 616-878-5554 878-5569
TF: 800-446-0682 ■ *Web:* www.ntbtrk.com

Navajo Express Inc 1400 W 64 Ave Denver CO 80221 303-287-3800 286-9661*
*Fax: Sales ■ *TF:* 800-525-1969 ■ *Web:* www.navajo.com

NE Finch Co 1925 S Darst St Peoria IL 61607 309-671-1433 671-1449
Web: nefinch.com

New England Motor Freight Inc 1-71 N Ave E. Elizabeth NJ 07201 908-965-0100 965-0795

New Penn Motor Express Inc 625 S Fifth Ave Lebanon PA 17042 717-274-2521 274-5593
TF Cust Svc: 800-285-5000 ■ *Web:* www.newpenn.com

Newark School District 100 E Miller St 4th Fl. Newark NY 14513 315-332-3230 332-3517
TF: 877-789-2613 ■ *Web:* www.newarkcsd.org

Newton Independent School District
720 Rusk St Newton TX 75966 409-379-8137 379-2189
Web: www.newtonisd.net

Nick Strimbu Inc 3500 PkwyRd Brookfield OH 44403 330-448-4046 448-4106
TF: 800-446-8785 ■ *Web:* www.nickstrimbu.com

North Park Transportation Co
5150 Columbine St. Denver CO 80216 303-295-0300 295-6244
Web: www.nopk.com

North Shore Central Illinois Freight Co
5101 S Lawndale Ave Summit IL 60501 708-496-8222 496-8449
Web: www.northshorelogistics.net

Northland Trucking Inc 1515 S 22nd Ave Phoenix AZ 85009 602-254-0007 254-0455
TF: 800-214-5564 ■ *Web:* www.northlandtrucking.com

Nussbaum Trucking Inc 19336 N 1425 East Rd Normal IL 61748 309-452-4426 452-4431
TF: 800-322-7305 ■ *Web:* www.nussbaum.com

O & S Trucking Inc 3769 E Evergreen St Springfield MO 65803 417-864-4780
TF: 855-861-9571 ■ *Web:* www.oandstrucking.com

Old Dominion Freight Line Inc
500 Old Dominion Way Thomasville NC 27360 336-889-5000
NASDAQ: ODFL ■ *TF:* 800-432-6335 ■ *Web:* www.odfl.com

Oliver Construction Co 1770 Executive Dr Oconomowoc WI 53066 262-567-6677
Web: www.oliverconstruction.com

Oliver Trucking Corp 1101 Harding Ct. Indianapolis IN 46217 317-787-1101 787-1102
TF: 888-561-4449 ■ *Web:* www.oltg.com

Online Transport System Inc
6311 W Stoner Dr. Greenfield IN 46140 317-894-2159 894-2160
TF: 866-543-1235 ■ *Web:* www.onlinetransport.com

Orcutt Union School District 500 Dyer St Orcutt CA 93455 805-938-8900 938-8919
Web: www.orcutt-schools.net

Ormsby Trucking Inc
888 W Railroad St PO Box 67 Uniondale IN 46791 260-543-2233 543-2842
Web: www.ormtrk.com

Osborn Transportation Inc
1245 West Grand Ave Rainbow City AL 35906 256-442-2514
TF: 866-215-3659 ■ *Web:* www.osborntransportation.com

Otto Trucking Inc 4220 E McDowell Ste 108 Mesa AZ 85215 480-641-3500 641-3550
Web: www.ottotrucking.com

Overland Express Co
5539 Harvey Wilson PO Box 262322 Houston TX 77207 713-672-6161 672-5040
TF: 800-929-7402 ■ *Web:* www.overlandexp.com

Ozark Motor Lines Inc 3934 Homewood Rd Memphis TN 38118 901-251-9711 375-8661
TF: 800-264-4100 ■ *Web:* www.ozark.com

P J Hoerr Inc 107 Commerce Pl. Peoria IL 61604 309-688-9567 688-9556
Web: www.pjhoerr.com

Palmetto State Transportation Company Inc
1050 Pk W Blvd Greenville SC 29611 864-672-3800
TF: 800-269-0175 ■ *Web:* www.palmettostatetrans.com

PAM Transportation Services Inc
297 W Henri De Tonti Blvd Tontitown AR 72770 479-361-9111 361-5338
NASDAQ: PTSI ■ *TF:* 800-879-7261 ■ *Web:* www.pamtransport.com

Paper Transport Inc 2701 Executive Dr. Green Bay WI 54304 800-317-3650 497-6230*
*Fax Area Code: 920 ■ *TF:* 800-317-3650 ■ *Web:* www.papertransport.com

Patriot Transportation Holding Inc
501 Riverside Ave Ste 500 Jacksonville FL 32202 904-396-5733
NASDAQ: PATI ■ *TF:* 877-704-1776 ■ *Web:* www.patriottrans.com

Peet Frate Line Inc
650 S Eastwood Dr PO Box 1129 Woodstock IL 60098 815-338-5500 338-1052
TF: 800-435-6909 ■ *Web:* www.peetfrateline.com

Penn's Best Inc PO Box 128. Meshoppen PA 18630 800-852-3243
TF: 800-852-3243 ■ *Web:* www.pennsbest.net

Peoples Bancshares-Pnt Coupee
805 Hospital Rd PO Box 747 New Roads LA 70760 225-638-3713
Web: www.thefriendlybank.com

Phoenix Transportation Services LLC
335 E Yusen Dr. Georgetown KY 40324 502-863-0108 863-0029
TF: 800-860-0889 ■ *Web:* www.phoenix-transportation.net

Pitt Ohio Express 15 27th St. Pittsburgh PA 15222 412-232-3015 232-0944
TF Cust Svc: 800-366-7488 ■ *Web:* works.pittohio.com

Phone Fax

Pleasant Trucking Inc
2250 Industrial Dr PO Box 778 Connellsville PA 15425 800-245-2402 628-5868*
*Fax Area Code: 724 ■ *TF:* 800-245-2402 ■ *Web:* www.pleasanttrucking.com

Pozas Bros Trucking Company Inc
8130 Enterprise Dr Newark CA 94560 510-742-9939 742-9979
TF: 800-874-8383 ■ *Web:* pozasbros.com

Predator Trucking Co 3181 Trumbull Ave McDonald OH 44437 888-773-3875
TF: 888-773-3875 ■ *Web:* www.predatortrucking.com

Prestera Trucking 19129 US Rt 52 South Point OH 45680 740-894-4770
TF: 855-761-7943 ■ *Web:* www.prestera.com

Pride Transport Inc 5499 W 2455 S Salt Lake City UT 84120 801-972-8890 972-1450
TF: 800-877-1320 ■ *Web:* pridetransport.com

Prime Inc PO Box 4208 Springfield MO 65808 417-866-0001
TF Cust Svc: 800-848-4560 ■ *Web:* w3.primeinc.com

Pritchett Trucking Inc
1050 SE Sixth St PO Box 311 Lake Butler FL 32054 386-496-2630 496-2883
TF: 800-486-7504 ■ *Web:* www.pritchetttrucking.com

Q Carriers Inc 1415 Maras St Shakopee MN 55379 952-445-8718 445-8794
Web: www.qcarriers.com

Quality Distribution Inc
4041 Pk Oaks Blvd Ste 200 Tampa FL 33610 800-282-2031
NASDAQ: QLTY ■ *TF:* 800-282-2031 ■ *Web:* www.qualitydistribution.com

Queensboro Co 113 E Broad St PO Box 467 Louisville GA 30434 478-625-2000 625-2008
TF: 800-236-2442 ■ *Web:* www.qnbtrust.com

R & R Trucking Inc 302 Thunder Rd PO Box 545 Duenweg MO 64841 417-623-6885 623-6479
TF: 800-625-6885 ■ *Web:* www.randrtruck.com

Ralph Moyle Inc (RMI) 55475 N Main St. Mattawan MI 49071 269-668-4531

Raven Transport Company Inc
6800 Broadway Ave Jacksonville FL 32254 904-880-1515 880-1913
Web: www.idriveraven.com

Rbx Inc PO Box 2118 Springfield MO 65802 800-245-5507
TF: 877-450-2200 ■ *Web:* www.rbxinc.com

Redwood Coast Trucking 2210 Peninsula Dr Arcata CA 95521 707-443-0857

Refrigerated Food Express Inc 57 Littlefield St. Avon MA 02322 508-587-4600 588-9655
TF: 800-342-8822 ■ *Web:* www.rfxinc.com

Relco Systems Inc 7310 Chestnut Ridge Rd Lockport NY 14094 716-434-8100 434-7229
TF: 800-262-1020 ■ *Web:* www.relcosystems.com

Riechmann Transport Inc
3328 W Chain of Rocks Rd. Granite City IL 62040 618-797-6700
TF: 800-844-4225 ■ *Web:* www.riechmanntransport.com

River City Petroleum Inc
840 Delta Ln West Sacramento CA 95691 916-371-4960
Web: rcpfuel.com

River Forest Public Schools 90
7776 Lake St. River Forest IL 60305 708-771-8282 771-8291
Web: www.district90.org

Roadtex Transportation Corp 13 Jensen Dr. Somerset NJ 08873 800-762-3839
TF: 800-762-3839 ■ *Web:* www.roadtex.com

Robert Bearden Inc
2601 Industrial Pk Dr PO Box 870 Cairo GA 39828 229-377-6928
TF: 888-298-6928 ■ *Web:* www.rbitrucking.com

Robert Heath Trucking Inc 1201 E 40th St. Lubbock TX 79404 806-747-1651 747-0339
Web: www.robertheath.com

Roehl Transport Inc
1916 E 29th St PO Box 750 Marshfield WI 54449 715-591-3795 387-1942
TF: 800-826-8367 ■ *Web:* www.roehl.jobs/corp

Roger Ward Inc 17275 Green Mtn Rd San Antonio TX 78247 210-655-8623 653-0919
TF General: 888-909-3147 ■ *Web:* www.wardnorthamerican.com

Ross Neely Systems Inc 1500 Second St Birmingham AL 35214 205-798-1137
Web: www.rossneely.com

Rountree Transport & Rigging Inc
2640 N Ln Ave Jacksonville FL 32254 904-781-1033 786-6229
TF: 800-342-5036 ■ *Web:* rountreetransport.com

Roy Bros Inc 764 Boston Rd Billerica MA 01821 978-667-1921 667-5091
TF Cust Svc: 800-225-0830 ■ *Web:* www.roybrosinc.com

Royal Trucking Co
1323 Eshman Ave N PO Box 387 West Point MS 39773 662-494-1637 495-1066
TF: 800-321-1293 ■ *Web:* www.royaltruck.com

RWH Trucking Inc 2970 Old Oakwood Rd Oakwood GA 30566 800-256-8119
TF: 800-256-8119 ■ *Web:* www.rwhtrucking.com

S & S Transport Inc PO Box 12579 Grand Forks ND 58208 800-726-8022 746-5665*
*Fax Area Code: 701 ■ *TF:* 800-726-8022 ■ *Web:* www.sstransport.com

S T Bunn Construction
1904 University Blvd PO Box 20109 Tuscaloosa AL 35401 205-752-8195 349-4288
TF: 800-297-6302 ■ *Web:* www.stbunn.com

S-j Transportation Co Inc PO Box 169 Woodstown NJ 08098 856-769-2741 769-9811
TF: 800-524-2552 ■ *Web:* www.sjtransportation.com

Salida Union School District 4801 Sisk Rd Salida CA 95368 209-545-0339 545-2270
Web: stancoe.org/scoe/districts/salida

Sammons Trucking 3665 W Broadway Missoula MT 59808 406-728-2600 549-4989
TF: 800-548-9276 ■ *Web:* www.sammonstrucking.com

Schilli Transportation Services Inc
6358 W US Hwy 24 Remington IN 47977 219-261-2100
Web: www.schilli.com

Security Van Lines LLC 100 W Airline Dr Kenner LA 70062 800-794-5961
TF: 800-218-6915 ■ *Web:* securitymayflower.com

Selland Auto Transport Inc 615 S 96th St Seattle WA 98108 206-767-5960 767-0604
Web: www.sellandauto.com

Seward Motor Freight Inc PO Box 126. Seward NE 68434 402-643-4503 643-3199
TF: 800-786-4468 ■ *Web:* www.sewardmotor.com

Shaffer Trucking Inc
49 E Main St PO Box 418 New Kingstown PA 17072 402-475-9521 795-5550*
*Fax Area Code: 717 ■ *TF Cust Svc:* 800-742-3337 ■
Web: cretecarrier.com/services-solutions/shaffer-refrigeration

Sheedy Drayage Company Inc
1215 Michigan St. San Francisco CA 94107 415-648-7171 648-1535
Web: sheedydrayage.com

Shelba D. Johnson Trucking Inc
PO Box 7287 High Point NC 27264 336-476-2000 476-0187
Web: www.sdjtrucking.com

Sherman Bros Trucking
32921 Diamond Hill Dr PO Box 706 Harrisburg OR 97446 541-995-7751 995-7742
TF: 800-547-8980 ■ *Web:* www.shermantrucking.com

Phone | Fax

Shetler Moving & Storage Inc
1253 E Diamond Ave .... Evansville IN 47711 812-421-7750 421-7759
TF: 800-321-5069 ■ *Web:* www.shetlermoving.com

Shippers Express Co 1651 Kerr Dr .... Jackson MS 39204 601-948-4251 948-5232
TF: 800-647-2480 ■ *Web:* shippersexpressinc.com

Short Freight Lines Inc
459 S River Rd PO Box 357 .... Bay City MI 48707 989-893-3505 893-3151
TF: 800-248-0625 ■ *Web:* www.shortfreightlines.com

Shuster's Transportation Inc 750 E Valley St .... Willits CA 95490 707-459-4131 459-1855

Simons Trucking Inc 920 Simon Dr PO Box 8 .... Farley IA 52046 563-744-3304 744-3726
TF: 800-373-2580 ■ *Web:* www.simonstrucking.com

Skinner Transfer Corp PO Box 438 .... Reedsburg WI 53959 608-524-2326 524-9660
TF: 800-356-9350 ■ *Web:* www.skinnertransfer.com

South Shore Transportation Inc
4010 Columbus Ave .... Sandusky OH 44870 419-626-6267 626-9640
TF: 888-428-0879 ■ *Web:* www.sshoretrans.com

Southeastern Freight Lines Inc
420 Davega Rd .... Lexington SC 29073 803-794-7300 939-3462*
**Fax:* Cust Svc ■ *TF:* 800-637-7335 ■ *Web:* www.sefl.com

Southern Pan Services Co (SPS)
2385 Lithonia Industrial Blvd .... Lithonia GA 30058 678-301-2400 301-2439
Web: www.southernpan.com

Southwest Freightlines 11991 Transpark Dr. .... El Paso TX 79927 915-860-8592 860-9606
TF General: 800-776-5799 ■ *Web:* www.swflines.com

Southwestern Motor Transport Inc
4600 Goldfield .... San Antonio TX 78218 210-661-6791 662-3295
Web: www.smtlines.com

Spectraserv Inc 75 Jacobus Ave. .... South Kearny NJ 07032 973-589-0277 589-0415
Web: www.spectraserv.com

Stahly Cartage Co 119 S Main St .... Edwardsville IL 62025 618-656-5070 656-0293

Star Fleet Inc 915 South Main St .... Middlebury IN 46540 888-281-8727
TF: 877-805-9547 ■ *Web:* www.starfleettrucking.com

Star Transportation Inc PO Box 100925 .... Nashville TN 37224 615-256-4336 255-9013*
**Fax:* Cust Svc ■ *TF Cust Svc:* 800-333-3060 ■ *Web:* www.startransportation.com

Steelman Transportation 2160 N Burton .... Springfield MO 65803 417-831-6300
TF: 800-488-6287 ■ *Web:* www.steelmantransport.com

Stevens Transport PO Box 279010 .... Dallas TX 75227 866-551-0337 647-3940*
**Fax Area Code:* 214 ■ *TF:* 800-233-9369 ■ *Web:* www.stevenstransport.com

Styer Transportation Co 7870 215th St W .... Lakeville MN 55044 952-469-4491 469-3422
TF: 800-548-9149 ■ *Web:* www.styertrans.com

Summitt Trucking LLC 1800 Progress Way .... Clarksville IN 47129 812-285-7777 285-8949
TF: 866-999-7799 ■ *Web:* www.summitttrucking.com

Sunco Carriers Inc 1025 N Chestnut Rd. .... Lakeland FL 33805 863-688-1948 680-1759
TF: 800-237-8288 ■ *Web:* www.suncocarriers.com

Superior Carriers Inc
711 Jory Blvd Ste 101-N .... Oak Brook IL 60523 630-573-2555 573-2570
TF: 800-654-7707 ■ *Web:* www.superior-carriers.com

Sweetwater County School District 1 (SCSD)
3550 Foothill Blvd PO Box 1089 .... Rock Springs WY 82901 307-352-3400 352-3411
TF: 888-503-7562 ■ *Web:* www.sweetwater1.org

Swift Transportation Company Inc
2200 S 75th Ave .... Phoenix AZ 85043 602-269-9700
NYSE: SWFT ■ *TF:* 800-800-2200 ■ *Web:* www.swifttrans.com

Swing Transport Inc 1405 N Salisbury Ave .... Salisbury NC 28144 704-633-3567
Web: www.swingtransport.com

T & T Trucking Inc 11396 N Hwy 99 .... Lodi CA 95240 209-931-6000 931-6156
TF Cust Svc: 800-692-3457 ■ *Web:* www.tttrucking.com

T-w Transport Inc 7405 S Hayford Rd .... Cheney WA 99004 509-623-4004
TF: 800-356-4070 ■ *Web:* www.twtrans.com

TanTara Transportation Corp
2420 Stewart Rd .... Muscatine IA 52761 563-262-8621 264-8998
TF: 800-650-0292 ■ *Web:* www.tantara.us

Taylor Made Transportation Services Inc
2901 Druid Pk Dr Ste 206 .... Baltimore MD 21215 410-728-1951
Web: www.tmtransportation.com

Taylor Truck Line Inc
31485 Northfield Blvd .... Northfield MN 55057 507-645-4531
TF: 800-962-5994 ■ *Web:* www.taylortruckline.com

Teal's Express Inc
22411 Teal Dr PO Box 6010 .... Watertown NY 13601 315-788-6437 788-5060
TF: 800-836-0369 ■ *Web:* www.teals.com

Telfer Oil Co 211 Foster St .... Martinez CA 94553 925-228-1515 229-3955
Web: telfercompanies.com

Tennessee Steel Haulers Inc PO Box 78189 .... Nashville TN 37207 615-271-2400
TF: 800-776-4004 ■ *Web:* www.tenh.com

Teresi Trucking Inc 900 1/2 Victor Rd. .... Lodi CA 95240 209-368-2472 369-2830
Web: www.teresitrucking.com

Texas Transeastern Inc 3438 Pasadena Blvd .... Pasadena TX 77503 281-604-3100
Web: www.texastranseastern.com

Tiger Lines LLC Lodi 927 Black Diamond Way .... Lodi CA 95241 209-334-4100 333-3725
TF: 800-967-8443 ■ *Web:* www.tigerlines.com

Total Package Express Inc 5871 Cheviot Rd .... Cincinnati OH 45247 513-741-5500
TF: 800-420-5505 ■ *Web:* tp-exp.com

TP Trucking LLC 5630 Table Rock Rd .... Central Point OR 97502 800-292-4399
TF: 800-292-4399 ■ *Web:* www.tptrucking.com

Trailer Bridge Inc
10405 New Berlin Rd E .... Jacksonville FL 32226 904-751-7100 751-7444
OTC: TRBRQ ■ *TF:* 800-554-1589 ■ *Web:* www.trailerbridge.com

Trailer Transit Inc 1130 E US 20 .... Porter IN 46304 219-926-2111 859-1191*
**Fax Area Code:* 877 ■ *TF:* 800-423-3647 ■ *Web:* www.trailertransit.com

Trans-Carriers Inc 5135 US Hwy 78 .... Memphis TN 38118 901-368-2900 368-0336
TF: 800-999-7383 ■ *Web:* www.transcarriers.com

Trans-Phos Inc PO Box 9004 .... Bartow FL 33831 863-534-1575 534-3200
TF: 800-940-1575 ■ *Web:* www.transphos.com

TransAm Trucking Inc 15910 S 169th Hwy .... Olathe KS 66062 913-782-5300 324-7063
TF: 800-800-5945 ■ *Web:* www.transamtruck.com

Transport Corp of America Inc
1715 Yankee Doodle Rd .... Eagan MN 55121 651-686-2500 686-2566
TF: 800-328-3927 ■ *Web:* www.transportamerica.com

Transport Distribution Co PO Box 306 .... Joplin MO 64802 417-624-3814 624-9767
TF: 800-866-7709 ■ *Web:* www.gotdc.com

Transport Inc 2225 Main Ave SE .... Moorhead MN 56560 218-236-6300 236-0227
TF: 800-598-7267 ■ *Web:* www.transport-inc.com

TransWood Carriers Inc PO Box 189 .... Omaha NE 68101 888-346-8092 341-2112*
**Fax Area Code:* 402 ■ *TF:* 888-346-8092 ■ *Web:* www.transwood.com

Tri Star Freight System Inc 5407 Mesa Dr. .... Houston TX 77028 713-631-1095 631-1099
TF: 800-229-1095 ■ *Web:* www.tristarfreightsys.com

Trinity Logistics Group Inc 4001 Irving Blvd .... Dallas TX 75247 214-589-7505 589-7529
Web: www.trinitytrucking.com

Triple Crown Services
2720 Dupont Commerce Ct Ste 200 .... Fort Wayne IN 46825 260-416-3600 416-3771
TF: 800-325-6510 ■ *Web:* www.triplecrownsvc.com

Truline Corp 9390 Redwood St .... Las Vegas NV 89139 702-362-7495 362-3215
TF: 800-634-6489 ■ *Web:* www.trulinecorp.com

Tryon Trucking Inc PO Box 68 .... Fairless Hills PA 19030 215-295-6622 295-7168
TF: 800-523-5254 ■ *Web:* www.tryontrucking.com

Underwood Transfer Company LLC
940 W Troy Ave .... Indianapolis IN 46225 317-783-9235 782-2769
TF: 800-428-2372 ■ *Web:* www.underwoodcompanies.com

United Road Services Inc 10701 Middlebelt Rd .... Romulus MI 48174 734-947-7900
TF: 800-221-5127 ■ *Web:* www.unitedroad.com

Universal Truckload Services Inc
12755 E Nine Mile Rd. .... Warren MI 48089 586-920-0100 920-0258
NASDAQ: UACL ■ *TF:* 800-233-9445 ■ *Web:* www.goutsi.com

Upper Township School District 525 Perry Rd .... Woodbine NJ 08270 609-628-3500 628-2002
Web: www.upperschools.org

US Xpress Enterprises Inc
4080 Jenkins Rd .... Chattanooga TN 37421 423-510-3000 510-4006
TF: 800-251-6291 ■ *Web:* www.usxpress.com

USA Truck Inc 3200 Industrial Pk Rd. .... Van Buren AR 72956 479-471-2500
NASDAQ: USAK ■ *TF:* 800-643-9691 ■ *Web:* www.usa-truck.com

USF Holland Inc 750 E 40th St .... Holland MI 49423 616-395-5000 392-3104
Web: www.yrcregional.com

V & S Midwest Carriers Corp
2001 Hyland Ave PO Box 107 .... Kaukauna WI 54130 920-766-9696
TF: 800-876-4330 ■ *Web:* www.vsmidwest.com

Van Eerden Foodservice Co
650 Ionia Ave SW .... Grand Rapids MI 49503 616-475-0900 475-0990
TF: 800-833-7374 ■ *Web:* www.vaneerden.com

Van Wyk Freight Lines Inc PO Box 70 .... Grinnell IA 50112 641-236-7551 236-4247
TF: 800-362-2595 ■ *Web:* www.middlewest.com

Venezia Transport Service Inc PO Box 909 .... Royersford PA 19468 610-495-5200
Web: www.veneziainc.com

Vitran Express Canada Inc
1201 Creditstone Rd .... Concord ON L4K0C2 416-798-4965 798-4753
NASDAQ: VTNC ■ *TF:* 800-263-9588 ■ *Web:* www.vitran.com

Vitran Express Inc 1600 W Oliver Ave .... Indianapolis IN 46221 317-803-4000
TF: 800-366-0150 ■ *Web:* www.vitranexpress.com

Volume Transportation Inc
6575 Marshall Blvd .... Lithonia GA 30058 770-482-1400
TF: 800-879-5565 ■ *Web:* www.volinc.com

Waggoners Trucking 5220 Midland Rd .... Billings MT 59101 406-248-1919 259-6924
TF: 800-999-9097 ■ *Web:* www.waggonerstrucking.com

Waller Truck Company Inc
400 S McCleary Rd .... Excelsior Springs MO 64024 816-629-3400 629-3460
TF: 800-821-2196 ■ *Web:* www.wallertruck.com

Walpole Inc PO Box 1177 .... Okeechobee FL 34973 863-763-5593 763-7874
TF: 800-741-6500 ■ *Web:* www.walpoleinc.com

Warren Transport Inc 210 Beck Ave .... Waterloo IA 50701 319-233-6113 235-6555
TF General: 800-553-2007 ■ *Web:* www.warrentransport.com

Watsontown Trucking Company Inc
60 Belford Blvd .... Milton PA 17847 570-522-9820 538-0254
TF: 800-344-0313 ■ *Web:* www.watsontowntrucking.com

WC McQuaide Inc 153 Macridge Rd .... Johnstown PA 15904 814-269-6000
TF: 800-456-0292 ■ *Web:* www.mcquaide.com

Weaver Bros Inc 2230 Spar Ave .... Anchorage AK 99501 907-278-4526 276-4316
Web: weaverbrothersinc.com

Wel Companies Inc 1625 S Broadway PO Box 5610 .... De Pere WI 54115 920-339-0110 983-2139
TF: 800-333-4415 ■ *Web:* www.welcompanies.com

Werner Enterprises Inc 14507 Frontier Rd .... Omaha NE 68138 402-895-6640 894-3927*
NASDAQ: WERN ■ **Fax:* Hum Res ■ *TF:* 800-228-2240 ■ *Web:* www.werner.com

Western Co-op Transport Assn
4501 72nd St SW .... Montevideo MN 56265 320-269-5531 269-5532
TF: 800-992-8817 ■ *Web:* www.westernco-op.com

Western Express Inc 7135 Centennial Pl. .... Nashville TN 37209 615-259-9920 350-9957
TF: 800-316-7160 ■ *Web:* westernexpress.publishpath.com

Westwood Contractors Inc 951 W Seventh St .... Fort Worth TX 76102 817-877-3800 877-4731
Web: www.westwoodcontractors.com

White Bros Trucking Co 4N793 School Rd .... Wasco IL 60183 630-584-3810
TF: 800-323-4762 ■ *Web:* whitebrotherstrucking.com

White Settlement Independent School District
401 S Cherry Ln .... Fort Worth TX 76108 817-367-1300
Web: www.wsisd.com

Whitefish Bay Schools
1200 E Fairmount Ave .... Whitefish Bay WI 53217 414-963-3901
Web: www.wfbschools.com

Wildwood Express Trucking
12416 E Swanson Ave .... Kingsburg CA 93631 559-897-1035 897-1038
Web: wildwoodex.com

Willis Shaw Express Inc 201 N Elm St .... Elm Springs AR 72728 479-248-7261
TF: 800-843-9904 ■ *Web:* mcttrans.com

Wilson Lines of Minnesota Inc
2131 Second Ave .... Newport MN 55055 651-459-2384 769-3050
TF General: 800-525-3333 ■ *Web:* www.wilsonlines.com

Wilson Trucking Corp 137 Wilson Blvd .... Fishersville VA 22939 540-949-3200 949-3205
TF: 866-645-7405 ■ *Web:* www.wilsontrucking.com

Wiseway Motor Freight Inc PO Box 838 .... Hudson WI 54016 800-876-1660
TF: 800-876-1660 ■ *Web:* www.wiseway.com

Woodruff Construction LLC 1890 Kountry Ln. .... Fort Dodge IA 50501 515-576-1118 955-2170
Web: www.woodruffcompanies.com

Woody Bogler Trucking Co PO Box 229 .... Rosebud MO 63091 573-764-3700 764-4200
TF: 800-899-4120 ■ *Web:* www.woodybogler.com

Wragtime Air Freight Inc 596 W 135th St. .... Gardena CA 90248 800-586-9701
TF: 800-586-9701 ■ *Web:* www.visionexpressltl.com

Wright Transportation Inc
2333 Dauphin Island Pkwy .... Mobile AL 36605 251-432-6390
TF: 800-342-4598 ■ *Web:* www.wrighttrans.com

	Phone	Fax
Wyatt Transfer Inc 3035 Bells Rd PO Box 24326 ... Richmond VA 23224 *Fax: Administration ■ TF: 800-552-5708 ■ Web: www.wyatttransferinc.com	804-743-3800	271-9598*
Wynne Transport Service Inc 2222 N 11th St ... Omaha NE 68108 TF: 800-383-9330 ■ Web: www.wynnetr.com	402-342-4001	342-4608
Yorkville Community Unit School District 115 602A Ctr Pkwy PO Box 579 ... Yorkville IL 60560 Web: www.y115.org	630-553-4382	553-4398
Young's Commercial Transfer 2075 W Scranton Ave PO Box 871 ... Porterville CA 93257 TF: 800-289-1639 ■ Web: www.yctinc.com	559-784-6651	784-5280
Yourga Trucking Inc 100 Shenango St ... Wheatland PA 16161 TF: 800-245-1722 ■ Web: www.yourga.com	724-981-3600	

781 TYPESETTING & RELATED SERVICES

See Also Graphic Design p. 2442; Printing Companies - Commercial Printers p. 2976

	Phone	Fax
A A Blueprint Company Inc 2757 Gilchrist Rd ... Akron OH 44305 TF: 800-821-3700 ■ Web: aablueprint.com	330-794-8803	
Adflex Corp 300 Ormond St ... Rochester NY 14605 Web: www.adflexcorp.com	585-454-2950	
Allied Bindery LLC 32501 Dequindre Rd ... Madison Heights MI 48071 Web: www.alliedbindery.com	248-588-5990	
Ano-Coil Corp 60 E Main St ... Rockville CT 06066 Web: www.anocoil.com	860-871-1200	872-0534
Aptara Inc 3110 Fairview Pk Dr ... Falls Church VA 22042 Web: www.aptaracorp.com	703-352-0001	352-8862
ARC Document Solutions (ARC) ARC 1981 N Broadway Ste 385 ... Walnut Creek CA 94596 NYSE: ARC ■ Web: www.e-arc.com	925-949-5100	949-5101
ARC Document Solutions 6300 Gulfton St ... Houston TX 77081 Web: www.e-arc.com	713-782-8580	
Artisan Colour Inc 8970 E Bahia Dr ... Scottsdale AZ 85260 Web: blog.artisanhd.com	480-948-0009	
As Soon As Possible Inc 1750 W 96th St ... Bloomington MN 55431 Web: www.asap.net	952-564-2727	
Auto-Graphics Inc 430 N Vineyard Ave ... Ontario CA 91764 TF: 800-776-6939 ■ Web: www4.auto-graphics.com	909-595-7004	595-3506
Bacompt Systems Inc 12742 Hamilton Crossing Blvd ... Carmel IN 46032 Web: www.bacompt.com	317-574-7474	
Bank-A-Count Corp 1666 Main St PO Box 167 ... Rudolph WI 54475 Web: www.bank-a-count.com	715-435-3131	
Bell Litho Inc 370 Crossen Ave ... Elk Grove Village IL 60007 Web: www.bell-litho.com	847-952-3300	
Blanks Printing & Imaging Inc 2343 N Beckley Ave ... Dallas TX 75208 TF: 800-325-7651 ■ Web: www.blanks.com	214-741-3905	741-6105
Boston Color Graphics LLC 755 Middlesex Tpke ... Billerica MA 01821 TF: 800-767-0067 ■ Web: www.bcgconnect.com	800-767-0067	
Carey Digital 1718 Central Pkwy ... Cincinnati OH 45214 TF: 800-767-6071 ■ Web: www.careydigital.com	513-241-5210	241-2205
Cohber Press PO Box 93100 ... Rochester NY 14692 TF: 800-724-3032 ■ Web: www.cohber.com	585-475-9100	475-9406
Color Communication Inc 4000 W Fillmore St ... Chicago IL 60624 *Fax Area Code: 773 ■ TF: 800-458-5743 ■ Web: www.ccicolor.com	800-458-5743	638-0887*
Color House Graphics Inc 3505 Eastern Ave SE ... Grand Rapids MI 49508 TF: 800-454-1916 ■ Web: www.colorhousegraphics.com	616-241-1916	
Color Technology 2455 NW Nicolai St ... Portland OR 97210 Web: www.colortechnology.com	503-294-0393	
Computer Composition Corp 1401 W Girard Ave ... Madison Heights MI 48071 Web: www.computercomposition.com	248-545-4330	544-1611
Container Graphics Corp 114 Edinburgh S Dr Ste 104 ... Cary NC 27511 Web: www.containergraphics.com	919-481-4200	469-4897
Continental Colorcraft 1166 W Garvey Ave ... Monterey Park CA 91754 Web: www.continentalcolorcraft.com	323-283-3000	283-3206
Dixie Graphics Co 636 Grassmere Pk ... Nashville TN 37211 Web: www.dixiegraphics.com	615-832-7000	832-7621
eBlueprint Holdings Inc 3666 Carnegie Ave ... Cleveland OH 44115 Web: www.eblueprint.com	216-281-1234	
ET Lowe Publishing Co 2920 Sidco Dr ... Nashville TN 37204 Web: www.etlowe.com	615-254-8866	254-8867
GGS Technical Publications Services 3265 Farmtrail Rd ... York PA 17406 TF: 800-927-4474 ■ Web: ggsinc.com	717-764-2222	767-0027
Global Fulfillment 4 S Idaho St ... Seattle WA 98134 Web: www.gloful.com	206-405-3350	
GotPrint 7651 N San Fernando Rd ... Burbank CA 91505 TF: 877-922-7374 ■ Web: gotprint.com	818-252-3000	
Graphic Solutions Group Inc 8575 Cobb Intl Blvd Nw ... Kennesaw GA 30152 Web: www.gsghome.com	770-424-2300	
Graphics Group 2800 Taylor St ... Dallas TX 75226 Web: www.graphicsgroup.com	214-749-2222	749-2252
Imtech Graphics Inc 545 Dell Rd ... Carlstadt NJ 07072 TF: 800-468-3240 ■ Web: imtechgraphics.com	800-468-3240	
Jackson Typesetting Company Inc 1820 W Ganson St ... Jackson MI 49202	517-784-0576	784-1200
Kramer Graphics Inc 2408 W Dorothy Ln ... Dayton OH 45439 Web: www.kramergraphics.com	937-296-9600	
Lasergraphics Inc 4 Squire Rd ... Revere MA 02151 Web: www.laserg.com	781-289-2022	289-2027
Ligature, The 4909 Alcoa Ave ... Los Angeles CA 90058 TF: 800-944-5440 ■ Web: www.theligature.com	323-585-6000	585-1737
Luminite Products Corp 148 Commerce Dr ... Bradford PA 16701 TF: 888-545-2270 ■ Web: luminite.com	814-817-1420	
Mark Trece Inc 2001 Stockton Rd ... Joppa MD 21085 Web: www.marktrece.com	410-879-0060	879-3438
Maryland Composition Co 14880 Sweitzer Rd ... Laurel MD 20707 Web: ags.com	240-295-5674	
MATRIX Publishing Co 36 N Highland Ave ... York PA 17404 Web: matrix508.com	717-764-9673	764-9672
New England Typographic Service Inc 206 W Newberry Rd ... Bloomfield CT 06002 Web: www.netype.com	860-242-2251	
Newtype Inc 447 Rte 10 E Ste 14 ... Randolph NJ 07869 Web: www.newtypeinc.com	973-361-6000	361-6005
Pacific Digital Image 333 Broadway ... San Francisco CA 94133 Web: www.pacdigital.com	415-274-7234	
Para Plate 15910 Shoemaker Ave ... Cerritos CA 90703 TF: 800-788-1556 ■ Web: paraplate.com	562-404-3434	
Presstek Inc 55 Executive Dr ... Hudson NH 03051 NASDAQ: PRST ■ TF: 800-422-3616 ■ Web: www.presstek.com	603-595-7000	
Printing Prep Inc 12 E Tupper St ... Buffalo NY 14203 TF: 877-878-7114 ■ Web: www.printleader.us	716-852-5011	852-3150
Progressive Information Technologies 315 Busser Rd ... Emigsville PA 17318 Web: www.pit-magnus.com	717-764-5908	767-4092
Quintessence Publishing Co 4350 Chandler Dr ... Hanover Park IL 60133 TF: 800-621-0387 ■ Web: www.quintpub.com	630-736-3600	
Reed Technology & Information Services Inc 7 Walnut Grove Dr ... Horsham PA 19044 Web: www.reedtech.com	215-441-6400	
Regency Infographics Inc (SED) 2867 E Allegheny Ave ... Philadelphia PA 19134 TF: 800-829-0020 ■ Web: www.sed.com/desktop-publishing.html	215-425-8800	425-9715
Richards Graphic Communications Inc 2700 Van Buren St ... Bellwood IL 60104 TF: 866-827-3686 ■ Web: www.rgcnet.com	708-547-6000	547-6044
Rpr Graphics Inc 87 Main St ... Mountainside NJ 07092 Web: www.rprgraphicsinc.com	908-654-8080	
Schawk Inc 1600 Sherwin Ave ... Des Plaines IL 60018 NYSE: SGK ■ Web: www.schawk.com	847-827-9494	
Southern Graphic Systems Inc 502 N Willow Ave ... Tampa FL 33606 TF: 800-777-6789 ■ Web: www.sgsintl.com	813-253-3427	254-2112
Southern Graphics Systems 7435 Empire Dr ... Florence KY 41042 TF: 800-777-6789 ■ Web: www.sgsintl.com	859-525-1190	647-8205
Spectragraphic Inc 4 Brayton Ct ... Commack NY 11725 Web: www.spectragraphic.com	631-499-3100	499-5255
Spry Enterprises Inc 53 Loveton Cir Ste 207 ... Sparks MD 21152 Web: www.spryinc.com	443-212-5072	
St. Assoc Inc 1 Teal Rd ... Wakefield MA 01880 Web: www.stassoc.com	781-246-4700	246-4218
State & Federal Communications Inc 80 S Summit St ... Akron OH 44308 TF: 888-452-9669 ■ Web: stateandfed.com	330-761-9960	
Stevenson The Color Company Inc 535 Wilmer Ave ... Cincinnati OH 45226 Web: www.stevensoncolor.com	513-321-7500	321-7502
Sunrise Hitek Service Inc 5915 N Northwest Hwy ... Chicago IL 60631 Web: www.sunrisehitek.com	773-792-8880	
Techniprint Co 2545 N Seventh St ... Phoenix AZ 85006 Web: www.techniprintaz.com	602-257-0686	
Total Works Inc 2240 N Elston Ave ... Chicago IL 60614 Web: www.totalworks.net	773-489-4313	
Typesetting Inc 1144 S Robertson Blvd ... Los Angeles CA 90035 Web: local.latimes.com	310-273-3330	273-0733
VT Graphics Inc 465 Penn St ... Yeadon PA 19050 Web: www.vtgraph.com	610-259-4090	259-7235
West Essex Graphics Inc (WEG) 305 Fairfield Ave ... Fairfield NJ 07004 *Fax Area Code: 973 ■ TF: 800-221-5859 ■ Web: www.westessexgraphics.com	800-221-5859	227-2906*

782 ULTRASONIC CLEANING EQUIPMENT

See Also Dental Equipment & Supplies - Mfr p. 2190

	Phone	Fax
Branson Ultrasonics Corp 41 Eagle Rd ... Danbury CT 06813 Web: www.emersonindustrial.com	203-796-0400	
Crest Ultrasonics Corp 10 Grumman Ave ... Trenton NJ 08628 TF: 800-992-7378 ■ Web: www.crest-ultrasonics.com	609-883-4000	
L & R Manufacturing Co 577 Elm St ... Kearny NJ 07032 Web: www.lrultrasonics.com	201-991-5330	991-5870
Sonicor Inc 82 Otis St ... West Babylon NY 11704 TF: 800-864-5022 ■ Web: www.sonicor.com	631-920-6555	920-6080
Sonics & Materials Inc 53 Church Hill Rd ... Newtown CT 06470 OTC: SIMA ■ TF: 800-745-1105 ■ Web: www.sonicsandmaterials.com	203-270-4600	270-4610
Sterigenics 2015 Spring Rd Ste 650 ... Oak Brook IL 60523 TF: 800-472-4508 ■ Web: www.sterigenics.com	630-928-1700	928-1701

783 UNITED NATIONS AGENCIES, ORGANIZATIONS, PROGRAMS

	Phone	Fax
United Nations 2 UN Plz Rm DC21950 ... New York NY 10017 *Fax: PR ■ Web: www.un.org	212-963-1234	963-4260*
Inter-American Development Bank 1300 New York Ave NW ... Washington DC 20577 TF: 877-782-7432 ■ Web: www.iadb.org	202-623-1000	623-3096
International Atomic Energy Agency (IAEA) 1 UN Plz Rm DC1-1155 ... New York NY 10017 *Fax Area Code: 917 ■ Web: www.iaea.org	212-963-6010	367-4046*

Organization	City	State	Zip	Phone	Fax
International Fund for Agricultural Development (IFAD) 1775 K St NW Ste 410 *Web:* www.ifad.org	Washington	DC	20006	202-331-9099	331-9366
International Labour Organization (ILO) 220 E 42nd St Ste 3101 *Web:* www.ilo.org	New York	NY	10017	212-697-0150	697-5218
International Monetary Fund (IMF) 700 19th St NW *Web:* www.imf.org	Washington	DC	20431	202-623-7000	623-4661
International Tsunami Information Ctr 737 Bishop St Ste 2200 *Web:* itic.ioc-unesco.org	Honolulu	HI	96813	808-532-6422	532-5576
United Nations Children's Fund (UNICEF) 3 United Nations Plz *Web:* www.unicef.org	New York	NY	10017	212-326-7000	888-7465
United Nations Development Programme 1 UN Plz *Web:* www.undp.org	New York	NY	10017	212-906-5000	906-5364
United Nations Educational Scientific & Cultural Organization (UNESCO) 2 UN Plz Ste 900 *Web:* en.unesco.org	New York	NY	10017	212-963-5995	963-8014
United Nations Environment Programme (UNEP) 900 17th St NW Ste 506 *Web:* www.rona.unep.org	Washington	DC	20006	202-785-0465	785-2096
United Nations Industrial Development Organization (UNIDO) 1 UN Plz *Web:* www.unido.org	New York	NY	10017	212-963-6890	963-7904
World Bank Group, The (WBG) 1818 H St NW *Web:* www.worldbank.org	Washington	DC	20433	202-473-1000	477-6391
World Intellectual Property Organization (WIPO) 2 UN Plz Ste 2525 *Web:* www.wipo.int	New York	NY	10017	212-963-6813	963-4801

784 UNITED NATIONS MISSIONS

See Also Embassies & Consulates - Foreign, in the US p. 2238

All of the missions listed here are permanent missions except the Holy See, which has the status of Permanent Observer Mission to the UN. Two member states, Kiribati and Palau, are not listed because they do not maintain offices in New York. Another member state, Guinea Bissau, has a New York office but is excluded from this list because no telephone number was available for it.

Mission	City	State	Zip	Phone	Fax
Afghanistan 633 Third Ave 27A Fl *Web:* www.afghanistan-un.org	New York	NY	10017	212-972-1212	972-1216
Albania 320 E 79th St	New York	NY	10075	212-249-2059	535-2917
Algeria 326 E 48th St *Web:* www.algeria-un.org	New York	NY	10017	212-750-1960	
Angola 820 Second Ave 12th Fl *Web:* www.un.int	New York	NY	10017	212-861-5656	861-9295
Antigua & Barbuda 305 E 47th St 6th Fl *Web:* antigua-barbuda.org	New York	NY	10017	212-541-4117	
Armenia 119 E 36th St *Web:* www.un.int	New York	NY	10016	212-686-9079	686-3934
Australia 150 E 42nd St 33rd Fl *Web:* unny.mission.gov.au	New York	NY	10017	212-351-6600	351-6610
Austria 600 Third Ave 31st Fl **Fax Area Code: 212* ■ *Web:* advantageaustria.org	New York	NY	10016	917-542-8400	949-1840*
Azerbaijan 866 UN Plz Ste 560 *Web:* www.un.int	New York	NY	10017	212-371-2559	371-2784
Bahrain 866 Second Ave 14th & 15th Fls	New York	NY	10017	212-223-6200	
Bangladesh Mission To the UN 227 E 45th St 14th Fl *Web:* www.un.int	New York	NY	10017	212-867-3434	972-4038
Belarus 136 E 67th St 4th Fl *Web:* www.un.int	New York	NY	10021	212-535-3420	734-4810
Belgium 885 Second Ave 41st Fl *Web:* www.diplomatie.be/newyorkun	New York	NY	10017	212-378-6300	681-7618
Belize 675 Third Ave Ste 1911 *Web:* www.belizemission.com	New York	NY	10017	212-986-1240	593-0932
Benin 125 E 38th St *Web:* www.un.int	New York	NY	10016	212-684-1339	684-2058
Bolivia 801 Second Ave 4th Fl, Rm 42	New York	NY	10017	212-682-8132	
Botswana 154 E 46th St *Web:* botswanaun.org	New York	NY	10017	212-889-2277	725-5061
Brazil 747 Third Ave 9th Fl *Web:* www.un.int	New York	NY	10017	212-372-2600	371-5716
Bulgaria 11 E 84th St	New York	NY	10028	212-737-4790	472-9865
Burkina Faso 866 UN Plz Ste 326 *Web:* www.burkina-onu.org	New York	NY	10017	212-308-4720	308-4690
Burundi 336 E 45th St 12th Fl *Web:* burundi-un.org	New York	NY	10017	212-499-0001	499-0006
Cameroon 22 E 73rd St *Web:* www.delecam.us	New York	NY	10021	212-794-2295	249-0533
Canada 885 Second Ave 14th Fl *TF:* 800-267-8376 ■ *Web:* www.canadainternational.gc.ca	New York	NY	10017	212-848-1100	848-1195
Cape Verde 27 E 69th St	New York	NY	10021	212-472-0333	794-1398
Chad Mission 129 E 36th St	New York	NY	10016	212-986-0980	
Chile Mission 885 Second Ave 40th Fl **Fax Area Code: 212*	New York	NY	10017	917-322-6800	832-0236*
China 350 E 35th St *Web:* www.china-un.org	New York	NY	10016	212-655-6100	634-7626
Colombia 140 E 57th St *Web:* www.colombiaun.org	New York	NY	10022	212-355-7776	355-7776
Comoros 866 UN Plz Ste 418 *Web:* www.un.int	New York	NY	10017	212-750-1637	750-1657
Consulate General of Liberia 866 UN Plz Ste 249 *Web:* www.liberianconsulate-ny.com	New York	NY	10017	212-687-1033	
Costa Rica 211 E 43rd St Rm 903	New York	NY	10017	212-986-6373	986-6373
Croatia 820 Second Ave 19th Fl	New York	NY	10017	212-986-1585	986-2011
Cuba 315 Lexington Ave *TF General:* 800-553-3210 ■ *Web:* un.org	New York	NY	10016	212-689-7215	689-9073
Cyprus 13 E 40th St *Web:* www.un.int	New York	NY	10016	212-481-6023	685-7316
Czech Republic 1109 Madison Ave *Web:* www.mzv.cz/un.newyork	New York	NY	10028	212-717-5643	717-5064
Democratic People's Republic of Korea 820 Second Ave 13th Fl *Web:* www.un.org	New York	NY	10017	212-972-3105	972-3154
Dominican Republic 144 E 44th St 4th Fl *Web:* www.un.int	New York	NY	10017	212-867-0833	297-2509
Ecuador 866 UN Plz Ste 516 *Web:* un.int	New York	NY	10017	212-935-1680	935-1835
Egypt 304 E 44th St *Web:* egyptembassy.net	New York	NY	10017	212-503-0300	
El Salvador 46 Pk Ave	New York	NY	10016	212-889-3608	725-3467
Eritrea 800 Second Ave 18th Fl *Web:* www.eritrea-unmission.org	New York	NY	10017	212-687-3390	687-3138
Estonia 305 E 47th St 6th Fl **Fax Area Code: 646* ■ *Web:* www.un.estemb.org	New York	NY	10017	212-883-0640	514-0099*
Ethiopia 866 Second Ave 3rd Fl	New York	NY	10017	212-421-1830	754-0360
Finland 866 UN Plz Ste 222 *Web:* www.finlandun.org	New York	NY	10017	212-355-2100	759-6156
France 1 Dag Hammarskjold Plaza # 36 *Web:* www.un.int	New York	NY	10017	212-371-0480	421-6889
Gambia 800 Second Ave Rm 400F *Web:* un.int	New York	NY	10017	212-949-6640	856-9820
Georgia 1 UN Plaza 26th Fl	New York	NY	10017	212-759-1949	
German Marshall Fund of the United States 1744 R St NW *TF:* 800-276-5680 ■ *Web:* www.gmfus.org	Washington	DC	20009	202-745-3950	
Germany 871 UN Plz *Web:* www.new-york-un.diplo.de	New York	NY	10017	212-940-0400	940-0402
Ghana 19 E 47th St *Web:* www.un.int/ghana	New York	NY	10017	212-832-1300	751-6743
Greece 866 Second Ave 13th Fl *Web:* www.mfa.gr	New York	NY	10017	212-888-6900	888-4440
Grenada 800 Second Ave Ste 400-K	New York	NY	10017	212-599-0301	
Guatemala 57 Pk Ave *Web:* www.un.int	New York	NY	10016	212-679-4760	685-8741
Guinea 140 E 39th St *Web:* www.un.int	New York	NY	10016	212-687-8115	687-8248
Guyana 801 Second Ave 5th Fl *Web:* www.guyana.org/govt/govt_offices.html	New York	NY	10017	212-573-5828	573-6225
Haiti 801 Second Ave Ste 600	New York	NY	10017	212-370-4840	661-8698
Holy See 25 E 39th St *Web:* www.holyseemission.org	New York	NY	10016	212-370-7885	370-9622
Honduras 866 UN Plz Ste 417 *Web:* www.un.int	New York	NY	10017	212-752-3370	223-0498
Hungary 223 E 52nd St *Web:* www.un.int	New York	NY	10022	212-752-0209	
Iceland 800 Third Ave 36th Fl *Web:* www.iceland.is	New York	NY	10022	212-593-2700	593-6269
India 235 E 43rd St *Web:* www.un.int	New York	NY	10017	212-490-9660	490-9656
Indonesia 325 E 38th St *Web:* www.indonesiamission-ny.org	New York	NY	10016	212-972-8333	972-9780
Iran 622 Third Ave 34th Fl *Web:* www.un.int	New York	NY	10017	212-687-2020	867-7086
Ireland 1 Dag Hammarskjold Plz # 885 *Web:* www.un.int	New York	NY	10017	212-421-6934	752-4726
Israel 800 Second Ave *Web:* embassies.gov.il	New York	NY	10017	212-499-5000	499-5515
Italy 885 Second Ave 49th Fl *Web:* www.italyun.esteri.it	New York	NY	10017	212-486-9191	486-1036
Jamaica 767 Third Ave 9th Fl *Web:* www.un.int	New York	NY	10017	212-935-7509	935-7607
Japan 866 UN Plz 2nd Fl *Web:* www.un.int	New York	NY	10017	212-223-4300	751-1966
Kenya 866 UN Plaza Rm 304 *Web:* www.kenyaun.org	New York	NY	10017	212-421-4740	
Korea Republic of 335 E 45th St *Web:* www.un.int	New York	NY	10017	212-439-4000	986-1083
Kuwait 321 E 44th St *Web:* www.kuwaitmission.com	New York	NY	10017	212-973-4300	
Lao People's Democratic Republic 317 E 51st St *Web:* www.un.int	New York	NY	10022	212-832-2734	750-0039
Latvia 333 E 50th St *Web:* mfa.gov.lv	New York	NY	10022	212-838-8877	838-8920
Lebanon 866 UN Plz Rm 531-533	New York	NY	10017	212-355-5460	838-2819
Lesotho 204 E 39th St *Web:* www.un.int	New York	NY	10016	212-661-1690	682-4388
Libyan Arab Jamahiriya 309-315 E 48th St *TF:* 800-253-9646 ■ *Web:* www.un.org	New York	NY	10017	212-752-5775	593-4787
Madagascar 820 Second Ave Ste 800 *Web:* un.int	New York	NY	10017	212-986-9491	986-6271
Malawi 866 UN Plz Ste 486 *Web:* www.un.int/malawi	New York	NY	10017	212-317-8738	317-8729
Malaysia 313 E 43rd St *Web:* www.un.int/malaysia	New York	NY	10017	212-986-6310	490-8576
Maldives 800 Second Ave Ste 400-E	New York	NY	10017	212-599-6194	661-6405
Mali 111 E 69th St	New York	NY	10021	212-737-4150	472-3778
Malta 249 E 35th St *Web:* www.foreign.gov.mt	New York	NY	10016	212-725-2345	779-7097
Marshall Islands 800 Second Ave 18th Fl	New York	NY	10017	212-983-3040	
Mauritania 116 E 38th St *Web:* www.un.int	New York	NY	10016	212-252-0113	252-0175
Mauritius 211 E 43rd St *Web:* mfa.govmu.org	New York	NY	10017	212-949-0190	
Mexico 3810 Ventor Ave *Web:* mexicorestaurantbar.com	Atlantic City	NJ	08401	609-344-0366	
Micronesia 300 E 42nd St Ste 1600 *TF:* 800-469-4828 ■ *Web:* www.fsmgov.org/fsmun	New York	NY	10017	212-697-8370	697-8295

Name / Address	City	State	Zip	Phone	Fax
Mission-Andorra To the UN 2 UN Plz 27th Fl	New York	NY	10017	212-750-8064	750-6630
Monaco 866 UN Plaza Ste 520 *Web:* www.monaco-un.org	New York	NY	10017	212-832-0721	832-5358
Mongolia 6 E 77th St *Web:* www.un.int/mongolia	New York	NY	10075	212-861-9460	861-9464
Mozambique 420 E 50th St *Web:* www.un.int	New York	NY	10022	212-644-6800	644-5972
Nepal 820 Second Ave Ste 17B	New York	NY	10017	212-370-3988	953-2038
Nicaragua 820 Second Ave Ste 801 *Web:* www.un.int	New York	NY	10017	212-490-7997	286-0815
Niger 417 E 50th St *Web:* www.un.int	New York	NY	10022	212-421-3260	753-6931
Norway 825 Third Ave 39th Fl *Web:* www.norway-un.org	New York	NY	10022	646-430-7510	
Oman 305 E 47th St 12th Fl *Web:* www.un.int/wcm/content/site/oman	New York	NY	10017	212-355-3505	644-0070
Pakistan 8 E 65th St *Web:* www.pakun.org	New York	NY	10065	212-879-8600	744-7348
Panama 866 UN Plz Ste 4030 *Web:* www.panama-un.org/en.html	New York	NY	10017	212-421-5420	421-2694
Paraguay 801 Second Ave Ste 702	New York	NY	10017	212-687-3490	818-1282
Permanent Mission of Cambodia 327 E 58th St	New York	NY	10022	212-336-0777	759-7672
Permanent Mission of Macedonia 866 UN Plaza *Web:* www.macedonianembassy.org	New York	NY	10017	212-308-8504	
Permanent Mission of Solomon Islands to the United Nations 800 Second Ave Ste 400L *Web:* www.un.int/wcm/content/site/solomonislands	New York	NY	10017	212-599-6192	661-8925
Permanent Mission of Sweden to the United Nations 885 Second Ave Fl 46 1 Dag Hammarskjold Plz *Web:* www.swedenabroad.com	New York	NY	10017	212-583-2500	583-2549
Permanent Mission of the Netherlands to the UN in New York United States 666 Third Ave 19th Fl *Web:* www.netherlandsmission.org	New York	NY	10017	212-519-9500	370-1954
Permanent Mission of the Republic of Seychelles to the United Nations 800 Second Ave Ste 400C *Web:* www.un.int/seychelles	New York	NY	10017	212-972-1785	972-1786
Permanent Mission of the Republic of the Union of Myanmar 10 E 77th St *Web:* mmnewyork.org	New York	NY	10075	212-744-1271	744-1290
Permement Mission of Argentina 1 UN Plz	New York	NY	10017	212-688-6300	980-8395
Permement Mission of Turkey 821 UN Plz 10th Fl	New York	NY	10017	212-682-8717	949-0086
Peru 820 Second Ave Ste 1600	New York	NY	10017	212-687-3336	972-6975
Philippines 556 Fifth Ave 5th Fl *Web:* www.un.int	New York	NY	10036	212-764-1300	840-8602
Poland 9 E 66th St Web: nowyjorkonz.msz.gov.pl	New York	NY	10065	212-744-2506	517-6771
Qatar 809 UN Plz 4th Fl *Web:* www.un.org	New York	NY	10017	212-486-9335	758-4952
Romania 573-577 Third Ave *Web:* www.un.int	New York	NY	10016	212-682-3273	
Russia 136 E 67th St *Web:* russiaun.ru	New York	NY	10065	212-861-4900	628-0252
Rwanda 124 E 39th St	New York	NY	10016	212-679-9010	679-9133
Saint Kitts & Nevis 414 E 75th St 5th Fl *Web:* www.stkittsnevis.org	New York	NY	10021	212-535-1234	535-6854
Saint Lucia 800 Second Ave Fl 5 *Web:* saintluciamissionun.org	New York	NY	10017	212-697-9360	697-4993
San Marino 327 E 50th St	New York	NY	10022	212-751-1234	751-1436
Senegal 238 E 68th St *Web:* www.un.int	New York	NY	10065	212-517-9030	517-3032
Serbia 854 Fifth Ave *Web:* www.un.int	New York	NY	10021	212-879-8700	879-8705
Sierra Leone 245 E 49th St *Web:* www.un.int/sierraleone	New York	NY	10017	212-688-1656	688-4924
Singapore 318 E 48th St *Web:* www.mfa.gov.sg/newyork	New York	NY	10022	212-223-3331	826-5028
Slovakia 801 Second Ave 12th Fl *Web:* www.mzv.sk/nyc	New York	NY	10017	212-286-8434	286-8439
Somalia 425 E 61st St Ste 702 *Web:* un.int	New York	NY	10065	212-688-9410	
South Africa 333 E 38th St 9th Fl *Web:* www.southafrica-newyork.net	New York	NY	10016	212-213-5583	692-2498
Spain 245 E 47th St 36th Fl *Web:* www.spainun.org	New York	NY	10017	212-661-1050	949-7247
Sudan 305 E 47th St 4th Fl *Web:* www.un.int/sudan	New York	NY	10017	212-573-6033	573-6160
Suriname 866 UN Plaza Ste 320 *Web:* www.un.int	New York	NY	10017	212-826-0660	980-7029
Switzerland 633 Third Ave 29th Fl *Web:* www.eda.admin.ch	New York	NY	10011	212-286-1540	599-4266
Syria 820 Second Ave 15th Fl *Web:* un.int	New York	NY	10017	212-661-1313	983-4439
Tanzania 307 E 53rd St 4th Floor	New York	NY	10022	212-697-3612	697-3618
Thailand 351 E 52nd St *Web:* www.thaicgny.com	New York	NY	10022	212-754-1770	688-3029
Tunisia 31 Beekman Pl	New York	NY	10022	212-751-7503	751-0569
Uganda 336 E 45th St *Web:* newyork.mofa.go.ug	New York	NY	10017	212-949-0110	687-4517
Ukraine 220 E 51st St	New York	NY	10022	212-355-9455	355-9455
UN Mission of Iraq 14 E 79th St	New York	NY	10075	212-737-4433	
United Arab Emirates 305 E 47th St 7th Fl *Web:* www.un.int/uae	New York	NY	10017	212-371-0480	371-4923
United Kingdom 1 Dag Hammarskjold Plz *Web:* www.gov.uk	New York	NY	10017	212-745-9200	745-9316
United States of America 799 United Nations Plz *Web:* www.un.int	New York	NY	10017	212-415-4000	415-4443
Uruguay 866 UN Plz Ste 322 *Web:* www.un.int/uruguay	New York	NY	10017	212-752-8240	593-0935
Vanuatu 800 E Second Ave *Web:* www.un.int	New York	NY	10017	212-661-4303	422-3427
Venezuela 335 E 46th St *Web:* www.un.int	New York	NY	10017	212-557-2055	557-3528
Vietnam 866 UN Plaza Ste 428 *Web:* www.un.int	New York	NY	10017	212-644-0594	644-5732
Zambia 237 E 52nd St *Web:* www.un.int	New York	NY	10022	212-888-5770	888-5213
Zimbabwe 128 E 56th St	New York	NY	10022	212-980-9511	308-6705

785 UNIVERSITIES - CANADIAN

Name / Address	City	Prov	Postal Code	Phone	Fax
Acadia University 15 University Ave *TF:* 877-585-1121 ■ *Web:* www2.acadiau.ca	Wolfville	NS	B4P2R6	902-542-2201	585-1081
Alberta College of Art & Design 1407 14th Ave NW *TF:* 800-251-8290 ■ *Web:* www.acad.ca	Calgary	AB	T2N4R3	403-284-7600	289-6682
Athabasca University 1 University Dr *TF:* 800-788-9041 ■ *Web:* www.athabascau.ca	Athabasca	AB	T9S3A3	780-675-6111	675-6174
Bethany Bible College 26 Western St *TF:* 888-432-4444 ■ *Web:* www.kingswood.edu	Sussex	NB	E4E1E6	506-432-4400	432-4425
Bishop's University 2600 College St *Web:* www.ubishops.ca	Sherbrooke	QC	J1M0C8	819-822-9600	822-9661
Brandon University 270 18th St *Web:* www.brandonu.ca	Brandon	MB	R7A6A9	204-728-9520	728-7346
Brescia University College 1285 Western Rd *Web:* www.brescia.uwo.ca	London	ON	N6G1H2	519-432-8353	858-5137
Brock University 1812 Sir Isaac Brock Way *Web:* www.brocku.ca	Saint Catharines	ON	L2S3A1	905-688-5550	988-5488
Campion College at the University of Regina 3737 Wascana Pkwy *TF:* 800-667-7282 ■ *Web:* www.campioncollege.sk.ca	Regina	SK	S4S0A2	306-586-4242	359-1200
Canadian College of Naturopathic Medicine 1255 Sheppard Ave E *TF:* 866-241-2266 ■ *Web:* www.ccnm.edu	Toronto	ON	M2K1E2	416-498-1255	
Canadian Memorial Chiropractic College 6100 Leslie St *TF:* 800-463-2923 ■ *Web:* www.cmcc.ca	Toronto	ON	M2H3J1	416-482-2340	482-9745
Cape Breton University 1250 Grand Lk Rd *TF:* 888-959-9995 ■ *Web:* www.cbu.ca	Sydney	NS	B1P6L2	902-539-5300	562-0119
Carleton University 1125 Colonel By Dr *TF:* 888-354-4414 ■ *Web:* www.carleton.ca	Ottawa	ON	K1S5B6	613-520-7400	520-3847
Columbia Bible College 2940 Clearbrook Rd *TF:* 800-283-0881 ■ *Web:* www.columbiabc.edu	Abbotsford	BC	V2T2Z8	604-853-3358	853-3063
Concordia University 1455 de Maisonneuve Blvd W *TF:* 866-333-2271 ■ *Web:* www.concordia.ca	Montreal	QC	H3G1M8	514-848-2424	848-2621
Concordia University College of Alberta 7128 Ada Blvd NW *TF:* 866-479-5200 ■ *Web:* www.concordia.ab.ca	Edmonton	AB	T5B4E4	780-479-9220	378-8460
Crandall University 333 Gorge Rd *TF:* 888-968-6228 ■ *Web:* crandallu.ca	Moncton	NB	E1G3H9	506-858-8970	858-9694
Dalhousie University 6299 S St Rm 125 Henry Hicks A&A Bldg *Web:* www.dal.ca	Halifax	NS	B3H4R2	902-494-3998	494-2839
Dominican University College 96 Empress Ave *Web:* udominicaine.ca	Ottawa	ON	K1R7G3	613-233-5696	233-6064
Emmanuel Bible College 100 Fergus Ave *Web:* emmanuelbiblecollege.ca	Kitchener	ON	N2A2H2	519-894-8900	894-5331
First Nations University of Canada					
Northern 1301 Central Ave *TF:* 800-267-6303	Prince Albert	SK	S6V4W1	306-765-3333	765-3330
Saskatoon 226 20th St E *TF:* 800-267-6303 ■ *Web:* fnuniv.ca	Saskatoon	SK	S7K0A6	306-931-1800	
Heritage College & Seminary 175 Holiday Inn Dr *TF:* 800-465-1961 ■ *Web:* heritagecambridge.com	Cambridge	ON	N3C3T2	519-651-2869	651-2870
Huntington University 935 Ramsey Lk Rd *TF:* 800-461-6366 ■ *Web:* www.huntington.laurentian.ca	Sudbury	ON	P3E2C6	705-673-4126	673-6917
Huron University College 1349 Western Rd *Web:* www.huronuc.on.ca	London	ON	N6G1H3	519-438-7224	438-3938
International Academy of Design & Technology					
Chicago 1 N State St Ste 500 *TF:* 888-318-6111 ■ *Web:* www.iadt.edu	Chicago	IL	60602	312-386-7681	
King's University College 9125 50th St *TF:* 800-661-8582 ■ *Web:* kingsu.ca	Edmonton	AB	T6B2H3	780-465-3500	465-3534
Lakehead University 955 Oliver Rd *Web:* www.lakeheadu.ca	Thunder Bay	ON	P7B5E1	807-343-8110	343-8023
Laurentian University 935 Ramsey Lake Rd *TF:* 800-461-4030 ■ *Web:* www.laurentian.ca	Sudbury	ON	P3E2C6	705-675-1151	675-4838
Laval University 2325 Rue University *TF:* 877-785-2825 ■ *Web:* www2.ulaval.ca	Quebec	QC	G1V0A6	418-656-2131	656-5216
McGill University 845 Sherbrooke St W *Fax: Admissions ■ *Web:* www.mcgill.ca	Montreal	QC	H3A2T5	514-398-4455	398-8939*
McMaster University 1280 Main St W *Web:* www.mcmaster.ca	Hamilton	ON	L8S4L8	905-525-9140	527-1105
Mount Allison University 62 York St *Web:* www.mta.ca	Sackville	NB	E4L1E2	506-364-2269	364-2272
Mount Royal College 4825 Mt Royal Gate SW *TF:* 877-440-5001 ■ *Web:* www.mtroyal.ca	Calgary	AB	T3E6K6	403-440-6111	440-6339
Mount Saint Vincent University 166 Bedford Hwy *TF:* 877-733-6788 ■ *Web:* www.msvu.ca	Halifax	NS	B3M2J6	902-457-6117	457-6498
Nipissing University 100 College Dr PO Box 5002 *TF:* 800-655-5154 ■ *Web:* nipissingu.ca	North Bay	ON	P1B8L7	705-474-3450	495-1772
Brantford 67 Darling St *Web:* www.nipissingu.ca	Brantford	ON	N3T2K6	519-756-8228	720-9996
NSCAD University 5163 Duke St *Web:* www.nscad.ca	Halifax	NS	B3J3J6	902-444-9600	425-2420

Phone Fax

Ontario College of Art & Design
100 McCaul St .... Toronto ON M5T1W1 416-977-6000 977-6006
Web: www.ocad.on.ca

Prairie Bible Institute
330 Fifth Ave NE PO Box 4000 .... Three Hills AB T0M2N0 403-443-5511 443-5540
TF: 800-661-2425 ■ *Web:* www.prairie.edu

Queen's University 99 University Ave. .... Kingston ON K7L3N6 613-533-2000 533-2068
Web: www.queensu.ca

Redeemer University College 777 Garner Rd E .... Ancaster ON L9K1J4 905-648-2131 648-2134
TF: 877-779-0913 ■ *Web:* www.redeemer.ca

Royal Military College of Canada
Stn Forces PO Box 17000 .... Kingston ON K7K7B4 613-541-6000 541-6599
Web: www.rmcc-cmrc.ca/en

Royal Roads University 2005 Sooke Rd .... Victoria BC V9B5Y2 250-391-2511 391-2500
TF: 800-788-8028 ■ *Web:* www.royalroads.ca

Ryerson University 350 Victoria St. .... Toronto ON M5B2K3 416-979-5000 979-5170
TF: 866-592-8882 ■ *Web:* www.ryerson.ca

Saint Francis Xavier University
PO Box 5000 .... Antigonish NS B2G2W5 902-863-3300 867-2329*
**Fax:* Admissions ■ *TF Admissions:* 877-867-7839 ■ *Web:* www.stfx.ca

Saint Jerome's University
290 Westmount Rd N .... Waterloo ON N2L3G3 519-884-8110 884-5759
Web: www.sju.ca

Saint Mary's University 923 Robie St .... Halifax NS B3H3C3 902-420-5756 420-5141
Web: www.smu.ca

Saint Paul University 223 Main St. .... Ottawa ON K1S1C4 613-236-1393 782-3014
TF: 800-637-6859 ■ *Web:* www.ustpaul.ca

Saint Thomas University 51 Dineen Dr .... Fredericton NB E3B5G3 506-452-0640
TF: 877-788-4443

Simon Fraser University (SFU)
Burnaby 8888 University Dr MBC 1150 .... Burnaby BC V5A1S6 778-782-2667 782-5496
Web: www.sfu.ca
Harbour Centre 515 W Hastings St .... Vancouver BC V6B5K3 778-782-5000 782-5219
Web: www.sfu.ca
Surrey 250 - 13450 102 Ave .... Surrey BC V3T0A3 778-782-7400 782-7403
Web: www.sfu.ca/campuses/surrey.html

Taylor University College & Seminary
11525 23rd Ave .... Edmonton AB T6J4T3 780-431-5200 436-9416
TF: 800-567-4988 ■ *Web:* www.taylor-edu.ca

Thompson Rivers University
900 McGill Rd PO Box 3010 .... Kamloops BC V2C5N3 250-828-5000 371-5960*
**Fax:* Admissions ■ *TF:* 800-663-1663 ■ *Web:* www.tru.ca

Thorneloe University 935 Ramsey Lake Rd .... Sudbury ON P3E2C6 705-673-1730 673-4979
TF General: 800-461-4030 ■ *Web:* thorneloe.laurentian.ca

Toronto Baptist Seminary & Bible College
130 Gerrard St E .... Toronto ON M5A3T4 416-925-3263 925-8305
Web: www.tbs.edu

Toronto School of Theology
47 Queen's Pk Crescent E .... Toronto ON M5S2C3 416-978-4039 978-7821
Web: www.tst.edu

Trent University 1600 W Bank Dr .... Peterborough ON K9J7B8 705-748-1011 748-1629
TF: 888-739-8885 ■ *Web:* www.trentu.ca

Trinity Western University 7600 Glover Rd .... Langley BC V2Y1Y1 604-888-7511 513-2064*
**Fax:* Admissions ■ *TF:* 888-468-6898 ■ *Web:* www.twu.ca

Universite de Moncton
Campus Shippagan 218 Blvd JD Gauthier .... Shippagan NB E8S1P6 506-336-3400 336-3604
TF: 800-363-8336 ■ *Web:* www.umoncton.ca
Edmundston 165 Blvd Hebert .... Edmundston NB E3V2S8 506-737-5051 737-5373
TF: 888-736-8623 ■ *Web:* www.umoncton.ca

Universite de Montreal
CP 6128 Succursale Centre Ville .... Montreal QC H3C3J7 514-343-6111 343-5788*
**Fax:* Admissions ■ *Web:* www.umontreal.ca

Universite de Sherbrooke
2500 boul de l'Universite .... Sherbrooke QC J1K2R1 819-821-8000 821-7966
TF: 800-267-8337 ■ *Web:* www.usherbrooke.ca

Universite du Quebec 475 Rue du Parvis .... Quebec QC G1K9H7 418-657-3551 657-2132
Web: www.uquebec.ca

Universite du Quebec a Trois-Rivieres
3351 Boul des Forges CP 500 .... Trois-Rivieres QC G9A5H7 819-376-5011 376-5210
TF: 800-365-0922 ■ *Web:* www.uqtr.ca

Universite Sainte Anne 1695 Rt 1 .... Pointe-de-l'Eglise NS B0W1M0 902-769-2114 769-2930
TF: 888-338-8337 ■ *Web:* www.usainteanne.ca

University of Alberta 116 St & 85 Ave. .... Edmonton AB T6G2R3 780-492-3111
Web: www.ualberta.ca
Augustana 4901-46th Ave .... Camrose AB T4V2R3 780-679-1100 679-1129
TF: 800-661-8714 ■ *Web:* www.augustana.ualberta.ca

University of British Columbia
2016-1874 E Mall .... Vancouver BC V6T1Z1 604-822-9836 822-3599
TF: 877-272-1422 ■ *Web:* www.ubc.ca
Okanagan 3333 University Way .... Kelowna BC V1V1V7 250-807-8000
Web: ok.ubc.ca

University of Calgary 2500 University Dr NW .... Calgary AB T2N1N4 403-220-5110 282-7298
Web: www.ucalgary.ca

University of Guelph 50 Stone Rd E .... Guelph ON N1G2W1 519-824-4120 766-9481
TF: 877-674-1610 ■ *Web:* www.uoguelph.ca

University of Lethbridge
4401 University Dr .... Lethbridge AB T1K3M4 403-329-2111 329-5159*
**Fax:* Admissions ■ *Web:* www.uleth.ca

University of Manitoba
65 Chancellors Cir 424 University Ctr .... Winnipeg MB R3T2N2 204-474-8880 474-7554
TF Admissions: 800-224-7713 ■ *Web:* www.umanitoba.ca

University of New Brunswick
100 Tucker Pk Rd PO Box 4400 .... Fredericton NB E2L4L5 506-453-4666 453-5016
Web: www.unb.ca
Saint John 100 Tucker Pk Rd PO Box 5050 .... Saint John NB E2L4L5 506-648-5500 648-5528
Web: www.unb.ca

University of Northern British Columbia
3333 University Way .... Prince George BC V2N4Z9 250-960-5555 960-6330
Web: www.unbc.ca

University of Ottawa 550 Cumberland St .... Ottawa ON K1N6N5 613-562-5800 562-5323
TF: 877-868-8292 ■ *Web:* www.uottawa.ca

University of Regina 3737 Wascana Pkwy .... Regina SK S4S0A2 306-585-4111 337-2525
TF: 800-644-4756 ■ *Web:* www.uregina.ca

Phone Fax

Luther College 3737 Wascana Pkwy .... Regina SK S4S0A2 306-585-5333 585-5267
Web: www.luthercollege.edu
Saint Thomas More College 1437 College Dr ..... Saskatoon SK S7N0W6 306-966-8900 966-8904
TF: 800-667-2019 ■ *Web:* www.stmcollege.ca

University of Toronto 315 Bloor St W .... Toronto ON M5S1A3 416-978-2190 978-7022*
**Fax:* Admissions ■ *Web:* www.utoronto.ca
Mississauga 3359 Mississauga Rd N .... Mississauga ON L5L1C6 905-828-5399 569-4301
Web: www.utm.utoronto.ca
Scarborough 1265 Military Trl. .... Toronto ON M1C1A4 416-287-8872 978-7022
Web: www.utsc.utoronto.ca
University of Trinity College 6 Hoskin Ave. .... Toronto ON M5S1H8 416-978-2522 978-2797
Web: www.trinity.utoronto.ca
Victoria University 140 Charles St .... Toronto ON M5S1K9 416-585-4524 585-4524
Web: www.vicu.utoronto.ca

University of Victoria
3800 Finnerty Rd Stn CSC PO Box 1700 .... Victoria BC V8P5C2 250-472-5416 472-5477
Web: www.uvic.ca

University of Waterloo 200 University Ave W .... Waterloo ON N2L3G1 519-888-4567 746-3242
Web: uwaterloo.ca

University of Western Ontario
1393 Western Rd Ste 6100 .... London ON N6A3K7 519-661-2111 661-3630*
**Fax:* Purchasing ■ *Web:* www.uwo.ca
King's University College 266 Epworth Ave .... London ON N6A2M3 519-433-3491 433-2227
TF: 800-265-4406 ■ *Web:* www.uwo.ca

University of Windsor 401 Sunset Ave .... Windsor ON N9B3P4 519-253-3000 973-7070
Web: www.uwindsor.ca

University of Winnipeg 515 Portage Ave. .... Winnipeg MB R3B2E9 204-786-9914 783-8910
Web: www.uwinnipeg.ca

Wilfrid Laurier University
75 University Ave W .... Waterloo ON N2L3C5 519-884-1970 886-9351
Web: www.wlu.ca

York University 4700 Keele St. .... Toronto ON M3J1P3 416-736-2100 736-5536
TF: 800-426-2255 ■ *Web:* www.yorku.ca

786 UNIVERSITY SYSTEMS

Listings are organized by state names.

Phone Fax

Alabama Higher Education Commission
100 N Union St PO Box 302000 .... Montgomery AL 36130 334-242-1998 242-0268
Web: www.ache.state.al.us

University of Alabama System
401 Queen City Ave .... Tuscaloosa AL 35401 205-348-5861 348-6301
TF: 800-638-6420 ■ *Web:* www.uasystem.ua.edu

University of Alaska System
910 Yukon Dr PO Box 775000 .... Fairbanks AK 99775 907-450-8000 450-8012
Web: www.alaska.edu

Arakansas Higher Education Dept (ADHE)
423 Main St Ste 400 .... Little Rock AR 72201 501-371-2000 371-2001
Web: www.adhe.edu

California State University
401 Golden Shore .... Long Beach CA 90802 562-951-4000 951-4899
TF: 800-325-4000 ■ *Web:* www.calstate.edu

University of California System
1111 Franklin St 12th Fl .... Oakland CA 94607 510-987-9074 987-9086
TF: 800-888-8267 ■ *Web:* www.ucop.edu

Colorado State University System
410 17th St Ste 2440 .... Denver CO 80202 303-534-6290 534-6298
Web: www.csusystem.edu

University of Colorado System
1800 Grant St Ste 800 .... Denver CO 80203 303-860-5600 860-5610
Web: www.cu.edu

Connecticut State University System
39 Woodland St .... Hartford CT 06105 860-493-0000 493-0085
Web: www.ct.edu

Delaware Higher Education Commission
401 Federal St Ste 2 .... Dover DE 19901 302-735-4000
Web: www.doe.state.de.us

State University System of Florida
325 W Gaines St Ste 1614 .... Tallahassee FL 32399 850-245-0466 245-9685
Web: www.flbog.edu

University System of Georgia
270 Washington St SW. .... Atlanta GA 30334 404-656-2250 657-6979
Web: www.usg.edu

University of Hawaii System 2500 Campus Rd .... Honolulu HI 96822 808-956-8111 956-3952
Web: www.hawaii.edu

Illinois Higher Education Board
431 E Adams St 2nd Fl .... Springfield IL 62701 217-782-2551 782-8548
Web: www.ibhe.org

University of Illinois System
506 S Wright St Ste 352 .... Urbana IL 61801 217-333-1920 244-2282
Web: www.uillinois.edu

Louisiana State University System
125 E Boyd Dr .... Baton Rouge LA 70803 225-578-3357
TF: 800-227-3002

University of Louisiana System
1201 N Third St Ste 7-300 .... Baton Rouge LA 70802 225-342-6950 342-6473
Web: ulsystem.edu

University of Maine System 16 Central St .... Bangor ME 04401 207-973-3200 973-3296
Web: www.maine.edu

University System of Maryland
3300 Metzerott Rd .... Adelphi MD 20783 301-445-2740 445-1931
Web: www.ums.edu

Massachusetts Higher Education Board
1 Ashburton Pl Rm 1401 .... Boston MA 02108 617-994-6950 727-6397
Web: www.mass.edu

University of Massachusetts System
225 Franklin St 33rd Fl .... Boston MA 02110 617-287-7050
Web: www.massachusetts.edu

University of Missouri System
321 University Hall .... Columbia MO 65211 573-882-2011 882-2721
TF: 800-225-6075 ■ *Web:* www.umsystem.edu

	City	State	ZIP	Phone	Fax
Montana University System 2500 E Broadway St. *Web:* www.mus.edu	Helena	MT	59601	406-444-6570	
Nebraska State College System 1115 K St Ste 102 *Web:* www.nscs.edu	Lincoln	NE	68508	402-471-2505	471-2669
University of Nebraska System 3835 Holdrege St Varner Hall *TF:* 800-542-1602 ■ *Web:* www.nebraska.edu	Lincoln	NE	68583	402-472-2111	472-1237
Nevada System of Higher Education 2601 Enterprise Rd *Web:* system.nevada.edu	Reno	NV	89512	775-784-4905	784-1127
New Jersey Higher Education Commission 20 W State St PO Box 542 *Web:* www.state.nj.us	Trenton	NJ	08625	609-292-4310	292-7225
New Mexico Higher Education Dept 2048 Galisteo St *TF:* 800-279-9777 ■ *Web:* www.hed.state.nm.us	Santa Fe	NM	87505	505-476-8400	476-8453
City University of New York (CUNY) 535 E 80th St *TF:* 877-769-7441 ■ *Web:* www.cuny.edu	New York	NY	10075	212-794-5555	794-5397
New York State Education Dept 89 Washington Ave 5N EB *Web:* www.highered.nysed.gov	Albany	NY	12234	518-474-3901	
State University of New York, The (SUNY) State University Plz *TF:* 800-342-3811 ■ *Web:* www.suny.edu	Albany	NY	12246	518-320-1888	
North Carolina Community College System 200 W Jones St *Web:* nccommunitycolleges.edu	Raleigh	NC	27603	919-807-7100	807-7164
University of North Carolina 910 Raleigh Rd PO Box 2688 *Web:* www.northcarolina.edu	Chapel Hill	NC	27515	919-962-1000	962-6725
North Dakota University System 600 E Blvd Ave Dept 215 10th Fl *Web:* www.ndus.edu	Bismarck	ND	58505	701-328-2960	328-2961
Ohio State University System 190 N Oval Mall 205 Bricker Hall *Web:* www.osu.edu	Columbus	OH	43210	614-292-2424	292-1231
Oklahoma State System of Higher Education 655 Research Pkwy Ste 200 *Web:* www.okhighered.org	Oklahoma City	OK	73104	405-225-9120	225-9235
Pennsylvania State System of Higher Education 2986 N Second St *TF:* 800-732-0999 ■ *Web:* www.passhe.edu	Harrisburg	PA	17110	717-720-4000	720-4011
South Carolina Commission on Higher Education 1122 Lady St Ste 300 *Web:* www.che.sc.gov	Columbia	SC	29201	803-737-2260	737-2297
University of South Dakota Foundation 1110 N Dakota St PO Box 5555 *TF:* 800-521-3575 ■ *Web:* www.onwardsd.org	Vermillion	SD	57069	605-677-6703	677-6717
Tennessee Higher Education Commission 404 James Robertson Pkwy Ste 1900 *Web:* www.state.tn.us	Nashville	TN	37243	615-741-3605	741-6230
University of Tennessee System 800 Andy Holt Tower 8th Fl *Web:* www.tennessee.edu	Knoxville	TN	37996	865-974-2241	974-3753
Texas A & M University System, The 200 Technology Way Ste 2043 *Web:* www.tamus.edu	College Station	TX	77845	979-458-6000	458-6044
Texas State University System (TSUS) 208 E Tenth St Ste 600 *Web:* www.tsus.edu	Austin	TX	78701	512-463-1808	463-1816
Texas Tech University System 124 Admin Bldg PO Box 42013 *Web:* www.texastech.edu	Lubbock	TX	79409	806-742-0012	742-8050
University of Texas System 601 Colorado St *TF:* 866-882-2034 ■ *Web:* www.utsystem.edu	Austin	TX	78701	512-499-4200	499-4215
Utah System of Higher Education 60 South 400 West *TF:* 800-418-8757 ■ *Web:* www.higheredutah.org	Salt Lake City	UT	84101	801-321-7100	366-8405
Vermont State Colleges 575 Stone Cutters Way *Web:* vsc.edu	Montpelier	VT	05601	802-224-3000	224-3035
Virginia Community College System 101 N 14th St 15th Fl *Web:* www.vccs.edu	Richmond	VA	23219	804-819-4901	819-4766
Washington Higher Education Coordinating Board 917 Lakeridge Way PO Box 43430 *Web:* www.wsac.wa.gov	Olympia	WA	98504	360-753-7800	753-7808
West Virginia Higher Education Policy Commission 1018 Kanawha Blvd E Ste 700 *TF:* 888-825-5707 ■ *Web:* wvhepc.com	Charleston	WV	25301	304-558-2101	
University of Wisconsin System 1220 Linden Dr 1720 Van Hise Hall *TF:* 800-442-6461 ■ *Web:* www.wisconsin.edu	Madison	WI	53706	608-262-2321	262-3985
Wyoming Community College Commission 2300 Capitol Ave Fl 5 Ste B *Web:* communitycolleges.wy.edu	Cheyenne	WY	82002	307-777-7763	777-6567

787 UTILITY COMPANIES

See Also Electric Companies - Cooperatives (Rural) p. 2206; Gas Transmission - Natural Gas p. 2350
Types of utilities included here are electric companies, water supply companies, and natural gas companies.

	City	State	ZIP	Phone	Fax
6D Global Technologies Inc 17 State St Ste 2550 *Web:* www.6dglobal.com	New York	NY	10004	646-681-4900	
889 Global Solutions 2501 Brookwood Rd *Web:* www.889globalsolutions.com	Columbus	OH	43209	614-235-8889	
A New Path 2527 Doubletree Rd *Web:* anewpathsite.org	Spring Valley	CA	91978	619-670-1184	
Acorn Energy Inc 3903 Centerville Rd *Web:* www.acornenergy.com	Wilmington	DE	19807	302-656-1708	
Acuren Group Inc 7450 - 18th St *Web:* www.acuren.com	Edmonton	AB	T6P1N8	780-440-2131	
AES Corp 4300 Wilson Blvd 11th Fl *NYSE: AES* ■ *Web:* www.aes.com	Arlington	VA	22203	703-522-1315	
AGL Resources Inc 10 Peachtree Pl PO Box 4569 *NYSE: GAS* ■ *TF Cust Svc:* 866-977-4278 ■ *Web:* www.aglresources.com	Atlanta	GA	30309	404-584-4000	
Alabama Gas Corp (Alagasco) 605 Richard Arrington Jr Blvd N *TF:* 800-292-4005 ■ *Web:* www.alagasco.com	Birmingham	AL	35203	205-326-8100	
Alameda County Water District 43885 S Grimmer Blvd *TF:* 866-275-3772 ■ *Web:* www.acwd.org	Fremont	CA	94537	510-668-4200	770-1793
Alaska Power & Telephone Co 193 Otto St PO Box 3222 *OTC: APTL* ■ *TF Cust Svc:* 800-982-0136 ■ *Web:* www.aptalaska.com	Port Townsend	WA	98368	360-385-1733	385-5177
Allegheny Power 800 Cabin Hill Dr *TF Cust Svc:* 800-255-3443 ■ *Web:* www.firstenergycorp.com	Greensburg	PA	15601	724-837-3000	
Alliant Energy Corp 4902 N Biltmore Ln Ste 1000 *NYSE: LNT* ■ **Fax Area Code:* 608 ■ *TF:* 800-255-4268 ■ *Web:* www.alliantenergy.com	Madison	WI	53718	800-255-4268	458-0100*
Alsco Inc 505 East South Temple *TF:* 800-408-0208 ■ *Web:* www.alsco.com	Salt Lake City	UT	84102	801-328-8831	
Ambit Energy LP 1801 N Lamar St Ste 200 *TF:* 877-282-6248 ■ *Web:* ww2.ambitenergy.com	Dallas	TX	75202	877-282-6248	
American Consumer Industries Inc (ACI) 1105 N Market St Ste 1150 *Web:* www.aciinc.net	Wilmington	DE	19801	303-495-2665	
American Emo Trans Inc 2600 Hutchison McDonald Rd *Web:* americanemotrans.com	Charlotte	NC	28219	704-359-0045	
American Municipal Power Inc 1111 Schrock Rd Ste 100 *Web:* www.amppartners.org	Columbus	OH	43229	614-540-1111	540-1113
Andretti Green Racing 7615 Zionsville Rd *Web:* www.andrettigreenracing.com	Indianapolis	IN	46268	317-872-2700	
Aqua America Inc 762 W Lancaster Ave *NYSE: WTR* ■ *TF:* 877-987-2782 ■ *Web:* www.aquaamerica.com	Bryn Mawr	PA	19010	877-987-2782	
Aquarion Co 835 Main St *TF:* 800-732-9678 ■ *Web:* www.aquarion.com	Bridgeport	CT	06604	203-336-7662	
AREVA Inc 4800 Hampden Ln Ste 1100 *Web:* www.areva.com	Bethesda	MD	20814	301-841-1600	
Arizona Public Service Co (APS) 400 N Fifth St PO Box 53999 *TF:* 800-253-9405 ■ *Web:* www.aps.com	Phoenix	AZ	85004	602-371-7171	
ATCO Gas & Pipelines Ltd 10035 - 105 St *Web:* www.atcogas.com	Edmonton	AB	T5J2V6	780-424-5222	
ATCO Ltd 700 909 11th Ave SW *TSE: ACO/X* ■ *TF:* 800-242-3447 ■ *Web:* www.atco.com	Calgary	AB	T2R1N6	403-292-7500	292-7532
Austin Tape & Label Inc 3350 Cavalier Trl *Web:* www.austintape.com	Stow	OH	44224	330-928-7999	
Authentidate Holding Corp 300 Connell Dr Fl 5 *Web:* www.authentidate.com	Berkeley Heights	NJ	07922	908-787-1700	
Avista Corp 1411 E Mission St *NYSE: AVA* ■ *TF:* 800-936-6629 ■ *Web:* www.avistacorp.com	Spokane	WA	99202	509-489-0500	
Avista Utilities 1411 E Mission St **Fax Area Code:* 509 ■ *TF:* 800-227-9187 ■ *Web:* www.avistautilities.com	Spokane	WA	99252	800-227-9187	495-8725*
Baltimore Gas & Electric Co 110 W Fayette St PO Box 1475 *TF:* 800-685-0123 ■ *Web:* www.bge.com	Baltimore	MD	21201	410-470-7433	
Bangor Hydro Electric Co PO Box 932 *TF:* 800-499-6600 ■ *Web:* emeramaine.com	Bangor	ME	04402	207-945-5621	
BCE Inc 1 CARREFOUR ALEXANDER-GRAHAM-BELL Bldg A, 4th Fl *Web:* www.bce.ca	Verdun	QC	H3E3B3	514-786-3891	
Berkshire Gas Company Inc 115 Cheshire Rd *TF:* 800-292-5012 ■ *Web:* www.berkshiregas.com	Pittsfield	MA	01201	413-442-1511	443-0546
Booth Creek Ski Holdings Inc 950 Red Sand Stone Rd Ste 43 *Web:* www.boothcreek.com	Vail	CO	81657	530-550-5100	
Brownstown Electric Supply Company Inc 690 E State Rd 250 PO Box L *TF:* 800-742-8492 ■ *Web:* www.brownstown.com	Brownstown	IN	47220	812-358-4555	358-2484
Cabot Oil & Gas Corp 840 Gessner Rd Ste 1200 *NYSE: COG* ■ *TF:* 800-434-3985 ■ *Web:* cabotog.com	Houston	TX	77024	281-848-2799	
Cadiz Inc 550 S Hope St Ste 2850 *NASDAQ: CDZI* ■ *Web:* www.cadizinc.com	Los Angeles	CA	90071	213-271-1600	271-1614
Caithness Corp 565 Fifth Ave 29Fl *Web:* www.caithnessenergy.com	New York	NY	10017	212-921-9099	921-9239
California ISO 151 Blue Ravine Rd PO Box 639014 *TF:* 800-220-4907 ■ *Web:* www.caiso.com	Folsom	CA	95630	916-351-4400	608-7222
California Water Service Group 1720 N First St *NYSE: CWT* ■ *TF:* 800-750-8200 ■ *Web:* www.calwater.com	San Jose	CA	95112	408-367-8200	367-8430
Calpine Corp 717 Texas Ave Ste 1000 *NYSE: CPN* ■ *TF:* 800-367-5690 ■ *Web:* www.calpine.com	Houston	TX	77002	713-830-2000	
Canadian Utilities Ltd 1400 909 - 11th Ave SW *TSE: CU* ■ *Web:* www.canadianutilities.com	Calgary	AB	T2R1N6	403-292-7500	292-7532
Carthage Water & Electric Plant PO Box 611 *Web:* www.cwepnet.com	Carthage	MO	64836	417-237-7300	237-7310
Cascade Natural Gas Corp (CNGC) 8113 W Grandridge Blvd *TF:* 888-522-1130 ■ *Web:* www.cngc.com	Kennewick	WA	99336	206-624-3900	624-7215
Central Hudson Gas & Electric Corp 284 S Ave *TF:* 800-527-2714 ■ *Web:* www.centralhudson.com	Poughkeepsie	NY	12601	845-452-2700	

	City	State	Zip	Phone	Fax
Central Iowa Power Cooperative 1400 Hwy 13 SE *Web:* www.cipco.net	Cedar Rapids	IA	52403	319-366-8011	
Central Maine Power Co 83 Edison Dr *TF:* 800-565-0121 ■ *Web:* www.cmpco.com	Augusta	ME	04336	207-623-3521	621-4778
Central Vermont Public Service Corp 2154 Post Rd *TF:* 800-649-2877 ■ *Web:* Www.account.greenmountainpower.com	Rutland	VT	05701	888-835-4672	
Chesapeake Utilities Corp 909 Silver Lk Blvd *NYSE: CPK* ■ *Web:* www.chpk.com	Dover	DE	19904	302-734-6799	734-6750
Chickasaw Holding Co 124 W Vinita *Web:* www.chickasawholding.com	Sulphur	OK	73086	580-622-2111	
Chorus Aviation Inc 3 Spectacle Lk Dr *Web:* www.flyjazz.ca	Dartmouth	NS	B3B1W8	902-873-5000	
Chubu Electric Power Co Inc 900 17th St NW Ste 1220 *Web:* www.chuden.co.jp	Washington	DC	20006	202-775-1960	331-9256
CI Financial Corp Twentieth 2 Queen St E Fl *Web:* www.theglobeandmail.com/globe-investor	Toronto	ON	M5C3G7	416-364-1145	
Citizens Gas & Coke Utility 2020 N Meridian St *TF:* 800-427-4217 ■ *Web:* www.citizensenergygroup.com	Indianapolis	IN	46202	317-924-3311	927-4395
City Public Service Board PO Box 1771 *TF:* 800-870-1006 ■ *Web:* www.cpsenergy.com	San Antonio	TX	78296	210-353-2222	
Cleco Corp 2030 Donahue Ferry Rd *TF Cust Svc:* 800-622-6537 ■ *Web:* cleco.com	Pineville	LA	71361	318-484-7400	
Colorado Springs Utilities 111 S Cascade Ave PO Box 1103 *TF:* 800-238-5434 ■ *Web:* www.csu.org	Colorado Springs	CO	80903	719-448-4800	668-7288
Columbia Gas of Ohio Inc 200 Civic Ctr Dr *TF:* 800-807-9781 ■ *Web:* columbiagasohio.com	Columbus	OH	43215	614-460-6000	
Columbia Gas of Virginia Inc 1809 Coyote Dr *TF Cust Svc:* 800-543-8911	Chester	VA	23836	800-543-8911	
Commissioners of Public Works 121 W Ct Ave *Web:* www.greenwoodcpw.com	Greenwood	SC	29646	864-942-8100	942-8114
Conergy Inc 2460 W 26th Ave Ste 280C **Fax Area Code:* 505 ■ *Web:* www.conergy.com	Denver	CO	80211	720-305-0700	473-3830*
Connecticut Light & Power Co 107 Selden St *TF Cust Svc:* 800-286-2000 ■ *Web:* www.cl-p.com	Berlin	CT	06037	860-665-5000	
Connecticut Natural Gas Corp (CNG) 76 Meadow St *Web:* www.cngcorp.com	East Hartford	CT	06108	860-727-3000	
Consumers Energy Co 1 Energy Plz **Fax:* Hum Res ■ *TF Cust Svc:* 800-477-5050 ■ *Web:* www.consumersenergy.com	Jackson	MI	49201	517-788-0550	788-2451*
Coulson Group of Companies 4890 Cherry Creek Rd *Web:* www.coulsongroup.com	Port Alberni	BC	V9Y8E9	250-724-7600	
Covanta Energy Corp 445 South St *NYSE: CVA* ■ *TF:* 800-950-8749 ■ *Web:* covanta.com	Morristown	NJ	07960	862-345-5000	
Cupric Canyon Capital LLC 7373 E Doubletree Ranch Rd Ste A-180 *Web:* www.cupriccanyon.com	Scottsdale	AZ	85258	480-607-6771	
Dakota Gasification Co PO Box 5540 *TF:* 866-747-3546 ■ *Web:* www.dakotagas.com	Bismarck	ND	58506	701-221-4400	557-5336
Dayton Power & Light Co PO Box 1247 *TF:* 800-433-8500 ■ *Web:* www.dpandl.com	Dayton	OH	45401	937-331-3900	331-3900
Delmarva Power PO Box 231 *TF Cust Svc:* 800-898-8042 ■ *Web:* www.delmarva.com	Wilmington	DE	19899	800-898-8042	
Delta Natural Gas Co Inc 3617 Lexington Rd *NASDAQ: DGAS* ■ *TF:* 800-262-2012 ■ *Web:* www.deltagas.com	Winchester	KY	40391	859-744-6171	744-3623
Dominion East Ohio PO Box 26532 *TF Cust Svc:* 800-362-7557 ■ *Web:* www.dom.com	Richmond	VA	23261	800-362-7557	
Dominion Hope 701 E Cary St *TF:* 866-366-4357 ■ *Web:* www.dom.com/dominion-hope	Richmond	VA	23219	888-366-8280	
Dominion North Carolina Power 701 E Cary St *TF:* 888-667-3000 ■ *Web:* www.dom.com	Richmond	VA	23219	757-857-2112	
Dominion Virginia Power 120 Tredegar St *TF:* 800-688-4673 ■ *Web:* www.dom.com	Richmond	VA	23219	800-688-4673	
Duke Energy Corp 550 S Tryon St Mail Drop WP 890 *TF:* 800-521-2232 ■ *Web:* m.duke-energy.com	Charlotte	NC	28202	713-627-5400	
Dynasty Import Co 2765 16th St *Web:* m.dynastygallery.com	San Francisco	CA	94103	415-864-5084	
Eastern Shore Natural Gas Co 1110 Forest Ave Ste 201 *TF:* 877-650-1257 ■ *Web:* www.esng.com	Dover	DE	19904	302-734-6720	
EGPI Firecreek Inc 6564 Smoke Tree Ln *Web:* www.egpifirecreek.com	Scottsdale	AZ	85253	480-948-6581	
El Paso Electric Co 100 N Stanton Stanton Tower *NYSE: EE* ■ *TF:* 800-351-1621 ■ *Web:* www.epelectric.com	El Paso	TX	79901	915-543-5711	521-4766
Elizabethtown Gas Co 1 Elizabethtown Plz *TF:* 800-242-5830 ■ *Web:* www.elizabethtowngas.com	Union	NJ	07083	908-289-5000	859-5307
Emerald Coast Utilities Authority (ECUA) 9255 Sturdevant St PO Box 15311 *Web:* www.ecua.fl.gov	Pensacola	FL	32514	850-476-0480	
Empire District Electric Co, The 602 Joplin St PO Box 127 *NYSE: EDE* ■ *TF:* 800-206-2300 ■ *Web:* www.empiredistrict.com	Joplin	MO	64802	417-625-5100	
Energy West Inc 1 First Ave S *TF:* 800-570-5688 ■ *Web:* www.ewst.com	Great Falls	MT	59401	406-791-7500	791-7560
ENMAX Corp 141 50 Ave SE *TF:* 877-571-7111 ■ *Web:* www.enmax.com	Calgary	AB	T2G4S7	403-514-3000	
Enpower Corp 2420 Camino Ramon Ste 101 *Web:* www.enpowercorp.com	San Ramon	CA	94583	925-244-1100	
ENSTAR Natural Gas Co 401 E International Airport Rd *Web:* www.enstargas.com	Anchorage	AK	99518	907-277-5551	
Entergy Arkansas Inc 425 W Capitol Ave *TF:* 800-368-3749 ■ *Web:* www.entergy-arkansas.com	Little Rock	AR	72201	800-368-3749	
Entergy Louisiana Inc 639 Loyola Ave *TF Cust Svc:* 800-368-3749 ■ *Web:* www.entergy.com	New Orleans	LA	70113	504-576-6116	
Entergy Mississippi Inc PO Box 1640 *Web:* www.entergy-mississippi.com	Jackson	MS	39215	601-969-2440	
Entergy New Orleans Inc 639 Loyola Ave *TF Cust Svc:* 800-368-3749 ■ *Web:* www.entergy-neworleans.com	New Orleans	LA	70113	800-368-3749	
Entergy Texas Inc 350 Pine St *TF:* 800-368-3749 ■ *Web:* www.entergy-texas.com	Beaumont	TX	77701	409-981-3245	
EQT Corp 625 Liberty Ave Ste 1700 *NYSE: EQT* ■ *TF:* 800-242-1776 ■ *Web:* www.eqt.com	Pittsburgh	PA	15222	412-553-5700	
Equitable Gas Co PO Box 6766 *TF:* 800-654-6335 ■ *Web:* www.peoples-gas.com/welcomeequitablegascustomers.aspx	Pittsburgh	PA	15212	800-654-6335	
Erie County Water Authority (ECWA) 295 Main St Rm 350 *TF:* 855-748-1076 ■ *Web:* www.ecwa.org	Buffalo	NY	14203	716-849-8484	849-8467
Eversource 1 Nstar Way NW200 *TF Cust Svc:* 800-592-2000 ■ *Web:* nstar.com	Westwood	MA	02090	781-441-8011	441-8167
Eversource 1 Federal St Bldg 111-4 *TF:* 800-286-2000 ■ *Web:* www.wmeco.com	Springfield	MA	01105	413-785-5871	
Far Bank Enterprises Inc 8500 NE Day Rd *Web:* www.farbank.com	Bainbridge Island	WA	98110	206-780-8767	
First Surgical Partners Inc 411 First St *Web:* www.firstsurgical.com	Bellaire	TX	77401	713-665-1111	
Florida City Gas (FCG) 955 E 25th St *TF:* 800-993-7546 ■ *Web:* www.floridacitygas.com	Hialeah	FL	33013	305-691-8710	
Florida Power & Light Co (FPL) 700 Universe Blvd *Web:* www.fpl.com	Juno Beach	FL	33408	561-697-8000	
Florida Public Utilities Co (FPUC) 401 S Dixie Hwy **Fax Area Code:* 561 ■ *TF:* 800-427-7712 ■ *Web:* www.fpuc.com	West Palm Beach	FL	33401	800-427-7712	833-0151*
Folkstone Capital Corp 1000 595 Burrard St., Stn Bentall Centre, PO Box 49290 *Web:* ca.finance.yahoo.com	Vancouver	BC	V7X1S8	905-467-5564	
Fys Group Corp 131 S Brent Cir *Web:* fysonline.com	Walnut	CA	91789	909-468-0072	
Garvey Group LLC, The 7400 N Lehigh Ave *Web:* www.thegarveygroup.com	Niles	IL	60714	847-647-1900	
Gas Co, The 515 Kamake'e St *TF:* 866-499-3941 ■ *Web:* www.hawaiigas.com	Honolulu	HI	96814	808-535-5933	535-5934
Gatco Inc 1550 Factor Ave *TF:* 800-227-5640 ■ *Web:* www.gatco-inc.com	San Leandro	CA	94577	510-352-8770	
Georgia Power Co 241 Ralph McGill Blvd NE *TF Cust Svc:* 866-506-5333 ■ *Web:* www.southernco.com	Atlanta	GA	30308	404-506-5000	
Ges USA Inc 101 W Elm St Ste 550 *Web:* services-ges.com	Conshohocken	PA	19428	610-940-6088	
Globalscale Technologies Inc 1200 N Van Buren St Ste D *Web:* globalscaletechnologies.com	Anaheim	CA	92807	714-632-9239	
Goleta Water District 4699 Hollister Ave *Web:* www.goletawater.com	Goleta	CA	93110	805-964-6761	
GolfBC Holdings Inc 1800-1030 W Georgia St *TF:* 800-446-5322 ■ *Web:* www.golfbc.com	Vancouver	BC	V6E2Y3	800-446-5322	
Green Brick Partners Inc 2805 Dallas Pkwy Ste 400 *Web:* greenbrickpartners.com	Plano	TX	75093	469-573-6755	
Green Mountain Energy Co PO Box 689008 *Web:* greenmountainenergy.com	Austin	TX	78768	512-691-6100	
Green Mountain Power Corp 163 Acorn Ln *TF:* 888-835-4672 ■ *Web:* www.greenmountainpower.com	Colchester	VT	05446	802-864-5731	655-8419
GridPoint Inc 2801 Clarendon Blvd Ste 100 *Web:* www.gridpoint.com	Arlington	VA	22201	703-667-7000	667-7001
HaloSource Inc 1631 220th St SE Ste 100 *Web:* www.halosource.com	Bothell	WA	98021	425-881-6464	882-2476
Harris, Harris, Bauerle & Sharma PA 1201 E Robinson St *Web:* www.hhbslaw.com	Orlando	FL	32801	407-843-0404	
Hawaiian Electric Industries Inc 1001 Bishop St Ste 2900 *TF:* 877-871-8461 ■ *Web:* www.hei.com	Honolulu	HI	96813	808-543-5662	
Hawaiian Telcom Holdco Inc 1177 Bishop St *Web:* www.hawaiiantel.com	Honolulu	HI	96813	808-546-4511	
Hazelett Strip-Casting Corp 135 W Lakeshore Dr PO Box 600 *Web:* www.hazelett.com	Colchester	VT	05446	802-863-6376	
Home Meridian International Inc 2485 Penny Rd Ste 310 *Web:* www.homemeridian.com	High Point	NC	27265	336-819-7200	
Hydro One Inc 483 Bay St 15th Fl *TF:* 888-664-9376 ■ *Web:* www.hydroone.com	Toronto	ON	M5G2P5	416-345-5000	
Idaho Power Co 1221 W Idaho St **Fax:* Hum Res ■ *TF:* 800-488-6151 ■ *Web:* www.idahopower.com	Boise	ID	83702	208-388-2200	388-6695*
Indianapolis Power & Light Co 1 Monument Cir *Web:* www.iplpower.com	Indianapolis	IN	46204	317-261-8261	
Intermountain Gas Co Inc 555 S Cole Rd *TF Cust Svc:* 800-548-3679 ■ *Web:* www.intgas.com	Boise	ID	83709	208-377-6840	377-6081
Inuvialuit Regional Corp Bag Service #21 *Web:* www.irc.inuvialuit.com	Inuvik	NT	X0E0T0	867-777-2737	
J S Redpath Limited 710 McKeown Ave *Web:* www.redpathmining.com	North Bay	ON	P1A7M2	705-474-2461	
Jackson Energy Authority 119 E College St *Web:* www.jaxenergy.com	Jackson	TN	38301	731-422-7500	422-7307
Jc Toys Group Inc 9590 Nw 40th St Rd *Web:* www.jctoys.com	Doral	FL	33178	305-597-7801	
Jfm Enterprises Inc 1301 W 22nd St Ste 1001 *Web:* www.jfm.net	Oak Brook	IL	60523	630-990-4555	
Kansas City Power & Light Co 1200 Main *TF:* 888-471-5275 ■ *Web:* www.kcpl.com	Kansas City	MO	64141	816-556-2200	654-1125
Kansas Gas Service 7421 W 129th St *TF:* 888-482-4950 ■ *Web:* www.kansasgasservice.com	Overland Park	KS	66213	888-482-4950	

Phone | Fax

Kimble Companies Inc 3596 State Rt 39 NW ... Dover OH 44622 330-343-1226
Web: www.kimblecompanies.com

Kinder Morgan Inc KN Energy Retail Div
370 Van Gordon St ... Lakewood CO 80228 303-989-1740
TF: 800-232-1627 ■ *Web:* www.kindermorgan.com

Kissimmee Utility Authority Inc (KUA)
1701 W Carroll St ... Kissimmee FL 34741 407-933-7777
TF: 877-582-7700 ■ *Web:* www.kua.com

KP Tissue Inc 1900 Minnesota Crt Ste 200 ... Mississauga ON L5N5R5 905-812-6900
Web: www.kptissueinc.com

Laclede Gas Co 720 Olive St ... Saint Louis MO 63101 314-342-0500
TF: 800-887-4173 ■ *Web:* www.lacledegas.com

Lad Global Enterprises Inc 1309 S Fountain Dr ... Olathe KS 66061 913-768-0888
Web: www.lad-global.com

Lake Haven Utility District
31627-1st Ave S PO Box 4249 ... Federal Way WA 98063 253-941-1516
Web: www.lakehaven.org

Lampton-Love Inc PO Box 1607 ... Jackson MS 39215 601-939-8304 939-8309
Web: www.lamptonlove.com

Laney's Inc 55 27 St S ... Fargo ND 58103 701-237-0543
Web: www.laneysinc.com

Lightyear Network Solutions LLC
1901 Eastpoint Pkwy ... Louisville KY 40223 502-244-6666
Web: www.lightyear.net

Lineage Power Corp 601 Shiloh Rd ... Plano TX 75074 972-244-9288
TF: 877-546-3243 ■ *Web:* geindustrial.com/products/critical-power

Long Island Power Authority
333 Earle Ovington Blvd Ste 403 ... Uniondale NY 11553 516-222-7700 222-9137
TF Cust Svc: 877-275-5472 ■ *Web:* www.lipower.org

Lord Electric Co Of Puerto Rico Inc
8 Simon Madera ... San Juan PR 00924 787-758-4040
Web: www.lordelectric.com

Lyondellbasell Industries Inc
1221 McKinney St LyondellBasell Tower
Ste 700 ... Houston TX 77010 713-309-7200
Web: www.lyondellbasell.com

Madison Gas & Electric Co 133 S Blair St ... Madison WI 53703 608-252-7000 252-7098
TF: 800-245-1125 ■ *Web:* www.mge.com

Marts & Lundy Inc 1200 Wall St W ... Lyndhurst NJ 07071 201-460-1660 460-0680
TF: 800-526-9005 ■ *Web:* www.martsandlundy.com

Mastercool Usa Inc 1 Aspen Dr ... Randolph NJ 07869 973-252-9119
Web: www.mastercool.com

Maxland International Inc
9457 Rush St ... South El Monte CA 91733 626-443-2443
Web: www.maxland.com

MEAG Power 1470 Riveredge Pkwy NW ... Atlanta GA 30328 770-563-0300 563-0004
TF: 800-333-6324 ■ *Web:* www.meagpower.org

Mel-Kay Electric Company Inc
1511 N Garvin St ... Evansville IN 47711 812-423-1128 423-5117
Web: www.mel-kayelectric.com

Memphis Light Gas & Water (MLGW)
220 S Main St PO Box 430 ... Memphis TN 38101 901-528-4011
Web: www.mlgw.com

Menasha Utilities 321 Milwaukee St PO Box 340 ... Menasha WI 54952 920-967-3400 967-3441
Web: www.menashautilities.com

Merrithew Corp 2200 Yonge St Ste 500 ... Toronto ON M4S2C6 416-482-4050
TF: 800-910-0001 ■ *Web:* www.merrithew.com

Meruelo Construction
9550 Firestone Blvd Ste 105 ... Downey CA 90241 562-745-2345
Web: merueloenterprises.com

Metromedia Energy Inc 6 Industrial Way W ... Eatontown NJ 07724 732-542-7575 542-8655
Web: www.metromediaenergy.com

Michael W Middleton PC (MWMPC)
3330 Longmire Dr ... College Station TX 77845 979-695-2726 695-2754
Web: www.mwmpc.com

Middle Tennessee Natural Gas Utility District (MTNG)
1036 W Broad St PO Box 670 ... Smithville TN 37166 615-597-4300 597-6331
TF: 800-880-6373 ■ *Web:* www.mtng.com

Middlesex County Utilities Authority Inc (MCUA)
2571 Main St PO Box 159 ... Sayreville NJ 08872 732-721-3800 721-0206
Web: www.mcua.com

Middlesex Water Co 1500 Ronson Rd PO Box 1500 ... Iselin NJ 08830 732-634-1500 638-7515
NASDAQ: MSEX ■ *TF:* 800-549-3802 ■ *Web:* middlesexwater.com

Miller-Eads Company Inc
4125 N Keystone Ave ... Indianapolis IN 46205 317-545-7101 545-4660
TF: 800-530-0684 ■ *Web:* www.miller-eads.com

Minnesota Power 30 W Superior St ... Duluth MN 55802 218-722-2625 720-2795
TF: 800-228-4966 ■ *Web:* www.mnpower.com

Missouri Gas Energy 3420 Broadway ... Kansas City MO 64111 816-756-5252 756-0595
TF: 800-582-1234 ■ *Web:* www.missourigasenergy.com

Mobile Gas Service Corp 2828 Dauphin St ... Mobile AL 36606 251-476-8052 471-2588*
**Fax:* Mktg ■ *Web:* www.mobile-gas.com

Monroe County Water Authority
475 Norris Dr PO Box 10999 ... Rochester NY 14610 585-442-2000 442-0220
TF: 866-426-6292 ■ *Web:* www.mcwa.com

Montana-Dakota Utilities Co (MDU)
400 N Fourth St ... Bismarck ND 58501 701-222-7900
TF: 800-638-3278 ■ *Web:* www.montana-dakota.com

Morgan-McClure Motorsports Inc
26502 Newbanks Rd ... Abingdon VA 24210 276-628-3683
Web: www.morgan-mcclure.com

Morris Products Inc 53 Carey Rd ... Queensbury NY 12804 518-743-0523
TF: 888-777-6678 ■ *Web:* www.morrisproducts.com

Morristown Utility Systems PO Box 667 ... Morristown TN 37815 423-586-4121 587-6590
Web: www.morristownutilities.org

Mount Carmel Public Utility Co
316 Market St PO Box 220 ... Mount Carmel IL 62863 618-262-5151
TF: 877-262-7036 ■ *Web:* www.mtcpu.com/home.php

MRC Global Inc 2 Houston Ctr ... Houston TX 77010 877-294-7574
TF: 877-294-7574 ■ *Web:* www.mrcglobal.com/global-region/default

National Fuel Gas Supply Corp
6363 Main St ... Williamsville NY 14221 716-857-7000 857-7206
TF Cust Svc: 800-365-3234 ■ *Web:* nationalfuelgas.com

National Fuel Resources Inc
165 Lawrence Bell Dr Ste 120 ... Williamsville NY 14221 716-630-6778 630-6798
TF: 800-839-9993 ■ *Web:* www.nfrinc.com

Neal Electri Corp 13250 Kirkham Way ... Poway CA 92064 858-513-2525 513-9488
Web: www.nealelectric.com

Nevada Irrigation District (NID)
1036 W Main St ... Grass Valley CA 95945 530-273-6185 271-6838
TF: 800-222-4102 ■ *Web:* nidwater.com

Nevada Power Co 6226 W Sahara Ave ... Las Vegas NV 89146 702-402-5555
NYSE: NVE ■ *TF Cust Svc:* 800-331-3103 ■ *Web:* www.nvenergy.com

New York Power Authority
123 Main St Ste 10-H ... White Plains NY 10601 914-681-6200
Web: www.nypa.gov

New York State Electric & Gas Corp
Corporate Dr PO Box 5240 ... Binghamton NY 13902 800-572-1111
TF: 800-572-1111 ■ *Web:* www.nyseg.com

NextEra Energy Resources LLC
NextEra Energy Resources LLC
700 Universe Blvd PO Box 14000 ... Juno Beach FL 33408 561-691-7171
TF: 888-867-3050 ■ *Web:* www.nexteraenergyresources.com

Nicor Gas 1844 Ferry Rd ... Naperville IL 60563 888-642-6748 983-6755*
**Fax Area Code:* 630 ■ *TF:* 888-642-6748

Nippon Kodo Inc 2771 Plz Del Amo Ste 805 ... Torrance CA 90503 310-320-8881
TF: 888-775-5487 ■ *Web:* www.nipponkodo.com

North Shore Gas Co 3001 Grand Ave ... Waukegan IL 60085 847-263-3200
TF: 866-556-6004 ■ *Web:* northshoregasdelivery.com

Northern Electric Inc 1275 W 124th Ave ... Denver CO 80234 303-428-6969 428-6669
TF: 877-265-0794 ■ *Web:* www.northernelec.com

Northern Kentucky Water District
2835 Crescent Springs Rd ... Erlanger KY 41018 859-578-9898 578-5456
TF: 800-772-4636 ■ *Web:* www.nkywater.org

Northwest Natural Gas Co 220 NW Second Ave ... Portland OR 97209 503-226-4211 220-2584
NYSE: NWN ■ *TF:* 800-422-4012 ■ *Web:* www.nwnatural.com

Nova Scotia Power Inc PO Box 910 ... Halifax NS B3J2W5 902-428-6230 428-6108
TF: 800-428-6230 ■ *Web:* www.nspower.ca

NRG Energy Inc 211 Carnegie Ctr ... Princeton NJ 08540 609-524-4500 524-4501
NYSE: NRG ■ *Web:* nrg.com

NSTAR Gas 1 N Star Way ... Westwood MA 02090 800-592-2000
TF: 800-592-2000 ■ *Web:* nstar.com

Ocean Embassy Panama Inc
6426 Milner Blvd Ste 101 ... Orlando FL 32809 407-852-9129
Web: www.oceanembassy.com

OG & E Electric Services PO Box 24990 ... Oklahoma City OK 73124 405-553-3000
TF: 800-272-9741 ■ *Web:* www.oge.com

Ohio Edison Co 76 S Main St PO Box 3637 ... Akron OH 44308 800-736-3402
TF: 800-736-3402 ■ *Web:* firstenergycorp.com

Oklahoma Natural Gas Co
401 N Harvey PO Box 401 ... Oklahoma City OK 73101 800-664-5463
TF: 800-664-5463 ■ *Web:* www.oklahomanaturalgas.com

Olympia Financial Group Inc
Ste 2300 125 - 9 Ave SE ... Calgary AB T2G0P6 403-261-0900
TF: 888-668-8384 ■ *Web:* www.olympiatrust.com

Oncor 1616 Woodall Rodgers Fwy Ste 2M-012 ... Dallas TX 75202 214-486-2000
TF: 888-313-6862 ■ *Web:* www.oncor.com

Orange & Rockland Utilities Inc
390 W Rte 59 ... Spring Valley NY 10977 877-434-4100
TF Cust Svc: 877-434-4100 ■ *Web:* www.oru.com

Orange Water & Sewer Authority (Inc)
400 Jones Ferry Rd ... Carrboro NC 27510 919-968-4421 968-4464
Web: www.owasa.org

Osaka Gas Energy America Corp
1 N Lexington Ave Ste 504 ... White Plains NY 10601 914-253-5500 328-4430
Web: www.osakagas.co.jp

Otter Tail Power Co 215 S Cascade St ... Fergus Falls MN 56537 218-739-8200 751-5151
TF: 800-257-4044 ■ *Web:* www.otpco.com

Pacific Data Electric Inc (PDE)
9970 Bell Ranch Dr Ste 109 ... Santa Fe Springs CA 90670 562-204-3550 204-0380
Web: www.pdeinc.com

Pacific Gas & Electric Co 77 Beale St ... San Francisco CA 94105 415-973-7000
TF Cust Svc: 800-743-5000 ■ *Web:* www.pge.com

Pacific Power & Light 825 NE Multnomah St ... Portland OR 97232 503-813-6666 800-2851*
**Fax Area Code:* 888 ■ **Fax:* Cust Svc ■ *TF Cust Svc:* 888-221-7070 ■ *Web:* www.pacificpower.net

PacifiCorp 825 NE Multnomah St ... Portland OR 97232 503-813-5000 813-6659*
**Fax:* Hum Res ■ *TF:* 888-221-7070 ■ *Web:* www.pacificorp.com

Paducah Power System 1500 Broadway ... Paducah KY 42001 270-575-4000 575-4027
Web: www.paducahpower.com

Park Water Co 9750 Washburn Rd ... Downey CA 90241 562-923-0711 861-5902
TF: 800-727-5987 ■ *Web:* www.parkwater.com

Parkway Electric Inc 11952 James St ... Holland MI 49424 616-392-2788 392-6880
TF: 800-574-9553 ■ *Web:* www.parkwayelectric.com

Passaic Valley Water Commission
1525 Main Ave ... Clifton NJ 07011 973-340-4300 340-5598
TF: 877-772-7077 ■ *Web:* www.pvwc.com

Pennichuck Corp 25 Manchester St ... Merrimack NH 03054 603-882-5191 913-2362
NASDAQ: PNNW ■ *TF:* 800-553-5191 ■ *Web:* www.pennichuck.com

Peoples Gas Light & Coke Co
130 E Randolph Dr ... Chicago IL 60601 312-240-4000
TF Cust Svc: 866-556-6001 ■ *Web:* northshoregasdelivery.com

Pepco Energy Services Inc
1300 N 17th St Ste 1600 ... Arlington VA 22209 703-253-1800 967-5820*
**Fax Area Code:* 301 ■ *TF:* 800-424-8028 ■ *Web:* www.pepco.com

Pepco Holdings Inc 701 Ninth St NW ... Washington DC 20068 202-872-2000
NYSE: POM ■ *Web:* www.pepcoholdings.com

PFB Corp 100-2886 Sunridge Way NE ... Calgary AB T1Y7H9 403-569-4300
Web: www.pfbcorp.com

Phalcon Ltd 505 Main St ... Farmington CT 06032 860-677-9797
Web: phalconusa.com

Philadelphia Gas Works (PGW)
800 W Montgomery Ave ... Philadelphia PA 19122 215-235-1000
Web: www.pgworks.com

Phillips 66 3010 Briarpark Dr ... Houston TX 77042 281-293-6600
Web: www.phillips66.com

				Phone	Fax
Piedmont Natural Gas 4720 Piedmont Row Dr PO Box 33068	Charlotte	NC	28233	704-364-3120	
NYSE: PNY ■ *TF:* 800-752-7504 ■ *Web:* www.piedmontng.com					
Pinnacle Gas Resources Inc 1 E Aalger St	Sheridan	WY	82801	307-673-9710	
Placer County Water Agency 144 Ferguson Rd PO Box 6570	Auburn	CA	95604	530-823-4850	
Web: www.pcwa.net					
Portland General Electric 121 SW Salmon St	Portland	OR	97204	503-464-8000	464-2676*
NYSE: POR ■ **Fax:* Hum Res ■ *TF:* 800-542-8818 ■ *Web:* www.portlandgeneral.com					
Portland Water District 225 Douglass St PO Box 3553	Portland	ME	04104	207-761-8310	761-8307
Web: www.pwd.org					
POWDR Corp 1790 Bonanza Dr Ste W201	Park City	UT	84060	435-658-5820	
Web: www.powdr.com					
Power Marketing Administrations *Bonneville Power Administration* 905 NE 11th Ave	Portland	OR	97232	503-230-3000	
TF: 800-282-3713 ■ *Web:* www.bpa.gov					
PowerSecure International Inc 1609 Heritage Commerce Ct	Wake Forest	NC	27587	919-556-3056	556-3596
NYSE: POWR ■ *TF:* 866-347-5455 ■ *Web:* www.powersecure.com					
PPL Electric Utilities Corp 2 N Ninth St	Allentown	PA	18101	610-774-5151	
TF Cust Svc: 800-342-5775 ■ *Web:* www.pplweb.com					
PPL Global LLC 2 N Ninth St	Allentown	PA	18101	610-774-5151	
NYSE: PPL ■ *TF:* 800-345-3085 ■ *Web:* www.pplweb.com					
Pratt Communications 2913 Tech Ctr	Santa Ana	CA	92705	714-540-6840	
TF General: 800-980-2323 ■ *Web:* www.prattcommunications.com					
PS Energy Group Inc 2987 Clairmont Rd Ste 500	Atlanta	GA	30329	404-321-5711	321-3938
TF: 800-334-7548 ■ *Web:* www.psenergy.com					
PSEG Power LLC 80 Pk Plz	Newark	NJ	07101	973-430-7000	
TF: 800-436-7734 ■ *Web:* www.pseg.com					
Public Service of New Hampshire 780 N Commercial St	Manchester	NH	03105	603-669-4000	
TF: 800-662-7764 ■ *Web:* www.psnh.com					
Public Works Commission of The City of Fayetteville North Carolina 955 Old Wilmington Rd PO Box 1089	Fayetteville	NC	28301	910-483-1382	
TF: 877-687-7921 ■ *Web:* www.faypwc.com					
Puget Sound Energy Inc 10885 NE Fourth St	Bellevue	WA	98004	425-452-1234	
TF: 888-225-5773 ■ *Web:* www.pse.com					
Quantum Utility Generation LLC 1401 McKinney St Ste 1800	Houston	TX	77010	713-485-8600	
Web: www.quantumug.com					
Questar Gas Co PO Box 45841	Salt Lake City	UT	84139	801-324-5111	
TF: 800-323-5517 ■ *Web:* questargas.com					
RedPrairie Holding Inc 20700 Swenson Dr	Waukesha	WI	53186	262-317-2000	
Web: www.redprairie.com					
Reliant Energy Retail Services LLC 1201 Fannin St	Houston	TX	77002	866-222-7100	488-4422*
**Fax Area Code:* 713 ■ *TF:* 866-660-4900 ■ *Web:* www.reliant.com					
RF Fisher Electric Co LLC 1707 W 39th Ave	Kansas City	KS	66103	913-384-1500	
Web: rffisher.com					
Roanoke Gas Co 519 Kimball Rd	Roanoke	VA	24030	540-777-4427	777-7952
Web: www.roanokegas.com					
Rochester Gas & Electric Corp 89 E Ave	Rochester	NY	14649	800-743-2110	
TF: 800-743-2110 ■ *Web:* www.rge.com					
Roland's Electric Inc 307 Suburban Ave	Deer Park	NY	11729	631-242-8080	242-6392
TF: 800-981-8010 ■ *Web:* www.rolandselectric.com					
S&W Contracting Company Inc 952 New Salem Rd	Murfreesboro	TN	37129	615-893-2511	895-2030
Web: www.sandwcontracting.com					
Salt River Project (SRP) 1521 N Project Dr	Tempe	AZ	85281	602-236-5900	236-2442
TF: 800-258-4777 ■ *Web:* www.srpnet.com					
San Diego Gas & Electric Co 101 Ash St	San Diego	CA	92101	619-696-2000	654-1755*
**Fax Area Code:* 858 ■ **Fax:* Cust Svc ■ *TF:* 800-411-7343 ■ *Web:* www.sdge.com					
San Jacinto River Authority 1577 Dam Site Rd	Conroe	TX	77304	936-588-1111	
Web: www.sanjacintoriverauthority.com					
SaveDaily Inc 3020 Old Ranch Pkwy Ste 140	Seal Beach	CA	90740	562-795-7500	
Web: www.savedailyinc.com					
SCANA Energy Marketing Inc 220 Operation Way	Cayce	SC	29033	803-217-9000	217-7344
TF: 800-472-1051 ■ *Web:* www.scana.com					
SemCAMS 521 Third Ave SW Ste 1200	Calgary	AB	T2P3T3	403-536-3000	
Web: www.semgroupcorp.com/businessunits/semcams.aspx					
SETEL UC 720 Cool Springs Blvd Ste 520	Franklin	TN	37067	615-874-6000	
TF: 800-743-1340 ■ *Web:* seteluc.com					
Shell Trading 909 Fannin St Plz Level 1	Houston	TX	77010	713-767-5400	
Web: www.shell.us					
Sid Richardson Carbon & Energy Cos 201 Main St	Fort Worth	TX	76102	817-390-8600	
Web: www.sidrich.com					
SilverSun Technologies Inc 5 Regent St Ste 520	Livingston	NJ	07039	973-758-6108	
Web: www.silversuntech.co					
Sims Recycling Solutions Holdings Inc 1600 Harvester Rd	West Chicago	IL	60185	630-231-6060	
Web: www.simsrecycling.com					
SourceGas 655 E Millsap Dr	Fayetteville	AR	72703	800-563-0012	
TF: 800-563-0012 ■ *Web:* www.sourcegasarkansas.com					
South Carolina Electric & Gas Co PO Box 100255	Columbia	SC	29202	803-635-4444	
TF: 800-251-7234 ■ *Web:* www.sceg.com					
South Coast Water District 31592 W St	Laguna Niguel	CA	92651	949-499-4555	499-4256
Web: www.scwd.org					
Southern California Edison Co 2244 Walnut Grove Ave	Rosemead	CA	91770	626-302-1212	
TF: 800-655-4555 ■ *Web:* www.sce.com					
Southern California Gas Co 555 W Fifth St	Los Angeles	CA	90013	909-305-8261	244-8293*
**Fax Area Code:* 213 ■ *TF:* 800-427-2200 ■ *Web:* www.socalgas.com					
Southern California Public Power Authority (SCPPA) 225 S Lake Ave Ste 1250	Pasadena	CA	91101	626-793-9364	793-9461
Web: www.scppa.org					
Southern Connecticut Gas (SCG) 60 Marsh Hill Rd	Orange	CT	06477	866-268-2887	
TF: 866-268-2887 ■ *Web:* www.soconngas.com					
Southwest Gas Corp 5241 Spring Mtn Rd PO Box 98510	Las Vegas	NV	89193	702-876-7237	
NYSE: SWX ■ *TF:* 877-860-6020 ■ *Web:* www.swgas.com					
Southwest Gas Corp Northern Nevada Div 400 Eagle Stn Ln	Carson City	NV	89701	877-860-6020	
TF: 877-860-6020 ■ *Web:* www.swgas.com					
Southwest Gas Corp Southern Arizona Div PO Box 98512	Las Vegas	NV	89193	877-860-6020	
TF: 877-860-6020 ■ *Web:* www.swgas.com					
Southwest Gas Corp Southern California Div 13471 Mariposa Rd	Victorville	CA	92395	877-860-6020	
TF: 877-860-6020 ■ *Web:* www.swgas.com					
Southwest Gas Corp Southern Nevada Div 5241 Spring Mtn Rd	Las Vegas	NV	89150	702-876-7011	
TF: 877-860-6020 ■ *Web:* www.swgas.com					
Southwest Water Co 12535 Reed Rd	Sugar Land	TX	77478	281-207-5800	
Web: www.swwc.com					
Southwestern Energy Co 2350 N Sam Houston Pkwy E Ste 300	Houston	TX	77032	832-796-1000	796-4818
NYSE: SWN ■ *TF:* 866-322-0801 ■ *Web:* www.swn.com					
Spectra Energy Corp 5400 Westheimer Ct	Houston	TX	77056	713-627-5400	
TF: 800-700-8744 ■ *Web:* m.duke-energy.com					
Spectra Plus Inc 638 Goodwin Dr	Richardson	TX	75081	972-437-5705	
Stream Gas & Electric Ltd 1950 Stemmons Fwy Ste 3000	Dallas	TX	75207	866-447-8732	
TF: 866-447-8732 ■ *Web:* mystream.com					
Summer Infant Inc 1275 Park E Dr	Woonsocket	RI	02895	800-268-6237	
TF: 800-268-6237 ■ *Web:* www.summerinfant.com					
Superior Water Light & Power 2915 Hill Ave PO Box 519	Superior	WI	54880	715-394-2200	
TF: 800-227-7957 ■ *Web:* www.swlp.com					
Sweetwater Authority PO Box 2328	Chula Vista	CA	91912	619-420-1413	425-7469
TF: 866-275-3772 ■ *Web:* www.sweetwater.org					
SWEPCo 1 Riverside Plz 13th Fl	Columbus	OH	43215	888-216-3523	
TF: 888-216-3523 ■ *Web:* www.swepco.com					
Synex International Inc 1444 Alberni St 4th Fl	Vancouver	BC	V6G2Z4	604-688-8271	
Web: www.synex.com					
System Engineering International Inc (SEI) 5115 Pegasus Ct Ste Q	Frederick	MD	21704	301-694-9601	694-9608
TF: 800-765-4734 ■ *Web:* www.seipower.com					
Tallgrass Energy Partners LP 6640 W 143rd St Ste 200	Overland Park	KS	66223	303-763-2950	
Web: www.tallgrassenergylp.com					
Telemark Diversified Graphics 411 Mckee St	Sturgis	MI	49091	269-651-7876	
Web: www.telemarkcorp.com					
Texarkana Water Utilities 801 Wood St	Texarkana	TX	75501	903-798-3800	791-0724
Web: txkusa.org					
Texas Gulf Supply Corp 10420 Rockley Rd	Houston	TX	77099	281-495-5500	
Web: www.texasgulfsupply.com					
Texas-New Mexico Power Co (TNMP) 577 N Garden Ridge Blvd	Lewisville	TX	75067	972-420-4189	
TF: 888-866-7456 ■ *Web:* www.tnmp.com					
Thompson Electric Co (TEC) 2300 Seventh St	Sioux City	IA	51105	712-252-4221	
Web: www.thompsonelectriccompany.com					
Tile Shop Holdings Inc 14000 Carlson Pkwy	Plymouth	MN	55441	888-398-6595	
TF: 888-398-6595 ■ *Web:* www.tileshop.com					
Tokyo Electric Power Company Inc 1901 L St NW Ste 720	Washington	DC	20036	202-457-0790	457-0810
Web: www.tepco.co.jp					
Toledo Edison Co PO Box 3687	Akron	OH	44309	800-447-3333	
TF: 800-447-3333 ■ *Web:* www.firstenergycorp.com/content/customer/toledo_edison					
Total Insight LLC 328 First Ave NW	Hickory	NC	28601	828-485-5240	
Web: www.totalinsight.com					
Trans-Tel Central Inc (TTC) 2805 Broce Dr	Norman	OK	73072	405-447-5025	447-5029
TF: 800-729-4636 ■ *Web:* www.trans-tel.com					
TransAlta Corp 110 12th Ave SW PO Box 1900 Stn M	Calgary	AB	T2P2M1	403-267-7110	
TSE: TA ■ *TF:* 877-700-9288 ■ *Web:* www.transalta.com					
Travel Leaders Group LLC 3033 Campus Dr Ste W320	Plymouth	MN	55441	763-744-3700	
Web: www.travelleadersgroup.com					
Tricomm Services Corp 1247 N Church St Ste 8	Moorestown	NJ	08057	856-914-9001	914-9065
TF: 800-872-2401 ■ *Web:* www.tricommcorp.com					
Trident Resources Corp 444 - 7 Ave SW Ste 1000	Calgary	AB	T2P0X8	403-770-0333	
Web: www.tridentexploration.ca					
Triple Peaks LLC 77 Okemo Heights	Ludlow	VT	05149	802-228-1947	
Web: www.okemo.com					
Trivascular Technologies Inc 3910 Brickway Blvd	Santa Rosa	CA	95403	707-543-8800	
Web: www.trivascular.com					
Tucker Technology Inc 300 Frank H Ogawa Plaza Ste 235	Oakland	CA	94612	510-836-0422	836-2625
Web: www.tuckertech.com					
Tucson Electric Power Co 1 S Church Ave Ste 100	Tucson	AZ	85701	520-571-4000	
TF: 800-430-4046 ■ *Web:* www.tep.com					
Twin Butte Energy Ltd Suite 410, 396 - 11 Ave. SW	Calgary	AB	T2R0C5	403-215-2045	
Web: www.twinbutteenergy.com					
TXU Electric 1601 Bryan St	Dallas	TX	75201	972-791-2888	812-2488*
**Fax Area Code:* 214 ■ *TF:* 800-242-9113 ■ *Web:* www.txu.com/us/ourbus/elecgas					
Underground Specialists Inc (USI) 570 SW 16th Terr	Pompano Beach	FL	33069	954-782-8740	782-1919
Web: www.usicable.com					
United Electric Supply Inc 10 Bellecor Dr	New Castle	DE	19720	302-322-3333	324-3333
TF: 800-322-3374 ■ *Web:* www.unitedelectric.com					
United Illuminating Co 157 Church St	New Haven	CT	06510	203-499-2000	499-5973*
**Fax:* Hum Res ■ *TF Cust Svc:* 800-722-5584 ■ *Web:* www.uinet.com					

Phone Fax

United States Information Systems Inc (USIS)
35 W Jefferson Ave....Pearl River NY 10965 845-358-7755 358-7882
TF: 866-222-3778 ■ *Web:* www.usis.net

Upland Software Inc
Frost Tower 401 Congress Ave, Ste 2950....Austin TX 78701 855-944-7526
TF: 855-944-7526 ■ *Web:* www.uplandsoftware.com

Upper Trinity Regional Water District
900 N Kealy St PO Box 305....Lewisville TX 75067 972-219-1228 221-9896
Web: www.utrwd.com

USlegal Inc 3720 Flowood Dr....Jackson MS 39232 601-896-0180
Web: www.uslegal.com

Viair Corp 15 Edelman....Irvine CA 92618 949-585-0011
Web: www.viaircorp.com

Virginia American Water Co (VAWC)
2223 Duke St....Alexandria VA 22314 703-706-3879
TF: 800-452-6863 ■ *Web:* www.amwater.com

Virginia Natural Gas Inc AGL Resources Inc
PO Box 4569....Atlanta GA 30302 404-584-4000 281-3184*
**Fax Area Code:* 484 ■ *TF:* 800-633-4236 ■ *Web:* www.aglresources.com

Volaris Group Inc 5800 Explorer Dr 5th Fl....Mississauga ON L4W5K9 905-267-5400
Web: www.volarisgroup.com

W Bradley Electric Inc 90 Hill Rd....Novato CA 94945 415-898-1400 898-5991
Web: www.wbeinc.com

Wachter Inc 16001 W 99th St....Lenexa KS 66219 913-541-2500 541-2529
TF: 800-462-9638 ■ *Web:* www.wachter.com

Walter Stern Inc 68 Sintsink Dr E....Port Washington NY 11050 516-883-9100
Web: www.waltersterninc.com

Wang Electric Inc 4107 E Winslow Ave Ste C....Phoenix AZ 85040 602-324-5350 324-5360
Web: www.wangelectric.com

Ward's Marine Electric Inc
617 SW Third Ave....Fort Lauderdale FL 33315 954-523-2815
TF: 800-545-9273 ■ *Web:* www.wardsmarine.com

Washington Gas & Light Co
6801 Industrial Rd....Springfield VA 22151 703-750-4440 624-6010*
**Fax Area Code:* 202 ■ *TF:* 800-752-7520 ■ *Web:* www.washingtongas.com

We Energies 231 W Michigan St PO Box 2046....Milwaukee WI 53203 414-221-2345
TF: 800-242-9137 ■ *Web:* www.we-energies.com

Weber Basin Water Conservancy District
2837 East Hwy 193....Layton UT 84040 801-771-1677
Web: www.weberbasin.com

Werklund Capital Corp
4500 DevonTower 400 Third rd Ave SW....Calgary AB T2P4H2 403-231-6545
Web: www.werklund.com

Westar Energy PO Box 758500....Topeka KS 66675 785-575-6300 575-1796
TF: 800-544-4857 ■ *Web:* www.westarenergy.com

Western Water Co 705 Mission Ave Ste 200....San Rafael CA 94901 415-256-8800 256-8803

Wisconsin Power & Light Co
4902 N Biltmore Ln PO Box 77007....Madison WI 53718 800-255-4268
TF: 800-255-4268 ■ *Web:* www.alliantenergy.com

Wisconsin Public Service Corp PO Box 19001....Green Bay WI 54307 800-450-7260 433-1527*
**Fax Area Code:* 920 ■ **Fax:* Mktg ■ *TF:* 800-450-7260 ■ *Web:* www.wisconsinpublicservice.com

Worldwide Energy & Mfg USA Inc
1675 Rollins Rd Unit F....Burlingame CA 94010 650-794-9888 794-9878
OTC: WEMU ■ *Web:* www.wwmusa.com

Xcel Energy Inc 414 Nicollet Mall....Minneapolis MN 55401 612-330-5500
NYSE: XEL ■ *TF:* 800-328-8226 ■ *Web:* www.xcelenergy.com

Xcel Energy Inc PO Box 840....Denver CO 80201 303-571-7511
NYSE: XEL ■ *TF:* 877-322-8228 ■ *Web:* www.xcelenergy.com

Y Ss Group Inc 8612 Nw 70th St....Miami FL 33166 305-436-7371
Web: yssgroup.com

Yankee Gas Services Co 107 Selden St....Berlin CT 06037 800-989-0900 841-8684
TF: 800-989-0900 ■ *Web:* www.yankeegas.com

York Water Co, The 130 E Market St PO Box 15089....York PA 17405 717-845-3601 845-3792
NASDAQ: YORW ■ *TF:* 800-750-5561 ■ *Web:* www.yorkwater.com

Yucaipa Valley Water District PO Box 730....Yucaipa CA 92399 909-797-5117 797-6381
TF: 800-272-8869 ■ *Web:* www.yvwd.dst.ca.us

788 VACUUM CLEANERS - HOUSEHOLD

See Also Appliances - Small - Mfr p. 1737

Phone Fax

Beam Industries 1700 W Second St....Webster City IA 50595 515-832-4620
TF: 800-369-2326 ■ *Web:* www.beamvac.com

Bissell Inc 2345 Walker NW....Grand Rapids MI 49544 616-453-4451 791-0662*
**Fax:* Hum Res ■ *Web:* www.bissell.com

CentralVac International
23455 Hellman Ave PO Box 259....Dollar Bay MI 49922 800-666-3133
TF: 800-666-3133 ■ *Web:* www.centralvac.com

Electrolux Home Care Products Inc PO Box 3900....Peoria IL 61612 800-282-2886
TF Cust Svc: 800-282-2886 ■ *Web:* www.eureka.com

Kirby Co 1920 W 114th St....Cleveland OH 44102 216-228-2400 529-6146
TF: 800-437-7170 ■ *Web:* www.kirby.com

Lindsay Manufacturing Inc PO Box 1708....Ponca City OK 74602 580-762-2457 762-9547
TF: 800-546-3729 ■ *Web:* www.lindsaymfg.com

Metropolitan Vacuum Cleaner Co Inc
1 Ramapo Ave PO Box 149....Suffern NY 10901 845-357-1600 357-1640
TF: 800-822-1602 ■ *Web:* www.metrovacworld.com

Oreck Corp 1400 Salem Rd....Cookeville TN 38506 800-289-5888
TF: 800-289-5888 ■ *Web:* www.oreck.com

Rexair Inc 50 W Big Beaver Rd Ste 350....Troy MI 48084 248-643-7222 643-7676
Web: www.rainbowsystem.com

Sanyo Fisher Co 21605 Plummer St....Chatsworth CA 91311 818-998-7322 717-2759

Sequoia Vacuum Systems Inc
164 Jefferson Dr....Menlo Park CA 94025 650-322-7281

789 VALVES - INDUSTRIAL

Phone Fax

Alkon Corp 728 Graham Dr....Fremont OH 43420 419-333-7000
Web: www.alkoncorp.com

American Cast Iron Pipe Co (ACIPCO)
1501 31st Ave N....Birmingham AL 35207 205-325-7701
TF: 800-442-2347 ■ *Web:* www.american-usa.com

American Valve & Hydrant Manufacturing Company LP
3525 Hollywood St....Beaumont TX 77701 409-832-7721
Web: www.avhmc.com

Anderson Brass Co 1629 W Bobo Newsome Hwy....Hartsville SC 29550 843-332-4111 332-3752
TF: 800-476-9876 ■ *Web:* www.andersonbrass.com

Armstrong International Inc
2081 SE Ocean Blvd 4th Fl....Stuart FL 34996 772-286-7175 286-1001
TF: 866-738-5125 ■ *Web:* www.armstronginternational.com

Automatic Valve Corp 41144 Vincenti Ct....Novi MI 48375 248-474-6700 474-6732
Web: www.automaticvalve.com

Balon Corp 3245 S Hattie Ave....Oklahoma City OK 73129 405-677-3321
Web: www.balon.com

Barksdale Inc 3211 Fruitland Ave....Los Angeles CA 90058 323-589-6181 589-3463
TF: 800-835-1060 ■ *Web:* www.barksdale.com

Bray International Inc 13333 Westland E Blvd....Houston TX 77041 281-894-5454
Web: www.bray.com

BS&B Safety Systems LLC 7455 E 46th St....Tulsa OK 74145 918-622-5950
Web: www.bsbsystems.com

C & D Valve Manufacturing Co
201 Nw 67th St....Oklahoma City OK 73116 405-843-5621
Web: www.cdvalve.com

Campbell Sevey Inc 15350 Minnetonka Blvd....Minnetonka MN 55345 952-935-2345
Web: www.campbell-sevey.com

Cash Acme Inc 2727 Paces Ferry Rd SE Ste 1800....Atlanta GA 30339 877-700-4242
TF: 877-700-4242 ■ *Web:* www.cashacme.com

Circle Seal Controls Inc 2301 Wardlow Cir....Corona CA 92880 951-270-6200 270-6201
TF: 800-991-2726 ■ *Web:* www.circle-seal.com

Clow Valve Co 902 S Second St....Oskaloosa IA 52577 641-673-8611 673-8269
TF: 800-829-2569 ■ *Web:* www.clowvalve.com

Continental Disc Corp 3160 W Heartland Dr....Liberty MO 64068 816-792-1500 792-2277
Web: www.contdisc.com

Conval Inc 265 Field Rd....Somers CT 06071 860-749-0761 763-3557
Web: www.conval.com

Crane Co 100 First Stamford Pl 4th Fl....Stamford CT 06902 203-363-7300
NYSE: CR ■ *Web:* www.craneco.com

Crane Company Stockham Div 2129 Third Ave SE....Cullman AL 35055 256-775-3800 775-3860
TF: 800-786-2542 ■ *Web:* www.cranecpe.com

Curtiss-Wright Flow Control Target Rock Div
1966 Broadhollow Rd....Farmingdale NY 11735 631-293-3800
Web: www.curtisswright.com

DeZurik Water Controls 250 Riverside Ave N....Sartell MN 56377 320-259-2000 259-2227
Web: www.dezurik.com

DFT Inc 140 Sheree Blvd....Exton PA 19341 610-363-8903
Web: www.dft-valves.com

Dynex Rivett Inc 770 Capitol Dr....Pewaukee WI 53072 262-691-0300 691-0312
Web: www.dynexhydraulics.com

Engineered Controls International Inc (ECII)
100 Rego Dr PO Box 247....Elon NC 27244 336-449-7707 449-6594
TF: 800-650-0061 ■ *Web:* www.regoproducts.com

Equilibar LLC 320 Rutledge Rd....Fletcher NC 28732 828-650-6590
Web: www.equilibar.com

Fike Corp 704 SW Tenth St....Blue Springs MO 64015 816-229-3405 228-9277
TF: 877-342-3453 ■ *Web:* www.fike.com

Fisher Controls International Inc
205 S Ctr St PO Box 190....Marshalltown IA 50158 641-754-3011 754-2830
Web: www2.emersonprocess.com/en-us/brands/fisher

Flowserve Corp 5215 N O'Connor Blvd Ste 2300....Irving TX 75039 972-443-6500 443-6800
NYSE: FLS ■ *TF:* 800-350-1082 ■ *Web:* www.flowserve.com

Fluid Flow Products Inc 2108 Crown View Dr....Charlotte NC 28227 704-847-4464
Web: www.fluidflow.com

FMC Technologies Inc 1803 Gears Rd....Houston TX 77067 281-591-4000 591-4102
NYSE: FTI ■ *TF:* 800-356-4898 ■ *Web:* www.fmctechnologies.com

GA Industries Inc
9025 Marshall Rd....Cranberry Township PA 16066 724-776-1020 776-1254
Web: www.gaindustries.com

Gemini Valve 2 Otter Ct....Raymond NH 03077 603-895-4761 895-6785
TF: 800-370-0936 ■ *Web:* www.geminivalve.com

Gemu Valves Inc 3800 Camp Creek Pkwy SW....Atlanta GA 30331 678-553-3400 344-9350*
**Fax Area Code:* 404 ■ *Web:* www.gemu-group.com/en_us

Girard Equipment Inc 531 Hwy 146 N....La Porte TX 77571 281-842-7500
Web: www.girardequip.com

Gonzales Inquirer, The
1000 Civic Ctr Loop....San Marcos TX 78666 830-672-2861 672-7029
TF: 800-210-5909 ■ *Web:* gonzalesinquirer.com

Goulds Pumps Inc Goulds Water Technologies Group
240 Fall St....Seneca Falls NY 13148 315-568-2811 568-2418
TF: 800-327-7700 ■ *Web:* www.gouldspumps.com

Groth Corp 13650 N Promenade Blvd....Stafford TX 77477 281-295-6800 295-6999
TF: 800-354-7684 ■ *Web:* www.grothcorp.com

High Vacuum Apparatus LLC (HVA) 12880 Moya Blvd....Reno NV 89506 775-359-4442 359-1369
TF: 800-551-4422 ■ *Web:* www.highvac.com

Hilton Valve 14520 NE 91st Ct....Redmond WA 98052 425-883-7000
Web: www.dezurik.com

Hoerbiger Corp of America Inc
3350 Gateway Dr....Pompano Beach FL 33069 954-974-5700 974-0964
Web: hoerbiger.com

Hudson Valve Company Inc
5301 Office Pk Dr Ste 330....Bakersfield CA 93309 661-869-1126 607-8731*
**Fax Area Code:* 800 ■ *TF:* 800-748-6218 ■ *Web:* www.hudsonvalve.com

Humphrey Products Co
5070 E N Ave PO Box 2008....Kalamazoo MI 49048 269-381-5500 381-4113
TF: 800-477-8707 ■ *Web:* www.humphrey-products.com

Hunt Valve Company Inc 1913 E State St....Salem OH 44460 330-337-9535 337-3754
Web: www.huntvalve.com

Hydroseal Valve Co Inc 1500 SE 89th St....Oklahoma City OK 73149 405-631-1533 778-1072*
**Fax Area Code:* 845 ■ *TF:* 800-398-2493 ■ *Web:* circorenergy.com

ITT Goulds Pumps Industries/Goulds Industrial Pumps Group
240 Fall St....Seneca Falls NY 13148 315-568-2811 568-2418
TF: 800-327-7700 ■ *Web:* www.gouldspumps.com

Company	City	State	ZIP	Phone	Fax
ITT Industries Inc Engineered Valves Div 33 Centerville Rd *TF:* 800-366-1111 ■ *Web:* www.engvalves.com	Lancaster	PA	17603	717-509-2200	509-2336
Jarecki Valves 6910 W Ridge Rd *Web:* jareckivalves.net	Fairview	PA	16415	814-474-2666	474-3645
Kennedy Valve 1021 E Water St *TF:* 800-782-5831 ■ *Web:* www.kennedyvalve.com	Elmira	NY	14902	607-734-2211	734-3288
KF Industries Inc 1500 SE 89th St *TF:* 800-398-2493 ■ *Web:* circorenergy.com	Oklahoma City	OK	73149	405-631-1533	631-5034
Kraft Fluid Systems Inc 14300 Foltz Pkwy *TF:* 800-257-1155 ■ *Web:* www.kraftfluid.com	Strongsville	OH	44149	440-238-5545	238-5266
Kupferle Foundry Co, The 2511 N Ninth St *Web:* hydrants.com	Saint Louis	MO	63102	314-231-8738	
Lee Co 2 Pellitaug Rd PO Box 424 **Fax:* Sales ■ *Web:* www.theleeco.com	Westbrook	CT	06498	860-399-6281	399-7058*
Leonard Valve Co 1360 Elmwood Ave *TF:* 800-222-1208 ■ *Web:* www.leonardvalve.com	Cranston	RI	02910	401-461-1200	941-5310
Leslie Controls Inc 12501 Telecom Dr *TF:* 800-323-8366 ■ *Web:* www.lesliecontrols.com	Tampa	FL	33637	813-978-1000	978-0984
Lourdes Industries Inc 65 Hoffman Ave *Web:* www.lourdesinc.com	Hauppauge	NY	11788	631-234-6600	
Mac Valves Inc 30569 Beck Rd *TF:* 800-622-8587 ■ *Web:* www.macvalves.com	Wixom	MI	48393	248-624-7700	624-0549
Marotta Controls Inc 78 Boonton Ave PO Box 427 *TF:* 888-627-6882 ■ *Web:* www.marotta.com	Montville	NJ	07045	973-334-7800	334-1219
Maxon Corp 201 E 18th St PO Box 2068 *Web:* www.maxoncorp.com	Muncie	IN	47307	765-284-3304	286-8394
McDantim Inc 3730 N Montana Ave *Web:* mcdantim.com	Helena	MT	59602	406-442-5153	
McKenzie Valve & Machining Co 145 Airport Rd *Web:* www.mckenzievalve.com	McKenzie	TN	38201	731-352-5027	352-3029
McWane Inc 2900 Hwy 280 Ste 300 *Web:* www.mcwane.com	Birmingham	AL	35223	205-414-3100	414-3170
Milwaukee Valve Company Inc 16550 W Stratton Dr *TF:* 800-348-6544 ■ *Web:* www.milwaukeevalve.com	New Berlin	WI	53151	262-432-2800	432-2801
Mueller Co 500 W Eldorado St **Fax:* Cust Svc ■ *TF:* 800-423-1323 ■ *Web:* www.muellerflo.com	Decatur	IL	62522	217-423-4471	425-7537*
Mueller Refrigeration Co Inc 121 Rogers St *TF Cust Svc:* 866-566-7233 ■ *Web:* www.muellerrefrigeration.com	Hartsville	TN	37074	615-374-2124	374-2080
Newdell Co, The 13750 Hollister Rd *TF:* 877-510-7853 ■ *Web:* www.newdellco.com	Houston	TX	77086	713-590-1312	
Newport News Industrial Corp 182 Enterprise Dr *TF:* 800-627-0353 ■ *Web:* nni.huntingtoningalls.com	Newport News	VA	23603	757-380-7053	688-3841
NIBCO Inc 1516 Middlebury St *TF:* 800-234-0227 ■ *Web:* www.nibco.com	Elkhart	IN	46515	574-295-3000	295-3307
Noranco Inc 1842 Clements Rd *Web:* www.noranco.com	Pickering	ON	L1W3R8	905-831-0100	
Ogontz Corp 2835 Terwood Rd *TF:* 800-523-2478 ■ *Web:* www.ogontz.com	Willow Grove	PA	19090	215-657-4770	657-0460
Parker Hannifin Corp Hydraulic Valve Div 520 Ternes Ave **Fax:* Sales ■ *TF:* 800-272-7537 ■ *Web:* www.parker.com	Elyria	OH	44035	440-366-5200	366-5253*
Parker Hannifin Corp Sporlan Div 711 Industrial Ave *Web:* parker.com	Washington	MO	63090	636-239-6524	
Parker Instrumentation Group 6035 Parkland Blvd *TF:* 800-272-7537 ■ *Web:* parker.com	Cleveland	OH	44124	216-896-3000	896-4022
Peter Paul Electronics Co Inc 480 John Downey Dr *TF:* 800-825-8377 ■ *Web:* peterpaul.com	New Britain	CT	06051	860-229-4884	223-1734
Plast-O-Matic Valves Inc 1384 Pompton Ave *TF:* 800-323-2710 ■ *Web:* www.plastomatic.com	Cedar Grove	NJ	07009	973-256-3000	256-4745
Plattco Corp 7 White St *TF:* 800-352-1731 ■ *Web:* www.plattco.com	Plattsburgh	NY	12901	518-563-4640	563-4892
Primore Inc 2304 W Beecher Rd *Web:* www.primore.com	Adrian	MI	49221	517-263-2220	265-6160
Red Valve Company Inc 600 N Bell Ave Bldg. 2 *Web:* www.redvalve.com	Carnegie	PA	15106	412-279-0044	
Richards Industries Inc 3170 Wasson Rd **Fax:* Sales ■ *TF Cust Svc:* 800-543-7311 ■ *Web:* www.richardsind.com	Cincinnati	OH	45209	513-533-5600	871-0105*
Robert H Wager Co 570 Montroyal Rd *TF:* 800-562-7024 ■ *Web:* www.wagerusa.com	Rural Hall	NC	27045	336-969-6909	969-6375
Rocker Solenoid Co 1500 W 240th St *Web:* www.rockerindustries.com	Harbor City	CA	90710	310-534-5660	
Salina Vortex Corp 1725 Vortex Ave *Web:* www.vortexvalves.com	Salina	KS	67401	785-825-7177	
Sealant Equipment & Engineering Inc 45677 Helm St PO Box 701460 *Web:* www.sealantequipment.com	Plymouth	MI	48170	734-459-8600	
Sedco 2304 W Beecher Rd PO Box 624 *Web:* www.sedco-prv.com	Adrian	MI	49221	517-263-2220	265-6160
Servotronics Inc 1110 Maple St PO Box 300 *NYSE:* SVT ■ *Web:* www.servotronics.com	Elma	NY	14059	716-655-5990	655-6012
Shan-Rod Inc 7308 Driver Rd *Web:* shanrodinc.com	Berlin Heights	OH	44814	419-588-2066	
Sherwood 2200 North Main St *TF:* 888-508-2583 ■ *Web:* www.sherwoodvalve.com	Washington	PA	15301	724-225-8000	225-6188
Snap-Tite Inc 8325 Hessinger Dr *Web:* www.snap-tite.com	Erie	PA	16509	814-838-5700	
Spence Engineering Company Inc 150 Coldenham Rd *Web:* www.spenceengineering.com	Walden	NY	12586	845-778-5566	778-1072
Tapco International Inc 990 W 15th St	Riviera Beach	FL	33404	561-844-2502	845-2410
Taylor Valve Technology Inc 8300 SW 8th *Web:* www.taylorvalve.com	Oklahoma City	OK	73128	405-787-0145	
Transtech Industries Inc 2025 Delsea Dr *OTC:* TRTI ■ *Web:* www.transtechindustries.com	Sewell	NJ	08080	856-481-4214	227-6578
Triangle Process Equipment Inc 2307 Industrial Park Dr Se *Web:* www.4tpe.com	Wilson	NC	27893	252-246-1089	
Tru Tech Valve LLC 577 W Pike St *Web:* www.ttvlv.com	Canonsburg	PA	15317	724-916-4805	
United Brass Works Inc 714 S Main St *TF:* 800-334-3035 ■ *Web:* www.ubw.com	Randleman	NC	27317	336-498-2661	498-4267
Valcor Engineering Corp 2 Lawrence Rd *Web:* www.valcor.com	Springfield	NJ	07081	973-467-8400	467-8382
Valvtechnologies Inc 5904 Bingle Rd *Web:* www.valv.com	Houston	TX	77092	713-860-0400	860-0499
Velan Inc 7007 Cote de Liesse *TSE:* VLN ■ *Web:* www.velan.com	Montreal	QC	H4T1G2	514-748-7743	748-8635
Watts Water Technologies Inc 815 Chestnut St *NYSE:* WTS ■ *Web:* www.wattswater.com	North Andover	MA	01845	978-688-1811	794-1848

790 VALVES & HOSE FITTINGS - FLUID POWER

See Also Carburetors, Pistons, Piston Rings, Valves p. 1892

Company	City	State	ZIP	Phone	Fax
Aero Kool Corp 1495 SE Tenth Ave *Web:* www.aerokool.com	Hialeah	FL	33010	305-887-6912	
Aero-craft Hydraulics Inc 392 N Smith Ave *Web:* www.aero-craft.com	Corona	CA	92880	951-736-4690	
Air-Way Manufacturing Co 586 N Main St *TF Cust Svc:* 800-253-1036 ■ *Web:* www.air-way.com	Olivet	MI	49076	269-749-2161	749-3161
Allen Orton LLC 15050 FAA Blvd Ste 200 *Web:* www.ortondirect.com	Fort Worth	TX	76155	770-986-9999	
Arkwin Industries Inc 686 Main St **Fax:* Sales ■ *TF:* 800-284-2551 ■ *Web:* www.arkwin.com	Westbury	NY	11590	516-333-2640	334-6786*
Bosch Rexroth PO Box 394 *TF:* 800-739-7684 ■ *Web:* www.boschrexroth.com/en/us	Wooster	OH	44691	330-263-3300	263-3333
Bosch Rexroth Corp 5150 Prairie Stone Pkwy *TF:* 800-860-1055 ■ *Web:* www.boschrexroth.com/en/us	Hoffman Estates	IL	60192	847-645-3600	645-6201
Brand Hydraulics Company Inc 2332 S 25th St *Web:* www.brand-hyd.com	Omaha	NE	68106	402-344-4434	
Carten Controls 604 W Johnson Ave *Web:* www.cartenus.com	Cheshire	CT	06410	203-699-2100	
Cashco Inc 607 W 15th St *Web:* www.cashco.com	Ellsworth	KS	67439	785-472-4461	472-3539
Civacon 4304 N Mattox Rd *TF Sales:* 888-526-5657 ■ *Web:* www.opwglobal.com/civacon	Kansas City	MO	64150	816-741-6600	741-1061
Clippard Instrument Lab 7390 Colerain Ave *TF:* 877-245-6247 ■ *Web:* www.clippard.com	Cincinnati	OH	45239	513-521-4261	521-4464
Control Flow Inc 9201 Fairbanks N Houston Rd *TF:* 800-231-9922 ■ *Web:* www.controlflow.com	Houston	TX	77064	281-890-8300	890-3947
Crissair Inc 28909 Avenue Williams *Web:* www.crissair.com	Valencia	CA	91355	661-367-3300	
Daman Products Co Inc 1811 N Home St *TF:* 800-959-7841 ■ *Web:* www.damanifolds.com	Mishawaka	IN	46545	574-259-7841	259-7665
Delta Power Co 4484 Boeing Dr *Web:* www.delta-power.com	Rockford	IL	61109	815-397-6628	397-2526
Deltrol Fluid Products 3001 Grant Ave **Fax:* Sales ■ *TF:* 800-477-9772 ■ *Web:* www.deltrolfluid.com	Bellwood	IL	60104	708-547-0500	547-6881*
Dynaquip Controls 10 Harris Industrial Pk *TF:* 800-545-3636 ■ *Web:* www.dynaquip.com	Saint Clair	MO	63077	636-629-3700	629-5528
E H Lynn Industries Inc 524 Anderson Dr *TF:* 800-633-2948 ■ *Web:* www.ehlynn.com	Romeoville	IL	60446	815-328-8800	
EA Patten Co 303 Wetherell St *Web:* eapatten.com	Manchester	CT	06040	860-649-2851	
EDN Aviation Inc 6720 Valjean Ave *Web:* www.ednaviation.com	Van Nuys	CA	91406	818-988-8826	904-6799
Faber Enterprises Inc 6606 Variel Ave *Web:* www.faberent.com	Canoga Park	CA	91303	818-999-1300	
Fresno Valves & Castings Inc 7736 E Springfield Ave PO Box 40 *TF:* 800-333-1658 ■ *Web:* www.fresnovalves.com	Selma	CA	93662	559-834-2511	834-2017
Gar-Kenyon Technologies 106 Evansville Ave PO Box 559 *Web:* www.garkenyon.com	Meriden	CT	06451	203-729-4900	729-4950
Hays Fluid Controls 114 Eason Rd *TF:* 800-354-4297 ■ *Web:* www.haysfluidcontrols.com	Dallas	NC	28034	704-922-9565	922-9595
Henry Pratt Co 401 S Highland Ave *TF:* 877-436-7977 ■ *Web:* www.henrypratt.com	Aurora	IL	60506	630-844-4000	844-4124
Hoke Inc 405 Centura Ct PO Box 4866 *Web:* www.hoke.com	Spartanburg	SC	29305	864-574-7966	
Hose Master LLC 1233 E 222nd St *Web:* www.hosemaster.com	Cleveland	OH	44117	216-481-2020	
Hunt Valve Company Inc 1913 E State St *Web:* www.huntvalve.com	Salem	OH	44460	330-337-9535	337-3754
HUSCO International Inc 2239 Pewaukee Rd *Web:* www.huscointl.com	Waukesha	WI	53188	262-513-4200	513-4514
Hydraforce Inc 500 Barclay Blvd *TF:* 877-237-9101 ■ *Web:* www.hydraforce.com	Lincolnshire	IL	60069	847-793-2300	793-0087
Hyson Products 10367 Brecksville Rd *TF:* 800-876-4976 ■ *Web:* hysonproducts.com	Brecksville	OH	44141	440-526-5900	838-7684
ITT Aerospace Controls 28150 Industry Dr *Web:* www.ittaerospace.com	Valencia	CA	91355	661-295-4000	294-1750
ITT Industries Inc 1133 Westchester Ave *NYSE:* ITT ■ *TF:* 800-254-2823 ■ *Web:* www.itt.com	White Plains	NY	10604	914-641-2000	696-2950
JD Gould Co Inc 4707 Massachusetts Ave **Fax Area Code:* 317 ■ *TF:* 800-634-6853 ■ *Web:* www.gouldvalve.com	Indianapolis	IN	46218	800-634-6853	547-5234*
Jetstream of Houston LLP 4930 Cranswick *TF:* 800-231-8192 ■ *Web:* www.waterblast.com	Houston	TX	77041	713-462-7000	462-5387
Kepner Products Co 995 N Ellsworth Ave *Web:* www.kepner.com	Villa Park	IL	60181	630-279-1550	279-9669

Phone | Fax

Kimray Inc 52 NW 42nd St....................Oklahoma City OK 73118 405-525-6601 525-7520
Web: www.kimray.com
LDI Industries Inc
1864 Nage Ave PO Box 1810....................Manitowoc WI 54221 920-682-6877 684-7210
Web: www.ldi-industries.com
Long Beach Hose & Coupling Coinc
1265 W 16th St....................Long Beach CA 90813 562-901-2970
Web: www.lbhose.com
McTurbine Inc 401 Junior Beck Dr....................Corpus Christi TX 78405 361-851-1290
Web: www.mcturbine.com/contact.shtml
Mead Fluid Dynamics Inc 4114 N Knox Ave....................Chicago IL 60641 773-685-6800 685-7002
TF Cust Svc: 877-632-3872 ■ *Web:* www.mead-usa.com
Morrison Bros Co 570 E Seventh St....................Dubuque IA 52001 563-583-5701 583-5028
TF: 800-553-4840 ■ *Web:* www.morbros.com
Norgren 5400 S Delaware St....................Littleton CO 80120 303-794-5000 795-9487*
**Fax:* Mktg ■ *TF:* 800-514-0129 ■ *Web:* norgren.com/us
Oilgear Co 2300 S 51st St PO Box 343924....................Milwaukee WI 53219 414-327-1700 327-0532
Web: www.oilgear.com
Omega Flex Inc 451 Creamery Way....................Exton PA 19341 610-524-7272 524-7282
NASDAQ: OFLX ■ *TF:* 800-355-1039 ■ *Web:* www.omegaflex.com
Ontic Engineering & Manufacturing Inc
4150 N Sam Houston E Pkwy....................Houston TX 77032 818-678-6555
Web: www.ontic.com
Parker Fluid Connectors Group
6035 Parkland Blvd....................Cleveland OH 44124 216-896-3000 896-4000
TF General: 800-272-7537 ■ *Web:* parker.com
Parker Hannifin Corp 6035 Parkland Blvd....................Cleveland OH 44124 216-896-3000 514-6738
Web: parker.com
Parker Hannifin Corp Brass Products Div
100 Parker Dr....................Otsego MI 49078 269-694-9411 694-4614
TF: 800-272-7537 ■ *Web:* www.parker.com
Parker Hannifin Corp General Valve Div
26 Clinton Dr Unit 103....................Hollis NH 03049 800-272-7537
TF: 800-272-7537 ■ *Web:* www.parker.com
Parker Hannifin Corp Instrumentation Pneutronics Div
26 Clinton Dr Ste 103....................Hollis NH 03049 603-595-1500 595-8080
Web: www.parker.com
Parker Hannifin Corp Pneumatic Div
8676 E M 89....................Richland MI 49083 269-629-5000 629-5385
TF: 877-321-4736 ■ *Web:* www.parker.com
Parker Hannifin Corp Skinner Valve Div
95 Edgewood Ave....................New Britain CT 06051 860-827-2300 827-2384
TF: 800-825-8305 ■ *Web:* www.parker.com
PBM Inc 1070 Sandy Hill Rd....................Irwin PA 15642 724-863-0550 864-9255
TF: 800-967-4726 ■ *Web:* www.pbmvalve.com
PerkinElmer Inc 940 Winter St....................Waltham MA 02451 203-925-4602 944-4904
NYSE: PKI ■ *Web:* www.perkinelmer.com
Pima Valve Inc 6525 W Allison Rd....................Chandler AZ 85226 520-796-1095 796-4012
Web: www.pimavalve.com
Plattco Corp 7 White St....................Plattsburgh NY 12901 518-563-4640 563-4892
TF: 800-352-1731 ■ *Web:* www.plattco.com
Precision Sensors Inc 50 Seemans Ln....................Milford CT 06460 203-877-2795
Web: www.precisionsensors.com
Rexarc Inc PO Box 7....................West Alexandria OH 45381 937-839-4604 839-5897
TF: 877-739-2721 ■ *Web:* www.rexarc.com
Richards Industries Inc 3170 Wasson Rd....................Cincinnati OH 45209 513-533-5600 871-0105*
**Fax:* Sales ■ *TF Cust Svc:* 800-543-7311 ■ *Web:* www.richardsind.com
Ritter Technology LLC 100 Williams Dr....................Zelienople PA 16063 724-452-6000 452-0766
Web: www.ritter1.com
Ross Controls 1250 Stephenson Hwy....................Troy MI 48083 248-764-1800 764-1850
TF: 800-438-7677 ■ *Web:* www.rosscontrols.com
Rupe's Hydraulics Sales & Service
725 N Twin Oaks Vly Rd....................San Marcos CA 92069 760-744-9350
TF: 800-354-7873 ■ *Web:* rupeshydraulics.com
Sedco 2304 W Beecher Rd PO Box 624....................Adrian MI 49221 517-263-2220 265-6160
Web: www.sedco-prv.com
SH Leggitt Co 1000 Civic Ctr Loop....................San Marcos TX 78666 512-396-2257
Web: shleggitt.com
Specialty Manufacturing Co
5858 Centerville Rd....................Saint Paul MN 55127 651-653-0599 653-0989
Web: www.specialtymfg.com
Sun Hydraulics Corp 1500 W University Pkwy....................Sarasota FL 34243 941-362-1200 355-4497
NASDAQ: SNHY ■ *Web:* www.sunhydraulics.com
Universal Valve Company Inc
478 Schiller St....................Elizabeth NJ 07206 908-351-0606
TF: 800-223-0741 ■ *Web:* www.universalvalve.com
Versa Products Co Inc 22 Spring Valley Rd....................Paramus NJ 07652 201-843-2400 843-2931
Web: versa-valves.com
Watts Regulator Co 815 Chestnut St....................North Andover MA 01845 978-688-1811 794-1848
Web: www.watts.com
Whitco Supply LLC 200 N Morgan Ave....................Broussard LA 70518 337-837-2440
Web: www.whitcosupply.com
Young & Franklin Inc (Y&F)
942 Old Liverpool Rd....................Liverpool NY 13088 315-457-3110 457-9204
Web: www.yf.com

791 VARIETY STORES

Phone | Fax

99 Cents Only Stores 4000 Union Pacific Ave....................Commerce CA 90023 323-980-8145 980-8160
TF: 888-582-5999 ■ *Web:* www.99only.com
AC Doctor LLC
2151 W Hillsboro Blvd Ste 400....................Deerfield Beach FL 33442 866-264-1479
TF: 866-264-1479 ■ *Web:* www.acdoctor.com
Alaska Textiles Inc 620 W Fireweed Ln....................Anchorage AK 99503 907-265-4880
Web: www.alaskatextiles.com
Albuquerque Winnelson Co
3545 Princeton Dr NE....................Albuquerque NM 87107 505-884-1553
Web: www.abqwinnelson.com
All Graphic Supplies 6691 Edwards Blvd....................Mississauga ON L5T2H8 905-795-2610
TF: 800-501-4451 ■ *Web:* www.allgraphicsupplies.com
Allen Tel Products Inc 30 TV5 Dr....................Henderson NV 89014 702-855-5700
Web: www.allentel.com
American Eagle Steel Corp 716 Giddings Ave....................Annapolis MD 21401 410-573-0335
Web: www.americaneaglesteel.com
American Key Products Inc 1 Reuten Dr....................Closter NJ 07624 201-767-8022
Web: www.akfponline.com
American Muscle 7 Lee Blvd....................Malvern PA 19355 610-251-2397
TF: 888-332-7930 ■ *Web:* www.americanmuscle.com
APEL International Inc 11201 Ampere Ct....................Louisville KY 40299 502-240-0443
Web: www.apelfilters.com
Armature Dns 2000 Inc 11001 Jean Meunier....................Montreal QC H1G4S7 514-324-1141
TF: 800-363-7996 ■ *Web:* www.dns-2000.com
AutoTruckToys.com 2814 W Wood St....................Paris TN 38242 731-642-3535
TF: 800-544-6194 ■ *Web:* www.autotrucktoys.com
B & B Discount Sales Co 712 S Broadway....................Oklahoma City OK 73109 405-232-3578 232-2848
Bearing Service & Supply Inc
1327 N Market....................Shreveport LA 71107 318-424-1447
Web: www.bearserco.com
Beere Precision Products Inc 4915 21st St....................Racine WI 53406 262-632-0472
TF: 800-348-0101 ■ *Web:* www.beere.com
Best Impressions Catalog Co 345 N Lewis Ave....................Oglesby IL 61348 815-883-3532
Web: www.bestimpressions.com
Big Lots Inc (BLI) 300 Phillipi Rd....................Columbus OH 43228 614-278-6800 278-8322
NYSE: BIG ■ *TF:* 877-998-1697 ■ *Web:* www.biglots.com
Black Forest Decor LLC PO Box 297....................Jenks OK 74037 800-605-0915
TF: 800-605-0915 ■ *Web:* www.blackforestdecor.com
Blocker & Wallace Service LLC
1472 Rogers Ave....................Memphis TN 38114 901-274-0708
Web: www.blockerandwallace.com
Bobcat of Atlanta 6972 Best Friend Rd....................Atlanta GA 30340 770-242-6500
Web: www.bobcatofatlanta.com
Bobcat of Boston Inc 20 Concord St....................North Reading MA 01864 978-664-3727
Web: www.bobcatboston.com
Bomgaars 1805 Zenith....................Sioux City IA 51103 712-226-5000 277-1247
Web: www.bomgaars.com
Boscogen Inc 11 Morgan Ste B....................Irvine CA 92618 949-380-4317
Web: www.boscogen.com
Building 19 Inc 319 Lincoln St....................Hingham MA 02043 781-749-6900
Web: www.building19.com
Busch Electronics 739 Kasota Ave SE....................Minneapolis MN 55414 651-288-2580
Web: www.buschelectronics.com
C W Rod Tool Company Inc 15050 Northgreen Dr....................Houston TX 77032 281-449-0881
Web: www.cwrodtool.com
Camping World RV Sales 8155 Rivers Ave....................Charleston SC 29406 888-586-5446
TF: 888-586-5446 ■ *Web:* www.campingworldofcharleston.com
CBS Builders Supply Inc 1000 Carroll St....................Clermont FL 34711 352-394-2116
Web: www.cbsbuilderssupply.com
Churchville Fire Equipment Corp
340 Sanford Rd S....................Churchville NY 14428 585-293-1688
Web: www.churchvillefire.com
Clubfurniture.com
11535 Carmel Commons Blvd Ste 202....................Charlotte NC 28226 888-378-8383
TF: 888-378-8383 ■ *Web:* www.clubfurniture.com
Coast Guard Exchange System
510 Independence Pkwy Ste 500....................Chesapeake VA 23320 800-572-0230
TF: 800-572-0230 ■ *Web:* shopcgx.com
Conserv FS Inc 1110 McConnell Rd....................Woodstock IL 60098 815-334-5950
Web: www.conservfs.com
CoolTronics 220 E Madison St Ste 1220....................Tampa FL 33602 813-259-4407
Web: www.cooltronics.com
Dana Safety Supply Inc 5221 W Market St....................Greensboro NC 27409 336-854-5536
Web: www.danasafetysupply.com
DeMesy & Company Ltd 300 Crescent Ct....................Dallas TX 75201 214-855-8777
Web: www.demesy.com
Dempsey Corp 47 Davies Ave....................Toronto ON M4M2A9 416-461-0844
Web: www.dempseycorporation.com
Diamond Attachments LLC 2801A S Mississippi....................Atoka OK 74525 580-889-6202
TF: 800-445-1917 ■ *Web:* www.diamondattachments.com
Dixie Aerospace Inc 473 Dividend Dr....................Peachtree City GA 30269 678-490-0140
Web: www.dixieaerospace.com
Dollar General Corp 100 Mission Ridge....................Goodlettsville TN 37072 615-855-4000
NYSE: DG ■ *TF:* 800-777-1410 ■ *Web:* www.dollargeneral.com
Dollar Tree Stores Inc 500 Volvo Pkwy....................Chesapeake VA 23320 877-530-8733
NASDAQ: DLTR ■ *TF:* 877-530-8733 ■ *Web:* www.dollartree.com
Drury Capital Inc 47 Hulfish St Ste 340....................Princeton NJ 08542 609-252-1230
Web: www.drurycapital.com
Dueber's Inc
300 Industrial Blvd....................Norwood Young America MN 55397 952-467-3085 467-3001
Easy Ice LLC 925 W Washington St Ste 100....................Marquette MI 49855 866-327-9423
TF: 866-327-9423 ■ *Web:* www.easyice.com
Echo Engineering & Production Supplies Inc
5406 W 78th St....................Indianapolis IN 46268 317-876-8848
Web: www.echosupply.com
Emitations.com 6162 Mission Gorge Rd Ste G....................San Diego CA 92120 619-528-9100
Web: www.emitations.com
Employee Owned Holdings Inc
5500 N Sam Houston Pkwy W Ste 100....................Houston TX 77086 281-569-7000
Web: www.eoh-inc.com
Exchange, The 3911 S Walton Walker Blvd....................Dallas TX 75236 800-527-2345 446-0163
TF: 800-527-2345 ■ *Web:* www.shopmyexchange.com
Exporting Commodities International Inc
12000 Lincoln Dr W Ste 108....................Marlton NJ 08053 856-797-2004
Web: www.eci-coal.com
Fabric Images Inc 325 Corporate Dr....................Elgin IL 60123 847-488-9877
Web: www.fabricimages.com
Family Dollar Stores Inc PO Box 1017....................Charlotte NC 28201 704-847-6961
NYSE: FDO ■ *TF:* 866-377-6420 ■ *Web:* www.familydollar.com
Fertilizer Company of Arizona Inc
2850 S Peart Rd....................Casa Grande AZ 85293 520-836-7477
Web: www.comptonag.com
Filtration Lab Inc
193 Rang De L Eglise....................Saint Ligouri QC J0K2X0 450-754-4222
TF: 800-738-0168 ■ *Web:* www.filtrationlab.com

Company	City	State	Zip	Phone	Fax
Fortune Metals Inc 330 Hwy 7 E Ste 201 *Web:* www.fortunemetals.com	Richmond Hill	ON	L4B3P8	905-707-0786	
Fusion Tech 218 20th Ave *Web:* www.ftiinc.org	Roseville	IL	61473	309-774-4275	
Ghost Armor LLC 1470 N Horne St *TF:* 888-960-2766 ■ *Web:* www.ghost-armor.com	Gilbert	AZ	85233	480-921-3161	
GK TechStar LLC 802 W 13th St *Web:* www.techstaris.com	Deer Park	TX	77536	281-542-0205	
Great Canadian Dollar Store (1993) Ltd 2957 Jutland Rd Ste 101 *TF:* 877-388-0123 ■ *Web:* www.dollarstores.com	Victoria	BC	V8T5J9	250-388-0123	388-9763
Greatlookz 4635 N Black Canyon Hwy *Web:* www.greatlookz.com	Phoenix	AZ	85015	602-218-5976	
Gulf States Engineering Inc 4110 Moffett Rd *Web:* www.gseeng.com	Mobile	AL	36618	251-460-4646	
Hanwha International LLC 2559 Rt 130 *Web:* www.hanwha-usa.com	Cranbury	NJ	08512	609-655-2500	
Herman Strauss Inc 35th & McColloch St *Web:* www.strauss-ind.com	Wheeling	WV	26003	304-748-0699	
Home Furniture Mart 5301 Sheila St *TF:* 888-936-6673 ■ *Web:* www.homefurnituremart.com	Commerce	CA	90040	909-627-5705	
Howell Tractor & Equipment LLC 480 Blaine St *TF:* 800-852-8816 ■ *Web:* www.howelltractor.com	Gary	IN	46406	800-852-8816	
Hubbard`s Impala Parts Inc 1676 Anthony Rd *Web:* www.impalaparts.com	Burlington	NC	27215	336-227-1589	
Intrepid Aviation Group Holdings LLC 263 Tresser Blvd One Stamford Plz *Web:* www.intrepidaviation.com	Stamford	CT	06901	203-905-4220	
JD Fields & Company Inc 55 Waugh Dr Ste 1250 *Web:* www.jdfields.com	Houston	TX	77007	281-558-7199	
K&D Pratt Group Inc 55 Akerley Blvd Burnside Industrial Park *Web:* www.kdpratt.com	Dartmouth	NS	B3B1M3	902-468-1955	
Karl Chevrolet Accessories 1101 Se Oralabor Rd *Web:* www.karlchevrolet.com	Ankeny	IA	50021	515-299-4300	
Kataman Metals LLC 7733 Forsyth Blvd Ste 300 *Web:* www.katamanmetals.com	St. Louis	MO	63105	314-863-6699	
Keenpac North America Ltd 25 Main St Ste 3 *Web:* keenpac.com	Goshen	NY	10924	845-291-8680	
Kelloggauto Supply 502 S Edgemoor St *Web:* www.poormanautosupply.com	Wichita	KS	67218	316-682-4525	
Kerley & Sears Inc 4331 Cement Vly Rd *TF:* 800-346-4381 ■ *Web:* www.kerleyandsears.net	Midlothian	TX	76065	972-775-3902	
Keystone Archery Inc 186 Path Vly Rd *Web:* www.keystonecountrystore.com	Fort Loudon	PA	17224	717-369-2970	
Kryptonite Kollectibles 1441 Plainfield Ave. *TF:* 877-646-1728 ■ *Web:* www.kryptonitekollectibles.com	Janesville	WI	53545	877-646-1728	
Leeco Steel LLC 1011 Warrenville Rd Ste 500 *Web:* www.leecosteel.com	Lisle	IL	60532	630-427-2100	
Little General Store Inc 17 Yellow Wood Way *Web:* lgstoreswv.com	Beckley	WV	25801	304-253-9592	
Lynch Metals Inc 1075 Lousons Rd *TF:* 888-272-9464 ■ *Web:* www.lynchmetals.com	Union	NJ	07083	908-686-8401	
Lynn Roberts International Inc 9100 F St *Web:* www.golynnroberts.com	Omaha	NE	68127	402-331-5400	
Mallory Sonalert Products Inc 4411 S High School Rd *Web:* www.mallory-sonalert.com	Indianapolis	IN	46241	317-821-0370	
Marden's 458 Kennedy Memorial Dr *Web:* www.mardenssurplus.com	Waterville	ME	04901	207-873-6112	680-2229
Materials Innovation Technologies LLC 320 Rutledge Rd *Web:* www.emergingmit.com	Fletcher	NC	28732	828-651-9646	
McVean Trading & Investments LLC 850 Ridge Lk Blvd Ste One *TF:* 800-374-1937 ■ *Web:* www.mcvean.com	Memphis	TN	38120	901-761-8400	
Middlesex Gases & Technologies Inc 292 Second St PO Box 490249 *Web:* www.middlesexgases.com	Everett	MA	02149	617-387-5050	
Midwest Manufacturing Resources Inc 1993 Case Pkwy N *Web:* www.hfomidwest.com	Twinsburg	OH	44087	330-405-4227	
Nashville Rubber & Gasket Company Inc 1900 Elm Tree Dr *Web:* www.nashvillerubber.com	Nashville	TN	37210	615-883-0030	
Navy Exchange Service Command (NEXCOM) 3280 Virginia Beach Blvd *TF:* 800-628-3924 ■ *Web:* www.mynavyexchange.com	Virginia Beach	VA	23452	757-463-6200	
NeedleTech Products Inc 452 John L Dietsch Blvd. *Web:* www.needletech.com	North Attleboro	MA	02763	508-431-4000	
Net Worth Solutions Inc 1410 Broadway 34th Fl. *Web:* www.networthsolutionsinc.com	New York	NY	10018	212-278-8200	
New Vitality 260 Smith St *TF:* 888-997-2941 ■ *Web:* www.newvitality.com	Farmingdale	NY	11735	888-997-2941	
Norquist Salvage Corp 2151 Professional Dr Ste 200 *Web:* www.thrifttown.com	Roseville	CA	95661	916-787-1070	
Ocean State Jobbers Inc 375 Commerce Pk Rd *Web:* www.oceanstatejoblot.com	North Kingstown	RI	02852	401-295-2672	885-0359
Ollie's Bargain Outlet Inc 6295 Allentown Blvd Ste 1 *Web:* www.ollies.us/home.html	Harrisburg	PA	17112	717-657-2300	
Overstock.com Inc 6350 South 3000 East *NASDAQ: OSTK* ■ *TF Cust Svc:* 800-843-2446 ■ *Web:* www.overstock.com	Salt Lake City	UT	84121	801-947-3100	944-4629
Palay Display Industries Inc 10901 Louisiana Ave S Ste 106 *Web:* www.palaydisplay.com	Bloomington	MN	55438	952-983-2026	
PB Hoidale Company Inc 3801 W Harry *Web:* www.hoidale.com	Wichita	KS	67213	316-942-1361	
Peach Trader Inc 6286 Dawson Blvd *TF:* 888-949-9613 ■ *Web:* www.acitydiscount.com	Norcross	GA	30093	404-752-6715	
Pet Supplies Inc Customer Service Return Ctr 1 Maplewood Dr *TF:* 800-738-7877 ■ *Web:* www.petsupplies.com	Hazleton	PA	18202	800-738-7877	
Playscripts 7 Penn Plz Ste 904 *TF:* 866-639-7529 ■ *Web:* www.playscripts.com	New York	NY	10001	866-639-7529	
PLH Products Inc 6655 Knott Ave. *TF:* 800-946-6001 ■ *Web:* www.healthmatesauna.com	Buena Park	CA	90620	714-739-6600	
Polyform Products Co 1901 Estes Ave *Web:* sculpey.com	Elk Grove Village	IL	60007	847-427-0020	
Premier Elevator Company Inc 230 Andrew Dr *Web:* www.premier-elevator.com	Stockbridge	GA	30281	770-389-4951	
Pride Products Corp 4333 Veterans Memorial Hwy **Fax Area Code:* 877 ■ *TF:* 800-898-5550 ■ *Web:* www.prideproducts.com	Ronkonkoma	NY	11779	631-737-4444	729-4749*
Pro Athlete Inc 10800 N Pomona Ave *Web:* www.beapro.com	Kansas City	MO	64153	816-587-6050	
Promoshop Inc 5420 McConnell Ave *Web:* www.promoshopinc.com	Los Angeles	CA	90066	310-821-1780	
Protective Group Inc, The 14100 NW 58th Ct *Web:* www.protectivegroup.com	Miami Lakes	FL	33014	305-820-4270	
Quadratec Inc 1028 Saunders Ln *Web:* www.quadratec.com	West Chester	PA	19380	610-701-3336	
R J Schinner Company Inc 16950 W Lincoln Ave *TF:* 800-234-1460 ■ *Web:* www.rjschinner.com	New Berlin	WI	53151	262-797-7180	797-7190
Rack Attack-car Rack & Hitch Center 745 Worcester Rd *Web:* www.rackattack.com	Framingham	MA	01701	508-879-1444	
Rakuten.com Shopping 85 Enterprise St. *Web:* www.rakuten.com	Aliso Viejo	CA	92656	949-389-2000	389-2800
Rally House & Kansas Sampler 9750 Quivira Rd. *TF:* 800-645-5394 ■ *Web:* www.rallyhouse.com	Lenexa	KS	66215	800-645-5394	
Regal Mold and Die 25208 Leer Dr *Web:* www.regalmold.com	Elkhart	IN	46514	574-262-4110	
Reliance Parts Corp 2535 Business Pkwy *TF:* 800-776-3113 ■ *Web:* www.relianceparts.com	Minden	NV	89423	800-776-3113	
Rennco LLC 300 Elm St *TF:* 800-409-5225 ■ *Web:* www.rennco.com	Homer	MI	49245	800-409-5225	
River Trading Company LTD 10900 89th Ave N. *Web:* www.rivertradingcompany.com	Maple Grove	MN	55369	763-463-3400	
Rogers Stereo Inc 525 Woodruff Rd. *Web:* www.rogersstereo.com	Greenville	SC	29607	864-288-9999	
Sawyer Products Inc 605 Seventh Ave N. *Web:* www.sawyer.com	Safety Harbor	FL	34695	727-725-1177	
Schwing Bioset Inc 350 SMC Dr *Web:* www.schwingbioset.com	Somerset	WI	54025	715-247-3433	
Scout Stuff PO Box 7143 *TF:* 800-323-0736 ■ *Web:* www.scoutstuff.org	Charlotte	NC	28241	800-323-0736	
SDB Trade International LP 817 Southmore Ave Ste 301 *Web:* thesdbgroup.com	Houston	TX	77502	713-475-0048	
SelecTransportation Resources LLC 9550 N Loop E *Web:* www.selectransportation.com	Houston	TX	77029	713-672-4115	
Shoplet.com 39 Broadway Ste 2030 *TF:* 800-757-3015 ■ *Web:* www.shoplet.com	New York	NY	10006	212-619-3353	617-3389
Skycraft Parts & Surplus Inc 2245 W Fairbanks Ave *Web:* www.skycraftsurplus.com	Winter Park	FL	32789	407-628-5634	
Slack Auto Parts 404 Main St Sw *Web:* www.slackautoparts.com	Gainesville	GA	30501	770-535-6000	
Southern Company of NLR Inc, The 1201 Cypress St *Web:* www.thesoco.com	North Little Rock	AR	72114	501-376-6333	
Speedway Motors 340 Victory Ln PO Box 81906 *TF:* 800-736-3733 ■ *Web:* www.speedwaymotors.com	Lincoln	NE	68528	402-323-3200	
Spot Trading LLC 440 S LaSalle St Ste 2800 *Web:* www.spottradingllc.com	Chicago	IL	60605	312-362-4550	
Stahl Peterbilt Inc 18020-118 Ave *TF:* 800-252-7981 ■ *Web:* www.stahlpeterbilt.com	Edmonton	AB	T5S2G2	780-483-6666	
SteelCon Supply Co 265 Industrial Dr *Web:* www.steelconsupply.com	Beckley	WV	25801	304-255-1416	
Store Supply Warehouse LLC 9801 Page Ave. *Web:* www.storesupply.com	St Louis	MO	63132	314-427-8887	
Store51 3653 Regent Blvd Ste 606 *Web:* www.store51.com	Jacksonville	FL	32224	904-998-2222	
Stowers Rental & Supply Inc 10644 Lexington Dr *Web:* www.stowerscat-inventory.com	Knoxville	TN	37932	865-218-8800	
Strato Inc 100 New England Ave *Web:* www.stratoinc.com	Piscataway	NJ	08854	732-981-1515	
Stylin Online 81900 Main St *Web:* www.stylinonline.com	Memphis	MI	48041	586-270-1086	
Sun Machinery Company Inc PO Box 789 *Web:* www.sunmachineryco.com	Lexington	SC	29071	803-359-1000	
Supply Chain Equity Partners 1300 East Ninth St *Web:* www.supplychainequity.com	Cleveland	OH	44199	216-925-4184	
Swain's General Store Inc 602 E First St *Web:* www.swainsinc.com	Port Angeles	WA	98362	360-452-2357	452-7561
Third Door Media Inc 279 Newtown Tpke *Web:* www.thirddoormedia.com	Redding	CT	06896	203-664-1350	

	City	State	Zip	Phone	Fax
Tiger Supplies Inc 27 Selvage St *TF:* 888-844-3765 ■ *Web:* www.tigersupplies.com	Irvington	NJ	07111	973-854-8636	
Trydor Industries (Canada) Ltd 19275 - 25th Ave *TF:* 800-567-8558 ■ *Web:* www.trydor.com	Surrey	BC	V3S3X1	604-542-4773	542-4776
Turbo International Inc 2151 Las Palmas Dr Ste E *Web:* www.turbointernational.com	Carlsbad	CA	92011	760-476-1444	
U-line Corp PO Box 245040 *TF:* 800-779-2547 ■ *Web:* www.u-line.com	Milwaukee	WI	53224	414-354-0300	
Unclaimed Baggage Ctr 509 W Willow St *Web:* unclaimedbaggage.com	Scottsboro	AL	35768	256-259-1525	
URELL Inc 86 Coolidge Ave *Web:* www.urell.com	Watertown	MA	02471	617-923-9500	
US-Japan High-Speed Rail LLC 1212 New York Ave NW Ste 700 *Web:* www.usjhsr.com	Washington	DC	20005	202-403-0437	
Valterra Products Inc 15230 San Fernando Mission Blvd Ste 107 *Web:* www.valterra.com	Mission Hills	CA	91345	818-898-1671	
Vanguard Steel Ltd 2160 Meadowpine Blvd *Web:* www.vanguardsteel.com	Mississauga	ON	L5N6H6	905-821-1100	
Vermeer Mid Atlantic Inc 10900 Carpet St *TF:* 800-768-3444 ■ *Web:* www.vermeermidatlantic.com	Charlotte	NC	28273	704-588-3238	
Vermeer Southeast Sales & Service Inc 4559 Old Winter Garden Rd *Web:* www.vermeersoutheast.com	Orlando	FL	32811	407-295-2020	
Waterfront Container Leasing Company Inc 888 N Point St *Web:* www.waterfrontcontainer.com	San Francisco	CA	94109	415-788-5667	
Weir Canada Inc 2360 Millrace Ct *Web:* www.global.weir/industries/power	Mississauga	ON	L5N1W2	905-812-7100	
West Springfield Auto Parts 92 Blandin Ave Ste C *TF:* 800-615-2392 ■ *Web:* www.wsaparts.com	Framingham	MA	01702	508-879-6932	
Western States Truck Centers LLC 3790 N Reserve St *Web:* www.westernstatestruckcenters.com	Missoula	MT	59808	406-543-3196	
Western United Electric Supply Corp 100 Bromley Business Pkwy *Web:* www.wue.coop	Brighton	CO	80603	303-659-2356	
Wild Bird Centers of America 4046 W 83rd St *Web:* www.wildbird.com	Prairie Village	KS	66208	913-381-5633	
World Trade Service Inc 1050 Nine N Dr Ste A *Web:* www.worldtradeservice.com	Alpharetta	GA	30004	770-521-0124	
WristWatch 109 S Main St *Web:* www.wristwatch.com	Mcallen	TX	78501	956-682-7132	
Yale Materials Handling-Green Bay Inc 2140 Hutson Rd *Web:* www.yalegb.com	Green Bay	WI	54303	920-494-8726	

792 VENTURE CAPITAL FIRMS

Companies listed here are investors, not lenders.

	City	State	Zip	Phone	Fax
AAVIN Equity Partners LP 1245 First Ave SE Ste 630 *Web:* www.aavin.com	Cedar Rapids	IA	52402	319-247-1072	
Aberdare Ventures 1 Embarcadero Ctr Ste 4000 *Web:* www.aberdare.com	San Francisco	CA	94111	415-392-7442	392-4264
ABS Capital Partners 400 E Pratt St Ste 910 *Web:* www.abscapital.com	Baltimore	MD	21202	410-246-5600	246-5606
ABS Ventures 950 Winter St Ste 2600 *Web:* www.absventures.com	Waltham	MA	02451	781-250-0400	
Accel Partners 428 University Ave *Web:* www.accel.com	Palo Alto	CA	94301	650-614-4800	
Adams Capital Management Inc 500 Blackburn Ave *Web:* www.acm.com	Sewickley	PA	15143	412-749-9454	749-9459
Adams Harkness Techventures 60 State St	Boston	MA	02109	617-788-1670	788-1663
Adams Street Partners LLC 1 N Wacker Dr Ste 2200 *Web:* www.adamsstreetpartners.com	Chicago	IL	60606	312-553-7890	553-7891
Adobe Ventures LP 345 Pk Ave *TF:* 877-722-7088 ■ *Web:* www.adobe.com	San Jose	CA	95110	408-536-6000	537-6000
Advanced Technology Ventures 500 Boylston St Ste 1380 *Web:* www.atvcapital.com	Boston	MA	02116	617-850-9700	
Advanced Technology Ventures 485 Ramona St *Web:* www.atvcapital.com	Palo Alto	CA	94301	650-321-8601	
Advantage Capital Partners 190 Carondelet Plz Ste 1500 *Web:* www.advantagecap.com	St Louis	MO	63105	256-883-8711	
Advent International Corp 75 State St *Web:* www.adventinternational.com	Boston	MA	02109	617-951-9400	
Alerion Partners 23 Old Kings Hwy S *Web:* www.alerionpartners.com	Darien	CT	06820	203-202-9900	202-9906
Alexander Hutton Venture Partners 1215 Fourth Ave Ste 900 *Web:* www.ahvp.com	Seattle	WA	98161	206-341-9800	341-9810
Allegis Capital 130 Lytton Ave Ste 210 *Web:* www.allegiscapital.com	Palo Alto	CA	94301	650-687-0500	687-0234
Alloy Ventures 400 Hamilton Ave 4th Fl *Web:* www.alloyventures.com	Palo Alto	CA	94301	650-687-5000	687-5010
Alpha Capital Partners Ltd 122 S Michigan Ave Ste 1700 *Web:* www.alphacapital.com	Chicago	IL	60603	312-322-9800	
Alta Communications 1000 Winter St S Entrance Ste 3500	Waltham	MA	02451	617-262-7770	262-9779
Alta Partners 1 Embarcadero Ctr 37th Fl *Web:* www.altapartners.com	San Francisco	CA	94111	415-362-4022	362-6178
Altira Group LLC 1675 Broadway Ste 2400 *Web:* www.altiragroup.com	Denver	CO	80202	303-592-5500	592-5519
Altos Ventures 2882 Sand Hill Rd Ste 100 *Web:* altos.vc	Menlo Park	CA	94025	650-234-9771	233-9821
Altotech Ventures LLC 205 De Anza Blvd Ste 14 *Web:* www.altotechventures.com	San Mateo	CA	94402	650-574-1870	
AM Pappas & Assoc 2520 Meridian Pkwy *Web:* www.pappasventures.com	Durham	NC	27713	919-998-3300	998-3301
American Bullion Inc 12301 Wilshire Blvd Ste 650 *TF:* 800-326-9598 ■ *Web:* www.americanbullion.com	Los Angeles	CA	90025	310-689-7720	
American Capital Group Inc 100 Spectrum Ctr Dr Ste 750 *TF:* 877-814-6871 ■ *Web:* www.acgcapital.com	Irvine	CA	92618	949-485-3005	271-5850
American River Ventures 2270 Douglas Blvd Ste 212 *Web:* www.arventures.com	Roseville	CA	95661	916-780-2828	
Ampersand Capital Partners 55 William St Ste 240 *TF:* 800-477-6834 ■ *Web:* www.ampersandcapital.com	Wellesley	MA	02481	781-239-0700	239-0824
Aperture Venture Partners 645 Madison Ave 20th Fl *Web:* www.aperturevp.com	New York	NY	10022	212-758-7325	319-8779
Apex Venture Partners 225 W Washington St Ste 1500 *Web:* www.apexvc.com	Chicago	IL	60606	312-857-2800	857-1800
Arbor Partners LLC 130 S First St *Web:* www.arborpartners.com	Ann Arbor	MI	48104	734-668-9000	669-4195
Arboretum Ventures 303 Detroit St *Web:* www.arboretumvc.com	Ann Arbor	MI	48104	734-998-3688	998-3689
ARCH Venture Partners 8725 W Higgins Rd Ste 290 *Web:* www.archventure.com	Chicago	IL	60631	773-380-6600	380-6606
Arete Corp PO Box 1299 *Web:* www.arete-microgen.com	Center Harbor	NH	03226	603-253-9797	253-9799
Ascension Health Ventures LLC 11775 Borman Dr Ste 310 *Web:* ascensionventures.org	Saint Louis	MO	63146	314-733-8100	
Ascent Venture Partners 255 State St 5th Fl *Web:* www.ascentvp.com	Boston	MA	02109	617-720-9400	720-9401
Asset Management Ventures 2100 Geng Rd Ste 200 *Web:* www.assetman.com	Palo Alto	CA	94303	650-621-8808	856-1826
Associated Venture Investors Management 130 Lytton Ave Ste 210 *Web:* pinnacleven.com	Palo Alto	CA	94301	650-687-0235	
ATA Ventures 4300 El Camino Real Ste 205 *Web:* www.ataventures.com	Los Altos	CA	94022	650-594-0189	594-0257
August Capital 2480 Sand Hill Rd Ste 101 *Web:* www.augustcap.com	Menlo Park	CA	94025	650-234-9900	234-9910
Aurora Funds 3100 Tower Blvd *Web:* www.aurorafunds.com	Durham	NC	27707	919-484-0400	484-0444
Austin Ventures 300 W Sixth St Ste 2300 *Web:* www.austinventures.com	Austin	TX	78701	512-485-1900	
Avansis Ventures LLC 12710 Popes Head Rd *Web:* www.avansis.com	Clifton	VA	20124	703-796-0222	935-0574
Bain Capital Inc 200 Clarendon St *Web:* baincapital.com	Boston	MA	02116	617-516-2000	516-2010
Battelle Ventures 100 Princeton S Corp Ctr Ste 150	Ewing	NJ	08628	609-921-1456	921-8703
Battery Ventures 1 Marina Pk Dr Ste 1100 *Web:* www.battery.com	Boston	MA	02210	617-948-3600	948-3601
Bay Partners 10600 N De Anza Blvd Ste 100 *Web:* www.baypartners.com	Cupertino	CA	95014	408-725-2444	446-4502
BCM Technologies 1709 Dryden Rd Ste 1790 *Web:* www.bcmtechnologies.com	Houston	TX	77030	713-795-0105	795-4602
Beecken Petty O'Keefe & Co 131 S Dearborn St Ste 2800 *Web:* www.bpoc.com	Chicago	IL	60603	312-435-0300	
Beringea LLC 32330 W 12 Mile Rd *Web:* www.beringea.com	Farmington Hills	MI	48334	248-489-9000	
Berkeley International Capital Corp 650 California St 26th Fl *Web:* www.berkeleyvc.com	San Francisco	CA	94108	415-249-0450	
BioAdvance 3711 Market St Fl 8 *Web:* www.bioadvance.com	Philadelphia	PA	19104	215-966-6214	
Bioventures Investors 70 Walnut St Ste 302 *Web:* www.bioventuresinvestors.com	Wellesley	MA	02481	617-252-3443	621-7993
Black River Asset Management LLC 9320 Excelsior Blvd *Web:* www.black-river.com	Hopkins	MN	55343	952-984-3863	
BlackRock Inc 601 Union St 56th Fl *NYSE: BLK* ■ **Fax Area Code:* 302 ■ *TF:* 800-441-7450 ■ *Web:* www.blackrock.com/corporate	Seattle	WA	98101	206-613-6700	797-2211*
Blue Chip Venture Co 312 Walnut St Ste 1120 *Web:* www.bcvc.com	Cincinnati	OH	45202	513-723-2300	
Blueprint Ventures 601 Gateway Blvd Ste 1140	South San Francisco	CA	94080	415-901-4000	
BlueRun Ventures 545 Middlefield Rd Ste 250 *Web:* brv.com	Menlo Park	CA	94025	650-462-7250	462-7252
Boldcap Ventures LLC 750 Lexington Ave 6th Fl **Fax Area Code:* 917 ■ *Web:* www.boldcap.com	New York	NY	10022	212-730-5498	591-0880*
Borealis Ventures 10 Allen St *Web:* www.borealisventures.com	Hanover	NH	03755	603-643-1500	
Boston Capital Ventures 84 State St Ste 320	Boston	MA	02109	617-227-6550	227-3847
Boston Millennia Partners 30 Rowes Wharf Ste 400 *Web:* www.bostonmillenniapartners.com	Boston	MA	02110	617-428-5150	428-5160
Brantley Partners 3550 Lander Rd Ste 300	Cleveland	OH	44124	216-464-8400	464-8405

					Phone	Fax
BTG International Inc	5 Tower Bridge 300 Barr Harbor Dr Ste 810 *Web:* www.btgplc.com	West Conshohocken	PA	19428	610-278-1660	278-1605
Burrill & Co	1 Embarcadero Ctr Ste 2700	San Francisco	CA	94111	415-591-5400	591-5401
BV Cornerstone Ventures LP	385 Interlocken Crescent Ste 250 *Web:* www.bvcv.com	Broomfield	CO	80021	303-410-2500	
Cambridge Innovations Inc	*Cambridge Innovation Ctr* 1 Broadway 14th Fl. *Web:* cic.us	Cambridge	MA	02142	617-758-4200	758-4101
Camp Ventures LLC	280 Second St Ste 280 *Web:* www.campventures.com	Los Altos	CA	94022	650-949-0804	618-1719
Capital Network Inc, The	281 Summer St 2nd Fl *Web:* www.thecapitalnetwork.org	Boston	MA	02210	781-591-0291	
Capital Resource Partners	31 State St 6th Fl *TF:* 800-623-2880 ■ *Web:* www.crp.com	Boston	MA	02109	617-478-9600	478-9605
Capital Southwest Corp	5400 Lyndon B Johnson Freeway Ste 1300 *NASDAQ: CSWC* ■ *Web:* www.capitalsouthwest.com	Dallas	TX	75240	214-238-5700	238-5701
Cardinal Partners	230 Nassau St *Web:* www.cardinalpartners.com	Princeton	NJ	08542	609-924-6452	683-0174
Cardinal Venture Capital	325 Sharon Pk Dr Ste 107 *Web:* www.cardinalvc.com	Menlo Park	CA	94025	650-289-4700	
Castile Ventures	65 William St Ste 205 *Web:* www.castileventures.com	Wellesley	MA	02481	781-890-0060	890-0065
Catamount Ventures	400 Pacific Ave 3rd Fl *Web:* www.catamountventures.com	San Francisco	CA	94133	415-277-0300	277-0301
Catterton	599 W Putnam Ave *Web:* www.catterton.com	Greenwich	CT	06830	203-629-4901	629-4903
CenterPoint Ventures	6300 Bridge Pt Pkwy Bldg 1 Ste 500 *Web:* www.cpventures.com	Austin	TX	78730	512-795-5800	795-5849
Charles River Ventures	1 Broadway 15th Fl *Web:* www.crv.com	Cambridge	MA	02142	781-768-6000	
Charter Venture Capital	525 University Ave Ste 1400 *Web:* www.charterventures.com	Palo Alto	CA	94301	650-325-6953	
Cherry Tree Investment Co	301 Carlson Pkwy Ste 103 *Web:* www.cherrytree.com	Minnetonka	MN	55305	952-893-9012	893-9036
Chevron Technology Ventures (CTV)	6001 Bollinger Canyon Rd *NYSE: CVX* ■ *Web:* www.chevron.com/technologyventures	San Ramon	CA	94583	925-842-1000	
CHL Medical Partners	1055 Washington Blvd 6th Fl *Web:* www.chlmedical.com	Stamford	CT	06901	203-324-7700	324-3636
Chrysalis Ventures	101 S Fifth St Ste 1650 *Web:* www.chrysalisventures.com	Louisville	KY	40202	502-583-7644	
CIBC Wood Gundy Capital	425 Lexington Ave *TF:* 800-999-6726 ■ *Web:* www.cibcwm.com	New York	NY	10017	212-856-4000	
CID Capital Inc	201 W 103rd St Ste 200 *Web:* www.cidcap.com	Indianapolis	IN	46290	317-818-5030	644-2914
CIVC Partners	191 N Wacker Dr Ste 1100 *Web:* www.civc.com	Chicago	IL	60606	312-873-7300	873-7300
Clearstone Venture Partners	1351 Fourth St 4th Fl *Web:* www.clearstone.com	Santa Monica	CA	90401	310-460-7900	
Code Hennessy & Simmons Inc	10 S Wacker Dr Ste 3175 *TF:* 888-603-5847 ■ *Web:* www.chsonline.com	Chicago	IL	60606	312-876-1840	876-3854
Columbia Capital	204 S Union St *Web:* www.colcap.com	Alexandria	VA	22314	703-519-2000	519-5870
Commons Capital LP	320 Washington St 4th Fl *Web:* www.commonscapital.com	Brookline	MA	02445	617-739-3500	
Commonwealth Capital Ventures	400 Cummings Park Dr Ste 1725 *Web:* www.commonwealthvc.com	Woburn	MA	01801	781-890-5554	
Connecticut Innovations Inc	865 Brook St 3rd Fl *TF:* 800-733-4763 ■ *Web:* www.ctinnovations.com	Rocky Hill	CT	06067	860-563-5851	563-4877
Cordova Ventures	70 Mansell Ct Ste 100 *Web:* www.cordovaventures.com	Roswell	GA	30076	678-942-0300	942-0301
Cornerstone Equity Investors LLC	281 Tresser Blvd 12th Fl *Web:* www.cornerstone-equity.com	Stamford	CT	06901	212-753-0901	826-6798
Court Square Ventures	455 Second St SE Ste 401 *Web:* courtsquareventures.com	Charlottesville	VA	22902	434-817-3300	
Covera Ventures	6836 Bee Caves Rd Ste275 *Web:* www.coveraventures.com	Austin	TX	78746	512-795-5870	
Crescendo Ventures	600 Hansen Way *Web:* www.crescendoventures.com	Palo Alto	CA	94304	650-470-1200	
Cross Atlantic Capital Partners	5 Radnor Corporate Ctr 100 Matsonford Rd Ste 555 *Web:* www.xacp.com	Radnor	PA	19087	610-995-2650	971-2062
Crosslink Capital	2 Embarcadero Ctr Ste 2200 *Web:* www.crosslinkcapital.com	San Francisco	CA	94111	415-617-1800	
Crosspoint Venture Partners	670 Woodside Rd *Web:* www.cpvp.com	Redwood City	CA	94061	650-851-7600	851-7600
Cutlass Capital LLC	229 Marlborough St *Web:* www.cutlasscapital.com	Boston	MA	02116	617-867-0820	
Davis Tuttle Venture Partners LP	110 W Seventh St *Web:* www.davistuttle.com	Tulsa	OK	74103	918-584-7272	582-3404
Defta Partners	111 Pine St *Web:* www.deftapartners.com	San Francisco	CA	94111	415-433-2262	
Delphi Ventures	160 Bovet Rd Ste 408 *Web:* www.delphiventures.com	San Mateo	CA	94402	650-854-9650	
Digital Power Capital	411 W Putnam Ave	Greenwich	CT	06830	203-862-7040	
Doll Capital Management	2420 Sand Hill Rd Ste 200 *Web:* www.dcm.com	Menlo Park	CA	94025	650-233-1400	854-9159
Dolphin Equity Partners	330 Madison Ave 9th Fl	New York	NY	10017	212-446-1600	
Domain Assoc	1 Palmer Sq Ste 515 *TF:* 866-803-9204 ■ *Web:* www.domainvc.com	Princeton	NJ	08542	609-683-5656	683-9789
Dominion Ventures	1646 N California Blvd *Web:* www.dominion.com	Walnut Creek	CA	94596	925-280-6338	
Draper Fisher Jurvetson (DFJ)	2882 Sand Hill Rd Ste 150 *Web:* www.dfj.com	Menlo Park	CA	94025	650-233-9000	
East Gate Capital Management	5050 El Camino Real Ste 104 *Web:* www.eg-group.com	Los Altos	CA	94022	650-325-5077	
Edelson Technology Partners	300 Tice Blvd *Web:* www.edelsontech.com	Woodcliff Lake	NJ	07677	201-930-9898	930-8899
EDF Ventures	425 N Main St *Web:* www.edfvc.com	Ann Arbor	MI	48104	734-663-3213	663-7358
Edison Venture Fund	281 Witherspoon St *Web:* edisonpartners.com	Lawrenceville	NJ	08540	609-896-1900	
EGL Holdings	3495 Piedmont Rd 11 Piedmont Ctr Ste 412 *Web:* www.eglholdings.com	Atlanta	GA	30305	404-949-8300	949-8311
El Dorado Ventures	702 Oak Grove Ave *Web:* www.eldorado.com	Menlo Park	CA	94025	650-854-1200	
EnerTech Capital	625 W Ridge Pk Bldg D Ste 105 *Web:* www.enertechcapital.com	Conshohocken	PA	19428	484-539-1860	539-1870
Enterprise Partners Venture Capital (EPVC)	2223 Avenida de la Playa Ste 300	La Jolla	CA	92037	858-731-0300	
Entrepia Ventures Inc	2975 Bowers Ave Ste 223 *Web:* www.entrepia.com	Santa Clara	CA	95051	408-492-9040	
Envest Ventures	2101 Parks Ave Ste 401 *Web:* www.envestventures.com	Virginia Beach	VA	23451	757-437-3000	
EQUUS Total Return Inc	700 Louisiana St 48th Fl **Fax Area Code: 212* ■ *TF:* 888-323-4533 ■ *Web:* www.equuscap.com	Houston	TX	77002	888-323-4533	671-1534*
Euclid SR Partners	45 Rockefeller Plaza Ste 1910	New York	NY	10111	212-218-6880	218-6877
Ferrer Freeman & Company LLC	10 Glenville St *Web:* www.ffandco.com	Greenwich	CT	06831	203-532-8011	532-8016
First Analysis Corp	1 S Wacker Dr Ste 3900 *Web:* firstanalysis.com	Chicago	IL	60606	312-258-1400	
Fisher Lynch Capital	2929 Campus Dr Ste 420 *Web:* www.fisherlynch.com	San Mateo	CA	94403	650-287-2700	287-2701
Flagship Ventures	1 Memorial Dr 7th Fl *Web:* www.flagshipventures.com	Cambridge	MA	02142	617-868-1888	868-1115
Fletcher Spaght Inc	222 Berkeley St 20th Fl *Web:* www.fletcherspaght.com	Boston	MA	02116	617-247-6700	247-7757
Focus Ventures	525 University Ave Ste 225 *Web:* www.focusventures.com	Palo Alto	CA	94301	650-325-7400	
Forward Ventures	4747 Executive Dr Ste 700 *Web:* www.forwardventures.com	San Diego	CA	92121	858-677-6077	
Foundation Capital	250 Middlefield Rd *Web:* www.foundationcapital.com	Menlo Park	CA	94025	650-614-0500	
Frazier Healthcare	601 Union 2 Union Sq Ste 3200 *Web:* www.frazierco.com	Seattle	WA	98101	206-621-7200	
Frontenac Co	135 S La Salle St Ste 3800 *Web:* www.frontenac.com	Chicago	IL	60603	312-368-0044	
G-51 Capital Management	900 S Capital of Texas Hwy Ste 151 *Web:* www.g51-amplify.com	Austin	TX	78746	512-929-5151	732-0886
Gabriel Venture Partners	999 Baker Way Ste 400 *Web:* www.gabrielvp.com	San Mateo	CA	94404	650-551-5000	551-5001
Gazelle Techventures	11611 N Meridian St Ste 310 *Web:* allosventures.com	Carmel	IN	46032	317-275-6800	
General Atlantic LLC	600 Steamboat Rd Ste 105 *Web:* www.generalatlantic.com	Greenwich	CT	06830	203-629-8600	622-8818
Geocapital Partners	1 Executive Dr Ste 160	Fort Lee	NJ	07024	201-461-9292	461-7793
GFI Energy Ventures LLC	333 S Grand Ave 28 Fl *Web:* www.oaktreecapital.com	Los Angeles	CA	90071	213-830-6300	830-6293
Globespan Capital Partners	1 Boston Pl Ste 2810 *Web:* www.globespancapital.com	Boston	MA	02108	617-305-2300	
GrandBanks Capital	65 William St Ste 330 *Web:* www.grandbankscapital.com	Wellesley	MA	02481	781-997-4300	997-4301
Great Hill Partners LLC	1 Liberty Sq *Web:* www.greathillpartners.com	Boston	MA	02109	617-790-9400	790-9401
Greenspring Assoc Inc	100 Painters Mill Rd Ste 700 *Web:* greenspringassociates.com	Owings Mills	MD	21117	410-363-2725	
Greer Capital Advisors LLC	2200 Woodcrest Pl Ste 309 *Web:* www.greercap.com	Birmingham	AL	35209	205-445-0800	445-1013
Grosvenor Funds	888 17th St NW Ste 214 *Web:* www.grosvenorfund.com	Washington	WA	20006	202-861-5650	861-5653
Grove Street Advisors	2221 Washington St Bldg 1 Ste 201 *Web:* grovestreet.com	Newton	MA	02462	781-263-6100	263-6101
GTCR Golder Rauner LLC	300 N Lasalle Ste 5600 *Web:* www.gtcr.com	Chicago	IL	60654	312-382-2200	
Hamilton BioVentures	990 Highland Dr Ste 302	Solana Beach	CA	92075	858-314-2350	314-2355

Firm	City	State	ZIP	Phone	Fax
HarbourVest Partners LLC 1 Financial Ctr *Web:* www.harbourvest.com	Boston	MA	02111	617-348-3707	350-0305
Harvard Management Company Inc 600 Atlantic Ave *Web:* www.hmc.harvard.edu	Boston	MA	02210	617-523-4400	
Harvest Partners 280 Pk Ave 25th Fl *TF:* 866-771-1000 ■ *Web:* harvestpartners.com	New York	NY	10017	212-599-6300	812-0100
HC Wainwright & Co Inc 430 Park Ave 4th Fl *Web:* www.hcwainwright.com	New York	NY	10022	212-356-0500	
Hercules Technology Growth Capital Inc 400 Hamilton Ave Ste 310 *NYSE: HTGC* ■ *Web:* htgc.com	Palo Alto	CA	94301	650-289-3060	473-9194
Highland Capital Partners 92 Hayden Ave *Web:* www.hcp.com	Lexington	MA	02421	781-861-5500	
HLM Venture Partners 222 Berkeley St 20th Fl *Web:* www.hlmvp.com	Boston	MA	02116	617-266-0030	
HMS Hawaii 841 Bishop St Ste 860 *Web:* www.hmshawaii.com	Honolulu	HI	96813	808-545-3755	
HO2 Partners 13455 Noel Rd 2 Galleria Tower Ste 1670 *Web:* www.ho2.com	Dallas	TX	75240	972-702-1107	702-8234
Housatonic Partners 800 Boylston St Ste 2220 *Web:* www.housatonicpartners.com	Boston	MA	02199	617-399-9200	267-5565
Hummer Winblad Venture Partners 1398 The Embarcadero Ste 200 *Web:* hwvp.com	San Francisco	CA	94111	415-979-9600	979-9601
Icon Ventures 505 Hamilton Ave Ste 310 *Web:* www.jafco.com	Palo Alto	CA	94301	650-463-8800	463-8801
Idealab 130 W Union St *Web:* www.idealab.com	Pasadena	CA	91103	626-585-6900	535-2701
IDG Ventures 1 Letterman Dr *Web:* www.idgvsf.com	San Francisco	CA	94129	415-439-4420	
IGNITE Group 255 Shoreline Dr	Redwood City	CA	94065	650-622-2005	
In-Q-Tel PO Box 749 *Web:* www.iqt.org	Arlington	VA	22216	703-248-3000	248-3001
Inflection Point Ventures (IPV) 1 Innovation Way Ste 302 *Web:* www.inflectpoint.com	Newark	DE	19711	302-452-1120	452-1122
InnoCal LP 650 Town Ctr Dr Ste 770 *Web:* www.innocal.com	Costa Mesa	CA	92626	714-850-6784	850-6798
Innovation Works Inc 2000 Technology Dr Ste 250 *Web:* www.innovationworks.org	Pittsburgh	PA	15219	412-681-1520	681-2625
Institutional Venture Partners 3000 Sand Hill Rd Bldg 2 Ste 250 *Web:* www.ivp.com	Menlo Park	CA	94025	650-854-0132	854-2009
Intelligent Systems Corp 4355 Shackleford Rd *NYSE: INS* ■ *Web:* www.intelsys.com	Norcross	GA	30093	770-381-2900	381-2808
InterWest Partners 2710 Sand Hill Rd 2nd Fl *TF:* 866-803-9204 ■ *Web:* www.interwest.com	Menlo Park	CA	94025	650-854-8585	854-4706
INVESCO Private Capital Inc 1166 Ave of the Americas 26th Fl *TF:* 800-959-4246 ■ *Web:* www.invesco.com	New York	NY	10036	212-278-9000	278-9822
Ironside Capital 945 Concord St *Web:* www.ironsidecapital.com	Framingham	MA	01701	781-622-5800	
iSherpa Capital LLC 6400 S Fiddlers Green Cir *Web:* isherpa.com	Greenwood Village	CO	80111	303-645-0500	
JatoTech Ventures 6300 Bridgepoint Pkwy *Web:* www.jatotech.com	Austin	TX	78730	512-795-5860	
JEGI Capital LLC 150 E 52nd St 18th Fl *Web:* www.jegi.com	New York	NY	10022	212-754-0710	
JH Whitney & Co 130 Main St *Web:* www.whitney.com	New Canaan	CT	06840	203-716-6100	716-6122
JK&B Capital 180 N Stetson Ave Ste 4500 *Web:* www.jkbcapital.com	Chicago	IL	60601	312-946-1200	946-1103
Johnson & Johnson Development Corp 1 Johnson & Johnson Plz *NYSE: JNJ* ■ *Web:* www.jnj.com	New Brunswick	NJ	08933	732-524-0400	
KB Partners LLC 600 Central Ave Ste 390 *Web:* www.kbpartners.com	Highland Park	IL	60035	847-681-1270	681-1370
KBL Healthcare Ventures 52 E 72nd St-PH *Web:* www.kblvc.com	New York	NY	10021	212-319-5555	319-5591
Kirtland Capital Partners 3201 Enterprise Pkwy Ste 200 *Web:* www.kirtlandcapital.com	Beachwood	OH	44122	216-593-0100	593-0240
Kleiner Perkins Caufield & Byers (KPCB) 2750 Sand Hill Rd *Web:* www.kpcb.com	Menlo Park	CA	94025	650-233-2750	233-0300
Kodiak Venture Partners 1000 Winter St Ste 3800 *Web:* www.kodiakvp.com	Waltham	MA	02451	781-672-2500	672-2501
Labrador Ventures 101 University Ave 4th Fl *Web:* www.labrador.com	Palo Alto	CA	94301	650-366-6000	366-6430
Lancet Capital 245 First St Ste 1800 *Web:* www.lancetcapital.com	Cambridge	MA	02142	617-444-8582	444-8405
Lee Munder Capital Group 200 Clarendon St *Web:* www.leemunderpim.com	Boston	MA	02116	617-380-5600	
Legacy Venture 180 Lytton Ave *Web:* www.legacyventure.com	Palo Alto	CA	94301	650-324-5980	324-5982
Life Sciences Greenhouse 225 Market St Ste 500 *Web:* www.lsgpa.com	Harrisburg	PA	17101	717-635-2100	
Lightspeed Venture Partners 2200 Sand Hill Rd Ste 100 *Web:* lsvp.com	Menlo Park	CA	94025	650-234-8300	234-8333
Lilly Ventures 115 W Washington St *Web:* www.lillyventures.com	Indianapolis	IN	46204	317-429-0140	759-2819
Lubar & Co 700 N Water St Ste 1200 *Web:* www.lubar.com	Milwaukee	WI	53202	414-291-9000	291-9061
Madison Dearborn Partners LLC (MDP) 70 W Madison Ste 4600 *Web:* www.mdcp.com	Chicago	IL	60602	312-895-1000	895-1001
Markpoint Venture Partners 15770 Dallas Pkwy Ste 800 *Web:* www.markpt.com	Dallas	TX	75248	972-490-1976	490-1980
Mason Wells Biomedical Fund 411 E Wisconsin Ave Ste 1280 *Web:* www.masonwells.com	Milwaukee	WI	53202	414-727-6400	727-6410
Massachusetts Capital Resource Co 420 Boylston St 5th Fl *Web:* www.masscapital.com	Boston	MA	02116	617-536-3900	
Massachusetts Growth Capital Corp (MGCC) 529 Main St Schrafft Ctr Ste 1M10 *Web:* www.mcdfc.com	Charlestown	MA	02129	617-523-6262	523-7676
Matrix Partners 1000 Winter St Bay Colony Corporate Ctr Ste 4500 *Web:* www.matrixpartners.com	Waltham	MA	02451	781-890-2244	890-2288
Maveron LLC 411 First Ave S Ste 600 *Web:* www.maveron.com	Seattle	WA	98104	206-288-1700	
Mayfield Fund 2484 Sand Hill Rd Quadrus Complex Bldg 4 *Web:* www.mayfield.com	Menlo Park	CA	94025	650-854-5560	854-5712
MCG Capital Corp 1001 19th St N 10th fl *NASDAQ: MCGC*	Arlington	VA	22209	703-247-7500	
McKellar & Co 311 E Rose Ln *Web:* mckellarandcompany.com	Phoenix	AZ	85012	602-277-1800	277-0429
MDT Advisors Inc 125 High St Oliver St Tower Ste 2100 *TF:* 800-685-4277 ■ *Web:* www.federatedinvestors.com	Boston	MA	02110	617-235-7100	235-7199
Menlo Ventures 2884 Sand Hill Rd Ste 100 *Web:* www.menlovc.com	Menlo Park	CA	94025	650-854-8540	854-7059
Mesirow Financial Private Equity 350 N Clark St *TF:* 800-453-0600 ■ *Web:* www.mesirowfinancial.com	Chicago	IL	60610	312-595-6000	595-4246
MidCoast Capital 259 N Radnor-Chester Rd Ste 210 *Web:* www.midcoastcapital.com	Radnor	PA	19087	610-687-8580	971-2154
Milestone Venture Partners 551 Madison Ave 7th Fl *Web:* www.milestonevp.com	New York	NY	10022	212-223-7400	223-0315
Mission Ventures 9255 Towne Ctr Dr Ste 350 *Web:* www.missionventures.com	San Diego	CA	92121	858-350-2100	
Mohr Davidow Ventures 3000 Sand Hill Rd Bldg 3 Ste 290 *Web:* www.mdv.com	Menlo Park	CA	94025	650-854-7236	854-7365
Montlake Capital 1200 Fifth Ave Ste 1800 *Web:* montlakecapital.com	Seattle	WA	98101	206-956-0898	956-0863
Morgan Stanley Venture Partners 1585 Broadway 38th Fl *TF:* 866-722-7310 ■ *Web:* www.morganstanley.com/institutional/venturepartners	New York	NY	10036	212-761-4000	
Morgenthaler 2710 Sand Hill Rd Ste 100 *Web:* www.morgenthaler.com	Menlo Park	CA	94025	650-388-7600	388-7601
Morgenthaler Ventures 600 Superior Ave Ste 2500 *Web:* www.morgenthaler.com	Cleveland	OH	44114	216-416-7500	416-7501
Mountaineer Capital LP 107 Capital St Ste 300 *Web:* www.mountaineercapital.com	Charleston	WV	25301	304-347-7519	347-0072
MPM Capital Offices 200 Clarendon St 54th Fl *TF:* 888-286-8010 ■ *Web:* www.mpmcapital.com	Boston	MA	02116	617-425-9200	425-9201
MRV Communications Inc 20415 Nordhoff St *OTC: MRVC* ■ *TF Sales:* 800-338-5316 ■ *Web:* www.mrv.com	Chatsworth	CA	91311	818-773-0900	773-0906
MVC Capital Inc 287 Bowman Ave 2nd Fl *NYSE: MVC* ■ *TF:* 800-322-2885 ■ *Web:* www.mvccapital.com	Purchase	NY	10577	914-510-9400	701-0315
Nautic Partners LLC 50 Kennedy Plz 12th Fl *Web:* www.nautic.com	Providence	RI	02903	401-278-6770	278-6387
NCA Partners Inc 1200 Westlake Ave N Ste 600 *Web:* www.nwcap.com	Seattle	WA	98109	206-689-5615	689-5614
NCIC Capital Fund 900 Kettering Tower *Web:* www.ncicfund.com	Dayton	OH	45423	937-222-4422	222-1323
Needham Capital Partners 445 Pk Ave *TF:* 800-625-7071 ■ *Web:* www.needhamcapital.com	New York	NY	10022	212-371-8300	371-2311
NeuroVentures Capital LLC Zero Ct Sq *Web:* www.neuroventures.com	Charlottesville	VA	22902	434-297-1000	
New Venture Partners LLC (NVP) 430 Mountain Ave Ste 404 *Web:* www.nvpllc.com	Murray Hill	NJ	07974	908-464-0900	464-8131
NewSpring Capital 555 E Lancaster Ave Ste 444 *Web:* www.newspringcapital.com	Radnor	PA	19087	610-567-2380	567-2388
Newtek Business Services Inc 1440 Broadway 17th Fl *NASDAQ: NEWT* ■ *TF Sales:* 866-820-8902 ■ *Web:* www.thesba.com	New York	NY	10018	212-356-9500	273-8252
Newton Technology Partners 550 Bryant St	Palo Alto	CA	94301	650-331-3992	
NGEN Partners LLC 1114 State St Ste 247 *Web:* www.ngenpartners.com	Santa Barbara	CA	93101	805-564-3156	
NJTC Venture Fund 1001 Briggs Rd Ste 280	Mount Laurel	NJ	08054	856-273-6800	787-9800
Noro-Moseley Partners 3284 Northside Pkwy NW Ste 525 *Web:* www.noromoseley.com	Atlanta	GA	30327	404-233-1966	
North Atlantic Capital 2 City Ctr 5th Fl *Web:* www.northatlanticcapital.com	Portland	ME	04101	207-772-4470	772-3257
North Bridge Venture Partners 950 Winter St Ste 4600 *Web:* www.northbridge.com	Waltham	MA	02451	781-290-0004	290-0999
North Hill Ventures 535 Boylston St 6th Fl *Web:* www.northhillventures.com	Boston	MA	02116	617-600-7050	
Northleaf Capital Partners 79 Wellington St W Sixth Fl PO Box 120 **Fax Area Code:* 416 ■ *TF:* 866-964-4141 ■ *Web:* www.northleafcapital.com	Toronto	ON	M5K1N9	866-964-4141	304-0195*
Northwood Ventures 485 Underhill Blvd Ste 205 *Web:* www.northwoodventures.com	Syosset	NY	11791	516-364-5544	364-0879

Firm	City	State	ZIP	Phone	Fax
Norwest Equity Partners 80 S Eigth St Ste 3600 *Web:* www.nep.com	Minneapolis	MN	55402	612-215-1600	215-1601
Norwest Venture Partners 525 University Ave Ste 800 *Web:* www.nvp.com	Palo Alto	CA	94301	650-321-8000	
Novak Biddle Venture Partners 7501 Wisconsin Ave E Tower Ste 1380 *Web:* www.novakbiddle.com	Bethesda	MD	20814	240-497-1910	223-0255
Noventi Ventures 8100 Jarvis Ave Ste 110 *Web:* www.noventivc.com	Newark	CA	94560	650-325-6699	
NTH Power Technologies Inc 1 Embarcadero Ctr Ste 1550 *Web:* www.nthpower.com	San Francisco	CA	94111	415-983-9983	
OCA Ventures 351 W Hubbard St Ste 600 *Web:* www.ocaventures.com	Chicago	IL	60654	312-327-8400	
Olympic Venture Partners 1010 Market St *Web:* www.ovp.com	Kirkland	WA	98033	425-889-9192	
Olympus Partners 1 Stn Pl Ste 1 *Web:* www.olympuspartners.com	Stamford	CT	06902	203-353-5900	
ONCAP 161 Bay St 48th Fl *Web:* www.oncap.com	Toronto	ON	M5J2S1	416-214-4300	216-1834
Onset Ventures 2400 Sand Hill Rd Ste 150 *Web:* www.onset.com	Menlo Park	CA	94025	650-529-0700	529-0777
Osprey Ventures LP 502 Waverley St	Palo Alto	CA	94301	650-473-9250	
Pacific Horizon Ventures 800 Fifth Ave Ste 4120 *Web:* www.pacifichorizon.com	Seattle	WA	98104	206-682-1181	682-8077
Palomar Ventures 233 Wilshire Blvd Ste 900 *Web:* www.palomarventures.com	Santa Monica	CA	90401	310-260-6050	
Pappajohn Capital Resources 666 Walnut St *Web:* www.pappajohn.com	Des Moines	IA	50309	515-244-5746	
Paul Capital Partners 575 Market St Ste 2500 *Web:* www.paulcapital.com	San Francisco	CA	94105	415-283-4300	
Peck's Management Partners Ltd 1 Rockefeller Plz Ste 1427	New York	NY	10020	212-332-1333	332-1334
Pfingsten Partners LLC 300 N LaSalle St Ste 5400 *Web:* www.pfingsten.com	Chicago	IL	60654	312-222-8707	222-8708
Pitango Venture Capital 540 Cowper St Ste 200 *Web:* www.pitango.com	Palo Alto	CA	94301	650-322-2201	
Pomona Capital 780 Third Ave 46th Fl *Web:* www.pomonacapital.com	New York	NY	10017	212-593-3639	
Primus Venture Partners 5900 Landerbrook Dr Ste 200 *Web:* www.primuscapital.com	Cleveland	OH	44124	440-684-7300	
Prince Ventures 6475 Bold Venture Tr *Web:* www.princeventures.com	Tallahassee	FL	32309	850-321-3353	
Prism Venture Management LLC 117 Kendrick St Ste 200 *Web:* www.prismventure.com	Needham	MA	02494	781-302-4000	
Private Capital Management 8889 Pelican Bay Blvd Ste 500 *TF:* 800-763-0337 ■ *Web:* www.private-cap.com	Naples	FL	34108	239-254-2500	254-2557
Prolog Ventures LLC 7701 Forsyth Blvd Ste 1095 *Web:* www.prologventures.com	Saint Louis	MO	63105	314-743-2400	
Prospect Venture Partners 435 Tasso St Ste 200 *Web:* www.prospectventures.com	Palo Alto	CA	94301	650-327-8800	324-8838
Provco Group 795 E Lancaster Ave Ste 200 *Web:* provcogroup.com	Villanova	PA	19085	610-520-2010	520-1905
Providence Equity Partners LLC 50 Kennedy Plz 18th Fl *Web:* www.provequity.com	Providence	RI	02903	401-751-1700	751-1790
Psilos Group Managers LLC 140 Broadway 51st Fl *Web:* www.psilos.com	New York	NY	10005	212-242-8844	242-8855
PureTech Ventures 501 Boylston St Ste 6102 *Web:* puretechhealth.com	Boston	MA	02116	617-482-2333	482-3337
Quaker BioVentures 2929 Arch St Cira Ctr *Web:* www.quakerbio.com	Philadelphia	PA	19104	215-988-6800	988-6801
Radius Ventures LLC 250 Park Ave Ste 1102 *Web:* www.radiusventures.com	New York	NY	10017	212-897-7778	397-2656
Rembrandt Venture Partners 600 Montgomery St 44th Fl **Fax Area Code:* 415 ■ *Web:* www.rembrandtvc.com	San Francisco	CA	94111	650-326-7070	528-2901*
Research Corp Technologies 101 N Wilmot Rd Ste 600 *Web:* www.rctech.com	Tucson	AZ	85711	520-748-4400	748-0025
Reynolds De Witt Securities 300 Main St	Cincinnati	OH	45202	513-241-6443	
Rho Capital Partners Inc 152 W 57th St 23rd Fl *Web:* www.rhoventures.com	New York	NY	10019	212-751-6677	751-3613
Richland Ventures 1201 16th Ave S	Nashville	TN	37212	615-383-8030	
Riordan Lewis & Haden 10900 Wilshire Blvd Ste 850 *Web:* www.rlhinvestors.com	Los Angeles	CA	90024	310-405-7200	405-7222
Rockport Capital Partners 160 Federal St 18th Fl *Web:* www.rockportcap.com	Boston	MA	02110	617-912-1420	912-1449
Rosewood Capital 1 Maritime Plz Ste 1575 *Web:* www.rosewoodcap.com	San Francisco	CA	94111	415-362-5526	362-1192
RRE Ventures LLC 130 E 59th St 17th Fl *Web:* www.rre.com	New York	NY	10022	212-418-5100	
Rustic Canyon Partners 100 Wilshire Blvd Ste 200 *Web:* rusticcanyon.com	Santa Monica	CA	90401	310-998-8000	
Safeguard Scientifics Inc 435 Devon Pk Dr Ste 800 *NYSE: SFE* ■ *Web:* www.safeguard.com	Wayne	PA	19087	610-293-0600	293-0601
Sail Venture Partners LP 3161 Michelson Dr Ste 750 *Web:* www.sailcapital.com	Irvine	CA	92612	949-398-5100	398-5101
Saints Ventures LLC 2020 Union St *Web:* www.saintscapital.com	San Francisco	CA	94123	415-773-2080	835-5970
Sanderling 400 S El Camino Real Ste 1200 *Web:* www.sanderling.com	San Mateo	CA	94402	650-401-2000	
Sapient Capital Management LLC 4020 Lk Creek Dr PO Box 1590 *Web:* www.sapientcapital.com	Wilson	WY	83014	307-733-3806	
Saugatuck Capital Co 187 Danbury Rd *Web:* www.saugatuckcapital.com	Wilton	CT	06897	203-348-6669	324-6995
Scale Venture Partners 950 Tower Ln Ste 700 *Web:* www.scalevp.com	Foster City	CA	94404	650-378-6000	378-6040
Selby Venture Partners PO Box Q Ste 200 *Web:* selbyventures.com	Menlo Park	CA	94025	650-300-5882	
Sequel Venture Partners 4430 Arapahoe Ave Ste 220 *Web:* www.sequelvc.com	Boulder	CO	80303	303-546-0400	546-9728
Sequoia Capital 2800 Sand Hill Rd Ste 101 *Web:* www.sequoiacap.com	Menlo Park	CA	94025	650-854-3927	
Sevin Rosen Funds 13455 Noel Rd Ste 1670 *Web:* www.srfunds.com	Dallas	TX	75240	972-702-1100	702-1103
Shasta Ventures 2440 Sand Hill Rd Ste 300 *Web:* www.shastaventures.com	Menlo Park	CA	94025	650-543-1700	
Shepherd Ventures 11722 Sorrento Valley Rd Ste G-2 *Web:* www.shepherdventures.com	San Diego	CA	92121	858-509-4744	509-3662
Sierra Ventures 1400 Fashion Island Blvd Ste 1010 *Web:* www.sierraventures.com	San Mateo	CA	94404	650-854-1000	
Sigma Partners 156 Diablo Rd Ste 320 *Web:* www.sigmapartners.com	Danville	CA	94526	650-853-1700	853-1717
Signal Peak 2795 E Cottonwood Pkwy Ste 520 *Web:* www.spv.com	Salt Lake City	UT	84121	801-942-8999	942-1636
Signature Capital LLC 100 Commercial St *Web:* www.signaturecapital.com	Portland	ME	04101	207-773-8123	
Siguler Guff & Co LLC 825 Third Ave 10th Fl *Web:* www.sigulerguff.com	New York	NY	10022	212-332-5100	332-5120
Sofinnova Ventures Inc 3000 Sand Hill Rd Bldg 4 Ste 250 *Web:* www.sofinnova.com	Menlo Park	CA	94025	650-681-8420	322-2037
Solstice Capital 81 Washington St Ste 303 *Web:* www.solcap.com	Salem	MA	01970	617-523-7733	
South Atlantic Capital Inc 614 W Bay St *Web:* www.southatlantic.com	Tampa	FL	33606	813-253-2500	253-2360
Spectrum Equity Investors LP 1 International Pl 35th Fl *Web:* www.spectrumequity.com	Boston	MA	02110	617-464-4600	464-4601
Split Rock Partners 1600 El Camino Real Ste 290 *Web:* www.splitrock.com	Menlo Park	CA	94025	952-995-7474	
Sprout Group 11 Madison Ave 13th Fl *Web:* www.sproutgroup.com	New York	NY	10010	212-538-3600	538-8245
Steamboat Ventures 801 N Brand Blvd Ste 665 *Web:* steamboatvc.com	Glendale	CA	91505	818-566-7400	566-7490
Sterling Venture Partners 650 S Exeter St # 10 *Web:* www.sterlingpartners.com	Baltimore	MD	21202	443-703-1700	703-1750
Storm Ventures 3000 Sand Hill Rd Bldg 4 Ste 301 *Web:* www.stormventures.com	Menlo Park	CA	94025	650-926-8800	
Strategic Investments & Holdings Inc (SIHI) 4445 N A1A Ste 247 *Web:* www.sihi.net	Vero Beach	FL	32963	716-857-6000	857-6490
Summit Partners 222 Berkeley St 18th Fl *TF:* 800-503-4611 ■ *Web:* www.summitpartners.com	Boston	MA	02116	617-824-1000	824-1100
Sutter Hill Ventures 755 Page Mill Rd Ste A-200 *Web:* www.shv.com	Palo Alto	CA	94304	650-493-5600	
SV Life Sciences (SVLS) 201 Washington St Ste 3900 *Web:* www.svlsa.com	Boston	MA	02108	617-367-8100	367-1590
TA Assoc Inc 200 Clarendon St 56th Fl *Web:* www.ta.com	Boston	MA	02116	617-574-6700	
TDF Ventures (TDF) 2 Wisconsin Cir Ste 920 **Fax Area Code:* 301 ■ *Web:* www.tdfventures.com	Chevy Chase	MD	20815	240-483-4286	907-8850*
Technology Crossover Ventures 528 Ramona St *Web:* www.tcv.com	Palo Alto	CA	94301	650-614-8200	614-8222
Technology Funding Inc 460 St Michael's Dr Ste 1000 *TF:* 800-821-5323 ■ *Web:* www.techfunding.com	Santa Fe	NM	87505	800-821-5323	
Technology Partners 550 University Ave *TF:* 800-747-3924 ■ *Web:* www.technologypartners.com	Palo Alto	CA	94301	650-289-9000	289-9001
TeleSoft Partners 950 Tower Ln Ste 1600 *Web:* www.telesoftvc.com	Foster City	CA	94404	650-358-2500	358-2501
TEOCO Corp 12150 Monument Dr Ste 400 *TF:* 888-868-3626 ■ *Web:* www.teoco.com	Fairfax	VA	22033	703-322-9200	322-9133
Texas Growth Fund 900 S Capital of Texas Hwy Ste 430 *Web:* www.tgfmanagement.com	Austin	TX	78746	512-322-3100	322-3101
TGap Ventures LLC 7171 Stadium Dr *Web:* www.tgapventures.com	Kalamazoo	MI	49009	269-217-1999	381-7620
Thoma Cressey Bravo Inc 600 Montgomery St 32nd Fl *Web:* www.thomabravo.com	San Francisco	CA	94111	415-263-3660	392-6480

				Phone	Fax
Thomas McNerney & Partners 1 Landmark Sq Ste 1920	Stamford	CT	06901	203-978-2000	978-2005
Web: www.tm-partners.com					
Thomas Weisel Partners Group LLC 1 Montgomery St	San Francisco	CA	94104	415-364-2500	364-2695
TF: 888-267-3700 ■ *Web:* www.tweisel.com					
TL Ventures 435 Devon Pk Dr	Wayne	PA	19087	610-971-1515	975-9330
Web: tl.ventures					
Topspin Partners LP 3 Expy Plaza	Roslyn Heights	NY	11577	516-625-9400	625-9499
Web: www.topspinpartners.com					
Tortoise Energy Capital Corp 11550 Ash St Ste 300	Leawood	KS	66211	913-981-1020	981-1021
NYSE: TYY ■ *TF:* 866-362-9331 ■ *Web:* www.tortoiseadvisors.com					
Trelys Funds PO Box 5066	Cary	NC	27512	919-459-4650	459-4670
Web: www.trelys.com					
Triathlon Medical Ventures (TMVP) 300 E Business Way Ste 200	Cincinnati	OH	45241	513-723-2600	247-6122
Web: www.tmvp.com					
Trident Capital 505 Hamilton Ave Ste 200	Palo Alto	CA	94301	650-289-4400	289-4444
Web: www.tridentcap.com					
Trillium Group LLC 1221 Pittsford Victor Rd	Pittsford	NY	14534	585-383-5680	
Web: www.trillium-group.com					
Trinity Ventures 2480 Sand Hill Rd Ste 200	Menlo Park	CA	94025	650-854-9500	
Web: trinityventures.com					
Triton Ventures 6300 Bridge Pt Pkwy Bldg 1 Ste 500	Austin	TX	78730	512-795-5820	
Web: www.tritonventures.com					
TVM Capital 101 Arch St Ste 1950	Boston	MA	02110	617-345-9320	
Web: www.tvm-capital.com					
Union Square Ventures 915 Broadway 19th Fl	New York	NY	10010	212-994-7880	994-7399
Web: www.usv.com					
UPS Strategic Enterprise Fund 55 Glenlake Pkwy NE Bldg 1 4th Fl	Atlanta	GA	30328	800-742-5877	
TF: 800-742-5877 ■ *Web:* www.ups.com/sef					
US Venture Partners (USVP) 1460 El Camino Real	Menlo Park	CA	94025	650-854-9080	854-3018
Web: www.usvp.com					
Valhalla Partners 8000 Towers Crescent Dr Ste 1050	Vienna	VA	22182	703-448-1400	448-1441
Web: www.valhallapartners.com					
VantagePoint Venture Partners 1001 Bayhill Dr Ste 300	San Bruno	CA	94066	650-866-3100	869-6078
Web: www.vpcp.com					
Vector Capital 1 Matket St Steuart Tower 23rd Fl	San Francisco	CA	94105	415-293-5000	293-5100
Web: www.vectorcapital.com					
Venrock Assoc 3340 Hillview Ave	Palo Alto	CA	94304	650-561-9580	561-9180
Web: www.venrock.com					
Venture Capital Fund of America 509 Madison Ave	New York	NY	10022	212-838-5577	838-7614
Web: www.vcfa.com					
Venture Investors LLC 505 S Rosa Rd Ste 201	Madison	WI	53719	608-441-2700	441-2727
Web: www.ventureinvestors.com					
Vertical Group 25 DeForest Ave	Summit	NJ	07901	908-277-3737	273-9434
Web: www.vertical-group.com					
Vesbridge Partners 601 Carlson Pkwy Ste 1160	Minnetonka	MN	55305	952-995-7499	995-7493
Web: www.vesbridge.com					
VIMAC Ventures LLC 177 Milk St	Boston	MA	02109	617-350-9800	350-9899
Web: www.vimac.com					
Vision Capital 700 Airport Blvd Ste 370	Burlingame	CA	94010	650-373-2720	373-2727
Web: www.visioncap.com					
VSP Capital 201 Post St Ste 1100	San Francisco	CA	94108	415-558-8600	
Walden Venture Capital 750 Battery St Ste 700	San Francisco	CA	94111	415-391-7225	
Web: www.waldenvc.com					
Warburg Pincus Ventures Co Inc 450 Lexington Ave	New York	NY	10017	212-878-0600	878-9351
Web: www.warburgpincus.com					
Washington Research Foundation 2815 Eastlake Ave E Ste 300	Seattle	WA	98102	206-336-5600	
Web: www.wrfcapital.com					
WayPoint Ventures					
RPM Ventures 320 N Main St Ste 400	Ann Arbor	MI	48104	734-332-1700	
Web: www.rpmvc.com					
Western Technology Investment (WTI) 104 La Mesa Dr Ste 102	Portola Valley	CA	94028	650-234-4300	234-4343
Web: www.westerntech.com					
Wicks Group of Cos LLC 405 Pk Ave Ste 702	New York	NY	10022	212-838-2100	223-2109
Web: www.wicksgroup.com					
Wind Point Partners 676 N Michigan Ave Ste 3700	Chicago	IL	60611	312-255-4800	255-4820
Web: www.wppartners.com					
Windjammer Capital Investors 610 Newport Ctr Dr Ste 1100	Newport Beach	CA	92660	949-721-9944	720-4222
Web: www.windjammercapital.com					
Windspeed Ventures 52 Waltham St	Lexington	MA	02421	781-860-8888	860-0493
Web: www.wsventures.com					
Woodside Fund 303 Twin Dolphin Dr Ste 600	Redwood Shores	CA	94065	650-610-8050	
Web: www.woodsidefund.com					
Zanett Inc 635 Madison Ave 15th Fl	New York	NY	10022	212-583-0300	583-0221
OTC: ZANE					
Zon Capital Partners 5 Vaughn Dr Ste 302	Princeton	NJ	08540	609-452-1653	452-1693
ZS Fund LP 1133 Ave of the Americas	New York	NY	10036	212-398-6200	398-1808
Web: www.zsfundlp.com					

793 VETERANS NURSING HOMES - STATE

See Also Veterans Hospitals p. 2527

Facility	City	State	Zip	Phone	Fax
Americor Management Services LLC N94W17900 Appleton Ave	Menomonee Falls	WI	53051	262-255-3606	
Web: harmonyresidence.net					
Andover Village Retirement Community Inc 486 S Main St	Andover	OH	44003	440-293-5416	
Web: www.andovervillage.com					
Angels of the Valley Hospice Care LLC 2511 Honolulu Ave	Montrose	CA	91020	818-542-3070	
Web: www.angelsofthevalley.com					
Apple Blossom Hill Inc 10150 Clyde Rd	Fenton	MI	48430	810-632-5590	
Web: appleblossomhill.com					
Arbor Rose Senior Care LLC 6063 E Arbor Ave	Mesa	AZ	85206	480-654-8200	
Web: www.arborroseseniorcare.com					
Arc Human Services Inc 201 S Johnson Rd	Houston	PA	15342	724-745-3010	
Web: www.aadvantageinc.org					
Arizona State Veterans Home 4141 N Third St	Phoenix	AZ	85012	602-248-1550	222-6687
Web: dvs.az.gov					
Arkansas State Veterans Home 4701 W 20th St	Little Rock	AR	72204	501-296-1885	
Baldomero Lopez State Veterans' Nursing Home 6919 Pkwy Blvd	Land O Lakes	FL	34639	813-558-5000	
Web: floridavets.org					
Barboursville Veterans Home 512 Water St	Barboursville	WV	25504	304-736-1027	736-1093
Web: veterans.wv.gov					
Charlotte Hall Veterans Home 29449 Charlotte Hall Rd	Charlotte Hall	MD	20622	301-884-8171	
Web: charhall.org					
Chelsea Soldiers Home 91 Crest Ave	Chelsea	MA	02150	617-884-5660	884-1162
Web: mass.gov					
Colorado State Veterans Nursing Home-Rifle 851 E Fifth St	Rifle	CO	81650	970-625-0842	625-3706
Web: colorado.gov					
DJ Jacobetti Home for Veterans 425 Fisher St	Marquette	MI	49855	906-226-3576	226-2380
TF: 800-433-6760 ■ *Web:* michigan.gov					
Eastern Nebraska Veterans Home 12505 S 40th St	Bellevue	NE	68123	402-595-2180	595-2234
Web: dhhs.ne.gov					
Emory L Bennett Memorial Veterans' Nursing Home 1920 Mason Ave	Daytona Beach	FL	32117	386-274-3460	274-3487
Floyd E Tut Fann State Veterans Home 2701 Meridian St	Huntsville	AL	35811	256-851-2807	851-2967
TF: 855-212-8028 ■ *Web:* www.va.state.al.us					
Georgia War Veterans Nursing Home 1101 15th St	Augusta	GA	30901	706-721-2824	721-3892
Grand Island Veterans' Home 2300 W Capital Ave	Grand Island	NE	68803	308-385-6252	385-6257*
**Fax:* Acctg ■ *TF:* 800-358-8802 ■ *Web:* dhhs.ne.gov					
Hastings Veterans Home 1200 E 18th St	Hastings	MN	55033	651-438-8500	
TF: 877-838-3803 ■ *Web:* mn.gov					
Hollidaysburg Veterans Home PO Box 319	Hollidaysburg	PA	16648	814-696-5201	
Web: www.portal.state.pa.us					
Holyoke Soldiers Home 110 Cherry St	Holyoke	MA	01040	413-532-9475	538-7968
Web: mass.gov					
Idaho State Veterans Home-Boise 320 Collins Rd	Boise	ID	83702	208-334-5000	334-4753
Web: veterans.idaho.gov					
Idaho State Veterans Home-Lewiston 821 21st Ave	Lewiston	ID	83501	208-799-3422	799-3414
TF: 877-222-8387 ■ *Web:* veterans.idaho.gov					
Idaho State Veterans Home-Pocatello 1957 Alvin Ricken Dr	Pocatello	ID	83201	208-236-6340	236-6343
TF: 877-222-8387 ■ *Web:* veterans.idaho.gov					
Illinois Veterans Home-Anna 792 N Main St	Anna	IL	62906	618-833-6302	833-3603
TF: 888-261-3336 ■ *Web:* illinois.gov					
Illinois Veterans Home-La Salle 1015 O'Connor Ave	La Salle	IL	61301	815-223-0303	
Web: www.vfwil.org/lasalle.asp					
Illinois Veterans Home-Manteno 1 Veterans Dr	Manteno	IL	60950	815-468-6581	
Web: vfwil.org					
Illinois Veterans Home-Quincy 1707 N 12th St	Quincy	IL	62301	217-222-8641	
Web: quincyivh.org					
Indiana Veterans Home 3851 N River Rd	West Lafayette	IN	47906	765-463-1502	
Web: in.gov					
Iowa Veterans Home 1301 Summit St Bldg 3465	Marshalltown	IA	50131	515-252-4698	727-3713
TF: 800-838-4692 ■ *Web:* va.iowa.gov					
Long Island State Veterans Home 100 Patriots Rd	Stony Brook	NY	11790	631-444-8500	
Louisiana War Veterans' Home 4739 Hwy 10	Jackson	LA	70748	225-634-5265	634-4057
Web: wwwprd.doa.louisiana.gov					
Luverne Veterans Home 1300 N Kniss Ave	Luverne	MN	56156	507-283-1100	
Web: mn.gov					
Lytton Gardens Inc 437 Webster St Ste	Palo Alto	CA	94301	650-617-7350	
Web: www.lyttongardens.org					
Maine Veterans Home-Augusta 310 Cony Rd	Augusta	ME	04330	888-684-4664	
TF: 888-684-4664 ■ *Web:* www.maineveteranshomes.org					
Maine Veterans Home-Bangor 44 Hogan Rd	Bangor	ME	04401	207-942-2333	
TF: 888-684-4665 ■ *Web:* www.maineveteranshomes.org					
Maine Veterans Home-Caribou 163 Van Buren Rd Ste 2	Caribou	ME	04736	207-498-6074	
TF: 888-684-4667 ■ *Web:* www.maineveteranshomes.org					
Maine Veterans Home-Scarborough 290 US Rt 1	Scarborough	ME	04074	207-883-7184	
TF: 888-684-4666 ■ *Web:* www.maineveteranshomes.org					
Maine Veterans Home-South Paris 477 High St	South Paris	ME	04281	207-743-6300	
TF: 888-684-4668 ■ *Web:* www.maineveteranshomes.org					

Phone Fax

ManagCare Inc 3553 W Peterson Ave Fl 3 . . . . Chicago IL 60659 773-463-1313
Web: www.managcare.com

Maple Lane Nursing & Retirement Home
60 Maple Ln . . . . Barton VT 05822 802-754-8575
Web: northernkarefacilitiesnetwork.com

Marian Manor Corp 2695 Winchester Dr Ste . . . . Pittsburgh PA 15220 412-563-6866
Web: www.marianmanor.com

Marion Regional Healthcare Systems
2829 E Hwy 76 . . . . Mullins SC 29574 843-431-2065
Web: www.marioncountyhfoundation.org

Masonic Villages of The Grand Lodge Of Pennsylvania
One Masonic Dr . . . . Elizabethtown PA 17022 717-367-1121
Web: www.masonicvillagespa.org

Mclean Fund 75 great pond rd . . . . Simsbury CT 60701 860-658-3700
Web: www.mcleancare.org

Medicalodges Inc 201 W 8th St . . . . Coffeyville KS 67337 620-251-6700
Web: www.medicalodges.com

Medway Country Manor 115 Holliston St . . . . Medway MA 02053 508-533-6634
Web: www.medwaymanor.com

Mega Care Inc 1020 Galloping Hill Rd . . . . Union NJ 07083 908-851-8355
Web: www.megacare.com

Mercy St Theresa Center Inc
7010 Rowan Hill Dr . . . . Cincinnati OH 45227 513-271-7010
Web: www.catholiccincinnati.org

Military Affairs 3000 Monroe Ave NW . . . . Grand Rapids MI 49505 616-364-5300 364-5397*

Miller's Health Systems Inc
1690 S County Farm Rd . . . . Warsaw IN 46581 574-267-7211
Web: www.millershealthsystems.com

Minnesota Veterans Home-Fergus Falls
1821 N Pk St . . . . Fergus Falls MN 56537 218-736-0400
Web: mn.gov

Minnesota Veterans Home-Minneapolis
5101 Minnehaha Ave S . . . . Minneapolis MN 55407 612-721-0600
TF: 877-838-6757 ■ *Web:* mn.gov

Minnesota Veterans Home-Silver Bay
45 Banks Blvd . . . . Silver Bay MN 55614 218-226-6300
TF: 877-729-8387 ■ *Web:* mn.gov

Mississippi State Veterans Home
120 Veterans Dr . . . . Oxford MS 38655 662-236-7641
Web: caremississippi.org

Mississippi State Veterans' Home Collins
3261 Hwy 49 S . . . . Collins MS 39428 601-765-0403
TF: 877-203-5632 ■ *Web:* www.vab.ms.gov

Mississippi State Veterans' Home Kosciusko
310 Autumn Ridge Dr . . . . Kosciusko MS 39090 662-289-7044 576-4868*
**Fax Area Code:* 601 ■ *TF:* 877-203-5632

Missouri Veterans Home-Cape Girardeau
2400 Veterans Memorial Dr . . . . Cape Girardeau MO 63701 573-290-5870 290-5909
TF: 800-392-0210 ■ *Web:* www.mo.gov

Missouri Veterans Home-Mount Vernon
1600 S Hickory . . . . Mount Vernon MO 65712 417-466-7103 466-4040
Web: mvc.dps.mo.gov

Missouri Veterans Home-Saint James
620 N Jefferson St . . . . Saint James MO 65559 573-265-3271 265-5771

Missouri Veterans Home-Saint Louis
10600 Lewis & Clark Blvd . . . . Saint Louis MO 63136 314-340-6389 340-6379
Web: mvc.dps.mo.gov

Montana Veterans Home 400 Veterans Dr . . . . Columbia Falls MT 59912 406-892-3256 892-0256
TF: 888-279-7532 ■ *Web:* dphhs.mt.gov

Morning Breeze Inc 950 N Lkview Dr . . . . Greensburg IN 47240 812-662-7778
Web: exceptionallivingcenters.com

Morrison Hospital Association 6 Ter St . . . . Whitefield NH 03598 603-837-2541
Web: www.morrisonnh.org

New Beacon Hospice Inc
201 Office Park Dr Ste 100 . . . . Birmingham AL 35223 205-939-8799
Web: www.newbeacon.org

New Hampshire Veterans Home 139 Winter St . . . . Tilton NH 03276 603-527-4400 527-4402
TF: 800-735-2964 ■ *Web:* www.nh.gov/veterans

New Mexico State Veterans Ctr
992 S Broadway St . . . . Truth or Consequences NM 87901 575-894-4200 894-4270
TF: 800-964-3976 ■ *Web:* nmhealth.org/about/ofm/ltcf/nmsvh

New Perspective Senior Living 4920 Lincoln Dr . . . . Edina MN 55436 952-746-3630
Web: www.npseniorliving.com

New Vista Nursing & Rehabilitation Center
8647 Fenwick St . . . . Sunland CA 91040 818-352-1421
Web: newvistanursing.com

New Vista Post Acute Care Center
1516 Sawtelle Blvd . . . . Los Angeles CA 90025 310-477-5501
Web: newvista.com

New York State Veterans Home at Batavia
220 Richmond Ave . . . . Batavia NY 14020 585-345-2000
Web: www.nysvets.org

New York State Veterans Home at Oxford
4207 New York 220 . . . . Oxford NY 13830 607-843-3100 843-3194

New York State Veterans Home at Saint Albans
178-50 Linden Blvd . . . . Jamaica NY 11434 718-990-0353
Web: veterans.ny.gov

NJ State Veteran's Memorial Home
132 Evergreen Rd PO Box 3013 . . . . Edison NJ 08837 732-452-4100
Web: nj.gov

Norfolk Veterans Home 600 E Benjamin Ave . . . . Norfolk NE 68701 402-370-3330 370-3190
Web: nebraska.gov

North Dakota Veterans Home 1600 Veterans Dr . . . . Lisbon ND 58054 701-683-6500 683-6550
Web: www.nd.gov

Nursing Center
3701 N Martin Luther King Jr Blvd . . . . Tulsa OK 74106 918-425-3583
Web: saintsimeons.org

Oak Brook HealthCare & Rehabilitation Centre
2013 Midwest Rd . . . . Oak Brook IL 60523 630-495-0220
Web: oakbrookcare.com

Ohio Veterans Home 3416 Columbus Ave . . . . Sandusky OH 44870 419-625-2454
TF Admissions: 800-572-7934 ■ *Web:* dvs.ohio.gov

Oklahoma Veterans Ctr Ardmore
1015 S Commerce . . . . Ardmore OK 73401 580-223-2266 221-5606
TF: 800-941-2160 ■ *Web:* www.ok.gov

Phone Fax

Oklahoma Veterans Ctr Claremore PO Box 988 . . . . Claremore OK 74018 918-342-5432 342-0835
Web: www.ok.gov

Oklahoma Veterans Ctr Clinton PO Box 1209 . . . . Clinton OK 73601 580-331-2200 323-4834
Web: www.ok.gov

Oklahoma Veterans Ctr Norman
1776 E Robinson St . . . . Norman OK 73071 405-360-5600
TF: 800-782-5218 ■ *Web:* www.ok.gov

Oklahoma Veterans Ctr Sulphur 200 E Fairlane . . . . Sulphur OK 73086 580-622-2144
Web: www.ok.gov

Oklahoma Veterans Ctr Talihina
10014 SE 1138th Ave PO Box 1168 . . . . Talihina OK 74571 918-567-2251 567-2950
TF: 800-941-2160 ■ *Web:* www.ok.gov

On-Call Nursing Agency and Associates of New Orleans Inc
7900 Earhart Blvd . . . . New Orleans LA 70125 504-866-0442
Web: www.oncallnursing.com

Oregon Veterans' Home 700 Veterans Dr . . . . The Dalles OR 97058 541-296-7190 296-7862
TF: 800-846-8460 ■ *Web:* oregon.gov

Palmyra Nursing Home Inc 341 N Railroad St . . . . Palmyra PA 17078 717-838-3011
Web: www.pennmed.com

Park Place Assisted Living 2305 Ives Ct . . . . Reno NV 89503 775-746-1188
Web: www.parkplaceassistedliving.com

Pearl City Nursing Home 919 Lehua Ave . . . . Pearl City HI 96782 808-453-1919
Web: pcnh.hawaiinursinghomes.com

Pleasant Care Corp 2258 Foothill Blvd . . . . La Canada CA 91011 818-248-9808
Web: www.pleasantcare.com

QuadMed LLC W227 N6103 Sussex Rd . . . . Sussex WI 53089 414-566-8100
Web: www.quad-med.com

Queens Boulevard Extended Care Facility Corp
61-11 Queens Blvd . . . . Woodside NY 11377 718-205-0287
Web: www.qbecf.com

Rhode Island Veterans' Home 480 Metacom Ave . . . . Bristol RI 02809 401-253-8000 254-1340

Richard M Campbell Veterans Home
4605 Belton Hwy . . . . Anderson SC 29621 864-261-6734 261-0453

Rocky Hill Veterans Home & Healthcare Ctr
287 W St . . . . Rocky Hill CT 06067 860-721-5891 721-5904
Web: www.ct.gov/ctva/cwp/view.asp?a=2005&q=482380

Seacrest Village Inc
1001 Ctr St . . . . Little Egg Harbor Twp NJ 08087 609-296-9292
Web: seacrestvillagenj.com

Tennessee State Veterans Home-Murfreesboro
345 Compton Rd . . . . Murfreesboro TN 37130 615-895-8850 895-5091
Web: tsvh.org

Thomson-Hood Veterans Ctr 100 Veterans Dr . . . . Wilmore KY 40390 859-858-2814 858-4039
TF: 800-928-4838 ■ *Web:* www.thvc.ky.gov

Vermont Veterans Home 325 N St . . . . Bennington VT 05201 802-442-6353 447-6466
Web: www.vvh.vermont.gov

Veterans Care Ctr 4550 Shenandoah Ave . . . . Roanoke VA 24017 540-982-2860 982-8667
Web: www.dvs.virginia.gov

Veterans Home of California-Barstow
100 E Veterans Pkwy . . . . Barstow CA 92311 760-252-6200
TF: 800-746-0606

Veterans Home of California-Chula Vista
700 E Naples Ct . . . . Chula Vista CA 91911 800-952-5626 205-1903*
**Fax Area Code:* 619 ■ *TF:* 800-952-5626 ■ *Web:* www.calvet.ca.gov

Veterans Home of California-Yountville
1227 O St . . . . Sacramento CA 95814 916-653-2573 944-4542*
**Fax Area Code:* 707 ■ *TF:* 800-952-5626

Washington Veterans Home
1141 Beach Dr PO Box 698 . . . . Retsil WA 98378 360-895-4700
Web: www.dva.wa.gov

Wisconsin Veterans Home N2665 County Rd QQ . . . . King WI 54946 715-258-5586 256-3207
TF: 877-944-6667 ■ *Web:* www.dva.state.wi.us

794 VETERINARY HOSPITALS

Phone Fax

Abita Trace Animal Clinic
69142 Hwy 59 Ste E . . . . Mandeville LA 70471 985-892-5656
Web: www.medi-vet.com

Alameda Animal Hospital 431 12th Ave Ne . . . . Norman OK 73071 405-360-0045
Web: www.myvetonline.com

All Creatures Animal Hospital
1894 State Rt 125 . . . . Amelia OH 45102 513-797-7387
Web: www.all-creatures.com

American Animal Care Center Salwan Shanima Dvm
37177 Fremont Blvd . . . . Fremont CA 94536 510-791-0464
Web: www.americananimalcare.com

Amherst Veterinary Hospital 313 Us Hwy 10 . . . . Amherst WI 54406 434-929-1010
Web: wi-net.com

Anchor Animal Hospital Inc
750 State Rd . . . . North Dartmouth MA 02747 508-996-3731
Web: anchoranimalhospital.com

Anchor Bay Veterinary Center PC
36755 Green St . . . . New Baltimore MI 48047 586-725-7700
Web: www.anchorbayvetcenter.com

Animal Ark Veterinary Clinic Pc
3235 N Kedzie Ave . . . . Chicago IL 60618 773-442-6500
Web: www.animalark.us

Animal Eye Specialty Clinic
3421 Forest Hill Blvd W . . . . Palm Beach FL 33406 772-220-8485

Animal Hospital Inc 5001 N 12th Ave . . . . Pensacola FL 32504 850-479-2900
Web: www.petcarehospital.com

Animal Hospital of Pittsford PC
2816 Monroe Ave Ste 2 . . . . Rochester NY 14618 585-271-7700
Web: www.pittsfordvet.com

Animal Medical Center of Somerset County Inc
1911 N Center Ave . . . . Somerset PA 15501 814-443-6979
Web: www.amcdocs.com

Animal Medical Center, The
510 E 62nd St Fl 2 . . . . New York NY 10065 212-838-8100
Web: www.amcny.org

	City	State	Zip	Phone	Fax
Animal Welfare Association 509 Centennial Blvd *Web:* www.awanj.org	Voorhees	NJ	08043	856-424-2288	
ARC Medical Devices Inc 2386 E Mall Ste 102 *Web:* arcmedicaldevices.com	Vancouver	BC	V6T1Z3	604-222-9577	
Aston Veterinarian Hospital 5200 Pennell Rd *Web:* www.astonvet.com	Media	PA	19063	610-494-5800	
Banfield the Pet Hospital 18101 SE 6th Way **Fax Area Code:* 503 ■ *TF:* 866-894-7927 ■ *Web:* www.banfield.com	Vancouver	WA	98683	866-894-7927	922-5000*
Barton Heights Veterinary Hospital 117 Terrace Dr *Web:* www.bartonheights.com	Stroudsburg	PA	18360	570-424-6773	
Bay Glen Animal Hospital P C 1616 Clear Lk City Blvd *Web:* www.bayglenvet.com	Houston	TX	77062	281-480-8800	
Best Friends Pet Care Inc 520 Main Ave *Web:* www.bestfriendspetcare.com	Norwalk	CT	06851	203-846-3360	
Best Friends Veterinary Center 2082 Cheyenne Ct *Web:* www.bestfriendsvet.com	Grafton	WI	53024	262-375-0130	
Bio Agri Mix LP 11 Ellens St *Web:* www.bioagrimix.com	Mitchell	ON	N0K1N0	519-348-9865	
BluePearl Veterinary Partners LLC 3000 Busch Lk Blvd *Web:* bluepearlvet.com	Tampa	FL	33614	813-933-8944	
Brook Farm Veterinary Center 2371 Route 22 *Web:* www.brookfarmveterinarycenter.com	Patterson	NY	12563	845-878-4833	
Burnham Park Animal Hospital 1025 S State St *Web:* www.chicagovet.net	Chicago	IL	60605	312-663-9200	
Canine Country Club Kennel & Pet Resort, The 33306 Tract 43 Rd *Web:* www.caninecountryclub.com	Los Fresnos	TX	78566	505-898-0725	
Caring Hands Animal Hospital of Arlington LLC 5659 Stone Rd *Web:* caringhandsvet.com	Centreville	VA	20120	703-830-5700	
Carolina Veterinary Specialists 2225 Township Rd *Web:* www.carolinavet.com	Charlotte	NC	28273	704-588-7015	
Carthage Veterinary Service Ltd 34 W Main St *Web:* www.hogvet.com	Carthage	IL	62321	217-357-2811	
Cat Doctor, The 535 N 22nd St *Web:* www.thecatdr.com	Philadelphia	PA	19130	215-561-7668	
Claremont Animal Hospital Inc 446 Charlestown Rd *Web:* www.claremontanimalhospital.com	Claremont	NH	03743	603-543-0117	
Clemson Univ Service 605 W Main St Ste 109	Lexington	SC	29072	803-785-8515	
Colorado River Animal Medical Center Inc 2079 Hwy 95 *Web:* www.cramcvet.com	Bullhead City	AZ	86442	928-763-7387	
Cresskill Animal Hospital 39 Spring St *Web:* www.cresskillanimalhosp.com	Cresskill	NJ	07626	201-568-7700	
Crysler Animal Hospital 12440 E 40 Hwy *Web:* www.crysleranimalhospital.com	Independence	MO	64055	816-358-2857	
Dove Lewis Emergency Animal Hospital Inc 1945 Nw Pettygrove St *Web:* www.dovelewis.org	Portland	OR	97209	503-228-7281	
Emergency Animal Clinic Properties Ltd 2260 W Glendale Ave *Web:* www.eac-az.com	Phoenix	AZ	85021	602-995-3757	
Family Friends Veterinary Hospital & Kennel 864 Massachusetts Ave *Web:* www.familyfriendsvetandkennel.com	Boxborough	MA	01719	978-263-3412	
Family Pet Animal Hospital 1401 W Webster Ave *Web:* familypetanimalhospital.com	Chicago	IL	60614	773-935-2311	
Five Mile Pet Clinic Ps 6825 N Country Homes Blvd *Web:* www.healthypets.com	Spokane	WA	99208	509-326-3465	
Forest Valley Veterinary Clinic 2555 Mosby Creek Rd *Web:* fvvet.com	Cottage Grove	OR	97424	541-942-9132	
Friedman Deborah s Dvm 1612 Washington Blvd *Web:* www.animaleyecare.com	Fremont	CA	94539	510-623-0444	
Friendship Hospital for Animals 4105 Brandywine St Nw *Web:* www.friendshiphospital.com	Washington	DC	20016	202-363-7300	
Garden District Animal Hospital, The 1302 Perkins Rd *Web:* www.gardendistrictanimalhospital.com	Baton Rouge	LA	70806	225-381-9661	
Gold Coast Animal Hospital 225 W Division St *Web:* www.goldcoastah.com	Chicago	IL	60610	312-337-7387	
Greenbriar Animal Hospital LLC 4307 N Green River Rd *Web:* www.greenbrieranimalhospital.com	Evansville	IN	47715	812-479-0867	
Gulf Coast Veterinary Avian 1111 W Loop S *Web:* www.gcvs.com	Houston	TX	77027	713-693-1133	
Hawthorne Animal Hospital 1516 Alarth Dr *Web:* glencarbonhawthorne.com	Troy	IL	62294	618-667-4900	
Healthy Pets of Westgate Inc 3588 W Broad St *Web:* healthypetsofohio.com	Columbus	OH	43228	614-279-8415	
Hickory Veterinary Hospital 2303 Hickory Rd *Web:* hickoryvet.com	Plymouth Meeting	PA	19462	610-828-3054	
Hopewell Veterinary Group Inc 230 Hopewell Pennington Rd *Web:* saintsbury.com	Hopewell	NJ	08525	609-466-0131	
Imex Veterinary Inc 1001 Mckesson Dr *TF:* 800-828-4639 ■ *Web:* www.imexvet.com	Longview	TX	75604	903-295-2196	
Janssen Clinic for Animals 1624 N High Point Rd *Web:* www.janssenclinic.com	Middleton	WI	53562	608-836-0600	
John Paul Pet Salon 32861 Camino Capistrano Ste F *TF:* 855-577-7669 ■ *Web:* johnpaulpetsalon.com	San Juan Capistrano	CA	92675	855-577-7669	
Look Ahead Veterinary Services 1451 Clark Rd *Web:* www.lookaheadvet.net	Oroville	CA	95965	530-534-0722	
Lyon Veterinary Clinic 21188 Pontiac Trl *Web:* lyonveterinaryclinic.com	South Lyon	MI	48178	248-486-8800	
Millburn Veterinary Hospital 147 Millburn Ave *Web:* millburnvet.com	Millburn	NJ	07041	973-467-1700	
Millhopper Veterinary Medical Center 4209 Northwest 37Th Pl *Web:* millhoppervet.com	Gainesville	FL	32606	352-373-8055	
Moore Lane Veterinary Hospital 30 Moore Ln *Web:* www.yellowstonevalleyvet.com	Billings	MT	59101	406-252-4159	
Mspca Animal Shelter 1577 Falmouth Rd *Web:* www.mspca.org	Centerville	MA	02632	508-775-0940	
National Veterinary Associates Inc 29229 Canwood St Ste 100 *TF:* 888-767-7755 ■ *Web:* www.nvaonline.com	Agoura Hills	CA	91301	805-777-7722	
Noah's Animal Hospitals 5510 Millersville Rd *Web:* noahsanimalhospital.com	Indianapolis	IN	46226	317-244-7738	
Noah's Ark Starr Animal Hospital Inc 422 Noth Euclid St *Web:* www.noahsarkfullerton.com	Fullerton	CA	92832	714-525-2202	
North Las Vegas Animal Hospital 2437 E Cheyenne Ave *Web:* www.huntco.com	North Las Vegas	NV	89030	702-642-5353	
Oak Knoll Animal Hospital Ltd 3113 41st St *Web:* oakknollanimalhospital.com	Moline	IL	61265	309-762-9474	
Ocean City Animal Hospital 11843 Ocean Gtwy *Web:* oceancityvet.com	Ocean City	MD	21842	410-213-1170	
Ocean State Veterinary Specialists Ltd 1480 S County Trl *Web:* www.osvs.net	East Greenwich	RI	02818	401-886-6787	
Oradell Animal Hospital Inc 580 Winters Ave *Web:* www.oradell.com	Paramus	NJ	07652	201-262-0010	
Parkside Animal Hospital 12962 Publishers Dr *Web:* parksidepets.com	Fishers	IN	46038	317-849-1440	
Penn Veterinary Supply Inc 53 Industrial Cir *TF:* 800-233-0210 ■ *Web:* pennvet.com	Lancaster	PA	17601	717-656-4121	
Perry Veterinary Clinic PLLC 3180 Rt 246 Perry *Web:* www.perryvet.com	New York	NY	14530	585-237-5550	
Pet Adoption Network, The 4261 Culver Rd *Web:* www.petadoptionnetwork.org	Rochester	NY	14622	585-338-9175	
Pet Vet Animal Hospitals 4520 Katy Fwy **Fax Area Code:* 713 ■ *Web:* www.petvethospitals.com	Houston	TX	77007	281-561-0276	629-7737*
Peterson & Smith Equine Hospital LLC 4747 SW 60th Ave *Web:* www.petersonsmith.com	Ocala	FL	34474	352-237-6151	
Petlovers Animal Hospital 6425 E Livingston Ave *Web:* petloversah.com	Reynoldsburg	OH	43068	614-866-1912	
Pipestone Veterinary Clinic LLC 1300 Hwy 75 S PO Box 188 *TF:* 800-658-2523 ■ *Web:* www.pipevet.com	Pipestone	MN	56164	507-825-4211	
Radiocat 32-A Mellor Ave **Fax Area Code:* 866 ■ *TF:* 800-323-9729 ■ *Web:* www.radiocat.com	Baltimore	MD	21228	800-323-9729	788-5201*
Ridgeview Animal Hospital 18146 Wright St *Web:* www.ridgeviewanimalhosp.com	Omaha	NE	68130	402-333-3366	
Rood Riddle & Partners PSC 2150 Georgetown Rd *Web:* www.roodandriddle.com	Lexington	KY	40511	859-233-0371	
Sage Centers 1410 Monument Blvd Ste 100 *Web:* sagecenters.com	Concord	CA	94520	925-627-7243	
Schafer Veterinary Consultants LLC 800 Helena Ct *Web:* schaferveterinary.com	Fort Collins	CO	80524	970-224-5103	
Spring Creek Animal Hospital 14837 Nacogdoches Rd *Web:* springcreekvet.com	San Antonio	TX	78247	210-599-2131	
Stone Mountain Pet Lodge 9935 Radisson Rd Ne *Web:* stonemountainpetlodge.com	Minneapolis	MN	55449	763-792-8929	
Summit Pet Product Distributors Inc 420 N Chimney Rock Rd *TF:* 800-323-2963 ■ *Web:* www.summitpet.com	Greensboro	NC	27410	336-294-3200	
Surrey Veterinary Clinic 5957 E Surrey Rd *Web:* www.surreyvetclinic.com	Clare	MI	48617	989-386-9200	
Tewksbury Animal Hospital 1098 Main St *Web:* tewksburyanimalhospital.com	Tewksbury	MA	01876	978-851-3626	
Trans Ova Genetics LC 2938 380th St *Web:* www.transova.com	Sioux Center	IA	51250	712-722-3586	
Tri-city Veterinary Clinic Inc 1929 W Vista Way *Web:* www.tricityvet.com	Vista	CA	92083	760-758-2091	
Twin City Animal Hospital 869 South St *Web:* www.twincityanimalhospital.com	Fitchburg	MA	01420	978-343-3049	
United Pet Care LLC 6232 N Seventh St Ste 202 *TF:* 877-872-8800 ■ *Web:* www.unitedpetcare.com	Phoenix	AZ	85014	602-266-5303	
Valley Cottage Animal Hospital Inc 202 Rt 303 *Web:* www.valleycottageanimalhospital.com	Valley Cottage	NY	10989	845-268-9263	268-0516
VCA Boston Road Animal Hospital 1235 Boston Rd *Web:* www.vcahospitals.com	Springfield	MA	01119	413-783-1203	
VDx Veterinary Diagnostics Inc 2019 Anderson Rd Ste C *TF:* 877-753-4285 ■ *Web:* vdxpathology.com	Davis	CA	95616	530-753-4285	

Phone | Fax

Vedco Inc 5503 Corporate Dr. .... Saint Joseph MO 64507 816-238-8840
Web: www.vedco.com

Vet Clinic of Palm Harbor Inc, The
35891 Us Hwy 19 N .... Palm Harbor FL 34684 727-781-7704
Web: thevetclinic.com

Vet Path Services Inc 6450 Castle Dr. .... Mason OH 45040 513-469-0777
Web: www.vetpathservicesinc.com

Vet-Stem Inc 12860 Danielson Court Ste B. .... Poway CA 92064 858-748-2004
Web: www.vet-stem.com

VetCor Inc 350 Lincoln Pl .... Hingham MA 02043 781-749-8151
Web: www.vetcor.com

Veterinary Specialists of the Southeast (CCVS)
3163 W Montague Ave .... North Charleston SC 29418 843-747-1507 747-7920
Web: www.ccvsllc.com

Veterinary Specialty and Emergency Hospital
3550 S Jason St .... Englewood CO 80110 303-874-7387
Web: www.vrcc.com

Veterinary Specialty Hospital of The Carolinas
6405 Tryon Rd Ste 100. .... Cary NC 27518 919-233-4911
Web: www.vshcarolinas.com

Veterinary Surgical Associates
1410 Monument Blvd Ste 100 .... Concord CA 94520 925-827-1777
Web: www.ccvec.com

Veterinary Transplant Services Inc
215 E Titus St. .... Kent WA 98032 253-520-0771
Web: www.vtsonline.com

Vets & Pets 3345 El Camino Real .... Santa Clara CA 95051 408-246-1893
Web: www.vcai.com

VetSelect Animal Hospital 2150 Old Novi Rd .... Novi MI 48377 248-624-1100 624-6542
TF: 800-462-8749 ■ *Web:* www.vetselect.com

Villa La PAWS LLC 3618 W Bell Rd Ste 1 .... Glendale AZ 85308 602-588-7833
Web: www.villalapaws.com

Western Veterinary Conference
2425 E Oquendo Rd .... Las Vegas NV 89120 702-739-6698
TF: 866-800-7326 ■ *Web:* www.wvc.org

Westfield Veterinary Hospital Pc
8789 Nw 54th Ave .... Johnston IA 50131 515-986-5738
Web: www.westfieldvet.com

Wild Animal Sanctuary, The
1946 County Rd 53. .... Keenesburg CO 80643 303-536-0118
Web: www.wildanimalsanctuary.org

795 VETERINARY MEDICAL ASSOCIATIONS - STATE

Phone | Fax

Alabama Veterinary Medical Assn
8116 Old Federal Rd Ste C .... Montgomery AL 36117 334-395-0086 270-3399
Web: www.alvma.com

Alaska State Veterinary Medical Assn (AKVMA)
1731 Bragaw St .... Anchorage AK 99508 907-563-3701
Web: www.akvma.org

Arizona Veterinary Medical Assn
100 W Coolidge St. .... Phoenix AZ 85013 602-242-7936 249-3828
Web: www.azvma.org

Arkansas Veterinary Medical Assn
PO Box 17687 .... Little Rock AR 72222 501-868-3036 868-3034
Web: www.arkvetmed.org

Colorado Veterinary Medical Assn 191 Yuma St. .... Denver CO 80223 303-318-0447 318-0450
TF: 800-228-5429 ■ *Web:* colovma.org/?

Connecticut Veterinary Medical Assn
PO Box 1058 .... Glastonbury CT 06033 860-635-7770 659-8772
Web: www.ctvet.org

Delaware Veterinary Medical Assn
937 Monroe Terr. .... Dover DE 19904 302-242-7014
Web: www.devma.org

District of Columbia Academy of Veterinary Medicine
PO Box 710477 .... Herndon VA 20171 703-733-0556 742-8745
Web: www.dcavm.org

Georgia Veterinary Medical Assn
233 Peachtree St NE Ste 2205 .... Atlanta GA 30303 678-309-9800 309-3361
TF: 800-853-1625 ■ *Web:* www.gvma.net

Idaho Veterinary Medical Assn (IVMA)
1841 W Secluded Ct. .... Kuna ID 83634 208-922-9431 922-9435
Web: www.ivma.org

Illinois State Veterinary Medical Assn
1121 Chatham Rd. .... Springfield IL 62704 217-546-8381 546-5633
Web: www.isvma.org

Indiana Veterinary Medical Assn
201 S Capitol Ave Ste 405 .... Indianapolis IN 46225 317-974-0888 974-0985
TF: 800-270-0747 ■ *Web:* www.invma.org

Iowa Veterinary Medical Assn
1605 N Ankeny Blvd Ste 110 .... Ankeny IA 50023 515-965-9237 965-9239
TF: 800-369-9564 ■ *Web:* www.iowavma.org

Kansas Veterinary Medical Assn
816 SW Tyler St Ste 200. .... Topeka KS 66612 785-233-4141 233-2534
TF: 888-545-5862 ■ *Web:* www.ksvma.org

Kentucky Veterinary Medical Assn
108 Consumer Ln. .... Frankfort KY 40601 502-226-5862 226-6177
TF: 800-552-5862 ■ *Web:* www.kvma.org

Louisiana Veterinary Medical Assn
8550 United Plz Blvd Ste 1001 .... Baton Rouge LA 70809 225-928-5862 408-4422
TF: 800-524-2996 ■ *Web:* www.lvma.org

Maine Veterinary Medical Assn (MVMA)
97A Exchange St Ste 305 .... Portland ME 04101 800-448-2772 612-0941*
**Fax Area Code:* 888 ■ *TF:* 800-448-2772 ■ *Web:* netforum.avectra.com

Maryland Veterinary Medical Assn
8015 Corporate Dr Ste A. .... Baltimore MD 21236 410-931-3332 931-2060
TF: 888-884-6862 ■ *Web:* www.mdvma.org

Massachusetts Veterinary Medical Assn
163Lakeside Ave. .... Marlborough MA 01752 508-460-9333 460-9969
Web: www.massvet.org

Michigan Veterinary Medical Assn (MVMA)
2144 Commons Pkwy. .... Okemos MI 48864 517-347-4710 347-4666
Web: www.michvma.org

Minnesota Veterinary Medical Assn
101 Bridgepoint Way Ste 100 .... South Saint Paul MN 55075 651-645-7533 645-7539
TF: 888-933-5363 ■ *Web:* www.mvma.org

Missouri Veterinary Medical Assn
2500 Country Club Dr .... Jefferson City MO 65109 573-636-8612 659-7175
TF: 800-632-6900 ■ *Web:* movma.org

Montana Veterinary Medical Assn PO Box 6322. .... Helena MT 59604 406-447-4259
Web: www.mtvma.org

Nebraska Veterinary Medical Assn
2727 W Second St Ste 332. .... Hastings NE 68901 402-463-4704 463-4705
Web: www.nvma.org

Nevada Veterinary Medical Assn PO Box 34420 .... Reno NV 89533 775-324-5344
Web: www.nevadavma.org

New Jersey Veterinary Medical Assn
390 Amwell Rd Ste 402 .... Hillsborough NJ 08844 908-281-0918 450-1286
Web: www.njvma.org

New Mexico Veterinary Medical Assn
60 Placitas Trls Rd .... Placitas NM 87043 505-867-6373 771-8963
Web: www.nmvma.org

New York State Veterinary Medical Society
100 Great Oaks Blvd Ste 127 .... Albany NY 12203 518-869-7867 869-7868
TF: 800-876-9867 ■ *Web:* www.nysvms.org

North Carolina Veterinary Medical Assn (NCVMA)
1611 Jones Franklin Rd Ste 108. .... Raleigh NC 27606 919-851-5850 851-5859
TF: 800-446-2862 ■ *Web:* www.ciclt.net

North Dakota Veterinary Medical Assn
921 S Ninth St Ste 120. .... Bismarck ND 58504 701-221-7740
Web: www.ndvma.com

Ohio Veterinary Medical Assn (OVMA)
3168 Riverside Dr. .... Columbus OH 43221 614-486-7253 486-1325
TF: 800-662-6862 ■ *Web:* www.ohiovma.org

Oklahoma Veterinary Medical Assn
PO Box 14521 .... Oklahoma City OK 73113 405-478-1002 478-7193
TF: 800-248-2862 ■ *Web:* www.okvma.org

Oregon Veterinary Medical Assn
1880 Lancaster Dr NE Ste 118 .... Salem OR 97305 503-399-0311 363-4218
TF: 800-235-3502 ■ *Web:* www.oregonvma.org

Rhode Island Veterinary Medical Assn
302 Pearl St Ste 108. .... Providence RI 02907 401-751-0944 780-0940
Web: www.rivma.org

South Carolina Assn of Veterinarians
PO Box 11766 .... Columbia SC 29211 803-254-1027 254-3773
TF: 800-441-7228 ■ *Web:* www.scav.org

Tennessee Veterinary Medical Assn
PO Box 803 .... Fayetteville TN 37334 931-438-0070 433-6289
TF: 800-697-3587 ■ *Web:* tvmanet.com

Texas Veterinary Medical Assn
8104 Exchange Dr .... Austin TX 78754 512-452-4224 452-6633
TF: 800-711-0023 ■ *Web:* www.tvma.org

Vermont Veterinary Medical Assn
88 Beech St .... Essex Junction VT 05452 802-878-6888 878-2871
Web: www.vtvets.org

Virginia Veterinary Medical Assn (VVMA)
3801 Westerre Pkwy Ste D .... Henrico VA 23233 804-346-2611 346-2655
TF: 800-937-8862 ■ *Web:* www.vvma.org

Washington State Veterinary Medical Assn
8024 Bracken Pl SE .... Snoqualmie WA 98065 425-396-3191
TF: 800-399-7862 ■ *Web:* www.wsvma.org

West Virginia Veterinary Medical Assn (WVVMA)
3801 Westerre Pkwy Ste D .... Henrico VA 23233 804-346-2611 346-2655
Web: www.wvvma.org

Wisconsin Veterinary Medical Assn (WVMA)
2801 Crossroads Dr Ste 1200 .... Madison WI 53718 608-257-3665 257-8989
TF: 888-254-5202 ■ *Web:* www.wvma.org

Wyoming Veterinary Medical Assn (WVMA)
1841 W Secluded Ct. .... Kuna ID 83634 208-922-9431 922-9435
TF: 800-272-1813 ■ *Web:* www.wyvma.org

796 VIATICAL SETTLEMENT COMPANIES

A viatical settlement is the sale of an existing life insurance policy by a terminally ill person to a third party in return for a percentage of the face value of the policy paid immediately.

Phone | Fax

Altrius Capital Management Inc
1323 Commerce Dr .... New Bern NC 28562 252-638-7598
Web: www.altrius-capital.com

Angel Baby Brokerage 26 Red Ball Trl .... Coffeen IL 62017 217-534-2557
Web: www.angelbabybrokerage.com

BRC Investment Management LLC
8400 E Prentice Ave Ste 1401. .... Greenwood Village CO 80111 303-414-1100
Web: www.brcinvest.com

Century Capital Management LLC
100 Federal St 29th Fl .... Boston MA 02110 617-482-3060
Web: www.centurycap.com

Chestnut Investment Advisory
402 Bethlehem Pk. .... Erdenheim PA 19038 215-836-4880
Web: www.regardingyourmoney.com

CMG Surety LLC 1016 Collier Ctr Way Ste 100. .... Naples FL 34110 239-597-0128
Web: www.cmgsurety.com

Cockrell Investment Group
700 Grand Ave Ste 14. .... Ridgefield CA 90805 562-984-7176
Web: cockrell-investment-group.hub.biz

Coventry First LLC 7111 Vly Green Rd .... Fort Washington PA 19034 877-836-8300 233-3201*
**Fax Area Code:* 215 ■ *TF:* 877-836-8300 ■ *Web:* www.coventry.com

Crystal Wealth Management System Ltd
3385 Harvester Rd Ste 200. .... Burlington ON L7N3N2 905-332-4414
TF: 877-299-2854 ■ *Web:* www.crystalwealth.com

Excel Funds Management Inc
2810 Matheson Blvd E Ste 800. .... Mississauga ON L4W4X7 905-813-7111
Web: www.excelfunds.com

Founders Financial Inc
1020 Cromwell Bridge Rd. .... Towson MD 21286 410-308-9988
Web: www.foundersfinancial.com

			Phone	Fax
Francis Investment Counsel LLC 21180 W Capitol Dr . . . Pewaukee	WI	53072	866-232-6457	
TF: 866-232-6457 ■ *Web:* www.francisinvco.com				
GlassRatner Advisory & Capital Group LLC Monarch Tower 3424 Peachtree Rd Ste 2150 . . . Atlanta	GA	30326	678-904-1990	
Web: www.glassratner.com				
Habersham Funding LLC 3495 Piedmont Rd NE Ste 910 . . . Atlanta	GA	30305	404-233-8275	233-9394
TF: 888-874-2402 ■ *Web:* www.habershamfunding.com				
iFuturistics Inc 1007 Orange St Nemours Bldg Ste 1414 . . . Wilmington	DE	19801	302-472-9271	
Web: www.ifuturistics.com				
Indiana Trust & Investment Management Co 4045 Edison Lakes Pkwy Ste 100 . . . Mishawaka	IN	46545	574-271-0374	
TF: 800-362-7905 ■ *Web:* www.indtrust.com				
Interis Consulting Inc 275 Slater St 20th Fl . . . Ottawa	ON	K1P5H9	613-237-9331	
Web: www.interis.ca				
Legacy Benefits Corp 350 Fifth Ave Ste 4320 . . . New York	NY	10118	800-875-1000	643-1180*
**Fax Area Code:* 212 ■ *TF:* 800-875-1000 ■ *Web:* www.legacybenefits.com				
Life Equity LLC 5611 Hudson Dr # 100 . . . Hudson	OH	44236	330-342-7772	342-7782
Web: www.lifeequity.net				
Life Partners Inc (LPI) 204 Woodhew Dr . . . Waco	TX	76712	254-751-7797	
TF: 800-368-5569 ■ *Web:* www.lifepartnersinc.com				
Life Settlement Solutions Inc 9201 Spectrum Ctr Blvd Ste 105 . . . San Diego	CA	92123	858-576-8067	576-9329
TF: 800-762-3387 ■ *Web:* www.lss-corp.com				
Life Trust LLC 330 Madison Ave 6th Fl . . . New York	NY	10017	212-653-0840	653-0844
Web: www.life-trust.net				
Lombardia Capital Partners LLC 55 S Lk Ave Ste 200 . . . Pasadena	CA	91101	626-568-2792	
Web: www.lombardiacapital.com				
Long Point Capital Inc 26700 Woodward Ave . . . Royal Oak	MI	48067	248-591-6000	
Web: www.longpointcapital.com				
Mcube Investment Technologies LLC 5240 Tennyson Pkwy Ste 102 . . . Plano	TX	75024	972-608-9919	
Web: www.mcubeit.com				
Meketa Investment Group 100 Lowder Brook Dr Ste 1100 . . . Westwood	MA	02090	781-471-3500	
Web: www.meketagroup.com				
Mercom Capital Group LLC 6836 Bee Cave Rd Ste 238 . . . Austin	TX	78746	512-215-4452	
Web: www.mercomcapital.com				
Nicola Wealth Management Ltd 1508 W Broadway 5th Fl . . . Vancouver	BC	V6J1W8	604-739-6450	
TF: 800-219-8032 ■ *Web:* www.nicolawealth.com				
Pabrai Investment Funds 1220 Roosevelt Ste 200 . . . Irvine	CA	92620	949-453-0609	
Web: www.pabraifunds.com				
Page & Assoc Inc 1979 Lakeside Pkwy Ste 200 . . . Tucker	GA	30084	800-252-5282	724-7373*
**Fax Area Code:* 770 ■ *TF:* 800-252-5282 ■ *Web:* www.thelifeline.com				
Pembroke Management Ltd 1002 Sherbrooke St W Ste 1700 . . . Montreal	QC	H3A3S4	514-848-1991	
TF: 800-667-0716 ■ *Web:* www.pml.ca				
Red Barn Investments 5215 Old Orchard Rd Ste 675 . . . Skokie	IL	60077	847-920-7100	
Web: www.redbarnllc.com				
Reilly Financial Advisors 7777 Alvarado Rd Ste 116 . . . La Mesa	CA	91942	619-698-0794	
Web: www.rfadvisors.com				
Reinhart Partners Inc 1500 W Market St Ste 100 . . . Mequon	WI	53092	262-241-2020	
Web: www.reinhart-partnersinc.com				
Sandalwood Securities Inc 101 Eisenhower Pkwy . . . Roseland	NJ	07068	973-228-5466	
Web: www.sandalwoodsecurities.com				
SDR Ventures Inc 5613 DTC Pkwy Ste 830 . . . Greenwood Village	CO	80111	720-221-9220	
Web: sdrventures.com				
Senior Settlements LLC 1000 S Lenola Rd Bldg 1 Ste 202 . . . Maple Shade	NJ	08052	856-235-2133	235-1294
TF: 800-834-0628 ■ *Web:* www.seniorsettlementsllc.com				
Tolleson Wealth Management Inc 5500 Preston Rd Ste 250 . . . Dallas	TX	75205	214-252-3250	
Web: www.tollesonwealth.com				
Vega Capital Group LLC 100 Bush St Ste 1428 . . . San Francisco	CA	94104	415-318-8740	
Web: www.vegacapital.com				
Weik Investment Services Inc 1075 Berkshire Blvd Ste 825 . . . Wyomissing	PA	19610	610-376-2240	
Web: weikinvest.com				
Winfield Associates Inc 700 W St Clair Ave Ste 404 . . . Cleveland	OH	44113	216-241-2575	
TF: 888-322-2575 ■ *Web:* www.winfieldinc.com				
Wright Investment Properties Inc 277 German Oak Dr . . . Cordova	TN	38018	901-755-9501	
Web: wrightinvestments.com				
Zesiger Capital Group LLC 460 Park Ave 22nd Fl . . . New York	NY	10022	212-508-6300	

797 VIDEO STORES

See Also Book, Music, Video Clubs p. 1867

			Phone	Fax
Amazon.com Inc 1200 12th Ave S Ste 1200 . . . Seattle	WA	98144	206-266-1000	
NASDAQ: AMZN ■ *TF Cust Svc:* 800-201-7575 ■ *Web:* www.amazon.com				
Best Buy Company Inc 7601 Penn Ave S . . . Minneapolis	MN	55423	612-291-1000	292-2323*
NYSE: BBY ■ **Fax:* Cust Svc ■ *TF:* 888-237-8289 ■ *Web:* www.bestbuy.com				
DVD Empire 2140 Woodland Rd . . . Warrendale	PA	15086	888-383-1880	
TF: 888-383-1880 ■ *Web:* www.dvdempire.com				
Facets Multimedia Inc 1517 W Fullerton Ave . . . Chicago	IL	60614	773-281-9075	929-5437
TF Cust Svc: 800-331-6197 ■ *Web:* www.facets.org				
Family Video 2500 Lehigh Ave . . . Glenview	IL	60026	847-904-9000	904-9009
TF: 888-332-6843 ■ *Web:* www.familyvideo.com				
NetFlix Inc 100 Winchester Cir . . . Los Gatos	CA	95032	408-540-3700	
NASDAQ: NFLX ■ *TF:* 800-290-8191 ■ *Web:* netflix.com				
Rainbo Record Manufacturing Corp 8960 Eton Ave . . . Canoga Park	CA	91304	818-280-1100	
Web: www.rainborecords.com				
Ross Video Ltd 8 John St . . . Iroquois	ON	K0E1K0	613-652-4886	
Web: www.rossvideo.com				
Videoflicks Canada 1701 Ave Rd . . . Toronto	ON	M5M3Y3	416-782-1883	
Web: www.myvideoflicks.ca				

798 VISION CORRECTION CENTERS

			Phone	Fax
Barnet-Dulaney Eye Ctr 4800 N 22nd St . . . Phoenix	AZ	85016	602-955-1000	
TF: 866-742-6581 ■ *Web:* www.goodeyes.com				
Carolina Eye Assoc PA 2170 Midland Rd . . . Southern Pines	NC	28387	910-295-2100	295-5339
Web: www.carolinaeye.com				
Center for Lasik Ophthalmology Consultants, The 5800 Colonial Dr Ste 103 . . . Margate	FL	33063	954-969-0090	977-8774
TF: 800-448-8770 ■ *Web:* www.bestvision.com				
Chicago Cornea Consultants Ltd 806 S Central Ave Ste 300 . . . Highland Park	IL	60035	847-882-5900	882-6028
Web: www.chicagocornea.com				
Eye Centers of Florida (ECOF) 4101 Evans Ave . . . Fort Myers	FL	33901	239-939-3456	936-8776
TF: 888-393-2455 ■ *Web:* www.ecof.com				
Gordon Binder Vision Institute 8910 University Ctr Ln Ste 800 . . . San Diego	CA	92122	858-455-6800	455-0244
John-Kenyon Eye Ctr 1305 Wall St . . . Jeffersonville	IN	47130	800-342-5393	
TF: 800-342-5393 ■ *Web:* www.johnkenyon.com				
Jones Eye Clinic 4405 Hamilton Blvd . . . Sioux City	IA	51104	712-239-3937	239-1305
TF: 800-334-2015 ■ *Web:* joneseye.com				
LaserVue Eye Ctr 3540 Mendocino Ave Ste 200 . . . Santa Rosa	CA	95403	707-522-6200	
TF: 888-527-3745 ■ *Web:* www.laservue.com				
LCA-Vision Inc 7840 Montgomery Rd . . . Cincinnati	OH	45236	513-792-9292	
NASDAQ: LCAV ■ *TF:* 800-688-4550 ■ *Web:* www.lasikplus.com				
Minnesota Eye Consultants PA 710 E 24th St Ste 100 . . . Minneapolis	MN	55404	612-813-3600	813-3601
TF: 800-526-7632 ■ *Web:* www.mneye.com				
Pacific Cataract & Laser Institute 2517 NE Kresky Ave . . . Chehalis	WA	98532	360-748-8632	748-3869
TF: 800-888-9903 ■ *Web:* www.pcli.com				
Prado Vision & Lasik Ctr 7522 N Himes Ave . . . Tampa	FL	33614	813-931-0500	
Web: www.pradovision.com				
South Penn Eye Care (SPECS) 250 E Walnut St . . . Hanover	PA	17331	717-632-6063	
Web: www.southpenneyecare.com				
Southwestern Eye Ctr 2610 E University Dr . . . Mesa	AZ	85213	480-892-8400	892-9533
TF General: 800-224-3339 ■ *Web:* www.sweye.com				
TLC Vision Corp 50 Burnhamthorpe Rd W Ste 101 . . . Mississauga	ON	L5B3C2	877-852-2020	
TF: 877-852-2020 ■ *Web:* www.tlcvision.com				
Will Vision & Laser Centers 8100 NE Pkwy Dr Ste 125 . . . Vancouver	WA	98662	360-885-1327	885-1333
TF: 877-542-3937 ■ *Web:* www.willvision.com				

799 VITAMINS & NUTRITIONAL SUPPLEMENTS

See Also Diet & Health Foods p. 2296; Medicinal Chemicals & Botanical Products p. 2748; Pharmaceutical Companies p. 2934; Pharmaceutical Companies - Generic Drugs p. 2936

			Phone	Fax
ADM Natural Health & Nutrition *Archer Daniels Midland Co* 4666 Faries Pkwy . . . Decatur	IL	62526	217-451-7231	451-4510*
**Fax:* PR ■ *TF:* 800-637-5843 ■ *Web:* www.adm.com				
AST Sports Science Inc 120 Capitol Dr . . . Golden	CO	80401	303-278-1420	278-1417
TF: 800-627-2788 ■ *Web:* www.ast-ss.com				
Atkins Nutritionals Inc 1050 17th St Ste 1000 . . . Denver	CO	80265	303-633-2840	633-2860
TF: 800-628-5467 ■ *Web:* www.atkins.com				
Beehive Botanicals Inc 16297 W Nursery Rd . . . Hayward	WI	54843	715-634-4274	634-3523
TF: 800-233-4483 ■ *Web:* www.beehivebotanicals.com				
Cc Pollen Co 3627 E Indian School Rd Ste 209 . . . Phoenix	AZ	85018	800-875-0096	381-3130*
**Fax Area Code:* 602 ■ *TF:* 800-875-0096 ■ *Web:* www.beepollen.com				
Celex Laboratories Inc 21600 Westminster Hwy Ste 115 . . . Richmond	BC	V6V0A2	604-231-6077	231-6078
Web: www.celexlaboratories.com				
Chattem Inc 1715 W 38th St PO Box 2219 . . . Chattanooga	TN	37409	423-821-4571	821-0395
Web: www.chattem.com				
CytoSport Inc 4795 Industrial Way . . . Benicia	CA	94510	707-751-3942	748-5732
TF: 888-313-1922 ■ *Web:* www.cytosport.com				
Douglas Laboratories Inc 600 Boyce Rd . . . Pittsburgh	PA	15205	800-245-4440	
TF: 800-245-4440 ■ *Web:* www.douglaslabs.com				
Edom Laboratories Inc 100 E Jefryn Blvd Ste M . . . Deer Park	NY	11729	631-586-2266	
TF: 800-723-3366 ■ *Web:* www.edomlaboratories.com				
Enzymatic Therapy 825 Challenger Dr . . . Green Bay	WI	54311	920-469-1313	469-4444
TF: 800-783-2286 ■ *Web:* www.enzymatictherapy.com				
Foodscience Corp 20 New England Dr Ste 10 . . . Essex Junction	VT	05452	802-878-5508	878-0549
TF: 800-451-5190 ■ *Web:* www.foodsciencecorp.com				
Fruitful Yield Inc 229 W Roosevelt Rd . . . Lombard	IL	60148	630-545-9098	
Web: www.fruitfulyield.com				
Futurebiotics LLC 70 Commerce Dr . . . Hauppauge	NY	11788	631-273-6300	273-1165
TF: 800-367-5433 ■ *Web:* www.futurebiotics.com				
Garden of Life Inc 5500 Village Blvd Ste 102 . . . West Palm Beach	FL	33407	866-465-0051	472-9298*
**Fax Area Code:* 561 ■ *TF:* 866-465-0051 ■ *Web:* www.gardenoflife.com				
GNC Inc 300 Sixth Ave 14th Fl . . . Pittsburgh	PA	15222	877-462-4700	
NYSE: GNC ■ *TF:* 877-462-4700 ■ *Web:* www.gnc.com				
Hammer Nutrition Ltd 4952 Whitefish Stage Rd . . . Whitefish	MT	59937	406-862-1877	862-4543
TF Cust Svc: 800-336-1977 ■ *Web:* www.hammernutrition.com				
Health Products Corp 1060 Nepperhan Ave . . . Yonkers	NY	10703	914-423-2900	
Web: www.hpc7.com				

				Phone	Fax
Herbalist, The 2106 NE 65th St. TF: 800-694-3727 ■ Web: store.theherbalist.com	Seattle	WA	98115	206-523-2600	522-3253
Integrated BioPharma Inc 225 Long Ave OTC: INBP ■ TF: 888-319-6962 ■ Web: www.chemintl.com	Hillside	NJ	07205	973-926-0816	
Irwin Naturals 5310 Beethoven St. TF: 800-297-3273 ■ Web: www.appliednutrition.com	Los Angeles	CA	90066	310-306-3636	
Jarrow Formulas Inc 1824 S Robertson Blvd. TF: 800-726-0886 ■ Web: www.jarrow.com	Los Angeles	CA	90035	310-204-6936	204-2520
Labrada Nutrition 403 Century Plz Dr Ste 440 *Fax Area Code: 281 ■ TF: 800-832-9948 ■ Web: www.labrada.com	Houston	TX	77073	800-832-9948	209-2135*
Maximum Human Performance Inc (MHP Inc) 21 Dwight Pl. TF: 888-783-8844 ■ Web: mhpstrong.com	Fairfield	NJ	07004	973-785-9055	785-9159
Mega-Pro International Inc 251 W Hilton Dr TF: 800-541-9469 ■ Web: www.mega-pro.com	Saint George	UT	84770	435-673-1001	673-1007
Natrol Inc 21411 Prairie St. TF: 800-262-8765 ■ Web: www.natrol.com	Chatsworth	CA	91311	818-739-6000	
Naturade Products Inc 2030 Main St Ste 630. *Fax Area Code: 714 ■ TF: 800-421-1830 ■ Web: www.naturade.com	Irvine	CA	92614	800-421-1830	935-9837*
Natural Alternatives International Inc 1185 Linda Vista Dr NASDAQ: NAII ■ TF: 800-848-2646 ■ Web: www.nai-online.com	San Marcos	CA	92078	760-744-7340	744-9589
Natural Factors Nutritional Products Ltd 1550 United Blvd *Fax Area Code: 800 ■ TF: 800-663-8900 ■ Web: www.naturalfactors.com	Coquitlam	BC	V3K6Y2	604-777-1757	663-2115*
Natural Factors Nutritional Products Ltd 14224 167th Ave SE. TF: 877-551-2179 ■ Web: www.naturalfactors.com	Monroe	WA	98272	360-243-3500	
Natural Organics Inc 548 Broadhollow Rd. TF: 800-645-9500 ■ Web: www.naturesplus.com	Melville	NY	11747	800-645-9500	
Naturally Vitamins 4404 E Elwood St. TF: 800-899-4499 ■ Web: www.naturally.com	Phoenix	AZ	85040	480-991-0200	991-0551
Nature's Way Products Inc 3051 W Maple Loop Dr Ste 125 TF: 800-962-8873 ■ Web: www.naturesway.com	Lehi	UT	84043	800-962-8873	688-3303
NBTY Inc 2100 Smithtown Ave. Web: www.nbty.com	Ronkonkoma	NY	11779	631-200-2000	
Nickers International Ltd PO Box 50066 TF: 800-642-5377 ■ Web: www.nickersinternational.com	Staten Island	NY	10305	718-448-6283	448-6298
Nutraceutical International Corp 1400 Kearns Blvd NASDAQ: NUTR ■ *Fax Area Code: 800 ■ TF: 800-669-8877 ■ Web: www.nutraceutical.com	Park City	UT	84060	435-655-6000	767-8541*
Nutrilite Products Inc 5600 Beach Blvd PO Box 5940. Web: www.nutrilite.com	Buena Park	CA	90621	714-562-6200	736-7610
Pacific Health Laboratories Inc 100 Matawan Rd Ste 150 TF General: 877-363-8769 ■ Web: www.pacifichealthlabs.com	Matawan	NJ	07747	732-739-2900	
Paragon Laboratories 20433 Earl St TF: 800-231-3670 ■ Web: www.paragonlabsusa.com	Torrance	CA	90503	310-370-1563	
Peak Nutrition Inc 1097 11th St PO Box 87 TF Sales: 800-600-2069 ■ Web: www.peaknutrition.com	Syracuse	NE	68446	402-269-2825	
Perrigo Co 515 Eastern Ave NYSE: PRGO ■ TF: 800-719-9260 ■ Web: www.perrigo.com	Allegan	MI	49010	269-673-8451	673-9128
Phibro Animal Health Corp 300 Frank W Burr Blvd Ste 21 TF: 800-223-0434 ■ Web: www.phibrochem.com	Teaneck	NJ	07660	201-329-7300	329-7399
Power Organics 301 S Old Stage Rd. TF: 877-769-3795 ■ Web: www.klamathbluegreen.com	Mount Shasta	CA	96067	530-926-6684	
Prolab Nutrition 21411 Prairie St TF: 800-776-5221 ■ Web: www.prolab.com	Chatsworth	CA	91311	818-739-6000	739-6001
Robinson Pharma Inc 3330 S Harbor Blvd Web: www.robinsonpharma.com	Santa Ana	CA	92704	714-241-0235	751-6066
Santa Cruz Nutritionals 2200 Delaware Ave *Fax: Sales ■ Web: www.santacruznutritionals.com	Santa Cruz	CA	95060	831-457-3200	454-0915*
Sportika Export Inc 225 Episcopal Rd Web: www.sportika.com	Berlin	CT	06037	860-828-9000	828-5962
SportPharma Inc 3 Terminal Rd TF: 800-872-0101 ■ Web: www.sportpharma.com	New Brunswick	NJ	08901	732-545-3130	509-0458
Swanson Health Products Inc PO Box 2803 TF: 800-824-4491 ■ Web: www.swansonvitamins.com	Fargo	ND	58108	701-356-2700	356-2708
Synutra International Inc 2275 Research Blvd Ste 500. NASDAQ: SYUT ■ TF: 866-405-2350 ■ Web: www.synutra.com	Rockville	MD	20850	301-840-3888	
Thayers Natural Pharmaceuticals Inc PO Box 56 *Fax Area Code: 203 ■ TF: 888-842-9371 ■ Web: www.thayers.com	Westport	CT	06881	888-842-9371	227-8183*
Tishcon Corp 50 Sylvester St. TF: 800-848-8442 ■ Web: www.tishcon.com	Westbury	NY	11590	516-333-3050	997-1052
Twinlab 600 E Quality Dr *Fax Area Code: 800 ■ TF: 800-645-5626 ■ Web: www.twinlab.com	American Fork	UT	84003	801-763-0700	723-5837*
Ultra-Lab Nutrition Inc 3100 NW Boca Raton Blvd	Boca Raton	FL	33431	561-367-1474	
USANA Health Sciences Inc 3838 West PkwyBlvd NYSE: USNA ■ TF: 888-950-9595 ■ Web: www.usana.com	Salt Lake City	UT	84120	801-954-7100	954-7300
Vitamins Inc 315 E Fullerton Ave. Web: www.vitamins-inc.com	Carol Stream	IL	60188	630-868-0300	
Wachters' Organic Sea Products Corp 550 Sylvan St TF: 800-682-7100 ■ Web: www.wachters.com	Daly City	CA	94014	650-757-9851	757-9858
Wakunaga of America Company Ltd 23501 Madero TF: 800-421-2998 ■ Web: www.kyolic.com	Mission Viejo	CA	92691	949-855-2776	458-2764
Windmill Health Products 6 Henderson Dr TF: 800-822-4320 ■ Web: www.windmillvitamins.com	West Caldwell	NJ	07006	973-575-6591	882-3256
Young Living Essential Oils 3125 Executive Pkwy TF: 866-203-5666 ■ Web: www.youngliving.com	Lehi	UT	84043	801-418-8900	418-8800

800 VOCATIONAL & TECHNICAL SCHOOLS

See Also Children's Learning Centers p. 1937; Colleges - Community & Junior p. 1950; Colleges - Culinary Arts p. 1965; Colleges - Fine Arts p. 1966; Colleges & Universities - Four-Year p. 1968; Language Schools p. 2626; Military Service Academies p. 2771; Universities - Canadian p. 3278

Listings in this category are organized alphabetically by states.

				Phone	Fax
Enterprise-Ozark Community College 1975 Ave C. TF: 877-701-0033 ■ Web: escc.edu	Mobile	AL	36615	251-438-2816	438-2816
Herzing College Birmingham 280 W Valley Ave *Fax: Admissions ■ TF: 800-425-9432 ■ Web: www.herzing.edu/birmingham	Birmingham	AL	35209	205-916-2800	916-2807*
ITT Technical Institute Birmingham 6270 Pk S Dr TF: 800-488-7033 ■ Web: www.itt-tech.edu	Bessemer	AL	35022	205-497-5700	
JF Drake State Technical College 3421 Meridian St N TF: 888-413-7253 ■ Web: www.drakestate.edu	Huntsville	AL	35811	256-539-8161	551-3142
Lawson State Community College *Bessemer* 1100 Ninth Ave SW TF: 800-373-4879 ■ Web: www.lawsonstate.edu	Bessemer	AL	35022	205-925-2515	929-3598
Lurleen B Wallace Community College *Andalusia* 1000 Dannelly Blvd PO Box 1418 *Fax: Admissions ■ TF: 877-382-4357 ■ Web: www.lbwcc.edu	Andalusia	AL	36420	334-222-6591	881-2201*
MacAurthur 1708 N Main St PO Box 910 TF: 877-382-4357 ■ Web: www.lbwcc.edu	Opp	AL	36467	334-493-3573	493-7003
Trenholm State Technical College 1225 Air Base Blvd TF: 800-917-2081 ■ Web: www.trenholmstate.edu	Montgomery	AL	36108	334-420-4200	420-4206
Virginia College *Birmingham* 488 Palisades Blvd Web: www.vc.edu	Birmingham	AL	35209	205-802-1200	
Huntsville 2021 Drake Ave SW Web: www.vc.edu	Huntsville	AL	35801	256-533-7387	533-7785
Wallace Community College Selma 3000 Earl Goodwin Pkwy TF: 855-428-8313 ■ Web: www.wccs.edu	Selma	AL	36703	334-876-9227	876-9250
DeVry University *Calgary* 2700 Third Ave SE TF General: 800-363-5558 ■ Web: www.cal.devry.edu	Calgary	AB	T2A7W4	403-235-3450	
Brown Mackie College Tucson 4585 E Speedway Blvd Ste 204 Web: www.brownmackie.edu	Tucson	AZ	85712	520-319-3300	
DeVry University Phoenix 2149 W Dunlap Ave. TF Cust Svc: 800-528-0250 ■ Web: www.phx.devry.edu	Phoenix	AZ	85021	602-870-9222	331-1494
ITT Technical Institute Tempe 5005 S Wendler Dr TF: 800-879-4881 ■ Web: www.itt-tech.edu	Tempe	AZ	85282	602-437-7500	
ITT Technical Institute Tucson 1455 W River Rd. TF: 800-870-9730 ■ Web: www.itt-tech.edu	Tucson	AZ	85704	520-408-7488	
Southwest Institute of Healing Arts 1100 E Apache Blvd TF: 888-504-9106 ■ Web: www.swiha.edu	Tempe	AZ	85281	480-994-9244	
Remington College *Little Rock* 10600 Colonel Glenn Rd Ste 100 TF: 800-323-8122 ■ Web: www.remingtoncollege.edu	Little Rock	AR	72204	501-312-0007	
Concorde Career Colleges Inc *San Bernardino* 201 E Airport Dr TF: 800-852-8434 ■ Web: www.concorde.edu	San Bernardino	CA	92408	909-884-8891	384-1768
San Diego 4393 Imperial Ave Ste 100 TF: 800-693-7010 ■ Web: www.concorde.edu	San Diego	CA	92113	619-688-0800	220-4177
DeVry University Fremont 6600 Dumbarton Cir *Fax: Admissions ■ TF: 800-363-5558 ■ Web: www.fre.devry.edu	Fremont	CA	94555	510-574-1200	284-1805*
DeVry University Long Beach 3880 Kilroy Airport Way TF: 800-597-1333 ■ Web: www.lb.devry.edu	Long Beach	CA	90806	562-997-5300	
DeVry University Pomona 901 Corporate Ctr Dr TF: 800-243-3660 ■ Web: www.pom.devry.edu	Pomona	CA	91768	909-622-8866	
DeVry University Sherman Oaks 15301 Ventura Blvd Bldg D-100. TF: 888-610-0800 ■ Web: www.devry.edu	Sherman Oaks	CA	91403	818-713-8111	
Everest College Alhambra 2215 W Mission Rd TF: 888-223-8556 ■ Web: www.everest.edu	Alhambra	CA	91803	626-979-4940	979-4960
Everest College Anaheim 511 N Brookhurst Ste 300 TF: 888-224-6684 ■ Web: www.everest.edu	Anaheim	CA	92801	714-953-6500	953-4163
Everest College City of Industry 12801 Crossroads Pkwy S TF: 888-224-6684 ■ Web: www.everest.edu	City of Industry	CA	91746	562-908-2500	
Everest College San Jose 1245 S Winchester Blvd Ste 102 TF: 888-223-8556 ■ Web: www.everest.edu	San Jose	CA	95128	408-246-4171	557-9874
Everest Institute Long Beach 2161 Technology Pl TF: 888-223-8556 ■ Web: www.everest.edu	Long Beach	CA	90810	562-624-9530	437-8111
Golden Gate University *Roseville* 7 Sierra Gate Plz Ste 101 TF: 800-448-4968 ■ Web: www.ggu.edu	Roseville	CA	95678	916-648-1446	
San Francisco 536 Mission St. *Fax: Admissions ■ TF: 800-448-4968 ■ Web: www.ggu.edu	San Francisco	CA	94105	415-442-7000	442-7807*
Heald College *Concord* 5130 Commercial Cir	Concord	CA	94520	925-288-5800	288-5896
Fresno 255 W Bullard Ave	Fresno	CA	93704	559-438-4222	437-4184*
Hayward 25500 Industrial Blvd *Fax Area Code: 510	Hayward	CA	94545	415-735-3146	783-3287*
Rancho Cordova 2910 Prospect Pk Dr.	Rancho Cordova	CA	95670	916-638-1616	414-2676
Salinas 1450 N Main St	Salinas	CA	93906	831-443-1700	443-1050

				Phone	Fax
San Jose 341 Great Mall Pkwy	Milpitas	CA	95035	408-876-5201	808-3005*
**Fax Area Code:* 415					
Stockton 1605 E March Ln	Stockton	CA	95210	209-473-5286	477-2739
ITT Technical Institute					
Lathrop 16916 S Harlan Rd	Lathrop	CA	95330	209-858-0077	
TF: 800-346-1786 ■ *Web:* www.itt-tech.edu					
Oxnard 2051 Solar Dr Ste 150	Oxnard	CA	93036	805-988-0143	
TF: 800-530-1582 ■ *Web:* www.itt-tech.edu					
Rancho Cordova 10863 Gold Ctr Dr	Rancho Cordova	CA	95670	916-851-3900	
TF: 800-488-8466 ■ *Web:* www.itt-tech.edu					
San Bernardino 670 Carnegie Dr	San Bernardino	CA	92408	909-806-4600	
TF: 800-888-3801 ■ *Web:* www.itt-tech.edu					
San Dimas 650 W Cienega Ave	San Dimas	CA	91773	909-971-2300	
TF: 800-414-6522 ■ *Web:* www.itt-tech.edu					
Sylmar 12669 Encinitas Ave	Sylmar	CA	91342	818-364-5151	
TF: 800-363-2086 ■ *Web:* www.itt-tech.edu					
Torrance 2555 W 190th St Ste 125	Torrance	CA	90504	310-965-5900	
Web: www.itt-tech.edu					
Shasta College					
11555 Old Oregon Trl PO Box 496006	Redding	CA	96049	530-242-7500	
Web: www.shastacollege.edu					
West Orange College					
12541 Brookhurst St Ste 100	Garden Grove	CA	92840	714-530-5000	
Westwood College Inland Empire					
20 W Seventh St	Upland	CA	91786	909-931-7550	
TF: 866-221-5632					
Wyotech Fremont 200 Whitney Pl	Fremont	CA	94539	510-490-6900	490-8599
Web: www.wyotech.edu					
Wyotech Sacramento					
980 Riverside Pkwy	West Sacramento	CA	95605	916-376-8888	721-4854*
**Fax Area Code:* 307 ■ **Fax:* Admissions ■ *TF:* 888-308-7158 ■ *Web:* www.wyotech.edu					
Bel-Rea Institute of Animal Technology					
1681 S Dayton St	Denver	CO	80247	303-751-8700	751-9969
TF: 800-950-8001 ■ *Web:* belrea.edu					
Colorado Technical University Denver					
1865 W 121st Ave Bldg C Ste 100	Westminster	CO	80234	303-362-2900	
TF: 877-250-9372 ■ *Web:* www.coloradotech.edu/denver					
Concorde Career Colleges Inc Denver					
111 N Havana St	Aurora	CO	80010	303-861-1151	839-5478
Web: www.concorde.edu					
Denver Academy of Court Reporting					
9051 Harlan St Ste 20	Westminster	CO	80031	303-427-5292	427-5383
TF: 866-712-2425 ■ *Web:* www.princeinstitute.edu					
Colorado Springs					
1175 Kelly Johnson Blvd	Colorado Springs	CO	80920	719-632-3000	
TF Help Line: 877-784-1997 ■ *Web:* www.devry.edu					
Denver					
6312 S Fiddlers Green Cr Ste 150E	Greenwood Village	CO	80111	303-329-3000	
Web: www.wes.devry.edu					
Everest College Aurora					
14280 E Jewell Ave Ste 100	Aurora	CO	80012	303-745-6244	745-6245
TF: 888-223-8556 ■ *Web:* www.everest.edu					
Everest College Thornton 9065 Grant St	Thornton	CO	80229	303-457-2757	457-4030
TF: 888-223-8556 ■ *Web:* www.everest.edu					
Lincoln College of Technology					
11194 E 45th Ave	Denver	CO	80239	303-722-5724	
TF: 800-254-0547 ■ *Web:* www.lincolntech.edu/campus/denver-co					
Redstone College					
Denver 10851 W 120th Ave	Broomfield	CO	80021	303-466-1714	
TF: 800-888-3995 ■ *Web:* www.redstone.edu					
Delaware Technical & Community College					
Owens 18800 Seashore Hwy PO Box 610	Georgetown	DE	19947	302-856-5400	
Web: www.dtcc.edu					
Stanton 400 Stanton-Christiana Rd	Newark	DE	19713	302-454-3900	292-3816*
**Fax:* Admissions ■ *Web:* www.dtcc.edu					
Terry 100 Campus Dr	Dover	DE	19904	302-857-1000	
Web: www.dtcc.edu/terry					
Acupuncture & Massage College					
10506 N Kendall Dr	Miami	FL	33176	305-595-9500	595-2622*
**Fax:* Admissions ■ *Web:* www.amcollege.edu					
Brown Mackie College Miami 3700 Lakeside Dr	Miramar	FL	33027	305-341-6600	
TF: 866-505-0335 ■ *Web:* www.brownmackie.edu					
Concorde Career Colleges inc Miramar					
10933 Marks Way	Miramar	FL	33025	954-731-8880	
TF: 800-693-7010 ■ *Web:* www.concorde.edu					
DeVry University Miramar 2300 SW 145th Ave	Miramar	FL	33027	954-499-9800	
Web: www.devry.edu					
DeVry University Orlando 4000 Millenia Blvd	Orlando	FL	32839	407-345-2800	370-3198*
**Fax:* Admissions ■ *TF:* 888-857-5757 ■ *Web:* www.devry.edu					
Everest University					
Brandon 3924 Coconut Palm Dr	Tampa	FL	33619	813-621-0041	
TF Cust Svc: 888-223-8556 ■ *Web:* www.everest.edu					
Jacksonville 8226 Phillips Hwy	Jacksonville	FL	32256	904-731-4949	731-0599
TF: 800-611-2101 ■ *Web:* www.everest.edu					
Lakeland 995 E Memorial Blvd Ste 110	Lakeland	FL	33801	863-686-1444	682-1077
TF: 888-223-8556 ■ *Web:* www.everest.edu					
Largo 1199 E Bay Dr	Largo	FL	33770	727-725-2688	373-4412
TF: 888-223-8556 ■ *Web:* www.everest.edu					
North Orlando 5421 Diplomat Cir	Orlando	FL	32810	407-628-5870	628-1344*
**Fax:* Admissions ■ *TF:* 888-223-8556 ■ *Web:* www.everest.edu					
Orange Park 805 Wells Rd	Orange Park	FL	32073	904-264-9122	264-9952
TF: 888-223-8556 ■ *Web:* www.everest.edu					
Pompano Beach 225 N Federal Hwy	Pompano Beach	FL	33062	954-783-7339	783-7964
TF: 888-223-8556 ■ *Web:* www.everest.edu					
South Orlando 9200 Southpark Ctr Loop	Orlando	FL	32819	407-851-2525	851-1477
TF: 800-611-2101 ■ *Web:* www.everest.edu					
Tampa 3319 W Hillsborough Ave	Tampa	FL	33614	813-879-6000	871-2483
TF: 888-223-8556 ■ *Web:* www.everest.edu					
Florida Technical College					
12900 Challenger Pkwy	Orlando	FL	32826	407-447-7300	447-7301
TF General: 888-678-2929 ■ *Web:* www.ftccollege.edu					
Full Sail University					
3300 University Blvd Ste 160	Winter Park	FL	32792	407-679-6333	
TF: 800-226-7625 ■ *Web:* www.fullsail.edu					
ITT Technical Institute Fort Lauderdale					
3401 S University Dr	Fort Lauderdale	FL	33328	954-476-9300	
TF: 800-488-7797 ■ *Web:* www.itt-tech.edu					
ITT Technical Institute Jacksonville					
7011 AC Skinner Pkwy Ste 140	Jacksonville	FL	32256	904-573-9100	
TF: 800-318-1264 ■ *Web:* www.itt-tech.edu					
ITT Technical Institute Miami					
7955 NW 12th St Ste 119	Miami	FL	33126	305-477-3080	
Web: www.itt-tech.edu					
ITT Technical Institute Tampa					
4809 Memorial Hwy	Tampa	FL	33634	813-885-2244	
TF: 800-825-2831 ■ *Web:* www.itt-tech.edu					
Kaplan University					
6301 Kaplan University Ave	Fort Lauderdale	FL	33309	866-527-5268	588-4127*
**Fax Area Code:* 800 ■ *TF:* 866-527-5268 ■ *Web:* www.kaplanuniversity.edu					
Keiser University					
Daytona Beach 1800 Business Pk Blvd	Daytona Beach	FL	32114	386-274-5060	274-2725
Web: www.keiseruniversity.edu					
Fort Lauderdale					
1500 W Commercial Blvd	Fort Lauderdale	FL	33309	954-776-4456	771-4894
TF: 800-749-4456 ■ *Web:* www.keiseruniversity.edu					
Melbourne 900 S Babcock St	Melbourne	FL	32901	321-409-4800	725-3766
TF: 888-534-7379 ■ *Web:* www.keiseruniversity.edu					
Sarasota 6151 Lk Osprey Dr	Sarasota	FL	34240	941-907-3900	907-2016
TF: 866-534-7372 ■ *Web:* www.keiseruniversity.edu					
Lincoln College of Technology					
2410 Metro Centre Blvd	West Palm Beach	FL	33407	561-842-8324	245-3238*
**Fax Area Code:* 850 ■ *TF:* 800-254-0547 ■ *Web:* www.lincolntech.edu					
Remington College Largo					
6302 E Dr Martin Luther King Jr Blvd Ste 400	Tampa	FL	33619	800-323-8122	
TF: 800-323-8122 ■ *Web:* www.remingtoncollege.edu					
Remington College Tampa 6302 E MLK Blvd Ste 400	Tampa	FL	33619	813-935-5700	
TF General: 800-323-8122 ■ *Web:* www.remingtoncollege.edu					
Stenotype Institute of Jacksonville					
3563 Phillips Hwy Bldg E Ste 501	Jacksonville	FL	32207	904-398-4141	398-7878
TF: 800-273-5090					
Athens Technical College (ATC) 800 US Hwy 29 N	Athens	GA	30601	706-355-5000	369-5756
Web: athenstech.edu					
Augusta Technical College					
3200 Augusta Tech Dr	Augusta	GA	30906	706-771-4000	771-4034*
**Fax:* Admissions ■ *Web:* www.augustatech.edu					
Brown College of Court Reporting & Medical Transcription (BCCR)					
1900 Emery St NW Ste 200	Atlanta	GA	30318	404-876-1227	876-4415
TF: 800-849-0703 ■ *Web:* www.bccr.edu					
Brown Mackie College Atlanta					
4370 Peachtree Rd NE	Atlanta	GA	30319	404-799-4500	
TF: 877-479-8419 ■ *Web:* www.brownmackie.edu					
Central Georgia Technical College					
3300 Macon Tech Dr	Macon	GA	31206	478-757-3400	757-3454
TF: 866-430-0135 ■ *Web:* centralgatech.edu					
Columbus Technical College					
928 Manchester Expy	Columbus	GA	31904	706-649-1800	
Web: www.columbustech.edu					
Gupton-Jones College of Funeral Service					
5141 Snapfinger Woods Dr	Decatur	GA	30035	770-593-2257	593-1891
TF: 800-848-5352 ■ *Web:* www.gupton-jones.edu					
Herzing College					
Atlanta 3393 Peachtree Rd Ste 1003	Atlanta	GA	30326	404-816-4533	816-5576
TF: 800-573-4533 ■ *Web:* www.herzing.edu/atlanta					
Imedex Inc 4325 Alexander Dr	Alpharetta	GA	30022	770-751-7332	751-7334
TF: 800-243-6969 ■ *Web:* www.imedex.com					
ITT Technical Institute Kennesaw					
2065 Baker Rd NW	Kennesaw	GA	30144	770-426-2300	706-3040*
**Fax Area Code:* 317 ■ *TF:* 800-564-9771 ■ *Web:* www.itt-tech.edu					
Savannah Technical College					
5717 White Bluff Rd	Savannah	GA	31405	912-443-5700	443-5705
TF: 800-769-6362 ■ *Web:* www.savannahtech.edu					
Westwood College Atlanta Northlake					
2309 Parklake Dr NE	Atlanta	GA	30345	770-743-3000	
TF: 800-227-5695 ■ *Web:* www.westwood.edu					
Argosy University Hawaii					
400 ASB Tower 1001 Bishop St	Honolulu	HI	96813	808-536-5555	536-5505
TF: 888-323-2777 ■ *Web:* www.argosy.edu					
Remington College Honolulu					
1111 Bishop St Ste 400	Honolulu	HI	96813	808-772-5978	
Web: www.remingtoncollege.edu					
Eastern Idaho Technical College					
1600 S 25th E	Idaho Falls	ID	83404	208-524-3000	525-7026
TF: 800-662-0261 ■ *Web:* www.eitc.edu					
ITT Technical Institute Boise					
12302 W Explorer Dr	Boise	ID	83713	208-322-8844	
TF: 800-666-4888 ■ *Web:* www.itt-tech.edu					
DeVry University Addison 1221 N Swift Rd	Addison	IL	60101	630-953-1300	
TF: 800-346-5420 ■ *Web:* www.devry.edu					
DeVry University Chicago 3300 N Campbell Ave	Chicago	IL	60618	773-929-8500	697-2710*
**Fax:* Admissions ■ *Web:* www.chi.devry.edu					
DeVry University Tinley Park					
18624 W Creek Dr	Tinley Park	IL	60477	708-342-3300	
Web: www.devry.edu					
Gem City College 700 State St	Quincy	IL	62301	217-222-0391	222-1557
Web: www.gemcitycollege.com					
ITT Technical Institute Mount Prospect					
3800 N Wilke RD	Arlington Heights	IL	60004	847-454-1800	
Web: www.itt-tech.edu					
ITT Technical Institute Orland Park					
11551 184th Pl	Orland Park	IL	60467	708-326-3200	
Web: www.itt-tech.edu					
Lexington College 310 S Peoria St	Chicago	IL	60607	312-226-6294	226-6405*
MacCormac College 29 E Madison St	Chicago	IL	60602	312-922-1884	922-4286
Web: www.maccormac.edu					
Midstate College 411 W Northmoor Rd	Peoria	IL	61614	309-692-4092	692-3893
TF: 800-251-4299 ■ *Web:* www.midstate.edu					
Morrison Institute of Technology					
701 Portland Ave	Morrison	IL	61270	815-772-7218	772-7584
Web: morrisontech.edu					

Phone Fax

Northwestern College Chicago Campus
4829 N Lipps Ave . . . . Chicago IL 60630 773-777-4220
TF: 888-205-2283 ■ *Web*: www.nc.edu

Westwood College O'Hare Airport
8501 W Higgins Rd Ste 100 . . . . Chicago IL 60631 773-380-6800
TF: 866-552-7536 ■ *Web*: www.westwood.edu

Worsham College of Mortuary Science
495 Northgate Pkwy . . . . Wheeling IL 60090 847-808-8444 808-8493
Web: www.worshamcollege.com

Brown Mackie College
Fort Wayne 3000 E Coliseum Blvd. . . . . Fort Wayne IN 46805 260-484-4400 484-2678
TF General: 866-433-2289 ■ *Web*: www.brownmackie.edu
Merrillville 1000 E 80th Pl Ste 205M. . . . . Merrillville IN 46410 219-769-3321 738-1076
TF: 800-258-3321 ■ *Web*: www.brownmackie.edu
Michigan City 1001 E US Hwy 20 . . . . Michigan City IN 46360 219-877-3100
TF: 800-519-2416 ■ *Web*: www.brownmackie.edu
South Bend 3454 Douglas Rd . . . . South Bend IN 46635 574-237-0774 237-3585
TF: 800-743-2447 ■ *Web*: www.brownmackie.edu

College of Court Reporting Inc
111 W Tenth St Ste 111 . . . . Hobart IN 46342 219-942-1459 942-1631
TF: 866-294-3974 ■ *Web*: www.ccr.edu

International Business College
5699 Coventry Ln . . . . Fort Wayne IN 46804 260-459-4500
TF: 800-589-6363 ■ *Web*: www.ibcfortwayne.edu

ITT Technical Institute Fort Wayne
2810 Dupont Commerce Ct . . . . Fort Wayne IN 46825 260-497-6200
TF: 800-866-4488 ■ *Web*: www.itt-tech.edu

ITT Technical Institute Indianapolis
9511 Angola Ct. . . . . Indianapolis IN 46268 317-875-8640
TF: 800-937-4488 ■ *Web*: www.itt-tech.edu

ITT Technical Institute Newburgh
10999 Stahl Rd. . . . . Newburgh IN 47630 812-858-1600
TF: 800-832-4488 ■ *Web*: www.itt-tech.edu

Ivy Tech Columbus College
Columbus 4475 Central Ave . . . . Columbus IN 47203 812-372-9925 372-0311
TF: 800-922-4838 ■ *Web*: www.ivytech.edu/columbus

Ivy Tech Community College
Bloomington 200 Daniels Way. . . . . Bloomington IN 47404 812-330-6137 330-6140
TF: 866-447-0700 ■ *Web*: www.ivytech.edu
Central Indiana
50 W Fall Creek Pkwy N Dr . . . . Indianapolis IN 46208 317-921-4800 921-4753
TF: 888-489-5463 ■ *Web*: www.ivytech.edu/indianapolis
Kokomo 1815 E Morgan St . . . . Kokomo IN 46901 765-459-0561 454-5111
TF: 800-459-0561 ■ *Web*: www.ivytech.edu/kokomo
Muncie 4301 S Cowan Rd . . . . Muncie IN 47302 765-289-2291 289-2292
TF: 800-589-8324 ■ *Web*: www.ivytech.edu/eastcentral
North Central 220 Dean Johnson Blvd. . . . . South Bend IN 46601 574-289-7001 236-7177
TF: 888-489-3478 ■ *Web*: www.ivytech.edu
Northwest 1440 E 35th Ave . . . . Gary IN 46409 219-981-1111 981-4415
TF: 888-489-5463 ■ *Web*: www.ivytech.edu
Richmond 2357 Chester Blvd . . . . Richmond IN 47374 765-966-2656 962-8741
TF: 800-659-4562 ■ *Web*: www.ivytech.edu
Southeast 590 Ivy Tech Dr. . . . . Madison IN 47250 812-265-2580 265-4028
TF: 800-403-2190 ■ *Web*: www.ivytech.edu
Southern Indiana 8204 old Indiana 311 . . . . Sellersburg IN 47172 812-246-3301 246-9905
TF: 800-321-9021 ■ *Web*: www.ivytech.edu
Southwest Indiana 3501 N First Ave . . . . Evansville IN 47710 812-426-2865 429-9878
Web: www.ivytech.edu
Wabash Valley 8000 S Education Dr . . . . Terre Haute IN 47802 812-298-2293 298-2294
TF: 888-489-5463 ■ *Web*: www.ivytech.edu

Lincoln College of Technology
7225 Winton Dr Bldg 128. . . . . Indianapolis IN 46268 317-632-5553 245-3238*
**Fax Area Code*: 850 ■ *TF*: 800-228-6232 ■ *Web*: www.lincolntech.edu

Mid-America College of Funeral Science (MACFS)
3111 Hamburg Pk. . . . . Jeffersonville IN 47130 812-288-8878 288-5942
TF: 800-221-6158 ■ *Web*: www.mid-america.edu

AIB College of Business 2500 Fleur Dr. . . . . Des Moines IA 50321 515-244-4221 244-6773
TF: 800-444-1921 ■ *Web*: www.aib.edu

Brown Mackie College Bettendorf
2119 E Kimberly Rd . . . . Bettendorf IA 52722 563-344-1500
TF: 888-420-1652 ■ *Web*: www.brownmackie.edu

Des Moines Unviersity 3200 Grand Ave . . . . Des Moines IA 50312 515-271-1400
Web: www.dmu.edu

Western Iowa Tech Community College
4647 Stone Ave . . . . Sioux City IA 51102 712-274-6400 274-6412
TF: 800-352-4649 ■ *Web*: witcc.edu

Brown Mackie College Lenexa 9705 Lenexa Dr . . . . Lenexa KS 66215 913-768-1900 495-9555
TF: 800-635-9101 ■ *Web*: www.brownmackie.edu

Brown Mackie College Salina 2106 S Ninth St. . . . . Salina KS 67401 785-825-5422
TF: 800-365-0433 ■ *Web*: www.brownmackie.edu/salina.aspx

Concorde Career Colleges
5800 Foxridge Dr Ste 500. . . . . Mission KS 66202 913-831-9977 831-6556
TF: 800-693-7010 ■ *Web*: www.concorde.edu

Wichita Area Technical College
301 S Grove St Bldg A . . . . Wichita KS 67211 316-677-9400 677-9555
TF: 866-296-4031 ■ *Web*: www.watc.edu

Bowling Green Technical College
1845 Loop Dr . . . . Bowling Green KY 42101 270-901-1000 901-1144
TF: 866-590-9238 ■ *Web*: www.bowlinggreen.kctcs.edu

Brown Mackie College Hopkinsville
4001 Ft Campbell Blvd. . . . . Hopkinsville KY 42240 270-886-1302 886-3544
TF: 800-359-4753 ■ *Web*: www.brownmackie.edu

Brown Mackie College Louisville
3605 Fern Vly Rd . . . . Louisville KY 40219 502-968-7191 357-9956
TF: 800-999-7387 ■ *Web*: www.brownmackie.edu

Brown Mackie College Northern Kentucky
309 Buttermilk Pk. . . . . Fort Mitchell KY 41017 859-341-5627 341-6483
TF: 800-888-1445 ■ *Web*: www.brownmackie.edu

Daymar College 3361 Buckland Sq. . . . . Owensboro KY 42301 270-926-4040
Web: daymarcollege.edu

Gateway Community & Technical College (GCTC)
1025 Amsterdam Rd. . . . . Covington KY 41011 859-441-4500 292-6415
TF: 855-346-4282 ■ *Web*: www.gateway.kctcs.edu

Phone Fax

ITT Technical Institute Lexington
3020 Old Todds Rd. . . . . Lexington KY 40509 859-246-3300
Web: www.itt-tech.edu

ITT Technical Institute Louisville
9500 Ormsby Stn Rd Ste 100 . . . . Louisville KY 40223 502-327-7424
TF: 888-790-7427 ■ *Web*: www.itt-tech.edu

Louisville Technical Institute
Sullivan College of Technology & Design
3901 Atkinson Sq Dr . . . . Louisville KY 40218 502-456-6509 456-2341
TF: 800-844-6528 ■ *Web*: www.sctd.edu

National College
Lexington 2376 Sir Barton Way . . . . Lexington KY 40509 859-253-0621
TF: 877-540-3494 ■ *Web*: national-college.edu

National College of Business & Technology Danville
115 E Lexington Ave. . . . . Danville KY 40422 859-236-6991
Web: national-college.edu

National College of Business & Technology Florence
8095 Connector Dr. . . . . Florence KY 41042 859-525-6510 525-8961
TF: 888-956-2732 ■ *Web*: www.national-college.edu

National College of Business & Technology Pikeville
50 National College Blvd . . . . Pikeville KY 41501 606-478-7200
TF: 800-664-1886 ■ *Web*: national-college.edu

National College of Business & Technology Richmond
125 S Killarney Ln . . . . Richmond KY 40475 859-623-8956
Web: national-college.edu

Owensboro Community & Technical College
4800 New Hartford Rd . . . . Owensboro KY 42303 270-686-4400 686-4496
TF: 866-755-6282 ■ *Web*: www.octc.kctcs.edu

Remington College Lafayette
303 Rue Louis XIV . . . . Lafayette LA 70508 337-981-4010
Web: www.remingtoncollege.edu

Andover College 265 Western Ave . . . . South Portland ME 04106 207-774-6126 774-1715
TF: 800-639-3110 ■ *Web*: kaplanuniversity.edu

Beal College 99 Farm Rd. . . . . Bangor ME 04401 207-947-4591 947-0208
TF: 800-660-7351 ■ *Web*: www.bealcollege.edu

Central Maine Community College
1250 Turner St . . . . Auburn ME 04210 207-755-5100 755-5493
TF Admissions: 800-891-2002 ■ *Web*: www.cmcc.edu

Central Maine Medical Ctr School of Nursing
70 Middle St. . . . . Lewiston ME 04240 207-795-2840 795-2849
Web: mchp.edu

Eastern Maine Community College 354 Hogan Rd . . . . Bangor ME 04401 207-974-4600
TF: 800-286-9357 ■ *Web*: www.emcc.edu

Northern Maine Community College (NMCC)
33 Edgemont Dr . . . . Presque Isle ME 04769 207-768-2700 768-2848
Web: nmcc.edu

Southern Maine Community College (SMCC)
2 Ft Rd . . . . South Portland ME 04106 207-741-5500 741-5760
TF: 877-282-2182 ■ *Web*: www.smccme.edu

ITT Technical Institute Owings Mills
11301 Red Run Blvd. . . . . Owings Mills MD 21117 443-394-7115
TF: 877-411-6782 ■ *Web*: www.itt-tech.edu

Maryland Bartending Academy
209 New Jersey Ave NE . . . . Glen Burnie MD 21060 410-787-0020
Web: www.marylandbartending.com

National Labor College
10000 New Hampshire Ave. . . . . Silver Spring MD 20903 301-431-6400 431-5411
TF: 888-427-8100 ■ *Web*: www.nlc.edu

Bay State College 122 Commonwealth Ave . . . . Boston MA 02116 617-217-9000 249-0400
TF: 800-815-3276 ■ *Web*: www.baystate.edu

Benjamin Franklin Institute of Technology
41 Berkeley St. . . . . Boston MA 02116 617-423-4630 482-3706
TF: 877-400-2348 ■ *Web*: www.bfit.edu

Boston Architectural College 320 Newbury St . . . . Boston MA 02115 617-585-0100 585-0100*
**Fax*: Admissions ■ *TF*: 877-585-0100 ■ *Web*: www.the-bac.edu

Cambridge College Inc
360 Merrimack St 4th fl . . . . Lawrence MA 01843 617-868-1000 349-3545
TF: 800-829-4723 ■ *Web*: www.cambridgecollege.edu

FINE Mortuary College LLC 150 Kerry Pl . . . . Norwood MA 02062 781-762-1211 762-7177
Web: www.fine-ne.com

ITT Technical Institute Wilmington
200 Ballardvale St Ste 200 . . . . Wilmington MA 01887 978-658-2636
TF: 800-430-5097 ■ *Web*: www.itt-tech.edu

Laboure College 303 Adams St. . . . . Milton MA 02186 617-322-3575 690-3730
Web: www.laboure.edu

National Aviation Academy 150 Hanscom Dr . . . . Bedford MA 01730 727-535-8727 274-8490*
**Fax Area Code*: 781 ■ *TF*: 800-659-2080 ■ *Web*: www.naa.edu

New England College of Business & Finance
10 High St Ste 204 . . . . Boston MA 02110 617-951-2350 951-2533
TF: 888-357-7332 ■ *Web*: www.necb.edu

Sanford-Brown College
Boston 126 Newbury St . . . . Boston MA 02116 617-578-7100
TF: 877-809-2444 ■ *Web*: www.sanfordbrown.edu

Academy of Court Reporting
Clawson 1055 W Maple Rd . . . . Clawson MI 48017 888-314-7780
TF: 888-314-7780 ■ *Web*: www.acr.edu

Cleary University 3601 Plymouth Rd . . . . Ann Arbor MI 48105 734-332-4477 332-4646
TF: 800-686-1883 ■ *Web*: www.cleary.edu
Livingston 3750 Cleary Dr. . . . . Howell MI 48843 517-548-3670 552-7805
TF: 800-686-1883 ■ *Web*: www.cleary.edu

Everest Institute 21107 Lahser Rd. . . . . Southfield MI 48033 248-799-9933 799-2912*
**Fax*: Admissions ■ *TF General*: 800-611-2101 ■ *Web*: www.everest.edu

ITT Technical Institute Canton
1905 S Haggerty Rd . . . . Canton MI 48188 734-397-7800
TF: 800-247-4477 ■ *Web*: www.itt-tech.edu

ITT Technical Institute Grand Rapids
1980 Metro Ct SW . . . . Wyoming MI 49519 616-406-1200
TF: 800-632-4676 ■ *Web*: www.itt-tech.edu

ITT Technical Institute Troy
1522 E Big Beaver Rd . . . . Troy MI 48083 248-524-1800
TF: 800-832-6817 ■ *Web*: www.itt-tech.edu

Anoka Technical College 1355 W Hwy 10. . . . . Anoka MN 55303 763-433-1100 576-7701*
**Fax*: Admissions ■ *TF*: 800-627-3529 ■ *Web*: www.anokatech.edu

Phone | Fax

Brown College
1345 Mendota Heights Rd — Mendota Heights MN 55120 — 651-905-3400
TF: 888-247-4238 ■ *Web:* www.browncollege.edu

Dakota County Technical College
1300 E 145th St — Rosemount MN 55068 — 651-423-8301 423-8775
TF: 877-937-3282 ■ *Web:* www.dctc.edu

Duluth Business University (DBU)
4724 Mike Colalilo Dr — Duluth MN 55807 — 218-722-4000 628-2127
TF: 800-777-8406 ■ *Web:* www.dbumn.edu

Dunwoody College of Technology
818 Dunwoody Blvd — Minneapolis MN 55403 — 612-374-5800 374-4128
TF: 800-292-4625 ■ *Web:* www.dunwoody.edu

Hennepin Technical College
9000 Brooklyn Blvd — Brooklyn Park MN 55445 — 952-995-1300 488-2944*
**Fax Area Code:* 763 ■ *TF:* 800-345-4655 ■ *Web:* www.hennepintech.edu

Northwest Technical Institute
950 Blue Gentian Rd Ste 500 — Eagan MN 55121 — 952-944-0080
Web: www.globeuniversity.edu/drafting-degree

Ridgewater College
Hutchinson 2 Century Ave SE — Hutchinson MN 55350 — 320-234-8500
TF: 800-722-1151 ■ *Web:* www.ridgewater.edu
Willmar 2101 15th Ave NW PO Box 1097 — Willmar MN 56201 — 320-222-5200 222-5216*
**Fax:* Admissions ■ *TF:* 800-722-1151 ■ *Web:* www.ridgewater.edu

Saint Cloud Technical & Community College
1540 Northway Dr — Saint Cloud MN 56303 — 320-308-5089 308-5981
TF: 800-222-1009 ■ *Web:* www.sctcc.edu

Saint Paul College 235 Marshall Ave — Saint Paul MN 55102 — 651-846-1600 846-1703
TF: 800-227-6029 ■ *Web:* www.saintpaul.edu

Virginia College Gulf Coast 920 Cedar Lk Rd — Biloxi MS 39532 — 228-392-2994 392-2039
Web: www.vc.edu

Virginia College Jackson 5841 Ridgewood Rd — Jackson MS 39211 — 601-977-0960
Web: www.vc.edu

Concorde Career Colleges inc Kansas City
3239 Broadway — Kansas City MO 64111 — 816-531-5223 756-3231
Web: www.concorde.edu

DeVry University Kansas City
1310 E 104th St 2nd Fl — Kansas City MO 64131 — 816-941-0430 943-7551
TF: 800-821-3766 ■ *Web:* www.kc.devry.edu

Everest College 1010 W Sunshine St — Springfield MO 65807 — 417-864-7220 864-5697
TF: 888-223-8556 ■ *Web:* www.everest.edu

ITT Technical Institute Arnold
1930 Meyer Drury Dr — Arnold MO 63010 — 636-464-6600
TF: 888-488-1082 ■ *Web:* www.itt-tech.edu

ITT Technical Institute Earth City
3640 Corporate Trl Dr — Earth City MO 63045 — 314-298-7800
TF: 800-235-5488 ■ *Web:* www.itt-tech.edu

ITT Technical Institute Kansas City
9150 E 41st Terr — Kansas City MO 64133 — 816-276-1400
TF: 877-488-1442 ■ *Web:* www.itt-tech.edu

Vatterott College Berkeley 8580 Evans Ave — Berkeley MO 63134 — 314-264-1000
TF: 888-202-2636 ■ *Web:* www.vatterott.edu

Vatterott College Joplin 809 Illinois Ave — Joplin MO 64801 — 417-781-5633 781-6437
TF: 866-200-1898 ■ *Web:* www.vatterott.edu

Vatterott College South County
12900 Maurer Industrial Dr — Saint Louis MO 63127 — 314-843-4200 843-1709
TF: 866-312-8276 ■ *Web:* www.vatterott.edu

Vatterott College Springfield
3850 S Campbell — Springfield MO 65807 — 417-831-8116 831-5099*
**Fax:* Admissions ■ *TF:* 844-244-3304 ■ *Web:* www.vatterott.edu

University of Montana 32 Campus Dr — Missoula MT 59812 — 406-243-6266 243-5711*
**Fax:* Admissions ■ *TF Admissions:* 800-462-8636 ■ *Web:* www.umt.edu
College of Technology 909 S Ave W — Missoula MT 59801 — 406-243-7852 243-7899
TF: 800-542-6882 ■ *Web:* www.mc.umt.edu
Helena College of Technology
1115 N Roberts St — Helena MT 59601 — 406-444-6800 444-6892
TF: 800-827-1000 ■ *Web:* www.umhelena.edu

ITT Technical Institute Omaha
1120 N 103rd Plz Ste 200 — Omaha NE 68114 — 402-331-2900
TF: 800-677-9260 ■ *Web:* www.itt-tech.edu

Kaplan University Lincoln 1821 K St — Lincoln NE 68508 — 800-987-7734
TF: 800-987-7734 ■ *Web:* www.kaplanuniversity.edu

Kaplan University Omaha 5425 N 103rd St — Omaha NE 68134 — 402-572-8500
TF: 800-987-7734 ■ *Web:* www.kaplanuniversity.edu

Nebraska College of Technical Agriculture
404 E 7th — Curtis NE 69025 — 308-367-4124 367-5203
TF: 800-328-7847 ■ *Web:* www.ncta.unl.edu

Southeast Community College
Beatrice 4771 W Scott Rd — Beatrice NE 68310 — 402-228-3468 228-2218*
**Fax:* Admissions ■ *TF:* 800-233-5027 ■ *Web:* www.southeast.edu
Milford 600 State St — Milford NE 68405 — 402-761-2131 761-2324
TF: 800-933-7223 ■ *Web:* www.southeast.edu

Vatterott College
Omaha 11818 I St — Omaha NE 68137 — 402-891-9411
Web: www.vatterott.edu

ITT Technical Institute Henderson
2300 Corporate Cir Ste 150 — Henderson NV 89074 — 702-558-5404
TF: 800-488-8459 ■ *Web:* www.itt-tech.edu

Berkeley College
Garrett Mountain 44 Rifle Camp Rd — Woodland Park NJ 07424 — 973-278-5400 278-9141
TF: 800-446-5400 ■ *Web:* www.berkeleycollege.edu
Paramus 64 E Midland Ave — Paramus NJ 07652 — 201-967-9667 265-6446
TF: 800-446-5400 ■ *Web:* www.berkeleycollege.edu
Woodbridge 430 Rahway Ave — Woodbridge NJ 07095 — 732-750-1800 750-0652
TF: 800-446-5400 ■ *Web:* www.berkeleycollege.edu

DeVry University North Brunswick
630 US Hwy 1 — North Brunswick NJ 08902 — 800-333-3879 729-3965*
**Fax Area Code:* 732 ■ **Fax:* Admissions ■ *TF:* 800-333-3879 ■ *Web:* www.nj.devry.edu

Divers Academy International 1500 Liberty Pl — Erial NJ 08081 — 800-238-3483
TF: 800-238-3483 ■ *Web:* www.diversacademy.edu

Central New Mexico Community College
10549 Universe Blvd NW — Albuquerque NM 87114 — 505-224-3000 224-3237
TF: 888-453-1304 ■ *Web:* www.cnm.edu

ITT Technical Institute Albuquerque
5100 Masthead St NE — Albuquerque NM 87109 — 505-828-1114
TF: 800-636-1114 ■ *Web:* www.itt-tech.edu

Navajo Technical College PO Box 849 — Crownpoint NM 87313 — 505-786-4100 786-5644
Web: www.navajotech.edu

Southwestern Indian Polytechnic Institute
9169 Coors Blvd NW PO Box 10146 — Albuquerque NM 87120 — 505-346-2306 346-2311
TF: 800-586-7474 ■ *Web:* www.sipi.edu

American Academy McAllister Institute of Funeral Service
619 W 54th St 2nd Fl — New York NY 10019 — 212-757-1190 765-5923
TF: 866-932-2264 ■ *Web:* www.funeraleducation.org

Berkeley College New York City 3 E 43rd St — New York NY 10017 — 212-986-4343 818-1079
TF: 800-446-5400 ■ *Web:* www.berkeleycollege.edu

Berkeley College White Plains
99 Church St — White Plains NY 10601 — 914-694-1122 328-9469
TF: 800-446-5400 ■ *Web:* www.berkeleycollege.edu

Bramson ORT College 69-30 Austin St — Forest Hills NY 11375 — 718-261-5800 575-5119
Web: www.bramsonort.org

Bryant & Stratton College Albany
1259 Central Ave — Albany NY 12205 — 518-437-1802 437-1048
Web: www.bryantstratton.edu

Bryant & Stratton College Amherst
3650 Millersport Hwy — Getzville NY 14068 — 716-625-6300
Web: www.bryantstratton.edu

Bryant & Stratton College Buffalo
465 Main St Ste 400 — Buffalo NY 14203 — 716-884-9120 884-0091
Web: www.bryantstratton.edu

Bryant & Stratton College Greece
150 Bellwood Dr — Rochester NY 14606 — 585-720-0660
Web: www.bryantstratton.edu

Bryant & Stratton College Henrietta
1225 Jefferson Rd — Rochester NY 14623 — 585-292-5627 292-6015
Web: www.bryantstratton.edu

Bryant & Stratton College Southtowns
200 Red Tail — Orchard Park NY 14127 — 716-677-9500 677-9599
Web: www.bryantstratton.edu

Bryant & Stratton College Syracuse
953 James St — Syracuse NY 13203 — 315-472-6603 474-4383
Web: www.bryantstratton.edu

Bryant & Stratton College Syracuse North
8687 Carling Rd — Liverpool NY 13090 — 315-652-6500 652-5500
TF: 800-836-5627 ■ *Web:* www.bryantstratton.edu

Champlain Valley Educational Services
PO Box 455 — Plattsburgh NY 12901 — 518-561-0100
Web: www.cves.org

Cochran School of Nursing 967 N Broadway — Yonkers NY 10701 — 914-964-4444
Web: www.riversidehealth.org

College of Westchester (CW)
325 Central Ave — White Plains NY 10606 — 800-660-7093 948-5441*
**Fax Area Code:* 914 ■ **Fax:* Admissions ■ *TF:* 800-660-7093 ■ *Web:* www.cw.edu

Commercial Driver Training
600 Patton Ave — West Babylon NY 11704 — 631-249-1330
TF: 800-649-7447 ■ *Web:* www.cdtschool.com

DeVry University Long Island City
3020 Thomson Ave — Long Island NY 11101 — 718-472-2728
TF: 888-713-3879 ■ *Web:* www.devry.edu

Helene Fuld College of Nursing
24 E 120th St — New York NY 10035 — 212-616-7200 616-7299
Web: www.helenefuld.edu

Institute of Design & Construction (IDC)
141 Willoughby St — Brooklyn NY 11201 — 718-855-3661 852-5889
Web: www.idc.edu

ITT Technical Institute Albany 13 Airline Dr — Albany NY 12205 — 518-452-9300
TF: 800-489-1191 ■ *Web:* www.itt-tech.edu

ITT Technical Institute Getzville
2295 Millersport Hwy — Getzville NY 14068 — 716-689-2200
TF: 800-469-7593 ■ *Web:* www.itt-tech.edu

ITT Technical Institute Liverpool
235 Greenfield Pkwy — Liverpool NY 13088 — 315-461-8000
TF: 877-488-0011 ■ *Web:* www.itt-tech.edu

Jamestown Business College
7 Fairmount Ave PO Box 429 — Jamestown NY 14702 — 716-664-5100 664-3144
TF: 877-557-2575 ■ *Web:* www.jamestownbusinesscollege.edu

Monroe College 2501 Jerome Ave — Bronx NY 10468 — 718-933-6700 364-3552*
**Fax:* Admissions ■ *TF:* 800-556-6676 ■ *Web:* www.monroecollege.edu

New York Career Institute 11 Pk Pl 4th Fl — New York NY 10007 — 212-962-0002 385-7574
Web: www.nyci.edu

Phillips Beth Israel School of Nursing
776 Ave of the Americas — New York NY 10001 — 212-614-6110 614-6109

Plaza College 74-09 37th Ave — Jackson Heights NY 11372 — 718-779-1430 779-7423
Web: www.plazacollege.edu

Simmons Institute of Funeral Service
1828 S Ave — Syracuse NY 13207 — 315-475-5142 475-3817

TCI College of Technology 320 W 31st St — New York NY 10001 — 212-594-4000
TF: 800-878-8246 ■ *Web:* www.tcicollege.edu

Utica School of Commerce 201 Bleecker St — Utica NY 13501 — 315-733-2307 733-9281
TF: 800-321-4872 ■ *Web:* www.uscny.edu

Wood Tobe-Coburn School 8 E 40th St — New York NY 10016 — 212-686-9040
TF: 800-394-9663 ■ *Web:* www.woodtobecoburn.edu

Forsyth Technical Community College
2100 Silas Creek Pkwy — Winston-Salem NC 27103 — 336-723-0371 761-2399
TF: 800-870-3676 ■ *Web:* www.forsythtech.edu

ITT Technical Institute High Point
4050 Piedmont Pkwy — High Point NC 27265 — 336-819-5900
TF: 877-536-5231 ■ *Web:* www.itt-tech.edu

South College-Asheville
140 Sweeten Creek Rd — Asheville NC 28803 — 828-398-2500
Web: www.southcollegenc.edu

Stanly Community College 141 College Dr — Albemarle NC 28001 — 704-982-0121 982-0819
TF: 877-275-4219 ■ *Web:* www.stanly.edu

United Tribes Technical College
3315 University Dr — Bismarck ND 58504 — 701-255-3285 530-0640
Web: www.uttc.edu

Academy of Court Reporting Cleveland
2044 Euclid Ave — Cleveland OH 44115 — 888-314-7780
TF: 888-314-7780 ■ *Web:* www.acr.edu

Phone | Fax

Academy of Court Reporting Columbus
150 E Gay St ... Columbus OH 43215 614-221-7770 221-8429
TF: 866-865-8067 ■ *Web:* www.miamijacobs.edu

Bradford School 2469 Stelzer Rd ... Columbus OH 43219 614-416-6200
TF: 800-678-7981 ■ *Web:* www.bradfordschoolcolumbus.edu

Brown Mackie College Akron 755 White Pond Dr ... Akron OH 44320 330-869-3600 869-3650
Web: www.brownmackie.edu

Brown Mackie College Canton
4300 Munson Ave NW ... North Canton OH 44718 330-494-1214 494-8112
Web: www.brownmackie.edu

Brown Mackie College Cincinnati
1011 Glendale-Milford Rd ... Cincinnati OH 45215 513-771-2424 771-3413
Web: www.brownmackie.edu

Brown Mackie College Findlay
1700 Fostoria Ave Ste 100 ... Findlay OH 45840 419-423-2211 423-0725
TF: 800-842-3687 ■ *Web:* www.brownmackie.edu

Bryant & Stratton College
Cleveland 3121 Euclid Ave ... Cleveland OH 44115 216-771-1700 771-7787
TF: 866-948-0571 ■ *Web:* www.bryantstratton.edu
Eastlake 35350 Curtis Blvd ... Eastlake OH 44095 440-510-1112 306-2015
Web: www.bryantstratton.edu
Parma 12955 Snow Rd ... Parma OH 44130 216-265-3151 265-0325
Web: www.bryantstratton.edu

Central Ohio Technical College
1179 University Dr ... Newark OH 43055 740-366-9494
Web: www.cotc.edu

Cincinnati College of Mortuary Science
645 W N Bend Rd ... Cincinnati OH 45224 513-761-2020 761-3333
TF: 888-377-8433 ■ *Web:* www.ccms.edu

Cleveland Institute of Electronics
1776 E 17th St ... Cleveland OH 44114 216-781-9400 781-0331
TF: 800-243-6446 ■ *Web:* www.cie-wc.edu

Davis College 4747 Monroe St ... Toledo OH 43623 419-473-2700 473-2472
TF: 800-477-7021 ■ *Web:* www.daviscollege.edu

DeVry University Dayton
3610 Pentagon Blvd Ste 100 ... Dayton OH 45431 937-320-3200
Web: www.devry.edu

Eastern Gateway Community College
4000 Sunset Blvd ... Steubenville OH 43952 740-264-5591 264-1338
TF: 800-682-6553 ■ *Web:* egcc.edu

ETI Technical College of Niles
2076 Youngstown-Warren Rd ... Niles OH 44446 330-652-9919 652-4399
Web: www.eticollege.edu

Hocking College 3301 Hocking Pkwy ... Nelsonville OH 45764 740-753-3591 753-7065
TF: 877-462-5464 ■ *Web:* www.hocking.edu

ITT Technical Institute Dayton
3325 S- Eight Rd ... Dayton OH 45414 937-264-7700
TF: 800-568-3241 ■ *Web:* www.itt-tech.edu

ITT Technical Institute Norwood
4750 Wesley Ave ... Norwood OH 45212 513-531-8300
TF: 800-314-8324 ■ *Web:* www.itt-tech.edu

ITT Technical Institute Strongsville
14955 Sprague Rd ... Strongsville OH 44136 440-234-9091
TF: 800-331-1488 ■ *Web:* www.itt-tech.edu

ITT Technical Institute Warrensville Heights
4700 Richmond Rd ... Warrensville Heights OH 44128 216-896-6500
TF: 800-741-3494 ■ *Web:* www.itt-tech.edu

ITT Technical Institute Youngstown
1030 N Meridian Rd ... Youngstown OH 44509 330-270-1600
TF: 800-832-5001 ■ *Web:* www.itt-tech.edu

James A Rhodes State College 4240 Campus Dr ... Lima OH 45804 419-995-8320 995-8098*
**Fax:* Admissions ■ *Web:* www.rhodesstate.edu

Marion Technical College 1467 Mt Vernon Ave ... Marion OH 43302 740-389-4636 389-6136
TF: 800-772-1213 ■ *Web:* www.mtc.edu

North Central State College
2441 Kenwood Cir ... Mansfield OH 44906 419-755-4800 755-4750
TF: 888-755-4899 ■ *Web:* www.ncstatecollege.edu

Northwest State Community College
22600 SR-34 ... Archbold OH 43502 419-267-5511 267-3688
Web: www.northweststate.edu

Remington College Cleveland
14445 Broadway Ave ... Cleveland OH 44125 216-502-3035
Web: www.remingtoncollege.edu

Stark State College of Technology
6200 Frank Ave NW ... North Canton OH 44720 330-494-6170 497-6313
TF: 800-797-8275 ■ *Web:* www.starkstate.edu

University of Northwestern Ohio 1441 N Cable Rd ... Lima OH 45805 419-998-3120 998-3139
Web: www.unoh.edu

Zane State College 1555 Newark Rd ... Zanesville OH 43701 740-454-2501 454-0035
TF: 800-686-8324 ■ *Web:* www.zanestate.edu

Indian Capital Technology Ctr
2403 N 41st St E ... Muskogee OK 74403 918-687-6383
TF: 800-757-0877 ■ *Web:* www.ictctech.com

Oklahoma State University
219 Student Union Bldg ... Stillwater OK 74078 405-744-5000 744-7092
TF: 800-852-1255 ■ *Web:* www.okstate.edu
Okmulgee 1801 E Fourth St ... Okmulgee OK 74447 918-293-4678 293-4650
TF: 800-722-4471 ■ *Web:* go.osuit.edu

Spartan College of Aeronautics & Technology
8820 E Pine St PO Box 582833 ... Tulsa OK 74115 918-836-6886 831-5287
TF Admissions: 800-331-1204 ■ *Web:* www.spartan.edu

ITT Technical Institute Portland
9500 NE Cascades Pkwy ... Portland OR 97220 503-255-6500
TF: 800-234-5488 ■ *Web:* www.itt-tech.edu

American College 270 S Bryn Mawr Ave ... Bryn Mawr PA 19010 610-526-1000 526-1300*
**Fax:* Admissions ■ *TF:* 888-263-7265 ■ *Web:* www.theamericancollege.edu

Aviation Institute of Maintenance
3001 Grant Ave ... Philadelphia PA 19114 215-676-7700
Web: www.aviationmaintenance.edu

Cambria-Rowe Business College (CRBC)
221 Central Ave ... Johnstown PA 15902 814-536-5168
TF: 800-639-2273 ■ *Web:* www.crbc.net

Central Pennsylvania College
600 Valley Rd PO Box 309 ... Summerdale PA 17093 717-732-0702 732-5254
TF: 800-759-2727 ■ *Web:* www.centralpenn.edu

Dean Institute of Technology
1501 W Liberty Ave ... Pittsburgh PA 15226 412-531-4433 531-4435
Web: www.deantech.edu

DeVry University Fort Washington
1140 Virginia Dr ... Fort Washington PA 19034 215-591-5700 591-5745
Web: www.devry.edu

DuBois Business College 1 Beaver Dr ... Du Bois PA 15801 814-371-6920 371-3974
TF: 800-692-6213 ■ *Web:* www.dbcollege.com

Erie Business Ctr
Erie 246 W Ninth St ... Erie PA 16501 814-456-7504 456-4882

Everest Institute 100 Forbes Ave Ste 1200 ... Pittsburgh PA 15222 412-261-4520 261-4546
Web: www.everest.edu

ITT Technical Institute Harrisburg
449 Eisenhower Blvd Ste 100 ... Harrisburg PA 17111 717-565-1700
TF: 800-847-4756 ■ *Web:* www.itt-tech.edu

Johnson College 3427 N Main Ave ... Scranton PA 18508 570-342-6404 348-2181*
**Fax:* Admissions ■ *TF:* 800-293-9675 ■ *Web:* www.johnson.edu

Lansdale School of Business
290 Wissahickon Ave ... North Wales PA 19454 215-699-5700 699-8770
TF: 800-219-0486 ■ *Web:* www.lsb.edu

Lincoln Technical Institute
5151 Tilghman St ... Allentown PA 18104 610-398-5300 395-2706
Web: www.lincolntech.edu

Lincoln Technical Institute
9191 Torresdale Ave ... Philadelphia PA 19136 215-335-0800 335-1443
Web: www.lincolntech.edu

Mixology Wine Institute 77 W Broad St ... Bethlehem PA 18018 610-814-2900
Web: mixologywine.com

Penn Commercial Inc 242 Oak Spring Rd ... Washington PA 15301 724-222-5330 222-4722
TF: 888-309-7484 ■ *Web:* www.penncommercial.edu

Penn Foster Career School 925 Oak St ... Scranton PA 18515 570-342-7701
TF: 800-275-4410 ■ *Web:* pennfoster.edu

Pennco Tech 3815 Otter St ... Bristol PA 19007 215-785-0111
TF General: 844-226-0975 ■ *Web:* www.penncotech.edu

Pennsylvania College of Technology
1 College Ave ... Williamsport PA 17701 570-326-3761 321-5551
TF Admissions: 800-367-9222 ■ *Web:* www.pct.edu

Pennsylvania Institute of Technology (PIT)
800 Manchester Ave ... Media PA 19063 610-892-1500 892-1533*
**Fax:* Admissions ■ *TF Admissions:* 800-422-0025 ■ *Web:* www.pit.edu

Philadelphia College of Osteopathic Medicine (PCOM)
4170 City Ave ... Philadelphia PA 19131 215-871-6100
TF Admissions: 800-999-6998 ■ *Web:* www.pcom.edu

Pittsburgh Institute of Aeronautics (PIA)
5 Allegheny County Airport ... West Mifflin PA 15122 412-346-2100 346-2170
TF: 800-444-1440 ■ *Web:* www.pia.edu

Pittsburgh Institute of Mortuary Science Inc
5808 Baum Blvd ... Pittsburgh PA 15206 412-362-8500 362-1684
TF: 800-933-5808 ■ *Web:* www.pims.edu

Pittsburgh Technical Institute (PTI)
1111 McKee Rd ... Oakdale PA 15071 412-809-5100 809-5121*
**Fax:* Admissions ■ *TF:* 800-784-9675 ■ *Web:* www.pti.edu

Thaddeus Stevens College of Technology (TSCT)
750 E King St ... Lancaster PA 17602 717-299-7701 391-6929
TF: 800-842-3832 ■ *Web:* www.stevenstech.org

Triangle Tech Inc
Du Bois PO Box 551 ... Du Bois PA 15801 814-371-2090 371-9227
TF: 800-874-8324 ■ *Web:* www.triangle-tech.edu
Erie 2000 Liberty St ... Erie PA 16502 814-453-6016 454-2818
TF: 800-874-8324 ■ *Web:* www.triangle-tech.edu
Greensburg 222 E Pittsburgh St ... Greensburg PA 15601 724-832-1050 834-0325
TF: 800-874-8324 ■ *Web:* www.triangle-tech.edu

Welder Training & Testing Institute
1144 N Graham St ... Allentown PA 18109 610-820-9551 820-0271
TF: 800-223-9884 ■ *Web:* www.welderinstitute.com

Williamson Free School of Mechanical Trades, The
106 S New Middletown Rd ... Media PA 19063 610-566-1776 566-6502
TF: 888-565-1095 ■ *Web:* www.williamson.edu

Wyotech Blairsville 500 Innovation Dr ... Blairsville PA 15717 724-459-9500 459-6499
Web: www.wyotech.edu

New England Institute of Technology
2500 Post Rd ... Warwick RI 02886 401-467-7744 738-5122
TF: 800-736-7744 ■ *Web:* www.neit.edu

Central Carolina Technical College
506 N Guignard Dr ... Sumter SC 29150 803-778-1961 778-6696
Web: www.cctech.edu

Denmark Technical College
1126 Solomon Blatt Blvd PO Box 327 ... Denmark SC 29042 803-793-5176 793-5942*
**Fax:* Admissions ■ *Web:* www.denmarktech.edu

Florence-Darlington Technical College
2715 W Lucas St ... Florence SC 29502 843-661-8324
TF: 800-228-5745 ■ *Web:* www.fdtc.edu

Horry-Georgetown Technical College
2050 E Hwy 501 ... Conway SC 29526 843-347-3186 347-4207
TF: 855-544-4482 ■ *Web:* www.hgtc.edu
Grand Strand Campus 743 Hemlock Ave ... Myrtle Beach SC 29577 843-477-0808 477-0775
TF: 855-544-4482 ■ *Web:* www.hgtc.edu

ITT Technical Institute Greenville
6 Independence Pointe
Independence Corporate Pk ... Greenville SC 29615 864-288-0777
TF: 800-932-4488 ■ *Web:* www.itt-tech.edu

Piedmont Technical College
620 N Emerald Rd ... Greenwood SC 29646 864-941-8324 941-8555
TF: 800-868-5528 ■ *Web:* www.ptc.edu

Spartanburg Community College
800 Brisack Rd PO Box 4386 ... Spartanburg SC 29305 864-592-4800 592-4564
TF: 866-591-3700 ■ *Web:* www.sccsc.edu

Tri-County Technical College 7900 Hwy 76 ... Pendleton SC 29670 864-646-8361 646-1890
TF: 866-269-5677 ■ *Web:* www.tctc.edu

Trident Technical College (TTC)
7000 Rivers Ave PO Box 118067 ... North Charleston SC 29406 843-574-6111 574-6483*
**Fax:* Admissions ■ *TF:* 877-349-7184 ■ *Web:* www.tridenttech.edu

Southeast Technical Institute
2320 N Career Ave ... Sioux Falls SD 57107 605-367-8355 367-4372*
**Fax:* Hum Res ■ *TF:* 800-247-0789 ■ *Web:* www.southeasttech.edu

Name / Address	City	State	Zip	Phone	Fax
Fountainhead College of Technology 3203 Tazewell Pk; *TF:* 888-218-7335 ■ *Web:* www.fountainheadcollege.edu	Knoxville	TN	37918	865-688-9422	688-2419
ITT Technical Institute Cordova 7260 Goodlett Farms Pkwy; *TF:* 866-444-5141 ■ *Web:* www.itt-tech.edu	Cordova	TN	38016	901-381-0200	
ITT Technical Institute Nashville 2845 Elm Hill Pk; *TF:* 800-331-8386 ■ *Web:* www.itt-tech.edu	Nashville	TN	37214	615-889-8700	
John A Gupton College 1616 Church St; *Web:* guptoncollege.edu	Nashville	TN	37203	615-327-3927	321-4518
Nashville State Community College (NSCC) 120 White Bridge Rd; **Fax:* Admissions ■ *TF:* 800-272-7363 ■ *Web:* www.nscc.edu	Nashville	TN	37209	615-353-3333	353-3243*
National College of Business & Technology Bristol 1328 Hwy 11 W; *TF:* 888-956-2732 ■ *Web:* www.national-college.edu	Bristol	TN	37620	423-878-4440	
National College of Business & Technology Nashville 1638 Bell Rd; *TF:* 855-800-1715 ■ *Web:* national-college.edu	Nashville	TN	37211	615-333-3344	
Northeast State Technical Community College 2425 Hwy 75 PO Box 246; *TF:* 800-836-7822 ■ *Web:* www.northeaststate.edu	Blountville	TN	37617	423-323-3191	323-0217
Remington College Memphis 2710 Nonconnah Blvd; *Web:* www.remingtoncollege.edu	Memphis	TN	38132	901-345-1000	
South College 3904 Lonas Dr; *TF:* 877-557-2575 ■ *Web:* www.southcollegetn.edu	Knoxville	TN	37909	865-251-1800	584-7339
Aviation Institute of Maintenance Houston 7651 Airport Blvd; *TF:* 888-349-5387 ■ *Web:* www.aviationmaintenance.edu	Houston	TX	77061	713-644-7777	644-0902
Court Reporting Institute of Dallas 1341 W Mockingbird Ln Ste 200-E; *TF:* 866-382-1284 ■ *Web:* www.cri.edu	Dallas	TX	75247	214-350-9722	
Court Reporting Institute of Houston 13101 NW Fwy Ste 100; *TF:* 866-996-8300 ■ *Web:* www.cri.edu	Houston	TX	77040	713-996-8300	
Dallas Institute of Funeral Service 3909 S Buckner Blvd; *TF:* 800-235-5444 ■ *Web:* www.dallasinstitute.edu	Dallas	TX	75227	214-388-5466	388-0316
DeVry University Houston 11125 Equity Dr; *TF:* 866-338-7934 ■ *Web:* www.devry.edu	Houston	TX	77041	713-973-3100	896-7650
DeVry University Irving 4800 Regent Blvd Ste 200; *TF:* 800-633-3879 ■ *Web:* www.devry.edu/universities/texas/irving-campus.html	Irving	TX	75063	972-929-6777	929-6778
Everest Institute San Antonio 6550 First Pk Ten Blvd; *Web:* www.everest.edu	San Antonio	TX	78213	210-732-7800	731-9313
ITT Technical Institute Arlington 551 Ryan Plz Dr; *TF:* 888-288-4950 ■ *Web:* www.itt-tech.edu	Arlington	TX	76011	817-794-5100	
ITT Technical Institute Austin 6330 Hwy 290 E Ste 150; *TF:* 800-431-0677 ■ *Web:* www.itt-tech.edu	Austin	TX	78723	512-467-6800	
ITT Technical Institute Houston 15651 N Fwy; *TF:* 800-879-6486 ■ *Web:* www.itt-tech.edu	Houston	TX	77090	281-873-0512	
ITT Technical Institute Richardson 2101 Waterview Pkwy; *TF:* 888-488-5761 ■ *Web:* www.itt-tech.edu	Richardson	TX	75080	972-690-9100	
ITT Technical Institute San Antonio 5700 NW Pkwy; *TF:* 800-880-0570 ■ *Web:* www.itt-tech.edu	San Antonio	TX	78249	210-694-4612	
Remington College Dallas 1800 Eastgate Dr; *Web:* www.remingtoncollege.edu	Garland	TX	75041	972-686-7878	
Wade College 1950 N Stemmons Fwy LB 562 Ste 4080; *TF:* 800-624-4850 ■ *Web:* www.wadecollege.edu	Dallas	TX	75207	214-637-3530	637-0827
ITT Technical Institute Murray 920 Levoy Dr; *TF:* 800-365-2136 ■ *Web:* www.itt-tech.edu	Murray	UT	84123	801-263-3313	
Latter Day Saints Business College 95 North 300 West; *TF:* 800-999-5767 ■ *Web:* www.ldsbc.edu	Salt Lake City	UT	84101	801-524-8100	524-1900
Sterling College PO Box 72; *TF:* 800-648-3591 ■ *Web:* www.sterlingcollege.edu	Craftsbury Common	VT	05827	802-586-7711	586-2596
Vermont Technical College PO Box 500; *TF:* 800-442-8821 ■ *Web:* www.vtc.edu	Randolph Center	VT	05061	802-728-1000	728-1321
Bryant & Stratton College Richmond 8141 Hull St Rd; *TF:* 866-948-0571 ■ *Web:* www.bryantstratton.edu	Richmond	VA	23235	804-745-2444	745-6884
Bryant & Stratton College Virginia Beach 301 Ctr Pt Dr; *Web:* www.bryantstratton.edu	Virginia Beach	VA	23462	757-499-7900	499-9977
DeVry University Crystal City 2450 Crystal Dr; *Web:* www.devry.edu	Arlington	VA	22202	703-414-4000	
Everest College 14555 Potomac Mills Rd Ste 200; *TF:* 888-223-8556 ■ *Web:* www.everest.edu	Woodbridge	VA	22192	571-408-2100	
ITT Technical Institute Norfolk 5425 Robin Hood Rd Ste 100; *TF:* 888-253-8324 ■ *Web:* www.itt-tech.edu	Norfolk	VA	23513	757-466-1260	
ITT Technical Institute Richmond 300 Gateway Centre Pkwy; *TF:* 888-330-4888 ■ *Web:* www.itt-tech.edu	Richmond	VA	23235	804-330-4992	
ITT Technical Institute Springfield 7300 Boston Blvd; *TF:* 866-817-8324 ■ *Web:* www.itt-tech.edu	Springfield	VA	22153	703-440-9535	
Jefferson College of Health Sciences 101 Elm Ave SE; *TF:* 888-985-8483 ■ *Web:* www.jchs.edu	Roanoke	VA	24031	540-985-8483	224-6703
National College of Business & Technology					
Charlottesville 3926 Seminole Trl; *Web:* national-college.edu	Charlottesville	VA	22911	434-295-0136	
Danville 336 Old Riverside Dr; *Web:* www.national-college.edu	Danville	VA	24541	434-793-6822	
Harrisonburg 1515 Country Club Rd; *Web:* an.edu	Harrisonburg	VA	22802	540-432-0943	
Lynchburg 104 Candlewood Ct; *Web:* national-college.edu	Lynchburg	VA	24502	434-239-3500	
Martinsville 905 N Memorial Blvd; *Web:* www.national-college.edu	Martinsville	VA	24112	276-632-5621	
Roanoke Valley 1813 E Main St; *TF:* 800-664-1886 ■ *Web:* www.national-college.edu	Salem	VA	24153	540-986-1800	
DeVry University Federal Way 3600 S 344th Way; *TF:* 877-923-3879 ■ *Web:* www.devry.edu	Federal Way	WA	98001	253-943-2800	
Highline Community College 2400 S 240th St; *Web:* www.highline.edu	Des Moines	WA	98198	206-878-3710	870-4855
ITT Technical Institute Seattle 12720 Gateway Dr Ste 100; *TF:* 800-422-2029 ■ *Web:* www.itt-tech.edu	Seattle	WA	98168	206-244-3300	
Everest Institute 5514 Big Tyler Rd; *Web:* www.everest.edu	Cross Lanes	WV	25313	304-776-6290	776-6262
Huntington Junior College 900 Fifth Ave; *TF:* 800-344-4522 ■ *Web:* www.huntingtonjuniorcollege.com	Huntington	WV	25701	304-697-7550	697-7554
West Virginia Junior College					
Charleston 1000 Virginia St E; *TF:* 800-924-5208 ■ *Web:* www.wvjc.edu	Charleston	WV	25301	304-345-2820	
Morgantown 148 Willey St; *Web:* www.wvjc.edu	Morgantown	WV	26505	304-296-8282	
West Virginia Junior College - Bridgeport 176 Thompson Dr; *TF:* 800-470-5627 ■ *Web:* www.wvjc.edu	Bridgeport	WV	26330	304-842-4007	842-8191
Blackhawk Technical College 6004 S County Rd G; *TF:* 800-498-1282 ■ *Web:* www.blackhawk.edu	Janesville	WI	53546	608-758-6900	743-4407
Bryant & Stratton College Milwaukee 310 W Wisconsin Ave Ste 500-E; *TF:* 866-948-0571 ■ *Web:* www.bryantstratton.edu	Milwaukee	WI	53203	414-276-5200	276-3930
Chippewa Valley Technical College 620 W Clairemont Ave; *TF:* 800-547-2882 ■ *Web:* www.cvtc.edu	Eau Claire	WI	54701	715-833-6200	833-6470
Fox Valley Technical College 1825 N Bluemound Dr PO Box 2277; *TF:* 800-735-3882 ■ *Web:* www.fvtc.edu	Appleton	WI	54912	920-735-5600	735-2484
Gateway Technical College 3520 30th Ave; *TF:* 800-247-7122 ■ *Web:* www.gtc.edu	Kenosha	WI	53144	262-564-2200	564-2201
Herzing College Madison 5218 E Terr Dr; *TF:* 800-582-1227 ■ *Web:* www.herzing.edu	Madison	WI	53718	608-249-6611	249-8593
ITT Technical Institute Greenfield 6300 W Layton Ave; *Web:* www.itt-tech.edu	Greenfield	WI	53220	414-282-9494	
Lakeshore Technical College 1290 N Ave; *TF:* 888-468-6582 ■ *Web:* www.gotoltc.com	Cleveland	WI	53015	920-693-1000	693-3561
Madison Area Technical College 1701 Wright St; *TF:* 800-322-6282 ■ *Web:* www.madisoncollege.edu	Madison	WI	53704	608-246-6100	246-6880
Milwaukee Area Technical College 700 W State St; *TF:* 866-211-3380 ■ *Web:* www.matc.edu	Milwaukee	WI	53233	414-297-6600	297-6496
Moraine Park Technical College 235 N National Ave; *TF:* 800-472-4554 ■ *Web:* www.morainepark.edu	Fond du Lac	WI	54935	920-922-8611	924-3421
Northcentral Technical College 1000 W Campus Dr; *TF:* 888-682-7144 ■ *Web:* www.ntc.edu	Wausau	WI	54401	715-675-3331	675-9776
Northeast Wisconsin Technical College PO Box 19042; *TF:* 800-422-6982 ■ *Web:* www.nwtc.edu	Green Bay	WI	54307	920-498-5400	
Southwest Wisconsin Technical College (SWTC) 1800 Bronson Blvd; *TF:* 800-362-3322 ■ *Web:* www.swtc.edu	Fennimore	WI	53809	608-822-3262	822-6019
Waukesha County Technical College 800 Main St; *Web:* www.wctc.edu	Pewaukee	WI	53072	262-691-5566	
Western Technical College 400 Seventh St N; *TF:* 800-322-9982 ■ *Web:* www.westerntc.edu	La Crosse	WI	54601	608-785-9200	789-6206
Wisconsin Indianhead Technical College					
New Richmond Campus 1019 S Knowles Ave; *TF:* 800-243-9482 ■ *Web:* www.witc.edu	New Richmond	WI	54017	715-246-6561	246-2777
Rice Lake Campus 1900 College Dr; *TF:* 800-243-9482 ■ *Web:* www.witc.edu	Rice Lake	WI	54868	715-234-7082	234-5172
Superior Campus 600 N 21 St; *TF:* 800-243-9482 ■ *Web:* www.witc.edu	Superior	WI	54880	715-394-6677	394-3771
WyoTech 4373 N Third St; *Web:* www.wyotech.com	Laramie	WY	82072	307-742-3776	

801 VOTING SYSTEMS & SOFTWARE

Name / Address	City	State	Zip	Phone	Fax
Avante International Technology Inc (AIT) 70 Washington Rd; *TF:* 800-735-5040 ■ *Web:* www.aitechnology.com	Princeton Junction	NJ	08550	609-799-9388	799-9308
Diebold Inc 5995 Mayfair Rd; *NYSE: DBD* ■ *TF:* 800-999-3600 ■ *Web:* www.diebold.com	North Canton	OH	44720	330-490-4000	
Dynapar 1675 Delany Rd; *TF General:* 800-873-8731 ■ *Web:* www.dynapar.com	Gurnee	IL	60031	800-873-8731	
Election Data Corp 29751 Vly Ctr Rd; *Web:* www.electiondata.com	Valley Center	CA	92082	760-751-1131	751-1141
Election Services Corp 70 Trade Zone Ct; *Web:* electionservicescorp.com	Ronkonkoma	NY	11779	516-248-4200	248-4770
Election Systems & Software Inc 11208 John Galt Blvd; *TF General:* 877-377-8683 ■ *Web:* essvote.com	Omaha	NE	68137	402-593-0101	593-8107

Phone Fax

Elections USA Inc 1927 E Saw Mill Rd. . . . . Quakertown PA 18951 215-538-0779 538-3283
TF: 800-789-8683 ■ *Web:* www.electionsusainc.com

Hart InterCivic
15500 Wells Port Dr PO Box 80649. Austin TX 78708 512-252-6400 252-6466
TF: 800-223-4278 ■ *Web:* www.hartintercivic.com

MicroVote General Corp
6366 Guilford Ave. . . . . .Indianapolis IN 46220 317-257-4900 254-3269
TF: 800-257-4901 ■ *Web:* www.microvote.com

UniLect Corp PO Box 3026 . . . . .Danville CA 94526 925-833-8660 833-8874
TF: 888-864-5328 ■ *Web:* www.unilect.com

802 WALLCOVERINGS

Phone Fax

Blonder Home Accents 3950 Prospect Ave . . . . Cleveland OH 44115 216-431-3561 431-4748

Blue Mountain Wallcoverings Inc
15 Akron Rd . . . . .Etobicoke ON M8W1T3 416-251-1678
Web: www.blmtn.com

Butler/Newco Printing & Laminating Inc
250 Hamburg Tpke . . . . .Butler NJ 07405 973-838-8550 838-1767
Web: www.butlerprinting.com

Fashion Wallcoverings 4005 Carnegie Ave. . . . . Cleveland OH 44103 216-432-1600
TF Orders: 800-362-9930 ■ *Web:* www.fashionwallcoverings.com

Goldcrest Wallcoverings PO Box 245. . . . . Slingerlands NY 12159 518-478-7214 478-7216
TF: 800-535-9513 ■ *Web:* www.wallcovering.com

J Josephson Inc 35 Horizon Blvd . . . . .South Hackensack NJ 07606 201-440-7000 440-7109*
**Fax:* Cust Svc ■ *Web:* www.jjosephson.com

Thibaut Inc 480 Frelinghuysen Ave . . . . Newark NJ 07114 973-643-1118 643-3050
TF: 800-223-0704 ■ *Web:* www.thibautdesign.com

York Wallcoverings Inc
750 Linden Ave PO Box 5166. . . . . .York PA 17405 717-846-4456 843-5624
TF: 800-375-9675 ■ *Web:* www.yorkwall.com

803 WAREHOUSING & STORAGE

See Also Logistics Services (Transportation & Warehousing) p. 2681

803-1 Commercial Warehousing

Phone Fax

Acme Distribution Centers Inc
18101 E Colfax Ave . . . . .Aurora CO 80011 303-340-2100 340-2424
TF: 800-444-3614 ■ *Web:* www.acmedistribution.com

All Source Security Container Mfg Corp
40 Mills Rd. . . . . .Barrie ON L4N6H4 705-726-6460 726-5017
TF: 866-526-4579 ■ *Web:* www.allsourcemfg.com

American Warehouses Inc
1918 Collingsworth St . . . . .Houston TX 77009 713-228-6381 228-5913
Web: www.americanwarehouses.com

ASW Global LLC 3375 Gilchrist Rd . . . . Mogadore OH 44260 330-733-6291
TF: 888-826-5087 ■ *Web:* www.aswglobal.com

ATCO Industries Inc
7300 Fifteen Mile Rd . . . . .Sterling Heights MI 48312 586-795-9595
Web: www.atcoindustries.com

Automated Records Management Systems Inc
1850 Enterprise Dr . . . . De Pere WI 54115 920-339-0135
Web: www.arms4rim.com

Barrett Distribution Centers Inc
15 Freedom Way. . . . . .Franklin MA 02038 508-553-8800
Web: www.barrettdistribution.com

Bay Logistics Inc 1202 Pontaluna Rd. . . . . .Spring Lake MI 49456 231-799-1015
Web: www.baylogistics.com

Brundage Management Co Inc
254 Spencer Ln . . . . .San Antonio TX 78201 210-735-9393 735-2061
Web: www.brundagemgt.com

Case Systems Inc 2700 James Savage Rd . . . . .Midland MI 48642 989-496-9510
Web: www.casesystems.com

Customized Distribution Services Inc
20 Harry Shupe Blvd. . . . . .Wharton NJ 07885 973-366-5090
Web: www.dsdcds.com

D & D Distribution Services Inc
789 Kings Mill Rd. . . . . .York PA 17403 717-845-1646 846-0414
TF: 877-683-3358 ■ *Web:* www.dd-dist.com

Dart Entities 1430 S Eastman Ave. . . . . .Los Angeles CA 90023 323-264-1011 264-6925
Web: www.dartentities.com

Datalok Co 5990 Malburg Way .Los Angeles CA 90058 323-582-6100 581-8285
Web: www.datalok.com

DD Jones Transfer & Warehouse Co Inc
2121 Old Greenbrier Rd . . . . .Chesapeake VA 23320 757-494-0225 494-0291
TF: 800-335-4787 ■ *Web:* www.ddjones.com

Derby Industries LLC 4451 Robards Ln . . . . .Louisville KY 40218 502-451-7373 451-6330
TF: 800-569-4812 ■ *Web:* www.derbyllc.com

Distribution Technology Inc
1701 Continental Blvd . . . . Charlotte NC 28273 704-587-5587 587-5591
Web: www.distributiontechnology.com

E L Hamm Assoc Inc
4801 Columbus St Ste 400. . . . . .Virginia Beach VA 23462 757-497-5000
Web: www.elhamm.com

Evans Distribution Systems
18765 Seaway Dr . . . . .Melvindale MI 48122 313-388-3200 388-0136
TF: 800-653-8267 ■ *Web:* www.evansdist.com

Federal Compress & Warehouse Company Inc (FCWI)
6060 Primacy Pkwy Ste 400. . . . . .Memphis TN 38119 901-524-4000 524-4050
Web: www.federalcompress.com

GSC Logistics Inc 530 Water St 5th Fl . . . . Oakland CA 94607 510-844-3700
Web: www.gschq.com

Gulf Compress 201 N 19th St .Corpus Christi TX 78408 361-882-5489
Web: www.gulfcompress.com

Gulf Winds International Inc 411 Brisbane St. . . . . .Houston TX 77061 713-747-4909 747-5330
TF: 866-238-4909 ■ *Web:* www.gwii.com

Phone Fax

Habco Beverage Systems Inc
501 Gordon Baker Rd . . . . .Toronto ON M2H2S6 416-491-6008 491-6982
TF: 800-448-0244 ■ *Web:* www.habcotech.com

Harley Marine Services Inc 910 SW Spokane St . . . . Seattle WA 98134 206-628-0051
Web: www.harleymarine.com

Holman Distribution Ctr of Oregon Inc
2300 SE Beta St . . . . Milwaukie OR 97222 503-652-1912
Web: holmanusa.com

Hyperlogistics Group Inc
9301 Intermodal Ct N Rickenbacker Global Logistics Pk
. . . . Columbus OH 43217 614-497-0800
Web: www.hyperlog.com

Iron Mountain 745 Atlantic Ave. . . . . .Boston MA 02111 800-899-4766
NYSE: IRM ■ *TF:* 800-899-4766 ■ *Web:* www.ironmountain.com

Kenco Group Inc 2001 Riverside Dr . . . . Chattanooga TN 37406 800-758-3289
TF: 800-758-3289 ■ *Web:* www.kencogroup.com

Longistics Transportation Inc
10900 World Trade Blvd. . . . . Raleigh NC 27617 919-872-7626 872-2883
TF: 800-289-0082 ■ *Web:* www.longistics.com

Mackinnon Transport Inc 405 Laird Rd . . . . .Guelph ON N1G4P7 519-821-2311 821-1834
TF: 800-265-9394 ■ *Web:* www.mackinnontransport.com

Mid-West Terminal Warehouse Company Inc
1700 Universal Ave. . . . . .Kansas City MO 64120 816-231-8811 231-0020
Web: www.mwtco.com

Monsoon Commerce Solutions Inc
1250 45th St Ste 100 . . . . Emeryville CA 94608 510-594-4500 652-2403
TF: 800-520-2294 ■ *Web:* www.monsooncommerce.com

MSI General Corp PO Box 7 . . . . Oconomowoc WI 53066 262-367-3661
Web: www.msigeneral.com

Murphy Warehouse Co 701 24th Ave SE. . . . . Minneapolis MN 55414 612-623-1200 623-9108
Web: www.murphywarehouse.com

Offshore International Inc 8350 E Old Vail Rd. . . . . Tucson AZ 85747 520-889-0022
Web: www.offshoregroup.com

Oilseeds International Ltd
8 Jackson St. . . . . .San Francisco CA 94111 415-956-7251
Web: www.oilseedssf.com

Pacific Storage Co PO Box 334. . . . . Stockton CA 95201 209-320-6600 465-9533
TF: 888-823-5467 ■ *Web:* www.pacificstorage.com

PenserSC 11001 Pritchard Rd . . . . .Jacksonville FL 32219 904-786-1811
Web: www.pensersc.com

Quality Logistics Systems Inc PO Box 5637 . . . . Meridian MS 39302 601-483-0265 483-7928
Web: www.qualitylogistics.com

Recall Inc
180 Technology Pkwy NW 180 Technology Pkwy . . . . Norcross GA 30092 770-776-1000
Web: www.recall.com

Robinson Terminal Warehouse Corp
1 Oronoco St . . . . .Alexandria VA 22314 703-836-8300 836-8307
Web: www.robinsonterminal.com

Security Storage Co 1701 Florida Ave NW . . . . .Washington DC 20009 202-234-5600 234-3513
TF: 888-903-7695 ■ *Web:* www.secor-group.com

SFI of Tennessee LLC 4768 Hungerford Rd. . . . . .Memphis TN 38118 901-363-1571
Web: www.sfifab.com

Shippers Group, The 8901 Forney Rd . . . . Dallas TX 75227 214-381-5050
Web: www.shipperswarehouse.com

Smart Warehousing LLC 18905 Kill Creek Rd. . . . . Edgerton KS 66021 913-888-3222
Web: www.smartwarehousing.com

SOPAKCO Inc 118 S Cypress St. . . . . Mullins SC 29574 843-464-7851 464-2096
Web: www.sopakco.com

Southern Warehousing & Distribution Inc
3232 N Pan Am Expy . . . . .San Antonio TX 78219 210-224-7771 226-9485
Web: www.southernwd.com

SRC Logistics Inc 2065 E Pythian. . . . . .Springfield MO 65802 417-864-4946
Web: www.srclogisticsinc.com

States Logistics Services Inc
5650 Dolly Ave. . . . . Buena Park CA 90621 714-521-6520
Web: www.stateslogistics.com

Tejas Logistics System PO Box 1339. . . . . .Waco TX 76703 254-753-0301 752-4452
TF: 800-535-9786 ■ *Web:* www.tejaswarehouse.com

Tri Union Express Inc 1939 N Lafayette Ct. . . . . .Griffith IN 46319 219-838-5400 838-1680
TF: 800-228-9098 ■ *Web:* www.triunion.com

Triad Manufacturing Inc 4321 Semple Ave . . . . Saint Louis MO 63120 314-381-5280 381-7786
Web: www.triadmfg.com

Vanderpol's Eggs Ltd 3911 Mt Lehman Rd . . . . .Abbotsford BC V2T5W5 604-856-4127
Web: www.vanderpolseggs.com

Verst Group Logistics Inc 300 Shorland Dr . . . . .Walton KY 41094 859-485-1212
Web: www.verstgroup.com

W O W Logistics Co 3040 W Wisconsin Ave . . . . Appleton WI 54914 920-734-9924 734-2697
TF: 800-236-3565 ■ *Web:* www.wowlogistics.com

Willis Day Storage Co
4100 Bennett Rd PO Box 676. . . . . .Toledo OH 43697 419-476-8000
Web: willisday.com

803-2 Refrigerated Storage

Phone Fax

American Growers Cooling Co 1225 Abbott St . . . . Salinas CA 93901 831-753-6555

Berkshire Refrigerated Warehousing
4550 S Packers Ave . . . . .Chicago IL 60609 773-254-2424

Burris Logistics 501 SE Fifth St PO Box 219 . . . . Milford DE 19963 302-839-5157 839-5175
TF: 800-805-8135 ■ *Web:* www.burrislogistics.com

MTC Logistics 4851 Holabird Ave. . . . . .Baltimore MD 21224 410-342-9300 522-1163
Web: mtccold.com

New Orleans Cold Storage & Warehouse Company Inc (NOCS)
3411 JouRdan Rd . . . . New Orleans LA 70126 504-944-4400
Web: www.nocs.com

Perley-Halladay Assn Inc 1037 Andrew Dr. . . . . .West Chester PA 19380 610-296-5800 647-1711
TF: 800-248-5800 ■ *Web:* www.perleyhalladay.com

United Freezer & Storage Co
650 N Meridian Rd . . . . Youngstown OH 44509 330-792-1739 792-2299
TF: 800-716-1416 ■ *Web:* www.unitedfreezer.com

				Phone	Fax
US Cold Storage Inc 201 Laurel Rd Ste 400 4 Echelon Plz *Web:* www.uscoldstorage.com	Voorhees	NJ	08043	856-354-8181	772-1876

803-3 Self-Storage Facilities

				Phone	Fax
A-American Self Storage Management Co Inc 11560 Tennessee Ave *TF:* 888-333-6479 ■ *Web:* www.aamericanselfstorage.com	Los Angeles	CA	90064	310-914-4022	914-4042
Derrel's Mini Storage 3265 W Ashlan Ave *Web:* www.derrels.com	Fresno	CA	93722	559-224-9900	224-1884
Devon Self Storage Holdings LLC 2000 Powell St Ste 1240 *Web:* www.devonselfstorage.com	Emeryville	CA	94608	510-450-1300	450-1325
Executive Self Storage Assoc Inc 5353 W Dartmouth Ave Ste 401 *Web:* www.executiveselfstorage.com	Denver	CO	80227	303-703-1289	703-1289
Hammond North Condominium Assn 5300 Hamilton Ave	Cincinnati	OH	45224	513-541-5252	
Lock Up Self Storage, The 800 Frontage Rd *Web:* www.thelockup.com	Northfield	IL	60093	847-441-7477	
Metro Storage LLC 13528 Boulton Blvd *Web:* www.metrostorage.com	Lake Forest	IL	60045	847-235-8900	235-8901
Olson Bros Contractors Inc 829 Chambers St	South Haven	MI	49090	269-637-4494	
Public Storage Inc 701 Western Ave *NYSE: PSA* ■ *TF Cust Svc:* 800-567-0759 ■ *Web:* www.publicstorage.com	Glendale	CA	91201	818-244-8080	
Shader Bros Corp 6325 Edgewater Dr *Web:* www.personalministorage.com	Orlando	FL	32810	407-297-3683	
Sovran Self Storage Inc 6467 Main St *NYSE: SSS* ■ *TF:* 800-242-1715 ■ *Web:* www.unclebobs.com	Buffalo	NY	14221	716-633-1850	
Stor-All Storage 1375 W Hillsboro Blvd *TF:* 877-786-7255 ■ *Web:* www.stor-all.com	Deerfield Beach	FL	33442	954-421-7888	426-1108

804 WASTE MANAGEMENT

See Also Recyclable Materials Recovery p. 3056; Remediation Services p. 3059

				Phone	Fax
Allied Waste Bettendorf 6449 Valley Dr *Web:* www.republicservices.com	Bettendorf	IA	52722	563-332-0050	
ARC Disposal & Recycling Company Inc 2101 S Busse Rd *Web:* www.republicservices.com	Mount Prospect	IL	60056	847-981-0091	981-9180
Aspen Waste Systems Inc 2951 Weeks Ave SE *Web:* www.aspenwaste.com	Minneapolis	MN	55414	612-884-8000	884-8010
Athens Services 14048 Valley Blvd *TF:* 888-336-6100 ■ *Web:* www.athensservices.com	La Puente	CA	91746	626-336-3636	
Avalon Holdings Corp 1 American Way *NYSE: AWX* ■ *Web:* www.avalonholdings.com	Warren	OH	44484	330-856-8800	856-8480
Basin Disposal Inc 2021 N Commercial Ave *TF:* 800-642-6447 ■ *Web:* www.basindisposal.com	Pasco	WA	99301	509-547-2476	547-8617
Bend Garbage & Recycling Inc 20835 NE Montana St PO Box 504 *Web:* www.bendgarbage.com	Bend	OR	97709	541-382-2263	383-3640
Bluebonnet Waste Control PO Box 223845 *Web:* www.bluebonnetwaste.com	Dallas	TX	75222	214-748-5221	748-6886
Boston Harbor Association, The 374 Congress St Ste 307 *Web:* www.tbha.org	Boston	MA	02210	617-482-1722	
Burrtec Waste Industries Inc 9890 Cherry Ave *TF:* 888-287-7832 ■ *Web:* www.burrtec.com	Fontana	CA	92335	909-429-4200	429-4291
CalMet Services Inc 9821 Downey Norwalk Rd *Web:* www.calmetservices.com	Downey	CA	90241	562-869-0901	529-7958
CalMet Services Inc 7202 Peterson Ln *TF:* 800-990-6387 ■ *Web:* www.calmetservices.com	Paramount	CA	90723	562-259-1239	529-7958
Casella Waste Systems Inc 25 Greens Hill Ln *NASDAQ: CWST* ■ *TF:* 800-227-3552 ■ *Web:* www.casella.com	Rutland	VT	05701	802-775-0325	
Catalytic Products International Inc 980 Ensell Rd *Web:* www.cpilink.com	Lake Zurich	IL	60047	847-438-0334	
Coalition for Buzzards Bay Inc, The 114 Front St *Web:* www.savebuzzardsbay.org	New Bedford	MA	02740	508-999-6363	
Community Waste Disposal Inc 2010 California Crossing *Web:* www.communitywastedisposal.com	Dallas	TX	75220	972-392-9300	392-9301
Consolidated Disposal Services Inc 12949 Telegraph Rd *TF:* 800-299-4898 ■ *Web:* republicservices.com	Santa Fe Springs	CA	90670	800-299-4898	
Curtis Bay Energy 3200 Hawkins Pt Rd *Web:* curtisbayenergy.com	Baltimore	MD	21226	410-354-3228	354-3591
Deffenbaugh Industries Inc 2601 Midwest Dr *TF:* 800-631-3301 ■ *Web:* deffenbaughinc.com	Kansas City	KS	66111	913-631-3300	667-8798
Dolphins Plus Inc 31 Corrine Pl *TF:* 866-860-7946 ■ *Web:* dolphinsplus.com	Key Largo	FL	33037	305-451-1993	
Duncan Disposal Co *Arlington* 1212 Harrison Ave *TF:* 800-766-1758 ■ *Web:* www.republicservices.com	Arlington	TX	76011	817-317-2000	860-0330
E J Harrison & Sons PO Box 4009 *TF:* 800-418-7274 ■ *Web:* www.ejharrison.com	Ventura	CA	93007	805-647-1414	644-7751
Edco Disposal Corp 6670 Federal Blvd *Web:* www.edcodisposal.com	Lemon Grove	CA	91945	619-287-7555	287-4073
EL Harvey & Sons Inc 68 Hopkinton Rd *TF:* 800-321-3002 ■ *Web:* www.elharvey.com	Westborough	MA	01581	508-836-3000	836-3040
EnergySolutions LLC 423 West Broadway Ste 200 *Web:* www.energysolutions.com	Salt Lake City	UT	84101	801-649-2000	321-0453
Exp Pharmaceutical Services Corp 48021 Warm Springs Blvd *TF:* 800-350-0397 ■ *Web:* www.expworld.com	Fremont	CA	94539	510-476-0909	933-1470
Gilton Solid Waste Management 755 S Yosemite Ave *Web:* www.gilton.com	Oakdale	CA	95361	209-527-3781	527-0422
Headwaters Inc 10653 Riverfront Pkwy Ste 300 *NYSE: HW* ■ *Web:* www.headwaters.com	South Jordan	UT	84095	801-984-9400	984-9410
Health & Environment Dept 130 S Market St Ste 6050 *TF:* 800-842-0078 ■ *Web:* www.kdheks.gov	Wichita	KS	67202	316-337-6020	
Heritage Environmental Services Inc 7901 W Morris St *Web:* www.heritage-enviro.com	Indianapolis	IN	46231	317-243-0811	486-5085
Homewood Disposal Service Inc 1501 W 175th St *Web:* mydisposal.com	Homewood	IL	60430	708-798-1004	798-7193
K B Recycling Inc PO Box 550 *Web:* www.kbrecycling.com	Canby	OR	97013	503-266-7903	
Kaiser Ventures LLC 3633 Inland Empire Blvd Ste 480	Ontario	CA	91764	909-483-8500	
Knox County Health Dept 11660 Upper Gilchrist Rd *Web:* www.knoxhealth.com	Mount Vernon	OH	43050	740-392-2200	
Little Rock Wastewater 11 Clearwater Dr *Web:* www.lrwu.com	Little Rock	AR	72204	501-376-2903	688-1409
Maine Coast Heritage Trust 1 Bowdoin Mill Island Ste 201 *Web:* www.mcht.org	Topsham	ME	04086	207-729-7366	
Metro Waste Authority 300 E Locust St Ste 100 *Web:* www.mwatoday.com	Des Moines	IA	50309	515-244-0021	244-9477
Modern Corp 4746 Model City Rd *TF:* 800-662-0012 ■ *Web:* www.moderncorporation.com	Model City	NY	14107	716-754-8226	754-8964
N-Viro International Corp 2254 Centennial Rd *OTC: NVIC* ■ *TF:* 800-336-2225 ■ *Web:* www.nviro.com	Toledo	OH	43606	419-535-6374	535-7008
Napa Recycling & Waste Services (NRWS) 820 Levitin Way PO Box 239 *Web:* www.naparecycling.com	Napa	CA	94559	707-256-3500	256-3565
National Serv-All Inc 6231 McBeth Rd *TF:* 800-876-9001 ■ *Web:* servall.com	Fort Wayne	IN	46809	260-747-4117	
Natural Capitalism Solutions Inc 11823 N 75th St *Web:* www.natcapsolutions.org	Longmont	CO	80503	720-684-6580	
Oakleaf Waste Management LLC 415 Day Hill Rd **Fax Area Code:* 860 ■ *TF:* 888-625-5323 ■ *Web:* wmsbs.wm.com	Windsor	CT	06095	713-512-6200	290-1251*
Oregon Environmental Council 222 Nw Davis St Ste 309 *Web:* www.oeconline.org	Portland	OR	97209	503-222-1963	
Palm Springs Disposal Services 4690 E Mesquite Ave *Web:* www.palmspringsdisposal.com	Palm Springs	CA	92264	760-327-1351	323-5132
Republic Services 1131 N Blue Gum St **Fax:* Hum Res ■ *TF:* 866-238-2444 ■ *Web:* republicservices.com	Anaheim	CA	92806	714-238-3300	238-3304*
Republic Services Inc 18500 N Allied *NYSE: RSG* ■ *Web:* www.republicservices.com	Phoenix	AZ	85054	480-627-2700	
Republic Services of Southern Nevada 770 E Sahara Ave *TF:* 800-752-4092 ■ *Web:* www.republicservices.com	Las Vegas	NV	89193	702-735-5151	
Rubatino Refuse Removal Inc 2812 Hoyt Ave *Web:* www.rubatino.com	Everett	WA	98201	425-259-0044	339-4196
Rumpke 10795 Hughes Rd **Fax Area Code:* 513 ■ *TF:* 800-582-3107 ■ *Web:* www.rumpke.com	Cincinnati	OH	45251	800-582-3107	742-2900*
San Luis Garbage Co 2945 McMillan St Ste 136 *Web:* wasteconnections.com	San Luis Obispo	CA	93401	805-543-0875	
Sanitary Services Co Inc 21 Bellwether Way Ste 404 *TF:* 888-333-9882 ■ *Web:* www.ssc-inc.com	Bellingham	WA	98225	360-734-3490	671-0239
Sanitation District 1 of Northern Kentucky 1045 Eaton Dr *Web:* www.sd1.org	Fort Wright	KY	41017	859-578-7450	
Sewerage & Water Board of New Orleans 625 Saint Joseph St Rm 140 *Web:* www.swbno.org	New Orleans	LA	70165	504-529-2837	
South Tahoe Refuse Co 2140 Ruth Ave *Web:* www.southtahoerefuse.com	South Lake Tahoe	CA	96150	530-541-5105	544-2608
Spirit Lake Tribe (SLT) PO Box 359 *Web:* www.spiritlakenation.com	Fort Totten	ND	58335	701-766-4221	766-4126
Stericycle Inc 28161 N Keith Dr *NASDAQ: SRCL* ■ *TF:* 866-783-9816 ■ *Web:* www.stericycle.com	Lake Forest	IL	60045	847-367-5910	
Sudbury Valley Trustees Inc 18 Wolbach Rd *Web:* www.sudburyvalleytrustees.org	Sudbury	MA	01776	978-443-5588	
Sunset Scavenger Co 250 Executive Pk Ste 2100 *Web:* www.sunsetscavenger.com	San Francisco	CA	94134	415-330-1300	
Synagro Technologies Inc 435 Williams Ct Ste 100 **Fax Area Code:* 410 ■ *TF:* 800-370-0035 ■ *Web:* www.synagro.com	Baltimore	MD	21220	443-489-9017	284-9220*
Tahoe Truckee Disposal Co 645 W Lk Blvd Ste 5 Sunnyside *Web:* waste101.com	Tahoe City	CA	96145	530-583-7800	
Texas Disposal Systems Inc (TDS) 12200 Carl Rd *TF:* 800-375-8375 ■ *Web:* www.texasdisposal.com	Creedmoor	TX	78610	512-421-1300	243-4123
Triumvirate Environmental 61 Innerbelt Rd *TF:* 800-966-9282 ■ *Web:* www.triumvirate.com	Somerville	MA	02143	617-628-8098	
Union Sanitary District (USD) 5072 Benson Rd PO Box 5050 *Web:* www.unionsanitary.com	Union City	CA	94587	510-477-7500	477-7501

Phone | Fax

Urban Services Systems
212 Van Buren St NW ... Washington DC 20012 202-543-2000 547-0159
Web: www.urbanssc.com

Ute Water Conservancy District
3975 Rapid Creek Rd ... Palisade CO 81526 970-464-5563
Web: www.utewater.org

Vallejo Sanitation & Flood Control District Financing Corp
450 Ryder St ... Vallejo CA 94590 707-644-8949
Web: www.vsfcd.com

Veolia Environmental Services
200 E Randolph St Ste 7900 ... Chicago IL 60601 312-552-2800 552-2866
Web: www.veolianorthamerica.com/en

Veolia Environmental Services
1980 N Hwy 146 ... La Porte TX 77571 713-307-2100
Web: www.veolianorthamerica.com/en

Waste Industries USA Inc
3301 Benson Dr Ste 601 ... Raleigh NC 27609 919-325-3000 872-1471*
**Fax:* Mktg ■ *TF:* 800-647-9946 ■ *Web:* www.wasteindustries.com

Waste Management Inc 1001 Fannin St Ste 4000 ... Houston TX 77002 713-512-6200 512-6299
NYSE: WM ■ *TF:* 800-633-7871 ■ *Web:* www.wm.com

Waste Services Inc
1122 International Blvd Ste 601 ... Burlington ON L7L6Z8 905-319-1237 319-9050
Web: www.wasteservicesinc.com

WCA Waste Corp 1330 Post Oak Blvd 30th Fl ... Houston TX 77056 713-292-2400
NASDAQ: WCAA ■ *Web:* www.wcawaste.com

Wheelabrator Technologies Inc 4 Liberty Ln W ... Hampton NH 03842 603-929-3000 929-3139
TF: 800-682-0026 ■ *Web:* www.wtienergy.com

York Waste Disposal Inc 3730 Sandhurst Dr ... York PA 17406 717-845-1557
Web: yorkwaste.com

805 WATER - BOTTLED

Phone | Fax

Absopure Water Co 8845 General Dr ... Plymouth MI 48170 765-449-4892
TF: 800-422-7678 ■ *Web:* www.absopure.com

Calistoga Beverage Co 865 Silverado Trl ... Calistoga CA 94515 800-365-4446
TF: 800-365-4446 ■ *Web:* www.calistogawater.com

Chester Water Authority PO Box 467 ... Chester PA 19016 610-876-8185
TF: 800-793-2323 ■ *Web:* www.chesterwater.com

Coca-Cola Enterprises Inc
2500 Windy Ridge Pkwy ... Atlanta GA 30339 770-989-3000
NYSE: CCE ■ *Web:* www.cokecce.com

Coca-Cola Export Corp, The
1 Coca Cola Plz Nw ... Atlanta GA 30313 404-676-2121
Web: www.coca-colacompany.com

Culligan International Co
9399 W Higgins Rd Ste 1100 ... Rosemont IL 60018 847-430-2800
TF: 800-285-5442 ■ *Web:* www.culligan.com

Distillata Co 1608 E 24th St ... Cleveland OH 44114 216-771-2900 771-1672
TF Cust Svc: 800-999-2906 ■ *Web:* www.distillata.com

DS Waters of America Inc
5660 New Northside Dr Ste 500 ... Atlanta GA 30328 800-201-6218
TF Cust Svc: 800-201-6218 ■ *Web:* www.water.com

Glacier Clear Enterprises Inc
3291 Thomas St ... Innisfil ON L9S3W3 705-436-6363 436-4949
TF Cust Svc: 800-668-5118 ■ *Web:* www.glacierclear.com

Mountain Valley Spring Co
150 Central Ave ... Hot Springs AR 71901 501-624-1635 623-5135
Web: www.mountainvalleyspring.com

Natural Springs Water Group
128 LP Auer Rd ... Johnson City TN 37604 423-926-7905 926-8210

Polar Beverages Inc 1001 Southbridge St ... Worcester MA 01610 508-753-4300 793-0813
TF Cust Svc: 800-734-9800 ■ *Web:* www.polarbev.com

Pure-Flo Water Co 7737 Mission Gorge Rd ... Santee CA 92071 619-448-5120 596-4154
TF Cust Svc: 800-787-3356 ■ *Web:* www.pureflo.com

Temple Bottling Company Ltd 3510 Pkwy Dr ... Temple TX 76504 254-773-3376 778-5414
Web: www.templebot.com

806 WATER TREATMENT & FILTRATION PRODUCTS & EQUIPMENT

Phone | Fax

Aqua-Aerobic Systems Inc 6306 N Alpine Rd ... Loves Park IL 61111 815-654-2501 654-2508
TF: 800-940-5008 ■ *Web:* www.aqua-aerobic.com

Aquion Water Treatment Products LLC
2080 E Lunt Ave ... Elk Grove Village IL 60007 847-437-9400 437-1594
Web: aquion.com

Atlas Water Systems Inc 301 Second Ave ... Waltham MA 02451 781-373-4700 244-5141*
**Fax Area Code:* 617 ■ *TF:* 888-877-0561 ■ *Web:* atlaswater.com

Beaufort-Jasper Water & Sewer Authority
6 Snake Rd ... Okatie SC 29909 843-987-9200
Web: www.bjwsa.org

Brentwood Industries Inc Polychem Systems Div
500 Spring Ridge Dr ... Reading PA 19610 610-374-5109
Web: brentwoodindustries.com/products/clarification/sludge-collectors

Brita Products Co 1221 Broadway ... Oakland CA 94612 510-271-7000 832-1463
TF: 800-242-7482 ■ *Web:* www.brita.com

Bucks County Water & Sewer Authority (BCWSA)
1275 Almshouse Rd ... Warrington PA 18976 215-343-2538 200-0339*
**Fax Area Code:* 267 ■ *TF:* 800-222-2068 ■ *Web:* www.bcwsa.net

Carolina Filters Inc 109 E Newberry Ave ... Sumter SC 29150 803-773-6842 775-6190
TF: 800-849-5646 ■ *Web:* www.carolinafilters.com

Clack Corp 4462 Duraform Ln ... Windsor WI 53598 608-846-3010 846-2586
Web: www.clackcorp.com

Court Thomas Wingert
11800 Monarch St PO Box 6207 ... Garden Grove CA 92841 714-379-5519 379-5549
Web: www.jlwingert.com

Culligan International Co
9399 W Higgins Rd Ste 1100 ... Rosemont IL 60018 847-430-2800
TF: 800-285-5442 ■ *Web:* www.culligan.com

Deepwater Chemicals Inc 1210 Airpark Rd ... Woodward OK 73801 580-256-0500 256-0575
TF: 800-854-4064 ■ *Web:* www.deepwaterchemicals.com

Dow Liquid Separations PO Box 1206 ... Midland MI 48642 989-636-1000 832-1465
TF: 800-447-4369 ■ *Web:* dow.com

East Valley Water District
3654 E Highland Ave Ste 18 ... Highland CA 92346 909-889-9501 889-5732
TF: 866-275-3772 ■ *Web:* www.eastvalley.org

Energy Recovery Inc 1717 Doolittle Dr ... San Leandro CA 94577 510-483-7370 483-7371
NASDAQ: ERII ■ *TF:* 888-455-2263 ■ *Web:* www.energyrecovery.com

Everpure LLC 1040 Muirfield Dr ... Hanover Park IL 60133 630-307-3000 307-3030
TF: 800-323-7873

Filterspun 624 N Fairfield St ... Amarillo TX 79107 806-383-3840
TF: 800-323-5431 ■ *Web:* www.serfilco.com

Filtra-Systems Co 23900 Haggerty Rd ... Farmington Hills MI 48335 248-427-9090 427-9895
Web: www.filtrasystems.com

GE Water & Process Technologies
4636 Somerton Rd ... Trevose PA 19053 215-355-3300
TF: 866-439-2837 ■ *Web:* www.gewater.com

Graver Technologies LLC 200 Lake Dr ... Newark DE 19702 302-731-1700 731-1707
TF: 800-249-1990 ■ *Web:* www.gravertech.com

Graver Water Systems
675 Central Ave Ste 3 ... New Providence NJ 07974 908-516-1400 516-1401
TF: 877-472-8379 ■ *Web:* www.graver.com

Hungerford & Terry Inc 226 N Atlantic Ave ... Clayton NJ 08312 856-881-3200 881-6859
Web: www.hungerfordterry.com

Infilco Degremont Inc
8007 Discovery Dr PO Box 71390 ... Richmond VA 23255 804-756-7600 756-7643
Web: www.degremont-technologies.com

Kinetico Inc 10845 Kinsman Rd ... Newbury OH 44065 800-944-9283 564-9541*
**Fax Area Code:* 440 ■ *TF:* 800-944-9283 ■ *Web:* www.kinetico.com

KX Technologies LLC 55 Railroad Ave ... West Haven CT 06516 203-799-9000 799-7000
Web: www.kxtech.com

Lancaster Pump Co 1340 Manheim Pk ... Lancaster PA 17601 717-397-3521 392-0266
TF: 800-442-0786 ■ *Web:* www.lancasterpump.com

Macon Water Authority 790 Second St PO Box 108 ... Macon GA 31202 478-464-5600 741-9146
Web: www.maconwater.org

MSC Filtration Technologies
198 Freshwater Blvd ... Enfield CT 06082 860-745-7475 745-7477
TF Cust Svc: 800-237-7359 ■ *Web:* www.mscfiltertech.com

National Water Purifiers Corp 1065 E 14th St ... Hialeah FL 33010 305-887-7065 887-6209

Pall Corp 2200 Northern Blvd ... East Hills NY 11548 516-484-5400 801-9754
NYSE: PLL ■ *TF:* 800-645-6532 ■ *Web:* www.pall.com

Pentair Inc 5500 Wayzata Blvd Ste 800 ... Minneapolis MN 55416 763-545-1730 656-5400
NYSE: PNR ■ *Web:* www.pentair.com

PEP Filters Inc 322 Rolling Hill Rd ... Mooresville NC 28117 704-662-3133 662-3155
TF: 800-243-4583 ■ *Web:* www.pepfilters.com

Polaris Pool Systems Inc 2620 Commerce Way ... Vista CA 92081 760-599-9600
TF: 800-822-7933 ■ *Web:* www.polarispool.com

Pro Products LLC 7201 Engle Rd ... Fort Wayne IN 46804 260-490-5970 490-9431
TF: 866-357-5063 ■ *Web:* www.proproducts.com

Pure & Secure LLC 4120 NW 44th St ... Lincoln NE 68524 402-467-9300
TF Cust Svc: 800-875-5915 ■ *Web:* www.mypurewater.com

Schreiber LLC 100 Schreiber Dr ... Trussville AL 35173 205-655-7466 655-7669
Web: www.schreiberwater.com

Severn Trent Services
580 Virginia Dr Ste 300 ... Fort Washington PA 19034 215-646-9201
Web: www.severntrentservices.com

Sharp Water Culligan 129 Columbia Rd ... Salisbury MD 21801 410-742-3333
Web: sharpwater.com

Siemens Water Technologies
181 Thorn Hill Rd ... Warrendale PA 15086 724-772-0044 772-1300
TF: 800-424-9300

Sydnor Hydro Inc
2111 Magnolia St PO Box 27186 ... Richmond VA 23261 804-643-2725 788-9058
TF: 800-552-7714 ■ *Web:* www.sydnorhydro.com

Taylor Technologies Inc 31 Loveton Cir ... Sparks MD 21152 410-472-4340 771-4291
TF Cust Svc: 800-837-8548 ■ *Web:* www.taylortechnologies.com

Tomco2 Equipment Co 3340 Rosebud Rd ... Loganville GA 30052 770-979-8000 985-9179
TF: 800-832-4262 ■ *Web:* www.tomcosystems.com

Walker Process Equipment 840 N Russell Ave ... Aurora IL 60506 630-892-7921 892-7951
TF: 800-992-5537 ■ *Web:* www.walker-process.com

Waterco USA Inc 1864 Tobacco Rd ... Augusta GA 30906 706-793-7291 790-5688
TF General: 800-277-4150 ■ *Web:* www.waterco.com.au

Westech Engineering Inc
3665 SW Temple ... Salt Lake City UT 84115 801-265-1000 265-1080
Web: www.westech-inc.com

Xylem Inc 227 S Div St ... Zelienople PA 16063 724-452-6300 452-1377
Web: www.xylem.com/treatment/us/brands/leopold

Zodiac Pool Systems Inc 2620 Commerce Way ... Vista CA 92081 800-822-7933 479-8324
TF: 800-822-7933 ■ *Web:* www.zodiacpoolsystems.com

807 WEAPONS & ORDNANCE (MILITARY)

See Also Firearms & Ammunition (Non-Military) p. 2285; Missiles, Space Vehicels, Parts p. 2776; Simulation & Training Systems p. 3186

Phone | Fax

Adams Arms Inc 612 Florida Ave ... Palm Harbor FL 34683 727-853-0550
Web: www.adamsarms.net

Addison Clark Management LLC
10 Wright St Ste 100 ... Westport CT 06880 203-222-4000
Web: www.leask.com

Amron LLC 920 Amron Ave ... Antigo WI 54409 715-623-4176 752-2544*
**Fax Area Code:* 608 ■ *Web:* www.nationaldefensecorp.com/amtec-corporation.html

ArmaLite Inc 745 S Hanford St ... Geneseo IL 61254 309-944-6939
Web: www.armalite.com

Armtec Defense Products Co 85-901 Ave 53 ... Coachella CA 92236 760-398-0143 398-3896
Web: esterline.com

Cammenga Company LLC 2011 Bailey St ... Dearborn MI 48124 313-914-7160
Web: www.cammenga.com

Colt Defense LLC 547 New Pk Ave ... West Hartford CT 06110 860-232-4489 244-1442
Web: www.colt.com

Dillon Aero Inc 8009 E Dillons Way ... Scottsdale AZ 85260 480-444-2919
Web: www.dillonaero.com

Company	City	State	Zip	Phone	Fax
Essex Industries Inc 7700 Gravois Rd *Web:* essexindustries.com	Saint Louis	MO	63123	314-832-4500	832-1633
FN America LLC 797 Old Clemson Rd *Web:* www.fnamerica.com	Columbia	SC	29229	803-736-0522	
General Dynamics Corp 2941 Fairview Pk Dr Ste 100 *NYSE: GD* ■ *Web:* www.generaldynamics.com	Falls Church	VA	22042	703-876-3000	876-3125
Kaman Aerospace Corp Old Windsor Rd PO Box 2 *Web:* www.kaman.com	Bloomfield	CT	06002	860-242-4461	243-7514
Keystone Sporting Arms LLC 155 Sodom Rd *Web:* www.keystonesportingarmsllc.com	Milton	PA	17847	570-742-2777	
Knight's Armament Co 701 Columbia Blvd *Web:* www.knightarmco.com	Titusville	FL	32780	321-607-9900	
Lilja Precision Rifle Barrel 81 Lower Lynch Creek Rd *Web:* www.riflebarrels.com	Plains	MT	59859	406-826-3084	
Magpul Industries Corp 400 Young Court Unit 1 *Web:* www.magpul.com	Erie	CO	80516	303-828-3460	
Manroy USA LLC 201 Lonnie E Crawford Blvd *Web:* www.manroy-usa.com	Scottsboro	AL	35769	256-259-9800	
Marvin Engineering Co 261 W Beach Ave *Web:* www.marvingroup.com	Inglewood	CA	90302	310-674-5030	673-9472
NAPCO International Inc 11055 Excelsior Blvd *Web:* www.napcointl.com	Hopkins	MN	55343	952-931-2400	931-2402
North American Arms Inc 2150 South 950 East *TF:* 800-821-5783 ■ *Web:* www.naaminis.com	Provo	UT	84606	801-374-9990	
Rock River Arms Inc 1042 Cleveland Rd *Web:* www.rockriverarms.com	Colona	IL	61241	309-792-5780	
Sai Industries Inc 631 Allen Ave *Web:* www.standardarmament.com	Glendale	CA	91201	818-842-6144	
Silencerco LLC 5511 South 6055 West *Web:* www.silencerco.com	West Valley City	UT	84118	801-417-5384	
Textron Systems Corp 201 Lowell St *Web:* textron.com	Wilmington	MA	01887	978-657-5111	657-6644
US Ordnance Inc 300 Sydney Dr *Web:* www.usord.com	Mccarran	NV	89434	775-343-1320	

808 WEB HOSTING SERVICES

See Also Internet Service Providers (ISPs) p. 2596

Companies listed here are engaged primarily in hosting web sites for companies and individuals. Although many Internet Service Providers (ISPs) also provide web hosting services, they are not included among these listings.

Company	City	State	Zip	Phone	Fax
Baillio's Inc 5301 Menaul Blvd NE *TF:* 800-540-7511 ■ *Web:* baillios.com	Albuquerque	NM	87110	505-883-7511	
Catalog.com Inc 14000 Quail Springs Pkwy Ste 3600 *TF:* 888-932-4376 ■ *Web:* www.webhero.com	Oklahoma City	OK	73134	405-753-9300	753-9353
CBS Interactive Inc 235 Second St *Web:* www.cbsinteractive.com	San Francisco	CA	94105	415-344-2000	
Coronado Unified School District 201 Sixth St *Web:* www.edline.net	Coronado	CA	92118	619-522-8900	
DataPipe 10 Exchange Pl **Fax Area Code:* 888 ■ *TF:* 877-773-3306 ■ *Web:* www.datapipe.com	Jersey City	NJ	07302	201-792-4847	749-5821*
Datarealm Internet Services Inc PO Box 1616 **Fax Area Code:* 602 ■ *TF:* 877-227-3783 ■ *Web:* www.datarealm.com	Hudson	WI	54016	877-227-3783	850-3660*
Fortress Integrated Technologies 100 Delawanna Ave *TF:* 888-734-9320	Clifton	NJ	07014	973-572-1070	572-1061
Freeservers.com 1253 N Research Way Ste Q-2500 *TF:* 800-396-1999 ■ *Web:* www.freeservers.com	Orem	UT	84097	800-396-1999	
Global Knowledge Group Inc (GKG) 302 N Bryan Ave *TF:* 866-776-7584 ■ *Web:* www.gkg.net	Bryan	TX	77803	866-776-7584	
Homestead Technologies Inc 180 Jefferson Dr *TF:* 800-797-2958 ■ *Web:* www.homestead.com	Menlo Park	CA	94025	650-944-3100	
Host Depot Inc 4613 N University Dr Ste 227 *TF:* 888-340-3527 ■ *Web:* www.hostdepot.com	Coral Springs	FL	33067	954-340-3527	340-3539
Hostcentric Inc 70 BlanchaRd Rd 3rd Fl *TF Tech Supp:* 866-897-5418 ■ *Web:* www.hostcentric.com	Burlington	MA	01803	602-716-5396	
Hostedware Corp 16 Technology Dr Ste 116 *TF:* 800-211-6967 ■ *Web:* www.hostedware.com	Irvine	CA	92618	949-585-1500	
Hostway Corp 100 N Riverside Plaza 8th Fl *TF:* 866-467-8929 ■ *Web:* www.hostway.com	Chicago	IL	60606	312-238-0125	236-1958
Hurricane Electric Internet Services 760 Mission Ct *Web:* www.he.com	Fremont	CA	94539	510-580-4100	580-4151
INetU Inc 744 Roble Rd *TF:* 888-664-6388 ■ *Web:* www.inetu.net	Allentown	PA	18109	610-266-7441	266-7434
LightEdge Solutions Inc 215 10th St Ste 1000 *TF:* 877-771-3343 ■ *Web:* www.lightedge.com	Des Moines	IA	50309	515-471-1000	471-1112
Media3 Technologies LLC 33 Riverside Dr N River Commerce Pk *TF:* 800-903-9327 ■ *Web:* www.media3.net	Pembroke	MA	02359	781-826-1213	996-4971
Microserve 276 Fifth Ave Ste 1011 *Web:* www.mserve.com	New York	NY	10001	212-683-2811	
NetNation Communications Inc 550 Burrard St Ste 200 *TF:* 888-277-0000 ■ *Web:* www.netnation.com	Vancouver	BC	V6C2B5	604-688-8946	688-8934
OLM LLC 4 Trefoil Dr *TF:* 877-265-6638 ■ *Web:* olm.net	Trumbull	CT	06611	203-445-7700	
Opsource Inc 5201 Great America Pkwy Ste 120 *TF:* 800-664-9973 ■ *Web:* cloud.dimensiondata.com/saas-solutions	Santa Clara	CA	95054	408-567-2000	982-8902
Pacific Internet 105 W Clay St *TF:* 888-722-8638 ■ *Web:* www.pacific.net	Ukiah	CA	95482	707-468-1005	468-5822
Radiant Communications Corp 1600-1050 W Pender St *CVE: RCN* ■ *TF:* 888-219-2111 ■ *Web:* www.radiant.net	Vancouver	BC	V6E4T3	888-219-2111	
Superb Internet Corp 999 Bishop St Ste 1850 *TF:* 888-354-6128 ■ *Web:* www.superb.net	Honolulu	HI	96813	808-544-0387	441-0952
Telus 1000 Rue de Serigny *TF:* 888-709-8759 ■ *Web:* www.telushealth.co	Longueuil	QC	J4K5B1	450-928-6000	928-6344
TierraNet Inc 14284 Dani Elson St *Web:* www.tierra.net	Poway	CA	92064	858-560-9416	560-9417
Verio Inc 8300 E Maplewood Ave Ste 400 *TF Sales:* 800-438-8374 ■ *Web:* www.verio.com	Greenwood Village	CO	80111	561-912-2555	
VPOP Technologies Inc 1772J Avenida de los Arboles Ste 374 *TF Sales:* 888-811-8767 ■ *Web:* www.vpop.net	Thousand Oaks	CA	91362	805-529-9374	
WorldPost Technologies Inc 5886 De Zavala Rd Ste 102/535 *Web:* www.worldpost.com	San Antonio	TX	78249	210-212-5600	212-5800

809 WEB SITE DESIGN SERVICES

See Also Advertising Agencies p. 1695; Advertising Services - Online p. 1706; Computer Systems Design Services p. 2039

Company	City	State	Zip	Phone	Fax
1020 Inc 184 Rose St *Web:* www.placecast.net	San Francisco	CA	94102	415-501-9759	
415 Productions Inc 2507 Bryant St *Web:* www.415.com	San Francisco	CA	94110	415-642-4200	
A C I Media 2485 S Marion Ave *Web:* www.acimedia.com	Lake City	FL	32025	386-758-2266	
A E Data Integration Inc 933 N Kenmore St Ste 318 *Web:* www.aediinc.com	Arlington	VA	22201	703-875-2095	
Aareas Interactive 1120 Finch Ave W *Web:* www.aareas.com	North York	ON	M3J3H7	416-661-2244	
Accelian Llc 1222 Earnestine St *Web:* www.accelianllc.com	Mc Lean	VA	22101	703-543-1616	
Acro Media Inc 2303 Leckie Rd Ste 103 *TF:* 877-763-8844 ■ *Web:* acromediainc.com	Kelowna	BC	V1X6Y5	250-763-8884	763-6936
AdvantageWare Inc 425 Madison Ave Ste 1700 *Web:* www.advantageware.com	New York	NY	10017	212-319-1903	
AeroInfo Systems Inc 200 -13575 Commerce Pky *Web:* www.aeroinfo.com	Richmond	BC	V6V2L1	604-232-4200	
Ajel Technologies Inc 45 Brunswick Ave Ste# 222 Ste *Web:* www.ajel.com	Edison	NJ	08817	732-476-6000	
AKQA Inc 3299 K St NW *Web:* www.akqa.com	Washington	DC	20007	202-337-2572	
Alan Weber and Associates Inc 13740 Research Blvd Ste N8 *Web:* www.alanweberassociates.com	Austin	TX	78750	512-366-9511	
Albano Systems Inc 360 Bloomfield Ave Ste 308 *Web:* www.albanosystems.com	Windsor	CT	06095	860-688-9555	
AlmondNet Inc 134 Spring St Ste 302 *Web:* www.almondnet.com	New York	NY	10012	212-219-5070	
Antenna House Inc 3844 Kennett Pk Ste 200 *Web:* rainbowpdf.com	Greenville	DE	19807	302-427-2456	
Apacheta Corp 75 W Baltimore Pk *Web:* www.apacheta.com	Media	PA	19063	610-558-5852	
Applied Logic Inc 1432 Strassner Dr *Web:* www.appliedlogicinc.com	St. Louis	MO	63144	314-918-8877	
Applied Statistics & Management Inc 31515 Rancho Pueblo Rd Ste 205 *Web:* www.mdstaff.com	Temecula	CA	92592	951-699-4600	
AppNeta Inc 285 Summer St Fourth Fl *Web:* www.appneta.com	Boston	MA	02210	781-235-2470	
Apprimus Inc 291 Rt 22 E Ste 20 *Web:* www.apprimus.biz	Lebanon	NJ	08833	908-236-8885	
AppWorx Corp 2475 140th Avene NE *Web:* www.automic.com	Bellevue	WA	98005	425-644-2121	
Aptech Systems Inc 30741 3rd Ave Ste 160 *Web:* www.aptech.com	Black Diamond	WA	98010	360-886-7100	
AQT Solutions Inc 1001 Second St Ste 245 *Web:* www.aqtsolutions.com	Napa	CA	94559	707-265-7800	
Aqumin LLC 7676 Woodway Dr Ste 325 *Web:* www.aqumin.com	Houston	TX	77063	713-781-2121	
Arc90 Inc 747 3rd Ave 30th Fl *Web:* www.arc90.com	New York	NY	10017	212-400-6296	
Arcot Systems Inc 455 W Maude Ave *Web:* www.arcot.com	Sunnyvale	CA	94085	408-969-6100	
Aries Computer Solutions Inc 2211 Sheridan Dr Ste 203 *Web:* www.customswebclearance.com	Buffalo	NY	14223	716-876-4004	
Armanta Inc 350 Mt. Kemble Ave *Web:* www.armanta.com	Morris Township	NJ	07960	973-326-9600	
Armen Computing Ltd 286 Bethany Ct *TF:* 800-372-6078 ■ *Web:* www.armencomp.com	Inman	SC	29349	800-372-6078	
AssetPoint LLC 770 Pelham Rd *Web:* assetpoint.com	Greenville	SC	29615	864-679-3415	
Aster Group Inc 434-B Copperfield Blvd *Web:* www.astergroup.com	Concord	NC	28025	704-262-9200	
Astoundry Inc 2441 Bartlett St *Web:* astoundry.com	Houston	TX	77098	713-520-6200	
At First Site Inc 4449 Easton Way 2nd Fl *Web:* www.afsweb.net	Columbus	OH	43219	614-479-0000	
ATAC Corp 755 N Mathilda Ave Ste 200 *Web:* www.atac.com	Sunnyvale	CA	94085	408-736-2822	
Atr Inc 6405 Cypresswood Dr Ste 250 *Web:* www.atrco.com	Spring	TX	77379	281-370-9540	

Company	City	State	ZIP	Phone	Fax
AutoManager Inc 7301 Topanga Canyon Blvd Ste 200 *Web:* www.automanager.com	Canoga Park	CA	91303	310-207-2202	
AXIOM Design Automation Inc 1900 McCarthy Blvd Ste 207 *Web:* www.axiom-da.com	Milpitas	CA	95035	408-433-9997	
B Line Express Inc 7065 Long View Rd *Web:* www.blinex.com	Columbia	MD	21044	301-596-9290	
B2i Technologies Inc 2000 N Central Expy Ste 209 *Web:* www.b2itech.com	Plano	TX	75074	972-234-9200	
Backupify Inc 17 Sellers St, *TF:* 800-571-4984 ■ *Web:* www.backupify.com	Cambridge	MA	02139	800-571-4984	
BankTEL Systems LLC 319 Park Creek Dr *Web:* banktel.com	Columbus	MS	39705	662-245-1007	
Base One International Corp 44 E 12th St Apt 3B *Web:* www.boic.com	New York	NY	10003	212-673-2511	
Battlespace Simulations Inc 26525 Harmony Hills *Web:* www.battlespacesims.com	San Antonio	TX	78260	210-179-2656	
Bayside Business Solutions Inc 415 S Topanga Canyon Blvd *Web:* www.baysidebiz.com	Topanga	CA	90290	310-455-7520	
Bellrock Media Inc 2917 Santa Monica Blvd. *Web:* www.bellrockmedia.com	Santa Monica	CA	90404	310-496-5105	
Berico Technologies LLC 1501 Lee Hwy, Ste 303 *Web:* www.bericotechnologies.com	Arlington	VA	22209	703-224-8300	
Bevilacqua Research Corp 4901 Corporate Dr NW *Web:* www.brc2.com	Huntsville	AL	35805	256-882-6229	
Bitwise Solutions Inc 569 Aviator Dr. *Web:* www.bitwise.com	Fort Worth	TX	76179	817-577-4866	
Bixler Inc 1600 Tysons Blvd Ste 800 *Web:* www.bixler.com	McLean	VA	22102	703-894-3000	894-3001
Blakeslee-Lane Inc 916 N Charles St *Web:* www.blakesleeadv.com	Baltimore	MD	21201	410-727-8800	
Boden Inc P.O. Box 258 *TF:* 866-291-3363 ■ *Web:* www.bodeninc.com	Helmetta	NJ	08828	866-291-3363	
Bold Planning Solutions Llc 1116 Sklar Dr E *Web:* www.boldplanning.com	Venice	FL	34293	941-497-3110	
Burgess Group LLC, The 1727 King St *Web:* www.burgessgroup.com	Alexandria	VA	22314	703-894-1800	
bx.com Inc 1 W Exchange St *TF:* 800-262-8138 ■ *Web:* www.bx.com	Providence	RI	02903	401-274-8991	
Cambria Corp 3723 Haven Ave Ste 130 *Web:* www.cambria.com	Menlo Park	CA	94025	650-328-9270	
Ccp Global Inc 6825 Hobson Valley Dr Ste 302 *Web:* www.ccpglobal.com	Woodridge	IL	60517	312-543-5030	
Cgi Interactive Communications Inc 76 Otis St *Web:* www.cgiinteractive.com	Westborough	MA	01581	508-898-2500	
Champions Way Enterprises Inc 980 1st St W *TF:* 877-774-5425 ■ *Web:* www.championsway.com	North Vancouver	BC	V7P3N4	877-774-5425	
Cityspan Technologies Inc 2437 Durant Ave Ste 206 *Web:* www.cityspan.com	Berkeley	CA	94704	510-665-1700	
Clerysys Inc 10600, W Higgins Rd O'Hare Corporate Towers Ste 711 *Web:* www.clerysys.com	Rosemont	IL	60018	847-376-2756	
CLR Group Ltd 8 Eagle Ctr Ste 5 *Web:* www.clrgroup.com	Ofallon	IL	62269	618-624-6799	
Computer Wrangler On-site Service 4937 320th St. *Web:* www.computerwrangler.net	Stacy	MN	55079	651-462-8809	
Consensus International LLC 10520 N.W. 26th St Ste C-101 *Web:* www.consensusintl.com	Doral	FL	33172	305-477-6269	
Cramer 425 University Ave *Web:* www.cramer.com	Norwood	MA	02062	781-278-2300	278-8464
Cravetek Llc 24509 E Louisiana Cir *Web:* www.cravetek.com	Aurora	CO	80018	303-364-8830	
Createthe Group Inc 116 W Houston St 5th Fl *Web:* www.createthegroup.com	New York	NY	10012	212-375-7900	
CustomerVision Inc 515 N 2nd St. *Web:* www.customervision.com	Des Moines	IA	50047	515-989-9900	
DAFCA Inc 10 Speen St *Web:* dafca.com	Framingham	MA	01701	774-204-0020	
Data Square LLC 733 Summer St Ste 601 *Web:* www.datasquare.com	Stamford	CT	06901	203-964-9733	
Data Technique Inc 3402 Airport Cir *Web:* www.datatechnique.com	Pittsburg	KS	66762	620-235-1000	
Delasoft Inc 630 Churchmans Rd Ste 108 *Web:* www.delasoft-inc.com	Newark	DE	19702	302-533-7913	
Digital Surgeons LLC 900 Grand Ave Ste C *Web:* www.digitalsurgeons.com	New Haven	CT	06510	203-672-6201	
Digital West Media Inc PO Box 270219 *Web:* www.dwmi.com	San Diego	CA	92198	760-740-1787	
E Walker Consulting Inc 4902 Crosspoint Dr *Web:* www.ewalkerconsulting.com	Doylestown	PA	18901	215-806-3537	
Echo Nest Corp, The 48 Grove St Davis Sq *Web:* the.echonest.com	Somerville	MA	02144	617-628-0233	
Equiom Inc 3181 156th Ave SE Ste 200 *Web:* www.equiom.com	Bellevue	WA	98007	425-818-3043	
Estimating EDGE, The 47 SE 5th Ave. *Web:* www.edgeestimating.com	Delray Beach	FL	33483	561-276-9100	
Etouch Federal Systems Llc 6167 Jarvis Ave Ste 281 *Web:* etouchfederal.com	Newark	CA	94560	510-764-2303	
eWareness Inc 2420 Minton Rd. *Web:* www.ewarenessinc.com	Melbourne	FL	32904	321-821-7483	
EZSolution Corp 3002 Hempland Rd *Web:* www.ezsolution.com	Lancaster	PA	17601	717-291-4689	
Fluid Innovation Inc 911 N RR 620 Ste 205 *TF:* 866-934-7779 ■ *Web:* www.fluidinnovation.com	Austin	TX	78734	866-934-7779	
Foraker Design LLC 5277 Manhattan Cir Ste 210 *Web:* www.foraker.com	Boulder	CO	80303	303-449-0202	
ForeSite Technologies Inc 99 E River Dr 7th Fl *Web:* www.foresitetech.com	East Hartford	CT	06108	860-528-1100	
Fortuna Technologies Inc 1270 A Lawrence Station Rd *Web:* www.fortuna.com	Sunnyvale	CA	94089	408-541-0200	
Forum One Communications Corp 2200 Mt Vernon Ave *Web:* www.forumone.com	Alexandria	VA	22301	703-548-1855	
Frontline Systems Inc 40 NE Loop 410 Ste 400 *Web:* www.front-line.com	San Antonio	TX	78216	210-822-0494	
Function Point Productivity Software Inc 2034 11th Ave W Ste 140 *Web:* www.functionpoint.com	Vancouver	BC	V6J2C9	604-731-2522	
Fusebox Inc 36 W 20th St *Web:* www.fusebox.com	New York	NY	10011	212-929-7644	929-7947
G&G Technologies Inc 140 Preston Executive Dr Ste 100 *Web:* www.gandgtech.com	Cary	NC	27513	919-461-9848	
Genex Interactive 800 Corporate Pointe *Web:* meredithxceleratedmarketing.com	Culver City	CA	90230	424-672-9500	
GNP Computers Inc 555 E Huntington Dr *Web:* www.gnp.com	Monrovia	CA	91016	626-305-8484	
GotData.com Inc 25431 Cabot Rd Ste 202	Laguna Hills	CA	92653	949-716-7500	269-9161
Hagerman & Company Inc 505 Sunset Ct *Web:* www.hagerman.com	Mount Zion	IL	62549	217-864-2326	
HazMat Systems Inc 501 Slaters Ln Ste 1024 *Web:* www.hazmatsystemsinc.com	Alexandria	VA	22314	703-652-4512	
Headquarters.Com Inc 625 Walnut Ridge Dr Ste 108	Hartland	WI	53029	262-369-0600	369-0800
Help Button, The 3109 W Market St *Web:* thehelpbutton.net	Akron	OH	44333	330-867-4357	
Higher Technology Solutions Inc 1547 Old Forge Rd Ste 1111 *Web:* www.htsglobal.com	Bartlett	IL	60103	630-830-7638	
Hostnet Inc 1301 E Arapaho Rd Ste 104 *Web:* www.hostnet.com.br	Richardson	TX	75081	214-800-5501	
IIF Data Solutions Inc 5885 Trinity Pkwy Ste 120 *Web:* www.iifdata.com	Centreville	VA	20120	703-531-1180	
Impact Technologies Group Inc 10735 David Taylor Dr University Research Park Ste 350 *Web:* www.impact-tek.com	Charlotte	NC	28262	704-549-1100	
In-Style Software Inc 315 Lemay Ferry Rd *Web:* www.inpulsedm.com	Saint Louis	MO	63130	314-631-6982	
Infopros Drakeley Inc 111 Natoma St *Web:* infopros.com	Folsom	CA	95630	916-458-6777	
Intersoft Corp 4300 Stevens Creek Blvd Ste 277 *Web:* www.intersoftusa.com	San Jose	CA	95129	408-987-5302	
Invaluable LLC 38 Everett St Ste 101 *Web:* www.invaluable.com	Allston	MA	02134	617-746-9800	
Jellyvision Inc 848 W Eastman St Ste 104 *Web:* www.jellyvision.com	Chicago	IL	60622	312-266-0606	
Keek Inc 1 Eglinton E Ste 300 *Web:* www.keek.com	Toronto	ON	M4P3A1	416-639-5335	
KT Consulting Inc 2545 W 10th St Ste A *Web:* www.ktc-ops.com	Antioch	CA	94509	925-755-3300	
Kuberre Systems Inc 805 TurnPk St *Web:* www.kuberresystems.com	North Andover	MA	01845	978-689-2353	
Lab Lite Llc 8 S Main St *Web:* www.lablite.com	New Milford	CT	06776	860-355-8817	
LabAnswer Government LLC 2277 Plz Dr Ste 275 *Web:* www.labanswer.com	Sugar Land	TX	77479	713-982-8030	
Langtech Systems Consulting Inc 733 Frnt St Ste 110 *Web:* www.langtech.com	San Francisco	CA	94111	415-364-9600	
Liquid Compass LLC 2399 BLk St Ste 180 *Web:* www.liquidcompass.net	Denver	CO	80205	303-839-9400	
Litehaus Systems Inc 7445 132nd St Ste 2010 *TF:* 866-771-0044 ■ *Web:* www.litehaus360lease.com	Surrey	BC	V3W1J8	866-771-0044	
LiveBlock Auctions International Inc 2125 11th Ave Ste 200 *Web:* www.liveblockauctions.com	Regina	SK	S4P3X3	306-584-1383	
Logical It Solutions 157 Park St Ste 36 *Web:* logicalsolutionsllc.com	Bangor	ME	04401	207-942-5487	
Lux Scientiae Inc 46 Central St *Web:* luxsci.com	Somerville	MA	02143	814-870-9250	
Macabe Associates Inc, The 110 Union St Ste 310 *Web:* www.macabe.com	Seattle	WA	98101	206-382-0924	
Make It Work Inc 3890 La Cumbre Plz Ln Ste 200 *Web:* www.makeitwork.com	Santa Barbara	CA	93105	805-695-8550	
ManTech MBI Inc 2250 Corporate Park Dr Ste 500 *Web:* www.mcdonaldbradley.com	Herndon	VA	20171	703-326-1000	
Mantis Technology Group Inc 12413 Willows Rd NE Ste 300 *Web:* www.mantis-tgi.com	Kirkland	WA	98034	425-250-0400	

Company	City	State	Zip	Phone	Fax
Marick Group, The 9100 Rexis Ave Ste 100 *Web:* www.marickgroup.com	Perry Hall	MD	21128	410-258-2390	
Marketing Evolution Inc 4364 Town Ctr Blvd Ste 320 *Web:* www.marketingevolution.com	El Dorado Hills	CA	95762	916-933-7500	
Mdr Associates Inc 6486 Little Falls Dr *Web:* mdrandassociates.com	San Jose	CA	95120	408-927-8302	
Mejia Technologies Ltd 2189 Spinningwheel Ln *Web:* www.mejiatechnologies.com	Cincinnati	OH	45244	513-231-1920	
Meritide Inc 2670 Patton Rd *Web:* www.meritide.com	Saint Paul	MN	55113	651-255-7300	
Msights Inc 9935 Rea Rd Ste D-301 *TF:* 877-267-4448 ■ *Web:* msights.com	Charlotte	NC	28277	877-267-4448	
MuseBox Media LLC 650 Broadway 4th Fl *Web:* www.themusebox.net	New York	NY	10012	646-237-0023	
NDS USA LLC 406 E Silver Springs Blvd *Web:* www.ndsusallc.com	Ocala	FL	34470	352-840-9593	
Netelligent Corp 16401 Swingley Ridge Rd Ste 500 *Web:* www.netelligent.com	Chesterfield	MO	63017	314-392-6900	
Netimpact Strategies Inc 24917 Castleton Dr *Web:* www.netimpactstrategies.com	Chantilly	VA	20152	703-327-7859	
Netsoft USA Inc 24 W 25th St 5th Fl *Web:* www.epam.com	New York	NY	10010	212-994-8181	
Network Alternatives Inc 3000 Cabot Blvd W Ste 3006 *Web:* www.network-alternatives.com	Langhorne	PA	19047	215-702-3800	
Neuric Technologies Llc 2929 Buffalo Speedway *Web:* neuric.com	Houston	TX	77098	713-553-1716	
Next IT Corp 12809 E. Mirabeau Pkwy *Web:* www.nextit.com	Spokane Valley	WA	99216	509-242-0767	
Next Wave Logistics Inc 28377 Davis Pkwy Ste 607A *Web:* www.nwlinc.com	Warrenville	IL	60555	630-393-0507	
NFA Group Inc 2002 A Guadalupe Ave Ste 118 *Web:* www.buydrm.com	Austin	TX	78705	512-377-1340	
NIEFERT Certified Solutions LLC 5850 Oberlin Dr *Web:* www.niefert.com	San Diego	CA	92121	858-450-9092	
Nimbix LLC 1432 Waverly St *Web:* www.nimbix.net	Houston	TX	77008	832-305-6365	
NinjaTrader LLC 1236 Clarkson St *Web:* www.ninjatrader.com	Denver	CO	80218	303-830-8003	
Niyamit Inc 13076 Monterey Estates Dr *Web:* www.niyamit.com	Herndon	VA	20171	703-981-0499	
Noregon Systems Inc 7009 Albert Pick Rd *Web:* www.noregon.com	Greensboro	NC	27409	336-768-4337	
Northwest Data Service LLC 1169 Hilltop Pkwy Unit 105 *Web:* northwestdata.com	Steamboat Springs	CO	80487	970-879-0734	
NSK & Associates Inc 2 Liberty Sq 7th Fl *Web:* www.nskinc.com	Boston	MA	02109	617-303-0480	
NSS Corp 264 S River Rd Ste 520 *Web:* www.nsscorp.com	Bedford	NH	03110	603-296-2900	
NVision Solutions Inc 13131 Hwy 603 Ste 301 *Web:* www.nvisionsolutions.com	Bay St. Louis	MS	39520	228-242-0010	
Oak Tree Systems Inc 694 Frnt St *Web:* www.oaktree-systems.com	Lovingston	VA	22949	434-263-6700	
obdEdge LLC 7117 Florida Blvd *Web:* www.obdedge.com	Baton Rouge	LA	70808	225-215-0079	
Object Research Systems Inc 760 St-Paul W Ste 101 *Web:* www.theobjects.com	Montreal	QC	H3C1M4	514-843-3861	
Oculus Technologies Corp 110 Broad St 2nd Fl *Web:* www.oculustech.com	Boston	MA	02110	617-426-4277	
OmniSYS-LLC 15950 Dallas Pkwy Ste 350 *Web:* careclaim.com	Dallas	TX	75248	903-455-0461	
Open Channel Solutions Inc Three Allied Dr Ste 303 *Web:* www.ocs.com	Dedham	MA	02026	781-407-3900	
Open Systems International Inc 3600 Holly Ln N Ste 40 *Web:* www.osii.com	Minneapolis	MN	55447	763-551-0559	
Openfirst LLC 300 N Jefferson St *Web:* www.openfirst.com	Milwaukee	WI	53202	414-347-4100	
OpenRoad Communications Ltd 12 Water St Ste 210 *Web:* www.openroad.ca	Vancouver	BC	V6B1A5	604-694-0554	
OpenRules Inc 75 Chatsworth Ct *Web:* openrules.com	Edison	NJ	08820	732-993-3131	
Optimal Networks Inc 15201 Diamondback Dr Ste 220 *Web:* www.optnw.com	Rockville	MD	20850	240-499-7900	
Orion Systems Integrators Inc 3759 US Hwy 1 S *Web:* www.orioninc.com	Monmouth Junction	NJ	08852	732-422-9922	
Orionnet Systems Llc 4141 Nw Expy Ste 300 *Web:* www.iorion.com	Oklahoma City	OK	73116	405-286-1674	
Oss Inc 2000 N Mays Ste 114 *Web:* www.ossjobs.com	Round Rock	TX	78664	512-255-2424	
OuterBox Solutions Inc 453 S High St Ste 103 *Web:* www.outerboxdesign.com	Akron	OH	44311	234-542-6503	
Outsource Testing Inc 1278 Ctr Ct Dr *Web:* www.outsourcetesting.com	Covina	CA	91724	909-592-8898	
Oxygen Ventures LLC 4601 Locust Ln Ste 306 *Web:* oxygenventures.com	Harrisburg	PA	17109	717-540-9730	
P s i Prime Inc 137 Jackson Ave *Web:* www.psiprime.com	Woodland Park	NJ	07424	973-225-9870	
Paloma Systems Inc 11250 Waples Mill Rd *Web:* www.palomasys.com	Fairfax	VA	22030	703-626-5024	591-0985
Panacore Corp 2015 E 8th St Ste 242 *Web:* www.panacore.com	Odessa	TX	79761	432-580-9933	
Pandora Data Systems Inc 10 Victor Sq Ste 250 *Web:* www.pandoradatasystems.com	Scotts Valley	CA	95066	831-429-8900	
Panoptic Development Inc 131 Wayland Ave *Web:* www.panopticdev.com	Providence	RI	02906	401-484-7812	
Paragon Employment Solutions Llc 108 3rd St Ste 200 *Web:* www.paragonitpros.com	Des Moines	IA	50309	515-288-2128	
Partner Software Inc 345 W Hancock Ave *Web:* www.partnersoft.com	Athens	GA	30601	706-354-1833	
Patel Consultants Corp 1525 Morris Ave *Web:* www.patelcorp.com	Union	NJ	07083	908-964-7575	964-3176
PayService Com Inc 910 Kenyon Ct Ste 110 *Web:* www.payservice.com	Charlotte	NC	28211	704-644-0019	
Pedigree Technologies L L C 1810 NDSU Research Cir N *Web:* www.pedigreetechnologies.com	Fargo	ND	58102	701-293-9949	
Persystent Technology Corp 3930 Premier N Dr Ste 235 *Web:* www.UtopicSoftware.com	Tampa	FL	33618	813-264-2999	
Pillar Technology Group LLC 5180 Washakie Trail Ste 3445 *Web:* www.pillartechnology.com	Brighton	MI	48116	614-890-0910	
Pinestar Technology Inc 400 Apgar Dr Ste 1 *Web:* www.pinestar.com	Somerset	NJ	08873	732-356-0070	
Pipeline Software Inc 2850 Red Hill Ave Ste 110 *Web:* www.pipelinesoftware.com	Santa Ana	CA	92660	949-296-8375	
Pixia Corp 45615 Willow Pond Plz *Web:* www.pixia.com	Sterling	VA	20164	571-203-9665	
Platinum Business Corp 14662 Cambridge Cir *Web:* www.platinumcorporation.com	Laurel	MD	20707	301-498-4149	
Poliac Research Corp 12233 Wood Lk Dr *Web:* www.poliac.com	Burnsville	MN	55337	952-882-1772	
Ponder Professional Services Inc 282 Moore Rd *Web:* www.ponderproserve.com	Griffin	GA	30223	770-490-2767	
PortBlue Corp 13323 Washington Blvd Ste 300 *Web:* www.portblue.com	Los Angeles	CA	90066	310-566-7222	
Portlogic Systems Inc First Canadian Pl, 100 King St. W Ste 5700 *Web:* www.portlogicsystems.com	Toronto	ON	M5X1K7	647-847-8350	
Positive Technology 8612 Wolftrap Rd *Web:* positek.net	Vienna	VA	22182	703-242-2362	
PowerPlan Corp 2130 Main St Ste 245 *Web:* www.powerplancorp.com	Huntington Beach	CA	92648	714-969-5353	
PPI Technical Communications Inc 32200 Solon Rd *Web:* www.ppitechcom.com	Cleveland	OH	44139	440-498-9254	
Premium Ware Inc 3210 Pleasant Valley Ln Ste A *Web:* www.premiumware.com	Arlington	TX	76015	817-375-9898	
Primestream Corp 15590 NW 15th Ave *Web:* primestream.com	Miami	FL	33169	305-868-9085	
PrintSoft Americas Inc 500 Park Blvd Ste 270 *Web:* www.printsoftamericas.com	Itasca	IL	60143	630-625-5400	
PrivaSys Inc 1153 Lawrence Dr *Web:* www.privasys.com	Newbury Park	CA	91320	805-498-2310	
Prn Computer Systems Inc 16435 Sw 2nd Dr *Web:* prncomp.com	Pembroke Pines	FL	33027	954-431-5071	
Proactive Performance Solution 560 Peoples Plz 139 *Web:* www.proactiveusa.com	Newark	DE	19702	302-375-0451	
Probaris Technologies Inc 1880 JFK Blvd Ste 1909 *Web:* www.probaris.com	Philadelphia	PA	19103	215-238-0510	
ProCare Pharmacy Benefit Manager Inc 1267 Professional Pkwy Ste 100 *TF:* 888-821-5516 ■ *Web:* www.procarerx.com	Gainesville	GA	30507	888-821-5516	
Process Integrity Inc 5840 W Interstate 20 Ste 150 *Web:* www.processintegrity.com	Arlington	TX	76017	817-561-6600	
Processmodel Inc 10602 S Cvered Bridge Cyn *Web:* www.processmodel.com	Spanish Fork	UT	84660	801-356-7165	
Projectbits Consulting Inc 236 Lead King Dr *Web:* www.projectbits.com	Castle Rock	CO	80108	720-319-8160	
ProLogic Inc 1000 Green River Dr Ste 201 *Web:* www.ultra-prologic.com	Fairmont	WV	26554	304-333-2680	
ProMost Inc 1616 16th St Ste 350 *Web:* www.promost.com	San Francisco	CA	94103	415-575-1350	
Prophetline Inc 2120 S Waldron Rd *Web:* www.prophetline.com	Fort Smith	AR	72903	479-452-6526	
Proplanner 2321 N Loop Dr Ste 107 *Web:* www.proplanner.com	Ames	IA	50010	515-296-9914	
Propylon Inc 3429 Derry St *Web:* www.propylon.com	Harrisburg	PA	17111	717-265-0400	
Protolink Inc 1755 N Collins Blvd Ste 550 *Web:* www.protolink.com	Richardson	TX	75080	972-644-9774	
PTC International Inc 1430 Joh Ave Bldg M *Web:* www.ptcintl.com	Baltimore	MD	21227	410-247-2345	
Pyramid Peak Design 2950 N Academy Blvd Ste 200 *Web:* pyramidpeak.com	Colorado Springs	CO	80917	719-598-1186	
Qiva Inc 299 Kansas St *Web:* www.qiva.com	San Francisco	CA	94103	415-762-6000	

Phone Fax

QuadriSpace Corp 705 N Greenville Ave Ste 800 Allen TX 75002 866-337-7223
TF: 866-337-7223 ■ *Web:* www.quadrispace.com

Quadros Systems Inc
10450 Stancliff Rd Ste 100 Houston TX 77099 832-351-2830
Web: quadros.com

QualCorp Inc 27240 Turnberry Ln Ste 200 Valencia CA 91355 661-799-0033
Web: qualcorp.com

Quality Systems Solutins Inc
6905 Zachary Dr Carpentersville IL 60110 847-426-9548
Web: www.qualitysystemssolutions.com

Quantech Corp 4528 21st St Long Island City NY 11101 718-433-1024
Web: quantech.net

Radianta Inc 2154 Michelson Dr Ste A Irvine CA 92612 866-467-9695
TF: 866-467-9695 ■ *Web:* www.radianta.com

Radsoft 322 E Sherman Ave Coeur D Alene ID 83814 208-665-0516
Web: www.radsoft.com

Rationale Technologies Corp
12949 Ridgemist Ln Fairfax VA 22033 703-388-9089
Web: rationaleinc.com

Ready At Dawn Studios LLC
7525 Irvine Ctr Dr Ste 150 Irvine CA 92618 949-724-1234
Web: www.readyatdawn.com

Rebel Interactive Inc 1217 S 13th St Omaha NE 68108 402-561-0520
Web: www.rebelinteractive.com

Redsson Ltd 1600 Madison Ave Toledo OH 43604 419-244-1111
Web: www.redsson.com

Rekon Technologies Inc
23 E Colorado Blvd Ste 203 Pasadena CA 91105 626-577-4350
Web: www.rekon.com

Requitest Inc 8614 N Bali Ct Ellicott City MD 21043 410-465-8637
Web: www.requitest.com

Resource Intelligence Inc 502 Abbey Ct Alpharetta GA 30004 770-667-2031
Web: www.resource-intelligence.com

Result Data Consulting Ltd
200 E Campus View Blvd Three Crosswoods
Ste 120 Columbus OH 43235 614-505-0770
Web: www.resultdata.com

RMS Telecommunications LLC
5600 Maggie Run Ln Fuquay Varina NC 27526 919-567-4620
Web: www.rms-telecomms.com

Rome Technologies Inc
412 Headquarters Dr Ste 4 Millersville MD 21108 410-923-2000
Web: rometech.com

Root Consulting Inc 2018 N Durham Durham Dr Houston TX 77008 713-523-8976
Web: www.rootcon.com

Ros Technology Services Inc
8500 Nw River Park Dr Ste 342 Parkville MO 64152 816-746-4100
Web: www.rosnet.com

ROW2 Technologies Inc
200 Lanidex Plz 2nd Fl Parsippany NJ 07054 973-581-6315
Web: www.row2technologies.com

Rusco Inc 450 Gravers Rd Plymouth Meeting PA 19462 610-313-9955
Web: www.ruscoservices.com

SafeData LLC 250A Ctrville Rd Warwick RI 02886 401-734-5866
Web: www.datastoragecorp.com

SageTV LLC 9800 S La Cienega Blvd Ste 905 Inglewood CA 90301 310-417-3075
Web: www.sagetv.com

Sai Ann International Inc
28428 Golf Pointe Blvd Farmington Hills MI 48331 248-324-1604
Web: www.saiann-inc.com

Sapient Corp 131 Dartmouth St 3rd Fl Boston MA 02116 617-621-0200 621-1300
NASDAQ: SAPE ■ *TF:* 866-796-6860 ■ *Web:* www.sapient.com

Sapphire Infotech Inc 200 Brown Rd Ste 200 Fremont CA 94539 510-360-0990
Web: www.sapphireinfotech.com

Sapta Global Inc 267 Amboy Ave Ste 125 Woodbridge NJ 07095 732-602-0240
Web: www.saptanet.com

Sauper Associates Inc 1317 Rt 73 Ste 205 Mount Laurel NJ 08054 856-778-3800
Web: sauper.com

Sawtooth Software Inc 1457 East 840 North Orem UT 84097 360-681-2300
Web: www.sawtoothsoftware.com

SBS Studios LLC
8400 Baymeadows Way Ste 4 Jacksonville FL 32256 904-352-2401
Web: www.sbsstudios.com

SciImage Inc 4916 El Camino Real Los Altos CA 94022 650-694-4858
Web: www.scimage.com

Sea Island Software Inc
330 Bampfield Dr Mount Pleasant SC 29464 843-881-0593
Web: www.hurrevac.com

Seal Systems Inc 17505 N 79th Ave Ste 201 Glendale AZ 85308 865-380-0005
Web: www.sealsystems.com

Seattle Lab Inc 11730 118th Ave NE Ste 400 Kirkland WA 98034 425-825-7000
Web: www.seattlelab.com

SECNAP Network Security Corp
6421 Congress Ave Ste 206 Boca Raton FL 33487 561-999-5000
Web: www.secnap.com

Securboration Inc 1050 W Nasa Blvd Ste 156 Melbourne FL 32901 321-409-5252
Web: www.securboration.com

Secure Passage
8400 W 110th St Ste 400 Shawnee Mission KS 66210 913-948-9575
Web: www.firemon.com

SecurLinx Holding Corp 150 Clay St Ste 440 Morgantown WV 26501 304-284-5020
Web: www.securlinx.com

SEIDCON Inc 145 Vallecitos De Oro Ste G San Marcos CA 92069 760-510-9800
Web: www.seidcon.com

Sengen Inc 1000 Briggs Rd Mount Laurel NJ 08054 856-793-9300
Web: www.sengen.com

Sensible Vision Inc 40376 Blue Star Hwy Ste 11 Covert MI 49043 269-932-4548
Web: www.sensiblevision.com

Sentinel Development Solutions Inc
4015 Beltline Rd Ste 100 Addison TX 75001 515-564-0585
Web: www.sentinelds.com

Sequoyah Technologies LLC
6666 S Sheridan Ste 210 Tulsa OK 74133 918-493-7200
Web: www.seqtek.com

Servant Systems Inc 13770 Is Lk Rd Chelsea MI 48118 734-475-1619
Web: servantsystems.com

Setu Inc 388 B Great Rd Ste 20 Acton MA 01720 978-263-0262
Web: www.setu.com

Sharp Innovations Inc 117 SW End Ave Lancaster PA 17603 717-290-6760
Web: www.sharpinnovations.com

ShiftWise Inc 1800 SW 1st Ave Ste 510 Portland OR 97201 503-548-2030
Web: www.shiftwise.net

Sierra Creative Systems Inc
7283 Bellaire Ave Ste 2 North Hollywood CA 91605 818-503-0691
Web: www.theaddressers.com

Sigma Business Solutions Inc 55 York St Toronto ON M5J1R7 855-594-1991
TF: 855-594-1991 ■ *Web:* www.sigma-sbs.com

Sigmetrix LLC 105 W Virginia St Mckinney TX 75069 972-542-7517
Web: www.sigmetrix.com

Silent Solutions Inc 8704 Lee Hwy Fairfax VA 22031 703-849-8246
Web: www.silentsolutions.com

Silicomm Corp 6302 Far Hills Ave Dayton OH 45459 937-310-3940
Web: www.silicomm.com

SimpleSolve Inc 1 Airport Pl Ste 3 Princeton NJ 08540 609-452-2323
Web: www.simplesolve.com

Sincera Consulting Llc 3735 Dohm Dr Charlevoix MI 49720 231-547-0478
Web: www.sincera.net

SiteStuff Inc
12401 Research Blvd Bldg 1 Ste 250 Austin TX 78759 512-514-7800
Web: www.sitestuff.com

Skelmier Llc 55 Davis Sq Somerville MA 02144 617-625-1551
Web: www.roaster.org

Skunk Studios LLC 463 Bryant St San Francisco CA 94107 415-777-0900
Web: www.skunkstudios.com

SkyZone Entertainment Inc 8400 River Rd North Bergen NJ 07047 201-453-1110
Web: www.skyzonemobile.com

Slight Edge Solutions Inc 28 Dominic Dr Monroe NJ 08831 646-342-9407
Web: www.itsses.com

Smartleaf Inc One Cambridge Ctr 7th Fl Cambridge MA 02142 617-453-0714
Web: www.smartleaf.com

Snap Surveys Ltd 210 Commerce Way Ste 200 Portsmouth NH 03801 603-610-8700
Web: www.snapsurveys.com

Softex Inc 9300 Jollyville Rd Ste 201 Austin TX 78759 512-452-8836
Web: www.softexinc.com

SoftLEAD Technology Partners Inc
100 S Citrus Ave Ste: 201 Ste Covina CA 91723 626-915-0001
Web: www.softlead.com

SoftThinks USA Inc Jollyville Rd Ste 225-S Austin CA 78759 512-258-5574
Web: www.softthinks.com

SoftVu LLC 12920 Metcalf Ste 200 Overland Park KS 66213 913-696-9700
Web: www.SoftVu.com

Software Folks Inc 50 Bridge St Metuchen NJ 08840 609-945-1737
Web: www.softwarefolks.com

Softwyre Inc 14916 Wade Blvd Maumelle AR 72113 501-734-0017
Web: www.softwyre.com

Sohar Inc 5601 W Slauson Ave Ste 257 Culver City CA 90230 310-338-0990
Web: www.sohar.com

Solidus Technical Solutions Inc
17 Forsythia Rd Leominster MA 01453 978-534-8363
Web: www.solidus-ts.com

Soltrix Technology Solutions Inc
16 Thomas Newton Dr Westborough MA 01581 774-293-1293
Web: www.soltrixsolutions.com

Solution Design Group Inc
Minnetonka Executive Plz 10275 Wayzata Blvd
Ste 300 Minnetonka MN 55305 952-278-2500
Web: solutiondesign.com

Sovereign Technologies Llc
11414 Gravois Rd Ste 301 Saint Louis MO 63126 314-537-5739
Web: www.sovereigntec.com

Spark Plug Games Llc 1011 Passport Way Cary NC 27513 919-651-0792
Web: www.sparkpluggames.com

SpecTec Inc 22500 SE 64th Pl Ste 230 Issaquah WA 98027 425-313-0154
Web: www.spectec.net

Spindustry Systems Corp
1370 Nw 114th St Ste 300 Clive IA 50325 515-225-0920
Web: www.spindustry.com

Spn Services Inc 5851 43rd Ave Flushing NY 11377 718-565-5954
Web: www.spnservices.com

Spokane Software Systems Inc 911 N Pines Rd Spokane WA 99206 509-252-4150
Web: sssonline.com

Sprocket Express LLC 23 W Bacon St Plainville MA 02762 508-695-3673
Web: www.sprocketexpress.com

Sproxil Inc 1 Fitchburg St C320 Somerville MA 02143 209-877-7694
Web: www.sproxil.com

Stauder Technologies Inc 114 Mexico Ct St Peters MO 63376 636-498-6658
Web: www.staudertech.com

SteelTorch Software Inc 423 Jamestown Rd Belmont NH 03220 866-705-2730
TF: 866-705-2730 ■ *Web:* www.steeltorch.com

SteepRock Inc 67 Lwr Church Hill Rd Washington Depot CT 06794 860-868-8075
Web: www.steeprockinc.com

Stepware Inc 320 Dakota Dr Grand Junction CO 81507 970-243-9390
Web: www.stepware.com

Stock Garber & Assoc Inc 1368 Manor Dr Ebensburg PA 15931 814-472-5158
Web: www.sgasoftware.com

STR Grants LLC 4103 Chain Bridge Rd 3rd Fl Fairfax VA 22030 703-460-9004
Web: www.strllc.com

StratBridge LLC
124 Mount Auburn St University Pl Ste 200 Cambridge MA 02138 978-772-4647
Web: www.stratbridge.com

Structure Networks Inc 17542 17th St Ste 105 Tustin CA 92780 714-505-0330
Web: www.structurenetworks.com

Submittal Exchange LLC 495 Alices Rd Waukee IA 50263 515-978-2060
Web: www.submittalexchange.com

Sunera Technologies Inc
631 E Big Beaver Rd Ste 109 Troy MI 48083 248-524-0222
Web: www.suneratech.com

Company	City	State	Zip	Phone	Fax
Sungard Bi-Tech Inc 890 Ftress St *Web:* bi-tech.com	Chico	CA	95973	530-891-5281	
Surgeworks 4609 South 2300 East Ste 103 *Web:* www.surgeworks.com	Holladay	UT	84117	801-272-9800	
Swb Consulting Inc 466 Green St Ste 303 *Web:* www.swb-consulting.com	San Francisco	CA	94133	415-543-5825	
Sybven Llc 440 Sawgrass Corporate Pkwy Ste 108-a *Web:* www.sybven.com	Sunrise	FL	33325	954-837-0078	
Symphony Corp 22 E Mifflin St Ste 400 *Web:* www.symphonycorp.com	Madison	WI	53703	608-294-4090	
Syntergy Inc 6515 El Camino Del Teatro *Web:* www.syntergy.com	La Jolla	CA	92037	858-964-3243	
SYO Computer Engineering Services Inc 42621 Garfield Rd Ste 108 *Web:* www.syo.com	Clinton Township	MI	48038	586-286-2557	
SYSTAP LLC 1737 Harvard St Nw *Web:* www.systap.com	Washington	DC	20009	801-328-3945	
Tactical Network Solutions LLC 8850 Stanford Blvd Ste 1600 *Web:* www.tacnetsol.com	Columbia	MD	21045	443-276-6990	
Tarsin Inc 916 Southwood Blvd Ste 3A *Web:* www.tarsin.com	Incline Village	NV	89451	775-833-0156	
Taxography Inc 6353 N Rosebury Ave *Web:* www.taxography.com	Saint Louis	MO	63105	314-863-9292	
TBD Networks Inc 2 N First St *Web:* www.tbdnetworks.com	San Jose	CA	95113	408-278-1590	
Team IA Inc 714 S Lk Dr Ste 110 *Web:* www.teamia.com	Lexington	SC	29072	803-356-7676	
Tech Hackers LLC 332 Springfield Ave *Web:* www.thi.com	Summit	NJ	07901	908-598-1460	
Techaspect Solutions Inc 6750 Fremont Blvd, Ste 204 *Web:* www.techaspect.com	Fremont	CA	94538	510-962-3200	
TechProse Inc 3685 Mt. Diablo Blvd Ste 340 *Web:* www.techprose.com	Lafayette	CA	94549	925-299-3900	
Techtonic Group Llc 142 Bonita Ave., Ste. 216 Ste *Web:* www.techtonicgroup.com	San Dimas	CA	91773	303-440-8772	
Tekgroup International Inc 1280 Sw 36th Ave Ste 204 *Web:* www.tekgroup.com	Pompano Beach	FL	33069	954-351-5554	
TeleBright Software Corp 1700 Research Blvd Ste 240 *Web:* www.telebright.com	Rockville	MD	20850	301-296-3800	
Telstar Associates Inc 2108 Amy Ave *Web:* www.telstarinc.net	Boise	ID	83706	208-343-3894	
Terrasage Technology Partners Llc 3313 Butler Ave *Web:* terrasage.com	Los Angeles	CA	90066	310-391-2015	
TerraSpark Geosciences L P 10955 Westmoor Dr *Web:* www.terraspark.com	Westminster	CO	80021	303-379-3050	
Teton Data Systems 125 S Kings St Ste G1 *Web:* www.tetondata.com/	Jackson	WY	83001	307-733-5494	
ThinkFire Services USA Ltd 1011 Rt 22W Ste 101 *Web:* www.thinkfire.com	Bridgewater	NJ	08807	908-991-9000	
Thinkgeo LLC 1617 Saint Andrews Dr *Web:* thinkgeo.com	Lawrence	KS	66047	785-727-4133	
Thylaksoft Llc 307 Elizabeth Sweetbriar Ln *Web:* www.thylaksoft.com	New Castle	DE	19720	302-355-0449	
Tip Technologies Inc N14 W24200 Twr Pl Ste 100 *Web:* www.tiptech.com	Waukesha	WI	53188	262-544-1211	
Tiva Software LLC 5200 Park Rd Ste 235 *Web:* www.tivasoftware.com	Charlotte	NC	28209	704-525-0005	
Tiversa Inc 144 Emeryville Dr Ste 300 Cranberry Township *Web:* www.tiversa.com	Cranberry Twp	PA	16066	724-940-9030	
Tk Interactive Inc 9 N Long St *Web:* www.tkinteractive.com	Williamsville	NY	14221	716-632-2967	
TMD Solutions Inc 938 E Swan Creek Rd Ste 270 *Web:* www.tmdx.com	Fort Washington	MD	20744	301-248-1465	
TMT Software Co 6114 Fayetteville Rd Ste 106 *Web:* www.tmtsoftware.com	Durham	NC	27713	919-493-4700	
Tnr Global Llc 277 Main St Ste 301 *Web:* www.tnrglobal.com	Greenfield	MA	01301	413-425-1499	
Tokenzone Inc 34 S Broadway Ste 712 *Web:* tokenzone.com	White Plains	NY	10601	914-997-1999	
Treefort Inc 6500 Barrie Rd Ste 10 *Web:* www.treefort.com	Minneapolis	MN	55435	612-285-5625	
Tri-bry Information Solutions 123 Harrison St *Web:* www.tribry.com	Hoboken	NJ	07030	201-798-5191	
Tricycle Inc 3001 Broad St 2nd Fl *Web:* www.tricycleinc.com	Chattanooga	TN	37408	423-648-6480	
Trinal Inc 329 W 18th St Ste 405 *Web:* www.trinalinc.com	Chicago	IL	60616	312-738-0500	
Triniti Corp 9999 Hamilton Blvd One Tek Park Ste 340 *Web:* www.triniti.com	Breinigsville	PA	18031	610-530-7268	
Trinity Information Technology Llc 17 Windmill Dr *Web:* www.trinityit.biz	Southampton	PA	18966	267-254-7421	
Tripod Technologies Llc 1050 Kings Hwy N Ste 102 *Web:* www.tripodtech.net	Cherry Hill	NJ	08034	856-755-1478	
TriTeal Corp 2011 Palomar Airport Rd *Web:* www.triteal.com	Carlsbad	CA	92009	760-827-5000	
Trivent Systems Inc 2274 Eldemere Cir *Web:* www.triventlegal.com	Macungie	PA	18062	610-832-1529	
Truefit Solutions Inc 800 Cranberry Woods Dr Ste 120 *Web:* www.truefitsolutions.com	Cranberry Township	PA	16066	724-772-5959	
TrueNorthLogic LLC 8160 S Highland Dr Ste A-5 *Web:* www.truenorthlogic.com	Sandy	UT	84093	801-453-0136	
TSG Solutions Inc 685 Carnegie Dr Ste 210 *Web:* www.tsginc.com	San Bernardino	CA	92408	909-475-4080	
Ultryx 8760 Orion Pl, Ste 200 *Web:* www.ultryx.com	Columbus	OH	43240	614-410-2020	
Unibased Systems Architecture Inc 14323 S Outer 40 Rd S Ste 300 *Web:* www.unibased.com	St. Louis	MO	63017	314-878-6050	
UNICOM Systems Inc 15535 San Fernando Mission Blvd UNICOM Plz Ste 310 *Web:* www.unicomglobal.com	Mission Hills	CA	91345	818-883-0606	
Uniplus Consultants Inc 8700 Centreville Rd Ste 300 *Web:* www.uniplus.com	Manassas	VA	20110	703-365-2227	
United Developers LLC 2019 N Lamar St Ste 240 *Web:* uniteddevelopersllc.com	Dallas	TX	75202	214-855-5955	
US Netcom Corp 710 S Maiden Ln *Web:* www.usnetcomcorp.com	Joplin	MO	64801	417-781-1185	
US Websoft Corp 2430, Birch Cove Rd *Web:* www.us-websoft.com	Herndon	VA	20171	703-318-0103	
Vel Micro Works Inc 726 Yorklyn Rd Ste 400 *Web:* www.velmicro.com	Hockessin	DE	19707	302-239-4661	
Velaro Inc 8174 Lark Brown Rd Ste 201 *TF:* 800-983-5276 ■ *Web:* www.velaro.com	Elkridge	MD	21075	800-983-5276	
Venarc Inc 2314 W Burbank Blvd *Web:* www.venarc.com	Burbank	CA	91506	818-524-2500	
Verge Solutions LLC 641 Royall Ave *Web:* verge-solutions.com	Mount Pleasant	SC	29464	843-628-4168	
Verient Inc 1190 Saratoga Ave Ste 220 *Web:* www.verient.com	San Jose	CA	95129	408-521-1660	
Verisma Systems Inc 510 W 3rd St Ste 200 *Web:* www.verismasystems.com	Pueblo	CO	81003	719-546-1849	
Vertex Computer Systems Inc 2245 Enterprise Pkwy E *Web:* www.vertexcs.com	Twinsburg	OH	44087	330-963-0044	
Viable Solutions Inc 2839 University Acres Dr *Web:* viable-solutions.com	Orlando	FL	32817	407-249-9200	
ViaTrack Systems LLC 2840 Hillcreek Dr *Web:* www.viatrack.com	Augusta	GA	30909	706-869-9960	
VIDA Diagnostics Inc 2500 Crosspark Rd W150 BioVentures Ctr *Web:* www.vidadiagnostics.com	Coralville	IA	52241	319-335-4740	
Vigilistics Inc 14 Bunsen Ste 100 *Web:* www.vigilistics.com	Irvine	CA	92691	949-900-8380	
Vision7 Software 4729 E Sunrise Dr Ste 201 *Web:* www.vision7.com	Tucson	AZ	85718	520-320-5442	
Visionpace Inc 17501 E US Hwy 40 *Web:* www.visionpace.com	Independence	MO	64055	816-350-7900	
VisionWare Inc 930 W 1st St Ste 200 *Web:* www.visionware-inc.com	Fort Worth	TX	76102	817-810-9109	
Vistem Solutions Inc 2102 Business Ctr Dr Ste 220 *Web:* www.vistem.com	Irvine	CA	92649	949-253-5729	
Vitalyst LLC One Bala Plz Ste 434 *Web:* www.pchelps.com	Bala Cynwyd	PA	19004	610-668-3516	
Vivid Image Inc 897 Hwy 15 S *Web:* www.vimm.com	Hutchinson	MN	55350	320-587-8974	
Vivisimo Inc 1710 Murray Ave *Web:* vivisimo.com	Pittsburgh	PA	15217	412-422-2499	
VoIP Group Inc 6161 Blue Lagoon Dr Ste 190 *Web:* www.voipgroup.com	Miami	FL	33126	305-264-2401	
Vortalsoft Inc 100 Davidson Ave Ste 300 *Web:* vortalsoft.com	Somerset	NJ	08873	732-748-1800	
Voxify Inc 1151 Marina Village Pkwy *Web:* www.voxify.com	Alameda	CA	94501	510-545-5000	
W 3 Edge Llc 12 Stoneholm St Apt 602 *Web:* w3-edge.com	Boston	MA	02115	617-375-6134	
W3health Solutions LLC 115 Franklin TurnPk Ste 352 *Web:* www.w3health.com	Mahwah	NJ	07430	201-701-0240	
Wasabi Systems Inc 500 E Main St Ste 1520 *Web:* www.wasabisystems.com	Norfolk	VA	23510	757-248-9601	
Waterford Technologies Inc 19700 Fairchild Ste 300 *Web:* www.waterfordtechnologies.com	Irvine	CA	92612	949-428-9300	
Wave Software LLC 300 S Orange Ave Ste 900 *Web:* www.discoverthewave.com	Orlando	FL	32801	407-325-5006	
Web Presence Architects LLC 10113 Meadowneck Ct *Web:* wpaconsulting.com	Silver Spring	MD	20910	301-587-3584	
Web.com 12808 Grand Bay Pkwy W *TF:* 800-338-1771 ■ *Web:* www.web.com	Jacksonville	FL	32258	904-680-6600	880-0350
Westtek 8585 154th Ave Ne *Web:* www.westtek.com	Redmond	WA	98052	425-861-8271	
WGAL LLC 6900 N Dallas Pkwy Ste 600 *Web:* www.wizetrade.com	Plano	TX	75024	972-387-4728	
Whiteboard Labs LLC 3100 Richmond Ave Ste 200 *Web:* www.whiteboardlabs.com	Houston	TX	77098	713-333-9944	
Willow Technology Inc 961 Red Tail Ln Ste 220 *Web:* www.willowtech.com	Bellingham	WA	98226	360-393-4962	
Wilson Hewitt & Associates Inc 355 Lancaster Ave Ste *Web:* www.wha.com	Haverford	PA	19041	610-649-2300	

Company	City	State	Zip	Phone	Fax
Winsoft Corp 1932 E. Deere Ave Alton Deere Plz, Ste 110 *Web:* www.winsoft.com	Santa Ana	CA	92705	949-428-4844	
Wipro Gallagher Solutions Inc 18001 Old Cutler Rd Ste 651 *Web:* wiprogallagher.com	Palmetto Bay	FL	33157	305-251-6654	
Wizards of Oztechs Llc, The 2099 Mt Diablo Blvd Ste 203 *Web:* www.oztechs.com	Walnut Creek	CA	94596	925-280-7400	
Wonderware Mobile Solutions Group 10111 Richmond Ave Ste 650 *Web:* www.sat-corp.com	Houston	TX	77042	713-344-2600	
XLPrint USA LLC 213 Rose Ave Ste 1 *Web:* www.usa.xlprint.com	Venice	CA	90291	310-829-7684	
Xpriori Llc 2864 S Cir Dr Ste 1200 *Web:* www.xpriori.com	Colorado Springs	CO	80906	719-527-1315	
XRiver Technologies LLC 5175 Parkstone Dr *Web:* www.xrivertech.com	Chantilly	VA	20151	703-480-0480	
Yale Software Solutions 9 Yale Dr *Web:* its.yale.edu	New City	NY	10956	845-304-8033	
Z-space Technologies Inc 26933 Westwood Rd Ste 400 *Web:* www.z-space.com	Cleveland	OH	44145	440-899-7370	
Zco Corp 41 Sagamore Park Rd *Web:* www.zco.com	Hudson	NH	03051	603-881-9200	
ZEH Software Inc 16420 Park Ten Pl Ste 520 *Web:* www.zeh.com	Houston	TX	77084	281-589-7757	
Zen Ventures LLC 3939 S 6th St Ste 201 *TF:* 888-936-2278 ■ *Web:* www.zen-cart.com	Klamath Falls	OR	97603	888-936-2278	
Zlantech Inc 16 Technology Dr Ste 321 *Web:* www.zlantech.com	Irvine	CA	92618	949-679-0465	
Zolon Tech Inc 13921 Park Ctr Rd Ste 350 *Web:* www.zolontech.com	Herndon	VA	20171	703-636-7370	
Zolon Tech Solutions Inc 21515 Ridgetop Cir Ste 350 *Web:* www.zolon.com	Sterling	VA	20166	703-378-6585	
Zoniac Inc 1613 S Main St Ste 104 *Web:* www.zoniac.com	Milpitas	CA	95035	408-719-9991	

810 WEIGHT LOSS CENTERS & SERVICES

See Also Health & Fitness Centers p. 2456; Spas - Health & Fitness p. 3187

Company	City	State	Zip	Phone	Fax
American Laser Skincare 24555 Hallwood Ct *Web:* www.americanlaser.com	Farmington Hills	MI	48335	248-426-8250	
Barix Clinics 135 S Prospect St *TF:* 800-282-0066 ■ *Web:* www.barixclinics.com	Ypsilanti	MI	48198	734-547-4700	
Companions & Homemakers Inc 613 New Britain Ave *TF:* 800-348-4663 ■ *Web:* www.companionsandhomemakers.com	Farmington	CT	06032	860-677-4948	
Fit America MD 4864 Arthur Kill Rd *TF:* 800-940-7546 ■ *Web:* fitamerica.com	Staten Island	NY	10309	718-227-4980	
Fuze Fit for a Kid 15405 Los Gatos Blvd Ste 103 *Web:* www.fuzefit.com	Los Gatos	CA	95032	408-358-7529	
Greenpath Inc 36500 Corporate Dr *TF:* 800-550-1961 ■ *Web:* www.greenpath.com	Farmington Hills	MI	48331	248-553-5400	699-1613
Indigo Integrative Studio 1304 Eighth Ave *Web:* www.indigo-pilates.com	Brooklyn	NY	11215	718-832-3464	
Jazzercise Inc 2460 Impala Dr *TF Cust Svc:* 800-348-4748 ■ *Web:* www.jazzercise.com	Carlsbad	CA	92010	760-476-1750	602-7180
Jenny Craig International Inc 5770 Fleet St *TF:* 800-443-2331 ■ *Web:* www.jennycraig.com	Carlsbad	CA	92008	760-696-4000	696-4506
JumpstartMD 595 Price Ave Ste 200 *Web:* www.jumpstartmd.com	Redwood City	CA	94063	650-701-1460	
Maria Paonessa Moda 2000 1500 N Wells St 2	Chicago	IL	60610	312-994-6747	
NutriSystem Inc 600 Office Center Dr Bldg 1 *NASDAQ: NTRI* ■ *TF:* 800-585-5483 ■ *Web:* www.nutrisystem.com	Fort Washington	PA	19034	215-706-5300	
Physicians Weight Loss Centers of America Inc 395 Springside Dr *TF:* 800-205-7887 ■ *Web:* www.pwlc.com	Akron	OH	44333	330-666-7952	666-2197
Primescape Solutions Inc 510A Herndon Pkwy *Web:* www.primescape.net	Herndon	VA	20170	703-650-1900	650-1901
Weight Management Centers 2605 W Swann Ave Ste 600 *Web:* www.weightmanagement.com	Tampa	FL	33609	813-876-7073	877-1277

811 WELDING & SOLDERING EQUIPMENT

Company	City	State	Zip	Phone	Fax
Acro Automation Systems Inc 2900 W Green Tree Rd *Web:* www.acro.com	Milwaukee	WI	53209	414-352-4540	352-1609
AGM Industries Inc 16 Jonathan Dr *TF:* 800-225-9990 ■ *Web:* www.agmind.com	Brockton	MA	02301	508-587-3900	587-3283
Alliance Winding Equipment Inc 3939 Vanguard Dr *Web:* www.alliance-winding.com	Fort Wayne	IN	46809	260-478-2200	
American Ultraviolet Co 40 Morristown Rd *TF:* 800-288-9288 ■ *Web:* www.americanultraviolet.com	Bernardsville	NJ	07924	908-696-1130	696-1131
Applied Fusion Inc 1915 Republic Ave *Web:* appliedfusioninc.com	San Leandro	CA	94577	510-351-4511	351-0692
Arc Machines Inc 10500 Orbital Way *Web:* www.arcmachines.com	Pacoima	CA	91331	818-896-9556	890-3724
Arcos Industries 1 Arcos Dr *TF:* 800-233-8460 ■ *Web:* www.arcos.us	Mount Carmel	PA	17851	570-339-5200	339-5206
Aro Welding 48500 Structural Dr *Web:* www.arotechnologies.com	Chesterfield	MI	48051	586-949-9353	949-4493
Automation International Inc 1020 Bahls St *Web:* www.automation-intl.com	Danville	IL	61832	217-446-9500	446-6855
Banner Welder Inc N 117 W 18200 Fulton Dr *Web:* www.bannerweld.com	Germantown	WI	53022	262-253-2900	
Bernard Welding Equipment 449 W Corning Rd *Web:* www.bernardwelds.com	Beecher	IL	60401	708-946-2281	
Bonal Technologies Inc 1300 N Campbell Rd *Web:* www.bonal.com	Royal Oak	MI	48067	248-582-0900	
BUG-O Systems Inc 161 Hillpointe Dr *TF:* 800-245-3186 ■ *Web:* www.bugo.com	Canonsburg	PA	15317	412-331-1776	331-0383
CK Worldwide Inc 3501 C St NE *TF:* 800-426-0877 ■ *Web:* www.ckworldwide.com	Auburn	WA	98002	253-854-5820	939-1746
Esab Welding & Cutting Products Inc 411 S Ebenezer Rd PO Box 100545 **Fax:* Hum Res ■ *TF:* 800-372-2123 ■ *Web:* www.esabna.com	Florence	SC	29501	843-669-4411	664-4258*
Eureka Welding Alloys Inc 2000 E Avis Dr *TF:* 800-962-8560 ■ *Web:* www.eurekaweldingalloys.com	Madison Heights	MI	48071	248-588-0001	585-7711
Eutectic Corp N 94 W 14355 Garwin Mace Dr *TF:* 800-558-8524 ■ *Web:* www.eutectic-na.com	Menomonee Falls	WI	53051	262-532-4677	255-5542
Forney Industries Inc 1830 LaPorte Ave *TF:* 800-521-6038 ■ *Web:* www.forneyind.com	Fort Collins	CO	80521	800-521-6038	
Gapco Inc 2151 Centennial Dr *Web:* www.gapco.com	Gainesville	GA	30504	770-534-7928	
Goss Inc 1511 William Flynn Hwy *TF:* 800-367-4677 ■ *Web:* www.gossonline.com	Glenshaw	PA	15116	412-486-6100	486-6844
Grossel Tool Co 34190 Doreka *Web:* www.grosseltool.com	Fraser	MI	48026	586-294-3660	294-7134
Harris Products Group 4501 Quality Pl **Fax:* Sales ■ *TF:* 800-733-4043 ■ *Web:* www.harrisproductsgroup.com	Mason	OH	45040	513-754-2000	754-8778*
Hobart Bros Co 101 Trade Sq E *TF:* 800-424-1543 ■ *Web:* www.hobartbrothers.com	Troy	OH	45373	937-332-4000	332-5178
Indalco Alloys Inc 939 Gana Ct *Web:* www.indalco.com	Mississauga	ON	L5S1N9	905-564-1151	564-1405
Industrial Welders & Machinists Inc 610 Opperman Dr *TF:* 800-455-4565 ■ *Web:* caselaw.findlaw.com	Eagan	MN	55123	800-455-4565	
Jetline Engineering 15 Goodyear St *Web:* www.jetline.com	Irvine	CA	92618	949-951-1515	951-9237
JWF Industries 84 Iron St PO Box 1286 *TF:* 800-225-9359 ■ *Web:* www.jwfi.com	Johnstown	PA	15907	814-539-6922	
Lincoln Electric Co 22801 St Clair Ave *TF:* 888-935-3878 ■ *Web:* www.lincolnelectric.com	Cleveland	OH	44117	216-481-8100	486-1751
M K Products Inc 16882 Armstrong Ave *TF:* 800-787-9707 ■ *Web:* www.mkprod.com	Irvine	CA	92606	949-863-1234	474-1428
Maine Oxy 22 Albiston Way *TF:* 800-639-1108 ■ *Web:* www.maineoxy.com	Auburn	ME	04210	207-784-5788	784-5383
Manufacturing Technology Inc (MTI) 1702 W Washington St *Web:* www.mtiwelding.com	South Bend	IN	46628	574-233-9490	233-9489
Merrill Mfg Corp 236 S Genesee St *TF:* 888-662-9473 ■ *Web:* www.merrill-mfg.com	Merrill	WI	54452	715-536-5533	536-5590
Milco Manufacturing Co 2147 E 10-Mile Rd *Web:* www.milcomfg.com	Warren	MI	48091	586-755-7320	755-7442
Miller Electric Mfg Co 1635 W Spencer St **Fax:* Sales ■ *TF:* 888-843-7693 ■ *Web:* www.millerwelds.com	Appleton	WI	54914	920-734-9821	735-4134*
NLC Inc 319 W Main St **Fax Area Code:* 800 ■ *TF Sales:* 800-594-3958 ■ *Web:* profaxlenco.com	Jackson	MO	63755	573-243-3141	232-3046*
Northern Stamping Corp 6600 Chapek Pkwy *Web:* northernstamping.com	Cleveland	OH	44125	216-883-8888	883-8237
Ogden Welding Systems Inc 372 Div St *Web:* www.ogdenwelding.com	Schererville	IN	46375	219-322-5252	865-1825
Palomar Technologies 2728 Loker Ave W *TF:* 800-854-3467 ■ *Web:* www.palomartechnologies.com	Carlsbad	CA	92010	760-931-3600	931-5191
Pandjiris Inc 5151 Northrup Ave *Web:* www.pandjiris.com	Saint Louis	MO	63110	314-776-6893	776-8763
Pia Group Inc 3520 Ibsen Ave *Web:* www.piagroup.com	Cincinnati	OH	45209	513-351-3300	
Research Inc 7128 Shady Oak Rd *Web:* pcscontrols.com	Eden Prairie	MN	55344	952-941-3300	941-3628
RoMan Manufacturing Inc 861 47th St SW *Web:* www.romanmfg.com	Grand Rapids	MI	49509	616-530-8641	530-8953
RWC Inc 2105 S Euclid Ave *Web:* www.rwcinc.com	Bay City	MI	48706	989-684-4030	684-3960
Sciaky Inc 4915 W 67th St *Web:* www.sciaky.com	Chicago	IL	60638	708-594-3800	594-9213
Smith Equipment Mfg Co 2601 Lockheed Ave *TF Cust Svc:* 866-931-9730 ■ *Web:* www.smithequipment.com	Watertown	SD	57201	605-882-3200	882-2100
Sonobond Ultrasonics Inc 1191 McDermott Dr *TF:* 800-323-1269 ■ *Web:* sonobondultrasonics.com	West Chester	PA	19380	610-696-4710	692-0674
Systematics Inc 1025 Saunders Ln PO Box 2429 *TF:* 800-222-9353 ■ *Web:* 800abcweld.com	West Chester	PA	19380	610-696-9040	430-8714
Taylor-Winfield Inc 3200 Innovation Pl *Web:* www.taylor-winfield.com	Youngstown	OH	44509	330-259-8500	259-8538
Thermatool Corp 31 Commerce St **Fax:* Cust Svc ■ *Web:* www.thermatool.com	East Haven	CT	06512	203-468-4100	468-4281*
Tuffaloy Products Inc 1400 S Batesville Rd *TF:* 800-521-3722 ■ *Web:* www.tuffaloy.com	Greer	SC	29650	864-879-0763	877-2212
Uniweld Products Inc 2850 Ravenswood Rd *TF:* 800-323-2111 ■ *Web:* www.uniweld.com	Fort Lauderdale	FL	33312	954-584-2000	587-0109
Vitronics Soltec Inc 2 Marin Way *Web:* www.vitronics-soltec.com	Stratham	NH	03885	603-772-7778	
Weld Mold Co 750 Rickett Rd *TF:* 800-521-9755 ■ *Web:* www.weldmold.com	Brighton	MI	48116	810-229-9521	229-9580
Western Enterprises Inc 875 Bassett Rd **Fax Area Code:* 440 ■ *TF:* 800-783-7890 ■ *Web:* www.westernenterprises.com	Westlake	OH	44145	800-783-7890	835-8283*

812 WHOLESALE CLUBS

Company	City	State	ZIP	Phone	Fax
Costco Wholesale Corp 999 Lake Dr. *NASDAQ:* COST ■ *TF Cust Svc:* 800-774-2678 ■ *Web:* www.costco.com	Issaquah	WA	98027	425-313-8100	
Marukai Wholesale Mart 2310 Kamehameha Hwy *Web:* www.marukaihawaii.com	Honolulu	HI	96819	808-845-5051	841-2379
PriceSmart Inc 9740 Scranton Rd *NASDAQ:* PSMT ■ *Web:* www.pricesmart.com	San Diego	CA	92121	858-404-8800	

813 WIRE & CABLE

Company	City	State	ZIP	Phone	Fax
Ace Wire & Cable Co Inc 7201 51st Ave *TF:* 800-225-2354 ■ *Web:* www.acewireco.com	Woodside	NY	11377	718-458-9200	335-6340
AFC Cable Systems Inc 272 Duchaine Blvd *TF:* 800-757-6996 ■ *Web:* www.afcweb.com	New Bedford	MA	02745	508-998-1131	998-1447
Allwire Inc 16395 Ave 24 1/2 PO Box 1000 *TF:* 800-255-3828 ■ *Web:* www.allwire.com	Chowchilla	CA	93610	559-665-4893	
AmerCable Inc 350 Bailey Rd *TF:* 800-643-1516 ■ *Web:* www.amercable.com	El Dorado	AR	71730	870-862-4919	862-9613
Astro Industries Inc 4403 Dayton-Xenia Rd *Fax: Sales ■ *TF:* 800-543-5810 ■ *Web:* www.astro-ind.com	Dayton	OH	45432	937-429-5900	429-4054*
Bekaert Corp 3200 W Market St Ste 303 *Web:* www.bekaert.com	Akron	OH	44333	330-867-3325	873-3424
Cerro Wire & Cable Company Inc 1099 Thompson Rd SE *TF:* 800-523-3869 ■ *Web:* www.cerrowire.com	Hartselle	AL	35640	256-773-2522	
Charter Wire 3700 W Milwaukee Rd *TF:* 800-436-9074 ■ *Web:* www.charterwire.com	Milwaukee	WI	53208	414-390-3000	390-3031
Cooner Wire Co 9265 Owensmouth Ave *Web:* www.coonerwire.com	Chatsworth	CA	91311	818-882-8311	709-8281
Cove West 195 E Merrick Rd *Web:* covewestusa.com	Freeport	NY	11520	714-525-2930	525-2928
Elektrisola Inc 126 High St *TF:* 800-325-2022 ■ *Web:* www.elektrisola.com	Boscawen	NH	03303	603-796-2114	
Encore Wire Corp 1329 Millwood Rd *NASDAQ:* WIRE ■ *TF:* 800-962-9473 ■ *Web:* www.encorewire.com	McKinney	TX	75069	972-562-9473	562-3644
Eubanks Engineering Co 3022 Inland Empire Blvd *TF:* 800-729-4208 ■ *Web:* www.eubanks.com	Ontario	CA	91764	909-483-2456	483-2498
Fiberwave Corp 140 58th St Bldg B Unit 6E *TF:* 800-280-9011 ■ *Web:* www.fiberwave.com	Brooklyn	NY	11220	718-802-9011	802-0116
Foerster Instruments Inc 140 Industry Dr *Web:* www.foerstergroup.com	Pittsburgh	PA	15275	412-788-8976	788-8984
Gehr Industries 7400 E Slauson Ave *TF:* 800-688-6606 ■ *Web:* gehr.com	Los Angeles	CA	90040	323-728-5558	728-1983
Hendrix Wire & Cable Inc 53 Old Wilton Rd *Web:* www.hendrix-wc.com	Milford	NH	03055	603-673-2040	673-1497
Insteel Industries Inc 1373 Boggs Dr *NASDAQ:* IIIN ■ *TF:* 800-334-9504 ■ *Web:* www.insteel.com	Mount Airy	NC	27030	336-786-2141	786-2144
Inter-Wire Products (IWP) 355 Main St *Web:* www.interwiregroup.com	Armonk	NY	10504	914-273-6633	273-6848
Kalas Manufacturing Inc 167 Greenfield Rd *Web:* www.kalaswire.com	Lancaster	PA	17601	717-336-5575	945-1002
Kerite Co 49 Day St *TF:* 800-777-7483 ■ *Web:* www.kerite.com	Seymour	CT	06483	203-888-2591	888-1987
Keystone Consolidated Industries Inc 7000 SW Adams St *Fax Area Code: 309 ■ *TF Sales:* 800-447-6444 ■ *Web:* www.redbrand.com	Peoria	IL	61641	800-447-6444	697-7120*
Leoni Wiring Systems Inc 2861 N Flowing Wells Rd Ste 121 *Web:* www.leoni.com	Tucson	AZ	85705	520-741-0895	741-0864
Major Custom Cable Inc 281 Lotus Dr *Fax Area Code: 573 ■ *TF:* 800-455-6224 ■ *Web:* www.majorcustomcable.com	Jackson	MO	63755	800-455-6224	243-1365*
Mercury Wire Products Inc 1 Mercury Dr *Web:* www.mercurywire.com	Spencer	MA	01562	508-885-6363	
Mid-South Wire Company Inc 1070 Visco Dr *TF:* 800-714-7800 ■ *Web:* www.midsouthwire.com	Nashville	TN	37210	615-743-2850	256-5836
Mount Joy Wire Corp 1000 E Main St *TF:* 800-321-2305 ■ *Web:* www.mjwire.com	Mount Joy	PA	17552	717-653-1461	653-0221
Nichols Wire 1547 Helton Dr *Fax Area Code: 256 ■ *TF:* 800-633-3156 ■ *Web:* investors.kaiseraluminum.com	Florence	AL	35630	800-873-2011	767-5152*
Okonite Co 102 Hilltop Rd *Web:* www.okonite.com	Ramsey	NJ	07446	201-825-0300	825-3524
Owl Wire & Cable Inc 3127 Seneca Tpke *TF:* 800-765-9473 ■ *Web:* www.owlwire.com	Canastota	NY	13032	315-697-2011	697-2123
Rea Magnet Wire Company Inc 3600 E Pontiac St *TF:* 800-732-9473 ■ *Web:* www.reawire.com	Fort Wayne	IN	46803	260-421-7321	
Ribbon Technology Corp 825 Taylor Stn Rd *TF:* 800-848-0477 ■ *Web:* www.ribtec.com	Gahanna	OH	43230	614-864-5444	864-5305
S & S Industries Inc 5 Odell Plz *Web:* www.sandsindustries.com	Yonkers	NY	10701	914-885-1500	885-1488
Seneca Wire & Manufacturing Co 319 S Vine St	Fostoria	OH	44830	419-435-9261	435-9265
Shaped Wire Inc 30000 Solon Rd *Web:* www.shapedwire.com	Solon	OH	44139	440-248-7600	248-5491
Sivaco Wire Group 800 Rue Ouellette *TF:* 800-876-9473 ■ *Web:* www.sivaco.com	Marieville	QC	J3M1P5	450-658-8741	460-2744
Southwestern Wire Inc PO Box CC *TF:* 800-348-9473 ■ *Web:* www.southwesternwire.com	Norman	OK	73070	405-447-6900	447-2830
Southwire Co 1 Southwire Dr *TF:* 800-444-1700 ■ *Web:* www.southwire.com	Carrollton	GA	30119	770-832-4242	832-4406
Spotnails 1100 Hicks Rd *TF:* 800-873-2239 ■ *Web:* www.spotnails.com	Rolling Meadows	IL	60008	847-259-1620	259-9236
Sumitomo Electric USA Inc 21241 S Western Ave Ste 120 *Web:* www.sumitomoelectricusa.com	Torrance	CA	90501	310-782-0227	782-0211
Superior Essex Inc Magnet Wire/Winding Wire Div 1601 Wall St PO Box 1601 *TF:* 800-551-8948 ■ *Web:* www.superioressex.com	Fort Wayne	IN	46802	260-461-4550	461-4690
TE's Rochester Wire & Cable product line 751 Old Brandy Rd *Web:* www.te.com/usa-en/products/families/rochester-cable.html	Culpeper	VA	22701	540-825-2111	825-2238
Techalloy Company Inc Baltimore Wire Div 2310 Chesapeake Ave *TF:* 800-638-1458 ■ *Web:* www.techalloy.com	Baltimore	MD	21222	410-633-9300	633-2033
Times Fiber Communications Inc 358 Hall Ave PO Box 384 *TF:* 800-677-2288 ■ *Web:* www.timesfiber.com	Wallingford	CT	06492	203-265-8500	265-8422
Tokusen USA Inc 1500 Amity Rd PO Box 446 *Web:* www.tokusenusa.com	Conway	AR	72033	501-327-6800	327-0231
Tree Island Steel 12459 Arrow Rt *TF:* 800-255-6974 ■ *Web:* treeisland.com/brands/tree-island	Rancho Cucamonga	CA	91739	909-594-7511	595-0439
WireCo WorldGroup 12200 NW Ambassador Dr *Web:* www.wirecoworldgroup.com	Kansas City	MO	64163	816-270-4700	270-4707
Wirerope Works Inc 100 Maynard St *TF Cust Svc:* 800-541-7673 ■ *Web:* www.wwwrope.com	Williamsport	PA	17701	570-326-5146	327-4274
Wrap-On Company Inc 5550 W 70th Pl *TF:* 800-621-6947 ■ *Web:* wrap-on.com	Chicago	IL	60638	708-496-2150	496-2154

814 WIRE & CABLE - ELECTRONIC

Company	City	State	ZIP	Phone	Fax
Alpha Wire Co 711 Lidgerwood Ave *TF:* 800-522-5742 ■ *Web:* www.alphawire.com	Elizabeth	NJ	07207	908-925-8000	925-5411
Belden Inc Americas Div 2200 US Hwy 27 S PO Box 1980 *TF:* 800-235-3362 ■ *Web:* www.belden.com	Richmond	IN	47375	765-983-5200	983-5294
C & M Corp 349 Lake Rd *Web:* www.cmcorporation.com	Dayville	CT	06241	860-774-4812	779-4330
Cable USA LLC 2584 S Horseshoe Dr *Web:* cableusallc.com	Naples	FL	34104	239-643-6400	643-4230
Cables to Go Inc 3599 Dayton Pk Dr *TF:* 800-826-7904 ■ *Web:* www.cablestogo.com	Dayton	OH	45414	937-224-8646	496-2666
Champlain Cable Corp 175 Hercules Dr *Fax Area Code: 802 ■ *Fax: Sales ■ *TF:* 800-451-5162 ■ *Web:* www.champcable.com	Colchester	VT	05446	800-451-5162	654-4224*
Cicoil Corp 24960 Ave Tibbitts *Web:* www.cicoil.com	Valencia	CA	91355	661-295-1295	295-0813
CommScope Inc 1100 Commscope Pl SE PO Box 339 *Fax: Cust Svc ■ *TF:* 800-982-1708 ■ *Web:* www.commscope.com	Hickory	NC	28603	828-324-2200	328-3400*
Compulink Inc 1205 Gandy Blvd N *TF:* 800-231-6685 ■ *Web:* www.compulink.com	Saint Petersburg	FL	33702	727-579-1500	578-8420
Comtran Corp 330A Turner St *Web:* comtrancorp.com	Attleboro	MA	02703	508-399-7004	399-8839
Consolidated Electronic Wire & Cable Co 11044 King St *TF:* 800-621-4278 ■ *Web:* www.conwire.com	Franklin Park	IL	60131	847-455-8830	455-8837
Corning Cable Systems 800 17th St NW *TF:* 800-743-2671 ■ *Web:* www.corning.com	Hickory	NC	28603	828-901-5000	325-5060
CXtec 5404 S Bay Rd PO Box 4799 *TF Orders:* 800-767-3282 ■ *Web:* www.cxtec.com	Syracuse	NY	13212	315-476-3000	455-1800
DC Electronics 1870 Little Orchard St *Web:* www.dcelectronics.com	San Jose	CA	95125	408-947-4500	947-4510
Dekoron WIre & Cable 1300 Industrial Blvd *Fax: Cust Svc ■ *Web:* www.dekoroncable.com	Mount Pleasant	TX	75455	903-572-3475	572-6153*
Fargo Assembly Co (FAC) 3300 Seventh Ave N PO Box 2340 *Web:* www.facnd.com	Fargo	ND	58102	701-298-3803	298-3806
Gallant & Wein Corp 11-20 43Rd Rd *Web:* www.galwein.com	Long Island	NY	11101	718-784-5210	937-6426
General Cable Corp 4 Tesseneer Dr *NYSE:* BGC ■ *TF:* 800-572-8000 ■ *Web:* www.generalcable.com	Highland Heights	KY	41076	859-572-8000	547-8072
Harbour Industries Inc 4744 Shelburne Rd PO Box 188 *TF:* 800-659-4733 ■ *Web:* www.harbourind.com	Shelburne	VT	05482	802-985-3311	985-9534
Judd Wire Inc 124 Tpke Rd *TF Cust Svc:* 800-545-5833 ■ *Web:* www.juddwire.com	Turners Falls	MA	01376	413-863-4357	863-2305
Lynn Products Inc 2645 W 237th St *Web:* www.lynnprod.com	Torrance	CA	90505	310-530-5966	530-8426
Madison Cable Corp 125 Goddard Memorial Dr *TF:* 877-623-4766 ■ *Web:* www.te.com	Worcester	MA	01603	508-752-2884	752-4230
National Wire & Cable Corp 136 N San Fernando Rd *Web:* www.nationalwire.com	Los Angeles	CA	90031	323-225-5611	225-4630
Nehring Electric Works Inc 1005 E Locust St *TF:* 800-435-4481 ■ *Web:* www.nehringwire.com	DeKalb	IL	60115	815-756-2741	756-7048
Oleco Inc 18683 Trimble Ct *TF:* 800-575-3282 ■ *Web:* globaltec.com	Spring Lake	MI	49456	616-842-6790	
Optical Cable Corp (OCC) 5290 Concourse Dr *NASDAQ:* OCC ■ *TF:* 800-622-7711 ■ *Web:* www.occfiber.com	Roanoke	VA	24019	540-265-0690	265-0724
Prestolite Wire Corp 200 Galleria Officentre Ste 212 *TF:* 800-498-3132 ■ *Web:* www.prestolitewire.com	Southfield	MI	48034	248-355-4422	386-4462
Rockbestos-Surprenant Cable Corp 20 Bradley Pk Rd *TF:* 800-327-7625 ■ *Web:* www.r-scc.com	East Granby	CT	06026	860-653-8300	
Siemon Co 101 Siemon Co Dr *TF:* 866-548-5814 ■ *Web:* www.siemon.com	Watertown	CT	06795	860-945-4200	945-4225
Superior Essex Inc 6120 Powers Ferry Rd Ste 150 *NASDAQ:* SPSX ■ *TF:* 800-551-8948 ■ *Web:* www.superioressex.com	Atlanta	GA	30339	770-657-6000	303-8883
Trilogy Communications Inc 2910 Hwy 80 E *TF:* 888-713-1414 ■ *Web:* www.trilogycoax.com	Pearl	MS	39208	601-932-4461	939-6637

815 WIRING DEVICES - CURRENT-CARRYING

Company	City	State	Zip	Phone	Fax
360 Electrical LLC 1935 E Vine Ste 360	Murray	UT	84121	801-364-4900	
Web: www.360electrical.com					
American Superconductor Corp 64 Jackson Rd	Devens	MA	01434	978-842-3000	
Web: www.amsc.com					
AMETEK Inc 485 Oberlin Ave, S.	Lakewood	NJ	08701	732-370-9100	
Web: www.ametek-ecp.com					
Amphenol Corp 358 Hall Ave.	Wallingford	CT	06492	203-265-8900	
NYSE: APH ■ *TF:* 877-267-4366 ■ *Web:* www.amphenol.com					
Arlington Industries Inc 1 Stauffer Industrial Pk	Scranton	PA	18517	570-562-0270	562-0646
TF: 800-233-4717 ■ *Web:* www.aifittings.com					
AVA Electronics Corp 4000 Bridge St	Drexel Hill	PA	19026	610-284-2500	259-8379
Backer Springfield Inc 4700 John Bragg Hwy	Murfreesboro	TN	37127	615-907-6900	
Web: backer-springfield.com					
Bizlink Technology Inc 3400 Gateway Blvd.	Fremont	CA	94538	510-252-0786	252-1178
TF: 800-326-4193 ■ *Web:* www.bizlinktech.com					
Brainin Advance Industries Inc 48 Frank Mossberg Dr	Attleboro	MA	02703	508-226-1200	226-8703
Web: www.pepbrainin.com					
Burndy LLC 47 E Industrial Park Dr.	Manchester	NH	03109	800-346-4175	
TF: 800-346-4175 ■ *Web:* www.burndy.com					
Carbide Probes Inc 1328 Research Park Dr	Dayton	OH	45432	937-429-9123	
Web: www.carbideprobes.com					
Carling Technologies Inc 60 Johnson Ave.	Plainville	CT	06062	860-793-9281	793-9231
TF: 800-243-8556 ■ *Web:* www.carlingtech.com					
Charles E Gillman Co 907 E Frontage Rd.	Rio Rico	AZ	85648	520-281-1141	281-1372
Web: www.gillman.com					
Checon Corp 30 Larsen Way	North Attleboro	MA	02763	508-809-5100	809-5163
Web: www.checon.com					
Cherry Corp 11200 88th Ave	Pleasant Prairie	WI	53158	262-942-6500	942-6566
TF: 800-510-1689 ■ *Web:* cherryamericas.com					
Cinch Connectors Inc 1700 Findley Rd.	Lombard	IL	60148	630-705-6000	705-6055
TF: 800-323-9612 ■ *Web:* www.cinch.com					
Cole Hersee Co 20 Old Colony Ave.	Boston	MA	02127	617-268-2100	268-9490
TF: 800-365-2653 ■ *Web:* www.colehersee.com					
Component Enterprises Co Inc 235 E Penn St PO Box 189	Norristown	PA	19401	877-232-7253	272-7040*
**Fax Area Code:* 610 ■ *TF:* 877-232-7253 ■ *Web:* componententerprises.com					
Connector Manufacturing Co 3501 Symmes Rd	Hamilton	OH	45015	513-860-4455	860-6114
Web: www.cmclugs.com					
Cooper Bussmann Inc 114 Old State Rd	Ellisville	MO	63021	636-394-2877	394-2877*
**Fax:* Cust Svc ■ *TF:* 855-287-7626 ■ *Web:* www.cooperindustries.com/content/public/en/bussmann.html					
Cooper Crouse-Hinds 1201 Wolf St.	Syracuse	NY	13208	315-477-5531	477-5531
TF: 866-764-5454 ■ *Web:* www.cooperindustries.com					
Cooper Industries 600 Travis St Ste 5400	Houston	TX	77002	713-209-8400	209-8995
NYSE: ETN ■ *TF:* 866-853-4293 ■ *Web:* www.cooperindustries.com					
Cooper Wiring Devices Inc 203 Cooper Cir.	Peachtree City	GA	30269	770-631-2100	631-2100
TF Cust Svc: 866-853-4293 ■ *Web:* www.cooperindustries.com					
Cord Sets Inc 1015 Fifth St N	Minneapolis	MN	55411	612-337-9700	337-0800
TF: 800-752-0580 ■ *Web:* www.cordsetsinc.com					
Cord Specialties Co 10632 Grand Ave.	Franklin Park	IL	60131	847-455-3503	
Web: www.cordspecialties.com					
Cristek Interconnects Inc 5395 E Hunter Ave	Anaheim	CA	92807	714-696-5200	696-5225
TF: 888-265-9162 ■ *Web:* www.cristek.com					
Curtis Industries Inc 2400 S 43rd St PO Box 343925	Milwaukee	WI	53219	414-649-4200	649-4279
TF: 800-657-0853 ■ *Web:* www.curtisind.com					
Ddh Enterprise Inc 2220 Oak Ridge Way	Vista	CA	92081	760-599-0171	599-9397
Web: www.ddhent.com					
Edwin Gaynor Corp 200 Charles St.	Stratford	CT	06615	203-378-5545	381-9019
TF: 800-342-9667 ■ *Web:* www.egaynor.com					
EECO Switch 1240 Pioneer St Ste A.	Brea	CA	92821	714-835-6000	
TF: 800-854-3808 ■ *Web:* www.eecoswitch.com					
Electri-Cord Mfg Co Inc 312 E Main St.	Westfield	PA	16950	814-367-2265	367-2314
TF: 888-278-8253 ■ *Web:* www.electri-cord.com					
Electro Adapter Inc 20640 Nordhoff St	Chatsworth	CA	91311	818-998-1198	
Web: www.electro-adapter.com					
Electronic Systems Packaging LLC (ESP) 1175 W Victoria St	Rancho Dominguez	CA	90220	310-639-2535	632-6666
Web: www.espbus.com					
Electroswitch 2010 Yonkers Rd	Raleigh	NC	27604	919-833-0707	833-8016
TF: 888-768-2797 ■ *Web:* www.electro-nc.com					
ERICO Products Inc 34600 Solon Rd.	Solon	OH	44139	440-248-0100	248-0723
TF: 800-248-2677 ■ *Web:* www.erico.com					
ETCO Inc 25 Bellows St.	Warwick	RI	02888	401-467-2400	467-9230
TF: 800-689-3826 ■ *Web:* www.etco.com					
Eureka Electrical Products Inc 79 Clay St	North East	PA	16428	814-725-9638	725-3670
Fastron Company Inc, The 11800 Franklin Ave.	Franklin Park	IL	60131	630-766-5000	
Web: www.fastron.com					
FTZ Industries Inc 515 Palmetto Dr	Simpsonville	SC	29681	864-963-5000	963-5352
Web: www.ftzind.com					
Glenair Inc 1211 Air Way.	Glendale	CA	91201	818-247-6000	500-9912
TF: 888-465-4094 ■ *Web:* www.glenair.com					
Group Dekko Services LLC 2505 Dekko Dr.	Garrett	IN	46738	260-357-3621	357-4293
TF: 800-829-3101 ■ *Web:* www.dekko.com					
Harger Inc 301 Ziegler Dr.	Grayslake	IL	60030	847-548-8700	
Web: www.harger.com					
Hi Rel Connectors Inc 760 Wharton Dr	Claremont	CA	91711	909-626-1820	399-0626
Web: www.hirelco.net					
Hoffman Products 9600 Vly View Rd	Macedonia	OH	44056	216-525-4320	896-3017*
**Fax Area Code:* 866 ■ *TF:* 800-645-2014 ■ *Web:* www.tpcwire.com					
Hubbell Premise Wiring Inc 23 Clara Dr	Mystic	CT	06355	800-626-0005	535-8328*
**Fax Area Code:* 860 ■ *TF:* 800-626-0005 ■ *Web:* www.hubbell-premise.com					
Hubbell Wiring Device-Kellems 40 Waterview Dr	Shelton	CT	06484	203-882-4800	882-4852*
**Fax:* Tech Supp ■ *TF Cust Svc:* 800-288-6000 ■ *Web:* www.hubbell-wiring.com					
ILSCO 4730 Madison Rd	Cincinnati	OH	45227	513-533-6200	533-6274
TF Sales: 800-776-9775 ■ *Web:* www.ilsco.com					
Independent Protection Company Inc 1607 S Main St.	Goshen	IN	46526	574-533-4116	534-3719
TF: 800-860-8388 ■ *Web:* www.ipclp.com					
JB Nottingham & Company Inc Duraline Div 1731 Patterson Ave.	DeLand	FL	32724	631-234-2002	234-2360
Web: jbn-duraline.com					
Kemlon Products & Development Co 1424 N Main St	Pearland	TX	77581	281-997-3300	997-1300
Web: www.kemlon.com					
Keystone Cable Corp 8200 Lynch Rd	Detroit	MI	48234	313-924-9720	924-0050
Web: www.keystonecable.net					
LL Rowe Co 66 Holton St	Woburn	MA	01801	781-729-7860	721-7264
Web: www.llrowe.com					
Lumens Light & Living 2028 K St	Sacramento	CA	95811	916-444-5585	
TF: 877-445-4486 ■ *Web:* www.lumens.com					
Marinco 2655 Napa Valley Corp Dr	Napa	CA	94558	707-226-9600	226-9670
TF: 800-307-6702 ■ *Web:* www.marinco.com					
McGill Electrical Product Group 9377 W Higgins Rd	Rosemont	IL	60018	847-268-6000	356-4714*
**Fax Area Code:* 800 ■ *TF:* 800-621-1506 ■ *Web:* www.emersonindustrial.com					
Metalor Electrotechnics 1003 Corporate Ln	Export	PA	15632	724-733-8332	733-8341
Web: www.metalor.com					
Midwest Manufacturing Inc 5311 Kane Rd	Eau Claire	WI	54703	715-876-5555	
Web: www.midwestmanufacturing.com					
Mill-Max Mfg Corp 190 Pine Hollow Rd.	Oyster Bay	NY	11771	516-922-6000	922-9253
TF: 800-333-4237 ■ *Web:* www.mill-max.com					
Minnesota Wire & Cable Co 1835 Energy Pk Dr	Saint Paul	MN	55108	651-642-1800	642-9286
TF: 800-258-6922 ■ *Web:* www.mnwire.com					
Nexus Inc 50 Sunnyside Ave	Stamford	CT	06902	203-327-7300	324-7623
Web: www.nexus.com					
Ohio Associated Enterprises LLC 1382 W Jackson St.	Painesville	OH	44077	440-354-3148	354-0687
TF: 888-637-4832 ■ *Web:* www.meritec.com					
Omnetics Connector Corp 7260 Commerce Cir E	Minneapolis	MN	55432	763-572-0656	572-3925
TF Cust Svc: 800-343-0025 ■ *Web:* www.omnetics.com					
Panduit Corp 17301 Ridgeland Ave.	Tinley Park	IL	60477	708-532-1800	532-1811
TF: 888-506-5400 ■ *Web:* www.panduit.com					
Pass & Seymour Inc 50 Boyd Ave PO Box 4822	Syracuse	NY	13221	315-468-6211	
Web: www.passandseymour.com					
Penn-Union Corp 229 Waterford St.	Edinboro	PA	16412	814-734-1631	734-4946
Web: www.penn-union.com					
Phoenix Co of Chicago Inc 555 Pond Dr	Wood Dale	IL	60191	630-595-2300	595-6579
Web: www.phoenixofchicago.com					
Preformed Line Products 660 Beta Dr	Cleveland	OH	44143	440-461-5200	442-8816
NASDAQ: PLPC ■ *TF:* 800-622-6757 ■ *Web:* www.preformed.com					
Shape LLC 2105 Corporate Dr	Addison	IL	60101	630-620-8394	620-0784
TF: 800-367-5811 ■ *Web:* www.shapellc.com					
Special Mine Services Inc PO Box 188	West Frankfort	IL	62896	618-932-2151	937-2715
Web: www.smsconnectors.com					
State Tool & Manufacturing Co 1650 E Empire Ave	Benton Harbor	MI	49022	269-927-3153	927-4230
Web: www.statetool.com					
Tower Manufacturing Corp 25 Reservoir Ave.	Providence	RI	02907	401-467-7550	461-2710
Web: www.towermfg.com					
Tripp Lite Inc 1111 W 35th St	Chicago	IL	60609	773-869-1111	869-1329
Web: www.tripplite.com					
Unlimited Services of Wisconsin Inc 170 Evergreen Rd	Oconto	WI	54153	920-834-4418	
Web: www.us-wire-harness.com					
Veetronix Inc 1311 W Pacific Ave	Lexington	NE	68850	308-324-6661	324-4985
TF General: 800-445-0007 ■ *Web:* www.veetronix.com					
Volex Inc 915 Tate Blvd SE Ste 130	Hickory	NC	28602	828-485-4500	485-4501
Web: www.volex.com					
Weidmuller Inc 821 Southlake Blvd	Richmond	VA	23236	804-794-2877	379-2593
TF Cust Svc: 800-849-9343 ■ *Web:* www.weidmuller.com					
Zierick Manufacturing Corp 131 Radio Cr.	Mount Kisco	NY	10549	914-666-2911	666-0216
TF: 800-882-8020 ■ *Web:* www.zierick.com					

816 WIRING DEVICES - NONCURRENT-CARRYING

Company	City	State	Zip	Phone	Fax
Adalet 4801 W 150th St	Cleveland	OH	44135	216-267-9000	267-1681*
**Fax:* Sales ■ *Web:* www.adalet.com					
Allied Moulded Products Inc 222 N Union St	Bryan	OH	43506	419-636-4217	636-2450
TF: 800-722-2679 ■ *Web:* www.alliedmoulded.com					
Aluma-Form Inc 3625 Old Getwell Rd.	Memphis	TN	38118	901-362-0100	794-9515
Web: www.alumaform.com					
Bedford Materials Co Inc 7676 Allegheny Rd	Manns Choice	PA	15550	800-773-4276	623-9199*
**Fax Area Code:* 814 ■ *TF:* 800-773-4276 ■ *Web:* www.bedfordmaterials.com					
Bridgeport Fittings Inc 705 Lordship Blvd	Stratford	CT	06615	203-377-5944	381-3488
Web: www.bptfittings.com					
Chalfant Manufacturing Co 11525 Madison Ave	Cleveland	OH	44102	216-521-7922	
Web: www.chalfantcabletray.com					
Chase & Sons Inc 295 University Ave.	Westwood	MA	02090	781-332-0700	
TF: 800-323-4182 ■ *Web:* www.chasecorp.com					
Conduit Pipe Products Co 1501 W Main St	West Jefferson	OH	43162	614-879-9114	879-5185
TF: 800-848-6125 ■ *Web:* www.conduitpipe.com					
Cooper B-Line Inc 509 W Monroe St	Highland	IL	62249	618-654-2184	356-1438*
**Fax Area Code:* 800 ■ *TF:* 800-851-7415 ■ *Web:* www.cooperindustries.com					
Cottrell Paper Company Inc 1135 Rock City Rd PO Box 35	Rock City Falls	NY	12863	518-885-1702	885-1702
TF: 800-948-3559 ■ *Web:* www.cottrellpaper.com					

Company	City	State	ZIP	Phone	Fax
Durham Co 722 Durham Rd *Web:* www.durhamcompany.com	Lebanon	MO	65536	417-532-7121	532-2366
EGS Electrical Group LLC 9377 W Higgins Rd *TF:* 800-621-1506 ■ *Web:* www.emersonindustrial.com	Rosemont	IL	60018	847-268-6000	
Electri-Flex Co 222 Central Ave *TF:* 800-323-6174 ■ *Web:* www.electriflex.com	Roselle	IL	60172	630-529-2920	529-0482
Flex-Cable Inc 5822 N Henkel Rd *TF:* 800-245-3539 ■ *Web:* www.flexcable.com	Howard City	MI	49329	231-937-8000	937-8091
Gaylord Manufacturing Co 1088 Montclaire Dr *TF:* 800-375-0091 ■ *Web:* www.gaylordmfg.com	Ceres	CA	95307	209-538-3313	
Gund Co 2121 Walton Rd *Web:* www.thegundcompany.com	Saint Louis	MO	63114	314-423-5200	423-9009
Hubbell Premise Wiring Inc 23 Clara Dr **Fax Area Code:* 860 ■ *TF:* 800-626-0005 ■ *Web:* www.hubbell-premise.com	Mystic	CT	06355	800-626-0005	535-8328*
Hubbell RACO 3902 W Sample St **Fax Area Code:* 800 ■ *TF:* 800-722-6437 ■ *Web:* www.hubbell-raco.com	South Bend	IN	46619	574-234-7151	722-6462*
Hubbell Wiegmann 501 W Apple St *Web:* www.hubbell-wiegmann.com	Freeburg	IL	62243	618-539-3193	539-5794
Hughes Bros Inc 210 N 13th St PO Box 159 *TF:* 800-869-0359 ■ *Web:* www.hughesbros.com	Seward	NE	68434	402-643-2991	643-2149
ICO-RALLY Corp 2575 E Bayshore Rd **Fax Area Code:* 800 ■ *Web:* www.icorally.com	Palo Alto	CA	94303	650-856-9900	856-2006*
Ideal Industries Inc 1375 Pk Ave *TF:* 800-435-0705 ■ *Web:* www.idealindustries.com	Sycamore	IL	60178	815-895-5181	
Joslyn Sunbank Co LLC 1740 Commerce Way **Fax:* Cust Svc ■ *TF:* 800-523-0727 ■ *Web:* www.sunbankcorp.com	Paso Robles	CA	93446	805-238-2840	238-0241*
Kortick Manufacturing Co 2230 Davis Ct *Web:* www.kortick.com	Hayward	CA	94545	510-856-3600	
LoDan Electronics Inc 3311 N Kennicott Ave *TF:* 800-401-4995 ■ *Web:* www.lodanelectronics.com	Arlington Heights	IL	60004	847-398-5311	398-5340
MacLean Power Systems 11411 Addison St **Fax:* Sales ■ *TF:* 855-677-7447 ■ *Web:* www.macleanpower.com	Franklin Park	IL	60131	847-455-0014	455-0029*
Monti Inc 333 W Seymour Ave *Web:* www.monti-inc.com	Cincinnati	OH	45216	513-761-7775	948-6858
MP Husky Corp 204 Old Piedmont Hwy PO Box 16749 *TF:* 800-277-4810 ■ *Web:* www.mphusky.com	Greenville	SC	29605	864-234-4800	234-4822
Mulberry Metal Products Inc 2199 Stanley Terr *Web:* www.mulberrymetal.com	Union	NJ	07083	908-688-8850	688-7294
Ngk-locke Polymer Insulators Inc 1609 Diamond Springs Rd *Web:* www.ngk-polymer.com	Virginia Beach	VA	23455	757-460-3649	460-3550
O-Z/Gedney 9377 W Higgins Rd **Fax Area Code:* 800 ■ *TF:* 800-621-1506 ■ *Web:* www.emersonindustrial.com	Rosemont	IL	60018	847-268-6000	356-4714*
Ohio Brass Co 1850 Richland Ave E *Web:* www.hubbellpowersystems.com	Aiken	SC	29801	803-648-8386	642-2959
Opti-Com Mfg Network Co Inc 259 Plauche St *TF:* 800-345-8774 ■ *Web:* opti-com.info	New Orleans	LA	70123	504-736-0331	733-9046
Rittal Corp 1 Rittal Pl *TF:* 800-477-4000 ■ *Web:* www.rittal.com/us-en/content/en/start	Springfield	OH	45504	937-399-0500	390-5599
Saginaw Control & Engineering Inc 95 Midland Rd *TF:* 800-234-6871 ■ *Web:* www.saginawcontrol.com	Saginaw	MI	48638	989-799-6871	799-4524
TJ Cope Inc 11500 Norcom Rd *TF:* 800-483-3473 ■ *Web:* copecabletray.com	Philadelphia	PA	19154	215-961-2570	961-2580
Varflex Corp 512 W Ct St *TF:* 800-648-4014 ■ *Web:* www.varflex.com	Rome	NY	13440	315-336-4400	336-0005
Virginia Plastics Co Inc 3453 Aerial Way Dr PO Box 4577 *TF:* 877-351-1699 ■ *Web:* www.vaplastics.com	Roanoke	VA	24018	540-981-9700	981-2022
Weidmann Electrical Technology 1 Gordon Mills Way PO Box 903 *Web:* weidmann-electrical.com	Saint Johnsbury	VT	05819	802-748-8106	748-8630

817 WOOD MEMBERS - STRUCTURAL

Company	City	State	ZIP	Phone	Fax
Alpine Engineered Products Inc 1100 Pk Central Blvd S Ste 2400 & 3800 *TF General:* 800-786-6086 ■ *Web:* www.alpeng.com	Pompano Beach	FL	33064	954-781-3333	973-2644
American Laminators 600 Applegate St PO Box 297 *Web:* www.americanlaminators.com	Drain	OR	97435	541-836-2000	836-7144
Armstrong Lumber Co Inc 2709 Auburn Way N *TF:* 800-868-9066 ■ *Web:* www.armstrong-homes.com	Auburn	WA	98002	253-833-6666	833-5878
Automated Bldg Components Inc 2359 Grant Rd *TF:* 800-837-2152 ■ *Web:* www.abctruss.com	North Baltimore	OH	45872	419-257-2152	257-2779
Automated Products Inc 1812 Karau Dr *Web:* apiebs.com	Marshfield	WI	54449	715-387-3426	387-6588
Buettner Bros Lumber Co 700 Seventh Ave SW *Web:* bblumber.net	Cullman	AL	35055	256-734-4221	
California TrusFrame 23665 Cajalco Rd *Web:* caltrusframe.com	Perris	CA	92570	951-657-7491	
Calvert Company Inc 3559 S Truman Rd *Web:* calvertglulam.com	Washougal	WA	98671	360-835-3110	
Chantiers Chibougamau Ltd 521 Chemin Merrill PO 216 *Web:* www.chibou.com	Chibougamau	QC	G8P2K7	418-748-6481	
East Coast Lumber & Supply Co 308 Ave A *Web:* www.eastcoastlumber.com	Fort Pierce	FL	34950	321-636-0411	
Enwood Structures Inc 5724 McCrimmon Pkwy PO Box 2002 *TF:* 800-777-8648 ■ *Web:* www.enwood.com	Morrisville	NC	27560	919-518-0464	469-2536
Fullerton Bldg Systems Inc (FBS) 34620 250th St PO Box 308 *TF:* 800-450-9782 ■ *Web:* www.fullertonbuildingsystems.com	Worthington	MN	56187	507-376-3128	376-9530
Giddings Manufacturing Company Inc 1426 Us Route 7 *Web:* giddingsvt.com	Pittsford	VT	05763	802-483-2292	
Giles & Kendall Inc 3470 Maysville Rd Ne PO Box 188 *Web:* cedarsafe.com	Huntsville	AL	35804	256-776-2978	
Goodfellow Inc 225 Goodfellow St *TF:* 800-361-6503 ■ *Web:* www.goodfellowinc.com	Delson	QC	J5B1V5	450-635-6511	635-3729
HM Stauffer & Sons Inc 33 Glenola Dr PO Box 567 *TF:* 800-662-2226 ■ *Web:* hmstauffer.com	Leola	PA	17540	717-656-2811	656-4392
J C Snavely & Sons Inc 150 Main St *Web:* www.jcsnavely.com	Landisville	PA	17538	717-898-2241	898-5208
Laminate Technologies Inc 161 Maule Rd **Fax Area Code:* 419 ■ *TF:* 800-231-2523 ■ *Web:* www.lamtech.net	Tiffin	OH	44883	800-231-2523	448-0811*
Laminated Wood Systems Inc (LWS) 1327 285th Rd PO Box 386 **Fax Area Code:* 402 ■ *TF:* 800-949-3526 ■ *Web:* www.lwsinc.com	Seward	NE	68434	800-949-3526	643-4374*
Laminators Inc 3255 Penn St *TF:* 877-663-4277 ■ *Web:* www.laminatorsinc.com	Hatfield	PA	19440	215-723-8107	721-4669
Molpus Co, The 502 Vly View Dr PO Box 59 *TF:* 800-535-5434 ■ *Web:* www.molpus.com	Philadelphia	MS	39350	601-656-3373	656-4947
Montgomery Truss & Panel Inc 803 W Main St *TF:* 800-942-8010 ■ *Web:* montgomerytruss.com	Grove City	PA	16127	724-458-7500	458-0765
Okaw Truss Inc 368 E St Rt 133 *Web:* www.okawtruss.com	Arthur	IL	61911	217-543-3371	
RedBuilt LLC 200 E Mallard Dr *Web:* www.redbuilt.com	Boise	ID	83706	208-364-1316	
Robbins Mfg Co 13001 N Nebraska Ave *TF:* 888-558-8199 ■ *Web:* www.robbinslumber.com	Tampa	FL	33612	813-971-3030	972-3980
Roof Structures Inc 3333 Yale Way *Web:* www.roofstructures.com	Fremont	CA	94538	510-226-7171	226-8989
Sentinel Structures Inc 477 S Peck Ave *Web:* www.sentinelstructures.com	Peshtigo	WI	54157	715-582-4544	582-4932
Shook Builder Supply Co 1400 16th St NE *Web:* shookbuildersupply.com	Hickory	NC	28601	828-328-2051	328-2425
Southern Components Inc 7360 Julie Frances Dr *TF:* 800-256-2144 ■ *Web:* www.socomp.com	Shreveport	LA	71129	318-687-3330	
Stow Co, The 3311 Windquest Dr *TF:* 800-562-4257 ■ *Web:* www.windquestco.com	Holland	MI	49424	616-399-3311	399-8784
Structural Wood Corp 4000 Labore Rd *TF:* 800-652-9058 ■ *Web:* www.structural-wood.com	Saint Paul	MN	55110	651-426-8111	426-6859
Structural Wood Systems 321 Dohrimier St *Web:* www.structuralwood.com	Greenville	AL	36037	334-382-6534	382-4260
Tacoma Truss Systems Inc 20617 Mtn Hwy E *Web:* www.tacomatruss.com	Spanaway	WA	98387	253-847-2204	
Trusco Inc 12527 Porr Rd *Web:* www.truscoinc.com	Doylestown	OH	44230	330-658-2027	658-4979
Trussway Ltd 9411 Alcorn Rd *Web:* www.trussway.com	Houston	TX	77093	713-691-6900	691-2064
Valley Best-Way Bldg Supply 118 S Union Rd	Spokane	WA	99206	509-924-1250	922-5420
Villaume Industries Inc 2926 Lone Oak Cir *TF Cust Svc:* 800-488-3610 ■ *Web:* www.villaume.com	Eagan	MN	55121	651-454-3610	454-8556

818 WOOD PRESERVING

Company	City	State	ZIP	Phone	Fax
Appalachian Timber Services Inc 393 EDGAR Givens Pkwy *Web:* www.atstimber.com	Sutton	WV	26601	304-765-7393	
Bell Lumber & Pole Co 778 First St NW PO Box 120786 *TF:* 877-633-4334 ■ *Web:* www.blpole.com	New Brighton	MN	55112	651-633-4334	633-8852
Biewer Lumber LLC 812 S Riverside *Web:* www.biewerlumber.com	Saint Clair	MI	48079	810-329-4789	
Brooks Mfg Co 2120 Pacific St *Web:* www.brooksmfg.com	Bellingham	WA	98229	360-733-1700	734-6668
Brown Wood Preserving Company Inc 6201 Camp Ground Rd *TF:* 800-537-1765 ■ *Web:* brownwoodpoles.com	Louisville	KY	40216	502-448-2337	448-9944
Building Products Plus 12317 Almeda Rd **Fax Area Code:* 713 ■ *TF:* 800-460-8627 ■ *Web:* www.buildingproductsplus.com	Houston	TX	77045	800-460-8627	433-7068*
Conrad Forest Products 68765 Wildwood Dr **Fax Area Code:* 541 ■ *TF:* 800-356-7146 ■ *Web:* www.conradfp.com	North Bend	OR	97459	800-356-7146	756-0131*
Cox Industries Inc 860 Cannon Bridge Rd PO Box 1124 *TF:* 800-476-4401 ■ *Web:* www.coxwood.com	Orangeburg	SC	29116	803-534-7467	534-1410
Culpeper Wood Preservers Inc 15487 Braggs Corner Rd PO Box 1148 *Web:* www.culpeperwood.com	Culpeper	VA	22701	540-825-5201	
Elder Wood Preserving Co Inc 334 Elder Wood Rd *TF:* 866-606-2470 ■ *Web:* greatsouthernwood.com	Mansura	LA	71350	318-964-2196	964-5276
Exterior Wood Inc 2685 Index St *TF:* 800-222-1222 ■ *Web:* www.exteriorwood.com	Washougal	WA	98671	360-835-8561	
Great Southern Wood Preserving Inc 1100 US Hwy 431 N *Web:* www.greatsouthernwood.com	Abbeville	AL	36310	334-585-2291	585-4353
Hoover Treated Wood Products Inc 154 Wire Rd *Web:* www.frtw.com	Thomson	GA	30824	706-595-1264	
JH Baxter & Co PO Box 5902 *TF:* 800-556-1098 ■ *Web:* www.jhbaxter.com	San Mateo	CA	94402	650-349-0201	570-6878
Koppers Inc 436 Seventh Ave *NYSE:* KOP ■ *TF:* 800-385-4406 ■ *Web:* www.koppers.com	Pittsburgh	PA	15219	412-227-2001	227-2333
Madison Wood Preservers Inc 216 Oak Park Rd *Web:* www.madwood.com	Madison	VA	22727	540-948-6801	
McFarland Cascade 1640 E Marc St PO Box 1496 *TF Cust Svc:* 800-426-8430 ■ *Web:* www.ldm.com	Tacoma	WA	98421	253-572-3033	627-0764
Osmose Inc 980 Ellicott St *TF:* 800-877-7653 ■ *Web:* www.osmose.com	Buffalo	NY	14209	716-882-5905	882-5139
Perma Treat Corp 74 Airline Dr	Durham	CT	06422	860-349-1133	349-1365
Professional Coaters Inc 100 Commerce Park Dr *TF:* 800-962-0344 ■ *Web:* www.procoatinc.com	Cabot	AR	72023	501-843-7509	

Company	City	State	ZIP	Phone	Fax
Robbins Mfg Co 13001 N Nebraska Ave	Tampa	FL	33612	813-971-3030	972-3980
TF: 888-558-8199 ■ *Web:* www.robbinslumber.com					
Shenandoah Wood Preserving Inc 301 E 16th St	Scotland Neck	NC	27874	252-826-4151	
Western Wood Preserving Co 1310 Zehnder St	Sumner	WA	98390	253-863-8191	
TF: 800-472-7714 ■ *Web:* www.westernwoodpreserving.com					
Wood Preservers Inc 15939 Historyland Hwy PO Box 158	Warsaw	VA	22572	804-333-4022	333-9269
TF: 800-368-2536 ■ *Web:* www.woodpreservers.com					

819 WOOD PRODUCTS - RECONSTITUTED

Company	City	State	ZIP	Phone	Fax
Aya Kitchens & Baths Ltd 1551 Caterpillar Rd	Mississauga	ON	L4X2Z6	905-848-1999	848-5127
TF: 866-292-4968 ■ *Web:* www.ayakitchens.com					
Cabinet Tronix LLC 290 Trousdale Dr Ste A	Chula Vista	CA	91910	866-876-6199	
TF: 866-876-6199 ■ *Web:* www.cabinet-tronix.com					
Duraflame Inc 2894 Mt Diablo Ave PO Box 1230	Stockton	CA	95201	209-461-6600	462-9412
Web: www.duraflame.com					
Geo Products LLC 8615 Golden Spike Ln	Houston	TX	77086	281-820-5493	
TF: 800-434-4743 ■ *Web:* www.geoproducts.org					
Homasote Co 932 Lower Ferry Rd PO Box 7240	West Trenton	NJ	08628	609-883-3300	883-3497
OTC: HMTC ■ *TF:* 800-257-9491 ■ *Web:* www.homasote.com					
Liberty Wood Products 874 Iotla Church Rd	Franklin	NC	28734	828-524-7958	369-7652
Web: www.libertywoodproducts.net					
Panel Processing Inc 120 N Industrial Hwy	Alpena	MI	49707	989-356-9007	356-9000
TF: 800-433-7142 ■ *Web:* www.panel.com					
Panolam Industries International Inc 20 Progress Dr	Shelton	CT	06484	203-925-1556	225-0051
TF: 877-391-4130 ■ *Web:* www.panolam.com					
Pasquier Panel Products Inc 1510 Puyallup St PO Box 1170	Sumner	WA	98390	253-863-6323	891-7993
Web: www.pasquierpanel.com					
Potlatch Corp 601 W First Ave Ste 1600	Spokane	WA	99201	509-835-1500	
NASDAQ: PCH ■ *Web:* www.potlatchcorp.com					
Potlatch Corp Wood Products Div 805 Mill Rd PO Box 1388	Lewiston	ID	83501	509-835-1500	
Web: www.potlatchcorp.com					
Rex Lumber Co 840 Main St	Acton	MA	01720	978-263-0055	263-9806
TF: 800-343-0567 ■ *Web:* www.rexlumber.com					
Tectum Inc 105 S Sixth St	Newark	OH	43055	740-345-9691	349-9305
TF: 888-977-9691 ■ *Web:* www.tectum.com					

820 WOOD PRODUCTS - SHAPED & TURNED

Company	City	State	ZIP	Phone	Fax
A&M Supply Corp 6701 90th Ave N	Pinellas Park	FL	33782	727-541-6631	546-3617
TF: 800-877-8551					
American Wood Fibers Inc 9841 Broken Land Pkwy Ste 302	Columbia	MD	21046	410-290-8700	
Web: www.awf.com					
Amorim Industrial Solutions Inc 26112 110th St	Trevor	WI	53179	262-862-2311	
Web: www.amorimcorkcomposites.com					
Art Connection Inc 2860 Ctr Port Cir	Pompano Beach	FL	33064	954-977-8177	
Web: www.artconnectionusa.com					
Art for Everyday Inc 420 Canarctic Dr	Toronto	ON	M3J2V3	416-645-5120	645-5121
Web: www.afe-inc.com					
Baker McMillen Co 3688 Wyoga Lk Rd	Stow	OH	44224	330-923-8300	
Web: www.baker-mcmillen.com					
Banks Hardwoods Inc 69937 M-103	White Pigeon	MI	49099	269-483-2323	
Web: www.bankshardwoods.com					
Brown Wood Products Co 7040 N Lawndale Ave	Lincolnwood	IL	60712	800-328-5858	884-0423
TF: 800-328-5858 ■ *Web:* www.brownwoodinc.com					
Burroughs-Ross-Colville Co 301 Depot St	McMinnville	TN	37110	931-473-2111	473-5350
Web: www.brclumber.com					
Carriage Works Inc 1877 Mallard Ln	Klamath Falls	OR	97601	541-882-0700	
Web: www.carriageworks.com					
Chicago Dowel Company Inc 4700 W Grand Ave	Chicago	IL	60639	773-622-2000	622-2047
TF: 800-333-6935 ■ *Web:* www.chicagodowel.com					
Circular Technologies 3275 Prairie Ave	Boulder	CO	80301	303-443-8512	
TF: 800-215-1831 ■ *Web:* www.circulartech.com					
Cochran Forest Products Inc 702 NE Okinawa St	Lake City	FL	32055	386-752-0335	755-5561
Web: www.cochranforestproducts.com					
Confluence Energy LLC 1809 Hwy 9	Kremmling	CO	80459	970-724-9839	
Web: www.confluenceenergy.com					
Davidson Plyforms Inc 5505 33rd St SE	Grand Rapids	MI	49512	616-956-0033	956-0041
TF: 800-505-4732 ■ *Web:* lpworkfurniture.com					
Del-Tin Fiber LLC 757 Del-Tin Hwy	El Dorado	AR	71730	870-309-3100	
Web: www.deltinfiber.com					
Dry Creek Products Inc 51 Edward St	Arcade	NY	14009	585-492-2990	
Web: www.drycreekproducts.com					
Empire Architectural 409 N Main St	Freeport	NY	11520	516-377-8545	
Web: www.empirearchitecturalproducts.com					
Enviva Lp 7200 Wisconsin Ave Ste 1100	Bethesda	MD	20814	301-657-5560	
Web: www.envivabiomass.com					
Flakeboard America Ltd 515 River Crossing Dr Ste 110	Fort Mill	SC	29715	905-475-9686	
Web: www.flakeboard.com					
Fox Lumber Sales Inc PO Box 1000	Hamilton	MT	59840	406-363-5140	
Web: www.foxlumber.com					
Frank Edmunds & Co 6111 S Sayre	Chicago	IL	60638	773-586-2772	586-2783
TF: 800-447-3516 ■ *Web:* www.frankedmunds.com					
Garick Corp 13600 Broadway Ave	Cleveland	OH	44125	216-581-0100	
Web: www.garick.com					
Geneva Wood Fuels LLC 30 Norton Hill Rd	Strong	ME	04983	207-684-3048	
Groupe de Scieries GDS Inc 207 Rt 295	Degelis	QC	G5T1R1	418-853-2566	
Web: www.groupgds.com					
Harbortown Industries Inc 28477 N Ballard Dr	Lake Forest	IL	60045	847-327-9900	
Web: www.harbortown.net					
Highwood USA LLC 87 Tide Rd	Tamaqua	PA	18252	570-668-6113	
Web: www.highwood-usa.com					
Horton Components 117 Milledgeville Rd	Eatonton	GA	31024	706-485-5480	
Web: www.hortoncomponents.com					
Humboldt Redwood Company LLC 108 Main St PO Box 565	Scotia	CA	95565	707-764-4472	
Web: www.getredwood.com					
Idaho Cedar Sales LLC 221 Main St	Troy	ID	83871	208-835-2161	
Web: www.cedar.idahotimber.com					
Intermountain Wood Products Inc 1948 SW Temple	Salt Lake City	UT	84115	801-486-5414	466-0428
Web: www.intermountainwood.com					
Jarden Home Brands 14611 W Commerce Rd	Daleville	IN	47334	765-557-3000	
TF Cust Svc: 800-240-3340 ■ *Web:* www.jardenhomebrands.com					
Lexington Manufacturing Inc 1330 115th Ave NW	Minneapolis	MN	55448	763-754-9055	
Web: www.lexingtonmfg.com					
Maine Wood Concepts Inc 1687 New Vineyard Rd	New Vineyard	ME	04956	207-652-2441	
Web: www.mainewoodconcepts.com					
Michigan Maple Block Co 1420 Standish Ave	Petoskey	MI	49770	231-347-4170	347-7975
New Century Picture Corp 2737 W Fulton St	Chicago	IL	60612	773-638-8888	
Web: newcenturybk.com					
Nomacorc LLC 400 Vintage Park Dr	Zebulon	NC	27597	919-460-2200	
Web: www.nomacorc.com					
Owens Handle Company Inc 4200 N Frazier St	Conroe	TX	77303	936-856-2981	856-2260
Pallet Logistics of America LLC 4100 Platinum Way	Dallas	TX	75237	972-850-5000	
Web: www.plofa.com					
Paramount Pallet Inc 1330 Martin Grove Rd	Toronto	ON	M9W4X3	416-742-6006	
Web: www.paramountpallet.com					
Price Companies Inc, The 218 Midway Route	Monticello	AR	71655	870-367-9751	
Web: www.thepricecompanies.com					
Saunders Bros LLC 256 Main St	Locke Mills	ME	04255	207-875-2853	875-2857
Web: www.saundersbros.com					
Sharut Furniture Inc 220 Passaic St	Passaic	NJ	07055	973-473-1000	
Web: www.furnitureinmotion.com					
Southern Filter Media LLC 2735 Kanasita Dr Ste A	Hixson	TN	37343	423-698-8988	
Web: www.southernfiltermedia.com					
TrimJoist Corp 5146 Hwy 182 E	Columbus	MS	39704	662-327-7950	
Web: www.trimjoist.com					
Wayne Kiltz Africa Imports 240 S Main St Unit A	South Hackensack	NJ	07606	201-457-1995	
TF: 800-500-6120 ■ *Web:* www.africaimports.com					
Western Excelsior Corp 901 Grand Ave	Mancos	CO	81328	970-533-7412	
Web: www.westernexcelsior.com					
Willi Hahn Corp - Wiha Tools 1348 Dundas Cir	Monticello	MN	55362	763-295-6591	
Web: www.wihatools.com					

821 WOODWORKING MACHINERY

Company	City	State	ZIP	Phone	Fax
Acrowood Corp 4425 S Third Ave PO Box 1028	Everett	WA	98203	425-258-3555	252-7622
Web: www.acrowood.com					
Baker Products 55480 Hwy 21 N PO Box 128	Ellington	MO	63638	573-663-7711	663-2787
TF: 800-548-6914 ■ *Web:* www.baker-online.com					
Capital Machine Company Inc 2801 Roosevelt Ave	Indianapolis	IN	46218	317-638-6661	636-5122
Web: www.capitalmachineco.com					
Corley Manufacturing Co PO Box 471	Chattanooga	TN	37401	423-698-0284	622-3258
Web: www.corleymfg.com					
Diehl Woodworking Mach Inc 981 S Wabash St PO Box 465	Wabash	IN	46992	260-563-2102	563-0206
Web: diehlmachines.com					
HMC Corp 284 Maple St	Contoocook	NH	03229	603-746-4691	746-4819
Web: www.hmccorp.com					
James L. Taylor Manufacturing Co 108 Parker Ave	Poughkeepsie	NY	12601	845-452-3780	452-0764
TF: 800-952-1320 ■ *Web:* www.jamesltaylor.com					
Jenkins Systems LLC 4336 Gateway Dr	Sheboygan	WI	53081	920-452-2110	
Web: www.jenkins-systems.com					
Kimwood Corp 77684 Oregon 99	Cottage Grove	OR	97424	541-942-4401	942-0719
TF: 800-942-4401 ■ *Web:* www.kimwood.com					
KVAL Inc 825 Petaluma Blvd S	Petaluma	CA	94952	707-762-7367	762-0621
TF: 800-553-5825 ■ *Web:* www.kvalinc.com					
McDonough Manufacturing Co 2320 Melby St PO Box 510	Eau Claire	WI	54702	715-834-7755	834-3968
Web: www.mcdonough-mfg.com					
Memphis Machinery & Supply Co Inc 2881 Directors Cove	Memphis	TN	38131	901-527-4443	
TF: 800-932-8376 ■ *Web:* machinery-sales.com					
Mereen-Johnson Machine Co 4401 Lyndale Ave N	Minneapolis	MN	55412	612-529-7791	529-0120
TF: 888-465-7297 ■ *Web:* www.mereen-johnson.com					
Michael Weining Inc 124 Crosslake Pk Dr PO Box 3158	Mooresville	NC	28117	704-799-0100	799-7400
TF: 877-548-0929 ■ *Web:* www.weinigusa.com					
Oliver Machinery Co 6902 S 194th St	Kent	WA	98032	253-867-0334	867-0387
TF: 800-559-5065 ■ *Web:* www.olivermachinery.net					
Pendu Manufacturing Inc 718 N Shirk Rd	New Holland	PA	17557	717-354-4348	355-2148
TF: 800-233-0471 ■ *Web:* www.pendu.com					
Premier Gear & Machine Works Inc 1700 NW Thurman St	Portland	OR	97209	503-227-3514	227-1611
Web: www.premier-gear.com					

Phone *Fax*

Safety Speed Cut Mfg Co Inc
13943 Lincoln St NE............................. Ham Lake MN 55304 763-755-1600 755-6080
TF: 800-772-2327 ■ *Web:* www.safetyspeed.com
Schutte Lumber Co 3001 SW Blvd................. Kansas City MO 64108 816-753-6262 753-7935
Web: www.schuttelumber.com
Selway Corp PO Box 287......................... Stevensville MT 59870 406-777-5471 777-5473
Web: www.selwaycorp.com
Thermwood Corp 904 Buffaloville Rd..................... Dale IN 47523 812-937-4476 937-2956
OTC: TOOD ■ *TF Mktg:* 800-533-6901 ■ *Web:* www.thermwood.com
USNR 1981 Schurman Way PO Box 310............... Woodland WA 98674 360-225-8267 225-8017
TF: 800-289-8767 ■ *Web:* www.coemfg.com
USNR Inc 558 Robinson Rd PO Box 310............... Woodland WA 98674 360-225-8267 225-8017
TF: 800-289-8767 ■ *Web:* www.usnr.com
Viking Engineering & Development Inc
5750 Main St NE .... Fridley MN 55432 763-571-2400 586-1319
TF Sales: 800-328-2403 ■ *Web:* www.vikingeng.com
Voorwood Co 2350 Barney St .... Anderson CA 96007 530-365-3311 365-3315
TF: 800-826-0089 ■ *Web:* www.voorwood.com
Yates-American Machine Company Inc
2880 Kennedy Dr.................................... Beloit WI 53511 608-364-6333
TF: 800-752-6377 ■ *Web:* www.yatesamerican.com

822 WORLD TRADE CENTERS

Phone *Fax*

Houston World Trade Ctr
Greater Houston Partnership
1200 Smith St Ste 700............................. Houston TX 77002 713-844-3600
Web: www.houston.org
Messe Frankfurt Inc 1600 Parkwood Cir Ste 615......... Atlanta GA 30339 770-984-8016 984-8023
Web: us.messefrankfurt.com
Montana World Trade Ctr
Gallagher Business Bldg Ste 257.................. Missoula MT 59812 406-243-6982
Web: www.mwtc.org
Northern California World Trade Ctr
1 Capitol Mall Ste 300............................ Sacramento CA 95814 855-667-2259 443-2672*
**Fax Area Code:* 916 ■ *TF:* 855-667-2259 ■ *Web:* www.norcalwtc.org
Ronald Reagan Bldg & International Trade Ctr
1300 Pennsylvania Ave NW....................... Washington DC 20004 202-312-1300 312-1310
Web: www.itcdc.com
San Diego World Trade Ctr 2980 Pacific Hwy......... San Diego CA 92101 619-615-0868 615-0876
Web: www.wtca.org/locations/world-trade-center-san-diego?locale=en
Seaport World Trade Ctr Boston
200 Seaport Blvd.................................. Boston MA 02210 617-385-4212 385-5090*
**Fax:* Sales ■ *TF:* 800-440-3318 ■ *Web:* www.seaportboston.com
State of Hawaii World Trade Ctr
250 S Hotel St PO Box 2359....................... Honolulu HI 96813 808-587-2750 586-2589
Web: hawaii.gov
World Trade Ctr 101 W Main St .... Norfolk VA 23510 757-627-9440 627-1548
World Trade Ctr Alaska
431 W Seventh Ave Ste 108....................... Anchorage AK 99501 907-278-7233 278-2982
Web: www.wtcak.org
World Trade Ctr Assn Los Angeles
350 S Figueroa St Ste 272....................... Los Angeles CA 90071 213-680-1888 680-1878
Web: laedc.org/wtc
World Trade Ctr Baltimore
401 E Pratt St Ste 232........................... Baltimore MD 21202 410-576-0022 576-0751
Web: www.wtci.org
World Trade Ctr Delaware 802 NW St .... Wilmington DE 19801 302-656-7905 656-7956
Web: www.wtcde.com
World Trade Ctr Denver 1625 Broadway Ste 680 .... Denver CO 80202 303-592-5760 592-5228
Web: wtcdenver.org
World Trade Ctr Detroit/Windsor
1200 Sixth St .... Detroit MI 48226 313-962-2345
Web: www.wtcdw.com
World Trade Ctr Miami
1007 N America Way Ste 500......................... Miami FL 33132 305-871-7910 871-7904
Web: worldtrade.org
World Trade Ctr Montreal
380 St Antoine St W Ste 6000 .... Montreal QC H2Y3X7 514-871-4000 871-1255
Web: www.ccmm.qc.ca
World Trade Ctr of New Orleans
365 Canal St Ste 1120 .... New Orleans LA 70130 504-529-1601 529-1691
Web: wtcno.org
World Trade Ctr Orlando 1600 E Amelia St............. Orlando FL 32803 407-894-5740 894-5740
Web: www.worldtradecenterorlando.org
World Trade Ctr Palm Beach
777 S Flagler Dr........................... West Palm Beach FL 33401 561-712-1443 712-1445
Web: www.wtcpalmbeach.com
World Trade Ctr Portland 121 SW Salmon St........... Portland OR 97204 503-464-8688 464-2300
Web: www.wtcpd.com
World Trade Ctr Saint Louis
7733 Forsyth Blvd Ste 2200...................... Saint Louis MO 63105 314-615-8141 615-8140
Web: www.worldtradecenter-stl.com
World Trade Ctr Seattle
2200 Alaskan Way Ste 410............................ Seattle WA 98121 206-441-5144 770-7923
Web: www.wtcseattle.com
World Trade Ctr Tacoma 950 Pacific Ave Ste 310 .... Tacoma WA 98402 253-396-1022 396-1033
Web: www.wtcta.org
World Trade Ctr Tampa Bay 1101 Channelside Dr........ Tampa FL 33602 813-330-2931
Web: www.wtctampa.com
World Trade Ctr Wisconsin
750 N Lincoln Memorial Dr .... Milwaukee WI 53202 414-274-3840
Web: www.wistrade.org

823 ZOOS & WILDLIFE PARKS

See Also Aquariums - Public p. 1739; Botanical Gardens & Arboreta p. 1870

Phone *Fax*

Abilene Zoological Gardens
2070 Zoo Ln Nelson Pk .... Abilene TX 79602 325-676-6085 676-6084
Web: www.abilenetx.com
African Lion Safari & Game Farm RR 1 Ste 1........ Cambridge ON N1R5S2 519-623-2620 623-9542
TF: 800-461-9453 ■ *Web:* www.lionsafari.com
African Safari Wildlife Park
267 S Lightner Rd............................... Port Clinton OH 43452 419-732-3606 734-1919
TF: 800-521-2660 ■ *Web:* www.africansafariwildlifepark.com
Akron Zoological Park 500 Edgewood Ave .... Akron OH 44307 330-375-2550 375-2575
Web: www.akronzoo.org
Alabama Gulf Coast Zoo, The
1204 Gulf Shores Pkwy .... Gulf Shores AL 36542 251-968-5732
Web: alabamagulfcoastzoo.org
Alaska Wildlife Conservation Ctr
Mile 79 Seward Hwy PO Box 949..................... Portage AK 99587 907-783-2025 783-2370
Web: www.alaskawildlife.org
Alaska Zoo 4731 O'Malley Rd .... Anchorage AK 99507 907-346-3242 346-2673
Web: www.alaskazoo.org
Alexandria Zoological Park
3016 Masonic Dr .... Alexandria LA 71301 318-441-6810 473-1149
Web: www.thealexandriazoo.com
Alligator Adventure
4604 Hwy 17 S Barefoot Landing........... North Myrtle Beach SC 29582 843-361-0789
Web: www.alligatoradventure.com
Amarillo Zoo
NE 24 Ave & Dumas Hwy Thompson Pk................ Amarillo TX 79105 806-381-7911 381-7901
Web: zoo.amarillo.gov
Animal Ark Wildlife Sanctuary & Nature Ctr
1265 Deerlodge Rd....................................... Reno NV 89508 775-970-3111 366-5771*
**Fax Area Code:* 866 ■ *TF:* 866-366-5771 ■ *Web:* www.animalark.org
Arkansas Alligator Farm & Petting Zoo
847 Whittington Ave .... Hot Springs AR 71901 501-623-6172
Web: www.alligatorfarmzoo.com
Assiniboine Park Zoo 55 Pavilion Crescent........... Winnipeg MB R3P2N6 204-927-8080
TF: 877-927-6006 ■ *Web:* www.assiniboinepark.ca/zoo
Audubon Nature Institute
6500 Magazine St............................. New Orleans LA 70118 504-581-4629
TF: 800-774-7394 ■ *Web:* audubonnatureinstitute.org
Austin Zoo 10807 Rawhide Trail......................... Austin TX 78736 512-288-1490 288-3972
Web: www.austinzoo.org
Beardsley Zoo 1875 Noble Ave..................... Bridgeport CT 06610 203-394-6565
Web: www.beardsleyzoo.org
Bergen County Zoological Park 216 Forest Ave .... Paramus NJ 07652 201-262-3771 986-1788
Web: co.bergen.nj.us
Binder Park Zoo 7400 Div Dr .... Battle Creek MI 49014 269-979-1351 979-8834
Web: www.binderparkzoo.org
Binghampton Zoo at Ross Park 60 Morgan Rd...... Binghamton NY 13903 607-724-5461
Web: www.rossparkzoo.com
Birmingham Zoo 2630 Cahaba Rd................. Birmingham AL 35223 205-879-0409 879-9426
Web: www.birminghamzoo.com
Blank Park Zoo 7401 SW Ninth St .... Des Moines IA 50315 515-285-4722
Web: www.blankparkzoo.com
Bolsa Chica Ecological Reserve
3842 Warner Ave .... Huntington Beach CA 92649 714-846-1114 846-4065
Web: www.bolsachica.org
Bowmanville Zoological Park Ltd
340 King St E .... Bowmanville ON L1C3K5 905-623-5655 623-0957
Web: www.bowmanvillezoo.com
Bramble Park Zoo 800 Tenth St NW PO Box 910....... Watertown SD 57201 605-882-6269 882-5232
Web: www.brambleparkzoo.com
Brandywine Zoo 1001 N Pk Dr .... Wilmington DE 19802 302-571-7747 571-7787
Web: www.brandywinezoo.org
BREC's Baton Rouge Zoo 3601 Thomas Rd......... Baton Rouge LA 70807 225-775-3877 775-3931
Web: www.brzoo.org
Brevard Zoo 8225 N Wickham Rd .... Melbourne FL 32940 321-254-9453 259-5966
TF: 800-435-7352 ■ *Web:* brevardzoo.org
British Columbia Wildlife Park
9077 Dallas Dr .... Kamloops BC V2C6V1 250-573-3242 573-2406
Web: www.bcwildlife.org
Bronx Zoo 2300 Southern Blvd.......................... Bronx NY 10460 718-220-5100
TF: 800-433-4149 ■ *Web:* www.bronxzoo.com
Brookfield Zoo 3300 Golf Rd...................... Brookfield IL 60513 708-485-0263
Buffalo Zoological Gardens 300 Parkside Ave........... Buffalo NY 14214 716-837-3900 837-0738
Web: www.buffalozoo.org
Busch Gardens Williamsburg
1 Busch Gardens Blvd .... Williamsburg VA 23185 800-343-7946 253-3399*
**Fax Area Code:* 757 ■ **Fax:* Mktg ■ *TF:* 800-343-7946 ■ *Web:* www.buschgardens.com
Butterfly Pavilion & Insect Ctr
6252 W 104th Ave .... Westminster CO 80020 303-469-5441 657-5944
Web: www.butterflies.org
Buttonwood Park Zoo 425 Hawthorn St............ New Bedford MA 02740 508-991-6178
Web: www.bpzoo.org
Caldwell Zoo 2203 ML King Blvd .... Tyler TX 75702 903-593-0121
Web: www.caldwellzoo.org
Calgary Zoo Botanical Garden & Prehistoric Park
1300 Zoo Rd NE .... Calgary AB T2E7V6 403-232-9300 237-7582
TF: 800-588-9993 ■ *Web:* www.calgaryzoo.com
Cameron Park Zoo 1701 N Fourth St .... Waco TX 76707 254-750-8400 750-8430
Web: www.cameronparkzoo.com
Capron Park Zoo 201 County St .... Attleboro MA 02703 508-222-3047 223-2208
Web: www.capronparkzoo.com
Caribbean Gardens 1590 Goodlette-Frank Rd .... Naples FL 34102 239-262-5409 262-6866
TF: 888-520-3756 ■ *Web:* napleszoo.org
Cat Tales Zoological Park 17020 Newport Hwy........... Mead WA 99021 509-238-4126 238-4126
Web: www.cattales.org
Central Florida Zoological Park
3755 NW Hwy 17-92 & I-4 PO Box 470309......... Lake Monroe FL 32747 407-323-4450 321-0900
TF: 800-435-7352 ■ *Web:* www.centralfloridazoo.org
Central Park Zoo Fifth Ave & 64th St .... New York NY 10065 212-439-6500 988-0286
Web: centralparkzoo.com
Chahinkapa Zoo Park & Carousel
1004 RJ Hughes Dr .... Wahpeton ND 58075 701-642-8709 642-9285
Web: www.wahpetonpark.com
Charles Paddock Zoo 9305 Pismo Ave .... Atascadero CA 93422 805-461-5080
Web: www.charlespaddockzoo.org
Chattanooga Zoo 301 N Holltzclaw Ave .... Chattanooga TN 37404 423-697-1322 697-1329
Web: chattzoo.org

Name / Address	City	State	Zip	Phone	Fax
Cherry Brook Zoo Inc 901 Foster Thurston Dr. *Web:* www.cherrybrookzoo.com	Saint John	NB	E2K5H9	506-634-1440	634-0717
Cheyenne Mountain Zoological Park 4250 Cheyenne Mtn Zoo Rd *Web:* www.cmzoo.org	Colorado Springs	CO	80906	719-633-9925	633-2254
Cincinnati Zoo & Botanical Garden 3400 Vine St. *TF:* 800-944-4776 ■ *Web:* www.cincinnatizoo.org	Cincinnati	OH	45220	513-281-4700	559-7790
Claws 'n' Paws Wild Animal Park 1475 Ledgedale Rd. *Web:* www.clawsnpaws.com	Lake Ariel	PA	18436	570-698-6154	
Cleveland Metroparks Zoo 3900 Wildlife Way *Web:* clevelandmetroparks.com/zoo/zoo.aspx	Cleveland	OH	44109	216-661-6500	
Clyde Peeling's Reptiland 18628 US Rt 15 *TF:* 800-737-8452 ■ *Web:* www.reptiland.com	Allenwood	PA	17810	800-737-8452	
Columbian Park Zoo 1915 Scott St *TF:* 800-438-9926 ■ *Web:* www.lafayette.in.gov	Lafayette	IN	47904	765-807-1540	807-1547
Columbus Zoo & Aquarium 4850 W Powell Rd *TF:* 800-666-5397 ■ *Web:* columbuszoo.org	Powell	OH	43065	614-645-3400	645-3465
Como Zoo & Conservatory 1225 Estabrook Dr *Web:* comozooconservatory.org	Saint Paul	MN	55103	651-487-8200	
Cosley Zoo 1356 N Gary Ave *Web:* www.cosleyzoo.org	Wheaton	IL	60187	630-665-5534	260-6408
Cougar Mountain Zoo 19525 SE 54th St *Web:* www.cougarmountainzoo.org	Issaquah	WA	98027	425-392-6278	392-1076
Dakota Zoo 602 Riverside Pk Rd *Web:* www.dakotazoo.org	Bismarck	ND	58504	701-223-7543	258-8350
David Traylor Zoo of Emporia 75 Soden Rd *Web:* www.emporiazoo.org	Emporia	KS	66801	620-341-4365	
Denver Zoo 2300 Steele St *Web:* www.denverzoo.org	Denver	CO	80205	303-376-4800	376-4801
Detroit Zoological Institute 8450 W Ten-Mile Rd *Web:* www.detroitzoo.org	Royal Oak	MI	48067	248-541-5717	
Dickerson Park Zoo 3043 N Ft *Web:* www.dickersonparkzoo.org	Springfield	MO	65803	417-833-1570	833-4459
Discovery Cove 6000 Discovery Cove Way *TF:* 877-434-7268 ■ *Web:* www.discoverycove.com	Orlando	FL	32821	407-370-1280	
Ecomuseum 21125 Ch Sainte-Marie *Web:* www.ecomuseum.ca	Sainte-Anne-de-Bellevue	QC	H9X3Y7	514-457-9449	457-0769
El Paso Zoo 4001 E Paisano Dr *Web:* www.elpasozoo.org	El Paso	TX	79905	915-521-1850	521-1857
Ellen Trout Zoo 402 Zoo Cir *Web:* cityoflufkin.com/zoo	Lufkin	TX	75904	936-633-0399	633-0311
Elmwood Park Zoo 1661 Harding Blvd *TF:* 800-652-4143 ■ *Web:* www.elmwoodparkzoo.org	Norristown	PA	19401	610-277-3825	292-0332
Erie Zoo 423 W 38th St *TF:* 877-371-5422 ■ *Web:* www.eriezoo.org	Erie	PA	16508	814-864-4091	864-1140
Everglades Alligator Farm 40351 SW 192nd Ave *Web:* www.everglades.com	Homestead	FL	33034	305-247-2628	248-9711
Everglades Safari Park 26700 SW 8th St *Web:* www.evergladessafaripark.com	Miami	FL	33194	305-226-6923	554-5666
Felix Neck Wildlife Sanctuary 100 Felix Neck Dr *TF:* 866-627-2267 ■ *Web:* massaudubon.org	Edgartown	MA	02539	508-627-4850	627-6052
For-Mar Nature Preserve & Arboretum 2142 N Genesee Rd *Web:* www.geneseecountyparks.org	Burton	MI	48509	810-789-8567	
Fort Wayne Children's Zoo 3411 Sherman Blvd *Web:* kidszoo.org	Fort Wayne	IN	46808	260-427-6800	427-6820
Fossil Rim Wildlife Ctr 2299 County Rd 2008 *Web:* www.fossilrim.com	Glen Rose	TX	76043	254-897-2960	
Franklin Park Zoo 1 Franklin Pk Rd *Web:* www.zoonewengland.org	Boston	MA	02121	617-541-5466	989-2025
Fresno Chaffee Zoo 894 W Belmont Ave *Web:* www.fresnochaffeezoo.org	Fresno	CA	93728	559-498-5910	
Gator Park 24050 SW Eigth St *TF:* 800-559-2205 ■ *Web:* www.gatorpark.com	Miami	FL	33194	305-559-2255	
Gatorland 14501 S Orange Blossom Trl *TF:* 800-393-5297 ■ *Web:* www.gatorland.com	Orlando	FL	32837	407-855-5496	
Gibbon Conservation Ctr 19100 Esguerra Rd *Web:* www.gibboncenter.org	Santa Clarita	CA	91350	661-296-2737	
Gladys Porter Zoo 500 Ringgold St *Web:* www.gpz.org	Brownsville	TX	78520	956-546-7187	541-4940
Glen Oak Park 2218 N Prospect Rd *Web:* www.peoriazoo.org	Peoria	IL	61603	309-686-3365	685-6240
Global Wildlife Ctr 26389 Hwy 40 *Web:* www.globalwildlife.com	Folsom	LA	70437	985-796-3585	796-9487
Good Zoo & Benedum Planetarium 465 Lodge Dr *TF:* 800-624-6988 ■ *Web:* www.oglebay-resort.com/goodzoo	Wheeling	WV	26003	304-243-4030	243-4110
Great Plains Zoo 805 S Kiwanis Ave *Web:* www.greatzoo.org	Sioux Falls	SD	57104	605-367-7059	367-8340
Greenville Zoo 150 Cleveland Pk Dr *TF:* 800-877-8339 ■ *Web:* www.greenvillezoo.com	Greenville	SC	29601	864-467-4300	467-4314
Grizzly & Wolf Discovery Ctr 201 S Canyon St *TF:* 800-257-2570 ■ *Web:* www.grizzlydiscoveryctr.org	West Yellowstone	MT	59758	406-646-7001	646-7004
Happy Hollow Park & Zoo 1300 Senter Rd *Web:* www.hhpz.org	San Jose	CA	95112	408-794-6400	
Harmony Park Safari 431 Clouds Cove Rd SE	Huntsville	AL	35803	256-723-3880	
Hattiesburg Zoo 107 S 17th Ave *Web:* www.hattiesburgms.com	Hattiesburg	MS	39401	601-545-4500	
Henry Doorly Zoo 3701 S Tenth St *Web:* www.omahazoo.com	Omaha	NE	68107	402-733-8401	733-7868
Henry Vilas Park Zoo 702 S Randall Ave *Web:* www.vilaszoo.org	Madison	WI	53715	608-266-4732	

Name / Address	City	State	Zip	Phone	Fax
Henson Robinson Zoo 1100 E Lake Dr *Web:* www.springfieldparks.org/facilities/hensonrobinsonzoo	Springfield	IL	62712	217-585-1821	529-8748
Honolulu Zoo 151 Kapahulu Ave *Web:* www.honoluluzoo.org	Honolulu	HI	96815	808-971-7171	
Houston Zoo Inc 1513 Cambridge *Web:* www.houstonzoo.org	Houston	TX	77030	713-533-6500	
Hutchinson Zoo 6 Emerson Loop E *TF:* 800-362-3247 ■ *Web:* hutchgov.com	Hutchinson	KS	67501	620-694-2693	694-1980
Indianapolis Zoo 1200 W Washington St *Web:* www.indianapoliszoo.com	Indianapolis	IN	46222	317-630-2001	630-5153
International Exotic Feline Sanctuary PO Box 637 *Web:* www.bigcat.org	Boyd	TX	76023	940-433-5091	433-5092
Jackson Zoological Park 2918 W Capitol St *Web:* www.jacksonzoo.org	Jackson	MS	39209	601-352-2580	352-2594
Jacksonville Zoo & Gardens 370 Zoo Pkwy *Web:* www.jacksonvillezoo.org	Jacksonville	FL	32218	904-757-4463	757-4315
John Ball Zoological Garden 1300 W Fulton St *Web:* www.jbzoo.org	Grand Rapids	MI	49504	616-336-4301	336-3907
Jungle Adventures 26205 E Colonial Dr *TF:* 877-424-2867 ■ *Web:* www.jungleadventures.com	Christmas	FL	32709	407-568-2885	568-0038
Jungle Cat World Inc 3667 Concession Rd 6 *Web:* www.junglecatworld.com	Orono	ON	L0B1M0	905-983-5016	983-9858
Jungle Island 1111 Parrot Jungle Trl *Web:* www.jungleisland.com	Miami	FL	33132	305-400-7000	400-7290
Kansas City Zoo 6800 Zoo Dr *Web:* www.kansascityzoo.org	Kansas City	MO	64132	816-595-1234	
Kentucky Horse Park 4089 Iron Works Pkwy *TF:* 800-678-8813 ■ *Web:* www.kyhorsepark.com	Lexington	KY	40511	859-233-4303	254-0253
Kisma Preserve PO Box 84 *Web:* www.kismapreserve.org	Mount Desert	ME	04660	207-667-3244	
Knoxville Zoological Gardens Inc 3500 Knoxville Zoo Dr *Web:* www.zooknoxville.org	Knoxville	TN	37914	865-637-5331	637-1943
Lake Superior Zoo 7210 Fremont St *Web:* lszooduluth.org	Duluth	MN	55807	218-730-4500	723-3750
Lee Richardson Zoo 312 E Finnup Dr *Web:* leerichardsonzoo.org	Garden City	KS	67846	620-276-1250	276-1259
Lincoln Children's Zoo 1222 S 27th St *Web:* www.lincolnzoo.org	Lincoln	NE	68502	402-475-6741	475-6742
Lincoln Park Zoo 2001 N Clark St PO Box 14903 *Web:* www.lpzoo.org	Chicago	IL	60614	312-742-2000	742-2299
Lion Country Safari 2003 Lion Country Safari Rd *Web:* www.lioncountrysafari.com	Loxahatchee	FL	33470	561-793-1084	793-9603
Little Rock Zoo 1 Zoo Dr *Web:* www.littlerockzoo.com	Little Rock	AR	72205	501-666-2406	666-7040
Living Desert Zoo & Gardens 47900 Portola Ave *Web:* www.livingdesert.org	Palm Desert	CA	92260	760-346-5694	568-9685
Los Angeles Zoo & Botanical Gardens 5333 Zoo Dr *Web:* www.lazoo.org	Los Angeles	CA	90027	323-644-4200	662-9786
Louisville Zoo 1100 Trevilian Way *TF:* 866-229-0502 ■ *Web:* www.louisvillezoo.org	Louisville	KY	40213	502-459-2181	459-2196
Lowry Park Zoo 1101 W Sligh Ave *Web:* www.lowryparkzoo.org	Tampa	FL	33604	813-935-8552	935-9486
Maryland Zoo in Baltimore 1876 Mansion House Dr *Web:* marylandzoo.org	Baltimore	MD	21217	410-396-7102	
Maymont 2201 Shields Dr *Web:* www.maymont.org	Richmond	VA	23220	804-358-7166	358-9994
Memphis Zoo 2000 Prentiss Pl *Web:* www.memphiszoo.org	Memphis	TN	38112	901-333-6500	333-6501
Mesker Park Zoo 1545 Mesker Pk Dr *Web:* meskerparkzoo.com	Evansville	IN	47720	812-435-6143	435-6140
Micke Grove Zoo 11793 N Micke Grove Rd *Web:* www.sjgov.org/mgzoo	Lodi	CA	95240	209-953-8840	331-7271
Minnesota Zoo 13000 Zoo Blvd *TF:* 800-366-7811 ■ *Web:* mnzoo.org	Apple Valley	MN	55124	952-431-9200	431-9300
Mobile Zoo 15161 WaRd Rd W *Web:* www.mobilezoo.cc	Wilmer	AL	36587	251-649-1845	
Monkey Jungle 14805 SW 216th St *Web:* www.monkeyjungle.com	Miami	FL	33170	305-235-1611	
Montgomery Zoo 2301 Coliseum Pkwy *Web:* www.montgomeryzoo.com	Montgomery	AL	36110	334-240-4900	240-4916
Nashville Zoo 3777 Nolensville Rd *Web:* www.nashvillezoo.org	Nashville	TN	37211	615-833-1534	333-0728
National Zoological Park (Smithsonian Institution) 3001 Connecticut Ave NW *Web:* www.nationalzoo.si.edu	Washington	DC	20008	202-633-4888	673-4836
Natural Bridge Wildlife Ranch 26515 Natural Bridge Caverns Rd *Web:* www.wildliferanchtexas.com	San Antonio	TX	78266	830-438-7400	438-3494
New York State Zoo 1 Thompson Pk *Web:* www.nyszoo.org	Watertown	NY	13601	315-782-6180	
North Carolina Zoological Park 4401 Zoo Pkwy *TF:* 800-488-0444 ■ *Web:* www.nczoo.org	Asheboro	NC	27205	336-879-7000	
Northeastern Wisconsin Zoo 305 E Walnut St Rm 102 PO Box 23600 *TF:* 888-844-8070 ■ *Web:* co.brown.wi.us/departments	Green Bay	WI	54301	920-448-6242	448-4054
Northwest Trek Wildlife Park 11610 Trek Dr E *Web:* www.nwtrek.org	Eatonville	WA	98328	360-832-6117	832-6118
Oakland Zoo 9777 Golf Links Rd *Web:* www.oaklandzoo.org	Oakland	CA	94605	510-632-9525	635-5719
Oklahoma City Zoological Park & Botanical Gardens 2101 NE 50th St *TF:* 800-891-2917 ■ *Web:* www.okczoo.org	Oklahoma City	OK	73111	405-424-3344	425-0297
Orange County Zoo 1 Irvine Pk Rd *Web:* www.ocparks.com	Orange	CA	92869	714-973-6847	

Phone Fax

Oregon Zoo 4001 SW Canyon Rd Portland OR 97221 503-226-1561
Web: www.oregonzoo.org
Out of Africa Wildlife Park
4020 N Cherry Rd Camp Verde AZ 86322 928-567-2840 567-2839
Web: www.outofafricapark.com
Oxbow Park 5731 County Rd 105 NW Byron MN 55920 507-775-2451 775-2544
Palm Beach Zoo at Dreher Park
1301 Summit Blvd West Palm Beach FL 33405 561-533-0887 585-6085
Web: www.palmbeachzoo.org
Parc Safari 280 Rang Roxham Saint-Bernard-de-Lacolle QC J0L1H0 450-247-2727 247-3563
Web: www.parcsafari.com
Parks at Chehaw 105 Chehaw Pk Rd Albany GA 31701 229-430-5275 430-3035
Web: www.chehaw.org
Philadelphia Zoo 3400 W Girard Ave Philadelphia PA 19104 215-243-1100 243-5385
Web: www.philadelphiazoo.org
Phoenix Zoo 455 N Galvin Pkwy Phoenix AZ 85008 602-273-1341 273-7078
Web: www.phoenixzoo.org
Pittsburgh Zoo & PPG Aquarium 1 Wild Pl Pittsburgh PA 15206 412-665-3640 665-3661
TF: 800-732-0999 ■ *Web:* www.pittsburghzoo.org
Pocatello Zoo 2900 S Second Ave Pocatello ID 83204 208-234-6264
Web: www.pocatellozoo.org
Point Defiance Zoo & Aquarium 5400 N Pearl St Tacoma WA 98407 253-591-5337 591-5448
Web: www.pdza.org
Potter Park Zoo 1301 S Pennsylvania Ave Lansing MI 48912 517-483-4222 316-3894
Web: www.potterparkzoo.org
Provincial Wildlife Park
149 Creighton Rd PO Box 299 Shubenacadie NS B0N2H0 902-758-2040 758-7011
Web: wildlifepark.novascotia.ca
Pueblo Zoo 3455 Nuckolls Ave Pueblo CO 81005 719-561-1452
Web: www.pueblozoo.org
Queens Zoo 53-51 111th St Flushing NY 11368 718-271-1500
Web: www.wcs.org
Racine Zoo 200 Goold St Racine WI 53402 262-636-9189 636-9307
Web: www.racinezoo.org
Red River Zoo 4255 23rd Ave S Fargo ND 58104 701-277-9240 277-9238
Web: www.redriverzoo.org
Reid Park Zoo 1100 S Randolph Way Tucson AZ 85716 520-791-3204 791-5378
Web: reidparkzoo.org
Riverbanks Zoo & Botanical Garden
500 Wildlife Pkwy Columbia SC 29210 803-779-8717 253-6381
Web: www.riverbanks.org
Riverside Zoo 1600 S Beltline Hwy W Scottsbluff NE 69361 308-630-6236
Roger Williams Park Zoo 1000 Elmwood Ave Providence RI 02907 401-785-3510 941-3988
Web: rwpzoo.org
Rolling Hills Wildlife Adventure
625 N Hedville Rd Salina KS 67401 785-827-9488 827-3738
Web: www.rollinghillswildlife.com
Roosevelt Park Zoo 1219 Burdick Expy Minot ND 58701 701-857-4166 857-4169
Web: www.rpzoo.com
Rosamond Gifford Zoo at Burnet Park
1 Conservation Pl Syracuse NY 13204 315-435-8511 435-8517
TF: 800-724-5006 ■ *Web:* rosamondgiffordzoo.org
Sacramento Zoo 3930 W Land Pk Dr Sacramento CA 95822 916-808-5888
TF: 866-570-7318 ■ *Web:* www.saczoo.org
Safari West Wildlife Preserve & Tent Camp
3115 Porter Creek Rd Santa Rosa CA 95404 707-579-2551 579-8777
TF: 800-616-2695 ■ *Web:* www.safariwest.com
Saint Augustine Alligator Farm
999 Anastasia Blvd Saint Augustine FL 32080 904-824-3337
Web: www.alligatorfarm.com
Saint Louis Zoological Park
1 Government Dr Saint Louis MO 63110 314-781-0900 647-7969
TF: 800-966-8877 ■ *Web:* www.stlzoo.org
Salisbury Zoological Park 755 S Pk Dr Salisbury MD 21804 410-548-3188 860-0919
Web: www.salisburyzoo.org
Salmonier Nature Park PO Box 190 Holyrood NL A0A2R0 709-229-3915 229-7078
Web: www.env.gov.nl.ca
San Antonio Zoological Gardens & Aquarium
3903 N St Mary's St San Antonio TX 78212 210-734-7184 734-7291
Web: www.sazoo-aq.org
San Diego Zoo 2920 Zoo Dr San Diego CA 92101 619-231-1515 231-0249
Web: www.sandiegozoo.org
San Diego Zoo Safari Park
15500 San Pasqual Valley Rd Escondido CA 92027 760-747-8702
TF Cust Svc: 877-363-6237 ■ *Web:* www.sdzsafaripark.org
San Francisco Zoo 1 Zoo Rd San Francisco CA 94132 415-753-7080
Web: www.sfzoo.org
Santa Ana Zoo 1801 E Chestnut Ave Santa Ana CA 92701 714-835-7484 550-0346
Web: www.santaanazoo.org
Santa Barbara Zoological Gardens
500 Ninos Dr Santa Barbara CA 93103 805-962-5339 962-1673
Web: www.sbzoo.org
Santa Fe Community College Teaching Zoo
3000 NW 83rd St Gainesville FL 32606 352-395-5604
Web: www.sfcollege.edu/zoo
Sarasota Jungle Gardens 3701 Bay Shore Rd Sarasota FL 34234 941-355-5305
TF: 877-681-6547 ■ *Web:* www.sarasotajunglegardens.com
Scovill Zoo 71 S Country Club Rd Decatur IL 62521 217-421-7435
Web: www.decatur-parks.org
Sedgwick County Zoo 5555 W Zoo Blvd Wichita KS 67212 316-660-9453 942-3781
Web: www.scz.org
Seneca Park Zoo 2222 St Paul St Rochester NY 14621 585-336-7200 342-1477
Web: www.senecaparkzoo.org
Sequoia Park Zoo 3414 W St Eureka CA 95503 707-441-4263
Web: www.sequoiaparkzoo.net
Sierra Safari Zoo 10200 N Virginia St Reno NV 89506 775-677-1101
Web: www.sierrasafarizoo.com
Smithsonian National Zoological Park
3001 Connecticut Ave NW Washington DC 20008 202-633-4888
Web: nationalzoo.si.edu
Spring River Park & Zoo
1306 E College Blvd PO Box 1838 Roswell NM 88201 575-624-6760
Web: www.museumsusa.org
Staten Island Zoo 614 Broadway Staten Island NY 10310 718-442-3101 981-8711
Web: www.statenislandzoo.org
Tautphaus Park Zoo 308 Constitution Way Idaho Falls ID 83402 208-612-8100
Web: www.idahofallsidaho.gov
Texas Zoo 110 Memorial Dr Victoria TX 77901 361-573-7681 576-1094
Web: www.texaszoo.org
Toledo Zoo 2700 Broadway Toledo OH 43609 419-385-5721 389-8670
TF: 866-900-1146 ■ *Web:* www.toledozoo.org
Topeka Zoological Park 635 SW Gage Blvd Topeka KS 66606 785-368-9180 368-9152
Web: topekazoo.org
Toronto Zoo 361-A Old Finch Ave Toronto ON M1B5K7 416-392-5900 392-5934
Web: www.torontozoo.com
Tracy Aviary 589 East 1300 South Salt Lake City UT 84105 801-596-8500
Web: www.tracyaviary.org
Trevor Zoo 131 Millbrook School Rd Millbrook NY 12545 845-677-3704
Web: www.millbrook.org/page/school-life/trevor-zoo
Tulsa Zoo 6421 E 36th St N Tulsa OK 74115 918-669-6600 669-6610
Web: tulsazoo.org
Tupelo Buffalo Park & Zoo 2272 N Coley Rd Tupelo MS 38803 662-844-8709 844-8850
TF: 866-272-4766 ■ *Web:* www.tupelobuffalopark.com
Utah's Hogle Zoo 2600 E Sunnyside Ave Salt Lake City UT 84108 801-582-1631
Web: www.hoglezoo.org
Utica Zoo 1 Utica Zoo Way Utica NY 13501 315-738-0472 738-0475
Web: www.uticazoo.org
Virginia Zoological Park 3500 Granby St Norfolk VA 23504 757-441-2374 441-5408
Web: www.virginiazoo.org
Waccatee Zoological Farm
8500 Enterprise Rd Myrtle Beach SC 29588 843-650-8500
Web: www.waccateezoo.com
West Virginia State Wildlife Ctr
PO Box 38 French Creek WV 26218 304-924-6211
Web: www.wvdnr.gov/wildlife/wildlifecenter.shtm
Wild Animal Safari 1300 Oak Grove Rd Pine Mountain GA 31822 706-663-8744 663-8880
TF: 800-367-2751 ■ *Web:* www.animalsafari.com
Wildlife Sanctuary of Northwest Florida
PO Box 1092 Pensacola FL 32591 850-433-9453 438-6168
Web: www.pensacolawildlife.com
Wildlife West Nature Park 87 N Frontage Rd Edgewood NM 87015 505-281-7655 281-7170
TF: 877-981-9453 ■ *Web:* www.wildlifewest.org
Wildlife World Zoo
16501 W Northern Ave Litchfield Park AZ 85340 623-935-9453
Web: www.wildlifeworld.com
Wilds, The 14000 International Rd Cumberland OH 43732 740-638-5030
Web: www.thewilds.org
Wonders of Wildlife 500 W Sunshine St Springfield MO 65807 417-890-9453 890-9278
TF: 877-245-9453 ■ *Web:* www.wondersofwildlife.org
Woodland Park Zoo 601 N 59th St Seattle WA 98103 206-548-2500 548-1536
Web: www.zoo.org
World of Reptiles & Birds Park
Edgartown-VineyaRd Haven Rd Edgartown MA 02539 508-627-5634
Web: www.reptilesandbirds.com
Zoo Atlanta 800 Cherokee Ave SE Atlanta GA 30315 404-624-5600 627-7514
Web: www.zooatlanta.org
Zoo Boise 355 Julia Davis Dr Boise ID 83702 208-384-4260 384-4194
Web: zooboise.org
Zoo in Forest Park, The
302 Sumner Ave PO Box 80295 Springfield MA 01138 413-733-2251 733-2330
Web: www.forestparkzoo.org
Zoo of Acadiana 5601 Hwy 90 E Broussard LA 70518 337-837-4325 837-4253
Web: www.zooofacadiana.org
Zoo, The 5701 Gulf Breeze Pkwy Gulf Breeze FL 32563 850-932-2229
Web: gulfbreezezoo.org
ZooAmerica North American Wildlife Park
100 W Hersheypark Dr Hershey PA 17033 717-534-3900 534-3151
Web: www.zooamerica.com
ZooMontana & Botanical Gardens
2100 S Shiloh Rd Billings MT 59106 406-652-8100
Web: www.zoomontana.org

Area Code and Zip Code Guide

The information provided in this Guide is organized **alphabetically by city name,** with area code(s) and zip code(s) shown to the right of the city name.

A

City	Area Code(s)	Zip Code(s)
Abbeville, AL	334	36310
Abbeville, GA	229	31001
Abbeville, LA	337	70510-70511
Abbeville, SC	864	29620
Abbotsford, WI	715, 534	54405
Abbott Park, IL	224, 847	60064
Aberdeen, ID	208	83210
Aberdeen, MD	410	21001
Aberdeen, MS	662	39730
Aberdeen, NC	910	28315
Aberdeen, SD	605	57401-57402
Aberdeen, WA	360	98520
Aberdeen Proving Ground, MD	410	21005, 21010
Abernathy, TX	806	79311
Abilene, KS	785	67410
Abilene, TX	915	79601-79608, 79697-79699
Abingdon, VA	276	24210-24212
Abington, MA	339, 781	02351
Abington, PA	215, 267	19001
Accident, MD	301	21520
Accokeek, MD	301	20607
Accomac, VA	757	23301
Accord, NY	845	12404
Ackerman, MS	662	39735
Acme, MI	231	49610
Acton, MA	351, 978	01718-01720
Acworth, GA	470, 770	30101-30102
Ada, MI	616	49301, 49355-49357
Ada, MN	218	56510
Ada, OH	419, 567	45810
Ada, OK	580	74820-74821
Adairsville, GA	470, 770	30103
Adams, MA	413	01220
Adams, OR	541, 458	97810
Adamstown, MD	301	21710
Adamstown, PA	717	19501
Adamsville, TN	731	38310
Addison, AL	256	35540
Addison, IL	331, 630	60101
Addison, TX	469, 972	75001
Addison, VT	802	05491
Adel, GA	229	31620
Adel, IA	515	50003
Adelanto, CA	760, 442	92301
Adelphi, MD	301	20783, 20787
Adrian, GA	478	31002
Adrian, MI	517	49221
Advance, NC	336	27006
Affton, MO	314	63123
Afton, OK	918	74331
Afton, WY	307	83110
Agawam, MA	413	01001
Agoura Hills, CA	818	91301, 91376-91377
Aguadilla, PR	787, 939	00603-00605
Ahoskie, NC	252	27910
Aiea, HI	808	96701
Aiken, SC	803	29801-29808
Ainsworth, NE	402	69210
Airway Heights, WA	509	99001
Aitkin, MN	218	56431
Ajo, AZ	520	85321
Akron, CO	970	80720
Akron, IN	574	46910
Akron, NY	585	14001
Akron, OH	234, 330	44301-44328, 44333-44334*
Akron, PA	717	17501
Alabaster, AL	205	35007, 35144
Alachua, FL	386	32615-32616
Alamance, NC	336	27201
Alameda, CA	510	94501-94502
Alamo, CA	925	94507
Alamo, GA	912	30411
Alamo, TN	731	38001

City	Area Code(s)	Zip Code(s)
Alamo, TX	956	78516
Alamogordo, NM	505	88310-88311
Alamosa, CO	719	81101-81102
Albany, CA	510	94706, 94710
Albany, GA	229	31701-31708
Albany, KY	606	42602
Albany, MN	320	56307
Albany, MO	660	64402
Albany, NY	518	12201-12214, 12220-12262*
Albany, OR	541, 458	97321
Albany, TX	915	76430
Albemarle, NC	704, 980	28001-28002
Albert Lea, MN	507	56007
Alberta, VA	434	23821
Albertson, NY	516	11507
Albertville, AL	256	35950-35951
Albia, IA	641	52531
Albion, IL	618	62806
Albion, IN	260	46701
Albion, MI	517	49224
Albion, NE	402	68620
Albion, NY	585	14411
Albion, PA	814	16401, 16475
Albuquerque, NM	505	87101-87125, 87131, 87153*
Alcoa, TN	865	37701
Alcorn State, MS	601, 769	39096
Alden, NY	585	14004
Alderson, WV	304	24910
Aledo, IL	309	61231
Alexander, AR	501	72002
Alexander, IA	641	50420
Alexander, NY	585	14005
Alexander City, AL	256	35010-35011
Alexandria, AL	256	36250
Alexandria, IN	765	46001
Alexandria, LA	318	71301-71309, 71315
Alexandria, MN	320	56308
Alexandria, SD	605	57311
Alexandria, TN	615	37012
Alexandria, VA	571, 703	22301-22315, 22320-22321*
Alexandria Bay, NY	315	13607
Alfred, ME	207	04002
Alfred, NY	607	14802
Algoma, WI	920	54201
Algona, IA	515	50511
Algona, WA	253	98001
Algonquin, IL	224, 847	60102, 60156
Alhambra, CA	626	91801-91804, 91841, 91896*
Alice, TX	361	78332-78333, 78342
Aliceville, AL	205	35442
Aliquippa, PA	724, 878	15001
Aliso Viejo, CA	949	92653-92656, 92698
Alledonia, OH	740	43902
Allegan, MI	616	49010
Allen, TX	469, 972	75002, 75013
Allen Park, MI	313	48101
Allendale, MI	616	49401
Allendale, NJ	201, 551	07401
Allendale, SC	803	29810
Allenhurst, NJ	732, 848	07709-07711
Allenstown, NH	603	03275
Allentown, NJ	609	08501
Allentown, PA	484, 610	18101-18109, 18175, 18195
Allenwood, NJ	732, 848	08720
Allenwood, PA	570	17810
Allgood, AL	205	35013
Alliance, NE	308	69301
Alliance, OH	234, 330	44601
Allison, IA	319	50602
Allison Park, PA	412, 878	15101
Allston, MA	617, 857	02134
Alma, GA	912	31510
Alma, KS	785	66401, 66501
Alma, MI	989	48801-48802
Alma, NE	308	68920
Alma, WI	608	54610

City	Area Code(s)	Zip Code(s)
Almena, WI	715, 534	54805
Almo, ID	208	83312
Almont, MI	810	48003
Alpena, MI	989	49707
Alpha, NJ	908	08865
Alpharetta, GA	470, 678, 770	30004-30005, 30009, 30022*
Alpine, CA	619	91901-91903
Alpine, TX	915	79830-79832
Alpine, UT	801, 385	84004
Alsip, IL	708	60803
Alta, UT	801, 385	84092
Altadena, CA	626	91001-91003
Altamahaw, NC	336	27202
Altamont, KS	620	67330
Altamont, TN	931	37301
Altamonte Springs, FL	321, 407	32701, 32714-32716
Altavista, VA	434	24517
Alto, GA	706, 762	30510, 30596
Alton, IL	618	62002
Alton, MO	417	65606
Altona, NY	518	12910
Altoona, IA	515	50009
Altoona, PA	814	16601-16603
Alturas, CA	530	96101
Altus, OK	580	73521-73523
Altus AFB, OK	580	73523
Alva, OK	580	73717
Alvarado, TX	682, 817	76009
Alvin, TX	281, 832	77511-77512
Alviso, CA	408	95002
Amado, AZ	520	85640, 85645
Amana, IA	319	52203-52204
Amarillo, TX	806	79101-79124, 79159, 79163*
Ambler, PA	215, 267	19002
Amboy, IL	815	61310
Amboy, WA	360	98601
Ambridge, PA	724, 878	15003
Amelia Court House, VA	804	23002
Amelia Island, FL	904	32034
American Falls, ID	208	83211
American Fork, UT	801, 385	84003
Americus, GA	229	31709-31710
Ames, IA	515	50010-50014
Amesbury, MA	351, 978	01913
Amherst, MA	413	01002-01004, 01059
Amherst, NH	603	03031
Amherst, NY	716	14051, 14068, 14221, 14226*
Amherst, TX	806	79312
Amherst, VA	434	24521
Amidon, ND	701	58620
Amite, LA	985	70422
Amityville, NY	631	11701, 11708
Amlin, OH	614	43002
Amory, MS	662	38821
Amsterdam, NY	518	12010
Anaconda, MT	406	59711
Anacortes, WA	360	98221-98222
Anadarko, OK	405	73005
Anaheim, CA	714	92801-92817, 92825, 92850*
Anaheim Hills, CA	714	92807-92809, 92817
Anahuac, TX	409	77514
Analomink, PA	570	18320
Anamosa, IA	319	52205
Anchorage, AK	907	99501-99524, 99540, 99599*
Ancora, NJ	609	08037
Andalusia, AL	334	36420
Anderson, CA	530	96007
Anderson, IN	765	46011-46018
Anderson, MO	417	64831
Anderson, SC	864	29621-29626
Anderson, TX	936	77830, 77875
Andersonville, GA	229	31711
Andover, KS	316	67002
Andover, ME	207	04216
Andover, MA	351, 978	01810-01812, 01899, 05501*
Andover, NJ	862, 973	07821

*Partial list of zip codes, including main range

City	Area Code(s)	Zip Code(s)
Andover, OH	440	44003
Andrews, TX	915	79714
Andrews AFB, MD	240, 301	20762
Angel Fire, NM	505	87710
Angels Camp, CA	209	95221-95222
Angie, LA	985	70426, 70467
Angleton, TX	979	77515-77516
Angola, IN	260	46703
Angola, LA	225	70712
Angoon, AK	907	99820
Angwin, CA	707	94508, 94576
Ankeny, IA	515	50015, 50021
Ann Arbor, MI	734	48103-48109, 48113
Anna, IL	618	62906
Annandale, MN	320	55302
Annandale, NJ	908	08801
Annandale, VA	571, 703	22003
Annapolis, MD	410, 443	21401-21405, 21411-21412
Annapolis Junction, MD	301	20701
Anniston, AL	256	36201-36207
Annona, TX	903	75550
Annville, PA	717	17003
Anoka, MN	763	55303-55304
Anson, TX	915	79501
Ansonia, CT	203	06401
Ansonia, OH	937	45303
Ansted, WV	304	25812
Anthony, KS	620	67003
Anthony, TX	915	79821
Antigo, WI	715, 534	54409
Antioch, CA	925	94509, 94531
Antioch, IL	224, 847	60002
Antioch, TN	615	37011-37013
Antlers, OK	580	74523
Antonito, CO	719	81120
Antrim, NH	603	03440
Anza, CA	951	92539
Apache, OK	580	73006
Apache Junction, AZ	480	85217-85220, 85278, 85290
Apalachicola, FL	850	32320, 32329
Apex, NC	919	27502
Apopka, FL	321, 407	32703-32704, 32712
Apple Valley, CA	760, 442	92307-92308
Apple Valley, MN	952	55124
Appleton, WI	920	54911-54915, 54919
Appomattox, VA	434	24522
Aptos, CA	831	95001-95003
Aquebogue, NY	631	11931
Arab, AL	256	35016
Arapaho, OK	580	73620
Arbor Vitae, WI	715, 534	54568
Arbuckle, CA	530	95912
Arcade, NY	585	14009
Arcadia, CA	626	91006-91007, 91066, 91077
Arcadia, FL	863	34265-34269
Arcadia, LA	318	71001
Arcadia, SC	864	29320
Arcadia, WI	608	54612
Arcata, CA	707	95518-95521
Archbold, OH	419, 567	43502
Archdale, NC	336	27263
Archer, FL	352	32618
Archer City, TX	940	76351
Arco, ID	208	83213
Arcola, IL	217	61910
Arcola, TX	281, 832	77583
Arden, NC	828	28704
Arden Hills, MN	651	55112
Ardmore, OK	580	73401-73403
Ardmore, PA	484, 610	19003
Ardsley, NY	914	10502
Arecibo, PR	787, 939	00612-00614
Argonne, IL	331, 630	60439
Argyle, MN	218	56713
Arkadelphia, AR	870	71923, 71998-71999
Arkansas City, AR	870	71630
Arkansas City, KS	620	67005
Arlington, MA	339, 781	02474-02476
Arlington, MN	507	55307
Arlington, TN	901	38002
Arlington, TX	682, 817	76001-76019, 76094-76096
Arlington, VT	802	05250
Arlington, VA	571, 703	22201-22230, 22234, 22240*
Arlington, WA	360	98223
Arlington Heights, IL	224, 847	60004-60006
Armada, MI	586	48005
Armonk, NY	914	10504
Armour, SD	605	57313
Armstrong, IA	712	50514
Arnett, OK	580	73832
Arnold, MD	410	21012
Arnold, MO	636	63010
Arnold, PA	724, 878	15068
Arnold AFB, TN	931	37389
Aromas, CA	831	95004
Arroyo Grande, CA	805	93420-93421
Artesia, CA	562	90701-90703
Artesia, NM	505	88210-88211
Artesian, SD	605	57314
Arthur, IL	217	61911
Arthur, NE	308	69121
Arthurdale, WV	304	26520
Arvada, CO	303, 720	80001-80007, 80021, 80403
Arvilla, ND	701	58214
Arvin, CA	661	93203
Arvonia, VA	434	23004
Asbury, NJ	908	08802
Asbury Park, NJ	732, 848	07712
Ash Flat, AR	870	72513
Ashaway, RI	401	02804
Ashburn, GA	229	31714
Ashburn, VA	571, 703	20146-20149, 22093
Ashdown, AR	870	71822
Asheboro, NC	336	27203-27205
Asheville, NC	828	28801-28806, 28810-28816
Ashford, AL	334	36312
Ashford, WA	360	98304
Ashippun, WI	920	53003
Ashland, AL	256	36251
Ashland, KS	620	67831
Ashland, KY	606	41101-41105, 41114
Ashland, ME	207	04732, 04737, 04759
Ashland, MA	508, 774	01721
Ashland, MS	662	38603
Ashland, MT	406	59003-59004
Ashland, NE	402	68003
Ashland, NH	603	03217
Ashland, OH	419, 567	44805
Ashland, OR	541, 458	97520
Ashland, PA	570	17921
Ashland, VA	804	23005
Ashland, WI	715, 534	54806
Ashland City, TN	615	37015
Ashley, ND	701	58413
Ashtabula, OH	440	44004-44005
Ashton, ID	208	83420, 83447
Ashton, IL	815	61006
Ashville, AL	205	35953
Ashville, NY	716	14710
Ashville, OH	740	43103
Asotin, WA	509	99402
Aspen, CO	970	81611-81612
Aspermont, TX	940	79502
Assumption, IL	217	62510
Aston, PA	484, 610	19014
Astoria, NY	347, 718	11101-11106
Astoria, OR	503	97103
Atascadero, CA	805	93422-93423
Atchison, KS	913	66002
Atco, NJ	856	08004
Atglen, PA	484, 610	19310
Athens, AL	256	35611-35614
Athens, GA	706, 762	30601-30612
Athens, OH	740	45701
Athens, TN	423	37303, 37371
Athens, TX	903	75751-75752
Athens, WV	304	24712
Atherton, CA	650	94027
Athol, ID	208	83801
Athol, MA	351, 978	01331, 01368
Atkinson, NH	603	03811
Atlanta, GA	404, 470, 678	30301-30380, 30384-30399*
Atlanta, MI	989	49709
Atlanta, TX	903	75551
Atlantic, IA	712	50022
Atlantic, NC	252	28511
Atlantic Beach, FL	904	32224, 32233
Atlantic Beach, NC	252	28512
Atlantic City, NJ	609	08400-08406
Atmore, AL	251	36502-36504
Atoka, OK	580	74525, 74542
Attalla, AL	256	35954
Attica, IN	765	47918
Attica, NY	585	14011
Attica, OH	419, 567	44807
Attleboro, MA	508, 774	02703
Attleboro Falls, MA	508, 774	02763
Atwater, CA	209	95301, 95342
Atwood, KS	785	67730
Au Gres, MI	989	48703
Auburn, AL	334	36830-36832
Auburn, CA	530	95602-95604
Auburn, IL	217	62615
Auburn, IN	219	46706
Auburn, KY	270	42206
Auburn, ME	207	04210-04212
Auburn, MA	508, 774	01501
Auburn, NE	402	68305
Auburn, NY	315	13021-13024
Auburn, WA	253	98001-98003, 98023, 98047*
Auburn University, AL	334	36849
Auburndale, FL	863	33823
Auburndale, MA	617, 857	02466
Audubon, IA	712	50025
Audubon, PA	484, 610	19403, 19407
Augusta, AR	870	72006
Augusta, GA	706, 762	30901-30919, 30999
Augusta, KS	316	67010
Augusta, ME	207	04330-04338
Augusta, MI	616	49012
Augusta, MT	406	59410
Auke Bay, AK	907	99821
Aumsville, OR	503, 971	97325
Aurora, CO	303, 720	80002, 80010-80019, 80040*
Aurora, IL	331, 630	60504-60507, 60568, 60572*
Aurora, IN	812	47001
Aurora, MN	218	55705
Aurora, MO	417	65605
Aurora, NE	402	68818
Aurora, NY	315	13026
Aurora, OH	234, 330	44202
Aurora, OR	503, 971	97002
Austell, GA	470, 770	30106, 30168
Austin, IN	812	47102
Austin, MN	507	55912
Austin, PA	814	16720
Austin, TX	512	73301, 73344, 78701-78774*
Austinburg, OH	440	44010
Autaugaville, AL	334	36003
Ava, MO	417	65608
Avalon, CA	310, 424	90704
Avenal, CA	559	93204
Avenel, NJ	732, 848	07001
Aventura, FL	305, 786	33160, 33180, 33280
Avery Island, LA	337	70513
Avoca, PA	570	18641
Avon, CO	970	81620
Avon, CT	860	06001
Avon, MA	508, 774	02322
Avon, MN	320	56310
Avon, OH	440	44011
Avon Lake, OH	440	44012
Avon Park, FL	863	33825-33826
Avondale, AZ	623	85323
Avondale, PA	484, 610	19311
Axis, AL	251	36505
Axtell, KS	785	66403
Axtell, NE	308	68924
Ayer, MA	351, 978	01432
Azle, TX	682, 817	76020, 76098
Aztec, NM	505	87410
Azusa, CA	626	91702

B

City	Area Code(s)	Zip Code(s)
Babson Park, FL	863	33827
Babson Park, MA	339, 781	02457
Babylon, NY	631	11702-11707
Bad Axe, MI	989	48413
Bagdad, KY	502	40003
Bagley, MN	218	56621
Baileys Harbor, WI	920	54202

*Partial list of zip codes, including main range

City	Area Code(s)	Zip Code(s)
Bainbridge, GA	229	31717-31718
Bainbridge Island, WA	206	98110
Baird, TX	915	79504
Baker, LA	225	70704, 70714
Baker, MT	406	59313, 59354
Baker, NV	775	89311
Baker City, OR	541, 458	97814
Bakersfield, CA	661	93301-93313, 93380-93390
Bakerstown, PA	724, 878	15007
Bakersville, NC	828	28705
Bal Harbour, FL	305, 786	33154
Bala Cynwyd, PA	484, 610	19004
Baldwin, GA	706, 762	30511
Baldwin, LA	337	70514
Baldwin, MI	231	49304
Baldwin, NY	516	11510
Baldwin, WI	715, 534	54002
Baldwin City, KS	785	66006
Baldwin Park, CA	626	91706
Baldwinsville, NY	315	13027
Ball Ground, GA	470, 770	30107
Ballinger, TX	915	76821
Ballston Spa, NY	518	12020
Ballwin, MO	636	63011, 63021-63024
Bally, PA	484, 610	19503
Balsam Lake, WI	715, 534	54810
Baltimore, MD	410, 443	21075, 21201-21244, 21250*
Bamberg, SC	803	29003
Bandera, TX	830	78003
Bangor, ME	207	04401-04402
Bangor, PA	484, 610	18010-18013, 18050
Bangor, WI	608	54614
Banner Elk, NC	828	28604, 28691
Banning, CA	951	92220
Bannock, OH	740	43972
Bannockburn, IL	224, 847	60015
Bar Harbor, ME	207	04609
Baraboo, WI	608	53913
Baraga, MI	906	49908
Barberton, OH	234, 330	44203
Barboursville, WV	304	25504
Barbourville, KY	606	40906
Bardstown, KY	502	40004
Bardwell, KY	270	42023
Barker, NY	716	14012
Barksdale AFB, LA	318	71110
Barnard, VT	802	05031
Barnardsville, NC	828	28709
Barnesville, GA	470, 770	30204
Barneveld, NY	315	13304
Barnstable, MA	508, 774	02630, 02634
Barnwell, SC	803	29812-29813
Barre, MA	351, 978	01005
Barre, VT	802	05641
Barrington, IL	224, 847	60010-60011
Barrington, NH	603	03825
Barrington, NJ	856	08007
Barron, WI	715, 534	54812
Barrow, AK	907	99723, 99734, 99759, 99789*
Barstow, CA	760, 442	92310-92312
Bartlesville, OK	918	74003-74006
Bartlett, IL	331, 630	60103, 60108, 60133
Bartlett, NE	308	68622
Bartlett, TN	901	38133-38135, 38184
Bartlett, TX	254	76511
Bartow, FL	863	33830-33831
Basalt, CO	970	81621
Basin, WY	307	82410
Basking Ridge, NJ	908	07920, 07939
Bassett, NE	402	68714
Bassett, VA	276	24055
Bastrop, LA	318	71220-71221
Bastrop, TX	512	78602
Batavia, IL	331, 630	60510, 60539
Batavia, NY	585	14020-14021
Batavia, OH	513	45103
Batesburg, SC	803	29006
Batesville, AR	870	72501-72503
Batesville, IN	812	47006
Batesville, MS	662	38606
Bath, ME	207	04530
Bath, NY	607	14810
Bath, OH	234, 330	44210
Bath, PA	484, 610	18014
Bath, SD	605	57427
Baton Rouge, LA	225	70801-70827, 70831-70837*
Battle Creek, MI	616	49014-49018
Battle Creek, NE	402	68715
Battle Ground, WA	360	98604
Battle Mountain, NV	775	89820
Baudette, MN	218	56623
Baxley, GA	912	31513-31515
Bay City, MI	989	48706-48708
Bay City, TX	979	77404, 77414
Bay Harbor, MI	231	49770
Bay Harbor Islands, FL	305, 786	33154
Bay Minette, AL	251	36507
Bay Pines, FL	727	33744
Bay Saint Louis, MS	228	39520-39521, 39525
Bay Shore, NY	631	11706
Bay Springs, MS	601, 769	39422
Bay Village, OH	440	44140
Bayamon, PR	787, 939	00956-00961
Bayard, NE	308	69334
Bayboro, NC	252	28515
Bayfield, WI	715, 534	54814
Bayonne, NJ	201, 551	07002
Bayou La Batre, AL	251	36509
Bayport, MN	651	55003
Bayport, NY	631	11705
Bayside, NY	347, 718	11359-11361
Baytown, TX	281, 832	77520-77522
Bayville, NJ	732, 848	08721
Beach, ND	701	58621
Beach Lake, PA	570	18405
Beachwood, OH	216	44122
Beacon, NY	845	12508
Beale AFB, CA	530	95903
Bean Station, TN	865	37708
Bear Creek, WI	715, 534	54922
Bear Mountain, NY	845	10911
Bearden, AR	870	71720
Beatrice, NE	402	68310
Beattyville, KY	606	41311
Beaufort, NC	252	28516
Beaufort, SC	843	29901-29906
Beaumont, CA	951	92223
Beaumont, TX	409	77657, 77701-77713, 77720*
Beaumont, VA	804	23014
Beaver, OK	580	73932
Beaver, PA	724, 878	15009
Beaver, UT	435	84713
Beaver, WV	304	25813
Beaver City, NE	308	68926
Beaver Creek, CO	970	81620
Beaver Dam, KY	270	42320
Beaver Dam, WI	920	53916-53917
Beaver Dams, NY	607	14812
Beaver Falls, NY	315	13305
Beaver Falls, PA	724, 878	15010
Beavercreek, OH	937	45410, 45430-45434, 45440
Beaverton, OR	503, 971	97005-97008, 97075-97078
Bechtelsville, PA	484, 610	19505
Beckley, WV	304	25801-25802, 25926
Bedford, IN	812	47421
Bedford, IA	712	50833
Bedford, KY	502	40006
Bedford, MA	339, 781	01730-01731
Bedford, NH	603	03110
Bedford, OH	440	44146
Bedford, PA	814	15522
Bedford, TX	682, 817	76021-76022, 76095
Bedford, VA	540	24523
Bedford Heights, OH	216	44128, 44146
Bedford Hills, NY	914	10507
Bedford Park, IL	708	60455-60459, 60499-60501*
Bedminster, NJ	908	07921
Beebe, AR	501	72012
Beech Creek, PA	570	16822
Beech Grove, IN	317	46107
Beeville, TX	361	78102-78104
Bel Air, MD	410	21014-21015
Belcamp, MD	410	21017
Belcourt, ND	701	58316
Belding, MI	616	48809, 48887
Belfast, ME	207	04915
Belgrade, MT	406	59714
Belhaven, NC	252	27810
Bell, CA	323	90201-90202, 90270
Bell Gardens, CA	562	90201-90202
Bella Vista, AR	479	72714-72715
Bellaire, MI	231	49615
Bellaire, TX	713, 832	77401-77402
Belle Chasse, LA	504	70037
Belle Fourche, SD	605	57717
Belle Glade, FL	561	33430
Belle Mead, NJ	908	08502
Belle Plaine, MN	952	56011
Belle Vernon, PA	724, 878	15012
Bellefontaine, OH	937	43311
Bellefonte, PA	814	16823
Bellerose, NY	347, 718	11426
Belleview, FL	352	34420-34421
Belleville, IL	618	62220-62226
Belleville, KS	785	66935
Belleville, MI	734	48111-48112
Belleville, NJ	862, 973	07109
Belleville, PA	717	17004
Belleville, WI	608	53508
Bellevue, IA	563	52031
Bellevue, NE	402	68005, 68123, 68147, 68157
Bellevue, OH	419, 567	44811
Bellevue, WA	425	98004-98009, 98015
Bellflower, CA	562	90706-90707
Bellingham, MA	508, 774	02019
Bellingham, WA	360	98225-98228
Bellmawr, NJ	856	08031, 08099
Bellmore, NY	516	11710
Bellows Falls, VT	802	05101
Bellport, NY	631	11713
Bells, TN	731	38006
Bellville, OH	419, 567	44813
Bellville, TX	979	77418
Bellvue, CO	970	80512
Bellwood, IL	708	60104
Bellwood, PA	814	16617
Belmont, CA	650	94002-94003
Belmont, MA	617, 857	02478-02479
Belmont, MS	662	38827
Belmont, NH	603	03220
Belmont, NY	585	14813
Belmont, NC	704, 980	28012
Beloit, KS	785	67420
Beloit, WI	608	53511-53512
Belpre, OH	740	45714
Belton, SC	864	29627
Belton, TX	254	76513
Beltsville, MD	301	20704-20705
Belvidere, IL	815	61008
Belvidere, NJ	908	07823
Belzoni, MS	662	39038
Bemidji, MN	218	56601, 56619
Bend, OR	541, 458	97701-97702, 97707-97709
Benicia, CA	707	94510
Benjamin, TX	940	79505
Benkelman, NE	308	69021
Bennettsville, SC	843	29512
Bennington, NH	603	03442
Bennington, VT	802	05201
Bensalem, PA	215, 267	19020-19021
Bensenville, IL	331, 630	60105-60106, 60399
Benson, AZ	520	85602
Benson, MN	320	56215
Benson, NC	919	27504
Benton, AR	501	72015-72018, 72022, 72158
Benton, IL	618	62812
Benton, KY	270	42025
Benton, LA	318	71006
Benton, MO	573	63736
Benton, PA	570	17814
Benton, TN	423	37307
Benton Harbor, MI	616	49022-49023
Bentonville, AR	479	72712, 72716
Berea, KY	859	40403-40404
Berea, OH	440	44017
Bergenfield, NJ	201, 551	07621
Berkeley, CA	510	94701-94712, 94720
Berkeley, IL	708	60163
Berkeley, MO	314	63134, 63140
Berkeley Heights, NJ	908	07922
Berkeley Springs, WV	304	25411
Berlin, CT	860	06037
Berlin, MD	410	21811
Berlin, NH	603	03570
Berlin, NJ	856	08009
Berlin, NY	518	12022
Berlin, OH	234, 330	44610
Berlin, PA	814	15530

*Partial list of zip codes, including main range

City	Area Code(s)	Zip Code(s)
Berlin, WI	920	54923
Berlin Heights, OH	419, 567	44814
Bernalillo, NM	505	87004
Bernardsville, NJ	908	07924
Berne, IN	260	46711, 46769
Berrien Springs, MI	616	49103-49104
Berryville, AR	870	72616
Berryville, VA	540	22611
Berwick, PA	570	18603
Berwyn, IL	708	60402
Berwyn, PA	484, 610	19312
Beryl, UT	435	84714
Bessemer, AL	205	35020-35023
Bessemer, MI	906	49911
Bessemer City, NC	704, 980	28016
Bethany, CT	203	06524
Bethany, MO	660	64424
Bethany, OK	405	73008
Bethany, WV	304	26032
Bethany Beach, DE	302	19930
Bethel, AK	907	99559, 99637, 99679-99680*
Bethel, CT	203	06801
Bethel, ME	207	04217, 04286
Bethel, MN	763	55005
Bethel, VT	802	05032
Bethel Park, PA	412, 878	15102
Bethesda, MD	240, 301	20810-20817, 20824-20827*
Bethlehem, GA	470, 770	30620
Bethlehem, PA	484, 610	18015-18020, 18025
Bethpage, NY	516	11714
Bettendorf, IA	563	52722
Beulah, MI	231	49617
Beulah, ND	701	58523
Beverly, MA	351, 978	01915
Beverly, NJ	609	08010
Beverly, OH	740	45715, 45721
Beverly Hills, CA	310, 323, 424	90209-90213
Bexley, OH	614	43209
Biddeford, ME	207	04005-04007
Big Bear Lake, CA	909	92315
Big Bend National Park, TX	915	79834
Big Cabin, OK	918	74332
Big Island, VA	434	24526
Big Lake, AK	907	99652
Big Lake, MN	763	55309
Big Lake, TX	915	76932
Big Pine Key, FL	305, 786	33043
Big Rapids, MI	231	49307
Big Rock, IL	331, 630	60511
Big Sky, MT	406	59716
Big Spring, TX	915	79720-79721
Big Stone Gap, VA	276	24219
Big Sur, CA	831	93920
Big Timber, MT	406	59011
Bigfork, MN	218	56628, 56639
Bigfork, MT	406	59911
Biglerville, PA	717	17307
Billerica, MA	351, 978	01821-01822, 01862
Billings, MT	406	59101-59117
Billings, OK	580	74630
Biloxi, MS	228	39530-39535, 39540
Bingen, WA	509	98605
Binger, OK	405	73009
Bingham Farms, MI	248, 947	48025
Binghamton, NY	607	13901-13905
Bird-in-Hand, PA	717	17505
Birdsboro, PA	484, 610	19508
Birmingham, AL	205	35201-35249, 35253-35255*
Birmingham, MI	248, 947	48009-48012
Birmingham, NJ	609	08011
Bisbee, AZ	520	85603
Biscoe, NC	910	27209
Bishop, CA	760, 442	93512-93515
Bishopville, SC	803	29010
Bismarck, ND	701	58501-58507
Bison, SD	605	57620
Bixby, OK	918	74008
Black Butte Ranch, OR	541, 458	97759
Black Creek, NC	252	27813
Black Earth, WI	608	53515
Black Hawk, CO	303, 720	80403, 80422
Black Mountain, NC	828	28711
Black River Falls, WI	715, 534	54615
Blackfoot, ID	208	83221
Blacksburg, SC	864	29702
Blacksburg, VA	540	24060-24063
Blackshear, GA	912	31516
Blackwell, OK	580	74631
Blackwood, NJ	856	08012
Bladensburg, MD	301	20710
Blaine, MN	763	55014, 55434, 55449
Blaine, WA	360	98230-98231
Blair, NE	402	68008-68009
Blairsville, GA	706, 762	30512-30514
Blairsville, PA	724, 878	15717
Blakely, GA	229	31723
Blakeslee, PA	570	18610
Blanchester, OH	937	45107
Bland, VA	276	24315
Blanding, UT	435	84511
Blandon, PA	484, 610	19510
Blasdell, NY	716	14219
Blauvelt, NY	845	10913
Blissfield, MI	517	49228
Blomkest, MN	320	56216
Bloomfield, CT	860	06002
Bloomfield, IN	812	47424
Bloomfield, IA	641	52537-52538
Bloomfield, MO	573	63825
Bloomfield, NJ	862, 973	07003
Bloomfield Hills, MI	248, 947	48301-48304
Bloomingdale, IL	331, 630	60108, 60117
Bloomingdale, IN	765	47832
Bloomington, CA	909	92316
Bloomington, IL	309	61701-61704, 61709-61710*
Bloomington, IN	812	47401-47408, 47490
Bloomington, MN	952	55420, 55425, 55431, 55435*
Bloomsburg, PA	570	17815, 17839
Bloomsbury, NJ	908	08804
Blountstown, FL	850	32424
Blountville, TN	423	37617
Blowing Rock, NC	828	28605
Blue Anchor, NJ	609	08037
Blue Ash, OH	513	45242
Blue Ball, PA	717	17506
Blue Bell, PA	215	19422-19424
Blue Earth, MN	507	56013
Blue Hill, ME	207	04614
Blue Island, IL	708	60406, 60827
Blue Mounds, WI	608	53517
Blue Mountain, MS	662	38610
Blue Ridge, GA	706, 762	30513
Blue Springs, MO	816	64013-64015
Bluefield, VA	276	24605
Bluefield, WV	304	24701
Bluegrove, TX	940	76352
Bluffton, IN	260	46714
Bluffton, OH	419, 567	45817
Bluffton, SC	843	29910
Blunt, SD	605	57522
Blythe, CA	760, 442	92225-92226, 92280
Blytheville, AR	870	72315-72319
Blythewood, SC	803	29016
Boardman, OH	234, 330	44512-44513
Boardman, OR	541, 458	97818
Boaz, AL	256	35956-35957
Boca Raton, FL	561	33427-33434, 33464, 33481*
Bodega Bay, CA	707	94923
Boerne, TX	830	78006, 78015
Bogalusa, LA	985	70427-70429
Bogart, GA	706, 762	30622
Bogota, NJ	201, 551	07603
Bohemia, NY	631	11716
Boiling Springs, NC	704, 980	28017
Boise, ID	208	83701-83735, 83744, 83756*
Boise City, OK	580	73933
Boley, OK	918	74829
Bolingbrook, IL	331, 630	60439-60440, 60490
Bolivar, MO	417	65613, 65727
Bolivar, TN	731	38008, 38074
Bolivia, NC	910	28422
Bolton, CT	860	06043
Bolton, MA	351, 978	01740
Bolton Landing, NY	518	12814
Bon Air, VA	804	23235
Bon Secour, AL	251	36511
Bon Wier, TX	409	75928
Bonham, TX	903	75418
Bonifay, FL	850	32425
Bonita, CA	619	91902, 91908
Bonita Springs, FL	239	34133-34136
Bonner Springs, KS	913	66012
Bonners Ferry, ID	208	83805
Bono, AR	870	72416
Boone, IA	515	50036-50037
Boone, NC	828	28607-28608
Booneville, AR	479	72927
Booneville, KY	606	41314
Booneville, MS	662	38829
Boonton, NJ	862, 973	07005
Boonville, IN	812	47601
Boonville, MO	660	65233
Boothbay Harbor, ME	207	04536-04538, 04570
Boothwyn, PA	484, 610	19061
Borden, IN	812	47106
Bordentown, NJ	609	08505
Borger, TX	806	79007-79008
Boring, OR	503, 971	97009
Borrego Springs, CA	760, 442	92004
Boscawen, NH	603	03303
Boscobel, WI	608	53805
Bossier City, LA	318	71111-71113, 71171-71172
Boston, MA	617, 857	02101-02137, 02163, 02196*
Bothell, WA	425	98011-98012, 98021, 98028*
Botkins, OH	937	45306
Bottineau, ND	701	58318
Bouckville, NY	315	13310
Boulder, CO	303, 720	80301-80310, 80314, 80321*
Boulder, MT	406	59632
Boulder City, NV	702	89005-89006
Bound Brook, NJ	732, 848	08805
Bountiful, UT	801, 385	84010-84011
Bourbon, MO	573	65441
Bourbonnais, IL	815	60914
Bovey, MN	218	55709
Bow, NH	603	03304
Bow, WA	360	98232
Bowbells, ND	701	58721
Bowdon, GA	470, 770	30108
Bowerston, OH	740	44695
Bowie, AZ	520	85605
Bowie, MD	301	20715-20721
Bowie, TX	940	76230
Bowling Green, FL	863	33834
Bowling Green, KY	270	42101-42104
Bowling Green, MO	573	63334
Bowling Green, OH	419, 567	43402-43403
Bowling Green, VA	804	22427-22428
Bowman, ND	701	58623
Bowmansville, NY	716	14026
Box Elder, MT	406	59521
Boxborough, MA	351, 978	01719
Boyden, IA	712	51234
Boydton, VA	434	23917
Boyertown, PA	484, 610	19512
Boylston, MA	508, 774	01505
Boyne Falls, MI	231	49713
Boynton Beach, FL	561	33424-33426, 33435-33437*
Boys Town, NE	402	68010
Bozeman, MT	406	59715-59719, 59771-59773
Bozrah, CT	860	06334
Brackenridge, PA	724, 878	15014
Brackettville, TX	830	78832
Bradbury, CA	626	91010
Braddock, PA	412, 878	15104
Bradenton, FL	941	34201-34212, 34280-34282
Bradford, PA	814	16701
Bradford, VT	802	05033
Bradley, IL	815	60915
Bradley, ME	207	04411
Bradley, WV	304	25818
Brady, TX	915	76825
Braham, MN	320	55006
Braidwood, IL	815	60408
Brainard, NE	402	68626
Brainerd, MN	218	56401, 56425
Braintree, MA	339, 781	02184-02185
Braithwaite, LA	504	70040, 70046
Branchburg, NJ	908	08876
Branchville, NJ	862, 973	07826-07827, 07890
Brandenburg, KY	270	40108
Brandon, FL	813	33508-33511
Brandon, MS	601, 769	39042-39043, 39047, 39232
Brandon, VT	802	05733
Branford, CT	203	06405
Branson, MO	417	65615-65616
Braselton, GA	470, 678, 770	30517

*Partial list of zip codes, including main range

City	Area Code(s)	Zip Code(s)
Brattleboro, VT	802	05301-05304
Brawley, CA	760, 442	92227
Braymer, MO	660	64624
Brazil, IN	812	47834
Brea, CA	714	92821-92823
Breckenridge, CO	970	80424
Breckenridge, MN	218	56520
Breckenridge, TX	254	76424
Brecksville, OH	440	44141
Breese, IL	618	62230
Breezy Point, MN	218	56472
Bremen, GA	470, 770	30110
Bremen, IN	574	46506
Bremen, OH	740	43107
Bremerton, WA	360	98310-98314, 98337
Brenham, TX	979	77833-77834
Brent, AL	205	35034
Brentwood, NH	603	03833
Brentwood, NY	631	11717
Brentwood, TN	615	37024-37027
Bretton Woods, NH	603	03575
Brevard, NC	828	28712
Brewer, ME	207	04412
Brewerton, NY	315	13029
Brewster, MA	508, 774	02631
Brewster, NE	308	68821
Brewster, NY	845	10509
Brewster, OH	234, 330	44613
Brewster, WA	509	98812
Brewton, AL	251	36426-36427
Briarcliff Manor, NY	914	10510
Briarwood, NY	347, 718	11435
Brick, NJ	732, 848	08723-08724
Brickeys, AR	870	72320
Bridgeport, AL	256	35740
Bridgeport, CA	760, 442	93517
Bridgeport, CT	203	06601-06615, 06650, 06673*
Bridgeport, NE	308	69336
Bridgeport, NJ	856	08014
Bridgeport, PA	484, 610	19405
Bridgeport, WV	304	26330
Bridgeton, MO	314	63044-63045
Bridgeton, NJ	856	08302
Bridgeview, IL	708	60455
Bridgeville, PA	412, 878	15017
Bridgewater, MA	508, 774	02324-02325
Bridgewater, NJ	908	08807
Bridgewater, VA	540	22812
Bridgewater Corners, VT	802	05035
Bridgman, MI	616	49106
Bridgton, ME	207	04009
Brigantine, NJ	609	08203
Brigham City, UT	435	84302
Brighton, CO	303, 720	80601-80603
Brighton, MA	617, 857	02135
Brighton, MI	810	48114-48116
Brighton, UT	801, 385	84121
Brillion, WI	920	54110
Brimfield, IL	309	61517
Brinkley, AR	870	72021
Brinson, GA	229	31725
Brisbane, CA	415, 650	94005
Bristol, CT	860	06010-06011
Bristol, FL	850	32321
Bristol, IN	574	46507
Bristol, PA	215, 267	19007
Bristol, RI	401	02809
Bristol, TN	423	37620-37621, 37625
Bristol, VT	802	05443
Bristol, VA	276	24201-24203, 24209
Bristol, WI	262	53104
Britton, SD	605	57430
Broadalbin, NY	518	12025
Broadus, MT	406	59317
Broadview, IL	708	60153-60155
Broadview Heights, OH	440	44147
Broadway, VA	540	22815
Brockport, NY	585	14420
Brockton, MA	508, 774	02301-02305
Brockway, PA	814	15824
Brocton, NY	716	14716
Brodhead, WI	608	53520
Brodnax, VA	434	23920
Broken Arrow, OK	918	74011-74014
Broken Bow, NE	308	68822
Broken Bow, OK	580	74728
Bronson, FL	352	32621

City	Area Code(s)	Zip Code(s)
Bronwood, GA	229	31726
Bronx, NY	347, 718	10451-10475, 10499
Bronxville, NY	914	10708
Brook Park, OH	216	44142
Brookfield, CT	203	06804
Brookfield, IL	708	60513
Brookfield, MO	660	64628
Brookfield, OH	234, 330	44403
Brookfield, WI	262	53005-53008, 53045
Brookhaven, MS	601, 769	39601-39603
Brookhaven, PA	484, 610	19015
Brookings, OR	541, 458	97415
Brookings, SD	605	57006-57007
Brookline, MA	617, 857	02445-02447
Brooklyn, CT	860	06234
Brooklyn, IA	641	52211
Brooklyn, MI	517	49230
Brooklyn, NY	347, 718	11201-11256
Brooklyn Center, MN	763	55428-55430, 55443-55444
Brooklyn Heights, OH	216	44109, 44131
Brooklyn Park, MN	763	55428-55429, 55443-55445
Brooks AFB, TX	210	78235
Brookshire, TX	281, 832	77423
Brooksville, FL	352	34601-34614
Brooksville, KY	606	41004
Brookville, IN	765	47012
Brookville, OH	937	45309
Brookville, PA	814	15825
Brookwood, AL	205	35444
Broomall, PA	484, 610	19008
Broomfield, CO	303, 720	80020-80021, 80038, 80234
Broussard, LA	337	70518
Brown Deer, WI	414	53209, 53223
Brownfield, TX	806	79316, 79376
Browning, MT	406	59417
Browns Mills, NJ	609	08015
Brownsboro, AL	256	35741
Brownsburg, IN	317	46112
Brownstown, IN	812	47220
Brownsville, KY	270	42210
Brownsville, PA	724, 878	15417
Brownsville, TN	731	38012
Brownsville, TX	956	78520-78526
Brownsville, VT	802	05037
Brownsville, WI	920	53006
Brownville, NY	315	13615
Brownwood, TX	915	76801-76804
Bruce, SD	605	57220
Bruceton Mills, WV	304	26525
Brunswick, GA	912	31520-31527, 31561
Brunswick, ME	207	04011, 04053
Brunswick, NC	910	28424
Brunswick, OH	234, 330	44212
Brush, CO	970	80723
Brusly, LA	225	70719
Bryan, OH	419, 567	43506
Bryan, TX	979	77801-77808
Bryantown, MD	301	20617
Bryce Canyon, UT	435	84717
Bryn Athyn, PA	215, 267	19009
Bryn Mawr, PA	484, 610	19010
Bryson City, NC	828	28713
Buchanan, GA	470, 770	30113
Buchanan, MI	616	49107
Buchanan, VA	540	24066
Buckeye, AZ	623	85326
Buckhannon, WV	304	26201
Buckingham, VA	434	23921
Bucyrus, OH	419, 567	44820
Buda, TX	512	78610
Budd Lake, NJ	862, 973	07828
Buellton, CA	805	93427
Buena, NJ	856	08310
Buena Park, CA	714	90620-90624
Buena Vista, CO	719	81211
Buena Vista, GA	229	31803
Buena Vista, VA	540	24416
Buffalo, MN	763	55313
Buffalo, MO	417	65622
Buffalo, NY	716	14201-14233, 14240-14241*
Buffalo, OK	580	73834
Buffalo, SD	605	57720
Buffalo, WY	307	82834, 82840
Buffalo Gap, TX	915	79508
Buffalo Grove, IL	224, 847	60089
Buford, GA	470, 678, 770	30515-30519

City	Area Code(s)	Zip Code(s)
Buhl, ID	208	83316
Buies Creek, NC	910	27506
Bullhead City, AZ	928	86426-86430, 86439-86442*
Bunker Hill, IN	765	46914
Bunker Hill, KS	785	67626
Bunn, NC	919	27508
Bunnell, FL	386	32110
Buras, LA	504	70041
Burbank, CA	818	91501-91510, 91521-91526
Burbank, IL	708	60459
Burgaw, NC	910	28425
Burgettstown, PA	724, 878	15021
Burien, WA	206	98146-98148, 98166-98168
Burke, SD	605	57523
Burke, VA	571, 703	22009, 22015
Burkesville, KY	270	42717
Burkeville, VA	434	23922
Burleigh, NJ	609	08210
Burleson, TX	682, 817	76028, 76097
Burley, ID	208	83318
Burlingame, CA	650	94010-94012
Burlington, CO	719	80807
Burlington, IL	224, 847	60109
Burlington, IA	319	52601
Burlington, KS	620	66839
Burlington, KY	859	41005
Burlington, MA	339, 781	01803-01805
Burlington, NJ	609	08016
Burlington, NC	336	27215-27220
Burlington, VT	802	05401-05407
Burlington, WA	360	98233
Burlington, WI	262	53105
Burnet, TX	512	78611
Burnham, PA	717	17009
Burns, OR	541, 458	97710, 97720
Burnsville, MN	952	55306, 55337
Burnsville, NC	828	28714
Burr Ridge, IL	331, 630	60525-60527
Burton, MI	810	48509, 48519, 48529
Burton, OH	440	44021
Burtonsville, MD	301	20866
Burwell, NE	308	68823
Bushkill, PA	570	18324, 18371-18373
Bushnell, FL	352	33513
Bushnell, IL	309	61422
Butler, AL	205	36904
Butler, GA	478	31006
Butler, IN	260	46721
Butler, MD	410	21023
Butler, MO	660	64730
Butler, NJ	862, 973	07405
Butler, PA	724, 878	16001-16003
Butler, WI	262	53007
Butner, NC	919	27509
Butte, MT	406	59701-59703, 59707, 59750
Butte, NE	402	68722
Butterfield, MN	507	56120
Buxton, NC	252	27920
Buzzards Bay, MA	508, 774	02532, 02542
Byfield, MA	351, 978	01922
Byhalia, MS	662	38611
Byrdstown, TN	931	38549
Byron, IL	815	61010
Byron, MN	507	55920
Byron Center, MI	616	49315

C

City	Area Code(s)	Zip Code(s)
Cabazon, CA	951	92230, 92282
Cabot, AR	501	72023
Cabot, PA	724, 878	16023
Cadillac, MI	231	49601
Cadiz, KY	270	42211
Cadiz, OH	740	43907
Cahokia, IL	618	62206
Cairo, GA	229	31728
Cairo, IL	618	62914
Calabasas, CA	818	91301-91302, 91372
Calabasas Hills, CA	818	91301
Calais, ME	207	04619
Caldwell, ID	208	83605-83607
Caldwell, NJ	862, 973	07006-07007
Caldwell, OH	740	43724
Caldwell, TX	979	77836
Caledonia, MN	507	55921

**Partial list of zip codes, including main range*

City	Area Code(s)	Zip Code(s)
Caledonia, NY	585	14423
Caledonia, WI	262	53108
Calexico, CA	760, 442	92231-92232
Calhoun, GA	706, 762	30701-30703
Calhoun, KY	270	42327
Calhoun, TN	423	37309
Calhoun City, MS	662	38916, 38955
Calico Rock, AR	870	72519
California, MD	301	20619
California, MO	573	65018, 65042
California, PA	724, 878	15419
Calipatria, CA	760, 442	92233
Calistoga, CA	707	94515
Callery, PA	724, 878	16024
Callicoon, NY	845	12723
Calmar, IA	563	52132
Calumet, MI	906	49913, 49918, 49942
Calumet City, IL	708	60409
Calumet Park, IL	708	60643, 60827
Camarillo, CA	805	93010-93012
Camas, WA	360	98607
Cambria, CA	805	93428
Cambridge, IL	309	61238
Cambridge, MD	410	21613
Cambridge, MA	617, 857	02138-02142, 02163, 02238*
Cambridge, MN	763	55008
Cambridge, NE	308	69022
Cambridge, OH	740	43725, 43750
Cambridge, WI	608	53523
Cambridge City, IN	765	47327
Cambridge Springs, PA	814	16403
Camden, AL	334	36726
Camden, AR	870	71701, 71711
Camden, DE	302	19934
Camden, IN	574	46917
Camden, ME	207	04843, 04847
Camden, MI	517	49232
Camden, NJ	856	08100-08110
Camden, NY	315	13316
Camden, NC	252	27921
Camden, SC	803	29020
Camden, TN	731	38320
Camdenton, MO	573	65020
Cameron, LA	337	70631
Cameron, MO	816	64429
Cameron, MT	760, 442	59720
Cameron, TX	254	76520
Cameron Park, CA	530	95682
Camilla, GA	229	31730
Camillus, NY	315	13031
Camp Douglas, WI	608	54618, 54637
Camp Hill, PA	717	17001, 17011-17012, 17089*
Camp Lejeune, NC	910	28542, 28547
Camp Pendleton, CA	760, 442	92054-92055
Camp Point, IL	217	62320
Camp Shelby, MS	601, 769	39401, 39407
Camp Springs, MD	301	20746-20748
Camp Verde, AZ	928	86322
Campbell, CA	408	95008-95011
Campbell Hall, NY	845	10916
Campbellsville, KY	270	42718-42719
Campton, KY	606	41301, 41342
Canadian, TX	806	79014
Canal Winchester, OH	614	43110
Canandaigua, NY	585	14424-14425
Canastota, NY	315	13032
Candler, NC	828	28715
Cando, ND	701	58324
Candor, NC	910	27229
Canfield, OH	234, 330	44406
Cannon AFB, NM	505	88101-88103
Cannon Beach, OR	503	97110
Cannon Falls, MN	507	55009
Canoga Park, CA	818	91303-91309, 91396
Canon City, CO	719	81212-81215, 81246
Canonsburg, PA	724, 878	15317
Canterbury, NH	603	03224
Canton, GA	470, 770	30114-30115
Canton, IL	309	61520
Canton, MA	339, 781	02021
Canton, MI	734	48187-48188
Canton, MS	601, 769	39046
Canton, MO	573	63435
Canton, NY	315	13617
Canton, OH	234, 330	44701-44714, 44718-44721*
Canton, PA	570	17724, 17743
Canton, SD	605	57013
Canton, TX	903	75103
Canyon, TX	806	79015-79016
Canyon City, OR	541, 458	97820
Canyonville, OR	541, 458	97417
Cape Canaveral, FL	321	32920
Cape Charles, VA	757	23310
Cape Coral, FL	239	33904, 33909-33910, 33914*
Cape Elizabeth, ME	207	04107
Cape Girardeau, MO	573	63701-63705
Cape May, NJ	609	08204
Cape May Court House, NJ	609	08210
Cape Vincent, NY	315	13618
Capitol Heights, MD	301	20731, 20743, 20753, 20790*
Capitola, CA	831	95010, 95062
Capron, VA	434	23829
Captain Cook, HI	808	96704
Captiva, FL	239	33924
Capulin, NM	505	88414
Carbondale, IL	618	62901-62903
Carbondale, PA	570	18407
Carefree, AZ	480	85377
Carey, OH	419, 567	43316
Caribou, ME	207	04736
Carle Place, NY	516	11514
Carlinville, IL	217	62626
Carlisle, IN	812	47838
Carlisle, KY	859	40311, 40350
Carlisle, PA	717	17013
Carlisle, SC	864	29031
Carlsbad, CA	760, 442	92008-92009, 92013, 92018
Carlsbad, NM	505	88220-88221
Carlstadt, NJ	201, 551	07072
Carlton, MN	218	55718
Carlyle, IL	618	62231
Carmel, CA	831	93921-93923
Carmel, IN	317	46032-46033, 46082
Carmel, NY	845	10512
Carmel Valley, CA	831	93924
Carmi, IL	618	62821
Carmichael, CA	916	95608-95609
Carnegie, PA	412, 878	15106
Carnesville, GA	706, 762	30521
Carneys Point, NJ	856	08069
Caro, MI	989	48723
Carol Stream, IL	331, 630	60116, 60125-60128, 60132*
Carolina, PR	787, 939	00979-00988
Carpentersville, IL	224, 847	60110
Carpinteria, CA	805	93013-93014
Carrabassett Valley, ME	207	04947
Carrington, ND	701	58421
Carrizo Springs, TX	830	78834
Carrizozo, NM	505	88301
Carroll, IA	712	51401
Carroll Valley, PA	717	17320
Carrollton, AL	205	35447
Carrollton, GA	470, 770	30112, 30116-30119
Carrollton, IL	217	62016
Carrollton, KY	502	41008, 41045
Carrollton, MS	662	38917
Carrollton, MO	660	64633
Carrollton, OH	234, 330	44615
Carrollton, TX	469, 972	75006-75011
Carson, CA	310, 424	90745-90749, 90810
Carson, ND	701	58529
Carson City, MI	989	48811
Carson City, NV	775	89701-89706, 89711-89714*
Carter Lake, IA	712	51510
Carteret, NJ	732, 848	07008
Cartersville, GA	470, 770	30120-30121
Carterville, IL	618	62918
Carthage, IL	217	62321
Carthage, MS	601, 769	39051
Carthage, MO	417	64836
Carthage, NC	910	28327
Carthage, TN	615	37030
Carthage, TX	903	75633
Caruthersville, MO	573	63830
Carver, MA	508, 774	02330, 02355, 02366
Cary, IL	224, 847	60013
Cary, NC	919	27511-27513, 27518-27519
Casa Grande, AZ	520	85222, 85230
Cascade, ID	208	83611
Cascade Locks, OR	509	97014
Casey, IL	217	62420
Cashiers, NC	828	28717
Cashmere, WA	509	98815
Casper, WY	307	82601-82605, 82609, 82615*
Casselberry, FL	321, 407	32707-32708, 32718-32719*
Cassopolis, MI	616	49031
Cassville, MO	417	65623-65625
Castaic, CA	661	91310, 91384
Castine, ME	207	04420-04421
Castle Dale, UT	435	84513
Castle Point, NY	845	12511
Castle Rock, CO	303, 720	80104
Castleton, VT	802	05735
Castro Valley, CA	510	94546, 94552
Castroville, CA	831	95012
Catalina, AZ	520	85738-85739
Catasauqua, PA	484, 610	18032
Catawba, VA	540	24070
Catawissa, PA	570	17820
Cathedral City, CA	760, 442	92234-92235
Cathlamet, WA	360	98612
Catlettsburg, KY	606	41129
Catonsville, MD	410	21228
Catoosa, OK	918	74015
Catskill, NY	518	12414
Cavalier, ND	701	58220
Cave Junction, OR	541, 458	97523, 97531
Cayce, SC	803	29033
Cazenovia, NY	315	13035
Cedar City, UT	435	84720-84721
Cedar Crest, NM	505	87008
Cedar Falls, IA	319	50613-50614
Cedar Falls, NC	336	27230
Cedar Grove, NJ	862, 973	07009
Cedar Grove, WI	920	53013
Cedar Hill, TX	469, 972	75104-75106
Cedar Knolls, NJ	862, 973	07927
Cedar Park, TX	512	78613, 78630
Cedar Rapids, IA	319	52401-52411, 52497-52499
Cedar Springs, GA	229	31732
Cedar Springs, MI	616	49319
Cedar Vale, KS	620	67024
Cedarburg, WI	262	53012
Cedartown, GA	470, 770	30125
Cedarville, OH	937	45314
Celebration, FL	321, 407	34747
Celina, OH	419, 567	45822, 45826
Celina, TN	931	38551
Centennial, CO	303, 720	80015-80016, 80111-80112*
Center, NE	402	68724
Center, ND	701	58530
Center, TX	936	75935
Center City, MN	651	55002, 55012
Center Hill, FL	352	33514
Center Line, MI	586	48015
Center Moriches, NY	631	11934
Center Point, TX	830	78010
Center Valley, PA	484, 610	18034
Centerburg, OH	740	43011
Centerport, NY	631	11721
Centerville, IA	641	52544
Centerville, MA	508, 774	02632-02636
Centerville, MO	573	63633
Centerville, OH	937	45458-45459
Centerville, TN	931	37033
Centerville, TX	903	75833
Centerville, UT	801, 385	84014
Central, SC	864	29630
Central City, CO	303, 720	80427
Central City, KY	270	42330
Central City, NE	308	68826
Central Falls, RI	401	02863
Central Islip, NY	631	11722, 11749, 11760
Central Point, OR	541, 458	97502
Centralia, IL	618	62801
Centralia, MO	573	65240
Centralia, WA	360	98531
Centre, AL	256	35960
Centre Hall, PA	814	16828
Centreville, AL	205	35042
Centreville, IL	618	62207
Centreville, MD	410	21617
Centreville, MI	616	49032
Centreville, MS	601, 769	39631
Centreville, VA	571, 703	20120-20122

Partial list of zip codes, including main range

City	Area Code(s)	Zip Code(s)
Centuria, WI	715, 534	54824
Century, FL	850	32535
Ceres, CA	209	95307
Cerritos, CA	562	90701-90703
Chadds Ford, PA	484, 610	19317
Chadron, NE	308	69337
Chaffee, NY	585	14030
Chagrin Falls, OH	440	44022-44023
Chalfont, PA	215, 267	18914
Challis, ID	208	83226-83229
Chalmette, LA	504	70043-70044
Chama, NM	505	87520
Chamberlain, SD	605	57325-57326
Chambersburg, PA	717	17201
Chamblee, GA	470, 770	30341, 30366
Champaign, IL	217	61820-61826
Champion, PA	814	15622
Chandler, AZ	480	85224-85226, 85244-85249
Chandler, IN	812	47610
Chandler, OK	405	74834
Chandlerville, IL	217	62627
Chanhassen, MN	952	55317
Channahon, IL	815	60410
Channelview, TX	281, 832	77530
Channing, TX	806	79018, 79058
Chantilly, VA	571, 703	20151-20153
Chanute, KS	620	66720
Chapel Hill, NC	919	27514-27517, 27599
Chapin, SC	803	29036
Chapmanville, WV	304	25508
Chappell, NE	308	69129
Chardon, OH	440	44024
Chariton, IA	641	50049
Charleroi, PA	724, 878	15022
Charles City, IA	641	50616, 50620
Charles City, VA	804	23030
Charles Town, WV	304	25414
Charleston, IL	217	61920
Charleston, ME	207	04422
Charleston, MS	662	38921, 38958
Charleston, MO	573	63834
Charleston, SC	843	29401-29425, 29492
Charleston, WV	304	25301-25339, 25350, 25356*
Charleston AFB, SC	843	29404
Charlestown, IN	812	47111
Charlestown, MA	617, 857	02129
Charlestown, NH	603	03603
Charlevoix, MI	231	49711, 49720
Charlotte, MI	517	48813
Charlotte, NC	704, 980	28201-28290, 28296-28299
Charlotte, TN	615	37036
Charlotte, VT	802	05445
Charlotte Court House, VA	434	23923
Charlotte Hall, MD	301	20622
Charlottesville, VA	434	22901-22911
Charlton City, MA	508, 774	01508
Chase City, VA	434	23924
Chaska, MN	952	55318
Chateaugay, NY	518	12920
Chatfield, MN	507	55923
Chatham, IL	217	62629
Chatham, MA	508, 774	02633
Chatham, NJ	862, 973	07928
Chatham, NY	518	12037
Chatham, VA	434	24531
Chatom, AL	251	36518
Chatsworth, CA	818	91311-91313
Chatsworth, GA	706, 762	30705
Chatsworth, IL	815	60921
Chattahoochee, FL	850	32324
Chattanooga, TN	423	37343, 37401-37424, 37450
Chautauqua, NY	716	14722
Chauvin, LA	985	70344
Cheboygan, MI	231	49721
Checotah, OK	918	74426
Cheektowaga, NY	716	14043, 14206, 14211-14215*
Chehalis, WA	360	98532
Chelan, WA	509	98816
Chelmsford, MA	351, 978	01824
Chelsea, MA	617, 857	02150
Chelsea, MI	734	48118
Chelsea, VT	802	05038
Cheltenham, PA	215, 267	19012
Cheney, KS	316	67025
Cheney, WA	509	99004
Cheraw, SC	843	29520
Cherokee, IA	712	51012
Cherokee, NC	828	28719
Cherokee, OK	580	73728
Cherry Hill, NJ	856	08002-08003, 08034
Cherry Point, NC	252	28533
Cherry Valley, IL	815	61016
Cherry Valley, MA	508, 774	01611
Cherryfield, ME	207	04622
Cherryville, NC	704, 980	28021
Chesapeake, VA	757	23320-23328
Chesapeake City, MD	410	21915
Cheshire, CT	203	06408-06411
Chester, CT	860	06412
Chester, GA	478	31012
Chester, IL	618	62233
Chester, MD	410	21619
Chester, MT	406	59522
Chester, NH	603	03036
Chester, NJ	908	07930
Chester, NY	845	10918
Chester, PA	484, 610	19013-19016, 19022
Chester, SC	803	29706
Chester, VA	804	23831, 23836
Chester, WV	304	26034
Chester Springs, PA	484, 610	19425
Chesterbrook, PA	484, 610	19087
Chesterfield, MI	586	48047, 48051
Chesterfield, MO	314, 636	63005-63006, 63017
Chesterfield, SC	843	29709
Chesterfield, VA	804	23832, 23838
Chesterfield Township, MI	586	48047, 48051
Chesterland, OH	440	44026
Chesterton, IN	219	46304
Chestertown, MD	410	21620, 21690
Chestertown, NY	518	12817
Chestnut Hill, MA	617, 857	02467
Chestnut Ridge, NY	845	10952, 10965, 10977
Cheswick, PA	724, 878	15024
Cheverly, MD	301	20781-20785
Chevy Chase, MD	301	20813-20815, 20825
Cheyenne, OK	580	73628
Cheyenne, WY	307	82001-82010
Cheyenne Wells, CO	719	80810
Cheyney, PA	484, 610	19319
Chicago, IL	312, 773	60601-60701, 60706-60707*
Chicago Heights, IL	708	60411-60412
Chickamauga, GA	706, 762	30707
Chickasaw, AL	251	36611
Chickasha, OK	405	73018, 73023
Chico, CA	530	95926-95929, 95973-95976
Chicopee, MA	413	01013-01014, 01020-01022
Chiefland, FL	352	32626, 32644
Childersburg, AL	256	35044
Childress, TX	940	79201
Chillicothe, IL	309	61523
Chillicothe, MO	660	64601
Chillicothe, OH	740	45601
Chilton, WI	920	53014
Chincoteague Island, VA	757	23336-23337
Chinle, AZ	928	86503, 86507, 86538, 86545*
Chino, CA	909	91708-91710
Chinook, MT	406	59523, 59535
Chipley, FL	850	32428
Chippewa Falls, WI	715, 534	54729, 54774
Chisholm, MN	218	55719
Chocorua, NH	603	03817
Choteau, MT	406	59422
Chowchilla, CA	559	93610
Christiana, PA	484, 610	17509
Christiansburg, VA	540	24068, 24073
Christmas, FL	321, 407	32709
Chuckey, TN	423	37641
Chula Vista, CA	619	91909-91915, 91921
Cicero, IL	708	60804
Cimarron, KS	620	67835
Cincinnati, OH	513	45201-45258, 45262-45280*
Cinnaminson, NJ	856	08077
Circle, MT	406	59215
Circle Pines, MN	763	55014
Circleville, OH	740	43113
Cisco, TX	254	76437
Citrus Heights, CA	916	95610-95611, 95621, 95662
City of Commerce, CA	323	90040, 90091
City of Industry, CA	626	90601, 91714-91716, 91732*
Clackamas, OR	503, 971	97015
Clairton, PA	412, 878	15025
Clallam Bay, WA	360	98326
Clanton, AL	205	35045-35046
Clare, MI	989	48617
Claremont, CA	909	91711
Claremont, NH	603	03743
Claremont, NC	828	28610
Claremore, OK	918	74017-74018
Clarence, NY	716	14031, 14221
Clarendon, AR	870	72029
Clarendon, TX	806	79226
Clarendon Hills, IL	331, 630	60514, 60527
Clarinda, IA	712	51632
Clarion, IA	515	50525-50526
Clarion, PA	814	16214
Clarissa, MN	218	56440
Clark, CO	970	80428
Clark, NJ	732, 848	07066
Clark, SD	605	57225
Clarkdale, AZ	928	86324
Clarkesville, GA	706, 762	30523
Clarks Summit, PA	570	18411
Clarksburg, MD	240, 301	20871
Clarksburg, WV	304	26301-26302, 26306, 26461
Clarksdale, MS	662	38614, 38669
Clarkston, MI	248, 947	48346-48348
Clarksville, AR	479	72830
Clarksville, IN	812	47129-47131
Clarksville, TN	931	37040-37044
Clarksville, TX	903	75426
Claude, TX	806	79019
Clawson, MI	248, 947	48017, 48398
Claxton, GA	912	30414-30417, 30438
Clay, WV	304	25043
Clay Center, KS	785	67432
Clay Center, NE	402	68933
Claymont, DE	302	19703
Clayton, AL	334	36016
Clayton, CA	925	94517
Clayton, DE	302	19938
Clayton, GA	706, 762	30525
Clayton, MO	314	63105, 63124
Clayton, NJ	856	08312
Clayton, NM	505	88415
Clayton, NC	919	27520
Clear Brook, VA	540	22624
Clear Creek, IN	812	47426
Clear Lake, IA	641	50428
Clear Lake, SD	605	57226
Clearfield, PA	814	16830
Clearfield, UT	801, 385	84015-84016, 84089
Clearwater, FL	727	33755-33769
Clearwater Beach, FL	727	33767
Cleburne, TX	682, 817	76031-76033
Cleghorn, IA	712	51014
Clementon, NJ	856	08021
Clements, CA	209	95227
Clements, MN	507	56224
Clemson, SC	864	29631-29634
Clermont, FL	352	34711-34713
Cleveland, GA	706, 762	30528
Cleveland, MS	662	38732-38733
Cleveland, OH	216, 440	44101-44149, 44177-44199
Cleveland, OK	918	74020
Cleveland, TN	423	37311-37312, 37320-37323*
Cleveland, TX	281, 832	77327-77328
Cleveland, WI	920	53015
Cleveland Heights, OH	216	44106, 44112, 44118-44121
Clewiston, FL	863	33440
Clifford, PA	570	18413
Cliffside, NC	828	28024
Cliffside Park, NJ	201, 551	07010
Cliffwood Beach, NJ	732, 848	07735
Clifton, AZ	928	85533
Clifton, KS	785	66937
Clifton, NJ	862, 973	07011-07015
Clifton, TN	931	38425
Clifton, TX	254	76634, 76644
Clifton Forge, VA	540	24422
Clifton Heights, PA	484, 610	19018
Clifton Park, NY	518	12065
Clifton Springs, NY	315	14432
Clines Corners, NM	505	87070
Clinton, AR	501	72031
Clinton, CT	860	06413
Clinton, IL	217	61727
Clinton, IN	765	47842

*Partial list of zip codes, including main range

City	Area Code(s)	Zip Code(s)
Clinton, IA	563	52732-52736, 52771
Clinton, KY	270	42031
Clinton, LA	225	70722
Clinton, ME	207	04927
Clinton, MD	301	20735
Clinton, MA	351, 978	01510
Clinton, MI	517	49236
Clinton, MN	320	56225
Clinton, MS	601, 769	39056-39060
Clinton, MO	660	64735
Clinton, NJ	908	08809
Clinton, NY	315	13323
Clinton, NC	910	28328-28329
Clinton, OK	580	73601
Clinton, SC	864	29325
Clinton, TN	865	37716-37717
Clinton Township, MI	586	48035-48038
Clintonville, WI	715, 534	54929
Clintwood, VA	276	24228
Clio, MI	810	48420
Clive, IA	515	50325
Cloquet, MN	218	55720
Closter, NJ	201, 551	07624
Cloudcroft, NM	505	88317, 88350
Clover, SC	803	29710
Clover, VA	434	24534
Cloverdale, VA	540	24077
Clovis, CA	559	93611-93613
Clovis, NM	505	88101-88103
Clute, TX	979	77531
Clyde, NY	315	14433
Clyde, NC	828	28721
Clyde Park, MT	406	59018
Coachella, CA	760, 442	92236
Coal Township, PA	570	17866
Coalgate, OK	580	74538
Coalinga, CA	559	93210
Coalmont, TN	931	37313
Coalville, UT	435	84017
Coatesville, PA	484, 610	19320
Cobleskill, NY	518	12043
Coburg, OR	541, 458	97408
Cochran, GA	478	31014
Cochranton, PA	814	16314
Cockeysville, MD	410	21030-21031
Cocoa, FL	321	32922-32927
Cocoa Beach, FL	321	32931-32932
Coconut Creek, FL	754, 954	33063-33066, 33073, 33097
Coconut Grove, FL	305, 786	33133-33134, 33146
Cody, WY	307	82414
Coeburn, VA	276	24230
Coeur d'Alene, ID	208	83814-83816
Coffeyville, KS	620	67337
Cogan Station, PA	570	17728
Cohasset, MA	339, 781	02025
Cohoes, NY	518	12047
Cokato, MN	320	55321
Coker, AL	205	35452
Colby, KS	785	67701
Colchester, CT	860	06415, 06420
Colchester, IL	309	62326
Colchester, VT	802	05439, 05446-05449
Cold Spring, KY	859	41076
Cold Spring, MN	320	56320
Cold Spring, NY	845	10516
Cold Spring Harbor, NY	516	11724
Cold Springs, NV	775	89506
Coldspring, TX	936	77331
Coldwater, KS	620	67029
Coldwater, MI	517	49036
Coldwater, OH	419, 567	45828
Coleman, FL	352	33521
Coleman, MI	989	48618
Coleman, OK	580	73432
Coleman, TX	915	76834
Colfax, IA	515	50054
Colfax, LA	318	71417
Colfax, WA	509	99111
College Corner, OH	513	45003
College Park, GA	404, 470	30337
College Park, MD	301	20740-20742
College Place, WA	509	99324
College Point, NY	347, 718	11356
College Station, TX	979	77840-77845
Collegedale, TN	423	37315
Collegeville, MN	320	56321
Collegeville, PA	484, 610	19426, 19473
Colleyville, TX	682, 817	76034
Collierville, TN	901	38017, 38027
Collingswood, NJ	856	08108
Collins, MS	601, 769	39428
Collins, NY	716	14034
Collinsville, IL	618	62234
Collinsville, OK	918	74021
Collinsville, VA	276	24078
Collinwood, TN	931	38450
Colman, SD	605	57017
Colmar, PA	215, 267	18915
Coloma, CA	530	95613
Coloma, MI	616	49038-49039
Colon, MI	616	49040
Colonial Heights, VA	804	23834
Colorado City, AZ	928	86021
Colorado City, TX	915	79512
Colorado Springs, CO	719	80901-80950, 80960-80962*
Colquitt, GA	229	31737
Colstrip, MT	406	59323
Colt, AR	870	72326
Colton, CA	909	92313, 92324
Columbia, IL	618	62236
Columbia, KY	270	42728, 42735
Columbia, LA	318	71418
Columbia, MD	410, 443	21044-21046
Columbia, MS	601, 769	39429
Columbia, MO	573	65201-65205, 65211-65218*
Columbia, NC	252	27925
Columbia, PA	717	17512
Columbia, SC	803	29201-29230, 29240, 29250*
Columbia, TN	931	38401-38402
Columbia City, IN	260	46725
Columbia Falls, MT	406	59912
Columbia Heights, MN	763	55421
Columbia Station, OH	440	44028
Columbiana, AL	205	35051
Columbiana, OH	234, 330	44408
Columbus, GA	706, 762	31829, 31901-31909, 31914*
Columbus, IN	812	47201-47203
Columbus, KS	620	66725
Columbus, MS	662	39701-39705, 39710
Columbus, MT	406	59019
Columbus, NE	402	68601-68602
Columbus, NC	828	28722
Columbus, ND	701	58727
Columbus, OH	614	43085, 43201-43236, 43240*
Columbus, TX	979	78934
Columbus, WI	920	53925
Columbus AFB, MS	662	39701
Columbus Grove, OH	419, 567	45830
Colusa, CA	530	95932
Colville, WA	509	99114
Comanche, TX	915	76442
Combined Locks, WI	920	54113
Commack, NY	631	11725
Commerce, CA	323	90040, 90091
Commerce, GA	706, 762	30529-30530, 30599
Commerce, TX	903	75428-75429
Commerce City, CO	303, 720	80022, 80037
Commerce Township, MI	248, 947	48382, 48390
Compton, CA	310, 424	90220-90224
Comstock, NY	518	12821
Comstock Park, MI	616	49321
Conception, MO	660	64433
Concord, CA	925	94518-94529
Concord, MA	351, 978	01742
Concord, NH	603	03301-03305
Concord, NC	704, 980	28025-28027
Concord, OH	440	44060, 44077
Concordia, KS	785	66901
Concordville, PA	484, 610	19331, 19339-19340
Condon, OR	541, 458	97823
Conejos, CO	719	81129
Conestoga, PA	717	17516
Congers, NY	845	10920
Conklin, NY	607	13748
Conneaut, OH	440	44030
Connell, WA	509	99326
Connellsville, PA	724, 878	15425
Connersville, IN	765	47331
Conover, NC	828	28613
Conrad, IA	641	50621
Conrad, MT	406	59425
Conroe, TX	936	77301-77306, 77384-77385
Conshohocken, PA	484, 610	19428-19429
Contoocook, NH	603	03229
Convent, LA	225	70723
Conway, AR	501	72032-72035
Conway, NH	603	03818
Conway, SC	843	29526-29528
Conyers, GA	470, 770	30012-30013, 30094
Cook, MN	218	55723
Cookeville, TN	931	38501-38506
Coolidge, AZ	520	85228
Coolidge, GA	229	31738
Coolidge, TX	254	76635
Coon Rapids, MN	763	55433, 55448
Cooper, TX	903	75432
Cooper City, FL	754, 954	33024-33026, 33328-33330
Coopersburg, PA	484, 610	18036
Cooperstown, NY	607	13326
Cooperstown, ND	701	58425
Coopersville, MI	616	49404
Coos Bay, OR	541, 458	97420
Copiague, NY	631	11726
Copley, OH	234, 330	44321
Coppell, TX	469, 972	75019, 75099
Copper Center, AK	907	99573
Copper Mountain, CO	970	80443
Copperas Cove, TX	254	76522
Coquille, OR	541, 458	97423
Cora, WY	307	82925
Coral Gables, FL	305, 786	33114, 33124, 33133-33134*
Coral Springs, FL	754, 954	33065-33067, 33071, 33075*
Coralville, IA	319	52241
Coraopolis, PA	412, 878	15108
Corbett, OR	503, 971	97019
Corbin, KY	606	40701-40702
Corcoran, CA	559	93212, 93282
Cordele, GA	229	31010, 31015
Cordell, OK	580	73632
Cordova, AK	907	99574, 99677
Cordova, TN	901	38016-38018, 38088
Core, WV	304	26529
Corinne, UT	435	84307
Corinth, MS	662	38834-38835
Corinth, TX	940	76208-76210
Cornelia, GA	706, 762	30531
Cornelius, NC	704, 980	28031
Cornelius, OR	503, 971	97113
Cornell, WI	715, 534	54732
Corning, AR	870	72422
Corning, CA	530	96021, 96029
Corning, IA	712	50841
Corning, NY	607	14830-14831
Cornish, NH	603	03745
Cornville, AZ	928	86325
Cornwall, NY	845	12518
Cornwall Bridge, CT	860	06754
Corona, CA	951	92877-92883
Corona, NY	347, 718	11368
Corona del Mar, CA	949	92625
Coronado, CA	619	92118, 92178
Corpus Christi, TX	361	78350, 78401-78419, 78426*
Corry, PA	814	16407
Corsicana, TX	903	75109-75110, 75151
Corte Madera, CA	415	94925, 94976
Cortez, CO	970	81321
Cortland, NY	607	13045
Cortlandt Manor, NY	845	10567
Corunna, MI	989	48817
Corvallis, MT	406	59828
Corvallis, OR	541, 458	97330-97333, 97339
Corydon, IN	812	47112
Corydon, IA	641	50060
Cos Cob, CT	203	06807
Coshocton, OH	740	43812
Costa Mesa, CA	714, 949	92626-92628
Cotati, CA	707	94926-94931
Cottage Grove, OR	541, 458	97424, 97472
Cottonport, LA	318	71327
Cottonwood, AZ	928	86326
Cottonwood, CA	530	96022
Cottonwood, ID	208	83522, 83533
Cottonwood, MN	507	56229
Cottonwood Falls, KS	620	66845
Cotuit, MA	508, 774	02635
Cotulla, TX	830	78001, 78014

*Partial list of zip codes, including main range

City	Area Code(s)	Zip Code(s)
Coudersport, PA	814	16915
Coulee City, WA	509	99115
Coulee Dam, WA	509	99116
Council, ID	208	83612
Council Bluffs, IA	712	51501-51503
Council Grove, KS	620	66846, 66873
Countryside, IL	708	60525
Coupeville, WA	360	98239
Courtland, VA	757	23837
Coushatta, LA	318	71019
Coventry, RI	401	02816
Covina, CA	626	91722-91724
Covington, GA	470, 770	30014-30016
Covington, IN	765	47932
Covington, KY	859	41011-41019
Covington, LA	985	70433-70435
Covington, TN	901	38019
Covington, VA	540	24426
Cowiche, WA	509	98923
Coxsackie, NY	518	12051, 12192
Cozad, NE	308	69130
Craftsbury Common, VT	802	05827
Craig, CO	970	81625-81626
Craigsville, VA	540	24430
Cranberry Township, PA	724, 878	16066
Cranbury, NJ	609	08512, 08570
Crandall, TX	469, 972	75114
Crandon, WI	715, 534	54520
Crane, TX	915	79731
Cranford, NJ	908	07016
Cranston, RI	401	02823, 02905-02910, 02920*
Craryville, NY	518	12521
Crater Lake, OR	541, 458	97604
Crawfordsville, IN	765	47933-47939
Crawfordville, FL	850	32326-32327
Crawfordville, GA	706, 762	30631
Crazy Horse, SD	605	57730
Creede, CO	719	81130
Creedmoor, NC	919	27522, 27564
Creighton, NE	402	68729
Crescent City, CA	707	95531-95532, 95538
Crescent Springs, KY	859	41017
Cresco, IA	563	52136
Cresco, PA	570	18326
Cresskill, NJ	201, 551	07626
Cresson, PA	814	16630, 16699
Cresson, TX	682, 817	76035
Cressona, PA	570	17929
Creston, IA	641	50801
Crestview, FL	850	32536-32539
Crestview Hills, KY	859	41017
Creswell, OR	541, 458	97426
Crete, IL	708	60417
Crete, NE	402	68333
Creve Coeur, IL	309	61610
Creve Coeur, MO	314	63141
Crewe, VA	434	23930
Cripple Creek, CO	719	80813
Crisfield, MD	410	21817
Crockett, CA	510	94525
Crockett, TX	936	75835
Crofton, MD	410	21114
Cromwell, CT	860	06416
Crookston, MN	218	56716
Crosby, ND	701	58730
Crosbyton, TX	806	79322
Cross City, FL	352	32628
Cross Lanes, WV	304	25313, 25356
Cross Plains, WI	608	53528
Crossett, AR	870	71635
Crossville, TN	931	38555-38558, 38571-38572
Croswell, MI	810	48422
Crow Agency, MT	406	59022
Crowell, TX	940	79227
Crowley, CO	719	81033-81034
Crowley, LA	337	70526-70527
Crown Point, IN	219	46307-46308
Crownsville, MD	410	21032
Croydon, PA	215, 267	19021
Crum Lynne, PA	484, 610	19022
Crystal, MN	763	55422, 55427-55429
Crystal Bay, NV	775	89402
Crystal City, MO	636	63019
Crystal City, TX	830	78839
Crystal Falls, MI	906	49920
Crystal Lake, IL	815	60012-60014, 60039
Crystal River, FL	352	34423, 34428-34429
Crystal Springs, MS	601, 769	39059
Cuba, NY	585	14727
Cudahy, CA	323	90201
Cudahy, WI	414	53110
Cuddy, PA	412, 878	15031
Cuero, TX	361	77954
Cullman, AL	256	35055-35058
Cullowhee, NC	828	28723
Culpeper, VA	540	22701
Culver, OR	541, 458	97734
Culver City, CA	310, 424	90230-90233
Cumberland, KY	606	40823
Cumberland, MD	301	21501-21505
Cumberland, OH	740	43732
Cumberland, RI	401	02864
Cumberland, VA	804	23040
Cumberland Gap, TN	423	37724, 37752
Cumming, GA	470, 770	30028, 30040-30041
Cupertino, CA	408	95014-95015
Currie, NC	910	28435
Currituck, NC	252	27929
Curtis, NE	308	69025
Cushing, OK	918	74023
Cusick, WA	509	99119
Cusseta, GA	706, 762	31805
Custer, SD	605	57730
Cut Bank, MT	406	59427
Cuthbert, GA	229	31740
Cuyahoga Falls, OH	234, 330	44221-44224
Cuyahoga Heights, OH	216	44105, 44125-44127
Cynthiana, KY	859	41031
Cypress, CA	714	90630
Cypress, TX	281, 832	77410, 77429, 77433

D

City	Area Code(s)	Zip Code(s)
Dade City, FL	352	33523-33526
Dadeville, AL	256	36853
Dafter, MI	906	49724
Dahlgren, VA	540	22448
Dahlonega, GA	706, 762	30533, 30597
Daingerfield, TX	903	75638
Dakota, IL	815	61018
Dakota City, IA	515	50529
Dakota City, NE	402	68731
Dakota Dunes, SD	605	57049
Dale, IN	812	47523
Dalhart, TX	806	79022
Dallas, GA	470, 770	30132, 30157
Dallas, NC	704, 980	28034
Dallas, OR	503, 971	97338
Dallas, PA	570	18612, 18690
Dallas, TX	214, 469, 972	75201-75254, 75258-75270*
Dallastown, PA	717	17313
Dalton, GA	706, 762	30719-30722
Dalton, MA	413	01226-01227
Dalton, OH	234, 330	44618
Daly City, CA	650	94013-94017
Damariscotta, ME	207	04543
Dammeron Valley, UT	435	84783
Dana Point, CA	949	92624, 92629
Danboro, PA	215, 267	18916
Danbury, CT	203	06810-06817
Danbury, NC	336	27016
Dandridge, TN	865	37725
Dania Beach, FL	754, 954	33004, 33312
Daniel, WY	307	83115
Danielson, CT	860	06239
Danielsville, GA	706, 762	30633
Dannemora, NY	518	12929
Danube, MN	320	56230
Danvers, MA	351, 978	01923
Danville, AR	479	72833
Danville, CA	925	94506, 94526
Danville, IL	217	61832-61834
Danville, IN	317	46122
Danville, IA	319	52623
Danville, KY	859	40422-40423
Danville, PA	570	17821-17822
Danville, VA	434	24540-24544
Daphne, AL	251	36526
Darby, MT	406	59829
Dardanelle, AR	479	72834
Darien, CT	203	06820
Darien, GA	912	31305
Darien, IL	331, 630	60561
Darien Center, NY	585	14040
Darlington, SC	843	29532, 29540
Darlington, WI	608	53530
Darrow, LA	225	70725
Dartmouth, MA	508, 774	02714, 02747-02748
Dassel, MN	320	55325
Dauphin Island, AL	251	36528
Davenport, FL	863	33836-33837, 33896-33897
Davenport, IA	563	52801-52809
Davenport, WA	509	99122
David City, NE	402	68632
Davidson, NC	704, 980	28035-28036
Davie, FL	754, 954	33024, 33312-33317, 33324*
Davis, CA	530	95616-95618
Davis, WV	304	26260
Davison, MI	810	48423
Daviston, AL	256	36256
Davisville, WV	304	26142
Dawson, GA	229	31742
Dawsonville, GA	706, 762	30534
Dayton, IA	515	50530
Dayton, NV	775	89403
Dayton, NJ	732, 848	08810
Dayton, OH	937	45390, 45401-45441, 45448*
Dayton, TN	423	37321
Dayton, TX	936	77535
Dayton, WA	509	99328
Daytona Beach, FL	386	32114-32129, 32198
Daytona Beach Shores, FL	386	32116
Dayville, CT	860	06241
De Funiak Springs, FL	850	32433-32435
De Kalb, MS	601, 769	39328
De Pere, WI	920	54115
De Queen, AR	870	71832
De Smet, SD	605	57231
De Witt, AR	870	72042
De Witt, IA	563	52742
Deadwood, SD	605	57732
Dearborn, MI	313	48120-48128
Dearborn Heights, MI	313	48125-48127
Death Valley, CA	760, 442	92328
Decatur, AL	256	35601-35603, 35609, 35699
Decatur, AR	479	72722
Decatur, GA	404, 470	30030-30037
Decatur, IL	217	62521-62527
Decatur, IN	260	46733
Decatur, MS	601, 769	39327
Decatur, TN	423	37322
Decatur, TX	940	76234
Decaturville, TN	731	38329
Deckerville, MI	810	48427
Declo, ID	208	83323
Decorah, IA	563	52101
Dedham, MA	339, 781	02026-02027
Deer Harbor, WA	360	98243
Deer Lodge, MT	406	59722
Deer Park, CA	707	94576
Deer Park, NY	631	11729
Deer Park, TX	281, 832	77536
Deer River, MN	218	56636
Deerfield, IL	224, 847	60015
Deerfield, MA	413	01342
Deerfield, WI	608	53531
Deerfield Beach, FL	754, 954	33064, 33441-33443
Deerwood, MN	218	56444
Defiance, OH	419, 567	43512
DeForest, WI	608	53532
DeGraff, OH	937	43318
DeKalb, IL	815	60115
Del City, OK	405	73115, 73135, 73165
Del Mar, CA	858	92014
Del Norte, CO	719	81132
Del Rey, CA	559	93616
Del Rio, TX	830	78840-78843, 78847
Delair, NJ	856	08110
Delanco, NJ	856	08075
DeLand, FL	386	32720-32724
Delano, CA	661	93215-93216
Delano, MN	763	55328
Delavan, MN	507	56023
Delavan, WI	262	53115
Delaware, OH	740	43015
Delaware City, DE	302	19706
Delaware Water Gap, PA	570	18327

Partial list of zip codes, including main range

City	Area Code(s)	Zip Code(s)
Delbarton, WV	304	25670
DeLeon Springs, FL	386	32130
Delhi, NY	607	13753
Dellroy, OH	234, 330	44620
Delmar, MD	410	21875
Delmar, NY	518	12054
Delmont, NJ	856	08314
Delmont, PA	724, 878	15626
Delphi, IN	765	46923
Delphos, OH	419, 567	45833
Delray Beach, FL	561	33444-33448, 33482-33484
Delta, CO	970	81416
Delta, UT	435	84624
Deming, NM	505	88030-88031
Demopolis, AL	334	36732
Demorest, GA	706, 762	30535, 30544
Demotte, IN	219	46310
Denham Springs, LA	225	70706, 70726-70727
Denison, IA	712	51442
Denison, TX	903	75020-75021
Denmark, SC	803	29042
Denmark, WI	920	54208
Denton, MD	410	21629
Denton, NC	336	27239
Denton, TX	940	76201-76210
Denver, CO	303, 720	80002, 80010-80014, 80022*
Denver, IA	319	50622
Denver, NC	704, 980	28037
Denver, PA	717	17517
Denville, NJ	862, 973	07834
Depew, NY	716	14043
Depoe Bay, OR	541, 458	97341
Deposit, NY	607	13754
Dequincy, LA	337	70633
Derby, CT	203	06418
Derby, KS	316	67037
Derby, NY	716	14047
DeRidder, LA	337	70634
Dermott, AR	870	71638
Derry, NH	603	03038
Derwent, OH	740	43733
Des Allemands, LA	504	70030
Des Arc, AR	870	72040
Des Moines, IA	515	50301-50340, 50347-50350*
Des Moines, WA	206	98148, 98198
Des Plaines, IL	224, 847	60016-60019
Descanso, CA	760, 442	91916
Desert Hot Springs, CA	760, 442	92240-92241
Deshler, NE	402	68340
DeSoto, KS	913	66018
DeSoto, TX	469, 972	75115, 75123
Destin, FL	850	32540-32541, 32550
Destrehan, LA	985	70047
Detroit, MI	313, 734	48201-48244, 48255, 48260*
Detroit, OR	503, 971	97342
Detroit Lakes, MN	218	56501-56502
Devault, PA	484, 610	19432
Devens, MA	351, 978	01432
Devils Lake, ND	701	58301
Devils Tower, WY	307	82714
Devon, PA	484, 610	19333
Dewey, OK	918	74029
Dewey Beach, DE	302	19971
DeWitt, NY	315	13214
Dexter, MI	734	48130
Dexter, MO	573	63841
Diamond, MO	417	64840
Diamond Bar, CA	909	91765
Diamond Point, NY	518	12824
Diboll, TX	936	75941
Dickens, TX	806	79229
Dickinson, ND	701	58601-58602
Dickinson, TX	281, 832	77539
Dickson, TN	615	37055-37056
Dighton, KS	620	67839
Dighton, MA	508, 774	02715
Dillingham, AK	907	99576
Dillon, MT	406	59725
Dillon, SC	843	29536
Dillwyn, VA	434	23936
Dimmitt, TX	806	79027
Dinosaur, CO	970	81610, 81633
Dinuba, CA	559	93618
Dinwiddie, VA	804	23841
Dix Hills, NY	631	11746

City	Area Code(s)	Zip Code(s)
Dixie, GA	229	31629
Dixmoor, IL	708	60406, 60426
Dixon, CA	707	95620
Dixon, IL	815	61021
Dixon, KY	270	42409
Dixon, MO	573	65459
Dobbs Ferry, NY	914	10522
Dobson, NC	336	27017
Dodge Center, MN	507	55927
Dodge City, KS	620	67801
Dodgeville, WI	608	53533, 53595
Dolgeville, NY	315	13329
Dolton, IL	708	60419
Donaldson, IN	574	46513
Donaldsonville, LA	225	70346
Donalsonville, GA	229	31745
Dongola, IL	618	62926
Doniphan, MO	573	63935
Dorado, PR	787, 939	00646
Doraville, GA	470, 770	30340, 30360-30362
Dorchester, MA	617, 857	02121-02125
Dorchester, NE	402	68343
Doswell, VA	804	23047
Dothan, AL	334	36301-36305
Double Springs, AL	205	35553
Douglas, AK	907	99824
Douglas, AZ	520	85607-85608, 85655
Douglas, GA	912	31533-31535
Douglas, MI	616	49406
Douglas, WY	307	82633
Douglassville, PA	484, 610	19518
Douglassville, TX	903	75560
Douglaston, NY	347, 718	11362-11363
Douglasville, GA	470, 770	30133-30135, 30154
Dove Creek, CO	970	81324
Dover, DE	302	19901-19906
Dover, FL	813	33527
Dover, NH	603	03820-03822
Dover, NJ	862, 973	07801-07806, 07869
Dover, OH	234, 330	44622
Dover, TN	931	37058
Dover AFB, DE	302	19902
Dover Plains, NY	845	12522
Dowagiac, MI	616	49047
Downers Grove, IL	331, 630	60515-60517
Downey, CA	562	90239-90242
Downieville, CA	530	95936
Downingtown, PA	484, 610	19335, 19372
Doylestown, OH	234, 330	44230
Doylestown, PA	215, 267	18901, 18933
Doyline, LA	318	71023
Dracut, MA	351, 978	01826
Dragoon, AZ	520	85609
Drain, OR	541, 458	97435
Draper, UT	801, 385	84020
Dravosburg, PA	412, 878	15034
Dresden, TN	731	38225
Dresher, PA	215, 267	19025
Dresser, WI	715, 534	54009
Drexel Hill, PA	484, 610	19026
Driggs, ID	208	83422
Drummond Island, MI	906	49726
Dry Ridge, KY	859	41035
Dryden, NY	607	13053
Du Bois, PA	814	15801
Duarte, CA	626	91009-91010
Dublin, CA	925	94568
Dublin, GA	478	31021, 31027, 31040
Dublin, NH	603	03444
Dublin, NC	910	28332
Dublin, OH	614	43016-43017
Dublin, VA	540	24084
Dubois, ID	208	83423, 83446
Dubois, WY	307	82513
Dubuque, IA	563	52001-52004, 52099
Duchesne, UT	435	84021
Duck, NC	252	27949
Duck Hill, MS	662	38925
Duck Key, FL	305, 786	33050
Dudley, GA	478	31022
Dudley, MA	508, 774	01571
Dudley, MO	573	63936
Dudley, NC	919	28333
Due West, SC	864	29639
Dugway, UT	435	84022
Dulles, VA	571, 703	20101-20104, 20163-20166*

City	Area Code(s)	Zip Code(s)
Duluth, GA	470, 678, 770	30026-30029, 30095-30099
Duluth, MN	218	55701, 55801-55816
Dumas, TX	806	79029
Dunbar, PA	724, 878	15431
Dunbar, WV	304	25064
Dunbar, WI	715, 534	54119
Dunbridge, OH	419, 567	43414
Duncan, AZ	928	85534
Duncan, OK	580	73533-73536, 73575
Duncan, SC	864	29334, 29390-29391
Duncannon, PA	717	17020
Duncansville, PA	814	16635
Duncanville, TX	469, 972	75116, 75137-75138
Dundalk, MD	410	21222
Dundee, FL	863	33838
Dundee, IL	224, 847	60118
Dundee, NY	607	14837
Dundee, OR	503, 971	97115
Dunedin, FL	727	34697-34698
Dunkirk, IN	765	47336
Dunkirk, MD	301	20754
Dunkirk, NY	716	14048, 14166
Dunlap, IL	309	61525
Dunlap, TN	423	37327
Dunmore, PA	570	18509-18512
Dunn, NC	910	28334-28335
Dunnell, MN	507	56127
Dunnellon, FL	352	34430-34434
Dunning, NE	308	68833
Dunseith, ND	701	58329
Dupont, WA	253	98327
Dupree, SD	605	57623
DuQuoin, IL	618	62832
Durand, MI	989	48429
Durand, WI	715, 534	54736
Durango, CO	970	81301-81303
Durant, OK	580	74701-74702
Durham, CT	860	06422
Durham, NH	603	03824
Durham, NC	919	27701-27717, 27722
Duryea, PA	570	18642
Dushore, PA	570	18614
Duxbury, MA	339, 781	02331-02332
Dwight, IL	815	60420
Dyer, NV	760, 442	89010
Dyersburg, TN	731	38024-38025
Dyersville, IA	563	52040
Dyess AFB, TX	915	79607

E

City	Area Code(s)	Zip Code(s)
Eads, CO	719	81036
Eagan, MN	651	55120-55123
Eagle, CO	970	81631
Eagle, WI	262	53119
Eagle Creek, OR	503, 971	97022
Eagle Grove, IA	515	50533
Eagle Nest, NM	505	87710, 87718
Eagle Pass, TX	830	78852-78853
Eagle River, AK	907	99577
Eagle River, MI	906	49950
Eagle River, WI	715, 534	54521
Eagle Rock, CA	323	90041
Eagleville, PA	484, 610	19403, 19408, 19415
Earle, AR	870	72331
Earlville, IL	815	60518
Early Branch, SC	803	29916
Earth City, MO	314	63045
Easley, SC	864	29640-29642
East Alton, IL	618	62024
East Amherst, NY	716	14051
East Aurora, NY	585	14052
East Bend, NC	336	27018
East Berlin, CT	860	06023
East Bernstadt, KY	606	40729
East Bloomfield, NY	585	14443, 14469
East Boston, MA	617, 857	02128, 02228
East Brunswick, NJ	732, 848	08816
East Canton, OH	234, 330	44730
East Chicago, IN	219	46312
East Cleveland, OH	216	44110-44112, 44118
East Derry, NH	603	03041
East Dubuque, IL	815	61025
East Dundee, IL	224, 847	60118

*Partial list of zip codes, including main range

City	Area Code(s)	Zip Code(s)
East Durham, NY	518	12423
East Earl, PA	717	17519
East Elmhurst, NY	347, 718	11369-11371
East Falmouth, MA	508, 774	02536
East Farmingdale, NY	631	11735
East Granby, CT	860	06026
East Grand Forks, MN	218	56721
East Grand Rapids, MI	616	49506, 49546
East Greenville, PA	215, 267	18041
East Greenwich, RI	401	02818
East Haddam, CT	860	06423
East Hampstead, NH	603	03826
East Hampton, CT	860	06424, 06447
East Hampton, NY	631	11937
East Hanover, NJ	862, 973	07936
East Hartford, CT	860	06108, 06118, 06128, 06138
East Haven, CT	203	06512-06513
East Hazel Crest, IL	708	60429
East Hills, NY	516	11548, 11576-11577
East Jordan, MI	231	49727
East Lansing, MI	517	48823-48826
East Liberty, OH	937	43074, 43319
East Liverpool, OH	234, 330	43920
East Longmeadow, MA	413	01028, 01116
East Meadow, NY	516	11554
East Millstone, NJ	732, 848	08873-08875
East Moline, IL	309	61244
East Montpelier, VT	802	05651
East New Market, MD	410	21631
East Northport, NY	631	11731
East Norwalk, CT	203	06855
East Orange, NJ	862, 973	07017-07019
East Palatka, FL	386	32131
East Palestine, OH	234, 330	44413
East Palo Alto, CA	650	94303
East Pembroke, NY	585	14056
East Peoria, IL	309	61611
East Petersburg, PA	717	17520
East Point, GA	404, 470	30344, 30364
East Providence, RI	401	02914-02916
East Rochester, NH	603	03868
East Rutherford, NJ	201, 551	07073
East Saint Louis, IL	618	62201-62208
East Stroudsburg, PA	570	18301
East Syracuse, NY	315	13057
East Taunton, MA	508, 774	02718
East Tawas, MI	989	48730
East Templeton, MA	351, 978	01438
East Texas, PA	484, 610	18046
East Troy, WI	262	53120
East Walpole, MA	508, 774	02032
East Weymouth, MA	339, 781	02189
East Windsor, CT	860	06016, 06088
East Windsor, NJ	609	08512, 08520
Eastaboga, AL	256	36260
Easthampton, MA	413	01027
Eastlake, MI	231	49626
Eastlake, OH	440	44095-44097
Eastland, TX	254	76448
Eastman, GA	478	31023
Easton, MD	410	21601, 21606
Easton, PA	484, 610	18040-18045
Eastpointe, MI	586	48021
Eastport, ME	207	04631
Eastsound, WA	360	98245
Eastville, VA	757	23347
Eaton, CO	970	80615
Eaton, IN	765	47338
Eaton, OH	937	45320
Eaton Rapids, MI	517	48827
Eatonton, GA	706, 762	31024
Eatontown, NJ	732, 848	07724, 07799
Eatonville, WA	360	98328
Eau Claire, WI	715, 534	54701-54703
Ebensburg, PA	814	15931
Edcouch, TX	956	78538
Eddyville, KY	270	42038
Eden, NC	336	27288-27289
Eden Prairie, MN	952	55343-55347
Edenton, NC	252	27932
Edgartown, MA	508, 774	02539
Edgefield, SC	803	29824
Edgeley, ND	701	58433
Edgerton, MN	507	56128
Edgerton, OH	419, 567	43517
Edgerton, WI	608	53534
Edgewater, FL	386	32132, 32141
Edgewater, MD	410, 443	21037
Edgewater, NJ	201, 551	07020
Edgewood, IA	563	52042-52044
Edgewood, MD	410	21040
Edgewood, NY	631	11717
Edgewood, WA	253	98371-98372, 98390
Edina, MN	952	55343, 55410, 55416, 55424*
Edina, MO	660	63537
Edinboro, PA	814	16412, 16444
Edinburg, TX	956	78539-78540
Edinburg, VA	540	22824
Edinburgh, IN	812	46124
Edison, CA	661	93220
Edison, NJ	732, 848	08817-08820, 08837, 08899
Edisto Beach, SC	843	29438
Edmeston, NY	607	13335
Edmond, OK	405	73003, 73013, 73034, 73083
Edmonds, WA	425	98020, 98026
Edmonton, KY	270	42129
Edmore, MI	989	48829
Edna, TX	361	77957
Edon, OH	419, 567	43518
Edwards, CA	661	93523-93524
Edwards, CO	970	81632
Edwardsburg, MI	616	49112, 49130
Edwardsville, IL	618	62025-62026
Edwardsville, KS	913	66111-66113
Edwardsville, PA	570	18704
Effingham, IL	217	62401
Egg Harbor, WI	920	54209
Egg Harbor City, NJ	609	08215
Egg Harbor Township, NJ	609	08234
Eglin AFB, FL	850	32542
Eielson AFB, AK	907	99702
Eighty Four, PA	724, 878	15330
Ekalaka, MT	406	59324
El Cajon, CA	619	92019-92022, 92090
El Campo, TX	979	77437
El Centro, CA	760, 442	92243-92244
El Cerrito, CA	510	94530
El Dorado, AR	870	71730-71731, 71768
El Dorado, KS	316	67042
El Dorado Hills, CA	916	95762
El Dorado Springs, MO	417	64744
El Monte, CA	626	91731-91735
El Paso, IL	309	61738
El Paso, TX	915	79821, 79901-79961, 79966*
El Reno, OK	405	73036
El Segundo, CA	310, 424	90245
El Sobrante, CA	510	94803, 94820
Elba, AL	334	36323
Elba, NY	585	14058
Elberfeld, IN	812	47613
Elberton, GA	706, 762	30635
Elbow Lake, MN	218	56531
Eldora, IA	641	50627
Eldorado, IL	618	62930
Eldorado, TX	915	76936
Eldorado Springs, CO	303, 720	80025
Eldridge, CA	707	95431
Eldridge, IA	563	52748
Eleele, HI	808	96705
Elephant Butte, NM	505	87935
Elgin, IL	224, 847	60120-60123
Elgin, SC	803	29045
Elizabeth, IL	815	61028
Elizabeth, IN	812	47117
Elizabeth, NJ	908	07201-07202, 07206-07208
Elizabeth, PA	412, 878	15037
Elizabeth, WV	304	26143
Elizabeth City, NC	252	27906-27909
Elizabethton, TN	423	37643-37644
Elizabethtown, IL	618	62931
Elizabethtown, KY	270	42701-42702
Elizabethtown, NY	518	12932
Elizabethtown, NC	910	28337
Elizabethtown, PA	717	17022
Elizabethville, PA	717	17023
Elk City, OK	580	73644, 73648
Elk Grove, CA	916	95624, 95758-95759
Elk Grove Village, IL	224, 847	60007-60009
Elk Point, SD	605	57025
Elk Rapids, MI	231	49629
Elk River, MN	763	55330
Elkader, IA	563	52043
Elkhart, IN	574	46514-46517
Elkhart, KS	620	67950
Elkhart Lake, WI	920	53020
Elkhorn, NE	402	68022
Elkhorn, WI	262	53121
Elkin, NC	336	28621
Elkins, WV	304	26241
Elkins Park, PA	215, 267	19027
Elkland, PA	814	16920
Elko, MN	952	55020
Elko, NV	775	89801-89803, 89815
Elkridge, MD	410	21075
Elkton, KY	270	42220
Elkton, MD	410	21921-21922
Elkton, OH	234, 330	44415
Ellaville, GA	229	31806
Ellendale, ND	701	58436
Ellensburg, WA	509	98926, 98950
Ellenville, NY	845	12428
Ellenwood, GA	404, 470	30294
Ellettsville, IN	812	47429
Ellicott City, MD	410	21041-21043
Ellicottville, NY	716	14731
Ellijay, GA	706, 762	30540
Ellington, CT	860	06029
Ellinwood, KS	620	67526
Ellis, KS	785	67637
Ellisville, MS	601, 769	39437
Ellisville, MO	636	63011, 63021, 63038
Ellsworth, KS	785	67439
Ellsworth, ME	207	04605
Ellsworth, WI	715, 534	54003, 54010-54011
Ellsworth AFB, SD	605	57706
Ellwood City, PA	724, 878	16117
Elm Grove, WI	262	53122
Elm Springs, AR	479	72728
Elma, NY	585	14059
Elma, WA	360	98541
Elmendorf AFB, AK	907	99505-99506
Elmer, NJ	856	08318
Elmhurst, IL	331, 630	60126
Elmhurst, NY	347, 718	11373, 11380
Elmira, NY	607	14901-14905, 14925
Elmira, OR	541, 458	97437
Elmira Heights, NY	607	14903
Elmont, NY	516	11003
Elmore, AL	334	36025
Elmore, OH	419, 567	43416
Elmsford, NY	914	10523
Elmwood, CT	860	06110, 06133
Elmwood Park, IL	708	60707
Elmwood Park, NJ	201, 551	07407
Elon, NC	336	27244
Elsah, IL	618	62028
Elsmere, KY	859	41018
Elverson, PA	484, 610	19520
Elwood, IN	765	46036
Elwood, NE	308	68937
Ely, MN	218	55731
Ely, NV	775	89301, 89315
Elyria, OH	440	44035-44039
Elysburg, PA	570	17824
Emerado, ND	701	58228
Emeryville, CA	510	94608, 94662
Emigrant, MT	406	59027
Emigsville, PA	717	17318
Eminence, KY	502	40019
Eminence, MO	573	65466
Emlenton, PA	724, 878	16373
Emmaus, PA	484, 610	18049, 18098-18099
Emmetsburg, IA	712	50536
Emmett, ID	208	83617
Emmitsburg, MD	301	21727
Emory, TX	903	75440
Emory, VA	276	24327
Empire, MI	231	49630
Emporia, KS	620	66801
Emporia, VA	434	23847
Emporium, PA	814	15834
Encinitas, CA	760, 442	92023-92024
Encino, CA	818	91316, 91335, 91416, 91426*
Endicott, NY	607	13760-13763
Enfield, CT	860	06082-06083
Enfield, NH	603	03748
Enfield, NC	252	27823
Engelhard, NC	252	27824
England, AR	501	72046

*Partial list of zip codes, including main range

City	Area Code(s)	Zip Code(s)
Englewood, CO	303, 720	80110-80112, 80150-80155*
Englewood, FL	941	34223-34224, 34295
Englewood, NJ	201, 551	07631-07632
Englewood, OH	937	45315, 45322
Englewood Cliffs, NJ	201, 551	07632
English, IN	812	47118
Englishtown, NJ	732, 848	07726
Enid, OK	580	73701-73706
Ennis, MT	406	59729
Ennis, TX	469, 972	75119-75120
Enola, PA	717	17025
Enon, OH	937	45323
Enoree, SC	864	29335
Enosburg Falls, VT	802	05450
Enterprise, AL	334	36330-36331
Enterprise, OR	541, 458	97828
Enumclaw, WA	360	98022
Ephraim, UT	435	84627
Ephrata, PA	717	17522
Ephrata, WA	509	98823
Epping, NH	603	03042
Epps, LA	318	71237
Epworth, IA	563	52045
Erdenheim, PA	215, 267	19038
Erie, CO	303, 720	80516
Erie, IL	309	61250
Erie, KS	620	66733
Erie, MI	734	48133
Erie, PA	814	16501-16515, 16522, 16530*
Erin, TN	931	37061
Erlanger, KY	859	41017-41018
Erving, MA	351, 978	01344
Erwin, TN	423	37650
Escalon, CA	209	95320
Escanaba, MI	906	49829
Escondido, CA	760, 442	92025-92033, 92046
Esopus, NY	845	12429
Espanola, NM	505	87532-87533
Essex, CT	860	06426
Essex, MD	410	21221
Essex Junction, VT	802	05451-05453
Essexville, MI	989	48732
Essington, PA	484, 610	19029
Estancia, NM	505	87009, 87016
Estero, FL	239	33928
Estes Park, CO	970	80511, 80517
Estherville, IA	712	51334
Estill, SC	803	29918, 29939
Euclid, OH	216	44117-44119, 44123, 44132*
Eudora, AR	870	71640
Eufaula, AL	334	36027, 36072
Eufaula, OK	918	74432, 74461
Eugene, OR	541, 458	97401-97408, 97412, 97440*
Euless, TX	682, 817	76039-76040
Eunice, LA	337	70535
Eureka, CA	707	95501-95503, 95534
Eureka, IL	309	61530
Eureka, KS	620	67045
Eureka, MO	636	63025
Eureka, MT	406	59917
Eureka, NV	775	89316
Eureka Springs, AR	479	72631-72632
Eustis, FL	352	32726-32727, 32736
Eutaw, AL	205	35462
Evans, GA	706, 762	30809
Evans City, PA	724, 878	16033
Evanston, IL	224, 847	60201-60204, 60208-60209
Evanston, WY	307	82930-82931
Evansville, IN	812	47701-47750
Evansville, WI	608	53536
Evansville, WY	307	82636
Eveleth, MN	218	55734
Everett, MA	617, 857	02149
Everett, PA	814	15537
Everett, WA	425	98201-98208
Evergreen, AL	251	36401
Evergreen, CO	303, 720	80437-80439
Evergreen Park, IL	708	60805
Ewa Beach, HI	808	96706
Ewing, NJ	609	08618, 08628, 08638
Excelsior, MN	952	55331
Excelsior Springs, MO	816	64024
Exeter, CA	559	93221
Exeter, NH	603	03833
Exeter, PA	570	18643
Exeter, RI	401	02822
Export, PA	724, 878	15632
Exton, PA	484, 610	19341, 19353
Eynon, PA	570	18403

F

City	Area Code(s)	Zip Code(s)
Fabens, TX	915	79838
Fair Haven, VT	802	05731, 05743
Fair Lawn, NJ	201, 551	07410
Fair Oaks, CA	916	95628
Fairbanks, AK	907	99701-99716, 99767, 99775*
Fairborn, OH	937	45324, 45431
Fairburn, GA	470, 770	30213
Fairbury, NE	402	68352
Fairchild AFB, WA	509	99011
Fairfax, SC	803	29827
Fairfax, VA	571, 703	20151-20153, 22030-22039
Fairfax Station, VA	571, 703	22039
Fairfield, AL	205	35064
Fairfield, CA	707	94533-94535, 94585
Fairfield, CT	203	06430-06432
Fairfield, ID	208	83322, 83327
Fairfield, IL	618	62837
Fairfield, IA	641	52556-52557
Fairfield, ME	207	04937
Fairfield, MT	406	59436
Fairfield, NJ	862, 973	07004
Fairfield, OH	513	45011-45014, 45018
Fairfield, PA	717	17320
Fairfield, TX	903	75840
Fairfield, VT	802	05455
Fairfield Glade, TN	931	38555-38558
Fairgrove, MI	989	48733
Fairhaven, MA	508, 774	02719
Fairhope, AL	251	36532-36533
Fairlawn, OH	234, 330	44313, 44333-44334
Fairlee, VT	802	05045
Fairless Hills, PA	215, 267	19030
Fairmont, MN	507	56031, 56075
Fairmont, MT	406	59711
Fairmont, WV	304	26554-26555
Fairplay, CO	719	80432, 80440, 80456
Fairport, NY	585	14450
Fairport Harbor, OH	440	44077
Fairton, NJ	856	08320
Fairview, NJ	201, 551	07022
Fairview, OK	580	73737
Fairview, OR	503, 971	97024
Fairview, PA	814	16415
Fairview Heights, IL	618	62208, 62232
Fairview Park, OH	440	44126
Fairview Village, PA	484, 610	19409
Fajardo, PR	787, 939	00738
Falconer, NY	716	14733
Falfurrias, TX	361	78355
Fall Creek, WI	715, 534	54742
Fall River, MA	508, 774	02720-02726
Fall River, WI	920	53932
Fallbrook, CA	760, 442	92028, 92088
Fallon, NV	775	89406-89407, 89496
Falls Church, VA	571, 703	22040-22047
Falls City, NE	402	68355
Fallsburg, NY	845	12733
Fallston, MD	410	21047
Falmouth, KY	859	41040
Falmouth, ME	207	04105
Falmouth, MA	508, 774	02540-02543
Fanwood, NJ	908	07023
Far Hills, NJ	908	07931
Far Rockaway, NY	347, 718	11096, 11690-11697
Fargo, ND	701	58102-58109, 58121-58126
Faribault, MN	507	55021
Farina, IL	618	62838
Farmers Branch, TX	469, 972	75234, 75244
Farmerville, LA	318	71241
Farmingdale, NJ	732, 848	07727
Farmingdale, NY	631	11735-11737, 11774
Farmington, CT	860	06030-06034, 06085
Farmington, ME	207	04911, 04938
Farmington, MI	248, 947	48331-48336
Farmington, MN	651	55024
Farmington, MO	573	63640
Farmington, NH	603	03835
Farmington, NM	505	87401-87402, 87499
Farmington, NY	585	14425
Farmington, PA	724, 878	15437
Farmington, UT	801, 385	84025
Farmington Hills, MI	248, 947	48331-48336
Farmingville, NY	631	11738
Farmville, NC	252	27828
Farmville, VA	434	23901, 23909, 23943
Farnhamville, IA	515	50538
Farragut, TN	865	37922
Farwell, TX	806	79325
Faulkner, MD	301	20632
Faulkton, SD	605	57438
Fayette, AL	205	35555
Fayette, IA	563	52142
Fayette, MS	601, 769	39069, 39081
Fayette, MO	660	65248
Fayetteville, AR	479	72701-72704
Fayetteville, GA	470, 770	30214-30215, 30232
Fayetteville, NY	315	13066
Fayetteville, NC	910	28301-28314
Fayetteville, PA	717	17222
Fayetteville, TN	931	37334
Fayetteville, WV	304	25840
Feasterville, PA	215, 267	19053
Federal Way, WA	253	98001-98003, 98023, 98063*
Federalsburg, MD	410	21632
Feeding Hills, MA	413	01030
Felton, DE	302	19943
Fennimore, WI	608	53809
Fenton, MI	810	48430
Fenton, MO	636	63026, 63099
Fenwick, WV	304	26202
Ferdinand, IN	812	47532
Fergus Falls, MN	218	56537-56538
Ferguson, MO	314	63135-63136, 63145
Fernandina Beach, FL	904	32034-32035
Ferndale, CA	707	95536
Ferndale, MI	248, 947	48220
Ferndale, WA	360	98248
Ferriday, LA	318	71334
Ferrisburg, VT	802	05456
Ferrum, VA	540	24088
Ferrysburg, MI	616	49409
Fessenden, ND	701	58438
Festus, MO	636	63028
Fillmore, UT	435	84631
Fincastle, VA	540	24090
Findlay, OH	419, 567	45839-45840
Finksburg, MD	410	21048
Finley, ND	701	58230
Finleyville, PA	724, 878	15332
Firebaugh, CA	559	93622
Firth, ID	208	83236
Fisher Island, FL	305, 786	33109, 33139
Fishers, IN	317	46038
Fishersville, VA	540	22939
Fishkill, NY	845	12524
Fiskeville, RI	401	02823
Fitchburg, MA	351, 978	01420
Fitzgerald, GA	229	31750
Flagler Beach, FL	386	32136, 32151
Flagstaff, AZ	928	86001-86004, 86011, 86015*
Flanders, NJ	862, 973	07836
Flandreau, SD	605	57028
Flasher, ND	701	58535
Flat Rock, NC	828	28731
Flatonia, TX	361	78941
Fleetwood, PA	484, 610	19522
Flemingsburg, KY	606	41041
Flemington, NJ	908	08822
Fletcher, NC	828	28732
Fletcher, OH	937	45326
Flint, MI	810	48501-48509, 48519, 48529*
Flintstone, GA	706, 762	30725
Flippin, AR	870	72634
Flora, IL	618	62839
Flora, MS	601, 769	39071
Floral Park, NY	516	11001-11005
Florence, AL	256	35630-35634
Florence, AZ	520	85232, 85279
Florence, CO	719	81226, 81290
Florence, KY	859	41022, 41042
Florence, MA	413	01062
Florence, MS	601, 769	39073
Florence, NJ	609	08518

**Partial list of zip codes, including main range*

City	Area Code(s)	Zip Code(s)
Florence, OR	541, 458	97439
Florence, SC	843	29501-29506
Florence, WI	715, 534	54121
Floresville, TX	830	78114
Florham Park, NJ	862, 973	07932
Florida, NY	845	10921
Florida City, FL	305, 786	33034
Florien, LA	318	71429
Florissant, CO	719	80816
Florissant, MO	314	63031-63034
Flourtown, PA	215, 267	19031
Flower Mound, TX	469, 972	75022, 75027-75028
Flowery Branch, GA	470, 770	30542
Flowood, MS	601, 769	39208, 39232
Floyd, VA	540	24091
Floydada, TX	806	79235
Flushing, MI	810	48433
Flushing, NY	347, 718	11351-11381, 11385-11386*
Fogelsville, PA	484, 610	18051
Folcroft, PA	484, 610	19032
Foley, AL	251	36535-36536
Foley, MN	320	56329, 56357
Folkston, GA	912	31537
Folsom, CA	916	95630, 95762-95763
Folsom, LA	985	70437
Folsom, NJ	609	08037
Fond du Lac, WI	920	54935-54937
Fonda, NY	518	12068
Fontana, CA	951	92334-92337
Fontana, WI	262	53125
Fontana Dam, NC	828	28733
Foothill Ranch, CA	949	92610
Ford, KS	620	67842
Fordland, MO	417	65652
Fords, NJ	732, 848	08863
Fordyce, AR	870	71742
Forest, MS	601, 769	39074
Forest, OH	419, 567	45843
Forest, VA	434	24551
Forest City, IA	641	50436
Forest City, NC	828	28043
Forest City, PA	570	18421
Forest Grove, OR	503, 971	97116
Forest Hill, MD	410	21050
Forest Hills, NY	347, 718	11375
Forest Lake, MN	651	55025
Forest Park, GA	404, 470	30297-30298
Forest Park, IL	708	60130
Forestville, CA	707	95436
Forestville, CT	860	06010
Forked River, NJ	609	08731
Forks, WA	360	98331
Forksville, PA	570	18616
Forman, ND	701	58032
Forrest City, AR	870	72335-72336
Forsyth, GA	478	31029
Forsyth, MO	417	65653
Forsyth, MT	406	59327
Fort Atkinson, WI	920	53538
Fort Belvoir, VA	571, 703	22060
Fort Benning, GA	706, 762	31905, 31995
Fort Benton, MT	406	59442
Fort Bliss, TX	915	79906-79908, 79916-79918
Fort Bragg, CA	707	95437, 95488
Fort Bragg, NC	910	28307-28310
Fort Buchanan, PR	787, 939	00920-00922, 00934-00936
Fort Calhoun, NE	402	68023
Fort Campbell, KY	270	42223
Fort Carson, CO	719	80913
Fort Collins, CO	970	80521-80528, 80553
Fort Davis, TX	915	79734
Fort Defiance, AZ	928	86504, 86549
Fort Deposit, AL	334	36032
Fort Dix, NJ	609	08640
Fort Dodge, IA	515	50501
Fort Dodge, KS	620	67801
Fort Drum, NY	315	13602-13603
Fort Edward, NY	518	12828
Fort Eustis, VA	757	23604
Fort Gaines, GA	229	31751
Fort Gibson, OK	918	74434
Fort Gordon, GA	706, 762	30905
Fort Harrison, MT	406	59636
Fort Hood, TX	254	76544
Fort Huachuca, AZ	520	85613, 85670
Fort Irwin, CA	760, 442	92310
Fort Jackson, SC	803	29207
Fort Jones, CA	530	96032
Fort Kent, ME	207	04741-04743
Fort Knox, KY	502	40121
Fort Laramie, WY	307	82212
Fort Lauderdale, FL	754, 954	33301-33340, 33345-33351*
Fort Leavenworth, KS	913	66027
Fort Lee, NJ	201, 551	07024
Fort Lee, VA	804	23801
Fort Leonard Wood, MO	573	65473
Fort Lewis, WA	253	98433
Fort Loramie, OH	937	45845
Fort Madison, IA	319	52627
Fort McPherson, GA	404, 470	30310, 30330
Fort Meade, MD	301	20755
Fort Meade, SD	605	57741
Fort Mill, SC	803	29708, 29715-29716
Fort Mitchell, KY	859	41017
Fort Monmouth, NJ	732, 848	07703
Fort Monroe, VA	757	23651
Fort Morgan, CO	970	80701, 80705, 80742
Fort Myer, VA	571, 703	22211
Fort Myers, FL	239	33901-33919, 33965, 33994
Fort Myers Beach, FL	239	33931-33932
Fort Oglethorpe, GA	706, 762	30742
Fort Payne, AL	256	35967-35968
Fort Pierce, FL	772	34945-34954, 34979-34988
Fort Pierre, SD	605	57532
Fort Polk, LA	337	71459
Fort Recovery, OH	419, 567	45846
Fort Richardson, AK	907	99504-99505
Fort Riley, KS	785	66442
Fort Rucker, AL	334	36362
Fort Sam Houston, TX	210	78234
Fort Scott, KS	620	66701
Fort Shafter, HI	808	96858
Fort Sill, OK	580	73503
Fort Smith, AR	479	72901-72908, 72913-72919
Fort Smith, MT	406	59035
Fort Snelling, MN	612	55111
Fort Stewart, GA	912	31313-31315
Fort Stockton, TX	915	79735
Fort Story, VA	757	23459
Fort Sumner, NM	505	88119
Fort Supply, OK	580	73841
Fort Thomas, KY	859	41075
Fort Totten, ND	701	58335
Fort Valley, GA	478	31030
Fort Wainwright, AK	907	99703
Fort Walton Beach, FL	850	32547-32549
Fort Washington, MD	301	20744, 20749-20750
Fort Washington, PA	215, 267	19034, 19048-19049
Fort Wayne, IN	260	46801-46809, 46814-46819*
Fort Worth, TX	682, 817	76101-76140, 76147-76150*
Fort Yates, ND	701	58538
Fortine, MT	406	59918
Fortuna, CA	707	95540
Forty Fort, PA	570	18704
Fossil, OR	541, 458	97830
Foster City, CA	650	94404
Fostoria, OH	419, 567	44830
Fountain Hills, AZ	480	85268-85269
Fountain Inn, SC	864	29644
Fountain Valley, CA	714	92708, 92728
Four Oaks, NC	919	27524
Fowler, CA	559	93625
Fowler, IN	765	47944, 47984-47986
Fowlerville, MI	517	48836
Fox Lake, WI	920	53933
Foxboro, MA	508, 774	02035
Foxborough, MA	508, 774	02035
Frackville, PA	570	17931-17932
Framingham, MA	508, 774	01701-01705
Francesville, IN	219	47946
Frankenmuth, MI	989	48734, 48787
Frankfort, IL	815	60423
Frankfort, IN	765	46041
Frankfort, KY	502	40601-40604, 40618-40622
Frankfort, MI	231	49635
Frankfort, NY	315	13340
Franklin, GA	706, 762	30217
Franklin, ID	208	83237
Franklin, IN	317	46131
Franklin, KY	270	42134-42135
Franklin, LA	337	70538
Franklin, MA	508, 774	02038
Franklin, NE	308	68939
Franklin, NH	603	03235
Franklin, NJ	862, 973	07416
Franklin, NC	828	28734, 28744
Franklin, OH	513	45005, 45342
Franklin, PA	814	16323
Franklin, TN	615	37064-37069
Franklin, TX	979	77856
Franklin, VA	757	23851
Franklin, WV	304	26807
Franklin, WI	414	53132
Franklin Furnace, OH	740	45629
Franklin Lakes, NJ	201, 551	07417
Franklin Park, IL	224, 847	60131, 60398
Franklin Springs, GA	706, 762	30639
Franklin Square, NY	516	11010
Franklinton, LA	985	70438
Franklinton, NC	919	27525
Franklinville, NY	585	14737
Franksville, WI	262	53126
Frankton, IN	765	46044
Franktown, CO	303, 720	80116
Fraser, MI	586	48026
Frazee, MN	218	56544
Frazer, PA	484, 610	19355
Frazeysburg, OH	740	43822
Frederic, MI	989	49733
Frederica, DE	302	19946
Frederick, CO	303, 720	80504, 80516, 80530
Frederick, MD	301	21701-21705, 21709
Frederick, OK	580	73542
Fredericksburg, PA	717	17026
Fredericksburg, TX	830	78624
Fredericksburg, VA	540	22401-22408, 22412
Fredericktown, MO	573	63645
Fredericktown, OH	740	43019
Fredonia, AZ	928	86022, 86052
Fredonia, KS	620	66736
Fredonia, NY	716	14063
Fredonia, WI	262	53021
Freeburg, IL	618	62243
Freeburg, MO	573	65035
Freedom, WY	307	83120
Freehold, NJ	732, 848	07728
Freeland, MI	989	48623
Freeland, PA	570	18224
Freeland, WA	360	98249
Freeport, IL	815	61032
Freeport, ME	207	04032-04034
Freeport, MI	616	49325
Freeport, NY	516	11520
Freeport, PA	724, 878	16229
Freeport, TX	979	77541-77542
Fremont, CA	510	94536-94539, 94555
Fremont, IN	260	46737
Fremont, MI	231	49412-49413
Fremont, NE	402	68025-68026
Fremont, OH	419, 567	43420
French Camp, CA	209	95231
French Creek, WV	304	26218-26219
French Lick, IN	812	47432
Frenchburg, KY	606	40322
Frenchtown, NJ	908	08825
Fresh Meadows, NY	347, 718	11365-11366
Fresno, CA	559	93650, 93701-93729, 93740*
Friday Harbor, WA	360	98250
Fridley, MN	763	55421, 55432
Friendship, WI	608	53927, 53934
Friendswood, TX	281, 832	77546-77549
Friona, TX	806	79035
Frisco, CO	970	80443
Frisco, TX	469, 972	75034-75035
Fritch, TX	806	79036
Front Royal, VA	540	22630
Frostburg, MD	301	21532
Frostproof, FL	863	33843
Fruita, CO	970	81521
Fruitland, ID	208	83619
Fruitport, MI	231	49415
Fullerton, CA	714	92831-92838
Fullerton, NE	308	68638
Fulton, AL	334	36446
Fulton, IL	815	61252
Fulton, MS	662	38843
Fulton, MO	573	65251

*Partial list of zip codes, including main range

City	Area Code(s)	Zip Code(s)
Fulton, NY	315	13069
Fultonville, NY	518	12016, 12072
Fuquay-Varina, NC	919	27526

G

City	Area Code(s)	Zip Code(s)
Gabriels, NY	518	12939
Gadsden, AL	256	35901-35907
Gaffney, SC	864	29340-29342
Gahanna, OH	614	43230
Gail, TX	806	79738
Gainesboro, TN	931	38562
Gainesville, FL	352	32601-32614, 32627, 32635*
Gainesville, GA	470, 678, 770	30501-30507
Gainesville, MO	417	65655
Gainesville, TX	940	76240-76241
Gaithersburg, MD	240, 301	20877-20886, 20898-20899
Galax, VA	276	24333
Galena, IL	815	61036
Galena, KS	620	66739
Galena, MD	410	21635
Galena, MO	417	65624, 65656
Galena Park, TX	713, 832	77547
Galesburg, IL	309	61401-61402
Galesburg, KS	620	66740
Galion, OH	419, 567	44833
Gallatin, MO	660	64640
Gallatin, TN	615	37066
Gallatin Gateway, MT	406	59730
Gallaway, TN	901	38036
Galliano, LA	985	70354
Gallipolis, OH	740	45631
Gallitzin, PA	814	16641
Galloway, NJ	609	08201, 08205
Gallup, NM	505	87301-87305, 87310, 87317*
Galt, CA	209	95632
Galveston, TX	409	77550-77555
Gambier, OH	740	43022
Ganado, AZ	928	86505, 86540
Gann Valley, SD	605	57341
Gap, PA	717	17527
Garden City, GA	912	31405-31408, 31415-31418
Garden City, KS	620	67846, 67868
Garden City, MI	734	48135-48136
Garden City, NY	516	11530-11531, 11535-11536*
Garden City, TX	915	79739
Garden City Park, NY	516	11040
Garden Grove, CA	714	92840-92846
Gardena, CA	310, 323, 424	90247-90249
Gardiner, ME	207	04345
Gardner, IL	815	60424
Gardner, KS	913	66030-66031
Gardner, MA	351, 978	01440
Gardners, PA	717	17324
Gardnerville, NV	775	89410
Garfield, NJ	862, 973	07026
Garfield Heights, OH	216	44105, 44125-44128
Garland, NC	910	28441
Garland, TX	469, 972	75040-75049
Garner, IA	641	50438
Garner, NC	919	27529
Garnett, KS	785	66032
Garretson, SD	605	57030
Garrett, IN	260	46738
Garrettsville, OH	234, 330	44231
Garrison, NY	845	10524
Garrison, ND	701	58540
Garwood, NJ	908	07027
Gary, IN	219	46401-46411
Garyville, LA	985	70051, 70076
Gaston, OR	503, 971	97119
Gastonia, NC	704, 980	28052-28056
Gate City, VA	276	24251
Gatesville, NC	252	27938
Gatesville, TX	254	76528, 76596-76599
Gatlinburg, TN	865	37738
Gautier, MS	228	39553
Gaylord, MI	989	49734-49735
Gaylord, MN	507	55334
Gearhart, OR	503, 971	97138
Geismar, LA	225	70734
Geneseo, IL	309	61254
Geneseo, NY	585	14454
Geneva, AL	334	36340
Geneva, IL	331, 630	60134
Geneva, NE	402	68361
Geneva, NY	315	14456
Geneva, OH	440	44041
Genoa, OH	419, 567	43430
Genoa City, WI	262	53128
Gentry, AR	479	72734
George, IA	712	51237
George West, TX	361	78022
Georgetown, CO	303, 720	80444
Georgetown, DE	302	19947
Georgetown, GA	229	31754
Georgetown, KY	502	40324
Georgetown, MA	351, 978	01833
Georgetown, NY	315	13072, 13129
Georgetown, OH	937	45121
Georgetown, SC	843	29440-29442
Georgetown, TX	512	78626-78628
Gering, NE	308	69341
Germantown, MD	301	20874-20876
Germantown, OH	937	45325-45327
Germantown, TN	901	38138-38139, 38183
Germantown, WI	262	53022
Gervais, OR	503, 971	97026
Gettysburg, PA	717	17325-17326
Gettysburg, SD	605	57442
Getzville, NY	716	14068
Geyserville, CA	707	95441
Gibbon, MN	507	55335
Gibbon, NE	308	68840
Gibbsboro, NJ	856	08026
Gibbstown, NJ	856	08027
Gibson, GA	706, 762	30810
Gibson City, IL	217	60936
Gibsonia, PA	724, 878	15044
Gibsonville, NC	336	27249
Giddings, TX	979	78942
Gig Harbor, WA	253	98329-98335
Gilbert, AZ	480	85233-85234, 85296-85299
Gilbertsville, KY	270	42044
Gilford, NH	603	03247-03249
Gillett, AR	870	72055
Gillette, WY	307	82716-82718, 82731-82732
Gilman, CT	860	06336
Gilmer, TX	903	75644-75645
Gilmore City, IA	515	50541
Gilroy, CA	408	95020-95021
Girard, KS	620	66743
Girard, OH	234, 330	44420
Girard, PA	814	16417
Girdwood, AK	907	99587, 99693
Gladstone, MI	906	49837
Gladstone, MO	816	64116-64119, 64155-64156*
Gladstone, NJ	908	07934
Gladwin, MI	989	48624
Gladwyne, PA	484, 610	19035
Glasgow, KY	270	42141-42142, 42156
Glasgow, MT	406	59230-59231
Glassboro, NJ	856	08028
Glassport, PA	412, 878	15045
Glastonbury, CT	860	06033
Glen Allen, VA	804	23058-23060
Glen Arbor, MI	231	49636
Glen Arm, MD	410	21057
Glen Burnie, MD	410	21060-21062
Glen Cove, NY	516	11542
Glen Dale, WV	304	26038
Glen Echo, MD	301	20812
Glen Ellen, CA	707	95442
Glen Ellyn, IL	331, 630	60137-60138
Glen Gardner, NJ	908	08826
Glen Head, NY	516	11545
Glen Jean, WV	304	25846
Glen Lyn, VA	540	24093
Glen Raven, NC	336	27215
Glen Riddle, PA	484, 610	19037, 19063
Glen Ridge, NJ	862, 973	07028
Glen Rock, NJ	201, 551	07452
Glen Rock, PA	717	17327
Glen Rose, TX	254	76043
Glencoe, IL	224, 847	60022
Glencoe, MN	320	55336
Glendale, AZ	623	85301-85313, 85318
Glendale, CA	818	91201-91210, 91214, 91221*
Glendale, CO	303, 720	80246
Glendale, NY	347, 718	11385
Glendale, WI	414	53209-53212, 53217
Glendale Heights, IL	331, 630	60139
Glendive, MT	406	59330
Glendora, CA	626	91740-91741
Glendora, NJ	856	08029
Gleneden Beach, OR	541, 458	97388
Glenelg, MD	410	21737
Glenmont, OH	234, 330	44628
Glenmoore, PA	484, 610	19343
Glennallen, AK	907	99588
Glennville, GA	912	30427
Glens Falls, NY	518	12801-12804
Glenshaw, PA	412, 878	15116
Glenside, PA	215, 267	19038
Glenview, IL	224, 847	60025-60026
Glenville, NY	518	12302, 12325
Glenville, WV	304	26351
Glenwillow, OH	440	44139
Glenwood, IL	708	60425
Glenwood, IA	712	51534
Glenwood, MN	320	56334
Glenwood Springs, CO	970	81601-81602
Glidden, IA	712	51443
Glide, OR	541, 458	97443
Globe, AZ	928	85501-85502
Glorieta, NM	505	87535
Gloucester, MA	351, 978	01930-01931
Gloucester, NJ	856	08030-08031
Gloucester, VA	804	23061
Gloucester Point, VA	804	23062
Gloversville, NY	518	12078
Gnadenhutten, OH	740	44629
Godfrey, IL	618	62035
Godwin, NC	910	28344
Goffstown, NH	603	03045-03046
Golconda, IL	618	62938
Golconda, NV	480	89414
Gold Beach, OR	541, 458	97444
Gold Canyon, AZ	480	85218-85219
Gold Hill, NV	775	89440
Gold Hill, OR	541, 458	97525
Gold River, CA	916	95670
Golden, CO	303, 720	80401-80403, 80419
Golden, MS	662	38847
Golden Valley, MN	763	55416, 55422, 55426-55427
Goldendale, WA	509	98620
Goldfield, NV	775	89013
Goldsboro, NC	919	27530-27534
Goldthwaite, TX	915	76844
Goleta, CA	805	93110-93111, 93116-93118*
Golf, IL	224, 847	60029
Goliad, TX	361	77963
Gonzales, CA	831	93926
Gonzales, LA	225	70707, 70737
Gonzales, TX	830	78629
Goochland, VA	804	23063
Goodfellow AFB, TX	915	76908
Goodfield, IL	309	61742
Gooding, ID	208	83330
Goodland, KS	785	67735
Goodlettsville, TN	615	37070-37072
Goodman, MS	662	39079
Goodrich, MI	810	48438
Goodwell, OK	580	73939
Goodyear, AZ	623	85338
Gordo, AL	205	35466
Gordon, NE	308	69343
Gordonsville, VA	540	22942
Gordonville, TX	903	76245
Gore, OK	918	74435
Gorham, ME	207	04038
Gorham, NH	603	03581
Goshen, IN	574	46526-46528
Goshen, NY	845	10924
Goulds, FL	305, 786	33170
Gouverneur, NY	315	13642
Gove, KS	785	67736
Gowanda, NY	716	14070
Grabill, IN	260	46741
Graceville, FL	850	32440
Gracewood, GA	706, 762	30812
Grady, AR	870	71644
Grafton, IL	618	62037
Grafton, MA	508, 774	01519
Grafton, ND	701	58237
Grafton, OH	440	44044
Grafton, WV	304	26354
Grafton, WI	262	53024

Partial list of zip codes, including main range

City	Area Code(s)	Zip Code(s)
Graham, NC	336	27253
Graham, TX	940	76450
Grain Valley, MO	816	64029
Grambling, LA	318	71245
Gramercy, LA	225	70052
Gramling, SC	864	29348
Grampian, PA	814	16838
Granada Hills, CA	818	91344, 91394
Granbury, TX	682, 817	76048-76049
Granby, CO	970	80446
Granby, CT	860	06035, 06090
Grand Blanc, MI	810	48439
Grand Canyon, AZ	928	86023
Grand Chenier, LA	337	70643
Grand Forks, ND	701	58201-58208
Grand Forks AFB, ND	701	58204-58205
Grand Haven, MI	616	49417
Grand Island, NE	308	68801-68803
Grand Island, NY	716	14072
Grand Junction, CO	970	81501-81506
Grand Junction, MI	616	49056
Grand Ledge, MI	517	48837
Grand Marais, MN	218	55604
Grand Marsh, WI	608	53936
Grand Portage, MN	218	55605
Grand Prairie, TX	469, 972	75050-75054
Grand Rapids, MI	616	49501-49518, 49523-49525*
Grand Rapids, MN	218	55730, 55744-55745
Grand Rapids, OH	419, 567	43522
Grand Terrace, CA	909	92313, 92324
Grandview, MO	816	64030
Grandview, WA	509	98930
Grandville, MI	616	49418, 49468
Granger, IN	574	46530
Granger, WA	509	98932
Grangeville, ID	208	83530-83531
Granite, OK	580	73547
Granite City, IL	618	62040
Granite Falls, MN	320	56241
Granite Falls, NC	828	28630
Granite Quarry, NC	704, 980	28072
Graniteville, SC	803	29829
Graniteville, VT	802	05654
Grant, CO	303, 720	80448
Grant, MI	231	49327
Grant, NE	308	69140
Grant City, MO	660	64456
Grantham, PA	717	17027
Grants, NM	505	87020
Grants Pass, OR	541, 458	97526-97528, 97543
Grantsboro, NC	252	28529
Grantsburg, WI	715, 534	54840
Grantsville, MD	301	21536
Grantsville, WV	304	26147
Grantville, PA	717	17028
Granville, IL	815	61326
Granville, MA	413	01034
Granville, NY	518	12832
Granville, OH	740	43023
Grapevine, TX	682, 817	76051, 76092, 76099
Grass Valley, CA	530	95945, 95949
Graterford, PA	484, 610	19426
Gratz, PA	717	17030
Grawn, MI	231	49637
Gray, GA	478	31032
Gray, KY	606	40734
Gray, LA	985	70359
Grayling, MI	989	49738-49739
Grayslake, IL	224, 847	60030
Grayson, KY	606	41143
Grayville, IL	618	62844
Great Barrington, MA	413	01230
Great Bend, KS	620	67530
Great Falls, MT	406	59401-59406
Great Falls, VA	571, 703	22066
Great Lakes, IL	224, 847	60088
Great Neck, NY	516	11020-11027
Greeley, CO	970	80631-80634, 80638-80639
Greeley, NE	308	68842
Green Bay, WI	920	54301-54313, 54324, 54344
Green Brook, NJ	732, 848	08812
Green Cove Springs, FL	904	32043
Green Forest, AR	870	72638
Green Island, NY	518	12183
Green Lake, WI	920	54941
Green Lane, PA	215, 267	18054
Green Pond, AL	205	35074

City	Area Code(s)	Zip Code(s)
Green River, UT	435	84515, 84525, 84540
Green River, WY	307	82935-82938
Green Springs, OH	419, 567	44836
Green Valley, AZ	520	85614, 85622
Greenbelt, MD	301	20768-20771
Greenbrae, CA	415	94904, 94914
Greencastle, IN	765	46135
Greencastle, PA	717	17225
Greendale, WI	414	53129
Greene, NY	607	13778
Greeneville, TN	423	37743-37745
Greenfield, IN	317	46140
Greenfield, IA	641	50849
Greenfield, MA	413	01301-01302
Greenfield, MO	417	65661
Greenfield, NH	603	03047
Greenfield, OH	937	45123, 45165
Greenfield, WI	414	53219-53221, 53227-53228
Greenland, NH	603	03840
Greenlawn, NY	631	11740
Greenport, NY	631	11944
Greens Farms, CT	203	06436
Greensboro, AL	334	36744
Greensboro, GA	706, 762	30642
Greensboro, NC	336	27401-27420, 27425-27429*
Greensburg, IN	812	47240
Greensburg, KS	620	67054
Greensburg, KY	270	42743
Greensburg, LA	225	70441
Greensburg, PA	724, 878	15601, 15605-15606
Greenup, KY	606	41144
Greenvale, NY	516	11548
Greenville, AL	334	36037
Greenville, DE	302	19807
Greenville, GA	706, 762	30222
Greenville, IL	618	62246
Greenville, KY	270	42345
Greenville, MI	616	48838
Greenville, MS	662	38701-38704, 38731
Greenville, MO	573	63944
Greenville, NC	252	27833-27836, 27858
Greenville, OH	937	45331
Greenville, PA	724, 878	16125
Greenville, RI	401	02828
Greenville, SC	864	29601-29617, 29698
Greenville, TX	903	75401-75404
Greenwell Springs, LA	225	70739
Greenwich, CT	203	06830-06832, 06836
Greenwood, AR	479	72936
Greenwood, DE	302	19950
Greenwood, IN	317	46142-46143
Greenwood, MS	662	38930, 38935
Greenwood, SC	864	29646-29649
Greenwood, WI	715, 534	54437
Greenwood Village, CO	303, 720	80110-80112, 80121, 80150*
Greer, SC	864	29650-29652
Gregory, SD	605	57533
Grenada, MS	662	38901-38902
Grenloch, NJ	856	08032
Gresham, OR	503, 971	97030, 97080
Gretna, LA	504	70053-70056
Gretna, NE	402	68028
Gretna, VA	434	24557
Greybull, WY	307	82426
Greystone Park, NJ	862, 973	07950
Griffin, GA	470, 770	30223-30224
Griffith, IN	219	46319
Griggsville, IL	217	62340
Grinnell, IA	641	50112, 50177
Groesbeck, TX	254	76642
Grosse Pointe, MI	313	48224, 48230, 48236
Grosse Pointe Farms, MI	313	48230, 48236
Grosse Pointe Park, MI	313	48215, 48224, 48230, 48236
Grosse Pointe Shores, MI	313	48230, 48236
Groton, CT	860	06340, 06349
Groton, MA	351, 978	01450, 01470-01471
Groton, VT	802	05046
Grove, OK	918	74344-74345
Grove City, OH	614	43123
Grove City, PA	724, 878	16127
Grove Hill, AL	251	36451
Groveland, FL	352	34736
Groveport, OH	614	43125, 43195-43199
Grover, NC	704, 980	28073
Grover Beach, CA	805	93433, 93483
Groves, TX	409	77619

City	Area Code(s)	Zip Code(s)
Groveton, TX	936	75845
Grovetown, GA	706, 762	30813
Grundy, VA	276	24614
Grundy Center, IA	319	50638
Gruver, TX	806	79040
Guayama, PR	787, 939	00784-00785
Guerneville, CA	707	95446
Guilderland, NY	518	12084
Guildhall, VT	802	05905
Guilford, CT	203	06437
Guilford, ME	207	04443
Guin, AL	205	35563
Gulf Breeze, FL	850	32561-32566
Gulf Shores, AL	251	36542, 36547
Gulfport, FL	727	33707, 33711, 33737
Gulfport, MS	228	39501-39507
Gun Barrel City, TX	903	75147
Gunnison, CO	970	81230-81231, 81247
Gunnison, UT	435	84634
Guntersville, AL	256	35976
Guntown, MS	662	38849
Gurdon, AR	870	71743
Gurnee, IL	224, 847	60031
Gustavus, AK	907	99826
Guthrie, OK	405	73044
Guthrie, TX	806	79236
Guthrie Center, IA	641	50115
Guymon, OK	580	73942
Gwynedd, PA	215, 267	19436
Gwynedd Valley, PA	215, 267	19437

H

City	Area Code(s)	Zip Code(s)
Hackensack, NJ	201, 551	07601-07602
Hackettstown, NJ	908	07840
Haddam, CT	860	06438
Haddonfield, NJ	856	08033
Hadley, MA	413	01035
Hagerman, ID	208	83332
Hagerman, NM	505	88232
Hagerstown, MD	240, 301	21740-21742, 21746-21749
Hahnville, LA	985	70057
Hailey, ID	208	83333
Haines, AK	907	99827
Haines City, FL	863	33844-33845
Hainesport, NJ	609	08036
Haledon, NJ	862, 973	07508, 07538
Hales Corners, WI	414	53130-53132
Haleyville, AL	205	35565
Half Moon Bay, CA	650	94019
Halifax, MA	339, 781	02338
Halifax, NC	252	27839
Halifax, PA	717	17032
Halifax, VA	434	24558
Hall, NY	585	14463
Hallandale, FL	754, 954	33008-33009
Hallettsville, TX	361	77964
Hallock, MN	218	56728, 56740, 56755
Hallowell, ME	207	04347
Halls, TN	731	38040
Halstad, MN	218	56548
Halstead, KS	316	67056
Haltom City, TX	682, 817	76111, 76117, 76137, 76148*
Ham Lake, MN	763	55304
Hamburg, AR	870	71646
Hamburg, NJ	862, 973	07419
Hamburg, NY	716	14075, 14219
Hamburg, PA	484, 610	19526
Hamden, CT	203	06514-06518
Hamel, MN	763	55340
Hamer, ID	208	83425
Hamilton, AL	205	35570
Hamilton, GA	706, 762	31811
Hamilton, IL	217	62341
Hamilton, MT	406	59840
Hamilton, NJ	609	08609-08611, 08619-08620*
Hamilton, NY	315	13346
Hamilton, OH	513	45011-45026
Hamilton, TX	254	76531
Hamilton Square, NJ	609	08690
Hamlet, NC	910	28345
Hamlin, NY	585	14464
Hamlin, TX	915	79520
Hamlin, WV	304	25523

*Partial list of zip codes, including main range

City	Area Code(s)	Zip Code(s)
Hammond, IN	219	46320-46327
Hammond, LA	985	70401-70404
Hammond, WI	715, 534	54002, 54015
Hammondsport, NY	607	14840
Hammonton, NJ	609	08037
Hampden-Sydney, VA	434	23943
Hampshire, IL	224, 847	60140
Hampstead, MD	410	21074
Hampstead, NH	603	03841
Hampton, AR	870	71744
Hampton, GA	470, 770	30228
Hampton, IA	641	50441
Hampton, NH	603	03842-03843
Hampton, SC	803	29913, 29924
Hampton, VA	757	23605, 23630-23631, 23651*
Hampton Falls, NH	603	03844
Hamptonville, NC	336	27020
Hamtramck, MI	313	48211-48212
Hana, HI	808	96713
Hanahan, SC	843	29406, 29410
Hanceville, AL	256	35077
Hancock, MI	906	49930
Hancock, MN	320	56244
Hancock, WI	715, 534	54943
Hanford, CA	559	93230-93232
Hannibal, MO	573	63401
Hannibal, OH	740	43931
Hanover, IN	812	47243
Hanover, MD	410	21075-21076, 21098
Hanover, NH	603	03755
Hanover, PA	717	17331-17334
Hanover, VA	804	23069
Hanover Park, IL	331, 630	60108, 60133
Hanscom AFB, MA	339, 781	01731
Hanson, MA	339, 781	02341, 02350
Harahan, LA	504	70123
Harbor Beach, MI	989	48441
Harbor City, CA	310, 424	90710
Harbor Springs, MI	231	49737-49740
Harborcreek, PA	814	16421
Harcourt, IA	515	50544
Hardin, IL	618	62047
Hardin, MT	406	59034
Hardinsburg, KY	270	40143
Hardwick, GA	478	31034
Hardwick, VT	802	05843
Hardy, VA	540	24101
Harkers Island, NC	252	28531
Harlan, IA	712	51537, 51593
Harlan, KY	606	40831, 40840
Harlem, GA	706, 762	30814
Harlem, MT	406	59526
Harleysville, PA	215, 267	19438-19441
Harlingen, TX	956	78550-78553
Harlowton, MT	406	59036
Harpers Ferry, IA	563	52146
Harpers Ferry, WV	304	25425
Harrells, NC	910	28444
Harriman, NY	845	10926
Harriman, TN	865	37748
Harrington, DE	302	19952
Harrington Park, NJ	201, 551	07640
Harris, MN	651	55032
Harris, NY	845	12742
Harrisburg, AR	870	72432
Harrisburg, IL	618	62946
Harrisburg, NE	308	69345
Harrisburg, NC	704, 980	28075
Harrisburg, PA	717	17101-17113, 17120-17130*
Harrison, AR	870	72601-72602
Harrison, ID	208	83833, 83842
Harrison, MI	989	48625
Harrison, NE	308	69346
Harrison, NJ	862, 973	07029
Harrison, NY	914	10528
Harrison, OH	513	45030
Harrison Township, MI	586	48045
Harrisonburg, LA	318	71340
Harrisonburg, VA	540	22801-22803, 22807
Harrisonville, MO	816	64701
Harrisville, MI	989	48740
Harrisville, WV	304	26362
Harrodsburg, KY	859	40330
Harrogate, TN	423	37707, 37752
Hart, MI	231	49420
Hartford, AL	334	36344
Hartford, CT	860	06101-06156, 06160-06161*
Hartford, KY	270	42347
Hartford, WI	262	53027
Hartford City, IN	765	47348
Hartington, NE	402	68739
Hartland, ME	207	04943
Hartland, WI	262	53029
Hartsdale, NY	914	10530
Hartselle, AL	256	35640
Hartsville, SC	843	29550-29551
Hartsville, TN	615	37074
Hartville, MO	417	65667
Hartville, OH	234, 330	44632
Hartwell, GA	706, 762	30643
Hartwick, NY	607	13348
Harvard, IL	815	60033
Harvey, IL	708	60426
Harvey, LA	504	70058-70059
Harwich, MA	508, 774	02645
Harwood Heights, IL	708	60656, 60706
Hasbrouck Heights, NJ	201, 551	07604
Haskell, NJ	862, 973	07420
Haskell, TX	940	79521
Hastings, MI	616	49058
Hastings, MN	651	55033
Hastings, NE	402	68901-68902
Hastings-on-Hudson, NY	914	10706
Hatboro, PA	215, 267	19040
Hatfield, MA	413	01038
Hatfield, PA	215, 267	19440
Hato Rey, PR	787, 939	00917-00919
Hattiesburg, MS	601, 769	39401-39407
Haughton, LA	318	71037
Hauppauge, NY	631	11749, 11760, 11788
Havana, IL	309	62644
Haverford, PA	484, 610	19041
Haverhill, MA	351, 978	01830-01835
Haverstraw, NY	845	10927
Havertown, PA	484, 610	19083
Haviland, KS	620	67059
Havre, MT	406	59501
Havre de Grace, MD	410	21078
Haw River, NC	336	27258
Hawaii National Park, HI	808	96718
Hawaiian Gardens, CA	562	90716
Hawesville, KY	270	42348
Hawkins, TX	903	75765
Hawkins, WI	715, 534	54530
Hawkinsville, GA	478	31036
Hawthorn Woods, IL	224, 847	60047
Hawthorne, CA	310, 424	90250-90251
Hawthorne, NV	775	89415
Hawthorne, NJ	862, 973	07506-07507
Hawthorne, NY	914	10532
Hay Springs, NE	308	69347, 69367
Hayden, AZ	520	85235
Hayden, ID	208	83835
Hayden Lake, ID	208	83835
Hayes Center, NE	308	69032
Hayesville, NC	828	28904
Hayesville, OH	419, 567	44838
Haynesville, VA	804	22472
Hayneville, AL	334	36040
Hays, KS	785	67601, 67667
Haysville, KS	316	67060
Hayti, MO	573	63851
Hayti, SD	605	57241
Hayward, CA	510	94540-94546, 94552, 94557
Hayward, WI	715, 534	54843
Hazard, KY	606	41701-41702
Hazel Crest, IL	708	60429
Hazel Park, MI	248, 947	48030
Hazelwood, MO	314	63042-63045, 63135
Hazen, ND	701	58545
Hazlehurst, GA	912	31539
Hazlehurst, MS	601, 769	39083
Hazlet, NJ	732, 848	07730
Hazleton, PA	570	18201-18202
Healdsburg, CA	707	95448
Healy, AK	907	99743, 99755
Healy, KS	620	67850
Heartwell, NE	308	68945
Heath, OH	740	43056
Heathrow, FL	321, 407	32746
Heathsville, VA	804	22473
Hebbronville, TX	361	78361
Heber, CA	760, 442	92249
Heber City, UT	435	84032
Heber Springs, AR	501	72543-72545
Hebron, IL	815	60034
Hebron, KY	859	41048
Hebron, NE	402	68370
Hebron, OH	740	43025, 43098
Hector, MN	320	55342
Hedgesville, WV	304	25427
Heflin, AL	256	36264
Helen, GA	706, 762	30545
Helena, AL	205	35080
Helena, AR	870	72342
Helena, GA	229	31037
Helena, MT	406	59601-59604, 59620-59626
Helena, OK	580	73741
Helenwood, TN	423	37755
Hellertown, PA	484, 610	18055
Hemet, CA	951	92543-92546
Hemphill, TX	409	75948
Hempstead, NY	516	11549-11551
Hempstead, TX	979	77445
Henderson, CO	303, 720	80640
Henderson, KY	270	42419-42420
Henderson, NE	402	68371
Henderson, NV	702	89009-89016, 89052-89053*
Henderson, NC	252	27536-27537
Henderson, TN	731	38340
Henderson, TX	903	75652-75654, 75680
Hendersonville, NC	828	28739, 28791-28793
Hendersonville, TN	615	37075-37077
Hennepin, IL	815	61327
Henniker, NH	603	03242
Henning, TN	731	38041
Henrietta, NY	585	14467
Henrietta, TX	940	76365
Henry, TN	731	38231
Henryetta, OK	918	74437
Henryville, IN	812	47126
Heppner, OR	541, 458	97836
Hercules, CA	510	94547
Hereford, AZ	520	85615
Hereford, TX	806	79045
Herkimer, NY	315	13350
Hermann, MO	573	65041
Hermiston, OR	541, 458	97838
Hermitage, MO	417	65668
Hermitage, PA	724, 878	16148
Hermitage, TN	615	37076
Hermleigh, TX	915	79526
Hermon, ME	207	04401
Hermosa, SD	605	57744
Hernando, FL	352	34442
Hernando, MS	662	38632
Herndon, PA	570	17830
Herndon, VA	571, 703	20170-20172, 20190-20195*
Herrin, IL	618	62948
Hershey, PA	717	17033
Hertford, NC	252	27930, 27944
Hesperia, CA	760, 442	92340, 92345
Hesston, KS	620	67062
Hettinger, ND	701	58639
Heuvelton, NY	315	13654
Hewitt, NJ	862, 973	07421
Hewitt, TX	254	76643
Heyburn, ID	208	83336
Hialeah, FL	305, 786	33002, 33010-33018, 33054
Hialeah Gardens, FL	305, 786	33010, 33016-33018
Hiawassee, GA	706, 762	30546
Hiawatha, IA	319	52233
Hiawatha, KS	785	66434
Hibbing, MN	218	55746-55747
Hickam AFB, HI	808	96853
Hickman, KY	270	42050
Hickory, KY	270	42051
Hickory, NC	828	28601-28603
Hicksville, NY	516	11801-11804, 11815, 11819*
Hidden Valley, PA	814	15502
Higginsville, MO	660	64037
High Point, NC	336	27260-27265
High Ridge, MO	636	63049
High Shoals, GA	706, 762	30645
Highgate Springs, VT	802	05460
Highland, CA	909	92346
Highland, IL	618	62249
Highland, IN	219	46322, 47854
Highland, KS	785	66035

*Partial list of zip codes, including main range

City	Area Code(s)	Zip Code(s)
Highland, NY	845	12528
Highland Heights, KY	859	41076
Highland Heights, OH	440	44143
Highland Hills, OH	216	44122, 44128
Highland Park, IL	224, 847	60035-60037
Highland Park, MI	313	48203
Highland Springs, VA	804	23075
Highlands, NJ	732, 848	07732
Highlands Ranch, CO	303, 720	80124-80130, 80163
Highmore, SD	605	57345
Hightstown, NJ	609	08520
Hildebran, NC	828	28637
Hill AFB, UT	801, 385	84056
Hill City, KS	785	67642
Hill City, SD	605	57745
Hilliard, OH	614	43026
Hillsboro, IL	217	62049
Hillsboro, KS	620	67063
Hillsboro, MO	636	63050
Hillsboro, NH	603	03244
Hillsboro, ND	701	58045
Hillsboro, OH	937	45133
Hillsboro, OR	503, 971	97123-97124
Hillsboro, TX	254	76645
Hillsboro, WV	304	24946
Hillsboro, WI	608	54634
Hillsboro Beach, FL	754, 954	33062
Hillsborough, NJ	908	08844
Hillsborough, NC	919	27278
Hillsdale, MI	517	49242
Hillsdale, NJ	201, 551	07642, 07676
Hillsgrove, PA	570	18619
Hillside, IL	708	60162-60163
Hillside, NJ	973	07205
Hillsville, VA	276	24343
Hilmar, CA	209	95324
Hilo, HI	808	96720-96721
Hilton, NY	585	14468
Hilton Head Island, SC	843	29915, 29925-29928, 29938
Hinckley, MN	320	55037
Hinckley, OH	234, 330	44233
Hindman, KY	606	41822
Hines, IL	708	60141
Hinesville, GA	912	31310-31315
Hingham, MA	339, 781	02018, 02043-02044
Hinsdale, IL	331, 630	60521-60523, 60570
Hinsdale, NH	603	03451
Hinton, OK	405	73047
Hinton, WV	304	25951
Hiram, OH	234, 330	44234
Hixson, TN	423	37343
Hobart, IN	219	46342
Hobart, OK	580	73651
Hobbs, IN	765	46047
Hobbs, NM	505	88240-88244
Hobe Sound, FL	772	33455, 33475
Hoboken, NJ	201, 551	07030
Hockessin, DE	302	19707
Hodgenville, KY	270	42748
Hodgkins, IL	708	60525
Hoffman, NC	910	28347
Hoffman Estates, IL	224, 847	60173, 60179, 60192-60195
Hohenwald, TN	931	38462
Hoisington, KS	620	67544
Holbrook, AZ	928	86025-86031
Holbrook, MA	339, 781	02343
Holbrook, NY	631	11741
Holden, MA	508, 774	01520
Holdenville, OK	405	74848
Holdingford, MN	320	56340
Holdrege, NE	308	68949, 68969
Holland, IN	812	47541
Holland, MI	616	49422-49424
Holland, NY	716	14080
Holland, OH	419, 567	43528
Hollandale, MS	662	38748
Hollidaysburg, PA	814	16648
Hollis, NH	603	03049
Hollis, OK	580	73550
Hollister, CA	831	95023-95024
Hollister, MO	417	65672-65673
Holliston, MA	508, 774	01746
Holloman AFB, NM	505	88330
Hollsopple, PA	814	15935
Holly, MI	248, 947	48442
Holly Hill, FL	386	32117
Holly Springs, MS	662	38634-38635, 38649
Hollywood, CA	323	90027-90028, 90038, 90068*
Hollywood, FL	754, 954	33019-33029, 33081-33084*
Holmdel, NJ	732, 848	07733, 07777
Holmen, WI	608	54636
Holstein, IA	712	51025
Holt, MI	517	48842
Holton, KS	785	66436
Holtsville, NY	631	00501, 00544, 11742
Holyoke, CO	970	80734
Holyoke, MA	413	01040-01041
Homer, AK	907	99603
Homer, GA	706, 762	30547
Homer, LA	318	71040
Homerville, GA	912	31634
Homestead, FL	305, 786	33030-33035, 33039, 33090*
Homestead, PA	412, 878	15120
Homewood, AL	205	35209, 35219, 35259
Homewood, IL	708	60430
Hominy, OK	918	74035
Homosassa Springs, FL	352	34447
Honaunau, HI	808	96726
Hondo, TX	830	78861
Honea Path, SC	864	29654
Honeoye, NY	585	14471
Honesdale, PA	570	18431
Honolulu, HI	808	96801-96830, 96835-96850
Hood River, OR	541, 458	97031
Hooker, OK	580	73945
Hooper, NE	402	68031
Hoosick Falls, NY	518	12090
Hoover, AL	205	35216, 35226, 35236, 35244
Hopatcong, NJ	862, 973	07843
Hope, AK	907	99605
Hope, AR	870	71801-71802
Hope Hull, AL	334	36043
Hope Valley, RI	401	02832
Hopedale, MA	508, 774	01747
Hopewell, VA	804	23860
Hopewell Junction, NY	845	12533
Hopkins, MI	616	49328
Hopkins, MN	952	55305, 55343-55345
Hopkins, SC	803	29061
Hopkinsville, KY	270	42240-42241
Hopkinton, MA	508, 774	01748
Hopkinton, NH	603	03229
Hopland, CA	707	95449
Hoquiam, WA	360	98550
Horn Lake, MS	662	38637
Hornell, NY	607	14843
Hornick, IA	712	51026
Horse Cave, KY	270	42749
Horseheads, NY	607	14844-14845
Horseshoe Bay, TX	830	78654-78657
Horsham, PA	215, 267	19044
Horton, KS	785	66439
Hot Springs, AR	501	71901-71903, 71909-71914
Hot Springs, SD	605	57747
Hot Springs, VA	540	24445
Hot Springs National Park, AR	501	71901-71903, 71909-71914*
Hot Sulphur Springs, CO	970	80451
Houghton, IA	319	52631
Houghton, MI	906	49921, 49931
Houghton, NY	585	14744
Houghton Lake, MI	989	48629
Houlka, MS	662	38850
Houlton, ME	207	04730, 04761
Houma, LA	985	70360-70364
Houston, MS	662	38851
Houston, MO	417	65483
Houston, TX	281, 713, 832	77001-77099, 77201-77293*
Houtzdale, PA	814	16651, 16698
Howard, KS	620	67349
Howard, SD	605	57349
Howard Lake, MN	320	55349, 55575
Howell, MI	517	48843-48844, 48863
Howell, NJ	732, 848	07731
Howes Cave, NY	518	12092
Howey in the Hills, FL	352	34737
Hoxie, KS	785	67740
Hubbard, OR	503, 971	97032
Huber Heights, OH	937	45424
Hudson, FL	727	34667-34669, 34674
Hudson, KS	620	67545
Hudson, MA	351, 978	01749
Hudson, MI	517	49247
Hudson, NH	603	03051
Hudson, NY	518	12534
Hudson, NC	828	28638
Hudson, OH	234, 330	44236-44238
Hudson, WI	715, 534	54016, 54082
Hudson Falls, NY	518	12839
Hueytown, AL	205	35022-35023
Hughesville, MD	301	20637
Hughson, CA	209	95326
Hugo, CO	719	80821
Hugo, MN	651	55038
Hugo, OK	580	74743
Hugoton, KS	620	67951
Hulbert, OK	918	74441
Hull, IA	712	51239
Hull, MA	339, 781	02045
Humacao, PR	787, 939	00791-00792
Humble, TX	281, 832	77325, 77338-77339, 77345*
Humboldt, IA	515	50548
Humboldt, KS	620	66748
Humboldt, TN	731	38343
Hummelstown, PA	717	17036
Hunlock Creek, PA	570	18621
Hunt, TX	830	78024
Hunt Valley, MD	410	21030-21031, 21065
Hunter, NY	518	12442
Huntersville, NC	704, 980	28070, 28078
Huntertown, IN	260	46748
Huntingburg, IN	812	47542
Huntingdon, PA	814	16652-16654
Huntingdon, TN	731	38344
Huntingdon Valley, PA	215, 267	19006
Huntington, IN	260	46750
Huntington, NY	631	11743
Huntington, UT	435	84528
Huntington, VT	802	05462
Huntington, WV	304	25701-25729, 25755, 25770*
Huntington Beach, CA	714	92605, 92615, 92646-92649
Huntington Park, CA	323	90255
Huntington Station, NY	631	11746-11750
Huntley, IL	224, 847	60142
Huntley, MT	406	59037
Huntsville, AL	256	35801-35816, 35824, 35893*
Huntsville, AR	479	72740
Huntsville, MO	660	65259
Huntsville, TN	423	37756
Huntsville, TX	936	77320, 77340-77344, 77348*
Hurley, WI	715, 534	54534, 54565
Huron, CA	559	93234
Huron, OH	419, 567	44839
Huron, SD	605	57350, 57399
Hurricane, WV	304	25526
Hurst, TX	682, 817	76053-76054
Hutchins, TX	469, 972	75141
Hutchinson, KS	620	67501-67505
Hutchinson, MN	320	55350
Huttonsville, WV	304	26273
Hyannis, MA	508, 774	02601
Hyannis, NE	308	69350
Hyattsville, MD	301	20781-20788
Hydaburg, AK	907	99922
Hyde Park, MA	617, 857	02136-02137
Hyde Park, NY	845	12538
Hyde Park, VT	802	05655
Hyden, KY	606	41749, 41762
Hyrum, UT	435	84319
Hysham, MT	406	59038, 59076

I

City	Area Code(s)	Zip Code(s)
Ida Grove, IA	712	51445
Idabel, OK	580	74745
Idaho City, ID	208	83631
Idaho Falls, ID	208	83401-83406, 83415
Idaho Springs, CO	303, 720	80452
Idyllwild, CA	951	92549
Imlay City, MI	810	48444
Immaculata, PA	484, 610	19345
Immokalee, FL	239	34142-34143
Imperial, CA	760, 442	92251
Imperial, MO	636	63052-63053
Imperial, NE	308	69033

*Partial list of zip codes, including main range

City	Area Code(s)	Zip Code(s)
Imperial Beach, CA	619	91932-91933
Ina, IL	618	62846
Incline Village, NV	775	89450-89452
Independence, CA	760, 442	93526
Independence, IA	319	50644
Independence, KS	620	67301
Independence, KY	859	41051
Independence, MO	816	64050-64058
Independence, OH	216	44131
Independence, OR	503, 971	97351
Independence, VA	276	24348
Indian, AK	907	99540
Indian Orchard, MA	413	01151
Indian Springs, NV	702	89018, 89070
Indian Trail, NC	704, 980	28079
Indian Wells, CA	760, 442	92210
Indiana, PA	724, 878	15701, 15705
Indianapolis, IN	317	46201-46260, 46266-46268*
Indianola, IA	515	50125
Indianola, MS	662	38749-38751
Indianola, PA	412, 878	15051
Indiantown, FL	772	34956
Indio, CA	760, 442	92201-92203
Inez, KY	606	41224
Ingalls, KS	620	67853
Inglewood, CA	310, 424	90301-90313, 90397-90398
Ingomar, PA	412, 878	15127
Inkster, MI	313	48141
Inman, SC	864	29349
Institute, WV	304	25112
Intercourse, PA	717	17534
Interior, SD	605	57750
Interlochen, MI	231	49643
International Falls, MN	218	56649
Inver Grove Heights, MN	651	55076-55077
Inverness, FL	352	34450-34453
Inwood, NY	516	11096
Iola, KS	620	66749
Iola, WI	715, 534	54945, 54990
Ione, CA	209	95640
Ionia, MI	616	48846
Iowa City, IA	319	52240-52246
Iowa Falls, IA	641	50126
Ipswich, MA	351, 978	01938
Ipswich, SD	605	57451
Irma, WI	715, 534	54442
Irmo, SC	803	29063
Iron Mountain, MI	906	49801-49802, 49831
Iron River, WI	715, 534	54847
Irondale, AL	205	35210
Ironton, MO	573	63650
Ironton, OH	740	45638
Ironwood, MI	906	49938
Irvine, CA	949	92602-92606, 92612-92623*
Irvine, KY	606	40336, 40472
Irvine, PA	814	16329
Irving, TX	214, 469, 972	75014-75017, 75037-75039*
Irvington, NJ	862, 973	07111
Irvington, NY	914	10533
Irvington, VA	804	22480
Irwin, PA	724, 878	15642
Irwindale, CA	626	91706
Irwinton, GA	478	31042
Iselin, NJ	732, 848	08830
Ishpeming, MI	906	49849, 49865
Islamorada, FL	305, 786	33036, 33070
Islandia, NY	631	11749, 11760
Isle of Palms, SC	843	29451
Isle of Wight, VA	757	23397
Islip, NY	631	11751
Isola, MS	662	38754
Issaquah, WA	425	98027-98029, 98075
Itasca, IL	331, 630	60143
Itasca, TX	254	76055
Ithaca, MI	989	48847
Ithaca, NY	607	14850-14853, 14882
Itta Bena, MS	662	38941
Iuka, MS	662	38852
Ivanhoe, CA	559	93235
Ivanhoe, MN	507	56142
Ivel, KY	606	41642
Ivins, UT	435	84738
Ivoryton, CT	860	06442
Ivyland, PA	215, 267	18974
Ixonia, WI	920	53036

J

City	Area Code(s)	Zip Code(s)
Jackman, ME	207	04945
Jackpot, NV	775	89825
Jacksboro, TN	423	37757
Jacksboro, TX	940	76458
Jackson, AL	251	36501, 36515, 36545
Jackson, CA	209	95642, 95654
Jackson, GA	470, 770	30233
Jackson, KY	606	41307, 41339
Jackson, LA	225	70748
Jackson, MI	517	49201-49204
Jackson, MN	507	56143
Jackson, MS	601, 769	39201-39218, 39225, 39232*
Jackson, MO	573	63755
Jackson, NH	603	03846
Jackson, NJ	732, 848	08527
Jackson, NC	252	27845
Jackson, OH	740	45640
Jackson, SC	803	29831
Jackson, TN	731	38301-38308, 38314
Jackson, WI	262	53037
Jackson, WY	307	83001-83002, 83025
Jackson Center, OH	937	45334
Jackson Heights, NY	347, 718	11372
Jackson Hole, WY	307	83001-83002
Jacksonville, AL	256	36265
Jacksonville, AR	501	72076-72078
Jacksonville, FL	904	32099, 32201-32250, 32254*
Jacksonville, IL	217	62650-62651
Jacksonville, NC	910	28540-28546
Jacksonville, TX	903	75766
Jacksonville Beach, FL	904	32227, 32240, 32250
Jaffrey, NH	603	03452
Jamaica, NY	347, 718	11405, 11411-11439, 11451*
Jamaica Plain, MA	617, 857	02130
Jamesburg, NJ	732, 848	08831
Jamestown, CA	209	95327
Jamestown, KY	270	42629
Jamestown, NY	716	14701-14704
Jamestown, NC	336	27282
Jamestown, ND	701	58401-58405
Jamestown, OH	937	45335
Jamestown, RI	401	02835
Jamestown, SC	843	29453
Jamestown, TN	931	38556
Janesville, IA	319	50647
Janesville, WI	608	53545-53547
Jarratt, VA	434	23867-23870
Jasper, AL	205	35501-35504
Jasper, AR	870	72641
Jasper, FL	386	32052
Jasper, GA	706, 762	30143
Jasper, IN	812	47546-47549
Jasper, MN	507	56144
Jasper, TN	423	37347
Jasper, TX	409	75951
Jay, FL	850	32565
Jay, ME	207	04239, 04262
Jay, OK	918	74346
Jay, VT	802	05859
Jayton, TX	806	79528
Jean, NV	702	89019, 89026
Jeanerette, LA	337	70544
Jeannette, PA	724, 878	15644
Jefferson, AR	870	72079
Jefferson, GA	706, 762	30549
Jefferson, IA	515	50129
Jefferson, LA	504	70121
Jefferson, NC	336	28640
Jefferson, OH	440	44047
Jefferson, OR	541, 458	97352
Jefferson, SD	605	57038
Jefferson, TX	903	75657
Jefferson, WI	920	53549
Jefferson City, MO	573	65101-65111
Jefferson City, TN	865	37760
Jefferson Valley, NY	914	10535
Jeffersontown, KY	502	40269, 40299
Jeffersonville, GA	478	31044
Jeffersonville, IN	812	47129-47134, 47144, 47199
Jeffersonville, NY	845	12748
Jeffersonville, OH	740	43128
Jekyll Island, GA	912	31527
Jelm, WY	970	82063, 82070-82072
Jena, LA	318	71342
Jenison, MI	616	49428-49429
Jenkintown, PA	215, 267	19046
Jenks, OK	918	74037
Jennerstown, PA	814	15547
Jennings, LA	337	70546
Jericho, NY	516	11753, 11853
Jermyn, PA	570	18433
Jerome, ID	208	83338
Jersey City, NJ	201, 551	07097, 07302-07311, 07399
Jerseyville, IL	618	62052
Jessup, MD	410, 443	20794
Jesup, GA	912	31545-31546, 31598-31599
Jetersville, VA	804	23083
Jetmore, KS	620	67854
Jewell, IA	515	50130
Jewett, TX	903	75846
Jim Thorpe, PA	570	18229
Johnson, KS	620	67855
Johnson, VT	802	05656
Johnson City, NY	607	13790
Johnson City, TN	423	37601-37605, 37614-37615
Johnson City, TX	830	78636
Johnston, IA	515	50131
Johnston, RI	401	02919
Johnston, SC	803	29832
Johnston City, IL	618	62951
Johnstown, NY	518	12095
Johnstown, OH	740	43031
Johnstown, PA	814	15901-15909, 15915, 15945
Joliet, IL	815	60431-60436
Jonesboro, AR	870	72401-72404
Jonesboro, GA	470, 770	30236-30238
Jonesboro, IL	618	62952
Jonesboro, LA	318	71251
Jonesborough, TN	423	37659
Jonesburg, MO	636	63351
Jonestown, MS	662	38639
Jonesville, LA	318	71343, 71377
Jonesville, VA	276	24263
Joplin, MO	417	64801-64804
Joppa, MD	410	21085
Jordan, MN	952	55352, 56071
Jordan, MT	406	59337
Jordan, NY	315	13080
Joshua Tree, CA	760, 442	92252
Jourdanton, TX	830	78026
Julesburg, CO	970	80737
Junction, TX	915	76849
Junction, UT	435	84740
Junction City, KS	785	66441-66442
Junction City, OR	541, 458	97448
Juneau, AK	907	99801-99803, 99811, 99821*
Juneau, WI	920	53039
Juno Beach, FL	561	33408
Jupiter, FL	561	33458, 33468-33469, 33477*

K

City	Area Code(s)	Zip Code(s)
Kadoka, SD	605	57543
Kahoka, MO	660	63445
Kahuku, HI	808	96731
Kahului, HI	808	96732-96733
Kailua, HI	808	96734
Kailua-Kona, HI	808	96739-96740, 96745
Kaiser, MO	573	65047
Kalaheo, HI	808	96741
Kalama, WA	360	98625
Kalamazoo, MI	616	49001-49009, 49019, 49024*
Kalaupapa, HI	808	96742
Kalida, OH	419, 567	45853
Kalispell, MT	406	59901-59904
Kalkaska, MI	231	49646
Kalona, IA	319	52247
Kamuela, HI	808	96743
Kanab, UT	435	84741
Kanawha, IA	641	50447
Kane, PA	814	16735
Kaneohe, HI	808	96744
Kankakee, IL	815	60901-60902

Partial list of zip codes, including main range

City	Area Code(s)	Zip Code(s)
Kannapolis, NC	704, 980	28081-28083
Kansas City, KS	913	66101-66119, 66160
Kansas City, MO	816	64101-64173, 64179-64199*
Kapaa, HI	808	96746
Kapolei, HI	808	96707-96709
Karnes City, TX	830	78118
Karthaus, PA	814	16845
Kasson, MN	507	55944
Katonah, NY	914	10536
Katy, TX	281, 832	77449-77450, 77491-77494
Kaufman, TX	469, 972	75142
Kaukauna, WI	920	54130-54131
Kaumakani, HI	808	96747
Keaau, HI	808	96749
Kealakekua, HI	808	96750
Kearney, MO	816	64060
Kearney, NE	308	68845-68849
Kearneysville, WV	304	25429-25430
Kearny, NJ	201, 551	07032, 07099
Keene, CA	661	93531
Keene, NH	603	03431, 03435
Keene, TX	682, 817	76059
Keesler AFB, MS	228	39534
Keizer, OR	503, 971	97303, 97307
Keller, TX	682, 817	76244, 76248
Kellogg, ID	208	83837
Kelly, WY	307	83011
Kelseyville, CA	707	95451
Kelso, WA	360	98626
Kemmerer, WY	307	83101
Kenai, AK	907	99611, 99635
Kenansville, NC	910	28349
Kendall, FL	305, 786	33156-33158, 33173-33176*
Kendallville, IN	260	46720, 46755
Kenedy, TX	830	78119, 78125
Kenilworth, NJ	908	07033
Kenmare, ND	701	58746
Kenmore, NY	716	14217, 14223
Kenmore, WA	425	98028
Kennebec, SD	605	57544
Kennebunk, ME	207	04043
Kennebunkport, ME	207	04046
Kennedy Space Center, FL	321	32815
Kenner, LA	504	70062-70065
Kennesaw, GA	470, 770	30144, 30152, 30156, 30160
Kennett, MO	573	63857
Kennett Square, PA	484, 610	19348
Kennewick, WA	509	99336-99338
Kenosha, WI	262	53140-53144, 53158
Kenova, WV	304	25530
Kensington, CT	860	06037
Kensington, MD	301	20891, 20895
Kent, CT	860	06757
Kent, OH	234, 330	44240-44243
Kent, WA	253	98031-98035, 98042, 98064
Kentfield, CA	415	94904, 94914
Kentland, IN	219	47951
Kenton, OH	419, 567	43326
Kentwood, MI	616	49506-49508, 49512, 49518*
Kenwood, CA	707	95452
Kenyon, MN	507	55946
Keokuk, IA	319	52632
Keosauqua, IA	319	52565
Kermit, TX	915	79745
Kernersville, NC	336	27284-27285
Kernville, CA	760, 442	93238
Kerrville, TX	830	78028-78029
Kershaw, SC	803	29067
Keshena, WI	715, 534	54135
Keswick, VA	434	22947
Ketchikan, AK	907	99901-99903, 99918-99919*
Ketchum, ID	208	83340
Kettering, OH	937	45409, 45419-45420, 45429*
Keuka Park, NY	315	14478
Kew Gardens, NY	347, 718	11415-11418
Kewanee, IL	309	61443
Kewanna, IN	574	46935, 46939
Kewaskum, WI	262	53040
Kewaunee, WI	920	54216
Key Biscayne, FL	305, 786	33149
Key Largo, FL	305, 786	33037
Key West, FL	305, 786	33040-33041, 33045
Keyser, WV	304	26726
Keystone, CO	970	80435
Keystone, SD	605	57751

City	Area Code(s)	Zip Code(s)
Keystone Heights, FL	352	32656
Keytesville, MO	660	65261
Kiamesha Lake, NY	845	12751
Kiawah Island, SC	843	29455
Kidron, OH	234, 330	44636
Kiel, WI	920	53042
Kihei, HI	808	96753
Kilgore, TX	903	75662-75663
Kill Devil Hills, NC	252	27948
Killbuck, OH	234, 330	44637
Killeen, TX	254	76540-76549
Killington, VT	802	05751
Kimball, NE	308	69145
Kimberly, OR	541, 458	97848
Kimberly, WI	920	54136
Kincheloe, MI	906	49784-49788
Kinder, LA	337	70648
Kinderhook, NY	518	12106
Kindred, ND	701	58051
King, NC	336	27021
King, WI	715, 534	54946
King City, CA	831	93930
King Ferry, NY	315	13081
King George, VA	540	22485
King of Prussia, PA	484, 610	19406, 19487
King Salmon, AK	907	99549, 99613
King William, VA	804	23086
Kingfisher, OK	405	73750
Kingman, AZ	928	86401-86402, 86411-86413*
Kingman, KS	620	67068
Kings Bay, GA	912	31547
Kings Mountain, NC	704, 980	28086
Kings Point, NY	516	11024
Kingsburg, CA	559	93631
Kingsford, MI	906	49801-49802
Kingsport, TN	423	37660-37665, 37669
Kingston, MA	339, 781	02364
Kingston, MO	816	64650
Kingston, NJ	609	08528
Kingston, NY	845	12401-12402
Kingston, OK	580	73439
Kingston, PA	570	18704
Kingston, RI	401	02881
Kingston, TN	865	37763
Kingston, WA	360	98346
Kingstree, SC	843	29556
Kingsville, MD	410	21087
Kingsville, MO	816	64061
Kingsville, TX	361	78363-78364
Kingwood, TX	281, 832	77325, 77339, 77345-77346
Kingwood, WV	304	26519, 26537
Kinnelon, NJ	862, 973	07405
Kinsale, VA	804	22488
Kinsley, KS	620	67547
Kinsman, OH	234, 330	44428
Kinston, NC	252	28501-28504
Kiowa, CO	303, 720	80117
Kirbyville, TX	409	75956
Kirkland, WA	425	98033-98034, 98083
Kirksville, MO	660	63501
Kirkville, NY	315	13082
Kirkwood, MO	314	63122
Kirtland, OH	440	44094
Kirtland AFB, NM	505	87116-87118
Kissimmee, FL	321, 407	34741-34747, 34758-34759
Kittanning, PA	724, 878	16201, 16215
Kittery, ME	207	03904
Klamath Falls, OR	541, 458	97601-97603, 97625
Knights Landing, CA	530	95645
Knightstown, IN	765	46148
Knox, IN	574	46534
Knoxville, IA	641	50138, 50197-50198
Knoxville, TN	865	37901-37902, 37909-37933*
Kodiak, AK	907	99615, 99619, 99697
Kohler, WI	920	53044
Kokomo, IN	765	46901-46904
Koloa, HI	808	96756
Kosciusko, MS	662	39090
Koshkonong, MO	417	65692
Kotzebue, AK	907	99752
Kountze, TX	409	77625
Kreamer, PA	570	17833
Kula, HI	808	96790
Kulpsville, PA	215, 267	19443
Kuna, ID	208	83634

City	Area Code(s)	Zip Code(s)
Kurten, TX	979	77862
Kutztown, PA	484, 610	19530

L

City	Area Code(s)	Zip Code(s)
La Belle, FL	863	33935
La Canada, CA	818	91011-91012
La Conner, WA	360	98257
La Crescenta, CA	818	91214, 91224
La Crosse, KS	785	67548, 67553
La Crosse, WI	608	54601-54603
La Fayette, GA	706, 762	30728
La Follette, TN	423	37729, 37766
La France, SC	864	29656
La Grande, OR	541, 458	97850
La Grange, IL	708	60525
La Grange, TX	979	78945
La Grange Park, IL	708	60526
La Habra, CA	562	90631-90633
La Jolla, CA	858	92037-92039, 92092-92093
La Junta, CO	719	81050
La Mesa, CA	619	91941-91944
La Mesa, NM	505	88044
La Mirada, CA	562, 714	90637-90639
La Moure, ND	701	58458
La Palma, CA	714	90623
La Pine, OR	541, 458	97739
La Plata, MD	301	20646
La Plume, PA	570	18440
La Porte, IN	574	46350-46352
La Porte, TX	281, 832	77571-77572
La Puente, CA	626	91744-91749
La Quinta, CA	760, 442	92253
La Rue, OH	740	43332
La Salle, IL	815	61301
La Union, NM	505	88021
La Vergne, TN	615	37086-37089
La Verne, CA	909	91750
La Veta, CO	719	81055
Lac du Flambeau, WI	715, 534	54538
Lacey, WA	360	98503-98509, 98513-98516
Lackawanna, NY	716	14218
Lackland AFB, TX	210	78236
Laclede, ID	208	83841
Lacon, IL	309	61540
Laconia, NH	603	03246-03249
Ladd, IL	815	61329
Ladysmith, WI	715, 534	54848
Lafayette, AL	334	36862
Lafayette, CA	925	94549, 94596
Lafayette, CO	303, 720	80026
Lafayette, IN	765	47901-47909, 47996
Lafayette, LA	337	70501-70509, 70593-70598
Lafayette, NJ	862, 973	07848
Lafayette, TN	615	37083
LaFox, IL	331, 630	60147
Lago Vista, TX	512	78645
LaGrange, GA	706, 762	30240-30241, 30261
LaGrange, IN	260	46761
LaGrange, KY	502	40031
Lagrangeville, NY	845	12540
Laguna Beach, CA	949	92607, 92637, 92651-92656*
Laguna Hills, CA	949	92637, 92653-92656
Laguna Niguel, CA	949	92607, 92677
Lahaina, HI	808	96761, 96767
Laie, HI	808	96762
Lake Alfred, FL	863	33850
Lake Andes, SD	605	57356
Lake Ariel, PA	570	18436
Lake Bluff, IL	224, 847	60044
Lake Buena Vista, FL	321, 407	32830
Lake Butler, FL	386	32054
Lake Charles, LA	337	70601-70616, 70629
Lake City, CO	970	81235
Lake City, FL	386	32024-32025, 32055-32056
Lake City, IA	712	51449
Lake City, MI	231	49651
Lake City, MN	651	55041
Lake City, PA	814	16423
Lake City, SC	843	29560
Lake Crystal, MN	507	56055
Lake Dallas, TX	940	75065
Lake Delton, WI	608	53940
Lake Elsinore, CA	951	92530-92532
Lake Forest, CA	949	92609, 92630

Partial list of zip codes, including main range

City	Area Code(s)	Zip Code(s)
Lake Forest, IL	224, 847	60045
Lake Geneva, WI	262	53147
Lake George, CO	719	80827
Lake George, NY	518	12845
Lake Grove, NY	631	11755
Lake Harmony, PA	570	18624
Lake Havasu City, AZ	928	86403-86406
Lake Helen, FL	386	32744
Lake Hiawatha, NJ	862, 973	07034
Lake Isabella, CA	760, 442	93240
Lake Jackson, TX	979	77566
Lake Junaluska, NC	828	28745
Lake Lillian, MN	320	56253
Lake Lure, NC	828	28746
Lake Mary, FL	321, 407	32746, 32795
Lake Mills, WI	920	53551
Lake Monroe, FL	321, 407	32747
Lake Odessa, MI	616	48849
Lake Orion, MI	248, 947	48359-48362
Lake Oswego, OR	503, 971	97034-97035
Lake Ozark, MO	573	65049
Lake Park, GA	229	31636
Lake Placid, FL	863	33852, 33862
Lake Placid, NY	518	12946
Lake Pleasant, NY	518	12108
Lake Powell, UT	435	84533
Lake Providence, LA	318	71254
Lake Saint Louis, MO	636	63367
Lake Stevens, WA	425	98258
Lake Success, NY	516	11020, 11042
Lake Toxaway, NC	828	28747
Lake View, SC	843	29563
Lake Village, AR	870	71653
Lake Wales, FL	863	33853-33859, 33867, 33898
Lake Worth, FL	561	33454, 33460-33467
Lake Zurich, IL	224, 847	60047
Lakehurst, NJ	732, 848	08733, 08755, 08759
Lakeland, FL	863	33801-33815
Lakeland, GA	229	31635
Lakeland, LA	225	70752
Lakeport, CA	707	95453
Lakeside, AZ	928	85929
Lakeside, CA	619	92040
Laketon, IN	260	46943
Lakeview, AR	870	72642
Lakeview, CA	909	92567
Lakeview, OR	541, 458	97630
Lakeville, CT	860	06039
Lakeville, MN	952	55044
Lakeville, PA	570	18438
Lakeway, TX	512	78734, 78738
Lakewood, CA	562	90711-90716, 90805
Lakewood, CO	303, 720	80033, 80123, 80214-80215*
Lakewood, NJ	732, 848	08701
Lakewood, NY	716	14750
Lakewood, OH	216	44107
Lakewood, WA	253	98439, 98492, 98497-98499
Lakin, KS	620	67860
Lakota, ND	701	58344
Lamar, CO	719	81052
Lamar, MO	417	64759
Lamberton, MN	507	56152
Lambertville, NJ	609	08530
Lame Deer, MT	406	59043
Lamesa, TX	806	79331
Lamoni, IA	641	50140
Lamont, CA	661	93241
Lampasas, TX	512	76550
Lanai City, HI	808	96763
Lanark, IL	815	61046
Lancaster, CA	661	93534-93539, 93584-93586
Lancaster, KY	859	40444-40446
Lancaster, MO	660	63548
Lancaster, NH	603	03584
Lancaster, NY	716	14043, 14086
Lancaster, OH	740	43130
Lancaster, PA	717	17601-17608, 17699
Lancaster, SC	803	29720-29722
Lancaster, TX	469, 972	75134, 75146
Lancaster, VA	804	22503
Lancaster, WI	608	53813
Lander, WY	307	82520
Landisburg, PA	717	17040
Landisville, PA	717	17538
Landover, MD	301	20785
Landrum, SC	864	29356
Lanett, AL	334	36863
Langdon, ND	701	58249
Langhorne, PA	215, 267	19047, 19053
Langley, WA	360	98260
Langley AFB, VA	757	23665
Langston, OK	405	73050
Lanham, MD	301	20703-20706, 20784
Lanham Seabrook, MD	301	20703-20706
Lansdale, PA	215, 267	19446
Lansdowne, PA	484, 610	19050
L'Anse, MI	906	49946
Lansford, PA	570	18232
Lansing, IL	708	60438
Lansing, KS	913	66043
Lansing, MI	517	48901, 48906-48924, 48929*
Lantana, FL	561	33460-33465
Lapeer, MI	810	48446
LaPlace, LA	985	70068-70069
Laporte, PA	570	18626
Laramie, WY	307	82051, 82063, 82070-82073
Larchmont, NY	914	10538
Laredo, TX	956	78040-78049
Largo, FL	727	33770-33779
Largo, MD	301	20774
Larkspur, CA	415	94939, 94977
Larned, KS	620	67550
Larose, LA	985	70373-70374
Las Animas, CO	719	81054
Las Cruces, NM	505	88001-88006, 88011-88012
Las Vegas, NV	702	89101-89164, 89170-89173*
Las Vegas, NM	505	87701, 87745
Latham, NY	518	12110-12111, 12128
Lathrop, CA	209	95330
Latrobe, PA	724, 878	15650
Latta, SC	843	29565
Latty, OH	419, 567	45855
Lauderdale-by-the-Sea, FL	754, 954	33062, 33308
Lauderhill, FL	754, 954	33311-33313, 33319-33321*
Laughlin, NV	702	89028-89029
Laughlin AFB, TX	830	78840-78843
Laurel, MD	240, 301	20707-20709, 20723-20726
Laurel, MS	601, 769	39440-39443
Laurel Hill, NC	910	28351
Laurelton, NY	347, 718	11413
Laurens, IA	712	50554
Laurens, SC	864	29360
Laurinburg, NC	910	28352-28353
Lava Hot Springs, ID	208	83246
LaVale, MD	301	21502-21504
Lawndale, CA	310, 424	90260-90261
Lawrence, KS	785	66044-66049
Lawrence, MA	351, 978	01840-01843
Lawrence, MI	616	49064
Lawrence, NY	516	11559
Lawrence, PA	724, 878	15055
Lawrenceburg, IN	812	47025
Lawrenceburg, KY	502	40342
Lawrenceburg, TN	931	38464
Lawrenceville, GA	470, 678, 770	30042-30049
Lawrenceville, IL	618	62439
Lawrenceville, NJ	609	08648
Lawrenceville, VA	434	23868
Lawton, MI	616	49065
Lawton, OK	580	73501-73507, 73558
Layton, NJ	862, 973	07851
Layton, UT	801, 385	84040-84041
Le Center, MN	507	56057
Le Grand, IA	641	50142
Le Mars, IA	712	51017, 51031
Le Roy, NY	585	14482
Le Sueur, MN	507	56058
Lead, SD	605	57754
Leadville, CO	719	80429, 80461
League City, TX	281, 832	77573-77574
Leakesville, MS	601, 769	39451
Leakey, TX	830	78873
Leander, TX	512	78641, 78645-78646
Leavenworth, KS	913	66043, 66048
Leavittsburg, OH	234, 330	44430
Leawood, KS	913	66206-66211, 66224
Lebanon, CT	860	06249
Lebanon, IL	618	62254
Lebanon, IN	765	46052
Lebanon, KY	270	40033
Lebanon, MO	417	65536
Lebanon, NH	603	03756, 03766
Lebanon, NJ	908	08833
Lebanon, OH	513	45036
Lebanon, OR	541, 458	97355
Lebanon, PA	717	17042, 17046
Lebanon, TN	615	37087-37090
Lebanon, VA	276	24266
Lebec, CA	661	93243
Lecanto, FL	352	34460-34461
Lee, MA	413	01238, 01264
Leechburg, PA	724, 878	15656
Leeds, AL	205	35094
Leeds, MA	413	01053
Lee's Summit, MO	816	64063-64065, 64081-64082*
Leesburg, FL	352	34748-34749, 34788-34789
Leesburg, GA	229	31763
Leesburg, NJ	856	08327
Leesburg, VA	571, 703	20175-20178
Leesville, LA	337	71446, 71459, 71496
Leesville, SC	803	29070
Lehi, UT	801, 385	84043
Lehigh Acres, FL	239	33936, 33970-33972
Lehigh Valley, PA	484, 610	18001-18003
Lehighton, PA	484, 610	18235
Lehman, PA	570	18627
Leicester, MA	508, 774	01524
Leicester, NY	585	14481
Leitchfield, KY	270	42754-42755
Leland, MI	231	49654
Leland, NC	910	28451
Lemmon, SD	605	57638
Lemon Grove, CA	619	91945-91946
Lemont, IL	331, 630	60439-60440, 60490
Lemoore, CA	559	93245-93246
Lemoyne, PA	717	17043
Lena, IL	815	61048
Lenexa, KS	913	66210-66220, 66227, 66285*
Lenni, PA	484, 610	19052
Lenoir, NC	828	28633, 28645
Lenoir City, TN	865	37771-37772
Lenox, MA	413	01240
Leola, PA	717	17540
Leola, SD	605	57456
Leominster, MA	351, 978	01453
Leon, IA	641	50144
Leonardtown, MD	301	20650
Leonia, NJ	201, 551	07605
Leoti, KS	620	67861
Lester, PA	484, 610	19029, 19113
Lester Prairie, MN	320	55354
Levelland, TX	806	79336-79338
Leverett, MA	413	01054
Levittown, NY	516	11756
Levittown, PA	215, 267	19054-19059
Lewes, DE	302	19958
Lewis Center, OH	740	43035
Lewis Run, PA	814	16738
Lewisberry, PA	717	17339
Lewisburg, PA	570	17837
Lewisburg, TN	931	37091
Lewisburg, WV	304	24901
Lewiston, ID	208	83501
Lewiston, ME	207	04240-04243
Lewiston, MI	989	49756
Lewiston, MN	507	55952
Lewiston, NY	716	14092
Lewiston, NC	252	27849
Lewistown, IL	309	61542
Lewistown, MO	573	63452
Lewistown, MT	406	59457
Lewistown, PA	717	17044
Lewisville, AR	870	71845
Lewisville, ID	208	83431
Lewisville, NC	336	27023
Lewisville, TX	469, 972	75022, 75027-75029, 75056*
Lexington, GA	706, 762	30648
Lexington, KY	859	40502-40517, 40522-40526*
Lexington, MA	339, 781	02420-02421
Lexington, MI	810	48450
Lexington, MS	662	39095
Lexington, MO	660	64067
Lexington, NE	308	68850
Lexington, NC	336	27292-27295
Lexington, OH	419, 567	44904
Lexington, OK	405	73051
Lexington, SC	803	29071-29073

*Partial list of zip codes, including main range

City	Area Code(s)	Zip Code(s)
Lexington, TN	731	38351
Lexington, VA	540	24450
Lexington Park, MD	301	20653
Libby, MT	406	59923
Liberal, KS	620	67901, 67905
Liberty, IN	765	47353
Liberty, KY	606	42539
Liberty, MS	601, 769	39645
Liberty, MO	816	64068-64069, 64087
Liberty, NC	336	27298
Liberty, SC	864	29657
Liberty, TX	936	77575
Liberty Corner, NJ	908	07938
Liberty Lake, WA	509	99019
Libertyville, IL	224, 847	60048, 60092
Licking, MO	573	65542
Lightfoot, VA	757	23090
Lighthouse Point, FL	754, 954	33064, 33074
Ligonier, PA	724, 878	15658
Lihue, HI	808	96766
Lilburn, GA	470, 770	30047-30048
Lillington, NC	910	27546
Lima, NY	585	14485
Lima, OH	419, 567	45801-45809, 45819, 45854
Lima, PA	484, 610	19037
Limerick, PA	484, 610	19468
Limon, CO	719	80826-80828
Lincoln, CA	916	95648
Lincoln, IL	217	62656
Lincoln, KS	785	67455
Lincoln, ME	207	04457
Lincoln, MA	339, 781	01773
Lincoln, MI	989	48742
Lincoln, NE	402	68501-68532, 68542, 68583*
Lincoln, RI	401	02802, 02865
Lincoln City, IN	812	47552
Lincoln City, OR	541, 458	97367
Lincoln Park, MI	313	48146
Lincoln Park, NJ	862, 973	07035
Lincoln University, PA	484, 610	19352
Lincolnshire, IL	224, 847	60069
Lincolnton, GA	706, 762	30817
Lincolnton, NC	704, 980	28092-28093
Lincolnwood, IL	224, 847	60645-60646, 60659, 60712
Lincroft, NJ	732, 848	07738
Linden, AL	334	36748
Linden, IN	765	47955
Linden, NJ	908	07036
Linden, TN	931	37096
Linden, TX	903	75563
Lindenhurst, NY	631	11757
Lindenwood, IL	815	61049
Lindon, UT	801, 385	84042
Lindsay, CA	559	93247
Lindsay, NE	402	68644
Lindsay, OK	405	73052
Lindsborg, KS	785	67456
Lindstrom, MN	651	55045
Linesville, PA	814	16424
Lingle, WY	307	82223
Linn, MO	573	65051
Linneus, MO	660	64653
Lino Lakes, MN	651	55014, 55038, 55110, 55126
Linthicum, MD	410	21090
Linthicum Heights, MD	410	21090
Linton, IN	812	47441
Linton, ND	701	58552
Linville, NC	828	28646
Linwood, KS	913	66052
Linwood, NJ	609	08221
Linwood, PA	484, 610	19061
Lionville, PA	484, 610	19353
Lipscomb, TX	806	79056
Lisbon, NH	603	03585
Lisbon, ND	701	58054
Lisbon, OH	234, 330	44432
Lisbon Falls, ME	207	04252
Lisle, IL	331, 630	60532
Litchfield, CT	860	06750, 06759
Litchfield, IL	217	62056
Litchfield, MI	517	49252
Litchfield, MN	320	55355
Litchfield Park, AZ	623	85340
Lithia, FL	813	33547
Lithia Springs, GA	470, 770	30122
Lithonia, GA	470, 770	30038-30039, 30058
Lititz, PA	717	17543
Little Chute, WI	920	54140
Little Compton, RI	401	02801, 02837
Little Elm, TX	469, 972	75068
Little Falls, MN	320	56345
Little Falls, NJ	862, 973	07424
Little Falls, NY	315	13365
Little Ferry, NJ	201, 551	07643
Little Neck, NY	347, 718	11362-11363
Little River, SC	843	29566
Little Rock, AR	501	72201-72227, 72231, 72260*
Little Rock AFB, AR	501	72076
Little Silver, NJ	732, 848	07739
Little Torch Key, FL	305, 786	33042
Little Valley, NY	716	14755
Littlefield, TX	806	79339
Littlerock, WA	360	98556
Littlestown, PA	717	17340
Littleton, CO	303, 720	80120-80130, 80160-80166
Littleton, MA	351, 978	01460
Live Oak, CA	530	95953
Live Oak, FL	386	32060, 32064
Livermore, CA	925	94550-94551
Livermore, CO	970	80536
Liverpool, NY	315	13088-13090
Livingston, AL	205	35470
Livingston, CA	209	95334
Livingston, LA	225	70754
Livingston, MT	406	59047
Livingston, NJ	862, 973	07039
Livingston, TN	931	38570
Livingston, TX	936	77351, 77399
Livingston Manor, NY	845	12758
Livonia, MI	734	48150-48154
Llano, TX	915	78643
Loa, UT	435	84747
Loch Sheldrake, NY	845	12759
Lock Haven, PA	570	17745
Lockhart, TX	512	78644
Lockport, IL	815	60441, 60446
Lockport, LA	985	70374
Lockport, NY	716	14094-14095
Locust Grove, VA	540	22508
Lodi, CA	209	95240-95242
Lodi, NJ	862, 973	07644
Logan, IA	712	51546, 51550
Logan, OH	740	43138
Logan, UT	435	84321-84323, 84341
Logan, WV	304	25601
Logansport, IN	574	46947
Loganville, GA	470, 770	30052
Loma Linda, CA	909	92350, 92354-92357
Lombard, IL	331, 630	60148
Lompoc, CA	805	93436-93438
London, KY	606	40741-40745
London, OH	740	43140
Londonderry, NH	603	03053
Lone Tree, CO	303, 720	80112, 80124
Lone Tree, IA	319	52755
Lone Wolf, OK	580	73655
Long Beach, CA	562	90745-90749, 90801-90815*
Long Beach, MS	228	39560
Long Beach, NY	516	11561
Long Beach, WA	360	98631
Long Branch, NJ	732, 848	07740
Long Grove, IL	224, 847	60047-60049
Long Island City, NY	347, 718	11101-11109, 11120
Long Pond, PA	570	18334
Long Prairie, MN	320	56347
Long Valley, NJ	908	07853
Longboat Key, FL	941	34228
Longmeadow, MA	413	01106, 01116
Longmont, CO	303, 720	80501-80504
Longview, TX	903	75601-75608, 75615
Longview, WA	360	98632
Longwood, FL	321, 407	32750-32752, 32779, 32791
Lonoke, AR	501	72086
Lookout Mountain, GA	706, 762	30750
Lookout Mountain, TN	423	37350
Loomis, CA	916	95650
Lorain, OH	440	44052-44055
Lordsburg, NM	505	88009, 88045, 88055
Lorenzo, TX	806	79343
Loretto, KY	270	40037
Loretto, PA	814	15940
Loretto, TN	931	38469
Loris, SC	843	29569
Lorman, MS	601, 769	39096
Lorton, VA	571, 703	22079, 22199
Los Alamitos, CA	562, 714	90720-90721
Los Alamos, NM	505	87544-87545
Los Altos, CA	650	94022-94024
Los Altos Hills, CA	650	94022-94024
Los Angeles, CA	213, 310, 323, 424	90001-90103, 90174, 90185*
Los Angeles AFB, CA	310, 424	90009
Los Banos, CA	209	93635
Los Gatos, CA	408	95030-95033
Los Lunas, NM	505	87031
Lostine, OR	541, 458	97857
Lotus, CA	530	95651
Loudon, NH	603	03307
Loudon, TN	865	37774
Loudonville, NY	518	12211
Loudonville, OH	419, 567	44842
Louisa, KY	606	41201, 41230
Louisa, VA	540	23093
Louisburg, NC	919	27549
Louisville, CO	303, 720	80027-80028
Louisville, GA	478	30434
Louisville, IL	618	62858
Louisville, KY	502	40201-40233, 40241-40245*
Louisville, MS	662	39339
Louisville, OH	234, 330	44641
Louisville, TN	865	37777
Loup City, NE	308	68853
Loveland, CO	970	80537-80539
Loveland, OH	513	45111, 45140
Lovell, WY	307	82431
Lovelock, NV	775	89419
Loves Park, IL	815	61111, 61130-61132
Lovingston, VA	434	22949
Lovington, NM	505	88260
Low Moor, VA	540	24457
Lowell, AR	479	72745
Lowell, FL	352	32663
Lowell, IN	219	46356
Lowell, MA	351, 978	01850-01854
Lowell, MI	616	49331
Lowellville, OH	234, 330	44436
Lower Burrell, PA	724, 878	15068
Lower Gwynedd, PA	215, 267	19002
Lower Waterford, VT	802	05848
Lowville, NY	315	13367
Loxahatchee, FL	561	33470
Loysville, PA	717	17047
Lubbock, TX	806	79401-79416, 79423-79424*
Lubec, ME	207	04652
Lucas, KY	270	42156
Lucasville, OH	740	45648, 45699
Lucedale, MS	601, 769	39452
Ludington, MI	231	49431
Ludlow, MA	413	01056
Ludlow, VT	802	05149
Ludowici, GA	912	31316
Lufkin, TX	936	75901-75904, 75915
Lugoff, SC	803	29078
Luke AFB, AZ	623	85307-85309
Lula, MS	662	38644
Luling, LA	985	70070
Lumber Bridge, NC	910	28357
Lumberton, NJ	856	08048
Lumberton, NC	910	28358-28360
Lumberton, TX	409	77657
Lumpkin, GA	229	31815
Lunenburg, MA	351, 978	01462
Lunenburg, VT	802	05906
Lunenburg, VA	434	23952
Luray, VA	540	22835
Lusk, WY	307	82225
Lutherville, MD	410	21093-21094
Lutsen, MN	218	55612
Luttrell, TN	865	37779
Luverne, AL	334	36049
Luverne, MN	507	56156
Luxemburg, WI	920	54217
Lykens, PA	717	17048
Lyman, SC	864	29365
Lyme, NH	603	03768
Lynbrook, NY	516	11563-11564
Lynchburg, TN	931	37352

**Partial list of zip codes, including main range*

City	Area Code(s)	Zip Code(s)
Lynchburg, VA	434	24501-24506, 24512-24515
Lyndhurst, NJ	201, 551	07071
Lyndon, KS	785	66451
Lyndonville, NY	585	14098
Lyndonville, VT	802	05851
Lynn, IN	765	47355
Lynn, MA	339, 781	01901-01905, 01910
Lynn Haven, FL	850	32444
Lynnfield, MA	339, 781	01940
Lynnwood, WA	425	98036-98037, 98046
Lynwood, CA	310, 424	90262
Lyon, MS	662	38645
Lyon Mountain, NY	518	12952-12955
Lyon Station, PA	484, 610	19536
Lyons, CO	303, 720	80540
Lyons, GA	912	30436
Lyons, KS	620	67554
Lyons, NJ	908	07939
Lyons, NY	315	14489
Lyons, OR	503, 971	97358

M

City	Area Code(s)	Zip Code(s)
Mableton, GA	404, 470	30126
Macclenny, FL	386	32063
MacDill AFB, FL	813	33608
Macedon, NY	315	14502
Macedonia, OH	234, 330	44056
Machesney Park, IL	815	61115
Machias, ME	207	04654, 04686
Machiasport, ME	207	04655
Mackay, ID	208	83251
Mackinac Island, MI	906	49757
Mackinaw City, MI	231	49701
Macomb, IL	309	61455
Macomb, MI	586	48042-48044
Macomb Township, MI	586	48042-48044
Macon, GA	478	31201-31221, 31294-31299
Macon, MS	662	39341
Macon, MO	660	63552
Macungie, PA	484, 610	18062
Macy, IN	574	46951
Macy, NE	402	68039
Maddock, ND	701	58348
Madeira Beach, FL	727	33708, 33738
Madelia, MN	507	56062
Madera, CA	559	93637-93639
Madill, OK	580	73446
Madison, AL	256	35756-35758
Madison, CT	203	06443
Madison, FL	850	32340-32341
Madison, GA	706, 762	30650
Madison, IL	618	62060
Madison, IN	812	47250
Madison, ME	207	04950
Madison, MN	320	56256
Madison, MS	601, 769	39110, 39130
Madison, NE	402	68748
Madison, NJ	862, 973	07940
Madison, NC	336	27025
Madison, OH	440	44057
Madison, SD	605	57042
Madison, TN	615	37115-37116
Madison, VA	540	22719, 22727
Madison, WV	304	25130
Madison, WI	608	53562, 53593, 53701-53719*
Madison Heights, MI	248, 947	48071
Madisonville, KY	270	42431
Madisonville, LA	985	70447
Madisonville, TN	423	37354
Madisonville, TX	936	77864
Madras, OR	541, 458	97741
Maggie Valley, NC	828	28751
Magna, UT	801, 385	84044
Magnolia, AR	870	71753-71754
Magnolia, MS	601, 769	39652
Mahanoy City, PA	570	17948
Mahnomen, MN	218	56557
Mahomet, IL	217	61853
Mahopac, NY	845	10541
Mahwah, NJ	201, 551	07430, 07495-07498
Maiden, NC	828	28650
Maiden Rock, WI	715, 534	54750
Maitland, FL	321, 407	32751, 32794
Makanda, IL	618	62958
Makawao, HI	808	96768
Malad City, ID	208	83252
Malden, MA	339, 781	02148
Malden, MO	573	63863
Malibu, CA	310, 424	90263-90265
Malinta, OH	419, 567	43535
Malone, FL	850	32445
Malone, NY	518	12953
Malta, ID	208	83342
Malta, IL	815	60150
Malta, MT	406	59538
Malta, NY	518	12020
Malvern, AR	501	72104-72105
Malvern, OH	234, 330	44644
Malvern, PA	484, 610	19355
Malverne, NY	516	11565
Mamaroneck, NY	914	10543
Mammoth Cave, KY	270	42259
Mammoth Lakes, CA	760, 442	93546
Mamou, LA	337	70554
Manahawkin, NJ	609	08050
Manalapan, FL	561	33462
Manalapan, NJ	732, 848	07726
Manasquan, NJ	732, 848	08736
Manassas, VA	571, 703	20108-20113
Manassas Park, VA	571, 703	20111
Manawa, WI	920	54949
Manchester, CT	860	06040-06045
Manchester, IA	563	52057
Manchester, KY	606	40962
Manchester, ME	207	04351
Manchester, MI	734	48158
Manchester, NH	603	03101-03111
Manchester, TN	931	37349, 37355
Manchester, VT	802	05254
Manchester Center, VT	802	05255
Manchester Village, VT	802	05254
Mancos, CO	970	81328
Mandan, ND	701	58554
Mandeville, LA	985	70448, 70470-70471
Mangum, OK	580	73554
Manhasset, NY	516	11030
Manhattan, KS	785	66502-66506
Manhattan Beach, CA	310, 424	90266-90267
Manheim, PA	717	17545
Manila, UT	435	84046
Manistee, MI	231	49660
Manistique, MI	906	49854
Manitou, OK	580	73555
Manitou Springs, CO	719	80829
Manitowoc, WI	920	54220-54221
Mankato, KS	785	66956
Mankato, MN	507	56001-56006
Manlius, NY	315	13104
Manning, IA	712	51455
Manning, ND	701	58642
Manning, SC	803	29102
Manor, TX	512	78653
Mansfield, AR	479	72944
Mansfield, CT	860	06250, 06268
Mansfield, LA	318	71052
Mansfield, MA	508, 774	02031, 02048
Mansfield, MO	417	65704
Mansfield, OH	419, 567	44901-44907, 44999
Mansfield, PA	570	16933
Mansfield, TX	682, 817	76063
Manson, NC	252	27553
Manteca, CA	209	95336-95337
Manteno, IL	815	60950
Manteo, NC	252	27954
Manti, UT	435	84642
Mantorville, MN	507	55955
Mantua, NJ	856	08051
Mantua, OH	234, 330	44255
Many, LA	318	71449
Maple Glen, PA	215, 267	19002
Maple Grove, MN	763	55311, 55369, 55569
Maple Heights, OH	216	44137
Maple Park, IL	331, 630	60151
Maple Plain, MN	763	55348, 55359, 55393, 55570*
Maple Shade, NJ	856	08052
Maple Valley, WA	425	98038
Mapleton, OR	541, 458	97453
Mapleville, RI	401	02839
Maplewood, MN	651	55109, 55117-55119
Maplewood, NJ	862, 973	07040
Maplewood, NY	518	12189
Mappsville, VA	757	23407
Maquoketa, IA	563	52060
Marana, AZ	520	85653
Marathon, FL	305, 786	33050-33052
Marathon, WI	715, 534	54448
Marble City, OK	918	74945
Marble Falls, TX	830	78654-78657
Marblehead, MA	339, 781	01945
Marblehead, OH	419, 567	43440
Marceline, MO	660	64658
Marcellus, NY	315	13108
Marco Island, FL	239	34145-34146
Marcus, IA	712	51035
Marcy, NY	315	13403
Marengo, IL	815	60152
Marengo, IA	319	52301
Marfa, TX	915	79843
Margate, FL	754, 954	33063-33068, 33073, 33093
Marianna, AR	870	72360
Marianna, FL	850	32446-32448
Maricopa, AZ	520	85239
Marietta, GA	470, 678, 770	30006-30008, 30060-30069*
Marietta, OH	740	45750
Marietta, OK	580	73448
Marietta, PA	717	17547
Marina, CA	831	93933
Marina del Rey, CA	310, 424	90291-90295
Marine City, MI	810	48039
Marinette, WI	715, 534	54143
Marion, AL	334	36756
Marion, AR	870	72364
Marion, IL	618	62959
Marion, IN	765	46952-46953
Marion, IA	319	52302
Marion, KS	620	66861
Marion, KY	270	42064
Marion, MA	508, 774	02738
Marion, NY	315	14505
Marion, NC	828	28737, 28752
Marion, OH	740	43301-43302, 43306-43307
Marion, SC	843	29571
Marion, SD	605	57043
Marion, VA	276	24354
Marion, WI	715, 534	54950
Mariposa, CA	209	95338
Marissa, IL	618	62257
Marked Tree, AR	870	72365
Markham, IL	708	60426
Markle, IN	260	46770
Markleeville, CA	530	96120
Marks, MS	662	38646
Marksville, LA	318	71351
Marlboro, NJ	732, 848	07746
Marlboro, VT	802	05344
Marlborough, MA	508, 774	01752
Marlin, TX	254	76661
Marlinton, WV	304	24954
Marlow Heights, MD	301	20746-20748
Marlton, NJ	856	08053
Marquette, MI	906	49855
Marrero, LA	504	70072-70073
Marriottsville, MD	410	21104
Mars, PA	724, 878	16046
Mars Hill, NC	828	28754
Marshall, AR	870	72650
Marshall, IL	217	62441
Marshall, MI	616	49068-49069
Marshall, MN	507	56258
Marshall, MO	660	65340
Marshall, NC	828	28753
Marshall, TX	903	75670-75672
Marshall, WI	608	53559
Marshalls Creek, PA	570	18335
Marshalltown, IA	641	50158
Marshfield, MA	339, 781	02020, 02041, 02047-02051*
Marshfield, MO	417	65706
Marshfield, WI	715, 534	54404, 54441, 54449, 54472
Marshville, NC	704, 980	28103
Marstons Mills, MA	508, 774	02648
Martin, SD	605	57551
Martin, TN	731	38237-38238
Martinez, CA	925	94553
Martinez, GA	706, 762	30907
Martins Ferry, OH	740	43935

*Partial list of zip codes, including main range

City	Area Code(s)	Zip Code(s)
Martinsburg, WV	304	25401-25402
Martinsdale, MT	406	59053
Martinsville, IN	765	46151
Martinsville, VA	276	24112-24115
Maryland Heights, MO	314	63043
Marylhurst, OR	503, 971	97036
Marysville, CA	530	95901-95903
Marysville, KS	785	66508, 66555
Marysville, MI	810	48040
Marysville, OH	937	43040-43041
Marysville, PA	717	17053
Marysville, WA	360	98270-98271
Maryville, IL	618	62062
Maryville, MO	660	64468
Maryville, TN	865	37801-37804
Mascot, TN	865	37806
Mashantucket, CT	860	06339
Mashpee, MA	508, 774	02649
Mason, MI	517	48854
Mason, OH	513	45040
Mason, TX	915	76856
Mason City, IA	641	50401-50402, 50467
Maspeth, NY	347, 718	11378
Massapequa, NY	516	11758
Massena, IA	712	50853
Massena, NY	315	13662
Massillon, OH	234, 330	44646-44648
Matador, TX	806	79244
Matawan, NJ	732, 848	07747
Mather, CA	916	95655
Mathews, LA	985	70375
Mathews, VA	804	23109
Matteson, IL	708	60443
Matthews, NC	704, 980	28104-28106
Mattoon, IL	217	61938
Mattoon, WI	715, 534	54450
Mauldin, SC	864	29662
Maumee, OH	419, 567	43537
Maumelle, AR	501	72113, 72118
Maunaloa, HI	808	96770
Maury, NC	252	28554
Mauston, WI	608	53948
Maxton, NC	910	28364
Maxwell AFB, AL	334	36112-36113
Mayaguez, PR	787, 939	00680-00682
Maybrook, NY	845	12543
Mayersville, MS	662	39113
Mayetta, KS	785	66509
Mayfield, KY	270	42066
Mayfield, PA	570	18433
Mayfield Heights, OH	440	44124
Mayfield Village, OH	440	44143
Mayhill, NM	505	88339
Maynard, IA	563	50655
Maynard, MA	351, 978	01754
Maynardville, TN	865	37807
Mayo, FL	386	32066
Mayport, FL	904	32227-32228
Mays Landing, NJ	609	08330
Maysville, KY	606	41056
Maysville, MO	816	64469
Mayville, NY	716	14757
Mayville, ND	701	58257
Mayville, WI	920	53050
Maywood, CA	323	90270
Maywood, IL	708	60153-60155
Maywood, NE	308	69038
Maywood, NJ	201, 551	07607
Mazama, WA	509	98833
Mazomanie, WI	608	53560
McAdenville, NC	704, 980	28101
McAfee, NJ	862, 973	07428
McAlester, OK	918	74501-74502
McAllen, TX	956	78501-78505
McArthur, OH	740	45651
McBee, SC	843	29101
McCall, ID	208	83635-83638
McCalla, AL	205	35111
McCaysville, GA	706, 762	30555
McChord AFB, WA	253	98438-98439, 98499
McClelland, IA	712	51548
McCloud, CA	530	96057
McClusky, ND	701	58463
McComb, MS	601, 769	39648-39649
McComb, OH	419, 567	45858
McConnell AFB, KS	316	67221
McConnellsburg, PA	717	17233
McConnellsville, NY	315	13401
McConnelsville, OH	740	43756
McCook, IL	708	60525
McCook, NE	308	69001
McCordsville, IN	317	46055
McCormick, SC	864	29835
McDermott, OH	740	45652
McDonough, GA	470, 770	30252-30253
McEwen, TN	931	37101
McFarland, WI	608	53558
McGraw, NY	607	13101
McGregor, IA	563	52157
McGregor, MN	218	55760
McGregor, TX	254	76657
McGuire AFB, NJ	609	08641
McHenry, IL	815	60050-60051
McHenry, MD	301	21541
McIntosh, SD	605	57641
McKee, KY	606	40447
McKees Rocks, PA	412, 878	15136
McKeesport, PA	412, 878	15130
McKenzie, TN	731	38201
McKinleyville, CA	707	95519-95521
McKinney, TX	469, 972	75069-75071
McLean, TX	806	79057
McLean, VA	571, 703	22101-22106
McLeansboro, IL	618	62859
McLeansville, NC	336	27301
McLeod, MT	406	59052
McLoud, OK	405	74851
McLouth, KS	913	66054
McMinnville, OR	503, 971	97128
McMinnville, TN	931	37110-37111
McMurray, PA	724, 878	15317
McPherson, KS	620	67460
McRae, GA	229	31055
McShan, AL	205	35471
McSherrystown, PA	717	17344
Mead, WA	509	99021
Meade, KS	620	67864
Meadow Lands, PA	724, 878	15347
Meadowbrook, PA	215, 267	19046
Meadville, MS	601, 769	39653
Meadville, PA	814	16335, 16388
Mebane, NC	919	27302
Mechanicsburg, IL	217	62545
Mechanicsburg, PA	717	17050, 17055
Mechanicsville, VA	804	23111, 23116
Mechanicville, NY	518	12118
Medaryville, IN	219	47957
Medfield, MA	508, 774	02052
Medford, MA	339, 781	02153-02156
Medford, NJ	609	08055
Medford, NY	631	11763
Medford, OK	580	73759
Medford, OR	541, 458	97501-97504
Medford, WI	715, 534	54451
Media, PA	484, 610	19037, 19063-19065, 19086*
Medical Lake, WA	509	99022
Medicine Lake, MT	406	59247
Medicine Lodge, KS	620	67104
Medina, MN	763	55340, 55357-55359
Medina, NY	585	14103
Medina, OH	234, 330	44215, 44256-44258
Medley, FL	305, 786	33166, 33178
Medora, ND	701	58645
Medway, MA	508, 774	02053
Meeker, CO	970	81641
Mehoopany, PA	570	18629
Melba, ID	208	83641
Melbourne, AR	870	72556
Melbourne, FL	321	32901-32912, 32919, 32934*
Melbourne Beach, FL	321	32951
Melfa, VA	757	23410
Melrose, MA	339, 781	02176-02177
Melrose, MN	320	56352
Melrose Park, IL	708	60160-60165
Melrose Park, PA	215, 267	19027
Melville, NY	516, 631	11747, 11775
Melvin, IL	217	60952
Melvindale, MI	313	48122
Memphis, MO	660	63555
Memphis, TN	901	37501, 38101-38152, 38157*
Memphis, TX	806	79245
Mena, AR	479	71953
Menahga, MN	218	56464
Menan, ID	208	83434
Menard, IL	618	62259
Menard, TX	915	76859
Menasha, WI	920	54952
Mendenhall, MS	601, 769	39114
Mendham, NJ	862, 973	07945
Mendocino, CA	707	95460
Mendon, IL	217	62351
Mendon, MA	508, 774	01756
Mendota, CA	559	93640
Mendota, IL	815	61342
Mendota Heights, MN	651	55118-55120
Menlo, GA	706, 762	30731
Menlo Park, CA	650	94025-94029
Menominee, MI	906	49858
Menomonee Falls, WI	262	53051-53052
Menomonie, WI	715, 534	54751
Mentone, CA	909	92359
Mentone, IN	574	46539
Mentone, TX	915	79754
Mentor, OH	440	44060-44061
Mequon, WI	262	53092, 53097
Merced, CA	209	95340-95344, 95348
Mercedes, TX	956	78570
Mercer, PA	724, 878	16137
Mercer Island, WA	206	98040
Mercersburg, PA	717	17236
Mercerville, NJ	609	08619
Meredith, NH	603	03253
Meriden, CT	203	06450-06454
Meridian, GA	912	31319
Meridian, ID	208	83642, 83680
Meridian, MS	601, 769	39301-39309
Meridian, TX	254	76665
Merion, PA	484, 610	19066
Merkel, TX	915	79536
Merriam, KS	913	66202-66204
Merrick, NY	516	11566
Merrifield, VA	571, 703	22081-22082, 22116-22120
Merrill, MI	989	48637
Merrill, WI	715, 534	54452
Merrillville, IN	219	46410-46411
Merrimac, MA	351, 978	01860
Merrimac, WI	608	53561
Merrimack, NH	603	03054
Merritt Island, FL	321	32952-32954
Mertzon, TX	915	76941
Mertztown, PA	484, 610	19539
Mesa, AZ	480	85201-85216, 85274-85277
Mesa Verde National Park, CO	970	81330
Mesilla Park, NM	505	88047
Mesquite, NV	702	89024-89027
Mesquite, TX	469, 972	75149-75150, 75180-75187
Metairie, LA	504	70001-70011, 70033, 70055*
Metamora, IL	309	61548
Metcalf, GA	229	31792
Methuen, MA	351, 978	01844
Metlakatla, AK	907	99926
Metropolis, IL	618	62960
Metter, GA	912	30439
Metuchen, NJ	732, 848	08840
Mexia, TX	254	76667
Mexico, MO	573	65265
Mexico, NY	315	13114
Meyersdale, PA	814	15552
Miami, FL	305, 786	33010-33018, 33054-33056*
Miami, OK	918	74354-74355
Miami, TX	806	79059
Miami Beach, FL	305, 786	33109, 33119, 33139-33141*
Miami Lakes, FL	305, 786	33014-33018
Miami Shores, FL	305, 786	33138, 33150-33153, 33161*
Miami Springs, FL	305, 786	33166, 33266
Miamisburg, OH	937	45342-45343
Micanopy, FL	352	32667
Micaville, NC	828	28755
Michigan City, IN	219	46360-46361
Middle Granville, NY	518	12849
Middle Island, NY	631	11953
Middle River, MD	410	21220
Middle Village, NY	347, 718	11379
Middleboro, MA	508, 774	02344-02349
Middlebourne, WV	304	26149

*Partial list of zip codes, including main range

City	Area Code(s)	Zip Code(s)
Middleburg, PA	570	17842
Middleburg, VA	540	20117-20118
Middleburg Heights, OH	440	44130
Middlebury, CT	203	06762
Middlebury, IN	574	46540
Middlebury, VT	802	05753
Middlefield, CT	860	06455
Middlefield, OH	440	44062
Middleport, NY	585	14105
Middlesboro, KY	606	40965
Middlesex, NJ	732, 848	08846
Middleton, MA	351, 978	01949
Middleton, NH	603	03887
Middleton, WI	608	53562
Middletown, CA	707	95461
Middletown, CT	860	06457-06459
Middletown, DE	302	19709
Middletown, NJ	732, 848	07748
Middletown, NY	845	10940-10943
Middletown, OH	513	45042-45044
Middletown, PA	717	17057
Middletown, RI	401	02840-02842
Middletown, VA	540	22645, 22649
Midland, GA	706, 762	31820
Midland, MI	989	48640-48642, 48667-48670*
Midland, NC	704, 980	28107
Midland, TX	915	79701-79712
Midland, VA	540	22728
Midland Park, NJ	201, 551	07432
Midlothian, IL	708	60445
Midlothian, TX	469, 972	76065
Midlothian, VA	804	23112-23114
Midvale, UT	801, 385	84047
Midway, FL	850	32343
Midway, GA	912	31320
Midway, KY	859	40347
Midway, UT	435	84049
Midwest City, OK	405	73110, 73130, 73140, 73145
Mifflinburg, PA	570	17844
Mifflintown, PA	717	17059
Milaca, MN	320	56353
Milan, GA	229	31060
Milan, IL	309	61264
Milan, MI	734	48160
Milan, MO	660	63556
Milan, OH	419, 567	44846
Milan, TN	731	38358
Milbank, SD	605	57252-57253
Milbridge, ME	207	04658
Miles City, MT	406	59301
Milford, CT	203	06460
Milford, DE	302	19963
Milford, IN	574	46542
Milford, IA	712	51351
Milford, MA	508, 774	01757
Milford, MI	248, 947	48380-48381
Milford, NE	402	68405
Milford, NH	603	03055
Milford, OH	513	45150
Milford, PA	570	18337
Mililani, HI	808	96789
Mill City, OR	503, 971	97360
Mill Run, PA	724, 878	15464
Mill Valley, CA	415	94941-94942
Millboro, VA	540	24460
Millbrae, CA	650	94030-94031
Millbrook, NY	845	12545
Millburn, NJ	862, 973	07041
Millbury, MA	508, 774	01527, 01586
Millbury, OH	419, 567	43447
Milldale, CT	860	06467
Milledgeville, GA	478	31059-31062
Millen, GA	478	30442
Miller, SD	605	57362
Millersburg, OH	234, 330	44654
Millersburg, PA	717	17061
Millersville, MD	410	21108
Millersville, PA	717	17551
Millersville, TN	615	37072
Millerton, NY	518	12546
Milligan College, TN	423	37682
Millington, TN	901	38053-38055, 38083
Millinocket, ME	207	04462
Millis, MA	508, 774	02054
Mills, WY	307	82604, 82644
Millville, NJ	856	08332
Millwood, VA	540	22646

City	Area Code(s)	Zip Code(s)
Milpitas, CA	408	95035-95036
Milroy, IN	765	46156
Milton, FL	850	32570-32572, 32583
Milton, MA	617, 857	02186
Milton, NY	845	12547
Milton, PA	570	17847
Milton, WV	304	25541
Milton, WI	608	53563
Milton-Freewater, OR	541, 458	97862
Milwaukee, WI	414	53201-53228, 53233-53237*
Milwaukie, OR	503, 971	97222, 97267-97269
Minden, LA	318	71055-71058
Minden, NE	308	68959
Minden, NV	775	89423
Mineola, NY	516	11501
Mineral, CA	530	96061-96063
Mineral Point, MO	573	63660
Mineral Wells, TX	940	76067-76068
Mineral Wells, WV	304	26120-26121, 26150
Minersville, PA	570	17954
Minerva, OH	234, 330	44657
Mineville, NY	518	12956
Mingo Junction, OH	740	43938
Minneapolis, KS	785	67467
Minneapolis, MN	612, 763, 952	55401-55450, 55454-55460*
Minnesota Lake, MN	507	56068
Minnetonka, MN	763, 952	55305, 55343-55345
Minnewaukan, ND	701	58351
Minonk, IL	309	61760
Minooka, IL	815	60447
Minot, ND	701	58701-58707, 58768
Minot AFB, ND	701	58704-58705
Minster, OH	419, 567	45865
Mio, MI	989	48647
Mira Loma, CA	951	91752
Miramar, FL	754, 954	33023-33029, 33083
Misenheimer, NC	704, 980	28109
Mishawaka, IN	574	46544-46546
Mishicot, WI	920	54228
Mission, KS	913	66201-66205, 66222
Mission, SD	605	57555
Mission, TX	956	78572-78573
Mission Hills, CA	818	91345-91346, 91395
Mission Viejo, CA	949	92675, 92690-92694
Mission Woods, KS	913	66205
Mississippi State, MS	662	39762
Missoula, MT	406	59801-59808, 59812
Missouri City, TX	281, 832	77459, 77489
Mitchell, IN	812	47446
Mitchell, NE	308	69357
Mitchell, SD	605	57301
Mitchells, VA	540	22729
Mitchellville, IA	515	50169
Mitchellville, MD	301	20716-20717, 20721
Moab, UT	435	84532
Moberly, MO	660	65270
Mobile, AL	251	36601-36633, 36640-36644*
Mocksville, NC	336	27028
Model City, NY	716	14107
Modesto, CA	209	95350-95358, 95397
Moffett Field, CA	650	94035
Mogadore, OH	234, 330	44260
Mohall, ND	701	58761
Mohawk, NY	315	13407
Mohnton, PA	484, 610	19540
Mojave, CA	661	93501-93502, 93519
Mokena, IL	708	60448
Molalla, OR	503, 971	97038
Moline, IL	309	61265-61266
Monaca, PA	724, 878	15061
Monahans, TX	915	79756
Monarch, CO	719	81227
Moncks Corner, SC	843	29430, 29461
Mondovi, WI	715, 534	54755, 54764
Monee, IL	708	60449
Monessen, PA	724, 878	15062
Monett, MO	417	65708
Monitor, WA	509	98836
Monmouth, IL	309	61462
Monmouth, OR	503, 971	97361
Monmouth Junction, NJ	732, 848	08852
Monona, IA	563	52159
Monongahela, PA	724, 878	15063
Monroe, CT	203	06468
Monroe, GA	470, 770	30655-30656
Monroe, IA	641	50170

City	Area Code(s)	Zip Code(s)
Monroe, LA	318	71201-71203, 71207-71213
Monroe, MI	734	48161-48162
Monroe, NC	704, 980	28110-28112
Monroe, OH	513	45050, 45073, 45099
Monroe, WA	360	98272
Monroe, WI	608	53566
Monroe Township, NJ	609	08831
Monroeville, AL	251	36460-36462
Monroeville, PA	412, 878	15140, 15146
Monrovia, CA	626	91016-91017
Monsey, NY	845	10952
Mont Alto, PA	717	17237
Montague, MI	231	49437
Montague, TX	940	76251
Montauk, NY	631	11954
Montclair, CA	909	91763
Montclair, NJ	862, 973	07042-07043
Monte Vista, CO	719	81135, 81144
Montebello, CA	323	90640
Montebello, NY	845	10901
Montecito, CA	805	93108, 93150
Montello, WI	608	53949
Monterey, CA	831	93940-93944
Monterey, VA	540	24465
Monterey Park, CA	323, 626	91754-91756
Montesano, WA	360	98563
Montevallo, AL	205	35115
Montevideo, MN	320	56265
Montezuma, IA	641	50171
Montezuma, KS	620	67867
Montgomery, AL	334	36101-36125, 36130-36135*
Montgomery, IL	331, 630	60538
Montgomery, NY	845	12549
Montgomery, PA	570	17752
Montgomery, TX	936	77316, 77356
Montgomery, WV	304	25136
Montgomery City, MO	573	63361
Montgomery Village, MD	301	20877-20879, 20886
Montgomeryville, PA	215, 267	18936
Monticello, AR	870	71655-71657
Monticello, FL	850	32344-32345
Monticello, GA	706, 762	31064
Monticello, IL	217	61856
Monticello, IN	574	47960
Monticello, IA	319	52310
Monticello, KY	606	42633
Monticello, MN	763	55362-55365, 55561-55565*
Monticello, MS	601, 769	39654
Monticello, MO	573	63457
Monticello, NY	845	12701, 12777
Monticello, UT	435	84535
Montour Falls, NY	607	14865
Montoursville, PA	570	17754
Montpelier, IN	765	47359
Montpelier, OH	419, 567	43543
Montpelier, VT	802	05601-05604, 05609, 05620*
Montreat, NC	828	28757
Montrose, CA	818	91020-91021
Montrose, CO	970	81401-81402
Montrose, MI	810	48457
Montrose, NY	845	10548
Montrose, PA	570	18801
Montross, VA	804	22520
Montvale, NJ	201, 551	07645
Montville, NJ	862, 973	07045
Monument, OR	541, 458	97864
Moodus, CT	860	06469
Moody, AL	205	35004
Moon Township, PA	412, 878	15108
Moonachie, NJ	201, 551	07074
Moore, OK	405	73153, 73160, 73170
Moore Haven, FL	863	33471
Moorefield, WV	304	26836
Moorestown, NJ	856	08057
Mooresville, IN	317	46158
Mooresville, NC	704, 980	28115-28117
Moorhead, MN	218	56560-56563
Moorhead, MS	662	38761
Moorpark, CA	805	93020-93021
Moose, WY	307	83012
Moose Lake, MN	218	55767
Mooseheart, IL	331, 630	60539
Moosic, PA	570	18507
Moosup, CT	860	06354
Mora, MN	320	55051
Mora, NM	505	87732
Moraga, CA	925	94556, 94570, 94575

**Partial list of zip codes, including main range*

City	Area Code(s)	Zip Code(s)
Moran, WY	307	83013
Moravia, NY	315	13118
Morehead, KY	606	40351
Morehead City, NC	252	28557
Morenci, AZ	928	85540
Morenci, MI	517	49256
Moreno Valley, CA	951	92551-92557
Morgan, GA	229	31766
Morgan, MN	507	56266
Morgan, UT	801, 385	84050
Morgan City, LA	985	70380-70381
Morgan Hill, CA	408	95037-95038
Morganfield, KY	270	42437
Morganton, NC	828	28655, 28680
Morgantown, KY	270	42261
Morgantown, PA	484, 610	19543
Morgantown, WV	304	26501-26508
Moro, OR	541, 458	97039
Moroni, UT	435	84646
Morrilton, AR	501	72110
Morris, AL	205	35116
Morris, IL	815	60450
Morris, MN	320	56267
Morris Plains, NJ	862, 973	07950
Morrison, CO	303, 720	80465
Morrison, IL	815	61270
Morristown, IN	765	46161
Morristown, NJ	862, 973	07960-07963
Morristown, OH	740	43759
Morristown, TN	423	37813-37816
Morrisville, NY	315	13408
Morrisville, NC	919	27560
Morrisville, PA	215, 267	19067
Morrisville, VT	802	05657, 05661
Morro Bay, CA	805	93442-93443
Morrow, GA	470, 770	30260, 30287
Morton, IL	309	61550
Morton, MN	507	56270
Morton, MS	601, 769	39117
Morton, TX	806	79346
Morton Grove, IL	224, 847	60053
Mosca, CO	719	81146
Moscow, ID	208	83843-83844
Moscow, TN	901	38057
Moselle, MS	601, 769	39459
Moses Lake, WA	509	98837
Mosinee, WI	715, 534	54455
Mosquero, NM	505	87733
Moss Beach, CA	650	94038
Moss Landing, CA	831	95039
Moss Point, MS	228	39562-39563, 39581
Motley, MN	218	56466
Mott, ND	701	58646
Moulton, AL	256	35650
Moultrie, GA	229	31768, 31776
Mound City, IL	618	62963
Mound City, KS	913	66056
Mound City, SD	605	57646
Moundridge, KS	620	67107
Mounds View, MN	763	55112
Moundsville, WV	304	26041
Mount Airy, NC	336	27030-27031
Mount Angel, OR	503, 971	97362
Mount Arlington, NJ	862, 973	07856
Mount Ayr, IA	641	50854
Mount Berry, GA	706, 762	30149
Mount Carmel, IL	618	62863
Mount Carmel, PA	570	17851
Mount Carroll, IL	815	61053
Mount Clemens, MI	586	48043-48046
Mount Crawford, VA	540	22841
Mount Crested Butte, CO	970	81225
Mount Dora, FL	352	32756-32757
Mount Freedom, NJ	862, 973	07970
Mount Gay, WV	304	25637
Mount Gilead, NC	910	27306
Mount Gilead, OH	419, 567	43338
Mount Holly, NJ	609	08060
Mount Holly, NC	704, 980	28120
Mount Hope, OH	234, 330	44660
Mount Ida, AR	870	71957
Mount Jackson, VA	540	22842
Mount Joy, PA	717	17552
Mount Juliet, TN	615	37121-37122
Mount Kisco, NY	914	10549
Mount Laurel, NJ	856	08054
Mount Lebanon, PA	412, 878	15228
Mount Marion, NY	845	12456
Mount Meigs, AL	334	36057
Mount Morris, IL	815	61054
Mount Morris, NY	585	14510
Mount Olive, MS	601, 769	39119
Mount Olive, NJ	862, 973	07828
Mount Olive, NC	919	28365
Mount Olive, WV	304	25185
Mount Olivet, KY	606	41064
Mount Pleasant, IA	319	52641
Mount Pleasant, MI	989	48804, 48858-48859
Mount Pleasant, NC	704, 980	28124
Mount Pleasant, PA	724, 878	15666
Mount Pleasant, SC	843	29464-29466
Mount Pleasant, TN	931	38474
Mount Pleasant, TX	903	75455-75456
Mount Pocono, PA	570	18344
Mount Prospect, IL	224, 847	60056
Mount Pulaski, IL	217	62548
Mount Royal, NJ	856	08061
Mount Shasta, CA	530	96067
Mount Solon, VA	540	22843
Mount Sterling, IL	217	62353
Mount Sterling, KY	859	40353
Mount Sterling, OH	740	43143
Mount Vernon, AL	251	36560
Mount Vernon, GA	912	30445
Mount Vernon, IL	618	62864
Mount Vernon, IN	812	47620
Mount Vernon, IA	319	52314
Mount Vernon, KY	606	40456
Mount Vernon, MO	417	65712
Mount Vernon, NY	914	10550-10553, 10557-10558
Mount Vernon, OH	740	43050
Mount Vernon, TX	903	75457
Mount Vernon, VA	571, 703	22121
Mount Vernon, WA	360	98273-98274
Mount Washington, KY	502	40047
Mount Wolf, PA	717	17347
Mountain City, TN	423	37683
Mountain Grove, MO	417	65711
Mountain Home, AR	870	72653-72654
Mountain Home, ID	208	83647
Mountain Home, TN	423	37684
Mountain Home AFB, ID	208	83648
Mountain Lakes, NJ	862, 973	07046
Mountain Pass, CA	760, 442	92366
Mountain Pine, AR	501	71956
Mountain Top, PA	570	18707
Mountain View, AR	870	72533, 72560
Mountain View, CA	650	94035, 94039-94043
Mountain View, MO	417	65548
Mountain View, WY	307	82939
Mountainair, NM	505	87036
Mountainside, NJ	908	07092
Mountlake Terrace, WA	425	98043
Moville, IA	712	51039
Moxee, WA	509	98936
Muenster, TX	940	76252
Mukilteo, WA	425	98275
Mukwonago, WI	262	53149
Mulberry, FL	863	33860
Muleshoe, TX	806	79347
Mullen, NE	308	69152
Mullica Hill, NJ	856	08062
Muncie, IN	765	47302-47308
Muncy, PA	570	17756
Mundelein, IL	224, 847	60060
Munfordville, KY	270	42765
Munhall, PA	412, 878	15120
Munising, MI	906	49862
Munroe Falls, OH	234, 330	44262
Munster, IN	219	46321
Murdo, SD	605	57559
Murdock, NE	402	68407
Murfreesboro, AR	870	71958
Murfreesboro, NC	252	27855
Murfreesboro, TN	615	37127-37133
Murphy, ID	208	83650
Murphy, NC	828	28906
Murphysboro, IL	618	62966
Murray, KY	270	42071
Murray, UT	801, 385	84107, 84117, 84121-84123*
Murray Hill, NJ	908	07974
Murrells Inlet, SC	843	29576
Murrieta, CA	951	92562-92564
Murrysville, PA	724, 878	15668
Muscatine, IA	563	52761
Muscle Shoals, AL	256	35661-35662
Muskego, WI	262	53150
Muskegon, MI	231	49440-49445
Muskegon Heights, MI	231	49444
Muskogee, OK	918	74401-74403
Mustang, OK	405	73064
Myerstown, PA	717	17067
Myrtle Beach, SC	843	29572-29579, 29587-29588
Mystic, CT	860	06355, 06388

N

City	Area Code(s)	Zip Code(s)
Nacogdoches, TX	936	75961-75965
Nageezi, NM	505	87037
Nags Head, NC	252	27959
Nahunta, GA	912	31553
Naknek, AK	907	99633
Nampa, ID	208	83651-83653, 83686-83687
Nanticoke, MD	410	21840
Nanticoke, PA	570	18634
Nantucket, MA	508, 774	02554, 02564, 02584
Nanuet, NY	845	10954
Napa, CA	707	94558-94559, 94581
Napanoch, NY	845	12458
Naperville, IL	331, 630	60540, 60563-60567
Naples, FL	239	34101-34120
Naples, NY	585	14512
Napoleon, ND	701	58561
Napoleon, OH	419, 567	43545
Napoleonville, LA	985	70390
Nappanee, IN	574	46550
Narberth, PA	484, 610	19072
Narragansett, RI	401	02874, 02879-02882
Naselle, WA	360	98638
Nashotah, WI	262	53058
Nashua, NH	603	03060-03064
Nashville, AR	870	71852
Nashville, GA	229	31639
Nashville, IL	618	62263
Nashville, IN	812	47448
Nashville, NC	252	27856
Nashville, TN	615	37201-37250
Nassau, NY	518	12123
Nassau Bay, TX	281, 832	77058, 77258
Nassawadox, VA	757	23413
Natchez, MS	601, 769	39120-39122
Natchitoches, LA	318	71457-71458, 71497
Nathrop, CO	719	81236
Natick, MA	508, 774	01760
National City, CA	619	91950-91951
Natrona Heights, PA	724, 878	15065
Natural Bridge Station, VA	540	24579
Naugatuck, CT	203	06770
Navarre, MN	952	55392
Navarre, OH	234, 330	44662
Navasota, TX	936	77868-77869
Navesink, NJ	732, 848	07752
Nazareth, PA	484, 610	18064
Nebo, NC	828	28761
Nebraska City, NE	402	68410
Nederland, TX	409	77627
Nedrow, NY	315	13120
Needham, MA	339, 781	02492-02494
Needham Heights, MA	339, 781	02494
Neenah, WI	920	54956-54957
Neillsville, WI	715, 534	54456
Neligh, NE	402	68756
Nellis AFB, NV	702	89191
Nelson, NE	402	68961
Nelsonville, OH	740	45764
Neodesha, KS	620	66757
Neosho, MO	417	64850-64853
Nephi, UT	435	84648
Neponset, IL	309	61345
Neptune, NJ	732, 848	07753-07754
Neptune Beach, FL	904	32266
Nespelem, WA	509	99155
Nesquehoning, PA	570	18240
Ness City, KS	785	67560
Netcong, NJ	862, 973	07857
Nettleton, MS	662	38858
Nevada, IA	515	50201
Nevada, MO	417	64772

*Partial list of zip codes, including main range

City	Area Code(s)	Zip Code(s)
Nevada City, CA	530	95959
Neversink, NY	845	12765
New Albany, IN	812	47150-47151
New Albany, MS	662	38652
New Albany, OH	614	43054
New Augusta, MS	601, 769	39462
New Baltimore, MI	586	48047, 48051
New Bedford, MA	508, 774	02740-02746
New Berlin, NY	607	13411
New Berlin, WI	262	53146, 53151
New Bern, NC	252	28560-28564
New Bethlehem, PA	814	16242
New Bloomfield, PA	717	17068
New Boston, TX	903	75570
New Braunfels, TX	830	78130-78135
New Bremen, OH	419, 567	45869
New Brighton, MN	651	55112
New Brighton, PA	724, 878	15066
New Britain, CT	860	06050-06053
New Brunswick, NJ	732, 848	08901-08906, 08922, 08933*
New Canaan, CT	203	06840-06842
New Carlisle, IN	574	46552
New Carlisle, OH	937	45344
New Castle, CO	970	81647
New Castle, DE	302	19720-19721
New Castle, IN	765	47362
New Castle, KY	502	40050
New Castle, PA	724, 878	16101-16108
New Castle, VA	540	24127
New Century, KS	913	66031
New City, NY	845	10956
New Columbia, PA	570	17856
New Concord, OH	740	43762
New Cumberland, PA	717	17070
New Cumberland, WV	304	26047
New England, ND	701	58647
New Enterprise, PA	814	16664
New Era, MI	231	49446
New Fairfield, CT	203	06812
New Freedom, PA	717	17349
New Glarus, WI	608	53574
New Gretna, NJ	609	08224
New Hampton, IA	641	50659-50661
New Hampton, NY	845	10958
New Harbor, ME	207	04554, 04558
New Hartford, CT	860	06057
New Hartford, NY	315	13413
New Haven, CT	203	06501-06525, 06530-06540
New Haven, IN	260	46774
New Haven, MI	586	48048-48050
New Hill, NC	919	27562
New Holland, PA	717	17557
New Hope, MN	763	55427-55428
New Hope, PA	215, 267	18938
New Hyde Park, NY	516	11040-11044, 11099
New Iberia, LA	337	70560-70563
New Kensington, PA	724, 878	15068-15069
New Kent, VA	804	23124
New Kingstown, PA	717	17072
New Knoxville, OH	419, 567	45871
New Lebanon, NY	518	12125
New Lenox, IL	815	60451
New Lexington, OH	740	43764
New Lisbon, NJ	609	08064
New Lisbon, WI	608	53950
New London, CT	860	06320
New London, IA	319	52645
New London, MO	573	63459
New London, NH	603	03257
New London, OH	419, 567	44851
New London, WI	920	54961
New Madrid, MO	573	63869
New Market, VA	540	22844
New Martinsville, WV	304	26155
New Milford, CT	860	06776
New Milford, NJ	201, 551	07646
New Orleans, LA	504	70112-70131, 70139-70190*
New Oxford, PA	717	17350
New Paltz, NY	845	12561
New Paris, IN	574	46553
New Philadelphia, OH	234, 330	44663
New Port Richey, FL	727	34652-34656
New Providence, NJ	908	07974
New Richmond, OH	513	45157
New Richmond, WI	715, 534	54017
New Roads, LA	225	70760
New Rochelle, NY	914	10801-10805
New Rockford, ND	701	58356
New Sharon, IA	641	50207
New Smyrna Beach, FL	386	32168-32170
New Springfield, OH	234, 330	44443
New Tazewell, TN	423	37824-37825
New Town, ND	701	58763
New Ulm, MN	507	56073
New Wilmington, PA	724, 878	16142, 16172
New Windsor, MD	410	21776
New Windsor, NY	845	12553
New York, NY	212, 646, 917	10001-10048, 10055, 10060*
New York Mills, MN	218	56567
New York Mills, NY	315	13417
Newark, CA	510	94560
Newark, DE	302	19702, 19711-19718, 19725*
Newark, NJ	862, 973	07101-07108, 07112-07114*
Newark, NY	315	14513
Newark, OH	740	43055-43058, 43093
Newaygo, MI	231	49337
Newberg, OR	503, 971	97132
Newberry, MI	906	49868
Newberry, SC	803	29108
Newburg, WI	262	53060
Newburgh, IN	812	47629-47630
Newburgh, NY	845	12550-12555
Newbury, OH	440	44065
Newbury Park, CA	805	91319-91320
Newburyport, MA	351, 978	01950-01951
Newcastle, WY	307	82701, 82715
Newcomerstown, OH	740	43832
Newell, SD	605	57760
Newell, WV	304	26050
Newfane, VT	802	05345
Newhall, CA	661	91321-91322, 91381-91382
Newington, CT	860	06111, 06131
Newington, NH	603	03801
Newington, VA	571, 703	22122
Newkirk, OK	580	74647
Newland, NC	828	28657
Newman Grove, NE	402	68758
Newnan, GA	470, 678, 770	30263-30265, 30271
Newport, AR	870	72112
Newport, DE	302	19804
Newport, IN	765	47966
Newport, KY	859	41071-41076, 41099
Newport, MN	651	55055
Newport, NH	603	03773
Newport, NC	252	28570
Newport, OR	541, 458	97365-97366
Newport, RI	401	02840-02841
Newport, TN	423	37821-37822
Newport, VT	802	05855
Newport, WA	509	99156
Newport Beach, CA	949	92657-92663
Newport News, VA	757	23600-23612, 23628
Newton, GA	229	31770
Newton, IL	618	62448
Newton, IA	641	50208
Newton, KS	316	67114-67117
Newton, MA	617, 857	02456-02468, 02495
Newton, NJ	862, 973	07860
Newton, NC	828	28658
Newton, TX	409	75966
Newton Center, MA	617, 857	02459
Newton Falls, OH	234, 330	44444
Newton Grove, NC	910	28366
Newton Upper Falls, MA	617, 857	02464
Newtonville, NY	518	12110, 12128
Newtown, CT	203	06470
Newtown, PA	215, 267	18940
Newtown Square, PA	484, 610	19073
Nezperce, ID	208	83543
Niagara Falls, NY	716	14301-14305
Niagara University, NY	716	14109
Niantic, CT	860	06357
Niceville, FL	850	32578, 32588
Nicholasville, KY	859	40340, 40356
Niles, IL	224, 847	60714
Niles, MI	616	49120-49121
Niles, OH	234, 330	44446
Ninety Six, SC	864	29666
Niota, TN	423	37826
Nipomo, CA	805	93444
Niskayuna, NY	518	12309
Nisswa, MN	218	56468
Nixon, TX	830	78140
Noble, OK	405	73068
Noblesville, IN	317	46060-46061
Nocona, TX	940	76255
Nogales, AZ	520	85621, 85628, 85648, 85662
Nokomis, FL	941	34274-34275
Nome, AK	907	99762
Norco, CA	951	92860
Norcross, GA	470, 678, 770	30003, 30010, 30071, 30091*
Norfolk, CT	860	06058
Norfolk, MA	508, 774	02056
Norfolk, NE	402	68701-68702
Norfolk, VA	757	23500-23523, 23529-23530*
Normal, AL	256	35762
Normal, IL	309	61761, 61790
Norman, OK	405	73019, 73026, 73069-73072
Norridge, IL	708	60634, 60656, 60706
Norristown, PA	484, 610	19401-19409, 19488-19489
North Adams, MA	413	01247
North Amityville, NY	631	11701
North Andover, MA	351, 978	01845
North Anson, ME	207	04958
North Attleboro, MA	508, 774	02760-02763
North Augusta, SC	803	29841-29842, 29860-29861
North Aurora, IL	331, 630	60542
North Babylon, NY	631	11703
North Baltimore, OH	419, 567	45872
North Barrington, IL	224, 847	60010
North Bay Village, FL	305, 786	33141
North Bend, OR	541, 458	97459
North Bend, WA	425	98045
North Bergen, NJ	201, 551	07047
North Berwick, ME	207	03906
North Billerica, MA	351, 978	01862
North Branch, MN	651	55056
North Branch, NJ	908	08876
North Branford, CT	203	06471
North Brookfield, MA	508, 774	01535
North Brunswick, NJ	732, 848	08902
North Canton, OH	234, 330	44709, 44720
North Charleston, SC	843	29405-29406, 29410, 29415*
North Chelmsford, MA	351, 978	01863
North Chicago, IL	224, 847	60064, 60086-60088
North Chili, NY	585	14514
North Clarendon, VT	802	05759
North Conway, NH	603	03860
North Dartmouth, MA	508, 774	02747
North Dighton, MA	508, 774	02764
North East, MD	410	21901
North East, PA	814	16428
North Easton, MA	508, 774	02356-02357
North Falmouth, MA	508, 774	02556, 02565
North Fort Myers, FL	239	33903, 33917-33918
North Grafton, MA	508, 774	01536
North Grosvenordale, CT	860	06255
North Haledon, NJ	862, 973	07508, 07538
North Haven, CT	203	06473
North Haverhill, NH	603	03774
North Hero, VT	802	05474
North Highlands, CA	916	95660
North Hills, CA	818	91343, 91393
North Hollywood, CA	818	91601-91618
North Huntingdon, PA	724, 878	15642
North Judson, IN	574	46366
North Kansas City, MO	816	64116
North Kingstown, RI	401	02852-02854, 02874
North Kingsville, OH	440	44068
North Lake, WI	262	53064
North Las Vegas, NV	702	89030-89036, 89084-89086
North Liberty, IA	319	52317
North Lima, OH	234, 330	44452
North Little Rock, AR	501	72113-72120, 72124, 72190*
North Logan, UT	435	84341
North Manchester, IN	260	46962
North Mankato, MN	507	56002-56003
North Miami, FL	305, 786	33161-33162, 33167-33169*
North Miami Beach, FL	305, 786	33160-33162, 33169, 33179*
North Monmouth, ME	207	04265
North Myrtle Beach, SC	843	29582, 29597-29598
North Newton, KS	316	67117
North Olmsted, OH	440	44070
North Palm Beach, FL	561	33403, 33408-33410
North Pekin, IL	309	61554

*Partial list of zip codes, including main range

City	Area Code(s)	Zip Code(s)
North Plains, OR	503, 971	97133
North Platte, NE	308	69101-69103
North Providence, RI	401	02904, 02908-02911
North Quincy, MA	617, 857	02171
North Redington Beach, FL	727	33708
North Richland Hills, TX	682, 817	76118, 76180-76182
North Ridgeville, OH	440	44035, 44039
North Riverside, IL	708	60546
North Royalton, OH	440	44133
North Saint Paul, MN	651	55109
North Salt Lake, UT	801, 385	84054
North Scituate, RI	401	02857
North Sioux City, SD	605	57049
North Smithfield, RI	401	02824, 02896
North Springfield, VT	802	05150
North Stonington, CT	860	06359
North Syracuse, NY	315	13212
North Tonawanda, NY	716	14120
North Vernon, IN	812	47265
North Versailles, PA	412, 878	15137
North Wales, PA	215, 267	19436, 19454-19455, 19477
North Warren, PA	814	16365
North Webster, IN	574	46555
North White Plains, NY	914	10603
North Wilkesboro, NC	336	28656-28659, 28674
Northampton, MA	413	01060-01063
Northampton, PA	484, 610	18067
Northborough, MA	508, 774	01532
Northbrook, IL	224, 847	60062-60065
Northeast Harbor, ME	207	04662
Northfield, IL	224, 847	60093
Northfield, MN	507	55057
Northfield, NJ	609	08225
Northfield, OH	234, 330	44056, 44067
Northfield, VT	802	05663
Northford, CT	203	06472
Northlake, IL	708	60164
Northport, AL	205	35473-35476
Northport, NY	631	11768
Northridge, CA	818	91324-91330, 91343
Northumberland, PA	570	17857
Northvale, NJ	201, 551	07647
Northville, MI	248	48167
Northwood, IA	641	50459
Northwood, OH	419, 567	43605, 43619
Norton, KS	785	67654
Norton, MA	508, 774	02766
Norton, OH	234, 330	44203
Norton, VA	276	24273
Norton Shores, MI	231	49441
Norwalk, CA	562	90650-90652, 90659
Norwalk, CT	203	06850-06860
Norwalk, OH	419, 567	44857
Norway, IA	319	52318
Norwell, MA	339, 781	02018, 02061
Norwich, CT	860	06351, 06360, 06365
Norwich, KS	620	67118
Norwich, NY	607	13815
Norwich, OH	740	43767
Norwood, MA	339, 781	02062
Norwood, MN	952	55368, 55383, 55554, 55583
Norwood, NJ	201, 551	07648
Norwood, NC	704, 980	28128
Norwood, OH	513	45207, 45212
Notre Dame, IN	574	46556
Nottingham, PA	484, 610	19362
Nottoway, VA	434	23955
Novato, CA	415	94945-94949, 94998
Novi, MI	248, 947	48374-48377
Nowata, OK	918	74048
Nucla, CO	970	81424
Nuevo, CA	951	92567
Nutley, NJ	862, 973	07110
Nyack, NY	845	10960
Nyssa, OR	541, 458	97913

O

City	Area Code(s)	Zip Code(s)
Oak Brook, IL	331, 630	60521-60523, 60527, 60561
Oak Creek, WI	414	53154
Oak Forest, IL	708	60452
Oak Grove, LA	318	71263
Oak Grove, OR	503, 971	97222, 97267-97268
Oak Grove, VA	804	22443
Oak Harbor, WA	360	98277-98278
Oak Hill, WV	304	25901
Oak Lawn, IL	708	60453-60459
Oak Park, IL	708	60301-60304
Oak Park, MI	248, 947	48237
Oak Ridge, NJ	862, 973	07438
Oak Ridge, TN	865	37830-37831
Oakbrook Terrace, IL	331, 630	60181
Oakdale, CA	209	95361
Oakdale, LA	318	71463
Oakdale, MN	651	55042, 55128
Oakdale, NY	631	11769
Oakdale, PA	412, 878	15071
Oakdale, WI	608	54649
Oakham, MA	508, 774	01068
Oakhurst, CA	559	93644
Oakhurst, NJ	732, 848	07755
Oakland, CA	510	94601-94627, 94643, 94649*
Oakland, MD	301	21550
Oakland, NJ	201, 551	07436
Oakland, TN	901	38060
Oakland City, IN	812	47660
Oakland Park, FL	754, 954	33304-33311, 33334
Oakley, CA	925	94513, 94561
Oakley, KS	785	67748
Oakmont, PA	412, 878	15139
Oaks, PA	484, 610	19456
Oakton, VA	571, 703	22124
Oakville, CA	707	94562
Oakville, IA	319	52646
Oakwood, GA	470, 770	30502, 30566
Oakwood, OH	419, 567	45409, 45419, 45873
Oakwood, VA	276	24631
Oakwood Village, OH	440	44146
Oberlin, KS	785	67749
Oberlin, LA	337	70655
Oberlin, OH	440	44074
Oblong, IL	618	62449
Ocala, FL	352	34470-34483
Ocean, NJ	732, 848	07712
Ocean City, MD	410	21842-21843
Ocean City, NJ	609	08226
Ocean Shores, WA	360	98569
Ocean Springs, MS	228	39564-39566
Oceano, CA	805	93445
Oceanport, NJ	732, 848	07757
Oceanside, CA	760, 442	92049-92058
Oceanside, NY	516	11572
Oceanville, NJ	609	08231
Ochopee, FL	239	34141
Ocilla, GA	229	31774
Ocoee, FL	321, 407	34761
Oconomowoc, WI	262	53066
Oconto, WI	920	54153
Oconto Falls, WI	920	54154
Odenton, MD	410	21113
Odessa, FL	813	33556
Odessa, MO	816	64076
Odessa, TX	915	79760-79769
Odessa, WA	509	99144, 99159
Odon, IN	812	47562
Odum, GA	912	31555
Oelwein, IA	319	50662
O'Fallon, MO	636	63366-63367
Offutt AFB, NE	402	68113
Ogallala, NE	308	69153
Ogden, UT	801, 385	84201, 84244, 84401-84415
Ogdensburg, NY	315	13669
Oglesby, IL	815	61348
Oglethorpe, GA	478	31068
Ogunquit, ME	207	03907
Oil City, PA	814	16301
Ojai, CA	805	93023-93024
Ojo Caliente, NM	505	87549
Ojus, FL	305, 786	33163, 33180
Okahumpka, FL	352	34762
Okanogan, WA	509	98840
Okarche, OK	405	73762
Okeechobee, FL	863	34972-34974
Okemah, OK	918	74859
Okemos, MI	517	48805, 48864
Oklahoma City, OK	405	73101-73173, 73177-73180*
Okmulgee, OK	918	74447
Olathe, KS	913	66051, 66061-66063
Old Bethpage, NY	631	11804
Old Bridge, NJ	732, 848	08857
Old Brookville, NY	516	11545-11548
Old Chatham, NY	518	12136
Old Forge, PA	570	18518
Old Fort, NC	828	28762
Old Greenwich, CT	203	06870
Old Hickory, TN	615	37138
Old Lyme, CT	860	06371
Old Orchard Beach, ME	207	04064
Old Saybrook, CT	860	06475
Old Town, ME	207	04468
Old Westbury, NY	516	11568
Oldwick, NJ	908	08858
Olean, NY	585	14760
Olive Branch, MS	662	38654
Olive Hill, KY	606	41164
Olivet, MI	616	49076
Olivet, SD	605	57052
Olivia, MN	320	56277
Olney, IL	618	62450
Olney, MD	301	20830-20832
Olney, TX	940	76374
Olustee, FL	386	32072
Olympia, WA	360	98501-98516, 98599
Olympia Fields, IL	708	60461
Olympic Valley, CA	530	96146
Olyphant, PA	570	18447-18448
Omaha, NE	402	68046, 68101-68147, 68152*
Omak, WA	509	98841
Onalaska, WI	608	54650
Onamia, MN	320	56359
Onawa, IA	712	51040
Onaway, MI	989	49765
Oneida, NY	315	13421
Oneida, TN	423	37841
Oneida, WI	920	54155
O'Neill, NE	402	68763
Oneonta, AL	205	35121
Oneonta, NY	607	13820
Onida, SD	605	57564
Onley, VA	757	23418
Only, TN	931	37140
Onsted, MI	517	49265
Ontario, CA	909	91758-91764, 91798
Ontario, NY	585	14519
Ontario, OR	541, 458	97914
Ontonagon, MI	906	49953
Ooltewah, TN	423	37363
Opa Locka, FL	305, 786	33014, 33054-33056
Opelika, AL	334	36801-36804
Opelousas, LA	337	70570-70571
Opheim, MT	406	59250
Opp, AL	334	36467
Oquawka, IL	309	61469
Oracle, AZ	520	85623
Oradell, NJ	201, 551	07649
Orange, CA	714	92856-92869
Orange, CT	203	06477
Orange, MA	351, 978	01355, 01364, 01378
Orange, NJ	862, 973	07050-07051
Orange, TX	409	77630-77632
Orange, VA	540	22960
Orange Beach, AL	251	36561
Orange City, IA	712	51041
Orange Cove, CA	559	93646, 93675
Orange Park, FL	904	32003-32006, 32065-32067*
Orange Village, OH	216	44022, 44122, 44128, 44146
Orangeburg, NY	845	10962
Orangeburg, SC	803	29115-29118
Orangevale, CA	916	95662
Orchard Lake, MI	248, 947	48323-48324
Orchard Park, NY	716	14127
Ord, NE	308	68862
Ordway, CO	719	81063
Orefield, PA	484, 610	18069
Oregon, IL	815	61061
Oregon, MO	660	64473
Oregon, OH	419, 567	43605, 43616-43618
Oregon, WI	608	53575
Oregon City, OR	503, 971	97045
Orem, UT	801, 385	84057-84059, 84097
Orestes, IN	765	46063
Orient, OH	614	43146
Oriental, NC	252	28571
Orinda, CA	925	94563
Orion, MI	248, 947	48359-48362
Oriskany, NY	315	13424

*Partial list of zip codes, including main range

City	Area Code(s)	Zip Code(s)
Orland, CA	530	95963
Orland Park, IL	708	60462, 60467
Orlando, FL	321, 407	32801-32839, 32853-32862*
Orleans, IN	812	47452
Orleans, MA	508, 774	02653
Ormond Beach, FL	386	32173-32176
Orofino, ID	208	83544
Orondo, WA	509	98843
Orono, ME	207	04469, 04473
Orosi, CA	559	93647
Oroville, CA	530	95915, 95940, 95965-95966*
Orrtanna, PA	717	17353
Orrville, OH	234, 330	44667
Ortonville, MI	248, 947	48462
Ortonville, MN	320	56278
Orwigsburg, PA	570	17961
Osage, IA	641	50454, 50461
Osage Beach, MO	573	65065
Osage City, KS	785	66523
Osawatomie, KS	913	66064
Osborne, KS	785	67473
Osceola, AR	870	72370
Osceola, IA	641	50213
Osceola, MO	417	64776
Osceola, NE	402	68651
Osceola, WI	715, 534	54020
Osceola Mills, PA	814	16666
Oscoda, MI	989	48750
Osgood, IN	812	47037
Osgood, OH	419, 567	45351
Oshkosh, NE	308	69154, 69190
Oshkosh, WI	920	54901-54906
Oskaloosa, IA	641	52577
Oskaloosa, KS	785	66066
Osseo, MN	763	55311, 55369, 55569
Ossining, NY	914	10562
Ossipee, NH	603	03864
Osterville, MA	508, 774	02655
Oswego, IL	331, 630	60543
Oswego, KS	620	67356
Oswego, NY	315	13126
Otisville, NY	845	10963
Otsego, MI	616	49078
Ottawa, IL	815	61350
Ottawa, KS	785	66067
Ottawa, OH	419, 567	45875
Ottawa Lake, MI	734	49267
Otter River, MA	351, 978	01436
Otter Rock, OR	541, 458	97369
Ottsville, PA	484, 610	18942
Ottumwa, IA	641	52501
Ouray, CO	970	81427
Overland Park, KS	913	66202-66215, 66221-66225*
Overton, NV	702	89040
Oviedo, FL	321, 407	32762-32766
Owasso, OK	918	74055, 74073
Owatonna, MN	507	55060
Owego, NY	607	13827
Owen, WI	715, 534	54460
Owensboro, KY	270	42301-42304
Owensville, MO	573	65066
Owenton, KY	502	40359
Owings Mills, MD	410	21117
Owingsville, KY	606	40360
Owosso, MI	989	48841, 48867
Oxford, AL	256	36203
Oxford, CT	203	06478
Oxford, GA	470, 770	30054
Oxford, ME	207	04270
Oxford, MI	248, 947	48370-48371
Oxford, MS	662	38655
Oxford, NY	607	13830
Oxford, NC	919	27565
Oxford, OH	513	45056
Oxford, PA	484, 610	19363
Oxford, WI	608	53952
Oxnard, CA	805	93030-93035
Oyster Bay, NY	516	11771
Ozark, AL	334	36360-36361
Ozark, AR	479	72949
Ozark, MO	417	65721
Ozawkie, KS	785	66070
Ozona, TX	915	76943
Ozone Park, NY	347, 718	11416-11417

P

City	Area Code(s)	Zip Code(s)
Pablo, MT	406	59855
Pace, FL	850	32571
Pacheco, CA	925	94553
Pacific, MO	636	63069
Pacific, WA	253	98047
Pacific Beach, CA	858	92109
Pacific Grove, CA	831	93950
Pacific Palisades, CA	310, 424	90272
Pacifica, CA	650	94044-94045
Packwood, IA	319	52580
Pacoima, CA	818	91331-91334
Paden City, WV	304	26159
Paducah, KY	270	42001-42003
Paducah, TX	806	79248
Page, AZ	928	86036, 86040
Pageland, SC	843	29728
Pagosa Springs, CO	970	81147, 81157
Pahoa, HI	808	96778
Pahokee, FL	561	33476
Pahrump, NV	775	89041, 89048, 89060-89061
Paicines, CA	831	95043
Paincourtville, LA	985	70391
Painesville, OH	440	44077
Paint Rock, TX	915	76866
Painted Post, NY	607	14870
Paintsville, KY	606	41240
Palatine, IL	224, 847	60038, 60055, 60067, 60074*
Palatine Bridge, NY	518	13428
Palatka, FL	386	32177-32178
Palestine, TX	903	75801-75803, 75882
Palisade, NE	308	69040
Palisades, NY	845	10964
Palisades Park, NJ	201, 551	07650
Palm Bay, FL	321	32905-32911
Palm Beach, FL	561	33480
Palm Beach Gardens, FL	561	33403, 33408-33412, 33418*
Palm Beach Shores, FL	561	33404
Palm City, FL	772	34990-34991
Palm Coast, FL	386	32135-32137, 32142, 32164
Palm Desert, CA	760, 442	92210-92211, 92255, 92260*
Palm Harbor, FL	727	34682-34685
Palm Springs, CA	760, 442	92262-92264, 92292
Palmdale, CA	661	93550-93552, 93590-93591*
Palmer, AK	907	99645
Palmer, MA	413	01069
Palmerton, PA	484, 610	18071
Palmetto, FL	941	34220-34221
Palmetto, GA	470, 770	30268
Palmyra, IN	812	47164
Palmyra, MO	573	63461
Palmyra, NJ	856	08065
Palmyra, NY	315	14522
Palmyra, PA	717	17078
Palmyra, VA	434	22963
Palmyra, WI	262	53156
Palo Alto, CA	650	94301-94310
Palo Pinto, TX	940	76484
Palos Heights, IL	708	60463
Palos Hills, IL	708	60465
Palos Verdes Peninsula, CA	310, 424	90274-90275
Pampa, TX	806	79065-79066
Pana, IL	217	62557
Panama City, FL	850	32401-32413, 32417, 32461
Panama City Beach, FL	850	32401, 32407-32408, 32413*
Panguitch, UT	435	84759
Panhandle, TX	806	79068
Panorama City, CA	818	91402, 91412
Pantego, NC	252	27860
Paola, KS	913	66071
Paoli, IN	812	47454
Paoli, PA	484, 610	19301
Paonia, CO	970	81428
Papaikou, HI	808	96781
Papillion, NE	402	68046, 68133, 68157
Paradise, CA	530	95967-95969
Paradise, PA	717	17562
Paragould, AR	870	72450-72451
Paramount, CA	562	90723
Paramus, NJ	201, 551	07652-07653
Parchman, MS	662	38738
Paris, ID	208	83261, 83287
Paris, IL	217	61944
Paris, KY	859	40361-40362
Paris, MO	660	65275
Paris, TN	731	38242
Paris, TX	903	75460-75462
Park City, KY	270	42160
Park City, UT	435	84060, 84068, 84098
Park Falls, WI	715, 534	54552
Park Forest, IL	708	60466
Park Hill, OK	918	74451
Park Hills, MO	573	63601, 63653
Park Rapids, MN	218	56470
Park Ridge, IL	224, 847	60068
Park Ridge, NJ	201, 551	07656
Parker, AZ	928	85344
Parker, CO	303, 720	80134, 80138
Parker, SD	605	57053
Parker, WA	509	98939
Parker City, IN	765	47368
Parker Ford, PA	484, 610	19457
Parkersburg, WV	304	26101-26106
Parksley, VA	757	23421
Parkville, MO	816	64151-64152
Parlier, CA	559	93648
Parlin, NJ	732, 848	08859
Parma, ID	208	83660
Parma, OH	216, 440	44129-44134
Parowan, UT	435	84761
Parshall, CO	970	80468
Parsippany, NJ	862, 973	07054
Parsons, KS	620	67357
Parsons, TN	731	38363
Parsons, WV	304	26287
Pasadena, CA	626	91050-91051, 91101-91110*
Pasadena, MD	410	21122-21123
Pasadena, TX	281, 713, 832	77501-77508
Pascagoula, MS	228	39562-39563, 39567-39569*
Pasco, WA	509	99301-99302
Pascoag, RI	401	02859
Paso Robles, CA	805	93446-93447
Passaic, NJ	862, 973	07055
Patagonia, AZ	520	85624
Patchogue, NY	631	11772
Paterson, NJ	862, 973	07501-07514, 07522-07524*
Paterson, WA	509	99345
Patrick AFB, FL	321	32925
Patterson, CA	209	95363
Patterson, GA	912	31557
Patterson, LA	985	70392
Patterson, NY	845	12563
Patton, CA	909	92369
Patuxent River, MD	301	20670
Paul, ID	208	83347
Paulding, OH	419, 567	45879
Pauls Valley, OK	405	73075
Paw Paw, MI	616	49079
Pawcatuck, CT	860	06379
Pawhuska, OK	918	74009, 74056
Pawleys Island, SC	843	29585
Pawling, NY	845	12564
Pawnee, OK	918	74058
Pawnee City, NE	402	68420
Pawtucket, RI	401	02860-02862
Paxton, IL	217	60957
Paxton, MA	508, 774	01612
Payette, ID	208	83661
Paynesville, MN	320	56362
Payson, AZ	928	85541, 85547
Payson, UT	801, 385	84651
Peabody, MA	351, 978	01960-01961
Peace Dale, RI	401	02879, 02883
Peach Glen, PA	717	17375
Peachtree City, GA	470, 770	30269
Peapack, NJ	908	07977
Pearce, AZ	520	85625
Pearisburg, VA	540	24134
Pearl, MS	601, 769	39208, 39218, 39232, 39288
Pearl City, HI	808	96782
Pearl Harbor, HI	808	96860
Pearl River, NY	845	10965
Pearland, TX	281, 832	77581-77584, 77588
Pearsall, TX	830	78061
Pearson, GA	912	31642
Pebble Beach, CA	831	93953
Pecos, NM	505	87552

*Partial list of zip codes, including main range

City	Area Code(s)	Zip Code(s)
Pecos, TX	915	79772
Peculiar, MO	816	64078
Peekskill, NY	845	10566
Pekin, IL	309	61554-61558
Pekin, IN	812	47165
Pelham, AL	205	35124
Pelham, GA	229	31779
Pelham, NH	603	03076
Pelham, NY	845	10803
Pelham Manor, NY	845	10803
Pelican Rapids, MN	218	56572
Pell City, AL	205	35125-35128
Pella, IA	641	50219
Pelzer, SC	864	29669
Pemberton, NJ	609	08068
Pembroke, GA	912	31321
Pembroke, MA	339, 781	02327, 02358-02359
Pembroke, NH	603	03275
Pembroke, NC	910	28372
Pembroke, VA	540	24136
Pembroke Park, FL	754, 954	33009, 33021-33023
Pembroke Pines, FL	754, 954	33019-33029, 33081-33084*
Pen Argyl, PA	484, 610	18072
Penacook, NH	603	03303
Penasco, NM	505	87553
Pender, NE	402	68047
Pendergrass, GA	706, 762	30567
Pendleton, IN	765	46064
Pendleton, OR	541, 458	97801
Pendleton, SC	864	29670
Penfield, NY	585	14526
Penfield, PA	814	15849
Peninsula, OH	234, 330	44264
Penland, NC	828	28765
Penn Yan, NY	315	14527
Penndel, PA	215, 267	19047
Pennington, NJ	609	08534
Pennsauken, NJ	856	08109-08110
Pennsburg, PA	215, 267	18073
Pennsville, NJ	856	08070
Penrose, CO	719	81240
Pensacola, FL	850	32501-32516, 32520-32526*
Pensacola Beach, FL	850	32561
Pentwater, MI	231	49449
Peoria, AZ	623	85345, 85380-85385
Peoria, IL	309	61601-61616, 61625-61644*
Peoria Heights, IL	309	61614-61616
Peosta, IA	563	52068
Peotone, IL	708	60468
Pepper Pike, OH	216	44122-44124
Pequannock, NJ	862, 973	07440
Perdue Hill, AL	251	36470
Perham, MN	218	56573
Perkasie, PA	215, 267	18944
Perkinston, MS	601, 769	39573
Perris, CA	951	92570-92572, 92599
Perry, FL	850	32347-32348
Perry, GA	478	31069
Perry, IA	515	50220
Perry, KS	785	66073
Perry, OH	440	44081
Perry, OK	580	73077
Perrysburg, OH	419, 567	43551-43552
Perrysville, OH	419, 567	44864
Perryton, TX	806	79070
Perryville, AR	501	72126
Perryville, MO	573	63747, 63775-63776, 63783
Perth Amboy, NJ	732, 848	08861-08863
Peru, IL	815	61354
Peru, IN	765	46970-46971
Peru, NE	402	68421
Pescadero, CA	650	94060
Peshastin, WA	509	98847
Peshtigo, WI	715, 534	54157
Petal, MS	601, 769	39465
Petaluma, CA	707	94952-94955, 94975, 94999
Peterborough, NH	603	03458
Petersburg, AK	907	99833
Petersburg, IL	217	62659, 62675
Petersburg, IN	812	47567
Petersburg, TX	806	79250
Petersburg, VA	804	23801-23806
Petersburg, WV	304	26847
Petersburgh, NY	518	12138
Peterson AFB, CO	719	80914
Petoskey, MI	231	49770
Pewaukee, WI	262	53072
Pewee Valley, KY	502	40056
Pflugerville, TX	512	78660, 78691
Pharr, TX	956	78577
Phelps, NY	315	14532
Phenix City, AL	334	36867-36870
Phil Campbell, AL	256	35581
Philadelphia, MS	601, 769	39350
Philadelphia, PA	215, 267	19019, 19092-19093, 19099*
Philip, SD	605	57567
Philippi, WV	304	26416
Philipsburg, MT	406	59858
Philipsburg, PA	814	16866
Phillips, WI	715, 534	54555
Phillipsburg, KS	785	67661
Phillipsburg, NJ	908	08865
Philmont, NY	518	12565
Philomath, OR	541, 458	97370
Philpot, KY	270	42366
Phoenix, AZ	480, 602	85001-85055, 85060-85087*
Phoenix, OR	541, 458	97535
Phoenixville, PA	484, 610	19453, 19460
Picayune, MS	601, 769	39466
Pickens, SC	864	29671
Pickerington, OH	614	43147
Pico Rivera, CA	562	90660-90665
Piedmont, AL	256	36272
Pierce, NE	402	68767
Pierre, SD	605	57501
Pierz, MN	320	56364
Piffard, NY	585	14533
Pigeon, MI	989	48755
Pigeon Forge, TN	865	37862-37864, 37868, 37876
Piggott, AR	870	72454
Pikesville, MD	410	21208, 21282
Pikeville, KY	606	41501-41502
Pikeville, TN	423	37367
Pilot Grove, IA	319	52648
Pima, AZ	928	85535, 85543
Pinckneyville, IL	618	62274
Pinconning, MI	989	48650
Pine Bluff, AR	870	71601-71603, 71611-71613
Pine Bluffs, WY	307	82082
Pine Brook, NJ	862, 973	07058
Pine City, MN	320	55063
Pine City, NY	607	14871
Pine Island, MN	507	55963
Pine Mountain, GA	706, 762	31822
Pine Plains, NY	518	12567
Pine River, MN	218	56456, 56474
Pinedale, WY	307	82941
Pinehurst, NC	910	28370, 28374
Pinellas Park, FL	727	33780-33782
Pinetops, NC	252	27864
Pineville, KY	606	40977
Pineville, LA	318	71359-71361
Pineville, MO	417	64856
Pineville, NC	704, 980	28134
Pineville, WV	304	24859, 24874
Piney Flats, TN	423	37686, 37699
Pinole, CA	510	94564
Pioche, NV	775	89043
Pioneer, OH	419, 567	43554
Pipersville, PA	215, 267	18947
Pipestem, WV	304	25979
Pipestone, MN	507	56164
Pippa Passes, KY	606	41844
Piqua, OH	937	45356
Piru, CA	805	93040
Piscataway, NJ	732, 848	08854-08855
Pismo Beach, CA	805	93420, 93433, 93448-93449
Pitman, NJ	856	08071
Pittsboro, MS	662	38951
Pittsboro, NC	919	27228, 27312
Pittsburg, CA	925	94565
Pittsburg, KS	620	66762-66763
Pittsburg, TX	903	75686
Pittsburgh, PA	412, 878	15122-15123, 15201-15244*
Pittsfield, IL	217	62363
Pittsfield, ME	207	04967
Pittsfield, MA	413	01201-01203
Pittsfield, NH	603	03263
Pittsford, NY	585	14534
Pittston, PA	570	18640-18644
Pittstown, NJ	908	08867
Pittsville, WI	715, 534	54466
Placentia, CA	714	92870-92871
Placerville, CA	530	95667
Plain, WI	608	53577
Plain City, OH	614	43064
Plainfield, IL	815	60544
Plainfield, IN	317	46168
Plainfield, NJ	908	07060-07063, 07069
Plainfield, VT	802	05667
Plainfield, WI	715, 534	54966
Plains, GA	229	31780
Plains, PA	570	18702-18705
Plains, TX	806	79355
Plainsboro, NJ	609	08536
Plainview, MN	507	55964
Plainview, NY	516	11803
Plainview, TX	806	79072-79073
Plainville, CT	860	06062
Plainville, KS	785	67663
Plainville, MA	508, 774	02762
Plainville, NY	315	13137
Plainwell, MI	616	49080
Plankinton, SD	605	57368
Plano, IL	331, 630	60545
Plano, TX	469, 972	75023-75026, 75074-75075*
Plant City, FL	813	33564-33567
Plantation, FL	754, 954	33311-33313, 33317-33318*
Plantsville, CT	860	06479
Plaquemine, LA	225	70764-70765
Plato, MN	320	55370
Platte City, MO	816	64079
Platteville, WI	608	53818
Plattsburg, MO	816	64477
Plattsburgh, NY	518	12901-12903
Plattsmouth, NE	402	68048
Pleasant Gap, PA	814	16823
Pleasant Grove, UT	801, 385	84062
Pleasant Hill, CA	925	94523
Pleasant Plains, IL	217	62677
Pleasant Prairie, WI	262	53142-53143, 53158
Pleasant Valley, NY	845	12569
Pleasanton, CA	925	94566-94568, 94588
Pleasanton, TX	830	78064
Pleasantville, NJ	609	08232-08234
Pleasantville, NY	914	10570-10572
Plentywood, MT	406	59254
Plover, WI	715, 534	54467
Plymouth, IN	574	46563
Plymouth, MA	508, 774	02345, 02360-02362
Plymouth, MI	734	48170
Plymouth, MN	763	55441-55442, 55447
Plymouth, NH	603	03264
Plymouth, NC	252	27962
Plymouth, VT	802	05056
Plymouth, WI	920	53073
Plymouth Meeting, PA	484, 610	19462
Pocahontas, AR	870	72455
Pocahontas, IA	712	50574
Pocatello, ID	208	83201-83209
Pocomoke City, MD	410	21851
Pocono Manor, PA	570	18349
Point Clear, AL	334	36564
Point Comfort, TX	361	77978
Point Lookout, MO	417	65726
Point Lookout, NY	516	11569
Point Marion, PA	724, 878	15474
Point of Rocks, MD	301	21777
Point Pleasant, WV	304	25550
Point Pleasant Beach, NJ	732, 848	08742
Point Richmond, CA	510	94801
Poland, OH	234, 330	44514
Polk City, FL	863	33868
Polk City, IA	515	50226
Polkton, NC	704, 980	28135
Pollocksville, NC	252	28573
Polson, MT	406	59860
Pomeroy, OH	740	45769
Pomeroy, WA	509	99347
Pomfret, CT	860	06258
Pomfret Center, CT	860	06259
Pomona, CA	909	91765-91769, 91797-91799
Pomona, NJ	609	08240
Pomona, NY	845	10970

*Partial list of zip codes, including main range

City	Area Code(s)	Zip Code(s)
Pompano Beach, FL	754, 954	33060-33077, 33093, 33097
Pompton Lakes, NJ	862, 973	07442
Pompton Plains, NJ	862, 973	07444
Ponca, NE	402	68770
Ponca City, OK	580	74601-74604
Ponce Inlet, FL	386	32127
Ponchatoula, LA	985	70454
Ponte Vedra Beach, FL	904	32004, 32082
Pontiac, IL	815	61764
Pontiac, MI	248, 947	48340-48343
Pontotoc, MS	662	38863
Pooler, GA	912	31322
Pope AFB, NC	910	28308
Poplar, MT	406	59255
Poplar Bluff, MO	573	63901-63902
Poplarville, MS	601, 769	39470
Poquoson, VA	757	23662
Port Allen, LA	225	70767
Port Angeles, WA	360	98362-98363
Port Aransas, TX	361	78373
Port Arthur, TX	409	77640-77643
Port Charlotte, FL	941	33948-33954, 33980-33983
Port Chester, NY	914	10573
Port Clinton, OH	419, 567	43452
Port Ewen, NY	845	12466
Port Gibson, MS	601, 769	39150
Port Hueneme, CA	805	93041-93044
Port Huron, MI	810	48060-48061
Port Isabel, TX	956	78578, 78597
Port Jefferson, NY	631	11777
Port Jefferson Station, NY	631	11776-11777
Port Jervis, NY	845	12771, 12785
Port Lavaca, TX	361	77972, 77979
Port Ludlow, WA	360	98365
Port Neches, TX	409	77651
Port Orange, FL	386	32118-32119, 32124-32129
Port Orchard, WA	360	98366-98367
Port Orford, OR	541, 458	97465
Port Saint Joe, FL	850	32410, 32456-32457
Port Saint Lucie, FL	772	34952-34953, 34983-34988
Port Sulphur, LA	504	70083
Port Tobacco, MD	301	20677
Port Townsend, WA	360	98368
Port Washington, NY	516	11050-11055
Port Washington, WI	262	53074
Portage, IN	219	46368
Portage, MI	616	49002, 49024, 49081
Portage, WI	608	53901
Portageville, MO	573	63873
Portales, NM	505	88123, 88130
Porter, IN	219	46304
Porterville, CA	559	93257-93258
Portland, AR	870	71663
Portland, CT	860	06480
Portland, IN	260	47371
Portland, ME	207	04101-04112, 04116, 04122*
Portland, MI	517	48875
Portland, OR	503, 971	97201-97242, 97251-97259*
Portland, TN	615	37148
Portola, CA	530	96122, 96129
Portola Valley, CA	650	94028
Portsmouth, NH	603	03801-03804
Portsmouth, OH	740	45662-45663
Portsmouth, RI	401	02871-02872
Portsmouth, VA	757	23701-23709
Portville, NY	585	14770
Post, TX	806	79356
Post Falls, ID	208	83854, 83877
Post Mills, VT	802	05058
Postville, IA	563	52162
Poteau, OK	918	74953
Potomac, MD	301	20854, 20859
Potosi, MO	573	63664
Potsdam, NY	315	13676, 13699
Pottsboro, TX	903	75076
Pottstown, PA	484, 610	19464-19465
Pottsville, PA	570	17901
Poughkeepsie, NY	845	12601-12604
Poughquag, NY	845	12570
Poulsbo, WA	360	98370
Poultney, VT	802	05741, 05764
Pound, VA	276	24279
Poway, CA	858	92064, 92074
Powderhorn, CO	970	81243
Powell, OH	614	43065
Powell, TN	865	37849
Powell, WY	307	82435
Powhatan, VA	804	23139
Prairie City, IL	309	61470
Prairie du Chien, WI	608	53821
Prairie du Sac, WI	608	53578
Prairie Grove, IL	815	60012, 60050
Prairie View, TX	936	77446
Prairie Village, KS	913	66202-66208
Prairieville, LA	225	70769
Pratt, KS	620	67124
Prattville, AL	334	36066-36068
Preble, IN	260	46782
Prentiss, MS	601, 769	39474
Prescott, AZ	928	86301-86305, 86313, 86330
Prescott, AR	870	71857
Prescott, WA	509	99348
Prescott, WI	715, 534	54021
Prescott Valley, AZ	928	86312-86314
Presidio of San Francisco, CA	415	94129
Presque Isle, ME	207	04769
Preston, GA	229	31824
Preston, ID	208	83263
Preston, MN	507	55965
Preston, WA	425	98050
Prestonsburg, KY	606	41653
Price, UT	435	84501
Prichard, AL	251	36610, 36617
Prides Crossing, MA	617, 857	01965
Primghar, IA	712	51245
Primm, NV	702	89019
Primos, PA	484, 610	19018
Prince Frederick, MD	410	20678
Prince George, VA	804	23875
Prince William, VA	571, 703	22193
Princess Anne, MD	410	21853
Princeton, ID	208	83857
Princeton, IL	815	61356
Princeton, IN	812	47670
Princeton, KY	270	42445
Princeton, MN	763	55371
Princeton, MO	660	64673
Princeton, NJ	609	08540-08544
Princeton, WV	304	24740
Princeton Junction, NJ	609	08550
Princeville, HI	808	96714, 96722
Princeville, IL	309	61559
Prineville, OR	541, 458	97754
Prinsburg, MN	320	56281
Prior Lake, MN	952	55372
Proctor, MN	218	55810
Proctor, VT	802	05765
Prophetstown, IL	815	61277
Prospect, CT	203	06712
Prospect, ME	207	04981
Prospect Harbor, ME	207	04669
Prospect Heights, IL	224, 847	60070
Prospect Hill, NC	336	27314
Prosperity, SC	803	29127
Prosser, WA	509	99350
Providence, RI	401	02901-02912, 02918, 02940
Provincetown, MA	508, 774	02657
Provo, UT	801, 385	84601-84606
Pryor, OK	918	74361-74362
Pueblo, CO	719	81001-81015
Pueblo West, CO	719	81007
Puerto Nuevo, PR	787, 939	00920-00921
Pulaski, NY	315	13142
Pulaski, TN	931	38478
Pulaski, VA	540	24301
Pulaski, WI	920	54162
Pullman, WA	509	99163-99165
Punta Gorda, FL	941	33950-33951, 33955, 33980*
Punxsutawney, PA	814	15767
Purcell, OK	405	73080
Purcellville, VA	540	20132-20134, 20160
Purchase, NY	914	10577
Purvis, MS	601, 769	39475
Put-in-Bay, OH	419, 567	43456
Putnam, CT	860	06260
Putney, VT	802	05346
Puunene, HI	808	96784
Puyallup, WA	253	98371-98375
Pyote, TX	915	79777

Q

City	Area Code(s)	Zip Code(s)
Quakertown, PA	215, 267	18951
Quanah, TX	940	79252
Quantico, VA	571, 703	22134-22135
Quapaw, OK	918	74363
Quarryville, PA	717	17566
Queens Village, NY	347, 718	11427-11429
Queensbury, NY	518	12801-12804
Queenstown, MD	410	21658
Quimby, IA	712	51049
Quinault, WA	360	98575
Quincy, CA	530	95971
Quincy, FL	850	32351-32353
Quincy, IL	217	62301, 62305-62306
Quincy, MA	617, 857	02169-02171, 02269
Quincy, PA	717	17247
Quincy, WA	509	98848
Quinlan, TX	903	75474
Quinter, KS	785	67752
Quitman, GA	229	31643
Quitman, MS	601, 769	39355
Quitman, TX	903	75783

R

City	Area Code(s)	Zip Code(s)
Racine, WI	262	53401-53408, 53490
Radcliff, KY	270	40159-40160
Radcliffe, IA	515	50230
Radford, VA	540	24141-24143
Radisson, WI	715, 534	54867
Radnor, PA	484, 610	19087
Raeford, NC	910	28361, 28376
Rahway, NJ	732, 848	07065
Raiford, FL	386, 904	32026, 32083
Rainsville, AL	256	35986
Raleigh, MS	601, 769	39153
Raleigh, NC	919	27601-27629, 27634-27636*
Ralls, TX	806	79357
Ralston, IA	712	51459
Ralston, NE	402	68127
Ramah, NM	505	87321, 87357
Ramona, CA	760, 442	92065
Ramona, OK	918	74061
Ramseur, NC	336	27316
Ramsey, MN	763	55303
Ramsey, NJ	201, 551	07446
Rancho Cordova, CA	916	95670, 95741-95743
Rancho Cucamonga, CA	909	91701, 91729-91730, 91737*
Rancho Dominguez, CA	310, 424	90220, 90224
Rancho Mirage, CA	760, 442	92270
Rancho Palos Verdes, CA	310, 424	90275
Rancho Santa Fe, CA	858	92067, 92091
Rancho Santa Margarita, CA	949	92688
Rancho Viejo, TX	956	78575
Rancocas, NJ	609	08073
Randallstown, MD	410	21133
Randleman, NC	336	27317
Randolph, MA	339, 781	02368
Randolph, NJ	862, 973	07869
Randolph, UT	435	84064
Randolph, VT	802	05060
Randolph, WI	920	53956-53957
Randolph AFB, TX	210	78148-78150
Randolph Center, VT	802	05061
Random Lake, WI	920	53075
Rangely, CO	970	81648
Ranger, TX	254	76470
Rankin, PA	412, 878	15104
Rankin, TX	915	79778
Rantoul, IL	217	61866
Rapid City, SD	605	57701-57703, 57709
Rapidan, VA	540	22733
Raritan, NJ	908	08869, 08896
Raton, NM	505	87740
Ravenna, MI	231	49451
Ravenna, OH	234, 330	44266
Ravenswood, WV	304	26164
Rawlins, WY	307	82301, 82310
Ray Brook, NY	518	12977
Raymond, ME	207	04071

*Partial list of zip codes, including main range

City	Area Code(s)	Zip Code(s)
Raymond, MS	601, 769	39154
Raymond, NH	603	03077
Raymond, WA	360	98577
Raymondville, TX	956	78580, 78598
Raymore, MO	816	64083
Rayne, LA	337	70578
Raynham, MA	508, 774	02767
Raytown, MO	816	64129, 64133, 64138
Rayville, LA	318	71269
Readfield, ME	207	04355
Reading, MA	339, 781	01867
Reading, PA	484, 610	19601-19612, 19640
Readville, MA	617, 857	02136-02137
Reamstown, PA	717	17567
Red Bank, NJ	732, 848	07701-07704
Red Bay, AL	256	35582
Red Bluff, CA	530	96080
Red Bud, IL	618	62278
Red Cloud, NE	402	68970
Red Feather Lakes, CO	970	80536, 80545
Red Hill, PA	215, 267	18073-18076
Red Lake Falls, MN	218	56750
Red Lion, PA	717	17356
Red Lodge, MT	406	59068
Red Oak, IA	712	51566, 51591
Red River, NM	505	87558
Red Rock, AZ	520	85245
Red Springs, NC	910	28377
Red Wing, MN	651	55066
Redding, CA	530	96001-96003, 96049, 96099
Redding, CT	203	06896
Redfield, SD	605	57469
Redford, MI	313	48239-48240
Redlands, CA	909	92373-92375
Redmond, OR	541, 458	97756
Redmond, WA	425	98052-98053, 98073-98074
Redondo Beach, CA	310, 424	90277-90278
Redstone, CO	970	81623
Redstone Arsenal, AL	256	35808-35809
Redwood, NY	315	13679
Redwood City, CA	650	94059-94065
Redwood Falls, MN	507	56283
Reed City, MI	231	49677
Reedley, CA	559	93654
Reedsburg, WI	608	53958-53959
Refugio, TX	361	78377
Rego Park, NY	347, 718	11374
Rehoboth Beach, DE	302	19971
Reidsville, GA	912	30453, 30499
Reidsville, NC	336	27320-27323
Reinbeck, IA	319	50669
Reisterstown, MD	410	21071, 21136
Rembert, SC	803	29128
Remington, IN	219	47977
Remus, MI	989	49340
Renick, WV	304	24966
Reno, NV	775	89501-89515, 89520-89523*
Rensselaer, IN	219	47978
Rensselaer, NY	518	12144
Renton, WA	425	98055-98059
Renville, MN	320	56284
Represa, CA	916	95671
Republic, MO	417	65738
Republic, WA	509	99166
Research Triangle Park, NC	919	27709
Reseda, CA	818	91335-91337
Reserve, NM	505	87830
Reston, VA	571, 703	20190-20196, 22096
Retsil, WA	360	98378
Revere, MA	339, 781	02151
Rexburg, ID	208	83440-83441, 83460
Reynolds, GA	478	31076
Reynoldsburg, OH	614	43068
Rhinebeck, NY	845	12572
Rhinelander, WI	715, 534	54501
Rhodes, MI	989	48652
Rialto, CA	909	92376-92377
Rice Lake, WI	715, 534	54868
Riceboro, GA	912	31323
Rich Square, NC	252	27869
Richardson, TX	214, 469, 972	75080-75085
Richfield, MN	612	55423
Richfield, OH	234, 330	44286
Richfield, UT	435	84701
Richfield, WI	414	53076
Richland, MI	616	49083
Richland, MS	601, 769	39208, 39218, 39232
Richland, PA	717	17087
Richland, WA	509	99352-99353
Richland Center, WI	608	53581
Richland Hills, TX	682, 817	76118, 76180
Richlands, VA	276	24641
Richmond, CA	510	94801-94808, 94820, 94850
Richmond, IL	815	60071
Richmond, IN	765	47374-47375
Richmond, KY	859	40475-40476
Richmond, MO	816	64085
Richmond, TX	281, 832	77406, 77469
Richmond, VA	804	23173, 23218-23242, 23249*
Richmond Heights, MO	314	63117
Richmond Heights, OH	216	44143
Richmond Hill, NY	347, 718	11418
Richvale, CA	530	95974
Rickreall, OR	503, 971	97371
Riddle, OR	541, 458	97469
Riderwood, MD	410	21139
Ridge, NY	631	11961
Ridge Spring, SC	803	29129
Ridgecrest, CA	760, 442	93555-93556
Ridgedale, MO	417	65739
Ridgefield, CT	203	06877-06879
Ridgefield, NJ	201, 551	07657
Ridgefield Park, NJ	201, 551	07660
Ridgeland, MS	601, 769	39157-39158
Ridgeland, SC	843	29912, 29936
Ridgeville, SC	843	29472
Ridgeway, SC	803	29130
Ridgeway, VA	276	24148
Ridgewood, NJ	201, 551	07450-07452
Ridgewood, NY	347, 718	11385-11386
Ridgway, CO	970	81432
Ridgway, PA	814	15853
Ridley Park, PA	484, 610	19078
Rifle, CO	970	81650
Rigby, ID	208	83442
Rillito, AZ	520	85654
Rindge, NH	603	03461
Ringgold, GA	706, 762	30736
Ringoes, NJ	908	08551
Ringwood, NJ	862, 973	07456
Rio, WI	920	53960
Rio Grande, NJ	609	08242
Rio Grande, OH	740	45674
Rio Grande City, TX	956	78582
Rio Rancho, NM	505	87124, 87174
Rio Rico, AZ	520	85648
Rio Verde, AZ	480	85263
Rio Vista, CA	707	94571
Ripley, MS	662	38663
Ripley, TN	731	38063
Ripley, WV	304	25271
Ripon, CA	209	95366
Ripon, WI	920	54971
Ririe, ID	208	83443
Rising Sun, IN	812	47040
Rising Sun, MD	410	21911
Rison, AR	870	71665
Ritzville, WA	509	99169
River Edge, NJ	201, 551	07661
River Falls, WI	715, 534	54022
River Forest, IL	708	60305
River Grove, IL	708	60171
River Rouge, MI	313	48218
Riverbank, CA	209	95367, 95390
Riverdale, GA	470, 770	30274, 30296
Riverdale, IL	708	60827
Riverdale, MD	301	20737-20738
Riverdale, NJ	862, 973	07457
Riverdale, NY	347, 718	10463, 10471
Riverdale, UT	801, 385	84405
Riverhead, NY	631	11901
Riverside, CA	951	92501-92509, 92513-92522
Riverside, MI	616	49084
Riverside, MO	816	64150-64151, 64168
Riverside, NJ	856	08075
Riverton, NJ	856	08076-08077
Riverton, UT	801, 385	84065, 84095
Riverton, WY	307	82501
Riverview, FL	813	33568-33569
Riverwoods, IL	224, 847	60015
Riviera Beach, FL	561	33403-33407, 33418-33419
Roanoke, IN	260	46783
Roanoke, VA	540	24001-24050
Roanoke Rapids, NC	252	27870
Roaring Spring, PA	814	16673
Robbins, NC	910	27325
Robbinsdale, MN	763	55422
Robbinsville, NJ	609	08691
Robbinsville, NC	828	28771
Robert Lee, TX	915	76945
Roberta, GA	478	31078
Roberts, IL	217	60962
Robertsdale, AL	251	36567, 36574
Robesonia, PA	484, 610	19551
Robins AFB, GA	478	31098
Robinson, IL	618	62454
Robinsonville, MS	662	38664
Robstown, TX	361	78380
Roby, TX	915	79543
Rochdale, MA	508, 774	01542
Rochelle, IL	815	61068
Rochelle Park, NJ	201, 551	07662
Rochester, IN	574	46975
Rochester, MI	248, 947	48306-48309
Rochester, MN	507	55901-55906
Rochester, NH	603	03839, 03866-03868
Rochester, NY	585	14601-14627, 14638-14653*
Rochester, PA	724, 878	15074
Rochester, VT	802	05767
Rochester, WA	360	98579
Rochester, WI	262	53167
Rochester Hills, MI	248, 947	48306-48309
Rock City Falls, NY	518	12863
Rock Creek, OH	440	44084
Rock Falls, IL	815	61071
Rock Hill, NY	845	12775
Rock Hill, SC	803	29730-29734
Rock Island, IL	309	61201-61204, 61299
Rock Port, MO	660	64482
Rock Rapids, IA	712	51246
Rock Spring, GA	706, 762	30739
Rock Springs, WY	307	82901-82902, 82942
Rockaway, NJ	862, 973	07866
Rockaway Beach, NY	347, 718	11693
Rockaway Park, NY	347, 718	11694
Rockford, AL	256	35136
Rockford, IL	815	61101-61114, 61125-61126
Rockford, MI	616	49341, 49351
Rockford, MN	763	55373
Rockford, TN	865	37853
Rockingham, NC	910	28379-28380
Rockland, ME	207	04841
Rockland, MA	339, 781	02370
Rockledge, FL	321	32955-32956
Rockleigh, NJ	201, 551	07647
Rocklin, CA	916	95677, 95765
Rockmart, GA	470, 770	30153
Rockport, IN	812	47635
Rockport, ME	207	04856
Rockport, MA	351, 978	01966
Rockport, TX	361	78381-78382
Rocksprings, TX	830	78880
Rockton, IL	815	61072
Rockville, CT	860	06066
Rockville, IN	765	47872
Rockville, MD	240, 301	20847-20859
Rockville Centre, NY	516	11570-11572, 11592
Rockwall, TX	469, 972	75032, 75087
Rockwell, NC	704, 980	28138
Rockwell City, IA	712	50579
Rockwood, MI	734	48173
Rocky Ford, CO	719	81067
Rocky Hill, CT	860	06067
Rocky Mount, NC	252	27801-27804
Rocky Mount, VA	540	24151
Roebuck, SC	864	29376
Rogers, AR	479	72756-72758
Rogers, CT	860	06263
Rogers City, MI	989	49779
Rogersville, AL	256	35652
Rogersville, TN	423	37857
Rogue River, OR	541, 458	97537
Rohnert Park, CA	707	94927-94928
Roland, AR	501	72135
Roland, IA	515	50236
Rolla, MO	573	65401-65402, 65409
Rolla, ND	701	58367
Rolling Fork, MS	662	39159
Rolling Hills Estates, CA	310, 424	90274-90275
Rolling Meadows, IL	224, 847	60008
Rome, GA	706, 762	30149, 30161-30165

**Partial list of zip codes, including main range*

City	Area Code(s)	Zip Code(s)
Rome, NY	315	13440-13442, 13449
Romeo, MI	586	48065
Romeoville, IL	815	60441, 60446
Romney, WV	304	26757
Romulus, MI	734	48174
Romulus, NY	315	14541
Ronceverte, WV	304	24970
Ronkonkoma, NY	631	11749, 11779
Roodhouse, IL	217	62082
Roosevelt, AZ	928	85545
Roosevelt, UT	435	84066
Rootstown, OH	234, 330	44272
Rosamond, CA	661	93560
Roscoe, IL	815	61073
Roscoe, PA	412, 878	15477
Roscommon, MI	989	48653
Rose Hill, NC	910	28458
Roseau, MN	218	56751
Rosebud, TX	254	76570
Roseburg, OR	541, 458	97470
Rosedale, MS	662	38769
Roseland, NJ	862, 973	07068
Roselle, IL	331, 630	60172
Roselle, NJ	908	07203
Roselle Park, NJ	908	07204
Rosemead, CA	626	91770-91772
Rosemont, IL	224, 847	60018
Rosemont, PA	484, 610	19010
Rosemount, MN	651	55068
Rosenberg, TX	281, 832	77471
Rosendale, WI	920	54974
Rosenhayn, NJ	856	08352
Roseville, CA	916	95661, 95678, 95746-95747
Roseville, MI	586	48066
Roseville, MN	651	55112-55113, 55126
Roseville, OH	740	43777
Rosiclare, IL	618	62982
Roslindale, MA	617, 857	02131
Roslyn, NY	516	11576
Roslyn Heights, NY	516	11577
Rosman, NC	828	28772
Rosslyn, VA	571, 703	22209
Rossville, GA	706, 762	30741-30742
Roswell, GA	470, 678, 770	30075-30077
Roswell, NM	505	88201-88203
Rothschild, WI	715, 534	54474
Round Lake, IL	224, 847	60073
Round Rock, TX	512	78664, 78680-78683
Roundup, MT	406	59072-59073
Rouses Point, NY	518	12979
Rowayton, CT	203	06853
Rowe, MA	413	01367
Rowlett, TX	469, 972	75030, 75088-75089
Rowley, MA	351, 978	01969
Roxboro, NC	336	27573
Roxbury, MA	617, 857	02118-02120
Roxbury Crossing, MA	617, 857	02120
Roy, NM	505	87743
Roy, UT	801, 385	84067
Roy, WA	360	98580
Royal Oak, MI	248, 947	48067-48068, 48073
Royal Palm Beach, FL	561	33411-33412, 33421
Royersford, PA	484, 610	19468
Rugby, ND	701	58368
Ruidoso Downs, NM	505	88346
Rumford, RI	401	02916
Running Springs, CA	909	92382
Rupert, ID	208	83343, 83350
Rural Hall, NC	336	27045, 27094, 27098-27099
Rush, NY	585	14543
Rush City, MN	320	55067-55069
Rushford, MN	507	55971
Rushville, IL	217	62681
Rushville, IN	765	46173
Rushville, NE	308	69360
Rusk, TX	903	75785
Ruskin, FL	813	33570-33573
Russell, KS	785	67665
Russellville, AL	256	35653-35654
Russellville, AR	479	72801-72802, 72811-72812
Russellville, KY	270	42276
Russia, OH	937	45363
Rustburg, VA	434	24588
Ruston, LA	318	71270-71273
Rutherford, CA	707	94573
Rutherford, NJ	201, 551	07070
Rutherfordton, NC	828	28139
Rutland, MA	508, 774	01543
Rutland, VT	802	05701-05702
Rutledge, TN	865	37861
Rydal, PA	215, 267	19046
Rye, NY	914	10580
Rye Brook, NY	914	10573
Ryegate, MT	406	59074

S

City	Area Code(s)	Zip Code(s)
Sabetha, KS	785	66534
Sac City, IA	712	50583
Saco, ME	207	04072
Sacramento, CA	916	94203-94211, 94229-94263*
Saddle Brook, NJ	201, 551	07663
Saegertown, PA	814	16433
Safety Harbor, FL	727	34695
Safford, AZ	928	85546-85548
Sag Harbor, NY	631	11963
Saginaw, MI	989	48601-48609, 48663
Sagle, ID	208	83809, 83860
Saguache, CO	719	81149
Sahuarita, AZ	520	85629
Saint Albans, VT	802	05478-05479
Saint Albans, WV	304	25177
Saint Ann, MO	314	63074
Saint Ansgar, IA	641	50472, 50481
Saint Anthony, ID	208	83445
Saint Anthony, MN	612	55418-55421
Saint Augustine, FL	904	32080, 32084-32086, 32092*
Saint Bonaventure, NY	585	14778
Saint Bonifacius, MN	952	55375
Saint Catharine, KY	859	40061
Saint Charles, IL	331, 630	60174-60175
Saint Charles, MI	989	48655
Saint Charles, MO	636	63301-63304
Saint Clair, MI	810	48079
Saint Clair, MN	507	56080
Saint Clair, MO	636	63077
Saint Clair, PA	570	17970
Saint Clair Shores, MI	586	48080-48082
Saint Clairsville, OH	740	43950
Saint Cloud, FL	321, 407	34769-34773
Saint Cloud, MN	320	56301-56304, 56372, 56387*
Saint Croix Falls, WI	715, 534	54024
Saint Davids, PA	484, 610	19087
Saint Francis, KS	785	67756
Saint Francis, WI	414	53207, 53235
Saint Francisville, IL	618	62460
Saint Francisville, LA	225	70775
Saint Gabriel, LA	225	70776
Saint George, SC	843	29477
Saint George, UT	435	84770-84771, 84782-84783*
Saint Helena, CA	707	94574
Saint Helena Island, SC	843	29920
Saint Helens, OR	503, 971	97051
Saint Henry, OH	419, 567	45883
Saint Hilaire, MN	218	56754
Saint Ignace, MI	906	49781
Saint James, LA	225	70086
Saint James, MN	507	56081
Saint James, MO	573	65559
Saint James, NY	631	11780
Saint Joe, IN	260	46785
Saint John, KS	620	67576
Saint Johns, AZ	928	85936
Saint Johns, MI	989	48879
Saint Johnsbury, VT	802	05819
Saint Joseph, LA	318	71366
Saint Joseph, MI	616	49085
Saint Joseph, MN	320	56374-56375
Saint Joseph, MO	816	64501-64508
Saint Leo, FL	352	33574
Saint Louis, MI	989	48880
Saint Louis, MO	314	63101-63151, 63155-63171*
Saint Louis Park, MN	952	55416, 55424-55426, 55436
Saint Maries, ID	208	83861
Saint Martin, OH	513	45118
Saint Martinville, LA	337	70582
Saint Marys, GA	912	31558
Saint Marys, OH	419, 567	45885
Saint Marys, PA	814	15857
Saint Marys, WV	304	26170
Saint Matthews, SC	803	29135
Saint Meinrad, IN	812	47577
Saint Michael, MN	763	55376
Saint Michaels, MD	410	21624, 21647, 21663
Saint Nazianz, WI	920	54232
Saint Paul, MN	651	55101-55129, 55133, 55144*
Saint Paul, NE	308	68873
Saint Pauls, NC	910	28384
Saint Pete Beach, FL	727	33706, 33736
Saint Peter, MN	507	56082
Saint Peters, MO	636	63303-63304, 63376
Saint Petersburg, FL	727	33701-33716, 33728-33743*
Saint Rose, LA	504	70087
Saint Simons Island, GA	912	31522
Sainte Genevieve, MO	573	63670
Salamanca, NY	716	14779
Salem, AR	870	72576
Salem, IL	618	62881
Salem, IN	812	47167
Salem, MA	351, 978	01970-01971
Salem, MO	573	65560
Salem, NH	603	03079
Salem, NJ	856	08079
Salem, OH	234, 330	44460
Salem, OR	503, 971	97301-97314
Salem, SC	864	29676
Salem, SD	605	57058
Salem, VA	540	24153-24157
Salem, WV	304	26426
Salida, CA	209	95368
Salida, CO	719	81201, 81227-81228, 81237*
Salina, KS	785	67401-67402
Salinas, CA	831	93901-93908, 93912-93915*
Saline, MI	734	48176
Salineville, OH	234, 330	43945
Salisbury, CT	860	06068, 06079
Salisbury, MD	410	21801-21804
Salisbury, MA	351, 978	01952
Salisbury, NC	704, 980	28144-28147
Sallisaw, OK	918	74955
Salmon, ID	208	83467
Salt Flat, TX	915	79847
Salt Lake City, UT	801, 385	84101-84153, 84157-84158*
Saltillo, MS	662	38866
Saltsburg, PA	724, 878	15681
Saluda, SC	864	29138
Saluda, VA	804	23149
Salyersville, KY	606	41465
San Andreas, CA	209	95249-95250
San Angelo, TX	915	76901-76909
San Anselmo, CA	415	94960, 94979
San Antonio, FL	352	33576
San Antonio, TX	210	78201-78270, 78275-78299
San Augustine, TX	936	75972
San Benito, TX	956	78586
San Bernardino, CA	909	92401-92427
San Bruno, CA	650	94066-94067, 94096-94098
San Carlos, CA	650	94070-94071
San Clemente, CA	949	92672-92674
San Diego, CA	619, 858	92101-92199
San Dimas, CA	909	91773
San Fernando, CA	818	91340-91346
San Francisco, CA	415	94101-94177, 94188
San Gabriel, CA	626	91775-91778
San Gregorio, CA	650	94074
San Jacinto, CA	951	92581-92583
San Joaquin, CA	559	93660
San Jose, CA	408	95101-95142, 95148-95164*
San Juan, PR	787, 939	00901-00902, 00906-00940*
San Juan Bautista, CA	831	95045
San Juan Capistrano, CA	949	92675, 92690-92694
San Leandro, CA	510	94577-94579
San Lorenzo, CA	510	94580
San Luis, CO	719	81134, 81152
San Luis Obispo, CA	805	93401-93412
San Marcos, CA	760, 442	92069, 92078-92079, 92096
San Marcos, TX	512	78666-78667
San Marino, CA	626	91108, 91118
San Mateo, CA	650	94401-94409, 94497
San Pablo, CA	510	94806
San Pedro, CA	310, 424	90731-90734
San Quentin, CA	415	94964, 94974
San Rafael, CA	415	94901-94904, 94912-94915
San Ramon, CA	925	94583
San Saba, TX	915	76877
San Ysidro, CA	619	92143, 92173

*Partial list of zip codes, including main range

City	Area Code(s)	Zip Code(s)
Sanborn, NY	716	14132
Sand Point, AK	907	99661
Sand Springs, OK	918	74063
Sanderson, FL	386	32087
Sanderson, TX	915	79848
Sandersville, GA	478	31082
Sandia Park, NM	505	87047
Sandpoint, ID	208	83862-83864, 83888
Sandston, VA	804	23150
Sandstone, MN	320	55072
Sandusky, MI	810	48471
Sandusky, OH	419, 567	44870-44871
Sandwich, MA	508, 774	02563, 02644
Sandy, UT	801, 385	84070, 84090-84094
Sandy Hook, CT	203	06482
Sandy Hook, KY	606	41171
Sandy Lake, PA	724, 878	16145
Sandy Spring, MD	301	20860
Sanford, FL	321, 407	32771-32773
Sanford, ME	207	04073
Sanford, NC	919	27237, 27330-27332
Sanger, CA	559	93657
Sangerfield, NY	315	13455
Sanibel, FL	239	33957
Santa Ana, CA	714, 949	92701-92712, 92725-92728*
Santa Ana Pueblo, NM	505	87004
Santa Barbara, CA	805	93101-93111, 93116-93121*
Santa Clara, CA	408	95050-95056
Santa Clarita, CA	661	91310, 91321-91322, 91350*
Santa Claus, IN	812	47579
Santa Cruz, CA	831	95060-95067
Santa Cruz, NM	505	87567
Santa Fe, NM	505	87500-87509, 87592-87594
Santa Fe Springs, CA	562	90605, 90670-90671
Santa Maria, CA	805	93454-93458
Santa Monica, CA	310, 424	90401-90411
Santa Paula, CA	805	93060-93061
Santa Rosa, CA	707	95401-95409
Santa Rosa, NM	505	88435
Santa Rosa, TX	956	78593
Santa Rosa Beach, FL	850	32459
Santa Teresa, NM	505	88008, 88063
Santa Ynez, CA	805	93460
Santee, CA	619	92071-92072
Santurce, PR	787, 939	00907-00916, 00936, 00940
Sapulpa, OK	918	74066-74067
Saraland, AL	251	36571
Saranac Lake, NY	518	12983
Sarasota, FL	941	34230-34243, 34260, 34276*
Saratoga, CA	408	95070-95071
Saratoga, WY	307	82331
Saratoga Springs, NY	518	12866
Sardinia, OH	937	45171
Sardis, MS	662	38666
Sarita, TX	361	78385
Sartell, MN	320	56377
Sasabe, AZ	520	85633
Satanta, KS	620	67870
Satsuma, AL	251	36572
Saugerties, NY	845	12477
Sauget, IL	618	62201
Saugus, CA	661	91350, 91390
Saugus, MA	339, 781	01906
Sauk Centre, MN	320	56378, 56389
Sauk City, WI	608	53583
Sauk Rapids, MN	320	56379
Saukville, WI	262	53080
Sault Sainte Marie, MI	906	49783, 49788
Sausalito, CA	415	94965-94966
Savage, MD	410, 443	20763
Savage, MN	952	55378
Savanna, IL	815	61074
Savannah, GA	912	31401-31422, 31498-31499
Savannah, MO	816	64485
Savannah, TN	731	38372
Savoy, IL	217	61874
Saxonburg, PA	724, 878	16056
Sayre, OK	580	73662
Sayre, PA	570	18840
Sayreville, NJ	732, 848	08871-08872
Scandia, KS	785	66966
Scandinavia, WI	715, 534	54977
Scappoose, OR	503, 971	97056
Scarborough, ME	207	04070, 04074
Scarsdale, NY	914	10583
Schaefferstown, PA	717	17088
Schaumburg, IL	224, 847	60159, 60168, 60173, 60192*
Schenectady, NY	518	12008, 12301-12309, 12325*
Schererville, IN	219	46375
Schertz, TX	210	78154
Schiller Park, IL	224, 847	60176
Schnecksville, PA	484, 610	18078
Schofield, WI	715, 534	54476
Schoharie, NY	518	12157
Schoolcraft, MI	616	49087
Schuyler, NE	402	68661
Schuylkill Haven, PA	570	17972
Schwertner, TX	254	76573
Scituate, MA	339, 781	02040, 02055, 02060, 02066
Scobey, MT	406	59263
Scooba, MS	662	39358
Scotch Plains, NJ	908	07076
Scotia, CA	707	95565
Scotia, NY	518	12302
Scotland Neck, NC	252	27874
Scotrun, PA	570	18355
Scott, AR	501	72142
Scott, LA	337	70583
Scott, MS	662	38772
Scott AFB, IL	618	62225
Scott City, KS	620	67871
Scott City, MO	573	63780
Scott Depot, WV	304	25560
Scottdale, GA	404, 470	30079
Scottdale, PA	724, 878	15683
Scotts Valley, CA	831	95060, 95066-95067
Scottsbluff, NE	308	69361-69363
Scottsboro, AL	256	35768-35769
Scottsburg, IN	812	47170
Scottsdale, AZ	480	85250-85271
Scottsville, KY	270	42164
Scottsville, NY	585	14546
Scottsville, TX	903	75688
Scottville, MI	231	49454
Scranton, PA	570	18501-18522, 18540, 18577
Sea Island, GA	912	31561
Seabrook, NH	603	03874
Seabrook, NJ	856	08302
Seabrook, TX	281, 832	77586
Seabrook Island, SC	843	29455
Seaford, DE	302	19973
Seagoville, TX	469, 972	75159
Seal Beach, CA	562	90740
Seale, AL	334	36875
Searcy, AR	501	72143-72145, 72149
Searsmont, ME	207	04973
Searsport, ME	207	04974
Seaside, CA	831	93955
Seaside, OR	503	97138
Seaside Heights, NJ	732, 848	08751
Seattle, WA	206	98101-98138, 98144-98191*
Sebastian, FL	772	32958, 32976-32978
Sebastopol, CA	707	95472-95473
Sebastopol, MS	601, 769	39359
Sebring, FL	863	33870-33876
Sebring, OH	234, 330	44672
Secaucus, NJ	201, 551	07094-07096
Sedalia, CO	303, 720	80135
Sedalia, MO	660	65301-65302
Sedalia, NC	336	27342
Sedan, KS	620	67361
Sedona, AZ	928	86336-86341, 86351
Sedro Woolley, WA	360	98284
Seeley Lake, MT	406	59868
Seffner, FL	813	33583-33584
Seguin, TX	830	78155-78156
Selah, WA	509	98942
Selby, SD	605	57472
Selden, NY	631	11784
Selinsgrove, PA	570	17870
Selkirk, NY	518	12158
Sellersburg, IN	812	47172
Sellersville, PA	215, 267	18960
Sells, AZ	520	85634
Selma, AL	334	36701-36703
Selma, CA	559	93662
Selma, TX	210	78154
Selmer, TN	731	38375
Seminole, FL	727	33772-33778
Seminole, OK	405	74818, 74868
Seminole, TX	915	79360
Semmes, AL	251	36575
Senatobia, MS	662	38665-38668
Seneca, KS	785	66538
Seneca, SC	864	29672, 29678-29679
Seneca Falls, NY	315	13148
Sequatchie, TN	423	37374
Seven Hills, OH	216	44131
Severn, MD	410	21144
Severn, NC	252	27877
Severna Park, MD	410	21146
Sevierville, TN	865	37862-37864, 37868, 37876
Seville, OH	234, 330	44273
Sewanee, TN	931	37375, 37383
Seward, AK	907	99664
Seward, NE	402	68434
Sewell, NJ	856	08080
Sewickley, PA	412, 878	15143, 15189
Seymour, CT	203	06478, 06483
Seymour, IN	812	47274
Seymour, TX	940	76380
Seymour Johnson AFB, NC	919	27531
Shady Grove, PA	717	17256
Shadyside, OH	740	43947
Shafter, CA	661	93263
Shaftsbury, VT	802	05262
Shaker Heights, OH	216	44118-44122
Shakopee, MN	952	55379
Shallotte, NC	910	28459, 28467-28470
Shamokin, PA	570	17872
Shamokin Dam, PA	570	17876
Shannock, RI	401	02875
Sharon, CT	860	06069
Sharon, MA	339, 781	02067
Sharon, PA	724, 878	16146-16148
Sharon, WI	262	53585
Sharon Center, OH	234, 330	44274
Sharon Springs, KS	785	67758
Sharonville, OH	513	45241
Sharpsburg, MD	301	21782
Sharpsville, PA	724, 878	16150
Sharptown, MD	410	21861
Shavertown, PA	570	18708
Shaw AFB, SC	803	29152
Shawano, WI	715, 534	54166
Shawnee, CO	303, 720	80448, 80475
Shawnee, KS	913	66203, 66214-66220, 66226*
Shawnee, OK	405	74801-74804
Shawnee Mission, KS	913	66201-66227, 66250, 66276*
Shawnee on Delaware, PA	570	18356
Shawneetown, IL	618	62984
Sheboygan, WI	920	53081-53083
Sheboygan Falls, WI	920	53085
Sheffield, AL	256	35660
Sheffield, IA	641	50475
Sheffield, MA	413	01257
Sheffield, PA	814	16347
Sheffield, TX	915	79781
Shelbina, MO	573	63468
Shelburne, VT	802	05482
Shelburne Falls, MA	413	01370
Shelby, MI	231	49455
Shelby, MT	406	59474
Shelby, NE	402	68662
Shelby, NC	704, 980	28150-28152
Shelby, OH	419, 567	44875
Shelby Township, MI	586	48315-48318
Shelbyville, IL	217	62565
Shelbyville, IN	317	46176
Shelbyville, KY	502	40065-40066
Shelbyville, MO	573	63469
Shelbyville, TN	931	37160-37162
Sheldon, IA	712	51201
Shell, WY	307	82441
Shell Lake, WI	715, 534	54871
Shelley, ID	208	83274
Shellman, GA	229	31786
Shelocta, PA	724, 878	15774
Shelton, CT	203	06484
Shelton, NE	308	68876
Shelton, WA	360	98584
Shenandoah, IA	712	51601-51603
Shenandoah, PA	570	17976
Shepherdstown, WV	304	25443
Shepherdsville, KY	502	40165
Sheppard AFB, TX	940	76311
Sherburne, NY	607	13460
Sheridan, AR	870	72150
Sheridan, IN	317	46069

*Partial list of zip codes, including main range

City	Area Code(s)	Zip Code(s)
Sheridan, MI	989	48884
Sheridan, OR	503, 971	97378
Sheridan, WY	307	82801
Sherman, MS	662	38869
Sherman, TX	903	75090-75092
Sherman Oaks, CA	818	91401-91403, 91411-91413*
Sherwood, AR	501	72116-72120, 72124
Sherwood, OR	503, 971	97140
Shickshinny, PA	570	18655
Shillington, PA	484, 610	19607
Shiloh, OH	419, 567	44878
Shiloh, TN	731	38376
Shiner, TX	361	77984
Ship Bottom, NJ	609	08008
Shippensburg, PA	717	17257
Shippenville, PA	814	16254
Shiprock, NM	505	87420, 87461
Shipshewana, IN	260	46565
Shirley, MA	351, 978	01464
Shirley, NY	631	11967
Shoals, IN	812	47581
Shoemakersville, PA	484, 610	19555
Shoreline, WA	206	98133, 98155, 98177
Shoreview, MN	651	55126
Shorewood, IL	815	60431, 60435-60436
Short Hills, NJ	862, 973	07078
Shoshone, ID	208	83324, 83352
Show Low, AZ	928	85901-85902, 85911
Shreveport, LA	318	71101-71110, 71115-71120*
Shrewsbury, MA	508, 774	01545-01546
Shrewsbury, NJ	732, 848	07702
Shrub Oak, NY	914	10588
Sibley, IA	712	51249
Sibley, MO	816	64088
Sidney, IA	712	51652
Sidney, MI	989	48885
Sidney, MT	406	59270
Sidney, NE	308	69160-69162
Sidney, NY	607	13838
Sidney, OH	937	45365-45367
Sierra Blanca, TX	915	79851
Sierra Madre, CA	626	91024-91025
Sierra Vista, AZ	520	85613, 85635-85636, 85650*
Signal Hill, CA	562	90804-90807
Signal Mountain, TN	423	37377
Sigourney, IA	641	52591
Sikeston, MO	573	63801
Siler City, NC	919	27344
Siloam Springs, AR	479	72761
Silsbee, TX	409	77656
Silver Bay, MN	218	55614
Silver City, NM	505	88022, 88036, 88053, 88061*
Silver Creek, NE	308	68663
Silver Creek, NY	716	14136
Silver Lake, IN	260	46982
Silver Lake, NH	603	03875
Silver Spring, MD	301	20901-20918, 20997
Silver Spring, PA	717	17575
Silver Springs, FL	352	34488-34489
Silverdale, WA	360	98315, 98383
Silverton, CO	970	81433
Silverton, OH	513	45236
Silverton, OR	503, 971	97381
Silverton, TX	806	79257
Silvis, IL	309	61282
Simi Valley, CA	805	93062-93065, 93093-93094*
Simpson, PA	570	18407
Simpsonville, KY	502	40067
Simpsonville, SC	864	29680-29681
Simsbury, CT	860	06070, 06081, 06089-06092
Singer Island, FL	561	33404
Sinking Spring, PA	484, 610	19608
Sinton, TX	361	78387
Sioux Center, IA	712	51250
Sioux City, IA	712	51101-51111
Sioux Falls, SD	605	57101-57110, 57117-57118*
Siren, WI	715, 534	54872
Sisseton, SD	605	57262
Sisters, OR	541, 458	97759
Sitka, AK	907	99835-99836
Skagway, AK	907	99840
Skaneateles Falls, NY	315	13119, 13153
Skillman, NJ	908	08558
Skokie, IL	224, 847	60076-60077
Skowhegan, ME	207	04976
Sky Valley, GA	706, 762	30537
Skytop, PA	570	18357
Slater, CO	970	81653
Slater, IA	515	50244
Slatersville, RI	401	02876
Slaton, TX	806	79364
Slayton, MN	507	56172
Sleepy Eye, MN	507	56085
Slidell, LA	985	70458-70461, 70469
Slippery Rock, PA	724, 878	16057
Smackover, AR	870	71762
Smethport, PA	814	16749
Smith Center, KS	785	66967
Smithfield, NC	919	27577
Smithfield, RI	401	02828, 02917
Smithfield, VA	757	23430-23431
Smithland, KY	270	42081
Smithton, PA	724, 878	15479
Smithtown, NY	631	11745, 11787-11788
Smithville, MO	816	64089
Smithville, OH	234, 330	44677
Smithville, TN	615	37166
Smithville, TX	512	78957
Smyrna, DE	302	19977
Smyrna, GA	404, 770	30080-30082, 30339
Smyrna, TN	615	37167
Sneads, FL	850	32460
Sneedville, TN	423	37869
Snellville, GA	770	30039, 30078
Snohomish, WA	360	98290-98291, 98296
Snoqualmie, WA	425	98065-98068
Snow Hill, MD	410	21863
Snow Hill, NC	252	28580
Snowbird, UT	801, 385	84092
Snowflake, AZ	928	85937, 85942
Snowmass Village, CO	970	81615
Snowshoe, WV	304	26209
Snyder, NE	402	68664
Snyder, TX	915	79549-79550
Social Circle, GA	470, 770	30025
Socorro, NM	505	87801
Soda Springs, ID	208	83230, 83276, 83285
Sodus, NY	315	14551
Solana Beach, CA	858	92075
Soldotna, AK	907	99669
Soledad, CA	831	93960
Solitude, UT	801, 385	84121
Solomon, KS	785	67480
Solomons, MD	410	20688
Solon, OH	440	44139
Solvang, CA	805	93463-93464
Somers, CT	860	06071
Somers, NY	914	10589
Somers Point, NJ	609	08244
Somerset, KY	606	42501-42503, 42564
Somerset, MA	508, 774	02725-02726
Somerset, NJ	732, 848	08873-08875
Somerset, PA	814	15501, 15510
Somerton, AZ	928	85350
Somerville, MA	617, 857	02143-02145
Somerville, NJ	908	08876
Somerville, TN	901	38060, 38068
Sonoita, AZ	520	85637
Sonoma, CA	707	95476
Sonora, CA	209	95370-95373
Sonora, TX	915	76950
Sonyea, NY	585	14556
Soperton, GA	912	30457
Sorrento, LA	225	70778
Souderton, PA	215, 267	18964
South Attleboro, MA	508, 774	02703
South Barre, VT	802	05670
South Barrington, IL	224, 847	60010
South Bay, FL	561	33493
South Beloit, IL	815	61080
South Bend, IN	574	46601-46604, 46612-46620*
South Bend, WA	360	98586
South Boston, VA	434	24592
South Brunswick, NJ	732, 848	08810
South Burlington, VT	802	05401-05407
South Canaan, PA	570	18459
South Carver, MA	508, 774	02366
South Casco, ME	207	04077
South Charleston, WV	304	25303, 25309
South Chicago Heights, IL	708	60411
South Deerfield, MA	413	01373
South Easton, MA	508, 774	02375
South El Monte, CA	626	91733
South Elgin, IL	224, 847	60177
South Euclid, OH	216	44118-44121
South Fallsburg, NY	845	12779
South Fork, PA	814	15956
South Fulton, TN	731	38257
South Gate, CA	323, 562	90280
South Hackensack, NJ	201, 551	07606
South Hadley, MA	413	01075
South Haven, MI	616	49090
South Hill, VA	434	23970
South Holland, IL	708	60473
South Houston, TX	713, 832	77587
South Jordan, UT	801, 385	84065, 84095
South Kearny, NJ	862, 973	07032
South Laguna, CA	949	92651
South Lake Tahoe, CA	530	96150-96158
South Lancaster, MA	351, 978	01561
South Lee, MA	413	01260
South Lyon, MI	248, 947	48178
South Miami, FL	305, 786	33143-33146, 33155-33156*
South Milwaukee, WI	414	53172
South Mountain, PA	717	17261
South Natick, MA	508, 774	01760
South Norwalk, CT	203	06854
South Orange, NJ	862, 973	07079
South Otselic, NY	315	13155
South Padre Island, TX	956	78597
South Paris, ME	207	04281
South Pasadena, CA	626	91030-91031
South Pittsburg, TN	423	37380
South Plainfield, NJ	908	07080
South Plymouth, NY	607	13844
South Point, OH	740	45680
South Portland, ME	207	04106, 04116
South River, NJ	732, 848	08877, 08882
South Saint Paul, MN	651	55075-55077
South Salt Lake, UT	801, 385	84107, 84115, 84119, 84123*
South San Francisco, CA	650	94080-94083, 94099
South Sioux City, NE	402	68776
South Weymouth, MA	339, 781	02190
South Whitley, IN	260	46787
South Williamson, KY	606	41503
South Williamsport, PA	570	17702
South Windham, CT	860	06266
South Windham, ME	207	04082
South Windsor, CT	860	06074
South Yarmouth, MA	508, 774	02664, 02673
Southampton, NY	631	11968-11969
Southampton, PA	215, 267	18954, 18966
Southaven, MS	662	38671-38672
Southborough, MA	508, 774	01745, 01772
Southbridge, MA	508, 774	01550
Southbury, CT	203	06488
Southern Pines, NC	910	28387-28388
Southfield, MI	248, 947	48034-48037, 48075-48076*
Southgate, MI	734	48195
Southington, CT	860	06489
Southlake, TX	682, 817	76092
Southold, NY	631	11971
Southport, CT	203	06490
Southport, NC	910	28461, 28465
Southwest Harbor, ME	207	04656, 04679
Southwick, MA	413	01077
Spalding, ID	208	83540, 83551
Spanaway, WA	253	98387
Spanish Fort, AL	251	36527, 36577
Sparkill, NY	845	10976
Sparks, MD	410	21152
Sparks, NV	775	89431-89436
Sparta, GA	706, 762	31087
Sparta, MI	616	49345
Sparta, NJ	862, 973	07871
Sparta, NC	336	28675
Sparta, TN	931	38583
Sparta, WI	608	54656
Spartanburg, SC	864	29301-29307, 29316-29319
Spearfish, SD	605	57783, 57799
Spearman, TX	806	79081
Spearville, KS	620	67876
Speedway, IN	317	46224
Spencer, IN	812	47460
Spencer, IA	712	51301, 51343
Spencer, MA	508, 774	01562
Spencer, NY	607	14883
Spencer, NC	704, 980	28159
Spencer, TN	931	38585

Partial list of zip codes, including main range

City	Area Code(s)	Zip Code(s)
Spencer, WV	304	25276
Spencerport, NY	585	14559
Spencerville, OH	419, 567	45887
Spiceland, IN	765	47385
Spindale, NC	828	28160
Spirit Lake, IA	712	51360
Spokane, WA	509	99201-99224, 99228, 99251*
Spotsylvania, VA	540	22553
Spring, TX	281, 832	77373, 77379-77393
Spring Arbor, MI	517	49283
Spring City, PA	484, 610	19475
Spring City, UT	435	84662
Spring Green, WI	608	53588
Spring Grove, IL	815	60081
Spring Hill, FL	352	34604-34611
Spring Hill, TN	931	37174
Spring Hope, NC	252	27882
Spring House, PA	215, 267	19477
Spring Lake, MI	231, 616	49456
Spring Lake, NJ	732, 848	07762
Spring Lake Park, MN	612, 763	55432
Spring Mills, PA	814	16875
Spring Valley, CA	619	91976-91979
Spring Valley, IL	815	61362
Spring Valley, MN	507	55975
Spring Valley, NY	845	10977
Spring Valley, WI	715, 534	54767
Springboro, OH	513	45066
Springdale, AR	479	72762-72766
Springdale, OH	513	45246
Springdale, PA	724, 878	15144
Springdale, UT	435	84767, 84779
Springer, NM	505	87729, 87747
Springer, OK	580	73458
Springfield, CO	719	81073
Springfield, GA	912	31329
Springfield, IL	217	62701-62709, 62713-62726*
Springfield, KY	859	40069
Springfield, MA	413	01101-01119, 01128-01129*
Springfield, MN	507	56087
Springfield, MO	417	65721, 65742, 65801-65810*
Springfield, NJ	862, 973	07081
Springfield, OH	937	45501-45506
Springfield, OR	541, 458	97477-97478, 97482
Springfield, PA	484, 610	19064, 19118
Springfield, SD	605	57062
Springfield, TN	615	37172
Springfield, VT	802	05156
Springfield, VA	571, 703	22009, 22015, 22150-22161
Springfield Gardens, NY	347, 718	11413
Springs, PA	814	15562
Springtown, TX	682, 817	76082
Springvale, ME	207	04083
Springview, NE	402	68778
Springville, AL	205	35146
Springville, UT	801, 385	84663
Spruce Pine, NC	828	28777
Stafford, TX	281, 832	77477, 77497
Stafford, VA	540	22554-22555
Stafford Springs, CT	860	06076
Stamford, CT	203	06901-06914, 06920-06928
Stamford, NY	607	12167
Stamps, AR	870	71860
Stanardsville, VA	434	22973
Stanberry, MO	660	64489
Standish, ME	207	04084
Standish, MI	989	48658
Stanfield, AZ	520	85272
Stanford, CA	650	94305, 94309
Stanford, KY	606	40484
Stanford, MT	406	59479
Stanhope, NJ	862, 973	07874
Stanley, NC	704, 980	28164
Stanley, ND	701	58784
Stanleytown, VA	276	24168
Stanton, CA	714	90680
Stanton, KY	606	40380
Stanton, MI	989	48888
Stanton, NE	402	68779
Stanton, ND	701	58571
Stanton, TX	915	79782
Stanwood, WA	360	98282, 98292
Staples, MN	218	56479
Stapleton, NE	308	69163
Star, NC	910	27356
Star City, AR	870	71667
Starbuck, MN	320	56381
Starke, FL	904	32091
Starkville, MS	662	39759-39760
State Center, IA	641	50247
State College, PA	814	16801-16805
State Farm, VA	804	23160
State University, AR	870	72467
Stateline, NV	775	89449
Staten Island, NY	347, 718	10301-10314
Statenville, GA	229	31648
Statesboro, GA	912	30458-30461
Statesville, NC	704, 980	28625, 28677, 28687
Staunton, VA	540	24401-24402, 24407
Stayton, OR	503, 971	97383
Steamboat Springs, CO	970	80477, 80487-80488
Stearns, KY	606	42647
Steele, ND	701	58482
Steeleville, IL	618	62288
Steelville, MO	573	65565-65566
Steilacoom, WA	253	98388
Stennis Space Center, MS	228	39522, 39529
Stephenville, TX	254	76401-76402
Sterling, CO	970	80751
Sterling, IL	815	61081
Sterling, KS	620	67579
Sterling, VA	571, 703	20163-20167
Sterling City, TX	915	76951
Sterling Heights, MI	586	48310-48314
Steubenville, OH	740	43952-43953
Stevens Point, WI	715, 534	54481, 54492
Stevensburg, VA	540	22741
Stevenson, AL	256	35772
Stevenson, CT	203	06491
Stevenson, MD	410	21153
Stevenson, WA	509	98648
Stevensville, MD	410	21666
Stevensville, MI	616	49127
Stewart, MN	320	55385
Stewartville, MN	507	55976
Stigler, OK	918	74462
Stillwater, ME	207	04489
Stillwater, MN	651	55082-55083
Stillwater, NY	518	12170
Stillwater, OK	405	74074-74078
Stilwell, OK	918	74960
Stinnett, TX	806	79083
Stirling, NJ	908	07980
Stockbridge, GA	470, 770	30281
Stockbridge, MA	413	01262-01263
Stockton, CA	209	95201-95215, 95219, 95267*
Stockton, KS	785	67669
Stockton, MO	417	65785
Stockville, NE	308	69042
Stone Creek, OH	234, 330	43840
Stone Mountain, GA	470, 770	30083-30088
Stone Ridge, NY	845	12484
Stoneham, MA	339, 781	02180
Stoneville, MS	662	38776
Stonington, CT	860	06378
Stony Brook, NY	631	11790, 11794
Stony Creek, VA	434	23882
Stony Point, NY	845	10980
Storm Lake, IA	712	50588
Stormville, NY	845	12582
Storrs, CT	860	06268
Stoughton, MA	339, 781	02072
Stoughton, WI	608	53589
Stow, OH	234, 330	44224
Stowe, PA	484, 610	19464
Stowe, VT	802	05672
Stoystown, PA	814	15563
Strafford, MO	417	65757
Strasburg, CO	303, 720	80136
Strasburg, OH	234, 330	44680
Strasburg, VA	540	22641, 22657
Stratford, CA	559	93266
Stratford, CT	203	06497, 06614-06615
Stratford, NJ	856	08084
Stratford, TX	806	79084
Stratford, WI	715, 534	54484
Stratham, NH	603	03885
Stratton, CO	719	80836
Stratton Mountain, VT	802	05155
Strausstown, PA	484, 610	19559
Strawberry Point, IA	563	52076
Streamwood, IL	331, 630	60107
Streator, IL	815	61364
Streetsboro, OH	234, 330	44241
Stringtown, OK	580	74569
Stromsburg, NE	402	68666
Strongsville, OH	440	44136, 44149
Stroudsburg, PA	570	18360
Stryker, OH	419, 567	43557
Stuart, FL	772	34994-34997
Stuart, VA	276	24171
Stuarts Draft, VA	540	24477
Studio City, CA	818	91602-91607, 91614
Sturbridge, MA	508, 774	01518, 01566
Sturgeon Bay, WI	920	54235
Sturgis, MI	616	49091
Sturgis, SD	605	57785
Sturtevant, WI	262	53177
Stuttgart, AR	870	72160
Subiaco, AR	479	72865
Sublette, KS	620	67877
Sublimity, OR	503, 971	97385
Succasunna, NJ	862, 973	07876
Sudbury, MA	351, 978	01776
Suffern, NY	845	10901
Suffield, CT	860	06078-06080, 06093
Suffolk, VA	757	23432-23439
Sugar Grove, IL	331, 630	60554
Sugar Land, TX	281, 832	77478-77479, 77487, 77496
Sugar Valley, GA	706, 762	30746
Sugarcreek, OH	234, 330	44681
Suitland, MD	301	20746, 20752
Sullivan, IL	217	61951
Sullivan, IN	812	47864, 47882
Sullivan, MO	573	63080
Sullivans Island, SC	843	29482
Sulphur, LA	337	70663-70665
Sulphur, OK	580	73086
Sulphur Springs, TX	903	75482-75483
Sultan, WA	360	98294
Summerdale, AL	251	36580
Summerdale, PA	717	17093
Summersville, WV	304	26651
Summerville, GA	706, 762	30747
Summerville, SC	843	29483-29485
Summit, IL	708	60501
Summit, MS	601, 769	39666
Summit, NJ	908	07901-07902
Summit, NY	518	12175
Summit Station, PA	570	17979
Summitville, OH	234, 330	43962
Sumner, WA	253	98352, 98390
Sumter, SC	803	29150-29154
Sumterville, FL	352	33585
Sun City, AZ	623	85351, 85372-85379, 85387
Sun City, CA	951	92584-92587
Sun City, FL	813	33586
Sun City Center, FL	813	33570-33573
Sun City West, AZ	623	85374-85379, 85387
Sun Lakes, AZ	480	85248
Sun Prairie, WI	608	53590-53591, 53596
Sun Valley, CA	818	91352-91353
Sun Valley, ID	208	83353-83354
Sunbury, OH	740	43074
Sunbury, PA	570	17801, 17877
Suncook, NH	603	03275
Sundance, WY	307	82729
Sunland, CA	818	91040-91041
Sunland Park, NM	505	88008, 88063
Sunman, IN	812	47041
Sunny Isles Beach, FL	305, 786	33160
Sunnyside, NY	347, 718	11104
Sunnyside, WA	509	98944
Sunnyvale, CA	408	94085-94090
Sunnyvale, TX	469, 972	75182
Sunrise, FL	754, 954	33304, 33313, 33319-33326*
Sunriver, OR	541, 458	97707
Superior, AZ	520	85273
Superior, MT	406	59872
Superior, WI	715, 534	54880
Supply, NC	910	28462
Surfside, FL	305, 786	33154
Surfside Beach, SC	843	29575, 29587
Surgoinsville, TN	423	37873
Surry, VA	757	23883
Susanville, CA	530	96127-96130
Sussex, NJ	862, 973	07461
Sussex, VA	434	23884

*Partial list of zip codes, including main range

City	Area Code(s)	Zip Code(s)
Sussex, WI	262	53089
Sutherlin, OR	541, 458	97479
Sutter, CA	530	95982
Sutton, MA	508, 774	01590
Sutton, WV	304	26601
Suttons Bay, MI	231	49682
Suwanee, GA	470, 678, 770	30024
Swainsboro, GA	478	30401
Swampscott, MA	339, 781	01907
Swannanoa, NC	828	28778
Swanquarter, NC	252	27885
Swansea, IL	618	62220-62226
Swansea, MA	508, 774	02777
Swanton, OH	419, 567	43558
Swanton, VT	802	05488
Swarthmore, PA	484, 610	19081
Swartz Creek, MI	810	48473
Swea City, IA	515	50590
Swedesboro, NJ	856	08085
Sweet Briar, VA	434	24595
Sweet Home, OR	541, 458	97386
Sweetwater, TN	423	37874
Sweetwater, TX	915	79556
Swepsonville, NC	336	27359
Swiftwater, PA	570	18370
Swissvale, PA	412, 878	15218
Swords Creek, VA	276	24649
Swoyersville, PA	570	18704
Sycamore, AL	256	35149
Sycamore, IL	815	60178
Sykesville, MD	410	21784
Sylacauga, AL	256	35150-35151
Sylmar, CA	818	91342, 91392
Sylva, NC	828	28779
Sylvania, GA	912	30467
Sylvania, OH	419, 567	43560
Sylvester, GA	229	31791
Syosset, NY	516	11773, 11791
Syracuse, IN	574	46567
Syracuse, KS	620	67878
Syracuse, NE	402	68446
Syracuse, NY	315	13201-13225, 13235, 13244*

T

City	Area Code(s)	Zip Code(s)
Tabor, SD	605	57063
Tabor City, NC	910	28463
Tacoma, WA	253	98401-98424, 98431-98433*
Taft, CA	661	93268
Taft, OK	918	74463
Taftville, CT	860	06380
Tahlequah, OK	918	74464-74465
Tahoe City, CA	530	96145-96146
Tahoka, TX	806	79373
Takoma Park, MD	301	20903, 20912-20913
Talbotton, GA	706, 762	31827
Talihina, OK	918	74571
Talladega, AL	256	35160-35161
Tallahassee, FL	850	32301-32318, 32395, 32399
Tallapoosa, GA	470, 770	30176
Tallassee, AL	334	36023, 36045, 36078
Tallevast, FL	941	34270
Tallmadge, OH	234, 330	44278
Tallulah, LA	318	71282-71284
Talmage, PA	717	17580
Taloga, OK	580	73667
Tama, IA	641	52339
Tamaqua, PA	570	18252
Tamarac, FL	754, 954	33309, 33319-33323, 33351*
Tamiment, PA	570	18371
Tamms, IL	618	62988, 62993
Tampa, FL	813	33601-33637, 33647-33651*
Taneytown, MD	410	21787
Tangent, OR	541, 458	97389
Tannersville, PA	570	18372
Taos, NM	505	87571
Tappahannock, VA	804	22560
Tarboro, NC	252	27886
Tarentum, PA	724, 878	15084
Tarpon Springs, FL	727	34688-34691
Tarrytown, NY	914	10591
Tarzana, CA	818	91335, 91356-91357
Taunton, MA	508, 774	02718, 02780-02783
Tavares, FL	352	32778
Tavernier, FL	305, 786	33070
Tawas City, MI	989	48763-48764
Taylor, MI	313, 734	48180
Taylor, NE	308	68879
Taylor, PA	570	18517
Taylor, TX	512	76574
Taylors, SC	864	29687
Taylorsville, KY	502	40071
Taylorsville, MS	601, 769	39168
Taylorsville, NC	828	28681
Taylorville, IL	217	62568
Tazewell, TN	423	37879
Tazewell, VA	276	24608, 24651
Teaneck, NJ	201, 551	07666
Teays, WV	304	25569
Tecumseh, MI	517	49286
Tecumseh, NE	402	68450
Tecumseh, OK	405	74873
Tehachapi, CA	661	93561, 93581
Tekamah, NE	402	68061
Telford, PA	215, 267	18969
Tell City, IN	812	47586
Telluride, CO	970	81435
Temecula, CA	951	92589-92593
Tempe, AZ	480, 602	85280-85289
Temperance, MI	734	48182
Temple, PA	484, 610	19560
Temple, TX	254	76501-76508
Temple City, CA	626	91780
Temple Hills, MD	301	20748, 20752, 20757, 20762
Temple Terrace, FL	813	33617, 33637, 33687
Templeton, CA	805	93465
Tenafly, NJ	201, 551	07670
Tenino, WA	360	98589
Tenstrike, MN	218	56683
Tequesta, FL	561	33469
Terminal Island, CA	310, 424	90731
Terra Bella, CA	559	93270
Terre Haute, IN	812	47801-47814
Terrell, TX	469, 972	75160-75161
Terry, MT	406	59349
Terryville, CT	860	06786
Teterboro, NJ	201, 551	07608
Teton Village, WY	307	83025
Teutopolis, IL	217	62467
Tewksbury, MA	351, 978	01876
Texarkana, AR	870	71854
Texarkana, TX	903	75501-75507, 75599
Texas City, TX	409	77590-77592
Thatcher, AZ	928	85552
The Colony, TX	469, 972	75034, 75056
The Dalles, OR	541, 458	97058
The Sea Ranch, CA	707	95445, 95497
The Villages, FL	352	32159-32162
The Woodlands, TX	281, 832	77380-77387, 77393
Thedford, NE	308	69166
Theodore, AL	251	36582, 36590, 36619
Thermopolis, WY	307	82443
Thibodaux, LA	985	70301-70302, 70310
Thief River Falls, MN	218	56701
Thiensville, WI	262	53092, 53097
Thomaston, CT	860	06778, 06787
Thomaston, GA	706, 762	30286
Thomaston, ME	207	04861
Thomasville, AL	334	36762, 36784
Thomasville, GA	229	31757-31758, 31792, 31799
Thomasville, NC	336	27360-27361
Thomasville, PA	717	17364
Thompson, CT	860	06277
Thompson, IA	641	50478
Thompson Falls, MT	406	59873
Thompsons Station, TN	615	37179
Thompsonville, MI	231	49683
Thomson, GA	706, 762	30824
Thorndale, PA	484, 610	19372
Thornton, CO	303, 720	80020, 80221, 80229, 80233*
Thornton, IL	708	60476
Thornville, OH	740	43076
Thornwood, NY	914	10594
Thorofare, NJ	856	08086
Thousand Oaks, CA	805	91319-91320, 91358-91362
Three Lakes, WI	715, 534	54562
Three Rivers, CA	559	93271
Three Rivers, MI	616	49093
Three Rivers, TX	361	78060, 78071
Throckmorton, TX	940	76483
Thurmont, MD	301	21788
Tiburon, CA	415	94920
Tie Siding, WY	307	82084
Tierra Amarilla, NM	505	87575
Tierra Verde, FL	727	33715
Tiffin, OH	419, 567	44883
Tifton, GA	229	31793-31794
Tigard, OR	503, 971	97223-97224, 97281
Tigerville, SC	864	29688
Tilden, TX	361	78072
Tillamook, OR	503	97141
Tillery, NC	252	27887
Tilton, NH	603	03276, 03298-03299
Timber Lake, SD	605	57656
Timberline Lodge, OR	503, 971	97028
Timmonsville, SC	843	29161
Timonium, MD	410	21093-21094
Tinker AFB, OK	405	73145
Tinley Park, IL	708	60477
Tinton Falls, NJ	732, 848	07724
Tionesta, PA	814	16353
Tipp City, OH	937	45371
Tipton, IN	765	46072
Tipton, IA	563	52772
Tipton, MO	660	65081
Tipton, OK	580	73570
Tipton, PA	814	16684
Tiptonville, TN	731	38079
Tishomingo, OK	580	73460
Titusville, FL	321	32780-32783, 32796
Titusville, NJ	609	08560
Titusville, PA	814	16354
Toa Baja, PR	787, 939	00949-00951
Toccoa, GA	706, 762	30577
Toccoa Falls, GA	706, 762	30598
Togo, MN	218	55723
Tok, AK	907	99776-99780
Tokeland, WA	360	98590
Toledo, IL	217	62468
Toledo, IA	641	52342
Toledo, OH	419, 567	43601-43624, 43635, 43652*
Tolland, CT	860	06084
Tolleson, AZ	623	85353
Tollhouse, CA	559	93667
Tolono, IL	217	61880
Toluca, IL	815	61369
Tomah, WI	608	54660
Tomball, TX	281, 832	77337, 77375-77377
Tombstone, AZ	520	85638
Tompkinsville, KY	270	42167
Toms River, NJ	732, 848	08753-08757
Tonalea, AZ	928	86044, 86053-86054
Tonawanda, NY	716	14150-14151, 14217, 14223
Tonkawa, OK	580	74653
Tonopah, NV	775	89049
Tontitown, AR	479	72770
Tooele, UT	435	84074
Topeka, IN	260	46571
Topeka, KS	785	66601-66629, 66634-66638*
Toppenish, WA	509	98948
Topsfield, MA	351, 978	01983
Topsham, ME	207	04086
Topton, PA	484, 610	19562
Torrance, CA	310, 424	90501-90510
Torrance, PA	724, 878	15779
Torrey, UT	435	84775
Torrington, CT	860	06790-06791
Torrington, WY	307	82240
Totowa, NJ	862, 973	07511-07512
Tougaloo, MS	601, 769	39174
Toulon, IL	309	61483
Toutle, WA	360	98645, 98649
Towaco, NJ	862, 973	07082
Towanda, PA	570	18848
Towner, ND	701	58788
Townsend, MA	351, 978	01469, 01474
Townsend, MT	406	59644
Townsend, TN	865	37882
Towson, MD	410	21204, 21284-21286
Tracy, CA	209	95304, 95376-95378, 95385*
Travelers Rest, SC	864	29690
Traverse City, MI	231	49684-49686, 49696
Travis AFB, CA	707	94535
Tremonton, UT	435	84337
Trenton, FL	352	32693
Trenton, GA	706, 762	30752
Trenton, ME	207	04605

*Partial list of zip codes, including main range

City	Area Code(s)	Zip Code(s)
Trenton, MI	734	48183
Trenton, MO	660	64683
Trenton, NE	308	69044
Trenton, NJ	609	08601-08611, 08618-08620*
Trenton, NC	252	28585
Trenton, OH	513	45067
Trenton, SC	803	29847
Trenton, TN	731	38382
Trevor, WI	262	53102, 53179
Trevose, PA	215, 267	19053
Triangle, VA	571, 703	22172
Tribune, KS	620	67879
Trinidad, CO	719	81074, 81082
Trinity, AL	256	35673
Trinity, NC	336	27370
Trinity Center, CA	530	96091
Trion, GA	706, 762	30753
Trotwood, OH	937	45406, 45415-45418, 45426*
Troutdale, OR	503, 971	97060
Troy, AL	334	36079-36082
Troy, ID	208	83871
Troy, IL	618	62294
Troy, KS	785	66087
Troy, MI	248, 947	48007, 48083-48085, 48098*
Troy, MO	636	63379
Troy, NY	518	12179-12183
Troy, NC	910	27371
Troy, OH	937	45373-45374
Troy, VA	434	22974
Truckee, CA	530	96160-96162
Truman, MN	507	56088
Trumann, AR	870	72472
Trumbauersville, PA	215, 267	18970
Trumbull, CT	203	06611
Trussville, AL	205	35173
Truth or Consequences, NM	505	87901
Tryon, NE	308	69167
Tryon, NC	828	28782
Tsaile, AZ	928	86556
Tualatin, OR	503, 971	97062
Tuba City, AZ	928	86045
Tuckahoe, NY	914	10707
Tucker, AR	501	72168
Tucker, GA	470, 678, 770	30084-30085
Tucson, AZ	520	85701-85754, 85775-85777
Tucumcari, NM	505	88401, 88416
Tukwila, WA	206, 425	98108, 98138, 98168, 98178*
Tulare, CA	559	93274-93275
Tulelake, CA	530	96134
Tulia, TX	806	79088
Tullahoma, TN	931	37388-37389
Tullytown, PA	215, 267	19007
Tulsa, OK	918	74101-74121, 74126-74137*
Tumacacori, AZ	520	85640, 85645-85646
Tumwater, WA	360	98501, 98511-98512
Tunica, MS	662	38676
Tunkhannock, PA	570	18657
Tupelo, MS	662	38801-38804
Turbeville, SC	843	29162
Turlock, CA	209	95380-95382
Turner, OR	503, 971	97359, 97392
Turners Falls, MA	413	01349, 01376
Turnersville, NJ	856	08012
Turpin, OK	580	73950
Turtle Creek, PA	412, 878	15145
Turtle Lake, WI	715, 534	54004, 54889
Tuscaloosa, AL	205	35401-35407, 35485-35487
Tuscola, IL	217	61953
Tuscola, TX	915	79562
Tuscumbia, AL	256	35674
Tuscumbia, MO	573	65082
Tuskegee, AL	334	36083
Tuskegee Institute, AL	334	36083, 36087-36088
Tustin, CA	714	92780-92782
Twentynine Palms, CA	760, 442	92277-92278
Twin Bridges, MT	406	59754
Twin Falls, ID	208	83301-83303
Twinsburg, OH	234, 330	44087
Two Harbors, MN	218	55616
Two Rivers, WI	920	54241
Tybee Island, GA	912	31328
Tyler, MN	507	56178
Tyler, TX	903	75701-75713, 75798-75799
Tylertown, MS	601, 769	39667
Tyndall, SD	605	57066
Tyndall AFB, FL	850	32403
Tyngsboro, MA	351, 978	01879
Tyrone, GA	470, 770	30290
Tyrone, PA	814	16686

U

City	Area Code(s)	Zip Code(s)
Ubly, MI	989	48475
Uhrichsville, OH	740	44683
Ukiah, CA	707	95418, 95482
Ullin, IL	618	62992
Ulm, MT	406	59485
Ulysses, KS	620	67880
Umatilla, OR	541, 458	97882
Una, SC	864	29378
Unadilla, GA	478	31091
Unadilla, NY	607	13849
Unalakleet, AK	907	99684
Unalaska, AK	907	99547, 99685, 99692
Uncasville, CT	860	06382
Union, IL	815	60180
Union, MO	636	63084
Union, NJ	908	07083
Union, SC	864	29379
Union, WA	360	98592
Union, WV	304	24983
Union City, CA	510	94587
Union City, GA	470, 770	30291
Union City, IN	765	47390
Union City, NJ	201, 551	07086-07087
Union City, PA	814	16438
Union City, TN	731	38261, 38281
Union Gap, WA	509	98901-98903
Union Grove, WI	262	53182
Union Lake, MI	248, 947	48387
Union Springs, AL	334	36089
Uniondale, NY	516	11553-11556, 11588
Uniontown, AL	334	36786
Uniontown, OH	234, 330	44685
Uniontown, PA	724, 878	15401
Unionville, MO	660	63565
Unity, ME	207	04988
Universal City, CA	818	91608, 91618
Universal City, TX	210	78148-78150
University, MS	662	38677
University Center, MI	989	48710
University City, MO	314	63124, 63130
University Heights, OH	216	44118, 44122
University of Richmond, VA	804	23173
University Park, IL	708	60466
University Park, IA	641	52595
University Park, PA	814	16802
Upland, CA	909	91784-91786
Upland, IN	765	46989
Upland, PA	484, 610	19013-19015
Upper Arlington, OH	614	43220-43221
Upper Black Eddy, PA	484, 610	18972
Upper Marlboro, MD	301	20772-20775, 20792
Upper Montclair, NJ	862, 973	07043
Upper Saddle River, NJ	201, 551	07458
Upper Saint Clair, PA	724, 878	15241
Upper Sandusky, OH	419, 567	43351
Upperville, VA	540	20184-20185
Upton, MA	508, 774	01568
Upton, NY	631	11973
Urbana, IL	217	61801-61803
Urbana, IN	260	46990
Urbana, IA	319	52345
Urbana, OH	937	43078
Urbandale, IA	515	50322-50323
Ursa, IL	217	62376
USAF Academy, CO	719	80841
Utica, MI	586	48315-48318
Utica, MS	601, 769	39175
Utica, NY	315	13501-13505, 13599
Uvalde, TX	830	78801-78802

V

City	Area Code(s)	Zip Code(s)
Vacaville, CA	707	95687-95688, 95696
Vail, CO	970	81657-81658
Valdese, NC	828	28690
Valdez, AK	907	99686
Valdosta, GA	229	31601-31606, 31698-31699
Vale, OR	541, 458	97918
Valencia, CA	661	91354-91355, 91380, 91385
Valencia, PA	724, 878	16059
Valentine, NE	402	69201
Valhalla, NY	914	10595
Vallejo, CA	707	94503, 94589-94592
Valley, AL	334	36854, 36872
Valley Center, CA	760, 442	92082
Valley Center, KS	316	67147
Valley City, ND	701	58072
Valley City, OH	234, 330	44280
Valley Cottage, NY	845	10989
Valley Falls, NY	518	12185
Valley Forge, PA	484, 610	19481-19485, 19493-19496
Valley Park, MO	636	63088
Valley Stream, NY	516	11580-11583
Valley View, OH	216	44125, 44131
Valley View, TX	940	76272
Valley Village, CA	818	91607, 91617
Valparaiso, IN	219	46383-46385
Valyermo, CA	661	93563
Van Alstyne, TX	903	75495
Van Buren, AR	479	72956-72957
Van Buren, MO	573	63965
Van Horn, TX	915	79855
Van Nuys, CA	818	91316, 91388, 91401-91416*
Van Wert, OH	419, 567	45891
Vanceburg, KY	606	41179
Vancouver, WA	360	98660-98668, 98682-98687
Vandalia, IL	618	62471
Vandalia, OH	937	45377
Vandenberg AFB, CA	805	93437
Vanderbilt, MI	989	49795
Vandergrift, PA	724, 878	15690
Vansant, VA	276	24656
Vashon, WA	206	98013, 98070
Vassar, MI	989	48768-48769
Vega, TX	806	79092
Vega Alta, PR	787, 939	00692
Velva, ND	701	58790
Venice, CA	310, 424	90291-90296
Venice, FL	941	34284-34293
Ventura, CA	805	93001-93009
Verdi, NV	775	89439
Vergennes, VT	802	05491
Vermillion, SD	605	57069
Vernal, UT	435	84078-84079
Vernon, AL	205	35592
Vernon, CA	323	90058
Vernon, CT	860	06066
Vernon, IN	812	47282
Vernon, NJ	862, 973	07462
Vernon, NY	315	13476
Vernon, TX	940	76384-76385
Vernon Hills, IL	224, 847	60061
Vernonia, OR	503, 971	97064
Vero Beach, FL	772	32960-32969
Verona, MS	662	38879
Verona, NY	315	13478
Verona, PA	412, 878	15147
Verona, VA	540	24482
Verona, WI	608	53593
Versailles, IN	812	47042
Versailles, KY	859	40383-40386
Versailles, MO	573	65084
Vesta, VA	276	24177
Vestal, NY	607	13850-13851
Vevay, IN	812	47043
Vicksburg, MI	616	49097
Vicksburg, MS	601, 769	39180-39183
Victor, ID	208	83455
Victor, NY	585	14564
Victoria, MN	952	55386
Victoria, TX	361	77901-77905
Victoria, VA	434	23974
Vidalia, GA	912	30474-30475
Vidalia, LA	318	71373
Vienna, GA	229	31092
Vienna, IL	618	62995
Vienna, MO	573	65582
Vienna, OH	234, 330	44473
Vienna, VA	571, 703	22027, 22124, 22180-22185
Vienna, WV	304	26101, 26105
Viera, FL	321	32940, 32955
Villa Park, IL	331, 630	60181

*Partial list of zip codes, including main range

City	Area Code(s)	Zip Code(s)
Villanova, PA	484, 610	19085
Ville Platte, LA	337	70586
Vinalhaven, ME	207	04863
Vincennes, IN	812	47591
Vincent, AL	205	35178
Vineland, NJ	856	08360-08362
Vineyard Haven, MA	508, 774	02568, 02573
Vinita, OK	918	74301
Vinton, IA	319	52349
Vinton, LA	337	70668
Vinton, VA	540	24179
Virginia, IL	217	62691
Virginia, MN	218	55777, 55792
Virginia Beach, VA	757	23450-23471, 23479
Virginia City, MT	406	59755
Virginia City, NV	775	89440
Viroqua, WI	608	54665
Visalia, CA	559	93277-93279, 93290-93292
Vista, CA	760, 442	92083-92085
Vivian, LA	318	71082
Vonore, TN	423	37885
Voorhees, NJ	856	08043
Voorheesville, NY	518	12186

W

City	Area Code(s)	Zip Code(s)
Wabash, IN	260	46992
Wabasha, MN	651	55981
Wabasso, FL	772	32970
Waco, TX	254	76701-76716, 76795-76799
Waconia, MN	952	55375, 55387
Waddington, NY	315	13694
Wadena, MN	218	56482
Wadesboro, NC	704, 980	28170
Wadley, AL	256	36276
Wadley, GA	478	30477
Wadsworth, OH	234, 330	44281-44282
Wagoner, OK	918	74467, 74477
Wahoo, NE	402	68066
Wahpeton, ND	701	58074-58076
Waianae, HI	808	96792
Waikoloa, HI	808	96738
Wailea, HI	808	96753
Wailuku, HI	808	96793
Waimanalo, HI	808	96795
Waipahu, HI	808	96797
Waite Park, MN	320	56387-56388
Wakarusa, IN	574	46573
Wake Forest, NC	919	27587-27588
WaKeeney, KS	785	67672
Wakefield, MA	339, 781	01880
Wakefield, MI	906	49968
Wakefield, RI	401	02879-02883
Wakulla Springs, FL	850	32327
Walbridge, OH	419, 567	43465
Walcott, IA	563	52773
Walden, CO	970	80430, 80480
Walden, NY	845	12586
Waldorf, MD	301	20601-20604
Waldron, AR	479	72924, 72958
Wales, WI	262	53183
Waleska, GA	470, 770	30183
Walhalla, SC	864	29691
Walker, MI	616	49544
Walker, MN	218	56484
Walkerton, IN	574	46574
Wall, NJ	732, 848	07719
Wall, SD	605	57790
Walla Walla, WA	509	99362
Wallace, ID	208	83873-83874
Wallace, NC	910	28466
Wallace, SC	843	29596
Walland, TN	865	37886
Walled Lake, MI	248, 947	48390-48391
Waller, TX	281, 832	77484
Wallingford, CT	203	06492-06495
Wallingford, PA	484, 610	19086
Wallington, NJ	862, 973	07057
Wallkill, NY	845	12589
Walls, MS	662	38680, 38686
Walnut, CA	909	91788-91789, 91795
Walnut, IL	815	61376
Walnut Creek, CA	925	94595-94598
Walnut Creek, OH	234, 330	44687
Walnut Ridge, AR	870	72476

City	Area Code(s)	Zip Code(s)
Walpole, MA	508, 774	02032, 02071, 02081
Walpole, NH	603	03608
Walsenburg, CO	719	81089
Walstonburg, NC	252	27888
Walterboro, SC	843	29488
Walters, OK	580	73572
Walthall, MS	662	39771
Waltham, MA	339, 781	02451-02455
Walthourville, GA	912	31333
Walton, IN	574	46994
Walton Hills, OH	440	44146
Walworth, WI	262	53184
Wamego, KS	785	66547
Wampsville, NY	315	13163
Wanamingo, MN	507	55983
Wanatah, IN	219	46390
Wantagh, NY	516	11793
Wapakoneta, OH	419, 567	45819, 45895
Wapato, WA	509	98951
Wapello, IA	319	52653
Wapiti, WY	307	82450
Wappingers Falls, NY	845	12590
Ward, CO	303, 720	80481
Ward Hill, MA	351, 978	01835
Warden, WA	509	98857
Ware, MA	413	01082
Wareham, MA	508, 774	02571
Warfordsburg, PA	301	17267
Warm Springs, GA	706, 762	31830
Warm Springs, MT	406	59756
Warm Springs, OR	541, 458	97761
Warm Springs, VA	540	24484
Warminster, PA	215, 267	18974, 18991
Warner, NH	603	03278
Warner, OK	918	74469
Warner Robins, GA	478	31088, 31093-31099
Warren, AR	870	71671
Warren, MI	586	48088-48093, 48397
Warren, MN	218	56762
Warren, NJ	908	07059
Warren, OH	234, 330	44481-44488
Warren, PA	814	16365-16369
Warren, RI	401	02885
Warren, VT	802	05674
Warrendale, PA	724, 878	15086, 15095-15096
Warrensburg, MO	660	64093
Warrensville Heights, OH	216	44122, 44128
Warrenton, GA	706, 762	30828
Warrenton, MO	636	63383
Warrenton, NC	252	27589
Warrenton, OR	503	97146
Warrenton, VA	540	20186-20188
Warrenville, IL	331, 630	60555
Warrington, PA	215, 267	18976
Warrior, AL	205	35180
Warroad, MN	218	56741, 56763
Warsaw, IN	574	46580-46582
Warsaw, KY	859	41095
Warsaw, MO	660	65355
Warsaw, NY	585	14569
Warsaw, NC	910	28398
Warsaw, VA	804	22572
Wartburg, TN	423	37887
Warwick, NY	845	10990
Warwick, RI	401	02818, 02886-02889
Wasco, IL	331, 630	60183
Waseca, MN	507	56093
Washburn, MO	417	65772
Washburn, ND	701	58577
Washburn, WI	715, 534	54891
Washington, CT	860	06777, 06793-06794
Washington, DC	202	20001-20020, 20024-20082*
Washington, GA	706, 762	30673
Washington, IL	309	61571
Washington, IN	812	47501
Washington, IA	319	52353
Washington, KS	785	66968
Washington, MO	636	63090
Washington, NJ	908	07882
Washington, NC	252	27889
Washington, PA	724, 878	15301
Washington, VA	540	22747
Washington, WV	304	26181
Washington Court House, OH	740	43160
Washington Green, CT	860	06793
Washington Island, WI	920	54246
Washington Navy Yard, DC	202	20374-20376, 20388-20391*

City	Area Code(s)	Zip Code(s)
Washingtonville, NY	845	10992
Washougal, WA	360	98671
Wasilla, AK	907	99652-99654, 99687, 99694
Wassaic, NY	845	12592
Watauga, TX	682, 817	76148
Water Valley, MS	662	38965
Waterbury, CT	203	06701-06712, 06716, 06720*
Waterbury, VT	802	05671, 05676
Waterbury Center, VT	802	05677
Waterford, CT	860	06385-06386
Waterford, MI	248, 947	48327-48330
Waterford, NY	518	12188
Waterford, PA	814	16441
Waterford, WI	262	53185
Waterloo, IL	618	62298
Waterloo, IN	260	46793
Waterloo, IA	319	50701-50707, 50799
Waterloo, NY	315	13165
Waterloo, WI	920	53594
Watertown, CT	860	06779, 06795
Watertown, MA	617, 857	02471-02472, 02477
Watertown, MN	952	55388
Watertown, NY	315	13601-13603
Watertown, SD	605	57201
Watertown, WI	920	53094, 53098
Waterville, ME	207	04901-04903
Waterville, OH	419, 567	43566
Waterville, WA	509	98858
Waterville Valley, NH	603	03215
Watervliet, NY	518	12189
Watford City, ND	701	58854
Watkins Glen, NY	607	14891
Watkinsville, GA	706, 762	30677
Watonga, OK	580	73772
Watrous, NM	505	87750-87753
Watseka, IL	815	60970
Watsonville, CA	831	95076-95077
Wauchula, FL	863	33873
Waucoma, IA	563	52171
Wauconda, IL	224, 847	60084
Waukegan, IL	224, 847	60079, 60085-60087
Waukesha, WI	262	53146, 53151, 53186-53189
Waukon, IA	563	52172
Waunakee, WI	608	53597
Waupaca, WI	715, 534	54981
Waupun, WI	920	53963
Wauregan, CT	860	06387
Waurika, OK	580	73573
Wausau, WI	715, 534	54401-54403
Wauseon, OH	419, 567	43567
Wautoma, WI	920	54982
Wauwatosa, WI	414	53210-53213, 53222, 53226
Waverly, FL	863	33877
Waverly, IA	319	50677
Waverly, OH	740	45690
Waverly, TN	931	37185
Waverly, VA	804	23890-23891
Wawaka, IN	260	46794
Waxahachie, TX	469, 972	75165-75168
Waycross, GA	912	31501-31503
Wayland, MA	508, 774	01778
Wayland, MI	616	49348
Wayland, NY	585	14572
Waymart, PA	570	18472
Wayne, MI	734	48184
Wayne, NE	402	68787
Wayne, NJ	862, 973	07470, 07474-07477
Wayne, PA	484, 610	19080, 19087-19089
Wayne, WV	304	25570
Waynesboro, GA	706, 762	30830
Waynesboro, MS	601, 769	39367
Waynesboro, PA	717	17268
Waynesboro, TN	931	38485
Waynesboro, VA	540	22980
Waynesburg, PA	724, 878	15370
Waynesville, MO	573	65583
Waynesville, NC	828	28738, 28785-28786
Wayzata, MN	763, 952	55391
Weatherford, OK	580	73096
Weatherford, TX	682, 817	76085-76088
Weaverville, CA	530	96093
Weaverville, NC	828	28787
Webb City, MO	417	64870
Webberville, MI	517	48892
Webster, MA	508, 774	01570
Webster, NY	585	14580
Webster, SD	605	57274

*Partial list of zip codes, including main range

City	Area Code(s)	Zip Code(s)
Webster, TX	281, 832	77598
Webster City, IA	515	50595
Webster Groves, MO	314	63119
Webster Springs, WV	304	26288
Wedowee, AL	256	36278
Weed, CA	530	96094
Weehawken, NJ	201, 551	07086-07087
Weidman, MI	989	48893
Weimar, CA	530	95736
Weirsdale, FL	352	32195
Weirton, WV	304	26062
Weiser, ID	208	83672
Welch, WV	304	24801
Welches, OR	503, 971	97067
Weldon, NC	252	27890
Wellesley, MA	339, 781	02457, 02481-02482
Wellesley Hills, MA	339, 781	02481
Wellesley Island, NY	315	13640
Wellfleet, MA	508, 774	02667
Wellington, CO	970	80549
Wellington, FL	561	33414, 33421, 33467
Wellington, KS	620	67152
Wellington, OH	440	44090
Wellington, TX	806	79095
Wells, ME	207	04090
Wells, MN	507	56097
Wells, NV	775	89835
Wellsboro, PA	570	16901
Wellsburg, NY	570	14894
Wellsburg, WV	304	26070
Wellsville, NY	585	14895
Wellsville, OH	234, 330	43968
Wellton, AZ	928	85356
Wenatchee, WA	509	98801-98802, 98807
Wendell, NC	919	27591
Wenham, MA	351, 978	01984
Wentworth, NC	336	27375
Wernersville, PA	484, 610	19565
Weslaco, TX	956	78596-78599
Wesley Chapel, FL	813	33543-33544
Wessington Springs, SD	605	57382
Wesson, MS	601, 769	39191
West Alexandria, OH	937	45381
West Allis, WI	414	53214, 53219, 53227
West Atlantic City, NJ	609	08232
West Babylon, NY	631	11704-11707
West Barnstable, MA	508, 774	02668
West Bath, ME	207	04530
West Belmar, NJ	732, 848	07719
West Bend, IA	515	50597
West Bend, WI	262	53090, 53095
West Bethesda, MD	301	20817, 20827
West Bloomfield, MI	248, 947	48322-48325
West Boylston, MA	508, 774	01583
West Branch, IA	319	52358
West Branch, MI	989	48661
West Brentwood, NY	631	11717
West Bridgewater, MA	508, 774	02379
West Burlington, IA	319	52655
West Caldwell, NJ	862, 973	07006-07007
West Carrollton, OH	937	45439, 45449
West Chester, OH	513	45069-45071
West Chester, PA	484, 610	19380-19383
West Chicago, IL	331, 630	60185-60186
West Columbia, SC	803	29033, 29169-29172
West Columbia, TX	979	77486
West Conshohocken, PA	484, 610	19428
West Covina, CA	626	91790-91793
West Deptford, NJ	856	08066
West Des Moines, IA	515	50265-50266, 50398
West Dover, VT	802	05351, 05356
West Dundee, IL	224, 847	60118
West Falmouth, MA	508, 774	02574
West Fargo, ND	701	58078
West Frankfort, IL	618	62896
West Franklin, NH	603	03235
West Glacier, MT	406	59921, 59936
West Greenwich, RI	401	02817
West Grove, PA	484, 610	19390
West Hartford, CT	860	06107-06110, 06117-06119*
West Haven, CT	203	06516
West Haverstraw, NY	845	10993
West Hazleton, PA	570	18202
West Helena, AR	870	72390
West Hempstead, NY	516	11552
West Henrietta, NY	585	14586
West Hills, CA	818	91304-91308
West Hollywood, CA	310, 323, 424	90038, 90046-90048, 90069
West Homestead, PA	412, 878	15120
West Hurley, NY	845	12491
West Islip, NY	631	11795
West Jefferson, OH	614	43162
West Jordan, UT	801, 385	84084, 84088
West Kennebunk, ME	207	04094
West Kingston, RI	401	02892
West Lafayette, IN	765	47906-47907, 47996
West Lafayette, OH	740	43845
West Lebanon, IN	765	47991
West Lebanon, NH	603	03784
West Liberty, IA	319	52776
West Liberty, KY	606	41472
West Liberty, WV	304	26074
West Long Branch, NJ	732, 848	07764
West Los Angeles, CA	310, 424	90025
West Mansfield, OH	937	43358
West Melbourne, FL	321	32904, 32912
West Memphis, AR	870	72301-72303
West Middlesex, PA	724, 878	16159
West Mifflin, PA	412, 878	15122-15123, 15236
West Milford, NJ	862, 973	07480
West Monroe, LA	318	71291-71294
West New York, NJ	201, 551	07093
West Nyack, NY	845	10994
West Olive, MI	616	49460
West Orange, NJ	862, 973	07052
West Palm Beach, FL	561	33401-33422
West Park, NY	845	12493
West Paterson, NJ	862, 973	07424
West Pittsburg, PA	724, 878	16160
West Plains, MO	417	65775-65776
West Point, GA	706, 762	31833
West Point, MS	662	39773
West Point, NE	402	68788
West Point, NY	845	10996-10997
West Point, PA	215, 267	19486
West Point, VA	804	23181
West Redding, CT	203	06896
West Roxbury, MA	617, 857	02132
West Sacramento, CA	916	95605, 95691, 95798-95799
West Saint Paul, MN	651	55107, 55118
West Salem, OH	419, 567	44287
West Salem, WI	608	54669
West Sayville, NY	631	11796
West Seneca, NY	716	14206, 14210, 14218-14220*
West Springfield, MA	413	01089-01090
West Tawakoni, TX	903	75474
West Terre Haute, IN	812	47885
West Trenton, NJ	609	08628
West Union, IA	563	52175
West Union, OH	937	45693
West Union, WV	304	26456
West Valley, NY	716	14171
West Valley City, UT	801, 385	84118-84120, 84128
West Warren, MA	413	01092
West Warwick, RI	401	02893
West Yellowstone, MT	406	59758
Westampton, NJ	609	08060
Westborough, MA	508, 774	01580-01582
Westbrook, CT	860	06498
Westbrook, ME	207	04092, 04098
Westbury, NY	516	11568, 11590-11597
Westby, WI	608	54667
Westchester, IL	708	60154
Westcliffe, CO	719	81252
Westerlo, NY	518	12055, 12193
Westerly, RI	401	02808, 02891
Westerville, OH	614	43081-43082, 43086
Westfield, IN	317	46074
Westfield, MA	413	01085-01086
Westfield, NJ	908	07090-07091
Westfield, NY	716	14787
Westfield, PA	814	16927, 16950
Westfield, VT	802	05874
Westfield Center, OH	234, 330	44251
Westford, MA	351, 978	01886
Westhampton Beach, NY	631	11978
Westlake, LA	337	70669
Westlake, OH	440	44145
Westlake, TX	682, 817	76262
Westlake Village, CA	805, 818	91359-91363
Westland, MI	734	48185-48186
Westminster, CA	714	92683-92685
Westminster, CO	303, 720	80003-80005, 80020-80021*
Westminster, MD	410	21157-21158
Westminster, MA	351, 978	01441, 01473
Westminster Station, VT	802	05159
Westmont, IL	331, 630	60559-60561
Westmont, NJ	856	08108
Westmoreland, KS	785	66426, 66549
Weston, CT	203	06883
Weston, FL	754, 954	33326-33327, 33331-33332
Weston, MA	339, 781	02493
Weston, MO	816	64098
Weston, WV	304	26452
Westover, MD	410	21871, 21890
Westport, CT	203	06880-06881, 06888-06889
Westport, MA	508, 774	02790
Westport, WA	360	98595
Westville, IN	574	46391
Westwego, LA	504	70094-70096
Westwood, KS	913	66205
Westwood, MA	339, 781	02090
Westwood, NJ	201, 551	07675-07677
Wethersfield, CT	860	06109, 06129
Wetumpka, AL	334	36092-36093
Wewahitchka, FL	850	32465
Wewoka, OK	405	74884
Wexford, PA	724, 878	15090
Weyers Cave, VA	540	24486
Weymouth, MA	339, 781	02188-02191
Wharton, TX	979	77488
Whately, MA	413	01093, 01373
Wheat Ridge, CO	303, 720	80002, 80033-80034, 80212*
Wheatland, IA	563	52777
Wheatland, PA	724, 878	16161
Wheatland, WY	307	82201
Wheaton, IL	331, 630	60187-60189
Wheaton, MD	301	20902, 20906, 20915
Wheaton, MN	320	56296
Wheeler, TX	806	79096
Wheeling, IL	224, 847	60090
Wheeling, WV	304	26003
Whippany, NJ	862, 973	07981-07983, 07999
Whiskeytown, CA	530	96095
White Bear Lake, MN	651	55110, 55115
White Castle, LA	225	70788
White City, OR	541, 458	97503
White Cloud, MI	231	49349
White Deer, PA	570	17887
White Haven, PA	570	18661
White Lake, MI	248, 947	48383-48386
White Oak, PA	412, 878	15131
White Oak, TX	903	75693
White Pigeon, MI	616	49099
White Plains, NY	914	10601-10610, 10650
White River, SD	605	57579
White River Junction, VT	802	05001, 05009
White Sands, NM	505	88002
White Sands Missile Range, NM	505	88002
White Stone, VA	804	22578
White Sulphur Springs, MT	406	59645
White Sulphur Springs, WV	304	24986
Whitefish, MT	406	59937
Whitehall, MI	231	49461-49463
Whitehall, PA	484, 610	18052
Whitehall, WI	715, 534	54773
Whitehouse, NJ	908	08888
Whitehouse, OH	419, 567	43571
Whitehouse Station, NJ	908	08889
Whitesburg, KY	606	41858
Whitestone, NY	347, 718	11357
Whiteville, NC	910	28472
Whiteville, TN	901	38075
Whitewater, WI	262	53190
Whitfield, MS	601, 769	39193
Whiting, IN	219	46394
Whiting, NJ	732, 848	08759
Whitinsville, MA	508, 774	01588
Whitley City, KY	606	42653
Whitsett, NC	336	27377
Whittier, AK	907	99693
Whittier, CA	562	90601-90612
Wibaux, MT	406	59353
Wichita, KS	316	67201-67236, 67251, 67256*
Wichita Falls, TX	940	76301-76311

*Partial list of zip codes, including main range

City	Area Code(s)	Zip Code(s)
Wickenburg, AZ	928	85358, 85390
Wickliffe, KY	270	42087
Wickliffe, OH	440	44092
Wiggins, MS	601, 769	39577
Wilber, NE	402	68465
Wilberforce, OH	937	45384
Wilbraham, MA	413	01095
Wilburton, OK	918	74578
Wilder, KY	859	41071, 41076
Wilder, VT	802	05088
Wildomar, CA	951	92595
Wildorado, TX	806	79098
Wildwood, FL	352	34785
Wildwood, NJ	609	08260
Wildwood Crest, NJ	609	08260
Wilkes-Barre, PA	570	18701-18711, 18761-18769*
Wilkesboro, NC	336	28697
Willard, OH	419, 567	44888-44890
Willard, UT	435	84340
Willcox, AZ	520	85643-85644
Williams Bay, WI	262	53191
Williamsburg, IA	319	52361
Williamsburg, KY	606	40769
Williamsburg, OH	513	45176
Williamsburg, PA	814	16693
Williamsburg, VA	757	23081, 23185-23188
Williamson, WV	304	25661
Williamsport, IN	765	47993
Williamsport, MD	301	21795
Williamsport, PA	570	17701-17705
Williamston, MI	517	48895
Williamston, NC	252	27892
Williamstown, KY	859	41097
Williamstown, MA	413	01267
Williamstown, NJ	856	08094
Williamstown, WV	304	26187
Williamsville, NY	716	14221, 14231
Willimantic, CT	860	06226
Willingboro, NJ	609	08046
Willis, TX	936	77318, 77378
Williston, FL	352	32696
Williston, ND	701	58801-58802
Williston, SC	803	29853
Williston, VT	802	05495
Willits, CA	707	95429, 95490
Willmar, MN	320	56201
Willoughby, OH	440	44094-44097
Willow Grove, PA	215, 267	19090
Willow Springs, MO	417	65793
Willow Street, PA	717	17584
Willowbrook, IL	331, 630	60527
Willows, CA	530	95988
Willsboro, NY	518	12996
Wilmerding, PA	412, 878	15148
Wilmette, IL	224, 847	60091
Wilmington, CA	310, 424	90744, 90748
Wilmington, DE	302	19801-19810, 19850, 19880*
Wilmington, MA	978	01887
Wilmington, NC	910	28401-28412
Wilmington, OH	937	45177
Wilmore, KY	859	40390
Wilson, NY	716	14172
Wilson, NC	252	27893-27896
Wilson, WY	307	83014
Wilsonville, OR	503, 971	97070
Wilton, CT	203	06897
Wilton, IA	563	52778
Wilton, ME	207	04294
Wilton, NH	603	03086
Wilton, NY	518	12831
Wimberley, TX	512	78676
Winamac, IN	574	46996
Winchester, IL	217	62694
Winchester, IN	765	47394
Winchester, KY	859	40391-40392
Winchester, MA	339, 781	01890
Winchester, NH	603	03470
Winchester, TN	931	37398
Winchester, VA	540	22601-22604, 22638
Wind Gap, PA	484, 610	18091
Windber, PA	814	15963
Winder, GA	470, 770	30680
Windermere, FL	321, 407	34786
Windham, NH	603	03087
Windom, MN	507	56101, 56118
Window Rock, AZ	928	86515
Windsor, CA	707	95492
Windsor, CT	860	06006, 06095
Windsor, NC	252	27983
Windsor, VT	802	05089
Windsor, VA	757	23487
Windsor, WI	608	53598
Windsor Locks, CT	860	06096
Winfield, AL	205	35594
Winfield, IL	331, 630	60190
Winfield, KS	620	67156
Winfield, WV	304	25213
Wingate, NC	704, 980	28174
Winlock, WA	360	98596
Winn, ME	207	04495
Winnebago, WI	920	54985
Winneconne, WI	920	54986
Winnemucca, NV	775	89445-89446
Winner, SD	605	57580
Winnetka, CA	818	91306, 91396
Winnett, MT	406	59084-59087
Winnfield, LA	318	71483
Winnsboro, LA	318	71295
Winnsboro, SC	803	29180
Winona, MN	507	55987-55988
Winona, MS	662	38967
Winona, MO	573	65588
Winona Lake, IN	219	46590
Winooski, VT	802	05404
Winslow, AZ	928	86047
Winslow, ME	207	04901
Winslow, NJ	609	08095
Winsted, CT	860	06063, 06094, 06098
Winston, OR	541, 458	97496
Winston-Salem, NC	336	27101-27109, 27113-27117*
Winter Garden, FL	321, 407	34777-34778, 34787
Winter Haven, FL	863	33880-33888
Winter Park, CO	970	80482
Winter Park, FL	321, 407	32789-32793
Winters, CA	530	95694
Winters, TX	915	79567
Winterset, IA	515	50273
Wintersville, OH	740	43952-43953
Winterthur, DE	302	19735
Winthrop, ME	207	04364
Winthrop, WA	509	98862
Winton, NC	252	27986
Wiscasset, ME	207	04578
Wisconsin Dells, WI	608	53965
Wisconsin Rapids, WI	715, 534	54494-54495
Wisdom, MT	406	59761
Wise, VA	276	24293
Wixom, MI	248, 947	48393
Woburn, MA	781	01801, 01806-01808, 01813*
Wolcott, CT	203	06716
Wolcott, IN	219	47995
Wolcott, NY	315	14590
Wolf, WY	307	82844
Wolf Point, MT	406	59201
Wolfe City, TX	903	75496
Wolfeboro, NH	603	03894
Womelsdorf, PA	484, 610	19567
Wood Dale, IL	331, 630	60191
Wood River, IL	618	62095
Woodbine, GA	912	31569
Woodbine, IA	712	51579
Woodbine, MD	301	21797
Woodbourne, NY	845	12788
Woodbridge, CT	203	06525
Woodbridge, NJ	732, 848	07095
Woodbridge, VA	571, 703	22191-22195
Woodburn, IN	260	46797
Woodburn, OR	503, 971	97071
Woodbury, CT	203	06798
Woodbury, MN	651	55125, 55129
Woodbury, NJ	856	08096-08097
Woodbury, NY	516	11797
Woodbury, TN	615	37190
Woodcliff Lake, NJ	201, 551	07677
Woodhaven, MI	734	48183
Woodhaven, NY	347, 718	11421
Woodinville, WA	425	98072
Woodland, CA	530	95695, 95776
Woodland, PA	814	16881
Woodland, WA	360	98674
Woodland Hills, CA	818	91302-91303, 91364-91367*
Woodridge, IL	331, 630	60517, 60540
Woodruff, SC	864	29388
Woodruff, WI	715, 534	54568
Woods Cross, UT	801, 385	84010, 84087
Woods Hole, MA	508, 774	02543
Woodsfield, OH	740	43793
Woodside, CA	650	94062
Woodside, NY	347, 718	11377
Woodstock, CT	860	06281
Woodstock, GA	470, 770	30188-30189
Woodstock, IL	815	60098
Woodstock, NY	845	12498
Woodstock, VT	802	05091
Woodstock, VA	540	22664
Woodstown, NJ	856	08098
Woodville, MS	601, 769	39669
Woodville, OH	419, 567	43469
Woodville, TX	409	75979, 75990
Woodville, WI	715, 534	54028
Woodward, IA	515	50276
Woodward, OK	580	73801-73802
Woolrich, PA	570	17779
Woonsocket, RI	401	02895
Woonsocket, SD	605	57385
Wooster, OH	234, 330	44691
Worcester, MA	508, 774	01601-01615, 01653-01655
Worcester, PA	484, 610	19490
Worland, WY	307	82401, 82430
Wormleysburg, PA	717	17043
Worth, IL	708	60482
Worthington, MN	507	56187
Worthington, OH	614	43085
Wrangell, AK	907	99929
Wray, CO	970	80758
Wrens, GA	706, 762	30818, 30833
Wrentham, MA	508, 774	02070, 02093
Wright, WY	307	82732
Wright City, MO	636	63390
Wright-Patterson AFB, OH	937	45433
Wrightstown, NJ	609	08562
Wrightsville, AR	501	72183
Wrightsville, GA	478	31096
Wrightsville, PA	717	17368
Wrightsville Beach, NC	910	28480
Wyalusing, PA	570	18853
Wyandanch, NY	631	11798
Wyandotte, MI	734	48192
Wyckoff, NJ	201, 551	07481
Wye Mills, MD	410	21679
Wylliesburg, VA	434	23976
Wyncote, PA	215, 267	19095
Wyndmoor, PA	215, 267	19038
Wynne, AR	870	72396
Wynnewood, PA	484, 610	19096
Wyoming, MI	616	49418, 49508-49509, 49548
Wyoming, MN	651	55092
Wyoming, PA	570	18644
Wyomissing, PA	484, 610	19610
Wysox, PA	570	18854
Wytheville, VA	276	24382

X

City	Area Code(s)	Zip Code(s)
Xenia, OH	937	45385

Y

City	Area Code(s)	Zip Code(s)
Yabucoa, PR	787, 939	00767
Yacolt, WA	360	98675
Yadkinville, NC	336	27055
Yakima, WA	509	98901-98909
Yakutat, AK	907	99689
Yale, IA	641	50277
Yanceyville, NC	336	27379
Yankton, SD	605	57078-57079
Yardley, PA	215, 267	19067
Yardville, NJ	609	08620
Yarmouth, ME	207	04096
Yates Center, KS	620	66783
Yazoo City, MS	662	39194
Yeadon, PA	484, 610	19050
Yellow Springs, OH	937	45387
Yellowstone National Park, WY	307	82190
Yellville, AR	870	72687

*Partial list of zip codes, including main range

City	Area Code(s)	Zip Code(s)
Yelm, WA	360	98597
Yerington, NV	775	89447
Yoakum, TX	361	77995
Yonkers, NY	914	10701-10710
Yorba Linda, CA	714	92885-92887
York, AL	205	36925
York, NE	402	68467
York, PA	717	17315, 17401-17407, 17415
York, SC	803	29745
York Harbor, ME	207	03910-03911
York Haven, PA	717	17370
York Springs, PA	717	17372
Yorktown, VA	757	23690-23693
Yorktown Heights, NY	914	10598
Yorkville, IL	331, 630	60560
Yorkville, NY	315	13495
Young America, MN	952	55394-55399, 55473, 55550*
Young Harris, GA	706, 762	30582
Youngstown, OH	234, 330	44501-44515, 44555, 44598*
Youngsville, LA	337	70592
Youngsville, NC	919	27596
Youngsville, PA	814	16371
Youngwood, PA	724, 878	15697
Yountville, CA	707	94599
Ypsilanti, MI	734	48197-48198
Yreka, CA	530	96097
Yuba City, CA	530	95991-95993
Yucaipa, CA	909	92399
Yucca Valley, CA	760, 442	92284-92286
Yukon, OK	405	73085, 73099
Yuma, AZ	928	85364-85369
Yuma, CO	970	80759

Z

City	Area Code(s)	Zip Code(s)
Zachary, LA	225	70791
Zachow, WI	715, 534	54182
Zanesville, OH	740	43701-43702
Zapata, TX	956	78076
Zebulon, GA	470, 770	30295
Zebulon, NC	919	27597
Zeeland, MI	616	49464
Zelienople, PA	724, 878	16063
Zellwood, FL	321, 407	32798
Zenda, WI	262	53195
Zephyrhills, FL	813	33539-33544
Zillah, WA	509	98953
Zion, IL	224, 847	60099
Zionsville, IN	317	46077
Zionsville, PA	484, 610	18092
Zolfo Springs, FL	863	33890
Zumbrota, MN	507	55992

**Partial list of zip codes, including main range*

Index to Classified Headings

Citations given in this index refer to the subject headings under which listings are organized in the Classified Section. The page numbers given for each citation refer to the page on which a particular subject category begins rather than to a specific company or organization name. "See" and "See also" references are included to help in the identification of appropriate subject categories.

A

B

C

D

E

H

I

J

K

L

M

N

O

S

T

U

V

W

X

Y

Z

How To Use This Directo

Illustrated here are the various symbols, terms, and other features typically found on the pages of this directory, t concise explanations of what those features represent. For more detailed information about what's included in t please refer to the introductory section also titled "How To Use This Directory."

PLEASE NOTE: Listing data printed here are for sample purposes only. Consult directory for actual entries.

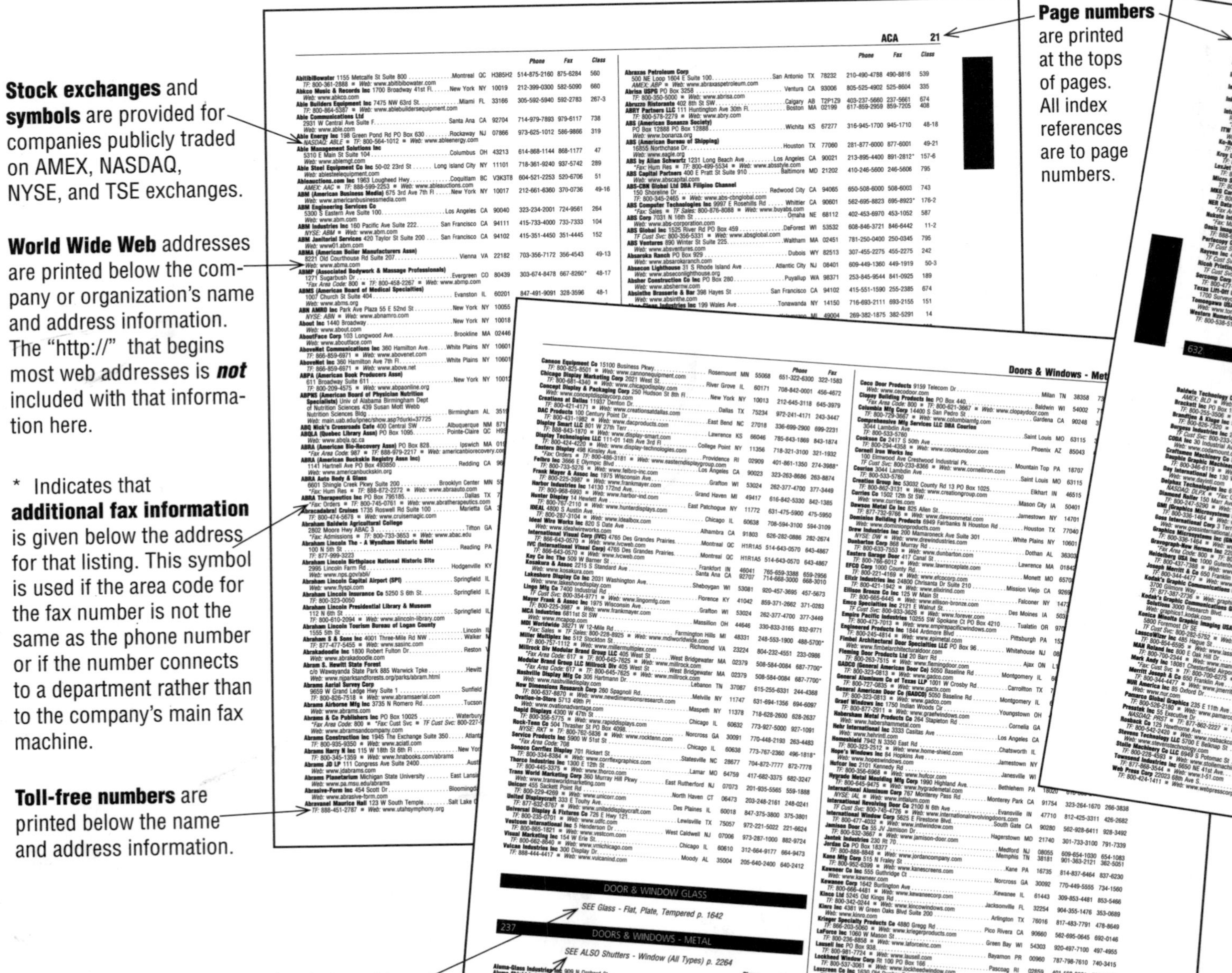

Stock exchanges and **symbols** are provided for companies publicly traded on AMEX, NASDAQ, NYSE, and TSE exchanges.

World Wide Web addresses are printed below the company or organization's name and address information. The "http://" that begins most web addresses is ***not*** included with that information here.

* Indicates that **additional fax information** is given below the address for that listing. This symbol is used if the area code for the fax number is not the same as the phone number or if the number connects to a department rather than to the company's main fax machine.

Toll-free numbers are printed below the name and address information.

Page numbers are printed at the tops of pages. All index references are to page numbers.

"SEE" references are included to help guide users to appropriate headings.

"SEE ALSO" indicates that similar or related types of information are printed under other classified headings.